CASSELL'S LATIN DICTIONARY

CASSELL'S
LATIN DICTIONARY

(Latin=English and English=Latin)

REVISED BY

J. R. V. MARCHANT, M.A.
Formerly Scholar of Wadham College, Oxford

AND

JOSEPH F. CHARLES, B.A.
Late Assistant Master at the City of London School

281ST THOUSAND

FUNK & WAGNALLS COMPANY
NEW YORK AND LONDON

PREFACE

In preparing a Revised Edition of the Latin-English part of this
Dictionary, the aim has been so to adapt the work that it may
be suited for the middle forms of public schools. It is above all
intended to be a Dictionary of Classical Latin, and thus a large
number of archaic, or post-Augustan words, have been omitted,
while nearly all the important articles have been entirely re-
written, chiefly with the view of introducing a greater number
of quotations to illustrate constructions and usage. The historical
and geographical notices have been largely increased in number
and lessened in size. Etymologies have been added, but mainly
those of an unambitious kind. It is hoped that the considerable
changes that have been made in type and classification will make
the work more intelligible, and so more useful.

EXPLANATION OF SIGNS AND ABBREVIATIONS
USED IN THIS WORK

ablat. ablative.

absol. absolute, absolutely, **i.e. without dependent case or adjunct.**

abstr. abstract.

accus. accusative.

act. active.

adj. adjective.

adv. adverb.

al. l. alia lectio or **alii legunt (a different** reading).

ap. followed by a proper noun, e.g., ap. Cic. = in the works of.

appellat. appellative (when a proper noun is used as a common noun, e.g. when Achilles = a brave, handsome man).

attrib. attribute or attributive.

a. Aug. ante-Augustan.

Aug. Augustan.

c. common.

conj. conjunction.

collect. collective.

compar. comparative.

concr. concrete.

conn. connected.

correl. correlative.

constr. construction.

contr. contraction or contracted.

cp. compare.

dat. dative.

decl. declension.

defect. defective.

demonstr. demonstrative.

dep. deponent.

desider. desiderative.

diff. different.

dim. diminutive.

dissyll. dissyllable.

distrib. distributive

dub. doubtful.

eccl. ecclesiastical

ed. edition.

e.g. exempli gratiā (for example).

ellipt. elliptical, elliptically.

enclit. enclitic.

Eng. English.

esp. especially.

etc. et cetera.

eth. dat. ethic dative.

etym. etymology.

euphem. euphemism or euphemistical.

euphon. euphonic, euphonically.

ex. exs. example, examples.

f. feminine.

fig. figurative or figure.

fin. or *ad fin.* at the end.

foll. followed by.

follg. following.

fr. from.

Fr. French.

freq. frequently or frequentative.

fut. future.

gen. general or generally.

genit. genitive.

geogr. geographical.

Germ. German.

Gr. Greek.

gram. grammatical.

heterocl. heteroclite.

heterog. heterogeneous.

ib. ibidem.

id. idem.

i.e. id est (that is).

imper. imperative.

imperf. imperfect.

impers. impersonal.

inanim. inanimate.

inchoat. inchoative, inceptive.

indecl. indeclinable.

indef. indefinite.

indic. indicative.

infin. infinitive.

init., in, or *ad init.* at the beginning.

intens. intensive.

interrog. interrogative.

SIGNS AND ABBREVIATIONS (*continued*)

intr. intransitive.
i.q. idem quod.
irreg. irregular.
It. Italian.
Lat. Latin.
lit. literal.
l. lectio (reading).
locat. casus locativus.
m. masculine.
mathem. mathematical.
med. medical or medically.
met. metaphorically.
meton. by metonymy.
mid. middle.
milit. military.
MS. manuscript.
MSS. manuscripts.
n. neuter.
naut. nautical.
neg. negative.
neut. neuter.
nom. nominative.
num. numeral.
object. objective or objectively.
onomatop. onomatopoeia or onomatopoeic.
opp. opposite to.
ord. ordinal.
orig. original or originally.
p. page.
p. adj. participial adjective.
p. Aug. post-Augustan.
partic. participle.
partit. partitive.
pass. passive.
perf. perfect.
pers. person, personal, or personally.
philosoph. philosophical or philosophy.
pleonast. pleonastical or pleonastically.
plur. plural.

pluperf. pluperfect.
poet. poetical or poetically.
polit. political or politically.
posit. positive.
preced. preceding.
prep. preposition.
pres. present.
prob. probably.
pron. pronoun.
prop. properly.
prov. proverb or proverbially.
q.v. quod or quae vide (which see).
refl. reflective or reflectively.
reg. regular or regularly.
rel. relative.
relig. religious.
rhet. rhetoric, rhetorical, or rhetorically.
Rom. Roman.
Sansc. Sanscrit.
sc. scilicet (that is to say, namely).
script. scriptor (writer).
sing. singular.
sq. sequens (and the following).
subj. subjunctive.
subject. subjective or subjectively.
subst. substantive.
suff. suffix.
sup. supine.
superl. superlative.
s.v. sub voce.
syl. syllable.
syncop. syncope or syncopated.
synonym. synonymous.
t.t. technical term.
transf. transferred.
transl. translation or translated.
trisyll. trisyllable.
v. verb, vide, or vox.
voc. vocative.

LATIN ABBREVIATIONS

A. Aulus, Augustus, absolvo, antiquo, annus.
a.d. Ante diem (in dates).
A.U.C. Anno urbis conditae, ab urbe condita.

B. Bonus or bene.
B.D. Bona Dea, bonum datum.
B.L. Bona lex.
B.O. Bono omine, bona omina.
B.P. Bono publico, bona possessio.
B.M. Bene merenti.
B.V.V. Bene vale, vale!

C. Cajus, conjux, condemno.
C. As num. sign = centum.
Cal. Calendae.
Cn. Cnaeus.
Corn. Cornelius.

D. Decimus, Divus, deus, dominus, decurio, dies, dabam.
D.D. Dono dedit.
D.D.D. Dat donat dedicat.
D.M. Diis manibus.
D.O.M. Deo optimo maximo.
D.P.S. De pecunia sua.
D.S. De suo.
D.N. Dominus noster.

E. Emeritus, evocatus.
E.M.V. Egregiae memoriae vir.
E.P. Equo publico.
E.Q.R. Eques Romanus.

F. Filius, fecit, fidelis, felix.
F.C. Faciendum curavit.
F.I. Fieri jussit.
Fl. Flavius.
Fl. P. Flamen perpetuus.

G. Gajus, Gallica, Gemina.
G.I. Germania Inferior.
G.S. Germania Superior.

H. Hic, etc., habet, hastata (cohors), heres, honos.
Har. Haruspex.
H.C. Hispania citerior.
Hor. Horatiā tribu.
H.S. Hic situs est.
H.S. (Mistake for IIS.), sestertius, sestertium.
H.S.S. Hic siti sunt.

I. In, infra, ipse.
I.D. Idus.
I.H.F.C. Ipsius heres faciendum curavit.
Im. Immunis.
Imp. Imperium, imperator.

K. Kaeso.
Kal. Kalendae.

L. Lucius, libra.
L. As num. sign = 50.

M. Marcus.
M'. Manius.
M. As num. sign = mille.

N. Numerius.
Non. Nonae.

O. Optimus, omnis.

P. Publius.
P.C. Patres conscripti.
P.M. Pontifex Maximus.
P.R. Populus Romanus.
P. VIII. Pedum octo.
Prid. Pridie.

Q. Quintus, que.

R. Rufus, Romanus, recte, regnum, reficiendum.

LATIN ABBREVIATIONS (*continued*)

R.P.   Respublica.

R.R.   Rationes relatae.

S.   Sextus, Senatus, semissis.

S. or Sp.   Spurius.

S.C.   Senatus consultum.

S.P.Q.R.   Senatus populusque Romanus.

T.   Titus tribunus.

Ti.   Tiberius.

Tr. pl.   Tribunus plebis.

U.   Urbs (Roma).

V.   Valeo, vir, vivus, vivens, votum.

X. = 10, and also in coins denarius.

X.V.   Decemvir.

XV.V.   Quindecimvir.

ABBREVIATIONS OF THE NAMES OF LATIN AUTHORS REFERRED TO IN THIS WORK.

App. Lucius Appuleius, philosopher, born about 130 B.C.

Auct. b. Afr. Auctor belli Africani.

Auct. b. Alex. Auctor belli Alexandrini.

Auct. b. Hisp. Auctor belli Hispani.

Caes. Caius Julius Caesar, historian, died 44 B.C.

Cat. C. Valerius Catullus, poet, born 87 B.C.

Cato. M. Porcius Cato, orator and historian, died 147 B.C.

Cic. M. Tullius Cicero, orator and philosopher, died 43 B.C.

Col. L. Jun. Moderatus Columella, writer on husbandry, of the 1st cent. A.D.

Enn. Q. Ennius, poet, died 169 B.C.

Eutr. Flavius Eutropius, historian of the 4th cent. A.D.

Hirt. Aulus Hirtius, historian, died 43 B.C.

Hor. Q. Horatius Flaccus, poet, died 8 B.C.

Juv. D. Junius Juvenalis, poet of the 1st cent. A.D.

Liv. T. Livius Patavinus, historian, died 16 B.C.

Lucan. M. Annaeus Lucanus, poet, died 65 A.D.

Lucr. T. Lucretius Carus, poet, died about 50 B.C.

Mart. M. Valerius Martialis, poet of the 1st cent. A.D.

Nep. Cornelius Nepos, writer of biographies of the 1st cent. A.D.

Ov. P. Ovidius Naso, poet, died 16 A.D.

Pers. A. Persius Flaccus, satirist, died 62 A.D.

Petr. T. Petronius Arbiter, satirist, died 67 A.D.

Phaedr. Phaedrus, fabulist of the 1st cent. A.D.

Plaut. M. Accius (or T. Maccius) Plautus, died 184 B.C.

Plin. C. Plinius Secundus (major), naturalist, died 79 A.D. C. Plinius Caecilius Secundus (minor), died about 100 A.D.

Prop. Sex. Aurelius Propertius, poet, died 15 B.C.

Q. Cic. Quintus Cicero, brother of M. Tullius.

Quint. M. Fabius Quintilianus, rhetorician of the 1st cent. A.D.

Sall. C. Crispius Sallustius, died 34 B.C.

Sen. L. Annaeus Seneca, philosopher, died 65 A.D.

Stat. P. Papinius Statius, poet of the 1st cent. A.D.

Suet. C. Suetonius Tranquillus, writer of biographies of the 1st and 2nd cent. A.D.

Tac. C. Cornelius Tacitus, historian, born between 50 and 60 A.D.

Ter. P. Terentius Afer, writer of comedies of the 2nd cent. B.C.

Tib. Albius Tibullus, poet, died 18 B.C.

Varr M. Terentius Varro, writer on husbandry, etc., born 82 B.C.

Vell. P. Velleius Paterculus, historian of the 1st cent. A.D.

Verg. P. Vergilius Maro, poet, died about 19 B.C.

Vitr. Vitruvius Pollio, writer on architecture, died about 14 B.C.

TABLE OF THE ROMAN CALENDAR.

Days of the Month.	January, August, December—31 days.	March, May, July, October—31 days.	April, June, Sept., November—30 days.	February—28 days, in leap year, 29.
1	Kal. Jan. Aug. Dec.	Kal. Mart. Mai. Jul. Oct.	Kal. Apr. Jun. Sept. Nov.	Kal. Febr.
2	a.d. (ante diem) IV. Non. (Jan., Aug., Dec.)	a.d. VI. Non. Mart. Mai. Jul. Oct.	a.d. IV. Non. Apr. Jun. Sept. Nov.	a.d. IV. Non. Febr.
3	a.d. III. „ „	a.d. V. „ „	a.d. III. „ „	a.d. III. „ „
4	Pridie „ „	a.d. IV. „ „	Pridie „ „	Pridie „ „
5	Non. Jan. Aug. Dec.	a.d. III. „ „	Non. Apr Jun. Sept. Nov.	Non. Febr.
6	a.d. VIII. Id. Jan. Aug. Dec.	Pridie „ „	a.d. VIII. Id. Apr. Jun. Sept. Nov.	a.d. VIII. Id. Febr.
7	a.d. VII. „ „	Non. Mart. Mai. Jul. Oct.	a.d. VII. „ „	ad. VII. „ „
8	a.d. VI. „ „	a.d. VIII. Id. Mart. Mai. Jul. Oct.	a.d. VI. „ „	a.d. VI. „ „
9	a.d. V. „ „	a.d. VII. „ „	a.d. V. „ „	a.d. V. „ „
10	a.d. IV. „ „	a.d. VI. „ „	a.d. IV. „ „	a.d. IV. „ „
11	a.d. III. „ „	a.d. V. „ „	a.d. III. „ „	a.d. III. „ „
12	Pridie „ „	a.d. IV. „ „	Pridie „ „	Pridie „ „
13	Id. Jan. Aug. Dec.	a.d. III. „ „	Id. Apr. Jun. Sept. Nov.	Id. Febr.
14	a.d. XIX. Kal. Febr. Sept. Jan. „	Pridie „ „	a.d. XVIII. Kal. Mai. Jul. Oct. Dec.	a.d. XVI. Kal. Mart.
15	a.d. XVIII. „ „	Id. Mart. Mai. Jul. Oct.	a.d. XVII. „ „	a.d. XV. „ „
16	a.d. XVII. „ „	a.d. XVII. Kal. Apr. Jun. Aug. Nov.	a.d. XVI. , „	a.d. XIV. „ „
17	a.d. XVI. „ „	a.d. XVI. „ „	a.d. XV. „ „	a.d. XIII. „ „
18	a.d. XV. „ „	a.d. XV. „ „	a.d. XIV. „ „	a.d. XII. „ „
19	a.d. XIV. „ „	a.d. XIV. „ „	a.d. XIII. „ „	a.d. XI. „ „
20	a.d. XIII. „ „	a.d. XIII. „ „	a.d. XII. „ „	a.d. X. „ „
21	a.d. XII. „ „	a.d. XII. „ „	a.d. XI. „ „	a.d. IX. „ „
22	a.d. XI. „ „	a.d. XI. „ „	a.d. X. „ „	a.d. VIII. „ „
23	a.d. X. „ „	a.d. X. „ „	a.d. IX. „ „	a.d. VII. „ „
24	a.d. IX. „ „	a.d. IX. „ „	a.d. VIII. „ „	a.d. VI. „ „
25	a.d. VIII „ „	a.d. VIII. „ „	a.d. VII. „ „	a.d. V. „ „
26	a.d. VII „ „	a.d. VII. „ „	a.d. VI. „ „	a.d. IV. „ „
27	a.d. VI. „ „	a.d. VI. „ „	a.d. V. „ „	a.d. III. „ „
28	a.d. V. „ „	a.d. V. „ „	a.d. IV. „ „	Pridie „ „
29	a.d. IV. „ „	a.d. IV. „ „	a.d. III. „ „	
30	a.d. III. „ „	a.d. III. „ „	Pridie , „	
31	Pridie „ „	Pridie „ „		

SIGNS AND ABBREVIATIONS PECULIAR TO THE ENGLISH-LATIN SECTION

I.—(a) Brackets ( ) enclosing the first syllable of a compound verb, denote that both the simple and compound forms of the verb are in use, as *(de)currĕre*. Lack of space, as a rule, has prevented the explanation of the difference in shades of meaning between the two forms. Where the student finds this a difficulty, a reference to the Latin-English section will at once relieve him. An English-Latin Dictionary serves its best purpose when it encourages the beginner to consult quotations from Roman authors in a good Latin Dictionary.

(b) Brackets enclosing a single letter denote that the word was written sometimes with and sometimes without that letter. Thus, *ex(s)pectare* shows that the two forms *exspectare* and *expectare* were both in use. The table at the beginning of Messrs. Lewis and Short's Latin Dictionary has frequently been consulted in respect to the spelling of doubtful words.

(c) Brackets enclosing a whole word denote that the word may be inserted or omitted according to the context. Thus for "tide," *aestus (maritimus)* implies that *aestus maritimus* is the full phrase, for which *aestus* alone may sometimes serve.

II.—Space has not allowed the insertion of much help in the way of declensions and conjugations, but the genitive of nouns in the fourth declension is given to distinguish them from those of the first. Where such a genitive occurs in a phrase, it is given thus, *aestus, -ūs, maritimus.* In a few other instances of doubtful words, genitives are also given.

III.— * prefixed to a word denotes that it is of modern or very late Latin origin. † appended to a word denotes that it is only used, in the Classical period, by poets.

IV.—

alqs	= *aliquis*	*alqm*	= *aliquem*
alqd	= *aliquid*	*alqam*	= *aliquam*
alcjs	= *alicujus*	*alqo*	= *aliquo*
alci	= *alicui*	*alqâ*	= *aliquâ*

Ante and Post Aug. = used by writers before and after the time of Augustus.

Circumloc. = circumlocution.

Class. = Classical, *i.e.* belonging to the best period of Latin literature.

Com. = used by the comic poets.

Comb. = in combination.

Eccl. = used by the ecclesiastical writers. The asterisk (*) is sometimes used to prevent a repetition of Eccl. after each of the derivatives in a single paragraph.

Gram. = used by the Latin grammarians.

Inscrip. = found in inscriptions.

Jct. = used by the Jurisconsults, or lawyers.

Late ; very late = used by authors after the Classical period.

Med. Lat. = Latin of the Middle Ages.

Opp. = in opposition to.

V.—Abbreviations of the names of authors peculiar to the English-Latin section of the Dictionary.

Ammian. Ammianus Marcellinus, historian, 4th cent. A.D.

Cels. A. Cornelius Celsus, writer on medicine, 1st cent. A.D.

Curt. Q. Curtius Rufus, historian, probably 1st cent. A.D.

Linn. Karl von Linné, or Linnaeus, modern botanist, 18th cent.

Prisc. Priscianus, grammarian, 5th cent. A.D.

Veget. Flavius Renatus Vegetius, military writer, 4th cent. A.D.

Val. Max. Valerius Maximus, compiler of anecdotes, 1st cent. A.D.

LATIN-ENGLISH

LATIN-ENGLISH DICTIONARY.

A

A a, the first letter of the Latin Alphabet.
a as an abbreviation, see the Table.

a, ah, interj. *Ah!* Verg.

ā, ăb, abs, prep. with abl. (a stands before consonants except h ; ab before vowels, h, and consonants ; abs only before c, q, t). Ab denotes motion in any direction from a fixed point (opp. ad). **I.** Lit., in space, **A.** Of motion, 1, *away from;* fuga ab urbe, Cic. ; 2, a, *from . . . to;* ad carceres a calce revocari, Cic. ; ab aliquo (esp. a me, a te, a se, a nobis, a vobis), *from the house of,* Cic. With verbs of taking, hearing, etc., such as accipio, emo, audio, cognosco, comperio ; a me, *from my purse,* Cic. ; of dependents or disciples, Zeno et qui ab eo sunt, *Zeno and his school,* Cic. ; b, *down from ;* suspendere columbam a malo, Verg. ; c, usque ab, *right away from ;* plausus usque ab capitolio excitatus, Cic. **B.** 1, of direction, *from ;* a supero mari Flaminia (via), ab infero Aurelia, Cic. ; 2, *on the side of;* a septentrionibus, *on the north,* Caes. ; a fronte, a tergo, a latere, a dextro cornu, Cic. ; **ab** novissimis, *in the rear,* Caes. **C.** Of distance, *from ;* 1, Lit., *from* a point, with such verbs as abesse, distare, and with procul, longe, prope ; ab millibus passuum, *a thousand paces distant,* Caes. ; 2, Transf., to express difference, with such verbs as differre, discrepare ; quantum mutatus ab illo, Verg. ; 3, of number or position, *after ;* quartus ab Arcesila, Cic. **II.** Transf., **A.** Of time, 1, with reference to duration, *from ;* ab hora tertia bibebatur, Cic. ; a pueris, *from boyhood,* Cic. ; 2, with reference to distance of time, *from ;* cujus a morte hic tertius et tricesimus annus, Cic. **B.** Of various relations implying the notion of starting from a point ; 1, of agency, with pass. and intrans. verbs, *by ;* reprehendi ab aliquo, Cic. ; interire ab aliquo, Cic. ; 2, of origin, *from, of ;* a, id facinus natum a cupiditate, Cic. ; b, of naming, puero ab inopia Egerio inditum nomen, Liv. ; 3, *in relation to ;* imparati quum a militibus tum a pecunia, Cic. ; 4, *from, out of* (of part of a number) ; nonnulli ab novissimis, Caes. ; 5, in relation to the part of the body with which a person serves ; servus a pedibus, *footman,* Cic. ; a manu servus, *amanuensis,* Suet.

ăbactus -a -um, partic. of abigo.

ăbăcus -i, m. (ἄβαξ). 1, *a counting-board,* Pers. ; 2, *a gaming-board divided into compartments,* Suet. ; 3, *a sideboard,* Cic. ; 4, in architecture, a, *mosaic panelling ;* b, *the square slab on the top of a column.*

ăbăliēnātĭo -ōnis, f. *alienation of property,* Cic.

ăbăliēno, 1. *to separate.* **A.** Lit., 1, *to separate,* Plaut. ; 2, *to alienate* (property) ; agros populi, Cic. **B.** Transf., 1, *to deprive ;* abalienati jure civium, Liv. ; 2, *to estrange ;* aliquem ab aliquo, Cic.

Ăbās -antis, m. *king of Argos, father of Acrisius ;* hence, a, adj., **Ăbantēus** -a -um ; b, **Ăbantĭădes** -ae, m. *a descendant of Abas, Acrisius* (*son of Abas*)*, Perseus* (*great-grandson of Abas*).

ăbăvus -i, m. *a great-great-grandfather,* Cic. ; and in general, *forefather,* Cic.

Abdēra -orum, n. plur. (Ἄβδηρα, τά). **I.** *a town in Thrace* (now *Polystilo* or *Asperosa*)*, birthplace of Protagoras and Democritus, noted for the stupidity of its inhabitants ;* hic Abdera, *here reigns stupidity,* Cic. ; also **Abdēra** -ae, f. Ov. **II.** *a town in Spain* (now *Adra*). **Abdērĭtēs** -ae (abl. -a), m. *an inhabitant of Abdera,* Cic.

abdĭcātĭo -ōnis, f. **1,** *disowning of a son,* Plin. ; **2,** *renouncing of an office ;* dictaturae, Liv.

1. abdĭco, 1. **1,** *to renounce, disown ;* aliquem patrem, Liv. ; **2,** *to abdicate* (a magistracy by a formal declaration)*,* se non modo consulatu sed etiam libertate, Cic. ; in Sall. and Liv. with simple accusative, magistratum, Sall. ; dictaturam, Liv. ; absol., ut abdicarent consules, Cic.

2. abdīco -dixi -dictum, 3. t. t. of augury, *to refuse assent to, disapprove of* (opp. addico) ; quum tres partes (vineae) aves abdixissent, Cic.

abdĭte, adv. *secretly,* Cic.

abdĭtīvus -a -um, *removed, separated,* Plaut.

abdĭtus -a -um, p. adj. (of abdo), *concealed, secret.* **I.** Lit., vis abdita quaedam, Lucr. **II.** Transf., res abditae et obscurae, Cic. ; neut. plur., abdita rerum, *deep thoughts,* Hor.

abdo -dĭdi -dĭtum, 3. **A.** Gen., *to put away, withdraw, remove ;* copias ab eo loco abditas, Caes. ; hence, 1, of a weapon, *to drive in ;* lateri capulo tenus ensem, Verg. ; 2, reflex., abdere se in aliquem locum ; *to withdraw oneself, to retire ;* in intimam Macedoniam, Cic. ; in bibliothecam ; in litteras (or litteris), Cic. **B.** *to secrete, to hide ;* ferrum veste, Liv. ; se in scalarum tenebras, Cic.

abdōmen -ĭnis, n. *the belly,* Plaut. ; especially as seat of the appetite, *gluttony ;* manebat insaturabile abdomen, Cic. ; natus abdomini suo, *whose god is his belly,* Cic. ; abdominis voluptates, *pleasures of appetite,* Cic.

abdūco -duxi -ductum, 3. *to lead* or *take away.* **I. A.** Lit., 1, aliquem e foro, Cic. ; 2, *to take away* for punishment ; collegam vi de foro, Liv. ; in lautumias, Cic. ; 3, *to elope with ;* filiam mimi Isidori, Cic. ; 4, *to steal ;* mancipia, Cic. ; armenta, Ov. **B.** Transf., *to seduce* a person from his allegiance ; equitatum Dolabellae ad se, Cic. **II.** In a wider sense, **A.** *to relieve ;* animum a sollicitudine, Cic. **B.** *to bring down, to lower ;* artem ad mercedem atque quaestum, Cic.

Ăbella -ae, f. *town in Campania* (now *Avella Vecchia*). Adj., **Ăbellānus** -a -um.

ăbĕo -ii -ĭtum -īre, *to go away.* **I. A.**
Lit., **1.** Gen., ex agris atque urbibus, Cic. ; ab
urbe, Liv. ; de Sicilia, Cic. ; comitio, Liv. ; si
abis periturus, *if you go to death,* Verg. ; imper., abi, a, *good, very well;* non es avarus, abi,
Hor. ; **b,** *be off with you,* so abin (for abisne) ;
abi in malam rem, *go to the devil,* Plaut. ; abi
hinc cum tribunatibus ac rogationibus tuis,
Liv. Of things, abeuntia vela, Ov. ; sol abit,
Plaut. ; cornus sub altum pectus abit, Verg. ;
2, Esp., a, *to come off* (e.g. from a battle);
Romani semper victores certamine abire, Liv. ;
nemo non donatus abibit, Verg. ; absol., abiturum
eum non esse, si accessisset, *he could not have
got off unpunished,* Cic. ; **b,** *to retire from* a
public office ; consulatu, Cic. ; **c,** of the dying,
to depart; ad deos, Cic. ; ad plures, *to "the
great majority,"* Petr. ; e vita, Cic. ; **d,** in auctions, *not to be knocked down to;* si res abiret
a mancipe, Cic. **B.** Transf., **1,** Gen., non longe
abieris, *you have not far to go* (for an example),
Cic. ; quorsum abeant, *on which side will they
range themselves?* Hor. ; **2.** Esp., of a discussion, *to digress;* illuc, unde abii, redeo, Hor. ; quid
ad istas ineptias abis? Cic. ; etiam tu hinc abis,
will you also go away? Cic. **II.** With notion of
disappearing ; **1,** of time, *to pass away ;* abiit
ille annus, Cic. ; **2,** of diseases, jam abiit pestilentia, Cic. ; **3,** of other things, *to disappear,
vanish;* sensus abit, Cic. ; timor, fides abiit,
Liv. ; **4,** of the consequences of an action, non
posse istaec sic abire, *be without consequences,*
Cic. **III.** With notion of transference from one
person or thing to another, **1,** *to go over ;* **a,** to
a person, ad sanos abeat tutela propinquos, Hor. ;
b, to a thing, vigor ingenii velocis in alas et pedes
abiit, Ov. ; **2,** *to change into;* sic deus in flammas
abiit, Ov.

ăbĕquĭto, 1. *to ride off,* Liv.

ăberrātĭo, -ōnis, f. *an escape or relief from
anything irksome,* Cic.

ăberro, 1. *to wander, lose one's way.* **I.**
Lit., pecore, Liv. ; aberrantes ex agmine naves,
Liv. **II.** Transf., **1,** *to deviate from;* a proposito,
Cic. ; **2,** *to free oneself from something irksome;*
a miseria quasi aberrare, Cic.

ăbhinc, adv. *from hence.* **I.** Of space, aufer
abhinc lacrimas, Lucr. **II.** Of time, reckoned from
the present moment backward ; annos tres, triennium, annis tribus abhinc, *three years ago,* Cic.

ăbhorrĕo, 2. I. Lit., *to shrink back from, to
be disinclined to* a pace, Caes. ; a ducenda uxore,
Cic. ; with abl. alone, spectaculorum oblecta-
mentis, Tac. ; absol., omnes aspernabantur, omnes
abhorrebant, Cic. **II.** Transf., *to be inconsistent
with* or *opposed to ;* oratio abhorret a persona hominis gravissimi, Cic. ; a fide, *to be incredible,* Liv. ;
spes ab effectu haud abhorrens, *hope capable of
being realised,* Liv. ; orationes abhorrent inter
se, *are inconsistent with one another,* Liv. ; with
simple abl., neque abhorret vero, Tac. ; with
dat., huic tam pacatae profectioni abhorrens mos,
Liv. Pres. part., as an adjective, *unseasonable,
inappropriate;* absurdae atque abhorrentes lacrimae, Liv.

ăbĭegnus -a -um (abies), *made of fir wood
or deal,* Cic.

ăbĭes -ĕtis, f. **I.** *the fir-tree* (Pinus picea,
Linn.), Caes. **II.** Meton., *anything made of deal ;
a letter,* because formerly written on wood, Plaut. ;
a ship, Verg. ; *a spear,* Verg. (Abiĕtis, ābiĕtĕ,
trisyll., Verg.)

ăbĭgo -ēgi -actum, 3. (ab and ago). **I.** Lit.,
A. Gen., *to drive away;* volucres et feras, Cic.
B. Esp., **1,** pecus, *to steal cattle,* Cic. ; **2,** partum
medicamentis, *to procure abortion,* Cic. ; **3,**
uxorem, *to divorce,* Suet. **II.** Fig., *to banish,*

get rid of; pauperiem epulis regum, Hor. Abacti
oculi, *deep-sunk eyes,* Stat.

ăbītĭo -ōnis, f. = abitus (q.v.).

ābĭto, 3. *to go away,* Plaut.

ăbĭtus -ūs, m. (abeo), **1,** *a going away, departure ;* post abitum hujus, Cic. ; **2,** *place of
egress* (opp. aditus), Verg.

abjectē, adv. *abjectly, in a spiritless and
cowardly manner,* Cic. ; *meanly,* Tac.

abjectĭo -ōnis, f. **I.** Lit., *a throwing away, rejection.* **II.** Transf., animi, *despondency, despair,*
Cic.

abjectus -a -um, p. adj. with compar. and
superl. (abjicio) ; **1,** of position, *low, common ;*
familia abjecta atque obscura, Cic. ; **2,** of
character, *cowardly, mean-spirited;* animus, Cic. ;
3, *despicable;* contemptus atque abjectus, Cic. ;
4, *without force, prosaic;* versus, Cic. ; oratio
humilis et abjecta, Cic.

abjĭcĭo -jēci -jectum, 3. (ab and jacio), *to
throw down, or away.* **I.** Lit., **1,** scutum, arma,
Cic. ; se ad pedes alicuius, Cic. ; **2,** *to throw down
violently;* aliquem ad tribunal, ad pedes tuos, ad
terram virgis et verberibus, Cic. ; so in battle, *to
strike to the ground,* Verg. **II.** Transf., **1,** *to pronounce carelessly, to break off abruptly;* versum,
Cic. ; ambitus non est abjiciendus, *the period
must not be broken off abruptly,* Cic. ; **2,** *to get
rid of, to dispose of;* pecuniam, Cic. ; **3,** *to give
up, to let go;* memoriam beneficiorum, Cic. ; *to
abandon;* Scaurum, Cic. ; **4,** *to dash to the
ground, to deprive of all power;* senatus auctoritatem, Cic. ; with reference to character, *to
dishearten;* se perculsum atque abjectum esse
sentit, Cic. ; abjecta metu filia, *desponding,* Cic. ;
5, Fig., *to throw away ;* cogitationes in rem tam
humilem, Cic. ; se abjicere, *to degrade oneself,* Cic.

abjūdĭco, 1. (opp. adjudico), as a judge, *to
give sentence against any one; to take away by a
judgment;* aliquid ab aliquo, Cic. ; sibi libertatem, Cic.

abjungo -junxi -junctum, 3. **I.** *to unharness;* juvencum, Verg. **II.** Transf., *to estrange,
detach ;* abjuncto Labieno, Caes. ; se ab hoc
dicendi genere, *to keep from,* Cic.

abjūro, 1. *to abjure, deny on oath;* pecuniam,
Cic. ; creditum, Sall.

ablātīvus -a -um, *ablative.* Subst., **ablātīvus** -i, m. (sc. casus), *the ablative, the sixth
case* of the Latin noun, Quint.

ablēgātĭo -ōnis, f. **I.** Gen., *a sending away ;*
juventutis ad bellum, Liv. **II.** Esp., *banishment,* = relegatio, Plin.

ablēgo, 1. I. Lit., *to send away, remove to a
distance ;* honestos homines, Cic. ; pueros vena-
tum, Liv. ; aliquem a penatibus suis, Liv. **II.**
Fig., **1,** haec (legatio) a fratris adventu me
ablegat, *prevents me from being present on my
brother's arrival,* Cic. ; **2,** milit. t. t., *to dislodge;*
aliquem, Liv.

ablĭgūrĭo, 4. *to consume in luxury;* patria
bona, Ter.

ablŏco, 1. *to let on lease,* Suet.

ablūdo, 3. Lit. *to be out of tune with,* hence
to be unlike; haec a te non multum abludit
imago, Hor.

ablŭo -lŭi -lūtum, 3. *to wash.* **I.** In the sense
of cleansing, pedes alicuius, Cic. ; pass., ablui,
to be washed clean, Cic. **II.** In the sense of
removing, *to wash away.* **A.** Lit., maculas e
veste, Plin. ; lacrimas, Tac. ; poet., sitis de corpore abluitur, *is quenched,* Lucr. **B.** Transf.,
omnis perturbatio animi placatione abluatur, Cic.

ablūtĭo -ōnis, f. *a washing away, ablution,*
Plin.

abnĕgo, 1. *to deny, refuse;* alicui conjugium et dotes, Verg.; nec comitem se abnegat, Hor.; absol., abnegat, Verg.

abnĕpos -ōtis, m. *great-great-grandson,* Suet.

abneptis -is, f. *a great-great-granddaughter,* Suet.

Abnŏba -ae, m. *a range of mountains in Germany, where the Danube rises.*

abnocto, 1. *to stay out all night,* Sen.

abnormis -e (ab and norma), *irregular, unconventional;* abnormis sapiens, *one of Nature's philosophers,* Hor.

abnŭo -nŭi -nŭĭtūrus, 3. *to refuse by a motion of the head or eye, deny;* manu abnuit quidquam opis in se esse, *gave a sign with his hand that he could not help,* Liv.; regi pacem, Sall.; nemo abnuit a se commissum esse facinus, Cic.; spes abnuit, *it does not admit of hope,* Tib.; of soldiers, *to refuse to fight,* Liv.

abnūto, 1. *to deny* (by a nod) *repeatedly,* Plaut.

ăbŏlĕo -ēvi -ĭtum, 2. *to destroy.* **I.** Lit., Poppaeae corpus non igni abolitum, Tac.; viscera undis, *to cleanse,* Verg. **II.** Fig., *to do away with;* magistratum, Liv.; dedecus armis, Verg.; ritus, sacrificandi disciplinam, Liv.

ăbŏlesco -ēvi, no sup., 3. *to perish;* non abolescet gratia facti, Verg.; nomen vetustate abolevit, Liv.

ăbŏlĭtĭo -ōnis, f. *a removing, abrogating, annulling, abolition;* legis, *repeal,* Suet.; tributorum, Tac.; facti, *amnesty,* Suet.

ăbolla -ae, f. *cloak of thick woollen cloth,* worn by soldiers; prov., facinus majoris abollae, *a crime on a larger scale,* Juv.

ăbŏmĭno = abominor (q.v.).

ăbŏmĭnor -atus (sum), 1. dep. (ab and omen), **1,** *to deprecate an unfavourable omen;* aliquid, Liv.; quod abominor, *God forbid,* Ov.; **2,** *to hate, detest, abominate* (opp. optare), Liv.; abominandus, *detestable,* Liv.; abominatus, *detested,* Hor.

Ăbŏrīgĭnes -um, m. (Ἀβοριγίνες), *the Aborigines,* an Italian tribe from whom the Latins were said to be descended; hence *original inhabitants of a country* (= αὐτόχθονες). Plin.

ăbŏrĭor -ortus (sum) 4. dep. (opp. exorior), **1,** of the heavenly bodies, *to set, to disappear,* Varr.; **2,** *to perish by untimely birth,* Plin.; **3,** poet., of the voice, *to fail,* Lucr.

ăbŏriscor = aborior (q.v.).

ăbortĭo -ōnis, f. *an untimely birth, miscarriage,* Cic.

ăbortīvus -a -um, *prematurely born;* Sisyphus, Hor.; ovum, *addled,* Mart. Subst., **ăbortĭvum** -i, n. (sc. medicamentum), *drug for procuring abortion,* Juv.

ăbortus -ūs, m. *a miscarriage,* Cic.

abrādo -rasi -rasum, 3. **I.** Lit., *to scrape off, shave;* supercilia, Cic. **II.** Transf., *to squeeze money out of a person, to extort;* nihil se ab A. Caecina posse litium terrore abradere, Cic.

abrĭpio -rĭpŭi -reptum, 3. (ab and rapio), *to snatch away, tear off, drag off.* **I. A.** Lit., abripi vi fluminis, Caes. **B.** Transf., Romulum si natura ad humanum exitum abripuit, Cic. **II. A.** *to rob;* non dona tantum sed simulacra numinum, Tac. **B.** 1, *to drag away;* Cappadocem de grege venalium, Cic.; **2,** *to drag away to punishment;* aliquem de convivio in vincula, Cic.; **3,** *to take away by force;* filios e complexu parentum, Cic.

abrōdo -si -sum, 3. *to gnaw off, away,* Pers.

abrŏgātĭo -ōnis, f. *an annulling or repealing;* legis, Cic.

abrŏgo, 1. **A.** 1, *to repeal a law wholly, to annul;* legem, Cic.; huic legi nec abrogari fas est, neque derogari ex hac aliquid licet neque tota abrogari potest, Cic.; **2,** *to deprive* (a magistrate of his office); si tibi magistratum abrogasset, Cic. **B.** Transf., *to take away;* fidem, *to take away a man's credit,* Cic.

abrŏtŏnum -i, n. and **abrŏtŏnus** -i, f. (ἀβρότονον), *southern-wood, an aromatic herb,* Lucr., Hor.

abrumpo -rūpi -ruptum, 3. **I.** *to break off, loosen, separate.* **A.** Lit., ramos, Ov.; vincula, Liv. **B.** Transf., se latrocinio Antonii, *to break away from,* Cic. **II.** *to tear off, to separate forcibly, to sever.* **A.** Lit., pontem, Tac. **B.** Transf., 1, *to violate;* fas, Verg.; 2, *to break off prematurely, to destroy;* vitam, Verg.; medium sermonem, *to break off in the middle of a speech,* Verg.

abruptĭo -ōnis, f. (abrumpo). **I.** *a tearing away;* corrigiae, *of a shoe-latchet,* Cic. **II.** Transf., *divorce,* Cic.

abruptus -a -um, p. adj. with compar. and superl. (abrumpo), *torn off;* hence, **I.** *steep, precipitous.* Subst., **abruptum** -i, n. *a steep ascent or descent;* sorbet in abruptum fluctus, Verg. **II.** Transf., **A.** Gen. only subst., abruptum -i, n. *a precipice, the precipice of danger, the road to ruin;* in abruptum tractus, Tac. **B.** Of character, *rough;* contumacia, Tac.

abscēdo -cessi -cessum, 3. *to go away, depart.* **I.** Lit., **A.** Of persons, a curia, e foro, Liv.; as milit. t. t., *to withdraw, retire;* a Capua, Liv.; impers., Regio abscessum est, Liv. **B.** Of things, *to retire;* quantum mare abscedebat, Liv. **II.** Transf., **A.** of persons, 1, *to retire from an office or employment;* non militaribus modo sed civilibus quoque muneribus, Liv.; **2,** *to desert one;* Pallada abscessisse mihi, Ov. **B.** Of things, 1, *to go away;* somnus ut abscessit, Ov.; **2,** *to desert;* cives earum urbium quae regno abscedunt, Liv.

abscessĭo -ōnis, f. (abscedo), *a going away, a separation,* Cic.

abscessus -ūs, m. (abscedo), *a going away;* 1, of persons, *going away* (especially in battle), *withdrawal;* Rutulum, Verg.; continuus abscessus, Tac.; 2, of inanimate objects, solis, Cic.

abscīdo -cīdi -cīsum. 3. (abs and caedo), *to cut off.* **I.** Lit., funes, Caes.; aquam, Liv.; caput, Liv. **II. A.** Transf., *to separate;* intersaeptis munimentis hostis pars parti abscisa erat, Liv.; abscisus in duas partes exercitus, Caes. **B.** *to take away;* regibus spem auxilii sui, Liv.

abscindo -scĭdi -scissum, 3. *to tear off, wrench away.* **I.** Lit., tunicam a pectore, Cic.; vestem humeris, Verg.; venas, *to open the veins,* Tac.; poet., abscissa comas, *with her hair torn,* Verg. **II.** Transf., **A.** *to divide;* terras Oceano, Hor. **B.** *to separate;* inane soldo, Hor. **C.** *to take away;* reditus dulces, Hor.

abscīsus -a -um, p. adj. (from abscido), *cut off,* hence *precipitous;* rupes, Liv.

abscondĭtē, adv. *obscurely, abstrusely,* Cic.

abscondo -condi (-condĭdi) -condĭtum (-consum), 3. **I.** *to conceal;* gladios, Cic. **II. A.** *to obscure;* galea frontem abscondit, Juv.; hence pass. of stars, *to set,* Verg. **B.** *to lose sight of;* Phaeacum arces, Verg. **C.** *to keep out of sight;* quod quo studiosius ab istis opprimitur et absconditur eo magis eminet et apparet, Cic.

absens -entis (absum), p. adj. *absent,* Cic.

absentia -ae, f. (absum), *absence*, Cic.

absilio 4. (ab and salio), *to spring forth*, or *away*, Lucr.

absimilis -e, *unlike;* non absimili forma, Caes.

absinthium -i, n. (ἀψίνθιον), *wormwood*, Lucr.

absisto -stiti, -stitum, 3. **1,** *to go away*, followed by ab or the abl. alone; limine, Verg.; ab signis, Caes.; absol., tandem abstiterunt, Liv.; of things, ab ore scintillae absistunt, Verg.; **2,** *to desist from;* with abl., obsidione, spe, Liv.; with infin., absiste moveri, *cease to be moved*, Verg.; with gerund, sequendo, *from following*, Liv.; accusator abstitit, *the accuser withdrew* (i.e. from his accusation), Tac.

absolute, adv. *perfectly, completely;* vivere feliciter, absolute, Cic.

absolutio -ōnis, f. (absolvo), **1,** *acquittal;* majestatis, *on the charge of treason*, Cic.; **2,** *perfection;* virtus quae rationis absolutio definitur, Cic.

absolutorius -a -um, *relating to acquittal;* tabella, *the voting-tablet that acquits*, Suet. Subst., **absolutorium** -ii, n. (sc. remedium), *means of escape from*, Plin.

absolutus -a -um, p. adj. with compar. and superl. (absolvo). **I.** *perfect, complete;* vita, Cic. **II.** *unfettered, unconditional, absolute;* causa, Cic.

absolvo -solvi -solutum, 3. **A.** Lit., *to loosen*. **B.** Transf., **1, a,** *to free;* se a Fannio judicio, Cic.; aliquem regni suspicione, Liv.; **b,** *to acquit;* improbitatis, Cic.; capitis, Nep.; reos culpa, Ov.; de praevaricatione, Cic.; **2,** *to dispose of in narration, to relate;* de Catilinae conjuratione paucis absolvam, Sall.; **3,** *to complete, to finish;* tectum, Cic.; opera, Caes.; absolve beneficium tuum, Liv.

absonus -a -um. **I.** Lit., *inharmonious;* vox, Cic. **II.** Transf., *disagreeing with, not correspondent with;* absoni a voce motus, Liv.; with dat., nihil absonum fidei divinae originis fuit, Liv.

absorbeo -ŭi, 2. *to swallow, to gulp down.* **I.** Lit., placentas, Hor; Oceanus vix videtur tot res absorbere potuisse, Cic. **II.** Transf., hunc absorbuit aestus gloriae, *carried him off*, Cic.; tribunatus absorbet meam orationem, *absorbs, engrosses*, Cic.

absque, prep. with abl. *without;* absque argumento, Cic.

abstemius -a -um (abs and temum = temetum), *one who abstains from intoxicating liquors, temperate, abstemious, moderate*, Ov., Hor.

abstergeo -tersi -tersum, 2. *to wipe off, to dry by wiping*. **I.** Lit., cruorem, Liv. **II.** Transf., *to remove something disagreeable;* omnes senectutis molestias, Cic.

absterreo -terrui -territum, **2.** *to frighten away, to drive away by fear.* **I.** Lit., hostes saxis, Liv.; neminem a congressu meo, Cic. **II.** Transf. *to frighten from, keep off from;* eos a tam detestabili consilio, Liv.; animos vitiis, *from vices*, Hor.; aliquem bello, Tac.

abstinens -entis, p. adj. with compar. and superl. (abstineo), *abstinent, continent, temperate*, Cic.; with genit., pecuniae, Hor.

abstinenter, adv. *abstinently, continently*, Cic.

abstinentia -ae, f. **I.** *abstinence, continence, self-denial, temperance;* absol., *fasting;* abstinentia vitum finire, Tac. **II.** *uprightness*, Cic.; *freedom from avarice*, Cic.

abstineo -tinui -tentum, 2. (abs and teneo), *to hold back, to keep away from.* **I.** Transf., manus, Liv.; gen. with a and the abl. or with the abl. alone, militem a praeda, Liv.; manus a se, *to abstain from suicide*, Cic. **II.** Reflex., abstinere se, or simply abstinere; **a,** with the abl. or with ab and the abl., se scelere, Cic.; a legatis violandis, Liv.; publico, *not to go out*, Tac.; **b,** with genit., irarum, Hor.; **c,** with acc., liberas urbes, Liv.; **d,** with acc. of thing and dat. of person, Aeneae Antenorique omne jus belli; **e,** with ne and the subj., Liv.; **f,** absol., non tamen abstinuit, Verg.

absto, 1. *to stand at a distance, stand aloof*, Hor.

abstraho -traxi, -tractum, 3. **I.** Lit., *to drag away;* aliquem de matris complexu, Cic.; naves e portu, Liv.; aliquem a penetralibus, Liv.; liberos in servitutem, Caes. **II.** Transf., **A.** aliquem ex tanto comitatu clarissimorum virum, *to exclude*, Cic.; animus a corpore abstractus, Cic.; a bono in pravum, Sall. **B. 1,** *to estrange;* copias a Lepido, Cic.; **2,** *to restrain;* ingressos in castra ab direptione abstrahere non poterat, Liv.; a rebus gerendis senectus abstrahit; **3,** *to draw away from;* a bonis, Cic.; se a sollicitudine, Cic.

abstrudo -trūsi -trūsum, 3. *to push away from any place, to hide.* **I.** Lit., se in silvam densam, Cic.; semina flammae abstrusa in venis silicis, Verg. **II.** Transf., penitus abstrusus animi dolor, *deep-seated grief*, Cic.

abstrusus -a -um, p. adj. with compar. (from abstrudo). **A.** Lit., *concealed, secret*, Plin.; **B.** Transf., **1,** *abstruse;* disputatio abstrusior, Cic.; **2,** of character, *reserved*, Tac.

absum (abfui, abesse, afui, afuturus, aforem, afore, etc., also occur). **I.** With regard to motion, *to be away, to be absent.* **A.** Gen., ab urbe or ex urbe, Cic. **B.** Esp., **1,** *to take no part in;* ab hoc concilio, Caes.; ab his studiis, Cic.; toto bello, Caes.; **2,** *not to help;* quo plus interat, eo plus aberas a me, *the more I needed you, the less you helped me*, Cic.; longe iis paternum nomen populi Romani afuturum, *would be of no avail*, Caes.; **3,** *to be wanting;* studium semper sit, cunctatio absit, Cic.; semper aves quod abest, Lucr.; neque corpus neque animus a vobis aberit, Sall.; abest historia nostris litteris, Cic. **II.** As regards position, **A.** Lit., *to be distant;* ab urbe milia passuum ducenta, Cic.; quatridui iter Laodicea, Cic. **B.** Transf., **1,** *to be far from;* longe a spe, Cic.; so the impers. phrase, tantum abest ut — ut, e.g. tantum abest ab eo ut malum sit mors ut verear, *so far is death from being an evil that I fear*, etc., Cic.; so haud multum, or procul abest, or paulum abest, or minimum abest quin, etc.; haud multum afuit quin interficeretur, *he was nearly killed*, Liv.; **2,** *to be free from* (a fault); a culpa, Cic.; a cupiditate pecuniae, Nep.; **3,** *to be far removed* (especially in phrases expressing a wish); procul absit gloria vulgi, Tib.; nomen ipsum crucis absit non modo a corpore civium Romanorum, etc., Cic.; **4,** *to be firmly opposed to;* a consilio fugiendi, Cic.; **5,** *to be inconsistent with;* quod certe abest a tua virtute et fide, Cic.

absumedo -inis, f. *consumption*, Plaut.

absumo -sumpsi -sumptum 3. *to take away.* **I. A.** *to lessen, destroy, consume;* res maternas atque paternas, Hor.; absumptis frugum alimentis, Liv. **B.** Of time, *to waste;* tempus dicendo, Cic. **II.** *to destroy utterly.* **A.** Of things, incendium domos absumpsit, Liv. **B.** Of living beings, *to kill;* multos pestilentia absumpsit, Liv.

absurde, adv. **1,** *harshly, discordantly;*

canere, Cic.; 2, *in bad taste*; absurde et aspere respondere verbis vultuque, Cic.

absurdus -a -um. **I.** Lit., *that which offends the ear, unmelodious, harsh*; vox, Cic. **II.** Transf., *foolish, unreasonable.* **A.** Of things, vestrae istae absurdae atque abhorrentes lacrimae, Liv.; haud absurdum est, *it is not out of place*, Sall. **B.** Of persons, *incapable*; homo, Cic.; ingenium haud absurdum, Sall.; absurdus ingenio, Tac.

Absyrtus -i, m. (Ἄψυρτος), *brother of Medea, killed by his sister on her flight from Colchis.*

ăbundans -antis, p. adj. with compar. and superl. (abundo). **I.** Lit., of rivers, *overflowing*; amnis abundantissimus, Cic. **II.** Transf., **A.** *abundant, rich*; with abl., locus fontibus abundans, Cic.; with genit., lactis, Verg. **B.** 1, *abounding in* (thoughts, devices, etc.); abundantior consilio, Cic.; 2, in a bad sense, *overloaded*; non erat abundans, non inops tamen oratio, Cic. **C.** *numerous*; abundante multitudine freti, Liv.; abundantes voluptates, Liv.

ăbundantĕr, adv. 1, *abundantly*; abundantius occurrere, Cic.; 2, of discourse, *copiously*; loqui, Cic.

ăbundantĭa -ae, f. 1, *abundance, richness, plenty*; omnium rerum quas natura desiderat, Cic.; voluptatum, Cic.; 2, *riches, wealth*, Tac.

ăbundē, adv. *copiously, excessively, extravagantly*; promittere, Lucr.; satisfacere, Cic.; with adj., abunde magnus, Sall.; tibi abunde est, *you are more than satisfied*, Plin.; abunde libertatem ratus, *thinking liberty more than enough*, Sall. Subst. with genit., terrorum ac fraudis abunde est, Verg.

ăbundo, 1. *to overflow.* **I.** Lit., flumina, Lucr.; abundat aqua, Liv. **II.** Transf., **A.** *to grow in abundance*; de terris abundant herbarum genera, Lucr. **B.** *to abound*; porco, Cic.; ingenio et doctrina, Cic.; absol., *to be rich*; quum ex reliquis vel abundare debeam, cogor mutuari, Cic.

ăbūsĭo -ōnis, f. (abutor), in rhetoric, *a false use of words*, Cic.

ăbusquĕ, prep. with abl. = usque ab, *from*; 1, as regards position, Oceano abusque, Tac.; 2, as regards time, Tiberio abusque, Tac.

ăbūsus -ūs, m. (abutor), *using up, wasting*, Cic.

ăbūtor -ūsus -sum, 3. dep., with abl. **I.** *to use*; nisi omni tempore, quod mihi lege concessum est, abusus ero, Cic. **II.** *to make full use of, to use fully.* **A.** In a good sense, sagacitate canum ad utilitatem nostram, Cic. **B.** In a bad sense, *to waste*; militum sanguine, Cic.; insolenter et immodice indulgentia populi Romani, Liv. **C.** *to use a word wrongly*; verbo, Cic.

Ăbȳdus (Abȳdos) -i, f. and **Ăbȳdum** -i, n. (Ἄβυδος). **I.** *a town in Asia Minor, on the Hellespont* (modern *Aïdos* or *Avido*). **II.** *a town in Egypt.* Adj., **Ăbȳdēnus** -a -um; juvenis or absol., *Leander*, Ov.; plur., **Abȳdēni** -orum, *the inhabitants of Abydos*, Tac.

Ăbȳla -ae, f. (Ἀβύλη), *a mountain on the African side of the Straits of Gibraltar, forming one of the so-called Pillars of Hercules* (now *Sierra Zimiera*).

ac, vid. atque.

Ăcădēmĭa -ae, f. (Ἀκαδήμεια), *the Academy, a grove near Athens where Plato taught*; hence, meton., *the Academic school of philosophy*, Cic.; hence, too, *a gymnasium on Cicero's estate at Tusculum*, called after the Athenian Academy.

Ăcădēmĭcus -a -um (Ἀκαδημικός). **I.** *belonging to the Academy at Athens*; philosophi,

Cic.; hence plur. subst., **Ăcădēmĭci** -orum, m. *the Academic philosophers.* **II.** *belonging to Cicero's gymnasium, called the Academy*; hence plur. subst., **Ăcădēmĭca** -orum, n. *a treatise of Cicero on the Academic philosophy.*

Ăcădēmus -i, m. (Ἀκάδημος), *a Greek hero*, after whom the Academia was named.

ăcălanthis -ĭdis, f. (ἀκαλανθίς) = acanthis, q.v.

Ăcămās -antis, m. (Ἀκάμας), 1, *son of Theseus and Phaedra*, Verg.; 2, *promontory in Cyprus*, Plin.

ăcanthis -ĭdis, f. (ἀκανθίς), *a small dark green bird, the thistle-finch*, Plin.

1. **ăcanthus** -i, m. (ἄκανθος), 1, *bear's foot, a plant*, Verg.; 2, *a thorny evergreen Egyptian tree*, Verg.

2. **Ăcanthus** -i, f. (Ἄκανθος), *a town in the Macedonian peninsula—Chalcidice.*

ăcapnŏs -ŏn (ἄκαπνος), *without smoke*; ligna, *burning without smoke*, Mart.

Ăcarnānes -um, m. (Ἀκαρνᾶνες), *Acarnanians*; Acarnanum amnis, *the Achelous*, Ov.; sing., **Ăcarnān** -anis, *an Acarnanian*, Verg.; hence **Ăcarnānĭa** -ae, *Acarnania, a country on the west of Greece, between Epirus and Aetolia.* Adj., **Ăcarnānĭcus** -a -um.

Ăcastus -i, m. (Ἄκαστος). **I.** *son of the Thessalian king Pelias, father of Laodamia, brother of Alcestis.* **II.** *a slave of Cicero.*

Acca Lārentia, *a Roman goddess of the fields, according to the legend, the wife of the herdsman Faustulus, and the nurse of Romulus and Remus.* **Lārentalia** or **Accalia** -ium, n. *her festival at Rome in December.*

accēdo -cessi -cessum, 3. (ad and cedo), *to approach, to come near.* **I.** Lit., **A.** Gen., 1, of persons, with the accusative and ad; ad urbem, Cic.; alicui ad aurem et dicere, *to approach any one to whisper*, Cic.; with in, in aedes, Cic.; in funus, *to join the funeral procession*, Cic.; with simple accusative, scopulos, Verg.; Jugurtham, Sall.; absol., *to approach*, Cic.; 2, of lifeless subjects, febris accedit, Cic. **B.** Esp., 1, *to come as a suppliant*; senatus supplex accedit ad Caesarem, Cic.; quo accedam aut quos appellem, Sall.; 2, *to come as an enemy*; usque ad castra, Caes.; with simple acc., loca hostiliter, Sall.; 3, *to come to an auction to bid*; ad illud scelus sectionis, Cic.; ad hastam, Liv.; 4, *to approach the city (Rome) as a candidate for a triumph*; ad urbem, Cic. **II.** Transf., **A.** Gen., 1, of persons, ad amicitiam Philippi, Nep.; sed propius accedam, de his nostris testibus dicam, Cic.; 2, of lifeless subjects, accedit manus extrema operibus, Cic.; fervor accedit capiti, *the wine mounts to his head*, Hor. **B.** Esp., 1, of time, *to approach*; quo propius ad mortem accedam, Cic.; 2, *to enter upon some work*; ad rem publicam, *to begin public life*, Cic.; ad vectigalia, *to engage in the collection of the taxes*, Cic.; 3, *to assent to*; ad conditiones, Cic.; 4, *to be added, to increase*; ad eas (naves) captivae Massiliensium accesserunt sex, Caes.; quo plus aetatis ei accederet, *the older he became*, Cic.; iis tantum fiduciae accessit ut, etc., Caes.; hence the phrases, huc accedit, eo accedit, huc accedit summus timor, Cic.; often followed by ut and quod, with the meaning of simply *moreover*; 5, *to fall to one's share, to come to one*; num tibi stultitia accessit, Plaut.; alicui animus accedit, Cic.; 6, *to approach, to become like*; propius ad deos, Cic.

accĕlĕro, 1. **I.** Trans., *to quicken, to accelerate*; iter, Caes.; consulatum alicui, Tac. **II.**

Intrans., *to hasten;* si accelerare volent, Cic. ; accelera, signifer, Liv.

accendo -cendi -censum 3. (ad and * cando, causat. of candeo), *to kindle, to set on fire.* **I. A.** Lit., faces, Cic. ; tus, Liv. **B.** Met., *to lighten up;* luna radiis solis accensa, Cic. **II.** Transf., **A.** Gen., *to kindle as a light;* virtutum quasi scintillulae e quibus accendi philosophi ratio debet, Cic. **B.** Esp., 1, *to inflame;* plebis animum, Sall. ; animos bello, *to excite to war,* Verg. ; ira accensus, Liv. ; 2, *to provoke;* spem invidiam, Liv. ; studia Numidarum in Jugurtham accensa, *the enthusiasm of the N. for J.*), Sall. ; 3, *to increase;* quum eo magis vis venti accensa esset, Liv.

accensĕo -censum, 2. *to reckon in addition;* accenseor illi, *I am his comrade,* Ov.

1. **accensus** -a -um, part. of accenseo. **I.** Generally used in plural, **accensi** -orum, lit. *those numbered with;* originally, *the fifth class of Roman citizens,* who in battle stood in the last ranks, and were also employed in constructing public roads, hence *the supernumeraries,* Liv. **II. accensus** -i, m. *a subordinate public officer* (in the service of the decemviri, consuls, and praetors), Cic.

2. **accensus** -a -um, partic. of accendo.

acceptĭo -ōnis, f. *a reception, acceptance,* Cic. ; frumenti, *receipt,* Sall.

accepto, 1. (intens. of accipio), *to receive,* Plaut.

acceptor -ōris, m. *one who approves,* Plaut.

acceptrix -īcis, f. *she who receives,* Plaut.

acceptus -a -um, p. adj. with compar. and superl. (from accipio), *welcome, pleasant, agreeable;* 1, of persons, with the dat., qui maxime plebi acceptus erat, Caes. ; 2, of things, nihil est deo acceptius quam, etc., Cic.

accerso = arcesso (q.v.).

accessĭo -ōnis, f. (accedo), *a going or coming to.* **I.** Lit., suis accessionibus, *by the audiences which he gave,* Cic. **II.** Transf., **A.** *increase; dignitatis,* Cic. ; pecuniae, Nep. **B.** *addition, appendage;* accessionem adjunxit aedibus, Cic. ; minima accessio semper Epirus regno Macedoniae fuit, Liv. **C.** *addition to a tax;* decumae, Cic.

accessus -ūs, m. (accedo) *an approach to.* **I.** Lit., **A.** ad urbem nocturnus, Cic. ; accessus stellarum et recessus, Cic. ; accessus et recessus aestuum, *ebb and flow,* Cic. **B.** *admittance* to a person ; dare alicui accessum, Ov. **C.** *means of approach, entrance;* omnem accessum lustrare, Verg. **II.** Transf., ad res salutares, *inclination to,* Cic. ; ad causam, *leading up to a subject,* Cic.

1. **accido** -cīdi -cisum, 3. (ad and caedo), 1, Lit., *to hew* or *hack at;* aut ab radicibus subruere aut accidere arbores, Caes. ; 2, Transf., *to weaken, ruin;* Latinorum etsi pariter accisae copiae sint, Liv. ; res accisae, Cic.

2. **accido** -cīdi, no sup. 3. (ad and cado), *to fall down, to fall to.* **I.** Lit., **A.** Gen., ad terram, Plaut. **B.** Esp., 1, of missiles, tela ab omni parte accidebant, Liv. ; 2, *to fall at the feet of, to ask assistance;* ad pedes omnium, Cic. ; 3, *to come to the ears* or *notice of;* vox accidit ad hostes, Liv. **II.** Transf., **A.** *to happen* (generally of misfortunes, opposed to evenio) ; si quid adversi accidisset, Caes. ; impers., 1, accidit, followed by ut, casu accidit ut id primus nuntiaret, Cic. ; by quod, accidit perincommode quod eum nusquam vidisti, Cic. ; by infinitive, nec acciderat mihi opus esse, Cic. ; 2, si quid alicui accidat, *if anything happens,* i.e. *if he dies,* Cic. **B.** *to fall out;* ut omnia contra opinionem acciderent, Caes.

acciĕo, 2. obs. form of accio (q.v.).

accingo -cinxi -cinctum 3. **I.** Lit., *to gird to* or *on;* ensem lateri, Verg. ; miles non accinctus, unarmed, Tac. **II.** Transf., *to equip, to arm;* reflex., se accingere, and pass. accingi ; a, *to arm one's self;* studio popularium accinctus, Tac. ; magicas accingier artes, Verg. ; b, *to make one's self ready;* accingi ad consulatum, *to strive for the consulship,* Liv. ; accingunt operi = se accingunt, Verg. (Infin. pass., accingier, Verg.)

accĭo -īvi (ii)-ītum, 4. *to call to, summon, fetch;* haruspices ex Etruria, Cic. ; aliquem in adoptionem, Tac. ; with double acc., aliquem doctorem filio, Cic.

accĭpĭo -cēpi -ceptum, 3. (ad and capio). **I.** *to take, receive.* **A.** Gen., 1, accipere pecuniam, Cic. ; 2, of business transactions, aliquid (alicui) accipere referre, *to enter on the credit side of an account book,* Cic. ; hence subst., **acceptum** -i, *what is received;* codex accepti et expensi, *an account book,* Cic. ; 3, where the thing received is a person, cujus abavi manibus esset accepta (Mater Idaea), Cic. ; 4, *to receive in* or on a part of the body ; alvus omne quod accepit cogit atque confundit, Cic. ; aliquem gremio, Verg. ; 5, *to receive in a friendly manner;* a, Romanos in arcem, Liv. ; in amicitiam, Cic. ; in deditionem, Caes. ; b, of places, pavidos Samnites castra sua accepere, Liv. ; c, *to receive as a guest;* hospitio, Cic. ; 6, *to treat,* a, *in a friendly way;* aliquem leniter clementerque, Cic. ; b, *in a hostile way;* aliquem verberibus ad necem, Cic. ; 7, with reference to the senses, *to hear;* orationem, Cic. ; pronis auribus accipi, *to be willingly listened to,* Tac. ; of the understanding, *to grasp;* quae parum accepi, Cic. ; of the judgment, *to take;* aliquid in bonum partem, *to take in good part,* Cic. ; verisimilia pro veris, Liv. ; with double acc., beneficium contumeliam, *to take a kindness for an insult,* Cic. **B.** *to accept, not to reject;* pacem, Liv. ; omen, Cic. ; legem, Cic. **II.** In a wider sense, *to get, receive, obtain;* 1, lucrum, Cic. ; adulterinos nummos pro bonis, Cic. ; 2, *to feel;* dolorem, Cic. ; 3, *to hear;* multa auribus accepisse, multa vidisse, Cic. ; ut accepi a senibus, Cic. ; 4, *to learn;* primas artes ab iisdem magistris, Ov. ; usum ac disciplinam ab aliquo, Caes.

accipiter -tris, m. **I.** Lit., *a hawk,* Cic. **II.** Transf., pecuniae, *an avaricious person,* Plaut.

accitus -ūs, m. *a summons,* Cic.

Accius -a -um, *name of a Roman gens, the most famous member of which was Accius, a celebrated dramatic poet* (born A.C. 170). Adj., **Accĭānus** -a -um, *of Accius;* versus, Cic.

acclāmātĭo -ōnis, f. *a loud cry;* 1, *an outcry against;* non modo ut acclamatione sed ut convicio et maledictis impediretur, Cic. ; 2, *a cry of approbation,* Liv., Cic.

acclāmo, 1. (ad and clamo), 1, *to cry out at* (in derision or disapproval) ; alicui, Cic. ; populus cum risu acclamavit ipsa esse, Cic. ; 2, *to cry out* in approval; omnes acclamarunt gratias se inter cetera etiam ob hoc agere, quod, etc., Liv. ; 3, with acc. of person, *to name by acclamation;* aliquem servatorem liberatoremque, Liv. ; si nocentem acclamaverant, Tac.

acclāro, 1. *to make clear, to reveal* (of omens), Liv. ; uti tu signa nobis certa acclarassis (for acclaraveris), Liv.

acclīnis -e. **I.** Lit., *leaning on anything;* trunco arboris, Verg. **II.** Transf., *inclined to;* acclinis falsis animus, Hor.

acclīno, 1. (ad and * clino). **I.** Lit., *to lean on anything;* se in illum, Ov. ; castra tumuli sunt acclinata, Liv. **II.** Transf., *to incline to;* haud gravate se acclinaturos ad causam senatus, Liv.

acclivis -e (ad and clivus), *gently inclined upwards;* pars viae, Cic. ; collis leniter ab infimo acclivis, Caes.

acclivitas -ātis, f. *acclivity, gentle inclination upwards,* Caes.

acclivus -a -um, vid. acclivis.

accŏla -ae, m. (ad and colo), *one who lives near, a neighbour;* Oceani, Liv. ; Cereris, *near the temple of Ceres,* Cic. ; as adj., pastor accola ejus loci, *dwelling near that place,* Liv. ; accolae fluvii, *neighbouring rivers,* Tac.

accŏlo -cŏlŭi -cultum, 3. *to live near;* locum, Cic. ; gentes quae Macedoniam accolunt, Liv.

accommŏdātē, adv. *agreeably to;* ad veritatem, Cic.

accommŏdātĭo -ōnis, f. 1, *a proportion or adjusting of one thing to another;* verborum et sententiarum ad inventionem acc., Cic. ; 2, *courteousness, complaisance;* ex liberalitate atque accommodatione magistratuum, Cic.

accommŏdātus -a -um, p. adj. with compar. and superl. (from accommodo), *adapted, suitable to;* 1, of things, with ad and the acc., puppes ad magnitudinem fluctuum tempestatemque accommodatae, Caes. ; with dat., oratio hominum sensibus ac mentibus accommodata, Cic. ; 2, of persons, with ad and the acc., homo ad Verris flagitia libidinesque accommodatus, Cic. ; with dat., servus vilissimus nec cuiquam serio ministerio accommodatus, Tac.

accommŏdo, 1. (ad and commodo), *to fit, put on.* I. Lit., insignia, Caes. ; coronam sibi ad caput, Cic. ; lateri ensem, Verg. II. Transf., *to make suitable, to adjust;* testes ad crimen, Cic. ; orationem auribus auditorum, Cic. ; in omnem eventum consilia, Liv. ; se accommodare or accommodari, *to adapt oneself;* ad voluntatem alicujus et arbitrium et nutum totum se fingere et accommodare, Cic.

accommŏdus -a -um, *fit, adapted to,* Verg.

accrēdo -dĭdi -dĭtum, 3. (ad and credo), *to believe, give credence to;* alicui, Hor. ; absol., vix accredens, Cic.

accresco -crēvi -crētum, 3. (ad and cresco), *to grow, to increase.* I. Lit., flumen subito accrevit, Cic. II. Transf., quum dictis factisque omnibus ad fallendum instructis varia accresceret fides, Liv. ; trimetris accrescere jussit nomen iambeis, *ordered to be joined to,* Hor.

accrētĭo -ōnis, f. (accresco), *increase;* luminis, Cic.

accŭbĭtĭo (accŭbātĭo) -ōnis, f. *the act of reclining at table,* Cic.

accŭbĭtus -ūs, m. = accubitio (q.v.).

accŭbo, 1. (ad and cubo), *to lie by the side of.* I. Gen., humi, Liv. ; of wine, Sulpiciis horreis, Hor. II. Esp., *to recline at table;* in convivio, Cic. ; cum aliquo, *next to,* Plaut. ; apud aliquem, *at the house of* (as a guest), Cic. ; accuba, *take your place,* Plaut.

accŭdo, 3. *to hammer together,* Plaut.

accumbo -cŭbui -cŭbĭtum, 3. (ad and *cumbo), *to lie down;* 1, in via, Plaut. ; 2, especially used of the Romans at the dinner table, where each person lay upon a sofa, supported on his left elbow ; in sinu alicujus, *to sit next to any one at table,* Liv. ; cum aliquo, *next to,* Mart. ; apud aliquem, *at the house of* (as a guest), Cic.

accŭmŭlātē, adv. *abundantly, copiously,* Cic.

accŭmŭlātor -ōris, m. *one who heaps together;* opum, Tac.

accŭmŭlo, 1. (ad and cumulo), *to heap up, to accumulate.* I. Lit., auget, addit, accumulat,

Cic. II. Transf., 1, *to heap on a person, give in abundance;* alienas res, Liv. ; alicui summum honorem, Ov. ; 2, *to overwhelm;* animam nepotis his donis, Verg. ; 3, *to increase;* caedem caede, Lucr. ; curas, Ov.

accūrātē, adv. *carefully, exactly, accurately;* aliquid studiose accurateque facere, Cic. ; perscribere, Cic. ; aedificare, Caes.

accūrātĭo -ōnis, f. *accuracy, carefulness,* Cic.

accūrātus -a -um, p. adj. with compar. and superl. (from accuro), *careful, exact, accurate;* oratio, Cic. ; accuratiorem delectum habere, Liv. ; accuratissima diligentia, Cic.

accūro, 1. (ad and curo), *to take care of, to prepare with care;* victum et cultum, Cic.

accurro -curri and -cucurri -cursum, 3. (ad and curro), *to run to, to run up, to hasten up;* ad praetorem, Cic. ; equo admisso ad aliquem, Caes. ; of things, *to occur;* istae imagines ita nobis dicto audientes sunt, ut, simulatque velimus, accurrant, Cic.

accursus -ūs, m. *a running to, concourse,* Tac.

accūsābĭlis -e, *blameworthy,* Cic.

accūsātĭo -ōnis, f. I. *an accusation;* accusationem factitare, Cic. ; comparare atque constituere, *to prepare with evidence,* Cic. ; plur., acres accusationes, Cic. II. Met., *the indictment;* accusationis quinque libri, *of the orations against Verres,* Cic.

accūsātor -ōris, m. 1, *an accuser* (strictly only in regard to state offences, while petitor is a plaintiff in a private suit) ; petitoris personam cupere, accusatoris deponere, Cic. ; 2, *an informer,* Juv.

accūsātōrĭē, adv. *after the manner of an accuser;* loqui, Cic.

accūsātōrĭus -a -um, *pertaining to an accuser;* lex, Cic.

accūsātrix -īcis, f. *a female accuser,* Plaut.

accūsĭto, 1. (freq. of accuso), *to accuse frequently,* Plaut.

accūso, 1. (ad and cansa), *to accuse* (generally in public cases) ; 1, aliquem ad populum (of the tribunes), Liv. ; a, with genit., of the offence, aliquem ambitus, Cic.; b, with abl., de veneficiis, Cic. ; c, with propter, propter injurias, Cic. ; d, with inter, inter sicarios, *of assassination,* Cic. ; e, with genit., of the punishment, capitis, on *a capital charge,* Cic. ; 2, *to blame, find fault with;* aliquem aspere et acerbe in senatu, Cic. ; followed by quod and the subj., and by cur with the subj., Cic.

1. **ăcer** -ĕris, n. *the maple tree,* Ov.

2. **ăcer** -cris -cre (from root AC, as acuo, acies, etc.), *sharp, cutting.* I. Lit., of sharp tools, hastas acri ferro, Tac. II. Transf., A. Of the senses ; 1, of taste, *biting;* rapula, Hor. ; 2, of touch, *sharp;* dolor corporis cujus morsus est acerrimus, Cic. ; 3, of hearing, *shrill;* vox, Lucr. ; flammae sonitus, *crackling,* Verg. ; 4, of smell, *penetrating;* unguenta summa et acerrima suavitate condita, Cic. ; 5, of sight, *keen;* acerrimus sensus videndi, Cic. B. Relating to the feelings ; 1, of emotions, *painful;* cura, Lucr. ; 2, of the understanding, *vigorous;* judicium acrius et certius, Cic. ; 3, of the character, a, *energetic;* homo ad perdiscendum acerrimus, Cic. ; in ferro, *brave in fight,* Cic. ; b, *passionate;* acerrima uxor, Plaut. ; so of the passions themselves, amor gloriae, Cic. ; c, hence of abstractions, supplicium, Cic. Subst., **acre** -is, n. *acrimony, severity* (opp. to ridiculum), Hor.

ăcerbē, adv. **I.** *bitterly, harshly;* accusare, Cic. ; acerbius invehi in aliquem, Cic. ; acerbissime dicere, Caes. **II.** *with difficulty or pain,* aliquid ferre, Cic.

ăcerbĭtas -ātis, f. **I.** Lit., *bitterness of taste,* Cic. **II.** Transf., 1, *harshness;* morum, Cic. ; 2, *painfulness;* temporis Sullani, Cic. ; in plur., *calamities,* Cic.

ăcerbo, 1. *to make bitter, to aggravate or heighten;* crimen, Verg.

ăcerbus -a -um. **I. A.** Lit., 1, *bitter in taste, sour,* used especially of unripe fruit ; hence = *raw, unripe, immature;* uva, Phaedr. ; partus, *premature,* Ov. **B.** Transf., 1, of the voice, *harsh;* stridor, Plin. ; acerba sonans, Verg. ; 2, of the sound, *rough;* frigus, Hor. ; 3, of the look, *dark, gloomy;* vultus acerbi, Ov. ; acerba tuens, *with angry look,* Verg. **II.** Fig., **A.** Of persons, *morose;* acerbos e Zenonis schola exire (of the Stoics), Cic. **B.** Of things, 1, *painful, severe, harsh;* acerbissima tributa, Cic. ; 2, of speech or writing, *bitter;* minaces et acerbae litterae, Cic. ; 3, of events, *painful;* incendium, Cic.

ăcernus -a -um (1. acer), *made of maple wood,* Verg., Hor.

ăcerra -ae, f. *a casket for keeping incense,* Cic.

Ăcerrae -ārum, f. *town in Campania, on the river Clanius* (now *Acerra*).

ăcersĕcŏmēs -ae, m. (ἀκερσεκόμης), *having unshorn hair,* Juv.

ăcervālis -e, *that which is heaped up* = σωρείτης, *an argument by accumulation,* Cic.

ăcervātim, adv. **I.** Lit., *in heaps,* Lucr. **II.** Transf., dicere, *to sum up, to speak comprehensively,* Cic. ; multa acervatim frequentans, *crowding together a number of thoughts,* Cic.

ăcervo, 1. *to heap up;* promiscue acervati cumuli hominum, Liv.

ăcervus -i, m. (connected with ἀγείρω), a *heap.* **I.** Lit., tritici, Cic. ; insepulti acervi civium, Cic. **II.** Transf., **A.** *a multitude ;* facinorum, Cic. **B.** Logical term, *argument by accumulation,* Cic.

ăcesco -ăcŭī, 3. (aceo), *to grow sour,* Hor.

Ăcesta -ae, f. (Ἀκέστη), *an old town in the north of Sicily,* also called Egesta and Segesta (now *Castel a Mare di Golfo*); hence **Acestenses** ĭum, *inhabitants of Acesta.*

Ăcestes -ae, m. *king in Sicily, of Trojan descent.*

ăcētum -i, n. (aceo). **I.** Lit., *vinegar,* Cic. **II.** Transf., *acuteness, wit;* Italo perfusus aceto, Hor.

Ăchaei -ōrum, m. (Ἀχαιοί). **I.** *the Achaeans, inhabitants of the Greek country of Achaia,* Liv. ; also, a, *the Greeks in general,* Plin. ; b, *the inhabitants of the Roman province of Achaia,* Cic. ; c, *inhabitants of a Greek colony on the Euxine,* Ov. **II.** Hence, 1, **Achaeus** -a -um, a, *belonging to the Greek country of Achaia,* Lucr. ; b, *Greek, belonging to the Roman province of Achaia,* Cic. ; 2, **Achaia** -ae, f. (Ἀχαία), or **Achaja** -ae, f. a, *the Greek country of Achaia, in the north of* the Peloponnese, Ov. ; b, after 146 B.C., *the Roman province of Achaia* (including the whole of Greece except Thessaly), Cic. ; 3, **Achaias** -ădis, f. *a Greek woman,* Ov. ; 4, **Achaicus** -a -um, *Greek,* Cic. ; 5, **Achais** -īdos, *an Achaean woman,* Ov. ; poet. = *Greece,* Ov. ; 6, **Achaius** -a -um, *Greek,* Verg. ; 7, **Achivi** -ōrum, m. *the Homeric Greeks* (genit. plur., Achivom and Achivum). Adj., **Achivus** -a -um, *Greek,* Ov.

Ăchaemĕnēs -is, m. (Ἀχαιμένης), *grandfather of Cyrus, and founder of the Persian line*

of the Achaemenidae. Hence **adj.**, **Achaemĕnĭus** -a -um, *Persian,* Ov.

Ăcharnae -ōrum, f. (Ἀχαρναί), *a town in Attica.* Hence adj., **Acharnānus** -a -um, *born at Acharnae.*

Ăchātes -ae, m. (Ἀχάτης), 1, *river in Sicily;* 2, *friend of Aeneas.*

Achĕlōus -i, m. (Ἀχελῶος), *a river between Acarnania and Aetolia;* hence, **A. Achĕlōĭas** -ădis, f. *daughter of the river-god Achelous, Parthenope,* Ov. **B. Achelōĭus** -a -um, *belonging to the river-god Achelous,* Ov. **C. Achelōĭdes** -um, f. *the Sirens,* Ov.

Achĕron -ontis, m. (Ἀχέρων), 1, *a river in Thesprotia, flowing through the swamp Acherusia* (now *Gurla,* or *river of Suli*); 2, *a river in Bruttii* (now *Mucone* or *Lese*); 3, Mythol., *river in the lower world,* hence *the lower world itself;* Acheronta movebo, Verg. ; fugere Acheronta, *to become immortal,* Hor.

Achĕrontĭa -ae, f. *a small town in Apulia,* Hor.

Achĕruns -untis, m. and f. Latin form of Acheron, *the lower world.* Hence adj., **Achĕrūsĭus** -a -um. Subst., **Acherusia** -ae, f. a, *a swamp in Thesprotia ;* b, *a lake in Campania ;* c, *a cavern in Bithynia.*

Achilles -is, m. (Ἀχιλλεύς), and **Achillēus** -ĕī, m. *a Greek hero, son of Peleus and Thetis;* appell., *a brave handsome man, a hero,* Verg. ; hence, 1, **Achillēus** -a -um, *relating to Achilles;* 2, **Achillides** -ae, m. (Ἀχιλλείδης), *a descendant of Achilles.*

Achivus -a -um = Achaeus (q.v.).

Achradĭna -ae, f. (Ἀχραδινή), *the most important part of the city of Syracuse,* Cic.

Ăcĭdălĭa -ae, f. (Ἀκιδαλία), *a surname of Venus,* from the fountain Acidalia in Boeotia, where the Graces, daughters of Venus, bathed. Adj., **Acĭdălĭus** -a -um, *belonging to Venus;* nodus, *the girdle of Venus,* Mart.

ăcĭdus -a -um (aceo), *sharp.* **I.** Lit., *sour in taste, acid,* Hor. **II.** Transf., *disagreeable, unpleasant,* Hor.

ăcĭes -ēi, f. (AC, root of acuo), *keenness, edge.* **I.** Lit., of a sharp instrument, securis, Cic. ; fig., patimur hebescere aciem horum auctoritatis, Cic. **II.** Transf., **A.** Of the eye, 1, *piercing look ;* ne vultum quidem atque aciem oculorum ferre potuisse, Caes. ; 2, *vision ;* bonum incolumis acies, malum caecitas, Cic. ; poet., *the twinkling* of the stars, Verg. ; 3, *the pupil of the eye,* Cic. ; met., *the eye itself,* Verg. ; hence, 4, of the mind, *insight, keenness;* animi, ingenii, mentis, Cic. **B.** Milit. t.t., 1, *an army drawn up in line of battle,* a, *a single line;* prima, Caes. ; novissima, Liv. ; and b, *the whole army;* aciem instruere, Cic. ; 2, *battle;* Pharsalica, Cic. ; in acie vincere, Caes. ; poet., Vulcania, *mass of fire,* Verg. Transf., *a battle in words,* Cic.

Acĭlĭus -a -um, *name of a Roman gens,* the most famous members of which were : 1, Man. *Acil.* Glabrio, Consul A.C. 192, *conqueror of Antiochus and the Aetolians;* 2, C. *Acil.* Glabrio, *author of a Roman history in Greek.*

Ăcilla, and **Ăcylla**, and **Ăcholla** -ae, f. *town of the Carthaginians in Byzacium* (near modern Elalia).

ăcĭnăces -is, m. (ἀκινάκης), *a short Persian sabre,* Hor.

ăcĭnus -i, m. and **ăcĭnum** -i, n. *a berry* (esp. *grape*), Cic.

ăcĭpenser -ĕris (ăcĭpensis -is), m. *a fish, highly prized by the Romans, the sturgeon* according to Cuvier, Cic.

Ācis -ĭdis, m. ('Ακις), 1, *a river in Sicily*, near Aetna, famous for its cold water (now *Fiume di Jaci*), Ov.; 2, Mythol., *a beautiful shepherd, lover of Galatea*, Ov.

āclys -ўdis, f. (perhaps shortened from ἀγκυλίς), *a small javelin*, Verg.

Acmōnĭa -ae, f. *a town of Phrygia*, on the road from Dorylaeum to Philadelphia (now *Ahatkoi*); hence **Acmōnensis** -e, *relating to Acmonia*.

Acmŏnĭdes -ae, m. ('Ακμονίδης), *one of the workmen of Vulcan*.

ăcŏnītum -i, n. (ἀκόνιτον), *a poisonous herb, monk's hood, aconite*, Plin.; poet. = poison, Verg.

acquĭesco -quĭēvi -quiētum, 3. (ad and quiesco), *to rest, repose;* 1, physically, a, of persons, tres horas, Cic.; euphem., *to die;* anno acquievit sexagesimo, Nep.; b, of things, aures in eo acquiescant, Cic.; rem familiarem acquiescere, not *to be seized*, Liv.; 2, mentally, a, mentis agitatio quae numquam acquiescit, Cic.; b, *to find rest or comfort in;* in his (litteris tuis) acquiesco, Cic.; c, *to be satisfied or pleased with;* in adolescentium caritate, Cic.; Clodii morte, Cic.

acquīro -quīsīvi -quīsītum, 3. (ad and quaero). I. *to add to, acquire*, as an increase to what is already possessed; dignitatem, Cic.; vires acquirit eundo, Verg. II. A. Gen., *to acquire, get;* triumphos de populis, Tac. B. Absol., *to amass money;* acquirendi insatiabile votum, Juv.

acra -ae, f. (ἀκρα), *a summit, height, promontory*, Plin.

Acraeus -a -um (ἀκραῖος), *that which is upon a height*, surname of Jupiter and Juno, Liv.

ăcrātŏphŏron -i, n. (ἀκρατόφορον), *a vessel for holding unmixed wine*, Cic.

ācrēdŭla -ae, f. *a bird* (variously explained as *the thrush, the owl*, or *the nightingale*), Cic.

ācrĭcŭlus -a -um (2. acer), *somewhat sharp, violent;* ille acriculus, Cic.

ācrĭmōnĭa -ae, f. 1, *sharpness of taste or pungency of smell*, Plin.; 2, *energy of speech and demeanour*, Cic.

Ācrīsĭus -ĭi, m. ('Ακρίσιος), *a king of Argos*, father of Danäe. Hence, 1, **Acrīsĭōnē** -es, f. *Danäe;* 2, **Ācrīsĭōnĭădes** -ae, m. *Perseus, son of Danäe;* 3, adj., **Acrīsĭōnēus** -a -um, arces, *Argos*, Ov.

ācrĭtĕr, adv. (2. acer), *sharply, violently, strongly;* 1, of the senses; a, of the sight, acriter intueri solem, *steadfastly, without being dazzled*, Cic.; b, of touch, *painfully;* caedunt acerrime virgis, Cic.; c, of hearing, *penetratingly*, Plin.; 2, of the mind, etc.; a, of the understanding, *with sharp insight;* videre vitia, Cic.; b, of action, *courageously;* se morti offerre, Cic.; c, of the passions, *passionately;* acerrime exspectare, *longingly*, Cic.; in speech, *violently;* vituperare, Cic.

ācrŏāma -ătis, n. (ἀκρόαμα), *that which is heard with pleasure;* Esp., 1, *an entertainment at table of reading or music*, Cic.; 2, Meton., *the person who conducts such an entertainment, a reader, actor*, or *singer*, Cic.

ācrŏāsis -is, f. (ἀκρόασις), *an assembly of persons to listen to reading aloud*, Cic.

Ācrŏcĕraunĭa -orum, n. 1, *part of the Ceraunian mountains*, v. Ceraunius; 2, appell., *a dangerous place;* haec Acroceraunia vita, Ov.

Ācrŏcŏrinthus -ĭ, f. ('Ακροκόρινθος), *the citadel of Corinth*, Liv.

1. **acta** -ae, f. (ἀκτή), *the sea-shore, the beach*, especially as a place of recreation, Cic.; hence, meton., *the pleasures of life at the seaside*, Cic.

2. **acta** -ōrum, n. (part. of ago), 1, *actions;* Caesaris non modo acta verum etiam cogitata, Cic.; 2, *public acts, ordinances;* servare, Cic.; especially *the register of these acts;* a, of the senate, Tac.; b, of the people, Cic.; c, of courts of justice, Cic.; acta diurna, *a kind of official gazette published daily in Rome*, Tac.

Actaeōn -ŏnis, m. ('Ακταίων), *son of Aristaeus, a hunter, who for seeing Diana while bathing was turned into a stag, and torn to pieces by his dogs*.

Actē -ēs, f. ('Ακτή), *coast land, an old name of Attica;* hence, a, **Actaeus** -a -um, *belonging to Attica or Athens;* subst., **Actaei** -orum, *the people of Attica;* b, **Actĭās** -ădis, f. *Attic*, Verg.

Actĭăcus -a -um, v. under Actium.

actĭo -ōnis, f. (ago). I. *motion*, hence *the action of the body;* 1, of an orator, *gesture*, Cic.; 2, of an actor, *action*, Cic. II. A. Gen., *doing, action;* gratiarum, *giving of thanks*, Cic.; primas ejus actiones horreo, Cic. B. Esp., *public action;* 1, *the action of any magistrate, proposal;* consularis, Cic.; actio de pace sublata est, Liv.; 2, *action in a court of justice;* a, *the bringing of an action;* inquieta urbs actionibus, Tac.; b, *the action itself;* actionem instituere, constituere, intendere, Cic.; and so, c, *the formula used in bringing an action;* actiones componere, *to draw statements of claim*, Cic.; and gen., *a legal formula;* actiones Hostilianae, Cic.; d, *the speech on an indictment;* actiones Verrinae, Cic.; e, *the permission or right to bring an action;* actionem habere, postulare, dare, accipere, restituere, Cic.; f, *the hearing of an action;* altera, tertia, Cic.

actĭto, 1. (freq. of ago), *to be busy in pleading or acting*, used of the theatres and courts of law; causas multas, Cic.; tragoedias, Cic.

Actĭum -ĭi, n. ('Ακτιον). I. *a promontory in Acarnania*, on which stood a temple of Apollo; hard by was fought the naval battle (A.C. 31) in which Augustus conquered Antony and Cleopatra. II. *a roadstead near Corcyra*. Hence adj., 1, **Actĭăcus** -a -um; frondes, *the leaves of the bay tree*, sacred to Apollo, Ov.; legiones, *those that fought at Actium*, Tac.; 2, **Actĭus** -a -um; bella, *the battle of Actium*, Verg.

actor -ōris, m. (ago), 1, *a driver;* pecoris, Ov.; 2, *an actor;* secundarum et tertiarum partium, Cic.; 3, a, *one who accomplishes anything;* rerum, Cic.; b, *a public speaker*, Cic.; c, *the plaintiff in an action*, Cic.; d, *the manager of property or finances;* actor publicus, *one who manages public property*, Tac.

Actŏrĭdēs -ae, m. ('Ακτορίδης), *a descendant of Actor*, e.g., *Menoetius* (son of Actor), or *Patroclus* (grandson of Actor), Ov.

actŭărĭŏla -ae, f. (dim. of aetuaria), *a small skiff*, Cic.

actŭărĭus -a -um (ago), *easily moved, swift;* actuaria navis, *a swift-sailing vessel*, Caes.; navigium actuarium, Caes. Subst., **actŭārĭa** -ae, f. Cic.

actŭōsē, adv. *actively, with energy*, Cic.

actŭōsus -a -um, *active;* virtus, Cic.; of a speech, *effective*, Cic.

actus -ūs, m. (ago). I. *motion;* fertur magno mons improbus actu, Verg. II. *putting in motion*. A. 1, *driving of cattle;* levi admonitu, non actu, inflectit illam feram, Cic.; 2, Meton., *right of way for driving cattle, carts, etc.*, Cic. B. *movement of the body*. C. Of an actor or orator, *gesture*, Liv.; 1, Esp., *presentation of a piece on the stage;* fabellarum, Liv.; 2, *division of a piece, an act;* in extremo actu corruere, Cic.; 3, Transf., extremus actus aetatis, Cic.

actūtum, adv. *immediately, directly*, Liv.

ăcŭlĕātus -a -um (aculeus). **I.** Lit., of plants and animals, *provided with prickles or stings*, Plin. **II.** Transf., *sharp pointed, stinging;* litterae, Cic. ; sophisma, *hair-splitting, subtle*, Cic.

ăcŭlĕus -i, m. (dim. of acus), *sting*. **I. A.** Of animals, apis, Cic. **B.** Of missiles, *point;* sagittae, Liv. **II.** Transf., especially in plur., **A.** *sarcasm;* aculei in C. Caesarem, Cic. **B.** *sting;* sollicitudinum, Cic. **C.** *deep impression* (of a speech); orator cum delectatione aculeos relinquit in animos, Cic.

ăcūmen -ĭnis, n. (acuo), *the sharp point of anything*. **I.** Lit., stili, Cic. **II.** Transf., **A.** *point* (of something witty); etiam interpretatio nominis habet acumen, Cic. **B.** *sharpness of understanding;* ubi est acumen tuum? Cic. **C.** *cunning, trickery;* argutiae et acumen ejus, Cic.

ăcŭo -ŭi -ūtum, 3. (AC, root of acus and acies), *to sharpen to a point*. **I.** Lit., *to whet* (a cutting instrument); gladios, Liv. **II.** Transf., *to sharpen, practise*. **A.** linguam exercitatione dicendi, *to make more fluent, incite;* ingenia adolescentium, Cic. **B.** *to inflame;* iram hostis ad vindicandas injurias, Liv. **C.** *to encourage, incite;* juventutem ad dicendum, Cic.

ăcus -ūs, f. (AC, root of acuo and acies), *a needle, a bodkin;* vulnus, quod acu punctum videtur, Cic. ; acu pingere, *to embroider*, Verg. ; acu rem tetigisti, *you have hit the right nail on the head*, Plaut.

ăcūtē, adv. (acutus), *keenly*. **I.** Of the senses, cernere, Lucr. ; of the voice, *shrilly;* sonare, Cic. **II.** Of the understanding, *keenly;* acute arguteque respondere, Cic.

ăcūtŭlus -a -um (dim. of acutus), *somewhat subtle*, Cic.

ăcūtus -a -um, p. adj. with compar. and superl. (from acuo), *sharpened, pointed, acute*. **I.** Lit., sagitta, Ov. ; of anything pointed, cornua lunae, Cic. **II.** Transf., **A.** Of physical sensations, 1, referring to particular senses ; a, of hearing, *shrill;* vox, Cic. ; acc. neut. as adv., resonare triste et acutum, Hor. ; b, of touch, *piercing;* gelu, Hor. ; 2, of the whole body, *painful;* morbus, Hor. ; poet., acuta belli, *the hardships of war*, Hor. **B.** Of mental perceptions, 1, *sharp, keen;* populi Romani oculos esse acres atque acutos, Cic. ; acc. neut. as adv., cernis acutum, *you have keen sight* (for the failings of others), Hor. ; 2, of persons, *keen-sighted, vigorous;* homo acutus magis quam eruditus, Cic. ; of orators, *effective;* orator, Cic.

ad, prep. with acc., expressing direction, *towards, to*. **I.** Of space, **A.** Lit., 1, of motion, *towards;* concurrere ad curiam, Cic ; ad Dianae venire, *to the temple of Diana* (sc. aedem), Ter. ; ad me, ad te, etc., *to my house*, Cic. ; so of extension, ab imis unguibus usque ad verticem summum, Cic. ; 2, of rest, *in the direction of, near;* sedere ad latus ejus, Cic. ; esse ad portas (of Roman generals waiting outside Rome for a triumph), Cic. ; esse ad aliquem, *to be on a visit to a person*, Cic. ; ad judicem, *before a judge*, Cic. ; ad tibiam, *to the sound of the flute*, Cic. **B.** Transf., 1, to express direction or extent ; a, of direction (a) esp. with verbs implying motion, as movere, ducere, etc. ; (β) of striving after an object, with such nouns as cupiditas, aviditas, etc., and such adjectives, as acer, propensus, etc. ; (γ) of aim or purpose, to, for ; adjutorem ad injuriam, Cic. ; so with adj. like natus, aptus, etc., and verbs as adjuvare, etc. ; ad id, *for that object*, Liv. ; quid ad rem ? *what is the object of this ?* Cic. ; quid ad me, *what has this to do with me ?* Cic. ; so (aa) of medicines, *for,*

against; radicum genera ad (*to cure*) morsus bestiarum, Cic. ; (ββ) of occupation, *to, for;* servos ad remum dare, Liv. ; (δ) *in relation to;* impiger ad labores belli, Cic. ; (ε) *in comparison with;* scuta ad amplitudinem corporum parum lata, Liv. ; b, of extent, *to, up to;* (α) virgis ad necem caedi, Cic. ; ad extremum, ultimum, *entirely;* homo non ad extremum perdĭtus, Liv. ; ad summam, *on the whole*, Cic. ; (β) of numbers, *to the amount of*, etc. ; ad unum omnes, *all to a man*, Cic. ; ad assem perdere, *to lose your last farthing*, Hor. ; (γ) *near to, about;* (fuimus) omnino ad ducentos, Cic. ; 2, a, *in addition to;* ad cetera hanc quoque plagam infligere, Cic. ; ad hoc, *besides*, Sall. ; b, *in consequence of;* ad famam belli novas legiones scribere, Liv. ; c, *according to* (some standard); ad istorum normam, Cic. ; ad verbum, *literally*, Cic. **II.** Of time, 1, a, of extent, *up to;* ab hora octava ad vesperum, Cic. ; ad hoc tempus, *till now*, Cic. ; quem ad finem ? *how long ?* Cic. ; b, of duration ; ad paucos dies, *for a few days;* 2, of point of time, a, *at, towards;* nos te hic ad mensem Januarium expectamus, Cic. ; ad lucem, *in the morning*, Cic. ; ad tempus, *in due time*, Cic. ; b, *within;* ad annum tribunum plebis fore, Cic.

ădactĭo -ōnis, f. (adigo), *a driving to, compulsion;* jurisjurandi (*obligation*), Liv.

ădactus -ūs, m. (adigo), *a bringing to;* dentis, *a bite*, Lucr.

ădaequē, adv. *in like manner*, Liv.

ădaequo, 1. **A.** Lit., *to make equal with;* moles moenibus, Caes. **B.** Transf., 1, *to equalise;* a, with cum and the abl., cum virtute fortunam, Cic. ; b, with dat., se virtute nostris, Cic. ; so *to compare;* formam, aetatem, genus mortis magni Alexandri fatis, Tac. ; 2, *to come near to;* altitudinem muri, Caes. ; deorum vitam, Cic.

ădămantēus -a -um, *hard as steel*, Ov.

ădămantĭnus -a -um (ἀδαμάντινος), *made of hard steel, adamantine*, Hor.

ădămas -antis, m. (ἀδάμας), 1, *the hardest steel, adamant;* nexae adamante catenae, Ov. ; poet., *anything that is firm, unyielding, and durable;* in pectore ferrum aut adamanta gerit, Ov. ; voce sua adamanta movere, *a heart of steel*, Mart. ; 2, *the diamond*, Plin.

ădambŭlo, 1. *to walk by or near anything*, Plaut.

ădămo, 1. **I.** *to fall in love with;* aliquem, Liv. **II.** *to find pleasure in;* equos, Cic. ; gloriam, Cic.

ădămussim, v. amussis.

ădăpĕrĭo -pĕrŭi -pertum, 4. *to open fully;* adapertae fores portae, Liv.

ădăpertĭlis -e, *that which is capable of being opened;* latus tauri, Ov.

ădapto, 1. *to fit to, adapt*, Suet.

ădăquo, 1. *to supply with water, to give to drink*, Plin.

ădăquor, 1. dep. *to fetch water; of soldiers*, Caes.

ădauctus -ūs, m. (adaugeo), *an increase*, Lucr.

ădaugĕo -auxi -auctum, 2. 1, *to increase, to augment;* bonum, Cic. ; 2, of sacrifices, *to devote*, Plaut.

ădaugesco, 3. *to begin to increase*, Cic. poet.

ădbĭbo -bĭbi -bĭbĭtum, 3. 1, Lit., *to drink, drink in*, Ter. ; 2, Transf., of the ears ; verba puro pectore, Hor.

adbīto, 3. *to go near*, Plaut.

addĕcet, v. impers. *it becomes, suits*, Plaut.

addensĕo, 2. and **addenso, 1.** *to make thick,* or *compact;* extremi addensent acies, Verg.

addīco -dixi -dictum, **3.** *to assent to;* **1,** t.t. in augury, *to promise favourably* (of the omens of birds), Liv. ; **2,** *to award;* **a.** of a judge, especially the praetor (whose formula was do, dico, addico); alicui bona, Cic. ; liberum corpus in servitutem, Liv. ; esp., *to award a debtor as a slave to his creditor;* ob creditam pecuniam addici, Liv.; addictus, *a debtor thus adjudged a slave,* Liv.; **b,** of an auctioneer, *to knock down to a bidder;* fundum alicui, Cic.; alicui aliquid nummo sestertio, or simply nummo, *to give* (by a fictitious sale), Cic., Hor. ; *to put up for sale* (of the vendor); aedes, Cic. ; transf., regna pecunia, Cic. ; **3,** *to give up* or *over,* alicuius bona in publicum, *to confiscate,* Cic. ; aliquem perpetuae servituti, Caes. ; so addictus, *bound, pledged;* nullius addictus jurare in verba ministri, Hor. ; se alicui, in a bad sense, *to give oneself up to slavishly;* se senatui, Cic.

addictĭo -ōnis, f. (addico), *the judge's award;* bonorum possessionumque, Cic.

addictus -a -um, v. addico.

addisco -dĭdĭcī, no sup. **3.** *to learn in addition;* artem, Cic.

addĭtāmentum -i, n. *an addition;* Ligus, additamentum inimicorum meorum, Cic.

addo -dĭdi -dĭtum, **3. I.** *to give to, to give, to place.* **A.** Lit., epistolas in fasciculum, Cic. ; soleam pedi, Ov. ; of persons, alicui comitem, Verg. **B.** Transf., *to inspire, to cause, produce;* alicui alacritatem scribendi, Cic. **II.** *to add, increase,* Liv. **A.** Lit., 1, unum granum, Cic. ; gradum, *to hasten,* Liv. ; **2,** of writing, *to add;* in orationem quaedam, *to make some additions,* Cic. ; **3,** of reckoning, *to add;* addendo deducendoque, *by addition and subtraction;* videre quae reliqui summa fiat, Cic. **B.** Transf., 1, hunc laborem ad quotidiana opera, Caes. ; sceleri scelus, Liv. ; **2,** *to give as a respite* (of time); paucos dies ad rem publicam gerendam, Cic.; **3,** *to add to something said, to say in addition;* addunt etiam de Sabini morte, Caes. ; with acc. and infin., addit etiam illud, equos non optimos fuisse, Cic. ; adde, or adde huc, or eo, with acc. subst. or quod, *add to this;* adde eo exsilia, luctus, Cic.

addŏcĕo, 2. *to teach in addition, to teach,* Hor.

addŭbĭto, 1. *to incline to doubt, to begin to doubt;* followed by de, in, num, an, utrum, quid ; res addubitata, *a question undecided,* Cic.

addūco -duxi -ductum, **3. I.** *to draw to oneself.* **A.** Gen., parvis colla lacertis (of children embracing their mother), Ov. **B.** Esp., 1, *to draw tight to oneself;* balistae et reliqua tormenta contenta atque adducta vehementius, Cic. ; **2,** *to draw together, to wrinkle;* adducit cutem macies, Ov. **II.** *to bring* (as a guide), or *lead* a thing or a person. **A.** Lit., 1, of persons, aliquem in conspectum populi, Liv. ; aliquem in jus or judicium, or simply aliquem, *to bring to justice,* Cic. ; **2,** of things, aurum secum, Liv.; esp. of bringing water (by an aqueduct, etc.), aquam, Cic. **B.** Transf., 1, *to bring to a certain condition;* aliquem in vituperationem, invidiam, Cic. ; eo adduxit eos ut, etc., Cic. ; se suumque regnum in ultimum discrimen, Liv. ; **2,** *to bring a person to a certain state of mind;* in fletum, in metum, Cic. ; adduci ad suspicandum, Cic.; followed by ut and the subj., adducis me ut tibi assentiar, Cic. ; with infin., in spem adducti, hunc ipsum annum salutarem civitati fore, Cic. ; with genit., in spem adductus conficiendi belli, Sall. ; so adductus, *influenced;* spe mercedis, Cic. ; absol., adducor igitur et prope modum assentior, Cic.

adductĭus, adv. compar. (adductus), *more severely,* Tac.

adductus -a -um, p. adj. (from adduco), of persons, *severe,* Tac.

ădĕdo -ēdi -ēsum, **3.** *to nibble, to gnaw.* **I.** A. Lit., adesi favi, Liv. **B.** Transf., scopulus adesus aquis, Ov. **II.** *to consume, waste away;* non adesa jam sed abundanti etiam pecunia, Cic.

ădemptĭo -ōnis, f. (adimo), *a taking away;* civitatis, Cic.

1. **ădĕo,** adv. (ad and eoi, old dat. of is), *to that point, so far.* **I.** Lit., **A.** Of space, *so far,* Ter. **B.** Of time, *so long,* used with usque and followed by dum, donec, quoad, Cic. **II.** Transf., of degree, **a,** *so much, so,* followed by ut, Cic. ; **b,** *even, what is more;* ducem hostium intra moenia atque adeo in senatu videmus, Cic. ; **c,** used enclitically with pron., *just;* id adeo, Cic.; with conj., si, nisi, sive, aut, vel, Cic. ; **d,** *to such an extent, so;* adeo prope omnis senatus Hannibalis fuit, Liv. ; **e,** with non, *much less,* Tac.

2. **ădĕo** -ĭi -ĭtum, **4.** *to go or come to, approach.* **I.** Lit., **A.** Gen., ad istum fundum, Cic. ; curiam, Liv. **B.** Esp., 1, adire in praetorem in jus ; or simply in jus, *to go to law,* Cic. ; **2,** *to travel to, to visit;* casas aratorum, Cic. ; **3,** *to go to some one* for counsel or help ; praetorem, Cic. ; or for consulting about the future ; magos, Cic. ; or for prayer for help ; aras, Cic. ; **4,** *to approach as an enemy;* ad quemvis numerum ephippiatorum equitum adire audere, Cic. **II.** Transf., 1, *to undertake some business;* ad causas privatas et publicas, Cic. ; ad rempublicam, *to enter public life,* Cic. ; **2,** *to come to some condition, to undergo, incur;* periculum capitis, Cic. ; **3,** legal t. t., adire hereditatem, *to enter on an inheritance,* Cic.

ădeps -ĭpis, c. (connected with ἀλείφω), *the soft fat of animals;* meton., Cassii adipem, *the corpulent Cassius,* Cic.

ădeptĭo -ōnis, f. (adipiscor), *attainment, obtaining;* filii; commodi, Cic.

ădēquĭto, 1. *to ride to;* with dat., ipsis portis, Liv. ; with ad, ad nostros, Caes. ; absol., Liv.

ădesdum, or ades dum, *come hither,* Ter.

ădēsŭrĭo, 4. *to hunger after anything.* Plaut.

adf, v. under aff . . .

adg, v. under agg . . .

ădhaerĕo -haesi -haesum, **2.** *to hang to, stick to, adhere.* **A.** Lit., manus oneri adhaerentes, *frozen to,* Tac. ; saxis, Liv. **B.** Transf., 1, *to border on, to be near;* modica silva adhaerebat, Tac. ; **2,** *to keep close to a person, to be always at the side of;* lateri adhaerere gravem dominum, *to sit on the neck of,* Liv. ; so nulli fortunae adhaerebat animus, *depended upon,* Liv. ; of things, cui canis cognomen adhaeret, *the nickname clings to him,* Hor. ; of an appendage, summusque in margine versus adhaesit, *was written on the edge for want of room,* Ov.; so, of persons, te vix extremum adhaesisse, Cic.

ădhaeresco -haesi -haesum, **3.** *to hang to, to adhere.* **A.** Lit., gravis lateri craterae limus adhaesit, Hor. ; of burning missiles, ad turrim, Caes. ; fig., in me uno consulares faces . . . in me omnia conjurationis tela adhaeserunt ; of shipwrecks, ad saxa sirenum, Cic. ; fig., ad quamcumque sunt disciplinam quasi tempestate delati, ad eam tam quam ad saxum adhaerescunt, Cic. **B.** Transf., 1, *to cling to, to remain;* in hic locis adhaerescere, Cic. ; justitiae honestatique, *not to swerve from,* Cic. ; ad omnium vestrum studium, *sympathise with,* Cic. ; 2, of an orator, *to stick fast, stop,* Cic.

ădhaesĭo -ōnis, f. (adhaereo), *clinging to;* atomorum, Cic.

ădhaesus -ūs, m. (adhaereo), *an adhering,* Lucr.

ădhĭbĕo -ŭi -ĭtum, 2. (ad and habeo), *to bring one thing to another, to apply to.* **I.** Gen., manus genibus, Ov.; manus vectigalibus, *to lay hands on, to seize,* Cic.; adhibete animos et mentes vestras, non solum aures, Cic. **II.** Esp., **A.** *to join, associate, add;* studio adhibito atque usu, Cic. **B.** 1, *to apply* something to some particular end or object; orationem ad vulgus, Cic.; alicui vim, Cic.; morbis remedia, Cic.; iambum in fabulis, Cic.; fidem, Cic.; 2, *to employ* or *call* a person to help or advise, etc.; aliquem in consilium, Cic.; aliquem in convivium, *to invite,* Cic.; medicum, Cic.; with double acc., aliquem patronum, Cic.; Siciliam testem, Cic.; with adv., *to treat;* aliquem liberaliter, Cic.

ădhinnĭo, 4. *to neigh after.* **I.** Lit., Ov. **II.** Transf., sic ad illius orationem adhinnivit, *neighed with joy at,* Cic.

ădhortātĭo -ōnis, f. *an exhortation,* Cic.

ădhortātor -ōris, m. *one who exhorts;* operis, Liv.

ădhortor, 1. dep. *to exhort, encourage* (especially of soldiers); omnes cohortes ordinesque, Caes.; in bellum, Tac.; ad defendendam republicam, Cic.

ădhūc, adv. (ad and huic, shortened to huc), *thus far, hitherto;* properly of place, but generally used of time, *hitherto;* 1, *up to the present time, till now;* **a,** of the actual present, usque adhuc, adhuc semper, adhuc dum, Cic.; used with unus, non, neque, nihil, nullus, Cic.; **b,** of the historic present, fluctuans adhuc animo, Liv.; 2, of something which is continuing, *still;* adhuc de consuetudine exercitationis loquor; nondum de ratione et sapientia, Cic.; followed by ut or qui with the subj. = *so far that,* Cic.

Ădĭăbēnē -ēs, f. (Ἀδιαβηνή), *a province of Assyria* (now *Kurdistan*). Adj., **Adĭăbēnus** -a -um, *Adiabenian.*

ădĭcĭo = adjicio (q.v.).

ădĭgo -ēgi -actum, 3. (ad and ago), *to drive to.* **A.** Lit., 1, of cattle, pecus e vicis longinquioribus, Caes.; 2, of men, aliquem fulmine ad umbras, Verg.; so legal t. t., arbitrum (old Lat. for ad arbitrum), adigere aliquem, *to summon before an arbiter,* Cic.; 3, of things, triremes per aestuaria, Tac.; quodam loco turri adacta, Caes. **B.** Transf., 1, *to drive to, to compel to;* ad mortem, Tac.; absol., adigit ita Postumia et Servius filius, Cic.; legal and milit. t. t., aliquem ad jusjurandum, Caes.; or jusjurandum, Cic.; or jurejurando, or sacramento, Liv., *to put a man on his oath, to swear in;* 2, *to fashion;* in faciem prorae pinus adacta novae, Prop.

ădĭmo -ēmi -emptum, 3. (ad and emo), *to take away;* 1, something painful; vincula canibus, Ov.; dolores, Hor.; 2, *to take away* (property); alicui pecuniam, vitam, Cic.; with a and the abl., Cic.; 3, *to take away* (a person), aliquem alicui, Cic.; esp. of death, hence ademptus, poet. *dead,* Hor.

ădĭpātus -a -um (adeps). **I.** Lit., *fatty, greasy.* Subst., **ădĭpāta** -orum n. *pastry made with grease,* Juv. **II.** Transf., of style, *bombastic;* adipatae dictionis genus, Cic.

ădĭpiscor -eptus, 3. dep. (ad and apiscor). **I.** *to come up to, to overtake;* fugientem, Liv. **II.** Transf., *to obtain;* laudem, Cic.; gloriam ex aliqua re, Nep.; quod adeptus est per scelus, Cic.; with genit., rerum adeptus, Tac.; part., adeptus, used passively, eandem accusant adeptam, *when reached,* Cic., De Sen. ii. 4.

ădītĭo -ōnis, f. *a going to, an approach,* Plaut.

ădītus -ūs, m. (2. adeo), *a going to, an approach, access.* **I. A.** Lit., 1, difficiles aditus aabere ad pastum, Cic.; 2, *right* or *possibility of entrance to;* aditus in id sacrarium non est viris, Cic.; of audience of a person, homo rari aditus, *difficult of access,* Liv.; faciles aditus ad eum privatorum, Cic.; aditus ad aliquem intercludere, Cic.; petentibus non dare, Nep.; ad aliquem postulare, Tac. **B.** Meton., *entrance to a place, approach;* aditus insulae muniti, Cic.; aditus templi, Cic.; ad castra, Caes.; in Siciliam, Cic.; omnes aditus claudere, or intercludere, Cic. **II.** Transf., *opportunity of obtaining;* ad honorem, Cic.; laudis, Cic.

adjăcĕo, 2. *to lie by the side of, to be adjacent;* ad ostium Rhodani, Caes.; with acc. alone, Etruriam, Liv.; with dat., agro Romano, Liv.; absol., adjacente Tibri, Tac. Subst., **adjăcěntĭa** -ium, n. *the neighbourhood,* Tac.

adjectĭo -ōnis, f. (adjicio), *an adding to;* adjectione populi Albani, Liv.; illiberali adjectione, *a paltry advance,* Liv.; Hispaniensibus familiarum adjectiones dedit, *incorporated new families,* Tac.

adjectus -ūs, m. (adjicio), *an adding to,* Lucr.

adjĭcĭo -jēci -jectum, 3. (ad and jacio), *to throw to.* **I. A.** Lit., telum, Caes. **B.** Transf. 1, *to cast* a longing look upon; oculum hereditati, Cic.; 2, *to direct* the thoughts to; dictis mentem, Ov. **II. A.** *to apply;* stimulos frementi, Ov. **B.** *to add;* 1, Lit., aggerem ad munitiones, Caes.; 2, Transf., a, ad belli laudem doctrinae et ingenii gloriam, Cic.; b, *to add* to what has been said, Liv.; 3, *to outbid* at an auction; supra adjecit Aeschrio, Cic.

adjūdĭco, 1. *to award as a judge, adjudicate, to decide as a judge.* **I.** Lit., causam alicui, in favour of any one, Cic.; regnum Ptolemaeo, *to assign* the kingdom to Ptolemy, Cic. **II.** Transf., Italis adjudicat armis, *assigns* to *the Roman power,* Hor.; alicui salutem imperii hujus atque orbis terrarum, Cic.

adjūmentum, -i, n. (adjuvo), *help, assistance;* alicuius rei, ad aliquid, alicui rei, in aliqua re, Cic.

adjunctĭo -ōnis, f. (adjungo), *a joining to.* **I.** *addition to, union;* **a,** naturae ad hominem, Cic.; **b,** a rhet. figure = συνεζευγμένον, where the predicate stands either at the beginning or the end of a clause. **II.** *a joining to, adding to, connexion, union;* **a,** verborum, Cic.; **b,** in rhet., *a limitation, restriction,* Cic.

adjunctor -ōris, m. (adjungo), *one who joins, connects;* ille Galliae ulterioris adjunctor (i.e., Pompeius, who caused Gallia Ulterior to be added to Caesar's province), Cic.

adjunctus -a -um, p. adj. (from adjungo), *bound to, belonging to;* propiora hujus causae et adjunctiora, Cic. Subst., **adjuncta** -ōrum, n. *things closely connected with,* or *suitable to,* anything, Cic.

adjungo -junxi -junctum, 3. *to join to, bind to.* **I.** Lit., 1, of animals, plostello mures, Hor.; 2, of vines, ulmis vites, Verg. **II.** Transf., *to join, add.* **A.** 1, of space; **a,** of things, parietem ad parietem communem, Cic.; adjunctus fundus, *neighbouring,* Cic.; **b,** of persons, belus adjuncto humano corpori, Cic.; juris scientiam eloquentiae tamquam ancillulam pedisequamque, Cic.; 2, of time, pass., *to be near in age;* ei proxime adjunctus Drusus frater fuit, Cic. **B.** *to express any connection* or *relation;* 1, of things, **a,** in speaking, *to join;* verba ad nomen adjuncta, *epithets,* Cic.; similitudines adjungens,

Cic. ; b, in argument, to connect; rebus praesentibus adjungere atque annectere futuras, Cic. ; c, of territory, to add; Ciliciam ad imperium populi Romani, Cic. ; agros populo, Cic. ; d, to connect in any kind of relation, to give, to attribute ; fidem visis, Cic. ; sibi auxilium, Cic. ; insolentiam honestati, Cic. ; animum ad aliquod studium, Ter. ; 2, of persons, a, to bring in as a participator ; aliquem ad suos sermones, Cic. ; b, to bind, unite ; urbem ad amicitiam, Liv. ; aliquem sibi socium, or simply socium, Cic. ; with double acc., se comitem fugae, Cic.

adjūro, 1. 1, to swear in addition, Liv. ; 2, to swear, to promise on oath; qui omnia adjurant, Cic. ; a, with acc. and infin., adjura sid te invito me non esse facturum, Cic. ; b, with per and the acc., per Jovem, Plaut. ; c, with the simple acc., adjuro Stygii caput implacabile fontis, Verg.

adjūtābĭlis -e, full of help, serviceable, Plaut.

adjūto, 1. to be serviceable, to help, Plaut., Ter.

adjūtor -ōris, m. (adjuvo), a helper ; 1, victoriae populi Romani, Cic. ; a, with in and the abl., in re gerenda, Cic. ; b, with ad and the acc., adjutores ad injuriam, Cic. ; c, with contra and the acc., his adjutor contra patriam inventus est nemo, Cic. ; 2, a regular assistant ; one who played secondary parts on the stage, Hor. ; esp., the assistant of a public officer, deputy ; P. Manlius in Hispaniam citeriorem adjutor consuli datus, Liv.

adjūtrix -īcis, f. (adjutor), 1, of persons, she that helps, a female assistant, a helper ; Minerva adjutrix consiliorum meorum, Cic. ; 2, of things, aid ; quae res Plancio in petitione fuisset adjutrix, Cic. ; 3, name of reserve legions under the empire, Tac.

adjūvo -jūvi -jūtum, 1. to help, assist, support. I. aliquem in aliqua re, Cic. ; ad bellum, Liv. ; followed by ut with the subj., Cic. ; maerorem nationis lacrimis suis, Cic. II. to be of service, to avail ; jam nihil te Neronis judicium adjuvat, Cic. ; philos. t. t., causae adjuvantes, mediate, Cic. ; impers., followed by the infin., nihil igitur adjuvat procedere et progredi in virtute, Cic.

adl, v. under all . . .

admātūro, 1. to hasten ; admaturari defectionem, Caes.

admētior -mensus, 4. dep. to measure out to ; frumentum alicui, Cic.

Admētus -i, m. (Ἄδμητος), 1, ruler of Pherae, in Thessaly, husband of Alcestis, who died for him ; 2, king of the Molossi, friend of Themistocles.

admigro, 1. to wander to, to come to, Plaut.

admĭnĭcŭlo, 1. to support, prop; vitem, Cic.

admĭnĭcŭlum -i, n. (ad and *mineo). I. Lit., a prop, a support, the pole on which a vine is trained, Cic. II. Transf., aid, help; ad aliquod tamquam adminiculum anniti, Cic. ; egere adminiculis, Tac.

administra -ae, f. (administer), she that helps; artes hujus administrae comitesque virtutis, Cic.

administrātĭo -ōnis, f. 1, the giving of help ; sine hominum administratione, Cic. ; 2, direction, government; navis, Caes. ; belli, Cic. ; mundi, rerum, reipublicae, Cic.

administrātor -ōris, m. an administrator, manager ; quidam belli gerendi, Cic.

administro, 1. 1, to help, assist, Plaut. ; 2, to manage, direct, administer ; rempublicam,

Cic. ; navem, to steer, Caes. ; of war, bellum cum Cimbris, Cic. ; exercitum, Cic. ; of other things, provinciam, Cic. ; leges et judicia, Cic. ; omnem mundum, Cic.

admĭrābĭlis -e, worthy of admiration, admirable ; 1, admirabilis et singularis sapientia, Cic. ; 2, astonishing, strange (to translate παράδοξα), Cic.

admĭrābĭlĭtas -ātis, f. admirableness, Cic. ; haec animi despicientia magnam admirabilitatem facit, excites wonder, Cic.

admĭrābĭlĭter, adv. 1, admirably, wonderfully ; laudari, Cic. ; 2, strangely (Gr. παραδόξως), Cic.

admĭrandus -a -um (admiror) = admirabilis, worthy of admiration ; homo, Cic.

admĭrātĭo -ōnis, f. 1, admiration; summam hominum admirationem excitare, Cic. ; habere, Cic. ; in magna admiratione esse, Cic. ; plur., admirationes, outbursts of admiration ; clamores et admirationes efficere, Cic. ; 2, wonder, astonishment ; tam atrocis rei, at so cruel a deed, Cic. ; admiratio consulem incessit quod, Liv. ; admiratio orta est, followed by acc. with infin., Liv. ; fit clamor et admiratio populi, followed by acc. with infin., Cic.

admĭror, 1. dep. 1, to admire ; res gestas, Cic. ; 2, to be astonished at ; with adv., leviter, vehementer, magnopere, etc., aliquid, Cic. ; nihil, Cic. ; in aliqua re, de aliquo, Cic. ; with acc. and infin., Cic. ; with quod, cur, quo pacto, unde, Cic.

admiscĕo -miscŭi -mixtum (-mistum), 2. I. to mix with, to add to by mixing. A. Lit., aquae admixtus calor, Cic. B. Transf., to join ; admiscerentur plebeii, Liv. ; ad id consilium admiscear, Cic. II. to mix with something. A. Lit., aër multo calore admixtus, Cic. B. Transf., urbes maritimae admiscentur novis sermonibus ac disciplinis, become familiar with, Cic.

admissārĭus -i, m. (admitto), a stallion ; fig., a lascivious man, Cic.

admissĭo -ōnis, f. an audience, esp. of a royal person, Plin.

admissum -i, m. a crime, Cic.

admitto -mīsi -missum, 3. to send to. I. to let go. A. Lit., 1, to let a horse go at full speed, to urge on, to put to a gallop ; equo admisso, Cic. ; 2, to hurry; admisso passu, with hurried step, Ov. B. Transf., to let go ; quod semel admissum coerceri reprimique non potest, Cic. II. to let in, to give access to. A. Lit., 1, aliquem ad capsas, Cic. ; 2, to give audience to ; aliquem, Cic. ; 3, to admit a person to share in an undertaking, etc. ; aliquem ad consilium, Cic. B. Transf., 1, of words, entreaties, etc., to allow to reach ; eas conditiones vix auribus, Liv. ; 2, of an act, to allow; litem, Cic. ; of omens, admittunt aves, the auguries allow it, Liv. ; 3, to commit a crime ; in te tantum facinus, Cic.

admixtĭo -ōnis, f. (admisceo), a mingling, an admixture; corporis, Cic.

admŏdĕrātē, adv. appropriately, Lucr.

admŏdĕror, 1. dep. to moderate, Plaut.

admŏdum adv. (ad and modum), up to the measure, up to the mark; hence, I. With numbers, about ; turres admodum CXX., Caes. II. Of degree, completely, quite ; A. Gen., 1, with adjectives or adverbs, forma admodum impolita et plane rudis, Cic. ; admodum raro, Cic. ; with nihil and nullus, litterarum admodum nihil sciebat, entirely ignorant of, Cic. ; of age, puer admodum, a mere boy, Liv. ; non admodum grandis natu, Cic. ; 2, with verbs, me admodum diligunt, Cic. B. In affirmative answer, certainly, Ter.

admoenĭo, 4. *to besiege,* Plaut.

admōlĭor, 4. dep. *to move to,* Plaut.

admŏnĕo -ŭi -ĭtum, 2. *to admonish, remind,* **a**ll *the attention to;* 1, aliquem alicuius rei, or de aliqua re, Cic. ; aliquem haec, eam rem, multa, Cic. ; followed by acc. and infin., Liv. ; or relative sentence with quantus, qui, Cic. ; 2, in business language, *to remind of a debt;* aliquem aeris alieni, Cic. ; 3, **a**, *to advise to do something;* followed by ut or ne and the subj., or by the simple subj., by ad or in and the acc., or by the infin., Cic. ; ad thesaurum reperiendum admoneri, Cic. ; **b**, *to urge* or *incite;* telo bijugos, Verg.

admŏnĭtĭo -ōnis, f. *a reminding;* 1, Gen., Cic. ; 2, *friendly admonition;* admonitio in consilio dando familiaris, Cic. ; in plur., nec precibus nec admonitionibus nostris reliquit locum, Cic.

admŏnĭtor -ōris, m. *one who reminds,* Cic.

admŏnĭtum -i, n. *an admonition, a calling to mind,* Cic.

admŏnĭtus -ūs, m. *a reminding;* 1, locorum admonitu, Cic. ; 2, *admonishing, warning;* amici tali admonitu, Cic. ; mortis, Ov.

admordĕo -morsum, 2. 1, *to bite at, to gnaw,* Prop. ; 2, *to fleece,* Plaut.

admōtĭo -ōnis, f. *a moving to;* digitorum, *playing on the harp,* Cic.

admŏvĕo -mōvi -mōtum, 2. *to move, bring to.* **A.** Gen., 1, fasciculum ad nares, Cic. ; alicui stimulos, Cic. ; manum operi, *to engage in a work,* Ov. ; manus nocentibus, *to lay hands on the guilty,* Liv. ; so manus vectigalibus, Cic. ; aspidem ad corpus, Cic. ; angues curribus, *to yoke,* Ov. ; with acc. alone, ignem, Cic. ; aurem, Cic. ; 2, *to direct, devote;* mentes suas, non solum aures, ad haruspicum vocem, Cic. ; 3, milit. t. t., *to bring up* war-machines ; opus ad turrim hostium, Caes. ; *to bring up* soldiers ; armatos muris, Liv. ; 4, of sacrifices, *to bring to the altar;* filiam victimam aris, Liv. ; 5, *to bring near, place near;* urbem ad mare, Cic. **B.** 1, *to apply;* curationem ad aliquem, Cic. ; orationem ad sensus animorum atque motus inflammandos, Cic. ; 2, of time, in the pass., *to draw near;* admotus supremis, *drawing near to death,* Tac. ; se admovere, *to draw near;* se applicare et propius admovere, Cic.

admūgĭo, 4. *to bellow after,* Ov.

admurmŭrātĭo -ōnis, f. *a murmuring* (either of approbation or disapprobation), Cic.

admurmŭro, 1. *to murmur at* (in approval or disapproval), Cic.

admŭtĭlo, 1. *to shear, shave;* hence, transf., *to fleece,* Plaut.

adn, v. agn or ann . . .

ădŏlĕo -ŭi, 2. 1, Intrans., *to smell,* Plaut. ; 2, Trans., *to make to smell, to set on fire, to burn* (of sacrifices) ; viscera tauri flammis, Ov. ; honores Junoni, *to honour by burning sacrifices to,* Verg. ; so of the altar itself, *to light up* with sacrificial fire ; altaria flammis, Lucr. ; flammis Penates (= focos), Verg. ; cruore captivo aras, *to feed the altars with,* etc., Tac.

ădŏlescens (ădŭlescens) -entis (part. of adolesco). **A.** Adj. (with compar.), *young;* admodum adolescens, Cic. ; adolescentior academia, Cic. **B.** Subst., 1, masc., *a young man* (without reference to any particular age) ; puer sive jam adolescens, Cic. ; adolescens vel puer potius, Cic. ; used (like junior in English) to distinguish a person from some one of the same name, but older ; P. Crassius adol., Caes. ; 2, fem., *a girl,* gen. as an attribute ; filia adol., Cic.

ădŏlescentĭa -ae, f. *youth;* citius adolescentiae senectus quam pueritiae adolescentia obrepit, Cic. ; ineunte adolescentia, Cic. ; ab adolescentia, **a** prima adol. ; ab ineunte adol., *from youth upward,* Cic. ; meton., *the young,* Cic.

ădŏlescentŭla -ae, f. *a very young girl,* used as a term of endearment, Plaut.

ădŏlescentŭlus -i, m. *a very young man;* applied by Cic. to himself in his 27th year, and by Sallust to Caesar when Caesar was about 33 or 35 ; ab adolescentulo, *from youth upward,* Cic.

1. **ădŏlesco** -ōlēvi -ultum, 3. *to grow, to grow up to maturity.* **A.** Lit., 1, of men, is qui adoleverit, Cic. ; 2, of plants, viriditas herbescens quae sensim adolescit, Cic. **B.** Transf., *to grow, increase;* of time, *to advance;* cum matura adoleverit aetas, Verg. ; ver donec adolesceret, Tac. ; of the mind, *to be developed, to come to maturity;* ratio quum adolevit atque perfecta est, Cic. ; ea cupiditas adolescit una cum aetatibus, Cic.

2. **ădŏlesco** -ēre (adoleo), *to blaze;* adolescunt ignibus arae, Verg.

Ădōneus -ĕi, m. = Adonis (q.v.).

Ădōnis -ĭdis (Ἄδωνις), and **Adōn** -ōnis, m. (Ἄδων), *a beautiful youth, son of Cinyras, king of Cyprus, beloved of Venus, slain by a wild boar, but changed after death by Venus into a flower* (adonium).

ădŏpĕrĭo -pĕrŭi -pertum, 4. 1, *to cover;* capite adoperto, Liv. ; humus floribus adoperta, Ov. ; 2, *to close,* adoperta lumina somno, Ov.

ădŏpīnor, 1. dep. *to guess,* Lucr.

ădoptātīcĭus -a -um, *adopted as a child,* Plaut.

ădoptātĭo -ōnis, f. = adoptio (q.v.).

ădoptĭo -ōnis, f. *the adoption of a child;* emancipare filium alicui in adoptionem, *to give in adoption,* Cic. ; ascire aliquem in or per adoptionem, *to adopt,* Tac.

ădoptīvus -a -um. **I.** *relating to adoption;* filius, pater, frater, soror, *adopted son,* etc., Suet. ; sacra, *the rites of the family into which the person was adopted,* Cic. ; nobilitas, Ov. **II.** Transf., of plants, *grafted,* Ov.

ădopto, 1. **I.** Gen. *to choose for one's self;* sibi aliquem patronum, Cic. ; of things, Etruscas opes, *to take to one's aid,* Ov. **II.** Esp., **A.** Lit., *to adopt* as child or grandchild (per aes et libram, *by a fictitious sale,* or testamento, *by will*); sibi filium, Cic. ; aliquem ab aliquo, *from the natural father,* Cic. ; in regnum, Sall. **B.** Transf. 1, in jest, C. Stalenus qui ipse se adoptaverat et de Staleno Aelium fecerat, *had changed his name by adopting himself,* Cic. ; frater, pater adde ; ut cuique est aetas, ita quemque facetus adopta, *adopt him by calling him brother, father,* etc., Hor. ; nomen or cognomen adoptare, Mart. ; 2, of plants, *to graft;* fac ramus ramum adoptet, Ov.

ădŏr -ōris, n. *a species of grain, spelt* (Triticum spelta, Linn.), Hor.

ădōrātĭo -ōnis, f. *a praying to, adoration,* Plin.

ădōrĕa (ădōrĭa) -ae, f. (adoro), *reward of valour, glory;* ille dies . . . qui primus alma risit adorea, Hor.

ădōrĕus -a -um (ador), *relating to spelt;* liba, Verg.

ădōrĭor -ortus, 4. dep. *to rise up.* **I.** *to attack;* **a**, aliquem fustibus, gladiis, Cic. ; a tergo, Cic. ; pagum, Caes. ; **b**, *to besiege with* entreaties, threats, etc. ; aliquem minis, Tac. ; aliquem tumultuosissime, Cic. **II.** *to attempt, undertake;* hoc ipsum, Cic. ; majus nefas, Verg. ; followed by infin., convellere ea, etc., Cic.

ădorno, 1. *to prepare, furnish, provide.* **I.** Gen., naves onerarias, Caes. ; Italiae duo maria maximis classibus firmissimisque praesidiis, Cic. ; accusationem, Cic. **II.** *to adorn.* **A.** Lit., forum magno ornatu, Cic. ; aliquem insigni veste, Liv. **B.** Transf., justi honores aliquem adornant, Liv.

ădŏro, 1. A. Gen., *to speak to.* **B.** Esp., 1, *to address* a deity, *to entreat, to ask for,* a, with acc. of person and acc. of thing ; pacem deum, Liv. ; b, followed by ut and the subj., Liv. ; 2, *to honour* ; Phoebum, Ov.

adp, v. under app.

adq, v. under acq.

adr, v. under arr.

ădrādo -rāsi -rāsum, **3.** *to scrape, shave;* adrasum quendam, Hor.

Adrămyttēum -i, n. (Ἀδραμύττειον), *town on the coast of Mysia, not far from the foot of Mount Ida* (now *Adramitti* or *Edremit*). Hence **Adramyttēnus** -i, m. *a native of Adramytteum.*

Adrastus -i, m. (Ἄδραστος), *king of Argos, father-in-law of Polynices and Tydeus, one of the Seven against Thebes, and the only one who escaped, afterwards one of those who destroyed Thebes in the war of the Epigoni.* Adj., **Adrastēus** -a -um.

Adria = Hadria (q.v.).

Adrūmētum (Hadrūmētum) -i, n. *town on the coast of the Roman province of Africa.*

ads, v. under ass.

adsc, v. under asc.

adsp, v. under asp.

adst, v. under ast.

adt, v. under att.

Adŭătŭci -ōrum, m. *people in Gallia Belgica,* in modern South Brabant, Caes.

ădūlātĭo -ōnis, f. **I.** *fawning* (of dogs), Cic. **II.** *cringing, flattery,* Cic., Liv. ; so of oriental prostration, humi jacentium adulationes, Liv. ; used with adversus or in and the acc. ; adversus superiores, Tac. ; patrum in Augustum, Tac.

ădūlātor -ōris, m. *a base flatterer,* Suet.

ădūlātōrĭus -a -um, *flattering;* dedecus, Tac.

ădūlescens, etc., v. adolescens.

ădūlo, 1. *to fawn;* pinnata cauda nostrum adulat sanguinem, *wipes off our blood fawningly* (of a dog), Lucr.

ădūlor, 1. dep. **A.** Lit., *to fawn* (of dogs and other animals) ; ferae adulantes, Ov. **B.** Transf., 1, *to greet with servile prostrations;* more adulantium procumbere, Liv. ; 2, *to flatter, to cringe before;* a, with acc., omnes, Cic. ; plebem, Liv. ; fortunam alterius, Cic. : b, with dat., plebi, Liv. ; c, absol., aperte adulans, Cic.

ădulter -ĕri, m., **ădultĕra** -ae, f. *an adulterer, adulteress.* **I.** Subst., sororis, Cic. ; in nepti Augusti, Tac. ; Dardanius adulter, *Paris,* Verg. ; Lacaena adultera, *Helen,* Hor. ; poet., *a gallant,* Hor. **II.** Adj., *adulterous;* virgo, Ov. ; crines, *the locks of an adulterer,* Hor. ; mens, Ov. ; clavis, Ov.

ădultĕrīnus -a -um (adulter), 1, *adulterous,* Plin. ; 2, *not genuine, forged;* nummus, Cic. ; signum, *a forged seal,* Cic. ; clavis, *a double key,* Sall.

ădultĕrĭum -ĭi, n. *adultery;* in adulterio deprehendi, Cic. ; Mutiliae, *adultery with,* Tac.

ădultĕro, 1. I. Intrans., *to commit adultery,* Cic. **II.** Trans., **A.** Of animals, adulteretur et columba miluo, *let the kite wed the dove,* Hor. ;

adulteratus nidus (of a nest where the cuckoo has laid its eggs), Plin. **B.** Transf., *to falsify, corrupt;* jus civile pecuniâ, Cic. ; faciem arte (of Proteus), *changes his form,* Ov.

ădultus -a -um, p. adj. with compar. (adolesco). **I.** *grown up, adult;* virgo, Cic. Plur. subst., **ădulti,** *adults,* Cic. **II.** Transf., **A.** Of time, puer aetate adulta, *near manhood,* Cic. ; aestas, *midsummer,* Sall., Tac. **B.** Fig., of growth; 1, in power, Athenae, Cic. ; pestis (of Catilina), Cic. ; Parthi nondum adulti, Tac. ; 2, of mental development, populus, Cic.

ădumbrātim, adv. *in outline,* Lucr.

ădumbrātĭo -ōnis, f. *a sketch,* Cic.

ădumbrātus -a -um, p. adj. (adumbro), 1, *sketched, imperfect;* imago gloriae, Cic. ; adumbratae intelligentiae rerum, *imperfect, confused notions,* Cic. ; 2, *shadowy, unreal;* opinio, Cic. ; laetitia, Tac.

ădumbro, 1. *to shade,* esp. *to sketch, to sketch in words;* fictos luctus dicendo, Cic.

ăduncĭtas -ātis, f. *a bending inwards;* rostrorum, Cic.

ăduncus -a -um, *bent inwards, crooked;* unguis, Cic. ; nasus, *an aquiline nose,* Ter.

ădurgĕo, 2. *to press to,* or *against;* poet., *to pursue closely;* aliquem remis, Hor.

ădūro -ussi -ustum, **3.** *to set fire to, to kindle, consume by burning;* sine gemitu aduruntur, Cic. ; candente carbone sibi capillum, *to singe,* Cic. ; panis adustus, *burnt bread,* Hor. ; of frost or wind, *to nip,* Verg. ; fig., of love, Venus non erubescendis adurit ignibus, Hor.

ădusquĕ = usque ad ; 1, prep. with acc. *as far as,* Verg. ; 2, adv. = usque, *thoroughly, entirely,* Ov.

ădustus -a -um, p. adj. with compar. (from aduro), *burnt by the sun, brown;* hominum color, Liv.

advectĭtĭus -a -um, *that which is brought from a distance, foreign;* vinum, Sall.

advecto, 1. (intens. from adveho), *to convey often;* rei frumentariae copiam, Tac.

advectus -ūs, m. *a conveying, carrying,* Tac.

advĕho -vexi -vectum, **3.** 1. *to carry, bring, convey to a place.* **I.** Act., frumentum ex agris Romam, Cic. ; ultrices unda advehit rates, Ov. ; frumentum Romam, Cic. **II.** Pass., advehi, *to be borne to* a place (on horseback, in a chariot, on a ship, etc.) ; advecta classis, Verg. ; e Pompeiano navi in Luculli hospitium, Cic. ; citato equo in eam partem, Liv. ; Corcyram insulam advehitur, *reaches,* Tac. ; with dat. of person, quum tibi tota cognatio serraco advehatur, Cic. ; with acc. of person, Dardanos, Verg. ; so ut quosque advectus erat, Tac.

advēlo, 1. *to draw a veil over;* poet., *to crown;* tempora lauro, Verg.

advĕna -ae, c. (advenio), 1, of men, *a stranger, foreigner* (opp. indigena), Cic. ; indigenae advenaeque, Tac. ; dei advenae, *foreign gods,* Cic. ; 2, of birds, *a bird of passage;* grus, Hor. ; 3, of things, Tibris, Ov. ; amor, *love for a foreigner,* Ov.

advĕnĭo -vēni -ventum, **4.** *to come to.* **A.** Lit., 1, of men, advenis modo? Cic. ; ex Hyperboraeis Delphos, Cic. ; in provinciam belli gerendi causa, Cic. ; with acc. only, Tyriam urbem, Verg. ; with dat., Tac. ; 2, of things, esp. of ships, a quibus adveniat navis Miletida sospes ad urbem, Ov. **B.** Transf., 1, of time, *to come;* interea dies advenit, Cic. ; 2, of events, *to happen, to come near, to break out;* urbi periculum advenit, Sall. ; morbi advenientes, Cic. ; **3.** of

acquisitions, *to come to;* res sua sponte mox ad eum advenit, Liv.

adventīcīus -a -um (advenio), *coming from without.* **A.** Gen., *outward;* externus et adventicius tepor, Cic. **B.** Esp., 1, *coming from a foreign country, foreign;* auxilia, Cic. ; doctrina transmarina atque adventicia, Cic. ; **2,** *casual, extraordinary, accidental;* pecunia, *money not inherited,* Cic.

advento, 1. (intens. of advenio), *to approach, arrive at,* gen. with notion of haste ; ad Italiam, Cic. ; with dat. of person, Parthis, Tac. ; in subsidium, Tac. ; of things and abstractions, quod fere jam tempus adventat, Cic.

adventor -ōris, m. (advenio), *one who arrives, a visitor,* Plaut.

adventus -ūs, m. (advenio). **I.** *an arrival;* nocturnus ad urbem, Cic. ; in plur., invitationes adventusque nostrorum hominum, Cic. ; of things, veris, Hor. ; in animos et introitus imaginum, Cic. **II.** Transf., malorum, Cic.

adversārīus -a -um (adversus), *turned towards.* **I.** Subst., **adversārīa** -orum, n. *(that which is always open,* or *lying in front of one), a day-book, journal, memorandum;* adversaria negligenter scribere, Cic. **II.** Adj., *opposed, contrary;* with dat., Cic. ; factio, Nep. Subst., **adversārīus** -ii, m. *adversary, rival, antagonist,* Cic. ; plur., *enemies,* Cic. ; **adversārīa** -orum, n. *the assertions of an opponent;* adversaria evertere, Cic.

adversor, 1. dep. (adversus), *to oppose, resist;* absol., of persons, non adversante collega, Cic. ; of things, adversante fortuna, Cic. ; with dat., alicui infestius, Cic. ; legi, Cic., Liv. ; cum duae causae perspicuis et evidentibus rebus adversentur, Cic.

1. adversus -a -um, p. adj. (adverto), *turned towards.* **A.** Lit., *fronting, opposite;* dentes, *the front teeth,* Cic. ; adversa vulnera, *wounds in the front,* Cic. ; solem adversum intueri, *to look straight at the sun,* Cic. ; adversos concitare equos, *to ride towards,* Liv. ; adversis hostibus occurrere, *to meet the enemy,* Caes. ; adverso colle, *on the front of the hill,* Caes. ; adverso flumine, *against the stream,* Caes. ; venti adversi, *contrary winds,* Liv. ; with prep., in adversum, *against,* Verg., Liv. ; ex adverso, *over against,* Liv. **B.** Transf., 1, of persons, *opposed,* adversus alicui, Cic., adverso Marte, Verg. ; adverso senatu, *against the will of the senate,* Liv. ; 2, of things, **a,** *unfavourable, unpropitious;* adversis auribus, Liv. ; valetudo, *ill health,* Liv. ; bellum, *cruel,* Hor. ; proelium, *unsuccessful,* Caes. ; res adversae, Cic., fortuna adversa, Verg., *misfortune;* with dat., res plebi adversa, Liv. ; **b,** *hated,* quis omnia regna adversa sunt, Sall. Subst., **adversum** -i, n. *misfortune;* si quid adversi acciderit, Cic.

2. adversus, adversum (adverto), *opposed to.* **I.** Adv., *against;* nemo adversus ibat, Liv. ; adversus arma ferre, Nep. **II.** Prep. with acc. **A.** Of direction, 1, as regards place, *towards;* adversus clivum, Caes. ; 2, of action, etc., *against;* adversus quem ibatur, Liv. ; adversus rempublicam facere, Caes. ; respondere adversus ea, *to answer to,* Liv. ; adversus legem, Cic. ; adversus quod . . . convenisset, *against the agreement,* Liv; adversus blanditias incorruptus, Tac. ; munitus adversum aliquem or aliquid, Sall. **B.** Of position, 1, as regards place, *over against;* adversus aedes publicas, Liv. ; 2, of comparison, quid autem esse duo prospera in tot saeclis bella Samnitium adversus tot decora populi Romani, *compared with,* Liv. ; 3, of behaviour, *in the presence of;* quonam modo me gererem adversus Caesarem, Cic. ; so of respect to, *towards;* reverentia adversus homines, Cic

adverto (advorto) -verti (-vorti) -versum (-vorsum), 3. *to turn towards.* **A.** agmen urbi, Verg. ; esp. used of ships, *to steer;* classem in portum, Liv. ; pass., notae advertuntur arenae, *they steer to,* Verg. ; Scythicas advertitur oras, Ov. **B.** Of the senses and thoughts, etc., *to direct;* 1, of the senses, especially the eyes, lumina in quamcunque aedis partem, Ov. ; of the gods, malis advertite numen, *direct your powers to,* Verg. ; aures ad vocem, Ov. ; 2, of the mind, animum, and (sometimes) mentem advertere ; **a,** *to direct one's attention to;* animos ad religionem, Lucr. ; with dat., animos monitis, Ov., followed by ne and the subj., animum animadvertant, ne quos offendant, *take care not to,* etc., Cic. ; absol., Cic. ; **b,** *to perceive;* animum in contione stantem, Cic. ; followed by acc. and infin., Cic. ; or relative clause, Cic. ; with animo or animis, animis advertite vestris, Verg. ; **c,** *to punish;* in aliquem, Tac. ; **d,** *to draw the attention of* some one else ; gemitus et planctus etiam militum aures oraque advertere, *roused the attention of,* Tac.

advespĕrascit -āvit, 3. (impers. and incept.), *evening approaches,* Cic.

advĭgĭlo, 1. *to watch by, to guard.* **I.** Lit., parvo nepoti, Tib. ; ad custodiam ignis, Cic. **II.** Fig., *to be vigilant,* Plaut.

advŏcātĭo -ōnis, f. *calling to one's aid.* **I.** *summoning persons to advise;* maximarum rerum, *on the most important points,* Cic. ; frequentissimae advocationes, Cic. **II.** Esp., 1, *legal advice;* advocationem postulare, petere, dare, consequi, Cic. ; 2, concr., *the bar,* Cic.

advŏcātus -i, m. *one who is called in to help in a legal process, whether as advocate or as witness,* Cic.

advŏco, 1. *to summon, to call.* **I.** Gen., contionem populi, Cic. ; aliquem in consilium, Cic. ; advocare ad obsignandum, Cic. ; with dat., advocari aegro, Ov. ; gaudiis, Hor. ; non desiderat fortitudo iracundiam advocatam, *called to its aid,* Cic. **II.** Esp., **A.** Legal t. t., of a judge, *to ask the opinion of a jurist,* Cic. ; of the parties to an action, *to consult an advocate;* aliquem contra aliquem, Cic. ; with dat., aliquem sibi, Plaut. ; absol., aderat frequens, advocabat, Cic. **B.** Of the gods, *to ask for help;* deum sibi, Cat. ; deos, Liv.

advŏlatus, abl. -ū, m. *a flying to,* Cic. poet.

advŏlo, 1. *to fly to.* **I.** Lit., of birds and insects, ad eas aves quae, etc., Cic. **II.** Transf., *to hasten towards, to fly to;* 1, of persons, absol., advolone an maneo, Cic. ; ad urbem, Cic. ; rostra, Cic. ; 2, of things, fama mali tanti advolat Aeneae, *flies to the ears of,* Verg.

advolvo -volvi -vŏlūtum, 3. *to roll to;* robora focis, *to the hearth,* Verg. ; ornos montibus, *from the mountains,* Verg. ; hence advolvi, *or* se advolvere, *to throw oneself at the feet of;* genibus alicuis, Liv. ; genua alicuius, Sall.

advorsum, advorsus, advorto = **adversum,** adversus, adverto (q.v.).

ădȳtum, -i, n. (ἄδυτον = not to be entered). **I.** Lit., gen. in plur., *the inmost and holiest portion of a temple; the shrine,* Verg., Hor. ; adytis ab imis, *from the bottom of a grave,* Verg. **II.** Transf., ex adyto tamquam cordis, *from the bottom of the heart,* Lucr.

Aeăcus -i, m. (Αἰακός), *a mythical king of Aegina, father of Peleus and Telamon, grandfather of Ajax and Achilles ; after his death judge in the infernal regions;* hence **Aeăcĭdes** -ae, m. *a descendant of Aeacus, one of his sons ; as Peleus or Phocus,* Ov.; *his grandson, Achilles,* Verg.; *his great-grandson, Pyrrhus* (Neoptolemus), Verg. ; *one of his remote descendants, Pyrrhus (king of Epirus),* Enn. ;

Perseus, king of Macedonia, Verg. **B. Acăcĭdēĭus** -a -um; regna (Aegina), Ov. **C. Aeăcĭdīnus** -a -um.

Aeaeē -ēs, f. (Αἰαίη νῆσος), *the island of the sorceress Circe,* or *of Calypso;* hence **Aeaeus** -a -um; **a,** surname of Circe, Verg.; Aeaeae artes, Aeaea carmina, *sorceries,* Ov.; Aeaeus Telegonus, *son of Circe,* Prop.; **b,** surname of *Calypso;* puella, Prop.

Aeās -antis, m. (Αἴας), *a river in Greece, flowing by Apollonia.*

Aebura -ae, f. *a town in Hispania Tarraconensis,* now *Cuerva,* Liv.

Aeculānum -i, n. *town of the Hirpini in Samnium,* Cic.

aedēs (aedis) -is, f.; originally, *a building.*
I. Sing., **A.** *a room,* Plaut. **B.** *a temple;* gen., where the context is not clear, with the name of some god, or with sacra; aedes sacra, Cic.; aedes Minervae, Cic.; in plur., complures aedes sacrae, Cic.; aedes alone, *the temple of the Palatine Apollo,* Hor. **II.** Plur., **A.** Lit., *a house,* Cic.; aedes liberae, *empty,* Liv. **B.** Meton., **1,** *the family,* Plaut.; **2,** Transf., **a,** *the cells of bees,* Verg.; **b,** *the chambers of the ears, the ears,* Plaut.

aedĭcŭla -ae, f. (dim. of aedes), *a small building;* **1,** *a small temple;* Victoriae, Liv.; also *a niche,* or *shrine* for the image of a god, Cic.; **2,** in plur., *a little house,* Cic.

aedĭfĭcātĭo -ōnis, f. (aedifico), *building;* **1,** Abstr., *the act of building;* consilium aedificationis, Cic.; aedificationem deponere or abjicere, *to give up building,* Cic.; **2,** Concr., *the building itself;* domus tua et aedificatio omnis, Cic.

aedĭfĭcātĭuncŭla -ae, f. (dim. of aedificatio), *a small building,* Cic.

aedĭfĭcātor -ōris, m. (aedifico), **1,** *a builder, architect;* fig., mundi, Cic.; **2,** *one who has a passion for building,* Juv.

aedĭfĭcĭum -i, n. (aedifico), *a building;* aedificia publica privata, sacra profana, Cic.; opposed to inhabited houses, aedes aedificiaque, Liv.; opposed to a number of houses together, vicis aedificiisque incensis, Caes.; opposed to the site, cujus (domus) amoenitas non aedificio sed silva constabat, Nep.; opposed to a palace, plebis aedificiis obseratis, patentibus atriis principium, Liv.

aedĭfĭco, 1. (aedes and facio). **I.** Lit., *to build, erect, establish;* villam, porticum, domum, urbem, navem, hortos, Cic. **II.** Fig., aedificare mundum, *to create,* Cic.; rempublicam, *to frame,* Cic.

aedĭlĭcĭus -a -um (aedilis), *relating to the aediles;* munus, Cic.; vectigal, *tax paid by the provinces for the shows of the aediles,* Cic. Subst., **aedilicius** -i, m. *one who has been aedile,* Cic.

aedīlis -is, m. (aedes), *an aedile, a public officer at Rome who had the superintendence of the buildings of the city, the roads, markets, theatres, dramatic performances, and police;* under the Republic there were four, two aediles curules (originally patricians, but afterwards patricians and plebeians), and two aediles plebis, or plebei, or plebeii.

aedīlĭtas -ātis, f. (aedilis), *the aedileship;* aedilitate fungi, Cic.

aedĭtĭmus (aeditumus) -i, m. an old form of aedituus (q.v.).

aedĭtŭens -entis, m. = aedituus (q.v.).

aedĭtŭus -i, m. (aedes), *the keeper* or *guardian of a temple,* Cic.

Aedŭi (Haedŭi) -ōrum, *a Gallic people between the Arar* (Saone) *and the Liger* (Loire), *whose chief town was Bibracte.*

Aeēta -ae, m., and **Aeētēs** -ae, m. (Αἰήτης),

king of Colchis, father of Medea; hence, **A. Aeētĭas** -ādis, f. *Medea,* Ov.; **B. Aeētĭnē** -ēs, f. *Medea,* Ov. **C. Aeētaeus** -a -um, *belonging to Colchis;* fines, *Colchis,* Cat.

Aefŭla -ae, f., and **Aefŭlum** -i, n. *town in Latium, north of Praeneste;* hence **Aefŭlānus** -a -um, *belonging to Aefula.*

Aegae (Aegaeae, Aegēae, Aegīae) -ārum, f. (Αἰγαί, Αἰγειαί), **1,** *town in Macedonia;* **2,** *town in Aeolis;* **3,** *town in Cilicia,* now *Castle of Ajas Kala.*

Aegaeōn -ŏnis, m. (Αἰγαίων), *another name for Briareus,* Verg.; *a sea-god,* Ov.

Aegaeus -a -um (Αἰγαῖος), *Aegaean;* mare, *the Aegaean Sea, the Archipelago,* Cic. Subst., **Aegaeum** -i, n. *the Aegaean Sea,* Hor.

Aegātes -ĭum, f., and **Aegātae** -ārum, f. (with or without insulae), *a group of three islands on the west coast of Sicily,* near which the decisive battle of the first Punic war was fought (241 B.C.).

aeger -gra -grum, *sick, ill.* **A.** Of physical illness; **1,** of persons; **a,** of persons themselves, homines aegri gravi morbo, Cic.; ex vulnere, Cic.; pedibus, Sall.; oculis, Liv.; manum, Tac. Subst., **aeger** -gri, m. *an invalid,* Cic.; **b,** of bodies or parts of the body, corpus, Cic.; dens, Mart.; so of states regarded as bodies; pars reipublicae, Cic.; civitas, Liv.; **c,** of bodily conditions, valetudo, Cic.; anhelitus, Verg.; **2,** of plants, seges, Verg.; **3,** of things, quid in toto terrarum orbe validum, quid aegrum, *unsound,* Tac. **B.** Of ailments of the mind, *ill* from any cause, love, hope, fear, sorrow, etc.; **1,** of persons, mortales aegri, Verg.; aegra amans, Verg.; aegra municipia, *mutinous,* Tac.; animo magis quam corpore aeger, Liv.; amore, Liv.; animi, *in mind,* Liv.; consilii, Sall.; **2,** of conditions, or relations, or abstractions, *painful;* amor, mors, Verg.; aegris oculis, *with envious eyes,* Tac.

Aegeus -ĕi, m. (Αἰγεύς), *king of Athens, father of Theseus;* hence **Aegĭdēs** -ae, m. *Theseus,* or *any one of the descendants of Aegeus.*

Aegĭmūrus -i, f., and **Aegĭmŏrŏs** -i, f. (Αἰγίμουρος and Αἰγίμορος), *an island near Carthage,* now *Al Djamur* or *Zimbra.*

Aegīna -ae, f. (Αἴγινα), *an island near Athens;* hence **Aeginensis** -e, *belonging to Aegina;* **Aeginenses** -ĭum, m. **Aeginētae** -ārum, m. *natives of Aegina.*

Aegīnĭum -ĭi, n. (Αἰγίνιον), *town in Macedonia, on the borders of Epirus,* now *Erkinia;* hence **Aeginĭenses** -ĭum, m. *the inhabitants of Aeginium.*

Aegĭon (Aegĭum) -ĭi, n. (Αἴγιον), *one of the twelve Achaean towns on the Corinthian Gulf,* now *Vostiza.*

aegis -ĭdis, f. (αἰγίς). **A.** *the aegis,* or *shield;* **1,** *of Jupiter,* Verg.; **2,** *of Minerva with the Medusa's head,* Ov. **B.** Transf., *a protection, bulwark,* Ov.

Aegīsos -i, f. (Αἴγισσος), *an old town in Moesia,* on the banks of the Danube, now *Isacze.*

Aegisthus -i, m. (Αἴγισθος), *son of Thyestes, murderer of Agamemnon, afterwards husband of Clytemnestra, himself murdered by Orestes,* Cic.

Aegĭum = Aegion (q.v.).

Aeglē -ēs, f. (Αἴγλη), *name of one of the Naiads.*

Aegŏcĕrōs -ōtis, m. (αἰγόκερως), *a sign of the zodiac, Capricorn,* Lucr.

aegrē, adv. with compar. and superl. (aeger).
I. *painfully;* aegre est mihi or meo animo, *I am grieved,* Plaut.; aegre ferre, *to be distressed.* **II.** **1,** *with difficulty;* aegre divelli, aegrius depelli, Cic.; **2,** *hardly, scarcely* (by itself and with vix);

æ tenere, Cic.; **3**, *unwillingly;* **ferre aliquid**, Cic.; aegre ferre, foll. by acc. and infin., *to take it ill that*, etc., Cic.

aegrĕo, 2. (aeger), *to be sick*, Lucr.

aegresco, 3. (aegreo), *to fall ill.* **I.** Lit., Lucr. **II.** Transf., **A.** *to become worse, more violent;* violentia Turni aegrescit medendo, Verg. **B.** *to be disturbed in mind, to trouble one's self;* longiore sollicitudine, Tac.

aegrĭmōnĭa -ae, f. (aeger), *grief, trouble of mind*, Cic.

aegrĭtūdo -ĭnis, f. (aeger), *sickness.* **I.** Of body, Plaut., Tac. **II.** Of mind, *grief;* se totum aegritudini dedere, Cic.; aegritudine emori, Cic.; in aegritudinem incidere, Cic.; aegritudinem levare, lenire, sedare, adimere alicui, depellere, efficere, Cic.; plur., aegritudines leniores facere, Cic.

aegror -ōris, m. (aeger), *sickness*, Lucr.

aegrōtātĭo -ōnis, f. (aegroto), *sickness.* **I.** Of body, Cic. **II.** Of the mind, Cic.

aegrōto, 1. (aegrotus), *to be sick or ill.* **I.** Lit., **A.** Of the body, graviter, vehementer diuque, leviter, periculose, Cic.; of cattle, Hor.; of plants, Plin. **B.** Of the mind, ea res ex qua animus aegrotat, Cic. **II.** Of abstractions, aegrotat fama vacillans, Lucr.

aegrōtus -a -um (aeger), *sick, ill;* **1**, in body, Cic.; **2**, in mind, Ter.; of abstract things, respublica, Cic.

Aegyptus -i (Αἴγυπτος). **A.** Mythol., m. *son of Belus, brother of Danaus.* **B.** Geogr., f. *Egypt.* Adj., 1, **Aegyptĭăcus** -a -um; 2, **Aegyptĭus** -a -um, *Egyptian*, Cic. Subst., **Aegyptĭus** -i, m. *an Egyptian*, Cic.

aelĭnos -i, m. (αἴλινος), *a dirge*, Ov.

Aemĭlĭānus -a -um, *relating to the gens Aemilia*, a surname of Scipio Africanus minor, the son of L. Aemilius Paulus, adopted by the elder Scipio Africanus.

Aemĭlĭus -a -um, gens, *name of one of the oldest and most distinguished patrician families of Rome;* Aemilia via, and simply Aemilia, *a road made by the consul M. Aem. Lepidus*, leading from Ariminum to Placentia; pons, *a bridge near the pons sublicius*, Juv.; ratis, *the ship in which the spoils of Perseus were brought home by Aem. Paulus*, Prop.; ludus, *a gladiatorial school founded by P. Aemilius Lepidus*, Hor.

Aemōnĭa, etc., v. Haemōnĭa.

aemŭlātĭo -ōnis, f. (aemulor), *a striving after or up to, emulation.* **I.** In a good sense, laudis, Nep.; gloriae, Liv. **II.** In a bad sense, *jealousy, envy, ill-natured rivalry*, Cic.; plur., *rivalries*, Cic.

aemŭlātor -ōris, m. (aemulor), *a rival;* Catonis aemulator, *an imitator*, Cic.

aemŭlātus -ūs, m. (aemulor) = aemulatio (q.v.).

aemŭlor, 1. dep. (aemulus), *to rival, emulate, strive to attain to.* **I.** In a good sense, aliquem, Nep.; ejus instituta, Cic.; Albanum vinum, *to come near to*, Plin. **II.** In a bad sense, *to envy;* with dat., alicui, Cic.; cum aliquo, Liv.; inter se, Tac.

aemŭlus -a -um, *emulous, vying with, rivalling.* **I.** In a good sense. **A.** Lit., gen. with genitive, mearum laudium, Cic.; with dat., dictator Caesar summis oratoribus aemulus, Tac. Subst., **aemulus** -i, m.; alicuius, Cic.; esp., *a zealous follower of a philosophical system;* cujus (Zenonis) inventorum aemuli Stoici nominantur, Cic. **B.** Transf., *coming near to, approaching to* (in excellence, etc.); tibia tubae aemula, Hor. **II.** In a bad sense, *zealous, rivalling;* Carthago aemula

imperii Romani, Sall.; aemula senectus, *jealous*, Verg. Subst., **aemŭlus** -i, m. and **aemŭla** -ae, f. *a rival in love*, Cic. and Ov.

Aemus = Haemus (q.v.).

Aenārĭa -ae, f. *a volcanic island on the west coast of Italy, opposite Campania* (now Ischia).

Aenēa -ae, f. (Αἴνεια), *a town in Chalcidice;* hence, **Aenēātes** -um, m. (Αἰνεᾶται), *inhabitants of Aenea.*

Aenēas -ae, m. (Αἰνείας), *son of Venus and Anchises*, hero of Vergil's Aeneid, myth. ancestor of the Romans; Aeneae mater, *Venus*, Ov.; Aeneae urbs, *Rome*, Ov.; hence **A. Aenĕădes** -ae, m. *descendant of Aeneas;* a, his son Ascanius, Verg.; b, *Augustus*, Ov.; plur., Aeneadae -arum, m.; a, *the companions of Aeneas*, Verg.; or *the Trojans*, Verg.; b, *the Romans*, Verg., Ov. **B. Aenēis** -ĭdos, f. *Vergil's Aeneid.* **C. Aenēĭus** -a -um, *relating to Aeneas.* **D. Aenīdēs** = Aeneades.

ăēnĕātor -ōris, m. (aeneus), *a trumpeter*, Suet.

ăēnĕus and **ăhēnĕus** -a -um (aenum, ahenum). **I.** Lit., **1**, *made of brass, copper, or bronze*, Cic.; **2**, *of a bronze colour*, Suet. **II.** Transf., **1**, *hard as metal;* murus, Hor.; **2**, aenea proles, *the brazen age*, Ov.

Aenĭānes -um, m. (Αἰνιᾶνες), *a Greek race in the south of Thessaly.*

aenigma -ătis, n. (αἴνιγμα), *a riddle.* **I.** Quint. **II.** Transf., *what is obscure, mystery;* somniorum, Cic.

ăēnĭpes (ăhēnĭpes) -pĕdis (ăēnĕus and pes), *brazen-footed*, Ov.

1. ăēnus (ăhēnus) -a -um (aes), **1**, *made of brass, copper, or bronze*, Verg. Subst., **ăēnum** -i, n. *a brazen vessel*, Verg.; **2**, *firm, inexorable;* manus, Hor.

2. Aenus -i **I.** Aenus (Aenŏs) -i, f. (Αἶνος), *a town in Thrace, at the mouth of the Hebrus*, now *Enos;* hence **Aenii** -orum, m. *its inhabitants.* **II. Aenus** -i, m. *a river between Vindelicia and Noricum* (now the Inn).

Aeŏles -um, m. *the Aeolians, one of the chief races of the Greeks*, the most important settlements of whom were in Boeotia and Lesbos; hence, a, **Aeŏlĭcus** -a -um, and b, **Aeŏlĭus** -a -um, *Aeolic*, with especial reference to Sappho, the Lesbian poetess.

Aeŏlĭa -ae, f. (Αἰολία), **1**, *the north part of the coast of Asia Minor, opposite to Greece*, Cic.; **2**, plur., **Aeŏlĭae insulae**, *a group of volcanic islands on the north coast of Sicily* (the Lipari isles); myth. seat of Aeolus and Vulcan.

Aeŏlis -ĭdis, f. (Αἰολίς), *a part of Mysia, in Asia Minor, north of the Hermus*, Liv.

Aeŏlus (Αἴολος) -i, m. (Αἴολος). **I.** *son of Hellen*, myth. *founder of the Aeolian race.* **II.** *son or grandson of Hippotas, ruler of the Aeolian islands and of the winds.* **III.** *a Trojan*, Verg.; hence, **A. Aeŏlĭdes** -ae, m. *a descendant of Aeolus;* **1**, his sons, Sisyphus, Ov.; Athamas, Ov.; Salmoneus, Ov.; his grandsons, Cephalus, Ov.; Ulysses, Verg. **B. Aeŏlis** -ĭdos, f. *female descendant of Aeolus;* **1**, his daughters, Canace, Ov.; Alcyone, Ov. **C. Aeŏlĭus** -a -um, *belonging to Aeolus;* **1**, *belonging to Aeolus* (**I.**); postes (of Athamas), Ov.; pecus, *the golden fleece*, Mart.; **2**, *belonging to Aeolus* (**II.**); virgo, *his daughter Arne*, Ov.; tyrannus, *Aeolus*, Ov.; antra, *the caves where the winds were kept*, Ov.; procellae, Verg.

aequābĭlis -e (aequo), *like, similar, equal;* **1**, praedae partitio, Cic.; **2**, *that which is equal to itself, uniform, equable;* amnis, Cic.; **3**, *fair, just;* nihil ea jurisdictione aequabilius, Cic.; of persons, cunctis vitae officiis aequabilis, Tac.; in suos, *affable*, Tac.

aequābĭlĭtas -ātis, f. (aequabilis), *uniformity, equability;* motus, Cic.; hence, a, juris, *impartiality,* Cic.; b, *equality of political rights,* Cic.; c, *equanimity,* Cic.

aequābĭlĭtĕr, adv. with compar. (aequabilis), *equably, uniformly, fairly;* praedam dispertire, Cic.; aequabilius provinciae regentur, Tac.

aequaevus -a -um (aequus and aevum), *of equal age,* Verg.

aequālis -e (aequo), *equal.* **I.** *level;* loca, Sall. **II.** *equal in height, size,* etc.; 1, *corresponding to;* with dat., pars pedis aequalis alteri parti, Cic.; with inter, virtutes sunt inter se aequales et pares, Cic.; 2, *of the same age with;* with dat., exercitus aequalis stipendiis suis, *that had served as many campaigns as he himself,* Liv.; with genit., calo quidam aeq. Hieronymi, Liv.; of things, aequali corpore nymphae, *of the same age and growth,* Verg.; with genit., sacrificium aequale hujus urbis, *contemporary with,* Cic.; with dat., cui (Ennio) si aequalis fuerit Livius, Liv.; with genit., Philistus aequalis temporum illorum, Cic.; memoria aequa illius aetatis, Cic. Subst., **aequālis** -is, c. *a comrade, person of the same age;* P. Orbius meus fere aequalis, Cic.; 3, *uniform;* imber lentior aequaliorque accidens auribus, Liv.; nihil aequale homini fuit illi, Hor.

aequālĭtas -ātis, f. (aequalis), 1, *evenness, smoothness,* Plin.; 2, *equality;* similitudo aequalitasque verborum (of a pun), Cic.; paterna, *complete harmony in thought,* etc., Cic.; *equality of age,* Cic.; 3, *equality of political privileges,* Tac.

aequālĭtĕr, adv. (aequalis), 1, *evenly;* collis ab summo aequaliter declivis, *gently sloping,* Caes.; 2, *equally;* distribuere, Cic.; 3, *uniformly;* oratio aequaliter constanterque ingrediens, *symmetrically,* Cic.

aequănĭmĭtas -ātis, f. (aequanimus, from aequus and animus), 1, *impartiality,* Ter.; 2, *calmness,* Plin.

aequātĭo -ōnis, f. (aequo), *a making equal;* bonorum, *communism,* Cic.; juris, Liv.

aequē, adv. (aequus), *in like manner, equally.* **I.** 1, duae trabes aeque longae, Caes.; aeque dolere, Cic.; with adv., aeque lubenter, Cic.; 2, *in comparison, just as, equally with;* a, foll. by et, atque, ac si, quam, quam ut, etc.; eosdem labores non esse aeque graves imperatori et militi, Cic.; hi coluntur aeque atque illi, Cic.; with cum and the abl., ut aeque mecum haec scias, Plaut.; with abl. alone, Plaut.; with compar., homo me miserior nullus est aeque, Plaut.; b, when the object of the comparison is to be understood, pauci quibuscum essem aeque libenter (sc. ac tecum), Cic. **II.** *fairly, justly;* societatem conditionis humanae munifice et aeque tuens, Cic.

Aequi (Aequĭcŭli, Aequĭcŏli, Aequĭcŭlāni) -ōrum, m. *a people in Latium,* with whom the Romans waged frequent wars; hence, a, **Aequĭcus** -a -um, *Aequian;* b, **Aequĭcŭlus** -a -um, *Aequian.*

aequĭlībrĭtas -ātis, f. *the equal distribution of natural forces* = ἰσονομία, Cic.

Aequĭmaelĭum -ĭi, n. *an open space in Rome, on the west side of the Capitol, where the cattle for the sacrifices were kept,* Cic.

aequĭnoctĭālis -e (aequinoctium), *equinoctial, relating to the equinox,* Cat.

aequĭnoctĭum -ĭi, n. (aequus and nox), *the equinox,* Cic.

aequĭpăro (aequĭpĕro), 1. (aequus and paro), 1, *to compare;* with ad and the acc., suas virtutes ad tuas, Plaut.; with dat., mari tranquillo quod ventis concitatur multitudinem Aetolorum,

Liv.; 2, *to equal,* aliquem, Liv.; nec calamis solum sed voce magistrum, Verg.

aequĭtas -ātis, f. (aequus), 1, *uniformity, symmetry;* membrorum, Suet.; 2, *equanimity* (with or without animi), Cic.; 3, *impartiality, equity, fairness, justice;* causae, Cic.; conditionum, Caes.; servare aequitatem, Cic.

aequo, 1. (aequus). **I.** *to make level;* locum, Caes.; aequata agri planities, Cic; aequare frontem, milit. t.t., *to form a line,* Liv. **II.** *to make equal with something else.* **A.** 1, *to distribute equally;* sortes, *to shake up the lots,* Cic.; pecunias, Cic.; aequato omnium periculo, Cic.; 2, *to make things of different kind equal;* a, of height, solo, *to level with the ground,* Liv.; fig., solo aequandae sunt dictaturae consulatusque, *must be abolished,* Liv.; machina aequata caelo, *as high as the heavens,* Verg.; fig., aliquem caelo laudibus, *to extol to the heavens,* Verg.; b, of number, qui (libri) se jam illis aequarunt, Cic.; per somnum vinumque dies noctibus, *to turn day into night by sleeping and drinking,* Liv.; nocti ludum, *to spend the whole night in play,* Verg.; c, of rights, *to make equal;* inventum est temperamentum quo tenuiores cum principibus aequari se putarent, Cic.; d, *to compare;* Hannibali Philippum, Liv. **B.** *to equal, to come up to;* Appii odium, Liv.; sagitta aequans ventos, Verg.; aliquem passibus, Verg.; aliquem equestri gloria, Liv.

aequor -ōris, n. (aequus), *a flat surface.* **I.** Gen., speculorum, Lucr. **II.** Esp., 1, *the flat surface of a plain* (with campi), camporum patentium aequor, Cic.; poet. (without campi), immensum aequor, *of a desert,* Verg.; 2, poet., *the flat surface of the sea, the sea;* with ponti or maris, vastum maris aequor, Verg.; oftener without maris, etc., Ionium, Lucr.; vastum, Verg.; plur., saeva aequora, Verg.; meton., *the sea-water in a ship;* aequor refundere in aequor, Ov.; rarely, *the surface of a river,* as the Tiber, Verg.

aequŏrĕus -a -um (aequor), *belonging to the sea;* genus, *fishes,* Verg.; rex, *Neptune,* Ov.; Britanni, *sea-girt,* Ov.; Achilles, *a son of Thetis,* Lucan.

aequus -a -um, adj. with compar. and superl. *equal.* **I.** *equal in itself.* **A.** Lit., 1, of the surface of the ground, *level;* aequus et planus locus, Cic.; ex aequo loco loqui, *to speak in the senate* (opp. to ex inferiore loco, *in the presence of the judges,* and ex superiore loco, *in the presence of the people*), Cic.; ex superiore et ex aequo loco sermones habitos, *public and private conversations,* Cic. Neut. subst., **aequum** -i, n. *level ground;* facile in aequo campi victoriam fore, Liv.; 2, of other things, *level;* aequa frons, milit. t.t., *a straight line,* Liv. **B.** Transf., 1, of places, *favourable, advantageous;* locum se aequum ad dimicandum dedisse, Caes.; et tempore et loco aequo instructos, Liv.; 2, of character, *quiet, contented;* concedo et quod animus aequus est et quia necesse est, Cic.; aequam rebus in arduis servare mentem, Hor.; esp. in the phrase aequo animo, *patiently, with resignation;* pati or ferre with acc., and acc. with infin., Cic.; tolerare, Sall.; accipere, Sall.; spectare, Cic.; animo aequissimo mori, Cic.; in plur., animis lubentibus aut aequis aliquid remittere, Cic. **II.** *equal to something else.* **A.** Lit., *equal,* in breadth, height, etc.; aequo fere spatio abesse, Caes.; sequitur patrem non passibus aequis, *with shorter steps,* Verg.; urbs nubibus aequa, *as high as the clouds,* Ov.; aequis portionibus or pensionibus (*equal payments*), dare, solvere, etc., Liv.; foll. by atque, quam, cum; aequo et pari cum civibus jure vivere, Cic.; quum aequam partem tibi sumpseris atque populo Romano miseris, Cic. **B.** Transf., 1, in aequa laude ponere, Cic.; aequa pugna, *an indecisive battle,* Liv.; so

aequo proelio or marte discedere, *to fight an inde-cisive battle*, Caes. ; so aequa manu, or aequis manibus, Tac. and Liv. ; adv., ex aequo, *equally ;* sol ex aequo meta distabat utraque, *was equally distant*, Ov. ; **2**, of behaviour, etc., *equal, impartial ;* **a**, of persons, *fair ;* se alicui aequum praebere, Cic. ; praetor, judex, testis, Cic. ; **b**, of things, judicia, Cic. ; lex, Cic. ; aequum est, *it is just ;* with the acc. and infin., aequum esse eum et officio meo consulere et tempori, Cic. Subst., **aequum** -i, n. *fairness ;* quid in jure (*strict law*) aut in aequo (*equity*) verum aut esset aut non esset, Cic. ; per aequa per iniqua, *by fair means or foul*, Liv. ; gravius aequo, *than is right*, Sall. ; aequum et bonum, *what is right, fit ;* reus magis ex bono aequoque quam ex jure gentium Bomilcar, Sall. ; as a legal formula, quod or quantum aequius melius, *as is more equitable*, Cic. ; so aequi bonique facere aliquid, *not to find fault with*, Cic. ; **3**, *favourable to others, propitious ;* nobilitate inimica, non aequo senatu, Cic. ; non aequa Pallas, Verg. ; minus aequis animis auditus est Scipio, Liv. ; mea aequissimis utuntur auribus, *I hear them with the greatest pleasure*, Cic. ; with dat., aequa Venus Teucris, Ov. ; ipsis est aer avibus non aequus, *harmful to*, Verg. Plur. subst., **aequi,** *friends* in the phrase aequi iniquique, *friends and enemies*, Cic.

āēr, āĕris, m. (ἀήρ), *the lower air, the atmosphere around us ;* crassus, Cic. ; purus et tenuis, Cic. ; temperatus, Cic. ; aer summus arboris, *the airy summit of a tree*, Verg. ; aere septus obscuro, *surrounded by a cloud*, Verg.

aera -ae, f. (αἶρα), *a weed growing among grain, darnel, tares*, Plin.

aerāmentum -i, n. *bronze or copper ware*, Plin.

aerāria -ae, f., v. aerarius, I. B. 2.

aerārĭum -ii, n., v. aerarius, II. B. 2.

aerārĭus -ii, m. (aes). **I.** *belonging to brass or copper.* **A.** Adj., lapis, *copper*, Plin. ; structurae, *copper mines*, Caes. **B.** Subst., **1**, **aerārĭus** -ii, m. *a worker in brass*, Plin. ; **2**, **aerāria** -ae, f. *smelting-works*, Plin. **II.** *belonging to money.* **A.** Adj., ratio, *standard of the copper coinage*, Cic. ; milites, *mercenaries*, Varr. ; illa vetus aeraria fabula, *the old tale about the copper coin that Vettius gave to Clodia*, Cic. **B.** Subst., **1**, **aerārĭus** -ii, m. gen. in plur., aerarii, *the citizens of the lowest class in Rome, who had no votes, but had to pay a certain sum for the expenses of the state*, a class to which citizens of the higher ranks might be degraded by the censors for punishment ; aliquem aerarium facere, *to degrade*, Liv. ; aliquem in aerarios referri jubere, Cic. ; **2**, **aerārĭum** -ii, n. **a**, *the exchequer, treasury*, Rome, under or behind the temple of Saturn, where the treasures and archives of the state were kept ; pecuniam in aerarium referre, inferre, deferre, redigere, Cic. ; decreta patrum ad aerarium deferre, Tac. ; meton., *the money in the treasury*, Cic. ; **b**, *any public treasury*, Cic.

aerātus -a -um (aes), **I.** 1, *covered or fitted with brass or bronze ;* navis, Caes. ; lecti, *with bronze feet*, Cic. ; poet., acies, *an armed line of troops*, Verg. ; 2, *provided with money, rich*, tribuni non tam aerati, quam ut appellantur aerarii (with a play on the words, vide aerarius II. B. 1), Cic. **II.** *made of brass or bronze ;* securis, Verg. ; transf., *as firm as brass ;* nodi, Prop.

aerĕus -a -um (aes), 1, *made of brass or copper, signa aerea et marmorea*, Liv. ; 2, *covered with brass ;* puppis, Verg.

aerĭfĕr -fĕra -fĕrum (aes and fero), *bearing brazen cymbals*, Ov.

aerĭfĭcē, adv. (aes and facio), *skilfully* (of work in brass), Varr.

aerīnus -a -um (αἴρινος), *made of darnel* or *tares*, Plin.

aerĭpes -pĕdis (aes and pes), *brazen-footed*, Verg. , Ov.

āĕrĭus (āĕrĕus) -a -um (āer), 1, *belonging to the air, airy ;* alterum (animantium genus), penigerum et aerium, *living in the air*, Cic. ; domus, *the heavens*, Hor. ; aerias vias carpere, *to fly through the air*, Ov. ; mel (from the belief that honey fell in dew from the sky), Verg. ; 2, *high in the air, lofty ;* Alpes, Verg.

aero -ōnis, *a wicker basket*, Plin

Āĕrŏpē -ēs, f. and **Āĕrŏpa** -ae, f. (Ἀερόπη) *mother of Agamemnon and Menelaus.*

aerōsus -a -um (aes), *rich in copper ;* aurum, *mixed with copper*, Plin.

aerūgĭnōsus -a -um (aerugo), *covered with verdigris or copper-rust*, Sen.

aerūgo -ĭnis, f. (aes). **I. A.** *the rust of copper, verdigris*, Cic. **B.** Meton. = *rusty money*, Juv. **II.** Transf., **1**, *envy*, Hor. ; **2**, *avarice*, Hor.

aerumna -ae, f. *hard labour, toil, hardship ;* Herculis perpeti aerumnas, Cic.

aerumnābĭlis -e (aerumna), *calamitous, pitiable*, Lucr.

aerumnōsus -a -um (aerumna), *full of hardship and calamity ;* Regulus, Cic.

aes, aeris, n. *copper.* **I.** Lit., *copper ore*, and *the alloy of copper, brass,* or *bronze ;* pedestris ex aere statua, Cic. ; poet., of the brazen age, ut inquina vitae re tempus aureum, Hor. **II.** Meton., *something made of bronze, etc.* **A.** Gen. (esp. in poets), *a vessel, statue,* etc., made of bronze, etc. ; aes cavum, *kettle*, Ov. ; aera aere repulsa, *cymbals*, Ov. ; Corybantia, *cymbals used in the service of Cybele*, Verg. ; ejus aera refigere, *the brazen tablets on which the laws were engraved*, Cic. ; aes publicum, *public inscriptions*, Tac. ; aere ciere viros, *with the trumpet*, Verg. ; dempto aere, *the helmet*, Ov. **B.** Esp. money, 1, *copper* or *brass money ;* aes grave, *the as* (of a pound weight), which was weighed instead of counted ; denis millibus aeris gravis reos condemnavit, Liv. ; quinquaginta millia aeris (for assium), Liv. ; argentum aere solutum est, *three-fourths of the debts were remitted by payment of a* (copper) *as for a* (silver) *sesterce*, Sall. ; *small change* (cf. Engl., *coppers*) ; aera dabant olim, Ov. ; 2, *money* generally, gravis aere dextra, Verg. ; pueri qui nondum aere lavantur (= *boys under four years, who use the baths without paying*), Juv. ; esp., **a**, aes meum, *my property ;* est aliquis in meo aere, *he is bound to me*, Cic. ; aes alienum, *debt ;* facere, contrahere, in aes alienum incidere, esse in aere alieno, Cic. ; solvere, Cic. ; so aes mutuum, Sall. ; **b**, pay, Juv. ; esp. *soldiers' pay ;* aera militibus constituere, dare, Liv. ; **c**, aes circumforaneum, *money borrowed from the money-changers, who had their booths round the forum*, Cic. ; **3**, plur., aera, *counters*, Cic.

Aesăcŏs and **Aesăcus** -i, m. (Αἴσακος), *son of Priam, husband of Asterope or Hesperia.*

Aesăr -ăris, n. *a river in Bruttii,* now *Esaro ;* hence adj., **Aesārĕus** -a -um, *belonging to the river Aesar.*

Aeschīnes -is and -i, m. (Αἰσχίνης), **I.** *an Athenian philosopher, disciple of Socrates.* **II.** *a Neapolitan philosopher, pupil of Carneades.* **III.** *the celebrated Athenian orator, opponent of Demosthenes.* **IV.** *an orator of Miletus, contemporary with Cicero.*

Aeschўlus -i, m. (Αἰσχύλος). **I.** *an Athenian tragic poet* (born about A.C. 525) ; hence **Aeschylēus** -a -um, *belonging to Aeschylus ;* cothurnus, Prop. **II.** *a rhetorician of Cnidos, contemporary with Cicero.*

Aescŭlāpĭum -ĭi, n. *a temple of Aesculapius.*

Aescŭlāpĭus -ĭi, m. (Ἀσκληπιός), *the god of medicine, son of Apollo and Coronis, worshipped at Epidaurus.*

aescŭlētum -i, n. (aesculus), *an oak forest,* Hor.

aescŭlĕus -a -um (aesculus), *relating to the winter oak,* Ov.

aescŭlus -i, f. *the winter* or *Italian oak,* Verg.

Aesernĭa -ae, f. *town in Samnium,* now *Isernia;* hence **Aesernīnus** -a -um, *belonging to Aesernia; surname of M. Marcellus, who was taken prisoner at Aesernia; name of a celebrated gladiator,* Cic.

Aesis -is, m. *river in Picenum,* now *Esino* or *Fiumesino;* hence adj., **Aesīnās** -ātis.

Aeson -ŏnis, m. (Αἴσων), *a Thessalian prince, father of Jason;* hence, a, **Aesŏnĭdes** -ae, m. *a descendant of Aeson (Jason),* Prop.; b, **Aesŏnĭus** -a -um, *relating to Aeson;* heros, *Jason,* Ov.

Aesōpus -i, m. (Αἴσωπος). **I.** *a celebrated Greek fabulist of Phrygia, supposed to have lived in the 6th cent.* B.C. **II.** Claudius (Clodius) Aesopus, *a tragic actor in Rome, contemporary and friend of Cicero.*

aestas -ātis, f. (connected with αἴθω = to burn, and aestus), *summer.* **I.** Lit., ineunte, Cic.; novâ, *at the beginning of summer,* Verg.; mediâ, Cic.; adultâ, Tac.; summâ, Cic.; exactâ, *at the end of,* Sall.; esp. used of the summer as *the time for military operations;* unis litteris totius aestatis (*summer campaign*) res gestas ad senatum perscribere, Cic.; so quae duabus aestatibus gesta, Tac. **II.** Meton., *clear summer weather,* Verg.; *summer heat,* Hor.

aestĭfer -fĕra -fĕrum (aestus and fero), *heat-bringing,* Verg.; ignis, Lucr.

aestĭmābĭlis -e (aestimo), *valuable,* Cic.

aestĭmātĭo -ōnis, f. (aestimo). **I.** Lit., *an appraising according to value in money;* aequam aestimationem facere, Caes.; census, *the valuation of the census,* Cic.; frumenti, *valuation of the corn allowance for the governor of a province, or the amount to be paid by the aratores of the province instead of this allowance,* Cic.; litis, *assessment of damages,* Cic.; so, multae, Liv.; possessionis, *valuation of property,* Cic.; praedia in aestimatione ab aliquo accipere, *to take estates at the higher valuation that prevailed before the civil war,* Cic. **II.** Transf., 1, *the valuation* of a thing, a person, *according to its true value;* honoris, Liv.; 2, as a philosoph. t. t. (Gr. ἀξία), propria aestimatio virtutis, *the absolute worth of virtue,* Cic.

aestĭmātor -ōris, m. (aestimo), 1, *one who estimates, an appraiser;* frumenti, Cic.; 2, *one who values a thing according to its worth;* fidei, Liv.

aestĭmātus -ūs, m. = aestimatio (q.v.).

aestĭmo (aestŭmo). 1. (aes), *to appraise, estimate the value of anything.* **I.** *to estimate pecuniary value;* frumentum (vid. aestimatio frumenti), Cic.; with abl. or gen., of value; aliquid ternis denariis, Cic.; ut liceat, quanti quisque velit, tanti aestimet, Cic.; with adv., tenuissime, *at a very low rate,* Cic.; with ex and abl., aliquid ex artificio, *according to the standard of workmanship,* Cic.; litem alicui or alicuius, legal t. t., *to assess the damages in a law-suit,* Cic.; pugnatum est ut lis haec capitis aestimaretur, *should be held a capital charge,* Cic. **II.** In a wider sense, 1, *to value according to any standard;* with abl. or gen., magno, Cic.; magni, Cic.; with adv., carius, Cic.; levius tempestatis quam

classis periculum, Caes.; **with ex and abl.**, vulgus ex veritate pauca, ex opinione multa aestimat, Cic.; virtutem annis, Hor.; satis aestimare, *to estimate at full value,* with acc. and infin., Tac.; 2, *to judge,* sicuti ego aestimo, Sall.

aestīva -ōrum, n., v. aestivus.

aestīvē, adv. (aestivus), *as in summer,* Plaut.

aestīvo, 1. (aestivus), *to pass the summer,* Plin.

aestīvus -a -um (aestus), *relating to summer;* tempora, Cic.; aura, Hor.; saltus, *summer pasturage of cattle,* Liv.; aurum, *the gold ring of the military tribunes, worn for six months,* Juv.; aestivum tonat, *it thunders as in summer,* Juv. Plur. subst., **aestīva** -orum, n. : a, (sc. castra), *a summer camp,* Cic.; meton. (because the ancients generally waged war only in the summer), *a campaign,* Cic.; b, *summer pastures for cattle,* Varr.; meton., *the cattle in summer pastures,* Verg.

aestŭārĭum -ĭi, n. (aestus). 1, *low ground covered by the sea at high water, morass;* itinera aestuariis concisa, Caes.; 2, *a firth, creek, or part of the river up which the tide flows;* in aestuario Tamesae, Tac.

aestŭo, 1. (aestus), *to boil, to be hot.* **I.** Of fire, aestuat ignis, Verg.; or the results of fire; ventis pulsa aestuat arbor, *is heated,* Lucr.; si dixeris "aestuo" (*I am warm*) sudat, Juv. **II. A.** Lit., of liquids, *to boil,* or (of the sea) *to rage;* gurges aestuat, Verg. **B.** Fig., of the passions, *to be inflamed* or *excited;* ut desiderio te nostri aestuare putarem, Cic.; nobilitas invidia aestuabat, Sall.; so of love, rex in illa aestuat, *burns with love for,* Ov.; aestuabat dubitatione, Cic.

aestŭōsē, adv. with compar. (aestuosus), *hotly,* Hor.

aestŭōsus -a -um, adj. with superl. (aestus), 1, *hot;* via, Cic.; 2, *agitated;* freta, Hor.

aestus -ūs, m. (αἴθω). **I.** *heat;* 1, of fire, propiusque aestus incendia volvunt, Verg.; 2, of the sun, meridiei aestus, Liv.; plur., *hot days,* Verg.; 3, of fever, aestu febrique jactari, Cic. **II.** 1, *seething and raging,* of the sea; ferventes aestibus undae, Ov.; minuente aestu, *the storm lessening,* Caes.; 2, Transf., a, *rage;* civilis belli, Hor.; of love, pectoris, Ov.; b, *fervour;* ne aestus nos consuetudinis absorbeat, Cic.; c, *unrest, anxiety;* qui tibi aestus, qui error, quae tenebrae erant, Cic.; magno curarum fluctuat aestu, Verg.

aetas -ātis, f. (contr. from aevitas, from aevum), *age.* **I. A.** *lifetime;* a, breve tempus aetatis, Cic.; aetatem agere, degere, conterere, consumere, Cic.; aetas mea, tua = *I, you,* Plaut.; b, *a generation* (gen., 30 years; sometimes, in poets, 100); tertiam jam aetatem hominum vivebat, Cic. **B.** *the age of a man;* 1, Lit., a, filius id aetatis, *of that age,* Cic.; sometimes, *youth;* qui aliquid formae aetatis artificiique habebant, Cic.; carus eris Romae donec te deseret aetas, Hor.; sometimes, *old age;* nusquam tantum tribuitur aetati, Cic.; sometimes, *manhood;* in aetatem pervenire, Liv.; b, with narrower meaning, iniens aetas, *youth,* Cic.; so flos aetatis, bona aetas, Cic.; ad tendum (magistratum) legitima aetas, Cic.; aetas militaris, *the seventeenth year,* Sall.; quaestoria, *the twenty-fifth,* Quint.; senatoria, *the twenty-fifth,* Tac.; consularis, *the forty-third,* Cic.; adulta, Cic.; ingravescens, Cic.; aestate jam affecta, *far advanced in years,* Cic.; 3, Meton., *the persons of a particular age;* vestra, Cic.; puerilis, boys, Cic.; senilis, *old men,* Cic. **II.** *the time at which a person lives;* clarissimus imperator suae aetatis, Liv.; nostra aetas, *the men of our time,* Liv.; verborum vetus aetas, *obsolete words,* Hor.; 2, used gen. for time; aurea, *the golden age,* Ov.; omnia fert aetas, Verg.

aetātŭla -ae, f. (dim. of aetas), *youthful age;* prima illa aetatula sua, Cic.

aeternĭtas -ātis, f. (aeternus). **I.** *eternity;* ex omni aeternitate verum esse, Cic. **II.** a, *immortality;* animorum, Cic.; alicui aeternitatem immortalitatemque donare, Cic.; b, in imperial times, *a title of the Emperor,* similar to majestas, divinitas, etc., Plin.

aeterno, 1. (aeternus), *to make eternal, to immortalize,* Hor.

aeternus -a -um, adj. with compar. (contr. from aeviternus), *eternal, immortal.* **I.** deus, Cic. **II.** *everlasting, lasting, undying;* bellum, Cic.; urbs, *Rome,* Tib.; amore aeterno, Cic.; in aeternum, *for ever,* Liv.; so aeternum, Verg.; aeterne, *everlastingly,* Plin.; neut. plur. subst., aeterna moliri, *to do deathless deeds,* Cic.

aether-ĕris,acc.-ĕra,m.(αἰθήρ). **I.A.** *the upper air,* Cic.; poet., *heaven;* Juppiter aethere summo despiciens, Verg.; meton., *the gods;* oneravit aethera votis, Verg. **B.** Poet. (= aer), *the lower air;* verberare aethera pennis, Verg.; *the upper world* (opposed to the infernal regions); aethere in alto, Verg. **II.** Proper name, **Aether,** *son of Erebus and Night, identified with Jupiter.*

aethĕrĭus (aethĕrĕus) -a -um (αἰθέριος). **I.** *ethereal, relating to the ether;* natura, Cic.; esp., *relating to the heavens as the abode of the gods, heavenly;* domus, *heaven,* Hor.; ignes, *heavenly inspiration,* Ov.; equi, *the horses of the sun,* Ov. **II.** 1, *belonging to the air;* aqua, *rain,* Ov.; 2, *belonging to the upper world* (as opposed to the lower world); vesci aura aetheria, *to live,* Verg.

Aethĭŏpes -um, acc. -as, m. (Αἰθίοπες), *the inhabitants of Aethiopia,* Cic.; sing., **Aethiops** -ŏpis, m. *a black man,* Juv.; cum stipite Aethiope, *stupid,* Cic.; hence,1, **Aethiŏpia** -ae, f. in wider sense, *all the land to the south of the world as known to the ancients;* in narrow sense, *the country south of Egypt;* 2, **Aethiŏpĭcus** -a -um, *Aethiopian;* 3, **Aethiŏpis** -ĭdis, f. *a plant, a kind of sage,* Plin.

1. **Aethra** -ae, f. (Αἴθρα). **I.** *daughter of king Pittheus of Troezen, mother of Theseus by Aegeus.* **II.** *daughter of Oceanus, mother of the Hyades and of Hyas.*

2. **aethra** -ae, f. (αἴθρα), *the upper air, the clear sky,* Verg.

Aetna -ae, f. (Αἴτνη). **I.** *Aetna, a volcano in Sicily,* according to one legend, the mountain that Jupiter cast on the giant Typhoeus (or Typhon), or Enceladus; so proverb, onus Aetna gravius, Cic.; according to another legend, the interior was the workshop of Vulcan and the Cyclopes, who there forged Jupiter's thunderbolts; hence **Aetnaeus** -a -um, *belonging to Aetna;* fratres, *the Cyclopes,* Verg.; pastor, *the Cyclops Polyphemus,* Ov.; meton., tellus, *Sicily,* Ov. **II.** *a town at the foot of Mount Aetna,* also called *Innesa;* hence **Aetnensis** -e, *belonging to the town of Aetna.*

Aetōli -ōrum, m. (Αἰτωλοί), *the Aetolians, the inhabitants of Aetolia.* Adj. **Aetōlus** -a -um, *Aetolian;* plagae (alluding to Meleager and the hunt of the Calydonian boar), Hor.; arma, cuspis (of the Aetolian Diomedes), Verg.; urbs or Arpi, a town in Apulia, said to have been founded by Diomedes, Verg.; hence, 1, **Aetōlia** -ae, f. *Aetolia, a country in the west of Greece, between Ozolian Locris and Acarnania;* 2, **Aetōlĭcus** -a -um, *Aetolian;* bellum, Liv.; 3, **Aetōlis** -ĭdis, f. *an Aetolian woman,* Deianira, *daughter of Oeneus king of Aetolia,* Ov.; 4, **Aetōlĭus** -a -um, heros, *Diomedes,* Ov

aevĭtas -ātis, f. old form of aetas.

aevum -i, n. (αἰών). **I.** *eternity;* in aevum, *for ever,* Hor. **II.** *time.* **A.** 1, *time of life;* degere, Cic.; perbrevis aevi Carthaginem esse, Liv.; 2, *a generation* (thirty years); ter aevo functus, Hor.; 3, *age;* a, flos aevi, *youth,* Lucr.; integer aevi, *in the bloom of youth,* Verg.; primo exstingui in aevo, *in early youth,* Ov.; b, esp., of old age, aevo macieque senescunt, Lucr.; aevi maturus, *far advanced in years,* Verg. **B.** 1, *time at which a person is living;* omnis aevi clari vivi, *of every age,* Liv.; 2, *time* in gen., veteris non inscius aevi, Ov.

Āfer, v. Afri.

affābĭlis -e, adj. with compar. (affor), *easy to be spoken to, affable;* in omni sermone affabilem et jucundum esse velle, Cic.

affābĭlĭtas -ātis, f. (affabilis), *affability;* comitas affabilitasque sermonis, Cic.

affābrē, adv. (ad and faber), *in a workmanlike way, skilfully;* factus, Cic.

affātim, adv. (ad and fatim), *sufficiently, enough;* satisfacere alicui, Cic. Subst. with genit., copiarum affatim esse, Liv.

affātus -ūs, m. (affor), *an address, speech, accosting,* Verg.

affectātĭo -ōnis, f. (affecto), *a violent desire and striving;* quietis, Tac.; Germanicae originis, *eagerness to pass for Germans,* Tac.

affectātor -ōris, m. (affecto), *one who strives after anything,* Quint.

affectātus -a -um, p. adj. (affecto), in rhet., *elaborate, studied,* Quint.

affectĭo -ōnis, f. (afficio). **I.** Active, *influence;* praesentis mali sapientis affectio nulla est, *the wise man is not affected by evil,* Cic. **II.** Passive, *condition;* 1, *relation;* quaedam ad res aliquas affectio, Cic.; 2, *state;* caeli, Cic.; 3, *condition;* a, of the body, firma corporis affectio, *good health,* Cic.; b, of the mind, with or without animi, *favourable disposition of the mind,* Cic.; nulla affectione animi, *without predilection,* Tac.

affecto (adfecto), 1. (afficio). **I.** *to grasp;* ubi nulla datur dextra affectare (navem) potestas, Verg.; viam, *to aim after,* Plaut.; eam rem, *to meddle with,* Liv.; regnum, *to obtain,* Liv. **II.** *to strive after;* 1, munditiam, non affluentiam, Nep.; spes potiendae Africae, *to entertain hopes,* Liv.; bellum Hernicum, *to try to get the command of the war,* etc., Liv.; imperium, Liv.; 2, *to affect;* in verbis effusiorem cultum, Quint.

1. **affectus** -ūs, m. (afficio), *a condition, disposition;* of the mind, 1, animi, Cic.; absol., *feeling;* veri affectus, Tac.; 2, *emotions, passions;* amoris, avaritiae, metus, Quint.; desire, Tac.; 3, *affection,* Plin.

2. **affectus** -a -um, p. adj. with superl. (afficio). **A.** *provided, furnished with;* virgis, Plaut.; virtutibus, vitiis, Cic. **B.** *disposed in any way* as to mind or body; 1, of the body, a, num manus recte affecta est quum in tumore est, Cic.; transf., quomodo affecto caelo compositisque sideribus quodque animal oriatur, *under what disposition of the stars,* Cic.; b, *indisposed, disordered;* Caesarem graviter affectum jam videram, Cic.; valetudine affectus, Caes.; transf., civitas aegra et affecta, Cic.; c, *near completion;* bellum affectum videmus et, ut vere dicam, paene confectum, Cic.; 2, of the mind, *disposed;* eodem modo erit sapiens affectus erga amicum, quo in se ipsum, Cic.

affĕro, attŭli, allātum, afferre (ad and fero), *to carry, or bring to.* **I.** Lit., **A.** Of persons, aliquid domum, Cic.; epistolam. litteras, *to* *bring a letter*, Cic. ; **is** qui litteras attulit, *the bearer of this letter*, Cic. **B.** Of things, si tantum notas odor attulit auras, Verg. **II.** Transf., **A.** Gen., *to bring*; animum vacuum ad res difficiles scribendas, Cic. ; manus affere alicui or alicui rei, *to seize*, Cic. ; manus sibi, *to commit suicide*, ap. Cic. ; manus suis vulneribus, *to tear open*, Cic. ; alicui vim, *to offer violence to*, Cic. **B.** Esp., **1,** *to bring news;* alicui non jucundissimum nuntium, Cic. ; eo de Hortensii morte mihi est allatum, *news was brought me*, Cic. ; foll. by acc. and infin., Caelium ad illum attulisse se quaerere, etc., Cic. ; **2,** *to bring as an excuse* or *reason;* rationes, cur hoc ita sit, Cic. ; aetatem, *to allege in excuse*, Cic. ; **3,** *to produce, cause;* alicui mortem, Cic. ; **4,** *to bring as a help;* ad bene vivendum aliquid, Cic. ; **5,** *to bring as an addition;* quis attulerit, *who added the clause to the bill*, Cic.

afficio -fēci -fectum, 3. (ad and facio). **I.** *to do something to;* in rhet., *to connect;* eae res quae quodammodo affectae sunt ad id de quo quaeritur, Cic. **II.** *to influence.* **A.** aliquem aliqua re, *to affect in any way;* aliquem maxima laetitia, Cic. ; quanta me molestia affecerit, Cic. ; cives Romani morte, cruciatu, cruce, Cic. ; aliquem sepultura, *to bury*, Cic. ; aliquem capitali poena, *to punish*, Liv. ; so in passive, morbo gravi et mortifero affectum esse, Cic. ; magna difficultate affici, *to be placed in a difficult position*, Caes. ; beneficio affici, *to be benefited*, Cic. ; pio dolore affectum, Cic. **B.** aliquem, *to affect the body* or *mind;* **1,** the body, exercendum corpus et ita afficiendum est ut, etc., Cic. ; aestus, labor, fames, sitis afficiunt corpora, *weaken*, Liv. ; **2,** of the mind, litterae tuae sic me affecerunt ut, etc., Cic.

affictio -ōnis, f. *an adding to*, Phaedr.

affīgo -fixi -fixum, 3. (ad and figo), *to fasten to, affix.* **I.** Lit., litteram illam (κ) ita vehementer ad caput, ut, etc., *to brand*, Cic. ; Prometheum Caucaso, Cic. ; cruci, Liv. ; of trophies of war, signa affixa delubris, Hor. **II.** Transf., a, Ithaca illa in asperrimis saxis tamquam nidulus affixa, Cic. ; alicui affixum esse tamquam magistro, *not to leave the side of*, Cic. ; b, of the mind, *to imprint*, ea maxime affigi animis nostris, Cic.

affingo -finxi -fictum, 3. (ad and fingo), *to form, feign, invent in addition, to add to.* **I.** Lit., of artists, partem corporis, Cic. **II.** Transf., *to invent;* qui nihil opinione affingat assumatque ad aegritudinem, Cic. ; multa rumore affingebantur, Caes.

affīnis -e (ad and finis). **I.** Lit., *neighbouring;* gens affinis Mauris, Liv. **II.** Transf., **1,** *related by marriage;* alter mihi affinis erat, Cic. Subst., **affinis** -is, m. *brother-, sister-, father-, mother-in-law;* cognati et affines, *blood relations and connections by marriage*, Cic. ; **2,** *connected with, privy to;* hujus suspicionis, Cic. ; huic facinori, Cic.

affīnitas -ātis, f. (affinis). **I.** *neighbourhood*, Varr. **II. A.** *relationship by marriage;* affinitate sese devincire cum aliquo, Cic. ; in affinitatem alicuius pervenire, Cic. ; plur., conjunctio hominum inter homines serpit sensim foras, cognationibus primum, deinde affinitatibus, deinde amicitiis, Cic. ; meton., *relations by marriage*, Plaut. **B.** *union* of any kind; litterarum, Quint.

affirmātō, adv. with superl. (affirmatus), *certainly, positively*, promittere aliquid, Cic.

affirmātĭo -ōnis, f. *asseveration, positive assertion*, Cic.

affirmo, 1. (ad and firmo). **I.** *to strengthen;* societas jurejurando affirmatur, Liv. **II.** a, *to support a statement, to prove;* quod breviter dictum est rationibus affirmatum, Cic. ; b, *to assert*

as true; quis rem tam veterem pro certo affirmet, Liv. ; omni asseveratione tibi affirmo (followed by acc. and infin.), Cic. ; with de and the abl., quid opus est de Dionysio tam valde affirmare.

affixus -a -um (p. adj. from affigo), *fixed to, closely joined to, affixed ;* Pyrenaeo, *closely adjacent to*, Plin.

afflātus -ūs, m. (afflo). **I.** *a blowing* or *a breathing on;* maris, *sea breeze*, Plin. ; deneget afflatus ventus et aura suos, Ov. ; used of the breath of men and animals, Ov. **II.** *inspiration ;* sine aliquo afflatu divino, Cic.

affleō -flēvi -flētum, 2. (ad and fleo), *to weep at*, Plaut.

afflictātĭō -ōnis, f. (afflicto), *bodily pain, torture*, Cic.

afflicto, 1. (intens. of affligo). **I.** *to strike* or *beat.* **A.** Lit., afflictare se, *to beat one's breast in grief*, Sall. **B.** Transf., afflictare se, or afflictari, *to be troubled;* de quibus vehementer afflictor, Cic. **II.** *to damage by striking.* **A.** Lit., onerarias (naves) tempestas afflictabat, Caes. **B.** Transf., *to harass, to torment;* gravius vehementiusque afflictari (morbo), Cic.

afflictor -ōris, m. (affligo), *a destroyer;* dignitatis et auctoritatis, Cic.

afflictus -a -um, p. adj. (affligo), **1,** *damaged, shattered ;* fortuna, amicitia, Cic. ; **2,** *broken down, spiritless, desponding;* aegritudine afflictus, debilitatus, jacens, Cic. ; **3,** *vile, contemptible;* homo afflictus et perditus, Cic.

affligo -flixi -flictum, 3. **I. A.** *to strike, dash against ;* vasa parietibus, Liv. **B.** *to dash to the ground ;* statuam, Cic. ; equi virique afflicti, *struck down in battle*, Sall. **II.** *to ill-treat, damage.* **A.** fusti caput alicuius, Tac. ; naves quae gravissime afflictae erant, Caes. **B.** Transf., *to weaken, discourage, injure;* non vitium nostrum sed virtus nostra nos afflixit, Cic. ; non plane me enervavit nec afflixit senectus, Cic. ; causam susceptam, *to drop a law suit*, Cic. ; vectigalia bellis affliguntur, *suffer through war*, Cic. ; animos affligere et debilitare metu, Cic.

afflo (ad-flo), 1. **I.** *to blow on.* **A.** Lit., afflabat acrior frigoris vis, Liv. ; odores qui affiarentur e floribus, Cic. **B.** Transf., **1,** Intrans., *to blow propitiously;* felix cui placidus leniter afflat amor, Tib. ; **2,** Trans., *to bring;* rumoris nescio quid afflaverat commissione Graecorum frequentiam non fuisse, Cic. ; **3,** *to breathe, to communicate secretly;* laetos oculis afflarat honores, Verg. **II. A.** *to breathe on ;* velut illis Canidia afflasset, Hor. ; nosque ubi primus equis Oriens afflavit anhelis, Verg. ; of fire and heat, saucii afflatique incendio, *scorched*, Liv. **B.** *to inspire;* afflata est numine quando jam propiore dei, Verg.

afflŭens -entis (p. adj. of affluo), *rich, affluent, abundant, plentifully provided with, full of;* opibus et copiis, Cic. ; omni scelere, Cic. ; **ex afflu**enti, *in abundance*, Tac.

afflŭentĕr, adv. with compar. (affluens), *richly, abundantly*, voluptate affluentius haurire, Cic.

afflŭentĭa -ae, f. (affluens), *overflow, abundance ;* omnium rerum, Cic.

afflŭo (ad-fluo) -fluxi -fluxum, 3. *to flow to* **A.** Lit., **1,** of rivers, Aufidus amnis utrisque castris affluens, Liv. ; **2,** a, of the concourse of atoms in the Epicurean philosophy, Lucr. ; b, of men, *to flock together ;* affluente quotidie multitudine ad famam belli spemque praedae, Liv. **B.** Transf., **1,** *to come ;* nihil ex istis locis non modo litterarum, sed ne rumoris quidem affluxit, Cic. ; **2,** *to abound;* quum domi otium et divitiae affluerent, Sall. ; unguentis affluens, *dripping with unguents*, Cic. ; voluptatibus, Cic.

affor (ad-for), 1. dep., *to accost, address*; versibus aliquem, Cic.; esp., *to say farewell* to the dead; affari extremum, Verg.; *to pray to*; deos, Verg. (1st pers. of pres. indic. not found; only used in the other persons of the pres. indic., the 1st pers. imperf. indic., the 2nd pers. imper., the infin., and partic.).

afformīdo, 1. *to be in fear*, Plaut.

affrīco -fricui -fricatum, 1. *to rub*, Plin.

affrictus -ūs, m. (affrico), *a rubbing on*, Plin.

affulgĕo -fulsi, 2. *to shine, glitter.* **A.** Lit., Venus (*the planet*), affulsit, Ov. **B.** Transf., 1, of a deity, *to look favourably upon;* vultus ubi tuus affulsit, Hor.; 2, of hope, *to appear;* consuli rei majoris spes affulsit, Liv.

affundo -fūdi -fūsum, 3. *to pour into.* **I.** Lit., venenum vulneri, Tac.; colonia amne affusa, *washed by a river*, Plin. **II.** 1, of men, *to add;* ut equitum tria millia cornibus affunderentur, Tac.; 2, affundere se or affundi, *to prostrate oneself on the ground;* affusaque poscere vitam, Ov.

Āfrānius -a -um, *name of a Roman plebeian gens*, the most famous of which were **I. L.** Afranius, *a Roman comic poet* (born probably about 130 A.C.), *contemporary of Terence.* **II. L.** Afranius, *dependent and legate of Cn. Pompeius, killed after the battle of Thapsus.*

Āfri -ōrum, m. *the dwellers in Africa*, especially in the narrow sense of the district round Carthage; sing., dirus **Afer**, *Hannibal*, Hor. Adj., **Āfĕr** -fra -frum; aqua, *sea between Sicily and Africa*, Ov.; avis, *guinea-fowl*, Hor.; sorores, *the Hesperides*, Juv. Hence **A. Āfrĭca** -ae, f. 1, in wider sense, *the continent of Africa*, Sall.; 2, in narrower sense, Africa propria or Africa provincia, *the country around and formerly belonging to Carthage;* and in a narrower sense still, *the district of Zeugis with its capital Carthage.* **B. Āfrĭcānus** -a -um, *belonging to Africa;* bellum, *Caesar's war against the Pompeians in Africa*, Cic.; gallinae, *guinea-fowl*, Varr. Subst., **Africanae** -arum, f. (sc. bestiae), *African wild beasts*, lions, etc., used in the circus at Rome, Liv. As a surname, Africanus, see Cornelius. **C. Āfrĭcus** -a -um, *African;* bellum, *the second Punic war*, Liv.; *Caesar's war against the Pompeians*, Caes.; mare, *south-west part of the Mediterranean sea*, Sall.; ventus Africus or Africus alone, *the S.W. stormy rain-wind;* praeceps, Hor.

Ăgămemnōn -ōnis, m. (Ἀγαμέμνων), *a king of Mycenae, leader of the Greek expedition to Troy;* hence, 1, **Agamemnōnĭdes** -ae, m., *a son or descendant of Agamemnon, Orestes*, Juv.; 2, **Agamemnōnius** -a -um, *relating to Agamemnon;* puella, *Iphigeneia*, Prop.

Ăgănippē -ēs, f. (Ἀγανίππη), *a fountain in Boeotia, sacred to the Muses*, Verg.; hence, 1, **Ăgănippis** -ĭdis, f. *Aganippean*, Ov.; 2, **Ăgănippēus** -a -um, *relating to Aganippe, sacred to the Muses;* lyra, Prop.

ăgāso -ōnis, m. (ago), *a horse-boy, groom*, Liv.; *donkey-driver*, Liv.; *awkward servant*, Hor.

Ăgăthŏclēs -is and -i, m. (Ἀγαθοκλῆς), 1, *a tyrant of Syracuse, born 361 A.C.;* 2, *a Greek philosopher and writer on husbandry;* 3, *a Greek historian.*

Ăgăthyrna -ae, f. (Ἀγάθυρνα), or **Ăgăthyrnum** -i, n. (Ἀγάθυρνον), *a town on the N. coast of Sicily, now S. Agatha.*

Ăgăthyrsi -ōrum, m. (Ἀγάθυρσοι), *a Scythian people living on the Maris, in modern Hungary, who tattooed themselves blue;* picti, Verg

Ăgāvē -ēs, f. (Ἀγαυή), *daughter of Cadmus, mother of Pentheus, whom she killed in a Bacchis frenzy.*

Ăgendĭcum -i, n. *capital of the Senones, in Gallia Lugdunensis, now Sens.*

Ăgĕlastus -i, m. (ἀγέλαστος, never laughing), *surname of M. Crassus, grandfather of the triumvir, said to have laughed only once in his life.*

ăgellus -i, m. (dim. of ager), *a little field*, Cic.

ăgēmă -ătis, n. (ἄγημα), *a corps in the Macedonian army*, Liv.

Ăgēnor -ōris, m. (Ἀγήνωρ), *a king of Phoenicia, father of Cadmus and Europa;* urbs Agenoris, *Carthage*, Verg.; Agenore natus, *Cadmus*, Ov.; hence, 1, **Ăgēnŏrīdes** -ae, m. *a son or descendant of Agenor, Cadmus*, Ov.; Perseus, *as descendant of Danaus, nephew of Agenor*, Ov.; 2, **Ăgēnŏrēus** -a -um, *relating to Agenor;* domus, *house of Cadmus*, Ov.; bos, *the bull that bore away Europa*, Ov.; aenum, *the kettle used for the Phoenician purple dye*, Mart.

ăgens -entis (partic. of ago), *lively, active;* acer orator, incensus et agens, Cic.

ăger, agri, m. (ἀγρός). **I.** 1, *land in cultivation, a field, piece of land;* colere, Cic.; homo ab agro remotissimus, *knowing nothing of agriculture*, Cic.; 2, *open country in opposition to the town;* vastati agri sunt, urbs assiduis exhausta funeribus, Liv.; 3, *the land opposed to the sea;* arx Crotonis una parte imminens mari, altera parte vergente in agrum, Liv.; 4, in agrum, *in depth* (opp. in frontem, *in length*), Hor. **II.** *the territory of a state*, Tusculanus, Cic.

Ăgēsĭlāus -i, m. (Ἀγησίλαος), *a king of Sparta who conquered the Persians on the Pactolus in Asia Minor* (A.C. 395), *and the Boeotians, Athenians, and other Greeks at Coronea in Boeotia.*

Ăgēsimbrŏtus -i, m. (Ἀγησίμβροτος), *commander of the Rhodian fleet against Philip of Macedon.*

Ăgēsĭpŏlis -pŏlĭdis, m. (Ἀγησἰπολις), *son of Cleombrotos and king of Sparta about 195 A.C.*

aggĕmo (ad-gemo), 3. *to groan at, to weep at*, Ov.

agger -ĕris, m. (2. aggero). **I.** *material brought together to form a heap or mound;* aggerem comportare, petere, Caes.; paludem aggere explere, Caes.; poet. moliri aggere tecta, *to build and fortify with a mound*, Verg. **II.** 1, *a mound, rampart;* apparare, jacere, facere, instruere, Caes.; agger Tarquinii, or simply agger, *a rampart said to have been built by Tarquinus Superbus to protect Rome;* 2, *a rampart to protect a harbour*, Verg.; *the bank of a river*, gramineus ripae agger, Verg.; *the causeway of a road;* agger viae, Verg.; 3, poet., *any kind of elevation;* tumuli ex aggere, Verg.; aggeres Alpini, Verg.; arenae, Verg.; *a funeral pile*, Ov.

1. **aggĕro** (ad-gero), 1. (agger), *to form a mound, to heap up.* **I.** Lit., Tac.; cadavera, Verg. **II.** Fig., *to increase;* dictis iras, Verg.

2. **aggĕro** (ad-gero) -gessi -gestum, 3. (ad and gero). **1.** Lit., *to carry to, bring to;* luta et limum, Cic.; with dat., aggeritur tumulo tellus, Verg. **II.** Fig., *to load, heap on;* probra, Tac.

aggestus -ūs, m. (2. aggero), *a carrying to, accumulation;* pabulae, materiae, lignorum, Tac.

agglŏmĕro (ad-glomero), 1. Lit. *to wind on a ball, to add;* addunt se socios et lateri agglomerant nostro, *throng to our side.* Verg.

agglūtĭno (ad-glutino), 1. *to glue to, to fasten to*, Cic.

aggrăvesco (ad-gravesco), 3. *to become severe, to grow worse* (of sickness), Ter.

aggrăvo (ad-gravo), 1. **I.** Lit., *to make heavier*, Plin. **II.** Transf., *to make worse;* inopiam sociorum, Liv. ; *to heighten;* summam invidiae ejus, Liv.

aggrĕdĭo, 3. active form of aggredior (q. v.).

aggrĕdĭor -gressus sum, 3. dep. (ad and gradior). **A.** 1, *to go to, approach;* ad aliquem, Plaut. ; non repellitur quo aggredi cupiet, Cic. ; 2, *to approach a person;* a, in a friendly manner, quem ego Romae aggrediar, Cic. ; aliquem pecunia, Sall. ; Venerem dictis, *to address*, Verg. ; b, in a hostile manner, *to attack;* eos impeditos et inopinantes, Caes. ; murum, Sall. **B.** Transf., *to begin, to undertake, to attempt;* ancipitem causam, Cic. ; facinus, *to begin*, Liv. ; with ad and the acc., ad causam, ad crimen, and disputationem, ad historiam, Cic. ; with ad and the gerund, ad dicendum, Cic. ; followed by the infin., oppidum altissimis moenibus oppugnare, Caes.

aggrĕgo (ad-grego), 1. *to add to, join with;* a, with adv., eodem ceteros undique collectos naufragos, Cic. ; b, with in and the acc., ego te in nostrum numerum aggregare soleo, Cic. ; c, with ad and the acc., se ad eorum amicitiam, Caes. ; d, with dat., se Romanis, Liv. ; e, absol., alius alia ex navi, quibuscumque signis occurrerat, se aggregabat, Caes.

aggressĭo -ōnis, f. (aggredior), *the introduction to a speech;* prima aggressione animos occupare, Cic.

ăgĭlis -e (ago). **A.** Of things, 1, *easily moved, light;* classis, Liv. ; 2, *quick;* rivus agilior, Plin. **B.** Of persons, 1, *light, nimble;* dea, *Diana*, Ov. ; Cyllenius, *Mercury*, Ov. ; 2, *active;* oderunt agilem gnavumque remissi, Hor. ; nunc agilis fio, *busy*, Hor.

ăgĭlĭtas -ātis, f. (agilis), *the power of being easily moved, quickness, agility, lightness;* navium, Liv. ; naturae, Cic.

Ăgis -ĭdis, m. (Άγις), *name of three kings of Sparta.*

ăgĭtābĭlis -e (agito), *easily moved, light;* aer, Ov.

ăgĭtātĭo -ōnis, f. (agito). **I.** Act., **A.** Lit., *motion;* anceps telorum armorumque, Liv. **B.** *management;* rerum magnarum agitatio atque administratio, Cic. **II.** Pass., *state of motion.* **A.** Lit., agitatio et motus linguae, Cic. ; tantas agitationes fluctuum, Cic. **B.** Transf., *activity;* numquam animus agitatione et motu esse vacuus potest, Cic.

ăgĭtātor -ōrĭs, m. (agito), 1, *one who sets in motion, a driver;* aselli, Verg. ; 2, *a charioteer, who contended for the prize in the circus*, Cic.

ăgĭtātus -ūs, m. = agitatio (q. v.).

ăgĭto, 1. (intens. of ago), *to put in constant motion, to drive about.* **I.** Lit., 1, of animals, *to drive;* spumantem equum, Verg. ; or *to hunt;* aquila insectans alias aves et agitans, Cic. ; 2, of the wind on the sea, *to agitate, toss up and down;* mare ventorum vi agitari atque turbari, Cic. ; 3, *to stir up in any way, to move hastily;* quod pulsu agitatur externo, Cic. ; corpora huc illuc, Sall. **II.** Transf., 1, *to vex, agitate, harass;* ut eos agitent insectenturque furiae, Cic. ; Tyrrhenam fidem aut gentes agitare quietas, to trouble, Verg. ; seditionibus tribuniciis atrociter res publica agitabatur, Sall. ; *to ridicule*, quas personas agitare solemus, non sustinere, Cic. ; 2, in speech, *to handle, treat of, argue, discuss;* agraria lex vehementer agitabatur, Cic. ; 3, in thought, *to think about, consider* (with or without in corde, in mente, in animo, or simply

animo or mente) ; in animo bellum, Liv. ; rem mente, Cic. ; a, with infin., aliquid invadere magnum mens agitat mihi, Verg. ; b, with de, de inferendo bello, Liv. ; c, with rel. sent., id plebes agitabat quonam modo, etc., Liv. ; 4, *to practise, exercise;* quibus agitatus et exercitatus animus, Cic. ; 5, of festivals, *to keep;* dies festos, Cic. ; 6, *to manage, observe, keep;* imperium, Sall. ; gaudium atque laetitiam, *to express*, Sall. ; praecepta parentis mei, *to observe* or *practise*, Sall. ; 7, of time, *to live;* sub legibus aevum, Verg. ; 8, (sc. se), *to pass time, stay;* laeti neque procul Germani agitant, Tac. ; Libyes propius mare agitant, Sall. ; 9, *to act* (on the stage), Plaut.

Aglăĭē -ēs, f. (Άγλαΐα and Άγλαΐη), *the oldest of the graces*, Verg.

aglaspis -ĭdis, m. (άγλαὴ ἀσπίς, *a bright shield*), *soldiers with bright shields, name of a division in the Macedonian army*, Liv.

agmĕn -ĭnis, n. (ago), *something driven or moved, a mass in movement.* **I.** Gen., **A.** Of things with life, 1, of men, *a band, a throng;* stipatus agmine patriciorum, Liv. ; Eumenidum agmina, Verg. ; 2, of animals, agmen ferarum, Ov. ; aligerum agmen, *swans*, Verg. ; graniferum agmen, *ants*, Ov. **B.** Of things without life, 1, *a large stream* of water, leni fluit agmine flumen, Verg. ; so of rain, immensum agmen aquarum, Verg. ; 2, of the atoms, Lucr. ; 3, of the clouds, Lucr. ; 4, of the movement of oars, Verg. ; 5, of the gliding of snakes, extremae agmina caudae, Verg. **II.** As milit. t. t., *an army.* **A.** Abstr., *the march of an army;* citato agmine, Liv. ; rudis agminum, Hor. **B.** Concr., 1, *the army on march;* a, of infantry, phalanx agmen magis quam acies (acies, *the army in line of battle*), Liv. ; agmine ingredi, ire, Liv. ; agmine instructo, *ready for march*, Liv. ; agmine facto, *in close marching order*, Verg. ; tripartito agmine, *a march in three columns*, Tac. ; agmen pilatum, Verg., or justum, *an army in close marching order*, Tac. ; quadratum, *a march in a hollow square*, Sall. ; primum, *the vanguard*, Caes. ; medium, *the centre*, Caes. ; extremum or novissimum, *the rear*, Cic. ; ducere, *to lead*, Cic. ; cogere, *to act as rearguard*, Caes. ; so fig., ut nec duces sumus nec agmen cogamus, Cic. ; b, of cavalry, equitum, Liv. ; 2, of a fleet, Liv. ; 3, of the baggage of an army, impedimentorum, Tac. ; rerum captarum, Liv. ; 4, Transf., of animals marching in order, decedens agmine magno corvorum exercitus, Verg. ; and so of things personified, venti velut agmine facto, qua data porta, ruunt, Verg. ; stellae quarum agmina cogit Lucifer, Ov.

agna -ae, f. (agnus), *a female lamb*, Hor.

Agnālĭa -ium = Agonalia (q. v.).

agnascor (ad-gnascor) -nātus, 3. *to be born in addition to*, legal t. t. of children born after their father's will, either in his lifetime or after his death, Cic.

agnātĭo -ōnis, f. (agnascor), *relationship reckoned through males only*, Cic.

agnātus -i, m. (agnascor), 1, *a relation descended from a common ancestor in the male line*, Cic. ; 2, *a child born into a family where a regular heir already exists*, Tac.

agnellus -i, m. (dim. of agnus), *a little lamb*, Plaut.

agnīnus -a -um (agnus), *relating to a lamb*, Plaut. Subst., **agnīna** -ae, f. (sc. caro), *lamb's flesh*, Hor.

agnĭtĭo -ōnis, f. (agnosco). 1, *recognition;* cadaveris, Plin. ; 2, *knowledge;* animi, *of the nature of the mind*, Cic.

2 *

agnōmen (ad-nomen) -ĭnis, n. *surname, name given to a man for some service*, e.g. Africanus, Asiaticus.

agnosco (ad-gnosco) -nōvi -nītum, 3. (ad and gnosco = nosco). **I.** *to perceive* (in its true character), *to recognise;* deum ex operibus suis, Cic. ; veterem Anchisen agnoscit amicum, Verg.; parvam Trojam, Verg. **II.** *to recognise as true* or *genuine, to acknowledge ;* filium quem ille natum non agnorat, eundem moriens suum dixerat, Nep. ; aliquem non ducem, Liv. ; of things, crimen, Cic. ; quod meum quoddammodo agnosco, Cic. ; with acc. and infin., et ego ipse me non esse verborum admodum inopem agnosco, Cic.

agnus -i, m. *a lamb ;* collect., abundare agno, Cic. ; prov., agnum lupo eripere velle, *to wish for the impossible*, Plaut.

ago, ēgi, actum (ἄγω), 3. *to set in motion.* **I.** Lit., **A.** *to drive,* **1,** cattle, etc. ; boves Romam, Liv. ; **2,** *to lead* or *drive* men, agmen agere, *to set an army in motion*, Liv. ; se agere, *to go*, Plaut. ; **3,** *to ride* a horse or *drive* a carriage, *to set* a ship *in motion*, equum, Tac. ; carpentum, Liv. ; naves, Liv. ; **4,** of things, *to put in motion, drive*, vineas turresque, Caes. ; nubes ventus agens, Lucr. **B. 1,** *to drive with force* or *violence ;* turba fugientium, actus, Liv. ; animam agere, *to give up the ghost,* Cic. ; glebis aut fustibus aliquem de fundo, Cic. ; **2,** Esp., *to plunder, to drive away cattle,* often with ferre or portare, res quae ferri agique possunt, Liv. ; **3,** *to construct, build, lay ;* fundamenta, Cic. ; **4,** of plants, *to strike root*, Plin. ; fig., vera gloria radices agit, Cic. **II.** Transf., **A.** Gen., as regards actions, *to drive, incite ;* in arma, Liv. ; aliquem in fraudem, Verg. ; se agere or agere absol., *to live ;* multo et familiariter cum aliquo, Sall. **B. 1,** of time, *to pass ;* quartum annum ago et octogesimum, *I am in my eighty-fourth year*, Cic. ; aetatem in litteris, Cic. ; **2,** *to act, to do ;* quid vos agitis? Cic. ; quid agam? Ter. ; absol., industria in agendo, Cic. ; male, bene, praeclare agere cum aliquo, *to treat a person well* or *badly*, Cic. ; nihil agere, Cic. ; id agere ut or ne, *to give attention to, to do one's best ;* id agunt ut viri boni esse videantur, Cic. ; **3,** of outward expression, **a,** of orators, *to declaim*, agere cum dignitate ac venustate, Cic. ; **b,** of actors, *to play, represent, deliver*, nunquam agit Roscius hunc versum eo gestu quo potest, Cic. ; fabulam, *to play in a piece* (comedy), Cic. ; primas partes, *to play leading parts*, Ter. ; agere aliquem, *to represent some character ;* ministrum imperatoris, Tac. ; **c,** *to express* gratitude; grates, Cic. ; **4, a,** of a festival, *to keep ;* festos dies anniversarios, Cic. ; **b,** *to keep, observe*, pacem, Sall. ; **c,** *to keep* watch, Sall. ; vigilias, Cic. ; **d,** *to hold* a meeting, *to execute* some function, *to transact ;* forum or conventum, *to hold the assizes*, Cic., Caes. ; esp. agere bellum, *to have the conduct of a war*, Liv. ; **5, a,** *to treat with ;* ut agerem cum Lucceio de vestra vetere gratia reconcilianda agente Servilia, *through the agency of Servilia*, Cic. ; **b,** in politics, *to bring questions* before the senate or people for decision ; in senatu de aliqua re, Ov. ; cum populo, Cic. ; nihil omnino actum est de nobis, Cic. ; agere causam alicuius, *to take the side of some politician*, Cic. ; **c,** in law, agere causam, *to plead some one's cause*, Cic. ; absol., agere, *to bring an action, to sue ;* ex syngrapha, Cic. ; non enim gladiis tecum sed litibus agitur, Cic. ; used esp. with jure and lege, agere lege in hereditatem, Cic. ; with genit. of accusation, furti, *to indict for theft*, Cic. ; qua de re agitur, *the point at dispute*, Cic. ; in quo agitur populi Romani gloria, *is at stake*, Cic. ; acta res est or actum est, *the transaction is finished*, so followed by de, *it is all over with ;* acta ne agamus, *act when it is too late.* Cic. Im-

perat., age, agite, used with dum, **as an interjection**, come *! well ! good !* Cic.

agōn -ōnis, m. (ἀγών), *a contest in the public games*, Plin., Suet.

Agōnālĭa -ĭum and -ōrum, n. *the festival of Janus ;* hence adj., **Agōnālis** -e, *relating to the Agonalia ;* Agonalis lux, *the day of the Agonalia,* Ov.

Agōnĭa -ōrum, n. **1,** *the animals for sacrifice ;* **2,** = Agonalia, Ov.

ăgŏrănŏmus -i, m. (ἀγορανόμος), *a market inspector in Greece*, Plaut.

ăgrārĭus -a -um (ager), *relating to land ;* lex, *law relating to the division of the public land*, Cic. ; res, *the division of public lands*, Cic. ; triumvir, *the officer who presided over the division*, Liv. Subst., **ăgrārĭi** -ōrum, m. *the agrarian party,* who proposed to distribute the public land among the people, Cic. ; **ăgrārĭa** -ae f. (sc. lex), *an agrarian law*, Cic.

ăgrestis -e (ager), *relating to the fields* or *country.* **A. 1,** *wild ;* taurus, Liv. ; **2,** *savage ;* vultus, Ov. **B. 1,** *belonging to the country, rustic ;* hospitium, Cic. ; homo, Cic. Subst., **ăgrestis** -is, m. *a countryman*, Cic. ; **2,** *rough, boorish, clownish ;* servi agrestes et barbari, Cic. ; rustica vox et agrestis, Cic. ; agrestiores Musae, *the muses of the coarser, practical arts*, e.g. eloquence, opposed to mansuetiores Musae, e.g. *philosophy*, Cic.

1. ăgrĭcŏla -ae, m. (ager and colo), *a tiller of the fields, farmer ;* agricola et pecuarius, Cic. ; deus agricola, Silvanus, Tib. ; caelites agricolae, *the gods of the country*, Tib.

2. Ăgrĭcŏla -ae, m. *Gnaeus Julius* (40–93 A.D.), *father-in-law of Tacitus, governor of Britain.*

ăgrĭcultĭo -ōnis, f. = agricultura (q.v.).

ăgrĭcultor -ōris, m. = agricola (q.v.).

ăgrĭcultūra -ae, f. *agriculture*, Cic.

Ăgrĭgentum -i, n. (Gr. Ἀκράγας and Lat. Acrāgās), *a flourishing Greek town on the south coast of Sicily.* Adj., **Agrigentīnus** -a -um, and **Acrăgantīnus** -a -um, *Agrigentine.*

ăgrĭpĕta -ae, m. (ager and peto), *a land-grabber*, Cic. ; *a settler* or *squatter*, Cic.

Agrippa -ae, m. **I.** *Roman family name.* **A.** Menenius Agrippa, the author of the fable of the belly and the members, by which he was said to have reconciled the plebeians and patricians, Liv. ii. 32. **B. 1,** M. Vipsanius Agrippa, (63–12 B.C.), the friend and adviser of Augustus, whose niece, Marcella, and daughter, Julia, he successively married, a celebrated general and statesman, who adorned Rome with many large buildings. **2,** Agrippa Postumus, son of the above, banished to Planasia by Augustus, said to have been murdered there at the beginning of Tiberius's reign. **II.** *Name of two kings of the Herod family in Judaea,* Herodes Agrippa I. and Herodes Agrippa II.

Agrippīna -ae, f. *the name of several Roman women.* **I. A.** daughter of M. Vipsanius Agrippa, by his first wife, wife of Tiberius. **B.** daughter of Agrippa by Julia, and wife of Germanicus, banished to Pandataria after her husband's death. **II.** The granddaughter of Agrippa, daughter of Germanicus and Agrippina (I. B.), gen. known as the Younger Agrippina, wife of her uncle, the Emperor Claudius, murdered by order of her son, the Emperor Nero ; hence **Colonia Agrippinensis**, *a town of Germany* (now Cologne), named in honour of Agrippina (II.).

Ăgyīeus -ěi or -ěos, m. (Ἀγυιεύς), *surname of Apollo, as protector of streets*, Hor.

Ăgylla -ae, f. (Ἀγυλλα), *Greek name of the*

Etruscan town Caere. Adj., a, **Agyllīnus -a** -um, *relating to Agylla*, urbs = Agylla, Verg. ; b, **Agylleūs** -ĕos, m. *epithet of Apollo, who had a temple at Agylla,* Hor.

Agȳrĭum -ĭi, n. ('Αγύριον), *a town in Sicily, birth-place of the historian Diodorus,* now *S. Filippo d'Argiro ;* hence **Agȳrīnensis** -e, *relating to Agyrium.*

ah, interj., *ah ! oh !*

Ahāla -ae, m., C. Servilius, *the master of the horse under the dictator Cincinnatus,* B.C. 439, *who slew Sp. Maelius.*

Aharna -ae, f. *a town in Etruria,* now *Bargiano.*

Ahenobarbus, v. Domitius.

ai (αῖ), *ah !* an interjection of grief, Ov.

Aiax -ācis, m. (Αῖας), *the name of two Homeric heroes :* 1, Aiax Telamonius, *son of Telamon, king of Salamis,* who committed suicide because he failed in the contest with Ulysses for the arms of Achilles ; 2, Aiax Oileus, *king of the Locri.*

āiens -entis (partic. of aio), *affirmative,* Cic.

āio, defective verb. **I.** *to say yes, to affirm* (opp. nego), Plaut. **II.** *to say, to assert, to state,* Cic. ; ut aiunt, *as the people say,* Cic. ; quid ais ? *what is your opinion?* Ter. ; ain', ais-ne, *do you really mean it ? is it possible?* Cic.

Āius Lŏquens or **Āius Locūtĭus,** m. (aio and loquor), *the speaker saying,* i.e. *the voice which is said to have warned the Romans of the coming of the Gauls, afterwards honoured as a god in a temple erected to it,* Cic.

āla -ae, f. (for ag-la, from ago). **I.** *a wing ;* of birds, galli plausu premunt alas, Cic. ; of gods, hic paribus nitens Cyllenius alis constitit, Verg. ; poet., of the oars of a ship, classis centenis remiget alis, Prop. ; or the sails, velorum pandīmus alas, Verg. ; and to express anything swift, fulminis ocior alis, Verg. ; used of death, Hor. ; of sleep, Tib. **II.** Transf., **A.** *the shoulders and armpits of a man ;* sub ala fasciculum portare librorum, Hor. **B.** Milit. t. t., *the cavalry* (originally disposed on both sides of the legions like wings) ; *a squadron* (generally composed of allied troops), Cic.

Ălăbanda -ae, f., and -orum, n. (ἡ and τὰ 'Αλάβανδα), *a town in Caria, near the Maeander,* famous for its wealth and luxury, founded by Alabandus, son of Eurippus and Callirrhoe ; hence, 1, **Ălăbandensis** -e, *belonging to Alabanda ;* 2, **Ălăbandeūs** -ĕos, m. *born at Alabanda.* Plur. Gr. nom., **Alabandis** ('Αλαβανδεῖς), *the inhabitants of Alabanda,* Cic.

Ălăbarches (Arabarches) -ae, m. ('Αλαβάρχης), *a magistrate of Arabia, a tax-gatherer, a nickname applied to Pompey, who largely increased the revenue by his Eastern conquests,* Cic.

ălăbaster -stri, m., and **ălăbastrum** -i, n. (ἀλάβαστρος and -ον), 1, *a pear-shaped perfume casket,* Cic. ; 2, *a rose-bud,* Plin.

ălăcer -cris -cre and (rarely) **ălăcris** -e, adj. with compar. **I.** Gen., *excited ;* multos alacres exspectare quid statuetur, Cic. **II.** *quick, cheerful, lively ;* a, of men, Catilina alacer atque laetus, Cic. ; with ad and the gerund, ad bella suscipienda Gallorum alacer et promptus est animus, Caes. ; voluptas, Verg. ; b, of animals, equus, Cic.

ălăcrĭtas -ātis, f. (alacer), *quickness, briskness, eagerness, alacrity ;* 1, of men, quae alacritas civitatis fuit? Cic. ; with genit., reipublicae defendendae, Cic. ; ad and gerund, mira alacritate ad litigandum, Cic. ; 2, of animals, canum tanta alacritas in venando, Cic.

Ălămanni (Ălămāni, Alĕmanni) -ōrum, m. *name of a German confederacy between the Danube and the Rhine.*

Ălāni -ōrum, m. *a Scythian race,* originally from the Caucasus.

ălăpa -ae, f. *a box on the ear,* Juv. ; given by a master to his slave on the manumission of the slave ; hence, multo majoris alapae mecum veneunt, *I sell freedom at a much higher price,* Phaedr.

ālărĭus -a -um, and **ālāris** -e (ala), *belonging to the wings* of an army ; equites, Liv. ; cohortes, Cic. ; hence **ālārii,** *allied troops,* Caes. See ala II. B.

ālātus -a -um (ala), *winged,* Verg.

ălauda -ae, f. (a Keltic word), *a lark.* **I.** Lit., Plin. **II.** Transf., *the name of a legion formed by Caesar in Gaul,* Suet. ; hence, *the soldiers of the legion ;* Alaudae, Cic.

ălāzōn -ōnis, m. (ἀλάζων), *a braggart, boaster,* Plaut.

Alba -ae, f. (connected with albus, ἀλφός, alp, *a high mountain*). **A.** *Alba Longa,* the oldest Latin town, according to the legend built by Ascanius on a ridge of the Mons Albanus, the mother city of Rome, said to have been destroyed by Tullus Hostilius ; hence, a, **Albānus** -a -um, *Alban ;* mons, *a holy mountain of the Latins* (now *Monte Cavo);* lacus, *the lake at the foot of mons Albanus* (now *Lago di Albano);* municipium, *a later town, not far from the site of Alba Longa ;* **Albanum** -i, n. (sc. praedium), *name of the villa of Pompeius,* and afterwards of Nero and Domitian ; b, **Albenses** populi, *the people of Latium,* who kept the feriae Latinae. **B.** *Alba Fucentis* or *Albensium Alba, a town of the Marsi,* afterwards a Roman colony, in Samnium ; hence **Albensis** -e, *belonging to Alba F.*

1. **Albāni,** sc. Alba.

2. **Albāni** -ōrum, m. *the Albanians,* inhabitants of Albania ; hence, a, **Albānĭa** -ae, f. *a country on the west of the Caspian sea* (now *Daghestan);* b, **Albānus** -a -um, *Albanian.*

albātus -a -um (albus), *clothed in white,* Cic.

albĕo, 2. (albus), *to be white ;* membra in eum pallorem albentia ut, etc., Tac. ; albente coelo, *at daybreak,* Caes.

albesco, 3. (albeo), *to become white ;* albescens capillus, Hor. ; lux albescit, *day dawns,* Verg.

albĭcērātus -a -um, or **albĭcēris** -e, or **albĭcērus** -a -um, *whitish yellow,* Plin.

albĭco, 1. (albus), 1, *to make white,* Varr. ; 2, *to be white ;* prata canis albicant pruinis, Hor.

albĭdus -a -um (albus), *whitish,* Ov.

Albĭnŏvānus -i, m. **I.** C. Pedo Albinovanus, *an epic poet,* contemporary and friend of Ovid. **II.** Celsus Albinovanus, *a secretary in the retinue of Tiberius, to whom* Horace addressed one of his Epistles.

Albīnus -i, m. *the name of a family of the Gens Postumia.* Aulus Postumius Albinus, *consul 151* B.C., *writer of a Roman history in Greek.*

Albĭon -ōnis, f. (from alb, i.e. *high), the "high" country, old name of Britain, from its cliffs,* Plin.

Albis -is, m. *the Elbe,* Tac.

albĭtūdo -ĭnis, f. (albus), *whiteness,* Plaut.

Albĭus -ĭi, m. *name of a Roman gens ;* 1, Albius Tibullus, *the celebrated Roman elegiac poet ;* 2, Statius Albius Oppianicus, *of Larinium, whom* Cluentius *was accused of murdering ;* hence adj., **Albiānus** -a -um, *relating to Albius.*

albŏr -ōris, m. (albus), *the white of an egg*, Plin.

albŭlus -a -um (dim. of albus), *whitish;* columbus, Cat.; freta, *foaming*, Mart.; hence as proper name, **I. Albŭla** -ae, f. (sc. aqua), *old name of the Tiber;* fluvius Albula quem nunc Tiberim vocant, Liv. **II. Albŭla** -ae, m. and f., or **Albŭlae** aquae, or **Albŭlae** -arum, f. *medicinal springs near Tiber* (Tivoli), now *Solfatara di Tivoli*, or *Acqua Zolfa.*

. **album** -i, n., v. albus.

Albŭnĕa -ae, f. *a prophetic nymph to whom was dedicated a fountain and grotto at Tibur.*

Alburnus -i, m. *a high mountain of Lucania, near Paestum* (now *Monte di Postiglione*).

albus -a -um (root ALB, connected with ἀλφός), *white, dead white* (opp. candidus = *glittering white*). **I.** Adj., **A.** Lit., 1, *white;* equi, Liv.; nuper in hanc urbem pedibus qui venerat albis, *slaves who came to Rome with feet chalked* to show they were for sale, Juv.; prov., alba avis, *a white bird, a rarity*, Cic.; albis dentibus deridere, *to laugh so as to show the teeth*, i.e. *heartily*, Plaut.; filius albae gallinae, *a lucky fellow*, Juv.; albis equis praecurrere, *to surpass greatly* (referring to the triumphing general whose car was driven by a white horse), Hor.; 2, *grey;* barba, Plaut. **B.** Esp., 1, *pale;* albus ora pallor inficit, Hor.; 2, *bright;* admisso Lucifer albus equo, Ov.; so *making bright;* notus, Hor.; and fig., *fortunate;* stella, Hor. **II.** Subst., **album** -i, n. **A.** *white colour;* alba discernere et atra non posse, Cic.; esp., 1, *white paint or cement;* columnas albo polire, Liv.; 2, *a white spot in the eye*, Col.; 3, album oculi, *the white of the eye*, Cels.; 4, album ovi, *the white of an egg*, Cels. **B.** *a white tablet*, esp., 1, *the tablet on which the pontifex maximus at Rome published the events of the year*, Cic.; 2, album (praetoris), *the tablet on which the praetor published his edict;* 3, album senatorium, *the list of senators*, Tac.; album judicum, *the jury-list*, Suet.

Alcaeus -i, m. (Ἀλκαῖος), *a Greek lyric poet of Mytilene, flourishing about 610–602 B.C.;* hence **Alcaïcus** -a -um, metrum, *a metre named after him.*

Alcămĕnēs -is, m. (Ἀλκαμένης), *a sculptor, scholar of Phidias.*

Alcăthŏē -ēs, f. (Ἀλκαθόη), *a mountain in Megara named after Alcathous*, poet. for the whole district of Megaris, Ov.

Alcăthŏus -i, m. (Ἀλκάθοος), *son of Pelops, rebuilder of Megara after it had been destroyed by the Cretans;* hence urbs Alcathoi, *Megara*, Ov.

Alcē -ēs, f. (Ἀλκη), *town of the Carpetani in Hispania Tarraconensis.*

alcēdo -ŏnis, f. (= alcyon, ἀλκυών), *the kingfisher*, Plaut.; hence **alcēdŏnĭa** -ōrum, n. (sc. tempora). **I.** *the fourteen days of winter, during which the kingfisher is hatching its eggs, and the sea was believed to be calm.* **II.** Transf., *quietness, calm*, Plaut.

alces -is, f. *the elk*, Caes.

Alcestis -tĭdis, f. and **Alcestē**-ēs f. (Ἀλκηστις or Ἀλκήστη), *wife of Admetus, king of Pherae*, whose life she was said to have saved by dying for him, sent back to life by Proserpina, or, as in another legend, rescued from Hades by Hercules.

Alcēus -ĕi and -ĕos, m. (Ἀλκεύς), *son of Perseus, father of Amphitryon, grandfather of Hercules;* hence **Alcĭdēs** -ae, m. *a descendant of Alceus, Hercules*, Verg.

Alcĭbĭădēs -is, m. (Ἀλκιβιάδης). **I.** *an Athenian, son of Clenias, cousin of Pericles, pupil of Socrates.* **II.** *a Lacedaemonian living at the time of the war of the Romans with the Achaeans.*

Alcĭdămas -antis, m. (Ἀλκιδάμας), *a Greek rhetorician of Elaea in Aeolis, pupil of Gorgias.*

Alcĭmĕdē -ēs, f. (Ἀλκιμέδη), *daughter of Autolycus, wife of Aeson, mother of Jason.*

Alcīnŏus-i, m. (Ἀλκίνοος), *king of the Phaeacians, the host of Odysseus*, noted for his gardens and orchards, hence poma dare Alcinoo, *to carry coals to Newcastle*, Ov.; Alcinoi sylvae, *orchards*, Verg.; juventus, *luxurious young men*, Hor.

Alcmăeŏ and **Alcmaeōn**, lengthened to **Alcŭmaeo** (Alcūmĕo, Alcĭmēo) -ŏnis, m., and **Alcŭmēus** -i, m. (Ἀλκμαίων). **I.** *son of Amphiaraus and Eriphyle*, who murdered his mother at the wish of his father and with the approval of the oracle, and was afterwards driven mad; hence adj., **Alcmaeŏnĭus** -a -um. **II.** *a Greek philosopher and physician of Crotona, pupil of Pythagoras.*

Alcmān -ānis, m. (Ἀλκμάν), *an old Greek poet of Sardis, in Lydia* (circ. 670–640 B.C.).

Alcmēna -ae, f., and **Alcmēnē** -ēs, f., lengthened to **Alcŭmēna** -ae, f. (Ἀλκμήνη), *wife of the Theban Amphitryon and mother of Hercules by Jupiter.*

Alco and **Alcōn** -ōnis, m. (Ἀλκων). **I.** *a son of Atreus*, Cic. **II.** *a sculptor of Sicily*, Ov. **III.** *a shepherd*, Verg. **IV.** *a slave's name*, Hor. **V.** *a Saguntine*, Liv.

alcyŏn, alcyŏnĭa = alcedo, alcedonia (q.v.).

Alcyŏnē -ēs, f. (Ἀλκυόνη), *daughter of Aeolus, who jumped into the sea on seeing her husband, Ceyx, drowned, and was changed with her husband into a kingfisher.*

ālĕa -ae, f. 1, *a game with dice, hazard;* ludere alea, Cic.; aleam exercere, Tac.; de alea condemnatus (dice-playing being forbidden at Rome by the Lex Titia et Publicia et Cornelia, except during the Saturnalia), Cic.; 2, Transf., *chance, risk, uncertainty;* rem in aleam dare, *to risk*, Liv.; subire, Cic.; in dubiam imperii servitique aleam ire, Liv.

ālĕātor -ōris, m. (alea), *a dicer, hazard-player*, Cic.

ālĕātōrĭus -a -um (aleator), *relating to a dicer;* damna, *losses at play*, Cic.

ālec (allec) -ēcis, n. *a sauce prepared from fish*, Hor., Plin.

Alectō (Allecto), acc. -ō, f. (Ἀληκτώ, or Ἀλληκτω), *one of the three furies.* (Only found in nom. and acc.)

āles, ālĭtis (gen. pl. alituum, Verg.) (ala). **I.** Adj., *winged.* **A.** Lit., *winged;* Pegasus, Ov.; deus, *Mercury*, Ov.; puer, *Cupid*, Hor. **B.** Transf., *swift, quick;* auster, Verg.; passu alite, Ov. **II.** Subst., f. *bird* (m. only in poetry), mostly of large birds; regia, *the eagle*, Ov.; Phoebeius, *the raven*, Ov.; Daulias, *the nightingale*, Ov.; Junonia, *the peacock*, Ov.; imitatrix, rara, *the parrot*, Ov.; sacer, *the hawk*, Verg.; cristatus, *the cock*, Ov.; Palladis, *the owl*, Ov.; Caystrius, *the swan*, Ov.; ales Maeonii carminis, *a poet of Homeric strain*, Hor. In augury, *birds whose flight was examined* (while oscines = *birds whose note was observed*), Cic.; hence, poet., *a sign, an omen;* so bona or secunda alite, *with favourable omen*, Hor.

ālesco, 3. (alo), *to grow up*, Lucr.

Alēsia -ae, f. *town of the Mandubii in Gallia Lugdunensis*, now *St. Reine d'Alise.*

Alēsus, v. Halesus.

Aletrĭum (Alatrium) -ĭi, n. *an old town of the Hernici in Latium*, afterwards a Roman colony 'and municipium, now *Alatri;* hence **Aletrīnās** -ātis, *relating to Aletrium.*

Ălēvās -ae, m. (Ἀλευάς), *a descendant of Her-zules who ruled in Larissa.*

Alexander-dri,m.(Ἀλέξανδρος). **I.** Mythol., *Paris, son of Priam, king of Troy.* **II.** Hist., 1, *Alexander of Pherae, tyrant in Thessaly from* 370-357 B.C. ; **2,** *Alexander, son of Neoptolemus, prince of the Molossi, uncle of Alexander the Great ;* **3,** *Alexander the Great* (b. 356, d. 323 B.C.), *king of Macedonia, who conquered the Persians and extended the Macedonian empire to the Indus ;* hence **A. Alexandrĭa** or **-ēa** -ae, f. (Ἀλεξάνδρεια), *name of several cities founded by Alexander, the most famous of which was the Egyptian city, at the Canopic mouth of the Nile, capital of the kingdom of the Ptolemies.* **B. Alexandrēus** -a -um. **C. Alexandrīnus** -a -um, *belonging to Alexandria.*

alga -ae, f. 1, *sea-weed,* Hor. ; *used for a thing of little worth ;* vilior algâ, Hor. ; **2,** *the sea-coast,* Juv.

algens -tis (partic. of algeo), *cold, cool,* Plin.

algĕo, alsi, 2 *to be cold,* Juv. ; transf., probitas laudatur et alget, i.e. *is neglected.*

algesco, alsi, 3. (inch. of algeo), *to become cold,* Ter.

1. **algĭdus** -a -um (algeo), *cold,* Cat.

2. **Algĭdus** -i, m. (sc. mons), *a range of mountains in Latium, from Tusculum to Praeneste* (now *Monte Compatri*); hence, a, **Algĭdum** -i, n. *a town of the Aequi on one of the mountains in this range ;* b, **Algĭdus** -a -um, *belonging to Algidus.*

algor -ōris, m. (algeo). **I.** *the sensation of cold,* Sall. **II.** *that which causes cold, frost,* Lucr.

algōsus -a -um (alga), *abounding in sea-weed,* Plin.

algus -ūs, m. = algor (q.v.).

ălĭā, adv. (alius), sc. via, *by another way,* Liv.

ălĭās (sc. vices), adv. **I.** *at another time,* Cic. ; alias . . . alias, *at one time . . . at another time,* Cic. ; alius alias, *one person at one time, another at another,* Cic. **II.** Transf., 1, *elsewhere,* Cic. ; **2,** non alias quam, *on no other condition than,* Tac. ; non alias nisi, *not otherwise than, as if,* Tac.

ălĭbī, adv. (alius), 1, *elsewhere, at another place,* Cic. ; alibi . . . alibi, *here . . . there,* Liv. ; alibi alius, *one here, the other there,* Liv. ; alibi atque alibi, *now here, now there,* Plin. ; **2,** *in other respects,* Liv.

ălĭca (hălĭca) -ae f. 1, *spelt, a kind of grain,* Plin. ; **2,** *a drink prepared from spelt,* Mart.

ălĭcārĭus (hălĭcārĭus) -a -um, *belonging to spelt.* Subst., a, **ălĭcārĭus** -ii, m. *one who grinds spelt ;* b, **ălĭcārĭa** -ae, f. *a prostitute ; one who sat before the spelt-mills,* Plaut.

ălĭcŭbī, adv. (aliquis and ubi), *anywhere, somewhere,* Cic.

ălĭcŭla -ae, f. (ἀλλιξ), *a light upper garment,* Mart.

ălĭcundĕ, adv. (aliquis and unde), *from anywhere, from somewhere,* Cic.

ălĭēnātĭo -ōnis, f. (alieno). **I.** Active, *a transference or alienation of property ;* sacrorum, *transfer of the sacra gentilicia from one gens to another,* Cic. **II.** Middle, 1, mentis, *mental alienation, loss of reason,* Plin. ; **2,** *a separation between persons, a desertion, enmity, alienation of feeling ;* tua a me alienatio, Cic.

ălĭēnĭgĕna -ae, m. (alienus and gigno), *strange, foreign ;* hostis, Cic. Subst., *a foreigner ;* quid alienigenae de vobis loqui soleant, Cic.

ălĭēnĭgĕnus -a -um (alienus and geno = gigno), *of different elements. heterogeneous.* Lucr.

ălĭēno, 1. (alienus), *to make something another's.* **I.** Lit., **A.** *to take away ;* usus fructus jam mihi harum aedium alienatus est, Plaut. **B.** 1, legal term, *to transfer property ;* vectigalia, Cic. ; **2,** *to sell a child or slave to a new family,* Liv. ; **3,** alicuius mentem, *to cause a person to lose his reason ;* Junonis iram ob spoliatum templum alienasse mentem ferebant, Liv. ; oftener in pass., alienari, *to go out of one's mind ;* mente alienata, Caes. ; velut alienatis sensibus, Plin. **II.** Transf., **A.** *to remove from the mind, to banish ;* alienatis a memoria periculi animis, *having forgotten danger,* Liv. **B.** *to estrange, put at variance ;* omnes a se bonos, Cic. ; with dat., alienati Romanis, Liv. ; alienari ab interitu, *to have a repugnance to, to shun,* Cic.

ălĭēnus -a -um, adj. with compar. and superl. (alius), *that which belongs or relates to another* (opp. meus, tuus, suus, proprius). **I.** Lit., **A.** Gen., domus, Cic. ; aes, *debt,* Cic. ; nomina, *debts contracted in the names of others,* Sall. ; alienis mensibus aestas, *the winter months,* Verg. ; alieno vulnere, *a wound meant for another,* Verg. Subst., **ălĭēnum** -i, n. *another man's property,* Cic. **B.** 1, *not related* (opp. propinquus) ; with dat., non alienus sanguine regibus, Liv. ; with a and the abl., alienissimus a Clodio, Cic. ; **2,** *foreign ;* domi atque in patria mallem, quam in externis atque alienis locis, Cic. Subst., **ălĭēnus** -i, m. a, *a stranger,* cives potiores quam peregrini, propinqui quam alieni ; b, *a foreigner,* Plin. **II.** Transf., **A.** Of persons, 1, *not at home in, not acquainted with, strange to ;* in physicis totus alienus est, Cic. ; **2,** *estranged, unfriendly ;* with ab and the abl., ab aliquo or ab aliqua re, Cic. ; with dat., homo mihi alienissimus, Cic. **B.** Of things, *unfavourable ;* alieno loco proelium committere, *in a disadvantageous place,* Caes. ; aliena verba, *unsuitable,* Cic. ; non alienum est, followed by the infin., *it is not out of place to,* etc., Cic. ; aliena loqui, *to talk nonsense,* Ov. ; with ab and the abl., labor alienus non ab aetate solum nostra, verum etiam a dignitate, Cic. ; with simple abl., dignitate imperii, Cic. ; with dat., quod maxime huic causae est alienum, Cic. ; with genit., aliena firmae et constantis assensionis, Cic. ; with ad and the acc., ad committendum proelium tempus alienum, Cic.

ălĭgĕr -gĕra -gĕrum (ala and gero), *winged ;* amor, Verg.

ălĭmentārĭus -a -um, *relating to food ;* lex, *with regard to a distribution of bread among the poor,* ap. Cic.

ălĭmentum -i, n. (alo), 1, *food* (gen. used in the plural) ; alimenta corporis, Cic. ; alimenta arcu expedire, *to get food by the bow,* Tac. ; used of fire, ignis, Liv. ; transf., seditionis, Tac. ; **2,** *maintenance,* hence (like Gr. τροφεῖα), *the return due by children to their parents for their bringing up,* Cic.

ălĭmōnĭum -ii, n. (alo), *nourishment,* Tac.

ălĭŏ, adv. (alius), *to another place.* **I.** Lit., si offendet me loci celebritas, alio me conferam, Cic. ; alius alio, *one in this direction, the other in that,* Cic. **II.** Transf., 1, *to another person ;* quo alio nisi ad nos socios confugerent, Liv. ; **2,** *for another end ;* nusquam alio natus quam ad serviendum, *born only for slavery,* Liv. ; **3,** *to another object ;* si placet sermonem alio transferamus, *to another topic,* Cic.

ălĭŏqui (ălĭŏquin), adv. (alius and quoi or qui, alius and quoine or quine). **I.** 1, *otherwise ; in other respects,* introducing an exception ; nunc pudore a fuga contineri, alioquin pro victis haberi, Liv. ; **2,** concessive, triumphatum de Tiburtibus, alioquin mitis victoria fuit, Liv. **II.**

yet, besides, moreover, else, in general; Caesar validus alioquin spernendis honoribus, Tac.

ălĭorsum and **ălĭorsus,** adv. (contr. from aliovorsum (alioversum) and aliovorsus (alioversus), 1, *in another direction, elsewhere;* mater ancillas jubet aliam aliorsum ire, *in different directions,* Plaut. ; 2, *in another manner,* Ter.

ălĭpēs -pĕdis (ala and pes), 1, *having wings on the feet;* deus, or absol., Mercury, Ov. ; 2, *swift of foot;* equi, Verg. Subst., **ălĭpĕdes,** *horses,* Verg.

Aliphēra -ae, f. (ʼΑλιφήρα or ʼΑλίφειρα), *a town of Arcadia not far from the border of Elis.*

ălipta -ae, m., and **ăliptēs** -ae, m. (ἀλείπτης), *the anointer in the wrestling-school or the baths;* hence *the master of the wrestling school,* Cic.

ălĭquā (aliquis), adv. **I.** *by some road;* evolare, Cic. **II.** *in some way;* nocere, Verg.

ălĭquamdĭū, adv. (aliqui and diu), *for a moderately long time,* Cic.

ălĭquammultus or **aliquam** (sc. partem) **multus** -a -um (aliqui and multus), *considerable* in number or quantity, *a pretty good many;* vestrum aliquam multi, Cic.

ălĭquandŏ, adv. (aliquis). **I.** 1, *at any time, at some time, once;* sero, verum aliquando tamen, Cic. ; si forte aliquando, *if by chance ever,* Cic. ; 2, *once;* dicendum aliquando est, Cic. ; 3, *sometimes, occasionally;* scribe aliquando ad nos quid agas, Cic. **II.** *at times, on some occasion;* aliquando . . . aliquando, *at times . . . at times,* Cic.

ălĭquantillus -a -um (dim. of aliquantus), *a very little,* Plaut.

ălĭquantispĕr, adv. (aliquantus and per), *a moderately long time,* Plaut.

ălĭquanto, ălĭquantum, v. aliquantus.

ălĭquantŭlus -a -um (dim. of aliquantus), *little, small.* Adv., **ălĭquantŭlum,** *a little,* Cic.

ălĭquantus -a -um (alius and quantus), *moderate, not small;* timor aliquantus, spes amplior, Sall. Subst., **ălĭquantum** -i, n. *a good deal;* nummorum, Cic. ; temporis, Cic. ; acc. aliquantum and abl. aliquanto, *considerably, somewhat;* qui processit aliquantum ad virtutis aditum, *had made considerable progress towards,* Cic. ; epulamur intra legem et quidem aliquando, *not sparingly,* Cic. ; esp. with comparative, aliquanto majorem locum occuparis, Cic. ; aliquanto post or ante, *some time after or before,* Cic.

ălĭquātĕnus, adv. (sc. parte; from aliquis and tenus), *to a certain degree, in some measure,* Sen.

ălĭqui, aliquae, aliquod (alius and qui), *some, any;* 1, masc., dolor aliqui, Cic. ; aliqui ex nostris, Caes. ; 2, fem., aliquae res, Lucr. ; 3, neut., simulacrum aliquod, Cic. (For other cases see aliquis.)

ălĭquis, aliqua, aliquid, pron. indef. (aliusquis), *some one, something, any one, anything.* **I.** Gen., 1, used by itself, **a,** subst., quisquis est ille, si modo aliquis, *if he be any one at all,* Cic. ; **b,** adj., aliquis deus, Cic. ; aliquā republicā, *if only the state is in existence at all,* Cic. ; 2, strengthened by alius, aliquid aliud videbimus, Cic. ; 3, by unus, aliquis unus pluresve dictiores Cic. ; 4, partitive with ex, aliquis ex vobis, Cic. ; 5, like the Gr. τις (Engl. *some*), to express an unascertained number, tres aliqui aut quatuor, Cic. ; 6, aliquid with genit. of a subst. or adj., aliquid virium, Cic. ; falsi aliquid, Cic. ; 7, with adj., aliquid divinum, Cic. ; 8, with si or nisi, acc. aliquid, *in any respect;* si in me

aliquid offendistis, Cic. **II.** Esp., 1, *some person or other;* dixerit hic aliquis, Cat. ; 2, *somebody or something great or significant;* si nunc aliquid assequi se putant, Cic. ; hence, **a,** esse aliquem or aliquid, *to be somebody, to be something,* Cic. ; est aliquid nupsisse Jovi, Ov. ; **b,** dicere aliquid, *to say something weighty,* Cic. ; Vestorio aliquid significes, *say something agreeable,* Cic.

ălĭquō, adv. (aliquis), *some* or *any whither;* aliquem secum rus aliquo educere, *in some direction or other,* Cic. ; aliquo concedere ab eorum oculis, Cic.

ălĭquŏt, numer. indef. indecl., *some, several;* aliquot epistolae, Cic. ; aliquot diebus ante, Cic.

ălĭquŏtĭēs, adv. (aliquot), *several times;* aliquoties ex aliquo audisse, Cic.

ălis, alid, old form of alius, aliud.

ălĭtĕr, adv. (from alis = alius), 1, *otherwise, in another way;* non fuit faciendum aliter, Cic. ; alius aliter, *in different ways,* Cic. ; in comparisons, aliter . . . atque, aliter rem cecidisse atque opinatus sis, *in a different way from what you expected,* Cic. ; so aliter . . . quam, Cic. ; aliter . . . atque ut, Cic. ; non (or haud) aliter . . . quam si, quam quom, ac si, *just as,* Ov. ; non aliter . . . nisi, Cic. ; quod certe scio longe aliter esse, *is far from being the case,* Cic. ; aliter evenire, *to happen differently,* Sall. ; 2, *otherwise, else;* jus semper est quaesitum aequabile neque enim aliter jus esset, Cic.

ălĭŭbĭ, adv. (alius and ubi), *elsewhere,* Plin.

ălĭundĕ, adv. (alius and unde), *from some other direction;* alii aliunde coibant, *from different directions,* Liv. ; aliunde quam, *from a different direction from,* Cic. ; aliunde . . . aliunde, Liv.

ălĭus -a -ud (genit. alīus), *another, other.* **I.** Lit., **A.** Gen., 1, distributively, *one, another;* aliud est maledicere, aliud accusare, Cic. ; alii . . . alii, *some . . . others,* Cic. ; also, alii . . . reliqui, Cic. ; alii . . . quidam, Liv. ; alii . . . pars, Sall. ; alii . . . alii quidam, Cic. ; aliud alio melius, *one is better than the other,* Cic. ; alius alia via, *the one in this way, the other in that,* Liv. ; alius ex alio, Cic. ; super alium, Liv. ; post alium, *one after another,* Sall. ; alius atque alius, *now this, now that,* Cic. ; 2, followed by ac, atque, et, after a negative by nisi, quam, praeter, or the abl. ; lux longe alia est solis et lychnorum, *there is a great difference between the light of the sun and of lamps,* Cic. ; alius essem atque nunc sum, Cic. ; nec quidquam aliud philosophia est praeter studium sapientiae, Cic. ; nec quidquam aliud libertate quaesisse, *anything else but liberty,* Cic. ; tribunatus Sestii nihil aliud nisi meum nomen causamque sustinuit, Cic. ; 3, plur., alia, subst., si alia desint, Liv. ; acc. plur., alia, *in other respects;* alia clarus, Tac. ; 4, aliud, subst. with genit., aliud commodi, Cic. **B.** Esp., 1, of auguries, alio die, si unus augur alio die dixerit, *if an augur pronounces the word "on another day,"* i.e. *postpones the comitia on the ground of unfavourable omens,* Cic. ; 2, *of another nature, different;* alium facere, *to change, transform,* Plaut. ; alium fieri, *to be transformed,* Cic. ; in alia omnia ire, discedere, transire, *to dissent from a proposition, be of a contrary opinion* (in the Roman senate), Cic. **II.** Transf., 1, *the rest;* Divitiaco ex aliis (Gallis) maximam fidem habebat, Caes. ; 2, = alter, *one of two;* alius Ariovistus, *a second Ariovistus,* Tac. ; duo Romani super alium alius corruerunt, Liv.

ălĭusmŏdĭ (alius and modus), *of another kind,* Cic.

allābor -lapsus, 3. *to glide to, come to, flow to;* angues duo ex occulto allapsi, Liv. ; with

iăt. and acc., antiquis allabimur oris, *we land on*, Verg. ; fama allabitur aures, Verg.

allăbŏro (ad-lăbŏro), 1. *to labour at*, Hor.

allăcrĭmo (ad-lăcrĭmo), 1. *to weep at*, Verg.

allapsus -ūs, m. (allabor), *a gliding approach*, Hor.

allātro (ad-lātro), 1. *to bark at;* fig., *to rail at;* magnitudinem Africani, Liv.

allaudābĭlis (ad-laudābĭlis)-e, *praiseworthy*, Lucr.

allaudo, 1. *to praise*, Plaut.

allec, v. alec.

allecto (allicio), 1. *to entice*, Cic.

allectus -a -um (partic. of 2. allego), plur., *members elected into any collegium*, Varr. ; under the empire, *persons raised by the emperor to a higher rank*, Plin.

allēgātĭo -ōnis, f. (1. allego), *a sending of a person on a mission;* quum sibi omnes ad istum allegationes difficiles viderent, Cic.

allēgātus, abl. -ū, m. (1. allego), *instigation*, Plaut.

1. **allēgo** (ad-lēgo), 1. **I. A.** *to send on private business, to commission* (lego of state business) ; aliquem ad aliquem or alicui, Cic. ; patrem allegando fatigare, *by sending messages*, Cic. ; allegati, *deputies*, Cic. **B.** *to instigate, to suborn*, Ter. **II.** Transf., *to adduce* or *allege in excuse;* munera, preces, mandata regis sui Scyrothemidi allegant, Tac.

2. **allēgo** (ad-lēgo) -lēgi -lectum, 3. *to choose, to elect;* de plebe omnes, Liv. ; with in and the acc., aliquem in senatum, Suet.

allēvāmentum -i, n. (allevo), *a means of alleviation*, Cic.

allēvātĭo -ōnis, f. **A.** Lit., *a lifting up*, Quint. **B.** Transf., *alleviation;* doloris, Cic.

allēvo (ad-lēvo), 1. **A.** Lit., *to lift up, to erect;* circumstantium humeris, Tac. **B.** Transf., *to lighten, to alleviate;* sollicitudines, Cic. ; pass., allevari, *to be cheered;* allevor, quum loquor tecum absens, Cic.

Allĭa (Alia) -ae, f. *river in Latium, flowing into the Tiber*, near which the Romans were defeated by the Gauls, B.C. 389 ; infaustum Alliae nomen, Verg. Adj., **Allĭensis** -e.

allĭcĕfăcĭo, 3. *to entice*, Sen.

allĭcĭo -lexi -lectum, 3 (ad and * lacio), *to allure, entice, draw to oneself;* ad se allicere et attrahere ferrum (of the magnet), Cic. ; fig., oratione benigna multitudinis animos ad benevolentiam, Cic.

allīdo -līsi -līsum, 3. (ad and laedo). **A.** Lit., *to strike against, dash against;* allidi ad scopulos, Caes. **B.** Transf., allidi, *to suffer damage;* in quibus (damnationibus) Servius allisus est, Cic.

Allĭfae -ārum, f. *a town of the Samnites on the left bank of the Vulturnus*, now *Alife* in the *Terra di Lavoro;* hence **Allĭfānus** -a -um, *relating to Allifae*. Subst., **Allĭfāna** -ōrum, n. (sc. pocula), *earthenware drinking-vessels of some size*, Hor.

allĭgo (ad-lĭgo), 1. *to tie to, bind to.* **I.** Lit. **A.** Gen., aliquem ad palum, *bind a criminal to the stake for punishment*, Cic. **B.** Esp., 1, *to make fast;* unco dente velut manu ferrea injecta alligavit alterius proram, Liv. ; unco non alligat (naves) ancora morsu, Verg. ; 2, *to bind by a fastening*, a, of a wound, vulnus, Cic. ; b, of fetters, Tac. **II.** Transf. **A.** Gen., *to fetter, bind;* videas civitatis voluntatem solutam, virtutem alligatam, Cic. ; tristi palus inamabilis unda alligat, *confines, imprisons*, Verg. **B.** Esp., 1, *to bind by friendship* or *obligations;* non modo

beneficio sed etiam benevolentia alligari, Cic. ; 2, in rhet., of the constraints of metre, ut verba neque alligata sint quasi certa lege versus, Cic. ; 3, *to bind by promise, oath*, etc. ; lex omnes mortales alligat, Cic. ; sacris alligari, *to pledge oneself to perform* the sacra gentilicia, Cic. ; alligare se scelere, *to become an accomplice in a crime*, Cic. ; alligatus, *implicated* or *involved* in a crime, Cic.

allĭno (ad-lĭno) -lēvi -lĭtum, 3. *to smear on*, or *over, to bedaub*, Cic.

allĭum -i, n. *garlic*, Plin.

Allŏbrŏges -um, m. *the Allobroges, a Gallic people between the Rhone and the Isère;* nom. sing., **Allŏbrox**, Hor. ; Ciceronem Allobroga (i.e., *speaking bad Latin*) dixit, Juv. Adj., **Allŏbrŏgĭcus** -a -um, as *a surname of Q. Fabius Maximus*, conqueror of the Allobroges.

allŏcūtĭo -ōnis, f. (alloquor), *an address, a speaking to*, Plin.

allŏquĭum -i, n. (alloquor), *exhortation, encouragement, consolation;* benigni voltus et alloquia, Liv. ; alloquio firmare militem, Tac.

allŏquor -lŏcūtus sum, 3. *to address, exhort, encourage*, Cic. ; aliquem benigne, leniter, Liv. ; patriam maesta voce ita miseriter, Cat.

allŭbesco, 3. inch. (ad and lubet), *to begin to please*, Plaut.

allŭcĕo -luxi, 2. *to shine at*, or *upon;* Fortuna faculam tibi allucet, *offers thee a favourable opportunity*, Plaut.

alludo (ad-lūdo) -lūsi -lūsum, 3. 1, *to jest at, to sport with;* Galba alludens varie et copiose, Cic. ; 2, of waves, *to play* or *dash upon;* alludentibus undis, Ov. ; quae fluctus salis alludebant, Cat.

allŭo (ad-lŭo) -ŭi, 3. *to wash;* used of the sea, alluuntur a mari moenia, Cic. ; fig., Massilia quum barbariae fluctibus alluatur, *exposed to barbarians*, Cic.

allŭvĭes -ēi, f. (alluo), *a pool caused by the overflow of a river*, Liv.

allŭvĭo -ōnis, f. (alluo), *alluvial land, earth deposited by water*, Cic.

Almo -ōnis, m. *a small brook on the south side of Rome*, now *Aquataccio*.

almus -a -um (alo), *nourishing;* ager, Verg. ; *fair, gracious, propitious, kind;* Venus, Hor.

alnus -i, f. *the alder.* **I.** Lit., Plin. **II.** Meton., *a ship of alderwood*, Verg.

ălo, ălŭi, altum and ălĭtum, 3. *to nourish, support.* **I.** Lit., **A.** Of living things, 1, *to rear;* altus educatusque inter arma, Liv. ; 2, *to keep;* anseres in Capitolio, Cic. ; magnum numerum equitatus suo sumptu, Caes. ; se alere or ali, with abl., or ex and the abl., *to support oneself;* se suosque latrociniis, *to live by brigandage*, Caes. **B.** Of things, 1, of land, etc., *to provide means of existence;* cum agellus eum non satis aleret, Cic. ; venatus viros pariter ac feminas alit, Tac. ; 2, of the earth, *to nourish;* tellus humida majores herbas alit, Verg. ; 3, *to support;* a, plants, gramen erat circa quod proximus humor alebat, Ov. ; b, of rivers, amnis imbres quem super notas aluere ripas, *have swollen*, Hor. ; idem (Libanus mons) amnem Jordanem alit funditque, Tac. ; c, of fire, flammas, Ov. ; 4, of the means that support the body, *to give strength to;* otia corpus alunt, Ov. **II.** Transf., *to increase, promote, advance;* honos alit artes, Cic. ; hos successus alit, *encourages*, Verg. ; civitatem, *promote the good of the state*, Caes. ; alere spem mollibus sententiis, Cic.

ălŏē -ēs, f. (ἀλόη), *the aloe;* transf., *bitterness;* plus aloes quam mellis habet, Juv.

Ălŏēus -ĕi, m. (Ἀλωεύς), *a giant, son of Neptune.* **Alŏīdae** -arum, m. *sons of Aloeus (Otus and Ephialtes), giants who tried to storm heaven.*

Alŏīdae -ārum, m. (Ἀλωεῖδαι), v. Aloeus.

Ălŏpē -ēs, f. (Ἀλόπη), *a town in Opuntian Locris.*

Alpēs -ĭum, f. (Keltic alb, alp = *height, high mountain*), *the Alps;* hence **A. Alpīnus** -a -um. **B. Alpĭcus** -a -um, *Alpine.*

alpha, indecl. n. (ἄλφα), *the name of the first letter in the Greek alphabet,* Juv.; prov., *the first,* Mart.

Alphēus -i, m. (Ἀλφειός), *the principal river of the Peloponnesus flowing through Elis to the sea;* the river-god Alpheus was said to have dived under the sea in pursuit of the nymph Arethusa, and to have come up in Sicily; hence **Alphēīas** -ădis, f. *surname of the nymph Arethusa.* Adj., **Alphēus** -a -um, *belonging to the river Alpheus,* Verg.

Alsĭum -ĭi, n. *one of the oldest towns in Etruria* (now the village *Palo*), near which Pompeius had an estate; hence adj., **Alsĭensis** -e, *belonging to Alsium,* villa (*of Pompeius*), Cic. Subst., **Alsĭense** -is, n. (sc. praedium), *the estate of Pompeius,* Cic.

alsĭus (alsus) -a -um, *frosty, cold,* Lucr., Cic.

altānus -i, m. *a S.W. wind,* Suet.

altārĭa -ĭum, n. (altus). **I.** *the slab upon the altar* (ara), *on which the fire is lighted,* Quint. **II.** *a high altar;* ecce duas tibi, Daphni, tuas altaria Phoebo, Verg.; *an altar,* Cic.

altē, adv. (altus). **I.** *on high, highly.* **A. Lit.,** cadere, *from a height,* Cic. **B.** Transf., spectare, *to have high aims,* Cic. **II.** *deeply.* **A.** Lit., sulcus altius impressus, Cic. **B.** Transf., quod verbum in Jugurthae pectus altius quam quisquam ratus erat descendit, Sall.; petere, *to seek far and wide,* Cic.; altius perspicere, *to see farther,* Cic.

altěr -těra -těrum (genit., altěrīus, in poetry also altěrīus; dat., alteri, *one of two, the one, the other.* **I.** Lit., **A.** Gen., consulum alter, Liv.; alter . . . alter, *the one . . . the other;* so alter . . . ille or hic or iste, or a subst.; in plur., alteri dimicant, alteri victorem timent, Cic.; with the second alter in a different case, alter alterius ova frangit, Cic. **B.** Esp., 1, alter ambove, S. E. V., a form in the senate, *one of the consuls, or both,* si eis videbitur, Cic.; 2, *the second;* fortunate puer, tu nunc eris alter ab illo, *you will be second to him,* Verg.; unus et alter dies, *one or two,* Cic.; 3, used appellat., *another, a second;* me sicut alterum parentem diligit, *a second parent,* Cic.; tamquam alter idem, *a second self,* Cic.; 4, *the other,* i.e. *the opposite;* ripa, Caes.; pars, *the opposite faction,* Cic.; quoties te speculo videris alterum, *changed,* Hor. **II.** Transf., *another,* in the sense of your *neighbour, fellow creature;* qui nihil alterius causa facit, Cic.

altercātĭo -ōnis, f. (altercor), 1, *a dispute, wrangling, debate;* magna non disceptatio modo, sed etiam altercatio, Liv.; 2, legal t. t., *cross-examination* in a court of justice, Cic.

altercātor -ōris, m. (altercor), *a disputant,* Quint.

altercor, 1, dep. (alter), *to dispute, contend in words, quarrel.* **I.** Gen., **A.** Lit., altercari cum aliquo, Caes. **B.** Transf., poet., altercante libidinibus pavore, *contending with,* Hor. **II.** Legal t. t. *to cross-examine, to cross-question;* in altercando invenit parem neminem, Cic.

alterno, 1. (alternus). **I.** Trans., *to do first one thing, then another;* fidem, *make at one time credible, at another not,* Ov.; vices, Ov. **II.**

Intrans., **A.** Lit. *to change;* illi alternantes magna vi proelia miscent, *changing sides,* Verg. **B.** Transf., *to hesitate;* haec alternanti potior sententia visa est, Verg.

alternus -a -um (alter). **I.** *one after the other, by turns, alternate, interchanging;* sermones, *dialogue,* Hor.; versibus, *in alternate song,* Verg.; alterni metus, *mutual fear,* Liv.; alterno pede terram quatiunt, *first with one foot then with another,* Hor.; alterna loqui cum aliquo, *to hold a conversation with,* Hor. **II., A.** Of metre, elegiac verse, where hexameter and pentameter alternate; pedes alternos esse oportebit, Cic.; canere alterno carmine, Ov. **B.** Legal t. t., rejicere alterna consilia or alternos judices (of plaintiff and defendant), *to challenge a number of jurors,* Cic.

altěrūter, altěr-utra (altera utra), alterutrum (alterum utrum); genit., altěrutrīus, *one of two,* Cic.

Althaea -ae, f. (Ἀλθαία), *wife of Oeneus, king of Calydon, mother of Meleager.*

altĭcinctus -a -um (altus and cingo), *high girt;* hence *busy,* Phaedr.

altĭlis -e (alo). **A.** Of domestic animals, *fattened, fed up;* hence subst., **altĭlis,** f. (sc. avis), *a fowl,* Hor. **B.** Transf., *rich,* Plaut.

altĭsŏnus -a -um (alte and sono). **I.** *sounding from on high;* Juppiter, Cic. **II.** Transf., *high-sounding, sublime;* Maronis altisoni carmina, Juv.

altĭtŏnans -tis, *thundering from on high,* Lucr.

altĭtūdo -ĭnis, f. (altus). **I.** *height.* **A.** Lit., montium, Cic. **B.** Transf., *sublimity;* orationis, Cic. **II.** *depth.* **A.** Lit., fluminis, Caes. **B.** Transf., altitudo animi, *secrecy, reserve,* Cic.

altĭuscŭlus -a -um (dim. of altius), *a little too high,* Suet.

altĭvŏlans -antis (altus and volo), *flying high,* Lucr.

altor -ōris, m. (alo), *a nourisher, a fosterfather;* omnium rerum seminator et sator et parens, ut ita dicam, atque educator et altor est mundus, Cic.

altrinsĕcŭs, adv. (alter and secus), *on the other side,* Plaut.

altrix -īcis, f. (altor), *a nurse, foster-mother;* terra altrix nostra, Cic.

altrŏvorsum, adv. (alter and versus), *on the other side,* Plaut.

altus -a -um (alo), **I.** *high.* **A.** Lit., Cic., Caes.; with acc. of measure, signum septem pedes altum, Liv. Subst., **altum** -i, n. *height;* a, aedificia in altum edita, Tac.; b, esp., *the height of the heavens;* ab alto, Verg. **B.** Transf., 1, of position, altior dignitatis gradus, Cic.; 2, of the voice, *shrill;* altiore voce, Quint.; 3, of gods and exalted persons, Apollo, Verg.; Caesar, Hor.; Aeneas, *high-born,* Verg.; 4, of speech, *elevated;* nimis altam et exaggeratam (orationem), Cic.; 5, of character or intellect, *lofty;* te natura excelsum quendam et altum genuit, Cic.; vultus, *a lofty mien,* Hor.; 6, *ancient;* altior memoria, Cic.; aliquid ex alto petere, Verg. **II.** *deep.* **A.** Lit., flumen, Caes.; with acc. of measure, quinquaginta cubita altum mare, Plin. Subst., **altum** -i, n. *depth,* esp. *the deep sea;* in portum ex alto provehi, Cic. **B.** Transf., 1, of quiet, etc., *deep;* somnus altus, Liv.; 2, *deep-seated;* pavor, Tac.; 3, *secret;* si altior istis sub precibus venia ulla latet, Verg.; 4, *depth* (of mind); ex alto dissimulare, *to dissimulate profoundly,* Ov.

ălūcĭnātĭo -ōnis, f. (alucinor), *hallucination, delusion,* Sen.

ālūcĭnor, 1. dep. (connected with ἀλύω), *to wander in mind, dream, to talk idly*; ego tamen suspicor, hunc, ut solet, alucinari, Cic.

ălumna -ae, f., v. alumnus.

ălumnus -a -um (alo), *a nursling, a foster-son*. **I**. Masc., **A**. Lit., *child of a country, inhabitant*, Verg.; Italia alumnum suum videret, Cic.; sutrinae tabernae, *a cobbler*, Tac.; legionum, *brought up in the camp*, Tac.; of animals, parvi alumni, *the young of the flock*, Hor. **B**. Transf., *pupil, disciple;* Platonis, Cic.; fig., ego, ut ita dicam, pacis alumnus, Cic. **II. A**. Fem., *foster-child;* nostra haec alumna et tua profecto filia, Plaut.; aquae dulcis alumnae, *frogs*, Cic. poet. **B**. Transf., bene constitutae civitatis quasi alumna quaedam eloquentia, Cic. **III**. Neut., numen alumnum, Ov.

Ălūntĭum (Haluntĭum) -ĭi, n. (Ἀλούντιον), *a town on the north coast of Sicily*, now *Caronia*. Adj., **Aluntīnus** -a -um.

ălūta, -ae, f. *a kind of soft leather*, Caes.; hence, meton., **1**, *a shoe*, Ov.; **2**, *a purse*, Juv.; **3**, *an ornamental patch*, Ov.

alvĕārĭum -ĭi, n. *a beehive*, Verg.

alvĕātus -a -um (alveus), *hollowed like a trough*, Cato.

alvĕŏlus -i, m. (dim. of alveus), **1**, *a little hollow, a tray, trough, bucket*, Juv., Liv.; **2**, *a gaming board*, Cic.

alvĕus -i, m. (connected with alo), *a hollow, an excavation;* **1**, *a trough*, Liv.; **2**, *a boat*, Verg.; *the hold of a ship*, Sall.; **3**, *a bathing-tub*, Ov.; **4**, *the bed of a stream;* quia sicco alveo transiri poterat, Liv.; **5**, *a beehive*, Tib.; vitiosae ilicis alveo, *the hollow of a tree in which bees settled*, Verg.; **6**, *a gaming-table*, Plin.

alvus -i, f. (alo). **I**. *the belly*. **A**. Lit., purgatio alvi, Cic. **B**. Transf., **1**, *the womb*, Cic.; **2**, *the stomach*, Cic. **II**. *the hold of a ship*, Tac. **III**. *a bee-hive*, Plin.

Ălỹattēs -is or -ĕi, m. (Ἀλυάττης), *king of Lydia, father of Croesus*.

Alyzĭa -ae, f. (Ἀλυζία), *a small town of Acarnania*, with a temple of Hercules, now *Porto Candello*.

ămābĭlis -e (amo), *amiable, lovable;* amabilior mihi Velia fuit, quod te ab ea amari sensi, Cic.; amabile carmen, *lovely*, Hor.

ămābĭlĭtās -ātis (amabilis), *amiableness*, Plaut.

ămābĭlĭtĕr, adv. (amabilis), **1**, *amiably*, Hor.; **2**, *lovingly*, Cic.

Ămalthēa -ae, f. (Ἀμάλθεια), *a nymph, the nurse of Jupiter in Crete*, according to others, the goat on the milk of which Jupiter was reared; the cornu Amaltheae or Copiae was placed among the stars; hence **Amalthēa** -ae, f., and **Amalthēum** or **Amalthīum** -i, n. *a sanctuary of Amalthea, in Epirus*, near to the estate of Atticus.

āmandātĭo -ōnis, f. (amando), *a sending away*, Cic.

āmando, 1. *to send away, to send to a distance;* aliquem Lilybaeum, Cic.; transf., natura res similes procul amandavit a sensibus, Cic.

āmans -antis, p. adj. (amo), **1**, *loving, fond, affectionate*. **I**. Adj., **A**. Lit., pater amantissimus, Cic.; with gen., amantissimus reipublicae, Cic. **B**. Transf., of things, mea fidelissima atque amantissima consilia, Cic. **II**. Subst., c. *a lover*, Cic.

ămantĕr, adv. (amans), *lovingly*, Cic.

Amantĭa -ae, f. (Ἀμαντία), *a town in Illyria*, now *Nivitza;* hence **Amantiāni** -ōrum, m. *the inhabitants of Amantia*.

āmānŭensis -is, m. = a manu servus, *a secretary, clerk*, Suet.

Āmānus -i, m. (Ἄμανος), *a range of mountains in Asia Minor, dividing Cilicia from Syria* (now *Alma Dagh*); hence **Amāniénses** -ium, m. *the mountaineers of Mount Amanus*.

ămārăcĭnus -a -um, *made of marjoram*. Subst., **ămārăcĭnum** -i, n. (sc. unguentum), *marjoram ointment*, Lucr.

ămārăcus -i, c., and **ămārăcum** -i, n. (ἀμάρακος), *marjoram*, Verg.

ămārantus -i, m. (ἀμάραντος, *unfading*), *the amaranth*, Ov.

ămārē, adv. (amarus), *bitterly*, Sen.

ămārĭtūdo -Inis, f. (amarus). **I**. Lit., *bitterness of taste*, Varr. **II**. Transf., a, *that which is bitter, unpleasant*, Plin.; b, in rhet., vocis, *an excessive vehemence, harshness of voice*, Quint.

ămāror -ōris, m. (amarus), *bitterness*, Lucr., Verg.

ămārus -a -um, *bitter*. **A**. Lit., **1**, of taste, Cic.; **2**, of smell, *pungent;* fumus, Verg.; **B**. Transf., **1**, *disagreeable, unpleasant;* historiae, *tedious*, Hor.; curae, Ov. Neut. plur., **ămāra** -ōrum, *what is unpleasant*, Hor.; **2**, *irritable, susceptible;* amariorem me senectus facit, Verg.; **3**, of speech, *biting, acrimonious;* lingua, Ov.

Ămăryllis -Idis, acc. -Ida, f. (Ἀμαρυλλίς), *name of a shepherdess*.

Ămărynthĭs -Idis, f. *surname of Diana*, from Amarynthos, a place in Euboea where Diana was worshipped.

Ămăsēnus -i, m. *a river in Latium*, now *Amaseno*.

Ămāsis, acc. -im, abl. -i, -e, or -Idĕ, m. (Ἄμασις), *one of the Egyptian Pharaohs*.

ămāsius -ĭi, m. (amo), *a lover*, Plaut.

Ămastris -Idis, f. (Ἄμαστρις), *a town in Paphlagonia*, now *Amasserah;* hence **Amastrĭācus** -a -um, *belonging to Amastris;* orae, *coasts of Pontus*, Ov.

Ămāta -ae, f. myth. *wife of king Latinus, mother of Lavinia*.

Ămăthūs -untis, f. (Ἀμαθοῦς), *a city of Cyprus*, famous for the worship of Venus; hence **Ămăthūsĭa**, *Venus;* **Ămăthūsĭācus** -a -um, *Amathusian*.

ămātĭo -ōnis, f. (amo), *love-making, intrigue*, Plaut.

ămātor -ōris, m. (amo), **1**, *one who loves, a friend;* vir bonus amatorque noster, Cic.; amatores huic (Catoni) desunt, *admirers, readers of his works*, Cic.; so of a thing, puri sermonis, Caes.; sapientiae, pacis, Cic.; **2**, *lover of a woman, paramour;* virginem ab amatorum impetu prohibere, Cic.

ămātorcŭlus -i, m. (dim. of amator), *a little lover*, Plaut.

ămātōrĭē, adv. (amatorius), *amorously*, Cic.

ămātōrĭus -a -um (amator), *loving, amorous;* sermo, Cic.; poesis (Anacreontis), Cic.; frui voluptate amatoria, Cic.

ămātrix -Icis, f. (amator), *a mistress, sweetheart*, Plaut.

Ămāzon -ōnis, f., gen. in plur. **Amāzŏnes** -um (Ἀμαζόνες), myth. *nation of female warriors;* hence, **1**, **Amāzŏnis** -Idis, f. = Amazon, Verg.; **2**, **Amāzŏnĭcus** -a -um, *Amazonian;* **3**, **Amāzŏnĭus** -a -um, *Amazonian;* vir, *Hippolytus*, son of an Amazon by Theseus, Ov.

amb, ambi, and **ambe**, an inseparable preposition, entering into the composition of words, *around, round about* (as in ambedo, etc.).

ambactus -i, m. *a vassal*, Caes.

ambădĕdo, 3. *to eat round, consume utterly*, Plaut.

ambāges, abl. -e, f. (of sing. only abl. found, complete in the plur.), *going round, roundabout way, winding*. **I.** Lit., variarum ambage viarum, *of a labyrinth*, Ov. **II.** Transf., **A.** *circumlocution;* missis ambagibus, *without circumlocution*, Hor. **B.** *obscurity, ambiguity;* ambages canere, of the Sibyll, Verg.; immemor ambagum, of the Sphinx, Ov.; **C.** *shifts, prevarication;* falsi positis ambagibus oris, Ov.

Ambarri -ōrum, m. *a Gallic people east of the Aedui, with whom they were related.*

ambĕdo -ēdi -ēsum, 3. *to eat round, consume*, Verg.

Ambiăni -ōrum, m. *people in North Gaul, on the Somme.*

Ambibarii -ōrum, m. *Gallic people in Normandy* (whence the modern *Ambières*).

ambĭgo, 3. (amb and ago). **I.** Lit., *to go about* or *round*. **II.** Transf., **A.** *to doubt, hesitate, be uncertain;* jus quod ambigitur, Cic.; ambigitur, impers., followed by de and the abl., or with relative or infinitive clause, or with negative followed by quin and the subj., quum de vero ambigetur, Cic. **B.** *to dispute, contend*, at law or otherwise; cum eo qui heres est, Cic.; de hereditate, Cic.

ambĭgŭē, adv. (ambiguus), **1**, *ambiguously;* scribere, Cic.; **2**, *indecisively;* equites ambigue certavere, Tac.

ambĭgŭitas -ātis, f. (ambiguus), *ambiguity;* verborum, Cic.

ambĭgŭus -a -um (ambigo). **I.** *moving from side to side, of doubtful nature;* Proteus, Ov.; virgo, Siren or Sphinx, Ov.; viri, Centaurs, Ov.; ambiguam promisit Salamina, *a second Salamis*, Hor. **II.** Transf., **A.** *uncertain, doubtful;* ambiguus tanti certaminis heres, Ov.; imperandi, *not resolved on*, Tac. Subst., **ambĭgŭum** -i, n. *uncertainty;* non habui ambiguum, *I had no doubt*, Cic.; relinquere in ambiguo, Lucr. **B.** Of speech, *ambiguous, obscure;* oracula, Cic. Subst., **ambĭgŭum** -i, n. *ambiguity;* ex ambiguo dicta, Cic. **C.** *uncertain, untrustworthy;* fides, Liv.; tribuni, Tac.; res possessionis haud ambiguae, *with a clear title*, Liv.; res, *insecure*, Tac.; aquae, *changing*, Ov.

Ambiliati -ōrum, m. *a Gallic people on the Somme.*

ambĭo -īvi and -ii -ītum, 4. (amb and eo, but conjugated regularly acc. to the 4th conjug. except imperf. ambibat, Liv.). **I.** *to go round.* **A.** Lit., ut terram lunae cursus proxime ambiret, Cic. **B.** Transf., *to surround;* silvas profunda palus ambibat, Tac.; vallum armis, Tac. **II.A.** *to go round canvassing for votes*, or *help;* ad id quod agi videbatur ambientes, Liv.; pass., populus facit eos a quibus est maxime ambitus, Cic.; **B.** *to address individuals;* reginam affatu, Verg.; te pauper ambit sollicita prece ruris colonus, *approaches with prayer*, Hor.

Ambĭŏrix -rigis, m. *prince of the Eburones in Gallia Belgica.*

ambĭtĭo -ōnis, f. (ambio). **A.** *a canvassing for office in a lawful manner;* opp. ambitus (q.v.); me ambitio et forensis labor ab omni illa cogitatione abstrahebat, Cic. **B.** Transf., *striving after honours;* **1**, after public office, *desire for office;* me ambitio quaedam ad honorum studium duxit, Cic.; **2**, *desire for fame, display, pomp;* funerum nulla ambitio, *no empty pomp*, Tac.; **3**, *factiousness;* non puto existimare te ambitione me labi, Cic.; **4**, *striving after something;* conciliandae provinciae ad novas spes, Tac.

ambĭtĭōsē, adv. (ambitiosus), **1**, *aspiringly;* petere regnum, Liv.; **2**, *with a view to one's interest, selfishly;* non vulgariter nec ambitiose scribere, Cic.

ambĭtĭōsus -a -um (ambitio). **1**, *twining around;* lascivis hederis ambitiosior, Hor.; ambitiosa ornamenta, *excessive*, Hor.; **2**, a, *eager for public office, ambitious;* patres mollem consulem et ambitiosum rati, Liv.; b, *vain, ostentatious, pretentious;* amicitiae, *interested*, Cic.; mors, *ostentatious, studied*, Tac.; c, *eager to win favour, seeking after popularity;* dux indulgens ambitiosusque, Liv.; rogationes, *meant to win popularity*, Cic.; d, *striving after anything;* Musa nec in plausus ambitiosa mea est, Ov.; amor, Ov.

ambĭtus -ūs, m. (ambio), *a going round.* **I.** Gen., **A.** Abstr., *circuit, revolution;* siderum, Cic. **B.** Concr., **1**, *course, orbit;* stellarum rotundi ambitus, Cic.; transf., *circumlocution;* multos circa unam rem ambitus facere, Liv.; **2**, *circle, edge;* extremus ambitus campi, Tac.; esp., *the space left round a house*, Cic.; **3**, *extent*, castra lato ambitu, Tac. **II.** *going round to entreat.* **A.** Lit., *illegal canvassing for office, bribery;* lex de ambitu, Cic.; ambitus aliquem accusare, damnare, Cic. **B.** Transf., *striving after honours*, Plin.; *popularity-hunting*, Tac. **C.** *striving for*, with genit., ambitu remanendi aut eundi, Tac.

Ambivareti -ōrum, m. *a Gallic people, allies of the Aedui.*

Ambivariti -ōrum, m. *a Gallic people on the Maas*, near modern Breda.

Ambĭvĭus, L. Ambivius Turpio, *a celebrated actor in Rome*, contemporary of Terence.

ambō -ae -ō (ἄμφω), *both, two together* (uterque, *two considered separately*); hic qui utrumque probat, ambobus debuit uti, Cic.

Ambrăcĭa -ae, f. (Ἀμβρακία), *town on the south border of Epirus, near the sea*, now *Arta;* hence, 1, adj., **Ambrăcĭensis** -e, *Ambracian;* 2, **Ambrăcĭus** -a -um, *Ambracian;* 3, subst., **Ambrăcĭōtēs** -ae, m. *inhabitant of Ambracia.*

Ambrōnes -um, m. *a Keltic people defeated by Marius in the war with the Cimbri.*

ambrŏsĭa -ae, f. (ἀμβροσία), **1**, *ambrosia, the food of the gods*, Cic.; orator ambrosia alendus, *of a distinguished orator*, Cic.; **2**, *a miraculous unguent, giving divine beauty and making immortal*, Verg.

ambrŏsĭus -a -um (ἀμβρόσιος), *divine, immortal, ambrosial;* dapes, Mart.; comae, *anointed with ambrosia*, Verg.

Ambrȳsus -i, f. *a town in Phocis*, now *Dystomo.*

ambūbājae -ārum, f. (Syrian abub, anbub, the flute), *Syrian music women and prostitutes in Rome*, Hor.

ambŭlācrum -i, n. *a walk shaded with trees*, Plaut.

ambŭlātĭo -ōnis, f. (ambulo), **1**, *a walk*, Cic.; **2**, *a place for walking, a promenade*, Cic.

ambŭlātĭuncŭla -ae, f. **1**, *a little walk*, Cic.; **2**, *a little promenade*, Cic.

ambŭlātor -ōris, m. (ambulo), *one who walks about, a lounger*, Cato; *pedlar*, Mart.

ambŭlātōrĭus -a -um (ambulo), *movable*, Plin.

ambŭlātrix -īcis, f. *a gadding woman*, Cato.

ambŭlo, 1. (dim. of ambio). **I.** *to go backwards and forwards, to walk*, Cic.; defessus sum ambulando, Ter.; bene ambula, *bon voyage*, Plaut.; ergo ambula, *be off with you*, Plaut.; ambulare in jus, *to go to law*, Plaut.; of soldiers, *to march;* eodem modo ambulat

Caesar ut, etc., Cic. ; *to travel over, to traverse ;* with acc., quum (Xerxes) maria ambulavisset, Cic. **II.** Transf., **A.** Of things, Nilus immenso longitudinis spatio ambulans, Plin. **B.** *to go for a walk,* in hortis cum Galba, Cic.

ambūro -ussi -ustum, 3. **I. A.** *to burn round, to scorch, to burn up ;* ille domi suae vivus *exustus* est ; hic sociorum ambustus incendio tamen ex illa flamma periculoque evasit, Cic. ; ambusta tigna, Liv. ; *of lightning, to scorch ;* ambustus Phaethon, Hor. Subst., **ambustum** -i, n. *a burn,* Plin. **B.** Of cold, *to nip, numb ;* ambusti multorum artus vi frigoris, Tac. **II.** Transf., *to injure;* ambustas fortunarum mearum reliquias, Cic. ; damnatione collegae et sua prope ambustus evaserat, Liv.

ambustus -a -um, partic. of amburo.

ămellus -i, m. *the purple Italian starwort,* Verg.

Āmēnānus -i, m. (Ἀμέναvος), *a river of Sicily,* now *Indicello;* also used as an adject., Amenana flumina, Ov.

āmens -entis, *mad, insane, senseless ;* metu, Liv. ; animi, *in mind,* Verg. ; homo audacissimus atque amentissimus, Cic. ; consilium amentissimum, Cic.

āmentĭa -ae, f. (amens), *insanity, madness, folly ;* in istam amentiam incidere, Cic.

āmento, 1. (amentum), *to furnish with a strap;* hastae, Cic. ; and (in a figure) hastae amentatae, *ready-made arguments,* Cic.

āmentum -i, n. (for agimentum). **I.** *a strap, thong,* Caes. **II.** *a shoe-tie,* Plin.

Ămĕrĭa -ae, f. *a town in Umbria,* now *Amelia;* hence adj., **Amĕrīnus** -a -um, *belonging to Ameria.*

Ămĕrĭola -ae, f. *a town in the Sabine country.*

āmĕs -itis, m. *a forked pole,* for suspending fowlers' nets, Hor.

Ămestrātus -i, f. (Ἀμήστρατος), *a town on the north coast of Sicily, on the Halaesus,* now *Mestretta ;* hence **Amestrātīnūs** -a -um, *belonging to Amestratus.*

ămĕthystĭnus -a -um, 1, *amethyst-coloured ;* vestes, Mart. Subst., **ămĕthystĭna** -ōrum, n. (sc. vestimenta), *dresses of that colour,* Juv. ; 2, *set with amethysts,* Mart.

ămĕthystus -i, f. (ἀμέθυστος), *an amethyst,* Plin.

amfractus = anfractus (q.v.).

ămīca -ae, f. (v. amicus).

ămīcē, adv. (amicus), *in a friendly manner ;* amice facis, Cic. ; amice pauperiem pati, *willingly,* Hor. ; with dat., vivere vitae hominum amice, *as the friend of man,* Cic.

ămīcĭo -īcui and -ixi -ictum, 4. 1, *to clothe, wrap round;* amictus toga, laena, pallio, Cic. ; 2, Transf., *to cover, conceal;* nube cava amictus, Verg. ; piper et quidquid chartis amicitur ineptis, *wrapped up in,* Hor.

ămīcĭtĕr = amice (q.v.).

ămīcĭtĭa -ae, f. (amicus), *friendship.* **I.** Lit., **A.** *friendship* between persons ; est mihi amicitia cum aliquo, Cic. ; amicitiam facere, jungere, gerere, dimittere, dissociare, dissolvere, Cic. **B.** In politics, *friendship* between states ; omni tempore in fide atque amicitia civitatis Aeduae fuisse, Caes. ; in amicitiam populi Romani venire, Liv. ; **C.** Of inanimate things, *sympathy,* Plin. **II.** Meton., *friends;* parcet amicitiis et dignitatibus, Cic.

ămīcĭtĭes -ēi. f. = amicitia (q.v.).

ămictus -ūs, m. (amicio). **A.** *putting on of* a *garment,* Cic. ; esp., *the manner of wearing the toga;* nihil est facilius quam amictum imitari alicuius aut statum aut motum, Cic. **B.** Meton., 1, *a garment,* Verg. ; 2, *covering ;* nebulae amictus, Verg.

ămĭcŭla -ae, f. v. amiculus.

ămĭcŭlum -i, n. (amicio), *a mantle, cloak,* Cic.

ămĭcŭlus -i, m., and **ămĭcŭla** -ae, f. (dim. of amicus), *a little friend,* Cic.

ămīcus -a -um (amo). **I.** *friendly, well-wishing, inclined, favourable to.* **A.** Absol., amicus amicissimus animus, Cic. ; homines sibi conciliare amiciores, Cic. **B.** With inter se, or erga aliquem, or dat., velim ut tibi amicus sit, Cic. ; amica luto sus, Hor. ; of things, silentia lunae, Verg. ; amicum est mihi, *it pleases me ;* secundum te nihil est mihi amicius solitudine, Cic. **II.** Subst., **A. amicus** -i, m., a, *a friend ;* intimus, Cic. ; veritatis, Cic. ; of states, socius atque amicus, Cic. ; b, in plur., *the retinue of a Roman governor,* Suet. ; *the courtiers of the emperor,* Suet. **B. amica** -ae, f. *a friend* or a *mistress,* Cic.

Āmĭnaeus -a -um, *belonging to Aminaea, a district of Picenum, famous for its wine,* Verg.

Amĭsĭa -ae. **I.** m. (ὁ Ἀμισίας), *a river in North Germany,* now the *Ems.* **II.** f. *a place at the mouth of the Ems.*

āmissĭo -ōnis, f. (amitto), *a loss;* oppidorum, Cic. ; esp. *of a loss through death;* liberorum, Cic.

āmissus -ūs, m. = amissio (q.v.).

Ămīsus (Ămīsŏs) -i, f. (Ἀμισος), and **Ămīsum** -i, n. *a town in Pontus,* now *Samsun.*

ămīta -ae, f. *a father's sister* (opp. matertera, q.v.), *an aunt,* Cic.

Ămĭternum -i, n. *a town in the Sabine country,* birthplace of the historian Sallust ; hence adj., **Amĭternīnus** -a -um, and **Amĭternus** -a -um, *Amiternian.*

āmitto -mīsi -missum, 3. *to send away, to let go.* **I. A.** Lit., Plaut. **B.** Transf., *to give up;* omnes has provincias, Cic. **II.** *to let go, to let slip.* **A.** Lit., praedam de manibus, Cic. ; occasionem, Cic. ; tempus, Cic. **B.** *to lose ;* vitam, Cic. ; litem, Cic. ; mentem, Cic. ; fidem, *credit,* Phaedr. ; esp. *to lose by death;* filium consularem, Cic.

Ammĭānus Marcellīnus -i, m. *historian of the fourth century* A.D., who wrote a history of Rome from Nerva to Valens (91–378 A.D.), the first books of which are lost.

Ammōn (Hammon) -ōnis, m. (Ἀμμων), *a Libyan deity,* with a temple in the Oasis of Siwah, worshipped in Rome under the name of Jupiter Ammon, Cic. Adj., **Ammōnĭăcus** -a -um.

amnĭcŏla -ae, c. (amnis and colo), *dwelling by the river-side;* salix, Ov.

amnĭcŭlus -i, m. (dim. of amnis), *a little river,* Liv.

amnis -is, m. (orig. apnis, from same root as Lat. aqua, Skr. ap). **A.** *a stream of water, a river;* non tenuis rivulus sed abundantissimus amnis, Cic. **B.** Poet., *the stream;* secundo amni, *down stream,* Verg. ; *the ocean,* Verg. ; *a torrent;* ruunt de montibus amnes, Verg. ; *water,* Verg.

ămo, 1. *to love from inclination* or *passion* (diligere, *to love from esteem*) ; me non diligi solum, verum etiam amari, Cic. ; 1, a, aliquem mirifice, Cic. ; b, amare se, *to love one-self selfishly,* Cic. ; c, aliquem de, or in aliqua re or quod, *to feel obliged* or *bound to a person;* te multum amamus, quod ea abs te diligenter parvoque curata sunt, Cic. ; amabo te, **or**

ămăbo, *please, be so good;* amabo te, advola, Cic.; d, *to lore something;* amavi amorem tuum prout ipse amabat litteras, Cic.; amat janua limen, *clings to,* Hor.; with infin., hic ames dici pater atque princeps, Hor.; e, *to be wont, accustomed;* quae ira fieri amat, Sall.; 2, *to love passionately, sensually;* ibi primum insuevit exercitus populi Romani amare, *to lust,* Sall.

ămoenē, adv. (amoenus), *pleasantly,* Plaut.

ămoenĭtas -ātis, f. (amoenus). I. Gen., *pleasantness.* II. Esp., a, *of situation,* hortorum, Cic.; urbium, Liv.; plur., amoenitates orarum ac litorum, Cic.; absol., *pleasant situation,* Cic.; b, *of other things,* vitae, Tac.; as a term of endearment, mea amoenitas, Plaut.

ămoenus -a -um. I. Gen., *pleasant, delightful.* II. Esp., a, *of place;* locus, Cic. Subst., ămoena -orum, n. *pleasant places,* Tac.; b, *of other things,* vita, Tac.; cultus, *luxurious, splendid,* Liv.; c, *of persons,* Venus, Plaut.

ămōlĭor, 4. dep. *to remove.* I. Lit., objecta onera, Liv.; se, *to take oneself off,* Plaut. II. *to get rid of.* A. Of persons, Octaviam uxorem, Tac. B. Of something unpleasant, *to remove;* dedecus, Tac. C. In speech, *to pass over;* amolior et amoveo nomen meum, Liv.

ămōmum -i, n. (ἄμωμον), *a shrub, from which a costly balsam was prepared,* Verg.

ămŏr (amos) -ōris, m. (amo), *love from inclination* (caritas, *love from esteem*). I. A. Lit., noster in te amor, Cic.; amplecti or prosequi aliquem amore, Cic.; habere aliquem in amore, Cic.; habere amorem erga aliquem, Cic.; in amore esse alicui, *to be loved by some one,* Cic.; in a bad sense, *passion;* amore perdita est, Plaut.; plur., amores hominum in te, Cic.; mihi est in amoribus, *he is loved by me,* Cic.; in a bad sense, amores et hae deliciae quae vocantur, Cic.; personif., *the god* Cupid, Verg. B. Meton., *the object of love, darling;* amor et deliciae generis humani (Titus), Suet.; esp. in plur., amores et deliciae tuae, Cic. II. *love for something, desire;* consulatus, Cic.; cognitionis, Cic.; scribendi, Hor.

ămōtĭo -ōnis, f. (amoveo), *a removing;* doloris, Cic.

ămŏvĕo -mōvi -mōtum, 2. *to move away, remove.* I. Lit., A. Gen., 1, *of things,* neque in amovendo neque in exportando frumento, Cic.; 2, *of persons,* aliquem ex istis locis, Cic.; aliquem ab altaribus, Liv.; amoto patre, *in the absence of the father,* Tac.; se amovere, *to depart,* Ter. B. Esp., 1, euphem, *to steal;* boves per dolum amotae, Hor.; 2, *to banish;* in insulam, Tac. II. Transf. A. Gen., *to remove something unpleasant;* ab se culpam, Liv. B. Partic., 1, *of things,* sensum doloris mei a sententia dicenda amovebo, Cic.; 2, *of persons, to remove from a post;* Saturnium quaestorem a sua frumentaria procuratione, Cic.

Amphĭărāus -i, m. (Ἀμφιάραος), *a celebrated Argive soothsayer, son of Oïcles* (or *Apollo*) *and Hypermnestra, wife of Eriphyle, father of Alcmaeon and Amphilochus,* participator against his will in the expedition of the Seven against Thebes; when flying from Polyclymenus he was, by the order of Zeus, taken up from the earth and made immortal; hence a, Amphĭărāĕus -a -um, *belonging to Amphiaraus;* b, Amphĭărĕĭădēs -ae, m. *son of Amphiaraus* = Alcmaeon, Ov.

amphĭbŏlĭa -ae, f. (ἀμφιβολία), *ambiguity, double meaning,* Cic.

Amphictyŏnes -um, m. (Ἀμφικτύονες), the *Amphictyons, a religious assembly of representatives of the Greek states,* held first at Thermopylae and afterwards at Delphi.

Amphĭlŏchi -ōrum, m. *a people in Acarnania;* hence Amphĭlŏchĭa -ae, f. *their country;* and Argos Amphĭlŏchĭum, or Amphĭlŏchĭcum -i, n. *its chief town,* now *Philokia.*

Amphĭon -ōnis, m. (Ἀμφίων), *king of Thebes, and husband of Niobe;* said to have raised the walls of Thebes by the magical power of his lyre; hence arces Amphionis, i.e. *Thebes,* Ov. Adj., Amphīŏnĭus -a -um, *belonging to Amphion.*

Amphĭpŏlis, acc. -im, f. (Ἀμφίπολις), *Athenian colony in Macedonia, on the Strymon.*

amphisbaena -ae, f. (ἀμφίσβαινα), *a kind of African snake,* Plin.

Amphissa -ae, f. (Ἄμφισσα), *a town of the Ozolian Locrians,* near modern Salona; hence Amphissĭus -a -um.

amphĭthĕātrālis -e (amphitheatrum), *belonging to the amphitheatre;* spectaculum, Plin.

amphĭthĕātrĭcus -a -um = amphitheatralis (q.v.).

amphĭthĕātrum -i, n. (ἀμφιθέατρον), *an amphitheatre, an oval building for gladiatorial shows and public spectacles,* Tac.

Amphĭtrītē -ēs, f. (Ἀμφιτρίτη), *the wife of Neptune, goddess of the sea;* hence, *the sea,* Ov.

Amphĭtryŏn and Amphĭtrŭo -ōnis, m. (Ἀμφιτρύων), *king of Thebes, and husband of Alcmaena, the mother of Hercules by Jupiter,* hence Amphĭtryŏnĭădēs -ae, m. *the son of Amphitryon,* i.e. *Hercules,* Verg.

amphŏra -ae, f. (ἀμφορεύς). A. *a two-handled vase, pitcher, or jug,* generally made of clay or glass, chiefly used for wine, Hor.; hence, meton., *wine,* Hor.; used also for honey, Cic., oil, Cato. B. 1, *a measure for liquids,* 2 urnae or 8 congii or 48 sextarii, about 5¾ gallons; 2, *measure of the tonnage of a ship,* as we use ton, about 80 Roman pounds; naves onerariae quarum minor nulla erat duum millium amphorum, Cic.

amphŏrālis -e (amphora), *containing an amphora,* Plin.

Amphrȳsŏs -i, m. (Ἀμφρυσός), *a stream in Phthiotis,* near which Apollo kept the flocks of Admetus; pastor ab Amphryso, *Apollo,* Verg. Adj., Amphrȳsĭus -a -um; Amphrysia vates, *the Sibyll* (beloved by Apollo), Verg.

amplē, adv. (amplus). I. *richly, amply;* amplissime dare agrum, *most liberally,* Cic. II. *magnificently, splendidly,* exornare triclinium, Cic.; of oratory, elate et ample loqui, *with dignity and weight,* Cic. Esp. in compar., amplĭus, I. *more;* amplius aequo lamentari, Lucr. II. A. Of space or time, *more, farther;* non luctabor tecum amplius, Cic.; a, amplius pronuntiare, *a judicial formula, to adjourn the hearing of a case;* quum consules re audita amplius de consilii sententia pronuntiavissent, Cic.; b, a formula in contracts, sales, etc., amplius non peti, *that no further claim is made,* Cic.; c, esp. of definite measures of time, with nom., acc., abl., genit., generally without quam; amplius centum annis Romani, Cic.; non amplius pedum DC., Caes.; triennio amplius, Cic.; absol., xvi. non amplius legiones, 16 *legions and no more,* Liv. B. *further, more, in addition;* quid est quod jam amplius exspectes, Cic.; hence the formulae, a, non dico amplius, *I say nothing further,* Cic.; b, hoc or eo amplius; besides, moreover; esp. t. t. in the senate, Servilio assentior et hoc amplius censeo, *I give my adhesion to Servilius' proposal, but make an addition to it,* Cic.

amplector -plexus sum -plecti, 3. dep. (amb and plecto). I. Lit. *to surround, encircle.* A. with the arms or hands, *to embrace;* 1, aram,

Tac. ; dextram,Verg. ; **2,** *to embrace lovingly,* Ov.
B. *to surround;* tellurem alis (of night), *to cover,*
Verg. ; hostium aciem, Liv. ; *of* fire, ignis proxima
quaeque et deinceps continua amplexus, Liv.
II. Transf., **A.** *to welcome, receive;* libenter talem
amicum, Cic. **B.** 1, *to love, esteem;* aliquem
amore, Cic. ; **2,** *to prize;* tanto amore suas possessiones, Cic. ; **3,** *to embrace in thought, to consider;* si judex non omnia amplectetur consilio,
Cic. ; **4,** *to embrace,* in the sense of *to include*
or *comprise;* quod idem interdum virtutis
nomine amplectimur, Cic. ; **5,** *to embrace* or
touch on in discourse; argumentum pluribus
verbis, Cic. ; omnia communiter, Liv.

amplexor, 1. dep. (intens. of amplector) ;
1, *to surround, encircle, embrace,* Cic. ; transf.,
Appius totum me amplexatur, Cic. ; **2,** *to
honour, esteem;* aequabilitatem juris, Cic.

amplexus -ūs, m. (amplector). **A.** *a surrounding, encircling, embrace;* draconis or serpentis, Cic. ; aliquem amplexibus necare (of a
snake), Ov. **B.** Transf., terrarum amplexu, (the)
circuit of the earth, Liv.

amplĭātĭo -ōnis, f. (amplio), *the adjournment
of a suit,* Sen.

amplĭfĭcātĭo -ōnis, f. (amplifico), *an enlarging, increasing.* **I.** Lit., rei familiaris, Cic. **II.**
Transf., **a,** *an enlarging, heightening;* honoris
et gloriae, Cic. ; **b,** in rhetoric, *enlargement, am-
plification,* Cic.

amplĭfĭcātor -ōris, m. (amplifico), *one who
enlarges;* dignitatis, Cic.

amplĭfĭco 1. (amplus and facio), *to enlarge.* **A.** Lit., civitatem, Cic.; divitias, Cic.
B. Transf., **1,** *to increase;* voluptatem, Cic. ;
2, in rhetoric, *to dilate upon, magnify;* aliquid
dicendo amplificare atque ornare, Cic.

amplĭo, 1. (amplus), *to make wide, enlarge,
increase.* **I.** Lit., civitatem, Liv. ; equitum
centurias, Liv. **II.** Transf., **a,** *to glorify;* nomen, Mart. ; **b,** legal t.t., *to adjourn the hearing
of a case* (see under ample II. A.a); causam, Cic.

amplĭter, adv. = ample (q.v.).

amplĭtūdo -ĭnis, f. (amplus), *breadth, size.*
A. Lit., simulacrum modica amplitudine, Cic.
B. Transf., **1,** amplitudines quaedam bonorum,
increase of property, Cic. ; **2,** *greatness;* nominis,
Cic. ; **3,** *dignity, grandeur;* maxima cum gloria
ad summam amplitudinem pervenire, Cic. ; **4,**
dignity of expression; Platonis, Cic.

amplus -a -um, adj. with compar. and
superl., *large, spacious, ample.* **A.** Lit., 1, of
space, size, etc. ; domus, Cic. ; 2, of number,
height, quantity, etc. ; pecunia amplissima, Cic. ;
ampliores copiae, Caes. Neut. subst., **amplius,** imponebat amplius quam ferre possent,
Cic. ; with genit., si amplius obsidum dare velit,
Caes. **B.** Transf., **1,** *great, important;* occasio,
Cic. ; ampla spes, Sall. ; **2,** *honourable;* praemia,
Cic. ; amplum Tuscis ratus, *thinking it an
honour for the Etruscans,* Liv. ; **3,** *excellent, highly
esteemed;* amplae et honestae familiae, Cic. ;
amplissimi viri, *men of the highest position,* Cic. ;
especially of public offices, amplissimus honor,
the consulship, Cic.

Ampsancti (sc. lacus), or **Ampsanctus**
-i, m. *a lake in the country of the Hirpini,* said
to be one of the entrances to the lower world.

ampulla -ae, f. (dim. of amphora; amp(h)-
orula, amporla, ampurla, ampulla). **A.** *a flask,
bottle,* Cic. **B.** Transf., *bombast;* projicit am-
pullas, Hor.

ampullācĕus -a -um (ampulla), *bottle-
shaped,* Plin.

ampullārĭus -i, m. (ampulla), *a bottle-
maker,* Plaut.

ampullor, 1. dep. (ampulla, **B.**), *to speak*
bombastically, Hor.

ampŭtātĭo -ōnis, f. (amputo), *a cutting off,
pruning,* Cic.

ampŭto, 1. *to cut off.* **A.** Lit., 1, of plants
or trees, *to lop* or *prune;* ramos inutiles, Hor. ;
fig., non solum ramos amputare miseriarum,
Cic. ; **2,** *to cut off a part of the body;* caput,
Tac. ; as medical t. t., *to amputate;* in corpore quidquid est pestiferum, Cic. **B.** 1, *to
shorten, diminish;* multitudinem sententiarum,
Cic. ; **2,** amputata loqui, *to speak disconnectedly,*
Cic.

Ampȳcus -i, m. ("Αμπυκος). **I.** *son of
Iapetus, a singer and priest of Ceres,* killed at
the wedding of Perseus by Pettalus. **II.** *one
of the Lapithae, father of Mopsus;* hence, **Am-
pȳcĭdēs** -ae, m. *a descendant of Ampycus,* i.e.
Mopsus.

Ampyx -pȳcis, m. ("Αμπυξ). **I.** *a comrade
of Phineus,* turned into stone *by the Medusa's head
at the wedding of Perseus.* **II.** *one of the Lapithae, killed by the centaur Oiclus at the wedding
of Pirithous.*

ămŭlētum -i, n. (Arab. hamalet = *a pendant*), *a charm, amulet,* Plin.

Ămūlĭus -ĭi, m. *king of Alba Longa,* who
drove his elder brother, Numitor, from the
throne, and exposed in the Tiber Numitor's
grandsons, Romulus and Remus.

ămurca -ae, f. (ἀμόργη), *the oil-lees,* Plin.

ămussis (acc. -im), f. *a carpenter's rule;* ad
amussim, *exactly,* Varr.

Amŷclae -arum, f. ('Αμύκλαι). **I.** *a town in
Laconia, south-east of Sparta;* myth., *home of
the Dioscuri and of Helena.* **II.** *an old town in
Latium* (said to have been founded from Amyclae I.). Adj. **Amŷclaeus** -a -um, *belonging
to Amyclae, Amyclaean;* pluma, *of the swan,* in
allusion to the story of Juppiter and Leda,
Mart. ; fratres, *the Dioscuri,* Verg. ; hence poet.
Laconian; canis, Verg.

ămygdălum -i. n. (ἀμύγδαλον), *an almond,*
Ov.

Ămȳmōnē -ēs, f. ('Αμυμώνη), *daughter of
Danaus, beloved by Neptune,* who in her honour
caused a fountain to spring out of the rock near
Argos.

Amyntas -ae, m. ('Αμύντας), *name of several
Macedonian kings,* the most famous of whom
was Amyntas II., *father of Philip of Macedon,
and grandfather of Alexander the Great;* hence
Amyntĭădēs -ae, m. *Philip.*

Ămyntŏr -ŏris, m. ('Αμύντωρ), *king of the
Dolopes, father of Phoenix;* hence **Amyntŏr-
ĭdēs** -ae, m. *a son of Amyntor = Phoenix,* Ov.

ămystis -ĭdis, f. (ἀμυστις), *the emptying of a
goblet at a draught,* Hor.

Ămȳthāōn -ōnis, m. ('Αμυθάων) *father of
Melampus, Bias, and Aeolia;* hence, **Amȳ-
thāŏnĭus** -a -um, *son of Amythaon.*

ăn, conj. or, *whether,* introduces the second
clause of a direct or indirect double question,
or of a sentence implying doubt. **I. A.** Of sentences implying doubt; **1,** after utrum, utrumne
and ne, honestumne factu sit an turpe, dubitant,
Cic. ; **2,** without a verb of doubt, or *rather;*
non plus duobus an tribus mensibus, Cic. **B.**
Elliptically, where the first clause is to be understood, dubito an, haud scio an, or nescio
an, *I don't know whether it is not, perhaps, possi-
bly;* haud scio an satis sit, eum qui lacesserit,
injuriae suae poenitere, Cic. ; with a negative,
I don't know whether it is; dubitat an turpe non
sit, *whether it is base,* Cic. **C.** Like num, *whether*

(poet. or in post-Augustan prose), quis scit an adjiciant hodiernae crastina summae tempora di superi, Hor. **II.** In direct or indirect questions. **A.** Where both sentences are expressed ; **1,** in direct questions, utrum ea vestra an nostra culpa est, Cic. ; **2,** in indirect questions, id utrum Romano more locutus sit an quo modo Stoici dicunt, postea videro, Cic. **B.** Elliptically, where the first part of the question is suppressed, often to express irony or astonishment, *or then ? ;* an etiam id dubium est? Cic. ; an censes nihil inter nos convenire? Cic.

ănăbāthrum -i, n. (ἀνάβαθρον), *a raised seat* Juv.

Ănăcharsis -ĭdis, m. (Ἀνάχαρσις), *a Scythian who, it was said, visited Athens in the time of Solon.*

Ănacrĕōn -ontis, m. (Ἀνακρέων), *a lyric poet of Teos in Ionia* (559—478 B.C.). Adj., **Anacrĕontius** -a -um, *Anacreontic.*

ănădēma -ătis, n. (ἀνάδημα), *an ornament or fillet for the head,* Lucr.

Ănagnĭa -ae, f. (Ἀναγνία), *a town in Latium, capital of the Hernici,* now *Anagni.* Adj., **Anagnīnus** -a -um, *belonging to Anagnia.*

ănăgnostēs -ae, m. (ἀναγνώστης), *a reader,* Cic.

ănălecta -ae, m. (ἀναλέγω), *a slave whose duty it was to collect and remove crumbs after a meal,* Mart.

ānălŏgĭa -ae, f. (ἀναλογία), *proportion, comparison, analogy,* Varr., Quint.

ănancaeum -i, n. (ἀναγκαῖον, *unavoidable*), *a large drinking cup, bumper,* Plaut.

ănăpaestus -a -um (ἀνάπαιστος), pes, or simply anapaestus, *a metrical foot, an anapaest* (∪ ∪ –), Cic. Subst., a, **anapaestus** -i, m. *a verse composed of anapaests,* Cic. ; b, **anapaestum** -i, n., *a poem in anapaestic verse,* Cic.

ănăphŏră -ae f. (ἀναφορά), **1,** *the rising of the heavenly bodies,* Plin. ; **2,** in rhetoric, *the repetition of a word at the beginning of several sentences* (as in Cic. Verr. ii. 26).

Ănăphē -ēs, f. (Ἀναφη), *an island east of Thera, one of the Sporades,* now *Namfi,* or *Anafi.*

Ănāpus, -i, m. (Ἄναπος), *a river in Sicily, near Syracuse,* now *Anapo.*

Anartes -ium, m. (Ἄναρτοι), *a people in Dacia.*

1. Ănās -ae, m. (Ἄνας), *a river in Spain,* now *Wadi-ana* or *Guadiana.*

2. ănas, ănătis, f. *a duck,* Cic.

ănătĭcŭla -ae, f. (dim. of anas), *a little duck,* Cic.

ănătŏcismus -i, m. (ἀνατοκισμός), *compound interest,* Cic.

Ănaxăgŏras -ae, m. (Ἀναξαγόρας), *a philosopher of the old Ionian school, friend and teacher of Pericles and Euripides.*

Ănaxarchus -i, m. (Ἀνάξαρχος), *a philosopher of Abdera.*

Ănaxĭmander -dri, m. (Ἀναξίμανδρος), *a philosopher of Miletus, pupil of Thales.*

Ănaxĭmĕnes -is, m. (Ἀναξιμένης), *a philosopher of Miletus, pupil of Anaximander.*

anceps -cĭpĭtis, abl. sing. -cipiti (an and caput). **I.** Lit., *two-headed ;* Janus, Ov. ; acumen montis, *two-peaked,* Ov. **II.** Transf., *with two sides.* **A.** *two-edged ;* securis, Ov. **B. 1,** *coming on both sides, behind and before ;* quum anceps hostis et a fronte et a tergo urgeret, Liv. ; anceps proelium, *a battle where the enemy attack on both sides,* Caes. ; anceps metus et ab cive et ab hoste, Liv. ; **2,** *of two natures :* bestiae quasi

ancipites, *amphibious,* Cic. ; anceps faciendi dicendique sapientia, Cic. **C. 1,** *ambiguous ;* oraculum, Liv. ; **2,** *uncertain, undecided ;* belli fortuna, Cic. ; proelium, Liv. ; **3,** *unsettled ;* Lucanus an Apulus anceps, *uncertain whether a Lucanian or an Apulian,* Hor. ; **4,** *dangerous,* hic locus tam anceps, Cic.

Anchĭalos (ūs) -i, f. (Ἀγχίαλος), *a small town of Thrace on the Pontus Euxinus,* now *Akiali.*

Anchīsēs -ae, m. (Ἀγχίσης), *son of Capys and father of Aeneas ;* hence **1,** adj., **Anchīsēus** -a -um, *belonging to Anchises ;* **2, Anchīsĭādēs** -ae, m. *a descendant of Anchises,* i.e. *Aeneas,* Verg.

ancīle -is, n. (connected with *ancus, curved*), **1,** *a shield which fell from heaven in the time of Numa, on the preservation of which the safety of the Roman empire was supposed to depend,* Liv. ; **2,** *any oval shield,* Verg. (heterocl. genit. plur. anciliorum, Hor.).

ancilla -ae, f. *a maid-servant, female slave,* Cic. ; used as an attrib., mulier ancilla, Sall.

ancillārĭŏlus -i. m. (ancilla), *a lover of maid-servants,* Mart.

ancillāris -e (ancilla), *relating to a maid-servant ;* artificium, Cic.

ancillor, 1, dep. (ancilla), *to serve as a maid-servant ;* hence, *to serve slavishly,* Plin.

ancillŭla -ae, f. (dim. of ancilla), *a little maid-servant,* Liv. ; fig., idcirco istam juris scientiam tamquam ancillulam pedisequamque adjunxisti, Cic.

ancīsus -a -um (amb and caedo), *cut round,* Lucr.

Ancōn -ōnis, f. (Ἀγκών, *elbow*), and **Ancōna** -ae, f. *a town in Picenum, on the Adriatic Sea ;* hence **Ancōnĭtānus** -i, m. *an inhabitant of Ancona.*

ancŏra -ae, f. (ἄγκυρα), *an anchor ;* ancoram jacere, Caes. ; figere, pangere, *to cast anchor,* Ov. ; tollere, *to weigh anchor,* Caes. ; consistere ad ancoram, in ancoris, *to lie at anchor,* Caes.

ancŏrāle -is, n. (ancora), *a cable,* Liv.

ancŏrārĭus -a -um (ancora), *belonging to an anchor ;* funis, Caes.

Ancus (see Marcius).

Ancўra -ae, f. (Ἀγκυρα). **I.** *the chief town of the Tectosages, capital of Galatia,* now *Angora ;* hence, **Ancўrānus** -a -um, *belonging to Ancyra ;* Ancyranum monumentum, *an inscription put up by Augustus at the entrance to his temple at Ancyra, relating the chief events of his life.* **II.** *a town in Phrygia, on the borders of Mysia and Lydia.*

andăbătă -ae, m. *a kind of gladiator who fought with a helmet that had no openings for the eyes,* Cic.

Andănĭa -ae, f. (Ἀνδανία), *an old town in Messenia, between Megalopolis and Messene,* now *Andorossa.*

Andecavi -ōrum, m. and **Andes** -ium, m. *a Gallic people on the Loire with a town of the same name,* now *Angers.*

1. Andes, v. Andecavi.

2. Andēs -ium, f. *town in the Mantuan country, birthplace of Virgil,* now *Pietola.*

Andraemōn -ōnis, m. (Ἀνδραίμων). **I.** *father of Amphissus, husband of Dryope.* **II.** (also Andremon) *king of Calydon, father of Thoas.*

Andrīscus -i, m. (Ἀνδρισκος), *a slave who gave himself out to be the son of the Macedonian king Perseus, and caused the Third Macedonian War, which ended with the reduction of Macedonia into a Roman province by Metellus.*

Andrŏgĕōs, or gĕus -i, m. (Ἀνδρόγεως), *son of Minos and Pasiphae, killed by the Athenians, who were consequently attacked and subdued by Minos, and forced to pay a tribute of youths and maidens to the Minotaur.*

andrŏgȳnus -i, m. (ἀνδρόγυνος), *a hermaphrodite,* Liv., Cic.

Andrŏmăchē -ēs and **-cha** -ae, f. (Ἀνδρομάχη), *wife of Hector, and, after the capture of Troy, the captive of Pyrrhus and subsequently wife of Helenus;* appell., *a young and beautiful wife,* Mart.

Andrŏmĕdē -ēs, f., and **-da** -ae, f. (Ἀνδρομέδη), *daughter of the Aethiopian king Cepheus and of Cassiopeia, exposed to a sea-monster, but rescued by Perseus* (acc. -an, Ov., Met., iv. 671, and Ars Am., i. 53.)

Andrŏnīcus -i, m. (Ἀνδρονίκος), L. or T., Livius, *the earliest of the Roman tragic poets, a native of Magna Graecia, the slave of M. Livius Salinator* (about 240 B.C.).

Andrŏs and **Andrus** -i, f. (Ἀνδρος), *the most northerly of the Cyclades, now Andro;* hence adj., **Andrius** -a -um, *Andrian;* subst., **Andria** -ae, f. *the Woman of Andros, name of one of Terence's comedies.*

ānellus -i, m. (dim. of anulus), *a little ring,* Hor.

ănēthum -i, n. (ἄνηθον), *dill, anise,* Verg.

anfractus -ūs, m. (an and frango). **A.** *a turning, bending;* solis, *revolution,* Cic.; anfractus curvus vallis, *winding,* Verg.; recta regione, si nullus anfractus intercederet, *no tortuous windings,* Caes. **B.** Transf., **a,** *legal intricacies;* judiciorum, Cic.; **b,** *prolixity,* Cic.

angellus -i, m. (dim. of angulus) *a little corner,* Lucr.

angīna -ae, f. (ἀγχόνη), *the quinsy,* Plaut.

angĭportum -i, n. and (rarely) **angĭportus** -ūs, m. (ango and portus), *a narrow street,* Cic.

Angĭtĭa (Ancĭtĭa, Anguĭtĭa) -ae, f. *a goddess of the dwellers round the lake Fucinus* (now *Lago di Celano*), *of the Marsi and Marrubii;* nemus Angitiae, *a grove on the west bank of lake Fucinus,* (now *Selva d'Albi*).

Anglĭi -orum, m. *a branch of the Suevi, living in modern Altmark.*

ango, 3. (root ANG, Gr. ΑΓΧ, whence angulus, angustus, ἄγχω). **I.** *to press together, to throttle;* **a,** guttur, Verg.; **b,** *to distress;* ea collisio mistorum omnis generis animantium odore insolito urbanos et agrestem confertum in arta tecta aestu ac vigiliis angebat, Liv. **II.** *to torment, make anxious;* alicujus animum and aliquem, Cic.; angebant ingentis spiritus virum Sicilia Sardiniaque amissae, Liv.; pass., angi animi or animo or simply angi, *to be grieved or troubled;* alicujus decessu, Cic.; de Statio manumisso et nonnullis aliis rebus, Cic.; me angit or angor, followed by quod, or the acc. and the infin., Cic.

angor -ōris, m. (ango). **I.** 1, *a pressing together of the gullet, throttling,* Plin.; 2, *physical distress;* aestu et angore vexata, Liv. **II.** *mental distress, anguish, trouble;* confici angoribus, Cic.

Angrivarĭi -ōrum, m. *a German tribe on the Weser.*

anguĭcŏmus -a -um (anguis and coma), *having snaky hair,* Ov.

anguĭcŭlus -i, m. (dim. of anguis), *a little snake,* Ov.

anguĭfer -fĕra -fĕrum (anguis and fero), *snake-bearing;* Gorgo, Prop.

anguĭgĕna -ae, c. (anguis and geno = gigno), *snake-born,* Ov.

anguilla -ae, f. *an eel,* Plaut.

anguĭmănus -ūs, m. *snake-handed;* elephantus (so called from the snake-like movements of its trunk), Lucr.

anguĭnĕus -a -um (anguis), *pertaining to a snake, snaky,* Ov.

anguīnus -a -um = anguineus (q.v.).

anguĭpes -pĕdis (anguis and pes), *snake-footed,* Ov.

anguis -is, c. (ango). **I.** *a snake,* Cic.; prov., frigidus latet anguis in herba, *there is danger,* Verg. **II.** 1, *the constellation Draco,* Verg.; 2, *the constellation Ophiuchus,* Ov. (abl. angue, rarely—but sometimes in Cicero—angui).

Anguĭtĕnens -entis, m. (anguis and teneo, translation of Gr. Ὀφιοῦχος) *the Snake-holder; the constellation Ophiuchus,* Cic.

Angŭĭtĭa, v. Angitia.

angŭlātus -a -um (angulus), *angular, cornered,* Cic.

angŭlōsus -a -um (angulus), *full of corners,* Plin.

angŭlus -i. m. (root ANG, Gr. ΑΓΧ, whence ango, angustus, ἄγχω). **A.** *a corner, angle,* Caes. **B.** 1, *an angle in mathematics,* Cic.; 2, *the extremity or corner of a country;* extremus angulus agri Bruttii, Liv.; 3, *a bastion,* Liv.; 4, *a retired spot;* in ullo angulo Italiae, Cic.; fig., ad istas verborum angustias et ad omnes litterarum angulos, Cic.

angustē, adv., with compar. and superl. (angustus) *narrowly, in a confined manner.* **I.** Lit., **A.** *of space,* sedere, Cic, **B.** Of number or quantity, *sparingly;* uti re frumentaria, Caes. **II. A.** *in a narrow, circumscribed manner;* angustius apud Graecos valere, Cic. **B.** *briefly;* dicere, Cic.

angustĭa -ae, f., gen. pl. **angŭstĭae** -ārum, f. (angustus), *narrowness.* **A.** Lit., fretorum, Cic.; spiritus, *shortness of breath,* Cic.; absol., *defiles, narrow passes,* Caes. **B.** Transf., 1, *obscure or narrow reasoning;* tantas in angustias et stoicorum dumeta (orationem) compellimus, Cic.; 2, *of time, shortness;* angustiae temporis, Cic.; 3, *of circumstances, straitened condition, poverty;* pecuniae, aerarii, rei familiaris, Cic.; absol., *poverty,* ap. Cic.; 4, *difficulty, distress;* in angustias adduci, Cic.; 5, *of disposition, narrow-mindedness,* Cic.

angustĭclāvĭus ii, m. (angustus and clavus), *wearing a narrow stripe of purple on his tunic;* epithet of a plebeian military tribune, Suet.

angustus -a -um (root ANG, Gr. ΑΓΧ, whence ango, ἄγχω, angulus), *narrow.* **A.** Lit., 1, of space, *narrow, strait* (opp. latus); pons, Cic.; 2, of other things, habenae, *tightly drawn,* Tib.; spiritus angustior, *short breath,* Cic. Subst., **angustum** -i, n. *a narrow space;* in angusto tendere, *to encamp in a narrow space,* Liv.; angusta viarum, Verg. **B.** Transf., 1, in angustum deducere perturbationes, *to bridle,* Cic.; in angustum concludere, *to confine, limit,* Cic.; 2, of time, *short;* nox, Ov.; 3, of circumstances, *straitened, poor, scarce;* res frumentaria, Caes.; angustas civium domos, Tac.; liberalitas angustior, Cic.; 4, of other things, *precarious, critical, uncertain;* res angustae, Cic.; fides angustior, Caes.; 5, of character, *narrow-minded;* alii minuti et angusti, Cic.; of perception, sensus, Cic.; 6, of speech, **a,** *concise;* disputationes, Cic.; **b,** *petty, narrow, subtle;* concertationes, Cic. Subst., **angustum** -i, n. *difficulty;* res est in angusto, Caes.

ănhēlātĭo -ōnis = anhelitus (q. v.).

ănhēlātŏr -ōris, m. (anhelo), *one who breathes with difficulty*, Plin.

ănhēlītus -ūs, m. (anhelo). **A.** *short, quick breathing, puffing, panting;* anhelitum ducere, Plaut. ; anhelitus moventur, Cic. ; *asthma*, Plin. **B.** Transf., 1, *breath*, Ov. ; 2, *exhalation, vapour;* terrae, Cic.

ănhēlo, 1. (am and helo). **I.** Intransit., *to draw a heavy breath, puff, pant.* **A.** Lit., Verg. **B.** Of lifeless objects, *to roar;* fornacibus ignis anhelat, Verg. **II.** Transit., **A.** *to produce with panting;* verba inflata et quasi anhelata gravius, Cic. **B.** *to pant for, desire eagerly;* scelus, Cic.

ănhēlus -a -um (anhelo) = anhelans. **I.** *puffing, panting;* equi, Verg. **II.** Meton., *causing to pant;* febris, Ov.

ănĭcŭla -ae, f. (dim. of anus), *a little old woman*, Cic.

Ănĭēn -ēnis, v. Anis.

Ăniensis, Ănĭēnus, v. Anio.

Ănĭgrŏs -i, m. ('Ανιγρος), *a river in Triphylia (Elis).*

ănīlis -e (anus), *belonging to or like an old woman;* vultus, Verg. ; rugae, Ov. ; esp. with the notion of superstition or folly, superstitio, Cic. ; fabellae, *old wives' tales*, Cic.

ănīlĭtas -ātis, f. (anilis), *old age* (of women), Cat.

ănīlĭtĕr, adv. (anilis), *like an old woman;* id dicitis superstitiose atque aniliter, Cic.

ănĭma -ae, f. (connected with ἄω, ἄημι). **I.** Lit. **A.** *wind;* impellunt animae lintea Thraciae, *the north winds*, Hor. ; quantum ignes animaeque valent, of Vulcan's bellows, Verg. **B.** 1, *the air as an element*, Cic. ; 2, *the breath;* animam ducere, Cic. ; continere, Cic. **II.** Transf., **A.** *the vital principle, the soul* (anima, *physical;* animus, *spiritual*) ; 1, Lit., a, neque in homine inesse animum vel animam nec in bestia, Cic. ; *the spirits of the dead*, Suet. ; *the vital principle in plants*, Plin. ; b, *life;* animam edere, *to give up the ghost*, Cic. ; animam agere, *to be in the agonies of death*, Cic. ; trahere, *to drag on existence*, Liv. ; dum anima est, *as long as he is alive*, Cic. ; of the blood as the seat of life, purpuream vomit animam, *life-blood*, Verg. ; 2, Meton., *a living being;* ova parire, non animam, Enn. ; used as a term of endearment, *soul;* vos meae carissimae animae, Cic. ; egregiae animae, Veig. **B.** (Like animus), *the rational soul;* anima rationis consiliique particeps, Cic.

ănĭmābĭlis, -e (animo), *animating, giving life;* natura, Cic.

ănĭmadversĭo -ōnis, f. (animadverto). **I.** *perception, observation;* excitare animadversionem et diligentiam ut ne, &c., Cic. **II.** Transf. **A.** *punishment;* censoria, Cic. ; Dolabellae in audaces sceleratos, Cic. ; vitiorum, Cic. ; used euphem. for *capital punishment*, Cic. **B.** *censure, blame*, Cic.

ănĭmadversor -ōris, m. (animadverto), *an observer*, Cic.

ănĭmadverto (**ănĭmadvorto**), -verti (-vorti), -versum (-vorsum), 3. (for animum adverto). **I.** *to take notice of, attend to;* animadverti in pace, Cic. ; followed by relat. sent. ; ut animadvertam quae fiant, Cic. ; by ut or ne and the subj., animadvertant ne callida assentatione capiantur, Cic. ; t.t., of the lictor, *to clear the road for the consul;* consul animadvertere proximum lictorem jussit, Liv. **II.** Transf. **A.** *to perceive:* ecquid animadvertis horum silentium, Cic. ; **with** acc. and infin., animadvertit

Caesar unos Sequanos nihil earum rerum facere, Caes. ; with rel. sent., animadvertant quid de religione existimandum sit, Cic. ; with quum and the subj., animadversum saepe est, quum cor animantis alicujus evulsum palpitaret, Cic. **B.** 1, *to take notice of,* i.e. *to take measures against, to punish;* generally followed by in ; in judices quosdam, Cic. ; res animadvertenda, Cic. ; euphem. *to punish with death*, Tac. ; 2, *to blame;* ea sunt animadvertenda peccata maxime, Cic.

ănĭmal -ālis, n. (for animale, from anima), 1, *a living being, animal;* quum inter inanimum atque animal hos maximum intersit, quod animal agit aliquid, Cic. ; 2, *an animal,* as opposed to a man, Cic. ; so contemptuously of an animal (like English *brute, beast*), funestum illud animal, Cic.

ănĭmālis -e (anima), 1, *consisting of air, airy;* natura, Cic. ; 2, *belonging to life, living;* intelligentia, Cic. ; exemplum, Cic.

ănĭmans -antis, (p. adj. from animo), *living.* **I.** Adj. ; mundus, Cic. **II.** Subst., masc., fem., and neut., *a living being, animal;* masc., alius animans, Cic. ; fem., ceterae animantes, Cic. ; neut., animantia omnia, Cic.

ănĭmātĭo -ōnis, f. (animo). **I.** Lit., *an animating.* Meton. (= animal), *a living being;* divinae animationis species, Cic.

1. **ănĭmātus** -a -um (p. adj. from animo), 1, *alive, animated;* anteponantur animata inanimis, Cic. ; 2, *disposed in mind, inclined;* a, morally or politically, Pompeius animatus melius quam paratus, Cic. ; with erga and acc., Cic. ; with in and acc., Cic. ; b, *courageously inclined, courageous*, Cic.

2. **ănĭmātus** -ūs, m. (animo), *life, animation*, Plin.

ănĭmo, 1. (anima and animus), 1, *to animate, give life to;* omnia animat, format, alit, Cic. ; animare in, with acc., *to change a lifeless into a living thing;* guttas animant in angues, Ov. ; 2, *to endow with a particular disposition;* pueros orientes animari atque formari, Cic.

ănĭmōsē, adv. (animosus), *courageously;* animose et fortiter facere aliquid, Cic.

ănĭmōsus -a -um (animus), *courageous, high-spirited, ardent, passionate, furious.* **I.** Gen., **A.** Lit., fortis et animosus vir, Cic. ; equus, Ov. **B.** Transf., of winds, poet., ventus, Ov. ; Euri, Verg. ; with abl., *proud of;* animosus spoliis, Ov. **II.** Esp., *intent on;* corruptor, *a briber who spares no expense*, Tac.

ănĭmŭla -ae, f. (dim. of anima). **I.** *a little soul,* ap. Cic. **II.** *a little life;* tuae litterae quae mihi quidquam quasi animulae instillarunt, *have refreshed me a little*, Cic.

ănĭmŭlus -i, m. (dim. of animus), *a term of endearment;* mi animule, *my life*, Plaut.

ănĭmus -i, m. (root AN, connected with anima and ἄνεμος). **I.** *the spiritual principle of life in man,* opposed to corpus, *the body,* and to anima, *the principle of physical life;* credo deos immortales sparsisse animos in corpora humana, Cic. ; rarely of animals, bestiae quarum animi sunt rationis expertes, Cic. **II. A.** *the soul as the seat of feeling;* 1, animus alius ad alia vitia propensior, Cic. ; genit. animi (almost pleonastic) with adj. or subst., aeger animi, Liv. ; dubius animi, Verg. ; animi metus, Cic. ; with animo or animi and a verb, animo tremere, Cic. ; animi or animis pendere, *to be anxious*, Cic. ; 2, *character, disposition;* apertus et simplex, Cic. ; esse angusti animi atque demissi, Cic. ; poet., transf., *nature;* exuerint silvestrem animum, Verg. ; 3, *inclination towards some* one; bono (or alieno) animo esse in aliquem, Caes. ; mi anime, *"my dear,"* Plaut. ; 4, *courage, confidence, spirit;* fac animo magno fortique sis, Cic. ; neutris animus est ad pugnandum, Liv. ; so in plur., animi cadunt, *courage sinks,* Cic. ; transf., *fire* or *vivacity* in a speech, quae vis, qui animus, quae dignitas illi oratori defuit, Cic. ; poet., of a top, dant animos plagae, Verg. ; so (esp. in plural) *pride, arrogance,* uxor, inflata adhuc regiis animis et muliebri spiritu, Liv. ; jam insolentiam noratis hominis, noratis animos ejus et spiritus tribunicios, Cic. ; pone animos, Verg. ; 5, *wish, desire;* militum animis expletis, Liv. ; animi voluptatisque causa, Caes. **B.** *the soul as the seat of the will;* ad omnia et animo et consilio paratus, Cic. ; eo ad te animo venimus ut, &c., *with the resolve to,* &c., Cic. ; habeo in animo, with infin., *I am resolved,* Cic. ; so in animum habeo, Liv. ; est mihi in animo, Cic. ; avet animus, with infin., Cic. ; inclinat animus, with ut and the subj., Liv. ; ex animo, *willingly,* Cic. **C.** *the soul as the seat of the thoughts;* 1, omnium mentes animosque perturbare, Caes. ; 2, *consciousness;* deficientibus animis, Liv. ; *thought,* memor in bene meritos animus, Cic.

Anĭo -ōnis (or -enis from original Sabine form **Anĭen**), m., poet., **Anĭēnus** -i, m. *the Anio, a river, tributary to the Tiber.* Adj., 1, **Anĭensis** -e, 2, **Anĭēnus** -a -um, *belonging to the Anio.*

Ănĭus -ĭi, m. *priest of Apollo, and king of the island of Delos, friend of Anchises and Aeneas.*

Anna -ae, f., a, *sister of Dido;* b, Anna Perenna, *a Roman goddess.*

annālis -e (annus). **I.** Adj., **A.** *lasting a year,* Varr. **B.** *relating to a year;* lex, *the law which determined the minimum age for the great offices of state,* Cic. **II.** Subst., **annālis** -is, m. (sc. liber) and plur. **annāles** -ium, m. (libri) *yearly records, annals,* in early times kept by the Pontifices (hence annales pontificum or annales maximi), in later times composed by the so-called annalists (as Q. Fabius Pictor), Cic.

annăto, 1. (ad-nato), 1. *to swim to,* Plin. ; 2, *to swim by the side of,* Sen.

annāvĭgo, 1. (ad-navigo), *to voyage to,* Plin.

annecto (ad-necto) -nexui -nexum, 3. *to bind to, connect with.* **I.** Lit., stomachus ad linguam annectitur, Cic. **II.** Transf., 1, physically, animos corporibus, Lucr. ; 2, *to connect,* in a speech, rebus praesentibus futuras adjungere atque annectere, Cic.

annexus -ūs, m. (annecto), *a binding to, connection,* Tac.

Annĭbal, v. Hannibal.

Annĭcĕrĭi -ōrum, m. ('Ἀννικέρειοι), *a sect of Cyrenaic philosophers.*

annĭcŭlus -a -um (annus), *one year old;* neptis, Nep.

annītor (ad-nitor) -nisus or -nixus, 3. dep. **I.** Lit., *to lean upon;* ad aliquod tamquam adminiculum, Cic. **II.** Transf., *to strive after;* de triumpho, Cic. ; with ad and the acc. of the gerund, ad obtinendum hesternum decus, Liv. ; foll. by ut or ne, with the subj., Liv. ; also by the infin., Liv.

Annĭus -a -um, gens, *an old plebeian family at Rome,* of which T. Annius Milo was a member, v. Milo. Adj. **Anniānus** -a -um, *belonging to an Annius or Annia.*

annĭversārĭus -a -um (annus and verto), *recurring every year;* sacra, Cic. ; arma, Liv.

1. **anno** (ad-no), 1. **I.** *to swim to,* or *near;* with acc., naves, Caes. ; with dat., vestris oris, Verg.; navibus, Liv.; generally with ad and

3*

the acc., ad eam urbem, Cic. **II.** *to swim with,* or *alongside of;* pedites annantes equis, Tac.

2. **Anno,** v. Hanno.

annōna -ae, f. (annus). **I.** *yearly produce, crop;* 1, Gen., Col. ; 2, *means of subsistence,* esp. *grain;* annonae caritas, *dearness,* Cic.; vilitas, *cheapness,* Cic. **II.** Meton., *price of provisions;* annona salaria, *price of salt,* Liv. ; esp. of corn; annonae varietas, *fluctuation in the price of corn,* Cic. ; esp. *high price of corn;* solatium annonae, Cic. ; annonam queri, *to complain of the high price of corn,* Liv. ; fig., vilis amicorum annona, *friends are to be had cheap,* Hor.

annōsus -a -um (annus), *full of years, long-lived;* cornix, Hor.

annŏtātĭo (ad-notatio) -ōnis, f. (annoto), *remark, annotation,* Plin.

annŏtātor -ōris, m. (annoto), *one who remarks, an observer,* Plin.

annŏtīnus -a -um (annus), *a year old, belonging to last year;* naves, Caes.

annŏto (ad-noto), 1. *to note down.* **I.** Lit., annotatum est, with acc. and infin., Tac. ; librum, *to make remarks on a book,* Plin. **II.** Transf. *to remark, take notice of,* Plin.

annŭmĕro (ad-numero), 1. **I.** *to count out, pay;* tibi denarios, Cic. **II.** *to reckon with;* with dat., aliquem his duobus, Cic. ; with in and the abl., aliquem patronorum in grege, Cic.

annuntĭo (ad-nuntio), 1. *to announce, tell, relate,* Plin.

annŭo (ad-nuo) -ŭi, 3. **I.** *to nod to;* simul atque sibi annuisset, Cic. **II. A.** *to assent by a nod* or *sign;* id toto capite, Cic. ; with dat., of person, petenti, Verg. ; of the thing, quibus (praemiis) etiam rex ipse annuerat, Liv. ; annue coeptis, *be favourable to our undertaking,* Verg. ; with fut. infin., quum annuisset se venturum, Liv. **B.** alicui aliquid, *to promise;* caeli arcem, Verg. **C.** *to point out by a sign;* quos iste annuerat, Cic.

annus -i, m. (root AN connected with anulus); *revolution of time,* hence *year.* **I.** Lit., exeunte anno, Cic. ; anno superiore, Cic. ; omnibus annis, *annually,* Caes. ; tempus anni, *time of the year, season,* Cic. ; adv. phrases, 1, anno, *a whole year,* Liv. ; *in each year, yearly,* Liv. ; so, in anno, *in each year,* Cic. ; annum, *a full year,* Cic. ; in annum, *for a year,* Liv. ; ad annum, *next year,* Cic. ; intra annum, *within the space of a year,* Liv. ; 2, of the years of a person's life; annos LXX natus, *seventy years old,* Cic. ; Hannibal annorum ferme novem, *when nine years old,* Caes. ; habere annos viginti, Cic. ; annum agere quartum et octogesimum, Cic. ; hence, like aetas, *old age,* confectus annis, Sall. ; 3, *the year of a person's life at which he could stand for a magistracy;* is enim erat annus, quo per legis ei consulem fieri liceret, Caes. ; annus meus, tuus, suus, Cic. ; so, *the year of office;* prorogare annum, Cic. ; 4, *a year* with relation to the weather, healthiness, &c.; locuples frugibus, Hor. ; gravissimus et pestilentissimus, Cic. ; 5, annus magnus, *a cycle of years,* Cic. **II.** Transf. (poet.), 1, *time of year:* pomifer, *autumn;* hibernus, *winter,* Hor. ; 2, *the growth of a year,* Cic.

annŭto (ad-nuto), 1. (intens. of annuo), *to nod to, make a sign to,* Plaut.

annūtrĭo (ad-nutrio), *to nourish at* or *near to,* Plin.

ānnŭus -a -um (annus). **I.** *lasting for a year;* magistratus, Caes. **II.** *returning every year, annual;* labor agricolarum, Cic. ; hence, subst., **ānnŭum** -i, n. or **ānnŭa** -orum, n. *a yearly salary, pension, annuity,* Plin.

anquīro -quisīvi -quisītum (an and quaero), 3. *to search carefully, to inquire after.* **I.** Lit., omnia quae sunt ad vivendum necessaria anquirere et parare, Cic. **II.** Transf., **A.** Transit., *to investigate;* mens semper aliquid anquirit aut agit, Cic. **B.** Intransit., *legal* t. t. *to set an inquiry on foot;* de perduellione, Liv. ; capite or capitis, *on a charge involving capital punishment,* Liv.

ansa -ae, f. *a handle, haft.* **I.** Lit., ansa poculi, canthari, Verg. ; crepidae, *the eye through which a shoe-tie is passed,* Tib. **II.** Transf., *occasion, opportunity;* habere reprehensionis ansam aliquam, Cic.

Ansancti, v. Ampsancti.

ansātus -a -um (ansa), *provided with a handle;* homo, *a man with handles,* i.e., *with arms akimbo,* Plaut.

1. **anser** -ēris, m. *a goose,* Cic.

2. **Anser** -ēris, m. *a wanton poet, friend of the triumvir Antonius.*

ansērīnus -a -um (anser), *relating or belonging to a goose,* Plin.

Antaeus -i, m. (Ἀνταῖος), *a powerful giant, ruler of Libya, who compelled all strangers coming to his country to wrestle with him, at last slain by Hercules, who, observing that each time Antaeus fell on the earth he gained new force, held him aloft in the air and so killed him.*

Antandros (us) -i, f. (Ἀντανδρος), *a town of Mysia,* now *Antandro;* hence adj., **Antandrīus** -a -um, *of Antandros.*

antĕ (old form, anti, whence antidea, antideo, connected with ἄντα, ἀντί, ἄντην), prep. & adv. *before.* **I.** Adv., **A.** Of place, ante aut post pugnare, Liv. **B.** Of time, **a,** *before;* multis ante saeculis, Cic. ; ante quam, *before that;* ut te ante videret quam a vita discederet, Cic. ; anno ante quam mortuus est, Cic. ; **b,** very rarely used as adj., neque ignari sumus ante malorum (= τῶν πρὶν κακῶν), *of former sufferings,* Verg. **II.** Prep., *before.* **A.** Of place, 1, Lit., ante pedes, Cic. ; causam ante aliquem dicere, *before a judge,* Cic. ; 2, Transf., of preference, quem ante me diligo, *whom I love more than myself,* Cic. ; so ante alios, Liv. ; ante omnes, Tac. **B.** of time, ante lucem, Cic. ; ante me, *before my time,* Cic. ; often with a partic., ante urbem conditam, *before the founding of the city,* Cic. ; esp. **a,** ante annum, *a year ago,* Plin. ; **b,** ante rem, *before the fight,* Liv. ; ante tempus, *before the right time,* Liv. ; **c,** ante diem, (α) *before the day,* Ov., (β) *before the day fixed by fate,* Ov. ; **d,** ante id tempus, *up to the present time,* Caes. ; **e,** ante certam diem, *within a fixed time;* equites ante certam diem decederent, Cic. ; **f,** so to mark the date, ante diem quartum Idus Martias (A.D. IV. Id. Mart.), *the fourth day before the Ides of March,* i.e. *the twelfth of March,* Cic.

antĕā (ante and abl. eā), adv., *before, formerly,* Cic. ; followed by quam, Cic.

antĕambŭlo -ōnis, m. (ante and ambulare), *a running footman to clear the way,* Mart.

antĕcānem (translation of προκύων), *a star, the little dog,* Cic.

antĕcāpio -cēpi -ceptum, 3. **I.** Lit., *to seize beforehand;* pontem Mosae fluminis, Tac. ; locum castris, Sall. **II.** Transf., **a,** *to anticipate, to prepare beforehand;* quae bello usui forent, Sall. ; *to excite,* or *provoke beforehand;* ea omnia (famem aut sitim, etc.) luxu, Sall. ; *to use beforehand;* noctem, *not to wait for,* Sall. ; **b,** philosoph. t. t., anteceptam animo rei quandam informationem, *preconceived idea,* Cic.

antĕcēdens -entis, p. adj. (from antecedo), *preceding.* **I.** Plin. **II.** Esp., philosoph. t. t.,

causa, *the antecedent cause.* Subst., **antĕcēdens**, *the antecedent cause;* oftener in plur. antecedentia, Cic.

antĕcēdo -cessi -cessum, 3. *to go before, precede.* **I.** Gen., **A.** Lit., in space, agmen, Caes. ; absol., stellae tum antecedunt, tum subsequuntur, Cic. **B.** Transf., in time (with dat. and acc.), alicui aetate paulum, Cic. **II.** Esp. *to hasten before, to overtake.* **A.** Lit., nuntios oppugnati oppidi famamque, Caes. **B.** Transf., *to excel;* with dat., quantum natura hominis pecudibus reliquisque bestiis antecedat, Cic. ; with acc., aliquem scientia atque usu nauticarum rerum, Caes. ; absol., et auctoritate et aetate et usu rerum, Cic.

antĕcello -ēre, no perf. or sup., *to distinguish oneself, excel;* 1, of persons, with dat. of person and acc. of thing, omnibus ingenii gloria, Cic. ; with acc. of the person and abl. of the thing, omnes fortuna, Tac. ; with abl. of thing alone, militari laude, Cic. ; 2, of things, duae aedes sacrae quae longe ceteris antecellant, Cic.

antĕcessio -ōnis, f. (antecedo), 1, *a preceding or going before;* quae in orbibus conversiones antecessionesque eveniunt, Cic. ; 2, *the antecedent cause;* homo causas rerum videt earumque praegressus et quasi antecessiones non ignorat, Cic.

antĕcessus -ūs, m. (antecedo), *a going before;* in antecessum, *in advance,* Sen.

antĕcursor -ōris, m. (antecurro), *one who runs before;* plur. *pioneers, advance guard of an army,* Caes.

antĕeo -īvi (and gen.) -īi, -īre (old form, antideo), *to go before.* **I.** Lit., alicui, Cic. ; aliquem, Hor. **II.** Transf., **A.** *to go before* in time ; alicui aetate, Cic. ; si anteiissent delicta, *had happened before,* Tac. **B.** 1, *to excel;* alicui sapientia, Cic. ; omnes intelligentia, Cic. ; absol., *to distinguish oneself;* operibus, *by actions,* Cic. ; 2, *to anticipate;* damnationem veneno Tac. (in poets and post-Augustan prose, the syllable after ante disappears, anteāt, Ov. ; antibo, Tac.).

antĕfĕro -tūli -lātum, -ferre. **I.** *to carry before;* viginti clarissimarum familiarum imagines, Tac. **II.** Transf., **A.** *to prefer;* longe omnibus unum Demosthenem, Cic. ; iniquissimam pacem justissimo bello, Cic. **B.** *to anticipate, consider beforehand;* quod est dies allatura, id consilio anteferre debemus, Cic.

antĕfixus -a -um, *fastened in front;* truncis arborum antefixa ora, Tac. Subst., **antĕfixa**, -ōrum, n. *ornaments fixed on the roofs and gutters of houses;* antefixa fictilia deorum Romanorum, Liv.

antĕgrĕdior -gressus -grĕdi, dep. (ante and gradior), *to go before.* **I.** Lit., stella Veneris antegreditur solem, Cic. **II.** Transf., causae antegressae, *antecedent causes,* Cic.

antĕhăbĕo, 2. *to prefer,* Tac.

antĕhāc (old form, antidhac), adv. (ante and abl. hāc), *before this time, formerly,* Cic.

antĕlātus -a -um, v. antefero.

antĕlūcānus -a -um (ante and lux), *happening before daybreak;* tempus, Cic. ; cena, Cic.

antĕmĕrīdiānus -a -um, *before noon,* Cic.

antĕmitto, more properly separated, ante and mitto q.v.

Antemnae -ārum, f. *Sabine town at the junction of the Anio with the Tiber;* hence, **Antemnātes** -ium, m. *the inhabitants of Antemnae.*

antenna (antemna) -ae, f. (an = ἀνά and tendere), *a sail-yard;* antennas ad malos destinare, Caes.

Antēnŏr -ŏris, m. (Ἀντήνωρ) *a Trojan, the legendary founder of Patavium* (Padua); hence, **1, Antēnŏrēus** -a -um, *belonging to Antenor, Patavian;* **2, Antēnŏrīdes** -ae, m. (Ἀντηνορίδης), *a descendant of Antenor.*

antĕpagmentum -i., n. *the lining of a door* or *post, a jamb,* Cato.

antĕpēs -pĕdis, m. *the forefoot,* Cic.

antĕpīlāni -ōrum, m. *the soldiers who fought in front of the pilani* or *triarii,* i.e. *the hastati and principes,* Liv.

antĕpōno -pŏsŭi -pŏsĭtum, 3. **I.** *to place before;* alicui prandium, Plaut. **II.** *to place in front.* **A.** Lit., equitum locos sedilibus plebis, Tac. **B.** Transf., *to prefer;* se alicui, Cic.; amicitiam omnibus rebus humanis, Cic.

antĕpŏtens -entis, *very powerful, very fortunate,* Plaut.

Antĕrōs -ōtis, m. (Ἀντέρως), 1, *the genius* or *avenger of slighted love,* Cic. ; 2, *a kind of amethyst,* Plin.

antes -ium, m. *rows* or *ranks,* e.g. of vines, Verg.

antĕsignānus -i, m. (ante and signum), plur. antesignani, *chosen soldiers who fought in front of the line to support the cavalry, skirmishers,* Caes. ; hence, sing., *a leader,* Cic.

antesto (antisto) -stĭti, 1. *to stand before;* transf., *to surpass;* with dat. of person and abl. of thing, multum omnibus (dat.) corporum viribus (abl.), Cic. ; absol., *to be prominent,* Cic.

antestor, 1. dep. (contr. from antetestor), legal t. t., *to call to witness,* Hor. The formula was "licet antestari?" used by the demandant, and the person whose witness was required held up the lap of his ear to express his consent: used once by Cicero without reference to judicial proceedings.

antĕvĕnĭo -vēni -ventum, 4. **I.** Lit., **A.** *to come before, to get the start of;* per tramites occultos exercitum Metelli, Sall. **II.** Transf., **A.** *to anticipate, prevent;* consilia et insidias hostium, Sall. **B.** *to excel;* per virtutem nobilitatem, Sall.

antĕverto, antĕvorto -verti (-vorti) -versum (-vorsum), 3. and dep. **antĕvortor** -vorti. **I.** Lit., *to come* or *go before, to precede;* stella tum antevertens tum subsequens, Cic. **II.** Transf., **A.** *to anticipate, hinder by anticipating;* atque id ipsum quum tecum agere conarer, Fannius antevertit, Cic. **B.** *to prefer;* Caesar omnibus consiliis antevertendum existimavit ut Narbonem proficisceretur, Caes.

Anthēdōn -ŏnis, f. (Ἀνθηδών), *town and state of the Boeotian league on the river Messapius,* now *Lukisi.*

Anthēmūsĭa -ae, f. and **Anthēmūsĭas** -ădis, f. *a town in Mesopotamia.*

anthĭās -ae, m. (ἀνθίας), *a sea-fish,* Ov.

anthŏlŏgĭca, genit. -ŏn, n. (ἀνθολογικά), *anthology, a collection of extracts and small poems,* Plin.

Antiānus, Antiās, v. Antium.

Antĭcāto -ōnis, m. *the Anticato, a work of C. Jul. Caesar in two books, in answer to Cicero's Cato,* Juv.

anticĭpātĭo -ōnis, f. (anticipo), *a preconception, innate idea,* Cic.

antĭcĭpo, 1. (ante and capio), 1, *to take* or *receive before, anticipate;* quod ita sit informatum anticipatumque mentibus nostris, Cic. ; viam, *to travel over before,* Ov. ; ludos, *to celebrate before their time,* Suet. ; 2, *to come before,* Lucr.

Antĭclēa and **-clīa** -ae, f. (Ἀντίκλεια),

daughter of Autolycus, wife of Laertes, mother of Ulysses.

antīcus -a -um (ante), *forward, in front* (opp. posticus), pars, Cic.

Antĭcȳra -ae, f. (Ἀντίκυρα), *a town in Phocis, famous for its hellebore,* now *Aspro Spiti,* Hor.

antidea, antideo, antidhac, v. antea, anteeo, antehac.

antĭdŏtum -i, n. (ἀντίδοτον), *an antidote,* Suet.

Antĭgĕnēs -is, m. (Ἀντιγένης). **I.** *a general of Alexander the Great,* Nep. **II.** *a shepherd,* Verg.

Antĭgĕnĭdas -ae, m. and **-īdēs** -ae, m. (Ἀντιγενίδης), *name of two celebrated flute-players, one of whom, a Theban, flourished about* 440 B.C., *the other, a son of Dionysius, about* 338 B.C.

Antĭgŏnē -ēs, f. and **Antĭgŏna** -ae, f. (Ἀντιγόνη). **I.** *daughter of Oedipus, sister of Polynices and Eteocles, put to death for burying her brother against the command of the king of Thebes.* **II.** *daughter of Laomedon, king of Troy, changed into a stork by Hera.*

Antĭgŏnēa -ae, f. (Ἀντιγόνεια or Ἀντιγονία) *name of several towns, the most important of which were—a, a town on the Celydnus, in Epirus;* hence, **Antĭgŏnensis** -e, *belonging to Antigonia;* b, *a town in Macedonia.*

Antĭgŏnus -i, m. (Ἀντίγονος), *name of several of the successors of Alexander the Great, the most celebrated of whom was* Antigonus I., *born* 385 B.C., *father of Demetrius Poliorcetes, ruler of Phrygia, and, after·Alexander's death, of Pamphylia and Lycia, killed at Ipsus* 301 B.C.

Antĭlĭbānus -i, m. (Ἀντιλίβανος) *a mountain range in Phoenicia. running parallel to Mount Libanus,* now *Dschebel Escharki.*

Antĭlŏchus -i, m. (Ἀντίλοχος), *son of Nestor, friend of Achilles.*

Antĭmachus -i, m. (Ἀντίμαχος), *a Greek poet, contemporary with Plato.*

Antĭnŏus -i, m. (Ἀντίνοος), *a beautiful youth, beloved by the emperor Hadrian, who gave him divine honours on his early death.*

Antĭochīa -ae, f. (Ἀντιόχεια), *name of several towns.* **I.** *Antiochia Epidaphnes* (ἡ ἐπὶ Δάφνης, Plin.), *capital of Syria, on the river Orontes,* now *Antakia.* **II.** *town of Caria, on the Maeander;* hence, adj., **Antĭochensis** -e and **Antĭochīnus** -a -um, *belonging to Antioch.*

Antĭochus -i, m. (Ἀντίοχος). **I.** *name of thirteen Syrian kings, the most important of whom were—a,* Antiochus III., *Magnus, protector of Hannibal in his exile, conquered by L. Corn. Scipio;* b, Antiochus IV., *Epiphanes, who was deterred by the Roman envoy, L. Popillius, from seizing Egypt;* c, Antiochus X., *whose son,* Antiochus XIII., *came to Rome with his brother to uphold their claims on Egypt.* **II.** *name of several kings of Commagene.* **III.** Antiochus *of Ascalon, the last philosopher of the Academic school of philosophers, teacher of Varro and Cicero;* hence 1, **Antĭochīus** -a -um, *belonging to the philosopher Antiochus.* Subst., a, **Antĭochii** -orum, m. *the disciples of Antiochus;* b, ista Antiochia, *the dogmas of Antiochus;* 2, **Antĭochīnus** -a -um, a, *belonging to Antiochus III.;* b, *belonging to the philosopher Antiochus.*

Antĭopa -ae, f. and **Antĭopē** -ēs, f. (Ἀντιόπη), 1, *daughter of Nycteus, mother of Amphion and Zethus;* 2, *mother of the Pierides.*

Antĭpătĕr -tri, m. (Ἀντίπατρος). **I.** *name of several kings of Macedonia, the most important of whom was the confidant of Philip and Alexander the Great. king of Macedonia after Alexan-*

der's death. **II.** *name of several Greek philosophers;* **a,** Antipater Cyrenaicus, *a disciple of the elder Aristippus;* **b,** Antipater of Tarsus, *a Stoic, teacher of Panaetius.* **III.** L. Caelius Antipater, **v.** Caelius.

Antĭpătrĭa -ae, f. (Ἀντιπατρία), *a town in Macedonia, on the border of Illyria.*

Antĭphătēs -ae, m. (Ἀντιφάτης). **I.** *ruler of the cannibal Laestrygones.* **II.** *a son of Sarpedon, killed by Turnus.*

Antĭphōn -ontis (Ἀντιφῶν), **1,** *a celebrated Athenian orator,* 479-411 B.C.; **2,** *a sophist, contemporary and adversary of Socrates;* **3,** *a freedman and actor.*

Antĭpŏlis -is, f. (Ἀντίπολις), *town of the Massilians in Gallia Narbonensis, now Antibes.*

antĭquārĭus -a -um (antiquus), *belonging to antiquity.* Subst., **antĭquārĭus** -ii, m. and **antĭquārĭa** -ae, f., *an antiquary,* Juv., Suet.

antĭquē, adv. (antiquus), *in an ancient manner,* Hor.

antĭquĭtas -ātis, f. (antiquus). **I.** *antiquity, ancient times,* Cic. **II.** Meton., **1,** *the history of ancient times,* Cic.; hence plur. *the ancients,* Cic.; **2,** *the good old times, primitive virtue, integrity,* Cic.; **3,** *great age;* generis, Cic.

antĭquĭtŭs, adv. (antiquus), **1,** *formerly, in ancient times,* Caes.; **2,** *from antiquity,* Liv.

antĭquo, **1.** (antiquus), *to leave in its former state;* hence, *to reject a bill;* legem, rogationem, Cic.

antĭquus -a -um (for anticus, from ante). **1.** *that which excels all other things in worth;* in compar. and superl., *more or most weighty, important, preferable;* id antiquius consuli fuit, *the consul preferred that,* Liv.; ne quid vita existimem antiquius, *more important,* Cic.; nihil ei fuisset antiquius quam (followed by the infin.), Cic.; navalis apparatus ei semper antiquissima cura fuit, Cic. **II.** *that which is before in point of time.* **A.** Relative, *old, ancient previous, once existing;* **a,** antiquae munitiones, Caes.; causa antiquior memoria tua, Cic.; subst., nam illa nimis antiqua praetereo, Cic.; **b,** esp. with the notion of what is *simple, pure, innocent;* antiqui homines, Cic. **B.** Absol., *having existed for a long time, old, ancient, venerable;* tuus antiquissimus amicus, Cic.; esp. of towns, urbs, Verg. Subst., **antiqui** -orum. m. *the people of old time, ancient authors, old statesmen, men of old,* Cic.

Antissa -ae, f. (Ἄντισσα), *a town on a small island near Lesbos;* hence, **Antissaei** -orum, m. *the Antissaeans.*

antistēs -stĭtis, c. (antisto). **I.** *a presiding priest or priestess;* sacrorum, Cic. **II.** Transf., *master in any art;* artis dicendi, Cic.

Antisthĕnēs -is and -ae, m. (Ἀντισθένης), *a Greek philosopher, founder of the Cynic school.*

antistĭta -ae, f. (antistes), *a presiding priestess,* Cic., Ov.

antisto, v. antesto.

antithĕton -i, n. (ἀντίθετον), *a figure of rhetoric, antithesis, opposition,* Cic.

Antĭum -ii, n. (Ἄντιον), *an old town of Latium on the sea-coast,* now Torre or Porto d'Anzio; hence, **1, Antĭānus** -a -um; **2, Antĭas** -ātis, *belonging to Antium.*

antlĭa -ae, f. (ἀντλίον), *a pump,* Mart.

Antōnĭaster -tri, m. *an imitator of the oratory of Antonius,* Cic.

Antōnīnus -i, m. *a name of several Roman emperors, the most notable of whom are,* **1,** Antoninus Pius, *ruled from* 138-161 A.D.; **2,** M. Aurelius

Antoninus Philosphus, *son-in-law and adopted son of the former, ruled from* 161-180 A.D; **3,** M. Aurelius Antoninus, v. Heliogabalus.

Antōnĭus -a -um, gens, *the name of a Roman family, the most distinguished members of which were:* (1) M. Antonius, *surnamed Orator, born* B.C. 144, *put to death by Marius and Cinna* 88; *introduced by Cicero as a speaker in the dialogue* De Oratore. (2) M. Antonius Creticus, *son of* (1) *despatched against the pirates of the eastern Mediterranean in* 74 B.C. (3) C. Antonius, *second son of the preceding, the accomplice of Catiline, colleague with Cicero in the consulship,* B.C. 63. (4) M. Antonius Triumvir, *son of* (2), *born* B.C. 83, *the bitter enemy of Cicero, after Caesar's death triumvir with Octavianus and Lepidus, defeated by Octavianus at the battle of Actium* (B.C. 81); *killed himself shortly after.* (5) Iulus Antonius, *son of* (4), *by Fulvia, brought up by the elder Octavia;* hence, adj., **Antōnĭānŭs** -a -um, *of or relating to Antonius.*

antrum -i, n. (ἄντρον), *a cave,* Ov., Verg.; transf., *the hollow of a tree;* exesae arboris antro, Verg.; *of a litter,* vehi clauso antro, Juv.

Anūbis -bĭdis, m. (Ἄνουβίς, Egyptian Anup, or Anupu), *an Egyptian god, represented with a dog's head;* latratur A., Verg.

ānūlārĭus -a -um (anulus), *belonging to a seal ring;* scalae, *a place in Rome,* Suet. Subst., **anularius** -i, m. *a ring maker,* Cic.

ānūlātus -a -um (anulus), *beringed, ornamented with rings;* aures, Plaut.

ānūlus, annŭlus -i, m. (1. anus), *a ring,* Esp. **I.** *a finger or signet ring;* in ejusmodi cera centum sigilla imprimere hoc anulo, Cic.; vilissima utensilium anulo clausa, *sealed up,* Tac.; anulus equestris, *the gold ring which was the sign of a knight in Rome,* Hor.; anulum invenire, *to be raised to the rank of a knight,* Cic. **II.** Of objects similar in form, **1,** *a curtain ring,* Plin.; **2,** *the link of a fetter,* Plin.; **3,** *a ringlet of hair,* Mart.

1. ānus -i, m. *the fundament,* Cic.

2. ānŭs -ūs, f. *an old woman,* Cic.; anus Cumaea, *the Sibyl,* Ov.; in apposition, *old;* sacerdos, Verg.; *of animals and things,* cerva, Ov.; amphora, Mart.; Appia via, Prop.

anxĭē, adv. (anxius), *anxiously,* Sall.

anxĭĕtas -ātis, f. (anxius). **I.** *anxiety, anxiousness, as a trait in a person's character,* while angor is the transitory feeling of anxiety, Cic.; also = angor, *grief, anguish,* Ov. **II.** Transf. *painful accuracy,* Quint.

anxĭfer -fĕra -fĕrum (anxius and fero), *causing anxiety,* Cic.

anxĭtūdo -ĭnis, f. (anxius), *anxiousness,* Cic.

anxĭus -a -um (ango). **I.** *anxious, uneasy;* anxii senes, Cic.; anxium habere aliquem, *to make anxious,* Tac.; anxius animo, Sall.; with abl. of cause, ira et metu, Sall.; with genit., furti, Ov.; with de and the abl., de successore, Suet.; with pro, pro mundi regno, Ov.; followed by ne, Sall.; an . . . an, Tac.; ne (enclitic) . . . an, Sall.; quonam modo, Tac.; unde, Hor. **II.** Transf., *causing anxiety or anguish;* aegritudines, Cic.

Anxur -ŭris, m. and n. **I.** m. Anxur (Axur), and Anxurus, *a deity of the Volscians, identified with the Etruscan Vejovis;* Anxurus Juppiter, Verg. **II.** n. *an old town of the Volsci, on the sea-coast, afterwards called Terracina.* Adj., **Anxŭrnās** -ātis, *belonging to Anxur.*

Aōn -ŏnis, m. (Ἄων), *son of Poseidon, an old Boeotian hero;* hence **1, Aōnes** -um, acc. -as, m. (Ἄονες), Boeotian; **2, Aōnĭa** -ae, f. (Ἀονία), *mythic name of Boeotia, in which were* *the mountain Helicon and the spring Aganippe, the resort of the Muses;* 3, **Aŏnĭdēs** -um, f. *the Muses;* 4, **Aŏnĭus** -a -um (Ἀόνιος) *belonging to Aonia;* vertex, *Helicon,* Verg.; vir, *Hercules, born at Thebes,* Ov.; juvenis, *Hippomenes,* Ov.; deus, *Bacchus,* Ov.; fons and aquae, *Aganippe,* Ov.; sorores, *the Muses,* Ov.; vates, *a poet,* Ov.

Aornos -i, m. and f. (ἄορνος, *without birds*), *the lake of Avernus,* Verg.

Aŏus -i, m. (Ἀῷος), *a river in Illyria, now Viosa or Vovussa.*

ăpăgĕ, interj., *away with thee! be off!* Ter., Plaut.

Ăpămēa and **-ĭa** -ae, f. (Ἀπάμεια), 1, *a town of Syria on the Orontes, now Afamiah or Famit;* 2, *a town of Phrygia on the Maeander;* 3, *a town of Bithynia.* Adj., **Ăpămensis** -e and **Ăpămēnus** -a -um, *belonging to Apamea.*

Ăpellēs -is, m. (Ἀπελλῆς), *one of the greatest Greek painters, friend of Alexander the Great.* Adj., **Ăpellēus** -a -um.

Ăpennīnĭcŏla -ae, c. (Apenninus and colo), *an inhabitant of the Apennines,* Verg.

Ăpennīnĭgĕna -ae, c. (Apenninus and gigno), *one born upon the Apennines,* Ov.

Ăpennīnus -i, m. (connected with Keltic Pen, a mountain-top), *the chain of the Apennines,* a mountain range running down through the centre of Italy.

ăper, apri, m. *a wild boar,* Cic.; prov., uno in saltu duos apros capere, *to kill two birds with one stone,* Plaut.; apros immittere liquidis fontibus, *to do something absurd and perverse,* Verg.

Ăperantĭi -ōrum, m. (Ἀπεραντοί). *a people in northern Aetolia;* hence **Ăperantĭa** -ae, f. *their country.*

ăpĕrio -pĕrui -pertum, 4. (ad-pario, from root PAR, whence pario). **I.** *to uncover, to lay bare, to expose to view.* **A.** Lit., caput, *to uncover,* Cic. **B.** Transf., occulta, *to make known,* Cic.; sententiam suam, *to pronounce,* Cic.; casus futuros, *to predict,* Ov.; refl., se aperire and middle aperiri, *to reveal one's true character;* studioque aperimur in ipso, Ov.; memet ipse aperio quis sim, Liv. **II.** *to open what was shut, to unclose.* **A.** Lit., fores, Cic.; epistolam, Cic.; fundamenta templi, *to excavate,* Liv.; fig., fontes eloquentiae, Cic. **B.** Transf., *to open up a country, render it accessible;* Pontum, Cic.; Syriam, Tac.; locum asylum, *to throw open as an asylum,* Liv; ludum, *to open a school,* Cic.; annum, *to begin the year* (poet., of the constellation Aries, because, on the entry of the sun into it the new year began for the farmer), Verg.

ăpertē, adv., with compar. and superl. (apertus), **a,** *openly;* mentiri, Cic.; **b,** *without concealment, straightforwardly;* scribere, Cic.; dicere, Cic.

ăperto, 1. (intens. of aperio), *to lay bare* Plaut.

ăpertus -a -um, p. adj., with compar. and superl. (from aperio), *open, uncovered.* **I. A.** Lit., aether, caelum, *clear,* Verg.; naut. t.t., naves, *undecked,* Cic.; milit. t.t., *undefended;* latus, humerus, *unshielded, exposed,* Caes. **B.** Transf. *clear, unconcealed, manifest;* **a,** actio, Cic.; apertum latrocinium,, Cic.; apertum est, *it is clear,* followed by acc. and infin., esse aliquod numen praestantissimae mentis, Cic.; in aperto esse, **a,** *to be evident;* quo ad cognoscendum omnia illustria magio magisque in aperto sint, Sall.; **b,** *to be practicable;* fessos hieme hostes aggredi, Tac.; **c,** of speech, *clear, intelligible, unconcealed;* narratio aperta, Cic.; apertis or apertissimis verbis, Cic.; **d,** of character, *frank, straightforward, open;* animus, Cic.; homo, Cic.

II. *unclosed, open, free, unhindered, accessible.* **A.** Lit., **a,** vastum atque apertum mare, Caes.; campi ad dimicandum aperti, Liv. Subst., **ăpertum** -i., n. *an open space;* in aperto castra locare, Liv.; **b,** milit. t.t., *open;* proelium, Liv. **B.** Transf. *open, accessible;* beate vivendi via, Cic.

ăpex -ĭcis, m. *the top* or *summit.* **I.** Gen., mentis, Ov.; flammae, Ov. **II.** Esp., **A.** *the top of the conical cap of the Roman flamines,* hence *the cap itself;* lanigeri apices, Verg.; apicem Dialem alicui imponere, *to make a person flamen of Jove,* Liv.; also *the tiara of eastern kings and satraps,* regum apices, Hor.; so fig., *crown;* apex senectutis est auctoritas, Cic. **B.** *a helmet,* Verg. **C.** Gramm., *the long mark over a vowel,* Quint.

ăphaerĕma -ătis, n. (ἀφαίρεμα), *a coarse kind of grits,* Plin.

Ăphăreus -ĕi, m. (Ἀφαρεύς). **I.** *a king of the Messenians, father of Lynceus and Idas;* hence **Ăpharēĭus** -a -um, *belonging to Aphareus.* **II.** *a Centaur, whose arm was broken by Theseus at the wedding of Pirithous.*

aphractus -i, f. (ἄφρακτος), *a long undecked boat,* Cic.

Ăphrŏdīsĭa -ōrum, n. (ἀφροδίσια), *the festival of Aphrodite,* Plaut.

Ăphrŏdīsĭas -ădis, f. (Ἀφροδισιάς), *name of several towns;* 1, *a town on the borders of Phrygia and Caria, now Gheira;* hence **Ăphrŏdīsĭenses** -ium, m. *the people of Aphrodisias;* 2, *a harbour in Cilicia, near Porto Cavaliere.*

ăpĭăcus -a -um (apium), *like parsley,* Cato.

ăpĭanus -a -um (apis), *relating or belonging to bees,* Plin.

ăpĭārĭus -ĭi, m. (apis), *a bee-keeper,* Plin.

ăpĭcātus -a -um (apex), *adorned with the priest's cap,* Ov.

Ăpĭcĭus -ĭi, m. *a Roman name;* M. Gabius Apicius, *a celebrated epicure in the time of Tiberius.*

Ăpĭdănus -i, m. (Ἀπιδανός), *a river in Thessaly, tributary of the Peneus.*

ăpīnae -arum, f. *trifles,* Mart.

Ăpīōlae -arum, f. *a town in Latium.*

Ăpĭōn -ōnis, m. *surname of Ptolemaeus, king of Cyrene.*

1. **ăpis** -is, f. (ἐμπίς), *a bee,* Cic., Verg.

2. **Ăpis** -is, acc. -im, m. (Ἆπις), *a sacred bull of the Egyptians at Memphis.*

ăpiscor, aptus, 3. dep. **I.** *to attain to, come up to, reach;* mare, Cic. **II.** Transf., 1, *to lay hold of, grasp,* Lucr.; 2, *to attain to* (the object of one's desire), cujus (finis bonorum) apiscendi causa, Cic.; summum honorem, Liv.; once in Tac., with genit., dominationis.

ăpium -ĭi, n. *parsley,* Hor.

ăplustrĕ -is, n. (ἄφλαστον), generally plur. aplustria -ium, n. and aplustra -ōrum, n. *the carved stern of a ship, with its ornaments,* Lucr.

ăpŏclēti -ōrum, m. (ἀπόκλητοι). *the supreme council of the Aetolian League,* Liv.

ăpŏdytērium -ĭi, n. (ἀποδυτήριον), *the dressing-room in a bath,* Cic.

Ăpollo -ĭnis (-ōnis), m. (Ἀπόλλων), *Apollo, son of Juppiter and Latona, brother of Diana, god of archery, music, poetry, prophesying, and the sun, born at Delos;* hence, Delius vates, Verg.; and simply Delius, Cic.; ad Apollinis (sc. aedem), *to the temple of Apollo,* Liv.; aperitur Apollo, *the temple of Apollo becomes visible,* Verg.; promontorium Apollinis, *a promontory north of Utica, over against Sardinia, now Cape Zibib,* Liv.; hence, **A.** Adj., **Ăpollĭnāris** -e, *sacred* *to Apollo* ; ludi, *games held in honour of Apollo on the 5th of July*, Cic. Subst., **Ăpollĭnāre**, -is, n. *a place sacred to Apollo*, Liv.; **B. Ăpollĭnĕus** -a -um, *pertaining to Apollo;* urbs, *Delos*, Ov. ; proles, *Aesculapius*, Ov. ; vates, *Orpheus*, Ov. ; ars, *prophecy* or *medicine*, Ov.

Ăpollŏdōrus -i, m. (Ἀπολλόδωρος), 1, *a rhetorician of Pergamum, teacher of Augustus ;* 2, *grammarian and mythological writer of Athens*, about 140 B.C.

Ăpollōnĭa -ae, f. (Ἀπολλωνία), 1, *citadel near Naupactus*, Liv. ; 2, *town in Illyria*, now *Polonia* or *Polina*, Cic. ; 3, *town in Macedonia*, now *Polina*, Liv. ; hence, a, **Ăpollōnĭātēs** -ae, m. *an inhabitant of Apollonia ;* b, **Ăpollōnĭensis** -e, *belonging to Apollonia.*

Ăpollōnis -idis,*f. (Ἀπολλωνίς), *a town in Lydia ;* hence **Ăpollōnĭdensis** -e, *belonging to Apollonis.*

Ăpollōnĭus -ĭi, m. (Ἀπολλώνιος), 1, Apollonius Alabandensis, *Greek rhetorician, living about* 120 B.C. ; 2, Apollonius Molo, *a Greek rhetorician, living about* 110 B.C. ; 3, Apollonius Rhodius, *author of the Argonautica ;* 4, Apollonius Tyaneus, *philosopher and magician in 1st cent.* A.D.

ăpŏlŏgus -i, m. (ἀπόλογος), *a narrative, a fable, in the manner of Aesop*, Cic.

ăpŏphŏrēta -ōrum, n. (ἀποφόρητα), *presents given to guests, especially at the time of the Saturnalia*, Suet.

ăpŏprŏegmĕna -ōrum, n. plur. (ἀποπροηγμένα), in the philosophy of the Stoics, *that which is to be rejected* (opp. to proegmena), Cic.

ăpŏthēca -ae, f. (ἀποθήκη), *a store-room, magazine, especially for wine*, Cic.

appărātē, adv. with compar. (apparatus), *with much preparation, splendidly ;* opipare et apparate edere et bibere, Cic.

appărātĭo -ōnis, f. (apparo), *preparation*, popularium munerum, Cic.

1. **appărātus** -ūs, m. (apparo). **I.** Abstr. *a preparation, preparing ;* operis, Cic. ; belli, Liv. ; **II.** Concr., *preparation, provision, equipment.* **A.** Gen. tenuiculus, Cic. ; omnis apparatus oppugnandarum urbium, Liv. ; plur. apparatus regii, Cic. **B.** Esp. *brilliant preparations, splendour, magnificence, pomp ;* 1, Lit. *pomp ;* regius, Cic. ; 2, Transf., of a speech, *display, parade ;* dixit causam illam nullo apparatu pure et dilucide, Cic.

2. **appărātus** -a -um, p. adj. with compar. and superl. (from apparo), *prepared, ready ;* of things, *well supplied, sumptuous, splendid ;* domus apparatior, Cic.

appārĕo (ad-părĕo) -ŭi -ĭtum, 2. *to become visible, to appear.* **I.** Gen. **A.** Lit. equus mecum demersus rursum apparuit, Cic. ; with dat. of person, anguis ille, qui Sullae apparuit immolanti, Cic. ; so *of appearance before a court of justice,* in his subselliis me apparere nollem, Cic. ; of daylight, stars, &c., Tib. **B.** Transf., 1, *to be visible, to show itself, be manifest ;* non apparere labores nostros, Hor. ; 2, res apparet and apparet, with acc. and infin. or relat. sentence, *it is clear, plain, manifest*, Cic. **II.** Esp. *to appear as a servant to some person in authority,* or *deity, to serve ;* a, saevi in limine regis apparent, Cic. ; b, *to serve* a magistrate, as lictor, clerk, &c. ; with dat. of person, consulibus, Liv. ; with dat. of thing, quaestioni, Cic.

appārĭo, 3. *to get, obtain*, Lucr.

appārĭtĭo -ōnis, f. (appareo, No. II.). **A.** *A waiting upon, serving*, Cic. **B.** Meton. plur. = apparitores, *servants*, Cic.

appārĭtor -ōris, m. (appareo, No. II.), *a servant ;* esp. *a public servant*, e.g., *a lictor*, etc.,Cic.

appăro (ad-păro), 1. *to prepare for, get ready for, provide ;* convivium, Cic. ; bellum, iter, ludos, Cic. ; crimina in aliquem, *get up charges*, Cic. ; foll. by infin., Caes.

appellātĭo -ōnis, f. (1. appello), *an addressing.* **I.** with words, *speaking to.* **A.** Gen. hanc nactus appellationis causam, Caes. **B.** Legal t.t., *appeal ;* tribunorum, *to the tribunes*, Cic. ; **II.** Of sounds. **A.** *Pronunciation*, litterarum, Cic. **B.** *Naming ;* hence, meton. = nomen, *name, title ;* inanis, Cic. ; plur., regum appellationes, Cic.

appellātor -ōris, m. (1. appello), *an appellant*, Cic.

appellĭto 1. (freq. of 1. appello), *to be accustomed to name*, Tac.

1. **appello** 1. (intens. of 2. appello). **I.** *to address, accost, with words.* **A.** Gen. 1, singulos appellare, Cic. ; nominatim, Caes. ; 2, *to ask a person to do something, to make a proposal to a person ;* a, aliquem, Cic. ; aliquem de proditione, Liv. ; b, legal t.t., *to appeal to ;* praetorem, Cic. ; tribunos, Liv. ; a praetore tribunos, Cic. ; de aestimatione et solutionibus, Caes. ; c, *to apply to for payment ;* aliquem de pecunia, Cic. ; d, *to sue ;* cavendum est ne iisdem de causis alii plectantur, alii ne appellentur quidem, Cic. ; **II.** Of sounds, 1, *to pronounce*, litteras, Cic. ; 2, *to name, entitle ;* aliquem sapientem, Cic. ; appellata est ex viro virtus, Cic. ; (Scipio) Africanus ob egregiam victoriam de Hannibale Poenisque appellatus, Liv. ; hence, *to mention by name ;* quos idcirco non appello hoc loco, Cic. ; aliquem nutu significationeque, *to make known*, Cic.

2. **appello** (ad-pello), -pŭli -pulsum, 3. *to drive to, bring to.* **I.** Gen. **A.** Lit. turres ad opera Caesaris, Caes. **B.** Transf., animum or mentem ad aliquid, *to direct the mind to something ;* mentem ad philosophiam, Cic. **II.** Esp., Nautical t.t., *to bring to land ;* navem ad ripam, Cic. ; classem in insulam, Liv. ; poet., aliquem, with dat., hinc me digressus vestris Deus appulit oris, Verg. ; pass., appelli, of the ship ; navis appellitur ad villam, Cic. ; of the persons in the ship, alios ad Siciliam appulsos esse, Cic. ; refl., se appellere, in portum classe, Liv. ; absol., huc appelle, *put in here*, Hor.

appendĭcŭla -ae, f., (dim. of appendix), *a little addition*, Cic.

appendix -ĭcis, f. (appendo), *an appendage, addition, an appendix to anything ;* vidit enim appendicem animi esse corpus, Cic. ; appendices Olcadum, *smaller contingents*, Liv.

appendo (ad-pendo), -pendi -pensum, 3. *to weigh to ;* aurum alicui, Cic. ; transf., non enim ea verba me annumerare, *pay out*, like small coin ; lectori putavi oportere, sed tanquam appendere, *weigh out*, like whole bars, Cic.

appĕtens -entis, p. adj. with compar. and superl. (from appeto), 1, *desirous of ;* gloriae, Cic. ; 2, *desirous of gold, avaricious ;* homo non cupidus neque appetens, Cic.

appĕtentĕr, adv. (appetens), *greedily*, Cic.

appĕtentĭa -ae, f. (appetens), *desire, longing ;* laudis, Cic.

appĕtītĭo -ōnis, f. (appeto). 1, *grasping at*, Cic. ; 2, *longing for, desire ;* with genit., principatus, Cic.

appĕtītus -ūs, m. (appeto), *a passionate longing, passion, appetite ;* voluptatis, Cic.

appĕto (ad-peto), -īvi and -ĭi -ĭtum, 3. *to reach to.* **I.** Gen. *to grasp at, seize on ;* **A.** Lit., solem manibus, Cic. ; haec enim ipsa sunt honorabilia, salutari, appeti, *to have their hands* *issed*, Cic. **B.** Transf., *to desire, seek;* regnum, Cic. ; with infin., ut appetat animus aliquid agere semper, Cic. **II.** Esp. **A.** *to make for* or *go to a place, to go to, arrive at;* Europam, Cic. ; mare terram appetens, *pressing on the land,* Cic. **B.** *to attack;* aliquem lapidibus, Cic.; transf., ignominiis omnibus appetitus, Cic. **C.** *to draw near,* of time : dies appetebat septimus, quem constituerat, Cic.

1. **Appĭa (Apĭa)** -ae, f. *a town in Phrygia;* hence **Appĭānus** -a -um, *of Appia, Appian.*

2. **Appĭa,** fem. of Appius.

appingo (ad-pingo) -pinxi -pictum, 3. *to point to,* or *upon.* **I.** Lit. delphinum silvis, Hor. **II.** Transf., *to write in addition;* aliquid novi, Cic.

Appĭus -ĭi, m., **Appĭa** -ae, f. *a Roman praenomen, common in the* gens *Claudia,* v. Claudius ; hence, 1, **Appĭus** -a -um, *Appian;* via, *the celebrated road from Rome to Capua, afterwards extended to Brundisium, constructed* A.U.C. 442 *by the Censor, App. Claudius Caecus;* aqua, *a conduit constructed by the same,* Liv.; Appii Forum, v. forum; 2, **Appĭas** -ădis, f. **a,** *the statue of a nymph which stood at the commencement of the above-mentioned aqueduct,* Ov. ; b, Appiades deae, *statues in the temple of Venus, which stood near this aqueduct,* Ov. : 3, **Appĭānus** -a -um, *belonging to an Appius, Appian;* libido (of the Decemvir App. Claudius), Liv.

Appĭĕtas -ātis, f. *the antiquity of the Appian family, a word invented by Cicero to flatter Appius.*

applaudo (ad-plaudo) -plausi -plausum, 3. **I.** Trans., *to strike upon, to clap;* cavis applauso corpore palmis, Ov. **II.** Intrans. *to applaud,* Plaut.

applĭcātĭo -ōnis, f. (applico). **I.** *inclination;* animi, Cic. **II.** jus applicationis, *the rights springing from the relation of patron and client,* Cic.

applĭcātus -a -um, p. adj. (from applico), *applied to, lying near,* Varr.

applĭco (ad-plico), -āvi -ātum and -ŭi -ĭtum, 1. **I.** *to add to, apply to, place to* or *near, join to,* put to. **A.** Lit., se ad flammam, Cic.; oscula feretro, *to kiss,* Ov.; ensem capulo tenus, *to drive in,* Verg.; milit. t.t., corpora corporibus, *to close up the ranks,* Liv.; b, in passive, esp. in partic. perf., *lying near, situated near, built near;* Leucas colli applicata, Liv. **B.** Transf., 1, *to connect;* voluptatem ad honestatem, Cic. ; 2, se ad and se alicui, *to attach oneself to;* se ad aliquem quasi patronum, Cic.; se ad alicujus familiaritatem, or amicitiam, or societatem, Cic. **II.** *to turn* or *direct towards.* **A.** Lit. nautical t.t., *to steer a ship towards, to bring to land;* naves ad terram, Caes. ; navem ad aliquem, Cic. ; absol., *to land;* quocumque litore applicuisse naves hostium audissent, Liv. **B.** Transf., *to devote oneself to;* se ad eloquentiam, Cic.; (perf. applicui, only once in Cic. ; sup. applicitum and partic. applicitus not used by Cic.).

apploro, 1. *to lament, deplore,* Hor.

appōno (ad-pono), -pŏsŭi -pŏsĭtum, 3. **I.** *to place near, to put to.* **A.** Gen. gladium, Cic. **B.** Esp., a, *to serve, put on the table;* patellam, Cic. ; apposita secunda mensa, Cic. ; b, in writing, *to place near;* notam ad versum, or epistolis, Cic. **II.** Transf. **A.** a, *to appoint;* custodem me Tullio, Cic. ; b, *to procure, suborn;* calumniatores, Cic. **B.** *to put to, add to;* 1, Gen., annos alicui, Hor. ; vitiis modum, Cic.; lucro, *reckon as a gain,* Hor. ; 2, *to add,* by way of command, aqua et igni interdictum reo appositumque, ut teneretur insulata, Tac.

apporrectus -a -um (ad and porrigo), *extended near,* Ov.

apporto (ad-porto), 1. *to carry, bring to;* lapidem, signa, Cic.

appōsco (ad-posco), 3. *to ask in addition,* Hor.

appŏsĭtē, adv. (appositus), *appropriately, appositely;* dicere apposite ad persuasionem, Cic.

appŏsĭtus -a -um, p. adj. with compar. and superl. (from appono), *placed near.* **I.** Lit., *situated,* or *lying near;* castellum flumini app., Tac. **II.** Transf., **A.** Gen., audacia fidentiae non contrarium sed appositum et propinquum, Cic. ; **B.** Esp., *fit, appropriate, apposite;* menses appositi ad agendum, Cic.; homo bene appositus ad istius audaciam, Cic.

appōtus (ad-pōtus)-a -um, *very drunk,* Plaut.

apprĕcor (ad-prĕcor), 1., dep. *to worship, pray to;* rite deos, Hor.

apprĕhendo (ad-prěhendo) -prěhendi -prěhensum, 3. and poet. **apprendo** (ad-prendo) -prendi -prensum, 3. *to seize, lay hold of.* **I.** Lit., **A.** Gen., claviculis adminicula tamquam manibus, Cic. **B.** Esp., *to take possession of;* Hispanias, Cic. **II.** Transf., of discourse, *to bring forward, allege;* ut quidquid ego apprehenderam, statim accusator extorquebat, Cic.

apprĭmē (apprimus), adv., *by far, above all, exceedingly,* Plaut., Nep.

apprĭmo -pressi, -pressum, 3. (ad and premo), *to press to;* dextram alicujus, Tac.

approbātĭo -ōnis, f. (approbo). **I.** *approbation, approval, assent,* Cic. **II.** Esp., philosoph. t.t., *proof;* quae (propositio) non indiget approbatione, Cic.

approbātor -ōris, m. (approbo), *one who approves* or *assents;* profectionis meae, Cic.

approbē, adv. (ad and probus), *very well;* illum novisse, Plaut.

approbo (ad-probo). 1. 1, *to approve of, assent to;* consilium alicujus, Cic. ; esp. of a deity, *to bless, approve of;* quod actum est dii approbent, Cic. ; 2, *to prove, to establish;* propositionem app. et firmare, Cic.

appromitto (ad-promitto) -mīsi -missum, 3. *to promise in addition,* i.e. *to promise also in one's own name,* Cic.

appropĕro (ad-propĕro) -āvi, ātūm, -āre. **I.** Trans., *to hasten;* coeptum opus, Liv.; **II.** Intrans., *to hasten;* approperate, Cic. ; appr. ad cogitatum facinus, Cic.

appropinquātĭo -ōnis, f. (appropinquo), *approach;* mortis, Cic.

appropinquo (ad-prŏpinquo), 1. *to approach, draw near.* **I.** Of place, ad summam aquam, Cic. ; with dat. januae, Liv.; Oceano, Caes. **II.** Transf., a, of time, hiems appropinquat, Caes. ; illi poena, nobis libertas appropinquat, Cic. ; b, of persons, qui jam appropinquat ut videat, *is near to seeing,* Cic.

appugno (ad-pugno), 1. *to storm, assault;* castra, Tac.

Appŭlējus, or **Āpŭlējus** -i, m. *a Roman name;* 1, L. Appulejus Saturninus, *tribune of the people,* 100 B.C.; 2, *a Roman writer, born about* 130 A.D., *at Madaura, in Africa.* Adj., 1, **Appŭlējus** -a -um, *of* or *belonging to Appulejus;* lex (de majestate) introduced by the tribune Appulejus; 2, **Appŭlējānus** -a -um, *of* or *belonging to Appulejus.*

Appūlĭa, Āpūlĭa -ae, f. *a country in the south of Italy.* Adj., a, **Appūlĭcus** -a -um, mare, *the Adriatic Sea,* Hor.; b, **Appūlus** -a -um, *Apulian.*

appulsus -ūs, m. (2. appello). **I.** *a driving towards.* **A.** *an approach;* quod pars earum (regionum) appulsu solis exarserit, Cic. **B.** *in-*

fluence produced by approach; caloris, Cic. **II.** *landing on, landing;* litorum, Liv.

ăprīcātĭo -ōnis, f. (apricor), *a basking in the sun,* Cic.

ăprīcĭtas -ātis, f. (apricus), *sunniness, sunshine, warmth,* Plin.

ăprĭcor, 1., dep. (apricus), *to sun oneself,* Cic.

ăprĭcus -a -um, adj. with compar. and superl. (for apericus, from aperio). **I.** Lit., Of places, *open to the sun, sunny;* locus, Cic. ; in apricum proferre, *to bring to light,* Hor. **II.** Transf., *loving the sun ;* flores, Hor. ; mergi, Verg. ; sensus, Pers.

Aprīlis -e (aperio), Aprilis mensis or subst., *the month of April,* Cic.

ăprīnus -a -um (aper), *relating or belonging to a wild boar,* Plin.

ăprŭgnus -a -um (aper), *belonging to a wild boar,* Plaut.

Apsus -i, m. ("Αψος), *a river of Illyria,* now *Berzatino.*

aptātus -a -um (partic. of apto), *fitted, appropriate,* Cic.

aptē, adv., with compar. and superl. (aptus), *fitly, appropriately;* facere, dicere, Cic.

apto, 1. (intens. of * apo), *to fit to, adapt to, adjust.* **I.** Gen., corpori arma, Liv. ; enses dexteris, Hor. **II.** *to prepare, get ready.* **A.** Lit., arma, Liv. ; classem velis, Verg. ; se armis, Liv. **B.** Transf., *to make fit or appropriate;* hoc verbum est ad id aptatum quod, etc., Cic.

aptus -a -um, 1. (partic. of obsolete verb, * apo). **I.** Partic., 1, Lit., *fastened to;* gladius e lacunari seta equina aptus, Cic. ; 2, Transf., *depending upon;* honestum ex quo aptum est officium, Cic. ; with abl. alone, rudentibus apta fortuna, Cic. **B.** *connected, joined, allied ;* 1, Lit., a, omnia inter se connexa et apta, Cic. ; b, *prepared, equipped, fitted out;* omnia sibi esse ad bellum apta et parata, Cic. ; caelum stellis fulgentibus aptum, Verg. ; 2, Transf., Thucydides verbis aptus et pressus, Cic. **II.** Adj., with compar. and superl., *suitable, appropriate, fitting;* with ad and the acc., milites minus apti ad hujus generis hostem, Cic. ; id pallium esse aptum ad omne anni tempus, Cic. ; with in and the acc., in quod (genus) minus apti sunt, Liv. ; with dat., haec genera dicendi aptiora sunt adolescentibus, Cic. ; absol., verbis quam maxime aptis, Cic.

ăpŭd (aput), prep., with acc. (root AP, whence apo, aptus, apud thus meaning *being fastened to, near to), at, near, by, with,* chiefly used of persons. **I.** Of nearness to persons, 1, apud aliquem sedere, *near,* Cic. ; plus apud me antiquorum auctoritas valet, Cic. ; hence a, apud me, *at my house,* Cic. ; apud se esse (fig.), *to be in possession of one's faculties,* Plaut. ; b, apud exercitum esse, *to be serving as a soldier,* Cic. ; 2, *before, in the presence of;* apud judices, Cic. ; 3, *with;* consequi gratiam apud bonos viros, Cic. ; hence, *with = in the time of;* apud patres nostros, Cic. ; 4, of an author, *in the works of;* apud Xenophontem, Cic. : 5, *to;* apud aliquem queri, Cic. **II.** Of places, 1, *in the neighbourhood of;* apud Alyziam, Cic. ; 2, *at, in;* apud villam, Cic.

Ăpŭlējus, v. Appulejus.

Ăpūlia, v. Appulia.

ăqua -ae, f. (akin to Keltic ach and Sanscrit apa = *water), water.* **I.** Lit., **A.** *water* in the broadest meaning of the word ; pluvia, Cic. ; marina, Cic. ; plur., aquae dulces, Cic. ; special phrases, a, aspergere alicui aquam, *to re-animate,* Plaut. ; b, aq iam praebere, *to entertain,* Hor. ; c, aqua et ignis, *the necessaries of life ;* non aqua, non

igni, ut aiunt, locis pluribus utimur quam amicitia, Cic. ; hence, (a) aqua et igni interdicere alicui, Cic. ; or aqua et igni aliquem arcere, Tac. ; *to banish ;* (β) aquam terramque petere or poscere ab aliquo, *to demand submission from the enemy,* a Persian custom, Liv. ; d, aqua haeret, *there is a difficulty* or *a hitch,* Cic. ; e, in aqua scribere, *to write in water,* Cat. **B.** *water* in a narrower sense ; 1, a, *the sea ;* ad aquam, *on the sea-coast,* Cic. ; b, *a lake,* Albanae aquae deductio, Cic. ; c, *a river,* secunda aqua, *down stream,* Liv. ; 2, *rain,* Hor. ; 3, plur., aquae ; a, *springs,* Verg. ; b, *hot medicinal springs;* ad aquas venire, Cic. ; hence as a proper name, Aquae Sextiae, &c. ; 4, of an aqueduct, aquam ducere non longe e villa, Cic. ; 5, *water in the water-clock;* hence, aquam dare, *to give time,* Plin. ; aquam perdere, *to lose time,* Quint. ; 6, *tears,* Prop. **II.** Transf., Aqua, *a constellation,* Cic. poet.

aquaeductus -ūs, m. ; 1, *an aqueduct,* Cic. ; 2, *the right of conveying water to a place,* Cic.

ăquālĭcŭlus -i, m. (dim. of aqualis), *a small water-vessel;* hence, *the belly,* Pers.

ăquālis -e (aqua), *watery.* Subst., **ăquālis** -is, c. *a wash-bowl,* Plaut.

ăquārĭus -a -um (aqua), *belonging to water.* **I.** Adj., provincia, *superintendence of the supply of water,* Cic. **II.** Subst., **ăquārĭus** -ii, m. 1, *a water-carrier,* Juv. ; 2, *an inspector of conduits,* ap. Cic. ; 3, *the constellation so called,* Hor.

ăquātĭcus -a -um (aqua). **I.** *living in water, aquatic;* lotos, Ov. **II.** *full of water, watery;* auster, *bringing rain,* Ov.

ăquātilis -e (aqua), *living or growing in the water,* Cic.

ăquātĭo -ōnis, f. (ạquor). **A.** *A fetching of water,* Caes. **B.** Meton., *a place whence water may be fetched, a watering-place,* Plin.

ăquātŏr -ōris, m. (aquor), *a person that fetches water,* Caes.

ăquĭla -ae, f. (perhaps fem. of aquilus), *an eagle.* **I.** Lit., in mythology, the bearer of the lightning of Jove, Cic. **II.** Transf., 1, *an eagle as the standard of each Roman legion,* Cic. ; Meton., a, *a legion,* Plin. ; b, *the post of standard-bearer,* Juv. ; 2, *the Eagle, a constellation,* Cic. ; 3, plur. aquilae, *the eagle on the front and rear of the temple of Jupiter Capitolinus, which seemed to support the gable,* Tac.

Ăquĭlēja -ae, f. *a town in the north of Italy,* now *Aquileja* or *Aglar ;* hence adj., **Ăquĭlējensis** -e, *of or belonging to Aquileja.*

ăquĭlĭfer -feri (aquila and fero), m. *an eagle* or *standard-bearer,* Cic.

ăquĭlīnus -a -um (aquila), *relating to an eagle,* Plaut.

Ăquĭlĭus -a -um, *name of a Roman gens, the most celebrated members of which were*—1, C. Aquilius Gallus, *friend of and colleague with Cicero in the praetorship* (66 B.C.), *a famous orator and jurist;* 2, Aquilius Regulus, *an informer under the empire;* hence, **Ăquĭlĭānus** -a -um, *belonging to Aquilius.*

ăquĭlo -ōnis, m. (connected with aquilus, *the black stormy one);* 1, *the north wind,* Cic. : meton., *the north,* Cic. ; 2, *Aquilo, as a myth. person, husband of Orithyia, father of Calais and Zetes.*

ăquĭlōnālis, -e (aquilo), *northern,* Cic.

Ăquĭlōnĭa -ae, f. *a town in the country of the Hirpini,* now *Carbonara.*

ăquĭlōnĭus -a -um, 1, *northern,* Cic. ; 2, *belonging to Aquilo* (2) ; proles, *Calais and Zeta,* Prop.

ăquĭlus -a -um, *dark-coloured, blackish,* Plaut.

Aquīnum -i, n. *town in Latium, now Aquino.* **Adj., Aquīnās** -ātis, *belonging to Aquinum.*

Āquītāni -ōrum, m. *inhabitants of Aquitania;* hence **Āquītānĭa** -ae, f. *Aquitania, the south-west part of Gaul, between the Garonne and the Pyrenees.*

ăquor, 1. dep. (aqua), *to fetch water,* Caes.

ăquōsus -a -um, adj. with compar. and superl. (aqua), *full of water, watery;* Orion, Verg.; Eurus, *rain-bringing,* Hor.; mater, *Thetis,* Ov.

ăquŭla -ae, f. (dim. of aqua), *a little water, a small stream,* Cic.

āra -ae, f. (connected with αἴρω, *I raise*); 1, *an elevation of earth, stone,* &c.; **a**, ara sepulcri, *a funeral pyre,* Verg.; 2, plur., arae, *rocks,* Verg.; 3, *a monument of stone;* virtutis, Cic.; 4, *an altar;* **a**, aram consecrare deo, Cic.; *pro* aris et foris, *for hearths and homes,* Cic.; fig., *a refuge, protection;* legum, Cic.; **b**, transf. *a constellation,* Cic. poet.

Ărăbarchēs -ae, m. ('Ἀραβάρχης), *an Egyptian magistrate, a superior tax-collector,* Juv.; used sarcastically of Pompey (who by his conquests increased the tribute paid to Rome), Cic.

Ărăbes -um, m. ('Ἀραβες), *the inhabitants of Arabia, the Arabs;* hence, 1, **Ărăbs** -ăbis, *Arabian;* 2, **Ărăbĭa** -ae, f. ('Ἀραβία), *the country of Arabia, in the south-west of Asia,* used loosely for any country inhabited by nomadic tribes akin to the Arabs; 3, **Ărăbĭcus** -a -um, *Arabian;* 4, **Ărăbĭus** -a -um, *Arabian;* 5, **Ărăbus** -a -um, *Arabian.*

ărābĭlis -e (aro), *that can be ploughed, arable.* Plin.

Ărachnē, -ēs, f. ('Ἀράχνη), *a Lydian maiden who entered into a contest in spinning with Minerva and was turned into a spider.*

Ārădus -i, f. ('Ἀραδος), *a Phoenician town, now Ruad.* Adj., **Ārădius** -a -um.

ărănĕa -ae f. (ἀράχνη), 1, *a spider;* 2, *the spider's web,* Plaut.

ărănĕŏla -ae. f. (dim. of aranea), *a little spider,* Cic.

ărănĕŏlus -i. m. (dim. of aranea), *a little spider,* Verg.

ărănĕōsus -a -um (aranea), 1, *full of cobwebs,* Cat.; 2, *like a cobweb,* Plin.

1. **ărănĕus** -i. m. *a spider,* Lucr.

2. **ărănĕus** -a -um, *relating to a spider,* Plin. Subst., **ărănĕum** -i, n. *a cobweb,* Phaedr.

Ărăr and **Ărăris**, -is, m. *a river in Gaul, the Saone.*

ărātĭo -onis, f. (aro). **I.** *ploughing, agriculture,* Cic. **II.** Meton., *a ploughed field,* Plaut.; esp., arationes = *the public domains let at a rent of one-tenth of their produce,* Cic.

ărător -ōris, m. 1, *a ploughman, a husbandman,* Cic.; appel. taurus, Ov.; 2, aratores, *tenants of the arationes,* q.v., Cic.

ărātrum -i, n. *the plough;* aratrum circumducere, Cic.; aliquem ab aratro arcessere, Cic.

Ăratthus -i, m. ('Ἀρατθος), *a river in Epirus, now Arta.*

Ărātus -i, m. ('Ἀρατος). **I.** *a Greek poet, born in Cilicia, whose astronomical poem Φαινόμενα was translated by Cicero.* Adj., **Ărātēus** and **Ărātīus** -a -um, *belonging to Aratus;* carmina, Cic.; and absol., nostra quaedam Aratea, Cicero's translation of the poem, Cic. **II.** *a celebrated Greek general, founder of the Achaean League.*

4

Ăraxēs -is, m. ('Ἀράξης), *a river in Armenia.*

arbĭtĕr -tri, m. (from ar = ad, and bitere, *to go*). **I.** *a witness, spectator, hearer;* locus ab arbitris remotus, Cic.; remotis arbitris, Cic. **II. A.** Legal t. t., *an umpire, arbitrator;* arbiter litis, Cic.; aliquem arbitrum adigere, Cic.; arbitrum dare, Cic.; sumere, Cic.; esse in aliquam rem arbitrum, Cic.; ad arbitrum confugere, Cic.; uti aliquo arbitro, Cic. **B.** Transf., 1, *a judge of any matter;* formae (of Paris), Ov.; armorum, Ov.; 2, *ruler, lord, master;* bibendi, Hor.; Adriae, *the south wind,* Hor.; elegantiae, Tac.

arbĭtra -ae, f. (arbiter) *a female witness,* Hor.

arbĭtrārius -a -um, *depending on the will, arbitrary, uncertain,* Plaut.

arbĭtrātus -ūs, m. *approval, will, choice, wish;* tuo arbitratu, Cic.; cujus arbitratu sit educatus, Cic.

arbĭtrĭum -i, n. **A.** *The umpire's decision;* aliud est judicium, aliud arbitrium; judicium est pecuniae certae, arbitrium incertae, Cic. **B.** Transf., 1, *any decision, judgment, free choice;* arbitrium eligendi, Tac.; libera arbitria de aliquo agere, Liv.; res ab opinionis arbitrio sejunctae, Cic.; arbitria funeris, *the expenses of a funeral,* Cic.; 2, *might, mastery, authority;* arbitrio suo, Cic.

arbĭtror, 1. dep. (pass. Plaut., Cic., arbitro, Plaut.). **I.** *to hear, perceive,* Plaut. **II.** Transf., *to express an opinion as witness,* Cic.; hence, *to think, be of opinion;* qui se natos ad homines juvandos arbitrantur, Cic.; with acc. and infin., ut quisque minimum in se esse arbitraretur, Cic.

arbŏr (arbos) -ŏris, f. *a tree.* **A.** Lit., fici, *a fig tree,* Cic.; Jovis, *the oak,* Ov.; Phoebi, *the laurel,* Ov.; Palladis, *the olive,* Ov. **B.** Meton., infelix, *the gallows,* Cic.; mali, *a mast,* Verg.; arbor, *an oar,* Verg.; *a ship,* Pelias, *the Argo,* Ov.

arbŏrĕus -a -um, *relating to trees,* Verg.; cornua, *branching,* Verg.

arbustum -i, n. (arbor), *a plantation, a vineyard planted with trees,* Cic.

arbustus -a -um, *full of trees;* ager, Cic.

arbŭtĕus -a -um, *relating to the arbutus,* Ov., Verg.

arbŭtum -i, n., 1, *the fruit of the wild strawberry or arbutus tree,* Verg.; 2, *the wild strawberry tree or arbutus,* Verg.

arbŭtus -i, f. *the wild strawberry or arbutus tree,* Verg.

arca -ae, f. (root ARC, whence also arceo). **I.** *a chest, box.* **A.** Gen., Cic. **B.** Esp., **a**, *a coffin,* Liv.; **b**, *money coffer,* Cic.; meton. = *the money in the coffer;* arcae nostrae confidito, Cic. **II.** *a cell for close imprisonment,* Cic.

Arcădĭa -ae, f. ('Ἀρκαδία), *a country of the Peloponnesus.* Adj., 1, **Arcădĭus** -a -um; 2, **Arcădĭcus** -a -um; deus, *Pan,* Prop.; juvenis, *a simpleton,* Juv.; virgo, *Arethusa,* Ov.; 3, **Arcăs** -ădis, tyrannus, *Lycaon,* Ov. Subst., **Arcăs**, -ădis, *Mercury,* Mart.; **Arcădes** -um, m. *the Arcadians,* Cic.

arcānō, adv., *secretly,* Cic.

arcānus -a -um (arca, arceo), 1, *silent;* homo, Plaut.; nox, Ov.; 2, *secret,* Cic.; arcana consilia, Liv.; sacra, Ov. Subst., **arcānum** -i. n. *a secret,* Liv., Juv.

Arcăs -ădis, m. ('Ἀρκάς), *son of Jupiter and Callisto, placed in the heavens as the star Arctophylax.*

arceo -cui, 2. (root ARC, whence arca). **I.** *to shut in, shut up;* alvus arcet et continet quod recipit, Cic. **II. A.** *to prohibit access to, to keep at a distance, to hinder, prevent;* copias hostium, Cic.; followed by ne with subj., Liv.; with the

acc. and **ab** with the abl., aliquem ab urbe, Cic.; with the acc. and abl. alone, hostem Gallia, Cic.; with dat., Verg. **B.** *to protect from;* aliquem periclis, Verg.

Arcĕsĭlās -ae, m. (Ἀρκεσίλας) and **Arcĕs-ĭlāus** -i, m. (Ἀρκεσίλαος), *a Greek philosopher of Pitane in Aeolia* (316–241 B.C.), *founder of the Middle Academy.*

Arcēsĭus -ĭi, m. (Ἀρκεισίος), *father of Laertes, and grandfather of Ulysses.*

arcessĭtor -ōris, m. *one who calls or fetches,* Plin.

arcessītus, abl. -ū, m. *calling for, summons;* ipsius rogatu arcessituque, Cic.

arcesso (accerso) -īvi -ītum, 3. (accedo), *to fetch* or *call to a place, to summon,* **I.** Gen. **A.** Lit., aliquem litteris Capua, Cic.; aliquem in senatum, Cic.; sacra ab exteris nationibus asciscere et arcessere, Cic. **B.** Transf., of a thought, *to bring, derive;* argumentum usque a capite, Cic.; hence arcessitus, *strained, far-fetched;* dictum, Cic. **II.** Esp. **1,** *to bring the dead from the lower world,* Verg.; **2,** *to bring the bride to the bridegroom's house,* Ter.; **3,** legal t. t., *to summon, bring before a court of justice;* aliquem judicio capitis, Cic.; aliquem capitis, Cic.

Archĕlāus -i, m. (Ἀρχέλαος). **I.** *a Greek philosopher of Miletus.* **II.** *King of Macedonia from* 413 B.C., *friend of Euripides.* **III.** *General of Mithridates.* **IV.** *Son of* **III.**, *husband of Berenice.* **V.** *the grandson of* **IV.**, *the last king of Cappadocia.*

archetўpus -a -um (ἀρχέτυπος), *original,* Juv.

Archĭās -ae, m. (Ἀρχίας). **I.** Aulus Licinius, *a Greek poet of Antioch, defended by Cicero.* **II.** *a celebrated cabinet-maker,* hence **Archĭācus** -a -um, *of or belonging to Archias.*

archĭgallus -i, m. *a high priest of Cybele,* Plin.

Archĭlŏchus -i, m. (Ἀρχίλοχος), *a Greek satiric poet, inventor of iambic verse.* Adj., *sharp, biting,* Cic.

archĭmāgīrus -i, m. (ἀρχιμάγειρος), *head cook,* Ov.

Archĭmēdes -is, m. (Ἀρχιμήδης), *celebrated mathematical and mechanical philosopher, killed on the capture of Syracuse by Marcellus* (212 B.C.).

archĭmīmus -i, m. (ἀρχίμιμος), *chief mime* or *buffoon,* Suet.

archĭpīrāta -ae, m. (ἀρχιπειρατής), *chief pirate,* Cic.

architectōn -ŏnis, m.(ἀρχιτέκτων), 1, *master-builder,* Plaut.; 2, *a master in cunning,* Plaut.

architector, 1. dep. **A.** *to build.* **B.** Transf., *to devise, to prepare, provide;* voluptates, Cic.

architectūra -ae, f. *architecture,* Cic.

architectus -i, m.(ἀρχιτέκτων), 1, *an archi-tect, master-builder;* architecti operum, Cic.; 2, Transf., *an inventor, author, maker;* hujus legis, Cic.; quasi arch. beatae vitae, Cic.

archōn -ontis, m. (ἄρχων), *an archon, one of the chief magistrates of Athens,* Cic.

Archўtās -ae, m. (Ἀρχύτας), *a philosopher of Tarentum* (about 400–365 B.C.).

arcĭtĕnens -entis (arcus and teneo), *holding the bow, epithet of Apollo and Diana,* Verg., Ov.

arct . . . = art . . . q.v.

Arctŏs -i, f. (ἄρκτος), 1, *the great and little bear,* Verg., Ov.; juncta Aquilonibus Arctos, *the North Pole,* Ov.; opacam excipere Arcton, *to be towards the North,* Hor.; 2, *the night,* Prop.

Arctōus -a -um (ἀρκτῷος) *belonging to the north pole, northern,* Mart.

Arctūrus -i, m. (ἀρκτοῦρος), 1, *the brightest star of the constellation Bootes,* Cic.; 2, *Bootes,* Verg.

arcŭātus -a -um (partic. of arcuo), *bent like a bow, curved;* currus, Liv.

arcŭla -ae, f. (dim. of arca), 1, *a casket for money, jewels,* or *perfume;* arculae muliebres, Cic.; 2, Transf., *rhetorical ornament;* omnes (Isocrati) discipulorum arculae, Cic.

arcŭlārĭus -i, m. *a casket maker,* Plaut.

arcŭo, 1. *to bend* or *shape like a bow,* Plin.

arcŭs -ūs, m. **I.** *a bow;* a, arcum intendere, Cic.; adducere, Verg.; arcus Haemonii, *the con-stellation Sagittarius,* Ov.; b, *the rainbow,* Cic.; c, *an arch, vault, triumphal arch,* Suet. **II.** Transf., 1, *anything arched* or *curved,* Verg., Ov.; 2, *a mathematical arc,* Sen.; *the parallel circles which bound the zones of the earth,* Ov.

1. **ardĕa** -ae, f. *a heron,* Verg.

2. **Ardĕa** -ae, f. (Ἀρδέα), *town of the Rutuli in Latium.* Adj., a, **Ardĕās** -ātis, b, **Ardĕ-ātĭnus** -a -um, *of or belonging to Ardea.*

ardēlĭo -ōnis, m. *a busybody,* Mart.

ardens -entis, p. adj. with compar. and superl. (ardeo), *hot, glowing.* **A.** Lit., lapides, Liv. **B.** Transf., a, of the eyes, *glowing;* oculi, Verg.; b, of colour, *glittering;* apes ardentes auro, Verg.; c, of wine, *strong, fiery;* Falernum, Hor.; d, of passions, &c., *burning, eager, hot;* odium, Liv.; avaritia, Cic.; ardentes in aliquem litterae, Cic.; ardentes equi, *spirited,* Verg.; e, of oratory, *fiery;* orator, Cic.; oratio, actio, Cic.

ardentĕr, adv., with compar. and superl. (ardens), *hotly, violently;* cupere, Cic.

ardĕo, arsi, arsum, 2. *to burn, glow, be on fire.* **I.** Lit., faces, Cic.; domus, Cic; mare arsit eo anno, Liv.; jam proximus ardet Ucalegon, *the house of U.,* Verg.; ardent altaria, Verg. **II.** Transf., 1, of the eyes, *to glow,* Cic.; 2, of colours, *to flash, sparkle, glow;* ardebat murice laena, Verg.; 3, of feelings, a, of the body, quum omnes artus ardere viderentur, *be in pain,* Cic.; b, of the mind, amore, dolore, furore, Cic.; ardere in proelia, *eagerly to desire fight,* Verg.; esp. in poets, *to burn with love;* ardere aliquā or in aliquā or aliquam, Hor., Verg., Ov.; ardere invidia, *to be heated,* Cic.; c, of conspiracies, wars, &c., *to burst out;* quum arderet conju-ratio, Cic.; quum arderet Syria bello, *be in a state of excitement,* Cic.

ardĕŏla -ae, f. (dim. of ardea), *a heron,* Plin.

ardesco, arsi, 3. (inch. of ardeo), *to take fire, kindle.* **I.** Lit., arsit arundo, Verg. **II.** Transf., 1, *to glitter;* fulmineis ignibus ardescunt undae, Ov.; 2, of the passions, *to become inflamed;* tuendo, Verg.; libidinibus, Tac.

ardŏr -ōris, m. *flame, burning, heat.* **I.** Lit., solis, Cic. **II.** Transf., 1, the glow of the eyes, oculorum, Cic.; 2, *gleam, glimmer;* stellarum, Cic.; 3, of the feelings or passions, *ardour, fierceness;* cupiditatum, Cic.; animorum et ar-morum, Cic.; pugnandi, *for fighting,* Liv.; with ad and the acc., mentis ad gloriam, Cic.; ad bellum armaque, Liv.; esp. *the passion of love,* Ov.; virginis, *for a maiden,* Ov.

Ardŭenna -ae, f. *a forest in Gallia Belgica,* now *the forest of Ardennes.*

ardŭus -a -um, adj. with compar. and superl. (root AR, Gr. AP, whence area, ἄραι), *steep.* **I.** Lit. **A.** collis, Liv.; ascensus diffi-cilis atque arduus, Cic. Subst., **ardŭum** -i, n. *a steep place;* per arduum ducuntur, Liv. **B.** Poet., *lofty;* aether, Ov.; nubes, Hor.; sese arduus infert (Turnus), *with proud mien,* Verg. **II.** Transf., *difficult to undertake* or *reach;* res

arduae ac difficiles, Cic. ; arduum videtur, or est followed by infin., Sall., Liv. Subst., **arduum** -i, n. *what is difficult to accomplish*, Hor., Ov.

ārĕa -ae, f. (Root AR, Gr. AP, whence arduus and ἄραι), *a high-lying open space, surface.* **I.** Gen. collemque super planissima campi area, Ov. **II.** Esp., 1, *an open space in a town*, Liv. ; 2, *a site for a house*, Cic. ; 3, *the court-yard*, Liv. ; 4, *threshing-floor*, Cic. ; 5, *the part of the circus where the games were held ;* fig., *sphere, scope*, Ov.

ārĕfăcĭo -fēci -factum, 3. *to make dry*, Lucr.

Ărĕlātĕ, n. and **Ărĕlās** -atis, f. *town in Gallia Narbonensis*, now *Arles.* Adj., **Ărĕlātensis** -e.

Ărĕmŏrĭcus -a -um (from Keltic are = *on*, and fior = *sea*), *lying on the sea ;* civitates, *Gallic states on the coast of the English Channel.*

ārēna -ae, f. *sand.* **I.** Lit., saxa globosa arenae immixta, Liv. ; arenae carae, *the sands of Pactolus*, Ov. ; prov., arenae mandare semina, *to sow the sand*, of a fruitless work, Ov. **II.** Meton., 1, *a sandy place ;* arenam aliquam aut paludes emere, Cic. ; 2, *the sea-shore ;* optata potiri arena, Verg. ; 3, *the arena in the amphitheatre* (covered with sand) ; promittere operas arenae, Tac. **III.** Transf., *the scene of any contention or struggle*, Plin.

ārēnārĭus -a -um, *relating to sand, sandy.* Subst., **ărēnārĭa** -ae, f. (sc. fodina), *a sand pit*, Cic.

ărēnōsus -a -um, *sandy*, Verg.

ārens -entis, p. adj. (areo), *dry.* **I.** Gen. rivus, Verg. **II.** *dry with thirst ;* ora, Ov. ; poet. sitis, Ov.

ārĕo, 2. **A.** *to be dry ;* aret ager, Verg. **B.** Esp., *to be dry with thirst*, Liv.

ārĕŏla -ae, f. (dim. of area), *a little open space*, Plin.

Ărĕŏpăgus -i, m. (Ἄρειος πάγος), *Mars' hill at Athens, upon which the court called Areopagus held its sittings*, Cic. ; hence, **Ărĕŏpăgītēs** -ae, m. *a member of the court*, Cic.

Ares -is, m. (Ἄρης), *the Greek god of war*, appell., *a warrior*, Plaut.

āresco, 3. (inch. of areo), *to become dry ;* cito arescit lacrima, Cic.

Ărestŏrĭdēs -ae, m. (Ἀρεστορίδης), *a descendant of Arestor*, i.e., *Argus, his son.*

ărĕtălŏgus -i, m. (ἀρεταλόγος), *a babbler about virtue, a kind of philosophical buffoon*, Juv.

Ărēthūsa -ae, f. (Ἀρέθουσα), *a fountain in the island of Ortygia at Syracuse ;* myth. *a Nereid beloved by the river Alpheus, who dived under the sea in pursuit of her.* Adj., 1, **Ărĕthūsis** -ĭdis ; 2, **Ărĕthūsĭus** -a -um, *of or belonging to Arethusa.*

Ărēus -a -um, *relating to Mars ;* judicium, *the Areopagus*, Tac.

Arganthōnĭus -ĭi, m. (Ἀργανθώνιος), *a king of Tartessus, who lived to a great age.*

Argēi -ōrum, m. 1, *chapels of local deities in Rome ;* 2, *figures of men, thrown into the Tiber every year on the Ides of May.*

Argentānum -i, n. *a town in Bruttium*, now *Argentino.*

argentārĭus -a -um, 1, *relating to silver ;* metalla, *silver mines*, Plin. ; 2, *relating to money ;* inopia, Plaut. ; taberna, *a banker's stall*, Liv. Subst., **A. argentārĭus** -ĭi, m. *a money-changer, banker*, Cic. **B. argentārĭa** -ae, f. 1, (sc. taberna), *a banker's office*, Liv. ; 2, (sc. ars), *a banker's trade*, Cic. ; 3, (sc. fodina), *a silver mine*, Liv.

argentātus -a -um, 1, *ornamented with silver ;* milites, *with silvered shields*, Liv. ; 2, *provided with money*, Plaut.

argentĕus -a -um, **I.** 1, *made of silver ;* aquila, Cic. ; nummus, Varr. ; denarius, Plin. ; or simply argenteus, Tac. ; 2, *ornamented or covered with silver ;* scena, Cic. ; 3, *of the colour of silver ;* anser, Verg. **II.** Transf., *belonging to the Silver Age ;* proles, Ov.

argentĭfŏdīna -ae, f. *a silver mine*, Varr., Plin.

argentōsus -a -um, *full of silver, rich in silver*, Plin.

argentum -i, n. (ἀργής), *silver ;* **I.** signatum, *stamped with a pattern*, Cic. ; **II.** Esp., 1, *silver plate*, Cic. ; 2, *silver coin*, and generally *money*, Cic., Liv.

Argĭlētum -i, n. *a part of Rome where were many booksellers' shops.* Adj., **Argĭlētānus** -a -um, *of or belonging to Argiletum.*

argilla, -ae, f. (ἄργιλλος), *white clay, potter's clay*, Cic.

argillācĕus -a -um, *clayey, of clay*, Plin.

Argĭnussae (Argĭnūsae) -arum, f. (Ἀργινοῦσαι), *islands on the coast of Aeolis, scene of a naval victory of the Athenians over the Spartans.*

Argō -ūs, f. (Ἀργώ), *the ship Argo, in which many Greek heroes sailed to Colchis, under Jason, to fetch the Golden Fleece.* Adj., **Argōus** -a -um.

Argŏnautae -ārum, m. (Ἀργοναῦται), *the Argonauts, the heroes who sailed in the Argo.*

Argŏs, n. and **Argi** -ōrum, m. **I.** *the capital of Argolis, a country of the Peloponnese.* Adj., **A. Argēus** -a -um. **B. Argīvus** -a -um ; Argive augur, Amphiaraus, Hor. ; plur. subst., Argivi -orum, and poet. -um, m. *the Argives.* **C. Argōlis** -ĭdis, f. 1, Adj., *Argolic ;* 2, Subst., *the district Argolis ;* hence adj., **Argŏlĭcus** -a -um, *Argolic.* **II.** Argos Amphilochium, *a town in Epirus.*

argūmentātĭo -ōnis, f. *the bringing forward of a proof ;* argumentatio est explicatio argumenti, Cic.

argūmentor, 1, dep. **I.** Intransit. *to bring forward a proof ;* quid porro argumenter, qua de re dubitare nemo possit, Cic. **II.** Transit. *to allege as a proof*, Liv.

argūmentum -i, n. (arguo), 1, *an argument, proof*, Cic. ; afferre argumenta, Cic. ; multis argumentis deos esse docere, Cic. ; argumenta atque indicia sceleris, Cic. ; 2, *subject, contents, matter ;* a, epistolae, Cic. ; b, *subject of a drama ;* fabulae, Ter. ; c, *a drama itself ;* explicare argumenti exitum, Cic. ; d, *subject of a work of art*, ex ebore diligentissime perfecta argumenta erant in valvis (*bas-reliefs*), Cic.

argŭo -ŭi -ūtum, 3. (connected with ἀργός), *to put in clear light.* **I.** Gen. **A.** Lit. *to maintain, prove ;* speculatores non legatos venisse, Liv. **B.** Transf., *to betray, prove ;* degeneres animos timor arguit, Verg. ; laudibus arguitur vini vinosus Homerus, Hor. **II.** Esp. **A.** *to charge, accuse, expose, convict ;* with gen., summi sceleris, Cic. ; with abl., hoc crimine te non arguo, Cic. ; with double acc., id quod me arguis, Cic. ; with infin., Roscius arguitur occidisse patrem, Cic. **B.** *to censure, complain of ;* culpa, quam arguo, Liv.

Argus -i, m. (Ἄργος), *the hundred-eyed guardian of Io, slain by Mercury.*

argūtǎtio -ōnis, f. *a rustling*, Cat.

argūtē, adv., with compar. and superl. (argutus), *sagaciously, acutely ;* callide arguteque dicere, Cic.

argūtĭae -ārum, f. 1, *liveliness, animation ;* digitorum, *quick movement of the fingers*, Cic. ;

2, a, *cleverness, subtlety, sagacity;* hujus orationes tantum argutiarum, tantum urbanitatis habent, Cic. ; **b,** in a bad sense, *cunning, quibbling,* Cic.

argūtor, 1. dep. *to chatter,* Plaut.

argūtŭlus -a -um, *somewhat acute;* libri, Cic.

argūtus -a -um, p. adj. with compar. and superl. (arguo), **1,** in relation to the senses : a, to the eye, *expressive, lively;* manus, oculi, Cic. ; **b,** to the ear, *piercing, penetrating, shrill;* hirundo, Verg. ; forum, *noisy,* Ov. ; poeta, *melodious,* Hor. ; **2,** relating to the mind, a, *significant, clear;* of omens, argutissima exta, Cic. ; **b,** of the understanding, *a,* in a good sense, *sagacious, acute;* argutus orator, Cic. ; *β,* in a bad sense, *sly, cunning;* meretrix, Hor.

argўraspĭdes -pĭdum m. (ἀργυράσπιδες), *name of a picked corps in the Macedonian army, the wearers of the silver shield,* Liv.

Arĭadna -ae, & **Arĭadnē** -ēs, f. (Ἀριάδνη), *daughter of Minos and Pasiphae, who helped Theseus to slay the Minotaur, but was deserted by him and then beloved by Bacchus.*

Arĭărāthēs -is, m. (Ἀριαράθης), *name of several kings of Cappadocia.*

Arīcĭa -ae, f. *town in Latium at the foot of the Alban Mount.* Adj. **Arīcīnus** -a -um, *belonging to Aricia.*

ārĭdŭlus -a -um (dim. of aridus), *somewhat dry,* Cat.

ārĭdus -a -um, adj. with compar. and superl. (areo), *dry, arid.* **I.** Lit., **1,** folia, Cic. ; poet. sonus, *a dry, crackling sound,* Verg. ; **2,** *dry with thirst;* viator, Verg. ; **3,** *shrivelled, fleshless;* crura, Ov. ; absol., exsiccati atque aridi, Cic. Subst., **arĭdum** -i, n. *dry ground;* naves in aridum subducere, Caes. **II.** Transf., **1,** of manner of living, *poor, meagre;* vita, Cic. ; **2,** *intellectually dry, jejune;* genus orationis, Cic. ; **3,** *avaricious,* Ter.

ărĭes -ĕtis, m. (ἄρϝν, ἄρρην). **I.** Lit. *a ram,* Cic. **II.** Transf. **A.** *a battering ram,* Caes. **B.** *a prop, beam,* Caes. **C.** *one of the signs of the zodiac,* Cic.

ărĭĕtātĭo -ōnis, f. *a butting like a ram,* Sen.

ărĭĕto, 1. *to butt like a ram,* Verg.

Arĭmĭnum -i, n. *town and river in Umbria.* Adj., **Arĭmĭnensis** -e, *belonging to Ariminum.*

Arĭŏbarzānēs -is, m. (Ἀριοβαρζάνης), *name of several kings of Cappadocia, and of one of Armenia.*

Arĭōn or **Arĭo** -ōnis, m. (Ἀρίων). **I.** Myth. *a harp-player, saved from drowning by a dolphin.* Adj., **Arĭŏnĭus** -a -um, *belonging to Arion.* **II.** *a Pythagorean philosopher, contemporary of Plato.*

Ariovistus -i, m. *a German prince, conquered by Caesar.*

Arisba -ae, and **Arisbē** -ēs, f. (Ἀρίσβη), *town in the Troad.*

ărista -ae, f. **I. A.** *the point of an ear of corn,* Cic. **B.** Meton., *the ear itself,* Verg. **II.** Transf., *bristly hair,* Pers.

Aristaeus -i, m. (Ἀρίσταιος), *son of Apollo and Cyrene, legendary introducer of bee-keeping.*

Aristarchus -i, m. (Ἀρίσταρχος), *a celebrated grammarian and critic of Alexandria;* appell. *a severe critic,* Cic.

Aristīdēs -is, m. (Ἀριστείδης). **I.** *a celebrated Athenian statesman and general, rival of Themistocles.* **II.** *a poet of Miletus.*

Aristippus -i, m. (Ἀρίστιππος), *a philosopher of Cyrene (about 380 B.C.) founder of the Cynic school.* Adj., **Aristippēus** -a -um, *of or belonging to Aristippus.*

Aristo and **Aristōn** -ōnis, m. (Ἀρίστων), *a philosopher of Chios, pupil of Zeno, contemporary with Caesar;* hence adj., **Aristōnēus** -a -um, *of or belonging to Aristo.*

Aristŏdēmus -i, m. (Ἀριστόδημος). **I.** *a tragic actor at Athens.* **II.** *a tyrant of Cumae in Campania, about 502 B.C.*

aristŏlŏchĭa -ae, f. (ἀριστολοχία), *a plant useful in childbirth,* Cic.

Aristŏphănēs -is, m. (Ἀριστοφάνης). **I.** *the great Athenian comic dramatist.* Adj., **Aristŏphăneus** -a -um, *of or relating to Aristophanes.* **II.** *a celebrated grammarian, pupil of Eratosthenes.*

Aristŏtĕlēs -is and -i, m. (Ἀριστοτέλης), *the celebrated Greek philosopher, founder of the Peripatetic school.* Adj., **Aristŏtĕlēus** -a -um, *of or relating to Aristotle.*

ărithmĕtĭca -ae and -ē -ēs, f. (ἀριθμητική, sc. τέχνη), *arithmetic,* Sen.

ărithmĕtĭca -ōrum, n. *arithmetic,* Cic.

ărītūdo -ĭnis, f. *dryness,* Plaut.

arma -ōrum, n. (Root AR, Greek AP, cf. τὰ ἄρμενα), *tools, implements.* **I.** Gen., arma equestria, *the fittings of a horse,* Liv. ; cerealia, *implements for grinding and baking corn,* Verg. ; *building tools,* Cic. **II.** *implements of war.* **A.** In the broadest sense, Liv. **B.** In a narrower meaning, *defensive armour* (tela, *offensive weapons*), **1,** Lit. arma his imperata, galea, clypeum, ocreae, lorica, omnia ex aere, Liv. ; arma capere, sumere, Cic. ; ad arma ire, Cic. ; armis decertare or decernere, Cic. ; in armis esse or stare, *to be under arms,* Liv. ; CL milia habere in armis, Liv. ; arma deponere, Liv. ; tradere, Liv. ; ad arma *"to arms,"* Caes. ; **2,** Meton., *war;* arma civilia, Cic. ; **3,** *military power;* Romana arma ingruere, Liv. ; **4,** *soldiers;* levia, *light-armed troops,* Liv. ; **5,** Fig. *defence;* arma prudentiae, Cic.

armamenta -ōrum, n. *implements, tackle;* esp. of a ship, vela armamentaque, Caes.

armāmentārĭum -i, n. *an armoury,* Cic.

armārĭŏlum -i, n. (dim. of armarium), *a little cupboard,* Plaut.

armārĭum -i, n. *a cupboard, chest,* Cic.

armātūra -ae, f. **A.** *equipment, armour;* Numidae levis armaturae, *light-armed,* Caes. **B.** Meton., *armed soldiers;* armatura levis, *light-armed troops,* Liv.

1. armatus, abl. -ū, m. *armour.* **A.** Lit., haud dispari armatu, Liv. **B.** Meton., *armed troops;* gravis, *heavy-armed troops,* Liv.

2. armatus -a -um, p. adj. with superl. (armo), *armed, equipped.* **A.** Lit., armatus togatusque, *both in war and in peace,* Liv. ; armatae classes, Verg. **B.** Transf., erat incredibili armatus audacia, Cic.

Armĕnĭa -ae, f. (Ἀρμενία), *a country in Asia;* hence, **Armĕnĭus** -a -um. **A.** Adj., *Armenian.* **B.** Subst., *an Armenian.*

armentālis -e, *belonging to a herd;* equae, Verg.

armentum -i, n. *cattle living in herds;* Esp. *oxen and horses;* **1,** sing. collective, *a herd;* Pan erat armenti custos, Ov. ; **2,** plur., *oxen;* greges armentorum reliquique pecoris, Cic.

armĭfĕr -fĕra -fĕrum (arma and fero), *bearing arms, warlike,* Ov.

armĭgĕr -gĕra -gĕrum (arma and gero), *bearing arms.* Subst., **a,** armiger -geri, m. *an armour-bearer,* Cic. ; Jovis, *the eagle,* Verg. ; Catilinae, *adherent,* Cic. ; **b,** armigera -ae, f. *a female armour-bearer,* Ov.

armilla -ae, f. *a bracelet,* worn by both men and women, Cic., Liv.

armillātus -a um, *adorned with a bracelet,* Suet. ; canes, *wearing a collar,* Prop.

armĭlustrĭum -ĭi, n. (arma and lustro), *a festival at which arms were consecrated,* celebrated at a spot in Rome called Armilustrum.

armĭpŏtens -entis, *mighty in arms, warlike,* Mars., Verg. ; diva, *Minerva,* Verg.

armĭsŏnus -a -um, *resounding with arms,* Verg.

armo, 1., **1,** *to provide with implements, to equip;* naves, Caes. ; **2,** *to arm, prepare for battle;* a, aliquem in rempublicam, Cic. ; milites, Caes. ; servum in or contra dominum, Cic. ; equum bello, *for battle,* Verg. : gladiis dextras, Liv. ; b, transf. *to supply, arm;* multitudinem auctoritate publica, Cic. ; se eloquentia, Cic.

armŏrācĭa -ae. f. (-cium -ii, n.), *horse-radish* (cochlearia armoracia, Linn.), Plin.

armus -i, m. (ἁρμός), **1,** *the shoulder-blade ;* latos huic hasta per armos tremit, Verg. ; in animals, *the shoulder ;* ex humeris armi fiunt, Ov. ; **2,** *the side of an animal,* Verg.

Arnus -i, m. (Ἄρνος), *the chief river of Etruria,* now the *Arno.* Adj., **Arnĭensis,** -e.

ăro, 1. (ἀρόω), *to plough.* **A.** Lit., 1, arare terram et sulcum altius imprimere, Cic. ; prov., non profecturis litora bubus aras, *to labour uselessly,* Ov. ; **2,** *to farm, cultivate;* Falerni mille fundi jugera, Hor. ; absol., cives Romani qui arant in Sicilia, *tenants of the domain-lands,* (cf. aratio), Cic. **B.** Transf., **1,** *to furrow, wrinkle;* rugae quae tibi corpus arent, Ov. ; **2,** of ships, *to plough the sea;* vastum maris aequor, Verg.

Arpi -ōrum, m. *a town in Apulia.* Adj., **Arpīnus** -a -um, *of or belonging to Arpi.*

Arpīnum, -i, n. *a town in Latium, birthplace of Cicero and Marius.* Adj., **Arpīnās** -ātis, **Arpīnus** -a -um, *of or belonging to Arpinum.*

arquātus, v. arcuatus.

arra, v. arrha.

arrectus, -a -um, p. adj. with compar. (from arrigo), *steep,* Liv.

arrēpo (ad-repo), -repsi, -reptum, 3. *to creep to, to glide gently to;* quibus rebus non sensim atque moderate ad amicitiam adrepserat, Cic.

Arrētĭum -ĭi, n. *a town in Etruria, birthplace of Maecenas.*

arrha -ae, f., and **arrhăbo** -ōnis, m. *earnest money,* Plaut., Ter.

arrīdĕo (ad-rīdĕo), -risi -risum, 2. *to laugh to;* **I.** *to laugh with;* ridentibus arrident, Hor. **II.** *to laugh at,* either in approval or ridicule. **A.** Lit., with dat. of pers., vix notis familiariter arridere, Liv. ; with acc. of the thing, video quid arriseris, Cic. **B.** Transf., **a,** *to be favourable;* quum tempestas arridet, Lucr. ; **b,** *to please;* "inhibere" illud tuum quod mihi valde arriserat, Cic.

arrĭgo -rexi -rectum, 3. (ad and rego). **A.** *to erect, lift up;* aures, comas, Verg. **B.** Transf., **a,** *to excite;* arrexere animos Itali, Verg. ; **b,** *to encourage, animate;* aliquem oratione, Sall.

arrĭpio -ripui -reptum, 3. (ad and rapio). **I.** *to seize on, lay hold of, snatch.* **A.** Gen. arma, Liv. ; cibum unguium tenacitate, Cic. ; aliquem manu, Liv. ; tabulam de naufragio, Cic. ; cohortes arreptas in urbem inducere, Liv. ; terram velis, *to sail quickly to,* Verg. **B.** Transf., **a,** *to seize upon, appropriate, take;* facultatem laedendi, quaecumque detur, Cic. ; maledicta ex trivio Cic. ; **b,** *to comprehend quickly;* celeriter res innumerabiles, Cic. ; litteras Graecas, *take to with zeal,* Cic. ; **II.** *to seize with violence ;* **a,** of diseases, &c., dolor, qui simul arripuit interficit, Cic. ; **b,** legal **t.t.** *to drag before a tribunal, accuse,* Cic. ;

c, transf., *to satirize;* primores **populi populumque,** Hor.

arrīsor -ōris, m. *one who smiles approvingly,* a *flatterer,* Sen.

arrōdo (ad-rōdo) -rōsi -rōsum, 3. *to gnaw at;* mures Antii coronam auream arrosere, Liv. ; fig., ut illa ex vepreculis extracta nitedula rempublicam conaretur arrodere, Cic.

arrŏgans -antis, p. adj. with compar. and superl. (from arrogo), *assuming, arrogant, haughty;* Indutiomarus iste minax atque arrogans, Cic.

arrŏgantĕr, adv. *arrogantly, haughtily;* dicere aliquid, Cic. ; scribere ad aliquem, Cic. ; facere, Caes.

arrŏgantia -ae, f. *arrogance, assumption, pride, haughtiness;* ex arrogantia odium, ex insolentia arrogantia oritur, Cic.

arrŏgo (ad-rŏgo), 1. **I.** 1, sibi aliquid, *to appropriate to oneself something to which one has no claim;* sibi sapientiam, Cic. ; **2,** alicui aliquid, *to claim, confer upon;* decus imperiis, Hor. **II.** 1, *to ask,* Plaut. ; **2,** *to associate one public officer with another;* cui unico consuli dictatorem arrogari haud satis decorum visum est patribus, Liv.

arrōsor -ōris, m. *one who gnaws at,* Sen

Arrūns (Ārŭns) -ūntis, m, *name of a younger son of Tarquinius Superbus.*

ars -tis, f. (stem AR, whence ar- -mus, ar- -tus; Gr. ΑΡΩ, ἀρτύω, ἀρετή). **I. A.** *a trade, profession, art;* disserendi, *dialectics,* Cic ; artes sordidae *mean occupations,* those of slaves, Cic. ; ingenuae, liberales, *honourable occupations,* Cic. ; urbanae, *jurisprudence and rhetoric,* Liv. ; artem aliquam factitare, Cic. ; exercere, *to practise, pursue,* Hor. **B.** Meton., 1, *art, knowledge, theory* (opp. *practice*): res mihi videtur esse facultate (*in practice*) praeclara, arte (*in theory*): mediocris, Cic. ; ex arte (dicere, scribere, &c.), *according to the rules of art,* Cic. ; hence as title of treatises on a subject, artes oratoriae, Cic. ; **2,** *skill, cleverness;* opus est vel arte vel diligentia, Cic. ; arte laboratae vestes, Verg. ; arte canere, Cic. ; **3,** plur., artes, *works of art,* Cic. ; **4,** Artes, *the Muses,* Phaed. **II.** Transf., 1, *conduct, character, method of acting, good or bad ;* bonae artes, *good qualities,* Sall. ; hac arte Pollux attigit arces igneas, Hor. ; **2,** absol., *cunning, deceit,* Verg.

Arsăcēs -is, m. (Ἀρσάκης), *the first king of the Parthians ;* hence, 1, **Arsăcĭdes** -ae, m. *a descendant of Arsaces;* **2, Arsăcĭus** -a -um, *Parthian.*

Artaxăta -ōrum, n. (-a -ae, f., Tac.), *capital of Armenia on the Araxes.*

Artaxerxēs -is, m. (Ἀρταξέρξης), *name of three Persian kings.*

artē (arctē), adv. with compar. and superl. (artus), *narrowly, tightly, closely.* **I.** Lit. artius complecti aliquem, Cic. ; signa artius collocare, Sall. ; fig., artius astringere rationem, Cic. **II.** Transf., **a,** *fast, soundly ;* dormire, Cic. ; **b,** *shortly;* artius appellare aliquem, *to cut a name short,* Ov. ; aliquem arte colere, *stingily,* Sall.

artērĭa -ae, f. (ἀρτηρία), 1, *the wind-pipe,* Cic. ; neut. plur., heterocl. arteria, Lucr. ; 2 *an artery,* Cic.

arthrītĭcus -a -um (ἀρθριτικός), *gouty,* Cic.

artĭcŭlāris -e, *relating to the joints;* morbus, *gout,* Suet.

artĭcŭlātim, adv. **A.** *limb by limb, piecemeal,* Plaut. **B.** Transf., *in a manner properly divided, distinctly;* articulatim distincteque dici, Cic.

artĭcŭlo, 1. *to articulate, speak distinctly,* Lucr.

artĭcŭlus -i, m. (dim. of artus). **I.** Lit. **1,** *a joint;* articulorum dolores, *gouty or rheumatic*

pains, Cic. **;** plur. meton., *the limbs,* esp., *the fingers,* Lucr., Ov.; 2, of plants, *a knob, knot,* Cic. **II.** Transf., 1, *a division of a discourse;* articuli membraque, Cic. ; 2, of time, *a moment, crisis;* in ipso articulo temporis, Cic. ; 3, of other abstractions, *part, division, point;* per eosdem articulos et gradus, Suet.

artĭfex -fĭcis, (ars and facio). **I.** 1, *an artist, artificer, painter, sculptor;* artifices scenici, *actors,* Cic. ; artifex equus, *a trained horse,* Ov. ; with genit. of gerund ; Graeci dicendi artifices et doctores, Cic. ; 2, *the maker, author, contriver;* probus ejus (mundi) artifex, Cic. ; 3, *a master of any art;* tractandi animos artifices, Liv. ; artifex conquirendae et comparandae voluptatis, Cic. ; artifices ad corrumpendum judicium, Cic. **II.** Of inanimate objects, 1, *active, clever, skilled;* artifex stilus, Cic. ; 2, passive, *skilfully wrought* or *made;* artifices boves, Prop.

artĭfĭciōsē, adv. *skilfully;* id multo artificiosius efficere, Cic.

artĭfĭciōsus -a -um. **A.** *skilful, accomplished;* rhetores artificiosissimi, Cic.; opus, Cic. **B.** Transf., *artificial* (opp. to natural) ; ea genera divinandi non naturalia, sed artificiosa dicuntur, Cic.

artĭfĭcĭum -i, n. **I.** *an occupation, handicraft;* ancillare, Cic. **II.** Esp., **A.** *theory, system;* componere artificium de jure civili, Cic. **B.** a, *cleverness, skill, art;* simulacrum Dianae singulari opere artificioque perfectum, Cic. ; b, *dexterity,* and in a bad sense, *cunning, craft;* artificio simulationis, Cic. ; c, *work of art;* haec opera atque artificia, Cic.

arto (arcto), 1. (artus), 1, *to press together, reduce to small compass,* Lucr. ; 2, *to abridge, curtail ;* in praemiis, in honoribus omnia artata, Liv.

artŏlăgănus -i, m. (ἀρτολάγανον), *a cake made of meal, wine, milk, oil, lard,* and *pepper,* Cic.

artŏpta -ae, m. (ἀρτόπτης), 1, *a baker,* Juv. ; 2, *a baker's vessel,* Plaut.

1. artus (arctus), -a -um, adj., with compar. and superl. (root AR, Gr. AP, whence 2. artus, arma, &c.), *narrow, tight, close.* **I.** Lit., catena, Ov. ; vinculum ad astringendam fidem artius, Cic. ; vallis, Liv. Subst., **artum** -i, n., *narrow space;* pugna in arto, Tac. **II.** Transf., a, *fast, sound;* somnus, Cic. ; b, *oppressed by care;* animus, Hor. ; c, *small, meagre;* numerus, Tac.; commeatus, Liv.; d, *difficult, distressing;* res, Ov. Subst., quum in arto res esset, Liv.

2. artŭs -ūs, m. (root A R, Gr. ἄρθρον), usually plur., artūs -ŭum, *the joints;* dolor artuum, *gout,* Cic. ; omnibus artubus contremisco, *I tremble in all my limbs,* Cic. ; fig., nervi atque artus sapientiae, Cic. ; poet., *limbs;* salsus per artus sudor iit, Verg.

ărŭla -ae. f., (dim. of ara), *a little altar,* Cic.

ărundĭfer -fĕra -fĕrum (arundo and fero), *reed-bearing;* caput, Ov.

ărundĭnĕus -a -um, *reedy;* canales, Verg. ; carmen, *a shepherd's song,* Ov.

ărundĭnōsus -a -um, *full of reeds,* Cat.

ărundo -ĭnis, f. *a reed.* **A.** Lit., crines umbrosa tegebat arundo, Verg. ; casae ex arundine textae, Liv. **B.** Meton., for an object made of reeds ; 1, *a fishing-rod;* moderator arundinis, *a fisherman,* Ov. ; 2, *limed twigs for catching birds,* Plaut. 3, *a pen;* tristis, *a severe style,* Mart. ; 4, *the shaft of an arrow,* Ov. ; poet., *the arrow itself,* Verg. ; 5, *a shepherd's pipe,* Verg. ; 6, *a flute,* Ov. ; 7, *a weaver's comb,* Ov. ; 8, *a scare-crow,* Hor. ; 9, *a plaything for children, a hobby-horse.* Hor.

arvĕho = adveho.

Arverni -orum, m. *a Gallic people in Aquitaine, in what is now Auvergne.* Adj., **Arvernus** -a -um, *Arvernian.*

arvīna -ae, f. *fat, lard,* Verg.

arvum -i, n. (aro), 1, *a ploughed* or *sown field,* Verg. ; 2, *a country, region;* arva laeta, Verg. ; arva Neptunia, *the sea,* Verg.

arvus -a -um, *ploughed,* Cic.

arx -cis, f. (from ARC, root of arceo), *a fortress, citadel, stronghold.* **I.** Lit., **A.** In the narrow sense ; ne quando arx hostium esset, Liv. ; at Rome the arx was *the S. W. height of the Capitol;* ne quis patricius in arce aut in Capitolio habitaret, Liv. ; used also of the whole hill ; Capitolina, Liv. ; *the stronghold* or *chief place of a town;* amisso oppido fugerat in arcem, Cic. ; *the stronghold of a kingdom;* ad caput arcemque regni Pergamum, Liv. ; prov., arcem facere e cloaca, *to make a mountain of a mole-hill,* Cic. ; **B.** In wider sense, *the height of heaven;* siderea arx, Ov. ; *temples of the gods,* Hor. ; (of towers), beatae arces, *Corinth,* Hor. ; *the height of a mountain;* Parnassi arx, Ov. **II.** Transf. **A.** *refuge, bulwark, protection;* haec urbs arx omnium gentium, Cic. **B.** *head-quarters, chief place;* ubi Hannibal sit, ibi caput atque arcem totius belli esse, Liv.

as, assis, m. (εἷς), *the whole* as *unity,* divided into twelve unciae, called uncia $\frac{1}{12}$, sextans $\frac{1}{6}$, quadrans $\frac{1}{4}$, triens $\frac{1}{3}$, quincunx $\frac{5}{12}$, semis $\frac{1}{2}$, septunx $\frac{7}{12}$, bes $\frac{2}{3}$, dodrans $\frac{3}{4}$, dextans $\frac{5}{6}$, deunx $\frac{11}{12}$. **A.** Gen., esp. in terms relating to inheritance, haeres ex asse, *sole heir,* Plin. **B.** Esp., 1, as a coin, *the* as, which originally consisted of a pound of copper, but was ultimately reduced to $\frac{1}{24}$ lb., and from the time of the second Punic war was worth a little over *a farthing;* hence prov., omnia ad assem perdere, *to the last farthing,* Hor. ; non assis facere, *not to estimate at a farthing,* Cat. ; 2, as a weight, *a pound,* Ov. ; 3, *an acre,* Plin.

asbestĭnum -i, n. sc. linum (ἀσβέστινον), *incombustible cloth,* Plin.

1. Ascănĭus -ĭi, m. *son of Aeneas and Creusa,* Verg. ; or *of Lavinia,* Liv.

2. Ascănĭus, -ĭi, m. *a river in Bithynia,* now *Tschatirgha Su.*

ascaules -is, m. (ἀσκαύλης), *a bag piper,* Mart.

ascendo -scendi -scensum, 3. (ad and scando), *to mount, ascend, go up.* **I.** Lit. with in and the acc., in murum, Cic. ; in equum, Cic. ; in concionem, *to go up to speak to the people,* Cic. ; with ad, ad Gitanas, Liv. ; with acc. alone, murum, Caes. ; ripam equo, Cic. **II.** Transf., *to rise,* in tantum honorem, Cic. ; altiorem gradum, Cic. ; gradatim ascendere vocem utile et suave est, *the voice rising higher and higher,* Cic.

ascensĭo -ōnis, f. *an ascent,* Plaut. ; transf., oratorum, *lofty flight,* Cic.

ascensus -ūs, m. *a going up, climbing up, ascent.* **I. A.** Lit., in Capitolium, Cic. **B.** Transf., primus ad honoris gradum, Cic. **II.** Meton., *the place for ascending;* difficilis atque arduus, Cic.

ascĭa -ae, f. *a carpenter's axe* or *adze,* ap. Cic.

ascĭo, (ad-scio), 4. *to take to oneself, adopt as one's own;* socios, Verg. ; asciri per adoptionem, Tac.

ascisco (adscisco), ascivi, ascitum, 3. (ascio) *to receive, admit.* **I.** Lit., with ad and the acc., ad hoc sceleris foedus, Cic. ; with in, aliquem in numerum civium, Cic. **;** with inter, inter patricios, Tac.; with dat., superis ascitus, Caesar, Ov.; with double acc., aliquem patronum, Cic. **II.** Transf. **A.** *to adopt*, hanc consuetudinem, Cic. **B.** *to approve of;* quas (leges) Latini voluerunt, asciverunt, Cic.; **2,** *to claim for oneself*, sibi sapientium, Cic.

1. ascītus -a -um (partic. of ascisco), *foreign, derived from without* (opp. nativus), Nep.

2. ascītus -us, m. *an acceptance, reception*, Cic.

ascŏpēra -ae, f. (ἀσκοπήρα), *a leather knapsack*, Suet.

Ascra -ae, f. (Ἄσκρα), *a small town in Boeotia, near Mount Helicon, the home of Hesiod.* Adj., **Ascraeus** -a -um; a, *Ascraean, of Ascra;* poeta, Prop.; senex, Verg.; simply Ascraeus = *Hesiod*, Ov.; b, carmen, *Hesiodic*, or *rural*, Verg.; c, fontes, *Heliconian*, Prop.

ascrībo (ad-scribo) -scripsi -scriptum, 3. (ad and scribo), *to write to*, or *in addition.* **A.** Lit. 1, with dat., poenam foederibus, Cic.; with in and the acc., aliquid in eandem legem, Cic.; 2, *to fix, appoint;* aliquem tutorem liberis, Cic.; 3, *to enrol;* aliquem in civitatem, Cic.; esp., a, *as a colonist*, colonos, Liv.; with acc., of the colony, colonos Venusiam, Liv.; β, *to enrol as a soldier;* urbanae militiae ascribi, Tac. **B.** Transf. 1, *to reckon under a class, include;* with ad or in and the acc., or with the dat., tu vero me ascribe in talem numerum, Cic.; aliquem ordinibus deorum, Hor.; with two acc., opinio socium me ascribit tuis laudibus, Cic.; 2, *to attribute, impute*, alicui incommodum, Cic.

ascriptīcĭus -a -um, *one who is enrolled as a member of a community*, Cic.

ascriptĭo -ōnis, f. *an addition in writing*, Cic.

ascriptīvus -a -um, *enrolled as a supernumerary*, Plaut.

ascriptor -ōris, m. *one who willingly adds his name, one who approves of;* legis agrariae, Cic.

Ascŭlum -i, n. *town of the Picentines.* Adj., **Ascŭlānus** -a -um, *of or belonging to Asculum.*

ăsella -ae, f. (dim. of asina), *a little she-ass*, Ov.

ăsellus -i, m. (dim. of asinus), *a little ass*, Cic.

Ăsĭa -ae, f. (Ἀσία). **I.** *the district in Lydia near the river Cayster.* **II.** *The continent of Asia.* **III.** *The peninsula of Asia Minor;* sometimes used specially for the kingdom of Pergamus (Liv.), or of the Troad (Ov.). **IV.** In the narrowest sense (the ordinary meaning of the word), *the Roman province of Asia, formed out of the kingdom of Pergamus;* hence, 1, **Ăsĭăgĕnes** -is, m. *surname of L. Corn. Scipio;* 2, **Ăsĭānus** -a -um, *belonging to the province of Asia.* Plur. subst., **Ăsĭani** -orum, m. *the farmers of the taxes of the province of Asia*, Cic.; 3, **Ăsĭātĭcus** -a -um, *Asiatic, surname of L. Corn. Scipio;* Asiatici oratores, *bombastic, ornate*, Cic.; 4, **Ăsĭs** -ĭdis, f. *Asiatic;* 5, **Ăsĭus** -a -um, palus, *the marsh round Ephesus*, Verg.

ăsĭlus -i, m. *the gad-fly*, Verg.

ăsĭna -ae, f. *a she ass*, Varr.

ăsĭnīnus -a -um, *belonging to an ass*, Plin.

Ăsĭnĭus -a -um, *name of a Roman gens, of which the most celebrated was* C. Asinius Pollio, *friend of J. Caesar and Augustus, statesman, orator, poet, historian.*

ăsĭnus -i, m. **A.** *an ass*, Cic. **B.** Transf., *a dolt, blockhead;* quid nunc te, asine, litteras doceam, Cic.

Ăsōpus -i, m. (Ἀσωπός). **I.** a, *a river in Boeotia;* b, *the river-god Asopus;* hence, **A.** **Ăsōpĭădēs** -ae, m. *a descendant of Asopus*

(Aeacus), Ov. **B.** **Ăsōpĭs** -ĭdis, f. 1, *Aegina, daughter of Asopus, mother of Aeacus by Jupiter*, Ov.; 2, *Euadne, daughter of Aegina*, Ov. **II.** *a river in Phthiotis.*

ăsōtus -i, m. (ἄσωτος), *a sensualist, libertine*, Cic.

aspărăgus -i, m. (ἀσπάραγος), *asparagus*, Suet.

aspargo, v. aspergo.

Aspāsia -ae, f. (Ἀσπασία), *the most celebrated of the Greek Hetaerae, mistress of Pericles.*

aspectābĭlis -e, *visible*, Cic.

aspecto, 1. **I.** *to look at earnestly*, or *with respect;* a, quid me aspectas, Cic.; b, of place, *to lie towards, to face;* mare quod Hiberniam insulam aspectat, Tac. **II.** *to observe, attend to;* jussa principis, Tac.

aspectus -us, m. **A.** Act. 1, *a seeing, looking, sight;* uno aspectu, Cic.; oculi mobiles ut aspectum quo vellent facile converterent, Cic.; 2, *view, limit of vision;* orbes qui aspectum nostrum definiunt, Cic.; 3, *power of vision;* omnia quae sub aspectum cadunt, Cic. **B.** Pass. 1, *sight, power of being seen;* patriam privare aspectu tuo, Cic.; situs Syracusarum laetus ad aspectum, Cic.; 2, *look, aspect, appearance;* pomorum jucundus aspectus, Cic.

aspello -puli -pulsum (abs and pello), 3. *to drive away*, Plaut.

Aspendus -i, f. (Ἄσπενδος), *a town in Pamphylia.* Adj., **Aspendĭus** -a -um, *of* or *belonging to Aspendus.*

asper -ěra -ěrum (-pra -prum, Verg.), *rough;* 1, physically, a, to the sense of touch; loca, *uneven*, Caes.; mare, *stormy*, Liv.; aspera caelo, *inclement in climate*, Liv. Subst., **aspěrum** -i, n. *roughness, a rough place*, Tac.; b, to the senses of taste and smell, *pungent, sour;* vinum, Ter.; c, to the sense of hearing, *harsh, grating*, Cic.; litera aspera, *the letter R*, Ov.; 2, morally, *rough, wild, harsh;* homo asper et durus, Cic.; of animals, *fierce*, anguis asper siti, Verg.; of events, *adverse, troublous, dangerous;* res, tempora, Cic.; sententia, *severe*, Liv.; of speech, *harsh, bitter;* facetiae, Cic.

aspěrē, adv. (asper), *roughly;* loqui, Cic.; scribere, Cic.

1. aspergo (aspargo) -spersi -spersum, 3. (ad and spargo). **I.** *to sprinkle;* a, guttam bulbo, Cic.; virus pecori, Verg.; b, *to cast upon, mingle with, add;* sapores huc, Verg.; transf., alicui molestiam, Cic. **II.** *to bespatter;* a, aram sanguine, Cic.; transf., *to sully, stain, asperse;* splendorem vitae maculis, Cic.; b, *to strew over;* olivam sale, Plin.; transf., aliquid mendaciunculis, Cic.

2. aspergo (aspargo) -ĭnis, f. *a sprinkling, besprinkling, spray;* aquarum, Ov.; salsa adspargo, Verg.

aspěrĭtas -ātis, f. *roughness.* **I.** Lit. 1, to the touch, *unevenness;* saxorum, Cic.; 2, to the taste, *sourness;* vini, Plin.; 3, to the ear, *harshness;* soni, Tac. **II.** Transf., 1, of character, *harshness, fierceness, severity, austerity;* Stoicorum, Cic.; 2, of inanimate things, *severity;* frigorum, *severe cold*, Sall.; of circumstances, *calamity, difficulty;* rerum, Cic.; of speech, *harshness;* judicialis verborum, Cic.

aspernātĭo -ōnis, f. *contempt*, Cic.

aspernor, 1. dep. *to despise, contemn, reject, spurn;* aspernatur dolorem ut malum, Cic.; amicitiam alicujus, Cic.; with a and the abl., proscriptionem nisi hoc judicio a vobis rejicitis atque aspernamini, Cic.

aspěro, 1. *to make rough.* **I.** Lit., a, glacialis hiems aquilonibus asperat undas, *make stormy*, Verg.; b, *to sharpen, whet;* sagittas

ossibus, Tac. II. Transf., *to excite, arouse;* aliquem in saevitiam, Tac.

aspersĭo -ōnis, f. *a sprinkling;* aquae, Cic.

aspersus -ūs, m. *a sprinkling,* Plin.

aspĭcĭo -spexi -spectum, 3. (ad and specio). **I.** *to look at, behold, see.* **A.** Lit., **1**, **a,** of persons, lucem aspicere vix possum, *endure the light of day,* live, Cic. ; **b,** of places, *to look towards, to face;* ea pars Britanniae quae Hiberniam aspicit, Tac. ; **2, a,** *to survey, inspect;* tabulas, Cic. ; **b,** *to look straight in the face, to withstand, confront;* aliquem in acie, Nep. ; hostem aspicere non possunt, Cic. **B.** Transf., **1,** *to weigh, consider;* neque tanta est in rebus obscuritas, ut eas non penitus vir ingenio cernat, si modo aspexerit, Cic. ; **2,** *to investigate;* res sociorum, Liv. **II.** Inchoative, *to perceive;* simulac Lentulum aspexit, Cic.

aspīrātĭo -ōnis, f. **1,** *a breathing;* aëris, Cic. ; **2,** *exhalation;* terrarum, Cic. ; **3,** *the pronunciation of the letter H, aspiration,* Cic.

aspīro, **1.** *to breathe, blow upon.* **I.** Intransit., *to breathe* or *blow upon.* **A.** Lit., pulmones se contrahunt aspirantes, *exhaling,* Cic. ; aspirant aurae in noctem, *towards evening,* Verg. **B.** Transf., *to be favourable to, assist;* aspiravit nemo eorum, Cic. ; with dat., vos, Calliope, aspirate canenti, Verg. ; **3,** *to approach,* Februario mense aspiravit in curiam, Cic. ; **4,** *to climb up to, to endeavour to obtain, to reach to* (in Cic. only with negatives), ex bellica laude ad Africanum aspirare nemo potest, Cic. **II.** Transit., *to breathe upon, blow on.* **A.** Lit., Juno ventos aspirat eunti, *give them a favourable wind,* Verg. **B.** Transf., *to infuse,* divinum amorem dictis, Verg.

aspis -ĭdis, f. (ἀσπίς), *an adder, asp,* Cic.

asportātĭo -ōnis, f. *a taking away, carrying off;* signorum, Cic.

asporto, 1. (abs and porto), *to carry off, take away;* multa de suis rebus secum, Cic. ; abreptam ex eo loco virginem secum, Cic.

asprētum -i, n. (asper), *a rough, uneven spot,* Liv.

Assărăcus -i, m. (Ἀσσάρακος), *a mythical king of Phrygia, son of Tros, brother of Ganymede, grandfather of Anchises;* Assaraci nurus, *Venus,* Ov. ; domus Assaraci, *the Romans,* Verg. ; Assaraci tellus, *Troy,* Hor.

assĕcla (assĕcŭla) -ae, m. (assequor), *a follower, servant, sycophant;* assentatores eorum atque asseculae, Cic.

assectātĭo -ōnis, f. *respectful attendance,* e.g., of a client on a patron, Cic.

assectātor -ōris, m., **1,** *a companion, follower;* cum ducibus ipsis, non cum comitatu assectatoribusque configant, Cic. ; **2,** *a disciple;* philosophiae, Plin.

assector, 1. dep., *to follow, attend assiduously* (esp. of friends of candidates); quum aedilitatem P. Crassus peteret eumque Ser. Galba assectaretur, Cic.

assensĭo -ōnis, **1,** *assent, agreement, applause;* popularis, Cic. ; rem assensione comprobare, Cic. ; plur., crebrae assensiones, Cic. ; **2,** as philosoph. t.t., *belief in the reality of sensible appearances* (Gr. συγκατάθεσις), Cic.

assensor -ōris, m. *one who assents* or *agrees;* quotidie commemorabam te unum in tanto exercitu mihi fuisse assensorem, Cic.

assensus -ūs, m. **I.** *assent, agreement;* assensu omnium dicere, Cic. **II.** Esp. **A.** Philosoph. t.t. *belief in the reality of sensible appearances;* assensum retinere, Cic. **B.** Poet., *echo;* nemorum, Verg.

assentātĭo -ōnis, f. *a flattering assent* or *ap-*

plause, *flattery;* faceta parasitorum, Cic. ; nullam in amicitiis pestem esse majorem quam adulationem, blanditiam, assentationem, Cic. ; plur., blanditiae et assentationes, Cic.

assentātĭuncŭla -ae, f. (dim. of assentatio), *trivial flattery,* Cic.

assentātor -ōris, m. (assentor), *a flatterer;* cavendum est ne assentatoribus patefaciamus aures, Cic.

assentātōrĭē, adv. (assentator), *flatteringly,* Cic.

assentātrix -trīcis, f. (assentator), *a female flatterer,* Plaut.

assentĭo -sensi -sensum, 4. and (gen. in classical authors) **assentĭor** -sensus sum, -sentiri (ad and sentio), *to assent to, agree with;* **a,** deponent form, gov. dat. of pers., de Vennonianis rebus tibi assentior, Cic. ; with dat. of the thing, ut ego assentior orationi, Cic. ; with acc. of obj., ego illud assentior Theophrasto, Cic. ; **b,** active form, cavendum est ne his rebus temere assentiamus, Cic. ; **c,** pass., neque percepta neque assensa, Cic. ; assentiendum temporibus, *we must accommodate ourselves to the times,* Cic.

assentor, 1. dep. (intens. of assentior), *to assent constantly, to flatter;* benevolentiam civium blanditiis et assentando colligere, Cic. ; with obj. in acc., ut nihil nobis assentati esse videamur, Cic. ; Baiae tibi assentantur, *wooes thee,* Cic.

assĕquor -cutus sum, 3. dep., *to follow* **I.** Lit., Porcius deinde assecutus cum levi armatura, Liv. **II.** Transf., *to reach by following, come up to, attain;* **a,** aliquem, Cic. ; merita alicujus non assequi, Cic. ; **b,** esp., *to gain* or *attain to something for which one strives;* eosdem honorum gradus, Cic. ; immortalitatem, Cic. ; foll. by ut or ne with the subj., Cic. ; or by the infin., Cic. ; **c,** of the mind, *to grasp, comprehend;* aliquid cogitatione, Cic.

asser -ĕris, m. (root ASS, whence also assis or axis) *a stake, a pole.* **A.** Gen., Caes. **B.** Esp., *a pole for carrying a litter,* Suet.

assercŭlum -i, n., or -us -i, m. *a small stake* or *pole,* Cato.

1. assĕro -sēvi -sītum 3. (ad and sero), *to plant at* or *near;* populus assita limitibus, Hor.

2. assĕro -sĕrŭi -sertum, 3. (ad and sero), *to join to.* **I.** Legal t. t., **A.** *to lay hold of a slave,* and thereby declare him free; aliquem in libertatem, Liv. ; aliquem manu liberali causa, Plaut. ; aliquem in liberali causa, Cic., ; asserui jam me, *I have freed myself,* Ov. **B.** *to claim as a slave;* aliquem in servitutem, Liv. **II.** Transf., **A.** *to set free from, protect;* se a mortalitate, Plin. **B.** *to claim;* alicui regnum, Liv. ; aliquem caelo, *declare the celestial origin of a person,* Ov.

assertĭo -ōnis, f. *a formal declaration as to freedom,* Suet.

assertor, -ōris, m. (2. assero), *one who asserts that another person is free* or *a slave.* **I.** Lit., **A.** *one who defends the liberty of another;* assertor libertatis, Plin. **B.** *one who asserts that another is a slave;* assertor puellae, Liv. **II.** Transf., *a liberator, saviour,* Ov.

asservĭo, 4. *to assist, help;* toto corpore contentioni vocis, Cic.

asservo, 1., **a,** *to preserve;* tabulas negligentius, Cic. ; aliquem domi suae, Cic. ; **b,** *to watch, observe;* oram, Caes. ; fig., *to attend to;* jus negligentius, Cic.

assessĭo -ōnis, f. (assideo), *a sitting by the side of one* (to console); quae tua fuerit assessio, oratio, confirmatio animi mei fracti, Cic.

assessor -ōris, m. (assideo), *one who sits by the side to assist;* Lacedaemonii regibus suis augurem assessorem dederunt; esp., *an assistant, a judicial assessor,* Suet.

assessus, abl. -ū, m. (assideo), *a sitting by the side of,* Prop.

assēvĕrantĕr, adv., with compar. (as-severans), *earnestly, emphatically;* loqui, Cic.

assēvĕrātĭo -ōnis, f. (assevero), 1, *earnest-ness in action;* multa asseveratione coguntur patres, Tac.; 2, *vehement assertion, asseveration;* omni asseveratione tibi affirmo (foll. by acc. with infin.), Cic.

assēvĕro, 1. (ad and severus), 1, *to act with earnestness;* bella ironia, si jocaremur; sin asse-veramus, vide ne, &c., Cic.; 2, *to assert confi-dently, strongly;* with acc. and infin., idque se facturum asseveravit, Cic.; with de and the abl., nemo de ulla re potest contendere neque asseverare, Cic.

assĭdĕo -sedi, -sessum, 2. (ad and sedeo), *to sit near,* or *by the side of.* **I.** Gen., **A.** Lit., Sthenius est, is qui nobis assidet, Cic. **B.** Transf., *to be next door to;* parcus assidet insano, Hor. **II.** Esp., **A.** *to sit at a person's side, to give comfort, advice, protection,* &c.; in carcere mater noctes diesque assidebat, Cic.; assidere aegro collegae, *to sit at the bedside of,* Liv.; quum, Cn. Pompeius Lentulo frequens assideret, Cic.; judiciis assidebat, *frequented,* Tac.; totā vitā litteris, *to devote oneself to,* Plin. **B.** Milit. t.t. *to besiege, blockade;* with dat., intactis muris, Liv.; assidens Casilino, Cic.

assīdo (ad -sīdo) -sēdi -sessum, 3. *to sit down;* in bibliotheca, Cic.; super aspidem, Cic.; prop-ter Tuberonem, Cic.; of an orator, *to break down in a speech;* subito assedit, Cic.

assĭdŭē, adv. (assiduus), *continuously, with-out remission;* voces quas audio assidue, Cic.; quibus (litteris) assidue utor, Cic.

assĭdŭĭtas -ātis, f. (assiduus). **I.** *continual presence, attention of friends, clients, candidates;* quotidiana amicorum assiduitas et frequentia, Cic.; medici, Cic. **II.** Transf., **A.** *constancy;* id assiduitate et virtute consequere, Cic. **B.** *con-stant repetition;* epistolarum, *unintermittent cor-respondence,* Cic.; molestiarum, Cic.; bellorum, Cic.

assĭduo = assidue, q.v.

assĭdŭus -a, -um (assideo). **I.** *sitting in a place constantly, established.* Political t.t., **assi-duus** -i, m. *a settled* and hence *a well-to-do, tax-paying citizen,* gen. in plur. assidui, *the citizens of the upper classes;* opp. to proletarii (who paid no taxes), Cic. **II.** *continuously in one place,* or *engaged in one occupation;* a, ruri assiduum semper vivere, Cic.; audivi Romae esse homi-nem et fuisse assiduum, Cic.; esp. of the friends who attended candidates and magistrates, me-cum fuit assiduus praetore me, Cic.; b, *con-stant, steady;* qui filios suos agricolas assiduos esse cupiunt, Cic.; c, of things, *constant, un-ceasing;* imbres, Cic.; homines labore assiduo et quotidiano assueti, Cic.

assignātĭo -ōnis, f. *assignment, allotment;* agrorum, Cic.

assigno, 1. *to assign to any one, allot.* **I. A.** Lit., inferiorem aedium partem alicui, Cic.; esp., of allotting lands to colonists, loca, Cic.; agros colonis, Cic.; agrum militibus, Cic. **B.** Transf., munus humanum a deo assignatum, Cic. **C.** *to ascribe;* hoc preceptum deo, Cic.; aliquid homini, non tempori, Cic. **II.** *to seal,* Pers.

assĭlio -silŭi, 4. (ad and salio), *to leap to,* or *on.* **I.** Gen., a, of persons moenibus, Ov.; b, of water, *to dash up;* assilien aqua, Ov. **II.** Transf., *to jump to;* neque assiliendum statim est ad genus illud orationis, Cic.

assĭmĭlis -e, *like, similar;* with dat., assim-ilis spongiis mollitudo, Cic.; with gen., Ov.

assĭmĭlĭtĕr, adv. (assimilis), *in like manner,* Plaut.

assĭmŭlātus -a -um (partic. of assimulo), 1, *similar,* Lucr.; 2, *feigned, pretended, simu-lated;* virtus, Cic.

assĭmŭlo, 1. *to make like.* **I. A.** deos in humani oris speciem, Tac.; litterae lituraeque omnes assimulatae, Cic. **B.** *to compare,* Cic.; formam totius Britanniae auctores oblongae scutulae vel bipenni assimulavere, Tac. **II.** *to imitate, counterfeit, pretend;* anum, Ov.; with acc. and infin., Plaut.; with quasi and the subj., Plaut.

assisto, astĭti, no sup., 3. *to place oneself, take up a position.* **I.** Lit., a, ad fores, Cic.; b, *to stand by;* foribus principum, Cic.; ad epulas regis, Cic. **II.** Transf. *to help,* Tac.

assŏlĕo, 2. *to be accustomed;* used only in the third person sing. and plur., deinde quae assolent (scribi), Cic.; ut assolet, *as is usual,* Cic.

assŏno, 1. *to answer with a sound;* plangen-tibus assonat echo, Ov.

assŭēfācĭo -fēci -factum, 3. (* assueo and facio), *to accustom to;* ad supplicia patrum ple-bem, Liv.; with abl., quorum sermone qui as-suefacti erant, Cic.; with dat., pedites operi aliisque justis militaribus, Liv.; with infin., equos eodem remanere vestigio, Caes.

assŭesco -suēvi -suetum, 3. (*assueo). **I.** Transit., *to accustom;* qui pluribus assuerit mentem, Hor. **II.** Intransit., *to accustom one-self;* assuevi, *I am wont,* Cic.; assuetus, *accus-tomed;* with in and the acc., in omnia familiaria jura assuetus, Liv.; with abl., homines labore assiduo et quotidiano assueti, Cic.; with dat., quaestui, Liv.; with acc., ne tanta animis as-suescite bella, Verg.; with infin., assueti vinci, Liv. (syncop. perf. forms assuesti, assuerim, assueram, assuesse).

assŭētūdo -inis, f. 1, *custom, use,* Liv.; 2, *carnal intercourse,* Tac.

assŭētus -a -um, adj. (from assuesco), 1, *used to, accustomed to;* assueta oculis regio, Liv.; 2, *usual;* assueti collis cultores, Liv.

assūgo -suctum, 3. *to suck,* Lucr.

assŭla -ae, f. *a shaving, chip,* Plaut

assŭlātim, adv. (assula), *in shivers* or *splinters,* Plaut.

assŭlōsē, adv. (assula), *splinter-wise,* Plin.

assulto, 1. (Intens. of assilio), *to leap vio-lently upon.* **I.** Gen., feminae assultabant ut sacrificantes aut insanientes Bacchae, Tac. **II.** Esp., *to attack, assault;* tergis pugnantium, Tac.; latera et frontem (agminis), Tac.

assultus -ū, m. (assilio), *a leaping upon, assault,* Verg.

assum (adsum), affŭi (ad-fŭi), adesse, *to be present, to be at.* **I.** Gen., **A.** Of persons, 1, of bodily presence, heri quum non adessetis, Cic.; omnes qui aderant, Caes.; mane ad portam adesse, Cic.; in foro, Liv.; ante oculos, Verg.; portis (dat.), Verg.; huc ades, *come here,* Verg.; 2, of the mind, in the phrase adesse animo *or* animis, *to attend;* adestote omnes animis, Cic.; also, *to be of good courage;* ades animo et omitte timorem, Cic. **B.** Of things, *to be near, at hand;* frumentum conferri, comportari, adesse, Caes.; tanti aderant morbi, Cic.; adesse Romanis ulti-mum diem, Liv. **II.** *to be present with a fixed object, to be in one's place.* **A.** 1, of men, primum me ipsum vigilare, adesse, Cic.; adversus hostes, Sall.; jam omnes feroces aderant, Sall.; num ades ad parendum vel ad imperandum potius, Cic.; 2, of deities, adsis placidusque j..ves, Verg.

rebus Romanis, *to be favourable to*, Liv.; si fortuna coeptis affuerit, Tac. **B.** Esp., 1, *to be present to witness, or to share in;* ad suffragium, Cic.; with dat., comitiis, Cic.; pugnae, Liv.; adesse scribendo senatus consulto *or* decreto, *to witness*, Cic.; 2, *to be present to help or advise;* semper absenti Deiotaro, Cic.; alicujus rebus, Cic.; alicui adesse in consilio, *to be an assessor to*, Cic.; *to support or defend in the lawcourts;* adesse Quinctio, Cic.; contra Satrium, Cic.; 3, *to be present in a court of justice;* a, *as the accused*, adesse juberi, Cic.; *or* b, *as the accuser*, adesse in judicio, Cic.

assūmo -sumpsi -sumptum, 3. *to take to oneself.* **A.** Lit. novas humeris alas, Ov.; plura sibi assumunt quam de se corpora mittunt, Lucr. **B.** Transf., 1, *to take for one's assistance;* a, of persons, legiones in Italia, Cic.; aliquem in societatem armorum, Liv.; aliquem in nomen familiamque, Tac.; b, of things, aliquantum noctis, Cic.; assumpta verba, *words borrowed from another source*, Cic.; 2, *to appropriate to oneself, to take;* a, regni insignia, Tac.; Cereris sacra de Graecia, Cic.; b, *to claim*, in eo sibi praecipuam laudem assumere, Liv.; 3, *to take in addition to;* a, si quis in aliqua arte excellens aliam quoque artem sibi assumpserit, Cic.; b, logical t.t. *to state the minor premises of a syllogism*, Cic.

assumptĭo -ōnis, f. (assumo), 1, *choice, adoption*, Cic.; 2, *the minor premises of a syllogism*, Cic.

assumptīvus -a -um (assumo), *which derives a defence from an extraneous cause;* causa, Cic.

assŭo, 3. *to sew on;* unus et alter assuitur pannus, Hor.

assurgo -surrexi -surrectum, 3. *to rise up, stand up.* **I.** Of persons, **A.** Gen., assurgentem regem umbone resupinat, Liv.; quae dum recitatur, vos quaeso, qui eam detulistis, assurgite, Cic.; assurgere alicui, *to rise up in the presence of*, as a sign of respect, Cic.; pass., haec ipsa sunt honorabilia, salutari, appeti, decedi, assurgi, Cic.; firmissima vina, Tmolius assurgit quibus et rex ipse Phanaeus, *yields the preference*, Verg. **B.** Esp., a, *to rise from a sick-bed;* ne assurrexisse quidem ex morbo, Liv.; b, *to rise to give more force to a blow;* quantus in clipeum assurgat, Verg.; c, *to rise into the air;* assurgere in auras, Verg.; d, querelis haud justis assurgis, *break out into*, Verg. **II.** Of things, *to rise.* **A.** colles assurgunt, Liv. **B.** *to appear, show itself;* non coeptae assurgent turres, Verg.

assus -a -um (from areo, as cassus from careo), *dried.* **I.** Lit., a, *roasted*, Plaut.; assum vitulinum, *roast veal*, Cic.; b, of bathing, sol, *basking in the sun* without being anointed, Cic.; balnearia assa, *a sweating bath*, Cic. **II.** Transf., nutrix, *a dry-nurse*, Juv.

Assўria -ae, f. (Ἀσσυρία), *a country in Asia, between Media, Mesopotamia, and Babylonia.* Adj., **Assўrius** -a -um, *Assyrian;* poet., for *Median, Phrygian, Phoenician, Indian,* &c.; **Assўrii** -orum, m. *the Assyrians.*

ast = at, q.v.

Asta -ae, f. (Ἄστα), *a town in Hispania Baetica*, now *Mesa de Asta;* hence adj., **Astensis** -e, *of or belonging to Asta.*

Astācus -i, m. *father of Melanippus;* hence, **Astăcĭdēs** -ae, m. *the son of Astacus.*

Astăpa -ae, f. *town in Hispania Baetica*, now *Estepa.*

Astĕria -ae, f., and -ĭē -ēs, f. (Ἀστερίη). **I.** *daughter of Coeus and Phoebe, changed into an island, first called Asteria, afterwards Ortygia, and later still Delos.* **II.** (Asterie), *a woman's name*, Hor.

asterno, 3. *to scatter upon;* pass. *to be stretched out;* asternuntur sepulchro, Ov.

astĭpŭlātĭo -ōnis, f., 1, *the assenting to, confirmation of*, Plin.

astĭpŭlātor -ōris m. **A.** Legal t.t., at Rome, *one who joined another* (the stipulator) *in the Roman contract called* stipulatio. **B.** Transf., *a supporter;* Stoici et eorum astipulator Antiochus, Cic.

astĭpŭlor, 1., dep. *to assent to*, Liv.

astĭtŭo -tui -tūtum, m. (ad and statuo), 3. *to put, or place somewhere*, Plaut.

asto -stĭti, no sup., 1. **I.** *to stand by.* **A.** Gen. alicui, Plaut.; astante et inspectante ipso, Caes.; astat in conspectu meo, Cic. **B.** *to stand by the side to help, to assist*, Plaut. **II.** *to stand upright*, Verg.

Astraea -ae, f. (Ἀστραία), *Astraea, goddess of justice, who left the earth in the iron age, and was placed among the stars under the name Virgo.*

astrĕpo (ad-strepo), -strĕpui -strĕpĭtum, 3., 1, *to make a noise at;* astrepebat vulgus, Tac.; 2, *to applaud,* ; haec dicenti, Tac.

astrictē, adv. (astrictus), of discourse, *concisely, briefly*, Cic.

astrictus -a -um, p. adj. with compar. (from astringo), *tight, compressed, drawn together.* **A.** Lit., limen, *shut*, Ov.; non astrictus soccus, *negligent, slatternly writing*, Hor.; frons, *wrinkled*, Mart.; aquae, *frozen*, Ov. **B.** Transf., 1, *closefisted, avaricious;* pater, Prop.; mos, Tac.; 2, of oratory, a, *bound by the limits of rhythm;* numero et astricto et soluto, Cic.; b, *concise;* contracta et astricta eloquentia, Cic.

astrĭfer -fĕra -fĕrum (astrum and fero), *starry, placed among the stars*, Mart.

astringo -strinxi -strictum, 3. **I.** Lit. *to tighten, draw together, compress, contract, bind together;* a, quae (vinculum) astringit, Cic.; aliquem ad statuam, Cic.; b, of cold, *to contract*, Ov. **II.** Transf., a, *to draw tight;* pater nimis indulgens quidquid ego astrinxi relaxat, Cic.; b, of writing or speech, *to compress;* breviter argumenta, Cic.; c, *to bind, fetter, oblige;* vel armis vel legibus totam Galliam sempiternis vinculis, Cic.; se videre astringere or astringi, *to commit oneself to, become guilty of*, Cic.

astrŏlŏgĭa -ae. f.(ἀστρολογία), *astronomy*, Cic.

astrŏlŏgus -i, m. (ἀστρολόγος), 1, *an astronomer*, Cic.; 2, *an astrologer*, Cic.

astrum -i, n. (ἄστρον), *a star, a constellation.* **A.** Lit., cognitio astrorum, Cic.; astrum natale, Hor.; poet., of a great height, turris educta ad astra, Verg. **B.** Transf., tollere in astra, *to exalt sky-high*, Cic.; ex astris decidere, *from the highest glory*, Cic.; sic itur ad astra, *thus is immortality gained*, Verg.

astrŭo (ad and strŭo), -struxi -structum, 3. **I.** Gen. *to build to or near, to build in addition;* gradus, Liv. **II.** Transf., *to add to;* formae animum, Ov.

astu (asty), only acc. and abl. astū, n. (ἄστυ), *the city* (only used of Athens), Cic.

astŭpĕo, 3. *to be astonished at*, Ov.

Astŭra -ae, f. (Ἀστυρα), *a river in Latium*, still called *Astura.*

asturco -ōnis, m. *an Asturian horse*, Plin.

Astŭres -um, m. (Ἄστυρες), *the Asturians, a people in Spain;* sing. **Astŭr** -ūris, m.; hence, a, **Astŭria** -ae, f. *the country of the Astures;* b, **Astŭricus** -a -um, *Asturian.*

astus -ūs, m. *cleverness, adroitness, cunning*, Verg., Liv.

astūtē, adv., with compar. and superl. (astutus), *cunningly, astutely*, Cic.

astūtĭa -ae, f. *adroitness, astuteness, craft,* Cic.

astūtus -a -um (astus), *adroit, clever, astute, cunning, crafty,* Cic.

Astўăges -is, m. (Ἀστυάγης). **I.** *King of Media, grandfather of the elder Cyrus.* **II.** *a companion of Phineus.*

Astўănax -actis, m. (Ἀστυάναξ). **I.** *son of Hector and Andromache.* **II.** *a tragic actor of Cicero's time.*

Astўpălaea -ae, f. (Ἀστυπάλεια), *island vear Crete.* Adj., 1, **Astўpălaeensis** -e; 2, **Astўpăleїus** -a -um, *belonging to Astypalaea.*

ăsўlum -i, n. (ἄσυλον), *a sanctuary, place of refuge, asylum,* Cic.; templa quae asyla Graeci appellant, Liv.

ăsymbŏlus -a -um (ἀσύμβολος), *one who contributes nothing to the cost of an entertainment,* Ter.

at (ast), conj., *but, moreover.* **I.** To introduce an idea different from, but not entirely opposed to, one that has gone before. **A.** una (navis) cum Nasidianis profugit, at ex reliquis una praemissa Massiliam, Cic. **B.** 1, in prayers, exhortations, etc., at videte hominis intolerabilem audaciam, Cic.; 2, in expressions of astonishment or impatience, at per deos immortales quid est quod dici possit, Cic. **II.** To express an idea entirely opposed to the preceding one. **A.** non cognoscebantur foris, at domi, Cic.; strengthened, at contra, Cic.; at etiam, Cic.; at vero, Cic. **B.** 1, to introduce an imaginary objection in an argument, factumne sit? at constat, Cic.; 2, *but at least, yet at least,* non est, inquit, in parietibus republica, at in aris et focis, Cic.

ătābŭlus -i, m. *a hot wind in Apulia, the sirocco,* Hor.

Ătălanta -ae and -ē -ēs, f. (Ἀταλάντη), *a maiden of Boeotia or Arcadia, famous for her speed in running; she refused to marry any one except the person who could beat her in a race; finally conquered by Milanion by the aid of Aphrodite.* Adj., **Ătălantaeus** -a, m. *of or belonging to Atalanta.*

ătăt, attat, attatae, attattatae, etc. (ἀτταταί), an interjection expressive of pain, astonishment, fear, warning, etc., *oh! ah! alas!* Plaut., Ter.

ătăvus -i, m. **I.** *the father of the abavus or great-great-grandfather,* Cic. **II.** atavi, plur. = *ancestors,* Maecenas atavis edite regibus, Hor.

Ătella -ae, f. *a very ancient city of Campania.* Adj., a, **Ătellānus** -a, -um; fabella, or gen. simply **Ătellāna** -ae, f. *a species of popular farce, long popular in Rome,* Liv.; Juv.; hence, a, **Ătellānus** -i, m. *a player in these dramas;* b, **Ătellānius** -a -um; **Ătellānĭcus** -a -um.

āter, atra, atrum, *black, dark (dead black,* while *niger* is *shining black).* **I.** Lit., nemus, Verg.; mare, *stormy,* Hor.; alba discernere et atra non posse, Cic.; poet. = atratus, *clothed in black;* lictores, Hor. **II.** Transf. **A.** *black,* as a sign of mourning, calamity, etc.; *dark, gloomy, sad, unfortunate,* mors, cura, Hor.; atri dies, *in the Roman calendar, those on which the republic had suffered a great misfortune,* Liv. **B.** *malicious, poisonous;* atro dente petere aliquem, Hor.

Ăthămānes -um, m. (Ἀθαμᾶνες), *the Athamanes, inhabitants of Athamania;* hence **Ăthămānia** -ae, f. *a country in the south of Epirus.*

Ăthămas -antis, m. (Ἀθάμας), *son of Aeolus and king of Thessaly, father of Phrixus and Helle, Melicerta and Learchus;* hence, a, **Ăthămantheūs** -a -um, aurum, *the golden fleece,* Mart.; b, **Ăthămantĭădes** -ae, m. Palaemon, Ov.; c, **Ăthămantis** -ĭdis, f. *Helle.* Ov.

Athēnae -ārum, f. (Ἀθῆναι). *Athens;* meton., *learning.* Juv.; hence, a, **Athēnaeus** -a -um; b, **Athēniensis** -e, *Athenian.* Subst., **Athēnienses** -ium, m. *the Athenians.*

Ăthēnĭo -ōnis, m. *a Sicilian shepherd, leader of the slaves in the 2nd Slave War* (102 B.C.).

ăthĕos and **ăthĕus** -i, m. (ἄθεος), *an atheist,* Cic.

Athĕsis, acc. -sim, abl. -si, m. (Ἄθεσις), *a river in Rhaetia,* now *Adiga, Etsch.*

athlēta -ae, m. (ἀθλητής), *one who contends in the public games, wrestler, athlete,* Cic.

athlētĭcus -a -um (ἀθλητικός), *relating to an athlete.*

Ăthōs, dat. -o, acc. -o, and -on, abl. -o (Ἄθως), and **Ătho** or **Ăthōn** -ōnis, m. *a rocky mountain at the end of the peninsula of Chalcidice.*

Ătĭlĭus -a -um, *name of a Roman gens:* 1, M. Atilius Regulus (see Regulus): 2, M. Atilius, *an early Roman poet.* Adj., **Ătĭlĭānus** -a -um.

Ătīna -ae, f. *a town in Latium,* still called *Atina;* hence **Ătīnas** -ātis, *belonging to Atina.*

Atlās -antis, m. (Ἄτλας), 1, *a high mountain in Africa, on which the sky was supposed to rest;* 2, *a mythical king and giant, son of Iapetus and Clymene, king of Mauretania, changed into a mountain by Perseus;* hence, a, **Atlantis** -ĭdis, f. *a female descendant of Atlas, Electra,* Ov.; *Calypso,* Tib.; plur., Atlantides, *the Pleiades and Hyades;* b, **Atlantĭcus** -a -um, mare, *the Atlantic ocean;* c, **Atlantēus** -a -um, finis, *Libyan,* Hor.; d, **Atlantĭădes** -ae, m. *a descendant of Atlas, Mercury (son of Maia, daughter of Atlas);* or *Hermaphroditus (son of Mercury and great-grandson of Atlas).*

ătŏmus -i, f. (ἄτομος), *that which is incapable of division, an atom,* Cic.

atque, or **ac** (ac only before consonants), *and, and also.* **A.** Joining single words; 1, Gen., spargere ac disseminare, Cic.; a, *and also;* nobiles atque ignobiles, Sall.; b, *and moreover, and even;* alii intra moenia atque in sinu urbis sunt hostes, Sall.; with the pron., hic, is, idem, etc., negotium magnum est navigare atque id mense Quintili, *and especially,* Cic.; so atque etiam, Cic.; 2, with comparisons; a, with words expressing comparison, as aeque, aequus, idem, item, juxta, par, proxime, similis, similiter, talis, totidem; or expressing dissimilarity, as aliter, aliorsum, alius, contra, contrarius, dissimilis, secus; b, with comparatives, for quam, artius atque hedera procera astringitur ilex, Hor.; c, simul atque, *as soon as,* Cic.; 3, with negatives, *and not rather* (also with potius); si hoc dissuadere est, ac non disturbare atque pervertere, Cic. **B.** Joining sentences, *and so;* 1, atque illi omnes sine dubitatione condemnant, Cic.; 2, to join a more important thought, *and especially;* id estne numerandum in bonis? Ac maximis quidem, Cic.; 3, to introduce an adversative clause, ac tamen, Cic.; 4, to introduce an objection raised by the speaker or writer himself, ac ne sine causa videretur edixisse, Cic.; 5, in narration, *and so;* atque iis, quos nominavi, Cic.; 6, at the end of a speech or treatise, ac de primo quidem officii fonte diximus, Cic. **C.** Particular connections and phrases; 1, alius atque alius, *now this, now that,* Liv.; 2, atque utinam, to express a wish, Cic.; 3, to make an assertion general, atque omnia, or omnes, atque haec omnia verbo continentur, Cic.; 4, with other conjunctions, after si, non minis et vi ac metu, Cic.; after que (Gr. τε . . . καί), submoverique atque in castra redigi, Liv.; with nec, Mart.; repeated in poetry, atque deos atque astra, Verg.

atqui, conj. (at and qui = quoi = quo), *nevertheless, notwithstanding.* **I.** Gen., atqui non ego te frangere persequor, Hor. ; *indeed, certainly,* Cic. **II.** Esp. in logical conclusions, to introduce the minor premise, *but now, now,* Cic.

ātrāmentum -i, n. (ater), **1,** *any black fluid;* sepiae, Cic. ; **2,** *ink,* Cic. ; **3,** *blue vitriol, shoemaker's black;* sutorium atramentum, Cic.

ātrātus -a -um (ater), *clothed in black, in mourning,* Cic.

Atrax -ācis ("Ατραξ), **1,** *a river in Aetolia;* **2,** *a city in Thessaly;* hence, **a, Atrācīdes** -ae, m. *the Thessalian Caeneus,* Ov. ; **Atrācis** -idis, f. *Hippodamia,* Ov.

Atrĕbătes -um, m. *a people in Gallia Belgica;* sing., **Atrĕbas** -bātis, m., Caes.

Atreus -ĕi, m (Ατρεύς), *son of Pelops, king of Argos and Mycenae, father of Agamemnon and Menelaus;* hence, **Atrīdes** -ae, m. *Agamemnon* or *Menelaus;* plur., Atridae, *Agamemnon and Menelaus.*

ātriensis -is, m. (atrium), *a head slave, steward,* Cic.

ātrĭŏlum -i, n. (dim. of atrium), *a little atrium,* or *fore-court,* Cic.

ātrĭtas -ātis, f. (ater), *blackness,* Plaut.

ātrĭum -ĭi, n. (ater), *the room blackened by smoke; the open court in a Roman house, into which opened the janua,* or *gate;* plur., atria -orum, n. = atrium, Verg. ; meton., *a house,* Ov. ; *the halls of the gods,* Ov. ; *the hall of a temple* or *public building;* atrium Libertatis, Cic. ; auctionarium, *an auctioneer's sale-room,* Cic.

ātrōcĭtas -ātis, f. (atrox). **A.** *fierceness, harshness, cruelty;* ipsius facti atrocitas aut indignitas, Cic. ; habet atrocitatis aliquid legatio, *has a threatening aspect,* Cic. **B.** Transf., *severity, barbarity;* invidiosa atrocitas verborum, Cic. ; atrocitas ista quo modo in veterem Academiam irruperit, Cic.

ātrōcĭtĕr, adv., with compar. and superl. (atrox), *severely, harshly, cruelly;* Verri nimis atrociter minitans, Cic.

Atrŏpŏs -i, f. (ἄτροπος, *not to be averted*), *one of the three Parcae.*

ātrox -ōcis (from ater, as ferox from ferus). **I.** Lit., *terrible, fearful, cruel, horrible;* res scelesta, atrox, nefaria, Cic. ; *of war,* proelium, Liv. ; *of the seasons,* hora flagrantis Caniculae, Hor. ; *of commands, threatening;* imperium, Liv. ; atrocissimae litterae, Cic. ; *of speeches, violent;* vehemens atque atrox orationis genus, Cic. **II.** Transf., *of persons and character, gloomy, morose, severe;* Agrippina semper atrox, Tac. ; animus Catonis, *unbending,* Hor.

Atta -ae, m. *a Roman surname;* C. Quintius Atta, *a comic poet* (d. 102 B.C.).

attactus -ūs, m. (attingo), *a touching, touch, contact,* Verg.

attăgēn -ēnis, m. (ἀτταγήν), *a woodcock,* Hor.

Attălus -i, m. (Ατταλος), *the name of several kings of Pergamos, the last of whom,* Attalus III., *left his territory to the Romans;* hence, **a, Attălĭcus** -a -um, *belonging to Pergamos;* agri, Cic. ; hence *rich, splendid;* conditiones, Hor. ; peripetasmata, *woven with threads of gold,* Cic. ; **b, Attălis** -ĭdis, f. (Ατταλίς), *name of a guild at Athens.*

attămĕn, conj. *but yet,* Cic.

attat = atat.

attĕgĭa -ae, f. *a hut,* Juv.

attempĕrātē, adv. (attemperatus), *in a fit or appropriate manner,* Ter.

attempĕro (ad and tempero), **1.** *to fit to, adjust to,* Sen.

attendo (ad and tendo) -tendi -tentum, **3.** *to stretch to;* animum, or absol., attendere; *to direct the attention towards, attend to;* with ad and the acc., attendite animos ad ea quae consequuntur, Cic. ; with acc., primum versum legis, Cic. ; with acc. and infin., non attendere superius illud ea re a se esse concessum, Cic. ; with rel. sent., si paulo diligentius, quid de his rebus dicat attenderis, Cic. ; with de and the abl., animus tamen erit sollicitus, ut nihil possit de officiis legationis attendere, Cic.

attentē, adv., with compar. and superl. (attentus), *attentively, carefully;* audire, Cic. ; cogitare, Cic.

attentĭo -ōnis, f. (attendo), *attentiveness, attention;* animi, Cic.

attento (ad-tento), or **attempto** (ad-tempto), **1.** *to strive after, to attempt;* **1,** ut praeteriri omnino fuerit satius quam attentatum deseri, Cic. ; **2,** *to tamper with, try to corrupt,* classem, Cic. ; **3,** *to attack;* aliquid lingua. Cic. ; aliquem vi, Tac.

attentus (ad-tentus) -a -um. **I.** Partic. of attendo and attineo. **II.** Adj. with compar. and superl. (attendo), **1,** *attentive;* animus, Cic. ; cogitatio, Cic. ; auditor, Cic. ; judex, Cic. ; **2,** *careful after one's property;* attentus quaesitis, Hor. ; paterfamilias, Hor. ; attenta vita et rusticana, Cic.

attĕnŭātē, adv. (attenuatus), *simply, without ornament;* dicere, Cic.

attĕnŭātus -a -um, p. adj. with superl. (from attenuo), *made weak;* *of discourse, abbreviated;* ipsa illa pro Roscio juveniilis abundantia multa habet attenuata, Cic. ; *over-refined;* ejus oratio nimia religione attenuata, Cic.

attĕnŭo (ad-tĕnŭo), **1.** *to make thin.* **A.** Lit., **1,** corpus, Ov. ; **2,** *of number, to lessen,* legio proeliis attenuata, Caes. ; **3,** *of strength, to weaken;* vires diutino morbo attenuatae, Liv. ; **4,** *of the voice, to make shrill,* Cic. **B.** Transf., curas, Ov. ; insignem, *degrade,* Hor.

attĕro (ad and tĕro) -trīvi (-tĕrŭi) -trītum, **3.** **A.** Lit., **1,** *to rub against;* leniter caudam, Hor. **2,** *to rub* or *wear away;* attrita ansa, Verg. **B.** Transf., *to weaken, ruin;* opes, Sall. ; aliquem, Sall.

attestor (ad and testor), **1.** dep. *to attest, bear witness to,* Phaedr.

attexo (ad and texo) -texŭi -textum, **3.** *to weave* or *plait on* or *to.* **A.** Lit., loricas ex cratibus, Caes. **B.** Transf., *to add,* vos ad id, quod erit immortale, partem attexitote mortalem, Cic.

Atthis -ĭdis, f. (Ατθίς), *Attic, Athenian,* Mart. Subst., f. **1,** *Attica,* Lucr. ; **2,** *nightingale* or *swallow,* Mart. ; **3,** *name of a friend of Sappho,* Ov.

Attĭca -ae, f. (Αττική), *Attica, the most celebrated country of Greece, with Athens for its capital.*

Attĭcē, adv. (Atticus), *in the Attic* or *Athenian manner,* dicere, Cic.

atticisso, **1.** (ἀττικιζω), *to imitate the Athenian mode of speaking,* Plaut.

Attĭcus -a -um (Αττικός), **1,** *belonging to Attica* or *Athens, Attic, Athenian;* virgo, i.e., *Canephoros,* Hor. ; pelex, *Philomela,* Mart. Plur. **Attĭci** -orum, m. *the Athenians,* Cic. ; **2,** *Attic, Athenian,* with reference to style, art, etc., stilus, *simple,* Cic. ; aures, *delicate,* Cic. ; hence Attici = *the Athenian orators,* Cic.

Attĭcus, T. Pomponius, *the intimate friend of Cicero,* who received his surname of Atticus from his long residence in Athens.

attĭneo -tĭnŭi -tentum, **2.** (ad and teneo). **I.** Transit., *to hold near, keep.* **A.** Lit., aliquem castris, carcere, publica custodia, Tac. **B.**

Transf., simul Romanum et Numidam spe pacis, *to amuse*, Sall. **II.** Intransit., *to pertain to, or concern*, only in 3rd person ; cetera quae ad colendam vitem attinebunt, Cic. ; esp. in the expression, quod attinet ad aliquem or aliquid, *in respect to ;* qui omnes, quod ad me attinet, vellem viverent, *as far as I am concerned*, Cic. ; nihil attinet me plura scribere, *it is of no use*, Cic.

attingo -tĭgi -tactum, 3. (ad and tango), *to touch.* **A.** Lit., **1**, digito se caelum attigisse putare, Cic. ; **2**, *to arrive at a place ;* Italiam, Cic. ; arces igneas, Hor. ; **3**, of places, *to touch upon, border upon,* Cappadocia regio ea quae Ciliciam attingit, Cic. ; **4**, *to attack ;* Sulla quem primum hostes attigerant, Sall. ; **5**, *to touch*, i.e., *to appropriate to oneself ;* de praeda mea nec teruncium attigit, Cic. ; **6**, *to strike*, si digito quem attigisset, poenas dedisset, Cic. ; **7**, *to embrace*, Ov. **B.** Transf., **1**, *to touch ;* of sensations, voluptas aut dolor aliquem attingit, Cic. ; **2**, *to have to do with, to touch, to reach to ;* corporis similitudo attingit naturam animi, Cic. ; attingere aliquem necessitudine, *to be closely connected with,* Cic. ; **3**, a, *to handle, manage, devote oneself to ;* rempublicam, Cic. ; Graecas litteras, Cic. ; rem militarem, Caes ; b, *to glance at cursorily ;* librum strictim, Cic. ; **4**, in writing or speech, *to mention;* illam injuriam non attingere, Cic.

Attis (Atthis and **Atys)** -ĭdis, m. *a Phrygian shepherd, beloved by Cybele.*

Attĭus -a -um, *name of a Roman gens, the most famous member of which was* P. Attius Varus, *a praetor in Africa at the time of the war between Caesar and Pompeius, a supporter of the latter ;* hence adj., **Attĭānus** -a -um, *Attian.*

attollo, no perf. or sup., 3. *to raise up, lift up.* **I.** Lit. **A.** vix prae lacrimis oculos, Liv. ; minas, iras (of a snake raising its head in anger), Verg. ; se attollere, or middle, attolli, *to raise oneself,* Verg. **B.** *to erect, raise;* molem, Verg. ; terra se attollere tandem visa, *to rise, appear,* Verg. **II.** Transf., *to raise, elevate;* a, vocem, Quint. ; b, *to elevate, excite, distinguish;* animos ad spem consulatus, Liv. ; rempublicam bello armisque, Tac.

attondĕo -tondi -tonsum, 2. **I.** Lit. *to shear, shave, cut ;* vitem, Verg. **II.** Transf., *to make less, diminish,* Cic., poet.

attŏnĭtus -a -um, p. adj. (from attono), *struck by thunder ;* hence, **1**, *stunned, terrified, senseless ;* magna pars integris corporibus attonitis concidunt, Liv. ; **2**, *inspired;* vates, Hor. ; attonitae Baccho matres, Verg.

attŏno -tŏnŭi -tŏnĭtum, 1. *to strike with thunder, stun, make senseless,* Ov.

attorquĕo, 2. *to whirl, swing upward,* Verg.

attrāctĭo -ōnis, f. (attraho), *a drawing to oneself ;* hence, litterarum, *assimilation,* Varr.

attrăho -traxi -tractum, 3. *to draw to, attract.* **I.** Lit. **A.** Of things, magnes lapis, qui ferrum ad se alliciat et attrahat, Cic. **B.** Of persons, *to drag ;* tribunos attrahi ad se jussit, Liv. **II.** Transf., **1**, *to attract ;* nihil esse quod ad se rem ullam tam alliciat et tam attrahat quam ad amicitiam similitudo, Cic. ; **2**, *to take with one ;* aliquem Romam, Cic.

attrectātus -ū, m. (attrecto), *a handling, touching,* ap. Cic.

attrecto, 1. (ad and tracto), *to touch, handle.* **I.** Gen., blanditia popularis aspicitur, non attrectatur, Cic. **II. A.** *to touch unlawfully, in an improper manner ;* libros (Sibyllinos) contaminatis manibus attrectare, Cic. **B.** *to lay hands on, to appropriate ;* gazas, Liv.

attrĕpĭdo, 1. *to stumble along,* Plaut.

attrĭbŭo -ŭi -ūtum, 3. *to allot to, assign to.* **A.** Lit. **1**, servos, pastores armat atque iis equos attribuit, Caes. ; **2**, of money, *to assign, lend ;* si modo attribuetur, quantum debetur, Cic. ; so of money paid from the public treasury ; pecunia attributa, numerata est, Cic. ; **3**, *to assign* (to some one to keep or do something) ; attribuit nos trucidandos Cethego, Cic. ; esp. of a military command, oppidam civibus Romanis, Caes. ; **4**, of a country, *to annex, subject ;* insulae, quae erant a Sulla Rhodiis attributae, Cic. **B.** Transf., **1**, *to add, give, cause;* summus timor quem mihi natura pudorque meus attribuit, Cic. ; **2**, gramm. t. t. *to add as an attribute,* Cic. ; **3**, *to ascribe, impute ;* bonos exitus diis immortalibus, Cic.

attrĭbūtĭo -ōnis, f. (attribuo), **1**, *the assignment of a debt,* Cic. ; **2**, rhet. t.t., *an accessory or attribute,* Cic.

attrĭbūtum -i, n. (attribuo), *the predicate,* Cic.

attrītus -a -um, p. adj., with compar. (from attero). **A.** *rubbed away, worn out,* Cic. **B.** Transf., frons, *shameless,* Juv.

Attus Navĭus, *a celebrated augur of the time of Tarquinius Priscus.*

Ătÿs (Attÿs) -ÿos, abl. -ÿe, m. ("Ατυς, "Αττυς). **I.** *a son of Hercules and Omphale, father of Tyrrhenus and Lydus,* myth. *ancestor of the Lydian kings.* **II.** *the founder of the gens Atia.*

au, interj., *oh! ha!* Plaut.

auceps -cŭpis, m. (for aviceps, from avis and capio). **I.** Lit., *a fowler, bird-catcher,* Plaut., Hor. **II.** Transf., peritissimum voluptatum aucupem sapientem esse, Cic. ; syllabarum, *a quibbling critic, caviller,* Cic.

auctārĭum -i, n. (augeo), *an increase.* Plaut.

auctĭo -ōnis, f. (augeo), **1**, *an auction ;* auctionem facere, constituere, *to appoint an auction,* Cic. ; praedicare, proscribere, Cic. ; proponere, *to announce publicly,* Quint. ; proferre, *to put off,* Cic. ; **2**, *that which is sold by auction ;* auctionem vendere, Cic.

auctĭonārĭus -a -um (auctio), *relating to an auction ;* atrium, *auction-room,* Cic.

auctĭonor, 1. (auctio) *to hold an auction,* Cic.

auctĭto, 1. (freq. of augeo), *to increase very much,* Tac.

aucto, 1. = auctito, Plaut., Lucr.

auctŏr -ōris, m. (augeo). **A.** *originator, causer, doer ;* incendii, Cic. ; vulneris, Verg. ; esp., **1**, *the producer of a work of art, artist ;* templi, *architect,* Liv. ; **2**, *the founder of a family, ancestor ;* praeclarus auctor nobilitatis tuae, Cic. ; **3**, *writer, author ;* carminis, Hor. **B.** *the originator of a proposal or undertaking, leader, beginner ;* nec auctor quamvis audaci facinori deerat, Liv. ; me auctore, *at my request,* Cic. ; auctor interficiendi alicuius, Cic. ; with dat., ille legibus Caecilii Metelli contra auspicia ferendis auctor, Cic. ; with ad and the acc., ad instituendam (rem), Cic. ; with in and the abl., in restituendo auctorem fuisse, Cic. ; alicui auctorem esse, *to advise, recommend,* semper senatui auctor pacis fui, Cic. ; foll. by ut or ne with the subj., Cic. **C.** *the author of a piece of information, warrant for its truth ;* a, certis auctoribus comperisse, Cic. ; b, *an authority;* malus auctor Latinitatis, Cic. ; Cratippo auctore, *on the authority of Cratippus,* Cic. ; non sordidus auctor naturae verique, *investigator,* Hor. ; c, *an author of note ;* Homerus optimus auctor, Cic. ; auctor rerum Romanarum, *historian,* Cic. ; hence, auctorem esse, *to answer for, state positively ;* nec pauci sunt auctores Cn. Flavium scribam libros protulisse, Cic. **D.** Esp., **1**, auctor legis or senatus consulti, *proposer*, Liv. ; 2, *supporter of a law*, multarum legum aut auctor aut dissuasor, Cic. ; 3, auctores fiunt patres, *the senators sanction a law*, Cic. ; 4, *defender, protector ; praeclarus iste* ᴜuctor suae civitatis, Cic. ; 5, *the guarantee of a right to an estate;* a malo auctore emere, Cic. ; 6, *of a guardian*, etc., *approver, sanctioner;* quod mulier sine tutore auctore promiserit, *without the approval of her guardian*, Cic.

auctōrāmentum -i, n. (auctoro), *the pay or hire for the performance of any duty*, Cic.

auctōrĭtas -ātis, f. (auctor), *continuance, a causing to continue.* **I. A.** *validity*, 1, in the case of property, usus et auctoritas, or simply auctoritas, *valid right to property arising from prescription;* usus et auctoritas fundi, Cic. ; 2, in case of an assertion, *attestation, security, authority;* publicarum tabularum, Cic. ; 3, *example*, majorum, Cic. ; alicuius auctoritatem sequi, Cic. **B.** *the origination of a proposal or proceeding, support, aid;* cuius auctoritas multum apud me valet, Cic. **C.** *the expression of approval or assent, resolve;* 1, hominum consilia et auctoritates, Cic. ; 2, of the will of the people, populi Romani, Cic. ; 3, of public bodies or magistrates, collegii, Liv. ; 4, of the senate, **a**, *a measure to which the senate has assented, the approval of the senate;* auctoritatem senatus, jussa populi Romani vendere, Cic. ; **b**, *a resolution of the senate*, prevented from being made a decree by the veto of the tribunes, si quis huic senatus consulto intercessisset, auctoris perscriberetur, Cic. **D.** *authorisation, full power*, legatos cum auctoritate mittere, Cic. ; hence, *power, might, command;* manere in alicuius auctoritate, Liv. **II.** *influence, authority;* 1, of a person, **a**, lit., auctoritatem habere apud aliquem, Cic. ; auctoritatem restituere, levare, amittere, Cic. ; **b**, meton., *a person in authority, an influential person*, Cic. ; 2, of things, legum, Cic. ; orationis, Cic.

auctōro, 1. (auctor). **I.** *to hire for money;* refl. auctorare se, or pass. *to hire, engage oneself.* Hor. **II.** Transf. *to bind oneself;* eo pignore velut auctoratum sibi proditorem ratus est, Liv.

auctumnālis -e (auctumnus), *autumnal*, Liv.

1. **auctumnus** -i. m. (augeo), *autumn*, Cic. ; meton., septem auctumni = *seven years*, Ov.

2. **auctumnus** -a -um (1. auctumnus), *au-ʼumnal ;* frigus, Ov.

1. **auctus** -a -um, p. adj. (from augeo), only ᴀsed in compar., *increased, enlarged, enriched;* majestas auctior, Liv. ; socii honore auctiores, Caes.

2. **auctus** -ūs, m. (augeo), *an increase, enlargement, growth;* corporis, Lucr. ; fluminum, Tac. ; imperii, Tac. ; maximis auctibus crescere, Liv.

aucŭpātĭo -ōnis, f. (aucupor), *fowling, bird-catching*, Quint.

aucŭpātōrĭus -a -um (aucupor), *relating to fowling*, Plin.

aucŭpĭum -i, n. (auceps), *bird-catching, fowling.* **I. A.** Lit., vitam propagare aucupio, Cic. **B.** Meton., *the birds caught*, Cat. **II.** Transf. *hunting after anything;* delectationis, *after pleasure*, Cic.; aucupia verborum, *cavilling, quibbling*, Cic.

aucŭpor, 1. dep. (auceps). **I.** Lit. *to catch birds*, Varr. **II.** Transf. *to chase, strive for, lie in wait for;* verba, Cic. ; errores hominum, Cic. ; inanem rumorem, Cic. ; tempestates, *to wait for finer weather*, Cic.

audācĭa -ae, f. (audax), 1, *courage, boldness, daring;* audacia in bello, Sall. ; 2, *audacity, impudence, temerity;* audacia et impudentia

fretus, Cic. ; alicuius audaciam debilitare, Cic. ; frangere, Liv. ; contundere et frangere, Cic. ; plur., audaciae, *audacious deeds*, Cic.

audācĭtĕr, and **audactĕr**, adv., with compar. and superl. (audax), *boldly* (in a good oɪ bad sense), *audaciously, rashly, impudently*, Cic.

audax -ācis, adj., with compar. and superl. (audeo), *daring* (in a good or bad sense), *bold, courageous, audacious, rash, foolhardy ;* a, of persons, Verres homo audacissimus atque amentissimus, Cic. ; paulo ad facinus audacior, Cic. ; **b**, of things, consilium prima specie temerarium magis quam audax, Liv.

audens -entis, p. adj., with compar. and superl. (from audeo), *daring, bold*, Verg.

audentĕr, adv. (audens), *boldly*, Tac.

audentĭa -ae, f. (audens), *boldness, courage*, Cic.

audĕo, ausus sum, 2. (connected with avidus), *to dare, venture;* audeo dicere, *I venture to assert*, Cic. ; with acc., tantum facinus, Liv. ; proelium, aciem, Tac. ; with in and the abl., ausurum se in tribunis, quod princeps familiae suae ausus in regibus esset, Liv. ; with pro and the abl., pro vita majora audere probavi, Verg. ; absol., quod sperant, quod audent, omne Caesari acceptum referre possunt, Cic. ; adversus Neronem ausus, Tac. ; audere in proelia, Verg.

audĭens -entis. **I.** Partic. of audio (q.v.). **II.** Subst. *a hearer*, Cic.

audĭentĭa -ae, f. (audio), *hearing, listening, attention;* alicui audientiam facere, *to get a hearing for any one by commanding silence*, Cic., Liv.

audĭo, 4. (connected with auris), *to hear.* **I.** *to have the power of hearing;* audiendi sensu carere, Cic. **II.** *to hear something.* **A.** clamorem, Caes. ; galli cantum, Cic. ; with double acc., te, ut spero, propediem censorem audiemus, Cic. ; with acc. and infin., saepe hoc majores natu dicere audivi, Cic. ; with acc. and partic., idque Socratem audio dicentem, Cic. ; with relative clause, audire enim cupio quid non probes, Cic. ; with de and the abl., multa falsa de me audierunt, Cic. ; the person from whom a thing is heard is put in the abl. with ab or de, Cic. Perf. part., as subst., **auditum** -i, n. *hearsay ;* nihil habeo praeter auditum, Cic. **B.** *to listen to ;* a, aliquem lubenter studioseque, Cic. ; of judges, *to hear a case;* audire de ambitu, Cic.; of pupils, *to listen to a master, to attend the classes or lectures of a professor;* annum jam audire Cratippum, Cic. ; **b**, *to listen to requests;* preces, Cic. ; **c**, of stories or persons, *to listen to*, i.e., *to give credence to;* si fabulas audire volumus, Cic. ; audio, *I believe it*, Cic. ; **d**, *to obey, to follow;* aliquem amicissime monentem, Cic. ; dicto audientem esse; with dat., *to obey;* non fore dicto audientes milites, Caes. **C.** *to be called* (like Gr. ἀκούω), Matutine pater, seu Jane libentius audis, Hor. ; bene audire, *to be well spoken of;* a propinquis, Cic.

audītĭo -ōnis, f. 1, (audio), *hearing, listening;* aliquid multa lectione atque auditione assequi, Cic. ; 2, *hearsay report;* levem auditionem habere pro re comperta, Cic. ; plur., fictae auditiones, Cic.

audītŏr -ōris, m. (audio), *a hearer, auditor, scholar ;* alicui auditorem venire, Cic.

audītōrĭum -i, n. (audio), *a place of audience, lecture-room, court of justice*, etc., Tac. ; *a school*, Quint. ; *circle of listeners*, Plin.

audītus -ūs, m. (audio). **I.** Gen., *hearing; the sense of hearing*, Cic. **II.** Esp., *listening*, Tac.

aufĕro, auferre, abstŭli, ablātum, 3. (ab and fero). **I.** *to carry away, carry off, remove.* **A.**

Lit., inter manus e convicio tamquam e proelio auferri, Cic. ; se e conspectu alicuius, Cic. ; auferor in scopulos, Ov. **B.** Transf., *to draw away from one's aim, seduce;* ne te auferant aliorum consilia, Cic. **II.** *to take away with, bear off;* sometimes in good, but oftener in bad sense, *to rob, steal.* **A.** Lit., **a,** of persons ; multa palam domum, Cic. ; auriculam mordicus, *to bite off,* Cic. ; **b,** of things ; hi ludi XV. dies auferent, Cic. ; mors Achillem abstulit, Hor. **B.** Transf., **1,** illa autem, quae contrariis commotionibus auferenda sunt, Cic. ; **2,** *to carry off,* i.e. *to gain, obtain;* tantum abstulit quantum petiit, Cic. ; responsum ab aliquo, Cic. ; **3,** *to lay aside, cease from;* aufer abhinc lacrimas, Lucr.

Aufīdēna -ae, f. *a town in Samnium,* now *Alfidena.*

Aufīdīus -a -um, *name of a Roman gens.*

Aufīdus -i, m. *a river in Apulia,* now *Ofanto.*

aufūgĭo -fūgi, 3. (ab and fugio), *to flee away,* Cic.

Augē -ēs, f. (Αὔγη), *daughter of Aleus and Neaera, mother of Telephus by Hercules.*

Augēas and **Augīas** -ae, m. (Αὐγείας), *king of the Epeans in Elis,* the cleansing of whose stable, which had not been cleansed for thirty years, was one of the labours of Hercules.

augĕo, auxi, auctum, 2. (connected with αὐξάνω), *to make to increase.* **I.** *to cause to grow, to fertilise;* aer humorem colligens terram auget imbribus, *makes fertile,* Cic. **II.** In a wide sense, *to make larger;* **a,** *to strengthen,* has munitiones, Caes. ; **b,** of rivers, *to cause to rise,* gen. in pass., augeri = *to be swollen;* amnis nimbis hiemalibus auctus, Ov. ; **c,** of number or quantity, *to increase;* numerum legatorum, Cic. ; **d,** of degree, vitium ventris et gutturis, Cic. ; populi Romani imperium, Cic. ; **e,** of moral or intellectual qualities or feelings, benevolentiam, Cic. ; luctum, Cic. ; **f,** in speech, *to extol, set forth;* hostium vim et copias et felicitatem, Cic. ; **g,** *to enrich, to honour;* cives suos copia rerum, Cic. ; augeri cognomento Augustae, Tac.

augesco, auxi, 3. (inch. of augeo), *to begin to grow, to increase;* **a,** quae (uva) et suco terrae et calore solis augescens primo est peracerba gustu, Cic. ; **b,** politically, *to increase in strength;* quum hostium res tantis augescere rebus cerneret, Liv.

augmĕn -ĭnis, n. (augeo), *an increase, growth,* Lucr.

augur -ŭris, c. *an augur, soothsayer, seer,* Cic.; aquae augur annosa cornix, *prophetess of rain,* Hor.

augŭrālis -e (augur), *relating to an augur or augury;* coena, Cic. Subst., **augŭrāle** -is, n. *the part of the Roman camp where the auguries were taken,* Tac.

augŭrātĭo -ōnis, f. (auguro), *divining, soothsaying,* Cic.

augŭrātus -ūs, m. (auguro), *the office of an augur,* Cic.

augŭrĭum -i, n. (augur), *the observation and interpretation of omens, augury.* **I. A.** Lit., augurium capere, Liv. ; salutis, *an augury in time of peace* (to inquire if it were permitted to pray to the gods de salute reipublicae), Cic. **B.** Transf., **a,** *any kind of prophecy;* o mea frustra semper verissima auguria rerum futurarum, Cic.; **b,** *presentiment;* inhaeret in mentibus quasi saeculorum quoddam augurium futurorum, Cic. **II.** Meton., **A.** Subject., *the science of augury;* Apollo augurium citharamque dabat, Verg. **B.** Object., **1,** *an omen;* augurium accipere, Liv. ; **2,** *a sign, token,* Ov.

augŭrĭus -a -um (augur), *relating to an augur,* jus, Cic.

augŭro, 1. (augur). **I.** *to act as an augur;* sacerdotes salutem populi auguranto, *take the auguries for,* etc., Cic. : pass., locus auguratur, *the place is consecrated by auguries,* Cic. ; augurato (abl. absol.), *after taking the auguries,* Liv. **II.** Transf. **A.** *to prophesy,* Cic. **B.** *to have a foreboding* or *presentiment;* praesentit animus et augurat quodammodo, quae futura sit suavitas Cic.

augŭror, 1. dep. (augur). **I.** *to perform the functions of an augur, to foretell by auguries;* ex passerum numero belli Trojani annos, Cic. **II.** Transf., **1,** *to foretell;* alicui mortem, Cic. ; **2,** *to guess;* quantum auguror conjectura aut opinione, Cic. ; quum ex nomine istius, quid in provincia facturus esset, perridicule homines augurarentur, Cic.

Augusta -ae, f. **I.** *name of the wife, daughter, mother,* or *sister of the Roman Emperor.* **II.** *name of several towns named after the emperor,* Augusta Taurinorum (*Turin*), Augusta Praetoria (*Aosta*), Augusta Treverorum (*Trèves*), Augusta Emerita (*Merida*), Augusta Vindelicum (*Augsburg*).

Augustālis -e (Augustus), *belonging to* or *in honour of the Emperor Augustus.*

augustē, adv. with compar. (augustus), *reverentially;* auguste et sancte venerari deos, Cic.

Augustŏdūnum -i, *town of the Aedui in Gaul,* now *Autun.*

1. augustus -a -um, adj. with compar. and superl. (augeo), **1,** *consecrated, holy;* Eleusis sancta illa et augusta, Cic. ; **2,** *majestic, dignified;* vestis augustissima, Liv.

2. Augustus -i, m. *surname of Octavianus after his elevation to the imperial power, and of all subsequent Roman emperors.*

3. Augustus -a -um, *relating to Augustus;* pax, Ov. ; mensis, *August,* formerly called Sextilis, changed to Augustus in honour of the emperor.

aula -ae, f. (αὐλή). **I.** *the fore-court in a building,* Hor. ; *yard for cattle,* Prop. **II.** = atrium, *an inner court,* Verg. **III.** *a palace.* **A.** Lit., aula Priami, Hor. ; so of the dwellings of the gods, illa se jactet in aula Aeolus, Verg. ; of the lower world, immanis janitor aulae (of Cerberus), Verg. ; of a bee-hive, Verg. **B.** Meton., **a,** *the court, courtiers;* puer ex aula, Hor. ; divisa et discors aula erat, Tac. ; **b,** *princely power;* auctoritate aulae constitutā, Cic.

aulaeum -i, n. (αὐλαία), usually plur., **1,** *curtain, tapestry;* aulaea superba, Verg. ; **2,** *a canopy,* Hor. ; **3,** *curtain of a theatre,* fastened below and let down at the beginning of a piece, and drawn up at the end ; aulaeum tollitur, Cic. ; **4,** *an embroidered upper garment,* Juv.

Aulerci -orum, m. *a people of Gallia Celtica,* divided into four branches ; **a,** Aulerci Eburovīces, in modern Normandy ; **b,** Aulerci Cenomani, in modern Dép. de la Sarthe ; **c,** Aulerci Brannovīces, on the Loire ; **d,** Aulerci Diablintes or Diablinti, in Modern Dép. de la Maine.

aulĭcus -a -um, (αὐλή), *belonging to the court, princely,* Suet. Subst., **aulici** -orum, m. *courtiers,* Nep.

Aulis -īdis, f. (Αὐλίς), *a port in Boeotia,* where the Greek fleet collected before sailing to Troy.

auloedus -i, m. (αὐλῳδός), *one who sings to the flute,* Cic.

Aulōn -ōnis, m. *a celebrated wine-district near Tarentum.*

Aulŭlārĭa -ae, f. *the title of a comedy of Plautus,* Verg

aura -ae, old genit. auräi (αὖρα), *air*. **A.** 1, *the motion of the air, wind*; nocturna aura uti (of ships), Caes.; venti et aurae cient mare, Liv.; 2, meton., plur. aurae, a, *the heavens*; cursum per auras dirigere, Verg.; stat ferrea turris ad auras, Verg.; b, *the world above*; venire superas ad auras, *the light of day*, Verg.; ferre sub auras, *to make known*, Verg.; 3, transf., *breath, sign*; rumoris, Cic.; aura popularis, *the breath of popular favour*, Cic.; 4, *the air that we breathe*; auris vitalibus vesci, Verg. **II.** 1, *smell*, Verg.; 2, *glitter*; auri, Verg.; 3, *echo*, Prop.

aurārius -a -um (aurum), *golden, relating to gold*, Plin. Subst., **auraria** -ae, f. (sc. fodina), *a gold mine*, Tac.

aurātus -a -um (aurum), *golden, gilt*; tecta, Cic.; vestis, Ov.

Aurēlius -a -um, *name of a Roman plebeian gens* (with the surnames Cotta, Orestes, Scaurus).

Aurelius, M., v. Antoninus.

aurĕŏlus -a -um (dim. of aureus). **A.** Lit., *golden*, Plaut. **B.** Transf., *glittering, splendid, beautiful*; libellus, Cic.

aurĕus -a -um (aurum), *golden*. **I.** 1, *made of gold*; a, lit., anulus, Cic.; nummus, and absol., *a golden coin*, Cic.; b, transf., *excellent, beautiful*; Venus, Verg.; mores, Hor.; 2, *gilt, ornamented with gold*; amiculum, Cic.; sella, Cic.; currus, *the triumphal car*, Cic.; Pactolus, *with golden sands*, Ov. **II.** *of the colour of gold*; color, Ov.; caesaries, Verg.

aurichalchum = orichalchum (q.v.).

aurĭcŏmus -a -um (aurum and coma). **I.** *golden-haired*, P. Aug. **II.** Transf., *golden-leaved*; fetus arboris, Verg.

aurĭcŭla -ae, f. (dim. of auris), *the lobe of the ear*, *the ear*. **I.** Lit., auricula infima, Cic.; auriculam mordicus auferre, Cic.; praeceptum auriculis instillare, Hor. **II.** Meton., plur. = *favourable hearing*, Pers.

aurĭfer -fĕra -fĕrum (aurum and fero). **I.** *gold-bearing, gold-producing*, arbor (of a tree in the garden of the Hesperides), Cic. poet. **II.** *bringing gold*; Tagus, Ov.; amnis, Cat.

aurĭfex -fĭcis, m. (aurum and facio), *a goldsmith*, Cic.

aurĭfŏdīna -ae, f. *a gold mine*, Plin.

auriga -ae, c. (from old aurea = *reins* and ago), *charioteer, driver*. **I.** Lit., Verg., Caes.; esp. *one who contends in the chariot race in the circus*, Cic. **II.** Transf., poet., *a helmsman*, Ov.

Aurigĕna -ae, c. (aurum and gigno), *begotten of gold*; epithet of Perseus, son of Danäe, Ov.

aurĭger -gĕra -gĕrum (aurum and gero), *gold-bearing*; taurus, *with gilt horns*, Cic. poet.

aurigo, 1. (auriga), *to be a charioteer, contend in the chariot race*, Suet.

aurĭpigmentum -i, n. *orpiment*, Plin.

auris -is, f. (connected with audio), *the ear*. **I. A.** Lit., aures; erigere, Cic., arrigere, Ter., *to prick up the ears*; adhibere, admovere, Cic., applicare, Hor., *to listen*; praebere aures conviciis adolescentium, Liv.; dare, Cic., *to give a hearing to*; accipere auribus, Cic.; aliquem admonere ad aurem, *to whisper advice in the ear*, Cic.; claudere aures alicui, Cic.; demittere aures (as a sign of submission), Hor.; diceran aurem alicui aliquid, Cic.; insusurrare ad aurem or in aures, Cic.; offendere aures, Cic.; aures refercire aliqua re, Cic.; aures respuunt aliquid, Cic.; servire alicuius auribus, *to speak according to the wish of*, Caes.; dormire in utramvis aurem, *to sleep soundly, be without anxiety*, Ter. **B.** Meton., a, *the hearing*, as judging of the merits of a speech, Atticorum aures teretes et religiosae,

Cic. **II.** Transf., aures; *the earth* or *mould-boards of a plough*, Verg.

auriscalpĭum -i, n. *an ear-pick*, Mart.

aurītŭlus -i, m. (dim. of auritus), *the long-eared one*, i.e., *the ass*, Phaedr.

aurītus -a -um (auris). **A.** Lit., *long-eared*; lepus, Verg. **B.** Transf., *attentive*, Hor.; testis auritus, *a hearsay witness*, Plaut.

aurōra -ae, f. (αὔως, ἀώς, ἠώς), *the break of day, redness of morning*. **I.** Lit., **A.** Gen., Verg., Liv. **B.** Personified, *Aurora, goddess of morning*, Ov. **II.** Meton., *the east*, Ov.

aurum -i, n. *gold*. **I. A.** Lit., Cic. **B.** Meton., *something made of gold, gold plate*, Lucr.; *a golden goblet*, Verg.; *chain, necklace*, Verg.; ring, Juv.; *bit*, Verg.; *the golden fleece*, Ov.; *gold coin, money*, Cic. **II.** Transf., **A.** *the colour or glittering of gold*, Ov. **B.** *the golden age*, Hor.

Aurunci -orum, m. *the people of Aurunca*; **Aurunca** -ae, f. *a town in Campania*. Adj., **Auruncus** -a -um, *Auruncian*.

Ausci -ōrum, m. *a people in Aquitania*.

auscultātĭo -ōnis, f. (ausculto); 1, *a listening*, Sen.; 2, *obedience*, Plaut.

auscultātor -ōris, m. (ausculto), *a listener*, Cic.

ausculto, 1. (for ausiculito, from ausicula = auricula). **I.** *to hear attentively*; populum, Cat. **II.** Esp., **A.** *to listen in secret, to overhear*, Plaut.; in a good sense, *to attend, wait at the door*, Hor. **B.** *to obey*; mihi ausculta; vide ne tibi desis, Cic.

Ausētāni -ōrum, m. *a Spanish people in modern Catalonia*; hence adj., **Ausētānus** -a -um, *Ausetanian*.

Ausŏnes -um, m. (Αὔσονες), *aborigines of Central and Southern Italy*; hence, **A. Ausŏnia** -ae, f. *Ausonia, Lower Italy*, Ov.; *Italy*, Verg. **B.** Adj., **Ausŏnĭus** -a -um; poet., *Italian*, Verg. Subst., **Ausŏnĭi** = Ausones, Verg. **C. Ausŏnĭda** -ārum, m. *the inhabitants of Ausonia, or generally of Italy*, Verg. **D. Ausŏnis** -ĭdis, *Ausonian, Italian*, Verg.

auspex -ĭcis, c. (for avispex, from avis and specio). **I.** *one who observes the habits of birds for purposes of divination*; latores et auspices legis curiatae (Caesar and Pompeius), Cic. **II.** Transf., **A.** *favourer, protector, leader*; Teucro duce et auspice Teucro, Hor. **B.** *a person who witnessed the marriage contract, best man, bridegroom's friend*, etc. (παράνυμφος), Cic.

auspĭcātō, adv. (lit. abl. absol. of auspico), *in a fortunate hour*; urbem condere, Cic.

auspĭcātus -a -um (auspico), 1, *consecrated by auguries*, Cic.; 2, *favourable, auspicious*; initium, Tac.

auspĭcĭum -ĭi, n. (for avispicium), *divination by means of birds*. **I. A.** Lit., in auspicio esse, *to act as augur*, Cic.; praeesse auspiciis, Cic.; adhibere aliquem in auspicium, Cic.; auspicio uti, Cic.; auspicia dissolvere, Cic.; esp., *the right to take auspices*, propraetores auspicia non habent, Cic.; auspicia ponere, *to lay down a magistracy*, Cic.; imperio atque auspicio alicuius, *under the command of* (in war the commander-in-chief alone had the right of taking the auspices), Liv. **B.** Transf., *control, protection, guidance*; suis auspiciis ducere vitam, Verg. **II.** Meton., *an omen, sign*; optimum, Cic.; aves auspicium ratum fecere, Cic.

auspĭco, 1. (auspex), *to take the auspices*; aliquid, *to accept as an omen*, Plaut.

auspĭcor, 1. dep. (auspex), 1, *to take the auspices*; auspicari oblitus est, Cic.; 2, *to begin under good auspices*, Tac.; *to begin*, Suet.

auster -stri, m. **I.** *the south wind,* Cic. **II.** Meton., *the south,* Verg.

austērē adv. (austerus), *severely, gravely, austerely,* Cic.

austērītas -ātis, f. (austerus). **I.** Lit., a, *harshness, sourness of taste,* Plin. ; b, *darkness of colour,* Plin. **II.** Transf., *strictness, austerity,* Quint.

austērus -a -um (αὐστηρός). **I.** *sour, harsh in taste,* Plin. **II.** Transf., 1, *strict, severe, austere;* illo austero more ac modo, Cic. ; 2, *sad, gloomy, melancholy, burdensome;* labor, Hor.

austrālis -e (auster), *southern,* Cic.

austrīnus -a -um (auster), *southern,* Verg.

ausum -i, n. (ausus, from audeo), *a daring deed, undertaking,* Verg.

aut, conj. disjunct., *or, or else, or rather,* Cic.; aut . . . aut, *either . . . or,* Cic.; neque . . . aut, = neque . . . neque, poet. ; aut vero, *or indeed* (used ironically), Cic.; aut certe, *or at least,* Cic. ; aut saltem, aut potius, aut etiam, Cic.

autem, conj. adversat. (αὖτε), *but, on the contrary, however, moreover;* never used at the beginning of a clause ; joined with adeo, porro, tum, ast, even with sed ; when used to correct a word before used = *did I say?* num quis testis Postumum appellavit? Testis autem? Num accusator? Cic.

authepsa -ae, f. (αὐτός and ἕψω), *a cooking-stove,* Cic.

autŏgrăphus -a -um (αὐτόγραφος), *written with one's own hand,* Suet.

Autŏlўcus -i, m. (Αὐτόλυκος), *son of Mercury, famous for his thefts.*

autŏmătus (ŏs) -a -um (-ŏn), adj. (αὐτόματος), *self-acting,* Petr. Subst., **autŏmăton** -i, n. *an automaton,* Suet.

Autŏmĕdōn -ontis, m. (Αὐτομέδων), *the charioteer of Achilles;* appell., *a charioteer,* Cic.

Autŏnŏē -ēs, f. (Αὐτονόη), *mother of Actaeon.* Adj., **Autŏnēius** -a -um, heros, *Actaeon,* Ov.

autumnus, etc., v. auctumnus.

autŭmo, 1. (orig. aitumo, from aio), *to say, assert,* Plaut., Ter.

auxĭlĭāris -e (auxilium), *giving help, assisting, auxiliary.* **I.** Gen., Ov. **II.** Esp., auxiliares, (sc. milites, cohortes), *auxiliary or allied troops,* Caes., Tac. ; hence, *belonging to the allied troops;* auxiliaria stipendia, Tac.

auxĭlĭārius -a -um (auxilium), 1, *helping, auxiliary,* Plaut. ; 2, milit. t. t., milites, *auxiliary troops,* Cic.

auxĭlĭātor -ōris, m. (auxilior), *a helper, assister,* Tac.

auxĭlĭātus -ūs, m. (auxilior), *help, assistance,* Lucr.

auxĭlĭor, 1. dep. (auxilium), *to help, assist, support;* alicui, Cic. ; especially used of medical aid, Ov.

auxĭlĭum -i, n. (augeo), *help, aid, assistance.* **I.** Gen., adjungere sibi auxilium, Cic. ; arcessere aliquem auxilio, *to help,* Caes. ; ad auxilium convenire, Caes. ; dare adversus aliquem auxilium, Liv. ; esse auxilio alicui, Caes. ; consuli adversus intercessionem collegae auxilio esse, Liv.; alicui nemo auxilio est, quin, etc., Liv. ; auxilio ei futurum ne causam dicat, Liv. ; expetere auxilium ab aliquo, Cic. ; exspectare vestrum auxilium, Cic. ; alicui ferre auxilium, Cic. ; ferre alicui auxilium contra tantam vim, Cic. ; implorare auxilium alicuius, Cic. ; aliquem auxilio mittere, Cic. ; petere auxilium ab aliquo, Cic. ; polliceri auxilium alicui rei, Cic. ; venire auxilio alicui, Caes. ; plur., illorum auxiliis uti, Cic.

II. Esp., plur., **a,** *military power;* equitum peditumque, Caes. ; b, auxilia, *auxiliary troops,* Cic., Caes.

ăvārē, adv. with compar. and superl. (avarus), *avariciously, covetously,* Cic.

Avārĭcum -i, n. *capital of the Bituriges Cubi in Aquitania,* now *Bourges.*

ăvārĭtĕr, adv. (avarus), *greedily,* Plaut.

ăvārĭtĭa -ae (**ăvārĭtĭēs** -ei, Lucr.), f. *avarice, cupidity, covetousness;* ardere avaritia, Cic. ; avaritia perire, Cic. ; plur., omnes avaritiae, *all kinds of avarice,* Cic.

ăvārus -a -um (connected with aveo and avidus). **I.** Gen., *covetous, greedy;* mare, Hor. ; with genit., publicae pecuniae avarus, Tac. **II.** Esp., *greedy after money, avaricious;* homo avarus et furax, Cic. Subst., **avarus** -i, m. *the avaricious man,* Hor.

ăvĕho -vexi -vectum, 3. *to carry off, bear away,* Verg., Liv. ; pass. *to ride off,* Liv.

ăvello -velli and -vulsi (-volsi) -vulsum (-volsum), 3. *to tear away, pluck away.* **I.** Lit., poma ex arboribus, cruda si sint, vi avelluntur, Cic.; sive secetur aliquid sive avellatur a corpore, Cic. **II.** *to take away with violence, separate.* **A.** Lit., de matris complexu avellere atque abstrahere, Cic. ; ex complexu avelli, Cic. ; avulsus a meis, Cic. **B.** Transf., aliquem convicio ab errore, Cic.

ăvēna -ae, f. **I.** a, *oats,* Verg. ; b, *wild oats,* Cic. ; steriles, Verg. **II.** Transf., *the shepherd's pipe,* Ov. ; plur., junctae avenae or structae avenae, *the Pan-pipes,* Ov.

ăvēnācĕus -a -um (avena), *oaten;* farina, Plin.

ăvēnārĭus -a -um, *relating or belonging to oats,* Plin.

Aventĭnum -i, n. and **Aventĭnus** -i, m. *the Aventine, one of the hills of Rome,* Cic. Adj., **Aventĭnus** -a -um, *of or belonging to the Aventine.*

1. **ăvĕo,** 2. (from ἄω or αὖω ἀέω), lit., *to pant after;* hence, *to desire;* aveo genus legationis, Cic. ; gen. with infin., valde aveo scire quid agas, Cic.

2. **ăvĕo** (**hăvĕo**), 2. *to be well;* found only in the imp. ave, aveto, avete, *hail! farewell!* a formula of greeting and farewell used by the Romans, Cic.

Avernus -a -um (ἄορνος), *without birds;* loca, *places where birds cannot live on account of the pestilential exhalations,* Lucr. Subst., **Avernus** -i, *the lake Avernus,* near Cumae, said to be the entrance to the infernal regions ; *the infernal regions themselves,* Ov. ; hence, adj., **Avernus** -a -um, **Avernālis** -e, *relating to Avernus,* or *the lower world.*

ăverrunco, 1. *to turn away, avert;* iram deorum, Liv.

āversābĭlis (aversor), *that from which one must turn away, horrible,* Lucr.

1. **āversor,** dep. (averto). **A.** *to turn away* (on account of shame, disgust, etc.) ; aversari advocati, vix etiam ferre posse, Cic. ; with acc., filium, Liv. **B.** Transf., *to repel, turn away, avoid, shun;* principes Syracusanorum, Liv. ; preces, Liv. ; aliquem ut parricidam liberum, Liv.

2. **āversor** -ōris, m. (averto), *an embezzler;* pecuniae publicae, Cic.

āversus -a -um, p. adj. (from averto). **A.** *turned away, backward, behind* (opp. adversus) ; adversus et aversus impudicus es, *before and behind,* Cic.; quendum actorem aversum *(turning his back on the people)* solitum esse dicere,

3

Cic. ; aversos boves in speluncam traxit, Liv. Plur. subst., **āversa** -orum, n. *the back parts;* urbis, Liv. **B.** *disinclined, unfavourable to, averse from;* aversus a vero, Cic. ; with dat., aversus mercaturis, Hor.

āverto (āvorto)-verti (-vorti)-versum (-vorsum), 3. *to turn away, turn off, remove.* **I.** Lit., **A.** Gen. Lepidus se avertit, Cic. ; aliquid ab oculis, Cic. ; flumina, *divert,* Cic. ; iter, Caes., Liv. ; hence, 1, pass., averti (as middle), aversus ab suo itinere, *turning away,* Liv. ; 2, active, as reflexive, prora avertit, Verg. **B.** Esp. 1, *to drive away by violence;* barbaros a portis castrorum, Caes. ; 2, *to carry off, appropriate to oneself, embezzle;* pecuniam publicam, Cic. ; hereditatem, Cic. ; quatuor tauros a stabulis, Verg. **II.** Transf., **A.** Gen., 1, *to keep off something dangerous;* pestem ab Aegyptiis, Cic. ; quod omen dii avertant, Cic. ; 2, *to keep something dangerous* or *disgraceful off some one;* qui me a tanta infamia averterit, Cic. **B.** Esp., 1, *to turn away, divert* (thoughts or wishes, etc.), Antonii furorem a pernicie reipublicae, Cic. ; cogitationem a miseriis, Cic. ; aliquem a consiliis pacis ; 2, *to estrange;* alicuius animum a se, Cic.

ăvĭa -ae, f. (avus), *a grandmother,* Cic.

ăvĭārĭus -a -um (avis), *relating to birds;* rete, Varr. Subst., **ăvĭārĭum** -ii, n., a, *a place where birds are kept, an aviary,* Cic. ; b, *the haunts of wild birds in the woods,* Verg.

ăvĭdē, adv. (avidus), *greedily;* exspectare, appetere, arripere, Cic.

ăvĭdĭtas -ātis (avidus), f. **A.** Gen., *vehement desire, avidity;* cibi, pecuniae, *for food, money,* Cic. ; legendi, Cic. **B.** Esp., *desire of money, avarice,* Cic.

ăvĭdus -a -um (1. aveo), *vehemently desiring, greedy.* **I. A.,** with genit., cibi, Ter. ; laudis, Cic. ; novarum rerum, Liv. ; belli gerendi, Sall. ; b, with infin., Verg. ; c, with in and the acc., Liv. ; d, with ad and the acc., Liv. ; e, with in and the abl., in pecuniis locupletium, Cic. **II.** Absol. **A.** Lit., a, *covetous, greedy of money;* heres, Hor. ; subst., *a miser,* Cic. ; b, *greedy in respect of food, gluttonous;* convivae, Hor. ; leones, *bloodthirsty,* Ov.; c, transf., aures avidae, *eager to hear,* Cic. ; libido, *insatiable,* Cic. ; mare, Hor. ; d, *hot, ardent, eager to fight;* legiones, Tac. **B.** Fig., *wide, large, vast,* Lucr.

ăvis -is, f. (connected with ἄημι). **I.** Gen., *a bird,* and coll. *the whole race of birds,* Cic. **II.** Esp., *omen,* as the chief method of divination among the Romans was by birds; avibus bonis Ov. ; secundis, Liv., *with good omens;* avi mala, Hor. ; sinistra, Plaut. ; adversa, *with bad omen.* Cic.

ăvītus -a -um (avus), *relating to a grandfather, ancestral;* bona paterna et avita, Cic. ; merum, *very old,* Ov.

āvĭus -a -um (a and via). **I.** *out of the right way, untrodden;* avii saltus montesque, Liv. Subst., **āvĭum** -i, n. *a by-way, a solitary place;* avia dum sequor, Verg. **II.** Poet., **A.** *out of the way, wandering, remote;* in montes se avius abdidit altos, Verg. **B.** Transf., *straying, wandering;* a vera ratione, Lucr.

ăvŏcātĭo -ōnis, f. (avoco), *a calling away from;* a cogitanda molestia, Cic.

āvŏco, 1. *to call away,* or *off.* **A.** Lit., populum ab armis, Liv. **B.** Transf., 1, *to withdraw, remove, divert;* Socrates videtur primus a rebus occultis avocasse philosophiam, Cic. ; senectus avocat a rebus gerendis, Cic. ; 2, *to relieve;* luctum lusibus, Sen.

āvŏlo, 1. *to fly away.* **A.** Lit., Cat. **B.**

Transf., *to hasten away;* experiar certe ut hinc avolem ; so of the dying, hinc avolare, Cic

ăvuncŭlus -i, m. (dim. of avus), *a mother's brother, uncle* (patruus, *a father's brother*) ; magnus, *a grandmother's brother, a great-uncle,* Cic

ăvus -i, m. *a grandfather,* Cic. ; generally *an ancestor,* Hor.

Axĕnus (ἄξενος, *inhospitable*), *earlier name of the Pontus Euxinus,* Ov.

1. **axis** -is, m. (root AC, AG, whence ago, Gr. ἄξων), *an axle-tree.* **I. A.** Lit., Verg. **B.** Meton., *a chariot, waggon,* Ov. **II.** Transf., **A.** *the axis of the earth;* terra circum axem se convertit, Cic. **B.** Meton., a, *the north pole,* Verg. ; b, *the heavens;* sub axe, *in the open air,* Verg. ; c, *a part of the heavens;* boreus, *the north,* Ov.

2. **axis** (assis) -is, m. (root AC, whence ἄγνυμι, ἄχμα), *a board, plank,* Caes.

Axōna -ae, m. *a river in Gallia Belgica,* now *the Aisne.*

B

B, b, the second letter of the Latin Alphabet, corresponding with the Greek beta (β).

băbae (βαβαί, or παπαῖ), an exclamation of astonishment or joy, *wonderful!* Plaut.

Băbylo -ōnis, m. *a Babylonian;* appell. = *a nabob,* Ter.

Băbylon -ōnis, f. (Βαβυλών), *a city of Asia on the Euphrates.* Hence, **A. Băbylōnia** -ae, f. *a tract of country extending between the Euphrates and the Tigris,* of which the aforenamed city was the capital. **B. Băbylōnĭcus** -a -um, *Babylonian;* Babylonica peristromata, *embroidered tapestry,* Plaut. **C. Băbylōnĭus** -a -um; numeri, *astrological calculations, for which the Babylonians* (or more properly the Chaldeans) *were noted,* Hor. ; Babylonii, *inhabitants of Babylon.* **D. Băbylōnĭensis** -e, *Babylonian*

bacca (băca) -ae, f. *a berry.* **I.** Lit., **A.** Gen., lauri baccae, Verg. **B.** Esp., *the fruit of the olive;* bicolor bacca Minervae, Ov. **II.** Transf., **A.** *any fruit of a round shape;* arborum baccae, Cic. **B.** *anything of the shape of a berry, a pearl,* Hor.

baccar (bacchar) -ăris, n. and **baccaris** -is, f. (βάκκαρις), the Valeriana Celtica of Linnaeus ; also called nardum rusticum, *a plant which yielded a kind of oil ; Celtic Valerian,* Verg.

baccātus -a -um, *set with pearls,* Verg.

Baccha -ae, f. *a Bacchante,* Ov.; Bacchis aliquem initiare, *to initiate any one into the festival of Bacchus,* Liv.

Bacchānal -is, n. *the place where the festival of Bacchus was held,* Plaut.; plur. **Bacchanalia,** *the (Greek) festival of Bacchus* (not to be confounded with the Roman feast of Liber), celebrated at Rome every three years, and suppressed by a decree of the senate, B.C. 186 ; Bacchanalia vivere, poet., *to live riotously* or *wantonly,* Juv.

bacchātĭo -ōnis, f. 1, *the celebration of the Bacchanalia,* P.Aug.; 2, *Bacchanalian revelling,* Cic.

Bacchēĭus -a -um, *belonging to Bacchus;* dona, Verg.

Bacchēus -a -um (Βακχεῖος), *belonging to Bacchus;* sacra, Ov.; ululatus, *of the Bacchantes,* Ov.

Bacchĭădae -ārum, m. (Βακχιάδαι), *the Bacchiadae, an ancient noble family of Corinth.*

Bacchis -ĭdis, f. = Baccha.

Bacchĭus -a -um, *belonging to Bacchus,* sacra, Ov.

bacchor, 1. dep. (Bacchus). **I.** Intransit., **A.** 1, *to celebrate the festival of Bacchus,* Plaut. ; partic. Bacchantes = Bacchae, Ov. ; 2, *to rage ;* tum baccharis, tum furis, Cic. ; quanta in voluptate bacchabere, Cic. **B.** *to run about in a furious manner, to rave ;* totam per urbem, Verg. ; of a fiery orator, eos furere et bacchari arbitraretur, Cic. ; of prophetic inspiration, in antro, Verg. ; of lifeless objects, the wind, Hor. ; rumour, fama bacchatur per urbem, Verg. **II.** Transit., **A.** *to raise the Bacchic cry ;* bacchari Evoë, Cat. **B.** Pass., of places, *to be made the scene of Bacchic revels ;* bacchata jugis Naxos, Verg. ; virginibus bacchata Lacaenis Taygeta, Verg.

Bacchus -i, m. (Βάκχος). **A.** *the god of wine, son of Jupiter and Semele.* **B.** Meton., 1, *the vine,* Verg. ; 2, more frequently, *wine,* Verg. ; 3, *the Bacchic cry* (Io Bacche); Baccho audito, Verg.

baccĭfer -fĕra -fĕrum, 1, *bearing berries,* Sen. ; 2, *bearing olive berries,* Pallas, Ov.

Bācēnis -is, f. *a forest in Germany,* probably the west part of the Thuringian Forest.

băcillum -i, n. (dim. of baculum), 1, *a little staff,* Cic. ; 2, *the lictor's staff,* Cic.

Bactră -ōrum n. (Βάκτρα), *the chief city of Bactria,* now *Balk ;* hence **Bactri** -ōrum, m. *inhabitants of Bactria ;* **Bactria** -ae, f. *the country of the Bactri ;* **Bactrĭānus** -a -um, **Bactrĭnus** -a -um, *Bactrian.*

băcŭlum -i, n. and **băcŭlus** -i, m. (connected with βάκτρον, from βάω, βάζω, *to go*), *a stick, staff,* Liv. ; *a shepherd's staff,* Ov. ; *an augur's staff,* Liv. ; *a walking-stick,* Liv.

bădĭsso, 1. (βαδίζω), *to walk, march,* Plaut.

Baebĭus -a -um, adj., *name of a plebeian Roman gens,* with the surnames Dives, Sulca, Tamphilus ; hence, lex Baebia (de praetoribus creandis).

Baecŭla ae, f. *a town in Hispania Baetica.*

Baetis -is, m. *a river in Spain, the Guadalquivir ;* hence, **Baetĭgĕna** -ae, *born on the Baetis ;* **Baetĭcŏla** -ae, *living near the Baetis ;* **Baetĭcus** -a -um, *relating to the Baetis ;* Baetica provincia, now *Andalusia and a part of Granada ;* **Baetĭci** -ōrum, m. *inhabitants of Baetica ;* **Baetĭcātus** -a -um, *clothed in Baetican wool,* Mart.

Băgōus -i, m. and **Băgōas** -ae, m. (Βαγώας), *a eunuch at the Persian court ;* hence *any person set to guard women,* Ov.

Băgrăda -ae, m. (Βαγράδας), *a river near Carthage.*

Bājae -ārum, f. **I.** *a town on the coast of Campania, a favourite resort of the Romans, celebrated for its baths.* **II.** Meton., *any watering place,* Cic. Adj., **Bājānus** -a -um, *belonging to Bajae.*

bājŭlo, 1. (bajulus), *to carry a burden,* Plaut.

bājŭlus -i, m. *a porter,* Plaut., Cic.

bālaena -ae, f. (φάλαινα), *a whale,* Ov.

bălănātus -a -um (balanus), *anointed with balsam, embalmed,* Mart.

bălănus -i, f. rarely m. (βάλανος), 1, *an acorn,* Plin. ; 2, *any fruit of similar form,* e.g. *a kind of large chestnut,* Plin. ; *a date,* Plin. ; *a fruit, the Arabian behen-nut,* from which an ointment was extracted, Hor. ; *or the tree which produces it,* usually called myrobalanus, Plin.

bălătro -ōnis, m. *a buffoon, jester,* Hor.

bālātus -us, m. (balo), *the bleating of sheep and goats,* Verg., Ov.

balbē, adv. (balbus), *in a stammering manner,* Lucr.

1. **balbus** -a -um (connected with balare), *stammering* (opp. planus) ; quum (Demosthenes) ita balbus esset ut, etc., Cic. ; verba balba, Hor.

2. **Balbus** -i, m. *surname of the Attii, Cornelii,* etc.

balbūtĭo, 4. (balbus). **I.** Intransit., **A.** *to stammer, stutter,* Cels. **B.** Transf., *to speak obscurely ;* desinant balbutire, aperteque et clara voce audeant dicere, Cic. **II.** Transit., *to stammer or stutter out ;* illum balbutit Scaurum, Hor.

Băleāres -ĭum, f. (Βαλιαρεῖς), insulae, or absol., *the Balearic Islands, Majorca, Minorca ;* hence, adj., **Băleāris** -e, **Băleāricus** -a -um.

bălĭnĕum or **balnĕum** -i, n., **bălĭnĕa** or **balnĕa** -ōrum, n. ; heteroclite pl. **bălĭnĕae** or **balnĕae** -ārum (βαλανεῖον), *a bath, bathing place,* Cic. ; a balineo or a balineis, *after bathing,* Plin.

Ballĭo -ōnis, m. *a worthless fellow,* from a character so named in the Pseudolus of Plautus, Cic.

ballista (bălista), -ae, f. (βάλλω). **A.** *a military engine for throwing large stones,* Cic., Caes. **B.** Transf., *the missiles thrown,* Plaut.

ballistārĭum -i, n. = ballista (q.v.).

balnĕae, v. balineum.

balnĕārĭus -a -um (balneum), *belonging to the bath ;* fur, *lurking about baths,* Cat. Subst., **balnĕāria** -ōrum, n. *baths, bathing-rooms,* Cic.

balnĕātor -ōris, m. (balneum), *the keeper of a bath,* Cic.

balnĕŏlum -i, n. (dim. of balneum), *a little bath,* Cic.

balnĕum, v. balineum.

bālo, 1. *to bleat,* Plaut. ; partic. balantes -ium and um, f. = oves, Verg.

balsămum -i n. (βάλσαμον), 1, *the sweet-smelling gum of the balsam-tree,* Verg, ; 2, *the tree itself,* Tac.

balteus -i. m. (-um -i, n.), *the girdle ;* a, esp., as serving to hold a weapon ; sutilis, Verg. ; b, *a woman's girdle,* Mart. (baltei dissyll., Verg. 10,496).

Bandŭsĭa -ae, f. *a fountain near Venusia, the birthplace of Horace.*

Bantĭa -ae, f. (Βαντία), *town of Apulia, near Venusia.* Adj., **Bantīnus** -a -um.

Baptae -arum, m. (Βάπται = baptists, from the rite of initiation), *priests of the Thracian goddess Cotytto,* Juv.

baptistērĭum -i, n. (βαπτιστήριον), *a cold plunging bath,* Plin.

bărăthrum -i, n. (βάραθρον). **A.** *the abyss, the lower world,* Plaut. ; barathro donare (*to squander*), Hor. **B.** Transf., barathrum maselli (of a greedy man), *the abyss of the market,* Hor.

bărăthrus -i, m. (βάραθρος), *worthless fellow,* Lucr.

barba -ae, f. *the beard.* **I.** Lit. **A.** of men, promittere barbam, *to let the beard grow,* Liv. ; barbam tondere, Cic. ; barbam ponere, Hor. **B.** of animals, lupi, Hor. **II.** Transf., of plants, nucum, Plin.

barbărē, adv. (barbarus), 1, *like a foreigner ;* loqui, Cic. ; 2, *cruelly, barbarously,* laedere oscula, Hor.

barbărĭa -ae, f. and **barbărĭēs,** acc. -em, abl. -e, f. (barbarus), **I.** *a foreign country,* as opposed to Greece and Rome ; a quo non solum Graecia et Italia sed etiam omnis barbaries commota est, Cic. ; Persia, Cic. ; Phrygia, Hor. ; Gallia, Cic. ; Scythia and Britannia, Cic. **II.** Meton., **A.** *want of culture, rudeness, roughness ;*

haec turba et barbaries forensis, Cic. ; so of mistakes in speech, nec eos aliqua barbaries domestica infuscaverat, Cic. **B.** *savageness ;* inveteratam quandam barbariam ex Gaditanorum moribus disciplina delevit, Cic.

barbărĭcus, -a -um, *foreign,* i.e., not Greek or Roman; supellex, Liv. ; esp., *eastern;* aurum, Verg. ; ope barbarica, Verg. ; manus (of the Phrygian Briseis), Ov.

barbărus -a -um (βάρβαρος). **I.** *foreign,* as opposed to Greek, *Italian, Roman,* poeta (Naevius), Plaut. ; used for *Phrygian,* carmen, Hor. ; for *Persian,* Nep. Subst., *a foreigner,* one strange to Greek or Roman life, Cic. **II.** Transf., **1,** *intellectually uncultivated, rough ;* homines barbari atque imperiti, Caes ; **2,** *morally rough, savage ;* homines feri ac barbari, Caes.

barbātŭlus -a -um (dim. of barbatus), *with a slight beard ;* juvenis, Cic.

barbātus -a -um (barba), *bearded.* **I.** Of living beings. **A.** Of men ; **1,** quos aut imberbes aut bene barbatos videtis, Cic. ; si quem delectet barbatum, *a man grown up,* Hor. ; **2,** esp., a, of men of the old Roman time, when the beard was worn, unus aliquis ex barbatis illis, Cic. ; **b,** barbatus magister, *a philosopher,* Pers. **B.** Of animals, hirculus, Cat. **II.** Transf., of plants, nux, Plin.

barbĭgĕr -gĕra, -gĕrum (barba and gero), *wearing a beard,* Lucr.

barbĭtŏs -i, m. and f. (βάρβιτος). **A.** *the lyre,* Hor. **B.** Meton., *the song sung to the lyre,* Ov.

barbŭla -ae, f. (dim. of barba), *a little beard,* Cic.

Barcās -ae, m. (Βάρκας, connected with Hebrew Barak, *lightning*), *the founder of the Barcine family of Carthage, to which belonged Hannibal and Hamilcar ;* hence, adj., **Barcīnus** -a -um, *Barcine.*

Barcē -ēs, f. (Βάρκη), *town in Cyrenaica;* **Barcaei** -ōrum, m. *the inhabitants of Barce.*

Bardaei -orum, m. *a people of Illyria.* Adj. **Bardăĭcus** -a -um, calceus, *a kind of soldier's boot,* in jest = *a centurion,* Juv.

bardŏcŭcullus -i, m. *a Gallic overcoat, with a hood made of wool,* Mart.

1. bardus -a -um (βραδύς), *stupid, slow, dull,* Cic.

2. bardus -i, m. *a bard, a poet among the Gauls,* Lucan.

Bargўlĭae -ārum, f. and **Bargўlĭa** -ōrum, n. (Βαργύλια), *a town in Caria.* Hence, a, **Bargўlētae** -ārum, m. *the inhabitants of Bargyliae ;* b, **Bargўlĭētĭcus** -a -um, *relating to Bargyliae.*

bāris -ĭdos, f. *a small Egyptian skiff,* Prop.

barĭtus v. barritus.

Bārĭum -ĭi, n. (Βάριον), *a port in Apulia, on the Adriatic.*

bāro -ōnis, m. *a blockhead, simpleton,* Cic.

barrĭo -īre (barrus), *to roar* (of elephants), Suet.

barrītus -ūs, m. (barrio), **1,** *the roar of an elephant;* **2,** *the cry of the Germans,* Tac.

barrus -i, m. (an Indian word), *the elephant,* Hor.

bascauda -ae, f. *a basket,* Mart., Juv.

bāsĭātĭo -ōnis, f. (basio), *kissing, a kiss,* Cat.

bāsĭātor -is, m. (basio), *a kisser,* Mart.

băsĭlĭcē, adv. (basilicus), *royally, splendidly,* Plaut.

băsĭlĭcus -a -um (βασιλικος). **I.** Adj. *royal, kingly, princely,* Plaut. ; vitis, *a kind of vine,*

Plin. **II.** Subst. **A.** **băsĭlĭcus** -i, m. (sc. jactus), *the best cast of the dice,* Plaut. **B.** **băsĭlĭca** -ae, f. (βασιλική sc. οἰκία or στοά), *a basilica, the name of a building* (in Rome and other towns) *usually adorned with a double row of columns, and situated near the forum, used as a meeting-place of merchants and for the administration of justice ;* qui forum et basilicas non spoliis provinciarum, sed ornamentis amicorum ornarent, Cic.; basili cam habeo, non villam, frequentia Formianorum (of a much-frequented place), Cic. **C. băsĭlĭcum** -i, n. *a splendid dress,* Plaut.

basilīscus -i, m. (βασιλίσκος), *a kind of lizard, a basilisk,* Plin.

băsĭo, l. *to kiss,* Cat., Mart.

băsis -is and ĕos, f. (βάσις), **1,** *a pedestal, base ;* statuae, Cic. ; **2,** *foundation, wall ;* villae, Cic. ; **3,** mathemat. t.t., trianguli, *base,* Cic.

băsĭum -ĭi, n. *a kiss,* either of the hand or lip, Cat. ; basia jactare, *to throw kisses,* Juv.

Bassăreus -ei, m. (Βασσαρεύς, from βασσάρα, *a fox-skin,* as forming part of the clothing of the Bacchantes), *a name of Bacchus,* Hor. ; hence, **Bassărĭcus** -a -um, adj., Prop.; **Bassăris** -ĭdis, f. *a Bacchante,* Pers.

Bastarnae and **Basternae** -ārum, m. *a German people near the mouths of the Danube.*

Bătāvia -ae, f. *the peninsula Batavia, Holland ;* **Bătāvi** -orum, m. *inhabitants of Batavia;* **Bătāvus** -a -um, *Batavian ;* Batavorum insula = *Batavia,* Tac.

bătillum (vatillum), -i, n. *a chafing-dish,* Hor.

bătĭŏla -ae, f. *a small drinking-vessel,* Plin.

battŭo (bātuo), 3. *to beat, knock,* Plaut.

Battus -i. m. (Βάττος), *the founder of the African city Cyrene ;* hence **Battĭădes** -ae, m. *an inhabitant of Cyrene ;* especially applied to the poet Callimachus, a native of Cyrene, Ov.

baubor, l. dep., *to bark,* Lucr.

bĕātē, adv. (beatus), *happily ;* bene et beate vivere, Cic.

bĕātĭtas -ātis, f. (beatus), *happiness, blessedness,* Cic.

bĕātĭtūdo -ĭnis, f. (beatus), *happiness, beatitude,* Cic.

bĕātŭlus -a -um (dim. of beatus), *somewhat happy,* Pers.

bĕātus -a -um, p. adj. (from beo), *happy, blessed.* **I.** Gen. **1,** of persons, qui beatus est, non intelligo quid requirat, ut sit beatior ; si est enim quod desit, ne beatus quidem est, Cic. ; agricolae parvo beati, *happy on little means,* Hor. ; **2,** of events or circumstances, beata mors, Cic. Neut. subst., **bĕātum** -i. *happiness,* Cic. **II.** Esp. **A.** *wealthy, prosperous ;* **1,** of persons, qui se locupletes, honoratos, beatos putant, Cic. ; **2,** of states, Dionysius tyrannus opulentissimae et beatissimae civitatis, Cic. ; **3,** of property, possessions, gazae beatae Arabum, Hor. **B.** beatorum insulae, *the islands of the blest,* Cic.

Bebrўces -um, m. (Βέβρυκες), *people in Bithynia.* Adj., **Bebrўcius** -a -um, *Bebrycian.*

Belgae -ārum, m. *the Belgae, a warlike people of German and Celtic race, inhabiting the north of Gaul.* Adj., **Belgĭcus** -a -um, *Belgic ;* hence, Gallia Belgica, or simply Belgica, *the country between the Rhine, the Seine, the Marne, and the German Ocean.*

bellārĭa -ōrum, n. (bellus), *dessert, including fruit, nuts, confectionery, sweet wine,* Plaut.

1 el ātor -ōris, m. (bello), *a warrior,* Cic.; used adj., *warlike, courageous ;* deus, Mars, Verg.; equus, Verg. ; also absol., *a war-horse,* Juv.

bellātōrĭus -a -um (bello), *skilled in carrying on war;* stilus, *a pugnacious, controversial style,* Plin.

bellātrix -īcis, f. (bellator), *a female warrior;* poet., adj., *warlike;* diva, *Pallas,* Ov.; Roma, Ov.; ira, Cic.

bellātŭlus -a -um (dim., jocosely formed from bellus), *pretty,* Plaut.

bellē, adv. (bellus), *finely, prettily, elegantly, neatly.* **I.** Gen. scribere, Cic.; dicere, Cic.; negare, *politely,* Cic.; bellissime navigare, Cic.; praediola belle aedificata, Cic. **II.** belle se habere, or esse, *to be in good health,* Cic.

Bellĕrŏphōn -ontis, m. (Βελλεροφῶν), or **Bellĕrŏphontēs** -ae, m. (Βελλεροφόντης), *the slayer of the Chimaera.* Adj., **Bellĕrŏphontēus** -a -um, equus, *Pegasus,* Prop.

bellĭcōsus -a -um (bellicus), *warlike, bellicose.* **A.** gentes immanes et barbarae et bellicosae, Cic. **B.** Transf., differre sibi consulatum in bellicosiorem annum, *a more warlike year,* Liv.

bellĭcus -a -um (bellum), *relating to war.* **I.** disciplina, Cic.; virtus, Cic. Subst., **bellĭcum** -i, n. *the signal for the attack;* **a,** bellicum canere, Cic.; **b,** transf., *to excite,* Cic. **II.** Transf., **1,** *vigorous, fiery* (of style), alter (Thucydides) incitatior fertur et de bellicis rebus canit etiam quodammodo bellicum, Cic.; **2,** *warlike;* dea, *Pallas,* Ov.

bellĭger -gĕra -gĕrum (bellum and gero), *warlike, fond of war;* poet., gentes, Ov.; of inanimate things, hasta, Mart.; manus, Ov.

bellĭgĕro, 1. (bellum and gero) *to wage war;* qui isti par in belligerando esse possit, Cic.

bellĭpŏtens -entis (bellum and potens), *mighty in war.* Poet., subst. = *Mars,* Verg.

bello, 1. (**bellor,** dep., Verg.). **A.** *to wage war;* cum aliquo, Cic.; adversus aliquem, Nep.; bellare bellum, Liv. **B.** Transf., *to fight;* pictis armis, Verg.

Bellōna -ae f. (bellum), *the goddess of war,* Verg.

Bellŏvăci -ōrum, m. *a people in Gallia Belgica, near modern Beauvais.*

bellŭa, v. belua.

bellŭlus -a -um (dim. of bellus), *pretty, elegant, beautiful.*

bellum -i, n. (old form, **duellum,** *a contest between two*) *war.* **I.** Lit. domesticum, Cic.; sociale, Liv.; piraticum, Cic.; civile, Cic.; navale, Cic.; terrestre, Liv.; concitare, excitare, suscitare, Cic.; movere, commovere, conflare, Cic.; parare or comparare, Cic.; in bellum incumbere, Caes.; instruere, Cic.; nuntiare, denuntiare, indicere, *to declare war,* Cic.; suscipere, Cic.; indicare, Cic.; alicui inferre, Cic.: inferre contra patriam, Cic.; prorogare, Cic.; alere, Cic.; trahere, *to prolong,* Cic.; ducere, Caes.; deponere, Cic.; componere, Cic.; conficere, Cic.; exstinguere, restinguere, delere, Cic.; renovare, Cic.; impendet, Cic.; oritur, Cic.; renascitur, Cic.; in bello, *in time of war,* Cic.; locative, belli, *in time of war,* Cic.; vel domi vel belli, Cic. **II.** Transf., a, tribunicium, *contest,* Liv.; **b,** bellum indicere philosophis, Cic. **III.** Fig., *contention, fight,* Sall.

bellus -a -um (contr. from benulus, dim. of benus, i.e., bonus), *pretty, handsome, charming, neat, agreeable;* homo, Cic.; epistola, Cic.; locus, Cic.; vultu et fronte, Cic. *cheerful,* Cic.; *cheerful from good health;* fac bellus revertare, Cic.

belŭa -ae, f. (stem FE, whence fera and θήρ), **1,** *any very large animal,* e.g. *the elephant, lion, whale;* quantum natura hominis pecudibus reliquisque beluis antecedat, Cic.; belua fera et im-

manis, Cic.; esp. of the elephant, Ov.; **2,** *as a* term of reproach, *monster, brute, beast;* taetram et pestiferam beluam, Caes.

belŭātus -a -um (belua), *covered with figures of animals,* of tapestry, Plin.

belŭōsus -a -um (belua), *full of monsters;* Oceanus, Hor.

Belus -i, m., Myth. *an Asiatic king, founder of Babylon, father of Danaüs and Aegyptus;* hence, **A. Bēlis** -īdis, f., gen. plur., **Bēlides** -um, *the grand-daughters of Belus, the Danaides,* Ov. **B. Bēlĭdēs** -ae, m. *Lynceus, son of Aegyptus,* Ov.

bĕnĕ, adv. (from benus for bonus), comp. melius, superl. optime. **I.** *well, rightly, honourably;* coenare, Hor.; habitare, Nep.; narrare, Cic.; promittere, Cic.; polliceri, Sall. **II.** Particular phrases. **A.** With verb, **1,** bene agere, *to act fairly,* Cic.; **2,** bene audire, cf. audio; **3,** bene dicere; **a,** *to speak well;* bene dicere, id est, Attice dicere, Cic.; **b,** *to speak words of good omen* (εὐφημεῖν), Plaut.; **c,** *to speak well* of a person, *to commend,* Cic.; absol., Hor.; **4,** bene facere; **a,** *to do well,* Cic.; hence, bene facta, *famous deeds;* **b,** med., *to be of good effect,* Cato; **c,** bene facis, *excellent, I am much obliged,* Plaut.; **d,** *to do good to,* Cic., hence bene facta, *benefits,* Plaut.; **5,** bene est or bene habet; **a,** alicui, *it is well with,* Pompeio melius est factum, *Pompeius is better in health,* Cic.; **b,** *it is well, I am pleased,* Cic.; si bene habet, bene agitur, Cic.; **6,** bene vivere, *to live well,* i.e., **a,** *luxuriously,* Ter.; **b,** *happily,* Cic.; vivitur parvo bene, Hor.; **7,** bene vocas, *you are very kind* (polite refusal), Plaut.; **8,** bene vendere, *to sell dear,* Plaut.; emere, *to sell cheap,* Plaut. **B.** As an exclamation, *good, excellent,* Cic.; with acc. and dat., *good health to you,* Plaut. **III.** With adj. and adv., *well, thoroughly,* bene robustus, Cic.; bene penitus, Cic.; bene mane, Cic.

bĕnĕdictum -i, n. (benedico), *praise,* Plaut.

bĕnĕfăcĭo -fēci, -factum, 3. v. bene.

bĕnĕfactum -i, n. v. bene.

bĕnĕfĭcentĭa -ae, f. (beneficus), *kindness, liberality, beneficence,* Cic.

bĕnĕfĭcĭārĭus -a -um (beneficium), *relating to a favour,* Sen. Subst., **bĕnĕfĭciārĭi** -ōrum, m. *soldiers who by favour of their commanders were exempt from the severer military labours,* as throwing up intrenchments, fetching wood, water, etc.; *privileged soldiers,* Caes.

bĕnĕfĭcĭum]-ii, n. (bene and facio), *a kindness, favour, benefit, service.* **I.** Gen. alicui beneficium dare, tribuere, Cic.; in aliquem conferre, Cic.; apud aliquem collocare, Cic.; aliquem beneficio afficere, complecti, ornare, *to do any one a service,* Cic.; beneficium accipere, *to receive a kindness,* Cic.; beneficium tueri, *to be mindful of a service,* Cic.; in beneficio, Liv.; in beneficii loco, beneficii causa, per beneficium, *as a kindness,* service, Cic.; beneficio tuo, *by your kindness,* Cic.; deorum beneficio, sortium beneficio, Caes. **II.** In political life. **A.** *a favour, grant, distinction, promotion;* populi, *favour of the people,* Cic.; centuriones sui beneficii, *his creatures,* Suet.; quum suo magno beneficio esset, *since he owed much to his recommendation,* Cic.; *used of military promotions,* tribuni militum quae antea dictatorum fuerant beneficia, Liv.; in beneficiis delatus est, *among those recommended for promotion,* Cic. **B.** *privilege, exemption;* liberorum, *exemption from the judicial office in consequence of having a specified number of children,* Suet.

bĕnĕfĭcus -a -um, comp. -entior, superl. -entissimus (beneficissimus, Cat.), (bene and facio) *kind, generous, obliging,* Cic.

Bĕnĕventum -i, n. *a town of the Hirpini in*

Samnium, seat of a Roman colony (modern *Benevento*); hence, **Bĕnĕventānus** -a -um, *belonging to Beneventum;* in plur. **Bĕnĕventāni** -orum, m. *the people of Beneventum.*

bĕnĕvŏlē, adv. (benevolus), *benevolently, kindly,* Cic.

bĕnĕvŏlēns -entis. **A.** Adj. *well-wishing, benevolent, obliging,* Plaut. **B.** Subst., *friend, patron,* Plaut., Ter.

bĕnĕvŏlentĭa -ae, f. (benevolens), *good-will, friendly disposition, kindness, friendship, benevolence;* alicui praestare, conferre, Cic. ; colligere, Caes. ; erga aliquem habere, conferre, Cic.

bĕnĕvŏlus -a -um (comp. -entior, superl. -entissimus), (bene and volo), *kind, obliging;* alicui, Cic. ; erga aliquem, Plaut. ; servus benevolus domino, *a faithful slave,* Cic.

bĕnignē, adv. (benignus), 1, *kindly, obligingly, willingly;* benigne respondere, Liv. ; benigne attenteque audire, Cic. ; arma capere, Liv. ; benigne dicis, or absol., benigne, *much obliged,* a phrase used either in accepting or refusing an offer, Cic. ; 2, *generously;* pecuniam praebere, Plaut. ; benigne facere alicui, *to confer benefits on a person,* Cic.

bĕnignĭtas -ātis, f. (benignus), 1, *kindness, mildness,* Cic. ; 2, *liberality, generosity,* Cic.

bĕnignĭter = benigne, q.v.

bĕnignus -a -um, adj. with compar. and superl. (contr. from benigenus, from bonus and genus). **I.** *kindly, friendly, mild, pleasing.* **A.** homines benefici et benigni, Cic. ; vultus benigni, Liv. ; dies, *fortunate,* Stat. **II.** *liberal, generous;* **A.** erga aliquem, Plaut. ; alicui, Plaut., Hor. ; vini somnique benignus, *indulging in wine and sleep,* Hor. ; *prodigal,* Plaut. ; **B.** *rich, abundant;* ager, Ov. ; daps, Hor.

bĕo, 1. (connected with benus, bonus), 1, *to bless, make happy;* beas or beasti, *that pleases me, I'm glad of it,* Ter. ; 2, *to make rich;* aliquem munere, Hor.

Bĕrĕcyntus -i, m. *a mountain of Phrygia, sacred to Cybele;* hence adj., **Bĕrĕcyntĭus** -a -um, mater, *Cybele,* Verg. ; heros, *Midas, son of Cybele,* Ov. ; tibia, *the flute used at the festivals of Cybele,* Hor.

Bĕrĕnīcē -ēs, f. (Βερενίκη), 1, *queen of Ptolemy Euergetes, whose hair was placed among the stars as a constellation;* 2, *daughter of the Jewish king Agrippa I., mistress of Titus.*

Bĕroea -ae, f. (Βέροια) *a town in Macedonia.* Hence, **Bĕroeaeus** -i, m..., and **Bĕroeensis** -is, m. *an inhabitant of Beroea.*

bēryllus -i, c. (βήρυλλος). **A.** *a beryl, a precious stone, of a sea-green colour, found in India,* Juv. **B.** Meton., *a ring set with a beryl,* Prop.

Bērȳtus -i, f. (Βηρυτός), *an old Phoenician town, afterwards a Roman colony, and under the empire seat of a law school,* modern *Beyrout.* Adj., **Bērȳtĭus** -a -um, and **Bērȳtensis** -e.

bēs, bessis, m. (for be -is = binae partes assis), *two-thirds* (= *eight* unciae) of any whole composed of twelve parts. **A.** Lit., a, *of a pound, eight ounces,* Plin. ; b, *of the as* (as a coin), fenus extriente Id. Quint. factum erat bessibus, *the interest was raised from one-third per cent. for the month to two-thirds per cent.*—i.e., from 4 per cent. for the year to 8 per cent., Cic. **B.** Meton. = *eight,* Mart.

bessālis -e (bes), *containing the number 8.*

Bessi -ōrum, m. (Βέσσοι), *a people in Thrace.* Adj., **Bessĭcus** -a -um.

Bessus -i, m. *satrap of Bactria, who murdered Darius Codomanus.*

bestĭa -ae, f. (from stem FE, whence **belua** and fera), *an animal without reason* (opp. homo), *beast.* **A.** Gen., bestiae mutae, Cic. ; mala bestia, as a term of reproach, Plaut. **B.** Particularly used of the animals exhibited in the amphitheatre ; aliquem ad bestias mittere, *to condemn to be devoured by the beasts of the amphitheatre,* Cic.

bestĭārĭus -a -um (bestia), *belonging to animals;* ludus, *a fight with wild beasts at a show,* Sen. Subst., **bestĭārĭus** -ii, m. *one who fought with wild beasts at the public shows,* Cic.

bestĭŏla -ae, f. (dim. of bestia), *a small animal,* Cic.

1. **bēta** -ae, f. *a vegetable, beet,* Cic.

2. **bēta,** indecl. (βῆτα), *the beta, the second letter in the Greek alphabet;* sometimes used prov. for *the second,* Mart.

bēto (baeto, bīto), 3. *to go,* Plaut.

Bĭās -antis, m. (Βίας), *a philosopher of Priene in Ionia, contemporary of Croesus of Lydia, one of the so-called seven wise men of Greece.*

bĭblĭŏpōla -ae, m. (βιβλιοπώλης), *a bookseller,* Plin.

bĭblĭŏthēca -ae, f., and **bĭblĭŏthēcē** -ēs, f. (βιβλιοθήκη), 1, *a collection of books, a library;* 2, *the place where books are kept,* Cic.

bĭbo, bĭbi, bĭbĭtum, 3. **I.** Lit., *to drink* (from natural desire); gemmā, *from a cup set with jewels,* Verg. ; sanguinem alicujus, Cic. ; dare bibere, *to give to drink,* Cic. **II.** Particular phrases, a, aut bibat aut abeat (transl. of Greek ἢ πίθι ἢ ἄπιθι), Cic. ; b, Graeco more, *to drink to one,* Cic. ; c, ad numerum, *according to the number of years that a person wishes to live,* Ov. ; d, poet., bibere flumen, *to live on the banks of a river,* Verg. ; Danuvium, *to dwell on the banks of the Danube,* Hor. **II. A.** Of things, *to drink in,* sat prata biberunt, Verg. ; hortus aquas bibit, Ov. ; arcus bibit, *the rainbow draws up water,* Verg. **B.** Of persons, fig., amorem, Verg. ; aure (of attentive listeners), *to drink in,* Hor.

Bĭbractē -is, n. *a town in Gaul, capital of the Aedui on the modern Mount Beubray.*

Bĭbrax -actis, f. *fortress of the Remi in Gaul.*

bĭbŭlus -a -um (bibo), *fond of drinking.* **I.** Act., *fond of drinking;* 1, with genit., Falerni, Hor. ; 2, of inanimate things, lapis, *sandstone,* Verg. ; lana, Ov. ; nubes, Ov. ; charta, *blotting paper,* Plin. **II.** Pass. *drinkable,* Falernum, Hor.

bĭceps -cĭpĭtis (bis and caput), *having two heads, two-headed.* **A.** Lit., puer, Cic. ; Janus, Ov. **B.** Poet., Parnassus, *double-peaked,* Ov.

bĭclīnĭum -i, n. (bis and κλίνη), *a dining sofa for the use of two persons,* Plaut.

bĭcŏlor -ōris (bis and color), *of two colours;* equus, Verg. ; myrtus, Ov.

bĭcorniger -gĕri, m. (bis and corniger), *two-horned,* an epithet of Bacchus, Ov.

bĭcornis -e (bis and cornu), *two horned,* Ov. ; poet., luna, *the new moon,* Hor. ; furcae bicornes, *two-pronged forks,* Verg. ; Rhenus, *with two mouths,* Verg.

bĭcorpor -ōris (bis and corpus), *having two bodies,* Cic. poet.

bĭdens -entis (bis and dens), *having two teeth;* forfex, Verg. ; ancora, Plin. Subst., a, m. *a hoe with two crooked teeth for breaking clods,* Verg. ; b, f. *an animal for sacrifice whose two rows of teeth were complete,* Verg., Ov. ; and esp., *a sheep,* Phaedr.

bĭdental -ālis, n. (bidens), *a place struck with lightning, which was afterwards consecrated by the sacrifice of a sheep* (bidens), *and enclosed,* Hor.

Bidis -is, f. *a town in Sicily, north-west of Syracuse.* Hence, **Bidīnus** -a -um, *belonging to Bidis.*

bĭduum -i, n. (bis and dies), *the space of two days;* in iis operibus consiliisque biduum consumitur, Caes.; aliquem biduum cibo tectoque prohibere, Cic.; abl. biduo, *in the course of two days,* Cic.; eo biduo, *in the course of these two days,* Cic.; biduo aut summum triduo, *in two days or three at the most,* Cic.; biduo post, *two days afterwards,* Caes.; biduo quo haec gesta sunt, *two days after this was done,* Caes.; bidui iter abesse, *to be two days' march distant,* Caes.; so bidui by itself (iter understood), castra quae aberant bidui, Cic.

biennĭum -ĭi, n. (bis and annus), *a space of two years;* biennio jam confecto fere, Cic.; biennium jam factum est postquam abii domo, *it is now two years since I left home,* Plaut.; acc., biennium, *for the space of two years;* biennium provinciam obtinere, Cic.; abl., biennio, with compar., biennio major natu Domitius, *older by two years,* Tac.; biennio proximo, *in the course of two years,* Tac.; biennio ante, *two years before,* Cic.

bĭfărĭam, adv. (acc. of bifarius, *double*), *in two parts;* distribuere, Cic.; castra bifariam facta sunt, Liv.

bĭfer -fĕra -fĕrum (bis and fero), *of a tree, bearing fruit twice a year,* Verg.

bĭfĭdus -a -um (bis and findo), *split into two parts,* Ov.

bĭfŏris -e (bis and foris); **1,** *having two doors, valves, or openings;* valvae, Ov.; **2,** *with two openings;* ubi biforem dat tibia cantum, *the changing deep and high notes of the flute,* Verg.

bĭformātus -a -um, Cic. poet., v. biformis.

bĭformis -e (**bĭformātus** -a -um), *of double form;* Janus, Ov.; vates, *the poet turned into a swan,* Hor.

bĭfrons -frontis (bis and frons), *with double forehead or countenance,* epithet of Janus, Verg.

bĭfurcus -a -um (bis and furca), *having two prongs, or forks;* valli, Liv.; ramus, Ov.

bīgae -ārum, f. and P. Aug. **bīga** -ae, f. (contr. from bijugae or bijuga), *a pair of horses,* Liv., Verg.

bĭgātus -a -um (bigae), *stamped with a pair of horses;* argentum, Liv. Subst., **bĭgāti** -orum, m. sc. nummi, *silver denarii so marked.*

bĭjŭgis -e, v. bijugus.

bĭjŭgus a- -um (bis and jugum), *yoked two together;* certamen, *a race between two-horse chariots,* Verg. Subst., **bĭjŭgi** -ōrum, m. *a pair of horses,* Verg.

bĭlĭbra -ae, f. (bis and libra), *a mass of two pounds weight,* Liv.

bĭlĭbris -e (bis and libra), **1,** *weighing two pounds;* offae, Plin.; **2,** *containing two pounds;* cornu, Hor.

bĭlinguis -e (bis and lingua), *having two tongues;* a, *speaking two languages;* canusini more bilinguis, Hor.; b, *double-tongued, treacherous,* Verg.

bīlis -is, f. *gall, bile.* **I.** Lit., Cic.; suffusa, *jaundice,* Plin. **II.** Fig., a, *anger, displeasure;* commovere, Cic.; b, atra bilis (Gr. μελαγχολία), *black bile*—i.e., *melancholy,* Cic.; *madness,* Plaut.

bĭlix -īcis (bis and licium), *only acc. sing.* bilicem found, *having a double thread,* Verg.

bĭlustris -e (bis and lustrum), *lasting ten years,* Ov.

bĭmăris -e (bis and mare), *lying on two seas;* Corinthus, Hor.; Isthmus, Ov.

bĭmarītus, m. (bis and maritus), *the husband of two wives,* ap. Cic.

bĭmātĕr -tris, m. (bis and mater), *having two mothers;* epithet of Bacchus, Ov.

bĭmātus -ūs, m. (bimus), *the age of two years* (of plants and animals), Plin.

bĭmembris -e (bis and membrum), *having double members, half man, half animal;* forma, used of the Centaurs, Ov.; bimembres, subst., *Centaurs,* Verg.

bĭmestris -e (bis and mensis), *lasting two months;* consulatus, ap. Cic.; porcus, *a pig two months old,* Hor.; stipendium, *pay for two months,* Liv.

bĭmŭlus -a -um (dim. of bimus), *two years old,* Cat., Suet.

bīmus -a -um (bis and annus), *two years old;* equus, Plin.; vix bimum hunc Tiberium Caesarem, Vell.; legio, *a legion that had served for two years,* Cic.; merum, Hor.; nix, *snow lying for two years,* Ov.; honor, *office conferred for two years,* Ov.; sententia, *a vote of the senate prolonging a governor's time to two years,* ap. Cic.

bīni -ae -a (sing., **bīnus** -a -um, Lucr.), *two by two,* Lucr.; **1,** *two apiece,* sometimes simply *two;* unicuique binos pedes assignare, *two feet each,* Cic.; binos imperatores, *two consuls a year,* Sall.; with substt. that are used only in the plur., or that have a different meaning in the plur., *two;* bina castra, Cic.; binae litterae, Cic.; with other numerals, bina millia passuum, *two miles,* Quint.; **2,** of things that match, boves, *a yoke of oxen,* Plin.; scyphi, *a pair of goblets,* Cic.; neut. plur. subst., findi in bina, *to be cleft in twain,* Lucr.; si bis bina quot essent didicisset, *if he had learnt that twice two is four,* Cic.

bĭnoctĭum -ĭi, n. (bis and nox), *a space of two nights,* Tac.

bĭnōmĭnis -e (bis and nomen), *having two names;* Ascanius (because also called Iulus), Ov.; Ister (because also called Danuvius), Ov.

Bĭōn -ōnis, m. (Βίων), *a satirical philosopher, first of the Cyrenaic, then of the Stoic school;* hence **Bĭōnēus** -a -um, sermones, *witty, caustic,* Hor.

bĭōs -ĭi, m. (βίος, *life,* cf. eau de vie), *a celebrated Greek wine,* Plin.

bĭpalmis -e (bis and palmus), *two palms or spans long or broad,* Liv.

bĭpartĭo, or bĭpertĭo -(-īvi), -ītum, 4. (bis and partio), *to divide into two parts,* Cic.

bĭpartītō, adv., from partic. of bipartio, *in two parts, in two ways;* distribuere, Cic.; inferre signa, Caes.

bĭpătens -entis (bis and patens), *doubly open; open in two directions;* portis bipatentibus, Verg.

bĭpĕdalis -e (bis and pedalis), *two feet long,* broad, thick, or high; trabes, Caes.

bĭpennĭfer -fĕra -fĕrum, *armed with a two-edged axe* (bipennis), Ov.

bĭpennis -e (bis and penna), **1,** *having two wings,* Plin.; **2,** transf., *double-edged;* ferrum, Verg. Subst., **bĭpennis** -is, f. (sc. securis), *a double-edged axe,* Verg., Hor.

bĭpēs -ēdis (bis and pes), *having two feet,* biped, Cic., Verg. Subst. plur., used contemptuously, *men;* omnium non bipedum solum, sed etiam quadrupedum impurissimus, Cic.

bĭrēmis -e (bis and remus). **I.** *two-oared,* Liv. Subst., **bĭrēmis** -is, f. *a skiff with two oars,* Lucan. **II.** *with two banks of oars;* used only as subst., *a ship with two banks of oars,* Cic.

bĭs, adv. *twice, in two ways;* bis terque, Cic.; bis terve, Cic.; *twice or thrice;* bis die, Cic.; bis consul, *a man who has been consul twice* (iterum consul, *a man who is consul for the second time*), Cic.; bis tanto or tantum, *twice as great,* Plaut.; with distributive numerals, bis bina, Cic.; with cardinal numerals, only in poet., bis quinque viri (the decem viri), Hor.; prov., bis ad eundem (sc. lapidem offendere), *to make the same mistake twice,* Cic.

Bistŏnes -um, m. (Βίστονες), *the Bistones, a Thracian people settled not far from Abdera;* used poet. for *Thracians;* hence adj., **Bistŏnĭus** -a -um, *Bistonian or Thracian;* tyrannus, *Diomedes,* Ov.; chelys, *the lyre of Orpheus,* Claud.; turbo, *violent north wind,* Lucan; Minerva, *goddess of the warlike Thracians,* Ov. Subst., **Bistŏnĭa** -ae, f. *Thrace;* **Bistŏnis** -ĭdis, f. *a Thracian woman =* Bacchante, Hor.; ales, *Procne, wife of the Thracian king Tereus,* Sen. poet.

bĭsulcis -e (bis and sulcus), *cloven.* **A.** bisulci lingua (anguis), Pac. **B.** Meton., *a double-tongued person, a hypocrite,* Plaut.

bĭsulcus -a -um (bis and sulcus), *split into two parts;* lingua, *forked,* Ov.; ungula, *cloven hoof,* Plin.; pes, Lucr., Plin. Subst., **bĭsulca** -ōrum, n. *animals with cloven hoofs* (opp. solipedes), Plin.

Bĭthȳnĭa -ae, f. *a country of Asia Minor, between the sea of Marmora and the Black Sea;* hence adj., **Bĭthȳnĭcus** -a -um, *surname of Pompeius, conqueror of the Bithynians, and of his son,* Cic.; **Bĭthȳnĭus** -a -um; **Bĭthȳnus** -a -um, *Bithynian;* **Bĭthȳnĭi** -ōrum, m., Plin.; **Bĭthȳni** -ōrum, m. *the Bithynians,* Tac.; **Bĭthȳnis** -ĭdis, f. *a Bithynian woman,* Ov.

bĭtūmen -ĭnis, n. *asphaltum, bitumen,* Verg., Ov.

bĭtūmĭnĕus -a -um (bitumen), *bituminous,* Ov.

Bĭtūrĭges -um, m. *a people of Aquitanian Gaul, near the modern town Bourges,* Caes.

bĭvĭum -ĭi, n. *a place where two roads meet,* Verg.; in bivio distineri, *to be distracted by a love for two persons,* Ov.

bĭvĭus -a -um, *having two ways or passages,* Verg.

blaesus -a -um (βλαισός), *lisping, indistinct;* lingua, sonus, Ov.; *used of the talk of a parrot,* Ov. Subst., madidi et blaesi, *drunken men,* Juv.

blandē, adv. (blandus), *caressingly, softly, tenderly, flatteringly;* rogare, Cic.; blandissime appellare hominem, Cic.

blandĭdĭcus -a -um (blande and dico), *flatteringly,* Plaut.

blandĭlŏquentŭlus -a -um, *talking flatteringly,* Plaut.

blandĭlŏquus -a -um (blande and loquor), *flattering, fair-spoken,* Plaut.

blandīmentum -i, n. (blandior). **I.** *flattery;* usually plur., blandimentis corrumpere, Cic.; blandimenta muliebria, Tac. **II.** 1, *whatever pleases the senses, an allurement;* sine blandimentis expellunt famem, *without sauces, delicacies,* Tac.; 2, *careful tending,* of a plant, Plin.

blandĭor, 4. dep. *to flatter, caress, coax.* **A.** Lit., governing the dative, mihi et per se et per Pompeium blanditur Appius, Cic.; Hannibalem pueriliter blandientem patri Hamilcari, ut duceretur in Hispaniam, Liv.; auribus, *to tickle the ears,* Plin.; sibi, *to deceive oneself,* Sen.; votis meis, *to delude oneself into believing what one wishes,* Ov. **B.** Transf., of things, blandiebatur coeptis fortuna, *fortune favoured his undertakings,* Tac.; voluptas sensibus blanditur, Cic.; blan-

diente inertia, *idleness pleasing him,* Tac. Hence past. partic., **blandĭtus** -a -um, *charming,* Prop.

blandĭter = blande (q.v.).

blandĭtĭa -ae, f. (blandus), *a caress, flattery,* used in both a good and a bad and not always in an invidious sense, as assentatio, and adulatio. **A.** Lit., popularis, Cic.; plur. benevolentiam civium blanditiis et assentando colligere, Cic.; adhibere, Ov.; muliebres, Liv. **B.** *that which is alluring or attractive;* blanditiae praesentium voluptatum, Cic.

blandĭtĭes -ei, f. = blanditia (q.v.).

blandus -a -um, *flattering, fondling, caressing;* 1, blandum amicum a vero secernere, Cic.; voluptates, blandissimae dominae, Cic.; with dat., blandiores alienis quam vestris, Liv.; 2, of things, *enticing, alluring, tempting;* litterae, Cic.; soni, Ov.; oculi, Plin.; otium consuetudine in dies blandius, *ease becoming by habit every day more attractive,* Liv.

blătĕro, 1. *to chatter, babble,* Hor.

blătĭo, 4. *to talk idly, babble;* nugas, Plaut.

blatta -ae. f. *a cockroach, chafer of uncertain species,* Verg., Hor.

blennus -i, n.. (βλεννός), *a stupid fellow,* Plaut.

blĭtum -i, n. (βλίτον), *a tasteless herb used in salad,* Plaut.; hence adj., **blĭtĕus** a- um, *insipid, silly,* Plaut.

bŏārĭus, and **bŏvārĭus** -a -um (bos), *relating to oxen;* forum, *the cattle market,* Liv.

Boccar -ăris m. *a king of Mauritania at the time of the second Punic war;* hence = *an African,* Juv.

Bocchus -i, 1, *king of Mauritania, the friend and afterwards the betrayer of Jugurtha;* 2, *a plant named after him,* Verg.

Boebe -ēs, f. (Βοίβη), *a lake in Thessaly and also a place on its shores;* hence **Boebēis** -ĭdis and Ĭdos, f. *the lake Boebe.* Adj., **Boebēius** -a um.

boeŏtarchēs -ae, m. (Βοιωτάρχης), *the highest magistrate of Boeotia,* Liv.

Boeŏti -ōrum, m. (Βοιωτοί), and **Boeŏtii** -ōrum, m. *the inhabitants of Boeotia, proverbial for their dullness;* hence **Boeŏtĭa** -ae, f. *a country in Greece, north-west of Attica;* **Boeŏtĭcus** -a -um, *Boeotian;* **Boeŏtĭs** -ĭdis, f. *Boeotia;* **Boeŏtĭus** -a -um, *Boeotian;* moenia, *Thebes,* Ov.; **Boeŏtus** -a -um, *Boeotian.*

Boëthĭus -ĭi, m. (Anicius Manlius Torquatus Severus), *a distinguished Roman philosopher and theologian of the post-classical period;* beheaded in prison (where he wrote his most celebrated work, De Consolatione Philosophiae Libri, v.) 524 A.D.

Bŏgud -ŭdis, m. *son of Bocchus and king of Mauritania Tingitana, ally of Caesar and afterwards of Antonius, taken prisoner by Agrippa and executed* (B.C. 31).

bŏjae -ārum, f. plur., *a species of collar, of wood or iron, for slaves and criminals,* Plaut.

Bŏji (Bŏii), and **Bŏi** -ōrum, m. *a Celtic people, settled partly in north Italy, partly in central Germany, partly in central Gaul.* Sing., **Bŏĭus** -i, m. *one of the Boii;* **Bŏĭa,** -ae, f. *a woman of the Boii;* hence, a, **Bŏja** -ae, f. *the country of the Boii;* b, **Bŏjohaemum** -i, n. (Germ. Boienheim), *the land of the Boii* (hence modern Bohemia).

Bŏla -ae, f. *a town of the Aequi in Latium, now Lugnano.* Hence **Bŏlānus** -a -um, *relating to Bola.*

Bolbĭtĭnē -ēs, f. (Βολβιτίνη), *town in Upper*

Egypt, now *Rosetta;* hence **Bolbĭtīnus** -a -um, *of Bolbitine;* ostium, *the Rosetta mouth of the Nile*, Plin.

bōlētus -i, m. (βωλίτης), *the best kind of mushroom*, Plin.

bŏlus -i, m. (βόλος), *a throw* (classical jactus); 1, of dice, Plaut. ; 2, of a fishing net, and hence a, *what is caught at one throw;* bolum emere, Suet. ; b, fig., *a good haul, gain;* is primus bolu 'st, Plaut. ; bolo tangere, or multare, or emungere aliquem, *to cheat a man of his game*, Plaut.

bombax, interj. (βόμβαξ), an exclamation of ironical astonishment ; *is it possible?* Plaut.

bombȳcĭnus -a -um (bombyx), *silken*, Plin. Plur. subst., **bombȳcīna** -ōrum, n. *silken garments*, Mart.

bombȳx -ȳcis, m. and f. (βόμβυξ). **I.** *the silkworm*, Plin. **II.** *silk, silk-stuff*, Prop.

Bŏna Dĕa, *the good goddess*, the deity of fertility, worshipped by the Roman women.

bŏnĭtas -ātis, f. (bonus), *goodness, excellence*. **I.** Of material things, agrorum, praediorum, vocis, Cic. **II. A.** Of abstract things, naturae bonitate, Cic. ; bonitas et aequitas causae, Cic. ; bonitas verborum, Cic. **B.** Of character, *goodness, kindness, integrity;* bonitas et beneficentia, Cic. ; facit parentes bonitas (*parental love*), non necessitas, Phaedr. ; with in or erga followed by the acc., bonitas in suos, Cic.; divina bonitate erga homines, Cic.

Bŏnōnĭa -ae, f. (Βονωνία), 1, *a town in Cisalpine Gaul* (now *Bologna*); hence adj. **Bŏnōnĭensis** -e ; 2, *a port in Gallia Belgica* (now *Boulogne*); 3, *a town on the Danube* (now *Banostor*).

bŏnum -i, n. *good*, material or moral; 1, material, generally plural, **bŏna** -ōrum, *property;* bona fortunaeque, Cic. ; bonorum omnium heres, *sole heir*, Liv. ; esse in bonis, *to be in possession*, Cic. ; 2, moral, bonum mentis est virtus, Cic. ; summum bonum, *the supreme good* (in philosoph. sense), Cic. ; bona pacis, *the blessings of peace*, Tac. ; bonum naturale, *inborn talent*, Cic. ; 3, *profit, advantage;* bonum publicum, *the common weal*, Liv. ; bono esse alicui, *to profit one*, Cic. ; cui bono fuisset, *for whose advantage*, Cic.

bŏnus -a -um (old form, **duonus**), compar. melior -ius, gen. -ōris, superl. optimus -a -um (from opto), *good*. **I.** Physically and mentally, 1, *good in itself;* nummi boni, *genuine coin*, Cic. ; bona voce, Plaut. ; dicta, *good things =* jests, Enn. ; bona indole, Cic. ; esp., a, *beautiful;* forma bona, Ter. ; cervix, Suet. ; b, *of good birth;* bono genere natus, Cic. ; c, *able, clever;* imperator, Cic. ; poeta, Cic. ; jaculo, *good at hurling the javelin*, Verg. ; hence, subst., **bŏni**, *able men*, Cic. ; d, in war, *brave;* vir pace belloque bonus, Liv. ; bonus militia, Sall. ; 2, *good* as regards the sensations, position, etc.; a, *physically*, of health, valetudo bona, Cic. ; mens bona, Liv.; bono animo, *of good courage*, Cic. ; b, of physical qualities, color, *good complexion*, Lucr.; aetas bona, *youth*, Cic. ; of the weather, bona tempestas, Cic. ; c, *pleasant to the senses;* bonae res, *good things, delicacies*, Nep.; d, of news, bona fama, *good news*, Cic. ; e, of human actions, etc., bonum exemplum, Tac. ; navigatio, *a good voyage*, Cic. ; mors, *a happy death*, Plin. ; bona gratia, *in all kindness*, Cic. ; bona venia, *with your permission*, Cic. ; bonae res, *good fortune*, Cic. ; in bonam partem accipere, *to take in good part*, Cic. ; f, of time, *lucky* (poet.); dies, Verg. ; g, of good omen, auspicium, Cic. ; bona verba, *auspicious words*, Cic. ; quod bonum felix faustumque sit, Cic. ; c, *good*, with regard

to some object ; aetas tironum plerumque melior, Cic. ; with ad, ad proelium boni, Tac. ; with dat., civitatibus suis, Cic. ; optimum factu, Cic. ; 4, as regards number or quantity, bona pars hominum, Hor. ; bonam partem sermonis, Cic. **II.** Morally, *honest, faithful.* **A.** Gen., vir boni est misereri, Cic. ; often ironical, homines optimi, Cic. ; bona atque honesta amicitia, Cic. ; in vocative, as a familiar greeting, O bone! *my good fellow*, Hor. **B.** Esp. a, with regard to the state, *patriotic, loyal;* bonus et fortis civis, Cic. ; and often in Cic. and Sall. boni = *conservatives, the supporters of the existing system;* b, *chaste;* femina, Cic. ; c, *kind;* bonus atque benignus, Hor.; di boni, *gracious gods!* Cic. ; with dat., tuis, Verg. ; with in and the acc., in me, Cic. ; d, name of Juppiter, Optimus Maximus, Cic.

bŏo, 1. (βοάω), *to shout, roar;* of places, *to echo;* redde meum ! toto voce boante foro, Ov.

Bŏōtes -ae and -is, m. (βοώτης, *the ox-driver*), *a constellation in the northern hemisphere*, also called Arctophylax.

Bŏrĕās -ae, m. (βορέας,). **A.** *the north wind*, Verg. (Class. Lat. aquilo). **B.** Meton., *the north*, Hor. **B.** Mythol., *the husband of Orithyia, and father of Calais and Zetes;* hence adj., **Bŏrēus** -a -um, *northern*.

bŏrĭa -ae, f. *a kind of jasper*, Plin.

Bŏrysthĕnēs -is, m. (Βορυσθένης), *a large river in Sarmatia* (now *the Dnieper*); hence **Bŏrysthĕnīdae** or **-ītae** -ārum, m. *dwellers on the Borysthenes;* **Bŏrysthĕnis** -idis, f. *a Greek colony on the Borysthenes;* **Bŏrysthĕnĭus** -a -um, *belonging to the Borysthenes*.

bōs, bŏvis, c. (βοῦς), 1, *ox, bullock, cow*, Cic., Liv. ; bos Luca, *an elephant*, Lucr. ; prov. bovi clitellas imponere, *to saddle an ox*, i.e. *to impose on any one an office for which he is not fit*, ap. Cic. ; 2, *a kind of flat fish*, Ov.

Bospŏrus (Bosphorus), -i, m. (Βόσπορος), 1, Bosporus Thracius, *the straits between Thrace and Asia Minor* (now *the Straits of Constantinople);* 2, Bosporus Cimmerius, *off the Crimea* (now *the Straits of Yenikale*); hence a, adj., **Bospŏrānus** -a -um, *belonging to the Bosphorus;* subst. a *dweller on the Bosphorus;* b, **Bospŏrĭus** -a -um, *belonging to the Bosphorus;* **Bospŏrēus** -a -um, *belonging to the Bosphorus.*

Bostra -ae, f. *capital of the Roman province of Arabia* (the Bozrah of the Bible); hence **Bostrēnus** -a -um, *of* or *belonging to Bostra.*

Bottĭaea -ae, f. (Βοττιαία), *a district of Macedonia;* hence **Bottĭaei** -ōrum, m. *the inhabitants of the district.*

Bŏvĭānum -i, n. (Βοϊανον), *town in Samnium* (now *Bojano*); hence adj., **Bŏvĭānĭus** -a -um.

bŏvīle = bubile (q.v.).

Bŏvillae -ārum, f. 1, *town in Latium, not far from Rome, near which Clodius was murdered by Milo;* hence adj., **Bŏvillānus** -a -um, pugna (with a play on the word bovillus), *the murder of Clodius*, Cic. ; 2, *town in the district of Arpinum.*

bŏvillus -a, -um (bos), an old form of bubulus, *relating to oxen;* grex, ap. Liv.

brăbeuta -ae, m. (βραβευτής), *a judge, umpire in the public games*, Suet.

brācae (**braccae**) -ārum, f. pl. (sing. once in Ov.), *breeches, trousers, hose;* originally worn by Persians, Gauls, and Germans, Tac., Ov.

brācātus (**braccātus**) -a -um (bracae). **I.** Lit., *wearing breeches.* **II.** Transf., **A.** *foreign, barbarian, effeminate;* natio, Cic. **B.** As geograph.

3 *

name = transalpinus, Gallia **bracata**, *Gaul on the north side of the Alps, the old name of Gallia Narbonensis*, Plin.; *cognatio bracata, kindred with people of Transalpine Gaul*, Cic.

braces, acc. -em, f. *a kind of corn*, Plin.

brăchĭālis -e (brachium), *belonging to the arm*, Plaut.

brăchĭŏlum -i, n. (dim. of brachium), *a small delicate arm*, Cat.

brăchĭum -ii, n. (βραχίων). **I.** *the arm from the elbow to the wrist* (lacertus = *the fore-arm*); brachia et lacerti, Ov. **II.** Gen., *the whole arm.* **A.** Lit., brachium frangere, Cic.; diu jactato brachio scutum emittere, Caes.; dare collo brachia, *to embrace*, Verg.; as used in speaking, porrectio brachii, Cic.; in dancing, brachia numeris movere, Ov.; prov., esp., brachia sua praebere sceleri, *to assist in a crime*, Ov.; levi brachio agere, *to act without energy*, Cic.; molli brachio objurgare, *to upbraid lightly*, Cic.; dirigere brachia contra torrentem, *to swim against the stream*, Juv. **B.** Transf., 1, *the limbs of animals, the claw of a crab*, Ov.; *the thigh of an elephant*, Plin.; *the leg of a lion*, Plin.; *the claw of the nautilus*, Plin.; used of the sign Cancer, Ov., and Scorpio, Verg.; 2, of things resembling the arm, *the branch of a tree*, Verg.; *arm of the sea*, Ov.; *the spur of a mountain chain*, Plin.; *the yard of a sail* = antenna, Verg.; *an outwork connecting two points of a fortification*, Liv.; *the long walls connecting Athens with the Piraeus*, Liv.

bractĕa (brattĕa) -ae, f. *a thin plate of metal, gold leaf*, Lucr., Verg., Ov.

bractĕātus -a -um. **A.** Lit. *covered with gold leaf.* **B.** Transf. 1, *gilt, glittering like gold, magnificent*; 2, *glittering, unreal, delusive*; felicitas, Sen.

bractĕŏla -ae, f. (dim. of bractea), *a little leaf of gold*, Juv.

Branchus -i, m. (Βράγχος), *a Greek to whom Apollo gave the gift of prophecy*; hence **Branchĭdae** -ārum, m. (Βραγχίδαι), *descendants of Branchus, the hereditary caste of priests at the temple of Apollo at Didyma, near Miletus.*

brassĭca -ae, f. *cabbage*, Plaut.

Bratuspantĭum -ii, n. *town in Gallia Belgica*, now ruins of *Bratuspante, near Breteuil.*

Brennus -i, m. (Βρέννος), 1, *leader of the Senonian Gauls who took and burned Rome*, B.C. 389; 2, *leader of a Gallic horde who invaded Greece.* Adj., **Brennĭcus** -a -um.

brĕvĭārĭus -a -um (brevis), *abridged.* Subst., **brĕvĭārĭum** -i, n. *short summary, report, epitome*; imperii, *statistical report*, Suet.

brĕvĭcŭlus -a -um (dim. of brevis), *somewhat short or little*, Plaut.

brĕvĭlŏquens -entis (brevis and loquor), *brief in speech*, Cic.

brĕvĭlŏquentĭa -ae, f. (breviloquens), *brevity of speech*, Cic.

brĕvis -e (βραχύς). **A.** In regard to space, 1, as to length and breadth (opp. to longus, latus), *short*; via, Verg.; in breve cogere, *to contract into a small space*, Hor.; 2, as to height (opp. to longus, altus, procerus), judex brevior quam testis, *of shorter stature*, Cic.; 3, as to depth (opp. to profundus), *shallow*; brevia rata, Verg. Subst., **brĕvia** -ium, n. *shallows*, Verg., Tac., and sing., *a shoal*, Tac. **B.** In regard to time (opp. to longus), 1, *short*; ad breve tempus, Cic.; brevi post, *shortly afterwards*, Liv.; *short, for a little time*, Ov.; 2, *of short duration*; vitae curriculum, Cic.; rosa, flos, lilium, *blooming only for a short time*, Hor.; breves populi

Romani amores, *short-lived*, Tac.; 3, of the quantity of syllables, *short*; syllaba, Cic.; 4, of discourse or writing, *short, concise*; breves litterae tuae, Cic.; brevis narratio, Cic.; brevi, *in a few words*, Cic.; breve faciam, *I will make it short*, Cic.; in breve cogere, *to shorten*, Cic.; so meton. of persons, quum se breves putent esse, longissimi sint, Cic.; brevis esse laboro, Hor.

brĕvĭtas -ātis, f. (brevis), *shortness.* **I.** Of space, 1, in regard to length or breadth, spatii, Caes.; 2, of height, brevitas nostra, *our short stature*, Caes. **II.** Of time. **A.** Lit., temporis, diei, Cic. **B.** Transf., a, of the quantity of syllables, syllabarum, Cic.; b, of speech and writing, *brevity, conciseness*; litterarum, Cic.; orationis, Cic.; brevitati servire, *to study brevity*, Cic.

brĕvĭtĕr, adv. (brevis), *shortly.* **I.** of space, Tib. **II.** Transf., a, of the quantity of syllables, Cic.; b, of conciseness in speaking or writing, *briefly*; rem breviter narrare, Cic.

Brĭăreus -ĕi, m. (Βριαρεύς), also called Aegaeon, *son of Uranus, a giant with a hundred arms and fifty heads*; centumgeminus, Verg. Hence **Brĭărēius** -a -um.

Brĭgantes -um, m. *a tribe in the north of Britain, in Northumberland or Cumberland*; hence adj., **Brĭgantĭcus** -a -um, *surname of Julius, nephew of Civilis.*

Brĭgantĭa -ae, f. *town of the Vindelici on the lake of Constance* (now *Bregenz*); hence adj., **Brĭgantīnus** -a -um, *Brigantine.*

Brīmo -ūs, f. (Βριμώ), *the terrible one*, epithet of Hecate, used of Proserpina, Prop.

Brĭtannĭa -ae, f. and plur. **Brĭtannĭae** -arum, used both of *Great Britain* and the *British Isles*; hence adj., 1, **Brĭtannĭcus** -a -um, herba, *the plant water-dock*, Plin.; 2, **Brĭtannus** -a -um, and subst., **Brĭtanni** -orum, m. *the Britons*, Caes.; plur. **Brĭtanni** -orum, m. *the Britons*, Caes.; **Brĭto** -onis, m. *a Briton*, Juv.; *a Breton, poet. for a Gaul*, Mart.

Brĭtannĭcus -i, m. *the son of Claudius and Messalina, born in* 42, so called from his father's pretended victories in Britain. He was set aside from the succession in favour of Nero, the son of his step-mother Agrippina, and murdered after Nero became Emperor.

Brĭtŏmartis -is, f. (Βριτόμαρτις), *a Cretan deity, afterwards identified with Diana.*

Brixĭa -ae, f. *town in Cisalpine Gaul* (now *Brescia*), *the mother-city of Verona.* Hence adj., **Brixĭānus** -a -um. *of or relating to Brixia.*

brocchĭtās -ātis, f. *projection of the teeth in animals*, Plin.

brocchus (brochus, bronchus), *projecting* (of teeth); of men and animals, *having projecting teeth*, Plaut.

Brŏmĭus -ii, m. (Βρόμιος, *the noisy*), *a surname of Bacchus*, Plaut., Ov.

Bructeri -ōrum, m. *a people of North Germany.*

brūma -ae, f. (for brevma, contracted from brevissima, sc. dies), *the time of the shortest day of the year, the winter solstice.* **I.** Lit., ante brumam, Cic.; sub bruma, Caes. **II.** Poet., *winter, wintry cold*; bruma recurrit iners, Hor.; **III.** Meton., *the year*, Mart.

brūmālis -e (bruma), 1, *relating to the shortest day*; dies, Cic.; signum, *Capricorn*, Cic.; 2, *wintry*; horae, Ov.; frigus, Verg.

Brundĭsĭum -i, n. *a town in Calabria, with an excellent harbour, the port most used by the Romans for journeys to Greece and the East* (now *Brindisi*); hence adj., **Brundĭsīnus** -a -um, *Brundisian.*

Bruttĭi (Brūtĭi, Brittĭi) -ōrum, m. *the Bruttii, the inhabitants of the southern extremity of Italy (now Calabria Ulteriore);* hence adj., **Bruttĭus** -a -um, *Bruttian.*

1. **brūtus** -a -um (connected with βαρύς and βριθύς), 1, *heavy, immoveable;* pondus, Lucr.; 2, *dull, insensible, without feeling or reason;* aliorum brutorum qui se cautos ac sapientes putant, Cic.

2. **Brūtus** -i., m. *a cognomen of the Roman Gens Junia.* 1, L. Junius Brutus, *relative of Tarquinius Superbus, feigned idiocy, freed Rome from the kingly power,* B.C. 509. 2, M. Junius Brutus, *nephew of Cato Uticensis, one of the murderers of Julius Caesar, intimate friend of Cicero, philosopher and orator.* 3, D. Junius Brutus, *fellow conspirator with* 2. Adj., **Brūtĭnus** -a -um. *belonging to* (M. Junius) *Brutus;* consilia Brutina, Cic.

Būbastis -is, f. (Βούβαστις), *an Egyptian goddess, represented with the head of a cat.*

būbĭle -is, n. (bos), *an ox-stall,* Plaut.

būbo -ōnis, m. (βύας, βύζα), *the screech owl,* Verg.

būbulcĭtor, 1. dep., and **būbulcĭto,** 1. *to be a cow-herd,* Plaut.

būbulcus -i, m. (bos), *one who ploughs with oxen,* Cic.

būbŭlus -a -um (bos), *relating to cows or oxen;* caro, Plin. Subst., **būbŭla** -ae, f. (sc. caro), *beef,* Plaut.

būcaeda -ae, m. (bos and caedo), *one who has been beaten with thongs of ox hide,* Plaut.

bucca -ae, f. *the cheek;* esp. when puffed out. **I.** Lit., buccas inflare, *to swell with rage,* Hor.; prov., quod in buccam venerit, scribito, *whatever comes into your mouth,* Cic. **II.** Meton., 1, *a declaimer, bawler,* Juv.; 2, *one who fills his mouth very full, a parasite,* Petr.; 3, *a mouthful,* Mart.; 4, *a person with swollen cheeks* (of a trumpeter), Juv.

buccella -ae, f. (dim. of bucca), *a little mouthful,* Mart.

buccĭna, buccĭnator, etc., v. bucina, etc.

bucco -ōnis, m. (bucca), *a babbling foolish fellow,* Plaut.

buccŭla -ae, f. (dim. of bucca); 1, *the cheek, jaw,* Plaut.; 2, *the beaver, the visor, the part of a helmet which covers the cheeks,* Liv.

buccŭlentus -a -um (bucca), *puffy-cheeked,* Plaut.

Būcĕphălās -ae, acc. -an, and **-us** -i, m. (Macedonian Βουκεφάλας, Gr. Βουκέφαλος), *the horse of Alexander the Great.* **Būcĕphăla** -ae, f. and **Būcĕphălē** -ēs, f. (Βουκεφάλη), *a town, founded in its honour on the Hydaspes.*

būcĕros -ōn, and **būcĕrĭus** -a -um, Lucr. (βούκερως), *having ox's horns,* Ov.

būcĭna -ae, f. (from the sound bu and cano, or contr. from bovicina, from bos and cano). **I.** *a crooked trumpet;* a, *the shepherd's horn,* Prop.; b, *a military trumpet,* Cic.; used as a signal for relieving guard, hence ad tertiam bucinam (= vigiliam), Liv.; c, *the trumpet used to summon the popular assemblies,* Prop. **II.** *Triton's horn,* Ov.

būcĭnātor -ōris, m. *a trumpeter,* Caes.

būcĭnum -i, n. 1, *the sound of a trumpet,* Plin.; 2, *a shell fish,* Plin.

būcŏlĭcus -a -um, and **-ŏs** -ē -ŏn (βουκολικός), *relating to shepherds, rural;* modi, Ov.

būcŭla -ae, f. (dim. of bos), *a heifer,* Verg., Cic.

būfo -ōnis, m. *a toad,* Verg.

bulbus -i, m. (βολβός), *an onion,* Ov.

būleutērĭon -ii, n. (βουλευτήριον), *the place of meeting of a Greek senate,* Cic.

bulla -ae, f. *a hollow swelling, a bladder, bubble.* **I.** Lit., *a water bubble;* ut pluvio perlucida caelo surgere bulla solet, Ov. **II.** Transf., **A.** *a boss, stud;* 1, on girdles, aurea bullis cingula, Verg.; 2, on doors, bullas aureas omnes ex his valvis non dubitavit auferre, Cic. **B.** bulla aurea, *a golden ornament, an amulet* (of Etruscan origin), *worn by triumphing generals and by boys of good family,* laid aside by the latter when the toga virilis was put on; hence dignus bulla = *childish,* Juv.

bullātus -a -um (bulla). **I.** *inflated, bombastic, or perishable, transitory,* Pers. **II.** Transf., 1, *furnished with a bulla,* in the sense of a *boss, knob,* cingulum, Varr.; 2, *wearing the bulla,* and consequently not yet arrived at years of discretion, heres, Juv.

bullĭo, 4. (bulla), *to well up, bubble up, boil up,* Pers.

Bullis (Byllis) -ĭdis, f. *an Illyrian town and district between Dyrrhachium and Apollonia;* hence **Bullĭdenses** -ium, m. *inhabitants of Bullis;* also **Bulĭenses** -ium, m. and **Bullīni** -ōrum, m.

būmastus -i, f. *a kind of vine bearing very large grapes,* Verg.

Būra -ae, f. (Βοῦρα), and **Būris -is,** f. *a town in Achaia, forty stadia from the sea.*

Burdĭgăla -ae, f. *a town in Aquitania* (now *Bordeaux).*

būris -is, m. *the crooked hinder part of the plough,* Verg.

Būsīris -rĭdis, m. (Βούσιρις), *an old king of Egypt who sacrificed all foreigners who came to his country.*

bustĭrăpus -i, m. (bustum and rapio), *a robber of tombs,* Plaut.

bustŭārĭus -a -um (bustum), *belonging to the place where corpses were burned;* gladiator, *one who fought at a funeral pile in honour of the dead,* Cic.

bustum -i, n. (from buro, old Lat. for uro). **I.** *the place where corpses where burned,* Lucr. **II.** *a grave, sepulchre.* **A.** Lit., Cic. **B.** Fig., tu bustum reipublicae, *the destroyer of the State,* Cic.; bustum miserabile nati, *Tereus who ate his own son,* Ov.

Buthrōtum -i, n. and **-tŏs** -i, f. (Βουθρωτόν and -τός), *a town on the coast of Epirus, opposite Corcyra,* now *Butrinto.*

būthўsĭa -ae, f. (βουθυσία), *a sacrifice of oxen,* Suet.

Butrōtus -i, m. *a river in Bruttium now Bruciano.*

Buxentum -i, n. *a town in Lucania,* now *Policastro.*

buxĭfer -a -um (buxus and fero), *producing the box-tree,* Cat.

buxus -i, f. and **buxum** i. n. (πύξος). **I.** 1, *the evergreen box-tree,* Ov.; 2, *box-wood,* Verg. **II.** Meton., *articles made of box-wood*—e.g., *flute,* Verg.; *top,* Verg.; *comb,* Ov.; *writing-tablets,* Prop.

Byrsa -ae, f. (Βύρσα), *the citadel of Carthage.*

Byzantĭum -ĭi, n. (Βυζάντιον), *Byzantium, a city in Thrace on the Bosphorus, opposite the Asiatic Chalcedon* (now *Constantinople*). Adj., **Byzantĭnus** -a -um, **Byzantĭus** -a -um, *Byzantine.*

C

C c, the third letter of the Latin Alphabet, corresponding in place and originally in sound with the Greek Γ, γ. At an early period it was substituted for K, which, except in a few instances, disappeared from the language.

căballīnus -a -um, *belonging to a horse;* fons (in jest) = *Hippocrene*, Pers.

căballus -i, m. *a pack-horse, nag*, Hor., Juv.

Căbillonum -i, n. *a town of the Aedui in Gallia Lugdunensis*, now *Châlons-sur-Saône*.

Căbīri -ōrum, m. (Κάβειροι), *gods honoured by secret rites in Lemnos and Samothrace*.

căchinnātĭo -ōnis, f. *a violent laughing, cachinnation*, Cic.

1. căchinno, 1. (cachinnus), *to laugh aloud;* ridere convivae, cachinnare ipse Apronius, Cic.

2. căchinno -ōnis, m. (cachinnus), *one who laughs heartily, a jester*, Plaut.; *scoffer*, Pers.

căchinnus -i. m. (καγχασμός), *loud laughter, jeering;* cachinnos irridentium commovere, Cic.; poet. transf., *the splashing of the sea*, Cat.

căco, 1. (κακάω), **1,** *to void the excrement*, Hor.; **2,** *to defile with excrement*, Cat.

căcoēthĕs -is, n. (κακόηθες), *an obstinate disease, an itch or incurable passion;* scribendi, *an incurable itch to write*, Juv.

căcŭla -ae, m. *a soldier's or officer's servant*, Plaut.

căcūmen -ĭnis, n. **1,** *the extreme point, top, summit;* montis, Cat.; arboris, Verg.; ramorum, Caes.; **2,** *height, perfection;* alescendi, *the greatest growth*, Lucr.

căcūmĭno, 1. (cacumen), *to point, make pointed*, Ov.

Căcus -i, m. (Κᾶκος), *son of Vulcan, an Italian cattle-robber slain by Hercules.*

cădāver -ĕris (cado), n. *a dead body, carcass*, of men or animals. **I.** Lit., Cic.; as a term of reproach, ab hoc ejecto cadavere quidquam mihi aut opis aut ornamenti expetebam, Cic. **II.** Transf., of the ruins of towns, cadavera oppidum, ap. Cic.

cădāvĕrōsus -a -um (cadaver), *like a corpse, cadaverous*, Ter.

Cadmus -i, m. (Κάδμος), *the son of Agenor, king of Phoenicia and brother of Europa; father of Polydorus, Ino, Semele, Autonoë, and Agave; founder of Thebes in Boeotia.* Adj., **Cadmēus** -a -um, *Thebae*, Prop.; hence subst., **Cadmēa** -ae, f. *the citadel of Thebes*, Nep.; **Cadmēis** -ĭdis, f. arx, *Theban*, Ov.; and subst., *a female descendant of Cadmus*, Ov.

cădo, cĕcĭdi, cāsum, 3. *to fall.* **I.** Gen. **A.** Lit., **1,** of lifeless things, arma alicui cadunt de manibus, Cic.; of weapons, levius, *with less violence*, Caes.; of thunderbolts, caelo cadunt fulmina, Petr.; of dice, ut (talus) cadat rectus, Cic.; of sails, vela cadunt, *are furled*, Verg.; of rain, snow, tears, and other liquids, guttae cadentes, Cic.; of shadows, altis de montibus, Verg.; of things which naturally fall—e.g., fruit, leaves, &c.; motis poma cadunt ramis, Ov.; barba cadit, Verg.; of the sun, stars, the day, etc., *to set;* sol cadens, poet., *the west;* juxta solem cadentem, Verg.; of winds, *to be lulled;* cadente jam euro, Liv.; of words, *to fall from the mouth;* verba cadentia tollit, Hor.; grammat. and rhet. **t. t.,** *to come to an end;* verba melius in syllabas longiores cadunt, Cic.; **2,** of living things, si prolapsus cecidisset, Liv.; in terram, Cic.; de equo, Cic. **B.** Transf., **1,** of payments, *to fall due;* in eam diem cadere nummos qui a Quinto

debentur, Cic.; **2,** of perception, *to fall to the notice of;* sub oculos, Cic.; **3,** *to fall under a certain class;* in idem genus orationis, Cic.; **4,** *to fall under;* in unius potestatem, Cic.; **5,** *to agree with, be consistent with;* non cadit in hos mores, non in hunc hominem ista suspicio, Cic.; **6,** *to happen;* si quid adversi casurum foret, Liv.; fortuito, Cic.; male, Caes.; cadere ad or in irritum, *to become of no effect*, Liv.; insperanti mihi cecidit ut, etc., Cic.; **7,** *to fall*, in power, honour, etc., tam graviter, Cic.; *to lose or be cast in a law-suit*, in judicio, Cic.; causa, Cic.; *to lose courage;* non debemus ita cadere animis quasi, etc., Cic. **II.** Esp., **A.** *to be destroyed;* non tota cadet Troja, Ov. **B.** Of persons, *to be killed;* pauci de nostris cadunt, Caes.; in acie, Cic.; sua manu, *to commit suicide*, Tac.; of the victims of a sacrifice, ovis cadit deo, Ov.

cādūcĕātor -ōris, m. (caduceus), *a herald*, Liv.

cādūcĕus -i, m. *a herald's staff*, Cic.; *the wand or staff of Mercury*, Suet.

cādūcĭfĕr -fĕri (caduceus and fero), *he that bears the caduceus*, surname of Mercury, Ov.; absol., Ov.

cādūcus -a -um (cado), *that which has fallen or is falling.* **I. A.** Lit., bello, *fallen in war*, Verg. **B.** Transf., legal t. t., bona, *a legacy rendered void by the death or legal incapacity of the legatee, which fell to other heirs or to the exchequer*, Cic.; legatum omne capis necnon et dulce caducum, Juv. **II. A.** Lit., *inclined or ready to fall;* **1,** gen., vitis, Cic.; flos, Ov.; **2,** esp., *destined to die, devoted to death;* juvenis, Verg. **B.** Transf., *frail, perishable, transitory;* res humanae fragiles caducaeque, Cic.

Cădurci -ōrum, m. *a Gaulish people in Aquitania, famous for their linen manufactures;* hence a, adj., **Cădurcus** -a, -um; b, subst., **Cădurcum** -i, n. (sc. stragulum). **A.** *a coverlet of Cadurcian linen.* **B.** Meton., *the marriage-bed*, Juv.

cădus -i, m. (κάδος), *a wine jar;* capite sistere, *to overturn*, Plaut.; meton., *wine*, Hor.; also used for other purposes, for honey, Mart.; = urna, *a funeral urn*, Verg.

Cădūsii -ōrum, m. (Καδούσιοι), *a warlike nation on the Caspian Sea.*

caecĭas -ae, m. (καικίας), *a north-east wind*, Plin.

caecĭgĕnus -a -um (caecus and gigno), *born blind*, Lucr.

Caecĭlĭus -a -um, *name of a celebrated plebeian gens, the most important family of which was the Metelli;* of these the most illustrious were: **1,** Qu. Caec. Metellus, *praetor* B.C. 148, surnamed Macedonicus, *for his conquests in Macedonia;* **2,** his son, Qu. Caec. Metellus, *consul* B.C. 123, surnamed Balearicus *for his victories over the Baleares;* **3,** Caecilia, *the daughter of Balearicus, the mother of the tribune Clodius;* **4,** C. Caecilius Statius, *Roman comic poet, contemporary of Ennius, died about* 168 B.C. Adj., **Caecĭlĭus** -a -um, *Caecilian*, lex (de ambitu), Cic.; **Caecĭlĭānus** -a -um, *fabula, of Caecilius Statius*, Cic.; senex, *in a play of the same*, Cic.

caecĭtas -ātis, f. (caecus), *blindness*, Cic.; fig., of the mind, ut tibi luminis obesset caecitas plus quam libidinis? Cic.

caeco, 1. *to make blind*, Lucr.; fig., largitione mentes imperitorum, Cic.; celeritate caecata oratio, *made obscure*, Cic.

Caecŭbum -i, n. and **Caecŭbus ager**, *a district in Latium, famed for its wine;* hence adj., **Caecŭbus** -a -um, *Caecuban;* vinum Caecubum and simply Caecubum, *wine of Caecubum*, Hor.

caecus -a -um, adj. with compar. **I.** Active. **A.** Lit., *blind, not seeing;* ille qui caecus factus est, Cic.; subst., apparet id etiam caeco, Liv. **B.** Transf., *intellectually* or *morally blind, blinded;* 1, of persons, caecus animi, Cic.; 2, of passions, timor, Cic. **II.** Passive. **A.** Lit., 1, of places that have no light, *dark;* domus, Cic.; 2, of objects, appearances, etc., *invisible, unseen;* fores, Verg.; pericula, Cic. **B.** Transf., 1, *dark, unintelligible, unknown;* fata, Hor.; 2, *blind, uncertain, objectless;* caeca expectatione, Cic.

caedes -is, f. (caedo). **A.** *a cutting off, a cutting down, killing, slaughter, carnage;* a, caedem facere, Cic.; plur. multae et atroces inter se caedes, Liv.; b, *killing of victims for sacrifice;* bidentium, Hor. **B.** Meton., a, *the persons slain;* caedis acervi, Verg.; b, *blood shed in slaughter,* (currus) respersus fraterna caede, Cat.

caedo, cĕcīdi, caesum, 3. *to hew, fell, cut down, hew in pieces, strike, beat.* **I. A.** januam saxis, Cic.; aliquem virgis, Cic.; silvam, Caes. **B.** Transf., testibus caedi, *to be hard pressed,* Cic. **II. A.** *to kill;* consulem exercituumque, Liv.; poet., caesi acervi, *heaps of the slain,* Cat.; caesus sanguis, *the blood of the slain,* Verg.; of sacrificial victims, hostias, Cic. **B.** *to cut out,* securibus humida vina (of wine when frozen), Verg.; latius (murus) quam caederetur ruebat, Liv.

caelāmĕn -ĭnis (caelo), n. *a bas-relief,* Ov.

caelātor -ōris, m. (caelo), *a chaser, graver,* or *carver,* Cic.

caelātūra -ae, f. (caelo), *the art of engraving* or *chasing,* chiefly in metals or ivory, Quint.; meton., *an engraving,* Suet.

caelebs -lĭbis, *unmarried, single* (of the man). **I. A.** Lit., se rectius viduam et illum caelibem esse futurum, Liv. **B.** Meton., *vita* (of an unmarried man), Hor. **II.** Transf., of trees, platanus, *to which no vine is trained,* Hor.

caelĕs -ĭtis (caelum), *heavenly;* regna, Ov. Subst., *a god,* Ov.; oftener in plur., **caelites,** *the gods,* Cic.

caelestis -e (caelum), a, *belonging to heaven, heavenly;* corpora, Cic.; hence subst., **caelestia** -ium, n. *things in heaven, the heavenly bodies,* Cic.; b, *coming from the heavens* or *seen in the heavens;* aqua, Hor.; spiritus, Cic.; c, *belonging to heaven as the seat of the gods, celestial, divine;* dii, Cic.; sapientia, Cic.; quem prope caelestem fecerint, *whom they almost deified,* Liv.; hence subst., **caelestis** -is, f. *a goddess,* Tib.; plur., m. and f. *the gods,* Cic.; transf. for what is excellent, *glorious, superhuman;* ingenium, Ov.

caelībātus -ūs, m. (caelebs), *celibacy,* Suet.

caelĭcŏla -ae, m. (caelum and colo), *a dweller in heaven;* poet., *a god,* Verg.

caelĭfĕr -fĕra -fĕrum, *bearing the heavens;* Atlas, Verg.

Caelius -a -um. **I.** *name of a Roman plebeian gens,* the most celebrated members of which were: 1, C. Caelius Caldus, *Roman orator and lawyer;* 2, L. Caelius Antipater, *annalist of the Second Punic War, contemporary of the Gracchi;* 3, M. Caelius Rufus, *intimate friend and client of Cicero.* **II.** Caelius Mons, *a hill in Rome south of the Palatine and east of the Aventine* (now the Lateran). Adj., **Caeliānus** -a -um, *Caelian.*

caelo, 1. (1. caelum), 1, *to engrave* or *chase metals* or *ivory, to carve in bas-relief;* speciem caelare argento, Cic.; vasa caelata, Cic.; 2, of poetry, caelatum novem Musis opus, *adorned by,* Hor.

1. caelum -i, n. (caedo), *the burin* or *engraving-tool,* Mart.

2. caelum -i, n. (connected with Gr. κοῖλος, *hollow*), 1, *the heavens;* caelum totum astris distinctum et ornatum, Cic.; non de caelo demissos, sed qui patrem ciere possent, Liv.; caelum ac terras miscere, Liv.; findere caelum aratro, *to do something impossible,* Ov.; hence, a, of a great height, it caelo clamor, Verg.; juncta caelo montium juga, Liv.; minari in caelum, Verg.; b, fig., as the height of joy, renown, etc., esse in caelo, Cic.; aliquem or aliquid ferre ad or in caelum, Cic.; 2, *the heavens,* a, as the home of light, clouds, etc., caelum nocte atque nubibus obscuratum, Sall.; de caelo cadere (of meteors), Liv.; caelum discedit, *light,* Cic.; ictus e caelo, Cic.; b, *the air,* caelum liberum, Cic.; of climate, gravitas huius caeli, *unhealthiness,* Cic.; caelum crassum, Cic.; 3, *heaven* as the home of the gods, de caelo delapsus, *a messenger of the gods,* Cic.; non ad mortem trudi, verum in caelum videri escendere, Cic.; quid me caelum sperare jubebas, *marriage with a god,* Verg.

Caelus -i, m. = Caelum *personified as a god, son of Aether and Dies.*

caementum -i, n. (caedo), *rough stone from the quarry,* Cic.

Caeneus -ĕi, m. (Καινεύς), *originally a maiden, daughter of Elatus, changed by Neptune into a boy and then into a bird.*

Caenina -ae, f. (Καινίνη), *town in Latium;* hence adj., **Caeninensis** -e and **Caeninus** -a -um, *of* or *belonging to Caenina.*

caenōsus -a -um (caenum), *muddy,* Juv.

caenum -i, n. (connected with in-quino), *mud, dirt, filth;* male olere omne caenum, Cic.; as a term of reproach, labes illa atque caenum, Cic.

caepa (cēpa) -ae, f. and **caepe** (cēpe) -is, n. *an onion,* Hor.

Caepĭo -ōnis, m. *the cognomen of a patrician branch of the gens Servilia.*

Caerĕ, n. indecl., and **Caerēs** -ĭtis or -ētis, f. *a very old city of Etruria, whose inhabitants received the Roman citizenship, except the right of voting;* hence, **Caerēs** -ĭtis and -ētis, *belonging to Caere;* subst., **Caerĭtes** or **Caerētes** -um, m. *the inhabitants of Caere;* Caerite cera (i.e., tabula) digni = *deserving of civic degradation,* Hor.

caerĭmōnĭa -ae, f. **I.** *holiness, sacredness;* deorum, Cic.; legationis, Cic. **II.** 1, *holy awe, reverence;* summa religione caerimoniaque sacra conficere, Cic.; 2, *religious usage, sacred ceremony* (gen. in plur.), Cic.

Caeroesi -ōrum, m. *a people in Gallia Belgica, near modern Luxemburg* or *Lüttich.*

caerŭlĕus (poet. **caerŭlus**) -a -um (connected with caesius). **I.** *dark-coloured, dark blue,* epithet of the sea and sky; a, of the sky, caerula caeli, or simply caerula, *the azure of the sky,* Lucr., Ov.; b, of the sea, aquae, Ov.; **caerŭla** -orum, n. *the sea,* Enn.; of sea-gods, deus, *Neptune,* Ov.; mater, *Thetis,* Ov.; equi, of *Triton,* Ov.; via, Ov.; puppis, Ov.; c, of rivers, Thybris, Verg.; d, of other things, angues, Verg.; Germanorum pubes, *blue-eyed,* Hor. Subst., **caerŭlĕum** -i, *a blue colour,* Plin. **II.** Poet., *dark green,* Ov.; *dark,* Verg.

Caesar -ăris, m. *a Roman family name of the gens Julia, the most famous of which were,* 1, C. Julius Caesar, *who conquered Pompeius, overthrew the power of the senate, was made Dictator with supreme power, and was murdered by Brutus and Cassius,* 44 B.C.; 2, *his nephew,* Octavius, *who took his name, with the addition of Octavianus, and established the empire. After him all the emperors bore the name of Caesar with the title Augustus,* till, under Hadrian, a distinction was made, and the reigning emperor was called Caesar Augustus, and the appointed heir Caesar. Adj., **A. Caesăreus** -a -um, *belonging to Julius Caesar; sang*uis, Ov. **B. Caesărĭanus** -a -um, *Caesarian;* subst. Caesariani, *the partisans of Caesar.* **C. Caesăriensis** -e, Mauritania, *the east part of Mauritania.* **D. Caesărīnus** -a -um, *of* (Julius) *Caesar;* celeritas, Cic.

Caesarēa -ae, f. (Καισάρεια), *name of several towns,* 1, *in Palestine;* 2, *in Mauritania Caesariensis;* 3, *in Cappadocia;* 4, *in Phoenicia.*

caesărĭātus -a -um (caesaries), *long-haired,* Plaut.

caesărĭes -ēi, f. *a bushy head of hair,* Verg.; barbae, *the hair of the beard,* Ov.

caesim, adv. (caedo). **A.** *with cutting, with the edge of the sword* (opp. to punctim, *with the point*), petere hostem, Liv. **B.** Transf., *of discourse, in short sentences;* membratim adhuc, deinde caesim diximus, Cic.

caesĭus -a -um, *bluish grey,* used of the colour of the eyes; caesios oculos Minervae, caeruleos Neptuni, Cic.; leo, *with grey eyes,* Cat.

caespes (cespes) -ĭtis (caedo), *grass that has been cut.* **I. A.** Lit. *turf,* used for altars, tombs, mounds; primum exstruendo tumulo caespitem Caesar posuit, Tac.; plur., gladiis caespites circumcidere, Caes.; non esse arma caespites neque glebas, Cic. **B.** Meton., **a,** *a hut of turf,* Hor.; **b,** *an altar of turf,* Hor.; **c,** *a clump of plants,* Verg. **II.** Transf. *grassy sward;* gramineus, Verg.

1. **caestus** -ūs, m. (caedo), *gauntlet for boxers,* made of leathern thongs, Cic.

2. **caestus** -i, m., v. cestus.

caeterus, etc. . . . . v. ceterus, etc.

Cāĭcus -i, m. (Κάϊκος), *a river in Mysia flowing into the Sinus Eleaticus.*

Cājēta -ae (and -ē -ēs), f. **I.** *the nurse of Aeneas.* **II.** *a town on the sea-coast, on the borders of Latium and Campania, now Gaëta.*

Cājus (poet. **Cāïus**), -i, m., and **Cāja** -ae, f., 1, *a common praenomen among the Romans.* At a wedding, the bride and bridegroom were called by these names, and the bride said ubi tu Cajus, ego Caja; 2, *the name of a celebrated Roman jurist,* more frequently written Gaius, who flourished under the Antonines at the beginning of the second century.

Călabri -ōrum, m. *inhabitants of Calabria;* hence, **Călāber** -bra -brum, *belonging to Calabria;* poet., Pierides, *the poems of Ennius,* Hor.; **Călabria** -ae, f. *the peninsula at the south-east extremity of Italy.*

Călactē -ēs, f. (Καλὴ ἀκτή), *a town on the north coast of Sicily;* hence, **Călactīnus** -a um, *of or belonging to Calacte.*

Călăgurris -is, f. *a town in Spain, now Loharre;* hence **Călăgurrĭtāni** -ōrum, m. *the inhabitants of Calagurris.*

Călāis, acc. -in, abl. -i, m. (Κάλαϊς) *son of Boreas and Orithyia, brothers of Zetes, who accompanied the Argonauts and drove off the Harpies.*

Călămis -mĭdis, m. (Κάλαμις), *one of the greatest sculptors of the age of Phidias.*

călămister -tri, m. and **călămistrum** -tri, n. (calamus). **A.** *a curling-iron for the hair;* frons calamistri notata vestigiis, Cic. **B.** Transf. *excessive ornament or flourish in discourse;* ineptis fortasse gratum fecit, qui volent illa calamistris inurere, Cic.

călămistrātus -a -um, *curled with the curling-iron;* coma, Cic.; saltator, Cic.

călămĭtas -ātis, f. **A.** *damage, loss, failure,* especially in agriculture, Cic. **B.** Transf. *misfortune, damage, calamity, loss;* calamitatem tolerare, Cic.; calamitate prohibere aliquem, Cic.; plur., calamitates reipublicae; especially *misfortune, reverse in war;* Cannensis illa calamitas, Cic.

călămĭtōsē, adv. (calamitosus), *unfortunately;* vivere, Cic.

călămĭtōsus -a -um (calamitas), 1, act., *causing loss, destructive;* tempestas, Cic.; bellum, *calamitous,* Cic.; 2, pass., *suffering great loss, miserable;* agri vectigal, *oppressive,* Cic.; homines miseri et fortuna magis quam culpa calamitosi, Cic.

călămus -i, m, (κάλαμος), **I.** *a reed.* **A.** Lit., Ov. **B.** Meton., various articles made of reed, *a writing reed, pen,* Cic.; *a reed-pipe, Pan-pipe,* Verg.; *an arrow,* Hor.; *a fishing-rod,* Ov.; *a limed twig for fowling,* Prop. **II.** *any reed-shaped stalk,* Verg.

călăthiscus -i, m. (dim. of calathus), *a small wicker basket,* Cat.

călăthus -i, m. (κάλαθος), 1, *a wicker basket,* used for fruit or flowers, Verg.; for spinning, Ov.; 2, *a vessel of similar form* of metal or wood; *a cheese-basket,* Verg.; *a wine-bowl,* Verg.

Călātĭa -ae, and **Călātĭae** -ārum, f. *a town in Campania.* Adj., **Călātīnus** -a -um, *Calatine.*

călātor -ōris, m. (1. calo), *a servant, attendant upon priests,* Suet.

călautĭca -ae, f. *a kind of female headdress with pendent lappets,* Cic.

calcănĕum -i, n. *the heel,* Verg. (?).

calcar -āris, n. (calx), *a spur.* **I.** Lit. equo calcaria subdere, Liv.; equum calcaribus concitare, Liv.; prov., addere calcaria sponte currenti, *to spur the willing horse,* Plin. **II.** Transf. *stimulus, incitement;* admovere, Cic.; gen. in plur., alter frenis eget, alter calcaribus, Cic.; calcaria adhibere, Cic.

calcĕāmentum -i, n. (calceo), *a covering for the foot;* calceamentum solorum callum, Cic.

calcĕārĭum -i, n. (calceus), *shoe money,* Suet.

calcĕātus -ūs, m. = calceamentum (q.v.).

calcĕo, 1. *to shoe, provide with shoes;* homines non satis commode calceati et vestiti, Cic.

calcĕŏlārĭus -i, m. (calceolus), *a shoemaker,* Plaut.

calcĕŏlus -i, m. (dim. of calceus), *a half shoe,* Cic.

calcĕus -i, m. (calx, *the heel*), *a shoe,* distinguished from the sandal (solea) as covering the whole foot, Cic.; calcei Sicyonii, *of Samian leather,* Cic.; (as the Romans took off their shoes when reclining at dinner), calceos poscere = *to rise from table,* Plin.; calceos mutare, *to become a senator* (from a particular kind of shoe worn only by senators), Cic.

Calchās (Calcās) -antis, acc. -antem and -anta, m. (Κάλχας), *son of Thestor, soothsayer to the Greeks before Troy.*

Calchēdon -ŏnis and -ŏnos, acc. -ŏnem and -ŏna, f. (Χαλκηδών), *town in Bithynia on the Propontis, opposite Byzantium.* Adj., **Calchēdŏnĭus** -a -um, *Calchedonian.*

calcio = calceo (q.v.).

calcĭtrātus -ūs, m. *a kicking,* Plin.

1. **calcĭtro,** 1. (calx). **A.** Lit. *to strike with the heel, kick,* Plin. **B.** Transf. *to oppose perversely and obstinately,* Cic.

2. **calcĭtro** -ōnis, m. (1. calcitro), *a kicker,* Varr.; of men, *a bully, blusterer,* Plin.

calco, 1. (1. calx), *to tread, to tread upon.* **I.** Gen. **A.** Lit. aliquem pede, Tac. **B.** Transf., **a**, *to trample under foot, conquer;* amorem, Ov.; **b**, *to mock, insult,* Prop. **II.** Esp. **A.** *to tread upon* (grapes) *in the wine-press;* uvas, Ov. **B.** *to stamp, compress,* Verg. **C.** *to visit* (a place); viam, Hor.

calcŭlātor -ōris, m. *a calculator, bookkeeper, accountant,* Mart.

calcŭlus -i, m. (dim. of 2. calx), *a little stone, pebble.* **I.** Gen., Cic.; collectively, *gravel,* Verg. **II.** Esp., **a,** *a piece used in the Roman game of* Latrunculi or Duodecim scripta; calculum reducere, *to retract a move,* Cic.; **b**, *a voting pebble,* a white one being thrown into the urn to acquit or to affirm, a black one to condemn or to negative; album calculum adjicere errori nostro, Plin.; **c**, *a counter for reckoning,* hence *a calculation;* ad calculos vocare aliquid, *to subject to a strict reckoning,* Cic.

caldus = calidus (q.**v.**).

Călēdŏnes -um, acc. -as, m. *the inhabitants of Caledonia.* Hence **A. Călēdŏnĭa** -ae, f. *the north-west of Scotland.* **B.** Adj., **Călēdŏnĭus -a** -um, *Caledonian.*

călĕfăcio (calfacio) -fēci -factum, 3., pass. **călĕfīo** (calfio) -factus sum -fieri. **A.** Lit., *to make warm, heat;* 1, of things, balineum calfieri jubebo, Cic.; **2**, of animals, corpus, Cic. **B.** Transf., *to disturb, excite;* Gabinium ad populum luculente calefecerat Mummius, Cic.; calefacta corda tumultu, Verg.

călĕfacto, 1. (intens. of calefacio), *to make warm, heat,* Hor.

Călendae (Kălendae) -ārum, f. (from calare, *to call,* the calends being the day on which the times of the Nones and the festivals were proclaimed), 1, *the first day of the month;* Cal. Februariae, *the first of February;* femineae Calendae, *the first of March, the day of the Matronalia, when Roman matrons sacrificed to Juno,* Juv.; on the calends, interest of money was paid; hence tristes Calendae — i.e., for debtors—Hor.; as there were no calends in the Greek year, ad Graecas Calendas solvere = *never to pay,* Suet.; **2,** *month,* Ov.

Cālēnus, v. Cales.

călĕo -ui, 2. (connected with καίω), *to be warm, hot, to glow.* **I.** Lit., **A.** Of physical heat, ignis calet, Cic.; centum Sabaeo ture calent arae, Verg.; terrae alio sole calentes, Hor. **B.** Of animal heat, os calet tibi, Plaut. **II.** Transf., **A.** Of persons, *to be inflamed, aroused, excited;* calebat in agendo, *he was all fire in acting,* Cic.; Romani calentes adhuc ab recenti pugna, Liv.; cupidine laudis, Ov.; so of love, *to be in love with;* juvene, femina, Hor. **B.** Of things, 1, *to be urged on zealously;* indicia calent, Cic.; res calet, *is ripe for execution,* Cic.; **2,** *to be yet warm, fresh of interest;* illud crimen de nummis caluit re recenti, Cic.

Căles -ium, f. *town in Campania, famous for its wine,* now *Calvi.* Adj., **Cālēnus -a** -um, *of* or *belonging to Cales.*

călesco, 3. (inch. of caieo), *to become warm, to grow hot;* calescere vel apricatione vel igni, Cic.; tunc primum radiis gelidi caluere triones, Ov.; fig., of love, quo propior nunc es, flamma propiore calesco, Ov.

Calēti -ōrum and **Calētes** -um, m. *a Gallic tribe in Normandy on the Seine.*

călĭandrum -i, n. v. caliendrum.

călĭdē, adv., with superl. (calidus), *warmly, speedily,* Plaut.

călĭdus (caldus) -a -um, *warm, hot.* **A.** Lit.,

dies, Cic. Subst., a, **călĭda** -ae, f. (sc. aqua), *warm water,* Plin.; b, **călĭdum** -i, n. *warm wine and water,* Plaut. **B.** 1, *hot, fiery, passionate, violent;* equus, Verg.; calidus juventa, Hor.; consilium calidum, Cic.; 2, *quick, speedy,* Plaut.

călĭendrum -i, n. *a head-dress of Roman women,* Hor.

călĭga -ae, f. (connected with calceus and calx, *heel*), *a stout shoe,* esp. *soldier's shoe,* Cic.

călĭgātus -a -um, *wearing the caliga;* caligatum venire, *booted and spurred,* Juv. Subst. m., *a common soldier,* Suet.

călĭgĭnōsus -a -um (1. caligo). **I.** Lit., *foggy, misty;* caelum nebulosum et caliginosum, Cic. **II.** Transf., *dark;* nox, *the unknown future,* Hor.

1. **cālīgo** -ĭnis, f. **I.** *fog, mist, vapour;* fulvae nubis caligo crassa, Verg. **II.** Meton., *darkness.* **A.** Lit., 1, gen., tetrae tenebrae et caligo, Cic.; 2, esp., *mist before the eyes;* aliquid cernere quasi per caliginem, Cic. **B.** Transf., 1, *mental darkness, dulness;* haec indoctorum animis offusa caligo, Cic.; 2, *calamity;* superioris anni caligo et tenebrae, Cic.; 3, *gloominess, sadness,* Cic.

2. **cālīgo**, 1. (1. caligo). **I.** *to spread a dark mist around,* Verg.; meton., caligantes fenestrae, *making dizzy,* Juv. **II.** *to be dark;* caligans lucus, Verg. **II.** Esp., of the eyes, *to be misty;* caligant oculi, Lucr.; transf., *to be in darkness,* Plin.; prov., caligare in sole, *to grope in daylight,* Quint.

Cālĭgŭla -ae, m. (dim. of caliga, lit., *a little soldier's shoe), nickname of C. Caesar, the third Roman Emperor, so called because when a boy in the camp of his father Germanicus he was dressed as a common soldier.*

călix -ĭcis, m. (κύλιξ), 1, *a goblet, drinking vessel;* calix mulsi, Cic.; 2, *a cooking vessel,* Ov.

Callaeci (Gallaeci) -ōrum, m. *a people in the north-west of Spain.* Hence **Callaecia** (Gallaecia) -ae, f., *the country of the Callaeci;* adj., **Callaecus -a** -um and **Callăĭcus -a** -um.

callĕo, 2. (callum). **I.** *to be thick-skinned,* Plaut. **II.** Transf., **A.** Intransit., *to be clever, experienced,* ap. Cic.; usu alicuius rei, Liv. **B.** Transit., *to know by experience, understand;* Poenorum jura, Liv.

Callicrătĭdās -ae, m. (Καλλικρατίδας), *a Spartan commander, killed at the battle of Arginusae.*

Callicŭla -ae, f. *a small hill in Campania.*

callĭdē, adv. (callidus), *in a good sense, cleverly;* in a bad sense, *cunningly, slyly;* callide arguteque dicere, Cic.; omnia decreta eius peritissime et callidissime venditare, Cic.

callĭdĭtas -ātis, f. **I.** In a good sense, *expertness, cleverness;* vincere omnes calliditate et celeritate ingenii, Nep. **II.** More frequently in a bad sense, *cunning, craft, artifice;* scientia quae est remota ab justitia calliditas potius quam sapientia appellanda, Cic.; *stratagem in war,* Liv.; in oratory, *artifice;* genus eiusmodi calliditatis atque calumniae, Cic.

callĭdus -a -um (calleo), 1, *clever by reason of experience, dexterous, skilful, sly, cunning;* a, absol., agitator (equi), Cic.; artifex, Cic.; legum scriptor peritus et callidus, Cic.; *a connoisseur in art,* Hor.; b, with ad and the acc., ad fraudem, Cic.; c, with in and the abl., in dicendo vehemens et callidus, Cic.; d, with the genit., rei militaris, Tac.; e, with the abl., homines callidi usu, Cic.; 2, of things, *cunningly* or *slyly devised;* audacia, Cic.; nimis callida juris interpretatio, *too subtle,* Cic.

Callifae -ārum, f. *a town in Samnium.*

Callĭmăchus -i, m. (Καλλίμαχος), *a celebrated Greek poet of Cyrene.*

Callĭŏpē -ēs, f. (Καλλιόπη, *the beautiful-voiced*), and **Callĭŏpēa** -ae, f. **I.** *Calliope, the Muse of epic poetry, or of poetry in general,* Hor., Ov. **II.** Meton., **1,** vos, O Calliope, etc., *all the Muses collectively,* Verg.; **2,** *poetry,* Ov.

Callĭpŏlis -is, f. (Καλλίπολις). **I.** *a town on the Thracian Chersonese, now Gallipoli.* **II.** *a town in the Tauric Chersonese.*

Callirrhŏē -ēs, f. (Καλιῤῥόη), **1,** *daughter of the river Achelous, wife of Alcmaeon;* **2,** *a well at Athens, on the south side of the Acropolis.*

callis -is, m. and (in prose, gen.) f. *a narrow track, footpath, cattle track;* Italiae calles et pastorum stabula, Cic.

Callisthĕnēs -is, m. (Καλλισθένης), *a philosopher of Olynthus, who accompanied Alexander the Great into Asia, and died a violent death there.*

Callistō -ūs, f. (Καλλιστώ), *daughter of the Arcadian king Lycaon, mother of Arcas by Jupiter, changed by Juno into a bear, and placed by Jupiter among the stars as Ursa Major or Helice.*

callōsus -a -um (callum), *having a hard skin, hard;* ova, Hor.

callum -i, n. and **callus** -i, m. **I.** *the hard skin of animals;* calceamentum callum solorum, Cic. **II.** Transf., *insensibility;* ipse labor quasi callum quoddam obducit dolori, Cic.; quorum animis diuturna cogitatio callum vetustatis obduxerat, Cic.

1. călo, 1. (καλῶ), *to call, summon;* t.t. of religious ceremonies, Quint.; comitia calata, *an assembly of the curiae for merely formal business,* Cic.

2. cālo -ōnis, m. (perhaps contr. for caballo, from caballus), *a horse-boy, groom, a litter-bearer,* Cic.; *a soldier's slave, camp-menial,* Caes.

1. călor -ōris, m. (caleo), *warmth, heat.* **I.** Phys., **A.** Gen., vis frigoris et caloris, Cic. **B.** Esp., *heat of the sun or day;* vitandi caloris causa Lanuvii tres horas acquieveram, Cic.; calores maximi, Cic.; mediis caloribus, *in full summer,* Liv. **C.** *heat of a hot wind;* calores austrini, Verg. **II.** *animal heat.* **A.** Lit., Tib. **B.** Transf., *love,* Ov., Hor.

2. Călor -ōris, m. *a river in Samnium, now Calore.*

Calpē -ēs, f. (Κάλπη), *one of the pillars of Hercules, now Gibraltar.*

Calpurnĭus -a -um, *name of a Roman plebeian gens, the families of which bore the names of* Flamma, Asprenas, Piso, Bestia, Bibulus. *The most remarkable of this gens were:* **1,** C. Calp. Piso, *praetor and propraetor in Spain,* 186 A.C.; **2,** L. Calp. Piso, *consul in* 112 A.C.; **3,** L. Calp. Frugi, *tribune* 149 A.C., *consul* 133 A.C.; **4,** L. Calp. Bestia, *tribune* 121, *consul* 111, *and general against Jugurtha;* **5,** L. Calp. Bibulus, *step-son of M. Brutus;* **6,** C. Calp. Piso, *son-in-law of Cicero;* **7,** L. Calp. Piso Caesonius, *father-in-law of Caesar;* **8,** Calpurnia, *wife of Caesar;* **9,** T. Calp. Siculus, *Roman bucolic poet of third century* A.C. Adj., *Calpurnian,* Calpurnia lex; **a,** de repetundis of L. Calp. Piso Frugi; **b,** de ambitu of the consul C. Calp. Piso.

caltha -ae, f. *a plant,* prob. *the common marigold,* Verg.

calthŭla -ae, f. (caltha), *a woman's robe of a yellow colour,* Plaut.

călumnia -ae, f. (Old Lat. calvĕre, connected with carpere), *trick, artifice, chicane, craft;* **a,** Gen., inimicorum calumnia, Cic.; religionis calumnia, *deceitful pretence,* Cic.; calumniam adhibere, Cic.; in hac calumnia timoris, mis-

giving caused by ill-grounded fear, Cic.; **b, esp.,** *false accusation, malicious prosecution;* calumnia litium alienos fundos petere, Cic.; calumniam jurare, *to swear that an accusation is not malicious,* Cic.; meton., *action for false accusation;* calumniam privato judicio non effugere, Cic.

călumnĭātor -ōris, m. (calumnior), *an intriguer, pettifogger; scriptum sequi calumniatoris esse; boni judicis, voluntatem scriptoris auctoritatemque defendere, Cic.*

călumnĭor, 1. dep. (calumnia), *to contrive tricks, to attack with artifices;* jacet res in controversiis isto calumniante biennium, Cic.; calumniabar ipse; putabam, etc., *I made myself unnecessarily anxious,* Cic.

calva -ae, f. (calvus), *the bald scalp of the head,* Cic.

calvĕo, 2. *to be bare of hair, bald,* Plin.

Calvĭsĭus -ĭi, m. *Roman name,* **1,** C. Calv. Sabinus, *legate of Caesar;* **2,** Calvisius, *the accuser of Agrippina, the mother of Nero.*

calvĭtĭēs -ēi, f. (calvus), *baldness,* Suet.

calvĭtĭum -ĭi, n. (calvus), *baldness,* Cic.

calvor, 3. dep. *to form intrigues, deceive,* Plaut.

calvus -a -um, *bald, without hair,* Plaut.

Calvus, *the name of a family of the Gens Licinia,* v. Licinius.

1. calx -cis, f. *the heel;* certare pugnis, calcibus, Cic.; calcem terere calce, *to tread close on the heels,* Verg.; calces remittere, *to kick,* Nep.; prov., adversus stimulum calces (sc. jactare), *to kick against the pricks,* Ter.

2. calx -cis, f. and (rarely) m. (χάλιξ), *a stone.* **I.** *a pebble used as a counter in various games,* Plaut. **II.** *lime, chalk;* lintribus in eam insulam materiam, calcem, caementa convehere, Cic.; as the goal in a racecourse was marked with chalk, meton.= *a goal, end* (opp. carceres, *the starting-point);* quibuscum tamquam e carceribus emissus sis, cum iisdem ad calcem, ut dicitur, pervenire, Cic.; ad carceres a calce revocari, *to turn back from the end to the beginning,* Cic.

Călȳcadnus -i, m. (Καλύκαδνος). **I.** *a river in Cilicia.* **II.** *promontory in Cilicia at the mouth of the river of the same name.*

Călȳdon -ōnis, f. (Καλυδών), *a very ancient city in Aetolia.* Hence adj., **1, Călȳdōnĭus** -a -um, *Calydonian;* heros, Meleager, Ov.; amnis, *the Achelous,* Ov.; regna, *the kingdom of Diomedes in Lower Italy,* Ov.; sus, aper, *the boar slain by Meleager,* Mart.; **2, Călȳdōnis** -ĭdis, f. *Calydonian;* subst.= Deianira, Ov.

Călȳpsō -ūs, acc. -o. f. (Καλυψώ), *a nymph, daughter of Atlas, who entertained Ulysses in the island of Ortygia, and kept him there seven years.*

cămăra = camera (q.v.).

Cămărīna (Cămĕrīna) -ae, f. (Καμαρίνα), *town in the south-west of Sicily,* now Camerina or Camarana.

Cambūnĭi montes, m. *mountains forming the boundary between Thessaly and Macedonia.*

Cambȳsēs -is, m. (Καμβύσης), **1,** *husband of Mandane, father of Cyrus the Elder;* **2,** *son and successor of Cyrus the Elder.*

camēlla -ae, f. (dim. of camera), *a kind of goblet,* Ov.

cămēlus -i, m. and f. (κάμηλος), *a camel,* Cic.

Camēna (Camoena) -ae, f. (from cano, orig. casmena, then carmena), gen. plur. *the prophesying goddesses of springs,* in later times identified with the Greek Muses; meton., *poetry,* Hor.

cămĕra (camara) -ae, f. (καμάρα), **1,** *a vaulted*

chamber, vault, Cic.; **2,** *a kind of flat covered boat,* Tac.

Cămērĭa -ae, f. and **Cămĕrĭum** -ĭi, n. *town in Latium.* Adj., **Cămĕrīnus** -a -um, *of or belonging to Cameria.*

Cămillus -i, m. *cognomen of several members of the gens Furia, the most famous of whom,* M. Furius Camillus, *took Veii, and freed Rome from the Gauls.* Appell., *a saviour of one's country;* novus Camillus, Liv.

cămīnus -i, m. (κάμινος), **1,** *a forge,* Ov.; prov., semper ardente camino, *with ceaseless industry,* Juv.; **2,** *a fire-place,* Hor.; meton., *fire;* luculentus, Cic.; prov., oleum addere camino, *to aggravate an evil,* Hor.

cammărus -i, m. (κάμμαρος), *a crab, lobster,* Juv.

Campānĭa -ae, f. (campus, cf. Fr. champagne, *the level country*), *a district of Central Italy, the capital of which was Capua,* now *Terra di Lavoro.* Adj., **Campānus** -a -um, *Campanian;* via, *a by-road connected with the via Appia,* Suet.; morbus, *a kind of wart on the face common in Campania,* Hor.; pons, *the bridge over the Savo (Saona),* Hor.; colonia, *Capua,* Cic.; arrogantia, Cic. Subst., **Campāni** -ōrum, m. *the inhabitants of Campania,* Cic.

campester -tris -tre (campus), **1,** *relating to level country, flat;* loca campestria, Liv.; iter, march in *a level country,* Caes.; hence subst., **campestria** -ium, n. *a plain,* Tac.; **2,** a, *relating to the Campus Martius and its gymnastic exercises;* ludus, Cic.; hence subst., **campestre** -is, n. (sc. velamentum), *a covering worn by wrestlers round their loins,* Hor.; b, *relating to the comitia;* certamen, Liv.; quaestus, Cic.

campus -i, m. (connected with κῆπος), **1,** a *flat spot, a plain;* campos et montes peragrare, Cic.; hence, *a meadow, field;* herbidus aquosusque, Liv.; *field of battle,* Liv.; poet., *a level surface of any kind, the sea,* Verg.; so of the level surface of a rock, Verg.; **2,** *the Campus,* or *Campus Martius at Rome, the place of meeting of the comitia centuriata;* hence meton., *the comitia,* fors domina campi, Cic.; also used as a place of exercise, Cic.; meton., *any free space, field,* or *theatre of action;* quum sit campus, in quo exsultare possit oratio, Cic.

Camulŏdūnum -i, n. *a town of the Trinobantes in Britain,* now *Colchester.*

cămŭr -a -um (connected with κάμπτω), *hooked, curved,* Verg.

Cănăcē -ēs, f. (Κανάκη), *daughter of Aeolus.*

Canae -ārum, f. *a coast town in Aeolis,* now *Kanot-Koei.*

cănālis -is, m. (orig. adj. of canna, *in the shape of a reed*), *a waterpipe, channel, canal,* Verg., Caes.

cănārĭus -a -um (canis), *relating to a dog, canine,* Plin. Adj. prop., **Cănārĭa** (insula), *one of the Happy Islands in the Atlantic;* plur. **Cănārĭae,** *the Canaries.*

cancelli -ōrum, m. (dim. of cancer), *a lattice, gruting,* or *trellis-work.* **A.** Lit., fori, *the bar of a tribunal,* Cic. **B.** Transf., *bounds, limits;* extra cancellos egredi, Cic.

cancer -cri, m. (connected with καρκίνος). **A.** *the crab, the sign of the zodiac in which the sun is at the summer solstice,* Ov. **B.** Meton., a, *the south,* Ov.; b, *summer heat,* Ov.

Candāvĭa -ae, f. (Κανδαονία), *a mountainous district of Illyria.*

candĕfăcĭo -fēci -factum (candeo and facio), *to make of a shining white,* Plaut.

candēla -ae, f. (candeo), **1,** *a wax* or *tallow candle, taper;* candelam apponere valvis, *to set the house on fire,* Juv.; **2,** *a rope coated with wax to preserve it from decay;* fasces involuti candelis, Liv.

candēlābrum -i, n. (candela), *a candlestick, candelabrum,* Cic.

candĕo -ŭi, 2. (from caneo as ardeo from areo). **A.** *to be of a shining white, to shine, glitter;* candet ebur soliis, Cat. **B.** Esp., *to glow with heat;* candente carbone, Cic.

candesco, 3. (inch. of candeo), **1,** *to begin to shine,* Ov.; **2,** *to begin to glow with heat,* Lucr.

candĭdātōrĭus -a -um, *relating to a candidate;* munus, Cic.

candĭdātus -a -um (candidus), *clothed in white,* Plaut. Subst., **candĭdātus** -i, m. *a candidate for office, who, among the Romans, was always clothed in white;* consularis, *for the consulship,* Cic.

candĭdē, adv. (candidus), **1,** *in white,* Plaut.; **2,** *clearly, candidly,* ap. Cic.

candĭdŭlus -a -um, (dim. of candidus), *shining, dazzling;* dentes, Cic.

candĭdus -a -um (candeo), *shining white, glittering white* (albus, *dead white*). **I.** Lit., a, lilia, Verg.; tunicae linteae, Liv.; tentoria, Ov.; candidum altā nive Soracte, Hor.; hence subst., **candĭdum** -i, n. *white colour,* Ov.; candidum ovi, *the white of the egg,* Plin.; b, of the hair or beard, *silver white, silver grey,* barba, Verg.; c, of the body, *snow-white,* corpora (Gallorum), Liv.; brachia candidiora nive, Ov.; of *dazzling beauty;* puer, Hor.; of animals, avis, *the stork,* Verg.; of deities, Bassareus, *of heavenly beauty,* Hor.; d, of the stars or the day, *bright;* luna, Verg.; dies, Ov.; e, of the white toga of candidates, Cic.; f, of a white stone, (a) candida sententia, *an acquittal,* Ov.; (β) *a sign of a lucky day;* candidiore or candidissimo calculo notare diem, Cat. **II.** Transf., a, of time, *happy;* hora, Ov.; b, of writing, *clear, lucid;* genus dicendi, Cic.; c, of character, *honest, straightforward;* pauperis ingenium, Hor.

candor -ōris m. (candeo), *dazzling white colour.* **I.** Of paint, fucati medicamenta candoris et ruboris, Cic. **II.** As a quality, *whiteness, lustre.* **A.** candor marmoreus, Lucr.; **1,** of the body, candor huius et proceritas, Cic.; **2,** of the sun or stars, solis, Cic.; of the Milky Way, via candore notabilis ipso, Ov. **B.** Transf., of character, *sincerity, candour;* animi, Ov.

canens -entis, partic. of caneo and cano.

cănĕo -ŭi, 2. (from canus, as albeo from albus), *to be white* or *hoary;* temporibus geminis canebat sparsa senectus, Verg.; gramina canent, *of dew,* Verg.; partic. canens, *hoary.*

cănēphŏros -i, f. (κανηφόρος), *a basket-bearer,* and plur. **cănēphŏroe** (κανηφόροι), *statues by Greek sculptors representing Athenian maidens bearing sacrificial baskets.*

cānesco, 3. (inch. of caneo), *to become white* or *hoary.* **I.** canescunt aequora, Ov. **II.** Transf., *to become old,* Ov.; fig., quum oratio nostra jam canesceret, Cic.

cănĭcŭla -ae, f. (dim. of canis). **I. A.** *a little dog,* Plin. **B.** Appell., *a violent woman,* Plaut. **II. A.** *the dog-star,* Sirius; canicula exoritur, Cic.; sitiens, Hor. **B.** *the worst throw upon the dice, all aces,* Pers.

cănīnus -a -um (canis). **A.** *relating to a dog, canine;* lac, Ov. **B.** Transf., **1,** littera, *the letter R,* Pers.; **2,** of character, *snarling, spiteful;* latrare canina verba in foro, Ov.

cănis -is, c. *a dog.* **I.** Lit., venaticus, Cic.; alere canes in Capitolio, Cic.; cave canem, *be* *ware of the dog*, inscription on a house-door, Varr.; prov., cane pejus et angue vitare, Hor. **II.** Transf., **a,** as a term of reproach, *a malicious, spiteful person;* of accusers, Cic.; *a parasite, hanger-on;* Clodianus canis, Cic.; **b,** as a star, canis major, Verg.; canis minor, Ov.; **c,** *the sea-dog,* Plin.; canes, *the dogs of Scylla,* Verg.; **d,** in dice, *the worst throw;* canes damnosi, Prop.

cānistra -ōrum, n. (κάναστρα), *a bread, fruit,* or *flower basket,* Cic.

cānĭtĭēs, acc. -em, abl. -e, f. (canus). **A.** *a whitish-grey colour,* esp. of the hair. **B.** Meton., *grey hair,* Verg.; *old age,* Hor.

canna -ae, f. (κάννα). **A.** *a reed;* palustris, Ov. **B.** Meton., *a reed-pipe,* Ov.; *a small boat,* Juv.

cannăbis -is, acc -im, abl. -i, f., (κάνναβις), **cannăbus** -i, m., **cannăbum** -i, n. *hemp,* Plin.

Cannae -ārum, f. *a small town in Apulia, near the Aufidus, scene of a defeat of the Romans by Hannibal* 216 A.C. Adj., **Cannensis** -e, *of* or *belonging to Cannae,* prov., pugna, *any disastrous slaughter* (e.g., *the proscription of Sulla*), Cic.

căno, cěcĭni, cantum, 3. *to sing.* **I.** Intransit. **A.** 1, of men, voce, Cic.; ad tibicinem, Cic.; in oratory of **a** sing-song delivery, inclinata ululantique voce more Asiatico canere, Cic.; **2,** of animals, of the cock, *to crow,* Cic.; of frogs, *to croak,* Plin. **B.** *to play;* 1, of men, fidibus, Cic.; canere receptui, *to sound the signal for retreat,* Liv.; **2,** of instruments, tubae cornuaque cecinerunt, Liv.; classicum canit, Liv. **II.** Transit., **A.** *to sing with the voice;* 1, carmen, Cic.; **2, a,** *to sing of, to celebrate in song;* ad tibiam clarorum virorum laudes atque virtutes, Cic.; **b,** of animals, *to give warning by a cry;* anser Gallos adesse canebat. **B.** *to play on a musical instrument;* signum canere, Liv.; prov., hoc carmen hic tribunus plebis non vobis, sed sibi intus canit, *thinks only of his own advantage,* Cic. **C.** Of gods, oracles, seers, *to prophesy;* ut haec quae fiunt canere dii immortales viderentur, Cic.; with acc and infin., te mihi mater, veridica interpres deum, aucturum caelestium numerum cecinit, Liv.; of fame, *to announce;* fama facta atque infecta canens, Verg.

Cănōpus -i, m. (Κάνωβος), *a city in Lower Egypt,* hence meton., *Lower Egypt,* Verg., and *Egypt* generally, Juv. Adj., **Cănōpēus** -a -um, *of* or *belonging to Canopus;* **Cănōpītae** -arum, m. *inhabitants of Canopus,* Cic.

cănor -ōris, m. (cano), *melody, song, sound;* Martius aeris rauci, Verg.

cănōrus -a -um (canor), *melodious, harmonious, sweet-sounding.* **I.** Neut., profluens quiddam habuit Carbo et canorum, Cic.; so of a fault in delivery, *of a sing-song pronunciation;* vox nec languens nec canora, Cic. Subst., **cănōrum** -i, n. *harmonious sound,* Cic. **II.** Act., of men, orator, Cic.; of animals, ales, *the swan,* Hor.; gallus, Cic.; of instruments, aes, *the trumpet,* Verg.

Cantăbri -ōrum, m. (Καντάβροι), *a people in the north of Spain, not subdued till the reign of Augustus.* Sing., **Cantăber** -bri, m. *Cantabrian;* hence, **Cantăbria** -ae, f. (Κανταβρία), *the country of the Cantabri;* adj., **Cantăbricus** -a -um, *Cantabrian.*

cantāmen -ĭnis, n. (canto), *incantation,* Prop.

cantātor -ōris, m. *a singer,* Mart.

cantērīnus (cantherīnus) -a -um (canterius), *relating to a horse, equine,* Plaut.

cantērĭus (cantherius) -i, m. (perhaps κανθήλιος), *a beast of burden, a gelding, nag,* Cic.;

cantherius in fossa, *a person in a helpless condition,* Liv.; meton., *an impotent person,* Plaut.

canthăris -ĭdis, f. (κανθαρίς), *a beetle, the Spanish fly,* Cic.

canthărus -i, m. (κάνθαρος), 1, *a large goblet with handles, a tankard,* Plaut.; **2,** *a kind of sea-fish,* Ov.

canthus -i, m. (κανθός), *the tire oj a wheel;* meton., *a wheel,* Pers.

cantĭcum -i, n. (cano), 1, *a scene in the Roman comedy, enacted by one person and accompanied by music and dancing,* Cic.; canticum agere, Liv.; 2, *a song,* Mart.; *a sing-song delivery in an orator,* Cic.

cantĭlēna -ae, f. *an old song, twaddle, chatter;* ut crebro mihi insusurret cantilenam suam, Cic.

cantĭo -ōnis, f. (cano), 1, *a song,* Plaut.; 2, *an incantation, enchantment;* veneficia et cantiones, Cic.

cantĭto, 1. (freq. of canto), *to sing repeatedly;* carmina in epulis, Cic.

Cantĭum -ĭi, n. (κάντιον), *a district on the south-east coast of Britain,* now *Kent.*

cantĭuncŭla -ae, f. (dim. of cantio), *a flattering, enticing song;* si cantiunculis tantus vir irretitus teneretur, Cic.

canto -āvi -ātum -are (intens. of cano), *to sing* or *play.* **I.** Intransit. **A.** Of the voice, *to sing;* 1, of men, ad manum histrioni, *to sing and play to the dumb-show of an actor,* Cic.; **2,** of birds, cantantes aves, Prop.; of the cock, *to crow,* Cic. **B.** *to play on an instrument;* avenis, Ov.; of the instrument itself, bucina cantat, Ov. **C.** *to sing an incantation,* Verg. **II.** Transit., **A.** *to sing* or *play;* 1, with cognate object, carmina, Hor.; doctum Catullum, *the songs of Catullus,* Hor.; 2, *to celebrate in singing;* convivia, Hor.; cantari dignus, *worthy to be celebrated in song,* Verg.; so *to praise;* nam ut scis, jampridem istum canto Caesarem, Cic.; 3, *to recite;* elegos, Juv. **B.** *to announce, tell;* vera cantas, Plaut. **C.** *to sing an incantation;* carmen, Ov.; hence, *to bewitch;* cantatae herbae, Ov.

cantor -ōris, m. (cano), 1, *a singer, poet;* cantor Apollo, *player on the harp,* Hor.; contemptuously, cantor formularum, Cic.; cantores Euphorionis, *eulogists,* Cic.; 2, *an actor,* esp. *the actor who cried* plaudite *at the end of the piece,* Hor.

cantrix -īcis, f. (cantor), *a female singer,* Plaut.

cantus -ūs, m. (cano). **I.** *song, melody, poetry,* Lucr. **II.** Concrete, *a song, a melody.* **A.** Gen., **a,** of persons, Sirenum, Cic.; **b,** of animals, avium, Cic.; **c,** of an instrument, *playing, music;* bucinarum, Cic. **B.** Esp., **a,** *prophecy;* veridici cantus, Cat.; **b,** *incantation,* Ov.

Canulējus -i, m. *name of a Roman plebeian gens, to which belonged* C. Canulejus, *tribune of the people* 445 B.C., *author of the law permitting marriages between plebeians and patricians.*

cānus -a -um. **I.** Lit., *whitish-grey, grey;* fluctus, Lucr.; lupus, Verg.; esp. of hair, capilli, Hor. Subst., **cāni** -ōrun (sc. capilli), *grey hair,* Cic. **II.** Meton., *old, aged;* senectus, Cat.

Cănŭsĭum -ĭi, n. *a town of Apulia* (now *Canosa*). Adj., **Cănŭsĭnus** -a -um, *Canusian;* lana, *Canusian wool,* which was very celebrated, Plin.; hence, **Cănŭsīna** -ae, f. (sc. vestis), *a garment of Canusian wool,* Mart.; **Cănŭsĭnātus** -a -um, *clothed in such a garment,* Suet.

căpācĭtas -ātis, f. (capax), *breadth, roominess,* Cic

Căpăneus -ĕi. acc. -ĕa, voc. -eu, m. (Καπα-νεύς), *one of the seven princes who besieged Thebes, killed by Jupiter with a thunderbolt.*

căpax -ācis (capio), *able to hold.* **I.** Lit., *able to hold much, broad, wide, roomy;* urbs, Ov.; with genit., circus capax populi, Ov.; cibi vinique capacissimus, Liv. **II.** Transf., *able to grasp, apt, capable, fit for;* aures avidae et capaces, Cic.; with genit., capax imperii, Tac.; with ad and the acc., animus ad praecepta capax, Ov.

căpēdo -ĭnis, f. (capis), *a bowl used in sacrifices,* Cic.

căpēduncŭla -ae, f. (dim. of capedo), *a small bowl,* Cic.

căpella -ae, f. (dim. of capra), 1, *a she-goat,* Cic.; 2, *a constellation so called,* Ov.

Căpēna -ae, f. *a town in Etruria, at the foot of Mount Soracte.* Adj., **Căpēnās** -ātis, **Căpēnus** -a -um, *of or belonging to Capena;* porta Capena, *a gate in Rome at the commencement of the via Appia.*

căper -ri, m. **A.** Lit., *a he-goat,* Verg. **B.** Meton., *the smell under the arm-pits,* Ov.

căpěro, 1. (caper), *to be wrinkled,* Plaut.

căpesso -ivi and -ii -itum, 3. (desider. of capio), *to seize, lay hold of eagerly.* **I. A.** Lit., arma, Verg.; cibum oris hiatu et dentibus (of animals), Cic. **B.** Transf., *to take to, to gain;* a, fugam, Liv.; libertatem, Cic.; **b**, *to take in hand, busy oneself with;* rempublicam, *to enter public life,* Cic.; so magistratus, imperium, honores, provincias, Tac.; bellum, Liv. **II.** *to strive to reach, to hasten, to make for;* omnes mundi partes medium locum capessentes, Cic.; animus superiora capessat necesse est, *aims after,* Cic.; Melitam, Cic.; Italiam, Verg.; reflex., se in altum, Plaut. (perf. infin., capessisse, Liv.).

Căphāreus and **Căphēreus**, or **Căphēreus** -ĕi and -ĕos, acc. -ĕa, voc. -eu, m. (ὁ Καφηρεύς), *a dangerous promontory on the south coast of Euboea, where the Greek fleet on returning from Troy was shipwrecked.* Adj., **Căphārēus** -a -um, *of or belonging to Caphareus.*

căpillātus -a -um (capillus), *hairy, having hair;* adolescens bene capillatus, Cic.; vinum capillato diffusum consule, *made when long hair was worn* (i.e., *very old*), Juv.

căpillus -i, m. (dim. form from root CAP, whence caput, and κεφαλή, prop. adj. sc. crinis). **A.** *the hair of the head or of the beard* (crinis, *any hair*); compositus, Cic.; plur., compti capilli, Cic. **B.** Transf., *the hair of animals,* Cat.

căpĭo, cēpi, captum, 3. (obs. fut. capso, Plaut.), **I.** *to take, to seize.* **A.** Lit., a, with the hand, arma, Cic.; **b**, *to take possession of,* esp. as milit. t.t., collem, Caes.; *to arrive at,* esp. of ships, portum, Caes.; *to select a place;* locum oculis, Verg.; locum castris, Liv.; so of auguries, templa ad inaugurandum, Liv. **B.** Transf., **a**, of acts, *to take in hand, to begin;* fugam, Caes.; consulatum, Cic.; **b**, of an opportunity, satis scite et commode tempus ad aliquem adeundi, Cic.; **c**, *to take* as an example or proof, documentum ex aliquo, Cic.; d, of a quality, *to take, adopt;* avi prudentiam, Cic.; **e**, *to take* as a companion, aliquem consiliis socium, Verg.; *to select out of a number,* in singulos annos sacerdotem Jovis sortito, Cic.; aliquem flaminem, *as a flamen,* Liv. **C.** *to take possession of by force, in a hostile manner;* 1, lit., a, lubido reipublicae capiundae, Sall.; **b**, in war, (a) *to take booty, etc.;* agros de hostibus, Cic.; (β) *to take a town, etc.;* urbem, castra hostium, Cic.; (γ) *to take prisoner;* belli nefarios duces, Cic.; partic. as subst., **captus** -i, m. (= captivus)

a captive, Nep.; **c**, *to take* animals; pisces, Cic.; 2, transf., **a**, *to seize, take possession of;* admiratio, metus capit aliquem, Liv.; nos post reges exactos servitutis oblivio ceperat, Cic.; **b**, esp., *to attack, to injure;* pass. capi, *to be injured* or *diseased;* oculis et auribus captus, *blind and deaf,* Cic.; captus mente, *distracted,* Cic.; **c**, *to deceive;* adolescentium animos dolis, Sall.; adversarium, Cic.; capere aliquem sua humanitate, Nep. **II.** *to take, receive.* **A.** Lit., **a**, with the hand, per aliquem aut honores aut divitias, Cic.; pecuniam, *to take money by force* or *bribery;* per vim atque injuriam, Cic.; legal t.t., *to take as heir,* ex hereditate nihil, Cic.; of tribute, pay, etc., stipendium jure belli, Caes.; **b**, *to receive into one's body;* cibum, Sall. **B.** Transf., *to receive, suffer, undergo;* somnum capere non posse, Cic.; aliquid detrimenti (esp. in the formula, videant consules ne quid respublica detrimenti capiat), Cic.; laetitiam, Cic. **III.** *to contain.* **A.** Lit., una domo capi non possunt, Cic. **B.** Transf., *to allow of, to comprehend;* nullam esse gratiam tantam quam non capere animus meus posset, Cic.

căpis -ĭdis, f. (capio), *a one-handled vessel,* used in sacrifices, Liv.

căpistro, 1. (capistrum), *to fasten with a halter,* Cic.

căpistrum -i, n. *a halter,* Verg.

căpĭtal -ālis, n. (capitalis), sc. facinus, *a capital crime,* Cic.

căpĭtālis -e (caput), 1, *relating to the head, relating to life, that which imperils a man's life,* or caput (i.e., *social position* and *civil rights* in Rome); esp. used of capital crimes, res, Cic.; inimicus, *a deadly enemy,* Cic.; odium, *mortal hatred,* Cic.; oratio, *dangerous,* Cic.; 2, *first, chief, distinguished;* Siculus ille capitalis, creber, acutus, Cic.; ingenium, Ov.

căpĭto -ōnis, m. (caput), *a man with a large head,* Cic.

Căpĭtōlĭum -ii, n. (caput), *the temple of Jupiter built upon the Tarpeian rock at Rome, the Capitol;* used often of the whole hill or mons Capitolinus. Adj., **Căpĭtōlīnus** -a -um, *Capitoline;* ludi, *in honour of Jupiter Capitolinus,* Liv.; hence subst., **Căpĭtōlīni** -ōrum, m. *the superintendents of these games,* Cic.

căpĭtŭlātim, adv. (capitulum), *briefly, summarily,* Nep.

căpĭtŭlum -i, n. (dim. of caput), *a little head,* Plaut.

Cappădŏces -um, m. (Καππάδοκες), *the inhabitants of Cappadocia;* sing., **Cappădŏx** -ŏcis, m. *a Cappadocian;* **Cappădŏcia** -ae, f. *a district of Asia Minor, the most eastern Asiatic province of the Romans.* Adj., **Cappădŏcius** and **Cappădŏcus** -a -um, *Cappadocian.*

capra -ae, f. (caper). **I.** *a she-goat.* **A.** Lit., Cic.; ferae, perhaps *chamois,* Verg. **B.** Meton., *the odour under the armpits,* Hor. **II.** Transf. **A.** *a constellation,* Cic. **B.** Caprae palus, *the place in Rome where Romulus disappeared,* Liv.

căprĕa -ae, f. (capra), *a roe, roebuck,* Verg.; prov., prius jungentur capreae lupis quam, etc. (of an impossibility), Hor.

Caprĕae -ārum, f. (Καπρέαι), *small island on the Campanian coast off Puteoli, to which Tiberius retired at the end of his life,* now *Capri.*

căprĕŏlus -i, m. (caper). **I.** *a roebuck,* Verg. **II.** Meton., plur., *props, supports,* Caes.

căprĭcornus -i, m. *a sign of the Zodiac, Capricorn,* Hor.

căprĭficus -i, m. *the wild fig-tree, and its fruit,* Pers.

căprĭgénus -a -um (caper **and** gigno), *born of goats,* Verg.

căprĭmulgus -i, m. (capra **and** mulgeo), *a goat-milker*—i.e., *a countryman,* Cat.

caprīnus -a -um (caper), *relating to a goat;* pellis, Cic.; prov., de lanâ caprinâ rixari, *to contend about trifles,* Hor.

căprĭpes -pĕdis (caper **and** pes), *goat-footed;* satyri, Hor.

1. **capsa** -ae, f. (capio), *a box* **or** *case for books,* Cic.

2. **Capsa** -ae, f. (Κάψα), *a town in Byzacium,* now *Kafsa* (south of Tunis); hence, **Capsenses** -ium, m. *the inhabitants of Capsa.*

capsārius -i, m. (capsa), *a slave who carried to school his young master's satchel,* Suet.

capsŭla -ae, f. (dim. of capsa), *a little chest,* Cat.

captātĭo -ōnis, f. (capto), *an eager seizing, a catching;* verborum, *quibbling, logomachy,* Cic.

captātor -ōris, m. (capto), *one who eagerly seizes;* aurae popularis, *eager after favour of the people,* Liv.; absol. *a legacy-hunter,* Hor., Juv.

captĭo -ōnis, f. (capio), *a, a cheat, deception;* in parvula re captionis aliquid vereri, Cic.; meton., *harm, loss;* mea captio est, si, etc., Cic.; **b,** *a fallacy, sophism;* quanta esset in verbis captio, si, etc., Cic.; captiones discutere, explicare, repellere, Cic.

captĭōsē, adv. (captiosus), *insidiously;* interrogare, Cic.

captĭōsus -a -um (captio), **1,** *deceitful;* societatem captiosam et indignam, Cic.; **2,** *sophistical, captious, insidious;* captiosissimo genere interrogationis uti, Cic. Subst., **captiōsa** -ōrum, n. *sophistries,* Cic.

captĭuncŭla -ae, f. (dim. of captio), *fallacy, quibble;* omnes captiunculas pertimescere, Cic.

captīvĭtas -ātis, f. (captivus), *captivity,* Tac.; urbium, *conquest,* Tac.

captīvus -a -um (captus, capio), *taken, captured.* **I.** *taken in war, captive;* **a,** of persons, cives Romani, Cic.; gen. subst., **captivus** -i, m.; **captīva** -ae, f. *a captive,* Cic.; poet., *relating to a prisoner;* sanguis, Verg.; crines, Ov.; **b,** used of inanimate things, *conquered, obtained as a prey;* naves, Caes.; agri, Tac. **II.** Gen. *captured, taken;* pisces, Ov.

capto, 1. (intens. of capio), *to seize, catch at, lay hold of, hunt.* **I.** Lit., feras, Verg. **II.** Transf. **A.** Gen. *to strive after, desire, seek;* sermonem alicuius, Plaut.; plausus, risus, Cic. **B.** Esp. *to seek to win, entice, allure craftily;* insidiis hostem, Liv.; testamenta, *to hunt for legacies,* Hor.

captus -ūs, m. (capio) **1,** *a catching, taking;* meton., *that which is taken,* Plin.; **2,** *power of comprehension, manner of comprehension, idea;* ut est captus hominum, Cic.; Germanorum, Caes.

Căpŭa -ae, f. (Καπύη), *chief town of Campania.* Adj., **Căpŭānus** -a -um.

căpŭlus -i, m. (capio). **I.** *a coffin;* ire ad capulum, *to go to the grave,* Lucr. **II.** *a handle.* **A.** Gen., aratri, Ov. **B.** Esp. *the hilt of a sword,* Cic.

caput -ĭtis, n. (root CAP, connected with κεφαλή), *the head.* **I.** Lit. and Meton. **A.** Of living things, **1,** of men, **a,** lit., *the head;* capite operto, obvoluto, involuto, Cic.; caput alicui auferre, abscidere, praecidere, percutere, Liv.; capita conferre, *to put their heads together* (of secret conversation), Liv.; per caputque pedesque ire praecipitem in lutum, *to go over head and heels,* Cat.; nec caput nec pedes (habere), prov., *of a business which one does not*

know how to begin with, Cic.; supra caput esse, of enemies, *to threaten,* Cic.; **caput** extollere, *to raise one's head again,* Cic.; **b,** meton., *a person;* caput liberum, Cic.; carum caput, Verg. and Hor.; in counting numbers, capitum Helvetiorum milia cclxiii., Caes.; exactio capitum, poll-tax, Cic.; of curses, quod illorum capiti sit, *may it fall on their heads,* ap. Cic.; **c,** *life, existence;* conjuratio in tyranni caput facta, Liv.; esp. in Rome, *a man's political and social rights;* judicium capitis, *a sentence involving loss of citizenship,* e.g., *exile;* so capitis damnare, Cic.; capite damnari, Cic.; capitis minor, *a person who has suffered a loss* of caput, Hor.; so capite deminui or minui, *to lose caput, to suffer a loss of status, to suffer a loss of political or social rights,* Cic.; **2,** of animals, jumenti, Nep.; belua multorum es capitum, Hor.; meton., *a head of cattle;* bina boum capita, Verg. **B.** Of things without life, *the top, summit, outside;* papaveris, Liv.; arcus capita, *the ends,* Verg.; capita aspera montis, Verg.; of rivers, *the source;* amnis, Verg.; Rheni, Caes.; fig., *the source;* quo invento ab eo quasi capite disputatio ducitur, Cic.; in ea est fons miseri arum et caput, Cic. **II.** Transf., **1,** of persons, *the head, chief;* omnium Graecorum concitandorum, Cic.; **2,** **a,** of things without life, *the chief, principal;* cenae, *the main dish,* Cic.; civilis prudentiae, *leading principle,* Cic.; **b,** in laws and writings, *the most important part;* legis, Cic.; **c,** of money, *capital,* de capite ipso demere, Cic.; **d,** of places, *the capital;* Roma caput orbis terrarum, Liv.

Căpȳs -yis, acc. yn, abl. -ȳe or -y, m. (Κάπυς), **1,** *son of Assaracus, father of Anchises;* **2,** *king of Alba;* **3,** *a companion of Aeneas;* **4,** *a king of Capua.*

Cărālis -is, f. (Κάραλις), and plur., **Cărăles** -ium, f. *a town and promontory of the same name in Sardinia,* now *Cagliari;* hence **Cărălĭtānus** -a -um, *of or belonging to Caralis.*

carbăsĕus -a -um (carbasus), *made of canvas;* vela, Cic.

carbăsus -i, m. (κάρπασος), plur. heterocl. gen., **carbăsa** -ōrum, *fine Spanish flax;* gen. meton., *articles produced from it, a linen garment, a sail,* Verg.

carbătīnus (carpatinus), -a -um (καρβάτινος), *of untanned leather;* crepidae, *rustic shoes,* Cat.

carbo -ōnis, m. **I.** *coal, charcoal;* candens, Cic.; fig., carbone notare, *to mark with black,* i.e., *think ill of any one,* Hor.; prov. carbonem pro thesauro invenire, *to find something of little value,* Phaedr. **II.** *cognomen of the Papirii.*

carbōnārius -ii, m. (carbo), *a charcoal burner,* Plaut.

carbuncŭlus -i, m. (dim. of carbo). **I.** Lit. *a little coal,* Plaut. **II.** Transf. **A.** *a kind of stone,* Plin. **B.** *a carbuncle,* Plin.

carcer -ĕris, m. (connected with arceo and Gr. ἕρκος), **1,** *a prison, jail, cell;* in carcerem ducere, condere, conjicere, contrudere, Cic.; emitti e carcere, Cic.; fig., qui e corporum vinculis tamquam e carcere evolaverunt, Cic.; meton., *the prisoners confined in a jail;* in me carcerem effudistis, *you have emptied the prison on me,* Cic.; **2,** gen. used in plur. carceres, *the starting-place of a racecourse* (opp. meta, calx); e carceribus emitti cum aliquo, Cic.; ad carceres a calce revocari, *to begin life anew,* Cic.

carcĕrārius -a -um (carcer), *belonging to a prison,* Plaut.

Carchēdŏnĭus -a -um (Καρχηδόνιος), *Carthaginian,* Plaut.

carchēsĭum -ĭi, n. (καρχήσιον), *a goblet with handles, contracted in the middle*, Verg.

cardăces -um, m. (Persian *carda*, *brave, warlike*), *a Persian troop*, Nep.

cardĭăcus -a -um (καρδιακός), *pertaining to the stomach*; of persons, *suffering from a disease of the stomach*; amicus, Juv. Subst., **cardĭăcus** -i, m. *one who so suffers*, Cic.

cardo -ĭnis, m. (connected with Gr. κραδάω, κραδαίνω, *to swing*). **I.** Lit. **A.** *the hinge of a door*; cardinem versare, *to open a door*, Ov. **B.** *the point round which anything turns, a pole of the heavens*; cardo duplex, *the ends of the earth's axle*, Cic. poet; *a point through which a line is drawn from north to south*, Liv.; quatuor cardines mundi, *the four cardinal points*, Quint. **II.** Transf. *a chief circumstance, or consideration upon which many others depend*; haud tanto cessabit cardine rerum, Verg.

cardŭus -i, m. *a thistle*, Verg.

cārē, adv. (carus), *dearly, at a high price*; aestinare, ap. Cic.

cārectum -i, n. (for caricetum, from carex), *a sedgy spot*, Verg.

cărĕo -ŭi -ĭtūrus, 2. *to be without, destitute of, to want*; gov. the abl. **I.** Gen. **A.** of persons, dolore, febri, Cic. **B.** of things, lege carens civitas, *lawless*, Cic. **II.** Esp. **A.** *to make no use of*; temeto, Cic.; hence, of a place, *to absent oneself from*; foro, senatu, publico, Cic.; patria, *to leave Rome*, Tac. **B.** *to be deprived of, to miss*; consuetudine amicorum, Cic.; libertate, Hor.; absol., quamquam non caret is qui non desiderat, Cic.

Cāres -um, m. (Κᾶρες), *inhabitants of Caria*; sing., **Căr**, Căris. Hence, **Cārĭa** -ae, f. (Καρία), *the most southerly district of Asia Minor.* **Cārĭcus** -a -um, *Carian.* Subst., **Cārĭca** -ae, f. (sc. ficus), *a kind of dried fig*, Cic.

cărex -ĭcis, f. *sedge*, Verg.

cărĭēs, acc. -em, abl. -e (other cases not found), f. *rottenness, decay*, Ov.

cărīna -ae, f. **I.** *the keel of a ship.* **A.** Lit., carinae aliquanto planiores quam nostrarum navium, Caes. **B.** Meton., *a ship, vessel*, Verg. **II.** Transf. plur., **Cărīnae** -ārum, f. *a spot in Rome on the Esquiline where Pompey's house stood.*

cărĭōsus -a -um (caries), *rotten, decayed, carious*; dentes, Plin.; transf., senectus, Ov.

cāris -ĭdis, f. (καρίς), *a kind of crab*, Ov.

cărĭstĭa = charistia (q.v.).

cārĭtas -ātis, f. (carus), *dearness, high price.* **I.** Lit., nummorum, *scarcity of money*, Cic.; absol. (sc. annonae), *high price of the necessaries of life*; annus in summa caritate est, *it is a very dear year*, Cic. **II.** Transf. *affection, love, esteem*; in caritate et honore esse, Liv.; complecti aliquem amicitia et caritate, Cic.; benevolentiā devincire homines et caritate, Cic.; civium, *esteem of the citizens*, Cic.; in pastores, Cic.; inter natos et parentes, Cic.; liberorum, *for one's children*, Cic.; in plur., omnes omnium caritates patria una complexa est, Cic.

carmen -ĭnis, n. (from cano and suffix -men, orig. canmen, then casmen, then carmen), *a song, tune*, either vocal or instrumental. **I.** Gen. carmina vocum, Cic.; *the song of the swan*, Ov.; *the screech of the owl*, Verg. **II.** Esp. **A.** *poetry, a poem of any kind*; a, fundere, condere, contexere, Cic.; componere, fingere, scribere, Hor.; facere, Verg.; b, *lyric poetry*, Hor.; amabile, *erotic poetry*, Hor.; c, *a part of a poem*, Lucr.; *a passage in a poem*; illud mollissimum carmen, Cic.; d, *a prediction, oracular declaration*, Liv. **B.** *incantation*, Verg. **C.** *a religious or legal formula*, in ancient times composed in verse; cruciatus, Cic.; lex horrendi carminis, Liv.

Carmentis -is, f., and **Carmenta** -ae, f. (carmen = *oracle*), *a prophetess, the mother of Evander, who came with him to Latium, prophesied on the Capitoline hill, and was afterwards reverenced as a deity.* Adj., **Carmentalis** -e, *of or belonging to Carmentis*; porta, *a gate of Rome near the temple of Carmentis, the right arch of which was called the* porta scelerata, *because the Fabii went through it on their journey to Cremera, where they were destroyed*; plur., **Carmentalia** -ium, n. *the festival of Carmentis.*

Carmo -ōnis, f. *town in Hispania Baetica*, now Carmone, *in Andalusia.*

Carna -ae, f. (caro), *the tutelary goddess of the nobler parts of the body, the heart*, etc., confused by Ovid with Cardea, *the goddess of hinges.*

carnārĭum -ĭi, n. (caro), *the larder, pantry*, Plaut.; *a frame provided with hooks to which provisions were hung*, Plaut.

Carnĕădes -is, m. (Καρνεάδης), *philosopher of Cyrene, founder of the third Academic school, opponent of Zeno.*

carnĭfex -ficis, m. (2. caro and facio), *the public executioner, hangman*, Cic.; used also as a term of reproach, *tormentor*, carnifex civium sociorumque, Cic.

carnĭfĭcīna -ae, f. (carnifex), 1, *the hangman's office*, Plaut.; 2, *place of torture*, Liv.; transf., *torture*, Cic.

carnĭfĭco, 1. (carnifex), *to slay, behead*, Liv.

Carnūtes -um, m. *people in the middle of Gaul, whose chief town was Genabum, the modern Orleans*, Caes.

1. **căro**, 3. *to card wool*, Plaut.

2. **căro**, carnis, f. *flesh.* **I.** Lit. **A.** lacte et carne vivere, Cic.; plur., carnes vipereae, Ov. **B.** Meton., used contemptuously of a man, ista pecus et caro putida, Cic. **II.** Transf. *the pulpy parts of fruit*, Plin. (old nom. cārnis, Liv.).

Carpăthus (-ŏs) -i, f. (Κάρπαθος), *an island in the Aegaean sea*, now *Scarpanto.* Adj., **Carpăthĭus** -a -um; vates, senex, *Proteus*, Ov.

carpentum -i, n. 1, *a two-wheeled carriage, a coach*; carpento in forum invehi, Liv.; 2, *a baggage waggon*; carpenta Gallica multa praeda onerata, Liv.

Carpētāni -ōrum, m. *the Carpetani, a Spanish tribe in modern Castile and Estremadura, with chief town Toletum* (now *Toledo*).

carpo -psi -ptum, 3. (connected with κάρφω, ἁρπάζω), **I.** *to pluck, pluck off.* **A.** Lit. 1, with the hand, flores ex arbore, Ov.; uvam de palmite, Verg.; pensum, *to spin*, Hor.; 2, with the mouth, a, *to take something as food*; gramen, *to graze*, of a horse, Verg.; thyma, of bees, *to suck*, Hor.; b, *to tear, pull to pieces*; cibum, Ov. **B.** Transf. 1, *to pluck off*; a, *to select, choose out*; flosculos, Cic.; paucos ad ignominiam, Cic.; b, poet., (a) *to enjoy*; diem, Hor.; auras vitales, Verg.; (β) of places, *to pass over, hasten over*; prata fuga, Verg.; mare, Ov.; 2, a, *to carp at, slander, calumniate*; aliquem maledico dente, Cic.; b, milit. t.t., *to annoy, harass*; equitatu agmen adversariorum, Caes.; c, *to weaken*; vires paulatim, Verg. **II. A.** Lit. *to rend*; jecur, Ov. **B.** Transf. *to separate, divide*; in multas parvasque partes exercitum, Liv.

carptim, adv., (carptus, carpo), 1, *in pieces, in single portions, in small parts*, Sall.; 2, *in different places*; aggredi, Liv.; 3, *at different times*; dimissi carptim et singuli, Tac.

carptor -ōris, m. (carpo), *one who carves food*, Juv.

carrūca -ae, f. *a kind of four-wheeled carriage*, Suet.

carrus -i., m. (carrum -i, n.), *a kind of four-wheeled baggage-waggon*, Caes.

Carsĕŏli (Carsĭŏli) -ōrum, m. (Καρσέολοι) *a town in Latium, now Arsoli;* hence, **Carsĕŏlānus** -a -um, *of or belonging to Carseoli.*

Cartēja -ae, f., **1**, *a town in Hispania Baetica;* hence, adj., **Cartējānus** -a -um; **2**, *town of the Olcades in Hispania Tarraconensis.*

Carthaea -ae, f. (Καρθαία), *town on the south coast of the island Cea;* hence adj., **Carthaeus** -a -um, and **Cartheus** -a -um, *of or belonging to Carthaea.*

Carthāgo -ĭnĭs, f., **1**, *the city of Carthage in N. Africa;* **2**, Carthago (Nova), *colony of the Carthaginians in Hispania Tarraconensis, now Carthagena.* Adj., **Carthāgĭnĭensis** -e, *Carthaginian.*

cărunc̆ŭla -ae, f. (dim. of caro), *a small piece of flesh,* Cic.

cārus -a -um, **1**, *high-priced, dear;* annona carior, annona carissima, Cic. ; **2**, *dear, beloved, esteemed;* patria, quae est mihi vita mea multo carior, Cic.; carum habere, *to love, esteem,* Cic.

Cărўae -ārum, f. (Καρύαι), *town in Laconia, with a temple to Artemis (Diana);* hence, **Cărўātĭdes**, acc. -ĭdas, f. *the Laconian maidens who served in the temple of Artemis;* hence, in architecture, *the figures of women in the place of pillars,* Vitr.

Cărystŏs -i, f. (Κάρυστος), **1**, *town on the south coast of Euboea, famous for its marble;* hence adj., **Cărystēus** -a -um, and **Cărystĭus** -a -um, *of or belonging to Carystos;* **2**, *town of the Ligurians.*

căsa -ae, f. (root CAS, whence castrum), *a hut, cottage, cabin,* Cic. ; *barrack,* Caes.

căsĕŏlus -i, m. (dim. of caseus), *a little cheese,* Verg.

căsĕus -i., m. (**căsĕum** -i, n., Plaut.), *a cheese;* caseum premere, *to make cheese,* Verg.; collect., villa abundat caseo, Cic.

căsia -ae, f. (κασία), **1**, *a tree with an aromatic bark, like cinnamon,* Verg. ; **2**, *the sweet-smelling mezereon,* Verg.

Căsĭlīnum, -i, n. *a town in Campania on the Volturnus;* hence, **Căsĭlīnātes** -um, and **Căsĭlīnenses** -ĭum, m. *inhabitants of Casilinum.*

Căsīnum -i, n. *a town in Latium.* Adj., **Căsīnās** -ātis, *of or belonging to Casinum.*

Caspĭum mărĕ or **pĕlăgus**, and **Caspĭus ŏcĕănus** (τὸ Κάσπιον πελαγος), *the Caspian Sea.* Adj., **Caspĭus** -a -um, *Caspian.*

Cassandra -ae, f. (Κασσάνδρα), *daughter of Priam, on whom the gift of prophecy was conferred by Apollo, with the reservation that no one should believe her.*

Cassandrēa and **īa**, ae, f. (κασσάνδρεια), *the town of Potidaea in Chalcidice, destroyed by Philĭp, re-built and re-named by Cassander;* hence, a, **Cassandrenses** -ĭum, m. *the inhabitants of Cassandrea;* b, **Cassandreus** -ĕi, m. (Κασσανδρεύς) = *Apollodorus, tyrant of Cassandrea,* Ov.

cassē, adv. (cassus), *in vain, without result,* Liv.

cassĭda -ae, f. *a helmet,* Verg.

1. **Cassĭŏpē** -ēs, f. (Κασσιόπη), *wife of Cepheus, mother of Andromeda, changed into a star.*

2. **Cassĭŏpē** -ēs, f. (Κασσιόπη), *town in Corcyra.*

1. **cassis** -ĭdis, f. **A.** *a metal helmet,* Caes. **B.** Meton., *war.* Juv.

2. **cassis** -is, gen. plur. **casses** -ĭum, m. *a net.* **I. A.** *a hunter's net;* casses ponere, Ov. **B.** Transf., *a trap, a snare,* Ov. **II.** *a spider's web,* Verg.

cassĭtĕrum -i, n. (κασσίτερος), *tin;* hence **Cassĭtĕrides** -um, f. (Κασσιτερίδες), *the tin islands, the Scilly Isles,* Plin.

Cassĭus -a -um, *name of a Roman gens, originally patrician, afterwards plebeian.* The most notable members were ; **1**, L. Cassius Longinus Ravilla, *celebrated as an upright judge, author of the lex tabellaria Cassia, that jurymen should vote by ballot;* hence **Cassĭānus** -a -um ; *Cassian; judex, an upright judge,* Cic. ; **2**, *the consul L. Cassius, conquered and killed by the Helvetii,* 107 A.C. ; **3**, C. Cassius Longinus, *one of the murderers of Caesar;* **4**, Cassius Parnensis, *a poet, another of Caesar's murderers;* **5**, C. Cassius Longinus, *a celebrated lawyer under Tiberius.*

cassus -a -um (perhaps from careo). **I.** Lit., *empty, hollow;* nux, Plaut. ; poet., *with* abl. or genit., *deprived of;* lumine cassus or aethere cassus, *dead,* Verg. **II.** Transf. *worthless, useless, vain;* cassum quiddam et inani vocis sono decoratum, Cic. ; in cassum, *in vain,* Liv.

Castālĭa -ae, f. (Κασταλία), *a spring on Mount Parnassus, sacred to Apollo and the Muses.* Adj., **Castālĭus** -a -um, and **Castālĭs** -ĭdis, f. *Castalian;* sorores, *the Muses,* Mart.

castănĕa -ae, f., **1**, *the chestnut-tree,* Col. ; **2**, *the chestnut;* castaneae nuces, Verg.

castē, adv. (castus). **I.** *purely, spotlessly;* caste et integre vivere, Cic. **II.** a, *innocently, chastely,* Cic. ; b, *piously, religiously;* caste ad deos adire, Cic.

castellānus -a -um (castellum), *relating to a fortress;* triumphi, *on the capture of fortresses,* Cic. Subst., **castellāni** -ōrum, m. *the garrison of a fortress,* Sall.

castellātim, adv. (castellum), *in single fortresses;* dissipati, Liv.

castellum -i, n. (dim. of castrum). **I. A.** *a castle, fortress, fort,* Cic. **B.** Transf. *protection, refuge;* omnium scelerum, Liv. **II.** *a dwelling on a height,* Verg.

castĕria -ae, f. *a portion of a ship, used as a resting-place for rowers,* Plaut.

castĭgābĭlis -e (castigo), *worthy of punishment,* Plaut.

castĭgātĭo -ōnis, f. (castigo), *punishment, chastisement, reproof;* afficere aliquem castigationibus, Cic. ; verborum, Liv.

castĭgātor -ōris, m. (castigo), *one who reproves or punishes,* Liv.

castĭgātōrĭus -a -um (castigo), *correcting,* Plin.

castĭgātus -a -um (partic. of castigo), *checked, restrained,* hence *small, neat,* as a term of praise; pectus, Ov.

castĭgo (castum-ago, as purgo = purum ago), **1**, *to reprove, chasten, punish.* **I.** Lit., *punish* verbis, verberibus, Cic. **II.** Transf., a, *to correct, amend;* carmen, Hor. ; b, *to check, restrain,* fig., examen in trutinā, *to amend one's opinion,* Pers.

castĭmōnĭa -ae, f. (castus), **1**, *bodily purity,* Cic. ; **2**, *moral purity,* Cic.

castĭtas -ātis, f. (castus), *abstinence from sensual pleasure, chastity,* Cic.

1. **castor** -ōris, m. (κάστωρ), *the beaver,* Cic.

2. **Castor** -ōris, m. (Κάστωρ), *the son of Tyndarus and Leda, twin-brother of Pollux and Helen.* Ecastor, mēcastor, *By Castor,* a common form of oath in Rome.

castŏrĕum, -i, n. *an aromatic secretion obtained from the beaver*, Verg.

castrensis -e (castra), *pertaining to a camp*, Cic.

castro, 1, *to castrate*, Plaut.

castrum -i, n. (root CAS, whence casa). **I.** Sing., *a castle, fort, fortress*, Nep. ; oftener in sing. as a proper name, e.g., Cas*t*rum Inui in Latium. **II.** Plur., **castra** -orum, n. **A.** Lit., 1, *a camp fortified by a ditch* (fossa) *and a mound* (agger) *surmounted by palisades* (vallum); stativa, *permanent*, Cic. ; aestiva, *summer quarters*, Suet. ; hiberna, *winter quarters*, Liv. ; navalia, *a naval encampment*, when the ships were drawn up on the beach and protected by an entrenchment, Caes. ; ponere, Liv. ; locare, facere, *to encamp*, Cic. ; movere, *to break up the camp*, Caes. ; promovere, *to advance*, Caes. ; removere, or movere retro, *to retreat*, Liv. ; hostem castris exuere, *to take the enemy's camp*, Liv. ; fig., like the English *camp*, of a party, in Epicuri nos adversarii nostri castra conjecimus, Cic. ; 2, esp., **a**, *the camp of the praetorian guard* at Rome ; praetoriana, Suet. ; **b**, as a proper name, Castra Cornelia, *a height near Utica*. **B.** Transf., of a bee-hive, cerea castra, Verg. **C.** Meton., 1, *a day's march*; tertiis castris pervenit, Liv. ; 2, *martial service*, magnum in castris usum habere, Caes.

castus -a -um (connected with Gr. καθαρός). **I.** *pure, spotless, innocent*; homo castissimus, Cic. **II.** Esp. **A.** 1, *temperate, unselfish*; homo castus ac non cupidus, Cic. ; 2, *chaste*; matronarum castissima, Cic. **B.** Transf., of things, Cassii castissima domus, Cic. **C.** of religion, *pious, religious, holy*; nepotes casti maneant in religione nepotes, Verg. ; castam contionem, sanctum campum defendo, Cic.

căsŭla -ae, f. (dim. of casa), *a little hut, cottage*, Plin.

căsus -us, m. (cado), *a falling, fall*, Liv. **I.** Gen. **A.** Lit., a, nivis, Liv. ; b, of a season, *end*; extremae sub casum hiemis, Verg. ; c, in grammar, *case*; casus rectus, *the nominative*, Cic. **B.** Transf., a, *fall*; quum gravis casus in servitium ex regno foret, Sall. ; b, *occasion, opportunity*; aut vi aut dolis se casum victoriae inventurum, Sall. ; c, *accident, event, occurrence*; novi casus temporum, Cic. ; abl. casu, *by chance*; evenire non temere nec casu, Cic. ; d, *disaster, mishap*; meus ille casus tam horribilis, tam gravis, etc., Cic. ; reipublicae, Sall. **II.** *destruction, ruin*; a, of things, urbis Trojanae, Verg. ; b, of persons, *violent death*; Saturnini atque Gracchorum casus (plur.), Caes.

Cătăbathmŏs -i, m. (Καταβαθμός), *a valley on the borders of Africa and Asia*, now *the valley of Akabah*.

cătădrŏmus -i, m. (κατάδρομος), *a rope for rope-dancing*, Suet.

Cătădūpa -ōrum, n. (κατάδουπα), *the Nile cataracts on the Ethiopian frontier*, now *cataracts of Wady Halfa*.

cătăgĕlăsĭmus -a -um (καταγελάσιμος), *serving as a subject of jest*, Plaut.

cătăgrăphus -a -um (κατάγραφος), *painted, parti-coloured*, Cat.

Cătămītus -i, m. *the Latin name for Ganymedes*.

Cătăŏnĭa -ae, f. *a district of the Roman province Cappadocia*.

cătăphractes -ae, m. (καταφρακτής), *a breast-plate of iron scales*, Tac. ; hence, adj., **cătăphractus** -a -um, *mail-clad*, Liv.

cătăplūs -i, m. (κατάπλους), *the arrival of a ship*; hence meton., *a ship that is arriving*, Cic.

cătăpulta -ae, f. (καταπέλτης), *an engine of war for throwing arrows, a catapult*, Liv.

cătăpultārĭus -a -um (catapulta), *relating to a catapult*, Plaut.

cătăracta (catarr.) -ae, f., and **cătăractes** -ae, m. (καταρράκτης), 1, *a waterfall*, esp. *a cataract of the Nile*, Sen. ; 2, *a sluice* or *floodgate*, Plin. ; 3, *a portcullis*, Liv.

cătasta -ae, f. (κατάστασις), *a stage upon which slaves were exposed in the market*, Pers.

cătē, adv. (catus), *skilfully, cleverly*, Cic.

cătēja -ae, f. *a kind of dart*, Verg.

1. **cătella** -ae, f. (dim. of catula), *a little bitch*, Juv.

2. **cătella** -ae, f. (dim. of catena), *a little chain*, Liv.

cătellus -i, m. (dim. of catulus), *a little dog*, Cic.

cătēna -ae f. (root CAT, CAS, whence cassis), 1, *a chain, fetter*; aliquem catenis vincire,, Liv. ; aliquem in catenas conjicere, Liv. ; alicui catenas injicere, Cic. ; in catenis tenere, Caes. ; fig., *restraint*; legum catenae, Cic. ; 2, *a chain, series*, Lucr.

cătēnātus -a -um (catena), *chained, bound*; Britannus, Hor. ; labores, *unremitting*, Mart.

căterva -ae, f. *crowd, troop*. **I.** Of men, **A.** Gen., magna togatorum, Cic. **B.** Esp., 1, *a troop of soldiers*, esp. of barbarian soldiers, of mercenaries as opp. to Roman legionaries, Hor., Tac. ; 2, *a company of actors*, Cic. ; 3, *the chorus in the drama*, Cic. **II.** Of animals, Verg.

cătervārĭus -a -um (caterva), *belonging to a troop*, Suet.

cătervātim, adv. (caterva), *in troops, in masses*, Sall., Lucr.

căthēdra -ae, f. (καθέδρα). **I. A.** *a chair*, principally used by ladies, Hor. ; also, *a litter for women*, Juv. **B.** Meton., cathedrae molles, *luxurious women*, Juv. **II.** *a professor's chair*, Juv.

Cătĭlīna -ae, m., L. Sergius, *a Roman of noble birth, who headed a conspiracy against the state, and was killed in battle at Faesulae*, B.C. 62; hence adj., **Cătĭlīnārĭus** -a -um, *Catilinarian*.

cătĭllo, 1. (catillus), *to lick plates*, Plaut.

1. **cătillus** -i, m. (dim. of catinus), *a small dish* or *plate*, Hor.

2. **Cătillus** -i, m. *son of Amphiaraus, one of the legendary founders of Tibur*.

Cătīna -ae, f. (Κατάνη), and **Cătănē** -ēs, f. *a town on the east coast of Sicily, at the foot of Mount Aetna*, now *Catania*. Adj., **Cătĭnensis** -e, *of* or *belonging to Catina*.

cătīnum -i, n. and **cătīnus** -i, m. *a broad, flat dish*, Hor.

Cătŏ -ōnis, m. **I.** *a cognomen belonging to the plebeian gens Porcia*. 1, M. Porcius Cato Censorius (235–147 B.C.), *celebrated for his uprightness and strenuous support of the old Roman simplicity and discipline, author of several works, among which the most noted are the* Origines *and* de Re rustica ; 2, M. Porcius Cato the younger, *leader of the senatorial party on the death of Pompeius, killed himself at Utica, B.C. 46, on the final ruin of his party* (hence called Uticensis). Adj., **Cătōnĭānus** -a -um, *Catonian*. Subst., **Cătōnīni** -orum, m. *the party of the younger Cato*. Plur., **Cătōnes**, *men of the old Roman type, like Cato*, Cic. **II.** M. Valerius Cato, *a freedman of Gaul, grammarian and poet in the time of Sulla*.

cătōnĭum -i, n. (κάτω), *the lower world*; with

a play on the word Cato, vereor ne in catonium Catoninos, Cic.

catta -ae, f. *cat* or *weasel*, Mart.

cătŭla -ae, f. *a little bitch*, Prop.

cătŭlīnus -a -um (catulus), *relating to a dog;* caro, Plaut. ; or subst., **cătŭlīna** -ae, f. *dog's flesh*, Plin.

Cătullus -i, m., Q. Valerius Catullus, *a celebrated Roman elegiac and epigrammatic poet, born in or near Verona*, B.C. 87. Adj., **Cătullĭānus** -a -um.

1. **cătŭlus** -i, m. (dim. of catus), *a young animal*, esp. of the dog or cat kind ; a, suis, Plaut. ; leonis, Hor. ; lupi, Verg. ; ursae, Ov. ; b, esp. *a young dog, whelp, puppy*, Cic.

2. **Cătŭlus** -i, m., *the name of a branch of the plebeian gens Lutatia.* **I.** C. Lutatius Catulus, *consul* B.C. 242, *who brought the First Punic War to a close by the victory of Aegusa*, B.C. 241. **II.** Q. Lutatius Catulus, *consul with Marius*, B.C. 102, *defeated the Cimbri at the battle of Vercellae; perished in the proscription of Sulla*, B.C. 87. **III.** Q. Lutatius Catulus, *son of the preceding, an honest and popular aristocratic statesman, contemporary with Cicero; consul*, B.C. 78 ; *died* B.C. 60.

cătus -a -um, 1, *sagacious, acute, clever* (opp. stultus), Cic. ; 2, *cunning, sly*, in a bad sense, Hor.

Caucăsus -i, m. (Καύκασος), *mountains separating Asia from Europe.* Adj., **Caucăsĭus** -a -um, *Caucasian.*

cauda -ae, f. *the tail of an animal;* 1, leonis, Cic. ; caudam trahere, *to wear a tail, a fool's cap*, Hor. ; 2, cauda Verrina, *the appendage to the name of Verres which was changed to Verrucius*, with a play on the word verres (boar).

caudĕus -a -um, *made of rushes*, Plaut.

caudex (codex) -ĭcis, m. *the stem or trunk of a tree*, Verg.

caudĭcālis -e (caudex), *relating to wood*, Plaut.

caudĭcārĭus, v. codicarius.

Caudĭum -ĭi, n. *an old city in Samnium, near the pass of the Caudine Forks, in which the Roman army was enclosed by the Samnites*, B.C. 321. Adj., **Caudīnus** -a -um, *Caudine;* furculae, Liv. ; proelium, Cic.

caulae -ārum, f. (contr. for cavillae, from cavus), 1, *a hole, opening*, Lucr. ; 2, *a sheep-fold*, Verg.

caulis -is, m. (connected with καυλός). **A.** *the stalk of a plant*, esp. *the cabbage-plant*, Plin. **B.** Transf., *anything of similar form;* pennae, *a quill*, Plin.

Caulōn -ōnis, m. and **Caulōnĭa** -ae, f. (Καυλών), *Italian town in Bruttii.*

Caunus (Caunŏs) -i, f. (Καῦνος), *a town in Caria.* Adj., **Caunĕus** or -ĭus -a -um.

caupo -ōnis, m. *a small shopkeeper*, or *innkeeper*, Cic.

caupōna -ae, f. (caupo), *a tavern, inn*, Cic., Hor.

caupōnĭus -a -um (caupo), *belonging to an innkeeper*, Plaut.

caupōnor, 1. dep. (caupo), *to trade in anything*, Enn.

caupōnŭla -ae, f. (dim. of caupo), *a little inn*, Cic.

caurus (cōrus), -i, m. *the north-west wind*, Verg., Caes.

causa (caussa) -ae, f. (cado), *a cause, reason, motive, inducement.* **A.** 1, magna, levis, justa, Cic. ; cum causa, *with good reason*, Cic. ; sine causa, *without reason*, Cic. ; with genit. causa

belli, Cic. ; with infin. (poet.), quae causa fuit consurgere in arma, Verg. ; ob eam causam quia, etc., Cic. ; quidnam esse causae cur, etc., Cic. ; propter hanc causam quod, etc., Cic. ; ea est causa ut (with subj.), Liv. ; quid est causae quin (with subj.), Cic. ; eis causis quominus (with subj.), Caes. ; in causa haec sunt, Cic. ; afferre causam, Cic. ; alicui inferre causam, Cic. ; alicui causam alicuius rei dare, Cic. ; causae esse, Caes. ; causam alicuius rei sustinere, *to bear the blame*, Cic. ; 2, *excuse;* causam accipere, Cic. ; 3, *pretext;* causas novarum postulationum quaerere, Cic. ; fingere causam, Cic. ; 4, *cause of a disease*, Cic. ; 5, abl., causa, *on account of;* joci causa, Cic. ; verbi causa, *for example*, Cic. ; mea causa, Cic. ; so tua, nostra, etc. **B.** 1, *case;* armis inferiores, non causa fiunt, Cic. ; 2, *situation, condition;* erat in meliore causa, Cic. ; 3, *side, party;* causa quam Pompeius susceperat, Cic. ; 4, *point in an argument, subject;* causam disserendi, Cic. ; 5, *lawsuit;* causa capitis, Cic. ; causae dictio, *pleading*, Cic. ; causam defendere, Cic. ; causam dicere, *to plead*, Cic. ; causam surripere, Cic. ; causam perdere or causa cadere, *to lose a suit*, Cic.

causārĭus -a -um (causa A. 4), *sickly, diseased*, Sen. ; hence subst., **causārĭi** -orum, m. milit. t.t., *invalided, discharged on account of illness*, Liv.

causĭa -ae, f. (καυσία), *a white broad-brimmed Macedonian hat*, Plaut.

causĭdĭcus -i, m. (causa and dico), *an advocate, barrister*, used contemptuously to denote one who pleads for money and without skill ; distinguished from orator, Cic.

causĭfĭcor, 1. (causa and facio), *to bring forward as a reason or pretext*, Plaut.

causor, 1. dep. (causa), *to give as a reason*, or *pretext; to plead, pretend;* multa, Lucr. ; consensum patrum, Liv. ; valetudinem, Tac.

caustĭcus -a -um (καυστικός), *burning, caustic.* Subst., **caustĭcum** -i, n. *caustic*, Plin.

causŭla -ae, f. (dim. of causa), 1, *a little lawsuit*, Cic. ; 2, *a slight occasion*, Auct. B. Afr.

cautē, adv. (cautus), *cautiously, carefully;* caute pedetemptimque dicere, Cic.

cautēs (cōtes) -is, f. *a rough sharp rock*, Caes., Verg.

cautim, adv. (cautus), *cautiously, carefully*, Ter.

cautĭo -ōnis, f. (contr. from cavitio, from caveo). **I.** *caution, care, foresight, precaution;* cautionem adhibere, Cic. ; hence, res cautionem habet, a, *the affair needs caution*, Cic. ; b, *allows of foresight*, Cic. **II.** Legal t.t., *security, bail, bond*, Cic. ; chirographi, *written*, Cic.

cautor -ōris, m. (caveo), 1, *one who is on his guard*, Plaut. ; 2, *one who gives bail for another*, Cic.

cautus -a um (caveo), 1, a, *cautious, wary, careful, circumspect;* parum putantur cauti providique fuisse, Cic. ; in scribendo, Cic. ; consilia cautiora, Cic. ; b, *sly;* vulpes, Hor. ; 2, of property, *made safe, secured;* quo mulieri esset res cautior, Cic.

căvaedĭum -i, n. = cavum aedium, *the open quadrangle formed by the inner walls of a house*, Plin.

căvĕa -ae, f. (cavus). **I.** *a hollow place, cavity*, Plin. **II.** Esp. **A.** *an inclosure, cage, den for wild animals*, Luc. ; esp. a, *a birdcage*, Cic. ; b, *a beehive*, Verg. **B.** a, *the seats in a theatre* or *amphitheatre;* prima, *the first tier, the place of honour where the knights sat;* media, summa, *less distinguished seats.* Cic. ; b, *the whole theatre*, Cic.

căvĕo, cāvi, cautum, 2. *to be on one's guard*, **I.** *to guard against, beware, avoid*; absol., nisi cavetis, Cic.; with ab, ab aliquo, Cic.; with acc., aliquem, *to be on one's guard against*, Cic.; pass., cavenda etiam gloriae cupiditas, *we must be on our guard against*, Cic.; with infin., in quibus cave vereri ne, etc., Cic.; with ne, ut ne, and the subj., quod ut ne accidat cavendum est, Cic.; with subj. alone, cave ignoscas, Cic.; with ut and the subj., Cic. **II.** *to take precautions.* **A.** With dat. of persons for whom, qui in Oratore tuo caves tibi per Brutum, Cic.; with ad, satis cautum tibi ad defensionem, Cic.; with ut and the subj., *to take care*, Cic. **B.** Esp., legal t.t., **1**, *to give security for;* praedibus et praediis populo, Cic.; **2**, *to get security;* ab sese caveat, Cic.; **3**, *to provide for in writing, to order;* a, by will, heredi velle cavere, Cic.; b, in a treaty, de quibus cautum sit foedere, Cic.; c, in a law, cautum est in legibus Scipionis ne, etc., Cic. (Imper. căvĕ sometimes in poet.)

căverna -ae, f. (cavus), *a hollow place, grotto, cavern*, Cic.; navis, *the hold*, Cic.; coeli, *the vault of heaven*, Lucr.

căvilla -ae, f. (dim. of cavus), *empty jesting, raillery, scoffing*, Plaut.

căvillātĭo -ōnis, f. (cavillor), *raillery, jesting, irony*, Cic.

căvillātor -ōris, m. (cavillor), *a jester, joker, humourist*, Cic.

căvillor, 1. dep. (cavilla), *to jest, joke, satirise, make game of;* **1**, cum aliquo, Cic.; in eo cavillatus est, Cic.; alicuius praetextam, Cic.; tribunos plebei cavilla s, Liv.; **2**, *to make captious objections;* cavillari tribuni, Liv.

căvillŭla -ae, f. (dim. of cavilla), *a little jest*, Plaut.

căvo, 1. (cavus), *to hollow, make hollow, excavate;* naves ex arboribus, Liv.; oppida cuniculis *to undermine*, Plin.; parmam gladio, *to pierce*, Verg.; luna cavans cornua, *waning*, Plin. Partic., **căvātus** -a -um, *hollowed out, hollow;* rupes, Verg.

căvum, i. n. (cavus), *a hole, cavity, cave*, Liv.

căvus -a -um, *hollow, concave* (opp. plenus). **I.** Lit., vena, Cic.; vallis, Liv.; nubes, Verg.; flumina, *deep-channelled*, Verg.; luna, *waning*, Plin. **II.** Meton., *empty;* imago formae, Verg.

Căystrus -i, m. (Κάϋστρος), *a river in Lydia, famous for its swans;* hence adj., **Căystrĭus** -a -um, *Caystrian;* ales, *the swan*, Ov.

cĕ, an inseparable particle joined on to pronouns and adverbs—e.g., hisce, Cic.

Cēa -ae, f. and **Cĕōs**, acc. Ceo (Κέως), *one of the Cyclades Islands, birthplace of the poet Simonides.* Adj., **Cēus** -a -um, *Cean*, Camenae, *the poetry of Simonides*, Hor.

Cebenna (Gebenna) nons, m. *a mountain-chain in Gaul* (now *the Cevennes*).

Cĕbrēn -ēnis, m. (Κεβρήν), *a river-god in Troas, father of Oenone and Hesperie.* Hence, **Cĕbrēnis** -ĭdis, f. *the daughter of Cebren, i.e., Hesperie*, Ov.

Cĕcrops -ŏpis, m. (Κέκροψ), *the first king of Attica, mythical founder of Athens;* hence adj., **Cĕcrŏpĭdēs** -ae, m. *descendant of Cecrops, e.g., Theseus*, Ov.; plur. *the Athenians*, Verg.; b, **Cĕcrŏpis** -ĭdis, f. *a female descendant of Cecrops*, e g., *Aglauros, daughter of Cecrops*, Ov.; *Procne and Philomela, daughters of Pandion*, Ov.; adj., terra, *Attica*, Ov.; ales, *Procne*, Ov.; c, **Cĕcrŏpĭus** -a -um, *Cecropian*, arx, Ov.; and subst., **Cĕcrŏpia** -ae, f. *the citadel of Athens*, Plin.; also, *relating to Attica and Athens; Athenian, Attic.*

1. cedo, cessi, cessum, 3. **I.** Gen., *to go, proceed.* **A.** Lit., per ora, Hor. **B.** Transf., **1**, *to come to something, to turn out, to happen;* alicui male, Ov.; **2**, *to fall to the lot of;* ut etiam is quaestus huic cederet, Cic.; res omnis Albana in Romanum cedit imperium, Liv.; **3**, *to change to, to become;* huc omnis aratri cessit honos, Verg. **II.** Esp., **A.** Lit., *to give ground, retire;* cedam atque abibo, Cic.; horae cedunt et dies, Cic.; e patria, or (simply) patria, Cic.; ab or de oppido, Cic.; e vita or vita, Cic.; e memoria or memoria, Liv.; with dat. of the person before whom one retreats, infenso hosti, Liv. **B.** Transf., **1**, *to submit, yield;* minis alicuius, Cic.; tempori, Cic.; precibus alicuius, Cic.; **2**, *to be inferior to;* alicui virtute, Caes.; **3**, *to give up a right* or *some property;* with abl. and dat., alicui possessione bonorum, Cic.; with acc., multa multis de jure, Cic.; *permitto* aliquid iracundiae tuae, *do* adolescentiae, *cedo* amicitiae, *tribuo* parenti, Cic.

2. cĕdŏ and plur. **cettĕ** (contracted from cedito and cedite), **1**, *here with it! give here;* cedo aquam manibus, Plaut.; cedo ut bibam, Plaut.; **2**, *out with it! let us hear, tell us;* also, cedo dum, Plaut., Ter.; **3**, *to call attention, see here;* cedo mihi leges Atinias, Furias, Cic.

cĕdrus -i, f. (κέδρος). **I.** *the cedar*, or *juniper tree*, Plin. **II.** Meton., **A.** *cedar-wood*, Verg. **B.** *cedar oil;* carmina linenda cedro, *worthy of immortality* (as the cedar oil preserved from decay), Hor.

Cĕlaenae -ārum, f. (Κελαιναί), *a town in Phrygia, near the Maeander*, Liv. Adj., **Cĕlaenaeus** -a -um, *Celaenean.*

Cĕlaeno -ūs, f. (Κελαινώ). **I.** *daughter of Atlas, placed in the sky as one of the Pleiades.* **II.** *one of the Harpies.* Appell., *a covetous woman*, Juv.

cēlātor -ōris, m. (celo), *a concealer*, Lucr.

cĕlĕber -bris -bre and **cĕlĕbris** -e, *numerous.* **I.** Of places, meetings, etc., **A.** Lit., *much frequented;* portus, Cic. **B.** Transf., **1**, *honoured;* funus fit regium, magis amore civium et caritate quam cura suorum celebre, Liv.; **2**, *renowned, distinguished, well-known;* a, of things, res tota Sicilia celeberrima atque notissima, Cic.; b, of persons, *famous;* clarissimarum urbium excidio celeberrimi viri, Liv. **II.** *often repeated;* vox celeberrima, Ov.

cĕlĕbrātĭo -ōnis, f. (celebro), **1**, *a numerous assembly;* quae celebratio quotidiana, Cic.; **2**, *numerous attendance upon a festival, celebration;* ludorum, Cic.

cĕlĕbrātor -ōris, m. (celebro), *one who praises* or *extols*, Mart.

cĕlĕbrātus -a -um, p. adj. (from celebro), **1**, *numerously attended;* a, of places, *much frequented;* forum rerum venalium totius regni maxime celebratum, Sall.; b, of festivals, *kept solemn, festive;* dies festus celebratusque per omnem Africam, Liv.; **2**, *known;* a, res celebratissimae omnium sermone, Cic.; b, *praised, honoured;* eloquentia, Tac.

cĕlĕbrĭtas -ātis, f. (celeber), **1**, *a frequenting in large numbers, numerous attendance at;* loci, Cic.; of a festival, *celebration;* supremi diei, *at a funeral*, Cic.; **2**, *a multitude, concourse;* virorum ac mulierum, Cic.; **3**, *fame, renown;* celebritatem sermonis hominum consequi, Cic.

cĕlĕbro, 1. (celeber), **1**, *to visit frequently*, or *in large numbers;* domum alicuius, Cic.; sepulcrum hominum conventu epulisque, Cic.; **2**, *to celebrate, solemnise;* festos dies ludorum, Cic; celebratur omnium sermone laetitiaque convivium, Cic.; **3**, *to publish, make known;* factum esse consulem Murenam nuntii litteraeque

celebrassent, Cic.; **4**, *to praise, honour;* egressum alicuius ornare atque celebrare, Cic.; nomen alicuius scriptis, Cic.; **5**, *to practise often, exercise;* artes, Cic.; nec unum genus est divinationis publice privatimque celebratum, Cic.

Cĕlemna -ae, f. *a town in Campania,* not far from Teanum.

cĕler -ĕris, -ĕre (root CEL, connected with cello, celox, κέλω, κέλης), *swift, quick, rapid.* **I.** Lit., navis, Ov. **II.** Transf., **A. 1**, in a good sense, mens qua nihil est celerius, Cic.; **2**, in a bad sense, *hasty, rash, precipitate;* consilia celeriora, *over hasty plans,* Liv.

cĕlĕrĕ, adv. (celer), *quickly, swiftly,* Plaut.

Cĕlĕres -um, m. (connected with κέλης), *the name of the body-guard of the Roman kings,* Liv.

cĕlĕrĭpes -pĕdis (celer and pes), *swift-footed,* Cic.

cĕlĕrĭtas -ātis, f. (celer), *quickness, swiftness, celerity.* **I.** Lit., equorum, Cic. **II.** Transf., orationis, Cic.; actionis, Cic.; animorum, Cic.

cĕlĕrĭtĕr, adv. (celer), *quickly, swiftly,* Cic.

cĕlĕro, 1. (celer). **I.** Transit., *to make quick, hasten, accelerate;* fugam, Verg. **II.** Intransit., *to hasten,* Lucr., Cat.

Cĕlĕus -i, m. (Κελεός), *king in Eleusis, who hospitably entertained Ceres, and was taught by her agriculture and the mysteries of her worship.*

cella -ae, f. *a room.* **I.** In a Roman house. **A.** Of a town-house, **1**, *a room for persons, esp. the servants' rooms,* Cic.; **2**, *a storehouse;* with or without penaria, Cic.; in cellam dare, imperare, emere, *to give out, order, buy things for the house,* Cic. **B.** Of a country-house, **1**, *storehouse;* penaria, *for corn,* olearia, *for oil,* vinaria, *for wine,* Cic.; transf., Capua cella atque horreum Campani agri, Cic.; **2**, *place for keeping birds,* Col. **C.** In a lodging-house, *a mean apartment,* Mart. **II.** In a temple, *the shrine of the god's image,* Cic. **III.** *the cell of a beehive,* Verg.

cellārĭus -a -um (cella), *relating to a store-room,* Plaut. Subst., **cellārĭus** -i, m. *a store-keeper, cellarer,* Plaut.

cellŭla -ae, f. (dim. of cella), *a little chamber,* or *cell,* Ter.

cēlo, 1. *to hide, conceal, keep secret;* sententiam suam, Cic.; dolorem vultu tegere et taciturnitate celare, Cic.; with acc. of the thing concealed and acc. of person from whom it is concealed; non te celavi sermonem T. Ampii, Cic.; with de and the abl. of the person; de insidiis te celare noluit, Cic.

celox -ōcis, f. (root CEL, v. celer), *a swift vessel,* or *yacht,* Liv.; publica, *packet-boat,* Plaut.

1. celsus -a -um (from * cello, lit. *driven up on high*), *high, upright.* **A.** Lit., natura homines humo excitatos celsos et erectos constituit, Cic. **B.** Transf., **1**, of rank, *eminent;* celsissima sedes dignitatis et honoris, Cic.; **2**, morally, *lofty, elevated;* celsus et erectus, Cic.; **3**, in a bad sense, *proud, haughty,* Cic.; celsi Ramnes, Hor.

2. Celsus -i, m. **A.** Cornelius, *a Latin writer on medicine.*

Celtae -ārum, m. *the Celts.* Adj., **Celtĭcus** -a -um. *Celtic*

Celtĭbēri -ōrum. m. *the Celtiberians, a race in the middle of Spain of mixed Celtic and Iberian blood.* Adj., **Celtĭber** -ēra -ērum and **Celtĭbērĭcus** -a -um. *Celtiberian.* Subst., **Celtĭbērĭa** -ae, f. *the land of the Celtiberi.*

cēna -ae, f. *the principal meal of the Romans, taken about three or four o'clock in the afternoon, dinner, supper.* **I.** Lit., cena recta, *a complete*

dinner of three courses, Suet.; caput cenae, *the chief dish,* Cic.; inter cenam, *at dinner-time,* Cic.; invitare ad cenam, *to ask to dinner,* Cic.; obire cenas, itare ad cenas, Cic.; cenam alicui dare, *to give any one a dinner,* Cic.; venire ad cenam, Cic.; redire a cena, Cic. **II.** Meton., a, *the courses at a dinner;* prima, altera, tertia, Mart., b, *the company invited;* ingens cena sedet, Juv.; c, *the place where the dinner is given,* Plin.

cēnācŭlum -i, n. (ceno), *literally an eating-room,* Varr.; and as these were often in the upper storey, *the upper storey of a house, the garret, attic;* Roma cenaculis sublata atque suspensa, Cic.; mutat cenacula, Hor.

Cēnaeum -i, n. (κηναιον ἄκρον), *the north-western promontory of Euboea, on which was a temple of Jupiter;* hence, adj., **Cēnaeus** -a -um, *of Cenaeum;* Juppiter, Ov.

cēnātĭcus -a -um (cena), *relating to dinner;* spes, Plaut.

cēnātĭo -ōnis, f. (cena), *an eating-room, dining-hall,* Plin.

cēnātōrĭus -a -um (cena), *relating to dinner.* Subst., **cēnātōrĭa** -ōrum n. *clothes to dine in,* Petr.

cēnātŭrĭo, 4. (ceno), *to wish to dine,* Mart.

cēnātus -a -um, v. ceno.

Cenchrĕae -ārum, f. (Κεγχρέαι), *port of the Corinthians on the Saronic gulf.* Adj., **Cenchrĕus** -a -um, *Cenchrean.*

cēnĭto, 1. (freq. of ceno), *to dine often, be accustomed to dine;* apud aliquem, Cic.

cēno, 1. (cena). **I.** Intransit., *to take the cena, to dine, sup, eat;* cenare bene, Cic.; cenare apud aliquem, Cic.; impers., quum cenaretur apud Vitellios, Liv.; partic. perf., cenatus, with a middle meaning, *having dined, after dinner;* cenati discubuerunt ibidem, Cic. **II.** Transit., *to dine on, to eat;* aprum, Hor.

Cenomāni -ōrum, *a Celtic people in Gaul.* Adj., **Cenomāni** -a -um, *Cenomanian.*

censeo -sŭi -sum, 2. (root CENS, CONS, whence consulo), *to give an opinion* **I.** Gen., *to appraise, estimate.* **A.** Lit., **1**, si censenda nobis atque aestimanda res sit, Cic.; **2**, esp. of the censor at Rome; a, *to take an account of the names and property of Roman citizens;* censores populi aevitates, suboles, familias pecuniasque censento, Cic.; capite censi, *the lowest class of Roman citizens,* whose persons only were counted, Sall.; sintne ista praedia censui censendo? *are those estates fit to be put on the censor's list?* (as the property of the possessors), Cic.; b, *to make a return to the censor;* in qua tribu denique ista praedia censuisti, Cic. **B.** Transf., censeri de aliquo, *to be regarded as belonging to a certain person,* Ov. **II. A.** *to express an opinion,* be *of an opinion;* ita prorsus censeo, Cic.; tibi igitur hoc censeo, Cic.; with ut and the subj., Cic.; with the subj. alone, magno opere censeo desistas, Cic.; with infin., delubra esse in urbibus censeo, Cic. **B.** *to vote, recommend by vote* or *advice;* captivos reddendos in senatu non censuit, Cic.; pars deditionem, pars eruptionem censebant, Caes. **C.** Of the senate (as jubere for the populus), *to resolve, order;* senatus censuit, etc., Caes.

censĭo -ōnis, f. (censeo). **A.** *an assessment, estimate,* esp. *the censor's estimate,* Plaut. **B.** Transf., in jest, bubula, *a scourging,* Plaut.

censor -ōris, m. (censeo), *the censor.* **I.** Lit., *a Roman magistrate, of whom two were elected, originally at intervals of five years, afterwards of one year and a half.* Their business was: a, *to hold the census;* b, *to punish persons for offences against morals by degradation* **to** **a**

lower rank; **c**, to look after the roads and bridges, public buildings, and the revenues of the state. **II**. Transf., *a severe judge, a rigid moralist, a censurer*, Cic.; castigator censorque minorum, Hor.

censōrĭus -a -um. **A.** *relating to the censor;* homo, *one who has filled the office of censor*, Cic.; tabulae, *the censor's lists*, Cic.; lex, locatio, *a contract relating to building* or *to the public revenue*, Cic.; opus, *a fault which was punished by the censor*, Cic. **B.** Transf., *rigid, severe*, Quint.

censūra -ae, f. (censor), *the censor's dignity, the censorship;* censuram gerere, Cic.

census -ūs, m. (censeo). **A.** *the enrolment of the names and the assessment of the property of all Roman citizens, the census;* censum habere, Cic.; agere, *to take a census*, Cic.; censu prohibere, Cic.; censu excludere, *to refuse to enrol in the census*, Liv.; censum perficere, Liv.; censum accipere, Liv.; censum alicuius augere, extenuare, Cic. **B.** Meton., **a**, *the censor's list*, Cic.; **b**, *the amount of property necessary for enrolment in a certain rank;* senatorius = 800,000 *sesterces*, Suet.; equester = 400,000 *sesterces*, Suet.; homo sine censu, *a poor man*, Cic.; dat census honores, Ov.

centaurēum -ēi, n. and **centaurĭum** -ĭi, n. (κενταύρειον), *the plant centaury*, Verg.

Centaurus -i, m. (Κένταυρος). **I.** *a centaur, a monster, half man and half horse*, Verg.; nobilis, *Chiron*, Hor.; hence adj., **Centaurēus** -a -um. **II.** f. *the name of a ship*, Verg.

centēnārĭus -a -um (centenus), *containing a hundred, relating to a hundred*, Varr., Plin.

centēnus -a -um (centum). **I.** Sing., used collectively, *a hundred;* centena arbore, Verg. **II.** Plur., num. distrib., *a hundred each*, Cic.

centēsĭmus -a -um, num. ordin. (centum), *the hundredth;* lux ab interitu Clodii, Cic. Subst., **centēsĭma** -ae, f. (sc. pars), *the hundredth part;* **a**, *a tax of one per cent.*, Cic.; **b**, of interest of money, *one per cent.* (reckoned at Rome by the month, therefore = 12 *per cent. per annum*); binae centesimae = 24 *per cent.;* quaternae, Cic.; perpetuae, *compound interest*, Cic.

centĭceps -cĭpĭtis (centum and caput), *hundred-headed;* belua, *Cerberus*, Hor.

centĭens or **centĭēs**, adv. (centum), *a hundred times;* HS. centies (sc. centena milia), *ten million sesterces*, Cic.

centĭmănus -a -um (centum and manus), *hundred-handed*, Hor., Ov.

centĭplex, v. centuplex.

cento -ōnis, m. (κέντρων), *patchwork, a covering of rags;* in war, *coverings to ward off missiles* or *extinguish fires*, Caes.

centum, indecl. numer., **1**, *a hundred*, Cic.; **2**, hyperbol., *any indefinitely large number;* centum puer artium, Hor.

centumgĕmĭnus -a -um, *hundred-fold;* Briareus, *hundred-armed*, Verg.

centumpondĭum -ĭi, n. *a weight of a hundred pounds*, Plaut.

centumvĭr -i, m., plur. **centumvĭri** -ōrum, m. *a college of 105 magistrates* (increased under the emperors to 180), *yearly elected at Rome, having jurisdiction over cases relating to inheritance*, Cic.

centumvĭrālis -e, *relating to the centumviri;* causa, *heard before the centumviri*, Cic.

centuncŭlus -i, m. (dim. of cento), *a little patch*, or *patchwork*, Liv.

centŭplex -ĭcis, *a hundred-fold*, Plaut.

centŭrĭa -ae, f. (centum), *a division of* 100;

1, *a company of soldiers*, originally 100, afterwards 60, Liv.; **2**, *a century, one of the* 193 *divisions into which Servius Tullius distributed the Roman people;* praerogativa, *the century which obtained by lot the privilege of first voting*, Cic.

centŭrĭātim, adv. (centuria), *by centuries* or *companies*, Caes., Cic.

1. centŭrĭātus -ūs, m. (1. centurio), *the division into companies* or *centuries*, Liv.

2. centŭrĭātus -ūs, m. (2. centurio), *the centurion's office*, Cic.

1. centŭrĭo, 1. (centuria), *to divide into centuries;* juventutem, Liv.; comitia centuriata, *the assembly in which the whole Roman people voted in their centuries* (e.g., at the election of a consul), Cic.; lex centuriata, *a law passed in such an assembly*, Cic.

2. centŭrĭo -ōnis, m. (centuria), *a commander of a century, a centurion*, Cic.

centŭrĭōnātus -ūs, m. (2. centurio), *the election of centurions*, Tac.

Centŭrĭpae -ārum, f. and **Centŭrĭpa** -ōrum, n. (τὰ Κεντόριπα), *a town in Sicily*, now *Centorbi;* hence, **Centŭrĭpīnus** -a -um, *of* or *belonging to Centuripa*.

centussis -is, m. (centum and as), *a hundred asses*, Pers.

cēnŭla -ae, f. (dim. of cena), *a little meal*, Cic.

cēnum, v. caenum.

Cēōs, v. Cea.

cēpa, v. caepa.

Cēphallēnĭa -ae, f. (Κεφαλληνία), *island in the Ionic Sea* (now *Cefalonia*); hence, **Cēphallēnes** -um, m. *inhabitants of Cephallenia*.

Cēphăloedis -ĭdis, f. (-ĭum -ĭi, n.), *town on the north coast of Sicily*. Adj., **Cēphăloedītānus** -a -um, *of* or *belonging to Cephaloedis*.

Cēphēnes -um, m. (Κηφῆνες), *a people of Aethiopia*, hence adj., **Cēphēnus** -a -um, *Cephenian*.

Cēpheus -ĕi, m. (Κηφεύς), *a mythical king of Aethiopia, husband of Cassiope, father of Andromeda*. Adj., **Cēphēïus** -a -um, *of* or *belonging to Cepheus;* virgo, *Andromeda*, Ov.; arva, *Aethiopia*, Ov.; **Cēphēus** -a -um, *Ethiopian;* also, **Cēphēïs** -ĭdos, f. *Andromeda*, Ov.

Cēphīsus or **Cēphissus** -i, m. (Κηφισός, Κηφισσός). **I.** *a river in Boeotia*, and, as a river-god, *the father of Narcissus;* hence, **Cēphīsĭus** -ĭi, m. = *Narcissus*, Ov. Adj., **Cēphīsis** -ĭdis, f. *of* or *belonging to Cephisus;* undae, Ov. **II.** *a river of Attica*, Ov. Adj., **Cēphīsĭas** -ădis, f. *of* or *belonging to the Cephisus*.

cēra -ae, f. (connected with κηρός), *wax*. **A.** Lit., mollissima, Cic.; ceras excudere (of bees making their hive), Verg. **B.** Meton., *articles made of wax;* **a**, *writing-tablets coated with wax*, Cic.; **b**, *a waxen seal*, Cic.; **c**, *a waxen image*, Sall.

Cĕrămĭcus -i, m. (Κεραμεικός), lit., *the pottery market, the name of two places at Athens, one within, the other without the wall, in the latter of which statues were erected to the heroes who fell in war*.

cērārĭum -ĭi, n. (cera), *a fee for sealing a document*, Cic.

cĕrastēs -ae, m. (κεράστης), *the horned snake*, Plin.

1. cĕrăsus -i, f. (κέρασος), **1**, *a cherry-tree*, Ov.; **2**, *a cherry*, Prop.

2. Cĕrăsus -untis, f. (Κερασοῦς), *a town in Pontus, whence came the cherry*.

cĕraunĭus -a -um (κεραύνιος), ceraunia gemma, or subst., **cĕraunĭum** -i, n., *a kind of precious stone*, Plin.

Cĕraunĭi montes, and alone **Cĕraunĭa** -ōrum, n. *mountains in Epirus.*

Cerbĕrŏs and -**us** -i, m. (Κέρβερος), *the three-headed dog at the gates of Tartarus.* Adj., **Cerbĕrĕus** -a -um, *of or belonging to Cerberus.*

Cercīna -ae, f. (Κερκίνα), *a large island off the African coast, now Kerkine or Cherkara or Zerbi.*

cercŏpĭthēcŏs and -**us** -i, m. (κερκοπίθηκος), *a kind of long-tailed ape*, Mart., Juv.

cercūrus -i., m. (κέρκουρος), 1, *a light species of vessel peculiar to Cyprus*, Liv.; 2, *a kind of sea-fish*, Ov.

Cercȳo -ōnis, m. (Κερκύων), *a brigand in Attica, killed by Theseus.* Adj., **Cercȳŏnēus** -a -um, *of or belonging to Cercyo.*

cerdo -ōnis, m. (κέρδος), *a handicraftsman, artizan*, Juv.; sutor cerdo, *a cobbler*, Mart.

cĕrĕbrōsus -a -um (cerebrum), *hot-brained, hot-tempered*, Hor.

cĕrĕbrum -i, n. **A.** *the brain*, Cic. **B.** Meton., **a,** *the understanding*, Hor.; **b,** *anger*, Hor.

Cĕrēs -ĕris (root CER, CRE, whence creo). **I.** *the Roman goddess of agriculture, the daughter of Saturn and Ops, sister of Jupiter and Pluto, and mother of Proserpina;* prov., Cereri has nuptias facere, i.e., *without wine*, Plaut. **II.** Meton., *grain, corn*, Verg., Hor.; whence the proverb, sine Cerere et Libero friget Venus, Ter. Adj., **Cĕrĕālis** -e, *relating to Ceres, relating to cultivation and agriculture*, Ov.; papaver, *the emblem of Ceres*, Verg.; cenae, *splendid, as at the festival of Ceres*, Plaut.; aediles, *who superintended the supply of provisions;* hence subst., **Cĕrĕālĭa** -ium, n. *the festival of Ceres.*

cērĕus -a -um (cera). **I.** *waxen*, Cic.; castra, *the cells of a hive*, Verg. Subst., **cērĕus** -i, m. *a wax taper*, Cic. **II.** Meton., 1, *wax-coloured;* pruna, Verg.; brachia Telephi, *smooth as wax*, Hor.; 2, *flexible like wax;* cereus in vitium flecti, Hor.

cērintha -ae, f. (κηρίνθη), *the wax flower, a plant of which bees are fond*, Verg.

cērĭnus -a -um (κήρινος), *wax-coloured*, Plin.

cerno, crēvi, crētum, 3. (Root CRE, CRI, Gr. ΚΡΙ, whence κρίνω, cribrum.) **I.** *to separate, sift;* aliquid in cribris, Ov. **II.** Transf. **A.** *to distinguish;* 1, with the senses, **a,** ut non sensu, sed mente cernatur, Cic.; **b,** esp. of the eyes, acies ipsa, qua cernimus, quae pupula vocatur, Cic.; with acc., Pompeianum non cerno, Cic.; with acc. and infin., cernebatur novissimo illorum premi, Caes.; 2, with the mind, **a,** *to perceive;* animus plus cernit et longius, Cic.; **b,** cerni in aliqua re, *to show oneself, to be shown;* fortis animus et magnus duobus rebus maxime cernitur, Cic. **B.** *to decide,* 1, in battle = *to contend;* magnis in rebus inter se, Lucr.; 2, *to resolve, determine;* quodcumque senatus creverit, agunto, Cic.; 3, as legal t.t., *to accept an inheritance;* hereditatem cernere, Cic.; fig., hanc quasi falsam hereditatem alienae gloriae, Cic.

cernŭus -a -um, *falling headlong, with the face towards the ground;* equus, Verg.

cēro, 1. *to smear or cover with wax*, gen. in perf. partic. pass., cerata tabella, Cic.

cērōma -ătis, n. (κήρωμα). **A.** *an ointment of oil and wax used by wrestlers*, Juv. **B.** Meton., **a,** *the arena for wrestling*, Plin.; **b,** *wrestling itself*, Mart.

cērōmătĭcus -a -um (κηρωματικός), *anointed with the ceroma*, Juv.

cerrītus -a -um (contracted from cerebritus, from cerebrum), *frantic, mad*, Plaut., Hor.

cerrus -i, m. *a kind of oak, the Turkey oak*, Plin.

certāmen -ĭnis, n. (2. certo), *contest;* **a,** *in gymnastics;* gladiatorium vitae, Cic.; **b,** *any kind of rivalry;* honoris et gloriae, Cic.; in certamen virtutis venire, Cic.; **c,** *a fight;* proelii, Cic.; vario certamine pugnatum est, Caes.; **d,** *contention, rivalry;* est mihi tecum pro aris et focis certamen, Cic.

certātim, adv. (certatus, from 2. certo), *emulously, eagerly, as if striving for a prize*, Cic.

certātĭo -ōnis, f. (2. certo), *a contest;* **a,** in games, corporum, Cic.; **b,** in words or actions, virtuti cum voluptate certatio, Cic.; **c,** *a legal contest;* multae poenae, *as to the amount of a fine to be inflicted*, Cic.; **d,** *emulation;* certatio honesta inter amicos, Cic.

certē, adv. (certus). **I.** **a,** *certainly, assuredly;* ea quae certe vera sunt, Cic.; in answers, *without doubt*, Cic.; **b,** certe scio, *certainly, I know it*, Cic. **II.** *at least, at all events;* mihi certe, Cic.; certe tamen, Cic.

1. **certō**, adv. (certus), *certainly, assuredly, undoubtedly;* nihil ita exspectare quasi certo futurum, Cic.; esp. in phrase, certo scio, *I am sure of it*, Cic.

2. **certo**, 1. (Root CER, whence cerno and cretus), *to contend, struggle* (with the idea of rivalry). **A.** Lit., de imperio cum populo Romano, Cic. **B.** Transf., 1, in words, verbis, oratione, Cic.; 2, of law, *to dispute;* inter se, Cic.; 3, *to vie with;* officiis inter se, Cic.; foll. by infin., vincere, Verg.

certus -a -um (cerno). **I.** Lit., *separated*, Cato. **II.** Transf., **A.** *certain, definite, fixed, decided;* 1, certum est mihi consilium, Plaut.; certum est (mihi, etc.), *I am resolved;* sibi certum esse a judiciis causisque discedere, Cic.; 2, of persons, certus mori, *determined to die*, Verg.; certus eundi, *determined to go*, Verg. **B.** 1, *certain, fixed;* certus ac definitus locus, Cic.; certi homines, *certain men*, Cic.; 2, *secure, to be depended on;* bona et certa tempestate, Cic.; certissima populi Romani vectigalia, Cic.; of persons, homo certissimus, *to be depended upon*, Cic.; 3, *true, undoubted, sure;* argumentum odii certius, Cic.; certum est, *it is certain;* est certum quid respondeam, Cic.; aliquid certi est, *something is certain;* si quicquam humanorum certi est, Liv.; certum scio, *I know it for certain;* quamdiu affutura sunt, certum sciri nullo modo potest, Cic.; certum habeo, *I have it for certain*, Cic.; certum inveniri non potest (followed by ne (enclit.) . . . an), Caes.; certum respondeo, Cic.; pro certo scio, Liv.; pro certo habeo, Cic.; pro certo puto, ap. Cic.; pro certo nego, Cic.; polliceor, Cic.; dico, Cic.; affirmo, Liv.; pono, Liv.; creditur, Sall.; ad certum redigere, *to make it certain*, Liv.; certum (as adv.), nondum certum constituerat, Cic.; of persons, certi patres, *undoubted*, Cic.; 4, *certain of a thing;* certi sumus perisse omnia, Cic.; certum facere aliquem, *to inform*, Verg.; in prose, certiorem facere aliquem; with genit., sui consilii, Cic.; with de, de Germanorum discessu, Caes.; with acc. and infin., P. Africanum simulacrum Dianae majoribus suis restituisse, Cic.; with rel. neut., quid egerim, Cic.; with subj. (without a particle), paulisper intermitteret proelium, *gives orders to*, etc., Cic.

cērŭla -ae, f. (dim. of cera), *a little piece of wax;* miniata, *a kind of red pencil for marking errors in MSS.*, Cic.; cerulas tuas miniatulas extimescebam, *criticisms*, Cic.

cerva -ae, f. (cervus), *a hind*, Liv.; poet., *deer*, Verg.

cervārĭus -a -um (cervus), *relating to deer*, Plin.

cervīcal -ālis n. (cervix), *a cushion for the head, a pillow, bolster*, Plin.

cervīcŭla -ae, f. (dim. of cervix), *a little neck*, Cic.

cervīnus -a -um (cervus), *relating to a stag;* pellis, Hor.; senectus, *extreme old age*, because the stag was believed to be very long-lived, Juv.

cervix -īcis, f. *the nape of the neck, the neck.* **I.** Of living beings, Cic.; alicui cervicem frangere, *to break the neck of any one*, Cic.; dare cervices alicui, *to submit to death*, Cic.; also, cervices securi subjicere, Cic.; fig., imponere in cervicibus alicuius sempiternum dominium, *to lay the yoke of mastery on*, Cic.; in cervicibus alicuius esse, *to be in burdensome and dangerous proximity*, Liv. **II.** Used of inanimate things, amphorae, Mart.; Peloponnesi, *the Isthmus of Corinth*, Plin.

cervus -i, m. (κεραός), *a stag.* **A.** Lit., Cic. **B.** Transf., cervi, military t.t., *branches of trees stuck in the ground as a palisade, to impede the advance of an enemy*, Caes.

cespes, v. caespes.

cessātĭo -ōnis, f. (cesso), **1**, *a delaying*, Plaut.; **2**, *inactivity, cessation, laziness, leaving off, idleness;* libera atque otiosa, Cic.

cessātor -ōris, m. (cesso), *one who loiters and lingers;* cessatorem esse solere, praesertim in litteris, Cic.

cessĭo -ōnis, f. (cedo), *a giving up, a cession;* legal t.t., in jure cessio, *a fictitious surrender*, Cic.

cesso, 1. (freq. of cedo). **I.** Lit., *to leave off, linger, delay, cease;* si tabellarii non cessarint, Cic. **II.** Transf., **1**, *to loiter, to be idle;* a, quid cessarent, Liv.; in suo studio atque opere, Cic.; **b**, *to be negligent in one's duty*, Hor.; **2**, a, *to rest, to take rest;* non nocte, non die unquam cessaverunt ab opere, Liv.; non cessare with infin., *not to cease;* ille in Achaia non cessat de nobis detrahere, Cic.; **b**, *to be idle, make holiday, do nothing;* cur tam multos deos nihil agere et cessare patitur, Cic.; cessasse Letoidos aras, *remained unvisited*, Ov.; of land, *to lie fallow;* alternis cessare novales, Verg.

cestrosphendŏnē -ēs, f. (κεστροσφενδόνη), *an engine for hurling stones*, Liv.

1. cestus -i, m. (κεστός), *a girdle*, esp. *the girdle of Venus*, Mart.

2. cēstus -ūs, m. v. caestus.

cētārĭus -a -um (cetus), *relating to sea-fish*, particularly *to the tunny-fish.* **I.** Adj., Tac. **II.** Subst. **A.** cētārĭus -ii, m. *a fishmonger, a dealer in sea-fish*, particularly *tunny-fish*, Ter. **B.** cētārĭa -ae, f. and cētārĭum -ii, n. (κητεία), *a bay in the sea where the tunny-fish collected and were caught*, Hor.

cēte, v. cetus.

cētĕrōqui or **cētĕrōquin**, adv. *otherwise, else*, Cic.

cētĕrus -a -um (= ἕτερος), *the other, the rest;* (sing. only used collectively, cetera classis, Liv.; nom. sing. masc. not found); usually found in the plur. **cētĕri** -ae -a; omnes ceterae res, Cic.; et cetera or simply cetera, *and so on*, Cic.; adv., ceterum, *for the rest, moreover*, Cic.; cetera, *besides*, Cic.; so, de cetero, Cic.; ad cetera, Liv.

Cĕthēgus -i, m. *the name of an old patrician family of the gens Cornelia, to which belonged C. Cornelius Cethegus, a conspirator with Catiline, put to death by Cicero.*

cētra -ae, f. *a small Spanish shield*, Verg., Liv.

cētrātus -a -um (cetra), *armed with the cetra*, Caes., Liv.

cette, v. cĕdo.

cētus (κῆτος), -i, m. and cētos, plur. cēte, n (κήτεα, contr. κήτη), *any large sea-fish, the whale, dolphin;* used esp. of *the tunny-fish*, Verg.

ceu, adv. (contr. from ce-ve, as neu from neve), *as, like as;* ceu quum, *as when*, Verg.; ceu si, *as if*, Verg.; esp. in comparison, *as if;* per aperta volans, ceu liber habenis, aequora, Verg.

Ceutrōnes -um, acc. -as, m. **1**, *a people in Gallia provincia;* **2**, *a people in Gallia Belgica.*

Cēyx -ўcis, m. (Κήϋξ). **I.** *king of Trachin, husband of Alcyone, changed with her into a kingfisher*, Ov. **II.** Plur., appel. **cēyces** -um, m., *the male kingfishers*, Plin.

Chaerōnēa -ae, f. (Χαιρώνεια), *a town in Boeotia, birth-place of Plutarch, scene of a victory of Philip of Macedon over the Athenians.*

Chalcĭoecŏs -i, f. (Χαλκίοικας, *with the brazen house*, name of the Greek Athena), *the temple of Minerva.*

Chalcĭŏpē -ēs, f. (Χαλκιόπη), *daughter of Aeetes, sister of Medea, wife of Phryxus.*

Chalcis -ĭdis, f. (Χαλκίς), *the chief city of Euboea, on the banks of the Euripus;* hence adj., **Chalcĭdĭcus** -a -um, *Chalcidian;* versus, *poems of Euphorion, born at Chalcis*, Verg.; arx, *Cumae, said to have been a colony of Chalcis*, Verg.; **Chalcĭdensis** -e, *Chalcidian.*

chalcītis -ĭdis, f. (χαλκῖτις), *copper ore*, Plin.

Chaldaea -ae, f. (Χαλδαία), *the south-west part of Babylonia from the Euphrates to the Arabian desert, the inhabitants of which were famous for astrology and soothsaying;* hence, a, **Chaldaeus** -a -um, *Chaldaean;* subst., **Chaldaei** -orum, m. (Χαλδαῖοι), *soothsayers*, Cic.; **b**, **Chaldaeĭcus** -a -um, *Chaldaic.*

chălўbēĭus -a -um, *made of steel*, Ov.

Chălўbes -um, m. (Χάλυβες), *a people in Pontus, famous for their steel.*

chălybs -ўbis, m. (χάλυψ). **A.** *steel;* vulnificus, Verg. **B.** Meton., *articles made of steel; a sword*, Sen.; *a horse's bit*, Lucr.; *the tip of an arrow*, Lucr.

chamaelĕon -ōnis and -ontis m. (χαμαιλέων), *the chamaeleon*, Plin.

Chāŏnes -um, m. (Χάονες), *a people of northwestern Epirus;* hence adj., **Chāŏnius** -a -um, *Epirote;* pater, *Jupiter, whose oracle was at Dodona*, Verg.; **Chāŏnis** -ĭdis, f. *Chaonian;* ales, *the pigeon of Dodona*, Ov.; arbos, *the oak*, Ov. **Chāŏnĭa** -ae, f. *the district of Chaonia.*

chăos, acc. chaos, abl. chao (other cases not found), n. (χάος), **1**, *the lower world*, Ov.; personified, *the father of Night and Erebus*, Verg.; **2**, *the shapeless mass out of which the universe was made, chaos*, Ov.

chara -ae, f. *a root, perhaps wild cabbage*, Caes.

Chărĭstĭa (cărĭstĭa) -ōrum, n. (χαρίστια), *a festival celebrated among the Romans on the 22nd of February, the chief object of which was the reconcilement of family disagreements*, Ov.

Chărĭtes -um, f. (Χάριτες), *the Graces* (pure Lat. Gratiae), *Aglaia, Euphrosyne, and Thalia*, Ov.

Charmădās -ae, m. (Χαρμάδας), *a disciple of Carneades, belonging to the Academic school* (teaching at Athens, 109 B.C.).

Chăron -ontis, m. (Χάρων), *Charon, the ferryman, who took the souls of the dead over the river Styx.*

Chărondās -ae, m. (Χαρώνδας), *a celebrated*

legislator of Catana, living about the middle of the seventh century B.C.

charta -ae, f. (χάρτης), *a leaf of the Egyptian papyrus, paper.* **I. A.** Lit., charta dentata, *smoothed*, Cic. **B.** Meton., a, *the papyrus plant*, Plin.; b, *that which is written upon it, a letter, poem*, etc.; ne charta nos prodat, Cic. **II.** Transf., *a thin leaf of any substance;* plumbea, Suet.

chartŭla -ae, f. (dim. of charta), *a little paper, a small writing*, Cic.

Chărybdis -is, f. (Χάρυβδις), *a dangerous whirlpool in the Sicilian straits, opposite the rock Scylla*, Cic.; fig., *anything voracious, greedy, or destructive;* Charybdim bonorum, voraginem potius dixerim, Cic.; quanta laborabas Charybdi, Hor.

Chatti (Catthi, Catti) -ōrum, m. (Χάττοι), *a German people* (in modern Hesse).

Chauci -ōrum, m. *a German people on the sea-coast.*

chēlē -ēs, f. (χηλή), plur. chelae, *the arms of the Scorpion in the signs of the Zodiac*, and (since these reach into the constellation of Libra) *Libra*, Verg.

Chĕlĭdŏnĭae insulae, *islands on the coast of Lycia* (lit. *swallow islands*), facing the Chelidoniarum or Chelidonium promontorium.

chĕlўdrus -i, m. (χέλυδρος), *an amphibious snake*, Verg.

chĕlys, acc. -ym and -yn, voc. -y, f. (χέλυς), 1, *the tortoise*, Petr.; and hence, 2, *the lyre made of its shell* (pure Latin, testudo), Ov.

Cherrŏnēsus and **Chersŏnēsus** -i, f. (Χερρόνησος), 1, *a peninsula*, Cic.; 2, Thracia, *the Thracian peninsula on the Hellespont*, Cic.

Chĕrusci -ōrum, m. *a people in North Germany.*

chĭlĭarchus -i, m. (χιλίαρχης), 1, *a commander of 1,000 soldiers*, Tac.; 2, among the Persians, *the chancellor*, or *prime minister*, Nep.

Chĭmaera -ae, f. (χίμαιρα, *a goat*), *a fire-breathing monster with the fore parts of a lion, the middle of a goat, and the hind parts of a dragon, killed by Bellerophon.* Adj., **Chĭmaereus** -a -um.

chĭmaerĭfĕr -fĕra, -fĕrum (Chimaera and fero), *producing the Chimaera, an epithet of Lycia.*

Chĭŏne -ēs, f. (Χιόνη), 1, *mother of Eumolpus by Neptune;* whence **Chĭŏnĭdes** -ae, m. = Eumolpus, Ov.; 2, *mother of Autolycus by Mercury.*

Chĭos or **Chĭus** -i, f. (Χίος), *an island in the Aegean Sea* (now Scio), *famous for its wine;* hence adj., **Chĭus** -a -um, *Chian;* vinum, Plaut.; or subst., **Chĭum** -i, n. *Chian wine*, Hor.; **Chĭi** -orum, m. *the Chians*, Cic.

chĭragra -ae, f. (χειράγρα), *the gout in the hands*, Hor., Mart.

chĭrŏgrăphum -i, n. (χειρόγραφον), *an autograph, a person's own handwriting;* alicuius chirographum imitari, Cic.

Chĭrōn, Chĭro -ōnis, m. (Χείρων), *a centaur, son of Saturn and Phillyra, the preceptor of Aesculapius, Jason, and Achilles, killed by Hercules.*

chĭrŏnŏmos -i, c., and **chĭrŏnŏmōn** -ontis, m. (χειρονόμος, χειρονομῶν), *one who uses the hands skilfully, a mime*, Juv.

chĭrurgĭa -ae, f. (χειρουργία), *surgery;* fig., sed ego diaetā curare incipio, chirurgiae taedet, *violent remedies*, Cic.

chlămўdātus -a -um (chlamys), *clothed in the chlamys*, Cic.

chlămys -ўd.s, f., and **chlamўda** -ae, f. (χλαμύς), *a large upper garment of wool, often of purple and gold, worn in Greece*, Cic., Verg.

Chlōris -ĭdis, f. (Χλῶρις, *the green one*), a, = Lat. Flora, *the goddess of flowers*, Ov.; b, *a Greek female name*, Hor.

Choerĭlus -i, m. (Χοιρίλος), *a poet who accompanied Alexander the Great in his Persian expedition.*

chŏrāgĭum -ĭi, n. (χορήγιον), *the training of a chorus*, Plaut.

chŏrāgus -i, m. (χορηγός), *he who supplies the chorus and all appurtenances*, Plaut.

chŏraulēs -ae, m. (χοραύλης), *a flute-player*, Mart.

chorda -ae, f. (χορδή), *string, cat-gut* (of a musical instrument), Cic.

chŏrēa -ae, f. (χορεία), *a dance to the sound of the dancers' voices*, Verg.

chŏrēus -i, m., and **chŏrius** -i, m. (χορεῖος) *the metrical foot* — ◡, *afterwards called a trochee* Cic.

chŏrŏcĭthăristēs -ae, m. (χοροκιθαριστής), *one who accompanies a chorus on the cithara*, Suet.

chŏrus -i, m. (χορός). **I.** *a dance in a circle, a choral dance;* agitare, exercere, Verg. **II.** Meton., *the persons singing and dancing, the chorus*, Cic. **A.** Lit., Dryadum, Verg.; Nereidum, Verg.; *the chorus of a tragedy*, Hor. **B.** Transf., *a crowd, troop of any kind;* Catilinam stipatum choro juventutis, Cic.

Chrēmes -mētis, m. *an old miser in several of the plays of Terence.*

Christĭānus -i, m. (Χριστιανός), *a Christian*, Tac.

Christus -i, m. (Χριστός), *Christ*, Tac., Plin

chrŏmis -is, m. (χρόμις), *a sea-fish*, Ov.

Chrȳsa -ae, f. and **Chrȳsē** -ēs, f. (Χρύση), *a town in Mysia, near which was a temple of Apollo Smintheus.*

Chrȳsās -ae, m. *a river in Sicily, now Dittaino.*

Chrȳsēs -ae, m. (Χρύσης), *the priest of Apollo at Chrysa, whose daughter was carried off by the Greeks;* hence, **Chrȳsēis** -ĭdos, f. (Χρυσηΐς). *the daughter of Chryses = Astynome.*

Chrȳsippus -i, m. (Χρύσιππος), 1, Stoic *philosopher of Soli in Cilicia*, b. 282, B.C.; 2, *a freedman of Cicero's.* Adj., **Chrȳsippeus** -a -um, *of or belonging to Chrysippus.*

Chrȳsis -ĭdis, f. (Χρυσίς), *name of one of the female characters in the Andria of Terence.*

chrȳsŏlĭthus -i, m. and f. (χρυσόλιθος), *chrysolite*, or *topaz*, Plin.

chrȳsŏphrys, acc. -yn, f. (χρύσοφρυς), *a kind of sea-fish with a golden spot over each eye*, Ov.

chrȳsos -i, m. (χρυσός), *gold*, Plaut.

chus, v. congius.

cĭbārĭus -a -um (cibus), *relating to food.* **A.** Lit., uva; *used for eating only*, not for wine, Plaut. Subst., **cĭbārĭa** -orum, n. *food, rations, fodder; corn allowed to provincial magistrates*, Cic.; *rations for soldiers*, Caes. **B.** Meton. (from the food usually given to servants), *ordinary, common;* panis, *black bread*, Cic.

cĭbātus -ūs, m. (cibo), *food nourishment*, Plaut.

cĭbo, 1. (cibus), *to feed*, Suet.

cĭbōrĭum -ĭi, n. (κιβώριον), and **cĭbōrĭa** -ae, f. literally, *the seed pod of the Egyptian bean;* and hence, *a large drinking-vessel of similar shape*, Hor.

cĭbus -i, m. *food for man and beast, nourishment, fodder.* **I.** Lit., **A.** Gen., cibum sumere, Nep.; subducere, Cic. **B.** Esp., **a,** animalis, *nourishment that the lungs draw from the air,* Cic.; **b,** *bait;* fallax, Ov. **II.** Transf., *sustenance;* quasi quidam humanitatis cibus, Cic.

Cĭbȳra -ae, f. (Κιβύρα), *a town in Pisidia;* hence, **A. Cĭbȳrātēs** -ae, c. *of Cibyra.* **B. Cĭbȳrātĭcus** -a -um, *of or belonging to Cibyra.*

cĭcāda -ae, f. *a cicada,* or *tree cricket,* Verg.; expectate cicadas, *summer,* Juv.

cĭcātrīcōsus -a -um (cicatrix), *covered with scars,* Plaut.

cĭcātrix -īcis, f. *a scar, cicatrice;* adverse or exceptae corpore adverso, *wounds received in front,* and therefore *honourable,* Cic.; *the marks of incisions in plants,* Verg.; *the patch upon an old shoe,* Juv.; fig., refricare obductam jam reipublicae cicatricem, Cic.

cĭccum -i, n. (κίκκος), *the core of a pomegranate;* hence *something worthless;* ciccum non interduim, Plaut.

cĭcer -ĕris, n. *a chick-pea,* Hor.

Cĭcĕro -ōnis, m. *name of a family of the gens Tullia,* to which belonged, **1,** M. Tullius Cicero, *the greatest Roman orator and writer, born* A.C. 106, *at Arpinum, murdered at the command of Antonius* A.C. 43; **2,** Qu. Tullius Cicero, *brother of the above.* Hence adj., **Cĭcĕrōnĭānus** -a -um, *Ciceronian.*

Cĭcōnes -um, m. (Κίκονες), *a Thracian people.*

cĭcōnĭa -ae, f. **1,** *a stork,* Hor., Ov.; **2,** *a gesture of ridicule, made by bending the fore-finger into the shape of a stork's neck,* Pers.

cĭcur -ŭris, *tame;* bestia, Cic.

cĭcūta -ae, f. **A.** *hemlock,* Hor. **B.** Meton., **1,** *poison extracted from the hemlock,* Hor.; **2,** *a shepherd's pipe, made from the hemlock stalk,* Verg.

cĭĕo, cīvi, cĭtum, 2. (connected with κίω, κινέω), *to cause to move, to move, shake.* **I. a,** natura omnia ciens et agitans motibus et mutationibus suis, Cic.; **b,** legal t.t., herctum ciere, *to divide the inheritance,* Cic.; **c,** pugnam ciere, *to give new impulse to the battle,* Liv.; **d,** *to disturb, agitate;* mare venti et aurae cient, Liv.; **e,** *to summon to battle;* aliquem ad arma, Liv.; **f,** *to summon to help;* nocturnos manes carminibus, Verg. **II. a,** *to excite, to arouse;* procellas proelia atque acies, Liv.; seditiones, Liv.; **b,** *to utter;* gemitus, Verg.; **c,** *to call by name;* aliquem magna voce, Verg.; patrem, *name one's father,* i.e., *prove one's free birth,* Liv.

Cĭlĭcĭa -ae, f. (Κιλικία), *a country of Asia Minor;* hence adj., **1, Cĭlix** -īcis, *Cilician;* pl. **Cĭlĭces** -um, m. *the Cilicians;* **Cĭlissa** -ae, f., *Cilician;* spica, *saffron,* Ov.; **2, Cĭlĭcĭus** -a -um, *Cilician.* Subst., **Cĭlĭcĭum** -ii, n. *a coarse cloth, or covering made of Cilician goats' hair.*

cĭlĭum -ii, n. *the eye-lid,* Plin.

Cilla -ae, acc. -an, f. (Κίλλα), *a town in Aeolis.*

Cilnĭus -a -um, Cilnia gens, *a distinguished Etruscan family, from which Maecenas was descended.*

Cimbri -ōrum, m. (Κίμβροι), *the Cimbrians, a German tribe who invaded the Roman Empire and were defeated by Marius;* sing., **Cimber** -bri, m. *a Cimbrian.* Adj., **Cimbrĭcus** -a -um, *Cimbrian.*

cīmex -īcis, m. *a bug,* Cat.; as a term of reproach, Hor.

Cīmĭnus -i, m. and **Cīmĭnĭus** lacus, *a lake in Etruria near to a mountain of the same name.*

Cimmĕrĭi -ōrum, m. (Κιμμέριοι). **I.** *a Thracian people, living on the Dnieper.* Adj., **Cimmĕrĭus** -a -um, *Cimmerian.* **II.** *a mythical people, living in the extreme west in darkness and mist.* Adj., **Cimmĕrĭus** -a -um, *Cimmerian* = *dark;* lacus, *the lower world,* Tib.

Cīmōlus -i, f. (Κίμωλος), *one of the Cyclades Islands.*

Cīmōn -ōnis, m. (Κίμων), *an Athenian general.*

cĭnaedĭcus -a -um (cinaedus), *unchaste,* Plaut.

cĭnaedus -i, m. (κίναιδος), *one who indulges in unnatural lust,* **a,** Plaut., Cat. Adj., **cĭnaedus** -a -um = *bold, shameless;* homo cinaeda fronte, Mart.; **b,** *a wanton dancer,* Plaut.

Cĭnăra -ae, f. (Κινάρα), **a,** *an island in the Aeguean Sea;* **b,** *a woman's name,* Hor.

1. cincinnātus -a -um (cincinnus), *having curled hair,* Cic.; *of comets, stellae eas quas Graeci cometas, nostri cincinnatas vocant,* Cic.

2. Cincinnātus -i, m. *the name of a patrician family of the gens Quinctia,* to which belonged L. Quinctius Cincinnatus, *a type of old Roman honesty and simplicity, consul 460* B.C., *in 458* B.C. *called from the plough to be dictator.*

cincinnus -i, m. (κίκιννος). **A.** *curled hair, a lock of hair,* Cic. **B.** Transf., *artificial rhetorical ornament,* Cic.

Cincĭus -a -um, *name of a Roman gens.* **I.** L. Cincius Alimentus, *annalist at the time of the Second Punic War.* **II.** M. Cincius Alimentus, *tribune of the people, 205* B.C., *author of the lex Cincia forbidding advocates to receive pay.*

cinctūra -ae, f. (cingo), *a girdle,* Suet.

cinctus -ūs, m. (cingo), *a girding;* **1,** Gabinus, *a particular way of wearing the toga, at religious festivals, in which one end was thrown over the head, and the other passed round the waist, so as to look like a girdle,* Liv.; **2,** *a girdle,* Suet.

cinctūtus -a -um (cinctus), *girded,* Hor., Ov.

cĭnĕfactus -a -um (cinis and facio), *changed into ashes,* Lucr.

cĭnĕrārĭus -ii, m. (cinis), *a slave who heated in hot ashes the irons for the hair-dresser,* Cat.

Cinga -ae, m. *a tributary of the Iberus in Hispania Tarraconensis,* now *Cinca.*

Cingĕtŏrix -rĭgis, m. **I.** *a prince of the Treveri in Gaul.* **II.** *a prince in Britain.*

cingo, cinxi, cinctum, 3. *to surround.* **I.** in a narrow sense, **1,** *to surround the body with a girdle, to gird;* pass. cingi, as middle, *to gird oneself;* **a,** cincta conjux Dialis, Ov.; **b,** *to gird oneself with a weapon;* ense, Ov.; gladio, Liv.; poet. with acc., inutile ferrum cingitur, Verg.; hence cingor, *to be prepared, ready,* Plaut.; **2,** *to surround the head with a chaplet, to crown;* cinge tempora lauro, Hor.; anuli cingunt lacertos, Mart. **II.** in a wider sense, *to surround, encircle;* **1,** of localities, *to surround, inclose;* tellus oras maris undique cingens, Lucr.; colles cingunt oppidum, Caes.; milit. t. t., *to surround with hostile intent or for protection;* hiberna castra vallo, Caes.; urbem obsidione, Caes.; transf., Sicilia multis undique cincta periculis, Cic.; **2,** *to surround a person in society, accompany;* cingere alicui latus, Liv.; **3,** *to circle round a place;* polum coetu (of swans), Verg.

cingŭla -ae, f. (cingo), *a girdle,* Ov.

1. cingŭlum -i, n. (cingo), *a girdle, a sword-belt* (plur.), Verg.

2. Cingŭlum -i, n. *a town in Picenum.*

cingŭlus -i, m. (cingo), *a girdle of the earth, a zone,* Cic.

cĭnĭflo -ōnis, m. = cinerarius, Hor.

cĭnis -ĕris, m., rarely f. (connected with κόνις), *ashes*. **I.** Lit., **A.** Gen., in cinerem dilabi, *to become ashes*, Hor.; from the use of ashes for scouring came the prov. huius sermo cinerem haud quaeritat, Plaut. **B.** Esp., 1, *the ashes of a corpse after being burned ;* cinis atque ossa alicuius, Cic.; 2, *ruins of a city that has been burnt ;* patriae cineres, Verg. **II.** Transf., as *a symbol of destruction ;* Troja virûm atque virtutum omnium acerba cinis, *the grave*, Cat.

Cinna -ae, m. *the name of a family of the Cornelii and Helvii.* **I.** L. Cornelius Cinna, *partisan of Marius in the civil war against Sulla, noted for his cruelty.* Adj., **Cinnānus** -a -um, *Cinnan.* **II.** *son of* I., *one of Caesar's murderers.* **III.** *son of* II., *twice pardoned by Augustus.* **IV.** C. Helvius Cinna, *a poet, the friend of Catullus.*

cinnămōmum or **cinnămum** -i, n. (κιννάμωμον, κίνναμον), *cinnamon*, Ov.; *as a term of endearment*, Plaut.

Cĭnyps -ўphis, m. (Κίνυψ), *a river in Libya, between the two Syrtes ;* hence adj., **Cĭnўphius** -a -um, 1, *relating or belonging to the Cinyps*, Verg.; 2, *African*, Ov.

Cĭnўras -ae, m. (Κινύρας), *a mythical king of Assyria or Cyprus, father of Myrrha, and by her of Adonis.* Adj., **Cĭnўrēĭus** -a -um, *Cinyrean ;* virgo, *Myrrha*, Ov.; juvenis, *Adonis*, Ov.

Cĭos and **Cĭus** -ii, f. (ἡ Κίος), *a town in Bithynia, now Ghio ;* hence, **Cĭāni** -ōrum, m. *the inhabitants of Cios.*

cippus -i, m. 1, *a tombstone or small tomb*, Hor.; 2, plur. milit. t. t., *palisades*, Caes.

circā (contr. for circum ea). **I.** Adv., *round about ;* gramen erat circa, Ov.; hence, circa esse, *to be round about, in the neighbourhood*, Liv.; sometimes directly connected with the subst. without esse, multarum circa civitatum, Liv.; omnia circa or circa undique, *all things around*, Liv. **II.** Prep. with acc., 1, of space, a, *around, at the side of ;* ligna contulerunt circa casam, Nep.; b, *round about to ;* legatos circa vicinas gentes misit, Liv.; c, *in the neighbourhood of, near to ;* templa circa forum, Cic.; d, *around or in company of a person ;* trecentos juvenes circa se habebat, Liv.; 2, of time, *about ;* circa eandem horam, Liv.; lucem, Suet.; Demetrium, *about the time of Demetrius*, Quint.; 3, of number = circiter, *about ;* ea fuere oppida circa septuaginta, Liv.; 4, *about, in respect to ;* circa bonas artes publica socordia, Tac.

circāmoerĭum -ii, n. = pomoerium (q.v.), Liv.

Circē -ēs and -ae, acc. -am, abl. -a, f. (Κίρκη), *an enchantress who lived in the neighbourhood of Circeji, where she turned her victims into swine, mother of Telegonus by Ulysses ;* hence adj., **Circaeus** -a -um, *Circean ;* poculum, *enchanted*, Cic.; moenia, *Tusculum, said to have been built by Telegonus*, Hor.; litus, *the promontory of Circeji*, Ov.

Circēji -ōrum, m. *the town of Circeji on a promontory of the same name in Latium.* Adj., **Circējensis** -e, *of or belonging to Circeji.*

circensis -e (circus), *belonging to the circus ;* ludi, *the games in the circus*, Cic. Subst., **circenses** -ium, m. (sc. ludi), *the circus games*, Sen.

circĭno, 1. (circinus), *to make round, to form into a circle*, Plin.; poet., easdem circinat auras, *flies through in a circle*, Ov.

circĭnus -i, m. (κίρκινος), *a pair of compasses for describing a circle*, Caes.

circĭtĕr, adv. (circus). **I.** Of place, *about, near*, Plaut. **II.** Transf., 1, of time, a, adv.

with abl., media circiter nocte, Caes.; b, prep. with acc., circiter Calendas, Cic.; 2, of number, *about ;* circiter CCXX naves, Caes.

circlus = circulus (q.v.).

circŭeo, v. circumeo.

circŭĭtĭo and **circŭmĭtĭo** -ōnis, f. (circueo, circumeo), 1, *a going round ;* milit. t. t. *patrol*, Liv.; 2, *a roundabout way of speaking or acting ;* quid opus est circumitione et amfractu, Cic.

circŭĭtus (circŭmĭtus), -ūs, m. (circueo = circumeo), *a going round in a circle, circuit, revolution.* **I.** Abstract., **A.** Lit., circuitus orbis, Cic. **B.** Transf., miri sunt orbes et quasi circuitus in rebus publicis commutationum et vicissitudinum, Cic. **II.** Concrete, a, *the path traversed in going round, a roundabout way, circuitous course ;* longo circuitu petere aliquem locum, Caes., Liv.; b, in rhetoric, *a period*, Cic.; c, *compass, circumference, extent ;* eius munitionis circuitus XI milia passuum tenebat, Caes.

circŭlātim, adv. (circulor), *circle-wise, in a circle*, Suet.

circŭlor, 1. dep. (circulus), a, *to gather in groups for conversation*, Caes.; b, *to enter a group, to converse*, Cic.

circŭlus (syncop. circlus) -i, m. (dim. of circus), *a circle, circular figure.* **I.** circulus aut orbis, qui κύκλος Graece dicitur, Cic.; priusquam hoc circulo excedas, Liv.; hence, *the orbit of a planet ;* stellae circulos suos orbesque conficiunt celeritate mirabili, Cic. **II.** Esp., a, *any circular body ;* flexilis obtorti circulus auri, poet. = a *golden collar*, Verg.; circulus muri exterior, Liv.; b, *a circle or group for conversation ;* circulos aliquos et sessiunculas consectari, Cic.

circum (prop. acc. of circus = κίρκος, *in a circle*). **I.** Adv. *round about, around ;* quae circum essent, Caes.; circum sub moenibus, Verg.; circum undique, *round about, on all sides*, Verg. **II.** Prep. with acc. **A.** *round about ;* terra circum axem se convertit, Cic. **B.** *round about, near, in the vicinity of, around ;* circum aliquem esse, *to be in any one's company*, Cic.; habere aliquem circum se, Sall.; circum haec loca commorabor, Cic.; *urbes quae circum Capuam sunt*, Cic.; circum pedes, *in attendance*, Cic.; used with verbs of motion, circum villulas nostras errare, Cic.; legatio circum insulas missa, Liv. (circum sometimes after the subst. which it governs, Cic., often in Verg.).

circumactus -a -um, partic. of circumago.

circŭmăgo -ēgi -actum, 3. **I. A.** *to drive or turn round, to drive in a circle*, hence a technical term for the manumission of a slave, because his master took him by the right hand, and turned him round, Sen. **B.** Transf., of time, circumagi or circumagere se, *to pass away, to be spent ;* annus se circumegit, Liv. **II.** *to turn or twist round.* **A.** Lit., equos frenis, Liv.; circumagente se vento, Liv. **B.** Transf., quo te circumagas? *how wilt thou evade the difficulty ?* Juv. **III.** *to lead or drive about from one place to another.* **A.** Lit., huc illuc clamoribus hostium circumagi, Tac.; nihil opus est te circumagi, *follow me about*, Hor. **B.** Transf.. *to drive about, distract, mislead ;* rumoribus vulgi circumagi, Liv.

circumăro, *to plough round*, Liv.

circumcaesūra ae, f. *the external outline of a body*, Lucr.

circumcīdo -cīdi -cīsum, 3. (circum and caedo), *to cut round, to cut, trim.* **A.** Lit., aras agricolarum quae circumcidat, Cic.; caespitem gladiis, Caes. **B.** Transf., *to make less, by cutting, diminish, cut off ;* multitudinem, Cic.; sumptus, Liv.

circumcircā, adv., *all round about*, ap. Cic., Plaut.

circumcisus -a -um, p. adj. (from circumcido), of localities, *abrupt, steep, inaccessible*, saxum, Cic.; collis ex omni parte circumcisus, Caes.

circumclūdo -clūsi -clūsum, 3. 1, *to shut in, enclose on all sides, surround;* cornua argento, Caes; 2, *to surround* in a hostile manner; circumcludi duobus exercitibus, Caes.; transf., Catilina meis praesidiis, meā diligentiā circumclusus, Cic.

circumcŏlo, 3. *to dwell around, dwell near,* Liv.

circumcurso, 1. (intens. of circumcurro), *to run round*, Plaut., Lucr., Cat.

circumdo -dĕdi -dătum, 1, *surround.* **I. A.** *to put something round something else;* with acc., of the thing placed, and dat., of the thing round which it is placed, tectis ac moenibus subjicere ignes circumdareque, Cic.; arma humeris, Verg.; in tmesis, collo dare brachia circum, Verg. **B.** Transf. *to supply,* paci egregiam famam, Tac. **C.** *to build* or *place round;* murum, Caes.; equites cornibus, Liv. **II.** *to surround something with something else;* with acc. and abl. **A.** Lit. animum corpore, Liv.; tempora vittis, Ov.; regio insulis circumdata, Cic. **B.** *to surround* in a hostile manner; omnem aciem suam redis et carris, Caes.; oppidum coronā, Liv. **C.** Transf., exiguis quibusdam finibus totum oratoris munus, Cic.

circumdūco -duxi -ductum, 3. **I.** *to lead round, move* or *drive round.* **A.** exercitum, Plaut.; aratrum (of the founding of a colony when a plough was driven around the site of the wall), Cic.; flumen ut circino circumductum, Caes. **B.** *to lead round, to lead by a round-about course;* 1, lit., cohortes quatuor longiore itinere, Caes.; absol., praeter castra hostium circumducit, *he marches round,* Liv.; 2, transf., a, *to lead astray, deceive,* Plaut.; b, of discourse, *to extend, amplify,* Quint. **II.** *to lead round about, to take round;* aliquem omnia sua praesidia circumducere, atque ostentare, Caes.

circumductĭo -ōnis, f. (circumduco), *cheating, deceiving,* Plaut.

circumductus -a -um, partic. of circumduco.

circŭmĕo (circŭĕo) -īvi or -ĭi -ĭtum -īre, *to go, travel,* or *walk round.* **I. A.** Gen., 1, *in a circle;* flagrantes aras, Ov.; hostium castra, Caes.; 2, a, *to go round in a curve;* metam ferventi rota, Ov.; b, transf., (a) *to cheat,* Ter.; (β) *to express by circumlocution;* Vespasiani nomen suspensi et vitabundi circumibant, *avoided mentioning,* Tac. **B.** *to enclose, surround;* aciem a latere aperto, Caes.; fig., in pass., circumiri totius belli fluctibus, Cic. **II.** *to go the round, gᵒ about.* **A.** ipse equo circumiens unum quemque nominans appellat, Sall.; urbem, Liv.; plebem, Liv.; praedia, *to visit,* Cic.; oram maris, Cic.; vigilias, Liv. **B.** Esp., *to go round to canvass* or *solicit;* senatum cum veste sordida, Liv.; circumire ordines et hortari, Caes.

circŭmĕquĭto, 1. *to ride round;* moenia, Liv.

circŭmerro, 1. *to wander round,* Sen.

circumfĕro -tŭli -lātum -ferre, *to carry round, bring round.* **I.** 1, circumferuntur tabulae inspiciendi nominis causa, Cic; poculum circumfertur, Liv.; 2, *to spread around;* circa ea omnia templa infestos ignes, Liv.; incendia et caedes et terrorem, Tac.; bellum, Liv.; 3, *to move round, turn in all directions* (of a part of the body, esp. the eyes); oculos, Liv.; 4,

to spread a report, disseminate news; quae se circumferat esse Corinnam, Ov. **II.** *to carry round* in a circle; 1, middle, sol ut circumferatur, revolves, Cic.; 2, religious t. t., *to lustrate, purify,* by carrying round consecrated objects; socios pura circumtulit unda, Verg.

circumflecto -flexi -flexum, 3. *to bend round, to turn about;* longos cursus, Verg.

circumflo, 1, *to blow round;* fig., ut ab omnibus ventis invidiae circumflari posse videatur, Cic.

circumflŭo -fluxi -fluxum, 3. **I.** *to flow round,* Ov. **II. A.** *to overflow;* fig., nec ea redundans tamen nec circumfluens oratio, *diffuse,* Cic. **B.** Transf. *to abound in;* circumfluere omnibus copiis, Cic.; gloria, Cic.

circumflŭus -a -um (circumfluo), 1, act., *flowing round, circumfluent;* humor, Ov.; 2, pass., *flowed round, surrounded by water;* insula, Ov.

circumfŏrānĕus -a -um (circum and forum), 1, *round the forum;* aes, *money borrowed from the bankers whose shops were round the forum = debt,* Cic.; 2, *attending at markets;* pharmacopola, Cic.

circumfundo -fūdi -fūsum, 3. *to pour around.* **I. A.** Lit., gen. in pass., circumfundi, or reflexive, se circumfundere, *to be poured round = to surround;* with dat., amnis circumfunditur parvae insulae, Liv. **B.** Transf., of persons, refl., se circumfundere, or simply circumfundere, *to flock round;* with dat., equites Hannoni Afrisque se circumfundere, Liv.; so pass., as middle, circumfunditur equitatus Caesaris, Caes.; of things, undique circumfusis molestiis or voluptatibus, Cic. **II.** *to encompass, surround.* **A.** Lit., 1, act., mortuum cera, Nep.; 2, pass., *to be washed by;* parva quaedam insula est circumfusa illo mari quem oceanum appellatis, Cic. **B.** Transf., *to surround, encircle, hem in;* praefectum castrorum et legionarios milites circumfundunt, Tac.; gen. in pass., multis circumfusus Stoicorum libris, Cic.

circumgĕmo, 3. *to growl round about;* ovile, Hor.

circumgesto, 1. *to carry round;* epistolam, Cic.

circumgrĕdĭor -gressus sum -grĕdi (circum and gradior), *to go round, travel round,* especially with hostile intent; exercitum, Sall.; terga, Tac.

circumĭcio = circumjicio (q.v.).

circuminjĭcĭo, 3. *to throw around;* vallum, Liv.

circumjăcĕo, 2. *to lie round about, adjoin;* quaeque circumjacent Europae, Liv.

circumjectus -ūs, m. (circumjicio). **I.** a *surrounding, enclosing;* qui (aether) tenero terram circumjectu amplectitur, Cic. **II.** Meton., ut ita munita arx circumjectu arduo niteretur, Cic.

circumjĭcĭo -jēci -jectum, 3. (circum and jacio); 1, *to throw round, put round;* multitudinem hominum totis moenibus, Caes.; hence of localities, **circumjectus** -a -um, *surrounding, adjacent;* nationes, Tac.; aedificia circumjecta muris, Caes.; 2, aliquid aliquā re, *to surround, enclose with anything,* Cic.; circumjicere extremitatem coeli rotundo ambitu, Cic.

circumlăvo -āre and -ĕre, *to wash round, to overflow round,* Sall.

circumlĭgo, 1. 1, *to bind round, bind to;* natam mediae hastae, Verg.; 2, *to bind round with;* ferrum stuppā, Liv.; circumligatum esse angui, Cic.

circumlĭno, no perf. -lĭtum, 3. and also

circumlĭnĭo -lĭvĭi, 4. 1, *to smear anything on anything;* sulfura taedis, Ov.; 2, *to besmear with anything, to cover;* circumlitus auro, Ov.; circumlita saxa musco, Hor.

circumlŭo, 3. *to wash round, flow round;* quo (mari) in paeninsulae modum pars major (arcis) circumluitur, Liv.

circumlustrans -antis, *illuminating all round,* Lucr.

circumlŭvĭo -ōnis, f. (circumluo), *the formation of an island by the encroachment of a river,* Cic.

circummitto -mīsi -missum, 3. **I.** *to send by a roundabout way, to send round;* tribuno cum duorum signorum militibus circummisso, Liv. **II.** *to send round about, to send in all directions;* legationes, Caes.

circummūnĭo (circummoenio, Plaut.), 4. *to fortify round, to wall round, to shut in by lines of circumvallation;* Uticam vallo, Caes.

circummūnītĭo -ōnis, f. (circummunio), *the investing or circumvallation of a fortress,* Caes.

circumpădānus -a -um, *round about the Po, near the river Po;* campi, Liv.

circumplaudo, 3. *to clap or applaud on all sides;* aliquem, Ov.

circumplector -plexus, 3. dep. *to embrace, enclose, surround;* domini patrimonium circumplexus quasi thesaurum draco, Cic.; collem opere, Caes.

circumplĭco, 1. *to fold round, wind round;* si anguem vectis circumplicavisset, Cic.

circumpōno -pŏsŭi -pŏsĭtum, 3. *to place or put round, encircle;* nemus stagno, Tac.; piper catillis, Hor.

circumpōtātĭo -ōnis, f. (circum and poto), *drinking round in succession,* ap. Cic.

circumrētĭo, 4. (circum and rete), *to enclose in a net, ensnare;* transf., aliquem, Lucr.; te circumretitum frequentiā populi Romani video, Cic.

circumrōdo -rōsi, 3. *to gnaw round;* escam, Plin.; transf., dudum enim circumrodo quod devorandum est, *I have long hesitated to speak out,* Cic.; qui dente Theonino quum circumroditur, *slandered,* Hor.

circumsaepĭo -saeptus, 4. *to hedge round, enclose;* corpus armatis, Liv.

circumscindo, 3. *to tear off, strip;* quo ferocius clamitabat, eo infestius circumscindere et spoliare lictor, Liv.

circumscrībo -scripsi -scriptum, 3. *to describe a circle round, to enclose in a circular line.* **I.** Lit., orbem, Cic.; stantem virgula, Cic. **II.** Transf. **A.** *to draw the outline of an object, to fix the boundaries of;* locum habitandi alicui, Cic. **B.** *to draw together, confine, limit, circumscribe, hamper, restrain;* tribunum plebis, Cic. **C.** 1, *to take in, deceive, circumvent, ensnare;* fallacibus et captiosis interrogationibus circumscripti, Cic.; 2, *to defraud;* adolescentulos, Cic.; vectigalia, *to embezzle,* Quint.; 3, *to put aside as invalid, invalidate, annul;* sententias, Cic.

circumscriptē, adv. (circumscriptus), *in rhetorical periods;* circumscripte numeroseque dicere, Cic.

circumscriptĭo -ōnis, f. (circumscribo), *encircling.* **I.** Lit., concrete, *circumference,* Cic. **II.** Transf. **A.** *outline, boundary;* 1, gen., terrae, Cic.; temporis, *limit,* Cic.; 2, in rhetoric, *a period,* Cic. **B.** *deceit, swindling, defrauding,* esp. in pecuniary matters; adolescentium, Cic.

circumscriptor -ōris, m. (circumscribo), *a cheat, swindler,* Cic.

circumscriptus -a -um, p. adj. (from circumscribo), *concise;* brevis et circumscripta quaedam explicatio, Cic.

circumsĕco -sectum, 1. *to cut round about;* aliquid serra, Cic.

circumsĕdĕo -sēdi -sessum, 2. **I.** Gen., *to sit round,* Sen. **II.** Esp., *to surround with hostile intent, besiege, beleaguer;* aliquem vallo, Cic.; transf., a lacrimis omnium circumsessus, assailed, Cic.

circumsessĭo -ōnis, f. (circumsedeo), *an encircling with hostile intent, a beleaguering,* Cic.

circumsīdo -sēdi, 3. *to sit down before c place, besiege;* oppidum, Sall.

circumsĭlĭo, 4. (circum and salio), *to leap,* or *jump round;* (passer) circumsiliens, Cat.; transf., *to surround;* morborum omne genus, Juv.

circumsisto -stĕti, or (more rarely) -stĭti, 3. *to place oneself round, to surround.* **A.** Gen., aliquem, Caes. **B.** Esp., *to surround hostilely, press round;* plures paucos circumsistebant, Caes.; sex lictores circumsistunt, Cic.

circumsŏno -sŏnŭi -sŏnātum, 1, a, *to sound around;* clamor hostes circumsonat, Liv.; b, *to echo with;* locus qui circumsonat ululatibus, Liv.; talibus aures tuas vocibus undique circumsonare, Cic.

circumsŏnus -a -um (circumsono), *sounding around;* turba canum, Ov.

circumspectātrix -īcis, f. (circumspecto), *a female who looks round about,* Plaut.

circumspectĭo -ōnis, f. (circumspicio), *foresight, circumspection, caution;* circumspectio aliqua et accurata consideratio, Cic.

circumspecto, 1. (freq. of circumspicio), *to look around.* **I.** Intransit., *to look round repeatedly;* circumspectant bestiae in pastu, Cic.; fig., dubitans, circumspectans, haesitans, Cic. **II.** Transit. **a,** *to look round at,* esp. with anxiety or suspicion; omnia, Cic.; patriciorum vultus, Liv.; **b,** *to look round to seek for something or somebody;* circumspectare omnibus fori partibus senatorem raroque usquam noscitare, Liv.; **c,** *to wait for, watch for;* defectionis tempus, Liv.

1. circumspectus -a -um, p. adj. with compar. and superl. (from circumspicio), 1, pass., of things, *deliberate, well considered;* verba circumspecta, Ov.; 2, active, of persons, *circumspect, cautious,* Sen.

2. circumspectus -ūs, m. (circumspicio), 1, *looking round,* Plin.; transf., *attention to;* detinere aliquem ab circumspectu rerum aliarum, Liv.; 2, *prospect, view on every side,* Cic.

circumspĭcĭo -spexi -spectum, 3. *to look round.* **I.** Intransit. **A.** qui in auspicium adhibetur nec suspicit nec circumspicit, Cic.; circumspicit (looks round anxiously), aestuat, Cic. **B.** Transf., *to consider;* circumspicite celeriter animo qui sint rerum exitus consecuti, Cic. **II.** Transit., *to look round at.* **A.** 1, lit., urbis situm, Liv.; 2, transf., *to consider carefully;* omnia pericula, Cic. **B.** *to look around for;* 1, lit., Caes.; saxum ingens, Verg.; 2, transf., *to look for, seek for;* externa auxilia, Tac.

circumsto -stĕti, 1. **I.** *to stand round* or *in a circle, to surround, encircle;* sellam, Liv.; hence partic. subst., circumstantes, *the bystanders,* Liv. **II.** *to surround with hostile intent, to beleaguer.* **A.** Lit., circumstare tribunal praetoris urbani, obsidere cum gladiis curiam, Cic. **B.** Transf., quum tanti undique terrores circumstarent, Liv.

circumstrĕpo -strĕpŭi -strĕpĭtum, 3. *to roar, make a noise round, shout clamorously around;* legatus clamore seditiosorum circumstrepitur, Tac.; with acc., quidam atrociora circumstrepebant, Tac.

circumstrŭo -struxi -structum, 3. *to build round*, Suet.

circumsurgens -entis, *rising round*, Tac.

circumtĕgo, 3. *to cover all round*, Lucr. (?).

circumtĕro, 3. *to rub against on all sides;* poet., *to crowd round*, Tib.

circumtextus -a -um, *woven all round;* circumtextum croceo velamen acantho, Verg.

circumtŏno -tŏnŭi, 1. *to thunder round;* qua totum Nereus circumtonat orbem, Ov.

circumtonsus -a -um, 1, *shaven or shorn all round*, Suet.; 2, transf., of discourse, *artificial*, Sen.

circumvādo -vāsi, 3. *to attack from every side, to surround.* **I.** Lit., immobiles naves circumvadunt, Liv. **II.** Transf., cum terror circumvasisset aciem, Liv.

circumvăgus -a -um, *wandering round, or in a circle;* Oceanus, Hor.

circumvăllo, 1. *to surround with a wall, or fortification, to blockade, beleaguer;* oppidum, Caes.; Pompeium, Cic.; fig., tot res repente circumvallant, Ter.

circumvectĭo -ōnis, f. (circumvehor), 1, *a carrying round of merchandise;* portorium circumvectionis, *transit dues*, Cic.; 2, solis, *circuit, revolution*, Cic.

circumvector, 1. dep. (intens. of circumvehor), 1, *to ride or sail round;* Ligurum oras, Liv.; 2, poet., *to go through, describe;* singula dum circumvectamur, Verg.

circumvĕhor -vectus, 3. dep., 1, *to ride or sail round;* jubet circumvectos (equites), ab tergo Gallicam invadere aciem, Liv.; navibus circumvecti, Caes.; with acc., cum classe Corsicae oram, Liv.; transf., frustra circumvehor omnia verbis, *try to describe at once*, Verg.; 2, *to ride or sail in every direction*, Liv.

circumvēlo, 1. *to veil or conceal on all sides;* aurato circumvelatur amictu, Ov.

circumvĕnĭo -vēni -ventum, 4. *to come round, surround, encircle.* **I.** Gen. **A.** Of persons, homines circumventi flamma, Caes. **B.** Of places, Rhenus modicas insulas circumveniens, Tac. **II.** *to surround with hostile intent.* **A.** Lit., 1, of persons, hostes a tergo, Caes.; 2, of things, cuncta moenia exercitu, Sall. **B.** Transf., 1, *to beset, oppress, assail;* aliquem judicio capitis, Cic.; 2, *to cheat;* innocentem pecunia, Cic.

circumversor, 1. dep., *to twist or turn round*, Lucr.

circumverto (-vorto) -verti (-vorti) -versum (-vorsum), 3. **A.** *to turn, twist round;* rota perpetuum qua circumvertitur axem, Ov.; mancipium, *to manumit*, Quint. **B.** Transf., *to defraud;* qui me argento circumvortant, Plaut.

circumvestĭo, 4. *to clothe all round*, poet., ap. Cic.

circumvincĭo -vinctus, 4. *to bind all round*, Plaut.

circumvīso, 3. *to look all round*, Plaut.

circumvŏlĭto, 1. 1, *to fly round;* lacus circumvolitavit hirundo, Verg.; 2, transf., *to rove about, hover round;* circumvolitant equites, Lucr.

circumvŏlo, 1. *to fly round;* aliquem atris alis (of death), Hor.

circumvŏlvo -volvi -vŏlūtum, 3. *to roll round;* sol magnum circumvolvitur annum, completes its annual course, Verg.

circus -i. m. (κίρκος). **I.** *a circular line;*

candens, *the milky way*, Cic. **II.** *a circus, hippodrome.* **A.** *in Rome;* 1, Circus Maximus, or Circus, *the great circus or racecourse in Rome, surrounded by galleries which accommodated 150,000 spectators*, Liv.; 2, Circus Flaminius, *outside the town*, Cic. **B.** *a circus in other places;* 1, Circus maritimus at Anagnia, Liv.; 2, *any circus or place where games are held*, Verg.

cīris -is, f. (κεῖρις), *a bird, into which Scylla, daughter of Nisus, was transformed*, Ov.

cirrātus -a -um (cirrus), *curled, crisped*, Mart.

Cirrha -ae, f. (Κίῤῥα), *a city of Phocis, the port of Delphi, sacred to Apollo;* hence, **Cirrhaeus** -a -um, *relating to Cirrha or Apollo.*

cirrus -i, m., 1, *a lock, curl, or ringlet of hair*, Juv.; 2, *the fringe of a garment*, Phaedr.

Cirta -ae, f. (Κίρτα), *a town of Numidia.*

cis, prep., with acc. (connected with is and hic, with demonstrative c prefixed), *on this side;* 1, of place, cis Taurum, Cic.; 2, of time, cis dies paucos, *within a few days*, Sall.

cisalpīnus -a -um, *on this side (the Roman)*, i.e., *the south side of the Alps;* Gallia, Caes.

cisĭum -ĭi., n. *a light two-wheeled gig*, Cic.

cisrhēnānus -a -um, *on this side the Rhine;* Germani, Caes.

Cisseus -ĕi, m. (Κισσεύς), *king of Thrace, father of Hecuba;* hence **Cisseïs** -ĭdis, f. (Κισσηΐς), *daughter of Cisseus, Hecuba.*

cista -ae, f. (κίστη), *a chest, casket for keeping money, fruit, books, etc.*, Cic.; for sacred utensils, Tib.; *a ballot-box*, Plin.

cistella -ae, f. (dim. of cista), *a little chest, or casket*, Plaut.

cistellātrix -īcis, f. (cistella), *the female slave whose business it was to keep the cash-box*, Plaut.

cistellŭla -ae, f. (dim. of cistella), *a little casket*, Plaut.

cisterna -ae, f. *a subterranean reservoir, a cistern;* piscinae cisternaeque servandis imbribus, Tac.

cistĭfer -fĕri, m. (cista and fero), *one who carries a box or chest*, Mart.

cistŏphŏrus -i, m. (κιστοφόρος), *an Asiatic coin worth about four drachmae, so called from the impression of a cista upon it;* in cistophoro in Asia habeo ad HS. bis et vicies, *in Asiatic coinage*, Cic.

cistŭla -ae, f. (dim. of cista), *a casket*, Plaut.

cĭtātim, adv. (citatus), *quickly, hastily*, Cic.

cĭtātus -a -um, p. adj. with compar. and superl. (from cito), *quick, rapid, speedy;* Rhenus per fines Trevirorum citatus fertur, Caes.; citato equo or citatis equis, *at full gallop*, Liv.

cĭtĕr -tra -trum (cis), *on this side.* **I.** Positive, Cato. **II.** Compar., **citĕrĭŏr** -us, genit. -ōris, *on this side.* **A.** Gallia, Cic. **B.** Transf., 1, ad haec citeriora veniam et notiora nobis, *more closely concerning us*, Cic.; 2, of time, *earlier;* citeriores nondum audiebamus, Cic. **III.** Superl., **cĭtĭmus** or **cĭtŭmus** -a -um, *very near, nearest;* stella ultima a caelo citima terris, Cic.

Cĭthaerōn -ōnis, m. (Κιθαιρών), *a mountain in the south-west of Boeotia, scene of the Bacchic orgies.*

cĭthăra -ae, f. (κιθάρα). **A.** *a four-stringed instrument*, Hor. **B.** Meton., 1, *the music of the cithara*, Hor.; 2, *the art of playing the cithara*, Hor.

cĭthărista -ae, m. (κιθαριστής), *a player on the cithara*, Ter.

cĭthărĭstrĭa -ae, f. (κιθαρίστρια), *a female player on the cithara*, Ter.

cĭthărĭzo, 1. (κιθαρίζω), *to play the cithara*, Nep.

cĭthăroedĭcus -a -um (κιθαρῳδικός), *relating to the citharoedus*, Suet.

cĭthăroedus -i, m. (κιθαρῳδός), *one who sings to the cithara*, Cic.

Cĭtium -ĭi, n. (Κίτιον), *a maritime city of Cyprus, birthplace of the Stoic philosopher, Zeno;* hence, **A. Cĭtĭensis** -e, *belonging to Citium.* **B. Cĭtĭeus** -a -um, *belonging to Citium.* **C. Cĭtĭŏus** -ĕi, m. *of Citium;* Zeno, Cic.

1. **cĭtŏ**, comp. **cĭtius**, sup. **cĭtissĭme**, adv. (citus). **A.** *quickly, speedily,* Cic. ; cito discere aliquid, Cic. **B.** Transf., a, non cito, *not easily,* Cic. ; b, compar., citius quam, *sooner than,* Cic.

2. **cĭto**, 1. (freq. of cio = cieo). **I.** *to put into violent motion,* hence *to cite, summon ;* a, *the senate ;* patres in curiam, Liv. ; b, *the people to vote ;* in campo Martio centuriatim populum, Liv. ; c, *the knights ;* "Cita," inquit Nero, "M. Livium," Liv. ; d, *the citizens to take the oath of military allegiance ;* citati milites nominatim apud tribunos militum in verba P. Scipionis juraverunt, Liv. ; e, in a court of justice, (a) *the jury ;* si Lysiades citatus judex non responderit, Cic. ; (β) *the prosecutor,or defendant ;* citat reum, non respondet ; citat accusatorem, Cic. ; omnes ii ab te capitis C. Rabirii nomine citantur, Cic. ; (γ) *a witness ;* in hanc rem te, Naevi, testem citabo, Cic. ; transf., quamvis citetur Salamis clarissimae testis victoriae, Cic. ; (δ) *the condemned ;* praeconis audita vox citantis nomina damnatorum, Liv. ; f, *to call upon a god for help ;* aliquem falso, Ov. **II.** a, *to shout out ;* paeanem, Cic. ; b, *to call forth, to produce ;* isque (animi) motus aut boni aut mali opinione citatur, Cic.

cĭtrā, adv. and prep. with acc. (from citer). **I.** *on this side ;* citra Veliam, Cic. ; citra Rhenum, Caes. **II.** Transf., **A.** *on this side of* (a certain boundary), *within, before ;* 1, of space, paucis citra milibus, Liv. ; citra tertiam syllabam, *before the third syllable,* Cic. ; 2, of time, *within ;* citra Trojana tempora, Ov. **B.** = sine, praeter, *without, except ;* citra vulnus, Plin.

cĭtrĕus -a -um (citrus), 1, *belonging to the citrus tree ;* mensa, *made of citrus wood,* Cic. ; 2, *belonging to the citron tree ;* citrea, *the citron tree,* Plin. ; citreum, *the citron,* Plin.

cĭtrō, adv. (citer), found only in combination with ultro ; ultro et citro, ultro citroque, ultro citro, ultro ac citro, *up and down, hither and thither,* Cic.

cĭtrum -i, n. *citrus wood,* Plin.

cĭtrus -i, m. *the citrus, a kind of African cypress,* from the aromatic timber of which the Romans manufactured costly articles of furniture (perhaps Thuia orientalis, Linn.), Plin.

cĭtus -a -um, p. adj. (from cieo), *quick, speedy ;* vox, Cic. ; incessus, Sall. ; pes, *the iambus,* Ov.

cīvĭcus -a -um (civis), *relating to a citizen, civic ;* bella, *civil war,* Ov. ; corona, and simply **cīvĭca** -ae, f. *the civic crown, a chaplet of oak leaves presented to one who had saved the life of a Roman citizen in war, bearing the inscription,* ob civem servatum, Cic.

cīvīlis -e (civis). **I.** *relating to a citizen, civic, civil.* **A.** Lit., conjuratio, Cic. ; discordia, Sall. ; quercus := corona civica (v. civicus), Verg. ; jus, either *the civil law of the Romans* (opp. jus naturale) or *the law of private rights* (opp. publicum), Cic. ; dies, *from midnight to midnight,* as opp. to the naturalis dies, *from sunrise to sunset,* Varr. **B.** Transf., a, *becoming a citizen, befitting a citizen ;* nulli civilis animus, Liv. ; b,

popular, affable, courteous ; quid civilius illo, Ov. **II.** *relating to public life or the state ;* a, scientia, Cic. ; civilium rerum peritus, Tac. ; b, *civil,* as opp. to military ; non militaria solum sed civilia quoque munera, Liv.

cīvīlĭtas -ātis, f. (civilis), 1, *the science oj politics,* used by Quint. as a translation of ἡ πολιτική ; 2, *politeness, condescension, civility,* Suet.

cīvīlĭtĕr, adv. (civilis), 1, *like a citizen ;* vivere, Cic. ; 2, *politely,* Ov.

cīvis -is, c. (from cio or cieo, summoned). **I.** *a citizen* (opp. hostis or peregrinus), civis Romanus, Cic. ; aliquem civem asciscere, Cic. ; fieri civem Romanum, Cic. ; fem., civis Attica, Ter. **II. A.** *fellow citizen ;* cives mei, Cic. **B.** *subject ;* imperare corpori ut rex civibus suis, Cic.

cīvĭtas -ātis, f. (civis). **I.** Abstr., *citizenship, the condition or rights of a citizen ;* civitatem dare alicui, Cic. ; amittere, Cic. ; aliquem civitate donare, Cic. ; aliquem in civitatem asciscere, Cic. ; in populi Romani civitatem suscipi, Cic. ; civitatem consequi, adipisci, habere, impetrare, adimere, Cic. ; civitate mutari, Cic. **II.** Concr. **A.** *a union of citizens, a state, commonwealth ;* civitates aut nationes, *civilised states or barbarous tribes,* Cic. ; civitatem instituere, condere, trare, Cic. ; civitates condere, Cic. **B.** Meton., *a town, city,* Cic.

clădēs -is, f. (connected with gladius), *destruction.* **I.** *destruction* of plants, etc., by hail or rain, *loss, damage,* Plaut. ; *loss of a limb ;* dextrae manus, Liv. **II. A.** *disaster, injury,* civitatis, Cic. **B.** Meton., *persons who cause the disaster ;* militum clades, Cic. ; geminos Scipiadas cladem Libyae, Verg. **C.** Esp., *misfortune in war, defeat ;* cladem inferre, Liv. ; facere, Sall. ; accipere, Liv. ; hosti inferre, Cic.

clam (old Lat. călam or călim, from root CAL, CEL, whence cel -o). **I.** Adv., *secretly* (opp. palam), *in secret ;* esse, *to remain incognito,* Liv. ; plura clam removere, Cic. **II.** Prep. a, with abl., clam vobis, Caes. ; clam istis, Cic. ; b, gen. with acc., clam me est, *it is unknown to me,* Cic.

clāmātor -ōris, m. (clamo), *a shouter, o bawler, noisy declaimer,* Cic.

clāmĭto, 1. (intens. of clamo), *to cry loudly, shout violently ;* 1, absol. or with acc., Cauneas clamitabat, *cried figs of Caunus,* Cic. ; of things, nonne ipsum caput et supercilia illa penitus abrasa clamitare calliditatem videntur, Cic. ; 2, followed by an exclamation in direct speech, ad arma ! clamitans, Liv. ; 3, foll. by acc. and infin. in indirect speech, saepe clamitans liberum se liberaeque civitatis esse, Caes. ; 4, with the acc., aliquem sycophantam, Ter.

clāmo, 1. (connected with καλέω). **I.** Intransit., *to shout, cry aloud.* **A.** Of men, loqui omnes et clamare coeperunt, Cic. ; de suo et uxoris interitu, Cic. **B.** Of animals, anseres qui tantummodo clamant, nocere non possunt, Cic. **II.** Transit., 1, *to call to or upon ;* comites, Ov. ; morientem nomine, Verg. ; with double acc., *to call aloud ;* aliquem furem, Hor. ; 2, *to proclaim aloud ;* a, with acc., hoc de pecunia, Cic. ; b, in direct speech, infantem Io triumphe ! clamasse, Liv. ; c, in indirect speech, clamare ille quum raperetur, nihil se miserum fecisse, Cic. ; d, with ut and the subj., clamare coeperunt, sibi ut haberet hereditatem, Cic.

clāmor -ōris, m. *a loud shouting, cry.* **A.** Of men, clamor populi infestus atque inimicus, Cic. ; clamorem edere, tollere, Cic. ; excitare, Liv. ; clamor oritur, Sall. ; auditur, Caes. ; esp., 1, *shout of applause ;* haec sunt, quae clamores et admirationes in bonis oratoribus efficiunt, Cic. ; 2, *wild cry ;* aliquem clamoribus et con-

viciis et sibilis consectari, Cic. **3,** *war-cry;* clamorem tollere, Caes.; **4,** *cry of sorrow;* lamentantium militum, Liv. **B.** Of animals, gruum, Lucr. **C.** *a sound of lifeless things;* montium, Hor.

clāmōsus -a -um (clamo), **1,** act., *noisy, clamorous,* Quint.; **2,** pass., *filled with noise;* circus, Mart.

clancŭlum, adv. (clam), *secretly, in secret,* Plaut., Ter.; prep. with acc., clanculum patres, Ter.

clandestīnus -a -um (clam), *secret, concealed, hidden, clandestine;* colloquia cum hostibus, Cic.

clangor -ōris, m. *a sound, clang, noise;* **1,** *the cry of birds,* Ov.; of the eagle, Cic. poet.; *the hissing of geese,* Liv.; **2,** *the sound of a trumpet,* Verg.

Clānis -is, m. *a river of Etruria.*

Clănĭus -ĭi, m. *a river of Campania.*

clārē, adv. (clarus). **I.** Lit., **A.** As regards sight, *clearly, brightly;* videre, Plaut.; fulgere, Cat. **B.** As regards hearing, *aloud;* plaudere, dicere, Plaut.; gemere, Cic. **II.** Transf. **A.** *clearly, distinctly;* apparere, ap. Cic.; ostendere, Quint. **B.** *illustriously;* explendescere, Nep.

clārĕo, 2. (clarus). **I.** *to be bright, to shine,* Cic. poet. **II.** Transf. **A.** *to be clear to the mind, be evident,* Lucr. **B.** *to be distinguished, illustrious,* Enn.

clāresco, clārŭi, 3. (inch. of clareo). **I. A.** *to become clear, bright,* Tac. **B.** *to sound or resound clearly;* clarescunt sonitus, Verg. **II.** Transf. **A.** *to become clear to the mind, become evident,* Lucr. **B.** *to become illustrious,* Tac.; ex gente Donitiā duae familiae claruerunt, Suet.

clārĭgātĭo -ōnis, f. (clarigo), **1,** *the demand of satisfaction and declaration of war by a Fetialis,* Plin.; **2,** *the fine imposed on a man caught beyond the limits within which he has been ordered to remain,* Liv.

clārĭgo (clare—i.e., clara voce—and ago), 1. *to declare war,* used of the Fetialis, Plin.

clārĭsŏnus -a -um (clarus and sono), *clearly sounding;* vox, Cat.

clārĭtas -ātis, f. (clarus). **I.** Lit. **A.** Of the sight, *clearness, brightness, brilliancy,* Plin. **B.** Of the voice, vocis, Cic. **II.** Transf. **A.** *clearness to the mind, plainness,* Quint. **B.** *fame, celebrity, renown;* hominis, Cic.

clārĭtūdo -ĭnis, f. (clarus), *clearness, brilliancy.* **I.** Lit., of the sight, deae (i.e., lunae), Tac. **II.** Transf., *fame, renown, celebrity,* Sall.

clāro, 1. (clarus). **I.** *to make clear, make bright,* Cic. poet. **II.** Transf. **A.** *to make plain, evident;* animi naturam versibus, Lucr. **B.** *to make illustrious, renowned,* Hor.

clāror -ōris, m. (clarus), *brightness,* Plaut.

Clărŏs, i, f. (Κλάρος), *a small town in Ionia, on a promontory near Colophon, famous for a temple and oracle of Apollo;* hence **Clărĭus** -a -um (Κλάριος), *Clarian, surname of Apollo,* Ov.; poeta, *the poet Antimachus, born at Claros.*

clārus -a -um (connected with κλεαινός), *clear, bright* (opp. obscurus, caecus). **I.** Lit. **A.** In regard to objects of sight, *bright, shining, brilliant;* lumina mundi, Verg.; locus, Cic.; poet., of the wind, *making clear, bringing fair weather;* aquilo, Verg. **B.** In regard to objects of hearing, *clear, loud;* voce, Cic. **II.** Transf. **A.** *clear, evident, plain;* luce sunt clariora nobis tua consilia, Cic. **B.** 1, *illustrious, renowned, distinguished;* a, of persons, vir clarissimus, Cic.; clarus gloria, Cic.; clarus in philosophia et nobilis, Cic.; ex doctrina nobilis et clarus,

Cic.; **b,** of things oppidum Cic.; victoria clarissima, Cic.; **2,** in a bad sense, *notorious;* illa oppugnatio fani antiquissimi quam clara apud omnes, Cic.; populus luxuriā superbiāque clarus, Liv.

classĭārĭus -i, m. (classis), **1** (sc. miles), *a soldier on board ship, a marine,* Tac.; **2** (sc. nauta), *a rower, or sailor, on board a war galley,* Caes.

classĭcŭla -ae, f. (dim. of classis), *a little fleet, flotilla,* Cic.

classĭcus -a -um (classis). **I. A.** *relating to the classes into which the Roman citizens were distributed;* hence, **classĭcus** -i, m. *a citizen of the first or highest class.* **B.** Transf., classicus scriptor, *an author of the first rank,* Gell. **II.** *relating to the army or the fleet.* **A.** *relating to the army;* Subst., **classĭcum** -i, n. *the signal of engagement given by a trumpet;* classicum canit, Liv.; or *the signal by which the classes were called to the comitia;* classico ad contionem convocat, Liv.; and meton., *the trumpet itself;* classicum inflare, Verg. **B.** *relating to the fleet;* milites, Liv.; bella, *naval war,* Prop.; and subst., **classĭci**-ōrum, m. *marines,* Tac.

classis -is, f. (connected with κλᾶσις, κλῆσω, from κλέω, and calo, to summon, lit. *the multitude summoned*). **I.** *a class.* **A.** Lit., *one of the divisions into which Servius Tullius divided the whole Roman people;* hence fig., quintae classis, *of the lowest rank,* Cic. **B.** Transf., *any division;* servorum, Petr. **II.** In milit. lang., *the forces.* **A.** *a land army;* Hortinae classes, Verg. **B.** *the fleet;* classem facere, comparare, aedificare, *to build a fleet,* Cic.; instruere atque ornare, *to fit out a fleet,* Cic.; classem appellere ad Delum, *to land,* Cic.; *a ship,* Hor., Verg.; hence, plur. classes = naves, Verg. Aen. ii. 30.

Clastĭdĭum -ĭi, n. *a town in Gallia Cispadana,* now *Casteggio or Chiateggio.*

Clăterna -ae, f., *stronghold in Cispadane Gaul* (now *Maggio*).

clātri -ōrum, m. and **clātra** -ōrum, n. (κλῆθρα), *a trellis or grating,* Hor.

clatro, 1. (clatri), *to provide or cover with a trellis or grating,* Plaut.

claudĕo -ēre, 2. and gen. **claudo,** clausurus, 3. (claudus), *to limp, halt, be lame;* gen. used fig., si (beata vita) una ex parte claudēret, Cic.; esp. of orators, in quacunque enim una (parte) plane claudēret, orator esse non posset, Cic.

Claudĭānus -i, m. (Claudius), *a Latin poet, who lived in the reigns of Theodosius the Great, and his sons Arcadius and Honorius.*

claudĭcātĭo -ōnis, f. (claudico), *a limping,* Cic.

claudĭco, 1. (claudus), *to limp, be lame;* graviter claudicare ex vulnere ob rempublicam accepto, Cic.; claudicat axis mundi, *inclines,* Lucr.; fig., *to halt, waver, be defective;* tota res vacillat et claudicat, Cic.; esp. of speech, nihil curtum, nihil claudicans, Cic.

Claudĭus (**Clōdĭus**) -a -um, *the name of a Roman family, both patrician and plebeian, of whom the most celebrated members were:*—**I.** Appius Claudius Sabinus Regillensis, *the founder of the family, a Sabine of Regillum, whose name was said to have been originally Attus Clausus.* **II.** Appius Claudius Crassus, *the most notorious of the decemvirs.* **III.** Appius Claudius Caecus, *censor* 312 B.C., *the builder of several great public works.* **IV.** Publius Clodius Pulcher, *tribune of the people, murdered by Milo,* B.C. 52. **V.** Tiberius Claudius Drusus Nero Germanicus, *the fourth Roman emperor.* Adj., **Claudĭānus** -a -um, **Claudĭālis** -e, **Clōdĭānus** -a -um *Claudian.*

1. claudo, clausi, clausum, **3.** and **clūdo,** clūsi, clusum, **3.** (root CLA, whence clavis, Gr. Dor. κλαΐς = κλείς). **I.** Gen., *to shut close* (opp. *aperire*). **A.** Lit., **1,** forem cubiculi, Cic.; portas alicui, Caes.; Janum, *to close the gates of the temple of Janus*, Liv.; fig., claudere aures alicui rei, Cic.; in ipsius consuetudinem, quam adhuc meus pudor mihi clausit, me insinuabo, Cic.; **2,** *to close up a road* or *a country, to make inaccessible;* omnes aditus claudentur, Cic.; quod clausae hieme Alpes essent, Liv.; adhuc clausum fuisse mare scio, Cic.; **3,** *to close up;* a, geograph. t. t., insula ea sinum ab alto claudit; **b,** milit. t. t., agmen claudere, *to bring up the rear*, Caes. Subst., **clausum** -i, n. *a bolt* or *lock;* clausa effringere, Sall.; **B.** Transf., **1,** *to bring to an end;* opus, Ov.; octavum lustrum, Hor.; **2,** of character, partic. clausus, *secret, close;* Tiberius, Tac. **II. A.** = intercludere, *to dam up, stop, intercept;* rivos, Verg.; commeatus, Liv.; horum ferocia vocem Evandri clausit, Liv. **B.** = concludere, includere; **1,** lit., a, *to shut up in;* aliquem in curiam or in curia, Liv.; b, milit. t. t., *to invest;* oppidum undique, Sall.; of hunting, nemorum saltus, Verg.; **c,** *to encompass, surround;* urbs loci natura terra marique clauditur, Cic.; **2,** transf., a, aliud clausum in pectore, aliud in lingua promptum habere; b, as rhet. t. t., sententias numeris, Cic.

2. claudo = claudeo (q.v.).

claudus (cludus) -a -um. **I.** Lit., *limping, halting, lame;* claudus altero pede, *lame on one foot*, Nep.; claudi ac debiles equi, Liv.; prov., iste claudus pilam, *one who can make proper use of nothing*, Cic. **II.** Transf. **A.** *crippled, defective, wavering;* naves, Liv.; poet., carmina alterno versu, *elegiac verse*, Ov. **B.** *wavering, insecure;* clauda nec officii pars erit ulla tui, Ov.

claustrum -i, n. (claudo), gen. plur. **I.** *a bolt, bar;* claustra revellere, Cic.; laxare, Ov.; relaxare, Ov.; fig., portarum naturae effringere, *to lay bare the secrets of nature*, Lucr. **II.** *a gate, inclosure, dam, limit, boundary;* a, venti circum claustra ferunt, Verg.; b, *custody, confinement;* of animals, *a den, cage;* diu claustris retentae ferae, Liv.; c, *a pass* or *narrow place;* claustra montium, Tac.; milit. t. t., *the key* or *critical point of a position;* terra claustra locorum tenet; claustra Aegypti, Liv.; fig., claustra ista (*barrier*) nobilitatis refregissem, Cic.

clausŭla -ae, f. (claudo), *the end, conclusion.* **A.** Gen., epistolae, Cic. **B.** Esp. **1,** *the closing scene* or *closing word* in a drama; in quo (mimo) quum clausula non invenitur, Cic.; **2,** in rhet., *the close of a period*, Cic.

clāva -ae, f. (clavus), *a knotty staff* or *cudgel,* Cic.; also *the staff used in the drill of recruits* or *in exercises in the use of weapons*, Cic.; *the club of Hercules*, Verg. Ov.

clāvārĭum -i, n. (clavus), *a gift of money to Roman soldiers*, Tac.

clāvātor -ōris, m. (clava), *one who carries the clava*, Plaut.

clāvĭcŭla -ae, f. (dim. of clavis, *a little key*), hence, *the twig* or *tendril by which the vine clings to its prop*, Cic.

1. clāvĭger -gĕri, m. (clava and gero), *the club-bearer*, epithet of Hercules, Ov.

2. clāvĭger -gĕri, m. (clavis and gero), *the key-carrier*, epithet of Janus as god of doors, Ov.

clāvis -is, f. (κλαΐς, κλείς), **1,** *a key;* adulterina portarum, *a false* or *skeleton key*, Sall.; claves adimere uxori, *to separate from one's wife*, Cic.; **2,** *a lock;* alias claves omnibus portis imponere, Liv.; **3,** clavis adunca trochi, *a stick for trundling a hoop*, Prop

clāvus -i-, m. *a nail.* **A.** Lit., clavis ferreis confixa transtra, Caes.; clavus trabalis, *a spike*, as a sign of firmness, an attribute of Necessitas, Hor.; hence, prov., trabali clavo figere, *to fix firmly*, Cic.; annalis, *the nail which on the ides of September every year was driven into the wall of the temple of Jupiter Capitolinus at Rome;* hence fig., ex hoc die clavum anni movebis, *reckon the beginning of the year*, Cic. **B.** Transf., **1,** a *helm, rudder*, Verg.; fig., clavum imperii tenere, Cic.; **2,** *a stripe of purple on the tunic, worn broad by the senators* (latus), *narrow by the knights* (angustus), latum clavum a Caesare impetravi, *I have become a senator*, Plin.; the latus clavus was also worn by the boys of noble families at Rome, Ov.; meton., clavus = *the tunic with the broad* or *narrow stripe*, Hor.

Clāzŏmĕnae -ārum, f. (Κλαζομεναί), *one of the twelve Ionic towns in Asia Minor.*

Clĕanthēs -is, m. (Κλεάνθης), *a Stoic philosopher, pupil of Zeno;* hence adj., **Clĕanthēus** -a -um, *Stoic*, Pers.

clēmens -entis, adj. with compar. and superl., *mild, placid, kind, merciful.* **I.** a, of persons, clementes judices et misericordes, Cic.; ab innocentia clementissimus, Cic.; b, of circumstances, events, etc., castigatio, Cic. **II.** Transf., a, of the weather, *mild;* flamen, Cat.; b, of water, *quiet, calm;* amnis clementissimus, *still*, Ov.

clēmentĕr, adv. with compar. and superl. (clemens), *mildly, gently, mercifully.* **I.** Lit., clementer facere or ferre aliquid, Cic.; clementer et moderate jus dicere, Caes.; clementer ductis militibus, *without plundering*, Liv. **II.** Transf., of places, *gently rising;* clementer editum jugum, Tac.

clēmentĭa -ae, f. (clemens). **A.** *mildness, mercy, clemency;* clementia mansuetudoque, Cic.; confugere in clementiam alicuius, Cic.; clementia uti, Cic. **B.** Transf., *mildness of weather;* aestatis, Plin.

Clĕombrŏtus -i, m. (Κλεόμβροτος), **1,** *a general of the Lacedaemonians;* **2,** *a Greek philosopher of Ambracia.*

Clĕon -ōnis, m. (Κλέων), *a celebrated Athenian demagogue.*

Clĕōnae -ārum, f. (Κλεωναί), *a city in Argolis, near Nemea;* hence adj., **Clĕōnaeus** -a -um, *Cleonean.*

Clĕōpătra -ae, f. **I.** *the daughter of Philip of Macedon and of Olympias, wife of Alexander I. of Epirus.* **II.** *the daughter of Ptolemy Auletes, queen of Egypt, the mistress of Antonius, whose forces allied with hers were overthrown by Augustus at Actium.*

clēpo, clepsi, cleptum, 3. (κλέπτω), *to steal,* ap. Cic.; se, *to conceal oneself*, Sen.

clepsȳdra -ae, f. (κλεψύδρα), *the water clock used to measure the time during which an orator spoke;* binas clepsydras petere, *to wish to speak for the length of two clepsydrae*, Plin.; dare, *to give leave to speak*, Plin.; cras ergo ad clepsydram, *rhetorical exercises*, Cic.; so, aliquem ad clepsydram latrare docere, Cic.

clepta -ae, m. (κλέπτης), *a thief*, Plaut.

clĭbănus -i, m. (κλίβανος), *an earthen* or *iron vessel perforated with small holes used for baking bread*, Plin.

clĭens -entis, m. (archaic cluens, from cluo, κλύω, *to hear*, lit. *a listener*). **I.** In Rome, *a client, dependant, one under the protection of a patronus.* **II.** Transf., **1,** in Gaul and Germany, *a vassal;* used of entire nations, *allies*, Caes.; **2,** *the worshipper of a god;* Bacchi, Hor.

clĭenta -ae, f. (cliens), *a female client.* Hor.

clĭentēla -ae, f. (cliens). **I. A.** *clientship, the relation between the client and his patron;* esse in alicuius clientela, Cic.; in alicuius clientelam se conferre, Cic. **B.** Meton. (gen. in plur.), *clients,* Cic. **II.** *the relation of a weaker nation to a more powerful one, dependence;* magnae eorum erant clientelae, Caes.; dicare se alicui in clientelam, Caes.

clĭentŭlus -i, m. (dim. of cliens), *a little client,* Tac.

clīnāmen -ĭnis, n. (* clino), *the inclination of a thing,* Lucr.

clīnātus -a -um (partic. from obsolete verb clino = κλίνω), *inclined, bent, leaning,* Lucr., Cic. poet.

Clĭnĭas -ae, m. (Κλεινίας), *the father of Alcibiades;* hence, **Clĭnĭādes** -ae, m. *Alcibiades.*

Clīŏ -ūs, f. (Κλειώ), 1, *the Muse of history;* 2, *a daughter of Oceanus.*

clĭpĕo (clupeo), 1. *to provide with a shield;* clipeata agmina, Verg. Subst., **clĭpĕāti** -ōrum, m. *soldiers bearing shields,* Liv.

clĭpĕus (clŭpĕus) -i, m. and **clĭpĕum** (clŭpĕum) -i, n. *the round metal shield of the Roman soldiers.* **I.** Lit., Cic.; prov., clipeum post vulnera sumere, *to do anything too late,* Ov. **II.** Transf., of objects resembling a shield in shape, **a,** *the disk of the sun,* Ov.; **b** (gen. clipeum), *a medallion portrait of a god or distinguished man,* Liv., Tac.

Clisthĕnēs -is, m. (Κλεισθένης), *an Athenian statesman.*

Clītarchus -i, m. (Κλείταρχος), *a Greek historian who accompanied Alexander the Great on his expeditions.*

clītellae -ārum, f. (* clino), *a pack saddle, a pair of panniers,* Cic.

clītellārĭus -a -um (clitellae), *belonging or relating to a pack saddle,* Cic.

Clĭternum -i, n. *a town of the Aequi.* Adj., **Cliternīnus** -a -um, *Cliternian.*

Clītŏmăchus -i, m. (Κλειτόμαχος), *an Academic philosopher, pupil of Carneades.*

Clītŏr -ŏris, m. (Κλείτωρ) and **Clītŏrĭum** -ĭi, n. *a town in Arcadia.* Adj., **Clitŏrĭus** -a -um, *Clitorian.*

Clītumnus -i, m. *a river in Umbria,* now *Clitunno.*

clĭvosus -a -um (clivus), *hilly, steep, precipitous,* rus, Verg.; Olympus, Ov.

clĭvus -i, m. (from root CLI, whence acclivis and declivis, and clino in acclino, etc.), *a gentle ascent or elevation, a hill;* lenis ab tergo clivus erat, Liv.; clivum mollire, Caes.; clivus Capitolinus, *the ascent from the forum to the Capitoline hill,* and *the Capitoline hill itself,* Liv.; so clivus sacer, Hor.; prov. for *an obstacle which is to be surmounted;* clivo sudamus in imo, Ov.

clŏāca -ae, f. (from cluo = I cleanse), **a,** *a sewer or drain;* fossas cloacasque exhaurire, Liv.; **b,** cloaca maxima, *the sewer constructed by Tarquinius Priscus, through which the filth of Rome was discharged into the Tiber,* Liv.

Clŏācina -ae, f. (from cluo, I cleanse), *the cleanser, surname of Venus whose image stood at the place where the Romans and Sabines were reconciled after the rape of the Sabine women, and where they purified themselves with myrtle boughs.*

Clōdĭus = Claudius (q.v.).

Cloelĭus (Cluilĭus) -a -um, *name of an Alban and afterwards of a Roman gens, the most celebrated of the name being:* 1, Cluilius or Cloelius, *the last king of Alba, who invaded the Roman territory and made the Cluilia fossa or* fossae Cloeliae, Liv.; 2, **Cloelĭa** -ae, f. *a Roman maiden, hostage to Porsena, who swam back across the Tiber to Rome.*

Clōthō -ūs, f. (Κλωθώ), *the spinner, one of the Parcae.*

clŭĕo, 2. (κλύω), *I hear myself called, I am called, am named;* quaecunque cluent, *whatever has a name,* Lucr.

clūnis -is, m. and f. *the buttocks, hinder parts,* Hor., Liv.

Clŭpĕa (Clўpĕa) -ae, f. and plur. **Clŭpĕae** -ārum, f. (translation of Gr. Ἀσπίς), *a promontory and town in Byzacium in Africa.*

Clūsĭum -ĭi, n. *a town of Etruria.* Adj., **Clūsīnus** -a -um, *of Clusium.*

Clūsĭus -ĭi, m. (cludo), *the shutter,* epithet of Janus.

Clўmĕne -ēs, f. (Κλυμένη), *the wife of the Aethiopian king Merops, and mother of Phaethon;* hence adj., **Clўmĕneīus** -a -um; proles, *Phaethon,* Ov.

clyster -ēris, m. (κλυστήρ), 1, *a clyster,* Suet.; 2, *syringe,* Suet.

Clўtaemnestra -ae, f. (Κλυταιμνήστρα), *daughter of Leda, sister of Helen, Castor, and Pollux, wife of Agamemnon and mother of Orestes, Electra, and Iphigenia, slew her husband with the help of Aegisthus.*

Clўtĭē -ēs, f. (Κλυτίη), *daughter of Oceanus, beloved by Apollo, changed into the flower heliotropium.*

Cnĭdus (-ŏs), or **Gnĭdus** (-ŏs) -i, f. (Κνίδος), *a town in Caria, famed for the worship of Venus.* Adj., **Cnĭdĭus** -a -um, *Cnidian.*

cŏăcervātĭo -ōnis, f. (coacervo), *a heaping up* (of proofs), Cic.

cŏăcervo, 1. *to heap up, accumulate;* pecuniae coacervantur, Cic.; transf., argumenta, Cic.

cŏăcesco -ācŭi, 3. *to become thoroughly sour;* ut enim non omne vinum, sic non omnis natura vetustate coacescit, Cic.; fig., quam valde eam (gentem Sardorum) putamus tot transfusionibus coacuisse, Cic.

cŏactĭo -ōnis, f. (cogo), *a collecting;* coactiones argentarias factitavit, Suet.

cŏacto, 1. (intens. of cogo), *to compel,* Lucr.

cŏactor -ōris, m. (cogo). **I.** Lit., **a,** *a collector of rents, money at auctions,* etc., Hor.; **b,** coactores agminis, *the rear-guard,* Tac. **II.** Transf., *one who compels,* Sen.

cŏactum -i, n. (cogo), *a coverlet of thick cloth,* Caes.

cŏactus -ūs, m. (cogo), *a compulsion, compelling;* coactu atque efflagitatu meo, Cic.

cŏaddo, 3. *to add in with,* Plaut.

cŏaedĭfĭco, 1. *to build on;* campum Martium, Cic.

cŏaequo, 1. *to level, make plain, even.* **A.** montes, Sall. **B.** Transf., omnia ad libidines suas, *placed on the same footing,* Cic.

cŏagmentātĭo -ōnis (coagmento), *a connection, binding together;* corporis, Cic.

cŏagmento, 1. (coagmentum), *to fix together, stick together, join together.* **I.** Lit., opus ipsa suum eadem, quae coagmentavit, natura dissolvit, Cic. **II.** Transf., verba compone et quasi coagmenta, Cic.; pacem, *to conclude,* Cic.

cŏagmentum -i, n. (cogo), *a joining together, a joint;* lapidum, Caes.

cŏagŭlum -i, n. (cogo), 1, *that which causes to curdle, rennet,* Plin.; 2, meton., *curds,* Plin.

cŏalesco -ălŭi, -ălĭtum, 3. (com and alesco),

1, *to grow together, to become one in growth, to coalesce, unite;* saxa vides sola coalescere calce, Lucr.; fig., sic brevi spatio novi veteresque (milites) coaluere, Sall.; ut cum Patribus coalescant animi plebis, Liv.; followed by in, in hunc consensum, Tac.; **2,** of plants, *to grow;* dum novus in viridi coalescit cortice ramus, Ov.; *to take root;* grandis ilex coaluerat inter saxa, Sall.; **3,** of wounds, *to close, be healed, grow together;* fig., vixdum coalescens foventis regnum, Liv.

cŏangusto, 1. *to narrow, limit, confine;* haec lex coangustari potest, Cic.

coarcto, etc. = coarto, etc. (q.v.).

cŏargŭo -gŭi -gūtum, but -gūiturus, 3. (com and arguo), *to show in a clear light.* **I.** Gen., *to demonstrate fully, to prove by evidence;* certum crimen multis suspicionibus, Cic.; perfidiam alicuius, Cic.; sin autem fuga laboris desidiam, repudiatio supplicum superbiam coarguit, Cic. **II. A.** *to prove to be false;* **1,** of things, id quidem coarguere nihil attinere ratus, Liv.; **2,** *to prove a person to be wrong, to convict a person of an error, to confute;* quo (decreto) maxime et refelli et coargui potest, Cic.. **B.** *to prove a person to be guilty, to convict of a crime;* aliquem, Cic.; with abl. of means, criminibus coarguitur, Cic.; with genit., of crime, aliquem avaritiae, Cic.

cŏartātĭo -ōnis, f. (coarto), *a drawing together, a confining* or *straightening in a small space,* Liv.

cŏarto, 1. *to confine, draw together* (opp. laxare, dilatare). **A.** Lit., Thermopylarum satum, ubi angustae fauces coartant iter, Liv. **B.** Transf., **1,** of discourse, *to compress, abbreviate;* ut quae coartavit, dilatet nobis, Cic.; **2,** of time, *to shorten;* consulatum aliorum, Tac.

cŏaxo, 1. (onomatop.), *to croak* (of a frog), Suet.

coccĭnātus -a -um (coccinus), *clad in scarlet,* Suet.

coccĭnĕus -a -um (coccum), *scarlet coloured,* Petr.

coccĭnus -a -um (coccum), *scarlet coloured,* Juv. Subst., **coccĭna** -orum, n. *scarlet clothes,* Mart.

coccum -i, n. (κόκκος). **A.** *the berry of the scarlet oak* (quercus coccifera, Linn.), used as a scarlet dye by the ancients (the real source of the dye has since been discovered to be an insect), Plin. **B.** Meton., **1,** *scarlet hue,* Hor.; **2,** *scarlet cloth* or *garments,* Suet.

cŏchlĕa -ae, f. (κοχλίας). **A.** *a snail,* Cic. **B.** Meton. *the snail shell,* Mart.

cŏchlĕar -āris, n. and **cochlĕārĭum** -ĭi, n. Plin., and **cochlĕāre** -is, n. Mart. (cochlea), *a spoon,* Mart.

Cocles -ĭtis, m. *the one-eyed man,* Plaut.; esp. Horatius Cocles, *the Roman who defended the bridge over the Tiber against the army of Porsena.*

coctana = cottana (q.v.).

coctĭlis -e (coquo), *baked;* lateres, Varr.; muri Babylonis, *made of burnt brick,* Ov.

Cōcytŏs and **ŭs,** -i, m. (Κώκυτος, *the stream of wailing*), *a river of the Lower World.* Adj., **Cōcytus** and **Cōcytĭus** -a -um, *Cocytian;* virgo, *Allecto,* Verg.

cōda = cauda, q.v.

cōdex -dĭcis, m. = caudex. **I.** *the trunk of a tree,* Ov. **II.** Meton., *a book, composed of wooden tablets, covered with wax.* **A.** Gen., *a book, writing, document,* c. falsus, Cic. **B.** Esp., codex accepti et expensi, *an account-book,* a *ledger* (adversaria, *a day-book,* the accounts

from which were entered into the **codex** every month), in codicem referre, Cic.

cōdĭcārĭus (**caudĭcārĭus**). **-a** -um (codex), *made of wooden blocks,* naves, Sall.

cōdĭcilli -ōrum, m. (dim. of codex), **1,** *small tablets upon which to make memoranda;* in codicillis exarare, Cic.; **2,** *something written on tablets;* a, *a letter,* Cic.; b, *a petition,* Tac.; c, *a codicil,* Tac.; d, *an imperial rescript* or *order,* Tac.

Codrus -i, m. (Κόδρος), *the last king of Athens, who was said to have voluntarily sought death in order to obtain victory for the Athenians over the Spartans.*

Coelē Sўrĭa -ae, f. (Κοίλη Συρία, *hollow Syria*), *the district between Libanus and Antilibanus.*

coelebs = caelebs.

coeles -ĭtis, v. caeles.

coelestis -e, v. caelestis.

coelĭcŏla -ae, v. caelicola.

coelĭfer, v. caelifer.

Coelius, v. Caelius.

coelo = caelo, q.v.

coelum -i, v. caelum.

cŏēmo -ēmi -emptum, 3. *to buy in large quantities, buy up,* te quae te delectarint coemisse, Cic.

cŏemptĭo -ōnis, f. (coemo), **1,** *a form of marriage which consisted in a reciprocal sale of the parties to one another,* Cic.; **2,** *a fictitious marriage to enable a woman to acquire certain rights,* Cic.

cŏemptĭōnālis -e (coemptio), *relating to a coemptio;* senex, *an old man used for a fictitious marriage,* Cic.

coena, &c., v. cena.

coenōsus -a -um, v. caenosus.

coenŭla -ae, f. v. cenula.

coenum, v. caenum.

cŏĕo -ĭi (rarely -ĭvi) -ĭtum, 4. (com and eo), *to go together, come together, assemble.* **I.** Gen., **A.** Of persons, **1,** as friends, Capuae, Liv.; **2,** as enemies, *to engage;* inter se coiisse viros et cernere ferro, Verg. **B.** Of things, vix memini nobis verba coisse decem, *that ten words have been exchanged between us,* Prop. **II.** *to unite so as to form a whole, to combine.* **A.** Of persons, **1,** milit. t. t., coire inter se, Caes.; in unum, Liv.; in orbem, Liv.; **2,** *to unite* in some relation; **a,** politically, cum hoc tu coire ausus es, ut, etc., Cic.; adversus rempublicam, Liv.; with acc., societatem vel periculi vel laboris, Cic.; in pass., societas coitur, Cic.; **b,** *to unite in marriage;* hac gener atque socer coeant mercede suorum, Verg. **B.** Of things, *to unite together;* **1,** ut placidis coeant immitia, Hor.; **2,** of wounds, neve retractando nondum coeuntia rumpam vulnera, Ov.; **3,** *to curdle;* coit formidine sanguis, Verg.; **4,** *to be frozen;* mentiar, an coeat duratus frigore pontus, Ov.

cŏepĭo, coepi, coeptum, 3. (the present tenses very rare and only A. Aug.; the perfect tenses more commonly used), v. transit. and intransit. (com and apio = apo) *to begin, commence.* **I.** Transit., **A.** Act., *to begin* quum talia vates, Verg.; dicere coepi, Cic.; si quae rapinae fieri coeperunt, Cic.; fut. partic., coepturus, with acc., Romanos omnibus instructiores rebus coepturos bellum, Liv. **B.** Pass., only in perf., lapides jaci coepti sunt, Caes.; postquam armis disceptari coeptum sit, Cic.; partic., coeptum bellum, Sall.; nocte coepta, Tac. **II.** Intransit., *to begin, arise;* quoniam coepit Graecorum mentio, Juv.; ubi dies coepit, Sall

coepto, 1. (intens. of coepi). **A**. Transit. *to begin* or *undertake eagerly;* with infin., coercere seditionem, Tac.; appetere ea, Cic. **B**. Intransit., coeptantem conjurationem disjecit, Tac.

coeptum -i, n. (coepi), *a beginning, undertaking,* Liv.

coeptus -ūs, m. (coepi), *a beginning, undertaking,* Cic.

coëpŭlōnus -i, m. *a fellow-reveller,* Plaut.

coërcĕo -cŭi -cĭtum, 2. (com and arceo). **I**. Gen., *to enclose on all sides and hold fast, to encompass, enclose;* mundus omnia complexu suo coercet et continet, Cic. **II**. Esp., 1, *to confine, restrain;* (aqua) jubetur coerceri, Cic.; quibus (operibus) intra muros coercetur hostis, Liv.; 2, *to keep in order;* virgā levem aureā turbam, Hor.; 3, *to prune;* vitem ferro amputans coercet, Cic.; 4, *to check, curb;* cupiditates, Cic.; seditionem, Liv.; 5, *to punish;* magistratus noxium civem multā, vinculis verberibusque coerceto, Cic.

coërcĭtĭo -ōnis, f. (coerceo), 1, *a confining, restraining;* profusarum cupiditatum, Tac.; 2, *punishing;* magistratus, Liv.

coeruleus = caeruleus (q.v.).

coetus -ūs, m. (for coitus, from coeo). **I**. *a meeting together,* Lucr. **II**. *a meeting, assemblage;* in a bad sense, *a seditious meeting;* coetus nocturni, Liv.; coetum or coetus celebrare, *to assemble in large numbers,* Verg., Cic. poet.

Coeus -i, m. (Κοῖος), *a Titan, father of Latona.*

cōgĭtātē, adv. (cogitatus, from cogito), *carefully, thoughtfully, with consideration;* scribere, Cic.

cōgĭtātĭo -ōnis, f. (cogito), *thinking.* **I**. Gen., **A**. Act., a, *the act of thinking, conception;* dicebas, speciem per percipi cogitatione, non sensu, Cic.; ea quae cogitatione depingimus, Cic.; b, *reflection, meditation, consideration, reasoning;* ad hanc causam non sine aliqua spe et cogitatione venerunt, Cic.; ad reliquam cogitationem belli se recepit, Caes. **B**. Pass., *a thought, idea;* num ullam cogitationem habuisse videantur ii, etc., Cic.; esp. in plur., mandare litteris cogitationes suas, Cic.; posteriores enim cogitationes sapientiores solent esse, Cic. **II**. Esp., 1, *a thinking of, intention, design;* accusationis cogitatio, Cic.; 2, pass., *a thought, plan, purpose;* minor cogitatio intervenit majori, Liv.; magnae cogitationis manifestis, Tac.; 3, *the faculty of thought and reflection;* homo solus particeps rationis et cogitationis, Cic.

cōgĭtātus -a -um (partic. of cogito). Subst., **cōgĭtāta** -orum, n. *thoughts, reflections, ideas,* Cic.

cōgĭto, 1. (co-igito, for com and agito), *to put together in the mind, to think, reflect, consider.* **A**. Gen., cui vivere est cogitare, Cic.; with acc., beneficia alicuius, Cic.; Scipionem, Cic.; with acc. and infin., homines ea si bis accidere posse non cogitant, Cic.; with de and the abl., de deo, Cic.; with relative sentence, cogita qui sis, Cic.; with ad and the acc., ad haec igitur cogita, Cic.; with ut or ne and the subj., Caes. **B**. a, *to think of, intend, plan;* nihil cogitant nisi caedes, nisi incendia, Caes.; qui noceri alteri cogitat, Cic.; de parricidio, Cic.; ellipt. (in letters), inde ad Taurum cogitabam, *I intended to go,* Cic.; b, *to be disposed to;* si humaniter et sapienter et amabiliter in me cogitare vis, Cic.

cognātĭo -ōnis, f. (com and gnascor = nascor). **I**. Lit., *relationship, connection by blood.* **A**. Lit., cognatio quae mihi tecum est, Cic.; cognatione cum aliquo conjunctam esse, Cic.; aliquem cognatione attingere, Cic. **B**. Meton., *persons related, kindred, family;* cognationis

magnae homo, *with a large connexion,* Caes. **II**. Transf., *connexion, agreement, resemblance;* studiorum et artium, Cic.

cognātus -a -um (gnatus = natus, from nascor). **A**. *related, connected by blood,* Cic. Subst., **cognātus** -i, m., **cognāta** -ae, f. *a relation either on the father or mother's side,* Cic. **B**. Transf., *related, similar, cognate;* nihil est tam cognatum mentibus nostris quam numeri, Cic.

cognĭtĭo -ōnis, f. (cognosco). **I**. *knowledge,* **A**. *knowledge of or acquaintance with a thing or person;* aliquem cognitione atque hospitio dignum habere, Cic. **B**. *knowledge of, study of;* 1, gen., cognitio contemplatioque naturae, Cic.; plur., meton., *an idea, a conception;* insitas deorum vel potius innatas cognitiones habemus, Cic.; 2, legal t. t., *a legal investigation;* consulibus cognitionem dare, Cic.; cognitionem de existimatione alicuius constituere, Cic. **II**. = agnitio, *recognition,* Ter.

cognĭtor -ōris, m. (cognosco). **I**. Legal t. t., 1, *a witness to the identity of a Roman citizen in a foreign country,* Cic. **II**. 1, *the procurator* or *attorney who took charge of an action at law,* Cic.; transf., huius sententiae, *voucher for,* Cic.; 2, *a kind of public prosecutor in fiscal matters,* Ov.

cognĭtus -a -um, p. adj. with compar. and superl. (from cognosco), *known, tried, proved;* homo virtute cognitā, Cic.

cognōmĕn -Inis, n. (com and gnomen = nomen). **A**. *a surname, family name, the name following the name of the gens* (e.g., Cicero); alicui cognomen Coriolano or Capitoni est, Cic., Liv.; cognomen habere sapientis, Cic.; cognomen sumere or trahere or sibi arripere ex aliqua re, Cic. **B**. *name of a place;* Hesperiam Graji cognomine dicunt, Verg.

cognōmentum -i, n. 1, *a surname,* Plaut.; 2, *a name,* Tac.

cognōmĭnātus -a -um (com and nominatus) = συνώνυμος, *of the same meaning;* verba, *synonyms.*

cognōmĭnis -e (cognomen), *having the same name;* gaudet cognomine terra, Verg.; with dat., cognomine Insubribus pago, Liv.

cognōmĭno, 1. (cognomen), *to give a surname to, call by a surname,* Varr.

cognosco -gnōvi -gnĭtum (com and gnosco = nosco), 3. *to become acquainted with, remark, notice, perceive, see;* and in the perf. tenses, *to know.* **I**. Gen., with acc., cognoscere naturam rerum, Cic.; aliquem bene cognovisse, Cic.; with abl. of means, aliquid experiendo magis quam discendo, Cic.; with per, homo per se cognitus, Cic.; with ab or ex, aliquem ex litteris alicuius, Cic.; with two accusatives, aliquem hominem pudentem et officiosum, Cic.; with acc. and infin., Attici nostri in valde studiosum esse cognovi, Cic.; abl. absol., cognito, *it being known,* cognito vivere Ptolemaeum, Liv.; with relative sentence, cognoscite nunc, quae potestas decemviris et quanta detur, Cic. **II**. a, *to recognise;* quum eum Syracusis amplius centum cives Romani cognoscerent, Cic.; b, *to study;* Demosthenem totum, Cic.; c, of judges, *to hear, decide;* causa cognita, Cic.; cognoscere de actis Caesaris, Cic.

cōgo, cŏēgi, cŏactum, 3. (coigo for com and ago). **I**. *to bring, drive,* or *draw to one point, to collect.* **A**. Lit., a, pecudes stabulis, Verg.; esp. as milit. t. t., exercitum magnasque copias, Caes.; b, political t. t., *to assemble a public body;* senatum, Cic.; judices, Cic.; comitium, Caes.; c, *to bring together* gifts or money; pecuniam ex decumis, Cic.; d, *to unite, gather together;* nubes imbres ventique coguntur, Cic.;

of liquids, **or of a thin material**, *to thicken;* frigore mella cogit hiems, Verg.; lac coactum, *curdled*, Ov.; subst., **cŏacta** -orum, n. *thick woven cloth*, *felt*, Caes.; **e**, milit. t. t., agmen cogere, *to bring up the rear*, Caes.; fig., *to be the last;* ut nec duces simus nec agmen cogamus, Cic. **B.** Transf., **a**, *to unite*, *collect;* jus civile in certa genera, Cic.; **b**, *to infer, conclude, prove;* hoc cogere volebat falsas litteras esse, Cic. **II.** *to drive, force into a narrow space.* **A.** Lit., **a**, vi et necessario sumus in portum coacti, Cic.; **b**, of liquids and places, *to confine;* in artissimas ripas Aous cogitur amnis, Liv. **B.** Transf., **a**, *to force;* Boios in jus judiciumque populi Romani, Liv.; **b**, *to compel to do something;* aliquem ad militiam, Sall.; with infin., te emere coegit, Cic.; with ut and the subj., cogere incipit eos ut absentem Heraclium condemnarent, Cic.; with acc. of the thing one is compelled to do, cogere cives id omnes, Cic.; partic., coactus, *constrained;* invitus et coactus, Cic.

cŏhaerentĭa -ae, f. (cohaereo), *a coherence, connexion;* mundi, Cic.

cŏhaerĕo -haesi -haesum, 2. **I. A.** *to adhere to, hang together, be closely connected with;* cohaerens cum corpore membrum, Cic.; nec equo mea membra cohaerent, Ov. **B.** Transf., haec ratio pecuniarum implicita est cum illis pecuniis Asiaticis et cohaeret, Cic. **II. A.** *to have cohaerence, subsist, hold together;* mundus ita apte cohaeret, ut dissolvi nullo modo queat, Cic. **B.** Transf., vix diserti adolescentis cohaerebat oratio, Cic.

cŏhaeresco -haesi, 3. (inchoat. of cohaereo), *to hang together, mutually adhere;* atomi inter se cohaerentes, Cic.

cŏhērēs -ēdis, m. *a coheir*, Cic.

cŏhĭbĕo -ŭi -ĭtum, 2. (com and habeo). **I.** *to hold, contain, hold together;* brachium togā, Cic.; omnes naturas ipsa (natura) cohibet et continet, Cic. **II.** *to confine, restrain.* **A.** Lit., ventos carcere, Ov.; crinem nodo, *to tie*, Hor. **B.** Transf., *to hinder, hold back, control, repress;* conatus alicuius, Cic.; manum, oculos, animum ab auro gazaque regia, Cic.; foll. by quominus and the subj., Tac.

cŏhŏnesto, 1. (com and honesto), *to honour or reverence;* statuas, Cic.

cŏhorresco -horrŭi, 3. (com and horresco), *to shudder or shiver;* quo (sudore) quum cohorruisset, Cic.; esp., *to shudder from fright*, *to be horrified at;* quem ut agnovi, equidem cohorrui, Cic.

cŏhors (cors, chors) -tis, f. (connected with χόρτος). **I.** *an enclosure for cattle*, Ov. **II.** Meton., **a**, *a troop, throng;* fratrum stipata, Verg.; febrium, Hor. **B.** Esp. milit. t. t., **1**, *a cohort, a division of the Roman army, being the tenth part of a legion*, Caes.; often = *the auxiliary forces of the allies*, Sall.; **2**, praetoria cohors, **a**, *a body-guard for the general*, Caes.; **b**, *the retinue of the governor of a province*, Cic.

cŏhortātĭo -ōnis, f. (cohortor), *an exhortation, encouragement;* cohortatio quaedam judicum ad honeste judicandum, Cic.

cŏhortĭcŭla -ae, f. (dim. of cohors), *a little cohort*, ap. Cic.

cŏhortor, 1. dep. (com and hortor), *to encourage, incite, exhort;* used esp. of the general's speech to his soldiers before a battle, aliquem ad virtutis studium, Cic.; exercitum more militari ad pugnam, Caes.; foll. by ut or ne with the subj., or by the subj. alone, Cic., Caes.; with ad and tae gerund, aliquem ad honorandum Serv. Sulpicium, Cic.

cŏinquĭno, 1. no perf., *to pollute, defile*, Col.

cŏĭtĭo -ōnis, f. (coeo), **1**, *a coming together, meeting*, Ter.; **2**, *a faction, party, coalition, conspiracy;* suspicio coitionis, Cic.; coitiones tribunorum adversus nobilium juventutem ortae, Liv.

cŏĭtus -ūs, m. (coeo), *a coming together, union, connexion*, Ov.

cŏlăphus -i, m. (κόλαφος), *a box on the ear;* colapho icere, or ferire aliquem, Plaut., Nep.

Colchis -ĭdis, f. (Κολχίς), *Colchis, a country on the eastern shore of the Black Sea;* hence adj., **Colchis** -ĭdis, f. *Colchian*, and used subst.= *Medea*, Hor.; **Colchus** -a -um, *Colchian*, venena (of Medea), Ov. Subst., **Colchus** -i, m. *a Colchian*, and appell. = *a barbarian*, Hor.

cŏlens -entis, p. adj. (colo), *honouring, reverent;* qui sunt religionum colentes (cives), Cic.

cŏlĕus -i, m. *a testicle*, Cic.

cōlĭphĭa (cōlȳphĭa) -ōrum, n. *a kind of nourishing food used by wrestlers*, Juv.

cōlis = caulis (q.v.).

collăbasco, 3. (com and labasco), *to begin to fall, to totter*, Plaut.

collăbĕfacto, 1. (com and labefacto), *to cause to totter*, Ov.; used also of the liquefaction of hard bodies, Lucr.

collăbĕfĭo -factus -fĭĕri (com and labefacio). **A.** Lit., *to be made to totter or fall;* altera (navis), praefracto rostro tota collabefieret, *was dashed to pieces;* igni collabefacta, *melted*, Lucr. **B.** Transf., a Themistocle collabefactus, *overthrown*, Nep.

collābor -lapsus sum, -labi, dep. (com and labor), *to fall down, sink down, collapse;* **a**, of buildings, towns, etc., collapsa quaedam ruinis sunt, Liv.; **b**, of persons, *to fall down in a swoon or death;* cecidit collapsus in artus, Verg.

collăcĕrātus -a -um (com and lacero), *very much lacerated or torn;* corpus, Tac.

collăcrĭmātĭo -ōnis, f. (collacrimo), *a weeping*, Cic.

collăcrĭmo, 1. (com and lacrimo), *to break out into tears*, Cic.; with acc. *to bemoan, weep for very much;* histrio casum meum totiens collacrimavit, Cic.

collactĕus -i, m. **-a** -ae, f. *a foster-brother, or sister*, Juv.

collāre -is, n. (collum), *an iron collar or chain for the neck*, Plaut.

Collātĭa -ae, f. *town of the Sabines near Rome;* hence, **Collātīnus** -a -um, *belonging to Collatia;* surname of L. Tarquinius, *the husband of Lucretia, native of Collatia.*

collātĭo -ōnis, f. (confero). **A.** Lit. *a bringing together;* **a**, signorum, *a hostile collision in the field*, Cic.; **b**, *a contribution, collection;* stipis aut decimae, Liv.; *a present for the emperor*, Tac. **B.** Transf. *comparison, simile;* collatio est oratio rem cum re ex similitudine conferens, Cic.

collātīvus -a -um (collatus), *brought together, united;* venter, *swollen*, Plaut.

collātor -ōris, m. (confero), *a contributor*, Plaut.

collātus a- -um, partic. of confero.

collaudātĭo -ōnis, f. (collaudo), *strong, or hearty praise*, Cic.

collaudo, 1. (com and laudo), *to praise very much;* orationem satis multis verbis, Cic.

collaxo, 1. (com and laxo), *to widen, extend*, Lucr.

collecta -ae, f. (collectus, from 1. colligo), *a contribution in money;* collectam a conviva exigere, Cic.

collectĭcĭus (collectītĭus) -a -um (1. colligo), *gathered together;* exercitus, *quickly levied,* Cic.

collectĭo -ōnis, f. (1. colligo). **I.** *a collecting, gathering together, collection;* membrorum, Cic. **II.** Transf., 1, in rhetoric, *a brief recapitulation,* Cic. ; 2, in logic, *a conclusion, inference,* Sen.

collectus -a -um, p. adj. with compar. and superl. (1. colligo), *contracted, concise, concentrated;* dicendi genus, Tac.

collēga -ae, m. (com and lēgo), 1, *one who is deputed with another, a colleague, partner in office;* alicuius collegam in questura fuisse, Cic. ; 2, *a comrade,* Juv.

collēgĭum -ĭi, n. (collega). **I.** Abstract, *colleagueship, the connexion between colleagues, between those who jointly fill the same office;* P. Decius per tot collegia expertus, Liv. **II.** Concrete, *persons united in colleagueship, a body, guild, corporation, college;* **a,** of magistrates, praetorum, tribunorum, Cic. ; **b,** of priests, pontificum, augurum, Cic. ; **c,** *a political club;* innumerabilia quaedam collegia ex omni faece urbis ac servitio constituta, Cic. ; **d,** *a trade guild;* mercatorum, Liv. ; **e,** *a band, body;* ambubajarum, Hor.

collībertus -i, m. (com and libertus), *a fellow freedman,* Cic.

collĭbet, or **collŭbet** -bŭit or -bĭtum est, 2. (com and lubet or libet), impers. *it pleases, is agreeable;* simul ac mihi collibitum sit de te cogitare, Cic.

collīdo -līsi -līsum (com and laedo), 3. *to strike together, dash together;* 1, humor ita mollis est, ut facile comprimi collidique possit, Cic.; 2, pass. *to come into hostile collision;* Graecia barbariae lento collisa duello, Hor.

collĭgātĭo -ōnis, f. (2. colligo), *a binding together, connexion;* causarum omnium, Cic.

1. **collĭgo** -lēgi -lectum, 3. (com and lĕgo), *to bring together, collect.* **I.** Lit., **a,** radices, Cic. ; vasa, *to pack up,* Liv. ; **b,** *to bring together, assemble;* ex agris ingentem numerum perditorum hominum, Cic. ; milites, Cic. ; **c,** *to gather into a smaller space, contract;* se colligere or colligi in arma, *to cover oneself with a shield,* Verg. **II.** Transf., **a,** *to gather together;* multa in conventu vitia in aliquem, Cic. ; **b,** *to gain, acquire;* ex hoc labore magnam gratiam magnamque dignitatem, Cic. ; **c,** colligere se, or animum, or mentem, *to compose oneself, gain courage;* se ex timore, Caes. ; **d,** in speech, *to bring together, tell of;* omnia belli civilia, Cic. ; **e,** *to think of;* quum maximarum civitatum veteres animo calamitates colligo, Cic.; **f,** of numbers, *to reckon;* centum et viginti anni ab interitu Ciceronis in hunc diem colliguntur, Tac. ; **g,** *to infer, conclude;* bene etiam colligit haec pueris et mulierculis esse grata, Cic.

2. **collĭgo,** 1. (com and ligo), *to bind, tie, fasten together.* **I. A.** Lit., manus, Cic. **B.** Transf., **a,** *to connect;* (mens) homines antea dissociatos jucundissimo inter se sermonis vinculo colligavit, Cic. ; gen. in pass., res omnes inter se aptae colligataeque, Cic. ; **b,** *to join together in writing;* ut verbis colligentur sententiae, Cic. ; **c,** *to join politically;* se cum multis, Cic. ; **d,** *to detain;* aliquem in Graecia, Cic. **II.** *to bind together* the parts of a thing. **A.** Lit., omne colligatum solvi potest, Cic. **B.** Transf., **a,** *to join together* in narration ; septingentorum annorum memoriam uno libro, Cic. ; **b,** *to hinder, stop;* impetum furentis vitae suae periculo, Cic.

collīnĕo, 1. (com and lineo), *to direct in a straight line;* hastam aut sagittam, Cic. ; absol., quis est enim qui totum diem jaculans non aliquando collineet. *hits the mark,* Cic.

collīno -lēvi -lĭtum, 3. (com and lino), *to besmear, daub;* aliquid aliqua re, Hor.

collīnus -a -um (collis). **I.** *hilly, relating to a hill, situate on a hill.* **II.** Esp. **Collīnus,** *of* or *on the Quirinal hill;* tribus, Cic. ; esp., porta Collina, *a gate of Rome near the Quirinal Hill,* Liv.; herbae, *growing near the Porta Collina,* Prop.

collĭquĕfactus -a -um (com and liquefio), *liquefied, melted,* Cic.

collis -is, m. *a hill, high ground,* Cic.

collŏcātĭo -ōnis, f. (colloco). **I.** Act., *a placing,* esp. *a giving in marriage;* filiae, Cic. **II.** Pass., *a position;* **a,** siderum, Cic. ; **b,** rhet. t. t., *position, arrangement, order;* verborum, Cic. ; argumentorum, Cic. ; bene structam collocationem dissolvere, Cic.

collŏco (con-loco), 1. *to place, lay, set.* **I.** Gen. **A.** Lit., 1, tabulas bene pictas in bono lumine, Cic. ; simulacrum Victoriae ante ipsam Minervam, Caes. ; aliquem in curru, Cic. ; 2, milit. t.t. *to station;* duas legiones et omnia auxilia in summo jugo, Caes. ; alicui insidias ante fundum suum, Cic. **B.** Transf., 1, *to place, lay, put;* res eae, quae agentur aut dicentur, suo loco collocandae, Cic. ; 2, *to place, cause to rest;* in aliquo magnam spem dignitatis suae, *to build hopes on,* Cic. ; 3, of time, *to pass;* adolescentiam suam in amore atque voluptatibus, Cic. **II.** Esp. **A.** Lit., 1, *to set up in a particular place, erect;* sedes ac domicilium, Cic. ; 2, chlamydem, ut pendeat apte, *to arrange,* Ov. ; 3, of persons, *to settle, station;* in eius tetrarchia unum ex Graecis comitibus suis, Cic. ; colonias, Cic. ; milit. t.t. *to billet, quarter;* exercitum in Aulercis Lexoviisque in hibernis, Caes. ; 4, *to settle in possession* or *property;* aliquem in patrimonio suo, Cic. **B.** Transf., 1, *to place;* aliquem in amplissimo consilio et in altissimo gradu dignitatis, Cic. ; 2, of women, *to settle in marriage;* aliquam in matrimonium, Cic.; alicuius filio filiam suam, Cic. ; 3, of money, *to invest;* pecuniam in praediis collocare, Cic. ; or *to employ, spend;* patrimonium in reipublicae salute, Cic. ; 4, *to arrange in proper order;* verba diligenter collocata, Cic. ; 5, *to direct, manage;* rem militarem, Cic.

collŏcŭplēto, 1. (com and locupleto), *to enrich exceedingly,* Ter.

collŏcŭtĭo -ōnis, f. (colloquor), *conversation;* collocutiones familiarissimae cum aliquo, Cic.

collŏquĭum -ĭi, n. (colloquor), *talk, conversation, colloquy, conference;* colloquia secreta serere cum aliquo, Liv. ; clandestina colloquia cum hostibus, Cic.; colloquium expetere, Caes.; dare, Liv. ; crebra colloquia inter se habere, Caes.; per colloquia de pace agere, Caes.; aliquem ad colloquium evocare, Cic. ; ad colloquium congredi, Liv.; dirimere, Caes.; interrumpere, Caes. ; in alicuius congressum colloquiumque pervenire, Cic.

collŏquor -cūtus or -quūtus sum, -loqui (com and loquor), 3. dep. *to speak, talk, converse with any one, to treat* or *negotiate with;* cum aliquo, Cic. ; inter se, Cic. ; cum aliquo per litteras, Cic.

collūcĕo, 2. (com and luceo), *to shine on all sides, to be completely illuminated.* **I.** Lit., sol qui tam longe lateque colluceat, Cic. ; collucent moenia flammis, Verg. **II.** Transf., vidi collucere omnia furtis tuis, Cic.

collūdo -lūsi -lūsum, 3. (com and ludo). **A.** Lit. *to play with;* paribus, Hor. **B.** Transf. *to have a secret understanding with another person, to act collusively,* Cic.

collum -i, n. (**collus** -i, m.), *the neck;* 1, of

men and animals, in collum invasit, *fell on his neck*, Cic.; collum torquere, *to drag before a tribunal*, or *to prison*, Liv.; posuit collum in pulvere, Hor.; **2**, *the neck* of a bottle, Phaedr.; of a poppy, Verg.

collŭo -lŭi -lūtum, 3. (com and luo), *to wash thoroughly, rinse;* os, Plin.; ora, *to quench the thirst*, Ov.

collus -i, m. = collum (q.v.).

collūsĭo -ōnis, f. (colludo), *collusion, a secret understanding;* cum aliquo, Cic.

collūsor -ōris, m. (colludo), **a**, *a play-fellow*, Juv.; **b**, *a fellow-gambler*, Cic.

collustro, 1. (com and lustro). **A**. *to illuminate on all sides;* sol omnia clarissima luce collustrans, Cic.; in picturis alios opaca, alios collustrata delectant, *brilliant colouring*, Cic. **B**. Transf., *to survey, look at on all sides;* omnia oculis, Cic.

collŭtŭlento, 1, *to dirty* or *defile all over*, Plaut.

collŭvĭo -ōnis, and **collŭvĭēs** -ēi, f. (colluo). **A**. *a flowing together*, or *collection of impurities, filth*, Plin. **B**. Transf., *rabble, medley, offscourings;* omnium scelerum, Cic.; quum ex hac turba et colluvione discedam, Cic.

collўbus -i, m. (κόλλυβος). **A**. *the agio* or *percentage charged in money-changing*, Cic. **B**. Transf., *the money-changer's occupation*, Cic.

collўra -ae, f. (κολλύρα), *a kind of cake* or *bun which was broken into broth*, Plaut.

collўrĭcus -a -um, jus, *the broth with which the* collyra *was eaten*, Plaut.

collўrĭum -ĭi, n. (κολλύριον), *eye-salve*, Hor.

cŏlo, cŏlui, cultum, 3. **I**. **1**, *to cultivate, till the ground, farm;* agrum, Cic.; praedia studiose, Cic.; vitem, Cic.; **2**, *to dwell in a place, inhabit;* urbem, Cic.; insulas, Liv.; absol., circa utramque ripam Rhodani, Liv. **II**. **1**, *to take care of, attend to;* formam augere colendo, Ov.; **2**, *to cultivate, practise, study;* studium philosophiae a prima adolescentia, Cic.; fidem virtutem, sapientiam, Cic.; **3**, *to pay respect to;* **a**, of deities, *to worship;* deos, Cic.; Musarum delubra, Cic.; templum miro honore, Verg.; **b**, of men, *to honour, reverence, court;* aliquem summa observantia, Cic.

cŏlŏcāsĭa -ae, f. and **cŏlŏcāsĭum** -ĭi, n. (κολοκασία), *the Egyptian bean*, Verg.

cŏlōna -ae, f. (colonus), *a country woman*, Ov.

Cŏlōnae -ārum, f. (Κολωναί), *a town in Troas*.

Cŏlōnēus -a -um, *belonging to the Attic deme Colonos;* Oedipus Coloneus, *a tragedy of Sophocles*.

cŏlōnĭa -ae, f. (colonus). **I**. *a farm, estate*, Col. **II**. *a colony*. **A**. Lit., constituere coloniam, Cic.; colonos deducere in colonias, Cic. **B**. Meton., *the colonists;* deducere, Cic.; mittere in locum, Cic.

cŏlōnĭcus -a -um (colonus), **1**, *relating* or *belonging to agriculture* or *a farm;* leges, Varr.; **2**, *relating* or *belonging to a colony, colonial;* cohortes, *levied in Roman colonies*, Caes.

cŏlōnus -i, m. (colo), **1**, *a farmer, agriculturist*, Cic.; **2**, *a colonist, inhabitant of a colony*, Cic.; poet. transf. = *inhabitant*, Verg.

Cŏlŏphōn -ōnis, f. (Κολοφὼν), *one of the twelve Ionian towns on the coast of Lydia, famed for its cavalry*. Adj., **Cŏlŏphōnĭăcus** -a -um, **Cŏlŏphōnĭus** -a -um, *Colophonian*.

cŏlor (colos) -ōris, m. (colo). **I**. Lit., **A**. Gen. *colour, tint, hue*, Cic.; colorem ducere, of the grape, *to become coloured*, Verg. **B**. Esp. **1**, *complexion;* verus, *real*, Ter.; fucatus, *artificial*,

Hor.; mutare, *to change colour*, Hor., **Ov.**; **2**, *beautiful complexion, beauty;* nimium ne crede colori, Verg. **II**. Transf., **1**, *outward show, external appearance;* civitatis, Cic.; **2**, esp. of oratory or speech, *cast, character, tone;* color urbanitatis, Cic.; **3**, *ornament, embellishment;* flos et color pigmentorum, Cic.; **4**, *an artful excuse*, or *colouring of a questionable action*, Juv.

cŏlōrātus -a -um (partic. of coloro), **1**, *coloured;* arcus, Cic.; **2**, *red, embrowned*, Tac.

cŏlōro, 1. (color). **A**. Lit., *to colour;* **a**, corpora, Cic.; **b**, *to tan* (of the sun); quum in sole ambulem natura fit ut colorer, Cic. **B**. Transf., *to give tone* or *colour to style;* urbanitate quadam quasi colorata oratio, Cic.

cŏlossēus -a -um (κολοσσαῖος), *colossal, gigantic*, Plin.

cŏlossĭcus -a -um (κολοσσικός), *colossal, gigantic*, Plin.

cŏlossus -i, m. (κολοσσός), *a colossus, a statue larger than life;* esp. applied to the gigantic statue of Apollo at the entrance of the harbour of Rhodes, Plin.

cŏlostra -ae, f. (**cŏlostra** -ōrum, n.), *the first milk after calving, biestings*, Mart.; used as a term of endearment, Plaut.

cŏlŭber -bri, m. *a serpent, snake*, Verg., Ov.

cŏlŭbra -ae, f. *a female serpent, a snake*, Hor.

cŏlŭbrĭfer -fěra -fěrum (coluber and fero), *snake-bearing, snaky-haired*, epithet of Medusa, Ov.

cŏlŭbrīnus -a -um (coluber), *snake-like;* transf., *cunning, wily*, Plaut.

cŏlum -i, n. *a colander, sieve, strainer*, Verg.

cŏlumba -ae, f. (columbus), *a pigeon, dove*, Cic.; Cythereiades (as sacred to Venus), Ov.

cŏlumbar -āris, n. (columba), *a kind of collar for slaves like a pigeon-hole*, Plaut.

cŏlumbīnus -a -um (columba), *relating* or *belonging to a pigeon;* pulli, Cic.

cŏlumbŭlus -i, m. (dim. of columbus), *a little pigeon*, Plin.

cŏlumbus -i, m. *a male dove* or *pigeon*, Hor.

1. cŏlŭmella -ae, f. (dim. of columna), *a little column*, Cic.

2. Cŏlŭmella -ae, m. L. Junius Moderatus, *a Roman writer upon agriculture, native of Cadiz, contemporary of Seneca and Celsus*.

cŏlŭmen -Inis, n. (* cello, *that which is raised on high*). **I**. *a height*. **A**. Lit., sub altis Phrygiae columinibus, *mountains*, Cat. **B**. Transf., of persons, *the chief, most distinguished;* columen amicorum Antonii Cotyla Varius, Cic. **II**. *a pillar*. **A**. Lit., Cic. poet. |**B**. Transf., columen reipublicae, *support*, Cic.

cŏlumna -ae, f. (connected with columen), *a pillar, column*. **A**. Lit., marmorea, Cic.; prov., incurrere amentem in columnas, *to run one's head against a stone wall*, Cic.; columna rostrata, *a column adorned with beaks of ships erected in honour of the victory of Duilius over the Carthaginians*, Quint.; columna Maenia, *a pillar in the Roman forum to which thieves and slaves were tied to receive punishment*, Cic.; hence, adhaerescere ad columnam, Cic.; ad columnam pervenire, Cic.; columnae, *the pillars in Rome round which books were exposed for sale*, Hor.; columnae Protei, *the boundaries of Egypt* (columns being used to mark boundaries), Verg.; columnae Herculis, *the mountains of Calpe and Abyla at the straits of Gibraltar*, Plin. **B**. Transf., **a**, *a support, pillar of the state;* injurioso ne pede promas stantem columnam, Hor.; **b**, *a water-spout*, Lucr.

cŏlumnārĭus -a -um (columna), *belonging*

to a pillar. Subst., **1, cŏlumnārĭi** -ōrum, m. *those who have been punished at the* columna Maenia (v. columna), *rascals, thieves,* ap. Cic.;

2, cŏlumnārĭum -ĭi, n. *a tax on pillars,* Cic.

cŏlumnātus -a -um (columna), *supported on columns,* Varr. ; os, *resting on the hand,* Plaut.

cŏlurnus -a -um (for corulnus, from corulus), *made of hazel wood ;* hastilia, Verg.

cŏlus -i and -ūs, abl. colo, f. (m. Cat., Ov.), *a distaff,* Cic.

com, old Latin = cum, in classical Latin; only found in composition.

cŏma -ae, f. (κόμη). **A.** Lit., *the hair of the head,* Cic. **B.** Transf., **1,** *the leaves of trees,* Hor.; **2,** *the wool of sheep,* ap. Cic.

cŏmans -antis (coma), *hairy ;* colla equorum, Verg. ; galea, *crested,* Verg. ; stella, *a comet,* Ov. ; narcissus sera comans, *covered with leaves,* Verg.

cŏmarchus -i, m. (κώμαρχος), *the mayor or chief officer of a village,* Plaut.

cŏmātus -a -um (coma), **1,** *hairy,* Mart. ; comata Gallia = *Transalpina,* Plin. ; **2,** silva, *in full leaf,* Cat.

1. combĭbo -bĭbi, 3. *to drink in, suck up, imbibe.* **A.** Lit., venenum corpore, Hor. **B.** Fig., quas (artes) si dum est tener combiberit, Cic.

2. combĭbo -ōnis, m. *a boon companion, comrade in drinking,* Cic.

Combultĕrĭa -ae, f. *town of the Samnites on the south-west borders of Campania.*

combūro -bussi -bustum, 3. (com and uro). **A.** Lit., *to burn up, consume entirely ;* libros, Caes. ; aliquem vivum, Cic. ; *of the burning of the dead,* aliquem in foro, Cic. **B.** Transf., aliquem judicio, *to ruin,* Cic. ; diem, *to consume in revelling,* Plaut.

combustum -i, n. *a burn or scald,* Plin.

Cŏmē -ēs, f. (κώμη, *village*). **I.** Hiera Come, *a place in Caria.* **II.** Xyline Come, *a place in Pisidia.* **III.** Antoridos Come, *a place in Phrygia.*

cŏmĕdo -ēdi -ēsum (-essum) or -estum, 3. *to eat up, consume entirely.* **A.** Lit., ex se natos (of Saturn), Cic. **B.** Transf., aliquem oculis, *to devour with one's eyes,* Mart. ; se, *to consume oneself in grief,* Cic. **C.** *to consume, waste, squander ;* patrimonium, Cic.

cŏmes -ĭtis, c. (com and eo or meo), **1,** *a companion, comrade, associate ;* seditionum, Tac. ; fugae, Cic. ; victoriae, Caes. ; esse comitem alicuius, Cic.; aliquem comitem habere, Cic. ; non praebere se comitem illius furoris sed ducem, Cic. ; *used of things and abstractions,* mortis comes gloria, Cic. ; **2,** esp. *an attendant ;* **a,** *the attendant or tutor of a boy,* Verg. ; **b,** plur., comites, *the retinue which accompanied a Roman magistrate into his province,* and generally, *any body of attendants ;* comites omnes magistratuum, Cic. ; in later times, *the body of courtiers, the imperial court,* Suet.

cŏmētēs -ae, m. (κομήτης), *a comet,* Cic.

cŏmĭcē, adv. (comicus), *in the manner of comedy ;* comice res tragicas tractare, Cic.

cŏmĭcus -a -um (κωμικός). **A.** Adj., **a,** *relating to comedy, comic ;* poeta, Cic. ; **b,** *represented in comedy ;* senes, Cic. ; adolescens, Cic. **B.** Subst., **a,** *an actor in comedy,* Plaut. ; **b,** *a comic poet,* Cic.

cominus = comminus (q.v.).

cŏmis -e (como), *courteous, kind, friendly, obliging, amiable ;* **a,** of persons, dominus, Cic. ; in amicis tuendis, Cic. ; erga aliquem, Cic. ; **b,** **of things,** comi hospitio accipi, Liv. ; sermo, Tac.

cōmissābundŭs -a -um (comissor), *revelling, rioting ;* temulento agmine per Indiam comissabundus incessit, Liv.

cōmissātĭo -ōnis, f. (comissor), *a revel, riotous feasting,* Cic.

cōmissātor -ōris, m. (comissor), *a reveller, riotous feaster,* Cic. ; transf., comissatores conjurationis, *accomplices,* Cic.

cōmissor (κωμάζω), 1, dep. *to make a joyful procession with music and dancing, to revel, feast riotously ;* comissatum ire ad aliquem, Liv.; comissari in domum Pauli, Hor.

cōmĭtas -ātis, f. (comis), *courtesy, friendliness, obligingness, civility* (opp. gravitas, severitas); comitas affabilitasque sermonis, Cic.

cōmĭtātus -ūs, m. (comitor), **1,** *attendance, companionship ;* optimorum et clarissimorum civium, Cic. ; transf., tanto virtutum comitatu (opus est), Cic. ; **2,** *a train, retinue, following ;* praedonis improbissimi societas atque comitatus, Cic. ; esp. **a,** in imperial times, *the court, imperial suite,* Tac. ; **b,** *a caravan, convoy ;* magnus, Caes.

cōmĭtĕr, adv. (comis), *courteously, civilly, kindly, affably,* Cic.

cōmĭtĭa, v. comitium.

cōmĭtĭālis -e (comitia), *relating to the comitia ;* dies, mensis, *when the comitia were held,* Cic.; homines, *men constantly in attendance on the comitia, and ready to sell their votes,* Plaut. ; morbus, *epilepsy, so called because its occurrence put a stop to the* comitia, Cels. ; hence subst., **cōmĭtĭālis** -is, m. *one afflicted with epilepsy,* Plin.

cōmĭtĭātus -ūs, m. (comitia), *the assembly of the people in the comitia,* Cic.

cōmĭtĭum -ĭi, n. (comeo = coeo). **I.** Sing. *an enclosed place in or near the Roman forum, where the comitia were held.* **II.** Plur. **cōmĭtĭa** -ōrum, n. *the assembly of the Roman people, under three distinct forms ;* centuriata, *an assembly according to the centuries instituted by Servius Tullius ;* curiata, *an assembly of the curies, in later times rarely held except formally ;* tributa, *the assembly of the people in their tribes ;* comitia habere, *to hold an assembly of the people,* Cic. ; consularia, *assembly for the purpose of electing a consul,* Liv. ; tribunicia quaestoria, Cic. ; comitia instituere, obire, dimittere, Cic.

cōmĭto, 1. = comitor, partic. comitatus, *accompanied ;* with abl., alienis viris, Cic.; dolore, Ov. ; abs. bene comitare, Cic.

cōmĭtor, 1. dep. (comes), **1,** *to join as a companion or follower, to accompany, to follow ;* aliquem, Caes. ; nautas fuga, Verg.; absol., magna comitante caterva, Verg.; with dat., tardis mentibus virtus non facile comitatur, Cic. ; **2,** *to follow to the grave ;* aliquem, Nep., Verg.

commācŭlo, 1. *to spot all over, pollute* **I.** Lit., manus sanguine, Verg. **II.** Transf., se isto infinito ambitu, Cic.

Commāgēnē -ēs, f. (Κομμαγηνή), *a province of Syria* (capital Samosata), now *Camash.* Adj., **Commāgēnus** -a -um, *Commagenian.*

commănĭpŭlāris -is, m. *a soldier belonging to the same maniple or company, a comrade,* Tac.

commĕātus -ūs, m. (commeo). **I.** *free passage, going and coming,* Plaut. **II.** Meton., **1,** *liberty to go unhindered ;* milit. t. t., *leave of absence, furlough ;* commeatum dare, Liv.; in commeatu esse, *to be on furlough,* Liv. ; cum commeatu Syracusis remanere, Cic ; **2,** *that which is going or coming ;* **a,** *a company of merchants, caravan ;* Londinium copiâ negotiatorum et commeatuum maxime celebre, Tac. ; **b,** *supply of provisions, food, forage ;* commeatum or commeatus

parare, Liv., Sall.; accipere, **arcessere**, convehere, advehere, portare, Liv.; petere, Caes.;
aliquem commeatu prohibere, Caes.; aliquem
commeatu et reliquis copiis intercludere, Cic.

commĕdĭtor, 1, dep. *to remind, call to remembrance*, Lucr.

commĕmĭni -isse, *to remember fully;* utrum
hoc tu parum commeministi, an ego non satis
intellexi? Cic.

commĕmŏrābĭlis -e (commemoro), *worthy
of remembrance, worthy of mention, memorable;*
pietas, Cic.

commĕmŏrātĭo -ōnis, f. (commemoro), *remembrance, mention, reminding;* officiorum, Cic.

commĕmŏro, 1. **I.** *to call to mind, recollect;*
quid quoque die dixerim, audierim, egerim, commemoro vesperi, Cic. **II. a,** *to remind another
person of something, to bring to another person's remembrance;* gratiam, amicitiam cognationemque,
Cic.; **b,** *to mention, relate, recount;* humanam
societatem, Cic.; Critolaus iste, quem cum Dio-
gene venisse commemoras, Cic.; de alicuius virtute, Cic.

commendābĭlis -e (commendo), *commendable, praiseworthy;* nec ullo commendabilis merito, Liv.

commendātĭcĭus -a -um (commendatus),
relating to a recommendation; literae, *a letter of
introduction,* Cic.

commendātĭo -ōnis, f. (commendo), 1,
recommendation, commendation; commendatio
nostra ceterorumque amicorum, Cic.; 2, *that
which recommends, excellence;* ingenii, liberalitatis, Cic.

commendātrix -īcis, f. (commendo), *that
which commends;* legem commendatricem virtutum, Cic.

commendātus -a -um, p. adj. (from commendo), 1, *recommended, commended;* quae (res)
commendatior erit memoriae hominum? Cic.; 2,
esteemed, prized, valued, Plin.

commendo, 1. (com and mando), *to commit
to the care, keeping,* or *protection of any one.* **I.**
Lit., tibi eius omnia negotia, Cic. **II.** Transf.,
A. Gen., nomen suum immortalitati, Cic.; aliquid literis, *to commit to writing,* ap. Cic. **B.**
Esp. **a,** *to recommend;* aliquem alicui diligenter, Cic.; se Caesari, Caes.; **b,** *to set off,
grace, render agreeable;* nulla re una magis oratorem commendari quam verborum splendore
et copia, Cic.

commensus, partic. of commetior.

commentārĭŏlum -i., n. (dim. of com-
mentarius), *a short treatise,* Cic.

commentārĭus -ii., m. and **commentārĭ-
um** -ii., n. (commentus, from comminiscor); 1, *a
memorandum,* or *note-book, a diary;* in commentarium referre, Cic.; commentarii belli Gallici,
the notes of Caesar on the Gallic war, Cic.; 2,
legal t. t., a brief, Cic.

commentātĭo -ōnis, f. (commentor), 1, *deep
reflection, careful consideration, meditation;* tota
philosophorum vita commentatio mortis est,
Cic.; 2, *practice, study of an orator;* commen-
tationes quotidianae, Cic.; 3, *a dissertation,* Plin.

commentīcĭus -a -um (commentus, from
comminiscor), *invented, fictitious;* nominibus
novis et commenticiis appellata, Cic.; civitas
Platonis, *ideal,* Cic.; crimen, *false,* Ov.

1. **commentor**, 1. dep. (com and MEN,
root of mens). **A.** *to consider thoroughly, reflect
upon deeply;* futuras secum miserias, Cic.; de
populi Romani libertate, Cic.; with rel. clause,
ut ante commentemur inter nos qua ratione
nobis traducendum sit hoc tempus, Cic. **B.**

Esp., *to study, practise, prepare for;* comment-
abar declamitans saepe cum M. Pisone et cum
Q. Pompeio quotidie, Cic.; with acc., commentari orationem in reum, Cic.; partic. perf. passive,
commentata oratio, Cic.; neut. plur. subst., sua
et commentata et scripta, Cic. **C.** *to sketch,
compose, write down;* mimos, Cic.

2. **commentor** -ōris, m. (comminiscor), *a
discoverer, inventor;* uvae, *Bacchus,* Ov.

commentum -i, n. (commentus from comminiscor), 1, *a fiction, an invention, contrivance;* opinionum commenta, *fancies,* Cic.;
miraculi, Liv.; 2, *a lie, falsehood;* millia rumorum commenta, Ov.

commĕo, 1. *to go up and down, come and go,
visit frequently;* vulgatum erat inter Vejos Rom-
amque nuncios commeare, Liv.; ut tuto ab
repentino hostium incursu etiam singuli commeare possent, Caes.; Delos quo omnes undique
cum mercibus atque oneribus commeabant, Cic.;
of ships, navis, quae ad ea furta, quae reliquisses,
commearet, Cic.; of the heavenly bodies, sursum deorsum, ultro citro, Cic.; of letters, crebro
enim illius litterae ab aliis ad nos commeant,
find their way to us, Cic.

commercĭum -ĭi, n. (com and merx). **I.
A.** *trade, commerce;* commercio prohibere aliquem, Sall. **B.** Meton., **a,** *the right of trade;*
commercium in eo agro nemini est, Cic.; salis
commercium dedit, Liv.; **b,** *an article of traffic,*
Plin.; **c,** *a place of trade, commercial depôt,* Plin.
II. *intercourse, communication, correspondence;*
commercium sermonum facere, Liv.; commercium belli, *negotiations as to ransom of prisoners,*
truces, etc., Tac.; habere commercium cum aliquo, Cic.

commercor, 1. dep. *to buy together, buy up;*
arma, tela alia, Sall.

commĕrĕo -ŭi -itum, 2. (commereor, dep.
Plaut.), 1, *to deserve fully;* aestimationem (poenae), Cic.; 2, *to commit a fault;* culpam, Plaut.

commētĭor -mensus, 4. 1, *to measure;* siderum ambitus, Cic.; 2, *to measure with anything,
compare;* negotium cum tempore, Cic

commēto, 1. (intens. of commeo), *to go frequently,* Ter.

commigro, 1. *to remove in a body, to migrate;*
in domum suam, Cic.

commīlĭtĭum -ĭi, n. (com and miles). **A.**
a companionship in war or *military service,* Tac.
B. Transf., *companionship, fellowship,* Ov.

commīlĭto -ōnis, m. (com and milito), *a
companion* or *comrade in war,* Cic.

comminātĭo -ōnis, f. (comminor), *a threatening, threat,* Cic.

commingo -minxi -minctum or -mictum, 3
to make water on, Hor.; transf., *to defile,* Cat.

commĭniscor -mentus, 3. dep. *to feign, invent;* monogrammos deos, Cic.; mendacium,
Plaut.; perf. partic. pass., *feigned, invented;*
commenta funera, Ov.

commĭnor, 1. dep. *to threaten;* comminati
inter se, Liv.; with acc., pugnam, obsidionem,
oppugnationem, Liv.

commĭnŭo -ŭi -ūtum, 3. **A.** *to make small,
lessen, break into small pieces, crush to pieces;*
statuam, anulum, Cic. **B.** Transf., *to lessen,
diminish, to weaken, deprive of strength;* opes
civitatis, Cic.; vires ingenii, Ov.

commĭnus, adv. (con and manus). **A.** Lit.,
a, milit. t. t. (opp. eminus), *hand to hand, in
close combat;* nec eminus hastis aut comminus
gladiis uteretur, Cic.; comminus acriter instare,
Sall.; manum comminus conserere, Liv.; of
hunting, comminus ire in apros, Ov.; **b,** gen.,

close at hand; comminus ad aliquem accedere, Cic. **B.** Transf., *face to face;* comminus aspicere aliquem, Ov.

commis, commi, cummis = gummi (q.v.).

commiscĕo -miscŭi -mixtum, or -mistum, 2. *to mix together, to mix up.* **A.** Lit., ignem Vestae cum communi urbis incendio, Cic.; commixta frusta mero cruento, Verg. **B. Transf.,** temeritatem cum sapientia, Cic.

commĭsĕrātĭo -ōnis, f. (commiseror), in rhetoric, *the part of an oration intended to excite pity,* Cic.; absol., *an affecting tone* (of voice), Cic.

commĭsĕresco, 3. *to pity,* Ter.

commĭsĕror, 1. dep. 1. *to pity, commiserate, bewail;* fortunam, Nep.; 2, of a speaker, *to excite pity;* quum commiserari, conqueri coeperit, Cic.

commissĭo -ōnis, f. (committo). **A.** *a contest or struggle for a prize,* Cic. **B.** Meton., *a showy declamation,* Sen.

commissum -i, n. (committo). **I.** *something undertaken, an undertaking;* supererat nihil aliud in temere commisso quam, etc., Liv.; esp., **a,** *a crime, fault, transgression;* factum aut commissum audacius, Cic.; **b,** *confiscation,* Quint. **II.** *a secret;* commissa enuntiare, Cic.

commissūra -ae, f. (committo). **A.** *a joining together, connection, joint, knot;* molles digitorum, Cic. **B.** Transf., *connexion of a speech, the thread of a discourse,* Quint.

committo -misi -missum, 3. *to unite, connect, combine.* **I.** Lit., duas noctes, Ov.; opera, Liv.; nondum commissa inter se munimenta, Liv. **II.** Transf., 1, **a,** *to begin, set on foot;* pugnam or pugnam cum aliquo, Cic.; proelium, Caes.; bellum, Liv.'; ludos, Cic.; **b,** *to commit a crime;* tantum facinus, Cic.; multa et in deos et in homines impie, Cic.; **c,** absol., *to commit a crime;* nemo enim committeret, Cic.; contra legem, Cic.; with ut and the subj., *to bring it about that;* non committam posthac ut me accusare de epistolarum negligentia possis, Cic.; **d,** *to incur a punishment;* poenam, Cic.; perf. partic., *forfeited;* hereditas Veneri Erycinae commissa, Cic.; **e,** *to entrust, commit to, reflex., to venture, risk oneself;* se in senatum, Cic.; se urbi, Cic.; aliquem fidei potestatique eius, Cic.; collum tonsori, Cic.; alicui rempublicam, Liv.; committere alicui, ut videat ne quid res publica detrimenti capiat, Cic.

commŏdē, adv. (commodus), **a,** *rightly, properly, fitly, appropriately;* dicere, Cic.; minus commode audire, *to have an indifferent reputation,* Cic.; **b,** *agreeably, pleasantly;* feceris igitur commode mihique gratum si, etc., Cic.; **c,** *satisfactorily;* navigare, Cic.

commŏdĭtas -ātis, f. (commodus). **I. a,** *proportion, symmetry;* corporis, Cic.; vitae, Cic.; **b,** *convenience;* ob commoditatem itineris, Liv.; **c,** *fitness, a fit occasion;* commoditas ad faciendum idonea, Cic.; **d,** *advantage;* qui ex bestiis fructus, quae commoditas percipi potest, Cic. **II.** of persons, *complaisance, kindness,* Ov.

commŏdo, 1. (commodus), 1, *to make fit, adapt, accommodate,* Plin.; 2, **a,** *to adapt oneself to suit another person, to please, oblige, serve;* ut eo libentius iis commodes, Cic.; **b,** with acc., *to furnish, lend, give;* nomen suum alicui, Cic.; reipublicae tempus, Liv.; alicui aurem, Ov.; *to lend* for a time; alicui aurum, Cic.

1. **commŏdum,** adv. (commodus), **a,** *at the right time, opportunely;* commodum enim egeram diligentissime, Cic.; **b,** with quum or postquam and the indic., *just;* commodum discesseras heri, quum Trebatius venit, Cic.

2 **commŏdum** -i, n. (commodus), **a,** *con-*

venience; nostro commodo, *at our convenience,* Cic.; commodo tuo, Cic.; per commodum, Liv.; quod commodo valetudinis tuae fiat, Cic.; commodo reipublicae facere aliquid, Cic.; commodum alicuius exspectare, Cic.; **b,** *use, advantage, convenience;* pacis, Cic.; sui commodi causa nocere alteri, Cic.; servire or consulere alicuius commodis, Cic.; plur., *favour, privileges, prerogatives;* tribunatus (militum) commoda, Cic.; **c,** *loan;* qui forum et basilicas commodis hospitum, non furtis nocentium ornarent, Cic.

1. **commŏdus** -a -um (com and modu_). **I. a,** *proper, fit, appropriate, convenient, satisfactory;* valetudine minus commoda uti, Caes.; litterae satis commodae de Britannicis rebus, Cic.; with dat., nulla lex satis commoda omnibus est, Cic.; commodum est, *it pleases, is agreeable;* si tibi erit commodum, Cic.; with acc. and infin., nihil duco esse commodius, quam de his rebus nihil jam amplius scribere, Cic.; **b,** *easy, convenient;* iter, Liv. **II.** *friendly, obliging, pleasant;* mores commodi, Cic.

2. **Commŏdus** -i, m. *Roman emperor from* 186–192 A.D.

commōlĭor, 4. dep. *to set in motion;* fulmina, Lucr.

commŏnĕfăcĭo -fēci -factum, 3., pass. **commŏnĕfīo** -factus sum, -fieri (commoneo and facio), *to remind, warn;* aliquem etiam atque etiam, Cic.; aliquem beneficii sui, Sall.; with acc. of thing, istius turpem calamitosamque praeturam, Cic.

commŏnĕo -ŭi -ĭtum, 2. *to remind, warn, impress upon, bring to one's recollection;* quod vos lex commonuit, Cic.; quin is unoquoque gradu de avaritia tua commoneretur, Cic.; non exprobrandi causa, sed commonendi gratia, Cic.; animos de periculo, Cic.; quum quidam ex illis amicis commonerent oportere decerni, Cic.

commonstro, 1. *to show fully and distinctly;* aurum alicui, Cic.

commŏrātĭo -ōnis, f. (commoror), *a delaying, loitering, lingering;* tabellariorum, Cic.; rhet. t.t., *the dwelling for some time on one point,* Cic.

commŏrĭor -mortuus, 3. dep. *to die together with;* with dat., hostibus, Sall.

commŏror, 1. dep. *to delay, linger, make a stay in any place, sojourn, tarry, remain;* **a,** Romae, Cic.; unam noctem ad Helorum, Cic.; apud aliquem, Cic.; fig., consilium tuum diutius in armis civilibus commorandi, Cic.; **b,** rhet. t.t. *to dwell on;* pluribus verbis in eo, Cic.

commōtĭo -ōnis, f. (commoveo), *an emotion, excitement;* animi, Cic.

commōtĭuncŭla -ae, f. (dim. of commotio), *a slight indisposition,* Cic.

commōtus -a -um, p. adj. (from commoveo), 1, *tottering, insecure, unsteady;* aes alienum, Tac.; genus (dicendi) in agendo, Cic.; 2, *moved in mind, excited;* animus commotior, Cic.

commŏvĕo -mōvi -mōtum, 3. **I.** Lit. *to move entirely or violently, to shake, to move from a place;* 1, se ex eo loco, Cic.; castra ex eo loco, *to cause the army to advance,* Cic.; sacra, *to carry about* (at festivals, etc.) *the statues of the gods and the sacred utensils,* Verg.; nummum, *to employ in commerce,* Cic.; columnas, *to carry off,* Cic.; 2, *to hunt;* cervum, Verg.; **b,** *to cause to yield or give way;* hostium aciem, Liv. **II.** Transf., 1, of the mind or the passions, *te move, influence, disturb;* his omnes, in quibus est virtutis indoles, commo ventur, Cic.; aut libidine aliqua aut metu commotum esse, Cic.; nova atque inusitata specie commotus, Caes.; eiusdem miseriis ac periculis commovetur, Cic.; quum esset ex aere alieno commota civitas, Cic.

2, *to call forth, produce, cause;* risum, Cic.; magnum et acerbum dolorem, Cic.; bellum aut tumultum, Cic.; 3, *to treat of,* nova quaedam, Cic. (contracted perf. forms commossem, commosset, commosse, Cic.).

commūnĭcātĭo -ōnis, f. (communico), 1, *a communicating, imparting;* consilii, Cic.; 2, *a rhetorical figure=*ἀνακοίνωσις, *in which the orator pretends to consult the audience,* Cic.

commūnĭco, 1. (communis), *to share, divide with, communicate;* 1, judicia cum equestri ordine communicata erant, Cic.; rem cum aliquo, Cic.; 2, *to communicate, impart, inform,* by speaking or writing; consilia, Caes.; de societate multa inter se, Cic; *to take counsel with, confer with;* cum aliquo de maximis rebus, Cic.; 3, *to join, unite;* quantas pecunias ab uxoribus dotis nomine acceperunt, tantas ex suis bonis aestimatione factā cum dotibus communicant, Caes.; 4, *to share something with one;* curam doloris sui cum aliquo, Cic.

1. **commūnĭo** -īvi or -ĭi -ītum, 4. *to fortify thoroughly on all sides;* castella, Caes.; transf., *to fortify, strengthen;* causam testimoniis, Cic.

2. **commūnĭo** -ōnis, f. (communis), *communion, mutual participation;* inter quos est communio legis, inter eos communio juris est, Cic.

commūnis -e (old form commoinis, from com and root MOIN, MUN, whence moenia, munus). **A.** *common, general, universal, ordinary, usual, public* (opp. proprius=*individual, private*); loca, *public places,* Cic.; loci, *philosophical or rhetorical commonplaces,* Cic.; with genit., communis hominum infirmitas, Cic.; with dat., mors omni aetati est communis, Cic.; with cum and the abl., quocum fuit et domus et militia communis Cic.; with inter se, multa sunt civibus inter se communia, Cic.; subst., **commūne** -is, n., 1, *the common property of a corporation;* quod jus statues communi dividundo, Cic.; 2, *state, commonwealth;* Siciliae, Cic.; in commune, adv., **a,** *for the public good, for common use;* in commune conferre, Cic.; b, *in general,* Tac. **B.** Transf., of persons, *affable, condescending;* Cyrum minorem communem erga Lysandrum atque humanum fuisse, Cic.

commūnĭtas -ātis, f. (communis). **I.** *community, fellowship;* nulla cum deo homini communitas, Cic. **II.** Transf., a, *the desire for human society,* Cic.; b, *condescension, affability,* Nep.

commūnĭtĕr, adv. (communis), *in common with others, jointly, generally,* Cic.

commurmŭror, 1., dep. *to mutter, murmur;* ut scriba secum ipse commurmuratus sit, Cic.

commūtābĭlis, -e (commuto), *changeable;* a, vitae ratio, Cic.; b, rhet. t. t., exordium, *such as could be easily adapted to a speech on the other side of the question,* Cic.

commūtātĭo -ōnis, f. (commuto), *a change, alteration;* temporum, Cic., aestuum, Caes.

commūtātus -ūs, m., *a change, alteration,* Lucr.

commūto, 1. **A.** *to change, alter entirely;* sursum, Cic.; iter, Caes.; tempora in horas commutantur, Cic.; reipublicae statum, Cic.; consilium, Caes.; sententiam, Cic.; nihil commutari animo, Cic. **B.** *to exchange, change something for something else;* gloriam constantiae cum caritate vitae, Cic.; fidem suam et religionem pecuniā, *to barter,* Cic.

cōmo, compsi, comptum, 3. (contr. from coemo), *to place together.* **I.** Gen., Lucr. **II.** *to place together in order, to arrange, adorn,* especially of the hair, *to comb, plait, adorn;*

capillos, Cic.; longas compta puella comas, Ov.; praecincti recte pueri comptique, Hor.

cōmoedĭa -ae, f. (κωμῳδία), *a comedy,* Cic.

cōmoedus -a -um (κωμῳδός), *relating to a comedy, comic;* natio, Juv. Subst., **cōmoedus** -i, m. *a comic actor,* Cic.

cōmōsus -a -um (coma), *hairy,* Phaedr.

compaciscor (compĕciscor),-pactus, or-pectus, -pacisci 3., dep. *to conclude an agreement, make a compact with any one,* Plaut.

compactĭo -ōnis, f. (compingo), *a putting or joining together;* membrorum, Cic.

compactum -i, n. (compaciscor), *a compact, agreement;* compacto, Cic., de compacto, Plaut., ex compecto, Suet., *according to agreement.*

compactus -a -um, p. adj. (from compingo), *thick-set, compressed, compact,* Plin.

compăges -is, f. (compingo). **I.** *a joining together, connexion;* lapidum, Ov.; quae (navis) per se ipsa omnibus compagibus aquam acciperet, Liv. **II.** Transf., dum sumus in his inclusi compagibus corporis, *bodily structure,* Cic.

compāgo -ĭnis, f. = compages (q.v.).

compar -păris, *like, similar;* postulatio Latinorum, Liv.; with dat., milites militibus compares, Liv. Subst., **compar** -păris, c. *a companion, equal, consort, spouse,* Hor.

compărābĭlis -e (2. comparo), *capable of comparison, comparable;* comparabile est, quod in rebus diversis similem aliquam rationem continet, Cic.

compărātē, adv. (2. comparo), *in comparison, by comparison,* Cic.

1. **compărātĭo** -ōnis, f. (1. comparo), *a preparing, preparation;* novi belli, Cic.; veneni, Liv.; criminis, *evidence necessary for an accusation,* Cic.

2. **compărātĭo** -ōnis, f. (2. comparo). **A.** *a comparing, comparison;* orationis suae cum scriptis alienis, Cic.; utilitatum, Cic.; comparatio quibus plurimum sit tribuendum, Cic. **B.** In rhet., comparatio criminis, *the set-off of a good motive against a crime,* Cic.

compărātīvus -a -um (2. comparo), *relating to comparison, containing a comparison, comparative;* judicatio, Cic.

comparco (comperco) -parsi, -parsum, 3. *to scrape together, to save up,* Ter.

compărĕo -pārŭi, 2, 1, *to appear, be visible;* cum subito sole obscurato non comparuisset (Romulus), Cic.; 2, *to be present, be in existence;* signa et dona comparere omnia, Cic.

1. **compăro,** 1. **A.** *to prepare, get ready, provide, furnish;* convivium magnifice et ornate, Cic.; se, *to make oneself ready,* Cic.; insidias alicui, Cic.; classem, Cic.; exercitum, Cic.; rem frumentariam, Caes.; animum auditoris idonee ad reliquam dictionem, Cic.; alicui a civitatibus laudationes per vim et metum, Cic.; bellum adversus aliquem, Caes. **B.** *to arrange, settle, dispose;* 1, of character, sic fuimus semper comparati ut, etc., Cic.; 2, of institutions, jura praeclara atque divinitus a nostris majoribus comparata, Cic.

2. **compăro,** 1. (compar). **I.** Lit., a, *to form into pairs, to unite in pairs,* Cic.; labella labellis, Plaut.; b, *to bring together for a contest, to match;* comparari cum Aesernino Samnite, cum patrono disertissimo, Cic. **II.** Transf., a, *to compare;* et se mihi comparat Ajax? Ov.; homo similitudines comparat, Cic.; Attico Lysiae Catonem nostrum, Cic.; meum factum cum tuo comparo, Cic.; b, comparare provincias inter se, or comparare provincias, **or simply**

comparare inter se (of magistrates), *to come to an agreement as to their several duties*, Liv.

compasco -pāvi -pastum, 3. *to feed* or *graze together;* si compascuus ager est, jus est compascere, Cic.

compascŭus -a -um, *relating to common pasturage;* ager, *pasturage held in common*, Cic.

compĕdĭo, 4. (compes), *to fetter*, Plaut.

compellātĭo -ōnis, f. (2. compello), *an accosting, rebuking, reprimanding;* crebrae vel potius quotidianae compellationes, Cic.

1. **compello** -pŭli -pulsum, 3. **I.** *to drive to one place, collect;* pecus totius provinciae, Cic. **II.** *to drive, force.* **A.** Lit., consules e foro in curiam, Liv.; naves in portum, Caes.; Romanos in castra, Liv.; omne Auruncum bellum Pometiam compulsum est, *confined to*, Liv. **B.** Transf., *to force* or *impel a person to an action, to compel;* aliquem ad bellum, Ov.; in eundem metum, Liv.; in hunc sensum et allici beneficiis hominum et compelli injuriis, Cic.

2. **compello**, 1. (intens. of 1. compello). **I.** Gen., *to address, accost, call by name;* aliquem voce, Verg. **II. A.** *to address with blame and reproach, chide, rebuke;* aliquem edicto, Cic. **B.** Legal t. t., *to accuse before a court of justice;* judicem, Cic.

compendĭārĭus -a -um (compendium), *short;* via, Cic.

compendĭum -ĭi, n. (com and pendo, *to weigh together*). **A.** *saving, parsimony,* and hence, *gain, profit, advantage* (opp. dispendium); privato compendio servire, Caes.; in re uberrima turpe compendium effugere, Cic. **B.** *a short way, a short cut;* per compendia maris assequi aliquem, Tac.

compensātĭo -ōnis, f. (compenso), *a balancing of an account, compensation;* incommoda commodorum compensatione leniunt, Cic.

compenso, 1. *to weigh together, to reckon one thing against another, to balance;* laetitiam cum doloribus, Cic.; summi labores nostri magnā compensati gloriā, Cic.

compĕrendĭnātĭo -ōnis, f. (comperendino), *a putting off a trial to the third day*, Tac.

compĕrendĭnātus -ūs, m. = comperendinatio (q.v.).

compĕrendĭno, 1. (com and perendinus), *to remand to the third day;* reum, Cic.; absol., ut ante primos ludos comperendinem, Cic.

compĕrĭo -pĕri -pertum, 4. (com and root PER, whence peritus, periculum, and reperio, experior), *to find out, discover, gain certain information of;* haec certis nuntiis, certis auctoribus comperisse, Cic.; partic. perf., *certain, undoubted;* levem auditionem pro re comperta habere, *for a certainty*, Caes.; ea dicimus quae comperta habemus, quae vidimus, Cic.; compertum narrare, Sall.; with acc. and infin., posteaquam comperit eum posse vivere, Cic.; abl. absol., comperto, *it having been discovered for certain;* satis comperto Eordaeam petituros Romanos, Liv.; with de and the abl., nihil de hoc comperi, Cic.; partic. perf., compertus (of persons), *convicted; probri*, Liv.

compĕrĭor = comperio.

compēs -pēdis, f. *a fetter* or *foot shackle*, gen. found in the plur, Plaut.; transf., qui in compedibus corporis semper fuerunt, Cic.; Telephum tenet puella grata compede vinctum, Hor.

compesco -pescŭi, 3. (connected with compes, compedio), *to hold in, restrain, check, curb;* equum angustis habenis, Tib.; seditionem exercitus verbo uno, Tac.; clamorem, Hor.; ramos, Verg.

compĕtītor -ōris, m. *a competitor*, Cic.

compĕtītrix -īcis, f. (competitor), *a female competitor*, Cic.

compĕto -petīvi and -petĭi -petītum 3. *to, come together, to meet.* **A.** Lit., Varr. **B.** Transf., 1, *to agree, coincide in point of time;* tempora cum Othonis exitu competisse, Tac.; 2, *to be equal to, capable of;* ut vix ad arma capienda aptandaque pugnae competeret animus, Liv.; neque oculis neque auribus satis competebant, Tac.

compīlātĭo -ōnis, f. (compilo), *a pillaging,* hence (contemptuously), *a compilation;* Chresti, Cic.

compīlo, 1. (com and pilo = ψιλόω), *to plunder, rob;* fana, Cic.; fig., ab ipsis capsis juris, consultorum sapientiam, Cic.

compingo -pēgi -pactum, 3. (com and pango). **A.** *to put together, construct;* part. perf., compactus, *constructed*, Cic., Verg. **B.** *to confine, hide, conceal;* se in Apuliam, Cic.; fig., in judicia et contiunculas tamquam in aliquod pistrinum detrudi et compingi, Cic.

compĭtālĭcĭus -a -um (compitalis), *relating to the Compitalia;* dies, Cic.; ludi, Cic.

compĭtālis -e (compitum), *relating* or *belonging to cross roads;* Lares, *the deities who presided over cross roads*, Suet., **Compĭtālĭa** -ĭum, n. *the festival in honour of these deities, celebrated on the cross roads on a day appointed by the praetor, shortly after the Saturnalia*, Cic.

compĭtum -i, n. (competo), *a place where two or more roads meet, a cross road*, Cic.

complācĕo -cŭi or -cĭtus sum, 2. 1, *to please several persons at once*, Ter.; 2, *to please exceedingly*, Plaut.

complāno, 1. *to level;* domum, *to raze*, Cic.

complector -plexus -plecti, 3. dep. (com and plecto). **I.** Lit., 1, *to embrace, encircle, surround, encompass;* aliquem manibus, Liv.; aliquem artius, Cic.; me artior somnus complexus est, Cic.; 2, *to enclose, surround;* collem opere, Caes.; animum mundi caelo, Cic. **II.** Transf., 1, *to hold fast, master;* quam (facultatem) quoniam complexus es, tene, Cic.; 2, *to attach oneself to, esteem;* quos fortuna complexa est, *the favourites of fortune*, Cic.; aliquem summa benevolentia, Cic.; 3, *of the mind, to embrace, grasp, comprehend;* omnia una comprehensione, Cic.; 4, *to unite in oneself* or *itself;* omnes omnium caritates patria una complexa est, Cic.

complēmentum -i, n. (compleo), *that which completes* or *fills up, a complement;* inania quaedam verba quasi complementa numerorum, Cic.

complĕo -plēvi -plētum, 2. *to fill up.* **I.** Lit., 1, fossas sarmentis et virgultis, Caes.; paginam, Cic.; multo cibo et potione completi, Cic.; with genit., convivium vicinorum quotidie compleo, Cic.; 2, milit. t. t., *to complete the number of an army, fleet,* etc.; classem Romanam sociis navalibus, Liv.; 3, *to fill a space with light, smell, shout, clamour,* etc.; omnia clamoribus, Liv.; sol cuncta sua luce lustrat et complet, Cic. **II.** Transf., 1, civitatem summa spe et voluntate, Caes.; 2, *to fulfil;* fata sua, Ov.; centum et septem annos complesse, Cic.; 3, *of a sum, to make up;* neque est adhuc ea summa (imperati sumptus) completa, Cic.; 4, *to complete, finish;* his rebus completis, Caes.

complētus -a -um, p. adj. (from compleo), *perfect, complete;* completus et perfectus verborum ambitus, Cic.

complexĭo -ōnis, f. (complector), 1, *connexion, combination;* complexiones atomorum

inter se, Cic.; **2**, of discourse, **a**, brevis totius
negotii, *a short summary of the whole matter*,
Cic.; **b**, verborum, or absol., *a period*, Cic.; **c**,
in logic, *the conclusion of a syllogism*, Cic.; **d**,
a dilemma, Cic.

complexus -ūs, m. (complector). **A. a**,
an embrace; aliquem de complexu matris avellere, Cic.; currere ad alicuius complexum, Cic.;
meton., *a loved object*; de complexu eius ac sinu,
from his favourites and bosom friends, Cic.; **b**,
combat; complexum armorum vitare, Tac.; **c**,
surrounding, encompassing; qui (mundus) omnia complexu suo coercet et continet, Cic. **B.**
Transf., *love for*; complexus totius gentis humanae, Cic.

complīco -āvi -ātum (-ŭi -ĭtum), 1. *to fold
together, fold up.* **I.** Lit., epistolam, Cic. **II.**
Transf., complicata notio, *confused, intricate*, Cic.

complōrātĭo -ōnis, f. (comploro), *a lamentation, a weeping and bewailing*; mulierum comploratio sui patriaeque, Liv.

complōrātus -ūs, m. = comploratio (q.v.).

complōro, 1. *to bewail* or *weep, to lament
loudly and violently*; mortem, Cic.; desperata
complorataque res est publica, Liv.

complūres, neut. **complūra**, and (rarely)
complūria -ium, n. *very many*, Cic. Subst.,
several; complures ex iis, Caes.

complūriens (complūriēs), adv. (complures), *many times, frequently*, Plaut.

complusculi -ae, -a (complures), *a good
many*, Plaut.

complŭvĭum -ii, n. (compluo, *to flow together*), *the quadrangular roofless space in the
centre of a Roman house, through which the water
collected on the roofs found its way to the* impluvium
below, Varr.

compōno -pŏsŭi -pŏsĭtum, 3. *to put, place,
lay, bring together.* **I.** Gen., 1, in quo (loco) erant
ea composita, quibus rex te munerare constituerat, Cic.; manibus manus atque oribus ora,
Verg.; **2**, **a**, *to place together as opponents*, Cic.;
pergis pugnantia secum pontibus adversis componere, Hor.; **b**, *to compare*; dignitati alicuius
suam, Cic. **II.** Esp. **A.** *to collect together a whole
from several parts, compose*; exercitus eius compositus ex variis gentibus, Sall.; venena, Ov.;
aggerem tumuli, Verg.; *of writers, to compose*;
volumen de tuenda sanitate, Cic.; oratio ad
conciliandos plebis animos composita, Liv. **B.**
1, *to compose, settle, arrange*; arma, Hor.; opes,
Verg.; cinerem, *the ashes of the dead*, Ov.; se
thalamis, Verg.; **2**, *to quiet, settle, reconcile*;
controversias regum, Caes.; Armeniam, Tac.;
amicos aversos, Hor. **C.** *to place in a certain
order, arrange*; **1**, sidera, Cic.; classiarios in
numeros legionis, Tac.; **2**, rhet. t. t., *to arrange
words in their order*; verba componere et quasi
coagmentare, Cic. **D.** 1, *to arrange, smooth;*
comas, Ov.; composito et delibuto capillo, Cic.;
togam, Hor.; vultum, Tac.; **2**, *to dispose,
settle in a particular way*; itinera sic ut, etc.,
Cic.; auspicia ad utilitatem reipublicae composita, Cic.; diem rei gerendae, Liv.; ex composito, *as we agreed*, Liv.; **b**, *to invent, feign*;
crimen et dolum, Tac.

comporto, 1. *to carry, bring together, collect;*
frumentum ab Asia, Caes.; arma in templum, Cic.

compŏs -pŏtis (com and potis), *having the
mastery* or *control of, possessed of, sharing in;*
animi, Ter.; mentis, *in full possession of mental
faculties*, Cic.; voti, *one whose wish is fulfilled*,
Hor., Liv.; scientiae compotem esse, *to be able
to know something*, Cic.; rationis et consilii
compos, Cic.; qui me huius urbis compotem
fecerunt, *enabled me to be in this city*, Cic.; tum
patriae compotem me numquam siris esse, Liv.

compŏsĭtē, adv. (compositus), **1**, *in an
orderly manner, in good order*; composite et apte
dicere, Cic.; **2**, *quietly*, Tac.

compŏsĭtĭo -ōnis, f. (compono), *a putting
together.* **I.** Gen., *a matching*; gladiatorum
compositiones, Cic. **II.** Esp. 1, *a composing*;
a, unguentorum, Cic.; **b**, of a book, juris ponti-
ficalis, Cic.; **2**, *a settlement of differences*; pacis,
concordiae, compositionis auctor esse non destiti, Cic.; **3**, *arrangement*; **a**, membrorum, Cic.;
b, anni, *of the calendar*, Cic.; **c**, rhet. t. t., *the
proper arrangement of words*; compositio apta,
Cic.

compŏsĭtor -ōris, m. (compono), *an arranger, adjuster*, Cic.

compŏsĭtūra -ae, f. (compono), *a connexion,
joining, a joint*, Lucr.

compŏsĭtus -a -um, p. adj. with compar.
and superl. (compono), *placed together*; **1**, *composed, quieted*; composito vultu, Tac.; **2**, *well
arranged*; composito agmine legiones ducere,
Tac.; so of oratory, oratio, Cic; and of the orator
himself, orator, Cic.; **3**, *peacefully governed,
settled*; respublica, Cic.; hence subst., **compŏ-
sĭta**, -orum, n. *the orderly condition of a state*,
Sall.; **4**, **a**, *prepared*; ut nemo unquam com-
positior ad judicium venisse videatur, Cic.;
b, *feigned, pretended, studied*; indignatio, Tac.

compŏtātĭo -ōnis, f. *a drinking party* (translation of συμπόσιον), Cic.

compŏtĭo, 4. (compos), *to make partaker of*,
Plaut.; passive, *to become partaker of*, Plaut.

compŏtor -ōris, m. *a drinking companion*,
Cic.

compŏtrix -īcis, f. (compotor), *a female
drinking companion*, Ter.

compransor -ōris, m. *a dinner companion*,
boon companion, Cic.

comprĕcātĭo -ōnis, f. (comprecor), *supplication of a deity*; haec sollemnis deorum com
precatio, Liv.

comprĕcor, 1., dep. *to pray to, supplicate;*
caelestūm fidem, Cat.; Cytherea, comprecor,
ausis assit, Ov.

comprĕhendo (comprendo) -prĕhendi
(-prendi) -prĕhensum (-prensum), 3. *to seize, lay
hold of.* **A.** Lit., **1**, quid opus est manibus si
nihil comprehendendum est? Cic.; ignem, *to
catch fire*, Verg.; ignis robora comprendit, *seizes
on*, Verg.; avidis comprenditur ignibus agger,
Ov.; without igne, comprehensa aedificia, Liv.;
2, as a suppliant, *to seize a person's hand*; com-
prehendunt utrumque et orant, Caes.; **3**, *to attack, lay hold of in a hostile manner, seize, capture*; **a**, persons, tam capitalem hostem, Cic.;
aliquem vivum in fuga, Caes.; aliquem in furto,
Cic.; **b**, animals, etc., *to seize, carry off*; redas
equosque, Caes.; **c**, *to seize a place*; aliis comprehensis collibus, Caes.; **4**, *to discover* or *reveal
a crime*; nefandum adulterium, Cic. **B.** Transf.,
1, *to embrace*; multos amicitia, Cic.; **2**, *to comprise, include*; cuae omnia una cum deorum
notione comprehendimus, Cic.; **3**, *to relate, express, tell in words* or *writing*; breviter comprehensa sententia, Cic.; ne plura consecter,
comprehendam brevi, Cic.; **4**, aliquid numero,
to count, express in numbers, Verg.; **5**, *to comprehend, perceive*; sensu or sensibus, Cic.;
animo intelligentiam alicuius rei, Cic.; intelligere et cogitatione comprehendere qualis sit
animus, Cic.; esse aliquid, quod comprehendi et
percipi posset, Cic.

comprĕhensĭbĭlis -e (comprehendo), *that
which can be comprehended, comprehensible*; natura non comprehensibilis, Cic.

comprĕhensĭo -ōnis, f. (comprehendo), *a
seizing with the hands, laying hold of.* **A.** Lit.,

1, Cic.; **2**, *a hostile seizing, apprehending;* sontium, Cic. **B.** Transf., **1**, *a perceiving, comprehending, comprehension;* complecti omnia una comprehensione, Cic.; **2.** *a period, sentence;* verba comprehensione devincire, Cic.

comprendo = comprehendo (q.v.).

compressē, adv. (compressus), *briefly, concisely, succinctly,* Cic.; compressius loqui, Cic.

compressĭo -ōnis, f. (comprimo), *compression of style, conciseness;* compressione rerum breves, Cic.

1. compressus -a -um, partic. of comprimo.

2. compressus, abl. -u, m. (comprimo), *a pressing together, pressure, embrace,* Cic.

comprĭmo -pressi -pressum. 3. (com and premo), *to press, squeeze together, compress.* **A.** Lit., **1**, quum digitos compresserat et pugnum fecerat, Cic.; prov., compressis manibus sedere, *to sit with folded hands, idle,* Liv.; **2**, *to press together, make closer or tighter;* ordines, *to close the ranks,* Liv. **B.** Transf., **1**, *to hold back;* a, frumentum, *to keep in the garner, not to sell,* Cic.; b, *to suppress;* delicta magna, Cic.; **2**, *to check;* plausus ipse admiratione compressus est, Cic.; gressum, Verg.; **3**, *to crush, subdue;* furentis hominis conatum atque audaciam, Cic.; seditionem, Liv.

comprŏbātĭo -ōnis, f. (comprobo), *approval,* Cic.

comprŏbātor -ōris, m. (comprobo), *one who approves,* Cic.

comprŏbo, 1., **1**, *to approve fully;* orationem omnium assensu, Liv.; istam tuam sententiam laudo vehementissimeque comprobo, Cic.; **2**, *to confirm, prove, establish;* patris dictum sapiens temeritas filii comprobavit, Cic.

comprōmissum -i, n. (compromitto), *a mutual agreement to abide by the decision of an arbitrator;* de hac pecunia compromissum facere, Cic.

comprōmitto -mīsi -missum, 3. *to agree to refer a cause to arbitration,* Cic.

Compsa -ae, f. *town of the Hirpini in Samnium* (now *Conza*); hence, **Compsānus** -a -um, *of or belonging to Compsa.*

1. comptus -a -um, p. adj. with compar. and superl. (from como), *ornamented, adorned;* oratio, Cic.

2. comptus -ūs, m. (como). **I.** *a head-dress,* Lucr. **II.** *a band, tie,* Lucr.

compungo -punxi -punctum, 3. *to prick, puncture on all sides.* **I.** Phaedr.; fig., ipsi se compungunt suis acuminibus, Cic. **II.** *to mark;* barbarus compunctus notis Threiciis, *tattooed,* Cic.

compŭto, 1. *to reckon together, calculate, compute;* rationem digitis, Plaut.; facies tua computat annos, *shows thy age,* Juv.; absol., computarat, pecuniam impetrarat, Cic.

compŭtresco -pūtrŭi, 3. *to putrefy,* Lucr.

Cōmum -i, n. (Κῶμον), *a town in Cisalpine Gaul,* now *Como.* Adj., **Cōmensis** -e, *of or belonging to Comum.*

con = com (q.v.).

cōnāmen -mĭnis, n. (conor), *an effort, endeavour,* Lucr., Ov.

cōnātum -i, n. (conor), *an undertaking;* gen. in plur., conata efficere, Cic.

cōnātus -ūs, m. (conor), a, *an attempt, effort, undertaking;* hoc conatu desistere, Cic.; compressi tuos nefarios conatus, Cic.; b, *trouble, difficulty, effort;* tumultus Gallicus haud magno conatu brevi oppressus est, Liv.; c, *impulse, inclination;* ut (beluae) conatum haberent ad naturales pastus capessendos, Cic.

concăco, 1. *to defile all over,* Phaedr.

concaedēs -ĭum, f. *a barricade of trees,* Tac.

concălĕfăcĭo (concalfacĭo) -fēci -factum, 3., and pass. **concălĕfĭo** (concalfīo), -factus sum, *to warm thoroughly;* brachium, Cic.

concălĕo, 2. *to be warm through and through,* Plaut.

concălesco -călŭi (inchoat. of concaleo), 3. **A.** Lit., *to become thoroughly warm;* corpora nostra ardore animi concalescunt, Cic. **B.** Transf., *to glow with love,* Ter.

concallesco -callŭi, 3. a, *to become practised;* tamquam manus opere, sic animus usu concalluit, Cic.; b, *to become callous or without feeling,* Cic.

Concāni -ōrum, m. (sing., **Concănus**, Hor.), *a savage tribe in Spain, who drank horses' blood.*

concastīgo, 1. *to punish, chastise severely,* Plaut.

concăvo, 1. (concavus), *to hollow out, make hollow or concave;* brachia geminos in artus, curves, bends, Ov.

concăvus -a -um, *hollow, vaulted, arched, concave;* cymbala, Lucr.; altitudines speluncarum, Cic.; aqua, *welling up,* Ov.

concēdo -cessi -cessum, 3. *to go away, depart, retire, withdraw.* **I.** Lit., superis ab oris, Verg.; ab alicuius oculis aliquo, Cic.; cum conjugibus ac liberis in arcem Capitoliumque, Liv.; docet unde fulmen venerit, quo concesserit, Cic.; concedere vita, *to die,* Tac.; so absol., quando concessero, Tac. **II.** Transf., **1**, *to cease;* tumor omnis et irae concessere deûm, Verg.; **2**, a, *to submit;* in alicuius ditionem, Liv.; b, *to pass over to some one's side or party or view;* in Attali sententiam, Liv.; **3**, *to yield;* a, intransit. (α) voluptas concedit dignitati, Cic.; concedere naturae, *to die a natural death,* Sall.; (β) *to give in to;* alicuius postulationi, Cic.; (γ) *to pardon;* alienis peccatis, Cic.; b, transit., (α) *to yield, give up;* alicui libertatem in aliqua re, Cic.; concedant, ut hi viri boni fuerint, *let them admit,* Cic.; alicui primas in dicendo partes, Cic.; (β) reipublicae dolorem atque amicitias suas, *sacrifice,* Cic.

concĕlĕbro, 1. **I.** Lit., *to visit a place often,* or *in large companies,* Lucr. **II.** Transf., **A.** Of any occupation, *to pursue eagerly, assiduously;* studia per otium, Cic. **B.** *to celebrate a festivity;* diem natalem, Plaut.; spectaculum, Liv. **C.** *to praise, extol;* fama et litteris eius diei victoriam, Cic.

concēnātĭo -ōnis, f. (conceno), *a supping together* (translation of Gr. σύνδειπνον), Cic.

concentĭo -ōnis, f. (concino), *a singing together, harmony,* Cic.

concentus -ūs, m. (concino). **A.** *a singing together, harmony;* avium, Cic.; tubarum ac cornuum, Liv. **B.** Transf., *agreement, harmony of opinion, unity, concord;* melior actionum sonorum concentus, Cic.

conceptĭo -ōnis, f. (concipio), **1**, a, *conception, a becoming pregnant,* Cic.; **2**, *the drawing up of legal formulae,* Cic.

conceptus -ūs, m. (concipio), *a conceiving, pregnancy,* Cic.

concerpo -cerpsi -cerptum, 3. (com and carpo), *to pull, pluck, tear in pieces.* **I.** Lit., epistolas, Cic. **II.** Transf., aliquem ferventissime, ap. Cic.

concertātĭo -ōnis, f. (concerto), *contest, strife;* **1**, magistratuum, Cic.; **2**, *contest in words, wrangling, dispute;* sine jejuna concertatione verborum, Cic.

concertātor -ōris, m. (concerto), *a rival*, Tac.

concertātōrĭus -a -um (concerto), *relating to a contest in words;* genus dicendi, Cic.

concerto, 1. *to strive eagerly;* 1, proelio, Cic.; 2, esp. of dispute in words, nunquam accidit ut cum eo verbo uno concertarem, Cic.

concessĭo -ōnis, f. (concedo), *a yielding, granting;* 1, agrorum, Cic.; 2, rhet. t. t., *an admission of a fault,* Cic.

concesso, 1. *to cease, leave off,* Plaut.

concessus -ūs, m. (concedo), *permission, leave;* gen. in abl., concessu omnium, Cic.

concha -ae, f. (κόγχη). I. Lit., 1, *a mussel,* Cic.; 2, *a mussel-shell,* Cic.; poet., *pearl,* conchae teretesque lapilli, Ov.; 3, *the shell-fish which yielded the purple dye,* Lucr.; poet., *purple dye,* Ov. II. Meton. *a vessel in the shape of a shell;* 1, concha salis puri, *salt-cellar,* Hor.; funde capacibus unguenta de conchis, Hor.; 2, *the horn of Triton,* Ov.

conchĕus -a -um (concha), *relating to a mussel-shell;* bacca, *a pearl,* Verg.

conchis -is, f. (κόγχος), *a kind of bean boiled with its pod,* Juv.

conchīta -ae, m. (κογχίτης), *a mussel gatherer,* Plaut.

conchȳlĭātus -a -um (conchylium), *purple;* peristromata, Cic.

conchȳlĭum -ĭi, n. (κογχύλιον), *a mussel,* or gen. *shell-fish.* I. Gen., Cic. II. Esp., 1, *an oyster,* Cic.; 2, *the shell-fish which yielded a purple dye,* Lucr.; meton., a, *purple dye;* vestis conchylio tincta, Cic.; b, *a purple garment,* Juv.

1. concīdo -īdi, 3. (com and cado), *to fall down, tumble to the ground, sink down.* A. Lit., 1, of things, concidat caelum omne necesse est, Cic.; repentinā ruinā pars eius turris concidit, Caes.; 2, of the winds, *to drop;* concidunt venti fugiuntque naves, Hor.; equus eius ante signum Jovis Statoris sine causā concĭdit, Cic.; in battle, ita pugnans concidit, Caes. B. Transf., 1, *to sink, perish, waste away;* neque enim tam facile opes Carthaginis tantae concidissent, Cic.; tum ferocia omnis concidit, Liv.; 2, of persons, a, *to be ruined, overthrown, to fail;* malas causas semper obtinuit, in optimā concidit, Cic.; at law, *to lose;* judicum vocibus fractus reus et una patroni omnes conciderunt, Cic.; b, ne unā plagā acceptā patres conscripti conciderent, *be disheartened,* Cic.

2. concīdo -cīdi -cīsum, 3. (com and caedo). I. *to cut up, cut in pieces, cut down, strike to the ground.* A. Lit., concisos equites nostros a barbaris nuntiabant, Cic. B. *to overthrow, annihilate;* Antonium decretis suis, Cic. II. A. *to beat severely, cudgel;* aliquem virgis, Cic. B. 1, a, *to cut in pieces;* nervos, Cic.; b, *to cut through;* magnos scrobibus montes, Verg.; pedestria itinera concisa aestuariis, Cic.; 2, rhet. t. t., *to divide too minutely,* Cic.; 3, logic. t. t., *to analyse,* Cic.

concĭeo -cīvi -cītum, 2. and (in prose gen.) (concio -īvi -ītum, 4.), *to stir up;* 1, Gen., a, *to move violently;* concita navis, Ov.; concita flumina, Ov.; b, of men, *to summon, bring together;* totam urbem, Liv.; exercitum ex tota insula, Liv.; 2, *to excite, disturb;* a, concita freta, Verg.; b, of men, *to rouse, stir up;* plebem contionibus, Liv.; immani concitus irā, Verg.; c, *to produce, cause, promote;* bellum in his provinciis, Liv.

concĭlĭābŭlum -i, n. (concilio), *a place of assembly, market place;* nundinas et conciliabula obire, Liv.

concĭlĭātĭo -ōnis, f. (concilio). I. *a uniting, joining;* 1, communem totius generis hominum conciliationem et consociationem colere, Cic.; 2, a, *a uniting in opinion, conciliating;* aut conciliationis causā leniter aut permotionis vehementer aguntur, Cic.; rhet. t. t. *the gaining the favour of the audience,* Cic.; b, *inclination;* prima est enim conciliatio hominis ad ea, quae sunt secundum naturam, Cic. II. *a procuring, acquiring;* gratiae, Cic.

concĭlĭātor -ōris, m. (concilio), *one who prepares, procures;* nuptiarum, *a match-maker,* Nep.; proditionis, Liv.

concĭlĭātrīcŭla -ae, f. (dim. of conciliatrix), *that which conciliates,* Cic.

concĭlĭātrīx -īcis, f. (conciliator). I. *one who unites, a match-maker,* Cic. II. Transf., *that which causes, promotes, brings about;* vis orationis conciliatrix humanae societatis, Cic.

1. concĭlĭātus -a -um, p. adj. with compar. and superl. (from concilio), 1, *beloved by,* Hamilcari conciliatus, Liv.; 2, *inclined to,* ut judex ad rem accipiendam fiat conciliatior, Cic.

2. concĭlĭātus abl. -ū, m. *the union, connexion of atoms,* Lucr.

concĭlĭo, 1. (concilium), *to bring together.* I. *to unite, connect.* A. corpora, Lucr. B. *to unite in sentiment, win over;* 1, gen., legiones sibi pecuniā, Cic.; animos plebis, Liv.; 2, *to recommend, make acceptable;* dictis artes conciliare suas, Ov. II. A. *to procure, prepare, provide, furnish;* 1, gen., pecunias, Cic.; 2, *to bring together, unite;* conciliari viro, Cat. B. *to bring about, cause, procure;* sibi amorem ab omnibus, Cic.; nuptias, Nep.

concĭlĭum -ĭi, n. (com and cio = cieo). I. *a union, connexion;* rerum, Lucr. II. 1, *a coming together, assembling;* Camenarum cum Egeria, Liv.; 2, *an assembly;* a, pastorum, Cic.; deorum, Cic.; b, *an assembly for deliberation, a council;* (a) outside Rome, Gallorum, Liv.; concilium Achaicum, *the Achaean League,* Liv.; constituere diem concilio, Caes.; cogere or convocare concilium, Caes.; aliquem adhibere ad concilium, Caes.; (β) in Rome, concilium sanctum patrum, Hor.; concilium plebis habere, *to hold a meeting of the comitia tributa,* Liv.; populi, of the comitia centuriata, Liv.

concinnē, adv. with compar. (concinnus), *elegantly, neatly, finely, tastefully;* rogare, Cic.; distribuere, *to arrange a speech artistically,* Cic.

concinnĭtas -ātis, f. (concinnus), *elegance and harmony of style;* verborum or sententiarum, Cic.

concinnĭtūdo -ĭnis, f. = concinnitas (q.v.).

concinno, 1. (concinnus). I. *to put or fit together carefully, to arrange;* munusculum alicui, ap. Cic. II. Transf., *to produce, cause;* amorem, Lucr.

concinnus -a -um, *well put together.* I. *pleasing, that which pleases on account of harmony and proportion, elegant, neat.* A. Gen., sat edepol concinna est virgo facie, Plaut.; tectorium, Cic.; helluo, *elegant,* Cic. B. Esp. of discourse, *tasteful, polished;* oratio, Cic.; concinnus et elegans Aristo, Cic. II. *suited, fit, appropriate, pleasing;* concinnus amicis, Hor.

concĭno -cĭnŭi -centum, 3. (com and canc). I. Intransit. A. Lit., *to sing in chorus, play instruments in concert;* concinunt tubae, Liv.; sic ad vada Maeandri concinit albus olor, Ov. B. Transf., a, *to join together in an utterance, to agree in saying;* ne juvet vox ista VETO, qua concinentes collegas auditis, Liv.; b, *to agree together, harmonise;* cum Peripateticis re concinere, verbis discrepare, Cic. II. Transit. A

Lit., haec quum concinuntur, Cic.; carmen **ad** clausas fores, Ov. **B.** Transf. *to celebrate*; laetos dies, Hor. **C.** *to prophesy;* tristia omina, Ov.

1. **concĭo** = concieo (q.v.).

2. **concĭo** -ōnis = contio (q.v.).

concĭōnabundus -a -um, v. contionabundus.

concĭōnālis -e, v. contionalis.

concĭōnārĭus -a -um, v. contionarius.

concĭōnātor, v. contionator.

concĭōnor, v. contionor.

concĭpĭo -cēpi -ceptum, 3. (com and capio), *to take together, hold together.* **I.** Gen. **A.** Lit. *to contain, hold;* multum ignem trullis ferreis, Liv. **B.** Transf., of words, *to express in a certain form;* verba, jusjurandum, Liv.; quod EX ANIMI SENTENTIA juraris, sicut concipitur more nostro, *according to our customary form,* Cic.; conceptis verbis jurare, Cic.; vadimonium, Cic.; **so, 1,** *to repeat words after another person,* Qu. Marcio Philippo praeeunte in foro votum, Liv.; preces, Ov.; **2,** *to publish, conclude;* foedus, Verg.; **3,** concipere summas, *to give the totals,* Liv. **II.** Esp. **A.** Lit., **1,** of fluids, *to take in, draw in, suck;* concipit Iris aquas, Ov.; terra caducas concepit lacrimas, Ov.; **2,** of fire, *to catch fire;* materies, quae nisi admoto igni ignem concipere possit, Cic.; fig., of love, quem mens mea concipit ignem, Ov.; **3,** of air, *to draw in;* pars (animae) concipitur cordis parte quadam, quem ventriculum cordis appellant, Cic.; **4,** *to conceive;* quum concepit mula, Cic.; fig., hoc quod conceptum respublica periculum parturit, Cic.; **5,** of physical qualities, *to take, gain;* alias aliasque vires, Ov. **B.** Transf., **1,** *to receive, incur, commit;* dedecus, Cic.; scelus, perpetrate, Cic.; **2,** *to feel;* iram intimo animo et corde, Cic.; spem regni, Liv.; **3,** *to fancy, imagine;* quid mirum si in auspiciis imbecilli animi superstitiosa ista concipiant, Cic.; **4,** *to comprehend, grasp;* rerum omnium quasi adumbratas intelligentias animo **ac** mente c., Cic.

concīsē, adv. (concisus), *in detached or minute portions;* hence, *concisely*, Quint.

concīsĭo -ōnis, f. (2. concido), rhet. **t. t**, *the breaking up of a clause into divisions,* Cic.

concīsus -a -um, p. adj. (from 2. concido), *divided into short sentences, brief, concise;* sententiae, Cic.

concĭtātĭo -ōnis, f. (concito), **1,** *quick movement;* remorum, Liv.; **2,** *tumult, sedition;* plebi contra patres concitatio et seditio, Cic.; **3,** *disturbance of the mind, passion;* ab omni concitatione animi semper vacare, Cic.

concĭtātor -ōris, m. (concito), *one who excites, stirs up;* seditionis, Cic.

concĭtātus -a -um, p. adj. with compar. and superl. (from concito), **1,** *quick, rapid;* conversio caeli, Cic.; quam concitatissimos equos immittere, *spur the horses to a full gallop,* Liv.; concitatior clamor, *louder,* Liv.; **2,** *excited, violent, passionate,* contio, Cic.

concĭto, 1. (freq. of concieo). **I. 1,** *to move quickly, violently, stir up, excite;* equum calcaribus, *to spur to a gallop,* Liv.; navem remis, Liv.; Eurus concitat aquas, Ov.; esp. *to summon by the voice;* servos ex omnibus vicis, Cic.; concitare aciem, *to move forward the army,* Liv.; se concitare in hostem, *to rush against the enemy,* Liv.; **2,** *to stir up, incite, impel;* Etruriam omnem adversus Romanos, Liv.; omnem Galliam ad suum auxilium, Caes.; animi quodam impetu concitatus, Cic. **II.** *to cause, produce;* seditionem ac discordiam, Cic.; invidiam in aliquem, Cic.

concĭtor -ōris, m. (concieo), *one who excites, stirs up;* belli, vulgi, Liv.

concĭuncŭla -ae = contiuncula (q.v.).

conclāmātĭo -ōnis, f. (conclamo), *an exclamation, shouting together;* universi exercitus, Caes.

conclāmĭto, 1. (intens. of conclamo), *to shout loudly, cry violently,* Plaut.

conclāmo, 1. **1,** *to shout together, in company;* ad arma, *to call to arms,* Liv.; vasa, *to give the signal for packing up baggage before a march,* Caes.; with acc. and infin., vos universi unā mente atque voce iterum a me conservatam esse rempublicam conclamastis, Cic.; with ut and the subj. *to demand loudly;* conclamaverunt, uti aliqui ex nostris ad colloquium prodirent, Caes; with indirect question, conclamavit, quid ad se venirent, Caes.; esp. **a,** of a shout of joy; ad quorum casum quum conclamasset gaudio Albanus exercitus, Liv.; with acc., conclamare victoriam, Caes.; **b,** of a cry of grief, aliquem conclamare, *to bewail the death of some one,* Verg.; **2,** *to call together;* conclamare socios, Ov.

conclāve -is, n. (com and clavis), *a room, chamber, a dining-room, a bedroom,* Cic.

conclūdo -clūsi -clūsum, 3. (com and cludo = claudo). **A.** Lit. *to shut up, inclose, confine;* bestias delectationis causā, Cic.; mare conclusum, *an inland sea,* Caes. **B.** Transf., **1,** *to include, compress, confine;* aliquem in angustissimam formulam sponsionis concludere, Cic.; quartus dies hoc libro concluditur, *is comprised,* Cic.; **2,** *to bring to an end;* epistolam, Cic.; perorationem inflammantem restinguentenve concludere, Cic.; **3,** rhet. *to close rhythmically, to round off in a period;* sententias, Cic.; **4,** philosoph. **t. t.** *to bring to a conclusion, to argue, infer;* deinde concludebas summum malum esse dolorem, Cic.; absol. argumenta ratione concludentia, *reasonable, logical proofs,* Cic.

conclūsē, adv. (conclusus, from concludo), *with well-turned periods;* concluse apteque dicere, Cic.

conclūsĭo -ōnis, f. (concludo). **A.** Lit. *a shutting, closing,* and in military language, *a blockade,* Caes. **B.** Transf. *a close, conclusion;* **a,** conclusio muneris ac negotii tui, Cic.; **b,** rhet. **t. t.,** *conclusion of a speech, peroration;* conclusio est exitus et determinatio totius orationis, Cic.; **c,** *a period;* verborum quaedam ad numerum conclusio, Cic.; **d,** philosoph. **t. t.** *conclusion in a syllogism, consequence;* rationis, Cic.

conclūsĭuncŭla -ae, f. (dim. of conclusio), *a foolish inference, paltry conclusion;* contortulae quaedam et minutulae conclusiunculae, Cic.

concoenātĭo -ōnis, f., v. concenatio.

concŏlor -ōris, *similar in colour;* humerus, Ov.; with dat., concolor est illis, Ov.

concŏquo -coxi -coctum, 3. **I.** Lit. *to boil together,* Lucr. **II.** *to digest.* **A.** Lit., cibum, Cic. **B.** Transf., **a,** *to bear, endure, stomach;* ut eius ista odia non sorbeam solum sed etiam concoquam, Cic.; aliquem senatorem (*as senator*) non concoquere, Liv.; **b,** *to consider maturely, deliberate upon;* tibi diu concoquendum est utrum, etc., Cic.; clandestina concocta sunt consilia, *have been concocted,* Liv.

1. **concordĭa** -ae, f. (concors), *agreement, union, harmony, concord, friendship, sympathy.* **I.** Lit., concordiam reconciliare, Liv.; concordiam confirmare cum aliqno, Cic.; concordiam conglutinare, Cic.; concordiam constituere, Cic.; meton., et cum Pirithoo felix concordia Theseus, *one heart and mind,* Ov. **II.** Transf., *harmony;* concordia discors, Ov.

2. **Concordia** -ae, f. *the goddess Concord,* to

whom several temples in Rome were dedicated, in one of which the senate frequently held its sittings, Cic.

concordĭtĕr, adv., with compar. and superl. (concors), *harmoniously, with concord, amicably;* concordissime vivere cum aliquo, Cic.

concordo, 1. (concors), *to agree, be in union;* quum animi judicia opinionesque concordant; with dat., concordant carmina nervis, Ov.

concors -dis, adj. with compar. and superl. (com and cor), *of one mind or opinion, concordant, agreeing, harmonious;* fratres concordissimi, Cic.; concordes animae, Verg.; of inanimate objects, moderatus et concors civitatis status, Cic.

concrēbresco -brŭi, 3. *to increase,* Verg.

concrēdo -dĭdi -dĭtum, 3. *to intrust, commit to;* rem et famam suam commendare et concredere alicui, Cic.

concrĕmo, 1. *to burn up, burn entirely;* omnia tecta, Liv.

concrĕpo -ŭi, 1. **I.** Intransit. *to rattle, creak, clash, grate;* scabilla concrepant, Cic.; concrepuere arma, Liv.; armis concrepat multitudo, Caes.; exercitus gladiis ad scuta concrepuit, Liv.; si digitis concrepuerit, *at the least sign,* Cic. **II.** Transit. *to rattle, strike upon;* aera, Ov.

concresco -crēvi -crētum. **A.** Gen. *to become stiff, to congeal, curdle, harden;* lac, Verg.; aer, Cic.; nive pruināque concrescit aqua, Cic; frigore sanguis, Verg.; quum claram speciem concreto lumine luna abdidit, *with darkened light,* Cic. **B.** *to grow, collect, increase, be formed;* aut simplex est natura animantis aut concreta est ex pluribus naturis, Cic.; de terris terram concrescere parvis, Lucr. (infin. perf. syncop. concresse, Ov.).

concrētĭo -ōnis, f. (concresco), **1,** *a growing together, congealing, condensing;* corporum, Cic.; **2,** *materiality, matter;* mortalis, Cic.

concrētus -a -um p. adj. (from concresco), *thickened, congealed, condensed, stiffened;* glacies, Liv.; lac, Verg.; dolor, *hard, tearless,* Ov.

concrŭcĭo, 1. *to torture violently,* Lucr.

concŭbīna -ae, f. (concubo), *a concubine.*

concŭbīnātus -ūs, m. (concubinus), *concubinage,* Plaut.

concŭbīnus -i. m. *a man living in a state of concubinage,* Tac.

concŭbĭtus -ūs, m. (concubo), **1,** *lying together* (at table), Prop.; **2,** *copulation,* Cic.

concŭbĭum -ii, n. (concubius), noctis, *the dead of night, the time at which men are in deep sleep,* Plaut.

concŭbĭus -a -um (concumbo), *relating to sleep,* found only in the phrase concubiā nocte, *at the time of men's first sleep, at dead of night,* Cic.

concŭbo, 1. = concumbo (q.v.).

conculco, 1. (com and calco). **A.** *to tread, trample under foot,* Cato. **B.** Transf., *to misuse, to despise;* miseram Italiam, Cic.; Macedonicam lauream, Cic.

concumbo -cŭbŭi -cŭbĭtum, 3. (com and * cumbo), *to lie with, have intercourse with,* Ov.

concŭpisco -pīvi or -pli -pītum, 3. (com and cupio), *to desire eagerly, covet, to endeavour after, aim at;* eandem mortem gloriosam, Cic.; signa, tabulas, supellectilem, vestem infinite, Cic.; with infin., ducere aliquam in matrimonium, Cic.

concurro -curri (rarely -cŭcurri) -cursum, **3. I.** *to run together, come together, flock to one* spot; tota Italia concurret, Cic.; ad arma, Caes.; ad curiam, Cic.; ad me restituendum Romam, Cic. **II.** 1, a, *to meet together;* ut neve aspere (verba) concurrerent neve vastius diducantur, Cic.; concurrit dextera laeva, *of clapping the hands for applause,* Hor.; b, *to happen at the same time;* quae ut concurrant omnia, optabile est, Cic.; **2,** a, *to run, dash, strike together;* ne prorae concurrerent, Liv.; b, *to meet in conflict, attack, engage;* concurrunt equites inter se, Caes.; omnia ventorum concurrere proelia vidi, Verg.; cum acie legionum rectā fronte, Liv.; with dat., concurrere equitibus, Liv.; adversus aliquem, Liv.; in aliquem, Sall.; transf., concurrentis belli minae, *war on the point of breaking out,* Tac.

concursātĭo -ōnis, f. (concurso), *a running together, concourse;* **1,** of persons, a, puerorum, Cic.; b, *going round;* concursatio regis a Demetriade nunc Lamiam in concilium Aetolorum nunc Chalcidem, Liv.; c, *skirmishing of light troops,* Liv.; **2,** of things without life, somniorum, Cic.

concursātor -ōris, m. (concurso), *a skirmisher* (opp. statarius), Liv.

concursĭo -ōnis, f. (concurro), **1,** *a running together, concourse;* atomorum, Cic.; **2,** *a figure of speech, in which the same word is frequently repeated* (Gr. συμπλοκή), Cic.

concurso, 1. **I.** Intransit. *to run about, rush hither and thither;* **1,** of persons, a, tum trepidare et concursare, Caes.; dies noctesque, Cic.; b, *to skirmish;* inter saxa rupesque, Liv.; c, *to travel about* (esp. of the magistrates of provinces), *to make official visits,* Cic.; **2,** of things, ignes concursant, Lucr. **II.** Transit. *to visit;* omnes fere domos omnium, Cic.

concursus -ūs, m. (concurro). **I.** *a running together, concourse;* **1,** concursus hominum in forum, Cic.; facere, *to cause a tumult or concourse;* **2,** of abstractions, *union;* honestissimorum studiorum, *co-operation in,* Cic. **II. A.** *a striking together, meeting;* corpusculorum, Cic.; verborum, Cic. **B.** *a dashing together;* **1,** navium, Caes., *a hostile encounter;* concursus utriusque exercitus, Caes.; **2,** fig., non posse sustinere concursum omnium philosophorum, Cic.; **3,** of disasters, concursus calamitatum, *attack,* Cic.

concussus, abl. -ū, m. (concutio), *a shaking, concussion,* Lucr.

concŭtĭo -cussi -cussum, 3. **I.** *to shake violently, agitate.* **A.** Gen., a, lit., caput, Ov.; terra concussa motu est, Liv.; b, transf., *to ipsum concute, search, examine yourself,* Hor. **B.** a, *to shatter, disturb, impair;* rempublicam, Cic.; b, *to alarm, trouble;* terrorem metum concutientem definiunt, Cic.; casu concussus acerbo, Verg.; c, *to urge, excite;* pectus, Verg. **C.** *to strike together,* frameas, Tac.

condĕcet, 2., impers. *it is proper, fit, decent;* capies quod te condecet, Plaut.

condĕcŏro, 1. *to adorn carefully;* ludos scenicos, Ter.

condemnātor -ōris, m. (condemno), *an accuser,* Tac.

condemno, 1. (com and damno). **I.** Of a judge, *to condemn, sentence.* **A.** Lit., Cic.; with genit., of the crime, aliquem injuriarum, Cic.; of the punishment, capitis, Cic.; with de, aliquem de alea, Cic.; with abl. of the penalty, denis millibus aeris, Liv. **B.** a, *to accuse;* aliquem impudentiae, Cic.; b, *to disapprove;* tuum factum non esse condemnatum judicio amicorum, Cic. **II.** Of an accuser, *to urge on effect the condemnation of a person;* condemnare aliquem uno hoc crimine, Cic.

condenseo = condenso (q.v).

condenso, 1. *to make thick, press close to-gether,* Varr.

condensus -a -um, *dense, thick;* puppes litore, Verg. ; vallis arboribus condensa, Liv.

condǐco -dixi -dictum, 1, *to make arrange-ment with, agree to, fix, appoint, settle;* diem, Plaut. ; 2, condicere alicui, *to invite oneself as a guest,* Cic.

condignus -a -um, *quite worthy, very worthy;* donum, Plaut.

condǐmentum -i., n. (condio), *spice, season-ing, sauce, condiment.* **A.** Lit. cibi condimentum est fames, potionis sitis, Cic. **B.** Transf., facet-iae omnium sermonum condimenta, Cic. ; seve-ritas alicuius multis condimentis humanitatis mitigatur, Cic.

condǐo -īvi or -ǐi -ītum, 4. *to pickle, to pre-serve.* **A.** Lit. **a,** in wine or vinegar, oleas, Cato ; **b,** in spice, *to make savoury;* herbas, Cic. ; hence, **c.** unguenta, *to make fragrant,* Cic. ; **c,** *to embalm;* mortuos, Cic. **B.** Transf. *to season, ornament, make pleasant;* orationem, Cic. ; *to soften, temper;* tristitiam temporum, Cic.

condiscǐpǔla -ae, f. *a female schoolfellow,* Mart.

condiscǐpǔlus -i, m. *a schoolfellow,* Cic.

condisco -dĭdĭci, 3. *to learn thoroughly;* modos, Hor. ; with infin., mihi paulo diligentius supplicare, Cic.

1. **condǐtǐo** -ōnis (condio), 1, *pickling* or *pre-serving of fruits,* Cic. ; 2, *a seasoning, making savoury;* ciborum, Ov.

2. **condǐtǐo** -ōnis, f. (condo), 1, *state, con-dition, external position, place, circumstances;* in-fima servorum, Cic. ; eā conditione nati sumus ut, etc., Cic. ; conditio imperii, Cic. ; parem cum ceteris fortunae conditionem subire, Cic. ; 2, *a condition, stipulation, provision, proviso;* non respuit conditionem, Caes. ; conditionem aequissimam repudiare, Cic. ; conditionem accip-ere, Cic. ; hāc, eā, istā conditione, his condi-tionibus, *on these terms,* Cic. ; armis conditione positis, *under conditions of peace,* Cic. ; 3, *esp. conditions of marriage, marriage contract, mar-riage;* and meton. *the person married;* aliam conditionem quaerere, Cic. ; conditionem filiae quaerere, Liv. ; nullius conditionis non habere potestatem, Nep. ; **in a bad sense,** *a gallant,* paramour, Cic.

condǐtor -ōris, m. (condo), *a founder, maker, contriver, composer, author;* Romanae arcis, Verg. ; Romanae libertatis, Liv. ; conditor et instructor convivii, Cic. ; conditor, Romani anni, chronicler), Ov.

condǐtōrǐum -ǐi, n. (condo), *the place in which a corpse or its ashes are preserved,* Suet.

1. **condǐtus** -a -um, partic. of condo.

2. **condǐtus** -a -um, p. adj., with compar. (from condio), *seasoned, savoury.* **I.** Lit. con-ditiora haec facit venatio, Cic. **II.** Transf. *sea-soned, ornamented;* oratio lepore et festivitate conditior, Cic.

condo -dĭdi -dĭtum, 3. **I. a,** *to put together, form, establish;* urbem Romam, Cic. ; Romanam gentem, Verg. ; collegium ad id novum, Liv. ; **b,** *to compose, write;* carmen, Cic. ; leges, Liv. ; hence, *to celebrate in song;* tristia bella, Verg. ; Caesaris acta, Ov. **II.** *to put in.* **A.** *to thrust, press in;* ensem in pectus, Ov. **B.** 1, *to preserve, collect;* pecuniam, Cic. ; litteras publicas in sanc-tiore aerario conditas habere, Cic. ; aliquid domi suae conditum jam putare, Cic. ; so esp. **a,** of wine, fruits, etc. *to store up;* frumentum, Cic. ; **dig., bonum in visceribus medullisque, Cic. ; of**

fruits, *to preserve, pickle;* corna condita in liquida faece, Ov. ; **b,** of persons, *to hide;* se deserto in litore, Verg. ; *to put, place;* aliquem in carcerem, Cic. ; **c,** *to bury;* aliquem in sepulcro, Cic. ; 2, transf., in causis conditae *(hidden);* sunt res futurae, Cic. ; 3, **a,** *to withdraw from sight;* caput inter nubila, Verg. ; of persons, condere diem, *to pass the day;* longos soles cantando, Verg. ; **b,** *to conceal, to cover;* caelum umbra, Verg. ; transf., iram, Tac.

condǒcěfǎcǐo -fēci -factum, 3 (condoceo and facio), *to train, instruct, teach;* beluas, Cic. ; animum, Cic.

condǒlesco -dǒlǔi (com and doleo), 3. *to suffer severely, to feel pain, to pain;* si pes con-doluit, si dens, Cic. ; latus ei dicenti condo-luisse, Cic.

condōnātǐo -ōnis, f. (condono), *a giving away;* bonorum possessionumque, Cic.

condōno, 1., 1, **a,** *to give away, present;* agros suis latronibus, Cic. ; consuli totam Achaiam, Cic. ; of the praetor, alicui hereditatem, *to award the inheritance,* Cic. ; **b,** *to give up to, sacrifice to;* se vitamque suam reipublicae, Sall. ; condonari libidini muliebri, Cic. ; 2, **a,** *to forgive a debt;* pecunias creditas debitoribus, Cic. ; **b,** hence, *to overlook, forgive a fault;* alicui crimen, Cic.; *to forgive an injury for the sake of a third party;* praeterita se Divitiaco fratri condonare dicit, Caes.

Condrūsi -ōrum, m. *a German people in Gallia Belgica.*

condūcǐbǐlis -e (conduco), *profitable, useful;* consilium ad eam rem, Plaut.

condūco -duxi -ductum, 3. **I.** Transit. **A.** *to bring* or *lead together, collect;* **a,** of persons, exercitum in unum locum, Caes. ; virgines unum in locum, Cic. ; **b,** of things, *to bring together, unite, connect;* partes in unum, Lucr. ; vineas, Cic. ; cortice ramos, Ov. ; transf., propositionem et assumptionem in unum, Cic. **B.** *to hire,* **a,** of persons, aliquem mercede, Cic. ; consulem ad caedem faciendam, Cic. ; esp. milit. t. t. *to hire soldiers;* homines, Caes. ; milites Gallos mercede, Liv. ; **b,** of things, *to hire for use* (opp. locare), domum, hortum, Cic. ; esp. *to farm the taxes;* portorium, Cic. ; **c,** *to undertake, contract for;* columnam faciendam, Cic. **II.** Intransit. *to be of use, to profit, to serve,* Cic. ; with dat., quae saluti tuae conducere arbitror, Cic. ; with ad and the acc., ad vitae commoditatem, Cic. ; with acc. and infin., hoc maxime reipublicae conducit Syriam Macedoniamque decerni, Cic.

conductǐcǐus -a -um (conduco), *hired;* ex-ercitus, *mercenary,* Nep.

conductǐo -ōnis, f. (conduco), 1, *a bringing together, uniting, recapitulation,* Cic. ; 2, *hiring, farming;* fundi, Cic.

conductor -ōris, m. (conduco), 1, *one who hires;* mercedes habitationum annuas conductor-ibus donare, Caes. ; 2, *a contractor;* operis, Cic.

conductus -a -um, partic. of conduco.

condǔplǐco, 1. *to double;* divitias, Lucr.

condūro, 1. *to harden, make quite hard;* ferrum, Lucr.

cōnecto, cōnexio, v. connecto, connexio.

cōnesto, v. cohonesto.

confābǔlor, 1., dep. *to talk, converse,* Plaut.

confarrěātǐo -ōnis, f. (confarreo), *an an-cient and solemn form of the marriage ceremony among the Romans, in which* panis farreus *was used,* Plin.

confarrěo, 1. (com and far), *to marry by the ceremony of* confarreatio; patricios confarreatis parentibus genitus, Tac.

confātālis -e, *determined by fate*, Cic.

confectĭo -ōnis, f. (conficio), 1, a, *a making ready, preparation, producing, composing, completing;* huius libri, Cic.; belli, Cic.; b, *exaction;* tributi, Cic.; 2, *consumption,* escarum, Cic.; valetudinis, *weakening,* Cic.

confector -ōris, m. (conficio), 1, *one who prepares, completes, finishes;* negotiorum, Cic.; 2, *a destroyer, consumer;* confector et consumptor omnium ignis, Cic.

confercĭo -fersi -fertum, 4. (com and farcio), *to press close together, compress, cram together;* confertae naves, Liv.

confĕro, contŭli, collātum (conlātum), conferre. I. *to bring together, collect;* 1, a, lit., sarcinas in unum locum, Caes.; b, transf., conferamus igitur in pauca, Cic.; 2, *to bring together money, contribute;* tributa quotannis ex censu, Cic.; quadragena talenta quotannis Delum, Nep.; 3, *to unite, to join, connect;* vires in unum, Liv.; 4, *to place together or near;* a, lit. (a) in a friendly manner, capita, Cic.; gradum, Verg.; (β) as milit. t. t., *to bring into hostile contact or collision;* Galli cum Fontejo ferrum ac manus contulerunt, Cic.; pedem cum pede, or conferre pedem, *to fight foot to foot,* Liv., Cic.; signa conferre, *to engage,* Cic.; se viro vir contulit, *man fought with man,* Verg.; absol., mecum confer, ait, *fight with me,* Ov.; conferre lites, *to contend,* Hor.; b, transf., of speech, *to interchange, exchange, discuss;* sermonem cum aliquo, Cic.; consilia, Liv.; tum si quid res feret, coram conferemus, Cic.; 5, *to compare;* Gallicum cum Germanorum agro, Caes.; cum illius vita P. Sullae vobis notissimam, Cic.; parva magnis, Cic. II. *to bring to a place;* 1, *to remove, transfer;* a, lit., suas rationes et copias in illam provinciam, Cic.; esp., se conferre; *to betake oneself, flee;* se in astu, Cic.; b, transf. (a) se conferre, *to devote oneself, join oneself to;* conferre se ad pontificem Scaevolam, Cic.; se ad studium scribendi, Cic.; (β) *to put off, postpone;* aliquid in longiorem diem, Caes.; 2, *to apply;* a, lit., pecuniam ad beneficentiam, Cic.; b, transf. (a) of thoughts, etc., *to direct, use;* curam ad philosophiam, Cic.; (β) *to hand over;* rem ad aliquem, Cic.; (γ) *to impute, attribute;* permulta in Plancium quae ab eo dicta non sunt, Cic.; culpam in aliquem, Cic.; (δ) confert, *it is profitable,* Quint.

confertim, adv. (confertus), *densely, thickly, compactly;* pugnare, Liv.

confertus -a -um, p. adj. with compar. and superl. (confercio), 1, *closely compressed, dense* (opp. rarus); confertae naves, Liv.; confertissima turba, Liv.; conferti milites, *in close formation,* Caes.; 2, *with abl., full of;* ingenti turbā conferta templa, Liv.; transf., vita, plena et conferta voluptatibus, Cic.

confervĕfăcĭo, 3. *to make very hot, to melt,* Lucr.

confervesco -ferbŭi, 3. *to begin to boil, begin to glow;* transf., mea quum conferbuit ira, Hor.

confessĭo -ōnis, f. (confiteor), *a confession, acknowledgment;* erranti sui, Cic.; captae pecuniae, Cic.; adducere aliquem ad ignorationis confessionem, Cic.; exprimere ab aliquo confessionem culpae, Liv.; ea erat confessio caput rerum Romam esse, Liv.

confessus -a -um (partic. of confiteor, with pass. meaning), *undoubted, acknowledged, certain;* res manifesta, confessa, Cic.; hence, ex confesso, *confessedly,* Quint.; in confesso esse, Tac.; in confessum venire, *to be generally acknowledged, universally known,* Plin.

confestim, adv., *immediately, without delay;* confestim huc advolare, Cic.; confestim consequi, Cic.; patres consulere, Liv.

conficĭens -entis, p. adj. (from conficio), *that which causes, effects, effecting, efficient;* causae, Cic.; with genit., cum civitate mihi res est acerrima et conficientissima litterarum, *that notes down everything carefully,* Cic.

conficĭo -fēci -fectum, 3. (com and facio), *to make together,* hence, I. *to finish, make ready, bring about, accomplish;* 1, a, soccos suā manu, Cic.; litteras, Cic.; sacra, Cic.; tantum facinus, Cic.; bellum, Cic.; his rebus confectis, Caes.; b, of business, *to conclude a bargain or transaction;* negotium ex sententia, Cic.; rem sine pugna et sine vulnere, Caes.; Cic.; pretium, *settle the price,* Cic.; absol., confice cum Apella de columnis, Cic.; c, of a journey, *to bring to an end;* cursum, Cic.; c. iter ex sententia, Cic.; incredibili celeritate magnum spatium paucis diebus, Cic.; d, of time, *to complete;* prope centum confecisse annos, Cic.; extremum vitae diem morte, Cic.; nondum hieme confecta, Caes.; 2, a, *to procure;* permagnam ex illa re pecuniam confici posse, Caes.; frumentum, Liv.; milit. t. t., *to get soldiers;* reliquas legiones, quas ex novo delectu confecerat, Cic.; exercitus maximos, Cic.; tribum suam necessariis, *to gain over,* Cic.; b, *to produce, cause;* (a) alicui reditum, procure, Cic.; motus animorum, Cic.; (β) philosoph. t. t., *to prove;* ex quo conficitur ut, etc., *it follows from this,* Cic. II. 1, *to consume;* a, of food, etc. (a) *to chew, eat;* escas, Cic.; plures jam pavones confeci, quam tu pullos columbinos, Cic.; (β) *to digest;* confectus et consumptus cibus, Cic.; b, *to waste, destroy;* patrimonium suum, Cic.; 2, *to destroy, kill;* haec sica nuper ad regiam me paene confecit, Cic.; 3, *to subdue;* Britanniam, Cic.; 4, *to weaken;* a, vitae cupiditas, quae me conficit angoribus, Cic.; often in pass., confici fame, frigore, lacrimis, curis, dolore, Cic.; confectus macie et squalore, Cic.; vulneribus, Caes.; b, of states, praevalentis populi vires se ipse conficiunt, Liv.

confictĭo -ōnis, f. (confingo), *a fabrication, invention;* criminis, Cic.

confīdens -entis, p. adj. with compar. and superl. (from confido), *confident, self-reliant,* gen. in a bad sense, *shameless, impudent,* Cic.

confīdenter, adv., with compar. and superl. (confidens), *boldly, confidently;* confidentius dicere, Cic.

confīdentĭa -ae, f. (confidens), a, *confidence;* confidentiam afferre hominibus, ap. Cic.; b, more frequently, *impudence, boldness, shamelessness;* confidentia et temeritas tua, Cic.

confīdo -fisus sum (confīdi(?), Liv.), 3. *to trust, be assured, confide;* a, absol., nimis confidere, Cic.; b, with dat., sibi, Cic.; c, with abl., militum virtute non satis, Cic.; d, with de, de salute urbis, Caes.; e, with acc. and infin., *to believe firmly;* id ita futurum esse confido, Cic.

configo -fixi -fixum, 3. 1, *to fasten together, nail together;* transtra clavis ferreis, Caes.; 2, *to pierce through, transfix with a weapon;* a, lit., filios suos sagittis, Cic.; b, transf., ducentis confixus senatus consultis, Cic.

confindo, 3. *to cleave asunder,* Tib.

confingo -finxi -fictum, 3. 1, *to construct;* nidos, Plin.; 2, *to fabricate, feign, invent;* crimen incredibile, Cic.; crimina in aliquem, Cic.

confīnis -e. A. Lit., *having the same boundary, conterminous, adjacent, near;* confines erant hi Senonibus, Caes.; caput confinis collo, Ov. Subst., **confīnis** -is, m. *a neighbour,* Mart. B. Transf., *nearly allied, similar;* studio confinia carmina vestro, Ov.

confīnĭum -ĭi, n. (confinis). A. Lit., *a*

confīne, common boundary, limit, border (of countries or estates); Trevirorum, Caes.; conveniet in omni re contrahenda vicinitatibus et confiniis aequum et facilem esse, Cic. **B.** Transf., *the bordering line, nearness, close connexion;* confinia noctis, *twilight,* Ov.; breve confinium artis et falsi, Tac.

confirmātĭo -ōnis, f. (confirmo), a, *an establishing, making firm;* confirmatio perpetuae libertatis, Cic.; b, esp., *consolation, encouragement, support;* neque enim confirmatione nostrā egebat virtus tua, Cic.; c, *confirming* or *verifying a fact;* perfugae, Caes.; d, rhet. t. t., *adducing of proofs,* Cic.

confirmātor -ōris, m. (confirmo), *one who confirms, establishes;* pecuniae, *a surety,* Cic.

confirmātus -a -um, p. adj. with compar. and superl. (from confirmo), 1, *encouraged, emboldened;* satis certus et confirmatus animus, Cic.; 2, *certain, credible;* in quibus (litteris) erat confirmatius idem illud, Cic.

confirmo, 1. **I.** Lit., *to establish, make firm, confirm, strengthen;* hoc nervos confirmari putant, Caes.; valetudinem, *to recover health,* Cic.; se confirmare, *to recover strength,* Cic. **II.** Transf., **A.** Gen., *to strengthen, make lasting;* pacem, Cic.; consilia, *to support,* Caes.; confirmatis rebus, *firmly established,* Caes.; se transmarinis auxiliis, Caes.; polit. t. t., *to ratify;* acta Caesaris, Cic. **B.** Esp. a, *to confirm persons in allegiance,* etc.; jure jurando inter se, Caes.; b, *to strengthen, encourage;* confirmare et excitare afflictos animos, Cic.; erige te et confirma, *take courage;* animos Gallorum verbis, Caes.; c, *to confirm* or *establish the truth of an assertion;* nostra argumentis ac rationibus, Cic.; d, *to affirm, assert positively;* id omne ego me rei publicae causā suscepisse confirmo, Cic.

confisco, 1. (com and fiscus), 1, *to lay up, preserve in a chest,* Suet.; 2, *to appropriate to the imperial treasury, to confiscate,* Suet.

contīsĭo -ōnis, f. (confido), *confidence, assurance;* fidentia, id est firma animi confisio, Cic.

confĭtĕor -fessus sum, 2. dep. (com and fateor). **I.** Lit., *to confess, allow, acknowledge;* with acc., hoc crimen, Cic.; with acc. and dat., amorem nutrici, Ov.; with double acc., se victos, Caes.; with acc. and infin., multa se ignorare, Cic.; with de, aliquid de veneno, Cic. Partic. perf., **confessus,** a, ⸺ct., *having confessed;* quinque homines comprehensi atque confessi, Cic.; b, pass., *confessed, acknowledged;* quam improbam, quam manifestam, quam confessam rem pecunia redimere conetur, Cic. **II.** Transf., *to reveal, make known;* se, Ov.; deam, *as a goddess,* Verg.

conflăgro, 1. *to be destroyed by fire, to be burnt up.* **A.** Lit., classis praedonum incendio conflagrabat, Cic.; fig., amoris flammā, Cic.; incendio invidiae, Cic. **B.** Transf., conflagrare invidiā, *to fall a victim to hatred,* Cic.

conflictĭo -ōnis, f. (confligo), *a striking together, collision, a conflict, combat;* transf., causarum, Cic.

conflicto, 1. (intens. of confligo), *to strike together violently;* thus pass., a, *to combat with, contend with;* conflictari cum adversā fortunā, Nep.; conflictari cum aliquo, Cic.; b, conflictari aliquā re, *to be grievously troubled, to suffer severely, to be harassed, tormented;* iniquissimis verbis, Cic.; magnā inopiā necessariarum rerum, Caes.; duriore fortunā, Cic.

conflictus -ūs, m. (confligo), *a striking together;* lapidum, Cic.

conflīgo -flixi -flictum, 3. **I.** Transit., *to strike, bring, join together;* corpora, Lucr.;

---

transf., *to bring together in order to compare;* factum adversarii cum scripto, Cic. **II.** Intransit., a, *to strike together;* illae (naves) graviter inter se incitatae confluxerunt, Caes.; b, *to struggle, fight, contend;* cum hoste, Cic.; contra or adversus aliquem, Nep.

conflo, 1. **I.** *to blow together, to blow up, to kindle.* **A.** Lit., quorum operā id conflatum incendium, Liv. **B.** Transf., *to excite;* seditionem, Cic. **II.** *to melt.* **A.** Lit., a, of metals, Plin.; falces in enses, *to forge,* Verg.; b, of money, *to coin;* aut flare aut conflare pecuniam, Cic. **B.** Transf., a, *to unite;* horum consensus conspirans et paene conflatus, Cic.; b, *to rivet together, forge, produce;* ut una ex duabus naturis conflata videatur, Cic.; c, *to get together;* exercitus perditorum civium clandestino scelere conflatus, Cic.; d, *to forge, invent;* crimen, Cic.; alicui periculum, Cic.; e, *to brood over, meditate;* judicia domi conflabant, pronuntiabant in foro, Liv.

conflŭens -entis or **conflŭentes** -ium, m. *the confluence* or *place of junction of two rivers;* Mosae et Rheni, Caes.

conflŭo -fluxi, 3. **A.** *to flow together;* in unum, Cic.; a confluente Rhodano castra movi, *from the confluence of the Rhone with the Arar,* ap. Cic. **B.** Transf., a, of a crowd, *to stream or flock together;* Athenas, Cic.; ad haec studia, Cic.; b, of abstractions, ad ipsos laus, honos, dignitas confluit, Cic.

confŏdĭo -fōdi -fossum, 3. a, *to dig thoroughly;* hortum, Plaut.; b, *to stab, pierce, wound;* jacentem, Liv.; (Ciceronem) de improviso domi suae, Sall.; fig., tot judiciis confossi praedamnatique, Liv.

conformātĭo -ōnis, f. (conformo). **A.** Lit., *a form, shape, forming, conformation;* lineamentorum, Cic. **B.** Transf., 1, gen., vocis, *expression;* verborum, *arrangement,* Cic.; 2, esp., a, philosoph. t. t., conformatio animi, or simply *conformatio, an idea,* Cic.; b, in rhet. t. t., *a figure of speech,* Cic.

conformo, 1. *to form symmetrically, form, arrange.* **A.** Lit., mundum a natura conformatum esse, Cic.; ad majora quaedam nos natura genuit et conformavit, Cic. **B.** Transf., *to arrange fittingly;* vocem secundum rationem rerum, Cic.; se ad voluntatem alicuius, Cic.

confossus -a -um, partic. of confodio.

confrăgōsus -a -um, *rugged, uneven;* loca, via, Liv.; neut. plur. as subst., *uneven places,* Liv.

confrĕmo -frĕmŭi, 3. *to murmur, roar, make a loud noise;* confremuere omnes, Ov.

confrĭco -frĭcŭi -frĭcātum, 1. *to rub;* caput atque os suum unguento, Cic.

confringo -frēgi -fractum, 3. (com and frango). **A.** Lit., *to break in two, break in pieces;* digitos, Cic. **B.** Transf., *to destroy, bring to naught;* consilia senatoria, Cic.

confŭgĭo -fūgi, 3. **A.** Lit., *to fly to, take refuge;* ad aliquem, ad or in aram, Cic.; in naves, Caes. **B.** Transf., a, ad alicuius misericordiam, Cic.; ad opem judicum, Cic.; b, *to have recourse to;* patrias ad artes, Ov.; confugit illuc ut neget, etc., Cic.

confŭgĭum -ii, n. (confugio), *a place of refuge,* Ov.

confulcĭo -fultus, 4. *to prop up,* Lucr.

confundo -fūdi -fūsum, 3. **I.** *to pour together, mingle, mix.* **A.** Lit., cum alicuius lacrimis lacrimas confundere nostras, Ov.; quum ignis oculorum cum eo igni qui est ob os offusus se confudit et contulit, Cic. **B.** Transf., 1, *to join together;* tantā multitudine confusā, Caes.; duo populi confusi in unum, Liv.; ea philosophia quae confundit vera cum falsis, Cic.; in hac confusā et universā defensione, *complicated*, Cic.; 2, a, *to confuse, throw into disorder;* signa et ordines peditum atque equitum, Liv.; jura gentium, Liv.; particulas minutas primum confusas, postea in ordinem adductas a mente divinā, Cic.; b, (a) *to obscure;* vultum Lunae, Ov.; (β) *to confuse, trouble, disturb;* confusa pudore, Ov.; audientium animos, Liv.; maerore recenti confusus, Liv. II. *to pour into;* cruor confusus in fossam, Hor.; per quas lapsus cibus in eam venam confunditur, Cic.; transf., est hoc quidem in totam orationem confundendum, nec minime in extremam, Cic.

confūsē, adv. with compar. (confusus), *confusedly, in a disorderly manner;* loqui, Cic.

confūsĭo -ōnis, f. (confundo), 1, *a mixture, union, connexion;* haec conjunctio confusioque virtutum,Cic.; 2, a, *confusion, disorder;* suffragiorum, *voting not in the centuries, but man by man,* Cic.; religionum, Cic.; b, oris, *blushing,* Tac.

confūsus -a -um, p. adj., with compar. and superl. (confundo), a, *disorderly, confused;* ita confusa est oratio, ita perturbata, nihil ut sit primum, nihil secundum, Cic.; strages, Verg.; b, *confused in appearance;* vultus, Liv.; confusus animo, Liv.

confūto, 1. *to check the boiling of a liquid;* hence transf., a, *to check, repress;* maximis doloribus affectus eos ipsos inventorum suorum memoriā et recordatione confutat, Cic.; b, esp. by speech, *to put down, silence, overthrow;* audaciam alicuius, Cic.; argumenta Stoicorum, Cic.

congĕlo, 1. I. Transit., *to freeze thoroughly.* A. Lit., Mart. B. Transf., *to harden, thicken;* rictus in lapidem, Ov. II. Intransit., *to freeze;* Ister congelat, Ov.; fig., congelasse nostrum amicum laetabar otio, *had become inactive,* Cic.

congĕmĭno, 1. *to double, redouble;* ictus crebros ensibus, Verg.

congĕmo -gĕmŭi, 3. I. Intransit. *to sigh* or *groan loudly;* congemuit senatus frequens, Cic. II. Transit., *to bewail, lament;* mortem, Lucr.

congĕr and **gongĕr** -gri, m. (γόγγρος), *a sea* or *conger eel,* Ov.

congĕrĭes -ēi, f. (congero). A. Gen., *a heap, mass;* lapidum, Liv. B. Esp., 1, *a heap of wood, a wood pile,* Ov.; 2, *the mass of chaos,* Ov.

congĕro -gessi -gestum, 3. A. Lit., *to carry together, bring together, collect;* 1, undique quod idoneum ad muniendum putarent, Nep.; salis magnam viam ex proximis salinis, Caes.; maximam vim auri atque argenti in regnum suum, Cic.; oscula, *to add one to another,* Ov.; 2, a, *to prepare;* alicui viaticum, Cic.; b, *to heap together;* auri pondus, Ov.; c, *to build;* aram sepulcri arboribus; so of birds, locus aeriae quo congessere palumbesa, *have built their nests,* Verg. B. Transf., a, in discourse, *to bring together, comprise;* turbam patronorum in hunc sermonem, Cic.; b, *to heap together;* ingentia beneficia in aliquem, Liv.; omnia ornamenta ad aliquem, Cic.; maledicta in aliquem, Cic.; omnes vastati agri periculorumque imminentium causas in aliquem, *to ascribe, impute,* Cic.

congestīcĭus -a -um (congero), *heaped up, artificially brought together;* agger, Caes.

congestus -ūs, m. (congero) *a collecting, heaping together.* I. Lit., a, gen., municipia congestu copiarum vastabantur, Tac.; b, esp. of birds, *building nests;* herbam (exstitisse) avium congestu, Cic. II. Meton., *that which is brought together, a heap, mass;* lapidum Tac.

congĭārĭum -ĭi, n. (sc. donum), *a donation distributed by the consuls and emperors among the people,* so called from the fact that it originally consisted of a congius of wine, oil, etc., Liv.; *a donation in money to the soldiery,* Cic.; or *to private friends,* Cic.

congĭus -ĭi, m. *a Roman measure for liquids, containing six* sextarii, Liv.

conglăcĭo, 1. I. Intransit., A. Lit., *to freeze;* frigoribus conglaciat aqua, Cic. B. Transf., Curioni nostro tribunatus conglaciat, *passes inactively,* ap. Cic. II. Transit., *to turn to ice,* Plin.

conglŏbātĭo -ōnis, f. (conglobo), *a heaping, pressing, crowding together,* Tac.

conglŏbo, 1. (com and globus), 1, *to form into a ball* or *sphere;* mare conglobatur undique aequabiliter, Cic.; figura conglobata, Cic.; 2, *to press together in a mass* or *crowd;* a, lit., catervatim uti quosque fors conglobaverat, Sall.; conglobata in unum multitudo, Liv.; b, transf., maxime definitiones valent conglobatae, *accumulated,* Cic.

conglŏmĕro, 1. *to roll, twist, entangle together,* Lucr.

conglūtĭnātĭo -ōnis, f. (conglutino), 1, *a sticking, cementing together,* Cic.; 2, *connexion, joining together;* verborum, Cic.

conglūtĭno, 1. A. *to stick together, cement together,* Plin. B. Transf., *to connect, bind closely;* amicitias, Cic.; voluntates nostras consuetudine, Cic.

congrātŭlor, 1. dep. *to wish joy, congratulate;* congratulantur libertatem concordiamque civitati restitutam, Liv.

congrĕdĭor -gressus, 3. dep. (com and gradior), 1, *to meet;* cum aliquo, Cic.; inter se, Liv.; 2, *to meet hostilely, in combat;* a, *to engage, contend;* locus, ubi congressi sunt, Cic.; congredi sua sponte cum finitimis proelio, Cic.; with dat., impar congressus Achilli, Verg.; b, *to dispute in words, argue;* congredi cum Academico, Cic.

congrĕgābĭlis -e (congrego), *sociable, inclined to collect;* examina apium, Cic.

congrĕgātĭo -ōnis, f. (congrego), *an assembling together, society, union;* nos ad congregationem hominum et ad societatem communitatemque generis humani esse natos, Cic.

congrĕgo, 1. (com and grex). I. Lit., A. *to collect into a flock;* oves, Plin.; refl., se congregare, or pass., congregari, in a middle sense *to form into flocks;* apium examina congregantur, *form themselves into swarms,* Cic. B. Of men, *to collect, gather together;* dispersos homines in unum locum, Cic.; refl., se congregare, and pass., congregari, in middle sense, *to assemble,* congregari in fano commentandi causa, Cic. II. Transf., of things, *to unite;* signa in unum locum, Tac.

congressĭo -ōnis, f. (congredior), 1, *a meeting,* Cic.; 2, *intercourse, society;* aliquem ab alicuius non modo familiaritate, sed etiam congressione prohibere, Cic.

congressus -ūs, m. (congredior), *a meeting;* 1, *a friendly meeting, social intercourse, conversation;* alicuius aditum, congressum, sermonem fugere, Cic.; often in plur., congressus hominum fugere atque odisse, Cic.; 2, *a hostile meeting, combat;* ante congressum, Cic.; primo congressu terga vertere nostros cogere, Caes.

congrŭens -entis, p. adj. (congruo), 1, *agreeing, fit, appropriate, suitable;* vultus et gestus congruens et apta, Cic.; with cum and the abl., gestus cum sententiis congruens, Cic.; with dat., actiones virtutibus congruentes, Cic.

2, *harmonious, accordant;* is concentus ex dissimillimarum vocum moderatione concors tamen efficitur et congruens, Cic.; clamor congruens, *unanimous,* Liv.

congrüentĕr, adv. (congruens), *aptly, agreeably, suitably;* congruenter naturae convenientˌerque vivere, Cic.

congrüentĭa -ae, f. (congruo), *agreement, harmony, symmetry, proportion,* Suet.

congruo -ŭi, 3. (com and *gruo, connected with ruo). **A.** Lit., *to run together, come together, meet;* ut vicesimo anno ad metam eandem solis, unde orsi essent, dies congruerent, Liv. **B.** Transf., **a,** of time, *to coincide;* qui suos dies mensesque congruere volunt cum solis lunaeque ratione, Cic.; **b,** *to be suited, fitted to, correspond with, agree;* sensus nostri ut in pace semper, sic tum etiam in bello congruebant, Cic.; with cum and the abl., eius sermo cum tuis litteris valde congruit, Cic.; with dat., non omni causae nec auditori neque personae neque tempori congruere orationis unum genus, Cic.; with inter se, multae causae inter se congruere videntur, Cic.

congrüus -a -um = congruens (q.v.).

cŏnĭcĭo = conjĭcĭo (q.v.).

cŏnĭfĕr -fĕra -fĕrum (conus and fero), *cone-bearing;* cyparissi, Verg.

cŏnĭgĕr (conus and gero) = conifer (q.v.).

cŏnĭtor = connitor (q.v.).

cŏnīvĕo = conniveo (q.v.).

conjectĭo -ōnis, f. (conjicio). **A.** *a hurling, throwing;* telorum, Cic. **B.** Transf., *conjectural interpretation;* somniorum, Cic.

conjecto, 1. (freq. of conjicio), *to throw together;* transf., *to conclude, infer, conjecture, surmise, guess at;* conjectantes iter, Liv.; rem eventu, Liv.; Caesar conjectans eum Aegyptum iter habere, Caes.

conjector -ōris, m. (conjicio), *an interpreter of dreams;* Isiaci conjectores, *the priests of Isis,* Cic.

conjectrix -īcis, f. (conjector), *a female interpreter of dreams,* Plaut.

conjectūra -ae, f. (conjicio), *a guess, conjecture, inference.* **I.** Gen., conjecturam adhibere, Cic.; aberrare conjecturā, *to be mistaken in,* Cic.; conjecturam facere or capere ex or de aliquā re, Cic.; afferre conjecturam, Cic.; conjectura assequi or consequi (foll. by relative clause), Cic.; quantum conjecturā auguramur, Cic. **II.** Esp. **1,** *interpretation of dreams and omens, divination, soothsaying;* facilis conjectura huius somnii, Cic.; **2,** rhet. t. t., *a part of the proof, conjecture, inference,* Cic.

conjectūrālis -e (conjectura), *relating to conjecture, conjectural;* controversia, Cic.

conjectus -ūs, m. (conjicio), *a throwing together.* **I.** Lit., **a,** materiai, Lucr.; **b,** *a throwing, casting, hurling;* lapidum, Cic.; venire ad teli conjectum, *to come within shot,* Liv.; ne primum quidem conjectum telorum ferre, Liv. **II.** Transf. *casting* or *directing towards;* vester in me animorum oculorumque conjectus, Cic.

conjĭcĭo -jēci -jectum, 3. (com and jacio). **I. A.** Lit., **1,** *to throw, bring together, collect;* sarcinas in medium, Liv.; sortes in hydriam, Cic.; sortem conjicere, *to cast lots,* Cic.; aggerem in munitionem, Caes. **2,** of missiles, *to throw, cast, hurl;* tela in nostros, Caes.; fig., petitiones ita ut vitari non possint, Cic. **B.** Transf., **1,** Gen., *to cast, direct;* oculos in aliquem, Cic.; maledicta in alicuius vitam, Cic.; **2, a,** *to conjecture, guess;* de matre suavianda ex oraculo acute arguteque, Cic.; partic. perf. subst., belle conjecta, *clever surmises,* Cic.; **b,** *to interpret*

conjecturally; omen, Cic. **II.** *to throw, to hurl.* **A.** Lit. **1,** quum haec navis invitis nautis vi tempestatis in portum conjecta sit, Cic.; aliquem in carcerem, Cic.; in vincula, Cic.; in lautumias, Cic.; se conjicere, *to betake oneself, flee;* se in portum, Cic.; se in fugam, Cic.; se in castra alicuius, Cic.; **2,** *to insert,* libellum in epistolam, Cic.; **3,** of a weapon, *to thrust;* gladium in adversum os, Caes. **B.** Transf., **1,** naves conjectae in noctem, *benighted,* Caes.; se in noctem, *to hasten away under cover of night,* Cic.; forensem turbam in quatuor tribus, *to divide,* Liv.; aliquem ex occultis insidiis ad apertum latrocinium, *to force,* Cic.; **2,** *to spend;* tantam pecuniam in propylaea, Cic.; **3,** *to introduce;* haec verba in interdictum, Cic.

conjŭgālis -e (conjux), *relating to marriage, conjugal;* amor, Tac.

conjŭgātĭo -ōnis, f. (conjugo), *the etymological connection of words,* Cic.

conjŭgātor -ōris, m. *one who connects, unites;* boni amoris, Cat.

conjŭgĭālis -e (conjugium), *relating to marriage, conjugal;* festa, Ov.

conjŭgĭum -ĭi, n. (conjungo), **1,** *a close connexion, union;* corporis atque animae, Lucr.; **2, a,** *marriage, wedlock;* Tulliae meae, Cic.; tota domus conjugio et stirpe conjungitur, Cic.; poet., of animals, Ov.; **b,** meton., *husband,* Verg.; *wife,* Verg.

conjŭgo, 1. (com and jugum), *to yoke together, to bind together, connect;* **a,** est ea jucundissima amicitia, quam similitudo morum conjugavit, Cic.; **b,** conjugata verba, *words etymologically connected,* Cic.

conjunctē, adv., with compar. and superl. (conjunctus), **1,** *conjointly, in connexion;* conjuncte cum reliquis rebus nostra contexere, Cic.; elatum aliquid, *hypothetically* (opp. simpliciter, *categorically*), Cic.; **2,** *intimately, on terms of friendship;* cum aliquo vivere conjunctissime et amantissime, Cic.

conjunctim, adv. (conjunctus), *conjointly, in common;* huius omnis pecuniae conjunctim ratio habetur, Caes.

conjunctĭo -ōnis, f. (conjungo), *uniting, joining together;* **1,** portuum, Cic.; **2, a,** of things, conjunctio confusioque naturae, Cic.; rhet. and philosoph. t. t. *connexion of ideas,* Cic.; grammat. t. t. *a connecting particle, conjunction;* quum demptis conjunctionibus dissolute plura dicuntur, Cic.; **b,** of persons, *union, connexion;* (a) gen. societas conjunctioque humana, Cic.; citius cum eo veterem conjunctionem dirimere quam novam conciliare, Cic.; Pompejum a Caesaris conjunctione avocare, Cic.; summa nostra conjunctio et familiaritas, Cic.; (β) *relationship through marriage,* or *relationship;* conjunctio sanguinis, Cic.; conjunctio affinitatis, Cic.

conjunctus -a -um, p. adj., with compar. and superl. (conjungo), *connected, joined;* **1,** sublicae cum omni opere conjunctae, Caes.; with dat. *bordering on, near;* theatrum conjunctum domui, Caes.; Paphlagonia conjuncta Cappadociae, Nep.; **2,** *contemporary with;* conjunctus igitur Sulpicii aetati P. Antistius fuit, Cic.; **3, a,** *connected with, agreeing with, proportioned to;* prudentia cum justitiā, Cic.; talis simulatio est vanitati conjunctior, *is more nearly allied,* Cic.; continuata conjunctaque verba, Cic.; subst., **conjunctum** -i, n. *connection,* Cic.; **b,** of persons, *connected, allied, friendly;* homines benevolentiā conjuncti, Cic.; homo mihi conjunctus fidissimā gratiā, Cic.; et cum iis et inter se conjunctissimos fuisse M'. Curium, Ti. Coruncanium, Cic.; tam conjuncta populo Romane cīvĭtas, Caes.; sanguine conjuncti, Nep.; civium Romanorum omnium sanguis conjunctus existimandus est, Cic.

conjungo -junxi -junctum, 3. *to join together* constr. with dat., cum and abl., inter se, or the abl. alone. **I.** Lit., navi onerariae alteram, Caes.; calamos plures cerā, Verg. **II.** Transf., *to unite*; 1, of space, a, of things, dextram dextrae, Ov.; eam epistolam cum hac epistola, Cic.; hunc montem murus circumdatus arcem efficit et cum oppido conjungit, Caes.; b, of persons, ut paulatim sese legiones conjungerent, Caes.; se Hannibali, Liv.; 2, of time, noctem diei, *to travel far into the night*, Caes.; 3, *to bring into connexion, unite, join;* a, causam alicuius cum communi salute, Cic.; conjungere bellum, *to undertake in common*, Cic.; b, *to unite in marriage, friendship, alliance*, etc.; filias suas filiis alicuius matrimonio, Liv.; me tibi studia communia conjungunt, Cic.; conjungere amicitias, Cic.

conjunx = conjux (q.v.).

conjūrātĭo -ōnis, f. (conjuro). **A.** *union confirmed by an oath;* conjuratio Acarnanica, Liv.; conjurationem nobilitatis facere, Caes. **B.** *a conspiracy, plot;* conjuratio Catilinae, Sall.; in ea conjuratione esse, *to be implicated in*, Sall.; conjurationem facere contra rempublicam, Cic. **C.** Meton. *the conspirators;* voces conjurationis tuae, Cic.

conjūrātus -a -um (conjuro), *united by oath, allied;* subst., **conjūrāti** -ōrum, m. *conspirators*, Cic.

conjūro, 1. *to swear together.* **I.** *to take the military oath;* ut omnes Italiae juniores conjurarent, Caes. **II.** *to unite together by oath.* **A.** Gen., barbari conjurare, obsides inter se dare coeperunt, Caes.; with acc. and infin., per suos principes inter se conjurant nihil nisi communi consilio acturos, Caes. **B.** Esp. *to plot, conspire;* conjurasse supra septem millia virorum ac mulierum, Liv.; with cum and the abl., or with inter se; ii, quibuscum conjurasti, Cic.; principes inter se conjurant, Sall.; with adversus or contra and the acc., contra rempublicam, Cic.; adversus patriam, Liv.; with de and the abl., de interficiendo Pompeio, Cic.; with in and the acc., cum aliquo in omne flagitium et facinus, Liv.; with infin., patriam incendere, Sall.; with ut and subj., urbem ut incenderent, Liv.

conjux (conjunx) -jŭgis, c. (conjungo), 1, *spouse, wife*, Cic.; more rarely, *husband*, Cic.; pl. *a married pair*, Cat.; 2, poet. *a betrothed virgin, bride*, Verg.; *a concubine*, Prop.

conl . . . . = coll . . . . (q.v.).

conm . . . = comm . . . (q.v.).

connecto -nexŭi -nexum, 3. *to fasten, tie together, connect, unite.* **A.** Lit. illae (apes) pedibus connexae ad limina pendent, Verg. **B.** Transf., 1, of space, Mosellam atque Ararim factā inter utrumque fossā, Tac.; 2, of time, persequere connexos his funeribus dies, *close-following*, Cic.; 3, *to unite;* amicitia cum voluptate connectitur, Cic.; esp. a, *to unite in discourse;* facilius est enim apta idonésve quam dissipata connectere, Cic.; b, of logical connexion, omne quod ipsum ex se connexum sit verum esse, Cic.; c, *of relationship;* alicui connexus per affinitatem, Tac.; partic. perf. subst., **connexum** -i, n. *logical conclusion*.

1. **connexus** -ūs, m. (connecto), *connexion, union*, Cic.

2. **connexus** -a -um, partic. of connecto.

connĭtor -nīsus or -nixus sum, 3. dep. **A.** Lit., 1, *to learn* or *push against with violence;* valido connixus corpore taurus, Cic. poet.; 2,

---

to climb up; in summum jugum, Caes.; **3,** *to bring forth;* gemellos, Verg. **B.** Transf., *to strive with all one's might;* with abl., quantum animo conniti potes, Cic.; with in and the acc., in unum locum connixi, Liv.; with ad and the acc., ad convincendum eum, Tac.; with infin., invadere hostem, Liv.; with ut and the subj., infantes connituntur, sese ut erigant, Cic.

connīvĕo -nīvi or -nixi, 2. *to close the eyes, to wink, blink with the eyes.* **A.** Lit., oculis somno conniventibus, Cic.; altero oculo, Cic.; poet., of the sun or moon, quasi connivent, Lucr. **B.** Transf., *to wink at, let pass unnoticed;* consulibus si non adjuvantibus, at conniventibus certe, Cic.; with in and the abl., quibusdam etiam in rebus conniveo, Cic.

connūbĭālis -e (connubium), *relating to marriage, connubial*, Ov.

connūbĭum -ii, n. (com and nubo), **1, a,** *a legal Roman marriage;* sequuntur connubia et affinitates, Cic.; poet., *marriage* in general, Pyrrhi connubia servare, Verg.; **b,** *intercourse*, Ov.; **2,** *the right of intermarriage;* connubium finitimis negare, Liv. (in poets often trisyll., connubjo, Verg., Aen. i. 73, vii. 96).

Cŏnōn -ōnis, m. (Κόνων), **1,** *an Athenian general;* **2,** *a mathematician and astronomer of Samos.*

cōnōpēum -i, n. (κωνωπεῖον) or **cōnōpĭum** -ii, n. *a net to keep off gnats or mosquitoes*, Hor.

cōnor, 1. dep. *to undertake, endeavour, attempt, exert oneself, strive;* with acc., opus magnum, Cic.; with infin., facere id quod constituerant, Caes.; ii qui haec delere conati sunt, Cic.

conp . . . = comp . . . (q.v.).

conquassātĭo -ōnis, f. (conquasso), *a violent shaking, shattering;* totius valetudinis corporis, Cic.

conquasso, 1. *to shake thoroughly, shatter;* quum Apulia maximis terrae motibus conquassata esset, Cic.; transf., conquassatas exteras nationes illius anni furore, Cic.

conquĕror -questus, 3. dep. *to bewail* or *complain loudly;* fortunas suas, Plaut.; bonorum direptiones, Cic.; de istius improbitate, Cic.

conquestĭo -ōnis, f. (conqueror), *a loud complaint, bewailing;* ubi nullum auxilium est, nulla conquestio, Cic.; in rhet., conquestio est oratio auditorum misericordiam captans, Cic.

conquestus, abl. -ū, m. (conqueror), *a loud complaint*, Liv.

conquĭesco -quiēvi -quiētum, 3. *to rest thoroughly, take rest, repose.* **A.** *to rest bodily;* videmus ut conquiescere ne infantes quidem possint, Cic.; haec (impedimenta) conquiescere vetuit, *to rest from a march*, Caes.; conquiescere, meridie, *to sleep*, Caes. **B.** *to be still, quiet, to take repose, stop;* **a,** imbre conquiescente, Liv.; conquiescit mercatorum navigatio, *is stopped*, Cic.; conquiescere a continuis bellis et victoriis, Cic.; **b,** *to find rest* or *recreation in;* in nostris studiis libentissime conquiescimus, Cic.

conquīro -quīsīvi -quīsītum, 3. (com and quaero), *to seek for, to bring together, to collect, get together.* **A.** Lit., sagittarios, Caes.; colonos Cic.; pecuniam, Cic.; aliquem totā provinciā, Cic. **B.** Transf., voluptatem conquirere et comparare, Cic.; solebat mecum interdum eiusmodi aliquid conquirere, Cic. (contr. fut. perf. form, conquisierit, Cic.).

conquīsītĭo -ōnis, f. (conquaero), 1, *search, collection;* pecuniarum, Tac.; talium librorum, Liv.; 2, *a pressing* or *forcible enlistment of soldiers, conscription;* exercitus durissimā conquisitione confectus, Cic.

conquīsītor -ōris, m. (conquiro), *a recruiting officer,* Cic.

conquīsītus -a -um, p. adj. with superl. (conquiro), *sought after, selected, chosen, costly, precious;* mensas conquisitissimis epulis extruere, Cic.

conr . . . = corr . . . (q.v.).

consaepĭo -saepsi, -saeptum, 4. *to fence round, to hedge in,* Suet.; gen., partic., **consaeptus** -a -um, *fenced round;* ager, Cic.; subst., **consaeptum** -i, n. *an inclosure,* Liv.

consălūtātĭo -ōnis, f. (consaluto), *a salutation of several persons;* forensis, Cic.

consălūto, 1. *to greet together, hail, salute;* inter se amicissime, Cic.; with double acc., aliquem dictatorem, Liv.; eam Volumniam, Cic.

consānesco -sānŭi, 3. *to become healthy, to get well;* illa quae consanuisse videbantur, Cic.

consanguĭnĕus -a -um, *related by blood, brotherly, sisterly;* umbrae, Ov. Subst., **consanguĭnĕus** -i, m. *brother,* Cic.; **consanguĭnĕa** -ae, f. *sister,* Cat.; plur., **consanguĭnĕi** -orum, m. *relations;* Aedui Ambarri necessarii et consanguinei Aeduorum, Caes.; transf., consanguineus Leti Sopor, Verg.

consanguĭnĭtas -ātis, f. (consanguineus), *relationship by blood, consanguinity,* Liv.

consaucĭo, 1. *to wound severely,* Suet.

conscĕlērātus -a -um, p. adj. with superl. (conscelero), *wicked, villainous, depraved;* consceleratissimi filii, Cic.; transf. of things, mens, Cic.

conscĕlěro, 1. *to defile with crime;* miseram domum, Cat.; oculos videndo, Ov.; aures paternas, Liv.

conscendo -scendi -scensum, 3. (com and scando). **A.** *to ascend, mount, go up;* with acc., equum, *to mount on horseback,* Liv.; vallum, Caes.; aequor navibus, Verg.; with in and the acc., in equos, Ov. **B.** Naut. t. t., *to go on board ship, embark;* with in and the acc., in navem, Caes.; with acc., navem, Caes.; absol., *to embark;* conscendere a Brundisio Cic.

conscensĭo -ōnis, f. (conscendo), *an embarking, embarkation;* in naves, Cic.

conscĭentĭa -ae, f. (conscio). **I. A.** *a joint knowledge with some other person, being privy to;* horum omnium, Cic.; conjurationis, Tac.; eiusmodi facinorum, Cic.; absol. conscientiae contagio, Cic.; aliquem in conscientiam assumere, Tac. **II.** *knowledge in oneself.* **A.** Gen., virium nostrarum ac suarum, Liv.; absol., nostra stabilis conscientia, Cic. **B.** *Consciousness of right or wrong;* **a,** conscientia bene actae vitae, Cic.; scelerum et fraudum suarum, Cic.; ex nullā conscientiā de culpā, Sall.; **b,** *conscience;* animi conscientiā excruciari, Cic.; praeclarā conscientiā, Cic.; absol., (*a*) *a good conscience;* mea mihi conscientia pluris est quam omnium sermo, Cic.; (β), *a bad conscience;* angor conscientiae, Cic.; conscientiā ictus, Liv.

conscindo -scĭdi -scissum, 3. *to tear or rend in pieces.* **I.** Lit., epistolam, Cic. **II.** Transf., conscissi sibilis, *hissed at,* Cic.

conscĭo, 4. *to be conscious of guilt;* nil conscire sibi, Hor.

conscisco -scīvi and -scĭi -scītum, 3. 1, *to agree on, resolve publicly, decree,* Cic.; bellum, Liv.; 2, *to bring or inflict upon oneself, inflict upon;* sibi mortem, or simply mortem, necem, *to kill oneself,* Cic.; sibi exsilium, Liv. (syncop. perfect forms conscisse, Liv.; conscisset, Cic.).

conscĭus -a -um (com and scio), 1, *having joint or common knowledge with another, privy to, cognisant of;* with genit., homo meorum in

te studiorum et officiorum maxime conscius, Cic.; conjurationis, *conspirator,* Sall.; poet., conscia fati sidera, Verg.; alicui conscium esse facinoris, Tac.; with dat., conscius facinori, Cic.; with in and the abl., conscius in privatis rebus, Cic.; with de and the abl., his de rebus conscium esse Pisonem, Cic.; absol., sine ullo conscio, Cic.; 2, *conscious to oneself;* a, with genit., si alicuius injuriae sibi conscius fuisset, Cic.; with acc. and infin., etsi mihi sum conscius me nimis cupidum fuisse vitae, Cic.; absol., conscii sibi, Sall.; poet., virtus conscia, Verg.; b, esp., *conscious of guilt;* animus, Sall.

conscrībillo, 1. (dim. of conscribo), *to scribble or scrawl all over,* Varr.; transf., nates, *to mark with bloody weals,* Cat.

conscrībo -scripsi -scriptum, 3. *to write together.* **I. A.** 1, milit. t. t., *to enrol, levy;* exercitus, Cic.; legiones, Caes.; 2, politic. t. t., a, *to enrol in a particular class;* centuriae tres equitum conscriptae sunt, Liv.; Collinam (tribum) novam delectu perditissimorum civium conscribebat, Cic.; b, *to enrol as a senator;* hence the phrase, patres conscripti (for patres et conscripti), *senators,* Cic.; sing., *a senator,* Hor.; c, *to enrol as colonists,* Liv. **B.** 1, *to put together in writing, write, compose;* librum de consulatu, Cic.; epistolam, legem, Cic.; absol., *to write a letter;* de Antonio quoque Balbus ad me cum Oppio conscripsit, Cic.; 2, esp. of physicians, *to prescribe;* pro salutaribus mortifera, Cic. **II.** *to write all over;* mensam vino, Ov.

conscriptĭo -ōnis, f. (conscribo), *a writing, composition, written paper;* falsae conscriptiones quaestionum, *forged minutes,* Cic.

conscriptus -a -um, partic. of conscribo.

consĕco -sĕcŭi -sectum, 1. *to cut in small pieces, dismember;* membra fratris, Ov.

consĕcrātĭo -ōnis, f. (consecro), 1, a, *a consecration;* aedium, Cic.; b, *a dedication to the infernal gods, execration, curse;* capitis, Cic.; 2, *deification of the emperors, apotheosis,* Tac.

consĕcro, (con-sacro), 1. **I. A.** *to consecrate, to dedicate to the service of a god;* totam Siciliam Cereri, Cic.; diem adventus alicuius, *make a feast-day,* Liv. **B.** *to consecrate to the gods below, to curse;* quum caput eius, qui contra fecerit, consecratur, Cic. **II. A.** *to deify, elevate to divine honours;* Liber quem nostri majores consecraverunt, Cic.; of the emperors, consecrare Claudium, Suet. **B.** Transf., *to make holy;* vetera jam ista et religione omnium consecrata, Cic. **C.** *to make immortal;* amplissimis monumentis memoriam nominis sui, Cic.

consectārĭus -a -um (consector), *following logically, consequent,* Cic. Subst., **consectārĭa** -orum, n. *logical conclusions, inferences,* Cic.

consectātĭo -ōnis, f. (consector), *the eager pursuit of anything, desire, effort, striving after;* concinnitatis, Cic.

consectātrix -īcis, f. (consectator), *an eager pursuer, devoted friend;* consectatrices voluptatis libidines, Cic.

consectĭo -ōnis, f. (conseco), *a cutting up, cleaving to pieces;* arborum, Cic.

consector, 1. dep. (freq. of consequor). **I.** **A.** Lit., *to follow, pursue eagerly,* Ter.; tardi in genii est rivulos consectari, fontes rerum non videre, Cic. **B.** Transf., *to pursue zealously, strive after, try to imitate or gain;* opes aut potentiam, Cic.; ubertatem orationis, Cic.; virtus de industriā, Cic. **II.** *to follow hostilely, pursue;* redeuntes equites, Caes.; aliquem et conviciis et sibilis, Cic.

consĕcūtĭo -ōnis, f. (consequor), 1, philosoph. t. t., *that which follows, an effect, conse-*

quence; causas rerum et consecutiones videre, Cic.; **2**, rhet. t. t., *order, connexion, arrangement;* verborum, Cic.

consĕnesco -sĕnŭi, **3.** **I.** *to become old, grow grey;* hac casā, Ov. **II.** In a bad sense, *to become old, to lose one's strength, to decay.* **A.** Lit., **1**, of persons, insontem, indemnatum in exsilio consenescere, Liv.; consenescere in Siciliā sub armis, Liv.; **2**, of bodily strength, *to decay;* consenescunt vires atque deficiunt, Cic. **B.** Transf., **1**, invidia habet repentinos impetus, interposito spatio et cognitā causā consenescit, Cic.; **2**, in politics, *to lose power;* omnes illius partis auctores ac socios nullo adversario consenescere, Cic.

consensĭo -ōnis, f. (consentio). **A.** Gen., *agreement, harmony, consent;* **a**, of persons, omnium gentium, Cic.; nulla de illis magistratuum consensio, Cic.; **b**, of things, *harmony;* naturae, Cic. **B.** In a bad sense, *a plot, conspiracy;* consensio scelerata, Cic.

consensus -ūs, m. (consentio). **I.** *agreement, unanimity, concord, agreement;* **a**, of persons, omnium, Cic.; optimus in rempublicam consensus, Cic.; abl., consensu, *unanimously, by general consent;* resistere, Liv.; **b**, of things, mirus quidam omnium quasi consensus doctrinarum concentusque, Cic. **II.** *a secret agreement, conspiracy;* consensus audacium, Cic.

consentānĕus -a -um (consentio), *agreeing to, agreeable with, consonant with, fit, suitable;* cum iis litteris, Cic.; gen. with dat., Stoicorum rationi, Cic.; impers., consentaneum est, with infin. or acc. and infin., *it agrees, is reasonable, suitable,* Cic.

Consentes Dii, *the advisers, the twelve superior deities of the Romans*—viz., *Jupiter, Juno, Vesta, Ceres, Diana, Minerva, Venus, Mars, Mercurius, Neptunus, Vulcanus, Apollo,* Varr.

Consentĭa -ae, f. *a town in Bruttii,* now *Consenza.* Adj., **Consentīnus** -a -um.

consentĭo -sensi -sensum, **4.** *to agree.* **I.** Lit., of persons. **A.** Gen., *to agree, to assent, to resolve unanimously;* absol., animi consentientes, Cic.; with dat. or cum and the abl., consentire superioribus judiciis, Cic.; cum populi Romani voluntatibus consentiant, Cic.; with de or in and the abl., Cic.; ad with the acc., Cic.; adversus with the acc., Liv.; cum aliquo de aliquā re, Cic.; with acc., Cic.; bellum, *to resolve upon war,* Liv.; with acc. and infin. or infin. alone, Cic. **B.** *to plot, conspire, form an unlawful union;* ad prodendam Hannibali urbem, Liv.; belli faciendi causa, Cic. **II.** Transf., of inanimate objects, *to agree, harmonise;* ratio nostra consentit, Cic.; pres. partic., **consentiens** -entis, *harmonious;* consentiens populi Romani universi voluntas, Cic.

consēpĭo = consaepio (q.v.).

consĕquens -quentis, p. adj. (consequor), **a**, grammat. t. t., *appropriate, of the right construction;* in conjunctis (verbis) quod non est consequens vituperandum est, Cic.; **b**, philosoph. t. t., *following logically, consequent;* consequens est, *it follows as a logical consequence,* Cic. Subst., **consĕquens** -quentis, n. *a logical consequence,* Cic.

consĕquentĭa -ae, f. (consequor), *a consequence, succession;* eventorum, Cic.

consĕquĭa -ae, f. = consequentia (q.v.).

consĕquor -sĕquŭtus (-sĕcūtus), **3.** dep. *to follow, go after.* **I.** Gen., **A.** Lit., **1**, aliquem vestigiis, *on foot,* Cic.; **2**, *to pursue;* consequi statim Hasdrubalem, Liv. **B.** Transf., **1**, *to follow in point of time;* mors, quae brevi consecuta est, Cic.; **2**, *quia libertatem pax consequebatur.* Cic.; **2**, **a**, *to follow as an effect or con-*

sequence, result from; quam eorum opinionem magni errores consecuti sunt, Cic.; **b**, *to follow as a logical consequence;* fit etiam quod consequitur necessarium, Cic.; **3**, *to follow a particular object or example;* consequi suum quoddam institutum, Cic. **II.** *to come up to by following, attain to, reach, obtain.* **A.** Lit., **1**, si statim navigas, nos Leucade consequere, Cic.; **2**, *to come up with in pursuit, overtake;* reliquos omnes equitatu, Caes. **B.** Transf., **1**, *to attain to, obtain, get;* cuius rei tantae tamque difficilis facultatem *consecutum esse* me non profiteor; *secutum esse* prae me fero, Cic.; opes quam maximas, Cic.; amplissimos honores, Cic.; fructum amplissimum ex reipublicae causa, Cic.; omnia per senatum, Cic.; fortitudinis gloriam insidiis et malitia, Cic.; foll. by ut or ne with the subj., Cic.; **2**, of objects, events, *to befall, happen to;* tanta prosperitas Caesarem est consecuta, Cic.; **3**, *to come up to in any respect, to equal;* **a**, verborum prope numerum sententiarum numero, Cic.; **b**, esp., *to express adequately in words;* alicuius laudes verbis, Cic.; **4**, *to come up to in speech or thought, to understand, grasp;* similitudinem veri, Cic.

1. consĕro -sēvi -sĭtum, **3.** **1**, *to sow, plant;* **a**, lit., agros, Cic.; **b**, transf., lumine arva (of the sun), Lucr.; **2**, *to plant, place in;* arborem, Liv.

2. consĕro -sĕrŭi -sertum, **3.** **I.** Gen., *to connect, tie, join, twine together;* lorica conserta hamis Verg.; exodia conserere fabellis potissimum Atellanis, Liv. **II.** *to join in a hostile manner.* **A.** Milit. t. t., manum or manus conserere, *to engage,* Cic.; cum aliquo, Cic.; inter se, Sall.; conserere pugnam, Liv.; proelium, Liv.; navis conseritur, *the ship is engaged,* Liv.; absol., conserere cum levi armatura, Liv. **B.** Legal. t. t., aliquem ex jure manum consertum vocare, *to commence an action concerning property by laying hands on it,* ap. Cic.

consertē, adv. (consertus from 2. consero), *connectedly,* Cic.

conserva -ae, f. *a fellow-servant,* Plaut.; transf., conservae fores, *in the same service,* Ov.

conservans -antis, p. adj. (conservo), *preserving;* with genit., ea quae conservantia sunt eius status, Cic.

conservātĭo -ōnis, f. (conservo), *a preservation, keeping, laying up;* **a**, frugum, Cic.; **b**, *observing, observance;* aequabilitatis, Cic.

conservātor -ōris, m. (conservo), *a preserver;* inimicorum, Cic.; reipublicae, Cic.

conservātrix -īcis, f. (conservo), *she who preserves;* natura, Cic. (?)

conservo, 1. *to keep, preserve, maintain;* **a**, of concrete objects, cives suos, Cic.; omnes salvos, Cic.; rempublicam, Cic.; rem familiarem, Cic.; **b**, of abstract objects, *to preserve, maintain, observe;* pristinum animum, Liv.; jusjurandum, *to keep,* Cic.

conservus -i, m. *a fellow slave, servant,* Cic.

consessor -ōris, m. (consido), *one who sits near or with,* in a court of justice, *an assessor,* Cic.; *a neighbour* at a feast or spectacle, Cic.

consessus -ūs, m. (consido), *an assembly* (of persons sitting together); in ludo talario, Cic.; praeconum, Cic.; ludorum gladiatorumque, Cic.; plur., consessus theatrales gladiatoriique, Cic.

considĕrātē, adv., with compar. and superl. (consideratus), *thoughtfully, carefully;* agere, Cic.

considĕrātĭo -ōnis, f. (considero), *consideration, contemplation, thought, reflection;* considerationem intendere in aliquid, Cic.

considĕrātus -a -um, p. adj. with compar.

and superl. (considero), a, pass., *thoroughly considered, well weighed, deliberate;* verbum, Cic.; considerata atque provisa via vivendi, Cic.; b, act., of persons, *cautious, wary, circumspect;* homo, Cic.

consĭdĕro, 1. (com and root SID, connected with ΕΙΔΩ, ΙΔΩ, VID-eo). **A.** Lit., *to look at, regard carefully, contemplate;* considerare opus pictoris, Cic. **B.** Transf., *to consider, weigh, reflect upon;* with secum, cum animo suo, secum in animo; considerare secum eos casus, in quibus, etc., Cic.; with rel. sent., consideres quid agas, Cic.; with de and the abl., nunc de praemiis consideremus, Cic.; absol., ille (ait) se considerare velle, Cic.

consĭdo -sēdi -sessum, 3. neut. **I.** Lit., *to sit down.* **A.** Of persons, hic in umbrā, Cic.; in molli herbā, Cic.; esp., **1,** *to sit down in a public assembly* or *court of justice;* ut primum judices consederant, Cic.; ad jus dicendum, Liv.; **2,** milit. t. t., a, *to take up one's position;* triarii sub vexillis considebant sinistro crure porrecto, Liv.; in insidiis, Liv.; b, more commonly, *to stop, encamp;* considere non longius mille passibus a nostris munitionibus, Caes.; **3,** *to stay,* and of passengers on board ship, *to land;* hic an Antii, Cic.; Tarquiniis, Liv. **B.** Of things, *to fall to the ground, settle, sink, subside;* quae (Alpes) jam licet considant, Cic.; Ilion ardebat neque adhuc consederat ignis, Ov. **II.** Transf. **A.** Of persons, considere in otio, *to rest,* Cic.; totam videmus consedisse urbem luctu, *sunk in grief,* Verg. **B.** Of things, **1,** *to stop, cease;* ardor animi consedit, Cic.; **2,** *to fall into neglect;* consedit utriusque nomen in quaestura, Cic.

consigno, 1. **1,** *to seal, to affix a seal as an authentication;* tabulas signis, Cic.; **2,** *to vouch for, authenticate;* aliquid litteris, Cic.; transf., antiquitas clarissimis monumentis testata consignataque, Cic.

consĭlĭārĭus -a -um (consilium), *relating to counsel, deliberating;* senatus, Plaut. Subst., **consĭlĭārĭus -ii,** m. *an adviser, an assessor, assistant judge;* consiliario et auctore Vestorio, Cic.; dari alicui consiliarium atque administrum, Cic.; consiliarii regis, Cic.

consĭlĭor, 1. dep. (consilium), *to hold a consultation, consult, take counsel;* difficilis ad consiliandum legatio, Cic.

consĭlĭum -ii, n. (connected with consulo). **I.** Act., **A. 1,** lit., *a deliberation, consultation, taking counsel;* consilium principum habere, *to hold a consultation with the chiefs,* Liv.; quasi consilii sit res, *as if the matter allowed of consideration,* Caes.; consiliis interesse, Cic.; esp. *the deliberation of a public body;* consilii publici participem fieri, Cic.; consilium habere, Cic.; adesse alicui in consilio, Cic.; **2,** meton., *the assembly of persons giving advice, council;* esp., a, *the senate;* senatus, id est, orbis terrae consilium, Cic.; b, *the body of judges;* ex senatu in hoc consilium delecti estis, Cic.; c, *a council of war;* consilium convocare, Caes.; rem ad consilium deferre, Caes. **B.** *understanding, foresight, prudence;* vir maximi consilii, Caes.; mulier imbecilli consilii, Cic. **II.** Pass., *the advice* or *counsel given; a resolution, plan, conclusion;* **1,** a, capere consilium, *to form a resolution,* Cic.; belli renovandi, Caes.; subito consilium cepi, ut antequam luceret exirem, Cic.; consilium consistit, *holds good,* Cic.; est consilium, foll. by infin., Cic.; quid sui consilii sit proponit, *he explains what his plan is,* Caes.; inire consilium senatus interficiendi, Cic.; abl., consilio, *intentionally, designedly,* Cic.; privato consilio, privatis consiliis (opp. **publico** consilio,

publicis consiliis), *in the interests of private persons,* Cic.; b, milit. t. t., *stratagem, device;* consilium imperatorium, Cic.; **2,** *advice, suggestion;* alicui consilium dare, Cic.; egere consilii or consilio, Cic.

consĭmĭlis -e, *like in all parts, exactly similar;* with genit., causa consimilis earum causarum quae, etc., Cic.; with dat., consimilis fugae profectio, Caes.; absol., laus, Cic.

consĭpĭo, 3. (com and sapio), *to be in one's senses, to have possession of one's faculties,* Liv.

consisto -stĭti, 3. *to put oneself in any place.* **I.** Gen., *to take one's stand, place oneself.* **A.** Lit., **1,** of persons, consistere ad mensam, Cic.; hi proximi constitere, Liv.; esp. a, as a listener, tota in illa contione Italia constitit, Cic.; b, milit. t. t., *to place oneself for battle, take one's place;* ne saucio quidem eius loci, ubi constiterat, relinquendi facultas dabatur, Cic.; **2,** of dice, *to fall;* quadringentis talis centum Venerios non posse casu consistere, Cic. **B.** Transf., *to agree with;* videsne igitur Zenonem tuum cum Aristone verbis consistere, re dissidere, Cic. **II.** Esp. *to stand still.* **A.** *to stop, halt;* **1,** lit., a, of persons, consistite! Ov.; consistere et commorari cogit, Cic.; esp., (a) *to stop for conversation;* viatores etiam invitos consistere cogunt, Caes.; (β) *to stop in wonder, curiosity,* etc.; bestiae saepe immanes cantu flectuntur et consistunt, Cic.; (γ) milit. t. t., *to halt;* prope hostem, Caes.; (δ) of travellers, fugitives, etc., *to halt, stop, stay;* consistere unum diem Veliae, Cic.; b, of things, vel concĭdat omne caelum omnisque natura consistat necesse est, Cic.; esp. of water, *to stop still;* ter frigore constitit Ister, *froze,* Ov.; **2,** transf., a, *to stop, dwell in speech;* in uno nomine, Cic.; b, *to rest, cease;* quum ad Trebiam terrestre constitisset bellum, Liv.; c, *to rest, fall upon;* in quo (viro) non modo culpa nulla, sed ne suspicio quidem potuit consistere, Cic.; d, *to consist, to be formed of;* major pars victus eorum in lacte, caseo, carne consistit, Caes. **B. 1,** *to stand firmly, keep one's ground, footing;* in fluctibus, Caes.; vertice celso aeriae quercus constiterunt, *were firmly rooted,* Verg.; **2,** transf. a, *to keep one's ground, to hold one's own;* in forensibus causis praeclare, Cic.; b, *to be firm;* neque mens, neque vox neque lingua consistit, Cic.

consĭtĭo -ōnis, f. (consero), *a sowing, planting;* plur., *different kinds of sowing* or *planting,* Cic.

consĭtor -ōris, m. (consero), *a sower, planter;* uvae, *Bacchus,* Ov.

consĭtūra -ae, f. (consero), *a sowing, planting;* agri, Cic.

consōbrīnus -i, m. and **consōbrīna -ae,** f. *cousin on the mother's side,* Cic.; *cousin,* Cic.; and in a more extended sense, *second, third cousin,* Suet.

consŏcer -cĕri, m. *a joint father-in-law,* Suet.

consŏcĭātĭo -ōnis, f. (consocio), *union, connexion, association;* hominum, Cic.

consŏcĭātus -a -um, p. adj. (from consocio), *united, harmonious;* consociatissima voluntas, Cic.

consŏcĭo, 1. *to unite, connect, share, associate, make common;* consilia cum aliquo, Cic.; injuriam cum amicis, Cic.; animos eorum, Liv.; nunquam tam vehementer cum senatu consociati fuistis, Cic.

consōlābĭlis -e (consolor), *consolable;* dolor, Cic.

consōlātĭo -ōnis, f. (consolor), *consolation, encouragement, comfort, alleviation;* **1,** communium malorum, Cic.; timoris, Cic.; adhibere aliquam modicam consolationem, Cic.; adhibere alicui consolationem, Cic.; num me una consolatio sustentat quod, etc., Cic.; uti hac consolatione alicuius (foll. by acc. and infin.), Cic.; **2**, *a consolatory treatise* or *discourse*, Cic.

consōlātor -ōris, m. (consolor), *a consoler*, Cic.

consōlātŏrĭus -a -um (consolator), *relating to consolation, consolatory*; litterae, Cic.

consōlor, 1. dep. **1**, of persons, *to console, comfort, to encourage*; se illo solatio quod, etc., Cic.; se his (foll. by acc. and infin.), Cic.; aliquem de communibus miseriis, Cic.; spes sola homines in miseriis consolari solet, Cic.; absol., consolando levare dolorem, Cic.; Caesar consolatus rogat (eum) finem orandi faciat, Caes.; **2**, of things, *to alleviate, lighten, solace*; dolorem, Cic.

consŏno -sŏnŭi, 1. **1**, *to sound together, sound loudly*; **a**, consonante clamore nominatim Quinctium orare ut, etc., Liv.; **b**, *to echo*; plausu fremituque virum consonat omne nemus, Verg.; **2**, transf., *to harmonise, agree, be consonant with*, Quint.

consŏnus -a -um. **A**. Lit., *sounding together, harmonious*; fila lyrae, Ov. **B**. Transf., *accordant, fit, suitable*; credo Platonem vix putasse satis consonum fore ut, etc., Cic.

consōpĭo, 4. *to lull to sleep, stupefy*; somno consopiri sempiterno, Cic.; Endymion a luna consopitus, Cic.

consors -sortis, **1**, *having an equal share with, sharing in, partaking of*; with genit., socius et consors gloriosi laboris, Cic.; mecum temporum illorum, Cic.; tribuniciae potestatis, Tac.; applied to inanimate objects, *common*; tecta, Verg.; **2**, *having an equal share in property*; tres fratres consortes, *tenants in common*, Cic.; poet., *brother* or *sister*; consors magni Jovis, Juno, Ov.; adj. = *brotherly, sisterly*; sanguis, Ov.

consortĭo -ōnis, f. (consors), *companionship, community, partnership*; humana, Cic.

consortĭum -ĭi, n. (consors), **1**, *community of goods*, Suet.; **2**, *fellowship, participation in*; si in consortio, si in societate reipublicae esse licet, Liv.

1. conspectus -a -um, p. adj. (from conspicio). **A**. Gen., *visible*; tumulus hosti conspectus, Liv. **B**. (with compar.) *striking, remarkable, distinguished*; conspectus elatusque supra modum hominis, Liv.; conspecta mors eius fuit, quia publico funere est elatus, Liv.; turba conspectior, Liv.

2. conspectus -ūs, m. (conspicio), *look, sight, view*. **I**. Act., **A**. Lit., dare se alicui in conspectum, *to allow oneself to be seen by*, Cic.; in conspectu alicuius esse, *to be within sight of*, Cic.; e conspectu abire, Caes.; adimere conspectum oculorum, Liv.; cadere in conspectum, Cic.; conspectus est in Capitolium, *the view is towards the Capitol*, Liv.; conspectum alicuius fugere, Caes.; privare aliquem omnium suorum consuetudine conspectuque, Cic.; of things, in conspectu alicuius loci, *in sight of*, Cic. **B**. Transf., *mental view, survey*; in hoc conspectu et cognitione naturae, Cic. **II**. Pass., *appearance*, Liv. **A**. Lit., conspectu suo proelium restituit, Liv. **B**. Meton., tuus jucundissimus conspectus, Cic.

conspergo (con-spargo), -spersi -spersum, 3. *to sprinkle, moisten by sprinkling*; me lacrimis, Cic.; transf., ut oratio conspersa sit quasi verborum sententiarumque floribus, *interspersed with*, Cic.

conspĭcĭendus -a -um, p. adj. (from conspicio), *worthy of being seen, noteworthy*; opus, Liv.; templum, Ov.

conspĭcĭo -spexi -spectum, **3**. (com and specio), **1**, *to look at, view, behold, to descry, perceive*; conspicere nostros equites, Caes.; infestis oculis omnium conspici, Cic.; milites in summo colle, Caes.; procul Ambiorigem suos cohortantem, Caes.; with acc. and infin., calones qui nostros victores flumen transisse conspexerant, Caes.; **2**, *to look at with attention*; Demetrium ut pacis auctorem cum ingenti favore conspiciebant, Liv.; locum insidiis, *for an ambush*, Verg.; in pass., conspici, *to attract notice, to be gazed at, to be distinguished*; vehi per urbem, conspici velle, Cic.

conspĭcor, 1. dep. (conspicio), *to catch sight of, perceive*; agmen Aeduorum, Caes.; ex oppido caedem et fugam suorum, Caes.

conspĭcŭus -a -um (conspicio), *visible*. **A**. Gen., conspicuus polus, Ov. **B**. *remarkable, striking, conspicuous*; conspicuus late vertex, Hor.; Romanis conspicuum eum novitas divitiaeque faciebant, Liv.

conspīrātĭo -ōnis, f. (conspiro), **1**, *unison, harmony, agreement, union*; omnium bonorum, Cic.; magnā amoris conspiratione consentientes amicorum greges, Cic.; **2**, in a bad sense, *conspiracy, plot*; conspiratio certorum hominum contra dignitatem tuam, Cic.

conspīrātus -a -um (partic. of conspiro), *sworn together, united by an oath*, Phaedr. Subst., **conspīrātī** -orum, m. *conspirators*, Suet.

conspīro, 1. (com and spiro), *to breathe together*. **I**. **A**. *to blow together, sound together*; aereaque assensu conspirant cornua rauco, Verg. **B**. *to agree, harmonise in opinion and feeling, to unite*; conspirate nobiscum, consentite cum bonis, Cic.; milites legionis nonae subito conspirati (*with one accord*) pila conjecerunt, Cic. **II**. In a bad sense, *to conspire, to form a plot*; priusquam plures civitates conspirarent, Caes.

consponsor -ōris, m. *a joint surety*, Cic.

conspŭo -spŭi -spūtum, 3. *to spit upon*, Plaut., Juv.

conspurco, 1. *to cover with dirt, defile*, Lucr.

conspūto, 1. (inchoat. of conspuo), *to spit upon contemptuously*; nostros, Cic.

constans -antis, p. adj. with compar. and superl. (consto), **a**, *steady, firm, unchanging, immovable, constant*; quae cursus constantes habent, Cic.; pax, Liv.; fides, Hor.; constans jam aetas, quae media dicitur, Cic.; **b**, of character, *firm, resolute, unchanging, constant*; sunt igitur firmi et stabiles et constantes (amici) eligendi, Cic.; **c**, *consistent, harmonious*; oratio, Cic.; **d**, *uniform, unanimous*; constanti famā atque omnium sermone celebrari, Cic.

constantĕr, adv. with compar. and superl. (constans), **a**, *firmly, consistently, constantly*; constanter in suo manere statu, Cic.; constanter et non trepide pugnare, Caes.; constanter et sedate ferre dolorem, Cic.; **b**, *uniformly, harmoniously*; constanter omnes nuntiaverunt manus cogi, Caes.; constanter sibi dicere, Cic.

constantĭa -ae, f. (constans), **a**, *unchangeableness*; dictorum conventorumque constantia, Cic.; **b**, *perseverance, firmness*; pertinacia aut constantia intercessoris, Cic.; **c**, *agreement, harmony*; testimoniorum, Cic.

consternātĭo -ōnis, f. (consterno), **1**, *fear, dismay, consternation, confusion*; pavor et consternatio quadrigarum, Liv.; pavor et consternatio mentis, Tac.; **2**, *a mutiny, tumult*; vulgi, Tac.; muliebris consternatio, Liv.

1. consterno -strāvi -strātum, 3. **A**. *to strew, scatter, cover by strewing*; tabernacula caespitibus, Caes.; omnia cadaveribus, Sall.; constrata navis, *a decked boat*, Caes.; subst., **constrāta**

-orum, **n.**, pontis, *the flooring* or *gangway over a bridge of boats*, Liv. **B.** *to throw down;* tempestas aliquot signa constravit, Liv.

2. consterno, 1. (intens. of 1. consterno), 1, *to cause confusion, consternation, fear, to frighten;* procella ita consternavit equos, Liv.; esp. in pass., equi consternati, *startled*, Liv.; pavida et consternata multitudo, Liv.; also, *to drive to flight by fear;* in fugam consternari, Liv.; **2**, *to excite to sedition* or *revolt;* metu servitutis ad arma consternati, Liv.

constĭpo, 1. *to press, crowd together;* tantum numerum hominum in agrum Campanum, Cic.

constĭtŭo --stĭtŭi -stĭtūtum, 3. (com and statuo). **I.** *to cause to stand, place, put;* hominem ante pedes Q. Manilii, Cic.; milit. t. t., **a**, *to draw up in line, place, station, arrange;* signa ante tribunal, *to set up the standards*, Liv.; legionem Caesar constituit, *drew up*, Caes.; naves in alto, Caes.; intra silvas aciem ordinesque, Caes.; **b**, *to halt;* signa haud procul porta, Liv.; agmen, Sall. **II.** *to put in a particular place;* **1**, *to station, post, settle;* **a**, praesidia in Tolosatibus circumque Narbonem, Caes.; plebem in agris publicis, Cic.; **b**, *to appoint to an office;* regem, Cic.; aliquem sibi quaestoris in loco, Cic.; with the acc., Commium regem ibi, Caes.; **2**, *to found, establish;* **a**, of buildings, towns, etc., turres, Caes.; oppidum, Caes.; nidos, Cic.; hiberna omnium legionum in Belgis, Caes.; **b**, of institutions, taxes, etc., vectigal, Cic.; of magistracies, quae (potestates, imperia, curationes) constituuntur ad populi fructum, Cic.; **c**, of an undertaking, auctionem, Cic.; actionem, *to begin an action*, Cic.; crimen in aliquo, Cic.; quaestionem, Cic.; **d**, of relations, *to establish;* concordiam, Cic.; exemplum justitiae in hostem, Cic.; **e**, of persons, tres legiones, *to form*, Caes.; **3**, *to arrange, appoint, dispose, establish firmly;* **a**, of the body, is cui corpus bene constitutum sit, Cic.; **b**, of the character, animus bene constitutus, Cic.; **c**, of condition, situations, etc., rem familiarem, Cic.; **d**, of the state, bene constituta civitas, Cic.; **4**, *to fix, settle upon;* **a**, (a) tempus, diem, Cic., Caes.; mercedem funeris, Cic.; pretium frumento, Cic.; diem cum aliquo, Caes.; with rel. sent., armorum quantum quaeque civitas quodque ante tempus efficiat constituit, Caes; with acc. and infin., me hodie venturum esse, Cic.; with ut and the subj., ut L. Bestia quereretur de actionibus Ciceronis, Cic.; **b**, absol., ut erat constitutum, Cic.; (β) of persons, *to appoint, agree upon;* accusatorem, Cic.; **b**, (a) *to settle, determine;* nondum satis constitui molestiaene an plus voluptatis attulerit Trebatius noster; (β) *to determine at law, settle, decide;* controversiam, Cic.; de perspicuo jure, Cic.; **c**, *to come to a determination, to resolve;* haec ex re et ex tempore constitues, Cic.; with infin., bellum cum Germanis gerere, Caes.; with ut and the subj., ut pridie Idus Aquini manerem, Cic.

constĭtūtĭo -ōnis, f. (constituo), 1, *constitution, condition, disposition, nature;* firma constitutio corporis, Cic.; reipublicae, Cic.; illa praeclara constitutio Romuli, Cic.; **2**, *fixing, determining;* **a**, *the definition* or *settling of something;* ea constitutio summi boni quae est praeposita, Cic.; **b**, rhet. t. t., *the point in dispute*, Cic.; **c**, *a regulation, order, ordinance;* cogebatur alia aut ex decreto priorum legatorum aut ex novā constitutione senatus facere, Cic.

constĭtūtum -i, n. (constitutus, from constituo), 1, *a fixed place* or *time of meeting, rendezvous;* V. Calend. igitur ad constitutum, Cic.; constitutum factum esse cum servis, ut venirent, Cic.; **2**, *an agreement, appointment, compact;* ad constitutum experiendi gratiā venire, Cic.

5

constĭtūtus -a- um, partic. of constĭtŭo.

consto -stĭti -stātūrus, 1. *to stand still.* **I.** Lit., Plaut. **II.** Transf., **A.** Gen., 1, a, *to exist;* unde omnis rerum nunc constet summa creata, Lucr.: b, *to consist;* ex animo constamus et corpore, Cic.; c, *to depend upon, rest upon;* monuit eius divi victoriam in earum cohortium virtute constare, Caes.; **2**, *to cost;* ambulatiuncula prope dimidio minoris constabit isto loco, Cic. **B.** 1, *to stand firm, remain;* a, milit. t. t. *to hold one's ground, stand firm;* postquam nullo loco constabat acies, Liv.; b, of looks, speech, etc. *to remain the same, to be unaltered;* adeo perturbavit ea vox regem, ut non color, non vultus ei constaret, Liv.; **2**, *to be in good order;* postquam cuncta videt caelo constare sereno, Verg.; esp., ratio constat, *the account is correct*, Cic.; **3**, *to remain in the same state, continue;* nullum est genus rerum, quod avulsum a ceteris per se ipsum constare possit, Cic.; uti numerus legionum constare videretur, Caes.; **4**, *to remain in the same thought* or *opinion;* a, *to remain constant;* nec animum eius satis constare visum, Liv.; constare sibi or alicui rei, *to be true to;* reliqui sibi constiterunt, Cic.; constat humanitati suae, Cic.; of resolves, *to be fixed, firm;* animo constat sententia, Verg.; alicui constat, *a person is resolved;* mihi quidem constat nec meam contumeliam nec meorum ferre, ap. Cic.; b, of evidence, facts, etc., *to be certain, sure, well-known;* eorum quae constant exempla ponemus, horum quae dubia sunt exempla afferemus, Cic.; quod omnibus constabat hiemari in Gallia oportere, Caes.; mihi plane non satis constit, utrum sit melius, Cic.; quum de Magio constet, Cic.

constrātum -i, n., v. 1. consterno.

constringo -strinxi -strictum, 3. **A.** Lit., a, *to draw, bind together;* sarcinam, Plaut.; b, *to confine, fetter;* corpora vinculis, Cic. **B.** Transf., a, *to strengthen, fortify;* constringere fidem religione potius quam veritate, Cic.; b, *to confine, limit, fetter, restrain;* orbem terrarum novis legibus, Cic.; c, of discourse, *to compress, abbreviate;* sententiam aptis verbis, Cic.

constructĭo -ōnis, f. (construo), 1, *a putting together, building, construction, making;* hominis, Cic.; **2**, rhet. t. t. *the proper connexion of words;* verborum apta et quasi rotunda, Cic.

construo -struxi -structum, 3., 1, a, *to heap up together;* acervos nummorum, Cic.; divitias, Hor.; b, *to construct, build up;* mundum, navem, aedificium, Cic.; **2**, *to arrange;* dentes in ore constructi, Cic.

constŭprātor -ōris, m. *a ravisher, defiler*, Liv.

constŭpro, 1, *to ravish, violate;* matronas, Liv.; fig., emptum constupratumque judicium, *corrupt*, Cic.

consuādĕo -si -sum, 2. *to advise earnestly*, Plaut.

Consŭālĭa, v. Consus.

consuāsor -ōris, m. (consuadeo), *an adviser*, Cic.

consūdo, 1. *to sweat profusely*, Plaut.

consŭēfăcĭo -fēci -factum, 3. (* consueo and facio), *to accustom, habituate*, (Gaetulorum) multitudinem ordines habere, Sall.

consŭesco -suēvi -suētum, 3. **I.** Transit., *to accustom to;* brachia, Lucr. **II.** Intransit., a, *to accustom oneself*, and often in perf. consuevi, *I am accustomed;* with infin., qui mentiri solet, pejerare consuevit, Cic.; with inanimate things as subjects, naves quae praesidii causā Alexandriae esse consuerant, Caes.; ut consuesti, *as you are accustomed*, Cic.; b, *to be intimate with;* cum aliquo, cum aliquā, Cic. (perf. forms often contr. consuesti, consuestis, consuemus, consuerunt, consueram, consuerim, consuesse).

consuētūdo -ĭnis, f. (consuesco). **I.** *custom, usage, habit;* **1,** mos consuetudoque civilis, Cic.; with genit. of subst., or gerund, consuetudo populi Romani, Cic.; consuetudo sermonis nostri, Cic.; consuetudo peccandi, Cic.; consuetudo bona, Cic.; adducere aliquem or se in eam consuetudinem ut, etc., Caes.; ab omnium Siculorum consuetudine discedere, Cic.; non est meae consuetudinis rationem reddere, Cic.; ut est consuetudo, *as is the usual practice,* Cic.; mutare consuetudinem dicendi, Cic.; obdurescere alicuius rei consuetudine, Cic.; tenere consuetudinem suam, Cic.; in consuetudinem venire, *to become customary,* Cic.; ex consuetudine, Caes.; consuetudine, *according to custom,* Cic.; **2,** a, *manner of living;* ad superiorem consuetudinem reverti, Cic.; **b,** *manner of speaking;* consuetudo indocta, Cic. **II.** *social intercourse, intimacy;* insinuare in consuetudinem alicuius, Cic.; esp. of lovers, stupri vetus consuetudo, *an intrigue of long standing,* Sall.

consuētus -a -um. **I.** Partic. of consuesco (q.v.). **II.** P. adj., *accustomed, customary, usual;* lubido, Sall.

consul -sŭlis, m. (root CONS, or from con and the root of salio, which is seen in praesul and exsul), *a consul,* pl. consules, *the consuls.* **I.** *the two chief magistrates of the Roman state, chosen by the comitia centuriata, originally from patricians only, but after* 365 B.C., *also from the plebeians;* consul ordinarius, *one elected at the usual time* (opp. consul suffectus, *one chosen in the course of the year to supply the place of a consul deceased),* Liv.; consul designatus, *consul elect,* so called between the election in July and entrance upon office on the 1st of January, Cic.; consul major, *the consul who had precedence of his colleague;* consul Flaminius consul iterum, Cic.; aliquem dicere consulem, Liv.; the year was generally called by the consuls' names, e.g., L. Pisone et A. Gabinio coss. (i.e. consulibus), i.e., 696 A.U.C., Caes.; consule Tullo, Hor.; the name of the consul stamped on the cork marked the age of wine; Bibuli consulis amphora, Hor.; pro consule, *an officer in the place of the consul, a governor of a country, province, a proconsul;* proconsule in Ciliciam proficisci, *to go as proconsul to Cilicia,* Cic. **II.** Transf., in the historians used instead of proconsul, Liv.

consŭlāris -e (consul), *relating to a consul, consular.* **A.** Adj., aetas, *the age (namely forty-three), at which a man might lawfully be chosen consul,* Cic.; fasces, Liv.; lictor, auctoritas, Cic.; candidatus, Cic.; familia, Cic.; imperium, Cic.; locus, *place in the senate,* Cic.; provincia, Caes. **B.** Subst., **consularis** -is, m. *one who had been a consul, an ex-consul,* Cic.; in the imperial period, *a governor of consular rank,* Tac.

consŭlārĭtĕr, adv. (consularis), *in a manner worthy of a consul;* vita omnis consulariter acta, Liv.

consŭlātus -ūs, m. (consul), *the office of consul, the consulship;* abdicare se consulatu, Cic.; abdicare consulatum, Cic.; abire consulatu, Liv.; adipisci consulatum, Cic.; afferre consulatum in eam familiam, Cic.; petere consulatum, Cic.; peracto consulatu, Caes.

consŭlo -sŭlŭi -sultum, 3. (root CONS, CENS, or from con and the root of salio). **I.** a, *to reflect, weigh, deliberate, consider, consult;* in commune, *for the common good,* Liv.; in longitudinem, *for the future,* Ter.; facto non consulto in tali periculo opus esse, Sall.; re consulta et explorata, Cic.; quid agant consulunt, Caes.; **b,** *to come to a conclusion, to take measures;* libere consulere ad summam rem, Caes.; quae reges at-

que populi male consuluerint, Sall.; obsecro ne quid gravius de salute et incolumitate tuā consulas, Caes.; consulere in, *to take measures against;* nihil in quemquam superbe ac violenter, Liv.; **c,** *to take counsel for some person or thing, to have regard for the interests of, look to;* with dat., parti civium consulere, parti negligere, Cic.; sibi, Cic.; dignitati alicuius, Cic.; alicui optime, Cic.; with ut, ne, or (with preced. negat.) quominus and the subj., Cic.; **d,** aliquid boni consulere, *to take in good part;* haec missa, Ov. **II.** *to ask the advice of, consult;* nec te id consulo, *consult about that,* Cic.; quod me de Antonio consulis, Cic.; quid mihi faciendum esse censeat, Cic.; **a,** *to ask the opinion of the senate, to bring a matter before the senate;* senatus a Bestiā consultus est, placeretne legatos Jugurthae recipi moenibus, Sall.; **b,** *to lay a matter before the people;* seniores de tribus consulendum dixerunt esse, Liv.; **c,** *to take legal advice;* qui de jure civili consuli solent, Cic.; **d,** *to consult an oracle, or deity;* haruspicem, Cic.; Phoebi oracula, Ov.; exta, Verg.; Apollinem Pythium quas potissimum regiones tenerent, Cic.; id possetne fieri, consuluit, Cic.

consultātĭo -ōnis, f. (2. consulto), **1,** *a full consideration, deliberation;* **a,** venit aliquid in consultationem, Cic.; consultationem raptim transigere, Liv.; **b,** *a case proposed for consideration,* Quint.; **2,** *an asking for advice, inquiry;* consultationi alicuius respondere, Cic.

consultē, adv., with compar. and superl. (consultus), *advisedly, after consideration;* caute ac consulte gerere aliquid, Liv.

1. consultō, adv. (abl. of consultum), *deliberately, designedly;* consulto fecisse aliquid, Cic.; non consulto sed casu in eorum mentionem incidere, Cic.

2. consulto, 1. (freq. of consulo). **I.** *to consider maturely, weigh, ponder.* **A.** Gen., de officio, Cic.; triduum ad consultandum dare, Liv.; in longius, *for the future,* Tac.; in medium, *for the common good,* Sall.; consultabat, utrum Romam proficisceretur, an Capuam teneret, Cic. **B.** alicui, *to consult for, provide for;* reipublicae, Sall. **II.** *to consult, ask advice of;* aliquem, Tib.; vates ad eam rem consultandam ex Etruria accire, Liv.

consultŏr -ōris, m. (consulo), **1,** *an adviser;* egomet in agmine, in proelio consultor idem et socius periculi vobiscum adero, Sall.; **2,** *one who asks advice,* especially legal advice, *a client;* consultoribus suis respondere, Cic.

consultrix -īcis, f. (consultor), *one who consults, cares for, provides;* natura consultrix et provida utilitatum, Cic.

consultum -i, n. (consultus, from consulo), *resolution, plan, decision;* **a,** consulto collegae, virtute militum victoria parta est, Liv.; facta et consulta fortium et sapientium, Cic.; **b,** esp. *a decree* of the senate at Rome, senatus consultum (shortened to S.C.); senatus consultum facere, Cic.; S.C. facere in aliquem, Liv.; S.C. facere ut, etc., Cic.; alicui senatus consulto scribendo adesse, Cic.; consulta patrum, Hor.; **c,** *the decree* of a Sicilian senate (βουλή), Cic.; **d,** *the answer of an oracle;* dum consulta petis, Verg.

1. consultus -a -um, p. adj. with compar. and superl. (consulo), **a,** *well considered, deliberated upon, well weighed;* omnia consulta ad nos et exquisita deferunt, Cic.; **b,** of persons, *experienced,* esp. in law; with genit., juris consultus (adj. or subst.), *some one learned in the law,* Cic.; consultissimus vir omnis divini et humani juris, Liv.; consultus insanientis sapientiae, Hor.; with abl., jure consultus, Cic. Subst., **consultus** -i, m. *a lawyer,* Hor.

2. consultus -ūs, m. (consulo) = consultum (q.v.).

consum -fui -futurum -fore, *to be, to happen,* Plaut., Ter.

consummātĭo -ōnis, f. (consummo), **1,** *a summing up, adding up,* Plin.; **2,** *a finishing, completion, consummation;* maximarum rerum, Sen.

consummātus -a -um, p. adj. with superl. (consummo). *complete, perfect, consummate;* eloquentia, Quint.; orator, Quint.

consummo, 1. (com and summa), **1,** *to add together, sum up;* transf., *to form a whole, complete;* quae consummatur partibus, una dies (of an intercalary day), Ov.; in suum decus nomenque velut consummata eius belli gloria, Liv.; **2,** *to complete, finish;* eam rem, Liv.

consūmo -sumpsi -sumptum, 3. *to take altogether, consume.* **A.** In doing something, *to spend, employ;* pecuniam in agrorum coemptionibus, Cic.; omne tempus in litteris, Cic.; ingenium in musicis, Cic.; omnem laborem, operam, curam, studium in salute alicuius, Cic. **B.** *to destroy, waste, bring to an end;* **a,** omnia tela, *to shoot away,* Caes.; of provisions, omne frumentum, Caes.; of property, patrimonia, Cic.; omnes fortunas sociorum, Caes.; of time, *to spend, pass;* magna diei parte consumpta, Caes.; aestatem in Treviris, Caes.; consumendi otii causa, Cic.; horas multas saepe suavissimo sermone, Cic.; of resources or activity, *to waste, consume in vain;* multam operam frustra, Cic.; **b,** *to waste,* or *wear away, destroy;* quum eam (quercum) tempestas vetustasve consumpserit, Cic.; in pass., consumi incendio, or flamma, *to be destroyed by fire;* quae (aedes) priore anno incendio consumptae erant, Liv.; of life, *to destroy, kill;* si me vis aliqua morbi aut natura ipsa consumpsisset, Cic.; totidem plagis hostem, Hor.; garrulus hunc consumet, *will be the death of him,* Hor.; fame consumi, *to die of hunger,* Caes.

consumptĭo -ōnis, f. (consumo), *a consumption, consuming, destroying,* Cic.

consumptor -ōris, m. (consumo), *a consumer, destroyer;* confector et consumptor omnium, Cic.

consŭo -sŭi -sūtum, 3. *to sew together, stitch together,* Plaut.

consurgo -surrexi -surrectum, 3. *to rise up, stand up.* **I.** Lit., **1,** of persons, **a,** lying down; consolatus (ad terram projectos) consurgere jussit, Caes.; **b,** sitting; senatus cunctus consurgit, Cic.; esp. of an orator, *to rise up to speak;* consurgit P. Scaptius de plebe et inquit, Liv.; *to rise up in honour of some one;* consurrexisse omnes et senem sessum recepisse, Cic.; **c,** of persons kneeling, paulisper addubitavit an consurgendi jam triariis tempus esset, Liv.; **d,** of persons fighting, *to raise oneself to give more force to a blow;* ad iterandum ictum, Liv.; **2,** of things without life, consurgunt venti, Verg.; consurgunt geminae quercus, Verg. **II.** Transf., **1,** of persons, *to rise for any action, join in an insurrection;* magno tumultu ad bellum, Liv.; **2,** of things, *to break out;* novum bellum, Verg.

consurrectĭo -ōnis, f. (consurgo), *a rising up from a seat;* judicum, Cic.

Consus -i, m. *an ancient Roman deity,* whose worship was said to have been introduced by Romulus; hence, **Consŭālĭa** -ium, n. *games in honour of Consus,* on the 21st of August and 15th of December.

consūsurro, 1. *to whisper together,* Ter.

contābĕfăcĭo, 3. *to consume, cause to waste away,* Plaut.

contābesco -tābŭi, 3. *to waste away, wear away gradually;* Artemisia luctu confecta contabuit, Cic.

contăbŭlātĭo -ōnis, f. (contabulo), *a covering with boards, planking, floor,* Caes.

contăbŭlo, 1. *to cover with boards, to plank;* turrem, Caes.

contābundus = cunctabundus (q.v.).

contactus -ūs, m. (contingo), **1,** *a contact, touching, touch;* sanguinis, Ov.; **2,** *a touching of something unclean, contagion;* contactus aegrorum vulgabat morbos, Liv.; transf., oculos a contactu dominationis inviolatos, Tac.

contāges -is, f. (contingo), *a touch, touching,* Lucr.

contāgĭo -ōnis, f. (contingo), *a touching, connexion;* **1,** gen., quum est somno sevocatus animus a societate et contagione corporis, Cic.; **2,** *a touching of something unclean, contagion, infection;* **a,** physical, contagio pestifera, Liv.; **b,** moral, *bad companionship, evil example;* turpitudinis, Cic.; furoris, Liv.

contāgĭum -ĭi, n. (contingo), **1,** *touch,* Lucr.; **2,** *infection, contagion;* **a,** physical, mala vicini pecoris contagia, Verg.; **b,** moral, contagia lucri, Hor.

contāmĭnātus -a -um, p. adj. with superl. (contamino), *unclean, contaminated,* Cic.

contāmĭno, 1. (com and TAG -o, tango), *to render unclean by contact or mixture, contaminate;* sanguinem, Liv.; se scelere, Cic.; veritatem aliquo mendacio, Cic.

contātĭo, contātus, etc. = cunctatio, cunctatus, etc. (q.v.).

contechnor, 1. dep. *to devise a trick,* Plaut.

contĕgo -texi -tectum, 3. *to cover.* **A.** Lit., **a,** locum linteis, Liv.; eos uno tumulo, *to bury,* Liv.; **b,** *to conceal;* corporis partes, quae aspectum sint deformem habiturae, contegere atque abdere, Cic. **B.** Transf., *to conceal;* libidines fronte et supercilio, non pudore et temperantiā, Cic.

contĕmĕro, 1. *to pollute, defile,* Ov.

contemno -tempsi -temptum, 3. *to think meanly of, despise, contemn.* **I.** Gen., casus humanos, Cic.; Romam prae sua Capua irridere atque contemnere, Cic.; with infin., contemnere coronari, Hor.; with acc. and infin., ut ipsum vinci contemnerent, Cic. **II.** Esp., *to ridicule, make little of;* Adherbalis dicta, Sall.; se non contemnere, *to have a high opinion of oneself,* Cic.

contemplātĭo -ōnis, f. (contemplor), *attentive or eager looking at, contemplation.* **A.** Lit., caeli, Cic. **B.** Transf., naturae, Cic.

contemplātor -ōris, m. (contemplor), *one who attentively looks at or contemplates;* caeli, Cic.

contemplātus, abl. -ū, m. (contemplor), *a looking at, contemplation,* Ov.

contemplor (contemplo), 1. dep. (com and templum), *to look at attentively or minutely, regard, contemplate.* **A.** Lit., coelum suspicere coelestiaque contemplari, Cic.; situm Carthaginis, Liv. **B.** Transf., *to consider carefully;* ut totam causam quam maxime intentis oculis, ut aiunt, acerrime contemplemini, Cic.

contemptim, adv. with compar. (contemptus), *contemptuously;* de Romanis loqui, Cic.

contemptĭo -ōnis, f. (contemno), *contempt, scorn, disdain;* pecuniae, Cic.

contemptor -ōris, m. (contemno), *one who contemns or despises;* divitiarum, Liv.; divum, Verg.; attrib., nemo tam contemptor famae est, Liv.; contemptor lucis animus, Verg.; contemptor animus, Sall.

1. **contemptus** -a -um, p. adj. with compar. and superl. (contemno), *despised, despicable, contemptible ;* **a,** of things, vita contempta ac sordida, Cic. ; **b,** of persons, homo contemptus et abjectus, Cic.

2. **contemptus** -ūs, m. (comtemno), *a mean opinion, contempt, disdain ;* **a,** pass., hominibus Gallis prae magnitudine corporum suorum brevitas nostra contemptui est, Caes. ; **b,** act., contemptus moriendi, Tac.

contendo -tendi -tentum, 3. **I.** Lit., *to stretch forcibly ;* arcum, Verg. ; ballistas lapidum et reliqua tormenta telorum contendere atque adducere, Cic. ; and hence of missiles, *to shoot, cast ;* tela, Verg. **II.** Transf., **A.** *to strive with all one's bodily* or *mental power, to strain, exert oneself ;* **1,** of the bodily powers, **a,** gen., (*a*) transit., summas vires, Lucr. ; (*β*) intransit., eniti et contendere debet ut vincat, Cic. ; fuga salutem petere contendunt, Caes. ; **b,** *to hasten on a journey, try to reach ;* Bibracte ire contendit, Caes. ; fig., si potuissemus, quo contendimus pervenire, Cic. ; **2,** of the mental powers, **a,** *to exert oneself ;* (*a*) transit., contendit omnes nervos Chrysippus ut, etc., Cic. ; (*β*) intransit., maximis laboribus et periculis ad summam laudem gloriamque, Cic. ; ob eam causam contendi, ut plura dicerem, Cic. ; **b,** *to strive to obtain something, strive for ;* non erat causa, cur hoc tempore aliquid a te contenderem, Cic. ; ab aliquo valde de reditu in gratiam, Cic. ; vehementer contendere ab aliquo ut, etc., Cic. ; **c,** *to assert with confidence, maintain ;* contendentes numquam eam urbem fuisse ex Triphylia, Liv. **B.** *to strive with some one else ;* **1,** a, cum victore, Caes. ; contra Paridem, Verg. ; pro vitulis contra leones, Cic. ; inter se de principatu, Caes. ; cum Libone de mittendis legatis, Caes. ; b, at an auction, *to bid against,* Cic. ; **2,** *to compare, contrast ;* ipsas causas, quae inter se configunt, Cic.

1. **contentē,** adv., with compar. and superl. (1. contentus), *eagerly, earnestly ;* contente pro se dicere, Cic.

2. **contentē,** adv. (2. contentus), *strictly, sparingly,* Plaut.

contentio -ōnis, f. (contendo), *the full exertise of the powers, effort, striving.* **I.** Gen., vocis, *the raising* or *straining of the voice,* Cic. ; animi, Cic. **II. 1,** *combat, contest, contention, strife ;* magna contentio belli, Cic. ; adversus procuratores contentio dicendi, Cic. ; in contentionem honoris incidere, *rivalry in seeking a public office,* Cic. ; contentiones habere cum aliquo, Caes. ; **2, a,** *a contrast, comparison ;* hominum ipsorum or fortunarum contentionem facere, Cic. ; **b,** rhet. t. t., *antithesis, juxtaposition of opposed ideas,* Quint.

contentiōsus -a -um (contentio), *pertaining to a contest, contentious, quarrelsome,* Plin.

1. **contentus** -a -um, p. adj. (contendo), *stretched, tense.* **A.** Lit., funis, Hor. **B.** Transf., **a,** onera contentis corporibus facilius feruntur, remissis opprimunt, Cic. ; **b,** *eager, zealous ;* ad tribunatum contento studio cursuque veniamus, Cic.

2. **contentus** -a -um, p. adj. with compar. (contineo), *contented, satisfied ;* with abl., suis rebus, Cic. ; ea victoria, Cic. ; contentus quod, etc., Cic. ; with infin, Ov.

contermĭnus -a -um, *having the same boundary, conterminous, near ;* contermina stabula ripae, Ov. Subst., **contermĭnum** -i, n. *an adjoining region, a confine,* Tac.

contĕro -trīvi -trītum, 3. **I.** In narrow sense, *to rub away, reduce to small portions by rubbing, to grind, pound ;* cornua cervi, Ov. **II.** In wider sense, **1,** *to destroy, wear away ;* eius

omnes injurias voluntariā quādam oblivione, Cic. ; reliqua conterere et contemnere, *trample under foot,* Cic. ; ferrum, *to wear away by using,* Ov. ; se in musicis, geometriā, astris, Cic. ; **2,** of time, *to consume, spend ;* omne otiosum tempus in studiis, Cic. ; bonum otium socordiā atque desidiā, Sall.

conterrĕo -terrŭi -terrĭtum, 2. *to terrify, frighten exceedingly ;* conterrere loquacitatem alicuius vultu ipso aspectuque, Cic. ; his nuntiis senatus conterritus, Liv.

contestātio -ōnis, f. (contestor), *an earnest supplication, eager request,* Cic.

contestor, 1. dep. 1, *to call to witness ;* deos hominesque, Cic. ; **2, a,** litem, *to set an action on foot, inaugurate an action by calling witnesses,* Cic. ; **b,** transf., virtus contestata, *approved,* Cic.

contexo -texŭi -textum, 3. **I.** Lit., *to weave together, twine together, connect, unite ;* lilia amaranthis, Tib. ; ovium villis contextis homines vestiuntur, Cic. **II.** Transf., **1,** *to connect, unite ;* extrema cum primis, Cic. ; **2,** *to continue ;* carmen longius, Cic. ; **3,** *to build, construct, put together ;* sic deinceps omne opus contexitur, Caes. ; equum trabibus acernis, Verg. ; **4,** *to devise, invent ;* crimen, Cic.

contextē, adv. (contextus), *in close connexion,* Cic.

1. **contextus** -a -um, p. adj. (from contexto), *interwoven, connected, united ;* **a,** contexta condensaque corpora, Lucr. ; **b,** perpetuae et contextae voluptates, *an unbroken series of pleasures,* Cic. ; **c,** contexta historia eorum temporum, *continuous,* Nep.

2. **contextus** -ūs, m. (contexo), *uniting, connexion ;* **a,** contextum corporum dissolvere, Lucr. ; **b,** of abstractions, mirabilis contextus rerum, Cic. ; **c,** of oratory, totus quasi contextus orationis, Cic.

conticesco -tĭcŭi, 3. (inchoat. of conticeo), *to become silent, to be dumb, silent.* **I.** Lit., **a,** of persons, conscientiā convictus repente conticuit, Cic. ; **b,** of personifications, neque ulla aetas de tuis laudibus conticescet, Cic. **II.** Transf., *to become still* or *quiet, to abate, cease ;* illae scilicet litterae conticuerunt forenses et senatoriae, Cic.

contignātio -ōnis, f. (contigno), *woodwork, a flooring, joists, storey,* Caes.

contigno, 1. (com and tignum), *to put planks together, to floor,* Cic.

contĭgŭus -a -um (contingo). **I.** Act., *that which touches another, contiguous, near ;* domus, Ov. ; pars circi quae Aventino contigua, Tac. ; Cappadoces, Tac. **II.** Pass. with dat., *within reach of ;* contiguus missae hastae, Verg.

contĭnens -entis, p. adj. with compar. (contineo). **I. 1,** *lying near, adjacent, bordering upon ;* praedia continentia huic fundo, Cic. ; continentibus diebus, *in the days immediately following,* Caes. ; **2, a,** *hanging together, unbroken ;* agmen, Liv. ; terra continens, *the mainland,* Cic. ; subst., **contĭnens** -entis, f. *a continent,* Caes. ; **b,** of time, *continuous, unbroken ;* e continenti genere, *in unbroken genealogical succession,* Cic. ; totius diei continens labor, Caes. ; continenti cursu, Liv. **II.** *temperate, continent ;* puer, Cic. ; ne continentior in vita hominum, quam in pecuniā fuisse videatur, Caes. **III.** Rhet. t. t., subst., **contĭnens** -entis, f. *the main point ;* causae, Cic.

contĭnentĕr, adv. (continens) **1, a,** of space, *in close succession ;* sedetis, Cat. ; **b,** of time, *continuously, without cessation ;* totā nocte ierunt, Caes. ; **2,** *continently, temperately ;* vivere, Cic.

contĭnentĭa -ae, f. (contineo), *continence, self-restraint, moderation, temperance ;* continentia in omni victu cultuque corporis, Cic.

contineo -tĭnui -tentum, 2. (com and teneo). **I.** *to keep together;* **1,** a, *to bind together, hold fast;* quum agger altiore aquā contineri non posset, Caes.; transf., nec enim ulla res vehementius rempublicam continet quam fides, Cic.; b, *to keep together, unseparated;* legiones uno in loco, Caes.; c, *to connect, join;* quod oppidum Genabum pons fluminis Ligeris continebat, Caes.; **2,** a, *to keep in, surround, contain, limit;* mundus qui omnia complexu suo coercet et continet, Cic.; *to confine;* beluas immanes saeptis, Cic.; milit. t. t., *to shut in;* Pompejum quam augustissime, Caes.; b, *to contain, comprehend, comprise;* tales res quales hic liber continet, Cic.; de summo bono quod continet philosophiam, *which is the main point in philosophy,* Cic.; status reipublicae maxime judicatis rebus continetur, *is involved in, depends upon,* Cic. **II.** *to keep, maintain;* **1,** a, *to keep firm;* naves minus commode copulis continebantur; b, *to keep what has been taken* or *received;* alvus arcet et continet quod recipit, Cic.; **2,** a, *to keep in a place* or *occupation;* milites sub pellibus, Caes.; se suo loco, Caes.; se in suis perennibus studiis, Cic.; Belgas in officio, *to maintain in allegiance,* Caes.; b, *to keep back, be silent about;* petimus ab Antonio, ut ea quae continet neque adhuc protulit explicet nobis, Cic.; **3,** *to restrain, confine, keep back;* a, lit., risum, Cic.; gradum, *to check,* Verg.; b, transf., *to keep some one from some thing;* suos a proelio, Caes.; contineo me ab exemplis, Cic.; *to keep obedient, hold in check;* et usus non tam armis, quam judiciorum terrore, Liv.; c, morally, *to restrain, curb, repress;* omnes cupiditates, Cic.; non posse milites contineri quin, etc., Caes.

1. contingo (contunguo), **3.** *to wet, moisten,* Lucr.

2. contingo -tĭgi -tactum, **3.** (com and tango). **I.** Transit., *to touch.* **A.** Lit., a, terram osculo, Liv.; paene terram (of the moon), Cic.; b, *to grasp;* dextram, Liv.; c, poet., *to touch, taste;* cibos ore, Ov.; d, *to sprinkle;* ora nati sacro medicamine, Ov.; e, *to reach to, touch;* nullas profecto terras caelum contingere, Liv.; esp. geograph. t. t., *to border on, touch;* quorum agri non contingunt mare, Cic.; f, *to reach;* (a) an aim with a missile, ex tantā altitudine contingere hostem non posse, Liv.; (β) an object desired, optatam cursu metam, Hor.; Italiam, Verg.; (γ) of the voice, *to reach the ear of;* nec contigit ullum vox mea mortalem, Ov. **B.** Transf., a, *to be related to;* aliquem sanguine ac genere, Liv.; *to concern, affect;* Romanos nihil (consultatio) contingit, nisi quatenus, etc., Liv.; b, *to pollute, defile;* milites contacti sacrilegio, Liv. **II.** Intransit., *to happen, to befall;* with dat., mihi omnia, quae opto, contingant, Cic.; with infin., celeriter antecellere omnibus ingenii gloriā contigit, Cic.; with ut and the subj., quoniam autem, tecum ut essem, non contigit, Cic.

continŭātĭo -ōnis, f. (continuo). **I.** Act., *an unbroken continuance, continuing;* tribunatus, Liv. **II.** Pass., **A.** *connexion, continuation, unbroken succession;* causarum, Cic.; rhet. t. t., *a period;* nimis longa continuatio verborum, Cic. **B.** *an unbroken succession, continuance in time;* imbrium, Caes.

continŭĭtas -ātis, f. (continuus), *continuity, unbroken succession,* Varr.

1. continŭŏ, adv. (continuus), **1,** *immediately, at once,* Cic.; **2,** in conjunction with a negative, *not immediately = not necessarily;* in a question = *perhaps then?* non continuo si me in gregem sicariorum contuli, sum sicarius, Cic.

2. continŭŏ, **1.** (continuus). **I.** Of space, *to bring into connexion, connect, unite;* aër mari continuatus est, Cic.; Suionibus Sitonum gentes continuantur, *are adjacent to,* Tac.; verba, *to form into a sentence,* Cic.; binas aut amplius domos, Sall.; aedificia moenibus, Liv.; agmen latissime, *to extend,* Cic. **II.** Of time, a, *to do in rapid succession, to keep on doing;* prope continuatis funeribus, *the funerals following close on one another,* Liv.; b, *to continue without interruption;* diem noctemque potando, *continue drinking day and night,* Tac.; iter die et nocte, Caes.; militiam, Liv.; magistratum, *to prolong,* Sall.; alicui consulatum, Liv.

continŭus -a -um (contineo), *connected with, hanging together, continuous, unbroken, uninterrupted.* **I.** Of space, a, Leucada continuam veteres habuere coloni, *connected with the main land,* Ov.; transf. of persons, Nerva, continuus principi, *standing next to,* Tac.; b, *unseparated, undivided;* Rhenus uno alveo continuus, Tac.; translationes, Cic. **II.** Of time, *successive, following on, uninterrupted;* secutae sunt continuos complures dies tempestates, Caes.; superiora continuorum annorum decreta, Cic.; oppugnatio, Liv.

contĭo -ōnis, f. (contr. from conventio), **1,** *an assembly of the people* or *of the soldiers, a public meeting;* contionem advocare, Cic.; advocare contionem populi or militum, Caes.; vocare ad contionem, Liv.; habere, Cic.; dimittere, Liv.; dare alicui contionem (of a magistrate, who called the meeting), Cic.; prodire in contionem, Cic.; producere aliquem in contionem, Liv.; aliquid in contione dicere, Cic.; in contionem ascendere or escendere, *to go up to the platform to speak,* Liv.; **2,** meton., *the speech made in such an assembly;* contiones turbulentae Metelli, temerariae Appii, furiosissimae Publii, Cic.; habere contiones in Caesarem graves, Caes.; funebris, *a funeral oration,* Cic.

contĭōnābundus -a -um (contionor), *haranguing, speaking in public,* Liv.

contĭōnālis -e (contio), *relating to a public assembly;* contionalis prope clamor senatus, Cic.; illa contionalis hirudo aerarii, *that bloodsucker and demagogue,* Cic.

contĭōnārius -a -um (contio), *relating to a public assembly;* ille contionarius populus, Cic.

contĭōnātor -ōris, m. (contionor), *a popular orator, demagogue,* Cic.

contĭōnor, **1.** dep. (contio), a, *to form, compose an assembly;* nunc illi vos singuli universos contionantes timent, Liv.; b, *to speak in public before an assembly;* apud milites, Caes.; superiore e loco, Cic.; also *to proclaim publicly, speak with a loud voice;* C. Cato contionatus est se comitia haberi non siturum, Cic.

contĭuncŭla -ae, f. (dim. of contio), **1,** *a small assembly,* Cic.; **2,** *a short harangue,* Cic.

contollo, **3.** (obsol. for confero), gradum, *to betake oneself,* Plaut.

contŏnat, impers. *it thunders violently,* Plaut.

contor = cunctor (q.v.).

contorquĕo -torsi -tortum, **2.** **I.** *to twist, whirl, turn violently, contort;* gubernaclum, Lucr.; membra quocunque vult, *to direct, turn,* Cic.; proram ad laevas undas, Verg. **II.** Esp. *to brandish, to hurl,* contorquere hastam in latus, Verg.; transf., verba, *to hurl forth,* Cic.

contortē, adv. with compar. (contortus), *in distorted order, in a constrained manner, ambiguously;* dicere, Cic.

contortĭo -ōnis, f. (contorqueo), *a swinging, twisting;* contortiones orationis, *distorted expressions,* Cic.

contortor -ōris, m. (contorqueo), *one who contorts* or *perverts;* legum, Ter.

contortŭlus -a -um (dim. of contortus), *somewhat intricate, obscure*, Cic.

contortus -a -um, p. adj. (from contorqueo), 1, *intricate, confused, complicated;* contortae et difficiles res, Cic.; 2, *powerful, vigorous;* oratio, Cic.

contrā (from com, as extra from ex). **I. Adv., A.** Of place, *opposite, over against, on the opposite side;* ulmus erat contra, Ov.; omnia contra circaque plena hostium erant, Liv. **B.** Of actions, 1, which answer to one another, *in return;* quum hic nugatur, contra nugari lubet, Plaut.; 2, which are opposed to one another, *on the other side, on the contrary;* alia aestimabilia, alia contra, Cic.; foll. by atque, or quam, simulacrum Jovis contra atque antea fuerat convertere, Cic.; quum contra fecerint quam polliciti sint, Cic.; 3, used of hostile opposition, *against;* pugnare, Lucr.; consistere, Caes.; dicere, Cic. **II.** Prep. with acc., 1, *opposite to, over against;* insula quae contra Brundusinum portum est, Caes.; 2, *against, in opposition to, contrary to;* vim atque impetum fluminis, Caes.; opinionem, Cic.; contra ea, *on the contrary, on the other hand,* Caes.; 3, *against, in the sense of* hostility; contra populum Romanum conjurasse, Caes.; contra deos disputare, Cic. (Contra occasionally is placed after its acc. in the case of a noun, Verg.; of a rel. pronoun, quos contra, Cic.)

contractĭo -ōnis, f. (contraho), *a drawing together, contraction.* **A.** Lit., contractio et porrectio digitorum, Cic.; frontis, Cic. **B.** Transf., 1, *abbreviation, shortness;* orationis, Cic.; syllabae, Cic.; 2, *anxiety, depression;* animi, Cic.

contractĭuncŭla -ae, f. (dim. of contractio), *dejection, sadness;* animi, Cic.

contractus -a -um, p. adj. with compar. (contraho), *drawn in, contracted, narrow;* a, of places, locus exiguus atque contractus, Verg.; b, of time, *shorter;* his jam contractioribus noctibus, Cic.; c, of the voice, contractum genus vocis, Cic.; d, of oratory, dialectica quasi contracta et astricta eloquentia putanda est, Cic.; e, of circumstances, *straitened;* paupertas, Hor.; f, *retired, quiet;* contractus leget, Hor.

contrādĭco -dixi -dictum, 3. *to gainsay, speak against, contradict;* sententiis aliorum, Tac.; nec contradici quin amicitia de integro reconcilietur, Liv.

contradictĭo -ōnis, f. (contradico), *a speaking against, contradiction,* Quint.

contrăho -traxi -tractum, 3. **I.** *to draw together, collect, unite* (opp. dissipare). **A.** Lit., a, milit. t. t., cohortes ex finitimis regionibus, Caes.; magnam classem, Nep.; Luceriam omnes copias, Cic.; omnes or omnia ad unum, Cic.; b, *to bring together for conversation,* etc.; Scipionem et Hasdrubalem ad colloquium dirimendarum simultatum causa, Liv. **B.** Transf., a, *to unite;* contrahit celeriter similitudo eos, Liv.; contrahere amicitiam, *to form friendship,* Cic.; b, *to complete a business arrangement;* rem, rationem, negotium, Cic.; contrahere magnam rationem cum Mauritaniae rege, Cic.; c, *to cause, bring on, bring about;* aes alienum, *to contract debt,* Cic.; bellum, Liv.; lites, Cic.; porca contracta, *due to expiate a crime,* Cic.; offensionem, Cic. **II.** *to draw together by way of shortening.* **A.** Lit., a, frontem, Cic.; collum, Cic.; pulmones se contrahunt, Cic.; contractum aliquo morbo bovis cor. Cic.; vela, *to furl one's sails,* fig., *to be moderate,* Cic.; b, of limbs, parts of the body, *to contract* (from cold, death, etc.); contracto frigore pigrae, *numbing,* Verg. **B.** Transf., *to shorten, reduce, draw in, draw together;* a, castra, Caes.; of the moon, orbem, Ov.; b, of speech, *to shorten;* orationem in verbum con-

trahere, Cic.; c, of appetites, *to repress;* appetitus omnes contrahere, Cic.; d, of courage, etc., *to lower, lessen;* animum, Cic.

contrārĭē, adv. (contrarius), *in an opposite direction or manner;* sidera contrarie procedentia, Cic.; verba relata contrarie, Cic.

contrārĭus -a -um (contra). **I.** Of place, *opposite, over against;* collis nascebatur adversus huic et contrarius, Caes.; vulnera, *wounds in front,* Tac. **II. A.** *coming from the opposite direction;* contrarius ictus, *a blow from an enemy,* Cic.; in contrarias partes fluere, Cic.; classi contraria flamina, *contrary winds,* Ov.; in comparison, followed by atque, qui versantur contrario motu atque caelum, Cic. **B.** 1, *opposed, contrary to;* contrariae epistolae, *contradictory,* Cic.; in contrarias partes disputare or disserere de aliquā re, *to speak for and against,* Cic.; with genit., huius virtutis contraria est vitiositas, Cic.; with dat., nihil malum esse, nisi quod virtuti contrarium esset, Cic.; subst., **contrārĭum** -ii, n. *the opposite;* in contrarium disputare, Tac.; followed by atque or a, contrarium decernebat ac paulo ante decreverat, Cic.; adv., ex contrario, *against, on the other side;* ut ego hoc ex contrario contendo, Cic.; plur., comparare contraria, Cic.; 2, esp. a, *opposed to in a hostile manner;* arma, Ov.; b, *injurious;* otium maxime contrarium esse, Caes.

contrectābĭlĭtĕr, adv. (contrectabilis), *with feeling,* Lucr.

contrectātĭo -ōnis, f. (contrecto), *a touching, handling,* Cic.

contrecto, 1. (contracto), *to touch, feel, handle.* **I. A.** Lit., vulnus, Ov. **B.** Transf., totaque mente contrectare varias voluptates, consider, Cic. **II.** *to dishonour,* Tac.

contrĕmisco (contrĕmesco), -trĕmŭi, 3. a, *to tremble violently, to quake;* contremiscere tota mente atque artubus omnibus, Cic.; b, *to tremble before, be afraid of;* periculum, Hor.

contrĕmo, 3. *to tremble violently, quake,* Lucr.

contrĭbŭo -tribŭi -trĭbūtum, 3., a, *to contribute to in common with others;* nec non Peneae nec Spercheides undae contribuere aliquid, Ov.; b, *to annex, incorporate with, unite;* Calagurritani qui erant cum Oscensibus contributi, Caes.; Ambracia quae tum contribuerat se Aetolis, Liv.

contristo, 1. (com and tristo), *to make sad, make sorrowful, sadden;* a, pluvio frigore caelum, *make gloomy,* Verg.; b, contristat haec sententia Balbum Cornelium, ap. Cic.

contrītus -a -um, p. adj. (from contero), *worn out, well-used, common, trite;* proverbium, Cic.

contrōversĭa -ae, f. (controversus), *debate, dispute, controversy;* hereditatis, *about an inheritance,* Cic.; controversiam habere de re cum aliquo, Cic.; controversia est inter aliquos de re, Cic.; in controversiā versari, esse, Cic.; rem adducere in controversiam, deducere in controversiam, vocare in controversiam, *to make matter of debate,* Cic.; sine controversiā, *without dispute,* Cic.; sine controversiā solvere, Cic.; sine controversiā vicimus, *we have undoubtedly conquered,* Cic.; controversia non erat quin, *there was no doubt that,* etc., Cic.

contrōversĭōsus -a -um (controversia), *controverted, strongly disputed;* res, Liv.

contrōversor, 1. dep. (controversus), *to contend, dispute, debate;* inter se de huiuscemodi rebus controversari, Cic.

contrōversus -a -um (contro, like contra, from com = with, against), 1, pass., *that which is a subject of debate, controverted;* res, Cic.; 2, act. *disputatious, fond of controversy;* gens, Cic.

contrŭcido 1. *to cut in pieces, cut down,*

hew down, slay ; debilitato corpore et contrucid-
ato, Cic; fig., rempublicam, Cic.

contrūdo -trūsi -trūsum, 3. 1, *to thrust, push
together ;* nubes in unum, Lucr. ; 2, *to thrust,
crowd into any place ;* aliquos in balneas, Cic.

contrunco, 1. *to cut in pieces ;* cibum, Plaut.

contŭbernālis -is, c. (com and taberna). **I.
a,** *a messmate, comrade, one who shares the same
tent ;* domi una eruditi, militiae contubernales,
Cic. ; **b,** *a young man who accompanied a general
to learn the art of war ;* fuit in Cretā postea
contubernalis Saturnini, Cic. ; so in public
affairs, *supporter ;* alicui contubernalem in consulatu fuisse, Cic. **II.** a, *comrade, mate, constant companion ;* habuisses non hospitem sed
contubernalem, Cic. ; **b,** *the husband* or *wife of
a slave,* Plin.

contŭbernĭum -i, n. (com and taberna).
I. Concr., 1, *a hut,* or *tent in which ten men and
an officer lodged ;* deponere in contubernio arma,
Caes. ; 2, *the common dwelling of a male and
female slave,* Tac. **II.** Abstr., 1, *a sharing in
the same tent, comradeship ;* militum, Tac. ; 2,
*the attendance of a young man on a general to learn
the art of war ;* contubernii necessitudo, Cic. ; 3,
companionship, intimacy, Suet. ; 4, esp. *the
living together of slaves as man and wife,* Col. ;
and gen. *concubinage,* Cic.

contŭĕor -tŭĭtus sum, 2. *to regard on all
sides, look at attentively.* **A.** Lit., aspicite ipsum,
contuemini os, Cic. **B.** Transf. *to consider, reflect
upon ;* quum (revocatio illa) a contuendis nos
malis avocat, Cic.

contŭĭtus, abl. -ū, m. (contueor), *a beholding, attentive looking at,* Plin.

contŭmācĭa -ae, f. (contumax), *stubbornness,
obstinacy, insolence, haughtiness ;* gen. in a bad
sense, insolentia, superbia, contumacia, Cic. ;
in a good sense, *firmness ;* libera contumacia (of
Socrates), Cic.

contŭmācĭtĕr, adv. (contumax), *obstinately,
stubbornly, insolently ;* scribere, Cic.

contŭmax -ācis (com and TEM -o, temno),
haughty, insolent, stubborn, obstinate ; quis con-
tumacior ? quis inhumanior ? quis superbior,
Cic. ; in a good sense, *firm, unyielding ;* contumax etiam adversus tormenta servorum fides,
Tac.

contŭmēlĭa -ae, f. (com and TEM -o,
temno), *insult, affront, outrage, contumely.* **I.**
Lit. **A.** contumeliam jacĕre in aliquem, Cic. ;
lacerare aliquem contumeliis, Cic. ; onerare aliquem contumeliis, Cic. ; vexare aliquem omnibus
contumeliis, Cic.; contumeliae causa aliquem describere, Cic. ; contumelia appellare aliquem per-
fugam, *insultingly,* Caes. ; vertere aliquid in contumeliam suam, *to take as an insult,* Caes. **B.**
dishonour, Cic. **II.** Transf. *damage, injury ;*
naves totae factae ex robore ad quamvis vim et
contumeliam perferendam, Caes.

contŭmēlĭōsē, adv., with compar. and
superl. (contumeliosus), *insolently, abusively ;*
contumeliose dicere, laedere, Cic.

contŭmēlĭōsus -a -um, adj., with compar.
and superl. (contumelia), *insulting, abusive ;*
epistolae in aliquem contumeliosae, Cic. ; id
contumeliosum est plebi (followed by acc. and
infin.), Liv.

contŭmŭlo, 1. 1, *to heap up in a mound,*
Plin. ; 2, *to bury, inter,* Ov.

contundo -tūdi -tūsum, 3. **I.** *to bruise,
crush, pound, break to pieces ;* allia serpyllumque,
Verg. **II.** *to crush, bruise, beat.* **A.** Lit., anum
saxis, Hor.; pugiles caestibus contusi, Cic. ;
contusi ac debilitati inter saxa rupesque, Liv.
B. 1, *to destroy, subdue, crush, demolish ;* feroc-

em Hannibalem, Liv. ; animum, Cic. ; *audaciam*
alicuius contundere et frangere, Cic. ; calumniam stultitiamque alicuius obterere ac contundere, Cic.

contŭo, contŭor, 3. = contueor (q.v.).

conturbātĭo -ōnis, f. (conturbo), *disorder,
confusion, perturbation of mind ;* mentis, Cic.

conturbo, 1., 1, *to disturb, throw into disorder, confusion ;* ordines Romanorum, Sall. ;
rempublicam, Sall. ; 2, *to disturb in mind, cause
anxiety ;* valetudo tua me valde conturbat, Cic. ;
rationes, or absol., conturbare, Cic., *to bring
money matters into confusion, to ruin, make bankrupt ;* conturbare putat sibi licere, Cic.

contus -i, m. (κοντός), 1, *a pole used for
pushing a boat along,* Verg. ; 2, *a long spear* or
pike, Tac.

cōnus -i, m. (κῶνος). 1, *a cone,* Cic. ; 2, *the
apex of a helmet,* Verg.

convălesco -vălŭi, 3. *to become strong.* **I.**
Gen. **A.** Lit., of things, postquam pestifer ignis
convaluit, *blazed up,* Ov. **B.** Transf., a, *to gain
strength ;* quum mala per longas convaluere
moras, *have become rooted,* Ov. ; b, of persons
or states, *to gain strength* or *power ;* Milo in dies
convalescebat, Cic. ; his ille (Caesar) rebus ita
convaluit ut, etc., Cic. ; nimis vicinas prope se
convalescere opes rati, Cic. **II.** Esp. **A.** *to
recover from a disease, gain strength, get well ;*
non aegri omnes convalescunt, Cic.; ex morbo,
Cic. **B.** Transf., ut tandem sensus convaluere
mei, Ov.

convallis -is, f. *a valley shut in on all sides,*
Cic.

convāso, 1. (com and vasa), *to pack up
baggage,* Ter.

convecto, 1. (intens. of conveho), *to bring
together, collect ;* praedam, Verg.

convector -ōris, m. (conveho), *a fellow-
voyager,* Cic.

convĕho -vexi -vectum, 3. *to bring together,
carry into one place ;* frumentum ex finitimis
regionibus in urbem, Caes. ; lintribus in eam
insulam materiem, calcem, caementa, arma, Cic.

convello -velli, -vulsi, and (rarely) -vulsi (-volsi)
-vulsum (-volsum), 3. *to tear, pluck, pull away,
wrench off.* **I.** Lit., 1, repagula, Cic. ; gradus
Castoris, Cic. ; Herculem ex suis sedibus convellere atque auferre, Cic. ; viridem ab humo
silvam, Verg. ; dapes avido dente, *devour,* Ov. ;
2, milit. t. t., convellere signa, *to pluck up
the standards, to decamp,* Cic. **II.** Transf. *to
weaken, overthrow, destroy ;* cuncta auxilia reipublicae labefactari convellique, Cic. ; si eam
opinionem ratio convellet, Cic. ; quo judicio con-
vulsam penitus scimus esse rempublicam, Cic.

convĕna -ae, c. adj. (convenio), *coming together,* Plaut. ; in plur. subst. *a concourse of
strangers, assembled multitude ;* pastores et con-
venas congregare, Cic.

convĕniens -entis, p. adj. (from convenio),
1, *agreeing, unanimous, concordant ;* bene conven-
ientes propinqui, Cic. ; 2, *fit for, appropriate,
suitable ;* conveniens decretis eius, Cic. ; oratio
tempori conveniens, Liv. ; nihil est enim tam
naturae aptum, tam conveniens ad res vel secundas vel adversas, Cic.

convĕnĭentĕr, adv. (conveniens), *agreeably
with, suitably to ;* convenienter cum naturā vivere, Cic. ; constanter convenienterque sibi dicere, Cic.

convĕnĭentĭa -ae, f. (conveniens), *agreement, harmony, conformity with ;* quaedam convenientia et conjunctio naturae, Cic.

convĕnĭo -vēni, -ventum, 4. **I.** Gen. **A.**
Intransit., 1, *to come together, collect ;* ex pro-

vinciā, Caes. ; **ad** hoc judicium, Cic. ; celeriter ad clamorem hominum circiter millia sex convenerant, Caes. ; uno tempore undique comitiorum ludorum censendique causā, Cic. ; **2,** civitates quae in id forum conveniunt, *who belong to that district,* Cic. ; **3,** legal t. t. convenire in manum (of the wife, *to come into the power of her husband by marriage*), Cic. **B.** Transit., *to visit, meet, call upon;* quotidie plurimos, Cic. ; convento Cn. Octavio Demetriade, Cic. ; tribuni plebis non desistebant clam inter se convenire, Cic. **II.** *to fit,* **A.** 1, Lit., si cothurni laus illa esset ad pedem apte convenire, Cic. ; 2, Transf., *to agree with, be congenial to, harmonise, be fitting;* haec tua deliberatio non convenit cum oratione Largi, Cic. ; non in omnes omnia convenire, Cic. ; with infin. or acc. and infin., illicone ad praetorem ire convenit? Cic. ; impers., minime miror caelum et terram, si tibi ita conveniat, dimittere, Cic. **B.** *to unite;* 1, lit., Lucr. ; 2, transf., **a,** res convenit, or impers., convenit, *a thing is agreed upon;* id signum quod convenerat, *which had been agreed upon,* Caes. ; pax convenit, Liv. ; pactum est quod inter jam inde per consules reliqua belli perfecta (esse), Liv. ; mihi cum Deiotaro convenit, ut ille in meis castris esset cum suis copiis, Cic. ; impers., quum de facto convenisset, Cic. ; **b,** bene (optime) convenit (alicui) cum aliquo, *to be on good terms with;* sororis vir, quicum optime convenisset, Cic.

conventīcĭum -ĭi, n. (convenio), sc. aes = τὸ ἐκκλησιαστικόν, *the money received by Greek citizens for attendance in the popular assembly,* Cic.

conventĭcŭlum -i, n. (dim. of conventus), **a,** *a coming together, assembly, association;* conventicula hominum, quae postea civitates nominatae sunt, Cic. ; **b,** *a place of meeting,* Tac.

conventĭo -ōnis, f. (convenio), 1, *an assembly,* Varr. ; 2, *an agreement, compact,* Cic.

conventum -i, n. (convenio), *a covenant, agreement, compact;* pactum, conventum, stipulatio, Cic.

conventus -ūs, m. (convenio). **I.** Lit., **A.** *a coming together, an assembly;* **a,** virorum mulierumque celeberrimus, Cic.; **b,** *an illegal assembly;* in nocturno conventu fuisse apud M. Laecam, Cic.; **c,** *a congress of states;* omnium sociarum civitatum, Liv.; **d,** *the assembly of the inhabitants of a province held by the praetor;* conventum agere, *to hold the assizes,* Cic. ; hence *the district of the province for which such an assembly was held;* homo omnium ex illo conventu quadruplatorum deterrimus, Cic. ; **e,** *the union of Roman citizens in a province forming a corporation;* conventus Syracusanus, Cic. **B.** Of atoms, *union,* Lucr.; **II.** Transf., *agreement,* Cic.

converbĕro, 1. *to beat violently,* Plin.

converro (-vorro) -verri (-vorri) -versum (-vorsum), 3. *to sweep together, brush out,* Plaut.; transf., hereditates omnium, *scrape together,* Cic.

conversātĭo -ōnis, f. (conversor). **I.** *frequent use, a frequent sojourn in a place,* Plin. **II.** *intercourse, conversation,* Tac.

conversĭo -ōnis, f. (converto). **A.** Lit., *a turning round;* coeli, Cic. ; mensium annorumque conversiones, *periodical return,* Cic. **B.** in rhet., 1, *the rounding off of a period;* ut (oratio) conversiones habeat absolutas, Cic. ; 2, *the repetition of the same word at the end of a clause,* Cic. ; 3, *change;* naturales esse quasdam conversiones rerum publicarum, Cic.

converso (intens. of converto), 1. *to turn round frequently;* animus se ipse conversans, Cic.

converto (-vorto) -verti (-vorti) -versum (-vorsum), **3.** *to turn round, whirl round.* **I.** Lit., **A.** *to turn round to the other side;* 1, palam anuli ad palmam, Cic. ; naves in eam partem, quo ventus fert, Caes. ; esp. milit. t. t., signa convertere, *to wheel round,* Caes. ; terga or se convertere, *to flee,* Caes. ; 2, **a,** in motion, *to turn round, change one's direction;* vox boum Herculem convertit, *makes Hercules turn round,* Liv. ; iter convertere, Caes. ; reflex., se ad montes Caes., or without se, cum paucis ad equites, Sall. ; **b,** convertere pecuniam publicam domum suam, *to embezzle,* Cic. ; 3, geograph. t. t., *to face, be directed towards, lie towards;* spelunca conversa ad aquilonem, Cic. **B.** *to turn round in a circle, to revolve;* quae (terra) circum axem se summa celeritate convertit et torquet, Cic. ; **II.** Transf., 1, *to direct towards;* convertere in se unum omnium vires, Liv. ; in ceteros ordines easdem vitae conditiones, Cic. ; 2, *to direct one's attention or looks towards;* video in me omnium vestrum ora atque oculos esse conversos, Cic. ; 3, *to direct one's inclination, mind,* etc., *towards;* omne studium curamque ad hanc scribendi operam, Cic.; reflex., se ad otium pacemque, Cic.; se in or ad aliquem, *to attach oneself to,* Cic. ; 4, *to devote to some object;* rationem in fraudem malitiamque, Cic. ; 5, *to convert, pervert;* alterum (auxilium) ad perniciem meam erat a vobis consulibus conversum, Cic. ; 6, **a,** *to change, alter;* mirum in modum conversae sunt omnium mentes, Caes.; convertere in graves inimicitias convertant se amicitiae, Cic.; Hecubam in canem esse conversam, Cic. ; **b,** librum e Graeco in Latinum, *to translate,* Cic.

convestĭo, 4. *to clothe.* **A.** Lit., Enn. **B.** Transf., *to cover, surround;* domus duobus lucis convestita, Cic.

convexĭtas -ātis, f. (convexus), *convexity;* mundi, Plin.

convexus -a -um (convehor), 1, *vaulted, arched, convex;* orbis lunae, Cic. Subst., **convexum** -i, n., and commonly in plur., **convexa** -orum, n. *an arch;* convexa coeli, Verg. ; 2, *sloping, steep;* iter, Ov.

convĭcĭātor -ōris, m. (convicior), *a railer, slanderer, reviler,* Cic.

convĭcĭor, 1. dep. (convicium), *to rail at, revile, reproach,* Liv.

convĭcĭum -ĭi, n. (= convocium, from com and vox), 1, *a loud cry, shout, clamour;* mulierum, Cic. ; 2, *violent reproach, reviling, insult;* clamore et conviciis et sibilis consectari, Cic. ; alicui convicium facere, Cic. ; non modo acclamatione sed convicio et maledictis impediri, Cic. ; verberavi te cogitationis tacito duntaxat convicio, Cic. ; meton., nemorum convicia, picae, *mocking-birds,* Ov.

convictĭo -ōnis, f. (convivo), *social intercourse, familiarity,* Cic.

convictor -ōris, m. (convivo), *one who lives with another, constant associate,* ap. Cic.

convictus -ūs, m. (convivo), 1, *a living together, constant intercourse;* conventus hominum ac societas, Cic. ; 2, *entertainment, feast,* Tac.

convinco -vīci -victum, 3. 1, *to convict of a crime or mistake;* aliquem summae negligentiae, Cic. ; multis avaritiae criminibus, Cic. ; convictus in hoc scelere, Cic. ; with infin., or acc. and infin., Liv., Sall. ; 2, *to prove conclusively, demonstrate;* errores Epicuri, Cic. ; inauditum facinus ipsius qui commisit voce convinci, Cic. ; with acc. and infin., Stoicos nihil de diis explicare convincit, Cic.

convīso, 3. *to behold attentively, examine;* omnia loca oculis, Cic. ; poet. (of the sun, etc.), *to beam upon,* Lucr.

convītĭātor, v. conviciator.

convītĭor, v. convicior.

convītĭum, v. convicium.

convīva -ae, c. (com and vivo), *a guest;* hilarus et bene acceptus, Cic.

convīvālis -e (convivïam), *relating to a feast* or *banquet,* Liv.

convīvātor -ōris, m. (convivor), *one who gives a feast, a host,* Hor., Liv.

convīvĭum -ĭi, n. (com and vivo). **A.** *a feast, entertainment, banquet;* accipere aliquem convivio, Cic.; adhibere aliquem convivio or in convivium, Cic.; convivium apparare opipare, Cic.; dimittere convivium, Liv.; discedere de convivio, Cic.; inire convivium publicum, Cic.; interesse in convivio, Cic.; producere convivium vario sermone ad multam noctem, Cic.; venire in convivium, Cic. **B.** Meton., *the company assembled, guests;* vinosa convivia, Ov.

convivor, l. dep. (conviva), *to eat and drink in company, feast, revel;* non solum in publico, sed etiam de publico, Cic.

convŏcātĭo -ōnis, f. (convoco), *a calling together;* populi Romani ad rempublicam defendendam, Cic.

convŏco, l. *to call together, assemble, convoke;* dissipatos homines, Cic.; principes ad se, Caes.; ad concionem, Liv.

convolněro, v. convulnero.

convŏlo, l. *to fly together, run together, come together hastily;* cuncta ex Italiā ad aliquem revocandum, Cic.

convolsus, v. convulsus.

convolvo -volvi -vŏlutum, 3. l, *to roll round;* sol se convolvens, Cic.; in lucem lubrica terga, Verg.; 2, *to cover;* testudo convoluta omnibus rebus, quibus ignis jactus et lapides defendi possent, Caes.

convŏmo, l. *to vomit all over,* Cic.

convulněro, l. *to wound severely,* Plin.

convulsus -a -um, partic. of convello.

cŏōlesco = coalesco (q.v.).

cŏōpěrĭo -pěrŭi -pertum, 4. (com and operio), *to cover entirely, envelop;* aliquem lapidibus, *to stone to death,* Cic.; Decii corpus coopertum telis, Liv.; transf., partic., coopertus, *overwhelmed;* flagitiis atque facinoribus, Sall.

cŏōptātĭo -ōnis, f. (coopto), *choice, election, co-optation;* collegiorum, Cic.; censoria, *filling up of the senate by the censors,* Cic.

cŏōpto (com and opto), l. *to choose, elect,* esp. to a public office or dignity, *to coopt;* senatores, Cic.; tres sibi collegas, Liv.; aliquem in paternum auguratus locum, Cic.; aliquem magistrum equitum, Liv.

cŏŏrĭor -ortus sum, 4. *to arise, come forth at once, appear.* **I.** a, of storms, etc., *to break out;* tum subito tempestates sunt coortae maximae, Lucr.; **b**, of fires, quod pluribus simul locis ignes coorti essent, Liv.; **c**, of disease, pestilentia coorta, minacior quam periculosior, Liv.; **d**, of political events, of war, sedition, etc., *to break out;* seditio tum inter Antiates Latinosque coorta, Liv.; **e**, of laughing or weeping, risus, Nep.; libero conquestu coortae voces sunt, Liv. **II.** *to rise for insurrection or fight;* sed adeo infensa erat coorta plebs ut, etc., Liv.; Volscos summa vi ad bellum coortos, Liv.

cŏortus -ūs, m. (coorior), *an arising, breaking forth,* Lucr.

Cŏos (Cŏus) -i, f., and **Cōs** -o, f. (Κόως and Κῶς), *a small island in the Aegean Sea, off the coast of Caria.* Adj., **Cōus** -a -um, *Coan;* poeta, Philetas, Ov.; artifex, Apelles, *whose picture of the Venus Anadyomene was at Coos,* Ov.; Venus, the

5 *

Venus Anadyomene of Apelles, Cic. Subst., **Cōum** -i, n. *Coan wine;* **Cōi** -orum, m. *the inhabitants of Coos;* **Cōa** -orum, n. *Coan garments.*

cōpa -ae, f. *the hostess of a wine-shop,* Verg.

Cōpāis -ĭdis, f. (Κωπαίς), palus, *a lake in Boeotia.*

cōphĭnus -i, m. (κόφινος), *a large basket or hamper,* Juv.

cōpĭa -ae. f. (cŏŏpia, from com and ops), *plenty, abundance.* **I.** Lit., **1**, **a**, of things, agri, vectigalium, pecuniae, Cic.; frumenti, Caes.; copia cum egestate confligit, Cic.; in plur., omnium rerum affluentes copiae, Cic.; milit. t. t., *supplies, provisions;* copias Dyrrhachii comparare, Caes.; **b**, of persons, virorum fortium atque innocentium tanta copia, Cic.; esp. milit. t. t., *troops, forces;* (a) sing., omnis armatorum copia, Cic.; augebatur illis copia, Caes.; (β) plur., copiae peditum equitumque, Liv.; terrestres navalesque, Liv.; copias magnas cogere, Caes.; comparare, Cic.; contrahere, Cic.; dimittere, Caes.; educere castris, e castris, Caes.; **2**, of abstractions, copia dicendi or orationis, *fulness of expression,* Cic. **II.** Transf., *ability, power, opportunity;* est alicui copia somni, Liv.; dimicandi cum hoste, Liv.; ab hoste copia pugnandi fit, Sall.; facere alicui consilii sui copiam, *to be accessible to a person asking one's advice,* Cic.; habere copiam alicuius, *to have some one in one's power,* Sall.

cōpĭōsē, adv. (copiosus), **1**, *abundantly, plentifully;* large et copiose comparare pastum, Cic.; senatorum urna copiose absolvit, *with a large majority,* Cic.; **2**, of discourse, *copiously;* dicere, Cic.

cōpĭōsus -a -um (copia), **1**, *richly provided, wealthy;* urbs celebris et copiosa, Cic.; copiosus a frumento locus, *rich in,* Cic.; opulenti homines et copiosi, Cic.; **2**, *copious of speech, eloquent;* homo copiosus ad dicendum, Cic.; oratio multa et varia et copiosa, Cic.; lingua copiosa, Cic.

cōpis -e = copiosus (q.v.).

cōpo, cōpona = caupo, caupona (q.v.).

cŏprěa (copria) -ae, m. (κοπρίας), *a low buffoon,* Suet.

copta -ae, f. (κόπτη), *a hard cake or biscuit,* Mart.

Coptos -i, f. (Κοπτός), *a town of Upper Egypt,* now *Coft* or *Keft.*

cōpŭla -ae, f. (com and * apio). **A.** *a rope, band, tie;* dura copula canem tenet, a leash, Ov.; plur., copulae, *fastenings, grapnels,* Caes. **B.** Transf., *a bond, connexion;* quos irrupta tenet copula, Hor.

cōpŭlātĭo -ōnis, f. (copula), *a union, connexion;* atomorum inter se, Cic.

cōpŭlātus -a -um, p. adj. (from copulo), *connected, united, coupled;* quaedam sunt in rebus simplicia, quaedam copulata, Cic.; transf., nihil est amabilius neque copulatius quam morum similitudo, *tending to unite,* Cic.

cōpŭlo, l. (copula), *to join together, connect, unite.* **A.** Lit., altera ratis huic copulata est, Liv. **B.** Transf., copulati in jus pervenimus, Cic.; copulare honestatem cum voluptate, Cic.; an haec inter se jungi copularique possint, Cic.; equester ordo qui tum cum senatu copulatus fuit, *were in harmony with,* Cic.

cŏqua -ae, f. (coquus), *a female cook,* Plaut.

cŏquĭno, l. (coquo), *to cook,* Plaut.

cŏquo, coxi, coctum, 3. *to cook, prepare food.* **I.** Lit., **1**, is qui illa coxerat, Cic.; cibaria, Liv.; **2**, *to bake, burn;* coquit glebas aestas matutinis solibus, Verg.; **3**, *to ripen;* poma matura et cocta, Cic.; **4**, *to warm;* calore et spiritu omnia cocta et confecta, Cic. **II.** Transf., **1**, *to think* *of, meditate, contrive ;* consilia secreto ab aliis, Liv.; **2**, *to disturb ;* femineae ardentem curaeque iraeque coquebant, Verg.

cŏquus (cocus) -i, m. (coquo), *a cook,* Cic.

cŏr, cordis, n. (root CORD, Gr. καρδ -ία). **I. A.** Lit., *the heart ;* cor palpitat, Cic. ; fig., a, *the heart as the seat of the feelings, the soul, feeling ;* exsultantia corda, Verg. ; cordi est aliquis or aliquid, *is dear to ;* quum audirem eam (sponsam) tibi cordi esse, Liv. ; idque eo mihi magis est cordi quod, etc., Cic. ; with acc. and infin., Liv.; b, *the heart as the seat of thought, the mind, judgment ;* qui propter haesitantiam linguae stuporemque cordis cognomen ex contumeliâ traxerit, Cic. **B.** Meton., *a person ;* lecti juvenes, fortissima corda, Verg. **II.** Transf., *the stomach,* Hor., Lucr.

Cŏra -ae, f. (Κόρα), *an old town in Latium,* now *Core* or *Cori.* Adj., **Cŏrānus** -a -um.

cŏrallĭum -ĭi, n. (κοράλλιον), *red coral,* Lucr.

cŏram (com and os, oris). **I.** Adv., **1**, *in presence oj, in face of, before ;* commodius fecissent, si quae apud vos de me deferunt, ea coram potius me praesente dixissent, Cic. ; **2**, *personally, in one's own person, oneself ;* intueri aliquid, *to behold with one's own eyes,* Cic.; agere, *to transact personally,* i.e., *not by letters,* Cic. ; quum coram sumus, *personally present,* Cic. **II.** Prep. with abl., *in presence of ;* genero meo, Cic. ; populo, Hor.

Corbĭo -ōnis, f. **1**, *a town of the Aequi ;* **2**, *a town in Hispania Tarraconensis.*

corbis -is, m. and f. *a wicker basket ;* messoria, Cic.

corbīta -ae, f. *a slow-sailing merchant vessel,* Cic.

corbŭla -ae, f. (dim. of corbis), *a little basket,* Plaut.

corcŭlum -i, n. (dim. of cor), *a little heart,* used as a term of endearment, Plaut.

Corcŷra -ae, f. (Κόρκυρα), *Corcyra, an island in the Ionian Sea,* identified with the Homeric Scheria, the home of Alcinous, now *Corfu ;* hence adj., **Corcŷraeus** -a -um, *Corcyraean ;* horti, *the gardens of Alcinous,* Mart.

cordātē, adv. (cordatus), *wisely, prudently,* Plaut.

cordātus -a -um (cor), *prudent, sagacious, wise,* Sen.

cordax -dācis (κόρδαξ), *a licentious dance,* Petr.; transf. of the trochaic rhythm, Cic.

cordŏlĭum -ĭi, n. (cor and doleo), *heartache,* Plaut.

Cordŭba -ae, f. *a town in Hispania Boetica,* now *Cordova.* Adj., **Cordŭbensis** -e.

cordŷla -ae, f. (κορδύλη), *the fry of the tunny fish,* Mart.

Corfīnĭum -ĭi, n. *a town of the Peligni in Samnium.* Adj., **Corfīnĭensis** -e, *Corfinian.*

Cŏrinna -ae, f. (Κόριννα), **1**, *a Greek poetess of Tanagra, contemporary with Pindar ;* **2**, *the feigned name of Ovid's mistress.*

Cŏrinthus -i, f. (Κόρινθος), *Corinth, a city of Greece on the Isthmus of Corinth.* Hence, **A.** Adj., **Cŏrinthĭus** -a -um, *Corinthian ;* aes, *a mixed metal of gold, silver, and copper,* greatly prized by the ancients, Cic. ; vasa, supellex, *made of Corinthian brass,* Cic. ; and absol., **Cŏrinthĭa** -orum, n. (sc. vasa), Cic. **B.** **Cŏrinthĭārĭus** -ĭi, m. *an artificer in Corinthian brass, a nickname of Augustus,* Suet. **C.** **Cŏrinthĭācus** -a -um, *Corinthian.* **D.** **Cŏrinthĭensis** -e, *Corinthian.*

Cŏrĭōli -ōrum, m. *a town of the Volsci in* *Latium.* Adj., **Cŏrĭōlānus** -a -um, *belonging to Corioli ;* Coriolanus, Cn. Marcius, *the capturer of Corioli ;* **Cŏrĭōlāni** -orum, m. *the inhabitants of Corioli.*

cŏrĭum (cŏrĭus) -ĭi, n. (χόριον), **1**, *hide, skin, leather ;* animantium aliae coriis tectae sunt, Cic.; petere corium, *to thrash,* Cic. ; prov., canis a corio nunquam absterrebitur uncto, *it is difficult to change a confirmed habit,* Hor. ; **2**, *a leathern thong, strap, lash,* Plaut.

Cornēlĭus -a -um, *name of a Roman gens, the most famous members of which were,* **1**, P. Corn. Scipio Africanus major, the conqueror of Hannibal ; **2**, P. Corn. Scipio Aemilianus Africanus minor, son of L. Aemilius Paulus, adopted by P. Corn. Scipio (son of Africanus major), the destroyer of Carthage ; **3**, Cornelia, the youngest daughter of Africanus major, wife of Tib. Sempronius Gracchus, the mother of the Gracchi ; **4**, Cornelia, the daughter of Qu. Metellus Scipio, wife first of P. Licin. Crassus, afterwards of Pompeius. Adj., **Cornēlĭānus** -a -um, *Cornelian.*

Cornēlĭus Nĕpos, v. Nepos.

cornĕŏlus -a -um (dim. of 1. corneus), *horny,* Cic.

1. **cornĕus** -a -um (cornu), **1**, *horny, made of horn ;* rostrum, Cic. ; **2**, a, *like horn, hard ;* cornea fibra, Pers. ; b, *horn-coloured,* Plin.

2. **cornĕus** -a -um (cornus), *relating or belonging to the cornel tree ;* virgulta, Verg.

cornĭcen -cĭnis, m. (cornu and cano), *a horn-blower,* Cic.

cornĭcor, 1. dep. (cornix), *to caw like a crow,* Pers.

cornĭcŭla -ae, f. (dim. of cornix), *a little crow,* Hor.

cornĭcŭlārĭus -ĭi, m. (corniculum), *a soldier who has been presented with the corniculum, an adjutant,* Suet.

1. **cornĭcŭlum** -i, n. (dim. of cornu), **1**, *a little horn,* Plin. ; **2**, *an ornament on the helmet given to deserving soldiers,* Liv.

2. **Cornĭcŭlum** -i, n. *a town in Latium.* Adj., **Cornĭcŭlānus** -a -um, *Corniculan.*

cornĭger -gĕra -gĕrum (cornu and gero), *horned,* Cic. Subst., **cornĭgera** -orum, n. *horned cattle,* Plin.

cornĭpēs -pĕdis (cornu and pes), *horn-footed, hoofed ;* equi, Verg.

cornix -īcis, f. (root COR, whence κορώνη), *crow ;* corvus, curvus, *crooked), the crow ;* natura cervis et cornicibus vitam diuturnam dedit, Cic. ; garrula, Ov. ; annosa, Hor. ; prov., cornicum oculos configere, and ellipt., qui cornici oculum, ut dicitur, *to deceive the sagacious,* Cic.

cornū -ūs and (rarely) -ū, n. (κέρας). **I.** Lit., **1**, *the horn of animals,* of the bull, ram, goat, stag, etc., Cic. ; Cornu Copiae (Cornucopia), *the horn of the goat Amalthea, the sign of plenty,* Hor. ; cornu, poet. for *strength, courage ;* tollere cornua in aliquem, Hor. ; cornua sumere, *gain courage,* Ov. ; **2**, a, *of things of similar material, a hoof,* Verg. ; *a beak of a bird,* Ov. ; b, *of things resembling a horn in shape, the elephant's tusk,* Varr. ; c, *of things made of horn, a bow,* Verg. ; *a large curved trumpet,* or *horn,* Cic. ; *a lantern,* Plaut. ; *an oil cruet,* Hor. ; *a funnel,* Verg. **II.** Transf., **A.** The horn as the point or end of anything, *the top of the helmet,* Verg. ; *the ends of the sail-yards,* Verg. ; *the ends of the staff round which parchments were rolled,* Ov. ; *the horns of the moon,* Cic. ; *the arm of a river,* Ov. ; *the end of a promontory,* Liv. ; *the corner or extremity of a country,* Liv. ; *the wing of an army,* dextrum, sinistrum, Caes. **B.** *a growth like a horn, a large wart on the head,* Hor. (acc. cornum, Ov.).

Cornūcōpĭa -ae, v. cornu

cornum -i, n. (cornus), **1**, *the fruit of the cornel*, Verg. ; **2**, *the wood of the cornel-tree;* meton. *a spear made of cornel-wood*, Ov.

cornus -i, and -ūs, f. (cornu), lit. *the horn-tree ;* **1**, *the cornel-tree* (cornus mascula, Linn.), so called from the toughness of its wood ; **2**, *the wood of the cornel-tree* and meton. *a javelin made of cornel-wood*, Ov.

cornūtus -a -um (cornu), *horned;* aves, Ov.

cŏrolla -ae, f. (dim. of corona), *a little crown*, Cat.

Cŏroebus -i, m. *a Phrygian, son of Mygdon.*

cŏrollārĭum -ĭi, n. (corolla), originally, *a garland of flowers*, then, *a garland of gilt or silvered flowers given away to actors*, etc., Varr. ; hence, *a present, douceur, gratuity*, Cic.

cŏrōna -ae, f. (κορώνη). **I.** Lit. *a wreath, garland, chaplet, crown*, Cic. ; castrensis, triumphalis, navalis, civica, obsidionalis, muralis, navalis, Cic. ; sub coronâ vendere, *to sell into slavery prisoners of war* who wore chaplets, Cic. ; also, sub coronâ venire, Liv. ; regni corona, *a diadem*, Verg. **II.** Transf., **1**, *a constellation, the northern crown*, Cic. ; **2**, *a circle, assembly of men*, Cic. ; milit. t.t. *the besiegers of a city;* (urbem) coronâ cingere, *to invest*, Caes. ; or, *the defenders of a city*, or *place;* coronâ vallum defendere, Liv. ; **3**, *the halo round the sun*, Sen.

cŏrōnārĭus -a -um (corona), *relating to a garland*, Plin. ; aurum, originally, *the golden crown sent by the provinces to a victorious general*, afterwards changed to *a sum of money*, Cic.

Cŏrōnē -ēs, f. (Κορώνη), *a town in Messenia.* Adj., **Cŏrōnaeus** -a -um, *Coronaean.*

Cŏrōnēa -ae, f. (Κορώνεια), *a town in Boeotia.* Adj., **Cŏrōnaeus** -a -um, *Coronaean.*

Cŏrōneus -ĕi, m. *king in Phocis, father of Corone.*

Cŏrōnis -ĭdis, f. (Κορωνίς), *daughter of Phlegyas, mother of Aesculapius;* hence **Cŏrōnĭdes** -ae, m. *Aesculapius.*

cŏrōno, 1. (corona). **I.** Lit. *to wreathe, crown with a garland;* aras, Prop. ; puppim, Ov. ; cratera, Verg. ; sequebantur epulae, quas inibant propinqui coronati, Cic. ; quis magna coronari contemnat Olympia, *to be crowned as conqueror at the Olympic games*, Hor. **II.** Transf. *to surround, enclose in the form of a circle;* coronant myrteta summum lacum, Ov. ; omnem abitum custode, Verg.

corpŏrālis -e (corpus), *relating to the body, corporeal*, Sen.

corpŏrĕus -a -um (corpus), **1**, *relating to the body, corporeal;* ille corporeus (ignis), Cic. ; **2**, *fleshy, consisting of flesh;* humerus, Ov.

corpŏro, 1. (corpus), *to form into a body, provide with a body;* mundus corporatus, Cic.

corpŭlentĭa -ae, f. (corpulentus), *fatness, corpulence*, Plin.

corpŭlentus -a -um, adj. with compar. (corpus), *fat, stout, corpulent*, Plaut.

corpus -pŏris, n. (root COR, as in cortex). **I.** Lit. **A.** Gen. **1**, *a body, substance* (opp. animus, anima), *the body of men and animals;* animi voluptates et dolores nasci e corporibus voluptatibus et doloribus, Cic. ; hence, *a person;* delecta virum corpora, Verg. ; unum vile atque infame corpus, Liv. ; **2**, *a lifeless substance, mass;* individua corpora, *the atoms*, Cic. **B.** Esp. **1**, *flesh;* ossa subjecta corpori, Cic. ; corpus amittere, *to lose flesh*, Cic. ; abiit corpusque colorque, Ov. ; **2**, *a corpse;* poet. *of the souls of the dead*, Verg. ; **3**, *the trunk*, Ov. **II.** Transf. *any whole like a body;* **1**, *the framework of a ship*, Caes. ;

2, *the "body politic;"* totum corpus reipublicae, Cic. ; **3**, *any whole, collection, mass;* a, of military works, Caes. ; b, of the world, universitatis corpus, Cic. ; c, of a book, corpus omnis juris Romani, Liv. ; d, *a collection of persons;* (α) of the state, eiusdem corporis, Liv. ; corpus nullum civitatis, Liv. ; (β) of a corporation, *a political union*, Liv.

corpuscŭlum -i, n. (dim. of corpus), *a little body, corpuscle, atom*, Cic.

corrādo -rāsi -rāsum, 3. (com and rado), *to scrape* or *rake together.* **A.** Lit., Lucr. **B.** Transf. *to scrape together money*, Plaut.

correctĭo -ōnis, f. (corrigo), **1**, *improvement, amendment;* correctio philosophiae veteris et emendatio, Cic. ; **2**, in rhet., *a figure of speech, in which an expression already used is replaced by a stronger one* (Gr. ἐπανόρθωσις), Cic.

corrector -ōris, m. (corrigo), *an improver, amender, corrector;* corrector atque emendator nostrae civitatis, Cic. ; emendator et corrector noster, Cic.

correpo -repsi -reptum, 3. (com and repo), *to creep or crawl together, to slink in;* in onerariam (navem), Cic. ; quoi non correpunt membra pavore, *whose limbs do not shrink with fear ?* Lucr.

correptē, adv. with compar. (correptus, from corripio), *shortly;* correptius exit syllaba, Ov.

corrīdĕo, 2. (com and rideo), *to laugh together, laugh loudly*, Lucr.

corrĭgĭa -ae, f. *a shoe-string, boot-lace*, Cic.

corrĭgo -rexi -rectum (com and rego), *to make straight, reduce to order, set right.* **I.** Gen. inde aegre cursum, Liv. **II.** a, *to correct, improve, amend;* praeterita magis reprehendi possunt quam corrigi, Liv. ; mores, Cic. ; alicuius sententiam, Cic. ; non modo superiores sed etiam se ipse correxerat, Cic. ; b, *of writing, to correct;* eas epistolas ego oportet perspiciam, corrigam, Cic. ; laudationem Porciae tibi correctam misi, Cic.

corrĭpĭo -rĭpŭi -reptum, 3. (com and rapio). **I.** *to seize violently, lay hold of, take up.* **A.** Lit., hominem corripi jussit, Cic. ; arcumque manu celeresque sagittas, Verg. ; se corripere, *to hasten away*, Verg. ; corpus corripere, *to start up*, Verg. **B.** Transf., a, *to plunder, carry off;* pecuniam, Cic. ; b, *to accuse, bring to trial;* statim corripit reum, Tac. ; c, *to blame, rebuke;* consules, Liv. ; voce magistri corripi, Hor. ; d, *of disease*, etc. *to attack;* nec singula morbi corpora corripiunt, Verg. ; e, of the passions, *to overcome;* visae correptus imagine formae, Ov. **II.** *to gather together;* **1**, of motion, *to hasten;* tarda necessitas teli corripuit gradum, Hor. ; viam, *to hasten over*, Verg. ; campum, Verg. ; **2**, of time, *to shorten;* numina corripiant moras, Ov.

corrōbŏro, 1. (com and roboro). **A.** Lit. *to strengthen, invigorate;* se corroborare, *to gain strength;* quum is se corroboravisset et vir inter viros esset, Cic. **B.** Transf., conjurationem non credendo corroborare, Cic.

corrōdo -rōsi -rōsum, 3. (com and rodo), *to gnaw away;* Platonis Politiam nuper apud me mures corroserunt, Cic.

corrōgo, 1. (com and rogo), *to bring together, collect by begging;* nummulos de nepotum donis, Cic. ; auxilia ab sociis, Liv.

corrūgo, 1. (com and rugo) *to wrinkle up ; ne sordida mappa corruget nares, make you turn up your nose in disgust*, Hor.

corrumpo -rūpi -ruptum, 3. **I.** *to destroy, annihilate;* sua frumenta corrumpere et aedificia incendere, Caes. ; vineas igni et lapidibus,

Sall.; res familiares, Sall.; libertatem, Tac.; multo dolore corrupta voluptas, Hor. **II.** *to spoil, mar, make worse, deteriorate;* **a**, physically, conclusa aqua facile corrumpitur, Cic.; Ceres corrupta undis, *corn spoiled by sea-water*, Verg.; of animals and men, *to weaken;* corrupti equi macie, Caes.; **b**, of pronunciation, *to corrupt;* nomen eorum paulatim Libyes corrupere, barbarā linguā Mauros pro Medis appellantes, Sall.; **c**, of writings, etc., *to falsify;* tabulas publicas municipii manu sua corrumpere, Cic.; **d**, morally, *to corrupt;* mores civitatis, Cic.; huius urbis jura et exempla corrumpere, Cic.; milites soluto imperio licentia atque lascivia corruperat, Sall.; corrumpere aliquem pecunia, *to bribe*, Cic.

corrŭo -rŭi, 3. (com and ruo). **I.** Intransit., *to fall to the ground, fall together, sink down.* **A.** Lit., **a**, corruerunt aedes, Cic.; conclave illud proxima nocte corruit, Cic.; **b**, of persons, paene ille timore, ego risu corrui, Cic.; esp., *to fall in battle;* ubi vero corruit telis obrutus, Liv. **B.** Transf., illa plaga pestifera qua Lacedaemoniorum opes corruerunt, Cic.; of persons, *to be ruined;* si uno meo fato et tu et omnes mei corruistis, Cic. **II.** Transit., *to throw down, overthrow;* hanc rerum summam, Lucr.

corruptē, adv. with compar. and superl. (corruptus) *corruptly, incorrectly;* neque depravate judicare neque corrupte, Cic.

corruptēla -ae, f. (corruptus), *the means of corruption, corruption, bribery, seduction;* mores hac dulcedine corruptelaque depravati, Cic.; pecuniosi rei corruptelam judicii molientes, Cic.

corruptĭo -ōnis, f. (corrumpo), *corruption, a corrupting;* corporis, Cic.; opinionum, Cic.

corruptŏr -ōris, m. (corrumpo), *a corrupter, seducer, briber;* juventutis, Cic.; tribus, *briber*, Cic.; exercitus, Liv.

corruptrix -īcis, f. (fem. of corruptor), *one that corrupts* or *seduces;* attrib. = *corrupting;* tam corruptrice provinciā, Cic.

corruptus -a -um, p. adj. with compar. and superl. (corrumpo), *spoiled, damaged, corrupted, corrupt.* **I.** Lit., physically, hordeum, Caes. **II.** Transf., morally, civitas, Sall.; judicia, Cic.; adulescentulus, Cic.

cors = cohors (q.v.).

Corsĭca -ae, f. *the island of Corsica in the Mediterranean Sea.* Adj., **Corsus** -a -um, and **Corsĭcus** -a -um, *Corsican.*

cortex -tĭcis, m. and f. *bark, rind, shell;* **a**, *the bark of trees;* obducuntur libro aut cortice trunci (liber = *the inner bark*), Cic.; **b**, esp., *the bark of the cork tree, cork*, Hor.; prov., nare sine cortice, *to swim without corks,* i.e., *to need no assistance*, Hor.; levior cortice, Hor.

cortīna -ae, f. **1**, *a round kettle* or *caldron*, Plaut.; esp. *the caldron-shaped Delphic tripod;* cortina Phoebi, *the oracle of Apollo*, Verg.; **2**, *anything in the shape of a caldron, a circle of hearers*, Tac.

Cortōna -ae, f. (Κόρτωνα), *Cortona, a town of Etruria.* Adj., **Cortōnensis** -e, *of* or *belonging to Cortona.*

cŏrŭlus = corylus (q.v.).

cŏrus = caurus (q.v.).

cŏrusco, 1. (connected with κορύσσω). **I.** *to butt with the horns*, Cic. **II. A.** Transit., *to move quickly, shake;* telum, Verg.; of snakes, linguas, Ov. **B.** Intransit., **a**, coruscant (apes) pennis, *flutter*, Verg.; coruscat abies, Juv.; **b**, *to shine, flash, glitter;* apes fulgore coruscant, Verg.

cŏruscus -a -um (corusco), **1**, *shaking, trembling;* silvae, Verg.; **2**, *gleaming, flashing;*

fulgura, Lucr.; sol, Verg.; juvenes auro corusci, Verg.

1. corvus -i, m. (κόραξ), *a raven*, Cic.; prov. in cruce corvos pascere, *to be food for the crows, to be crucified*, Hor.

2. Corvus -i, m. *a surname of a family of the* gens Valeria, Cic.

Cŏrўbās -bantis, m. (Κορύβας), gen. in plur., **Cŏrўbantes** -ium, m. *priests of Cybele.* Adj., **Cŏrўbantĭus** -a -um, *Corybantian.*

Cŏrўcĭdes, nymphae, (Κωρυκίδες), *daughter of Plistus.*

1. Cŏrўcĭus -a -um (Κωρύκιος), *belonging to the Corycian caves on Mount Parnassus.*

2. Cŏrўcĭus -a -um, v. Corycos, 1.

1. Cŏrўcos or **-us** -i, f. (Κώρυκος), **1**, *a mountain and city of Cilicia, celebrated for a cave and the cultivation of saffron;* hence adj., **Cŏrўcĭus** -a -um, *Corycian;* crocum, Hor.; senex, *Cilician*, Verg.; **2**, *a promontory on the coast of Ionia.*

2. cŏrўcus -i, m. (κώρυκος), *a sand-bag in the palaestra, which the athletes struck to exercise their strength;* fig., corycus laterum et vocis meae, Bestia, Cic.

cŏrўlētum -i, n. (corylus), *a hazel copse*, Ov.

cŏrўlus -i, f. (*κόρυλος), a hazel tree*, Verg., Ov.

cŏrymbĭfĕr -fĕra -fĕrum (corymbus and fero), *carrying bunches of ivy berries*, epithet of Bacchus, Ov.

cŏrymbus -i, m. (κόρυμβος), *a bunch of flowers* or *fruit*, esp. *a cluster of ivy berries*, Verg.

cŏrўphaeus -i, m. (κορυφαῖος), *the leader, chief, head;* Epicureorum Zeno, Cic.

Cŏrўthus -i (Κόρυθος), **1**, f. *a town in Etruria*, afterwards Cortona; **2**, m. *the legendary founder of Corythus.*

cŏrўtus -i, m. (γωρυτός), *a quiver*, Verg.

1. cōs, cōtis, f. *any hard, flinty stone*, Cic.; esp. *a whetstone, grindstone*, Hor., Cic.

2. Cōs, v. Coos.

Cōsa (**Cossa**) -ae, f. (Κόσσα) and **Cossae** -ārum, f. (Κόσσαι), **1**, *a town in Etruria.* Adj., **Cōsānus** -a -um, *Cosan;* **2**, *a town in Lucania.*

cosmētēs -ae, m. (κοσμήτης), *the slave who had charge of his mistress's wardrobe and toilet*, Juv.

cosmĭcos -ŏn (κοσμικός), *belonging to the world.* Subst., *a citizen of the world*, Mart.

Cossўra (**Cōsўra**) and **Cossūra** (**Cōsūra**) -ae, f. (Κόσσυρα), *a small island between Sicily and Africa*, now *Pantalaria.*

costa -ae, f. **1**, *a rib*, Verg.; **2**, *a side;* aeni, Verg.

costum -i, n. (κόστος), *an eastern aromatic plant*, employed in the preparation of unguents, Hor.

Cōsūra and **Cōsўra** = Cossyra (q.v.).

cŏthurnātus -a -um (cothurnus), *provided with a buskin*, hence *sublime, tragic;* deae, Ov.

cŏthurnus -i, m. (κόθορνος). **I.** *a large hunting boot, reaching to the calf, and laced up the front*, Verg. **II.** *the thick-soled boot worn by tragic actors.* **A.** Lit., cothurnus tragicus, Hor.; cothurnus major, minor, Cic. **B.** Transf., **a**, *tragedy*, Hor.; **b**, *a tragic, elevated style;* sola Sophocleo tua carmina digna cothurno, Verg.

cotidianus, cotidie = quotidianus etc (q.v.).

Cōtōnĕus, v. Cydonea.

Cotta -ae, m. *a cognomen of a family of the* gens Aurelia, Cic.

cottăbus -i, m. (κότταβος), *a game played by throwing heeltaps of wine into a brazen basin;* hence, from the similarity of sound, *the crack of a whip,* Plaut.

cottăna (cotŏna, coctŏna, coctăna) -ōrum, n. (κόττανα), *a kind of small Syrian fig,* Juv.

Cottius -ii, m. *name of the kings of two Ligurian peoples in the Cottian Alps,* so called after them. Adj., **Cottiānus** -a -um, *Cottian.*

cŏtŭla or **cŏtўla** -ae, f. (κοτύλη), *a measure of capacity, half a sextarius,* Mart.

cŏturnix -icis, f. *a quail,* Ov.

Cŏtўs -tўis, acc. -tyn, voc. -tў, abl. tўe, m. (Κότυς), **1,** *name of several Thracian princes;* **2,** *brother of Mithridates, prince of the Bosporus.*

Cŏtyttŏ -ūs, f. (Κοτυττώ), *the goddess of unchastity, originally worshipped in Thrace, afterwards in Athens and Corinth also.* **Cŏtyttĭa** -ōrum, n. *the festival of Cotytto,* Hor.

cŏvīnārĭus and **cŏvinnārĭus** -ii, m. *one who fights from a war chariot,* Tac.

cŏvīnus (cŏvinnus), i., m. (a Celtic word), **1,** *the war-chariot of the ancient Britons and Belgians,* Luc.; **2,** *a travelling-chariot,* Mart.

cŏxa -ae, f. *the hip-bone,* Plin.

coxendix -icis, f. (coxa), *the hip, the hipbone,* Plin.

Crabra or **Aqua Crabra,** *a small river near Tusculum.*

crabro -ōnis, m. *a hornet,* Verg.

Crăgus -i., m. (Κράγος), *a promontory of Lycia.*

crambē -ēs, f. (κράμβη), *cabbage,* Plin.; crambe repetita, *cold cabbage warmed up,* i.e. *stale repetitions,* Juv.

Crănōn (Crannōn) -ōnis, f. (Κρανών, or Κραννών), *a town in Thessaly.* Adj. **Crănōnĭus** (Κρανώνιος) -a -um, *Cranonian.*

Crantor -ōris, m. **I.** Myth., *the armourbearer of Peleus.* **II.** Hist., *a philosopher of the old Academy.*

Cranĭi -ōrum, m. *a town on the island of Cephallenia.*

crāpŭla -ae, f. (κραιπάλη), *intoxication, drunkenness, drunken revel;* crapulam edormire et exhalare, Cic.

cras, adv., **1,** *to-morrow;* scies igitur fortasse cras, Cic.; subst., cras istud, quando venit, Mart.; **2,** *in the future;* quod sit futurum cras, fuge quaerere, Hor.

crassē, adv., with compar. (crassus), *grossly, rudely, roughly;* crasse compositum poema, Hor.

crassĭtūdo -inis, f. (crassus), *thickness;* parietum, Caes.; aëris, *density,* Cic.

1. crassus -a -um, *thick, dense, solid.* **A.** Lit., unguentum, Hor.; aër, *misty,* Cic.; filum, Cic.; toga, *coarse-grained,* Hor.; ager, *fruitful,* Cic. **B.** Transf., Ofellus rusticus crassâ Minervâ, *of sound common sense,* Hor.; turba, *rude, uncultivated,* Mart.

2. Crassus -i, m. *name of a family of the gens Licinia* (q.v.).

crastīnus -a -um (cras), *relating to to-morrow;* dies crastinus, Cic.; die crastinâ, *to-morrow,* Liv. Subst., **crastīnum** -i, n. *the morrow;* in crastinum differre aliquid, Cic.

Crătaeis -idis, f. (Κραταιίς), *mother of Scylla, a nymph.*

crātēr -ēris, m. (κρατήρ) = cratera (q.v.).

crātēra -ae, f. **I.** Lit., *a large bowl in which wine was mixed with water,* Cic. **II.**

Transf., **1,** *an oil-cruet,* Verg.; **2,** *the crater of a volcano,* Lucr., or *a volcanic fissure in the earth,* Ov.; **3,** *a constellation, the cup,* Ov.

Crătērus -i, m. (Κρατερός), **1,** *a general of Alexander the Great;* **2,** *a celebrated physician in the time of Cicero;* appellat. = *a skilled physician,* Hor.

Crāthis -thidis, m. (Κράθις), *a river near Thurii, between Lucania and Bruttium,* now *Crati.*

Crătīnus -i, m. (Κρατῖνος), *an Athenian comic poet, contemporary of Aristophanes.*

Crătippus -i, m. (Κράτιππος), *a peripatetic philosopher of Athens, teacher of Cicero's son.*

crātis -is. **A.** Lit. *a frame or basket made of hurdles;* also, *a harrow,* Verg.; milit. t.t, *fascines,* Caes.; sub crate necari, *an old method of capital punishment, by which the accused was placed under a hurdle, and pressed to death with great stones,* Liv. **B.** Transf., favorum, *honeycomb,* Verg.; spinae, *the joints of the backbone,* Ov.

crĕātĭo -ōnis, f. (creo), *choice, election,* magistratuum, Cic.

crĕātor -ōris, m. (creo), *the creator, maker, founder;* huius urbis Romulus creator, Cic.; *father,* Ov.

crĕātrix -icis, f. (creator), *she who brings forth or produces, a mother;* natura rerum, Lucr.; diva, Verg.

crēber -bra -brum, adj. with compar. and superl. (root CRE, whence creo, cresco). **I.** Of space, *thick, crowded together, close, pressed together;* a, creberrima aedificia, Caes.; creberrima grando, Liv.; crebri ignes, Sall.; b, *thick with, full of;* with abl., creber arundinibus lacus, Ov.; qui (Thucydides), ita creber est rerum frequentiâ, Cic. **II.** Of time, *repeated, numerous, frequent;* a, crebra inter se colloquia habere, Caes.; crebri ictus, Verg.; creberrimus sermo, Cic.; b, creber pulsat, *he beats repeatedly,* Verg.; Africus creber procellis, *abounding in,* Verg.; in scribendo multo essem crebrior quam tu, Cic.

crēbresco (crēbesco), -brŭi (-brŭi), 3. (creber), *to become frequent, increase, gather strength, extend;* seditio crebrescens, Tac.; horror, Verg.; crebrescunt optatae aurae, Verg.; crebrescit vivere Agrippam, *the report is spread abroad that,* etc., Tac.

crēbrĭtas -ātis, f. (creber), *thickness, closeness, frequency;* sententiarum, Cic.; officiorum, Cic.

crēbro, adv., with compar. crebrius and superl. creberrime (creber), *repeatedly, frequently, very often;* ad aliquem crebrius litteras mittere, Cic.; crebro respicere Romam, Ov.

crēdĭbĭlis -e, adj. with compar. (credo), *credible, worthy of belief;* narrationes credibiles sint, Cic.; credibile est (fit, videtur), followed by acc. and infin., ita fit credibile deorum et hominum causâ factum esse mundum, Cic.; vix credibile est, Hor.

crēdĭbĭlĭter, adv. with compar. (credibilis), *credibly,* Cic.

crēdĭtor -ōris, m. (credo), *a creditor;* tabulae creditoris, Cic.; fraudare creditores.

crēdĭtum -i, n. (credo), *a loan,* Sall.

crēdo -didi -ditum, 3. **I.** *to trust;* **1,** *to confide, trust in, rely upon, place confidence in;* with dat. of person, credere eorum nemini, Cic.; with dat. of thing, praesenti fortunae non credere, Liv.; **2,** *to believe, give credence to;* his auctoribus temere credens, Caes.; often parenthetic, mihi crede or crede mihi, *believe me, take my advice;* venies, mihi crede, exspectatus, Cic.; with dat. of thing, fabulis, Cic.; lacrimis, Ov.; somniis

Cic.; with de, non credis de numero militum, Cic. II. *to trust*, in relation to something; 1, *to entrust, commit, trust something to some one;* a, arma militi, Liv.; alicui res omnes, Cic.; se perfidis hostibus, Ov.; aciem campo, Verg.; b, *to entrust to the secrecy of some one;* alicui arcanos sensus, Verg.; c, *to lend;* alicui pecuniam, Cic.; absol., *to lend;* credendi modum constituere, Cic.; often in partic. perf., pecunia credita or res creditae, *loans,* Cic.; 2, *to believe something;* a, *to be convinced of as true;* fere libenter homines id quod volunt credunt, Caes.; esp. parenthetic, quod quidem magis credo, Cic.; with acc. and infin., Caes., Cic., or relative sentence, lior.; b, *to think, to be of the opinion;* with acc. and infin., credo ego vos, judices, mirari, Cic.; moesti (crederes victos) redeunt in castra, *you would think,* Liv.; in pass., with nom and infin., pro certo creditur necato filio vacuam domum scelestis nuptiis fecisse, Sall.; with acc. and infin., quorum neminem nisi juvante deo talem fuisse credendum est, Cic.; parenthetic, credo, *I believe, I think;* male, credo, mererer de meis civibus, si, etc., Cic.

crēdŭlĭtas -ātis, f. (credulus), *credulity;* ap. Cic.

crēdŭlus -a -um (credo). **A.** Act. *believing easily, credulous, confiding;* alicui, Verg.; in aliquid, Ov.; stultus et credulus auditor, Cic. **B.** Pass. *easily believed,* fama, Tac.

Crĕmēra -ae, m. *a river in Etruria, near which 300 Fabii were killed.* Adj., **Crĕmērensis** -e.

crĕmo, 1. *to burn, consume by fire;* a, libros in conspectu populi, Liv.; regalia tecta, Ov.; b, esp., of the burning of the bodies of the dead, Sulla primus e patriciis Corneliis igni voluit cremari, Cic.; corpus alicuius, Cic.; c, of sacrifices, crematos igni vitulos, Ov.

Crĕmōna -ae, f. *Cremona, a town in N. Italy.* Adj., **Crĕmōnensis,** -e, *of Cremona.*

Crĕmōnis jugum, *a mountain range in the Pennine Alps.*

crĕmor -ōris, m. *the thick juice obtained from animal or vegetable substances, pulp, cream,* etc., Ov.

1. **crĕo,** 1. (root CER, CRE, whence cresco), *to make, create, produce.* **I.** Gen., a, omnes res quas et creat natura et tuetur, Cic.; alicui periculum, Cic.; b, *to beget a child,* Cic.; pass. partic., creatus with abl., of father or mother = *daughter* or *son,* Telamone creatus, Ov. **II.** a, *to institute an office or magistracy;* tribuniciam potestatem, Liv.; b, *to elect a magistrate or priest;* consules, Cic.; with double acc., Ancum Marcium regem populus creavit, Liv.

2. **Crĕo** -ōnis, and **Crĕōn** -ontis, m. *king of Corinth, whose daughter Creusa was betrothed to Jason.*

crĕper -pĕra -pĕrum (Sabine word connected with κνέφας), *dark, obscure, uncertain,* Lucr.

crĕpīda -ae, f. (κρηπίς), *a sandal,* Cic.; prov. ne sutor ultra crepidam, *shoemaker, stick to your last,* Plin.

crĕpīdātus -a -um (crepida), *wearing sandals,* Cic.

crĕpīdo -ĭnis, f. (κρηπίς), 1, *a base, foundation, pedestal,* Cic.; 2, *a quay, pier,* Cic.

crĕpītācillum -i, n. (dim. of crepitaculum), *a little rattle,* Lucr.

crĕpītācŭlum -i, n. (crepito), *a rattle,* Quint.

crĕpīto, 1. (freq. of crepo), *to rattle, creak, crackle, rustle, clatter;* crepitantia arma, Ov.; lenis crepitans auster, *rustling,* Verg.; multā grandine nimbi culminibus crepitant, Verg.

crĕpītus -ūs, m. (crepo), *a rattling, creaking, rustling, clattering;* digitorum, *snapping the*

fingers, Mart.; pedum, Cic.; dentium, Cic.; aeris, Liv.; viridis materiae flagrantis, Liv.; alarum, Liv.

crĕpo -pŭi -pĭtum, 1. **I.** Intransit., *to creak, rattle, rustle, crackle;* digiti crepantis signa, *a snapping of the fingers to call a servant's attention,* Mart.; acuto in murice remi obnixi crepuere, *crashed,* Verg.; crepat in mediis laurus adusta foris, *crackle,* Ov. **II.** Transit. a, *to cause to resound, rattle;* quum populus frequens laetum theatris ter crepuit sonum, Hor.; *to talk much of, chatter about, prate about;* sulcos, Hor.; b, immunda ignominiosaque verba, Hor.; post vina gravem militiam aut pauperiem, Hor.

crĕpundĭa -ōrum, n. (crepo), *child's playthings, rattle;* naevo aliquo aut crepundiis aliquem cognoscere, Cic.

crĕpuscŭlum -i, n. (creper), *twilight.* **I.** Gen., dubiae crepuscula lucis, Ov. **II.** Esp., *evening twilight;* inducunt obscura crepuscula noctem, Ov.

Crēs -ētis, m., v. 1. Creta.

cresco, crēvi, crētum, 3. (inchoat. from root CER, whence creo, creare). **I.** *to grow up, spring forth, arise;* quaecunque e terrā corpora crescunt, Lucr.; crescentes segetes, Ov.; in past partic., cretus, *sprung from;* mortali semine, Ov.; Trojano a sanguine, Verg. **II.** *to grow, increase in size;* 1, a, fruges, arbusta, animantes, Lucr.; in longitudinem, Plin.; ut cum lunā pariter crescant pariterque decrescant, Cic.; b, esp. of boys, *to grow up;* toti salutifer orbi cresce puer, Ov; 2, *to increase in height, number,* etc.; Roma interim crescit Albae ruinis, Liv.; quum Albanus lacus praeter modum crevisset, Cic.; luna crescens, *waxing,* Cic.; crescit in dies singulos hostium numerus, Cic.; crescentes morbi, Cic.; crescebat in eos odium, Cic.; 3, *to grow great, increase in fame, power,* etc.; pater per se crevisset, Caes.

1. **Crēta** -ae, f. and **Crētē** -ēs, f. (Κρήτη), *the Mediterranean island of Crete,* now *Candia;* hence, 1, **Crēs** -ētis, m., *Cretan;* subst., *a Cretan,* plur., **Crētes** -um, m. *the Cretans;* 2, **Cressa** -ae, f. *Cretan;* Cressa nota, *of Cretan chalk,* Hor.; bos, *Pasiphaë,* Prop.; subst., Ariadne, Aerope, Ov.; 3, **Crēsĭus** -a -um, *Cretan;* 4, **Crētaeus** -a -um, *Cretan;* subst., Epimenides, Prop.; 5, **Crētānus** -i, m. *a Cretan;* 6, **Crētensis** -is, *Cretan;* 7, **Crētĭcus** -a -um, *Cretan;* subst., *the surname of Q. Metellus from his conquest of the island;* 8, **Crētis** -tidis, f. *Cretan.*

2. **crēta** -ae, f. (prop. adj. of 1. Creta), *Cretan earth, chalk,* or *a kind of fuller's earth,* used for cleansing garments, Plaut.; used also for painting the face, Hor.; for seals, Cic.

crētātus -a -um (2. creta), *chalked;* fascia, Cic.; transf., ambitio, *the canvassing of the white-robed candidates,* Prop.

crētĕus -a -um (2. creta), *made of chalk or Cretan earth,* Lucr.

crētĭo -ōnis, f. (cerno), *a declaration of an heir accepting an inheritance.*

crētŭla -ae, f. (dim. of creta), *white clay for sealing,* Cic.

Crĕūsa -ae, f. (Κρέουσα), 1, *daughter of Creon, king of Corinth, wife of Jason;* 2, *daughter of Priam, wife of Aeneas;* 3, *a port in Boeotia.*

cribrum -i, n. (from root CRE, CRI, whence also cerno), *a sieve,* Cic.

crimen -ĭnis, n. (from root CRE, CRI, Gr. KPI, whence cerno, κρίνω). **I. A.** Lit., *accusation, complaint, reproach, calumny;* esse in crimine, *to be accused,* Cic.; dare alicui aliquid crimini,

Cic.; propulsare, defendere, *to repel, confute*, Cic. **B.** Meton., *an object of reproach*; perpetuae crimen posteritatis eris, Ov. **II.** *the fault, guilt, crime, with which a person is charged*. **A.** Lit., haec causa est omnium horum scelerum atque crininum, Cic. **B.** Meton, a, *an object representing a crime*; pictas caelestia crimina vestes, Ov.; b, *cause of crime*; se causam clamat crimenque caputque malorum, Verg.

crĭmĭnātĭo -ōnis, f. (criminor), *an accusation, calumny, charge*; illa criminatio quā in me absentem usus est, Cic.

crĭmĭnātor -ōris, m. (criminor), *an accuser, calumniator*, Tac.

crĭmĭnor, 1. dep. (crimino, Plaut.; criminor, pass., Cic. ?); **1**, *to accuse, charge a person with a crime, to calumniate*; patres apud populum, Liv.; nihil Sistium, Cic.; Q. Metellum apud populum Romanum criminatus est bellum ducere, Cic.; **2**, *to charge with, to lay something to the blame of some one, to complain of*; non licet omnia criminari, Cic.; contiones quibus quotidie meam potentiam invidiose criminabatur, Cic.; with acc. and infin., me esse gratum criminaris, Cic.; absol., *to reproach*; argumentando criminari, Cic.

crĭmĭnōsē, adv., with compar. and superl. (criminosus), *by way of accusation, reproachfully*; qui suspiciosius aut criminosius diceret, Cic.

crĭmĭnōsus -a -um (crimen), *reproachful, calumnious, slanderous*; ille acerbus criminosus popularis homo ac turbulentus, Cic.; criminosum nomen, Cic.; iambi, Hor.; criminosum est or fit or habetur, *blameworthy*, Cic.

Crīmissus (Crīmĭsus) -i, m. (Κριμισσός, Κριμισός), *a river in the south-west of Sicily*.

crīnālis -e, (crinis), *relating to the hair*; vitta, Ov. Subst., **crīnāle** -is, n. *a hair-band*; curvum, *a diadem*, Ov.

crīnis -is, m. (root CER, CRE, whence cerno, creo, cresco). **A.** *the hair*, esp. of the head, Cic.; crines sparsi, Liv.; crinibus passis, Liv. **B.** Transf., *the tail of a comet*, Verg.

crīnītus -a -um (crinis), *provided with hair, hairy, with long hair*. **A.** Lit., Apollo, Verg. **B.** Transf., stella crinita, *a comet*, Cic.

crispĭsulcans -antis (crispus and sulco), *serpentine*, ap. Cic.

crispo, 1. (crispus), **1**, *to curl, crisp*; capillum, Plin.; **2**, *to move rapidly up and down, brandish*; hastilia manu, Verg.

crispŭlus -a -um (dim. of crispus), *curlyhaired, curly*, Mart.

crispus -a -um, **1**, *curly, curly-headed*, Plaut., Ter.; **2**, *in trembling motion, trembling, quivering*; latus, Verg.; pecten, Juv.

crista -ae, f. (connected with cresco, crinis), **1**, *the crest of a bird, the comb of a cock*, Juv.; **2**, *the crest or plume of a helmet*, Verg., Liv.

cristātus -a -um, (crista), *crested*; a, draco, Ov.; aves, cocks, Mart.; b, *having a crest or plume*; galeae, Liv.

Crithōtē -ēs, f. (Κριθωτή), *a town on the east coast of the Thracian Chersonese*.

Crĭtīas -ae, m. (Κριτίας), *one of the Thirty Tyrants at Athens*.

crĭtĭcus -i, m. (κριτικός), *a critic*, Cic.

Crĭto -ōnis, m. (Κρίτων), *a disciple and friend of Socrates*.

Crĭtŏbūlus -i, m. (Κριτόβουλος), *a disciple of Socrates*.

Crĭtŏlāus -i, m. (Κριτόλαος), **1**, *a peripatetic philosopher, ambassador from Athens to Rome*, 155 B.C.; **2**, *a general of the Achaean League*.

crŏcĕus -a -um (crocus), **1**, *belonging to saffron, saffron*; odores, Verg.; **2**, *saffron-coloured, golden, yellow*; flores, Verg.

crŏcĭnus -a -um (κρόκινος), *belonging to saffron, saffron-coloured, yellow*; tunica, Cat. Subst., **crŏcĭnum** -i, n. (sc. oleum), *saffron oil*, Prop.

crŏcĭo, 4. (κρώζω), *to caw like a crow*, Plaut.

crŏcŏdīlus -i, m. (κροκόδειλος), *a crocodile*, Cic.

crŏcŏta -ae, f. (sc. vestis, Gr. ὁ κροκωτός, sc. χιτών), *a saffron-coloured robe worn by women*, Cic.

crŏcŏtŭla -ae, f. (dim. of crocota), *a little saffron-coloured robe*, Plaut.

crŏcus -i, m., **crŏcum** -i, n. (κρόκος and κρόκον). **I.** *saffron*, used by the ancients not only as a spice and in medicine, but in the preparation of perfumes, Ov.; personified, Crocus, *a young man changed into a saffron-flower*, Ov. **II.** Meton., *the colour of saffron, yellow*, Verg.

Croesus -i, m. (Κροῖσος), *a king of Lydia famous for his wealth*; appell. = *a rich man*, Ov. Adj., **Croesius** -a -um, *of Croesus*.

Crŏmyŏn -ōnis, f. (Κρομυών), *a village in Megaris*.

crŏtālĭa -ōrum, n. (κροτάλια), *an earring consisting of several pendant pearls*, Pers.

crŏtālistrĭa -ae, f. *a female dancer and performer on the castanets*, Prop.

crŏtălum -i, n. (κρόταλον), *a castanet*, Verg.

Crŏto (Crŏtōn) -ōnis, c. (Κρότων), *a town on the east coast of Bruttium*, now Crotone. Hence **1**, **Crŏtōnĭātes** -ae, m. (Κροτωνιάτης), *an inhabitant of Crotona*; **2**, adj., **Crŏtōnĭensis** -e, *of Crotona*.

Crŏtōpĭădes -ae, m. (Κροτωπιάδης), *the poet Linus, grandson, on the mother's side, of Crotopus, king of Argos*, Ov.

crŭcĭāmentum -i, n. (crucio), *torture, torment*, Cic.

crŭcĭātus -ūs, m. (crucio), *torture, torment, execution*; omnes animi cruciatus et corporis, Cic.; per cruciatum interficere, Caes.; quin tu abi in malam pestem malumque cruciatum, *go and be hanged*, Cic.

crŭcĭo, 1. (crux), *to torture, torment*; quum vigiliis atque fame cruciaretur, Cic.; aliquem, Cic.

crŭdēlis -e (crudus), *unfeeling, unmerciful, cruel, inhuman, hardhearted*; a, of persons, crudelissimus tyrannus, Cic.; Lepidus crudelis in liberos, Cic.; in hominis consularis calamitate crudelis, Cic.; b, of things, funus, Verg.; bellum, Cic.; consilia crudelissima, Cic.

crŭdēlĭtas -ātis, f. (crudelis), *cruelty, inhumanity*; importuna in me crudelitas, Cic.

crŭdēlĭter, adv. (crudelis), *cruelly, inhumanly*; imperare, Caes.; aliquem crudelissime interficere, Cic.

crŭdesco -dŭi, 3. *to become hard, violent*; crudescit morbus, Verg.; seditio, Tac.

crŭdĭtas -ātis, f. (crudus), *overloading of the stomach, indigestion*, Cic.

crŭdus -a -um (contr. from cruidus, from root CRU, whence cruor), *raw*. **I.** Lit., **1**, *not prepared by fire, uncooked, raw*; exta cruda victimae, Liv.; **2**, *not ripened by the sun, unripe*, poma, Cic.; **3**, a, *undigested*; pavo, Juv.; b, *suffering from indigestion*; Roscius crudior fuit, Cic.; **4**, *raw, not healed*; vulnera, Ov.; **5**, *unprepared, rough*; cortice crudo hasta, Verg. **II.** Transf., **1**, *not ready, immature, fresh*; servitium, Tac.; **2**, *vigorous, fresh*; senectus cruda viridisque, Verg.; **3**, *rough, cruel*; Getae, Ov.; ensis, Verg.

crŭento, 1. (cruentus), *to make bloody, to stain with blood;* manus sanguine, Nep.; gladium, Cic.; fig., haec te lacerat, haec cruentat oratio, *wounds,* Cic.

crŭentus -a -um (cruor), *bloody.* **I.** Gen. a, *mixed with blood;* guttae imbrium quasi cruentae, Cic.; b, *blood-red;* myrta, Verg. **II.** In a bad sense, *bloody through murder.* **A.** Lit., *covered, stained, spotted with blood, bloody;* cruentus sanguine civium Romanorum, Cic.; cadaver, Cic.; gaudens Bellona cruentis, *in the shedding of blood,* Hor. **B.** Transf., a, *wounding;* dens, Hor.; b, *rejoicing in blood, bloodthirsty, cruel;* ira, Hor.

crŭmēna -ae, f. *a leathern pouch for money, carried by a strap round the neck.* **A.** Lit., Plaut. **B.** Transf., *money;* non deficiente crumēna, Hor.

crŭor -ōris, m. (root CRU, whence also crudus), *the blood which flows from a wound, gore;* cruor inimici recentissimus, Cic.; fig., *murder, slaughter;* cruor Cinnanus, *the slaughter of Cinna,* Cic.; castus a cruore civili, Cic.; ad caedem et cruorem abstrahi, Cic.

cruppellārii -ōrum, m. *Gaulish gladiators, who fought in full armour,* Tac.

crūs, crūris, n. 1, *the shin, shin-bone, leg;* frangere alicui crus or crura (of persons crucified), Cic.; rigida crura, Cic.; succidere crura equo, Liv.; 2, plur., *the supports of a bridge,* Cat.

crusta -ae, f. 1, *the crust, rind, shell, bark of any substance;* concrescunt subitae currenti in flumine crustae, *coating of ice,* Verg.; 2, *mosaic, inlaid work on walls, bas-relief,* or *embossing on silver plate,* Cic.

crustŭlum -i, n. (dim. of crustum), *a little cake,* Hor.

crustum -i, n. (crusta), *anything baked, bread, cake,* Verg.

Crustŭmĕrĭa -ae, f. (Κρουστομερία) (-mĕrĭum -ii, n., -mĕrĭi -ōrum, m. -mĭum -ii, n.), *a town of the Sabines, near the sources of the Allia.* Hence adj., 1, **Crustŭmīnus** -a -um, 2, **Crustŭmĭus** -a -um, *of Crustumeria.*

crux, crŭcis, f. *a cross;* agere aliquem in crucem, Cic.; affigere aliquem cruci, Liv.; detrahere aliquem ex cruce, Cic.; minari alicui crucem, Cic.; rapere aliquem in crucem, Cic.; abi in malam crucem, *go and be hanged!* Plaut.

crypta -ae, f. (κρύπτη), *a subterranean gallery, vault, crypt, grotto,* Juv.

crystallĭnus -a -um (κρυστάλλινος), *crystalline, made of crystal,* Plin. Subst., **crystallĭna** -ōrum, n. (sc. vasa), *crystal vases,* Juv.

crystallus -i, f. and (rarely) m. (κρύσταλλος) (heterocl. plur., crystalla). **A.** Lit., *crystal.* **B.** Meton., a, *a crystal drinking vessel,* Mart.; b, *the glittering, precious stone in a ring,* Prop.

Ctēsĭphōn -phontis, m. (Κτησιφῶν), *an Athenian statesman, friend of Demosthenes, who defended him when accused by Aeschines.*

cŭbĭcŭlāris -e (cubiculum), *relating to a sleeping-room;* lectus, Cic.

cŭbĭcŭlārĭus -a -um (cubiculum), *belonging to a sleeping-room.* Subst., **cŭbĭcŭlārĭus** -ii, m. *a chamber-servant,* Cic.

cŭbĭcŭlum -i, n. (cubo), *a sleeping-room, bedroom,* Cic.

cŭbīle (cubo), 1, *a bed, esp. the marriagebed;* 2, *the resting-place of animals, lair, den;* ferarum bestiarum, Liv.; rimosa cubilia, of bees, hives, Verg.; construere sibi cubilia nidos, Verg.; fig., *the seat of an evil;* ut omnes mortales istius avaritiae non jam vestigia, sed ipsa cubilia videre possint, Cic.

cŭbĭtal -tālis, n. (cubitum), *an elbow cushion,* Hor.

cŭbĭtālis -e (cubitum), *of the length of a cubit;* cubitalis fere cava, Liv.

cŭbĭto, 1. (freq. of cubo), *to lie down often, be accustomed to lie,* Cic.

cŭbĭtum -i, n. and **cŭbĭtus** -i, m. (cubo). 1, *the elbow;* cubito remanere presso, Hor.; 2, *a cubit, an ell,* Cic.

cŭbo -ŭi -itum, 1. 1, a, *to lie down, recline;* in lectica, Cic.; b, esp. *to lie down to sleep;* cubitum ire, *to go to bed,* Cic.; c, *to recline at table;* quod meminisset quo eorum loco quisque cubuisset, Cic.; d, *to lie down from illness, to lie in bed ill;* cubantem disputare de aliqua re, Cic.; 2, applied to inanimate objects, partic. cubans, *sloping;* Ustica, Hor.

cŭcullus -i, m. *a hood, cowl,* Juv.

cŭcūlus -i, m. (κόκκυξ), *the cuckoo,* Plaut.; as a term of reproach, Plaut., Hor.

cŭcŭmis -mĕris, m. *a cucumber,* Verg.

cŭcurbĭta -ae, f. 1, *a gourd,* Plin.; 2, *a cupping-glass,* Juv.

cūdo, 3. 1, *to beat, pound;* fabas, *to thresh;* prov., istaec in me cudetur faba, *I shall suffer for that,* Ter.; 2, of metals, *to stamp, beat out, coin;* plumbeos nummos, Plaut.

cuicuimodi = cujus-cujus-modi, *of what kind soever,* Cic.

cūjās -ātis and **cūjātis** -is (cujus from qui), *of what country? whence?* Cic.

cūjŭs -a -um, 1. (cujus from qui), 1, interrog. pron. *to whom belonging? whose?* cujum pecus? *whose flock?* Verg.; 2, relat. pron. *whose,* is cuja res sit, Cic.

cūjuscĕmŏdi (qui, ce, and modus), *of whatever kind,* Cic.

cūjusdam-mŏdi, *of a certain kind,* Cic.

cūjusmŏdi (quis and modus), *of what kind?* Cic.

cūjusquĕmŏdi (quisque and modus), *of every kind,* Cic.

culcĭta -ae, f. (calco), *a mattress, bolster, pillow;* plumea, Cic.

cŭlēus (cullēus) -i, m. (root CU, whence cupa), *a large leathern sack,* Nep.; aliquem insuere in culeum (the punishment of parricides), Cic.

cūlex -icis, m. *a gnat, midge,* Hor.

cŭlīna -ae, f. (contr. from coquilina), a, *a kitchen;* tua (philosophia) in culina, mea in palaestra est, Cic.; b, meton., *food, fare, victuals;* Murena praebente domum, Capitone culinam, Hor.

cullĕus, v. culeus.

culmen -inis, n. (for columen from * cello), *the top, summit.* **I. A.** Lit., 1, culmen Alpium, Caes.; 2, *the ridge of a roof;* culmen tecti, Verg. **B.** Transf., *summit;* summum culmen fortunae, Liv. **II.** Poet. = culmus, *haulm,* Ov.

culmus -i, m. (from * cello, like culmen), a *stalk, haulm,* esp. of grain, Cic.; *thatch;* Romuleo recens horrebat regia culmo, Verg.

culpa -ae, f. *fault, error.* **I.** Lit., 1, culpa delicti, Cic.; a, abl., culpā, *by one's own fault,* Cic.; so meā culpā, tuā culpā, etc.; abesse a culpa or culpa, Cic.; non abhorrere a tali culpa, Cic.; uni culpam attribuere, Cic.; committere culpam, Cic.; dare alicui summam laudem vitio et culpae, Cic.; est culpa mea, Cic.; est culpa in aliquo or in aliqua re, Cic.; esse in culpa, Cic.; extra culpam esse, Cic.; liberare aliquem culpa, Cic.; b, praestare culpam, *to make oneself responsible for,* Cic.; in se suscipere istius culpam, Cic.; vacare culpa, Cic.; 2, esp. a, *the*

ault of negligence, Hor. ; b, *unchastity*, Ov. **II.**
Meton., *the cause of error or sin;* culpam ferro
compesce, Verg.

culpātus -a -um, p. adj. (from culpo), *blame-worthy;* Paris, Verg.

culpo, 1. (culpa), **1**, *to blame, find fault with,
accuse, disapprove;* laudatur ab his, culpatur
ab illis, Hor. ; **2**, *to lay blame on;* arbore nunc
aquas culpante, Hor.

cultē, adv. with compar. (1. cultus), *elegantly;* loqui, Ov.

cultellus -i, m. (dim. of culter), *a little
knife*, Hor.

culter -tri, m. (connected with Skr. kar, *to
wound,* and Gr. κείρω), *a knife;* cultri tonsorii,
razors, Cic. ; *a ploughshare, coulter,* Plin. ; prov.,
me sub cultro linquit, *leaves me under the knife,*
i.e., *in the greatest peril,* Hor.

cultor -ōris, m. (colo), *a cultivator, planter,
labourer.* **I.** Lit., **A.** Gen., terrae, Cic. ; agrorum, Liv. **B.** 1, absol., *husbandman,* Sall. ; **2**,
with genit., *an inhabitant, occupier ;* eius terrae,
Sall. **II.** Transf., 1, gen., *a friend, supporter;*
bonorum (*of the optimates*), Liv. ; veritatis, Cic. ;
2, esp., *a worshipper;* deorum, Hor. ; religionum, Liv.

cultrix -īcis, f. (cultor), **1**, *she who tends
or takes care of,* Cic. ; **2**, *inhabitant;* nemorum
Latonia virgo, Verg.

cultūra -ae, f. (colo), *culture, cultivation.*
I. Lit., **1**, gen., agri, Cic. ; vitis, Cic. ; **2**, *agriculture, husbandry,* Hor. **II.** **1**, *mental culture,
cultivation;* animi, Cic. ; **2**, *reverence, respect,
courting ;* potentis amici, Hor.

1. cultus -a -um, p. adj. with compar. and
superl. (colo). **A.** *cultivated, tilled, planted ;* loci
culti, Cic. ; ager cultissimus, Cic. Subst., **culta**
-orum, n. *cultivated land ;* an culta ex silvestribus facere potui ? Liv. **B.** a, *ornamented,
adorned;* femina cultissima, Ov. ; b, *polished,
elegant;* sonum linguae et corporum habitum
et nitorem cultiora quam pastoralia esse, Liv. ;
culta carmina, Ov.

2. cultus -ūs, m. (colo). **I.** *cultivation ;*
agrorum, Liv., Cic. **II. A.** *physical or mental
cultivation ;* **1**, a, *physical cultivation, care,
tending ;* corporis, Cic. ; b, *adornment, dress ;*
culticus Punicus habitusque, Liv. ; **2**, *mental
culture, training, education ;* animi, ingenii, Cic.
B. *reverence, respect, worship;* a, *of the gods,*
cultus deorum, Cic. ; b, *respect paid to men ;* be-
nevolis officium et diligens tribuitur cultus, Cic.

cŭlullus -i, m. *a drinking-vessel,* Hor.

cūlus -i, m. *the fundament,* Cat.

1. cum, conj. = quum (q.v.).

2. cum, prep. with abl. *with.* **I.** In space, **1**,
together with; esse, vivere, agitare, habitare,
cessare, dormire, ire, abire, redire, mittere cum
aliquo ; cum impedimentis venire, Caes. ; esp.
a, *in the company of a general ;* cum Magone
equites Hispanorum praemissos, Liv. ; b, *of some
office held in common with some one else,* unum
imperium unumque magistratum habere cum
ipsis, Liv. ; **c**, *in relation with, in company with ;*
cum aliquo se delectare, Cic. ; **2**, *adorned with,
provided with ;* cum pallio purpureo versabatur
in conviviis, Cic. ; legatos cum auctoritate mittere, Cic. **II.** Of time, **1**, *at the same time with ;*
cum primā iuce Pomponii domum venire, Cic. ;
2, *together with ;* aliquid magno cum gemitu
civitatia suferre, Cic. ; cum eo quod, ut, or ne,
on the condition that ; sit sane sed tamen cum eo,
credo, quod sine peccato meo fiat, Cic. (Cum,
when used with the personal pronoun, is always,
and when used with relative pronouns generally,
placed after its case, mecum, quocum, etc.)

Cūmae -ārum, f. (Κύμη), *an ancient city of
Campania, famous as the residence of the Sibyl.*
Adj. **Cūmānus** -a -um ; **Cūmæus** -a -um,
Cumaean; virgo, *the Sibyl,* Ov.

cumba = cymba (q.v.).

cŭmĕra -ae, f. *a corn-chest,* Hor.

cŭmīnum -i, n. (κύμινον), *the herb cummin,*
Hor.

cummi, v. gummi.

cumprīmis, v. primus.

cumque (cunque, quomque), an adverb
usually found in composition, e.g., quicumque,
ubicumque, etc., signifying *however, whatever,
whenever ;* sometimes standing by itself ; quae
demant quomque dolorem, *pain in general,* Lucr.;
mihi cumque salve rite vocanti, *whenever I call,*
Hor.

cŭmŭlātē, adv. with compar. and superl.
(cumulatus), *abundantly, copiously ;* gratias
agere, Cic.

cŭmŭlātus -a -um, p. adj. with compar. and
superl. (cumulo), **1**, *heaped up, increased, enlarged ;* Hesiodus eādem mensurā reddere jubet,
quā acceperis, aut etiam cumulatiore, si possis,
Cic. ; **2**, *perfect ;* hoc sentire et facere perfectae
cumulataeque virtutis est, Cic.

cŭmŭlo, 1. (cumulus). **I. A.** Lit., *to heap up,
pile up;* cetera omnis generis arma in acervum,
Liv. **B.** Transf., quum aliae super alias clades
cumularentur, Liv. ; omnes in aliquem honores,
Tac. **II.** a, *to fill by heaping up, fill up, overload;*
fossas corporibus, Tac. ; altaria donis, Verg. ;
b, confiteor me cumulari maximo gaudio, Cic. ;
cumulatus laude, *loaded with praise,* Cic. ; **c**, *to
increase, heighten;* invidiam, Liv. ; cumulare eloquentiā bellicam gloriam, Cic. ; **d**, *to bring to
perfection ;* cumulata erant officia vitae, *perfectly
fulfilled,* Cic.

cŭmŭlus -i, m. (connected with culmen and
culmus). **A.** Lit., *a heap, pile, mass ;* hostium
coacervatorum, Liv.; aquarum, Ov. **B.** Transf.,
addition, increase, surplus, summit ; commenda-
tionis tuae, Cic. ; alicui afferre cumulum gaudii,
Cic.

cūnābŭla -ōrum, n. (cunae). **A.** Lit., *a
cradle ;* a, esse in cunabulis, Cic. ; b, *the bed
of the young of bees,* Verg. **B.** Meton., *the earliest
abode;* gentis, Verg.

cūnae -ārum, f. (cubo, * cumbo), *a cradle ;* a,
in cunis dormire, Cic. ; primis cunis, *in earliest
childhood,* Ov. ; b, *the nest of young birds,* Ov.

cunctābundus -a -um (cunctor), *loitering,
delaying, dilatory,* Liv., Tac.

cunctans -antis, p. adj. with compar. (cunctor), *loitering, lingering, slow,* Plin.; ilex glebae,
tenacious, Verg.

cunctantĕr, adv. with compar. (cunctans),
slowly, lingeringly, Liv.

cunctātĭo -ōnis, f. (cunctor), *a delay, lingering, hesitation ;* invadendi, Liv. ; sine cunctatione, Cic. ; abjecta omni cunctatione, Cic.

cunctātor -ōris, m. (cunctor), *one who de-
lays, lingers, hesitates ;* cunctatorem ex acerrimo
bellatore factum, Liv.; *a surname of the dictator,*
Q. Fabius Maximus.

cunctor, 1. dep. *to delay;* **1**, of motion, *to stay,
tarry ;* cunctari diutius in vitā, Cic. ; tardum
cunctatur olivum, *drops slowly,* Lucr. ; **2**, of action, *to hesitate, linger, be slow ;* sedendo et cunc-
tando bellum gerebat, Liv. ; with infin., non est
cunctandum profiteri hunc mundum animal esse,
Cic. ; non cunctor, foll. by quin and the subj. ;
non cunctandum existimavit, quin pugnā decer-
taret, *there ought to be no delay in,* etc., Caes.
impers. pass., nec cunctatum apud latera, Tac.

cunctus -a -um (contr. from conjunctus or

convinctus), *all, all collectively, the whole;* a, sing., senatus, Cic.; b, orbis terrarum, Verg.; b, plur., **cuncti** -ae -a, cives, Cic.; in poet. sometimes foll. by genit., hominum, Ov.

cŭnĕātim, adv. (cuneo), *in shape of a wedge,* Caes.

cŭnĕātus -a -um, p. adj. with compar. (cuneo), *pointed like a wedge;* jugum in angustum dorsum cuneatum, Liv.

cŭnĕo, 1. (cuneus), *to drive in a wedge, to wedge in,* Plin.

cŭnĕŏlus -i, m. (dim. of cuneus), *a little wedge,* Cic.

cŭnĕus -i, m. *a wedge.* **I.** Lit., **A.** cuneis scindere fissile lignum, Verg. **B.** *a wedge as a triangular figure;* Britannia in cuneum tenuatur, *is narrowed in the shape of a wedge,* Tac. **II.** Transf., **A.** *troops drawn up in form of a wedge, a wedge;* cuneum facere, Caes. **B.** *the wedge-shaped compartments into which the seats of the amphitheatre were divided,* Verg.; cuneis omnibus, *to all the spectators,* Phaed.

cŭnĭcŭlōsus -a -um (cuniculus), *full of holes and caverns,* Cat.

cŭnĭcŭlus -i, m. 1, *a rabbit, cony,* Cat.; 2, *an underground passage;* omne genus cuniculorum apud eos notum atque usitatum est, Caes.; esp. milit. t. t., *a mine;* agere cuniculum, Caes.; aperire cuniculum, Caes.

cunnus -i, m. = pudendum muliebre; meton., *a prostitute,* Hor.

cūpa -ae, f. (root CU, whence **culeus**), *a cask* or *butt,* Cic.

cŭpēdĭa -ae, f. *daintiness, fondness for dainties,* Cic.

cŭpĭdē, adv. with compar. and superl. (cupidus), *eagerly, passionately, hotly, vehemently, warmly;* cupide appetere aliquid, Cic.; cupide proficisci, Cic.; cupidius aliquid dicere, Cic.; ego vero cupide et libenter mentiar tuā causā, Cic.

cŭpĭdĭtas -ātis, f. (cupidus), *eager desire,* and in a bad sense, *passionate longing, vehement desire.* **I.** Gen., cupiditas inexplebilis, insana, nimia, Cic.; with obj. genit., pecuniae, Cic.; dominandi, Cic.; with ad, tanta cupiditas ad reditum, Cic.; ardere cupiditate, Cic.; coercere cupiditates, Cic.; explere cupiditates, Cic.; incitare aliquem cupiditate imitandi, Cic.; servire cupiditatibus, Cic. **II.** Esp., a, *ambition;* popularis (of a demagogue), Cic.; b, *desire for money, avarice;* sine cupiditate vixisse, Cic.; c, *factiousness, party spirit;* cupiditatis atque inimicitiarum suspicio, Cic.

cŭpīdo -ĭnis, f. (m. only in poet.) (cupio), *longing, desire.* **I.** Gen., Sall.; with genit., auri, Tac.; pecuniae, honoris, Sall.; flagrare cupidine regni, Liv.; Hannibalem ingens cupido incesserat Tarenti potiendi, Liv. **II.** Esp., a, *physical desire;* somni, Sall.; b, *love;* cupido visae virginis, Ov.; hence personified, **Cŭpīdo** -ĭnis, m. *Cupid, the god of love, son of Venus,* Cic.; plur., **Cŭpīdĭnes,** *Cupids;* c, *avarice;* cupido sordidus, Hor.; d, *ambition;* ita cupidine atque irā, pessimis consultoribus, grassari, Sall.

cŭpĭdus -a -um, adj. with compar. and superl. (cupio), *desirous, wishful, eager, fond.* **I.** Gen., a, absol., consul non cupidus, Cic.; b, with genit. of object, pecuniae, Cic.; novarum rerum, Cic.; te audiendi, Cic.; c, with in and the abl., in perspiciendā cognoscendāque rerum naturā, Cic. **II.** Esp., a, *longing for, loving,* Ov.; b, *avaricious;* homo non cupidus neque appetens, Cic.; c, (a) in a good sense, *devoted to;* homo tui cupidus, Cic.; (β) in a bad sense,

factious, partial; quaestores vehementer istius cupidi, Cic.; absol., judex cupidus, Cic.

cŭpĭens -entis, p. adj. with compar. and superl. (cupio), *desiring, longing, wishing, eager;* novarum rerum, Tac.; cupientissimā plebe, Sall.

cŭpĭentĕr, adv. (cupiens), *eagerly,* Plaut.

cŭpĭo -īvi or -ĭi, -ītum, 3. *to desire, long for, wish for.* **I.** Gen., a, with acc., is quem cupimus optamusque vestitus, Cic.; pacem, Liv.; partic. perf., res cupita, Liv.; b, with infin., cupiens ad suos redire, Cic.; c, with acc. and infin., equidem cupio Antonium haec quam primum audire, Cic. **II.** Esp., alicui or alicuius causae, *to favour, support, wish well to;* quid? ego Fundanio non cupio? non amicus sum? Cic.

cŭpītor -ōris, m. (cupio), *one who desires;* matrimonii, Tac.

cuppēdĭa, v. cupedia.

cŭpressētum -i, n. (cupressus), *a cypress wood,* Cic.

cŭpressĕus -a -um (cupressus), *made of cypress wood;* signa Junonis, Liv.

cŭpressĭfer -fĕra -fĕrum (cupressus and fero), *cypress-bearing,* Ov.

cŭpressus -i, f. -ūs, m. (κυπάρισσος). **A.** *the cypress,* sacred to Pluto, used at funerals, Verg. **B.** Meton., *a casket of cypress wood,* Hor.

cŭprĕus -a -um, v. cypreus.

cūr (orig. quoirei, cuirei, then cuire, cuir, cur), adv. *why? wherefore? for what reason?* 1, rel., quae sunt causae, cur, etc., Cic.; 2, interrog., cur non assum? Cic.

cūra -ae, f. *care.* **I. A.** Gen., *carefulness, solicitude, pains, trouble* (opp. negligentia), *attention;* magnā cum curā et diligentiā scribere aliquid, Cic.; with genit., rerum alienarum cura (difficilis) est, Cic.; cura colendi, Verg.; with de, studium tuum curaque de salute meā, Cic.; verbal constructions, adhibere curam in capris et ovibus parandis, Cic.; agere curam civium, Liv.; conferre magnam curam in alicuius salutem, Cic.; non dimittere istam curam, Cic.; maxima erat cura duci ne, etc., Liv.; salutem eius regis senatui populoque Romano magnae curae esse, Cic.; imprimis tibi curae sit ne mihi tempus prorogetur, Cic.; habere curam rerum divinarum, Liv.; incumbe in eam curam, *devote yourself to,* Cic.; ponere curam alicuius rei, *to lay aside,* Liv.; ponere curam in aliquā re, *to devote one's attention to,* Cic.; suscipere curam, Cic.; sustinere maximam curam belli, Cic. **B.** *care for something, attending, caring, minding;* 1, of husbandry, quae cura boum, Verg.; 2, *the adornment of the body;* cura cultusque feminarum, Liv.; 3, *healing, cure;* simplex illa jam cura doloris tui, Cic.; 4, *the worship of the gods;* deorum, Liv.; 5, *taking care of a person;* suum sororisque filios in eādem curā habere, Liv.; meton., *the object of attention;* tua cura, palumbes, Verg.; 6, *care for, management, administration;* esp. of public affairs, cura reipublicae, Liv.; cura navium, *of the fleet,* Tac.; meton., *business, administration;* quum sumus necessariis negotiis curisque vacui, Cic. **II.** *care, anxiety, solicitude, disquiet;* 1, sine curā, Cic.; afferre alicui curam, Cic.; afficere aliquem aliquā curā, Cic.; confici curis, Cic.; priusquam ea cura decederet patribus Romanis, Liv.; liberare aliquem curā, Cic.; et curā vacare et negotio, Cic.; 2, of the disquiet of love, juvenum curae, Hor.; meton., *the object of love;* tua cura, Lycoris, Verg.

cūrābĭlis -e (cura), *exciting care* or *fear;* vindicta, Juv.

cūrālĭum -ĭi = corallium (q.v.).

cūrātē, (curatus), adv. *carefully,* compar., curatius legi, *between the lines.* Tac.

cūrătĭo -ōnis, f. (curo). **I.** Gen., *a taking care*, Plaut. **II.** Esp. *attention, management ;* **1,** a, with genit., curatio corporis, Cic. ; b, *medical attention, healing, cure ;* curatio medici, Cic. ; curatio valetudinis, Cic. ; adhibere curationem, Cic. ; praescribere curationem, Cic. ; **2,** *management, administration ;* esp. of a public office, curatio Nemeorum, *of the Nemean games*, Liv. ; Asiatica curatio frumenti, *commission to buy corn*, Cic. ; curatio agraria, *commission to divide land*, Cic. ; curationem suscipere, Cic. ; aedes Telluris est curationis meae, Cic.

cūrător -ōris, m. (curo), *one who takes care ;* **1,** *a guardian, overlooker, curator ;* viae Flaminiae Cic. ; muris reficiendis sunto aediles curatores urbis annonae ludorumque sollemnium, Cic. ; legibus agrariis curatores constituere, Cic. ; **2,** legal t. t., *guardian of a minor or idiot or prodigal ;* alicui curatorem dare (of the praetor), Hor.

cūrātus -a -um, p. adj. (curo), *carefully prepared ;* curatissimae preces, Tac.

curcŭlĭo -ōnis, m. *a weevil, corn-worm*, Verg.

Cŭrēs -ium, f. *an ancient town of the Sabines ;* meton., *the inhabitants of Cures*, Ov. Hence **A.** Adj., **Cŭrensis** -e, *of Cures*. **B. Cŭres** -ētis, m. *an inhabitant of Cures.*

Cŭrētes -um, m. (Κουρῆτες), *the ancient inhabitants of Crete, who celebrated a frantic worship of Jupiter, like that of Cybele by the Corybantes.* Adj., **Cŭrētis** -ĭdis, poet. = *Cretan*, Ov.

cūrĭa -ae, f. (connected with Quiris). **I.** *a curia, one of thirty divisions into which the Roman patricians were distributed by Romulus*, Liv. **II.** Meton., **A.** *the meeting-place of a curia*, Tac. **B.** a, *the building in which the senate met*, usually the Curia Hostilia, afterwards the Curia Pompeja or Curia Julia ; b, Curia Saliorum, *the house of the Salii on the Palatine*, Cic. ; c, *the senate ;* aliquem in curiam introducere, Liv. ; d, *the senate-house of non-Roman nations*—e.g., at Salamis, Cic. ; Syracuse, Cic. ; Troy, Ov. ; Athens, *the Areopagus*, Juv.

cūrĭālis -e (curia), *belonging to the same curia*, Cic.

cūrĭātim, adv. (curia), *by curiae ;* populum consuluit, Cic.

Cŭrĭātĭi -ōrum, m. *name of an Alban gens, three of which fought with the Horatii.*

cūrĭātus -a -um (curia), *relating to the curiae ;* comitia curiata, *the original assembly of the Roman people, in which they voted by curiae*, Cic. ; lex, *a law passed in the comitia curiata*, Cic.

Cŭricta -ae, f. *an island on the Illyrian coast, now Veglia.*

1. cūrĭo -ōnis, m. (curia), **1,** *the priest of a curia*, Varr. ; maximus, *the head of the college formed by the thirty curiones*, Liv. ; **2,** *a herald, crier*, Mart.

2. Cŭrĭo -ōnis, m. *the name of a family of the gens Scribonia.*

cūrĭōsē, adv., with compar. and superl. (curiosus), **1,** *carefully ;* conquirere ista curiosius, Cic. ; **2,** *inquisitively ;* curiosius id faciunt quam necesse est, Cic.

cūrĭōsĭtas -ātis, f. (curiosus), *inquisitiveness, curiosity.*

Curiosolites -um, m. *a people in Brittany, near modern Corseult.*

cūrĭōsus -a -um, adj. with compar. and superl. (cura), *careful ;* **1,** *attentive, diligent ;* curiosis oculis perspici non posse, Cic. ; permulta alia colligit Chrysippus, ut est in omni historia curiosus, Cic. ; **2,** *inquisitive, curious ;* isti curiosi, Cic.

cŭris -is, f. (a Sabine word) = hasta, *a lance, or javelin*, Ov.

Cŭrĭus -a -um, *name of a plebeian gens, of which the most illustrious member was* M'. Curius Dentatus, *the conqueror of the Sabines, Samnites, and of Pyrrhus, celebrated for his temperance ;* hence appell. *a brave and temperate man*, Hor. Adj., **Cŭriānus** -a -um, *of or belonging to Curius.*

cūro, 1. (cura). **I.** Gen. *to care for, pay attention to, tend ;* a, with acc., negotia aliena, Cic. ; b, with acc. and gerundive, in Siciliā frumentum emendum et ad urbem mittendum curare, *to get bought and sent*, Cic. ; c, with infin., qui res istas scire curavit, Cic. ; non curare, *not to care, to decline, refuse ;* in Siciliam ire non curat, Cic. ; d, followed by ut, ne, ut ne and the subj., or the subj. alone, Cic. ; so in letters, cura ut valeas, Cic. ; e, with de, Quintus de emendo nihil curat hoc tempore, Cic. **II.** Esp., **1,** *to attend to, take care of ;* se, Cic. ; membra, Hor. ; *to attend to, cure an invalid, or a disease ;* curare corpora, Cic. ; curari non posse, Caes. ; **2,** *to attend to religious observances ;* sacra, Cic. ; **3,** *to provide or procure a sum of money ;* jube sodes nummos curari, Cic. ; **4,** *to administer, manage ;* res Romae, Liv. ; absol. *to command ;* curare Romae, Tac. (Archaic forms, coiravi, coirandi, ap. Cic.).

currĭcŭlum -i, n. (curro). **I.** Act., **A.** Abstr., **1,** *running*, Plaut. ; **2,** esp. a, *a contest in running, a race*, Cic. ; b, *a course, orbit of heavenly bodies ;* solis et lunae, Cic. **B.** Concr., *the chariot used in races ;* in curriculum quadrigarum incurrere, Cic. **II.** Pass. *the raceground ;* athletae se in curriculo exercentes, Cic. ; often fig., exiguum vitae curriculum natura circumscripsit, immensum gloriae, Cic.

curro, cŭcurri, cursum, 3. *to run, hasten ;* pass. impers., curritur, *one runs*, Cic. ; curritur ad praetorium, Cic. ; pro se quisque currere ad sua tutanda, Liv. ; with cognate acc., eosdem cursus currere, Cic. ; prov., currentem hortari, incitare or instigare, *to spur the willing horse*, Cic. ; esp. a, *to run in a race ;* currere bene, Ov. ; with acc. of place, qui stadium currit, Cic. ; b, of ships, *to sail ;* per omne mare, Hor. ; with acc., currere cavā trabe vastum aequor, Verg. ; c, of a wheel, si mea sincero curreret axe rota, Ov. ; d, of water, currentes aquae, Ov. ; e, of the heavenly bodies, libera currebat et inobservata per annum sidera, Ov. ; f, of the hem of a garment, quam plurima circum purpura Maeandro duplici Meliboea cucurrit, Verg. ; g, of fright, cold, shame, etc., varius per ora cucurrit Ausonidum turbata fremor, Verg. ; h, of time, *to pass ;* currit ferox aetas, Hor. ; i, fig., of discourse, *to march easily ;* perfacile currens oratio, Cic.

currus -ūs, m. (curro). **I. A.** *a chariot, car*, esp. *a triumphal car ;* escendere in currum, Cic. ; flectere currum de foro in Capitolium, Cic. ; invehi curru Capitolium, Cic. **B.** Meton., a, *the horses, the team ;* neque audit currus habenas, Verg. ; b, *triumph ;* quem ego currum aut quam lauream cum tuā laudatione conferrem ? Cic. **II.** *a plough with wheels*, Verg. **III.** *a ship*, Cat. (syncop. genit. plur. currum, Verg., Aen. vi. 653).

cursim, adv. (curro), *hastily, quickly ;* cursim agmen agere, Liv. ; cursim dicere aliena, Cic.

cursĭto, 1. (intens. of curso), *to run up and down ;* huc et illuc (of the atoms), Cic.

curso, 1. (freq. of curro), *to run hither and thither ;* ultro et citro, Cic.

cursor -ōris, m. (curro). **I.** Lit. **A.** *a runner*, especially for a prize, Cic. ; *one who contends in the chariot race*, Ov. **B. 1,** *a messenger* *postman*, Tac.; **2,** *a slave who ran before his master's carriage, a running footman,* Suet. **II.** Transf. *surname of* L. Papirius, *the conqueror of the Samnites.*

cursus -ūs, m. (curro), *a running, rapid motion on horseback, in a carriage,* or *ship;* milites cursu exanimatos, Caes.; cursus equorum, Verg.; longarum navium, Caes.; cursu tendere ad aliquem or ad locum, Liv.; in cursu esse, *to travel in haste,* Cic.; esp. a, *chariot or horse-race;* cursus certamen, Ov.; fig. *the race for office, honour,* etc.; in eodem cursu fuisse a Sullā dictatore ad eosdem fere consules, Cic.; **b,** *course, march, journey;* cursus maritimus, Cic.; mihi cursus in Graeciam per tuam provinciam est, Cic.; cursus dirigere, Liv.; cursum secundum habere, Caes.; cursum tenere, Cic.; fig., reliquus vitae cursus, Cic.; **c,** *the course of water;* quosdam exaruisse amnes aut in alium cursum contortos et deflexos videmus, Cic.; **d,** of heavenly bodies, annui cursus solis, Cic.; **e,** of the voice, his per omnes sonos vocis cursus, Cic.

Curtius -a -um, *name of a Roman gens, the most noted members of which were:* a, M. Curtius, *a Roman youth, said to have jumped into a chasm in the Roman forum, which then closed;* **b,** C. Curtius Postumus, *an adherent of Caesar's;* Q. Curtius Rufus, *the author of a Latin history of Alexander the Great, probably contemporary with Vespasian.* Hence, Curtius lacus, *the chasm in the forum into which M. Curtius was said to have jumped.*

curto, 1. (curtus), *to abridge, abbreviate, lessen,* Hor,

curtus -a -um. *shortened, mutilated, cut short;* res, Ov.; mulus, Hor.; transf., of discourse, *cut short;* curta sentiunt nec amant redundantia, Cic.

cŭrūlis -e (currus), *relating to a chariot;* equi. *the team of four horses provided out of the public purse for the Circensian games,* Liv.; sella, *the curule chair adorned with ivory, the official seat of the consuls, praetors, and curule aediles,* Cic.; curulis aedilis, *a curule aedile,* Liv.

curvāmen -Inis, n. (curvo), *a curving, vaulting, arching,* Ov.

curvātūra -ae, f. (curvo), *a vault, arch,* Plin.; rotae, *the rim,* Ov.

curvo, 1. (curvus), *to bend, bow, curve;* curvare brachia longo circuitu, Ov.; quum nux plurima curvabit ramos, *makes to bend,* Verg.; tollimur in caelum curvato gurgite, Verg.; curvare genua sua, Verg.; Hadria curvans Calabros sinus, Hor.; transf., *make to bend, move;* nec te vir Pieria pellice saucius curvat, Hor.

curvus -a -um (κυρτός), *bent, bowed, arched, curved, crooked;* arbor, *bent with the weight of fruit,* Ov.; aratrum, Verg.; naves, Ov.; litus, Hor.; flumen, *winding,* Verg.; cursus arator, *bowed down,* Verg.; curva senecta, Ov.; subst., **curvum** -i, n. *what is crooked;* curvo dignoscere rectum, Hor.

cuspis -Idis, f. **A.** Lit. *a point,* esp. *the point* or *head of a spear;* asseres pedum XII cuspidibus praefixi, Caes.; of the sting of a bee, Plin.; of a scorpion, Ov. **B.** Meton. a, *a lance, javelin;* infestis cuspidibus uti, Liv.; **b,** *Neptune's trident;* cuspis triplex, Ov.; **c,** *a spit,* Mart.

custōdĭa -ae, f. (custos). **I.** *a watching, guarding, custody, care.* **A.** Lit. a, canum, Cic.; aliquem diligenti custodia asservare, Liv.; **b,** milit. t.t. *keeping guard, watching;* custodiae classium, Caes.; committere custodiam corporis feris barbaris, Cic. **B.** Meton., 1, *the watch, sentinels;* a, sing., in prose only collective, custodiam ex suis ac praesidium sex milia hominum unā reliquerunt, Caes.; **b,** plur., frequens cus-

todiis locus, Liv.; circumdare horribiles custodias, Cic.; disponere custodias diligentius, Caes.; **2,** *the station of the guard, post;* haec mea sedes est, haec vigilia, haec custodia, Cic. **II.** Esp. *custody, safe-keeping;* custodia libera, *liberation on parole,* Liv.; dare aliquem in custodiam, Cic.; esse in custodiā publicā, Cic.; necari in custodiā, Caes.

custōdĭo, 4. (custos). **I.** Gen. *to guard, watch, keep;* tuum corpus domumque, Cic.; se diligentissime, Cic.; custodire salutem alicuius, Cic.; poma, of a dragon, Ov. **II.** Esp. a, *to keep in sight, observe, watch;* aliquem custodire ne quid auferat, Cic.; A. Terentius Varro ad custodiendum iter eorum missus, Liv.; **b,** *to take care of;* liber tuus a me custoditur diligentissime, Cic.; custodire aliquid litteris, Cic.; **c,** *to keep in prison, hold captive;* ducem praedonum, Cic.; obsides, Caes.

custos -ōdis, c. **I.** Gen. *a guardian, watchman, keeper, preserver, attendant;* a, portae, Liv.; custos defensorque provinciae, Cic.; custos urbis, Cic.; fortitudo custos dignitatis, Cic.; **b,** *the guardian of a young man;* custos incorruptissimus, Hor.; **c,** *the guardian of a woman;* nimium servat custos Junonius Io, Ov.; d, *the officer in charge of the voting-tablets;* custodes tabellarum, Cic.; **e,** milit. t.t. *a sentinel, guard;* custodes dare, Cic.; disponere, Caes. **II.** a, *an overseer, overlooker, spy;* custos ac vindex cupiditatum, Cic.; **b,** *the gaoler, guard of a prisoner;* jugulari a custodibus, Nep.

cŭtĭcŭla -ae, f. (dim. of cutis), *the skin, cuticle,* Juv.

Cŭtĭliae -ārum, f. *an old town in the country of the Sabines.*

cūtis -is, f. (root CUT, Gr. KYT, whence κύτος), *the skin,* Hor.; *hide, leather,* Mart.

Cўănē -ēs, f. (Κυάνη), *a nymph changed into a fountain for her grief at the loss of Proserpine.*

Cўănēē -ēs, f. (Κυανέη), *daughter of Maeander, mother of Caunus and Byblis.*

cўăthus -i, m. (κύαθος), **1,** *a ladle for filling the goblets* (pocula) *with wine out of the crater,* Hor.; **2,** *a measure of capacity* = one-twelfth of a sextarius, Hor.

cўbaeus -a -um, navis and absol., **cўbaea** -ae, f. *a kind of transport* or *merchantman,* Cic.

Cўbĕlē or **Cўbēbē** -ēs, f. (Κυβέλη, Κυβήβη), **1,** *a Phrygian goddess, afterwards worshipped at Rome under various names* (Rhea, Ops, Magna Mater, etc.), *whose priests were called Galli;* adj., **Cўbĕlēĭus** -a -um, *belonging to Cybele;* **2,** *a mountain in Phrygia.*

Cўbistra -ōrum, n. (τὰ Κύβιστρα), *a town in Cataonia, at the foot of Mount Taurus.*

1. cўclas -ădis, f. (κυκλάς), *a female robe of state, having a border of purple* or *gold embroidery,* Juv.

2. Cўclas -ădis, f. (sc. insula), gen. in plur. **Cyclădes** -um, f. (Κυκλάδες), *a group of islands in the Aegean Sea.*

cўclĭcus -a -um (κυκλικός), *cyclic;* scriptor, *an epic poet whose works formed a complete cycle of history,* Hor.

Cўclops -clōpis, m. (Κύκλωψ, *round-eyed*), *a Cyclops,* gen. in plur., **Cўclōpes** -clōpum, m. *the Cyclopes, a gigantic one-eyed race, the workmen of Vulcan;* sing., *the Cyclops Polyphemus,* Hor. Adj., **Cўclōpĭus** -a -um, saxa, *Sicilian,* Verg.

Cycnēius -a -um, *belonging to the Boeotian Cycnus;* Tempe, Ov.

cycnēus -a -um (κύκνειος), *belonging to the swan;* plumae, Ov.; tamquam cycnea fuit divini hominis vox et oratio, *his swan's song,* Cic.

1. cȳcnus -i, m. (κύκνος), *the swan, famed in legend for its death-song, sacred to Apollo*, Cic.; metòn. = *poet;* Dircaeus cycnus, *Pindar*, Hor.

2. Cȳcnus -i, m. 1, *king of Liguria, son of Sthenelus, changed into a swan;* 2, *the son of Neptune by Calyce, changed into a swan.*

Cȳdōnēa -ae, f. (Κυδωνεια), *an ancient city on the north coast of Crete;* hence, 1, **Cȳdōn** -ōnis, m. *a Cydonian;* 2, **Cȳdōniātae** -ārum, m. *inhabitants of Cydonia;* 3, **Cȳdōnius** -a -um, poet. for *Cretan*, Verg.; 4, **Cȳdōnēus** -a -um, poet. for *Cretan*.

cygn . . . v. cycn . . .

cȳlindrus -dri, m. (κύλινδρος), 1, *a cylinder*, Cic.; 2, *a roller for levelling the ground*, Verg.

Cyllărŏs and **-ŭs** -i, m. (Κύλλαρος), 1, *a Centaur;* 2, *the horse of Castor or Pollux.*

Cyllēnē -ēs and -ae, f. (Κυλλήνη). **I.** *a high mountain in north-east Arcadia, where Mercury was born and reared.* Hence, adj., 1, **Cyllēnius** -a -um, *Cyllenian and Mercurian;* proles, *Mercury*, Verg.; also *Cephalus, son of Mercury,* Ov.; ignis, *the planet Mercury*, Verg.; subst., **Cyllenius** -ii, m. *Mercury*, Verg.; 2, **Cyllēnēus** -a -um, *Cyllenian or Mercurian;* fides, *the lyre*, Hor.; 3, **Cyllēnis** -ĭdis, f. *Cyllenian or Mercurian.* **II.** *a town in the north of Elis.*

cymba -ae, f. (κύμβη), *a small boat, skiff*, Cic.; esp. *the boat of Charon*, Verg.

cymbălum -i, n. (κύμβαλον), *a cymbal,* usually found in the plur., Cic.

cymbĭum -ii, n. (κυμβίον), *a small drinking-vessel*, Verg.

Cȳmē -ēs, f. (Κύμη). **A.** *a town in Aeolis, mother-city of Cumae in Campania.* Adj., **Cȳmaeus** -a -um, *Cymaean.* **B.** = Cumae (q.v.).

Cȳnăpēs, m. *a river in Asia, falling into the Black Sea.*

Cȳnĭcus -i, m. (Κυνικός), *a Cynic philosopher, a Cynic.* Adj., **Cȳnĭcus** -a -um, *Cynic.*

cȳnŏcĕphălus -i, m. *an ape with a head like a dog's*, Cic.

Cȳnŏs and **-ŭs** i, f. (Κῦνος), *a town in Locris.*

Cȳnŏsargēs -is, n. (Κυνόσαργις), *a gymnasium outside Athens, sacred to Hercules.*

Cȳnoscĕphălae -ārum, f. (Κυνὸς κεφαλαί, *dogs' heads), two hills near Scotussa in Thessaly where the Romans defeated the Macedonians.*

Cȳnŏsūra -ae, f. (κυνόσουρά), *the constellation of the Little Bear, the pole star*, Cic. Adj., **Cȳnŏsūris** -ĭdis, ursa, *the Little Bear*, Ov.

Cȳnŏsūrae -ārum, f. (Κυνόσουρα), *a promontory in Attica.*

Cynthus -i, m. (Κύνθος), *a mountain in Delos, the birthplace of Apollo and Diana;* hence, **Cynthĭus** -ii, m. *Apollo;* **Cynthĭa** -ae, f. *Diana.*

1. Cȳpărissus -i, m. *a youth beloved by Apollo, changed into a cypress.*

2. cȳpărissus = cupressus (q.v.).

Cȳprus and **-ŏs** -i, f. (Κύπρος), *the island of Cyprus;* hence adj., **Cȳprius** -a -um, *Cyprian;* Cyprium aes, or subst., **Cȳprium** -ii, n. *copper*, Plin. Subst., **Cȳpria** -ae, f. *Venus*, Tib.; **Cȳprii** -orum, m. *the Cypriotes.*

Cypsĕlus -i, m. (Κύψελος), *a tyrant of Corinth.*

Cȳrēnē -ēs (**-ae** -ārum), f. **I.** *a city of North Africa, birthplace of the poet Callimachus and of the philosopher Aristippus, founder of the Cyrenaic school.* Hence 1, adj., **Cȳrēnaeus** -a -um,

Cyrenaic; **Cȳrēnaei** -orum, m. *the Cyrenai, philosophers;* 2, **Cȳrēnăĭcus** -a -um, *Cyrenaic;* **Cȳrēnăĭci** -orum, *the Cyrenaic philosophers;* 3, **Cȳrēnensis** -e, *Cyrenaic.* **II. Cȳrēnē** -es, f. *daughter of Hypseus, mother of Aristaeus by Apollo.*

Cyrnŏs (Cyrnus) -i, f. (Κύρνος), *the island of Corsica.* Adj., **Cyrnaeus** -a -um, *Corsican.*

Cyrtaei or **Cyrtĭi** -ōrum, m. *a people in Persis and Media.*

Cȳrus -i, m. (Κῦρος), 1, *the founder of the Persian Empire;* 2, *Cyrus minor, second son of Ochus, who fought with his brother, Artaxerxes Memnon, and was killed at Cunaxa;* 3, *an architect at Rome in the time of Cicero;* hence, **Cȳrēa** -ōrum, n. *the works of Cyrus*, Cic.; 4, *a youth mentioned by Horace.*

Cȳtae -ārum, f. (Κύται), *a city in Colchis, birthplace of Medea.* Adj., 1, **Cȳtaeus** -a -um, *Cytaean* = Colchian; 2, **Cȳtaeis** -ĭdis, f. *the Cytaean,* i.e., *Medea.*

Cȳthēra -ōrum, n. (Κύθηρα), *the island Cythera, sacred to Venus, now Cerigo;* hence 1, **Cȳthērēa** -ae, f. *Venus;* 2, **Cȳthērēïus** -a -um, *Cytherean;* subst., **Cȳthērēïa** -ae, f., *Venus;* 3, **Cȳthērēïs** -ĭdis, f. *the Cytherean, Venus;* 4, **Cȳthērĭacus** -a -um, and 5, **Cȳthērēïas** -ādis, f. *sacred to Venus.*

Cythnŏs (Cythnus) -i, f. (Κύθνος), *an island in the Aegean Sea, now Thermia.*

cȳtĭsus -i, c. and **cȳtĭsum** -i, n. (κύτισος), *a kind of clover or trefoil much valued by the ancients*, Verg.

Cȳtōrus -i, m. (Κύτωρος), *a mountain and city in Paphlagonia, famous for box-trees.* Adj., **Cȳtōrĭăcus** -a -um, *Cytorian;* pecten, *made of boxwood*, Ov.

Cȳzĭcus (-ŏs) -i, f. (Κύζικος) and **Cȳzĭcum** -i, n. *a town on the Propontis.* Adj., **Cȳzĭcēnus** -a -um, *Cyzicene.*

D

D d, *the fourth letter of the Latin alphabet, corresponding in sound and alphabetical position with the Greek* Δ, δ. For its meaning as an abbreviation, see Table of Abbreviations.

Dāci -ōrum, m. *the Dacians, a warlike people on the Lower Danube;* hence, 1, **Dācia** -ae, f. *their country, Dacia;* 2, **Dācĭcus** -i, m. (sc. nummus), *a gold coin of Domitian, the conqueror of the Dacians.*

dactȳlĭcus -a -um (δακτυλικός), *dactylic;* numerus, Cic.

dactȳlĭŏthēca -ae, f. (δακτυλιοθήκη), 1, *a casket for rings*, Mart.; 2, *a collection of seal rings and gems*, Plin.

dactȳlus (-ŏs) -i, m. (δάκτυλος) (lit. *a finger), a metrical foot, consisting of one long, followed by two short syllables* ($\_ \cup \cup$), *a dactyl*, Cic.

Daedăla -ōrum, n. *a stronghold in Caria.*

1. daedălus -a -um (δαίδαλος), 1, act., *artful, full of art;* Circe, Verg.; 2, pass., *artfully constructed;* tecta, Verg.

2. Daedălus -i, m. (Δαίδαλος), *a celebrated Athenian artificer, builder of the Cretan labyrinth;* hence adj., **Daedălēus** -a -um, *Daedalean;* iter, *the labyrinth*, Prop.

Dăhae -ārum, m. (Δάαι), *a Scythian tribe on the east side of the Caspian Sea.*

Dalmătae (Delmătae) -ārum, m. (Δαλ-μάται), *the Dalmatians, inhabitants of Dalmatia.* Hence **1, Dălmătĭă** -ae, f. *the country of Dalmatia on the east side of the Adriatic Sea ;* **2,** adj., **Dalmătĭcus** -a -um, *Dalmatian* ; subst., **Dalmătĭcus** -i, m. *surname of Metellus, conqueror of the Dalmatians.*

dāma -ae, f. (in Verg. m.), *a fallow-deer,* Hor.

Dămascus -i, f. (Δαμασκός), *the Syrian city of Damascus.* Adj., **Dămascēnus** -a -um, *Damascene* ; pruna, *damsons,* Plin.

Dămăsippus -i, m. *cognomen in the gens* Licinia.

damma = dama (q.v.).

damnātĭo -ōnis, f. (damno), *condemnation ;* ambitus, *for bribery,* Cic. ; tantae pecuniae, *to pay,* etc., Cic.

damnātōrĭus -a -um (damno), *relating to condemnation, condemnatory,* Cic. ; judicium, Cic.

damno, 1. (damnum). **I.** *to condemn, declare guilty, sentence.* **A.** Lit. legal t.t., alicuius ministros sociosque, Cic. ; with acc. of the cause, causa judicata atque damnata, Cic. ; with acc. of person, aliquem inauditum, Tac. ; damnari inter sicarios, *to be condemned as an assassin,* Cic.; damnari per arbitrum, Cic. ; daṃnari nullam aliam ob causam, Cic. ; with perf. infin. act., aut dabis aut contra edictum fecisse damnabere, Cic.; with quod, A. Baebius unus est damnatus, quod milites Romanos praebuisset ad ministerium caedis, Liv.; with abl. of the motive, inutili pudore causam suam damnare, Liv. ; with abl. of the accusation, damnari eo crimine, Cic. ; with abl. of the law or formula, damnari suā lege, Cic. ; with the abl. of the court, damnari populi judicio, Cic. ; with abl. of the punishment, damnari aliquem capite, *to loss of civil rights,* Cic.; with genit. of the crime, ambitus, Cic. ; with genit. of the punishment, damnari octupli, Cic. ; with de, damnari de vi, Cic. ; with ad, damnari ad mortem, Tac. **B.** Transf., a, of deities, damnare aliquem voti or voto, *to grant a person's wish, and thereby compel him to keep his vow* ; damnabis tu quoque votis, *you will grant prayer, and thereby bind the suppliant to keep his vow,* Verg. ; gen. in pass., damnari voti or voto, *to attain one's wish ;* bis eiusdem voti damnata republica, Liv. ; b, of a testator, *to bind the heir,* Hor. ; c, *to sentence* to endure or suffer ; damnare aeterna lumina nocte, Ov. ; d, *to condemn a person on account of, to inculpate ;* aliquem summae stultitiae, Cic. ; e, *to blame, disapprove of ;* nec mihi mens dubia est, queri te tuā numinā damnent, Ov. ; f, *to assign, devote to* (for destruction), Ilion, mihi castaeque damnatum Minervae, Hor. **II.** *to procure the condemnation of a person ;* hoc uno crimine illum, Cic.

damnōsē, adv. (damnosus), *ruinously ;* bibere, *to the host's loss,* Hor.

damnōsus -a -um, adj. with compar. and superl. (damnum), *causing loss or damage, mischievous, ruinous, detrimental ;* bellum sumptuosum et damnosum Romanis, Liv.

damnum -i, n. (old form dampnum, from root DAP, connected with daps, Gr. ΔΑΠ, whence δαπάνη, or else from dare = *the thing given as a punishment), loss, damage, injury* (opp. lucrum). **I.** Gen. contrahere, facere, *to suffer injury,* Cic. ; pati, Liv. ; damna caelestia lunae, *the waning of the moon,* Hor. ; maximis damnis affici, Cic. ; dare damnum, *to cause loss,* Cic. ; damnum naturae, *a natural defect,* Liv. ; stomachum suum damno Tulli (*to the injury o)* explere, Cic. **II.** Esp., **1,** *loss in war, defeat ;*

damna Romano accepta bello, Liv. ; **2,** *a fine,* pecuniary mulct, Cic.

Dămŏclēs -is, m. (Δαμοκλῆς), *a friend of Dionysius, tyrant of Syracuse, who, on praising the tyrant's prosperity, was placed by Dionysius at a sumptuous feast, and a sword was let down so as to hang by a hair over his head.*

Dāmōn -ōnis, m. (Δάμων), **1,** *a Pythagorean, famous for his friendship with Phintias ;* **2,** *a celebrated Athenian musician, teacher of Socrates.*

Dănăē -ēs, f. (Δανάη), *daughter of Acrisius, mother of Perseus by Zeus, who visited her in a shower of gold when shut up in a tower by her father ;* hence, adj., **Dănăēĭus** -a -um ; heros, *Perseus,* Ov.

Dănăus -i, m. (Δαναός), *son of Belus, brother of Aegyptus, and father of the fifty Danaïdes, the mythical founder of Argos ;* hence, **1,** adj., **Dănăus** -a -um, *Greek, Argive* ; pl. **Dănăi** -ōrum, m. *the Greeks ;* **2, Dănăĭdes** -um, f. *the daughters of Danaus.*

Dānŭbĭus (Dānŭvĭus) -ĭi, m. *the Danube* (in the upper part of its course ; the lower part was called Ister).

dăno, v. do.

Daphnē -ēs, f. (Δάφνη), **1,** *the daughter of the river-god Peneus, changed into a laurel tree ;* **2,** *a grove and temple to Apollo and Diana near Antiochia in Syria.*

Daphnis -nĭdis, acc. -nim and -nīn (Δάφνις), *son of Mercury, a Sicilian shepherd, inventor of pastoral poetry, and the favourite of Pan.*

daphnōn -ōnis, m. (δαφνών), *a grove of laurels,* Mart.

daps, dăpis, f. (root DAP, Gr. ΔΑΠ, whence δάπτω, δαπάνη), **1,** *a sacrificial feast, religious banquet ;* ergo obligatam redde Jovi dapem, Hor.; **2,** *a meal, feast, banquet ;* amor dapis, Hor. ; humanā dape (*with human flesh*) pascere equos, Ov. ; plur., dapibus epulari opimis, Verg.

dapsĭlis -e (δαψιλής), *sumptuous, plentiful, richly provided,* Plaut.

Dardăni -ōrum, m. (Δάρδανοι), *a people in Upper Moesia, the modern Servia.*

Dardănus -i, m. (Δάρδανος), *son of Jupiter and Electra of Arcadia, the mythical ancestor of the royal family of Troy ;* hence **1, Dardănus** -a -um, *Trojan* ; subst., **Dardăni** -ōrum, m. *the Trojans;* **2, Dardănĭus** -a -um, *Trojan ;* subst., **Dardănĭa** -ae, f. *Troy:* **3, Dardănĭdes** -ae, m. *a descendant of Dardanus, Aeneas,* Verg. ; *a Trojan,* Verg. ; **4, Dardănis** -ĭdis, f. *a Trojan woman,* Ov. ; *Creusa,* Verg.

Dărēs -rētis, m. (Δάρης), *a companion to Aeneas, a boxer.*

Dārēus and **Dārĭus** -i, m. (Δαρεῖος), *name of several Persian kings ;* **1,** Darius Hystaspis, *died* 485 B.C. ; **2,** *son of Xerxes ;* **3,** Darius Ochus or Nothus, *died* 404 B.C. ; **4,** Darius Codomannus, *the last Persian king.*

dătĭo -ōnis, f. (do), **1,** *a giving ;* legum, Cic. ; **2,** *the legal right of alienation,* Liv.

Dātis -tĭdis, acc. -tim, m. (Δᾶτις), *a Mede, general of Darius Hystaspis, defeated with Artaphernes at Marathon.*

dător -ōris, m. (do), *a giver ;* laetitiae, *Bacchus,* Verg.

Daulis -ĭdis, f. (Δαυλίς), *a city in Phocis ;* adj., **Daulĭas** -ădis, f. *Daulian ;* ales, Procne, Ov. ; Dauliades puellae, *Procne and Philomela,* Verg.

Daunus -i, m. *a mythical king of Apulia, father (or ancestor) of Turnus, and father-in-law of Diomedes ;* hence **1, Daunĭus** -a -um. *Daunian ;*

heros, *Turnus*, Verg.; gens, *the Rutulians, of whom Turnus was king*, Verg.; dea, *Juturna, sister of Turnus*, Verg.; Camena, *the Roman muse*, Hor.; caedes, *Roman*, Hor.; **2, Daunīas** -ădis, f. *Apulia*, Hor.

dē, prep., with abl., *from*. **I.** In space, *from, away from, down from;* de alterā parte agri Sequanos decedere juberet, Caes.; de manibus effugere, Cic.; de digito anulum detrahere, Cic. **II.** Transf., **A.** Of time, 1, *in the course of, during;* de nocte venire, Cic.; de die, *in the day-time*, Hor.; de mense Decembri navigare, Cic.; **2,** *from, immediately after;* statim de auctione venire, Cic.; diem de die differre, proferre, *to put off from day to day*, Liv. **B.** 1, *from,* of the place from which a person comes; copo de viā Latinā, Cic.; rabula de foro, Cic.; Libyca de rupe Leones, *African lions*, Ov.; **2,** to denote a body of persons *out of* which some one is taken; hominem certum misi de comitibus meis, Cic.; esp. **a,** of the birth, origin, class to which a person belongs, homo de plebe, Cic.; **b,** in the place of the partitive genit., de duobus honestis utrum honestius, Cic.; **3,** *out of*, to express the material out of which a thing is made, de eodem oleo et operā exarare aliquid, Cic.; esp. **a,** of the change of one thing to another, de templo carcerem fieri, Cic.; **b,** *from*, of the property which bears the cost of anything, de meo, de tuo, etc., *from my property;* de publico, *at the public expense*, Cic.; **c,** of the part of the body which suffers punishment, de tergo satisfacere, Cic.; **4,** of the ground, cause of a thing, *on account of*, gravi de causā, Cic.; quā de causā, *on account of which*, Cic.; **5,** *in accordance with, in obedience to some form or example;* vix de meā sententiā concessum est, Cic.; **6,** *with relation to, concerning;* recte non credis de numero militum, Cic.; **7,** with adj., to form an adverbial phrase, de improviso, *unexpectedly*, Cic.; de integro, *anew*, Cic.

dĕa -ae, f. (dat. and abl. pl., diis, deis, deābus), *a goddess*, Cic.; triplices, *the Parcae*, Ov.; deae novem, *the Muses*, Ov.

dĕalbo, 1. *to whitewash, plaster;* columnas, Cic.

dĕambŭlo, 1. *to take a walk*, Suet.

dĕarmo, 1. *to disarm;* quibus dearmatus exercitus hostium, Liv.

dēbacchor, 1. dep. *to rave, rage furiously;* debacchantur ignes, Hor.

dēbellātor -ōris, m. (debello), *a conqueror;* ferarum, Verg.

dēbello, 1. **I.** Intransit. *to wage war to the end, finish a war;* neque priusquam debellavero absistam, Liv.; proelio uno debellatum est, Liv. **II.** Transit., **a,** *to fight out;* rixa super mero debellata, Hor.; **b,** *to conquer, overcome;* superbos, Verg.

dēbĕo -ŭi -ĭtum, 2. (for dehibeo, from de and habeo, *to have from a person, i.e. to be bound to restore something*). **I.** Lit. *to owe, be indebted;* alicui pecuniam, Cic.; talenta CC, Cic.; illi quibus debeo, *my creditors*, Cic.; absol. ii qui debent, *debtors*, Cic.; subst., **dēbĭtum** -i, n. *a debt;* debitum alicui solvere, Cic.; debito fraudari, Cic. **II.** Transf., **A.** *to remain indebted;* quod praesenti tibi peste subnegaram, non tribueram certe, id absenti debere non potui, Cic. **B.** *to owe, to be bound to repay;* **1,** morally, with acc., alicui gratiam Cic.; with infin. *to be bound, to be pledged;* homines, qui te et maxime debuerunt et plurimum juvare potuerunt, Cic.; partic. **dēbĭtus** -a -um, *bound, owed;* debitae poenae, Cic.; **2,** *to be bound or obliged by fate or circumstances;* tu, nisi ventis debes ludibrium, *if you are not bound to become*, Hor.; debitus destinatusque morti, Liv.; vita quae fato debetur, Cic.; **3,**

to owe, to have to thank a person for, to be indebted to a person for; alicui beneficium, Cic.; alicui vitam, Ov.

dēbĭlis -e, adj. with compar. (orig. dehibilis, from de and habilis), *feeble, weak.* **A.** Lit., corpus, Cic.; senex, Cic.; ferrum, Verg. **B.** Transf., mancam ac debilem praeturam futuram suam, Cic.

dēbĭlĭtas -ātis, f. (debilis), *weakness, feebleness, debility.* **A.** Lit., bonum integritas corporis, miserum debilitas, Cic.; linguae, Cic. **B.** Transf., animi, Cic.

dēbĭlĭtātĭo -ōnis, f. (debilito), *a weakening, weakness;* animi, Cic.

dēbĭlĭto, 1. (debilis), *to lame, weaken, cripple, disable.* **A.** Lit. **a,** membra lapidibus, fustibus, Cic.; gen. in pass., esp. in partic. perf., debilitatum corpus et contrucidatum, Cic.; **b,** of things, quae (hiems) nunc oppositis debilitat pumicibus mare Tyrrhenum, Hor. **B.** Transf. *to enervate, break the force of, disable;* audaciam debilito, sceleri resisto, Cic.; tribunicios furores, Cic.; debilitatum metu, Cic.

dēbĭtĭo -ōnis, f. (debeo), *an owing, debt;* pecuniae, Cic.

dēbĭtor -ōris, m. (debeo), *one who owes, a debtor.* **A.** Lit., addicere Futidium creditorem debitoribus suis, Cic. **B.** Transf., mercede solutā non manet officio debitor ille tuo, Ov.; *owing his life to*, Ov.

dēbĭtum -i, n. v. debeo.

dēcanto, 1. **I.** Transit., 1, *to sing, repeat in singing;* elegos, Hor.; 2, *to repeat over and over again;* pervulgata praecepta, Cic. **II.** Intransit., *to leave off singing;* sed jam decantaverant fortasse, Cic.

dēcēdo -cessi -cessum, 3. **I.** Lit., *to go forth, go away, depart.* **A.** Gen., **a,** ex nostrā provinciā, Cic.; decedere Italiā, Sall.; of animals, decedere e pastu, Verg.; **b,** de viā decedere, *to depart from one's course*, Cic.; naves imprudentiā aut tempestate paululum suo cursu decesserunt, Cic.; fig., se nullā cupiditate inductum de viā decessisse, Cic.; alicui de viā decedere, *to make way for*, as a sign of respect, Plaut.; salutari appeti, decedi, *to have persons make way for you*, Cic.; decedere canibus de viā, *to get out of the way of*, Cic.; *to yield to, get out of the way for, cease on account of;* serae decedere nocti, Verg.; calori, Verg.; **c,** milit. t. t., *to march away, to evacuate;* decedere atque exercitum deducere ex his regionibus, Caes.; pugnā, Liv.; **d,** of the magistrate of a province, *to leave on the expiration of his term;* de or ex or (simply) provinciā, Cic.; **e,** of actors, decedere de scenā, Cic. **B.** Esp., **a,** *to depart from life, to die;* decedere de vitā, Cic.; or absol., decedere, Cic.; pater nobis decessit a. d. III. Cal. Dec., Cic.; **b,** of things without life, (α) of water, *to retire;* quum decessisse inde aquam nuntiatum esset, Liv.; (β) of the sun and moon, *to set;* sol decedens, Verg.; (γ) of diseases, *to cease;* alteram quartanam mihi dixit decessisse, Cic. **II.** Transf., **A.** Gen., **a,** *to abandon property;* de possessione, Cic.; **b,** *to abandon a plan or opinion;* de sententiā, Cic.; **c,** *to swerve from duty;* de officio et dignitate, Cic.; **d,** *to yield place to;* with dat., vivere si recte nescis, decede peritis, Hor. **B. a,** *to decrease;* ut de causā periculi nihil decederet, Cic.; **b,** *to cease;* postquam invidia decesserat, Sall.

Dĕcēlēa (-ĭa) -ae, f. (Δεκέλεια), *a town in Attica on the Boeotian border.*

dĕcem (δέκα), ten. **A.** Lit., Cic. **B. Meton.,** *an indefinite number;* decem vitia, Hor.

Dĕcember -bris -bre, abl. -bri, (decem), **1,** mensis December, *the tenth month of the Roman year reckoned from March, December*, Cic.; subst.,

Dĕcember -bris, m. *December ;* 2, *belonging to the month December ;* kalendae, Cic. ; libertate Decembri utere, *the licence of December,* i.e., *of the Saturnalia,* Hor.

dĕcempĕda -ae, f. (decem and pes), *a measuring rod ten feet in length,* Cic.

dĕcempĕdātor -ōris, m. (decempeda), *one who uses the decempeda, a land surveyor ;* aequissimus agri privati et publici decempedator, Cic.

dĕcemplex -ĭcis (decem and plex, from plico), *ten-fold,* Nep.

dĕcemprīmi -ōrum, m. (often written in two words), *the ten chief men in the senate of a* municipium or colonia, Cic.

dĕcemscalmus -a -um (decem and scalmus), *having ten thowls or rowlocks ;* actuariolum, Cic.

dĕcemvir -i, m., gen. plur., **dĕcemvĭri** -ōrum or -um, m. *a college of ten magistrates at Rome ;* 1, decemviri legibus scribendis, *the magistrates who drew up the XII. Tables ;* 2, decemviri sacrorum or sacris faciundis, *the guardians of the Sibylline Books ;* 3, decemviri stlitibus (litibus) judicandis, *a judicial body who judged in cases affecting freedom and citizenship ;* 4, decemviri agris metiendis dividendisque, *commissioners for dividing public land.*

dĕcemvĭrālis -e (decemvir), *relating to the decemvirs ;* annus, Cic. ; potestas, Liv.

dĕcemvĭrātus -ūs, m. (decemvir), *the office or dignity of a decemvir,* Cic.

dĕcens -entis, p. adj. with compar. and superl. (decet), 1, *seemly, becoming, decent ;* amictus, Ov. ; quid verum atque decens curo atque rogo, Hor. ; 2, *well-formed, handsome, comely ;* facies, forma, Ov. ; malae, Hor. ; Venus, Hor.

dĕcentĭa -ae, f. (decet), *comeliness, decency ;* figurarum venustas atque ordo, et ut ita dicam, decentia, Cic.

dĕcerno -crēvi -crētum, 3. **I.** *to decide.* **A.** *peacefully ;* 1, qui sine manibus et pedibus constare deum posse decreverunt, Cic. ; 2, a, *to decide judicially ;* quod iste aliter atque edixisset decrevisset, Cic. ; b, of the senate, etc., or of individual members of the senate, *to decree, propose ;* si hic ordo (*the senate*) placere decreverat te ire in exsilium, obtemperaturum te esse dicis, Cic. ; pecunias ad templum monumentumque alicuius, Cic. ; D. Junius Silanus primus sententiam rogatus supplicium sumendum decreverat, Sall. ; senatus decrevit, darent operam consules, ne quid respublica detrimenti caperet, Sall. ; alicui triumphum, Cic. ; 2, *to decide in a hostile manner ;* decernere pugnam, Liv. ; proelium, Cic. ; decernere armis, Cic. ; crastino die bene juvantibus diis acie decernamus, Liv. **II.** *to resolve, form a resolution, settle ;* gen. with infin., Caesar his de causis Rhenum transire decreverat, Caes. ; decreram cum eo familiariter vivere, Cic. (syncop. perf. forms, decrerim, decreram, decrero, decresset, decresse).

dĕcerpo -cerpsi -cerptum, 3. **A.** Lit., *to pluck off, pluck away ;* arbore pomum, Ov. **II.** 1, transf., humanus animus decerptus ex mente divinâ, *a scion of,* Cic. ; 2, *to take away ;* ne quid jocus de gravitate decerperet, Cic.

dĕcertātĭo -ōnis, f. (decerto), *a contest ;* harum rerum omnium, Cic.

dĕcerto, 1. *to contend, struggle vehemently, fight to a decision ;* proeliis cum acerrimis nationibus, Cic. ; pugnâ, Caes. ; armis, Caes. ; mecum contentione dicendi is locus, ubi Demosthenes et Aeschines inter se decertare soliti sunt, Cic. ; quâ de re jure decertari oporteret, armis non contendere, Cic.

dĕcessĭo -ōnis, f. (decedo), *a going away,*

departure (opp. accessio). **A.** Gen., tua decessio, Cic. **B.** Esp. 1, *the departure of a governor from his province* at the expiration of his year of office, Cic. ; 2, *lessening, diminution ;* non enim tam cumulus bonorum jucundus esse potest quam molesta discessio, Cic.

dĕcessor -ōris, m. (decedo), *one who retires from an office, a predecessor ;* successori decessor invidit, Cic.

dĕcessus -ūs, m. (decedo), *a going away, departure.* **I.** Gen., Dionysii, Nep. **II.** Esp. **A.** *the retirement of a magistrate from office ;* post M. Bruti decessum, Cic. **B.** 1, *death ;* amicorum, Cic. ; 2, of water, *ebb ;* aestus, Caes.

dĕcet -cŭit, 2. (root DEC or DIC, whence also dignus), *it becomes, it fits.* **A.** Lit., quem decet muliebris ornatus, Cic. ; quem tenues decuere togae nitidique capilli, Hor. **B.** Transf., *it beseems, it is fitting, it suits ;* id enim maxime quemque decet, quod est cuiusque maxime suum, Cic. ; et quod decet honestum est et quod honestum est decet, Cic. ; oratorem irasci minime decet, Cic. ; with infin., exemplis grandioribus decuit uti, Cic. ; absol., quo majorem spem habeo nihil fore aliter ac deceat, Cic.

Decetĭa -ae, f. *a town of the Aedui on the Liger,* now *Decize.*

1. **dĕcĭdo** -cĭdi, 3. (de and cado), *to fall down ;* absol. or with ex, ab, de, or abl. alone. **A.** Lit., of things, a, of water, si decidit imber, Hor. ; b, of things that fall naturally, poma, si matura et cocta, decidunt, Cic. ; fig., ficta omnia celeriter tamquam flosculi decidunt, Cic. ; c, of buildings, *to fall down ;* celsae graviore casu decidunt turres, Hor. ; 2, of persons, a, decidere equo, Caes. ; in praeceps, *headlong,* Ov. ; fig., ex astris decidere, *to fall from the height of happiness,* Cic. ; b, *to die ;* scriptor abhinc annos centum qui decidit, Hor. **B.** Transf., *to sink, fall ;* postquam a spe societatis Prusiae decidit, Liv. ; in hanc fraudem tuam tam scelestam ac tam nefariam decidisti, Cic.

2. **dĕcīdo** -cīdi -cīsum, 3. (de and caedo). **A.** Lit., *to hew off, cut off ;* aures, Tac. ; pennas, Hor. **B.** Transf., a, *to cut short ;* post decisa negotia, Hor. ; b, *to decide or determine a dispute ;* quibus omnibus rebus actis atque decisis, Cic. ; per te, C. Aquili, decidit P. Quinctius quid liberis eius dissolveret, Cic. ; sine me cum Flavio decidisti, Cic.

dĕcĭes (-ĭens), adv. (decem), *ten times,* Cic.

dĕcĭma (dĕcŭma) -ae, f. (decimus), *a tenth part, tithe ;* a, as an offering to the gods, Oresti nuper prandia in semitis decumae nomine magno honori fuerunt, Cic. ; b, *a tax paid by landowners in the provinces ;* decima hordei, Cic.

dĕcĭmānus (dĕcŭmānus) -a -um (decimus, decumus). **I.** 1, *relating to the provincial tax of a tenth ;* ager, *the land paying a tenth,* Cic. ; frumentum, *a tithe of corn,* Cic. ; subst., **dĕcĭmānus** -i, m. *the farmer of such a tax,* Cic. ; mulier decimana or simply decimana -ae, f. (sarcastically), *the wife of a farmer of the taxes,* Cic. ; 2, milit. t. t., a, *belonging to the tenth legion,* Tac. ; b, *belonging to the tenth cohort ;* porta, *the gate of a Roman camp farthest from the enemy,* so called because the tenth cohorts of the legions were there stationed. **II.** Meton., *large, immense ;* acipenser, ap. Cic.

dĕcĭmo (dĕcŭmo), 1. (decimus) *to select every tenth man for punishment, to decimate,* Suet.

dĕcĭmus (dĕcŭmus), -a -um. **A.** Lit., *the tenth,* Cic. ; adv., decimum, *for the tenth time,* Liv. **B.** Meton., *large, vast, great ;* unda, Ov. Subst., **dĕcĭmum** -i, n. *tenfold ;* ager efficit or effert cum decimo, Cic.

dĕcĭpĭo -cēpi -ceptum, 3. (de and capio). **I**

to cheat, cozen, deceive; novem homines honest-issimos, Cic.; exspectationes, Cic. **II.** Esp. of time, *to beguile;* sic tamen absumo decipioque diem, Ov.

dĕcīsĭo -ōnis, f. (2. decido), *a decision;* decisionem facere, Cic.

Dĕcĭus -a -um, *name of a Roman gens, the most famous members of which,* P. Decius Mus, father and son, *devoted themselves to death in battle to save the state.*

dēclāmātĭo -ōnis, f. (declamo), 1, *loud, violent speaking, declamation;* non placet mihi declamatio (candidati) potius quam persalutatio, Cic.; 2, *practice in oratory;* quotidiana, Cic.

dēclāmātōrĭus -a -um (declamator), *relating to declamation, declamatory, rhetorical,* Cic.

dēclāmĭto, 1. (freq. of declamo), a, *to speak loudly, declaim;* Graece apud Cassium, Cic.; b, *to practise;* causas, *to plead for the sake of practice,* Cic.

dēclāmo, 1. 1, *to speak loudly and violently;* contra me, *to declaim against,* Cic.; 2, *to practise speaking in public;* a, intransit., ad fluctum aiunt declamare solitum Demosthenem, Cic.; b, transit., *to declaim;* quae mihi iste visus est ex aliā oratione declamare, quam in alium reum commentaretur, Cic.

dēclārātĭo -ōnis, f. (declaro), *a declaration, revealing;* animi tui, Cic.

dēclāro, 1. *to make clear or distinct, reveal, declare.* **A.** Lit., a, praesentiam saepe divi suam declarant, Cic.; b, *to declare, pronounce, proclaim;* aliquem consulem, Cic.; Numa declaratus rex, Liv. **B.** transf., *to explain, make clear, declare;* a, volatibus avium res futuras declarari, Cic.; with infin., quod plurimis locis perorationes nostrae voluisse nos atque animo contendisse declarant, Cic.; with relat. sent., declaravit quanti me faceret, Cic.; absol., res declarat, Cic.; b, *to signify, mean;* verba idem declarantia, *synonyms,* Cic.

dēclīnātĭo -ōnis, f. (declino). **A.** Lit., *a bending away, a turning aside;* tuas petitiones parvā quādam declinatione effugi, Cic.; declinatio atomi, Cic. **B.** Transf., a, *an avoiding, declining, turning away from;* appetitio et declinatio naturalis, Cic.; b, rhet. t. t., *a digression,* declinatio brevis a proposito, Cic.

dēclīno, 1. *to bend aside, turn away.* **I.** Gen., **A.** Lit., a, transit., si quo ego inde agmen declinare voluissem, Liv.; b, intransit., Cumanae cohortes declinavere paululum, Liv.; declinare de viā, Cic.; esp. of atoms, declinare dixit atomum perpaulum, Cic. **B.** Transf., 1, transit., ut declinet a proposito deflectatque sententiam, Cic.; 2, intransit., a, de statu suo, Cic.; a religione officii, Cic.; b, of orators, writers, *to digress;* aliquantum a proposito, Cic. **II.** *to avoid, shun;* 1, lit., urbem unam mihi amoenissimam, Cic.; 2, transf., vitia, Cic.

dēclīvis -e (de and clivus), *bent or inclined downwards, sloping;* collis aequaliter declivis ad flumen, Caes.; ripa, Ov. Subst., **dēclīve** -is, n. *a declivity;* per declive se recipere, Caes.

dēclīvĭtas -ātis, f. (declivis), *a declivity,* Caes.

dēcoctor -ōris, m. (decoquo), *a spendthrift, bankrupt,* Cic.

dēcollo, 1. (de and collum), *to behead,* Suet.

dēcŏlor -ōris, *discoloured.* **A.** Lit., decolor ipse suo sanguine Rhenus, Ov. **B.** Transf., *deteriorated;* deterior paulatim ac decolor aetas, Verg.

dēcŏlōrātĭo -ōnis, f. (decoloro), *a discolouring,* Cic.

dēcŏlōro, 1. (decolor), *to discolour;* quod mare Dauniae non decoloravere caedes, Hor.

dēcŏquo -coxi -coctum, 3. **I.** *to boil;* olus, Hor. **II. A.** Lit., of metals, *to melt away;* pars quarta argenti decocta erat, Liv.; fig., suavitas decocta, *insipid, washy,* Cic. **B.** Transf., absol., *to become bankrupt;* tenesne memoria praetextatum te decoxisse, Cic.

dĕcor -ōris, m. (decet), 1, *grace, elegance;* mobilibus decor naturis dandus et annis, Hor.; 2, *beauty;* te decor iste,quod optas,esse vetat,Ov.

dĕcōrē, adv. (decorus). 1, *properly, fitly, becomingly;* ad rerum dignitatem apte et quasi decore loqui, Cic.; 2, *beautifully,* Cic. poet.

dĕcŏro, 1. (decus). **A.** Lit., *to adorn, decorate;* oppidum monumentis, Cic.; templa novo saxo, Hor. **B.** Transf., *to honour;* quem populus Romanus singularibus honoribus decorasset, Cic.; haec omnia vitae decorabat dignitas et integritas, Cic.

dĕcōrus -a -um (decor). **A.** *fitting, seemly, becoming, decorous;* with infin., ut vix satis decorum videretur eum plures dies esse in Crassi Tusculano, Cic.; with dat., color albus praecipue decorus deo est, Cic.; with ad, ad ornatum decoras, Cic. Subst., **dĕcōrum** -i, n. *what is fitting, fitness, propriety;* πρέπον appellant hoc Graeci, nos dicamus sane decorum, Cic. **B.** *beautiful, graceful, handsome, adorned;* aedes, facies, Hor.; arma, Sall.

dēcrĕpĭtus -a -um, *very old, infirm, decrepit;* aetas, Cic.

dēcresco -crēvi -crētum, 3. *to lessen, become gradually smaller, decrease;* ostreis et conchyliis omnibus contingere, ut cum lunā pariter crescant pariterque decrescant, Cic.; decrescentia flumina, Hor.; cornua decrescunt, *become smaller and smaller, disappear,* Ov.; tantum animorum nobis in dies decrescit, Liv.

dēcrētum -i, n. (decerno), 1, *a resolve, resolution, decree;* consulis, Liv.; senatus, Cic.; decreta facere, Cic.; 2, philosoph. t. t. = δόγμα, *doctrine, principle,* Cic.

dĕcūmānus, v. decimanus.

dĕcŭmātes -ium (decimus), *relating to tithes;* agri, *lands on which the tithe or land-tax was paid,* Tac.

dēcumbo -cūbŭi, 3. (de and * cumbo), 1, *to lie down,* either to sleep or at table, Cic.; 2, *to fall, fall down,* used of a vanquished gladiator, Cic.

dĕcŭria -ae, f. (decem), 1, *a body of ten men,* Varr.; 2, *a class, division,* esp. of jurors; judicum, Cic.; scribarum, Cic.

dĕcŭrĭātĭo -ōnis, f. (1. decurio), *a dividing into decuriae,* Cic.

dĕcŭrĭātus -ūs, m. (1. decurio), *a dividing into decuriae,* Liv.

1. **dĕcŭrĭo**, 1. (decuria), *to divide into bodies of ten;* equites decuriati, centuriati pedites conjurabant, Liv.; decuriare tribules, Cic.

2. **dĕcŭrĭo** -ōnis, m. (decuria), 1, *the captain of a body of ten;* decurio equitum Gallorum, Caes.; 2, *a senator of a municipium or colonia,* Cic.

dēcurro -curri (more rarely -cucurri) -cursum, 3. **I.** Lit., *to run down, hasten down;* summā decurrit ab arce, Verg.; ad naves, Caes.; decurro rus, Cic.; esp., 1, milit. t. t., *to make an evolution towards a lower place;* a, in practice or at a festival, *to manœuvre, charge;* pedites ordinatos instrue॰o et decurrendo signa sequi et servare ordines docuit, Liv.; mos erat lustrationis sacro peracto decurrere exercitum, Liv.; b, *to charge the enemy, to run down;* ex Capitolio in hostem, Liv.; ex omnibus partibus

Caes.; **2,** *to run in a race, run towards the goal;* nunc video calcem, ad quam quum sit decursum, nihil sit praeterea extimescendum, Cic.; quasi decurso spatio, Cic.; **3,** of ships, *to sail;* ego puto te bellissime cum quaestore Mescinio decursurum, Cic.; **4,** of water, *to run down;* monte decurrens velut amnis, Hor. **II.** Transf., a, *to have recourse to, take refuge in;* decurrere ad istam cohortationem, Cic.; ad miseras preces, Hor.; **b,** *to finish;* prope acta jam aetate decursaque, Cic.; inceptum unā decurre laborem, Verg.; quae abs te breviter de urbe decursa sunt, *treated,* Cic.

dēcursĭo -ōnis, f. (decurro), *a military evolution* or *manœuvre, charge,* ap. Cic.

dēcursus -ūs, m. (decurro). **I.** Lit., *a running down;* in rus decurro atque in decursu, Cic.; esp., **1,** milit. t. t., a, *a manœuvre;* alios decursu edere motus, Liv.; **b,** *a charge, attack;* subitus ex collibus decursus, Liv.; **2,** of water, *running down;* aquarum, Ov. **II.** Transf., *the completion of an office;* decursu honorum, *after filling every public office,* Cic.

dēcurto, 1. *to cut off, abridge, curtail;* transf., of discourse, mutila sentit quaedam et quasi decurtata, Cic.

dĕcus -ŏris, n. (decet), *that which adorns or beautifies, an ornament, honour, glory, grace.* **I.** Gen., **A.** Lit., a, of things, decora atque ornamenta fanorum, Cic.; hominis decus ingenium, Cic.; civitatis dignitatem et decus sustinere, Cic.; **b,** of persons, *pride, glory;* imperii Romani decus ac lumen (of Pompey), Cic. **B.** Meton., esp. plur., decora, *exploits in war,* Liv.; renowned ancestors, Tac. **II.** Philosoph. t. t., *moral dignity, virtue,* Cic.

dĕcusso, 1. (decussis, *the intersection of two lines*), *to divide cross-wise in the shape of the letter* X, Cic.

dēcŭtĭo -cussi -cussum, 3. (de and quatio), *to shake down, shake off, throw down, knock off.* **I.** Lit., papavrum capita baculo, Liv.; rorem, Verg.; turres fulminibus, Liv.; ariete decussi ruebant muri, Liv. **II.** Transf., cetera aetate jam sunt decussa, *laid aside,* ap. Cic.

dēdĕcet -dĕcŭit, 2. *it is unbecoming, unsuitable to, unfitting,* gen. with a negative. **A.** Lit., neque te ministrum dedecet myrtus neque me, etc., Hor. **B.** Transf., *it is unseemly, unfitting;* with infin., simulare non dedecet, Cic.; falli, errare, labi, tam dedecet quam, etc., Cic.; of persons, *to dishonour;* Pomponius Atticus Claudiorum imagines dedecere videbatur, Tac.

dēdĕcor -ŏris, adj. *unseemly, shameful, vile,* Sall.

dēdĕcŏro, 1. (dedecus), *to dishonour, bring shame upon;* se flagitiis, Sall.; et urbis auctoritatem et magistri, Cic.

dēdĕcōrus -a -um, *shameful, dishonourable,* Tac.

dēdĕcus -ŏris, n. *shame, dishonour, disgrace.* **I.** Gen., **A.** Lit., alicui dedecori esse or fieri, *to bring shame upon,* Cic.; dedecus concipere, Cic. **B.** Meton., *the crime, cause of disgrace;* nullo dedecore se abstinere, Cic.; dedecora militiae alicui objicere, *dishonourable conduct in the field,* Liv. **II.** Esp., philosoph. t. t., *evil, vice* (opp. decus), Cic.

dēdĭcātĭo -ōnis, f. (dedico), *a consecration, dedication;* aedis, Liv.

dēdĭco, 1. *to declare;* **1,** naturam eius, Lucr.; **2,** *to make a return of property to the censor;* haec praedia in censu, Cic.; **2,** *to consecrate, dedicate a temple;* templum alicui, Cic.; Junonem, *to dedicate the temple of Juno,* Cic.

dēdignor, 1. dep. *to disdain, scorn, reject as unworthy;* dedignari maritum, Ov.; Nomades

maritos, *as husbands,* Verg.; with infin., sollicitare, Ov.

dēdisco -dĭdĭci, 3. *to unlearn, forget;* nomen disciplinamque populi Romani, Caes.; with infin., eloquentia loqui paene dediscit, Cic.

dēdĭtīcĭus -a -um (deditio), *relating to capitulation* or *surrender;* plur., dediticii, *the subjects of Rome, those who had surrendered unconditionally* or *had no rights* (opp. socii), Caes.

dēdĭtĭo -ōnis (dedo), *surrender, capitulation;* aliquem in deditionem accipere, Caes.; in deditionem venire, Liv.; facere deditionem, Caes.; compellere in deditionem, Liv.; deditionis conditio, Liv.; agere de deditione, *to treat,* Caes.; fit ad Poenos deditio, Liv.

dēdĭtus -a -um (p. adj. with compar. and superl.), *given to, devoted to, zealous for, addicted to;* Coepio nimis equestri ordini deditus, Cic.; adolescentulus mirifice studiis deditus, Cic.; nimis voluptatibus esse deditum, Cic.; ventri atque somno deditus, Sall.

dēdo -dĭdi -dĭtum, 3. **I.** Lit. *to give up;* a, aliquem ad supplicium, Liv.; aliquem telis militum, Cic.; aliquem trucidandum populo Romano, Liv.; b, of the conquered, *to give up, surrender;* esp., dedere se, or pass. as middle, dedi, *to surrender;* dedere se populo Romano, Caes.; se in arbitrium ditionemque populi Romani, Liv.; se suaque omnia Caesari, Caes. **II.** Transf. *to give up to, dedicate, devote;* aures suas poetis, Cic.; filiam libidini Ap. Claudii, Cic.; se, *to devote oneself, give up oneself to;* se totum Catoni, Cic.; se ei studio, Cic.; deditā operā, *designedly, intentionally,* Cic.

dēdŏcĕo, 2. *to cause to unlearn, to unteach;* aut docendus is est aut dedocendus, Cic.; virtus populum falsis dedocet uti vocibus, *teaches them not to use,* Hor.

dēdŏlĕo -dŏlŭi, 2. *to make an end of grieving,* Ov.

dēdūco -duxi -ductum, 3. **I.** *to lead* or *bring down.* **A.** Lit., 1, aliquem de rostris, Caes.; ramos pondere suo, *to weigh down,* Ov.; pectine crines, *to comb down,* Ov.; **2,** milit. t. t., *to lead down;* aciem in planum, Sall.; **3,** naut. t. t., a, *to spread sail;* tota carbasa malo, Ov.; b, *to drag a ship down to the sea;* naves in aquam, Liv.; **4,** of enchantment, *to bring down;* Jovem caelo, Ov. **B.** Transf., *to reduce;* universitatem generis humani ad singulos, Cic. **II.** *to lead away.* **A.** Lit., 1, aliquem ex eā viā, Cic.; aliquem in arcem, Liv.; deducere atomos in viā, Cic.; **2,** milit. t. t. *to remove;* praesidia ex iis oppidis, Cic.; legiones in hibernā, Caes.; **3,** *to conduct, escort, accompany a person;* a, to an audience, transfuga deductus (se) traditurum urbem promittit, Liv.; b, *to accompany a person from the provinces to Rome* (aliquem secum Romam, Liv.; aliquem deducere ex ultimis gentibus, Cic.; c, *to take to a house as a guest;* aliquem ad Janitorem quemdam hospitem, Cic.; d, *to take under an escort* or *guard;* deducere Lentulum in carcerem, Sall.; e, *to accompany* (as a sign of respect) *a statesman from his house to the forum* or *senate;* haec ipsa sunt honorabilia assurgi, deduci, reduci, Cic.; magnam affert opinionem, magnam dignitatem quotidiana in deducendo frequentiā, Cic.; aliquem ad forum, Cic.; f, *to accompany a bride to the house of a bridegroom;* virginem ad aliquem, Liv.; **4,** *to lead forth, conduct colonists, to found a colony;* coloniam, Cic.; deducere colonos lege Julia Capuam, Caes.; **5,** *to bring before a court of law;* aliquem ad hoc judicium, Cic.; **6,** of water, *to bring;* aquam Albanam ad utilitatem agri suburbani, Cic.; **7,** *to dispossess;* ex eā possessione Antiochum, Liv.; esp. as legal t. t., moribus deducere; *to make an entry on land for the sake of having the right to* *possession tried;* aliquem de fundo (with or without moribus), Cic. **B.** Transf., a, *to lead away from, turn away from;* aliquem ab humanitate, Cic.; aliquem de sententia, Cic. ; b, of things, *to bring to;* deducere rem ad arma, Caes. ; c, *to derive one's origin;* nomen ab Anco, Ov. **C.** a, *to deduct, subtract;* centum nummos, Cic.; b, *to spin;* levi pollice filum, Ov. ; transf., *to compose* (of writing), tenui deducta poemata filo, Hor.

dēductĭo -ōnis, f. (deduco), *a leading down.* **I.** Gen., 1, *the quartering* or *billeting of soldiers;* in oppida militum crudelis et misera deductio, Cic.; 2, *a conducting of colonists, a colonising;* quae erit in istos agros deductio, Cic.; 3, *a fictitious ejectment from disputed property,* Cic. ; 4, *a bringing down of water;* rivorum a fonte, Cic. **II.** *a lessening, deduction,* Cic.

dēductor -ōris, m. (deduco), *a client or friend who accompanies a candidate,* ap. Cic.

dēductus -a -um, p. adj. with compar. (deduco), *thin, fine, slender;* carmen, *light, unambitious,* Verg.

dēerro, 1. *to wander from the right path, lose one's way.* **A.** Lit., in itinere, Cic. ; in navigando a ceteris, Sall. **B.** Transf., magno opere a vero longe, Lucr.

dēfătĭgātĭo -ōnis, f. (defatigo), *weariness, fatigue;* membrorum, Cic. ; hostium, Caes.

dēfătīgo, 1. *to weary, fatigue, tire;* a, physically, exercitum quotidianis itineribus, Caes. ; gen. in partic. pass., defatigatis in vicem integri succedunt, Caes. ; b, mentally, te nec animi neque corporis laboribus defatigari, Cic.; non modo censores, sed etiam judices omnes potest defatigare, Cic.

dēfătiscor = defetiscor (q.v.).

dēfectĭo -ōnis, f. (deficio), 1, *a desertion, defection, rebellion;* a, lit., defectio a populo Romano, Cic.; facere defectionem, Liv.; sollicitare aliquem ad defectionem, Liv. ; sociorum, Cic. ; b, transf., a tota ratione defectio, Cic.; 2, *a ceasing, failure, vanishing, disappearing;* a, virium, Cic. ; b, of light, defectiones solis et lunae, *eclipses,* Cic. ; c, *weakness;* defectio manifesta, Tac.

dēfector -ōris, m. (deficio), *a rebel, deserter,* Tac.

1. **dēfectus** -a -um, partic. of deficio.

2. **dēfectus** -ūs, m. (deficio), *a failing, ceasing, disappearing;* a, aquarum, Liv. ; b, *a failing of light, eclipse;* lunae, Cic.

dēfendo -fendi -fensum, 3. (de and * fendo). **I.** *to repel, repulse, ward off, drive away;* defendere ictus ac repellere, Caes.; nimios solis ardores (from the vines), Cic.; defendere civium pericula, Cic. ; proximus a tectis ignis defenditur aegre, Ov. **II.** *to defend, protect, guard, watch over.* **A.** rempublicam, Cic. ; se telo, Cic. ; vitam ab inimicorum audaciā telisque, Cic. ; castra, Caes. ; senatum contra Antonium, Cic. **B.** In writing or speaking, *to defend;* 1, a, acta illa Caesaris, Cic. ; b, (a) *to defend before a court of law,* Sex. Roscium parricidii reum, Cic.; defendere crimen, *to defend a person on a charge of,* etc. ; defendere crimen istius conjurationis, Cic. ; aliquem de ambitu, *on a charge of,* Cic. ; aliquem in capitis periculo, Cic. ; (β) *to maintain* or *assert in defence;* id aliorum exempla se fecisse defendit, Cic. ; c, *to maintain a proposition or statement;* defendere sententiam, Cic. ; 2, transf. *to sustain a part;* vicem rhetoris atque poetae, Hor. ; defendere commune officium censurae, Cic.

dēfēnĕro, 1. *to plunge into debt;* dimissiones libertorum ad defenerandas diripiendasque provincias, Cic.

dēfensĭo -ōnis, f. (defendo), *a defence;* a, by

---

arms, castrorum, Caes.; b, in speech or writing, defensio miserorum, Cic.; id ad suam defensionem offerre, Cic.; defensionem alicuius or alicuius rei suscipere, Cic. ; c, *the speech* or *writing itself, defence;* defensionem causae suae scribere, Cic.

dēfensĭto, 1. (freq. of defenso), *to be wont to defend, defend frequently;* causas, Cic.; haec non acrius accusavit in senectute quam antea defensitaverat, Cic.

dēfenso, 1. (intens. of defendo), *to protect, defend;* Italici, quorum virtute moenia defensabantur, Sall.

dēfensor -ōris. m. (defendo), 1, *one who wards off* or *averts,* periculi, Cic. ; 2, *a defender;* a, in war, murus defensoribus nudatus, Caes. ; b, *a defender, protector;* esp. in a court of law, adoptare sibi aliquem defensorem sui juris, Cic.; fieri defensorem alicuius, Cic.

dēfĕro -tŭli -lātum -ferre. **I.** *to bring, bear, carry down.* **A.** Gen. amoeno ex Helicone perenni fronde coronam, Lucr. ; esp., a, of rivers, *to carry down with them;* excipere dolia quae amnis defert, Liv. ; b, *to change, remove to a lower place;* aedes suas sub Veliam, Cic. ; acies in campos delata est, Liv. **B.** Esp. *to carry down, bear down with violence;* ruinā tota prolapsa acies in praeceps deferri, Liv. ; praeceps aerii speculā de montis in undas deferor, Verg. **II.** *to bear* or *bring from one place to another.* **A.** Lit., 1, gen., a, ad causas judicia jam facta domo, Cic. ; commeatum in viam, Liv. ; alicui epistolam, Cic. ; b, polit. t.t., deferre sitellam, de M. Octavio, *to bring the balloting-box for voting,* i.e. *to have the vote taken about,* etc., Cic. ; deferre ex aerario or in aerarium, *to bring from* or *to the treasury* (where the standards, decrees of the senate, public accounts, etc., were kept), Liv.; deferre rationes, *to give in the accounts,* Cic ; deferre censum Romam, *to send the census-lists from the colonies to Rome,* Liv. ; 2, esp., a, *to take away violently from one place to another, to drive, carry;* hic rumor est Asinium delatum (esse) vivum in manus militum, Cic. ; b, as naut. t.t. *to drive away, carry;* aliquem ex alto ignotas ad terras et in desertum litus, Cic. **B.** Transf., 1, *to offer, hand over, refer;* si quid petet, ultro defer, Hor. ; alicui praemium dignitatis, Cic. ; totius belli summa ad hunc omnium voluntate defertur, Caes. ; rem ad amicos, Cic. ; rem ad senatum, Cic. ; 2, *to communicate, report, tell;* deferre falsum equitum numerum, Caes. ; vehementer te esse sollicitum multi ad nos quotidie deferunt, Cic.; esp., a, as legal t.t., nomen alicuius, or alicuius rei, or nomen alicui, *to inform against, to set a prosecution on foot;* deferre nomen venefici cuiusdam, Cic.; deferre crimen, *to bring a charge,* Cic.; deferre aliquid, or de aliqua re, or de aliquo, *to inform,* Cic. ; deferre aliquem, *to accuse,* Tac. ; b, polit. t.t., ad aerarium deferre, *to register;* nomina judicium, Cic. ; aliquem in beneficiis ad aerarium deferre, or simply deferre aliquem, *to recommend for reward,* Cic.

dēfervesco -fervi or -ferbŭi, 3. *to cease boiling;* of the heat of passion, *to cease to rage, diminish in violence;* quum adolescentiae cupiditates defervissent, Cic.

dēfessus, v. defetiscor.

dēfĕtiscor (dēfătiscor) -fessŭs, 3. dep. *to become tired, grow weary;* gen. found in perf. partic., **dēfessus** -a -um, *weary, tired;* defessus cultu agrorum, Cic.

dēfĭcĭo -fēci -fectum 3. (de and facio). **I.** Intransit. or reflex., 1, *to rebel, revolt;* a, lit., ab rege, Sall.; a republica, Cic.; ad Poenos, *to go over to the Carthaginians,* Liv.; b, transf., ab amicitia, Cic.; a virtute, Liv. ; 2, *to fail, cease, become less;* a, of the sun or moon, *to become eclipsed;* sol deficiens, Cic.; of fire, *to go out;* ubi ignem deficere extremum videbat, Verg. ; of water, *to retire, fail;* utcumque exaestuat aut deficit mare, *flows or ebbs,* Liv.; deficiunt laesi carmine fontis aquae, Ov. ; **b,** of number, quantity, etc. *to become less, fail;* non materia, non frumentum deficere poterat, Caes. ; nec vero levitatis Atheniensium exempla deficiunt, Cic.; **c,** of time, *to fail, to be too short for;* dies deficiat, si velim paupertatis causam defendere, Cic.; **d,** of strength, etc. *to fail, become weak;* ne vox viresque deficerent, Cic. ; nisi memoria defecerit, Cic. ; et simul lassitudine et procedente jam die fame etiam deficere, Liv. ; animo deficere, *to lose heart,* Caes., Cic. ; absol. *to be disheartened ;* ne unā plagā acceptā patres conscripti conciderent, ne deficerent, Cic. **II.** Transit., a, act., *to abandon, leave, fail;* quoniam me Leontina civitas atque legatio propter eam quam dixi causam deficit, Cic.; ipsos res frumentaria deficere coepit, Caes.; dolor me non deficit, Cic. ; **b,** pass. defici, *to be abandoned by, to be wanting in;* defici a viribus, Caes.; mulier abundāt, audaciā consilio et ratione deficitur, Cic. ; sanguine defecti artus, *bloodless,* Ov.

dēfīgo -fixi -fixum, 8. *to fix or fasten into.* **I.** Lit., sudes sub aqua, Caes. ; sicam in consulis corpore, Cic.; tellure hastas, Verg. **II.** Transf., **a,** *to fix the eyes* or *the mind on something ;* omnes vigilias, curas, cogitationes in reipublicae salute defigere, Cic.; Lilybae defixit lumina regnis, Verg.; in cogitatione defixum esse, *to be deep in thought,* Cic. ; **b,** *to make fast;* virtus est una altissimis radicibus defixa, Cic. ; **c,** *to fix in amazement, make motionless* with astonishment, etc. ; defixerat pavor cum admiratione Gallos, Liv.; partic., defixus, *motionless with astonishment, fear,* etc. ; quum silentio defixi stetissent, Liv. ; **d,** *to imprint firmly;* in oculis omnium sua furta atque flagitia defixurus sum, Cic. ; **e,** religious t.t. *to declare, denounce;* quae augur injusta, nefasta, vitiosa, dira defixerit, Cic. ; **f,** of enchantment, *to bind by a spell, to curse,* regis Iolciacis animum defigere votis, Verg.

dēfingo -finxi -fictum, 8. *to form, mould, fashion,* Hor.

dēfīnīo, 4. *to inclose within limits, to bound.* **A.** Lit. eius fundi extremam partem oleae directo ordine definiunt, Cic. **B.** Transf., 1, *to fix, define, determine;* ii qui mala dolore, bona voluptate definiunt, Cic. ; esp. **a,** logical t.t. *to define, give a definition of;* rem definire verbis, Cic. ; **b,** *to fix;* suum cuique locum, Caes. ; 2, *to confine within limits, restrain;* non vagabitur oratio mea longius atque eis fere ipsis definietur viris, etc., Cic.

dēfīnītē, adv. with superl. (definitus), *definitely, distinctly;* lex Gellia et Cornelia quae definite potestatem Pompejo civitatem donandi dederat, Cic.

dēfīnītīo -ōnis, f. (definio), *a definition;* **a,** verborum omnium definitiones, Cic; **b,** *a fixing;* judiciorum aequorum, Cic.

dēfīnītīvus -a -um (definio), *relating to definition* or *explanation, explanatory;* constitutio, Cic.

dēfīnītus -a -um, p. adj. (from definio), *definite, distinct;* constitutio, Cic. ; causa, Cic.

dēfīo -fieri, pass. of deficio, *to fail;* numquamne causa defiet, cur victi pacto non stetis, Liv. ; lac mihi non aestate novum, non frigore defit, Verg.

dēfīagrātīo -ōnis, f. (deflagro), *a burning, consuming by fire;* terrarum, Cic.

dēfīagro, 1. *to be burnt down, to be consumed by fire.* **A.** Lit., quum curia Saliorum deflagrasset, Cic. ; Phaethon ictu fulminis deflagravit, Cic. ; part. pass., deflagratus, *consumed,* Cic. **B.** Transf., *to cease burning, to abate, cool ;*

interdum spes animum subibat deflagrare iras vestras, Liv. ; deflagrante paulatim seditione, Tac.

dēfīecto -flexi -flexum, 3. **I.** Transit., **A.** Lit., **a,** *to bend down;* tenerum prono pondere corpus, Cat. ; **b,** *to turn aside;* amnes in alium cursum, Cic. **B.** Transf., declinare a proposito et deflectere sententiam, Cic. **II.** Intransit., *to turn aside, turn away;* **a,** de via, Cic. ; a veritate, Cic. ; **b,** of speech, *to digress;* oratio redeat illuc unde deflexit, Cic.

dēfīeo -flēvi -flētum, 2. 1, *to bewail, weep for;* impendentes casus inter se, Cic. ; alicuius mortem, Cic. ; 2, *to speak with tears;* haec ubi deflevit, Verg.

dēfīoresco -flōrŭi, 3. **A.** Lit., *to shed blossom, to fade;* idem (flos) quum tenui carptu's defloruit ungui, Cat. **B.** Transf., *to lose bloom, wither;* cum corporibus vigere et deflorescere animos, Liv. ; meton., amores mature et celeriter deflorescunt, Cic.

dēfīŭo -fluxi, 3. **I.** *to flow down.* **A.** Lit., **a,** of water, etc., sudor a capite, Cic. ; humor saxis, Hor. ; Rhenus in plūres defluit partes, Caes. ; **b,** of things not liquid, *to float;* dolia medio amni defluxerunt, Liv. ; *to swim down ;* secundo amni, Verg. ; *to sail down ;* cum paucis navigiis secundo amni, Liv. **B.** Transf., *to fall down, descend, glide down;* 1, quum ipsae defluebant coronae, Cic. ; of dress, hair, etc., *to fall ;* pedes vestis defluxit ad imos, Verg.; rusticius tonso toga defluit, Hor. ; of horsemen, moribundus Romanus labentibus super corpus armis ad terram defluxit, Liv. ; 2, abstr., **a,** *to be derived;* quodsi inest in hominum genere mens, fides, virtus, concordia, unde haec in terras nisi a superis defluere potuerunt, Cic.; **b,** *to fall to the lot of;* multaque merces tibi defluat aequo ab Jove Neptunoque, Hor. ; **c,** *to change to;* a necessariis artificiis ad elegantiora defluximus, Cic. **II.** *to flow away, disappear, be lost;* **a,** of hair, etc., extemplo tristi medicamine tactae defluxere comae, Ov.; **b,** of persons, ex novem tribunis unus me absente defluxit, *has proved false to me,* Cic. ; **c,** of time, *to disappear, cease;* ubi salutatio defluxit, Cic.

dēfōdīo -fōdi -fossum, 3. **I.** 1, *to dig in, to cover with earth;* signum septem pedes altum in terram defodi, Liv. ; 2, *to conceal by digging, bury;* thesaurum sub lecto, Cic.; aliquem humo, Ov. ; Menucia Vestalis viva defossa est scelerato campo, Liv. **II.** *to dig up;* terram, Hor.

dēformātīo -ōnis, f. (deformo), *a deforming, disfiguring.* **I.** Lit., corporis et coloris, Cic. **II.** Transf., tantae majestatis, *degradation,* Liv.

dēformis -e, adj. with compar. and superl. (de and forma), **I.** *deformed, misshapen, ugly.* **A.** Lit., **a,** of persons or animals, *deformed in body;* deformem natum esse, Cic. ; jumenta parva atque deformia, Caes.; **b,** of things, *ugly, disgusting ;* foeda omnia ac deformia visa, Liv. ; aspectus deformis atque turpis, Cic. **B.** Transf., **a,** *disgraced, disgraceful;* patriae solum deformis belli malis, Liv. ; **b,** *hateful, foul, shameful ;* ira, deforme malum, Ov.; deforme est, foll. by infin., Cic. **II.** *formless, shapeless;* deformes animae, Ov.

dēformĭtas -ātis, f. (deformis), *deformity, ugliness.* **I.** Lit., corporis, Cic. ; oris, Tac. **II.** Transf., *disgrace, dishonour;* illius fugae negligentiaeque deformitas, Cic.

1. **dēformo,** 1. *to form, fashion, delineate;* transf., ille quem supra deformavi, *whom I have formerly described,* Cic.

2. **dēformo,** 1. (de and forma). **A.** Lit., *to bring out of form and shape, disarrange;* **a,** of persons, deformatus corpore, *deformed in body*

Cic.; **b,** of things, parietes nudos ac deformatos reliquit, Cic. **B.** Transf., *to disgrace, dishonour;* victoriam clade, Liv.; homo vitiis deformatus, Cic.

dēfraudo, 1. *to deceive, defraud, cheat;* **I.** Of space. **A.** Lit., Tac. **B.** Transf., of the aures, Cic.; aliquem, with abl. of thing, aliquem ne andabatā quidem, Cic.

dēfrēnātus -a -um (de and freno), *unbridled, unrestrained;* cursus, Ov.

dēfrīco -frīcŭi -frīcātum, and -frictum, 1. *to rub, rub hard;* dentes, Ov.; fig., urbem sale multo, *to satirise, lash,* Hor.

dēfringo -frēgi -fractum, 3. (de and frango), *to break off;* ramum arboris, Cic.; ferrum ab hasta, Verg.

dēfrūtum -i, n. (for defervitum sc. mustum), *must* or *new wine boiled down to a small portion of its original quantity,* Verg.

dēfŭgĭo -fūgi, 3. **I.** Intransit., *to flee away;* armis abjectis totum sinistrum cornu defugit, Liv. **II.** Transit., *to fly from, avoid, get out of the way of;* proelium, Caes.; judicia, Cic.; auctoritatem consulatus sui, Cic.; eam disputationem, Cic.

dēfundo -fūdi -fūsum, 3. *to pour down, pour out;* a, vinum, Hor.; aurea fruges Italiae pleno defundit Copia cornu, Hor.; **b,** *to pour a libation;* defunde merum pateris, Hor.

dēfungor -functus sum, 3. dep. *to finish, complete, discharge, perform, be relieved of an office or duty;* a, defunctus honoribus, *having filled all public offices,* Cic.; periculis, Cic.; proelio, bello, Liv.; laboribus, Hor.; defunctum bello barbiton, *discharged from the warfare of love,* Hor.; **b,** vitā defungi, *to die,* Verg.; absol., defuncta (est) virgo Vestalis Laelia, Tac.

dēgĕnĕr -ēris (de and genus). **A.** Lit., *unworthy of one's race, not genuine, degenerate;* Neoptolemus, *unworthy of his father,* Verg.; hi jam degeneres sunt, mixti et Gallograeci vere, quod appellantur, Liv. **B.** Transf., *morally degenerate, unworthy, ignoble;* patriae non degener artis, Ov.; non degener ad pericula, Tac.; ceterorum preces degeneres fuere ex metu, Tac.

dēgĕnĕro, 1. (degener). **I.** Intransit., *to become unlike one's race* or *kind, to fall off, degenerate.* **A.** Lit., Macedones in Syros Parthos Aegyptios degenerarunt, Liv.; poma degenerant sucos oblita priores, Verg. **B.** Transf., *to degenerate morally;* ab hac perenni contestataque virtute majorum, Cic.; in Persarum mores, Liv. **II.** Transit., a, *to cause to degenerate;* ni degeneratum in aliis huic quoque decori offecisset, Liv.; **b,** *to dishonour, stain by degeneracy;* propinquos, Prop.

dēgo, dēgi, 3. (for deigo, from de and ago), *to pass* time; omne tempus aetatis sine molestia, Cic.; vitam in egestate, Cic.; in beatorum insulis immortale aevum, Cic.; senectam turpem, Hor.; absol., *to live;* ille potens sui laetusque deget, Hor.

dēgrandĭnat, impers. *it ceases to hail,* Ov.

dēgrăvo, 1. **A.** Lit., *to press down, oppress;* degravat Aetna caput, Ov.; quae (duo millia) illatis ex transverso signis degravabant prope circumventum cornu, Liv. **B.** Transf., *to weigh down, impede, distress;* quia vulnus degravabat, Liv.

dēgrĕdĭor -gressus, 3. dep. (de and gradior), *to step, march, walk down;* degressus ex arce, Liv.; monte, colle, Sall.; in aequum, Liv.; in campum, Liv.; ad pedes, *to dismount,* Liv.

dēgusto, 1. **A.** Lit., *to taste;* a, of persons, inde, Sall.; nec degustanti lotos amari fuit, Ov.; **b,** of things, celeri flammā tigna trabesque (of fire), *to lick,* Lucr.; of a weapon, *to graze;* summum vulnere corpus, Verg. **B.** Transf., *to try, make a trial of;* genus hoc exercitationum,

Cic.; *to sound,* eorum, apud quos aliquid aget auf erit acturus, mentes sensusque degustet, Cic.

dĕhinc, adv. *from here, hence, henceforth.* **I.** Of space. **A.** Lit., Tac. **B.** Transf., of the order of succession, *hereupon,* Hor. **II.** Of time, a, *from this time, henceforth;* me L. Tarquinium Superbum quācumque dehinc vi possum exsecuturum, Liv.; **b,** *thereupon;* Eurum ad se Zephyrumque vocat; dehinc talia fatur, Verg.; c, *then;* corresponding with primum, *in the second place,* Sall. (dehinc sometimes one syllable, Verg. Ov.).

dĕhisco -hīvi or hīi, 3. *to gape, open, split;* terra dehiscat mihi, *may the earth swallow me up,* Verg.; dehiscens intervallis hostium acies, Liv.

dĕhŏnestāmentum -i, n. (dehonesto), *a blemish, deformity, disgrace;* corporis, Sall.; amicitiarum, Tac.

dĕhŏnesto, 1. *to dishonour, disgrace;* famam, Tac., Liv.

dĕhortor, 1. dep. *to advise to the contrary, to dissuade;* aliquem, Cic.; aliquem ab aliquo, Sall.; with infin., plura scribere dehortatur me fortuna, Sall.

Dēĭănīra -ae, f. (Δηϊάνειρα), *daughter of Oeneus, sister of Meleager, wife of Hercules, whose death she caused by sending him a garment poisoned with the blood of Nessus.*

deicio, v. dejicio.

Dēĭdămīa -ae, f. (Δηϊδάμεια), *daughter of Lycomedes, king in Scyrus, mother of Pyrrhus by Achilles.*

dĕin, v. deinde.

dĕinceps, adv. (dein and capio), *one after another, successively;* a, *in space;* tres deinceps turres cum ingenti fragore prociderunt, Liv.; **b,** *in time;* quos (tres fratres) video deinceps tribunos plebis per triennium fore, Cic.; c, *in order of succession;* P. Sulpicius qui deinceps eum magistratum petiturus putabatur, Cic.; corresponding to primus, primum est officium ut se conservet in naturae statu, deinceps ut, etc., Cic. (deinceps, dissyll., Hor., Sat. ii. 8.80).

dĕindĕ and **dĕin** (for dein, from de and locat. suff. -im), adv. a, of space, *thereupon, from that place;* via tantum interest perangusta, deinde paulo latior patescit campus, Liv.; **b,** of time, *thereafter, thereupon, then, afterwards;* Cimbrum Gambrinium statim ad me vocavi, deinde item accessitur, etc., Cic.; correspond ing with primum, principio (initio), prius, inde, post, postremo, etc., Caesar primum suo, deinde omnium ex conspectu remotis equis, Caes.; with other adverbs, tum deinde, Liv.; deinde postea, Cic., etc.; c, in narration or order of succession, *then, next;* at a prima congressione maris ac feminae, deinde a progenie, etc., Cic.; corresponding with primum, primum . . . deinde, Cic. (ei, in classical poets, one syllable).

Dēĭŏnĭdes -ae, m. (Δηϊονίδης), *son of Deione and Apollo, i.e., Miletus.*

Dēĭŏpēa -ae, f. (Δηϊόπεια), *one of the nymphs of Juno.*

Dēĭphŏbē -ēs, f. (Δηϊφόβη), *daughter of Glaucus.*

Dēĭphŏbus -i, m. (Δηΐφοβος), *son of Priam, husband of Helen after the death of Paris.*

dējectĭo -ōnis, f. (dejicio), *a throwing down,* legal t.t. *ejectment from property,* Cic.

1. **dējectus** -a -um, p. adj. (from dejicio), **1,** *low-lying;* equitatus noster dejectis locis constiterat. Caes.; **2,** *dispirited, dejected,* Verg.

2. **dējectus** -ūs (dejicio), **1,** *a throwing down, hurling down;* arborum, Liv.; **2,** *declivity, depression;* collis, Caes.

dejĕro = dejuro (q.v.).

dējĭcĭo -jēci -jectum, 3 (de and jacio), *to throw, cast, hurl down.* **I.** Lit. **A.** Gen., aliquem de ponte in Tiberim, Cic. ; librum in mare, Cic. **B.** Esp. **l**, se dejicere, or pass. dejici, *to rush down;* venti ab utriusque terrae praealtis montibus subiti ac procellosi se dejiciunt, Liv. ; **2,** *to throw to the ground;* of trees, *to fell,* Liv. ; of statues, *to throw down,* Cic. ; of buildings, *to pull down;* turrim, Caes. ; **3,** *to throw lots into an urn;* quum dejecta in id sors esset, Liv. ; **4,** milit. t.t. *to drive from a position;* nostros loco, Caes.; **5,** pass., dejici, naut. t.t. *to be driven away;* ad inferiorem partem insulae, Caes. ; **6,** of the head, eyes, &c. *to let fall;* dejecto in pectora mento, Ov. ; vultum, Verg.; **7,** legal t.t. *to eject, dispossess;* aratores, Cic.; aliquem de possessione fundi, Cic. ; **8,** *to kill;* paucis dejectis, Caes. **II.** Transf., **l,** aliquem de sententia, *make a person change his opinion,* Cic. ; **2, a,** aliquem de honore, *to deprive,* Cic. ; **b,** uxore dejectā, *carried off,* Tac.

Dējŏtărus -i, m. *one of the tetrarchs of Galatia, defended by Cicero on a charge of murder.*

dējungo -junxi -junctum, 3. *to separate, sever,* Tac

dējūro, 1. *to swear solemnly, attest by an oath;* verbis conceptis dejurare ausim neminem inimicum tantum molestiae mihi tradidisse, Nep.

dēlābor -lapsus sum, 3. dep. **I.** *to glide down, fall down, sink;* **a,** signum de caelo delapsum, Cic. ; ex equo, Liv. ; **b,** *of a deity, to come down from heaven;* caelo, Verg., Liv. ; aliquis de caelo delapsus, *a person who comes unexpectedly to one's assistance,* Cic. ; **c,** of liquids, *to flow down;* ex utraque parte tecti aqua delabitur, Cic. **II.** *to glide away;* hence **l,** *to proceed from, be derived from;* illa sunt ab his delapsa plura genera (sc. vocum), Cic. ; **2,** *to fall away* from the right path, *to fall away, to fall, to come to;* **a,** in eas difficultates, ut etc., Cic. ; in hoc vitium scurrile, Tac. ; **b,** *to digress;* nescio quo pacto ad praecipiendi rationem delapsa est oratio mea, Cic. ; *a sapientium familiaritatibus ad vulgares amicitias oratio nostra delabitur,* Cic. ; **3,** *to fall into* unobserved; medios in hostes, Verg.

dēlāmentor, 1. dep. *to bewail, lament;* natam ademptam, Ov.

dēlasso, 1. *to weary, tire out;* cetera de genere hoc loquacem delassare valent Fabium, Hor.

dēlātĭo -ōnis, f. (defero), *an information against any one, accusation, denunciation;* nominis, Cic. ; absol., dare alicui delationem, Cic.

dēlātor -ōris, m. (defero), *an accuser, informer, spy;* criminum auctores delatoresque, Liv. ; majestatis, *of high treason,* Tac.

dēlēbĭlis -e (deleo), *that can be obliterated* or *destroyed;* liber, Mart.

dēlectābĭlis -e, adj. with compar. (delecto), *pleasant, delightful, agreeable;* cibus, Tac.

dēlectāmentum -i, n. (delecto), *delight, pleasure, amusement;* inania ista sunt delectamenta puerorum, Cic.

dēlectātĭo -ōnis, f. (delecto), *delight, pleasure;* mira quaedam in cognoscendo suavitas et delectatio, Cic. ; magnam delectationem habere, Cic.

dēlecto, 1. (intens. of delicio), *to delight, cause pleasure* or *enjoyment;* **a,** act., ista me sapientiae fama delectat, Cic. ; with abl., of the cause, aut libris me delecto aut fluctus numero, Cic. ; with in and the abl., ille me delectat in omni genere, Cic. ; with infin., quam delectabat eum defectiones solis et lunae multo ante nobis praedicere, Cic. ; **b,** pass., *to take delight in;* with abl., jumentis, Caes. ; filiolā tuā **te** delectari

laetor, Cic. ; criminibus inferendis, Cic. ; with in and the abl., in hac inani prudentiae laude delector, Cic. ; in hoc admodum delector, Cic. ; in hoc admodum delector quod, etc., Cic. ; with infin., Hor.

dēlectus -ūs, m. (1. deligo). **I.** Gen. *a choosing, choice, selection;* verborum, *a choice of language,* Cic. ; sine ullo delectu, *without any choice,* Cic. **II.** Milit. t.t., *a levy, recruiting of troops, conscription;* delectum habere, Cic. ; conficere, Liv. ; delectus provincialis, *a levy in the provinces,* Cic.

dēlēgātĭo -ōnis, f. (2. deligo), *an assignment of a debt;* a mancipe annuā die, Cic.

dēlēgo, 1, *to transfer, give in charge, to entrust, assign.* **I.** Gen., ad senatum, Liv. ; infantem nutricibus, Tac. ; hunc laborem alteri, ap. Cic. **II.** Esp. **l,** mercantile t.t. *to assign a debt* or *to nominate some one else to pay a debt;* alicui, Cic. ; **2,** *to impute, attribute, ascribe a merit* or *a fault to any one;* crimen alicui, Cic.; servati consulis decus ad servum, Liv.

dēlēnĭmentum -i, n. (delenio), *anything that coaxes, soothes, caresses, a charm, blandishment;* delenimentum animis Volani agri divisionem obici, Liv.

dēlēnĭo, 4. *to soothe, win, coax, caress, charm;* mulierem non nuptialibus donis, sed filiorum funeribus, Cic. ; aliquem blanditiis voluptatum, Cic. ; animos, Cic.

dēlēnĭtor -ōris, m. (delenio), *one who soothes, cajoles, wins over;* cuius (judicis) delenitor esse debet orator, Cic.

dēlĕo -lēvi -lētum, 2. *to destroy, annihilate, abolish.* **I.** Of things, **A.** Gen., urbes, Liv. ; Volscum nomen, Liv. ; bella, *to bring to an end,* Cic. ; leges, Cic. ; improbitatem, Cic.; ignominiam, Liv. **B.** Esp. *to efface* or *erase something engraved* or *written,* Cic. ; digito legata, Cic. **II.** Of persons, *to destroy, annihilate;* paene hostes, Caes. ; senatum, Cic. ; rarely of a single person, C. Curionem delere voluisti, Cic. ; hostes, Caes.

dēlētrix -trīcis (deleo), *that which destroys;* sica paena deletrix huius imperii, Cic.

Dēlia, v. Delos.

dēlībĕrābundus -a -um (delibero), *carefully considering, deliberating;* consules velut deliberabundi capita conferunt, Liv.

dēlībĕrātĭo -ōnis, f. (delibero), *consideration, consultation, deliberation;* consilii capiundi, Cic. : res habet deliberationem, *admits of,* cadit in deliberationem, Cic. ; habere deliberationes de aliqua re, Cic.

dēlībĕrātīvus -a -um (delibero), *relating to consideration* or *deliberation;* genus, Cic.

dēlībĕrātor -ōris, m. (delibero), *one who deliberates,* Cic.

dēlībĕrātus -a -um, p. adj. (from delibero), *decided, resolved, certain,* Cic.

dēlībĕro, 1. (de and libra), *to weigh carefully, consider, consult about.* **I.** Lit., maxima de re, Cic. ; deliberare de Corintho cum imperatore Romano, Liv. ; with rel. clause, utri potissimum consulendum sit, deliberetur, Cic. **II.** Transf. **A.** *to ask advice,* esp. of an oracle, Nep. **B.** *to resolve, decide as a consequence of deliberation;* quod iste certe statuerat ac deliberaverat, non adesse, Cic.

dēlĭbo, 1. *to take away a little, to taste.* **I.** Lit., sol humoris parvam delibet partem, Lucr. ; oscula, Verg. ; fig., ut omnes undique flosculos carpam et delibem, Cic. **II.** Transf. **A.** Gen., *to take from, to derive,* or *to enjoy;* ex universa mente divina delibatos animos habemus, Cic. ; novum honorem, Liv. **B.** Esp., *to diminish, take away;* aliquid de gloria sua, Cic.

dēlībro 1. (de and liber), *to bark, peel the bark off*, Caes.

dēlībŭo -ŭi -ūtum, 3. (de and root LIB, Gr. ΔIII, whence λίπος, ἀλείφω), *to besmear, anoint;* multis medicamentis delibutus, Cic. ; delibutus capillus, Cic.

dēlĭcātē, adv. with compar. (delicatus), *luxuriously ;* delicate ac molliter vivere, Cic.

dēlĭcātus -a -um (adj. with compar. and superl. (deliciae). **I.** *delightful, charming, alluring, luxurious ;* connitatus, convivium, voluptas, Cic. **II.** *soft, tender, delicate, voluptuous, luxurious.* **A.** Lit., adolescens, Cic. ; capella, Cat. ; pueri, juventus, Cic. **B.** Transf., *fastidious, dainty, nice ;* est fastidii delicatissimi, Cic.

dēlĭcĭae -ārum, f. (delicio, *to allure*), *pleasure, delight, charm, luxury.* **A.** Lit., multarum deliciarum comes est extrema saltatio, Cic. ; ecce aliae deliciae (*pretensions*) equitum vix ferendae. Cic. **B.** Transf. *the beloved object, darling, sweetheart ;* amores ac deliciae tuae Roscius, Cic.

dēlĭcĭŏlae -ārum, f. (dim. of deliciae), *a darling ;* Tullia, deliciolae nostrae, Cic.

dēlictum -i, n. (delinquo), *a fault, crime, delinquency ;* quo delictum majus est, eo poena est tardior, Cic.

1. **dēlĭgo** -lēgi -lectum, 3 (de and lego), **1,** *to pick, pluck ;* tenui primam ungue rosam, Ov. ; **2,** *to choose, select ;* a, magistratus, consulem, Cic. ; aliquem potissimum generum, Cic. ; ad eas res conficiendas Orgetorix deligitur, Caes. ; optimum quemque, Cic. ; locum castris, Caes. ; b, *to pick out, send away ;* longaevos senes ac fessas aequore matres, Verg.

2. **dēlĭgo,** 1. *to bind, fasten, bind up ;* naviculam ad ripam, Caes. ; aliquem ad palum, Cic.

dēlĭno (-lēvi) -lītum, 3. *to wipe off ;* ex qua tantum tectorium vetus delitum sit, Cic.

dēlinquo -līqui -lictum, 3. *to fail, be wanting,* esp. *to fail in duty, commit a crime ;* hac quoque in re eum deliquisse, Cic. ; ut nihil adhuc a me delictum putem, Cic. ; si quid deliquero, Cic. ; (miles) in bello propter hostium metum deliquerat, Cic.

dēlĭquesco -licŭi, 3. *to melt, dissolve ;* ubi delicuit nondum prior (nix) altera venit, Ov. ; transf., *to vanish, disappear ;* nec alacritate futili gestiens deliquescat, Cic.

dēlīrātĭo -ōnis, f. (deliro), *folly, silliness, dotage ;* ista senilis stultitia, quae deliratio appellari solet, Cic.

dēlīro, 1. (de and lira, lit. *to draw the furrow awry in ploughing*), *to be crazy, mad, insane, to rave ;* delirare et mente captum esse, Cic. ; quidquid delirant reges plectuntur Achivi, *the people suffer for the mad acts of their kings,* Hor.

dēlīrus -a -um, adj. with compar. (deliro), *silly, crazy, doting ;* senex, Cic.

dēlĭtesco -tŭi, 3. (de and latesco), *to conceal oneself, lurk, lie hid.* **A.** Lit., hostes noctu in silvis delituerant, Caes. ; in ulva, Verg. ; in cubilibus, Cic. **B.** Transf., *to take refuge ;* in alicuius auctoritate, Cic. ; in frigida calumnia, Cic. ; sub tribunicia umbra, Liv.

dēlĭtĭgo, 1. *to scold furiously,* Hor.

Dēlĭus, v. Delos.

Dēlos -i, f. (Δῆλος), *an island of the Aegean Sea, one of the Cyclades, and the birthplace of Apollo and Diana ;* hence **1,** adj., **Dēlĭus** -a -um, *Delian ;* folia, *the laurel,* Hor. ; tellus, *Delos,* Ov. ; subst., **Dēlĭus** -ĭi, m. *Apollo,* Ov.; **Dēlĭa** -ae, f. *Diana,* Verg. ; **Dēlĭum** -ĭi, n. *a place on the Boeotian coast where stood a temple of Apollo ;* **2, Dēlĭăcus** -a -um, *Delian ;* vasa,

Cic. ; gallinarius Deliacus (the people of Delium being celebrated for their brazen vessels and for their poultry), Cic.

Delphi -ōrum, m. (Δελφοί), *a town of Phocis, celebrated for its oracle of Apollo ;* hence adj., **Delphĭcus** -a -um, *Delphian,* and subst., **Delphĭcus** -i, m. *Apollo,* Ov.

delphīnus -i and **delphin** -īnis, m. (δελφίς), **1,** *a dolphin,* Cic. ; **2,** *a constellation so called,* Ov.

Deltōton -i, n. (Δελτωτόν), *the constellation called the Triangle,* Cic. poet.

dēlūbrum -i, n. (de and luo), *a temple, shrine,* as *a place for expiation ;* noctu ex delubro audita vox, Liv. ; gen. in plur., *shrines, holy places ;* deorum templa ac delabra, Cic.

dēlūdo -lūsi -lūsum, 3. *to mock, cheat, delude, deceive ;* corvum hiantem, Hor. ; et quae sopitos deludunt somnia sensus, Verg. ; absol., aliquanto lentius agere atque deludere, Cic.

dēlumbis -e (de and lumbus), *nerveless, weak,* Pers.

dēlumbo, 1. *to make weak and nerveless;* sententias, Cic.

dēmādesco -mădŭi, 3. *to become wet,* Ov.

dēmando, 1. *to entrust, give in charge ;* pueros curae alicuius, Liv.

Dēmărātus -i, m. (Δημάρατος), *a Corinthian exile, father of Tarquinus Priscus.*

dēmens -mentis, adj., with compar. and superl., *out of one's mind, insane, foolish, senseless ;* a, of persons, summos viros desipere, delirare, dementes esse dicebas, Cic. ; subst., in tranquillo tempestatem adversam optare dementis est, Cic. ; b, transf., of things, dementissimum consilium, Cic. ; minae, Hor.

dēmentĕr, adv. (demens), *foolishly, senselessly, madly,* Cic.

dēmentĭa -ae, f. (demens), *foolishness, madness, insanity,* Cic.

dēmentĭo, 4. (demens), *to be mad, insane, to rave,* Lucr.

dēmĕrĕo and dep. **dēmĕrĕor,** 2. *to deserve well of, to oblige ;* demerendi beneficio tam potentem populum occasio, Liv. ; servos, Ov.

dēmergo -mersi -mersum, 3. **A.** Lit., *to sink, to plunge into, dip under ;* **1,** in water, a, C. Marius in palude demersus, Cic. ; se demergere, Cic. ; b, of ships, *to sink ;* tredecim capere naves, decem demergere, Liv.; **2,** dapes avidam in alvum, *to swallow,* Ov. ; plebs in fossas cloacasque exhauriendas demersa, Liv. **B.** Transf., est enim animus caelestis ex altissimo domicilio depressus et quasi demersus in terram, Cic. ; plebs aere alieno demersa, *over head and ears in debt,* Liv.

dēmētĭor -mensus sum, 4. dep. *to measure, measure out ;* ut verba verbis quasi demensa et paria respondeant, Cic.

dēmēto -messŭi -messum, 3. *to mow, reap, cut down,* or *off ;* fructus, Cic.; frumentum, Liv.; huic ense caput, Ov. ; agros, Cic.

dēmētor, dep. 1. *to measure off,* Cic.

dēmīgrātĭo -ōnis, f. (demigro), *emigration,* Nep.

dēmigro, 1. **1,** *to migrate, emigrate, remove* or *depart from a place ;* ex his aedificiis, Caes.; ex agris in urbem, Liv. ; in alia loca, Cic. ; **2,** transf., hinc demigrare, *to die,* Cic. ; de meo statu demigro, Cic.

dēmĭnŭo -mĭnŭi -mĭnūtum, 3. **A.** Lit., **1,** *to diminish, make less, lessen ;* militum vir s inopia frumenti deminuerat, Caes. ; aliquid de tempore, Cic. ; **2,** *to alienate,* praedia, Cic. **B.** Transf., a, gen., aliquid de jure, de libertate,

Cic. ; **b**, esp. legal t. t., *capite se deminuere or capite deminui*, *to suffer a loss of civil rights*, Cic.

dēmĭnūtĭo -ōnis, f. (deminuo), *a lessening, diminution.* **A.** Lit., **1**, gen., accretio et deminutio luminis, Cic. ; deminutio vectigalium, Cic. ; **2**, legal t. t., *right of alienation ;* utique Fecenniae Hispalae datio deminutio esset, Liv. **B.** Transf., **1**, gen., deminutio sui, *loss of honour, dignity*, etc., Tac. ; **2**, *loss of civil rights ;* deminutio libertatis, Cic.

dēmīror, 1. dep. *to wonder at, to wonder ;* quod demiror, Cic. ; with acc. and infin., nihil te ad me postea scripsisse demiror, Cic.

dēmissē, adv., with compar. and superl. (demissus). **A.** Lit., *low, near the ground ;* volare, Ov. **B.** Transf., *modestly, lowly, humbly, abjectly, meanly ;* suppliciter demisseque respondere, Cic. ; humiliter demisseque sentire, Cic.

dēmissĭo -ōnis, f. (demitto). **A.** Act., *a sinking, lowering ;* storiarum, Caes. **B.** Pass. *dejection ;* animi, Cic.

dēmissus -a -um, p. adj. (demitto). **I.** Lit., **a**, *hanging down ;* aures, Verg. ; **b**, *sunken, low-lying ;* loca demissa ac palustria, Caes. **II.** Transf., **a**, *feeble, weak ;* demissā voce loqui, Verg. ; **b**, *unassuming, modest ;* sermo demissus atque humilis, Cic. ; **c**, *down-cast, dispirited ;* animus, Cic. ; **d**, *poor, needy ;* qui demissi in obscuro vitam habent, Sall.

dēmītĭgo, 1. *to make mild, soften ;* pass., *to become mild ;* nosmet ipsi quotidie demitigamur, Cic.

dēmitto -mīsi -missum, 3. *to send down, to lower, let down, cast, thrust, throw, put down, cause to hang down.* **I.** Lit., **A.** Gen., se manibus, *to let oneself down by the hands*, Liv. ; per manus, Caes. ; aliquem per tegulas, Cic. ; equum in flumen, Cic. ; imbrem caelo, Verg. ; caput ad fornicem, *to bend*, Cic. ; vultus, oculos, *to let fall, lower*, Ov. ; aures, Hor. ; fasces, *to lower*, Cic. **B.** Esp., **1**, demittere agmen, exercitum, etc. ; *to lead an army to a lower position ;* agmen in inferiorem campum, Liv. ; demittere se, *to march down*, Caes. ; **2**, naut. t. t., demittere antennas, *to lower sail*, Sall. ; **3**, navem demittere, *to sail down* (a river), Liv. ; **4**, se demittere or demitti, *to flow down ;* quo se demittere rivi assuerant pluvialis aquae, Ov. ; **5**, *to let the hair or beard grow long ;* demissi capilli, Ov. ; **6**, of dress, *to let droop ;* usque ad talos demissa purpura, Cic. ; tunica demissa, *hanging down, not girt up*, Hor. ; **7**, *to let fall to the ground ;* sublicas in terram, Caes. ; **8**, *to plunge into* (of a weapon) ; ferrum in pectus, Tac. ; **9**, of places, *to let down, to cause to slope down ;* molli jugum demittere clivo, Verg. **II.** Transf., **a**, se animo, Caes., animum, Cic., mentem, Verg., *to lose heart, become discouraged ;* aliquid in pectus, *to impress on one's mind*, Liv. ; se in causam, *to engage in*, Cic. ; **b**, demitti ab aliquo, *to be descended from ;* ab alto demissum genus Aeneae, Verg.

dēmĭurgus -i, m. (δημιουργός), *the highest magistrate in certain Greek states*, Liv.

dēmo, dempsi, demptum, 3. (for deimo, from de and emo), *to take away.* **A.** 1, lit., Publicola secures de fascibus demi jussit, Cic. ; barbam, Cic. ; 2, transf., sollicitudinem, Cic. **B.** Esp., *to take away* from a whole, *to subtract, make less ;* **1**, lit., partem solido de die, Hor. ; de capite medimna DC, Cic. ; **2**, transf., plus additum ad memoriam nominis nostri, quam demptum de fortuna.

Dēmŏcrĭtus -i, m. (Δημόκριτος), *a celebrated philosopher of Abdera, author of the Atomic theory ;* hence adj., **Dēmŏcrĭtēus** (īus) -a -um, *Democritean ;* subst., **a**, **Dēmŏcrĭtēa** -ōrum, n. *the doctrines of Democritus*, Cic. ; **b**, **Dēmŏcrĭtĭi** -orum, m. *the disciples of Democritus*, Cic.

dēmōlĭor, 4. dep. **A.** Lit., *to throw down, to destroy utterly, demolish ;* domum, parietem, statuas, Cic. **B.** Transf., demolientes Bacchanalia, Liv.

dēmōlĭtĭo -ōnis, f. (demolior), *a tearing down, demolition ;* statuarum, Cic.

dēmonstrātĭo -ōnis, f. (demonstro). **I.** Lit., *a pointing out* (by the hand, by gestures, etc.), Cic. **II.** Transf. **A.** Gen., *a representation, description*, Cic. **B.** Esp., rhet. t. t., *a laudatory style of oratory*, Cic.

dēmonstrātīvus -a -um (demonstro) = ἐπιδεικτικός, *laudatory or declamatory ;* genus orationis, Cic.

dēmonstrātor -ōris, m. (demonstro), *one who points out or indicates ;* Simonides dicitur demonstrator uniuscuiusque sepeliendi fuisse, Cic.

dēmonstro, 1. *to show, indicate, point out.* **I.** With the hand or by gesture, figuram digito, Cic. ; itinera, Cic. **II.** *to point out by signs or words, indicate, describe, show.* **A.** Gen., demonstrare rem, Cic. ; demonstravi haec Caecilio, Cic. ; ad ea castra quae supra demonstravimus contendit, Caes. ; with acc. and infin., mihi Fabius demonstravit te id cogitare facere, Cic. ; with rel. sent., quanta praedae faciendae facultas daretur, demonstraverunt, Caes. ; esp. in parenthetic sentences, ut supra or ante demonstravimus, ut demonstratum est, Caes. **B.** Esp., **1**, legal t. t., demonstrare fines, *to show a purchaser the extent of property and hand it over to him*, Cic. ; **2**, *to express, signify ;* verba proprie demonstrantia ea quae significari ac declarari volemus, Cic.

dēmŏrĭor -mortŭus, 3. dep. *to die, die off* (used of one among a number) ; quum esset ex veterum numero quidam senator demortuus, Cic. ; in demortui locum censor sufficitur, Liv.

dēmŏror, 1. dep. **A.** Intransit., *to delay, loiter ;* ille nihil demoratus (*without delay*) exsurgit, Tac. **B.** Transit., *to stop, hinder, delay, retard ;* aliquem diutius, Cic. ; iter, Caes. ; agmen novissimum, Caes. ; inutilis annos demoror, *drag on a useless existence*, Verg. ; Teucros quid demoror armis, *to restrain from battle*, Verg.

Dēmosthĕnēs -is and -i, m. (Δημοσθένης), *the celebrated Athenian orator.*

dēmŏvĕo -mōvi -mōtum, 2. *to move away, remove.* **I.** Gen., demoveri et depelli de loco, Cic. ; aliquem de sententia, *make a person change his opinion*, Cic. **II.** Esp. **A.** Milit. t. t. or of gladiators, gradu aliquem, *make a person give ground*, Liv. ; aliquem suo loco, Cic. **B. a**, *to dispossess, remove from one's property ;* populum Romanum de suis possessionibus, Cic. ; **b**, *to remove a person from an office ;* aliquem praefectură, Tac.

dēmūgītus -a -um (de and mugio), *filled with the noise of lowing ;* paludes, Cic.

dēmulcĕo -mulsi -mulsum or -mulctum, 2. *to stroke down, caress by stroking ;* dorsum (of horses), Liv.

dēmum, adv. (from de, connected with Gr. δή), *at length, at last*, **1**, with particles relating to time, nunc demum, *now at length*, Cic. ; jam demum, *now at last*, Ov. ; tum demum, *then indeed, then at length*, Caes. ; **2**, to express a climax or emphasis, esp. with pron., ea demum firma amicitia est, *that and that alone*, Sall. ; hac demum terra, Verg.

dēmurmŭro, 1. *to murmur or mutter over ;* ter novies carmen magico ore, Ov.

dēmūtātĭo -ōnis, f. (demuto), *change, alteration ;* morum, *deterioration*, Cic.

dēmūto, 1. *to change ;* animum, Plaut.

dēnārĭus -a -um (deni), *containing the number ten;* nummus or subst., **denarius** -ii, m. *a Roman silver coin, originally equivalent to ten, but afterwards to sixteen asses, worth about 8½d. of English money;* alicui ad denarium solvere, *to pay in Roman currency,* Cic.; ecquae spes sit denarii, *of being paid in denarii,* Cic.

dēnarro, 1. *to narrate, tell, relate;* matri denarrat ut, etc. Hor.

dēnăto, 1. *to swim down;* Tusco alveo, Hor.

dēnĕgo, 1. 1, *to deny, say no;* Aquilium non arbitramur qui denegavit et juravit morbum, Cic.; 2, more frequently, *to deny, refuse, reject a request;* operam reipublicae, Liv.; id antea petenti denegavisse, Caes.; potest enim mihi denegari occupatio tua, Cic.

dēni -ae -a, num. distrib. (decem), 1, *ten by ten, ten at a time, by tens;* uxores habent deni duodenique inter se communes, Caes.; 2, *ten;* bis deni, Verg.

dēnĭcālis -e (de and nex), *relating to death;* feriae, *a funeral feast* or *solemnity among the Romans* (at which the family of the person dead was purified), Cic.

dēnĭque, adv. I. 1, *in the order of succession, at last, at length,* Cic.; 2, to express a climax, qui non civium, non denique hominum numero essent, *even,* Liv.; 3, *in fine, in short;* omnia denique, Cic. II. Like demum, nunc denique, *now indeed;* tum denique, *then indeed,* Cic.

dēnōmĭno, 1. *to name;* hinc (ab Lamio) Lamias ferunt denominatos, Hor.

dēnormo, 1. (de and norma), *to make irregular;* o si angulus ille proximus accedat, qui nunc denormat agellum, Hor.

dēnŏto, 1. *to mark out, denote, designate precisely;* quum ei res similes occurrant, quas non habeat denotatas, Cic.; cives necandos denotavit, Cic.

dens, dentis, m. (connected with Gr. ὀδούς). A. 1, *a tooth;* aprorum, Ov.; dens eburneus, Liv.; dentes genuini, *the grinders,* Cic.; dentibus manditur atque extenuatur cibus, Cic.; 2, fig., a, *envy, ill-will, slander;* hoc maledico dente carpunt, Cic.; dens invidus, *the tooth of envy,* Hor.; atro dente aliquem petere, Hor.; b, of time, vitiata dentibus aevi, Ov. B. Transf., of things resembling a tooth, dens ancorae, Verg.; dens vomeris, Verg.; dens uncus, *mattock,* Verg.; dens Saturni, *the sickle,* Verg.

densē, adv., with compar. and superl. (densus), 1, *densely,* Plin.; 2, of time, *frequently,* Cic.

denseo = denso (q.v.).

Denselētae, v. Dentheleti.

denso, and **densĕo,** 2. (densus), *to make thick, to thicken, condense, press together.* I. Gen., male densatus agger, Liv. II. Esp., a, t. t. of weaving, *to make thick* with the reed, Ov.; b, milit. t. t., *to press close together;* scuta super capita, Liv.; ordines, Liv.; catervas, Verg.; c, mixta senum ac juvenum densentur funera, *are crowded together,* Hor.

densus -a -um, adj., with compar. and superl., *thick, close, dense* (opp. rarus). A. Gen., silva, Cic.; litus, Ov.; imber densissimus, Verg.; caput densum caesarie, Ov. B. *crowded together, closely packed;* 1, aristae, Verg.; apes, Verg.; frutices, Ov.; 2, of time, *following closely, uninterrupted, frequent;* ictus, Verg.; amores, Verg.; 3, *vehement;* densa frigoris asperitas, Ov.

dentālĭa -ium, n. (dens), *ploughshare,* Verg.

1. **dentātus** -a -um (dens). I. *provided with teeth, toothed.* A. Lit., si male dentata puella est, Ov. B. *toothed, spiked, pronged;* ex omni parte dentata et tortuosa serrula, Cic. II. *smoothed with a tooth;* charta, Cic.

2. **Dentatus,** v. Curius.

Denthēlēti -ōrum (Δανθηλῆται) and **Denselētae** -ārum, m. *a Thracian people living near the sources of* Strymon.

dentiscalpĭum -ii. n. (dens and scalpo), *a toothpick,* Mart.

dēnŭbo -nupsi -nuptum, 3. *to be married, to marry* (of the woman); nec Caenis in ullos denupsit thalamos, Ov.; Julia, quondam Neronis uxor, denupsit in domum Rubellii Blandi, Tac.

dēnŭdo, 1. *to lay bare, uncover, denude;* 1, ne Verres denudetur a pectore, Cic.; transf., mihi suum consilium, Liv.; 2, *to rob, plunder;* cives Romanos, ap. Cic.; transf., suo eam (juris scientiam) concesso et trdito (ornatu) spoliare atque denudare, Cic.

dēnuntĭātĭo -ōnis, f. (denuntio), *an announcement, intimation, declaration, threat.* I. Gen., periculi, Cic. II. Esp., a, polit. t. t., denuntiatio belli, *declaration of war,* Cic.; b, legal t. t., *summoning of a witness,* Cic.; c, *warning;* quae est enim a dis profecta significatio et quasi denuntiatio calamitatum, Cic.

dēnuntĭo, 1. I. Gen. *to announce, intimate, declare, threaten, denounce;* proscriptionem, Cic.; alicui mortem, Cic.; illa arma, centuriones, cohortes non periculum nobis, sed praesidium denuntiant, Cic.; with acc. and infin., Gorgias se ad omnia esse paratum denuntiavit, Cic.; with ut or ne with the subj., or subj. alone, Lupus mihi denuntiavit ut ad te scriberem, Cic.; with rel. sent., ut denuntiet quid caveant, Cic. II. Esp. a, polit. t. t., bellum denuntiare, *to declare war,* Cic.; b, milit. t.t. *to give order;* denuntiare ut arma capiant, Liv.; c, legal t.t., of the prosecutor, (a) alicui testimonium denuntiare, *to summon a person as witness,* Cic.; (β) denuntiare alicui, *to give notice of an action;* de isto fundo Caecinae, Cic.; (γ) denuntiare in judicium, *to give notice to one's witnesses, friends, etc., to be present at the trial;* d, *to give warnings of, to forewarn;* qui (Hector) moriens propinquam Achilli mortem denuntiat, Cic.; quibus portentis magna populo Romano bella perniciosaeque caedes denuntiabantur, Cic.

dēnŭo, adv. (for de novo), *anew, again;* 1, = iterum, *again, a second time;* rebellare, Liv.; 2, = rursus, of that which is repeated any number of times; recita denuo, Cic.

Dēŏis -ĭdis, f. (Δεωίς), *daughter of Deo* (Δηώ, *Ceres*), i.e., *Proserpina,* Ov.

Dēŏĭus -a -um, *sacred to Ceres;* quercus, Ov.

dĕŏnĕro, 1. *to unload, disburden;* transf., ex illius invidia deonerare aliquid et in te trajicere coepit, Cic.

dĕorsum, adv. (for de -vorsum), *downwards* (opp. sursum), indicating motion; sursum deorsum, *up and down, backwards and forwards;* naturis sursum deorsum, ultro citro commeantibus, Cic.

dēpăciscor (depēciscor) -pactus, 3. dep. *to bargain for, make an agreement;* ipse tria praedia sibi depactus est, Cic.; depacisci cum aliquo ut, etc., Cic.

depango -pactum, 3. *to drive into the ground, to drive, fix in;* fig., vitae depactus terminus alte, Lucr.

dēpasco -pāvi, -pastum, 3., 1, *to feed off, eat down;* saltus, Ov.; luxuriem segetum, Verg.; 2, *to feed, graze, pasture* (found also in the dep. form, **depascor** -pastus), agros, Cic.; Hyblaeis apibus florem depasta salicti saepes, Verg.; depasta altaria, poet. = *food on the altars,* Verg.;

transf., depascere luxuriem orationis stilo, *to prune down extravagance of language*, Cic. ; artus depascitur arida febris, Verg.

dēpĕciscor, v. depaciscor.

dēpecto -pexi -pexum, 3. *to comb, comb down;* crines buxo, Ov. ; vellera foliis tenuia, *to comb off*, Verg.

dēpĕcūlātor -ōris, m. (depeculor), *one who robs or embezzles;* aerarii, Cic.

dēpĕcūlor, 1. dep. (de and peculium), *to rob, plunder;* fana, Cic. ; aliquem omni argento spoliare atque depeculare, Cic. ; cur pro isto qui laudem honoremque familiae vestrae depeculatus est pugnas, Cic.

dēpello -pŭli -pulsum, 3. **I.** *to drive away* (of shepherds), teneros fetus Mantuam, Verg. **II.** *to drive down, cast down, expel, remove.* **A.** Lit., 1, gen., simulacra deorum depulsa, Cic. ; aliquem ex urbe, Cic. ; 2, esp. **a**, milit. t.t. *to dislodge ;* hostem loco, Caes. ; **b**, *to wean ;* ab ubere matris, Cic.; aliquem, Verg.; **c**, naut. t.t., *to drive out of one's course;* aliquem obvii aquilones depellunt, Tac. **B.** Transf. *to drive away, keep off, turn away;* famem sitimque, Cic. ; suspicionem a se, Cic. ; aliquem de causa suscepta, Cic. ; de spe conatuque depulsus, Cic. ; aliquem tribunatu, Cic.

dēpendĕo, 2. **A.** Lit. *to hang down, hang from ;* ex humeris dependet amictus, Verg.; laqueo dependentem invenere, Liv. **B.** Transf. *to depend upon ;* **a**, fides dependet a die, Ov. ; **b**, *to be etymologically derived from ;* huius et augurium dependet origine verbi, Ov.

dēpendo -pendi -pensum, 3. *to weigh out.* **A.** Lit. *to pay ;* dependendum tibi est quod mihi pro illo spopondisti, Cic. **B.** Transf., poenas reipublicae, Cic.

dēperdo -perdĭdi -perdĭtum, 3. 1, *to spoil, ruin ;* deperditus fletu, *exhausted*, Cat. ; deperditus in aliquā, *desperately in love with*, Cat. ; 2, *to lose ;* non solum bona sed etiam honestatem, Cic. ; paucos ex suis, Caes.

dēpĕrĕo -pĕrĭi -pĕrĭtūrus, 4. *to perish or be ruined utterly ;* tempestate deperierant naves, Caes.; si servus deperisset, Cic. ; esp., deperire amore alicuius, *to be desperately in love with*, Liv. ; so aliquem (aliquam), Cat.

dēpĭlo, 1. *to deprive of hair, make bald*, Mart.

dēpingo -pinxi, -pictum, 3. **A.** Lit. *to paint, represent in painting, depict;* pugnam Marathoniam, Nep. **B.** Transf., 1, *to draw or depict in words;* vitam huius, Cic. ; nimium depicta, *too elaborately delineated*, Cic. ; 2, *to picture to oneself in thought*, Cic.

dēplango -planxi -planctum, 3. *to bewail, lament*, Ov.

dēplexus -a -um, *clasping, embracing*, Lucr.

dēplōro, 1. **I.** Intransit. *to weep violently, to lament ;* de suis incommodis, Cic. **II.** Transit. **A.** *to lament, bewail;* alicuius interitum, Cic. **B.** Transf. *to regard as lost, give up;* agros, Liv.; spem Capuae retinendae deploratam apud Poenos esse, Liv.

dēplŭo, 3. *to rain down*, Tib.

dēpōno, -pŏsŭi -pŏsĭtum, 3. *to put, place, lay down, put away, put aside.* **I.** Gen. **A.** Lit., caput terrae, Ov. ; mentum in gremio, Cic. ; onus, Cic. ; arma, Caes. ; comas, *to cut the hair*, Mart. ; plantas sulcis, Verg. ; aliquam, *to give birth to*, Cat. ; vitulam *lay as a wager or as a prize*, Verg. **B.** Transf., **a**, *to renounce, lay aside, put an end to ;* amicitias, simultates, Cic. ; adeundae Syriae consilium, Cic. ; memoriam alicuius rei, or aliquid ex memoria, *to forget*, Cic. ; **b**, *to lay down an office;* imperium, Cic. ; **c**, *to deprive of an*

honour or *office;* triumphum, Liv. **II.** Esp., *to deposit, lay up for preservation, commit to the charge of.* **A.** Lit., pecuniam in delubro, Cic. ; obsides apud eos, Caes.; pecuniam apud aliquem, Cic. **B.** Transf., jus populi Romani in vestra fide ac religione depono, Cic. ; hence **dēpŏsĭtus**, *laid out dead;* ut depositi proferret fata parentis, Verg. ; jam prope depositus, Ov.

dēpŏpŭlātĭo -ōnis, f. (depopulor), *a laying waste, plundering;* aedium sacrarum publicorumque operum, Cic.

dēpŏpŭlātor, -ōris, m. (depopulor), *one who ravages or lays waste;* fori, Cic.

dēpŏpŭlor, 1. dep. *to lay waste, ravage ;* Ambiorigis fines, Caes. ; agros, Cic. (pass. depopulatis agris, Caes. ; late depopulato agro, Liv.).

dēporto, 1. *to bear, carry away, remove, convey away.* **I.** Gen., **a**, *of persons and ships*, frumentum in castra, Caes. ; Tertiam secum, Cic.; Pleminium legatum vinctum Romam, Liv.; **b**, *of rivers*, Nilus magnam vim seminum secum frumenti similium dicitur deportare, Cic. **II.** Esp. **a**, *to bring home from a province;* victorem exercitum, Cic. ; si nihil aliud de hac provincia nisi illius benevolentiam deportassem, Cic. ; **b**, *to banish for life* (with loss of civil rights and property), in insulam Amorgum deportari, Tac.; Italiā, Cic.

dēposco -pŏposci, 3. *to ask, beg, beseech, demand earnestly.* **I.** Gen., certas sibi deposcit naves, Caes. ; unum ad id bellum imperatorem deposci atque expeti, Cic. **II.** Esp. 1, *to ask an office or duty for oneself;* sibi id muneris, Caes. ; sibi partes istas, Cic. ; 2, *to demand for punishment;* Hannibalem, Liv. ; aliquem ad mortem, Caes. ; aliquem morti, Tac.; aliquem, Cic.; 3, *to challenge to combat;* aliquem sibi, Liv.

dēprāvātē, adv. (depravo), *unjustly, iniquitously ;* judicare, Cic.

dēprāvātĭo -ōnis, f. (depravo), *a perverting, distorting.* **A.** Lit., oris, Cic. **B.** Transf., animi, *depravity*, Cic.

dēprāvo, 1. (de and pravus), *to pervert, distort, disfigure.* **A.** Lit. quaedam contra naturam depravata habere, Cic. ; depravata imitatio, *caricature*, Cic. **B.** Transf. *to spoil, corrupt, deprave;* puer indulgentiā nostrā depravatus, Cic. ; mores dulcedine depravati, Cic. ; plebem consiliis, Liv.

dēprĕcābundus -a -um (deprecor), *earnestly entreating*, Tac.

dēprĕcātĭo -ōnis, f. (deprecor), 1, *a warding off or averting by entreaty, deprecating;* periculi, Cic. ; in religious language, *an imprecation, curse;* deorum, *invoking the curse of the gods*, Cic. ; 2, *an entreaty for forgiveness ;* eius facti, Cic.

dēprĕcātor -ōris, m. (deprecor), *one who begs off, an intercessor ;* huius periculi, Cic. ; eo deprecatore, *at his intercession*, Caes.

dēprĕcor, 1. dep. **I.** *to pray earnestly to some person or for something.* **A.** Gen., **a**, aliquem, Cic. ; deprecari patres ne festinarent, Liv. ; non deprecor, foll. by quominus, Liv.; **b**, aliquid, *to beg for, entreat for;* pacem, Cic. ; with ne and the subj., unum petere ac deprecari ne, etc., Caes. ; primum deprecor ne putetis, etc., Cic. ; nihilum deprecans quin, etc., Liv.; with infin. = *to allege in excuse;* errasse regem, Sall.; **c**, aliquid ab aliquo, *to beg for;* multorum vitam ab aliquo, Cic. ; civem a civibus, Cic. ; **d**, absol., *to intercede;* pro aliquo, Cic. **B.** *to execrate, curse*, Cat. **II.** *to avert by entreaty, beg off ;* mortem, Caes. ; poenam, Liv.

dēprĕhendo and **deprendo** -prĕhendĭ (prendi), -prĕhensum (-prensum), 3. *to seize, lay*

hold of, catch. **I.** Lit., **A.** Gen., tabellarios deprehendere litterasque intercipere, Caes.; naves, Caes.; of storms, deprensis nautis, *caught in a storm*, Verg. **B.** Esp., *to surprise, catch, detect*, esp. in a crime or fault; deprehendi in manifesto scelere, Cic.; aliquem in adulterio, Cic. **II.** Transf., **A.** *to perceive, observe, mark;* res magnas saepe in minimis rebus, Cic. **B.** Pass., deprehendi, *to be surprised, embarrassed;* se deprehensum negare non potuisse, Cic.

dēprěhensĭo -ōnis, f. (deprehendo), *detection;* veneni, Cic.

dēpressus -a -um, p. adj., with compar. and superl. (deprimo), *low-lying, sunk down;* domus, Cic.; convallis, Verg.

dēprĭmo -pressi -pressum, 3. (de and premo), *to sink down, press down, depress.* **I.** Lit., **A.** Gen., altero ad frontem sublato, altero ad mentum depresso supercilio, Cic.; depresso aratro (sc. in terram), Verg. **B.** Esp. **1,** *to plant or place deep in the ground, dig deep;* saxum in mirandam altitudinem depressus, Cic.; **2,** of ships, *to sink;* naves, Caes.; classem, Cic. **II.** Transf., **A.** Gen., *to press down, depress, oppress;* fortunam meam, Cic.; spes illius civitatis, Cic. **B.** Esp. *to put down by words;* multorum improbitate depressa veritas, Cic.

dēproelĭor, 1. *to contend violently;* ventos aequore fervido deproeliantes, Hor.

dēprōmo -prompsi -promptum, 3. *to bring forth, produce, fetch out;* pecuniam ex aerario, Cic.; Caecubum cellis, Hor.; transf., orationem ex jure civili, Cic.; verba domo patroni, Cic.

dēprŏpěro, *to hasten;* alicui coronas, *weave quickly,* Hor.

dēpŭdet -pŭduit, 2. impers. *to cease to be ashamed, to be shameless,* Ov.

dēpŭgis = depygis (q.v.).

dēpugno, 1. *to fight, struggle, contend violently;* ut acie instructā depugnarent, Caes.; cum Hectore, Cic.; transf., voluptas depugnat cum honestate, Cic.

dēpulsĭo -ōnis, f. (depello), **1,** *driving away, driving off;* luminum, Cic.; doloris, Cic.; **2,** in rhet., *defence,* Cic.

dēpulsor -ōris, m. (depello), *one who drives away, a destroyer;* dominatus, Cic.

dēpŭto, 1. *to prune, cut off;* umbras, *branches,* Ov.

dēpÿgis -is, *thin buttocked,* Hor.

deque, v. susque deque.

Dercětis -is, f. and **Dercětō** -ūs, f. (Δερκετώ), *a Syrian goddess* (also called Atargatis), *identified with the Greek Aphrodite.*

dērēlictĭo -ōnis, f. (derelinquo), *a deserting, forsaking;* communis utilitatis, Cic.

dērēlinquo -līqui -lictum, 3. *to forsake, desert entirely, abandon.* **A.** Lit., totas arationes derelinquere, Cic.; naves ab aestu derelictae, Caes. **B.** Transf., derelictus ab amicis, Cic.

dērěpentě, adv., *suddenly,* ap. Cic.

dērēpo -repsi, 3. *to creep, crawl down,* Phaedr.

dērīděo -rīsi -rīsum, 2. *to laugh at, mock, deride, scoff at;* aliquem, Cic.; absol., deridet, quum, etc., Cic.

dērīdĭcŭlus -a -um (derideo), *very ridiculous, very laughable;* alterum deridiculum esse se reddere rationem, Liv.; subst., **deridicŭlum** -i, n. *ridicule, ridiculousness;* esse or haberi deridiculo, *to be an object of ridicule,* Cic.

dērīgesco (dīrigesco) -rĭgŭi, 3. *to grow quite stiff, rigid;* derigescit cervix, Ov.; deriguere oculi, Verg., Ov.

dērĭpĭo -rĭpŭi -reptum, 3. (de and rapio),

to tear down, snatch away; ensem vaginā, Verg.; aliquid de manu, Cic.; aliquem de provincia, Cic.; (id) alteri, Cic.; transf., quantum de mea auctoritate deripuisset, *curtailed,* Cic.

dērīsor -ōris, m. (derideo), *one who mocks, derides, a mocker,* Hor.

dērīsus -ūs, m. (derideo), *mockery, derision,* Phaedr., Tac.

dērīvātĭo -ōnis, f. (derivo), *a turning or drawing off of water;* aquae Albanae, Liv.; derivationes fluminum, Cic.

dērīvo, 1. **A.** *to turn, draw off water;* aquam ex flumine, Caes. **B.** Transf., *to turn off, divert;* crimen, Cic.; responsionem alio, Cic.; culpam in aliquem, Cic.; partem curae in Asiam, Cic.

dērŏgātĭo -ōnis, f. (derogo), *the partial repeal of a law;* plur., legum derogationes, Cic.;

dērŏgo, 1. **A.** Lit., *to repeal part of the provisions of a law, to restrict, modify a law;* huic legi nec obrogari fas est neque derogari ex hac aliquid licet neque tota abrogari potest, Cic. **B.** Transf., *to diminish, take away, derogate from;* de honestate quiddam, Cic.; fidem alicui or alicui rei, Cic.

dērōsus -a -um (partic. of an unused verb derodo), *gnawed away;* clipeos esse a muribus, Cic.

dērŭo -rŭi -rŭtum, 3. *to cast down, overturn;* fig., cumulum de laudibus Dolabellae, Cic.

dēruptus -a -um (*derumpo), *broken off;* hence, of places (conf. abruptus), *precipitous, steep;* ripa, Liv.; collis, Tac. Subst., **dērupta** -orum, n. *precipices,* Liv.

dēsaevĭo -ĭi -ītum, 4. *to rage violently;* pelago desaevit hiems, Verg.; toto Aeneas desaevit in aequore, Verg.

dēscendo -scendi -scensum, 3. (de and scando), *to step down, come down, descend* (opp. ascendo). **I.** Of persons, **A.** Lit., **1,** gen., ex equo or equo, Sall.; de rostris, Cic.; monte, Verg.; coelo ab alto, Verg.; in ambulationem, Cic.; ad naviculas, Cic.; **2,** esp., **a,** descendere in or ad forum, or simply descendere, in Rome *to come down into the Forum,* in order to attend the Comitia, etc.; hodie non descendit Antonius, Cic.; **b,** of an army, *to descend from a height into the plain;* ex superioribus locis in planitiem, Caes.; in aequum, Liv. **B.** Transf., *to lower oneself, to have recourse to, to condescend to, agree to, give way to;* senes ad ludum adolescentium descendant, Cic.; ad vim atque ad arma, Caes.; in preces omnes, Verg. **II.** Of things, **A.** Lit., **a,** of weapons, *to pierce, to penetrate;* ferrum in corpus descendit, Liv.; **b,** of mountains, *to slope down;* Caelius ex alto quā mons descendit in aequum, Ov.; of the voice, *to sink,* Cic. **B.** Transf., quod verbum in pectus Jugurthae altius quam quis ratus erat descendit, *sank deeper,* Sall.

dēscensĭo -ōnis, f. (descendo), *a going down, descending, descent;* Tiberina, *voyage down the Tiber,* Cic.

dēscensus -ūs, m. (descendo), *a descending, descent.* **I.** Lit., descensus difficilis et artae viae, Liv.; poet. with dat., facilis descensus Averno, Verg. **II.** Meton., *a descending way;* descensus ripae utriusque in alveum trecentorum ferme passuum, Liv.

dēscisco -scīvi or -scĭi -scītum, 3. **A.** Lit., *to revolt from, desert to;* multae civitates ab Afranio desciscunt, Caes.; desciscere a populo Romano, Liv.; a senatu, Cic.; ab Latinis ad Romanos, Liv. **B.** *to withdraw, depart, diverge from, fall off from;* a pristina causa, Cic.; a veritate, Cic.; a se, *to be untrue to oneself,* Cic.;

hence, *to fall into, degenerate to ;* ad inclinatam fortunam, Cic.

dēscrībo -scripsi -scriptum, 3. **I.** *to transcribe, copy ;* quintum "de Finibus" librum, Cic. **II.** *to describe, delineate,* or *represent in writing* or *by signs.* **A.** Lit., geometricas formas in arena, Cic.; carmina in foliis or in cortice, Verg. **B.** Transf., **1,** *to represent in words, to describe ;* **a,** of things, hominum sermones moresque, Cic.; regionem aut pugnam, Cic.; flumen Rhenum, Hor.; **b,** of persons, *to portray ;* conjugem sine contumelia, Cic.; **2,** *to define, explain ;* describere officia, Cic.; **3,** *to mark out, arrange, classify ;* rationem totius belli, Cic.; jus civile generatim in ordines aetatesque, Cic.; **4,** *to impose, appoint, fix, allot ;* civitatibus pro numero militum pecuniarum summas, Cic.; suum cuique munus, Cic.; duodena in singulos homines jugera, Cic.; **5,** *to divide, distribute ;* populum censu, ordinibus, aetatibus, Cic.

dēscriptē, adv. (descriptus), *in order, systematically ;* descripte et electe digerere, Cic.

dēscriptĭo -ōnis, f. (describo). **I.** *a copy ;* descriptio imagoque tabularum, Cic. **II.** *a representation by writing* or *signs.* **A.** Lit., *a description, representation ;* descriptis aedificandi, plans, Cic.; numeri aut descriptiones, *geometric figures,* Cic. **B.** Transf., **1,** *a representation in words, a description ;* regionum, Cic.; **2,** *a definition ;* nominis brevis et aperta, Cic.; **3,** *fixing, limiting ;* expetendarum fugiendarumque rerum, Cic.; **4,** *distribution ;* possessionum, Cic.; **5,** *arrangement, settling, division ;* magistratuum, civitatis, Cic.

dēscriptus -a -um, p. adj. with compar. (from describo), *properly arranged ;* ordo verborum, Cic.

dēsĕco -sĕcŭi -sectum, 1. *to hew off, cut off ;* partes ex toto, Cic.; aures, Caes.; segetem, Liv.

dēsĕnesco -sĕnŭi, 3. *to grow weaker by age ;* ira belli, Sall.

dēsĕro -sĕrŭi -sertum, 3. (de and sero, *to sever one's connexion with*), *to desert, forsake, abandon, leave.* **I.** Gen., **1,** inamabile regnum desere, Ov.; **2,** *to leave uninhabited ;* agros latos ac fertiles deserere, Cic.; insulas desertas, Cic. **II.** *to abandon, be untrue to, desert.* **A.** Lit., **1,** gen., cum amici partim deseruerint me, partim etiam prodiderint, Cic.; pass., with abl. alone, deseror conjuge, Ov.; desertus suis, Cic.; **2,** esp., milit. t. t., *to desert ;* exercitum, Cic.; exercitum ducesque, Caes.; castra, Liv. **B.** Transf., *to neglect, disregard ;* **1,** gen., **a,** of persons, deserere officium, Cic.; curam belli, Liv.; nec fratris preces nec Sextii promissa nec spem mulieris, Cic.; **b,** of things or abstractions, multo tardius fama deseret Curium Fabricium, Cic.; a mente deseri, *to lose one's head,* Cic.; **2,** esp., **a,** of religious rites, *to neglect ;* publica sacra et Romanos deos in pace, Liv.; **b,** legal t. t., vadimonium, *to fail to appear,* Cic.

dēsertĭo -ōnis, f. (desero), *neglect,* Liv. (?)

dēsertor -ōris, m. (desero), **1,** *one who forsakes, abandons, a deserter ;* amicorum, Cic.; desertor communis utilitatis, Cic.; **2,** in milit. t. t., *a deserter,* Caes.; poet., *a fugitive,* Ov., Verg.

dēsertus -a -um, p. adj., with compar. and superl. (desero), *forsaken, abandoned, deserted ;* locus, regio, Cic.; loca, Caes.; deserta siti regio, Sall. Subst., **dēserta** -ōrum, n. *deserts, wildernesses,* Verg.

dēservĭo, 4. *to serve zealously ;* **a,** *to serve a person ;* alicui, Cic.; cuivis, Cic.; **b,** *to be devoted to a thing ;* divinis rebus, Cic.; in a bad sense, *to be a slave to ;* corpori, Cic.

dēsĕs -sĭdis, m. (desideo), *idle, lazy, slothful, inactive ;* sedemus desides domi, Liv.; nec rem Romanam tam desidem umquam fuisse atque imbellem, Liv.

dēsĭdĕo -sēdi -sessum, 2. *to sit idle, to be idle, slothful,* Ter.

dēsīdĕrābĭlis -e, adj., with compar. (desidero), *desirable ;* nihil enim desiderabile concupiscunt, Cic.

dēsīdĕrātĭo -ōnis, f. (desidero), *a desire, longing for anything,* Cic. (?)

dēsīdĕrĭum -ii, n. (desidero). **I.** *desire* or *longing, yearning, grief for the absence* or *loss of a person* or *thing ;* miserum me desiderium urbis tenet, Cic.; esse in desiderio rerum sibi carissimarum, Cic.; me tanto desiderio afficis ut, etc., Cic.; desiderio tabescere, Cic.; desiderio alicuius mortuum esse, Cic.; meton., *the object of desire ;* desiderium meum, Cic. **II.** Esp. **A.** *natural desire ;* cibi atque potionis, Liv. **B.** *a wish, desire ;* militum, Tac.

dēsīdĕro, 1. (like considero, from root SID, Gr. 1Δ, ΕΙΔ, *to look eagerly at*), *to long for some person* or *thing that is absent* or *lost, to wish for.* **I.** Gen., **a,** of persons, aliquid, Cic.; aliquid ab aliquo, Cic.; aliquid in aliquo, Cic.; with infin., haec scire desidero, Cic.; **b,** of things, *to require, need ;* res non modo tempus sed etiam animum vacuum desiderat, Cic. **II.** Esp., **1,** with the notion of a fault, *to miss ;* ex me audis quid in oratione tua desiderem, Cic.; **2,** *to lose ;* in eo proelio CC milites desideravit, Caes.; quarta (legio) victrix desiderat neminem, Cic.

dēsĭdĭa -ae, f. (deses), *sloth, idleness, inactivity ;* ne languori se desidiaeque dedat, Cic.

dēsĭdĭōsē, adv. (desidiosus), *slothfully, idly,* Lucr.

dēsĭdĭōsus -a -um, adj. with compar. and superl. (desidia), *slothful, idle, lazy ;* **a,** of persons, qui nolet fieri desidiosus, amet, Ov.; **b,** of things, *causing sloth ;* illecebrae, Cic.; delectatio, Cic.; inertissimum et desidiosissimum otium, Cic.

dēsīdo -sēdi and -sīdi, 3. *to sink down, subside, settle ;* terra, Cic.; transf., *to diminish, deteriorate ;* mores, Liv.

dēsignātĭo -ōnis, f. (designo). **I.** Lit., *a marking out, designing, describing ;* personarum et temporum, Cic. **II.** **1,** *arrangement, order ;* totius operis, Cic.; **2,** *appointment to an office ;* annua designatio, *nomination of consuls,* Tac.

dēsignātor -ōris, m. (designo), *one who arranges, an umpire at the public games,* Cic.

dēsigno, 1. *to mark out, trace out.* **I.** Lit., **a,** urbem aratro, Verg.; fines templo Jovis, Liv.; **b,** *to point out by signs ;* aliquem digito, Ov.; notare et designare aliquem oculis ad caedem, Cic.; **c,** *to sketch, delineate ;* Maeonis elusam imagine tauri Europam, Ov. **II.** Transf., **A.** Gen., *to signify, allude to ;* hac oratione Dumnorigem designari, Caes. **B.** Esp., **1,** *to contrive, perpetrate ;* quid non ebrietas designat? Hor.; **2,** *to arrange, regulate ;* constituere et designare, Cic.; **3,** polit. t. t., *to nominate to an office, elect ;* ut ii decemviratum habeant, quos plebs designaverit, Cic.; esp., designatus, *elect ;* consul designatus, *consul elect,* Cic.; tribunus plebis, Cic.; civis designatus (of a child not born), Cic.

dēsĭlĭo -sĭlŭi -sultum, 4 (de and salio), *to leap down ;* de navibus, Caes.; ex navi, Caes.; ab equo, Verg.; ad pedes, *dismount,* Caes.; of things, *to desilientis aqua,* Ov.

dēsĭno -sii -sĭtum, 3. *to leave off, cease, give over, desist* (opp. coepi). **I.** Transit., artem, Cic.; versus, Verg.; poet. (for deserere), *to abandon ;*

dominam, Ov. ; with infin. *to cease to;* desiit defendere, Cic. ; illud timere desino, Cic. ; with abl., desine quaeso communibus locis, Cic. ; with genit., tandem mollium querelarum, Hor. ; des-init in lacrimas, *ends by weeping,* Ov. ; pass. impers., si esset factitatum, non esset desitum, Cic. **II.** Intransit. *to cease, stop, end;* in piscem, Ov. ; rhet., of the close of a period, quae similiter desiuunt aut quae cadunt *similiter,* Cic.

dēsĭpĭens -entis, p. adj. (desipio), *foolish,* Cic

dēsĭpĭentĭa -ae, f. (desipiens), *foolishness, stupidity,* Lucr.

dēsĭpĭo -sĭpŭi, 3. (de and sapio), *to be foolish, silly, to act foolishly;* summos viros desipere, Cic. ; dulce est desipere in loco, Hor.

dēsisto -stĭti -stĭtum, 3. *to desist, leave off, cease;* de illa mente, Cic. ; a defensione, Caes.; conatu, Caes.; with infin. destiti stomachari, Cic.

dēsōlo, 1. *to leave solitary, to forsake;* ingentes agros, Verg. ; frequently in perf. partic., **dēsōlātus** -a -um, *forsaken, desolate;* desolatae terrae, Ov.

despectĭo -ōnis, f. (despicio), *a looking down;* transf. *contempt;* humanarum opinionum, Cic.

despecto, 1. (intens of despicio), *to regard from above, look down upon.* **I.** Lit., a, of persons, terras, Verg. ; b, of places, *to overlook;* quos despectant moenia Abellae, Verg. **II.** Transf., *to despise;* liberos ut multum infra, Tac.

1. **despectus** -a -um, p. adj., with compar. *despised, despicable,* Cic.

2. **despectus** -ūs, m. (despicio). **A.** *a looking down, downward view;* erat ex oppido Alesia despectus in campum, Caes. **B.** Transf., *contempt, despising;* alicui despectui esse, Tac.

despērantĕr, adv. (despero), *despairingly, hopelessly;* loqui, Cic.

dēspērātĭo -ōnis, f. (despero), *hopelessness, despair;* vitae, Cic. ; recuperandi, Cic.

despērātus -a -um, p. adj. with compar. and superl. (despero), *desperate, hopeless;* aegrota ac paene desperata res publica, Cic. ; morbi, Cic. ; senes, Cic. ; desperatissimo perfugio uti, Cic.

despēro, 1. *to be without hope, to despair, give up;* de republica, Cic. ; honores, Cic. ; sibi, Cic. ; suis fortunis, Caes. ; with acc. and infin. ; ista vera esse, Cic. ; often in pass. desperatis nostris rebus, Caes. ; desperatur turpiter quidquid fieri potest, Cic.

despĭcātĭo -ōnis, f. (despicor), *contempt;* in plur., odia, invidia, despicationes adversantur voluptatibus, Cic.

1. **despĭcātus** -a -um, p. adj. with superl. (despicor), *despised, despicable;* homo despicatissimus, Cic.

2. **despĭcātus** -ūs, m. (despicor), *contempt;* si quis despicatui ducitur, Cic.

despĭcientĭa -ae, f. (despici), *contempt;* rerum humanarum, Cic.

despĭcĭo, -spexi -spectum, 3. **I.** *to look down, regard from above.* **A.** Lit., a, intransit., de vertice montis in valles, Ov. ; a summo caelo in aequora, Ov. ; b, transit., Juppiter aethere summo despiciens mare, Verg. ; varias gentes et urbes despicere et oculis collustrare, Cic. **B.** Transf., *to look down upon, despise;* despicere et contemnere aliquem, Cic. ; partic. with gen., despiciens sui, Cic. **II.** Intransit., *to look away from,* Cic.

despōlĭo, 1. *to plunder, despoil;* aliquem, Cic. ; despoliandum templum Dianae, Cic.

despondĕo -spondi -sponsum, 2. **I.** *to promise.* **A.** Gen., Syriam homini, Cic. **B.** Esp.,

to promise a maiden in marriage, betroth; filiam alicui, Cic. **II.** Transf., **A.** Gen., *to promise, give up;* quaecumque (spes) est, ea despondetur anno consulatus tui, Cic. **B.** Esp., *despondere animos, to lose courage, despond,* Liv.

despūmo, 1. *to skim off;* foliis undam aheni, Verg.

despŭo -spŭi -spūtum, 3. **A.** Intransit., *to spit out* (a superstitious usage for averting evil); sacellum ubi despui religio est, Liv. **B.** Transit. fig., *to reject, abhor;* preces nostras, Cat.

desquāmo, 1. *to take off the scales, to scale,* Plaut.

desterto -tŭi, 3. *to finish snoring;* poet. *to finish dreaming,* Pers.

destillo, 1. *to drop down, distil;* lentum distillat ab inguine virus, Verg.

destĭnātĭo -ōnis, f. (destino), *a fixing, determination, resolution;* partium, quibus cessurus aut non cessurus esset, Liv.

destĭno, 1. (from root STAN, whence στανύω, ἱστάνω, lit. *to fix firm.*) **A.** *to make fast, bind, fasten;* antennas ad malos, Caes. **B.** Transf., a, *to fix, determine, settle;* tempus locumque ad certamen, Liv.; aliquem ad mortem, Liv. ; debiti destinatique morti, Liv. ; certae destinataeque sententiae, Cic. ; with infin. *to resolve to do;* quae agere destinaverat, Caes. ; quas urbes direpturos se destinaverant, Liv. ; b, *to aim at with a missile;* locum oris, Liv. ; c, *to fix upon, intend to buy,* Cic. ; d, *to betroth, fix upon as a wife for some one;* Lepida destinata quondam uxor L. Caesari, Tac. ; e, *to select, fix upon for an office;* destinare aliquem consulem, Liv.

destĭtŭo -stĭtŭi -stĭtūtum, 3. (de and statuo), *to set.* **I.** *to set down, to place.* **A.** aliquem ante tribunal regis, Liv. **B.** Transf., quum in hac miserrima fortuna destitutus sit, Cic. **II.** *to place on one side;* 1, *to leave, abandon;* nudos in litore pisces, Verg. ; aliquem in convivio, Cic. ; 2, *to leave in the lurch, forsake, desert;* aliquem in ipso discrimine periculi, Liv. ; nudus paene est destitutus, Cic.; deos mercede pactā, *to cheat,* Hor. ; spes destituit, Liv. ; partic. perf. *abandoned;* ab omne spe destitutus, Liv.

destĭtūtus -a -um, partic. of destituo.

destĭtūtĭo -ōnis, f. (destituo), *a forsaking, abandoning,* Cic.

districtus -a -um, p. adj. with compar. (destringo), *sharp, severe;* districtior accusator, Tac.

destringo -strinxi, -strictum, 3, **I.** *to strip off.* **A.** Gen., Quint. **B.** *to draw or bare the sword;* gladium, Cic. **II.** *to touch lightly, graze.* **A.** Lit., aequora alis, Ov.; pectora summa sagittā, Ov. **B.** Transf., *to satirise, censure;* aliquem mordaci carmine, Ov.

destrŭo -struxi -structum, 3. *to pull down.* **A.** Lit. *to destroy* (opp. construo); aedificium, Cic.; moenia, Verg. **B.** Transf. *to destroy, ruin;* jus destruere ac demoliri, Liv. ; hostem, Tac.

dēsŭbĭto, adv. *suddenly,* Cic.

dēsūdo, 1. *to sweat violently;* transf. *to exert oneself, labour hard;* in aliqua re, Cic.

dēsŭefăcĭo -fēci -factum (*desueo and facio), *to disuse, make unaccustomed to;* multitudo desuefacta a contionibus, Cic.

dēsuesco -suēvi -suētum, 3. **A.** Transit. *to disuse, bring into disuse;* res desueta, Liv. **B.** Intransit. *to become unaccustomed to;* and in perf. *unused to;* desuetus triumphis, Verg.

dēsuētūdo -ĭnis, f. (desuesco), *disuse;* armorum, Liv.

dēsultor -ōris, m. (desilio), *a circus rider who leaped from one horse to another while both* *were at full speed*, Liv.; transf. *an inconstant person*; amoris, Ov.

dēsultōrǐus -a -um (desultor), *relating to a desultor*, Cic.

dēsum -fŭi -esse, *to be absent, away, wanting, to fail*. **I.** Gen. omnia deerant quae, etc., Caes.; with dat., tibi nullum officium a me defuit, Cic.; with in and the abl., desunt (verba) in C. Laenia commendando, Cic.; deesse, or non deesse, foll. by quominus and the subj., duas sibi res, quominus in vulgus et in foro diceret defuisse, Cic.; nihil deest, foll. by quin, si tibi ipsi nihil deest, quod in forensibus civilibusque rebus versetur quin scias, Cic. **II.** Esp. **A.** *not to be present at*; convivio, Cic. **B.** *to fail, be wanting, not to keep, to leave in the lurch*; nullo loco deesse alicui, Cic.; sibi, Cic.; officio, Cic.; non deesse, foll. by quin, deesse mihi nolui, quin te admonerem, Cic.; absol., nos consules desumus, *are wanting in our duty*, Cic.

dēsūmo -sumpsi -sumptum, 3. *to choose, select*; sibi hostes, Liv.

dēsŭpĕr, adv. *from above, above*, Caes.

dēsurgo -surrexi -surrectum, 3. *to rise up, stand up*; coenā, Hor.

dētĕgo -texi -tectum, 3., 1, *to uncover, lay bare*; aedem, Liv.; caput, Verg.; quia possit fieri, ut (illa) patefacta et detecta mutentur, Cic.; 2, *to detect, disclose, betray*; insidias, consilium, Liv.; culpam, Ov.

dētendo (-tendi) -tensum, 3. *to unstretch*; tabernacula, *to strike the tents*, Caes.

dētergĕo, -tersi -tersum, 2. **I.** *to wipe off, wipe away*; lacrimas, Ov.; primo anno LXXX detersimus, *got together*, Cic. **II.** *to cleanse by wiping*; cloacas, Liv. **III.** *to strip off, break off*; remos, Caes.

dētĕrĭor -ĭus, genit. -ōris, compar. adj., with superl. dēterrimus (connected with detero), *worse, inferior, poorer*; vectigalia, Caes.; aetas, Verg.; peditatu, *weaker*, Nep.; homo deterrimus, Cic.; neut. subst., in deterius, *for the worse*; in deterius mutare, Tac.

dētĕrius, adv. (deterior), *worse, in an inferior manner*; de male Graecis Latine scripta deterius, Cic.

dētermǐnātǐo -ōnis, f. (determino), *a boundary, end*; mundi, Cic.; transf., orationis, Cic.

dētermǐno, 1. *to bound, fix the limits of, determine*. **I.** Lit., augur regiones ab oriente ad occasum determinavit, Liv. **II.** Transf., id quod dicit spiritu non arte determinat, Cic.

dētĕro -trīvi -trītum, 3. **A.** Lit., *to rub off, rub away, wear out*; detrita tegmina, Tac. **B.** *to lessen in strength, to weaken*; laudes egregii Caesaris et tuas, Hor.; si quid ardoris ac ferociae miles habuit, popinis et comissationibus et principis imitatione deteritur, Tac.

dēterrĕo -terrŭi -terrǐtum, 2. *to frighten from anything, deter by fear, discourage*; homines a scribendo, Cic.; Stoicos de sententia, Cic.; aliquem a dimicatione, Cic.; aliquem multis verbis ne (with subj.), Caes.; aliquem non deterrere quominus (with subj.), Cic.; nihil deterreri quominus, etc., Liv.; aliquem non deterrere quin, etc., Caes.; simply with acc., aliquem, Caes.; with acc. of thing, *to ward off*; vim a censoribus, Liv.

dētestābǐlis -e (detestor), adj., with compar. (detestor), *abominable, detestable, horrible*; omen, Cic.

dētestātǐo -ōnis, f. (detestor), 1, *cursing, execration, horror, detestation*, Liv.; 2, *a warding off, averting*; scelerum, Cic.

dētestor, 1. dep. **I.** 1, relig. t. t., *to invoke the curse of a god*; minas periculaque in alicuius caput, Liv.; 2, *to execrate, abominate*,

detest; Ambiorigem, Caes.; exitum belli civilis, Cic.; partic. perf. (pass.), bella matribus detestata, Hor. **II.** Transf., *to avert, ward off*; o dii immortales, avertite et detestamini hoc omen, Cic.

dētexo -texŭi -textum, 3. **A.** *to plait, make by plaiting*; aliquid viminibus mollique junco, Verg. **B.** Transf., *to finish (of discourse)*; detexta prope retexere, Cic.

dētǐnĕo -tinŭi -tentum, 2. (de and teneo), *to hold away, hold back, detain*. **I.** Lit., novissimos proelio, Caes.; Romano bello in Italia detineri, Liv.; aliquem, Caes. **II.** Transf., 1, *to hold fast, fetter*; me gratā detinuit compede Myrtale, Hor.; 2, *to occupy, engage*; in alienis negotiis detineri, Cic.; aliquem de or ab aliqua re, *to detain from*; ab circumspectu aliarum rerum, Liv.; 3, detinere se, *to support existence*; se miserandis alimentis nonum ad diem, Tac.; 4, *to detain possession of property*; pecuniam, Tac.

dētondĕo -tondi -tonsum, 2. *to shear, clip*. **A.** Lit., crines, Ov. **B.** Transf., detonsae frigore frondes, *made leafless*, Ov.

dētŏno -tŏnŭi, 1. **I.** Lit., *to thunder, thunder down*; hic (Juppiter) ubi detonuit, Ov. **II.** *to cease to thunder*, transf. = *cease to rage*; dum detonet omnis (nubes belli), Verg.

dētorquĕo -torsi -tortum, 2. 1, *to turn away, bend aside*; a, lit., ponticulum, Cic.; habenas, Verg.; in dextram partem, Cic.; proram ad undas, Verg.; b, transf., voluptates animos a virtute detorquent, Cic.; 2, *to twist anything out of its proper shape, distort*; corporis partes detortae, Cic.; transf., calumniando omnia detorquendoque suspecta et invisa efficere, Liv.

dētractǐo -ōnis, f. (detraho), *a drawing away, withdrawal, taking away*. **I.** In a good sense, **A.** Lit., 1, gen., doloris, Cic.; 2, esp. medic. t. t., *a purging*, Cic. **B.** Transf., *a taking away, withdrawal*; cuius loci detractionem fieri velit, Cic. **II.** *taking away (in a bad sense)*; detractio atque appetitio alieni, *of another person's property*, Cic.

dētracto = detrecto (q.v.).

dētractor -ōris, m. (detraho), *one who makes less, a detractor*; sui, Tac.

dētrăho -traxi -tractum, 3. **I.** *to take down*. **A.** Lit., aliquem de curru, Cic.; aliquem equo, Liv.; muros coloniae, Tac. **B.** *to lower, humiliate*; regum majestatem difficilius ad mediam detrahi, etc., Liv. **II.** *to take away*. **A.** 1, lit., alicui de digito anulum, Cic.; torquem hosti, Cic.; vestem, Cic.; pellem, Hor.; 2, transf., a, *to remove*; de homine sensus, Cic.; b, milit. t. t., *to detach*; ex tertia acie singulas cohortes, Caes.; c, numerically, *to subtract from a sum* (de tota summa binas quinquagesimas, Cic.; d, *to take away some mental or moral evil or good*; alicui calamitatem, Cic.; detracta opinione probitatis, Cic. **B.** *to take away, remove*; transf., a, inimicum ex Gallia, Cic.; b, *to compel*; aliquem ad hanc accusationem, Cic. **C.** *to drag away, take from*; 1, lit., spolia hostium templis porticibusque, Liv.; 2, transf., a, alicui debitum honorem, Cic.; multa de suis commodis, Cic.; de honestate et de auctoritate alicuius, Cic.; b, *to calumniate, slander*; de aliquo, Cic.; absol., absentibus detrahendi causā maledice contumelioseque dicere, Cic.

dētrectātǐo -ōnis, f. (detrecto), *a refusal*; militiae, Liv.

dētrectātor -ōris, m. (detrecto), *a disparager, detractor*; laudum suarum, Liv.

dētrecto, 1. (de-tracto), 1, *to decline, refuse*; militiam, Caes.; certamen, Liv.; 2, *to disparage, detract from, depreciate*; virtutes, Liv.; bene facta, Ov.

dētrīmentōsus -a -um (detrimentum), *detrimental, hurtful;* ab hoste discedere detrimentosum esse existimabat, Caes.

dētrīmentum -i, n. (detero), *damage, injury, detriment;* **a,** gen., detrimentum capere or accipere or facere, *to suffer,* Cic.; alicui ornamento et praesidio non detrimento esse, Caes.; **b,** polit. t. t., videant (provideant) consules or videat (consul) ne quid respublica detrimenti capiat or accipiat, Cic.; **c,** milit. t. t., *loss, defeat;* magna detrimenta inferre, Caes.; **d,** *loss of money, property,* etc.; aestimando cuiusque detrimento quatuor progeneri Caesaris delecti, Tac.

dētrītus -a -um, partic. of detero.

dētrūdo -trūsi -trūsum, 3. **I.** Lit., **A.** Gen. *to push away, push down, thrust down;* naves scopulo, Verg.; scutis tegumenta, Caes. **B.** Esp. **1,** milit. t. t., *to dislodge an enemy from his position;* impetu conari detrudere virum, Liv.; **2,** legal t. t., *to dispossess, eject;* ex praedio vi, Cic. **II.** Transf., **1,** *to force, compel;* aliquem de sua sententia, Cic.; **2,** *to postpone;* comitia in mensem Martium, Cic.

dētrunco, 1. **1,** *to lop or cut off;* arbores, Liv.; **2,** *to mutilate, behead;* gladio detruncata corpora, Liv.

dēturbo, 1. *to drive away with violence, cast down.* **I.** Lit., **A.** Gen., aliquem de tribunali, Caes.; aliquem tabula, Cic.; alicuius statuam, Cic. **B.** Esp., milit. t. t., *to dislodge, drive off;* nostros de vallo lapidibus, Caes. **II.** Transf., **A.** *to deprive;* aliquem de sanitate ac mente, Cic.; deturbari ex magna spe, Cic. **B.** Esp., legal t. t., *to eject, dispossess;* aliquem possessione, Cic.

Deucālĭōn -ōnis, m. (Δευκαλίων), *son of Prometheus, king of Phthia in Thessaly, was saved alone with his wife Pyrrha from the deluge, repeopled the world by throwing stones behind his back, which stones became men, while the stones that Pyrrha threw became women.* Adj., **Deucālĭōnēus** -a -um, *Deucalionian,* undae, *the deluge,* Ov.

dĕunx -uncis, m. (de and uncia), *eleven-twelfths of unity;* heres ex deunce, Cic.

dĕūro -ussi -ustum, 3. **1,** *to burn down, burn utterly;* agros vicosque, Liv.; **2,** of cold, *to destroy, nip;* hiems arbores deusserat, Liv.

dĕus -i, m., nom. plur. dei, dii, and di, genit. deorum or deum, dat. deis, diis, and dis, voc. sing. deus (connected with Ζεύς), *a god, a deity.* **A.** Lit., aliquem ut deum colere, Cic.; dii hominesque, *the whole world,* Cic.; of female deities, ducente deo, *Venus,* Verg.; nec dextrae erranti deus afuit, *Allecto,* Ov.; esp. phrases, di or dii boni, Cic.; (pro) dii immortales, Cic.; pro deum atque hominum fidem, Cic.; dii meliora (ferant), Cic.; si dii volunt, Cic.; si diis placet, Cic. **B.** Transf., **a,** of distinguished persons, audiamus Platonem quasi quemdam deum philosophorum, Cic.; **b,** of patrons, protectors, etc., P. Lentulus cuius pater deus ac parens fortunae ac nominis mei, Cic.

dĕūtor -ūti -ūsus, 3. dep. *to misuse,* Nep.

dēvasto, 1. *to lay waste, devastate;* agrum, fines, Liv.

dēvĕho -vexi -vectum, 3. *to bear, carry away, convey away;* legionem equis, Caes.; frumentum in Graeciam, Liv.; pass., used as middle, devehi (sc. navi), *to sail;* Veliam devectus, Cic.

dēvello -velli -vulsum, 3. *to pull, pluck, tear away;* ramum trunco, Ov.

dēvēlo, 1. *to unveil, uncover;* ora, Ov.

dēvĕnĕror, 1. dep. *to venerate, worship;* deos cum prece, Ov.

dēvĕnĭo -vēni -ventum, 4. *to come to, arrive at, reach.* **I.** Lit., ad senatum, Cic.; poet. with acc., speluncam, Verg. **II.** Transf., in victoris manus, Cic.; ad juris studium, Cic.; in medium certamen, Cic.

1. dēversor, 1. dep. *to lodge as a guest or stranger;* apud aliquem, Cic.; in ea domo, Cic.; absol., parum laute, Cic.

2. dēversor -ōris, m. (deverto), *a guest,* Cic.

dēversōrĭŏlum -i, n. (dim. of deversorium), *a small lodging,* Cic.

dēversōrĭus -a -um (deverto), *relating to the accommodation of strangers;* taberna, Plaut. Subst., **dēversōrĭum** -ii, n. *an inn, lodging;* peropportunum, Cic.; emere deversorium Tarracinae, Cic.; transf., *a place of resort, resting-place;* studiorum deversorium esse non libidinum, Cic.

dēvertĭcŭlum (dēvortĭcŭlum) -i, n. (deverto). **I. A.** Lit., *a by-way, by-path;* quae deverticula flexionesque quaesivisti, Cic. **B.** Transf., *a digression,* Liv. **II. a,** *an inn, lodging-place,* Liv.; **b,** *a place of refuge, hiding-place,* Cic.

dēverto (dēvorto) -verti (-vorti) -versum (-vorsum), 3. **I.** Transit., pass. (in present tenses), devertor, with middle signification, *to turn aside from the way, betake oneself;* si qui Ebromago deverterentur, Cic.; esp. *to stay, lodge;* ut locum publice pararet, ubi deverteretur, Liv.; fig., quid ad magicas deverteris artes, *have recourse to,* Ov. **II.** Intransit., *to turn aside;* **a,** cum perpaucis via, Liv.; transf., of discourse, *to digress;* redeamus ad illud unde devertimus, Cic.; **b,** *to lodge, stay with, go to;* ad hospitem, Cic.; ad villam alicuius, Cic.

dēvexus -a -um, adj. with compar. (de and veho), *going aside.* **I.** Of motion, *moving away from, rolling from;* **a,** of space, amnis devexus ab Indis, Hor.; Orion devexus, *sinking,* Hor.; **b,** of time, aetas jam a diuturnis laboribus devexa ad otium, *inclining to,* Cic. **II.** Of position, *sloping downwards, shelving, steep;* lucus devexus in novam viam, Cic.

dēvincio -vinxi -vinctum, 4. *to bind, tie fast.* **A.** Lit., aliquem fasciis, Cic. **B.** Transf., *to bind, fasten, connect;* **a,** gen., illud vinculum quod primum homines inter se reipublicae societate devinxit, Cic.; **b,** rhet. t. t., *to connect;* verba comprehensione, Cic.; **c,** *to fetter, bind* (by power, eloquence, etc.); urbem praesidiis, Cic.; animos eorum, qui audiant, voluptate, Cic.; **d,** morally, *to bind, pledge;* aliquem beneficio, Cic.; se scelere, Cic.

dēvinco -vīci -victum, 3. **I.** *to conquer thoroughly, subjugate;* Galliam Germaniamque, Caes.; Poenos classe, Cic. **II.** Transf., Catonis sententia devicit, ut in decreto perstaretur, Liv.

dēvinctus -a -um, p. adj. (from devincio), *bound to, devoted to;* iis studiis, Cic.; devinctior alicui, Hor.

dēvītātĭo -ōnis, f. (devito), *an avoiding;* legionum, Cic.

dēvīto, 1. *to avoid;* procellam, Cic.; dolorem, Cic.

dēvĭus -a -um (de and via). **A.** Lit., **a,** *removed from the straight road, out of the way;* iter, Cic.; oppidum, Cic.; **b,** *living out of the way, retired, secluded;* devia et silvestris gens, Liv.; esse devios, Cic.; poet., *wandering;* mihi devio, Hor.; uxores, *goats,* Hor. **B.** Transf., *out of the way, erroneous, unreasonable;* homo in omnibus consiliis praeceps et devius, Cic.

dēvŏco, 1. **I.** *to call down;* suos ab tumulo, Liv.; Jovem deosque ad auxilium, Liv.; transf., philosophiam e caelo, Cic. **II.** *to call away, call* *off, recall;* aliquem de provincia ad gloriam, Cic.; transf., non avaritia ab instituto cursu ad praedam aliquam devocavit, Cic.; sese suas exercitusque fortunas in dubium non devocaturum, Caes.

dēvŏlo, 1. **I.** *to fly down.* **A.** Lit., per caelum, (of Iris), Verg. **B.** Transf., *to hasten down;* alii praecipites in forum devolant, Liv. **II.** *to fly away to.* **A.** Lit., turdus devolat illuc, ubi, etc., Hor. **B.** Transf., ad florentem (amicitiam), Cic.

devolvo -volvi -vŏlūtum, 3. **A.** Lit. a, *to roll down;* saxa in musculum, Caes.; corpora in humum, Ov.; pass. with middle signification, *to roll down, fall headlong;* veluti monte praecipiti devolutus torrens, Liv.; **b,** *to roll off;* pensa fusis, *to spin off,* Verg. **B.** Transf., per audaces nova dithyrambos verba, Hor.; pass., devolvi as middle, *to fall into;* ad spem estis inanem pacis devoluti, Cic.

dēvŏro, 1. **I.** Lit., *to swallow, gulp down, devour;* id quod devoratur, Cic. **II.** Transf., **A.** Of persons, a, *of property, to consume, waste;* pecuniam publicam, Cic.; patrimonium, Cic.; **b,** *to swallow, suppress;* lacriuas, Ov.; c, *to devour, consume;* devorare spe et opinione praedam, Cic.; **d,** *to devour eagerly* mentally; illos libros, Cic.; **e,** *to swallow down, hear without understanding;* eius oratio a multitudine et a foro devorabatur, Cic.; **f,** *to swallow anything unpleasant, to endure;* hominum ineptias ac stultitias, Cic. **B.** Of things, me Zanclaea Charybdis devoret, Ov.

devortĭcŭlum, v. deverticulum.

dēvortĭum -ĭi, n. (deverto), *a by-way, by-path;* itinerum, Tac.

dēvōtĭo -ōnis, f. (devoveo), 1, *a consecrating, devoting* (esp. to the infernal gods); vitae or capitis, Cic.; P. Decii consulis, Liv.; plur. Deciorum devotiones, Cic.; 2, *a curse,* Nep., esp. *an enchantment, an incantation,* Tac.; 3, *a vow;* eius devotionis esse convictum, Cic.

dēvōto, 1. (intens. of devoveo), *to consecrate, devote to death;* quae vis patrem Decium, quae filium devotavit, Cic.

dēvōtus -a -um, p. adj. with compar. and superl. (devoveo), *devoted;* 1, to the infernal gods, *accursed;* arbor, sanguis, Hor.; 2, *devoted to any one, faithful, affectionate;* cliens, Juv.; subst., **dēvōti** -ōrum, m. *faithful followers,* Caes.

dēvŏvĕo -vōvi -vōtum, 2. *to consecrate, devote.* **I.** Relig. t. t., *to devote to a deity.* **A.** Gen., Dianae quod in suo regno pulcherrimum natum esset, Cic.; Marti ea quae ceperunt, Caes. **B.** Esp. 1, *to devote to the infernal gods, to devote to death;* se diis immortalibus pro republica, Cic.; devota corpora (Deciorum), Liv.; 2, a, *to curse, execrate;* aliquem, Nep.; b, *to bewitch, enchant,* Tib. **II.** Transf., 1, *to devote, give up;* devovere animam alicui, *for another,* Verg.; 2, se devovere alicui or alicui rei, *to devote, attach oneself;* se alicuius amicitiae, Caes.

dextans -antis, m. (de and sextans), *five-sixths,* Suet.

dextella -ae, f. (dim. of dextra), *a little right hand;* Quintus filius Antonii est dextella, Cic.

dexter -tĕra -tĕrum, or more freq. -tra -trum, comp. **dextĕrĭor** -ius, superl. **dextĭmus** -a -um (δεξιτερός). **I.** Lit., **A.** Adj., *right, on the right hand, on the right side;* manus, Cic.; latus, Hor.; ab dextra parte, Caes.; rota dexterior, Ov. **B.** Subst., 1, **dextera** or **dextra** -ae, f. (sc. manus), *the right hand;* a, lit., ad dextram, *to the right,* Cic.; a dextra, *on the right,* Caes.; dexterā or dextrā, *on the right,* Caes.; dextram dare, *to give the right hand* (as pledge of faith), Liv.; **b,** fig. (a) *fidelity;* dominorum

dextras fallere, *fidelity towards masters,* Verg.; (β) dextram alicui tendere or porrigere, *to help,* Cic.; (γ) meā dextrā, *by my right hand,* i.e., *power, bravery,* Ov., Hor.; 2, **dextera** or **dextra** -orum, n. *what is on the right, the right side,* Cic. **II.** Transf., a, *propitious;* dexter adi, Verg.; b, *skilful;* rem dexter egit, Liv.

dextĕrē or **dextrē,** adv. with compar. (dexter), *dexterously, skilfully;* apud regem, liberaliter dextreque obire officia, Liv.

dextĕrĭtas -ātis, f. (dexter), *skilfulness, dexterity, readiness,* Liv.

dextrorsum and **dextrorsus,** adv. (from dextrovorsum), *on the right hand, towards the right,* Hor.

Dĭa -ae, f. (Δῖα), *old name of the island of Naxos.*

Diablintes -um and **Diablinti** -ōrum, m. *people in Gallia Lugdunensis, in what is now Dep. de la Maine.*

dĭădēma -ătis, n. (διάδημα), *a royal head-dress, diadem;* diadema alicui or capiti alicuius imponere, Cic.; diadema ponere, Cic.

dĭaeta -ae, f. (δίαιτα), *a way of living prescribed by a physician, regimen, diet;* sed ego diaetā curare incipio; chirurgiae taedet, Cic.

Dĭăgŏras -ae, m. (Διαγόρας), 1, *a poet and philosopher of Melos, contemporary with Pindar and Simonides;* 2, *an athlete of Rhodes, contemporary with Pindar.*

1. **dĭălectĭcē,** adv. (dialecticus), *dialectically,* Cic.

2. **dĭălectĭcē** -ēs, f. (διαλεκτικὴ sc. τέχνη), *the art of dialectic, logic.*

dĭălectĭcus -a -um (διαλεκτικός) *relating to discussion, dialectical;* captiones, Cic.; subst., a, **dĭălectĭca** -ae f. (sc. ars), *the art of dialectic,* Cic.; b, **dĭălectĭca** -orum, n. *dialectical discussion,* Cic.; c, **dĭălectĭcus** -i, m. *a dialectician, logician,* Cic.

Dĭālis -e (Δίς = * Dis in Diespiter), *relating to Jupiter;* flamen, Cic.; or simply Dialis, Tac., *the priest of Jupiter;* conjux sancta, *the wife of the priest of Jupiter,* Ov.

dĭălŏgus -i, m. (διάλογος), *a philosophical dialogue or conversation,* Cic.

Dĭāna -ae, f. (old form for Jana, or Διώνη = *the daughter of Zeus,* orig. Diviana = Diva Jana), *an Italian goddess, identified with the Greek Artemis, daughter of Jupiter and Latona, sister of Apollo, the virgin goddess of the moon and of hunting,* tria virginis ora Dianae, *the three forms of Diana;* Luna *in heaven,* Diana *on earth,* Hecate *in the lower world,* Verg.; meton. *the moon,* Ov.; *the chase,* Mart. Adj. **Dĭānĭus** -a -um, *belonging to Diana,* Ov. Subst., **Dĭānĭum** -ĭi, n. a, *a place dedicated to Diana;* b, *a promontory in Spain, now Denia,* Cic.

dĭārĭum -ĭi, n. (dies), *a day's allowance of provisions* for soldiers, Cic.; slaves, Hor.

dĭbăphus -um (later) -a -um (δίβαφος), *double-dyed;* purpura, Cic. Subst., **dĭbăphus** -i, f. (sc. vestis), *the purple-striped robe of the higher magistrates at Rome;* Curtius dibaphum cogitat, *is longing for office,* Cic.

dĭca -ae, f. (δίκη), *a law-suit, action* in a Greek court; dicam scribere alicui, *to bring an action against,* Cic.; dicam sortiri, *to select the jury by lot,* Cic.

dĭcācĭtas -ātis, f. (dicax), *pungent wit, satire, raillery,* Cic.

dĭcātĭo -ōnis, f. (1. dico), *settling as a citizen in another state,* Cic.

dĭcax -ācis, adj. with compar. and superl.

(2. dico), *witty, satirical, ironical, sarcastic;* Demosthenes non tam dicax fuit quam facetus, Cic.

dichŏrēus -i, m. (διχορειος), *a double trochee,* Cic.

dĭcis, genit. (from unused nom. dix, from dico), found only in the phrases, dicis causā, dicis gratiā, *for form's sake, for appearance sake,* Cic.

1. **dĭco**, 1. (intens. of 2. dico). **A.** Lit., *a, religious t. t., to consecrate, dedicate, devote to the gods;* donum Jovi dicatum, Cic.; aram, Jovi, Liv.; templum, Ov.; b, *to deify, place among the gods;* inter numina dicatus Augustus, Tac. **B.** Transf., a, *to devote, give up to;* hunc totum diem tibi, Cic.; b, se alicui, *to devote oneself to;* se Crasso, Cic.; se alicui in clientelam, Caes.; se civitati or in civitatem, *to become a citizen of another state,* Cic.

2. **dĭco**, dixi, dictum, 3. (root DIC or DEC, whence also dic-nus (dignus), dec-eo, δείκνυμι), *to say, relate, tell, mention.* **I.** Gen., ille, quem dixi, *he whom I have mentioned,* Cic.; illa quae dixi, Cic.; Hilarum dico, *I mean Hilarus,* Cic.; ne dicam, *not to say;* crudelem ne dicam sceleratum, Cic.; dicet aliquis, *one might say,* Cic.; nisi quid dicis, *if you have nothing to say against it,* Cic.; causam, *to plead a cause, answer an accusation,* Cic.; causas in foro, *to plead as an advocate,* Cic.; jus dicere, *to administer justice,* Cic.; sententiam (of a senator), *to vote,* Cic.; ut dixi, Cic.; ut dictum est, Caes.; foll. by ut or ne and the subj., *to command,* Cic.; pass., dicor, diceris, dicitur, etc., *it is said, the report is;* with nom. and infin., Aesculapius dicitur obligavisse, Cic.; dicto citius, *quicker than can be said, in a trice,* Verg. **II.** Esp. a (intransit.), *to speak, deliver an oration;* ars dicendi, *the art of eloquence,* Cic.; dicere pro reo, Cic.; contra aliquem pro aliquo apud centum viros, Cic.; b, *to name, call;* orbis qui κύκλος Graece dicitur, Cic.; with acc. of name, cui Ascanius parentes dixere nomen, Liv.; with double acc., quem dixere chaos, Ov.; c, *to sing, describe, celebrate in verse, compose;* versus, carmen, Verg., Hor.; carmina in imperatorem, Liv.; alicuius facta, Verg.; d, *to nominate, appoint;* dictatorem et magistrum equitum, Cic.; with double acc., aliquem dictatorem, Caes.; e, *to fix, appoint, settle;* diem operi, Cic.; f, *to say yes, affirm* (opp. nego); quem esse negas, eundem esse dico, Cic. (syncop. perf. dixti = dixisti, Cic., Ov.).

dicrŏtum -i, n. (δίκροτον), *a vessel having two banks of oars,* Cic.

dictamnum -i, n. and **dictamnus** -i, f. (δίκταμνον and -ος), *dittany, a plant found on Mount Dicte and Mount Ida* (Origanum dictamnum, Linn.), Cic.

dictāta -ōrum, n. (dicto), *that which is dictated by a teacher, precepts, rules;* iisdem de rebus semper quasi dictata decantare, Cic.

dictātor -ōris, m. (dicto). **I.** *a commander, dictator;* a, *the chief magistrate in the Latin towns,* Cic., Liv.; b, in Rome, *dictator, an extraordinary magistrate, elected in times of great emergency for six months, superseding all other magistrates, and armed with absolute power.* **II.** Transf., *the chief magistrate of Carthage, a suffete,* Liv.

dictātōrĭus -a -um (dictator), *relating or belonging to a dictator, dictatorial;* gladius, Cic.; invidia, *against the dictator,* Liv.; juvenis, *son of the dictator,* Liv.

dictātūra -ae, f. (dictator), *the office of dictator, dictatorship;* dictaturam gerere, Cic.; dictaturā se abdicare, Caes.; dictaturam abdicare, Liv.

Dictē -ēs, f. (Δίκτη), *a mountain in Crete on which Jupiter was reared;* adj., **Dictaeus** -a

-um, arva, *Cretan,* Verg.; rex, *Jupiter,* Verg.; Minos, Ov.

dictĭo -ōnis, f. (2. dico). **I.** Gen., **A.** *a saying, speaking, uttering;* sententiae, Cic.; causae, defence, Cic.; multae, *fixing,* Cic. **B.** Meton., a, *the answer of an oracle,* Liv.; b, *conversation,* Tac. **II.** Esp. **A.** *declamation, elocution;* dictioni operam dare, Cic. **B.** Meton., 1, *a speech;* dictiones subitae, *extemporised,* Cic.; 2, *diction;* Attica, Cic.

dictĭto, 1. (freq. of 2. dico), 1, *to say often;* reiterate, assert repeatedly; ut dictitabat, Caes.; quod levissimi ex Graecis dictitare solent, Liv.; with acc. and infin., Catilinam Massiliam ire, Cic.; with double acc., aliquem sanum recteque valentem, Hor.; 2, esp. dictitare causas, *to plead causes frequently,* Cic.

dicto, 1. (intens. of 2. dico), *to reiterate, repeat, say often, to dictate to an amanuensis, pupil,* etc.; quod non modo tironi dictare, sed ne ipse quidem auderem scribere, Cic.; epistolam, Cic.; versus, Hor.; carmina Livii, Hor.

dictum -i, n. (2. dico), *a word, saying, speech.* **I.** Gen., nullum meum dictum, non modo factum, intercessit, quod, etc., Cic.; dicta tristia, *complaints, wailing,* Ov.; mutua dicta reddere, *to converse,* Liv. **II.** Esp., 1, *a maxim, sentence, saying;* Catonis est dictum, *it is a maxim of Cato's,* Cic.; 2, *a witty saying, a bon-mot;* dicta dicere in aliquem, Cic.; 3, *a command, order;* dicto paruit consul, Liv.; 4, *watch-word, pass-word,* Nep.

Dictynna -ae, f. (Δίκτυννα), *surname of Artemis.* Hence, **Dictynnēum** -i, n. *temple of Artemis Dictynna, near Sparta.*

1. **Dīdō** -ūs or (gen.) -ōnis, f. (Διδώ), *the founder of Carthage, daughter of Belus, king of Tyre, sister of Pygmalion, wife of Sichaeus;* also called Elisa or Elissa.

2. **dīdo**, dĭdĭdi, dĭdĭtum, 3. (dis and do), a, *to divide, distribute;* dum munia didit, Hor.; b, *to spread, disseminate;* diditur hic subito Trojana per agmina rumor, Verg.

dīdŭco -duxi -ductum, 3. (dis and duco). **I.** *to draw apart, stretch out, expand;* pugnum, Cic.; rictum, Hor.; fores, Tac. **II.** *to separate, divide.* **A.** Gen., 1, a, assem in partes centum, Hor.; b, milit. t. t. (a) *to divide, distribute;* aciem in cornua, Liv.; (β) *to scatter the enemy, disperse;* adversariorum manus, Caes.; 2, transf., oratio rivis diducta est, non fontibus, Cic.; vastius diducuntur verba, Cic. **B.** Esp., 1, *to separate forcibly;* aliquem ab aliquo, Cic.; 2, transf., animus varietate rerum diductus, *distracted,* Cic.

dīductĭo -ōnis, f. (diduco), *a separating,* Cic.

dīēcŭla -ae, f. (dim. of dies), *a little day;* dieculam ducere, Cic.

dĭes -ēi, m. and f. in sing. (in Cic. fem. only when it applies to a fixed time or period of time or in the date of a letter), in plur. only masc. **I.** Gen., **A.** Lit., *a day;* hesterno, hodierno, crastino die, Cic.; postero die, Cic.; postera die, Sall.; diem de die, Liv., or diem ex die, Caes., *from day to day;* in dies, *daily,* Cic.; ad diem or ad certam diem, *for the appointed day,* Caes.; multo die, *late in the day,* Caes.; ad multum diem or ad multum diei, *till late in the day,* Liv.; bis in die, *twice a day,* Cic.; die et nocte, *a day and a night,* Cic.; noctes et dies, *night and day,* Cic.; so diem noctem, Cic. **B.** Meton., *the business or events of the day;* diei poenas dare, Cic.; exercere diem, *the day's work,* Verg.; daylight, Verg.; transf., videre diem, *to see the light of day,* Ov.; *a day's march;* diem plus triginta in longitudinem patere, Liv. **II.** Esp., **A.** 1, gen., *a fixed day or time;* pecuniae, *pay-day,* Cic.; prodicere, *to put off a fixed day,* Liv.; diem

ex die ducŏre, *to put off from one day to another,* Caes.; diem perexiguam postulavi, Cic.; diem **obire**, *to wait for*, Cic.; alios non solvere, aliorum diem nondum esse, *day for payment not arrived*, Cic.; **2**, esp., *birthday;* dies meus, Cic.; **3**, *the day of death;* obire diem supremum, Nep.; **4**, *date of a letter;* in altera dies erat ascripta Nonarum Aprilium, etc., Cic. **B**. *time;* quod est dies allatura, Cic.

Diespĭter -tris, m. (Umbrian = Δὶς πατήρ), *Jupiter*, Hor.

diffāmo, 1. (dis and fama), *to spread abroad an evil report, to defame;* viros illustres procacibus scriptis, Tac.

diffĕrens -entis, v. differo.

diffĕrentĭa -ae, f. (differo), *difference, distinction;* honesti et decori, Cic.

diffĕrĭtas -ātis, f. (differo), *difference*, Lucr.

diffĕro, distŭli, dīlātum, differre, 2. (dis and fero). **I**. Transit., **A**. *to carry in different directions, spread abroad, scatter;* **1**, lit., ulnos in versum, *to plant*, Verg.; ignem, *to spread*, Caes.; 2, transf., a, (α) rumorem, *to spread*, Liv.; (β) aliquem variis rumoribus, *to malign*, Tac.; b, of time, *to put off, delay, postpone;* tempus, Cic.; bellum, Liv.; aliquem in tempus aliud, Cic.; rem in aliud tempus, Caes.; se differre, *to tarry*, Ov.; with infin., nec differret obsides ab Arretinis accipere, Liv. **B**. *to separate violently, disperse, scatter;* aquilo differt nubila, Verg.; classem vis venti distulit, Hor. **II**. Intransit. (without perf. or supine), *to differ, be different;* inter se, Cic.; ab aliquo or ab aliqua re, Cic.; cum aliqua re, Cic.; nihil differt inter deum et deum, Cic.

differtus -a -um (dis and farcio), *stuffed full, crammed, full;* provincia differta praefectis atque exactoribus, Caes.

diffĭcĭlis -e, adj. with compar. and superl. (dis and facilis), *difficult.* **A**. Lit., res arduae ac difficiles, Cic.; of places, *difficult, dangerous;* iter, Sall.; aditus, Caes.; of time, *critical, dangerous;* tempus anni difficillimum, Cic.; est difficile with infin., est difficile confundere, Cic.; with ad, difficilius ad eloquendum, Cic. **B**. Transf., of character, *hard to please, surly, morose, captious, obstinate;* parens in liberos difficilis, Cic.; difficilis alicui, Liv.

diffĭcĭlĭtĕr, adv. with compar. difficilius and superl. difficillimē (difficilis), *with difficulty*, Cic.

diffĭcultas -ātis, f. (difficilis), *difficulty, need, peril, trouble, distress.* **A**. Lit., dicendi, navigandi, Cic.; loci, Sall.; magnam haec Caesari difficultatem ad consilium afferebat si, etc., Caes.; nummaria, *pecuniary embarrassment*, Cic.; domestica, *distressed circumstances*, Cic. **B**. Transf., *obstinacy, moroseness*, Cic.

diffĭcultĕr, adv. (difficilis), *with difficulty*, Caes.

diffīdens, p. adj. (diffido), *distrustful, diffident*, Sall.

diffīdentĕr, adv. (diffidens), *diffidently, without confidence;* altera timide et diffidenter attingere, Cic.

diffīdentĭa -ae, f. (diffidens), *want of confidence, diffidence, distrust, despair;* fidentiae contrarium est diffidentia, Cic.; diffidentiam rei simulare, Sall.

diffīdo -fisus sum, 3. (dis and fido), *to have no confidence, mistrust, be hopeless, despair;* sibi, Cic.; suis rebus, Caes.; virtuti militum, Sall.; with acc. and infin., rem posse confici diffido, Cic.; absol., jacet, diffidit, abjecit hastas, Cic.

diffindō -fidi -fissum, 3. (dis and findo), *to split, cleave.* **A**. Lit., saxum, Cic.; portas muneribus, *open*, Hor. **B**. Transf., a, equidem

nihil huic diffindere possum, *I have nothing to say against your opinion, I must agree to it*, Hor.; b, legal t. t., diem, *to postpone*, Liv.

diffingo -finxi -fictum, 3. (dis and fingo), *to form again, forge anew;* ferrum incude, Hor.; fig., *to change*, Hor.

diffĭtĕor -ēri, 2. dep. (dis and fateor), *to deny, disavow*, Ov.

difflŭo -fluxi -fluxum, 3. (dis and fluo). **A**. Lit., *to flow in different directions;* ut nos quasi extra ripas diffluentes coerceret, Cic. **B**. a, juvenes sudore diffluentes, *dripping with sweat*, Phaedr.; transf., otio, *to give oneself up to*, Cic.; luxuria, Cic.; b, *to dissolve, melt away;* diffluit acervus, Lucr.; transf., uti per socordiam vires tempus, ingenium diffluxere, Sall.

diffŭgĭo -fūgi -fŭgĭtum, 3. (dis and fugio), *to fly apart, fly in different directions, to disperse;* metu perterriti repente diffugimus, Cic.

diffŭgĭum -ĭi, n. (diffugio), *a dispersion*, Tac.

diffundo -fūdi -fūsum, 3. (dis and fundo), **I**. Lit., **A**. *to pour out on all sides, pour forth;* vina, Hor.; sanguis per venas in omne corpus diffunditur, Cic. **B**. *to spread, scatter, diffuse;* pass., diffundi, used as middle, lux diffusa toto caelo, Cic.; diffusis capillis, Ov. **II**. Transf., **A**. Gen., Claudia nunc a quo diffunditur et tribus et gens per Latium, *spread abroad*, Verg.; error longe lateque diffusus, Cic. **B**. Esp., *to brighten up, gladden;* diffundere animos munere Bacchi, Ov.; ut bonis amici quasi diffundantur et incommodis contrahantur, Cic.

diffūsē, adv. (diffusus), *copiously, diffusely;* dicere aliquid, Cic.

diffūsĭlis -e (diffundo), *easily extending itself, diffusive;* aether, Lucr.

diffūsus -a -um, p. adj. with compar. (diffundo), *spread out, extensive, wide.* **A**. Lit., platanus diffusa ramis, Cic. **B**. Transf., jus civile quod nunc diffusum (*prolix*) est dissipatum est, in certa genera coacturum, Cic.

dĭgamma, n. indecl. (δίγαμμα), or **dĭgamma** -ae, f., or **dĭgammon** -i, n. (δίγαμμον) and **dĭgammos** -i, f. **I**. *the Aeolic digamma* (ϝ). **II**. (In jest) = *rental or investment book*, from F, the first letter of Fenus; tuum digamma viderai, Cic.

Dĭgentĭa -ae, f. *a brook flowing through Horace's estate into the Anio, now Licenza.*

dĭgĕro -gessi -gestum, 3. (dis and gero), *to carry apart in different directions, to separate, sunder, divide.* **I**. Lit., 1, *to plant out;* vacuos si sit digesta per agros (arbor), Verg.; 2, *to arrange, put in order;* capillos, Ov. **II**. Transf., 1, *to divide;* septem digestus in cornua Nilus, Ov.; 2, *to arrange;* jus civile in genera, Cic.; rempublicam bene, Cic.; nomina in codicem accepti et expensi, Cic.; 3, *to count;* qui matris digerit annos, Ov.

dĭgestĭo -ōnis, f. (digero), rhet., fig. = μερισμος, *distribution*, Cic.

dĭgestus -a -um, v. digero.

dĭgĭtŭlus -i, m. (dim. of digitus), *a little finger*, Cic.

dĭgĭtus -i, m. (conn. with δέχομαι). **I**. Lit. **A**. *the finger;* pollex, *the thumb*, Caes.; index, Hor.; digitos comprimere pugnumque facere, Cic.; digitos extendere, Cic.; concrepare digitis, Cic.; digito se caelum attigisse putare, *to think himself almost in heaven*, Cic.; tuos digitos novi, *thy skill in counting*, Cic.; liceri digito, *to bid at an auction*, Cic.; ne digitum quidem alicuius rei causā porrigere, *not to move a finger*, Cic.; digito aliquem attingere, *to touch gently*,

Cic.; primoribus labris gustasse hoc genus vitae et extremis, ut dicitur, digitis attigisse, Cic. **B.** *the toe;* insistere digitis, *to tread on the toes,* Ov.; constitit in digitos arrectus, Verg. **II.** Meton. **A.** As a measure, *a finger's breadth, an inch, the sixteenth part of a Roman foot;* quatuor patens digitos, Caes.; prov., ab hac (regula) mihi non licet transversum, ut aiunt, digitum discedere, Cic.

dĭglădĭor, 1. dep. (dis and gladius), **A.** Lit., *to fight for life and death, struggle fiercely;* inter se sicis, Cic. **B.** Transf., *to dispute in words;* inter se de aliqua re, Cic.; cum aliquo, Cic.

dignātĭo -ōnis, f. (dignor), *dignity, reputation, honour,* Liv.

dignē, adv. (dignus), *worthily;* quis de tali cive satis digne umquam loquetur? Cic.

dignĭtas -ātis, f. (dignus). **I.** *worth, worthiness, merit;* honos dignitate impetratus, Cic. **II.** Meton. **A.** *the consequence of worth;* **1,** *esteem, reputation, honour;* **a,** civitatis dignitatem et decus sustinere, Cic.; **b,** *rank in the state, position;* altus dignitatis gradus, Cic.; aliquem ad summam dignitatem perducere, Caes.; **c,** *an office of honour,* Cic.; **d,** dignitates, *men of rank and position,* Cic.; **2,** *honour, dignity;* agere cum dignitate, Cic. **B.** Transf., of things that bring honour, **a,** of persons, *a dignified, seemly exterior;* in formis aliis dignitatem esse, aliis venustatem, Cic.; **b,** of buildings, etc., *imposing appearance;* porticus, Cic.; **c,** of expression, *dignity;* orationis, Tac.

digno, 1. *to consider worthy;* quae consimili laude dignentur, Cic.

dignor, 1. dep. (dignus), **1,** *to consider worthy;* haud equidem tali me dignor honore, Verg.; **2,** *to regard as worthy of oneself, to deign,* and with a neg., *to disdain,* Verg.

dignosco -nōvi, 3. (dis and nosco), 3. *to recognise as different, to distinguish;* rectum curvo, Hor.; non civem hoste, Hor.; geminos inter se similes vix dignoscere posse, Ov.

dignus -a -um, adj. with compar. and superl. (dic-nus, root DIC or DEK, whence deceo), *worthy, deserving.* **I.** With abl. laude, Cic.; memoriā, Cic.; with supine, dictu, Liv.; followed by a relative, qui aliquando imperet dignus, *worthy to command,* Cic.; with ut and the subj., quos ut socios haberes dignos duxisti, Liv.; poet. with infin., puer cantari dignus, Verg.; with ad, amicus dignus huic ad imitandum, Cic.; absol., diligere non dignos, Cic. **II.** Transf., *worthy of a person* or *thing, becoming, suitable, fitting;* with abl., facere quid docto homine et amico dignum fuerit, Cic.; with pro, quidnam pro offensione hominum dignum eloqui possim, Cic.; absol., *fitting, suitable, sufficient;* qui maeror dignus in tanta calamitate inveniri potest, Cic.; dignum est, foll. by infin. or acc. with infin., Cic.

dĭgrĕdĭor -gressus sum -grĕdi, (dis and gradior), 3. dep. **A.** Lit., *to go apart, go asunder, separate, depart;* Luna tum congrediens cum sole, tum digrediens, Cic.; ab aliquo, Cic.; a Corcyra, Liv.; ex loco, Caes.; in urbem, Tac.; viā, Liv.; **B.** Transf., *to deviate;* **a,** de causa, Cic.; a causa, Cic.; **b,** of discourse, *to digress;* digredi ab eo quod proposueris, Cic.

dĭgressĭo -ōnis, f. (digredior), **1,** *a separation, departure,* Cic.; **2,** *a digression in discourse;* a proposita oratione, Cic.

dĭgressus -ūs, m. (digredior), *a separation, departure;* digressus et discessus, Cic.; digressus (lunae a sole), Cic.

dĭjūdĭcātĭo -ōnis, f. (dijudico), *an adjudication, decision,* Cic.

dĭjūdĭco, 1. (dis and judico), **1,** *to decide, adjudicate, determine;* controversiam, Cic.; litem, Hor.; *to decide by arms;* dijudicata belli fortunā, Caes.; **2,** *to distinguish, discern a difference;* vera et falsa, Cic.; vera a falsis dijudicare et distinguere, Cic.

dijun . . . v. disjun **. . .**

dĭlābor -lapsus sum, 3. dep. (dis and labor). **I.** *to glide apart.* **A.** Lit., **a,** of houses, bodies, etc., *to fall to pieces, fall down;* aedis Jovi vetustate dilapsa, Liv.; **b,** of fluids, *to melt, dissolve, disappear;* eadem (aqua conglaciata) admixto colore liquefacta et dilapsa, Cic. **B.** Transf., *to fall to decay, be ruined, disappear;* rem familiarem dilabi sinere, Cic.; dilapsa esse robora corporum animorumque, Liv. **II.** *to glide away from.* **A.** Lit., *to slip away,* esp. of soldiers, *to escape, disappear;* exercitus brevi dilabitur, Sall.; nocte in sua tecta, Liv.; of rivers, *to glide away;* Fibrenus rapide dilapsus, Cic. **B.** Transf., *to vanish, disappear;* **1,** sunt alii plures fortasse sed de mea memoria dilabuntur, Cic.; **2,** esp. of time, *to go by;* dilapso tempore, Sall.

dĭlăcĕro, 1. (dis and lacero), *to tear in pieces.* **A.** Lit., aliquem, Ov. **B.** Transf., rempublicam, Cic.

dĭlāmĭno, 1. (dis and lamina), *to split in two,* Ov.

dĭlănĭo, 1. (dis and lanio), *to tear in pieces;* cadaver, Cic.

dĭlargĭor, 4. dep. (dis and largior), *to lavish abroad, give liberally;* qui omnia quibus voluit dilargitus est, Cic.

dĭlātĭo -ōnis, f. (differo), *a putting off, delaying, postponing;* temporis, Cic.; belli, Liv.; sine dilatione, Liv.; res dilationem non recipit or non patitur, Liv.

dĭlāto (dis and latus), 1. *to spread out, extend.* **I.** Lit., manum, Cic.; aciem, Liv. **II.** Transf., **A.** Gen., nomen in continuentibus terris, Cic.; legem in ordinem cunctum, *to extend,* Cic. **B.** Esp. **1,** litteras, *to pronounce broadly,* Cic.; **2,** of speech, *to enlarge, amplify;* orationem, Cic.

dĭlātor -ōris (differo), m. *a dilatory person, a loiterer,* Hor.

dĭlātus, v. differo.

dĭlaudo, 1. (dis and laudo), *to praise highly;* libros, Cic.

1. dĭlectus -a -um, p. adj. with compar. and superl. (from diligo), *beloved, dear;* dilecti tibi poetae, Hor.

2. dĭlectus -ūs = delectus (q.v.).

dĭlĭgens -entis, p. adj. with compar. and superl. (from diligo). **I.** Gen., *assiduous, accurate, careful, sedulous, diligent* (opp. negligens), **a,** of persons, omnibus in rebus, Cic.; with genit., diligentissimus omnis officii, Cic.; with dat., Corinthios publicis equis assignandis fuisse diligentes, Cic.; with ad and the gerund, ad custodiendum, Cic.; **b,** of things which bear marks of attention, assidua ac diligens scriptura, Cic. **II.** Esp. *careful in housekeeping, economical, saving;* homo frugi ac diligens, Cic.; in re hereditaria, Cic.

dĭlĭgentĕr, adv. with compar. and superl. (diligens), *carefully, assiduously, accurately, diligently;* aliquem benigne et diligenter audire, Cic.; iter caute diligenterque facere, Caes.

dĭlĭgentĭa -ae, f. (diligo). **A.** Gen. *carefulness, attentiveness, accuracy, diligence;* with obj. genit., testamentorum, Cic.; with in and the abl., pro mea summa in republica diligentia, Cic.; non mediocrem adhibere diligentiam, Caes.; diligentiam adhibere ut or ne (with the subj.) Cic.; adhibere ad considerandas res et tempus

et diligentiam, Cic.; omnia acerbissimā diligentiā perpendere, Cic. **B.** Esp. *care in management of a household, frugality;* res familiaris conservari (debet) diligentiā atque parsimoniā, Cic.

dīlĭgo -lexi -lectum, 3. (dis and lego, to *choose), to prize, love, esteem highly;* aliquem, Cic.; aliquem diligere et carum habere, aliquem colere atque diligere, Cic.; se ipsum, Cic.; inter se, Cic.; of things, hunc locum, Cic.; alicuius consilia, officia, *to be satisfied with,* Cic.

dīlōrīcō, 1. (dis and lorico), *to tear open;* tunicam, Cic.

dīlūcĕo, 2. (dis and luceo), *to be clear, evident;* dilucere deinde fraus coepit, Liv.

dīlūcesco -luxi, 3. (inchoat. of diluceo), *to grow light, become day;* a, pers., omnem crede diem tibi diluxisse supremum, Hor.; **b,** impers., quum jam dilucesceret, Cic.

dīlūcĭdē, adv. with compar. and superl. (dilucidus), *clearly, plainly, lucidly;* plane et dilucide or dilucide planeque dicere, Cic.

dīlūcĭdus -a -um, *clear, lucid, plain;* oratio, Cic.; dilucidis verbis uti, Cic.

dīlūcŭlum -i, n. (diluceo), *the break of day, dawn;* primo diluculo, Cic.; diluculo, *at dawn,* Cic.

dīlūdĭum -ii, n. (dis and ludus), *the period of rest for gladiators between the days of public exhibition;* transf., diludia posco, *breathing-time, rest,* Hor.

dīlŭo -lŭi -lūtum, 3. (dis and luo), *to wash away, to dissolve.* **A.** Lit., a, ne canalibus aqua immissa lateres diluere posset, Caes.; unguenta lacrimis, Ov.; **b,** *to dilute, temper;* vinum, Mart.; venenum, Liv. **B.** Transf., a, *to weaken the force of, lessen, impair;* molestias, Cic.; curam multo mero, Ov.; **b,** *to expose the falseness of a statement, refute;* crimen, Cic.; diluere aliquid et falsum esse docere, Cic.

dīlūtus -a -um, v. diluo.

dīlŭvĭes -ēi, f. (diluo), *a washing away, inundation,* Hor.

dīlŭvĭo, 1. (diluvium), *to overflow,* Lucr.

dīlŭvĭum -ii, n. (diluo), *a flood, deluge, inundation,* Verg.

dīmāno, 1. (dis and mano), *to flow in different directions, spread itself abroad;* fig. meus hic forensis labor vitaeque ratio dimanavit ad existimationem hominum, Cic.

dīmensĭo -ōnis, f. (dimetior), *a measuring;* quadrati, Cic.

dīmētĭor -mensus, 4. dep. (dis and metior), *to measure out.* **I.** Lit. **A.** Gen., a, act., atque ego ista sum dimensus, Cic.; **b,** pass., a quo essent illa dimensa atque descripta, Cic.; tigna dimensa ad altitudinem fluminis, Caes. **B.** Esp. a, milit. t.t., *to measure out a place for a camp;* opere dimenso, Caes.; **b,** astronom. t.t., caelum atque terram, Cic.; pass., certis dimensus partibus orbis, Verg.; c, metric. t.t., syllabas, Cic.; versum, Cic. **II.** Transf., audiam civem digitis peccata dimetientem sua, Cic.

dīmēto, 1. (dis and meto), and dep. **dīmētor,** 1. *to measure the boundaries of,* Cic.; locum castris dimetari jussit, Liv.; dep., eorum cursus (acc.) dimetati, Cic.

dīmĭcātĭo -ōnis, f. (dimico), 1, *a fight, struggle, contest in arms;* proelii, Cic.; 2, *any contest or struggle;* vitae, *for life and death,* Cic.; capitis, Cic.

dīmĭco -āvi or ŭi, 1. (dis and mico). **A.** *to fight, contend, struggle in arms;* pro patria, Cic.; proelio, Caes. **B.** Transf., *to struggle, contend, strive;* omni ratione erit dimicandum ut, etc., Cic.; de fama, de civitate, Cic.

dīmĭdĭātus -a -um (dimidium), *halved, divided, half;* mensis, Cic.; partes versiculorum, Cic.

dīmĭdĭus -a -um (dis and medius), *halved, divided in half;* gen. with pars, dimidia pars, *the half,* Cic.; terrae, Cic.; of persons, frater meus dimidius major est quam totus, Cic. Subst., **dīmĭdĭum** -ii, n. *the half;* pecuniae, Cic.; dimidio with a compar., stultior, *by half,* Cic.; prov., dimidium facti, qui coepit, habet, *well begun is half done,* Hor.

dīmĭnūtĭo, v. dēminutio.

dīmissĭo -ōnis, f. (dimitto), 1, *a sending out;* libertorum ad provincias, Cic.; 2, *a dismissing, discharging;* remigum, Cic.

dīmitto -mīsi -missum, 3. (dis and mitto). **I.** *to send forth, send in different directions;* pueros circum amicos, Cic.; litteras per omnes provincias, Caes.; nuntios in omnes partes, Caes.; aciem (oculorum) in omnes partes, Ov. **II.** *to send away from oneself, let go.* **A.** Lit. 1, gen., a, legatos, Liv.; tabellarium, Cic.; hostem ex manibus, Caes.; regem spoliatum, Cic.; b, of things, *to let drop;* signa ex metu, Caes.; librum e manibus, Cic.; 2, esp. a, of persons, (a) *to adjourn a meeting, dismiss;* senatum, Cic.; (β) milit. t.t., *to discharge;* exercitum, Caes.; b, of things, *to give up;* provinciam, Liv. **B.** Transf. 1, gen., quare istos sine ulla contumelia dimittamus, Cic.; 2, esp. *to let drop, give up, renounce, abandon, leave;* oppugnationem, Caes.; quaestionem, Cic.; injuriam ignominiamque nominis Romani inultam impunitamque, Cic.

dīmŏvĕo -mōvi -mōtum, 2. (dis and moveo), *to move asunder, part, separate, divide.* **A.** Lit., terram aratro, *to plough,* Verg.; aquam corpore, Ov. **B.** *to separate, remove, to take away;* a, spes societatis equites Romanos a plebe dimovet, Sall.; b, statu sua sacra, Liv.

Dīnarchus -i, m. (Δείναρχος), *an Athenian orator, contemporary with Demosthenes.*

Dindymus -i. m. and **Dindȳma** -ōrum, n. (Δίνδυμος, Δίνδυμα τὰ), *a mountain in Mysia, sacred to Cybele;* hence **Dindȳmēnē** -ēs, f. Cybele, Hor.

dīnosco = dignosco (q.v.).

dīnŭmĕrātĭo -ōnis, f. (dinumero), *an enumeration;* dierum ac noctium, Cic.

dīnŭmĕro, 1. (dis and numero), *to count up, enumerate.* **A.** Gen., stellas, Cic.; regis annos, Cic. **B.** Esp. *to count money, to pay;* centuriat Capuae, dinumerat, *counts out the gold,* Cic.

Dĭōdōrus -i, m. (Διόδωρος). **I.** *a philosopher, contemporary of Ptolemaeus Soter.* **II.** *a peripatetic philosopher, of Tyre, flourishing about* 109 B.C. **III.** (Siculus), *a Greek historian.*

dĭoecēsis -ĕos and -is, f. (διοίκησις), *the district of a magistrate,* Cic.

dĭoecētes -ae, m. (διοικητής), *a finance officer or treasurer,* Cic.

Dĭŏgĕnēs -is, m. (Διογένης), *the name of several Greek philosophers, the most notorious of whom was the Cynic philosopher of Sinope.*

Dĭŏmēdes -is, m. (Διομήδης), 1, *a hero of the Trojan war, son of Tydeus, prince of Calydon, said to have subsequently settled in Apulia, and to have founded Arpi;* hence, adj., **Dĭŏmēdēus** -a -um, *relating to Diomedes;* 2, *king of the Bistones in Thrace, who gave his captives as food to his horses.*

Dĭōn -ōnis, m. (Δίων), *brother-in-law of Dionysius I., tyrant of Syracuse, killed by a conspiracy.*

Dĭōne -ēs, f. and **Dĭōna** -ae, f. (Διώνη), 1, *the mother of Venus, daughter of Oceanus and Tethys* or *of Aether and Gaea;* 2, *Venus.* Adj.,

Dīōnaeus -a -um, *relating to Dione,* or *Venus, mater,* i.e. *Venus,* Verg. ; *Caesar* (by the legend), *descendant of Aeneas, son of Venus,* Verg. ; *antrum, sacred to Venus,* Hor.

Dĭönỹsĭus -ii, m. (Διονύσιος), **1**, *the Elder, Tyrant of Syracuse* 406–367 A.C. ; **2**, *his son and successor, tyrant,* 367–356, A.C.

Dĭönỹsus -i, m. (Διόνυσος), *the Greek name of Bacchus;* hence **Dĭönỹsĭa** -ōrum, n. *the feast of Dionysus.*

dīöta -ae f. (διώτη). *a two-handled wine-jar,* Hor.

Dĭphĭlus -i, m. (Δίφιλος), *a comic poet of Sinope, contemporary of Menander and Philemon, imitated by Plautus.*

diplōma -ătis, n. (δίπλωμα), literally, *a folded letter;* **1**. under the republic, *a circular letter of introduction given to travellers by the government, in order to facilitate their journey,* Cic. ; **2**, under the empire, *a government document conferring privileges on the persons to whom it was addressed,* Tac.

Dĭpỹlŏn, -i, n. (Δίπυλον), *the double door, name of the Thriasian gate at Athens.*

Dircē -ēs, f. (Δίρκη). **I**. *the wife of Lycus king of Thebes, bound to a bull by Amphion and Zethus, and thrown* (or *changed*) *into the fountain named after her.* **II.** *the fountain of Dirce, to the north-west of Thebes.* Adj., **Dircaeus** -a -um, *Dircean, Boeotian; cygnus, Pindar,* Hor.

directē, adv. with compar. (directus), *straightforward, in a straight line;* **1**, horizontally, Cic. ; transf., dicere, *directly,* Cic. ; **2**, perpendicularly; directe ad perpendiculum, Caes.

directō, adv. (directus), *in a straightforward way, directly,* Cic.

directus -a -um, p. adj. with compar. (dirigo), **1**, *straight, direct,* either in a horizontal or perpendicular direction ; paries, Cic. ; iter, Cic. ; trabes, Caes. ; **2**, *straightforward, plain, simple;* verba, Cic. ; homo, Cic.

diremptus -ūs, m. (dirimo), *a separation,* Cic.

direptĭo -ōnis, f. (diripio), *a plundering, pillaging;* urbs relicta direptioni, Cic. ; bonorum direptio, Cic.

direptor -ōris, m. (diripio), *a plunderer, pillager,* Cic.

dīrĭbĕo -ŭi -ĭtum, 2. (for dis -hibeo, from habeo), *to sort the voting tickets which were cast into the balloting urn;* tabellas, Cic.

dīrĭbĭtĭo -ōnis, f. (diribeo), *the sorting of the voting tickets,* Cic.

dīrĭbĭtor -ōris, m. (diribeo), *the officer whose duty it was to sort the voting tickets,* Cic.

dīrĭgo -rexi -rectum, 3. (dis and rego). **I**. *to set straight, arrange in a straight line;* pass. dirigi, *to proceed in a straight line;* transf., dirigitur (argumentatio) quum proposuit aliquid quod probaret, Cic. **II.** *to arrange, direct.* **A**. Lit., **1**, as regards motion, **a**, *of* ships, carriages, journeys, etc., *to direct;* ad castra Corneliana vela, Caes. ; cursum eo (quo), Cic. ; iter ad Mutinam, Cic. ; **b**, *of* weapons, *to aim, direct;* hastam in aliquem, Ov. ; **c**, *of* the sight, aciem ad aliquem, Cat. ; **2**, *of* position, **a**, *to arrange, order, dispose;* (α) in quincuncem ordines (arborum), Cic. ; (β) milit. t. t., *to draw up;* aciem, Caes. ; naves in pugnam, Liv. ; (γ) *to raise, erect;* opera, Caes. **B**. Transf., **a**, *to direct, guide;* dirige vatis opus, Ov. ; intransit. *to lead;* ad veritatem saepissime dirigit, Cic. ; **b**, *to direct the thoughts, attention,* etc., *to something;* suas cogitationes ad aliquid, Cic. ; **c**, *to direct a speech to, to address;* orationem ad aliquid, Cic. ; **d**, *to settle, arrange, fix,* dis-

pose; vitam ad certam rationis normam, Cic. ; utilitate officium magis quam humanitate, Cic.

dīrĭmo -ēmi -emptum, 3. (dis and emo). **I.** 1, *to part, separate, sunder, divide;* Sabinae mulieres ex transverso impetu facto dirimere infestas acies, dirimere iras, Liv. ; **2**, *to interrupt, hinder, disturb, put off, break off;* **a**, an assembly or conversation, actum est de eo nihil ; nox diremit, Cic. ; ea res colloquium ut diremisset, Caes. ; esp. of omens, bellum inter Philippum Liv. ; a war, contention, bellum inter Philippum atque Aetolos, Liv. ; **c**, an alliance, league, *to break up;* veterem conjunctionem civium, Cic. **II.** *to divide;* quae urbs Volturno flumine dirempta Falernum a Campano agro dividit, Liv.

dīrĭpĭo -rĭpŭi, -reptum, 3. (dis and rapio), **I.** *to tear to pieces.* **A**. Lit., Hippolytum, Ov. **B**. Transf. *to plunder, pillage, destroy;* socios, Cic. **II.** *to tear away;* a pectore vestem, Ov. ; res pulcherrimas ex tota Asia, Cic.

dīrĭtas -ātis, f. (dirus), **1**, *misfortune, disaster,* Cic. poet.; **2**, *cruelty, fierceness;* quanta in altero diritas, in altero comitas, Cic.

dīrumpo -rūpi -ruptum, 3. *to break in pieces, shatter.* **I**. Lit., tenuissimam quamque partem (nubis) dividere atque dirumpere, Tac. ; (homo) diruptus, *ruptured,* Cic. **II.** Transf., **a**, dirupi me paene in judicio Galli Caninii, *shouted myself hoarse in defending,* etc., Cic. ; middle, dirumpi, *to burst with envy, grief, anger,* etc. ; dirumpi plausu alicuius, *to burst with envy at the applause given to some one else,* Cic. ; dolore, Cic. ; **b**, *to sever, break up;* amicitiam, Cic. ; societatem, Cic.

dīrŭo -ŭi -ŭtum, 3. (dis and ruo), *to pull down, raze to the ground, destroy.* **A**. Lit., urbem, Cic. ; agmina vasto impetu, *to scatter,* Hor. **B**. Transf., aere dirui, *to be mulcted of one's pay,* Plin. ; in quibus (castris), quum frequens esset, tamen aere dirutus est, *ruined by gambling,* Cic. ; homo diruptus dirutusque, *bankrupt,* Cic.

dīrus -a -um (connected with δεινός), *fearful, horrible, dire.* **A**. Of unfavourable omens, omen, Ov. ; subst., **dirae** -arum, f. *unlucky omens,* Cic. ; so **dīra** -orum, n., Cic. **B**. Transf., *horrible, cruel, frightful;* **a**, of things, exsecratio, Verg. ; venena, Hor. ; subst., **dīrae** -arum, f. *curses;* diris agam vos, Hor. ; contingere funebribus diris signa tela arma hostium, Liv. ; **b**, of persons, *cruel, terrible;* dea, Circe, Cic. ; Hannibal, Hor. ; subst., personif., **Dira** -ae, f. *a Fury,* Verg. ; gen. plur. often with ultrices, *Furies,* Verg.

1. dis, inseparable particle, meaning *away from,* takes the form of dis-, di-, and dir-.

2. Dis, Ditis, m. *a name of Pluto, god of the lower world,* Cic. ; domina Ditis, Proserpina, Verg.

3. dīs, ditis, adj. with compar. and superl., *rich.* **A**. Lit., dis hostis, Liv. ; apud Helvetios ditissimus fuit Orgetorix, Caes. ; with genit., ditissimus agri, Verg. **B**. Transf. *richly provided, making rich;* ditia stipendia, Liv.

discēdo -cessi -cessum, 3. **I**. *to go asunder, part, separate;* in duas partes, Cic. ; caelum discedit, *the heavens open,* Cic. ; transf., omnis Italia animis discedit, *is divided,* Sall. **II. A**. Lit., **1**, gen., *to depart, go away;* e Gallia, Cic. ; de foro, Cic. ; finibus Ausoniae, Ov. ; used impersonally, a contione disceditur, Caes. ; **2**, esp. **a**, milit. t. t. (α) of troops, *to march away;* a Brundisio, Caes. ; as signis, *to break the ranks, leave the line of battle,* Caes. ; ab armis, *to lay down arms,* Caes. ; (β) *to come out of a contest, to come off;* victor, Caes. ; victus, Sall. ; aequo Marte cum Volscis. *to have a drawn battle with,*

Liv.; so *to come out of any contest* (e.g., in a *court of law*); *superior discedit*, Cic.; turpissime, *to come off with disgrace*, Cic.; **b**, *to abandon, desert*; ab amicis, Cic.; ab aliquo duce (of soldiers), Caes. **B**. Transf., **1**, gen., ex vita tamquam ex hospitio, Cic.; a vita, Caes.; a re, *to digress* (of an orator), Cic.; nunquam ex animo meo discedit illius viri memoria, Cic.; **2**, esp. **a**, *to abandon a duty, deviate, swerve from principles*, etc.; ab officio, Cic.; a consuetudine, Cic.; **b**, polit. t. t. of the senate, in aliquam sententiam discedere, *to support a resolution*; in alia omnia discedere, *to be quite of the contrary opinion*, Cic.; **c**, discedere ab aliquo or ab aliqua re, *to except*; quum a vobis discesserim, *you excepted*, Cic.

disceptātĭo -ōnis, f. (discepto), **1**, *a debate, discussion, controversy*; cum quibus omnis fere nobis disceptatio contentioque est, Cic.; with genit., disceptatio juris, Cic.; **2**, *a judicial decision, award*; disceptationem ab rege ad Romanos revocabant, Liv.

disceptātor -ōris, m. (discepto), *an arbitrator, judge of a controversy*; domesticus, Cic.; juris, Cic.

disceptātrix -trīcis, f. (disceptator), *one who decides*, Cic.

discepto. 1. (dis and capto), **1**, *to decide a suit* or *cause, adjudicate, determine*; controversias, Cic.; inter populum et regem, Liv.; **2**, *to dispute, debate, discuss*; verbis de jure, Liv.; de controversiis apud se potius quam inter se armis, Caes.; de jure publico armis, Cic.; transf., in uno proelio omnis fortuna reipublicae disceptat, *depends upon*, Cic.

discerno -crēvi -crētum, 3. **A**. *to sever, separate*; mons qui fines eorum discerneret, Sall.; duae urbes magno inter se maris terrarumque spatio discretae, Liv.; discretae sedes piorum, *set apart*, Hor. **B**. Transf., *to distinguish, discern*; alba et atra discernere non posse, Cic.; with rel. sent., animus discernit, quid sit eiusdem generis, quid alterius, Cic.

discerpo -cerpsi -cerptum, 3. (dis and carpo). **A**. Lit. *to pluck to pieces, tear in pieces, dismember*; membra gruis, Hor.; animus nec dividi nec discerpi potest, Cic. **B**. Transf., in a discourse, *to separate, divide*; qui quae complecti tota nequeunt, haec facilius divulsa et quasi discerpta contrectant, Cic.

discessĭo -ōnis, f. (discedo), **1**, *a going away, departure*, Tac.; **2**, polit. t. t., *voting, division in the senate* (by going over to one side or the other); senatus consultum facere per discessionem, *without discussion*, Cic.; discessionem facere, *to vote*, Cic.; facta est discessio in sententiam alicuius, Cic.

discessus -ūs, m. (discedo), **1**, *a parting, separation*; caeli, *lightning*, Cic.; **2**, *a departure, going away*; ab urbe, Cic.; e vita, Cic.; esp., **a**, milit. t.t. *marching off*, Caes.; ab Dyrrhachio discessus exercituum, Cic.; **b**, euphem. *banishment*, Cic.

discĭdĭum -ĭi, n. (discindo). **I**. *a tearing away, dividing*; nubis, Lucr. **II**. *separation, division, parting*. **A**. Lit., conjugis miserae, *from a wife*, Cic.; esp., of the parting of lovers or of divorce, Cic.; divortia atque affinitatum discidia, Cic. **B**. Transf. *separation in feelings, dissension*; belli discidio, Cic.; deorum odia, discidia, discordiae, Cic.

discĭdo. 3. (dis and caedo), *to cut in pieces, hew in pieces*, Lucr.

discinctus -a -um (p. adj. of discingo), *careless, reckless, dissolute, extravagant*; nepos, Hor.; otia, Ov.

discindo -scĭdi -scissum, 3. (dis and scindo),

1, *to cleave asunder, split*; cotem novaculā, Cic.; transf., amicitias, Cic.; **2**, *to tear open*; tunicam, Cic.

discingo -cinxi -cinctum, 3. *to take off the girdle, ungird*; Afros, *to disarm*, Juv.

disciplīna -ae, f. (discipulus). **I**. *instruction, teaching*. **A**. Lit., litterae reliquaeque res quarum est disciplina, Cic.; novum aliquem alicui in disciplinam tradere. Cic.; ab aliquo disciplinam accipere, Cic.; subj. gen., disciplina majorum, Cic.; obj. gen., disciplina virtutis, Cic. **B**. Meton., *that which is taught, learning, knowledge, science*; **a**, gen., bellica, *the art of war*, Cic.; navalis, Cic.; habere quasdam etiam domesticas disciplinas, Cic.; juris civilis, Cic.; **b**, *a philosophical school, a system*; philosophiae disciplina, Cic.; **c**, *a rhetorical school* or *system*; Hermagorae, Cic. **II**. In a wider sense, *training, education*. **A**. Lit., **a**, gen., disciplina puerilis, *of boys*, Cic.; disciplina familiae, *of slaves*; gravis et constans, Cic.; **b**, esp. *military training*; militaris, Liv.; militiae, Cic. **B**. Meton., *the result of training, custom, habit, order*; **a**, gen., disciplinae sanctitas, Liv.; certa vivendi disciplina, Cic.; **b**, *the ordering of a state, constitution*; disciplina reipublicae, Cic.; disciplinam dare, Cic.; o morem praeclarum disciplinamque quam a majoribus accepimus, Cic.

discĭpŭla -ae, f. (discipulus), *a female scholar*, Hor.

discĭpŭlus -i., m. (disco), *a scholar, pupil, disciple*, Cic.

disclūdo -clūsi -clūsum, 3. (dis and claudo), *to shut up apart, to separate, divide*. **I**. Nerea ponto, Verg.; tigna, *keep at the proper distance*, Caes.; mons qui Arvernos ab Helviis discludit, Caes. **II**. Transf., morsus roboris, *to loosen*, Verg.

disco, dĭdĭci, 3. **I**. *to learn*. **A**. Gen., litteras Graecas, Cic.; jus civile aut rem militarem, Cic.; id quod ex pluribus testibus prioribus actionibus didicistis, Cic.; ab eo Stoico dialecticam didicerat, Cic.; apud aliquem litteras, Cic.; in castris per laborem usum militiae, Sall.; with infin., saltare, Cic.; Latine loqui, Sall.; quinquennes gubernare didicisse, Cic.; with rel. clause, plures discent quem ad modum haec fiant quam quem ad modum his resistatur, Cic.; ita didicisse a majoribus ut, etc., *to have so learnt to be accustomed to*, Caes.; disco fidibus, *to learn to play on the lyre*, Cic.; absol., valent pueri, studiose discunt, diligenter docentur, Cic.; voluntas discendi, Cic. **B**. Esp., discere causam, legal t.t., *to get up the facts of a case*, of an advocate, Cic. **C**. **II**. *to become acquainted with*; **1**, gen., me peritus discet Hiber Rhodanique potor, Hor.; **2**, *to become acquainted with a fact, learn, find out*; didici ex tuis litteris te omnibus in rebus habuisse rationem, Cic.

discŏlor -ōris. **A**. *of different colours; signa*, Cic.; miles, *black and white* (of the men at draughts), Ov. **B**. Transf., *different from, unlike to*; matrona meretrici dispar atque discolor, Hor.

disconvĕnĭo, 4. *to disagree, not to harmonise*; vitae ordine toto, Hor.; impers., eo disconvenit inter meque et te, Hor.

discordĭa -ae, f. (discors). **I**. **a**, *dissension, disagreement, discord*; haec discordia non rerum sed verborum, Cic.; **b**, *dissension, sedition*, Tac. **II**. Personif., Discordia, *the Goddess of Discord*, Verg.

discordĭōsus -a -um (discordia), *full of discord, mutinous*; vulgus seditiosum atque discordiosum fuit, Sall.

discordo. 1. (discors), **1**, *to be at discord, to disagree*; cum Cheruscis, Tac.; inter se dis-

sidere atque discordare, Cic.; animus a se dissidens secumque discordans, Cic.; of soldiers, *to be mutinous*, Tac.; **2**, *to be unlike*; quantum discordet parum avaro, Hor.

discors -cordis (dis and cor), 1. **1**, *disagreeing, inharmonious, discordant*; civitas secum ipsa discors, Liv.; of inanimate objects, venti, Verg.; bella, Ov.; **2**, *unlike, dissimilar, different*; tam discordia inter se responsa Liv.

discrĕpantĭa -ae, f. (discrepo), *disagreement, difference*; scripti et voluntatis, Cic.

discrĕpātĭo -ōnis, f. (discrepo), *disagreement, disunion*; inter consules, Liv.

discrĕpĭto, 1. (intens. of discrepo), *to be entirely dissimilar, to be quite unlike*, Lucr.

discrĕpo -pāvi, 1. *not to sound together.* **A**. Lit., *to be out of time, to be discordant*; in fidibus aut in tibiis, Cic. **B**. Transf., *to disagree, be different, be unlike*; cum aliquo or cum aliqua re, Cic.; ab aliqua re, Cic.; sibi, Cic.; inter se, Cic.; nunc in re, Cic.; with dat., quantum simplex hilarisque nepoti discrepet, Hor.; impers., discrepat, *there is a disagreement, people are not agreed*; discrepat inter scriptores, Liv.; illud haudquaquam discrepat, Liv.; with acc. and infin., Liv.; non or haud discrepat quin, etc., Liv.

discrībo = describo (q.v.).

discrīmen -ĭnis, n. (discerno), *that which divides.* **I**. Lit., **A**. Concr., *the dividing line*; quum pertenui discrimine (duo maria) separarentur, Cic. **B**. Abstr., **a**, *the space between*; spatium discrimina fallit, Ov.; **b**, in music, *interval*; septem discrimina vocum (of the lyre with seven strings), Verg. **II. a**, *separation, distinction, difference*; delectu omni et discrimine remoto, Cic.; **b**, *turning-point, critical moment*; ea res nunc in discrimine versatur utrum possitne ... an, Cic.; in discrimen adductum esse, Cic.; **c**, *crisis, hazard, danger*; in tanto discrimine periculi, Liv.; ad ipsum discrimen eius temporis, Cic.; res esse in summo discrimine, Caes.

discrīmĭno, 1. (discrimen), *to separate, sunder, divide*; Etruriam discriminat Cassia, Cic.; vigiliarum somnique nec die nec nocte discriminata tempora, Liv.

discrīptĭo -ōnis, f. (discribo), *a division*, Cic.

discrŭcĭo, 1. *to torture vehemently, torment*; of bodily torture, discruciatos necare, Cic.; of mental anguish, refl. or pass., *to torment oneself, make oneself miserable*, Cic.

discumbo -cŭbŭi -cŭbĭtum, 3. *to lie down*; **a**, *to recline at table*; discubuimus omnes praeter illam, Cic.; impers., discumbitur, *one goes to the table*, Cic.; **b**, *to sleep, go to bed*; cenati discubuerunt ibidem, Cic.

discŭpĭo -īvi -ītum, 3. *to desire vehemently*, Cat.

discurro -cŭcurri and -curri -cursum, 3. *to run in different directions, run about, run to and fro*; in muris, Caes.; circa deum delubra, Liv.; ad arma, Liv.; impers., totā discurritur urbe, Verg.; of things, diversa ruens septem discurrit in ora, Verg.; quum mens discurrit utroque, Ov.

discursus -ūs, m. (discurro), *a running up and down, a running about, running to and fro*; militum, Liv.; lupi, Ov.; of things, liber inter ordines discursus, of a ship, *unhindered motion*, Liv.

discus -i, m. (δίσκος), *a quoit*; discum audire quam philosophum malle, Cic.

discŭtĭo -cussi -cussum, 3. (dis and quatio), *to strike asunder.* **I**. *to shatter, break down*: tribus arietibus aliquantum muri, Liv. **II. 1**, *to*

disperse, *scatter*; nubem, Ov.; umbras, Verg.; discussa est caligo, Cic.; **2**, *to frustrate, bring to nought, suppress*; eam rem, Liv.; caedem, Cic.; eorum captiones, Cic.; eorum advocationem manibus, ferro, lapidibus, Cic.

disertē, adv. with superl. (disertus), *clearly, plainly, eloquently*; dicere, Cic.

disertus -a -um, p. adj. with compar. and superl. (dissero), *eloquent, well-expressed*; **a**, of the language, oratio, Cic.; historia, Cic.; **b**, of the person speaking, homo, Cic.; disertissimūs orator, Cic.

disĭcio = disjicio (q.v.).

disjecto, 1. (intens. of disjicio), *to cast about scatter*, Lucr.

1. **disjectus** -a -um, v. disjicio.

2. **disjectus** -ūs, m. (disjicio), *a scattering, dispersing*, Lucr.

disjĭcĭo -jēci -jectum, 3. (dis and jacio), *to cast asunder.* **I**. Lit., **A**. Gen., **a**, of buildings, etc., *to throw down, destroy*; disjecta tempestate statua, Liv.; disjecta aedificia, Caes.; **b**, *to scatter, disperse*; naves or classem, Liv.; disjecta comas, *with dishevelled hair*, Ov.; disjecta membra poetae, Hor.; disjecta manus, Cic.; milit. t.t., *to scatter*; phalangem, Caes. **II**. Transf., *to bring to naught, frustrate*; consilia ducis, Liv.

disjunctĭo -ōnis, f. (disjungo), *separation*. **I**. Lit., meorum, Cic. **II**. Transf., 1, gen., *difference*; animorum, Cic.; 2, esp., **a**, in logic, *a disjunctive proposition*, Cic.; **b**, in rhet. *a series of sentences without connecting particles, asyndeton*, Cic.

disjunctus -a -um, p. adj. with compar. and superl. (disjungo), *separated, sundered, distant.* **I**. Lit., quae (Aetolia) procul barbaris disjuncta gentibus, Cic. **II**. Transf., **A**. Gen., *remote from*; homines Graeci longe a nostrorum hominum gravitate disjuncti, Cic. **B**. Esp., **1**, in logic, *disjunctive*; **2**, in rhet., *disconnected*, Cic.

disjungo -junxi -junctum, 3. *to unbind, loosen, separate.* **I**. Lit., **a**, *to unyoke* or *unharness*; jumenta, Cic.; **b**, *to separate, sunder, remove*; intervallo locorum et tempore disjuncti sumus, Cic.; Italis disjungimur oris, Verg. **II**. Transf., **A**. Gen., *to separate*; aliquem ab aliquo, Cic. **B**. Esp., *to distinguish*; insaniam a furore, Cic.

dispālor, 1. dep. *to wander about, to stray*, Nep.

dispando -pandi -pansum, 3. *to expand, extend, stretch out*, Lucr.

dispar -păris, *unlike, different, dissimilar, unequal*; fortuna, Cic.; tempora, Cic.; with dat., illa oratio huic dispar, Cic.; with genit., quidquam dispar sui atque dissimile, Cic.

dispargo, v. dispergo.

dispărĭlis -e, *unlike, dissimilar, different, unequal*; disparilis exspiratio terrarum, Cic.

dispăro, 1. *to separate, part, divide*; seniores a junioribus divisit eosque ita disparavit ut, etc., Cic.; partic. subst., **dispărātum** -i, n., rhet. t. t., *the contradictory proposition* (e.g., sapere, non sapere), Cic.

dispartio = dispertio (q.v.).

dispello -pŭli -pulsum, 3. **I**. *to drive in different directions*; pecudes, Cic. **II**. *to scatter, dispel*; umbras, Verg.; transf., ab animo tamquam ab oculis caliginem, Cic.

dispendĭum -ĭi, n. (dispendo), *expenditure, expense, loss*; facere, *to suffer loss*; transf., dispendia morae, *loss of time*, Verg.

1. **dispendo** = dispando (q.v.).

2. **dispendo** -pensum, 3. *to weigh out*, Varr.

dispenno = dispando (q.v.).

dispensātĭo -ōnis, f. (dispenso), **1**, *management, economical administration;* aerarii, Cic.; annonae, Liv.; **2**, *the office of a dispensator,* Cic.; regia, *the office of treasurer to a king,* Cic.

dispensātor -ōris, m. (dispenso), *a steward, bailiff, treasurer,* Cic.

dispenso, 1. (intens. of 2. dispendo). **I.** *to weigh out* or *pay away money,* Plaut.; *to divide, distribute;* oscula per natos, Ov.; laetitiam inter impotentes populi animos, Liv.; in rhet., inventa non solum ordine, sed etiam momento quodam atque judicio, Cic. **II.** a, gen., *to arrange;* annum intercalariis mensibus interponendis ita dispensavit ut, etc., Liv.; **b**, esp., *to manage a household;* res domesticas, Cic.

disperdĭtĭo -ōnis, f. (disperdo), *a total destruction, ruin,* Cic.

disperdo -dĭdi -dĭtum, 3. *to destroy, ruin, annihilate;* possessiones, Cic.

dispĕrĕo -ĭi, 4. *to perish utterly, be entirely ~uined;* fundūs disperit, Cic.; dispeream, si, or nisi, *may I perish if* or *except,* Cat., Hor.

dispergo -spersi -spersum, 3.(dis and spargo), *to scatter, spread abroad, disperse;* **a**, tam multa pestifera terrā marique, Cic.; *to disperse an army,* Caes.; **b**, rumores, *to spread abroad reports,* Tac.

dispersē and **dispersim**, adv. (dispersus), *in different places, dispersedly, here and there,* Cic.

dispersĭo -ōnis, f. (dispergo), *a scattering, destruction,* Cic.

dispertĭo (dis-partio) -īvi and -ĭi -ītum, 4. *to separate, divide, distribute.* **A.** Lit., pecuniam judicibus, Cic.; exercitum per oppida, Liv. **B.** Transf., tempora voluptatis laborisque, Cic.; dep., **dispertĭor** -īri, aliquid in infinita, Cic.; administrationem inter se, Liv.

dispĭcĭo -spexi -spectum, 3. (dis and specio). **I.** *to open the eyes and begin to see;* catuli qui jam dispecturi sint, Cic. **II. A.** *to catch sight of, perceive;* 1, lit., Lucr.; 2, transf., populus Romanus libertatem jam ex diutina servitute dispiciens, Cic. **B.** 1, *to perceive mentally;* si dispicere quid coepero, Cic.; with rel. sent., sed ego quod sperem non dispicio, Cic.; **2**, *to reflect upon, consider;* res Romanas, Cic.

displĭcĕo -plĭcŭi -plĭcĭtum, 2. (dis and placeo), *to displease* (opp. placeo, complaceo); alicui, Cic.; alicui de aliquo, Cic.; nihi or alicui displicet, with infin., Cic.; displicere sibi, *to be dissatisfied with oneself, to be melancholy, out of spirits,* Cic.

displōdo -plōsi -plōsum, 3. *to spread out, dilate, burst,* Hor.

dispōno -pŏsŭi -pŏsĭtum, 3. (dis and pono), *to put in different places, to distribute.* **I.** Gen., **A.** Lit., pocula Bacchi, Ov.; signa ad omnes columnas, omnibus etiam intercolumniis, in silva denique disposita sub divo, Cic.; milit. t. t., portis stationes, Liv.; praesidia ad ripas, Caes. **B.** Transf., a, *to distribute on a definite plan;* imperii curas, Tac.; **b**, rhet. t. t., verba ita, ut pictores varietatem colorum, Cic. **II.** *to arrange, dispose, set in order.* **A.** Lit., Homeri libros antea confusos, Cic.; bene dispositae comae, Ov. **B.** Transf., disposita ad honorem studia, Cic.

dispŏsĭtē, adv. (dispositus), *in proper order, methodically;* accusare, Cic.

dispŏsĭtĭo -ōnis, f. (dispono), *a regular arrangement* or *order in a speech,* Cic.

dispŏsĭtūra -ae, f. (dispono), *arrangement, order,* Lucr.

1. **dispŏsĭtus** -a -um, p. adj. (dispono), *arranged,* Plin.

2. **dispŏsĭtus** -ūs, m. (dispono), *arrangement,* Tac.

dispŭtātĭo -ōnis, f. (disputo), *an arguing, debating, argument, debate;* hāc in utramque partem disputatione habitā, Cic.

dispŭtātor -ōris, m. (disputo), *a debater, disputant,* Cic.

dispŭto, 1. *to discuss, weigh, debate, argue;* aliquid, Cic.; de aliqua re, Cic.; ad aliquam rem de aliqua re, Cic.; pro omnibus et contra omnia, Cic.; contra propositum, Cic.; disputari in utramque partem, *for and against,* Cic.; with rel. sent., ego enim quid desiderem, non quid viderim disputo, Cic.

disquiro, 3. (dis and quaero), *to inquire into, investigate,* Hor.

disquīsītĭo -ōnis (disquiro), *an inquiry, investigation,* Cic.

dissaepĭo -saepsi -saeptum, 4. *to hedge off, separate, divide;* aliquid tenui muro, Cic.

dissaeptĭo -ōnis, f. (dissaepio), *a partition,* Liv. (?).

dissaeptum -i, n. (dissaepio), *a barrier, partition,* Luc.

dissēmĭno, 1. *to spread abroad, disseminate;* sermonem, Cic.; malum, Cic.

dissensĭo -ōnis, f. (dissentio), *disagreement, variance.* **I.** Of persons, a, in a friendly manner, inter homines de jure, Cic.; est quaedam inter nos parva dissensio, Cic.; **b**, in a hostile manner, *dissension, disunion; dissensio ac discidium,* Cic.; dissensio civilis, Caes. **II.** Of abstractions, *opposition;* utilium cum honestis, Cic.

dissensus -ūs, m. (dissentio), *disunion, disagreement,* Verg.

dissentānĕus -a -um (dissentio), *disagreeing, different* (opp. consentaneus); alicui rei, Cic.

dissentĭo -sensi -sensum, 4. *to be of a different opinion, not to agree.* **I.** Lit., Of persons, a, in a friendly manner, ab aliquo, Cic.; ab aliqua re, Cic.; de aliqua re, Cic.; cum aliquo, Cic.; inter se, Cic.; with dat., conditionibus foedis, Hor.; **b**, in a hostile manner, *to be at variance;* acerrime dissentientes cives, Cic. **II.** Transf., of things, *to be opposed, different;* a more, Cic.; quid ipsum a se dissentiat, Cic.

dissēp . . . v. dissaep . . .

dissĕrēnascit -avit, impers. (inchoat. of disserenat, *it clears up* (of the weather); quum undique disserenavisset, Liv.

dissĕrēnat, impers. (dis and serenat), *it clears up,* Plin.

1. **dissĕro** -sēvi -sĭtum, 3., 1, *to scatter seed,* Plin.; 2, *to plant at a distance in the ground;* taleas, Caes.

2. **dissĕro** -sĕrŭi -sertum, 3. *to examine, treat of, discuss a subject;* with acc., ista, Cic.; with acc. and infin., Cic.; with relative sentence (quomodo, qui, quid), Cic.; with de, quae Socrates supremo vitae die de immortalitate animorum disseruisset, Cic.

disserpo, 3. *to creep in different directions, spread imperceptibly;* late disserpunt tremores, Lucr.

disserto, 1. (intens. of 2. dissero), *to treat of discuss, argue;* aliquid, Tac.

dissĭdĕo -sēdi -sessum, 2. (dis and sedeo), lit., *to sit apart.* **I.** *to be drawn apart;* si toga dissidet impar, *sits unevenly,* Hor. **II.** *to be distant, to be separated.* **A.** Lit., of places, quantum Hypanis Veneto dissidet Eridano, Prop. **B.** Transf., *not to agree;* **a**, of persons, *to disagree, dissent, be of a different opinion;* inter se,

Cic.; **ab** aliquo, Cic.; cum aliquo, Cic.; de aliqua, Cic.; with dat., dissidens plebi virtus, Hor.; in a hostile sense, *to be at variance*, Cic.; **b**, of things, *to be opposed, contrary;* scriptum a sententia dissidet, Cic.; cupiditates inter se dissident et discordant, Cic.

dissĭdĭum -ĭi, n. (dissideo), *disagreement, disunion*, Cic.

dissĭlĭo -sĭlŭi -sultum, 4. (dis and salio), *to leap apart, burst asunder.* **A.** Lit., haec loca dissiluisse ferunt, Verg.; dissilit omne solum, Ov. **B.** Transf., gratia sic fratrum geminorum dissiluit, *was broken up*, Hor.

dissĭmĭlis -e, adj. with compar. and superl., *unlike, dissimilar;* with genit., verum tamen fuit tum sui dissimilis, Cic.; with dat., quies est tam dissimilis homini, qui non, etc., Cic.; with inter se, duo fuerunt per idem tempus dissimiles inter se, Cic.; with inter se and the genit., qui sunt et inter se dissimiles et aliorum, Cic.; with atque (ac) quam and et, dissimilis est militum causa et tua, Cic.; absol., naturae dissimiles, Cic.

dissĭmĭlĭtĕr, adv. (dissimilis), *differently, in a different manner*, Liv.

dissĭmĭlĭtūdo -ĭnis, f. (dissimilis), *unlikeness, difference;* locorum, Cic.; habet ab illis rebus dissimilitudinem, Cic.; dissimilitudinem non nullam habet cum illius administratione provinciae, Cic.; quum tanta sit inter oratores bonos dissimilitudo, Cic.

dissĭmŭlantĕr, adv. (dissimulo), *secretly, in a dissembling manner;* verba non aperte sed dissimulanter conclusa, Cic.; non or ne dissimulanter, *without dissembling*, Cic.

dissĭmŭlātĭo -ōnis, f. (dissimulo), *a concealing, dissembling, dissimulation*, Cic.; esp. *of irony* (in the Socratic sense), Cic.

dissĭmŭlātor -ōris, m. (dissimulo), *a dissembler, concealer;* opis propriae, Hor.

dissĭmŭlo, 1. *to make unlike.* **I.** *to conceal, to hide;* Achilles veste virum longā dissimulatus erat, *concealed his manhood beneath a woman's robe*, Ov. **II.** *to act* or *to speak as if a thing which is were not.* **A.** *to dissemble, disguise, keep secret;* aliquid silentio, Cic.; dissimulata deam, *concealing her divinity*, Ov.; with acc. and infin., Cic.; with ut and the subj., Cic.; non dissimulare, followed by quin, Cic.; dissimulare non sinit quin delecter, Cic.; absol., *to dissemble;* non dissimulat, Cic. **B.** *to ignore, leave unnoticed*, Tac.; dissimulare consulatum alicuius, Tac.

dissĭpābĭlis -e (dissipo), *that can be scattered;* ignis et aer, Cic.

dissĭpātĭo -ōnis, f. (dissipo). **I.** *scattering;* civium, Cic. **II. A.** *dispersion by sale;* praedae, Cic. **B.** Rhet. t. t., *the analysis of an idea*, Cic.

dissĭpātus -a -um, p. adj. (dissipo), *scattered, disconnected;* oratio, Cic.

dissĭpo, 1. (dis and *sipo). **I.** *to scatter, disperse, spread abroad.* **A.** Lit., membra fratris, Cic.; aliud alio, Cic. **B.** Transf., **1**, ea contrahere amicitiam, dissipare discordiam, *put an end to*, Cic.: **2**, famam, *spread abroad*, Cic. **II.** *to scatter by violence.* **A.** Lit., **1**, milit. t.t. *to rout, scatter;* hostes, Cic.; dissipata fuga, Liv.: **2**, *to pull down, destroy;* statuam, Cic.; tecta, Liv.; **3**, of property, *to squander, destroy;* patrimonium, Cic.; reliquias reipublicae, Cic.

dissĭtus, partic., v. 1. dissero.

dissŏcĭābĭlis -e (dissocio), **1**, act. *that which separates;* oceanus, Hor.; **2**, pass., *that which cannot be united;* res, Tac.

dissŏcĭātĭo -ōnis, f. (dissocio), *a separation, parting;* spiritus corporisque, Tac.

dissŏcĭo, 1. **I.** *to separate, sever, divide* friendships, etc.; morum dissimilitudo dissociat amicitias, Cic.; disertos a doctis, Cic. **II.** Of places, *to separate, divide;* ni (montes) dissocientur opacā valle, Hor.

dissŏlūbĭlis -e (dissolvo), *dissoluble, separable;* mortale omne animal et dissolubile et dividuum sit necesse est, Cic.

dissŏlūtē, adv. (dissolutus), **1**, *disconnectedly, loosely;* dissolute dicere, *without connecting particles*, Cic.; **2**, *carelessly, negligently, without energy;* minus severe quam decuit, non tamen omnino dissolute, Cic.

dissŏlūtĭo -ōnis, f. (dissolvo). **I.** Lit. *breaking up, dissolution, destruction, annihilation;* naturae, *death*, Cic.; navigii, *shipwreck*, Tac. **II.** Transf., **1**, *destruction, abolition;* legum, judiciorum, Cic.: **2**, *refutation of* a charge; criminum, Cic.; **3**, *want of energy, weakness;* remissio animi ac dissolutio, Cic.; **4**, in rhet., *want of connexion*, Cic.

dissŏlūtus -a -um, p. adj. with compar. and superl. (dissolvo). **I.** *not bound together, loosened;* navigium, *leaky*, Cic. **II.** Transf., **1**, rhet. t. t., *disconnected, loose*, Cic.; **2**, *wanting in energy, lax;* poterone esse in eum dissolutus qui, etc., Cic.; **3**, *profligate, dissolute;* dissolutissimus hominum, Cic.

dissolvo -solvi -sŏlūtum, 3. **I.** *to loosen, unloose.* **A.** Lit., **1**, gen., scopas, clipeum, Cic.; **2**, esp. *to melt;* aes, Lucr. **B.** Transf., **1**, gen., *to break up, destroy;* societatem, amicitiam, Cic.; leges, Cic.; **2**, esp. a, rhet. t. t., *to divide;* orationem, Cic.; **b**, *to refute an assertion, charge*, etc.; criminationem, Cic. **II.** *to pay, discharge* a debt; aes alienum, Cic.; pecuniam publicam ulli civitati, Cic.

dissŏnus -a -um. **A.** *discordant, inharmonious, dissonant;* clamores, Liv. **B.** Transf., *different, disagreeing;* dissonae gentes sermone moribusque, Liv.

dissors -sortis, *having a different lot* or *fate;* ab omni milite dissors gloria, *not shared with*, Ov.

dissuādĕo -suāsi -suāsum, 2. *to advise against, oppose by argument;* legem agrariam, Cic.; de captivis, Cic.; with acc. and infin., Cic.; absol., dissuasimus nos, *I spoke against it*, Cic.

dissuāsĭo -ōnis, f. (dissuadeo), *advising to the contrary, speaking against;* rogationis eius, Cic.

dissuāsor -ōris, m. (dissuadeo), *one who advises to the contrary, one who speaks against;* rogationis, Cic.; legis agrariae, Liv.; transf., of things, Auster quasi dissuasor consilii mei, Cic.

dissuāvĭor, 1. dep. *to kiss eagerly*, ap. Cic.

dissulto, 1. (intens. of dissilio), *to leap apart, burst asunder;* nec fulmine tanti dissultant crepitus, Verg.; dissultant ripae, Verg.

dissŭo -sŭi -sūtum, 3. **A.** Lit., *to unstitch.* **B.** Transf., *to open wide;* sinum, Ov.; *to loosen gently* or *by degrees;* tales amicitiae dissuendae magis quam discindendae, Cic.

distantĭa -ae, f. (disto), *difference, diversity;* morum studiorumque, Cic.

distendo -tendi -tentum and -tensum, 3. *to stretch apart, expand, extend.* **I.** Gen., aciem, Caes.; brachia, Ov. **II.** **1**, *to fill full, distend;* ubera cytiso, Verg.; horrea plena spicis, Tib.; **2**, a, milit. t. t., *to divide, to distract the attention of the enemy by attacks in different places;* copias hostium, Liv.; **b**, *to distract, perplex;* distendit ea res animos Samnitium, Liv.

1. **distentus** -a -um, p. adj. (distendo), *distended, full;* ubera, Hor.

2. **distentus** -a -um, p. adj. with superl. (distineo), *busy, occupied;* tot tantisque negotiis, Cic.

distermĭno, 1. *to separate by a boundary, divide,* Cic. poet. ; quod (flumen) Dahas Ariosque disterminat, Tac.

distĭchus -a -um (δίστιχος), *consisting of two rows;* subst. **distichum** (-on) -i, n. *a poem of two lines, a distich,* Mart.

distinctē, adv. with compar. (distinctus), *clearly, definitely, distinctly;* dicere, Cic.

distinctĭo -ōnis, f. (distinguo), 1, *a separation in space;* solis lunae siderumque omnium, *different orbits,* Cic. ; 2, a, *distinguishing, discriminating;* facilis est distinctio ingenui et illiberalis joci, Cic.; lex est justorum injustorumque distinctio, Cic. ; b, rhet. t. t., *a distinguishing between the same word used in different ways,* or *between ideas nearly alike,* Cic. ; 3, a, *distinction, difference;* modo intelligatur, quae sit causarum distinctio et dissimilitudo, Cic.; b, rhet. t. t., *a pause, division,* Cic.

1. **distinctus** -a -um, p. adj. (distinguo), *separated, distinct;* urbs delubris distinctis spatiisque communibus, Cic.

2. **distinctus**, abl. -ū, m. (distinguo), *difference, distinction,* Tac.

distĭnĕo -tĭnŭi, -tentum, 2. (dis and teneo). I. A. Lit., *to hold asunder, keep apart, separate, divide;* tigna binis utrimque fibulis distinebantur, Caes. B. Transf., a, gen., duae senatum distinebant sententiae, Liv. ; b, esp., *to delay;* pacem, Cic. II. *to prevent uniting together.* A. Milit. t. t., *to prevent the union of forces ;* Caesaris copias, Cic.; Volscos, Liv. B. *to prevent the concentration of one's thoughts, to distract ;* maximis occupationibus distineri, Cic.

distinguo -stinxi -stinctum, 3. (from dis and *stigo, stinguo, connected with στίζω). I. *to separate, divide.* A. Lit., onus numero distinxit eodem, Ov. B. Transf., 1, *to separate, distinguish ;* distinguere voces in partes, Cic. ; vera a falsis, Cic. ; impers., quid inter naturam et rationem intersit non distinguitur, Cic. ; 2, grammat. t.t., *to punctuate,* Quint. II. Meton. A. *to point out, mark out ;* nigram medio frontem distinctus ab albo, Ov. B. *to decorate, adorn;* pocula ex auro quae gemmis erant distincta clarissimis, Cic. ; of oratory, oratio distinguitur atque illustratur aliquā re, Cic. C. *to vary, change, give variety to ;* historiam varietate locorum, Cic.

disto, 1. (dis -sto). I. *to be apart, separate, distant ;* 1, of space, quae turres pedes LXXX inter se distarent, Caes. ; 2, of time, quantum distet ab Inacho Codrus, Hor. II. Transf., *to differ, be distinct ;* inter se, Cic. ; ab aliquo, Cic. ; scurrae (dat.), Hor. ; impers., distat, *there is a difference,* Cic.

distorquĕo -torsi -tortum, 2. *to twist apart, distort ;* ora cachinno, Ov. ; oculos, Hor.

distortĭo -ōnis, f. (distorqueo), *distortion ;* membrorum, Cic.

distortus -a -um, p. adj. with compar. and superl. (distorqueo), *distorted, deformed.* A. Lit., crura, Hor.; of persons, distortus Gallus, Cic. B. Transf., of discourse, *perverse;* nullum (genus enuntiandi) distortius, Cic.

distractĭo -ōnis, f. (distraho), 1, *a dividing, separating;* humanorum animorum, Cic. ; 2, *disunion, dissension;* nulla nobis societas cum tyrannis et potius summa distractio est, Cic.

distrăho -traxi -tractum, 3. I. *to pull apart, tear asunder, tear in pieces.* A. Lit., 1, gen., vallum, Liv.; corpus, Cic.; equis distrahi, Verg.; acies distrahitur, *is divided,* Caes.; fuga distrahit aliquos, Cic. ; 2, esp., a, *to sell property by auction, to put up for sale;* agros, Tac.; b,

grammat. t. t., *to leave a hiatus in a verse;* voces, Cic. B. Transf. 1, distrahi in contrarias partes (or sententias), Cic. ; oratoris industriam in plura studia, *to distract,* Cic. ; 2, esp., a, *to dissolve a league* or *union;* omnem societatem civitatis, Cic. ; concilium Boeotorum Liv. ; distrahi cum aliquo, *to fall out with some one,* Cic. ; b, *to bring to naught;* hanc rem, Caes. ; c, *to settle a dispute;* controversias, Cic. II. *to tear from something.* A. Lit., aliquem a complexu suorum, Cic. B. Transf., *to estrange;* aliquem ab aliquo, Cic.

distrĭbŭo -ŭi -ūtum, 3. *to distribute, divide.* I. Gen., populum in quinque classes, Cic. ; pecunias exercitui, Caes. II. Esp., *to arrange* or *divide logically;* causam in crimen et in audaciam, Cic.

distrĭbūtē, adv. with compar. (distributus), *methodically, with logical arrangement;* scribere, Cic.

distrĭbūtĭo -ōnis, f. (distribuo), a, *a division, distribution,* Cic. ; b, *logical arrangement of ideas,* Cic.

distrĭbūtus -a -um, p. adj. (distribuo), *logically arranged;* expositio, Cic.

districtus -a -um, p. adj. (from distringo), a, *busy, occupied, engaged;* contentione ancipiti, Cic. ; b, *severe,* Tac.

distringo -strinxi -strictum, 3. A. Lit., *to draw apart, stretch out;* radiis rotarum districti pendent, Verg.; fig., districtus enim mihi videris esse, *to be on the rack,* Cic. B. Transf., *to engage an enemy at different points, divert, occupy;* Hannibalem in Africam mittere ad distringendos Romanos, *to make a diversion,* Liv.

disturbātĭo -ōnis, f. (disturbo), *destruction;* Corinthi, Cic.

disturbo, 1. *to drive apart, separate with violence, throw into confusion.* I. Lit., A. Gen., contionem gladiis, Cic. B. *to destroy, raze to the ground;* domum meam, Cic.; aedes, Lucr. II. Transf., *to bring to naught, frustrate, ruin;* societatem, Cic.; legem, Cic.

dītesco, 3. (3. dis), *to become rich,* Hor.

dĭthўrambĭcus -a -um (διθυραμβικός), *dithyrambic;* poëma, Cic.

dĭthўrambus -i, m. (διθύραμβος), *a dithyrambic poem* (originally in honour of Bacchus), Cic.

dītĭo (dĭcĭo) -ōnis, f. *power, sovereignty, authority;* esse in ditione alicuius, *to be in the power of,* Cic.; facere ditionis suae, Liv.; redigere bellicosissimas gentes in ditionem huius imperii, Cic.; urbes multas sub imperium populi Romani ditionemque subjungere, Cic.; rem Nolanam in jus ditionemque dare Poeno, Liv.

dītĭor, dītissĭmus, v. 3. dis.

1. **ditis**, v. 3. dis.

2. **Ditis**, v. 2. dis.

dīto, 1. (3. dis), *to enrich, make wealthy;* praemiis belli socios, Liv.; militem ex hostibus, Liv.; pass., ditari as *middle, to become rich,* Liv.; transf., sermonem patrium, Hor.

1. **dĭū**, adv. (old abl. of dies). I. *by day;* diu noctuque, Tac. II. 1, *a long time, a long while, lasting for a long time;* tam diu, jam diu, Cic.; diu multumque or multum diuque, Cic. ; 2, *a long time ago;* jam diu, Cic. Compar., diutius, a, *longer,* Cic.; b, *too long,* Cic.; paulo diutius abesse, Liv. Superl., diutissime, Cic., Caes.

2. **dĭū**, v. dius.

dĭurnus -a -um (for diusnus, from dies). I. *lasting for a day;* opus, a day's work, Cic.; cibus, rations, Liv. Subst., a, **diurnum** -i, n. *journal, account-book of house expenditure kept by**

ɪ slave, **ɪev.**; b, **dĭurna** -orum, v. acta **II.** happening by day ; magna diurna nocturnaque itinera, Caes.; metus diurni nocturnique, Cic.

dĭus -a -um (archaic and poet. form of divus), god-like. **I.** Adj., **A.** Lit., dius Fidius, v. Fidius. **B.** Transf., 1, noble; dia Camilla, Verg.; 2, beautiful, fine; sententia dia Catonis, Hor. **II.** Subst., **dium** -ii, n., sub dio, and (archaic) sub diu, in the open air, Lucr.

dĭūtĭnus -a -um (diu), lasting a long time, long ; servitus, Cic.

dĭūtĭus, dĭūtissĭmē, v. 1. diu.

dĭūturnĭtas -ātis, f. (diuturnus), long duration ; temporis, Cic.; belli, Caes.

dĭūturnus -a -um (1. diu), lasting a long time, of long duration; gloria, bellum, Cic.; of persons, quae nupsit, non diuturna fuit, did not live long, Ov.; non potes esse diuturnus, you cannot remain long in your position, Cic.

dīvārĭco, 1. to stretch apart, spread out; hominem, Cic.

dīvello -velli -vulsum (-volsum), 3. **I.** to pluck apart, tear asunder, separate by force. **A.** Lit., suos artus lacero morsu, Ov. **B.** Transf., 1, res a natura copulatas, Cic.; commoda civium, Cic.; 2, to break up, destroy; affinitatem, Cic.; somnum, interrupt, Hor. **II.** to tear away, remove, separate. **A.** Lit., liberos a complexu parentum, Cic.; se ab hoste, Liv. **B.** Transf., divelli, to tear oneself away from; ab otio, a voluptate, Cic.

dīvendo (-vendĭdi) -vendĭtum, 3. to sell in separate lots; bona populi Romani, Cic.

dīverbĕro, 1. to strike apart, cleave, divide; volucres auras sagittā, Verg.

dīverbĭum -ii, n. (dis and verbum), a dialogue on the stage, Liv.

dīversē, adv. with compar. and superl. (diversus), in different directions, differently, diversely; inconstans est, quod ab eodem de eadem re diverse dicitur, Cic.

dīversĭtas -ātis, f. (diversus), 1, contrariety, disagreement; inter exercitum imperatoremque, Tac.; 2, difference, diversity; supplicii, Tac.

dīversōrĭum, v. deversorium.

dīversus -a -um, p. adj. with compar. and superl. (diverto), turned in different directions. **I. A.** Lit., diversam aciem in duas partes constituere, Caes.; diversi abeunt, they go different ways, Liv.; ubi plures diversae semitae erant, leading different ways, Liv. **B.** Transf., inconstant, irresolute, wavering, indecisive; metu ac libidine diversus agebatur, Sall.; in diversum auctores trahunt utrum . . . an, are not agreed, Liv. **C.** separate, isolated; legatos alium ex alio diversos aggreditur, Sall.; ex locis tam longinquis tamque diversis, Cic. **II.** turned away from, in a different direction. **A.** Lit., 1, quo diversus abis, Verg.; diversis a flumine regionibus, Caes.; 2, lying out of the way, remote; de Achaiae urbibus regionis a se diversae, Liv.; arva colebat diversa Aetnae, Ov.; 3, in an opposite direction; equi in diversum iter concitati, Liv.; anguli maxime inter se diversi, Cic. **B.** different, opposed; a, hostile; acies, Tac.; b, different, opposed in character or nature; with a or ab, haec videntur esse a proposita ratione diversa, Cic.; with inter se, diversa inter se mala, luxuria atque avaritia, Sall.; absol., varia et diversa studia et artes, Cic.; of persons, different in character; ab aliquo, Cic.

dīverto (dīvorto) -verti (-vorti),[3. to turn away, to diverge from, differ, Plaut.

dīves -vĭtis, compar. **dīvĭtĭor** -ĭus, genit. **ōris,** superl. **dīvĭtissĭmus,** rich, wealthy.

I. Lit., **a,** of persons, ex pauperrimo dives factus est, Cic.; with abl., agris, Hor.; with genit, pecoris, Verg.; b, of things, terra dives amomo, Ov. **II.** Transf., rich ; a, epistola, containing much, Ov.; lingua, eloquent, Hor.; divitior fluxit dithyrambus, Cic.; b, precious, costly; cultus, rich dress, Ov.

dīvexo, 1. (dis and vexo), to tear asunder, destroy, plunder ; agros civium optimorum, Cic.

dīvĭdo -vīsi -vīsum, 3. (from dis and root VID, whence viduus). **I.** to separate, divide. **A.** Lit., **1,** gen., omne animal secari ac dividi potest, Cic.; 2, to destroy; muros, Verg. **B.** Transf., 1, a, to divide into parts; exercitum in duas partes, Caes.; Gallia est omnis divisa in partes tres, Caes.; populum in duas partes, Cic.; b, of logical division, genus universum in species certas partiri et dividere, Cic.; c, polit. t. t., sententiam; to divide a resolution into parts so that each part can be voted on, Cic.; 2, a, to divide among persons, distribute, allot; agrum, bona viritim, Cic.; praedam per milites, Liv.; b, to separate a multitude into different places; in hiberna exercitum Magnesiam et Tralles Ephesumque, Liv.; c, poet., imbelli cithară carmina, to sing, Hor. **II.** to separate two wholes from one another. **A.** Gen., a, lit., to divide; Gallos ab Aquitania Garumna dividit, Caes.; b, transf., to distinguish; legem bonam a mala, Cic. **B.** to adorn; gemma fulvum quae dividit aurum, Verg.

dīvĭdŭus -a -um (divido), 1, divisible, Cic.; 2, divided, parted ; aqua, Ov.

dīvīnātĭo -ōnis, f. (divino), 1, the gift of prophecy, divination, Cic.; 2, legal t. t., the selection of a prosecutor out of several, Cic.

dīvīnē, adv. (divinus), 1, by divine inspiration, prophetically, Cic.; 2, divinely, admirably, excellently, Cic.

dīvīnĭtas -ātis, f. (divinus). **I.** a divine nature, divinity, Cic. **II. A.** the power of prophecy or divination, Cic. **B.** excellence, surpassing merit (of an orator), Cic.

dīvīnĭtus, adv. (divinus). **I.** Lit., divinely, by divine influence, Cic. **II.** Transf., **A.** by inspiration, by means of divination, Cic. **B.** ad mirably, nobly, divinely; loqui, Cic.

dīvīno, 1. (divinus), to foretell, prophesy, forebode, divine the future; with acc., hoc, Cic.; with rel. sent., quid futurum sit latrocinio tribunorum non divino, Cic.; absol., quiddam praesentiens atque divinans, Cic.

dīvīnus -a -um, adj. with compar. and superl. (divus). **I.** belonging or relating to a deity, divine ; res divina, the service of the gods, Cic.; so res divinae, but res divinae (also) = natural objects as opp. to res humanae, and natural law as opp. to res humanae, positive law, Cic. Subst., **dīvīnum** -i, n. a sacrifice, Liv.; plur., divina, divine things, Liv.; the attributes of the gods, Cic. **II.** Transf., **A.** divinely inspired, prophetic; vates, a poet, Hor.; subst., **dīvīnus** -i, m. a seer, Cic. **B.** divine, excellent, noble, admirable ; divinus ille vir, Cic.

dīvīsĭo -ōnis, f. (divido), 1, division ; **a,** orbis terrae, Sall.; b, rhet. t.t., division of a subject, Cic.; 2, distribution ; agrorum, Tac.

dīvīsor -ōris, m. (divido), 1, a divider, distributor, esp. of lands in a colony, Cic.; 2, a hired bribery agent, Cic.

1. **dīvīsus** -a -um, partic. of divido.

2. **dīvīsus** -ūs, m. (divido), division ; Macedonia divisui facilis, Liv.

dīvĭtĭae -ārum, f. (dives), riches, wealth. **I.** Lit., superare Crassum divitiis, Cic. **II.** Transf., ingenii, Cic.

divortĭum -ĭi, n. (diverto or divorto). **I.** Of things, a, of places, *the poi t where roads, etc. separate, cross-roads;* divortia nota, Verg.; **b,** *the boundary line between two continents* or *countries;* artissimum inter Europam Asiamque divortium, Tac. **II.** Of persons, a, *a divorce;* divortium facere cum aliqua, Cic.; **b,** *separation* generally, Cic.

divorto, v. diverto.

dīvulgātus -a -um, p. adj. (from divulgo), *spread abroad, made common;* magistratus levissimus et divulgatissimus, Cic.

dīvulgo (divolgo), 1. (dis and vulgo or volgo), 1, *to make public, publish, spread abroad;* librum, Cic.; rem sermonibus, Cic.; 2, *to make common;* cuius primum tempus aetatis palam fuisset ad omnium libidines divulgatum, Cic.

dīvus -a -um (from deus). **I.** Adj., *belonging to the deity, divine;* diva parens, Verg **II.** Subst. **A. dīvus** -i, m. *a god,* Cic.; **diva** -ae, f. *a goddess,* Liv.; in imperial times divus was the epithet of the deified emperors, divi genus, of Octavianus, Verg. **B. dīvum** -i, n. *the sky;* only in the phrase, sub divo, *in the open air,* Cic.

do, dĕdi, dătum, dăre. **I.** *to give, offer.* **A.** aliquid; 1, lit., dare donum, Cic.; populo Romano arma, Cic.; of letters, *to send, despatch;* tres epistolae eodem abs te datae tempore, Cic.; dare poenas, *to suffer punishment,* Cic.; dare lora, *to let the reins loose,* Verg.; vela dare ventis, *to sail,* Verg.; dare alicui cervices, *to offer the neck for punishment,* Cic.; 2, transf., *to give, lend, bestow, offer;* alicui vitam, Cic.; nomen alicui rei, Liv.; dare alicui fasces, *consular power,* Cic.; eum locum colloquio, *to fix,* Liv.; accipio quod datur, *what is offered,* Cic.; corpori omne tempus, Cic.; id misericordiae, *to grant, give up,* Cic.; dare alicui contionem, Cic.; dare urbem excidio ac ruinis, Liv. **B.** aliquem (also corpus, membra, animum); 1, lit., dare arbitrum, Cic.; natam genero, Verg.; 2, transf., aliquam in matrimonium, Caes.; aliquem morti, Hor.; 3, dare se or pass. dari, *to give oneself up;* se dare alicui in conspectum, Cic.; *to throw oneself;* se in viam, Cic.; dare se (alicui) obvium, *to meet,* Liv.; dare se somno, Cic.; se labori et itineribus, Cic. **C.** *to give something from oneself;* 1, lit., clamorem, *to utter,* Verg.; dare (alicui) responsum, Cic.; dare litem secundum aliquem, *to decide in one's favour,* Cic.; impetum in aliquem, Liv.; 2, transf., alicui dolorem, Cic.; documenta dare, Cic.

dŏcĕo, dŏcŭi, doctum, 2. (DOC -eo, causative of DIC-sco—i.e., disco), *to teach, instruct.* **I.** Gen., with acc., aliquem, Cic.; aliquem equo armisque, Liv.; aliquem fidibus, Cic.; with ad, ad quam (legem) non docti, Cic.; with adv., aliquem Latine, Cic.; jus civile, Cic.; with double acc., aliquem litteras, Cic.; de aliqua re, with infin., aliquem sapere, Cic.; absol., quum doceo et explano, Cic. **II.** Esp., a, theatr. t.t., docere fabulam, like διδάσκειν δρᾶμα. (lit., *to teach a play to the actors*), *to bring out, exhibit,* Cic.; **b,** *to bring a matter before a public body or patron;* judices de injuriis, Cic.

dochmĭus -ĭi, m. (δόχμιος, sc. πούς), *a species of foot in poetry, the dochmiac foot* (∪ – – ∪ –), Cic.

dŏcĭlis -e, adj. with compar. (doceo), *teachable, docile, attentive;* attentus judex et docilis, Cic.; docilis ad hanc disciplinam, Cic.; with genit., modorum, Hor.

dŏcĭlĭtas -ātis, f. (docilis), *teachableness, docility,* Cic.

doctē, adv. with compar. and superl. (doctus), *learnedly, skilfully;* luctari, Hor.

doctor -ōris, m. (doceo), *a teacher;* eiusdem sapientiae doctores, Cic.

doctrīna -ae, f. (doceo), 1, *teaching, instruction;* puerilis, Cic.; honestarum rerum, Cic.; 2, *that which is imparted in teaching, knowledge, learning;* Piso Graecis doctrinis eruditus, Cic.; animos nostros doctrinā excolere, Cic.

doctus -a -um, p. adj. with compar. and superl. (from doceo), 1, a, of persons, *learned, instructed, well-informed;* Graecis litteris et Latinis, Cic.; ex disciplina Stoicorum, Cic.; subst., **docti** -orum, *learned men;* with genit., fandi, Verg.; with acc., dulces modos, Hor.; b, of things that show learning, ars, Ov.; sermones, Cic.; 2, *experienced, clever, shrewd;* doctus usu, Caes.; aetate et usu, Liv.

dŏcŭmen -ĭnis, n. = documentum (q.v.).

dŏcŭmentum -i, n. (doceo), *example, pattern, warning, proof;* P. Rutilius documentum fuit hominibus nostris virtutis, Cic.; alicui documento esse, Caes.; documentum sui dare, Liv.

Dōdōna -ae and -ē -ēs, f. (Δωδώνη), *a city of Epirus, renowned for its oak groves and oracle;* hence adj., 1, **Dōdōnaeus** -a -um, *of Dodona;* 2, **Dōdōnis** -ĭdis, f. *of Dodona.*

dodrans -antis, m. (de and quadrans), *three-fourths;* 1, gen., aedificii reliquum dodrantem emere, Cic.; heres ex dodrante, *heir to three-fourths of the property,* Suet.; 2, esp., a, as a superficial measure = *three-fourths of an acre,* Liv.; b, as a measure of length, *nine inches, three-fourths of a foot,* Plin.

dodrantārĭus -a -um (dodrans), *belonging to three-fourths;* tabulae, *the register of debts introduced by the lex Valeria feneratoria, whereby the debts were reduced to one-fourth,* Cic.

dogma -ătis, n. (δόγμα), *a philosophical doctrine, principle, dogma,* Cic.

Dolabella -ae, m. *a Roman family name of the gens Cornelia, the best known member of which is* P. Cornelius Dolabella, *the son-in-law of Cicero.*

dŏlābra -ae, f. (1. dolo), *an axe, hatchet, a military implement,* Liv.

dŏlenter, adv. with compar. (doleo), *painfully, sorrowfully;* hoc dicere, Cic.

dŏlĕo -dŏlŭi, fut. partic. dŏlĭturus, 2. *to suffer pain.* **I.** Of bodily pain, pes, caput dolet, Cic. **II.** Mentally, 1, of persons, *to suffer pain, to grieve, bewail;* de Hortensio, Cic.; meum casum luctumque doluerunt, Cic.; with acc. and infinit., se a suis superari, Cic.; foll. by quod, Caes.; si, Hor.; absol., aeque dolendo, Cic.; 2, of things, a, *to grieve;* injecta monstris terra dolet suis, Hor.; b, *to cause pain;* nihil cuiquam doluit, Cic.

dōlĭŏlum -i, n. (dim. of dolium), *a little cask,* Liv.

dōlĭum -ĭi, n. *a large earthenware jar or wooden cask,* in which new wine was placed; de dolio haurire, *to drink new wine,* Cic.

1. **dŏlo,** 1. **I.** *to hew with an axe;* robur, Cic.; transf., alicuius caput lumbosque saligno fuste, *to cudgel,* Hor. **II.** *to work with an axe;* non est (homo) e saxo sculptus aut e robore dolatus, Cic.; transf., illud opus, *to work roughly,* Cic.

2. **dŏlo** or **dŏlōn** -ōnis, m. (δόλων), 1, *a wooden staff with an iron point,* Verg.; transf., *the sting of a fly,* Phaedr.; 2, *a small foresail,* Liv.

Dŏlops -lŏpis and plur. **Dŏlŏpes** -um, acc. -as, m. (Δόλοπες), *the Dolopes, a people in Thessaly.* Hence, **Dŏlŏpĭa** -ae, f. (Δολοπία), *the country of the Dolopes.*

dŏlor -ōris, m. (doleo). **I.** *bodily pain,*

anguish; pedum, Cic.; laterum, Hor. **II.** *mental
pain, grief, sorrow.* **A.** Lit., **1,** gen., injuriae,
Caes.; dolorem accipere aliquā re or ex aliqua
re, Cic.; tanto dolore affici ut, etc., Cic.; dolorem alicui facere or efficere, or dare, or afferre,
Cic.; hoc est mihi dolori, Cic.; **2,** *rancour,
animosity,* Cic.; quo dolore exarsit, Caes. **B.**
Meton., **a,** *the cause of sorrow,* Ov.; **b,** in rhet.,
pathos, Cic.

dŏlōsē, adv. (dolosus), *deceitfully, craftily;*
agi dolose, Cic.

dŏlōsus -a -um (dolus), *crafty, deceitful,
cunning;* consilia, Cic.

dŏlus -i, m. (δόλος). **I.** Legal t. t., dolus
malus, *fraud;* quum ex eo quaereretur quid
esset Dolus malus, respondebat quum esset
aliud simulatum, aliud actum, Cic. **II. A.**
fraud, deceit, guile; fraus ac dolus, Cic.; ut
magis virtute quam dolo contenderent, Caes.
B. Meton., *trick;* dolos (= retia) saltu deludit,
Ov.

dŏmābĭlis -e (domo), *that can be tamed, tame-
able;* Cantaber, Hor.

dŏmestĭcus -a -um (domus). **I.** *belonging
to the house* or *the family, domestic;* luctus, Cic.;
difficultas, *poverty,* Cic.; tempus, *spent at home,*
Cic.; domesticus homo, Cic., and subst. domesticus, Ov., *a friend of the house, member of a
family;* plur., **dŏmestĭci** -ōrum, m. *the inmates of one's house, members of one's family,* Cic.
II. Transf., *private, domestic, native* (opp. to
foreign or *public*); crudelitas, *towards citizens,*
Cic.; si superavissent vel domesticis opibus vel
externis auxiliis, Caes.; bellum, *civil war,* Cic.

dŏmĭcĭlĭum -ii, n. (domus), *a place of residence, dwelling.* **A.** Lit., aliud domicilium,
alias sedes parant, Caes.; domicilium collocare
in aliquo loco, Cic. **B.** Transf., imperii, *Rome,*
Cic.; superbiae, Cic.

dŏmĭna -ae, f. (dominus). **I.** *the mistress of
a household, lady,* Verg. **II.** *mistress, queen,
lady.* **A.** Lit., **a,** as a term of respect to goddesses, of Venus, Ov.; of Cybele, Verg.; **b,** like
English mistress, *a sweetheart,* Tib. **B.** Transf.,
ruler, controller; justitia domina virtutum, Cic.;
Fors domina campi, Cic.

dŏmĭnātĭo -ōnis, f. (dominor), *irresponsible
power, despotism, arbitrary government.* **I.** Lit.,
A. unius, Cic.; Cinnae, Cic. **B.** Meton. = do-
minantes, *absolute rulers,* Tac. **II.** Transf.,
governing; temperantia est rationis in libidinem
firma et moderata dominatio, Cic.

dŏmĭnātŏr -ōris, m. (dominor), *ruler,
governor;* rerum Deus, Cic.

dŏmĭnātrix -īcis, f. (fem. of dominator), *a
despotic mistress;* transf., caeca ac temeraria
animi cupiditas, Cic.

dŏmĭnātus -ūs, m. (dominor), **1,** *absolute
power;* dominatus regius, Cic.; **2,** *rule;* dominatus cupiditatum, Cic.

dŏmĭnĭum -ii, n. (dominus), **1,** *rule, power,*
Sen.; **2,** *a feast, banquet;* huius argento dominia
vestra ornari, Cic.

dŏmĭnor, **1.** dep. (dominus), *to rule, be lord*
or *master, to domineer;* in adversarios, Liv.;
summā arce, Verg.; dominari Alexandriae, Cic.;
in suos, Cic.; in nobis, Cic.; in capite fortunisque hominum honestissimorum, Cic.; in
judiciis, Cic.; transf., dominatur libido, Cic.;
quod unum in oratore dominatur, *wherein the
strength of the orator consists,* Cic.

dŏmĭnus -i, m. (domus). **I.** *the master of a
house, the head of the household, lord, master;*
plur., domini, *master and mistress,* Cic. **II.**
A. Lit., **1,** *master, owner, possessor;* aedificii,
navis, Cic.; **2,** *lord, ruler;* in aliquem, Cic.;

gentium, Cic.; rei (of the judge), Cic.; esp., **a,**
a lover, Ov.; **b,** attrib., *belonging to a master;*
poet., manus dominae, Ov.; **3,** *the arranger, a
person that orders something;* of gladiatorial
games, Cic.; of an auction, Cic.; with or without convivii or epuli, *the person who arranges a
feast, host,* Cic. **B.** Transf., *ruler;* vitae necisque, *over life and death,* Liv.; comitiorum dominum esse, Cic.

dŏmĭporta -ae, f. (domus and porto), *she
who carries her house upon her back, the snail,*
ap. Cic.

Dŏmĭtĭānus -i, m. *T. Flavius Domitianus
Augustus, son of Vespasian, brother of Titus,* born
51 A D., Emperor of Rome from 81 A.D. to 96 A.D.

Dŏmĭtĭus -a -um, *name of a plebeian gens at
Rome, the most famous members of which were:—*
Cn. Domitius Calvinus, *consul* 53 A.C.; Cn. Domitius Ahenobarbus, *consul* 122 A.C., *conqueror
of the Allobroges;* Cn. Domitius Ahenobarbus,
tribune 104 A.C., *proposer of the lex Domitia de
sacerdotiis (by which the priesthoods were filled up
by the votes of 17 tribes chosen by lot);* L. Domitius
Ahenobarbus, *consul* 54 A.C., *general and adherent of Pompeius;* Cn. Domitius Ahenobarbus,
father of the Emperor Nero; Cn. Domitius Cor-
bulo, *successful general in Germany and Armenia
under the Emperors Claudius and Nero.* Adj.=
Domitian; via, *road in Gaul made by Domitius
Ahenobarbus, the conqueror of the Allobroges,* Cic.
Hence, **Dŏmĭtĭānus** -a -um, *of Domitius;*
milites, *the soldiers of L. Domitius Ahenobarbus,*
Caes.

dŏmĭto, **1.** (intens. of domo), *to tame, subdue;*
boves, Verg.

dŏmĭtŏr -ōris, m. (domo), *a tamer.* **I.** Lit.,
a, of animals, equorum, *a horse-breaker,* Cic.;
b, of men, *conqueror, victor;* domitor Persarum,
Cic. **II.** Transf., Saturnius domitor maris alti,
Verg.

dŏmĭtrix -īcis, f. (fem. of domitor), *she who
tames;* Epidaurus domitrix equorum, Verg.;
clava domitrix ferarum, Ov.

dŏmĭtus, abl. -ū, m. (domo), *taming;* effi-
cimus domitu nostro quadrupedum vectiones, Cic.

dŏmo, dŏmŭi, dŏmĭtum, **1.** *to tame, break in.*
I. Lit., **a,** animals, beluas, Cic.; equos stimulo
et verbere, Ov.; **b,** men, peoples, countries,
&c. *to conquer, subdue;* hasta pugnantem, Ov.;
maximas nationes virtute, Cic. **II.** Transf., **a,**
concrete objects, ipsius fluminis vim, Liv.;
arbores multā mercede, Verg.; uvas prelo, *to
press,* Hor.; **b,** abstract objects, domitas habere
libidines, Cic.; invidiam, Hor.

dŏmŭs -ūs, f. (cf. Gk. root ΔEM, δέμ-ω, whence
δόμος). **I. A.** Lit., *a house* (as a dwelling-place,
as a home, seat of family, etc., while aedes =
house as a building), as opp. to insula (which
was let out in flats or lodgings; domus = *a
house with its outbuildings and garden;* domum
aedificare, Cic.; aliquem tecto et domo invitare,
Cic.; used adverbially, domi, *at home, in the
house,* Cic.; meae domi (tuae, suae, nostrae, etc.), *at
my house,* Cic.; alienae domi, *in the house of another,*
Cic.; domi aliquid habere, *to have at home, to
possess, be provided with,* Cic.; domum, *home,
towards home, homeward,* Cic.; domo, *from home,
out of the house,* Cic. **B.** Transf., poet. *a dwelling-place,* of birds, Verg.; of the gods, Verg.; of
the spirits of the dead, Verg.; of the labyrinth,
Verg. **II.** Meton., **A. 1,** *inmates of a house,
household,* Cic.; **2,** *a philosophical school or sect,*
Cic.; Socratica domus, Hor. **B.** *a household,
management of a house,* Cic. **C.** *home, native
country;* domi, *at home, in one's own country,*
Cic.; domi militiaeque, Cic., belli domique, Liv.,
in peace and in war (archaic genit. or locat.

domi, in classical writers only = *at home ;* dat. domui, abl. generally domo, also domu ; plur. nom. domus, acc. domus and domos, genit. domuum and domorum, dat. and abl. domibus).

dōnārĭum -ĭi, n. (donum), 1, *temple, shrine, altar,* Verg., Ov. ; **2,** *a votive offering,* Liv.

dōnātĭo -ōnis, f. (dono), *a giving, gift, present, donation,* Cic.

dōnātīvum -i, n. (dono), *an imperial largess, or donative to the soldiery,* Tac.

dōnĕc, conj. (shortened from doneque, donique), 1, *as long as, while,* Liv. ; donec gratus eram tibi, Hor. ; 2, *until,* Cic. ; with usque eo, Cic. ; or eo usque, Liv.

dōno, 1. (donum). **I.** (alicui aliquid), *to give as a present, to present.* **A.** Gen., 1, lit., non pauca suis adjutoribus, Cic. ; 2, transf., a, *to grant, bestow ;* alicui aeternam immortalitatem, Cic.; poet., with infin., alicui divinare, Hor.; b, *to sacrifice, give up to ;* inimicitias reipublicae, Caes. **B.** Esp., 1, lit. *to remit a debt or obligation ;* alicui aes alienum, Cic. ; 2, transf. *to forgive, pardon* (for the sake of someone else), noxae damnatus donatur populo Romano, Liv. **II.** (aliquem aliquā re), *to present a person with something ;* cohortem militaribus donis, Caes.

dōnum -i, n. (dare), *a gift, present ;* 1, gen., dona nuptialia, Cic. ; dono dare, *to give as a present,* Ter. ; 2, esp., *a gift to the gods, a votive offering,* Cic.

Dōnūsa -ae, f. (Δονουσία), *an island in the Aegean Sea, east of Naxos.*

dorcas -ădis, f. (δορκάς), *a gazelle, antelope,* Mart.

Dōres -um, m. (Δωριεῖς), *the Dorians, one of the Hellenic races ;* hence, 1, adj., **Dōrĭcus** a -um, poet.= *Greek,* Verg. ; 2, **Dōrĭus** -a -um, *Dorian ;* 3, **Dōris** -ĭdis, f. *Dorian ;* subst., a, *Doris, a country in the north of Greece ;* b, *the wife of Nereus, and mother of the fifty Nereids ;* meton. *the sea,* Verg.

1. **Dōris,** v. Dores.

2. **Dōris** -ĭdis, f. (Δωρίς), *wife of Dionysius I. of Syracuse.*

dormĭo -īvi or -ĭi, -ītum, 4. 1, *to sleep ;* se dormitum conferre, Cic. ; ad dormiendum proficisci, Cic.; dormientem excitare, Cic. ; innumerabilia saecula dormisse, Cic.; 2, *to rest, be inactive ;* beneficia dormientibus deferuntur, Cic.

dormīto, 1. (dormio), *to be sleepy, to begin to sleep.* **A.** Lit., dormitanti mihi epistola illa reddita, Cic. ; jam dormitante lucernā, *just going out,* Ov. **B.** *to dream, be lazy, inactive ;* ista oscitans et dormitans sapientia Scaevolarum, Cic. ; quandoque bonus dormitat Homerus, *nods,* Hor.

dormītor -ōris, m. (dormio), *a sleeper,* Mart.

dorsum -i, n. (**dorsus** -i, m.). **A.** Lit., *the back,* either of men or animals ; dorso onus subire, Hor. ; dorsum demulcere equis, Liv. **B.** Transf. *any elevation of similar form ;* duplex (dentalium), *the projecting irons of a ploughshare,* Verg. ; immane dorsum, *a rock in the sea,* Verg. ; of mountains, *slope ;* jugi, Caes.

Dŏrÿlaeum -i, n. (Δορύλαιον), *a town in Phrygia.* Hence, **Dŏrÿlenses** -ĭum, m. *the inhabitants of Dorylaeum.*

dŏrÿphŏrŏs -i, m. (δορυφόρος), *the lance-bearer,* the name of a celebrated statue by Polycletus, Cic.

dōs, dōtis, f. (δώς). **A.** Lit. *a dowry, portion ;* accipere pecuniam ab uxore dotis nomine, Caes. ; filiae nubili dotem conficere non posse, Cic. **B.** Transf., a, *a gift ;* cuius artem quum indotatam esse et incomptam videres, verborum eam dote

locupletasti et ornasti, Cic. ; **b,** *a quality, endowment ;* dotes ingenii, Ov.

dōtālis -e (dos), *relating or belonging to a dowry ;* praedium, Cic.

dōtātus -a -um, p. adj. (from doto), *richly dowered.* **A.** Lit., Aquilia, Cic. **B.** Transf., *richly endowed ;* Chione dotatissima formā, Ov.

dōto, 1. (dos), *to provide with a dowry, endow ;* sanguine Trojano et Rutulo dotabere, virgo, Verg.

drachma -ae, f. (δραχμή), 1, *a small Greek coin, a drachm, about equal in value to a Roman denarius,* Cic. ; 2, as a weight, ⅛ *of an uncia,* Plin.

1. **drăco** -ōnis, m. (δράκων), **A.** *a kind of snake, dragon,* Cic. **B.** Meton., *a constellation so called,* Cic.

2. **Drăco** -ōnis, m. (Δράκων), *Draco, an Athenian legislator.*

drăcōnĭgĕna -ae, c. (draco and gigno) = δρακοντογενής, *dragon-born, sprung from dragon-seed ;* urbs, *Thebes,* Ov.

Drĕpănum -i, n. (Δρέπανον), and **Drĕpăna** -ōrum, n. (Δρέπανα), *a town on the west coast of Sicily* (now *Trapani*). Adj. **Drĕpănĭtānus** -a -um, *of or belonging to Drepanum.*

drŏmas -ădis, m. (δρομάς), *a dromedary,* Liv.

drŏmos -i, m. (δρόμος), *the race-course of the Spartans,* Liv.

Drŭentĭa -ae, f. *a river in Gallia flowing into the Rhone,* now *the Durance.*

Drŭĭdes -um, m., and **Drŭĭdae** -ārum, m. (*deruydd* or *dryod,* old British = *wise man*), *the Druids, the priests of the Celtic nations,* Ov.

Drūsus -i, m. *a cognomen of the Gens Livia and Claudia.* (1) M. Livius Drusus, *murdered for attempting to revive some of the Gracchan laws ;* (2) Nero, *son of the Empress Livia, by her first husband, Tiberius Claudius Nero.* Hence a, adj., **Drūsĭānus** -a -um and **Drūsĭnus** -a -um, *of or belonging to Drusus ;* b, subst. **Drūsilla** -ae, f. *name of several females of the gens Livia.*

1. **Drÿăs** -ădis, f. (Δρυάς), *a wood nymph, Dryad ;* gen. plur. Dryades, Verg.

2. **Drÿas** -antis, m. (Δρυας), *father of Lycurgus, king of Thrace.* Hence **Drÿantĭdes** -ae, m. *the son of Dryas,* i.e. *Lycurgus,* Ov.

Drÿŏpes -um (Δρύοπες), *a Pelasgic people, who were driven southwards by the Dorians, and settled in Messenia.*

dŭbĭē, adv. (dubius), 1. **A.** *doubtfully, hesitatingly ;* inter confessum dubie dubieque negantem, Ov. **B.** *doubtfully, uncertainly ;* ut aliquod signum dubie datum pro certo sit acceptum, Cic.; hence, haud dubie, nec dubie, non dubie, *certainly, without doubt,* Cic.

Dūbis -is, m. *river in Gallia Belgica,* now *the Doubs.*

dŭbĭtābĭlis -e (dubito), *doubtful, uncertain,* Ov.

dŭbĭtantĕr, adv. (dubito), 1, *doubtingly ;* dubitanter unum quodque dicemus, Cic. ; 2, *hesitatingly ;* illud verecundi et dubitantes recepisse, Cic.

dŭbĭtātĭo -ōnis, f. (dubito) **I.** *doubt, uncertainty ;* sine ulla dubitatione, *certainly,* Cic. ; res non habet dubitationem, *the matter admits of no doubt,* Cic. ; with obj. genit., dubitatio adventus legionum, *doubt as to the coming,* Cic.; with de, illa Socratica dubitatio de omnibus rebus, Cic.; with rel. sent., si quando dubitatio accidit, quale sit id, etc., Cic. ; followed by quin when a negative precedes, hic locus nihil habet dubitationis quin, etc. *admits of no doubt that,* Cic.; nulla dubitatio est quin, etc., Cic. ; nisi dubitationem affert quin, etc., Cic. **II.** *hesitation, wavering, irresolution;* dubitatio belli, *as to the conduct of the war,* Cic.; angunt me dubitationes tuae, Cic.

dŭbĭto, 1. (dubius). **I.** *to doubt, waver in opinion, be uncertain;* de hoc, Cic.; haec, Cic.; utrum sit utilius an, etc., Cic.; honestumne factu sit an turpe, Cic.; non dubito quid, etc.; non dubito quin, etc., *I have no doubt that,* Cic. **II.** *to waver in resolution, hesitate;* a, of persons, quid dubitas, Caes.; dubito, foll. by infin., Cic.; non dubito, foll. by infin., Cic.; non dubito, foll. by quin, Cic.; **b,** of things, dubitavit aciei pars, Sall.

dŭbĭus -a -um (duo). **I.** Subject., *doubting.* **A.** *wavering in opinion, doubting, doubtful, uncertain,* Cic.; with genit., sententiae, Cic.; haud dubius, foll. by acc. and infin., *confident that,* Liv. **B.** *wavering in resolve, hesitating, uncertain, irresolute;* dubius an transiret, Liv. **II.** Object., *doubted, doubtful.* **A.** *undecided, uncertain, doubtful;* genus causae, Cic.; victoria, Caes.; caelum, *cloudy,* Ov.; non est dubium quin, *there is no doubt that,* Cic.; dubiumne est or cui dubium est quin? Cic.; num or nemini dubium est, with acc. and infin., Cic.; neut. subst., generally with a prepos., in dubium vocare or revocare, *to make doubtful,* Cic.; sine dubio, Cic.; procul dubio, *without doubt,* Liv. **B.** Meton. *doubtful, dubious, dangerous, critical;* res dubia, Sall.; tempora, Hor.

dŭcēni -ae, -a (distrib. of ducenti), *two hundred each,* Liv.

dŭcentēsĭma -ae, f. (fem. of ducentesimus, from ducenti, sc. pars), *the two hundredth part, as a tax, one-half per cent.,* Tac.

dŭcenti -ae, -a (duo and centum), 1, *two hundred,* Cic.; 2, *generally any large number,* Hor.

dŭcentĭēs, adv. (ducenti), *two hundred times,* Cic.

dūco, duxi, ductum, 3. **I.** *to draw.* **A.** Gen., frena manu, Ov. **B.** Esp., 1, *to drag behind;* sidera crinem ducunt, Verg.; 2, *to draw towards oneself;* a, lit., ducere remos, *to row,* Ov.; colorem, *to get a darker colour,* Verg.; b, transf., (α) *to charm, attract;* fabellarum auditione ducuntur, Cic.; (β) *to draw away, mislead;* errore duci, Cic.; (γ) *to draw to, influence;* me ad credendum tua ducit oratio, Cic.; 3, *to draw in;* aëra spiritu, Cic.; poet., somnos, *to sleep,* Verg.; *to quaff;* pocula Lesbii, Hor.; 4, *to draw out;* ferrum vaginā, Ov.; sortes, Cic.; aliquid or aliquem sorte, Cic.; 5, *to draw out, extend, make, build, fashion;* parietem, Cic.; murum, Liv.; vallum, Caes.; ocreas argento, Verg.; 6, *to draw out a thread;* lanas, *to spin,* Ov.; transf., of a poet, carmina, *to make verses,* Hor.; 7, *to prolong;* a, *to pass;* aetatem in litteris, Cic.; b, *to delay, protract;* bellum, Cic.; aliquem diem ex die, *to put off,* Caes.; 8, *to distort;* os, Cic.; 9, *to draw down;* transf., a, *to derive;* nomen ex aliqua re, Cic.; etymolog., ab eundo nomen (Jani) est ductum, Cic.; b, *to begin;* ab eodem verbo ducitur saepius oratio, Cic.; 10, *to count, reckon;* fenus quaternis centesimis, Cic; aliquem in hostium numero, Caes.; aliquid parvi, *to esteem little,* Cic.; pluris, Cic.; pro nihilo, Cic.; aliquem despicatui, *to despise,* Cic.; with accus. and infin., *to consider;* qui se regem esse ducebat, Cic. **II.** *to lead.* **A.** Gen., 1, of persons, ducere equum, Liv.; 2, of things, duxit via in leniter editum collem, Liv. **B.** Esp., 1, polit. and legal t.t., *to lead before a court of justice,* or *to lead away for punishment;* aliquem in jus, Liv.; in carcerem, in vincula, Cic.; 2, a, milit. t.t., *to march;* cohortes ad munitiones, Caes.; absol., ad hostem, Liv.; b, *to command;* exercitus, Caes.: transf., familiam. *to be the most*

celebrated of, Cic.; 3, uxorem ducere, *to marry,* ducere uxorem alicuius filiam, Cic.; absol., ducere ex plebe, *to marry from among the plebs,* Liv.; 4, *to lead by the nose, cheat,* Ov.; 5, of water, *to conduct;* aquam in urbem, Liv.; 6, *to take with one;* suas mulierculas secum, Cic.; 7, *to order, arrange;* alicui funus, Cic.

ducto, 1. (intens. of duco), *to lead;* exercitum, Sall.

ductor -ōris, m. (duco), *a leader, commander,* Cic.; ordinum ductor, *a centurion,* Liv.

ductus -ūs, m. (duco) **I.** *drawing;* a, oris, *the lineaments of the face,* Cic.; b, muri, *building,* Cic. **II.** *leading;* 1, milit. t.t., *command, leadership;* alicuius ductu, Cic.; se ad ductum Pompeii applicare, Cic.; 2, *conducting of water;* aquarum, Cic.

dūdum, adv. (from diu = die and dum), 1, *a little while ago, not long since;* quod tibi dudum (*just now*) videbatur, Cic.; 2, a, quam dudum, *as long as;* quam dudum nihil habeo quod ad te scribam, Cic.; b, jam dudum, *now for a long time;* quem jam dudum Cotta et Sulpicius expectat, Cic.

dŭellum, dŭellĭcus, dŭellātor = bellum, bellicus, bellator, q.v.

Dŭīlĭus -a -um, *name of a Roman gens, of which the most celebrated was* C. Duilius, cons. 261 A.C., *who gained a great naval victory over the Carthaginians, near the Liparean Islands.* The victory was commemorated by the erection in the forum of a column, adorned with the prows of ships (columna rostrata).

dulcĕ, adv. (dulcis), *sweetly;* canere, Hor.

dulcēdo -ĭnis, f. (dulcis). **I.** Lit., *a sweet taste;* sanguinis, Ov. **II.** Transf., a, *sweetness, pleasantness, charm;* dulcedine quadam gloriae commoti, Cic.; dulcedine orationis, Cic.; b, *desire;* dulcedo invasit plebeios creandi, Liv.

dulcesco, 3. (dulcis), *to become sweet,* Cic.

dulcĭcŭlus -a -um (dim. of dulcis), *somewhat sweet;* potio, Cic.

dulcis -e, adj. with compar. and superl. (connected with γλυκύς). **I.** Lit. *sweet* (opp. amarus), vinum, Hor.; unda, *fresh water,* Ov. Subst., **dulce** -is, n. *what is sweet,* Ov.; **dulcia** -ium, n. *sweet things,* Cic. **II.** Transf. **A.** *sweet, pleasant, delightful, agreeable;* nomen libertatis, Cic.; poemata, Hor.; orator, Cic. **B.** *friendly, dear, beloved;* amici, Cic.; used in addresses, dulcissime Attice, Cic.

dulcĭter, adv.(dulcis), with compar. dulcius, superl. dulcissime, *sweetly,* Cic.

dulcĭtūdo -ĭnis, f. (dulcis), *sweetness,* Cic.

Dŭlĭchĭum -ĭi, n. (Δουλίχιον), *an island in the Ionian Sea, forming part of the kingdom of Ulysses.* Adj. **Dŭlĭchĭus** -a -um, *Dulichian,* poet., *belonging to Ulysses;* rates, Verg.; dux, Ulysses, Ov.

dum (like quum and tum, the acc. of a lost pronoun). **I.** Adv., joined as an enclitic with other words, a, with non, nullus, haud vix, etc., nondum, *not yet,* Cic.; so necdum, Liv.; nequedum, Cic.; nullusdum, *no one yet,* Liv.; vixdum, *scarcely yet,* Cic.; nihildum, *nothing yet,* Cic.; nedum (sc. dicam), *not to say,* Cic.; b, with imperat. *then;* age dum, Cic.; itera dum, Cic. **II.** Conj., 1, *while;* generally with indicat., Cic.; 2, *as long as;* with indicat., Cic.; 3, *until, till;* with subj., Cic.; 4, *in so far as, if only, provided that;* with the subj., Cic.; strengthened by modo, dummodo, Cic.; dumne, *provided that not,* Cic.; dummodo ne, Cic.

dūmētum -i. n. (dumus), *a thorn bush, thicket,* Cic.; fig., cur eam tantas in angustias et Stoicorum dumeta compellimus. Cic.

dummŏdo, v. dūm.

Dumnŏrix -īgis, m. *brother of the Aeduan Divitiacus.*

dūmōsus -a -um (dumus), *covered with thorn bushes, bushy,* Verg.

dumtaxăt = duntaxat, q.v.

dūmus -i, m. *a thorn bush, bramble,* Cic.

duntaxăt (dumtaxat), adv. (dum and taxo), *exactly, according to the right measure, not more and not less.* **I.** nos animo duntaxat vigemus, *as far as the mind is concerned,* Cic. **II.** a, *only, merely,* Cic.; non duntaxat . . . sed, *not only . . . but,* Liv.; b, *at least,* Cic. **III.** *in so far;* exceptis duntaxat iis gentibus, quae regnantur, Tac.

dŭŏ -ae, -ŏ (δύο), *two,* Cic.

dŭŏ-dĕcĭēs, adv., *twelve times,* Cic.

dŭŏ-dĕcĭm (duo and decem), *twelve;* tabulae, *the twelve tables,* Cic. sometimes simply duodecim, *the Twelve.*

dŭŏ-dĕcĭmus -a -um (duodecim), *the twelfth,* Caes.

dŭŏ-dēni -ae, -a, **1,** *twelve each,* Cic.; **2,** *twelve,* Verg.

dŭŏ-dē-quădrāgēsĭmus, *thirty-eighth,* Liv.

dŭŏ-dē-quădrāginta, *thirty-eight,* Cic.

dŭŏ-dē-quinquāgēsĭmus -a -um, *the forty-eighth,* Cic.

dŭŏ-dē-trīcĭens (-trĭcĭes) adv., *twenty-eight times,* Cic.

dŭŏ-dē-trīginta, *twenty-eight,* Liv.

dŭŏ-dē-vīcēni -ae, -a, *eighteen each,* Liv.

dŭŏ-dē-vīginti, *eighteen,* Cic.

dŭŏ-et-vīcēsĭmāni -ōrum, m. *soldiers of the 22nd legion,* Tac.

dŭŏ-et-vīcēsĭmus -a -um, *the twenty-second,* Tac.

dŭplex -plĭcis (duo and plico), **1,** *double, two-fold;* amiculum, Nep., amictus, Verg., pannus, Hor., *a garment folded twice round the body;* palmae, *both hands,* Verg.; **2,** a, *doubled, twice as much;* frumentum, stipendium, Caes.; b, *double-faced, false, deceitful,* Hor.

dŭplĭcārĭus -a -um (duplex), miles, *a soldier who gets double rations,* Liv.

dŭplĭcĭtĕr, adv. (duplex), *doubly,* Cic.

dŭplĭco, 1. (duplex). **I.** Lit., *to fold in two, double up;* duplicatque virum (hasta), transfixā dolore, Verg. **II.** Transf., 1, a, *to double;* numerum dierum, Cic.; b, duplicare verba, *to repeat,* Cic.; 2, a, *to lengthen,* crescentes umbras (of the sun), Verg.; b, *to increase;* duplicari sollicitudines, Cic.

dŭplus -a -um (duo), *twice as much, double;* 1, adj., pars, Cic.; pecunia, Liv.; 2, subst., **dŭplum** -i, n. *the double,* esp. *a double penalty;* poenam dupli subire or in duplum ire, Cic.; judicium dare in duplum, Cic.

dŭpondĭus -ĭi, m. (= duo asses pondo), *a coin of two asses,* Cic.

dūrābĭlis -e (duro), *lasting, durable,* Ov.

dūrāmen -ĭnis, n. (duro) *hardness;* aquarum, *ice,* Lucr.

dūrătĕus -a -um (δουράτεος), *wooden,* applied only to the Trojan horse, Lucr.

dūrē, and **dūrĭtĕr,** adv. with compar. dūrĭus, superl. dūrissimē (durus), *hardly.* **I.** Lit., a, *with respect to hearing, unpleasantly;* pleraque dure dicere, Hor.; b, *of works of art, rudely, roughly;* quid sculptum infabre, quid fusum durius esset, Hor. **II.** Transf., a, in demeanour. *awkwardly;* durius incedit, Ov.; b,

in conduct, harshly, severely; durius in deditos consulere, Liv.; durius aliquid accipere, Cic.

dūresco dūrŭi, 3. (durus), *to grow hard;* frigoribus durescit humor, *freezes,* Cic.

dūrĭtas -ātis, f. (durus), *harshness, unfriendliness,* Cic.

dūrĭter = dure (q.v.).

dūrĭtĭa, -ae, f. and **dūrĭtĭēs** -ēi, f. (durus) *hardness.* **I.** Lit., of nature, atrae pellis, Ov. **II.** Transf., a, *hardness, austerity;* duritia virilis, Cic.; ab parvulis labori ac duritiae studere, Caes.; b, *harshness, severity;* animi, Cic.; c, *severity, oppressiveness;* operum, Tac.; caeli militiaeque, Tac.

dūro, 1. (durus). **I.** Transit. **A.** Lit., *to make hard;* 1, gen., caementa calce, Liv.; enses in scopulos, Ov.; 2, esp., *to dry up, make dry;* terram (by heat), Verg.; Albanam fumo uvam, Hor. **B.** Transf., 1, *to make hardy, inure;* se labore, Caes.; in a bad sense, *to render callous;* ad omne facinus duratus, Tac.; 2, *to endure;* laborem, Verg.; imperiosius aequor, Hor. **II.** Intransit. **A.** Lit. *to become hard* or *dry;* durare solum, Verg. **B.** Transf., 1, *to become hard* or *callous;* in nullius unquam suorum necem durravit, Tac.; 2, *to endure;* unam hiemem in castris, Liv.; sub Jove, Ov.; 3, *to last, remain, continue;* durat simulacrum, Verg.; totidem durare per annos, Verg.

dūrus -a -um, adj. with compar. and superl. *hard.* **I.** Lit., a, *hard to the touch;* ferrum, Hor.; b, *harsh to the taste;* sapor Bacchi, Verg.; c, *harsh to the ear;* vocis genus, Cic.; oratio, Cic.; d, *rough to the eye, hard;* signa dura sed tamen molliora quam Canachi, Cic.; e, of feeling, *hard, rough;* poeta durissimus, Cic. **II.** Transf., 1, *strong, enduring;* Scipiadae duri bello, Verg.; 2, *in demeanour;* a, *awkward, uncouth;* ut vitā sic oratione durus, incultus, horridus, Cic.; b, *shameless;* os, Ov.; 3, a, *hardy, austere;* homo durus ac priscus, Cic.; b, *without taste for;* C. Marius, qui durior ad haec studia videbatur, Cic.; 4, *feelingless, stern, severe;* Varius est habitus judex durior, Cic.; 5, a, *of weather, severe;* tempestates, Caes.; b, of the soil, *hard, difficult to work;* glebae, Verg.; c, of work, *hard, difficult;* subvectio, Caes.; d, *hard, painful, unfavourable, adverse;* conditio durior, Verg.; pauperies, Hor.

dŭumvir and **dŭŏvir** -vĭri, m. gen. plur., duumviri or duoviri, *a pair of magistrates.* **I.** In Rome. **A.** duumviri perduellionis, *the magistrates who tried cases of* perduellio, Liv. **B.** duumviri sacrorum or sacris facundis, *keepers of the Sibylline books* (afterwards increased to ten, and then to fifteen), Liv. **C.** duumviri aedi faciendae or locandae or dedicandae, *a commission for building* or *dedicating a temple,* Liv. **D.** duumviri navales, *a commission for looking after the fleet,* Liv. **II.** In the Roman municipia and coloniae, duumviri (juri dicundo), *the highest magistrates,* Cic.

dux, dŭcis, c. **I.** *a leader, guide, conductor;* locorum, Liv.; armenti, Ov.; transf., impietatis, Cic.; diis ducibus, *under the direction of the gods,* Cic. **II.** *a ruler.* **A.** Gen., superum, *Jupiter,* Verg. **B.** Esp., 1, *a military* or *naval commander;* dux praefectusque classis, Cic.; 2, *the emperor,* Ov.

Dȳmās -mantis, m. (Δύμας), *father of Hecuba.* Hence Dymantis probes, or subst. **Dȳmantis** -tĭdis, f. *Hecuba,* Ov.

Dȳmē -ēs, f. (Δύμη), and **Dȳmae** -ārum, f. *a town in Achaia.* Adj. **Dȳmaeus** -a -um, *of* or *belonging to Dyme.*

dȳnastes -is, m. (δυνάστης), *ruler, prince,* Cic.

Dyr 185 edi

Dyrrăchĭum-ĭi, n. (Δυρράχιον), *later name of Epidamnus, in Illyria, the port where ships landed coming from Brundisium to Greece, now Durazzo.* Hence **Dyrrachini** (- ēni) -ōrum, m. *the people of Dyrrachium.*

E

E̊ **e,** the fifth letter of the Latin alphabet, corresponding in the Greek alphabet both to ε and η. For the meaning of E as an abbreviation, see Table of Abbreviations. .

ē, prep. = ex (q.v.).

ĕā, adv. (abl of is, sc. parte), *there,* **Liv.**

ĕădem, adv. (abl. of idem, sc. viā), *by the same road,* Cic.

ĕā-propter = propterea.

ĕātĕnus = ea tenus (parte), adv., *so far ;* foll. by qua, quoad, Cic. ; by ut and the subj., Cic.

ĕbĕnus -i, m. (ἔβενος), *the ebony tree, ebony,* Verg.

ēbĭbo -bĭbi -bĭtum, 3. **I.** Gen., *to drink up;* amnes (of the sea), Ov. **II.** 1, Nestoris annos, *to drink as many cups as the years of Nestor's age,* Ov. ; 2, *to squander;* ut haec ebibat, Hor.

ēblandĭor, 4., dep., *to obtain by flattery;* omnia, Liv. ; enitere, elabora, vel potius eblandire, efficit ut, etc., Cic. ; partic. passive, eblandita illa non enucleata esse suffragia, Cic.

ēbrĭĕtas -ātis, f. (ebrius), *drunkenness, revelling,* Cic.

ēbrĭōsĭtas -ātis, f. (ebriosus), *the love of drink, habit of drunkenness,* Cic.

ēbrĭōsus -a -um, (ebrius), *drink-loving,* Cic.

ēbrĭus -a·-um, 1, *drunk, intoxicated,* Cic. ; 2, transf., *intoxicated with, full of;* dulci fortunā, Hor.

ēbullĭo, 4. **I.** Intransit., *to boil up,* Sen. **II.** Transit., *to cause to boil up;* transf., *to boast of;* virtutes, Cic.

ēbŭlum -i, n. (-us, i., f.), *the dwarf elder-tree* (sambucus ebulus, Linn.), Verg.

ēbur -ŏris, n. **A.** Lit., *ivory;* signum ex ebore, Cic. **B.** Meton., a, of things made of ivory, *a statue,* Verg. ; *a flute,* Verg. ; *the sheath of a sword,* Ov. ; *the curule chair,* Hor. ; b, *the elephant,* Juv.

ĕburnĕŏlus -a -um (dim. of eburneus), *made of ivory;* fistula, Cic.

ĕburnĕus (ĕburnus) -a -um (ebur). **A.** *made of ivory, ivory;* signum, Cic. ; dens (of the elephant), Liv. **B.** Meton., *white as ivory;* brachia, cervix, Ov.

Ebŭrōnes -um, m. *a German people in Gallia Belgica.*

Ebŭsus and **-ŏs** -i, f., *an island in the Mediterranean, off the Spanish coast, now Iviza or Yviça.*

ĕcastor, v. Castor.

eccĕ, adv. (for ence, from en and ce), *behold! lo! see!* ecce tuae litterae, Cic. ; ecce tibi exortus est Isocrates, Cic. ; ubi . . . ecce, Verg. ; dum . . . ecce, Hor. ; ecce autem, Cic.

ecdĭcus -i, m. (ἔκδικος), *among the Greeks, a public attorney or prosecutor,* Cic.

Ecĕtra -ae, f. *capital of the Volsci.* Hence **Ecetranus** -i, m. *an inhabitant of Ecetra.*

ecf . . ., v. eff . . .

Echecrătes -ae, m. (Ἐχεκράτης), *a Pythagorean philosopher, contemporary with Plato.*

ĕchĕnēis -ĭdis, f. (ἐχενηΐς), *a sucking fish, remora* (echeneis remora, Linn.), Ov.

ĕchidna -ae, f. (ἔχιδνα). **I.** *the viper, adder, as an attribute of the Furies,* Ov. **II.** Proper noun, **A.** Echidna Lernaea, *the Lernaean hydra killed by Hercules,* Ov. **B.** *a monster of the lower world, mother of Cerberus and of the Lernaean hydra,* Ov. Adj. **Echidnēus**-a-um, canis echidneus, *Cerberus,* Ov.

Echĭnādes -um (Ἐχινάδες, Urchin Islands), *a group of five islands in the Ionian Sea at the mouth of the Achelous.*

ĕchinus i., m. (ἐχῖνος). 1, *the edible sea-urchin* (echinus esculentus, Linn.), Hor. ; 2, *a brazen dish used for washing goblets,* Hor.

Echĭon -ŏnis, m. (Ἐχίων). **I.** *one of the Theban heroes who sprang from the dragon's teeth sown by Cadmus, husband of Agave, father of Pentheus ;* Echione natus, *Pentheus,* Ov. Hence, 1, **Echĭonĭdes** -ae, m. *a son of Echion*—i.e., *Pentheus,* Ov. ; 2, **Echĭonĭus** -a -um, *Echionian,* and poet.= *Cadmeian, Theban,* Verg. **II.** *son of Mercury, one of the Argonauts.* Hence adj., **Echĭonĭus** -a -um, *of or belonging to Echion.*

ēchō -ūs, f. (ἠχώ), 1, *an echo,* Plin. ; 2, personif., *Echo, a wood-nymph,* Ov.

eclŏgărĭi -orum, m. = loci electi, *select passages or extracts,* Cic.

ec-quando, adv., 1, *ever,* used in an impassioned interrogation, ecquando te rationem factorum tuorum redditurum putasti? Cic. ; 2, *ever,* indefinite, after nisi, Cic.

ec-qui, ecquae or ecqua, ecquod, pronoun interrog. adj.= numqui, *any,* used in an impassioned interrogation; ecqui pudor est? ecquae religio, Verres? Cic. ; quaeris ecqua spes sit, Cic.

ec-quis, ec-quid, pron. interrog. subst. *whether any? any one? any thing?* in impassioned interrogation, ecquis retulit aliquid ad conjugem ac liberos, praeter odia? Liv. ; with nam, ecquisnam tibi dixerit, Cic. ; adj. = ecqui, ecquis Latini nominis populus defecerit ad nos? Liv. ; used adverbially, a, ecquid, *whether; fac sciam* ecquid venturi sitis, Cic. ; b, ecqui = num aliqui, Cat. ; c, ecquo, *whither? ecquo te tua virtus provexisset?* Cic.

ĕcŭlĕus = equuleus (q.v.).

ĕdācĭtas -ātis, f. (edax), *greediness, gluttony,* Cic.

ĕdax -ācis, f. (1. edo), 1, *greedy, gluttonous;* hospes, Cic. ; 2, transf., *destructive, consuming;* ignis, Verg. ; curae edaces, *"eating cares,"* Hor. ; tempus edax rerum, Ov.

Edessa ae, f. (Ἔδεσσα), 1, *town in Macedonia, residence of the old Macedonian kings.* Hence adj., **Edessaeus** -a -um, *of or belonging to Edessa;* 2, *capital of the province of Oshroene in Mesopotamia.*

ēdĭco -dixi -dictum, 3. 1, *to make known, publish, order, appoint;* hoc simul, Hor. ; foll. by a rel. sent., Cic. ; 2, esp. *to publish openly* (by a herald or otherwise), *to decree, ordain by proclamation* (of magistrates); diem comitiis, Liv. ; with acc. and infin., Cic. ; with ut or ne and the subj., Cic. ; with subj. alone, Cic.

ēdictum -i. n. (edico), *a decree, edict ;* a, of a magistrate, general, king, etc., Archilochia in illum edicta Bibuli, Cic. ; edictum constituere or proponere, Cic. ; praemittere, Caes. ; b, *the proclamation by a praetor on his entering office in which he published the principles that would govern his judicial decisions,* Cic.

ēdisco -dĭdĭci, 3. **1,** *to learn thoroughly, learn off by heart;* aliquid ad verbum, *word for word,* Cic. ; magnum numerum versuum, Caes. ; **2,** *to learn, study;* istam artem, Cic.

ēdissĕro -sĕrŭi -sertum, 3. *to explain, set forth, relate fully;* res gestas, Liv. ; neque necesse est edisseri a nobis, quae finis funestae familiae fiat, Cic.

ēdisserto, 1. (intens. of edissero), *to set forth, explain, relate exactly;* neque aggrediar narrare quae edissertanda minora vero faciam, Liv.

ēdītĭcĭus -a -um (2. edo), *put forth, announced, proposed;* judices, *the panel of 125 judices (jury), of which the accused could reject 75,* Cic.

ēdītĭo -ōnis, f. (2. edo), **1,** *the publishing of a book;* maturare libri huius editionem, Tac. ; **2,** *a statement;* in tam discrepante editione, Liv. ; **3,** legal t. t., editio tribuum, *the proposal of four tribes by the plaintiff or prosecutor, out of which the jury were to be chosen.*

ēdĭtus -a -um, p. adj. with compar. and superl. (2. edo), **1,** *high, lofty;* collis, Caes. ; locus, Cic. ; subst., **ēdĭtum** -i, n. *a lofty situation, height,* Tac. ; **2,** transf., viribus editior, mightier, Hor.

1. ēdo, ēdi, ēsum, edere or esse (ἔδω), **1,** *to eat;* nec esuriens Ptolemaeus ederat jucundius, Cic. ; multos modios salis simul edendos esse, ut amicitiae munus expletum sit, *many bushels of salt must be eaten together,* i.e. *the friendship must be of long standing,* Cic. ; **2,** *of inanimate things, to consume, eat away, corrode;* culmos edit or est robigo, Verg. ; si quid est animam, Hor. (contracted forms, es, est, estis ; subj. essem, infin. esse.)

2. ēdo -dĭdi -dĭtum, 3. *to give out.* **I.** Gen., animam or extremum vitae spiritum, *to breathe one's last, to die,* Cic. ; of things, cuniculus armatos repente edidit, *brought to light,* Liv. **II.** Esp., **1,** *to bring into the world, to bring forth, give birth to;* partum, Cic. ; aliquem, Tac. ; edi in lucem, *to be brought into the world,* Cic. ; partic., Maecenas atavis edite regibus, *descended from,* Hor. ; of things, *to produce;* (terra) edit innumeras species, Ov. ; **2,** *to give forth from oneself, to utter;* clamorem majorem, Cic. ; **3,** *to make known;* **a,** of writing, *to publish;* illos de republica libros, Cic. ; **b,** *to spread a report;* quae opinio erat edita in vulgus, Cic. ; **c,** *to set forth, relate, tell, divulge;* ede illa quae coeperas, Cic. ; consilia hostium, Liv. ; esp. (α) of the oracles, *to state, answer;* Apollo oraculum edidit Spartam perituram, Cic. ; (β) legal t.t. *to fix, determine;* judicium, Cic. ; tribus, *to nominate the tribes out of which the jury were to be chosen,* Cic. ; aliquem sibi socium, in etc., *to propose,* Cic. ; (γ) *to command;* ederet consul quid fieri vellet, Liv. ; partic. subst., **ēdĭta** -ōrum, n. *commands,* Ov. ; **4,** *to bring about, cause, furnish;* **a,** ruinas, Cic. ; annuam operam, *to serve for a year,* Liv. ; magnam caedem, Liv. ; **b,** of magistrates, *to provide games for the people;* ludos, spectaculum, Tac. ; **5,** of time, *to close, bring to an end;* vitam, Cic.

ēdŏcĕo -dŏcŭi -doctum, 2. *to teach, instruct thoroughly, to inform fully;* generally with double acc., juventutem multa facinora, Sall. ; with relat. sent., quos ille edocuerat quae fieri vellet, Caes. ; with infin., omnia venalia habere edocuit, Sall. ; with acc., of things, omnia ordine, Liv. ; freq. in partic. perf. pass. with acc., edoctus artes belli, Liv. ; of abstractions, with ut and the subj., edocuit ratio ut videremus, etc., Cic.

ēdŏlo, 1. *to hew out with an axe, to bring into shape, complete;* quod jusseras edolavi, Cic.

ēdŏmo -dŏmŭi -dŏmĭtum, 1. *to tame thoroughly,*

entirely subdue; vitiosam naturam doctrinā, Cic. ; orbem (terrarum), Ov.

Ēdōni -ōrum (Ἠδωνοί), *a Thracian people, famed for the worship of Bacchus.* Adj., 1, **Ēdōnus** -a -um, poet., *Thracian,* Verg. ; 2, **Ēdōnis** -nĭdis, f. poet., adj., *Thracian,* Ov. ; subst., *a Bacchanal,* Prop.

ēdormĭo, 4. *to have one's sleep out.* **I.** Intransit., *to sleep away, to sleep one's fill;* quum (vinolenti) edormiverunt, Cic. **II.** Transit., **a,** *to sleep off;* crapulam, Cic. ; **b,** Fufius Ilionam edormit (of an actor), *sleeps through the part of Iliona,* Hor.

ēdŭcātĭo -ōnis, f. (educo), *bringing up, training, education;* of children, educatio liberorum, Cic. ; institutus liberaliter educatione doctrināque puerili, Cic.

ēdŭcātor -ōris, m. (educo), *one who trains or brings up;* **a,** *a foster-father,* Cic. ; **b,** *a tutor,* Tac.

ēdŭcātrix -īcis, f. (educator), *a foster-mother, nurse;* transf., earum (rerum) parens est educatrixque sapientia, Cic.

1. ēdŭco, 1. (intens. of 2. educo), *to bring up, rear, educate;* **a,** of human beings, aliquem, Cic.; caelum quo natus educatusque essem, Liv. ; homo ingenuus liberaliterque educatus, Cic. ; ad turpitudinem educatur, Cic. ; **b,** of animals, in educando perfacile apparet aliud quiddam iis (bestiis) propositum, Cic. ; **c,** of things, transf., educata huius nutrimentis eloquentia, Cic.

2. ēdūco -duxi -ductum, 3. **I.** *to draw out, lead out.* **A.** *to draw out;* **1,** gen., gladium e vagina, Cic. ; **2,** esp., t. t. of drawing lots, sortem, Cic. ; aliquem ex urna, Cic. **B.** *to lead out;* **1,** gen., hominem de senatu, Cic. ; aliquem in provinciam, Cic. ; esp., **a,** milit. t. t., *to march troops out;* cohortes ex urbe, Caes. ; exercitum in expeditionem, Cic. ; **b,** legal t. t., *to lead before a court of law;* aliquem in jus, Cic. ; aliquem ad consules, Cic., or simply educere aliquem, Cic. ; **c,** naut. t. t., *to take a ship out of port,* naves ex portu, Caes. ; **d,** *to lead out of a country;* equos ex Italia, Liv. ; **e,** *to bring water* (by aqueduct); lacum, Cic. ; **f,** *to build a wall on to a river;* moles quam eductam in Rhenum retulimus, Tac. **II.** *to raise up.* **A.** Lit., aliquem superas sub auras, Verg. ; fig., in astra, *to praise sky high,* Hor. **B.** Transf., **a,** turris summis sub astra educta tectis, Verg. ; **b,** to *bring up, rear a child;* aliquem, Cic. **III.** Of time, *to live, spend;* pios annos, Prop.

ēdūlis -e (1. edo), *eatable,* Hor.

ēdūro, 1. *to last, endure,* Tac.

ēdūrus -a -um, *very hard;* pirus, Verg. ; transf., eduro ore negare, Ov.

Eētĭon -ōnis, m. (Ἠετίων), *father of Andromache, prince of Thebae in Cilicia.* Hence adj., **Eētĭōnēus** -a -um, *of or belonging to Eetion.*

effarcĭo -fersi -fertum, 4. (ex and farcio), *to stuff full;* intervalla grandibus saxis, Caes.

effātum -i, n. (n. of partic. of effor), **1,** *an announcement, prediction;* fatidicorum et vatum, Cic. ; **2,** *an axiom,* Cic.

effectĭo -ōnis, f. (efficio), **1,** *a doing, practising;* artis, Cic. ; **2,** *an efficient cause,* Cic.

effector -ōris, m. (efficio), *one who produces, causes, originates;* effector mundi molitorque deus, Cic. ; of things, stilus optimus et praestantissimus dicendi effector ac magister, Cic.

effectrix -trīcis, f. (effector), *she that causes or produces;* terra diei noctisque effectrix, Cic.

1. effectus -a -um, partic. of efficio.

2. effectus -ūs, m. (efficio). **I.** Act., *doing,*

effecting, execution, performance; **1,** gen., conatus tam audax trajiciendarum Alpium et effectus, Liv.; in effectu esse, Cic.; postquam ad effectum operis ventum est, Liv.; **2,** esp., *the working;* quarum (herbarum) causam ignorare, vim et effectum videres, Cic. **II.** Pass., *effect, consequence;* effectus eloquentiae est audientium approbatio, Cic.; sine ullo effectu, Liv.

effēmǐnātē, adv. (effeminatus), *effeminately,* Cic.

effēmǐnātus -a -um, p. adj. with compar. and superl. (from effemino), *effeminate, womanish;* corpora, Liv.; opinio, Cic.; effeminatissimus languor, Cic.

effēmǐno, l. (ex and femina), **1,** *to make into a woman;* effeminarunt eum (aërem) Junonique tribuerunt, Cic.; **2,** *to make effeminate, to enervate;* virum in dolore, Cic.; effeminari cogitationibus mollissimis.

effērātus -a -um, p. adj. with compar. and superl. (1. effero), *wild, savage;* mores ritusque, Liv.; gentes, Cic.

effercǐo, v. effarcio.

effērǐtas -ātis, f. (efferus), *wildness, savageness,* Cic.

1. effĕro, l. (efferus), *to make wild, make savage.* **A.** Lit., barba et capilli efferaverant speciem oris, Liv.; terram immanitate beluarum efferari, Cic. **B.** Transf., animos, Liv.; odio iräque efferati, Liv.

2. effĕro (ecfĕro), extŭli, ēlātum, efferre (ex and fero). **I.** *to bear, carry out, bring out.* **A.** Gen., **1,** lit., tela ex aedibus alicuius, Cic.; deam in terram, Liv.; esp., **a,** pedem or se efferre, *to betake oneself;* pedem portā non efferre, Cic.; **b,** milit. t.t., efferre signa (vexilla, arma), *to march out;* signa portis or extra urbem, Liv.; **c,** *to carry to the grave, bury;* aliquem, Cic.; pass., efferri, *to be borne out, buried,* Cic.; fig., ingens periculum manet ne libera respublica efferatur, Liv.; **d,** *to bring forth, bear;* uberiores fruges, Cic.; cum decimo, *tenfold,* Cic.; **2,** transf., *to utter,* **a,** *to express;* si graves sententiae inconditis verbis efferuntur, Cic.; **b,** *to publish, make known;* aliquid in vulgus, Cic.; ne has meas ineptias efferatis, Cic.; **c,** se, *to show itself;* volo enim se efferat in adolescente fecunditas, Cic. **B.** *to carry away;* **1,** lit., Messium impetus per hostes extulit ad castra, Liv.; **2,** transf., *to carry away, drive to;* si me efferet ad gloriam animi dolor, Cic.; se efferri aliquā re (laetitiā, dolore, studio, iracundiā), *to be carried away,* Cic. **II.** *to raise up, lift up.* **A.** Lit., **a,** scutum super caput, Liv.; **b,** *to make to appear;* lucem, Verg. **B.** Transf., **a,** *to raise;* aliquem ad summum imperium, Cic.; **b,** *to praise, extol;* aliquem or aliquid laudibus, Cic.; **c,** efferri or se efferre, *to pride oneself on, to be puffed up by;* efferre se insolenter, Cic.; partic., elatus, *puffed up;* recenti victoriā, Caes.

effertus -a -um, p. adj. (from effarcio), *stuffed full, full;* nimbus effertus tenebris, Lucr.

effĕrus -a -um (ex and ferus), *very wild, savage;* facta tyranni, Verg.

effervesco -ferbŭi and -fervi, 3. *to boil up, foam up, effervesce.* **A.** Lit., eae aquae, quae effervescunt subditis ignibus, Cic.; poet. of the stars, at the creation of the world, *to swarm forth, to break out into a glow,* Ov. **B.** Transf., **a,** Pontus armatus, effervescens in Asiam atque erumpens, *bursting forth,* Cic.; **b,** *to rage,* Cic.; esp. of an orator, *to be passionate,* Cic.

effervo, 3. (ex and fervo). **I.** *to boil up or over;* effervere in agros vidimus undantem Aetnam, Verg. **II.** *to swarm forth,* Verg.

effētus -a -um (ex and fetus, *having given*

birth to young), *weakened, exhausted, effete;* corpus, Cic.; vires, Verg.; innumeris effetus laniger annis, Ov.; effeta veri senectus, *incapable of truth,* Verg.

effǐcācǐtas -ātis, f. (efficax), *efficacy, efficiency,* Cic.

effǐcācǐtĕr, adv. with compar. and superl. (efficax), *effectively, efficaciously;* id acturos efficacius rati, Liv.

effǐcax -ācis, adj. with compar. and superl. (efficio), *effective, efficient, efficacious;* **a,** of things, scientia, Hor.; with ad, quae maxime efficaces ad muliebre ingenium preces sunt, Liv.; with in and the abl., in quibus (rebus) peragendis continuatio ipsa efficacissima esset, Liv.; with infin., amara curarum eluere efficax, Hor.; **b,** of persons, Hercules, *active,* Hor.

effǐcǐens -entis, p. adj. (from efficio), *efficient, effective;* res, Cic.; causa, *efficient cause,* Cic.; with genit., efficiens voluptatis, *cause of,* Cic.

effǐcǐentĕr, adv. (efficiens), *efficiently, powerfully,* Cic.

effǐcǐentǐa -ae, f. (efficiens), *efficiency,* Cic.

effǐcǐo -fēci -fectum, 3. (ex and facio). **I.** *to produce, effect, make.* **A.** Gen., mundum, Cic.; magnas rerum commutationes, Caes. **B.** Esp., **a,** *to build, erect;* columnam, Cic.; **b,** of land, *to bear;* plurimum, Cic.; cum octavo, *eight-fold,* Cic.; **c,** of number, *to make up;* pass., effici, come to; ea tributa vix in fenus Pompeii quod satis est efficiunt, Cic.; **d,** *to bring together;* magnum cratium numerum, Caes.; duas legiones, Caes.; **e,** philosoph. t. t., *to prove, show;* minutis interrogationibus quod proposuit efficit, Cic.; ex quibus vult efficere, with acc. and infin., Cic.; ita efficitur ut, etc., Cic.; **f,** *to make;* Catilinam consulem, Cic.; hostes ad pugnam alacriores, Caes. **II.** *to bring to an end, accomplish, execute, complete;* **1,** omne opus, Caes.; sphaeram, Cic.; hoc id illud efficere ut, etc., Cic.; simply efficere ut, Cic.; non effici potest quin, etc., Cic.; **2,** *to accomplish* (of a march), quantumcumque itineris equitatu efficere potuerat, Caes.

effǐgǐēs -ēi, f. or **effǐgǐa** -ae, f. (effingo). **I.** Lit., **1,** *an image, likeness, effigy, portrait;* quaedam effigies spirantis mortui, Cic.; hanc pro Palladio effigiem statuere, Verg.; **2,** *form, shape;* **a,** simulacrum deae non effigie humana, Tac.; **b,** *a shade, ghost;* effigies, immo umbrae hominum, Liv. **II.** *abstract, copy, imitation, image;* et humanitatis et probitatis, Cic.; effigies justi imperii, *ideal,* Cic.

effingo -finxi -fictum, 3. (ex and fingo), **1,** *to wipe off, wipe out;* e foro sanguinem spongiis effingere, Cic.; **2,** **a,** *to form, fashion;* oris lineamenta, Cic.; **b,** *to represent;* (natura) speciem ita formavit oris ut in ea penitus reconditos mores effingeret, Cic.; *so to express in words;* alicuius mores, Cic.; **c,** *to imitate, strive to reach;* illum imitando, Cic.; *to conceive;* ea effingenda animo, Cic.

efflǐo -fǐěri, pass. of efficio (q.v.).

efflāgǐtātǐo -ōnis, f. (efflagito), *an urgent demand;* efflagitatio ad coëundam societatem, Cic.

efflāgǐtātus -ūs, m. (efflagito), *an urgent request;* coactu atque efflagitatu meo, Cic.

efflāgǐto, l. (ex and flagito), *to ask earnestly, demand, entreat;* nostram misericordiam, Cic.; ab ducibus signum pugnae, Liv.; epistolam, Cic.; ut se ad regem mitteret, Cic.

efflīgo -flixi -flictum, 3. (ex and fligo), *to kill, murder, slay;* Pompeium, Cic.

efflo, l. (ex and flo), **1,** transit., *to blow out, breathe out;* ignes ore et naribus, Ov.; **2,** intransit., *to breathe forth*, Lucr.; animam, Cic.; extremum halitum, *to die*, Cic.

efflōresco -flōrŭi, 3. (ex and floresco), *to blossom, break into bloom, flourish* ; huic efflorescunt genera partesque virtutum, Cic.; si quidem efflorescit (illa aetas) ingenii laudibus, Cic.

efflŭo (ecflŭo) -fluxi, 3. (ex and fluo), 3. *to flow out.* **A.** una cum sanguine vita, Cic.; aër effluens huc et illuc ventos efficit, Cic. **B.** 1, *to vanish* ; tanta est enim intimorum multitudo, ut ex iis aliquis potius effluat quam novo sit aditus, Cic.; 2, a, *to vanish out of thought, to be forgotten* ; effluere ex animo alicuius, Cic.; absol., quod totum effluxerat, Cic.; b, of thought, *to be lost, fail;* alicui ex tempore dicenti solet effluere mens, Cic.; c, of time, *to disappear* ; ne effluat aetas, Cic.; 3, *to come to light, become known* ; effluunt multa ex vestra disciplina, quae etiam ad nostras aures saepe permanent, Cic.

efflŭvĭum -ii, n. (effluo), *flowing out, outlet;* convivium effluvio lacus appositum, Tac.

effŏdĭo -fōdi -fossum, 3. (ex and fodio). **I.** *to dig out.* **A.** Gen., ferrum e terrā, Cic. **B.** Esp., 1, *to gouge out;* oculos, Cic.; 2, *to make by digging, to excavate;* portus, Verg. **II.** *to dig up.* **A.** Gen., terram, Liv. **B.** *to rummage;* domibus effossis, Caes.

effor (ecfor), 1. dep. (ex and for). **I.** Gen., *to speak out, express, speak;* verbum, Cic.; nefanda, Liv.; tum ferunt ex oraclo ecfatam esse Pythiam, Cic. **II.** Esp., **A.** In logic, *to state a proposition,* Cic. **B.** T. t. of augury, *to fix or determine a place;* templum, Cic.; partic., effatus (pass.), *fixed, determined by the augurs,* Cic.

effrēnātē, adv. with compar. (effrenatus), *unrestrainedly, violently,* Cic.

effrēnātĭo -ōnis, f. *unbridled impetuosity;* animi impotentis, Cic.

effrēnātus -a -um, p. adj. with compar. and superl. (from effreno, P. Aug., *to let loose*), *unbridled.* **A.** Lit., equi, Liv. **B.** Transf., *unrestrained, unchecked, violent;* furor, cupiditas, homo, Cic.; effrenatior vox, Cic.; effrenata insolentiā multitudo, Cic.

effrēnus -a -um (ex and frenum), *unbridled;* 1, lit., equus, Liv.; 2, transf., *unrestrained;* amor, Ov.

effringo -frēgi -fractum (ex and frango), 1, *to break open;* fores, Cic.; januam, Cic.; 2, *to break off;* crus, Sall.

effŭgĭo -fūgi -fŭgĭtum, 3. (ex and fugio). **I.** Intransit., *to flee, fly away, escape, get off;* e praelio, Cic.; a quibus (iudis) vix vivus effugit, Cic. **II.** Transit., *to escape from, avoid, flee from, shun;* equitatum Caesaris, Caes.; alicuius impias manus, Cic.; with ne and the subj., propinquae clade urbis ipsi, ne quid simile paterentur, effugerunt, Liv.; me effugit, *it escapes me, escapes my observation,* Cic.

effŭgĭum -ii, n. (effugio), *a flying away, flight.* **I.** Lit., Lucr. **II.** Meton., **A.** *an outlet for flight;* si effugium patuisset in publicum, Liv. **B.** *the means or opportunity of flight;* mortis, Cic.; effugia pennarum habere, Cic.

effulgĕo -fulsi, 2. (ex and fulgeo), *to shine out, glitter.* **A.** Lit., nova lux oculis effulsit, Verg.; auro, *glitter with gold,* Verg. **B.** Transf., effulgebant Philippus ac magnus Alexander, Liv.

effultus -a -um (ex and fulcio), *resting upon, supported by;* velleribus, Verg.

effundo -fūdi -fūsum, 3. (ex and fundo), *to pour out, pour forth, shed.* **I.** 1, of liquids, lacrimas, Cic.; Tiberis effusus super ripas, Liv.; imber effusus nubibus, Verg.; 2, of things not fluid, *to pour out, pour forth ;* saccos nummorum,

to empty, Hor. **II. A.** 1, *to throw down* ; aliquem solo, Verg.; esp. of horses, *to throw their riders;* effundere consulem super caput, Liv.; 2, *to drive out* ; excutiat Teucros vallo atque effundat in aequum, Verg. **B.** 1, *to loosen, let go;* iterum sinum, *unfold the toga,* Liv.; navibus omnes habenas, Verg.; 2, *to pour, throw;* of weapons, telorum omnis generis vis ingens effusa est in eos, Liv.; of other objects, primum impetum quem fervido ingenio et caecā irā effundunt, Liv.; 3, *to send forth* (a number of men), auxilium castris, Verg.; reflex., se effundere, middle effundi, *to stream forth, pour forth;* cunctum senatum, totam Italiam esse effusam, Cic.; Celtiberi omnes in fugam effunduntur, Liv.; 4, *to pour forth, give forth;* a, of sounds, tales voces, Verg.; vox in coronam turbamque effunditur, Cic.; b, of fruits, *to bring forth in abundance;* segetes effundunt fruges, Cic.; 5, of property, *to spend, squander;* patrimonia effundere largiendo, Cic. **III.** Transf., **A.** *to pour out, tell, impart;* effudi vobis omnia quae sentiebam, Cic.; in a bad sense, omnem suum vinolentum furorem in aliquem, *pour forth on,* Cic. **B.** Esp. reflex. and middle, *to give oneself up to, indulge in;* effundere se in aliqua libidine, Cic.; nimio successu in tantam licentiamque socordiamque effusus, Liv. **C.** 1, *to use, expend, make full use of;* omnia reipublicae remedia, Cic.; ibi omnis effusus labor, *wasted,* Verg.; 2, *to breathe forth;* spiritum extremum in victoria, *to die,* Cic.

effūsē, adv. with compar. and superl. (effusus). **I.** *far and wide;* ire, *in disorder,* Sall.; vastare, Liv. **II.** Transf., 1, *profusely, lavishly;* donare, Cic.; 2, *unrestrainedly, immoderately;* exsultare, Cic.

effūsĭo -ōnis, f. (effundo). **I.** Act. 1, *a pouring forth;* tutantur se atramenti effusione sepiae, Cic.; 2, *extravagance, prodigality;* hae pecuniarum effusiones, Cic.; absol., liberalitatem effusio imitatur, Cic. **II.** Middle, 1, lit., a, aquae, Cic.; b, *pouring out of people;* effusiones hominum ex oppidis, Cic.; 2, transf., *exuberance of spirits, excessive hilarity;* effusio animi in laetitia, Cic.

effūsus -a -um, p. adj. with compar. and superl. (effundo), *poured forth.* **I.** Lit., 1, *let loose;* effusae comae, Ov.; effuso cursu, *at full speed,* Liv.; 2, *wide-spread;* mare late effusum, Hor.; 3, of soldiers, *disorderly* (in march), effuso agmine, Liv.; fuga effusa, Liv. **II.** Transf., a, *extravagant;* in largitione, Cic.; b, *unrestrained, immoderate;* licentia, Liv.

effūtĭo, 4. (ex and * futio, from root, FUD, FUT, whence fundo, futilis), *to blab out, chatter;* aliquid, Cic.; de mundo, Cic.; absol., ex tempore, Cic.

effūtŭo -ŭi, 3. *to squander in debauchery,* Cat.

egĕlĭdus -a -um, 1, *with the chill off, lukewarm, tepid;* tepores, Cat.; 2, *cool, somewhat cold;* flumen, Verg.

ĕgens -entis, p. adj. with compar. and superl. (egeo), *poor, needy, indigent* (opp. locuples); egens quidam calumniator, Cic.; with genit., verbum non egens, *not deficient in,* Cic.

ĕgēnus -a -um (egeo), *needy, wanting, in need of;* with genit., omnium egena corpora, Liv.; of condition, *poor;* in rebus egenis, poverty, Verg.

ĕgĕo -ŭi, 2. **I.** *to want, be in need, be destitute, be needy, poor;* a, absol., egebat? immo locuples erat, Cic.; b, *to be in want of something;* with abl., medicinā, Cic.; with genit., auxilii, Caes. **II.** Transf., 1 (= careo), *to be without, not to have;* with abl., auctoritate, *to have no authority,* Cic.; with genit., classis, Verg.; 2,

(= desidero), *to desire, wish for, want;* with abl., pane, Hor.

Ēgĕrĭa -ae, f. *an Italian nymph, the instructress of Numa Pompilius.*

ēgĕro -gessi -gestum, 3. *to carry, bear, bring, get out.* **A.** Lit., **1,** gen., tantum nivis, Liv.; **2,** esp., a, *to carry off,* as plunder, praedam ex hostium tectis, Liv.; b, dapes, *to vomit,* Ov. **B.** Transf., expletur lacrimis egeriturque dolor, *is expelled,* Ov.

ĕgestas -ātis, f. (for egentas from egeo). **I.** *extreme poverty, indigence, need.* **A.** Lit., ista paupertas vel potius egestas ac mendicitas, Cic. **B.** Transf., animi, Cic. **II.** *want of, deficiency in;* frumenti, Sall.

ēgigno, 3. *to produce out of,* Lucr.

Egnātĭa (Gnātĭa) -ae, f. *a town in Apulia Peucetia.*

ĕgŏ (ἐγώ), pron. pers. genit. mei, dat. mihi, acc. me, abl. me; plur. nom. nos, genit. nostrum and nostri, dat. nobis, acc. nos, abl. nobis, I, plur. *we.* **I.** Lit., **1,** gen., alter ego, *my second self,* Cic.; genit. nostrum partitive and possessive, nostri, objective, Cic.; **2,** esp., nos for ego, nobis consulibis, Cic. **II.** Meton., **A.** ad me, *to me, to my house,* Cic. **B.** a me, *from my property, at my expense;* se a me solvere, Cic. (ego, etc., strengthened by -met in all cases except genit. plur., egomet, etc.).

ēgrĕdĭor -gressus, 3. dep. (ex and gradior). **I.** Intransit. **A.** *to go out, pass out;* **1,** Lit., a, e cubiculo; b, milit. t.t., (a) *to leave the ranks;* egredi ordine, Sall.; (β) *to march out of camp;* e castris, Caes., or simply castris, Caes.; ad proelium, Caes.; b, naut. t.t. (a) egredi ex navi or simply navi, Cic., *to disembark;* so egredi in terram, Cic.; absol., Caes.; (β) egredi ex portu, *to sail away,* Cic.; **2,** in discourse, *to digress;* a proposito, Cic. **B.** *to go up, ascend;* ad summum montis, Sall. **II.** Transit., **A.** *to go out of;* urbem, Liv. **B.** Lit., **1,** *to pass beyond;* munitiones, Caes.; **2,** transf., *to overstep, pass;* modum, Tac.; *to go out of;* fines, Caes.

ēgrĕgĭē, adv. (egregius), *excellently, admirably, singularly;* with verbs, pingere, loqui, Cic.; with adjectives, egregie fortis imperator, Cic.; egregie subtilis scriptor et elegans, Cic.

ēgrĕgĭus -a -um, (ex and grex, lit., *not belonging to the common herd), admirable, excellent, extraordinary, distinguished;* civis, Cic.; with in and the abl., Laelius in bellica laude, Cic.; with ad, vir ad cetera egregius, Liv.; with abl., bello, Verg.; with genit., animi, Verg. Subst., **ēgrĕgĭa** -ōrum, n. *distinguished actions,* Sall.

ēgressus -ūs, m. (egredior). **I.** *a going out, departure;* vester, Cic.; ventos custodit et arcet Aeolus egressu, Ov. **II. A.** *a landing from a ship, disembarkation;* egressus optimus, Caes. **B.** *a passage out;* egressus obsidens, Tac.; poet., *the mouth of a river,* Ov.

ĕheu, interj., expressing grief or pain, *alas! woe!* eheu me miserum; often followed by quam, Hor. (ēheu in epic and lyric poets).

ei (hei), interj., expressing pain, *ah! woe! ei mihi conclamat,* Ov.

ēĭa and **hēĭa** (εἶα), interj., exclamation of joy and surprise, *hallo! well then!* heia vero! Cic.; eia age, of exhortation, *quick! come then!* Verg.

ēĭcĭo = ejicio (q.v.).

ējăcŭlor, 1. dep., *to throw out, hurl out;* aquas, Ov.

ējectāmentum -i, n. (ejecto), *that which is thrown up;* maris, Tac.

ējectĭo -ōnis, f. (ejicio), *banishment, exile,* Cic.

ējecto, 1. (intens. of ejicio), *to throw, cast, hurl out, eject;* **1,** arenas, favillam, Ov.; **2,** *to vomit forth;* cruorem ore, Verg.

ējectus -ūs, m. (ejicio), *a casting out,* Lucr.

ējĭcĭo -jēci -jectum, 3. (ex and jacio), *to throw out, cast out, drive out, drive away, eject.* **I.** Gen., **A.** Lit., aliquem ex oppido, Caes.; multos sedibus ac fortunis, Cic.; se in terram e navi, Cic.; fig., si quidem hanc sentinam huius urbis ejecerit, Cic. **B.** Transf., amorem ex animo, Cic. **II.** Esp., **A.** *to cast forth, utter;* vocem, Cic. **B.** Milit. t.t., **a,** *to drive away;* cohortes, Caes.; b, se ejicere, *to rush forth;* se ex oppido, Caes. **C.** *to drive away;* **a,** from house or property, aliquem domo, Cic.; absol., damnato et ejecto, Cic.; of the wife (with or without domo), *to divorce,* Cic.; b, *to banish;* aliquem ex patria, Cic.; or simply ejicere aliquem, Cic.; c, *to remove from a magistracy, guild,* etc.; aliquem de collegio, Cic.; e senatu, Cic. **D.** Naut. t.t., a, *to bring to shore;* navem in terram, Caes.; b, in pass., *to be cast ashore, stranded;* classis ad Baleares ejicitur, Liv.; ejici in litore, Caes.; ejectus, *a shipwrecked person,* Cic. **E.** *to throw out a dead body, leave unburied;* ne corpus ejiciatur, Cic. **F.** 1, *to stretch forth, thrust out;* linguam, Cic.; **2,** *to dislocate;* armum, Verg. **G.** *to hiss an actor off the stage,* Cic.; so transf., *to reject, disapprove of;* Cynicorum ratio tota est ejicienda, Cic.

ējŭlātĭo -ōnis, f. (ejulo), *wailing, a lamentation;* illa non virilis, Cic.

ējŭlātus -ūs, m. (ejulo), *a wailing, lamenting;* ejulatus ne mulieri quidem concessus est, Cic.

ējŭlo, 1, *to wail, lament;* magnitudine dolorum ejulans, Cic.

ējūro and **ējĕro,** 1. *to refuse* or *deny on oath.* **I.** Legal t.t., bonam copiam, *to swear that one is insolvent,* Cic.; forum sibi iniquum, provinciam sibi iniquam, aliquem (judicem) iniquum, *to declare by oath that a court or judge is partial, to challenge,* Cic.; magistratum, imperium, *to resign, abdicate, with an oath that the duties have been duly performed,* Tac. **II.** Transf., *to give up, abjure, abandon, disown;* patriam, Tac.

ējusdemmŏdi or **ējusdem mŏdi** (idem and modus), *in the same manner,* Cic.

ējusmŏdi or **ējus mŏdi** (is and modus). **I.** *of this kind, such;* genus belli est ejusmodi, Cic. **II.** = ita, so, quam viam tensarum atque pompae ejusmodi exegisti, ut, etc., Cic.

ēlābor -lapsus, 3. dep., *to glide out of, slide away from, escape, slip away.* **I.** Lit., **A.** Gen., anguis ex columna lignea elapsus, Liv.; quum se convolvens sol elaberetur et abiret, Cic. **B.** Esp., *to slip away, escape;* e manibus curantium, Liv.; animi corporibus elapsi, Cic.; with acc., custodias, Tac. **II.** Transf., **A.** Gen., disciplina elapsa est de manibus, Cic. **B.** Esp., *to be acquitted, escape from punishment, get off;* ex tot tantisque criminibus, Cic.

ēlăbōro, 1. **I.** Intransit., *to labour hard, strive, take pains;* generally with in and the abl., in litteris, Cic.; with ut and the subj., in eo quoque elaborare ut, etc., Cic. **II.** Transit., *to labour on, work out, elaborate, produce;* causae diligenter elaboratae et tanquam elucubratae, Cic.; versus ornati elaboratique, *carefully worked out,* Cic.; as opp. to natural, *artificial;* elaborata concinnitas, Cic.

Ēlaea -ae, f. (Ἐλαία), *a town in Aeolis.*

ēlāmentābĭlis -e, *very lamentable;* gemitus Cic.

ēlanguesco -gŭi, 3. *to become weak, be relaxed, become languid;* alienā ignaviā, Liv.; differendo deinde elanguit res, Liv.

ēlargĭor, 4. *to lavish, give liberally,* Pers.

ēlātē, adv. (elatus), 1, *loftily ;* loqui, Cic. ; 2, *arrogantly ;* se gerere, Nep.

Ēlătēïus -a -um, *of* or *belonging to Elatus.* Subst., *son of Elatus,* i.e., *Caeneus.*

ēlātĭo -ōnis, f. (effero), 1, *flight, soaring ;* elatio et magnitudo animi, Cic. ; elatio atque altitudo orationis suae, Cic. ; 2, *elevation ;* parium comparatio nec elationem habet nec summissionem, Cic.

ēlātro, 1. *to bark out, cry out,* Hor.

ēlātus -a -um (partic. of 2. effero), *elevated, exalted ;* of discourse, verba, Cic. ; of the mind, animus magnus elatusque, Cic.

Ēlăvĕr -ĕris, n. *a tributary of the Liger,* now *the Allier.*

Ēlĕa -ae, f. ('Ελέα), *town in Lower Italy* (Lat. *Velia), birthplace of Parmenides and Zeno, the founders of the Eleatic school of philosophy.* Hence,

Ēlĕătēs -ae, m. *Zeno,* Cic. Adj., Ēlĕātĭcus -a -um, *Eleatic ;* philosophi, Cic.

ēlectē, adv. with compar. (electus) *choicely, selectly ;* digerere, Cic.

ēlectĭo -ōnis, f. (eligo), *choice, selection ;* a, of persons, senatus electionem (legatorum) Galbae permiserat, Tac. ; b, of things, judicium electioque verborum, Cic. ; iis trium conditionum electionem ferre, Liv.

Ēlectra -ae, f. ('Ηλέκτρα), 1, *daughter of Atlas, one of the Pleiades, mother of Dardanus by Jupiter ;* 2, *daughter of Agamemnon, wife of Pylades, sister of Orestes and Iphigenia.*

ēlectrum -i, n. (ἤλεκτρον), 1, *amber,* Verg. ; 2, *an alloy of gold and silver, resembling amber in colour,* Verg.

1. ēlectus -a -um, p. adj. with compar. and superl. (eligo), *chosen, select ;* a, of persons, manus, Tac. ; b, of things, verba electissima, *choice,* Cic.

2. ēlectus -ūs, m. (eligo), *choosing, choice ;* necis, Ov.

ēlĕgans -antis, adj. with compar. and superl. (for eligens, from eligo), *choice, fine, neat, tasteful, elegant ;* a, of persons, non parcus solum, sed etiam elegans, Cic. ; subst., elegantes, *fine folk,* Cic. ; b, of things, *tasteful ;* artes, Cic. ; c, of oratory and diction, *fine, correct, elegant ;* elegans in dicendo, Cic. ; subst., elegantes. *fine orators,* Cic. ; epistola elegantissima, Cic.

ēlĕgantĕr, adv. with compar. and superl. (elegans), *tastefully, choicely, neatly, elegantly ;* scribere, Cic. ; scribere, psallere et saltare elegantius quam necesse est, Sall. ; Latine loqui elegantissime, Cic.

ēlĕgantĭa -ae, f. (elegans), a, *taste, refinement, grace, elegance ;* integritas et elegantia alicuius, Cic. ; elegantia vitae, Cic. ; doctrinae, Cic. ; b, of oratory or diction, *grace, correctness, elegance, neatness ;* elegantia loquendi, Cic. ; disserendi, Cic.

ēlĕgī -ōrum, m. (ἔλεγοι), *elegiac verses,* Hor.

ēlĕgīa -ae, f. (ἐλεγεία), *a poem written in elegiac verse,* Ov.

Ēlĕleus -ĕi, m. ('Ελελεύς, from ἐλελεῦ, the Bacchic cry), *a surname of Bacchus,* Ov. ; hence, Ēlĕlēïdes -um, f. *Bacchantes,* Ov.

ēlĕmentum -i, n. I. *an element, first principle,* Plin. ; oftener in plur., Cic. II. Transf., plur. elementa. A. *the letters of the alphabet,* and *the alphabet itself,* Suet. B. *the rudiments* or *elements ;* a, *in reading* or *writing,* pueros elementa docere, Hor. ; b, *the elements of any science* or *art ;* loquendi, Cic. ; c, *the beginnings of other things ;* prima Romae, Ov.

ēlenchus -i, m. (ἔλεγχος), *a pearl pendant worn as an earring,* Juv.

Ēlĕphantĭnē -ēs, f. ('Ελεφαντίνη) and Ēlĕphantis -tĭdis ('Ελεφαντίς), *an island in the Nile in Upper Egypt, opposite Syene.*

ēlĕphantus -i, c. (in classical prose commoner than elephas in oblique cases), *an elephant ;* elephanto beluarum nulla prudentior, Cic. ; meton., *ivory,* Verg.

ēlĕphās (-ans) -phantis, m. (ἐλέφας). A. Lit., *the elephant,* Liv. B. Meton., *the disease elephantiasis,* Lucr.

Ēlēus -a -um, v. Elis.

Ēleusin -īnis, f. (Ελευσίν), *an ancient city in Attica, famous for the worship of Ceres, and for the mysteries there celebrated.* Adj., Ēleusīnĭus -a -um, Eleusina mater, *Ceres,* Verg.

Ēleuthĕrĭus -a -um ('Ελευθέριος), *making free.* Subst. I. m. *the Liberator, a surname of Jupiter.* II. Ēleuthĕrĭa -ōrum, n. (sc. sacra) *the festival of Jupiter Liberator,* Plaut.

ēlĕvo, 1. (ex and levo). I. Lit., *to lift up, raise, elevate ;* contabulationem, Caes. II. Transf., *to lessen ;* a, in a bad sense, *to weaken, impair, disparage ;* adversarium, Cic. ; res gestas, Liv. ; b, in a good sense, *to alleviate, lighten ;* suspiciones offensionesque, Cic.

ēlĭcĭo -lĭcŭi -lĭcĭtum, 3. (ex and LAC -io), *to allure, entice out.* I. Gen., A. Lit., 1, *hostem ex paludibus silvisque,* Caes. ; 2, *to invoke the presence of a god* or *departed spirit ;* inferorum animas, Cic. B. *to invite, allure, induce ;* aliquem ad disputandum, Cic. II. *to bring forth to the light of day.* A. Lit., 1, gen., ferrum e terrae cavernis, Cic. ; 2, esp., *to produce, cause ;* lapidum ictu ignem, Cic. B. Transf., 1, *to win from, gain ;* alias litteras ab aliquo, Cic. ; 2, *to search out, find out ;* causam alicuius rei, Cic. ; sententiam meam, Cic. ; 3, *to awake ;* misericordiam, Liv.

Ēlĭcĭus -ĭi, m. (elicio), *a surname of Jupiter, he from whom a heavenly sign is called forth,* Liv.

ēlīdo -līsi -līsum, 3. (ex and laedo), *to strike, thrust, drive out.* I. Lit., aurigam e curru, Cic. ; morbum, *to expel,* Hor. II. *to dash to pieces, shatter ;* naves, Caes. ; aliquem, Cic. ; caput pecudis saxo, Liv. ; fig., nervos omnes virtutis, *to break,* Cic.

ēlĭgo -lēgi -lectum, 3. (ex and lego). I. *to pick out, to choose, select ;* amicos, Cic. ; ut de tribus Antoniis eligas quem velis, Cic. ; ex multis Isocratis libris triginta fortasse versus, Cic. ; hunc urbi condendae locum, Liv. II. *to root out ;* fig., superstitionis stirpes omnes eligere, Cic.

ēlīmĭno, 1. (ex and limen), *to carry over the threshhold ;* dicta foras, *to blab,* Hor.

ēlīmo, 1. (ex and lima), *to file off, smoothe, polish.* A. Lit., graciles ex aere catenas retiaque et laqueos, Ov. B. Transf., *to polish, elaborate, perfect ;* σχόλιον aliquod ad aliquem, Cic.

ēlinguis -e (ex and lingua), 1, *speechless,* Cic. ; 2, *without eloquence,* Cic. ; mutus atque elinguis, Liv.

Ēlis -ĭdis, f. ('Ηλις), *a territory of Western Peloponnesus, in which the Olympic games were solemnized ;* hence adj., 1, Ēlēus -a -um and Ēlīus -a -um, *Elean, Olympic ;* amnis, *the Alpheus,* Ov. ; 2, Ēlēis -ĭdis, f. *Elean ;* 3, Ēlĭas -ādis, f. *Elean, Olympic ;* equa, *a horse running in the Olympic games,* Verg.

Ēlissa (Ēlīsa) -ae, f. ('Ελισσα), *another name of Dido.*

ēlix -ĭcis, m. (elicio), *a deep furrow, to with-draw moisture from the roots of plants*, Ov.

ēlixus -a -um (ex and lix), *boiled*, Hor.

ellĕbŏrus (hellĕbŏrus) -i, m. (ἐλλέβορος and ἐλλέβορος), and gen. **ellĕborum (hellĕbŏrum)** -i, n. *hellebore*, a plant supposed to be a remedy for madness ; expulit elleboro morbum bilemque meraco, Hor.

ēlŏco, 1. *to let, let on hire ;* fundum, Cic.

ēlŏcūtĭo -ōnis, f. (eloquor), *oratorical delivery, elocution* (= φράσις), Cic.

ēlŏgĭum -ĭi, n. 1, *a short maxim, apophthegm;* Solonis, Cic. ; 2, *an inscription on a gravestone, epitaph*, Cic. ; 3, *a clause in a will, a codicil*, Cic.

ēlŏquens -entis, p. adj. with compar. and superl. (from eloquor), *eloquent ;* omnium eloquentissimi Ti. et C. Sempronii, Cic.

ēlŏquentĭa -ae, f. (eloquens), *the art of speaking well, eloquence*, Cic.

ēlŏquĭum -ĭi, n. (eloquor), 1, *expression of thought, speech;* tulit eloquium insolitam facundia praeceps, Hor. ; 2, *eloquence ;* qui licet eloquio fidum quoque Nestora vincat, Ov.

ēlŏquor (ex-lŏquor), -lŏcūtus (-lŏquūtus) sum 3. dep., *to speak out, say out, express ;* id quod sentit, Cic. ; cogitata praeclare, Cic.

Ēlōrus (Hēlōrus) -i, m. (Ἔλωρος) and **Ēlōrum (Hēlōrum)** -i. n. (Ἔλωρον), *river on the east coast of Sicily and a town of the same name*. Adj., 1, **Ēlōrĭus (Hēl.)** -a -um, *of or belonging to Elorus ;* 2, **Ēlōrīni** -ōrum, m. *inhabitants of the town*.

Elpēnōr -ŏris, m. (Ἐλπήνωρ) *one of the companions of Ulysses, changed by Circe into a hog*.

ēlūcĕo -luxi, 2. (ex and luceo), *to beam forth, shine out, glitter*. **A.** Lit., splendidissimo candore inter flammas elucens circulus, Cic. **B.** Transf., quae (scintilla ingenii) jam tum elucebat in puero, Cic.

ēluctor, 1. dep. **I.** Intransit., *to struggle out, burst forth*. **A.** Lit., aqua eluctabitur omnis, Verg. **B.** Transf., velut eluctantia verba, Tac. **II.** Transit., *to struggle out of, surmount a difficulty*. **A.** Lit., quum tot ac tam validae manus eluctandae essent, Liv. ; nives, Tac. **B.** Transf., locorum difficultates, Tac.

ēlūcŭbro, 1. *to compose by lamplight ;* causae diligenter elaboratae et tanquam elucubratae, Cic. Dep. form, **ēlūcŭbror**, 1 ; epistolam, Cic.

ēlūdo -lūsi -lūsum, 3. (ex and ludo). **I.** Intransit., *to dash forth, play* (of the waves of the sea) ; ipsum autem mare sic terram appetens litoribus eludit, Cic. ; litus qua fluctus eluderet, Cic. **II.** Transit., 1, *to parry a blow ;* absol., quasi rudibus eius eludit oratio, Cic. ; 2, *to evade, try to escape ;* pugnam, Liv. ; 3, *to mock, ridicule*, Cic. ; aliquem omnibus contumeliis, Liv.

ēlūgĕo -luxi, 2. **I.** Intransit., *to mourn for any one during the prescribed period*, Liv. **II.** Transit., *to mourn for ;* patriam, ap. Cic.

ēlumbis -e (ex and lumbus), *weak in the loins ;* transf., of orators, *weak, feeble*, Tac.

ēlŭo -lŭi -lūtum, 3. *to wash out, wash clean, rinse, cleanse*. **A.** Lit., corpus, Ov. ; sanguinem, Cic. **B.** Transf., *to wash away, efface, remove, get rid of ;* maculas furtorum, Cic. ; crimen, Ov. ; amicitias remissione usus, *gradually loosen*, Cic.

ēlūtus -a -um, p. adj. with compar. (from eluo) *washed out, watery, insipid ;* irriguo nihil est elutius horto, Hor.

ēlŭvĭes -ēi, f. (eluo). **I.** Middle, *a washing away, inundation, flood ;* maris, Tac. ; eluvie mons est deductus in aequor, Ov. ; fig., illa labes atque eluvies civitatis, *impurity*, Cic. **II.** Pass., 1, *filth ;* siccare eluviem, Juv. ; 2, *a puddle, pond ;* in proxima eluvie pueros exponunt, Liv.

ēlŭvĭo -ōnis, f. (eluo), *an inundation*, Cic. ; plur. aquarum eluviones, Cic. ; eluviones et exustiones terrarum, Cic.

Ēlymāis -māĭdis, f. (Ἐλυμαΐς), *a Persian district to the west of the present province of Iran*. Adj., **Ēlymaeus** -a -um, *Elymaean*.

Ēlȳsium -ĭi, n. (Ἠλύσιον πεδίον), *Elysium, the abode of the blessed ;* hence adj., **Ēlȳsĭus** -a -um, *Elysian*, campi, Verg. Subst., **Ēlȳsĭi**, m. *the Elysian fields*, Mart.

em, interj., *ha ! indeed !* Cic.

ēmancĭpo (ēmancŭpo) 1. **I.** *to release or emancipate a son from the* patria potestas, Liv. ; **II. A.** *to transfer a son to the power of another ;* filium alicui in adoptionem. **B.** Transf., *to make over, give up, transfer ;* emancipatum esse alicui, Cic.

ēmāno (ex and mano). **A.** Lit., *to flow out*, Lucr. **B.** Transf., 1, *to arise, spring, emanate from ;* alii quoque alio ex fonte praeceptores dicendi emanaverunt, Cic. ; 2, *to spread abroad ;* a, mala quae a Lacedaemoniis profecta emanarunt latius, Cic. ; b, of speech, ne per nos his sermo tum emanet, Cic. ; consilia tua emanare, Liv. ; foll. by acc. and infin., Liv.

Ēmăthĭa -ae, f. (Ἠμαθία), *an old name for Macedonia*, Verg. ; *a district of Macedonia*, Liv. ; poet., *Thessaly*, Verg. ; hence adj., 1, **Ēmăthĭus** -a -um, *Emathian, Macedonian ;* dux, *Alexander*, Ov. ; 2, **Ēmăthĭs** -ĭdis, f. *Macedonian ;* Emathides, *the Muses*, Ov.

ēmātūresco -tūrŭi, 3. **A.** Lit., *to become ripe*, Plin. **B.** Transf., *to become mild, be softened ;* ira, Ov.

ĕmax -ācis (emo), *fond of buying*, Cic.

emblēma -ātis, n. (ἔμβλημα), 1, *inlaid or mosaic work*, ap. Cic. ; 2, *raised or relief ornaments*, Cic.

embŏlĭum -ĭi, n. (ἐμβόλιον), *a dramatic interlude*, Cic.

ēmendābĭlis -e (emendo), *that may be amended ;* error, Liv.

ēmendātē, adv. (emendatus), *correctly, faultlessly ;* pure et emendate loqui, Cic.

ēmendātĭo -ōnis, f. (emendo), *improvement, emendation, amendment ;* correctio philosophiae veteris et emendatio, Cic.

ēmendātor -ōris, m. (emendo), *an amender, corrector ;* quasi emendator sermonis usitati, Cic.; emendator nostrae civitatis, Cic.

ēmendātrix -īcis, f. (emendator), *she who corrects or amends ;* vitiorum emendatricem legem esse oportet, Cic. ; o praeclaram emendatricem vitae poeticam, Cic.

ēmendātus -a -um, p. adj. with compar. and superl. (from emendo), *free from mistakes, faultless, perfect ;* a, intellectually, locutio, Cic. ; carmina, Hor. ; b, morally, mores, Cic.

ēmendo, 1. (ex and mendum), *to free from errors, emend, correct, improve ;* a, intellectually, alicuius annales, Cic. ; b, morally, civitatem, Cic. ; conscius mihi sum corrigi me et emendari castigatione posse, Liv. ; consuetudinem vitiosam, Cic. ; res Italias legibus, Hor.

ēmentĭor -ītus, 4. dep., *to devise falsely, counterfeit, falsify, pretend ;* auspicia, Cic. ; falsa naufragia, Liv. ; with acc. and infin., eo me beneficio obstrictum esse ementior, Cic. ; absol., *to make false statements ;* in aliquem, Cic.

partic. perf. (pass.), auspicia ementita, Cic.; neut. plur. subst., ementita et falsa, Cic.

ēmĕrĕo -ŭi -ĭtum, 2. and **ēmĕrĕor** -ĭtus, 2. dep. **I.** a, *to deserve*, foll. by infin., Ov.; b, *to deserve well of a person;* aliquem, Ov. **II.** *to serve;* stipendia, Liv.; partic., emeritus, *a soldier that has served his time, a veteran*, Suet.; transf., *old, disused;* aratrum, Ov.; pass., annuae operae emerentur, Cic.; tempus emeritum, *ended*, Cic.

ēmergo -mersi, -mersum (ex and mergo), 3. **I.** Transit., *to cause to rise up;* emergere se or emergi, *to rise up, emerge.* **A.** Lit., serpens se emergit, Cic.; emersus e flumine, Cic. **B.** Transf., *to free oneself, to rise;* emergere se ex malis, Nep. **II.** Intransit., *to come forth, come up, emerge.* **A.** Lit., equus ex flumine emersit, Cic. **B.** Lit., **1,** *to extricate oneself, get clear, emerge;* emergere ex judicio peculatus, Cic.; ex paternis probris ac vitiis, Cic.; **2,** *to come to light, appear;* emergit rursum dolor, Cic.; ex quo magis emergit, quale sit decorum illud, Cic.

ēmĕrĭtus -a -um (partic. of emereo).

ēmētĭca -ae, f. (ἐμετική). *an emetic;* ap. Cic.

ēmētĭor -mensus sum, 4. **I.** *to measure out.* **A.** Lit., spatium oculis, Verg. **B.** Transf., a, *to pass over, traverse;* una nocte aliquantum iter, Liv.; partic. perf. pass., toto emenso spatio, Caes.; b, *to pass through a space of time;* tres principes, *live through the reigns of,* Tac.; partic. perf. pass., emensae in lucem noctes, Ov. **II.** *to measure out, bestow;* ego autem voluntatem tibi profecto emetiar, Cic.

ēmĕto (-messŭi) -messum, 3. *to reap, mow;* plus frumenti, Hor.

ēmĭco -mĭcŭi -mĭcātum, 1. *to spring out, leap forth, appear quickly, dart forth.* **I.** **A.** Lit., **1,** of lightning, flame, etc., flamma emicat ex oculis, Ov.; **2,** of water, blood, etc.; scaturigines tenues emicant, Liv. **B.** Transf., a, *to break out;* alicui pavor emicat, Tac.; b, *to shine forth, be distinguished;* inter quae verba forte si emicuit decorum, Hor. **II.** **1,** of weapons, missiles, etc., *to whiz forth;* telum excussum velut glans emicabat, Liv.; **2,** of persons, *to jump out;* in litus, Verg. **III.** *to rush up;* **1,** of things, in superos ignes, Ov.; **2,** of persons, *to jump up;* solo, Verg.

ēmĭgro, 1. *to remove from a place, wander forth, migrate, emigrate;* huc ex illa domo praetoria emigrabat, Cic.; domo, Caes.; transf., e vita, *to die,* Cic.

ēmĭnens -entis, p. adj. (from emineo). **A.** Lit., *prominent, projecting, lofty;* promontoria, Caes.; oculi, *standing out,* Cic.; genae leniter eminentes, Cic. **B.** Transf., *illustrious, distinguished, eminent;* oratores, Tac. Subst., **ēmĭnentes** -ium, m. *remarkable persons,* Tac.

ēmĭnentĭa -ae, f. (emineo), a, *protuberance, prominence;* nec habere ullam soliditatem nec eminentiam, Cic.; b, **ĭn** painting, *the lights of a picture,* Cic.

ēmĭnĕo -mĭnŭi, 2. (ex and mineo). **I.** Lit., **1,** *to project, stand out;* ex terra nihil eminet quod, etc., Cic.; eminentibus oculis, *with projecting eyes,* Cic.; jugum directum eminens in mare, Caes.; **2,** of the lights of a picture, *to stand out;* magis id, quod erit illuminatum, exstare atque eminere videatur, Cic. **II.** Transf., **1,** *to appear, become visible;* toto ex ore crudelitas eminebat, Cic.; eminente animo patrio inter publicae poenae ministerium, Liv.; **2,** *to be conspicuous, remarkable, eminent;* Demosthenes unus eminet inter omnes in omni genere dicendi, Cic.; tantum eminebat peregrina virtus, Liv.

ēmĭnus, adv. (e and manus, opp. comminus), **1,** milit. t. t., *at a distance, from a distance;*

eminus hastis aut comminus gladiis uti, Cic.; eminus pugnare, Caes.; **2,** *at a distance, from afar,* Ov.

ēmĭror, 1. dep., *to wonder at exceedingly, be astonished at;* aequora, Hor.

ēmissārĭum -ĭi, n. (emitto), *an outlet for water,* Cic.

ēmissārĭus -ĭi, m. (emitto), *a person sent out to gain intelligence, an emissary, a spy,* Cic.

ēmissĭo -ōnis, f. (emitto), *a sending forth;* **1,** of missiles, balistae lapidum et reliqua tormenta eo graviores emissiones habent, quo sunt contenta atque adducta vehementius; **2,** *letting loose;* anguis, serpentis, Cic.

ēmissus -ūs, m. (emitto), *sending forth,* Lucr.

ēmitto -mīsi -missum, 3. (ex and mitto). **I.** *to send forth, send out.* **A.** Gen., equitatus pabulandi causa emissus, Caes. **B.** Esp., **1,** milit. t.t., *to send out against an enemy;* cohortes ex statione et praesidio, Caes.; equites in hostem, Liv.; **2,** a, *to drive away;* aliquem ex domo, Cic.; b, *to hurl forth;* hastam in fines eorum, Liv.; **3,** *to send forth from oneself;* si nubium conflictu ardor expressus se emiserit, id esse fulmen, Cic.; varios sonitus linguae, Lucr.; **4,** of fluids, *to let forth;* aquam ex lacu Albano, Liv.; lacum, *to draw off,* Cic.; **5,** of a book, *to publish;* si quando aliquid dignum nostro nomine emisimus, Cic. **II.** *to let go, let loose.* **A.** Gen., **1,** lit., aliquem noctu per vallum, Caes.; manu arma, Caes.; **2,** transf., aliquem de manibus, *to let slip,* Cic.; emissa de manibus res est, Liv. **B.** Esp., **1,** in the circus, *to start, send away;* quibuscum tanquam e carceribus emissus sis, Cic.; **2,** a, *to let out of prison;* aliquem e or de carcere, Cic.; b, *to let go;* anguem, Cic.; aliquem ex obsidione, Liv.; aliquem sub jugum, *to send under the yoke,* Liv.; legal t. t., of slaves, aliquem manu, *to free,* Liv.; of a debtor, librā et aere liberatum emittit, Liv.

ĕmo, ēmi, emptum, 3. *to buy, purchase.* **A.** Lit., domum de aliquo, Cic.; aedes ab aliquo, Cic.; with abl. or genit. (with adjectives and pronouns), of price, emere grandi pecunia, Cic.; magno, *dear,* Cic.; parvo, *cheap,* Cic.; emere domum prope dimidio carius quam aestimabatur, Cic.; bene, *cheap,* Cic.; male, *dear,* Cic.; minoris, *cheaper,* Cic.; pluris, *dearer,* Cic.; bona de aliqua duobus millibus nummûm, Cic. Subst., **emptum** -i, n. *the contract of sale;* ex empto, Cic. **B.** Transf., *to bribe, buy;* judices, Cic.; emptum judicium, Cic.; empta dolore voluptas, Hor.

ēmŏdĕror, 1. dep., *to moderate;* dolorem verbis, Ov.

ēmŏdŭlor, 1. dep., *to sing, praise in verse;* Musam per undenos pedes, Ov.

ēmŏlīmentum = emolumentum (q.v.).

ēmollĭo -ĭvi, -ĭtum, 4. (ex and mollio), *to soften.* **A.** Lit., fundas et amenta, Liv. **B.** Transf., a, in a good sense, *to make mild, soften;* mores, Ov.; b, in a bad sense, *to make effeminate;* exercitum, Liv.

ēmŏlŭmentum -i, n. (emolior, *to work out),* **1,** *effort, labour, exertion,* Caes.; **2,** *the result of effort, gain, advantage;* emolumento esse, Cic.; emolumenta rerum, Liv.

ēmŏnĕo, 2. *to warn, admonish;* aliquem ut, etc., Cic.

ēmŏrĭor -mortŭus sum, -mori, dep., *to die.* **A.** Lit. Of persons, pro aliquo, Cic.; non miserabiliter, Cic.; per virtutem, *bravely,* Sall. **B.** Transf., *to perish;* laus emori non potest, Cic.

ēmŏvĕo -mōvi -mōtum, 2. **I.** *to move out,*

move away, remove. **A.** Lit., multitudinem e foro, Liv.; aliquos senatu, Liv. **B.** Transf., curas dictis, Verg. **II.** *to shake, shatter;* muros fundamentaque, Verg.

Empĕdŏcles -is, m. (Ἐμπεδοκλῆς), *a poet and philosopher of Agrigentum;* hence adj., **Empĕdŏclēus** -a -um, *Empedoclean;* sanguis (acc. to the doctrines of Empedocles), *the soul,* Cic. Subst., **Empĕdŏclēa** -ōrum, n. *the doctrines of Empedocles,* Cic.

empīrĭcus -i, m. (ἐμπειρικός), *an unscientific physician, empiric,* Cic.

Empŏrĭae -ārum, f. (Ἐμπορίαι), *town in Hispania Tarraconensis, colony of the Phocaeans,* now *Ampurias.*

empŏrĭum -ĭi. n. (ἐμπόριον), *a place of trade, mart, emporium;* celebre et frequens emporium, Liv.

emptĭo -ōnis, f. (emo). **A.** *a buying, purchasing;* ista falsa et simulata emptio, Cic. **B.** Meton., *a purchase;* prorsus existis emptionibus nullam desidero, Cic.

emptĭto, 1. (freq. of emo), *to buy up, to buy,* ap. Tac.

emptor -ōris, m. (emo), *a buyer, purchaser;* emptor fundi, Cic.; emptores bonorum, Cic.; transf., dedecorum pretiosus emptor, Hor.

ēmulgĕo -mulsum, 2. *to milk out;* poet., transf., *to drain out, to exhaust;* paludem, Cat.

ēmungo -munxi -munctum, 3. (e and *mungo). **A.** Lit., *to blow the nose,* Juv. **B.** Transf., a, homo emunctae navis, *with a keen scent for other persons' faults,* Hor.; b, *to cheat, defraud, swindle;* aliquem, Hor.

ēmūnĭo -mūnīvi or -mūnĭi -mūnītum, 4. 1, *to fortify, strengthen, make safe;* locum, murum, Liv.; 2, *to make ready, prepare, make accessible;* silvas ac paludes, Tac.

ēn, interj., 1, demonstr. with nom. or acc., *lo! behold! see!* en ego vester Ascanius, Verg.; en quatuor aras, Verg.; en causa, Cic.; absol., en, cui tu liberos committas, Cic.; with aspice, en aspice, Ov.; 2, interrog., en, quid ago? Verg.; with unquam, en unquam futurum, etc., Liv.

ēnarrābĭlis -e (enarro), *that can be narrated or told,* Verg.

ēnarro, 1. *to tell, narrate;* enarrare alicui somnium, Cic.

ēnascor -nātus sum, 3. dep., *to grow out of, spring forth, arise from;* lauream in puppi navis longae enatam, Liv.

ēnăto, 1. *to swim from, escape by swimming.* **A.** Lit., si fractis enatat exspes navibus, Hor. **B.** Transf., *to extricate oneself from a difficulty;* reliqui habere se videntur angustius; enatant tamen, Cic.

ēnāvātus -a -um, *performed, finished,* Tac.

ēnāvĭgo, 1. **I.** Intransit., *to sail away,* fig., e quibus tanquam e scrupulosis cotibus enavigavit oratio, Cic. **II.** Transit., *to sail over, sail through;* undam, Hor.

Encĕlădus -i, m. (Ἐγκέλαδος), *one of the giants, slain by the lightning of Jupiter, and buried beneath Aetna.*

endo, archaic = in.

endrŏmis -idis, f. (ἐνδρομίς), *a coarse woollen cloak worn after exercise in the palaestra,* Juv.

Endўmĭōn -ōnis, m. (Ἐνδυμίων), *son of Aëthlius or of Zeus and Calyce, father of Aetolus, beloved by Selene and taken to Mount Latmos in Caria, and there lulled to perpetual sleep;* appell., *a beautiful youth,* Juv.

ēnĕco -nˣcŭi -nectum, 1. *to torment, torture;* siti enectus Tantalus, Cic.; fame, frigore, illuvie,

squalore enecti, Liv.; provinciam enectam tradere, *exhausted,* Cic.

ēnervātus -a -um, p. adj. (enervo), *enervated, powerless, effeminate;* a, of persons. Cic.; b, of things, mollis et enervata oratio, Cic.; enervata muliebrisque sententia, Cic.

ēnervis -e (ex and nervus), *nerveless, powerless, weak;* orator, Tac.

ēnervo, 1. (enervis), *to render weak, powerless, effeminate, to enervate;* of age, aliquem, Cic.; of sleep, wine, etc., Liv.; bellum, Cic.; ut enervetur oratio compositione verborum, Cic.

Engyŏn -i, n. (Ἔγγυον), *a town in Sicily;* hence, **Engŭinus** -a -um, *of or belonging to Engyon.*

ēnĭco = eneco (q.v.).

ĕnim, conj. (from e and nam), *for;* 1, to explain a previous statement or word, de corpusculorum (ita enim appellat atomos) concursione fortuita, Cic.; often where a sentence is to be understood, tum Socrates, non enim paruisti mihi revocanti, *that is not to be wondered at for,* etc., Cic.; 2, to strengthen a previous statement, *truly, certainly;* in his est enim aliqua securitas, Cic.; with other conj., at enim, sed enim, *but then,* Cic. (enim generally the second or third word in its clause).

ĕnimvēro, 1, *to be sure, certainly,* Cic.; 2, *but indeed;* stronger than at (to introduce an objection), Cic.

Enĭpeus -pĕi and -pĕos, m. (Ἐνιπεύς), 1, *a river in Thessaliotis, flowing into the Apidanus;* 2, *a river in Pieria,* Liv.

ēnīsus, v. enixus and enitor.

ēnĭtĕo -ŭi, 2. *to shine out, shine forth, to glitter.* **A.** Lit., enitet campus, Verg. **B.** Transf., *to be conspicuous;* quo in bello virtus enituit egregia M. Catonis, Cic.

ēnĭtesco -tŭi, 3. (inchoat. of eniteo), *to gleam, shine forth.* **A.** Lit., enitescit pulchrior multo, Hor. **B.** Transf., bellum novum exoptabat, ubi virtus enitescere posset, Sall.

ēnītor -nīsus or -nixus, 3. dep. **I.** Intransit., **A.** *to work one's way up, to struggle up, ascend;* per adversos fluctus ingenti labore remigum, Liv.; in altiora, Tac. **B.** *to strive, struggle, make an effort;* with ut and the subj., Cic.; eniti et contendere, eniti et efficere ut, etc., Cic.; with ne and the subj., Sall.; pugnare et eniti ne, Cic.; with neut. acc., quod quidem certe enitar, Cic.; quid eniti et quid efficere possim, Cic.; with infin., Sall.; absol., in aliqua re, Cic.; ad dicendum, Cic. **II.** Transit., 1, *to bring forth, bear;* partus plures, Liv.; 2, *to climb;* aggerem, Tac.

ēnixē, adv. with compar. and superl.(enixus), *eagerly, strenuously, zealously;* enixe aliquem juvare, Caes.; enixe operam dare ut, etc., Liv.; enixe obstare, Liv.

ēnixus (enīsus) -a -um, p. adj. (enitor), *strenuous, eager, zealous;* enixo studio, Liv.

Enna = Henna (q.v.).

Ennĭus -ii, m. *the most celebrated of the ante-Augustan poets, born at Rudiae in Calabria,* B.C. 239, *died* 169, *the creator of Roman epic poetry.*

Ennŏsĭgaeus -i, m. (Ἐννοσίγαιος), *the Earthshaker, surname of Neptune,* Juv.

ēno, 1. **A.** Lit., *to swim out;* 1, e concha, Cic.; 2, *to escape by swimming;* in terram, Liv. **B.** Transf., *to fly away;* insuetum per iter gelidas enavit ad Arctos, Verg.

ēnōdātē, adv. (enodatus), *clearly, plainly;* narrare, Cic.

ēnōdātĭo -ōnis, f. (enodo, *an untying), explanation, exposition;* cognitio enodationis in

7

ĭigens, Cic.; explicatio fabularum et enodatio nominum, Cic.

ēnōdātus -a -um, p. adj. (from enodo), *freed from knots, untied*, hence, *made clear, explained;* praecepta enodata diligenter, Cic.

ēnōdis -e (ex and nodus), *without knots;* truncus, Verg.; abies, Ov.

ēnōdo, 1. *to take out the knots;* transf., *to make clear, explain, expound;* nomina, Cic.

ēnormis -e (ex and norma), **1,** *irregular, unusual;* vici, Tac.; **2,** *very large, immense, enormous;* hasta, gladius, Tac.

ēnōtesco -nōtŭi, 3. *to become known, be made public;* quod ubi enotuit, Tac.

ensĭfer -fĕra -fĕrum (ensis and fero), *sword-bearing;* Orion, Ov.

ensis -is, m. *a sword*, Liv., Verg.

Entella -ae, f. (Ἔντελλα), *a town in the interior of Sicily*, now *Entella*. **Entellīnus** -a -um, *of or belonging to Entella*.

enthȳmēma -ătis, n. (ἐνθύμημα), *a syllogism in which one of the three terms is unexpressed*, Cic.

ēnūbo -nupsi -nuptum, 3. *to marry out of one's rank;* e patribus, Liv.; *from one town to another*, Liv.

ēnuclĕātē, adv. (enucleatus), *clearly, plainly, concisely* (opp. ornate), Cic.

ēnuclĕātus -a -um, p. adj. (from enucleo), *of discourse, clear, plain, unadorned;* genus dicendi, Cic.

ēnuclĕo, 1. (ex and nucleus), *to take out the kernel;* transf., acu quaedam enucleata argumenta, Cic.; eblandita illa, non enucleata esse suffragia, *given from conviction, free from corrupt motives*, Cic.; haec nunc enucleare non ita necesse est, *explain in detail*, Cic.

ēnŭmĕrātĭo -ōnis, f. (enumero), **1,** *a counting up, enumeration;* singulorum argumentorum, Cic.; **2,** in rhetoric, *recapitulation*, Cic.

ēnŭmĕro, 1. **1,** *to reckon, count up, enumerate;* pretium, *to compute, pay*, Cic.; **2,** *to count up, enumerate in discourse, recapitulate;* multitudinem beneficiorum, Cic.

ēnuntĭātĭo -ōnis, f. (enuntio), *enunciation, proposition*, Cic.

ēnuntĭātum -i, n. (enuntio), *a proposition*, Cic.

ēnuntĭo, 1. **1,** *to tell, divulge, disclose;* consilia adversariis, Cic.; enuntiare mysteria, Cic.; silenda, Liv.; rem Helvetiis per indicium, Caes.; with rel. sent., plane quid sentiam enuntiabo apud homines familiarissimos, Cic.; **2,** *to declare, announce, express in words;* **a,** aliquid verbis, Cic.; **b,** logic. t.t., *to state a proposition, to predicate*, Cic.

ēnuptĭo -ōnis, f. (enubo), *marriage out of one's own condition;* gentis, *out of one's gens*, Liv.

ēnūtrĭo -īvi -ītum, 4. *to nourish, rear, bring up;* puerum Ideis sub antris, Ov.

1. ĕo, īvi and ĭi, ĭtum, 4. (connected with Gr. εἶμι). **I.** *to go.* **A.** Of living beings, **1,** gen., domum, Plaut.; ad forum, Plaut.; subsidio suis, Caes.; novas vias, *to make a journey in unknown lands*, Prop.; pedibus, *to go by land*, Liv.; maximis itineribus, *to make forced marches*, Liv.; cubitum, *to go to bed*, Cic.; equis, *to ride*, Liv.; puppibus, *to make a voyage*, Ov.; **2,** esp., **a,** ad arma, ap. Cic., and ad saga, Cic., *to fly to arms, prepare for war;* **b,** in sententiam (with or without pedibus), *to support a motion in the senate*, Cic.; in alia omnia, *to oppose a motion, vote in the negative*, Cic.; **c,** ire in aliquem, *to attack*, Liv.; **d,** in poenas, *to punish*, Ov.; in

scelus, *to commit a fault*, Ov.; **ire in duplum**, *to give a double penalty*, Cic.; ierat in causam praeceps, Liv.; **e,** ire per aliquid, *to go over;* ire per laudes tuorum, Ov. **B.** of things, **a,** clamor it ad aethera, Verg.; pugna it ad pedes, *they fight afoot*, Liv.; **b,** *to move;* nec pes ire potest, Ov.; **c,** of missiles, *to go, pierce;* iit hasta, Verg.; **d,** of liquids, *to flow;* it naribus ater sanguis, Verg. **II.** 1, *to pass away;* eunt anni, Ov.; sic eat quaecumque Romana lugebit hostem, Liv.; **2,** *to go, to happen;* incipit res melius ire, Cic.; **3,** *to last;* si non tanta quies iret, Verg.; **4,** ire in aliquid, *to be changed to;* sanguis it in sucos, Ov. (perf. it, Verg. Aen. 9, 418; Ov. Met. 8, 349).

2. ĕō, adv. **I.** Old dat. of is, **a,** *thither, to that place;* pervenire, Cic.; **b,** *so far, to such a pitch;* eo rem adducam ut, etc., Cic.; with genit., eo consuetudinis adducta res est, Liv.; eo usque, *to that point*, Cic. **II.** Abl., **a,** *on that account;* eo quod, Cic.; eo quia, Cic.; eo ut, etc., Cic.; non eo, dico, quo, Cic.; **b,** with comparatives, eo magis, *the more*, Cic.; **c,** *in that place;* eo loci, *at that very place*, Cic.

ĕōdem, adv. **I.** Old dat. of idem, *to the same place, just so far;* eodem mittere, Caes.; transf., eodem pertinere, Cic. **II.** Abl., res est eodem loci ubi reliquisti, *in the same condition*, Cic.

ĕopse = eo ipso.

Ēŏs (ἠώς) and **Ēōs** (Ἔως) (occurs only in nom.), f. *the red of the morning, dawn;* hence adj., **Ēŏus** and **Ēōus** -a -um, *belonging to the morning or belonging to the East, eastern.* Subst., **Ēŏus** -i, m. **a,** *the morning star*, and meton., *the East or a dweller in the East*, Ov.; **b,** *one of the horses of the sun*, Ov.

Ĕpămĭnōndas -ae, m. (Ἐπαμεινώνδας), *a celebrated general of the Thebans, killed in the hour of victory at Mantinea.*

ĕpastus -a -um (pascor), *eaten up;* escae, Ov.

Ĕpĕŏs and **-ĕus** (**Ĕpīus**) -i, m. (Ἐπειός), *son of Panopeus, builder of the Trojan horse.*

ĕphēbus -i, m. (ἔφηβος), *a youth from his sixteenth to his twentieth year* (generally of Greeks), Cic.

ĕphēmĕris -ĭdis, f. (ἐφημερίς), *a journal, diary*, Cic.

Ĕphĕsus -i, m. (Ἔφεσος), *one of the twelve Ionic towns in Asia Minor, famous for its temple of Diana and school of rhetoric.* Hence, **Ĕphĕsĭus** -a -um, *Ephesian.*

ĕphippĭātus -a -um (ephippium), *provided with an ephippium.*

ĕphippĭum -i, n. (ἐφίππιον), *a horse-cloth, housing, saddle*, Cic.; prov., optat ephippia bos piger, optat arare caballus, *no one is content with his condition*, Hor.

1. ĕphŏrus -i, m. (ἔφορος), *the ephor, a Spartan magistrate*, Cic.

2. Ĕphŏrus -i, m. (Ἔφορος), *a Greek historian of Cyme in Asia Minor, flourishing about 340 B.C.*

Ĕphȳra -ae, and **Ĕphȳrē** -ēs, (Ἐφύρα), f. **I.** *a sea-nymph*, Verg. **II.** *the ancient name of Corinth;* hence, **Ĕphȳrēĭus** -a -um, *Corinthian*, Verg.

Ĕpĭcharmus -i, m. (Ἐπίχαρμος), *a philosopher and poet of Cos, and afterwards of Syracuse, disciple of Pythagoras.*

Ĕpĭclēros -i, f. (Ἐπίκληρος), *"the Heiress," name of a comedy of Menander.*

ĕpĭcōpus -a -um (ἐπίκωπος), *provided with oars;* phaselus, Cic.

Ĕpĭcūrus -i, m. ('Επίκουρος), *an Athenian philosopher, founder of the Epicurean school, which held that pleasure was the highest good.* Hence adj., **Ĕpĭcūrēus** (-ius) -a -um, *Epicurean.* Subst., **Ĕpĭcūrēi** -ōrum, m. *the disciples of Epicurus,* Cic.

ĕpĭcus -a -um (ἐπικός), *epic;* poeta, Cic.; poema, Cic.

Ĕpĭdaphna -ae, f., and **Ĕpĭdaphnēs**, *a place near Antioch in Syria.*

Ĕpĭdauros -i, f. ('Επίδαυρος), 1, *a town in Dalmatia;* 2, *a town in Laconia;* 3, *a town in Argolis, where Aesculapius was worshipped in the form of a serpent.* Adj. **Ĕpĭdaurĭus** -a -um, *Epidaurian.* Subst., **Ĕpĭdaurĭus** -ĭi, m. *Aesculapius,* Ov.

Ĕpĭgŏni -ōrum, m. ('Επιγόνοι), *the after-born, sons of the Seven against Thebes, who renewed the war of their fathers; name of a tragedy of Aeschylus and of one of Accius.*

ĕpĭgramma -ătis, n. (ἐπίγραμμα), 1, *an inscription on the base of a statue,* Cic.; 2, *an epigram,* Cic.

ĕpĭlŏgus -i, m. (ἐπίλογος), *a conclusion, peroration, epilogue,* Cic.

Ĕpĭmĕnĭdes -is, m. ('Επιμενίδης), *a Cretan, a poet contemporary with Solon.*

Ĕpĭmētheus -ĕi and -ĕos, m. ('Επιμηθεύς), *father of Pyrrha, son of Iapetus and brother of Prometheus.* Hence **Ĕpĭmēthis** -thĭdis, f. ('Επιμηθίς), *daughter of Epimetheus*—i.e., *Pyrrha,* Ov.

ĕpĭrēdĭum -ĭi, n. (ἐπί and reda or raeda), *the strap by which a horse was fastened to a vehicle, trace,* Juv.

Ēpīrus -i, f. ("Ηπειρος), *a country of Greece, between Macedonia, Thessaly, and the Ionian Sea, part of the present Albania.* Hence, 1, **Ēpīrensis** -e, *of Epirus;* 2, **Ēpīrōtes** -ae, m. ('Ηπειρώτης), *an Epirote;* 3, **Ēpīrōtĭcus** -a -um, *of Epirus.*

ĕpistŏla -ae, f. (ἐπιστολή), *a written communication, letter, epistle;* epistola ab aliquo, Cic.; ad aliquem, Cic.; epistolam dare, *to send off* or *to deliver,* Cic.; epistola Graecis litteris conscripta, Caes.; epistolam inscribere alicui, Cic.

ĕpistŏlĭum -ĭi, n. (ἐπιστόλιον), *a little letter, note,* Cat.

ĕpĭtăphĭus -ĭi, m. (ἐπιτάφιος), *a funeral oration,* Cic.

ĕpĭtŏma -ae, and **ĕpĭtŏmē** -ēs, f. (ἐπιτομή), *an abridgment, epitome,* Cic.

ĕpŏdes -um, m. *a kind of salt-water fish,* Ov.

Ĕpŏna -ae, f. (epus = equus), *the protecting goddess of horses, asses,* etc., Juv.

ĕpops -ōpis, m. (ἔποψ), *the hoopoe,* Verg.

Ĕpŏrĕdĭa -ae, f. *a Roman colony in Gallia Transpadana,* now *Yvrea.*

ĕpos, indecl. n. (ἔπος), *an epic poem, epos,* Hor.

ĕpōto -pōtāvi -pōtus and -pōtātūrus 1. (ex and poto), a, *to drink up, drink out* (in class. Lat. only in partic. perf.); poculo epoto, Cic.; epoto medicamento, Liv.; b, poet., *to suck up, swallow up;* terreno Lycus est epotus hiatu, Ov.

ĕpŭlae -ārum, f. *food, dishes.* **I.** Gen., mensae conquisitissimis epulis exstruebantur, Cic. **II.** Esp., *banquet, feast;* quotidianae epulae, Cic.; funestas epulas fratri comparare, Cic.; ad epulas regis assistere, Cic.; alicui epulas dare, Tac.; fig. (pars animi) saturata bonarum cogitationum epulis, Cic.

ĕpŭlāris -e (epulae), *relating* or *belonging to a banquet;* accubitio amicorum, Cic.; sacrificium, Cic.

ĕpŭlātĭo -ōnis, f. (epulor), *a feasting, revelling,* Cic.

ĕpŭlo -ōnis, m. (epulum), 1, *a reveller, feaster,* Cic.; 2, Tresviri (and subsequently) Septemviri epulones, *a college of priests who had charge of the sacrificial feasts,* Cic.; so simply epulones, Cic.

ĕpŭlor, 1. dep. (epulae), *to feast, eat.* **I.** Intransit., unā, *together,* Cic.; cum aliquo, Cic.; modice, Cic.; Saliarem in modum, *splendidly,* Cic.; with abl., dapibus opimis, Verg. **II.** Transit., aliquem epulandum ponere mensis, *to place on the table to be eaten,* Verg.

ĕpŭlum -i, n. *a solemn* or *public banquet, feast, entertainment;* epuli dominus, Cic.; epulum populi Romani, Cic.; alicui epulum dare nomine alicuius, Cic.

ĕqua -ae, f. *a mare,* Cic. (dat. and abl. plur. generally equis).

ĕques -ĭtis, c. (equus). **I.** Gen., *a horseman, rider;* illum equitem sex dierum spatio transcurrisse longitudinem Italiae, Liv. **II.** Esp., **A.** *a horse-soldier,* Caes. (opp. pedes), and used collectively, *cavalry,* Liv. **B.** equites, *the knights, a distinct order in the Roman commonwealth, between the senate and the plebs,* Cic.

ĕquester -stris -stre (equus). **I.** 1, *relating to horsemen and horsemanship, equestrian;* statuae, Cic.; 2, *relating to horse soldiers and cavalry;* proelium, Caes.; pugna, Cic. **II.** *relating to the knights;* ordo, Cic.; locus, Cic.; census, Cic. Subst., **ĕquester** -stris, m. *a knight,* Tac.

ĕquĭdem (strengthened form of quidem by addition of demonstrative prefix e-, cf. enim and nam), *a demonstrative particle, generally used with the first person,* 1, *indeed, truly;* nihil, inquit, equidem novi, Cic.; equidem ego, Cic.; certe equidem, Verg.; 2, *in a concessive sense, of course, certainly;* with sed, verum, sed tamen, Cic.

ĕquīnus -a -um (equus), *relating to horses, equine;* seta, Cic.; nervus, Verg.

ĕquĭrĭa -um or -ōrum, n. (equus), *horse-races in honour of Mars, which took place at Rome, in the Campus Martius, every 27th of February and 14th of March,* Ov.

ĕquĭtātus -ūs, m. (equito), 1, *cavalry* (opp. peditatus), Cic.; 2, *the equestrian order,* Cic.

ĕquĭto, 1. (eques). **A.** Lit., *to ride on horseback;* in equuleis, Cic. **B.** Transf., of winds, *to rush;* Eurus per Siculas equitavit undas, Hor.

ĕquŭlĕus -i, m. (dim. of equus). **A.** *a young horse, colt,* Cic. **B.** *a wooden rack in the shape of a horse,* Cic.

ĕquŭlus -i, m. (dim. of equus), *a colt,* Cic.

ĕquus -i, m. (ἵππος), *a horse.* **I. A.** Lit., equorum domitores, Cic.; equus bellator, *a war-horse,* Verg.; equus publicus, *given by the state,* Liv.; equum conscendere, Cic.; in equum ascendere (opp. ex equo descendere), Cic.; in equum insilire, Liv.; sedere in equo, Cic.; vehi in equo, Cic.; equis insignibus et aurato curru reportari, *to ride in triumph,* Cic.; merere equo, *to serve in the cavalry,* Caes.; ad equum rescribere, *to make some one a knight,* Caes.; equus Trojanus, *the Trojan horse,* Verg.; fig., *of a secret conspiracy,* Cic. **B.** Meton., plur., equi; 1, *a chariot,* Verg.; 2, *cavalry;* equi virique, Liv.; so prov., equis viris or viris equisque; *with all one's might,* Cic. **II.** Transf., *of things like a horse.* **A.** equus bipes, *the sea-horse,* Verg. **B.** *the constellation Pegasus,* Cic. poet. (genit. plur., equûm, Verg.)

Equus Tŭtĭcus -i, m. *a small town in the country of the Hirpini in Lower Italy.*

ērādo -rāsi -rāsum, 3. *to scratch out, to strike off.* **A.** Lit., aliquem albo senatorio, *from the senatorial list,* Tac. **B.** Transf., *to destroy, eradicate;* elementa cupidinis pravi, Hor.

Ērăna -ae, f. (Ἔρανα), *capital of the Eleutherocilices on Mount Amanus.*

Ērāsīnus -i, m. (Ἐρασῖνος), *river in Argolis,* now *Kephalari.*

Ērātō -ūs, f. (Ἐρατώ), *the muse of amorous poetry,* Ov.; appell., *muse,* Verg.

Erătosthĕnēs -is, m. (Ἐρατοσθένης), *a Greek philosopher and poet.*

ercisco, erctum = hercisco, herctum (q.v.).

Erĕbus -i, m. (Ἔρεβος), **1,** *a god of the lower world, son of Chaos and brother of Nox,* Cic.; **2,** *the lower world,* Verg. Adj., **Erĕbēus** -a -um, *belonging to the lower world.*

Erechtheus -ĕi, m. (Ἐρεχθεύς), *a mythical king of Athens, father of Orithyia and Procris;* hence, **1,** adj., **Erechthēus** -a -um, *m. Athenian,* Ov.; **2, Ěrecthĭdae** -arum, m. *the Athenians,* Ov.; **3, Ěrechthis** -ĭdis, f. *Orithyia,* Ov.; *Procris,* Ov.

ērectus -a -um, p. adj. with compar. (from erigo), *set up.* **I.** Lit., *upright, erect;* status, Cic. **II.** Transf., **A.** Gen., *high, elevated;* a, in a good sense, celsus et erectus, Cic.; b, in a bad sense, *proud;* erectus et celsus, Cic. **B.** Esp., a, *anxious, intent, with minds on the stretch;* judices, Cic.; quum civitas in foro exspectatione erecta staret, *on the tiptoe of expectation,* Liv.; b, *resolute, lively, cheerful;* alacri animo et erecto, Cic.

ērēpo -repsi -reptum, **1,** *to creep through;* agrum, Juv.; **2,** *to climb;* montes quos nunquam erepsemus (= erepsissemus), Hor.

ēreptĭo -ōnis, f. (eripio), *a taking by force, seizure,* Cic.

ēreptor -ōris, m. (eripio), *one who takes away by force, a robber;* bonorum, Cic.; libertatis, Cic.

Ěrētrĭa -ae, f. (Ἐρετρία). **I.** *a town near Pharsalus in Phthiotis.* **II.** *a town in the island of Euboea, native town of the philosopher Menedemus, founder of the Eretrian school of philosophy.* Adj., **Ěrētrĭcus** -a -um; subst., **Ěrētrĭci** -ōrum, m. *the philosophers of the Eretrian school,* Cic.; so **Ěrētrĭăci** -ōrum, m. Cic.; b, **Ěrētrĭensis** -e, *Eretrian.*

Ěrētum -i, n. (Ἤρητον), *an old Sabine town on the Tiber,* now *Cretona.* Adj., **Ěrētinus** -a -um, *Eretine.*

ergā, prep. with acc. (root ERG, whence ἔργω), *towards;* **1,** *in relation to;* ea prima Tiberio erga pecuniam alienam diligentia fuit, Tac.; **2,** *in relation to, towards* (of one's feelings or attitude towards a person or thing); a, in a good sense, erga nos amice et benevole collegisti, Cic.; amor erga te suus, Cic.; benevolentia erga aliquem, Cic.; b, in a bad sense, odium erga aliquem, Nep.; invidia erga aliquem, Tac.

ergastŭlum -i, n. *a house of correction for slaves;* ille ex compedibus atque ergastulo, Cic.; aliquem in ergastulum dare or ducere, Liv.; apud aliquem in ergastulo esse, Cic.; ergastula solvere, Caes.

ergō, adv. (ἔργω). **I.** With a genit. preceding it, *on account of;* victoriae, non valetudinis ergo, Liv. **II.** Absol., *consequently, therefore, accordingly, then.* **A.** Gen., Cic.; itaque ergo, Liv. **B.** Esp., a, of logical consequences, *therefore;* ergo etiam, Cic.; b, with questions,

then; quid ergo? *why then?* Cic.; c, with imperatives, *then, now,* Cic.; d, to resume something that had been dropped, *well then, as I was saying,* Cic. (sometimes ergō in meaning No. II.).

Erichthō -ūs, f. (Ἐριχθώ), *a Thessalian witch consulted by Pompey;* transf., *a witch,* Ov.

Erichthŏnĭus -ĭi, m. (Ἐριχθόνιος), **1,** *a mythical king of Athens, the first to yoke four horses in a chariot;* adj., **Erichthŏnĭus** -a -um, *Athenian;* **2,** *a mythical king of Troy, son of Dardanus, father of Tros;* hence, **Erichthŏnĭus** -a -um, *Trojan.*

ērĭcĭus -ĭi, m. (*a hedgehog*); milit. t. t., *a beam thickly studded with iron spikes, chevaux-de-frise,* Caes.

Erĭdānus -i, m. (Ἠριδανός), **1,** myth. and poet. *name of the river Padus;* **2,** *a constellation,* Cic. poet.

ērĭgo -rexi -rectum, 3. (ex and rego), *to set up, place upright, lift up, erect.* **I.** Lit., **A.** Gen., scalas ad moenia, Liv.; malum, *a mast,* Cic.; oculos, *to raise,* Cic.; aures, *to prick up the ears,* Cic. **B.** Esp., **1,** *to raise in height;* a, of places, *to make higher;* donec erecta in arcem via est, Liv.; so middle, *to rise;* insula Sicanium juxta latus erigitur, Verg.; b, *to raise, erect a building,* etc.; turrem, Caes.; **2,** milit. t. t., *to march a body of soldiers up a height;* agmen in adversum clivum, Liv.; aciem in collem, Liv. **II.** Transf., **A.** Gen., *to arouse, excite;* animum ad audiendum, Cic.; auditor erigatur, *be attentive,* Cic. **B.** Esp., *to raise up, encourage, cheer;* aliquem, Cic.; aliquem ad spem belli, Tac.; animum, Cic.; se erigere ad *to encourage oneself, be encouraged;* erigere se in spem legis, Liv.; so pass., erigimur, Hor.

Erĭgŏnē -ēs, f. (Ἠριγόνη), *the daughter of Icarus, transformed into the constellation Virgo;* hence adj., **Erĭgŏnēĭus** -a -um, *belonging to Erigone;* canis, *the dog of Icarus, Maera, changed into the constellation Canicula.*

Erĭgŏnus -i, m. (Ἐρίγων), *a tributary of the Axius in Macedonia,* now *Tzerna.*

Erillus (Hērillus) -i, m. (Ἤριλλος), *a Stoic philosopher of Carthage.* **Erillĭi** -ōrum, m. *the disciples of Erillus.*

Erinnys (Erīnys)-ўos, f. (Ἐριννύς). **I.** one of the Furies; plur., Erinnyes, the Furies. **II.** Transf., **A.** *scourge, curse;* patriae communis Erinys, Verg. **B.** *fury, madness;* quo tristis Erinys, quo fremitus vocat, Verg.

Erĭphŷla -ae, f. and **Erĭphŷlē** -ēs, f. (Ἐριφύλη), *daughter of Talaus and Lysimache, wife of Amphiaraus, whom she betrayed to Polynices for a golden necklace, for which she was slain by her son Alcmaeon.*

ērĭpĭo -rĭpŭi -reptum, 3. (ex and rapio), *to snatch away, tear out, pluck out, take away;* constr. with ex, ab, de with the abl. or the abl. alone, or with the dat.(of the person). **I.** Gen., ensem vaginā, Verg.; aliquem ex equo, Liv. **II.** Esp., **A.** In a bad sense, *to tear away, snatch away by violence;* aliquem ex manibus populi Romani, Cic.; hereditatem ab aliquo, Cic.; aurum Gallis, Liv.; Scipio quamquam est subito ereptus, *snatched away by death,* Cic.; alicui vitam, Sall.; omnem usum navium, Caes. **B.** In a good sense, *to free, tear away;* aliquem e manibus hostium, *to rescue,* Caes.; filium a morte, Cic.; se ab illa miseria, Cic.; aliquem ex servitute, Sall.; alicui timorem, Cic.; eripe te morae, *away with delay,* Hor.; eripe fugam, *snatch the opportunity of flight,* Verg.

ērōdo -rōsi -rōsum, 3. (ex and rodo), *to gnaw away, gnaw into, eat into;* vites, Cic.

ĕrŏgātĭo -ōnis, f. (erogo), *payment, expenditure ;* pecuniae, Cic.

ĕrŏgo, 1. (ex and rogo), *to pay from the public treasury ;* pecuniam ex aerario, Cic. ; pecuniam in classem, Cic.

errābundus -a -um (1. erro), *wandering ;* of persons, nunc errabundi domos suos pervagarentur, Liv. ; of animals, etc., vestigia bovis, Verg. ; odor, Lucr.

errātĭcus -a -um (1. erro), *wandering, erratic ;* Delos, Ov. ; vitis serpens multiplici lapsu et erratico, Cic.

errātĭo -ōnis, f. (1. erro), *a wandering, straying ;* nulla in caelo erratio, Cic. ; eum (caeli motum) ab omni erratione liberavit, Cic.

errātum -i, n. (1. erro), *a fault, error ;* 1, technically, erratum fabrile, Cic. ; erratum meum, tuum, etc., *mistake in reckoning,* Cic. ; 2, morally, errata aetatis meae, *of my youth,* Cic.

errātus -ūs, m. (1. erro), *wandering about, straying ;* longis erratibus actus, Ov.

1. **erro,** 1. **I.** *to wander, stray, rove.* **A.** Lit., 1, intransit., quum vagus et exsul erraret, Cic. ; of inanimate objects, stellae errantes, Cic. ; 2, transit., terrae erratae, *wandered over,* Verg. ; litora errata, Verg. **B.** Transf., ne vagari et errare cogatur oratio, Cic. ; ne tuus erret honos, Ov. ; sententia errans et vaga, *uncertain,* Cic. **II.** *to wander from the right path, lose one's way.* **A.** Lit., errare viā, Verg. **B.** Transf., *to err, be in error, be mistaken ;* vehementer, valde, Cic. ; si erratur in nomine, Cic. ; cui, errato, nulla venia, *when a mistake is made,* Cic.

2. **erro** -ōnis, m. (1. erro), *a wanderer, rover, vagabond ;* esp. of slaves, Hor.; of unfaithful lovers, Ov.

error -ōris, m. (1. erro), *a wandering about.* **I.** Gen., **A.** Lit., error ac dissipatio civium, Cic. **B.** Transf., *wavering, uncertainty ;* qui tibi aestus, qui error, quae tenebrae erunt, Cic. **II.** Esp., *wandering from the right way.* **A.** Lit., errore viarum, Liv. ; cursus errore facili, Cic. **B.** Transf., 1, *error, deception ;* errore duci, Cic. ; in errorem induci, rapi, Cic. ; mentis, Cic. ; 2, *mistake ;* ferendus tibi in hoc meus error, Cic.

ĕrŭbesco -rŭbŭi, 3. *to grow red, blush ;* a, erubuere genae, Ov. ; b, *to grow red from shame, be ashamed ;* ubi erubuit, Cic. ; with in and the abl., Cic. ; with abl., Liv. ; with ut and the subj., Cic. ; with infin., Cic. ; **ĕrŭbescendus** -a -um, *of which one should be ashamed ;* ignes, Hor.

ĕrūca -ae, f. *a kind of colewort,* Hor.

ĕructo, 1. *to belch forth, throw up, vomit.* **A.** Lit., saniem, Verg. ; fig., sermonibus suis caedem, *to talk of,* Cic. **B.** *to cast out, emit, eject ;* arenam, Verg.

ĕrŭdĭo -ivi and -ii -itum, 4. (ex and rudis), *to instruct, teach, educate ;* aliquem, Cic. ; with abl., aliquem artibus, Cic. ; with in and the abl., aliquem in jure civili, Cic. ; filios omnibus artibus ad Graecorum disciplinam, Cic. ; with two acc., aliquem damnosas artes, Ov. ; with infin., Ov.

ĕrŭdītē, adv., only used in compar. and superl. (eruditus), *learnedly ;* eruditius disputare, Cic.

ĕrŭdītĭo -ōnis, f. (erudio), 1, *teaching, instruction,* Cic. ; 2, *knowledge, learning, erudition ;* eruditione atque doctrina, Cic.

ĕrŭdītŭlus -i, m. (dim. of eruditus), *somewhat skilled,* Cat.

ĕrŭdītus -a -um, p. adj. with compar. and superl (from erudio), *learned, instructed, polished, erudite ;* homo, Cic. ; eruditior litteris, Cic. ; eruditissimus disciplinā juris, Cic. Subst.,

ĕrŭdītī -orum, m. *men of education,* Cic. ; transf., of things, tempora, saecula, oratio, Cic.

ĕrumpo -rūpi -ruptum, 3. *to break out, break forth.* **I.** Transit., **A.** *to cause to burst forth ;* 1, lit., gen. reflex., se erumpere, or pass., erumpi, *to burst forth ;* portis se erumpere foras, Cic. ; 2, transf., *to vent, discharge ;* stomachum in aliquem, Cic. **B.** *to break through ;* nubem, Verg. **II.** Intransit., *to burst forth, break out with violence.* **A.** Lit., ignes ex Aetnae vertice erumpunt, Cic. ; milit. t. t., *to rush forth ;* ex castris, Caes. ; impers., duabus simul portis erumpitur, Liv. **B.** Transf., a, erumpat enim aliquando vera et me digna vox, Cic. ; erupit deinde seditio, Liv. ; b, *to break out into ;* with in or ad and the acc., ad minas, Tac. ; c, *to break out against ;* sentire potuit sermones iniquorum in suum potissimum nomen erumpere, Cic. ; d, *to come to light ;* si illustrantur, si erumpunt omnia, Cic. ; e, *to turn out, result ;* haec quo sit eruptura timeo, Cic. ; ad perniciem civitatis, Cic.

ĕrŭo -rŭi -rŭtum, 3. *to dig out.* **I.** Gen., **A.** Lit., 1, gen., mortuum, Cic. ; aurum terrā, Ov. ; 2, esp., a, *to dig up ;* humum, Ov. ; missā latus hastā, *to pierce,* Ov. ; b, *to tear out, pluck away ;* eruitur oculos, *his eyes are torn out,* Ov. **B.** Transf., a, memoriam alicuius ex annalium vetustate, *to bring forth,* Cic. ; b, *to bring to the light of day, to search out, rummage out ;* si quid indagaris, inveneris, ex tenebris erueris, Cic. ; with rel. sent, mihi, sicunde potes, erues qui decem legati Mummio fuerint, Cic. **II.** *to destroy utterly, raze ;* urbem, Verg.

ĕruptĭo -ōnis, f. (erumpo), *a bursting or breaking forth.* **A.** Gen., eruptio Aetnaeorum ignium, Cic. **B.** Milit. t. t., *sally, attack ;* eruptio ex oppido simul duabus portis, Liv. ; eruptionem facere, Caes.

Ĕrўcīna -ae, f. v. Eryx.

Ĕrўmanthŏs -i, m. (Ἐρύμανθος). **I.** *a mountain in Arcadia, where Hercules slew the Erymanthian boar.* Hence, 1, **Ĕrўmanthis** -ĭdis, f. (Ἐρυμανθίς), *Erymanthian ;* custos ursae Erymanthidos (Callisto), i.e., *Bootes,* Ov. ; 2,

Ĕrўmanthĭus -a -um (Ἐρυμάνθιος), *Erymanthian.* **II.** *a river on the borders of Elis, falling into the Alpheus.*

Ĕrўsicthōn -thōnis, m. (Ἐρυσίχθων), *the son of the Thessalian king Triopas, who was cursed by Ceres with a raging hunger for having cut down one of her groves, and who finally devoured his own flesh.*

Ĕrўthēa (-ĭa) -ae, f. *a small island near Gades, where Hercules stole the oxen of Geryon.* Hence, **Ĕrўthēis** -thēĭdis, f. *Erythean ;* praeda, *the oxen of Geryon,* Ov.

ĕrўthĭnus -a -um (ἐρυθῖνος), *a kind of red barbel or mullet,* Ov.

Ĕrўthrae -ārum, f. (Ἐρυθραί), 1, *a town in Boeotia ;* 2, Erythrae Aetolorum, *a town in Aetolia ;* 3, *one of the twelve Ionian towns in Asia Minor.* Hence adj., **Ĕrўthraeus** -a -um, *Erythrean ;* Erythraea terra, or simply **Ĕrўthraca** -ae, f. *the district of Erythrae.*

ĕrўthraeus -a -um (ἐρυθραῖος), *reddish ;* mare Erythraeum, *the Indian Ocean,* Plin.

Ĕryx -rўcis, m. (Ἔρυξ), *a mountain (also called Erycus mons), with a city of the same name on the north-west coast of Sicily, with a famous temple of Venus.* Adj., **Ĕrўcīnus** -a -um, *of or belonging to Eryx,* Venus Erycina, Cic. ; Erycina alone, *Venus,* Hor.

esca -ae, f. (1. edo), 1, *food, victuals, both of*

men and animals. Cic.; **2**, *bait*, Ov.; transf., voluptas esca malorum, Cic.

escārĭus -a -um, (esca), *relating or belonging to food.* Subst., **escāria** -orum, n. *eating utensils,* Juv.

escendo -scendi -scensum, **3.** (ex and scando). **I.** Intransit., *to climb up, ascend;* **1**, in rotam, Cic.; in rogum ardentem, Cic.; in tribunal, Liv.; in currum, Cic.; **2**, *to go up from the sea-coast inland;* Ilium a mari, Liv. **II.** Transit., *to ascend;* Oetam, Liv.; rostra, Tac.

escensĭo -ōnis, f. (escendo), *landing, disembarkation;* escensionem facere ab navibus in terram, Liv.

escensus, abl. -ī, m. (escendo), *climbing;* capta escensu munimenta, Tac.

escit, escunt = erit, erunt, v. sum.

escul . . . v. aescul . . .

escŭlentus -a -um (esca), *relating to eating, edible, esculent;* frusta, Cic.; subst., **escŭlenta** -orum, n. *eatables,* Cic.

Esquĭlĭae -ārum, f. (ex and colere, lit., *the outer town, the suburb), the most considerable of the hills on which Rome was built,* now *the height of S. Maria Maggiore;* hence, **1**, adj., **Esquĭlĭus** -a -um; **2**, **Esquĭlīnus** -a -um, *Esquiline;* subst., **Esquĭlīna** -ae, f. *the Esquiline gate,* Cic.; **3**, **Esquĭlĭārĭus** -a -um, *Esquiline.*

essĕda -ae, f. = essedum (q.v.).

essĕdārĭus -ĭi, m. (esseda), *a fighter in a British* or *Gallic war-chariot,* Caes.

essĕdum -i, n. (a Keltic word), *a war-chariot used among the Gauls and Britons, and afterwards adopted by the Romans in their public games,* Caes.; *a travelling chariot,* Cic.

ēsŭrĭo, 4. (desider. of 1. edo). **A.** *to be hungry, desire food,* Cic. **B.** Transf., *to desire eagerly, long for;* nil ibi, quod nobis esuriatur, erit, Ov.

ēsŭrītĭo -ōnis, f. (esurio), *hunger,* Cat.

ēsus -a -um, partic. of 1. edo.

ĕt, conj. (cf. Gr. ἔτι). **I.** *and* (joining single words and sentences), **1**, et . . . et, *both* . . . *and;* et in patre et in filios, Cic.; so et . : . que, Cic.; or que . . . et, Liv.; **2**, nec (neque) . . . et, *not only not* . . . *but;* nec miror et gaudeo, Cic.; et . . . nec (neque), *not only* . . . *but also not,* Cic.; **3**, et quidem, *and indeed;* duo milia jugerum, et quidem immania, Cic.; so et alone, *and indeed;* magna vis est conscientiae, et magna in utramque partem, Cic.; **4**, et etiam, *and also;* auctoritate et consilio et etiam gratia, Cic.; **5**, et vero, *and truly,* Cic.; **6**, et non, *and not, and not rather;* dicam eos miseros, qui nati sunt, et non eos, qui mortui sunt, Cic.; **7**, et deinde, *and then,* Liv. **II.** *also;* addam et illud etiam, Cic. **III.** *but;* nullane habes vitia? imo alia, et fortasse minora, Hor.

ĕtĕnim, conj., **1** (explanatory) *namely,* Cic.; **2** (strengthening a previous assertion), *truly, and indeed,* Cic.

Ĕtĕŏclēs -is and -ĕos, n. (Ετεοκλῆς), myth., *son of Oedipus, brother of Polynices, killed in the siege of Thebes.*

ĕtēsĭae -ārum, f. (ἐτησία, sc. ἄνεμοι), *winds which blow for forty days every year about the dog-days, Etesian winds,* Cic.

ĕtēsĭus -a -um, *Etesian,* Lucr.

ēthŏlŏgus i, m. (ἠθολόγος), *one who mimics in sport the peculiarities of others;* mimi ethologi, Cic.

ĕtĭam, conj. (= et jam), lit. *and already.* **I.** (to express duration of time), *as yet, still;*

nondum etiam, vixdum etiam, *not yet, scarcely yet,* Cic.; quum iste etiam cubaret, *when he was still,* &c., Cic. **II.** 1, in answer, *certainly, yes, indeed;* aut etiam aut non respondere, *to answer yes or no,* Cic.; **2**, *certainly, by all means;* etiam, inquit, beatam, sed non beatissimam, Cic.; **3**, to express a climax, *even, nay even;* voce, motu, forma etiam magnifica, Cic.; non solum . . . sed (or verum) etiam, *not only . . . but also,* Cic.; tum (or quum) . . . tum etiam, *as well . . . as,* Cic.; **4**, *even, nay;* tabulas nihil profuturas, etiam plus suspicionis futurum, Cic. **III.** *again;* dic etiam clarius, Cic.; etiam atque etiam, *again and again,* rogare, considerare, Cic.

ĕtĭam-num and **ĕtĭam-nunc**, adv., *yet, still, till now;* de materia loqui orationis etiam-nunc, non ipso de genere dicendi, Cic.; nihil etiam nunc, *nothing further,* Cic.

ĕtĭam-sī, conj., *even if, although,* Cic.

ĕtĭam-tum and **ĕtĭam-tunc**, adv., *even then, till that time, till then,* Cic.

Etrūrĭa -ae, f. *a country in Central Italy,* now *Tuscany.* Adj., **Etruscus** -a -um, *Etruscan.*

et-sī, conj. 1, *although, yet;* foll. by tamen, at, certe, etc.; etsi non sapientissimi, at amicissimi hominis auctoritate, Cic.; **2**, *and yet, notwithstanding;* do poenas temeritatis meae; etsi quae fuit ista temeritas, Cic.

ĕtўmŏlŏgĭa -ae, f. (ἐτυμολογία), *etymology,* Cic.

eu (εὖ), interj., *good! well done!* an exclamation of joy and approval (sometimes ironical), Hor.

Euadnē -ēs, f. (Εὐάδνη), myth., *wife of Capaneus, one of the seven who fought against Thebes.*

Euandĕr -dri, and **Euandrus**, -i, m. (Εὔανδρος), myth., *son of Hermes and Carmentis, who led a colony from Pallantium in Arcadia, and built a town on the Palatine hill.* Adj., **Euandrĭus** -a -um, *Evandrian;* ensis, *of Pallas, son of Evander.*

Euboea -ae, f. (Εὔβοια), *an island in the Aegean Sea;* hence adj., **Euboïcus** -a -um, a, *Euboean;* cultor aquarum, *the sea-god Glaucus,* Verg.; b, poet., *belonging to Cumae, a colony from Euboea;* urbs, *Cumae,* Ov.

Euclīdēs -is, m. (Εὐκλείδης), **1**, *a philosopher of Megara, founder of the Megarian school of philosophy;* **2**, *a mathematician of Alexandria.*

Euēnus -i, m. (Εὔηνος), myth., *king of Aetolia, father of Marpessa, drowned in the river Lycormas, which received the name of Euenus.* Adj., **Euēninus** -a -um, *of or belonging to the* (river) *Euenus.*

Eugănĕi -ōrum, m. *a people in Upper Italy, living near Patavium and Verona.* Adj., **Eugănēus** -a -um, *Euganean.*

euge, interj. (εὖγε), *well done!* (sometimes ironical), Pers.

euhan (euan), interj. (εὐάν or εὖ ἄν), *shout of the Bacchanals;* euhan euhoe euhium, Enn.; personif., Iacchus et Euhan, Ov.

euhans (euans), -antis = εὐάζων, *shouting euhan,* of the Bacchanals; with acc., euhantes orgia, *celebrating the orgies of Bacchus,* Verg.

Euhēmĕrus -i, m. (Εὐήμερος), *Greek philosopher and historian of Agrigentum,* flourishing about 315 A.C.

Euhĭas (Euĭas), -ădis, f. (εὐϊάς), *a Bacchante.*

Euhĭus (Euĭus), -ĭi, m. (Εὔιος), *surname of Bacchus.*

euhoe, interj. (εὐοῖ), *shout of the Bacchantes;* euhoe Bacche, Verg.

Eumĕnēs -is, m. (Εὐμένης), *general of Alexander the Great, after his death governor of Cappadocia.*

Eumĕnĭdes -um. f. (Εὐμενίδες), *Eumenides, the gracious ones, euphem.* name for the Furies.

Eumolpus -i, m. (Εὔμολπος), myth., *son of Poseidon and Chione, a Thracian priest of Demeter, founder of the Eleusinian mysteries.* Hence,

Eumolpĭdae -ārum, m. (Εὐμολπίδαι), *a family in Athens from which the priests of Demeter were chosen.*

eunūchus -i, m. (εὐνοῦχος), *a eunuch,* Cic.

Euphorbus -i, m. (Εὔφορβος), *a Trojan, whose soul Pythagoras believed to have descended to himself.*

Euphŏrīon -ōnis, m. (Εὐφορίων), *a Greek poet of Chalcis in Euboea, flourishing about 220* A.C.

Euphrātes -is (also -i and -ae), m. (Εὐφράτης), *the Euphrates, a river in Western Asia, rising in Armenia, joining the Tigris, and flowing into the Persian Gulf;* meton. *the dwellers on the Euphrates,* Verg.

Eupŏlis -pŏlĭdis, m. (Εὔπολις), *an Athenian comic poet, contemporary with Aristophanes.*

Eurīpĭdes -is and -i, m. (Εὐριπίδης), *the celebrated Athenian tragic poet.* Adj., **Eurīpĭdēus** -a -um, *of Euripides.*

Eurīpus -i, m. (Εὔριπος), 1, *a channel, strait,* esp. *the strait between Euboea and the main land,* Cic. ; 2, *an artificial canal or water-course,* Cic. ; *the ditch or moat constructed round the Circus Maximus,* Suet.

Eurōpa -ae, f., and **Eurōpē** -ēs, f. (Εὐρώπη). I. Myth., *daughter of Agenor, king of Phoenicia, mother of Sarpedon and Minos by Jupiter, who in the form of a bull carried her off to Crete.* II. Geogr., *the continent of Europe, said to have been named after Europa.* Adj., **Eurōpaeus** -a -um, *belonging to Europa;* dux, *Minos,* Ov.

Eurōtas -ae, m. (Εὐρώτας), *the chief river of Lacedaemonia, now Basilipotamo.*

eurōus -a -um (eurus), *eastern,* Verg.

eurus -i, m. (εὖρος), *a south-east wind,* Verg. ; *an east wind.* Ov. ; poet., *wind in general,* Verg.

Eurўdĭcē -ēs, f. (Εὐρυδίκη), *wife of Orpheus, killed by a serpent's bite, recovered from Hades by Orpheus, but lost again by his looking back at her against his agreement with Pluto.*

Eurўmĕdōn -ontis, m. (Εὐρυμέδων), *river in Pamphylia,* now *Kapri-Su.*

Eurўmĭdes -ae, m. (Εὐριμίδης), *son of Eurymus,* i.e., *Telephus.*

Eurўnŏmē -ēs, f. (Εὐρυνόμη), *daughter of Oceanus and Tethys, mother of Leucothoë.*

Eurўpўlus -i, m. (Εὐρύπυλος), 1, *a son of Hercules, and king of Cos;* 2, *son of Euaemon, one of the Greek commanders before Troy.*

Eurystheus -ĕi, m. (Εὐρυσθεύς), myth., *son of Sthenelus, king in Mycenae, who imposed on Hercules his twelve labours.*

Eurўtus -i, m. (Εὔρυτος), myth., *king in Oechalia, father of Iole and Dryope.* Hence, **Eurўtis** -ĭdis, f. *daughter of Eurytus,* i.e., *Iole.*

Euterpē -ēs, f. (Εὐτέρπη), *the muse of harmony,* Hor.

Eutrŏpĭus -ĭi, m. *Flavius, a Roman historian of the fourth century* A.D.

Euxīnus -a -um (Εὔξεινος = *hospitable*), *an epithet of the Black Sea;* esp. in the phrase Pontus Euxinus ; mare, aquae, Ov.

ēvādo -vāsi -vāsum, 3. *to go out, go forth.* I. Intransit., A. Lit., 1, gen., ex balneis, Cic. ; oppido, Sall. ; per praeruptum saxum in Capitolium, Liv. ; 2, esp., *to escape, get off;* e manibus hostium, Liv. ; e periculo, Cic. B. Transf., a, *to turn out, issue, become;* quos judicabat non

posse oratores, evadere, Cic. ; b, *to result, turn out;* quo evasura sint, Cic. II. Transit., 1, *tc climb, ascend;* gradus altos, Verg. ; 2, *to pass, travel over;* ripam, Verg. ; evaserant media castra, Liv. ; 3, *to escape;* flammam, Verg. (syncop. perf., evasti, Hor.).

ēvăgor, 1. dep. I. Intransit., *to wander, stray away.* A. Lit., a, of plunderers, effuse, Liv. ; b, milit. t. t., *to wheel to the right* and *left, manœuvre;* nullo ad evagandum relicto spatio, Liv. B. Transf., appetitus longius evagantur, Cic. II. Transit., *to overstep;* ordinem rectum, Hor.

ēvălesco -vălŭi, 3. *to grow strong;* 1, in tumultum, *to grow into a tumult,* Tac. ; 2, *to prevail, come into vogue;* nationis nomen evaluisse paullatim, Tac. ; 3, *to have power, to be able;* with infin., sed non Dardanidae medicari cuspidis ictum evaluit, Verg.

ēvan, v. euhan.

Ēvander, v. Euander.

ēvānesco -vānŭi, 3. A. *to vanish, disappear, pass away;* evanescunt vinum et salsamentum vetustate, Cic. B. Transf., evanescit memoria alicuius, Cic. ; spes, Cic. ; rumor, Liv.

ēvānĭdus -a -um (evanesco), *vanishing, passing away;* pectora in tenues abeunt evanida rivos, Ov.

ēvans, v. euhans.

ēvasto, 1. *to devastate, lay waste utterly;* agrum, vallem, Liv.

ēvectus -a -um, partic. of eveho.

ēvĕho -vexi -vectum, 3. I. *to carry out, bear out.* A. Lit., aliquid plaustris ex fanis, Cic. ; aquas ex planis locis, Liv. ; pass., evehi (used as a middle) ; 1, of ships, *to sail away;* in altum, Liv. ; 2, se evehere and evehi, *to ride away;* se incaute, Liv. B. Transf., middle evehi ; a, e Piraeo eloquentia evecta est, Cic. ; b, *to be carried away;* spe varnā, Liv. ; c, fames eius evecta insulas, *spread abroad,* Tac. II. *to raise, lift up;* aliquem ad deos, *raises to the heaven,* Hor. ; evehere aliquem ad consulatum, Tac.

ēvello -velli -vulsum, 3. I. *to tear out, pluck out.* A. Lit., alicui linguam, Cic. ; arborem, Cic. B. Transf., *to tear out, erase, remove;* consules non modo e memoria sed etiam ex fastis evellendi, Cic. ; alicui ex animo scrupulum, Cic. II. *to tear away;* emblema, Cic.

ēvĕnĭo -vēni -ventum, 4. *to come out, come forth.* I. Lit., merses profundo, pulchrior evenit, Hor. II. Transf., 1, a, *to turn out, result;* bene, Cic. ; alicui feliciter, Caes. ; vides omnia fere contra ac dicta sint evenisse, Cic. ; b, *to fall to the lot of;* provincia (sorte) evenit alicui, Liv. ; 2, *to happen, befall, occur;* pax evenit, Sall. ; ut plerumque evenit, Cic. ; forte evenit ut, etc., Cic.

ēventum -i, n. (evenio), 1, *the issue, consequence of an action;* causarum cognitio cognitionem eventi facit, Cic. ; 2, *an event, occurrence;* causae eventorum magis me movent quam ipsa eventa, Cic.

. **ēventus** -ūs, m. (evenio). I. *consequence, issue, result;* 1, gen., eventus rei, Caes. ; eventus rerum qui acciderunt, Cic. ; eius diei, Caes. ; belli eventus prosper, Liv. ; 2, esp., a, *issue, end, catastrophe;* (α) of a drama, semper ad eventum festinat, Hor. ; (β) of persons, impiorum fratrum, Liv.; b, *favourable issue, success;* casus eventusque rerum, Tac. ; nec eventus defuit, Tac. II. *an occurrence, event,* Cic. ; *fate,* auditur Decii eventus, Liv.

ēverbĕro, 1. *to strike violently, flap;* clypeum alis, Verg. ; cauda pendentem escam, Ov.

ēvergo, 3. *to send out, send forth;* nullos apertos rivos, Liv.

ēverrĭcŭlum -i, n. (everro), *a fishing-net, drag-net;* fig., quod umquam huiuscemodi everriculum ulla in provincia fuit (with a pun on the name of Verres), Cic.; everriculum malitiarum omnium, judicium de dolo malo, Cic.

ēverro -verri -versum, 3. (*to sweep out*); transf., *to plunder;* quod fanum non eversum atque extersum reliqueris (with a pun on the name of Verres), Cic.

ēversĭo -ōnis, f. (everto), 1, *an overturning;* columnae, Cic.; 2, transf., *a destruction, ruin;* vitae, Cic.; patriae, rerum publicarum eversiones, Cic.

ēversor -ōris, m. (everto), *an overturner, destroyer;* civitatis, Cic.

ēverto -verti -versum, 3. **I. A.** *to overturn, throw down;* 1, lit., navem, Cic.; arborem,Verg.; hence, of a city, *to demolish, raze to the ground;* Carthaginem, Cic.; 2, transf., *to overthrow, destroy;* funditus civitates, Cic.; constitutam philosophiam, Cic.; aliquem, *to ruin politically,* Cic. **B.** *to expel* or *eject from one's property;* aliquem bonis, Cic.; perfidum fortunis patriis, Cic. **II.** *to raise up;* aequora ventis, Verg.

ēvestīgātus -a -um, *tracked out, discovered;* ingeniis evestigata priorum, Ov.

Ēvĭas, v. Euhias.

ēvĭdens -entis, adj. (ex and video), 1, *visible;* mensura quaedam, Cic.; 2, transf., *clear, plain, evident;* res, Cic.; evidentior causa victoriae, Liv.; quid est evidentius? Cic.

ēvĭdentĕr, adv. (evidens), *visibly, manifestly;* evidenter praenitere, Liv.

ēvĭdentĭa -ae, f. (evidens), *distinctness of language,* Cic.

ēvĭgĭlo, 1. **I.** Intransit., *to watch, be vigilant;* in quo evigilaverunt curae et cogitationes meae? Cic. **II.** Transit., a, *to watch through, pass in watching;* nox evigilanda, Tib.; b, *to elaborate carefully;* libros, Ov.; consilia evigilata cogitationibus, Cic.

ēvīlesco -vīlŭi, 3. *to become vile, worthless, contemptible,* Tac.

ēvincĭo -vinxi -vinctum, 4. *to bind, bind round;* diademate caput Tiridatis evinxit, Tac.; viridi evinctus oliva, Verg.

ēvinco -vīci -victum, 3. *to conquer entirely, utterly subdue.* **I.** Lit., imbelles Aeduos, Tac.; evicit omnia assuetus praedae miles, Liv.; platanus caelebs evincet ulmos, *will get the better of, drive away,* Hor.; oppositas gurgite moles, *to get past* or *through,* Verg. **II.** Transf., **A.** Gen., a, *to prevail upon a person;* lacrimis, dolore, precibus evinci, Verg.; b, *to conquer a passion* or *feeling;* evicit miseratio justa sociorum superbiam ingenitam, Liv. **B.** a, *to bring it about that;* with ut and the subj., summa ope evicerunt, ut M. Furius Camillus crearetur, Liv.; b, *to prove irresistibly;* si puerilius his ratio esse evincet amare, Hor.

ēvīro, 1. (ex and vir), *to castrate,* Cat.

ēviscĕro, 1. (ex and viscus), *to take out the bowels, eviscerate, tear in pieces;* (columbam) pedibus eviscerat uncis (of the hawk), Verg.; evisceratum corpus patris, Cic.

ēvītābĭlis -e (evito), *that can be avoided;* telum, Ov.

ēvīto, 1. *to avoid, shun;* suspicionem, Cic.

Ēvĭus, v. Euhius.

ēvŏcātor -ōris, m. (evoco), *one who calls to arms;* servorum et civium perditorum, Cic.

ēvŏcātus -a -um (partic. of evoco); subst., *a veteran who had served his time but was liable to be called upon in an emergency,* Caes.

ēvŏco, 1. *to call out.* **I.** Lit., **A.** Gen., aliquem e curia, Liv.; mercatores undique ad se, Caes.; aliquem litteris, Cic. **B.** Esp., 1, relig. t. t., a, *to summon the spirits of the dead;* aliquem ab inferis, Cic.; b, *to call forth a deity from a besieged and hostile city by promising a temple at Rome;* evocare deos, Liv.; 2, *to summon;* a, of magistrates, etc., aliquem ad se, Cic.; aliquem ad colloquium, Liv.; b, *to summon for military service;* legiones ex hibernis, Caes.; c, *to summon to a place of honour;* aliquem ad eum honorem, Caes.; 3, *in a hostile manner, to call upon the enemy to come out to fight;* magna cum contumelia verborum nostros ad pugnam, Caes. **II.** Transf., a, alicuius familiam abjectam et obscuram tenebris in lucem, Cic.; b, *to call forth, produce;* misericordia tua nullius oratione evocata, Cic.

ēvoe, v. euhoe.

ēvŏlo, 1. **I.** *to fly out, fly away.* **A.** Lit., ex quercu, Cic. **B.** Transf., *to come forth quickly, rush forth, hasten away;* ex corporum vinculis tanquam e carcere, Cic.; e senatu, Cic.; e conspectu, Cic.: fig., ex alicuius severitate, e poena, *to escape,* Cic. **II.** *to fly up;* concussisque levis pennis se evolat ales, Ov.

ēvŏlūtĭo -ōnis, f. (evolvo), *the unrolling,* and hence, *reading of a book;* poetarum, Cic.

ēvolvo -volvi -vŏlūtum, 3. **I. A.** Lit., *to roll out, roll forth;* 1, per humum evolvi, Tac.; 2, of a river, se evolvere in mare, Verg.; 3, fig., evolutus illis integumentis dissimulationis, *unmasked,* Cic. **B.** Transf., 1, *to extricate;* se ex his turbis, Tac.; 2, *to deprive;* illos ex praeda clandestina, *make to disgorge,* Liv.; 3, of news, evolvi, *to spread;* ad aures quoque militum dicta ferocia evolvebantur, Liv. **II.** *to roll apart, open, unwind.* **A.** Lit., 1, gen., volumen epistolarum, Cic.; 2, a, of the fates, *to spin;* fusos meos, Ov.; b, *to read, study;* librum, Cic. **B.** Transf., 1, *to make clear, narrate;* aliquid accuratius in litteris, Cic.; 2, *to find out;* exitum criminis, Cic.; 3, *to think over, reflect upon;* haec sub antris, Verg.

ēvŏmo -ŭi -ĭtum, 3. *to vomit forth.* **A.** Lit., conchas, Cic. **B.** Transf., a, *to vomit forth, cast out;* quae (urbs) tantam pestem evomuit forasque projecit, Cic.; in quo tu, accepta et devorata pecuniā, evomere non poteras, *disgorge,* Cic.; b, of speech, in aliquem absentem orationem ex ore impurissimo, Cic.

ēvulgo, 1. *to publish, make known;* jus civile, Liv.; Octaviae injurias, Tac.

ēvulsĭo -ōnis, f. (evello), *a pulling out, plucking out;* dentis, Cic.

ex, prep. with abl. (ἐξ, ἐκ), e before b, d, g, j, l, m, n, r, v, *from* or *out of.* **I.** 1, In space, *out of, from;* exire ex urbe, e vita, Cic.; milites ex eo loco deducere, Cic.; delabi ex equo, Liv. thus a, it follows verbs of taking, perceiving, questioning, and the like—e. g., sumere, percipere, accipere, auferre, colligere, quaerere, percunctari, discere, intelligere, etc.; b, so the phrase, ex persona alicuius, *under the mask—i.e., in the character of any one;* ex sua persona, *in one's own name, for oneself,* Cic.; 2, to denote position; a, ex aequo colloqui, Caes.; qui nihil ex occulto agendum putant, Cic.; b, laborare ex pedibus, *to suffer in the feet,* Cic. **II.** Of time, 1, *since;* ex eo tempore, Cic.; esp., ex quo, *from which time, since,* Liv.; 2, on. at: hunc judicem ex Kal. Jun. non habebimus, Cic.; 3, *after, immediately upon;* Cotta ex consulatu est profectus in Galliam, Cic.; aliud ex alio, *one* *after another*, Cic.; diem ex die, *day after day*, Cic. **III.** To denote origin, *from, out of, of ;* **1,** a, quidam ex Arcadia hospes, Nep.; virgines ex sacerdotio Vestae, *of the priesthood of Vesta*, Ter.; b, of etymological derivation, urbem quam e suo nomine Romam jussit nominari, Cic.; **2,** to denote the whole out of which any part is taken, unus ex meis intimis, Cic.; e numero, *of the number*, Cic.; hence, **a,** Q. Vettius Vettianus e Marsis, *a Marsian*, Cic.; b, in place of the genit., to denote that to which anything belongs, puppes e barbaris navibus, Caes.; **3,** to denote the material of which anything is made or compounded, pocula ex auro, Cic.; so of the source from which anything is paid or gained ; largiri ex alieno, Liv.; vivere e rapto, Ov.; **4,** to denote the cause or occasion of anything, *from, on account of, by reason of ;* ex eadem causa, Cic.; Demetrius e doctrina clarus, Cic.; esp. with conj. in the phrase, ex eo quod, ex eo quia, *on that account, because*, Cic.; ex eo factum est quod, *hence it came about that*, Cic.; ex quo, e quibus, *on account of which*, Cic.; e vulnere mori, Liv.; **5,** to denote a change from one condition or occupation to another, ex oratore arator factus, Cic.; **6,** *according to, in accordance with ;* ex edicto, Cic.; ex decreto, Cic.; ex foedere, Liv.; ex re et ex tempore, *according to time and circumstance*, Cic.; esp. a, ex mea, tua re, *for my, thy advantage*, Cic.; e republica, *for the benefit of the republic*, Cic.; ex usu esse, to be *useful*, Cic.; b, ex animo, *heartily, earnestly*, Cic.; ex sententia, *satisfactorily*, Cic.; **7,** *in regard to, with respect to ;* e ratione libertatis ; e nostra dignitate, Cic. **IV.** Adv. phrases, ex industria, *designedly*, Cic.; e memoria, *from memory*, Cic.; ex parte, *in part*, Cic.; e vestigio, *forthwith*, Caes.; e regione, *opposite to*, Cic.; ex inopinato, *unexpectedly*, Cic.

exăcerbo, 1. *to irritate, provoke, exasperate, embitter ;* contumeliis hostes, Liv.

exactĭo -ōnis, f. (exigo), **I.** *a driving out, expulsion ;* regum, Cic. **II.** 1, *a demanding, exacting, collecting of debts, tribute,* etc.; **a,** act., nominum, Cic.; capitum, *poll-tax*, Cic.; b, pass., *that which is collected, income ;* exactio prior, Cic.; **2,** *management, direction ;* operum publicorum, Cic.

exactor -ōris, m. (exigo), **I.** *one who drives out, expels ;* regum, Liv. **II.** 1, *one who demands or exacts, a collector of taxes*, Caes.; **2,** *an inspector, superintendent, overseer ;* quum ipse imperator et exactor ; circumiret, Liv.

exactus -a -um, p. adj. with compar. and superl. (from exigo), *accurate, precise, exact ;* numerus, Liv.

exăcŭo -ŭi -ūtum, 3. *to sharpen to a point, make sharp.* **A.** Lit., furcas, Verg.; fig., mucronem aliquem tribunicium in nos, Cic. **B.** Transf., **a,** quum animus exacuerit illam, ut oculorum, sic ingenii aciem, Cic.; b, *to excite, stir up, inflame ;* aliquem, Cic.; animos in bella, Hor.; irā exacui, Nep.

exadversum or **exadversus,** prep. with acc., *opposite ;* exadversus eum locum, Cic.

exaedĭfĭcatĭo -ōnis, f. (exaedifico), *a building up ;* fig., of an oration, ipsa autem exaedificatio posita est in rebus et verbis, Cic.

exaedĭfĭco, 1. *to build, build up, erect, finish building ;* Capitolium, Cic.; domos et villas, Sall.; fig., *to finish ;* exaedificare id opus quod instituisti, Cic.

exaequatĭo -ōnis, f. (exaequo), *a making equal, equality*, Liv.

exaequo, 1. **a,** *to place on a level, make equal ;* jura, Cic.; facta dictis sunt exaequanda, *must be related in an adequate manner*, Sall.; **b,**

7*

to compare ; se cum aliquo, Cic.; exaequari **alicui,** Cic.; c, *to equal ;* aliquem, Ov.

exaestŭo, 1. **I.** Intransit., *to boil up, foam up ;* mare, Liv.; unda ima verticibus, Verg.; transf., mens exaestuat irā, Verg. **II.** Transit., *to give forth ;* hos igitur tellus omnes exaestuat aestus, Lucr.

exaggĕratĭo -ōnis, f. (exaggero), *elevation, exaltation ;* amplitudo et quasi quaedam exaggeratio quam altissima animi, Cic.

exaggĕro, 1. *to heap up.* **I.** Gen., **A.** Lit., Plin. **B.** Transf., *to raise, elevate ;* animus virtutibus exaggeratus, Cic. **II.** *to heap up, increase ;* **1,** gen., rem familiarem, Cic.; **2,** esp., by words, *to heighten, exalt, magnify ;* beneficium verbis, Cic.; virtutem, Cic.

exăgĭtātor -ōris, m. (exagito), *one who blames, a censurer ;* omnium rhetorum, Cic.

exăgĭto, 1. **I.** Lit., *to drive anything from its position ;* **a,** of animals, *to hunt, chase ;* et lepus 'nic aliis exagitatus erit, Ov.; b, of winds, *to raise ;* quum vis (venti) exagitata foras erumpitur, Lucr. **II.** Transf., 1, *to harass, disquiet, disturb, persecute ;* exagitati istius injuriis, Cic.; ab Suebis complures annos exagitati bello premebantur, Caes.; quos illa quaestio exagitabat, Sall.; **2,** *to scold, blame, reproach, censure, criticise ;* aliquem, Cic.; omnes eius fraudes, Cic.; *to disapprove of ;* qui hanc dicendi exercitationem exagitarent atque contemnerent, Cic.; **3,** *to excite, irritate ;* plebem, Sall.; maerorem, Cic.

exalbesco -bŭi, 3. *to grow white, turn pale with fright*, Cic.

exāmen -ĭnis, n. (for exagimen, from ex and ago). **I.** *a swarm.* **A.** Lit., of bees, Cic.; of wasps, Liv. **B.** Transf., *a throng, crowd, shoal ;* servorum, Cic. **II. A.** *the tongue of a balance*, Verg. **B.** Transf., *testing, consideration, investigation ;* examina legum servare, *to apply*, Ov.

exāmĭno, 1. (examen), *to weigh.* **A.** Lit., ad certum pondus, Caes.; non aurificis staterā, sed quādam populari trutinā examinari, Cic. **B.** Transf., *to weigh, consider ;* **a,** diligenter verborum omnium pondera, Cic.; with abl., haec meis ponderibus, Cic.; b, of judges, male verum examinat omnis corruptus judex, Hor.

ex-ămussim, *according to the square or rule, exactly, accurately*, Plaut.

exanclo, 1. *to exhaust, empty.* **A.** Lit., vinum poculo, Plaut. **B.** Transf., *to bear to the end, suffer, endure ;* labores, Cic.

exănĭmātĭo -ōnis, f. (exanimo), *fright, terror*, Cic.

exănĭmis -e and gen. **exănĭmus** -a -um (ex and anima), 1, *lifeless, dead*, Verg., Liv.; 2, *lifeless, senseless with terror*, Verg.

exănĭmo, 1. (ex and anima or animus). **I.** *to deprive of breath.* **A.** 1, lit., duplici cursu exanimari, Caes.; milites cursu exanimati, *breathless*, Caes.; **2,** transf., *to make breathless with fear, to stun ;* te metus exanimat, Cic. **B.** *to deprive of life, kill ;* 1, lit., aliquem, Cic.; **2,** transf., *to exhaust, weaken ;* aliquem querelis, Hor. **II.** *to breathe out ;* nolo verba exiliter exanimata exire, Cic.

exantlo = exanclo (q.v.).

exaptus -a -um, *fastened, attached*, Lucr.

exardesco -arsi -arsum, 3. **I.** Lit., 1, *to take fire, kindle, burn up ;* nulla materia tam facilis ad exardescendum est quae etc., Cic.; 2, *to become hot, to glow ;* aetherioque recens exarsit sidere limus, Ov. **II.** Transf., 1, of persons, *to be violently excited, be inflamed ;* iracundiā ac stomacho, Cic.; ad spem libertatis' Cic.; of love, *to burn ;* imis tota exarsit medullis,

Cat.; 2, of things, *to break out;* **exarsit bellum,** Cic.

exāresco -ārŭi, 3. *to dry, become quite dry.* **A.** Lit., exarescunt amnes, Cic.; fontes, Caes.; lacrimae, Cic. **B.** Fig., *to dry up, become exhausted;* exaruit facultas orationis, Cic.; vides enim exaruisse jam veterem urbanitatem, Cic.

exarmo, 1. *to disarm, deprive of arms;* cohortes, Tac.

exăro, 1. **I.** *to plough up, dig up;* puerum, Cic. **II.** *to gain by ploughing;* plus quam decem medimna ex agro, Cic. **III.** *to plough;* a, lit., Varr.; b, transf., frontem rugis, Hor.; c, meton., *to write* or *note on waxen tablets;* exaravi ad te harum exemplum in codicillis, Cic.

exaspĕro, 1. *to make rough.* **A.** Lit., a, Plin.; b, of the sea, *to make stormy;* exasperato fluctibus mari, Liv. **B.** Transf., a, *to make savage;* durati tot malis exasperatique, Liv.; b, *to irritate, excite;* animos, Liv.

exauctōro, 1. *to dismiss from military service, discharge;* aliquem, Liv.; se exauctorare, *to leave the service,* Liv.

exaudĭo, 4. **I.** *to hear plainly;* maximā voce, ut omnes exaudire possint, dico, Cic.; non exaudito tubae sono, Caes. **II.** *to hear favourably, listen to;* a, aliquid, *to listen to prayers;* vota precesque, Verg.; b, aliquem, *to obey;* monitor non exauditus, Hor.

exaugĕo, 2. *to increase exceedingly;* radiorum ictum, Lucr.

exaugŭrātĭo -ōnis, f. (exauguro), *a profaning, desecrating;* sacellorum exaugurationes, Liv.

exaugŭro, 1. *to desecrate, profane;* fana, Liv.

excaeco, 1. *to make blind.* **A.** Lit., aliquem, Cic. **B.** Transf., *to stop a river* or *channel;* flumina, Ov.

excandescentĭa -ae, f. (excandesco), *heat, irascibility,* Cic.

excandesco -dŭi, 3. *to become hot with passion, to glow, burn;* absol., id postquam nesciit, excanduit, ap. Cic.; with abstractions, risi irā excanduerit fortitudo, Cic.

excanto, 1. *to charm out, bring forth by incantations;* sidera excantata voce Thessalā, Hor.

excarnĭfĭco, 1. *to tear to pieces;* aliquem, Cic.

excăvo, 1. *to hollow out, excavate;* ex una gemma praegrandi trullā excavatā, Cic.

excēdo -cessi -cessum, 3. **I.** Intransit., **A.** *to go out, go away, go from;* 1, lit., viā, Liv.; oppido, Caes.; urbe, Cic.; ex proelio, proelio, Caes.; 2, transf., a, ex ephebis, e pueris, *to pass out of the age of boyhood,* Cic.; e memoria, *to pass out of memory,* Cic.; e vita or simply vitā, *to die,* Cic.; excedere palmā, *to resign the prize,* Verg.; b, *to digress;* paullum ad enarrandum quam etc., Liv. **B.** *to go beyond, exceed;* 1, lit., ut nulla (pars) excederet ultra, Cic.; 2, transf., a, *to attain to;* eo laudis excedere quo, etc., Tac.; b, *to result in, turn to;* ne in altercationem excederet res, Liv.; c, *to pass beyond;* quum libertas non ultra vocem excessisset, Liv.; d, of events, *to happen;* insequentia excedunt in eum annum, etc., Liv. **II.** Transit. **A.** Gen., *to leave;* curiam, urbem, Liv. **B.** *to pass beyond;* modum, Liv.; tempus finitum, Liv.

excellens -entis, p. adj. with compar. and superl. (excello), *high, lofty, excellent, distinguished, remarkable;* Brutus excellens omni genere laudis, Cic.; excellens pulchritudo muliebris formae, Cic.; una excellentissima virtus, justitia, Cic.

excellentĕr, adv. (excellens), *excellently;* quae magno animo fortiter excellenterque gesta sunt, Cic.

excellentĭa -ae, f. (excellens), *excellence, distinguished merit;* animi excellentia magnitudoque, Cic.; absol., propter excellentiam, *pre-eminently,* Cic.

excello (excellĕo), 3. *to excel, be distinguished, be eminent;* illud excellit regium nomen, Cic.; with abl., animi magnitudine, Cic.; with in and the abl., in qua parte excello ipse, Cic.; with inter, inter quos posset excellere, Cic.; with praeter, in eo genere praeter ceteros, Cic.; with super, quia super ceteros excellat, Liv.; with dat. (of person excelled), ita figuratum esse corpus ut excellat ceteris, Cic.; in quibus tu longe aliis excellis, Cic.

excelsē, adv. with compar. and superl. (excelsus), *loftily;* dicere, *in a lofty style,* Cic.

excelsĭtas -ātis, f. (excelsus), *height;* transf., animi, *elevation,* Cic.

excelsus -a -um, p. adj. with compar. and superl. (excello), *lofty, high, elevated.* **A.** Lit., mons, Caes.; locus, Cic. Subst., **excelsum** -i, n. *a lofty place* or *situation,* Cic. **B.** Transf., *elevated above the common;* 1, of position, *distinguished, eminent, illustrious;* in excelso et illustri loco sita laus tua, Cic.; subst., **excelsum** -i, n. *high dignity, lofty position;* a, sing., in excelso vitam agere, Sall.; b, plur., excelsa et alta sperare, *high honours,* Liv.; 2, of the mind, *dignified, elevated;* magnus homo et excelsus, Cic.; animus excelsus, Cic.; 3, of the style of a writer or speaker, *lofty, elevated;* orator grandior et quodammodo excelsior, Cic.

exceptĭo -ōnis, f. (excipio), 1, *an exception, restriction, limitation;* cum exceptione, Cic.; sine exceptione, Cic.; quodsi exceptionem facit ne, etc., Cic.; 2, *an exception to the plaintiff's statement of a case tendered by the defendant;* exceptionem alicui dare, Cic.; exceptione excludi, Cic.

excepto, 1. (intens. of excipio), *to take out, catch up;* 1, barbatulos mullos de piscina, Cic.; singulos, Caes.; 2, auras, *to snuff up,* Verg.

excerno -crēvi -crētum, 3. *to separate, sift, sort;* Saguntinos ex captorum numero, Liv.; haedi excreti, *separated from their mothers,* Verg.

excerpo -cerpsi -cerptum, 3. (ex and carpo), *to pick out.* **I.** Lit., semina pomis, Hor. **II.** Transf. **A.** *to gather out, choose;* excerpere ex malis si quid inesset boni, Cic.; excerpere nomina omnium ex juniorum tabulis, Liv. **B.** *to put on one side, separate;* de numero, Cic.; se numero illorum, Hor.

excessus -ūs, m. (excedo), *departure from life, death;* vitae, Cic.; e vita, Cic.; absol., laeti excessu principis, Tac.

excētra -ae, f. *a snake,* Cic. poet.; transf., *a spiteful woman,* Liv.

excidĭum -ĭi, n. (excīdo = exscindo), *destruction, annihilation;* a, of places, Libyae, Verg.; excidia urbium relictarum, Liv.; b, of persons, excidium meorum, Verg.; legionum, Tac.

1. **excīdo** -cīdi, 3. (ex and cado), *to fall out, fall down.* **I.** Lit., **A.** Gen., sol excidisse mihi e mundo videtur, Cic.; gladii de manibus exciderunt; poet., vinclis excides, *escape,* Verg. **B.** Esp., 1, of a lot, *to fall out;* ut cuiusque sors exciderat, Liv.; 2, *to fall out, be lost;* litteras excidisse in via, Cic. **II.** Transf., **A.** Gen., ut quodammodo victoria e manibus excideret, *slipped out,* Cic.; in vitium libertas excidit, Hor. **B.** Esp., 1, *to slip out unawares, escape;* verbum ex ore alicuius or alicui, Cic.; libellus me imprudente et invito excidit, Cic.; 2, *to vanish, disappear, pass away;* a, vultus, oratio, mens denique excidit, Cic.; excidit illa metu, *lost consciousness.* Ov.; b, esp., *to pass*

away from memory or *thought, be forgotten;* Carthaginem excidisse de memoria, Liv.; nomen tuum mihi excidit, Ov.; cogitatio mihi non excidit, Cic.; **3,** *to fail;* magnis excidit ausis, Ov.

2. excīdo -cīdi -cīsum, 3. (ex and caedo), *to cut out.* **I.** Lit., **A.** Gen., lapides e terra, Cic.; arbor excisa, non evulsa, Cic. **B.** Esp., a, *to hew out, excavate;* saxum, Cic.; b, *to destroy;* of places, portas, *force open,* Caes.; domos, Cic.; of persons, *to annihilate;* Sugambros, Tac. **II.** Transf., *to root out, banish;* illud tristissimum tempus ex anno, Cic.; causas bellorum, Tac.

excĭĕo -cīvi -cītum, 2. and (gen.) **excĭo** -cīvi and -cii -cītum, 4. *to call forth, summon out.* **I.** Of persons, **A.** Lit., **1,** gen., ea res ab stativis excivit Mettium, Liv.; artifices e Graecia, Liv.; animas imis sepulcris, Verg.; **2,** esp., *to summon to help;* Romanos ad auxilium urbis obsessae, Liv.; auxilia e Germania, Tac. **B.** Transf., **1,** *to provoke;* hostem ad dimicandum acie, Liv.; **2,** with or without somno or e somno, *to arouse, awake,* Liv., Sall.; **3,** *to frighten, alarm;* conscientia mentem excitam vastabat, Sall. **II.** Of things, **1,** *to call forth, excite, produce;* tumultum in portis, Liv.; timorem, Liv.; **2,** *to shake;* pulsuque pedum tremit excita tellus, Verg.

excĭpĭo -cēpi -ceptum, 3. (ex and capio). **I.** *to take out.* **A.** Lit., aliquem e mari, Cic. **B.** Transf., a, *to except;* hosce homines excipio et secerno, Cic.; excipere aliquem or excipi, foll. by ne, Cic.; non excipi quominus, Cic.; b, *to make a condition, state expressly;* lex exciperet ut, etc., Cic. **II.** *to take up, catch up.* **A.** Of things, **1,** sanguinem paterā, Cic.; **2,** *to catch up by listening,* *to listen, overhear,* Cic.; **3,** a, *to receive;* vulnera, Cic.; b, *to undertake;* labores magnos, Cic.; c, *to suffer, endure;* omnem diu collectam vim improborum, Cic. **B.** Of persons, **1,** *to catch;* moribundum, Liv.; se pedibus or in pedes, *to spring to the ground,* Liv.; **2,** *to catch* (in a hostile manner); a, lit., servos in pabulatione, Caes.; b, transf., *to snatch at;* voluntates hominum, Cic. **III.** *to receive.* **A.** Lit., **1,** excipi ab omnibus clamore, Cic.; **2,** *to entertain;* aliquem, Cic.; **3,** of places, illam (patriam) ubi excepti sumus, Cic.; **4,** *to attack;* a, Orestes excipit incautum, Verg.; b, *to wound;* aliquem in latus, Verg. **B.** Transf., **1,** *to hear, receive;* motus futuros, Verg.; assensu populi excepta vox, Liv.; **2,** *to await;* qui quosque eventus exciperent, Caes.; **3,** *to follow, succeed;* orationem Tullii exceperunt preces multitudinis, Liv.; Herculis vitam immortalitas excipit, Cic.; hunc excipit Labienus, *speaks next,* Caes.; **4,** *to continue, prolong;* memoriam viri, Cic.; **5,** poet., *to lie towards;* porticus excipit Arcton, Hor.

excīsĭo -ōnis (excīdo), *destruction;* tectorum, Cic.; urbium, Cic.

excītātus -a -um, p. adj. with compar. and superl. (from excito), *lively, animated, vigorous, loud;* sonus, Cic.; clamor, Liv.

excīto, 1. **I.** *to rouse forth.* **A.** Of living creatures, **1,** feras, Cic.; **2,** *to call forth by shouting, to summon;* clamore excitatum praesidium Romanorum, Liv.; aliquem a mortuis or ab inferis, Cic.. **B.** Transf., of things, alicui memoriam caram, *to renew,* Cic. **II.** *to rouse up.* **A.** of persons, **1,** a, lit., universi rursus prociderunt, tandem excitati curiā excesserunt, Liv.; b, transf., *to console, raise up;* animum amici jacentem, Cic.; afflictos, Cic.; **2,** *to summon;* triarios, Liv.; recitatores, lectores, Cic.; testes, Cic.; **3,** a, *to arouse from sleep;* aliquem e somno or somne, Cic.; b, *to arouse, animate;* trepido nuntio excitatus, Liv.; aliquem ad laborem et laudem, Cic. **B.** Of things, **1,** *to raise,*

erect; turrem, Caes.; sepulcrum, Cic.; transf., excitata fortuna, *favourable,* Cic.; **2,** of a fire, *to kindle, inflame;* ignem, Caes.; incendium, Cic.; **3,** a, *to provoke, produce, call forth;* plausum, Cic.; fletum alicui, Cic.; b, *to provoke, cause;* amores, Cic.; indomitas iras, Verg.

exclāmātĭo -ōnis, f. (exclamo), in rhet., *an exclamation,* Cic.

exclāmo, 1. **I.** Intransit., *to shout, cry aloud;* in stadio cursores exclamant quam maxime possunt, Cic.; contiones saepe exclamare vidi, quum apte verba concidissent, Cic. **II.** Transit, **1,** *to shout out, call aloud by name;* Ciceronem, ap. Cic.; **2,** *to shout out;* mihi libet exclamare; pro Deum, etc., Cic.; with objective clause, quum magnā voce exclamasset ut, etc., Liv.

exclūdo -clūsi -clūsum, (ex and claudo), 3. **I.** *to shut out, exclude.* **A.** Lit., a, of persons, aliquem a domo sua, Cic.; aliquem moenibus, Cic.; ejicere nos magnum fuit, excludere facile, Cic.; b, of a place, *to cut off, separate;* locum, Liv. **B.** Transf., a, *to exclude;* ab hereditate paterna, Cic.; his praemiis et honoribus, Cic.; b, *to remove;* aliquem a republica, Cic.; c, *to prevent, hinder;* Romanos ab re frumentaria, shut off, Caes. **II.** of birds, *to hatch;* pullos suos in nido, Cic.

exclūsĭo -ōnis, f. (excludo), *a shutting out, exclusion,* Ter.

excōgĭtātĭo -ōnis, f. (excogito),*a contriving, devising;* illa vis quae tandem est, quae investigat occulta, quae invenio atque excogitatio dicitur, Cic.

excōgĭto, 1. *to scheme, devise, contrive, invent;* mira quaedam genera furandi, Cic.; with dat. of gerund. or ad with acc. (to express the object of the invention), alia tuendis urbibus excogitata, Cic.; excogitare multa ad avaritiam, Caes.; with relat. sentence, excogitat, sane acute quid decernat, Cic.; absol., ad haec igitur cogita, mi Attice, vel potius excogita, Cic.

excŏlo -cŏlŭi -cultum. 3. **A.** Lit., *to tend or cultivate carefully;* arva, Mart.; lanas rudes, *to spin,* Ov. **B.** Transf., a, *to adorn, polish, ennoble, refine;* Tuditanus omni vitā atque vitae excultus, Cic.; animos doctrinā, Cic.; vitam per artes, Verg.; b, *to serve, honour;* quaeque tu, est pietas, ut te non excolat ipsum, Ov.

excŏquo -coxi -coctum, 3. *to boil down;* **1,** *to melt down, refine;* vitium metallis, Ov.; omne per ignes vitium, Verg.; **2,** *to bake, make hard;* terram sol excoquit, Lucr.

excors -cordis (ex and cor), *foolish, silly, without intelligence;* anus, Cic.; hoc qui non videt, excors est, Hor.

excrēmentum -i, n. (excerno), *excrement;* oris, *spittle,* Tac.; narium, Tac.

excresco -crēvi -crētum, 3. *to grow up, spring up;* in hos artus, in haec corpora, quae miramur, excrescunt, Tac.

excrētus -a -um, partic. of excerno or of excresco.

excrŭcĭābĭlis -e (excrucio), *deserving of torture,* Plaut.

excrŭcĭo, 1. *to torture, torment exceedingly.* **A.** Lit., servos fame vinculisque, Caes.; excruciare aliquem vinculis ac verberibus atque omni supplicio, Cic. **B.** Transf., a, of physical pain, fumo excruciatus, Cic.; b, of mental torture, meae me miseriae magis excruciant quam tuae, Cic.

excŭbĭae -ārum, f. (excubo). **A.** Lit., *a keeping watch, keeping guard;* o excubias tuas, o flebiles vigilias, Cic.; excubias agere alicui, *to keep watch over,* Tac.; of animals, excubiae vigilum canum, Hor.; poet., excubiae divûm

aeternae, *the everlasting fire*, Verg. **B.** Meton., *the persons who keep watch, watchmen, guard*, Cic.

excŭbĭtor -ōris, m. (excubo) *a sentinel, watchman, guard*, Caes. ; of birds, excubitor ales, *the cock*, Verg.

excŭbo -bŭi -bĭtum, 1, *to lie, or sleep out of doors.* **I.** Gen., in agris, Cic. **II.** *to stand sentinel, keep watch.* **A.** Lit., in armis, Caes. ; pro castris, Caes. ; ad portum, Caes. **B.** Transf., a, Cupido excubat in genis, Hor. ; b, *to be watchful, vigilant ;* excubabo vigilaboque pro vobis, Cic.

excūdo -cūdi -cūsum, 3. **I. A.** Lit., *to strike out ;* scintillam silici, Verg. **B.** Transf., *to hatch*, pullos ex ovis, Cic. **II.** *to make ready by striking.* **A.** *to hammer, forge ;* spirantia mollius aera, Verg. ; of bees, *to mould ;* recentes ceras, Verg. **B.** Transf., *to compose* (of writing), aliquid, Cic.

exculco, 1. (ex and calco), *to trample firm, tread hard, stamp firm ;* singuli ab intimo solo pedes terra exculcabantur, Cic.

excurro -cŭcurri and -curri -cursum, 3. **I.** *to run out, hasten forth.* **A.** Gen., 1, lit., excurrat aliquis (sc. domo), Cic. ; 2, transf., quorum animi spretis corporibus evolant atque excurrunt foras, Cic. ; campus in quo excurrere virtus possit, *show itself*, Cic. **B.** Esp. 1, milit. t.t., *to attack, make a sortie ;* omnibus portis, Liv. ; ex Africa, Cic. ; 2, transf., *to make a digression ;* longius, Cic. **II.** of places, *to run out, to project ;* promontorium in altum excurrens, Liv. ; productiora alia et quasi immoderatius excurrentia, Cic.

excursĭo -ōnis, f. (excurro), 1, *a stepping forward* (of an orator), excursio moderata eaque rara, Cic. ; 2, *an attack, assault, sally ;* excursionem facere ex oppido, Caes. ; excursiones et latrocinia hostium, Cic. ; fig., prima excursio orationis, Cic.

excursor -ōris, m. (excurro), *a scout, skirmisher*, Cic.

excursus -ūs, m. (excurro), 1, *a running forth ;* excursusque breves tentant (of bees), Verg. ; 2, milit. t.t., *an attack, sally, assault ;* excursus militum, Caes.

excūsābĭlis -e (excuso), *excusable, deserving of excuse ;* delicti pars, Ov.

excūsātĭo -ōnis (excuso). **I.** *an excuse ;* 1, gen., with subject. genit., Pompeii, Cic. ; with object. genit., peccati, Cic. ; excusationem excipere, Cic. ; stultitia excusationem non habet, *finds no excuse*, Cic. ; excusationem probare, Cic. ; justā et idoneā uti excusatione intermissionis litterarum, Cic. ; plur., *grounds of excuse ;* nullae istae excusationes sunt, Cic. ; 2, esp., *refusal, declining ;* excusatio Serv. Sulpicii legationis, Cic. **II.** *plea, defence ;* excusationem oculorum accipere, Cic. ; excusatione uti temporis or valetudinis, *to allege in excuse*, Cic.

excūso, 1. (ex and causa). **I.** *to excuse ;* se apud aliquem or se alicui, Cic. ; se de aliqua re, Caes. ; tarditatem litterarum, Cic. ; excusare aliquem or se quod, etc., Cic. ; si Lysiades excusetur Areopagites esse, *is excused on the ground that he is* etc., Cic. **II.** *to allege in excuse, to plead ;* 1, morbum, Cic. ; valetudinem, aetatem, Liv. ; 2, *to decline ;* reflex., se excusare or pass., excusar with abl., *to be excused from, relieved from a duty*, etc., Tac.

excussus -a -um, partic. of excutio.

excŭtĭo -cussi -cussum, 3. (ex and quatio). **I.** *to shake out, strike out, throw out, drive out.* **A.** Gen., 1, lit., ancoram e nave, Liv. ; litteras in terram, Cic. ; 2, transf., *to remove, drive away ;* metum de corde, Ov. ; alicuius voces, *to pay no*

more heed to, Verg. **B.** Esp., 1, *to tear away ;* agnam ore lupi, Ov. ; transf., studia de manibus, Cic. ; 2, a, of weapons, *to shoot ;* glandem, Liv. ; b, *to throw* (of a horse, etc.), equus excussit equitem, Liv. ; c, *to drive away ;* aliquem patriā, Verg. ; 3, *to press out ;* sudorem, Nep. ; transf., risum, *to force*, Hor. ; 4, *to destroy, make void ;* foedus, Verg. ; 5, somno excuti, *to be disturbed from sleep*, Verg. ; 6, *to spread out ;* brachia, Ov. **II.** *to shake violently.* **A.** caesariem, Ov. **B.** 1, *to search, examine* (by shaking a person's garments), non excutio te, si quid forte ferri habuisti, Cic. ; 2, *to test, examine, weigh ;* omnes eorum delicias, omnes ineptias, Cic.

exec . . . v. exsec.

exĕdo -ēdi -ēsum, 3. *to eat up, devour, consume.* **I.** Lit., Plaut. **II.** *to consume, destroy*, esp. of the action of time, rust, etc. ; a, lit., exesis posterioribus partibus versiculorum, Cic. ; b, transf., of the mind, *to wear away, eat into, exhaust ;* aegritudo exest animum, Cic.

exĕdra -ae, f. (ἐξέδρα), *a room,* or *hall for conversation* or *debate*, Cic.

exĕdrĭum -ii, n. (ἐξέδριον), *a sitting-room*, Cic.

exemplar -āris, n. (**exemplāre** -is, n., Lucr.). **I. A.** *a copy, transcript*, Cic. **B.** *a pattern, model, exemplar, example*, Cic. **II.** *an image, likeness*, Cic.

exemplāris -e (exemplum), *serving as a copy.* Subst., **exemplāres**, *copies ;* omnium litterarum, Tac.

exemplum -i, n. (for exempulum, from eximo, orig. *something chosen from a number of the same kind*). **I.** *something similar ;* 1, *a copy, transcript ;* Caesaris litterarum exemplum tibi misi, Cic. ; 2, *manner, fashion ;* quaestionem haberi eodem exemplo quo M. Pomponius praetor habuisset, Liv. **II.** *something to be imitated.* **A.** Artistically, *an original, pattern ;* in rerum simulacrum ab animali exemplo transfertur, Cic. **B.** Morally, 1, *a copy, model ;* exemplum innocentiae, pudicitiae, Cic. ; exemplum cupere or petere ab aliquo, Cic. ; 2, *an example to be imitated* or *avoided ;* aliquid aliorum exemplo institutoque facere, Cic. ; plus exemplo quam peccato nocent, Cic. ; 3, *a warning and deterring example, exemplary punishment ;* exemplum severitatis edere, Cic. ; exemplum statuere in aliquem or in aliquo, Cic. **III.** *that which illustrates* or *explains, instance, example, proof ;* magna exempla casuum humanorum, Liv. ; exempli causā, or gratiā, or in exemplum, *for example*, Cic.

exemptus -a -um, partic. of eximo.

exĕo -ii (-īvi) -ĭtum, 4. **I.** Intransit., *to go out, go away, go forth.* **A.** Lit., 1, ex urbe, Cic. ; ab urbe, Liv. ; de triclinio, Cic. ; domo, Cic. ; 2, of things, a, of lots, quum de consularibus mea prima sors exisset, Cic. ; b, *to spring up, sprout forth ;* de stamine pampinus exit, Ov. ; c, *to rise in the air, ascend ;* curribus auras in aetherias, Verg. **B.** Transf., 1, gen., de or e vita, *to die*, Cic. ; e patriciis, *to lose one's rank as a patrician*, Cic. ; exisse ex or de potestate (mentis), *to lose control over oneself*, Cic. ; 2, esp., a, *to come out of ;* aere alieno, Cic. ; b, *to become known ;* exit oratio, Cic. ; c, of time, *to come to an end, pass away ;* quinto anno exeunte, Cic. **II.** Transit., 1, *to pass over, beyond ;* Avernas valles, Ov. ; transf., modum, Ov. ; 2, *to ward off ;* vim viribus, Verg.

exeq . . . v. ex-seq . . .

exercĕo -ŭi -ĭtum, 2. (ex and ARC-eo), *to work thoroughly, fatigue, weary.* **I.** Lit., a, equos aequore campi, *to exercise*, Verg. ; indomitas qualis undas exercet Auster, Hor. ; b, *to occupy*, *employ the limbs in work;* assiduis brachia telis, Ov.; **c,** of slaves, animals, etc., *to employ in work;* famulas ad lumina longo penso, Verg.; **d,** *to work hard at;* solum presso sub vomere, *to cultivate diligently,* Verg. **II.** Transf., **A.** Gen., *to harass, trouble;* meos casus in quibus me fortuna vehementer exercuit, Cic.; exerceri poenis, Verg. **B.** *to occupy in some activity, to exercise, practise;* **a,** of the body, hoc vocem et vires suas, Cic.; milit. t. t., *to exercise in arms, drill;* copias, Caes.; reflex., se exercere and middle exerceri, *to practise, exercise;* of athletes, se in curriculo, Cic.; **b,** of the mind, memoriam, Cic.; adolescentes ad copiam rhetorum, Cic.; reflex., se exercere, or middle, exerceri, *to practise;* se quotidianis commentationibus acerrime, Cic. **C.** *to make use of* an instrument or weapon, *to employ, use;* **1,** gen., **a,** arma, Verg.; diem, *to do one's day's work,* Verg.; **b,** of politics, *to use, practise;* facilitatem et lenitudinem animi in aliquo, Cic.; graves inimicitias cum aliquo, Sall.; libidinem et avaritiam in socios, Liv.; **2,** esp., **a,** of land, *to cultivate;* praedia rustica, Liv.; of mines, *to work;* metalla auri atque argenti, Liv.; **b,** *to practise an art,* etc., medicinam, Cic.; **c,** legal t. t., *(a) to preside over, to conduct;* qui exercet judicium, Cic.; quaestionem inter sicarios, Cic.; *(β)* vectigalia, *to manage,* Cic.; *(γ) to bring a law into execution;* legem confestius exerceri, Liv.

exercĭtātĭo -ōnis, f. (exercito), *practise, exercise;* **a,** of the body, corpora nostra motu atque exercitatione recalescunt, Cic.; **b,** of the mind, with genit., dicendi, Cic.; juris civilis, Cic.; **c,** *practice;* virtutis, scelerum, Cic.

exercĭtātus -a -um, p. adj. with compar. and superl. (from exercito), **1,** *busied;* agris subigendis, Cic.; **2,** *practised, exercised;* **a,** of the body, homines in armis exercitati, Cic.; exercitatus in uxoribus necandis, Cic.; **b,** of the mind, in arithmeticis satis exercitatus, Cic. **II.** *troubled, harassed;* Syrtes exercitatae Noto, Hor.; curis agitatus et exercitatus animus, Cic.

exercĭtĭum -ĭi, n. (exerceo), *practice, exercise;* equitum, Tac.

exercĭto, 1. (intens. of exerceo), *to practise,* Varr.

1. exercĭtus -a -um, p. adj. (exerceo), 1, *trained, schooled;* militiā, bello, Tac.; 2, *severe, vexatious,* Tac.; 3, *tried, harassed,* Cic.

2. exercĭtus -ūs, m. (exerceo), **a,** *a trained body of soldiers, army;* exercitus terrestris, navalis, Liv.; ducere exercitum, Cic.; conscribere, Cic.; parare or comparare, Cic.; conficere, Cic.; cogere, Caes.; repente conflare, Cic.; paucis diebus facere, Cic.; accipere, Cic.; exercitus alere, Cic.; exercitum ex castris educere, Caes.; exercitum exponere, *put on ship,* Caes.; esp., *the infantry;* exercitus equitatusque, Caes., Liv.; his omnibus diebus exercitum castris continuit, equestri proelio quotidie contendit, Caes.; **b,** poet., *crowd, swarm;* corvorum, Verg.

exēsor -ōris, m. (exedo), *one who gnaws or eats away,* Lucr.

exhālātĭo -ōnis, f. (exhalo), *an exhalation, vapour;* exhalationes terrae, Cic.

exhālo, 1. **I.** Transit., *to exhale, emit vapour,* **a,** of things, nebulam, Verg.; odores, Lucr.; **b,** of persons, vitam, Verg.; animam, Ov.; crapulam or vinum, Cic. **II.** Intransit., *to breathe forth,* Ov.

exhaurĭo -hausi -haustum, 4. **I.** *to draw out.* **A.** 1, of fluids, sentinam, Cic.; 2, gen., *to take out;* terram manibus, Caes.; omnem pecuniam ex aerario, Cic. **B.** Transf., *to take away;* partem ex tuis laudibus, Cic. **II.** *to empty out.* **A.** Lit., fossas cloacasque, Liv.; puteos,

poculum, vinum, *to empty by drinking,* Cic.; aerarium, Cic. **B.** Transf., **1,** *to exhaust, impoverish;* facultates patriae, Cic.; homines, Cic.; **2,** *to weaken, exhaust;* sermo hominum exhaustus est, Cic.; **3,** *to bring to an end, complete;* mandata, Cic.; **4,** *to endure, suffer;* labores, Liv.

exhērēdo, 1. (exheres), *to disinherit;* aliquem, Cic.

exhērēs -ēdis, *disinherited;* with genit., paternorum bonorum exheres, Cic.

exhĭbĕo -hĭbŭi -hĭbĭtum, 2. (ex and habeo). **I.** Gen., **a,** *to produce, bring forth;* esp., *to produce in a court of justice;* pupillum, fratres, Cic.; *to produce for proof,* etc., exhibe librarium illud legum vestrarum, Cic.; **b,** *to hand over, deliver;* omnia alicui integra, Cic. **II.** 1, *to show, display, exhibit;* **a,** dea formam removit anilem Palladaque exhibuit, Ov.; **b,** populo Romano philosophiam, *set forth, present,* Cic.; 2, *to make, to cause;* alicui negotium, *to cause trouble,* Cic.; so alicui molestiam, Cic.; 3, *to grant, allow;* toros, Ov.; exhibe liberam contionem vel Argis vel Lacedaemone, Liv.

exhĭlăro, 1. *to make cheerful;* miraris tam exhilaratam esse servitutem nostram, Cic.

exhorresco -horrŭi, 3. **I.** Intransit., *to shudder exceedingly, be terrified;* aequoris instar, Ov.; metu, Cic.; in aliquo, Cic. **II.** Transit., *to tremble at, to dread;* vultus, Verg.

exhortātĭo -ōnis, f. (exhortor), *exhortation, encouragement;* ducum, Tac.

exhortor, 1. dep., *to exhort, encourage;* natum, Verg.; foll. by ut and the subj., Tac.

exĭgo -ēgi -actum, 3. (ex and ago). **I.** *to drive out, drive away.* **A.** Lit., 1, of living beings, reges ex civitate, Cic.; servam e montibus, Liv.; 2, of things, **a,** sacer admissas exigit Hebrus aquas, *pours into the sea,* Ov.; **b,** agrorum fructus, *to sell,* Liv. **B.** Transf., otium, *to banish,* Hor. **II.** *to drive in, to thrust;* ensem per juvenem, Verg. **III.** *to complete, finish;* **a,** monumentum aere perennius, Hor.; opus, Ov.; **b,** of time, *to spend, pass;* exacto per scelera die, Tac.; *to complete, bring to an end;* exactis mensibus, Verg.; exactā aetate, *at the end of life,* Cic. **IV.** *to exact, demand.* **A.** Lit., **a,** of money, pecunias, Cic.; vectigalia, Cic.; **b,** of work, aedes privatas velut publicum opus, *superintend the execution of,* Liv.; esp., *(a) to require the building or making of something;* viam, Cic.; *(β) to make a requisition or demand for something;* equitum peditumque certum numerum a civitatibus, Caes. **B.** Transf., *to demand, require;* jusjurandum, Liv.; veritatem a teste, Cic.; promissum ab aliquo, Cic. **V.** *to measure, weigh, examine.* **A.** Lit., columnas ad perpendiculum, Cic. **B.** Transf., 1, ad illam summam veritatem legitimum jus, Cic.; 2, *to consider, reflect upon;* tempus secum ipsa opusque exigit, Verg.; non satis exactum quid agam, *not certain,* Cic.

exĭgŭē, adv. (exiguus), 1, *sparingly, scantily, scarcely;* frumentum exigue dierum xxx habere, Caes.; nimis exigue et exiliter ad calculos revocare amicitiam, *too narrowly,* Cic.; 2, *briefly;* exigue scripta est (epistola), Cic.

exĭgŭĭtas -ātis, f. (exiguus), 1, of space, *smallness;* castrorum, Caes.; 2, of number, *paucity;* copiarum, Cic.; 3, of time, *shortness;* ut temporis exiguitas postulabat, Caes.

exĭgŭus -a -um (exigo), *small, little, scanty.* **I.** Of quantity, **A.** Of space, *small, little;* castra, Caes.; pars terrae, Cic.; neut. subst., **exĭgŭum** -i, n. *smallness;* spatii, Liv. **B.** Of number, *scanty, small;* numerus oratorum, Cic. **C.** Of time, *short, scanty;* vita, Cic. **II.** Of quality,

1, *thin, meagre;* corpus, Nep.; 2, *sparing, scanty;* toga, Hor.; laus, Cic.; 3, of strength, *weak;* vires, Verg.; vox, Ov.

exilis -e (for exiglis, from exigo), *little, thin, slender, meagre, poor;* 1, of number, legiones, *weak, not of their proper number,* Cic.; 2, of quality, a, *thin, slender, meagre;* cor, Cic.; femur, Hor.; b, of discourse, *meagre, dry;* genus sermonis, Cic.; c, *poor, insignificant, scanty;* solum, Cic.; domus, Hor.

exilitas -ātis, f. (exilis), *thinness, meagreness, weakness;* in dicendo, Cic.

exiliter, adv. (exilis), *thinly, poorly, meagrely;* a, *sparingly, parsimoniously;* nimis exigue et exiliter ad calculos revocare amicitiam, Cic.; b, *uninterestingly;* annales sane exiliter descripti, Cic.; c, of strength, *weakly;* nolo verba exiliter exanimata exire, Cic.

eximiē, adv. (eximius), *uncommonly, extraordinarily, extremely;* diligere, Cic.; templum eximie ornatum, Liv.

eximius -a -um (eximo). **I.** *excepted;* tu unus eximius eo, in quo hoc praecipuum ac singulare valeat, Liv.; te illi unum eximium cui consuleret fuisse, Cic. **II.** *exceptional, distinguished, extraordinary, uncommon;* facies, ingenium, spes, Cic.; ironic., istae vestrae eximiae pulchraeque virtutes, Cic.

eximo -ēmi -emptum, 3. (ex and emo), *to take out, take away.* **I.** Lit., unam spinam de pluribus, Hor.; aliquid tamquam e vinculis alicuius rei, Cic. **II.** Transf., *to take away;* 1, a, aliquid ex rerum natura, Cic.; unum diem ex mense, Cic.; moram certaminis hosti, Liv.; b, of time, *to delay, procrastinate, waste;* diem dicendo, Cic.; c, of persons, aliquem ex or de reis, Cic.; 2, *to take away from some evil;* a, aliquid de, *to free from;* agrum de vectigalibus, Cic.; b, aliquid alicui, *to take something away from;* alicui curas, Ov.; c, of persons, aliquem ex with the abl., or with the abl. alone, *to free from;* aliquem ex culpa, Cic.; aliquem alicui rei, *to take away from;* aliquem vitae, Tac.; Syracusas in libertatem, *to free,* Liv.; d, *to except;* aliquem, Cic.

exin = exinde (q.v.).

exinānĭo -īvi -ītum, 4. *to empty;* navem, Cic.; agros, gentes, *to plunder,* Cic.

exindĕ (exin), adv. **I.** Of place, *from there, thence, thereupon, next;* mari finitimus aër, Cic. **II.** Of time, 1, *thereupon, after that, then,* Cic.; 2, in the enumeration of a series of facts, *then, next,* Verg., Liv.

existimātĭo -ōnis, f. (existimo). **I.** *the opinion that a man has of a thing* or *person, judgment;* non militis de imperatore existimationem esse, Liv. **II.** *the opinion that other persons have of a man,* esp. morally, *reputation, good name, honour, character;* bona, integra, magna, Cic.; alicuius existimationem offendere **or** oppugnare, Cic.; venisse in eam existimationem, Cic.

existimātor -ōris, m. (existimo), *one who forms* or *gives an opinion, a critic,* Cic.

existimo (exaestŭmo, existŭmo), 1. *to judge a thing according to its value.* **I.** *to consider, hold, regard, esteem, deem;* with predic. acc., existumare aliquem avarum, Cic.; aliquem sapientem et appellare et existumare, Cic.; in pass., homo, ut existimabatur, avarus et furax; with in and the abl., in hostium numero existimari, Cic. **II.** Transf., **A.** *to think, be of opinion, hold;* with acc. and infin., non possum existimare plus quemquam a se ipso quam me a te amari, Cic.; Africano vim attulisse existimatus est, Cic.; with pronoun acc., quod ego nullo modo exis-

timo; impers., ita intelligimus vulgo existimari, Cic. **B.** *to judge, decide, pass judgment;* esp. of critical judgment on literary works, with de and the abl., de scriptoribus, qui nondum ediderunt, existimare non possumus, Cic.; bene or male de aliquo, Cic.; with rel. sent., existimari non potest, vix existimari potest utrum . . . an, etc., Caes., Liv.; absol. partic. subst., **existimantes** -ium, m. *the critics,* Cic.

exitĭābĭlis -e (exitium), *deadly, destructive;* bellum, Cic.; tyrannus, Liv.

exitĭālis -e (exitium), *destructive, fatal, deadly;* exitus, Cic.; donum Minervae, Verg.

exitĭōsus -a -um, adj. with compar and superl. (exitium), *destructive, fatal, deadly;* conjuratio, Cic.; exitiosum esse reipublicae, Cic.

exitium -ĭi, n. (exeo, lit., *a going out* or *away), destruction, ruin;* 1, lit., huius urbis, Cic.; exitio esse alicui, *to be fatal to,* Cic.; omnia exitia publica, Cic.; 2, meton., *the cause of destruction,* Hor.

exitus -ūs, m. (exeo), *a going out, a going forth.* **I. A.** Lit., reditum mihi gloriosum injuria tua dedit; non exitum calamitosum, Cic.; omni exitu et pabulatione interclusi, Caes.; with ab, ne exitus inclusis ab urbe esset, Liv. **B.** Meton., *a place of going out, exit;* quod (posticum) devium maximi atque occultissimi exitus erat, Liv. **II.** Transf., **A.** Gen., quae plurimos exitus dant ad eiusmodi digressionem, *opportunities for digression,* Cic. **B.** Esp., 1, *the end;* adducta ad exitum quaestio est, Cic.; hic fuit exitus oppugnationis, Caes.; tristes exitus habere, Cic.; esp., a, of a tragedy, *the catastrophe;* ut tragici poetae, quum explicare argumenti exitum non potestis, Cic.; b, *the end of life;* humanus, Cic.; 2, *the result, consequence;* disceptatio sine exitu fuit, Liv.; 3, *issue, result;* eventus atque exitus rerum, Cic.; exitus futuri temporis, Hor.

exlex -lēgis, *lawless, bound by no law;* exlegem esse Sullam, Cic.

exmŏvĕo = emoveo (q.v.).

exōdium -ĭi, n. (ἐξόδιον), *a comic afterpiece,* Liv., Juv.

exōlesco -lēvi -lētum, 3. **I.** *to grow to full size;* only in perf. partic., exoletus, Plaut. **II.** *to pass away from use, be out of date, obsolete;* ne vetustissima Italiae disciplina per desidiam exolesceret, Tac.; exoletum jam vetustate odium, Liv.

exōlētus -a -um, partic. of exolesco.

exŏnĕro, 1. **A.** Lit., *to unload, disburden;* a, Plaut.; plenas colos, *to spin off,* Ov.; b, *to remove, send away;* multitudinem in proximas terras, Tac. **B.** Transf., *to free, release, relieve;* civitatem metu, Liv.; regnum praegravante multitudine, Liv.

exoptātus -a -um, p. adj. with compar. and superl. (exopto), *desired, wished for;* nuntius, Cic.; nihil exoptatius adventu meo, Cic.; exoptatissimus gratulatio, Cic.

exopto, 1. *to desire eagerly, earnestly wish for;* exoptare ea maxime, Cic.; Samnitium adventum, Liv.; tibi pestem exoptant, *wish you,* Cic.; with infin., Cic.; with ut and the subj., Cic.

exōrābĭlis -e, adj. with compar. (exoro), *easily entreated, placable,* Cic., Hor.

exordĭor -orsus sum, 4. dep., 1, *to lay a warp, begin to weave;* fig., pertexe quod exorsus es, Cic.; 2, *to begin;* bellum ab causa tam nefanda, Liv.; without acc., of orators, *to begin,* ab ipsa re, Cic.; with infin., dicere, Cic. Partic subst., **exorsa** -ōrum, n. *the beginning,* Cic.

exordium -ĭi, n. (exordior), 1, *the warp*

of a web, Quint. ; **2, a,** *the beginning ;* vitae, Cic.; plur., revocare exordia prima pugnae,Verg.; **b,** esp., *the beginning of a speech ;*in dicendi exordio permoveri, Cic.; as a part of **a speech,** *the introduction,* Cic.

exŏrĭor -ortus sum -ŏrīri, dep. 3. and 4. **I.** *to rise, rise up.* **A.** Lit., omnes exorti, *sprang up,* Liv. ; esp. of the sun, moon, and stars ; post solstitium Canicula exoritur, Cic. **B.** Transf., **1,** *to appear, step forward, make one's appearance ;* repentinus Sulla nobis exoritur, Cic. ; exortus est servus, *as an accuser,* Cic. ; of abstractions, exoritur Antipatri ratio ex altera parte, Cic. ; **2,** *to rise up from a misfortune, breathe again ;* ego nunc paulum exorior, Cic. **II.** *to arise, proceed, take rise.* **A.** exoritur ingens per litora flatus, Verg. **B.** Transf., **1,** exoritur fama alicuius rei or de aliqua re ; with accus. and infin., Lucr. ; **2,** *to proceed from ;* honestum quod ex virtutibus exoritur, Cic.

exornātĭo -ōnis, f. (exorno), *adorning, ornament.* **A.** Lit., Cic. **B.** *embellishment of a speech,* Cic.

exornātor -ōris, m. (exorno), *one who adorns, an embellisher ;* ceteri non exornatores rerum, sed tantummodo narratores fuerunt, Cic.

exorno, 1. *to furnish with, provide plentifully ;* **1,** vicinitatem armis, Sall. ; **2,** *to ornament, adorn ;* a, lit., domum, Cic. ; triclinium, Cic. ; **b,** transf., Cic. ; Graeciam praestantissimis artibus, Cic. ; philosophiam falsā gloriā ; of speech, orationem, Cic.

exŏro, 1. **I.** *to entreat earnestly, obtain by entreaty, prevail upon ;* exora supplice prece deos, Ov. ; exorare pacem divūm, Verg. ; with ut and the subj., denique exoravit tyrannum ut abire liceret, Cic. **II.** *to propitiate, move ;* carmina exorant deos, Ov. ; exorare aliquem or exorari foll. by ut or ne and the subj., Cic. ; non exorari by quin, Cic. ; absol., viri non esse neque exorari neque placari, Cic.

1. **exorsus** -a -um, partic. of exordior.

2. **exorsus** -ūs, m. (exordior), *a beginning ;* orationis meae, Cic.

exos -ossis, *without bones,* Lucr.

exoscŭlor, 1., dep., *to kiss frequently ;* alicuius manum, Tac.

exosso, 1. (exos), *to bone, take out the bones,* Ter. ; exossatum pectus, *boneless, flexible,* Lucr.

exostra -ae, f. (ἐξώστρα), a*theatrical machine, by which the inside of a house was revealed to the spectators,* Cic.

exōsus -a -um (ex and odi), *hating exceedingly ;* exosus Trojanos, Verg. ; templa oculos exosa viriles, Ov.

exōtĭcus -a -um (ἐξωτικός), *foreign, outlandish, exotic,* Plaut.

expallesco -lŭi, 3. *to become very pale, to grow white ;* toto ore, Ov. ; poet., with acc., Pindarici fontis haustus, *to dread,* Hor.

expando -pansi, -pansum and -passum, 3. *to stretch out, expand, spread out.* **A.** Lit., expassae delubri fores, *opened,* Tac. **B.** Transf., *to explain ;* rerum naturam dictis, Lucr.

expătro, 1. *to squander,* Cat.

expăvesco -pāvi, 3. *to be exceedingly terrified ;* ad id, Liv. ; with acc., ensem, *to dread exceedingly,* Hor.

expĕdĭo -īvi and -ĭi -ītum, 4. (ex and pes). **I.** *to disengage, disentangle, set free.* **A.** Lit., se ex laqueo, Cic. **B.** Transf., *to free, help out, bring off ;* se ab omni occupatione, Cic. ; a, Claudias manus per acuta belli, *lead successfully,* Hor. ; jaculum trans finem, *to throw,* Hor. ; **b,** *to despatch, settle, execute ;* negotia, Cic. ; rem

frumentariam, Caes. ; **c,** *to explain, show ;* omnem expediat morbi causam, Verg. ; priusquam huiusmodi rei initium expediam, Sall. ; ea de re quam verissime expediam, Tac. **II. A.** *to bring forth, provide ;* **1,** lit., virgas, Cic. ; Cererem canistris, Verg. ; **2,** transf., a, milit. t. t., *to make ready ;* naves or classem, Caes. ; se ad pugnam, Liv. ; **b,** *to find out, discover ;* alicui vicarium, Liv. **B.** res expedit, or impers. expedit, *it is expedient, useful, advantageous ;* non quominus expediat quidquam Caesari ad diuturnitatem dominationis, Cic. ; with acc. and infin. or the infin. simply, omnibus bonis expedit salvam esse rempublicam, Cic. ; with ut and the subj., Tac.

expĕdītē, adv. with compar. and superl. (expeditus), **1,** *quickly ;* expeditius navigare, Cic. ; **2,** *without difficulty, easily ;* explicare, Cic.

expĕdītĭo -ōnis, f. (expedio), *an undertaking against an enemy, expedition ;* milites ex hibernis in expeditionem evocare, Sall.; milites equitesque in expeditionem mittere, Caes. ; in expeditionem exercitum educere, Cic.

expĕdītus -a -um, p. adj. (from expedio). **I.** *unimpeded, unshackled ;* a, *lightly clad ;* Clodius, Cic. ; jaculatores, Liv. ; hence, subst., **expĕdītus** -i, m. *a light-armed foot-soldier,* Caes. ; expediti, *not burdened with baggage,* Liv. ; **b,** *without obstacles, easy ;* via, Liv. ; locus, Caes. ; **c,** *not hindered by obstacles, easy, quick ;* ad suos receptus, Caes. ; expedita et facile currens oratio, Cic. ; **d,** *not hindered by business, free ;* ut expeditus in Galliam proficisci posset, Cic. ; **e,** *ready, prepared ;* expeditus homo et paratus, Cic. ; ad dicendum, Cic. ; of soldiers, *ready for fight ;* copiae, Caes. ; copias in expedito habere ad, etc., Liv. **II.** *disentangled ;* a, *put in order, settled ;* negotia, Cic. ; **b,** *decisive ;* victoria, Caes.

expello -pŭli -pulsum, 3. *to drive out, away.* **I.** Of animals, pecus portā Esquilinā, Liv. **II. 1,** *to drive away, expel, throw away ;* a, lit., genis oculos, *to tear,* Ov. ; b, transf., naturam furcā, Hor. ; **2,** *to drive forth, thrust forth ;* a, lit., ab litore naves in altum, Liv. ; sagittam arcu, Ov. ; aliquem aethere toto, Ov. ; (*a*) esp. milit. t.t., *to drive out ;* aliquem ex oppido, Caes.; Romanos castris, Caes. ; (β) *to drive out of* a house or country, *to banish ;* aliquem domo suā, Cic. ; patriā, Cic. ; ex urbe, Cic. ; aliquem bonis, *from one's property,* Cic. ; *to drive out* kings, tyrants, etc., aliquem regno, Cic. ; (γ) *to divorce ;* filiam ex matrimonio, Cic. ; b, transf., (*a*) aliquem vitā, *to bring about a person's death,* Cic. ; (β) *to drive away, banish ;* omnem dubitationem, Caes. ; somnum or quietem, Verg.

expendo -pendi -pensum, 3. *to weigh.* **I. A.** Lit., ut jam expendantur non numerentur pecuniae, Cic. **B.** Transf., *to weigh, examine, test ;* expendere atque aestimare voluptates, Cic. ; testem, Cic. **II.** *to weigh out, pay out money, to pay.* **A.** Lit., auri pondo centum, Cic. ; esp., ferre alicui expensum, *to put down in one's account book a payment to some one else,* Cic. **B.** Transf., *to pay ;* poenas scelerum, Verg.

expergĕfăcĭo -fēci -factum, 3. *to wake up.* **I.** Lit., Suet. **II.** Transf., *to rouse, excite ;* se, Cic.

expergiscor -perrectus sum, 3. dep., *to awake, wake up, rise from sleep.* **A.** Lit., si dormis, expergiscere, Cic. **B.** Transf., *to awake, rouse oneself ;* experrecta nobilitas, Cic.

expĕrĭens -entis, p. adj. with compar. and superl. (from experior), *active, industrious, enterprising, experienced in ;* promptus homo et experiens, Cic. ; with genit., experiens laborum, Ov.

expĕrĭentĭa -ae, f. (experior), **1,** *trial, ex-*

periment; with genit., patrimonii amplificandi, Cic.; **2**, *the knowledge gained by experiment, experience*; multarum rerum experientiā **cognitus,** Tac.

expĕrĭmentum -i, n. (experior), *trial, experiment*; hoc maximum est experimentum, Cic.; Metello experimentis cognitum erat genus Numidarum perfidum esse, Sall.

expĕrĭor -pertus sum, 4. dep. (ex and root PER, whence com -perio or -perior, peritus, periculum). **I. A.** *to try, test, prove, put to the test*; **1**, gen., alicuius amorem, Cic.; vim veneni in servo, Cic.; amicos, Cic.; **2**, esp., *to try in a hostile manner, to measure one's strength with another*; **a,** in battle, si iterum experiri velint, iterum paratum esse decertare, Caes.; **b,** in a court of law, *to litigate*; cum aliquo, Cic. **B.** *to try the success of something, to risk, hazard, make a trial of*; **1,** gen., experiri id nolent quod se assequi posse diffidant, Cic.; rei eventum experiri, Caes.; ultima audere atque experiri, Liv.; with ut and the subj., experiar certe ut hinc avolem, Cic.; **2,** esp., experiri jus, *to go to law*, Cic.; experiri judicium populi Romani, *to leave it to the decision of the Roman people*, Liv. **II.** *to experience, find, or know by experience*; **1,** omnia quae dico expertus in nobis, Cic.; with predic. acc., deos constantes inimicos, Ov.; with acc. and infin., jam antea expertus sum parum fidei miseris esse, Sall.; equidem in me ipso saepissime experior, ut exalbescam in principio dicendi, Cic.; with relat. sent., experiri libet quantum audeatis, Liv.; de me experior, *I experience it in myself*, Cic.; **2,** *to experience something unpleasant*; nondum alteram fortunam expertus, Liv. (pass., libertatis dulcedine nondum expertā, Liv.).

experrectus -a -um, partic. of expergiscor.

expers -pertis (ex and pars). **A.** *having no part in, not sharing in*; with genit, periculorum, publici consilii, Cic. **B.** Transf., *wanting in, destitute of*; with genit., omnis eruditionis, Cic.; viri, *without a husband*, Ov.; with abl., famā atque fortunis, Sall.

expertus -a um, p. adj. with compar. and superl. (from experior), *that which has been often tested, tried, approved*; exercitus, Liv.; with genit., expertus belli, Verg., Tac.; with abl., expertus tribuniciis certaminibus, Liv.

expĕtendus -a -um, p. adj. (expeto), *to be desired, desirable*; gloriam expetendam putare, Cic.

expĕtesso, 3. (expeto), *to desire, wish for*, Plaut.

expĕto -ivi -itum, 3. **I.** Transit., *to desire, wish, or long for*; vitam alicuius, Cic.; auxilium ab aliquo, Cic.; with infin., vincere illi expetunt, Cic.; with acc. and infin., nostram gloriam tuā virtute augeri expeto, Cic.; with ut and the subj., Tac.; of things, mare medium terrae locum expetens, *encroaching on*, Cic. **II.** Intransit., *to fall upon, befall*; ut in eum omnes expetant huiusce clades belli, Liv.

expĭātĭo -ōnis, f. (expio), *atonement, expiation*; scelerum, Cic.

expīlātĭo -ōnis, f. (expilo), *a plundering, robbing*; sociorum, Cic.

expīlātor -ōris, m. (expilo), *a plunderer, robber*, Cic.

expĭlo, 1. *to plunder, rob*; aerarium, Cic.

expingo -pinxi -pictum, 3. *to paint, describe, depict in writing*, Cic.

expĭo, 1. **I.** *to propitiate, appease.* **A.** poenis manes mortuorum, Cic. **B.** *to avert an omen, or sign of the wrath of the gods*; prodigium, Liv. **II. A.** *to purify*; forum a sceleris vestigiis, Cic.; religionem aedium suarum, Cic. **B.**

to atone for; **1**, lit., scelus supplicio, Cic.; tua scelera dii in nostros milites expiaverunt, *have avenged on our soldiers*, Cic.; **2**, transf., *to atone for, make amends for*; incommodum virtute, Caes.

expiscor, 1, dep., *to fish out*; transf., *to search out, find out*; omnia ab aliquo, Cic.

explānātē, adv. with compar. (explanatus), *clearly, plainly*, Cic.

explānātĭo -ōnis, f. (explano), **1**, gen., *a making clear, explanation*; naturae, Cic.; **2**, esp., **a,** *interpretation*; portentorum, Cic.; **b,** rhet. t.t., *illustration*, Cic.

explānātor -ōris, m. (explano), *one who explains, an interpreter, expositor*; oraculorum et vaticinationum, Cic.

explānātus -a -um, p. adj. (from explano), *clear, plain*; vocum impressio, Cic.

explāno, 1. (ex and planus), *to explain, expound, make clear*: **1**, ille tibi omnia explanabit, Cic.; **2, a,** *to interpret*; carmen, Liv.; **b,** *to set forth, state*; de cuius hominis moribus pauca prius explananda sunt, Sall.

explaudo = explodo (q.v.).

explĕo -plēvi -plētum, 2. *to fill, fill up, complete by filling.* **I.** Lit., paludem cratibus atque aggere, Caes.; rimas, Cic. **II.** Transf., **1**, gen., sententias mollioribus numeris, Cic.; **2**, esp., **a,** *to amount to, make up*; aurum quod summam talenti Attici expleret, Liv.; milit. t.t., trium milium numerum, Liv.; **b,** *to fulfil, discharge*; munus, Cic.; **c,** *to satisfy, quench, appease*; sitim, Cic.; vereor ne non scribendo te expleam, Cic.; with genit., animum ultricis flammae, Cic.; **d,** *to make good*; ea damna, Liv.; **e,** *to fill up, complete the number of*; centurias, tribus, Liv.; legiones, Caes.; **f,** *to complete, perfect*; vitam beatam cumulate, Cic.; **g,** of time, *to complete, finish*; expletum annum habeto, Cic.

explētĭo -ōnis, f. (expleo), *satisfying*; naturae, Cic.

explētus -a -um, p. adj. (from expleo), *perfect, complete*; expletus omnibus suis partibus, Cic.

explĭcātē, adv. (explicatus), *plainly, clearly*, Cic.

explĭcātĭo -ōnis, f. (explico). **A.** *an unfolding, uncoiling*; rudentis, Cic. **B.** Transf., *explanation, exposition, interpretation*; in disserendo mira explicatio, Cic.; explicatio fabularum, Cic.

explĭcātor -ōris, m. (explico), *an expounder, interpreter, explainer*; rerum explicator prudens, Cic.

1. explĭcātus -a -um, p. adj. with compar. and superl. (explico). **I.** *ordered, arranged*; provincia quam maxime apta explicataque, Cic. **II.** *plain, clear*; litterae tuae, quibus nihil potest esse explicatius, Cic.

2. explĭcātus -ūs, m. (explico), *explanation, exposition*; difficiles habere explicatus, Cic.

explĭcĭtus -a -um, p. adj. (from explico), *straightforward, easy*; ex duobus consiliis propositis explicitius videbatur Ilerdam reverti Caes.

explĭco -āvi -ātum, and (not in Cicero) -ŭi -itum, 1. *to unfold, unroll, disentangle.* **I.** Lit., **A.** volumen, Cic.; suas pennas, Ov.; frontem, *to unwrinkle*, Hor. **B.** *to spread out, extend, expand*; forum laxare et usque ad atrium Libertatis explicare, Cic.; esp. as milit. t.t., *to extend the ranks, deploy*; agmen, aciem, ordines, Liv. **II.** Transf., **A.** 1, explica atque excute intelligentiam tuam, Cic.; **2,** *to provide, arrange*; rem frumentariam, Caes.; **3,** *to set free*; numquam laborant, quem ad modum se probent, sed quem ad modum se explicent dicendo, Cic.; **4,** t.

accomplish, execute, bring about; rationes meas, accounts, Cic. ; alicuius negotia, Cic. ; mandata, Cic. ; of a debt, *to pay off;* nomen, Cic. ; **5,** *to explain in discourse, expound, interpret;* causas rerum, Cic.; with relat. sent., explicare breviter quae mihi sit ratio et causa cum Caesare, Cic. ; absol., explicare, de rerum natura, Cic. ; *6, to discover, find out;* ut explicarem quid optimum esset factu, Cic.

explōdo (explaudo) -plōsi -plōsum, 3. **I.** *to drive off with a noise,* Sen. **II.** *to hiss a player off the stage;* histrionem exsibilare et explodere, Cic.; transf., *to reject, disapprove;* sententiam, Cic.

explōrātē, adv. with compar. (exploratus), *certainly, surely, definitely;* ad te explorate scribo, Cic.

explōrātĭo -ōnis, f. (exploro), *an exploring, investigation;* occulta, Tac.

explōrātor -ōris, m. (exploro), *one who investigates, an explorer, scout, spy,* Caes.

explōrātus -a -um, p. adj. with compar. and superl. (exploro), *established, confirmed, certain, sure;* spes, Cic. ; victoria, Caes. ; de quo mihi exploratum est, *I am convinced, am sure,* foll. by acc. and infin., Cic.

explōro, 1. **I.** *to seek out, search out, investigate, explore.* **A.** Africam, Cic. **B.** Esp. 1, milit. t. t., *to gain intelligence, spy out, reconnoitre;* hostium iter, Caes. ; in abl. absol., explorato or explorato ante, *after intelligence had been gained,* Liv. ; **2,** transf., a, *to search out, examine, investigate;* rem totam, Cic. ; b, *to spy out for something;* fugam domini, Cic. **II.** *to test, try, put to proof;* explorat robora fumus, Verg. ; epulas, cibos potusque, Tac.

explōsĭo -ōnis, f. (explodo), *a hissing off the stage,* ap. Cic.

expŏlĭo -īvi -ītum, 4. *to smooth, polish, to polish, refine;* Dionem Plato doctrinis omnibus expolivit, Cic. ; partes non eādem ratione, Cic.

expŏlītĭo -ōnis, f. (expolio), *a smoothing, polishing.* **A.** Lit., urbana, *of a town-house,* Cic. **B.** Transf., of discourse, *polishing, embellishing;* inventi artificiosa, Cic.

expŏlītus -a -um, p. adj. with compar. and superl. (expolio), **1,** *smooth, polished;* deus expolitior, Cat. ; **2,** *polished, refined;* vir omni vitā excultus atque expolitus, Cic.

expōno -pŏsŭi -pŏsĭtum, 3. *to put out, place out, set out.* **I.** Lit., **A.** Gen., scalas, *put up,* Verg. ; expositus, of places, *lying towards, placed near;* expositae prope in ipsis litoribus urbes, Liv. ; super exposta (= exposita) ponto, Verg. **B.** Esp., 1, *to put on land;* a, *to throw on the land;* os Orphei peregrinis arenis, Ov. ; b, naut. t.t., *to land, disembark;* exponere frumentum, Cic.; esp. of troops, milites navibus, Caes.; **2,** *to expose openly;* aliquid venditioni, Tac. ; esp. for show, vasa Samia, Cic. ; aliquem populo videndum, Ov. ; copias in omnibus collibus, *place openly,* Caes. ; **3,** *to expose a child;* in proxima alluvie pueros, Liv. **II.** Transf., 1, *to show, place before one;* praemia alicui, Cic. ; per urbes benigne commeatus, Liv.; **2,** of discourse, *to set forth, exhibit, explain;* vitam alicuius totam, Cic. ; with rel. sent. (with qui, quid, quemadmodum, etc.), Cic. ; **3,** *to expose, leave unprotected;* mare nimia propinquitate ad pericula classium externarum expositum, Liv. ; libertas exposita ad injurias Masinissae, Liv. (syncop. perf. partic., expostus (for expositus), Verg.)

exporrĭgo -rexi -rectum, 3. *to stretch out, expand, extend,* Ter.

exportātĭo -ōnis, f. (exporto), *exportation;* earum rerum quibus abundaremus, Cic.

exporto, 1. *to carry out.* **I.** Gen., omnia signa ex fanis plaustris evecta exportataque, Cic. **II.** Esp., a, *to export;* aurum ex Italia quotannis Hierosolyma, Cic.; b, *to banish, drive away;* portentum in ultimas terras exportandum, Cic.

exposco -pŏposci, 3. **I.** *to demand vehemently, entreat earnestly.* **A.** Gen., signum proelii, Caes.; misericordiam, Cic. ; with infin., Verg., Tac.; with acc. and infin., Verg. ; with acc. of pers. and subj., precibus exposcere plebem, unum sibi civem donarent, Liv. ; absol., exposcentibus militibus, Caes. **B.** Esp., 1, *to ask of the gods, to pray for;* victoriam a diis, Caes. ; 2, *to demand the delivery of a person;* aliquem ad poenam, Tac. **II.** *to demand, require;* nec opes exposcere magnas, Ov.

expŏsĭtĭo -ōnis, f. (expono), of discourse, *a statement, setting forth, exposition, narration;* expositio sententiae suae, Cic.; plur., expositiones rerum, Cic.

expŏsĭtus -a -um, p. adj. (from expono), *exposed, open, accessible.* **A.** Lit., of places, mollibus expositum Zephyris Lilybaeon, Ov. **B.** Transf., *accessible;* domus patens atque adeo exposita cupiditati et voluptatibus, Cic. **C.** *vulgar,* Juv.

expostŭlātĭo -ōnis, f. (expostulo). **I.** *a demand;* bonorum, Cic. **II.** *complaint, expostulation;* expostulationem facere, Cic.; fuerunt nonnullae expostulationes cum absente Pompeio, Cic.

expostŭlo, 1. **I.** *to desire, demand earnestly.* **A.** Gen., aliquid ab aliquo, Cic.; foll. by ut or ne and the subj., Tac. ; by acc. and infin., Tac. **B.** *to demand the delivery of a person;* aliquem ad supplicium, Tac. **II.** *to make a complaint, to expostulate;* cum aliquo de aliqua re, Cic. ; cum aliquo aliquid or aliquem, *concerning a thing or person,* Cic. ; expostulare et queri, foll. by acc. and infin., Cic.

expostus = expositus, v. expono.

expōtus = epotus (q.v.).

expressus -a -um, p. adj. with compar. (from exprimo). **I.** Of pronunciation, *clear, distinct,* Quint. ; in a bad sense, *affected;* litterae neque expressae neque oppressae, Cic. **II.** *plain, evident, visible.* **A.** Lit., litterae lituraeque expressae, Cic. **B.** Transf., expressa sceleris vestigia, Cic.

exprĭmo -pressi -pressum, 3. (ex and premo), *to press out, force out.* **A.** Lit., **1,** sucina solis radiis expressa, Tac.; corporis pondere conisa tenuem jam spiritum expressit, Tac. ; vestis exprimens singulos artus, *showing,* Tac. ; 2, of pronunciation, *to articulate distinctly;* exprimere litteras putidius, Cic. **B.** Transf., *to extort, wrest, squeeze out;* nummos ab aliquo blanditiis, Cic.; expressi ut negaret, *made him deny,* Cic. **II.** *to express, model, portray, represent.* **A.** Lit., expressi vultus per ahenea signa, Hor. **B.** 1, *to express in words;* a, *describe;* mores alicuius oratione, Cic. ; with rel. sent., qui crebro dicat diligenter oportere exprimi, quae vis subjecta sit vocibus, Cic. ; b, *to translate;* aliquid Latine, Cic. ; verbum e verbo, Cic. ; ad verbum de Graecis, Cic. ; 2, *to imitate, copy;* alicuius vitam et consuetudinem, Cic. **III.** *to raise up;* quantum his quotidianus agger expresserat, Caes.

exprŏbrātĭo -ōnis, f. (exprobro), *reproach, upbraiding;* alicui veteris fortunae, Liv.

exprŏbro, 1. (ex and probrum), *to reproach, twit with, lay to the charge of;* with acc., officia, Cic.; ea (vitia) in adversariis, Cic. ; with acc and dat., haec hosti, Liv. ; with dat. and de, with the abl., de uxore mihi exprobrare, Nep. ;

with acc. and infin., exprobrare nihilo plus sanitatis in curia quam in foro esse, Liv.; with quod and the subj., quasi exprobrare quod in vita maneam, Cic.; absol., circumstabant armati hostes exprobrantes eludentesque, Liv.

exprōmo -prompsi -promptum, 3. *to bring forth, produce.* **I.** Lit., omnes apparatus supplicii, Liv. **II.** Transf., 1, *to fetch out, utter;* maestas voces, Verg.; 2, *to exhibit, display;* a, crudelitatem suam in aliquo, Cic.; b, *to pronounce, set forth, state;* leges de religione, Cic.; causas et ordinem belli, Liv.; with rel. sent., quanta vis sit (eius) eloquentiae expromere, Cic.

expromptus -a -um, partic. of expromo.

expugnābĭlis -e (expugno), *that may be besieged or captured;* urbs, Liv.

expugnātĭo -ōnis, f. (expugno), *the taking or capturing of any place by storm;* urbis, Caes.; plur., expugnationes urbium, Cic.

expugnātor -ōris, m. (expugno), *a taker, capturer;* urbis, Cic.; transf., pudicitiae, violator, Cic.

expugno, 1. *to take, take by storm, capture, conquer, overcome.* **A.** Lit., urbes, naves, Caes.; urbem obsidione, Caes.; tyrannos eius, non ipsam urbem, Liv.; of things, fames obsessos expugnavit, *compelled to surrender,* Liv. **B.** Transf., a, *to overcome, subdue;* animum, Cic.; pertinaciam legatorum, Liv.; b, *to destroy, violate;* quaestiones, thwart, Liv.; pudicitiam, violate, Cic.; c, *to force, compel;* legationem, Cic.; with ut and the subj., *bring it about that,* etc., Cic.; d, *to accomplish;* coepta, Ov.

expulsĭo -ōnis, f. (expello), *a driving out, expulsion;* Laenatis, Cic.; plur., expulsiones vicinorum, Cic.

expulso, 1. (intens. of expello), *to drive out, drive back,* Mart.

expulsor -ōris, m. (expello), *one who drives out or expels;* iste homo acerrimus, bonorum possessor, expulsor, ereptor, Cic.

expultrix -trīcis, f. (expulsor), *one who expels;* philosophia expultrix vitiorum, Cic.

expungo -punxi -punctum, 3. *to strike out, blot out, expunge,* Plaut.

expurgātĭo -ōnis, f. (expurgo), *a vindication, justification,* Plaut.

expurgo, 1. *to cleanse, purify.* **A.** Lit., quae poterunt unquam satis expurgare cicutae, Hor. **B.** Transf., a, expurgandus est sermo, Cic.; b, *to justify, defend;* dissimulandi causa aut sui expurgandi, Sall.

expŭto, 1. *to comprehend,* ap. Cic.

exquaero = exquiro (q.v.).

Exquĭlĭae -ārum = Esquilae (q.v.).

exquīro -quisīvi -quisītum, 3. (ex and quaero). **I.** *to seek out;* 1, a, lit., antiquam matrem, Verg.; iter per aliquem, Caes.; b, transf., veritatem, verum, Cic.; with rel. sent., quid in omni genere vitae optimum et verissimum sit exquirere, Cic.; c, *to ask, inquire;* exquirere palam pretia, Cic.; a te nihil certi exquiro, Cic.; ex aliquo causas alicuius rei, Cic.; with rel. sent., quid iis de quoque officii genere placeat exquirere, Cic.; partic. subst., **exquisīta** -ōrum, n. *inquiries,* Cic.; 2, *to choose, select;* verba ad (*according to*), sonum, Cic. **II.** *to search through.* **A.** Lit., vescendi causā mari terraque omnia, Sall. **B.** *to search, test;* facta alicuius ad antiquae religionis rationem, Cic. **III.** *to ask for;* alicuius consilium, Cic.

exquīsītē, adv. with compar. and superl. (exquisitus), *accurately, carefully, admirably;* de eo crimine accurate et exquisite disputare, Cic.

exquīsītus -a -um, p. adj. with compar.

and superl. (exquiro), 1, *carefully sought, choice, exquisite, excellent, admirable;* sententiae, Cic.; exquisitius dicendi genus, Cic.; exquisitissimis verbis laudare, Cic.; 2, *artificial, far-fetched;* munditia exquisita nimis, Cic.

exsăcrĭfĭco, 1. *to sacrifice,* ap. Cic.

exsaevĭo, 4. *to rage to an end, cease to rage;* dum reliquum tempestatis exsaeviret, Liv.

exsanguis -e, *bloodless, without blood.* **I.** Lit., umbrae, Verg. **II.** Transf., a, *lifeless;* corpora mortuorum, Cic.; b, *pale as a corpse, deathly pale,* Cic.; color, Sall.; c, *exhausted, weak,* Cic.; of voice, speech, etc., Calvus exsanguis et aridus, Tac.; d, act., *making pale;* cuminum, Hor.

exsarcĭo -(s)artūrus, 4. *to patch up, make good, repair,* Ter.

exsātĭo, 1. *to satisfy thoroughly, satiate.* **A.** Lit., vino ciboque, Liv. **B.** Transf., morte alicuius exsatiari, Liv.

exsătŭrābĭlis -e (exsaturo), *that can be satiated;* non exsaturabile pectus, Verg.

exsătŭro, 1. *to satisfy, satiate.* **A.** Lit., belua exsaturanda visceribus meis, Ov. **B.** Transf., eius cruciatu atque supplicio pascere oculos animumque exsaturare, Cic.

exscendo = escendo (q.v.).

exscensĭo = escensio (q.v.).

exscensus = escensus (q.v.).

exscindo -scīdi -scissum, *to destroy utterly, raze to the ground;* Numantiam, Cic.; of persons, *to destroy;* hostem, Tac.

exscrĕo, 1. *to cough or hawk out;* totiens clausas ante fores, Ov.

exscrībo -scripsi -scriptum, 3. 1, *to copy;* litteras, Cic.; 2, *to note down, register;* ei sacra omnia exscripta exsignataque attribuit, Liv.

exsculpo -sculpsi -sculptum, 3. 1, *to scratch out, erase;* versus, Nep.; 2, *to cut out with a chisel, carve or scoop out;* aliquid e quercu, Cic.

exsēco -sĕcŭi -sectum, 1. *to cut out;* 1, linguam, Cic.; fig., vitiosas partes reipublicae, Cic.; transf., quinas hic capiti mercedes exsecat, *deducts from the principal,* Hor.; 2, *to castrate,* Cic.

exsĕcrābĭlis -e (exsecror), 1, *deserving curses;* fortuna, Liv.; 2, *cursing, execrating;* carmen, Liv.; hence, *deadly;* ira atque odium, Liv.

exsĕcrātĭo -ōnis, f. (exsecror), 1, *a curse, execration,* Cic.; 2, *an oath containing an imprecation,* Cic.

exsĕcrātus -a -um, p. adj. (from exsecror), *cursed, execrated;* exsecratus populo Romano, Cic.

exsĕcror, 1. dep. (ex and sacer), *to curse, execrate;* 1, a, aliquem, Cic.; consilia Catilinae, Sall.; b, *to utter a curse;* in caput alicuius, Liv.; exsecratur primum ut naufragio pereat, Cic.; 2, *to swear with an imprecation;* haec exsecrata civitas, Hor.

exsĕctĭo -ōnis, f. (exseco), *a cutting out;* linguae, Cic.

exsĕcūtĭo -ōnis, f. (exsequor), *performance, accomplishment;* negotii, Tac.; executio Syriae, *administration of,* Tac.

exsĕquĭae -ārum, f. (exsequor), *a funeral procession;* justa exsequiarum, *ceremonies of,* Cic.; exsequias alicuius funeris prosequi, Cic.; exsequias celebrare, Liv.

exsĕquĭālis -e (exsequiae), *relating or belonging to a funeral procession;* carmina, Ov.

exsĕquor -sĕcūtus sum, 3. dep. **I.** *to follow a corpse to the grave,* Cic. poet. **II. A.** *to follow;* suam quisque spem, sua consilia, communibus deploratis, **exsequentes**, Liv. **B. 1,** *to accomplish, execute*; **a,** mandata vestra, Cic.; officia, Cic.; **b,** *to assert, maintain*; jus suum armis, Caes.; **2,** *to follow revengefully, to avenge, punish*; jura violata, dolorem, Liv.; rem tam atrocem, Liv.; **3,** *to relate, describe, explain*; ea vix verbis exsequi posse, Cic.; viam consili. scelerati, Liv.; alicuius or alicuius rei laudes, *to spread abroad*, Liv.; with rel. sent., exsequebatur inde, quae sollemnis derivatio esset, Liv.; **4,** *to prosecute, carry out*; aliquid usque ad extremum, Cic.; **5,** *to ascertain, find out*, Liv.; **6,** *to suffer, endure*; cladem illam fugamque, Cic.

exsĕro -sĕrŭi -sertum, 3. **I.** Lit., **a,** *to stretch out, thrust out*; linguam, Liv.; caput ponto, Ov.; **b,** *to bare*; brachia, Ov.; Amazon unum exserta latus pugnae, Verg. **II.** Transf., *to free*; se aere alieno, Cic. (?)

exserto, 1. (intens. of exsero), *to stretch out*; ora, Verg.

exsertus -a -um, partic. of exsero.

exsībĭlo, 1. *to hiss an actor off the stage*, Cic.

exsiccātus -a -um, p. adj. (from exsicco), *dry, jejune*; genus orationis, Cic.

exsicco, 1. **1,** *to dry thoroughly*; arbores, Cic.; **2,** *to drain dry, to empty* by drinking; vina culullis, Hor.

exsigno, 1. *to put a mark upon, mark*; sacra omnia exscripta exsignataque, Liv.

exsĭlĭo -sĭlŭi -sultum, 4. (ex and salio), **1,** *to leap out, spring out*; in siccum (of a snake), Verg.; oculi exsiluere, Ov.; **2,** *to leap up, spring up*; de sella, Cic.; gaudio, *for joy*, Cic.; exsiluere loco silvae, Ov.

exsĭlĭum -ĭi, n. (exsul), **1,** lit., *banishment, exile*; exsilii poena, Cic.; aliquem exsilio afficere or multare, Cic.; in exsilium ire or pergere, Cic.; aliquem in exsilium mittere, Liv.; aliquem in exsilium ejicere or pellere, Cic., or agere, Liv.; aliquem reducere de exsilio, Cic.; **2,** meton., **a,** *the place of exile*, Cic.; **b,** exsilia = exules, plenum exsiliis mare, Tac.

exsisto (existo) -stiti -stitum, 3. *to arise, come forth, appear.* **I.** ab ara, Cic.; of soldiers, *to start up*; e latebris, Liv.; of things, ab aede Junonis ex arce (of a voice), Cic. **II.** *to spring, arise, come into existence.* **A.** Lit., ex stirpe quadam, Cic.; in statuae capite, Cic. **B.** Transf., ut tyranni existerent, Cic.; exsistit motus, Caes.; ex luxuria existit avaritia, Cic.; with predic. nomin., ego huic causae patronus exstiti, Cic.; with ut and the subj. (of logical consequence), ex quo existet, ut de nihilo quippiam fiat, Cic.; with acc. and infin., exsistit illud, multa esse probabilia quae, Cic.

exsolvo -solvi -sŏlūtum, 3. **I.** *to loosen, unloose, untie, unbind.* **A.** Lit., glaciem, *to dissolve*, Lucr.; fig., nodum huius erroris, Liv. **B.** Transf., exsoluti plerique legis nexus, Tac.; famem, *drive away*, Ov. **II.** *to set free, release.* **A.** Lit., se corpore, Verg. **B.** Transf., **1,** *to free*; plebem aere alieno, Liv.; se occupationibus, Cic.; **2, a,** *to pay*; nomina, Cic.; stipendium praeteritum cum fide, Tac.; **b,** *to discharge, to fulfil an engagement, perform a promise* or *something due*; quod promiserat, Liv.; jurandum, Liv.; poenas morte, Tac.

exsomnis -e (ex and somnus), *sleepless, wakeful*, Verg.

exsorbĕo -sorbŭi, 2. *to suck up, suck in.* **A.** Lit., sanguinem, Cic.; gustaras civilem sanguinem vel potius exsorbueras, Cic. **B.** Transf., **a,** *to endure*; multorum difficultatem, Cic.; **b,** *to swallow up, devour*; quantas iste Byzantiorum praedas exsorbuit, Cic.

exsors -sortis, *without lot*; **1,** *that for which*

no lot has been cast, specially chosen*; ducunt exsortem Aeneae (equum), Verg.; **2,** *having no share in, deprived of*; with genit., dulcis vitae, Verg.; amicitiae, Liv.

exspătĭor, 1. dep., *to digress from the path, deviate from the course*; exspatiantur equi, Ov.; of rivers, exspatiata ruunt per apertos flumina campos, Ov.

exspectābĭlis -e (exspecto), *that which is expected, probable*, Tac.

exspectātĭo -ōnis, f. (exspecto), *a waiting for, looking for, expectation*; with subj. genit., exspectatione hominum majore quam spe, Liv.; with obj. genit., exspectationem sui facere or concitare, Cic.; with de, quantum tu mihi moves exspectationem de sermone Bibuli, Cic.; with rel. sent., summa omnium exspectatio, quidnam sententiae ferrent judices, Cic.; abscl., obscurā spe et caecā exspectatione pendere, Cic.

exspectātus -a -um, p. adj. with compar. and superl. (exspecto), *expected, wished for, welcome*; carus omnibus exspectatusque venies, Cic.; exspectati ad amplissimam dignitatem, *expected to arrive at the highest rank*, Cic.; litterae exspectatae, Cic.

exspecto, 1. *to wait for, look for, expect.* **I. 1,** gen., transitum tempestatis, Cic.; partic. perf. subst., ante exspectatum, *before it was expected*, Verg., Ov.; with rel. sent., exspecto quid tribunus plebis excogitet, Cic.; exspectare quam mox, etc., Cic.; with dum, exspectas fortasse dum dicat, Cic.; with quoad, Nep.; with si, Caes.; with ut and the subj., nisi forte exspectatis ut illa diluam, Cic.; non exspectare foll. by quin, Caes.; abscl., *to wait, loiter*; ad portam, Cic.; **2,** esp., **a,** *to wait for a person* or *thing* (till it is ready or finished); oratores multas horas, Cic.; **b,** *to await*; me tranquilla senectus exspectat, Hor. **II.** *to wait with longing, fear, hope, desire,* etc., *to hope for, long, dread*; testamenta, Cic.; aliquid ab or ex with abl., a te hoc civitas vel potius omnes cives non exspectant solum sed etiam postulant, Cic.; with acc. and infin., quum exspectaret effusos omnibus portis Aetolos in fidem suam venturos (esse), Liv.

exspergo (ex-spargo), -spersum, 3. *to scatter*, Lucr.

exspes, adj. (only in nom. sing.), *without hope, hopeless*; erret inops, exspes, Ov.; with genit., exspes vitae, Tac.

exspīrātĭo -ōnis, f. (exspiro), *an exhalation*; terrae, Cic.

exspīro, 1. **I.** Transit., *to breathe out, exhale*; **a,** flammas pectore, Verg.; **b,** of the dying, animas, auras, Verg. **II.** Intransit., **1,** *to give up the ghost, to die*; in pugna et in acie, Liv.; fig., quid? si ego morerer, mecum exspiratura respublica erat, Liv.; **2,** *to blow forth, rush forth*; vis ventorum exspirare cupiens, Ov.

exspŏlĭo, 1. *to plunder, rob, despoil*; fana atque domos, Sall.; exercitu et provinciā Pompeium, Cic.

exspŭo -spŭi -spūtum, 3. *to spit out*; transf., *to get rid of, cast away*; hamum (of fishes), Ov.; rationem ex animo, Lucr.

externo, 1. *to frighten, terrify*, Ov., Cat.

exstillo, 1. *to drop moisture, drip, trickle*, Plaut., Ter.

exstĭmŭlātor -ōris, m. (exstimulo), *an inciter, instigator*; rebellionis, Tac.

exstĭmŭlo, 1. *to goad, to excite, instigate*; virum dictis, Ov.

extinctĭo -ōnis. f. (extinguo), *annihilation, extinction*, Cic.

exstinctor -ōris, m. (exstinguo), **1.** *one who*

extinguishes; incendii, Cic.; **2**, *one who destroys,*
annihilates; patriae, Cic.

exstinguo -stinxi ·stinctum, 3. **I.** Lit., *to*
put out, extinguish; incendium, Cic.; middle,
exstingui, *to go out ;* consumptus ignis exstinguitur, Cic. **II.** Transf., 1, *to dry up;* aquam
rivis, Liv. ; 2, *to quench;* sitim, Ov. ; 3, *to kill;*
invictum bello juvenem fortuna morbo exstinxit,
Liv. ; middle, exstingui, *to die,* esp. suddenly or
prematurely, Cic. ; 4, *to abolish, destroy, anni-*
hilate; exstincto senatu, Cic. ; gratiam alicuius,
Cic. ; esp., *to blot out the memory of something, to*
bring into oblivion; memoriam publicam, crimina sua, Cic. ; middle, exstingui, *to be for-*
gotten; rumor exstinguitur, Cic. (syncop. pluperf., exstinxem, for exstinxissem, Verg.).

exstirpo, 1. (ex and stirps) *to tear up by the*
root; transf., *to root out, extirpate;* vitia, Cic. ;
humanitatem ex animo, Cic.

exsto (exto), 1. *to stand out, project.* **I.** Lit.,
milites capite solo ex aqua exstant, Caes. ; quo
altius ab aqua exstaret, Liv. **II.** Transf., **A.**
Gen., quo magis id quod erit illuminatum exstare
atque eminere videatur, Cic. **B.** 1, *to be visible,*
show itself, appear, exist ; exstant huius fortitudinis vestigia, Cic. ; exstat, impers. with acc.
and infin., Cic.; apparet atque exstat, utrum
. . . an, etc., Cic. ; **2**, *to be still in existence, to*
be extant; exstant epistolae Philippi, Cic. ; non
exstat alius, Liv.

exstructĭo -ōnis, f. (exstruo), *a building up,*
erection; ea exstructio quae, etc., Cic. ; plur.,
exstructiones tectorum, Cic.

exstrŭo -struxi -structum, 3. *to heap up,*
pile up. **I.** Lit., rogum, Cic. ; magnum acervum
librorum Dicaearchi sibi ante pedes, Cic. ; divitias in altum, Hor. ; focum lignis, Hor. ; mensae
conquisitissimis epulis exstruebantur, Cic. ;
mensae exstructae, *piled up with food,* Cic. **II.**
Transf., exstrue animo altitudinem excellentiam-
que virtutum, *build up,* Cic. ; accurate non modo
undata, verum etiam exstructa disciplina, Cic.

exsuctus -a -um, partic. of exsugo.

exsūdo, 1. **I.** Intransit., *to come out in*
sweat, exude; inutilis humor, Verg. **II.** Transit.,
to sweat out. **A.** Lit., Plin. **B.** Transf., *to sweat*
through, toil through, perform with great labour ;
novum de integro laborem, Liv. ; certamen ingens, Liv.

exsūgo -suxi -suctum, *to suck out, suck up;*
ostrea vacuis exsucta medullis, Juv.

exsul -sŭlis, c. (from ex and the root of salio ;
cf. con-sul, prae-sul). **A.** *a banished or exiled*
person, an exile; quum vagus et exsul erraret,
Cic.; exsules reducuntur, Cic.; num qui exsules
restituti, Cic. ; with genit., patriae, Hor. ; with
abl., exsul patriā, domo, Sall. **B.** Transf., *de-*
prived of; with genit., exsul mentisque domus-
que, Ov.

exsŭlo (exŭlo), 1. (exsul), *to be banished,*
live in exile. **A.** Lit., Romae, *at Rome,* Cic.; apud
Prusiam, Cic.; in Volscos exsulatum abire, Liv.;
aptis sinus ad exsulandum locus, Cic. **B.**
Transf., meo discessu exsulasse rempublicam,
Cic.

exsultātĭo -ōnis, f. (exsulto), *a leaping up.*
I. Lit., Plin. **II.** Transf., *exultation, excessive*
rejoicing ; illa exsultatio Athamantis, Cic.

exsultim, adv. (exsilio) *friskingly,* Hor.

exsulto (exulto), 1. (freq. of exsilio), *to leap*
up frequently or violently. **I.** Lit., a, of living
subjects, equi ferocitate exsultantes, Cic. ; in
numerum, *to dance,* Lucr. ; medias inter caedes
exsultat Amazon, Verg. ; b, of things, vada
exsultant, *dash up,* Verg. **II.** Transf., **A.** appetitus quasi exsultantes sive cupiendo sive
fugiendo, Cic. **B.** Esp. 1, *to rejoice exceedingly,*

triumph; laetitiā or gaudio, Cic. ; in ruinis al
terius, Cic.; Graeci exsultant quod, etc., Cic.;
2, **a**, of orators and of discourse, *to run riot;*
audacius, Cic. ; verborum audaciā exsultans,
Cic. ; b, of discourse, *to move freely ;* campus
in quo exsultare possit oratio, Cic.

exsŭpĕrābĭlis -e (exsupero), *that can be*
conquered or overcome; non exsuperabile saxum
(of Sisyphus), Verg.

exsŭpĕrantĭa -ae, f. (exsupero), *superiority,*
pre-eminence; virtutis, Cic.

exsŭpĕro, 1. **I.** Intransit., **A.** Lit., *to*
mount up, appear above; flammae, Verg. **B.**
Transf., 1, *to be prominent, excel;* quantum feroci
virtute exsuperas, Verg. ; 2, in battle, *to get the*
upper hand, prevail; si non poterunt exsuperare,
cadant, Ov. **II.** Transf., *to surmount something.*
A. Lit., 1, *to surmount a height, to pass over or*
beyond; jugum, Verg.; an jam omnes angustiae
exsuperatae, Liv. ; 2, *to project above;* angues
exsuperant undas, Verg. **B.** Transf., 1, a, *to*
exceed; magnitudo sceleris omnium ingenia ex-
superat, *surpasses all thought,* Sall. ; b, *to sur-*
pass, go beyond; omnes Tarquinios superbiā,
Liv. ; 2, *to overcome;* consilium caecum, Cic.

exsurdo, 1. (ex and surdus), *to deafen.* **I.**
Lit., Plin. **II.** Transf., of taste, *to make dull*
or blunt; palatum, Hor.

exsurgo -surrexi -surrectum, 3. *to rise up,*
lift oneself up, stand up. **I.** Lit., 1, of persons,
quum exsurgeret, simul arridens, etc., Cic. ; exsurgit facem attollens, Verg. ; esp., *to raise one-*
self to one's full height to give force to a blow;
altior exsurgens, Verg. ; 2, of things (Roma)
tota simul exsurgere aedificiis, Liv. **II.** Transf.,
1, *to rise up, to regain strength;* exsurgere atque
erigere se, Cic. ; auctoritate vestrā respublica
exsurget, Cic. ; 2, of political risings, invidiā
eorum exsurgere rursus plebem, Liv.

exsuscĭto, 1. **I.** Lit., a, *to awaken from*
sleep; te (juris consultum) gallorum, illum (imperatorem) bucinarum cantus exsuscitat, Cic. ;
b, *to kindle fire;* flammam aurā, Ov. **II.** Transf.,
to excite, arouse; quae cura etiam exsuscitat
animos, Cic. ; se exsuscitare, *to arouse oneself,*
make an effort, Cic.

exta -ōrum, n. *the entrails of animals,* esp.,
the heart, lungs, liver, etc., used by the Romans
for divination ; exta inspicere, Cic. ; si est in
extis aliqua vis, quae declaret futura, Cic.

extābesco -tābŭi, 3. *to waste away entirely.*
A. Lit., corpus macie extabuit, ap. Cic. **B.**
Transf., *to vanish, disappear;* opiniones vetus-
tate extabuisse, Cic.

extemplo, adv. (ex and templum), *immed-*
iately, directly, straightway, Cic.

extempŏrālis -e (ex and tempus), *extem-*
porary, without preconsideration ; oratio, actio,
Quint.

extempŭlo = extemplo (q.v.).

extendo -tendi -tensum and -tentum, 3. *to*
stretch out, expand, extend. **I.** Lit. **A.** a, brachium, Cic. ; extentum funem, *tight rope,* Hor. ;
rigidā cervice et extento capite currere (of horses),
Liv. ; milit. t. t., *to extend in order of battle ;*
aciem in radicibus montis, Liv. ; b, of time, *to*
extend, prolong; ab hora tertia ad noctem pugnam, Liv.; middle, *to last;* tamquam non
longius, quam vitae humanae spatium est, cupiditas gloriae extenditur, Liv. **B.** 1, *to stretch*
on the ground; aliquem arenā, Verg. ; toto ingens
extenditur (Cerberus) antro, *is stretched,* Verg. ;
2, *to increase;* agros, Hor. **II.** Transf., 1, *to*
exert; se supra vires, Liv. ; itinera, *to march at*
great speed, Liv. ; avidos cursus, *to hasten eagerly,*
Verg.; 2, *to extend;* nomen in ultimas iras,

Hor.; in Asiam quoque cognitionem, Liv.; famam factis, to spread abroad, Verg.

extento, 1. (intens. of extendo), to stretch out, to extend; nervos, Lucr.

extentus a -um, p. adj. with superl. (from extendo), extended, wide; stagna latius extenta Lucrino lacu, Hor.; castra quam extentissimā potest valle locat, Liv.

extĕnŭātĭo -ōnis, f. (extenuo). **I.** a making thin, Plin. **II.** Rhet. t. t., a figure of speech, a diminution, lessening (Gr. μείωσις, opp. exaggeratio), Cic.

extĕnŭātus -a -um, p. adj. (from extenuo), weak, poor, slight; vestigia, Cat.; copiolae extenuatissimae, ap. Cic.

extĕnŭo, 1. to make thin or small, to reduce, diminish. **I.** Lit., 1, aër extenuatus, rarefied, Cic.; dentibus extenuatur et molitur cibus, Cic.; extenuari in aquas, dissolves into, Ov.; 2, milit. t. t., to extend a line or column, make thin; angustiae extenuabant agmen, Liv.; extenuatā suorum acie, Sall. **II.** Transf., 1, to lessen, weaken, diminish; sumptus, Cic.; spem, crimen, Cic.; 2, in speech, etc., to disparage, depreciate; suum munus, Cic.; famam belli, Liv.

exter and **extĕrus** -a -um (from ex), outward, foreign, strange. **I.** Posit., jus nationum exterarum, Cic. **II.** Compar., **extĕrior,** n. -ius, genit. -ōris; ortus, Cic.; hostis, Cic.; exteriorem ire alicui, to go on the left side, Hor. **III.** Superl. **A. extrēmus** -a -um, the outermost; 1, lit., subst., **extrēmum** -i, n., a, that which is outermost; caelum quod extremum atque ultimum mundi est, Cic.; b, the outermost, last; pars, Cic.; vitae dies, Cic. Subst., **extrēmum** -i. n., the end; extremum habet, has an end, Cic.; aestatis, Sall.; per extremum vitae, death, Verg.; ad extremum, adv., to the end; ad extremum reservatus, Cic.; at the end, Cic.; entirely; ad extremum perditus, Liv.; extremum, adv., at the end, Ov.; for the last time; extremum affari or alloqui aliquem, Verg.; extremo, at the end, Nep.; in extremo, at the end of a letter, Cic.; plur., **extrēma** -orum, the end; agri, Cic.; 2, transf., a, extreme—i.e., only used in the greatest need; senatus consultum, Caes.; b, extreme, greatest, most dangerous, most difficult; tempora, extreme need, Cic.; extremum bonorum, malorum, the highest good, evil, Cic.; neut. subst., vitam ipsam in extremum adductam, Tac.; extrema pati, the worst extremities, Verg.; with genit., quotiens in extrema periculorum ventum, Liv.; c, the lowest, worst; hāud Ligurum extremus, Verg.; extremi ingenii (of the lowest understanding) est qui, etc., Liv. **B. extĭmus** -a -um, the outermost; orbis, Cic.

extĕrĕbro, 1. to bore out, extract by boring; ex eo auro, quod exterebratum esset, Cic.

extergĕo -tersi -tersum, 2. to wipe off, wipe dry; transf., to strip clean, plunder; fanum quod non eversum atque extersum reliqueris, Cic.

extĕrior, exterius, v. exter.

extermĭno, 1. (ex and terminus), to drive beyond the boundaries; hence, 1, to drive out, expel, banish; aliquem ex urbe, Cic.; or urbe, Cic.; de civitate, Cic.; 2, to put aside, remove; auctoritatem senatus e civitate, Cic.

externus -a -um (exter). **I.** that which is outside, external; tepor, Cic. Subst., **externa** -ōrum, n. outward appearances, Cic. **II.** foreign, strange; hostis, Cic.; amor (of a foreigner), Ov.; timor, terror (of a foreign enemy), Liv. Subst., a, **externus** -i, m. a foreigner, Liv.; a stranger; canum odium in externos, Cic.; b, **externa** -ōrum, n. that which is foreign or strange; externa (foreign examples), libentius in tali re quam domestica recordor, Cic.

extĕro -trīvi -trītum, 3. to rub out, rub off, Lucr.

exterrĕo -terrŭi -territum, 2. to frighten suddenly, to terrify; periculo suo aliquem, ut, etc., Liv.; in pass., praeter modum exterreri, Cic.; partic., exterritus aspectu, Cic.; of things, exterritus amnis, Verg.

extĕrus, v. exter.

extĭmesco -tĭmŭi, 3. **I.** Intransit., to be greatly afraid, to be terrified; de fortunis communibus extimescere, Cic.; foll. by ne and the subj., Cic. **II.** Transit., to be greatly afraid of, to dread; with acc. of the thing, adventum tuum, Cic.; with ne and the subj., unum illud extimescebam ne quid turpiter facerem, Cic.; with acc. of the person, victorem orbis terrarum, Cic.

extĭmus, v. exter.

extispex -spĭcis, m. (exta and *specio), a soothsayer who predicts from the entrails of victims, Cic.

extollo, extŭli, and rarely exsustŭli, 3. to lift up, raise up. **I.** Lit., cruentum pugionem, Cic. **II.** Transf., 1, extollere animum or aliquem, to raise, elevate, exalt; extollere animos, to become insolent, Cic.; se extollere, Cic.; aliquem secundā oratione, Sall.; 2, in words, to raise; aliquid verbis in majus, to exaggerate, Liv.; to praise, celebrate, extol; fortunam alicuius, Cic.; aliquem ad caelum, Cic.; 3, to adorn; hortos a Lucullo coeptos insigni magnificentiā extollere, Tac.; 4, to raise to rank, power, etc.; jacentem, Cic.

extorquĕo -torsi -tortum, 2. to twist out, wrest away, wrench out. **I.** Gen., **A.** Lit., arma e manibus civium, Cic.; alicui sicam de manibus, Cic. **B.** Transf., to obtain by force, extort; a Caesare per Herodem talenta Attica L., Cic.; alicui veritatem, errorem, Cic.; ex animis cognitiones verborum, Cic.; with ut and the subj., extorsisti ut faterer, Cic. **II.** Esp., to dislocate, put out of joint; prava extortaque puella, deformed, Juv.; to torture, Liv.

extorris -e (ex and terra), driven from the country, exiled, banished; huic CXXXII patres familias extorres profugerunt, Cic.; with abl., agro Romano, Liv.; patriā, Sall.

extrā (= exterā sc. parte, from exter). **I.** Adv. **A.** Lit., outside (opp. intus); quae extra sunt, Cic.; quum extra et intus hostem haberent, Caes.; compar., exterius sitae (urbes), Ov. **B.** Transf., except; extra quam, extra quam si, except, unless, Cic. **II.** Prep. with acc., **A.** Lit., beyond, outside of, without; provinciam, Caes. **B.** a, except, with the exception of; extra ducem, Cic.; b, beyond, outside; extra modum, Cic.; extra ordinem, Cic.; c, without; extra jocum, joking apart, Cic.; esse extra culpam, Cic.

extrăho -traxi -tractum, 3. **I.** to draw out, extract. **A.** Lit., telum e corpore, Cic.; telum de vulnere, Ov.; vivum puerum alvo, Hor.; velut ab inferis extractus, Liv. **B.** Transf., a, to extricate, free; urbem ex periculis, Cic.; b, to destroy, root out; religionem ex animis, Cic. **II.** to draw forth, 1, lit., aliquem turbā oppositis humeris, Hor.; aliquem vi in publicum, Liv.; aliquem domo, Cic.; milit. t. t., hostes invitos in aciem, Liv.; 2, a, to bring to light; scelera in lucem, Liv.; b, to bring out; aliquem ad honorem, Liv. **II.** Of time, 1, to prolong, delay, protract; res variis calumniis, Cic.; certamen usque ad noctem, Liv.; aliquem, to put off, Liv.; 2, to waste; aestatem sine ullo effectu, Liv.

extrānĕus -a -um (extra), that which is outside. **I.** not belonging to a thing or subject, extraneous; res extraneae, Cic.; ornamenta, Cic. **II.** not belonging to a house, family, or country, *foreign, strange;* exercitatio forensis et extranea, Cic. Subst., **extrānĕus** -i, m. *a foreigner, stranger;* si extraneus deest, domi hostem quaerunt, Liv.

extrā-ordĭnārĭus -a -um, *extraordinary, anomalous, irregular;* petitio consulatus, Cic.; pecunia, *obtained by gift, legacy,* etc., Cic.; cupiditates, *unnatural,* Cic.; imperium, Cic.; milit. t. t., equites, cohortes, or simply extra-ordinarii, *picked troops of the auxiliary forces,* Liv.; porta, (= praetoria, near which the extra-ordinarii had their tents), Liv.

extrārĭus -a -um (extra), 1, *outward, external, extrinsic;* utilitas aut in corpore posita est aut in extrariis rebus, Cic.; 2, *strange, foreign.* Subst., **extrārĭus** -i, m. *a stranger,* Ter.

extrēmĭtas -ātis, f. (extremus), *the end, farthest portion, extremity;* mundi, Cic.

extrēmus -a -um, v. exter.

extrīco, 1. (ex and tricor), *to disentangle, extricate.* **A.** Lit., cervam plagis, Hor. **B.** Transf., *to procure with difficulty;* nummos, Hor.

extrīnsĕcus, adv. (extra and secus), 1, *from without, from the outside,* Cic.; 2, *on the outside, outwardly;* columna extrinsecus inaurata, Cic.

extrūdo -trūsi -trūsum, 3. *to push out, thrust out, extrude;* a, of persons, te in viam, Cic.; extrudi a senatu in Macedoniam, Cic.; b, of things, mare aggere, *to dam out,* Caes.

extundo -tūdi, 3. **I.** *to beat out.* **A.** Lit., *to form by beating with a hammer;* lapsa ancilia caelo extuderat, Verg. **B.** *to invent, devise;* alicui artem, Verg. **II.** *to beat out, force;* transf., *to drive away;* quum labor extuderit fastidia, Hor.

extŭrbo, 1. *to drive away, thrust out.* **A.** Lit., homines e possessionibus, Cic.; aliquem provinciā, Cic.; aliquem e fortunis omnibus, Cic. **B.** Transf., omnem spem pacis, Liv.; mentem alicuius, *to put out of countenance,* Cic.

exūbĕro, 1. **A.** Lit., of fluids, *to overflow;* alte spumis exuberat umbra, Verg. **B.** Transf., *to abound;* si luxuriā foliorum exuberat amnis, Verg.; pomis exuberat annus, Verg.; tam lato te fenore exuberat, Tac.

exul, v. exsul.

exulcĕro, 1. **I.** *to make sore,* Plin. **II.** Transf., 1, *to make worse, aggravate;* ea quae sanare nequeunt, exulcerant, Cic.; 2, *to irritate, embitter;* ut in exulcerato animo facile fictum crimen insideret, Cic.

exŭlŭlo, 1. *to howl out, howl loudly,* Ov.; **exŭlŭlātus** -a -um; a, *having howled,* Ov.; b, *invoked with howlings;* mater Cybeleia, Ov.

exundo, 1. 1, *to overflow, to flow out or over;* tura balsamaque vi tempestatum in adversa litora exundant, Tac.; 2, *to overflow, abound;* largus et exundans ingenii fons, Juv.

exungo -unctus and **exungor** -ungi, 3. *to anoint, besmear with unguents,* Plaut.

exŭo -ŭi -ūtum, 3. (connected with ind—uo). **I.** *to draw out or off, to take out.* **A.** se jugo, Liv.; unum exuta pedem vinclis, Verg.; se ex his laqueis, Cic. **B.** Transf., a, hominem ex homine, *deprive of all human feeling,* Cic.; mihi ex animo exui non potest esse deos, *I cannot but believe,* etc., Cic.; b, *to deprive;* aliquem agro paterno, Liv.; milit. t. t., *to strip an enemy of;* hostem impedimentis, castris, armis, praedā, Caes., Liv. **II.** *to lay aside, put off, take off.* **A.** Lit., ensem or pharetram, Verg., Ov. **B.** Transf., a, *to lay aside;* torvam faciem, Verg.; hominem, *human shape,* Ov.; b, *to lay aside, remove, divest oneself of;* humanitatem omnem,

Cic.; servitutem muliebrem, Liv.; **magistros** *get rid of,* Tac.

exūro -ussi -ustum, 3. **I.** *to burn out;* aliis scelus exuritur igni, Verg. **II.** *to burn up, consume entirely;* aliquem vivum, Cic.; classem, Verg.; exustus ager, *dried up,* Verg. **III.** *to burn;* 1, sol graciles exurit artus, Tib.; 2, of thirst, *to burn;* sitis exurit miseros, Lucr.; exustus flos siti veteris ubertatis exaruit, Cic.; 3, *to heat;* a, antra positis exusta caminis, Ov.; b, *to inflame with love,* Tib.

exustĭo -ōnis, f. (exurc), *a burning up, conflagration;* terrarum, Cic.

exŭvĭae -ārum, f. (exuo), *that which is taken off from the body.* **I.** Of men, a, *dress;* has enim exuvias mihi perfidus ille reliquit, Verg.; b, *spoils taken from the enemy, arms,* etc.; nauticae, Cic.; tu ornatus exuviis huius, Cic. **II.** Of animals, a, *the skin or slough which is laid aside* (naturally); exuvias ponere, Verg.; b, *the skin captured and taken off, the hide;* leonis, Verg.

F.

F f, the sixth letter of the Latin Alphabet, corresponding in form with the Aeolic digamma (Ϝ), though in sound most nearly represented by Φ, φ. For the meaning of this letter when used as an abbreviation, see Table of Abbreviations.

fāba -ae, f. *a bean,* Cic.; prov., isthaec in me cudetur faba, *I shall have to suffer for this,* Ter.

fābālis -e (faba), *of or relating to beans;* stipulae, Ov.

Făbăris -is, m., *a tributary of the Tiber in the Sabine country,* also called Farfarus, now *Farfa.*

făbella -ae, f. (dim. of fabula). **I.** *a little story, little narrative;* fabellarum auditione duci, Cic. **II.** Esp., a, *a fable,* Hor.; b, *a little drama,* Cic.

1. **făber** -bri, m. (perhaps shortened for faciber from facio); 1, *a worker,* esp. *in any hard material;* tignarius, *a carpenter,* Cic.; in the army, fabri, *the engineers,* Caes.; praefectus fabrum, *commander of the engineers,* Caes.; 2, *a fish,* perhaps *the dory,* Ov.

2. **făber** -bra -brum, *ingenious, skilful;* ars, Ov.

Făbĭus -a -um, *name of a Roman gens, of which the most famous were:* 1, Numerius Fabius Pictor, *Roman annalist at the beginning of the Second Punic war;* 2, Qu. Fabius Maximus Cunctator, *the opponent of Hannibal in the Second Punic war;* 3, Qu. Fabius Maximus Aemilianus, *son of L. Aemilius Paullus, consul 144 A.C.;* 4, Qu. Fabius Maximus Allobrogicus, *son of the preceding, conqueror of the Allobroges, builder of a triumphal arch on the sacra via* (called fornix Fabii, fornix Fabius, fornix Fabianus, Cic.); 5, Servius Fabius Pictor, *celebrated lawyer, praetor* 145 A.C. Adj., **Fabius** -a -um, *Fabian.* Hence, **Făbĭānus** -a -um, *of or belonging to Fabius.*

Făbrātĕrĭa -ae, f. *town of the Volsci on the river Trerus.* Hence, **Făbrāternus** -a -um, *of or belonging to Fabrateria.*

fabrē, adv. (2. faber), *skilfully,* Plaut.

făbrĕfăcĭo -fēci -factum, 3. *to make* or *fashion skilfully;* ex aere multa fabrefacta, Liv.

făbrĭca -ae, f. (faber). **I.** (sc. ars), *the art of a faber;* pictura et fabrica, *architecture,* Cic. **II.** *the work of a faber, working, making;* **fabrica**

aeris et ferri, Cic. **III.** (sc. officina), *the work-shop of a* faber, Cic.

făbrĭcātĭo -ōnis, f. (fabrico), 1, *making, framing, construction;* hominis, Cic.; 2, *artifice, device;* ne illa quidem traductio in verbo quandam fabricationem habet, Cic.

făbrĭcātor -ōris, m. (fabrico), *a maker, artificer, framer;* tanti operis, Cic.; ipse doli fabricator Epēos, Verg.

Făbrĭcĭus -a -um, *name of a Roman gens of which the most distinguished was* C. Fabricius, *consul* 282 *and* 278 B.C., *conqueror of Pyrrhus and the Samnites, famed for the simplicity of his life and the rigour of his censorship.* Adj., *Fabrician;* pons, *a bridge in Rome.* Hence, **Făbrĭcĭānus** -a -um, *of or belonging to Fabricius.*

făbrĭco, 1. (faber), *to form, make, forge out of hard materials;* arma, Hor.; pocula fago fabricata, Ov.

făbrĭcor, 1. dep. (faber), 1, *to frame, make, forge out of a hard material;* gladium, fulmen, signa, Cic.; Capitolii fastigium, Cic.; 2, *to fashion, form;* hominem, Cic.; verba, *invent new words,* Cic.

făbrīlis -e (faber), *relating or belonging to an artificer;* erratum, Cic.; scalprum, Liv.; opera, Verg.; neut. plur. subst., **făbrīlĭa** -ium, n., *tools,* Hor.

făbŭla -e, f. (fari). **I.** *talk;* fabulam fieri or esse, *to be the common talk,* Cic.; *conversation;* fabulae conviviales, Tac. **II.** *a tale, narrative, story, fable.* **A.** Gen., 1, lit., fabula tantum cine auctore edita, Liv.; 2, transf., fabulae manes, *the empty shades,* Hor. **B.** Esp., *the plot, story, of a drama,* Hor.; *a drama;* in iis quae ad scenam componuntur fabulis, Cic.

făbŭlor, 1. dep. (fabula), *to talk, converse, chatter;* quid Ser. Galba fabuletur, Liv.

făbŭlōsus -a -um (fabula), *renowned in story, fabled;* Hydaspes, Hor.; palumbes, Hor.

făcesso, făcessi, 3. (intens. of facio). **I.** Transit., *to do eagerly, perform, fulfil, accomplish;* jussa, Verg.; negotium, *to give trouble to,* Cic.; alicui periculum, Cic. **II.** Intransit., *to be off, go away, depart;* ab omni societate, reipublicae, Cic.; ex urbe, Liv.; urbe finibusque, Liv.

făcētē, adv. (facetus), *wittily, humorously;* si (contumelia) facetius jactatur, urbanitas dicitur, Cic.

făcētĭa -ae, f. (facetus). **I.** Sing., *wit,* Plaut. **II.** Plur., *wit, facetiousness, drollery, humour;* Scipio omnes sale facetiisque superabat, Cic.

făcētus -a -um (root FA, Skr. bha, Gk. φα, *shine,* whence also facies), 1, *fine, elegant;* orator, Cic.; sermo, Cic.; 2, *witty, facetious,* Cic.

făcĭes -ēi, f. (root FA). **I.** Abstr., 1, *the external form* or *figure;* a, of persons, quem ne de facie quidem nosti, Cic.; b, of things, ceterum facies totius negotii varia, incerta, foeda atque miserabilis, Sall.; 2, esp., a, *manner, kind;* in faciem hederae (*after the fashion of*), frondescere, Ov.; non una pugnae facies, Tac.; b, *beautiful exterior, beauty;* Tyndaridis, Verg. **II.** Concr., 1, *figure, form;* Homeri, Cic.; se in omnes facies vertere, Verg.; 2, *the face, countenance,* Cic.

făcĭlĕ, adv. (facilis). **I.** *easily, without difficulty;* 1, gen., haec facile ediscere, Cic.; 2, esp., *easily, indisputably, certainly;* facile primus, facile princeps, *indisputably first,* Cic.; facile doctissimus, Cic.; non facile or haud facile, *not easily, hardly,* Cic. **II.** *willingly;* pati, Cic.; facillime audiri, Cic.

făcĭlis -e (facio). **I.** Pass., 1, *that which is easy to be done, easy;* ascensus, Caes.; aditus,

Cic.; with ad and the acc., faciles ad receptum angustiae, Liv.; esp. with gerund, illud autem facile ad credendum est, Liv.; with in and the acc., altera crepido haud facilior in ascensum, Liv.; with the supine in u, or the abl., res cognitu facilis, Cic.; with infin., facile est perficere ut, etc., Cic.; with ut and the subj., quod ei fuit facillimum, ut in agrum Rutulorum procederet, Cic.; with dat., *suitable;* campus operi facilis esse, *to be easy,* Liv.; e or ex facili, *easily,* Ov.; 2, of circumstances, fortune, etc., *favourable;* quae (res et fortunae) quotidie faciliores mihi et meliores videntur, Cic. **II.** Act., **A.** 1, *that which does a thing easily, facile, skilful;* manu facili, Ov.; 2, *dexterous, clever;* facilis et expeditus ad dicendum T. Junius, Cic. **B.** *ready, willing, inclined;* 1, with dat., commercio facilis, Liv.; with ad, facili feminarum credulitate ad gaudia, Tac.; poet., with infin., Prop.; 2, esp. of character, *courteous, accessible, affable, easy, good-natured;* facilis et liberalis pater, Cic.; mores facillimi, Cic.; with ad and the gerund, facilis ad concedendum, Cic.; with in and the abl., facilis in hominibus audiendis, Cic.; with in and the acc., si faciles habeas in tua vota deos, Ov.; with dat., si mihi di faciles et sunt in amore secundi, Ov.; with abl., facilis amicitiā, Sall.

făcĭlĭtas -ātis, f. (facilis). **I.** Pass., *easiness, ease;* facilitas camporum, *for marching,* Tac. **II.** Act., 1, *readiness, disposition,* Cic.; 2, *willingness, friendliness, affability, good-nature, courteousness;* facilitas in audiendo, Cic.

făcĭnŏrōsus -a -um (facinus), *full of shameful deeds, wicked, atrocious, nefarious;* vir, Cic.; vita, Cic.; plur. subst., facinorosi, *abandoned men,* Cic.

făcĭnus -ŏris, n. (facio), 1, *a deed, action* (good or bad), pulcherrimum, Cic.; indignum, Cic.; 2, *a bad deed, crime, villainy* (not so strong a word as scelus, which = *infamy*); facinus est vinciri civem Romanum, scelus verberari, Cic.; facinus facere, obire, committere, Cic.; in se admittere, Caes.; patrare, Sall.; meton., a, *the instrument of crime;* facinus excussit ab ore, *the poisoned cup,* Ov.; b, *a criminal;* omnium flagitiorum atque facinorum circum se stipatorum catervae, Cic.

făcĭo, fēci, factum, 3. **I.** Transit. **A.** 1, *to make, prepare, build;* alicui anulum, Cic.; castra, Caes.; hence, a, *to write down;* litteras ad aliquem, Cic.; b, *to perform some action of the body;* gradum, Cic.; impetum in hostes, *to attack,* Liv.; 2, *to produce;* ignem ex lignis viridibus, Cic.; hence (of an orator, poet, etc.), *to compose;* orationem, versus, poema, Cic.; 3, *to gain;* praedam, Caes.; lucrum, manubias sibi ex, etc., Cic.; stipendia, *to serve in war,* Sall.; 4, *to raise, levy;* tributum, Cic.; auxilia mercede, Tac. **B.** 1, *to do, perform, accomplish, execute;* ego plus quam feci facere non possum, Cic.; caedem, furtum, fraudem, Cic.; alicui medicinam, *to cure,* Cic.; indutias, pacem, bellum, Cic.; fugam, *to take to flight,* or *to put to flight,* Sall., Liv.; facere de aliquo or de aliqua re, aliquo or aliquā re, alicui or alicui rei, cum aliqua re, *to do with,* or *do to;* quid hoc homine, or huic homini facias, Cic.; 2, a, *to manage* or *hold a ceremony;* ludos, Cic.; sacra, or sacrificium, or res divinas, *to sacrifice,* Cic.; b, *to practise a profession;* praeconium, Cic.; 3, *to procure;* orationi audientiam, Cic.; silentium, Liv.; 4, *to grant;* potestatem, permission, Cic.; 5, *to arouse* (some feeling, etc.); alicui dolorem, Cic.; spem, Cic.; 6, *to cause, bring it about;* with ut and the subj., facis ut rursus plebes in Aventinum sevocanda esse videatur, Cic.; with subj. alone; di facerent, sine patre forem I Ov.; fac sciam, *let me know,* Cic.; facio, with ne or quo and the subj., nor facere foll. by quin or quominus and the subj., facere non possum quin quotidie ad te mittam (litteras), *I cannot but,* Cic. ; poet. with acc. and infin., illum forma timere facit, Ov.; **7,** *to make, represent ;* with acc. and infin. (of artists and poets), quem tamen Homerus apud inferos conveniri facit ab Ulysse, Cic. ; **8,** *to suppose, assume ;* with acc. and infin., esse deos faciamus Cic. ; **9,** with double acc., *to make;* aliquem consulem, Cic. ; me unum ex iis feci qui, etc., *made myself out to be, etc.,* Cic. ; with adj., aliquem sanum, disertum, Cic.; aliquem certiorem, **v.** certus ; **10,** *to make something the property of some one, to bring into the power of;* with genit., tota Asia populi Romani facta est, Cic.; facere aliquid potestatis or ditionis suae, Cic.; with pron. possess., aliquam terram suam, *to subject,* Caes.; **11,** *to esteem, value;* with genit., parvi, minimi, pluris, maximi, nihili, Cic.; aequi bonique facere aliquid, *to be content with,* Cic. ; **12,** *to suffer;* naufragium facere, Cic.; damnum, detrimentum facere, *to suffer loss,* Cic. ; **13,** *to do,* referring to another verb, me ut adhuc fecistis audiatis (where fecistis = audivistis), Cic. **II.** Intransit., **1,** *to act;* humaniter, bene, amice, Cic.; **2,** facere cum, or ab aliquo, *to act on the side of, support, be of the same party;* contra nos, *to be of the opposite party,* Cic. ; **3,** *to sacrifice;* Junoni Sospitae, Cic. ; **4,** *to be suited for;* Medeae faciunt ad scelus omne manus, Ov. ; **5,** *to be serviceable, advantageous to, to suit, to be of service;* nec caelum nec aquae faciunt nec terra nec aurae, Ov. (archaic fut. perf. forms, faxo = fecero, Verg., Ov.; faxis, Hor.; faxit, ap. Liv.; faxitis, ap. Liv.; faxint, Cic.; faxitur, ap. Liv. The passive of facio is fio, q.v.).

factĕŏn, a word formed from facio, in imitation of the Greek = faciendum, Cic.

factĭo -ōnis, f. (facio). **I.** *a making, doing;* **1,** lit., Plaut. ; **2,** transf., *the right of making or doing;* factionem testamenti non habere, *to be incapable of making a will,* Cic. **II. 1,** *a political party, faction, side;* populus paucorum factione oppressus, Caes. ; triginta illorum consensus et factio, Cic.; **2, a,** *a faction or party in a theatre or circus,* Suet.; **b,** *the parties into which the charioteers in the circus were divided,* Suet.

factĭōsus -a -um (factio), *fond of power, factious;* adolescens nobilis, egens factiosus, Sall. ; exsistunt in republica plerumque largitores et factiosi, Cic.

factĭto, 1. (freq. of facio). **I.** *to make, do frequently, be accustomed to make or do;* verba compone et quasi coagmenta, quod ne Graeci quidem veteres factitaverunt, Cic. **II. a,** *to declare openly, to make or do;* quem palam heredem semper factitarat, Cic.; **b,** *to follow a trade, practise a profession, make a trade of;* accusationem, Cic.; delationem, Cic. ; **c,** *to celebrate usually;* sacrificia gentilicia illo ipso in sacello stato loco anniversaria, Cic.

factum -i, n. (facio), *that which has been done, a deed, act, exploit;* bene facta, *good deeds,* Cic.; recte facta, Liv.; poet., facta boum, *the works of oxen*—i.e., *a ploughed field,* Ov.

factus -a -um, p. adj. (facio), **1,** *wrought, worked ;* argentum factum, *silver plate,* Cic.; **2,** *polished, refined* (of persons) ; qui illuc factus institutusque venisset, Cic. ; homo ad unguem factus, Hor.

fācŭla -ae, f. (dim. of fax), *a little torch,* Prop.

făcultas -ātis, f. (Old Lat. facul = facile). **I. A.** *capacity, power, ability, capability;* facultas dicendi et copia, Cic. ; ingenii, Cic. **B.** *Esp., eloquence, oratorical power;* facultatis timor, Cic. **II. A.** *possibility, opportunity, power, means;* Miloni manendi nulla facultas, Cic.;

dare alicui facultatem irridendi sui, Cic.; habere efficiendi facultatem, Cic.; res mihi videtur esse facultate (*in practice*) praeclara, arte (*in theory*), mediocris, Cic.; alicui facultatem dare, offerre, concedere with ut and the subj., Cic. **B.** Transf., **a,** *abundance, great number;* omnium rerum in oppido summa facultus, Caes. ; **b,** *means, resources;* gen. in plur., Cic.

fācundē, adv. with compar. and superl. (facundus) ; *eloquently, fluently;* alloqui hostem, Liv.

fācundĭa -ae, f. (facundus), *eloquence, readiness of speech;* Romae Memmi facundia clara pollensque fuit, Sall.

fācundus -a -um, adj. with compar. and superl. (fari), *eloquent, fluent, ready of speech;* ingenia hominum sunt ad suam cuique levandam culpam nimio plus facunda, Liv. ; lingua, Hor.; oratio, Sall.

faecŭla -ae, f. (dim. of faex), *the tartar or crust of wine,* used either as a drug or condiment, Lucr., Hor.

Faesŭlae -ārum, f. *town in Etruria, at the foot of the Apennines,* now *Fiesole.* Hence adj., **Faesŭlānus** -a -um, *of or belonging to Faesulae.*

faex, faecis, f. **A.** *the dregs or refuse of any liquid,* Lucr., Hor. ; *the tartar or crust of wine,* Hor.; *the brine of pickles,* Ov. **B.** Transf., *the dregs, the lower orders;* faex populi or plebis, Cic.; in Romuli faece, Cic.

făgĭnĕus -a -um (fagus), *beechen;* frons, Ov.

făgĭnus -a -um (fagus), *beechen;* pocula, Verg.

fāgus -i, f. (φηγός), *the beech tree,* Caes.,Verg.

fāla -ae, f. *a wooden tower from which missiles were thrown into a besieged city,* Plaut. ; **2,** *one of the seven wooden pillars on the spina or barrier of the circus,* Juv.

fălărĭca (phălārĭca) -ae, f. **1,** *a huge spear hurled with the hand,* Verg. ; **2,** *a missile covered with tow and pitch, hurled from the catapult,* a brand, Liv.

falcārĭus -ii, m. (falx), *a scythe or sickle-maker;* inter falcarios, *the street of the scythe-makers,* Cic.

falcātus -a -um (falx), **1,** *furnished with scythes;* currus, quadrigae, Liv. ; **2,** *scythe-shaped;* ensis, Ov.; sinus, *a bay,* Ov.

falcĭfer -fĕra -fĕrum (falx and fero), *carrying a scythe or sickle;* senex, Saturnus, Ov.

Fălĕrĭi -ōrum, m. *the capital of the Falisci.*

Fălernus ager, *the Falernian country, at the foot of Mount Massicus, in Campania.* Adj., **Fălernus** -a -um, *Falernian;* vites, uvae, Hor. Subst., **Fălernum** -i, n. *Falernian wine,* Hor.

Fălisci -ōrum, m. *a people in Etruria.* Adj., **Făliscus** -a -um, *Faliscan.* Subst., **Făliscum** -i, n., *the territory of the Falisci.*

fallācĭa -ae, f. (fallax), *deceit, trick, fraud, artifice, craft;* sine fuco ac fallaciis, Cic.

fallācĭlŏquus -a -um (fallax and loqui), *speaking falsely or deceitfully,* ap. Cic.

fallācĭtĕr, adv. (fallax), *deceitfully, craftily, fallaciously,* Cic.

fallax -lācis, adj. (fallo), *deceitful, treacherous, false, fallacious;* homines, Cic.; herbae non fallaces, *not disappointing the farmer,* Cic.; spes, Cic. ; fallaces et captiosae interrogationes, Cic.

fallo, fĕfelli, falsum, 3. (σφάλλω). **I.** *to make to slip;* glacies fallit pedes, Liv. **II.** Transf., **a,** *to make invisible;* signa sequendi, Verg.; longe fallens sagitta, *coming unnoticed from afar,* Verg.; aetas labitur occulte fallitque, *glides un-*

noticed, Ov.; **b,** *to make ineffective, to drive away,*
beguile; infandum amorem, Verg.; curam vino
et somno, Ov.; **c,** *to break a promise,* etc.;
foedus ac fidem, Liv.; fidem hosti datam, Cic.;
d, *to escape the notice of, be concealed from;* custodias, Liv.; non fefellere insidiae, Liv.; aliquem fallit or non fallit, with acc. and infin.,
Cic.; aliquem non fallit quin, Caes.; esp. (like
Gr. λανθάνω) with a partic., hostis fallit incedens,
comes unnoticed, Liv.; **e,** *to lead astray, to de-*
ceive; pass., fallor as middle, *to make a mistake;*
fallere alicuius spem or opinionem, Cic.; fallit
me tempus, dies, *I am mistaken in,* Cic.; nisi
me forte fallo, Cic.; non in sortitione fallere,
Cic.; si fallo (in oaths), *if I do not keep my word,*
Cic.; impers., me fallit, *I am mistaken, err;*
quantum nos fefellerit, vides, Cic.; pass., potest
fieri ut fallar, *I may be mistaken,* Cic.

falsē, adv. (falsus), *falsely,* Cic.

falsĭpărens -entis (falsus and parens),
having a putative father; Amphitryoniades,
Hercules, Cat.

falsō, adv. (falsus), *falsely, wrongly, errone-*
ously, untruly, Cic.

falsus -a -um, p. adj. (from fallo). **I.** *invented,*
feigned, false, untrue, spurious, made up; gaudium, Cic.; Caesaris commentarii, Cic.; voculae,
falsetto, Cic.; ora non falsa, *genuine,* Ov. Subst.,
falsum -i, n. *an untruth, something false, a lie;*
ad te falsum scripseram, Cic.; falsum jurare,
Cic.; falso, adv., *falsely,* Cic. **II.** *deceitful, false,*
hypocritical; in amore, Tac.; lingua, Ov. Subst.,
falsum -i, n., **a,** *deceit, hypocrisy,* Tac.; **b,** tela
in falsum jacere, *at random,* Tac.

falx, falcis, f. **1,** *a scythe, sickle, bill-hook,*
pruning-hook, Cic.; **2,** *a sickle-shaped implement*
of war, used for tearing down stockades, etc., Caes.

fāma -ae, f. (fari). **I.** *talk, tradition, a re-*
port, rumour, intelligence, unauthenticated news;
nulla adhuc fama venerat, Cic.; fama est, *there*
is a rumour, Liv.; fama emergit, Cic.; fama
nuntiabat, Cic.; fama manat, foll. by acc. and
infin.; fama accipere, *to hear by rumour,* Caes.;
personif., Fama, *a goddess, daughter of Terra,*
Verg. **II.** *the opinion of the crowd, public*
opinion. **A.** contra famam opinionemque omnium, Cic.; fama popularis, *popular favour,* Cic.;
bona fama, *good opinion,* Cic.; mala fama, Sall.;
fama sapientiae, Cic. **B.** *reputation;* **1,** *good*
name; famae consulere, Cic.; famam sororis
defendere, Cic.; **2,** *evil reputation;* moveri fama,
Verg.

fāmātus -a -um (fama), *having an ill reputa-*
tion, Cic. (?).

fămēlĭcus -a -um (fames), *suffering hunger,*
hungry, famished; armenta, Juv.

fămes -is, f. *hunger.* **I.** Gen., **A.** Lit., cibi
condimentum esse famem, Cic.; aliqua re famem
tolerare, Caes.; aliqua re famem depellere, *to*
satisfy, Cic.; explere, Cic.; famem ab ore civium
propulsare, Liv. **B.** Transf., **1,** *insatiable de-*
sire; auri sacra fames, Verg.; **2,** *poverty of ex-*
pression; jejunitas et fames, Cic. **II.** *famine,*
time of famine; in fame frumentum exportare,
Cic.

fămĭlĭa -ae (-as after the words pater,
mater, filius, filia), f. (from root FAM, whence
famulus). **I.** *a household of slaves, household;* **a,**
familiam intelligamus, quae constet ex servis
pluribus, Cic.; emere eam familiam a Catone,
Cic.; **b,** *a band of gladiators;* gladiatoria, Sall.;
comparare familiam, Cic.; familiam ducere, *to*
be a the head, to take the first place, Cic.; **c,** *the*
dependents, vassals of a noble, Caes.; **d,** *the slaves*
of a temple. **II.** Transf., **A.** *the entire household*
or *family;* hence, paterfamilias, *the head of the*
household or *family;* materfamilias, *a married*

woman who had passed in manum viri, or *an*
unmarried woman whose father was dead, Cic.;
filiusfamilias, *the son still under his father's*
power, Cic. **B.** *a family;* **1,** lit., **a,** in a wide
sense, *race* (syn. with gens); familiam unam (sc.
gentem Claudiam) subisse civitatis onus, Liv.;
b, in a narrower sense, *a family,* as a subdivision of a gens; Laeliorum et Muciorum familiae,
Cic.; **2,** transf., *sect;* tota Peripateticorum, Cic.

fămĭlĭāris -e (familia). **I.** *belonging to the*
slaves of a house, Plaut. Subst., **fămĭlĭāris**
-is, m., *a servant,* plur., *the servants in a house,*
Liv. **II.** *belonging* or *relating to a family* or
household. **A.** Lit., **a,** *belonging to a household;*
lares, Cic.; copiae, Liv.; res familiaris; (a) *the*
household, Liv.; (β) *property,* Cic.; **b,** *belonging*
to a family; funus, *a death in the family,* Cic.
B. Transf., **a,** with compar. and superl., *known*
in the house or *family, intimate, friendly;*
biduo factus est mihi familiaris, Cic.; subst.,
fămĭlĭāris -is, m. *a friend;* so familiaris -is, **f.,**
a female friend; exclamat familiaris tua, Cic.;
of things, *ordinary, familiar, confidential;* sermo,
Cic.; aditus familiarior, Liv.; **b,** t. t. of augury,
fissum familiare or pars familiaris, *the part of*
the entrails relating to the persons sacrificing,
Cic., Liv.

fămĭlĭārĭtas -ātis, f. (familiaris), **1,** *con-*
fidential friendship, intimacy, familiarity; in
alicuius familiaritatem venire or intrare, or **se**
dare, Cic.; mihi cum aliquo familiaritas est or
intercedit, Cic.; **2,** meton., *familiar friends;* **e**
praecipua familiaritate Neronis, Tac.

fămĭlĭārĭter, adv. with compar. and superl.
(familiaris), *confidentially, familiarly, intimately;*
familiariter cum aliquo vivere, Cic.

fāmōsus -a -um, adj. with compar. and superl.
(fama). **I.** Pass., **a,** in a good sense, *much spoken*
of, renowned; urbs (of Jerusalem), Tac.; mors,
Hor.; **b,** in a bad sense, *infamous, notorious;*
si qua erat famosa, Cic. **II.** Act., *libellous, de-*
famatory; versus, Hor.; libelli, Tac.

fămul, fămŭla, v. famulus.

fămŭlāris -e (famulus), *relating* or *belonging*
to servants or *slaves;* vestis, Cic.; jura famularia
dare, *to make slaves,* Ov.

fămŭlātus -ūs, m. (famulor), *service, servi-*
tude, slavery, Cic.; transf., quam miser virtutis
famulatus servientis voluptati, Cic.

fămŭlor, 1. dep. (famulus), *to be a servant,*
to serve any one, Cic.; alicui, Cat.

fămŭlus -a -um (root FAM), *serving, servile;*
vertex, Ov. Subst., **a, fămŭlus** -i, m. *a serv-*
ant, slave; of a man, Cic.; of a deity, Cic.;
ante-class. form, famul, Lucr.; **b, fămŭla**
-ae, f. *a female slave, handmaid,* Verg., Ov.;
transf., virtus famula fortunae est, Cic.

fānātĭcus -a -um (fanum), *inspired by a*
deity, enthusiastic, raving. **A.** Lit., of persons,
Galli fanatici, Liv.; isti philosophi superstitiosi
et paene fanatici, Cic. **B.** Transf. of things,
vaticinantes carmine fanatico, Liv.; fanaticus
error, Hor.

Fannĭus -a -um, *name of a Roman gens, of*
which the most famous were C. Fannius, *an his-*
torian, and his uncle, C. Fannius, *an orator, con-*
temporaries of Scipio Aemilianus. Hence adj.,
Fannĭānus -a -um, *of or relating to Fannius.*

fānum -i, n. (fari). **I. a,** *a place solemnly*
consecrated to a god, Cic.; **b,** *a temple with the*
land round it, a holy place; in sing. generally
with the name of the deity, Apollinis, Cic.; fana
spoliare, Cic. **II.** Proper name, **Fānum** -i, n.
town on the coast of Umbria, now *Fano.*

fār, farris, n. **I.** Lit., *spelt* (triticum spelta
Linn.), farris seges, Liv.; farris acervus, Verg

II. Transf., **a,** *meal;* percontor quanti olus et far, Hor.; esp. as used in sacrifices, far pium, Hor.; **b,** *bread;* una farris libra, Hor.

farcĭo, farsi, fartum, 4. (root FARC, Gr. ΦΡΑΓ, φράγ-νυμι, φράττω), *to fill full, stuff full;* pulvinus rosā fartus, Cic.

Farfărus, v. Fabaris.

fārīna -ae, f. (far), *meal, flour,* Plin.; hence, *dust* or *powder of any kind,* Plin.; fig., nostrae farinae, *of our kind* or *sort,* Pers.

fārīnārĭus -a -um (farina), *relating to meal, made of meal,* Plin.

farrācĕus (ĭus) -a -um (far), *of* or *belonging to spelt,* Plin.

farrāgo -ĭnis, f. (far), **1,** *mixed fodder for cattle,* Verg.; **2,** transf., *a medley, mixture;* nostri libelli, Juv.

farrārĭus -a -um (far), *relating to spelt* or *to grain generally,* Cato.

farrātus -a -um (far), **1,** *provided with grain,* Pers.; **2,** *made of corn;* neut. plur. subst., farrata, *porridge,* Juv.

farrĕus -a -um (far), *made of spelt* or *corn generally.* Subst., **farrĕum** -i, n. *a spelt-cake,* Plin.

fartor -ōris, m. (farcio), *a fattener of fowls,* Hor.

fartum -i, n. and **fartŭs** -us, m. (farcio), *the stuffing, the inside,* Plin.

fās, n. indecl. (root FA, Gr. ΦΑ-Ω, whence also fari, fatum), *something spoken.* **I.** *divine law and right* (opp. jus, *human law and right*), *divine command;* jus ac fas omne delere, Cic.; contra jus fasque, Cic.; personif., audi Juppiter, audite fines, audiet fas, Liv. **II. A.** Gen., *that which is allowed, permitted, lawful, right* (opp. nefas); per omne fas et nefas aliquem sequi, Liv.; fas est, *it is allowed, is lawful;* quod aut per naturam fas esset aut per leges liceret, Cic.; si fas est, with infin., Cic.; with supine, si hoc fas est dictu, Cic.; fas est or non fas est, with infin., Cic.; fas putare, with infin., Caes. **B.** *fate, destiny;* fas obstat, Verg.; fas est, with infin. or acc. and infin.; si cadere fas est, *if I am destined to fall,* Ov.

fascĭa -ae, f. *a bandage, band.* **I.** Lit., **1,** *a surgical bandage,* Cic.; **2,** esp., **a,** *a woman's girdle,* Ov.; **b,** *a bed-girth,* Cic. **II.** Transf., *a streak of cloud in the sky,* Juv.

fascĭcŭlus -i, m. (dim. of fascis), *a little bundle* or *packet;* epistolarum, Cic.; librorum, Hor.; florum, *a nosegay,* Cic.

fascĭno, 1. (βασκαίνω), *to bewitch;* agnos, Verg.

fascĭnum -i, n. and **fascĭnus** -i, m. (βάσκανον). **I.** *an enchanting, bewitching,* Plin. **II.** = membrum virile, Hor.

fascĭŏla -ae, f. (dim. of fascia), *a little bandage,* Hor.; purpureae fasciolae, *bandages round the ankle worn by women,* Cic.

fascis -is, m. *a bundle, packet.* **I.** Gen., sarmentorum, Liv.; ego hoc te fasce levabo, Verg. **II.** Esp., plur. **A.** Lit., fasces, *bundles of sticks with an axe projecting, carried by lictors before the chief Roman magistrates;* fasces praeferre, Liv.; habere, Cic.; dare alicui fasces, *the consulate,* Cic.; summittere fasces, *to lower as a sign of respect,* Liv.; fig., alicui, *to yield the preference to,* Cic.; demissi populo fasces, *lowered before the people,* Cic. **B.** Meton., *high office,* esp. *the consulate,* Verg., Hor.

fāsēlus, fāsĕŏlus, etc. = phaselus, etc. (q.v.).

fasti -ōrum, m., v. fastus -a -um.

fastīdĭo -īvi -ītum, 4. (fastidium), *to loathe, feel distaste* or *disgust.* **I.** Lit., of physical loath-

ing, olus, Hor.; omnia praeter pavonem rhombumque, Hor. **II.** Transf., *to be averse to, dislike, loathe;* etiam in recte factis saepe fastidiunt, Cic.; preces alicuius, Liv.; with infin., ne fastidieris nos in sacerdotum numerum accipere, Liv.; with acc. and infin., est aliquis, qui se inspici, aestimari fastidiat, Liv.

fastīdĭōsē, adv. with compar. (fastidiosus), **1,** *with loathing, dislike;* huic ego jam stomachans fastidiose, immo ex Sicilia, inquam, Cic.; **2, a,** *fastidiously, daintily;* quam diligenter et quam paene fastidiose judicamus, Cic.; **b,** *disdainfully, contemptuously;* fastidiosius ad hoc genus sermonis accedere, Cic.

fastīdĭōsus -a -um, adj. with compar. and superl. (fastidium), *full of loathing.* **I.** *feeling, loathing.* **A.** Lit., *squeamish,* Varr. **B.** Transf., **a,** *sick of, disgusted with, impatient of;* with genit., Latinarum (litterarum), Cic.; terrae, Hor.; **b,** esp., *nice, dainty, fastidious;* fastidious facilis in causis recipiendis erat, fastidiosior Crassus, sed tamen recipiebat, Cic.; **c,** *contemptuous, disdainful,* Plin. **II.** *causing loathing, disgusting, ioatksome,* Hor.

fastīdĭum -ii, n. (FAST-idium, of same root as 1. fastus), *loathing.* **I.** Lit., *the loathing* of food; cibi satietas et fastidium, Cic. **II.** Transf., **A.** *dislike, aversion, disgust;* domesticarum rerum, Cic. **B. a,** *fastidiousness, hyper-criticism, fault-finding;* delicatissimum, Cic.; audiendi, Cic.; **b,** *scorn, haughtiness, pride;* fastidium et superbia, fastidium arrogantiaque, fastidium et contumacia, Cic.; fastidium alicuius non posse ferre, Cic.

fastīgātē, adv. (fastigatus), *slantingly,* Caes.

fastīgātus -a -um, partic. of fastigo.

fastīgĭum -ii, n. (FAST -igium, connected with ἄ-φλαστον). **I.** *a slope, declivity, descent;* ab oppido locus tenui fastigio vergebat, Caes. **II.** *the extremity, either above* or *below.* **A.** Lit., **1,** *above, height;* **a,** gen., *height, summit;* pari altitudinis fastigio, Caes.; **b,** esp., *the summit of a roof;* both, (a) *the whole of the roof,* Cic.; and (β) *the gable end, pediment;* fastigium Capitolii, Cic.; operi inchoato, prope tamen absoluto, tamquam fastigium imponere, *put the last touch to,* Cic.; **2,** *below, depth,* Caes. **B.** Transf., **1,** *dignity, rank, position;* dictaturae altius fastigium, Liv.; **2,** *principal point* (in writing); summa sequar fastigia rerum, Verg.

fastīgo, 1. (fastigium), *to sharpen to a point,* **1,** upwards, collis est in modum metae in acutum cacumen a fundo satis lato fastigatus, Liv.; **b,** *to slope down,* only in partic., fastigatus collis leniter fastigatus, Caes.

fastōsus -a -um (fastus), *proud, haughty,* Mart.

1. fastus -ūs, m. *pride, haughtiness, arrogance;* stirpis Achilleae fastus (plur.), Verg.; fastu erga patrias epulas, Tac.

2. fastus -a -um (root FA, Gr. ΦΑ-ω, whence fatum, φάσκω, φημί), dies fastus, gen. plur. dies fasti, or simply fasti, *the days on which the praetor could administer justice* (opp. nefasti); ille dies nefastus erit, per quem tria verba (do, dico, addico) silent; fastus erit per quem lege licebit agi, Ov.; *a list of these days, with the festivals, magistrates, chief events,* etc., *the Roman calendar;* fasti memores, Hor.; *a poetical form of this calendar composed by Ovid;* fasti consulares or magistratuum, *a list of the highest magistrates at Rome from the earliest times,* Cic.

fātālis -e (fatum), *relating to destiny* or *fate.* **I. a,** *fated, destined by fate;* necessitas, Cic.; annus ad interitum huius urbis fatalis, Cic.; **b,** *fateful, connected with the fate of a person* or *thing;* pignora, the *Palladium,* Ov.; libri, *the*

Sibylline books, Liv.; bellum, Cic.; deae, *the fates*, Ov. **II.** In a bad sense, *deadly, fatal;* telum, Verg.; jaculum, Ov.

fātālĭtĕr, adv. (fatalis), *according to fate or destiny;* definitum esse, Cic.

fătĕŏr, fassus sum, 2. dep. (root FA-, Gr. Φᾱ-ω, whence also fari, φᾰτίζω), 1, *to confess, admit, allow;* verum, Cic.; de facto turpi; with acc. and infin., si quis se amici causā fecisse fateatur, Cic.; 2, *to discover, make known;* iram vultu, Ov. (pass., qui (ager) publicus esse fateatur, Cic.).

fătĭcănus -a -um and **fătĭcĭnus** -a -um (fatum and cano), *prophetic,* Ov.

fătĭdĭcus -a -um (fatum and dico), *announcing fate, prophesying, prophetic;* vates, Verg.; anus, Cic.; subst., *a soothsayer,* Cic.

fătĭfĕr -fĕra -fĕrum (fatum and fero), *death-bringing, deadly, fatal;* arcus, Verg.

fătĭgātĭo -ōnis, f. (fatigo), *weariness, fatigue;* cum fatigatione equorum atque hominum, Liv.

fătĭgo, 1. (perhaps connected with fatis, whence also affatim). **I.** *to weary, tire, fatigue;* cervos jaculo cursuque, Verg.; se atroci pugnā, Liv.; itinere, magno aestu fatigati, Caes. **II.** Transf., *to vex, harass.* **A.** Of the body, verberibus, tormentis, igni fatigati, Cic. **B.** Of the mind, 1, *animum,* Sall.; se, Sall.; qui punit aliquem aut verbis fatigat, Cic.; 2, esp., *to tease, worry with entreaties,* etc.; aliquem precibus, Liv.; Vestam prece, Hor.

fătĭlŏquus -a -um (fatum and loqui), *announcing fate, prophetic.* Subst., *a prophet, prophetess;* Carmenta mater . . . quam fatiloquam miratae hae gentes fuerant, Liv.

fătis -is, f. whence acc. fatim, *sufficiently,* post-Aug.

fătisco, 3. and **fătiscor,** 3. dep. (χατέω, χατίσκω), 1, *to chink, gape, crack, open, part asunder;* naves rimis fatiscunt, Verg.; 2, *to become weak, droop, decrease;* seditio fatiscit, Tac.; dum copiā fatiscunt, Tac.

fătŭĭtas -ātis, f. (fatuus), *foolishness, simplicity,* Cic.

fātum -i, n. (for, fari), *an utterance.* **I.** *the expressed will of a god, prophecy, prediction;* fata Sibyllina, Cic. **II.** 1, *destiny, fate, the appointed order of the world, the fate, lot, or destiny of man;* omnia fato fieri, Cic.; fato rerum prudentia major, Verg.; alicui fatum est, with infin., Cic.; alicuius or alicui fatum est, with acc. and infin., Cic.; fuit hoc sive meum sive rei publicae fatum ut, etc., Cic.; *the will of a god;* sic fata Jovis poscunt, Verg.; and personif., Fata, the Parcae or Fates, Prop.; 2, a, *the natural term of life;* maturius exstingui quam fato suo, Cic.; fato cedere, Liv.; fato fungi, Ov.; fato obire, *to die a natural death,* Tac.; fata proferre, *to prolong life,* Verg.; b, *misfortune, ruin, calamity;* impendet fatum aliquod, Cic.; meton., *a cause of calamity* or *destruction;* duo illa reipublicae paene fata, Gabinius et Piso, Cic.

fătŭus -a -um, *foolish, idiotic, fatuous;* a, of persons, puer, Cic.; fatuus et amens es, Cic. Subst., **fătŭus** -i, m. *a fool, idiot,* Cat.; b, of things, *foolish, insipid, perverse;* primas illas rabiosulas (litteras) sat fatuas dedisti, Cic.

Faunus -i, m. (root FAV-, faveo), *a mythic king of Latium, revered as a god of woods and fields;* subsequently identified with Pan; hence, **Fauni** = *forest gods,* Ov.

faustē, adv. (faustus), *happily, fortunately;* evenire, Cic.

faustĭtas -ātis, f. (faustus), *prosperity;* personif. as a goddess of the fields, Hor.

Faustulus -i, m. (root FAV-, whence faus-

tus), myth., *the herdsman of the Alban king Amulius, who saved and brought up Romulus and Remus.*

faustus -a -um (root FAV-, faveo). **I.** *bringing luck* or *good fortune, fortunate, lucky, auspicious;* dies faustus alicui, Cic. **II.** As a proper name, Faustus, *a Roman surname;* L. Corn. Sulla Faustus, *son of the dictator Sulla;* Fausta, *daughter of the dictator Sulla, wife of Milo.*

fautor -ōris, m. (orig. favitor, from faveo), *a favourer, protector, patron, promoter;* dignitatis, Cic.; bonorum, Liv.; absol., *an applauder,* Hor.

fautrix -trīcis, f. (fautor), *a favourer, protector, promoter;* voluptatum, Cic.; regio suorum fautrix, Cic.

faux, faucis, f. (usually plur. **fauces** -ĭum, f.). **I.** Lit., *the jaws, gullet, throat;* arente fauce, Hor.; sitis urit fauces, Hor.; fig., quum inexplebiles populi fauces exaruerunt libertatis siti Cic.; Catilina cum exercitu faucibus urguet, *is at our throats,* Sall.; quum faucibus premeretur, *when the knife was at his throat,* Cic.; premit fauces defensionis tuae, *strangles, makes impossible,* Cic.; urbem ex belli ore ac faucibus ereptam esse, Cic. **II.** Transf., only in plur., 1, *jaws, chasm;* patefactis terrae faucibus, Cic.; 2, *entrance;* portus, Caes.; macelli, Cic.; 3, *a narrow pass, defile;* angustae, Liv.; artae, Tac.; Etruriae, Cic.; 4, a, *isthmus, neck of land;* artae fauces (Isthmi), Liv.; Graeciae, Cic.; b, *straits;* Hellesponti, Liv.

făvĕo, fāvi, fautum, 2. **I.** *to favour, be favourable* or *inclined to, help, protect;* with dat. of person or party, faveas tu hosti, Cic.; si tibi dei favent, Cat.; favere suis, Cic.; with dat. of thing, favere enim pietati fideique deos, Liv.; favere et reipublicae et dignitati ac gloriae alicuius, Cic.; isti sententiae, Cic.; impers., non modo non invidetur illi aetati, verum etiam favetur, Cic.; with pro and the abl., or contra and the acc., hac pro parte, Ov.; qui Parthorum quoque contra Romanum nomen gloriae favent, Liv.; with acc. and infin., Ov.; with neut. acc. (as regards), quod quidem ego favisse me tibi fateor, Cic.; absol., dum favet nox et Venus, Hor.; multitudo audiens favet, odit, Cic. **II.** Esp., *to favour* with the mouth, heart, etc., hence *to be silent,* favete linguis, Cic.; ore favete, Verg., *be silent;* absol., celebrate faventes, Verg.

făvilla -ae, f. (faveo), *glowing ashes,* esp. *the still glowing ashes of the dead;* reliquias vino et bibulam lavēre favillam, Verg.

făvĭtor -ōris, m. = fautor (q.v.).

făvōnĭus -ii, m. *the west wind* or *zephyr which blew at the beginning of spring,* Cic.

făvor -ōris, m. (faveo). **I.** *favour, goodwill, partiality, inclination;* with subject. genit., populi, Cic.; with object. genit., nominis, Liv.; with in and the acc., Liv.; amplecti aliquem favore, Liv.; in favorem alicuius venire, Liv. **II.** Esp., *a, attention at a religious ceremony;* pium praestare et mente et voce favorem, Ov.; b, *applause at the theatre, approbation, acclamation;* quod studium et quem favorem in scenam attulit Panurgus, Cic.

făvōrābĭlis -e, adj. with compar. (favor), *favour, popular, beloved, pleasing;* oratio, Tac.

făvus -i, m. *a honeycomb;* fingere favos, Cic., poet., favos dilue Baccho, *honey,* Verg.

fax, făcis, f. *a torch.* **I. A.** Lit., faces incidere, Liv.; faces nuptiales, Cic.; *a funeral torch,* Verg.; faces incendere, Cic.; fig., eius omnium incendiorum fax, Antonius, Cic.; attribute of Cupid and the Furies, Ov., Verg. **B.** Fig., 1, gen., faces dicendi, *fiery eloquence,* Cic.; alicui ad libidinem facem praeferre, *to minister to*, Cic.; facem bello praeferre, *to kindle the flame of war*, Tac.; me torret face mutuâ Calais, *with the flame of love*, Hor.; 2, esp., *that which provokes or causes, the author;* subjicere faces invidiae alicuius, Cic. **II.** Transf., 1, *the light of the moon;* crescentem face Noctilucam, Hor.; 2, *a fiery meteor, shooting star*, etc.; faces caelestes or caeli, Cic.

faxim, faxo = fecerim, fecero, v. facio.

febrīcŭla -ae, f. (dim. of febris), *a slight fever, feverishness;* febricula incipit, Cic.; febriculam habere, Cic.

febrīcŭlōsus -a -um (febricula), *feverish*, Cat.

febris -is, f., acc. -em or -im, abl. -ě or -ī (for ferbis, from ferveo), *fever;* in febrim subito incidere, Cic.; febrim habere, Cic.; febri carere, Cic.; Romam venisse cum febre, Cic.; Febris personif. as a goddess, with three temples in Rome.

februārius -a -um (februus, februo, *to purify*), *relating to cleansing;* a, mensis Februarius or simply Februarius, *the cleansing month* (so called because of the purificatory sacrifices in its second half), up to 450 B.C. the last month of the year, in the time of Cicero the second; b, *belonging to the month February;* Kalendae Februariae, *the 1st of February*, Cic.

februus -a -um, *purifying* (in the religious sense); subst. **februum** -i, n. *a means of religious purification;* hence, **Februa** -ōrum, n. *the feast of purification held by the Romans at the end of February.*

fecialis = fetialis (q.v.).

fecunditas -ātis, f. (fecundus), *fruitfulness, fecundity.* **I.** Lit., a, of persons, mulieris, Cic.; b, of the earth, aquarum inductionibus terris fecunditatem damus, Cic.; c, of the intellect, volo se efferat in adolescente fecunditas, Cic. **II.** Transf., *abundance*, Plin.

fecundo, 1. (fecundus), *to fructify, fertilise;* viridem Aegyptum nigrâ arenâ, Verg.

fecundus -a -um, p. adj. with compar. and superl. (FE-o, whence fetus, femina, fenus), *fruitful, prolific.* **I. A.** Lit., terra, Cic.; conjux, Hor. **B.** Fig., *rich, abounding in;* with genit., saecula fecunda culpae, Hor.; with abl., gens inter accolas latrociniis fecunda, Tac. **II.** Transf., 1, *abundant, full, plentiful;* quaestus, Cic.; calices, Hor.; with abl. (specus) uberibus fecundus aquis, Ov.; 2, *making fruitful;* fecundae verbera dextrae, Ov.

fel, fellis, n. *the gall, the gall-bladder.* **A.** Gen., 1, lit., fel gallinaceum, Cic.; 2, fig., a, *bitterness*, Tib.; b, *anger;* atrum fel, Verg. **B.** Esp., *the venom of a serpent;* vipereo spicula felle linunt, Ov.

feles (faeles) -is, and **felis (faelis)** -is, f. *a cat*, Cic.

felicitas -ātis, f. (felix). **I.** *fertility*, Plin. **II.** Transf., a, *happiness, felicity, good fortune, success;* perpetuâ quâdam felicitate usus ille excessit e vita, Cic.; plur., incredibiles felicitates, Cic.; personif., Felicitas, *Good Fortune as a goddess*, with a temple in Rome; b, *success*, esp. in war; Helvetiorum, Caes.

feliciter, adv. (felix), 1, *fruitfully;* illic veniunt felicius uvae, Verg.; 2, *happily;* a, vivere, navigare, Cic.; b, in a wish, *auspiciously, favourably;* precatus sum ut ea res mihi, populo plebique Romanae bene atque feliciter eveniret, Cic.; c, *good luck!* feliciter velim, Cic.

felis = feles (q.v.).

felix -icis (root FE-o, cf. fecundus). **I.** *fruitful, fertile;* arbor, Liv.; regio, Ov. **II. A.** *fortunate, favourable, propitious, lucky;* 1, gen.,

Sulla felicissimus omnium, Cic.; with genit., cerebri, Hor.; with ad and the acc., ad casum fortunamque felix, Cic.; with abl., morte felix, Verg.; with abl. gerund., tam felix vobis corrumpendis fuit, Liv.; with in and the abl. gerund., si minus felices in diligendo fuissemus, Cic.; with ab and the abl., ille Graecus ab omni laude felicior, Cic.; with infin., felicior ungers tela manu, Verg.; Felix, *the Lucky One, surname of Sulla*, Liv.; 2, esp., a, *rich;* tam felix esse, Ov.; b, *successful;* seditio, Liv.; arma, Verg. **B.** Act., a, *bringing good luck;* omen, Ov.; so the formula, quod bonum, faustum, felix fortunatumque sit, Cic.; b, *blessed with healing power;* malum, Verg.; c, *making joyful;* poma, Ov.; d, *making fruitful;* limus, Verg.

femella -ae, f. (dim. of femina), *a young woman, a girl*, Cat.

femen = femur (q.v.).

femina -ae, f. (root FE-o, cf. fecundus), lit., *any female animal that bears young;* a, of human beings, *a woman*, Cic.; b, of animals, *the female;* porcus femina, Cic.

femineus -a -um (femina), 1, *relating to a woman, female, feminine;* calendae, *the 1st of March, when the Matronalia were celebrated*, Juv.; curae iraeque, Verg.; 2, *womanish, effeminate;* amor, Verg.; fuga, Ov.

femur -ŏris or (from femen) -ĭnis, n. (FE-o, cf. fecundus), *the upper part of the leg, the thigh*, Cic.; femur utrumque, Caes.

fenebris -e (fenus), *relating to interest;* leges, Liv.

feneratio -ōnis, f. (fenero), *lending at interest, usury*, Cic.

fenerator -ōris, m. (fenero), *one who lends money at interest, money-lender, usurer;* fenerator acerbissimus, Cic.

fenero (faenero), 1. (fenus), *to lend money at interest;* ne fenerare liceret, Liv.

feneror (faeneror), 1. dep. (fenus), *to lend money at interest;* pecuniam binis centesimis, at twenty-four per cent. per annum, Cic.; provincias, *to despoil by usury*, Cic.; fig., beneficium, *to trade in*, Cic.

fenestella -ae, f. (dim. of fenestra), *a little opening*, (porta) Fenestella, *a little gate in Rome.*

fenestra -ae, f. (connected with φαίνω), a, *a window*, Cic.; b, *an opening;* lato dedit ore fenestram, Verg.; esp., *a loophole for shooting;* fenestras ad tormenta mittenda in struendo reliquerunt, Caes.

feneus -a -um (fenum), *made of hay;* homines, *men of straw*, Cic.

feniculārius -a -um (feniculum), *belonging to fennel;* hence **Feniculārius** campus, *a district in Spain*, Cic.

feniculum -i, n. *fennel*, Plaut.

fenilia -ium, n. plur. (fenum), *a hay-loft*, Verg.

feniseca -ae, m. (fenum and seco), *a mower;* transf., *a countryman*, Pers.

fenum (faenum, foenum) -i, n. (root FE-o), *hay;* fenum alios esse oportere, *must eat hay*, i.e., *be dolts*, Cic.; prov., fenum habet in cornu, *he is dangerous* (the horns of vicious cattle were bound with hay), Hor.

fenus (faenus) -ŏris, n. (root FE-o), lit., *that which is produced.* **I.** *interest of money;* pecuniam alicui dare fenore, *to lend at interest*, Cic.; pecuniam accipere fenore, *to borrow*, Liv.; pecuniam occupare grandi fenore, *to invest*, Cic. **II.** Meton., 1, *debt, indebtedness;* fenore obrui, mersum esse, laborare, Liv.; 2, *capital;* duas fenoris partes in agris collocare, Tac.; 3, *usury;* fenore trucidare patrimonium or plebem, Cic.

fēra -ae, f. v. ferus.

fērācĭtĕr, adv. with compar. (ferax), *fruitfully;* velut ab stirpibus laetius feraciusque renata urbs, Liv.

fērālis -e (root FER, whence also Feronia, in-fer-nus). **I.** *relating to the dead, funereal;* cupressus, Verg.; tempus or dies, = feralia, Ov. Subst., **fērālia** -ium, n., a, *the festival of the dead on the 10th of February,* Cic.; b, *things relating to the dead* or *to burial,* Tac. **II.** Transf., *death-bringing, deadly, fatal;* dona, Ov.; annus, Tac.

fērax -ācis (fero), *fruitful, fertile, prolific.* **A.** Lit., agri, Cic.; with genit., Iberia ferax venenorum, Hor.; with abl., feracior uvis, Ov.; **B.** Transf., nullus feracior in philosophia locus est quam de officiis, Cic.; with genit., illa aetate qua nulla virtutum feracior fuit, Liv.

ferbĕo, v. ferveo.

fercŭlum and **fērĭcŭlum** -i, n. (fero), a *litter, bier, tray;* a, for carrying the spolia opima and the trophies at a triumph, Liv.; b, for carrying the images of the gods in processions, Cic.; c, for bringing in dishes; hence, meton., *a course,* Prop.

fērē, adv. (root FER-o), *almost, nearly.* **A.** Gen., totius fere Galliae legati, Caes.; omnes fere, Cic.; a, esp. with expression denoting time, quintā fere horā, Cic.; eādem fere horā quā veni, *about the same hour,* Cic.; b, with negatives, *scarcely, hardly;* aetates vestrae nihil aut non fere multum differunt, Cic. **B.** = semper fere, *nearly always, usually;* fit enim fere ut, etc., Cic.; with a negative, *seldom,* Cic.

fērentārĭus -ĭi, m. (fero), a *light-armed soldier who fought with missiles,* Sall.

Fĕrentīnum -i, n. **I.** a *town of the Hernici on the Via Latina,* now *Ferento;* adj., a, **Fĕrentīnus** -a -um, *Ferentine;* caput aquae Ferentinae, or simply caput Ferentinum, *the source of a stream running near Ferentinum,* Liv.; subst., **Fĕrentīna** -ae, f. a *goddess of Ferentinum;* b, **Fĕrentīnās** -ātis, *Ferentine.* **II.** a *town in Etruria,* now *Ferentino.*

Fērētrĭus -ĭi, m. (feretrum, fero), a *surname of Jupiter, to whom the spolia opima were dedicated,* Liv.

fērētrum -i, n. (fero), a *bier for carrying a corpse to the grave,* Ov., Verg.

fērĭae -ārum, f. for fesiae, same root as festus, *days of rest, holidays.* **I.** Lit., novendiales, Cic.; ferias agere, Liv. **II.** Transf., *rest,* Hor.

fērĭātus -a -um, p. adj. (from ferior), *keeping holiday, idle unoccupied, disengaged, at leisure;* deus feriatus torpet, Cic.; with ab, feriatus a negotiis publicis, Cic

fērĭcŭlum = ferculum

fērīnus -a -um (ferus), *relating to a wild beast, wild;* caro, Sall.; vellera, Ov. Subst., **fērīna** -ae, f. *flesh of wild animals, game,* Verg.

fērĭo, 4. *to strike, knock, beat, hit, smite.* **I.** **A.** Lit., murum arietibus, Sall.; frontem, Cic.; ferire mare, *to row,* Verg.; absol., contra ferire, Sall.; ferit sidera vertice, *reaches to the stars,* Hor. **B.** Transf., *to hit;* multa patent in eorum vita quae fortuna feriat, *influences,* Cic.; medium ferire, *to keep the middle of the road,* Cic. **II.** 1, *to strike dead, slay, kill;* hostem, Sall.; humilem agnam, Hor.; and hence, foedus, *to make a treaty* (because a sow was then slain), Cic.; 2, *to cut in pieces;* stricto retinacula ferro, Verg.; 3, *to bring out, utter;* verba palato, Hor. (syncop. imperf. feribant, Ov.).

fērĭor, 1. (feriae), *to keep holiday,* Varr.

fērĭtas -ātis, f. (ferus), *wildness, savageness;* hominis, Cic.; leonis, Ov.; loci, Ov.

fermē, adv. (superl. of fere = ferin.e), *almost, nearly, within a little.* **I.** haec ferme gesta, Liv.; a, of numbers, *about;* sex millia ferme passuum, Liv.; b, with negatives, *hardly, scarcely,* Cic. **II.** = semper ferme, *nearly always, usually;* ut ferme evenit, Cic.

fermento, 1. (fermentum), *to cause to ferment,* Plin.

fermentum -i, n. (for fervimentum, from ferveo), 1, *that which causes fermentation, leaven,* yeast, Tac.; transf., *anger,* or *the cause of anger,* Plaut.; 2, meton., a *kind of beer,* Verg.

fĕro, tŭli, lātum, ferre (root FER, Gr. ΦΕΡ, perf. tuli, from old form tulo, supine latum, orig. tlatum from old tlao, τλάω), *to bear, bring, carry.* **I.** Gen., **A.** Lit., a, *to bear;* faces in Capitolium, Cic.; (a) *to carry on one's person;* cervice jugum, Hor.; (β) ventrem, *to be pregnant,* Liv.; (γ) milit. t. t., arma contra aliquem, Cic.; signa in aliquem, *to attack,* Liv.; b, *to bring;* venenum, Liv.; alicui osculum, Ov.; alicui tributum, Liv.; *to offer* (to the gods); sacra divis, Verg. **B.** Transf., a, *to bear;* (a) nomen Aemilii Pauli, Liv.; aliquem in oculis or oculis, *to be very fond of,* Cic.; prae se ferre aliquid, *to display, make public,* Cic.; obscure ferre, *to conceal,* Cic.; (β) *to endure, submit to, bear;* contumaciam alicuius, Cic.; ea vina quae vetustatem ferunt, *which keep for a long time,* Cic.; with pers. obj., optimates quis ferat? Cic.; with acc. and infin., ferunt aures hominum illa laudari, Cic.; absol., non feram, non patiar, non sinam, Cic.; with adv., aliquid ferre aegre, moleste, graviter molesteque, *to take it ill, be vexed at,* Cic.; aequo or iniquo animo, Cic.; facile, clementer, fortiter ac sapienter, Cic.; with acc. and infin., si quis aegre ferat se pauperem esse, Cic.; partic., non ferendus, *intolerable;* facinus, Cic.; non ferendum, with acc. and infin., Cic.; b, *to bring;* (a) opem, auxilium, Cic.; alicui fraudem, Cic.; ferre responsa Turno, Verg.; conditionem ferre, *to propose terms,* Cic.; aliquam, *to propose some one as a wife,* Cic.; legal t. t., suffragium, *to vote,* Cic.; legem, *to propose a law,* Cic.; so ferre de aliqua re ut, etc., *to propose that,* Cic.; (alicui) judicem, *of the prosecutor, to propose a judge to the defendant,* Cic.; (β) of abstractions, *to demand, require, allow;* si ita res feret, Cic.; ut mea fert opinio, Cic. **II.** Esp., **A.** expensum ferre, *to set down in an account-book as paid,* Cic. **B.** *to spread abroad, report, speak of;* ferre haec omnibus sermonibus, Caes.; ferunt or pass. fertur, feruntur, *people say,* it is *reported,* with acc. and infin. or in pass. nom. and infin.; fama fert, *the story goes,* with acc., Liv.; ferre, with double acc., *to give a person out to be;* si te petitorem fero, Cic. **C.** *to think over, consider;* id consilio ante ferre debemus, Cic. **D.** *to carry off;* 1, in a good sense, veniam peto feroque, Liv.; non tacitum feres, *I will not be silent about it,* Cic.; fructus ex republica, Cic.; gratiam (*thanks*) alicuius rei, Liv.; polit. t. t., repulsam (a populo), Cic.; centuriam, tribus, *to gain the votes of,* Cic.; 2, in a bad sense, *to carry off violently;* te fata tulerunt, Verg.; ferre et agere, *to plunder,* Liv. **E.** *to bring forth;* terra fruges ferre potest, Cic. **F.** *to put in motion;* 1, *to drive away, lead;* ferre se or middle ferri, *to hasten, rush,* and of things, *to flow, mount, sink;* a, lit., inde domum pedem, Verg.; milit. t. t., signa ferre, *to march away,* Liv.; se ferre alicui obviam, Cic.; se ferre aliquem, *to act as, to profess to be, to declare oneself to be;* libertum se populi Romani, Liv.; ad eum omni celeritate ferri, Caes.; Rhenus citatus fertur per, etc., *rushes quickly,* Caes.; b, transf., aliquem in or ad caelum laudibus, *to praise sky-high,* Cic.;

eloquentia quae cursu magno sonituque fertur, Cic. ; ferri aliquā re, *to be borne away by, to be possessed by* ; crudelitate et scelere, Cic. ; **2,** of a road, etc., *to lead to* ; via fert Verruginem, Liv.; transf., si qua ad verum via ferret inquirentem, Liv. (archaic redupl. perf. tetulit, ap. Cic.).

fērōcĭa -ae, f. (ferox), **a,** in a good sense, *high spirit, courage,* Cic. ; **b,** in a bad sense, *fierceness, ferocity,* Cic. ; transf., vini, *harshness, roughness,* Plaut.

fērōcĭtas -ātis, f. (ferox), **a,** *courage, untamed spirit,* Cic. ; **b,** in a bad sense, *fierceness, haughtiness,* Cic.

fērōcĭtĕr, adv. (ferox), **a,** in a good sense, *courageously, bravely,* Liv.; **b,** in a bad sense, *rudely, roughly, fiercely,* Cic.

Fērōnĭa -ae, f. (root FER, cf. feralis), *an old Italian goddess, patroness of freedmen.*

fērox -ōcis (connected with ferus and Gr. θήρ. **I.** In a good sense, *courageous, high-spirited, warlike, brave* ; juvenis ferocissimus, Liv.; feroces ad bellandum viri, Liv. **II.** In a bad sense, *wild, unbridled, proud* ; with abl., stolide ferox viribus suis, Liv. ; with genit., linguae, Tac. ; victoria eos ipsos ferociores impotentioresque reddit, Cic.; of things, ferox aetas, Hor. ; oratio, Cic.

ferrāmentum -i, n. (ferrum), *any instrument or tool,* esp. in agriculture, *made of iron,* Cic.

ferrārĭa -ae, f., v. ferrarius.

ferrārĭus -a -um (ferrum), *relating or belonging to iron* ; faber, *a blacksmith,* Plaut. Subst., **ferrārĭa** -ae, f. *iron mine,* Caes.

ferrātus -a -um (ferrum). **I.** *furnished or covered with iron,* Liv.; hasta, Liv.; agmina, *iron-clad,* Hor. **II.** *of iron, iron* ; obices portarum, Tac.

ferrĕus -a -um (ferrum), *iron.* **A.** Lit., *made of iron* ; clavi, Caes. **B.** Meton., *like iron* ; **1,** *hard, stern, unfeeling, cruel* ; Aristo Chius, praefractus, ferreus, Cic. ; os, Cic. ; **2,** *lasting like iron, immovable, unyielding, firm* ; corpus animusque Catonis, Liv. ; **3,** *hard, oppressive* ; sors vitae, Ov. ; somnus, *death,* Verg.

ferrūgĭnĕus -a -um (ferrugo), *iron-coloured, dusky* ; hyacinthus, Verg. ; cymba, Verg.

ferrūgĭnus -a -um = ferrugineus (q.v.).

ferrūgo -Inis, f. (from ferrum, as aerugo from aes), **1,** *iron rust,* Plin. ; **2,** *the colour of iron rust, dusky* (iron grey, dark blue, steel blue) *colour* ; viridis ferrugine barba, Ov.

ferrum -i, n. **I.** *iron in its rough state, ore.* **A.** Lit., Cic. **B.** Transf., *hard-heartedness, insensibility, cruelty* ; in pectore ferrum gerit, Ov. **II.** *iron worked up,* meton. **A.** Gen., *any iron instrument, the plough,* Verg.; *an axe,* Hor. ; a *stylus for writing,* Ov. ; *scissors for hair-cutting,* Ov. ; *curling-irons,* Verg. **B.** Esp., *a sword* ; ferrum stringere, Liv. ; aliquem cum ferro invadere, Cic. ; urbes ferro atque igni vastare, Liv. ; haec omnia flamma ac ferro delere, Cic.

ferrūmen -Inis, n., *cement,* Plin.

ferrūmĭno, 1. (ferrumen), *to cement, bind together,* Plin.

fertĭlis -e (fero), *fruitful, prolific, fertile* ; **1,** agri, Cic. ; with genit., multos fertiles agros alios aliorum fructuum, Cic. ; with abl., insula agro fertilis, Liv.; transf., pectus, Ov. ; **2,** *fertilising, making fruitful* ; dea, Ceres, Ov. ; Bacchus, Hor.

fertĭlĭtas -ātis, f. (fertilis), *fruitfulness, fertility* ; with subject. genit., agrorum, Cic. ; of persons, indoluit fertilitate suā, Ov.

fertum (ferctum) -i, n., *a kind of sacrificial cake,* Pers.

fertus a -um (fero), *fruitful* ; arva, ap. Cic.

fērŭla -ae, f. (fero), **1,** *the herb fennel* ; **2,** a *rod used to punish slight offences of slaves and children,* a *ferule,* Hor. ; *used as* **a** *goad for cattle,* Ov.

fērus -a -um (root FER, connected with θήρ, Aeolic φήρ). **I.** Lit., *wild, untamed, uncultivated* ; bestiae, Cic. ; montes, Verg. ; silvae, Hor. Subst., **a,** **fera** -ae, f. (sc. bestia), *a wild animal* (as opp. to cicur, a domesticated animal) ; ferarum ritu, Liv. ; feras agitare, Cic. ; transf., of constellations, magna minorque ferae, *the Great and Little Bear,* Ov. ; **b,** **ferus** -i, m., *a wild beast, a wild boar,* Ov. ; *an ox,* Ov. ; *horse,* Verg.; *stag,* Verg. **II.** Transf., *wild, rough, savage, uncivilised, cruel* ; gens, Cic. ; hostis, Cic. ; facinus, Liv.

fervĕfăcĭo -fēci -factum, 3. (ferveo and facio), *to make hot, heat, boil, melt* ; pix fervefacta, Caes. ; jacula fervefacta, Caes.

fervens -entis, abl. -enti, p. adj. (from ferveo), *glowing, hot, heated.* **I.** Lit., aqua, Cic.; rota, Ov. **II.** Transf., **a,** ira, Ov. ; **b,** of character, *impetuous, fiery* ; fortis animus ferventior est, Cic.; Cassi rapido ferventius amni ingenium, Hor.

ferventĕr, adv. (fervens), *hotly, warmly* ; loqui, ap. Cic.

fervĕo, ferbŭi, -ēre and (poet) **fervo,** fervi -ēre. **I. A.** Lit., *to be boiling hot, to boil, seethe, glow,* Cic. ; validum posito medicamen aeno fervet, Ov. **B.** Transf., **a,** *to glow with passion,* etc., *to be heated* ; fervet avaritiā pectus, Hor. ; qui usque fervet ferturque avaritiā ut etc. Cic. ; **b,** *to be carried on briskly* ; fervet opus, Verg. ; **c,** *to glitter* ; jam fervēre litora flammis, Verg. **II.** 1, *to rage, foam, seethe, hiss* ; **a,** lit., fervet fretis spirantibus aequor, Verg. ; **b,** transf., of a poet, monte decurrens velut amnis fervet (Pindarus), rages, Hor. ; **2,** *to be in quick movement* ; **a,** of a crowd, *to swarm forth* ; fervēre quum videas classem lateque vagari, Verg. ; **b,** of places, *to swarm with* ; instructo Marte videres fervere Leucaten, Verg.

fervesco, 3. (ferveo), *to become hot, begin to glow, begin to boil,* Lucr.

fervĭdus -a -um (ferveo). **I.** *boiling, seething.* **A.** 1, lit., humor, Ov. ; 2, transf., of orators, *passionate, excited* ; paulo fervidior erat oratio, Cic. **B.** *burning, glowing, hot* ; **1,** lit., pars mundi, Cic. ; vina, Hor. ; 2, transf., *fiery, hot* ; fervidi animi vir, Liv. ; with abl., fervidus irā, Verg. **II.** *raging, foaming* ; vada, Verg.

fervo = ferveo (q.v.).

fervor -ōris, m. (ferveo). **I.** *boiling heat, raging heat.* **A.** Lit., mediis fervoribus, *in the heat of noon,* Verg. ; mundi, Cic. **B.** Transf., *heat, ardour, passion* ; mentis, animi, Cic. **II.** *raging, foaming* ; Oceani, maris, Cic.

Fescennĭa -ae, f., and **Fescennĭum** -ĭi, n., *a town in Etruria famous for the Fescennini versus.* Adj., **Fescennīnus** -a -um, *Fescennine,* Fescennini versus, *rude satirical verses* ; hence licentia Fescennina, Hor.

fessus -a -um (fatiscor), *weary, tired, exhausted* ; de via, Cic. ; militiā, Hor. ; plorando, Cic. ; corpus fessum vulnere, Liv. ; in the genit., fessi rerum, Verg. ; fessa aetas, *old age,* Tac. ; res fessae, *distress,* Verg.

festĭnantĕr, adv. (festino), *hastily, rapidly, quickly* ; nimium festinanter dictum, Cic.

festĭnātĭo -ōnis, f. (festino), *haste, speed, hurry* ; festinatio praepropera, Cic. ; with object. genit., adipiscendi honoris, Cic. ; omni festinatione properare in patriam, Cic. ; plur., quid afferebat festinationum, Cic.

festĭnāto, adv. (festino), *hastily, rapidly,* Plin.

festīno, 1. (festinus). **I**. Intransit., *to be in rapid motion, to hasten, hurry;* plura scripsissem nisi tui festinarent, Cic.; with ad and the acc., **ad** effectum operis, Liv. **II**. Transit., *to hasten, accelerate;* profectionem, Sall.; fugam, Verg.; partic., festinatus, *hastened;* iter, Ov.: with infin., tanto opere migrare, Cic.

festīnus -a -um (fero), *hastening, hasty;* cursu festinus anhelo, Ov.

fēstīvē, adv. (festivus), *humorously, facetiously, wittily;* belle et festive, Cic.

festīvītas -ātis, f. (festivus). **I**. Object., **A**. *gaiety, pleasure*, Plaut. **B**. Esp., festivitates, *embellishments, ornaments* (of discourse), iis festivitatibus insolentius abutitur, Cic. **II**. Subject., *cheerfulness, humour, pleasantry;* lepos et festivitas, festivitas et facetiae, Cic.

festīvus -a -um (festus). **I**. Gen., 1, *pleasant, agreeable, pretty;* poema, Cic.; copia librorum, Cic.; 2, of places, *bright, pleasant*, Plaut. **II**. Esp., 1, of character, *good-humoured, cheerful;* puer, Cic.; 2, of discourse, or of speakers, *lively, bright, droll, amusing, humorous, witty;* oratio, Cic.; festivus homo, Cic.

festūca -ae, f. (fero). **A**. Lit., *a stalk, straw*, Plin. **B**. Transf., *the rod with which slaves were touched in the ceremony of manumission*, Plaut.

1. festus -a -um (root FE, whence also februus), *sacred, hallowed, devoted to festivals, festive;* dies, Cic.; chori, Ov.; lux (= dies), Ov.; tempus, Hor.; dies festos anniversarios agere, Cic. Subst., **festum** -i, n. *a feast*, Ov.

2. Festus -i, m. Sext. Pompeius, *a Latin grammarian, who lived probably at the end of the fourth century* A.D., *author of a work in twenty books,* "De Verborum Significatione."

fetīālis -is, m. *a fetial*, plur. **fetīāles**, *a college of heralds whose business it was to demand redress of grievances, declare war*, etc., Cic.; in sing., legatus fetialis, Liv. Adj., **fetīālis** -e, *belonging to the fetiales;* jus fetiale, Cic.

fetūra -ae, f. (fetus). **A**. *the bearing or bringing forth of young, breeding*, Cic. **B**. Meton., *the young brood, offspring*, Ov., Verg.

1. fētus (foetus) -a -um (partic. of * feo). **I**. Pass., **A**. Lit., 1, *pregnant;* pecus, Verg.; 2, transf., a, *fruitful, fertile;* terra feta frugibus, Cic. **B**. Poet., *full of;* machina feta armis, Verg. **II**. Middle, *that has brought forth, newly delivered;* ursa, lupa, Ov.

2. fētus -ūs, m. (* feo, whence also fecundus), **I**. *the bearing, bringing forth, or hatching of young;* labor bestiarum in fetu, Cic.; of the soil, *bearing, producing;* quae frugibus atque baccis terrae fetu profunduntur, Cic.; fig., nec ullā aetate uberior oratorum fetus fuit, Cic. **II**. Meton., *that which is brought forth;* a, *offspring, brood;* Germania quos horrida parturit fetus, Hor.; fetus suis (*sucking-pig*), Verg.; b, of plants, *fruit, produce, shoot;* nucis, Verg.; meliores et grandiores fetus edere (of land), Cic.; fig., ex quo triplex ille animi fetus exsistet, Cic.

fīber -bri, m., *a beaver*, Plin.

fībra -ae, f. (findo). 1, *a fibre, filament*, in animals or plants; stirpium, radicum, Cic.; 2, *the entrails of an animal;* bidentis, Ov.

Fībrēnus -i, m., *a river in Latium, near Arpinum, flowing into the Liris, now Fibreno*.

fībrīnus -a -um (fiber), *of or belonging to the beaver*, Plin.

fībŭla -ae, f. (contr. for figibula from figo), *a buckle, brooch, clasp*, Verg., Liv.; *an iron clamp fastening beams together*, Caes.

Ficāna -ae, f., *a town in Latium on the road to Ostia*.

fīcēdŭla -ae, f. (ficus), *a small bird, the becafico*, Plin.

fictē, adv. (fictus), *falsely, fictitiously;* ficte et fallaciter, Cic.

fictĭlis -e (fingo), *earthen, made of clay;* vasa, Cic.; figurae, Cic. Subst., **fictile** -is, n., usually plur., *earthenware, earthen vessels;* omnia (ponuntur) fictilibus, Ov.

fictor -ōris, m. (fingo), 1, *an image-maker, a statuary;* pictores fictoresque, Cic.; 2, *a feigner;* fandi fictor Ulysses, *master in deceit*, Verg.

fictrix -īcis, f. (fictor), *she that forms cr fashions;* materiae fictrix et moderatrix divina est providentia, Cic.

fictūra -ae, f. (fingo), *a forming, fashioning*, Plaut.

fictus, partic. of fingo.

fīcŭla -ae, f. (dim. of ficus), *a little fig*, Plaut.

Fĭcŭlĕa (**Fĭculnĕa**) -ae, f. *town in the country of the Sabines on the* Via Nomentana. Adj., **Fīcŭlensis** -e, *Ficulean*.

fīcŭlnus (**fīculnĕus**) -a -um (ficula), *of or relating to the fig-tree;* truncus, Hor.

fīcus -i and -ūs, f. (perhaps from fio, feo), 1, *the fig-tree;* arbor fici, Cic.; 2, *a fig*, Hor.

fīdē, adv. (fidus), *faithfully*, Cic.

fīdēĭcommissum -i, n. (fides and committo), legal t. t., *a trust*, Quint.

fīdēlē, adv. (fidelis), *faithfully*, Plaut.

fīdēlia -ae, f. *an earthenware pot or vase*, Plaut.; *a pot for whitewash;* prov., duo parietes de eadem fidelia dealbare, *to kill two birds with one stone*, ap. Cic.

fīdēlis -e (1. fides), *that can be trusted or relied upon, true, steadfast, faithful*. **A**. Of persons, socius, amicus, Cic.; alicui or in aliquem, Cic.; in amicitiis, Cic. Subst., **fīdēles** -ium, m. *confidants, faithful friends*, Cic. **B**. Transf., of inanimate objects, consilium fidele, Cic.; lacrimae, *genuine*, Ov.; meton., *durable, lasting, strong;* lorica, Verg.

fīdēlĭtas -ātis, f. (fidelis), *faithfulness, trustworthiness, fidelity*, Cic.; erga patriam, ap. Cic.

fīdēlĭtĕr, adv. with compar. and superl. (fidelis). 1, *faithfully, trustworthily, honestly, surely*, Cic.; per quorum loca fideliter (*free of danger*) mihi pateret iter, Cic.; 2, meton., *properly, well;* ingenuas didicisse fideliter artes, Ov.

Fīdēnae -ārum, f. and **Fīdēna** -ae, f. *a town in Latium, now Castro Giubileo*. Adj., **Fīdēnas** -ātis, *of or belonging to Fidenae*.

fīdens -entis, abl. -enti, p. adj. (from fido), *without fear, confident, courageous;* homo, animus, Cic.; with genit., animi, Verg.; with abl., fidens et animo et viribus, Liv.

fīdentĕr, adv. with compar. (fidens), *confidently, courageously*, Cic.

1. fīdentĭa -ae, f. (fido), *confidence, courage boldness*, Cic.

2. Fīdentĭa -ae, f. *town in Gallia Cispadana*.

1. fīdes -ĕi, f. (fido), *trust, confidence, reliance, credence, belief, faith*. **I**. Lit., **A**. Gen., fidem decipere, Liv., or fallere, Cic.; alicui or alicui rei fidem habere, *to place confidence in*, with acc. and infin., Cic.; alicui rei fidem tribuere, adjungere, Cic.; fidem facere, *to awake confidence*, Cic.; nuntiabantur haec eadem Curioni; sed aliquamdiu fides fieri non poterat, *no reliance was placed in the news*, Caes. **B**. Esp., mercantile t. t., *credit;* quum fides totā Italiā esset angustior, *impaired*, Caes.; fidem moliri, Liv.; fides concidit, *has fallen*, Cic.; fides de foro sublata est, Cic.; fidem renovare, Cic.; often with res, *property*, res et fides, Sall.;

ubi res eos jam pridem, fides nuper deficere coepit, Cic.; homo sine re, sine fide, sine spe, Cic.; transf., segetis certa fides meae, *produce, return*, Hor. **II.** Meton., **A.** *that which produces confidence, faithfulness, fidelity, conscientiousness, honesty, credibility, truthfulness;* 1, gen., exemplum antiquae probitatis ac fidei, Cic.; fidem praestare, *to be loyal*, Cic.; *of faithfulness in treaties and political alliances*, pro vetere ac perpetua erga Romanum fide, Caes.; a, in appeals and oaths, fidem vestram oro atque obsecro, judices, Cic.; pro deum atque hominum fidem, Cic.; **b**, legal t. t., ex bona fide or bonâ fide, *in good faith, sincerely, honestly*, Cic.; judicia de mala fide, *dishonesty*, Cic.; Fides personif. as a goddess, Cic.; 2, esp., a, *a promise, assurance, word of honour, engagement;* fidem fallere, frangere, violare, *to break a promise*, Cic.; dare alicui, Cic.; obligare, *to make an engagement*, Cic.; liberare, servare, *to keep a promise*, Cic.; fidem prodere, Cic.; fide meâ, *on my word of honour*, Cic.; **b**, fides publica or simply publica, *a promise of protection in the name of the state, a safe-conduct;* fidem publicam postulare, Cic.; Lusitani contra interpositam fidem interfecti, Cic.; fide acceptâ venerat in castra Romana, Liv.; **c**, *faithful protection, constant help;* conferre se in alicuius fidem et clientelam, in alicuius amicitiam et fidem, Cic.; se suaque omnia in fidem atque potestatem populi Romani permittere, Cic.; venire in alicuius fidem, Liv., or in alicuius fidem ac potestatem, Caes.; alicuius fidem sequi, Caes.; aliquem in fidem recipere, Cic.; in alicuius fide et clientela esse, Cic. **B.** *credibility, trustworthiness,* of reports, statements, etc.; 1, fidem facit aliquid judicii mei, Cic.; tabularum, Cic.; 2, a, *proof;* manifesta fides publicâ ope Volscos hostes adjutos, Liv.; **b**, *certainty;* verba fides sequitur, Ov.

2. **fĭdes** -is, f., usually plur. **fĭdes** -ium (σφίδη, or perhaps from findo), lit. *a gut-string for a musical instrument;* hence, *a lyre, lute, harp;* discere, Cic.; fidibus Latinis Thebanos aptare modos, Hor.; sing., fides Teïa, Hor.

fĭdĭcen -cĭnis, m. (2. fides and cano), *a player on the harp, lyre, lute*, Cic.; poet., *a lyric poet;* lyrae Romanae, Hor.

fĭdĭcĭna -ae, f. (fidicen), *a female player on the lute* or *harp*, Plaut.

fĭdĭcĭnus -a -um (fidicen), *relating or belonging to harp-playing*, Plaut.

fĭdĭcŭla -ae, f. and gen. plur. **fĭdĭcŭlae** -ârum, f. (dim. of 2. fides), 1, *a little lyre or lute*, Cic.; 2, *an instrument for torturing slaves*, Suet.

Fĭdīus -ĭi, m. (connected with fides, fido), in full Dius Fidius, *a Roman deity, personification of faith;* me Dius Fidius and medius fidius (ellipt. = ita me Dius Fidius juvet), *So help me God!* Cic.

fīdo, fīsus sum, 3. (root FID, Gr. ΠΙΘ, πείθ-ω, πείθ-ομαι), *to trust, believe, confide in;* with dat. or abl., sibi, Cic.; nocti, Verg.; prudentiâ, Cic.; with acc. and infin., Liv.

fĭdūcĭa -ae, f. (fido). **I.** Lit., a, *confidence, trust, reliance, assurance;* alicuius, *in some one*, Cic.; sui, *in oneself*, Liv.; arcae nostrae, Cic.; **b**, *self-confidence, self-reliance, courage, bravery*, Caes. **II.** Legal t. t., *a contract by which a man temporarily transfers property to another, a pledging, pawning, mortgaging*, etc.; formula fiduciae, Cic.; fiducia accepta, Cic.

fĭdūcĭārĭus -a -um (fiducia), *entrusted, committed, given in trust;* urbs, Liv.; opera, Caes.

fĭdus -a -um (fido), *true, faithful, trusty, certain, sure;* 1, *of persons*, amici fidi, Cic.; with dat., Abelux fidus ante Poenis, Liv.; with genit., regina tui fidissima, Verg.; 2, *of inanimate*

objects, tam fida canum custodia, Cic.; static male fida carinis, *an insecure anchorage for ships*, Verg.

figlīnus (**fĭgŭlīnus**) -a -um (figulus), *of* or *belonging to a potter*, Plin. Subst., 1, **figlīna** -ae, f. a, *a potter's art* or *craft*, Plin.; **b**, *a potter's workshop, pottery*, Plin.; 2, **figlīnum** -i, n. *earthenware*, Plin.

fīgo, fixi, fixum, 3. **I.** *to fix, fasten, make fast, make firm, attach, affix.* **A.** Lit., a, aliquem in cruce, Cic.; caput legis in poste curiae, Cic.; arma ad postem, Cic.; **b**, *to build;* moenia, Ov.; **c**, oscula, *to imprint*, Verg. **B.** Transf., a, nequitiae modum suae, *to set a limit*, Hor.; **b**, vestigia, *to check one's steps*, Verg.; **c**, *to fix, make fast;* fixum et statutum est, Cic. **II. A.** Lit., a, *to thrust in, drive in;* mucronem in hoste, Cic.; **b**, *to transfix;* aliquem sagittâ, Tac. **B.** Transf., a, aliquem maledictis, *attack with reproaches*, Cic.; **b**, *to fix;* oculos in terram, Liv.; **c**, *to fix in one's attention;* illud fixum in animis vestris tenetote, Cic.

fĭgŭlāris -e (figulus), *relating or belonging to a potter*, Plaut.

fĭgŭlīnus = figlinus (q.v.).

fĭgŭlus -i, m. (root FIG, whence fingo), *a worker in clay, a potter;* a figulis munitam urbem, *Babylon, made of brick*, Juv.

fĭgūra -ae, f. (fingo). **I.** *form, shape, figure;* a, hominis, Cic.; **b**, *an atom*, Lucr.; **c**, *shade of a dead person*, Verg. **II.** a, *kind, nature, species, form;* negotii, Cic.; **b**, in rhet., *a figure of speech*, Cic.

fĭgūrātus -a -um, partic. of figuro.

fĭgūro, 1. (figura), *to form, mould, shape;* 1, ita figuratum corpus ut excellat aliis, Cic.; 2, transf., os tenerum pueri balbumque poeta figurat, Hor.

fĭlātim, adv. (filum), *thread by thread*, Lucr.

fīlĭa -ae, f. (filius), *a daughter*, Cic.; virgo filia, Cic.; poet. transf., pinus silvae filia nobilis, Hor.

fĭlĭcātus -a -um (filix), *adorned with ferns;* paterae, *embossed* or *chased with fern leaves*, Cic.

fīlĭŏla -ae, f. (dim. of filia), *a little daughter*, Cic.; sarcastically of an effeminate man, duce filiolâ Curionis, Cic.

fīlĭŏlus -i, m. (dim. of filius), *a little son*, Cic.

fīlĭus -ĭi, (voc. sing. fili), m. (feo, whence fecundus, etc.), *son*, Cic.; terrae, *a man of mean origin, unknown person*, Cic.; fortunae, *a child of fortune*, Hor.

fīlix -icis, f. *fern*, Verg.

fīlum -i, n. (figo), *a thread.* **I.** Lit., a, *of wool, linen*, etc., velamina filo pleno, Ov.; prov., pendere filo (tenui), *to hang by a thread, be in great danger*, Ov.; b, *a woollen fillet round the cap of the flamen;* capite velato filo, Liv.; **c**, *of other things*, deducit aranea filum pede, Ov.; d, *the thread of life* spun by the Parcae; sororum fila trium, Hor. **II.** Transf., a, *the form, shape of anything*, Lucr.; **b**, *the manner, form, thread of discourse*, Cic.

fimbrĭae -ârum, f. plur., *fringe, border, edge;* madentes cincinnorum fimbriae, *extremities*, Cic.

Fimbrĭa -ae, m. (G. Flavius), *friend of Marius, general in the Mithridatic war.*

fīmus -i, m. and **fīmum** -i, n. *dung, excrement, dirt*, Liv., Verg.

findo, fidi, fissum, 3. *to split, cleave, separate, divide;* lignum, Verg.; findere agros sarculo, Hor.; hâc insulâ quasi rostro finditur Fibrenus, Cic.

fingo, finxi, fictum, 3. (root FIG, whence figulus). **I.** *to stroke;* manus aegras manibus amici, Ov. **II. A.** *to fashion, form, mould;* **1**, lit., **a,** mollissimam ceram ad nostrum arbitrium formare et fingere, Cic.; **b,** imago ficta, *a statue,* Cic.; natura fingit hominem, Cic.; **2,** transf., **a,** *to imagine, conceive;* fingite igitur cogitatione imaginem huius conditionis meae, Cic.; with acc. and infin., finge aliquem fieri sapientem, Cic.; **b,** *to invent, fabricate, devise;* crimina, opprobria in aliquem, Cic.; partic., fictus, *invented, feigned;* ficta fabula, Cic.; hence subst., **fictum** -i, n. *something invented, a lie;* ficta loqui, Ov.; **c,** *to feign;* nihil fingam, nihil dissimulem, Cic. **B.** *to arrange, order;* **1,** lit., **a,** crinem fronde premit fingens, Verg.; **b,** fingere vultum, *to put on a friendly look,* Ov., or *to put on a brave look,* Caes.; ficto pectore fatus, Verg.; **2,** transf., *to form;* oratorem, Cic.; se totum ad arbitrium alicuius, Cic.

fīnĭens -entis (partic. of finio), sc. orbis or circulus, *the horizon,* Cic.

fīnĭo, 4. (finis). **I.** Transit., *to bound, limit, enclose within limits.* **A.** Lit., imperium populi Romani, Caes.; lingua finita dentibus, Cic. **B.** Transf., **1,** *to enclose within bounds, restrain;* an potest cupiditas finiri? Cic.; **2,** *to define, determine, prescribe, appoint;* sepulcris novis modum, Cic.; with ne and the subj., potuisse finire senatus consulto ne, etc., Liv.; **3, a,** gen., *to put an end to, conclude, end, finish;* bellum, Caes.; labores, Cic.; and pass., *to end, cease;* **b,** (a) finiri (middle), *to die,* Cic. poet.; finitā Claudiorum domo, *having become extinct,* Tac.; (β) *to finish speaking;* omnia finierat, Ov.; (γ) *to bring a period to a close;* ut sententiae verbis finiantur, Cic. **II.** Intransit., **a,** *to die;* sic Tiberius finivit, Tac.; **b,** *to finish speaking;* finierat Telamone satus, Ov.; *to bring a period to a close;* illi philosopho placet ordiri a superiore paeone, posteriore finire, Cic.

fīnis -is, m. and f. (findo). **I.** *the boundary, limit, border.* **A.** Lit., eius loci, Cic.; provinciae Galliae, Liv.; plur., *territory;* iter in Santonum fines facere, Caes. **B.** Transf., **a,** *boundary, limit;* mihi fines terminosque constituam, extra quos egredi non possum, Cic.; **b,** *term, limit;* ad eum finem, *so far,* Cic.; fine (fini), with genit., *as far as,* fine genûs, Ov. **II.** *the end;* **a,** finis vitae, Cic.; ad finem venire, Liv.; finem facere, with genit. bellandi, Caes.; sollicitudinis, Cic.; finem facere, with dat. pretio, Cic.; finem capere, *come to an end,* Cic.; **b,** esp., (a) *death;* Neronis, Tac.; (β) *the highest, the extremity;* bonorum, malorum, *greatest good, greatest evil,* Cic.; **c,** *object, end, aim;* domus finis et usus, Cic. (abl. sing. fine and finī).

fīnītē, adv. (finitus, from finio), *moderately, within bounds,* Cic.

fīnītĭmus (fīnĭtŭmus) -a -um (finis), *neighbouring, adjacent.* **A.** Lit., Galli Belgis, Caes.; aër mari finituma, Cic. Subst., **fīnītĭmi** -ōrum, m. *neighbours, neighbouring states,* Cic. **B.** Transf., *related to, resembling, similar;* vicina eius atque finitima dialecticorum scientia, Cic.; with dat., huic generi historia finitima est, Cic.

fīnītor -ōris, m. (finio), *one who determines boundaries, a land surveyor,* Cic.

fīnītŭmus = finitimus (q.v.).

fīnītus -a -um, partic. of finio.

fĭo, factus sum, fieri (connected with φύω), pass. of facio. **I.** Lit., *to be made;* hic ubi fit doctā multa corona manu, Ov. **II.** Transf. **A.** Gen., **a,** *to be done, to arise;* fit clamor, Cic.; id ei loco nomen factum, Liv.; per aliquem fit quominus, etc., Cic.; **b,** *to happen;* (a) Pompeio melius est factum, Cic.; esp. with abl., quid illo fiet, *what will happen with him?* Cic.; with **de,** quid de Tulliola mea fiet? Cic.; ut fit, ut

fieri solet, *as usual, as is often the case;* ut fit plerumque, Cic.; fit saepe ut non respondeant ad tempus, Cic.; potest fieri ut fallar, *I may be deceived,* Cic.; fieri non potest quin, etc., Cic.; ita fit ut, etc., Cic.; (β) *to follow;* ita fit ut sapientia sanitas sit animi, Cic.; (γ) *to be;* nec potest fieri me quidquam superbius, Cic. **B.** Esp., **a,** *to become something;* consules facti sunt, Cic.; **b,** *to be esteemed;* me a te plurimi fieri, Cic.; **c,** *to be sacrificed;* quum pro populo fieret, Cic.

firmāmen -ĭnis, n. (firmo), *support, prop,* Ov.

firmāmentum -i, n. (firmo), *a means of support, a prop;* **1,** lit., transversaria tigna quae firmamento esse possint, Cic., Caes.; **2,** transf., **a,** reipublicae, Cic.; **b,** in rhet., *the main point of an argument,* Cic.

firmātor -ōris, m. (firmo), *one who makes firm or establishes,* Tac.

firmē, adv. (firmus), *firmly, steadfastly;* aliquid comprehendere, Cic.; firmissime asseverare, Cic.

firmĭtas -ātis, f. (firmus), *firmness, durability.* **A.** Lit., corporis, Cic. **B.** *firmness, strength of mind, constancy;* animi, Cic.

firmĭtĕr, adv. (firmus), *firmly, strongly;* firmiter insistere, Caes.; firmiter stabilire aliquem, Cic.

firmĭtūdo -dĭnis, f.(firmus), *firmness, strength.* **A.** Lit., operis, Caes. **B.** Transf., *strength, firmness, constancy;* animi, Cic.

firmo, 1. (firmus), *to make firm, strengthen.* **I.** Lit., urbem colonis, Cic.; castra munimentis, Liv. **II.** Transf., **a,** *to make durable, to make secure;* (a) vestigia pinu, *steady his steps by,* Verg.; (β) politically, rempublicam, Cic.; **b,** *to make strong, to strengthen;* (a) physically, vires, Verg.; vocem, Cic.; (β) morally, animum adolescentis nondum consilio et ratione firmatum, Cic.; (γ) *to encourage, cheer, animate;* nostros, Caes.; aliquem alloquio, Tac.; **c,** *to prove, establish;* aliquid rationibus or jurejurando, Cic.

Firmum -i, n. *a town in Picenum,* now *Fermo.* Adj., **Firmānus** -a -um, *of or belonging to Firmum.*

firmus -a -um, *firm, strong, stout.* **I.** Lit., ramus, Cic.; with dat., area firma templis ac porticibus sustinendis, Cic. **II.** Transf., **1,** *physically strong, powerful, healthy;* **a,** corpus, Cic.; **b,** milit., *strong;* equitatus et peditatus, Cic.; ad dimicandum, Caes.; **2,** of time, *durable, lasting;* firmissima vina, *which keep,* Verg.; transf., *lasting, valid;* acta Caesaris, Cic.; **3,** *morally and mentally strong;* **a,** *steadfast, firm, immovable;* animus, Cic.; accusator, Cic.; contra pericula, Sall.; firmior in sententia, Cic.; **b,** *sure, firm, to be relied upon;* litterae, Cic.; spes, Cic.; with abl., copiae et numero et genere et fidelitate firmissimae, Cic.; with ad and the acc., firmos (eos) milites ad tuendas nostras res efficere, Cic.

fiscella -ae, f. (dim. of fiscina), *a small rush or wicker basket,* Verg.

fiscĭna -ae, f. (fiscus), *a small basket of wickerwork,* Cic.

fiscus -i, m. *a wicker basket;* **1,** *a money-basket, money-bag, purse,* Cic.; meton. = *money,* Juv.; **2,** *the state treasury,* Cic.; **3,** under the empire, *the emperor's private purse* (opp. aerarium, *the state treasury*), Tac.

fissĭlis -e (findo), *that can be cloven or split;* lignum, Verg.

fissĭo -ōnis, f. (findo), *a splitting, cleaving, dividing;* glebarum, Cic.

fissum -i, n. (findo), *a split, cleft;* in augury, *a divided liver,* Cic.

8

fistūca or **festūca** -ae, f. *a rammer, mallet,* Caes.

fistŭla -ae, f. **I.** Lit., *a tube, pipe;* esp. *a water-pipe,* usually of lead; fistulas, quibus aqua suppeditabatur Jovis templis, praecidere, Cic. **II.** Transf., 1, *a reed-pipe, a shepherd's pipe, a reed;* eburneola, *a pitch-pipe of ivory,* Cic.; 2, *a kind of ulcer, fistula,* Nep.

fistŭlātor -ōris, m. (fistula), *one who plays upon the reed-pipe, one who gives a note with the pitch-pipe,* Cic.

fixus -a -um, p. adj. (from figo), *firm, fixed, immovable;* vestigia, Cic.; fixum est, *it is fixed determined,* Cic.; decretum, Cic.

flābellum -i, n. (dim. of flabrum), *a small fan,* Prop.; fig., cuius linguā quasi flabello seditionis illa tum est egentium contio ventilata, Cic.

flābĭlis -e (flo), *airy,* Cic.

flābrum -i, n. (flo), gen. in plur. **flābra** -ōrum, *blasts of wind, breezes,* Verg.

flaccĕo, 2. (flaccus), *to be faint, weak, languid;* transf., *to fail* or *flag in an undertaking;* Messala flaccet, Cic.

flaccesco, 3. (inch. from flacceo), *to begin to fade, to become faint, weak, languid;* flaccescebat oratio, Cic.

flaccĭdus -a -um (flaccus), *withered, flabby, flaccid, weak, languid,* Lucr.

1. **flaccus** -a -um, 1, *flabby, flaccid,* Varr.; 2, of men, *flap-eared,* Cic.

2. **Flaccus,** Q. Horatius, v. Horatius.

3. **Flaccus,** C. Valerius, v. Valerius.

flăgello, 1. (flagellum), *to whip, scourge, beat;* robora parte caudae, Ov.

flăgellum -i, n. (dim. of flagrum), *a whip, scourge.* **I.** Lit., a, Cic., Hor.; fig., *the scourge of conscience,* Juv., Lucr.; b, *a riding-whip,* Verg. **II.** Transf., **A.** *the thong of a javelin,* Verg. **B.** *a young sprout, vine-shoot,* Verg. **C.** Plur., flagella, *the arms of a polypus,* Ov.

flăgĭtātio -ōnis, f. (flagito), *an earnest demand* or *entreaty,* Cic.

flăgĭtātor -ōris, m. (flagito), *one who earnestly demands* or *entreats,* Cic.; *with* genit., pugnae, Liv.

flăgĭtiōse, adv. (flagitiosus), *shamefully, basely, disgracefully, infamously;* impure ac flagitiose vivere, Cic.; sumus flagitiose imparati, Cic.; alicuius amori flagitiosissime servire, Cic.

flăgĭtiōsus -a -um (flagitium), *shameful, disgraceful, infamous;* flagitiosa atque vitiosa vita, Cic.; flagitiosum est, with acc. and infin., Sall.; flagitiosum duco, with infin., Liv.

flăgĭtium -ii, n. (root FLAG, whence flagito), **I.** *a disgraceful action, shameful crime, shame, disgrace, infamy;* factum flagitii plenum et dedecoris, Cic.; ista flagitia Democriti, *shameful expressions,* Cic. **II.** Meton., *scoundrel, rascal;* flagitia atque facinora, Cic.

flăgĭto, 1. (root FLAG, whence also flag-ro) = flagranter posco, *to entreat, ask, demand earnestly.* **I.** Gen., a, of persons, alicuius auxilium, Cic.; mercedem gloriae ab aliquo, Cic.; with double acc., aliquem frumentum, Cic.; with ut and the subj., semper flagitavi ut convocaremur, Cic.; with infin., Hor.; absol., flagitat tabellarius, Cic.; b, of abstract subjects, quae tempus flagitat, Cic. **II.** Esp., a, *to demand to know;* posco atque adeo flagito crimen, Cic.; b, *to demand;* filium ab aliquo, Cic.; c, *to summon before a court of justice;* aliquem peculatorem, Tac.

flăgrans -antis, p. adj. (from flagro), *burning.* **I.** Gen., **A.** Lit., telum, *lightning,* Verg.; flagrantissimus aestus, Liv. **B.** Transf., *glowing*

with passion, eager, vehement, ardent; cupiditas, Cic.; multitudo, Cic. **II.** Esp., a, of the eyes, *glowing;* oculi, Ov.; ὁ, *of colour, glittering;* flagrans sidereo clipeo, Verg.

flăgrantěr, adv. (flagrans), *eagerly, ardently, vehemently;* cupere, Tac.

flăgrantĭa -ae, f. (flagro), *glowing;* oculorum, Cic.

flăgro, 1. (root FLAG, Gk. ΦΛΕΓ-ω, connected with FLA-re), *to blaze, burn, glow, flame.* **I.** Lit., 1, *to burn;* onerariae flagrantes, Cic.; 2, *to glow, glitter;* flagrant lumina nymphae, Ov. **II.** Transf., 1, of concrete subjects, esp. of persons, a, Italia flagrans bello, Cic.; invidiā propter interitum C. Gracchi, Cic.; b, *to glow* or *burn with passion, to be eager, vehement;* desiderio, amore, cupiditate, odio, studio dicendi, Cic.; 2, of abstract subj., flagrabant vitia libidinis apud illum, Cic.

flăgrum -i, n. (root FLAG, Gr. ΠΛΗΓ or ΠΛΗΚ, πλήσσω), *a scourge, whip,* used for punishing slaves; flagro caedi, Liv.

1. **flāmen** -ĭnis, m. *the priest of some particular deity;* there were three flamines majores, Dialis, *of Jupiter* (the highest in rank), Martialis, *of Mars,* and Quirinalis, *of Romulus,* and twelve flamines minores (Vulcani, Florae, etc.); flaminem inaugurare, Liv.

2. **flāmen** -ĭnis, n. (flo). **I.** *a blowing, blast;* flamina venti, Lucr. **II.** Meton., **A.** *the wind;* ferunt sua flamina classem, Verg. **B.** (like πνεύματα αὐλῶν) flamina tibiae, *the notes of a flute,* Hor.

flāmĭnĭca -ae, f. (sc. uxor), *the wife of a flamen;* flaminica Dialis, Tac.

Flāmĭnīnus, *a surname of the patrician Gens Quinctia;* v. Quinctius.

flāmĭnium -i, n. (flamen, sc. sacerdotium or munus), *the office* or *dignity of a flamen,* Cic.

Flāmĭnius -a -um, *name of a Roman gens, the most celebrated member of which was C. Flaminius, who, when censor, built a circus and made one of the chief military roads in Italy, and who, when consul, was defeated by Hannibal at the battle of Lacus Trasimenus.* Adj., *Flaminian.* Hence, **Flāmĭniānus** -a -um, *of* or *belonging to Flaminius.*

flamma -ae, f. (for flag-ma, from root FLAG, whence flag-ro), *a flame, blaze, blazing fire.* **I.** Lit., **A.** Gen., effusa flamma pluribus loris reluxit, Liv.; se flammā eripere, Cic.; flammam concipere, *to catch fire,* Caes.; prov., prius undis flamma (sc. misceatur), *sooner will fire mingle with water,* of something impossible, ap. Cic. **B.** Meton., a, *a flaming star, lightning,* Verg.; b, *glitter;* galea flammas vomens, Verg. **II.** Transf., **A.** Gen., belli, invidiae, Cic. **B.** Esp., *the fire* or *glow of passion,* esp. of love; amoris, Cic.; gulae, *raging hunger,* Cic.; ultrix flamma, *burning revenge,* Cic.

flammĕŏlum -i, n. (dim. of flammeum), *a small bridal veil,* Juv.

flammesco, 3. (flamma), *to become inflamed,* Lucr.

flammĕus -a -um (flamma), *fiery, flame-like, flaming.* **I.** Adj., **A.** Lit., stella, Cic. **B.** Transf., *flame-coloured, fiery-red;* corpora, Lucr.; vestigia, *in hot haste,* Cat. **II.** Subst., **flammĕum** -i, n. *a flame-coloured bridal veil;* flammeum capere, Cat.

flammĭfer -fĕra -fĕrum (flamma and fero), *flame-bearing, flaming, fiery,* Ov.

flammo, 1. (flamma). **I.** Intransit., *to flame, blaze, burn;* flammantia lumina, *glittering,* Verg. **II.** Transit., *to set on fire, inflame.* **A.** Lit., ut interirent crucibus affixi aut flammandi,

Tac. **B.** Transf., flammato **corde,** *with angry passion,* Verg.

flammŭla -ae, f. (dim. of flamma), *a little flame,* Cic.

flātus -ūs, m. (flo), *a blowing, blast.* **I.** Gen., Alpini boreae, Verg.; fig., prospero flatu fortunae uti, Cic. **II.** *breathing.* **A.** Lit., 1, flatus, *the breath,* Verg.; **2,** a, *snorting;* equorum, Verg.; b, *blowing on a flute,* Hor. **B.** Transf., *haughtiness, arrogance,* gen. in plur., Verg.

flāvĕo, 2. (flavus), *to be yellow* or *gold-coloured;* partic., flavens, *yellow, golden;* coma, Verg.; arena, Verg.

flāvesco, 3. (flaveo), *to become yellow* or *gold-coloured;* campus flavescet aristā, Verg.

Flāvīna -ae, f. *a town in Etruria.* Adj., **Flāvīnīus** -a -um, *of* or *belonging to Flavina.*

Flāvĭus -a -um, *name of a Roman gens, to which the Emperors Vespasian, Titus, and Domitian belonged;* hence Flavius = Domitian, Juv.; Cn. Flavius, *a freedman of Appius Claudius Caecus, who first published the formulae used in law-suits.* Hence 1, **Flāvĭālis** -is, m. (with or without flamen), *the flamen of the gens Flavia;* 2, adj., **Flāvĭānus** -a -um, *Flavian.*

flāvus -a -um (root FLA, whence fla-gro), *golden-yellow, gold-coloured, yellow;* arva, Verg.; crines, Verg., aurum, Verg.; decem flavi, *ten gold pieces,* Mart.

flēbĭlis -e (fleo) **I.** Pass., *lamentable, wretched, deserving tears;* illa species, Cic. **II.** Act., *causing lamentation* or *tears, tearful, doleful;* a, of things, gemitus, Cic.; b, of persons, *weeping;* Ino, Hor.

flēbĭlĭtĕr, adv. (flebilis), *tearfully, dolefully,* Cic.

flecto, flexi, flexum, 3. **I.** Transit., *to bend, bow, twist, curve.* **A.** 1, lit., membra, Cic.; iter suum or viam, *to diverge from one's march* or *journey,* Liv.; **2,** transf., a, *to modulate* (the voice), vocem, Cic.; flexus sonus, *a melancholy tone,* Cic.; b, *to change, alter;* vitam, Cic.; fata deum, Verg.; *to move, to make a person change his opinion;* animum or aliquem, Cic.; flecti misericordiā, Liv.; nihil flexerunt animos quin collem defenderent, Liv. **B.** *to bend, turn, direct;* 1, lit., equos, Caes.; currum de foro in Capitolium, Cic.; acies (= oculos) huc, Verg.; middle, flecti in gyrum, *to turn round in a circle,* Ov.; transf., of places, flectere se or middle flecti, *to turn towards;* hinc (silva) se flectit sinistrorsus, Caes.; **2,** transf., *to turn from, dissuade from;* aliquem a proposito, Liv.; a studio ad imperium, Cic. **C.** *to double, sail round;* Leucatam, Cic. **II.** Intransit., **A.** *to turn, go;* ad Oceanum, Liv. **B.** Transf., ad sapientiam, Tac.

flĕo, flēvi, flētum, 2. **I.** Intransit., a, *to weep;* de filii morte, Cic.; lapides flere et lamentari cogere, Cic.; b, of fluids, *to trickle down,* Lucr. **II.** Transit., *to weep for, lament, bewail.* **A.** Lit., juvenem, Ov.; filii necem, Tac.; with acc. and infin., Verg.; flendus, *worthy of being lamented,* Ov.; fletus, *wept for, lamented,* Verg. **B.** Transf., cavā testudine amorem, *sing mournfully of,* Hor. (Syncop. perf. forms flesti, Ov.; flerunt, Verg.; flesse, Liv.).

1. **flētus** -a -um (partic. of fleo).

2. **flētus** -ūs, m. (fleo), *a weeping, bewailing;* prae fletu, Cic.; clamore et fletu omnia complere, Cic.; urbe totā fletus gemitusque fieret, Cic.

flexănĭmus -a -um (flecto and animus), 1, *moving, affecting;* oratio, Cic.; 2, *affected, touched, moved;* ap. Cic.

flexĭbĭlis -e (flecto), *that can be bent, flexible.* **A.** Lit., materia rerum, Cic. **B.** Transf., a, of

the voice, vocis genus, Cic.; b, of speech, nihil est tam flexibile quam oratio, Cic.; c, of persons, *pliant, tractable,* or in a bad sense, *changeable;* aetas, Cic.; quid potest esse tam flexibile, Cic.

flexĭlis -e (flecto), *flexible, pliant, supple;* cornu, Ov.

flexĭlŏquus -a -um (flexus and loquor), *having two meanings, equivocal, ambiguous,* Cic.

flexĭo -ōnis, f. (flecto), *bending,* **I.** Gen., virili laterum flexione, Cic.; transf., vocis or modorum, *modulation of the voice,* Cic. **II.** Esp., *turning, winding;* deverticula flexionesque, Cic.

flexĭpes -pĕdis (flexus and pes), *crooked-footed;* hederae, *twining,* Ov.

flexŭōsus -a -um (flexus), *full of windings and turnings, crooked;* iter (of the ear), Cic.

flexūra -ae, f. (flecto), *a bending,* Lucr.

1. **flexus** -a -um, partic. of flecto.

2. **flexus** -ūs, m. (flecto), *a bending.* **I.** Middle, *bending oneself, turning, winding.* **A.** Gen., 1, lit., a, cervicis, Ov.; b, *a turning of a road, by-path;* in quo flexus est ad iter Arpinas, Cic.; 2, *variation, modification, change;* rerum publicarum, Cic. **B.** In the circus, *the turning round of the chariots towards the goal;* fig., in hoc flexu quasi aetatis, Cic. **II.** Pass., *being turned, turning, winding;* duros introitus habent (aures) multis cum flexibus, Cic.; flexus vallium, Liv.

flictus -ūs, m. (fligo), *a striking together, dashing against;* cavae dant sonitum flictu galeae, Verg.

flīgo, 3. *to beat* or *dash down,* Lucr.

flo, flāvi, flātum, 1. **I.** Intransit., of winds, *to blow;* qui ventus in his locis flare consuevit, Cic.; ita belle nobis ab Epiro flavit Onchesmites, Cic.; of persons, scintillam levem flando accenderunt, Liv.; of the flute, protinus inflexo Berecyntia tibia cornu flabit, Ov. **II.** Transit., **A.** a, *to blow forth from the mouth;* flammam, Lucr.; b, *to blow an instrument;* furiosa tibia flatur, Ov. **B.** *to cast metals, to make into coin, to coin;* flare pecuniam, Cic.

floccus -i, m., *a lock of wool,* Varr.; non flocci facere, *to think nothing of,* Cic.

Flōra -ae, f. (flos), *the goddess of flowers.* Adj., **Flōrālis** -e, *belonging to Flora;* subst., **Flōrālĭa** -ium *and* -īorum, n. *the festival of Flora on the 27th of April;* **Flōrālĭcĭus** -a -um, *relating to the festival of Flora.*

flōrens -entis, p. adj. (from floreo), *blooming;* 1, *fresh, fine, vigorous;* a, of orators, etc., florens orationis genus, Cic.; b, of age, aetas, Cic.; 2, *glittering, splendid, prosperous, flourishing;* (α) florens fortuna, Caes.; res publica florentissima, Cic.; (β) with abl., *distinguished for;* gratiā atque hospitiis florens hominum nobilissimorum, Cic.

Flōrentĭa -ae, f. *a town in Etruria,* now Florence. Adj., **Flōrentīnus** -a -um, *Florentine.*

flōrĕo -ŭi, 2. (flos). **I.** *to bloom, flower.* **A.** Lit., haec arbor ter floret, Cic. **B.** Fig., a, of things, verborum vetus interit aetas, et juvenum ritu florent modo nata virentque, Cic.; b, of persons, *to be in one's prime, to prosper, be flourishing, be in high repute;* floret Epicurus, Cic.; with abl., gratiā et auctoritate, Cic.; honoribus, Cic. **II.** Transf., **A.** Poet., *to be full of;* tibi pampineo gravidus auctumno floret ager, Verg. **B.** *to glitter;* florentes aere catervae, Verg. **C.** Of wine, *to froth,* Ov.

flōresco, 3. (inchoat. of floreo), *to begin to blossom, come into flower.* **A.** Lit., Cic. **B.** Transf., *to begin to flourish;* Sulpicius ad summam gloriam florescens, Cic.

flōrĕus -a -um (flos), 1, *made of flowers;* serta, Tib.; 2, *rich in flowers, flowery;* rura, Verg.

flōrĭdŭlus -a -um (dim. of floridus), *somewhat blooming,* Cat.

flōrĭdus -a -um (flos), *flowery.* **I.** Lit., a, *blossoming;* ramuli, Cat.; b, *made of flowers;* serta, Ov.; plur. subst., florida et varia, Cic.; c, *rich in flowers;* Hybla, Ov. **II.** Transf., a, of age, *flourishing;* aetas, Cat.; b, of expressions, *flowery, florid;* Demetrius est floridior, Cic.

flōrĭfer -fĕra -fĕrum (flos and fero), *flower-bearing,* Lucr.

flōrĭlĕgus a -um (flos and lego), *culling flowers;* apes, Ov.

Flōrus -i, m. *a Roman historian of the time of Trajan and Hadrian, who composed an epitome of Roman history from the foundation of the city to the age of Augustus.*

flos, flōris (connected with φλόος), *a flower, blossom.* **I. A.** Lit., florum omnium varietas, Cic. **B.** Meton., *flores, the juice of flowers,* Verg. **II.** Transf., **A.** *the prime, flower;* 1, gen., Graeciae, Cic.; virium, Liv.; 2, esp., flos aetatis, *the flower of youth,* Cic.; so flos juventae, Liv. **B.** *the flower = the best, the finest, the pride;* 1, gen., flos totius Italiae ac robur, Cic.; florem et colorem defuisse, *grace of expression,* Cic.; Bacchi, *strength,* Lucr.; 2, esp., flos juvenilis, *the first beard, down,* so simply flos, Verg.; flammae, *glitter,* Lucr.

floscŭlus -i, m. (dim. of flos), *a little flower.* **I.** Lit., ficta onmia tamquam flosculi decidunt, Cic.; omni ex genere orationis flosculos carpam, Cic. **II.** *pride;* o qui flosculus es Juventiorum, Cat.

fluctĭfrăgus -a -um (fluctus and frango), *wave-breaking,* Lucr.

fluctŭātĭo -ōnis, f. (fluctuo), *a moving backwards and forwards, fluctuation;* transf., *indecision;* animorum, Liv.

fluctŭo, 1. (fluctus). **I.** *to be in wave-like motion, move up and down.* **A.** Lit., mare, Plaut. **B.** 1, *to heave, undulate;* fluctuat tellus aere renidenti, *shimmers,* Verg.; 2, *to rage;* ira fluctuat, Verg. **II.** *to move up and down in the sea, to be tossed about.* **A.** Lit., of men and ships, Cic. **B.** Transf., 1, *to waver;* acies fluctuans, Liv.; of speech, oratio quasi fluctuans, Cic.; 2, *to waver in resolve, to vacillate;* in suo decreto, Cic.

fluctŭor -ātus sum, 1. dep., *to waver, vacillate;* fluctuatus animo est, utrum . . . an, Liv.

fluctŭōsus -a -um (fluctus), *full of waves, stormy;* mare, Plaut.

fluctus -ūs, m. (fluo). **I.** *a streaming, flowing,* Lucr. **II.** *a wave, wave of the sea, billow;* a, sing., fluctu operiri, Cic.; b, plur., fluctus sedare, Cic.; prov., excitare fluctus in simpulo, *to make much ado about nothing,* Cic.; fig., commotion, disturbance;* fluctus contionum, Cic.; viarum, Verg.

flŭens -entis -p. adj. (fluo). **I. A.** *flowing, easy, fluent;* tracta quaedam et fluens oratio, Cic. **B.** *unrestrained, diffuse;* ut ne aut dissoluta aut fluens sit oratio, Cic. **II.** *hanging down, flabby;* baccae fluentes, Cic.

flŭentĕr, adv. (fluo), *in a flowing manner,* Lucr.

flŭentĭsŏnus -a -um (fluentum and sono), *resounding with waves,* Cat.

flŭentum -i, n. (fluo), *running water, a stream;* rauca Cocyti, Verg.

flŭĭdus -a -um (fluo), *flowing, fluid.* **A.** Lit., cruor, Verg. **B.** Transf., a, *lax, languid, flaccid;* frondes, Lucr.; pendere lacertos, Ov.; b, *dissolving;* calor, Ov.

flŭĭto, 1. (intens. of fluo), *to flow hither and thither.* **A.** Lit., a, of streams, waves, etc., fusile per rictus aurum fluitare videres, Ov.; b, of ships, etc., *to float, move up and down, be tossed about on the water;* navem fluitantem in alto tempestatibus, Cic. **B.** Transf., a, *to waver;* fluitans testudo, Tac.; b, *to flutter, flap about;* fluitantia vela, Ov.; c, *to be uncertain, to vacillate, to be doubtful;* mobilia et caecā fluitantia sorte, Hor.

flūmen -īnis, n. (fluo), *flowing water, a stream.* **I.** Lit., **A.** Gen., flumine vivo, *running water,* Verg.; flumine secundo, *downstream,* Caes. **B.** Esp., *a river, a stream,* Cic.; Garumna flumen, Caes. **II.** Transf., 1, *a stream of anything;* of blood, Cic.; of tears, Verg.; 2, of the mind, a, *outpouring, flow;* nullius tantum flumen est ingenii, Cic.; b, of oratory, etc., *flood, flow, stream;* flumen orationis aureum, Cic.

Flūmentāna porta (flumen), *the river-gate, a gate in Rome near the Campus Martius.*

flūmĭnĕus -a -um (flumen), *of or relating to a river,* Ov.

flŭo, fluxi, fluxum, 3. *to flow.* **I.** Gen., **A.** Lit., of fluids and fluid bodies, 1, ut flumina in contrarias partes fluxerint, Cic.; fluit de corpore sudor, Ov.; 2, *to flow, drip with any liquid;* cruore, Ov.; sudore, Ov. **B.** Transf., 1, *to flow;* a, of air, wind, etc., venti fluunt, Lucr.; b, of clothes, *to flow down;* fluens vestis, Ov.; c, of the neck, *to sink;* ad terram fluit cervix, Verg.; d, of branches, *to spread;* ramos compesce fluentes, Verg.; 2, *to stream forth;* multa a luna manant et fluunt, Cic.; of a crowd, turba fluit castris, Verg. **C.** Fig., 1, *to be spread abroad;* Pythagorae doctrina quum longe lateque flueret, Cic.; 2, *to be derived from;* haec omnia ex eodem fonte fluxerunt, Cic.; 3, *to flow down;* a, *to proceed without interruption;* in rebus prosperis et ad voluntatem fluentibus, Cic.; b, *to tend to;* res fluit ad interregnum, Cic.; c, of oratory, *to be diffuse, lax,* Cic. **II. A.** *to dissolve, become weak;* mollitie or mollitiis, Cic.; fluunt sudore et lassitudine membra, Liv. **B.** 1, *to fall down;* fluent arma de manibus, Cic.; 2, *to disappear, fall gradually;* a, lit., poma, Ov.; b, fig., *to vanish;* fluit voluptas corporis, Cic.

flŭto, 1. (for fluito), *to flow, float, swim,* Lucr.

flŭvĭālis -e (fluvius), *of or belonging to a river;* undae, Verg.; anas, Ov.

flŭvĭātĭlis -e (fluvius), *of or belonging to a river;* testudo, Cic.

flŭvĭdus -a -um (fluo), *flowing, fluid,* Lucr.

flŭvĭus -īi, m. (fluo), 1, *flowing water,* Verg.; 2, *stream, river;* fluvius Eurotas, Cic.

fluxĭo -ōnis, f. *a flowing, flood,* Cic.

1. **fluxus** -a -um, p. adj. (fluo), *flowing.* **A.** *waving, fluttering, loose;* crines, Tac.; habena, Liv. **B.** Transf., a, *uncertain, inconstant, changeable;* gloria, Sall.; b, of character, *vacillating;* animus, Sall.; c, *decaying, declining, tottering;* murorum aevo fluxa, Tac.; res, Cic.

2. **fluxus** -ūs, m. (fluo), *a flowing,* Plin.; transf., autumni, *the passing away of autumn,* Tac.

fŏcāle -is, n. (for faucale, from faux), *a wrapper for the neck,* Hor.

fŏcŭlus -i, m. (dim. of focus), 1, *a small stove for cooking, brazier,* Juv.; 2, *a small altar,* Cic.

fŏcus -i, m. (root FO, whence also foveo), *a fireplace.* **A.** Gen., Ov. **B.** Esp., 1, *the fireplace in a house, hearth;* a, lit., Cic.; b, meton., *house, family, home;* domo et focis patriis aliquem ejicere, Cic.; 2, *an altar,* Ov.; 3, *the fire of a funeral pile,* Verg.

fŏdĭco, 1. (fodio), *to dig, pierce;* latus, *to dig in the ribs,* Hor.; transf., fodicantibus iis rebus quas malas esse opinemur, *troubling, vexing,* Cic.

fŏdĭo, fōdi, fossum, 3. (root FOD, Gr. BOΘ, whence βόθρος), *to dig.* **I.** Intransit., fodit, invenit auri aliquantum, Cic. **II.** Transit., **A.** *to dig;* 1, humum, Verg.; 2, *to dig out;* argentum, Liv.; *to excavate;* puteum, Caes.; absol., fodientes, *miners,* Liv. **B.** *to pierce;* 1, a, pectora telis, Ov.; aversos (elephantos) sub caudis, Liv.; b, *to gouge out;* lumina, Ov.; 2, transf., *of grief,* pungit dolor . . . fodiat sane, Cic.

foecundus, foecundo = fecundus, fecundo (q.v.).

foedē, adv. (1. foedus), *foully, horribly, cruelly;* foede exercere victoriam, Liv.; foedius pulsi, Liv.; foedissime agere causam, Cic.

foedĕrātus -a -um (2. foedus), *confederate, allied;* civitates, Cic.

foedĭfrăgus -a -um (2. foedus and frango), *treaty-breaking;* Poeni, Cic.

foedĭtas -ātis, f. (1. foedus), *foulness, hideousness, filthiness;* **a,** physical, odoris intolerabilis foeditas, Cic.; vestitus, Cic.; b, moral, turpificati animi, Cic.; decreti, Liv.

foedo, 1. (1. foedus) *to make foul, make filthy, defile, pollute, deform, disfigure.* **A.** Lit., pectora pugnis, Verg.; canitiem pulvere, Ov.; aliquid sanguine, Ov.; serenos vultus, Verg.; agri foedati, *laid waste,* Liv. **B.** Transf., *to dishonour, disgrace;* aliquem nefario scelere, Cic.

1. **foedus** -a -um, *foul, filthy, horrible, abominable, detestable;* **a,** physically, monstrum foedissimum, Cic.; foedi oculi, *staring, bloodshot,* Sall.; with dat., pestilentia foeda homini, Liv.; with supine, rem non modo visu foedam sed etiam auditu, Cic.; b, morally, bellum foedissimum, Cic.; ludos vero non facere, quid foedius? Cic.; with supine, foedum inceptu, Liv.

2. **foedus** -ĕris, n. *a league.* **I.** Lit., a, between states, foedus facere cum aliquo, or icere, or ferire, Cic.; foedus frangere, rumpere, violare, Cic.; b, *a compact, covenant, agreement between individuals;* amorum, Cic.; scelerum, Cic. **II.** Poet., *a law,* Verg.

foem . . ., foen . . . v. fem . . ., fen . . . :

foetĕo, 2. *to have a bad smell,* Plaut.

foetĭdus (faetĭdus, fētĭdus) -a -um, adj. with compar. (foeteo), *having a bad smell, stinking, fetid;* os, Cic.

foetor -ōris, m. (foeteo), *a bad smell, stink,* Cic.

foetus, v. fetus.

Fōlĭa -ae, f. *a witch of Ariminum.*

fŏlĭātum -i, n. (folium), *a salve or oil of spikenard leaves,* Juv.

fŏlĭum -ii, n. (connected with φύλλον, as alius with ἄλλος), *a leaf;* Sibyllae, *a prophecy, oracle written on leaves,* Juv.

follĭculus -i, m. (dim. of follis), *a little sack or bag,* Cic.

follis -is, m. *a leather bag.* **I.** Gen., Plaut. **II.** Esp., 1, *a pair of bellows,* Cic.; follis fabrilis, Liv.; transf., of the lungs, folles spirant mendacia, Juv.; 2, *a leathern purse,* Juv.

fōmentum -i, n. (for fovimentum, from foveo); 1, *a poultice, fomentation,* Hor.; 2, transf., *alleviation;* summorum malorum, Cic.

fōmes -itis, m. (foveo), *touchwood, tinder,* Verg.

1. **fons** -fontis, m. (orig. funs, from fundo), 1, *a spring, well, fountain,* Cic.; meton. poet., *fresh* or *spring water,* Verg.; 2, transf., *spring, origin, fountain, source;* philosophiae, Cic; juris, Liv.

2. **Fons**, Fontis, m., and **Fontus** -i, m. *the son of Janus, god of fountains.* Adj., **Fontĭnālis** -e, *belonging to Fons;* porta, *a gate in Rome on the Quirinal, near the Campus Martius,* Liv.

fontānus -a -um (fons), *belonging* or *relating to a spring* or *fountain;* unda, Ov.

Fontējus -a -um, *name of a Roman gens.*

fontĭculus -i, m. (dim. of fons), *a little fountain* or *spring,* Hor.

Fontĭnālis, v. 2. Fons.

for, fātus, 1., dep. (φάω, φῶ), *to speak, say;* esp. of gods, oracles, seers, &c. **A.** Gen., *to speak, say;* ad aliquem, Cic.; aliquid, Verg.; fando audire, *hear by report,* Cic.; partic. **fandus** -a -um, *that which may be spoken,* hence, *right, lawful;* respersae fando nefandoque sanguine arae, Liv. **B.** Esp., a, of poets, *to sing of,* Prop.; b, *to prophesy,* Verg. (The forms which are found are fatur, fantur, fabor, fabitur, farer; partic. perf. fatus; perf. fatus sum and eram; imper. fare; infin. fari (farier, Verg.); gerund fandi, fando; supine fatu; partic. pres. fans).

fŏrābĭlis -e (foro), *that can be bored through, penetrable, vulnerable,* Ov.

fŏrāmen -ĭnis, n. (foro), *a hole, aperture, opening;* a, natural; foramina terrae, Lucr.; foramina illa quae patent ad animum a corpore, Cic.; b, artificial; convexa foramina retis, Ov.

fŏras, adv. (connected with foris), *out of doors, forth, out;* ire foras, Ov.; aliquem projicere foras, Cic.; portis se foras erumpere, Cic.; ea scripta foras dare, Cic.; quae (vestigia) ubi omnia foras versa vidit, Liv.

forceps -cĭpis, m. and f. *a pair of tongs, pincers,* Ov.

fordus -a -um (fero), *pregnant,* Ov. Subst. **forda** -ae, f. (sc. bos), *a cow in calf,* Ov.

fŏre, fŏrem, -es, etc. (for fuerem from old fuo, φύω, Cic.). **I.** forem, 1, = essem, Sall.; 2, = fuissem, Ov. **II.** Infin. fore, 1, = futurum (-am, -os, etc.) esse, Cic.; 2, = esse, Cic.

fŏrensis -e (forum), *relating to the market* or *forum.* **A.** Gen., 1, *relating to the forum;* factio, turba, Liv.; vestitus, *dress worn out of doors, state dress,* Liv.; 2, *relating to the forum as a place for administration of justice, legal;* causa, Cic.; Mars, *eloquence,* Ov.

Fŏrentum -i, n. *town in Apulia,* now *Forenzo,* Hor.

forfex -fĭcis, c. *a pair of shears* or *scissors,* Mart.

fŏrĭca -ae, f. = ἀφεδρών, Juv.

1. **fŏris** -is, f. (connected with 2. foris), 1, *a door;* and plur., fores, *folding-doors;* claudere forem cubiculi, Cic.; fores aperire, Cic.; ad fores assistere, Cic.; 2, *opening, entrance;* equi aenei, Cic.

2. **fŏris**, adv. (from obsolete nom. fora) **I.** *out of doors, outside, without.* **A.** Gen., aliquid quaere foris, Cic. **B.** Esp., a, *not at home;* foris cenare or cenitare, Cic.; foris valde plauditur, *among the people,* Cic.; foris esse Gabinium, *in debt,* Cic.; b, *outside the senate,* Cic.; c, *outside the state, outside Rome,* Cic. **II.** *from without, from abroad;* aliquid foris petere, Cic.

forma -ae, f. (fero), *form, figure, shape.* **I. A.** Lit., 1, gen., corporis, Cic.; 2, esp. a, *the face;* forma nostra reliquaque figura, Cic.; b, *beauty,* Cic. **B.** Transf., 1, *form = government, constitution;* forma rerum publicarum, Cic.; in formam provinciae redigere, Liv.; 2, esp. *character, form, nature, kind, manner;* forma insolitae pugnae, Liv. **II.** *figure, image, likeness.* **A.** Lit., formae virorum, Cic.; formae quas in pulvere descripserat, Liv. **B.** Transf., a, *outline, sketch;* totius negotii, Cic.; **b,** in logic, *species,* Cic. **III.** *form as a model;* **a,** *a shoe-last,* Hor.; **b,** *a mould, stamp for coining,* Ov.

formāmentum -i, n. (formo), *shape, form,* Lucr.

formātūra -ae, f. (formo), *a form, forming, formation,* Lucr.

Formīae -ārum, f. *town on the coast of Latium, famed for its wine,* now *Mola di Gaëta.* Adj., **Formiānus** -a -um, *of or belonging to Formiae.* Subst., **Formiānum** -i, n. (sc. praedium), *an estate near Formiae,* Cic.

formīca -ae, f. (connected with μύρμηξ), *an ant,* Cic.

formīdābĭlis -e (formido), *exciting terror, fearful, formidable;* lumen, Ov.

1. **formīdo,** 1. (perhaps connected with horreo), *to fear, be frightened, terrified, to dread;* omnia, Cic.; with the infin., naribus uti, Hor.; with ut and the subj., Tac.

2. **formīdo** -ĭnis, f. (1. formido). **I.** Lit., **A.** *fear, dread, terror;* Stoici definiunt formidinem metum permanentem, Cic.; formidinem alicui injicere, Cic. **B.** Esp., *religious awe;* existunt horribiles formidines, Cic. **II.** Meton., *that which causes fear,* Cic.; and esp. *a scarecrow,* Hor.

formīdōlōsē, adv. (formidolosus), *fearfully, terribly,* Cic.

formīdōlōsus -a -um (2. formido). **I.** Act., *exciting fear, terrible, fearful;* tempora, Cic.; bellum formidolosissimum, Cic. **II.** Neut., *fearful, timid;* with obj. genit., formidolosior hostium, Tac.

formo, 1. (forma). **I.** *to form, shape, fashion.* **A.** Lit., materiam, Cic.; orationem, Cic. **B.** Transf., **1,** *to arrange, order, regulate;* formatis omnibus ad belli et pacis usus, Liv.; **2,** *to fashion by education and habit, to accustom, shape;* novos collegas in suos mores, Liv.; **3,** *to dispose, prepare;* animos, Cic. **II.** *to fashion out of something.* **A.** Lit., of sculptors, etc., signum in muliebrem figuram, Cic.; classem, *to build,* Cic.; personam novam, of actors, *to represent,* Hor. **B.** Transf., *to produce, form;* quatuor modis formatas in animis hominum deorum esse notiones, Cic.

formons . . . v. formos .

formōsē, adv. (formosus), *beautifully, gracefully,* Prop.

formōsĭtas -ātis, f. (formosus), *beauty,* Cic.

formōsus -a -um (forma), *beautifully formed, beautiful;* virgines formosissimae, Cic.; of abstractions, tempus, *spring,* Ov.; virtute nihil est formosius, Cic.

formŭla -ae, f. (dim. of forma), **1,** *a rule, pattern, scheme;* dicendi, Cic.; ad formulam vivere, Cic.; **2,** esp., a, *the form of an agreement between the Roman senate and its allies;* Lampsacenos in sociorum formulam referre, Liv.; **b,** *the rating of the censor;* censum agere ex formula, Liv.; **c,** legal t. t., *form of words, formula;* postulationum, testamentorum, Cic.

fornācālis -e (fornax), *relating to an oven;* dea, *the goddess of ovens* (Fornax), Ov. Subst., **Fornācālia** -ium, n. *the festival of the goddess Fornax, said to have been instituted by Numa.*

fornācŭla -ae, f. (dim. of fornax), *a little oven,* Juv.

fornax -ācis, f. (root FOR, connected with fer-veo, θερ-μός), **1,** *an oven, furnace, kiln;* ardens, Cic.; poet., Aetnae, *the crater,* Verg.; **2,** personif., Fornax, *the goddess of ovens,* Ov.

fornĭcātus -a -um (fornix), *arched, vaulted;* paries, Cic.; via, Liv.

fornix -ĭcis, m. *an arch, vault.* **I.** Gen., parietis, Cic. **II.** Esp., **A.** Fornix Fabii, *a triumphal arch erected by Q. Fabius Maximus.* **B.** Milit. t. t., **a,** *an arched sally-port,* Liv.; **b,** *a covered way,* Liv. **C.** *a brothel,* Hor.

fornus = furnus (q.v.).

foro, 1. (cf. Engl. bore), *to pierce,* Plaut.

fors, abl. forte, f. (fero), only in nom. and abl. sing., *chance, luck.* **I.** 1, gen., sed haec ut fors tulerit, Cic.; **2,** esp., a, abl., forte, *by chance,* used with si, sin, ne, nisi, etc., Cic.; **b,** adv. fors = fortasse, *by chance,* Verg.; **3,** fors fortuna, *good luck;* casu aut forte fortunā, Cic. **II.** Personif. as a deity, dea Fors, Ov.; esp., Fors Fortuna, Liv.

forsăn, adv. (= fors sit an), *perhaps,* Liv.

forsit, adv. (fors sit), *perhaps,* Hor.

forsĭtăn, adv. (fors sit an), *perhaps,* Cic.

fortassĕ, adv. (fors), *perhaps;* a, with verbs, dolent fortasse et anguntur, Cic.; with subj., fortasse dixerit quispiam, Cic.; **b,** with adj. and adv., res fortasse verae, Cic.; incondite fortasse, Cic.; **c,** with numbers, *about;* triginta fortasse versus, Cic.

fortĕ, v. fors.

fortĭcŭlus -a -um (dim. of fortis), *tolerably strong, brave, courageous,* Cic.

fortis -e (old form forctis = forectis, from fero, orig. *one that can endure much*), *strong, powerful, durable.* **I.** Lit., physically, *strong, durable, powerful, robust, stout;* ligna fortissima, Caes.; coloni, Verg. **II.** Transf., mentally, *brave, courageous, stout, steadfast;* 1, of persons, horum omnium fortissimi sunt Belgae, Caes.; fortior in dolore, Cic.; vir fortissimus contra audaciam, Cic.; fortis ad pericula, Cic.; prov., fortes fortuna adjuvat, *fortune favours the brave;* so elliptically, fortes fortuna, Cic. 2, of things, *courageous, energetic;* sententia, Cic.; genus dicendi, Cic.

fortĭtĕr, adv. (fortis), **1,** *strongly, firmly;* fortius attrahere lora, Ov.; **2,** *bravely, courageously, steadfastly;* ferre dolorem, Cic.

fortĭtūdo -ĭnis, f. (fortis), *bravery, courage, steadfastness, firmness, fortitude,* Cic.; plur., fortitudines, *deeds of bravery,* Cic.

fortŭĭto (fortŭĭtū), adv. (fortuitus), *by chance, by accident, fortuitously,* Cic.

fortŭĭtus -a -um (fors), *accidental, casual, fortuitous;* concursus atomorum, Cic.; subita et fortuita oratio, *unpremeditated,* Cic. Subst., **fortŭĭta** -ōrum, n. *chance occurrences,* Tac.

fortūna -ae, f. and plur. **fortūnae** -ārum, f. (fors), *chance, fate, lot, luck, fortune.* **I.** Gen., **A.** a, sing., prospera, secunda, *good fortune,* Cic.; adversa, *misfortune,* Cic.; fortunae se or omnia committere, Cic.; **b,** plur., fortunae secundae, Cic. **B.** Personif., Fortuna, *the goddess of chance,* Cic.; filius Fortunae, *a favourite of fortune,* Hor. **II.** Esp., **A.** Without an epithet, **1,** = fortuna secunda, Cic.; fortunam sibi ipsum facere, Liv.; per fortunas! *by thy good fortune! for Heaven's sake!* Cic.; **2,** = fortuna adversa, contra fortunam paratus armatusque, Cic. **B.** 1, lit., a, *lot, condition, state, mode of life;* infima servorum, Cic.; magna, *a high position,* Liv.; **b,** of things, bona belli, Cic.; **2,** meton., a, *lot, share;* cui cessit triplicis fortuna novissima regni, Ov.; **b,** *property, possessions;* gen. plur., alicui bona fortunasque adimere, Cic.

fortūnātē, adv. (fortunatus), *happily, fortunately;* vivere, Cic.

fortūnātus -a -um, p. adj. (fortuno), *happy, lucky, fortunate.* **I.** Gen., homo, Cic.; respublica, Cic.; insulae, *the islands of the blest, Elys-ium,* Plin.; so fortunata nemora, *Elysium,* Verg. Subst., **fortūnātus** -i, m. *a favourite of for-tune,* Cic. **II.** Esp., *well off, wealthy, rich,* Cic.

fortūno, 1. (fortuna), *to make happy, bless, prosper;* tibi patrimonium dei fortunent, Cic.

1. **fŏrŭli** -ōrum, m. (dim. of forus), *a book-case,* Juv.

2. **Fŏrŭli** -ōrum, m. *a place in the Sabine country,* now *Civita Tommasa.*

fŏrum -i, n. (connected with foras and foris), *an open space.* **I.** *in front of a tomb,* ap. Cic. **II. A.** *an open square, market-place,* Liv.; esp. at Rome, **1, a,** forum Romanum, or magnum, or vetus, or simply forum, *an open place at the foot of the Palatine and Capitoline hills, where legal, political, and commercial business was transacted,* Cic.; **b,** forum Caesaris, *founded by J. Caesar,* Suet.; **c,** forum Augusti, *built by Augustus,* Ov.; **d,** forum Trajani, *built by Trajan;* **2,** as mere market-places, **a,** forum bovarium or boarium, *the cattle-market,* Cic.; **b,** forum olitorium, *vege-table market,* Liv.; **c,** forum piscarium or pisca-torium, *fish-market,* Liv.; **3,** in reference to pub-lic business, law, and mercantile transactions, verba de foro arripere, *to use common and vulgar expressions,* Cic.; annos jam triginta in foro versaris, *thou hast been in business thirty years already,* Cic.; forum attingere, *to begin to apply oneself to public business,* esp. legal, Cic. **B.** Transf., **1,** *a place of trade,* Vacca, forum rerum venalium totius regni maxime celebratum, Sall.; **2,** *the chief place* or *market-town of a district;* civitates quae in id forum convenerant, *which are in that district,* Cic.; forum agere, *to hold an assize,* Cic. Hence, the name of several towns, **a,** Forum Appii, *on the Via Appia in Latium;* **b,** Forum Aurelium, *in Etruria, on the Via Aurelia,* now *Monte Alto;* **c,** Forum Cornelii, *in Gallia Cispadana,* now *Imola;* **d,** Forum Julii or Julium, *in Gallia Narbonensis,* now *Frejus;* **e,** Forum Voconii, *in Gallia Narbonensis.*

fŏrus -i, m. **1,** *the gangway of a ship,* Cic.; **2,** plur., *a row of seats in the theatre,* Liv.; **3,** plur., *the cells of bees,* Verg.

Fosi -ōrum, m. *a German people near the modern Hildesheim,* Tac.

fossa -ae, f. (fodio), *a ditch, trench;* **a,** fossam ducere, Caes.; facere, fodere, Liv.; obducere, praeducere, Cic.; vallo et fossā cingere, Cic.; fossas implere, Cic.; **b,** *canal, bed of a river;* Rheni, Cic.; fossae Cluiliae, Liv.

fossĭo -ōnis, f. (fodio), *a digging, excavation,* Cic.

fossor -ōris, m. (fodio), *a digger, delver,* Verg.; poet., *a boor, clown,* Cat.

fossūra -ae, f. (fodio), *a digging,* Suet.

fōtus, partic. of foveo.

fŏvĕa -ae, f. *a pit as a trap for catching game, a pitfall;* in foveam incidere, Cic.

fŏvĕo, fōvi, fōtum, 2. (root FO, whence fomes, fomentum), *to warm, keep warm.* **I. A.** Lit., **1,** esp. of a bird keeping warm its eggs or young, pullos pennis, Cic.; **2,** *to bathe, foment* a wound or part of the body; vulnus lymphā, Verg.; poet., **a,** *to heal;* ora, Verg.; **b,** *to sup-port;* colla, Verg. **B.** Meton., **1,** *to stay con-stantly in a place;* castra, Verg.; **2,** hiemem inter se luxu, *pass the winter,* Verg. **II.** Transf., **1,** *to foster;* spem, Liv.; **2,** *to cherish;* aliquem, Cic.; **3,** *to support, favour;* voluntatem patrum, Liv.

fractus -a -um, p. adj. (frango), *weak, power-less;* animus, *broken, down, spiritless,* Cic.

fraeno, fraenum = freno, frenum (q.v.).

frāga -ōrum, n. *strawberries,* Verg.

frăgĭlis -e (frango). **I. A.** Lit., *easily broken, fragile;* rami, Verg. **B.** Meton., *crackling;* laurus, Verg. **II.** Transf., **a,** *frail, transitory;* corpus, Cic.; res humanae, Cic.; **b,** *weak, nerveless;* anni, Ov.; Pediatia, Hor.

frăgĭlĭtas -ātis, f. (fragilis), *frailty, weak-ness;* humani generis, Cic.

fragmen -mĭnis, n. (frango), *a piece broken off, fragment;* in plur., *ruins;* ingens montis, Verg.; fragmina navigii, Ov.; *fragments, remains, ruins,* Verg., Ov.

fragmentum -i, n. (frango), *a piece broken off, fragment;* plur., *ruins;* lapidis, Cic.; frag-menta saeptorum, Cic.

frăgor -ōris, m. (frango), **1,** *breaking in pieces,* Lucr.; **2,** *a loud noise, crash of falling houses,* Liv.; *noise of the sea,* Verg.; of thunder, Ov.; fragorem dare, *to crash,* Ov.

frăgōsus -a -um (fragor). **I.** *fragile;* **A.** Lit., Lucr. **B.** Transf., *rough, uneven;* silva, Ov. **II.** *crashing, roaring;* torrens, Verg.

fragrans -antis, p. adj. (fragro), *sweet-scented;* mella, Verg.

fragro, 1. *to smell sweet, be fragrant;* un-guento, Sall.

frāgum, v. fraga.

frango, frēgi, fractum, 3. (root FRAG, con-nected with ῥήγνυμι), *to break, break in pieces, shatter, dash to pieces.* **I. A.** Lit., **1,** domum lapidum conjectu, Cic.; compluribus navibus fractis, *dashed to pieces,* Caes.; gulam laqueo, *to strangle,* Sall.; glebas rastris, *to break small,* Verg.; **2,** esp., **a,** *to grind;* fruges saxo, Verg.; **b,** *to break* (a limb); brachium, Cic. **B.** Transf., **a,** reflex. se frangere, *to break up* (of weather, cold, heat, etc.), Cic.; **b,** *to shorten time;* diem morantem mero, Hor. **II.** Fig., **1,** *to weaken;* se laboribus, Cic.; **2, a,** *to master, tame, sub-due;* nationes, cupiditates, impetum, Cic.; **b,** *to discourage, dispirit, humble;* Clodium, Cic.; frangi animo or frangi, *to be discouraged,* Cic.; **3,** *to bend, touch, move;* te ut ulla res frangat, Cic.; **4,** *to break, violate;* fidem, Cic.

frāter -tris, m., *a brother.* **I.** Lit., fratres gemini, *twin-brothers,* Cic.; *Castor and Pollux,* Ov.; fratres gemelli, Ov.; germanus, *own brother,* Cic. **II. A.** fratres (like ἀδελφοί), *brothers and sisters,* Tac. **B. a,** frater patruelis, Cic., and simply frater, *cousin,* Cic.; **b,** *brother-in-law,* Liv. **C.** *brother* (as term of endearment), *friend,* Cic. **D.** fratres, of things alike, positi ex ordine fratres (of writings), Ov.

frātercŭlus -i, m. (dim. of frater), *a little brother* (as term of endearment); ap. Cic.

frāternē, adv. (fraternus), *in a brotherly manner, like a brother.* **A.** Lit., facere, Cic. **B.** Transf., *heartily;* ab aliquo amari, Cic.

frāternĭtas -ātis, f. (fraternus), *brotherhood, fraternity,* Tac.

frāternus -a -um (for fraterinus, from frater), *brotherly, fraternal.* **I.** Lit., hereditas, *coming from a brother,* Cic.; lyra, *received by Apollo from his brother Mercury,* Hor.; nex, *murder of a brother,* Hor. **II.** Transf., **A.** *related;* sanguis, Verg.; fraterna peto, *the arms of my cousin Achilles,* Ov. **B.** *friendly;* amor in nos, Cic.

frātrĭcīda -ae, m. (from frater and caedo), *one who kills a brother, a fratricide,* Cic.

fraudātĭo -ōnis, f. (fraudo), *deceit, fraud,* Cic.

fraudātor -ōris, m. (fraudo), *a deceiver, defrauder;* creditorum, Cic.

fraudo, 1. (fraus), *to cheat, defraud, deceive.* **A.** Lit., with abl., Caecilium magnā pecuniā, Cic.; milites praedā, Liv.; creditores, Cic.;

aliquem in hereditaria societate, Cic.; **partic. subst., fraudāta** -ōrum, n. *ill-gotten gains;* fraudata restituere, Caes.; **B.** Transf., *to steal, embezzle;* stipendium equitum, Caes.

fraudŭlentĭa -ae, f. (fraudulentus), *deceitfulness*, Plaut.

fraudŭlentus -a -um (fraus), *deceitful, fraudulent;* Carthaginienses, Cic.; venditio, Cic.

fraus, fraudis, f. *deceit, deception, fraud.* **I. A.** Lit., 1, fraus odio digna majore, Cic.; sine fraude, *honourably*, Caes.; fraudem facere legi, Liv., or contra legem, Liv., or senatus consulto, Cic.; 2, *self-deception, error;* in fraudem incidere, delabi, Cic. **B.** Meton., *injury, damage, loss, caused by deception;* alicui fraudem ferre, or alicui fraudi esse, *to cause loss to*, Cic. **II.** *a crime, offence;* fraudem suscipere, Cic.; fraudem capitalem admittere or audere, Cic. (genit. plur. fraudium and fraudum).

fraxĭnĕus -a -um (fraxinus), *of ash-wood, ashen;* trabes, Verg.

1. **fraxĭnus** -a -um = fraxineus, Ov.

2. **fraxĭnus** -i, f. 1, lit., *an ash-tree*, Verg.; 2, meton., *a spear* or *javelin, the shaft of which was made of ash-wood*, Ov.

Frĕgellae -ārum, f. *town of the Volsci, in Latium, on the Liris*, now *Ceprano.* Adj., **Frĕgellānus**, -a -um, *Fregellan.*

Fregēnae -ārum, f. *town of Etruria.*

frĕmēbundus -a -um (fremo), *growling, muttering, murmuring*, Ov.

frĕmĭdus -a -um (fremo), *raging*, Ov.

frĕmĭtus -ūs, m. (fremo), *a low murmuring, muttering, growling noise, murmur, roar;* murmurantis maris, Cic.; terrae, Cic.; egentium, Cic.; equorum, Liv.; apum, Verg.

frĕmo -ŭi -ĭtum, 3. (βρέμω), *to roar, murmur, growl.* **I.** Intransit., a, of animals and things, leo, equus, Verg.; fremunt ripae, *rustle*, Verg.; b, of persons, laetitiā fremunt, Verg.; adversus injuriam decreti fremere, Liv. **II.** Transit., 1, *to murmur out something, express in secret, grumble, complain;* uno omnes eadem ore fremebant, Verg.; with acc. and infin., falsas esse et a scriba vitiatas (litteras) fremebant, Liv.; haec fremuit plebs, Liv.; jam vero Arrius consulatum sibi ereptum fremit, Cic.; 2, *to demand, call for with tears* or *rage;* arma, Verg.

frĕmor -ōris, m. (fremo), *murmuring;* varius, Verg.

frendo, frēsum (fressum), 3., 1, intransit., with or without dentibus, *to gnash the teeth*, Cic.; 2, transit., *to crush, bruise, grind;* fabam, Varr.

frēni -ōrum, m. v. frenum.

frēno, 1. (frenum), *to bridle, curb;* 1, lit., equos, Verg.; 2, transf., *to curb, restrain, check, hold in;* cursus aquarum, Verg.; furores, Cic.

Frentāni -ōrum, m. *a Samnite people on the east coast of Italy.* Hence, adj., **Frentānus** -a, -um, *Frentanian.*

frēnum -i, n., plur. **frēna** -ōrum, n., and **frēni** -ōrum, m. (frendo), *bridle, reins, bit;* frena remittere, *to give the reins to*, Ov.; so frena dare, Ov.; frenos inhibere, *to draw in*, Liv.; fig., frenos dare impotenti naturae, *to give full liberty to*, Liv.; alicui frenos adhibere, *to bridle*, Cic.; frenos recipere, *to submit to the rein*, Cic.; frenum mordere, *to chafe against restraint*, Cic. (in prose, nom. pl. freni and acc. plur. frenos commoner than frena).

frĕquens -entis. **I.** of space, **A.** Act., of a crowd, etc., *numerous, crowded;* legatio, Liv.; senatus, Cic. **B.** Pass., of places, *full, frequented, filled, populous;* theatrum, Cic.; municipium, Cic.; with abl., frequens custodiis locus Liv.

II. of time, **A.** Act., *frequent, constant;* Platonis auditor, Cic.; cum aliquo frequentem esse, *to be often in a person's company*, Cic. **B.** Pass., *frequently used, numerous;* pocula, Cic.

frĕquentātĭo -ōnis, f. (frequento), *frequency, frequent use;* argumentorum, Cic.

frĕquentātus -a -um (partic. of frequento), *full of, abounding in;* genus sententiis frequentatum, Cic.

frĕquentĕr, adv. (frequens), *frequently, numerously, in large numbers.* 1, quum ad eum frequenter per eos dies ventitaturos se esse dixissent, Cic.; 2, *frequently, often;* adhibenda frequentius etiam illa ornamenta rerum sunt, Cic.

frĕquentĭa -ae, f. (frequens), 1, *a large concourse, numerous assembly;* civium, Cic.; frequentiā crescere, *to increase in population*, Liv.; 2, *a large number, abundance;* sepulcrorum, Cic.

frĕquento, 1. (frequens). **I. A.** a, of persons, *to collect in large numbers;* de domo scribas ad aerarium, Cic.; b, transf., of things, multa acervatim, Cic. **B.** *to visit in large numbers;* a, *to attend upon a person in large numbers;* Marium, Sall.; b, *to celebrate a festivity in large numbers;* ferias, Cic.; c, *to make a place populous, to people;* urbes, Cic.; solitudinem Italiae, Cic. **II. A.** *to visit frequently, to frequent;* domum, Cic. **B.** *to repeat constantly;* verbi translationem, Cic.

frēsus (fressus) -a -um, v. frendo.

trētum -i, n., and **frētus** -ūs, m. (connected with ῥέειν and ῥεῖθρον), 1, a, lit., *the sea;* fretus Hadriae, Hor.; b, *the spring* (as the time of transition from cold to heat), Lucr.; c, *heat, violence, raging;* aetatis, Lucr.; 2, *a strait, sound, firth, channel;* gen., a, Siciliense, *the Straits of Messina*, Cic.; nostri maris et oceani, *the Straits of Gibraltar*, Sall.; b, esp., *the Straits of Messina*, Cic.

1. **frētus** -a -um (from unused freo = I strengthen), *strengthened*, hence *relying on, confiding in, trusting, depending on;* with the abl., vobis, Cic.; intelligentiā vestrā, Cic.; with dat., nulli rei, Liv.; with acc. and infin., satis fretus esse etiamnunc tolerando certamini legatum, Liv.

2. **frētus** -ūs, m. = fretum (q.v.).

frĭco, frĭcŭi, frictum, and frĭcātum, 1. *to rub, rub down;* (sus) fricat arbore costas, Verg.

frĭgĕo, 2. (ῥιγέω). **I.** *to be cold, be stiff with cold* (opp. calere), corpus frigentis (of a dead person), Verg. **II.** Transf., **A.** *to be inactive, lifeless, languid, to flag;* quum omnia consilia frigerent, Cic. **B.** *to be coldly received, fail of exciting approbation;* itaque (contio) frigebat, Cic.

frĭgĕro, 1. (frigus), *to cool, refresh*, Cat.

frĭgesco, frixi, 3. (frigeo). **I.** Lit., *to become cold;* pedes manusque, Tac. **II.** Transf., *to become languid, inactive;* ap. Cic.

frĭgĭdē, adv. (frigidus), *coldly;* hence transf., *languidly, feebly;* aliquid agere, ap. Cic.

frĭgĭdŭlus -a -um (dim. of frigidus), 1, *somewhat cold*, Verg.; 2, transf., *somewhat faint, languid*, Cat.

frĭgĭdus -a -um (frigeo), *cold, frigid, cool.* **I. A.** Lit., flumen, Cic.; rura, Verg.; annus, *winter*, Verg. Subst. plur., **frĭgĭda** -ōrum, n. *cold*, Cic.; of the chill of death or fright, Verg. **B.** Transf., 1, *cold, inactive, remiss, indolent;* accusator frigidissimus, Cic.; litterae, Cic.; 2, of discourse, *frigid, dull;* calumnia, Cic. **II.** Act., *causing cold;* sidera, Ov.; mors, Verg.; rumor, *chilling, causing fright*, Hor.

frĭgo, frixi, frictum, 3. (φρύγω), *to roast, parch*, Hor.

frĭgus -ŏris, n. (ῥῖγος), *cold, coolness, coldness.*

I. Lit., A. *physical cold;* 1, gen., vis frigoris et caloris, Cic.; 2, esp., a, *the cold of winter;* propter frigora, Caes.; b, meton., (a) *winter,* Verg.; (β) *a cold place;* frigus non habitabile, Ov. **B.** *animal cold;* a, of death, Verg.; b, of fright, Verg. **II.** Transf., a, *coldness in action, indolence, remissness,* ap. Cic.; b, *coldness in behaviour, coolness, disfavour,* Hor.

frĭgūtĭo (frĭguttĭo), 4. 1, *to twitter, chirp,* Suet.; 2, *to stammer,* Plaut.

frĭo, 1. *to rub, crumble,* Lucr.

Frĭsĭi -ōrum, m. *the Frisians.* Adj., **Frĭs-ĭus** -a -um, *Frisian.*

frĭtillus -i, m. *a dice-box,* Juv.

frĭvŏlus -a -um (frio), *silly, trifling, miserable, worthless,* Plin. Subst., **frĭvŏla** -ōrum, n. *wretched furniture,* Juv.

frondātor -ōris, m. (1. frons), *one who cuts off leaves, a pruner of trees,* Verg.

frondĕo, 2. (1. frons), *to be in leaf, be leafy, green with leaves;* nunc frondent silvae, Verg.

frondesco, 3. (inchoat. of frondeo), *to come into leaf, put forth leaves,* Cic.

frondĕus -a -um (1. frons), *leafy, full of leaf, covered with leaves;* nemus, Verg.; tecta, *leafy coverts = trees in full leaf,* Verg.

frondĭfer -fĕra -fĕrum (1. frons and fero), *leaf-bearing, leafy,* Lucr.

frondōsus -a -um (1. frons), *full of leaves, leafy;* ramus, Verg.

1. frons, frondis, f. **A.** *a leaf, leafy twig or branch, foliage;* via interclusa frondibus et virgultis, Cic. **B.** Meton., *a chaplet or crown of leaves,* Hor.

2. frons, frontis, f. *the forehead, brow.* **I.** Lit., a, frontem contrahere, *to frown,* Cic.; explicare, *to unwrinkle the brow, become cheerful,* Hor.; frontem ferire or percutere, Cic.; b, *the forehead as a sign of the feelings;* laeta, Verg.; sollicita, proterva, Hor.; fronte occultare sententiam, Cic. **II.** Transf., *the outside;* 1, gen., tabernae, Cat.; 2, esp., *the edge of a roll or volume,* Ov. **B.** *the front, forepart;* 1, gen., frons adversa (montis), Verg.; 2, esp. milit. t. t., a, *the van;* et a fr.ate et a tergo circumire hostem, Caes.; a fronte instare, Liv.; b, *the front line in battle;* frontem aequare, Liv. **C.** *frontage* (in measuring land), Hor.

frontālĭa -ĭum, n. (2. frons), *the frontlet of a horse,* Liv.

fronto -ōnis, m. (2. frons). **I.** *a man with a broad forehead,* Cic. **II.** Fronto, *a Roman surname.*

fructŭārĭus -a -um (fructus), *fruit-bearing, fruitful;* agri quos fructuarios habent civitates, *for which a portion of the produce is paid,* ap. Cic.

fructŭōsus -a -um (fructus), *fruit-bearing, fruitful, fertile.* **A.** Lit., ager, Cic. **B.** Transf., tota philosophia frugifera et fructuosa, Cic.; fructuosum est, with infin., Cic.

fructus -ūs, m. (fruor). **I.** Abstr., *enjoyment, enjoying.* **A.** Lit., Plaut. **B.** Transf., ad animi mei fructum, *for my intellectual enjoyment,* Cic. **II.** Concr., *the proceeds, profit, produce, fruit, income.* **A.** Lit., praediorum, Cic.; fructus percipere, demetere, Cic.; fructui esse alicui, *to bring profit to,* Cic.; in fructu habere, *to consider profitable,* Cic. **B.** Transf., *advantage, gain, profit;* verae virtutis, Cic.; fructum ferre, or capere, or percipere ex aliqua re, Cic.

frugālis -e (frux), *frugal, sparing, economical, worthy, excellent;* colonus frugalissimus, Cic. (positive not used in class. Latin, frugi instead).

frugālĭtas -ātis, f. (frugalis), *frugality, eco-*

nomy, worth, excellence, Cic.; cognomen Frugalitatis, *the surname Frugi,* Cic.

frūgālĭtĕr, adv. (frugalis), *frugally, economically, worthily, honourably,* Cic.

frūgi, v. frux.

frūgĭfer -fĕra -fĕrum (frux and fero). **A.** Lit., *fruit-bearing, fruitful, fertile;* ager, Cic.; numen, *making fruitful,* Ov.; with abl., alimentis frugifera insula, Liv. **B.** Transf., *profitable, advantageous;* tota philosophia frugifera et fructuosa, Cic.

frūgĭfĕrens -entis (frux and fero), *fruitful, fertile,* Lucr.

frūgĭlĕgus -a -um (frux and lego), *collecting fruit;* formicae, Ov.

frūgĭpărus -a -um (frux and pario), *fruitful, prolific,* Lucr.

frūĭtus, frūĭtūrus, v. fruor.

frūmentārĭus -a -um (frumentum), *relating or belonging to grain or corn;* res, *the supply of corn,* Cic.; lex, *relating to the price of grain,* Cic. Subst., **frūmentārĭus** -ii, m. *a corn-merchant,* Cic.

frūmentātĭo -ōnis, f. (frumentor), *a foraging,* Caes.

frūmentātor -ōris, m. (frumentor), *a forager, provider of corn,* Liv.

frūmentor, 1. dep. (frumentum), *to forage, fetch corn;* frumentari in propinquo agro, Liv.

frūmentum -i, n. (fruor), *grain, corn,* Cic.

frŭor, fructus and frūĭtus sum, 3. dep. 1, *to enjoy, to delight in, to derive advantage from;* with abl., vitā, Cic.; voluptate, Cic.; votis, *to obtain one's wishes,* Ov.; amicitiae recordatione, *to take delight in,* Cic.; absol., jucundius est carere quam frui, Cic.; 2, *to have the use and enjoyment of;* fundis certis, Cic.

Frūsĭno -ōnis, m. *town of the Volsci in Latium,* now *Frosinone.* Hence, **Frūsĭnās** -ātis, *of or belonging to Frusino.*

frustrā (for frustera, abl. of *frusterus, connected with fraudo), 1, *in error;* frustra esse, *to be deceived, mistaken,* Sall.; 2, *in vain, uselessly, without effect, unnecessarily,* Cic.; frustra esse (alicui), *to fail,* Sall.; frustra tempus contero, Cic.

frustrātĭo -ōnis, f. (frustro), *failure, disappointment;* tantae rei, Liv.

frustro, 1. and dep. **frustror,** 1. (frustra), *to cheat, deceive, trick;* nos falsā atque inani spe, Liv.; Coccejus vide ne frustretur, Cic.

frustum -i, n. (fruor), *a bit, piece, morsel of food;* frusta esculenta, Cic.; in frusta secare, Verg.

frŭtex -tĭcis, m. (perhaps connected with βρύω), 1, *a shrub, bush,* Ov.; 2, as a term of reproach, *blockhead,* Plaut.

frŭtĭcētum -i, n. (frutex), *a thicket,* Hor.

frŭtĭco and **frŭtĭcor,** 1. dep. (frutex), *to shoot out, become bushy;* quam fruticetur (arbor), vides, Cic.

frŭtĭcōsus -a -um, adj. with compar. and superl. (frutex), *bushy, thick with leaves, full of bushes,* Ov.

frux, frūgis (fruor). **A.** Lit., *fruit, produce;* non omnem frugem neque arborem in agro reperire, Cic.; plur., terrae fruges bacaeve arborum, Cic. **B.** Transf., a, *fruit;* fruges industriae, Cic.; bonam frugem libertatis ferre, Liv.; b, *moral excellence, virtue;* ad bonam frugem se recipere, *to improve oneself,* Cic.; **frūgi** used as an adj., *useful, worthy, honest, discreet, moderate, temperate;* homo, Cic.; permodestui et bonae frugi, Cic.

fūcātus -a -um (p. adj. of fuco), *painted, counterfeited, simulated;* nitor, Cic. ; omnia fucata et simulata a sinceris atque veris (secernere), Cic.

Fūcīnus -i, m. *a lake in Southern Italy, in the country of the Marsi,* now *Lago di Celano.*

fūco, 1. (1. fucus), **1,** *to colour, dye;* vellera hyali colore, Verg. ; **2,** *to paint, rouge,* Ov. ; transf., iisdem ineptiis fucata sunt illa omnia, Cic.

fūcōsus -a -um (1. fucus), *painted, simulated, counterfeited;* merx, Cic.

1. fūcus -i, m. (φῦκος), **1,** *red or purple colour,* Hor., Ov. ; **2,** = propolis, *the reddish substance with which bees stop up the entrance to their hives, bee-glue,* Verg. ; **3,** *rouge;* **4,** transf., *deceit, dissimulation, pretence;* sine fuco ac fallaciis, Cic.

2. fūcus -i, m. *a drone bee,* Verg.

Fūfius -a -um, *name of a Roman gens.*

fūga -ae, f. (φυγή). **I. A.** Lit., **1,** gen., *flight, running away;* fuga ab urbe turpissima, Cic. ; ex fuga se recipere, Caes. ; esse in fuga, Cic. ; hostes in fugam convertere, or dare, or conjicere, Caes. ; in fugam se dare, se conferre, se conjicere, Cic. ; fugae se mandare, Caes. ; or dare, Cic. ; fugam dare, *to flee,* Verg. ; or, *to let flee,* Verg., Hor. ; fugam facere, *to flee,* Sall., Liv. ; or *to make to flee,* Cic., Liv. ; fugam sistere, *to stop,* Liv. ; plur., quantae in periculis fugae proximorum, Cic. ; **2,** esp., *flight from one's country, exile, banishment;* fuga Metelli, Cic. ; meton., *the place of exile,* Ov. **B.** Transf., *disinclination to, avoidance of, aversion to;* laboris, bellandi, Cic. **II.** *flying, swift course,* Verg. ; of a ship, facilem fugam exspectare, Verg. ; transf., fuga temporum, *hastening,* Hor.

fūgācius, adv. in compar. (fugax), *in a manner more inclined to flight;* utrum a se audacius an fugacius ab hostibus geratur bellum, Liv.

fūgax -ācis (fugio), **1,** *ready to flee, flying, hastening;* Parthus, Ov. ; fugacissimus hostis, Liv. ; **2,** transf., a, *fleeting, transitory;* anni, Hor. ; haec omnia brevia, fugacia, caduca existima, Cic. ; b, with genit., *avoiding;* conditionis, Ov.

fūgiens -entis, p. adj. (from fugio) *flying from, avoiding;* with genit., laboris, Caes.

fūgio, fūgi, fūgitum, 3. (φεύγω). **I.** Intransit. **A.** *to flee, take to flight, run away;* **1,** gen., a, lit., longe, Ov. ; poet., of a bird, in auras, Verg. ; b, transf., omne animal appetit quaedam et fugit a quibusdam, Verg. ; **2,** esp. a, of soldiers, ex proelio, Cic. ; b, of fugitives, a Troja (of Aeneas), Cic. ; esp. of exiles, a patria, Ov. ; c, of slaves, *to run away,* Hor. **B.** 1, *to hasten away, depart quickly;* fugientia flumina, Hor. ; Camilla super amnem fugit, Verg. ; 2, *to pass away, vanish, disappear;* fugiunt cum sanguine vires, Ov. ; vinum fugiens, *becoming flat,* Cic. **II.** Transit. *to flee from.* **A.** *to run away from;* cerva fugiens lupum, Liv. ; velut qui currebat fugiens hostem, Hor. ; patriam, Verg. **B.** 1, *to avoid, shun;* a, lit., concilia conventusque hominum, Caes. ; b, transf., (a) ignominiam et dedecus, Cic. ; (β) *to decline, renounce, reject;* aliquem judicem, Liv. ; neque illud fugerim dicere, Cic. ; fuge quaerere, *do not seek,* Hor. ; 2, *to escape from;* Acheronta, Hor. ; scientiam alicuius, Cic. ; aliquid aliquem fugit, *escapes the notice of,* Cic. ; with infin., de Dionysio fugit me ad te antea scribere, Cic.

fūgitans -antis, p. adj. (from fugito) *flying from, avoiding,* Ter.

fūgitīvus -a -um (fugio), 1, adj., *flying, fugitive;* a dominis, Cic. ; 2, subst., *a fugitive,* esp. *a fugitive slave,* Cic.

fūgito, 1. (intens. of fugio), *to fly from, avoid, shun;* quaestionem, Cic.

fūgo, 1. (fuga), **1,** *to put to flight, chase away, drive away;* homines inermes, Cic. ; fundere atque fugare, Sall. ; **2,** *to drive away;* a, aliquem, Cic. ; b, esp., *to drive into exile,* Ov.

fulcīmen -ĭnis, n. (fulcio), *a prop, support, pillar,* Ov.

fulcio, fulsi, fultum, 4. **I.** *to prop up, support;* 1, lit., porticum, Cic. ; vitis fulta, Cic. ; 2, transf., *to support, stay, uphold;* amicum, Cic. ; labantem rempublicam, Cic. ; Thermum litteris, Cic. **II.** *to strengthen, secure;* postes, Verg. ; januam serā, Ov.

fulcrum -i, n. (fulcio), **1,** *a post* or *foot of a couch,* Verg. ; **2,** meton., *a couch,* Juv.

Fulfŭlae -ārum, f. *a town of the Samnites.*

fulgěo, fulsi, 2. (root FUL, whence also fulvus). **I.** *to lighten;* Jove, or caelo, fulgente, Cic. **II.** Transf., **A.** Of Pericles, as a powerful orator, compared to Jupiter, fulgere, tonare, Cic. **B.** 1, lit., *to shine, gleam, glitter;* auro, Cic. ; fulgebat luna, Hor. ; 2, transf., *to be distinguished, to shine;* virtus intaminatis fulget honoribus, Hor.

fulgĭdus -a -um (fulgeo), *shining, gleaming, glittering,* Lucr.

Fulgĭnia -ae, f. *a town in Umbria,* now *Foligno.* Adj., **Fulgĭniātis,** *of Fulginia.*

fulgo, 3. = fulgeo (q.v.).

fulgor -ōris, m. (fulgeo), **1,** *lightning;* fulgores et tonitrua, Cic. ; **2,** *glitter, brilliancy, brightness;* armorum, Hor. ; candelabri, Cic. ; 3, transf., *brightness, glory;* nominis, Ov. ; honoris, Tac.

fulgŭr -ŭris, n. (fulgeo), **1,** *lightning,* Cic. ; **2,** *a thunderbolt,* Ov. ; condere fulgur, *to bury an object which has been struck by lightning,* Juv. ; **3,** poet. = fulgor, *brightness, brilliancy;* solis, Lucr. ; rapidum Aetnaeo fulgur ab igne jaci, Ov. (plur. fulgora, Cic.).

fulgŭrālis -e (fulgur), *relating* or *belonging to lightning;* libri, *treating of the* (religious) *significance of lightning,* Cic.

fulgŭrātor -ōris, m. (fulguro), *a haruspex who interpreted the omens from lightning,* Cic.

fulgŭrītus -a -um (fulgur), *struck by lightning,* Plaut.

fulgŭro, 1. (fulgur), *to lighten;* Jove fulgurante, ap. Cic.

fŭlĭca -ae, f. *a coot,* Verg.

fūlīgo -ĭnis, f. (root FU, whence also fumus), 1, *soot,* Cic. ; 2, *a powder used for darkening the eyebrows,* Juv.

fūlix -ĭcis, f. = fulica (q.v.).

fullo -ōnis, m. *a fuller, cloth-fuller,* Plaut.

fulmen -ĭnis, n. (orig. fulcmen, from fulgeo, and suffix -men). **I.** *a flash of lightning which strikes something, a thunderbolt;* fulmine percussus, Cic. ; ictu fulminis deflagrare, Cic. **II.** Transf., **A.** *a thunder-bolt, crushing calamity;* fortunae, Cic. ; duo fulmina domum perculerunt, Liv. **B.** *mighty* or *irresistible power;* verborum, Cic. ; so of heroes, duo fulmina imperii nostri, *the two Scipios,* Cic.

fulmĭnĕus -a -um (fulmen). **A.** Lit., *relating to lightning;* ignes, Ov. ; ictus, Hor. **B.** Transf., *slaying, murderous, destructive;* ensis, Verg. ; os apri, Ov.

fulmĭno, 1. (fulmen), *to lighten, to thunder and lighten;* Juppiter fulminans, Hor. ; impers., boreae de parte trucis quum fulminat, Verg. ; transf., Caesar fulminat bello, Verg.

fultūra -ae, f. (fulcio), *a support, prop, stay* (of food), Hor.

Fulvĭaster, v. Fulvius.

Fulvĭus -a -um, *name of a Roman gens of which the most celebrated members were* M. Fulvius Flaccus, *supporter of C. Gracchus,* and Fulvia, *wife of Clodius, and afterwards of Antonius.* **Fulvĭaster** -stri, m. *an imitator of* Fulvius (Postumius), Cic.

fulvus -a -um (root FUL, whence fulgeo), *dark* or *reddish yellow, tawny, yellowish brown* (of lions, wolves, sand, gold), Verg. ; caesaries, Verg.; aquila or ales Jovis (because of its yellow eyes), Verg.

fūmĕus -a -um (fumus), *smoky, full of smoke,* Verg.

fūmĭdus -a -um (fumus), *smoky, full of smoke;* taeda, Verg. ; altaria, Ov.

fūmĭfer -fĕra -fĕrum (fumus and fero), *smoke-bearing, smoky;* ignes, nox, Verg.

fūmĭfĭcus -a -um (fumus and facio), *causing smoke,* Ov.

fūmo, 1. (fumus), *to smoke, steam;* agger fumat, Caes. ; domus fumabat, *reeked with the odours of feasts,* Cic. ; equûm fumantia colla, Verg.

fūmōsus -a -um (fumus), *full of smoke, smoky, steaming, smoked;* arae, Ov. ; imagines, *figures of ancestors,* Cic.

fūmus -i, m. (root FU, whence also fuligo), *smoke, steam, vapour;* fumus ganearum, Cic. ; fumo excruciari, Cic. ; fumo dare signum, Liv. ; plur., fumi incendiorum procul videbantur, Caes. ; prov., vertere omne in fumum et cinerem, *to squander, consume,* Hor.

fūnālis -e (funis), *relating* or *belonging to a rope.* Subst., **fūnāle** -is, n., **1,** *the thong of a sling,* Liv. ; **2,** *a wax-torch,* Cic.

fūnambŭlus -i, m. (funis and ambulo), *a rope-dancer,* Ter.

functĭo -ōnis, f. (fungor), *a performance, performing, executing;* muneris, Cic.

funda -ae, f. (2. fundo), **1,** *a sling,* Caes. ; fundâ mittere glandes et lapides, Liv. ; **2,** *a casting-net,* Verg.

fundāmen -ĭnis, n. (1. fundo), *a foundation, base;* ponere or jacêre, Verg.

fundāmentum -i, n. (1. fundo), **1,** lit., *a foundation, base;* fundamenta jacere, Cic. ; a fundamentis diruere Pteleum, Liv. ; **2,** transf., *foundation, basis;* pietas fundamentum est omnium virtutum, Cic.

Fundānĭus -a -um, *name of a Roman gens.*

fundātor -ōris, m. (1. fundo), *a founder;* urbis, Verg.

fundātus -a -um (p. adj. from 1. fundo), *firm, durable;* fundatissima familia, Cic.

fundĭtor -ōris, m. (funda), *a light-armed soldier, furnished with a sling, a slinger;* gen. in plur., Caes. ; sing. collective, funditor Balearis, Liv.

fundĭtŭs, adv. (fundus). **I.** *from the ground,* **A.** Lit., monumenta delere, Cic. **B.** Transf., *completely, entirely;* evertere amicitiam, Cic. **II.** *at the bottom, below,* Lucr.

1. fundo, 1. (fundus). **I.** *to lay the foundation of, to found;* arces, Verg. ; urbem colonis, Verg. ; dente tenaci ancora fundabat naves, *fastened to the ground,* Verg. **II.** Transf., **A.** *to found;* accurate non modo fundata verum etiam exstructa disciplina, Cic. **B.** *to make firm, to strengthen;* urbem legibus, Verg. ; nostrum imperium, Cic.

2. fundo, fūdi, fūsum, 3. (root FUD, connected with χέω, χεύσω), *to pour, pour out.* **I.** Lit., **1,** of liquids, sanguinem e patera, Cic.; liquorem de patera, Hor. ; lacrimas, Verg. ; middle, *to pour;* ingentibus procellis fusus imber, Liv. ;

2, of bodies not liquid, **a,** *to pour out;* segetem in Tiberim, Liv. ; **b,** of metals, *to melt, cast;* quid fusum durius, Hor. ; **c,** *to sprinkle;* tempora multo mero, Tib. **II.** Transf., **A.** 1, *to throw to the ground,* often in partic., *thrown down, lying;* fusi sub remis nautae, Verg. ; **2,** milit. t. t., *to rout, defeat, scatter, put to flight;* hostes, Liv. ; middle, *to rush away;* turpi fugâ fundi, Liv. **B.** *to let loose;* **1,** middle, fundi, *to spread;* vitis funditur, Cic. ; **2, a,** *to discharge missiles;* tela, Verg. ; **b,** luna per fenestram se fundebat, *streamed through,* Verg. ; **3,** of persons, reflex., *to rush out;* plenis se portis, Verg. ; **4, a,** *to pour forth from the mouth, to utter;* sonos inanes, Cic.; esp. of poets, *to pour forth, compose;* versus hexametros ex tempore, Cic. ; **b,** *to give forth, to produce;* terra fundit fruges, Cic. ; quem Maia fudit, *gave birth to,* Verg. ; **c,** *to squander;* opes, Hor. **III.** Fig., **a,** middle, fundi, *to spread;* utrumque eorum fundi quoddamodo et quasi dilatari, Cic. ; **b,** *to pour forth;* multo vitam cum sanguine, Verg.

fundus -i, m. *the bottom* or *base of anything.* **I.** Gen., **1, a,** lit., armarii, Cic. ; aequora ciere fundo, *from the bottom,* Verg.; **b,** transf., largitio non habet fundum, *knows no bounds,* Cic. ; fundum fieri legis, *to sanction, authorise,* Cic. **II.** Esp., *the soil, a farm, estate,* Cic.

fūnēbris -e (funus), **1,** *relating* or *belonging to a funeral, funereal;* epulum, contio, Cic. ; subst., **fūnēbria** -ĭum, n. *funeral ceremonies,* Cic. ; **2,** *deadly, destructive, cruel, fatal;* bellum, Hor. ; munera, Ov.

fūnĕrĕus -a -um (funus), **1,** *relating to a funeral, funereal;* faces, Verg. ; **2,** *of that which causes* or *betokens death;* dextra, Ov. ; bubo, *ill-omened,* Ov.

fūnĕro, 1. (funus), **1,** *to bury solemnly, inter with funeral rites,* Plin. ; **2,** *to kill,* Hor.

fūnesto, 1. (funestus), *to defile* or *pollute with murder;* aras ac templa hostiis humanis, Cic.

fūnestus -a -um (funus). **I.** *filled with mourning, defiled by death;* agros funestos reddere, *to pollute with blood,* Lucr.; familia funesta, *in mourning,* Liv. **II.** *calamitous, mournful, disastrous, deadly;* tribunatus, Cic. ; fax, Cic. ; with dat., funesta reipublicae pestis, Cic.

fungor, functus sum, 3. dep. *to be busy, occupy oneself, be engaged with anything, to perform, execute, accomplish.* **I.** Gen., **a,** with abl., muneribus corporis, Cic. ; virtute fungi, *to show bravery,* Hor. ; munere aedilicio, *discharge the office of aedile,* Cic. ; vice cotis, *to serve instead of,* Hor. ; dapibus, *to take food,* Ov. ; sepulcro, *to bury,* Ov.; **b,** with acc., hominum officia, Tac. **II. a,** *to suffer;* mala multa, Lucr. ; **b,** *to complete, finish;* gen., functum esse morte, *to die,* Ov.

fungus -i, m. (σφόγγος, σπόγγος), **1,** *a mushroom, fungus,* Cic.; as a term of reproach applied to *a dull, stupid fellow,* Plaut. ; **2,** *a thief in the wick of a candle, a candle-snuff,* Verg.

fūnĭcŭlus -i, m. (dim. of funis), *a thin rope, cord, string;* funiculus a puppi religatus, Cic.

fūnis -is, m. (fem. Lucr. 2, 1154), *a rope, cord, line;* per funem demitti, Verg.; of ship's ropes, ancorarius funis, Caes. ; funes qui antennas ad malos religabant, Caes. ; *the rope of a rope-dancer;* per extentum funem ire, Hor. ; prov., ne currente retro funis eat rota, *that all your labour may not be wasted,* Hor. ; ducere, *to guide the rope*—i.e., *to command,* Hor. ; sequi, *to follow, obey,* Hor. ; reducere, *to change one's mind,* Pers.

fūnus -ĕris, n. *a funeral, obsequies, interment.* **I. A.** Lit., funus quo amici conveniunt ad exsequias cohonestandas, Cic.; funus alicui facere,

Cic.; ducere, Cic.; in funus venire, Cic.; funus celebrare, Liv. **B.** Meton., 1, *the corpse;* lacerum, Verg.; 2, *death;* crudeli funere exstinctus, Verg.; edere funera, *to kill,* Verg. **II.** Transf., *destruction, ruin;* reipublicae, Cic.; meton., *the persons who cause ruin;* paene funera reipublicae, *destroyers,* Cic.

fŭo, fŭi, fŭtūrus, etc., v. sum.

fūr, fūris, c. (φώρ), *a thief;* non fur, sed erepter, Cic.; fur nocturnus, Cic.; as a term of reproach to slaves, Verg.

fūrācĭtĕr, adv. (furax), *thievishly;* domos furacissime scrutari, Cic.

fūrax -ācis (1. furor), *inclined to steal, thievish;* homo avarus et furax, Cic.

furca -ae, f. (fero). **I.** *a two-pronged fork, pitch-fork;* furcā detrudere aliquem, Liv.; prov., naturam expellas furcā, tamen usque recurret, Hor. **II.** Transf., **A.** *a fork-shaped prop or pole;* valli furcaeque bicornes, Verg.; furcae duodenos ab terra spectacula alta sustinentes pedes, Liv. **B.** *an instrument of punishment put over the neck, to the two prongs of which the arms were tied, used to punish slaves and parricides,* Liv.; fig. ire sub furcam, Hor. **C.** *a narrow pass;* Furcae Caudinae, v. Caudium.

furcĭfer -fĕra -fĕrum (furca and fero), *one who carries the furca as a punishment,* a term of reproach usually applied to slaves, *gallows-bird,* Cic.

furcilla -ae, f. (dim. of furca), *a little fork;* prov., furcillā extrudi, *to be expelled by force,* Cic.

furcŭla -ae, f. (dim. of furca), 1, *a fork-shaped prop,* Liv.; 2, *a narrow pass;* furculae Caudinae, Liv.

fŭrentĕr, adv. (furens), *furiously;* irasci, Cic.

furfur -ŭris, m. 1, *bran,* Plaut.; 2, *scales, scurf on the skin,* Plin.

fŭrĭa -ae, f., usually plur. (furo). **I.** *rage, madness, passion, fury;* muliebres furiae, Liv.; ventorum furiae, Verg. **II.** Personif., **Fŭrĭa** -ae, f. and gen. plur., **Fŭrĭae** -ārum, f. **A.** *the* Furies (Alecto, Megaera, Tisiphone), *the deities who avenged crimes and tormented criminals,* esp. *parricides;* eos (parricidas) agitent Furiae, Cic. **B.** Transf., of persons, a, illa Furia, *Clodius,* Cic.; b, *inciter to crime;* hunc juvenem tamquam furiam facemque huius belli, Liv.

fŭrĭālis -e (furia), 1, *furious, raging, terrible;* vox, Cic.; incessus, Liv.; Erichtho, *inspired with Bacchic fury,* Ov.; 2, *belonging to the Furies;* membra, Verg.

fŭrĭālĭtĕr, adv. (furialis), *furiously, madly,* Ov.

fŭrĭbundus -a -um (furo), 1, *raging, furious;* furibundus homo ac perditus, Cic.; 2, *inspired;* praedictio, Cic.

Fŭrīna -ae, f. *an ancient Roman goddess;* hence adj., **Fŭrīnālis** -e, *of or belonging to* Furina; subst., **Fŭrīnālĭa** -ĭum, n. *the festival of Furina.*

fŭrĭo, 1. (furia), *to make furious, cause to rage, infuriate;* matres equorum, Hor.; partic., furiatus, *raging;* mens, Verg.

fŭrĭōsē, adv. (furiosus), *furiously, madly;* aliquid furiose facere, Cic.

fŭrĭōsus -a -um, adj. with compar. and superl. (furia), *raging, raving, mad, furious;* mulier jam non morbo sed scelere furiosa, Cic.; transf., of things, cupiditas, Cic.; tibia, *inspiring,* Ov.

Fŭrĭus -a -um, *name of a Roman gens, the most famous member of which was* M. Furius Camillus, *who freed Rome from the Gauls.* Adj., **Fŭrĭānus** -a -um, *of or belonging to* Furius.

furnārĭa -ae, f. (furnus), *the trade of a baker,* Suet.

furnus -i, m. (root FOR, cf. fornus), *an oven, a bakehouse,* Ov., Hor.

fŭro, 3. (connected with θύω). **I.** *to rage, rave, be mad;* furere se simulavit, Cic. **II.** Transf., **A.** Of persons, a, *to rage, be furious;* Catilina furens audaciā, Cic.; furens Neptunus, *the raging waves,* Hor.; with acc., furorem, Verg.; with acc. and infin., (Clodius) furebat a Racilio se contumaciter urbaneque vexatum, Cic.; b, *to give oneself up to any violent passion,* esp. *love;* libidinibus inflammatus et furens, Cic.; furere aliquā, *to be madly in love with,* Hor. **B.** Of inanimate objects, tempestas or ignis furit, Verg.

1. fŭror, 1. dep. (fur), 1, *to steal, pilfer;* haec quae rapuit et furatus est, Cic.; librum ab aliquo, (of plagiarists), Cic.; 2, transf., a, *to obtain by stealth;* civitatem, Liv.; b, *to withdraw secretly;* oculos labori, Verg.; c, *to make secret attacks,* Tac.

2. fŭror -ōris, m. (furo). **I.** *madness, raving, insanity;* ira furor brevis est, Hor. **II.** Transf., **A.** Of persons, 1, a, of the Bacchic fury, majorem orsa furorem, Verg.; fig., versatur mihi ante oculos aspectus Cethegi et furor in vestra caede bacchantis, Cic.; b, *inspiration, inspired rage;* negat sine furore Democritus poetam magnum esse posse, Cic.; c, of martial rage, sic animis juvenum furor additus, Verg.; personif., Furor, as an attendant of Mars, Verg.; d, *the rage of anger;* tum regia Juno acta furore gravi, Verg.; e, *passionate love;* intus erat furor igneus, Ov.; meton., *the object of passion;* sive mihi Phyllis, sive esset Amyntas, seu quicumque furor, Verg.; 2, *delusion, frenzy, rage;* a, idem furor et Cretenses lacerabat, Liv.; b, *rage, tumult, sedition, revolt;* furor multitudinis, Cic.; alicuius furorem frangere, Cic. **B.** Of inanimate objects, furores et rabies tanta caeli marisque, Verg.

furtim, adv. (fur), *by stealth, stealthily, secretly* (opp. palam), Cic.

furtīvē, adv. (furtivus), *stealthily, secretly, furtively,* Ov.

furtīvus -a -um (furtum), 1, *stolen;* strigilis, Hor.; 2, *secret, concealed, furtive;* iter per Italiam, Cic.; amor, Verg.

furtum -i, n. (fur). **I. A.** Lit., *a theft;* furtum facere alicuius rei, Cic.; furti damnari, Cic. **B.** Meton., *the thing stolen;* furta reddere, Cic. **II.** Transf. **A.** *anything secret or concealed, hidden trick or deceit;* furto laetatus inani, Verg.; hence furto, adv.= furtim, *secretly,* Verg. **B.** 1, *secret or stolen love,* Verg.; 2, in war, *a stratagem, secret attack;* parva furta per occasionem temptantes, Liv.

fŭruncŭlus -i, m. (dim. of fur), *a little thief, a little rascal,* Cic.

furvus -a -um (from root FUR, whence also fuscus, connected with fumus, fuligo), *dark-coloured, dark, black;* a, gen., equus, Ov.; b, of the lower world and things relating to it, antrum, Ov.; Proserpina, Hor.

fuscĭna -ae, f. (connected with furca), *a three-pronged fork, trident,* Cic.

fusco, 1. act. (fuscus), *to make dark, darken, blacken;* dentes, Ov.

fuscus -a -um (orig. furscus, from root FUR, whence furvus), 1, *dark-coloured, dark, black;* cornix, Cic.; purpura paene fusca, Cic.; 2, applied to the voice, *hoarse, rough;* genus vocis, Cic.

fūsē, adv. with compar. (fusus), *at length, copiously, diffusely;* dicere, Cic.

fūsĭlis -e (2. fundo), *melted, molten, liquid;* aurum, Ov.; ferventes fusili (*softened*), ex argilla glandes, Caes.

fūsĭo -ōnis, f. (2. fundo), *a pouring-out, out-pouring;* mundum esse eius (dei) animi fusionem universam, Cic.

fustis -is, abl. -i and -e, m. *a stick, staff, cudgel, club,* Cic.

fustŭārĭum -ĭi, n. (sc. supplicium, from fustis), *beating to death with sticks, the military punishment for desertion;* fustuarium merere or mereri, Cic.

1. **fūsus** -a -um (p. adj. of 2. fundo), *spread out, extended;* 1, a, of places, campi fusi² in omnem partem, Verg.; b, of bodies, sunt fusa et candida corpora, *fleshy,* Liv.; 2, *let loose;* a, *flowing free;* crines, Verg.; b, of discourse, *diffuse;* genus sermonis, Cic.

2. **fūsus** -i, m., *a spindle;* fusum versare, Ov.; as an attribute of the Parcae, suis dixerunt, currite fusis, Verg.

fūtĭlis -e (connected with 2. fundo), 1, *that cannot hold* or *contain;* glacies, brittle, Verg.; 2, *vain, worthless, futile, good for nothing;* haruspices, Cic.; sententiae, Cic.

fūtĭlĭtas -ātis, f. (futilis), *worthlessness, folly, silliness,* Cic.

fūtūrus -a -um (partic. fut. of fuo, used as the partic. of sum), *future, about to be;* res, Cic.; tempus, Cic. Subst., **fūtūrum** -i, n. *the future;* haud ignara futuri, Verg.; videre in futurum, Liv.; plur., **fūtūra** -ōrum, n. *the future;* futura prospicere, Cic.

G.

G, g, the seventh letter of the Latin alphabet, originally represented by C, introduced into the Latin alphabet about the time of the Second Punic War. For the use of this letter in abbreviations, see Table of Abbreviations.

Găbăli -ōrum, m. and **Găbăles** -um, m. *a people in the south-east of Gallia Aquitania.*

Găbĭi -ōrum, m. *a very ancient city of Latium, between Rome and Praeneste.* Adj., **Găbīnus** -a -um, *Gabinian;* via, *from Gabii to Rome,* Liv.; Juno, *honoured in Gabii,* Verg.; cinctus, *a particular mode of wearing the toga, in which one end was passed over the head, and the other round the waist,* Liv.

Găbīnĭus -a -um, *name of a Roman gens, the most celebrated member of which was* A. Gabinius, *who restored the Egyptian king Ptolemaeus Auletes to his kingdom;* hence adj., *Gabinian; lex, a law giving extraordinary military power to Pompeius.* Adj., **Găbīnĭānus** -a -um, *of or belonging to Gabinius.*

Gādēs and **Gādis** -ĭum, f. *a town in the south-west of Spain, now Cadiz.* **Gādītānus** -a -um, *of or belonging to Gades.*

gaesum -i, n. *a very strong and heavy javelin, originally a Gaulish weapon,* Caes.

Gaetūli -ōrum, m. *a people in north-west Africa.* Adj., **Gaetūlus** -a -um, poet., *African, Libyan.*

Gāius and **Gāia**, v. Caius.

Gălaesus -i, m. *a river in the south of Italy, now Galaso.*

Gălătae -ārum, m. *a Celtic people settled in a part of Phrygia.* Hence, **Gălătĭa** -ae, f. *the country of the Galatae.*

Galba -ae, m. *a cognomen of the Sulpician gens.*

galbănĕus -a -um (galbanum), *of or relating to galbanum,* Verg

galbănum -i, n. (χαλβάνη), *the resinous sap of a Syrian plant* (bubon galbanum, Linn.), Plin.

galbănus -a -um, *greenish yellow, yellowish,* Juv.

galbĕum -i, n. *a kind of fillet* or *bandage for the arm,* Suet.

galbĭnus -a, -um, *greenish-yellow;* subst., **galbĭnum** -i, n. *a greenish-yellow garment,* Juv.

gălĕa -ae, f. *a helmet* (orig. of leather, opp. cassis, of metal), Caes., Cic.

gălĕo, 1. (galea), *to put on a helmet;* partic., galeatus, *armed with a helmet;* Minerva, Cic.

Gălĕōtae -ārum, m. (Γαλεῶται), *a body of Sicilian seers,* Cic.

gălērĭcŭlum -i, n. (dim. of galerum), 1, *a scull-cap,* Mart.; 2, *a wig,* Suet.

gălērĭtus -a -um (galerus), 1, *wearing a skull-cap of fur,* Prop.; 2, transf., galerita avis, *the crested lark* (alauda cristata, Linn.)

gălērum -i, n. (**gălērus** -i, m.), 1, *a cap of fur, skull-cup,* Verg.; 2, *a wig,* Juv.

Galesus = Galaesus (q.v.).

galla -ae, f. *the gall-nut, oak-apple,* Verg.

Galli -ōrum, m. *the Gauls, a Celtic people, living to the west of the Rhine and in the north of Italy as well as in Phrygia;* sing., **Gallus** -i, m. *a Gaul,* and **Galla** -ae, f. *a Gaulish woman.* Hence, **A. Gallĭa** -ae, f. *Gaul, the land of the Gauls;* cisalpina, or ulterior, Lombardy; transalpina, or ulterior, *Gaul north of the Alps,* Caes. **B. Gallĭcānus** -a -um, *belonging to Gallia provincia, the south-east part of Gaul.* **C. Gallĭcus** -a -um, *Gaulish.*

gallĭambus -i, m. *a song of the priests of Cybele,* Mart.

gallīna -ae, f. (1. gallus), *a hen, fowl,* Cic.

gallīnācĕus -a -um (gallina), *relating to poultry;* gallus, Cic.; m. *a cock.*

gallīnārĭus -a -um (gallina), *relating* or *belonging to poultry.* Subst., **gallīnārĭus** -ii, m. *one who has the care of poultry,* Cic.

Gallograecĭa -ae, f. = Galatia (q.v.). Hence, **Gallograecus** -a -um, *Galatian.*

1. **gallus** -i, m. *a cock, dunghill cock;* gallorum cantus, *cock-crowing,* Cic.

2. **Gallus** -i, m. *a Gaul,* v. Galli.

3. **Gallus** -i, m. (Γάλλος), 1, *a Phrygian river, now Kadshasu;* hence, adj., **Gallĭcus** -a -um, poet. = Phrygian, Trojan, Prop.; 2 (hence), **Galli** -ōrum, m. *the priests of Cybele;* sing., **Gallus** -i, m. and **Galla** -ae, f.; hence, adj., **Gallĭcus** -a -um, turba, *the priests of Isis,* whose worship resembled that of Cybele, Ov.

4. **Gallus** -i, m. Cornelius (69–26 B.C.), *a poet and orator, friend of Vergil.*

Gāmēlĭon -ōnis, m. (Γαμηλιών), *the seventh month of the Attic year, corresponding to our January,* Cic.

gānĕa -ae, f. and **gānĕum** -i, n. (connected with γάνος, γάνυμαι), *a low eating-house;* meton., *debauchery,* Cic.

gānĕo -ōnis, m. (ganea or ganeum), *a profligate person, debauchee, glutton,* Cic.

Gangărĭdae and **Gangărĭdes** -um, m. *a people in India, on the Ganges.*

Gangēs -is, m. (Γάγγης), *the river Ganges.* Adj., **Gangētĭcus** -a -um, and **Gangētis** -ĭdis, f. poet. = *Indian,* Ov.

gannĭo, 4. *to yelp, whine, to snarl, growl, grumble,* Plaut., Ter.

gannītus -ūs, m. (gannio), 1, *a barking,*

yelping, snarling of dogs, Lucr.; **2,** applied to men, Mart.

Gănўmēdēs -is, m. (Γανυμήδης), *son of the Trojan king Tros, carried off on account of his beauty to heaven by an eagle, and made the cup-bearer of Jove.*

Gărămantes -um, m. (Γαράμαντες), *a people in the interior of Africa.* Hence, **Gărămantis** -Idis, f.= *African,* Verg.

Gargānus -i, m. *a mountain of Apulia,* now *Monte di S. Angelo.* Adj., **Gargānus** -a -um, *of or belonging to Garganus.*

Gargăphīē -ēs, f. (Γαργαφία), *a valley of Boeotia, sacred to Diana.*

Gargăra -ōrum, n. (Γάργαρα), *the highest peak of Mount Ida in Mysia, with a town of the same name.*

Gargettus -i, m. (Γαργηττός), *a deme in Attica, birthplace of Epicurus,* hence called Gargettius.

Gargĭlĭus -ĭi, m. *a Roman name.*

găron = garum (q.v.).

garrĭo -īvi and -ĭi -ītum, 4. (connected with γηρύω), *to chatter, prate, babble;* a, intransit., in iis philosophi garrire coeperunt, Cic.; b, transit., quicquid in buccam (sc. venerit), Cic.

garrŭlĭtas -ātis, f. (garrulus), *chattering,* of magpies, garrulitas rauca, Ov.

garrŭlus -a -um (garrio). **I.** Lit., 1, of men, *talkative, garrulous, chattering, babbling;* garrula lingua, Ov.; 2, applied to animals, cornix, Ov.; hirundo, Verg. **II.** Transf., *noisy, sounding;* rivus, Ov.; lyra, Tib.

Gărumna -ae, f. *a river in Gaul,* now *the Garonne.* Hence, **Gărumni** -ōrum, m. *the people living on the Garonne.*

gărum (găron), -i, n. *a costly fish-sauce,* Ov.

Gates -um, m. *a people in Aquitania.*

gaudĕo, gāvīsus sum, 2. (root GA, ΓΑ, whence γαίω, γαῦρος, γηθέω), *to rejoice, find pleasure or delight in anything, be glad, delight in.* **I.** Lit., **A.** Gen., a, intransit., si est nunc ullus gaudendi locus, Cic.; poet. with partic., gaudent scribentes, *write with pleasure,* Hor.; mihi gaudeo, *rejoice for my part,* Cic.; gen. with abl. of cause, correctione gaudere, Cic.; b, transit., gen. with acc. and infin., quae perfecta esse gaudeo, Cic.; poet. with infin. alone, laedere gaudes, Hor.; with quod, sane gaudeo quod te interpellavi, Cic. **B.** Esp., 1, in sinu gaudere, *to rejoice in secret,* Cic.; 2, infin., gaudere as a salutation, Celso gaudere refer, *take my greeting to Celsus,* Hor. **II.** Transf., of inanimate objects, *to delight in;* scena gaudens miraculis, Liv.

gaudĭum -ĭi, n. (gaudeo), *joy, gladness, delight* (as an inward feeling, while laetitia denotes the external expression). **I.** Lit., gaudio, (*for joy*) lacrimare, triumphare, Cic.; exsultare, Cic.; aliquem gaudio afficere, Liv.; gaudia corporis, Sall. **II.** Meton., *that which produces delight;* sua gaudia, Verg.

Gaurus -i, m. *a mountain in Campania,* now *Monte Gauro.*

gausăpa -ae, f., and **gausăpē** -is, n., and **gausăpum** -i, n., and **gausăpes** -is, m. (γαυσάπης), *a woollen cloth, with a long nap on one side, frieze,* Ov., Hor.

gāza -ae, f. *the royal treasure of Persia, treasure generally, riches, wealth;* regia, Cic.

Gĕla -ae, f. (Γέλα), *town on the south coast of Sicily.* Hence, 1, adj., **Gĕlōus** -a -um, *of or belonging to Gela;* 2, **Gĕlenses** -ĭum, m. *the inhabitants of Gela.*

Gĕlās -ae, voc. Gela, m. (Γέλας), *a river on the south coast of Sicily.*

gĕlăsĭnus -i, m. (γελασῖνος), *a dimple or the cheek,* Mart.

gĕlĭdē, adv. (gelidus), *coldly, languidly, feebly,* Hor.

gĕlĭdus -a -um (gelu), *cold, icy-cold, frosty, icy.* **I.** Lit., aqua, Cic.; humor, *ice,* Verg. Subst., **gĕlĭda** -ae, f. *ice-cold water,* Hor. **II.** Transf., applied to the chill of old age, fear, death, etc.; sanguis, Verg.; mors, Hor.; metus, Ov.

Gellĭus -a -um, *name of a Roman gens, the most famous member of which was A.* Gellius, *a grammarian of the second century* A.D., *one of whose works,* Noctes Atticae, *is still extant.*

gĕlo, 1. (gelu). **I.** Transit., *to cause to freeze, to freeze;* pavido gelantur pectore, Juv. **II.** Intransit., *to freeze,* Plin.

Gĕlōni -ōrum, m. (Γελωνοί), *a Scythian or Sarmatian people on the Borysthenes, who tattooed themselves.* Sing., **Gĕlōnus** -i, m., coll. *the Geloni,* Verg.

gĕlu, n., **gĕlus** -ūs, m., **gĕlum** -i, n., 1, *frost, icy cold;* rura gelu claudit hiems, Verg.; 2, *the chill of age, death, fear,* etc., Verg.

gĕmĕbundus -a -um (gemo), *groaning, sighing,* Ov.

gĕmellĭpăra -ae, fem. adj. (gemelli and pario), *twin-bearing;* dea, or diva, Latona, Ov.

gĕmellus -a -um (dim. of geminus), *twin, twin-born.* **A.** Lit., fratres, proles, Ov.; hence subst., **gĕmellus** -i, m., *a twin,* Cat.; plur., gemelli, *twins,* Ov. **B.** Transf., a, *paired, double;* quam (legionem) factam ex duabus gemellam appellabat, Caes.; b, *resembling each other like twins, similar;* par nobile fratrum nequitiā et nugis pravorum et amore gemellum, Hor.

gĕmĭnātĭo -ōnis, f. (gemino), *a doubling;* verborum, Cic.

gĕmĭno, 1. (geminus). **I.** Transit., 1, *to double;* victoriae laetitiam, Liv.; aera, *to strike together,* Hor.; partic., **gĕmĭnātus** -a -um, *doubled;* sol, Cic.; 2, *to repeat, unite closely;* geminata ac duplicata ponantur, Cic.; *to pair;* serpentes avibus, Hor. **II.** Intransit., *to be double,* Lucr.

gĕmĭnus -a -um (perhaps from geno = gigno), *twin, twin-born.* **I.** Lit., fratres, Cic. Subst., **gĕmĭni** -ōrum, m. *twins,* especially *the twins* Castor *and* Pollux. **II.** Transf., **A.** a, *doubled, of double nature;* Chiron, *the Centaur, half man and half horse,* Ov.; Cecrops, *half Greek and half Egyptian,* Ov.; b, *doubled = two;* lumen, Cic.; acies, Verg. **B.** *similar, alike;* geminus et simillimus nequitiā, Cic.

gĕmĭtus -ūs, m. (gemo), *a sigh, groan.* **I.** **A.** Lit., gemitus fit, Cic.; gemitum or gemitus dare, Ov. **B.** Meton., *pain,* Verg. **II.** Transf., *a groaning, roaring;* pelagi, Verg.

gemma -ae, f. (probably connected with γέμω). **I.** *a bud or eye of a plant,* Cic. **II.** a *jewel, gem, precious stone.* **A.** Lit., Cic. **B.** Meton., 1, *a thing made of or adorned with jewels;* a, *a goblet;* bibere gemmā, Verg.; b, a *seal-ring, seal;* gemmā signari, Ov.; 2, gemmae, *the eyes in a peacock's tail,* Ov.

gemmātus -a -um (gemma), *set or adorned with jewels;* monilia, Ov.

gemmĕus -a -um (gemma), *made or set with jewels, gemmed;* trulla, Cic.

gemmĭfer -fĕra -fĕrum (gemma and fero), *bearing or producing jewels;* mare, Prop.

gemmo, 1. (gemma). **I.** *to bud;* vites, Cic.

II. A. *to be set with jewels;* sceptra gemmantia, Ov. **B.** *to glitter like jewels;* herbae gemmantes rore recenti, Lucr.

gĕmo -ŭi -ĭtum, 3. **I.** Intransit., **A.** Lit., *to sigh, groan;* desiderio alicuius, Cic. **B.** poet., transf., a, of animals, of the lion, *to roar,* Lucr.; of the turtle-do7e, *to coo,* Verg.; b, of inanimate objects, *to groan, creak;* gementis litora Bospori, Hor.; gemuit sub pondere cymba, Verg. **II.** Transit., *to sigh or groan over, lament, bemoan;* aliquid, Cic.; Ityn, Hor.

Gĕmōniae -ārum, f. (sc. scalae), or more rarely Gemoniae scalae, *a flight of steps from the Aventine hill to the Tiber, down which the dead bodies of malefactors were thrown.*

gĕna -ae, f. usually plur. (cf. γένυς). **I.** *the cheek,* Cic. **II.** Meton., a, *the eyelid,* Enn.; b, *the eye-hole,* Ov.; c, *the eyes;* et patiar fossis lumen abire genis, Ov.

Gĕnăbum -i, n. *a town in Gaul, the capital of the Carnutes, now Orleans.* Adj., **Gĕnăbensis** -e, *of or belonging to Genabum.*

Gĕnauni -ōrum, m. (Γεναῦνοι), *a people in Vindelicia.*

Genāva -ae, f. *a town of the Allobroges on the borders of the Helvetii, now Geneva.*

gĕnĕālŏgus -i, m. (γενεαλόγος), *a genealogist,* Cic.

gĕner -ĕri, m. *a son-in-law,* Cic.; *grand-daughter's husband,* Tac.; sometimes = *brother-in-law,* Nep.

gĕnĕrālis -e (genus), 1, *relating or belonging to a kind or genus, generic;* constitutio, Cic.; 2, *general;* quoddam decorum, Cic.

gĕnĕrālĭtĕr adv. (generalis), *in general, generally,* Cic.

gĕnĕrasco, 3. (genero), *to be generated, to be produced,* Lucr.

gĕnĕrātim, adv. (genus), 1, *according to kinds or classes;* copias generatim constituere, Caes.; 2, *in general, generally;* loqui de aliqua re, Cic.

gĕnĕrātor -ōris, m. (genero), *a begetter, producer;* nosse generatores suos optime poterant, Cic.

gĕnĕro, 1. (genus), *to beget, produce, create, cause to exist, bring to life, generate;* deus hominem generavit, Cic.; Herculis stirpe generatus, Cic.; quale portentum nec Jubae tellus generat, Hor.

gĕnĕrōsē, adv. (generosus), *nobly;* perire, Hor.

gĕnĕrōsus -a -um (genus). **A.** 1, *of noble birth, noble;* virgo, Cic.; 2, applied to animals, plants, or inanimate objects, *excellent in kind, noble, of superior quality, well-bred;* pecus, Verg.; vinum, Hor.; of abstractions, ortus amicitiā, Cic. **B.** Transf., *noble, magnanimous;* virtus, Cic.; mens, Ov.

gĕnĕsis -is, f. (γένεσις), *the constellation which presides over one's birth,* Juv.

gĕnĕtīvus (gĕnĭtīvus) -a -um (geno = gigno), 1, *inborn, innate;* imago, Ov.; nomina, *family names,* Ov.; 2, casus, *the genitive case.*

gĕnĕtrix -trīcis, f. (genitor). **A.** *one who brings forth or bears, a mother;* magna deum genetrix, Cybele, Verg. **B.** Transf., *she that produces;* frugum, Ceres, Ov.

gĕniālis -e (genius), *of or belonging to the genius.* **I.** *relating to the genius of marriage, nuptial;* lectus, *the marriage-bed,* and subst. **gĕniālis** -is, m. (sc. torus), *the marriage-bed,* Liv. **II.** *relating to the genius as partaking in enjoyment, pleasant, joyful, gay, delightful;* festum, Ov.; hiems, Verg.

gĕnĭālĭtĕr, adv. (genialis), *jovially, gaily,* Ov.

gĕnĭcŭlātus -a -um (geniculum), *knotty, full of knots;* culmus, Cic.

gĕnĭcŭlum -i, n. (dim. of genu), 1, *the knee,* Varr.; 2, *a knot of a plant,* Plin.

gĕnista (gĕnesta) -ae, f. *the plant broom,* Verg.

gĕnĭtābĭlis -e (geno = gigno), *relating to production or birth, fruitful, productive,* Lucr.

gĕnĭtālis -e (geno = gigno), *belonging to birth, generation, generating, producing, fruitful;* 1, dies, *birthday,* Tac.; 2, subst., **Gĕnĭtālis** -is, f. *surname of Diana as presiding over births,* Hor.

gĕnĭtālĭtĕr, adv. (genitalis), *in a fruitful manner,* Lucr.

gĕnĭtīvus, v. gĕnĕtīvus.

gĕnĭtor -ōris, m. (geno = gigno), 1, *a begetter, father,* Cic.; deûm, Jupiter, Ov.; urbis, Romulus, Ov.; 2, *producer;* quae genitor produxerit usus, Hor.

gĕnĭtūra -ae, f. (geno = gigno), 1, *a begetting, engendering, bringing forth,* Plin.; 2, *the constellation which presides over a birth,* Suet.

gĕnĭus -ii, m. (geno = gigno), 1, *the guardian spirit of a man or place, a genius;* genium piare or placare, Hor.; genium curare vino, *to enjoy oneself with,* Hor.; December geniis acceptus (because of rest from toil in the fields), Ov.; 2, *talent, genius,* Juv.

gĕno = gigno (q.v.).

gens, gentis, f. (geno, old form of gigno). **I.** *a clan, a number of families connected together by a common descent and the use of the same gentile name* (orig. only patrician, after the establishment of connubium between patricians and plebeians, plebeian also). **A.** a, lit., vir patriciae gentis, Cic.; gens Cornelia, Liv.; Peruvius, sine gente, *of low origin,* Hor.; patricii majorum (*senators appointed by Romulus*), et minorum (*appointed by Tarquin*), gentium, Cic.; *a breed or species of animals,* Cic.; b, transf., dii majorum gentium, *the supreme or superior gods,* Cic.; dii minorum gentium, *the inferior,* Cic. **B.** (Poet.) Meton., *offspring, descendant;* vigilasne, poeta gens, Aenea? Verg. **II.** *a people, tribe, nation,* **A.** 1, lit., exterae nationes et gentes, Cic.; Suevorum, Caes.; 2, transf., a, *a district, canton;* ipsum in eam gentem iturum, Liv.; b, partitive genit., ubinam gentium sumus? *where in the world are we?* Cic. **B.** gentes, *foreigners,* Tac. **III.** = genus, gens humana, *the human race,* Cic.

gentĭcus -a -um (gens), *belonging to a nation, national,* Tac.

gentīlĭcĭus -a -um (gentilis), *belonging to a particular gens;* sacra, Liv.; sacrificia, Cic.

gentīlis -e (gens). **I.** *belonging to a gens, gentile;* manus, *of the 300 Fabii,* Ov. Subst., **gentīlis** -is, m. *a clansman, a person of the same gens,* Cic.; plur., Cic. **II.** *belonging to the same country, national;* religio, Tac.

gentīlĭtas -ātis, f. (gentilis), *relationship between the members of a gens,* Cic.

gĕnu -ūs, n. (γόνυ), *the knee,* Cic.; accidere genibus alicuius, Liv.; attingere alicuius genu, Liv.

Gĕnŭa -ae, f. *coast-town in Liguria, now Genoa.*

gĕnŭāle -is, n. (genu), *a knee-band, garter,* Ov

1. **gĕnŭīnus** -a -um (geno = gigno), *natural, innate;* genuinae domesticaeque virtutes. Cic.

2. gĕnŭīnus -a -um (genae), *relating or belonging to the cheek* or *jaw;* dentes, *the back-teeth,* Cic. Subst., **gĕnŭīnus** -i, m. *a jaw-tooth,* Juv.

1. gĕnus -ĕris, n. (root GEN, whence geno = gigno and γένος). **I.** *birth, descent, origin,* esp. *of high birth;* generis auctor, *father,* Ov.; genus patricium, Liv.; plebeium, Liv.; maternum, paternum, Cic.; of animals, Ov. **II.** *race.* **A.** 1, *nation, stock;* Hispanum, Liv.; 2, a, *family, house;* genus Aemilium, Fabium, Liv.; genere regio natum esse, Cic.; b, *offspring, descendant,* and collectively, *descendants;* genus deorum (of Aeneas), Verg.; 3, *sex;* genus virile, muliebre, Cic. **B.** 1, of living beings, a, *race, kind;* genus humanum, Cic.; b, (a) of persons, *class, sort, kind;* omnis generis homines, Cic.; (β) of animals, *species, class;* multa genera ferarum, Caes.; 2, of things, a, lit., *kind, variety, sort;* omne genus frugum, Liv.; id genus imperii, Cic.; philosoph. t. t., *genus* in logic, genus universum in species certas partiri, Cic.; b, *fashion, manner, way;* tota domus in omni genere diligens, Cic.

2. gĕnus -ūs = genu (q.v.).

Gĕnŭsus -i, m. *a river on the borders of Macedonia,* now *Iskumi.*

gĕŏgrăphĭa -ae, f. (γεωγραφία), *geography,* Cic.

gĕŏmĕtres -ae, m. (γεωμέτρης), *a geometer,* Cic.

gĕŏmĕtrĭa -ae, f. (γεωμετρία), *geometry,* Cic.

gĕŏmĕtrĭcus -a -um (γεωμετρικός), *geometrical;* formae, *figures,* Cic. Subst., **gĕŏmĕtrĭca** -ōrum, n. *geometry;* geometrica didicisse, Cic.

gĕŏrgĭcus -a -um (γεωργικός), *agricultural.* Subst., **Gĕŏrgĭca** -ōrum, n. *the Georgics of Vergil.*

Gĕraestĭcus portus, *a harbour near Teos, in Ionia.*

Gĕraestŏs and -ŭs -i, f. (Γεραιστός), *seaport town in Euboea.*

Gergŏvĭa -ae, f. *town of the Arverni in Gallia Aquitania.*

Germălus (Cermălus) -i, m. *a part of the Palatine Hill at Rome.*

germānē, adv. (germanus), *faithfully, honestly;* rescribere, Cic.

Germāni -ōrum, m. *the Germans;* hence, 1. **Germānus** -a -um, *German;* 2. **Germānĭa** -ae, f. *Germany;* superior, inferior, Tac.; plur., Germaniae, Tac.; 3. **Germānĭcus** -a -um, *German.* Subst., **Germānĭcus** -i, m. as a surname (on account of his victories over the Germans), Germanicus Caesar, *son of Drusus, and nephew of Tiberius.*

germānĭtas -ātis (germanus), 1, *the relationship between brothers and sisters, brotherhood, sisterhood,* Cic.; 2, *the connexion between cities which are colonies of the same mother-city,* Liv.

1. germānus -a -um (like germen, from geno = gigno). **A.** *having the same parents or at least the same father;* frater, soror, Cic. Subst., a, **germānus** -i, m. *own brother;* b, **germāna** -ae, f. *own sister,* Verg. **B.** Transf., a, *brotherly, sisterly;* in germanum modum, Plaut.; b, *genuine, real, true;* scio me asinum germanum fuisse, Cic.; justitia, Cic.

2. Germānus -a -um, v. Germani.

germen -ĭnis, n. (perhaps from geno = gigno and suffix -men, orig. genmen, then gesmen, germen, cf. carmen), 1, *a bud, sprout, twig,* Verg.; 2, *offspring,* Ov.

germĭno, 1. (germen), *to sprout forth,* Hor.

1. gĕro, gessi, gestum, 3. *to carry.* **I.** Gen., **A.** Lit., saxa in muros, Liv. **B.** Transf., 1, se gerere, *to behave oneself, to conduct oneself;* se honeste, Cic.; with pro (= as) and the abl., ita se jam tum pro cive gessisse, Cic.; 2, *to conduct, manage;* quid negotii geritur, Cic.; negotium, or rem, bene, or male gerere, Cic.; rem or res gerere (of generals), *to hold the command;* Cnaeus terrā, Publius navibus rem gereret, Liv.; also rem gerere, *to fight,* Liv.; res gestae, *exploits,* esp., *warlike exploits,* Cic.; negotii gerentes, *business people,* Cic.; esp., a, *to hold some public office, to hold, to manage;* rempublicam gerere atque administrare, Cic.; magistratum, Cic.; b, *bellum gerere, to wage war,* cum aliquo, or adversus aliquem, or in aliquem, Cic.; 3, prae se gerere = prae se ferre, *to exhibit, manifest;* utilitatem, Cic. **II.** Esp., *to carry on oneself, to have.* **A.** Lit., 1, gen., hastam, Verg.; 2, *to bear, produce;* platani malos gessere, Verg. **B.** Transf., 1, personam alicuius gerere, *to act the part of,* Cic.; 2, amicitiam, *to entertain,* Cic.

2. gĕro -ōnis, m. (1. gero), *a carrier,* Plaut.

Gĕrōnĭum -ĭi, n. *town in Apulia Daunia* or *Samnium.*

gerrae -ārum, f. (γέῤῥα), *wattled twigs,* Varr.; transf., *trifles, nonsense,* Plaut.

gerro -ōnis, m. (gerrae), *a trifler, idler,* Ter.

gĕrŭlus -i, m. (1. gero), *a porter, carrier,* Hor.

Gēryōn (Gēryo) -ōnis, m. and **Gēryŏnes** -ae, m. (Γηρυών and Γηρυόνης), myth., *a king with three bodies, living in the island of Erythia, whose oxen were carried off by Hercules.*

gestāmen -ĭnis, n. (gesto), 1, *that which is carried either as a burden or an ornament;* clipeus gestamen Abantis, Verg.; 2, *that in or on which anything is carried, a litter,* Tac.

gestĭcŭlor, 1. dep. (from gesticulus, dim. of gestus), *to make pantomimic gestures, gesticulate, to represent* or *express by pantomime,* Suet.

1. gestĭo -ōnis, f. (1. gero), *management, performance;* negotii, Cic.

2. gestĭo -ivi and -ĭi -ītum, 4. (gestus), 1, *to exult, to be cheerful, lively, to be transported;* laetitiā, Cic.; voluptate, Cic.; animus gestiens rebus secundis, Liv.; 2, *to desire passionately, be eager;* with infin., scire omnia, Cic.; absol., studio lavandi, Verg.

gestĭto, 1. (freq. of 1. gero), *to carry often, carry much, be accustomed to carry,* Plaut.

gesto, 1. (intens. of 1. gero), *to carry, bear, carry about one, wear;* clavos manu, Hor.; caput in pilo, Cic.

gestor -ōris, m. (1. gero), *a tale-bearer, gossip,* Plaut.

gestus -ūs, m. (1. gero), 1, *the carriage of the body;* corporis, Cic.; 2, esp., *the studied gestures* or *gesticulation of an actor* or *orator;* histrionum nonnulli gestus, Cic.; in gestu peccare, Cic.

Gĕtae -ārum, m. (Γέται), *a people of Thrace living near the Danube.* Sing., **Gĕta** -ae, m., and **Gĕtēs** -ae, m., gen. collect., *the Getae;* hence, a, adj., **Gĕtes** -ae, m. *Getic;* b, **Gĕtĭcus** -a -um, poet. = *Thracian;* c, adv., **Gĕtĭcē,** *after the Getic fashion;* loqui, Ov.

Gĕtŭlus, etc. = Gaetulus, etc. (q.v.).

gibber -ĕra -ĕrum, *hump-backed,* Suet.

gibbus -i, m. (connected with κύπτω, κυφός), *a hump, hunch,* Juv.

Gĭgas -gantis, m. (Γίγας), *a giant;* gen. plur., Gigantes, *sons of Terra, who stormed the heavens, but were killed by the lightning of Jupiter.*

Adj., Gĭgantēus -a -um, *relating to the giants, gigantic,* Verg.

gigno, gĕnŭi, gĕnĭtum, 3. (geno, connected with γίνομαι, γίγνομαι), *to beget, bear, bring forth.* **A.** Lit., Herculem Juppiter genuit, Cic.; Hecuba Alexandrum genuit, Cic. **B.** Transf., *to cause;* permotionem animorum, Cic.

gilvus -a -um, *pale yellow,* Verg.

gingīva -ae, f. *the gum,* Cat.

gĭnĭtrix = genetrix (q.v.).

glăber -bra -brum, *without hair, smooth-skinned,* Plaut.

glăcĭālis -e (glacies), *relating* or *pertaining to ice, icy;* hiems, Verg.; frigus, Ov.

glăcĭes -ēi, f. 1, *ice;* dura et alte concreta glacies, Liv.; plur., glacies Hyperboreae, Verg.; 2, *hardness;* aeris, Lucr.

glăcĭo, 1. (glacies), *to freeze;* nives, Hor.

glădĭātor -ōris, m. (gladius), *one who was hired to fight at public shows, funerals,* etc., *a gladiator.* **A.** Lit., Cic.; as a term of reproach, *bandit, brigand,* Cic. **B.** Meton., gladiatores = *gladiatorial exhibition;* dare, Cic.; abl., gladiatoribus, *at the gladiatorial games,* Cic.

glădĭātōrĭus -a -um (gladiator), a, *relating* or *pertaining to gladiators, gladiatorial;* ludus, Cic.; familia, *a troop* or *band of gladiators,* Cic.; locus, *the place of exhibition,* Cic.; consessus, *the assembled spectators,* Cic.; munus, *spectaculum,* Cic.; b, transf., totius corporis firmitas, Cic. Subst., **glădĭātōrĭum** -ĭi, n. *the pay of gladiators,* Liv.

glădĭātūra -ae, f. (gladiator), *a combat of gladiators,* Tac.

glădĭus -ĭi, m. (root CLAD, whence also clades), *a sword, a short sword* (ensis, *a longer one*). **A.** Lit., gladius vaginā vacuus, *a naked sword,* Cic.; gladium stringere, Caes.; destringere, Cic.; educere, Caes.; nudare, *to draw the sword,* Ov.; aliquem gladio insequi, Cic.; alicui gladium intentare, Liv.; transfigere aliquem gladio per pectus, Liv.; prov., plumbeo gladio jugulari, *to be defeated with little trouble,* Cic. **B.** Meton., *that which is done by the sword;* tanta gladiorum impunitas, *of murder,* Cic.

glaeba = gleba (q.v.).

glaesum (glēsum) -i, n. *amber,* Tac.

glandĭfer -fĕra -fĕrum (glans and fero), *acorn-bearing;* quercus, Cic.

glans, glandis, f. (βάλανος), 1, *an acorn,* and gen. *any fruit of similar shape,* Hor.; 2, *a bullet discharged from a sling;* glandes fundis in casas jacěre, Caes.

glārěa -ae, f. *gravel,* Cic.

glārěōsus -a -um (glarea), *gravelly, full of gravel;* saxa, Liv.

glaucōma -ătis, n. (γλαύκωμα), *a disease of the eye,* Plin.

1. **glaucus** -a -um (γλαυκός), *bluish-grey;* salix, Verg.; amictus Arethusae, Verg.

2. **Glaucus** -i, m. (Γλαῦκος), 1, *a fisherman of Anthedon, changed into a sea-god, the prophet of the Nereids;* 2, *son of Sisyphus, torn to pieces by his own horses.*

glēba (glaeba) -ae, f. (connected with globus and glomus). **I.** *a lump* or *clod of earth,* Cic.; met., *land, soil;* terra potens ubere glebae, Verg. **II.** Transf., *a piece, lump of any substance;* picis, Caes.; turis, Lucr.

glēbŭla -ae, f. (dim. of gleba, *a little clod*), l, *a little farm* or *estate,* Juv.; 2, *a small lump* or *bit of any substance,* Plin.

glēsum = glaesum (q.v.).

glīs, glīris, m. *a dormouse,* Plin.

glisco, 3., 1, *to grow up, swell up, blaze up* ad juvenilem libidinem copia voluptatum glisci; illa, ut ignis oleo, Cic.; ignis sub pectore gliscens, Lucr.; 2, *to increase, swell, spread;* ne glisceret negligendo bellum, Liv.; gliscente in dies seditione, Liv.; multitudo gliscit immensum, *increases very much,* Tac.

glŏbo, 1. (globus), 1, *to form into a ball,* Plin.; 2, *to form into a mass, to crowd together,* Plin.

glŏbōsus -a -um (globus), *spherical, globe-shaped;* terra, Cic.

glŏbŭlus -i, m. (dim. of globus), *a little round ball, globule,* Plin.

glŏbus -i, m. 1, *a round ball, globe, sphere;* stellarum, Cic.; terrae, Cic.; 2, a, *a round heap* or *mass;* flammarum, Verg.; b, *a troop, crowd, mass of people;* globus circumstans consulis corpus, Liv.

glŏmĕrāmen -ĭnis, n. (glomero), *a round mass, globe,* Lucr.

glŏmĕro, 1. (glomus). **I.** Lit., **A.** *to wind round, make a ball, form into a sphere;* lanam in orbes, Ov. **B.** Of food, *to roll into a ball;* frusta mero glomerata, Ov. **II.** Transf., **A.** Of horsemen, superbos gressus, *to make a horse curvet or prance,* Verg. **B.** *to gather together, collect, form into a mass;* agmina, Verg.; glomerantur apes in orbem, Verg.

glŏmus -ĕris, n. (akin to globus), *clue, skein, ball of thread;* lanae, Hor.

glōrĭa -ae, f. (root CLU, CLO; Gk. ΚΛΥ, ΚΛΕ, whence Latin laus, Gk. κλέος), *fame, renown, glory.* **I.** Lit., doctrinae et ingenii, Cic.; in summam gloriam venire, Cic.; gloriam habere, consequi, capere, acquirere, Cic.; gloriam sequi, Cic.; aliquem gloriā afficere, *to honour,* Cic.; plur., gloriae, *opportunities for fame,* Sall. **II.** Meton., **A.** a, *a glorious deed,* Tac.; b, *pride, glory;* taurus pecoris, or armenti, gloria, Ov. **B.** In a bad sense, *vain-glory, boasting, ambition, pride,* Cic.

glōrĭātĭo -ōnis, f. (glorior), *a glorying, boasting,* Cic.

glōrĭŏla -ae, f. (dim. of gloria), *a little glory;* hisce eum ornes gloriolae insignibus, Cic.

glōrĭor, 1. dep. (gloria), *to glory in, boast of, pride oneself on anything;* 1, absol., hic tu me gloriari vetas, Cic.; with adverbs, nimis, Cic.; insolenter, Cic.; with adversus and the acc., ne adversus te quidem gloriabor, Liv.; with in and the abl., in victoria vel ignavis gloriari licet, Sall.; 2, with abl., nominibus veterum, Cic.; suā victoriā tam insolenter, Caes.; 3, with de and the abl., de tuis beneficiis intolerantissime gloriaris, Cic.; 4, with acc. and infin., is mihi etiam gloriabitur se omnes magistratus sine repulsa assecutum, Cic.; 5, with pronoun acc., vellem equidem idem posse gloriari quod Cyrus, Cic.; partic. fut. pass., gloriandus, *glorious, worthy to be boasted of;* beata vita glorianda et praedicanda est, Cic.

glōrĭōsē, adv. (gloriosus), 1, *with glory, gloriously;* aliquid gloriosissime et magnificentissime conficere, Cic.; 2, *vauntingly, boastingly;* mentiri, Cic.

glōrĭōsus -a -um (gloria). **I.** Object, *famous, glorious;* mors, Cic.; gloriosissimum factum, Cic. **II.** Subject, a, *ambitious,* Cic.; b, *pretentious, boastful;* miles, Cic.

glūbo, glupsi, gluptum, 3. 1, *to peel, take off the rind* or *bark,* Varr.; 2, transf., *to rob;* magnanimos Remi nepotes, Cat.

glūten -tĭnis, n. *glue,* Verg.

glūtĭnātor -ōris, m. (glutino), *one who glues together books. a bookbinder,* Cic.

glūtĭno, 1. (gluten), *to glue* or *paste together,* Plin.

glūtĭo (gluttĭo) -īvi or -ĭi -ītum, **4.** *to swallow, gulp down;* epulas, Juv.

glūto (glutto) -ōnis, m. (glutio), *a glutton,* Pers.

Glўcĕra -ae, f. (Γλυκέρα), *a woman's name.*

Glўco and **Glўcōn** -ōnis, m. (Γλύκων), **1,** *a celebrated athlete,* Hor.; **2,** *a physician,* Cic.

Gnaeus -i, m. *a Roman name,* shortened Cn.

gnārĭtas -ātis, f. (gnarus), *knowledge,* Sall.

gnārus -a -um (root GNA, whence also gnavus = navus), **1,** *knowing, having knowledge of, acquainted with;* with genit., reipublicae, Cic.; Latinae linguae, Liv.; with rel. sent., eum gnarum fuisse, quibus orationis modis quaeque animorum partes pellerentur, Cic.; with acc. and infin., Hasdrubal satis gnarus Hannibalem transitus quosdam pretio mercatum (esse), Liv.; **2,** pass., *known;* gnarum id Caesari, Tac.

Gnătho -ōnis, m. *the name of a parasite in the Eunuchus of Terence;* hence = *parasite,* Cic.; **Gnăthōnĭci** -ōrum, m. *parasites like Gnatho,* Ter.

Gnătĭa = Egnatia (q.v.).

gnātus, gnāvus = natus, navus (q.v.).

Gnīdus = Cnidus (q.v.).

Gnōsus (Gnossus) -i, f. (Κνωσός, Κνωσσός), *an ancient city of Crete, the residence of Minos;* hence adj., **1, Gnōsĭus** -a -um, *Gnosian, Cretan;* stella coronae, *crown of Ariadne,* Hor.; subst., **Gnōsĭa** -ae, f. *Ariadne,* Prop.; **2, Gnōsĭăcus** -a -um, *Gnosian;* rex, *Minos,* Ov.; c, **Gnōsĭas** -adis, f. *Gnosian,* poet.= *Cretan;* and subst.= *Ariadne;* d, **Gnōsis** -ĭdis, f., corona, *the constellation of Ariadne's crown,* Ov.; subst., *Ariadne.*

gōbĭus (cōbĭus) -ĭi, m. and **gōbĭo** -ōnis, m. (κωβιός), *a gudgeon,* Ov.

Gomphi -ōrum, m. (Γόμφοι), *a town in Thessaly, on the Peneus.* Hence **Gomphenses** -ĭum, m. *the inhabitants of Gomphi.*

gonger, v. conger.

Gordĭum -ĭi, n. (Γόρδιον), *town in Phrygia.*

Gordĭus -ĭi, m. (Γόρδιος), *a Phrygian king, famed for a knot on his chariot, the unfastener of which, according to a legend, would be the ruler of Asia. Alexander the Great cut the knot.*

Gordĭutĭchos, n. indecl. (Γορδίου τεῖχος), *a place in Caria.*

Gorgĭās -ae, m. (Γοργίας), **1,** *a Greek sophist of Leontini, contemporary of Socrates;* **2,** *a rhetorician at Athens, contemporary of Cicero.*

Gorgō -gōnis, or -gūs, f. (Γοργώ); plur., Gorgones, *the three daughters of Phorcus (Stheno, Euryale,* and *Medusa), monsters with snakes for hair, whose look turned persons to stone, the chief of whom, Medusa, was slain by Perseus, and her head set in Minerva's shield.* Adj., **Gorgōnĕus** -a -um, *Gorgon;* equus, *the horse Pegasus,* Ov.

Gorgobīna -ae, f. *town of the Boii on the borders of Aquitania.*

Gorgon, v. Gorgo.

Gortўna -ae, f. (Γόρτυνα), *chief town of the island of Crete.* Adj., **Gortўnius** -a -um, and **Gortўnĭăcus** -a -um, *Gortynian.*

Gŏthĭni (Gŏtĭni) -ōrum, m. *a German people on the river March.*

Gŏthōnes (Gŏtōnes) -um, m. *a German people.*

grăbātus -i, m. (κράββατος, a Macedonian word), *a low couch, a common, mean bedstead,* Cic.

Gracchus -i, m. *the name of a family of the* Gens Sempronia, *the most famous members of which were* Tib. and C. Sempronius Gracchus, *sons of* Tib. Sempronius Gracchus *and* Cornelia, *daughter of the elder Scipio Africanus.* Adj., **Gracchānus** -a -um, *Gracchan.*

grăcĭlis -e, *slender, thin, slim;* **1,** lit., puer, Hor.; capella, Ov.; **2,** transf., of discourse, *simple, without ornament;* materia, Ov.

grăcĭlĭtas -ātis, f. (gracilis), *thinness, slimness, slenderness;* corporis, Cic.

grăcŭlus -i, m. *a jackdaw,* Phaedr.

grădātim, adv. (gradus), *step by step, by gradations, gradually, by degrees,* Cic.

grădātĭo -ōnis, f.(gradus), in rhet.,*climax,*Cic.

grădĭor, gressus sum, grădi, dep., *to step, walk,* Cic.

Grădīvus -i, m. (gradior, *he that walks in battle), a surname of Mars,* Liv., Verg.

grădus -ūs, m. (gradior). **I.** *a step.* **A.** Gen., **1,** lit., gradum facere, *to make a step,* Cic.; celerare, Verg.; corripere, Hor.; addere, *to hasten,* Liv.; gradu citato, pleno, *at quick march,* Liv.; gradum referre, *to go back,* Liv.; gradum inferre in hostes, *to advance against,* Liv.; gradum conferre, *to come to close combat,* Liv.; **2,** fig., a, *a step towards something;* primus gradus imperii factus est, Cic.; gradum fecit ad censuram, Liv.; b, *step, approach;* quem mortis timuit gradum, Hor. **B.** *station, position, post* (of a combatant), aliquem gradu movere or demovere, *to drive from one's ground,* Liv.; fig., aliquem de gradu dejicere or gradu depellere, Cic. **II.** Meton., *step, stair, round of a ladder.* **A.** Lit., a, gradus templorum, Cic.; b, esp., gen. in plur., *the rows of seats in a theatre,* etc., Tac.; sing., at Novius collega gradu post me sedet uno, Hor. **B.** Transf., a, music. t. t., *the gradations of sound;* sonorum gradus, Cic.; b, *degree, stage;* a virtute ad rationem video te venisse gradibus, by *stages,* Cic.; omnes gradus aetatis, Cic.; c, *degree of relationship;* necessitudinum gradus, Cic.; d, *rank, position;* gradus senatorius, Cic.; infimus fortunae gradus, Cic.

Graeci -ōrum, m. (Γραικοί), *the Greeks;* sing., **Graecus** -i, m. *a Greek,* Cic., and **Graeca** -ae, f. *a Greek woman,* Liv. Hence **A. Graecus** -a -um, *Greek;* ad Graecas Calendas, v. Calendae; subst., **Graecum** -i, *Greek language* or *literature;* adv. **Graece,** *in the Greek language.* **B. Graecia** -ae, f. *Greece* (Ἑλλάς), **1,** *Greece in the narrow sense;* **2,** Magna Graecia, *the Greek colonies in the south of Italy.* **C. Graecŭlus** -a -um, dim. adj., *Greek* (gen. used ironically) Subst., **Graecŭlus** -i, m. *a little Greek,* used contemptuously of the Greek philosophers and rhetoricians in the houses of the rich at Rome, Cic.

graecor, 1. dep. (Graecus), *to live in Greek fashion,* Hor.

Graecostăsis -is, f. (Γραικόστασις), *a building in the Roman Forum, erected for the purpose of lodging Greek and other foreign ambassadors,* Cic.

Grāii -ōrum (and poet. -ûm), m.= Graeci, *the Greeks,* Cic.; sing., **Grāius** -i, m. *a Greek.* Hence, **Grāius** -a -um, *Greek.*

Grāiocĕli -ōrum, m. *a Gallic people in the Graian Alps.*

Grāiŭgĕna -ae, m. (Graius and geno = gigno), *a Greek by birth, a Greek,* Verg.

grāmen -ĭnis, n. (root GER, CER, whence cresco), **1,** *grass, turf,* Liv., Verg.; **2,** *plant, herb,* Verg.

grāmĭnĕus -a -um (gramen). **I.** *made of grass.* **A.** Gen., corona obsidionalis, Liv. **B.** *made of cane* or *bamboo ;* hasta, Cic. **II.** *grassy ;* campus, Verg.

grammătĭca, v. grammaticus.

grammătĭcus -a -um (γραμματικός). **I.** Adj., *relating to grammar, grammatical ;* tribus grammaticas adire, *the company of grammarians,* Hor. **II.** Subst., a, **grammătĭcus** -i, m. *a grammarian,* Cic. ; b, **grammătĭca** -ae, f. and **grammătĭcē** -ēs, f. *grammar, philology,* Cic. ; c, **grammătĭca** -ōrum, n. *grammar, philology,* Cic.

grammătista -ae, m. (γραμματιστής), *a teacher of grammar, teacher of languages,* Suet.

Grampĭus Mons, *a mountain in Scotland,* now *the Grampians.*

grānārĭum -ĭi, n. (granum), *a granary ;* gen. in plur., Cic.

grandaevus -a -um (grandis and aevum), *very old ;* Nereus, Verg.

grandēsco, 3. (grandis), *to become great, increase in size,* Cic.

grandĭfer -fĕra -fĕrum (grandis and fero), *producing great profit or service,* Cic.

grandĭlŏquus -a -um (grandis and loquor), 1, *speaking grandly,* Cic. ; 2, in a bad sense, *boastful, grandiloquent,* Cic.

grandĭnat, impers. *it hails,* Sen.

grandĭo, 4. (grandis). **I.** Transit., *to make great, increase,* Plaut. **II.** Intransit., *to become great,* Cato.

grandis -e. **I.** Lit., *great, large.* **A.** In extent, 1, epistola, Cic. ; 2, in stature, *tall,* puer, Cic. **B.** Of weight, etc., *large ;* pondus argenti, Cic. **C.** Of time, *old ;* grandis natu, Cic. **II.** Transf., **A.** *great, important ;* res grandiores, Cic. **B.** Esp., of style, *high, lofty, grand, elevated, sublime ;* genus dicendi, Cic. ; oratores grandes verbis, Cic.

grandĭtas -ātis, f. (grandis), *of discourse, loftiness, sublimity ;* verborum, Cic.

grando -ĭnis, f. *hail, hail-storm,* Cic.

Grānĭcus -i, m. (Γρανικός), *river in Mysia, famous for one of Alexander's victories.*

grānĭfer -fĕra -fĕrum (granum and fero), *grain-carrying ;* agmen, ants, Ov.

grānum -i, n. *a grain or seed ;* uvae, Ov. ; fici, Cic.

grăphĭārĭus -a -um (graphium), *relating to the graphium,* Suet.

grăphĭum -ĭi, n. (γραφίον), *a style or sharp-pointed instrument for writing on waxen tablets,* Ov.

grassātor -ōris, m. (grassor), 1, *an idler,* Cato ; 2, *a nocturnal vagabond or rioter,* Cic.

grassor, 1. dep. (gradior). **I. 1,** *to advance, proceed ;* ad gloriam virtutis viā, Sall. ; in possessionem agri publici, Liv. ; 2, a, *to go to work, to proceed ;* jure, non vi, Liv. ; veneno, Tac. ; b, esp., *to proceed violently, to rage ;* ut paucorum potentia grassaretur, Tac. **II.** *to go about idly in the streets, to loiter, riot ;* juventus grassans in Suburra, Liv.

grātē, adv. (gratus), 1, *willingly, with pleasure,* Cic. ; 2, *thankfully ;* et grate et pie facere, Cic.

grātes, acc. grates, abl. gratibus, f. (gratus), *thanks,* esp. to the gods ; alicui grates agere, Cic. ; laudes et grates alicui habere, Tac.

grātĭa -ae, f. (gratus), *agreeableness, pleasantness.* **I. A.** Lit., *that which is pleasing, charm ;* gratia non deest verbis, Prop. ; hence personif., Gratiae, *the Graces, daughters of Zeus and Eury-*

nome (Euphrosyne, Aglaia, and Thalia,) *the goddesses of grace, charm, agreeableness,* etc.). **B.** Transf., 1, *favour, grace ;* a, petivit in beneficii loco et gratiae, Cic. ; gratiam dicendi facere, *to allow to speak,* Liv. ; in gratiam alicuius, *to please some one,* Liv. ; abl., gratiā, *on account of ;* hominum gratiā, *for example,* Cic. ; b, *indulgence* (towards an offence) ; delicti gratiam facere, *to be indulgent to,* Sall. ; 2, *thankfulness, thanks ;* gratiam ferre alicuius rei, Liv. ; gratiam persolvere diis, Cic. ; gratias agere, *to thank,* Cic. ; alicui pro suo summo beneficio gratias agere, Cic. ; gratiarum actio, *giving thanks,* Cic. ; gratiam habere, *to be thankful,* Cic. ; gratiam referre, *to make a return,* Cic. ; gratiam reddere, Sall. ; dis gratia or gratia dis, *thank God !* Ov. ; abl. plur., gratiis or gratis, *without recompense, for nothing, gratis ;* gratiis exaedificari atque effici navem, Cic. **II. A.** *favour with other persons, credit, influence ;* gratiam alicuius sibi conciliare, Cic. ; gratiam inire ab aliquo, Cic. ; apud or ad aliquem, Liv. ; in gratia esse, *to be beloved,* Cic. **B.** Transf., 1, *friendship, regard ;* in gratiam redire cum aliquo, Cic. ; cum bona gratia aliquem demittere, Cic. ; 2, *power, dignity,* Cic.

grātĭfĭcātĭo -ōnis, f. (gratificor), *complaisance, obligingness, showing kindness ;* Sullana, *of Sulla to his soldiers,* Cic. ; impudens, Cic. ; gratificatio et benevolentia, Cic.

grātĭfĭcor, 1. dep. (gratus and facio), 1, *to act so as to please any one, to oblige, gratify, do a favour to ;* alicui, Cic. ; with de aliqua re, *to communicate ;* qui de eo quod ipsis superat, aliis gratificari volunt, Cic. ; 2, with acc. of thing, *to give, present to ;* populo aliena et sua, Cic.

grātĭīs, v. gratia.

grātĭōsus -a -um (gratia), 1, *enjoying favour, favoured, beloved ;* apud omnes ordines, Cic. ; in provincia, Cic. ; 2, *showing favour, complaisant ;* gratiosi scribae sint in dando et cedendo loco, Cic.

grātis, v. gratia.

Grātĭus -ĭi, m. (Faliscus), *a Roman poet, contemporary of Ovid.*

grātor, 1. dep. (gratus), 1, *to manifest joy, to congratulate any one ;* alicui, Verg. ; sibi, Ov. ; gratatur reduces (sc. eos esse), Verg. ; 2, *to rejoice ;* Jovis templum gratantes ovantesque adire, Liv.

grātŭīto, adv. (gratuitus), *without payment, gratuitously ;* alicui gratuito civitatem impertire, Cic.

grātŭītus -a -um, *not paid for, gratuitous, free, spontaneous, voluntary ;* suffragia, comitia, unbribed, Cic. ; amicitia, Cic. ; probitas, liberalitas, Cic.

grātŭlābundus -a -um (gratulor), *congratulating,* Liv.

grātŭlātĭo -ōnis, f. (gratulor), 1, *a wishing joy, congratulation ;* civium, Cic. ; laudis nostrae, *because of,* Cic. ; in sua gratulatione, *when he was being congratulated,* Cic. ; 2, *a thanksgiving festival ;* reipublicae bene gestae, Cic.

grātŭlor, 1. dep. (gratus), 1, *to manifest joy, to wish a person joy, congratulate ;* alicui de reditu, Cic. ; alicui in aliqua re, Cic. ; with acc., alicui recuperatam libertatem, Cic. ; with acc. of respect and infin., Cic. ; alicui quod, etc., Cic. ; with or without sibi, *to rejoice, wish oneself joy,* Cic. ; 2, *to give solemn thanks to a deity,* Cic.

grātus -a -um (root CRA, Gr. XAP, whence χαρτός, χάρις, χαίρω), *pleasing.* **I.** *charming, pleasant, agreeable ;* Venus, Hor. ; gratissima tellus, Delos, Verg. **II.** 1, a, *agreeable, welcome, beloved ;* conviva, Hor. ; gratissima victoria, Cic. ;

b, *grateful, deserving thanks;* veritas etiamsi jucunda non est, mihi tamen grata est, Cic.; gratum est, with infin., Cic.; **2,** *grateful;* gratus in or erga aliquem, Cic. Subst., **grātus** -i, m. *grateful man,* Cic.

grăvantĕr, adv. (gravans, from gravor), *with difficulty;* reguli Gallorum haud gravanter ad Poenum venerunt, Liv.

grăvātē, adv. (gravor), *with difficulty, unwillingly;* gravate ille primo, Cic.

grăvēdĭnōsus -a -um (gravedo), *subject to cold or catarrh,* Cic.

grăvēdo -ĭnis, f. (gravis), *heaviness of the limbs and head, cold, catarrh,* Cic.

grăvĕŏlens -lentis (grave and oleo), *strong-smelling, rank,* Verg.

grăvesco, 3. (gravis), **1,** *to become grievous, grow worse;* aerumna, Lucr.; **2,** *of animals, to become pregnant,* Plin.; transf., nemus fetu gravescit, *is laden with fruit,* Verg.

grăvĭdĭtas -ātis, f.(gravidus), *pregnancy,*Cic.

grăvĭdo, 1. (gravidus), *to fructify;* terra gravidata seminibus, Cic.

grăvĭdus -a -um (gravis), *pregnant.* **A.** Lit., Cic. **B.** *laden, filled, full;* with abl., pharetra sagittis, Hor.; urbs bellis, Verg.; tempestas fulminibus, Lucr.

grăvis -e. **I.** *heavy, weighty, burdensome* (opp. levis). **A.** Lit., onus armorum, Caes.; cibus, *heavy, hard to digest,* Cic.; agmen, *heavy-armed,* Liv.; aes grave, *heavy coin, according to the old reckoning, in which an as weighed a pound,* Liv. **B.** Transf., a, *of sound, low, deep* (opp. acutus); vox, sonus, Cic.; b, *of persons or things relating to persons, weighty, important;* testis, auctor, Cic.; *of style, elevated, dignified;* genus epistolarum severum et grave, Cic.; c, *grievous, painful, hard, harsh, severe, unpleasant;* tempestas, Cic.; vulnus, Caes.; ne quid gravius in fratrem statueret, *take harsh measures against,* Caes.; d, (α) *of smell, strong, fetid;* odor caeni gravis, Verg.; (β) *unwholesome, unhealthy;* anni tempus, Cic.; (γ) *oppressive, troublesome, sad;* senectus, Cic.; grave est, with infin., Cic. **II.** *loaded with, laden with.* **A.** Lit., agmen praedā grave, Liv. **B.** Transf., a, *pregnant,* Verg.; b, *heavy with sleep, food, wine,* etc.; graves somno epulisque, Liv.; c, *weak, ill;* morbo, Verg.; d, *advanced in age;* gravis aetate, Liv.

Grăviscae -ārum, f. *a town in Etruria.*

grăvĭtas -ātis, f. (gravis). **I.** *weight.* **A.** Lit., armorum, Caes. **B.** Transf., a, *weight, consequence, importance;* sententiarum, Cic.; b, *dignity, sublimity;* oris, Liv.; esp. of style, dicendi, Cic.; c, *authority, seriousness, sternness, gravity;* cum gravitate et constantia vivere, Cic.; d, (α) *high price;* annonae, Tac.; (β) *unhealthiness;* caeli, Cic.; (γ) *unpleasantness of smell;* odoris, Tac. **II.** a, *pregnancy,* Ov.; b, *dulness, heaviness, faintness;* corporis, Cic.; linguae, Cic.

grăvĭtĕr, adv. (gravis), a, *of sound, deeply;* sonare, Cic.; b, *impressively, with dignity;* orationem graviter habere et sententiose, Cic.; c, *violently, vehemently;* graviter aegrotare, Cic.; queri, conqueri, Cic.; gravissime dolere, Caes.; d, *in an unhealthy condition;* se non graviter habere, Cic.; e, *irritably, hardly;* aliquid graviter accipere, ferre, *to be vexed with,* Cic.

grăvo, 1. (gravis). **I.** Act., *to load, burden.* **A.** Lit., aliquem sarcinis, Tac. **B.** Transf., a, *to heighten, exaggerate, increase;* invidiam matris, Tac.; b, *to oppress, burden, trouble;* gravari injuriis militum, Liv. **II.** Pass., gravor used as dep., *to bear or do unwillingly, to be troubled, annoyed, to refuse, decline;* with infin., rogo ut ne graveris ●●aedificare id opus quod instituisti, Cic.

grĕgālis -e (grex). **I.** *belonging to a herd* Plin. **II.** Transf., **A.** *belonging to the same company;* as subst. plur., **grĕgāles** -ĭum, m. *companions, associates, accomplices;* Catilinae, Cic. **B.** *common, of a common kind;* amiculum, *of a private soldier,* Liv.

grĕgārĭus -a -um (grex), *belonging to the herd, common;* miles, *a private soldier,* Liv.

grĕgātim, adv. (grex). **I.** *in flocks or herds,* Plin. **II.** Transf., *in troops or crowds;* videtis cives gregatim conjectos, Cic.

grĕmĭum -ĭi, n. *the lap.* **A.** Lit., in gremio matris sedere, Cic.; fig., abstrahi e gremio patriae, Cic. **B.** Transf., *centre, middle;* medio Graeciae gremio, Cic.

gressus -ūs, m. (gradior), *a step, course, way;* gressum tendere ad moenia, Verg.; transf., of a ship, huc dirige gressum, Verg.

grex, grĕgis, m. **I.** *a herd, flock of any animals;* equarum, Cic.; avium, Hor. **II.** Transf., **A.** Of human beings, **1,** gen., *troop, band, company,* sometimes contemptuously, *a herd;* amicorum, Cic.; praedonum, Cic.; **2,** esp., a, *a philosophical sect;* philosophorum, Cic.; b, *of soldiers, a troop;* often grege facto, *in close order,* Liv. **B.** Of things without life, hyadum, Ov.

grunnĭo (grundĭo) -īvi or -ĭi -ītum, 4. *to grunt like a pig,* Plin.

grunnītus (grundītus) -ūs, m. (grunnio), *the grunting of a pig,* Cic.

grus, grŭis, m. and (gen.) f. *a crane,* Cic.

gryllus -i, m. (γρύλλος), *a cricket, grasshopper,* Plin.

Grȳnēus -a -um, v. Grynia.

Grȳnia -ae, f. (Γρύνεια), and **Grȳnĭum** -ĭi, n. (Γρύνιον), *a town in Aeolis,* with a temple and oracle of Apollo. Hence, **Grȳnēus** -a -um, *Grynean.*

gryps, grȳpis (grȳphis), m. (γρύψ), *a griffin,* Verg.

gŭbernācŭlum (gŭbernāclum) -i, n. (guberno), *a rudder, helm;* **1,** lit., ad gubernaculum accedere, Cic.; **2,** transf., *direction, management, government;* esp. of the state, accedere ad republicae gubernacula, Cic.; ad aliquem gubernacula reipublicae deferre, Cic.; ad gubernacula reipublicae sedere, Cic.; gubernacula reipublicae tractare, Cic.; senatum a gubernaculis dejicere, Cic.

gŭbernātĭo -ōnis, f. (guberno), **1,** lit., *steering, the art of steering,* Cic.; **2,** transf., *direction, government;* tantarum rerum, Cic.

gŭbernātor -ōris, m. (guberno), **1,** *helmsman, steersman, pilot,* Cic.; **2,** transf., *leader, director, governor;* civitatis, Cic.

gŭbernātrix -īcis, f. (gubernator), *she that leads, directs, governs;* ista praeclara gubernatrix civitatum, eloquentia, Cic.

gŭberno, 1. (κυβερνῶ). **A.** *to steer a ship,* Cic.; prov., e terra, *from a place of safety to direct those who are in danger,* Liv. **B.** Transf., a, intransit., *to sit at the helm, to steer;* jam pridem gubernare me taedebat, Cic.; b, transit., *to guide, direct, govern;* rempublicam, Cic.

gŭbernum -i, n. = gubernaculum (q.v.).

gŭla -ae, f. **1,** lit., *the gullet, throat;* obtorta gula, Cic.; gulam laqueo frangere, *to strangle,* Sall.; **2,** meton., *greediness, gluttony,* Cic.; irritamenta gulae, Sall.; o gulam insulsam, Cic.

gŭlōsus -a -um (gula), *gluttonous, greedy, dainty,* Mart.

gŭmĭa -ae, c. *an epicure, gourmand;* ap. Cic.

gummi, n. indecl. (κόμμι), *gum,* Plin.

gurges -ĭtis, m. (from root GAR, *to swallow*, whence also gula). **I.** *a whirlpool, eddy, abyss*; a, lit., Rheni, Cic. ; **b**, fig., gurges libidinum, Cic. ; gurges ac vorago patrimonii, *squanderer*, Cic. ; tu gurges atque helluo, Cic. **II.** poet. transf., *any deep water, a stream, flood, sea*; Carpathius, Verg.

1. gurgŭlĭo -ōnis, f. (see gurges), *the windpipe*, Cic.

2. gurgŭlĭo -ōnis, m. v. curculio.

gurgustĭum -ĭi, n. *a hut, hovel*, Cic.

gustatus -ūs, m. (gusto), **1**, *taste, as one of the senses*, Cic. ; fig., verae laudis gustatum non habere, *to have no taste for*, Cic. ; **2**, *the taste, flavour of anything*; pomorum, Cic.

gusto, 1. *to taste, take a little of.* **A.** Lit., aquam, Cic. ; gustare sanguinem alicuius, Cic. ; absol., quorum nemo gustavit cubans, Cic. **B.** Transf., *to partake of, enjoy*; amorem vitae, Lncr. ; lucellum, Hor. ; Metrodorum, *listen to for a time*, Cic.

gustus -ūs, m. (root GU-o, ΓΥ-ω, whence also gusto, γεύω, γεύομαι, γεῦσις), **1**, *the tasting*; gustu explorare cibum, potum alicuius, Tac. ; **2**, meton., **a**, *the whet or relish taken before a meal*, Mart. ; **b**, *the taste or flavour of anything*, Plin.

gutta -ae, f. **A.** Lit., *a drop of any liquid*; guttae imbrium quasi cruentae, Cic. **B.** Transf., guttae, *spots or marks on animals, stones*, Verg., Ov.

guttur -ŭris, n. *the windpipe, throat*; **1**, lit., guttur alicui frangere, *to break a person's neck*, Hor. ; **2**, meton., *gluttony*, Juv.

guttus -i, m. (gutta), *a narrow-necked jug*, Hor., Juv.

Gўăros -i, f. (Γύαρος), and **Gўăra** -ōrum, n. (Γύαρα), *an island in the Aegean Sea, one of the Cyclades*, now *Chiura*, or *Jura*.

Gўās -ae, acc. -an, and **Gўes** -ae, acc. -en, m. (Γύης), **1**, *a giant with a hundred arms*; **2**, *a companion of Aeneas*.

Gўgēs -is and -ae, acc. -en, m. (Γύγης), **1**, *a favourite of Candaules, king of Lydia, whom he murder ed and succeeded as king.* Adj., **Gўgaeus** -a -um, *of or belonging to Gyges.* **2**, *a youth mentioned by Horace.*

gymnăsĭarchus -i, m. (γυμνασίαρχος), *the master of a gymnasium*, Cic.

gymnăsĭum (**gumnăsĭum**) -ĭi, n. (γυμνάσιον), *a public school of gymnastics, gymnasium* (among the Greeks), Cic. ; the gymnasia in Greece were frequented by philosophers and sophists, hence *a place for philosophical discussion*, Cic.

gymnastĭcus -a -um (γυμναστικός), *relating to gymnastic exercises*, Plaut.

gymnĭcus -a -um (γυμνικός), *gymnastic*; ludi, Cic. ; certamen, Cic.

gўnaecēum -i, n., and **gўnaecīum** -i, n. (γυναικεῖον), *the women's apartments in a Greek house*, Cic.

gўnaecōnitis -ĭdis, f. (γυναικωνῖτις) = gynaeceum (q.v.), Nep.

Gўndēs -is, m. (Γύνδης), *a river in Assyria*, now *Kerah*, or *Karah Su.*

gypso, 1. (gypsum), *to cover with gypsum*; partic. **gypsatus** -a -um, *covered with gypsum*; pes (the feet of slaves for sale being marked with gypsum), Ov. ; gypsatissimis manibus, *with hands whitened with gypsum* (as of actors who played women's parts), Cic.

gypsum -i, n. (γύψος), **1**, *gypsum*, Plin. ; **2**, meton., *a gypsum, or plaster figure*, Juv.

Gўrton -ōnis, f. (Γυρτών), and **Gyrtōnē** -ēs, f. (Γυρτώνη), *a town in Thessaly.*

gȳrus -i, m. (γῦρος), *a circle, circular course*; a, gyrum trahere (of a snake), Verg. ; gyros per aera ducere, *to wheel through the air* (of birds), Ov. ; volat ingenti gyro (telum), Verg. ; esp. of a horse, gyros dare, *to career, curvet*, Verg. ; fig., in gyrum rationis et doctrinae duci, *to make a wide digression*, Cic. ; ex ingenti quodam oratorem immensoque campo in exiguum gyrum compellere, Cic. ; **b**, poet. (of time), *circuit*; bruma nivalem interiore diem gyro trahit, Hor.

Gythēum and **-īum** (Γύθειον), and **Gythĭum** -ĭi, n. (Γύθιον), *town in Laconia, the port of Sparta*, now *Paleopolis.*

H.

H, h, the eighth letter of the Latin Alphabet, corresponding to the Greek spiritus asper. Its position at the beginning of a word is often uncertain, as, for instance, we find aruspex for haruspex ; and on the contrary, honus for onus, etc. In combination, h before t is sometimes changed into c, as traho, tractus, and with following s forms x, as traxi, vexi.

ha! an exclamation, *ha! hold! stop! ha! ha!* Plaut.

hăbēna -ae, f. (habeo), *that by which anything is held.* **I.** *a thong*, of a sling, Verg. ; *a whip*, Hor. **II.** Esp., *the reins* (gen. in plur.). **A. 1**, lit., habenas fundere, dare, *to give the rein, to let loose the rein*, Verg. ; habenas adducere, or premere, *to tighten*, Verg. ; **2**, poet., transf., of sails, immittit habenas classi, *crowds on sail*, Verg. **B.** Fig., **1**, amicitiae habenas adducere, remittere, Cic. ; **2**, *government, guidance*; rerum (of the state), Verg.

hăbĕo -ŭi -ĭtum, 2. (root HAB, connected with ἍΠ-ω, ἅπτω), *to have, hold.* **I.** Lit., **A. 1**, *to have*, in the hand or on the neck, etc. ; *to carry, wear*; a, coronam in capite, Cic. ; vestis bona quaerit haberi, *to be worn*, Ov. ; of inanimate objects, altera vestes ripa meas habuit, *my clothes lay upon the other bank*, Ov. ; **b**, *to have as part of oneself*; feminae duplices papillas habent, Cic. ; **2**, of places, *to hold, have, contain, keep*; Tartara habent Panthoiden, Hor. ; **3**, of the contents of a writing or book, nihil enim (epistola) habebat, quod, etc., Cic. **B.** In a wider sense, **1**, *to have possession of, have power over*; **a**, *to inhabit a place*; Capuam, *to inhabit*, Liv. ; **b**, of an enemy, *to occupy*; hostis habet muros, *is in possession of*, Verg. ; **c**, *to have as a ruler, to rule*; Romam a principio reges habuere, Tac. ; animus habet cuncta neque ipse habetur, Sall. ; *to have property in actual possession*; gemmas, argentum, Hor. ; absol., *to possess property, to be wealthy*; habere in Bruttiis, Cic. ; habet idem in nummis, habet in praediis urbanis, Cic. ; habendi amor, Verg. ; aliquid sibi, *to possess or keep for oneself*; sibi haberent honores, Cic. ; hence the formula of divorce, res tuas tibi habeas (habe), Plaut. ; istam suas res sibi habere jussit, *divorced*, Cic. ; **e**, *to keep cattle, animals*; pecus, *to keep or possess a flock*, Verg. ; so domi divisores, Cic. ; **2**, *to keep constantly in some position, maintain*; **a**, *around oneself, to keep a person for a particular purpose*; aliquem secum, *to keep near oneself*, Nep. ; catervas flagitiosorum circum se, Sall ; **b**, *to keep in some place*; milites in castris, *to keep the soldiers in camp*, Sall. ; arma procul, *to keep arms at a distance*, i.e., *to avoid war*, Tac. ; **c**, *to confine, to keep fast*; senatum in curia inclusum, Cic. ; aliquem in vinculis, Sall. ; in custodiam haberi, *to be placed in confinement*, Liv. **II.** Transf., **A.** In ᴀ narrower sense, **1,** generally, aliquid in manibus, *to have in hand,* Cic.; aliquid in animo, *to have in the mind, intend;* with infin., Cic.; aliquem in animo, *to have in one's thoughts,* Sall.; **2,** of the condition of the mind or body; **a,** vulnus, *to be wounded,* Ov.; febrem, Cic.; animum fortem, Cic.; bonum animum, *to be of good courage,* Sall.; odium in aliquem, *to cherish hatred,* Cic.; **b,** *to possess as a quality;* modestiam, Sall.; Caesar hoc habebat, *had this custom,* Cic.; **c,** *to draw after as a consequence, have as a result, to cause;* beneficium habet querelam, Cic.; misericordiam, *to cause pity,* Cic.; **3, a,** *to bring into a certain condition;* mare infestum, *to make unsafe,* Cic.; aliquem sollicitum, *to make anxious,* Cic.; **b,** *to treat, behave towards;* aliquem liberalissime, Cic.; plebes servorum loco habetur, Cic.; exercitum luxuriose, Sall.; **c,** *to have or keep for some object;* aliquem ludibrio, *to make a mock of,* Cic.; rempublicam quaestui, Cic.; **4,** *to have, hold, consider, regard;* aliquem parentem, *in the light of a parent,* Cic.; aliquem pro hoste, *as an enemy,* Liv.; aliquid pro certo, Cic.; (in) numero hostium, Cic.; aliquid religioni, *to make a matter of conscience of,* Cic.; paupertas probro haberi coepit, *to be considered a disgrace,* Sall.; **5, a,** *to set about, order, hold, arrange;* concilium plebis, *to hold a council of the people,* Cic.; iter Aegyptum, *to go to Egypt,* Cic.; **b,** of speech, *to utter, deliver, propound;* orationem in senatu, *to deliver a speech,* Cic.; sermonem cum aliquo, *to hold a conversation with,* Cic.; habere verba, *to speak,* Cic.; habere dialogum, *to compose,* Cic.; **c,** of time, *to pass, spend;* aetatem, Sall.; **6,** *to keep, observe;* ordines, Sall.; **7,** alicui honorem, *to pay honour to,* Cic.; **8,** reflex., se habere, or simply habere, *to fare, to be circumstanced, situated;* **a,** of persons, graviter se habere, *to be very ill,* Cic.; singulos (saucios) ut se haberent rogitans, Liv.; **b,** of things, res sic or ita se habet, or simply sic or ita se habet, Cic. **B.** In ᴀ wider sense, **1,** gen., **a,** *to have, possess;* dimidium facti qui coepit habet, Hor.; **b,** *to have, be informed of;* habes consilia nostra, Cic.; **2,** *to have, experience;* nonnullam invidiam ex eo quod, etc., Cic.; **3,** *to have in some relation or condition;* digni sumus quos habeas tui consilii participes, Cic.; habeo aliquem acerbum, Cic.; with pass. partic., domitas habere libidines, Cic.; **4, a,** nisi quid habes ad hanc, *have something to say,* Cic.; **b,** *to be able, to be in a condition to;* habeo etiam dicere, Cic.; nihil habeo quod incusem senectutem, Cic,

hăbĭlis -e (habeo). **I.** *easily managed, handy, supple;* arcus, Verg.; currus, Ov. **II.** Transf., *suitable, fit, convenient;* **a,** physically, *vigor,* Verg.; with ad, calceus habilis et aptus ad pedem, Cic.; with dat., gens equis tantum habilis, Liv.; **b,** mentally *skilful;* with dat. of gerund, habilis capessendae reipublicae, Tac.

hăbĭlĭtas -ātis, f. (habilis), *aptitude, ability,* Cic.

hăbĭtābĭlis -e (habito), *habitable;* regio, Cic.

hăbĭtātĭo -ōnis, f. (habito), *dwelling, habitation;* sumptus habitationis, Cic.

hăbĭtātŏr -ōris, m. (habito), *one who dwells or inhabits;* **a,** of a house, habitatorem in hac caelesti ac divina domo, Cic.; **b,** *dweller in a country;* sunt e terra homines non ut incolae et habitatores sed quasi, etc., Cic.

hăbĭto, 1. (freq. of habeo). **I.** Transit., *to inhabit;* urbes, Verg.; in pass., *to be inhabited;* vix pars dimidia (urbis) habitabatur, Liv. **II.** Intransit. **A.** *to dwell;* alibi, Liv.; ad or apud aliquem, Cic.; cum aliquo, Cic.; in via, Cic.; impers. pass., habitari sunt Xenocrates, in luna, Cic.; partic. subst., habitantes, *the inhabitants,* Ov.; fig., metus habitat in vita beata, Cic. **B.**

Transf., **a,** *to dwell, to be always in a place, to frequent;* in foro, Cic.; *quorum in vultu habitant oculi mei,* Cic.; **b,** *to dwell on a subject;* in ec genere rerum, Cic.

hăbĭtūdo -ĭnis f. (habeo), *form, appearance; corporis,* Ter.

1. hăbĭtus -a -um, p. adj. (from habeo), *formed, constituted,* Ter.

2. hăbĭtus -ūs, m. (habeo). **I.** Lit., *the condition of the body, appearance.* **A.** Gen., corporis, Cic.; oris, Cic. **B.** Esp., *the appearance of the dress of the body;* habitus atque vestitus, Cic.; and meton., *dress itself,* Tac. **II.** Transf., **A.** *the nature, condition;* pecuniarum, Cic.; Italiae, Cic. **B.** *disposition;* virtus est animi habitus naturae modo atque rationi consentaneus, Cic.

hāc, adv. (abl. of hic, sc. parte, or viā), *here. this way, by this side,* Cic.

hāctĕnus, adv. (lit., hāc parte tenus), *so far.* **I.** Lit., of place, *up to this point;* hactenus dominum est illa secuta suum, Ov. **II.** Transf., **A.** In writing, discourse, etc., **1,** *up to this point;* hactenus mihi videor de amicitia quid sentirem potuisse dicere, Cic.; often elliptically, to close a discussion, sed haec haectenus, Cic.; or to pass on to something new, sed · haec hactenus; nunc ad ostenta veniamus, Cic.; **2,** *only so far, only this, only so much;* quare tibi hactenus mando, etc., Cic.; **3,** *in so far as;* with quoad, quod, etc.; or with ut or ne, Cic. **B.** Of time, *till now, hitherto,* Liv.

Hadrĭa (Adria) -ae, f., **1,** *a town in Picenum,* now *Atri;* **2,** *a town in the north of Italy between the Padus and the Athesis,* now *Adria;* **3,** generally masculine, *the Adriatic Sea.* Hence, Adj. **1, Hadrĭācus (Adriācus),** -a -um, *Hadriatic;* **2, Hadrĭānus** -a -um, *belonging to Hadria* (No. 2.); **3, Hadrĭātĭcus** -a -um, *Adriatic.*

1. Hadrĭānus -a -um, v. Hadria.

2. Hadrĭānus -i, m., P. Aelius Hadrianus, *Roman Emperor from* 117 *to* 138 ᴀ.ᴅ.

Hadrūmētum, v. Adrumetum.

haedīnus -a -um (haedus), *of or pertaining to a kid;* pelliculae, Cic.

haedŭlĕa -ae, f. (dim. of haedus), *a little kid,* Hor.

haedŭlus -i, m. (dim. of haedus), *a little kid,* Juv.

haedus -i, m. **1,** *a kid, young goat,* Cic.; **2,** haedi, *the Kids, two stars of the constellation Auriga,* Cic.

Haemŏnĭa -ae, f. (Αἱμονία), Haemonia, *an old name of Thessaly.* Adj. **1, Haemŏnĭus** -a -um, *Thessalian;* puppis, *the ship Argo,* Ov.; juvenis, *Jason,* Ov.; puer or heros, *Achilles,* Ov.; meton., as Thessaly was notorious for witches, artes, *arts of enchantment,* Ov.; **2, Haemŏnis** -nĭdis, f. *a Thessalian woman,* Ov.

haerĕdĭtas = hereditas (q.v.).

haerĕo, haesi, haesum, 2. *to hang to, stick to, cleave to, adhere.* **I.** Gen., **A.** Lit., haerere in equo, Cic.; or equo, Hor.; terra radicibus suis haereat, Cic.; fig., haerere visceribus civitatis, Liv. **B.** Transf., **a,** *to remain in a place;* hic haereo, Cic.; **b,** haerere alicui, *to keep close to a person, cleave to,* Verg.; in a hostile sense, haerere in tergo, or in tergis, or simply tergis hostium, *to hang upon the rear of an enemy,* Liv.; **c,** *to remain fixed, to keep firm, not to leave;* haerere in jure ac praetorum tribunalibus, Cic.; memoria rei in populo haerebit, Cic. **II.** *to be rooted to a spot, to stand still.* **A.** Lit., aspectu territus haesit continuitque gradum, Verg. **B.** Transf.,

a, *to be retarded, to cease;* Aeneae manu victoria haesit. Verg.; **b.** *to be in perplexity, to be embarrassed;* hacrere homo, versari, rubere, Cic.

haeres = heres (q.v.).

haeresco, 3. (haereo), *to adhere, cleave, stick,* Lucr.

haerĕsis -ĕos, f. (αἵρεσις), *a philosophical sect,* Cic.

haesĭtantĭa -ae, f. (haesito), *a sticking fast;* linguae, *stammering,* Cic.

haesĭtātĭo -ōnis, f.(haesito), 1, *a sticking fast, hesitation in speech, stammering;* quanta haesitatio tractusque verborum, Cic.; 2, *perplexity, embarrassment, hesitation,* Cic.

haesĭto, 1. (intens. of haereo), *to stick fast, remain fast.* **I.** Lit., in vadis, Liv.; absol., Caes. **II.** Transf., *to stop.* **A.** Of the tongue, linguā, *to stammer,* Cic. **B.** *to be perplexed, embarrassed, to hesitate, be at a loss;* non haesitans respondebo, Cic.

Hălaesa, v. Halesa.

Hălaesus, v. Halesus.

halcēdo, v. alcedo.

halcўon, v. alcyon.

Halcўōnē, v. Alcyone.

hālec, v. alec.

Hales -lētis, m. *river in Lucania,* now *Alento.*

Hălēsa (Hălaesa) -ae, f. (Ἅλαισα), *a town in Sicily.* Adj., **Hălēsīnus** -a -um, *of or belonging to Halesa.*

Hălēsus (Ălēsus) -i, m., *a descendant of Agamemnon.*

hālex, v. alec.

Hălĭacmōn (Ălĭacmōn) -mŏnis, m. *a river in Macedonia,* now *Vistriza.*

hălĭāĕtos and **hălĭaeĕtos** -i, m. (ἁλιαίετος), *the sea-eagle, osprey,* Ov.

Hălĭartus -i, f. (Ἁλίαρτος), *town in Boeotia on the lake Copais.* Hence, **Hălĭartii** -ōrum, m. *the inhabitants of Haliartus.*

Hălĭcarnassos -i, f. (Ἁλικαρνασσός), *town in Caria, birthplace of Herodotus, Hecataeus, and Callimachus.* Hence, 1, **Hălĭcarnassenses** -ium, m. *the inhabitants of Halicarnassus;* 2, **Hălĭcarnassĕus** -ĕi, m. (Ἁλικαρνασσεύς), *born in Halicarnassus;* 3, **Hălĭcarnassii** -ōrum, m. *inhabitants of Halicarnassus.*

Hălĭcўae -ārum, f. (Ἁλικύαι), *town in Sicily, near Lilybaeum,* now *Salemi.* Hence adj., **Hălĭcўensis** -e, *of or belonging to Halicyae.*

hălĭeutĭca -ōn, n. (ἁλιευτικά), *the title of a poem of Ovid's on fishing.*

hālĭtus -ūs, m. (halo), *breath, exhalation,* Cic.

hallex, v. alec.

hālo, 1. **I.** Intransit., *to breathe, exhale, be fragrant;* arae sertis halant, Verg. **II.** Transit., *to breathe forth;* nectar, Lucr

hālūc . . . v. aluc . . .

Hăluntĭum, v. Aluntium.

Hălus -i, f. *town in Assyria.*

Hălўattēs, v. Alyattes.

Hălўs -lўos, acc. -lyn, m. (Ἅλυς), *river in Asia Minor,* now *the Kisil-Irmak.*

hāma (āma), -ae, f. (ἄμη), *a bucket, esp. a fireman's bucket,* Juv.

Hămādrўas (Ămādrўas) -ădis, f. (Ἁμαδρυάς), *a wood-nymph, hamadryad,* Verg.

hāmātus -a -um (hamus), 1, *provided with hooks, hooked;* ungues, Ov.; 2, *curved like a hook, hooked, crooked;* corpora, Cic.

Hămilcăr -căris, m. (Ἀμίλκας), *name of several Carthaginians,* (1) *the son of Gisgo, captured and killed by Agathocles;* (2) Hamilcar Barca, *Carthaginian general in the First Punic War, father of Hannibal.*

Hammon, v. Ammon.

hāmus -i, m. (perhaps from habeo, "*that which holds*"), *a hook.* **I.** Lit., **A.** Gen., hami ferrei, Caes.; hamis auroque trilix, *the links of a coat of mail,* Verg. **B.** Esp., *a fish-hook,* Cic. **II.** Transf., **a,** *the talons of a hawk,* Ov.; **b,** *a thorn,* Ov.

Hannĭbăl -bălis, m. (Ἀννίβας), *name of several Carthaginians, the most famous being Hannibal, son of Hamilcar Barca, general of the Carthaginians in the Second Punic War, defeated by Scipio at Zama.*

hăra -ae, f. *a pen or coop for domestic animals, a pig-sty,* Cic.

hărēna, v. arena.

hărĭŏlātĭo (ărĭŏlātĭo) -ōnis, f. *soothsaying,* ap. Cic.

hărĭŏlor (ărĭŏlor), 1. dep. (hariolus), 1, *to utter prophecies, predict,* Cic.; 2, *to talk nonsense, foolishness,* Plaut.

hărĭŏlus (ărĭŏlus) -i, m. (dim. of *hariolus, ἱερεύς), a soothsayer, prophet,* Cic.

1. **harmŏnĭa** -ae, f. (ἁρμονία), 1, *the agreement or skilful blending of sounds, harmony* (= concentus), Cic.; 2, *concord, harmony,* Lucr.

2. **Harmŏnĭa** -ae, f. (Ἁρμονία), *daughter of Mars and Venus, wife of Cadmus, mother of Semele and Ino.*

harpăgo -ōnis, m. (ἁρπάγη), *a large hook, a drag, a grappling-iron,* Caes.; transf., *a rapacious person,* Plaut.

harpē -ēs, f. (ἅρπη), *a curved or sickle-shaped sword,* Ov.

Harpŏcrătes -is, m. (Ἁρποκράτης), *an Egyptian deity, the god of silence;* aliquem reddere Harpocratem, *to impose silence upon,* Cat.

Harpўiae (trisyll.) -ārum, f. (Ἅρπυιαι, *the snatchers*), *the Harpies, mythical monsters, half bird and half woman.*

Harūdes -um, m. *a German people between the Rhine, the Main, and the Danube.*

hărund . . . v. arund.

hăruspex (ăruspex) -spĭcis, m. (ἱερός, Boeotian ἱαρός, Etruscan harus and * specio), 1, *a soothsayer, one who foretold the future from the inspection of entrails, or from the interpretation of natural phenomena, as thunder, lightning,* etc., Cic.; 2, gen., *a seer, prophet,* Prop.

hăruspĭcīnus -a -um (haruspex), *relating to the inspection of entrails,* Cic. Subst., **hăruspĭcīna** -ae, f. (sc. ars), *the art of the haruspex, the art of inspecting entrails;* haruspicinam facere, *to practise the art of haruspex,* Cic.

hăruspĭcĭum -ii, n. (haruspex), *the inspection of entrails, divination,* Cat.

Hasdrŭbăl (Asdrŭbăl) -bălis, m. *name of several Carthaginians,* esp., 1, *son of Mago, twelve times general, died 480* A.C.; 2, *son-in-law of Hamilcar Barca;* 3, *son of Hamilcar Barca, brother of Hannibal, killed at the battle of the Metaurus;* 4, *Carthaginian general in the Third Punic War.*

hasta -ae, f. 1, *a spear, a pike, javelin;* amentata, *furnished with a thong to assist in throwing it,* Cic.; eminus hastis aut comminus gladio uti, Cic.; prov., hastas abjicere, *to lose* *courage*, Cic.; **2, a**, a spear stuck in the ground was the token of a public auction; hence, sub hasta vendere, *to sell by auction*, Liv.; emptio **ab** hasta, Cic.; hasta venditionis, Cic.; **b**, *a small spear, with which the bride's hair was parted on the wedding-day*, Ov.

hastātus -a -um (hasta), **1**, *armed with a spear*, Tac.; **2**, subst., **hastāti** -ōrum, m. *the first line of the Roman army when drawn up in order of battle, the first rank, vanguard*; hence, primus, secundus, etc., hastatus (sc. ordo), *the first, second*, etc., *of the companies into which the* hastati *were divided*, Liv.

hastīlĕ -is, n. (hasta), **1**, *the shaft of a spear*, Cic.; **2**, *the spear itself*, Verg.; **3**, *a piece of wood in the form of a shaft, a shoot, a prop for vines*, Verg.

hau, interj. *oh!* an exclamation of pain, Plaut.

haud (haut), adv. (an emphatic negative), *not, not at all, by no means*; **1**, gen., **a**, with verbs, haud dubito, Cic.; haud scio, Cic.; haud scio an, etc., Cic.; **b**, with adjectives, haud mediocris, Cic.; **c**, with pronouns, haud alius, Liv.; **d**, with subst., with or without a prep., haud injuriā, Liv.; **e**, with adverbs, haud dubie, Sall.; haud secus, Liv.; haud longe, Caes.; **2**, in antitheses, haud . . . sed, Cic.; sed ut . . . ita haud, Cic.; **3**, corresponding with other particles, haud . . . tam, Liv.

hauddum (hautdum), adv. *not at all as yet, not yet*, Liv.

haudquāquam (hautquāquam), adv. *by no means, not at all*, Cic.

haurĭo, hausi, haustum (fut.partic.hausurus, Verg.), 4. (connected with ἁρύω and ἐπανρέω), *to draw up, draw out*. **I.** Gen., **A.** Of fluids, **1**, lit., *to draw water*; aquam de puteo, Cic.; **2**, transf., **a**, *to draw or fetch a sigh*; suspiratus, Ov.; **b**, *to tear up*; terram, Ov.; **c**, *to shed blood*; sanguinem, Cic.; **d**, *to collect together*; pulvis haustus, Ov.; **3**, fig., **a**, hauris de faece, *you draw from the dregs, quote the worst orators*, Cic.; **b**, *to take away*; sumptum ex aerario, Cic. **B.** Meton., *to drain dry, empty*; **1**, lit., pocula ore, Ov.; **2**, transf., **a**, *to pierce*; latus gladio, Ov.; **b**, *to squander*; sua, Tac.; **c**, *to accomplish*; caelo medium sol igneus orbem hauserat, Verg.; **3**, fig., **a**, *to oppress*; exsultantia haurit corda pavor pulsans, Verg.; **b**, *to exhaust, weaken*; Italiam et provincias immenso fenore, Tac.; **c**, *to suffer*; calamitates, Cic. **II.** Esp., *to draw into oneself*; **1**, lit., alveus haurit aquas, Ov.; **2**, transf., **a**, *to devour, consume*; multos hausit flamma, Liv.; **b**, *to devour with the eyes or ears, to drink in*; vocem his auribus hausi, Verg.; **3**, fig., **a**, aliquid cogitatione, Cic.; animo spem inanem, *drink in*, Verg.; animo haurire, *to intend*, Tac.; **b**, *to drink the cup of pleasure or pain*; voluptates, Cic.; dolorem, Cic.

haustrum -i, n. (haurio), *a machine for drawing water*, Lucr.

haustus -ūs, m. (haurio), *a drawing of water*; **1**, legal t.t., aquae, *the right of drawing water from a well*, Cic.; **2**, *drawing in*; **a**, of air, *inhaling*; apibus esse haustus aetherios, Verg.; **b**, *drinking* and concrete, *a draught*; aquae, Liv.; fontis Pindarici, Hor.; **c**, *a handful*; arenae, Ov.

haut = haud (q.v.).

hăvĕo, v. aveo.

hĕautontīmōrūmĕnos-i, m.(ἑαυτὸν τιμωρούμενος), *the self-tormentor, the title of one of* Terence's comedies.

hebdŏmas -ădis, f. (ἑβδομάς), *the seventh day of a disease* (supposed to be a critical period), Cic.

Hēbē -ēs, f. (Ἥβη, *youth*), *the daughter of Jupiter, cup-bearer of the gods, wife of Hercules.*

hĕbēnus, v. ebenus.

hĕbĕo, 2. **1**, *to be blunt, dull*; ferrum, Liv.; **2**, transf., *to be dull, heavy, inactive*; sanguis hebet, Verg.; sic mihi sensus hebet, Ov.

hĕbĕs -ĕtis, *blunt, dull*. **I.** Lit., **a**, Cic.; gladius, Ov.; **b**, *blunted, stumpy*; lunae cornua, Cic.; **c**, hebeti ictu, *a blow that bruises and does not pierce*, Ov. **II.** Transf., **a**, of the senses, *dull*; aures, Cic.; acies oculorum, Cic.; **b**, of action, *sluggish, weak*; hebes ad sustinendum laborem miles, Sall.; **c**, of colour, *dull*; color non hebes, Ov.; **d**, *mentally dull, heavy, stupid*; hebeti ingenio esse, Cic.; homines hebetes, Cic.

hĕbesco, 3. (inch. from hebeo), *to become dull, blunt, dim*; mentis acies, Cic.; auctoritatis acies, Cic.

hĕbĕto, 1. (hebes), *to make dull, blunt*. **A.** Lit., hastas, Liv. **B.** Transf., *to make dull, blunt, to deaden, dim*; flammas, Ov.; alicui visus, Verg.

Hēbraeus -a -um, *Hebrew, Jewish*, Tac.

Hebrus -i, m. (Ἕβρος), *the chief river of Thrace, flowing into the Aegean Sea.*

Hĕcăbē, v. Hecuba.

Hĕcălē -ēs, f. (Ἑκάλη), *a poor old woman who entertained Theseus.*

Hĕcătē -ēs, f. (Ἑκάτη) and **Hĕcăta** -ae, f. *"she that works from afar," the goddess of magic and enchantment, often identified with Diana and Luna.* Hence, adj., **1**, **Hĕcătēïus** -a -um, and **2**, **Hĕcătēïs** -ĭdis, f. *Hecatean*; hence= *magical*, Ov.

hĕcătombē -ēs, f. (ἑκατόμβη), *a hecatomb, sacrifice of a hundred oxen*, Juv.

Hector -tŏris, m. (Ἕκτωρ), *son of Priam, husband of Andromache, the bravest of the Trojans, killed by Achilles.* Adj., **Hectŏrĕus** -a -um (Ἑκτόρεος), *belonging to Hector*; poet.= *Trojan*, Verg.

Hĕcŭba -ae, f. and **Hĕcŭbē (Hĕcăbē)** -ēs, f. (Ἑκάβη), *wife of Priam.*

hĕdĕra -ae, f. *ivy, a plant sacred to Bacchus*, Caes., Hor.

hĕdĕrĭger -gĕra -gĕrum (hedera and gero), *ivy-bearing, ivy-crowned*, Cat.

hĕdĕrōsus -a -um (hedera), *ivied, full of ivy*, Prop.

Hĕdessa, v. Edessa.

hĕdўchrum -i, n. (ἡδύχρουν), *a fragrant salve*, Cic.

hei, interj., *alas!* hei mihi, *woe is me*, Ov.

Hĕlĕna -ae, f. and **Hĕlĕnē** -ēs, f. (Ἑλένη), *daughter of Leda and Jupiter, sister of Castor, Pollux, and Clytemnestra, mother of Hermione, wife of Menelaus, carried off by Paris to Troy, and thus the cause of the Trojan war.*

Hĕlĕnus -i, m. (Ἕλενος), *son of Priam, a soothsayer.*

Hēlĭădes -um, f. (Ἡλιάδες), *the daughters of the Sun, who, at the death of their brother Phaëthon, were changed into poplars, and their tears into amber*; hence, nemus Heliadum, *a poplar grove*, Ov.; Heliadum lacrimae, *amber*, Ov.; gemmae, *amber*, Mart.

hĕlīca -ae, f. (ἑλίκη), *winding*, Cic.

Hĕlīcē -ēs, f. (Ἑλίκη), **1**, *a town in Achaia, destroyed by an earthquake*, 372 A.C.; **2**, *a constellation, the Great Bear*, Cic.

Hĕlĭcon -ōnis, m. (Ἑλικών), *a hill of Boeotia, sacred to Apollo and the Muses*; Heliconia alumnae, *the Muses*, Ov. Hence, **1**, adj., **Hĕlĭcōnĭus** -a -um, *Heliconian*; **2**, **Hĕlĭ-**

cŏnĭădes -um, f. and 3, Hĕlĭcŏnĭdes -um, f. *the Muses.*

Hĕlĭŏdōrus -i, m. (Ἡλιόδωρος), *a celebrated rhetorician in the time of Horace.*

Hĕlĭŏpŏlis -ĕos, f. (Ἡλιόπολις), 1, *a town in Coelesyria, now Baalbek;* 2, *a town in Lower Egypt.*

Hellē -ēs, f. (Ἕλλη), *daughter of Athamas and Nephele, who fled from her step-mother Ino on a golden ram; and was drowned in the Hellespont, so named after her.*

hĕlix -ĭcis, f. (ἕλιξ), *a kind of ivy,* Plin.

hellĕborus, v. elleborus.

Hellespontus -i, m. (Ἑλλήσποντος), 1, *the Hellespont, Dardanelles;* 2, transf., *the coast on both sides of the Hellespont;* meton., *the inhabitants of this coast,* Nep. Hence, adj., a, Hellespontĭus -a -um, and b, Hellespontĭăcus -a -um, *of or belonging to the Hellespont.*

hĕlops (ĕlops, ellops), -ŏpis, m. (ἔλλοψ), *a savoury fish, perhaps the sturgeon,* Ov.

Hēlōtes, v. Hilotae.

hēlŭātĭo (hēllŭātĭo) -ōnis, f. (heluor), *gluttony,* Cic.

hēlŭo (hēllŭo) -ōnis, m. *a glutton, gormandiser,* Cic.

hēlŭor (hēllŭor), 1. dep. (heluo), *to guzzle, gormandise,* Cic.; transf., *cum aliquo reipublicae sanguine,* Cic.

helvella -ae, f. *a small pot-herb,* Cic.

Helvētĭi -ōrum, m. *the Helvetii, the inhabitants of the part of Gallia now called Switzerland.* Hence, adj., Helvētĭus and Helvētĭcus -a -um, *Helvetian.*

Helvĭi (Helvi) -ōrum, m. *a people in Gallia Provincia.*

hem, interj. *ah! oh! well! only see! just look!* hem causam, Cic.

hēmĕrŏdrŏmus -i, m. (ἡμεροδρόμος), *a special courier, express,* Liv.

hēmĭcillus -i, m. (ἥμισυς and κιλλός), *half an ass, a term of reproach,* Cic.

hēmĭcyclĭum -ĭi, n. (ἡμικύκλιον), *a semicircular settee for conversation,* Cic.

hēmīna -ae, f. (ἡμίνα), *a measure of capacity, half a sextarius, nearly half a pint English,* Plaut.

hendĕcăsyllăbi -ōrum, m. (ἐνδεκασύλλαβοι), *verses of eleven syllables,* Cat.

Hĕnĕti -ōrum, m., v. Veneti.

Hĕnĭŏchi -ōrum, m. (Ἡνίοχοι), *a people of Asiatic Sarmatia.* Hence adj., Hĕnĭŏchĭus and Hĕnĭŏchus -a -um, *Heniochian.*

Henna (Enna) -ae, f. (Ἕννα), *an ancient city of Sicily, celebrated for a temple of Ceres.* Hence adj., Hennensis -e, and Hennaeus -a -um, *of or belonging to Henna.*

Hēphaestĭo -ōnis, m. (Ἡφαιστίων), *a general and friend of Alexander the Great.*

heptēris -is, f. (ἑπτήρης), *a galley with seven banks of oars,* Liv.

1. hĕra (ĕra) -ae, f. (herus), 1, *the mistress of a house,* Plaut., Ter.; 2, *mistress, queen, female ruler,* Cat., Ov.

2. Hēra -ae, f. (Ἥρα), *the Greek goddess identified with the Roman Juno;* hence, Hēraea -ōrum, n. (Ἡραία), *the festival of Hera,* Liv.

Hērăclēa (-ĭa) -ae, f. (Ἡράκλεια), *the city of Heracles (Hercules), name of several Greek towns;* 1, *a colony of the Tarentines in the south of Italy, on the rivir Siris;* 2, *a town in Phthiotis, near Thermopylae;* 3, *a town in Bithynia on the Black*

Sea, now Herakle or *Erekli;* 4, *a town in Sicily on the Halycos, also called Minoa;* 5, *Heraclea Sintica, a town in Paeonia on the Strymon.* Hence, a, Hērăclĕenses -ĭum, *the inhabitants of Heraclea;* b, Hērăclĕōtes -ae, m. *belonging to Heraclea;* plur., Hērăclĕōtae -ārum, m. *the inhabitants of Heraclea.*

Hērăclēum -i, n. (Ἡράκλειον), *a town in Macedonia, on the borders of Thessaly.*

Hērăclĭa, v. Heraclea.

Hērăclīdēs -ae, m. (Ἡρακλείδης), Ponticus, *a Greek philosopher.*

Hērăclītus -i, m. (Ἡράκλειτος), *a Greek philosopher of Ephesus.*

1. Hēraea -ōrum, v. Hera.

2. Hēraea -ae, f. (Ἡραία), *town in Arcadia on the Alpheus.*

herba -ae, f. (φέρβ-ω, φορβ-ή, orig. ferb-a, whence also febra, fibra), *a plant with stalks, grass, plant, herb* (sing. often collective). I. Gen., stirpes et herbae, Cic.; sing. collective, in herba se abjicere, Cic. II. Esp., a, *the stalk of wheat,* Cic.; b, *tares;* officiant laetis ne frugibus herbae, Verg.

herbĭdus -a -um (herba), *full of grass, grassy;* campus, Liv.

herbĭfer -fĕra -fĕrum (herba and fero), *full of herbage, grassy;* colles, Ov.

herbĭgrădus -a -um (herba and gradior), *going through the grass,* epithet of a snake, ap. Cic.

Herbĭta -ae, f. (Ἑρβιτα), *town in the interior of Sicily, now Nicosia.* Hence, adj., Herbĭtensis -e, *of or belonging to Herbita.*

herbōsus -a -um (herba), *full of herbage, grassy;* campus, Hor.

herbŭla -ae, f. (dim. of herba), *a little herb,* Cic.

Hercēus -a -um (Ἑρκεῖος), *a surname of Jupiter as the protector of the house, courtyard,* etc.

hercisco (ercisco), 3. (herctum), *to divide an inheritance,* Cic.

Hercle, v. Hercules.

herctum -i, n. (probably connected with heres), *an inheritance, found only in the phrase* herctum ciere, *to divide an inheritance,* Cic.

Hercŭlānĕum -i, n. I. *town in Campania, destroyed by an eruption of Vesuvius, under the emperor Titus.* Hence, adj., 1, Hercŭlānensis -e, *of Herculaneum.* Subst., in Herculanensi, *in the district of Herculaneum;* 2, Hercŭlānĕus and Hercŭlānus -a -um, *of Herculaneum.* II. *town in Samnium.*

Hercŭles -is and -i, m. (Ἡρακλῆς), *the son of Jupiter and Alcmena, husband of Deianira and (after his deification) of Hebe, the national hero of the Boeotians; the performer of twelve labours imposed upon him by Eurystheus; regarded as the giver of riches and the guide of the Muses.* Vocat. sing., Hercules or Hercule and Hercle (an oath of the Romans), *by Hercules,* Cic.; also mehercules or mehercule, Cic.; Hercle sane, Cic. Hence adj., Hercŭlĕus -a -um, *Herculean;* arbor, *the poplar,* Verg.

Hercȳnĭa silva -ae, f. *the Hercynian forest, in Central Germany;* also, Hercȳnĭa -ae, f. *the Hercynian forest,* Tac.

Herdōnĭa -ae, f. *town in Apulia, destroyed by Hannibal.*

hēre = heri (q.v.).

hērēdĭtārĭus -a -um (heres), 1, *relating to an inheritance;* auctio, Cic.; 2, *inherited, hereditary;* cognomen. Cic.; controversia. Cic.

hērēdĭtas -ātis, f. (heres), *inheritance.* **A.** Lit., hereditate possidere, Cic.; hereditatem adire or cernere, Cic. **B.** Transf., hereditas gloriae, Cic.

Herennĭus -a -um, *name of a Roman gens.* Adj., **Herenniānus** -a -um, *Herennian.*

hērēdĭum -ĭi, n. (heres), *a patrimony,* Nep.

hēres (haeres) -ēdis, c. (connected with hir, Greek χείρ), *an heir.* **I.** Lit., heres esse alicui or alicuius, Cic.; aliquem heredem scribere, facere, instituere, *to make a person one's heir,* Cic.; secundus, *a person named to receive the inheritance if the original heir cannot inherit,* Cic. **II.** Transf., *successor;* veteris Academiae, Cic.

hĕrī (hĕrĕ), adv. (χθές, Lat. HES, whence, first hesi, then heri), 1, *yesterday,* Cic.; 2, *lately,* Cat.

hĕrĭfŭga -ae, m. (herus and fugio), *a fugitive, runaway,* Cat.

hĕrīlis -e (herus), *of or relating to the master* or *mistress of the house;* mensa, Verg.

Hermaeum -i, n. (Ἑρμαιον), lit., *a temple* *of Hermes; a coast-town of Boeotia.*

Hermăgŏrās -ae, m. (Ἑρμαγόρας), *a Rhodian rhetorician of about the second half of the second century* A.C.

hermaphrŏdītus -i, m. (ἑρμαφρόδιτος), *an hermaphrodite,* Ov.

Hermāthēna -ae, f. (Ἑρμαθήνη), *a double bust of Hermes and Athena, on the same pedestal,* Cic.

Hermēracles -is, m. (Ἑρμηρακλῆς), *a double bust of Hermes and Hercules,* Cic.

Hermes -ae, m. (Ἑρμῆς, *the god Hermes, Mercury), a post, the top of which was carved into a head, placed in the streets, esp. of Athens.*

Hermĭŏnē -ēs, f. and **Hermĭŏna** -ae, f. (Ἑρμιόνη), 1, *daughter of Menelaus and Helena, wife of Orestes;* 2, *town in Argolis, now Kastri.* Hence, adj., **Hermĭŏnĭcus** -a -um, *of or belonging to Hermione.*

Hermĭŏnes -um, m. *a people of Germany.*

Hermundūri -ōrum, m. *a German tribe near the source of the Elbe.*

Hermus -i, m. (Ἑρμος), *a river in Lydia.*

Hernĭci -ōrum, m. *a people in Latium.* Adj., **Hernĭcus** -a -um, *Hernican.*

Hērō -ūs, f. (Ἡρώ), *a priestess of Aphrodite at Sestos, beloved by Leander.*

Hērōdes -is, m. (Ἡρώδης), *Herod the Great, king of Judaea.*

Hērŏdŏtus -i, m. (Ἡρόδοτος), *the first great Greek historian, born 484* A.C.

hērŏĭcus -a -um (ἡρωικός), *relating to the heroes, heroic;* tempora, Cic.; personae, Cic.

hērŏīnē -ēs, f. (ἡρωίνη), *a demigoddess, heroine,* Prop.

hērŏīs -ĭdis, f. (ἡρωΐς), *a demigoddess, heroine,* Ov. (Gr. dat. plur., heroisin, Ov.).

Hērŏphĭle -ēs, f. (Ἡροφίλη), *a priestess of Apollo.*

hērŏs -ōis, m. (ἥρως), 1, *a demigod, hero,* Cic.; 2, *a distinguished man, hero;* noster Cato, Cic.

hērōus -a -um (ἡρῷος), *relating to a hero, heroic;* pes, versus, *epic verse* (hexameter), Cic.

Hersĭlĭa -ae, f. *wife of Romulus.*

hĕrus (ĕrus) -i, m. 1, *the master* or *head of a household,* Cic.; 2, *master, owner, lord,* Hor.

Hēsĭŏdus -i, m. (Ἡσίοδος), *the oldest Greek poet after Homer.* Adj., **Hēsĭŏdēus** -a -um, *Hesiodean.*

Hēsĭŏna -ae, f. and **Hēsĭŏnē** -ēs, f. (Ἡσιόνη), *daughter of Laomedon, king of Troy, rescued by Hercules from a sea-monster.*

Hespĕris -ĭdis, f. (Ἑσπερίς), *western; aquae,* Italian, as Italy was to the west of Greece, Verg. Subst., **Hespĕrĭdes** -um, f. (αἱ Ἑσπερίδες Νύμφαι), *the Hesperides, daughters of the Evening, living in an island in the extreme west, in a garden with golden apples, guarded by a dragon.*

Hespĕrĭus -a -um (ἑσπέριος), *western;* terra, Italy, Verg. Subst., **Hespĕrĭa** -ae, f. *the western land,* Italy, Verg.; *Spain,* Hor.

Hespĕrus or **-os** -i, m. (Ἕσπερος), *the Evening Star,* Cic.

hesternus -a -um (from root HES, whence heri), *of or relating to yesterday;* dies, Cic.

hesterno, adv. (hesternus), *yesterday,* Cic.

hĕtaerĭcŏs -ē -ŏn (ἑταιρικός -ή -όν), *relating to comradeship,* Nep.

heu! interj. *an exclamation of pain, oh! alas! woe!* heu! heu! me miserum, Cic.

heus! interj. *hallo! ho there! hark!* heus tu quid agis! Cic.

hexămĕtĕr -tra -trum (ἑξάμετρος), *with six feet* (of metre); hexameter versus, or versus hexameter, *a hexameter, a verse of six feet,* Cic.

hexēris -is, f. (ἑξήρης), *a galley with six banks of oars,* Liv.

hĭātus -ūs, m. (hio). **A.** *a cleft, opening;* oris, Cic.; terrae, Cic.; absol., *the opening of the mouth, the open jaws,* Verg.; quid dignum tanto feret hic promissor hiatu, *of such pompous language,* Hor. **B.** Transf., a, *desire after;* praemiorum, Tac.; b, in grammar, *a hiatus, the meeting of two vowels,* Cic.

Hĭbēres -um ('Ἴβηρες), or generally **Hĭbēri** -ōrum, m. *the Hiberians* (Iberians), 1, *the inhabitants of Hiberia in Spain;* sing., **Hĭber,** Hor.; 2, *the inhabitants of Hiberia, in Asia.* Hence, **A. Hĭbērĭa** -ae ('Ἰβηρία), 1, *a part of Spain;* 2, *a district in Asia, now Georgia,* Hor. **B.** Adj., 1, **Hĭbērĭcus** -a -um, and 2, **Hĭbērus** -a -um, *Hiberian,* poet. = *Spanish;* gurges (of the Western Ocean), Verg.; piscis, *the scomber,* Hor.; pastor triplex, Geryon, Ov.; vaccae or boves, *belonging to Geryon,* Ov.

hiberna -ōrum, n., v. hibernus.

hĭbernācŭlum -i, n. (hiberno), plur., hibernacula, *tents* or *huts for winter quarters,* Liv.

Hibernĭa -ae, f. *Ireland.*

hĭberno, 1. (hibernus), *to winter, spend the winter;* 1, gen., in sicco (of ships), Liv.; 2, esp. as milit. t.t., *to keep in winter quarters,* Cic.

hĭbernus -a -um (hiems). **I.** Lit., *wintry, winterly;* tempus, mensis, Cic.; annus, *time of winter,* Hor.; Alpes, *cold,* Hor.; castra, *winter quarters,* Liv. Subst., **hĭberna** -ōrum, n. (sc. castra), *winter quarters;* dies hibernorum, *time for going into winter quarters,* Caes.; hiberna aedificare, Liv.; cohortes in hiberna mittere, Cic.; ibi hiberna habere, Liv.; ex hibernis discedere, egredi, Cic. **II.** Transf., *stormy;* mare, Hor.; ventus, Verg.

1. **Hĭbērus** -i, m. (Ἴβηρ), *a river in Spain,* now *the Ebro.*

2. **Hĭbērus**, v. Hiberes.

hĭbiscum -i, n. (ἰβίσκος), *the marsh-mallow,* Verg.

hĭbrĭda (hybrĭda) -ae, c., 1, *of animals, a hybrid,* Plin.; 2, *of men, the offspring of a Roman by a foreign woman,* or *of a freeman by a slave,* Hor.

1. **hic**, haec, hŏc, pron. demonstr. (from pro

nominal stem I, whence also is, with demonstrative suffix ce), *this*. **A.** Gen., hic avunculus, Cic.; hic ipse, hic ille, hic iste, hic talis, quidam hic, Cic.; **hic** . . . ille, hic . . iste, hic referring to the object which may be the remoter one in the sentence, but is the nearer in the speaker's thoughts; hoc, subst. with genit., hoc commodi est, quod, etc., Cic.; absol. plur., haec, a, *this town, this state;* haec delere, haec vastare, Cic.; **b,** *the whole visible world,* Cic. **B.** Esp., a, hunc hominem = *me,* Hor.; **b,** of time, *this, the present;* his temporibus, Cic.; absol. plur., haec, *the present state of affairs,* Cic.

2. hic and **heic,** adv. *here.* **I.** Lit., *in this place, in this spot,* Cic. **II.** Transf., **A.** *herein, in this matter, on this occasion,* Cic. **B.** Of time, *hereupon, here,* Cic.

hīce, haece, hōce, pron. demonstr. (a more emphatic form of hic, haec, hoc), *this;* a, Cic.; in questions with -ne, hicine, haecine, hocine, Cic.; b, of time, *the present;* huncine solem tam nigrum surrexe mihi, Hor.

Hīcĕtāon -ŏnis, m. (Ἱκετάων), *son of Laomedon, king of Troy.* Adj., **Hīcĕtāŏnĭus** -a -um, Thymoetes, *son of Hicetaon,* Verg.

Hīcĕtas -ae, m. (Ἱκέτας), *a Pythagorean of Syracuse.*

hicine, v. hice.

hĭĕmālis -e (hiems), **1,** *wintry, winterly;* tempus, Cic.; **2,** *stormy;* navigatio, Cic.

hĭĕmo, 1. (hiems). **A.** *to winter, spend the winter;* a, mediis in undis, Hor.; b, esp. of soldiers, *to keep in winter quarters;* hiemare in Gallia, Caes. **B.** Transf., *to be stormy;* mare hiemat, Hor.

hĭems (hĭemps) -ĕmis, f. (χειμών). **I.** *rainy, stormy weather, storm;* hiemis magnitudo, Cic.; dum pelago desaevit hiems, Verg.; **II. A.** *the rainy season, winter;* Arabes campos hieme et aestate peragrantes, Cic.; personif., glacialis Hiems, Ov. **B.** Meton., **1,** *cold;* letalis hiems in pectora venit, Ov.; **2,** *year;* post certas hiemes, Hor.

Hiĕro, and **Hiĕrōn** -ōnis, m. (Ἱέρων), **1,** Hiero I., *ruler of Syracuse* (477—467 A.C.); **2,** Hiero II., *ruler of Syracuse* (269—215 A.C.). Adj. **Hiĕrōnicus** -a -um, *of Hiero.*

Hiĕrōcles -is, m. (Ἱεροκλῆς), *a Greek rhetorician, contemporary of Cicero.*

Hiĕrōnўmus -i, m. (Ἱερώνυμος), **1,** *a ruler of Syracuse, successor of Hiero II.;* **2,** *a Greek peripatetic philosopher.*

Hiĕrŏsŏlўma -ōrum, n. (Ἱεροσόλυμα), *the capital of Judaea.* Hence, **Hiĕrŏsŏlўmārius,** *nickname of Pompey,* "*the hero of Jerusalem*" (*because of his priding himself on his oriental victories*).

hiĕto, 1. (intens. of hio for hiato), *to open the mouth, gape,* Plaut.

hĭlārē, adv. (hilarus), *cheerfully, merrily, blithely;* vivere, Cic.; hilarius loqui, Cic.

hĭlāris -e, and **hĭlărus** -a -um (ἱλαρός), *cheerful, merry, blithe, gay, jocund, jovial;* animus, vita, Cic.; esse vultu hilari atque laeto, Cic.; hilariores litterae, Cic.

hĭlărĭtas -ātis, f. (hilaris), *cheerfulness, mirth, gaiety, hilarity,* Cic.

hĭlărĭtūdo -ĭnis, f. = hilaritas (q.v.).

hĭlăro, 1. (hilaris), *to make joyful, cheerful, to cheer up, exhilarate;* huius suavitate maxime hilaratae Athenae sunt, Cic.; multo convivia Baccho, Verg.

hĭlărŭlus -a -um (dim. of hilarus), *somewhat cheerful,* Cic.

hilla -ae, f. (dim. of hira), **1,** generally in plur., *the smaller intestines of all animals;* **2,** *a kind of sausage,* Hor.

Hīlōtae, and **Īlōtae** -ārum, m. (Εἱλῶται), *the Helots, slaves of the Spartans.*

hīlum -i, n. (another form of filum), *a trifle;* neque (nec) hilum, *not a whit, not in the least,* Lucr.

Hĭmella -ae, f. *a stream in the Sabine country.*

Hĭmĕra -ae, f. (Ἱμέρα), **1,** *name of two rivers in Sicily;* **2,** *town on one of these rivers.*

hinc, adv. *from here, hence.* **I. A.** Lit., a nobis hinc profecti, Cic. **B.** Transf., **1,** *from this cause,* Cic.; hinc illae lacrimae, Ter.; *from this matter;* hinc quantum cui videbitur decidere, Cic.; **2,** of time, a, *henceforth;* quisquis es, amissos hinc jam obliviscere Graios, Verg.; b, *thereupon;* hinc toto praeceps se corpore ad undas misit, Verg. **II.** *on this side, in this direction;* hinc atque illinc, *on this side and on that,* Cic.

hinnĭo, 4. *to neigh, whinny,* Lucr.

hinnītus -ūs, m. (hinnio), *a neighing,* Cic.

hinnŭlĕus (hinnŭlus) -i, m. (hinnus), *a young hind or fawn,* Hor.

hinnus -i, m. (ἵννος), *a mule, the offspring of a stallion and a she-ass* (mulus = *the offspring of a he-ass and a mare*), Varr.

hĭo, 1. (connected with χαίνω, χάσκω). **I.** Intransit., *to open, stand open, gape.* **A.** Gen., **1,** lit., concha hians, Cic.; **2,** transf., *of discourse, to be badly put together, hang together badly;* hiantia loqui, Cic. **B.** Esp., *to open wide the mouth or jaws;* **1,** lit., Verg.; **2,** transf., a, *to desire with open mouth, long for;* Verrem avaritiā hiante atque imminente fuisse, Cic.; b, *to open the mouth in astonishment,* Verg. **II.** Transit., *to pour forth;* carmen lyrā, Prop.

hippăgōgoe -ōn, acc. -ūs, f. (αἱ ἱππαγωγοί), *transports for cavalry,* Liv.

Hippĭas -ae, m. (Ἱππίας), **1,** *son of Pisistratus, tyrant of Athens;* **2,** *a sophist of Elis, contemporary with Socrates.*

Hippo -ōnis, m. (Ἱππών), **1,** Hippo regius, *town in Numidia, now Bona;* **2,** *town in Hispania Tarraconensis.*

hippŏcentaurus -i, m. (ἱπποκένταυρος), *a centaur,* Cic.

Hippŏcrātes -is, m. (Ἱπποκράτης), *a physician of Cos* (flourishing about 436 A.C.).

Hippŏcrēnē -ēs, f. (ἵππου κρήνη), *a fountain on Mount Helicon, produced by a blow from the hoof of Pegasus.*

Hippŏdămē -ēs, f., and **Hippŏdămēa** or -īa -ae, f. (Ἱπποδάμη, -δάμεια), **1,** *daughter of Oenomaus, king of Pisa in Elis;* **2,** *wife of Pirithous.*

Hippŏdămus -i, m. (Ἱππόδαμος), *the horse-tamer*—i.e., Castor; poet. = *rider,* Mart.

hippŏdrŏmos -i, m. (ἱππόδρομος), *a hippo-drome, or racecourse for horses and chariots,* Plaut.

Hippŏlўtē -ēs, f., and **Hippŏlўta** -ae, f. (Ἱππολύτη), **1,** *Queen of the Amazons, taken prisoner by Theseus;* **2,** *wife of Acastus, King of Magnesia.*

Hippŏlўtus -i, m. (Ἱππόλυτος), *son of Theseus and Hippolyte, or Antiope.*

hippŏmănes, n. (ἱππομανές), **1,** *a slimy humour which flows from a mare when in heat,* Verg.; **2,** *a membrane on the head of a new-born foal,* Plin.; *both* 1 *and* 2 *were used for love-potions,* Juv.

Hippŏmēnēs -ae, m. (Ἱππομένης), **1**, *the husband of Atalanta ;* **2**, *father of Limone ; whence* **Hippŏmēnēis** -nēīdis, f. = *Limone.*

Hippōnax -nactis, m. (Ἱππώναξ), *a Greek satirical poet of the sixth century* B.C. Hence adj., **Hippōnactēus** -a -um, *biting, satirical;* praeconium, Cic.; Hipponacteos effugere vix posse, Cic.

hippŏpŏtamus -i, m. (ἱπποπόταμος), *a river-horse, hippopotamus,* Plin.

Hippŏtădes -ae, m. (Ἱπποτάδης), *descendant of Hippotes, Aeolus (grandson of Hippotes).*

hippŏtoxŏta -ae, m. (ἱπποτοξότης), *a mounted archer,* Caes.

hippūrus, or **-ŏs**, -i, m. (ἵππουρος), *a fish,* perhaps *the gold fish,* Ov.

hir and **īr**, indecl. (connected with χείρ), *the hand,* ap. Cic.

hīra -ae, f. *a gut, intestine,* Plaut.

hircīnus -a -um (hircus), *of or relating to a he-goat ;* folles, *made of goat skins,* Hor.

hircōsus -a -um (hircus), *smelling like a goat, goatish,* Plaut.

hircŭlus -i, m. (dim. of hircus), *a little goat,* Cat.

hircus -i, m. *a he-goat,* Verg.; olere hircum, *to smell like a goat,* Hor.; used as a term of reproach, *an old goat,* Cat.

hirnĕa -ae, f. *a can or jug,* Plaut.

hirnŭla -ae, f. (dim. of hirnea), *a little can or jug,* Cic.

Hirpīni -ōrum, m. *a Samnite people of Lower Italy ;* adj., **Hirpīnus** -a -um, *Hirpine.*

hirquus, hirquīnus = hircus, hircīnus (q.v.).

hirsūtus -a -um (conn. with hirtus), **1**, *covered with hair, hairy, hirsute, rough, shaggy, prickly ;* supercilium, Verg.; crines, Ov.; aliae (animantium) spinis hirsutae, Cic.; **2**, *rough, un-adorned ;* nihil est hirsutius illis (annalibus), Ov.

Hirtius -a -um, *name of a Roman gens, the most celebrated member of which was* A. Hirtius, *the friend and follower of* C. Julius Caesar, *slain at the battle of Modena, the author of the Eighth book of Caesar's* Bell. Gall. Hence, adj., **Hirtīnus** -a -um, *of or belonging to Hirtius.*

hirtus -a -um (root HIR), **1**, *shaggy, rough, hairy, prickly ;* setae, Ov.; capellae, Ov.; **2**, transf., *rough, uncultivated ;* ingenium, Hor.

hīrūdo -ĭnis, f. *a leech,* Plin.; transf., aerarii, Cic.

hīrundĭnīnus -a -um (hirundo), *of or relating to swallows,* Plaut.

hīrundo -dĭnis, f. (χελιδών), *a swallow,* Verg.

hisco, 3. (contr. for hiasco), **1**, *to open, split open, gape,* Ov.; **2**, especially, *to open the mouth, to mutter ;* respondebisne ad haec aut omnino hiscere audebis? Cic.

Hispăl -pălis, n. and (more commonly) **Hispălis** -is, f. *town in Spain, now Seville.* Hence, **Hispālienses** -ĭum, *the inhabitants of Hispalis.*

Hispāni -ōrum, m. *the Spaniards ;* hence, **A. Hispānia** -ae, f. *the whole of the Spanish peninsula (including Portugal) divided into* citerior, *the eastern part* (later Hisp. Tarraconensis), *and* ulterior, *the southern and western part* (later Lusitania and Baetica); hence plur. Hispaniae. **B. Hispāniensis** -e, and **C. Hispānus** -a -um, *Spanish.*

hispĭdus -a -um, *rough, shaggy, hairy, bristly ;* facies, Hor.; ager, *wild,* Hor.

1 hister = histrio (q.v.).

2. Hister -tri, m. (Ἱστρος), *name of the lower part of the Danube,* binominis (as the upper part was called Danuvius), Ov.

histŏria -ae, f. (ἱστορία), **1**, *historical narrative, history ;* historia Graeca, *Roman history written in Greek,* Cic.; historia Italici belli et civilis, Cic.; historiam scribere, Cic.; **2**, *narrative, narration ;* historiā dignum, *worthy of narration,* Cic.

histŏrĭcus -a -um (ἱστορικός), *relating or belonging to history, historical ;* genus, Cic.; subst., **histŏrĭcus** -i, m. *an historian,* Cic.

Histri -ōrum (Ἱστροι), *Istrians, inhabitants of Istria ;* hence, **A. Histria** -ae, f. (Ἱστρία), *Histria, a country near Illyria.* **B. Histrĭcus** -a -um, *Histrian.*

histrĭcus -a -um (hister), *of or relating to actors,* Plaut.

histrio -ōnis, m. *an actor,* Cic.

histrĭōnālis -e (histrio), *of or relating to actors,* Tac.

hĭulcē, adv. (hiulcus), *in a disconnected manner ;* loqui, Cic.

hĭulco, 1. (hiulcus), *to cause to gape, to split,* Cat.

hĭulcus -a -um (for hiulicus, from hio), *gaping, cleft, open.* **I.** Lit., hiulca siti arva, Verg. **II.** Transf. a, of discourse, *ill put together, disconnected ;* concursus verborum, Cic.; **b**, *eager, longing,* Plaut.

hŏdĭē, adv. (hodie = hoc die), *to-day* (opp. cras, heri). **I.** Lit., hodie sunt nonae Sextiles, Cic. **II.** Transf. a, *at the present time,* Cic.; **b**, *now, at present ;* si hodie hanc gloriam atque hoc orbis terrae imperium teneremus, Cic.; *up to to-day, up to the present time ;* quem vivere hodie aiunt, Cic.; **c**, = *at once, directly,* Cic.

hŏdĭernus -a -um (hodie), *of or relating to to-day ;* dies, Cic.; edictum, Cic.; ad hodiernum diem, *up to to-day,* Cic.

hoedus, hoedīnus, etc. = haedus, haedinus, etc. (q.v.).

Hŏmērus -i, m. (Ὅμηρος), *the celebrated Greek epic poet ;* hence, adj., **Hŏmērĭcus** -a -um, *Homeric.*

hŏmĭcīda -ae, c. (homo and caedo). **I.** Lit., *a murderer, murderess, homicide,* Cic. **II.** In a good sense (Gk. ἀνδροφόνος), of Hector, *slayer of men,* Hor.

hŏmĭcīdĭum -ĭi, n. (homicida) *murder, man-slaughter, homicide,* Tac.

hŏmo -ĭnis, m. (old Latin hĕmo), *a human being, man.* **I.** Gen., *man,* as opp. to the beasts (vir, *man* as opp. to woman); in plur., homines, *men in general, people,* Cic.; homo nemo, or nemo homo, *not a soul, no one,* Cic.; odium hominis, *a hateful man,* Cic.; inter homines esse, **a**, *to live,* Cic.; **b**, *to mix in society, be in the world,* Cic. **II.** Esp., **A.** a, *a man,* in the better sense of the word ; nihil hominis esse, *to be without the better qualities of a man ;* hominem ex homine tollere or exuere, *to take from a man that which constitutes a man,* Cic.; si quidem homo esset, *if he had the feelings of a man,* Cic.; homines visi sumus, Cic.; virum te putabo . . . hominem non putabo, *I must praise your patience and not your taste,* Cic.; **b**, *a man as liable to error, a mortal ;* quia homo est, Cic. **B.** Used in place of pronouns, valde hominem diligo, (where it stands for hunc, eum, or illum), Cic.; hic homo = ego, Hor. **C.** *a slave, servant ;* Quintii, *Quintius's man,* Cic. **D.** Plur., hŏmĭnes *infantry* (opp. equites), Caes.

hŏmoeŏmĕria -ae, f. (ὁμοιομέρεια), *similarity of parts,* Lucr.

Hŏmŏlē -ēs, f. (Ὁμόλη), a mountain in Thessaly, where Pan was worshipped.

hŏmullus -i, m. (dim. of homo), a little man, manikin, Cic.

hŏmuncĭo -ōnis, m. (dim. of homo), a little man, manikin, Cic.

hŏmuncŭlus -i, m. (dim. of homo), a little man, manikin, Cic.

hŏnestas -ātis, f. (honestus). **I.** honourable reputation, honour, respectability; honestatem amittere, Cic.; appetens honestatis, Cic.; honestates civitatis, notabilities, Cic. **II.** worth, virtue, honourable character, probity; 1, vitae, Cic.; hinc (pugnat) honestas, illinc turpitudo, Cic.; transf., of things, beauty; testudinis, Cic.; 2, philosoph. t. t., virtue, Cic.

hŏnestē, adv. (honestus), 1, honourably, creditably, respectably; cenare, Cic.; se gerere, Cic.; in pugna honeste cadere, Cic.; 2, honourably, nobly; honeste geniti, of noble birth, Liv.

hŏnesto (honestus), to honour, distinguish, adorn, dignify; aliquem laude, honore, Cic.; domum, curiam, Cic.

hŏnestus -a -um (honor). **I.** honourable, reputable, glorious; 1, gen., victoria, Liv.; dies honestissimus, Cic.; with sup., honestumne factu sit an turpe, Cic.; honestum est with acc. and infin., Cic.; subst., **hŏnestum** -i, n. morality, virtue, Cic.; 2, esp., a, fine, beautiful, Ter.; subst., **hŏnestum** -i, n. beauty, Hor.; b, specious, fine-sounding; honestum et probabile nomen, Cic. **II.** worthy of honour, distinguished; familia, Cic.; honesto loco natus, Cic.; vir honestus or honestissimus (title of the knights), Cic.; subst., **hŏnesti** -ōrum, m. people of distinction, Hor.

hŏnor = honos (q.v.).

hŏnōrābĭlis -e (honor), honourable; haec ipsa sunt honorabilia, salutari, appeti, decedi, assurgi, etc., Cic.

hŏnōrārĭus -a -um (honor), done or given in honour of, honorary; vinum, frumentum, Cic.; opera, Cic.; delectare honorarium (est), done out of respect for the audience, Cic.

hŏnōrātē, adv. (honoratus), with honour, honourably, Tac.

hŏnōrātus -a -um, p. adj. with compar. and superl. (honoro), 1, honoured, distinguished, respected; viri, Cic.; nusquam est senectus honoratior, Cic.; 2, honoured by a public office, placed in a high position, in office; honorati quatuor filii, Cic.

hŏnōrĭfĭcē, adv., comp. honorificentius, superl. honorificentissime (with honorificus), with honour, in an honourable or respectful manner; honorificentissime aliquem appellare, Caes.; aliquem honorificentissime tractare, Cic.

hŏnōrĭfĭcus -a -um, compar. honorificentior, superl. honorificentissimus (honor and facio), causing honour, honourable, honouring; senatus consultum, Cic.; senectus, Cic.

hŏnōro, 1. (honor), 1, to honour, show honour to; aliquem, Cic.; 2, to adorn, dignify, honour with; aliquem sellā curuli, Liv.

hŏnōrus -a -um (honor), honourable, Tac.

hŏnŏs and **hŏnŏr** -ōris, m. **I.** honour, honourable distinction. **A.** Gen., honorem alicui habere, tribuere, Cic.; praestare, Ov., honore aliquem afficere, to show honour to, Cic.; honore aliquem augere, Caes.; in honore habere, Cic.; esse, Cic.; esse alicui summo honori, to prove honourable to, Cic.; aliquid in honorem adducere, to bring to honour, Cic.; honori ducitur, it is considered an honour, Sall.; honorem

praefari or dicere, to say "by your leave," Cic.; honoris causā or gratiā, out of respect; quem honoris causā or gratiā nomino, Cic.; honoris Divitiaci et Aeduorum causā, Cic.; so, ad honorem alicuius, Cic.; ad honorem atque amplitudinem tuam, Cic.; supremus honos (the last honour = burial), Verg.; communi in morte honore carere, Cic.; mortis honore carere, Verg.; **B.** Esp., a, an office of dignity, a public office; ad honores ascendere, Cic.; honoribus amplissimis perfunctus, Cic.; b, a title of honour; honos militaris, Liv.; c, a reward, fee; honos medici, Cic.; d, honour rendered to the gods, sacrifice, Verg. **C.** Personif., Honor, the god of honour. **II.** Poet. transf., beauty, grace, ornament; honorum ruris, crops, Hor.; silvarum, foliage, Verg.

1. hōra -ae, f. (ὥρα). **I.** time in gen.; numquam te crastina fallet hora, Verg. **II.** a definite space of time. **A.** a time of the year, season; verni temporis hora, Hor. **B.** a time of the day, hour; 1, lit., in horam vivere, to live for the moment, Cic.; horā amplius, more than an hour, Cic.; in hora, in an hour, Cic.; in horas, hourly, Cic.; hora quota est? what's o'clock? Hor.; horae legitimae, hours fixed as limits to a speech, Cic.; 2, meton., **hōrae** -ārum, f. a clock, dial, mittere ad horas, Cic.

2. Hōra -ae, f. the name of Hersilia when deified, the celestial wife of Quirinus.

Hōrae -ārum, f. (Ὧραι), the Hours, goddesses who presided over the changes of the seasons, attendants on the sun-god.

Hŏrātĭus -a -um, name of a Roman gens to which belonged, 1, the three Horatii, who fought against the three Alban Curiatii; 2, Horatius Cocles, who defended the bridge over the Tiber against the army of Porsena; 3, Qu. Horatius Flaccus, son of a freedman of the Horatian gens (65-8 A.C.), the celebrated Roman lyric poet.

hordĕācĕus and **-cĭus** -a -um (hordeum), of or relating to barley, Plin.

hordĕārĭus -a -um (hordeum), of or relating to barley, Plin.

hordēĭus -a -um = hordeaceus (q.v.).

hordĕum (ordĕum) -i, n. barley, Liv., Caes.

hŏrĭa (ōrĭa) -ae, f. a small fishing-boat, Plaut.

hŏrĭŏla (ōrĭŏla) -ae, f. (dim. of oria), a small fishing-boat, Plaut.

hŏrĭor, 4. (connected with ὄρνυμι), to urge, incite, encourage, Enn.

hŏrizon -ontis, m. (ὁρίζων), the horizon, Sen.

hornō, adv. (hornus), this year, Plaut.

hornŏtĭnus -a -um (hornus), of or relating to the present year; frumentum, Cic.

hornus -a -um (for horinus, from hora), of this year, this year's; vina, Hor.

hōrŏlŏgĭum -ĭi, n. (ὡρολόγιον), a clock, sundial, or water-clock, Cic.

hōroscŏpŏs -ŏn, m. (ὡροσκόπος), a horoscope, Pers.

horrendus -a -um (partic. of horreo), 1, horrible, horrid, frightful, dreadful; monstrum, Verg.; Sibylla, Verg.; neut. as adv., horrendum stridens belua, Verg.; 2, worthy of reverence, venerable; virgo, Verg.

horrĕo, 2. **I.** to bristle. **A.** Lit., a, horret seges aristis, Verg.; b, to be hard and rough with frost; terram uno tempore florere deinde vicissim horrere, Cic. **B.** Of hair, to stand on end; comae horrent, Ov.; partic., horrens, prickly, rough; rubi, Verg. **II.** Of persons, to shiver or shudder with cold or fright. **A.** Intransit., horreo animo, Cic. **B.** Transit., to *shudder at ;* crimen, Cic.; with infin., non horreo in hunc locum progredi, Cic.

horresco, horrŭi, 3. (horreo), **1,** *to stand on end, bristle, be rough ;* horrueruntque comae, Ov.; mare coepit horrescere, *to be stormy,* Cic. ; **2,** *to tremble, begin to shudder, begin to dread,* Cic.; horresco referens, Verg.; with acc., morsus futuros, Verg.

horrĕum -i, n. *a barn, storehouse, magazine, granary ;* Capua horreum Campani agri, Cic.; poet., *a bee-hive,* Verg. ; *an ant-hill,* Ov.

horrĭbĭlis -e (horreo), **1,** *horrible, frightful, dreadful, fearful ;* pestis reipublicae, Cic. ; horribile est, with infin., Cic.; **2,** *astonishing, wonderful ;* horribili vigilantiā, Cic.

horrĭdē, adv. (horridus), **1,** *roughly, without embellishment ;* dicere, Cic. ; horridius utetur ornamentis, Cic. ; **2,** *roughly, harshly ;* alloqui, Tac.

horrĭdŭlus -a -um (dim. of horridus), **1,** *somewhat rough, projecting,* Plaut. ; **2,** transf., *somewhat rough, unadorned ;* orationes, Cic.

horrĭdus -a -um (horreo). **I.** *rough, shaggy, bristly.* **A.** Lit., barba, Cic. ; sus, Verg. **B.** Transf., a, *rough, wild, savage ;* campus, Cic.; b, *rough, without refinement, unpolished, uncouth ;* Tubero vitā et oratione horridus, Cic. **II. 1,** *shuddering, trembling with cold ;* si premerem ventosas horridus Alpes, Ov.; **2,** *dreadful, horrible ;* procella, Verg.

horrĭfer -fĕra -fĕrum (horror and fero), *causing dread, bringing fear, terrible ;* boreas, Ov.; Erinys, Ov.

horrĭfĭcē, adv. (horrificus), *with dread,* Lucr.

horrĭfĭco, 1. (horrificus), **1,** *to make rough,* Cat. ; **2,** *to terrify,* Verg.

horrĭfĭcus -a -um (horror and facio), *causing terror, horrible ;* letum, Verg.

horrĭsŏnus -a -um (horreo and sono), *sounding horribly ;* fremitus, Verg.

horror -ōris, m. (horreo), **1,** *a shaking, shivering with cold, ague-fit ;* quoniam jam sine horrore est, spero esse, ut volumus, Cic. ; **2,** *trembling ;* a, from dread, *terror, horror ;* qui me horror perfudit, Cic.; b, *religious dread, awe ;* perfusus horrore venerabundusque, Liv.

horsum, adv. (contr. for hucvorsum), *in this direction, hitherward,* Plaut.

Horta -ae, f. *town in Etruria, now Orte.* Adj., **Hortīnus** -a -um, *of Horta.*

hortāmen -ĭnis, n. (hortor), *an encouragement, incitement, exhortation,* Liv.

hortāmentum -i, n. (hortor), *encouragement, incitement,* Sall.

hortātio -ōnis, f. (hortor), *exhortation, encouragement ;* hortatione agere cum aliquo, Cic.; plur., contiones hortationesque, Cic.

hortātor -ōris, m. (hortor), *an exhorter, encourager ;* absol., isto hortatore, Cic. ; with genit., studii, *to study,* Cic.; with ad and the acc. gerund, auctores hortatoresque ad me restituendum, Cic. ; with ut and the subj., Cic.; esp., as milit. t. t., *one who exhorts the soldiers,* Liv.

hortātus -ūs, m. (hortor), *incitement, exhortation ;* id fecisse aliorum consilio, hortatu, Cic.

Hortensĭus -a -um, *name of a Roman gens, the most famous member of which was* Qu. Hortensius Hortalus, *an orator of the time of Cicero.* Adj., **Hortensĭānus** -a -um, *Hortensian.*

hortor, 1. dep. (contr. from horitor, intens. of horior, *to encourage,* from the same root **as** ὄρνυμι), *to exhort, incite, encourage.* **I.** Gen., **a,** *of persons,* aliquem, Cic. ; with ut and the **subj.,** magno opere te hortor ut, etc. ; with

ne and the subj., hortatur eos **ne animo defic'** iant, Caes.; with subj. alone, hortatur non solum ab eruptionibus caveant, etc., Caes. ; **with** infin., hortamur fari, Verg. ; with ad, populum ad vindicandum, Sall.; with in and the **acc.,** Gentium in amicitiam secum et cum Macedonibus jungendam, Liv.; with de, de Aufidiano nomine nihil te hortor, Cic.; with acc. of thing, pacem, Cic. ; prov., hortari currentem, *to spur the willing horse,* Cic. ; **b,** of inanimate subjects, multae res ad hoc consilium Gallos hortabantur, Caes.; with infin., reipublicae dignitas minora haec relinquere hortatur, Cic. **II.** Esp., *to harangue soldiers before a battle ;* suos, Caes.

hortŭlus -i, m. (dim. of hortus), *a little garden,* Cat.; gen. plur., hortuli, *grounds, a small park,* Cic.

hortus -i, m. (χόρτος), *garden ;* Epicuri, (where Epicurus taught), Cic.; meton., *garden produce,* Hor.

hospes -pĭtis, c. (akin to hostis), *a stranger, foreigner ;* hence, *a guest, guest friend,* Cic.; transf.= *unknown, inexperienced in ;* nec peregrinum atque hospitem in agendo esse debere, Cic.

hospĭtālis -e (hospes), **1,** *relating to a guest or host ;* cubiculum, *guest-chamber,* Liv.; sedes, Cic.; caedes, *murder of a guest,* Liv.; Juppiter, *protector of guests,* Cic.; **2,** *friendly, hospitable ;* domo hospitalissimus, Cic.; with in and the acc., Cimonem in suos curiales Laciadas hospitalem Cic.

hospĭtālĭtas -ātis, f. (hospitalis), *hospitality,* Cic.

hospĭtālĭtěr, adv. (hospitalis), *hospitably,* Liv.

hospĭtĭum -ĭi, n. (hospes). **I.** *hospitality, the relation between host and guest ;* mihi cum aliquo hospitium est, Cic., or intercedit, Caes. ; alicuius hospitio usus sum, Caes. ; hospitium cum aliquo facere, Cic. ; jungere, Liv. **II.** *hospitality, friendliness, hospitable reception.* **A.** aliquem hospitio magnificentissimo accipere, Cic. ; aliquem hospitio invitare, Cic. **B.** Meton., *a guest-chamber, guest's lodging, inn ;* hospitium parare, Cic.; cohortes per hospitia dispersae, *billeted,* Tac. ; transf., *the resting-place of animals,* Verg.

hospĭtus -a -um (hospes). **I.** *strange, foreign ;* navis, Ov.; aequora, Verg.; conjux hospita Teucris, Verg. Subst., **hospĭta** -ae, f. *a foreigner,* Cic. **II.** *hospitable ;* terra, Verg. Subst., **hospĭta** -ae, f. *the hostess,* Cic.

hostĭa -ae, f. (from 2. hostio, Lit., *the thing struck), an animal slain in sacrifice, a sin-offering ;* humana, Cic.; hostias immolare, Cic., or mactare, Verg.

hostĭātus -a -um (hostia), *provided with animals for sacrifice,* Plaut.

hostĭcus -a -um (hostis), *relating or belonging to the enemy, hostile ;* ager, Liv. Subst., **hostĭcum** -i, n. *the enemy's territory ;* in hostico, Liv.

hostĭfĭcus -a -um (hostis and facio), *hostile,* Cic.

hostīlis -e (hostis), **1,** *of or relating to th* enemy, *hostile ;* expugnatio, Cic. ; in augury, pars (opp. familiaris), *the part of the entrails said to refer to the enemy,* Lucan.; **2,** *like an enemy, unfriendly, hostile ;* hostili odio et crudelitate, Cic.; multa hostilia audere, Tac.

hostīlĭtěr, adv. (hostilis), *hostilely, like an* enemy; quid ille fecit hostiliter, Cic.

Hostīlĭus -ĭi, m. Tullus, *third king of Rome.* Adj., **Hostīlĭus** -a -um, *Hostilian ;* curia, *built by Tullus Hostilius,* Liv.

hostīmentum -i, n. (1. hostio), *compensation, requital*, Plaut.

1. hostĭo, 4, to *requite, recompense*, Plaut.

2. hostĭo, 4. *to strike*, Plaut.

hostis -is, c. originally *a stranger*, but afterwards *an enemy, a public foe* (opp. inimicus, *a private enemy*). **A.** Lit., cives hostesque, Liv.; omnes nos statuit ille non inimicos sed hostes, Cic.; populo Romano, adversus Romanos, Liv.; hostem aliquem judicare, *to denounce as an enemy to his country*, Cic.; sing. collect., capta hostis, *the female captives*, Liv. **B.** Transf., 1, *a bitter foe in private life*; hostis omnium hominum, Cic.; **2**, *a rival in love*, Ov.

hūc, adv. (hic), *hither, to this place*, **1**, of space, huc ades, *come hither*, Verg.; tum huc tum illuc, Cic.; nunc huc nunc illuc, Verg.; huc et illuc, huc, illuc, Cic.; huc atque illuc, *hither and thither*, Cic.; **2**, not referring to place, *hither, thus far, to this point*; rem huc deduxi, Cic.; huc te pares, *for this object*, Cic.; accedat huc, Cic.

hūcīne, adv. *so far? as far as this?* hucine tandem omnia reciderunt? Cic.

hŭi, interj., exclamation of astonishment, ridicule, etc., *eh! hallo!* hui, quam timeo quid existimes, Cic.

hūjusmŏdi or **hūjuscĕmŏdi**, *of this kind, of such a kind, such*; ex hujusmodi principio, Cic.

hūmānē, adv. (humanus), **1**, *humanly, like a human being*; morbos toleranter et humane ferre, Cic.; **2**, *humanely, kindly, courteously*; fecit humane, Cic.

hūmānĭtas -ātis, f. (humanus). **I.** *humanity, human nature, human feeling*; omnem humanitatem exuere, Cic.; fac, id quod est humanitatis tuae (*what you owe to yourself as a man*), ne quid aliud cures hoc tempore nisi ut quam commodissime convalescas, Cic. **II.** Esp., **A.** *humanity, human kindness, kindness, philanthropy, mildness*; edictorum, Cic. **B.** *refinement of education and taste, good breeding, mental cultivation, culture*; communium litterarum ac politioris humanitatis expers, Cic.

hūmānĭtĕr, adv. (humanus), **1**, *humanly, in a way becoming human nature*; vivere, Cic.; **2**, *politely, courteously, kindly*; litterae humaniter scriptae, Cic.

hūmānĭtŭs, adv. (humanus), *after the manner of men*; si quid mihi humanitus accidisset, i.e. *if I should die*, Cic.

hūmānus -a -um (homo), *human, of or relating to human beings*. **I.** Gen., genus, *the human race*, Cic.; facies, Cic.; res humanae, *human affairs*, Cic., or *things happening to man*, Cic.; hostia, *human sacrifice*, Cic.; scelus, *against men*, Liv.; humanum est, it is *human*, Cic.; subst., **a**, **humanus** -i, m. *one of the human race*, Ov.; **b**, **humana** -ōrum, n. *human affairs*; humana miscere divinis, Liv., or *things happening to man, the fate of man*; omnia humana tolerabilia ferre, Cic. **II.** Esp., **A.** *humane, kind, philanthropic*; erga aliquem, Cic. **B.** *civilised, refined*; gens humana atque docta, Cic.

hŭmātĭo -ōnis, f. (humo), *a burying, interment*, Cic.

hūmecto, 1. *to wet, moisten, water*; qua niger humectat flaventia culta Galesus, Verg.; vultum largo flumine, Verg.

hūmĕo, 2. *to be moist, wet*, Ov.; partic. pres., **hūmens** -entis, *moist, wet, dewy*; umbra, Verg.; oculi, Ov.

hŭmĕrus -i, m. *the shoulder*, **a**, of men, sagittae pendebant ab humero, Ov.; puerum in humeros suos efferre, Cic.; fig., comitia humeris suis sustinere, Cic.; **b**, of animals, *the shoulder, fore-quarter*, Cic.

hūmesco, 3. (humeo), *to become wet, grow moist*, Verg.

hūmĭdŭlus -a -um (dim. of humidus), *somewhat wet, moist*, Ov.

hūmĭdus -a -um (humeo), *wet, moist, humid*; ligna, Cic.; mella, *liquid*, Verg.; Ide, *rich in streams*, Ov. Subst., **hūmĭdum** -i, n. *a wet place*, Tac.; humida -ōrum, n. *wet parts*, Cic.

hūmĭfer -fĕra -fĕrum (humor and fero), *containing moisture, moist*, Cic. poet.

hŭmĭlĭs -e (humus), *low*. **I.** Lit., **a**, *low* (as opposed to high), arbores et vites et quae sunt humiliora, Cic.; statura humilis, Nep.; **b**, (as opposed to deep), *shallow*; fossa, Verg. **II.** Transf., **A.** Of position, rank, etc., *low, mean, humble, poor, insignificant*; humilibus parentibus natus, Cic.; humillimus de plebe, Liv.; subst., **humilis** -is, m. *a person of low rank*, Hor. **B.** Of character, **a**, *abject, base*; humili animo ferre, Cic.; **b**, *submissive, humble*; obsecratio humilis, Cic. **C.** Of expression, *mean, without elevation*; oratio humilis et abjecta, Cic.

hŭmĭlĭtas -ātis, f. (humilis). **I.** *smallness, lowness, nearness to the ground*; animalium, Cic. **II.** Transf., **A.** *lowness of birth or station, insignificance, obscurity*; alicuius humilitatem despicere, Cic. **B.** *humility of disposition, submissiveness, abjectness*; humilitas et obsecratio, Cic.

hŭmĭlĭtĕr, adv. with compar. and superl. (humilis), *humbly, meanly, abjectly*; sentire, Cic.; servire, Liv.

hŭmo, 1. (humus), **1**, *to cover with earth, bury*; aliquem, Cic.; **2**, transf., *to perform the funeral rites over a corpse (burn, etc.)*, Nep.

hūmor -ōris, m. (akin to χυμός, *a liquid*), *moisture, liquid, fluid*. **I.** Gen. Bacchi, *wine*, Verg.; lacteus, *milk*, Ov.; circumfluus, *the sea*, Ov.; humor in genas labitur, *tears*, Hor.; plur., humores marini, Cic. **II.** Esp., *the sap of plants*, Verg.

hŭmus -i, f. (akin to χαμ-αί), *the ground, earth, soil*. **I.** Lit., humus injecta, Cic.; humi, *on the ground, on the floor*; jacere, Cic.; stratus humi, Cic.; humo, **a**, *from the ground*; surgere, Ov.; **b**, *on the ground*; sedere, Ov.; **c**, *out of the ground*; fundit humo facilem victum justissima tellus, Verg.; **d**, *in the ground*; figere plantas, Verg. **II.** Meton., *land, country*; Punica, Pontica, Ov.

hyăcinthĭnus -a -um (ὑακίνθινος), *hyacinthine, belonging to the hyacinth*; flos, Cat.

1. Hўăcinthus (-ŏs) -i, m. (Ὑάκινθος), *a beautiful Spartan youth, beloved of and accidentally killed by Apollo; from his blood sprang the flower called by his name*; hence, **Hўăcinthĭa** -ōrum, n. *a festival celebrated at Sparta*.

2. hўăcinthus -i, m. (ὑάκινθος), *a flower, the hyacinth* (not the flower so called by us), Verg.

Hўădes -um, f. (Ὑάδες), *the Hyades, a group of seven stars in the constellation Taurus*, Verg.

hўaena -ae, f. (ὕαινα), *the hyena*, Ov.

hўălus -i, m. (ὕαλος), *glass*; color hyali, *glassgreen*, Verg.

Hўampŏlis -pŏlis, f. (Ὑάμπολις), *a city in the E. of Phocis*.

Hўantes -ĭum, m. (Ὕαντες), *an old name for the Boeotians*; adj., **a**, **Hўantēus** -a -um, *Boeotian*, Ov.; aqua, *Castalia*, Mart.; **b**, **Hўantĭus** -a -um, *Boeotian*; subst., **Hўantĭus** -ĭi, m. *Actaeon, grandson of Cadmus*, Ov.

Hўas -antis, m. (῞Υας), *son of Atlas, and brother* (or *father*) *of the Hyades;* sidus Hyantis, *the Hyades,* Ov. (acc. sing., Hyan, Ov.).

Hỹbla -ae, f. and **Hỹblē** -ēs, f. (῞Υβλα), 1, *a mountain of Sicily, famed for its bees;* adj., **Hyblaeus** -a -um, *Hyblaean;* 2, *name of three towns in Sicily* (parva, major, and minor); hence **Hyblenses** -ĭum, m. *the inhabitants of Hybla.*

Hỹdaspēs -pis, m. (῾Υδάσπης), 1, *a river in India,* now *Behut* or *Djelun;* 2, *name of an Indian slave.*

hỹdra -ae, f. (ὕδρα), 1, *the many-headed water-snake of the Lernaean Lake, slain by Hercules;* 2, *a constellation also called* Anguis; 3, *a monster of the lower world with fifty heads.*

hydraulus -i, m. (ὕδραυλος), *a water organ,* Cic.

hydrĭa -ae, f. (ὑδρία), *an urn, water-jar,* Cic.

hydrŏchŏus -i, m. (ὑδροχόος), *the constellation Aquarius,* Cat.

hydrōpĭcus -a -um (ὑδρωπικός), *dropsical,* Hor.

hydrops -ōpis, m. (ὕδρωψ), *the dropsy,* Hor.

1. **hydrus** -i -m (ὕδρος), *a water-snake, hydra,* Verg.; *applied to the hair of Medusa and the Furies,* Verg.

2. **Hydrūs** -druntis, f. (῾Υδροῦς), and **Hydruntum** -i, n. *town on the E. coast of Calabria,* now *Otranto.*

hўems, hўĕmālis, etc. = hiems, etc. (q.v.)

Hўlaeus -i, m. (῾Υλαῖος), *a centaur slain by Atalanta.*

Hўlās -ae, m. (῞Υλας), *son of Thiodamas, a beautiful youth, the friend and companion of Hercules on the Argonautic expedition, carried off by the water-nymphs in Mysia.*

Hyllus -i, m. (῞Υλλος), *son of Hercules and Deianira.*

Hўmēn -ěnis, m. (῾Υμήν), 1, *the god of marriage,* Ov.; 2, *the marriage song,* Ov.

hўmĕnaeŏs or -ŭs -i, m. (ὑμέναιος). **I.** *the marriage-song.* **A.** Lit., hymenaeon canere, Ov.; canere hymenaeos, Verg. **B.** (gen. plur.) meton., *the wedding,* Verg.; transf., *the pairing of animals,* Verg. **II.** *Hymen, the god of marriage,* Ov.

Hўm<ettŏs and **Hўmettus** -i, m.(῾Υμηττός), *a mountain in Africa, famous for its bees and marble.* Adj., **Hўmettius** -a -um., *Hymettian.*

Hymnis -ĭdis, f. (῾Υμνίς), *name of a comedy of Caecilius Statius.*

Hўpaepa -ōrum, n. (τὰ ῞Υπαιπα), *a town in Lydia,* now *Birghe* or *Beréki.*

Hўpănis -is, m. (῞Υπανις), *river in European Sarmatia,* now *the Bog.*

Hўpăta -ae, f. (῞Υπατα), *town in Thessaly.* Adj., 1, **Hўpataeus** -a -um; 2, **Hypatensis** -e, *of or belonging to Hypata.*

Hўperbŏrěi -ōrum, m. (῾Υπερβόρεοι), *the Hyperboreans, a fabulous people, dwelling at the extreme north;* hence, adj., **Hўperbŏrěus** -a -um, *lying to the north, northern,* Verg.

Hўpěrīdes -ae, n. (῾Υπερείδης), *an Athenian orator, contemporary with Demosthenes.*

Hўpěrīon -ŏnis, m. (῾Υπερίων), 1, *Hyperion, a Titan, father of the Sun;* 2. *the Sun god himself;* hence, 1, **Hўpěrīŏnĭus** -a -um, *of or belonging to Hyperion;* 2, **Hўpěrĭŏnis** -ĭdis, f. *Aurora,* Ov.

Hўpermnestra -ae, and -ē, -ēs, f. (῾Υπερμνήστρα), *the youngest of the Danaides, the only one who did not kill her husband* (Lynceus).

hўpŏdĭdascălus -i, m. (ὑποδιδάσκαλος), *an under-teacher,* Cic.

hўpomnēma -mătis, n.(ὑπόμνημα), *a memorandum, note,* ap. Cic.

hўpŏthēca -ae, f. (ὑποθήκη), *a pledge, security, mortgage,* Cic.

Hypsĭpўlē -ēs, f. and **Hypsĭpўla** -ae, f. (῾Υψιπύλη), *queen of Lemnos; saved her father when the women of Lemnos killed all the men; received the Argonauts.*

Hyrcāni -ōrum, m. (῾Υρκανοί), *the inhabitants of Hyrcania.* Hence 1, adj., **Hyrcānus** -a -um, *Hyrcanian;* 2, subst., **Hyrcānĭa** -ae, f. *the land of the Hyrcani in Asia, between Media, Parthia, and the Caspian Sea.*

Hўrĭē -ēs, f. (῾Υρίη), *town and lake in Boeotia.*

Hўrĭeus -ěi, m. (῾Υριεύς), *father of Orion.* Adj., **Hўrĭeus** -a -um, *proles, Orion,* Ov.

Hyrtăcīdēs -ae, m. (῾Υρτακίδης), *the son of Hyrtacus,* i.e. *Nisus.*

Hystaspēs -is, m. (῾Υστάσπης), *father of the Persian king, Darius.*

I.

I, *i, the ninth letter of the Latin alphabet.* For meaning of I as an abbreviation, see Table of Abbreviations.

Ĭacchus -i, m. (῎Ιακχος), 1, *a name of Bacchus;* 2, meton., *wine,* Verg.

1. **Ĭālўsus** -i, m. (᾽Ιάλυσος), *town in Rhodes,* now *Jaliso.* Hence, **Ĭālўsĭus** -a -um, poet. = *Rhodian,* Ov.

2. **Ĭālўsus** -i m., *son of Sol.*

ĭambēus -a -um (ἰαμβεῖος), *iambic,* Hor.

ĭambus -i, m. (ἴαμβος), 1, *an iambus, a metrical foot* (∪ —), Hor.; 2, *an iambic poem, iambic poetry,* Cic.

ĭanthĭnus -a -um (ἰάνθινος), *violet-coloured,* Plin. Subst., **ĭanthĭna** -ōrum, n. *violet-coloured clothes,* Mart.

Ĭăpĕtus -i, m. (᾽Ιαπετός), *a giant, father of Atlas, Epimetheus, and Prometheus;* genus Iapeti, *Prometheus,* Hor. Hence, **Ĭăpĕtīŏnĭdēs** -ae. m. *a son of Iapetus,* i.e. *Atlas,* Ov.

Ĭāpўdes -um, m. (᾽Ιάπυδες), *a people in north-west Illyria.* Hence, 1, **Ĭāpys** -pўdis, *Iapydian;* 2, **Ĭāpўdĭa** -ae, f. *Iapydia.*

Ĭāpyx -pўgis, m. (᾽Ιάπυξ). **I.** *the son of Daedalus, who reigned in a part of Southern Italy, thence called Iapygia.* **II. A.** *a west-north-west wind, favourable for crossing from Brundusium to Greece.* **B.** *a river in Apulia;* Iapygis arva, *Apulia,* Ov. **C.** Adj., *Iapygian.* Hence, **Ĭāpўgĭa** -ae, f. (᾽Ιαπυγία), *a district of Magna Graecia, part of Calabria,* now *Terra d'Otranto.*

Ĭarba, and **Ĭarbas** -ae, m. *an African king, rival of Aeneas.* Hence, **Ĭarbīta** -ae, m.=a *Mauretanian,* Hor.

Ĭardănis -nĭdis, f. *a daughter of Iardanus,* i.e., *Omphale,* Ov.

Ĭāsĭus -ĭi, m. (᾽Ιάσιος), 1, *an Argive king, father of Atalanta;* 2, *a Cretan, beloved by Ceres* (also called Iāsīon). Hence, 1, **Ĭāsĭdes** -ae, m. (᾽Ιασίδης), *a descendant of Iasius;* 2, **Ĭāsis** -sĭdos, f. *a daughter of Iasius,* i.e. *Atalanta.*

Ĭāsōn -ŏnis, m. ('Ιάσων). **I.** *son of Aeson, king in Thessaly, leader of the expedition of the Argonauts to Colchis to fetch the golden fleece.* Adj.,

Ĭāsŏnĭus -a -um, *Jasonian; carina, the Argo,* Prop.; remex, *the Argonauts,* Ov. **II.** *a tyrant of Pherae, contemporary with Epaminondas.*

ĭaspis -ĭdis, f. (ἰασπις), *a jasper,* Verg.

Ĭassus (Ĭāsus) -i, f. ('Ιασσος), *a town in Caria;* hence, **Ĭassenses** -ĭum, m. *the inhabitants of Iassus.*

Ĭāzȳges -um, m. ('Ιάζυγες), *a Sarmatian tribe on the Danube.* Sing., **Ĭazyx** -zȳgis, used as an adjective, *Iazygian.*

Ĭbēr . . . v. Hiber . . .

ĭbī, adv. (from pron. root I, whence is). **I.** *there, at that place,* Cic. **II.** Transf. **A.** Of time, *then, thereupon;* ibi infit, Liv. **B.** *in that thing, in that matter,* Cic.

ĭbīdem, adv. (ibi and demonstrat. suffix -dem, as in i-dem), **1,** *in the same place, in that very place;* hic ibidem, *on this very place,* Cic.; **2,** *moreover,* Cic. (Ibīdem, Juv.).

ĭbis, genit. ibis and ibĭdis, f. (ἰβις), *the ibis, a sacred bird among the Egyptians,* Cic.

ĭbiscum, ibrĭda = hibiscum, hibrida (q.v.).

Ĭbўcus -i, m. ('Ιβυκος), *a Greek lyric poet, flourishing about 540 A.C.*

Ĭcădĭus -ĭi, m. ('Ικάδιος), *a notorious pirate.*

Ĭcărĭus -ĭi, m. ('Ικάριος), *the father of Penelope.* Hence, **Ĭcărĭōtis** -ĭdis, f., and **Ĭcăris** -ĭdis, f. *Penelope.*

Ĭcărus -i, m. ('Ικαρος). **I.** *the son of Daedalus, drowned in the Aegean Sea, whilst flying from Crete with wings made by his father.* Hence adj., **Ĭcărĭus** -a -um, *Icarium mare,* or absol., **Ĭcărĭum** -ĭi, n. *the Icarian Sea, a part of the Aegean Sea.* **II.** *the father of Erigone, changed into the constellation Arcturus,* or *Bootes.* Adj., **Ĭcărĭus** -a -um, *Icarian;* canis, *the constellation Canis Major,* Ov.

iccirco = idcirco (q.v.).

Ĭcĕlos -i, m. (ἰκελος, *like*), *brother of Morpheus.*

Icēni -ōrum, m. *a people in Britain.*

ichneumon -ŏnis, m. (ἰχνευμων), *the ichneumon,* Cic.

ĭcĭo, or **ĭco,** ĭci, ictum, 3. *to strike, hit, smite, stab.* **I. A.** Lit., lapide ictus, Caes.; e caelo ictus, *struck by lightning,* Cic. **B.** Meton., icere foedus, *to make a treaty,* Cic. **II.** Transf., partic., ictus, *affected, touched, moved, struck;* conscientiā ictus, Liv.; desideriis icta, Hor. (pres. also **ĭco,** Lucr.).

Ĭcŏnĭum -ĭi, n. ('Ικόνιον), *town in Lycaonia.*

ictĕrĭcus -a -um (ἰκτερικός), *suffering from jaundice, jaundiced,* Juv.

ictus -ūs, m. (ico), *a blow, stroke, stab, hit, thrust.* **I.** Gen., a, lit., gladiatorius, Cic.; sagittarum ictus, Liv; lapidum, Caes. ; apri, Ov.; pollicis, *the striking of the lyre,* Hor.; fulminis, *lightning-stroke,* Cic.; solis, *a sunbeam,* Hor.; b, transf., *blow;* novae calamitatis, Cic. **II.** Esp., **A.** *the charge or assault of an enemy;* sub ictum dari, *to be exposed to the attacks of the enemy,* Tac. **B.** In music, *beating time, beat,* Hor.

Ĭda -ae, f., and **Ĭdē** -ēs, f. ("Ιδα, "Ιδη). **I.** *a woman's name,* Verg. **II. A.** *a mountain near Troy.* **B.** *a mountain in Crete, where Jupiter was nursed.* Adj., **Ĭdaeus** -a -um, a, *relating to Mount Ida in Phrygia;* parens deum, Verg., or mater, Cic., *Cybele;* naves, *Trojan,* Hor.;

pastor, Cic., or judex, or hospes, Ov., *Paris;* b, *relating to Mount Ida in Crete.*

Ĭdălĭē -ēs, f. ('Ιδαλίη), *a surname of Venus, from Idalium.*

Ĭdălĭum -ĭi, n. ('Ιδάλιον), *promontory and town in Cyprus, with a temple of Venus.* Hence l, adj., **Ĭdălĭus** -a -um, poet., *belonging to Cyprus,* Venus, Cic.; **2,** subst., **Ĭdălĭa** -ae, f. (sc. terra), *the neighbourhood of Idalium.*

idcirco (iccirco), adj. (id and circa), *on that account, for that reason;* absol., Cic.; followed by quod or quia, Cic.; by si, Cic.; by ut or ne and the subj., Cic.; by qui and the subj., Cic.; by quo facilius and subj., Caes.

idem, ĕădem, ĭdem (from is and suffix -dem), *the same;* idem velle atque idem nolle, *to have the same likes and dislikes,* Sall.; amicus est tamquam alter idem, *a second self,* Cic.; sometimes to be translated by *also;* suavissimus et idem facillimus, Cic.; followed by qui, atque (ac) et, ut, quam, quasi, cum, etc., eadem virtus, quae in proavo, Cic.; foll. by dat., idem facit occidenti, *he acted like,* etc., Hor.; neut. subst., idem juris, *the same right,* Cic.; eodem loci, *on the very spot,* Cic.; with et or que = *and indeed;* certissimi et iidem acerrimi, Cic. (abl. **ēōdem-que, ēādemque,** trisyll., Verg.

identĭdem, adv. (idem -ti -dem), *repeatedly, again and again,* Cic.

ĭdĕō, adv. *on that account, therefore,* Cic.; followed by quod, quia, quoniam, by ut, or ne with the subj., Cic., or by quin with the subj., Liv.

ĭdĭōta (ĭdĭōtes) -ae, m. (ἰδιώτης), *an ignorant, uncultivated man,* Cic.

Idmōn -mŏnis, m. ('Ιδμων), *father of Arachne.* Adj., **Idmŏnĭus** -a -um, *Arachne, daughter of Idmon,* Ov.

Ĭdŏmĕneus -ei, m. ('Ιδομενεύς), *son of Deucalion, king of Crete.*

ĭdōnĕē, adv. (idoneus), *fitly, appropriately,* Cic.

ĭdōnĕus -a -um, *fit, appropriate.* **I.** Act., *fit to do something, capable, qualified, suitable;* constr., a, with dat., with ad or in and the acc., castris idoneum locum, Caes.; idonei ad hoc negotium, Cic.; idonei in eam rem, Liv.; b, with infin., fons rivo dare nomen idoneus, Hor.; c, absol., verba minus idonea, Cic.; of persons, *sufficient, satisfactory;* idonei auctores, Cic.; with infin., idoneum visum est dicere. Sall. **II.** Pass., *fit to suffer* or *receive something, worthy;* constr., a, gen., with qui and the subj. (like dignus), tibi fortasse nemo fuit quem imitere, Cic.; b, absol., minus idoneum praemio afficere, Cic.

Ĭdūmē -ēs, f. and **Ĭdūmaea** -ae, f. ('Ιδουμαία), *a district in Palestine, bordering on Judaea and Arabia Petraea.* Hence, **Ĭdūmaeus** -a -um, *Idumaean.*

idus -ŭum, f. (root ID, VID, whence viduus and divido, *the dividing*), *the Ides, the middle of the Roman month, the fifteenth day in March, May, July, October;* *the thirteenth in the other months;* idus Martiae, *the 15th of March,* Cic.

Ĭdȳĭa -ae, f. ('Ιδυια), *the mother of Medea.*

Ĭgĭlĭum -ĭi, n. *a small island on the coast of Etruria, now Giglio.*

ĭgĭtur, adv. (from is and suffix -tur = -tus, as ita from i -s and suffix -ta), *then.* **A.** Of logical consequences, *so, therefore, then, accordingly;* si mentiris, mentiris. Mentiris autem; igitur mentiris, Cic. **B.** In asking questions, *then?* in quo igitur tua disciplina? Cic.; ironically, haec igitur est tua disciplina? Cic. **C.** With imperatives, *then, so then;* fac igitur quod, etc., Cic.

9

D. After digressions, parentheses, etc. to resume the argument, *so, as I was saying;* scripsi etiam (nam ab orationibus disjungo me fere), scripsi igitur, Cic. **E.** In a climax, *then;* pro imperio, pro exercitu, pro provincia, etc., pro his igitur omnibus rebus, Cic. (Igitur stands most frequently second or third in its clause, but sometimes first, esp. in Sallust).

ignārus -a -um (in and gnarus), **1,** *ignorant of, unacquainted with, inexperienced in;* with genit., faciendae orationis, Cic.; mariti, *unmarried,* Hor.; with acc. and infin., non sumus ignari multos studiose contra esse dicturos, Cic.; with rel. sent., ignaro populo Romano quid ageretur, Cic.; quid virtus valeret, Cic.; multos esse dicturos, Cic.; absol., Liv.; **2,** pass., *unknown;* with dat., proles ignara parenti, Ov.; regio hostibus ignara, Sall.; absol., ignari montes, Verg.

ignāvē and **ignāvĭtĕr,** adv. (ignavus), *lazily, slothfully, without spirit;* dicere, Hor.; facere, Cic.

ignāvĭa -ae, f. (ignavus), *idleness, laziness, listlessness, sloth, cowardice;* contraria fortitudini ignavia, Cic.

ignāvĭter = ignave (q.v.).

ignāvus -a -um (in and gnavus). **I.** *idle, slothful, listless, inactive* (opp. strenuus). **A.** Lit., a, homo, senectus, Cic.; with genit., legiones operum et laboris ignavae, Tac.; with ad and the acc., ignavissimus ad opera ac muniendum hostis, Liv.; **b,** *cowardly,* miles, Cic.; hostis, Liv.; subst., **ignāvus** -i, m. *a coward, poltroon,* Sall.; plur., Cic. **B.** Transf., of inanimate objects, *inert, sluggish;* nemus, *unfruitful,* Verg.; lux, *a day in which one is lazy, an idle day,* Juv.; gravitas, *immovable,* Verg. **II.** Act., *causing sloth and idleness;* frigus, Ov.; genus interrogationis, Cic.

ignesco, 3. (ignis). **A.** *to kindle, catch fire,* Cic. **B.** Transf., *to burn, glow with passion;* Rutulo ignescunt irae, Verg.

ignĕus -a -um (ignis), *fiery, burning, glowing with heat.* **I.** Lit., a, sidera, Cic.; sol, Cic.; b, *glowing like flame;* astra, Verg. **II.** Transf., **A.** Of colours, *flaming, glowing,* Plin. **B.** Fig., *glowing with passion, love, anger,* etc.; furor, Ov.; vigor, Verg.; Tarchon, Verg.

ignĭcŭlus -i, m. (dim. of ignis), *a little fire, little flame, spark.* **A.** Lit., Plin. **B.** Transf., a, *ardour;* desiderii, Cic.; b, *a spark, beginning;* virtutum, Cic.; desiderii tui, *the ardour, glow,* Cic.; ingenii, *sparks of talent,* Quint.

ignĭfer -fĕra -fĕrum (ignis and fero), *fire-bearing, fiery;* aether, Lucr.; axis, Ov.

ignĭgĕna -ae, m. (ignis and geno = gigno), *born of fire,* epithet of Bacchus, Ov.

ignĭpes -pĕdis (ignis and pes), *fiery-footed;* equi, Ov.

ignĭpŏtens -entis (ignis and potens), *mighty in fire, ruler of fire,* epithet of Vulcan, Verg.

ignis -is, m. *fire.* **I.** Lit., **A.** 1, gen., ignem concipere, comprehendere, *to catch fire,* Cic.; accendere, Verg.; ignem ab igne capere, *to kindle,* Cic.; operibus ignem inferre, Caes.; aliquem igni cremare, necare, interficere, Caes.; **2,** esp., a, *conflagration;* pluribus simul locis, et iis diversis, ignes coorti sunt, Liv.; b, *a watch-fire;* ignibus exstinctis, Liv.; c, *a fire-brand;* ignibus armata ingens multitudo, Liv.; d, *the flames of the funeral pile;* ignes supremi, Ov.; e, *lightning;* ignis coruscus, Hor.; f, *light of the stars;* ignes curvati lunae, Hor. **B.** a, *glow, heat;* solis, Ov.; b, *glitter, fire,* of the eyes, Cic.; c, *redness;* sacer ignis, *St. Anthony's fire,* Verg. **II.** Transf., **1,** huic ordini novum ignem sub-

jeci, *ground for hatred,* Cic.; **2,** *glow of the passions of love* or *anger,* and meton., for the person beloved, meus ignis, Verg.

ignōbĭlis -e (in and gnobilis = nobilis), **1,** *unknown, obscure, inglorious;* civitas, Caes.; **2,** *of low birth, of mean extraction, ignoble;* familia, Cic.; vulgus, Verg.

ignōbĭlĭtas -ātis, f. (ignobilis), **1,** *inglorious-ness, obscurity,* Cic.; **2,** *mean birth;* generis, Cic.

ignōmĭnĭa -ae, f. (in and gnomen = nomen), *the deprivation of one's good name, disgrace, dishonour, ignominy;* ignominiam accipere, Cic.; alicui injungere, inferre, Liv.; inurere, Cic., ignominia aliquem afficere, Cic.; ignominia notare, Cic.; ignominiam habere, Cic.; per ignominiam, Cic.; with subj. genit., senatūs, *inflicted by the senate,* Cic.

ignōmĭnĭōsus -a -um (ignominia), *full of disgrace, ignominious, disgraceful;* dominatio, Cic.; fuga, Liv.

ignōrābĭlis -e (ignoro), *unknown,* Cic.

ignōrans -antis (partic. of ignoro), *ignorant,* Caes.

ignōrantĭa -ae, f. (ignoro), *want of knowledge, ignorance;* loci, Caes.; absol., Cic.

ignōrātĭo -ōnis, f. (ignoro), *want of knowledge, ignorance;* locorum, Cic.; sui, Cic.; absol., Cic.

ignōrātus -a -um (partic. of ignoro), *unknown;* ignoratum a Syracusanis sepulcrum, Cic.

ignōro, 1. (ignarus), *to be without knowledge, ignorant of, not to know;* a, with acc., causam, Cic.; alicuius faciem, Sall.; aliquem, Cic.; b, with infin., Cic.; c, with acc. and infin., Cic.; d, with rel. sent., quum id quam vere sit ignores, Cic.; e, with de and the abl., Cic.; f, absol., Cic.

ignoscens -entis, (p. adj. of ignosco), *forgiving, placable,* Ter.

ignosco -nōvi -nōtum, 3. (in and gnosco = nosco, *not to take notice of*), *to overlook, forgive, pardon;* with dat., haesitationi meae, Cic.; orat ut sibi ignosceret, Caes.; with neut. acc., hoc, Cic.; with si or quod, *that,* Cic.

1. ignōtus -a -um, partic. of ignosco.

2. ignōtus -a -um (in and gnotus = notus). **I. 1,** *unknown;* with dat., plurimis ignotissimi gentibus, Cic.; jus obscurum et ignotum, Cic.; subst., **ignōtus** -i, m. *an unknown person,* Cic.; **2,** *ignoble, obscure* (opp. generosus); mater, Hor.; hic ignotissimus Phryx, Cic. **II.** Act., *ignorant,* Cic.

Ĭgŭvĭum -ĭi, n. *a town in Umbria,* now *Gubbio* or *Eugubio.* Hence, **1, Ĭgŭvīni** -ōrum, m. and **2, Ĭgŭvīnātes** -ĭum, m. *the inhabitants of Iguvium.*

Ĭlerda -ae, f. *town in Hispania Tarraconensis.*

Ĭlergăŏnes -um, m. and **Illurgavonenses** -ĭum, m. *a people in the east of Hispania Tarraconensis.*

Ĭlergētes -um, m. *a people in Hispania Tarraconensis.*

īlex -ĭcis, f. *the holm-oak,* Verg.

1. īlĭa -ĭum, n. **1,** *the part of the body between the ribs and thighs, the flank;* suffodere ilia equis, Liv.; ima longo ilia singultu tendere, Verg.; ducere, *to draw the flanks together, to become broken-winded,* Hor.; rumpere, *to burst,* Verg.; **2,** *the intestines of animals,* Hor.

2. Īlĭa -ae, f. v. Ilion.

Īlĭăcus, v. Ilion.

īlĭcet (= ire licet). **I. A.** Lit., *let us go, you may go,* a form of dismissal anciently used ᴀt the close of a meeting, Ter. **B**. Transf., *it is all over, all is lost*, Plaut., Ter. **II**. *immediately, forthwith, straightway*, Verg.

īlĭcētum -i, n. (ilex), *an ilex-grove*, Mart.

īlĭcō = illico.

Īlĭensis, v. Ilion.

īlignus -a -um (ilex), *belonging to the ilex;* glans, Hor.

Īlĭŏn or **Īlĭum** -ĭi, n. ('Ιλιον) and **Īlĭŏs** -ĭi, f. ('Ιλιος), *Troy;* hence, 1, adj., **Īlĭus** -a -um, *Trojan;* subst., a, **Īlĭi** -ōrum, m. *the Trojans;* b, **Īlĭa** -ae, f. *the Trojan woman* = *Rhea Sylvia, mother of Romulus and Remus*, Verg., and hence, **Īlĭădēs** -ae, m. *the descendant of Ilia* = *Romulus* or *Remus*, Ov.; 2, **Īlĭăcus** -a -um, *Trojan;* carmen, *on the Trojan war*, Hor.; 3, **Īlĭenses** -ĭum, m. *the inhabitants of Ilium;* 4, **Īlĭădēs** -ae, m. *Ganymede*, Ov.; 5, **Īlĭăs** -ădis, f. a, *a Trojan woman*, Verg.; b, *the Iliad of Homer*, Cic.

Īlĭŏna -ae, f. and **Īlĭŏnē** -ēs, f. 1, *the eldest daughter of king Priam, wife of Polymnestor, king in Thrace;* 2, = *Hecuba*, Cic.; Ilionam edormit, *the part of Hecuba*, Hor.

Īlīthyīa -ae, f. (Ειλείθυια), *the goddess who aided women in child-birth.*

Iliturgi (Illiturgi) -ōrum, m. *a place in Hispania Baetica*. Hence, **Īlĭturgĭtāni** -ōrum, m. *the inhabitants of Iliturgi.*

illā (ille), adv. 1 (abl. of ille, sc. parte), *at that place*, Plaut., Tac.; 2 (dat. illai, sc. parti), *to that place*, Ov.

illăbĕfactus -a -um (in and labefacio), *unshaken, firm*, Ov.

illăbor -lapsus, 3. dep. (in and labor), *to fall, glide, fall into, fall down;* 1, lit., si fractus illabatur orbis, Hor.; in stomacho illabuntur ea quae accepta sunt ore, Cic.; 2, transf., pernicies illapsa civium in animos, Cic.

illăbōro, 1. (in and laboro), *to work upon, labour at;* domibus, *in building houses*, Tac.

illāc, adv. (illic). **I**. (lit. abl.), *there, at this place;* hac atque illac, hac illac, Ter. **II**. (lit. dat.), *to that place;* transf., illac facere, *to stand on that side, belong to that party*, Cic.

illăcessītus -a -um (in and laᴚesso), *unattacked, unprovoked*, Tac.

illăcrĭmābĭlis -e (in and lacrimabilis), 1, *unwept;* omnes illacrimabiles urgentur, Hor.; 2, *not to be moved by tears, pitiless;* Pluto. Hor.

illăcrĭmo, 1. (in and lacrimo), *to weep, bewail;* with dat., errori, Liv.; absol., ebur maestum illacrimat templis, Verg.

illăcrĭmor, 1. dep. (in and lacrimor), *to weep over, bewail;* morti, Cic.

illaesus -a -um (in and laedo), *unhurt, uninjured*, Ov.

illaetābĭlis -e (in and laetabilis), *sorrowful, gloomy, cheerless;* ora, Verg.

illăquĕo (in and laqueo), *to entrap, ensnare, entangle;* fig., illaqueatus omnium legum periculis, Cic.

illaudātus -a -um (in and laudatus), *unpraised, obscure;* Busiris, Verg.

illautus = illotus (q.v.).

ille, illa, illud, genit. illīus, demonstr. pron. (perhaps for is-le, from is), *that;* a, ista beatitas cur aut in solem il*lum* aut in *hunc* mundum cadere non potest, Cic.; of time, qui illorum temporum historiam reliquerunt, Cic.; b, *that glorious* or *notorious;* ille Epaminondas, Cic.;

illa Medea, Cic.; hic ille, *this glorious*, etc.; hic nunc ille annus egregius, Cic.; c, ille quidem, *he indeed*, Cic.; non ille . . . sed hic, Cic.; d, referring to and preparing for what comes after, illud perlibenter audivi te esse, etc., Cic.; e, hic et (atque) ille, *the one and the other*, Hor.; ille aut (vel) ille, *this* or *that*, Cic.

illĕcĕbra -ae, f. (illicio), 1, *an allurement, enticement, attraction, charm;* voluptas est illecebra turpitudinis, Cic.; 2, meton., *an enticer, a decoy-bird*, Plaut.

1. **illectus** -a -um (in and lectus, from lego), *unread*, Ov.

2. **illectus** -ūs (illicio), m. *seduction, allurement*, Plaut.

3. **illectus** -a -um, partic. of illicio.

illĕpĭdē, adv. (illepidus), *ungracefully, inelegantly*, Plaut.

illĕpĭdus -a -um (in and lepidus), *ungraceful, inelegant, rude, unmannerly;* parens avarus, illepidus, in liberos difficilis, Cic.

1. **illex** -lĭcis (illicio), *alluring;* subst., f. a *decoy-bird*, Plaut.

2. **illex** -lēgis (in and lex), *lawless*, Plaut.

illĭbātus -a -um (in and libo), *undiminished, uncurtailed, unimpaired;* divitiae, Cic.

illĭbĕrālis -e (in and liberalis), 1, *unworthy of a free man, ignoble;* te in me illiberalem putabit, Cic.; 2, transf., *low, mean;* quaestus, Cic.; genus jocandi, Cic.

illĭbĕrālĭtas -ātis, f. (illiberalis), *illiberality, stinginess, meanness;* illiberalitatis avaritiaeque suspicio, Cic.

illĭbĕrālĭtĕr (illiberalis), 1, *ignobly, meanly;* patris diligentiā non illiberaliter institutus, Cic.; 2, *in a sordid, niggardly manner;* facere, Cic.

1. **illīc**, illaec, illūc, pron demonstr. (ille -ce), *that there;* in interrogative sentences, illiccine, Plaut.; illanccine, Ter.

2. **illīc**, adv. (l. illic), 1, *there, at that place*, Caes.; 2, transf., a, *on that side*, Tac.; b, *in that case*, Liv.

illĭcĭo -lexi -lectum, 3. (in and *lacio), *to entice, seduce, allure, decoy, inveigle;* conjugem in stuprum, Cic.; aliquem ad bellum, Sall.; with ut and the subj., Liv.

illĭcĭtātor -ōris, m. *a sham bidder at an auction, a puffer*, Cic.

illĭcĭtus -a -um (in and licitus), *not allowed, illicit, illegal;* exactiones, Tac.

illĭco (ĭlĭco), adv. (in loco), 1, *on the spot, in that very place*, Ter.; 2, transf., *on the spot, immediately*, Cic.

illīdo -līsi -līsum, 3. (in and laedo), 1, *to strike, knock, beat, dash against;* lateri algam, Verg.; saxeam pilam vadis, Verg.; illidere dentem, Hor.; 2, *to shatter, crush, dash to pieces;* serpens illisa morietur, Cic.

illĭgo, 1. (in and ligo), *to bind, tie, fasten.* **I**. **A**. aratra juvencis, Hor.; Mettium in currus, Liv. **B**. Transf., *to bind, to connect with oneself, bind to oneself;* aliquem pignoribus, Cic. **II**. **A**. *to fasten, attach;* a, lit., crustas in aureis poculis, Cic.; b, transf., sententiam verbis, Cic. **B**. *to entangle, impede;* a, lit., illigatur praedā, Tac.; b, transf., angustiis et concisis disputationibus illigati, Cic.

illim, adv. = illinc, *from there, from that place*, Cic.

illĭmis -e (in and limus), *free from mud, clear;* fons, Ov.

illinc, adv. (illim -ce). **I**. *from that place,* fugit illinc, Cic. **II**. Transf. *from that side,* *from that person, thence,* Cic.

illĭno -lēvi -lĭtum, 3. (in and lino), *to smear, daub, spread over ;* **1,** aurum vestibus illitum, Hor. ; quodcumque semel chartis illeverit, *has written, scribbled,* Hor. ; **2,** *to cover with ;* pocula ceris, Ov. ; fig., color venustatis non fuco illitus, Cic.

illĭquĕfactus -a -um (in and liquefacio), *molten, liquefied,* Cic.

illītĕrātus -a -um (in and literatus), *unlearned, ignorant, illiterate ;* **a,** of persons, vir non illiteratus, Cic. ; **b,** of things, multa . . . nec illiterata dicuntur, Cic.

illō, adv. (orig. illoi, dat. of ille), **1,** *to that place, thither,* Cic. ; **2,** transf., *to that matter or thing ;* haec omnia eodem illo pertinere, Caes.

illōc, adv. (1. illic), *thither,* Ter.

illōtus (illautus, illūtus) -a -um (in and lotus, or lautus, from lavo), **1,** *unwashed, unclean, impure,* Hor. ; **2,** *not washed off ;* sudor, Verg.

illūc, adv. (ille). **I.** Of space, *thither, to that place.* **A.** Lit., huc atque illuc, Cic. **B.** Transf., *to that matter, or person ;* ut illuc revertar, Cic. **II.** Of time, *up to that time,* Tac.

illūcesco (illūcisco) -luxi, 3. (in and lucesco or lucisco). **I.** *to become light, begin to shine.* **A.** Lit., quum tertio die sol illuxisset, Cic. ; illucescet aliquando ille dies, Cic. **B.** Transf., *to show oneself, appear ;* quum in tenebris vox consulis illuxerit, Cic. **II.** Impers., illucescit, *it grows light, is daylight ;* ubi illuxit, Liv.

illūdo -lūsi -lūsum, 3. (in and ludo). **I.** *to play with, sport with ;* chartis, *to play with paper,* i.e. *amuse oneself with writing,* Hor. **II.** In a bad sense, **1,** *to mock at, laugh at, make a mock of ;* **a,** with dat., capto, Verg. ; alicuius dignitati, Cic. ; rebus humanis, Hor. ; **b,** with the acc., miseros illudi nolunt, Cic. ; eam artem, Cic. ; absol., illudens, *ironically, in ridicule,* Cic. ; **2,** *to deceive ;* Cretensus omnes, Nep. ; illusi pedes, *staggering,* Hor. ; **3,** *to destroy, ruin, disgrace ;* cui (frondi) silvestres uri illudunt, Verg.

illūmĭnātē, adv. (illumino), *luminously, clearly ;* dicere, Cic.

illūmĭno, 1. (in and lumino). **A.** *to make light, enlighten, illuminate,* Cic. ; luna illuminata a sole, Cic. **B.** Of discourse, *to make clear, set off, adorn ;* orationem sententiis, Cic.

illūsĭo -ōnis, f. (illudo), *irony,* as a rhetorical figure, Cic.

illustris -e (in and lustro), *light, full of light, bright, brilliant.* **A.** Lit., stella ; lumen ; locus, Cic. **B.** Transf., **a,** *clear, plain, evident ;* oratio, res, Cic. ; **b,** *distinguished, celebrated, illustrious, famous, renowned ;* illustriori loco natus, Caes. ; nomen illustrius, Cic. ; **c,** *remarkable ;* res illustrior, Caes.

illustrĭus, adv. compar. and **illustrissĭmē,** adv. superl. (illustris), *more clearly, more distinctly ;* dicere, Cic.

illustro, 1. (illustris), *to enlighten, make light.* **I.** Lit., sol cuncta suā luce illustrat, Cic. **II.** Transf., **1,** *to bring to light, make known ;* consilia, Cic. ; **2,** *to explain, illustrate, elucidate ;* jus obscurum, Cic. ; **3,** *to adorn ;* **a,** of speech, orationem sententiis, Cic. ; **b,** *to make illustrious, celebrate, do honour to ;* aliquem laudibus Cic. ; aliquid Musā, Hor.

illŭvĭes -ēi, f. (illuo), **a,** *an inundation, flood,* Tac. ; **b,** *dirt, mud ;* morbo illuvieque peresus, Verg.

Illўrĭï -ōrum, m. *a people on the Adriatic Sea, in the modern Dalmatia and Albania.* Hence **1,** adj., **Illўrĭus** -a -um, *Illyrian ;* **2,** subst.,

Illўrĭa -ae, f. *Illyria ;* **3, Illўrĭcus** -a -um, *Illyrian ;* subst., **Illўrĭcum** -i, n. *Illyria ;* **4, Illўris** -ĭdis, f. *Illyrian ;* subst., *Illyria,* Ov.

Ilōtae -ārum = Hilotae (q.v.).

Ilus -i, m. (Ἶλος), **1,** *son of Tros, father of Laomedon, builder of Troy ;* **2,** = *Iulus.*

Ilva -ae, f. *an island to the west of Etruria,* now *Elba.*

Imăchăra -ae, f. *town on the east of Sicily,* now *Maccara.* Adj., **Imăchărensis** -e, *belonging to Imachara.*

im = **eum.**

imăgĭnārĭus -a -um (imago), *imaginary ;* fasces, Liv.

imăgĭnātĭo -ōnis, f. (imaginor), *imagination, fancy ;* provincias Orientis secretis imaginationibus agitare, Tac.

imăgĭnor, 1. dep. (imago), *to imagine, conceive, picture to oneself ;* pavorem, Tac.

imāgo -ĭnis, f. (root IM, whence also imitor and sim -ilis). **I.** Objective, **A.** Lit., **1, a,** gen., *an image, representation, portrait, figure, bust, statue ;* ficta, *a statue,* Cic. ; picta, *painted bust,* Cic. ; *a portrait engraved on a seal-ring ;* est signum notum, imago avi tui, Cic. ; **b,** esp., imagines (majorum), *waxen figures, portraits of ancestors* who had held curule offices, placed in the atria of Roman houses, and carried in funeral processions, Cic. ; **2, a,** *a likeness, counterfeit ;* imago animi et corporis tui, filius tuus, Cic. ; imago animi vultus est, Cic. ; **3, a,** *the shade or ghost of a dead man ;* imagines mortuorum, Cic. ; **b,** *a dream ;* somni, noctis, *a dream,* Ov. ; **c,** in the Epicurean philosophy, *the mental idea or representation of a real object,* Cic. ; **4,** *an echo ;* laus bonorum virtuti resonat tamquam imago, Cic. ; **5,** in discourse, *a metaphor, simile, image ;* hac ego si compellor imagine, Hor. **B.** Transf., *the appearance, pretence ;* pacis, Tac. ; decoris, Liv. ; imaginem reipublicae nullam reliquerunt, *they left no shadow or trace of the republic,* Cic. **II.** Subjective, **1,** *the appearance,* imago venientis Turni, Verg. ; **2,** *the image, idea, conception, mental representation of any object or event ;* tantae caedis, Ov. ; tantae pietatis, Verg.

imbēcillis, v. imbecillus.

imbēcillĭtas -ātis, f. (imbecillus), *weakness, imbecility, feebleness.* **A.** Lit., corporis, Cic. **B.** Transf., consilii, Cic. ; animi, Caes.

imbēcillĭus, adv. compar. (imbecillus), *somewhat weakly, feebly ;* assentiri, Cic.

imbēcillus -a -um, *weak, feeble.* **A.** Lit., filius, Cic. ; imbecillior valetudine, Cic. **B.** Transf., **a,** regnum, Sall. ; **b,** of the mind, *weak, without energy ;* animus, Cic. ; accusator, Cic.

imbellis -e (in and bellum). **I.** *unwarlike ;* **1,** multitudo, Liv. ; telum, *feeble,* Verg. ; dii, *Venus and Cupid,* Ov. ; **2,** *cowardly ;* res, cowardly behaviour, Cic. **II.** *without war, peaceful, quiet ;* annus, Liv.

imber -bris, m. (ὄμβρος), *a shower or storm of rain, pelting rain* (pluvia, *gentle, fertilising rain*). **I.** Lit., magnus, maximus, Cic. ; so also lactis, sanguinis, lapidum, Cic. **II.** Transf., **A.** *a storm, rain-cloud ;* super caput astitit imber, Verg. **B.** *water or any fluid ;* fluminis imber, Ov. ; tortus, *hail,* Verg. **C.** Of a shower of missiles, ferreus ingruit imber, Verg.

imberbis -e and **imberbus** -a -um (in and barba), *beardless,* Cic.

imbĭbo -bĭbi, 3. (in and bibo), **1,** *to drink in, conceive ;* de vobis malam opinionem animo, Cic. ; **2,** *to resolve, to determine upon any thing ;* memor eius quod initio consulatus imbiberat, Liv.

imbrex -ĭcis, c. (imber), *a hollow tile* (to keep the rain off), *used in roofing*, Verg.

imbrĭfer -fĕra -fĕrum (imber and fero), *rain-bringing ;* ver, Verg. ; auster, Ov.

Imbros and **Imbrus** -i, f. (Ἴμβρος), *an island in the Aegean Sea, near to Lemnos,* now *Embro.* Hence adj., **Imbrĭus** -a -um, *Imbrian.*

imbŭo -ŭi -ūtum, 3. (in and root BU, connected with BI in bibo), *to moisten, wet, steep, saturate.* **I.** Lit., vestem sanguine, Ov. ; imbuti sanguine gladii, Cic. **II.** Transf., **A.** *to fill, stain, taint;* imbutus maculā sceleris, Cic. ; imbutus superstitione, Cic. **B.** *to accustom, inure, initiate, instruct;* pectora religione, Cic. ; imbutus cognitionibus verborum, Cic. ; *with* ad and the acc., ad quam legem non instituti sed imbuti sumus, Cic. **C.** Poet., *to begin, make an essay of;* imbue opus tuum, Ov.

imĭtābĭlis -e (imitor), *that can be imitated, imitable;* orationis subtilitas, Cic.

imĭtāmen -ĭnis, n. (imitor), *an imitation, representation; image,* Ov.

imĭtāmentum -i, n. (imitor), *an imitating, imitation;* lacrimae vel dolorum imitameɔta, Tac.

imĭtātĭo -ōnis, f. (imitor), *an imitation;* virtutis, Cic.

imĭtātor -ōris, m. (imitor), *an imitator;* principum, Cic.

imĭtātrix -īcis, f. (imitator), *she that imitates;* imitatrix boni, voluptas, Cic.

imĭtor, 1. dep. (root IM, whence also imago). **I.** *to imitate, copy.* **A.** Lit., amictum alicuius aut statum aut motum, Cic. ; praeclarum factum, Cic. ; *of* things, *to be like, to resemble;* humor potest imitari sudorem, Cic. **B.** Transf., poet., *to replace, or supply by something similar;* pocula vitea acidis sorbis, Verg. **II.** *to represent, depict, express;* aliquid penicillo, Cic. ; capillos aere, Hor.

immădesco -măduĭ, 3. (in and madesco), *to become moist or wet;* lacrimis immaduisse genas, Ov.

immānē, adv. (immanis), *frightfully, dreadfully, savagely;* leo immane hians, Verg.

immānis -e (in and root MA, whence also manus (= bonus), Manes, etc.). **I.** *enormous, vast, immense, monstrous;* corporum magnitudo, Caes. ; ingens immanisque praeda, Cic. ; antrum, Verg. ; immane quantum discrepat, *differs to an enormous extent,* Hor. **II.** Transf., *frightful, savage, horrible, inhuman, fierce;* hostis gens, Cic. ; belua, Cic. ; flumen, Verg.

immānĭtas -ātis, f. (immanis), *savageness, fierceness, inhumanity, cruelty, barbarity, frightfulness;* vitiorum, facinoris, Cic. ; meton., in hac tanta immanitate versari, *in the midst of these inhuman persons,* Cic.

immansuĕtus -a -um (in and mansuetus), *untamed, unrestrained, wild;* gens, Cic.

immātūrĭtas -ātis, f. (immaturus), *immaturity,* hence = *untimely haste,* Cic.

immātūrus -a -um (in -maturus), 1, lit., *unripe, immature,* Plin. ; 2, transf., *untimely;* mors, Cic. ; interitus C. Gracchi, Cic. ; si filius immaturus obiisset, Hor.

immĕdĭcābĭlis -e (in and medicabilis), *that cannot be healed;* vulnus, Ov. ; telum, *the wound from which cannot be healed,* Verg.

immĕmor -mŏris (in and ɔemor), *unmindful, forgetful;* with genit., mandati, Cic. ; nec Romanarum rerum immemor, *familiar with Roman history,* Cic. ; libertatis, Liv. ; poet., equus immemor nerbae, *paying no heed to,* Verg.; absol., ingenium, Cic.

immĕmŏrābĭlis -e (in and memorabilis), 1, *indescribable;* spatium, Lucr. ; versus, *unworthy of representation,* Plaut. ; 2, *silent, uncommunicative,* Plaut.

immĕmŏrātus -a -um (in and memoro), *not mentioned, not narrated.* Plur. subst., **immĕmŏrāta** -ōrum, n. *new things, things not yet related,* Hor.

immensĭtas -ātis, f. (immensus), *immeasurableness, immensity;* latitudinum, altitudinum, Cic.

immensus -a -um (in and metior), *immeasurable, immense, vast, boundless;* magnitudo regionum, Cic. ; mare, Cic. Subst., **immensum** -i, n. *immense size, immeasurable space, immensity;* altitudinis, immeasurable *depth,* Liv. ; in immensum, *to an immense height,* Sall. ; ad immensum, *to a vast extent;* augere, Liv. ; immensum est dicere, *it is an endless task to tell,* Ov. ; adv., immensum, *enormously;* crescere, Ov.

immĕrens -entis (in and mereo), *not deserving, innocent,* Ov.

immergo -mersi -mersum, 3. (in and mergo), 1, lit., *to dip into, plunge into, immerse;* manus in aquam, Plin. ; aliquem undā, Verg. ; immersus in flumen, Cic. ; 2, transf., immergere se in consuetudinem alicuius, *to insinuate oneself into,* Cic.

immĕrĭto, v. immeritus.

immĕrĭtus -a -um (in and mereo), **1**, act., *not deserving or meriting, innocent ;* gens, Verg. ; mori, *that has not deserved to die,* Hor. ; **2**, pass., *undeserved, unmerited ;* laudes haud immeritae, Liv. **immĕrĭto,** adv. *undeservedly,* Cic.

immersābĭlis -e (in and merso), *that cannot be sunk;* adversis rerum immersabilis undis, *not to be overwhelmed by,* Hor.

immĕtātus -a -um (in and meto), *unmeasured ;* jugera, Hor.

immĭgro, 1. (in and migro). **A.** Lit., *to remove into;* in domum et in paternos hortos, Cic. **B.** Transf., ut ea (translata) verba non irruisse in alienum locum, sed immigrasse in suum diceres, *to have fallen naturally into their place,* Cic.

immĭnĕo, 2. (in and mineo), *to hang, bend, incline over, project over, overhang.* **I.** Lit., quercus ingens arbor praetorio imminebat, Liv.; populus antro imminet, Verg. ; collis urbi imminet, Verg. ; carcer imminens foro, Liv. ; lunā imminente, *by the light of the moon,* Hor. **II.** Transf. **A. a,** of evils, *to hang over threateningly, be imminent, threaten;* mors quae quotidie imminet, Cic. ; imminentium nescius, *ignorant of the immediate future,* Tac. ; **b,** *to be near with hostile intent, threaten;* castra Romana Carthaginis portis immineant, Liv. ; videt hostes imminere, Caes. ; gestus imminens, *threatening demeanour,* Cic. **B. a,** *to threaten, to be on the point of attacking;* imminent duo reges toti Asiae, Cic. ; **b,** *to be on the watch for, to look out for;* in victoriam, Liv. ; ad caedem, Cic.

immĭnŭo -ŭi -ūtum, 3. (in and minuo), *to lessen, diminish.* **I.** Gen., **A.** Lit., copias, Cic.; verbum imminutum, *abbreviated,* Cic. **B.** Transf., *to lessen, curtail;* imminuitur ɛ.ʔquid de voluptate, Cic. **II. A.** *to weaken;* corpus otio, animum libidinibus, Tac. **B.** Transf., *to weaken, destroy, injure;* majestatem, Liv. ; auctoritatem, Cic.

immĭnūtĭo -ōnis, f. (imminuo), *a lessening, diminishing, weakening;* 1, corporis, Cic. ; 2 transf., **a,** dignitatis, Cic. ; **b,** a rhet. figure = λιτότης (e.g., non minime for maxime), Cic.

immiscĕo -miscŭi -mixtum or -mistum, 2, (in and misceo), *to mix in, mingle with, inter-*

mix. I. Lit., **a,** of things, nives caelo prope immixtae, Liv.; poet., immiscent manus manibus, *they fight hand to hand,* Verg.; **b,** of persons, togati immisti turbae militum, Liv.; se mediis armis, Verg. **II.** Transf., *to join with, unite together;* **a,** of things, vota timori, Verg.; scrtern regni cum rebus Romanis, Liv.; **b,** of persons, se colloquiis montanorum, Liv.

immĭsĕrābĭlis -e (in and miserabilis), *unlamented, unpitied,* Hor.

immĭsĕrĭcors -cordis (in and misericors), *unmerciful,* Cic.

immissĭo -ōnis, f. (immitto), *a letting grow;* sarmentorum, Cic.

immītis -e (in and mitis), *sour, harsh.* **I.** Lit., uva, Hor. **II.** Transf., *rough, harsh, cruel, wild, pitiless, inexorable, stern;* tyrannus, Verg.; immites oculi, Ov.; lupus immitis, Ov.; ara, *on which human sacrifices were offered,* Ov.

immitto -mīsi -missum, 3. (in and mitto). **I.** *to send in, cause* or *allow to go in.* **A.** Lit., **1,** servos ad spoliandum fanum, Cic.; corpus in undam, Ov.; naves pice completas in classem Pompeianam, *let loose against,* Caes.; **2,** esp., **a,** milit. t. t., *to despatch, let go;* equitatum, Caes.; se in hostes, *to attack,* Cic.; **b,** *to discharge, shoot;* tela in aliquem, Caes.; **c,** *to sink into, let into;* tigna machinationibus in flumen, Caes.; **d,** *to conduct, convey;* aquam canalibus, Caes.; **e,** *to engraft;* feraces plautas, Verg.; **f,** *to work in;* lentum filis aurum, Ov.; **g,** legal t. t., *to put into possession of property;* tu praetor in mea bona quos voles immittes? Cic. **B.** Transf., **1,** hic corrector in eo ipso loco, quo reprehendit, immittit imprudens ipse senarium, *lets slip in,* Cic.; **2,** esp., **a,** *to send, incite;* immissus in rempublicam, Cic.; **b,** *to cause;* Teucris fugam atrumque timorem, Verg. **II. A.** *to let free;* juga, Verg.; frena, Verg.; habenas classi, *to crowd on sail,* Verg. **B.** *to let grow;* palmes laxis immissus habenis, Verg.; capilli, Ov.

immissus -a -um (immitto), *long, uncut;* barba, Verg.

immixtus or **immistus,** v. immisceo.

immŏ (īmŏ), adv. (for ipsimo), *yea, yes,* or *nay rather;* often with etiam, vero, enimvero, magis, potius, etc.; vivit! immo in senatum venit, *nay more, he comes into the senate,* Cic.; causa non bona est? immo optima, *yea, the very best,* Cic.; familiarem? immo alienissimum, *nay, but rather,* Cic.; non necesse esse? immo prorsus ita censeo, *nay, on the contrary,* Cic.

immōbĭlis -e (in and mobilis), **1,** *immovable;* terra, Cic.; **2,** transf., precibus, *inexorable,* Tac.; Ausonia, *not agitated by war,* Verg.

immŏdĕrātē, adv. (immoderatus), **1,** *without rule* or *measure;* moveri immoderate et fortuito, Cic.; **2,** *immoderately, intemperately;* vivere, Cic.

immŏdĕrātĭo -ōnis, f. (immoderatus), *want of moderation, excess, intemperance;* efferri immoderatione verborum, Cic.

immŏdĕrātus -a -um (in and moderatus), **1,** *without measure, immeasurable, endless;* cursus, Cic.; **2,** transf., *immoderate, intemperate, unbridled, unrestrained;* libertas, Cic.; oratio, Cic.

immŏdestē, adv. (immodestus), *immoderately, unbecomingly;* immodice immodesteque gloriari Hannibale victo a se, Liv.

immŏdestĭa -ae, f. (immodestus), **1,** *intemperate conduct;* publicanorum, Tac.; **2,** *insubordination;* militum vestrorum, Nep.

immŏdestus -a -um (in and modestus), *intemperate, unbridled;* genus jocandi, Cic.

immŏdĭcē, adv. (immodicus), *immoderately, intemperately;* hac potestate immodice ac superbe usum esse, Liv.

immŏdĭcus -a -um (in and modicus), *immoderate, excessive;* **1,** lit., frigus, Ov.; **2,** transf., *unrestrained, unbridled;* **a,** of persons, with in and the abl., in augendo numero, Liv.; with abl., immodicus linguā, Liv.; with genit., laetitiae, Tac.; **b,** of things, imperia, Liv.; cupido, Liv.

immŏdŭlātus -a -um (in and modulatus), *inharmonious,* Hor.

immoenis, v. immunis.

immŏlātĭo -ōnis, f. (immolo), *a sacrificing, immolation;* in ipso immolationis tempore, Cic.

immŏlātor -ōris, m. (immolo), *a sacrificer,* Cic.

immŏlītus -a -um (in and molior), *built up, erected;* quae in loca publica inaedificata immolitave privati habebant, Liv.

immŏlo, 1. (in and molo), orig., *to sprinkle with sacred meal;* hence, *to sacrifice, immolate.* **A.** Lit., bovem Dianae, vitulum Musis, Cic.; with abl. of the victim, Jovi singulis bubus, Liv.; absol., in Capitolio, Liv. **B.** Transf., *to devote to death, slay;* aliquem, Verg.

immŏrĭor -mortŭus, 3. dep. (in and morior), *to die in* or *upon;* sorori, *on his sister's body,* Ov.; Euxinis aquis, Ov.; transf., studiis, *to work oneself to death over,* Hor.

immŏror, 1. (in and moror), *to stay, remain, linger in a place,* Plin.

immorsus -a -um (in and mordeo). **I.** *bitten into, bitten;* immorso collo, Prop. **II.** Transf., *macerated* (by sharp, biting food); stomachus, Hor.

immortālis -e (in and mortalis), *deathless, immortal.* **A.** Lit., dii, Cic.; subst., **immortālis** -is, m. *an immortal,* Cic. **B.** Transf., **a,** *everlasting, imperishable;* memoria et gloria, Cic.; amicitiae immortales, inimicitiae mortales esse debent, Liv.; **b,** *happy beyond measure, divinely blessed,* Prop.

immortālĭtas -ātis, f. (immortalis). *immortality;* **1,** lit., animorum, Cic.; **2,** transf., **a,** *everlasting renown, an immortality of fame;* gloriae, Cic.; immortalitati commendare or tradere, *to make immortal,* Cic.; **b,** *the highest happiness,* Ter.

immortālĭtĕr, adv. (immortalis), *infinitely;* gaudeo, Cic.

immōtus -a -um (in and motus), *unmoved, motionless.* **I.** Lit., **a,** of things, arbores, *undisturbed,* Liv.; dies, *calm, windless,* Tac.; with ab and the abl., portus ab accessu ventorum immotus, Verg.; **b,** of persons, stat gravis Entellus nisuque immotus eodem, Verg.; esp. of soldiers in battle, adversus incitatas turmas stetit immota Samnitium acies, Liv. **II.** Transf., **a,** *unchanged, unbroken;* pax, Tac.; **b,** *fixed, firm, steadfast;* mens, fata, Verg.

immūgĭo, 4. (in and mugio), *to bellow, roar, resound in;* immugiit Aetna cavernis, Verg.

immulgĕo, 2. (in and mulgeo), *to milk into;* teneris immulgens ubera labris, Verg.

immundĭtĭa -ae, f. (immundus), *uncleanness, impurity,* Plaut.

immundus -a -um (in and 1. mundus), *unclean, impure, foul;* humus, Cic.; canis, Hor.; transf., dicta, Hor.

immūnĭo, 4. (in and munio), *to fortify,* Tac.

immūnis -e (in and munis, from root MUN, whence also munus, munia), *free, exempt;* **1,** with reference to the state, ager, *tax-free,* Cic.; militiā, *exempt from military service,* Liv.; with genit., portoriorum, Liv. ; immunes militarium operum, Liv. ; 2, gen., a, *free from work;* with genit., immunis operum, Ov. ; b, *contributing nothing;* fucus, Verg.; non ego te meis immunem meditor tingere poculis, Hor. ; quem scis immunem Cynarae placuisse rapaci, *without gifts,* Hor. ; c, *inactive,* Cic. ; d, *free from;* with genit., mali, Ov.; absol., manus, *stainless,* Hor.

immūnǐtas -ātis, f. (immunis), 1, *exemption from public offices or burdens;* with genit., omnium rerum, Caes. ; plur., immunitates dare, Cic. ; 2, *immunity, exemption;* magni muneris, Cic.

immūnītus -a -um (in and munitus), 1, *unfortified;* oppida castellaque, Liv. ; 2, *unpaved;* via, Cic.

immurmŭro, 1. (in and murmuro), *to murmur in* or *at;* silvis inmurmurat Auster, Verg.

immūtābǐlis -e (in and mutabilis), *immutable, unchangeable;* aeternitas, Cic.

immūtābǐlǐtas -ātis, f. (immutabilis), *immutability,* Cic.

immūtātǐo -ōnis, f. (immuto), 1, *a change, alteration;* ordinis, Cic. ; 2, *metonymy,* Cic.

1. **immūtātus** -a -um (in and muto), *unchanged,* Cic.

2. **immūtātus** -a -um, partic. of immuto.

immūto, 1. (in and muto), 1, *to change, alter;* ordinem verborum, Cic. ; aliquid de institutis priorum, Cic. ; of persons, prosperis rebus immutari, Cic. ; 2, a, in rhetoric, *to use by way of metonymy;* Ennius pro Afris immutat Africam, Cic. ; b, *to use allegorically;* immutata oratio, *allegory,* Cic.

īmo = immo (q. v.).

impācātus -a -um (in and pacatus), *warlike, disinclined to peace, restless,* Verg.

impallesco, -pallŭi, 3. (in and pallesco), *to grow pale over;* nocturnis chartis, Pers.

impar -păris (in and par), 1, a, *unequal, uneven;* par et impar ludere, *to play at odd and even,* Hor. ; modi impares, *hexameter and pentameter,* Ov. ; si toga dissidet impar, *sits awry,* Hor.; numeri impares an aequales, Cic. ; b, transf., *different,* Cic. ; 2, a, *unequal in strength, not a match for;* impar congressus Achilli, Verg.; certamen, Ov. ; b, *of unequal birth, of inferior birth;* maternum genus impar, Tac. (abl. sing. gen. impari, but impare, Verg. Ecl. 8. 75).

impărātus -a -um (in and paratus), *unprepared;* quum a militibus, tum a pecunia, *unprovided, with,* Cic. ; inermis atque imparatus, Caes.

impărǐtěr, adv. (impar), *unevenly, unequally,* Hor.

impartǐo, impartǐor = impertio, impertior (q. v.).

impastus -a -um (in and pasco), *unfed, hungry;* leo, Verg.

impătībǐlis (impětībǐlis) -e (in and patibilis), *intolerable, insufferable;* dolor, Cic.

impătǐens -entis (in and patiens), *unable to bear* or *to endure, impatient;* a, of persons, laborum, Ov. ; vulneris, Verg. ; solis, Tac. ; irae, *wrathful,* Tac. ; b, applied to inanimate objects, cera impatiens caloris, Ov. ; absol., impatiens animus, Ov.

impătǐentěr adv. (impatiens), *impatiently, unwillingly,* Tac.

impătǐentǐa -ae f. (impatiens), *impatience, inability to endure;* silentii impatientiam, Tac.

impăvǐdē, adv. (impavidus), *fearlessly, undauntedly,* Liv.

impăvǐdus -a -um (in and pavidus), *fear-*

---

less, courageous, undaunted; vir, Hor. ; pectora, Liv.

impēdīmentum -i, n. (impedio). **I.** *a hindrance, impediment;* impedimentum alicui facere, inferre, Cic. ; afferre, Tac. ; esse impedimenti loco, or impedimento, Caes. ; Gallis magno ad pugnam erat impedimento quod, etc., Caes. **II.** Esp., in plur., *the heavy baggage of an army* or *traveller, carried in waggons* or *on beasts of burden* (sarcina, *the soldier's knapsack*) ; impedimenta et sarcinas invadere, Liv. ; impedimenta exspectanda sunt quae Anagniā veniunt, Cic.

impēdǐo -īvi and -ǐi -ītum, 4. (in and PED, ΠΕΔ, whence also ped-s (pes), πος-ς (πούς), πεδ -άω). **I.** *to entangle, ensnare.* **A.** Lit. crura visceribus ; esp., *to render a place impassable;* saltum munitionibus, Liv. **B.** Transf., 1, *to embarrass, involve,* Tac. ; mentem dolore, Cic. ; 2, *to hinder, impede, prevent, obstruct;* aliquem, Cic. ; iter, Liv. ; with ab and the abl., se a suo munere non impedit, Cic. ; with abl., ne me dicendo impediat, Cic.; non or nihil impedire, foll. by quominus and the subj., Cic.; impedire, foll. by ne and the subj., Cic. ; aliquid aliquem impedit, with infin., Cic. ; with ad and the acc. gerund, Caes. ; with in and the abl., Caes. **II.** *to surround, wrap round;* caput myrto, Hor. ; equos frenis, *to bridle,* Ov.

impēdītǐo -ōnis, f. (impedio), *a hindering, hindrance;* animus liber omni impeditione curarum, Cic.

impēdītus -a -um (impedio), *hindered, impeded.* **I.** Lit., a, esp. as milit. t. t., *hindered by baggage, not ready for battle* (opp. expeditus); miles, Caes. ; b, of places, *impassable, difficult of access;* silva, Caes. **II.** Transf., a, *hindered, encumbered;* solutio, Cic. ; impeditis animis, busy, Caes.; b, *troublesome;* impeditus ancillarum puerorumque comitatus, Cic. ; c, *embarrassed;* tempora reipublicae, Cic.

impello -pŭli -pulsum, 3. (in and pello). **I.** *to strike, strike upon;* chordas, Ov. ; maternas impulit aures luctus Aristaei, Verg. **II.** *to push forward.* **A.** *to set in motion, drive on;* 1, lit., navem remis, Verg. ; aliquem in fugam, Cic.; 2, transf., a, aliquem in hunc casum, Cic.; b, *to incite, urge on, impel;* aliquem ad scelus, Cic.; aliquem ut, etc., Cic.; aliquem with infin., Liv. **B.** *to throw to the ground;* 1, esp. as milit. t. t., *to make to yield, to rout;* hostes, Liv. ; 2, transf., aliquem praecipitantem, *to give a push to some one falling, to complete a person's ruin,* Cic.

impendĕo, 2. (in and pendeo), *to hang over, overhang.* **A.** Lit., cervicibus, Cic. ; saxum impendere Tantalo, Cic. **B.** Transf., *to impend* or *hang over menacingly, to threaten, be close at hand;* in me terrores impendent, Cic. ; omnibus terror impendet, Cic. ; magnum etiam bellum impendet a Parthis, Cic.

impendǐo, adv. (impendium), *much, very much;* with comparatives, magis, *far more,* Cic.

impendǐum -ǐi, n. (impendo), 1, *expense, expenditure, outlay, cost;* impendio publico, *at the public expense,* Liv. ; sine impendio, Cic. ; 2, *interest of money,* Cic.

impendo -pendi -pensum, 3. (in and pendo), *to expend, lay out;* 1, lit., pecuniam in aliquam rem, Cic. ; 2, transf., ad incertum casum et eventum certus quotannis labor et certus sumptus impenditur, Cic.

impěnětrābǐlis -e (in and penetrabilis), 1, *impenetrable;* silex impenetrabilis ferro, Liv. ; tegimen adversus ictus impenetrabile, Tac. ; 2, *unconquerable, invincible,* Tac.

impensa -ae, f. (impensus -a -um from

impendo), *expense, outlay, cost;* **1**, lit., impensam facere in aliquid, Cic. ; nullā impensā, Cic.; **2**, transf., *applied to other than pecuniary outlay,* cruoris, Ov. ; operum, Verg.

impensē, adv. (impensus). **I.** *at great cost,* Pers. **II.** Transf., *urgently, eagerly, pressingly;* orare, Liv. ; nunc eo facio id impensius, Cic.

impensus -a -um, p. adj. (from impendo), **1**, lit., of price, *considerable, great;* impenso pretio, Cic. ; absol., impenso, *at a high price,* Hor. ; **2**, transf., *strong, vehement;* voluntas erga aliquem, Liv. ; voluntas bonorum, (ic.

impĕrātor -ōris, m. (impero), *a commander, leader.* **I.** Lit., **A.** Gen., populus est imperator omnium gentium, Cic. ; vitae, Sall. **B.** *the commander-in-chief of an army,* Cic. ; hence, a title given to a general after a great success by the army and senate, Cic. ; added as a title to the name, e.g. Cn. Pompeio Cn. F. Magno imperatori, Cic. **II.** Transf., **A.** name of Jupiter, Cic. **B.** after Julius Caesar, a name of the Roman emperors ; imperator Augustus, Suet.; and absol., = *the Roman emperor,* Suet.

impĕrātōrius -a -um (imperator), **1**, *of or relating to a general;* nomen, Cic. ; jus, laus, labor, Cic. ; **2**, *imperial;* uxor, Tac.

impĕrātrix -īcis f. (imperator), *a female ruler* or *commander;* (sarcastically), *a general in petticoats,* Cic.

imperceptus -a -um (in and percipio), *unperceived, unknown;* fraus, Ov.

impercussus -a -um (in and percutio), *not struck;* impercussos nocte movere pedes, *noiseless,* Ov.

imperdītus -a -um (in and perdo), *not slain, undestroyed,* Verg.

imperfectus -a -um (in and perficio), *incomplete, unfinished, imperfect;* verba, Ov. ; reliquum corpus imperfectum ac rude relinquere, Cic.; neut. subst., imperfecto nec absoluto simile pulchrum esse nihil potest, Cic.

imperfossus -a -um (in and perfodio), *unstabbed, unpierced;* ab omni ictu, Ov.

impĕrĭōsus -a -um (imperium), **1**, *powerful, mighty, potent;* populus, Cic. ; virga, *the fasces,* Ov.; sibi, *master of oneself,* Hor.; **2**, *masterful, imperious, tyrannical;* philosophus, Cic. ; cupiditas, Cic.

impĕrītē, adv. with compar. and superl. (imperitus), *unskilfully, ignorantly, clumsily;* imperite absurdeque fictum, Cic. ; quid potuit dici imperitius, Cic.

impĕrītĭa -ae, f. (imperitus), *want of skill and knowledge, inexperience, ignorance;* with subject. genit., juvenum, Tac.

impĕrīto, 1. (intens. of impero). **I.** Transit., *to command;* aequam rem imperito, Hor. **II.** Intransit., *to have power over;* si Nero imperitaret, Tac. ; with dat., oppido, Liv.

impĕrītus -a -um (in and peritus), *unskilled, inexperienced, ignorant;* with genit., juris civilis non imperitus, Cic. ; absol., homines imperiti, Cic.

impĕrĭum -ĭi, n. (impero). **I.** *an order, command;* accipere, *to receive,* Liv. ; exsequi, *to execute,* Verg. **II.** *the right* or *power of commanding, power, mastery, command.* **A.** Gen., domesticum, Cic. ; animi imperio, corporis servitio magis utimur, *the mind as a master, the body as a slave,* Sall. **B.** Esp., **1**, *the government* or *supreme authority in a state;* cadere sub P. R. imperium, Cic. ; sub P. R. imperium redigere, Cic. ; de imperio decertare, dimicare, Cic.; of magistracies, in imperio esse, *to hold an office,* Cic. ; cum imperio esse, *to have un-*

limited power, Cic. ; **2**, *military power* or *command;* summum imperium, Cic. ; maritimum, *chief naval command,* Caes. ; imperia magistratusque, *civil and military honours,* Nep. ; alicui imperium prorogare, Cic. **C.** Meton., **1**, *the person* or *persons exercising authority;* erat plena lictorum et imperiorum provincia, Caes. ; imperia et potestates, *military and civil authorities,* Cic. ; **2**, *the country governed, an empire;* finium imperii nostri propagatio, Cic.

imperjūrātus -a -um (in and perjuro), *that by which no one has sworn* or *dares to swear falsely;* aquae, *the Styx,* Ov.

impermissus -a -um (in and permitto), *forbidden,* Hor.

impĕro, 1. (in and paro), *to order, command.* **I.** Gen., with acc., quae imperarentur facere dixerunt, Caes. ; partic. subst., **impĕrātum** -i, n. *that which has been commanded;* imperatum, or imperata facere, Caes. ; with infin., flectere iter sociis, Verg. ; pass. infin., in easdem lautumias etiam ex ceteris oppidis deduci imperantur, Cic. ; with acc. and infin., esp. with acc. and pass. infin., Cic. ; with ut and the subj., Cic. ; ne and the subj., Caes. ; with the subj. alone, stringerent ferrum imperavit, Liv. **II.** Esp., **A.** **1**, *to rule over, govern, command;* Jugurtha omni Numidiae imperare parat, Sall. ; adesse ad imperandum, Cic. ; fig., sibi, Cic. ; cupiditatibus, Cic. ; **2**, transf., of agriculture, *to work at;* arvis, *compel to produce crops,* Verg. **B.** *to order some action;* **1**, of private life, cenam, Cic. ; **2**, polit. and milit. t.t., *to enjoin, prescribe, make a requisition for;* frumentum sibi in cellam, Cic. ; arma, Caes. ; (archaic form imperassit = imperaverit, Cic.).

imperterrĭtus -a -um (in and perterreo), *undaunted, fearless,* Verg.

impertĭo (in-partio) -īvi and -ĭi -ītum (impertior, dep.), 4. *to impart, communicate, share, bestow, give;* a, alicui de aliqua re or aliquid, indigentibus de re familiari, Cic. ; alicui civitatem, Cic. ; tempus cogitationi, Cic. ; b, aliquem aliquā re, Plaut., Ter. ; partic. subst., **impertĭta** -ōrum, n. *favours, concessions,* Liv.

imperturbātus -a -um (in and perturbo), *undisturbed, calm;* os, Ov.

impervĭus -a -um (in and pervius), *impassable, impervious;* iter, Tac. ; amnis, Ov.

impes -pĕtis, m. (in and peto) = impetus, *attack, onset, force;* impete vasto ferri, Ov.

impĕtĭbĭlis -e = impatibilis (q.v.).

impĕtrābĭlis -e (impetro), **1**, pass., *easy of attainment, attainable;* venia, Liv. ; pax, Liv. ; **2**, act., *that obtains easily, successful;* orator, Plaut. ; transf., dies, *on which wishes have been fulfilled,* Plaut.

impĕtrātĭo -ōnis, f. (impetro), *an obtaining by asking,* Cic.

impĕtrĭo, 4. (desider. of impetro). *to seek to obtain a good omen, to obtain by favourable omens,* Cic.

impĕtro, 1. (in and patro), *to get, obtain, accomplish, effect,* as a result of effort or entreaty; optatum, *to get one's wish,* Cic. ; alicui civitatem (*citizenship*) a Caesare, Cic. ; with ut and the subj., impetrabis a Caesare, ut tibi abesse liceat, Cic. ; absol., haec si tecum patria loquatur, nonne impetrare debeat? Cic.

impĕtus -ūs, m. (impes), *violent impulse, rapid motion, violence.* **I.** quinquereinis praelata impetu, Liv. **II.** *attack, assault, charge.* **A.** Lit., **1**, impetum facere in hostes, Caes.; excipere, sustinere, ferre, *to receive an attack,* Caes. ; impetum dare, *to attack,* Liv. ; prime impetu pulsi, Caes. ; **2**, of things, *force, vio-*

lence; in magno impetu maris atque aperto, Caes. **B.** Transf., **1**, of persons, **a,** *impulse, force;* impetus divinus, *inspiration,* Cic. ; b, *inclination, violent desire;* imperii delendi, Cic. ; **c,** *violence;* impetu magis quam consilio, Liv. ; **2,** of things, tanti belli impetus, Cic.

impexus -a -um (in and pecto), **1,** *uncombed,* Verg. ; **2,** transf., *rude, uncouth,* Tac.

impĭē, adv. (impius), *impiously, wickedly;* aliquid impie scelerateque committere, Cic.

impĭĕtas -ātis, f. (impius), *impiety, irreligion, ungodliness;* a, gen., Cic. ; **b,** esp., *treason against the emperor,* Tac.

impĭger -gra -grum (in and piger), *unslothful, diligent, active;* in scribendo, Cic.; ad labores belli, Cic. ; militiā, Liv. ; with genit., militiae, Tac. ; with infin., hostium vexare turmas, Hor.

impĭgrē, adv. (impiger), *actively, quickly;* impigre promittere auxilium, Liv.

impĭgrĭtas -ātis, f. (impiger), *activity, quickness,* Cic.

impingo -pēgi -pactum, 3. (in and pango), *to strike, beat, dash, drive, push against.* **I.** Lit., uncum alicui, Cic. ; litoribus impactus, Tac. **II.** Transf., **A.** *to press upon one, to thrust into one's hand;* alicui calicem mulsi, Cic. ; alicui epistolam, Cic. **B.** *to drive against;* agmina muris, Verg. ; hostes in vallum, Tac.

impĭo, 1. (impius), *to render sinful, defile with sin;* se, *to sin,* Plaut.

impius -a -um (in and pius), *impious, godless, reprobate, undutiful, unpatriotic.* **I.** Lit., civis, Cic. ; subst., nefarius impiusque, Cic. **II.** Transf., of things, bellum, Cic. ; arma, Verg.

implācābĭlis -e (in and placabilis), *implacable, irreconcileable;* alicui, Liv. ; in aliquem, Cic. ; of things, iracundiae, Cic.

implācābĭlĭus, adv. in compar. (implacabilis), *more implacably;* implacabilius alicui irasci, Tac.

implācātus -a -um (in and placo), *unappeased, unsatisfied;* Charybdis, Verg.

implăcĭdus -a -um (in and placidus), *rough, rude, harsh, savage, fierce;* genus, Hor.

implecto -plexi -plexum, 3. (in and plecto), *to interweave, weave, or twist with, or into;* 1, lit., implexae crinibus angues Eumenides, *whose hair is interwoven with serpents,* Verg. ; 2, transf., vidua implexa luctu continuo, *plunged in,* Tac.

implĕo -plēvi -plētum, 2. (in and * pleo), *to fill, fill up, fill full.* **I. A.** Gen., a, lit., fossas, Liv. ; with abl., gremium frustis, Cic. ; mero pateram, Verg. ; with genit., ollam denariorum, Cic. ; with de, voluminia de istis rebus, Cic. ; b, transf., urbem lamentis, Liv. ; implere aures alicuius Liv. **B.** Esp., **1,** *to fill with food, satiate;* implentur veteris Bacchi pinguisque ferinae, Verg.; **2,** *to make pregnant,* Ov. ; **3,** *to fill a certain measure, to complete a number;* impleta ut essent sex milia armatorum, Liv. ; of the moon, luna quater junctis implerat cornibus orbem, *had completed its circle,* Ov. **II.** Fig. **A.** omnia terrore, Liv. **B.** Esp., **1,** *to satisfy, content;* sese regum sanguine, Cic. ; **2,** *to complete;* quater undenos decembres, *to have lived through,* Hor. ; **3,** *to occupy a position;* locum principem, Tac. ; **4,** *to fulfil, perform;* officium scribendi, Cic. ; fata, Liv.

implexus -a um, partic. of implecto.

implĭcātĭo -ōnis,f.(implico), *an intertwining, interweaving;* 1, lit., nervorum, Cic. ; 2, transf., **a,** *a weaving together;* locorum communium, Cic. ; **b,** *embarrassment;* rei familiaris, Cic.

implĭcātus -a -um, p. adj. (from implico), *confused, entangled;* partes orationis, Cic.

implĭciscor, 3. dep. (implico), *to become confused, disordered,* Plaut.

implĭcĭtē, adv. (implicitus), *confusedly,* Cic.

implĭco -plĭcŭi -plĭcĭtum and -plĭcavi -plĭcātum, 1. (in and plico). **I.** *to enfold, enwrap, entangle.* **A.** Gen., 1, lit., se dextrae, *to cling to,* Verg. ; implicari remis, Liv. ; 2, transf., implicari or implicare se aliquā re, *to be entangled in, engaged in;* implicari morbo or in morbum, *to be attacked by,* Caes. ; negotiis, Cic. ; se societate civium, Cic. **B.** *to confuse, perplex;* a, implicare ac perturbare aciem, Sall. ; b, aliquem incertis responsis, Liv. **II. A.** *to twine around;* brachia collo, Verg. **B.** *to weave around, to surround;* tempora ramo, Verg.

implōrātĭo -ōnis, f. (imploro), *an imploring for help;* with subject. genit., illius, Cic. ; with object. genit., deûm, Liv.

implōro, 1. (in and ploro). **I.** *to call upon with tears or entreaties.* **A.** Gen., nomen filii, Cic. **B.** Esp., *to beseech, implore;* deos, Cic. ; alicuius auxilium, fidem, misericordiam, Cic. **II.** *to ask for;* auxilium ab aliquo, Cic., Caes.; with ne and the subj., Caes.

implūmis -e (in and pluma), *unfledged;* pulli, Hor. ; fetus (avis), Verg.

implŭo -plŭi, 3. (in and pluo), *to rain upon;* with dat., Peneus summis aspergine silvis impluit, Ov.

implŭvĭum -ĭi, n. (impluo), *a square basin in the floor of the atrium of a Roman house, in which the rain-water, coming through the compluvium, was received,* Cic.

impōlītē, adv. (impolitus), *plainly, without ornament;* dicere, Cic.

impōlītus -a -um (in and polio), *rough, unpolished, unrefined, inelegant;* forma ingenii admodum impolita et plane rudis, Cic. ; res, *unfinished,* Cic.

impollūtus -a -um (in and polluo), *unpolluted, undefiled,* Tac.

impōno -pŏsŭi -pŏsĭtum, 3. (in and pono). **I.** *to put, set, lay, place in;* aliquem sepulcro, *to bury,* Ov. ; coloniam in agro Samnitium, Liv.; praesidium Abydi, *at Abydos,* Liv. **II.** *to put, lay, place upon.* **A.** Lit., 1, gen., alicui coronam, Cic. ; dextram in caput, Liv.; aliquem in rogum, Cic., rogo, Verg. ; 2, esp. as naut. t. t., *to put on ship, to embark;* aliquem in naves or imponere, *to put on naves,* Caes.; exercitum Brundisii, Cic. **B.** Transf., **1,** *to put over as master;* regem Macedoniae, consulem populo, Cic. ; **2,** *to lay upon as a burden,* impose; frenos animo alicuius, Liv. ; alicui onus, Cic. ; invidiam belli consuli, Sall. ; **3,** *to impose upon, cheat, deceive;* with dat., Catoni egregie, Cic. **III.** *to place on.* **A.** Lit., claves portis, Liv. **B.** Transf., 1, manum extremam (summam, supremam) alicui rei, *to put the last touch to,* Verg. ; finem imponere alicui rei, Liv. ; modum alicui rei, *to put bounds to,* Liv. ; 2, *to add;* a, alicui nomen imponere (with genit. or acc. of the name); b, in a bad sense, *to cause;* alicui vulnus, Cic. (partic. perf. syncop. impostus, Verg.).

importo, 1. (in and porto), **1,** *to bring in, import;* vinum ad se importari omnino non sinunt, Caes. ; 2, transf., a, *to bring in, introduce;* importatis artibus, *foreign,* Cic. ; b, *to bring upon, cause;* alicui detrimentum, Cic.

importūnē, adv. (importunus), *unseasonably, rudely, violently;* insistere, Cic.

importūnĭtas -ātis, f. (importunus), *rudeness, impoliteness, insolence, incivility;* animi Cic.

9 *

importūnus -a -um (in and POR-o, PORT-o, whence portus, porta, etc.), 1, lit., *unsuitable, ill-adapted;* loca machinationibus, Sall.; 2. transf., **a,** of time, *unfavourable;* tempus, Cic.; **b,** of circumstances, *troublesome, burdensome, oppressive;* pauperies, Hor.; **c,** *rude, uncivil, unmannerly, churlish, savage;* mulier, hostis, libido, Cic.

importŭōsus -a -um (in and portuosus), *without harbours;* mare, Sall.; litus, Liv.

impos -pŏtis (in and POT, whence also potis), *having no power over;* animi, Plaut.

impŏsĭtus -a -um, partic. of impono.

impŏtens -entis (in and potens). **I.** *weak, impotent, having no power;* homo, Cic.; plur. subst. **impŏtentes** -ium, *the weak,* Cic. **II.** *having no power over, not master of.* **A.** Gen. with genit., equi regendi, Liv.; irae, Liv. **B.** *unable to command one's passions, violent, unrestrained, furious, outrageous;* a, lit., homo, Cic.; animus, Cic.; **b,** transf., of the passions themselves, *unbridled;* injuria, Liv.; laetitia, Cic.

impŏtentĕr, adv. (impotens), 1, *weakly, powerlessly;* elephantos impotentius jam regi, Liv.; 2, *intemperately, passionately,* Liv.

impŏtentĭa -ae, f. (impotens). **I.** *impotence,* Ter. **II.** *passionateness, ungovernableness, intemperance, extravagant passion;* animi, Cic.

impraesentĭārum (for in praesentiā rerum), *in present circumstances, for the present, at present,* Nep., Tac.

impransus -a -um (in and pransus), *that has not breakfasted, fasting,* Hor.

imprĕcor, 1. dep. (in and precor), *to wish any thing for any one, to call down upon, to imprecate;* litora litoribus contraria, Verg.; alicui diras, Tac.

impressĭo -ōnis, f. (imprimo), 1, in rhetoric, a, *a distinct expression, emphasis, stress of voice;* explanata vocum impressio, Cic.; b, impressiones, *raising and lowering of the voice,* Cic.; 2, philosoph. t. t., *the impressions of outward things received through the senses,* Cic.; 3, a *pressing-in-upon, an attack, assault;* non ferre impressionem Latinorum, Liv.; of political contests, me vi et impressione evertere, Cic.

imprīmis, adv. (in and primus), *especially, first of all, principally,* Cic.

imprĭmo -pressi -pressum, 3. (in and premo), *to press in or on.* **I.** Gen., *to press upon, press into;* impresso genu, Verg. **II. a,** *to press into, impress, drive in;* aratrum muris, Hor.; sulcum altius, Cic.; **b,** esp., *to stamp, make a mark;* sigillum in cera, Cic.; **c,** transf., as philosoph. t. t., of ideas, etc., *to impress on the mind;* quum visa in animis imprimantur, Cic.; **d,** *to seal;* signo suo impressae tabellae, Liv.; **e,** *to inlay, cover;* cratera impressum signis, chased, embossed, Verg.; **f,** fig., quae quum viderem tot vestigiis impressa, Cic.

imprŏbātĭo -ōnis, f. (improbo), *disapprobation, blame;* improbatione hominis uti, Cic.

imprŏbē, adv. (improbus), 1, *wrongly, dishonestly, wickedly;* dicere, facere, Cic.; 2, *wantonly, impudently;* improbissime respondere, Cic.

imprŏbĭtas -ātis, f. (improbus), *badness, wickedness, depravity;* alicuius, Cic.; applied to animals, simiae (*roguery*), Cic.

imprŏbo, 1. (in and probo), *to disapprove, blame, find fault with, reject;* multorum opera, Cic.; with double acc., aliquem testem, Cic.

imprŏbŭlus -a -um (dim. of improbus), *somewhat bad, wicked,* Juv.

imprŏbus -a -um (in and probus). **I.** *bad,*

poor; 1, lit., defensio, Cic.; 2, transf., *morally bad, wicked, depraved, reprobate;* homo, Cic.; lex, Cic.; subst., *a rogue,* Cic. **II.** *beyond measure;* a, *beyond the usual size, enormous, immense;* labor, *never-ending,* Verg.; rabies ventris, *insatiable hunger,* Verg.; anser, anguis, voracious, Verg.; **b,** transf. (*a) mischievous;* puer, Verg.; (β) *bold;* Aeneas, Verg.; shameless, *impudent;* siren, Hor.; (γ) *lascivious, lewd;* carmina, Ov.

imprŏcērus -a -um (in and procerus), *small, low of stature;* pecora, Tac.

impromptus -a -um (in and promptus), *not ready, not quick;* linguā, *slow of speech,* Liv.

imprŏpĕrātus -a -um (in and propero), *not hasty, slow;* vestigia, Verg.

improsper -ēra -ērum (in and prosper), *unfortunate, unprosperous;* claritudo, Tac.

improspĕrē, adv. (improsper), *unprosperously, unluckily,* Tac.

imprōvĭdē, adv. (improvidus), *without forethought, improvidently,* Liv.

imprōvĭdus -a -um (in and providus). **I.** *not foreseeing;* improvidos incautosque hostes opprimere, Liv.; with genit., improvidus futuri certaminis, Liv. **II.** *without forethought, incautious, heedless, improvident;* duces, Cic.; improvidi et creduli senes, Cic.; with genit., improvidus futuri, Tac.; transf., of things, improvida aetas (puerorum), Cic.

imprōvīso, adv. (improvisus), *suddenly, unexpectedly,* Cic.

imprōvīsus -a -um (in and proviso), *unforeseen, unanticipated, unexpected, sudden;* res, Cic.; adventus, Cic.; de or ex improviso, or improviso, *suddenly, unexpectedly,* Cic.

imprūdens -entis (in and prudens). **I.** *not foreseeing, not expecting, not knowing;* aliquem imprudentem aggredi, *to attack unawares,* Caes.; imprudente Sullā, *without the knowledge of Sulla.* **II. a,** *ignorant of, not acquainted with;* legis, Cic.; maris, Liv.; b, *unwise, rash, imprudent,* Tac.

imprūdentĕr, adv. (imprudens), 1, *ignorantly, unwittingly, unawares, through ignorance,* Cic.; 2, *imprudently, inconsiderately;* nihil imprudenter facere, ap. Cic.

imprūdentĭa -ae. f. (imprudens). **I.** *absence of design;* teli missi, Cic.; quo ne imprudentiam quidem oculorum adjici fas fuit, *cast a look unawares,* Cic. **II.** 1, *ignorance of;* eventus, Liv.; 2, *want of foresight, imprudence, inadvertence;* per imprudentiam, *from imprudence,* Cic.; propter imprudentiam labi, Caes.

impūbes -bēris and **impūbis** -e (in and pubes), *below the age of puberty, under age, youthful;* filius, Cic.; anni, Ov.; genae, *beardless,* Verg.; qui diutissime impuberes permanserunt, *retained their chastity,* Caes.; plur., impuberes or impubes, *boys,* Liv., Caes.

impŭdens -entis (in and pudens), *not ashamed, shameless, impudent;* tu es impudens! Cic.; transf., mendacium, Cic.; impudentissimae literae, Cic.

impŭdentĕr, adv. with compar. and superl. (impudens), *shamelessly, impudently;* mentiri, Cic.

impŭdentĭa -ae, f. (impudens), *shamelessness, impudence,* Cic.

impŭdīcĭtĭa -ae, f. (impudicus), *lewdness, incontinence, unchastity,* Tac.

impŭdīcus -a -um (in and pudicus), *unchaste, lewd, incontinent;* homo, Cic.; transf., P. Clodii imperatoris impudentia, Cic.

impugnātĭo -ōnis, f. (impugno), *an assault, attack,* Cic.

impugno, 1. (in and pugno), *to attack as*

sault, assail. **I.** Lit., as milit. t. t., terga *hostium,* Liv. ; absol., Caes. **II.** Transf., a, *to contend, struggle against any one, attack, assail;* regem, Sall. ; b, *to assail with words;* dignitatem alicuius, Cic. ; sententiam, Tac.

impulsĭo -ōnis, f. (impello), 1, *an external influence* or *force, an impression* or *impulse from without,* Cic. ; 2, *an instigation, incitement, impulse;* omnis ad omnem animi motum impulsio, Cic.

impulsor -ōris, m. (impello), *an instigator, inciter;* profectionis meae, Cic. ; Caesare impulsore atque auctore, Cic.

impulsus -ūs, m. (impello). **I.** *an outward force, shock, pressure;* scutorum, Cic. **II.** 1, *an incitement, instigation;* impulsu meo, suo, vestro, Cic. ; 2, *an inward impulse, sudden passion,* Cic.

impūnĕ (impunis, from in and poena), adv. *with impunity, without punishment.* **A.** Lit., facere, Cic. ; ferre, *to go unpunished,* Cic. ; non impune abire, Caes. **B.** Transf., *without peril, safely;* in otio esse, Cic. ; revisere aequor, Hor.

impūnĭtas -ātis, f. (impunis). **A.** Lit., *impunity, exemption from punishment;* peccandi, Cic. ; alicui veniam et impunitatem dare, Cic. ; impunitas non modo a judicio, sed etiam a sermone, Cic. **B.** Transf., *freedom, licence;* flagitiorum, Cic. ; superfluens juvenili quādam impunitate et licentiā, Cic.

impūnītē, adv. (impunitus), *with impunity,* Cic.

impūnītus -a -um (in and punitus). **A.** *unpunished, exempt from punishment;* multorum impunita scelera ferre, Cic. ; si istius haec injuria impunita discesserit, Cic. ; aliquem impunitum dimittere, Sall. **B.** Transf., *unbridled, unrestrained;* mendacium, Cic. ; omnium rerum libertas, Cic.

impūrātus -a -um (impuro), *vile, abandoned, infamous,* Plaut., Ter.

impūrē, adv. (impurus), *impurely, vilely, infamously, shamefully;* multa facere, Cic. ; vivere, Cic.

impūrĭtas -ātis, f. (impurus), *moral impurity,* Cic.

impūrus -a -um (in and purus), 1, lit., *unclean, stained, impure,* Ov. ; 2, usually in a moral sense, *impure, defiled, vile, shameful, infamous;* homo, Cic. ; animus, Sall. ; historia, Ov.

1. **impŭtātus** -a -um (in and puto), *unpruned, untrimmed;* vinea, Ov.

2. **impŭtātus** -a -um, partic. of impūto.

impŭto, 1. (in and puto), *to impute to, lay to the charge of any one, as a fault* or *merit, to account, reckon as a fault* or *merit;* a, as a merit, quis mihi plurimum imputet, Tac. ; b, as a fault, alicui natum, Ov.

īmŭlus -a -um (dim. of imus), *lowest,* Cat.

īmus -a -um, superl. from inferus (q.v.).

1. **ĭn,** prep. with acc. = *into,* with abl. = *in.* **I.** With the acc. **A.** Of space, *into;* ad urbem vel potius in urbem exercitum adducere, Cic. **B.** Of time ; 1, *to;* dormire in lucem, Hor. ; aliquid in omne tempus perdidisse, *for ever,* Cic. ; 2, *for, to;* magistratum creare in annum, Liv. ; in multos annos praedicere, Cic. ; in diem, a, *for a short time, for the day;* in diem vivere, *to live for the moment,* Cic. ; b, *daily;* in diem rapto vivere, Liv. ; c, *for the future;* in diem poenas praesentis fraudis dii reservant, Cic. ; in dies or in singulos dies, (a) *from day to day,* Cic. ; (β) *daily,* Cic. ; in horas, *hourly,* Hor. ; in singulos annos, *from year to year,* Liv. **C.** Of other relations ; 1, of dimension, *in;* murum in

altitudinem pedum sedecim fossamque perdúcit, Caes. ; 2, of division, *into;* Gallia est omnis divisa in tres partes, Caes. ; describere censores binos in singulas civitates, *two for each state,* Cic. ; 3, of object, *for;* nullam pecuniam Gabinio, nisi in rem militarem datam, Cic. ; in hoc, *for this purpose,* Hor. ; 4, of manner, *according to;* tradere regnum in fidem alicuius, *on the word of,* Sall. ; in eandem sententiam loqui, Cic. ; jurare in verba alicuius, Hor. ; in universum, *in general,* Liv. ; in vicem, Cic., Caes., or in vices, Ov., *in turns;* 5, of direction, a, *to, in the presence of, before;* de servis quaere in dominos, Cic. ; b, *towards;* amor in patriam, Cic. **D.** Pregnant constr., aliquem in carcerem asservari jubere, *to be taken to prison and kept there,* Liv. ; in Tusculanum futurum esse, *to wish to come to,* Cic. **II.** With abl., *in.* **A.** Of space ; 1, esse in Sicilia, Cic. ; in oculis esse, *to be before one's eyes,* Cic. ; 2, esp. of dress, etc., esse in veste domestica, Ov. ; excubare in armis, Caes. **B.** of time ; 1, *in the course of;* in sex mensibus, Cic. ; in bello, Cic. ; in deliberando, *during,* Cic. ; 2, *at;* in tali tempore, Liv. ; in eo est ut, etc., *on the point of,* Liv. ; in tempore, *at the right time,* Liv. **C.** Of other relations ; 1, of the condition in which one is, *in;* in hac solitudine, Cic. ; with persons, *in the case of;* in hoc homine non accipio excusationem, Cic. ; 2, of action, etc., *in;* in motu esse, Cic. ; 3, of the subjects of education, *in;* erudire in jure civili, Cic. ; 4, *amongst the number of;* in quibus Catilina, Sall.

2. **in,** inseparable particle, with adjectives and participles, *without, not,* e.g., indoctus.

ĭnaccessus -a -um (in and accedo), *inaccessible;* lucus, Verg.

ĭnăcesco -ācŭi, 3. *to become sour;* transf., haec tibi per totos inacescant omnia sensus, Ov.

Ĭnăchus(Ĭnăchos)-i,m.('Ιναχος),*a mythical king of Argos, father of Io, after whom the river Inachus in Argolis was named;* hence 1, adj., **Ĭnăchĭus** -a -um ; a, *relating to Inachus;* juvenca, Io, Verg. ; b, *Greek;* urbes, Verg. ; 2, **Ĭnăchĭdēs** -ae, m. *a descendant of Inachus, Perseus,* Ov. ; *Epaphus,* Ov. ; 3, **Ĭnăchis** -ĭdis, f. *relating to Inachus;* ripa, *of the river Inachus,* Ov. ; subst., *a daughter of Inachus, Io,* Prop.

ĭnădustus -a -um (in and aduro), *unburnt, unsinged,* Ov.

ĭnaedĭfĭco, 1. 1, *to build in* or *upon;* sacellum in domo, Cic. ; aliquid in locum, Liv. ; 2, *to build up, block up, barricade;* vicos plateasque, Caes.

ĭnaequābĭlis -e, a, *uneven;* solum, Liv. ; b, *unequal, varying;* motus, Cic.

ĭnaequābĭlĭtĕr, adv. (inaequabilis), *unequally, variously,* Suet.

ĭnaequālis -e. **I.** *unequal, uneven, unlike, various;* 1, lit., loca, Tac. ; calices, *now full, now half full,* Hor. ; 2, transf., varietas, Cic. **II.** Act., *making unequal;* tonsor, Hor. ; procellae, *disturbing the level of the sea,* Hor.

ĭnaequālĭtas -ātis, f. (inaequalis), *inequality, dissimilarity, irregularity,* Varr.

ĭnaequālĭtĕr, adv. (inaequalis), *unequally, unevenly;* inaequaliter eminentes rupes, Liv.

ĭnaequo, 1. *to make even* or *level;* haec levibus cratibus terrāque inaequat, Caes.

ĭnaestĭmābĭlis -e, 1, a, *that cannot be estimated;* nihil tam incertum nec tam inaestimabile quam animi multitudinis, Liv. ; b, *priceless, inestimable;* gaudium, Liv. ; 2, *having no (relative) value* (Gr. ἀπαξίαν ἔχον), Cic. ; in a bad sense, *unworthy of being valued,* Cic.

ĭnaestŭo, 1. *to boil, rage in;* fig., *si meis* inaestuat praecordiis bilis, Hor.

ĭnaffectātus -a -um (in and affecto), *natural, unaffected*, Plin.

ĭnalpīnus -a -um, *Alpine, dwelling in the Alps;* subst., **Ĭnalpīni** -ōrum, *the dwellers in the Alps,* ap. Cic.

ĭnămābĭlis -e, *unpleasant, hateful, unlovely, odious;* palus (of the Styx), Verg.

ĭnămāresco, 3. *to become bitter,* Hor.

ĭnambĭtĭōsus -a -um, *not ambitious, unpretentious,* Ov.

ĭnambŭlātĭo -ōnis, f. (inambulo), *a walking up and down,* Cic.

ĭnambŭlo, 1. *to walk up and down;* cum Cotta in porticu, Cic.

ĭnămoenus -a -um, *unpleasant, unlovely, dismal;* regna umbrarum, Ov.

ĭnānĭae -ārum, f. (inanis), *emptiness,* Plaut.

ĭnānĭlŏquus (ĭnānĭlŏgus) -a -um (inanis and loquor), *speaking in vain* or *emptily,* Plaut.

ĭnănĭmālis -e, *lifeless, inanimate;* animalia inanimaliaque omnia, Liv.

ĭnănĭmātus -a -um, *lifeless, inanimate,* Cic.(?).

ĭnănĭmentum -i, n. (inanio), *emptiness,* Plaut.

ĭnănĭmus -a -um (in and anima), *lifeless, inanimate;* neut. subst., quum inter inanimum et animal hoc intersit, Cic.

ĭnānĭo -īvi -ītum, 4. (inanis), *to empty, make void,* Lucr.

ĭnānis -e, *empty, void, vacant* (opp. plenus, completus, confertus). **I.** Lit., **A.** Gen., vas, domus, Cic.; equus, *without rider,* Cic.; navis, *unloaded,* Caes.; corpus, *soulless, dead,* Cic.; lumina, *blind,* Ov.; galea, *taken from the head,* Verg.; with genit., Hor.; with abl., epistola inanis aliquā re utili et suavi, Cic.; subst., **ĭnāne** -is, n. *space, empty space,* Cic. **B.** 1, esp., *empty-handed;* a, redire, Cic.; b, *poor, indigent;* civitas, Cic.; 2, *empty-bellied, hungry,* Hor. **II.** Transf., 1, *empty, void of;* with genit., inanissima prudentiae, Cic.; elocutio, Cic.; subst., **ĭnāne** -is, n. *vanity, emptiness,* Hor.; 2, *groundless, vain;* motus, Cic.; 3, *vain, useless;* contentiones, Cic.; 4, *vain, conceited;* animus, Cic.

ĭnānĭtas -ātis, f. (inanis), 1, *emptiness, empty space,* Cic.; 2, transf., *worthlessness, inanity,* Cic.

ĭnānĭtĕr, adv. (inanis), *emptily, vainly, uselessly,* Cic.

1. **ĭnărātus** -a -um (in and aro), *unploughed, fallow,* Verg.

2. **ĭnărātus,** partic. of inaro.

ĭnardesco -arsi, 3. **I.** *to burn on;* humeris Herculis, Hor. **II.** *to begin to glow, to kindle.* **A.** Lit., nubes inardescit solis radiis, Verg. **B.** Transf., of passions, *to glow, burn;* amor specie praesentis inarsit, Ov.; specie juvenis, Ov.

ĭnăresco -ārŭi, 3. *to become dry;* vi solis, Tac.

ĭnargentātus -a -um, *silvered, plated with silver,* Plin.

Ĭnărīmē -ēs, f. = Aenaria.

ĭnăro, 1. *to plough, to cultivate,* Plin.

ĭnassuētus -a -um, *unaccustomed;* equus, Ov.

ĭnattĕnŭātus (in and attenuo), *undiminished, unimpaired;* fames, *unappeased,* Ov.

ĭnaudax -ācis, *timid, fearful,* Hor.

ĭnaudĭo, 4. *to hear;* particularly, *to hear news, to hear a secret;* aliquid de aliquo, Cic.; de aliqua re ex aliquo, Cic.

1. **ĭnaudītus** -a -um (in and audio), *unheard of;* 1, a, inaudita criminatio, Cic.; b, *unheard of, unusual;* agger inauditus, Caes.; nomen est, non dico inusitatum, verum etiam inauditum, Cic.; 2, *unheard, without a hearing* (before a judge); aliquem inauditum et indefensum damnare, Tac.

2. **ĭnaudītus** -a -um, partic. of inaudio.

ĭnaugŭrāto, adv. (inauguro), *after having taken the auguries,* Liv.

ĭnaugŭro, 1. **I.** Intransit., *to take the auguries, to divine;* Palatium Romulus, Remus Aventinum ad inaugurandum templa capiunt, Liv.; with rel., sent., inaugura fierine possit, quod nunc ego mente concipio, Liv. **II.** Transit., *to consecrate, instal, inaugurate;* templum, Cic.; flaminem, Cic.

ĭnaures -ium, f. (in and aures), *earrings,* Plaut.

ĭnauro, 1. **I.** *to gild, cover with gold;* gen. in partic., **ĭnaurātus** -a -um, *gilt;* statua, Cic.; vestis, *gold-worked,* Ov. **II.** Transf. (in jest), *to gild, enrich,* Cic.

ĭnauspĭcāto, adv. (inauspicatus), *without consulting the auspices,* Cic.

ĭnauspĭcātus -a -um. **I.** *without auspices;* lex, *adopted without auspices,* Liv. **II.** Transf., *unlucky, inauspicious,* Plin.

ĭnausus -a -um (in and audeo), *not dared, not attempted;* ne quid inausum aut intractatum sceleris dolive fuisset, Verg.

incaedŭus -a -um, *not cut down, unfelled;* lucus, Ov.

incălesco -călŭi, 3. *to glow, become warm;* a, of things, incalescente sole, Liv.; b, of persons, *to glow with wine or passion;* vino, Liv.; esp. of love; vidit et incaluit pelagi deus, Ov.

incalfăcĭo, 3. *to heat, warm, make hot,* Ov.

incallĭdē, adv. (incallidus) *not cleverly, without ingenuity;* non incallide (= *skilfully*) tergiversari, Cic.

incallĭdus -a -um, *not clever, without ingenuity;* servus non incallidus, Cic.

incandesco -candŭi, 3. *to begin to glow with heat, become very hot;* incandescit eundo (plumbum), Ov.

incānesco -cānŭi, 3, *to become white;* ornusque incanuit albo flore piri, Verg.

incantāmentum -i, n. (incanto), *a charm, incantation,* Plin.

incanto, 1. *to consecrate with charms* or *spells;* vincula, Hor.

incānus -a -um, *quite grey;* menta, Verg.

incassum, adv. (v. cassus), *in vain, vainly, uselessly,* Verg.

incastīgātus -a -um (in and castigo), *unchastised, uncorrected,* Hor.

incautē, adv. (incautus), *incautiously, carelessly;* incaute et stulte, Cic.; compar., incautius sequi, Caes.

incautus -a -um, 1, *incautious, careless, heedless, unwary, inconsiderate;* homo incautus et rusticus, Cic.; with ab and the abl., incautus a fraude, Liv.; with genit., futuri, Hor.; 2, *not guarded against* or *that which cannot be guarded against, unforeseen, unexpected, uncertain, unprotected;* repente incautos agros invasit, Sall.; iter hostibus incautum, Tac.

incēdo -cessi -cessum, 3. **I.** Intransit., *to walk, go, march, step in, enter.* **A.** Lit., a, pedes, *on foot,* Liv.; molliter, *with a light step,* Ov.; quā cumque incedĕret, Cic.; **b,** as milit. **t. t.,** *to march, advance;* usque ad portas, Liv.; in perculsos Romanos, *to come on,* Sall. **B.** Transf., **a,** *to come on, break out;* postquam tenebrae incedebant, Liv.; incessit in ea castra vis morbi, Liv.; **b,** of news, reports, etc.; occultus rumor incedebat (with acc. and infin.), Tac.; **c,** of political events, *to take place, arise, spread abroad;* incessit timor Sabini belli, Liv.; with dat. pers., *to seize on;* gravis cura patribus incessit, ut, etc., Liv. **II.** Transit. **1,** *to walk on;* scenam, Tac.; **2,** *to happen to, come to, befall;* aliquem valetudo adversa incessit, Tac.

incĕlĕbrātus -a -um (in and celebro), *not made known, not spread abroad,* Tac.

incendiārĭus -a -um (incendium), *relating to a conflagration, incendiary;* hence, subst., **incendiārĭus** -ĭi, m. *an incendiary,* Tac.

incendĭum -ĭi, n. (incendo), *a conflagration, fire.* **I.** 1, lit., incendium facere, excitare, Cic.; conflare, Liv.; **2,** meton. *fire-brand;* incendia poscit, Verg. **II.** Transf., **1,** *fire, glow, heat* (of the passions); cupiditatum, Cic.; **2,** *danger, destruction, ruin;* civitatis, Cic.

incendo -cendi -censum, 3. (in and *cando), *to kindle, set fire to, burn.* **I. A.** Lit., **a,** tus et odores, Cic.; **b,** *to set on fire;* urbem, Cic.; **c,** medic. t. t., incensi aestus, *the burning heat of fever,* Verg. **B.** Meton., **1,** *to kindle fire upon;* altaria, Verg.; **2,** *to make bright, brilliant, to enlighten;* solis incensa radiis luna, Cic. **II.** Transf., **1,** *to set on fire with passion, incite, excite, stir up, irritate, incense;* **a,** animos judicium in aliquem, Cic.; desine me incendere querelis, Verg.; esp., *to excite to love;* aliquem, Verg.; incendi, *to burn, to glow, to be irritated, incensed;* amore, desiderio, Cic.; incensus irā, Cic.; **b,** of abstract objects, *to arouse;* cupiditatem, odia, Cic.; **2,** *to enhance, raise, increase;* luctum, Verg.; **3,** *to fill* (as with fire); caelum clamore, Verg.

incensĭo -ōnis, f. (incendo), *a burning, conflagration,* Cic.

1. **incensus** -a -um (in and censeo), *not enrolled by the censor, unassessed,* Cic.

2. **incensus. I.** Partic. of incendo. **II.** P. adj., fig., of orators, *fiery;* vehemens et incensus, Cic.

inceptĭo -ōnis, f. (incipio), *a beginning, undertaking;* tam praeclari operis, Cic.

incepto, 1. (intens. of incipio), *to begin, undertake,* Plaut., Ter.

inceptor -ōris, m. (incipio), *a beginner,* Ter.

inceptum -i, n. (incipio), *an undertaking, beginning, enterprise;* inceptum non succedebat, Liv.; incepta patrare, Sall.; ab incepto desistere, Liv.

inceptus -ūs, m. = inceptum (q.v.).

incerno -crēvi -crētum, 3. *to sift upon, to bestrew by sifting;* piper album cum sale nigro incretum, Hor.

incēro, 1. *to cover with wax;* in jest, genua deorum, *to cover with votive wax tablets,* i.e., *to beseech, implore,* Juv.

1. **incertō,** adv. (incertus), *not certainly, doubtfully,* Plaut.

2. **incerto,** 1. (incertus), *to make uncertain or doubtful,* Plaut.

incertus -a -um, *uncertain, doubtful, not sure.* **I. A.** casus, Cic.; responsum, Liv.; rumores, Caes. **B.** Esp., **a,** *not clearly visible, dim, dark;* luna, Verg.; **b,** *not sure* (of a blow); securis, Verg.; **c,** *disorderly;* crines, Ov.; vultus, *disturbed,* Cic. **II. A.** *undetermined;* os, *stammering,* Ov.; with rel. sent., incerti socii an hostes

essent, Liv.; subst., **incertum** -i, n. *that which is uncertain, uncertainty;* ad or in incertum revocare, *to make uncertain,* Cic.; plur., incerta belli, *the uncertainties of war,* Liv. **B.** Transf., of persons, *uncertain, hesitating;* quum incertus essem ubi esses, Cic.; with genit., rerum omnium, Liv.

incesso -cessi or -cessīvi, 3. (intens. of incedo), *to attack, assail, fall upon.* **A.** Lit., aliquem jaculis saxisque, Liv. **B.** Transf., *to assail with reproaches;* reges dictis protervis, Ov.; aliquem criminibus, Tac.

incessus -ūs, m. (incedo), *the gait, mode of walking.* **I.** Lit., **A.** Gen., rarus incessus nec ita longus, Cic.; incessus citus modo, modo tardus, Sall. **B.** Esp., *a hostile attack, assault;* primo incessu solvit obsidium, Tac. **II.** *entrance, approach;* alios incessus hostis claudere, Tac.

incestē, adv. (incestus), *impurely, sinfully,* Cic.

incesto, 1. (incestus), **1,** *to defile, pollute;* classem funere, Verg.; **2,** *to defile, dishonour,* Verg.

incestum -i, n., v. incestus.

1. **incestus** -a -um (in and castus), *impure, sinful, impious.* **I.** Gen., os, Cic.; manus, Liv.; subst., incestus, *a sinful person,* Hor. **II.** Esp., *unchaste, lewd;* **a,** of persons, judex (of Paris), Hor.; **b,** of things, flagitium, Cic.; subst., **incestum** -i, n. *unchastity, lewdness, incest;* incestum facere, Cic.

2. **incestus** -ūs, m. (1. incestus), *unchastity, incest,* Cic.

inchŏo, 1. *to begin, commence.* **A.** Gen., novum delubrum, Cic.; res quas (communis intelligentia) in animis nostris inchoavit, Cic. **B.** Esp., **1,** *to introduce, begin to treat of;* philosophiam multis locis, Cic.; **2,** *to bring a matter before the senate;* inchoante Caesare de, etc., Tac.; **3,** partic. perf., **inchŏātus** -a -um, *only begun, not finished, incomplete;* cognitio, officium, Cic.

1. **incĭdo** -cĭdi, 3. (in and cado), *to fall in or on.* **I.** Accidentally. **A.** Lit., foveam, Cic.; with dat., capitibus nostris, Liv. **B.** Transf., **1,** *to fall into, to light upon;* in insidias, Cic.; incidere alicui or in aliquem, *to meet unexpectedly,* Cic.; **2,** of time, *to fall upon, happen on;* in hunc diem incidunt mysteria, Cic.; **3,** *to fall into a disease or some evil;* in morbum, Cic.; in aes alienum, *to run into debt,* Cic.; **4,** *to fall upon by chance;* **a,** of persons, casu in eorum mentionem, Cic.; in Diodorum, *to fall in with the opinion of,* Cic.; **b,** of things, incidit mihi in mentem, *it comes into my mind,* Cic.; **5,** *to happen, occur;* incidunt saepe tempora quum, etc., Cic.; si qua clades incidisset, Liv.; forte incidit ut with subj., Liv.; with dat. pers., *to happen to;* multis tales casus inciderunt, Cic. **II.** Purposely. **A.** Lit., into a place, *to burst into;* castris, Liv.; in hostem, *to attack,* Liv. **B.** Transf., *to fall upon, seize;* terror incidit exercitui, Caes.

2. **incĭdo** -cĭdi -cīsum, 3. (in and caedo). **I.** *to cut into, make an incision, cut open;* **1,** gen., arbores, Caes.; pulmo incisus, Cic.; **2,** esp., **a,** *to inscribe, engrave an inscription;* leges in aes, Cic.; notum est carmen incisum in sepulcro, Cic.; **b,** *to make by cutting;* faces, Verg.; **c,** *to clip, prune, cut;* pinnas, Cic. **II.** *to cut through.* **A.** Lit., linum, Cic. **B.** Transf., **1,** *to cut short, bring to an end, break off;* poema quod institueram, Cic.; sermonem, Liv.; genus vocis in cidens, *broken off, interrupted;* **2,** *to take away;* spem omnem, Liv.

inciens -entis (connected with ἐγκύμων, ἔγκυος), *pregnant, with young,* Plin.

incīlis -e (for incidilis from incīdo), *cut;* subst., **incīle** -is, n. *a ditch or canal for carrying off water;* fig., tamquam in quodam incili jam omnia adhaeserunt, ap. Cic.

incīlo, 1. *to blame, scold, rebuke,* Lucr.

incingo -cinxi -cinctum, 3. *to surround, engirdle;* incinctus cinctu Gabino, Liv.; transf., urbes moenibus, Ov.

incīno, 3. (in and cano), *to sing,* Prop.

incĭpĭo -cēpi -ceptum, 3. (in and capio), *to begin, commence.* **I.** Transit., **A.** Gen. with acc., pugnam, Liv.; with infin., bella gerere, Cic.; absol., ut incipiendi ratio fieret, Cic. **B.** *to begin to speak;* sic statim rex incipit, Sall. **II.** Intransit., *to commence;* tum incipere ver arbitrabatur, Cic.

incĭpisso, 3. (incipio), *to begin, commence,* Plaut.

incīsē and **incīsim,** adv. (incīdo), *in short, disconnected sentences;* dicere, Cic.

incīsĭo -ōnis, f. (incīdo), *a division or clause of a sentence,* Cic.

incīsum -i, n. (incīdo), *a division of a sentence,* Cic.

incīsūra -ae, f. (incīdo), *a cutting into, incision,* Plin.

incĭtāmentum -i, n. (incito), *an incitement, inducement, incentive;* incitamentum periculorum et laborum, Cic.

incĭtātē, adv. (incitatus), *hastily, violently;* incitatius ferri, fluere, of speech, Cic.

incĭtātĭo -ōnis, f. (incito), *an inciting, instigating, exciting.* **I.** Act., languentis populi, Cic. **II.** Pass. **A.** *violent motion;* sol tantā incitatione fertur, Cic. **B.** Transf., *excitement, ardour, energy, vehemence;* animi, Caes.; mentis, Cic.

incĭtātus -a -um, p. adj. (from incito). **A.** *rapid, vehement;* equo incitato, *at full gallop,* Cic. **B.** Transf., cursus in oratione incitatior, Cic.

incĭto, 1. *to put into rapid motion, urge on, to hasten.* **I. A.** Lit., equos, Caes.; prov., incitare currentem, *to spur the willing horse,* Cic.; refl., se incitare, or middle incitari, *to quicken one's pace, to hasten;* alii ex castris se incitant, Caes. **B.** Transf., *to incite, rouse, urge, spur on;* 1, animos, ingenium, Cic.; Caesarem ad id bellum, Caes.; 2, a, *to inspire;* terrae vis Pythiam incitabat, Cic.; b, *to incite, make hostile, stir up;* aliquem in aliquem, Cic. **II.** *to increase;* 1, amnis incitatus pluviis, Liv.; 2, *to enhance;* eloquendi celeritatem, Cic.

1. **incĭtus** -a -um (in and cieo), *in rapid motion, rapid, swift,* Verg.

2. **incĭtus** -a -um (in and cieo), *immovable;* esp. used of a piece in the game of draughts, Plaut.

incīvīlis -e, *unjust, tyrannical,* Eutr.

inclāmĭto, 1. (intens. of inclamo), *to call out against,* Plaut.

inclāmo, 1. *to call upon loudly;* 1, generally, aliquem nomine, Liv.; comitem suum semet et saepius, Cic.; with dat., Albanus exercitus inclamat Curiatiis, uti opem ferant fratri, Liv.; 2, *to call upon for help;* nemo inclamavit patronum, Cic.

inclāresco -clārŭi, 3. *to become illustrious,* Tac.

inclēmens -entis, *unmerciful, not clement, harsh, rough;* dictator, Liv.; inclementiori verbo appellare, Liv.

inclēmentĕr, adv. with compar. (inclemens), *harshly, unmercifully, rigorously;* inclementius invehi in aliquem, Liv.

inclēmentĭa -ae, f. (inclemens), *unmercifulness, rigour, harshness;* divûm, Verg.

inclīnātĭo -ōnis, f. (inclino), *a leaning, bending, inclination.* **I.** Lit., **A.** corporis, Cic. **B.** *change of the voice,* Cic. **II.** Transf., 1, *a mental leaning, inclination;* ad meliorem spem, Cic.; 2, a, *inclination of will, good-will, liking;* voluntatis, Cic.; b, *change, alteration;* temporum, Cic.

inclīnātus -a -um, p. adj. (from inclīno), *sunk.* **I.** Lit., of the voice, *low, deep;* vox, Cic. **II.** Transf., 1, *sunken, fallen;* fortuna, Cic.; 2, *inclined towards, favourable to;* ad pacem, Liv.

inclīno, 1. (in and clino = κλίνω), *to bend, bow, lean, incline.* **I.** Act., **A.** Lit., genua arenis, Ov.; malos, *the masts,* Liv. **B.** Transf., 1, *to incline, turn away;* omnem culpam in aliquem, *to lay the blame on,* Cic.; haec animum inclinant ut credam, *induce me to believe,* Liv.; 2, a, *to cause to decline, change for the worse;* omnia simul inclinante fortunā, Liv.; b, *to decide, give a decisive turn to;* fraus rem inclinavit, Liv. **II.** Refl., se inclinare or simply inclinare, or middle inclinari, *to bend, incline.* **A.** Lit., 1, of an army, *to waver, yield;* acies inclinatur or inclinat, Liv.; 2, of the sun, or of time; inclinato in pomeridianum tempus die, *turning towards evening,* Cic. **B.** Transf., 1, paululum inclinari timore, *to waver,* Cic.; 2, a, *to incline in opinion;* ad Stoicos, Cic.; sententia senatus inclinat ad pacem, Cic.; with ut and the subj., Liv.; b, *to be favourable to;* pluribus hisce, Hor.

inclūdo -clūsi -clūsum, 3. (in and cludo, claudo). **I.** *to shut up, shut in, enclose.* **A.** Of personal objects, parietibus deos, Cic.; aliquem in cella Concordiae, Cic. **B.** Of inanimate objects, 1, a, *to insert;* emblemata in scaphis aureis, Cic.; verba versu, Cic.; b, *to surround;* suras auro, Verg.; *to insert as an episode;* aliquid orationi, Cic. **II.** *to obstruct, hinder, stop;* vocem, Cic.

inclūsĭo -ōnis, f. (includo), *a shutting up, confinement,* Cic.

inclўtus (inclŭtus, inclītus) -a -um (in and clueo), *celebrated, famous, renowned;* populi regesque, Liv.; leges Solonis, Liv.

1. **incoctus** -a -um (in and coquo), *uncooked, raw,* Plaut.

2. **incoctus** -a -um, partic. of incoquo.

incōgĭtābĭlis -e, *thoughtless, inconsiderate,* Plaut.

incōgĭtans -antis, *inconsiderate,* Ter.

incōgĭtantĭa -ae, f. (incogitans), *thoughtlessness, heedlessness,* Plaut.

incōgĭtātus -a -um, *inconsiderate,* Plaut.

incōgĭto, 1. *to contrive, plan;* fraudem socio, Hor.

incognĭtus -a -um. **I.** *unknown.* **A.** ne incognita pro cognitis habeamus, Cic. **B.** Legal t.t., *not examined;* incognitā re judicare, Cic. **II.** *unclaimed,* Liv.

incŏhĭbĕo, 2. *to hold together,* Lucr.

incŏla -ae, c. (incolo), *an inhabitant, dweller in any place.* **I.** Gen. **A.** Of persons, Pythagorei incolae paene nostri, *our fellow-countrymen,* Cic.; with genit., mundi, Cic.; poet., incola turba, *natives,* Ov. **B.** Of animals, aquarum incolae, Cic. **C.** Of winds, *native;* aquilones, Hor. **II.** Esp. = μέτοικος, *a resident without full civic rights,* Cic.

incŏlo -cŏlŭi, -cultum, 3. **I.** Transit., *to inhabit, dwell in;* eas urbes, Cic.; partic. subst., **incŏlentes** -ium, m. *the inhabitants,* Liv. **II.** Intransit., *to dwell;* inter mare Alpesque, Liv.

incŏlŭmis -e (in and *columis,* from *cello*)

uninjured, *safe and sound, without damage*, Cic.; naves, Caes.; *with* ab *and the* abl., incolumis a calamitate, Cic.

incŏlŭmĭtas -ātĭs, f. (incolumis), *safety, soundness, good condition, preservation;* mundi, Cic.; incolumitatem deditis polliceri, Caes.

incŏmĭtātus -a -um (in and comitor), *unaccompanied, without retinue, alone*, Verg.

incommendātus -a -um, *given up to, abandoned;* tellus incommendata ventis, Ov.

incommŏdē, adv. (incommodus), *inconveniently, unfitly, unsuitably, unseasonably;* venire, Cic.; incommodius mecum actum est, Cic.; incommodissime navigare, Cic.

incommŏdĭtas -ātis, f. (incommodus), *inconvenience, unsuitableness, disadvantage;* incommoditas alienati illius animi, Cic.; temporis, *unseasonableness*, Liv.

incommŏdo, 1. (incommodus), *to be unpleasant, burdensome, troublesome to any one, to incommode;* with dat., inimicis, Cic.; nihil alteri, Cic.

incommŏdum, v. incommodus.

incommŏdus -a -um, *inconvenient, unsuitable, unfit, troublesome, disagreeable.* **I.** Adj., a, of things, valetudo, *ill-health*, Cic.; compar., non incommodiore loco quam, etc., Cic.; superl., res eius incommodissimae, Cic.; b, of persons, *troublesome, annoying;* alicui incommodum esse, Cic. **II.** Subst., **incommŏdum** -i, n., a, *disadvantage;* incommodo tuo, Cic.; b, *injury, misfortune;* commoveri incommodo valetudinis tuae, Cic.; incommodo affici, Cic.; alicui incommodum ferre, Cic.; incommodum capere *or* accipere, Cic.

incommūtābĭlis -e, *unchangeable;* reipublicae status, Cic.

incompărābĭlis -e, *incomparable*, Plin.

incompertus -a -um (in and comperio), *unknown, not ascertained, uncertain;* inter cetera vetustate incomperta, Liv.

incompŏsĭtē, adv. (incompositus), *in a disorderly manner;* hostis negligenter et incomposite veniens, Liv.

incompŏsĭtus -a -um, *disordered, disorderly, irregular;* 1, agmen, Liv.; hostes, Liv.; 2, transf., of style, nempe incomposito pede currere versus Lucili, Hor.

incomprĕhensĭbĭlis -e, *that cannot be understood, incomprehensible*, Quint.

incomptus -a -um, a, *untended, untrimmed;* capilli, Hor.; b, *rude, artless*, Tac.; of style, *without ornament, rude, rough;* oratio, Cic.; versus, Verg.

inconcessus -a -um (in and concedo), *not allowed, forbidden;* hymenaei, Verg.

inconcĭlĭo, 1, *to win artfully to one's own side*, Plaut.

inconcinnus -a -um, *awkward, inelegant;* qui in aliquo genere inconcinnus et stultus est, Cic.

inconcussus -a -um, *unshaken, firm;* pax, Tac.

incondĭtē, adv. (inconditus), *confusedly;* versus Graecos dicere, Cic.

inconditus -a -um (in and condo), *disorderly, confused, irregular;* acies, Liv.; jus civile, *unarranged*, Cic.; genus dicendi, Cic.

incongrŭens -entis, *not agreeing, unsuitable*, Plin.

inconsīdĕrantĭa -ae, f. (in and considero), *thoughtlessness, inconsiderateness*, Cic.

inconsīdĕrātē, adv. (inconsideratus), *without consideration, rashly, inconsiderately;* agere, Cic.; dicere, Cic.

inconsīdĕrātus -a -um, 1, *thoughtless, inconsiderate*, Cic.; 2, *unadvised, unconsidered;* cupiditas, Cic.

inconsōlābĭlis -e, *inconsolable;* transf., vulnus, *incurable*, Ov.

inconstans -stantis, *changeable, unstable, inconstant;* mihi ridicule es visus esse inconstans, Cic.

inconstantĕr, adv. (inconstans), *inconstantly, inconsistently, capriciously;* loqui, Cic.; haec inconstantissime dicuntur, Cic.

inconstantĭa -ae, f. (inconstans), *changeableness, instability, inconstancy;* mentis, Cic.

inconsultē, adv. (inconsultus), *inconsiderately, unadvisedly;* inconsulte ac temere, Cic.

1. inconsultus -a -um (in and consulo), 1, *not consulted;* inconsulto senatu, Liv.; 2, *without advice, unadvised;* inconsulti adeunt, Verg.; 3, *inconsiderate, imprudent, indiscreet;* homo inconsultus et temerarius, Cic.; ratio, Cic.

2. inconsultus -ūs, m. (in and consulo), *the not asking advice*, Plaut.

inconsumptus -a -um, *unconsumed, undiminished*, Ov.

incontāmĭnātus -a -um, (in and contamino), *unspotted, unpolluted, uncontaminated*, Liv.

incontentus -a -um (in and contendo), *not stretched;* fides, *out of tune*, Cic.

incontĭnens -entis, *incontinent, immoderate, intemperate;* Tityos, Hor.; manus, Hor.

incontĭnentĕr, adv. (incontinens), *immoderately, incontinently;* nihil incontinenter facere, Cic.

incontĭnentĭa -ae, f. (incontinens), *incontinence, intemperance*, Cic.

incontrōversus -a -um, *uncontroverted, undisputed*, Cic.

inconvĕnĭens -entis, *not agreeing with, dissimilar;* facta, ap. Cic.

incŏquo -coxi -coctum, 3. *to boil in or with.* **A.** radices Baccho, Verg. **B.** *to dye, colour;* vellera Tyrios incocta rubores, Verg.

incorrectus -a -um, *unamended, unimproved*, Ov.

incorruptē, adv. (incorruptus), *incorruptly, justly, impartially;* judicare, Cic.

incorruptus -a -um, *not corrupted.* **I.** Lit., sanguis, Cic.; templa, *not destroyed*, Liv.; incorruptā sanitate esse, Cic. **II.** Transf., *incorrupt, unbribed, genuine, uninjured, unimpaired;* testis, Cic.; virgo, *pure*, Cic.; judicium, *upright*, Liv.; integritas Latini sermonis, Cic.

incrēbresco -crēbrŭi, 3., **and increbresco** -crēbŭi, 3. *to become frequent, strong, prevalent; to increase, prevail;* ventus, Cic.; proverbio, *to become a proverb*, Liv.; quum hoc nescio quo modo increbruisset, *with* acc. *and* infin., Cic.

incrēdĭbĭlis -e, 1, a, *incredible;* auditu, Cic.; dictu, Cic.; memoratu, Sall.; b, *extraordinary;* fides, Cic.; vis ingenii, Cic.; 2, *not worthy of belief* (of persons), Plaut.

incrēdĭbĭlĭtĕr, adv. (incredibilis), *incredibly, extraordinarily;* delectari, Cic.; pertimescere, Cic.

incrēdŭlus -a -um, *incredulous*, Hor.

incrēmentum -i, n. (incresco), *the growth of plants or animals.* **I. A.** Lit., vitium, Cic. **B.** Transf., urbis, Liv. **II.** Meton., 1, *that from or by which anything grows, increase;* incremento multitudinis, Liv.; dentes populi incrementa futuri, *the seed*, Ov.; **2**, poet.= *off-spring;* Jovis, Verg.

incrĕpĭto, 1. (intens. of increpo). **I.** Intransit., *to call loudly to any one;* tum Bitiae dedit increpitans, Verg. **II.** Transit., *to cry to, reproach, chide;* aliquem, Verg.; increpitare vocibus quod, etc., Caes.; increpitare Belgas qui (with subj.), Caes.; pertinaciam praetoris, Liv.

incrĕpo -ŭi (-āvi) -ĭtum (-ātum), 1. **I.** Intransit. **A.** *to rustle, rattle, whiz, rush, make a noise;* 1, discus increpuit, Cic.; **2**, *to be noised abroad, become known;* simulatque increpuit suspicio tumultūs, Cic.; quicquid increpuerit, Catilinam timeri, Cic. **B.** *to call upon;* increpat ultro, Verg. **C.** With in and the acc., *to slander, revile;* in Fulvi similitudinem nominis, Liv. **II.** Transit., **A.** *to cause to sound, cause to be heard;* lyram, Ov.; tubā ingentem sonitum, Verg. **B.** a, *to exclaim against, to blame, upbraid, chide, reproach, rebuke, reprove;* Tullium nomine, Liv.; aliquem graviter quod, etc., Liv.; with acc. and infin., *to shout out insultingly;* simul increpante qui vulneraverat habere quaestorem, Liv.; with rel. sent., quum undique duces, victisne cessuri essent, increparent, Liv.; b, *to animate, excite;* morantes aeris rauci canor increpat, Verg.; c, *to throw in one's teeth, to reproach a person with, to blame for;* perfidiam, Cic.

incresco -crēvi, 3. **I.** *to grow in anything;* squamae cuti increscunt, Ov. **II.** *to grow.* **A.** (ferrea seges) jaculis increvit acutis, Verg. **B.** Transf., increscit certamen, Liv.

incrētus -a -um, partic. of incerno.

incrŭentātus -a -um (in and cruento), *not bloody, not stained with blood,* Ov.

incrŭentus -a -um, *bloodless;* proelium, victoria, Liv.; exercitus, *that has lost no soldiers,* Sall.

incrusto, 1. *to cover with a rind, encrust;* vas sincerum, *to bedaub,* Hor.

incŭbātĭo -ōnis, f. (incubo), *a sitting upon eggs, incubation,* Plin.

incŭbo -āvi -ātum and -ŭi -ĭtum, 1. *to lie in* or *on.* **I.** Gen., stramentis, Hor.; cortici, Liv. **II. A.** *to pass the night in a temple to receive a divine message* or *cure of a disease;* in Pasiphaae fano, Cic. **B.** 1, lit, *of birds, to sit on* or *hatch eggs, to brood;* nidis, Ov.; **2**, transf., *to brood over, earnestly watch over;* pecuniae, Cic.; auro, divitiis, Verg. **C.** *to stay in a place;* Erymantho, Ov. **D.** Transf., ponto nox incubat atra, *settles on,* Verg.

incŭdo -cŭdi -cūsum, 3. *to forge, fabricate;* lapis incusus, *a sharpened stone for a handmill,* Verg.

inculco, 1. (in and calco), *to trample in.* **A.** *to foist in, mix in;* Graeca verba, Cic. **B.** Transf., 1, *to impress upon, inculcate;* tradatur vel etiam inculcetur, Cic.; with ut and the subj., Cic.; **2**, *to force upon, obtrude upon;* se alicuius auribus, Cic.

inculpātus -a -um (in and culpo), *unblamed, blameless,* Ov.

incultē, adv. (1. incultus), 1, *roughly, rudely;* vivere, Cic.; incultius agere or agitare, Cic.; **2**, of orators, *inelegantly, without refinement;* dicere, Cic.

1. incultus -a -um, *uncultivated, untilled.* **I.** Lit., **A.** ager, Cic. Subst., **inculta** -ōrum, n. *wastes, deserts,* Verg. **B.** *unarranged, disordered, untidy;* comae, *uncombed,* Ov.; homines intonsi et inculti, Liv. **II.** Transf., *unpolished, unrefined, unadorned, rude;* homo, *without education,* Sall.; inculta atque rusticana parsimonia, Hor.; versus, *rough, unpolished,* Hor.

2. incultus -ūs, m. *neglect, want of cultiva-*

tion; suos honores desertos per incultum et negligentiam, Liv.

incumbo -cŭbŭi -cŭbĭtum, 3. *to lie upon, recline* or *lean upon, bend to.* **I.** Lit., **A.** remis, *to ply,* Verg.; cumulatis in aqua sarcinis insuper, Liv.; in gladium, Cic.; ejecto (equiti), *to rush on,* Verg. **B.** Esp., 1, a, milit. t. t., *to throw oneself upon the enemy;* suo et armorum pondere in hostem, Liv.; b, *to press hard on;* in aliquem, Cic.; **2**, of things, a, *to overhang;* laurus incumbens arae, Verg.; b, *to burst upon, attack;* tempestas incubuit silvis, Verg. **II.** Transf., **A.** *to apply oneself to anything, exert oneself, take pains with, bend one's mind to;* in bellum, Caes.; in aliquod studium, Cic.; ad laudem, Cic.; novae cogitationi, Tac.; with neut. acc., haec incumbe, Cic.; with infin., Verg.; with subj., Liv. **B.** *to press heavily upon;* ut jam inclinato (judici) reliqua incumbat oratio, Cic.

incūnābŭla -ōrum, n. **I.** *swaddling-clothes,* Plaut. **II.** Meton., 1, *birthplace;* incunabula nostra, Cic.; **2**, *origin, commencement, beginning;* incunabula nostrae veteris puerilisque doctrinae, Cic.

incūrātus -a -um, *uncared for, unhealed;* ulcera, Hor.

incūria -ae, f. (in and cura), *carelessness, neglect, negligence, indifference;* alicuius rei, Cic.

incūriōsē, adv. with compar. (incuriosus), *negligently, carelessly;* agere, Liv.

incūriōsus -a -um. **I.** Act., *careless, negligent;* serendis frugibus, Tac. **II.** Pass., *neglected, careless;* finis, Tac.

incurro -curri (-cŭcurri) -cursum, 3. **I.** *to run purposely against something.* **A.** Lit., 1, incurrere in columnas, prov., *to run one's head against a stone wall,* Cic.; **2**, as milit. t. t., a, *to assail, attack;* in Romanos, Liv.; with dat., levi armaturae hostium, Liv.; with simple acc., hostium latus, Liv.; b, *to make an incursion into;* in Macedoniam, Liv. **B.** Transf., *to attack, to inveigh against;* in tribunos militares, Liv. **II.** *to run accidentally against.* **A.** Lit., incurrere atque incidere in aliquem, Cic. **B.** Transf., 1, in oculos, *to meet the eye,* Cic.; **2**, of places, *to border on;* privati agri, qui in publicum Cumanum incurrebant, Cic.; **3**, of persons, a, *to stumble on something;* in aliquid, Cic.; b, *to fall into any evil* or *misfortune;* in morbos, Cic.; in odia hominum, *to incur the hatred of men,* Cic.; **4**, of time, events, etc., a, *to happen, occur;* incurrunt tempora, Cic.; *to happen, happen to;* casus qui in sapientem potest incidere, may fall to the lot of the wise, Cic.; nec ulla est disputatio, in quam non aliquis locus incurrat, *does not occur,* Cic.; b, *to fall on a certain time;* in aliquem diem, Cic.

incursĭo -ōnis, f. (incurro), 1, *a running against, collision;* atomorum, Cic.; **2**, *a hostile attack;* incursio atque impetus armatorum, Cic.; as milit. t. t., *an inroad, invasion;* incursionem facere in fines Romanos, Liv.

incurso, 1. (intens. of incurro). **I.** *to run against, strike against, attack.* **A.** Lit., in agmen Romanum, Liv.; agros Romanos, *to make an incursion into,* Liv. **B.** Transf., incursabat in te dolor, Cic. **II.** *to run against;* rupibus, Ov.

incursus -ūs, m. (incurro), *an attack, assault, a pressing upon, incursion, influx.* **I.** Lit., a, of things, aquarum, Ov.; b, of persons and animals, *hostile attack;* luporum, Verg.; esp. as milit. t. t., aditus atque incursus ad defendendum, Caes. **II.** Transf., incursus animus varios habet, *efforts, plans,* Ov.

incurvo, 1. (incurvus), *to bend, curve, make*

crooked; bacillum, Cic.; arcum, Verg.; membra incurvata dolore, Ov.

incŭrvus -a -um, *bent, curved, crooked;* bacillum, Cic.

incus -cūdis, f. (incudo), *an anvil,* Cic.; prov., uno opere eandem incudem noctem diemque tundere, *to be always hammering at the same thing, to be always engaged in the same occupation,* Cic.

incūsātĭo -ōnis, f. (incuso), *blame, reproach, accusation,* Cic.

incūso, 1. (in and causa), *to accuse, blame, reproach, find fault with;* aliquem, Caes.; quietem Africani nostri somniantis, Cic.; with acc. and infin., Liv.; in pass., with nom. and infin., Tac.; with rel. sent., Verg.

incussus, only in abl. -ū, m. (incutio), *a beating* or *dashing against;* armorum, Tac.

incustōdītus -a-um (in and custodio). **I.** *unwatched, unguarded;* ovile, Ov.; urbs, Tac. **II.** Transf., **1,** *not observed, neglected;* observatio dierum, Tac.; **2,** *unconcealed;* amor, Tac.

incŭtĭo -cussi -cussum, 3. (in and quatio), *to strike, dash, beat against.* **I.** Lit., scipionem in caput alicuius, Liv. **II. A.** *to throw, hurl;* tela saxaque, Tac. **B.** *to strike into, inspire with, excite, produce;* terrorem alicui, Cic.; religionem animo, Liv.; desiderium urbis, Hor.

indāgātĭo -ōnis, f. (1. indago), *an inquiry, investigation;* veri, Cic.; initiorum, Cic.

indāgātor -ōris, m. (1. indago), *an investigator, explorer,* Plaut.

indāgātrix -trīcis, f. (indagator), *she who searches into* or *explores;* philosophia indagatrix virtutis, Cic.

1. indāgo, 1. **1,** *to follow a trail* or *scent, to track;* canis natus ad indagandum, Cic.; **2,** transf., *to search out, explore, investigate;* indicia, Cic.; with rel. sent., quid cuique esset necesse, Cic.

2. indāgo -ĭnis, f. **1,** *a surrounding of any spot with nets* or *beaters so as to enclose the game;* saltus indagine cingere, Verg.; velut indagine dissipatos Samnites agere, Liv.; **2,** *investigation, research, inquiry,* Plin.

indĕ, adv. (from is, with adverbial ending), *thence, from there, from that place.* **I.** Of space, non exeo inde ante vesperum, Cic. **II.** Transf., **A. a,** *from thence, from that cause;* inde (i.e., ex audacia) omnia scelera gignuntur, Cic.; **b,** *from thence,* of persons, quod inde oriundus erat, Liv. **B.** Of time, **a,** *then, thereupon,* Caes.; **b,** *from that time forth,* Cic.; **c,** with ab and the abl., *from;* jam inde a principio, Liv.

indēbĭtus -a -um (in and debeo), *that which is not owed, not due;* non indebita posco, Verg.

indĕcens -centis, *unbecoming, unseemly, ugly, unsightly,* Mart.

indĕcentĕr, adv. (indecens), *unbecomingly, indecently,* Mart.

indēclīnātus -a -um (in and declino), *unchanged, firm;* amicitia, Ov.

indĕcōrē, adv. (indecorus), *unbecomingly, indecorously;* facere, Cic.

indĕcōris -e, *unbecoming, inglorious, shameful,* Verg.

indĕcōro, 1. *to disgrace, dishonour,* Hor.

indĕcōrus -a -um, *unbecoming;* **a,** of outward appearance, *unseemly, unsightly;* motus, Liv.; **b,** morally, *indecorous, disgraceful;* si nihil malum, nisi quod turpe, inhonestum, indecorum, pravum, Cic.; indecorum est, with infin., Cic.

indēfensus -a -um (in and defendo), *un-*

defended, unprotected; Capua deserta indefensaque, Liv.

indēfessus -a -um, *unwearied, untired,* Verg.

indēflētus -a -um (in and defleo), *unwept,* Ov.

indējectus -a -um (in and dejicio), *not thrown down,* Ov.

indēlēbĭlis -e (in and deleo), *imperishable, indelible;* nomen, Ov.

indēlĭbātus -a -um (in and delibo), *untouched, uninjured, undiminished,* Ov.

indemnātus -a -um (in and damnatus, from damno), *uncondemned;* cives, Cic.

indēplōrātus -a -um (in and deploro), *unwept, unlamented,* Ov.

indēprĕhensus (indēprensus) -a -um (in and deprehendo or deprendo), *undiscovered, unobserved;* error, Verg.

indēsertus -a -um, *not forsaken,* Ov.

indestrictus -a -um (in and destringo), *untouched, unhurt,* Ov.

indētōnsus -a -um (in and detondeo), *unshorn,* Ov.

indēvītātus -a -um (in and devito), *unavoided;* telum, Ov.

index -dĭcis, c. (indĭco). **I.** Lit., **A.** *one who informs* or *discloses,* Cic. **B.** In a bad sense, *an informer, traitor, spy,* Cic. **II.** Transf., **A.** Of things, *that which informs, a sign, token;* vox index stultitiae, Cic.; index digitus, Hor., or simply index, Cic., *the fore-finger.* **B.** 1, *the title* or *inscription on a book;* libri, Cic.; also on a statue, Liv.; **2,** *a touch-stone,* Ov.

Indi -ōrum, m. (Ἰνδοί), *the inhabitants of India, the Indians;* sing., **Indus** -i, m. *an Indian;* collective, Verg., Ov., and = *an elephant-driver, mahout,* Liv.; poet., **a,** = *Aethiopian,* Verg.; **b,** = *Arabian,* Ov. Hence, **A. India** -ae, f. (Ἰνδία), *India.* **B. Indĭcus** -a -um (Ἰνδικός), *Indian.* **C. Indus** -a -um (Ἰνδός), *Indian;* dens, *ivory,* Ov.; conchae, *pearls,* Prop.

indĭcātĭo -ōnis, f. (indico), *a setting a price upon anything, a valuing,* Plaut.

1. indĭcens -entis (in and dīco), *that does not say;* me indicente, *without my saying a word,* Liv.

2. indĭcens, partic. of indico.

indĭcĭum -ĭi, n. (index). **I.** *a discovery, disclosure.* **A.** Lit., conjurationis, Cic.; indicia exponere et edere, Cic.; profiteri, *to make a confession before the judge,* Sall. **B.** Transf., **a,** *permission to confess;* indicium postulare, Cic.; **b,** *a reward for giving evidence;* partem indicii accipere, Cic. **II.** *a mark, sign, token, evidence;* sceleris, Cic.; indicio esse, *to be a sign of, serve to show,* Nep.

1. indĭco, 1.(intens. of 2. indico), *to disclose, declare, reveal, make known, betray, show, indicate.* **I.** Gen., rem dominae, Cic.; dolorem lacrimis, Cic.; vultus indicat mores, Cic.; se indicare, *to reveal one's own nature,* Cic.; in pass., with nom. and infin., Cic.; with rel. sent., Cic. **II. A.** *to inform against, give evidence about;* conscios, Cic. **B.** *to put a price on, value;* fundum alicui, Cic.

2. indĭco -dixi -dictum, 3. *to make publicly known, announce, proclaim, fix, appoint.* **A.** Gen., alicui bellum, *to declare war,* Cic.; comitia, Liv.; diem comitiis, Liv.; exercitum Aquileiam, *order to,* Liv.; with ut and the subj., Liv. **B.** *to impose;* tributum, Liv.

1. indictus -a -um (in and dico), *not said, unsaid.* **A.** Lit., indictis carminibus nostris,

ınsung, Verg. **B.** Esp., *without a trial, without a hearing;* aliquem capitis condemnare, Cic.

2. indictus -a -um, partic. of 2. indico.

indícus -a -um, v. Indi.

indĭdem, adv. (inde and idem), 1, *from the same place, from that very place;* indidem Ameriā, Cic.; 2, transf., *from the same matter,* Cic.

indiffĕrens -entis (in and differo), *indifferent* (= ἀδιάφορον), *neither good nor bad,* Cic.

indĭgĕna -ae, c. (indu and geno), *native, belonging to one's own country;* and subst. (opp. advena), *a native;* ne majores quidem eorum indigenas, sed advenas Italiae cultores, Liv.; of animals, bos, aper, Ov.

indĭgens, v. indigeo.

indĭgentĭa -ae, f. (indigeo), 1, *want, need,* Cic.; 2, *insatiable desire,* Cic.

indĭgĕo -ŭi, 2. (indu = in and egeo). **I.** *to want, need, stand in need of, suffer want of;* with genit., Nep.; with abl., iis rebus quae ad oppugnationem castrorum sunt usui, Caes. Subst., **indigens** -entis, m. *a needy person,* Cic. **II.** *to need, require;* with genit., tui consilii, Cic.; with abl., cohortatione non indigere, Cic.

1. Indĭges -gĕtis, m. (indu = in and geno), *a native deity,* esp. *Aeneas and the descendants of Aeneas, the fabled ancestors of the Romans.* Sing., Aeneas, Verg.; plur., *the descendants of Aeneas,* Liv., Verg.

2. indĭges -is (indigeo), *needy,* ap. Cic.

indĭgestus -a -um (in and digero), *disordered, confused, unarranged;* chaos rudis indigestaque moles, Ov.

Indĭgĕtes -um, m., v. Indiges.

indignābundus -a -um (indignor), *filled with indignation, greatly indignant,* Liv.

indignandus -a -um (partic. of indignor), *deserving indignation, to be scorned,* Ov.

indignans -antis, p. adj. (from indignor), *impatient, indignant;* verba, Ov.

indignātĭo -ōnis, f. (indignor), 1, *indignation, disdain;* indignationem movere, Liv.; 2, *the rhetorical exciting of indignation,* Cic.

indignē, adv. (indignus). **I.** *unworthily, disgracefully, dishonourably, undeservedly;* indignissime cervices frangere civium Romanorum, Cic. **II.** *impatiently, unwillingly, indignantly;* indigne pati, with acc. and infin., Cic.; indigne ferre, with quod and the subj., Cic.

indignĭtas -ātis, f. (indignus), 1, *unworthiness, vileness;* hominis, accusatoris, Cic.; 2, transf., a, *unworthy behaviour, meanness, indignity, baseness;* hominum insolentium, Cic.; omnes indignitates perferre, Cic.; b, meton., *indignation at unworthy treatment,* Cic.

indignor, 1. dep. (indignus), *to consider as unworthy or unbecoming, take as an indignity, be offended, indignant at;* aliquid, Cic.; pro aliquo, Ov.; foll. by quod, Caes.; by acc. and infin., Caes.; transf. of things, pontem indignatus Araxes, Verg.

indignus -a -um. **I.** *unworthy, not deserving;* a, with abl., omni honore indignissimus, Cic.; b, with genit., magnorum avorum, Verg.; c, with supine, id auditu dicere indignum esse, Liv.; d, with rel. sent., indigni erant qui impetrarent, *to obtain,* Cic.; e, with ut and the subj., Liv.; f, with infin., Ov., Hor.; g, absol., divitias quivis, quamvis indignus, habere potest, Cic. **II.** Transf., *unworthy, unbecoming;* a, with abl., indignum est sapientis gravitate et constantiā defendere, Cic.; b, absol., *unworthy = disgraceful, shameful;* hoc uno sol non

quidquam vidit indignius, Cic.; indignum est, with infin. or acc. and infin., *ıt is unsuitable, inappropriate;* non indignum videtur memorare, Sall.; *it is unworthy, disgraceful, shameful;* indignum facere a pari vinci aut superiore, Cic.; facinus indignum or indignum facinus, with infin. ᴏʀ acc. and infin. as an exclamation, *it would be disgraceful;* facinus indignum ! epistolam neminem reddidisse, Cic.

indĭgus -a -um (indigeo), *needy, in want of;* with genit., nostrae opis, Verg.; with abl., auxilio, Lucr.

indīlĭgens -entis, *neglectful, negligent, heedless,* Caes.

indīlĭgentĕr, adv. with compar. (indiligens), *carelessly, heedlessly, negligently,* Cic.

indīlĭgentĭa -ae, f. (indiligens), *carelessness, negligence;* Aeduorum, Caes.; litterarum amissarum, Cic.; veri, *in the investigation of truth,* Tac.

indĭpiscor -deptus sum, 3. dep. (indu and apiscor), 1, *to reach, grasp, attain;* indeptum esse navem manu ferreā injectā, Liv.; 2, *to obtain, attain, get,* Plaut.

indireptus -a -um (in and diripio), *unpillaged,* Tac.

indiscrētē, adv. (indiscretus), *without difference or distinction,* Plin.

indiscrētus -a -um (in and discerno), 1, *unsevered, undivided,* Tac.; 2, *undistinguished, indistinguishable, without difference;* proles indiscreta suis, Verg.

indĭsertē, adv. (indisertus), *ineloquently,* Cic.

indĭsertus -a -um, *ineloquent;* homo, Cic.

indispŏsĭtus -a -um, *disorderly, unarranged, confused,* Tac.

indissŏlūbĭlis -e, *indissoluble;* immortales et indissolubiles, Cic.

indissŏlūtus -a -um (in and dissolvo), *undissolved,* Cic.

indistinctus -a -um, 1, *not separated, not arranged,* Cat.; 2, transf., *unarranged, confused, indistinct, obscure,* Tac.

indivĭdŭus -a -um, 1, *indivisible;* corpora, *atoms, monads of the Democritean system,* Cic.; subst., **individŭum** -i, n. *an atom,* Cic.; 2, *inseparable,* Tac.

indivīsus -a -um (in and divido), *undivided,* Plin.

indo -dĭdi -dĭtum, 3. **I.** *to put in or on, set or place in or on.* **A.** Lit., aliquem lecticae, Tac. **B.** Transf., 1, *to introduce;* novos ritus, Tac.; 2, *to cause, occasion;* alicui pavorem, Tac. **II.** *to place on something.* **A.** Lit., castella rupibus, Tac. **B.** *to give, impose a name;* with dat. of the name, Superbo ei Romae inditum cognomen, Liv.

indŏcĭlis -e. **I. A.** *that cannot be taught, that learns with difficulty, unteachable, indocile;* 1, lit., homo, Cic.; with infin., pauperiem pati, Hor.; 2, *ignorant, inexperienced;* genus, Cic. **B.** *that cannot be learned;* usus disciplina, Cic. **II.** *untaught, unshown;* via, Prop.; numerus, artless, Ov.

indoctē, adv. (indoctus), *ignorantly, in an unlearned or inexperienced manner;* facere, Cic.

indoctus -a -um, *untaught, unlearned, unskilled,* Cic.; with genit., pilae discive, Hor.; with infin., juga ferre nostra, Hor.; canet indoctum, *without art,* Hor.

indŏlentĭa -ae, f. (in and doleo), *freedom from pain, absence of pain,* Cic.

indŏles -is, f. (indu and alo), 1, *natural constitution or quality, nature;* servare indolem (of plants), Liv.; 2, of men, *natural disposition,* *kalents, inclination ;* adolescentes bonâ **indole** praediti, Cic. ; indoles virtutis or ad virtutem, Cic.

indŏlesco -dŏlŭi, 3. (in and doleo), *to be pained, grieved at any thing,* Cic. ; with acc. and infin., tam sero se cognoscere, Cic. ; with abl., nostris malis, Ov. ; with neut. acc., id ipsum indoluit Juno, Ov. ; with quod or quia, Ov.

indŏmābĭlis -e, *that cannot be tamed, indomitable,* Plaut.

indŏmĭtus -a -um (in and domo), 1, *untamed, unrestrained, wild ;* a, of persons, pastores, Caes. ; Mars, *furious fight,* Verg. ; b, transf., of things, cupiditas, furor, libido, Cic. ; 2, *untameable, invincible ;* mors, Hor. ; Falernum, *indigestible,* Pers. ; ira, Verg.

indormĭo -īvi -ītum, 4. *to sleep in* or *on anything ;* with dat., congestis saccis, Hor. ; fig. *to go to sleep over any occupation, be negligent in ;* with dat. or in and the abl., tantae causae, Cic. ; huic tempori, Cic. ; in isto homine colendo tam indormivisse diu, Cic.

indōtātus -a -um, *without a dowry, portionless.* **I.** Lit., soror, Hor. **II.** Transf., corpora, *without funeral honours,* Ov. ; ars, *unadorned, poor, without the gift of eloquence,* Cic.

indŭ, archaic form of in (q.v.).

indŭbĭtātē, adv. (indubitatus), *undoubtedly,* Liv.

indŭbĭtātus -a -um (in and dubito), *undoubted, not doubtful, certain,* Plin.

indŭbĭto, 1. *to doubt of;* with dat., suis viribus, Verg.

indŭbĭus -a -um, *not doubtful, certain,* Tac.

indūcĭae = inductae (q.v.).

indūco -duxi -ductum, 3. **I.** *to draw over.* **A.** *to draw something over something else in order to cover it ;* 1, gen., tectorium, Cic. ; varias plumas membris, Hor. ; 2, *to put on articles of clothing, arms,* etc. ; manibus caestus, Verg. ; poet. pass. with acc., toga inducitur artus, Verg. **B.** *to cover;* 1, scuta pellibus, Caes. ; 2, *to erase writing on tablets, to draw a line through ;* nomina, Cic. ; *to revoke, make invalid ;* senatus consultum, locationem, Cic. **C.** *to bring in, to reckon in one's account-book ;* pecuniam in rationem, Cic. **II.** *to lead* or *bring in.* **A.** Lit., 1, milites in pugnam, Liv. ; 2, esp. a, *to bring into a dwelling ;* in regiam habitandi causâ, Caes. ; b, *to introduce* or *bring upon the stage* or *circus, produce on the stage ;* gladiatores, Cic. **B.** Transf., 1, gen., aliquem in errorem, Cic. ; discordiam in civitatem, *to introduce,* Cic. ; 2, animum, or in animum ; a, *to bring one's mind to, to resolve ;* potuit inducere animum, ut patrem esse sese obliviceretur, Cic. ; b, *to direct one's attention to ;* in spem cogitationemque meliorem, Cic. ; 3, *to induce, move, excite, persuade ;* ad misericordiam, ad pigendum, Cic. ; with ut and the subj., aliquem ut mentiatur, Cic. ; with infin., Tac. ; absol., inductus spe, cupiditate, *influenced by,* Cic. ; 4, *to bring in, introduce, represent in speaking* or *writing ;* hinc ille Gyges inducitur a Platone, Cic. ; 5, *to bring in, introduce a custom ;* morem novum judiciorum in rempublicam, Cic.

inductĭo -ōnis, f. (induco), *a leading* or *bringing to a place.* **A.** Lit., 1, *into the arena ;* juvenum armatorum, Liv. ; 2, of water, inductiones aquarum, Cic. **B.** Transf., 1, animi, *resolve, determination, intention,* Cic. ; 2, erroris, *misleading,* Cic. ; 3, personarum ficta inductio, *feigned introduction of persons in a composition,* Cic. ; 4, *induction,* Cic.

inductor -ōris, m. (induco), *one who stirs up* or *rouses, a chastiser,* Plaut.

1. **inductus** -a -um (partic. of induco).
2. **inductus** -ū, m. (induco), *inducement instigation ;* huius persuasu et inductu, Cic.

indŭgrĕdĭor = ingredior (q.v.).

indulgens -entis, p. adj. (from indulgeo), *kind, tender, indulgent ;* peccatis, Cic. ; in captivos, Liv. ; irarum indulgentes ministri, Liv.

indulgentĕr, adv. (indulgens), *kindly, tenderly, obligingly, indulgently ;* nimis indulgentei loqui, Cic.

indulgentĭa -ae, f. (indulgens), *kindness, tenderness, indulgence,* with obj. genit. ; corporis, Cic. ; with in and the acc., in captivos, Liv.

indulgĕo -dulsi -dultum, 2. (in and dulcis). **I.** Intransit., **A.** *to be complaisant, forbearing, indulgent, to indulge, gratify ;* sibi, Cic. ; sic sibi indulsit, *he allowed himself so many liberties,* Nep. **B.** Transf., 1, *to give oneself up to, indulge in ;* novis amicitiis, Cic. ; vino, Verg. ; ordinibus, *to enlarge,* Verg. ; 2, *to care for, attend to ;* valetudini, Cic. ; hospitio, Verg. **II.** Transit., *to give, to grant, allow, concede ;* alicui sanguinem suum, Liv. ; largitionem, Tac.

indŭo -dŭi -dūtum, 3. (= ἐνδύω), *to put on.* **I.** Lit., alicui tunicam, Cic. ; pass. with abl., socci quibus indutus esset, Cic. ; indutus duabus quasi personis, *with two masks,* i.e., *playing a double part,* Cic. **II.** Transf., **A.** 1, *to clothe, surround, cover ;* dii induti specie humanâ, *clothed in human form ;* homines in vultus ferarum, *to change,* Verg. ; arbor induit se in florem, Verg. ; cratera coronâ, *to crown with a garland,* Verg. ; 2, *to put on, assume ;* personam judicis, Cic. ; proditorem et hostem, *to play the part of,* Tac. ; societatem, seditionem, *to engage in,* Tac. ; sibi cognomen, Cic. **B.** 1, se in aliquid or alicui rei, *to fall into, fall on ;* se hastis, Verg. ; 2, transf., *to entangle oneself in, become involved with ;* se in captiones, Cic. ; pass., indui confessione suâ, *to be entangled in his own confession,* Cic.

indŭpĕdĭo, indŭpĕrātor = impedio, imperator (q.v.).

indūresco -dūrŭi, 3. *to become hard.* **I.** Lit., stiria induruit, Verg. **II.** Transf., miles induruerat pro Vitellio, *had become confirmed in attachment for Vitellius,* Tac.

indūro, 1. *to make hard, to harden.* **I.** Lit., nivem indurat Boreas, Ov. **II.** Transf., *to harden, to steel ;* induratus resistendo hostium timor, Liv.

1. **Indus,** v. India.
2. **Indus** -i, m. (Ἰνδός), 1, *a river of India,* now *Sind ;* 2, *a river of Phrygia and Caria.*

industria -ae, f. (industrius), *industry, diligence ;* in agendo, Cic. ; industriam in aliqua re ponere, Cic. ; de industria, Cic., ex industria, Liv., *on purpose, purposely, intentionally.*

industrĭē, adv. (industrius), *industriously, diligently, actively,* Caes.

industrĭus -a -um (for indu-starius, from industo = insto), *diligent, active, zealous, industrious, assiduous,* Cic.

indūtĭae -ārum, f. (from induo = tempus indutum, or insertum), *a truce, armistice, suspension of hostilities ;* indutias facere, Cic. ; dare, Liv. ; violare, Caes. ; rumpere, Liv. ; postulare, Sall. ; petere ab aliquo, Nep. ; tollere, Liv. ; per indutias, *during,* Sall.

Indutĭŏmārus -i, m. *prince of the Treveri.*

indūtus, only in dat. -ŭi, abl. plur. -ĭbus, m. (induo), *a putting on a dress ;* ea, quam indutui gerebat, vestis, Tac.

indŭvĭae -ārum, f. (induo), *clothes, clothing,* Plaut.

ĭnēbrĭo, 1., 1, *to intoxicate, inebriate,* Plin.

2, *to saturate with;* aurem, *to fill full of idle talk,* Juv.

ĭnēdĭa -ae, f. (in and edo), *fasting, abstinence from food;* vigiliis et inediā necatus, Cic. ; inediā consumi, Cic.

ĭnēdĭtus -a -um (in and edo), *not published or made known;* juvenes, quorum inedita cura (*work, i.e. writings*), Ov.

ĭneffābĭlis -e, *unutterable,* Plin.

ĭnēlĕgans -antis, *inelegant, not choice, tasteless, not beautiful;* gen. with negative, orationis copia, non inelegans, Cic.

ĭnēlĕgantĕr, adv. (inelegans), *inelegantly, tastelessly;* historia non ineleganter scripta, Cic. ; ineleganter dividere, *illogically,* Cic.

ĭnēluctābĭlis -e, *that cannot be successfully struggled against, inevitable;* fatum, Verg.

ĭnēmŏrĭor -ēmŏri, 3. dep., *to die in or at;* spectaculo, Hor.

ĭnemptus (ĭnemtus) -a -um (in and emo), *unbought;* dapes, Verg.

ĭnēnarrābĭlis -e, *indescribable, inexpressible;* labor, Liv.

ĭnēnarrābĭlĭtĕr, adv. (inenarrabilis), *indescribably,* Liv.

ĭnēnōdābĭlis -e, (in and enodo), *inextricable;* res, *inexplicable,* Cic.

ĭnĕo -ii (-īvi) -ĭtum, 4. **I.** Intransit., *to go in, enter.* **A.** Lit., in urbem, Liv. **B.** Transf., of time, *to begin, commence;* iniens aetas, *youth,* Cic. ; ab ineunte aetate, *from youth,* Cic. **II.** Transit., *to go in, enter.* **A.** Lit., domum, Cic. ; viam, *to enter upon, begin a journey,* Cic. **B.** Transf., 1, *to commence a period of time;* initā aestate, *at the beginning of,* Caes. ; 2, of some kind of action, *to begin, to enter upon;* magistratum, Cic. ; proelium, Cic. ; 3, *to undertake;* numerum, *to enumerate,* Liv. ; inire rationem, *to make an estimate,* Cic., and transf., *to consider,* Cic. ; societatem cum aliquo, *to enter into a league with,* Cic. ; consilium, *to form a plan,* Caes. ; gratiam ab aliquo, *to earn thanks from, conciliate the favour of,* Cic. (perf. init = iniit, Lucr. 4,314).

ĭneptē, adv. (ineptus), *unsuitably, inappropriately, absurdly, foolishly;* dicere, Cic.

ĭneptĭae -ārum, f. (ineptus), *foolish behaviour, silliness, absurdity, foolery;* hominum ineptiae ac stultitiae, Cic. ; ut eos partim scelerum suorum, partim etiam ineptiarum poeniteat, Cic.

ĭneptĭo, 4. (ineptus), *to talk foolishly, talk nonsense,* Cat.

ĭneptus -a -um (in and aptus), *unsuitable, inappropriate, tasteless, foolish, absurd, silly;* negotium, Cic. ; Graeculus, Cic. ; subst. plur., ĭnepti -ōrum, *pedants,* Cic. ; compar., nam quid est ineptius quam, etc., Cic.

ĭnermis -e, and ĭnermus -a -um (in and arma), *unarmed, weaponless.* **I.** Lit., a, gen., Cic. ; gingiva, *toothless,* Juv. ; milites, Caes. ; b, of countries, *undefended by troops;* ager, Liv. **II.** Transf., in philosophia, *not well versed in,* Cic. ; carmen, *inoffensive, offending no one,* Ov.

1. ĭnerrans -antis (in and erro), *not wandering, fixed;* stellae inerrantes, Cic.

2. ĭnerrans -antis, partic. of inerro.

ĭnerro, 1. *to rove or wander about,* Plin.

ĭners -ertis (in and ars). **I.** *simple, unskilful;* poeta iners, Cic. **II.** *inactive, lazy, idle, inert, sluggish, slothful.* **A.** a, homo, senectus, Cic. ; b, transf. of things and abstractions, (a) gen., otium, Cic. ; aqua, *stagnant,* Ov. ; aequora, *undisturbed by wind,* Lucr. ; stomachus, *not digesting,* Ov. ; terra, *immovable,* Hor. ; querelae,

useless, Liv. ; (β) of time during which nothing is done, *idle;* hora, Hor. ; tempus, Ov. ; (γ) of food, caro, *insipid,* Hor. ; (δ) act., *making idle or slothful;* frigus, Ov. **B.** *cowardly,* Cic.

ĭnertĭa -ae, f. (iners), 1, *unskilfulness, want of skill,* Cic. ; 2, *slothfulness, sluggishness;* laboris, *aversion to labour,* Cic.

ĭnērŭdītus -a -um, *unlearned, illiterate, ignorant,* Cic.

ĭnesco, 1. *to allure with a bait;* transf., *to entice, deceive;* nos caeci specie parvi beneficii inescamur, Liv.

ĭnēvectus -a -um (in and eveho), *raised upon, borne upon,* Verg.

ĭnēvītābĭlis -e, *inevitable, unavoidable;* fulmen, Ov.

ĭnexcĭtus -a -um (in and excieo), *unmoved, quiet,* Verg.

ĭnexcūsābĭlis -e, *without excuse, inexcusable,* Hor.

ĭnexercĭtātus -a -um (in and exercito), *unexercised, unpractised;* miles, *undrilled,* Cic. ; histrio, Cic. ; prompti et non inexercitati ad dicendum, Cic.

ĭnexhaustus -a -um (in and exhaurio), *unexhausted, inexhaustible;* metalla, Verg. ; pubertas, *unenfeebled,* Tac.

ĭnexōrābĭlis -e, *inexorable, not to be moved by entreaty;* a, of persons, in ceteros, Cic. ; adversus te, Liv. ; delictis, Tac. ; b, of things, disciplina, *severe,* Tac.

ĭnexpĕdītus -a -um, *hampered;* pugna, Liv.

ĭnexperrectus -a -um (in and expergiscor), *not awakened,* Ov.

ĭnexpertus -a -um. **I.** Act., *inexperienced, unpractised, unacquainted with;* with genit., lasciviae, Tac. ; with dat., bonis inexpertus atque insuetus, Liv. ; with ad and the acc., animus ad contumeliam inexpertus, Liv. **II.** Pass., 1, *untried, unattempted;* ne quid inexpertum relinquat, Verg. ; 2, *untried, untested;* a, of persons, legiones bello civili inexpertae, Tac. ; b, of things, puppis, Ov. ; fides, Liv.

ĭnexpĭābĭlis -e (in and expio), 1, *inexpiable;* scelus, Cic. ; 2, *implacable, irreconcileable;* homo, Cic. ; bellum, *obstinate,* Cic.

ĭnexplēbĭlis -e (in and expleo), *insatiable, that cannot be satisfied;* 1, lit., Sen. ; 2, transf., a, of things, cupiditas, Cic. ; populi fauces, Cic. ; epularum foeda et inexplebilis libido, Tac. ; b, of persons, with genit., vir inexplebilis virtutis veraeque laudis, *with an insatiable desire for,* Liv.

ĭnexplētus -a -um (in and expleo), *unfilled, insatiate, insatiable;* inexpletus lacrimans, *that cannot be satisfied with weeping,* Verg.

ĭnexplĭcābĭlis -e (*that cannot be untied*) transf., 1, *intricate, impracticable, difficult;* inexplicabiles continuis imbribus viae, *impassable,* Liv. ; legatio, *impracticable,* Cic. ; res difficilis et inexplicabilis, Cic. ; facilitas, *leading to no result,* Liv. ; 2, *inexplicable;* haec inexplicabilia esse dicitis, Cic.

ĭnexplōrātō, adv. (inexploratus), *without exploring, without reconnoitring;* proficisci, Liv.

ĭnexplōrātus -a -um (in and exploro), *unexplored, uninvestigated;* stagni vada, Liv.

ĭnexpugnābĭlis -e, *unconquerable, impregnable.* **I.** Lit., a, arx, Liv. ; b, gramen, *that cannot be rooted out,* Ov. ; via, *inaccessible,* Liv. **II.** Transf., with dat., inexpugnabile amori pectus, Ov. ; of persons, volumus eum qui beatus sit tutum esse, inexpugnabilem, saeptum atque munitum, Cic.

ĭnexspectātus -a -um, *unlooked for, unexpected*, Cic.

ĭnexstinctus -a -um (in and exstinguo), *unextinguished, inextinguishable* ; **1**, lit., ignis, Ov. ; **2**, transf., fames, libido, *insatiable*, Ov. ; nomen, *immortal*, Ov.

ĭnexsŭpĕrābĭlis -e, *that cannot be passed over or crossed, insurmountable.* **A.** Lit., Alpes, Liv. ; paludes, Liv. **B.** Transf., a, *unsurpassable*, Liv. ; b, *insuperable* ; vis fati, Liv.

ĭnextrīcābĭlis -e (in and extrico), *that cannot be disentangled, inextricable* ; error, *mazes out of which it is impossible to find one's way*, Verg.

infăbrē, adv. *unskilfully, in an unworkmanlike manner* ; vasa non infabre facta, Liv.

infăbrĭcātus -a -um (in and fabrico), *unwrought, unfashioned* ; robora, Verg.

infăcētē (**infĭcētē**), adv. (infacetus), *tastelessly, coarsely, without humour*, Suet.

infăcētĭae (**infĭcētĭae**) -ārum, f. (infacetus), *coarse jests, poor wit*, Cat.

infăcētus and **infĭcētus** -a -um (in and facetus), *coarse, rude, unmannerly, unpolished, without humour or wit* ; homo non infacetus, Cic. ; transf., mendacium non infacetum, Cic.

infācundus -a -um, *not eloquent* ; vir acer nec infacundus, Liv. ; compar., quia infacundior sit, Liv.

infāmĭa -ae, f. (infamis), *ill report, shame, dishonour, disgrace, ignominy, infamy* ; **1**, lit., infamiam inferre, Cic. ; movere, to cause, Liv. ; infamiā aspergi, *to come into bad repute*, Nep. ; infamiā flagrare, Caes. ; infamiam habere, Caes. ; subire infamiam sempiternam, Cic. ; **2**, meton., *the cause of ill repute and infamy* ; nostri saecli, *the disgrace of our age*, Ov. ; infamia silvae (of Cacus), Ov.

infāmis -e (in and fama), **1**, *of ill repute, disreputable, infamous* ; homines vitiis atque dedecore infames, Cic. ; vita, Cic. ; **2**, *bringing into ill repute, disgraceful* ; nuptiae, Cic.

infāmo, **1**. (infamis), **1**, *to bring into ill repute, make infamous, defame* ; aliquem, Nep. ; aliquid, Cic. ; **2**, *to blame, accuse, find fault with* ; rem, Cic.

infandus -a -um (in and fari), *unutterable, unspeakable, unheard of, unnatural, abominable* ; corpus eius impurum et infandum, Cic. ; caedes, Liv. ; dolor, labores, dies, Verg. Subst., **infanda** -ōrum, n. *unheard-of enormities*, Liv. ; infandum or infanda ! *abominable !* Verg.

infans -fantis (in and fari). **I. A.** *dumb, speechless*, Cic. **B.** Of children, *not able to speak* ; adj.= *young*, subst.= *a little child* ; **1**, a, lit., filius, Cic. ; infantibus parcere, Caes. ; b, meton., (a) poet., *belonging to a child* ; pectora infantia, Ov. ; (β) *childish, foolish* ; omnia fuere infantia, Cic. **II.** *without the gift of speech, devoid of eloquence* ; infantes et insipientes homines, Cic. ; transf., pudor, *embarrassed*, Hor. ; meton., historia, Cic.

infantĭa -ae, f. (infans). **I. A.** *inability to speak* ; linguae, Lucr. **B.** *childhood* (up to the age of seven) ; prima ab infantia, Tac. **II.** Transf., *want of eloquence, slowness of speech*, Cic.

infarcĭo (**infercĭo**) -farsi (-fersi) -farsum (-fersum) and -fartum (-fertum), **4**. (in and farcio), *to stuff in, cram in, stuff full of* ; fig., neque inferciens verba quasi rimas expleat, Cic.

infătĭgābĭlis -e, *that cannot be wearied, indefatigable*, Plin.

infătŭo, **1**. (in and fatuus), *to make a fool of, infatuate* ; aliquem mercede publicā, Cic.

infaustus -a -um, *unlucky, unfortunate* ; auspicium, Verg. ; dies, Tac.

infector -ōris, m. (inficio), *a dyer*, Cic.

1. infectus -a -um (in and facio). **I.** *unworked, unwrought* ; argentum, Liv. ; aurum, Verg. **II. A.** *undone, unfinished, incomplete* ; pro infecto habere, *to consider as having never taken place*, Cic. ; infectā re (*without having accomplished the business*) discedere, Caes., abducere exercitum, Liv. ; infecto negotio, Sall. ; infectā victoriā, Liv. ; infectā pace, Liv. ; infecto bello, Liv. ; reddere infectum, *to make void*, Hor. **B.** Transf., *impracticable, impossible* ; rex nihil infectum Metello credens, Sall.

2. infectus, partic. of inficio.

infēcundĭtas -ātis, f. (infecundus), *barrenness, sterility* ; terrarum, Tac.

infēcundus -a -um, *unfruitful, barren, sterile* ; ager, Sall. ; fig., fons (ingenii), Ov.

infēlīcĭtas -ātis, f. (infelix), *ill-luck, unhappiness, misfortune* ; haruspicum, Cic. ; alicuius in liberis, Liv.

infēlīcĭtĕr, adv. (infelix), *unluckily, unfortunately* ; totiens infeliciter temptata arma, Liv.

infēlīco, infēlīcĭto, 1. (infelix), *to make miserable*, Plaut.

infēlix -īcis. **I.** *unfruitful, barren* ; tellus frugibus infelix, Verg. **II.** Transf., **A.** *unlucky, unhappy, miserable* ; a, of persons, homo miserrimus atque infelicissimus, Cic. ; infelicior domi quam militiae, Liv. ; with genit., animi, *in mind*, Verg. ; with abl., operis summā, Hor. ; b, of things, patria, Verg. **B.** Act., *causing unhappiness, unfortunate, unlucky* ; **1**, gen., a, of persons, qui reipublicae sit infelix, Cic. ; b, of things, cousilium, Liv. ; **2**, esp., infelix arbor, *the gallows*, Cic.

infensē, adv. (infensus), *hostilely, acrimoniously* ; infense invectus, Tac. ; quis Isocrati est adversatus infensius, Cic.

infenso, 1. (infensus), *to treat in a hostile manner* ; Armeniam bello, *to attack*, Tac.

infensus -a -um (in and * fendo), *hostile, full of hate and bitterness, enraged* ; a, of persons, rex irā infensus, Liv. ; with dat., infensus alicui, Verg. ; with in and the acc., eo infensior in se quam in illum judicibus, Liv. ; b, of things, animus, Cic. ; opes principibus infensae, *dangerous*, Tac.

infer -a -um, **inferī** -ōrum, v. inferus.

infĕrĭae -ārum, f. (inferi), *sacrifices or offerings in honour of the dead* ; alicui inferias afferre, Cic.

infercĭo, v. infarcio.

infĕrĭor, v. inferus.

infĕrĭus, 1, adv., v. infra. ; 2, neut. adj., v. inferus.

infernē, adv. (infernus), *on the lower side, beneath, below*, Lucr.

infernus -a -um (infer), *that which is below, lower.* **I.** Gen., partes, Cic. **II.** Esp., a, *underground* ; gurges, Ov. ; b, *of or relating to the lower world, infernal* ; rex, Pluto, Verg. ; Juno, Proserpine, Verg. ; palus, *the Styx*, Ov. Hence subst., a, **infernī** -ōrum, m. *the inhabitants of the lower world*, Prop. ; b, **inferna** -ōrum, n. *the lower world, infernal regions*, Tac.

infĕro, intŭli, illātum, inferre, *to bring, bear, carry in, to put or place on.* **I.** Lit., **A.** Gen. templis ignes inferre, *to set fire to*, Cic. ; aliquid in ignem, Caes. ; in equum, *to put on horseback*, Caes. **B.** Esp., a, *to bury, inter*, Cic. ; b, *to give in an account* ; rationes, Cic. ; sumptum civibus, *to charge, put to the account of* ; c, *to sacrifice, pay* ; honores Anchisae, Verg. ; d, manus alicui or in aliquem, *to lay hands on*, Cic. ; alicui vim, *to do violence to*, Cic. ; e, signa in hostem, *to attack*, *charge*, Caes.; **f**, bellum alicui, or contra aliquem, *to make war on, levy war against*, Cic.; **g**, pedem, *to enter*, Cic.; in a hostile meaning, *to attack;* alicui, Liv.; so gradum, Liv.; **h**, reflex. and middle; (*a*) reflex., se inferre, *to betake oneself, to go*, lucus quo se persaepe inferebat, Liv.; *to charge the enemy;* effusi se stantibus vobis intulerint, Liv.; (*β*) middle, inferri in urbem, Liv. **II.** Transf., **A.** se in periculum, *to fall into*, Cic. **B.** a, *to produce, bring forward;* sermonem, *to speak*, Cic.; mentionem, *to mention*, Liv.; **b**, *to cause, occasion;* spem alicui, Caes.; hostibus terrorem, Cic.; periculum civibus, Cic.; **c**, *to excite or seek to excite;* misericordiam, invidiam, Cic.; **d**, *to infer, conclude*, Cic.

infersus and **infertus**, v. infarcio.

inferus -a -um (connected with ἔνεροι), and **infer** -a -um, compar. **inferior**, superl. **infimus** and **imus** -a -um. **I.** Positive, **inferus** -a -um, 1, *that which is below, lower* (opp. superus); mare, *the Etruscan Sea* (opp. mare Superum, *the Adriatic*), Cic.; 2, *that which is in the lower world;* inferi dii, Cic. Subst., **inferi** -ōrum and -ûm, m. *the departed, the dead, the lower world;* ab inferis exsistere, *to rise from the dead*, Liv.; apud inferos, *in the lower world*, Cic.; elicere animas inferorum, Cic., ab inferis excitare or revocare, *to raise from the dead*, Cic. **II.** Compar., **inferior**, neut. **inferius**, genit. -ōris, *the lower* (opp. superior), 1, of position, labrum, *the under-lip*, Caes.; ex inferiori loco dicere, *to speak from the body of the court* (opp. ex superiori loco, *from the tribunal*), Cic.; 2, transf., a, of order, versus, *the pentameter*, Ov.; b, of time, *later, younger;* aetate inferiores, Cic.; c, of number, inferior numero navium, *weaker*, Caes.; d, of rank, *lower, meaner, of less importance;* gradus, Cic.; inferioris juris magistratus, Liv.; e, of power, *weaker;* with abl., inferior animo, Caes.; fortunâ, *in fortune*, Cic.; in jure civili, Cic. **III.** Superl., **A. infimus (infumus)** -a -um, *the lowest* (opp. summus); 1, lit., a, solum, Caes.; b, ad infimos montes, *at the bottom of the mountains*, Nep.; ab infima ara, *from the bottom of the altar*, Cic.; 2, transf., of position, *lowest, meanest;* infimo loco natus, Cic.; faex populi, Cic.; precibus infimis, *with abject prayers*, Liv. **B. imus** -a -um, *the lowest;* 1, lit., a, sedes ima, Cic.; ab imo, *from the bottom*, Caes.; ab imo suspirare, *to sigh deeply*, Ov.; neut. plur., **ima** -ōrum, *the lower world*, Ov.; b, ab imis unguibus ad verticem summum, Cic., gurges, *the bottom of*, Ov.; 2, transf., a, of tone, *deepest, lowest;* vox ima, Hor.; b, of position, superi imique deorum, Ov.; *the last;* mensis, Ov.; ad imum, *to the end*, Hor., and *at the end*, Hor.

infervesco -ferbŭi, 3. *to begin to boil, grow hot, to be boiled down;* hoc ubi confusum sectis inferbuit herbis, Hor.

infeste, adv. (infestus), *in a hostile manner*, Liv.; compar., infestius atque inimicius, Liv.; superl., inimicissime atque infestissime, Cic.

infesto, 1. (infestus), *to attack, harass, disquiet;* latus dextrum, Ov.

infestus -a -um (in and *fendo). **I.** Act., *hostile, inimical, dangerous, troublesome;* 1, of things, **a**, provincia Gallia, Cic.; with dat., alicui invisus infestusque, Cic.; with in and the acc., infestus in suos, Cic.; b, milit. t. t., *with hostile intent, in hostile array, prepared for battle;* a Tibure infesto agmine profecti, Liv.; 2, of things, infestis oculis conspici, Cic.; infestis signis, *in hostile array*, Caes.; hastâ infestâ, *with lance couched*, Liv.; infestis pilis, *ready for the throw*, Caes. **II.** Pass., made

dangerous, unsafe, insecure, molested; iter, etc.; mare infestum habere, Cic.; with abl., via illa incursionibus barbarorum infesta, Cic.

inficetus, inficēte = infacetus, infacete (q.v.).

inficio -fēci -fectum, 3. (in and facio). **I.** *to put or dip into anything;* hence, *to tinge, dye, stain, colour;* 1, lit., a, se vitro, Caes.; rivos sanguine, Hor.; ora pallor albus inficit, *makes colourless*, Hor.; b, *to mix with;* hoc (dictamno) fusum labris splendentibus amnem inficit, Verg.; 2, transf., *to imbue, instruct;* (puer) jam infici debet in artibus, etc., Cic. **II.** 1, *to poison;* Gorgoneis Alecto infecta venenis, Verg.; 2, transf., *to taint, infect, corrupt;* ut cupiditatibus principum et vitiis infici solet tota civitas, Cic.; poet., infectum scelus, *the crime with which they are stained*, Verg.

infidelis -e, *unfaithful, untrue, perfidious, faithless*, Cic.; superl., infidelissimi socii, Cic.

infidelitas -tātis, f. (infidelis), *unfaithfulness, faithlessness;* amicitiarum, Cic.

infideliter, adv. (infidelis), *unfaithfully, faithlessly*, Cic.

infidus -a -um, *unfaithful, faithless, untrue;* a, of persons, amici, Cic.; b, of things, societas regni, Liv.; nihil est enim stabile quod infidum est, Cic.

infigo -fixi -fixum, 3. *to fix, fasten to, or in, to thrust in.* **I.** Lit., gladium hosti in pectus, Cic.; hasta infigitur portae, Verg. **II.** Transf., *to imprint, impress, fix;* cura erit infixa animo, Cic.; animus infixus est in patriae caritate, Cic.; in hominum sensibus positum atque infixum est, Cic.; infixum est, *it is fixed, finally resolved*, Tac.

infimatis -is, m. (infimus), *a person of the lowest condition*, Plaut.

infimus -a -um, superl. of inferus (q.v.).

infindo -fīdi -fissum, 3. *to cut in, cleave;* sulcos telluri, Verg.; poet., sulcos mari, *to sail through the sea*, Verg.

infinitas -tātis, f. (in and finis), *infinity, endlessness;* infinitas locorum, Cic.; in infinitatem omnem peregrinari, Cic.

infinite, adv. (infinitus), *infinitely, boundlessly, endlessly;* partes secare et dividere, Cic.; concupiscere, Cic.

infinitio -ōnis, f. (infinitus), *infinity*, Cic.

infinitus -a -um (in and finio). **I.** 1, lit., of space, altitudo, Cic.; 2, transf., a, of time, *endless, unceasing;* tempus, Cic.; odium, Cic.; b, of number, *countless;* infinita corporum varietas, Cic.; c, of extent, size, degree, *boundless, immense;* magnitudo, Caes.; silva, Cic.; infinitum est, with infin., Cic.; subst., **infinitum** -i, n. *that which is boundless*, Cic. **II.** *indefinite, general;* infinitior distributio, Cic.

infirmatio -ōnis, f. (infirmo), 1, *a refuting;* rationis, Cic.; 2, *invalidating;* rerum judicatarum, Cic.

infirme, adv. (infirmus), *weakly, faintly;* socii infirme animati, Cic.

infirmitas -tātis, f. (infirmus), *weakness, powerlessness, infirmity;* 1, corporis, Cic.; valetudinis, Cic.; 2, transf., a, *mental weakness;* hominum, Cic.; animi, *want of spirit, want of courage*, Cic.; b, *instability, unsteadiness of character;* Gallorum, Caes.

infirmo, 1. (infirmus), *to weaken;* 1, lit., legiones, Tac.; 2, transf., a, *to shake;* fidem testis, Cic.; b, *to refute;* res leves, Cic.; c, *to annul;* acta illa atque omnes res superioris anni, Cic.

infirmus -a -um, *weak, feeble, infirm.* **I.**

Lit., *physically*, vires, Cic.; classis, Cic.; in-firmi homines ad resistendum, Caes. **II.** Transf., a, *weak*; res infirma ad probandum, Cic.; b, *mentally and morally*, *weak*, *timorous*; animo infirmo esse, Cic.; *superstitious*, Hor.

infit, defective verb = incipit, **1**, *he* or *she begins*; with infin., Verg.; esp., **2**, *he* or *she begins to speak*, Verg.

infĭtĭae, f. (in and fateor), *a denial*; found only in acc., infitias ire aliquid, *to deny anything*, Liv.; with acc. and infin., infitias eunt, *they deny*, mercedem se belli Romanis inferendi pactos (esse), Liv.

infĭtĭālis -e (infitiae), *negative*, *containing a denial*; quaestio, Cic.

infĭtĭātĭo -ōnis, f. (infitior), *a denying*; negatio infitiatioque facti, Cic.

infĭtĭātor -ōris, m. (infitior), *one who denies* or *disavows a debt* or *deposit*, Cic.

infĭtĭor, **1**. dep. (in and fateor), *to deny*, *disavow*, *not to confess*; **1**, with acc., verum, Cic.; with acc. and infin., neque ego in hoc me hominem esse infitiabor unquam, Cic.; **2**, *to deny a debt*, *refuse to restore a deposit*; quid si infitiatur? Cic.

inflammātĭo -ōnis, f. (inflammo), *a fire*, *conflagration*; inferre inflammationem tectis, Cic.; transf., animorum, *fire*, *inspiration*, Cic.

inflammo, **1**. **A**. *to light up, kindle, set fire to*; taedas, Cic.; classem, Cic. **B**. Transf., *to inflame, excite, stir up, stimulate*; populum in improbos, Cic.; inflammari ad cupiditates, Cic.; inflammatus ipse (orator) et ardens, *fiery*, Cic.

inflātĭo -ōnis, f. (inflo), of the body, *a puffing up, blowing out, flatulence*; inflationem magnam habere, *to cause flatulence*, Cic.

inflātĭus, adv. in compar. (inflatus), *too pompously, proudly, haughtily*; haec ad eum latius atque inflatius perscribebat, Cic.

1. **inflātus** -a -um, p. adj. (from inflo). **A**. *swelling, swollen*; collum, Cic. **B**. Transf., a, *scornful*; animus, Cic.; b, *haughty, proud*; laetitiā, spe, Cic.

2. **inflātus** -ūs, m. (inflo), **1**, *a blowing into*; primo inflatu tibicinis, *at the first blast*, Cic.; **2**, *inspiration*; divinus, Cic.

inflecto -flexi -flexum, **3**. *to bend, bow, curve*. **I**. Lit., bacillum, Cic.; quum ferrum se inflexisset, Caes.; inflectere nullum unquam vestigium sui cursus, Cic.; oculos, Cic.; middle, inflecti, *to curve*; sinus ab litore in urbem inflectitur, Cic. **II**. Transf., a, jus civile, *to warp*, Cic.; b, *to modulate the voice*; inflexā ad miserabilem sonum voce, Cic.; c, *to alter a name*; suum nomen ex Graeco, Cic.; d, of persons, *to change, move, affect*; aliquem leviter, Cic.; sensus animumque labantem, Cic.

inflētus -a -um (in and fleo), *unwept, unlamented*, Verg.

inflexĭbĭlis -e, *that cannot be bent, inflexible*, Plin.

inflexĭo ōnis, f. (inflecto), *a bending, swaying*; laterum inflexio fortis ac virilis, Cic.

inflexus -ūs, m. (inflecto), *a bending, curving*, Juv.

inflīgo -flixi -flictum, **3**. **I**. *to strike, knock, dash against*; alicui securim, Cic.; puppis inflicta vadis, *dashed on*, Verg. **II**. *to inflict, cause hurt* or *damage*; mortiferam plagam, Cic.; alicui turpitudinem, Cic.

inflo, **1**. **I**. *to blow on* or *in*; a, *to play on wind instruments*; calamos leves, Verg.; tibias, Cic.; and absol., *to give a blast*; simul inflavit tibicen, Cic.; b, *to produce by blowing*; sonum, Cic. **II**. *to blow out*; **1**, lit., a, *to puff out, to*

swell; ambas buccas, Hor.; amnis inflatus (aquis), Liv.; b, *to blow out a sound fully*; aliquid extenuatur, inflatur, Cic.; **2**, transf., *to puff up, make proud* or *arrogant, elate*; animos falsā spe, Liv.; inflatus laetitiā, Cic.

inflŭo -fluxi -fluxum, **3**. *to flow in, stream in*. Caes. **A**. Lit., non longe a mari, quo Rhenus influit, Rhenus in Oceanum influit, Caes.; with simple acc., lacum, Caes. **B**. Transf., **1**, *to come in unavares, to steal in*; in aures, Cic.; in animos, Cic.; **2**, *to stream in, rush in, flow in*; in Italiam Gallorum copiae, Cic.

infŏdĭo -fōdi -fossum, **3**. *to dig in, bury*; corpora terrae, Verg.; taleas in terram, Caes.

informātĭo -ōnis, f. (informo), *a conception, idea*; Dei, Cic.; antecepta animo rei, *an à priori idea*, Cic.

informis -e (in and forma), **1**, *formless, unformed*; alvei, Liv.; **2**, *unshapely, misformed, deformed, hideous*; cadaver, Verg.; hiems, Hor.

informo, **1**. *to give form and shape to, to form, fashion*. **I**. Lit., clipeum, Verg. **II**. Transf., a, *to form*; animus a natura bene informatus, Cic.; b, *to form by instruction, instruct*; artes quibus aetas puerilis ad humanitatem informari solet, Cic.; c, *to sketch, represent, depict*; oratorem, Cic.; causam, Cic.; d, *to form an idea, conception, image of anything*; eos (deos) non conjecturā quidem informare posse, *form a conjectural idea of*, Cic.

infortūnātus -a -um, *unfortunate, unhappy, miserable*; nihil me infortunatius, Cic.

infortūnĭum -ĭi, n. (in and fortuna), *misfortune, ill luck*, Hor., Liv.

infrā (for inferā, sc. parte, from inferus). **I**. Adv., **1**, lit., a, gen. (a) posit. *on the under side, below, beneath*; innumeros supra infra, dextra sinistra deos esse, Cic.; *in writing*, earum (litterarum) exemplum infra scripsi or scriptum est, Cic.; (β) compar. inferius, *lower down*; inferius suis fraternos currere Luna admiratur equos, Ov.; b, *in the lower world*, Tib.; **2**, transf., *below* (in rank), nec fere unquam infra ita descenderent ut ad infimos pervenirent, Liv. **II**. Prepos. with acc.; **1**, lit., in space, *beneath, below*; mare infra oppidum, Cic.; infra eum locum ubi pons erat, Caes.; **2**, transf., a, of size, hi sunt magnitudine paulo infra (*less than*) elephantos, Caes.; b, of time, *later than*; Homerus non infra superiorem Lycurgum fuit, Cic.; c, *beneath, below*, in rank, estimation; res humanas infra se positas arbitrari, Cic.

infractĭo -ōnis, f. (infringo), *breaking*; transf., animi, *dejection*, Cic.

infractus -a -um (p. adj. from infringo), **1**, *broken*, Plin.; **2**, a, *broken, exhausted*; animos, *dejected*, Liv.; b, infracta loqui, *to speak disconnectedly*, Cic.

infrăgĭlis -e, **1**, *not fragile, that cannot be broken*, Plin.; **2**, *strong*; vox, Ov.

infrĕmo -frĕmŭi, **3**. *to roar, growl*; aper, Verg.

1. **infrēnātus** -a -um (in and freno), *without bridle*; equites, *riding without a bridle*, Liv.

2. **infrēnātus** -a -um, partic of infreno.

infrendĕo, **2**. *to gnash with the teeth*; dentibus, Verg.

infrēnis -e and **infrēnus** -a -um (in and frenum), *without bridle, unbridled*; equus, Verg.; Numidae, *riding without bridle*, Verg.

infrēno, **1**. **1**, lit., *to bridle*; equos, Liv.; currus, *to harness the horses to the chariot*, Verg.; **2**, transf., *to restrain, hold back, check*; horum alterum sic fuisse infrenatum conscientiā scelerum et fraudium suarum ut, etc., Cic.

infrēquens -entis, *infrequent.* **I.** Of space. **A.** *not numerous, few in number ;* hostes, Liv.; copiae infrequentiores, Caes.; senatus infrequens, Cic. **B.** Of places, *not full, scantily populated ;* pars urbis infrequens aedificiis erat, Liv.; causa, *attended by few hearers,* Cic.; subst., infrequentissima urbis, *the least populous parts of the city,* Liv. **II.** Of time ; of persons, *not doing a thing often, infrequent, occasional ;* deorum cultor, Hor.

infrēquentĭa -ae, f. (infrequens), 1, *fewness, scantiness of number, thinness ;* senatus, Cic. ; 2, *solitude, loneliness ;* locorum, Tac.

infrĭco -frĭcŭi -frictum and -frĭcātum, 1. *to rub in* or *on,* Plin.

infringo -frēgi -fractum, 3. (in and frango). **I.** *to break, break off, break in pieces.* **A.** Lit., remum, Cic. ; hastam, Liv. **B.** Transf., *to break, destroy, impair, check, enfeeble, cast down ;* vim militum, Caes. ; spem, Cic. ; conatus adversariorum, Caes. ; animum, Liv. ; Samnitium vires, Liv. **II.** *to knock against ;* liminibus lumbos, Hor.

infrons -frondis, *leafless ;* ager, *treeless,* Ov.

infructŭōsus -a -um, *unfruitful,* transf., *unproductive, fruitless, useless ;* militia, Tac. ; laus, Tac.

infūcātus -a -um (in and fuco), *rouged, painted ;* fig. vitia, Cic.

infŭla -ae, f. *a band* or *fillet made of locks of wool, knotted at intervals, worn by priests and Vestal virgins, and used to decorate victims,* altars, etc., Cic.; also worn by suppliants, Caes.; hence, *something holy ;* his insignibus atque infulis imperii Romani venditis, *the inalienable public land,* Cic.

infŭlātus -a -um (infula), *adorned with* or *wearing the infula,* Suet.

infulcĭo -fulsi -fultum, 4. *to stuff in, cram in,* Suet.

infundo -fūdi -fūsum, 3. **I.** *to pour in* or *on.* **A.** Lit., 1, aliquid in vas, Cic. ; 2, *to administer ;* alicui venenum,Cic.; alicui poculum, *to present,* Hor. **B.** Transf., a, of a crowd of people, gen. reflex., se infundere or passive infundi as middle = *to pour in, stream in ;* infusus populus, *collected in large numbers,* Verg.; b, of wind, sound, etc., *to pour into, to allow to penetrate ;* passive as middle = *to penetrate,* Cic.; vitia in civitatem, Cic. **II.** *to pour on* or *over.* **A.** Lit., a, of liquids, largos humeris rores, Verg.; b, of bodies not liquid, ignis infusus, Liv. **B.** Transf., infusus with dat., *spread, lying on ;* gremio, Verg.

infusco, 1. *to make dark* or *black ; to obscure, blacken.* **I.** Lit., vellera, arenam, Verg. **II.** Transf., *to disfigure, corrupt, stain ;* vicinitas non infuscata malevolentiā, Cic. ; eos barbaries infuscaverat, Cic.

infūsĭo -ōnis, f. (infundo), *a pouring in* or *on, infusion,* Plin.

Ingaevōnes -um, m. *a German tribe on the shores of the North Sea.*

Ingauni -ōrum, m. *a Ligurian tribe.*

ingĕmĭno, 1. **I.** Transit., *to double, redouble ;* ictus, voces, Verg. **II.** Intransit., *to become double, to increase ;* imber, clamor, Verg.

ingĕmisco (ingĕmesco) -gĕmŭi, 3. **I.** Intransit., *to sigh* or *groan ;* absol., nemo ingemuit, Cic. ; with in and the abl., in quo tu quoque ingemiscis, Cic. ; with dat., eius minis, Liv. **II.** Transit., *to sigh* or *groan over ;* with acc., quid ingemiscis hostem Dolabellam, Cic.

ingĕmo, 3. *to sigh, groan over ;* with dat., laboribus, Hor. ; aratro, Verg.

ingĕnĕro, 1. **I.** *to implant in, generate, produce ;* natura ingenerat amorem, Cic.; partic., **ingĕnĕrātus** -a -um, *implanted by nature, innate, natural ;* familiae frugalitas, Cic. **II.** *to create ;* animum esse ingeneratum a Deo, Cic.

ingĕnĭātus -a -um (ingenium), *endowed by nature,* Plaut.

ingĕnĭōsē, adv.(ingeniosus), *acutely, cleverly, ingeniously ;* ista tractare, Cic.

ingĕnĭōsus -a -um (ingenium), 1, *naturally clever, talented, acute, able, ingenious ;* quo quisque est sollertior et ingeniosior, Cic. ; 2, of inanimate objects, *fit for, adapted to ;* terra colenti, Ov.; ad segetes ager, Ov.

ingĕnĭtus -a -um, partic. of ingigno.

ingĕnĭum -ĭi, n. (in and geno = gigno), *nature, natural constitution.* **I.** Of things, arvorum, Verg. **II.** Of men. **A.** *natural disposition, temperament, character ;* ingenio suo vivere, *after one's own inclination,* Liv. **B.** a, esp., *cleverness, talent, mental power, genius ;* docilitas, memoria, quae fere appellantur uno ingenii nomine, Cic. ; tardum, acerrimum, acutum, magnum, Cic. ; ad fingendum, Cic.; b, meton., *a man of genius, a genius,* Cic.

ingens -entis (in and geno = gigno ; lit., *grown to a great size*), *vast, immense, enormous.* **I.** Lit., pecunia, campus, numerus, Cic. **II.** Transf., exitus, Verg.; bellum, Ov.; with abl., ingens viribus, Liv.; with genit., femina ingens animi, Tac.

ingĕnŭē, adv. (ingenuus), 1, *nobly, liberally ;* educatus, Cic. ; 2, *freely, frankly ;* confiteri, Cic.

ingĕnŭĭtas -tātis, f. (ingenuus), 1, *the condition of a freeman, free-birth,* Cic. ; ornamenta ingenuitatis, Cic. ; 2, *noble-mindedness, uprightness, frankness,* Cic.

ingĕnŭus -a -um (in and geno). **I.** *native, not foreign ;* fons, Lucr. **II.** *natural, innate, color,* Prop. **III.** *free-born, of free birth.* **A.** Lit., Cic. **B.** Transf., a, *that which becomes a free man, noble, honourable ;* vita, artes, Cic. ; b, *frank, sincere ;* homo, Cic. ; c, *weak, delicate,* Ov.

ingĕro -gessi -gestum, 3. **I.** Lit., *to carry, throw, put, pour in* or *upon ;* ligna foco,Tib.; hastas in tergum fugientibus,Verg. ; saxa in subeuntes, *to hurl at,* Liv. **II.** Transf., a, *to heap on, to utter ;* probra, Liv.; convicia alicui, Hor. ; b, *to press upon, force upon ;* alicui nomen, Tac.; aliquem (*as judge*), Cic.

ingestābĭlis -e, *unbearable, intolerable ;* onus, Plin.

ingigno -gĕnŭi -gĕnĭtum, 3. *to implant by birth* or *nature ;* natura cupiditatem homini ingenuit veri videndi, Cic. ; partic., **ingĕnĭtus** -a -um, *innate, inborn ;* ut habeat quiddam ingenitum quasi civile atque populare, Cic.

inglōrĭus -a -um (in and gloria), *without fame* or *glory, inglorious ;* vita, Cic. ; rex apum, *undistinguished,* Verg.

inglŭvĭes -ēi, f. (for ingulvies from in and gula), 1, *the craw* or *crop of birds, the maw of animals,* Verg. ; 2, meton., *gluttony,* Hor.

ingrātē, adv. (ingratus), 1, *unpleasantly,* Ov. ; 2, *ungratefully,* Cic.

ingrātĭa -ae, f. (ingratus), *unthankfulness,* in class. Lat. only in abl., ingratiis (ingratis), *against the will of, unwillingly,* Cic.

ingrātīs, v. ingratia.

ingrātus -a -um, 1, *unpleasant, unpleasing ;* ne invisa diis immortalibus oratio nostra aut ingrata esse videatur, Cic. ; 2, a, *unthankful, ungrateful ;* homo, Cic. ; ingrati animi crimen horreo, Cic. ; with in and the acc., ingratus in Democritum, Cic. ; with genit., salutis, or account of, Verg.; with in and the abl., ingratus in referenda gratia, Caes.; of things, ingluvies, *insatiable*, Hor.; b, *unprofitable, thankless*; labor, Sall.; pericula, Verg.

ingrăvesco, 3. 1, lit., *to become heavy,* Plin.; 2, transf., a, in a good sense, hoc (philosophiae), studium cotidie ingravescit, *is followed more seriously*, Cic.; b, in a bad sense; (a) *to become annoying, troublesome;* annona ingravescit, *becomes dearer*, Cic.; ingravescit in dies malum intestinum, Cic.; (β) *to be oppressed, wearied ;* corpora exercitationum defatigatione ingravescunt, Cic.

ingrăvo, 1. *to make heavy, to oppress, trouble, aggravate, render worse;* illa (conjugis imago) meos casus ingravat, Cic.; ingravat haec Drances, Verg.

ingrĕdĭor -gressus sum, 3. (in and gradior). **I.** Intransit. **A.** *to enter, go in;* a, lit., in navem, in templum, in fundum, Cic.; intra munitiones, Caes.; b, transf., *to enter on;* in bellum, Cic.; in eam orationem, Cic.; in spem libertatis, Cic. **B.** *to go forth, walk;* tardius, Cic.; per nudam infra glaciem, Liv. **II.** Transit. **A.** *to enter ;* domum, Cic.; curiam, Liv. **B.** Of time, *to begin ;* a, iter, Cic.; b, *to commence ;* orationem, Cic.; with infin., dicere, Cic.

ingressĭo -ōnis, f. (ingredior), 1, *an entering, going in ;* a, lit., fori, Cic.; b, transf., *a beginning*, Cic.; 2, *gait, pace*, Cic.

ingressus -ūs, m. (ingredior). **I.** *a going into, an entering.* **A.** Lit., *a hostile entrance, an inroad ;* ingressus hostiles praesidiis intercipere, Tac. **B.** Transf., *a beginning ;* ingressus capere, *to begin*, Verg. **II.** *walking, going, stepping;* ingressus, cursus, accubitio, inclinatio, sessio, Cic.; ingressu prohiberi, *not to be able to move*, Caes.

ingrŭo -ŭi, 3. (in and *gruo, connected with ruo), a, of persons, *to break in, fall upon violently ;* ingruit Æneas Italis, Verg.; b, transf., of things, *to assault, attack ;* periculum, bellum ingruit, Liv.; morbi ingruunt in remiges, Liv.; si nullus ingruat metus, Plin.

inguen -guĭnis, n. *the groin*, Verg.

ingurgĭto, 1. (in and gurges), 1, *to plunge ;* se in tot flagitia, *to plunge into the whirlpool of vice*, Cic.; 2, esp. refl., se ingurgitare, *to glut or gorge oneself, to gormandise*, Cic.

ingustābĭlis -e (in and gusto), *that cannot be tasted*, Plin.

ingustātus -a -um (in and gusto), *untasted, not tasted before ;* ilia rhombi, Hor.

inhăbĭlis -e. **I.** *that cannot be handled or managed, unmanageable ;* navis, Liv.; telum ad remittendum inhabile imperitis, Liv. **II.** *useless, unfit for, ill adapted to ;* tegimen inhabile ad resurgendum, Tac.; multitudo inhabilis ad consensum, Liv.

inhăbĭtābĭlis -e, *uninhabitable ;* maximae regiones inhabitabiles, Cic.

inhăbĭto, 1. *to inhabit ;* eum secessum, Ov.

inhaerĕo -haesi -haesum, 2. *to stick in, cleave to, remain fast to ;* 1, lit., ad saxa, Cic.; visceribus, Cic.; sidera sedibus suis inhaerent, Cic.; 2, transf., inhaeret in mentibus quoddam augurium, Cic.; virtutes semper voluptatibus inhaerent, *are always connected with*, Cic.; semper alicui, *to be always in the company of*, Ov.

inhaeresco -haesi -haesum, 3. (inchoat. of inhaereo), *to remain fast, to cleave to ;* in mentibus, Cic.

inhālo, 1. *to breathe upon ;* quum isto ore foetido teterrimam nobis popinam inhalasses, Cic.

inhĭbĕo -ŭi -ĭtum, 2. (in and habeo). **I.** *to hold in, hold back, check, restrain ;* tela, Liv.; equos, Ov.; si te illius acerba imploratio et vox miserabilis non inhibebat, Cic.; as naut. t. t., inhibere remis, Cic., or navem retro inhibere, Liv., *to row a boat backwards, to row a boat stern first, to back water.* **II.** *to exercise, practise, use, employ ;* supplicia nobis, Cic.; imperium in deditos, Liv.

inhĭbĭtĭo -ōnis, f. (inhibeo), *a restraining ;* remigum, *a rowing backwards*, Cic.

inhĭo, 1. **I.** *to gape, gape with wonder ;* tenuit inhians tria Cerberus ora, Verg. **II.** *to gape for, open the mouth with desire ;* Romulus lactens uberibus lupinis inhians, Cic.; fig. with dat., *to covet, desire, long for ;* alicuius hortis, opibus, Tac.; varios pulchrā testudine postes, *look with desire upon*, Verg.

inhŏnestē, adv. (inhonestus), *dishonourably, disgracefully ;* aliquem accusare, Cic.

inhŏnesto, 1. (inhonestus), *to disgrace, dishonour ;* palmas, Ov.

inhŏnestus -a -um, 1, *dishonourable, shameful, disgraceful ;* homo, Cic.; vulnera, Ov.; inhonestissima cupiditas, Cic.; 2, *ugly, unsightly ;* vulnus, Verg.

inhŏnōrātus -a -um, 1, *not honoured, honoured by no public office, private, retired ;* vita, Cic.; honoratus atque inhonoratus, Liv.; inhonoratior triumphus, Liv.; 2, *unrewarded, without gifts;* aliquem inhonoratum dimittere, Liv.

inhŏnōrus -a -um, 1, *unhonoured, undistinguished*, Plin.; 2, *ugly, unsightly*, Tac.

inhorrĕo -ŭi, 2. *to bristle ;* haud secus quam vallo saepta inhorreret acies, Liv.

inhorresco -horrŭi, 3. **I.** *to begin to bristle, to bristle up ;* a, aper inhorruit armos, Verg.; spicea jam campis messis inhorruit, Verg.; inhorruit unda tenebris, Verg.; b, *to be rough with frost;* quum tristis hiems aquilonis inhorruit alis, Ov. **II.** *to shudder, shiver, from cold, fever, fright,* etc.; 1, lit., dicitur inhorruisse civitas, Cic.; 2, transf., of things, *to shake, tremble;* aer, Ov.

inhospĭtālis -e, *inhospitable ;* Caucasus, Hor.

inhospĭtālĭtas -tātis, f. (inhospitalis), *want of hospitality*, Cic.

inhospĭtus -a -um, *inhospitable ;* tecta, Ov.; Syrtis, Verg.

inhūmānē, adv. (inhumanus), *inhumanly ;* inhumanius dicere, Cic.

inhūmānĭtas -tātis, f. (inhumanus), 1, *cruelty, inhumanity*, Cic.; 2, a, *incivility, discourtesy, disobligingness*, Cic.; b, *stinginess, niggardliness*, Cic.

inhūmānĭtĕr, adv. (inhumanus), *uncivilly, rudely, discourteously*, Cic.

inhūmānus -a -um, 1, *cruel, barbarous, inhuman ;* homo, scelus, Cic.; quis inhumanior? Cic.; 2, a, *rude, uncourteous, uncivil, unmannerly*, Cic.; b, *uncultivated ;* aures, Cic.

inhŭmātus -a -um (in and humo), *unburied*, Cic.

inhŭmo, 1. *to cover with earth*, Plin.

inĭbī, adv. 1, of place, *therein, in that place, in that matter*, Cic.; 2, of time, *almost, nearly, on the point of ;* inibi est, *it is on the point of taking place ;* aut inibi esse aut jam esse confectum, Cic.

inĭcĭo = injicio.

inĭmīcē, adv. (inimicus), *hostilely, in an unfriendly manner ;* insectari aliquem, Cic.

inimicitia -ae, f. (inimicus), *enmity*, Cic.; gen. in plur., cum aliquo mihi inimicit 'e sunt, or intercedunt, Cic.; inimicitias gerere, Cic., exercere, Cic., suscipere, Cic.

inimico, 1. (inimicus), *to make hostile, set at enmity;* ira miseras inimicat urbes, Hor.

inimicus -a -um (in and amicus). **I.** Act., *unfriendly, inimical, adverse.* **A.** Lit., a, adj., inimicus alicui, Cic.; inimicus cenis sumptuosis, Cic.; of inanimate objects, *hurtful, prejudicial;* odor nervis inimicus, Hor.; b, subst., **inimicus** -i, m, *an enemy, foe,* Cic.; **inimica** -ae, f. *a female foe,* Cic.; inimicissimi Sthenii, *the bitterest foes of S.,* Cic. **B.** Poet., transf. = hostilis; terra inimica, Verg. **II.** Pass. = *hated;* gener invisus inimici soceri, Tac.

intelligens -entis, *unintelligent,* Cic.

inique, adv. (iniquus), 1, *unequally;* iniquissime comparatum est, Cic.; 2, *unfairly, unjustly,* Cic.

iniquitas -tatis, f. (iniquus). **I.** *unevenness;* a, lit., loci, Caes.; b, transf., *unfavourableness, difficulty, unpropitiousness;* temporis, Cic.; rerum, Caes. **II.** *unfairness, injustice, unreasonableness;* hominis, Cic.; iniquitates maximae, Cic.

iniquus -a -um (in and aequus). **I.** *uneven;* 1, lit., locus, Liv.; 2, transf., a, *unfavourable, disadvantageous;* locus, Caes.; defensio angustior et iniquior, *on unfavourable ground,* Cic.; b, of time, *unpropitious;* tempus, Liv.; c, of character, *impatient, discontented;* animo iniquo ferre, with acc., *to be vexed at,* Cic.; animo iniquissimo mori, *to die most reluctantly,* Cic. **II.** *unequal;* 1, lit., *too great;* pondus, Verg.; sol, *too hot,* Verg.; 2, transf., a, *unjust, unfair;* pacem iniqua conditione retinere, Cic.; b, *hostile, adverse;* animo iniquissimo infestissimoque aliquem intueri, Cic.; subst., **iniqui** -orum, m. *enemies,* Cic.; aequi iniqui, or aequi iniquique, *friends and foes,* Liv.

initio, 1. (initium), *to initiate into a secret worship;* aliquem Cereri, Cic.; aliquem Bacchis, *as one of the Bacchantes,* Liv.

initium -ii, n. (ineo), *a beginning, commencement.* **I.** Gen., initium dicendi sumere, Cic.; initium caedis or confligendi facere, Cic.; initium capere ab or ex, etc., Cic.; ab initio, *from the beginning,* Cic.; initio, *in the beginning, at the commencement,* Cic. **II.** Esp., gen. in plur. **A.** *the elements* or *first principles of a science;* initia mathematicorum, Cic. **B.** In natural philosophy, *elements,* Cic. **C.** *the beginning of a reign;* initiis Tiberii auditis, Tac. **D.** *a principle;* initium cognoscendi, Cic. **E.** In plur., *a secret worship, hidden rites, mysteries,* Cic.; and meton., *things used in such rites,* Cat.

initus -us, m. (ineo), 1, *an arrival, entrance,* Lucr.; 2, *a beginning,* Lucr.; 3, *copulation,* Ov.

injectio -onis, f. (injicio), *a laying on;* manus, Quint.

injectus -us, m. (injicio), 1, *a throwing on, throwing over;* injectu multae vestis, Tac.; 2, *a putting in, inserting,* Lucr.

injicio -jeci -jectum, 3. (in and jacio). **I.** *to throw in* or *into, cast* or *put in* or *into;* 1, lit., manum foculo, Liv.; se in medios hostes, *to throw oneself into the midst of the enemy,* Cic.; 2, transf., a, *to cause, inspire, infuse, occasion;* alicui timorem, Cic.; alicui mentem, ut audeat, etc., Cic.; b, in conversation, *to mention,* let drop, throw in; alicui nomen cuiuspiam, Cic.; quum mihi in sermone injecisset, with acc. and infin., Cic. **II.** *to throw* or *place on.* **A.** pontem flumini, Liv.; brachia collo, *to embrace,* Cic.

B. Esp., 1, *to throw* or *cast on;* pallium al, ui, Cic.; sibi vestem, Ov.; vincula animo, Cic.; 2, transf., injicere alicui manus, *to lay hands in;* fig., mihi veritas manum injecit, Cic.; esp., *to lay hands on in order to appropriate what is one's own, to take possession of;* manum virgini venenti, Liv.; fig., manum Parcae, Verg.

injucunde, adv. only in compar. (injucundus), *unpleasantly, in an unfriendly manner;* res injucundius actae, Cic.

injucunditas -tatis, f. (injucundus), *unpleasantness;* ne quid habeat injucunditatis oratio, Cic.

injucundus -a -um, *unpleasant, displeasing;* minime nobis injucundus labor, Cic.; adversus malos injucundus, *unfriendly,* Cic.

injudicatus -a -um (in and judico), *untried, uncondemned, undecided,* Quint.

injungo -junxi -junctum, 3. **I.** *to join to, fasten to;* tignos in asseres, Liv. **II. A.** Lit., *to join, unite, connect with;* vineas et aggerem muro, Liv. **B.** Transf., 1, *to cause;* alicui injuriam, Liv.; 2, *to inflict upon, occasion, bring upon, to lay* or *impose upon, charge, enjoin;* alicui munus, Liv.; civitatibus servitutem, Caes.; alicui laborem, onus, leges, Liv.

injuratus -a -um, *unsworn, not having taken an oath,* Cic.

injuria -ae, f. (injurius), *an injury, injustice, wrong.* **I.** Lit., **A.** injuriam alicui inferre, imponere, facere, Cic.; in aliquem immittere, jacere, *to commit, inflict an injury on,* Cic.; accipere, *to suffer wrong,* Cic.; propulsare, Cic., defendere, Caes., *to repel,* etc.; per injuriam, *wrongfully,* Cic.; injuria, Cic. **B.** 1, *an insult;* spretae formae, Verg.; 2, *legal t.t., damage, harm, injury, affront;* actio injuriarum, Cic. **II.** Meton., 1, *a possession wrongfully obtained;* pertinaces ad obtinendam injuriam, Liv.; 2, *revenge for an affront;* consulis, Liv.

injuriose, adv. (injuriosus), *illegally, wrongfully, injuriously;* in magistratu decernere, Cic.; mercatores injuriosius tractare, Cic.

injuriosus -a -um (injuria), *acting wrongfully, unjust, wrongful, unlawful;* vita, Cic.; injuriosi in proximos, Cic.

injurius -a -um (in and jus), *wrongful, unjust;* quia sit injurium, Cic.

injurus -a -um = injurius (q.v.).

1. **injussus** -a -um (in and jubeo), *uncommanded, unbidden, spontaneous;* gramina virescunt, *without cultivation,* Verg.

2. **injussus**, m. found only in abl. injussu, *without orders;* injussu imperatoris, Cic.; injussu suo, Cic., or simply injussu, *e.g.,* pugnare, Liv.

injuste, adv. (injustus), *unjustly, unfairly;* facere, Cic.

injustitia -ae, f. (injustus), *injustice, unjust proceeding;* totius injustitiae nulla est capitalior, Cic.

injustus -a -um, 1, *unfair, unjust;* homo, Cic.; noverca, *harsh, severe,* Verg.; regna, *unjustly acquired,* Ov.; subst., **injustum** -i, n. *injustice;* metu injusti, Hor.; 2, *heavy, burdensome, oppressive;* onus, Cic.; fascis, Verg.

inl . . . v. ill . . .

inm . . . v. imm . . .

innabilis -e (in and no), *that cannot be swum in;* unda, Ov.

innascor -natus, 3. dep. **I.** *to be born, grow, arise* or *upon;* neglectus filix innascitur agris, Hor.; salicta innata ripiis, Liv. **II.** Transf., *to be produced, arise;* in hac elatione animi cupiditas innascitur, Cic.; partic., **in-**

nātus -a -um, *innate, inborn;* insita quaedam vel potius innata cupiditas, Cic.

innăto, 1. **I.** *to swim into;* in concham hiantem, Cic. **II. A.** *to swim* or *float in* or *upon;* with dat., lactuca acri innatat stomacho, Hor.; with acc., undam innatat alnus, Verg. **B.** Transf., *to flow into* or *over;* innatat unda dulcis freto, Ov.

innātus, partic. of innascor.

innävĭgābĭlis -e, *not navigable,* Liv.

innecto -nexŭi -nexum, 3. *to tie, bind, fasten, weave together.* **I.** Lit., comas, Verg.; fauces laqueo, Ov.; palmas armis, Verg.; inter se innexi rami, Tac. **II.** Transf., **A.** causas morandi, *to bring forward one after the other,* Verg. **B.** Esp., **1,** *to entangle, implicate;* innexus conscientiae alicuius, Tac.; **2,** *to connect;* Hyrcanis per affinitatem innexus erat, Tac.

innitor -nixus sum, 3. dep. *to lean upon, rest upon, support oneself by.* **I.** Lit., scutis, Caes.; hastā, Liv.; alis, *to fly,* Ov. **II.** Transf., univiro, Messio, fortuna hostium innititur, Liv.

inno, 1. *to swim in* or *on.* **I.** fluitantes et innantes beluae, Cic.; with dat., aquae, Liv.; with acc., fluvium, Verg. **II.** a, *to flow over,* Hor.; b, *to sail over, navigate;* Stygios lacus, Verg.

innŏcens -entis, *harmless, not hurtful.* **I.** Lit., innocentis pocula Lesbii, Hor. **II.** Transf., **A.** epistola, Cic. **B.** *innocent, harmless, inoffensive, blameless;* innocens is dicitur qui nihil nocet, Cic.; factorum, Tas.

innŏcentĕr, adv. (innocens), *innocently, blamelessly, inoffensively, irreproachably;* innocentius agere, Tac.

innŏcentĭa -ae, f. (innocens). **I.** *harmlessness;* ferorum animalium, Plin. **II.** *innocence, blamelessness, inoffensiveness, disinterestedness,* Cic.; meton., = *the innocent;* innocentiam judiciorum poenā liberare, Cic.

innŏcŭē, adv. (innocuus), *harmlessly, innocently;* vivere, Ov.

innŏcŭus -a -um. **I.** Act., *innocuous, harmless.* **A.** Lit., herba, Ov.; litus, *safe,* Verg. **B.** Transf., *innocent, harmless, blameless;* homo, Ov. **II.** Passive, *unhurt, unharmed;* carinae, Verg.

innŏtesco -nōtŭi, 3. *to become known* or *noted;* nostris innotuit illa libellis, Ov.; quod ubi innotuit, Liv.

innŏvo, 1. *to renew;* se ad suam intemperantiam, *to return to,* Cic.

innoxĭus -a -um. **I.** Act. **A.** *innoxious, harmless;* anguis, Verg. **B.** Transf., *innocent;* criminis innoxia, Liv. **II.** Pass., **A.** *unhurt, unharmed;* ipsi innoxii, Sall. **B.** *undeserved;* paupertas, Tac.

innūbĭlus -a -um, *unclouded, clear,* Lucr.

innūbo -nupsi -nuptum, 3. *to marry into, connect oneself with by marriage;* quo innupsisset Liv.

innūbus -a -um (in and nubo), *unmarried, without a husband;* Sibylla, Ov.; laurus (because Daphne, while still a virgin, was changed into a laurel), Ov.

innŭmĕrābĭlis -e, *that cannot be counted, innumerable;* multitudo, Cic.

innŭmĕrābĭlĭtas -atis, f. (innumerabilis), *an infinite number, innumerableness;* mundorum, Cic.

innŭmĕrābĭlĭtĕr, adv. (innumeraBilis), *innumerably,* Cic.

innŭmĕrālis -e, *countless, innumerable,* Lucr.

innŭmĕrus -a -um, *countless, innumerable;* gentes, Verg.

innŭo -ŭi, 3. *to give a nod to, make a sign ot signal to;* alicui, Plaut., Ter.; ubi innuerint, Liv.

innuptus -a -um (in and nubo), 1, *unmarried, having no husband,* Verg.; subst., **innupta** -ae, f. *a virgin, young damsel,* Verg.; 2, meton., nuptiae innuptae (γάμος ἄγαμος), *a marriage that is no marriage, an unhappy marriage;* ap. Cic.

innūtrĭo, 4. *to bring up, educate with* or *among;* innutritus pessimis, Tac.

Īnō -ūs and -ōnis, f. (Ἰνώ), *daughter of Cadmus, wife of Athamas;* adj., **Īnōus** -a -um, *of* or *belonging to Ino.*

ĭnoblītus -a -um (in and obliviscor), *mindful, not forgetful,* Ov.

ĭnobrŭtus -a -um (in and obruo), *not overwhelmed,* Ov.

ĭnobservābĭlis -e, *not to be observed, imperceptible,* Cat.

ĭnobservantĭa -ae, f. *negligence, carelessness, inattention,* Suet.

ĭnobservātus -a -um, *unobserved, unperceived;* sidera, Ov.

ĭnŏcŭlātĭo -ōnis, f. *an engrafting,* Plin.

ĭnŏdōror, 1. dep., *to trace out anything, to smell out,* Cic. (?).

ĭnŏdōrus -a -um, *without smell, inodorous,* Pers.

ĭnoffensus -a -um, *without stumbling, unrestrained, unhindered, unobstructed;* mare, Verg.; cursus honorum, *uninterrupted,* Tac.

ĭnoffĭcĭōsus -a -um, 1, *contrary to* or *neglectful of duty;* testamentum, *in which the nearest relatives are passed over,* Cic.; 2, *disobliging;* in aliquem, Cic.

ĭnōlens -entis, *without smell, inodorous,* Lucr.

ĭnōlesco -ŏlēvi -ŏlĭtum, 3. *to grow in* or *on;* 1, lit., udo libro, Verg.; 2, transf., penitusque necesse est multa (mala) diu concreta modis inolescere miris, Verg.

ĭnōmĭnātus -a -um (in and omen), *illomened, unlucky,* Hor.

ĭnŏpĭa -ae, f. (inops). **I.** *want, need;* in Rhodiorum inopia (*want of food*) et fame, Cic.; frumentaria, Caes.; with genit., frugum, Cic.; transf., consilii, Cic. **II.** *helplessness,* Cic.

ĭnŏpīnans -antis, *not expecting, unexpected, unawares;* aliquem inopinantem aggredi, Caes.

ĭnŏpīnantĕr (inopinans), *unexpectedly,* Suet.

ĭnŏpīnātō, adv. (inopinatus), *unexpectedly,* Liv.

ĭnŏpīnātus -a -um. **I.** Pass., *unexpected, unlooked for;* res, Cic.; malum, Caes.; subst., **ĭnŏpīnātum** -i, n. *an unexpected event,* Cic.; ex inopinato, Cic., inopinato, Liv., *unexpectedly.* **II.** Act., *not expecting;* inopinatos invadere, Liv.

ĭnŏpīnus -a -um (in and opinus, from opinor), *unexpected, unlooked for;* visus, Ov.; quies, Verg.

ĭnŏpĭōsus -a -um (inopia), *needy, in want of;* consilii, Plaut.

ĭnopportūnus -a -um, *inopportune, unseasonable,* Cic.

ĭnops -ŏpis. **I.** *without means.* **A.** *poor;* 1, a, lit., aerarium inops et exhaustum, Cic.; b, transf., *poor in words* or *thoughts;* lingua, oratio, Cic.; 2, *poor in something, wanting in;* with genit. or abl., or ab and the abl., pecuniae, Liv.; verborum, verbis, Cic.; amicorum, ab amicis, Cic.; transf., humanitatis, Cic. **B.** *powerless, weak,* Liv. **II.** *helpless;* inopes relicti a duce, Cic.

ĭnōrātus -a -um (in and oro), *not formally brought forward and heard;* re inoratā, Cic.

ĭnordĭnātus -a -um, *disorderly, in confusion;* dispersi, inordinati exibant, Liv.; subst., **ĭnordĭnātum** -i, n. *disorder;* ex inordinato in ordinem adducere, Cic.

ĭnŏrĭor, 4. dep., *to arise, appear,* Tac (?)

ĭnornātus -a -um, *unadorned.* **I.** Lit., mulieres, Cic. **II.** Transf., **A.** orator, Cic. **B.** *unpraised, uncelebrated,* Hor.

inp . . . = imp . . . (q.v.).

inquam -is -it, perf., inquii, v. def. (connected with ἐνέπω), *I say;* a, in quoting the words of a speaker, est vero, inquam, signum, Cic.; with dat., inquit mihi, Cic.; b, in repetition, for the sake of emphasis, hunc unum diem, hunc unum, inquam, diem, Cic.; c, in objections, non solemus, inquit, ostendere, Cic. (The forms found are: inquam, Cic.; inquit, Cic.; inquimus, Hor.; inquiunt, Cic.; inquiebat, Cic.; inquii, Cat.; inquisti, Cic.; inquies, Cat.; inquiet, Cic.; inque, Plaut.; inquito, Plaut.)

1. **inquĭes** -ētis, f. *disquiet, want of rest,* Plin.

2. **inquĭes** -ētis, *unquiet, restless;* homo, Sall.; nox, dies, Tac.

inquĭēto, 1. (inquietus), *to disquiet, disturb;* victoriam, Tac.

inquĭētus -a -um, *unquiet, restless.* **I.** Lit., Hadria, *stormy,* Hor.; nox inquieta, Liv. **II.** Transf., a, *restless in disposition;* inquietus animus, Liv.; b, *politically restless,* Liv.

inquĭlīnus -i, m. *one who dwells in a place not his own, a tenant, lodger;* transf., inquilinus civis Romae (said of Cicero, who was not born in Rome), Sall.

inquĭnātē, adv. (inquinatus), *filthily, impurely;* loqui, Cic.

inquĭnātus -a -um, p. adj. (from inquino), *dirtied, befouled, defiled, polluted, contaminated, sordid, shameful;* homo vita omni inquinatus, Cic.; sermo inquinatissimus, Cic.

inquĭno, 1. (connected with coenum), *to befoul, pollute, defile, stain, contaminate;* 1, lit., aqua turbida et cadaveribus inquinata, Cic.; aquas venenis, Ov.; 2, transf., *to corrupt, defile;* omnem splendorem honestatis, Cic.; se parricidio, Cic.

inquīro -quīsīvi -quīsītum, 3. (in and quaero). **I.** *to seek for, search for;* corpus alicuius, Liv. **II. A.** *to investigate, inquire into;* diligenter in ea, Cic.; in eum quid agat, quem ad modum vivat, inquiritur, Cic.; omnia ordine, Liv. **B.** Legal t. t., *to search for evidence against any one;* in competitores, Cic. (pluperf. subj., inquisissent, Liv.; perf. infin., inquisisse, Liv.).

inquīsītĭo -ōnis, f. (inquiro). **I.** *a searching after, looking for;* corporum, Plin. **II. A.** *investigation, inquiry;* veri inquisitio atque investigatio, Cic. **B.** Legal t. t., *the search for evidence against any one;* candidati, *against a candidate,* Cic.

inquīsītor -ōris, m. (inquiro), *an inquirer.* **I.** *a spy,* Suet. **II. A.** Philosoph. t. t., *an investigator;* rerum, Cic. **B.** *one who searches for evidence to support an accusation,* Cic.

inr . . . v. irr . . .

insălūbris -e, 1, *unhealthy,* Plin.; 2, *unserviceable, unprofitable,* Plin.

insălūtātus -a -um, *ungreeted, of whom no farewell has been taken;* in the tmesis, inque salutatam linquo, Verg.

insānābĭlis -e, *incurable;* 1, lit., morbus, Cic.; 2, transf., contumeliae, Cic.

insānē, adv. (insanus), *madly, insanely;* in silvam ne ligna feras insanius, Hor.

insānĭa -ae, f. (insanus), *madness, loss of reason, insanity;* 1, a, lit., nomen insaniae significat mentis aegrotationem et morbum, Cic.; concupiscere aliquid ad insaniam, *madly,* Cic.; b, transf., *mad desire, mad, senseless excess, senseless extravagance;* libidinum, Cic.; 2, *poetical rapture or inspiration;* amabilis, Hor.

insānĭo -īvi and -ĭi -ītum, 4. (insanus), *to rage, be seized with madness or frenzy;* a, lit. ex injuria, Liv.; nisi ego insanio, Cic.; of things, insaniens Bosporus, *raging,* Hor.; b, transf., *to act like a madman, to rave;* insanit statuas emendo, Hor.; with acc., similem (errorem), Hor.; sollemnia, *to be fashionably mad,* Hor.

insānĭtas -ātis, f. (insanus), *mental disease, insanity,* Cic.

insānus -a -um. **I.** *of unsound mind, mad, insane.* **A.** Lit., Cic. **B.** 1, *acting like a madman, raging, senseless;* homo flagitiis insanus, Cic.; contio, Cic.; of things, a, *raging;* fluctus Verg.; b, *of great size or violence;* moles, Cic.; cupiditas insanior, Cic.; 2, *inspired;* vates, Verg. **II.** Act., *making mad;* aqua, Ov.

insătĭābĭlis -e (in and satio). **I.** Pass., *that cannot be satisfied, insatiable;* cupiditas, Cic. **II.** Act., *that does not satiate, uncloying, unwearying;* pulchritudo, Cic.; insatiabilior species, Cic.

insătĭābĭlĭtĕr, adv. (insatiabilis), *insatiably,* Lucr.

insătĭĕtas -ātis, f. *insatiableness,* Plaut.

insătūrābĭlis -e (in and saturo), *insatiable;* abdomen, Cic.

insătūrābĭlĭtĕr, adv. (insaturabilis), *insatiably,* Cic.

inscalpo, 1. *to engrave,* Plin.

inscendo -scendi -scensum, 3. (in and scando), *to ascend, mount, go up;* in rogum ardentem, Cic.; navem, Plaut.

inscensĭo -ōnis, f. (inscendo), *a going on board;* in navem, Plaut.

inscĭens -entis, *ignorant, unaware;* me insciente factum, *done without my knowledge,* Cic.

inscĭentĕr, adv. (insciens), *ignorantly, stupidly, foolishly;* facere, Cic.

inscĭentĭa -ae, f. (insciens), 1, *ignorance, inexperience, want of acquaintance with;* inscientia mea, nostra, Cic.; foll. by genit. of the subject, vulgi, Caes.; of the object, locorum, Caes.; dicendi, Cic.; 2, philosoph. t. t., *want of certain knowledge* (opp. scientia), Cic.

inscītē, adv. (inscitus), *clumsily, awkwardly, unskilfully;* inscite aliquid comparare cum aliqua re, Cic.

inscītĭa -ae, f. (inscitus), 1, *clumsiness, awkwardness, inexperience, ignorance;* with genit. of subject, barbarorum, Cic.; of object, negotii gerendi, Cic.; disserendi, Cic.; 2, *ignorance, stupidity;* legionum, Tac.; erga domum suam, Tac.

inscītus -a -um, *ignorant, unskilful, absurd, silly;* quid autem est inscitius quam, etc., Cic.

inscĭus -a -um, *ignorant, not knowing;* medici inscii imperitique, Cic.; followed by gen., omnium rerum, Cic.; culpae, *free from,* Verg.; equus inscius aevi, *not confident of its strength,* Verg.; with rel. sent., inscii quid in Aeduis gereretur, Caes.

inscrībo -scripsi -scriptum, 3. **I.** *to write in or on, inscribe;* 1, lit., aliquid in basi tropaeorum, Cic.; nomen monumentis, Cic.; librum, *to give a title to a book,* Cic.; fig., *to impress;* orationem in animo, Cic.; 2, transf., a, *to assign;* sibi nomen philosophi, *to assume*, Cic. ; b, *to ascribe ;* deos sceleri, *to charge the gods with crime*, Ov. II. A. *to give an inscription or title to ;* inscribo epistolam patri, *to address*, Cic. ; liber qui Oeconomicus inscribitur, *is entitled*, Cic. ; flores inscripti nomina regum, *marked with*, Verg. ; versā pulvis inscribitur hastā, *is marked with*, Verg. B. *to brand*, Juv.

inscriptĭo -ōnis, f. (inscribo), *a writing in or upon ;* 1, nominis, Cic. ; 2, *the inscription on a statue, the title of a book*, Cic.

1. **inscriptus** -a -um (in and scribo), *unwritten*, Quint.

2. **inscriptus** -a -um, partic. of inscribo.

insculpo -sculpsi -sculptum, 3. *to cut or carve in, engrave ;* 1, lit., summam patrimonii saxo, Hor. ; foedus columnā aeneā, Liv. ; 2, transf., *to impress ;* natura insculpsit in mentibus, Cic.

insĕcābĭlis -e, *that cannot be cut, inseparable, indivisible*, Quint.

insĕco -sĕcŭi -sectum, 1. *to cut into, cut to pieces ;* gurguliones, Cic. ; cutem, *to make an incision in*, Liv.

insectātĭo -ōnis, f. (insector), 1, lit., *a following, pursuit*, Liv. ; 2, transf., *railing at, deriding, insulting ;* alicuius, Liv.

insectātor -ōris, m. (insector), *a pursuer, persecutor ;* plebis, Liv.

insector, 1. dep., *to follow, pursue ;* 1, lit., aquila insectans alias aves, Cic. ; 2, transf., *to pursue with harsh words, reproach, inveigh against, rail at ;* aliquem maledictis, Cic. ; audaciam improborum, Cic.

insēdābĭlĭtĕr, adv. (in and sedo), *inextinguishably, unquenchably*, Lucr.

insĕnesco -sĕnŭi, 3. *to grow old at or among ;* libris et curis, Hor.

insensĭlis -e, *insensible, imperceptible*, Lucr.

1. **insĕpultus** -a -um (partic. of insepelio).

2. **insĕpultus** -a -um (in and sepelio), *unburied ;* acervi civium, Cic. ; aliquem insepultum projicere, Liv. ; sepultura, *burial without the customary solemnities*, Cic.

insĕquor -sĕcūtus or -sĕquūtus sum, 3. *to follow after, follow on, succeed.* I. A. Lit., insequitur acies ornata armataque, Liv. ; with acc., temere insecutae Orphea silvae, Hor. B. Transf., a, mors insecuta est Gracchum, *overtook*, Cic. ; b, of time, *to follow ;* hunc proximo saeculo Themistocles insecutus est, Cic. ; annus insequens, Liv. ; c, *to pursue a subject ;* insequar longius, Cic. II. *to follow or pursue with hostile intent.* A. Lit., aliquem gladio stricto, Cic. ; clamore et minis, Cic. B. Transf., a, *to press hard ;* homines benevolos contumeliā, Cic. ; b, *to censure, reproach, attack ;* aliquem irridendo, Cic. ; vitae eius turpitudinem, Cic.

1. **insĕro** -sēvi -situm, 3. 1, *to sow in, plant in*, Plin. ; 2, *to implant ;* inserit novas opiniones, evellit insitas, Cic. ; partic., **insĭtus** -a -um, *implanted, innate, inborn ;* insitus menti cognitionis amor, Cic. ; 3, *to unite ;* corpora animis, Cic.

2. **insĕro** -sĕrŭi -sertum, 3. *to put, place, set in, insert.* I. Lit., collum in laqueum, Cic. ; oculos in alicuius pectora, *to fix the gaze upon*, Ov. II. Transf. A. Meton., *to introduce, insert into, intermingle with ;* jocos historiae, Ov. ; deos minimis rebus, Liv. ; se alicui rei, *to meddle with*, Ov. B. *to incorporate with, place among ;* aliquem vatibus, Hor.

insertim, adv. *by insertion*, Lucr.

inserto, 1. (intens. of 2. insero), *to insert, put into ;* clypeo sinistram, Verg.

inservĭo, 4. *to serve.* I. Lit., *as a vassal or subject*, reges inservientes, Tac. II. Transf., *to serve.* A. *to be devoted to, to pay attention to ;* alicui, Cic. ; nihil est inservitum a me temporis causā, Cic. B. *to be devoted to a thing, to take care of ;* inservi (valetudini), Cic.

insessus, partic. of insideo and insido.

insĭbĭlo, 1. *to hiss, pipe, whistle in*, Ov.

insĭdĕo -sēdi -sessum, 2. (in and sedeo). I. Intransit., *to sit upon.* A. Lit., a, with dat., or abl., immani et vastae beluae, Cic. ; equo, Cic. ; b, *to have one's seat or place* (of the Penates), Cic. B. Transf., a, insidens capulo manus, *resting upon*, Tac. ; b, *to be settled, to dwell, remain ;* insidet quaedam in optimo quoque virtus, Cic. II. Transit., a, *to take possession of, occupy ;* locum, Liv. ; b, *to inhabit ;* ea loca, Tac.

insĭdĭae -ārum, f. (insideo), *an ambush.* I. Lit., a, insidias locare, Liv. ; collocare, Caes. ; b, of the place of ambush, milites in insidiis collocare, Caes. II. Transf., a, *a snare, trap, treachery, deceit, plot ;* insidias vitae ponere or facere, Cic. ; insidias ponere contra aliquem, Cic. ; insidias alicui parare, Cic. ; insidias opponere, tendere, collocare, struere, adhibere, comparare, Cic. ; insidias componere, Tac. ; per insidias, ex insidiis, or insidiis, *treacherously*, Cic. ; b, *illusion, deception ;* noctis, Verg.

insĭdĭātor -ōris, m. (insidior), *a spy, waylayer, lurker, traitor*, Cic. ; viae, Cic.

insĭdĭor, 1. dep. (insidiae). I. *to lie in ambush against, lie in wait for*, Caes. ; hostibus, Ov. ; ovili, Verg. II. a, *to plot against the life of ;* alicui, Cic. ; b, *to watch for, wait for ;* somno maritorum, Cic. ; tempori, *to wait for the fitting opportunity*, Liv.

insĭdĭose, adv. with superl. (insidiosus), *deceitfully, treacherously, insidiously*, Cic.

insĭdĭōsus -a -um (insidiae), *deceitful, cunning, treacherous, full of snares ;* a, of inanimate objects, insidiosus et plenus latronum locus, Cic. ; clementia alicuius, Cic. ; b, of persons, quis insidiosior ? Cic.

insīdo -sēdi -sessum, 3. *to sit, settle, perch upon.* I. floribus (of bees), Verg. ; digitos membris, *sink into*, Ov. II. A. *to settle, dwell ;* jugis, Verg. ; with acc., cineres patriae, Verg. B. 1, *to beset a place, take up one's post at ;* with dat., silvestribus locis, Liv. ; with acc., tumulos, Liv. ; of things, semen in locis insedit, *takes root in*, Cic. ; 2, transf., *to sink deep ;* in animo, Cic.

insignē -is, n. (insignis), *a signal, token.* A. Gen., Cic. ; nocturnum, *a night-signal*, Liv. B. Esp., 1, *the official badge of a magistracy ;* insigne regium, Cic. ; more commonly plur., insignia, *badges, insignia ;* imperatoris, Caes. ; sacerdotum, Liv. ; regia, Cic. ; transf., insignia virtutis, laudis, Cic. ; 2, orationis lumina et quoddammodo insignia, *beauties*, Liv.

insignĭo, 4. (insignis), 1, *to put a mark, sign, or token upon, to impress ;* in animis tamquam insignitae notae veritatis, Cic. ; 2, a, *to distinguish ;* aliquem notā, Liv. ; cum omnis annus funeribus et cladibus insigniretur, *was remarkable for*, Tac. ; b, *to adorn ;* agros tropaeis, Verg. ; clipeum Io auro insignibat, Verg.

insignis -e (in and signum), *distinguished by a token, remarkable, noted, notable ;* 1, lit., bos maculis insignis, Verg. ; uxores insignes auro et purpurā, Liv. ; Phoebus insignis crinibus, Ov. ; insignis ad deformitatem, *remarkably ugly*, Cic. ; 2, transf., *remarkable, eminent, distinguished, extraordinary ;* improbitas, Cic. ; virtus Scipionis, Cic. ; insigne ad irridendum vitium, Cic.

insignītē, adv. with compar. (insignitus), *remarkably, extraordinarily*, Cic.

insignĭtĕr, adv. with compar. (insignis), *remarkably, extraordinarily,* Cic.

insignītus -a -um (p. adj. from insignio), **1,** *marked so as to be known, noticeable, plain;* imago, Cic.; notae veritatis, Cic.; **2,** *striking, remarkable, unexampled;* imagines, Cic.; insignitior contumelia, Liv.

insĭlĕ -is, n. *the spool* or *bobbin* on which the yarn was twisted in weaving, Lucr.

insĭlĭo -sĭlŭi -sultum, 4. (in and salio), *to leap, spring, jump in* or *on;* in phalangas, Caes.; in equum, Liv.; tergo, Ov.; with accus., Aetnam, Hor.; undas, Ov. (perf. insilivit, Liv.)

insĭmŭlātĭo -ōnis, f. (insimulo), *an accusation, charge;* probrorum, Cic.

insĭmŭlo, 1. *to charge, accuse, blame;* with acc. of pers., aliquem falso, Cic.; with accus. and infin., quod eos insimulemus omnia incerta dicere, Cic.; with acc. of pers. and genit., se peccati quod, etc., Cic.; with simple acc., quod ego insimulo, Cic.

insincērus -a -um, *tainted, putrefying;* cruor, Verg.

insĭnŭātĭo -ōnis, f. (insinuo), rhet. t.t., *the gaining the favour of the audience,* Cic.

insĭnŭo, 1. *to introduce by windings* or *turnings, to insinuate.* **A.** Lit., Romani quacumque data intervalla essent, insinuabant ordines suos, *pushed forward their files into the gaps of the enemy,* Liv.; refl., se insinuare, or simply insinuare, and middle insinuari, *to penetrate, work one's way in, to insinuate oneself,* insinuare in forum, Cic.; se inter equitum turmas, Caes.; qua se inter valles flumen insinuat, Liv. **B.** Transf., se in familiaritatem alicuius, Cic.; insinuare se in philosophiam, Cic.; se insinuare, or insinuare alicui, *to gain the good will of,* Cic.; penitus in causam, *to get to know thoroughly,* Cic.

insĭpĭens -entis (in and sapiens), *foolish, stupid,* Cic.

insĭpĭentĕr, adv. (insipiens), *foolishly, stupidly,* Plaut.

insĭpĭentĭa -ae, f. (insipiens), *foolishness, stupidity,* Cic.

insisto -stĭti, 3. **I.** *to stand on, set foot on, tread on, place oneself on.* **A.** Lit., **1,** cingulus lunae in quo qui insistunt, etc., Cic.; digitis, *to stand on the tip of one's toes,* Ov.; limen, Verg.; pedum primis vestigia plantis, Cic.; insistere vestigiis alicuius, *to tread in the steps of* (fig.), Cic.; **2,** esp., **a,** *to enter on a journey, pursue;* iter, Liv.; **b,** *to follow hard on;* referentibus pedem, Liv. **B.** Transf., **1,** perge tenere istam viam quam institisti, Cic.; **2,** esp., *to follow any object* or *occupation eagerly, persist in;* totus et mente et animo in bellum insistit, Caes.; with acc., rationem belli, *to follow out the plan of the war,* Caes.; munus, Cic.; with dat., ei rei, Liv. **II.** *to remain still, stand still.* **A.** Lit., stellae insistunt, Cic. **B.** Transf., **1, a,** *to stop, pause;* in speech, quae quum dixisset paulumque institisset, "Quid est," inquit, Cic.; **b,** *to pause over, dwell upon;* singulis peccatorum gradibus, Cic.; **2,** *to be fixed* or *obstinate in;* importune, Cic.; crudelitati, Tac.; with infin., sequi, Cic.; **3,** *to be at a stand* = *to doubt;* in reliquis rebus, Cic.

insĭtĭcĭus -a -um (1. insero), *engrafted, foreign,* Plin.

insĭtĭo -ōnis, f. (1. insero), **1,** *a grafting, budding;* plur., insitiones, *the kinds of grafting,* Cic.; **2,** meton., *the grafting season,* Ov.

insĭtīvus -a -um (1. insero), *grafted, engrafted;* **1,** lit., pira, Hor.; **2,** transf.. **a.**

foreign; quaedam disciplinae, Cic.; **b,** *suppositiuous, not genuine,* Phaedr.

insĭtor -ōris, m. (1. insero), *a grafter,* Prop.

insĭtus -a -um, partic. of 1. insero.

insŏcĭābĭlis -e, *that cannot be joined together, unsociable, unsocial;* gens, Liv.; with dat., homines generi humano insociabiles, Liv.

insōlābĭlĭtĕr, adv. (in and solor), *inconsolably,* Hor.

insŏlens -entis (in and soleo). **I.** *unusual, contrary to custom;* quid tu Athenas insolens? Ter. **II. A.** *unaccustomed to, unused to;* infamiae, Cic.; in dicendo, Cic. **B. 1,** *unusual, extravagant;* verbum, Cic.; **2,** of behaviour, **a,** *prodigal;* non fuisse insolentem in pecunia, Cic.; **b,** *proud, haughty, arrogant, insolent;* exercitus, *flushed with victory,* Hor.; ostentatio, Cic.

insŏlentĕr, adv. (insolens), **1,** *unusually, in a way contrary to custom;* evenire vulgo soleat, an insolenter et raro, Cic.; **2, a,** *immoderately, excessively;* his festivitatibus insolentius abuti, Cic.; **b,** *haughtily, arrogantly, insolently;* se efferre, Cic.

insŏlentĭa -ae, f. (insolens). **I.** *the not being accustomed to a thing, inexperience in, strangeness;* huius disputationis, Cic. **II. A.** *strangeness, affectation, novelty of diction;* verborum, Cic. **B.** *extravagance, profuseness,* Cic. **C.** *pride, arrogance, insolence,* Cic.

insŏlesco, 3. (in and soleo), **a,** *to behave extravagantly;* magis insolescente Plancinā, Tac.; **b,** *to become haughty* or *insolent, be elated;* per licentiam insolescere animum humanum, Sall.

insŏlĭdus -a -um, *weak, soft, tender;* herba, Ov.

insŏlĭtus -a -um. **I.** Act., *unaccustomed to;* ad laborem, Caes.; with genit., rerum bellicarum, Sall. **II.** Pass., **a,** *unusual, strange;* haec insolita mihi ex hoc loco ratio dicendi, Cic.; **b,** *uncommon, unusual;* insolita mihi loquacitas, Cic.; verbum, Cic.

insŏlūbĭlis -e, **1,** *that cannot be paid,* Sen.; **2,** *incontrovertible, indubitable,* Quint.

insomnĭa -ae, f. (insomnis), *sleeplessness, loss of sleep;* gen. in plur., insomniis carere, Cic.

insomnis -e (in and somnus), *sleepless;* insomnes magis quam pervigiles, Tac.; draco, Ov.; of things, nox, Verg.

1. insomnĭum -ĭi, n. (in and somnus), *sleeplessness,* Plin.

2. insomnĭum -ĭi, n. (in and somnus), *a dream;* sing., Tac.; plur., Verg.

insŏno -sŏnŭi -sŏnĭtum, 1. **I.** Intransit., *to make a noise, in sound, resound;* insonuere cavernae, Verg.; flagello, *to crack a whip,* Verg. **II.** Transit., *to make to sound;* verbera, Verg.

insons -sontis, 1, *innocent, guiltless;* insontes sicut sontes circumvenire, Sall.; 2, poet., transf., *harmless;* Cerberus, Hor.

insŏpītus -a -um (in and sopio), *not lulled to sleep, wakeful, watchful;* draco, Ov.

inspargo = inspergo (q.v.).

inspecto, 1. (intens. of inspicio), *to look at* or *in, observe, view;* inspecta spolia Samnitium, Liv.; inspectante exercitu interfici, Cic.

inspērans -antis (in and spero), *not hoping, not expecting;* insperanti mihi sed valde optanti cecidit ut, etc., Cic.

inspērātō, adv. (insperatus), *unexpectedly,* Plaut.

inspērātus -a -um (in and spero), *unhoped for, unexpected;* pecuniae, Cic.; malum. Cic.; ex insperato, *unexpectedly,* Liv.

inspergo and **inspargo**, -spersi (-sparsi), -spersum (-sparsum), 3. (in and spargo). **I.** *to strew, sprinkle in* or *on;* molam et vinum, Cic. **II.** *to besprinkle,* Plin.

inspĭcĭo -spexi -spectum, 3. (in and specio). **I.** *to look, see in* or *on.* **A.** Lit., **1,** faciem, Ov.; speculum, Phaedr. ; **2,** *to look into, read;* leges, Cic.; verba, Ov. **B.** Transf., *to examine, look into, become acquainted with;* aliquem a puero, Cic. **II.** *to contemplate, view, observe;* **1,** gen., signum publicum, Cic. ; **2,** esp., a, as buyer, *to inspect;* candelabrum, Cic. ; b, as a messenger, *to investigate;* sociorum res, Liv. ; c, as an inspector, milit. t. t., *to inspect;* arma militis, Cic. ; viros, Liv. ; d, as a sacrificer, fibras, Ov. ; e, as a spy, domos, Verg.

inspĭco, 1. *to sharpen a point,* Verg.

inspīro, 1. 1, intransit., *to breathe upon, to blow upon;* conchae, Ov. ; 2, transit., a, lit., *to breathe, blow in* or *on ;* venenum morsibus, Verg. ; b, transf., *to breathe into, inspire, rouse, inflame;* alicui occultum ignem, Verg.

inspŏlĭātus -a -um (in and spolio), *not despoiled, not plundered ;* arma, Verg.

inspŭo -spŭi -spūtum, 3. *to spit in* or *upon,* Plin.

inspūto, 1. *to spit upon,* Plaut.

instăbĭlis -e. **I.** Act., **A.** *that does not stand firm, unstable, tottering ;* pedes instabilis ac vix vado fidens, Liv. **B.** Transf., a, *unsteady, not keeping its ground;* hostis instabilis ad conferendas manus, Liv. ; b, *unstable, inconstant, changeable ;* motus, Caes.; animus, Verg. **II.** Pass., *on which it is impossible to stand, insecure;* tellus, Ov.

instăbĭlĭtas -ātis, f. (instabilis), *instability,* Plin.

instans -antis, p. adj. (from insto), **1,** *present ;* subst., **instans** -antis, n. *the immediate present,* Cic. ; **2,** *pressing, urgent ;* instantior cura, Tac.

instantĕr, adv. (instans), *urgently, earnestly, vehemently ;* instantius concurrere, Tac.

instantĭa -ae, f. (insto), *the present time,* Cic.

instar, n. indecl., *an image, likeness, picture, sketch ;* a, quantum instar in ipso l *what an imposing presence,* Verg.; gen. with genit., *like to, as great as, after the fashion of ;* navis cybaea maxima triremis instar, Cic. ; instar montis equus, Verg. ; instar alicuius or alicuius rei esse, *instar habere, instar obtinere, to be like, to be as good as, to be in the place of ;* Erana quae fuit non vici instar sed urbis, Cic. ; Plato mihi unus est instar omnium, Cic. ; alicuius rei instar putare or reri, *to think a thing as good as, consider it equal to ;* idque si accidat, mortis instar putemus, Cic. ; b, of number, *as many as, as large as ;* cohortes quaedam quod instar legionis videretur, Caes.

instaurātĭo -ōnis, f. (instauro), *repetition, renewal ;* ludorum, Cic.

instaurātīvus -a -um (instauro), *renewed, repeated ;* ludi, Cic.

instauro, 1. (in and *stauro from sto, stare). **I.** *to renew, repeat, begin anew ;* 1, a, of public solemnities and ceremonies, sacrificium, Cic. ; b, of any kind of action, scelus, caedem, Cic. ; novum de integro bellum, Liv.; 2, a, *to reanimate, restore ;* instaurati (sunt) animi, Verg. ; b, *to repay, requite ;* talia Graiis, Verg. **II.** *to set about, prepare ;* choros, Verg.

insterno -strāvi -strātum, 3. **I.** *to strew over, cover over ;* equum, *to saddle* or *cover with a saddle-cloth,* Liv. **II.** *to spread over ;* modicis tignis, Hor.

instīgātor -ōris, m. (instigo), *an instigator, stimulator ;* sibi quisque dux et instigator, Tac.

instīgātrix -trīcis, f. (instigator), *she that instigates,* Tac.

instigo, 1. (in and STIG-o = στίζω whence also instinguo), *to instigate, incite, stimulate;* aliquem in aliquem, Liv. ; absol., instigante te, *at your instigation,* Cic.

instillātĭo -ōnis, f. (instillo), *a dropping into,* Plin.

instillo, 1. *to drop in, pour in by drops;* oleum lumini, Cic. ; transf., *to instil ;* praeceptum auriculis, Hor.

instĭmŭlātor -ōris, m. (instimulo), *an instigator ;* seditionis, Cic.

instĭmŭlo, 1. *to stimulate, arouse, incite,* Ov.

instinctor -ōris, m. (instinguo), *an inciter, instigator ;* sceleris, Tac.

instinctus -ūs, m. (instinguo), *instigation, incitement ;* instinctu divino, Cic.

instinguo -stinxi -stinctum, 3. (in and STIG-o = στίζω, whence also instigo), *to instigate, incite ;* gen. in partic., **instinctus** -a -um, *incited, impelled ;* furore, Cic.

instĭpŭlor, 1. dep., *to stipulate* or *bargain for,* Plaut.

instĭta -ae, f. *a seam, border,* or *flounce on a lady's robe ;* meton., *a lady ;* nulla, Ov.

institĭo -ōnis, f. (insisto), *a standing still ;* stellarum, Cic.

instĭtor -ōris, m. (insto), *a broker, factor, huckster, pedlar ;* mercis, Liv.

instĭtōrĭum -ii, n. (institor), *the business of a hawker,* Suet.

instĭtŭo -ŭi -ūtum, 3. (in and statuo). **I.** *to put* or *place into ;* vestigia nuda sinistri pedis, Verg. **II.** *to arrange.* **A.** Lit., **1,** milit. t. t., *draw up in order ;* aciem duplicem, Caes. ; **2,** *to prepare, make ready, build, construct ;* turrim, pontes, naves, Caes. ; vineas, Cic. ; dapes, Verg. **B.** Transf., **1,** *to make arrangements for, begin, undertake ;* historiam, Cic. ; iter, Cic. ; with infin., *to resolve upon, determine ;* oppidum oppugnare, Cic. ; historias scribere, Nep. ; **2,** a, *to appoint, ordain, establish, introduce, institute ;* portorium, Cic. ; dies festos, Liv. ; ludos, Ov. ; with ut and the subj., *to arrange that,* etc., Cic. ; with infin., Caes. ; b, *to settle, to administer ;* civitates, Cic. ; c, *to instruct, teach, educate for a particular purpose ;* aliquem ad dicendum, Cic.

instĭtūtĭo -ōnis, f. (instituo), **1,** *arrangement ;* rerum, Cic. ; institutionem suam conservare, *method,* Cic. ; **2,** *instruction ;* doctoris, Cic. ; Cynica, *the principles of the Cynic philosophy,* Tac.

instĭtūtum -i, n. (instituo), **1,** *an undertaking, purpose ;* non ad nostrum institutum pertinet, Cic. ; **2,** *an old-established custom, arrangement, institution ;* majorum, Cic. ; institutum vitae capere, *to adopt a rule of life,* Cic. ; ex instituto, *according to custom, order,* Liv. ; **3,** *instruction, precept ;* philosophiae, Cic.

insto -stĭti -stātūrus, 1. **I.** *to stand in* or *on ;* rectam instas viam, Plaut. **II. A.** *to be close to, follow closely ;* 1, lit., vestigiis, Liv. ; 2, transf., a, *to press upon, pursue eagerly, urge, harass ;* absol., Cic. ; with dat., adversario, Cic. ; hosti, Liv. ; b, currum, *to be zealous in building,* Verg. ; *to pursue* or *devote oneself eagerly to anything ;* operi, Verg. ; with following infin., *to persist, not to cease, to persevere ;* poscere recuperatores, Cic. ; c, *to persist, insist, ask pressingly ;* alicui instare ut, with subj., Cic. ; d, of time, *to approach, draw nigh, threaten ;* dies instat quo, etc., Cic. **B.** *to stand upon, be fixed ;* jugis, Verg.

1. instrātus -a -um (in and sterno), *unovered*, Verg.

2. instrātus, partic. of insterno.

instrēnŭus -a -um, *inactive, lazy, idle*, Plaut.

instrĕpo -ŭi -ĭtum, 3. *to make a noise, rattle, clatter, creak;* sub pondere axis instrepat, Verg.

instringo -strinxi -strictum, 3. *to bind;* instricta fides gemmis, Ov.

instructē, adv. with compar. (instructus), *with great preparation;* ludos instructius fecit, Liv.

instructĭo -ōnis, f. (instruo), *a setting in array, drawing up in order;* militum, Cic.

instructor -ōris, m. (instruo), *a preparer;* convivii, Cic.

1. instructus -a -um, p. adj. (from instruo), **1**, *provided with, furnished;* Graecia instructa copiis, Cic.; **2**, *instructed, learned;* in jure civili, Cic.; instructior a jure civili, Cic.

2. instructus -ūs, m. (instruo), *a preparation, provision;* fig. = *matter* (in a speech), while ornatus=*rhetorical ornament*, quocumque (oratio) ingreditur, eodem est instructu ornatuque comitata, Cic.

instrūmentum -i, n. (instruo). **I.** *a tool, implement, instrument;* **a,** sing., instrumentum villae, *implements of husbandry*, Cic.; militare, Caes.; belli, Cic.; **b,** plur., instrumenta anilia, *dress*, Ov. **II.** Transf., **1,** *store, stock;* oratoris, Cic.; **2,** *means to an end;* instrumenta ad obtinendam sapientiam, Cic.

instrŭo -struxi -structum, 3. **I.** *to build in or into;* contabulationes in parietes, Caes. **II. A.** *to set up, build;* muros, Nep. **B.** *to arrange, prepare;* **a,** lit., apud aliquem epulas instruere, Liv.; **b,** transf., instruere fraudem, Liv. **C.** *to furnish, equip, provide;* **1,** gen., **a,** lit., domum suam in provincia, Cic.; domus instructa or aedes instructae, *a furnished house*, Cic.; **b,** transf., accusationem et petitionem adornare atque instruere, Cic.; of persons, aliquem mandatis, Liv.; **2,** esp., **a,** milit. t. t., (α) *to arm;* exercitum, Liv.; (β) *to draw up in order of battle, to post;* exercitum, aciem, Cic.; **b,** *to teach, instruct;* aliquem ad omne officii munus, Cic.

insuāvis -e, *not sweet, unpleasant, disagreeable;* littera insuavissima, *ill-sounding*, Cic.; homo, Hor.; vita, Cic.

Insŭbres -ium and -um, m. *the Insubrians, a people in Cisalpine Gaul*, whose capital was Mediolanum (*Milan*); sing., **Insŭbĕr** -bris, m. *an Insubrian.* Adj., **Insŭbĕr** -bris -bre, *Insubrian.*

Insŭbĕr, v. Insubres.

insŭdo, 1. *to sweat in or at;* libellis insudat manus, Hor.

insŭefactus -a -um (in -sueo and facio), *accustomed to, inured to*, Caes.

insuesco -suēvi -suētum, 3. **I.** Intransit., *to accustom oneself to, to become used tc;* corpori, Tac.; ad disciplinam, Liv.; with infin., victoriā frui, Liv. **II.** Transit., *to accustom, habituate any one to;* insuevit pater hoc me, Hor.

1. insuētus -a -um (in and suesco), **1,** *unaccustomed to, unused to;* with genit., laboris, Caes.; with dat., moribus Romanis, Liv.; with infin., vera audire, Liv.; **2,** pass., *unusual, unwonted;* solitudo, Liv.; poet., insueta (neut. plur.) as adv., *unusually;* rudere, Verg.

2. insuētus -a -um, partic. of insuesco.

insŭla -ae, f. **1,** *an island*, Cic.; **2,** *a detached house* or *building, let out to several poor families*, Cic.; *a hired lodging*, Tac., Suet.

insŭlānus -i, m. (insula), *an islander*, Cic.

insulsē, adv. (insulsus), *insipidly, tastelessly, sillily, absurdly;* loqui, Cic.

insulsĭtas -ātis, f. (insulsus), *insipidity, tastelessness, absurdity;* Graecorum, Cic.

insulsus -a -um (in and salsus), **1,** *unsalted, insipid;* O gulam insulsam, *pleased with tasteless food*, Cic.; **2,** *insipid, tasteless, absurd, foolish;* genus ridiculi, Cic.; adolescens, Cic.

insulto, 1. (intens. of insilio), **1,** *to leap at* or *on;* busta, Hor.; nemora, *dance through*, Verg.; **2,** *to scoff at, revile, insult, deride;* alicui in calamitate, Cic.; multos bonos, Sall.; in rempublicam, Cic.

insultūra -ae, f. (insilio), *a leaping at* or *on anything*, Plaut.

insum -fŭi -esse, *to be in* or *on;* **1,** lit., comae insunt capiti, Ov.; ferrum quale hastis velitaribus inest, Liv.; **2,** transf., *to be in, tc be contained in, to belong to;* with in and the abl., superstitio in qua inest inanis timor, Cic.; vitium aliquod inesse in moribus, Cic.; with dat., cui virile ingenium inest, Sall.

insūmo -sumpsi -sumptum, 3. *to take for anything, expend;* teruncium in aliquem, Cic.; sumptum in rem, Cic.; paucos dies reficiendae classi, Tac.; operam libellis accusatorum, Tac.

insŭo -sŭi -sūtum, 3. *to sew in, sew up, sew on;* aliquem in culeum, Cic.; insutum vestibu aurum, *embroidered, sewn on*, Ov.

insŭpĕr. I. Adv. **A.** Lit., **1,** *above, over, overhead;* insuper injicere centones, Caes.; **2,** *from above;* jugum insuper imminens, Liv. **B.** Transf., *over and above, in addition, moreover, besides;* insuper etiam, Liv.; insuper quam, Liv. **II.** Prepos. with acc., Cato.

insŭpĕrābilis -e, **1,** *insurmountable, impassable;* via, Liv.; **2,** transf., *unconquerable;* genus insuperabile bello, Verg.; fatum, *inevitable*, Ov.

insurgo -surrexi -surrectum, 3. *to rise up, raise oneself up.* **I.** Lit. **A.** Of persons, *to rise to one's full height*, in order to give more force to some action of the body; arduus insurgens, Liv.; of rowers, insurgite remis, *put all your strength into the stroke*, Verg. **B.** Of things, inde colles insurgunt, Liv.; of the wind, aquilo, Hor.; of water, vastius insurgens dominae ruit impetus undae, Ov. **II.** Transf., **a,** *to increase in power;* Caesar paulatim insurgere, Tac.; **b,** *to rise up against;* suis regnis, Ov.

insŭsurro, 1. *to whisper, whisper in the ear;* **a,** intransit., alicui, Cic.; in aurem alicuius, Cic.; **b,** transit., alicui cantilenam, Cic.

intābesco -tābŭi, 3. **1,** *to pine, waste, wither away gradually;* diuturno morbo, Cic.; **2,** *to become liquid, melt;* cera igni, Ov.

intactĭlis -e, *that cannot be touched*, Lucr.

1. intactus -a -um (in and tango), *untouched.* **I.** Gen., nix, *virgin*, Liv.; cervix juvencae, *untouched by the yoke*, Verg.; Britannus, *unconquered*, Hor.; intactum Graecis carmen, *not attempted by*, Hor. **II.** Esp., **a,** *unhurt;* prope intacti evasere, Liv.; **b,** *pure, chaste;* Pallas, Hor.; **c,** intactus aliquā re or ab aliqua re, *free from;* infamiā, cupiditate, Liv.

2. intactus -ūs, m. *intangibility*, Lucr.

intāmĭnātus -a -um (in and *tamino*, whence also contamino), *unstained, unspotted;* honores, Hor.

1. intectus -a -um, **1,** *uncovered, unclothed, unarmed;* pedes, Tac.; dux, Tac.; **2,** *open, frank*, Tac.

2. intectus -a -um, partic. of intego.

intĕgellus -a -um (dim. of integer), *tolerably uninjured, pretty safe*, Cic.

intĕger -gra -grum (for intager, from in and TAG-o, tango), *whole, entire, undiminished.* **I.** Physically, a, *unharmed, unwounded*, Cic.; integros pro sauciis accessere, Sall.; b, of food, *fresh, untainted;* aper, Hor.; c, *unhurt, undiminished, whole;* sublicae quarum pars inferior integra remanebat, Caes.; opes integrae, Hor.; existimatio, Cic.; d, *unmixed, pure;* fontes, Hor.; e, of strength, *fresh, unweakened, unexhausted, vigorous;* integris viribus repugnare, Caes.; f, *chaste, pure;* virgo, Cat.; g, of health or age, *sound, blooming;* valetudo, Cic.; integer aevi, *in the prime of life*, Verg.; h, of time, *entire;* annus, Cic.; i, *undiminished, fresh;* integram famem ad ovum affero, Cic.; de integro, *anew*, Cic.; so ab integro, Cic.; as legal t. t., in integrum restituere, *to restore a thing to its former condition;* praedia, Cic. **II.** Morally and intellectually. **A.** Intellectually, a, *undecided, undetermined;* rem integram relinquere, Cic.; causam integram reservare alicui, Cic.; in integro mihi res est, or integrum est mihi, *I am fully at liberty*, Cic.; foll. by infin. or ut and the subj., Cic.; sibi integrum reservare de aliquo or de aliq ia re, *to reserve one's freedom of action*, Cic.; dare, *to leave* or *grant full liberty*, Cic.; b, *inexperienced;* rudem me et integrum discipulum accipe, Cic.; c, *intellectually whole, unbiassed, impartial, free from prejudice;* integri testes, Cic.; integrum se servare, Cic. **B.** Morally, a, *uncorrupted;* se integros castosque conservare, Cic.; b, *blameless, innocent, pure;* nemo integrior, Cic.; integer vitae scelerisque purus, Hor.; c, *inviolate;* fides, Tac.; jus, Cic.

intĕgo -texi -tectum, 3. *to cover;* turres coriis, Caes.

intĕgrasco, 3. (integro), *to break out afresh*, Ter.

intĕgrātĭo -ōnis, f. (integro), *a renewing, renewal*, Ter.

intĕgrē, adv. (integer). **I.** *purely, correctly;* dicere, Cic. **II.** a, *honestly, uprightly, impartially;* judicare, Cic.; b, *disinterestedly;* in privatorum periculis caste integreque versari, Cic.

intĕgrĭtas -ātis, f. (integer). **I.** a, *unimpaired condition, soundness, health;* corporis, Cic.; valetudinis, Cic.; b, *purity, correctness;* incorrupta quaedam sermonis Latini integritas, Cic. **II.** *honesty, uprightness, integrity;* integritas vitae, Cic.

intĕgro, 1. (integer). **I.** a, *to renew, repeat, begin afresh;* pugnam, Liv.; lacrimas, Liv.; b, *to heal;* elapsos in pravum artus, Tac. **II.** *to refresh;* animus integratur, Cic.

intĕgŭmentum -i, n. (intego). **I.** *a covering;* laux cum integumentis, Liv. **II.** Transf., *a cloak, disguise;* haec flagitiorum integumenta, Cic.; evolutum illis integumentis dissimulationis tuae, Cic.

intellectus -ūs, m. (intelligo). **I.** *a perceiving, perception, sensation*, Plin. **II.** *an understanding, comprehension;* boni, mali, Tac.; intellectum habere, *to be understood*, Tac.

intellĭgens -entis, p. adj. (from intelligo), **1.** *intelligent, understanding* or *well acquainted with anything;* a, of persons, vir, Cic.; cuiusvis generis eius intelligens, Cic.; b, of things, judicium, Cic.; **2.** *a connoisseur;* homo ingeniosus et intelligens (opp. idiota), Cic.; in hisce rebus intelligens esse, Cic.

intellĭgentĕr, adv. (intelligens), *intelligently, with understanding;* audiri, Cic.

intellĭgentĭa -ae, f. (intelligens). **I.** *a conception, idea*, Cic. **II.** *insight, intelligence,*

knowledge. **A.** quia difficilis erat animi, quid aut qualis esset intelligentia, Cic.; intelligentiam juris habere, Cic. **B.** a, *the knowledge of a connoisseur in some art, taste*, Cic.; b, *understanding;* fretus intelligentiā vestrā, Cic.; quod in nostram intelligentiam cadit, Cic.; res sub intelligentiam cadentes, Cic.

intellĭgo (**intellĕgo**) -lexi -lectum, 3. (inter and lego), *to understand, comprehend.* **I.** By the senses or understanding, *to mark, perceive, observe, feel;* de gestu intelligo quid respondeas, Cic.; intellexi ex tuis litteris, te audisse, Cic.; ex quo intelligitur or intelligendum est, or intelligi potest, with acc. and infin. or rel. sent. (with quam, quantus, etc.), Cic. **II.** *to form an idea* or *conception, to think, to understand.* **A.** corpus quid sit intelligo, Cic.; with acc. and infin., *to be of the opinion, to think;* ipsi intelligamus naturā gigni sensum diligendi, Cic. **B.** Esp., **1,** *to be a connoisseur;* tamen non multum in istis rebus intelligo, Cic.; **2,** *to understand a person's character, judge, appreciate;* aliquis falsus intelligitur, Tac. (syncop. perf., intellexti, Cic.)

Intĕmĕlĭi (**Intĭmĕlĭi**) -ōrum, m. *a people on the east side of the Alps*, a branch of the Ligurians. Hence, **Intĕmĕlĭum** -ii, n. *the chief town of the Intemelii.*

intĕmĕrātus -a -um (in and temero), *unspotted, undefiled, inviolate;* fides, Verg.

intempĕrans -antis, 1, *extravagant, immoderate, intemperate;* intemperantis est, with infin., Cic.; in augendo eo intemperantior, Liv.; of things, libertas, gloria, Cic.; **2,** esp., *incontinent;* in aliqua re, Cic.; of things, intemperantissimae perpotationes, Cic.

intempĕrantĕr, adv. (intemperans), *immoderately, extravagantly, intemperately;* intemperantius opibus suis uti, Cic.

intempĕrantĭa -ae, f. (intemperans), **a,** *want of moderation, immoderateness, excess, intemperance;* libidinum, Cic.; vini, *immoderate indulgence in*, Liv.; b, *insubordination, insolence, haughtiness, arrogance*, Cic.

intempĕrātē, adv. (intemperatus), *intemperately;* vivere, Cic.

intempĕrātus -a -um, *intemperate, immoderate;* intemperata quaedam benevolentia, Cic.; intemperatā nocte, *in the dead of night*, Ov.

intempĕrĭae -ārum, f. (intempero), *inclement, unfavourable weather;* transf., quae te intemperiae tenent? *are you crazy?* Plaut.

intempĕrĭes -ēi, f. **I.** *inclement, unseasonable weather;* caeli, Liv.; aquarum, *excessive fall of rain*, Liv. **II.** Transf., **A.** *intemperate behaviour, outrageous conduct, insubordination;* amici, Cic.; cohortium, Tac. **B.** *incontinence, intemperance;* unius ex illis viris, Cic.

intempestīvē, adv. (intempestivus), *unseasonably;* accedere, Cic.

intempestīvus -a -um, *unseasonable, untimely, inopportune;* epistola, Cic.

intempestus -a -um (in and tempus or tempestas), 1, *unseasonable;* intempesta nox, *the dead of night*, Cic.; personified, Nox intempesta, *the mother of the Furies*, Verg.; 2, *unwholesome, unhealthy;* Graviscae, Verg.

intendo -tendi -tentum, 3. **I.** *to stretch out, extend.* **A.** Lit., 1, dextram ad statuam, Cic.; 2, of weapons, *to aim, direct;* tela, Cic. **B.** Transf., 1, transit. a, *to move in any direction, to direct towards;* iter in or ad locum, *to direct one's course towards*, Liv.; b, *to apply the mind, direct the thoughts to;* animum eo, Cic.; animum

10

ɔr mentem in aliquid, Cic.; oculos mentesque ad pugnam, Caes.; c, *to direct with hostile intention, to excite;* eo bellum, Liv.; periculum alicui or in aliquem, Cic.; alicui litem, Cic.; 2, intransit. or reflex., a, *to direct one's course;* quo intenderat in Manliana castra pervenit, Cic.; b, *to direct one's efforts;* quocumque intenderat, res adversae erant, Sall.; c, *to devote oneself to;* ad publicas curas, Tac. **II.** *to stretch.* **A.** Lit., arcum, Cic.; vincula stupea collo, *stretch round,* Verg.; tabernacula carbaseis velis, *to pitch,* Cic. **B.** Transf., 1, *to exert;* se ad firmitatem, Cic.; 2, *to intend;* quod animo intenderat, Cic.; 3, *to raise;* vocem, Verg.; 4, *to maintain, try to prove;* id quod intenderat confirmare, Cic.

1. **intentātus** -a -um (in and tento), *untouched, untried;* nil intentatum nostri liquere poëtae, *unattempted,* Hor.

2. **intentātus** -a -um, partic. of intento.

intentē, adv. (intentus), *carefully, diligently, attentively, vigorously;* aliquem intentius admonere, Liv.

intentĭo -ōnis, f. (intendo). **I.** *a directing, attention,* absol., Cic.; with subject. genit., vultus, Tac.; with object. genit., lusus, Liv. **II.** *stretching;* a, *corporis,* Cic.; b, of the mind, *an effort, exertion;* animi cogitationum, Cic.; c, *intention;* adversariorum, Cic.

intento, 1. (intens. of intendo), 1, *to stretch towards or against, to stretch out threateningly;* manus in aliquem, Liv.; sicam alicui, Cic.; 2, *to threaten with hostile purpose;* arma Latinis, *to threaten with war,* Cic.

1. **intentus** -ūs, m. (intendo), *a stretching out;* palmarum, Cic.

2. **intentus** -a -um. **I.** Partic. of intendo. **II.** P. adj. (from intendo), a, *anxious, intent, full of expectation;* omnes milites intenti pugnae proventum exspectabant, Caes.; with ad or adversus aliquid, or with dat., *attentive to, waiting eagerly for;* in omnem occasionem, Liv.; b, with dat., or ad, or in with the acc., *attentive to, intent upon, busied with, zealous in;* operi agresti, Liv.; esp. of soldiers, *ready for battle;* paratus et intentus, Liv.; c, *active, unceasing, vigorous;* intentissima cura, Liv.; d, *rigorous;* disciplina, Tac.

intĕpĕo, 2. *to be lukewarm,* Prop.

intĕpesco -tĕpŭi, 3. (inchoat. of intepeo), *to become lukewarm, grow gradually warm,* Ov.

intĕr (in with adverbial ending ter), prep. with acc. *between, among, amid.* **A.** Of space, 1, of rest, moror inter aras, templa, Cic.; quum (Hercules) inter homines esset, *among the number of,* Cic.; inter falcarios, *in the street of the sickle-makers,* Cic.; 2, of motion, inter stationes hostium emissi, Liv. **B.** Transf., of time, 1, *between;* inter horam tertiam et quartam, Liv.; 2, *during, in the course of;* inter decem annos, Cic.; inter cenam, Cic.; inter agendum, Verg. **C.** 1, *among a class;* adolescens inter suos, Cic.; 2, *between* (parties, adversaries, etc.); inter Marcellos et Claudios patricios judicare, Cic.; 3, of division, portion, inter se, *between one another,* Cic.; 4, *between* (of friendship, hostility, etc.); amicitiam nisi inter bonos esse non posse, Cic.; 5, with pronouns, inter se, inter nos, inter vos, inter ipsos, *between one another, mutually;* amare inter se, *to love one another,* Cic. **D.** Particular phrases, a, inter sicarios accusare, *to accuse of murder,* Cic.; b, inter pauca and inter paucos, *especially, particularly,* Liv.; c, inter cuncta, *before all,* Hor.; d, inter haec, *meanwhile,* Liv. (inter sometimes put after its case, quos inter, Cic.).

intĕrāmenta -ōrum, n. (inter), *the woodwork of a ship,* Liv.

Intĕramna -ae, f., 1, *a town in Umbria* now *Terni;* 2, *a town in Latium,* now *Teramo,* Hence, adj., 1, **Intĕramnānus** -a -um; 2, **Intĕramnās** -ātis, *belonging to Interamna.* Subst., **Intĕramnātes** -ium, m. *the people of Interamna.*

intĕrāresco, 3. *to become dry, to dry up, decay,* transf., Cic.

interbĭbo, 3 *to drink up,* Plaut.

interbīto, 3. *to perish,* Plaut.

intercălāris -e (intercalo), *intercalary;* calendae, *the first day of an intercalary month,* Cic.

intercălārĭus -a -um (intercalo), *intercalary;* mensis, Cic.

intercălo, 1. (lit., *to call out that something is inserted*), 1, *to insert or intercalate a day or month in the calendar;* si scies Romae intercalatum sit necne, Cic.; 2, *to defer, put off;* poenam, Liv.

intercăpēdo -ĭnis, f. (intercapio), *an interval, intermission, pause, respite;* molestiae, Cic.

intercēdo -cessi -cessum, 3. *to go between, come between.* **I.** Lit., inter singulas legiones impedimentorum magnum numerum intercedere, Caes. **II.** Transf., **A.** a, of places, *to stand or lie between;* palus quae perpetua intercedebat, Caes.; b, hence of time, *to intervene;* nox nulla intercessit, Cic.; c, of events, *to happen between;* saepe in bello parvis momentis magni casus intercedunt, Caes.; d, of relations, *to be between;* inter nos vetus usus intercedit, Cic. **B.** Of persons, *to step between;* a, by way of hindrance, *to interpose, withstand, protest against* (of the tribunes when they exercised their veto); legi, Cic.; alicui, Cic.; b, as a mediator, *to interpose;* quum vestra auctoritas intercessisset ut, etc., Cic.; in money transactions, *to stand surety;* pro aliquo, Cic.; magnam pecuniam pro aliquo, *in a large sum for,* Cic.

interceptĭo -ōnis, f. (intercipio), *a taking away;* poculi, Cic.

interceptor -ōris, m. (intercipio), *one who takes away, an embezzler;* praedae, Liv.

intercessĭo -ōnis, f. (intercedo), 1, *an intercession, interposition, suretyship for any one,* Cic.; 2, *a protest or exercise by the tribunes* of their veto, Cic.

intercessor -ōris, m. (intercedo), 1, *a surety,* bail, Cic.; 2, *one who protests against, opposes, withstands* (of a tribune in the exercise of his veto); legis, Cic.

1. **intercīdo** -cīdi -cīsum, 3. (inter and caedo), *to cut off, cut asunder;* pontem, *to demolish, pull down,* Liv.; montem, *to cut through,* Cic.

2. **intercĭdo** -cĭdi, 3. (inter and cado), 1, *to fall between,* Liv.; 2, transf., a, *to happen, occur;* si quae interciderunt, Cic.; b, *to become lost, decay, perish;* inimici, ap. Cic.; memoriā, *be forgotten,* Liv.; intercidit mihi aliquid, *I have forgotten something,* Hor.

intercĭno, 1. (inter and cano), *to sing between;* medios actus, Hor.

intercĭpĭo -cēpi -ceptum 3. (inter and capio), *to take by the way, intercept.* **I.** Lit. litteras, Cic.; commeatus, Liv. **II.** Transf., 1, *to deprive of, rob, steal;* agrum ab aliquo, Liv.; aliquem neci, Ov.; 2, *to snatch away, carry off prematurely;* aliquem veneno, Tac.; 3, *to cut off;* iter, Liv.

intercīsē, adv. (intercisus), *confusedly, interruptedly;* dicere, Cic.

interclūdo -clūsi -clūsum, 3. (inter and cludo, claudo). **I.** *to block up, hinder;* alicui fugam, Cic.; fig., omnes seditionum vias. Cic.

II. A. *to cut off, separate from;* aliquem ab exercitu, Caes.; aliquem re frumentariā, Caes.; fig., intercludor dolore quominus, etc., *I am prevented by grief,* Cic. **B.** *to enclose, shut in;* aliquem in iis insidiis quas, etc., Cic.; angustiis intercludi, Caes.

interclūsĭo -ōnis, f. (intercludo), *a stopping* or *blocking up;* animae, Cic.

intercŏlumnĭum -ĭi, n. (inter and columna), *the space between two columns,* Cic.

intercurro -cŭcurri and -curri -cursum, 3. **I.** 1, *to run between,* Lucr.; 2, fig., **a,** *to step between, intercede,* Cic.; **b,** *to run along with, be among, mingle with;* his laboriosis exercitationibus et dolor intercurrit, Cic. **II.** *to run* or *hasten to in the meanwhile;* Veios ad confirmandos militum animos, Liv.

intercurso, 1. (intens. of intercurro), *to run between,* Liv.

intercursus -ūs, m. (intercurro), *a running between, interposition;* intercursu consulum, suorum, Liv.

intercus -cŭtis (inter and cutis), *under the skin;* aqua, *the dropsy,* Cic.

interdātus -a -um, partic. of interdo.

interdīco -dixi -dictum, 3. **I.** *to forbid, prohibit.* **A.** Gen. **a,** alicui aliquā re or aliquo; Romanis omni Galliā, Caes.; **b,** alicui aliquid; alicui orbem, Ov.; **c,** with or without dat. of person, foll. by ne or ut, etc., and the subj., interdicit atque imperat Cassivellauno ne Mandubracio noceat, Caes.; in pass., Pythagoreis interdictum ne fabā vescerentur, Cic. **B.** Esp., 1, as legal t. t., interdicere alicui aquā et igni, *to banish,* Cic.; 2, sacrificiis interdicere, Caes. **II.** *to order, command;* 1, with ut and the subj., familiae valde interdicere ut uni dicto audiens sit, Cic.; 2, of the praetor, *to make a provisional* or *interlocutory decree;* de vi, Cic.; praetor interdixit ut unde dejectus esset eo restitueretur, Cic.

interdictĭo -ōnis, f. (interdico), *a forbidding, prohibition;* aquae et ignis, *banishing,* Cic.

interdictum -i, n. (interdico), 1, *a prohibition;* with subject. genit., Caesaris, Cic.; 2, *a praetor's interdict* or *provisional order,* Cic.

interdĭu (interdĭus), adv. *in the daytime, by day;* nocte an interdiu, Liv.

interdo -dĭdi -dătum, 1. *to give between, distribute,* Lucr.

interdŭătim = interdum (q.v.).

interductus -ū, m. (*interduco), *inter-punctuation,* Cic.

interdum, adv. 1, *sometimes, occasionally, now and then;* interdum . . . interdum, Cic.; 2, *meanwhile,* Tac.

interdŭo = interdo (q.v.).

intĕrĕā, adv. (inter and abl. eā), 1, *in the meantime, meanwhile,* Cic.; interea quum, Cic.; 2, *nevertheless, notwithstanding,* Cic.; quum interea, Cic.

intĕremptĭo -ōnis, f. (interimo), *slaughter, slaying,* Cic.

intĕrĕo -ĭi -ĭtum, 4. *to perish, to be lost among.* **I.** Lit., muriae stilla interit magnitudine maris, Cic. **II.** Transf., *to perish, be destroyed, be lost;* **a,** of things, intereunt sacra, Cic.; **b,** of men, *to die;* fame aut ferro, Caes. (syncop. perf. forms, interisse, interissent, Cic.).

intĕrĕquĭto, 1. *to ride between;* ordines, Liv.

interfātĭo -ōnis, f. (interfor), *a speaking between, interruption in discourse,* Cic.

interfectĭo -ōnis, f. (interficio), *a slaying,* ap. Cic.

interfector -ōris, m. (interficio), *a murderer, slayer,* Cic.

interfectrix -trīcis, f. (interfector), *a murderess,* Tac.

interfĭcĭo -fēci -fectum, 3. (inter and facĭo), *to destroy, put an end to, bring to naught;* **a,** of things, messes, Verg.; herbas, Cic.; **b,** of persons, *to murder, to slay, kill;* aliquem insidiis, Cic.; Crassum suāpte interfectum manu, Cic.

interfīo -fĭĕri (pass. of interficio = interficior), *to perish,* Plaut.

interflŭo -fluxi -fluxum, 3. *to flow between;* Naupactum et Patras, Liv.

interflŭus -a -um (interfluo), *flowing between,* Plin.

interfŏdĭo -fōdi -fossum, 3. *to dig into, pierce,* Lucr.

interfor -fātus sum, 1. dep., *to speak between, interrupt in discourse;* aliquem, Liv.; or absol., Liv., Verg. (1st pers. pres. not found).

interfŭgĭo, 3. *to flee between,* Lucr.

interfulgens -entis, *shining* or *gleaming among* or *between,* Liv.

interfundo -fūdi -fūsum, 3. *to pour between;* middle, interfundi, *to flow between;* noviens Styx interfusa, Verg.; transf., maculis interfusa genas, *stained with,* Verg.

intĕrĭbi, adv., *meanwhile, in the meantime,* Plaut.

intĕrĭcĭo = interjicio (q.v.).

intĕrim, adv., 1, *meanwhile, in the meantime,* Cic.; 2, *however,* Cic.

intĕrĭmo -ēmi -emptum, 3. (inter and emo), *to take away out of the midst;* 1, of things, *to destroy, annihilate, make an end of;* sacra, Cic.; 2, of persons, *to put out of the way, to kill, slay, murder;* aliquem, Cic.; stirpem fratris virilem, Liv.; se, *to commit suicide,* Cic.; transf., me examinant et interimunt hae voces Milonis, Cic.

intĕrĭor, intĕrĭus -ōris, compar. adj.; **intĭmus** -a -um, superl. (in-ter). **I.** Compar. interior. **A.** Lit., 1, *inner, interior;* pars aedium, Cic.; interiore epistolā, *in the middle of the letter,* Cic.; Falernum interiore notā, *from the depth of the cellar,* Hor.; interior ictibus, *within shot,* Liv.; 2, *a, remote from the sea, inland;* nationes, Cic.; interiora regni, *the interior of the kingdom,* Liv.; **b,** *nearer, shorter* (of the racecourse); gyrus, *on the inside of the course,* Hor.; cursus, *shorter,* Cic. **B.** Transf., 1, interior periculo vulneris, *too near to be in danger of a wound,* Liv.; 2, **a,** *more secret, more confidential;* amicitia, Cic.; **b,** *deeper* (s) timor, Cic.; (β) *more erudite, profound;* interiores et reconditae litterae, Cic. **II.** Superl., intimus -a -um, *inmost.* **A.** Lit., intima Macedonia, *the very centre of Macedonia,* Cic. **B.** Transf., 1, *deepest, most profound;* disputatio, philosophia, Cic.; 2, *most secret, confidential, intimate;* amicus, Cic.; intimus alicui, Cic.; familiaritas, Nep. Subst., **intĭmus** -i, m. *an intimate friend,* Cic.

intĕrĭtĭo -ōnis, f. (intereo), *destruction, ruin;* aratorum, Cic.

intĕrĭtus -ūs, m. (intereo), *destruction, ruin, annihilation;* **a,** of things, legum, Cic.; **b,** of persons, consulum, Cic.; with abl., exercitus nostri interitus ferro, fame, frigore, Cic.

intĕrĭus, 1, compar. adj., v. interior; **2,** compar. of intra, v. intra.

interjăcĕo, 2. *to lie between* or *among;* absol., interjacebat campus, Liv.; with dat., campus interjacens Tiberi ac moenibus Romanis, Liv.

interjectus -ūs, m. (interjicio), *a putting between ;* a., of place, interpositu interjectuque terrae, *between the sun and the moon,* Cic. ; b, of time, *an interval ;* interjectu noctis, *after an interval of a night,* Tac.

interjĭcĭo (interjăcĭo) -jēci -jectum, 3. *to throw, cast, place, put among,* or *between.* I. Lit., legionarias cohortes, Caes. Partic., **interjectus** -a -um, *interposed, thrown between ;* nasus, quasi murus oculis interjectus, Cic. II. Transf., 1, idque interjecit inter individuum atque id, etc., Cic. ; interjectus inter philosophos et eos, *standing between,* Cic. ; 2, a, of time, *to put in between ;* moram, Tac. ; anno interjecto, *after the interval of a year,* Cic. ; b, of words, *to intermingle ;* pleraque Latino sermone, Cic.

interjungo -junxi -junctum, 3. *to join together, unite, connect ;* dextras, Liv.

interlābor -labi, 3. dep., *to glide, fall, flow between ;* in tmesis, inter enim labentur aquae, Verg.

interlĕgo, 3. *to pluck, gather here and there,* Verg.

interlĭno -lēvi -lĭtum, 3. I. *to daub between ;* caementa interlita luto, Liv. II. *to erase, cancel, to falsify by erasure ;* testamentum, Cic.

interlŏquor -lŏcūtus (-loquūtus) sum, 3. dep., *to interrupt a person speaking,* Ter.

interlūcĕo -luxi, 2. I. *to shine, gleam between ;* terrena quaedam atque etiam volucria animalia plerumque interlucent (in amber), Tac. ; impers., noctu interluxisse, *there had been intervals of light,* Liv. II. A. *to shine forth ;* quibus inter gradus dignitatis et fortunae aliquid interlucet, Liv. B. *to be transparent, capable of being seen through* (on account of small numbers) ; interlucet corona (militum), Verg.

interlūnĭum -ĭi, n. (inter and luna), *the change of the moon, time of new moon,* Hor.

interlŭo -ŭi, 3. *to flow between, wash between ;* fretum quod; Capreas et Surrentum interluit, Tac.

intermenstrŭus -a -um, *between two months ;* intermenstruo tempore, *at the time of the change of the moon,* Cic. ; subst., **intermenstrŭum** -i, n. (sc. tempus), *the time of the new moon,* Cic.

1. **interminātus** -a -um (in and termino), *unbounded, boundless ;* magnitudo regionum, Cic.

2. **interminātus** -a -um, v. interminor.

interminor, 1. dep., *to threaten, forbid with threats,* Plaut. ; partic. perf. pass., cibus interminatus, *forbidden with threats,* Hor.

intermiscĕo -miscŭi -mixtum, 2. *to mix with, intermix ;* with dat., turbam indignorum intermiscere dignis, Liv. ; intermixti hostibus, Liv.

intermissĭo -ōnis, f. (intermitto). I. *leaving off ;* epistolarum, Cic. ; officii, Cic. II. *respite, interruption, interval ;* verborum, Cic.; sine ulla temporis intermissione, Cic.

intermissus -a -um, partic. of intermitto.

intermitto -mīsi -missum, 3. I. Transit., A. *to place between ;* trabes paribus intermissae spatiis, Caes. B. *to leave a space between, leave free, unoccupied, unsurrounded ;* 1, lit., pars oppidi a flumine intermissa, Caes. ; loca custodibus intermissa, Liv. ; 2, transf., a, *to leave off for a time, give over, break off, interrupt, neglect ;* studia, Cic. ; proelium, Caes. ; with infin., alicui litteras mittere, Cic. ; vento intermisso, *the wind having*

dropped, Caes. ; verba ab usu quotidiani sermonis intermissa, *obsolete,* Cic. ; b, of time, *to let pass ;* ne quem diem intermitterem, Cic. ; with ab and the abl., ut reliquum tempus ab labore intermitteretur, Caes. ; with ad and the acc., nulla pars nocturni temporis ad laborem intermittitur, Caes. ; with a negat. foll. by quin and the subj., neque ullum fere diem intermittebat quin perspiceret, *without examining,* Cic. ; c, *to discontinue, suspend an office ;* intermissis magistratibus, Cic. II. Intransit., *to cease, leave off ;* quā flumen intermittit, Caes.

intermŏrĭor -mortŭus sum, 3. dep., *to die, perish, decay ;* 1, lit., Suet. ; 2, transf., a, intermoriuntur reliquiae conjurationis, Cic. ; civitas intermoritur, Liv. ; contiones intermortuae, *lifeless,* Cic. ; b, *to faint away,* Liv.

intermundĭa -ōrum, n. (inter and mundus), *spaces between the worlds* (according to Epicurus, *the abode of the gods),* Cic.

intermūrālis -e, *between walls ;* amnis, Liv.

internascor -nātus sum, 3. dep., *to grow between ;* internata virgulta, Liv.

internĕcīnus -a -um, v. internecivus.

internĕcĭo (internĭcĭo) -ōnis, f. (interneco), *entire destruction, extermination, massacre, carnage ;* civium, Cic. ; ad internecionem adducere gentem, *to annihilate,* Liv.

internĕcīvus (internĕcīnus) -a -um (interneco), *murderous, mortal, deadly, internecine ;* bellum, Cic.

internĕco, 1. *to destroy utterly, exterminate ;* hostes, Plaut.

internecto, 3. *to bind together, to bind up ;* ut fibula crinem auro internectat, Verg.

internĭcĭo = internecio (q.v.).

internĭtĕo -nĭtŭi, 2. *to shine among, gleam through,* Plin.

internōdĭum -ĭi, n. (inter and nodus), *the space between two knots* or *joints,* Ov.

internosco -nōvi -nōtum, 3. *to distinguish between ;* geminos, Cic. ; quae internosci a falsis non possunt, Cic.

internuntia, v. internuntius.

internuntĭo, 1. *to send messengers between two parties,* Liv.

internuntĭus -a -um, adj., used as subst., *a messenger, negotiator, go-between ;* a, masc., Jovis interpretes internuntiique (of the augurs), Cic. ; b, fem., aves internuntiae Jovis, Cic.

internus -a -um, *inward, internal, civil ;* discordiae, Tac.

intĕro -trīvi -trītum, 3. *to rub, crumble, pound in anything,* Plin.

interpellātĭo -ōnis, f. (interpello), *interruption, hindrance, disturbance,* especially in a speech, Cic.

interpellātor -ōris, m. (interpello), *an interrupter, disturber,* Cic.

interpello, 1. (inter and *pello -are, intens. of pello -ĕre), 1, to interrupt a speaker ;* crebro dicentem, Cic. ; 2, *to disturb, hinder, impede ;* a, of persons, aliquem in jure suo, Cic.; aliquem ne, etc., Liv. ; comitia, Liv. ; b, of things, haec tota res interpellata bello, Cic.

interpōlātĭo -ōnis, f. (interpolo), *an alteration,* Plin.

interpŏlis -e (inter and polio), *furbished, vamped up, repaired ;* hence, *not genuine,* Plaut. Plin.

interpŏlo, 1. (interpolis), 1, *to alter, furbish, repair, vamp up ;* togam praetextam, *to re-dye,* Cic. ; 2, *to spoil, corrupt, falsify ;* semper aliquid demendo, mutando, interpolando, Cic.

interpōno -pŏsŭi -pŏsĭtum, 3. *to put, place,
way between* or *among, interpose.* **I.** Lit., 1,
elephantos, Liv.; 2, a, *to insert, intercalate;*
menses intercalarios, Liv.; b, *to insert in discourse;* ne inquam saepius interponeretur, Cic.
II. Transf., **A.** Of *time, to allow an interval to
pass between;* spatium ad recreandos animos,
Caes.; spatio interposito, *after some time,* Cic.;
moram, Cic., cunctationem, Tac., *to interpose,
delay.* **B.** *to cause to come between, to interpose;*
operam, studium, laborem, *to use, apply,* Cic.
C. *to introduce, bring forward;* a, judicium,
edictum, *to bring forward,* Cic.; b, *to bring
forward, allege as a reason* or *pretext;* gladiatores interpositi sunt, Cic.; c, *to pledge one's
word;* in aliquid or in aliqua re fidem suam,
Caes. **D.** *to admit as a helper, participator,* etc.;
1, judices, testes, Cic.; 2, se interponere in aliquid or alicui, *to engage in, have to do with, meddle;* se in pacificationem, Cic.; se audaciae alicuius, Cic. **E.** *to falsify;* rationes populorum, Cic.

interpŏsĭtĭo -ōnis, f. (interpono), 1, *a bringing forward, introducing* (in a speech); multarum
personarum, Cic.; 2, *a putting in, insertion,* Cic.

interpŏsĭtus, abl. -ū, m. (interpono), a
putting between, interposition; luna interpositu
terrae deficit, Cic.

interpres -prĕtis, c. (inter and PRET,
ΦΡΑΔ, φράζω). **I.** *a negotiator, mediator, messenger;* judicii corrumpendi, Cic.; divûm, *Mercury,* Verg. **II. A.** *an expounder, explainer;*
juris, Cic.; poetarum, Cic.; divûm, *prophet,
prophetess,* Verg., Liv.; interpretes comitiorum,
*the haruspices, who declare whether the comitia
have been rightly held,* Cic. **B.** a, *an interpreter;*
appellare or alloqui aliquem per interpretem,
Cic.; b, *a translator;* nec converti (orationes)
ut interpres, sed ut orator, Cic.

interprĕtātĭo -ōnis, f. (interpretor). **I.**
explanation, exposition, interpretation. **A.** Gen.,
juris, Cic.; verborum, Cic. **B.** Esp., *translation,* Plin.; concr. = *that which is translated;*
foederis, Cic. **II.** *meaning, understanding;* nec
interpretatio est facilis, Liv.

interprĕtor, 1. dep. (interpres), *to explain,
expound, interpret, translate.* **A.** Lit., 1, jus
alicui, Cic.; fulgura, somnia, Cic.; 2, *to translate;*
epistolam, scriptores, Cic. **B.** Transf., 1, *to put
an interpretation on, to understand in a certain
manner;* male, Cic.; aliquid mitiorem in partem,
Cic.; with acc. and infin., reditu in castra liberatum se esse jurejurando interpretabatur, Cic.;
2, *to understand, grasp, comprehend;* recte
alicuius sententiam, Cic.; 3, *to decide, determine;*
neque, recte an perperam, interpretor, Cic.
(pass., Cic., esp. in perf. partic.)

interpunctĭo -ōnis, f. (interpungo), *punctuation;* verborum, Cic.

interpungo -punxi -punctum, 3. *to punctuate, point;* narratio interpuncta, *well-divided,*
Cic.; partic. subst., clausulae atque interpuncta
verborum, *divisions,* Cic.

interquĕror -questus sum, 3. dep., *to interrupt with complaints,* Liv. (?)

interquĭesco -quiēvi -quiētum, 3. *to pause
between, rest in the mean time;* quum haec dix-
issem et paulum interquievissem, Cic.

interregnum -i, n. *a period between two
reigns, an interregnum,* Cic.; under the republic
at Rome, *the time during the absence of the consuls,* or *between the death* or *retirement of the
consuls and the choice of successors,* Cic.

interrex -rēgis, m. *a regent, person temporarily invested with royal authority,* Cic.; in later
times, *a person appointed in the absence of the
consuls to hold the comitia for the election of their
successors,* Cic.

interrĭtus -a -um (in and terreo), *unterrified,
undaunted,* Verg.

interrŏgātĭo -ōnis, f. (interrogo), *a question,
questioning, interrogation,* Cic.; esp. a, legal t.t.,
the examination of witnesses; testium, Tac.;
absol., Cic.; b, logic. t.t., *an argument, syllogism;*
aptâ interrogatione concludere, Cic.

interrŏgātĭuncŭla -ae, f. (dim. of interrogatio), *a short syllogism* or *argument;* minutae
interrogatiunculae, Cic.

interrŏgo, 1. **I.** *to ask, question, interrogate;*
te eisdem de rebus, Cic.; interrogabat suos quis
esset, Cic.; interrogans solerentne veterani
milites fugere, Caes.; with double acc., pusi-
onem quendam interrogavit quaedam geometrica,
Cic.; interrogatus sententiam, *being asked his
opinion,* Liv.; partic. subst., **interrŏgātum**
-i, n. *a question;* ad interrogata respondere,
Cic. **II.** Esp., a, *to interrogate judicially, tc
examine;* testem, Cic.; b, *to accuse, bring an
action against;* aliquem legibus ambitus, Sall.

interrumpo -rūpi -ruptum, 3. *to break
down, break in the middle, break asunder.* **I. A.**
pontem, Caes.; aciem hostium, Liv. **B.** *to
separate;* interrupti ignes, isolated, Verg.; interruptae vocis, *broken,* Cic. **II.** Transf., *to interrupt, disturb;* a, gen., iter amoris et officii,
Cic.; b, *to interrupt a speech;* orationem, Cic.

interruptē, adv. (interruptus from interrumpo), *interruptedly, disconnectedly;* non in-
terrupte narrare, Cic.

intersaepĭo -saepsi -saeptum, 4. *to hedge* or
fence in, inclose, hem in, block up. **I.** Lit., foramina, Cic.; quaedam operibus, Liv. **II.** Transf.,
cut off, separate; urbem vallo ab arce, Liv.;
iter, Cic.

interscindo -scĭdi -scissum, 3. *to cut* or *hew
asunder.* **I.** Lit., pontem, Cic.; venas, *to open,*
Tac. **II.** Transf., *to cut off, separate;* Chalcis
arcto interscinditur freto, Liv.

intersēpĭo = intersaepio (q.v.).

1. **intersĕro** -sēvi -sĭtum, 3. *to sow* or *plant
between,* Lucr.

2. **intersĕro,** 3. *to put* or *place between;*
oscula mediis verbis, Ov.; transf., causam inter-
serens, *alleging,* Nep.

interspīrātĭo -ōnis, f. *a breathing between,*
a taking breath, Cic.

1. **interstinguo** -stinctus, 3. *to cover with
spots* or *speckles;* facies interstincta medicamini-
bus, Tac.

2. **interstinguo,** 3. *to extinguish;* ignem,
Lucr.

interstrĕpo, 3. *to roar, make a noise in the
midst of,* Verg.

interstringo, 3. *to squeeze tight;* alicui
gulam, *to throttle,* Plaut.

intersum -fŭi -esse. **I. A.** *to be between;*
a, of space, ut Tiberis inter eos interesset, Cic.;
b, of time, *to intervene;* inter primum et sextum
consulatum XLVI anni interfuerunt, Cic. **B.**
to be different, be distinguished from; ut inter eos
ne minimum quidem intersit, Cic.; inter hominem et beluam hoc maxime interest, Cic.; quod ab
eo nihil intersit, Cic. **C.** *to be present, take part in;*
with in and the abl., in convivio, Cic.; with
dat., convivio, Cic. **II.** Impers., *interest, it
concerns, it imports, it is of importance;* constr.;
(α) with genit. of person or thing, or with the
fem. abl. of the possess. pron., meâ, tuâ, suâ,
nostrâ, vestrâ, cujâ, nam eorum quoque vehementer interest, Cic.; vestrâ hoc maxime interest,
Cic.; (β) with ad and the acc. of the thing, ad
nostram laudem non multum interesse, Cic.;
(γ) with the neut., multum, quantum, tantum,
plus, plurimum, or with adv., maxime, ve-

hementer, magnopere, or with genit. of value, magni, parvi, minoris, pluris, magni, Cic.; (δ) with infin., or acc. and infin., or ut or ne, or with rel. sent., magni interest meā unā nos esse, Cic.; illud magni meā interest ut te videam, Cic.; nunquam enim interest uter sit eorum in pede extremo, Cic.

intertexo -texŭi -textum, 3. *to weave together, interweave;* flores hederis intertexti, Ov.; chlamys auro intertexta, Verg.

intertrăho -traxi, 3. *to take away,* Plaut.

intertrīmentum -i, n. (inter and tero). **I.** *loss by friction, loss in working gold and silver;* argenti, Liv. **II.** Transf., *loss, damage;* sine ullo intertrimento, Cic.

interturbātĭo -ōnis, f. *disturbance, disquiet,* Liv.

intervallum -i, n. (inter and vallus), *a space between two palisades;* hence, **I. A.** *an intervening space, interval, distance;* pari intervallo, *at an equal distance,* Caes.; locorum, Cic. **B.** *an interval of time;* literarum, Cic.; sine intervallo loquacitas, *without intermission,* Cic.; longo intervallo, *after a long time,* Cic. **II.** *difference, unlikeness,* Cic.; as t. t. of music, intervalla = *distinctions between high and low notes,* Cic.

intervello -vulsi -vulsum, 3. *to pull or pluck out here and there, to thin,* Plin.

intervĕnĭo -vēni -ventum, 4. *to come between, come up while anything is doing, to intervene.* **I.** verens ne molesti vobis interveniremus, Cic.; huic orationi, Liv. **II.** Transf., a, of time, *to intervene, to interrupt;* with dat., nox intervenit proelio, Liv.; b, of events, *to happen while something else is being done, and so to interrupt;* with dat., intervenit deinde his cogitationibus avitum malum, Liv.; exigua fortuna intervenit sapienti, *opposes,* Cic.

interventor -ōris, m. (intervenio), *an interrupter, a visitor;* magis vacuo ab interventoribus die, Cic.

interventus -ūs, m. (interventio), *intervention, interposition, interference;* hominis, Cic.; noctis, Caes.

interverto (-vorto) -verti (-vorti) -versum (-vorsum), 3. *(to turn aside), to embezzle, appropriate to one's own use, purloin;* 1, regale donum, Cic.; 2, transf., *to take away, deprive of, defraud of;* promissum et receptum (consulatum) intervertere et ad se transferre, Cic.; 3, *to spend, lavish,* Tac.

intervīso -vīsi -vīsum, 3. 1, *to look after, inspect secretly;* crebro interviso, Cic.; 2, *to visit from time to time;* aliquem, Cic.

intervŏlĭto, 1. *to fly about among,* Liv.

intervŏmo, 3. *to pour forth among,* Lucr.

intestābĭlis -e, *disqualified from being a witness or from making a will;* hence *dishonourable, disgraceful, infamous, execrable,* Hor., Sall.; perjurium, Liv.

intestātus -a -um, 1, *having made no will, intestate;* adv., intestato or ab intestato, *intestate;* mori, Cic.; 2, *not convicted by witnesses,* Plaut.

intestīnum -i, v. intestinus.

intestīnus -a -um (intus). **I.** *inward, internal;* subst., **intestīnum** -i, n. *an intestine;* and plur., **intestīna** -ōrum, n. *the intestines;* intestinum medium, Cic.; ex intestinis laborare, *to have a pain in the bowels,* Cic. **II.** a, *domestic, internal, civil;* intestinum ac domesticum malum, Cic.; bellum, Cic.; b, *subjective* (opp. civatus, *objective),* Cic.

intexo -texŭi -textum, 3. **I.** *to weave in, plait in, interweave;* 1, lit., purpureas notas

filis, Ov.; vimina, Caes.; **2, a,** *to interlace,* venae toto corpore intextae, Cic.; b, *to interweave in discourse;* parva magnis, Cic. **II.** *to weave around, to wind around, to surround;* hastas foliis, Verg.; hederae solent intexere truncos, Ov.

intĭbum (intўbum, intŭbum) -i, n. and **intĭbus (intўbus, intŭbus)** -i, c. *endive, succory,* Verg.

intĭmē, adv. (intimus), 1, *confidentially, intimately,* Nep.; 2, *cordially, strongly;* commendari ab aliquo, Cic.

intĭmus, superl. from interior (q.v.).

intingo (intinguo) -tinxi -tinctum, 3. *to dip in;* faces sanguine, Ov.

intŏlĕrābĭlis -e, *unbearable, intolerable;* frigus, dolor, Cic.; saevitia, Liv.

intŏlĕrandus -a -um, *unbearable, unendurable,* Cic.

intŏlĕrans -antis. **I.** Act., *impatient of, unable to bear;* with genit., corpora intolerantissima laboris, Liv. **II.** Pass., *unbearable, intolerable;* subjectis intolerantior, Tac.

intŏlĕrantĕr, adv. (intolerans), *immoderately, excessively, impatiently;* dolere, Cic.; intolerantius se jactare, Cic.; intolerantissime gloriari, Cic.

intŏlĕrantĭa -ae, f. (intolerans), *intolerable, insufferable conduct, insolence;* regis, Cic.; illa superbia atque intolerantia, Cic.

intŏno -tŏnŭi -tŏnātum, 1. **I.** Intransit., *to thunder.* **A.** Lit., pater omnipotens ter caelo clarus ab alto intonuit, Verg. **B.** Transf., a, *to thunder, make a thundering noise,* especially of a speaker; jam hesternā concione intonuit vox perniciosa tribuni, Cic.; b, *to clash;* Aeneas horrendum intonat armis, Verg. **II.** Transit., a, *to thunder forth;* quum haec intonuisset plenus irae, Liv.; minas, Ov.; b, *to make to roar upon;* Eois intonata fluctibus hiems, raging on, Hor. (partic. perf. pass., intonatus, Hor.)

intonsus -a -um (in and tondeo), *unshorn.* **I.** Lit., caput, Ov.; of animals, intonsa bidens, Verg.; of persons, *with long hair or beard;* deus, Apollo, Ov.; of the old Romans, intonsi avi, Ov.; Numa, Ov.; Cato, Hor.; of savage nations, homines intonsi et inculti, Liv.; intonsi Getae; Ov. **II.** *wooded, leafy, not cleared of trees;* montes, Verg.

intorquĕo -torsi -tortum, 2. **I.** *to twist or turn round.* **A.** Gen. 1, paludamentum circum brachium, Liv.; 2, *to wind;* rudentes intorti, Ov. **B.** *to hurl;* telum in hostem, Verg.; transf., ardentes oculos, *to roll,* Verg.; intorquentur inter fratres gravissimae contumeliae, Cic. **II.** *to twist aside, turn, writhe.* **A.** intorti capillis Eumenidum angues, Hor.; navis vertice retro intorta, Liv. **B.** *to distort, turn away;* mentum in dicendo, Cic.

intortus -a -um (partic. of intorqueo).

intrā (for interā sc. parte, from *interus -a -um). **I.** Adv. (compar. intĕrĭus, superl. intĭmē), *within;* compar., rapiat sitiens interiusque recondat, Verg. **II.** Prepos. with acc., *within.* **A.** Lit., of space; 1, intra parietes, Cic.; 2, *into;* ingredi intra finem loci, Cic. **B.** Transf., 1, of time, *within, in the space of;* intra tot annos, Cic.; intra annos XIV, Caes.; foll. by quam, intra decimum diem quam Pheras venerat, *in less than ten days after his arrival,* Liv.; 2, with numerals, intra centum, *less than a hundred,* Liv.; 3, of other words expressing boundary, etc., cedere intra finem juris, Liv.; intra legem epulari, *within the bounds prescribed by law,* Cic.

intrābĭlis -e (intro), *that can be entered, accessible;* amnis os multis simul venientibus haud sane intrabile, Liv.

intractābĭlis -e, *unmanageable, intractable, ungovernable, rough;* genus intractabile bello, *unconquered,* Verg. ; bruma, *rough,* Verg.

intractātus -a -um, *not handled.* **I.** Lit., equus intractatus et novus, Cic. **II.** Transf., *unattempted;* scelus, Verg.

intrĕmisco -trĕmŭi, 3. (inchoat. of intremo), *to begin to tremble;* genua timore intremuere,Cic.

intrĕmo, 3. *to tremble, quake,* Verg.

intrĕpĭdē, adv. (intrepidus), *without trembling, undauntedly, intrepidly,* Liv.

intrĕpĭdus -a -um. **I.** *not trembling, undaunted, intrepid;* dux, Ov.; with dat., intrepidus minantibus, Tac. **II.** *free from care or alarm;* hiems, *undisturbed by war,* Tac.

intrīco, 1. (in and tricae), *to confuse, entangle, bring into confusion;* Chrysippus intricatur, Cic.

intrinsĕcŭs, adv. (intra and secus), *inside, inwardly, internally,* Cato.

1. intrītus -a -um (in and tero), *not worn away;* transf., *unexhausted;* cohortes intritae ab labore, Caes.

2. intrītus -a -um, partic. of intero.

1. intrō, adv. (for intero sc. loco from *interus -a -um), *within;* intro ire, Caes. ; filiam intro vocare, Cic.

2. intro, 1. (*interus), *to go into, enter.* **A.** Lit., regnum, pomoerium, Cic. ; in hortos, Ov. ; ad munimenta, Liv. ; intra praesidia, Caes. **B.** Transf., a, *to enter, penetrate;* in rerum naturam, Cic. ; in alicuius familiaritatem, Cic. ; b, of things, quo non modo improbitas sed ne imprudentia quidem possit intrare, Cic.

intrōdūco -duxi -ductum, 3. *to lead or conduct into.* **I.** Lit., copias in fines Bellovacorum, Caes. ; exercitum in Ligures, Liv. **II.** Transf., **A.** *to bring in, introduce;* philosophiam in domos, Cic. ; consuetudinem, Cic. **B.** 1, *to introduce in speech;* introducta rei similitudo, Cic. ; 2, *to maintain;* with acc. and infin., Cic.

intrōductĭo -ōnis, f. (introduco), *bringing in, introduction;* adolescentulorum, Cic.

intrŏĕo -ivi and -ĭi -ĭtum, 4. *to go into, enter;* in urbem, Cic. ; domum, Cic. ; portā, *by the gate,* Cic. ; transf., in vitam, Cic.

intrōfĕro -tŭli -ferre, *to bear, carry in;* liberis cibum, Cic.

intrōgrĕdĭor -gressus sum, 3. dep. (intro and gradior), *to enter,* Verg.

intrŏĭtus -ūs, m. (introeo), *an entrance.* **I.** 1, lit., Smyrnam, Cic. ; in urbem, Cic. ; 2, transf., *beginning, introduction, preamble;* fabulae Clodianae, defensionis, Cic. **II.** Meton., *a place of entrance, passage,* Cic.

intrōmitto -mīsi -missum, 3. *to send in, cause to enter;* legiones, Caes.

introrsŭs (introrsum), adv. (for introversus), 1, *towards the inside, inwards,* Caes. ; 2, *inwardly, internally,* Hor., Liv.

intrōrumpo -rūpi -ruptum, 3. *to break in, enter by force;* eā, Caes.

introspĭcĭo -spexi -spectum, 3. (intro and specio), *to look into, look within;* 1, lit., domum tuam, Cic. ; 2, transf., *to look attentively, observe, examine;* in omnes reipublicae partes, Cic. ; introspice in mentem tuam ipse, *cast a look within,* Cic. ; aliorum felicitatem, Tac.

intrōversus = introrsus (q.v.).

intrōvŏco, 1. *to call in, call within,* Cic.

intrūdo -trūsi -trūsum, 3. *to thrust in; se, to intrude,* Cic.

intŭbum -i, n., **intŭbus** -i, m., v. intibum.

intŭĕor -tŭĭtus sum, 2. dep. *to look at attentively, gaze at.* **I.** Lit., solem, Cic. ; in aliquem contra, *right in the face,* Liv. **II. A.** *to consider, contemplate, pay attention to;* aliquid, Cic. **B.** *to look with astonishment or admiration at;* Pompeium, Cic.

intŭĭtus -a -um, partic. of intueor.

intŭmesco -tŭmŭi, 3. *to swell, swell up.* **I. A.** Lit., intumuit venter, Ov. **B.** Transf., vox, Tac. ; intumescente motu, Tac. **II.** Fig., a, *to swell with pride;* superbiā, Tac. ; b, *to swell with anger, be angry;* intumuit Juppiter, Ov.

intŭmŭlātus -a -um (in and tumulo), *unburied,* Ov.

intŭor, 3. dep. = intueor (q.v.).

inturbĭdus -a -um, 1, pass., *undisturbed, quiet;* annus, Tac. ; 2, act., *not turbulent;* vir, Tac.

intŭs, adv. (in and -tus, cp. ἐντός), *within, inside.* **I.** 1, ea quae sunt intus in corpore, Cic. ; poet., with abl., tali intus templo, Verg. ; 2, transf., *within the heart;* intus in animis inclusae (cupiditates), Cic. **II.** With verbs of motion, *into, to the inside;* duci intus, Ov.

intūtus -a -um, *unprotected, unsafe.* **I.** Pass., castra, Liv. ; intuta moenium, *the unprotected parts of the walls,* Tac. **II.** Act., *unsafe, insecure;* latebrae, Tac. ; amicitia, Tac.

ĭnŭla -ae, f. *the plant elecampane,* Hor.

ĭnultus -a -um (in and ulciscor). **I.** *unavenged; injuriae,* Cic. ; ne inultus esset, Cic. **II.** *unpunished;* aliquem inultum sinere, or inultum esse pati, Cic.

ĭnumbro, 1. *to shade, overshadow, cover with shade;* vestibulum, Verg. ; inumbrante vesperā, *as the shades of evening were coming on,* Tac. ; ora coronis, Lucr.

ĭnunctĭo -ōnis, f. (inungo), *an anointing with salve or ointment,* Plin.

ĭnundātĭo -ōnis, f. (inundo), *an inundation, flood;* inundatio ex lacu Albano, Liv.

ĭnundo, 1. **I.** Transit., *to overflow, inundate.* **A.** Lit., hanc (terram) inundat aqua, Cic. ; vestro sanguine Enna inundabitur, Liv. **B.** Transf., *to stream over like a torrent;* hinc densi cursus inundant Troes, Verg. **II.** Intransit., *to overflow with;* inundant sanguine fossae,Verg.

ĭnungo -unxi -unctum, 3. *to anoint, smear with ointment;* oculos, Hor.

ĭnurbānē, adv. (inurbanus), *unpolitely, inelegantly, without wit or humour,* Cic.

ĭnurbānus -a -um, *rude, unpolished, rough, clownish, boorish;* 1, in demeanour, Cic. ; 2, in speech, *unrefined,* Cic.

ĭnurgĕo -ursi, 2. *to push, thrust against,* Lucr.

ĭnūro -ussi -ustum, 3. **I.** *to burn in.* **A.** Lit., notam, Verg. **B.** Transf., *to imprint indelibly, brand;* notam turpitudinis vitae alicuius, Cic. ; alicui dolorem, Cic. ; inuri notā censoriae severitatis, Cic. **II.** a, *to burn, burn up;* vulnere sanguis inustus, Ov. ; b, *to burn or singe with the curling-irons, to curl;* fig., illa calamistris, *to adorn elaborately,* Cic.

ĭnŭsĭtātē, adv. (inusitatus), *unusually, strangely;* inusitate loqui, Cic. ; inusitatius contrahere, Cic.

ĭnūsĭtātus -a -um, *unusual, strange, uncommon;* res inusitata ac nova, Cic. ; species navium inusitatior, Cic. ; with dat., inusitatas nostris oratoribus lepos, Cic. ; inusitatum est with infin., or with ut and the subj., Cic.

ĭnustus -a -um, partic. of inuro.

ĭnūtĭlis -e. **I.** *useless, unserviceable, unprofitable;* homo, Cic.; with dat., valetudine aut aetate inutiles bello, Caes.; with ad and the acc., ad usus civium non inutile, Cic.; inutile est with infin., Cic. **II.** *hurtful, injurious, harmful;* seditiosus et inutilis civis, Cic.; oratio inutilis sibi et civitati suae, Liv.

ĭnūtĭlĭtas -ātis, f. (inutilis), *uselessness, unprofitableness,* Cic.

ĭnūtĭlĭtĕr, adv. (inutilis), **1,** *uselessly, unprofitably,* Liv.; **2,** *hurtfully, injuriously,* Cic.

invādo -vāsi -vāsum, 3. **I.** *to go in, enter, come in;* **a,** in eas urbes, Cic.; with simple acc., portum, Verg.; tria milia stadiorum, *to advance,* Tac.; **b,** transf., *to undertake boldly;* aliquid magnum, Verg. **II. A.** *to attack, assault, fall upon, assail, invade;* **1,** lit., **a,** of persons, in hostem, Cic.; urbem, Verg.; **b,** of inanimate objects, *to penetrate, attack;* quocumque ignis invasit, Cic.; **2,** transf., **a,** with words, *to attack, assault;* aliquem minaciter, Tac.; **b,** of diseases, pestilentia populum invasit, Liv.; **c,** of passions and other evils, *to attack, befall;* pestis in vitam invasit, Cic.; furor invaserat improbis, Cic.; aliquem lubido invadit, Sall. **B.** *to fall upon in order to get possession of, usurp, seize;* in alicuius praedia, Cic.

invălesco -vălŭi, 3. (inchoat. of invaleo), *to gather strength, become strong;* tantum opibus invaluit, Cic.

invălētūdo -ĭnis, f. *indisposition,* Cic.

invălĭdus -a -um, **1,** *weak, powerless, feeble, impotent, indisposed, ill;* milites, Liv.; with ad and the acc., ad munera corporis senectā invalidus, Liv.; **2,** transf., *weak to resist;* exercitus, Liv.; moenia invalida adversus irrumpentes, Tac.

invectĭo -ōnis, f. (inveho), **1,** *importation,* Cic.; **2,** *an inveighing against, invective,* Cic.

invĕho -vexi -vectum, 3. **I.** Act., *to carry, bear, bring in;* **1,** lit., **a,** pecuniam in aerarium, Cic.; **b,** *to import;* vinum in Galliam, Liv.; **2,** transf., *to introduce, bring along with;* quae (mala) tibi castus invexerat, Liv.; divitiae avaritiam invexere, Liv. **II.** Middle, invehi. **A.** *to ride or travel on horseback, in a vehicle, in a ship;* curru in capitolium, Cic.; equo, Liv.; flumine, *to sail on,* Cic. **B.** Refl., se invehere and middle invehi, *to penetrate, burst into, attack;* **1,** lit., Romana se invexit acies, Liv.; quum utrinque invehi hostem nunciaretur, Liv.; **2,** transf., in aliquem or aliquid, *to attack with words, assail, inveigh against;* petulanter in aliquem, Cic.

invendĭbĭlis -e, *unsaleable,* Plaut.

invĕnĭo -vēni -ventum, 4. **I.** *to come or light upon, find, meet with.* **A.** Lit., **1,** aliquem, Cic.; naves, Caes.; **2,** *to find written, come upon in reading;* de aliqua re nulla littera in veteribus libris invenitur, Cic. **B.** Transf., **1,** *to find out;* ipsis durior inventus est, Caes.; **2,** *to procure, acquire, get, earn;* hoc cognomen, Cic.; gloriam ex culpa, Sall. **II.** *to find out, discover.* **A.** Lit., argenti venas, Cic. **B.** Transf., **1,** *to effect, bring about;* per me inventa salus, Cic.; **2,** *to find out from others, learn;* conjurationem, Cic.; inventum est with acc. and infin., Cic.; with rel. sent., non inveniebat quomodo, etc., Cic.; dolor se invenit, *shows itself,* Ov.

inventĭo -ōnis, f. (invenio), **1,** *invention,* Cic.; **2,** *the inventive faculty,* Cic.

inventor -ōris, m. (invenio), *an inventor, finder out;* novorum verborum, Cic.

inventrix -trīcis, f. (inventor), *she that finds out;* oleae Minerva inventrix, Verg.; illae omnium doctrinarum inventrices Athenae, Cic.

inventum -i, n. (invenio), *an invention, discovery,* Cic.

invĕnustē, adv. (invenustus), *ungracefully, inelegantly,* Plin.

invĕnustus -a -um, **1,** *inelegant, ungraceful,* Cic.; **2,** *unhappy in love,* Ter.

invĕrēcundus -a -um, *shameless, impudent;* deus, Bacchus, Hor.

invergo, 3. *to pour upon;* fronti vina, Verg.

inversĭo -ōnis, f. (inverto), *irony,* Cic.

inversus -a -um, partic. of inverto.

inverto -verti -versum, 3. *to turn over, turn about.* **I.** Lit., **A.** in locum anulum, Cic.; poet., inversum contristat Aquarius annum, *completed,* Cic. **B.** Esp., **1,** *to turn over;* **a,** of the plough, vomere terras graves, Verg.; **b,** of the winds, *to upturn,* Hor.; **2,** *to turn upside down, empty;* vinaria tota, Hor. **II.** Transf., **A.** *to invert, turn upside down, change, transpose, alter, pervert;* ordinem, Cic.; inversi mores, Hor. **B.** *to pervert, give a different meaning to;* verba, Cic.

invespĕrascit, 3. impers. *it grows dark, becomes twilight,* Liv.

investĭgātĭo -ōnis, f. (investigo), *an inquiring into, investigation;* veri, Cic.

investĭgātor -ōris, m. (investigo), *an inquirer, investigator;* antiquitatis, Cic.; conjurationis, Cic.

investĭgo, 1. *to search out, track out.* **I.** Of dogs, canum tam incredibilis ad investigandum sagacitas narium, Cic. **II.** Of men; **a,** aliquem, Cic.; **b,** conjurationem, Cic.; verum, Cic.

invĕtĕrasco -āvi, 3. (invetero), *to become old, grow old.* **I. a,** *to grow old in;* inveteraverunt hi omnes compluribus Alexandriae bellis, Caes.; **b,** *to become obsolete;* si (res) inveteravit, actum est, Cic. **II.** *to become old, become established, become fixed, to be rooted;* inveteravit jam opinio, Cic.; with dat., quorum nomen et honos inveteravit et huic urbi et hominum famae et sermonibus, Cic.; of persons, *to be firmly established;* exercitum hiemare atque inveterascere in Gallia, Caes.

invĕtĕrātĭo -ōnis, f. (invetero), *a becoming old, an inveterate disease or mistake,* Cic.

invĕtĕro, 1. *to allow to become old;* and pass., *to grow old, become old.* **I.** conglutinatio inveterata, *of long standing,* Cic. **II.** Middle, inveterari, *to become established, firmly rooted;* opinio inveterari potuisset, Cic.; often in partic., **invĕtĕrātus,** *old established;* amicitia, Cic.; ira, Cic.

invĭcem, adv. (in and vicis), *by turns, alternately.* **I.** hi rursus invicem anno post in armis sunt, illi domi remanent, Caes. **II.** Transf., **a,** *mutually, reciprocally;* invicem inter se gratantes, Liv.; **b,** *on both sides;* multae invicem clades, Tac.

invictus -a -um (in and vinco), *unconquered, unsubdued, unconquerable, invincible;* a labore, Cic.; ad laborem, Liv.; adversum aliquid, Tac.; Hannibal armis invictus, Liv.; absol., imperator, Cic.; defensio, *unanswerable,* Cic.

invĭdentĭa -ae, f. (invideo), *envying, envy,* Cic.

invĭdĕo -vīdi -vīsum, 2. **I.** *to look upon with the evil eye,* Cic. **II.** *to envy, grudge, be envious of;* **a,** with dat., paribus aut inferioribus, Cic.; honori, Cic.; in impers. pass., superioribus saepe invidetur, Cic.; **b,** alicui aliquid or simply aliquid; alicui honorem, Hor.; quoad id ipsi invidere dei, Liv.; **c,** alicui in aliqua re; in qua tibi invideo, Cic.; **d,** alicui aliqua re; non invideo laude sua mulieribus, Liv.; **e,** poet., alicui alicuius rei; illi ciceris, Hor.; **f,** with infin., or acc. and infin., Liburnis deduci triumpho, Hor. ; **g,** with ut or ne and the subj., Verg. ; **h,** absol., Cic.

invĭdĭa -ae, f. (invidus). **I.** envy, grudging, Nep. **II. 1, a,** hatred, jealousy, ill-will, odium, unpopularity ; invidiam alicui facere, conflare, to excite ill-will against, Cic. ; habere, to be unpopular, Cic. ; in invidiam venire, Cic. ; invidiam in aliquem commovere, concitare, excitare, Cic. ; invidiam lenire, Cic. ; absit invidia verbo, Liv. ; **b,** meton. (a) jealous or envious persons, Verg. ; (ß) something envied ; invidiae aut pestilentiae possessores, Cic. ; **2,** reproach ; invidiae erat amissum Cremerae praesidium, Liv.

invĭdĭōsē, adv. (invidiosus), enviously, jealously, bitterly, Cic.

invĭdĭōsus -a -um (invidia). **I.** full of envy ; **1,** envious ; omnes malevoli, iniqui, invidiosi, Cic. ; **2,** causing envy, envied ; invidiosae opes, Tac. ; non invidiosa voluptas, Ov. **II.** full of hate ; **1,** feeling hate, hating, Ov. ; **2, a,** causing hate, producing odium or ill-feeling ; crimen, Cic. ; with in and the acc., ut invidiosum sit in eos, Cic. ; with dat., hoc ipsis judicibus invidiosissimum futurum, Cic. ; **b,** hateful, detested ; senatus potentia, Cic.

invĭdus -a -um (invideo), envious; **I.** Lit., Cic. ; subst., an envier; laudis, Cic.; obtrectatores et invidi Scipionis, Cic. **II.** Transf., of things, cura, aetas, Hor. ; nox coeptis invida nostris, unfavourable to, Ov.

invĭgĭlo, 1. to watch in or over, be watchful or wakeful over; give great attention and care to; venatu, Verg. ; reipublicae, Cic.

inviŏlābĭlis -e, inviolable, that cannot be injured; pignus, Verg.

inviŏlātē, adv. (inviolatus), inviolately; memoriam nostri pie inviolateque servabitis, Cic.

inviŏlātus -a -um, **1,** uninjured, unhurt; invulnerati inviolatique vixerunt, Cic.; inviolatā vestrā amicitiā, Cic. ; **2,** inviolable; tribunus plebis, Liv.

invĭsĭtātus -a -um, not seen; hence, unusual, strange; magnitudo, Cic.; forma, Cic.; nova acies, Liv.

inviso, 1. **I.** to go to see, to visit. **A.** domum nostram quoad poteris invisas, Cic. **B.** to visit a person or place; aliquem, Cic. ; suos, Liv. ; Delum, Verg. **II.** to perceive, get a sight of, Cat.

1. invīsus -a -um (in and video), unseen, secret; sacra occulta et maribus non solum invisa sed etiam inaudita, Cic.

2. invīsus -a -um (invideo). **I.** Pass., hated; **a,** of persons, Cic. ; with dat., invisus deo, Cic.; **b,** of things, cupressi, negotia, Hor. ; judicium invisum etiam judicibus, Liv. **II.** Act., hating, hostile; invisum quem tu tibi fingis, Verg.

invītāmentum -i, n. (invito), an invitation, attraction, allurement; with subject. genit., naturae, Cic. ; with object. genit., temeritatis invitamenta, Liv. ; with ad and the acc., multa ad luxuriam invitamenta perniciosa, Cic.

invītātĭo -ōnis, f. (invito), invitation; with subject. genit., hospitum, Cic. ; in Epirum, Cic. ; ut biberetur, Cic. ; ad dolendum, Cic.

invītātus -ū, m. (invito), an invitation; invitatu tuo, Cic.

invītē, adv. (invitus), unwillingly, involuntarily, against one's will; invite cepi Capuam, Cic. ; vel pudentius vel invitius ad hoc genus sermonis accedere, Cic.

invīto, 1. to invite, request;civilly. **I.** Lit., **A.** aliquem in legationem to invite one to undertake an embassy, Cic. **B.** Esp., to invite as a guest; **a,** aliquem ad cenam, Cic. ; aliquem domum

suam, Cic. ; aliquem tecto ac domo, Cic. ; **b,** invitare se, to take one's fill; se cibo vinoque, Sall. **II.** to invite, allure, entice; aliquem praemiis ad rem, Cic. ; somnos, to invite, allure to sleep, Hor.

invītus -a -um. **I.** unwilling, against one's will; invitus facio ut, etc., Cic. ; eum invitissimum dimisi, Cic. ; me, te, se invito, against my, thy will, etc. ; invitissimis Stoicis, spite of the opposition of the Stoics, Cic. ; of things, invitā lege agere, Cic. **II.** Poet., given unwillingly ; invitā ope, Ov.

invĭus -a -um (in and via), impassable; saltus, Liv.; maria invia Teucris, Verg. ; invia virtuti nulla est via, Ov. Subst., **invĭa** -ōrum, n., impassable places, Liv. ; poet., lorica invia sagittis, impenetrable, Mart.

invŏcātĭo -ōnis, f. (invoco), a calling upon, invocation; deorum, Quint.

1. invŏcātus -a -um (in and voco), uncalled, Cic.

2. invŏcātus -a -um, partic. of invoco.

invŏco, 1. to call in, call upon, call for help, invoke; Junonem, Cic. ; aliquem advocatum ad communem imperatorum fortunam defendendam, Cic.

invŏlātus -ūs, m. (involo), a flying, flight, Cic. (only found in abl. sing.).

invŏlĭto, 1. to fly in ; transf., of the hair, to float or wave over; comae involitant humeris, Hor.

invŏlo, 1., **1,** to fly at, attack furiously; castra, Tac. ; **2,** to seize or pounce upon, take possession of; in possessionem quasi caducam ac vacuam, Cic. ; provinciam, Cic.

invŏlūcre -is, n. (involvo), a napkin, Plaut.

invŏlūcrum -i, n. (involvo), a wrapper, cover, case ; **1,** lit., candelabri, Cic. ; **2,** transf., involucris simulationum tegi,;Cic.

invŏlūtus -a -um, p. adj. (from involvo), obscure, confused, involved; res involutas definiendo explicare, Cic.

involvo -volvi -vōlūtum, 3. **I.** to roll in; igni suo involvunt, Tac. **II.** to roll along; silvas armenta virosque, Verg. **III.** to roll over; cupae involutae labuntur, Caes. ; with dat., to roll upon; Olympum Ossae, Verg. **IV. a,** to roll up, wrap up, cover; sinistras sagis, Caes. ; nox involvit umbrā diem, Verg. ; **b,** transf., se litteris, to bury oneself in, devote oneself to; se suā virtute, Hor. ; bellum pacis nomine involutum, concealed under, Cic.

invŏlvŭlus -i, m. (involvulo), a caterpillar which wraps itself up in leaves, Plaut.

invulgo, 1. to depose, give evidence, Cic.(?)

invulnĕrātus -a -um (in and vulnero), unwounded, Cic.

1. Ĭo, interj., an exclamation of joy and triumph, hurrah! Verg., Hor. ; or of pain, oh! Ov.

2. Ĭo (Ĭon) -ūs and -ōnis, f. (Ἰώ), daughter of the Argive king, Inachus, beloved by Jupiter, changed by Juno into a cow; identified with the Egyptian goddess, Isis.

Ĭŏlāus -i, m. (Ἰόλαος), son of Iphiclus, the constant companion of Hercules.

Ĭolcus (-ŏs) -i, f. (Ἰωλκός), town in Thessaly, the home of Jason. Hence, adj., **Ĭolcĭăcus** -a -um, of or belonging to Iolcus.

Ĭŏlē -ēs, f. (Ἰόλη), daughter of Eurytus, given by Hercules to his son Hyllus.

1. ĭon, -ĭi, n. (ἴον), **1,** the blue violet, Plin. ; **2,** a precious stone of similar colour, Plin.

2. Ĭon -ōnis, f., v. Io.

Ĭōnes -um, m. (Ἴωνες), the Ionians, a people of Greece, one of the four Greek races; hence, **1,**

adj., **Ĭŏnĭăcus** -a -um, *Ionian:* 2, **Ĭŏnĭcus** -a -um, *Ionian;* 3, **Ĭŏnĭus** -a -um, *Ionian, Ionic;* mare Ionium, *the sea between Italy and Greece*, Liv.; so aequor Ionium, Ov.; sinus Ionius, Hor., or simply Ionium -ĭi, n., Verg. Subst., **Ĭŏnĭa** -ae, f. *a district in Asia Minor between Caria and Aeolis.*

Ĭŏta n. indecl. (*ἰῶτα*), *the name of the Greek vowel*, I, ι, Cic.

Īphĭănassa -ae, f. = Iphigenia, Lucr.

Īphĭăs -ădis, f. (*Ἰφιάς*), *daughter of Iphis, i.e., Euadne.*

Īphĭgĕnĭa -ae, f. (*Ἰφιγένεια*), *daughter of Agamemnon, sacrificed by her father to appease the wrath of Diana;* or, according to another legend, *saved by Diana, and carried away, and made her priestess in Tauris.*

ipse -a -um, genit. ipsīus (poet., ipsĭus), self. ipsi (is and -pse), *self.* **I.** Gen., ille ipse, etc., Cic.; ego ipse, *I myself,* Cic.; ipse interviso, Cic.; in me ipso probavi, *in myself,* Cic.; et ipse, *also, too;* victor ex Aequis in Volscos transiit et ipsos bellum molientes, *who on their side were preparing war,* Liv. **II.** Esp., **A.** *very, identical, exactly;* **a,** eaque ipsa causa belli fuit, *and that very thing was the cause of the war,* Liv.; natali suo ipso die, *just on her birthday,* Cic.; **b,** with numerals = *just, exactly;* ipso vicesimo anno, Cic.; eā ipsā horā, Cic. **B.** ipse, ipsa, used emphatically of a *master, mistress, teacher,* etc.; ipse dixit, *the master* (i.e. *Pythagoras*) *has said it,* Cic. **C.** = *spontaneously, of one's own accord;* valvae se ipsae aperuerunt, Cic. **D.** *alone, with oneself;* genitor secum ipse volutat, Verg.; ipse per se, and simply ipse, *of himself, by himself, alone;* moventur ipsa per se, Cic. **E.** Used for the reflexive pronoun, quem si parum pudor ipsius defendebat, Cic.; ipse with suffix met, ipsimet (nom. plur.), Cic. (Superlative, ipsissimus, *one's very self,* Plaut.).

īra -ae, f. **I.** *wrath, anger, ire,* Cic.; iram evomere in aliquem, Tac.; irae indulgere, Liv.; irae caelestes, *divine wrath,* Liv.; with genit. of the cause of anger, dictatoris creati, Liv.; ira adversus Romanos, Liv.; veteres in populum Romanum irae, Liv.; transf., of inanimate objects, *violence, rage;* belli, Sall. **II.** Meton., *the cause of anger,* Ov.

īrācundē, adv. with compar. (iracundus), *wrathfully, angrily, passionately,* Cic.

īrācundĭa -ae, f. (iracundus). **I.** *an angry disposition, passionateness, irascibility,* Cic. **II.** *anger, fury, wrath;* iracundiam cohibere, Cic.; excitare, Cic.; plur., iracundiae implacabiles, Cic.

īrācundus -a -um (irascor), *inclined to anger, irascible, passionate, angry, wrathful,* Cic.; in aliquem, Cic.

īrascor, 3. dep. (ira), *to be angry, wrathful;* alicui, Cic.; of a bull, in cornua, *to charge wrathfully with the horns,* Verg.

īrātē, adv. (iratus), *angrily,* Phaedr.

īrātus -a -um (irascor), *angry, full of wrath;* alicui, *with any one;* iratior, iratissimus alicui, Cic.; quam iratus de judicio, Cic.; of inanimate objects, *raging;* mare, venter, Hor.

Īris -rĭdis, f. (*Ἶρις*), *the messenger of the gods, the goddess of the rainbow* (acc. Irim, Verg.; voc. Iri, Verg., Ov).

irnĕa = hirnea (q.v.).

īrōnĭa -ae, f. (*εἰρωνεία*), *irony,* Cic.

Irpīni = Hirpini (q.v.).

irrāsus -a -um (in and rado), *unshaved,* Plaut.

irraucesco, or **irraucĭo** -rausi, 3. (in and raucus), *to become hoarse,* Cic.

irrĕlĭgātus -a -um (in and religo), *unbound;* croceas irreligata comas, Ov.

irrĕlĭgĭōsē, adv. with compar. (irreligiosus), *irreligiously, impiously,* Tac.

irrĕlĭgĭōsus -a -um (in and religiosus), *irreligious, impious;* irreligiosum ratus, with infin., Liv.

irrĕmĕābĭlis -e (in and remeabilis), *from which there is no return;* unda, Verg.

irrĕpărābĭlis -e (in and reparabilis), *that cannot be restored, irreparable, irrecoverable;* tempus, Verg.

irrĕpertus -a -um (in and reperio), *not discovered, not found out;* aurum, Hor.

irrēpo -repsi -reptum, 3. *to creep, crawl in;* interim (Gabinius) ipso decimo die irrepsit, *came creeping in,* Cic.; transf., *to creep in, insinuate oneself into;* in mentes hominum, Cic.; in testamenta locupletium, Cic.

irrĕprĕhensus -a -um (in and reprehendo), *unblamed, blameless,* Ov.

irrĕquiētus -a -um (in and requietus), *restless, troubled;* Charybdis, Ov.

irrĕsectus -a -um (in and reseco), *uncut;* pollex, Hor.

irrĕsŏlūtus -a -um (in and resolvo), *not loosed, not slackened;* vincula, Ov.

irrētĭo, 4. (in and *retio, from rete), *to catch, entangle in a net;* a, lit., aliquem, Cic.; b, fig., aliquem corruptelarum illecebris, *to ensnare,* Cic.

irrĕtortus -a -um (in and retorqueo), *not turned or twisted back;* oculo irretorto, Hor.

irrĕvĕrentia -ae, f. (irreverens from in and reverens), *want of respect, irreverence;* juventutis, Tac.; adversus fas nefasque, Tac.

irrĕvŏcābĭlis -e (in-revocabilis), *that cannot be called back, irrevocable.* **I.** Lit., aetas, Lucr.; verbum, Hor. **II.** Transf., **A.** *unalterable;* casus, Liv. **B.** *implacable,* Ov.

irrĕvŏcātus -a -um (in and revoco), **1,** *not called back,* i.e., *not asked to repeat anything,* Hor.; **2,** *not to be called or held back,* Ov. (?)

irrīdĕo -rīsi -rīsum, 2. (in and rideo). **I.** Intransit., *to laugh at, jeer at,* Cic. **II.** Transit., *to mock, ridicule, deride;* deos, Cic.

irrīdĭcŭlē, adv. (in and ridicule), *without wit or humour;* non irridicule dixit, Caes.

irrīdĭcŭlum -i, n. (irrideo), *a laughing-stock;* irridiculo haberi (esse), *to be made game of,* Plaut.

irrĭgātĭo -ōnis, f. (irrigo). *a watering, irrigation;* agri, Cic.

irrĭgo (in-rīgo), 1. **I.** *to conduct water or any other liquid to any place;* imbres, Verg.; transf., *to diffuse,* per membra quietem, Verg. **II.** *to water, irrigate;* Aegyptum Nilus irrigat, Cic.; hortulos fontibus, Cic.; transf., fessos sopor irrigat artus, *overspreads, refreshes,* Verg.

irrĭgŭus -a -um (irrigo). **I.** Act., *watering, irrigating;* fons, Verg.; transf., somnus, *strengthening, refreshing,* Pers. **II.** Pass., *watered;* hortus, Hor.; corpus irriguum mero, *soaked,* Hor.

irrīsĭo -ōnis, f. (irrideo), *a laughing at, mocking, derision;* with subject. genit., omnium, Cic.

irrīsor -ōris, m. (irrideo), *a laugher, mocker, derider;* with object. genit., huius orationis, Cic.

irrīsus -ūs, m. (irrideo), *laughter, mockery, derision;* irrisui esse, *to be a laughing-stock,* Caes.; ab irrisu (*in derision*) linguam exserere, Liv.

irrītābĭlis -e (irrito), *irritable, easily roused;*

irritabiles sunt animi optimorum, Cic.; **genus** vatum, Hor.

irritāmen -ĭnis, n. (irrito), *an incitement, inducement;* amoris, Ov.

irritāmentum -i, n. (irrito), *incitement, inducement, provocation, incentive;* with object. genit., certaminum, Liv.; libidinum, Tac.; with dat., luxui, Tac.

irritātĭo -ōnis, f. (irrito), *a stirring up, provoking, irritating, irritation;* with subject. genit., nullis conviviorum irritationibus, Tac.; irritatio quidem animorum ea prima fuit, Liv.

irritātus -a -um, partic. of irrīto.

irrīto, 1. (in and *rito). **I.** *to stir up, stimulate, incite, excite;* aliquem ad certamen, Liv.; iram et odium, Liv. **II.** *to excite to anger, irritate;* aliquem, Cic.; animos barbarorum, Liv.

irritus -a -um (in and ratus). **I.** *void, invalid;* testamentum facere irritum, Cic. **II.** *vain;* a, of things, *vain, ineffectual, without effect;* inceptum, Liv.; dona, tela, Verg.; remedium, Tac.; subst., **irritum** -i, n. *that which is vain;* spes ad irritum cadit, *is disappointed,* Liv.; b, transf., of persons, *without doing anything;* irriti legati remittuntur, Tac.; with genit. of the object., legationis, Tac.

irrŏgātĭo -ōnis, f. (irrogo), *the imposing of a fine or penalty;* multae, Tac.

irrŏgo (in-rŏgo), 1. **I.** *to propose to the people a measure against anyone;* alicui legem, privilegium, Cic.; alicui multam, poenam, Cic. **II.** *to inflict, impose;* poenas peccatis, Hor. (irrogassit = irrogaverit, Cic.).

irrōro (in-rōro), 1. *to moisten with dew.* **I.** *to wet, moisten;* crinem aquis, Ov.; lacrimae irrorant foliis, *trickle down upon,* Ov. **II.** *to sprinkle upon;* liquores vestibus et capiti, Ov.

irrumpo -rūpi -ruptum, 3. (in and rumpo), *to break in, burst into, rush in.* **I.** Lit., 1, in castra, Cic.; with dat., thalamo, Verg.; with acc., portam, Sall.; 2, *to rush into, seize upon;* in nostrum patrimonium, Cic. **II.** Transf., luxuries quam in domum irrupit, Cic.; imagines in animos per corpus irrumpunt, Cic.; *to break in upon, seek to prevent;* in nostrum fletum irrumpes, Cic. (?)

irrŭo (in-rŭo) -rŭi, 3. *to rush into, rush upon.* **A.** Lit., 1, in aciem, Liv.; in aliquem, Cic.; 2, *to rush and seize upon, take possession of;* in alienas possessiones, Cic. **B.** Transf., ne quo irruas, *make some blunder,* Cic.; in odium offensionemque populi Romani, *rush blindly into,* Cic.

irruptĭo -ōnis, f. (irrumpo), *a breaking, bursting into, irruption;* etiamsi irruptio nulla facta est, Cic.

irruptus -a -um (in and rumpo), *unbroken, unsevered;* copula, Hor.

Ĭrus -i, m. ('Ιρος), *the name of a beggar in Ithaca;* appell. = *a poor man* (opp. to Croesus), Ov.

is, ĕa, ĭd. I. *he, she, it; this* or *that person or thing* (the demonstrative pronoun chiefly used to refer to something already mentioned). **A.** a, subst., mihi venit obviam puer tuus; is mihi literas reddidit, Cic.; b, adj., in eum locum, Caes.; ob eam causam, Nep. **B.** a, referring to a following subst., ea libera conjectura est, Liv.; b, used pleonastically for the sake of emphasis (a) with the relat., quod ne id facere posses, Cic.; esp. in apposition to a clause, si nos, id quod debet, nostra patria delectat, Cic.; (β) with a noun, urbem novam, conditam vi et armis, jure eam condere parat, Liv.; c, id subst.; id temporis, id aetatis, *at that age,* Cic.; **Id** gaudeo, *I rejoice because of that,* Cic.; in eo **est,** or **res** in eo est, *it is on the point of,* etc.,

Liv.; **d,** id est, *that is,* in explanation, hodie, id est, Cal. Oct., Cic.; **e,** et is, isque, atque is, *and that too, and indeed;* Antonius cum una legione, eāque vacillante, *and that vacillating,* Cic. **II.** *that,* as the correlative of qui, quae, quod, is qui physicus appellatur, Cic. **III.** *such, of such a kind;* a, subst., neque is es, qui, quid sis, nescias, Cic.; b, cuius ea stultitia ut, etc., Cic.

Ĭsăra -ae, f. *a river in Gaul,* now *the Isère.*

Ĭsauri -ōrum, m. (Ίσαυροι), *the Isaurians.* Hence, **A. Ĭsaurĭa** -ae, f. (Ίσαυρία), *a mountainous country of Asia Minor, north of Cilicia.* **B. Ĭsaurĭcus** -a -um, *surname of P. Servilius Vatia, the conqueror of the Isauri.* **C. Ĭsaurus** -a -um, *Isaurian.*

Ĭsis -Idis, f. (Ίσις), *the Egyptian goddess Isis.* Adj., **Ĭsĭăcus** -a -um, *of* or *belonging to Isis.*

Ismărus -i, m. (Ίσμαρος), and **Ismăra** -ōrum, n. *a mountain in Thrace.* Adj., **Ismărĭus** -a -um, poet. = *Thracian;* tyrannus, *Tereus,* Ov.

Ismēnus (-ŏs) -i, m. (Ίσμηνός), *a river in Boeotia.* Hence, **A. Ismēnis** -Idis, f. poet. = *a Theban woman.* **B. Ismēnĭus** -a -um, poet. = *Theban.*

Ĭsŏcrătēs -is, m. (Ίσοκράτης), *a celebrated Athenian orator.* Adj., **Ĭsŏcrătēus** and **Ĭsŏcrătĭus** -a -um, *Isocratean.*

Issa -ae, f. (Ίσσα), *an island in the Adriatic Sea, off the coast of Dalmatia,* now *Lissa.* Adj., **A. Issensis** -e. **B. Issaeus** -a -um. **C. Issăĭcus** -a -um, *of* or *belonging to Issa.*

istac, adv. *by that way,* Ter.

istactĕnus, adv. *thus far,* Plaut.

istĕ, ista, istūd, pron. demonstr. (is and -te), *this* or *that person* or *thing* (applies to the person spoken to). **I.** Gen., quid quod adventu tuo ista subsellia (*those seats where you sit*), vacuefacta sunt, Cic. **II.** a, in letters, *relating to places* or *conditions in which the person addressed is, perfer istam militiam, your military service,* Cic.; b, emphatic, *referring to something said by the person addressed,* Att. "Platonem videlicet dicis." M. "*istum* ipsum," Cic.; ista quae dicitis, Cic.; c, in speeches, *referring to the accused,* Cic.; d, ironical or contemptuous, ex quibus generibus hominum istae copiae comparentur, Cic.

Ister = Hister.

Isthmus, i, m. (ἰσθμός), *an isthmus;* a, *the isthmus on which Cyzicus was situated,* Prop.; b, especially *the Isthmus of Corinth,* Caes. Adj., **Isthmĭus** -a -um, *Isthmian;* labor, *in the Isthmian games,* Hor.; plur. subst., **Isthmĭa** -ōrum, n. *the Isthmian Games,* Liv.

isti, adv. (iste), *there,* Verg.

1. **istĭc (isthĭc),** istaec, istŏc or istŭc (iste and hic), *this same, this very person* or *thing;* istic labor, Plaut.; subst., istuc considerabo, Cic.; in interrogative sentences, istice, etc., Plaut.

2. **istĭc (isthĭc),** (iste and adv. hic), 1, *there,* denotes *the place of the person spoken to, here, there;* quoniam istic sedes, Cic.; scribite quid istic (= *in Rome*) agatur, Cic.; 2, *in this matter, in this affair,* Cic.; istic sum, *I am all ears,* Cic.

istim, adv. (iste), *from there,* Cic.

istinc (isthinc), adv. (iste and hinc), *thence, from thence.* **A.** Lit., *alludes to the place where the person spoken to may be;* qui istinc veniunt, Cic. **B.** Transf., *of that thing, thence,* Hor.

istiusmŏdi, *of that kind* or *sort, such;* ratio istiusmodi Cic.

istō, adv. (iste). **I.** *thither, to that place, to the place where you are;* venire, Cic. **II.** Transf., *thereunto, into that thing;* admiscere aliquem, Cic.

istōc, adv. (1. istic). **I.** *thither,* Plaut. **II.** *from that place,* Ter.

istorsum, adv. (istoversum), *thitherwards, in that direction,* Ter.

Istri, v. Histri.

1. **istŭc**, n. of 1. istic (q.v.).

2. **istūc** (**isthūc**), adv. (iste and huc), *thither;* venire, Cic.

ĭtă, adv. (i-s and -ta), *so, thus, in such wise.* **I.** Gen., a, te ita velle certe scio, Cic.; b, introducing a following thought, with acc. and infin., Cic.; c, est ita, or factum est ita, in answers, *so it is,* Cic.; ita prorsus, ita plane, *certainly,* Cic.; d, interrogative, itane? *really?* Cic.; quid ita? *why so?* Cic. **II.** Esp., **A.** With comparisons; a, gen. with ut, more rarely with quemadmodum, quomodo, quasi, etc. *so . . . . as, in such a manner . . . as;* me consulem ita fecistis quomodo pauci facti sunt, Cic.; b, in assertions and adjurations, ita vivam ut maximos sumptus facio, Cic.; saepe, ita me dii juvent, te desideravi, Cic. **B.** *of such a kind, such, in such a condition;* ita sunt res nostrae, Cic. **C.** *and so, consequently, and then;* aliquot dies aegrotasse et ita esse mortuum, Cic. **D.** To express condition or limitation, ita . . . ut, *to the extent that, only that;* ita tamen ut tibi nolim molestus esse, Cic. **E.** *with the object that,* duobus consulibus ita missis, ut alter Mithridatem persequeretur, Cic. **F.** To express degree, *so, to such an extent;* ita mendose scribuntur, Cic.

Ĭtăli -ōrum and -ûm, m. *the inhabitants of Italy, the Italians.* Hence, **A.** **Ĭtālĭa** -ae, f. *Italy.* **B.** **Ĭtālĭcus** -a -um, *Italian;* subst., **Ĭtălĭca** -ae, f. *a town in Hispania Baetica.* **C.** **Ĭtălus** -a -um, *Italian.* **D.** **Ĭtālĭs** -ĭdis, f., *Italian.* Plur., Italides = *Italian women,* Verg.

ĭtăquĕ, adv., 1, *and thus, and so,* Cic.; 2, *therefore, for that reason, on that account,* Cic.; 3, after a digression, to resume the thread of discourse, *so,* Cic.

ĭtem, adv. (i-s and -tem). **I.** *also, likewise, in like manner;* Romulus augur cum fratre item augure, Cic. **II. A.** In comparisons, *in like manner, as;* fecisti item ut praedones, Cic. **B.** et item, itemque, *and also, and even;* solis defectiones itemque lunae, Cic.

ĭtĕr, ĭtĭnĕris, n. (connected with ire, itum). **I.** *a going, walk, way.* **A.** 1, in diversum iter equi concitati, Liv.; 2, a, *a going, a journey, a march;* iter facere in Apuliam, Cic.; iter ingredi, Cic.; in itinere, *on the march,* Caes.; b, *a march,* considered as a measure of distance; cum abessem ab Amano iter unius diei, *one day's journey,* Cic.; quam maximis itineribus potest, *with the longest possible stages,* Caes.; 3, a, *a legal right of way,* Cic.; b, *permission to march;* negat se posse iter ulli per provinciam dare, Caes. **B.** Fig., defessus labore atque itinere disputationis, Cic. **II.** Concrete. **A.** Lit., *a way, road;* iter angustum et difficile, Caes. **B.** Fig., 1, *way, course;* iter amoris nostri et officii mei, Cic.; 2, *method;* naturam suo quodam itinere ad ultimum pervenire, Cic.

ĭtĕrātĭo -ōnis, f. (itero), *a repetition, iteration;* verborum, Cic.

ĭtĕro, 1, *to do a second time, repeat.* 1. pugnam, *to renew,* Liv.; aequor, *to take ship again,* Hor. **II. A.** *to plough again;* agrum non semel arare sed iterare, Cic. **B.** *to repeat* (words); verba, Cic.

ĭtĕrum, adv. **I.** a, *again, a second time;* C. Flaminius consul iterum, Cic.; b, of repeated actions, semel atque iterum, Cic.; iterum atque iterum, *again and again,* Hor.; c, in order ot events, *secondly,* semel . . . iterum, Cic. **II.** *on the other hand;* pares iterum accusandi causas esse, Tac.

Ĭthăca -ae, and **Ĭthăcē** -ēs, f. (Ἰθάκη), *an island in the Ionian Sea, the home of Ulysses.* Hence, adj., **A.** **Ĭthăcensis** -e, *Ithacan.* **B.** **Ĭthăcus** -a -um, *Ithacan.* Subst., **Ĭthăcus** -i, m. *Ulysses,* Verg.

ĭtĭdem, adv. (item-dem), *in like manner, likewise,* Cic.

ĭtĭo -ōnis, f. (eo), *a going, travelling;* domum itio, Cic.

Ĭtius portus, *a port of the Morini from which Caesar crossed over to Britain, perhaps Wit-Sand, Sandgatte, or Boulogne.*

ĭto, 1. (intens. of eo), *to go;* ad coenas, Cic.

Ĭtonē -ēs, f. (Ἰτώνη) and **Ĭtōnus** -i, m. (Ἰτωνος), *a town in Boeotia, with a temple oj Athene.* Hence, adj., **Ĭtōnĭus** -a -um, *Itonian.*

Ĭtūraei -ōrum, m. (Ἰτουραῖοι), *a people in the north-east of Palestine.* Hence, adj., **Ĭtūraeus** -a -um, *Ituraean.*

ĭtus -ūs, m. (eo), *a going, departure;* noster itus, reditus, Cic.

Ĭtўlus -i, m. (Ἴτυλος), *son of the Theban king Zetheus and Aedon, killed by his own mother.*

Ĭtўs -tўos, dat. -ty, acc. -tyn and -tym, abl. -ty, m. (Ἴτυς), *son of Tereus and Procne, killed by his mother and served up for food to his father.*

Ĭulēus = Julius. **I.** *named after Iulus, son of Aeneas,* avi, Ov. **II.** *belonging to Julius Caesar;* Calendae, *1st of July,* Ov.

Ĭulus -i, m. *son of Aeneas,* also called *Ar canius.*

Ixīon -ōnis, m. (Ἰξίων), *king of the Lapithae in Thessaly, father of Pirithous; for an insult to Juno he was hurled down to Tartarus, and bound to a perpetually revolving wheel.* Hence, **A.** Adj., **Ixīonius** -a -um, *of Ixion.* **B.** **Ixīonĭdes** -ae, m. (Ἰξιονίδης), *a son of Ixion, Pirithous,* Ov.

J.

J, j, a consonant, originally written with the same sign as the vowel I, i, yet recognised by the ancients as a different letter.

jăcĕo -cŭi -cĭtūrus, 2. (akin to jacio), *to lie* (opp. stare, pendere). **I.** Lit., **A.** Gen., humi, Cic.; in limine, Cic.; lecto, Ov.; super corpus alicuius, Ov.; ad alicuius pedes, Cic. **B.** Esp., 1, *to lie resting;* a, of persons, *to sleep;* in lecto, Cic.; b, *to recline at table,* Ov.; c, *to lie sick, be ill;* te jacente, *while you are ill in bed,* Cic.; 2, *to lie thrown to the ground;* a, Arge, jaces, Ov.; b, *to lie dead, be slain;* pro patria, Ov.; 3, *to lie or remain for a long time;* Brundusii, Cic.; 4, a, *to lie geographically, be situate;* jacet inter eos campus, Liv.; b, *to lie low, be flat;* domus depressa, caeca, jacens, Cic.; c, *to lie in ruins;* jacet Ilion ingens, Ov.; d, of clothes, *to hang loosely, be loose;* praeverrunt latas veste jacente vias, Ov.; e, *to be cast down;* vultus attolle jacentes, Ov. **II.** Fig., **A.** priora tempora in ruinis reipublicae nostrisque jacuerunt, *were united with* Cic. **B.** 1, *to be sunk*

in; in maerore, Cic.; **2, a,** *to be overcome, powerless;* (a) jacere Caesarem offensione populari, Cic.; (β) *to be hopeless, dispirited;* jacet, diffidit, abjecit hastas, Cic.; (γ) *to be neglected or despised;* philosophia jacuit usque ad hanc aetatem, Cic.; **b,** *to be overthrown, put out of court;* jacent hi suis testibus, Cic.; jacet igitur tota conclusio, Cic.; **c,** *to cease;* judicia jacebant, Cic.; **d,** *to be low in price;* jacent pretia praediorum, Cic.; **3,** of words, *to be in common use;* (verba) jacentia, Cic.

Jăcĕtāni -ōrum, m. *a people in the north of Hispania ulterior.*

jăcĭo, jēci, jactum, 3. *to throw, cast, hurl.* **I. A.** Lit., **1,** gen., in aliquem scyphum, Cic.; materiam de muro in aggerem, Caes.; se in profundum, Cic.; **2,** esp., **a,** *to throw dice;* talum, Cic.; **b,** *to throw out an anchor;* ancoram, Caes.; **c,** *to fling away;* vestem procul, Ov.; **d,** *to scatter, diffuse;* flores, Verg. **B.** Fig., **1,** *to throw, cast;* contumeliam in aliquem, Cic.; **2,** *to let fall in speaking, to utter;* assiduas ore querelas, Cic.; suspicionem, Cic.; de habitu cultuque et institutis eius, Tac. **II.** *to lay, build, erect;* aggerem, Caes.; fundamenta urbi, Liv.; fig., fundamenta pacis, Cic.

jactans -antis, p. adj. (from jacto), *boastful, vainglorious,* Cic.

jactantĕr, adv. with compar. (jactans), *boastfully, vaingloriously,* Tac.

jactantĭa -ae, f. (jacto), *boasting, bragging, vainglory;* sui, *about oneself,* Tac.

jactātĭo -ōnis, f. (jacto). **I.** Act., *a throwing, shaking, violently moving up and down;* **a,** corporis, Cic.; **b,** *extolling, belauding;* cultus, Tac. **II.** Pass., **1,** *being tossed about, tossing;* **a,** navis, Cic.; **b,** transf., *violent emotions,* Cic.; **2,** *applause;* jactationem habere in populo, Cic.; **3,** *vainglory;* alicuius, Cic.

jactātor -ōris, m. (jacto), *a boaster, ostentatious person,* Cic.

jactātus -ūs, m. (jacto), *a shaking, moving quickly up and down;* pennarum, Ov.

jactĭto, 1. (intens. of jacto), *to produce in public, to utter;* ridicula, Liv.

jacto, 1. (intens. of jacio), *to throw, cast.* **I. A.** Lit., **1,** gen., faces in vicinorum tecta, Cic.; vestem de muro, Caes.; **2, a,** *to cast dice;* numeros eburnos, Ov.; **b,** *to throw away;* arma multa passim, Liv.; **c,** *to diffuse, spread, scatter;* odorem late, Verg. **B.** Transf., *to throw, utter, hurl;* minas, Cic.; jocosa dicta in adversarios, Liv. **II.** *to move up and down, throw about, drive about, toss.* **A.** Lit., **1,** brachia, Ov.; cerviculam, Cic.; cum adversā tempestate in alto jactarentur, Cic.; aestu febrique jactari, Cic.; **2,** esp., *to throw about gesticulating;* se, Cic. **B.** Transf., **1,** gen., *to drive hither and thither;* curas pectore, Verg.; middle, jactabatur nummus, *fluctuated,* Cic.; refl., se jactare or middle jactari; se in causis centumviralibus, *to busy oneself with,* Cic.; **2,** esp., **a,** *to torment, disquiet;* jactatur domi suae, Cic.; **b,** *to talk about repeatedly, discuss, speak of;* rem in contione, Cic.; **c,** *to boast of, vaunt;* gratiam urbanam, Caes.; genus et nomen, Hor.; **d,** reflex., jactare se; (a) *to boast, brag,* Cic.; (β) *to behave oneself in a certain way;* se magnificentissime, Cic.

jactūra -ae, f. (jacio). **I.** *a throwing, throwing away;* in mari jacturam facere, *to throw overboard,* Cic. **II.** Transf., **A.** *loss, sacrifice;* jacturae rei familiaris erunt faciendae, Cic.; jacturam criminum facere, *to forego, pass over,* Cic. **B.** *cost, expense,* Cic.

jactus -ūs, m. (jacio), *a throwing, cast, throw.* **I.** fulminum, Cic.; intra teli jactum, *within*

shot, Verg. **II.** *the throw of the dice;* tesserarum prosper jactus, Liv.

jăcŭlābĭlis -e (jaculor), *that can be thrown or cast;* telum, Ov.

jăcŭlātĭo -ōnis, f. (jaculor), *a throwing, hurling,* Plin.

jăcŭlātor -ōris, m. (jaculor), **1,** *a thrower, hurler,* Cic.; **2,** *a javelin-man, a light-armed soldier,* Liv.

jăcŭlātrix -īcis, f. (jaculator), *she that hurls, the huntress (Diana),* Ov.

jăcŭlor, 1. (jaculum). **I.** Intransit., **1,** lit., *to throw a javelin;* totum diem jaculari, Cic.; **2,** transf., *to make an attack with words;* probris procacibus in aliquem, Cic. **II.** Transit., **A.** *to cast, hurl;* **1,** lit., ignes, Verg.; silicem in hostes, Ov.; **2,** transf., verbum, Lucr. **B.** *to shoot at;* **1,** lit., cervos, Hor.; **2,** transf., *to aim at, strive after;* multa, Hor.

jăcŭlum -i, n. (jacio, *the thing thrown*), **1,** *a dart, javelin;* fervefacta jacula in castra jacēre, Caes.; **2,** *a casting-net,* Ov.

jam, adv. (is), *now, already.* **I.** Temporal, **A. a,** of the immediate present, *just now;* non quia jam sint, sed quia saepe sint, Cic.; jam jamque, *directly,* Cic.; jam nunc, *just now,* Cic.; jam tum, *just then,* Cic.; **b,** of time just passed, *just lately;* illa his quae jam posui consequentia, Cic.; **c,** of future time, *immediately, directly, presently;* quam pulchra sint ipse jam dicet, Cic.; thus (a) *soon;* jam te premet nox, Hor.; (β) of commands, *now, at once;* sed jam age, carpe viam, Verg. **B. a,** *till now, up to the present time;* septingentos jam annos amplius unis moribus vivunt, Cic.; jam diu, jam dudum, jam pridem, *now for a long time,* Cic.; **b,** *from now;* jam concedo non esse miseros qui mortui sunt, Cic.; jam non, *not from this time,* Cic. **C.** To express something that happens unexpectedly early or late; **a,** *already;* omnes jam istius generis legationes erant constitutae, Cic.; **b,** *at last;* te aliquando jam rem transigere, Cic. **II.** Of other relations. **A.** *then certainly, now certainly;* da mihi hoc, jam tibi maximam partem defensionis praecideris, Cic.; thus used to express the consequence of something, *now indeed, so indeed;* id tu jam intelliges quum in Galliam veneris, Cic. **B.** To introduce some thing new, *further, moreover;* et aures . . . itemque nares . . . jam gustatus, Cic. **C.** To emphasise or limit statements, *just, indeed;* **a,** with pronoun, jam illud non sunt admonendi, Cic.; **b,** with adj., non scire quidem barbarum jam videtur, Cic.; **c,** of numerals, *just;* sunt duo menses jam, Cic.; **d,** with particles, non jam, *not indeed,* Cic.; nunc jam, *even now,* Cic.; tum jam, *just then,* Cic.

jamdūdum, jamprīdem, v. jam.

Jānālis, v. Janus.

Jānĭcŭlum -i, n. (Janus), *one of the hills of Rome, on the left side of the Tiber.*

Jānĭgĕna -ae, c. (Janus and gigno), *child of Janus,* Ov.

jānĭtor -ōris, m. (janua), *a door-keeper, porter.* **I.** Gen., janitor carceris, Cic. **II.** Esp., **A.** Of Janus, coelestis aulae, Ov. **B.** Of Cerberus, janitor immanis aulae, Hor.

jānĭtrix -īcis, f. (janitor), *a portress,* Plaut.

jānŭa -ae, f. (see Janus), **1,** *the outer door of a house;* januam claudere, Cic.; quaerere aliquem a janua, *to ask at the door for some one,* Cic.; **2,** transf., *entrance, passage;* Ditis, Verg.; maris gemini, *of the Bosphorus,* Ov.; eam urbem sibi Asiae januam fore, Cic.; fig., quā nolui januā sum ingressus in causam, Cic.

Jānŭārĭus -a -um (Janus), *belonging to*

Janus; Januarius mensis, *the month January*, Cic., or simply Januarius, Caes.; calendae Januariæ, *the 1st of January*, Cic.

Jānus -i, m. (root i, *to go*, whence also janua). **I.** *an old Italian deity, the god of the year*, represented with two faces looking in opposite directions. **II.** 1, *a covered passage*, esp. **a,** *one at the foot of the Argiletum, adorned with statues of Janus;* **b,** *one of the portals of the porta Carmentalis*, Liv.; **c,** *one of the arcades in the forum at Rome,* of which there were three, Janus summus, imus, and medius, where the merchants, bankers, and booksellers had their shops; 2, poet., *the month of January*, Ov. Hence, adj., **Jānālis** -e, *belonging to Janus*.

jĕcur, genit. jĕcŏris and jĕcĭnŏris, n., and **jŏcŭr,** genit. jŏcĭnĕris, n., *the liver*, Cic.; as *the seat of the passions* (according to the belief of the ancients); fervens difficili bile tumet jecur, Hor. (Varro and Cic. use the form jecoris, Livy jocineris.)

jĕcuscŭlum (jŏcuscŭlum) -i, n. (dim. of jecur), *a little liver*, Cic.

jējūnē, adv. (jejunus), *of style, dryly, meagrely, frigidly, without energy or taste;* de aliqua re jejune et exiliter disputare, Cic.; haec dicuntur fortasse jejunius, Cic.

jējūnĭōsus -a -um (jejunium), *hungry, fasting*, Plaut.

jējūnĭtas -ātis, f. (jejunus). **I.** *hungriness, emptiness*, Plaut. **II.** Transf., of *discourse, dryness, meagreness, frigidity, plainness;* inopia et jejunitas, Cic.

jējūnĭum -ĭi, n. (jejunus). **I.** *a fast, abstinence from food;* 1, lit., jejunium Cereri instituere, Liv.; 2, *hunger;* jejunia pascere, satiare, solvere, sedare, placare, *to satisfy hunger*, Ov. **II.** Transf., *leanness*, Verg.

jējūnus -a -um, *fasting*. **I.** 1, lit., ita jejunus ut ne aquam quidem gustarim, Cic.; 2, meton., **a,** *hungry*, Cic.; **b,** *thirsty*, Prop.; 3, **a,** *empty;* corpora suco jejuna, Lucr.; **b,** *unfruitful;* ager, Cic.; **c,** *scanty;* sanies, Verg. **II.** Fig., **A.** jejunae huius orationis aures, *unacquainted with*, Cic. **B. a,** *poor, mean;* calumnia, Cic.; **b,** *dry, meagre, weak,* oratio, Cic.; **c,** *pitiful, insipid;* illud vero pusilli animi et ipsâ malevolentiâ jejuni et inanis, Cic.

jentācŭlum -i, n. (jento), *a breakfast*, Plaut.

jento, 1. *to breakfast*, Suet.

jŏcātĭo -ōnis, f. (jocor), *a joke, jest*, Cic.

jŏcor, 1. dep. (jocus). **I.** Intransit., *to joke, jest;* cum aliquo per litteras, Cic.; me appellabat jocans, Cic. **II.** Transit., *to say in jest;* haec jocatus sum, Cic.

jŏcōsē, adv. (jocosus), *in jest;* jocosius scribere, Cic.

jŏcōsus -a -um (jocus), *jocose, humorous, witty, sportive, merry, facetious;* Maecenas, Hor.; res, Cic.; transf., imago (vocis), *the sportive echo,* Hor.

jŏcŭlāris -e (joculus), *jocular, laughable, ludicrous;* licentia, Cic.; subst., n. pl., **jŏcŭlāria** -ium, n. *jests*, Hor.

jŏcŭlārĭter, adv. (jocularis), *jocularly, jestingly*, Plin.

jŏcŭlātor -ōris, m. (joculor), *a joker, jocular person*, Cic.

jŏcŭlor, 1. dep. (joculus), *to joke, jest, speak jocosely;* quaedam militariter joculantes, *making rude soldier-jests*, Liv.

jŏcŭlus -i, 1. (dim. of jocus), *a little joke, or jest*, Plaut.

jŏcur, v. jecur.

jŏcus -i, m. (plur. joci and joca). **I.** *a joke, jest;* joci causâ, *for the jest's sake*, Cic.; per jocum, *in jest*, Cic.; extra jocum, remoto joco, *joking apart*, Cic. **II.** Transf., **a,** *a game*, Ov.; **b,** *toying*, Ov.; **c,** *a subject for jesting*, Hor.

1. **jŭba** -ae, f., 1, *the mane of any animal*, Cic.; 2, *the crest of a helmet*, Verg.

2. **Jŭba** -ae, m, ('Ιόβας), *son of Hiempsal, king of Numidia, one of the supporters of Pompeius.*

jŭbar -āris, n. (= jubare (sc. lumen) from jubar), *a beaming light, radiance,* esp. of the heavenly bodies, **a,** lit., *the light of the sun*, Ov.; *of the moon*, Ov.; *of fire*, Ov.; **b,** meton., *a star,* esp., *the morning star*, Varr.

jŭbātus -a -um (juba), *having a mane, crested;* anguis, Liv.

jŭbĕo, jussi, jussum, 2. *to order, command*. **I.** Gen. constr., **a,** with accus. and infin., Caesar te sine cura esse jussit, *told you not to be troubled*, Cic.; Dionysium jube salvere, *greet*, Cic.; pontem jubet rescindi, Caes.; in pass. with infin. alone, consules jubentur scribere, Liv.; **b,** with infin. alone, receptui canere jubet, Caes.; **c,** with ut and the subj., jubere ut haec quoque referret, Caes.; **d,** with subj. alone, Tac.; **e,** with accus. alone, fratris necem, Tac.; **f,** absol., defessa jubendo est saeva Jovis conjux, Ov. **II. A.** Of physicians, *to prescribe;* aegrotus qui jussus sit vinum sumere, Cic. **B.** As political t.t., **a,** of the Roman senate and people, *to order;* senatus decrevit populusque jussit, Cic.; senatus dictatorem dici jussit, Cic.; legem, Cic.; populus jussit de bello, Liv.; **b,** transf., of a law, lex jubet aut vetat, Cic.

jūcundē (jōcundē), adv. (jucundus), *pleasantly, agreeably, delightfully;* vivere, Cic.; jucundius bibere, Cic.

jūcundĭtas (jōcundĭtas) -ātis, f. (jucundus), *pleasantness, agreeableness, delightfulness, pleasure;* vitae, Cic.; dare se jucunditati, *to give oneself up to pleasure*, Cic.

jūcundus (jōcundus) -a -um (for juvicundus, from juvo), *pleasant, agreeable, delightful, pleasing;* est mihi jucunda in malis vestra erga me voluntas, Cic.; comes alicui jucundus, Cic.; verba ad audiendum jucunda, Cic.

Jūdaea -ae, f. ('Ιουδαία), *Judaea* or (sometimes) *Palestine;* hence, 1, adj., **Jūdaeus** -a -um, *Jewish,* and subst., **Judaei** -ōrum, m. *the Jews;* 2, **Jūdăĭcus** -a -um, *Jewish.*

jūdex -ĭcis, m. (jus dicere = judicare), *a judge.* **I.** selecti judices, *chosen by the praetor*, Cic.; judex quaestionis, *a judge chosen to preside at a trial*, Cic.; dare judicem, *to appoint a judge* (said of the praetor), Cic.; judicem alicui ferre, *of the plaintiff, to propose a judge*, Cic.; judicem dicere, *of the defendant*, Liv.; aliquem judicem sumere, or habere, Cic.; judices rejicere, *to object to*, Cic.; apud judicem causam agere, Cic.; judicem esse de aliqua re, Cic.; used with feminine nouns, dialectica veri et falsi quasi disceptatrix et judex, Cic.; hac judice, Ov. **II.** Transf., of a person who judges or decides on anything, aequissimus eorum studiorum aestimator et judex, Cic.

jūdĭcātĭo -ōnis, f. (judico), 1, *a judicial investigation*, Cic.; in a speech, *the examination of the defendant's plea*, Cic.; 2, *a judgment, opinion*, Cic.

jūdĭcātum -i, n. (judico), *a decided case, judgment, decision;* judicatum non facere, Cic.; judicatum negare, Cic.

jūdĭcātus -ūs, m. (judico), *the office or business of a judge*, Cic.

jūdĭcĭālis -e (judicium), *relating to a court of justice, judicial;* causa, Cic.

jūdĭcĭārĭus -a -um (judicium), *relating to a court of justice;* quaestus, Cic.

jūdĭcĭum -ĭi, n. (judex). **I.** 1, *a trial, legal investigation;* judicium dare or reddere, Cic.; qui judicium exercet, i.e., *the praetor,* Cic.; 2, meton., a, *a law-suit,* Cic.; b, *the judicial office,* Sall.; c, *the place of trial,* Nep.; d, *the judges;* judicium sortiri, Cic. **II.** *judgment, decision.* **A.** Lit., of an authority or superior, Cic.; senatus, Caes. **B.** Transf., 1, *opinion, view;* judicium facere, *to decide,* Cic.; meo judicio, *in my opinion,* Cic.; 2, a, *the judgment, power of judging, discernment, understanding;* intelligens, Cic.; subtile, Hor.; b, *reflection, consideration;* judicio aliquid facere, Cic.

jūdĭco, 1. (jus dico). **I.** *to investigate judicially, to be a judge,* Cic.. **II.** *to judge, decide.* **A.** Lit., rem, Cic.; lites, Cic.; aliquid contra aliquem, Cic.; with acc. and infin., deberi dotem, Cic.; judicata res, *a decided case,* Cic. **B.** Transf., 1, *to determine, decide;* judicatum est, Cic.; 2, *to judge;* a, ii quos ego posse judicare arbitrarer, Cic.; b, *to esteem, value;* prudentem non ex ipsius habitu sed ex aliqua re externa, Cic.; c, *to be of an opinion;* quod ante judicaram, Cic.; with acc. and infin., judico neminem tanta habuisse ornamenta, Cic.; or in pass., with nom. and infin.; nos bene emisse judicati sumus, Cic.; d, *to declare openly;* Dolabellā hoste judicato, Cic.

jŭgālis -e (jugum), *yoked together;* a, subst., **jŭgāles** -ĭum, m. *a team* or *yoke,* Verg.; b, *matrimonial, nuptial;* vinculum, Verg.; dona, Ov.

Jŭgārĭus vicus, *a part of Rome, at the foot of the capitol, named after Juno Juga, who had an altar there.*

jŭgātĭo -ōnis, f. (jugo), *the training of vines on a trellis,* Cic.

jūgĕrum -i, n., plur. according to the 3rd declension (jugis), 1, *a plot of land* 240 *feet long by* 120 *broad, and containing therefore* 28,000 *square feet,* Cic.; 2, *as a translation of the Greek πλέθρον, a measure of length, containing* '00 *Greek or* 104 *Roman feet,* Plin.

jūgis -e (jungo), *joined together;* a, *juge auspicium, an auspice marred by the dunging of yoked oxen,* Cic.; b, *perpetual, continuous, never-failing;* aqua, Cic.; puteus, Cic.

jūglans -glandis, f. (=Jovis glans), *a walnut,* Cic.

jūgo, 1. (jugum), *to bind together, connect;* a, virtutes inter se jugatae sunt, Cic.; b, *to marry, give in marriage,* Verg.; aliquem or aliquam alicui, Verg.

jŭgōsus -a -um (jugum), *mountainous,* Ov.

jŭgŭlae -ārum, f. (*jugulus = junctus), *the three stars which form the belt of the constellation Orion,* Plaut.

jŭgŭlo, 1. (jugulum), *to cut the throat, slay, kill.* **I.** Lit., suem, Cic.; cives optimos, Cic. **II.** *to ruin, destroy;* aliquem factis decretisque, Cic.; jugulari suā confessione, Cic.

jŭgŭlum -i, n. and **jŭgŭlus** -i, m. (jungo). **I.** *the collar-bone,* Plin. **II.** *the hollow above the collar-bone, the throat;* jugula concava, Cic.; jugulum dare (alicui), Cic., or porrigere, Hor.; of the defeated gladiator, *to present his throat to his adversary's stroke.*

jūgum -i, n. (root JUG, whence also jungo, Gk. ZΥΓ, whence ζυγόν, ζεύγνυμι). **I.** *a yoke passing over the necks of two oxen, a horse's collar.* **A.** 1, lit., juga imponere bestiis, Cic.; 2, meton., a, *a team* or *yoke of oxen,* Cic.; b, *a team of horses,* Verg.; c, transf., *a pair, a couple;* impiorum (of Antonius and Dolabella), Cic. **B.** Fig., 1, ferre jugum pariter, *to love in*

adversity as well as in prosperity, Hor.; 2, a, *the marriage-tie,* Ov.; b, *the yoke of slavery;* jugum accipere, Liv. **II.** 1, *the yoke under which the Romans compelled their vanquished enemies to pass in token of submission;* mittere sub jugum, Cic., Liv. 2, a, *the constellation Libra,* Cic.; b, *the beam of a pair of scales,* Liv.; 3, *the beam of a weaver's loom,* Ov.; 4, juga, *the rowers' benches,* Verg.; 5, *a ridge* or *summit of a mountain;* summum jugum montis, Caes.

Jŭgurtha -ae, m. *king of Numidia, who carried on a long war with the Romans, and was conquered by Marius.* Hence, adj., **Jŭgurthīnus** -a -um, *Jugurthine.*

Jūlĭus -a -um, *name of a Roman gens, the most celebrated members of which were* a, C. Julius Caesar; b, *his adopted son* Octavius; and c, Julia, *daughter of Augustus, wife of Marcellus, Agrippa, and Tiberius.* Adj., *Julian;* lex, *of Julius Caesar,* Cic.; mensis Julius or simply Julius, *the month of July,* so called in honour of Julius Caesar, formerly called Quinctilis.

jūmentum -i, n. (= jugmentum from jungo, as examen = exagmen), *an animal used for carrying* or *drawing, beast of burden,* Cic.

juncĕus -a -um (juncus), *of* or *relating to rushes, made of rushes;* vincula, Ov.

juncōsus -a -um (juncus), *full of rushes, rushy;* litora, Ov.

junctim, adv. (junctus), *successively, both together,* Suet.

junctĭo -ōnis, f. (jungo), *a joining, connexion;* eorum verborum, Cic.

junctūra -ae, f. (jungo), *a joining.* **A.** Lit., *a joint;* tignorum, Caes.; laterum, Verg. **B.** Transf., 1, generis, *relationship,* Ov.; 2, rhetorical combination, putting together, Hor.

junctus -a -um, p. adj. (from jungo), *joined together, yoked together, connected, united.* **I.** junctior cum exitu, Cic. **II.** 1, *joined by affection, relationship,* etc.; junctissimus, *most nearly connected, very intimate,* Ov.; 2, rhet. t. t., *well put together;* oratio, Cic.

juncus -i, m. (σχοῖνος), *a rush, bulrush;* limosus, Verg.; junci palustres, Ov.

jungo, junxi, junctum, 3. (root JUG, Gk. ZΥΓ, whence ζεύγνυμι, ζυγόν), *to join, unite, connect.* **I.** Lit., **A.** res inter se, Cic.; aliquid cum aliqua re, Cic.; oscula, *to kiss,* Ov.; fluvium ponte, Liv.; pontem, Tac.; *to throw a bridge over a river.* **B.** Esp., 1, *to yoke;* equos curru (dat.), Verg.; 2, of places, in passive, *to border on;* Jano loca juncta, Ov.; 3, milit. t. t., *to unite troops;* socia arma Rutulis, Liv. **II.** Transf., **A.** cum hominibus consuetudinis jungebat, Cic.; with abl., improbitas scelere juncta, Cic.; with dat., indignatio juncta conquestioni, Cic. **B.** Esp., 1, *to unite in marriage;* aliquem secum matrimonio, Liv.; alicui, Ov.; se alicui, Ov.; 2, *to connect by affection, relationship, friendship;* se ad aliquem, Cic.; amicitiam cum aliquo, *to form,* Cic.; 3, *to unite politically;* foedere or societate alicui jungi, Liv.; 4, *to connect grammatically;* juncta verba, Cic.

jūnĭor, v. juvenis.

jūnĭpērus -i, f. *the juniper-tree,* Verg.

Jūnĭus -a -um, *the name of a Roman gens, the most famous members of which were* L. Junius Brutus *and the two* Bruti, M. Jun. Brutus *and* D. Jun. Brutus, *the murderers of Caesar;* adj., *Junian;* mensis Junius or simply Junius, *the month of June.*

Jūno -ōnis, f. (= Jovino), *the goddess Juno, daughter of Saturn, sister and wife of Jupiter;* Juno inferna, *Proserpine,* Verg.; so Juno Averna,

Ov.; urbs Junonis, *Argos*, Ov. Hence, **A. Jūnōnālis** -e, *relating or belonging to Juno; tempus, the month of June*, Ov. **B. Jūnōnius** -a -um, *Junonian;* hospitia, *Carthage*, Verg.; ales, *the peacock*, Ov.; custos, *Argus*, Ov.; mensis, *June*, Ov. **C. Jūnōnĭcŏla** -ae, c. *a worshipper of Juno.* **D. Jūnōnĭgĕna** -ae, m. *son of Juno, of Vulcan*, Ov.

Juppĭter, Jŏvis, m. (prop., Diuspater, Diuspiter, Diespiter, *the father of the heavens*), *Jupiter,* 1, *the supreme god among the Romans, brother and husband of Juno, corresponding to the* Zεύς *of the Greeks;* Jovis satelles, Cic., ales, *the eagle*, Ov.; Juppiter Stygius, *Pluto*, Verg.; 2, transf., a, *the planet Jupiter*, Cic.; b, *air, sky, heavens;* sub Jove, *in the open air*, Ov.

Jūra -ae, m. *a mountain-chain extending northwards from the banks of the Rhone.*

jūrandum -i, n. (juro), *an oath*, Ter.

jūrātor -ōris, m. (juro), *a sworn assessor, assistant of the censor*, Liv.

1. **jūrātus** -a -um, partic. of juro.

2. **jūrātus** -a -um (jus), *sworn, bound by an oath;* jurati judices, Cic.

jūrĕconsultus = jurisconsultus (q. v.).

jūrĕjūro, 1. (jus and juro), *to swear by an oath*, Liv.

jūrĕpĕrītus = jurisperitus (q. v.).

jurgĭum -ĭi, n. (jurgo), *altercation, verbal contention, strife, quarrel, brawl;* jurgio saepe contendere cum aliquo, Cic.

jurgo, 1. (= jure ago). **I.** Intransit., *to quarrel, contend in words, brawl*, Cic. **II.** Transit., *to scold*, Hor.

jūrĭdĭcĭālis -e (juridicus), *relating to right* or *justice;* constitutio, Cic.

jūrisconsultus -i, m. *one learned in the law, a lawyer*, Cic.

jūrisdictĭo -ōnis, f. **I.** *the administration of justice by the praetor, judicial authority*, Cic.; jurisdictio urbana et peregrina (of the praetor urbanus and peregrinus), Liv.; jurisdictio in libera civitate contra leges senatusque consulta, Cic. **II.** Meton., *a place where justice is administered, an assize-town*, Tac.

jūrispĕrītus -i, m. *one skilled* or *experienced in the law*, Cie.

jūro, 1. (2. jus). **I.** Intransit., *to swear, take an oath.* **A.** ex animi mei sententia, Cic.; per deos, Sall.; pro aliquo, *in the place of some one*, Liv. **B.** in verba alicuius, *to swear after a certain formula*, Liv.; in certa verba, Cic.; in legem, *to swear to*, Cic.; omnis exercitus in se quisque jurat, *each soldier took the oath separately*, Liv. **II.** Transit., **A.** *to swear;* juravi verissimum jusjurandum, Cic. **B.** *to affirm on oath, to swear to;* morbum, *to the fact that one is ill*, Cic.; falsum jurare, Cic.; id in litem, *in support of a suit*, Cic.; with acc. and infin., Cic. **C.** *to call the gods to witness;* deos, Ov. **D.** *to deny on oath;* calumniam in aliquem, Liv.

jūror -ātus sum, dep. 1. (= juro), *to swear;* quid juratus sit, Cic.; partic. juratus, *sworn on oath;* si diceret juratus, Cic. (only used in perf. and partic. perf.).

1. **jūs,** jūris, n. (connected with ζύος, from ζέω, ζύω), *broth, soup*, Cic.

2. **jūs,** jūris, n. (from the same root as jubeo, lit. = jussum), *right, law.* **I. A.** As contained in statutes, etc., principia juris, Cic.; jus ac fas omne delere, Cic.; jura dare, *to give laws*, Liv. **B.** 1, *law, as comprising rights;* jus hominum, *natural law*, Cic.; jus gentium, Cic.; jus civile, *the common law*, Cic.; 2, a, *law, as*

opposed to equity; summum jus, summa injuria, Cic.; jus dicere, *to declare the law, to decide judicially* (said of the praetor), Cic.; b, meton., *a court of justice;* in jus vocare, Cic.; adire, Cic. **II.** Transf., **A.** *right, law, as common to mankind;* divina ac humana jura, Cic.; uxores eodem jure sunt quo viri, *have the same rights as*, Cic.; jure optimo, *by the best of rights*, Cic.; jus est, with infin., *it is right*, Cic. **B.** 1, *right, privilege;* jus civitatis, Cic.; jus auxilii sui, Liv.; 2, *legal right, authority;* jus agendi cum plebe, Cic.; sui juris esse, *to be independent*, Cic.

jusjūrandum, jūrisjūrandi, n. *an oath;* alicui jusjurandum dare, foll. by acc. and infin., *to promise on oath*, Cic.; jusjurandum accipere, *to take an oath*, Caes.; jusjurandum violare, Cic.; consecrare, Cic.; fidem astringere jurejurando, Cic.; aliquem jurejurando obstringere, with acc. and infin., Caes. (Sometimes separated, e.g., jus igitur jurandum, Cic.)

jussum -i, n. (jubeo), gen. in plur. **I.** *a command, order*, Cic.; jussa efficere, Sall. **A.** *the prescription of a physician*, Ov. **B.** *the command of the Roman people;* perniciosa et injusta jussa, Cic.

jussus -ū, m. (jubeo), *a command, commanding;* vestro jussu, *by your order*, Cic.

justē, adv. (justus), *justly, rightly;* imperare, Cic.; facilius fieri potuerit et justius, Cic.; immo justissime, Cic.

justĭfĭcus -a -um (justus and facio), *acting justly*, Cat.

justĭtĭa -ae, f. (justus), *justice, love of justice, equity;* justitiam colere, Cic.; justitia erga deos, Cic.; in hostem, Cic.

justĭtĭum -ĭi, n. (juris -stitium, from jus and sisto), *a suspension of business in the courts of law.* **I.** a, justitium indicere, edicere, *to proclaim a suspension of legal business;* justitium remittere, *to close*, Liv.; b, transf., *a pause, cessation, suspension;* omnium rerum, Liv. **II.** *a public mourning*, Tac.

justus -a -um (jus). **I.** Of persons, *just, upright, impartial;* judex, Cic. **II.** Of objects, **A.** *just, equitable, fair;* supplicium, Cic.; bellum, Liv.; hostis, *having the right on his side*, Cic.; subst., justum colere, *to do what is right*, Cic. **B.** Transf., 1, *well grounded, justifiable;* causa, Cic.; ira, Cic.; 2, *regular, proper, perfect, complete, suitable;* proelium, Liv.; victoria, Cic.; 3, *fitting, right, sufficient;* numerus, Liv.; altitudo, Caes.; neut. subst., plus justo, *more than is right*, Hor.; so longior justo, Ov.; plur., **justa** -orum, a, *what is fitting;* justa praebere servis, Cic.; b, *due forms and observances, esp. funeral rites;* justa facere alicui, Cic.

Jūturna -ae, f. (juvo), *the nymph of a spring in Latium, sister of Turnus, worshipped at Rome and sacrificed to in times of scarcity of water; a spring near the river Numicius, also worshipped.*

1. **jŭvĕnālis** -e (juvenis), *youthful;* corpus, Verg.; ludus, Liv.

2. **Jŭvĕnālis** -is, m., D. Junius, *a Roman writer of satires, contemporary of Domitian and Trajan.*

jŭvĕnālĭtĕr, adv. (1. juvenalis), *like a young man, with the strength of a young man*, Ov.

jŭvencus -a -um (for juvenicus, from juvenis), *young.* **I.** Adj., equus, Lucr. **II.** Subst., **A.** **jŭvencus** -i, m., a, *a young man*, Hor.; b, *a young bullock* or *ox*, Verg. **B.** **jŭvenca** -ae, f., a, *a young woman, a maiden*, Hor.; b, *a young cow, heifer*, Verg. (genit. plur., juvencûm, Verg.).

jŭvĕnesco -vĕnŭi, 3. (juvenis), **1**, *to grow up to youth;* vitulus, Hor.; **2**, *to become young again;* juvenescit homo, Ov.

jŭvĕnīlis -e (juvenis), *youthful, juvenile;* licentia, Cic.; redundantia, Cic.

jŭvĕnīlĭtĕr, adv. (juvenilis), *youthfully, like a youth;* Annibal juveniliter exsultans, Cic.

jŭvĕnis -is (juvo). **I.** Adj., *young, youthful;* anni, Ov.; compar., junior, Liv. **II.** Subst., **jŭvĕnis** -is, c., *a young man, young woman, one in the prime of life* (generally from the twentieth to the fortieth year), Cic.

jŭvĕnor, 1. dep. (juvenis), *to act like a youth, with youthful indiscretion and impetuosity,* Hor.

jŭventa -ae, f. (juvenis), *youth.* **I.** 1, lit., *the time of youth;* flos juventae, Liv.; 2, meton., (a) *the youth = the young;* imbellis, docilis, Hor.; (β) prima juventa, *the down on a young man's cheeks,* Verg.; (γ) abstract, *the force of youth;* virtus et juventa, Liv. **II.** Personif., *the goddess of youth,* Ov.

jŭventas -ātis, f. (juvenis). **I.** *youth, the time of youth;* 1, lit., Verg.; 2, meton., a, prima juventas, *the down on a young man's cheeks,* Verg.; b, *the vigour of youth,* Hor. **II.** Person., *the goddess of youth,* Hebe, Cic.

jŭventus -ūtis, f. (juvenis), *youth, the period of life between the twentieth and the fortieth year.* **A.** Lit., ea quae juventute geruntur et viribus, Cic. **B.** Meton., *young men;* juventus Romana, Liv.; legendus est hic orator juventuti, Cic.; princeps juventutis, in republican times, *the first among the knights,* Cic.

jŭvo, jūvi, jūtum, fut. partic., jŭvātūrus, 1. **I.** *to help, assist, aid, be of service;* aliquem in aliqua re, Cic.; aliquem auxilio laboris, Cic.; hostes frumento, Caes.; juvante deo, diis juvantibus, *with God's help,* Cic. **II.** *to delight, please, gratify;* ut te juvit coena? Hor.; ita se dicent juvari, Cic.; often impers., juvat, with infin., *it delights, it pleases;* juvit me tibi tuas literas profuisse, Cic.; forsan et haec olim meminisse juvabit, Verg.

juxtā (connected with jungo). **I.** Adv., **A.** Of space, *close to, by the side of, near, hard by;* legio quae juxta constiterat, Caes.; sellam juxta ponere, Sall. **B.** Transf., *in like manner, equally;* vitam mortemque juxta aestimo, Sall.; aliaque castella juxta ignobilia, Liv.; juxta ac si hostes adessent, Liv.; juxta quam, Liv.; with dat., res parva ac juxta magnis difficilis, Liv.; with cum and the abl., juxta mecum omnes intelligitis, Sall. **II.** Prep. with acc. **A.** Of space, 1, lit., *near to, hard by;* juxta murum castra posuit, Caes.; 2, transf., *immediately after or upon, next to;* juxta deos in tuā manu positum est, Tac. **B.** Of time, *just before;* juxta finem vitae, Tac.

juxtim, adv. (connected with jungo), *near, close by,* Lucr.

K.

K, The letter K, k, was originally a part of the Latin Alphabet, but afterwards almost entirely disappeared from it, and was replaced by C. K was only used in abbreviations, as K. = Kaesar, Kal. = Kalendae.

Kălendae = Calendae (q.v.).
Karthāgo = Carthago (q.v.).

L.

L, l, corresponds to the Greek lambda (Λ, λ). For its use as an abbreviation, v. Table of Abbreviations.

lābasco, 3. (labo), **1**, *to totter, threaten to fall,* Lucr.; **2**, *to give way,* Ter.

lābea -ae, f., *the lip* = labia (q.v.).

lābēcŭla -ae, f. (dim. of labes), *a little spot or stain, a slight disgrace,* Cic.

lābĕfăcĭo -fēci -factum, 3., pass., lăbĕfīo, -factus sum -fĭĕri (labo and facio). **I.** *to make to totter, shake, loosen;* partem muri, Caes.; charta sit a vinclis non labefacta suis, not opened, Ov. **II.** Transf., 1, a, *to weaken;* corpora aestus impatientia labefecit, Tac.; b, politically, *to shake, impair;* jura plebis, Cic.; 2, *to cause to shake or waver;* quem nulla unquam vis, nullae minae, nulla invidia labefecit, Cic.

lābĕfacto, 1. (intens. of labefacio), *to cause to totter, shake violently.* **I.** Lit., signum vectibus, Cic. **II.** Transf., 1, a, animam sedibus intus, Lucr.; b, *to injure, weaken, destroy;* alicuius fidem pretio, *to corrupt,* Cic.; amicitiam aut justitiam, Cic.; vitas hominum, *to disturb, disquiet,* Cic.

1. **lābellum** -i, n. (dim. of 1. labrum), *a little lip,* Cic.

2. **lābellum** -i, n. (dim. of 2. labrum), *a small bathing-vessel,* Cic.

Lăbĕrĭus -a -um, *name of a Roman gens,* the most famous member of which was D. Laberius, *a knight and writer of mimes, contemporary of Jul. Caesar.*

lābes -is, f. (1. labor), *a falling in, sinking in.* **I.** Lit., esp. of the earth, multis locis labes factae sint, Cic. **II.** Transf., **A.** prima labes mali, *the first mischance,* Verg. **B.** 1, *ruin, destruction;* innocentiae labes aut ruina, Cic.; applied to a person, labes atque pernicies provinciae Siciliae, Cic.; 2, *a spot, stain, blemish;* a, physical, sine labe toga, Ov.; victima labe carens, Ov.; b, moral, *mark of disgrace, stain of infamy, disgrace, dishonour, ignominy;* illa labes atque ignominia reipublicae, Cic.; alicui labem inferre, Cic.

lābĭa (lābĕa) -ae, f. and **lābĭum** -ĭi, n. (lambo), *a lip,* Plaut.

Lăbīci (Lāvĭci) -ōrum, m. and **Lăbīcum** -i, n. *an old Latin town, fifteen miles south-east of Rome.* Hence, adj., **Lăbīcānus** -a -um, *of or belonging to Labicum;* subst., a, **Lăbīcānum** -i, n. *the territory of Labicum;* b, **Lăbīcāni** -orum, m. *the inhabitants of Labicum.*

Lăbĭenus -i, m., T., *a legate of Julius Caesar, who deserted to Pompeius at the breaking out of the Civil War.*

lăbĭōsus -a -um (labium), *with large lips,* Lucr.

lăbĭum -ĭi, n. = labia (q.v.).

lābo, 1. *to totter, waver, be about to fall, begin to sink.* **I.** Lit., signum labat, Cic.; labat ariete crebro janua, Verg.; labantem unā parte aciem, *wavering,* Liv. **II.** Transf., 1, *to waver, totter;* omnes reipublicae partes aegras et labantes sanare et confirmare, Cic.; memoria labat, *is uncertain,* Liv.; 2, *to waver in fidelity or opinion;* scito labare meum consilium, Cic.; fides sociorum labare coepit, Liv.

1. **lābor,** lapsus sum, 3. dep. *to glide, slide, fall down, slip.* **I.** 1, lit., ex equo, Liv.; humor in genas furtim labitur, Hor.; stellas praecipites coelo labi, Verg.; lapsi de fontibus amnes, Ov.!

juia continenter laberentur et fluerent omnia, Cic. ; 2, transf., a, *to glide, to run, to flow;* sed labor longius, ad propositum revertat, *I wander from the point,* Cic. ; oratio sedate placideque labitur, *flows along,* Cic. ; of time, *to pass away;* labuntur tempora, Hor. ; b, *to incline to, fall into;* labor eo ut assentiar Epicuro, *I feel myself drawn into,* etc., Cic. ; civitatum mores lapsi ad mollitiem, Cic. II. A. *to glide down, glide off, deviate from;* ne adjectae voces laberentur atque errarent, Cic. ; hac spe lapsus, *deceived,* Cic. B. *to slip, to stumble;* 1, lit., agaso pede lapsus, Hor. ; 2, transf., a, *to make a slip, to make a mistake;* erravit, lapsus est, non putavit, Cic. ; in aliqua re, Cic. ; per errorem, Cic. ; propter imprudentiam, Cic. ; in officio, Cic. ; b, *to be on the point of falling;* labentem et prope cadentem rempublicam, Cic. C. *to glide out, to fall out;* viscera lapsa, Ov. ; of persons, *to slip away;* custodiā, Tac. D. *to fall to the ground;* calor ossa reliquit, labitur, Verg. ; labentes deorum aedes, Hor. ; transf., *to fall, be destroyed;* lapsum genus, Verg.

2. **lăbor** -ōris, m. *work, labour, toil, effort.* I. Lit., a, gen., res est magni laboris, *is difficult,* Cic. ; capere tantum laborem, Cic. ; impenditur labor ad incertum casum, Cic. ; laborem hominum periculis sublevandis impertire, Cic. ; laborem interponere pro aliquo, Cic. ; labor est, with infin., *it is a work of difficulty,* Liv. ; b, *activity, industry, capacity for work;* homo magni laboris, Cic. ; 2, meton., a, *work, result of labour;* multorum mensium labor interiit, Caes. ; b, *deed, undertaking;* belli, Verg. II. a, *hardship, fatigue, need, distress, difficulty;* cuius erga me benevolentiam vel in labore meo vel in honore perspexi, Cic. ; poet., labores solis, *eclipse of the sun,* Verg. ; Lucinae, *pains of labour,* Verg.; b, *sickness,* Plaut.

lăbōrĭfer -fĕra -fĕrum (labor and fero), *bearing toil and hardship;* Hercules, Ov.

lăbōrĭōsē, adv. (laboriosus), *laboriously, with toil and fatigue;* quo quisque est ingeniosior, hoc docet iracundius et laboriosius, Cic. ; diligentissime laboriosissimeque accusare, Cic.

lăbōrĭōsus -a -um (2. labor). I. *full of toil, hardship, trouble, laborious;* a, vitae genus laboriosum sequi, Cic. ; b, of persons, *industrious,* Cic. II. *troubled, harassed, undergoing trouble and hardship;* laboriosa cohors Ulixei, Hor. ; quid nobis duobus laboriosius, Cic.

lăbōro, 1. (2. labor). I. Intransit. A. a, *to work, toil, labour, strive;* sibi et populo Romano, non Verri laborare, Cic. ; in aliqua re, Cic. ; de aliqua re, Cic. ; de aliquo, Cic. ; in aliquid, Liv. ; with ut or ne and the subj., Cic. ; non laboro, with infin., Cic. ; b, *to be troubled about, to be distressed, to care;* quorsum recidat responsum tuum, non magno opere laboro, Cic. B. *to suffer, labour under anything, be oppressed with, afflicted with;* morbo, *to be ill,* Cic. ; ex intestinis, pedibus, renibus, *to suffer pain in,* Cic. ; ex invidia, Cic. ; a re frumentaria, Caes. ; in re familiari, Cic. ; absol., *to be in danger;* illi laboranti subvenire, Caes. ; of things, quod vehementer eius artus laborarent, *as he suffered from gout,* Cic. ; digitorum contractio nullo in motu laborat, *finds no difficulty in,* Cic. ; quum luna laboret, *is eclipsed,* Cic. II. Transit., *to work out, to elaborate, prepare, form;* arte laboratae vestes, Verg. ; dona laboratae Cereris, *corn made into bread,* Verg.

lăbos -ōris, m. = 2. labor (q.v.).

Lăbrōs -i, m. (Λάβρος), *name of a dog,* Ov.

1. **lăbrum** -i, n. (lambo), *a lip;* superius, *the upper lip,* Caes. ; prov., primis labris gustasse physiologiam, *to have only a superficial*

knowledge of, Cic. ; meton., *the edge, rim, lip;* fossae, Caes.

2. **lābrum** -i, n. (lavo), a, *a basin, vessel, tub,* Verg. ; b, especially, *a bathing-vessel,* Cic. ; meton. poet., labra Dianae, *bath,* Ov.

lābrusca -ae, f. *the wild vine,* Verg.

lābruscum -i, n. *the fruit of the wild vine,* Verg.

lăburnum -i, n. *the laburnum tree* (Cytisus Laburnum, Linn.), Plin.

lăbўrinthēus -a -um (labyrinthus), *labyrinthine,* Cat.

lăbўrinthus -i, m. (λαβύρινθος), *a labyrinth,* esp. *the labyrinth in Crete constructed by Daedalus,* Verg.

lac, lactis, n. (akin to γάλα, γάλακτος), *milk.* I. Lit., Cic. II. Transf., *the milky sap of plants,* Ov.

Lăcaena -ae, f. (Λάκαινα), Spartan, Lacedaemonian; virgo, Verg. ; subst., *a Spartan woman;* esp., *Helen,* Verg. ; *Leda,* Mart.

Lăcĕdaemon -ōnis, f. (Λακεδαίμων), *the city* Lacedaemon or *Sparta;* hence, adj., **Lăcĕdaemŏnĭus** -a -um, *Lacedaemonian;* Tarentum, *built by a colony from Sparta,* Hor.

lăcer -cĕra -cĕrum. I. Pass., *torn, maimed, dismembered, torn to pieces;* corpus, Sall.; vestis, Tac. II. Act., *tearing to pieces;* morsus, Ov.

lăcĕrātĭo -ōnis, f. (lacero), *a tearing to pieces, maiming, mangling, laceration;* corporis, Cic.

lăcerna -ae, f. *a mantle worn over the toga on a journey or in bad weather,* Cic.

lăcernātus -a -um (lacerna), *clad in the lacerna,* Juv.

lăcĕro, 1. (lacer), *to tear to pieces, maim, mangle, lacerate.* I. Lit., alicuius corpus lacerare atque vexare, Cic.; lacerare aliquem omni cruciatu, Cic.; pontes, *to destroy,* Liv. II. Transf., 1, *to wound deeply, ruin, destroy;* lacerare rempublicam, Cic.; patriam scelere, Cic.; esp., a, *to squander;* pecuniam, Cic.; b, *to distress, torture;* meus me moeror quotidianus lacerat, Cic.; 2, *to wound with words, rail at, asperse, attack, rend;* haec te lacerat, haec cruentat oratio, Cic.; aliquem probris, Liv.

lăcerta -ae, f. I. *a lizard,* Hor. II. *a sea-fish,* Cic.

lăcertōsus -a -um (lacertus), *muscular, powerful;* centuriones, Cic.

1. **lăcertus** -i, m., gen. plur. = *the muscles.* I. Gen., 1, lit., lacertos exercitatio expressit, Quint. ; 2, fig., of oratorical vigour, in Lysia sunt lacerti, Cic. II. 1, *the muscles of the upper part of the arm* (from the shoulder to the elbow), Milo Crotoniates nobilitatus ex lateribus et lacertis suis, Cic. ; 2, fig., of oratorical vigour, a quo quum amentatas hastas acceperit, ipse eas oratoris lacertis viribusque torquebit, Cic.

2. **lăcertus** -i, m. = lacerta (q.v.).

lăcesso -īvi and -ii -ītum, 3. (intens. of *lacio), to provoke, stimulate, excite, exasperate, irritate;* a, virum ferro, Cic. ; aliquem proelio, bello, Caes. ; aliquid ad pugnam, Liv. ; me scripto, *provoke me to write again,* Cic. ; so ad scribendum, Cic. ; aliquem injuriā, Cic. ; deos precibus, Hor. ; pelagus carinā, *to sail over,* Hor. ; b, with acc. of thing, *to begin, occasion;* pugnam, Liv. ; sermones, Cic.

Lăcĕtāni -ōrum, m. (Λακετανοί), *a people in Hispania Tarraconensis.* Hence, **Lăcĕtānĭa** -ae, f. *the country of the Lacetani.*

Lăchēs -ētis, m. (Λάχης), *son of Melampus, general of the Athenians, slain at Mantinea* (418 B.C.).

Lăchĕsis -is, f. (Λάχεσις), *the one of the three Parcae that spun the thread of life.*

lăchrĭma (lăchrўma), v. lacrima.

lăchrĭmo (lăchrўmo) and -or, v. lacrimo.

Lăcĭădēs -ae, m. (Λακιάδης), *belonging to the Lacian deme (in Attica)*, Cic.

lăcĭnĭa -ae, f. (λακίς), *a lappet or flap of a garment;* prov., aliquid obtinere lacinĭā, *to hold by the extreme end, to have but an insecure hold,* Cic.; in lacinia servare ex mensa secunda semina, ap. Cic.

Lăcĭnĭum -ĭi, n. (Λακίνιον ἄκρον), *a promontory in Bruttium, near Crotona,* where Juno Lacinia had a famous temple. Hence, adj., **Lăcĭnĭus** -a -um, *Lacinian;* diva Lacinia, *the Lacinian goddess (Juno);* meton. = *the temple of Juno Lacinia,* Verg.

Lăco (Lăcōn) -ōnis, m. (Λάκων), *a Spartan, Lacedaemonian;* fulvus Laco, *a Spartan hound,* Hor.; plur., **Lăcōnes** -um, m. *the Lacedaemonians.* Hence, 1, adj., **Lăcōnĭcus** -a -um, *Laconian.* Subst., a, **Lăcōnĭca** -ae, f. or **Lăcōnĭcē** -es, f. (Λακωνική), *the country of Laconia,* Nep.; b, **Lăcōnĭcum** -i, n. (sc. balneum), *a sweating-room in a bath,* Cic.; 2, **Lăcōnis** -ĭdis, f. *Spartan;* mater, Ov.

lăcrĭma (lăcrŭma, lăchrĭma, or **lăchrўma)** -ae, f. (δάκρυ, δάκρυμα). **I.** *a tear;* multis cum lacrimis, *with a flood of tears,* Cic.; lacrimas profundere, *to shed tears,* Cic.; prae lacrimis *(for tears)* loqui non possum, Cic.; debilitor lacrimis, *unmanned by,* Cic.; lacrimis gaudio effusis, Liv. **II.** *the exudation from certain plants;* turis, Ov.; Heliadum, *amber,* Ov.

lăcrĭmābĭlis (lăcrŭmābĭlis) -e (lacrimo), *deplorable, lamentable, woeful;* tempus, Ov.; bellum, Verg.

lăcrĭmābundus -a -um (lacrimo), *breaking into tears, weeping,* Liv.

lăcrĭmo (lăchrўmo, lăcrŭmo), 1. *to weep, shed tears.* **I.** Lit., ecquis fuit quin lacrimaret? Cic. **II.** Of plants, *to exude, to drip, drop down;* partic. pass., lacrimatae cortice myrrhae, *dripping from,* Ov.

lăcrĭmōsus (lăcrŭmōsus) -a -um (lacrima). **I.** *tearful, shedding tears;* lumina vino lacrimosa, Ov.; voces, Verg. **II.** a, *causing tears;* fumus, Hor.; b, *mournful, piteous;* bellum, Hor.

lăcrĭmŭla -ae, f. (dim. of lacrima), *a little tear,* Cic.

lăcrŭma, etc., v. lacrima, etc.

lactĕo, 2. (lac). **I.** *to suck;* lactens Romulus, Cic.; lactens hostia, Cic. Subst., **lactentes** -ium, f. (sc. hostiae), *unweaned animals,* as victims for a sacrifice; lactentibus rem divinam facere, Liv. **II.** *to be milky, juicy, contain milk, to be full of sap;* frumenta, Verg.

lactĕŏlus -a -um, adj. (dim. of lacteus), *milk-white,* Cat.

lactes -ium, f. (lac), *the small intestines, guts,* Plaut.

lactesco, 3. (lacteo), *to become milk, be changed into milk;* omnis fere cibus matrum lactescere incipit, Cic.

lactĕus -a -um (lac). **I.** Lit., 1, *milky;* humor, Ov.; 2. *full of milk;* ubera, Verg. **II.** Meton., *milk-white;* cervix, Verg.; via lactea, Ov., or orbis lacteus, Cic., *the Milky Way.*

1. **lacto,** 1. (lac), *to give milk, to be full of milk,* Ov.

2. **lacto,** 1. (intens. of *lacio, to entice), to allure, wheedle, dupe, deceive, cajole,* Plaut.

lactūca -ae, f. (lac), *a lettuce,* Hor.

lăcūna -ae, f. (for lacuina, from lacus). **I.** *a cavity, hollow, cavern;* 1, a, lacunae salsae, *the salt depths of the sea,* Lucr.; b, in the body of animals, sint modici victus parvaeque utrimque lacunae, *dimples,* Ov.; 2, *a pool, pond, ditch;* vastae lacunae Orci, Lucr.; cavae lacunae, Verg. **II.** Transf., *a gap, defect, loss;* ut illam lacunam rei familiaris expleant, Cic.

lăcūnar -āris, n. (lacuna), *a panelled ceiling,* Cic.; prov., spectare lacunar, *to gaze at the ceiling,* i.e., *to pretend not to see what is going on,* Juv.

lăcūno, 1. (lacuna), *to work in panels, to panel,* Ov.

lăcūnōsus -a -um (lacuna), *full of hollows or gaps;* nihil lacunosum, *defective,* Cic.

lăcus -ūs, m. (root LAC, whence also λάκκος, lacuna). **I.** *a lake,* Cic.; used poet. for *any large body of water,* Verg., Ov. **II.** *a water-trough or basin,* Hor.; *a blacksmith's trough,* Verg. **III.** *any large tank, vat, tub,* especially that into which the wine flows when pressed from the grapes; transf., nova ista quasi de musto ac lacu fervida oratio, Cic.

Lăcўdēs -is, m. (Λακύδης), *an academic philosopher, founder of the New Academy.*

Lādās -ae, m. (Λάδας), *a Laconian athlete, whose speed in running was proverbial in antiquity,* Juv.

Lādōn -ōnis, m. (Λάδων), *a river in Arcadia.*

laedo, laesi, laesum, 3. *to hurt, injure, damage.* **I.** Lit., cursu aristas, Verg.; frondes, Ov.; zonā laedere collum, *to strangle,* Hor. **II.** Transf., *to trouble, offend, annoy, vex, calumniate, attack;* aliquem perjurio suo, Cic.; famam alicuius gravi opprobrio, Cic.

Laelĭus -a -um, *name of a Roman gens, the most prominent members of which were:* C. Laelius, *the friend of* Scipio, and D. Laelius, *a supporter of Pompeius.* Hence, adj., **Laelĭānus** -a -um, *Laelian.*

laena -ae, f. (χλαῖνα), *an upper garment of thick cloth,* Cic.

Lāĕrtēs -ae, m. (Λαέρτης), *the father of Ulysses;* hence, 1, adj., **Lāĕrtĭus** -a -um, *Laertian;* regna, *Ithaca,* Verg.; heros, *Ulysses,* Ov.; 2, **Lāĕrtĭădes** -ae, m. *the son of Laertes, i.e., Ulysses,* Hor.

laesĭo -ōnis, f. (laedo), rhet. t.t., *an oratorical attack,* Cic.

Laestrўgŏnes -um, m. (Λαιστρύγονες), myth., *a race of cannibals in Sicily;* sing., **Laestrўgōn** -ŏnis, m. *a Laestrygonian;* urbs Lami Laestrygonis (i.e., *Formiae),* Ov. Hence, adj., **Laestrўgōnĭus** -a -um, *Laestrygonian;* domus, *Formiae,* Ov.

laetābĭlis -e (laetor), *joyful, gladsome, joyous,* Cic.

laetātĭo -ōnis, f. (laetor), *a rejoicing, joy,* Caes.

laetē, adv. (laetus), *joyfully, gladly;* aliquid laete atque insolenter ferre, Cic.

laetĭfĭco, 1. (laetificus). **I.** *to cheer, gladden, delight, make joyful;* sol terram laetificat, Cic. **II.** *to fertilise;* agros aquā, Cic.

laetĭfĭcus -a -um (laetus and facio), *causing joy, gladdening, cheering, joyous,* Lucr.

laetĭtĭa -ae, f. (laetus). **I.** *joy, expressed and unrestrained gladness, delight;* laetitiam capere, percipere ex aliqua re, Cic.; dare alicui laetitiam, Cic.; laetitiam alicui afferre, Cic.; laetitiā frui maximae praeclarissimaeque pugnae, Cic. **II.** *a pleasing appearance, beauty, grace;* orationis, Tac.

laetor, 1. dep. (laetus), *to rejoice, be joyful take delight, be glad;* a, with abl., bonis rebus.

Cic.; b, with in and the abl., in omnium gemitu, Cic.; c, with de and the abl., de communi salute, Cic.; d, with ex and the abl., Sall.; e, with acc. of the neut. pron., utrumque laetor, Cic.; f, with acc. and infin., filiolā tuā te delectari laetor, Cic.; g, with quod, se laetari, quod effugissem duas maximas vituperationes, Cic.; absol., laetanti animo, Cic.

Laetŏrĭus -a -um, *name of a Roman plebeian gens.*

laetus -a -um, *joyful, glad.* **I.** a, lit., of persons, hi vagantur laeti atque erecti passim toto foro, Cic.; with abl., minime laetus origine novae urbis, Liv.; with genit., laetus laborum, Verg.; b, transf., of things, oratio, Liv.; vultus, Cic. **II. A.** *making joyful, pleasing, agreeable;* omnia erant facta laetiora, Cic. **B.** Transf., 1, *favouring, fortunate, propitious;* augurium, Tac.; 2, a, *fruitful;* pascua, Liv.; laetae segetes, *rich,* Cic.; b, of animals, *fat,* Verg.; c, of orators, *copious, fluent, delightful;* nitidum quoddam genus est verborum et laetum, Cic.

laevē, adv. (laevus), *on the left hand,* hence *awkwardly,* Hor.

laevus -a -um (λαιός), *left.* **I.** Lit., a, adj., manus, Cic.; amnis, *the left bank,* Tac.; b, subst., (a) **laeva** -ae, f. (sc. manus), *the left hand, the left;* ad laevam, *to the left,* Cic.; (β) **laevum** -i, n. *the left side;* in laevum flectere cursus, Ov.; plur., **laeva** -ōrum, *places lying to the left,* Ov. **II.** Transf., 1, *left-handed, foolish, silly;* mens, Verg.; et ego laevus! *what a fool I am!* Hor.; 2, *unsuitable;* tempus, Hor.; 3, *unlucky, unpropitious;* picus, Hor.; 4, in augury, *favourable,* as the Roman augurs, looking south, had the east or lucky side on their left hand; laevum intonuit, *on the left,* Verg.

lăgănum -i, n. (λάγανον), *a cake made of flour and oil,* Hor.

lăgēna = lagoena (q.v.).

lăgēos -ēi, f. (λάγειος), *a Greek kind of vine,* Verg.

lăgoena -ae, f. (λάγηνος), *a large earthen jar* or *bottle with handles and a narrow neck,* Cic.

lăgōis -idis, f. (λαγωίς), *a bird,* perhaps a *heathcock* or *grouse,* Hor.

lăguncŭla -ae, f. (dim. of lagoena), *a little bottle* or *flask,* Plin.

Lăgus -i, m. *the father of Ptolemy, king of Egypt.* Hence, adj., **Lăgēus** -a -um, poet. = *Egyptian,* Mart.

Lăïs -idis and -idos, f. (Λαΐς), *a celebrated Corinthian beauty.*

Lăïus, or **Lăjus** -i, m. (Λάϊος), *son of Labdacus, father of Oedipus.* Hence, **Lăïădēs** -ae, m. *son of Laius,* i.e. *Oedipus,* Ov.

lăma -ae, f. (perhaps connected with lacuna, lacus), *a bog, slough, ditch,* Hor.

lambo, lambi, lambĭtum, 3. *to lick;* a, of animals, tribunal meum, Cic.; b, poet., transf., of things, quae loca fabulosus lambit Hydaspes, *bathes, washes,* Hor.; of fire, flamma summum properabat lambere tectum, Hor.

lāmentābĭlis -e (lamentor). **I.** *lamentable, deplorable;* regnum, Verg. **II.** *doleful, mournful;* vox, Cic.; mulierum comploratio, Liv.

lāmentātĭo -ōnis, f. (lamentor), *a lamenting, weeping, wailing, lamentation;* plangore et lamentatione complere forum, Cic.

lāmentor, 1, dep. **I.** Intransit., *to weep, wail, lament;* flebiliter in vulnere, Cic. **II.** Transit., *to bewail, weep over, lament;* caecitatem, Cic.; with acc. and infin., Hor.

lāmentum -i, n. *a wailing, weeping, lament-*

ation; gen. in plur., se lamentis muliebritea lacrimisque dedere, Cic.

1. **lămĭa** -ae, f. (λαμία), gen. plur., lamiae, *witches believed to suck children's blood, vampires,* Hor.

2. **Lămĭa** -ae, m. *a cognomen of the Aelian gens.*

3. **Lămĭa** -ae, f. (Λαμία), *a town in Thessaly* (now *Zeitun* or *Zeituni*).

lāmĭna and **lamna** -ae, f. (perhaps connected with latus, *broad*), *a plate* or *thin piece of metal* or *marble,* etc. **I.** Lit., 1, aenea, Liv.; 2, a, *uncoined gold and silver;* inimicus lamnae, Hor.; b, *a plate of iron, heated and used for torture;* laminae ardentes, Cic.; c, *the blade of a sword,* Ov.; d, *the blade of a saw,* Verg. **II.** *a nutshell,* Ov.

lampas -pădis, acc. -păda, acc. plur. -pădes and -pădas, f. (λαμπάς), *a torch.* **I.** Lit., Verg.; *a wedding-torch,* Ter.; also used at the torchrace when one runner delivered his torch to another; hence, quasi cursores vitae lampada tradunt, *end the course of their life,* Lucr. **II.** Meton., *brightness, brilliance;* Phoebaea, *the light of the sun,* Verg.

Lampsăcum -i, n. and **Lampsăcus (-os)** -i, f. (Λάμψακος), *a town of Mysia on the northeast part of the Hellespont.* Hence, adj., **Lampsăcēnus** -a -um, *of* or *belonging to Lampsacus.*

Lāmus -i, m. (Λάμος), *king of the Laestrygones, founder of the town Formiae;* urbs Lami Formiae, Ov.

lāmȳrus -i, m. (λάμυρος), *an unknown seafish,* Ov.

lāna -ae, f. (λῆνος, Doric λᾶνος), *wool.* **I.** Of animals, 1, a, lit., lanam ducere, Ov., trahere, *to spin,* Juv.; lanam sufficere medicamentis quibusdam, Cic.; b, meton., *wool-spinning;* lanae dedita, Liv.; 2, *woolly hair;* prov., rixari de lana caprina, *to quarrel about nothing,* Hor. **II.** *the down on leaves, fruit,* etc., Verg.

lānārĭus -a -um (lana), *of* or *relating to wool, woollen,* Plin.

lānātus -a -um (lana), *wool-bearing, woolly;* 1, lit., capras lanatas quibusdam factas (esse), Liv.; subst., **lānātae** -ārum, f. *sheep,* Juv.; 2, *downy, covered with down,* Plin.

lancĕa -ae, f. *a light spear* or *lance, with a leathern thong attached to it,* Lucr.

lancĭno, 1. *to tear to pieces, mangle, rend in pieces;* 1, lit., Plin.; 2, transf., paterna bona, *to squander,* Cat.

lānĕus -a -um (lana), *made of wool, woollen;* 1, lit., pallium, Cic.; 2, *soft as wool,* Cat.

Langŏbardi -ōrum, m. *a people in north Germany, on the west side of the Elbe.*

languēfăcĭo, 3. (langueo and facio), *to make languid* or *faint,* Cic.

languĕo -gŭi, 2. *to be faint, weak, languid.* **I.** Physically, quum de via languerem, *weary with the journey,* Cic.; partic., languens, *weak, faint, languid;* vox, Cic. **II.** Transf., *to be languid, inert, inactive;* otio, in otio, Cic.; languent vires, Cic.; partic., languens, *inactive, inert;* languens labensque populus, Cic.

languesco, langŭi, 3. (langueo), *to become faint, weak, languid,* *to languish.* **I.** Lit., 1, corpore, Cic.; senectute, Cic.; Bacchus languescit in amphora, *becomes milder,* Hor.; 2, *to become weak through illness;* nec mea consueto languescent corpora lecto, Ov. **II.** *to become languid, inactive, listless,* Cic.

languĭdē, adv. (languidus), *faintly, languidly, feebly;* negant ab ullo philosopho quid quam dictum esse languidius, Cic.

languĭdŭlus -a -um, (dim. of languidus), *somewhat faint, languid, limp,* Cic.

languĭdus -a -um (langueo), *faint, weak, languid, dull.* **I.** Physically, 1, gen., a, of persons, vino vigiliisque languĭdus, Cic.; b, of things, ventus, *gentle,* Ov.; aqua, *with gentle current,* Liv.; 2, esp., of wine stored up, *mild, mellow,* Hor. **II.** Of activity, *sluggish, inactive ;* a, pass., senectus non modo languida et iners non est, Cic.; studium, Cic.; b, act., languidae voluptates, *enervating,* Cic.

languor -ōris, m. (langueo), *faintness, languor, weariness, feebleness.* **I.** Physical, 1, corporis, Cic. ; 2, *languor, weakness arising from ill-health, ill-health ;* aquosus, *dropsy,* Hor. **II.** *listlessness, inactivity, idleness, sluggishness ;* se languori dedere, Cic. ; languorem alicui afferre, Cic.

lănĭātus -ūs, m. (lanio), *a mangling, tearing in pieces ;* with subj. genit., ferarum, Cic. ; fig., si recludantur tyrannorum mentes posse aspici laniatus et ictus, Tac.

lănĭcĭum, v. lanitium.

lănĭēna -ae, f. (lanius), *a butcher's shop, shambles,* Liv

lănĭfĭcus -a -um (lana and facio), *working in wool, spinning* or *weaving wool ;* ars, Ov. ; sorores, *the Parcae,* Mart.

lănĭger -gĕra -gĕrum (lana and gero), *woolbearing.* **I.** Adj., bidens, Verg. ; poet., apices, *woollen,* Verg. **II.** Subst., **lănĭger** -gĕri, m. *a ram,* Ov.

lănĭo, 1. *to tear* or *cut to pieces, mangle, lacerate ;* hominem, Cic. ; aliquem bestiis, Liv. ; crinem manibus, Ov. ; transf., et tua sacrilegae laniarunt carmina linguae, Ov.

lănista -ae, m., 1, *a trainer of gladiators,* Cic. ; 2, *an instigator, inciter,* Cic., Liv.

lănĭtĭum -ĭi, n. (lana) *wool,* Verg.

lănĭus -ĭi, m. (lanio), *a butcher,* Liv.; transf., *a hangman, executioner,* Plaut.

lanterna (**lāterna**) -ae, f. (conn. with λάμπω, λαμπάς), *a lantern, lamp,* Cic.

lanternārĭus -ĭi, m. (lanterna), *a lanternbearer ;* Catilinae, Cic.

lānūgo -ĭnis, f. (lana), *the down of plants,* Plin. ; *the first soft down of the beard ;* flaventem primā lanugine malas, Verg.

Lānŭvĭum -ĭi, n. *a town in Latium, fortyeight miles south-east of Rome.* Hence, adj., **Lānŭvinus** -a -um, *belonging to Lanuvium ;* subst., **Lānŭvĭnum** -i, n. *an estate near Lanuvium,* Cic.

lanx, lancis, f., 1, *a plate, platter, a large flat dish,* Cic. ; 2, *the scale of a balance,* Cic.

Lāŏcŏōn -ontis, m. (Λαοκόων), *a priest of Neptune in Troy, who with his two sons was devoured by serpents.*

Lāŏdămīa -ae, f. (Λαοδάμεια), *daughter of Acastus and wife of Protesilaus, on whose death she slew herself.*

Lāŏdĭcēa -ae, f. (Λαοδίκεια), *name of several towns :* 1, *a town in Phrygia Major, now Eski-Hissar ;* 2, *a town in Seleucis in Syria, now Lddikiyeh.* Hence, adj., **Lāŏdĭcensis** -e, *Laodicean.*

Lāŏmĕdōn -ontis, m. (Λαομέδων), *a king of Troy, father of Priam ;* hence, 1, adj., **Lāŏmĕdontēus** -a -um, *Laomedontean, poet.* = *Trojan,* Verg. ; 2, **Lāŏmĕdontĭus** -a -um, *Laomedontian ;* 3, subst., **Lāŏmĕdontĭădēs** -ae, m. *a male descendant of Laomedon (Priam),* Verg. ; plur., Laomedontiadae, *the Trojans,* Verg.

lăpăthum -i, n. and **lăpăthus** -i, f. (λάπαθον), *sorrel,* Hor.

lăpĭcīdīnae -ārum, f. (lapis and caedo), *the stone quarries as a place of punishment,* Cic.

lăpĭdārĭus -a -um (lapis), *of* or *relating to stone,* Plaut.

lăpĭdātĭo -ōnis, f. (lapis), *a throwing of stones ;* facta est lapidatio, Cic.

lăpĭdātor -ōris, m. (lapido), *a thrower of stones,* Cic.

lăpĭdĕus -a -um (lapis), *made of stone, stone ;* murus, Liv. ; imber, *a shower of stones,* Cic.

lăpĭdo, 1. (lapis), 1, *to throw stones at,* Suet. ; 2, impers., lapidat, *it rains stones ;* Veiis de caelo lapidaverat, Liv.

lăpĭdōsus -a -um (lapis), 1, *full of stones, stony ;* montes, Ov. ; 2, *as hard as stone ;* panis, Hor.

lăpillus -i, m. (dim. of lapis), *a little stone, pebble.* **I.** lapilli crepitantes, Ov. ; white stones were used to mark lucky, and black stones unlucky days, hence, dies signanda melioribus lapillis, Mart. **II.** 1, *a precious stone, gem ;* nivei viridesque lapilli, *pearls and emeralds,* Hor. ; 2, *a pebble used at trials* (a white one for acquittal, a black one for condemnation) ; lapilli nivei atrique, Ov.

lăpis -ĭdis, m. (λᾶας), *a stone.* **I.** Gen., often collective, bibulus, *pumice-stone,* Verg. ; ardens, *a meteoric stone,* Liv. ; aliquem lapidibus prosequi, Cic. ; lapidibus aliquem cooperire, obruere, Cic. ; lapidibus pluit, *it rains stones from the sky,* Liv. ; lapide candidiore diem notare, *to mark a day as lucky* (cf. lapillus I.), Cat. **II.** Esp. 1, *a boundary-stone,* Liv. ; 2, *a grave-stone,* Prop. ; 3, *a precious stone, jewel,* esp., *a pearl,* Hor. ; 4, *marble ;* Parius, Verg. ; albus, *a table of white marble,* Hor. ; 5, *a piece of mosaic,* Hor. ; 6, *a mile-stone ;* intra vicesimum lapidem, Liv. ; 7, *the stone,* or *platform of stone on which the praeco stood at the slave-auctions ;* duos de lapide emptos tribunos, Cic. ; 8, Juppiter lapis, *a stone held in the hand as a symbol of Jupiter, and sworn by ;* Jovem lapidem jurare, Cic.

Lăpĭthēs -ae, m., plur., Lapithae (Λαπίθαι), *the Lapithae,* myth., *a savage mountain race, living near Olympus and Pelion in Thessaly, famous for their fight with the Centaurs at the wedding of Pirithous.* Hence, adj., 1, **Lăpĭthaeus** -a -um ; 2, **Lăpĭthēĭus** -a -um, *or belonging to the Lapithae.*

lappa -ae, f. *a bur,* Verg.

lapsĭo -ōnis, f. (1. labor), *a gliding, an inclination, tendency towards,* Cic.

lapso, 1. (intens. of 1. labor), *to totter ;* Priamus lapsans, Verg.

lapsus -ūs, m. (1. labor). **I.** *a gradual motion, gliding, sliding,* Verg. ; *the flowing of water ;* si lacus emissus lapsu et cursu suo in mare profluisset, Cic. ; *the flight of birds ;* volucrum lapsus atque cantus, Cic. ; *the gliding of a snake,* Verg. **II.** *a falling, fall ;* 1, lapsus terrae, Cic. ; 2, *a moral fall, fault, error ;* quum sint populares multi variique lapsus, Cic.

lăquĕar -āris and **lăquĕāre** -is, n. (laqueus), n. *a panel in a ceiling, panelled ceiling ;* gen. plur., laquearia tecti, Verg.

lăquĕo, 1. (laqueus), *to adorn with a panelled ceiling ;* only in partic. perf., laqueatus, laqueata tecta, Cic.

lăquĕus -i, m. *a noose, snare, trap ;* 1, lit., collum inserere in laqueum, Cic. ; laqueo gulam frangere, Sall., or premere, Hor.; 2, transf., *a snare, noose ;* alicui laqueos ponere, *to lay snares for,* Ov ; in laqueos cadere, Ov. ; laquei legum, interrogationum, Cic.

1. Lar or **Lars**, Lartis, m. *an Etruscan title*

signifying lord, found as a praenomen; **Lars** Tolumnius, Cic. ; Lars Porsena, Liv.

2. **Lăr,** Lăris, m., usually plur., **Lăres** -um and (more rarely) -ium, *tutelary deities among the Romans;* Lares praestites, Ov. ; Lares domestici, familiares, privati, patrii, *domestic deities, the gods of the hearth,* Ov. ; permarini, *deities of the sea,* Liv. ; rurales, agri custodes, *guardians of agriculture,* Cic. ; meton., *hearth, dwelling, home;* ad larem suum reverti, *home,* Cic.

Lăra and **Lărunda** -ae, f. *a nymph whom Jupiter deprived of her tongue because of her loquacity.*

Larcĭus -a -um, *name of a celebrated Roman gens, the most celebrated member of which was the first dictator,* T. Larcius Flavus, Cic.

lardum (lărĭdum) -i, n. (connected with λαρινός), *the fat of bacon, lard,* Ov.

Lărentālĭa -ium, n. *a feast in honour of Acca Larentia.*

Lărentia, v. Acca.

1. **Lăres,** v. 2. Lar.

2. **Lăres,** acc. Lares, abl. Laribus, f. *a town in Numidia,* now *Larbuss* or *Lorbus.*

largē, adv. (largus), *largely, plentifully, abundantly;* dare, Cic. ; large atque honorifice aliquid promittere, Cic.; senatus consultum large factum, *with sweeping provisions,* Tac.

largĭfĭcus -a -um (largus and facio), *bountiful, liberal,* Lucr.

largĭflŭus -a -um (large and fluo), *flowing with full stream,* Lucr.

largĭlŏquus -a -um (large and loquor), *talkative, loquacious,* Plaut.

largĭor, 4. dep. (largus). **I.** *to give abundantly, bestow liberally, impart;* qui eripiunt aliis quod aliis largiantur, Cic.; absol., *to give liberal presents,* esp. for the purpose of bribing ; ex alieno largiendo aliquid parare, *by means of bribery,* Cic. **II.** Transf., *to give, bestow, grant;* populo libertatem, Cic. ; alicui civitatem, Cic.; patriae suum sanguinem, Cic.

largĭtas -ātis, f. (largus), *liberality, bountifulness;* terra cum maxima largitate fruges fundit, Cic.

largĭtĕr, adv. (largus), *abundantly, plentifully, largely;* posse, *to be powerful,* Caes. ; de judicio largiter esse remissum, Cic.

largĭtĭo -ōnis, f. (largior), *a giving freely, liberality, spending freely, lavishing;* 1, lit., a, in cives, Cic. ; largitione benevolentiam alicuius consectari, Cic.; prov., largitio non habet fundum, *giving has no limits,* Cic. ; b, *giving or spending in order to gain the favour of others, bribery;* largitionis suspicionem recipere, Cic. ; 2, *granting, bestowing;* civitatis, Cic.; aequitatis, Cic.

largĭtor -ōris, m. (largior), *a liberal giver, spender;* praedae erat largitor, Liv. ; absol., as attrib. = *generous,* Liv. ; in a bad sense, *a briber,* Cic.

largus -a -um. **I.** *abundant, plentiful, numerous, copious;* quum sol terras largā luce compleverit, Cic. ; imbres, Verg. ; with genit., *rich in, abounding in;* opum, Verg. **II.** *liberal in giving and spending, bountiful, profuse;* qui si largissimus esse vellet, Cic. ; plur. subst., largi, *generous persons,* Cic. ; with abl., largus animo, *of a generous disposition,* Tac. ; promissis, *liberal in promises,* Tac. ; with infin., spes donare novas, Hor.

lărĭdum -i, n. = lardum (q.v.).

Lărīnum -i, n. *town in Lower Italy,* now *Larino.* Hence, adj., **Lărīnās** -ātis, *of or belonging to Larinum.*

Lārīsa (Lārissa) -ae, f. (Λάρισα, Λάρισσα), **I.** *town in Pelasgiotis, in Thessaly,* now *Larisse.* Hence, a, **Lărīsaeus (Lārīssaeus)** -a -um, *Larissean* = *Thessalian,* Cic., Verg.; b, **Lārīsenses** -ium, m. *the inhabitants of Larisa.* **II.** Larisa Cremaste, *town in Phthiotis, in Thessaly.* **III.** *a fortress of Argos.*

Lārĭus -ii m. *name of a lake in north Italy,* now *Lago di Como.* Hence, adj., **Lārĭus** -a -um, *of or belonging to Larius.*

lărix -ĭcis, f. (λάριξ), *the larch,* Plin.

Lars, v. 1. Lar.

Lărunda, v. Lara.

larva -ae, f. (2. Lar), 1, *a ghost, spectre,* Plaut.; 2, *a mask,* Hor.

Lās, acc. Lān, f. (Λᾶς), *a town in Laconia, south-west of Gytheum.*

lăsănum -i, n. (λάσανον), *a cooking-utensil,* Hor.

lascīvē, adv. (lascivus), *lasciviously, wantonly,* Mart.

lascīvĭa -ae, f. (lascivus), 1, in a good sense, *playfulness, sportiveness, frolicsomeness;* hilaritas et lascivia, Cic. ; 2, in a bad sense, *wantonness, licentiousness, lasciviousness, insolence;* quos soluto imperio licentia atque lascivia corruperat, Sall. ; lasciviam a vobis prohibetote, Liv.

lascīvĭbundus -a -um (lascivio), *wanton, sportive,* Plaut.

lascīvĭo -ii -ītum, 4. (lascivus), *to sport, play, be sportive, wanton, to be insolent;* agnus lascivit fugā, Ov. ; plebs lascivit, Liv.

lascīvus -a -um, 1, in a good sense, *playful, sportive, frolicsome;* puella, Verg. ; aetas, Hor. ; 2, in a bad sense, *wanton, licentious, lascivious, insolent, overbearing;* Epicrates, Cic. ; puella, Ov.

lăserpĭcĭfer -fĕra -fĕrum, *producing the plant laserpitium,* Cat.

lăserpĭcĭum (lăserpītĭum) -ii, n. *a plant called silphium,* used in medicine and in cooking, Plin.

lassĭtūdo -ĭnis, f. (lassus), *weariness, lassitude,* Cic. ; lassitudine exanimari, confici, Caes.

lasso, 1. (lassus), *to make weary, tire, exhaust;* corpus, Ov.

lassŭlus -a -um (dim. of lassus), *somewhat weary, rather tired,* Cat.

lassus -a -um, *weary, tired, exhausted, faint, languid;* a, of persons, itinere atque opere castrorum et proelio fessi lassique erant, Sall. ; ab equo domito Hor. ; with genit., maris et viarum, Hor. ; b, applied to inanimate things, fructibus assiduis lassa humus, Ov. ; lasso papavera collo, *drooping,* Verg.

lātē, adv. (latus). **I.** *broadly, widely;* longe lateque, *far and wide,* Cic. ; vagari, *to wander far and wide,* Caes. ; populus late rex, Verg. **II.** Transf., 1, ars late patet, Cic. ; fidei bonum nomen latissime manat, Cic. ; 2, *at length, amply, copiously;* fuse lateque dicere de aliqua re, Cic.

lătēbra -ae, f. (lateo). **I.** *a concealment, hiding;* in quibus non invenio quae latebra togatis hominibus esse possit, Cic. ; lunae, *an eclipse of the moon,* Lucr. **II.** Concr. **A.** Lit. *hiding-place, lurking-place, covert;* latebrae ferarum, Cic. ; latebra teli, *the place where the arrow is embedded in the body,* Verg. **B.** Transf., 1, *hidden place, secret retreat;* quum in animis hominum tantae latebrae sint, Cic. ; 2, *a subterfuge, pretence, shift;* latebra mendacii, Cic.

lătĕbrĭcŏla -ae, c. (latebra and colo), *one who dwells in concealment,* Plaut.

lătēbrōsē, adv. (latebrosus), *secretly, in a corner,* Plaut.

lătēbrōsus -a -um (latebra), *full of hiding-places, secret, retired;* via, Cic.; pumex, *porous,* Verg.

lătens -entis, p. adj. (from lateo), *concealed, hidden;* res, Cic.; causa, Verg.

lătentĕr, adv. (lateo), *secretly,* Cic.

lătĕo -tŭi, 2. (connected with λανθάνω). **I.** *to be hid, be concealed;* **1,** gen., in occulto, Cic.; abdite, Cic.; latet anguis in herba, Verg.; navis latet portu, Hor.; latet sub classibus aequor, *is concealed, covered,* Verg.; portus latet, *is screened from the winds,* Cic.; **2,** esp., **a,** *to keep out of sight, in order not to appear in a court of justice,* Cic.; **b,** *to live in obscurity;* bene qui latuit, bene vixit, Ov. **II.** Transf., **1,** *to be concealed;* scelus latere inter tot flagitia, Cic.; **2,** *to be concealed or safe from misfortune;* sub umbra amicitiae Romanae, Liv.; in tutela ac praesidio bellicae virtutis, Cic.; **3,** *to be unknown;* **a,** aliae (causae) sunt perspicuae, aliae latent, Cic.; **b,** res latet aliquem, *it is concealed from, unknown to, a secret to,* Verg.; so res latet alicui, Cic.

lăter -tĕris, m. *a brick, tile,* Cic., Caes.

lătĕrāmen -ĭnis, n. (later), *an earthen vessel,* Lucr.

Lătĕrānus -a -um, *family name in the gentes Claudia, Sextia, and Plautia.*

lătercŭlus -i, m. (dim. of later), *a brick, tile,* Caes.

lătĕricĭus -a -um (later), *brick, built of brick;* turris, Caes.

Lătĕrĭum -ĭi, n. *an estate of Qu. Cicero at Arpinum,* Cic.

lāterna, v. lanterna.

lāternārius, v. lanternarius.

lătesco, 3. (lateo), *to hide oneself, be concealed,* Cic.

lătex -tĭcis, m. *a fluid, liquid;* used of water, occulti latices, Liv.; securi latices, Verg.; frugum laticumque cupido, *hunger and thirst,* Lucr.; also of wine, meri, Ov.; Lyaeus or Lenaeus, or simply latex, Verg.; latex absinthii, *wormwood juice,* Lucr.

Lătĭālis -e, v. Latium.

Lătĭāris -e, v. Latium.

lătĭbŭlum -i, n. (lateo), *a hiding-place, a lurking-place.* **I.** Lit., **a,** *of animals, quum etiam ferae latibulis se tegant,* Cic.; **b,** *of men,* latibula locorum occultorum, Cic. **II.** Transf., latibulum aut perfugium doloris mei, Cic.

lātĭclāvĭus -a -um, *having a broad purple stripe* (the distinguishing peculiarity of senators, equestrian military tribunes, and sons of noble families); tribunus, Suet.

lātĭfundĭum -ĭi, n. (latus and fundus), *a large landed estate,* Plin.

Lătīnē, v. Latium.

Lătīnĭensis, v. Latium.

Lătīnĭtas -ātis, f. (Latinus), **1,** *a pure Latin style, Latinity,* Cic.; **2,** = jus Latii, *Latin right, a condition intermediate between Roman citizenship and the condition of aliens,* Cic.

1. Lătīnus -a -um, v. Latium.

2. Lătīnus -i, m., *a king of the Laurentians, who received Aeneas hospitably, and gave him his daughter in marriage.*

lātĭo -ōnis, f. (fero), *a bringing.* **I.** auxilii, *rendering assistance,* Liv. **II. a,** legis, *a proposing, bringing forward,* Cic.; **b,** suffragii, *voting,* Liv.

lătĭto, 1. (intens. of lateo), *to lie hid, be concealed;* **a,** extrahitur domo latitans Oppianicus a Manlio, Cic.; invisae atque latitantes res, Caes.; **b,** esp., *to conceal oneself, so as not to appear in court,* Cic.

lătĭtūdo -ĭnis, f. (latus). **I.** *breadth;* **a,** fossae, Caes.; **b,** *extent, great size;* possessionum, Cic. **II.** *a broad pronunciation;* verborum, Cic.

Lătĭum -ĭi, n. **I.** *a district of Italy, in which Rome was situated.* **II.** Meton., **1,** *the Latins;* jus Latii (v. Latinitas), Tac.; **2,** = jus Latii or Latinitas, Tac. Hence, **a, Lătĭus -a -um,** *belonging to Latium, Latin,* poet. = *Roman;* forum, Ov.; **b, Lătīnus -a -um,** *Latin;* convertere in Latinum, *to translate into Latin,* Cic.; feriae Latinae, or simply Latinae, *the Latin games,* Liv.; **c,** adv., **Lătīnē,** *in Latin;* Latine loqui, Cic.; **d, Lătīnĭensis -e,** *Latin;* **e, Lătĭālis -e,** *Latin;* **f, Lătĭāris -e,** *Latin;* Juppiter, *as patron of the Latin league.* Hence, **Lătĭar -āris,** n. *a feast of Jupiter Latiaris.*

Latmus -i, m. (Λάτμος), *a mountain in Caria, where Selene laid Endymion to sleep.* Hence, adj., **Latmĭus -a -um,** *Latmian.*

Lătō -ūs, f. and **Lătōna -ae,** f. (Δητώ), *the mother of Apollo and Diana, whom she bore to Jupiter in the Island of Delos;* hence, **a, Lătōnĭus -a -um,** *Latonian,* Latonia virgo or simply Latonia, *Diana,* Verg.; **b, Lătōnĭgĕna -ae,** c. (Latona and gigno), *offspring of Latona,* Ov.; **c, Lătōĭus** and **Lētōĭus -a -um,** *Latonian;* proles, *Apollo and Diana,* Ov. Subst., **Lătōĭus -ĭi,** m. *Apollo,* and **Lătōĭa -ae,** f. *Diana,* Ov.; **d, Lătōis** or **Lētōis -ĭdis,** f., *Latonian,* Calaurea, *sacred to Latona,* Ov.; subst., *Diana,* Ov.; **e, Lătōus -a -um,** *Latonian.*

Latobrigi -ōrum, m. *a Gallic people, neighbours of the Helvetii.*

Lātōna, etc., v. Lato.

lātor -ōris, m. (fero), *the proposer of a law;* legis Semproniae, Cic.

Lātōus, v. Lato.

lātrātor -ōris, m. (1. latro), *a barker;* poet = *dog,* Verg.

lātrātus -ūs, m. (1. latro), *a barking,* Verg.

1. lātro -āvi, 1. *to bark, bay.* **I.** Intransit., **1,** lit., quod si luce quoque canes latrent, Cic.; partic. subst., latrans, *a barker,* i.e., *a dog,* Ov.; **2,** transf., **a,** of men, *to bark, brawl, rant;* latrare ad clepsydram, Cic.; **b,** of inanimate objects, *to roar;* undae latrantes, Verg.; stomachus, *rumbling,* Hor. **II.** Transit., **1,** *to bark at;* senem, Hor.; **2,** transf., of men, *to shout out;* canina verba in foro, Ov.

2. lātro -ōnis, m. (Λάτρις). **I.** *a hired servant, a mercenary soldier,* Plaut. **II.** Transf., **a,** *a robber, freebooter, bandit, brigand;* insidiosus et plenus latronum locus, Cic.; **b,** *a hunter,* Verg.; **c,** *a piece on a draught-board,* Ov.

lātrōcĭnĭum -ĭi, n. (latrocinor). **I.** *military service,* Plaut. **II. 1,** *robbery, highway robbery, piracy;* **a,** lit., incursiones hostium et latrocinia, Cic.; transf. *villany, roguery;* quid futurum sit latrocinio tribunorum, Cic.; **b,** meton., *a band of robbers;* unus ex tanto latrocinio, Cic.; **2,** *a game of draughts,* Ov.

lātrōcĭnor, 1. dep. (2. latro). **I.** *to serve as a mercenary soldier,* Plaut. **II.** *to practise robbery, piracy, brigandage,* Cic.

lātruncŭlus -i, m. (dim. of 2. latro), *a highwayman, freebooter, bandit,* Cic.

1. lătus -a -um, v. partic. of fero.

2. lātus -a -um (orig. stlatus = *broadened out, extended*), *broad, wide* (opp. angustus). **I.** Lit.,

a, fossa XV. pedes lata, Caes.; **via,** Cic.; **in latum** crescere, *to grow broad,* Ov.; **b,** *extensive, wide, large;* locus, Cic.; latissimae solitudines, Caes.; **c,** of persons, *proud, haughty;* latus ut in circo spatiere, Hor. **II.** Transf., **a,** of pronunciation, *broad;* cuius tu illa lata non numquam imitaris, Cic.; **b,** *diffuse, copious, full, rich;* oratio, disputatio, Cic.

3. **lătus** -ĕris, n. *the side, flank.* **I.** Of a **b**ody; **1, a,** of men, lateris dolor, Cic.; in the **.**ction of an orator, virili laterum inflexione, Cic.; latus dare, *to expose the side to* (*in boxing*), Tib.; malo latus obdere apertum, Hor.; ab alicuius latere numquam discedere, Cic.; artifices lateris, *dancers who make pantomimic gestures,* Ov.; **b,** of animals, cuius (equi aenei) in lateribus fores essent, Cic.; **2,** esp., **a,** *the side,* as the seat of the bodily strength, neque enim ex te nobilitatus es sed ex lateribus et lacertis tuis, Cic.; **b,** meton. = *the body;* latus fessum longā militiā, Hor. **II.** Of an object, *side, flank* (opp. frons, tergum); **1,** latus castrorum, Caes.; insula, cuius unum latus est contra Galliam, Caes.; prora avertit et undis dat latus, Verg.; **2,** milit. t. t., *the flank of an army;* nostros latere aperto aggressi, Caes.; a latere, a lateribus, *on the flank,* Caes.

lătuscŭlum -i, n. (dim. of 2. latus), *a little side,* Cat.

laudābĭlis -e (laudo), **1,** *praiseworthy, laudable;* vita, Cic.; orator, Cic.; **2,** *good in its kind, excellent;* vinum, Plin.

laudābĭlĭter, adv. (laudabilis), *laudably, in a praiseworthy manner;* vivere, Cic.

laudandus -a -um, p. adj. (from laudo), *deserving praise, laudable,* Ov.

laudātĭo -ōnis, f. (laudo), *praise.* **I.** com-**mendation;** laudatio tua, Cic. **II. 1,** in a court of justice, *a testimony to character;* gravissima atque ornatissima, Cic.; **2,** *a funeral oration or panegyric;* nonnullae mortuorum laudationes, Cic.; **3,** *a vote of thanks to a provincial governor sent to the Roman senate,* Cic.

laudātīvus -a -um (laudo), *laudatory,* Quint.

laudātor -ōris, m. (laudo). **I.** *a praiser;* temporis acti, Hor.; pacis semper laudator, Cic. **II. 1,** *a witness who bears favourable testimony to character,* Cic.; **2,** *one who delivers a funeral panegyric,* Liv.

laudātrix -īcis, f. (laudator), *a praiser;* vitiorum laudatrix fama popularis, Cic.

laudātus -a -um, p. adj. (from laudo), *praiseworthy, esteemed, excellent;* vir, Cic.; vultus, Ov.

laudo, 1. (laus), *to praise, laud, extol, commend.* **I.** Lit., **A.** aliquem, Cic.; laudibus, Cic.; foll. by infin., exstinxisse nefas laudabor, Verg. **B.** Esp., **a,** *to bear favourable testimony to any one's character,* Cic.; **b,** *to deliver a funeral panegyric over some one;* aliquem, Cic.; **c,** *to call happy, consider fortunate;* agricolam laudat juris peritus, Hor. **II.** Transf., *to name, mention, cite, quote;* aliquem auctorem, Cic.

laurĕa -ae, f., v. laureus.

laurĕātus -a -um (laurea), *crowned with laurel, laurelled* (esp. as a sign of victory), imago, Cic.; fasces, lictores, Cic.; literae, *bringing tidings of victory,* Liv.

Laurentum -i, n. *town in Latium, between Ostia and Lavinium.* Hence, adj., **a, Laurens** -entis, *Laurentine;* **b, Laurentĭus** -a -um, *Laurentine.*

laurĕŏla -ae, f. (dim. of laurea), *a laurel* **b**ranch, *laurel crown,* and meton., *triumph,* Cic.; prov., laureolam in mustaceo quaerere, *to seek fame in trifles,* Cic.

Laurētum -i, n. (laurus), *a grove of laurels, the name of a spot on the Aventine Hill,* Suet.

laurĕus -a -um (laurus), *of* or *relating to the laurel.* **I.** Adj., corona, Cic. **II.** Subst., **laurea** -ae, f. **1,** *the laurel tree,* Liv.; **2, a,** *the laurel crown* or *laurel branch, as a sign of victory;* decemviri laureā coronati, Liv.; **b,** meton., *triumph, victory;* quam lauream cum tua laudatione conferrem, Cic.

lauricŏmus -a -um (laurus and coma), *covered with laurel-trees,* Lucr.

laurĭger -gĕra -gĕrum (laurus and gero), *crowned with laurels, wearing laurels,* Ov.

laurus -i, f. *the laurel* or *bay-tree, sacred to Apollo, with which poets, triumphant generals, and, on certain occasions, flamens and ancestral busts were crowned,* Cic.; hence, meton., *triumph, victory,* Cic. (abl., lauru, Hor.; nom. and acc. plur., laurus, Verg.).

laus, laudis, f. *praise, fame, glory, commendation.* **A.** Lit., adipisci laudem, Cic.; canere ad tibiam clarorum virorum laudes, Cic.; capere (*to earn*) ex hac una re maximam laudem, Cic.; celebrare alicuius laudes, Cic.; cumulare aliquem omni laude, Cic.; efferre aliquem laudibus ad caelum, Cic.; in laude vivere, Cic.; alicuius laudes dicere, Verg.; hoc in tua laude pono, *I consider this praiseworthy in thee,* Cic.; non laudem habet de me, *he has nothing to boast of as far as I am concerned,* Ov. **B.** Meton., **a,** *a praiseworthy action;* hae tantae summis in rebus laudes, Cic.; **b,** plur., laudes = *praiseworthy qualities;* quarum laudum gloriam adamaris, Cic.

lautē, adv. (lautus), *splendidly, brilliantly, magnificently;* lautius res domesticas tueri, Cic.; **2,** *admirably, excellently, thoroughly;* hodie me emunxeris lautissime, ap. Cic.

lautĭa -ōrum, n. (connected with lavo), *the entertainment given to foreign ambassadors at Rome,* Liv.

lautĭtĭa -ae, f. (lautus), *splendour, elegance, magnificence in one's manner of living;* mea nova lautitia, Cic.

Lautŭlae (Lautŏlae) -ārum, f. *a place of the Volscians between Anxur and Fundi.*

lautŭmĭae (lātŏmĭae) -ārum, f. (λατομίαι), *a stone-quarry,* Plaut.; *a prison or dungeon cut out of rock at Syracuse and Rome,* Cic., Liv.

lautus -a -um, p. adj. (from lavo), lit., *washed, bathed;* and hence, **1,** *splendid, brilliant, elegant, sumptuous;* supellex, Cic.; **2,** *illustrious, distinguished, grand;* homines lauti et urbani, Cic.; lauta liberalitas, Cic.

lăvābrum -i, n. (lavo), *a bath,* Lucr.

lăvātĭo -ōnis, f. (lavo). **I.** *a washing, bathing,* Cic. **II.** Meton., **1,** *bathing apparatus,* Phaedr.; **2,** *water for bathing,* Cic.

Lăverna -ae, f. *the goddess of gain* (just or unjust); hence, *protectress of thieves and cheats;* hence, adj., **Lăvernālis** -e, *belonging to Laverna.*

Lavernĭum -ĭi, n. *a place in Latium, near Formiae.*

Lăvĭci, etc., v. Labici.

Lăvīnĭa -ae, f. *daughter of Latinus, wife of Aeneas.*

Lăvīnĭum -ĭi, n. *a town in Latium, built by Aeneas, and named after his wife Lavinia* (now *Pratica*). Hence, adj., **Lăvīnĭus** -a -um, and **Lāvīnus** -a -um, *Lavinian.*

lăvo, lāvi, lautum, partic. lautus and lōtus, lavēre, and lăvātum and lăvātŭrus, lăvāre (λούω), *to wash, bathe.* **I.** Gen., **1, a,** transit.. manus, Cic.; **b,** intransit. lavare and passi lavari, *to wash oneself, bathe;* cur te lautum

voluit, cenatum noluit occidere, Cic.; **2**, *to moisten, wet, bathe;* vultum lacrimis, Ov. **II.** *to wash away;* mala vino, *to drive away,* Hor.

laxāmentum -i, n. (laxo), *a widening, extending;* **1**, lit., gen.; **2**, transf., *a relaxing, mitigation, alleviation, respite;* si quid laxamenti a bello Samnitium esset, Liv.; laxamentum dare legi, *to release,* Cic.

laxē, adv. (laxus). **I.** *widely, spaciously, at wide intervals;* **1**, lit., habitare, Cic.; **2**, transf., of time, laxius proferre diem, *to put farther off,* Cic. **II.** *loosely;* **1**, lit., aliquem vincire, Liv.; **2**, transf., *loosely, without restraint;* vivere, Liv.

laxĭtas -ātis, f. (laxus), *wideness, roominess;* in domo clari hominis adhibenda cura est laxĭtatis, Cic.

laxo, 1. (laxus). **I.** *to widen, extend, enlarge;* forum, Cic.; manipulos, *to extend, leave a space between,* Caes. **II.** *to unloose, unfasten, slacken, relax;* **1**, vincula epistolae, Nep.; claustra, Verg.; **2**, *to set free from;* elatum pedem ab stricto nodo, Liv.; **3**, a, *to unbend, relax, refresh, amuse;* animos curamque, Cic.; quum laxati curis sumus, *free from,* Cic.; b, *to mitigate, relax, remit;* aliquid laboris, Liv.; annonam, *to lower the price of,* Liv.; intransit., annona haud multum laxaverat, *fallen in price,* Liv.; ubi laxatam pugnam vidit, Liv.

laxus -a -um. **I.** *wide, spacious;* **1**, lit., annulus, Ov.; spatium, Liv.; **2**, transf., of time, diem statuo satis laxum, *sufficiently distant,* Cic. **II.** *loose, lax, relaxed;* **1**, lit., arcus, Verg.; habenae, Verg.; funis, Hor.; male laxus in pede calceus haeret, Hor.; janua, *open,* Ov.; fig., laxissimas habenas habere amicitiae, Cic.; **2**, transf., annona laxior, *a lower price of provisions,* Liv.; milites laxiore imperio habere, Sall.

lĕa -ae, f. (leo), *a lioness,* Ov.

lĕaena -ae, f. (λέαινα), *a lioness,* Cic.

Lĕander and **Lĕandrus** -i, m. (Λείανδρος), *a youth of Abydos who swam nightly across the Hellespont to visit Hero at Sestos, till he was drowned in a storm.*

Lĕarchus -i, m. (Λέαρχος), *the son of Athamas and Ino, killed by his father in a fit of madness.* Hence, **Lĕarchēus** -a -um, *of or belonging to Learchus.*

Lĕbādīa -ae, f. (Λεβάδεια), *a town in Boeotia, famous for the Oracle and Grotto of Trophonius* (now *Livadia*), Cic.

Lĕbĕdŏs (-us) -i, f. (Λέβεδος), *a town in Ionia.*

lĕbēs -ētis, m. (λέβης), **1**, *a bronze kettle or cauldron,* often given as a prize in games, Verg.; **2**, *a metal vessel used for washing the hands,* Ov.

Lĕchaeum -i, n. (Λέχαιον), *the port of Corinth on the Corinthian Gulf.*

lectĭca -ae, f. (lectus), *a palanquin or litter;* lecticā octophoro ferri, *a litter borne by eight slaves,* Cic.; cubare in lectica, Cic.

lectĭcārĭus -ĭi, m. (lectica), *a litter-bearer, porter, chairman,* Cic.

lectĭcŭla -ae, f. (dim. of lectica), *a small litter;* **1**, gen., lecticulā in curiam deferri, Cic.; **2**, *a bier,* Nep.

lectĭo -ōnis, f. (2. lego). **I.** *a picking out, selecting;* judicum, Cic. **II. A.** *a reading, perusal;* librorum, Cic.; lectio sine ulla delectatione, Cic. **B.** lectio senatus, *a reading out or calling over of the names of the senators* (by the censor, who at the same time struck from the list the names of those he considered unworthy), Liv.

lectisternĭum -ĭi, n. (lectus and sterno), *a feast offered to the gods, in which their images were placed on couches in the streets, and food put before them,* Liv.

lectĭto -i, n. (intens. of 2. lego), *to read often, to read with eagerness and attention;* Platonem studiose, Cic.

lectĭuncŭla -ae, f. (dim. of lectio), *a short reading,* Cic.

Lecton and **Lectum** -i, n. (Λεκτόν), *a promontory in Mysia.*

lector -ōris, m. (2. lego), **1**, *a reader of a book;* aptus ad delectationem lectoris, Cic.; **2**, *a person who reads aloud,* Cic.

lectŭlus -i, m. (dim. of lectus), *a small bed, a bed, couch.* **I.** For sleeping, in lectulis suis mori, Cic. **II.** *a couch for resting on;* a, for reading, Cic.; b, for dining, stravit pelliculis haedinis lectulos Punicanos, Cic.; c, *a funeral bed, bed of state,* Tac.

1. **lectus** -a -um, p. adj. (from 2. lego), **1**, *chosen, selected;* verba, Cic.; **2**, transf., *choice, excellent;* adulescens, Cic.; femina lectior, Cic.; femina lectissima, Cic.

2. **lectus** -i, m. (2. lego), *a bed, couch.* **I.** For sleeping, *a bed;* **1**, gen., cubicularis, Cic.; lecto teneri, *to keep one's bed,* Cic.; **2**, *the marriage-bed;* genialis, Cic. **II.** *a couch for resting on;* **1**, *a dining-couch,* Cic.; **2**, *a funeral couch,* Tib.

Lēda -ae, f. and **Lēdē** -ēs, f. (Λήδη), *the wife of Tyndarus, who bore to Zeus Pollux and Helena, Castor and Clytemnestra.* Hence, adj., **Lēdaeus** -a -um, *of or belonging to Leda;* dei, *Castor and Pollux,* Ov.; poet. = *Spartan;* Helena, Verg.

lēgātārĭus -ĭi, m. (legatum), *a legatee,* Suet.

lēgātĭo -ōnis, f. (1. lego). **I.** *the sending of an embassy;* **1**, *the office of an ambassador, embassy, legation;* legationem suscipere, *to undertake,* Caes.; obire, Cic.; libera legatio, *permission given to a senator to travel with the privileges, yet without the duties, of an ambassador,* Cic.; votiva, *a libera legatio, which had for its object the fulfilment of a vow,* Cic.; **2**, meton., a, *the message or answer of an ambassador;* legationem renuntiare, Cic.; or referre, Liv.; b, *the persons attached to an embassy;* legatio Romam venit, Cic. **II.** *the office of legatus* (with a general or provincial governor); legationem obire, Cic.

lēgātor -ōris, m. (1. lego), *a testator, one who leaves something by will,* Suet.

lēgātōrĭus -a -um (legatus), *relating to an ambassador or legatus;* provincia, Cic.

lēgātum -i, n. (1. lego), *a legacy, bequest,* solutio legati, Cic.

lēgātus -i, m. (1. lego). **I.** *an ambassador;* legatos mittere, Cic. **II.** *a legate;* a, *a lieutenant, adjutant, second in command to a general,* Caes.; b, *the chief officer of the governor of a province;* legatum sibi legare, Cic.; c, in imperial times, *the general or governor sent by the emperor to take command of a province,* Tac.

lēgĭfer -fĕra -fĕrum (lex and fero), *law-giving;* Minos, Ov.

lēgĭo -ōnis, f. (2. lego), *a legion, a division of the Roman army, consisting of ten cohorts of infantry, with an auxiliary force of 300 cavalry, altogether between 4,200 and 6,000 men,* Cic.; duas legiones ibi conscribere, Caes.; transf., a, of the troops of other nations, Liv.; b, *an army,* Verg.

lēgĭonārĭus -a -um (legio), *belonging or relating to a legion;* milites, Caes.; plur. subst., **lēgĭonārii** -ōrum, m. *legionary troops,* Liv.

lēgĭtĭmē, adv.(legitimus), **1**, *lawfully, legally,* Cic.; **2**, *rightly, properly,* Tac.

lēgĭtĭmus -a -um (lex). **I.** *lawful, legal, legitimate; dies comitiis habendis,* Cic.; *controversiae, legal, decided by law,* Cic. Subst., **lēgĭtĭma** -ōrum, n. *legal usages,* Nep. **II.** Transf., *right, fit, proper, just, appropriate;* numerus, Cic.; poema, Hor.

lēgĭuncŭla -ae, f. (dim. of legio), *a small legion,* Liv.

1. lēgo, 1. (lex). **I. A.** *to send an ambassador;* aliquem, Cic. **B.** *to appoint as legate or second in command;* aliquem Caesari, Cic.; aliquem sibi, Cic. **II.** *to bequeath, leave as a legacy;* aliquid alicui ab aliquo, *to leave a legacy to be paid to the legatee by the heir,* Cic.; alicui pecuniam, Cic.

2. lēgo, lēgi, lectum, 3.(λέγω), *to collect, gather together, to pick.* **I.** Lit., 1, nuces, Cic.; spolia caesorum, Liv.; mala ex arbore, Verg.; *legere ossa, to collect the bones after a body has been burned,* Cic.; 2, a, fila, of the Parcae, *to wind up, spin,* Verg.; vela, *to furl the sails,* Verg.; b, *to steal;* sacra divum, Hor.; 3, a, *to pass or wander through a place;* saltus legit, Ov.; vestigia alicuius, *to follow or trace the footsteps of any one,* Verg.; tortos orbes, *to wander through,* Verg.; of ships, *to coast along;* oram Italiae, Liv.; b, *to choose, select, pick out;* judices, Cic.; viros ad bella, Ov.; aliquem in senatum, Cic. **II.** Transf., 1, *to catch sight of, look at, regard;* omnes adversos, Verg.; 2, a, *to read, peruse;* eos libros, Cic.; apud Clitomachum, *in the works of Clitomachus,* Cic.; partic. subst., **lĕgens** -entis, m. *a reader,* Ov.; b, *to read aloud, recite;* volumen suum, Cic.; hence, senatum legere, *to call over the senate, to go over the list of senators* with a view to erase the names of the unworthy, Liv.

lēgŭlējus -i, m. (lex), *a pettifogging lawyer,* Cic.

lēgūmen -ĭnis, n. (lego), *pulse,* or *any leguminous plant,* Cic.; esp., *the bean,* Verg.

Lĕlĕges -um, m. (Λέλεγες), *a people, scattered in different places over Greece and Asia Minor.* Hence, a, **Lĕlĕgēĭs** -ĭdis, f. *Lelegean;* b, **Lĕlĕgēĭus** -a -um, *Lelegean;* litora, *coasts of Megara,* Ov.; moenia, *Megara,* Ov.

Lĕmannus (Lĕmānus) -i, m. (with or without lacus), *a lake in the country of the Helvetii, now the Lake of Geneva.*

lembus -i, m. (λέμβος), *a small, swift vessel, cutter, felucca,* Liv.

Lemnĭcŏla -ae, c. (Lemnus and colo), *an inhabitant of Lemnos* (of Vulcan); *Lemnicolae stirps,* i.e., *Erichthonius,* Ov.

lemnĭscātus -a -um (lemniscus), *adorned with ribbons;* palma, *a palm-branch ornamented with ribbons, the reward of a victor,* Cic.

lemnĭscus -i, m.(λημνίσκος), *a fillet,* or *ribbon given in token of honour,* usually affixed to a crown, palm-branch, etc., Liv.

Lemnŏs (-us) -i, f. (Λῆμνος), *the island of Lemnos in the Aegean Sea, the abode of Vulcan.* Hence, a, adj., **Lemnĭus** -a -um, *Lemnian;* Lemnius pater, Verg., and subst., Lemnius, *Vulcan,* Ov.; furtum, *that of Prometheus, who stole fire from Vulcan at Lemnos,* Cic.; b, **Lemnĭăs** -ădis, f. *a Lemnian woman,* Ov.; Greek dat. plur., Lemniasi, Ov.

Lemonia tribus, *a Roman country tribe on the via Latina.*

Lĕmŏvĭces -um, m. *a Celtic people in the modern Limousin.*

lĕmŭres -um, m. *the shades* or *spirits of the dead, ghosts, spectres,* Hor. Hence, **Lĕmŭria** -ōrum, n. *a festival held, to appease departed spirits, on the ninth of May,* Ov

lēna -ae, f. (leno), 1, *a procuress, bawd,* Ov.; 2, *she that entices;* natura quasi sui lena, *enticing persons to her,* Cic.

Lēnaeus -a -um (Ληναῖος), *Bacchic;* latices, *wine,* Verg.; Lenaeus pater, or simply Lenaeus, *Bacchus,* Verg.

lēnĕ, adv. (lenis)=leniter, *gently, softly;* lene sonantis aquae, Ov.

lēnīmen -ĭnis, n. (lenio), *a means of alleviation, mitigation, assuaging;* testudo laborum dulce lenimen, Hor.

lēnīmentum -i, n. (lenio), *a mitigation, alleviation,* Tac.

lēnĭo -īvi and -ĭi, -ītum, 4. (lenis), *to make mild, alleviate, mitigate, assuage, soothe, relieve.* **I.** Lit., stomachum latrantem, Hor.; vulnera, Prop. **II.** Transf., se consolatione, Cic.; aliquem iratum, Cic.; desiderium crebris epistolis, Cic. (imperf., lenibat, lenibant, Verg.).

lēnis -e, *smooth, soft, mild, gentle.* **I.** Lit., sensus judicat lene asperum, Cic.; venenum, *slight,* Cic.; vinum, *mellow,* Hor.; ventus lenissimus, Cic.; clivus, *rising gradually,* Liv.; stagnum, *flowing gently,* Liv. **II.** Transf., **A.** Populus Romanus in hostes lenissimus, Cic.; leniorem sententiam dicere, Caes. **B.** Of discourse, *mild, calm;* oratio placida, submissa, lenis, Cic.

lēnĭtas -ātis, f. (lenis), *gentleness, softness, mildness.* **I.** Lit., vocis, Cic.; Arar in Rhodanum influit incredibili lenitate, *slowness, gentleness,* Caes. **II.** Transf., **A.** *gentleness, lenity;* animi, Cic.; legum, Cic. **B.** Of discourse, *mildness, calmness;* verborum, Cic.

lēnĭtĕr, adv. (lenis), *softly, gently, gradually, mildly, quietly.* **I.** Lit., arridere, Cic.; iter facere, *slowly,* Caes.; collis leniter editus, or acclivis, *rising gradually,* Caes. **II.** Transf., **A.** *gently, mildly;* alloqui, *in a friendly manner,* Liv. **B.** Of discourse, dicere, Cic.

lēnĭtūdo -ĭnis, f. (lenis), *gentleness, mildness;* in aliquem, Cic.

lēno -ōnis, m. (lenio), *a procurer, pander, allurer, seducer,* Cic.

lēnōcĭnĭum -ĭi, n. (leno). **I.** *the trade of a procurer* or *bawd,* Cic. **II.** Transf., 1, *an enticement, allurement,* Cic.; 2, *finery in dress;* Cic.; 3, of discourse, *meretricious ornament,* Tac.

lēnōcĭnor, 1. dep. (leno), *to pursue the trade of a procurer;* hence, transf., 1, *to flatter basely, be meanly subservient to;* alicui, Cic.; 2, *to advance, promote, increase;* feritati arte, Tac.

lēnōnĭus -a -um (leno), *relating or belonging to a procurer,* Plaut.

lens, lentis, f. *a lentil,* Verg.

lentē, adv. (lentus), 1, *slowly;* proceditur, Caes.; curritur, Ov.; 2, transf., a, *without animation, calmly, coolly, patiently;* aliquid ferre, Cic.; respondere, aliquid phlegmatically, Cic.; b, *deliberately;* lente ac fastidiose probare, Cic.

lentesco, 3. (lenteo), 1, *to become pliant, soft, sticky;* tellus picis in morem ad digitos lentescit habendo, Verg.; 2, *to slacken, relax, flag;* lentescunt tempore curae, Ov.

lentĭcĭfer -fĕra -fĕrum (lentiscus and fero), *producing the mastich-tree,* Ov.

lentĭscus -i, f., and **lentĭscum** -i, n. *the mastich-tree* (Pistacia lentiscus, Linn.), Cic.

lentĭtūdo -ĭnis, f. (lentus), 1, *slowness, sluggishness,* Tac.; 2, *insensibility, apathy,* Cic.

lento, 1. (lentus), *to make flexible, to bend;* lentandus remus in unda, *must be plied,* Verg.

Lentŭlĭtas -ātis, f., v. Lentulus.

1. lentŭlus -a -um (dim. of lentus), *somewhat slow (in paying)*, Cic.

2. Lentŭlus -i, m. *the name of one of the families of the patrician gens Cornelia, the most famous of the members of which were:* 1, P. Cornelius Lentulus Sura, *a fellow-conspirator with Catiline;* 2, P. Cornelius Lentulus Spinther, *who proposed the recall of Cicero from exile.* Hence, **Lentŭlĭtas** -ātis, f. *the family pride of the Lentuli* (a word coined in jest by Cic.).

lentus -a -um, *tough.* **I.** 1, gen., radix, Verg.; 2, a, *pliant, flexible;* brachia, Hor.; lentior salicis ramis, Ov.; b, *sticky, clammy, tenacious;* gluten pice lentius, Cic.; 3, fig., lentus abesto, *remain long away*, Ov. **II.** Transf., 1, *slow, motionless, inactive;* marmor (of the sea), *unruffled*, Verg.; lento igne, Ov.; pugna lenta, Liv.; lentiorem facere spem, Ov.; 2, a, *drawling;* in dicendo, Cic.; b, *lingering;* infitiator, *a bad payer*, Cic.; c, of character, *sluggish, apathetic, phlegmatic, insensible;* judex, Cic.; nihil illo lentius, Cic.; lentissima pectora, Ov.

lēnuncŭlus -i, m. (for lembunculus, dim. of lembus), *a small boat*, or *skiff*, Caes.

1. lĕo -ōnis, m. (λέων), *a lion;* 1, lit., vis leonis, Cic.; 2, transf., *the constellation Leo*, Hor.

2. *lĕo -ēre, *to blot out;* the root of deleo, letum, etc.

Lĕŏcŏrĭon -ii, n. (Λεωκόριον), *temple at Athens to the three daughters of Leos, who sacrificed their lives for their country.*

Lĕon -ontis, m. (Λέων), *a place in Sicily not far from Syracuse.*

Lĕōnĭdās -ae, m. (Λεωνίδας), *king of Sparta, killed at the defence of the pass of Thermopylae.*

lĕōnīnus -a -um (leo), *of or relating to a lion, leonine*, Plaut.

Lĕonnātus -i, m. (Λεοννάτος), *a general of Alexander the Great.*

Lĕontīni -ōrum, m. (Λεοντῖνοι), *a town on the east coast of Sicily.* Hence, adj., **Lĕontīnus** -a -um, *Leontine.*

Lĕontĭum -ii, f. (Λεόντιον), *an Athenian hetaira,* friend of Epicurus.

lĕpĭdē, adv. (lepidus). **I.** *pleasantly, agreeably, charmingly, capitally, prettily;* lepidissime, *excellently*, Plaut. **II.** Of style, *smartly, wittily*, Cic.

1. lĕpĭdus -a -um, 1, *pleasant, charming, agreeable, elegant, neat, pretty*, Ter., Plaut.; in a bad sense, *nice, effeminate;* hi pueri tam lepidi ac delicati, Cic.; 2, esp. of discourse, *witty, humorous;* dictum, Hor.

2. Lĕpĭdus -i, m. *the name of a family of the patrician gens Aemilia, the most famous members of which were:* 1, M. Aemilius Lepidus, *praetor in Sicily,* consul B.C. 79, *the bitter enemy of Sulla, whose measures he proposed to annul, and thereby brought about a civil war;* 2, M. Aemilius Lepidus, *Triumvir with Antonius and Octavianus,* B.C. 43.

Lĕpontii -ōrum, m. *an Alpine people in Cisalpine Gaul* (in modern *Val Leventina*).

lĕpor and **lĕpos** -ōris, m. 1, *pleasantness, agreeableness, charm,* Cic.; 2, of discourse, *pleasantry, wit, humour;* scurrilis, Cic.

lĕpos -ōris = lepor (q.v.).

Leptis -ptis, f. (Λέπτις), *Leptis, the name of two cities on the coast of Africa:* 1, Magna, now *Lebida;* 2, Minor, between Hadrumetum and Thapsus. Hence, **Leptĭtāni** -ōrum, m. *the inhabitants of Leptis.*

lĕpus -ōris, m. and c. (akin to λαγώς), 1, *a hare*, Verg.; prov.. aliis leporem agitare, *to*

labour for another's advantage, Ov.; 2, *the constellation Lepus*, Cic.

lepuscŭlus -i, m. (dim. of lepus), *a little hare*, Cic.

Lerna -ae, f. and **Lernē** -ēs, f. (Λέρνη), *a marsh in Argolis, inhabited by the Lernaean Hydra slain by Hercules;* belua Lernae, Verg.; hence, adj., **Lernaeus** -a -um, *Lernaean.*

Lesbos -i, f. (Λέσβος), *an island in the Aegean Sea, birthplace of Pittacus, Alcaeus, Theophrastus, Arion, and Sappho, famous for its wine.* Hence, adj., a, **Lesbĭăcus** -a -um, *Lesbian;* libri (*dialogues of Dicaearchus*), Cic.; b, **Lesbĭas** -ădis, f. *Lesbian;* subst., *a Lesbian woman*, Ov.; c, **Lesbis** -ĭdis, f. *Lesbian;* lyra, *of Arion*, Ov.; Lesbis puella, or simply Lesbis, *Sappho*, Ov.; d, **Lesbĭus** -a -um, *Lesbian;* civis, *Alcaeus*, Hor.; plectrum, *lyric*, Hor.; pes, *lyric poetry*, Hor.; vates, *Sappho*, Ov.; subst., **Lesbĭum** -ii, n. *Lesbian wine*, Hor.; e, **Lesbōus** -a -um, *Lesbian.*

lessus, acc. -um (found only in acc. sing), m. *a mournful cry, lamentation for the dead*, ap. Cic.

lētālis -e (letum), *deadly, mortal, fatal;* arundo, Verg.

lēthargĭcus -a -um (ληθαργικός), *drowsy, lethargic.* Subst., **lēthargĭcus** -i, m. *a drowsy, lethargic person*, Hor.

lēthargus -i, m. (λήθαργος), *drowsiness, lethargy*, Hor.

Lēthē -ēs, f. (Λήθη), *a river in the infernal regions, the drinking of the waters of which produced complete forgetfulness of the past.* Hence, adj., **Lēthaeus** -a -um, 1, *relating to Lethe or the infernal regions generally;* Lethaea vincula abrumpere alicui, *to restore to life*, Hor.; 2, *causing forgetfulness;* somnus, Verg.; sucus, Ov.

lethum, v. letum.

lētĭfer -fĕra -fĕrum (letum and fero), *deathbringing, deadly, fatal, mortal;* arcus, Verg.; locus, *a place on the body where a wound is fatal*, Ov.

lēto, 1. (letum), *to kill, slay*, Ov.

Lētōis, Lētōĭus = Latois, Latoius (v. under Lato).

lētum -i, n. (*leo, whence deleo), 1, *death;* turpi leto perire, Cic.; letum sibi parĕre manu, *to commit suicide*, Verg.; leto adimere aliquem, *to save from death*, Hor.; 2, transf., of things, poet., *ruin, annihilation;* Teucrûm res eripe leto, Verg.

Leucădĭa -ae, f. (Λευκαδία), and **Leucăs** -ădis, f. (Λευκάς), *an island of the Ionian Sea, with a temple to Apollo* (now *S. Maura*). Hence, adj., **Leucădĭus** -a -um, *Leucadian;* deus, *Apollo*, Ov.; more Leucadio (in allusion to the Leucadian custom of throwing a man every year from a rock into the sea), Ov.; subst., **Leucădĭa** -ae, f. *name of a play of Turpilius*, Cic.; **Leucădĭi** -ōrum, m. *the Leucadians*, Liv.

Leucăs -ădis, f. (Λευκάς), 1, *the island of Leucadia or its capital;* 2, = Leucatas.

leucaspĭs -ĭdis, f. (λεύκασπις), *having white shields;* phalanx, Liv.

Leucātās -ae, m. and **Leucătēs** -ae, m. (Λευκάτας), and **Leucăs** -cădis, f. *a promontory of the island Leucadia*, now *Capo Ducato.*

Leucē -ēs, f. (Λευκή), *a town in Laconia.*

Leuci -ōrum, m. *a people in Gallia Belgica.*

Leucippus -i, m. (Λεύκιππος). **I.** Myth. *father of Phoebe and Hilaira, who were carried off by Castor and Pollux.* Hence. **Leucippis**

-Idis, f. *a daughter of Leucippus.* **II.** Hist., *a Greek philosopher, disciple of Zeno the Eleatic.*

Leucŏpĕtra -ae, f. *a promontory in Bruttium,* now *Cap dell'Armi.*

Leucŏphrўna -ae, f. (Λευκοφρύνη, i.e. *with white eyebrows), a surname of Diana among the Magnesians.*

Leucōsĭa -ae, f. (Λευκωσία), *an island near* Paestum, now *Licosia.*

Leucŏthĕa -ae, f. and **Leucŏthĕē** -ēs, f. {Λευκοθέα, i.e. *the white goddess), name of Ino, daughter of Cadmus, after she had been turned into a sea-deity, afterwards identified with the old Italian goddess,. Matuta.*

Leucŏthŏē -ēs, f. *daughter of the eastern king Orchamus and Eurynome, beloved by Apollo.*

Leuctra -ōrum, n. (Λεῦκτρα), *a small town in Boeotia, where Epaminondas defeated the Spartans.* Hence, **Leuctrĭcus** -a -um, *Leuctrian.*

lĕvāmen -ĭnis, n. (1. levo), *a mitigation, alleviation, consolation, solace;* quod si esset aliquod levamen, id esset in te uno, Cic.

lĕvāmentum -i, n. (1. levo), *alleviation, mitigation, solace;* miseriarum, Cic.

lĕvātĭo -ōnis, f. (1. levo), 1, *an alleviation, mitigation;* invenire levationem molestiis, Cic.; 2, *a diminution;* vitiorum, Cic.

1. **lĕvātus** -a -um, v. 1. levo.

2. **lĕvātus (laevatus)** -a -um, v. 2. levo.

lĕvĭcŭlus -a -um (dim. of 1. levis), *somewhat vain, light-minded;* leviculus noster Demosthenes, Cic.

lĕvĭdensis -e (1. levis), *lightly made, of thin texture;* transf., *slight, poor;* munusculum, Cic.

lĕvĭpes -pĕdis (1. levis and pes), *light-footed;* lepus, Cic.

1. **lĕvis** -e, *light, not heavy* (opp. gravis). **I.** Lit., 1, as regards weight; pondus, Ov.; levis armatura, *light armour,* Caes., and concr. = *light-armed soldiery,* Cic.; 2, *light or quick in movement, rapid, swift;* cervus, Verg.; hora, *transitory,* Ov.; 3, *gentle, soft, mild;* somnus, Hor. **II.** Transf., 1, *light, trifling, unimportant, insignificant, of small value;* a, dolor, Cic.; periculum levius, Caes.; auditio, *a trifling, unfounded report,* Caes.; subst., in levi habere, *to regard as a trifle,* Tac.; b, of poetry, *light, unambitious* (of love songs, etc.); Musa, Ov.; c, *trivial, slight, insufficient;* levis causa belli, Liv.; pecunia levissima, Cic.; of persons, levis pauper, *whose credit is gone,* Hor.; 2, *light, mild, gentle;* reprehensio levior, Cic.; 3, *light, fickle, light-minded, unstable, unsteady;* homo, Cic.; amicitia, Cic.

2. **lēvis (laevis)** -e (λεῖος), *smooth* (opp. asper). **I.** Lit., 1, corpuscula, Cic.; 2, a, *polished;* pocula, Verg.; b, poet., *smooth, beardless;* juventas, Hor.; senex, *bald,* Ov.; hence = *youthful;* pectus, Verg.; vir, *decked out, spruce,* Ov.; c, *slippery;* sanguis, Verg. **II.** Of style, *flowing, smooth, polished,* oratio, Cic.

lĕvĭsomnus -a -um (1. levis and somnus), *lightly sleeping,* Lucr.

1. **lĕvĭtas** -ātis, f. (1. levis), *lightness.* **I.** Lit., 1, *lightness of weight;* armorum, Caes.; 2, *lightness in movement,* Lucr. **II.** Transf., 1, *lightness, levity, fickleness, changeableness, inconstancy;* levitatem alicuius experiri, Cic.; levitatem insectari, Cic.; 2, *groundlessness;* opinionis, Cic.

2. **lēvĭtas** -ātis, f. (2. levis), 1, *smoothness;* speculorum, Cic.; 2, *smoothness, polish (of style);* Aeschini, Cic.

lĕvĭtĕr, adv. (1. levis). **I.** *lightly, not*

heavily, softly; levius casura pila sperabat, Caes. **II.** Transf., 1, *slightly, not much, somewhat;* saucius, Cic.; aegrotare, Cic.; ut levissime dicam, *to speak in the mildest way,* Cic.; 2, *lightly, with equanimity;* ferre, Cic.

1. **lĕvo,** 1. (1. levis), *to raise, lift up, elevate.* **I.** Lit., se attollere ac levare, Liv.; de caespite virgo se levat, Ov. **II.** Transf., 1, *to lighten, make light, relieve from a weight;* ego te fasce levabo, Verg.; aliquem metu, Cic.; se aere alieno, *to free,* Cic.; 2, *to relieve, support, console, alleviate, mitigate;* curam et angorem animi mei, Cic.; 3, *to refresh, strengthen;* fessos corporis artus, Hor.; 4, *to diminish, weaken, impair;* fidem, Hor.; auctoritatem, Cic.

2. **lēvo,** 1. (2. levis), *to make smooth, polish;* corpus, Cic.; transf., of discourse, aspera, Hor.

lēvor -ōris, m. (2. levis), *smoothness,* Lucr.

lex, lēgis, f. (2. lego), *a set form of words.* **I.** *a proposition made by a magistrate to the people, bill.* **A.** Lit., legem ferre, rogare, *to propose a bill to the people,* Cic.; sciscere, jubere (of the people), *to accept or pass a bill,* Cic.; repudiare, antiquare, *to reject, throw out a bill,* Cic.; promulgare, *to publish,* Cic. **B.** *a law, legal enactment;* 1, a, legem ferre, *to pass a law, enact,* Liv.; abrogare, *to repeal,* Cic.; leges duodecim tabularum, *the laws of the Twelve Tables, drawn up by the Decemvirs,* Cic.; lege, legibus, used adv. = *legally, according to law,* Nep.; lege agere, (α) of the lictor, *to execute a sentence,* Liv.; (β) *to bring an action,* Cic.; lex est Lacedaemoniis or apud Rhodios* (foll. by ut. and the subj.), Cic.; b, meton., (a) *law as written* (opp. mores, consuetudo), Cic.; (β) *law generally,* including positive and natural law, Cic.; 2, *a law set by a man to himself;* legem sibi statuere, Cic.; 3, a, *a rule, principle, precept;* leges philosophiae, historiae, Cic.; versibus est certa lex, Cic.; b, *manner, way, nature, kind;* ex lege loci, Ov.; c, *order;* sine lege, *without order, irregularly;* equi sine lege ruunt, Ov. **II. A.** *a formula;* Manilianas venalium vendendorum leges ediscere, Cic. **B.** *a contract, covenant, agreement;* lex operi faciundo, *a building contract,* Cic.; legem alicui scribere, Cic.; leges pacis, *conditions of peace,* Liv.; homines eā lege natos, *on these terms, on this condition,* Cic.

Lexŏvĭi -ōrum, m. *a people of Gallia Lugdunensis on the Sequana (Seine),* whence the modern *Lisieux.*

lībāmen -ĭnis, n. (libo), 1, *a libation, offering of wine made to the gods at a sacrifice,* Verg. 2, transf., *what is first taken, a sample, specimen;* tu nova servatae carpes libamina famae, Ov.

lībāmentum -i, n. (libo), *a libation,* Cic.

lībātĭo -ōnis, f. (libo), *a libation,* Cic.

lībella -ae, f. (dim. of libra). **I.** 1, *a small coin, 1-10th of a denarius, equal in value to the as;* prov., *a very small sum of money, a farthing, a mite;* hence, ad libellam, *exactly,* Cic.; 2, transf., heres ex libella, *heir to the whole property* (cp. ex asse), Cic. **II.** *a carpenter's level,* Plin.

lībellus -i, m. (dim. of liber), *a little book.* **I.** scripsi etiam illud quodam in libello, Cic.; pl. meton., = *a bookseller's shop,* Cat. **II.** Esp., a, *a note-book, memorandum-book, diary;* retulit in libellum, Cic.; b, *a memorial, a petition;* libellum composuit, Cic.; c, *a note of invitation, programme;* gladiatorum libelli, Cic.; d, *a placard, hand-bill,* e.g., announcing the sale of goods, dejicere libellos, *to put off the sale,* Cic.; e, *a letter,* Cic.; f, *a satire, a libel,* Suet.

lībens and **lŭbens** -entis, p. adj. (libet), 1, *willing, with good-will, with pleasure;* libenti animo, *willingly*, Cic.; me libente, *with my goodwill*, Cic.; **2**, *joyful, pleased, glad*, Plaut., Ter.

lĭbentĕr (lŭbentĕr), adv. (libens, lubens), *willingly, with pleasure;* libenter uti verbo Catonis, Cic.; nusquam libentius cenare, *with better appetite*, Cic.; libentissime dare, Cic.

lĭbentĭa (lŭbentĭa) -ae, f. (libens, lubens), *cheerfulness, gladness*, Plaut.; personif., **Lĭbentĭa** -ae, f. *the goddess of mirth*, Plaut.

Lĭbentīna (Lŭbentīna) -ae, f. (libens, lubens), *a name of Venus, as the goddess of sensual pleasure.*

1. lĭber -ĕra -ĕrum, *free.* **I. A.** *of free birth* (opp. servus), aliquem non liberum putare, Cic.; of states, *free, independent;* civitas, Caes.; subst., **lĭber** -eri, m. *a freedman*, Cic. **B.** Transf., **1**, *free from tax or tribute;* agri, Cic.; **2**, of houses and places, *free from inhabitants;* aedes, *uninhabited*, Liv.; **3**, *unencumbered with debt;* ut rei familiaris liberum quidquam sit, Cic. **II.** *free from fetters.* **A.** Lit., Plaut. **B.** Transf., **1**, *free from anything, without;* a delictis, Cic.; curā, Cic.; **2**, *free from restraint, unbridled;* **a**, adolescentia, Cic.; toga, vestis, *the toga virilis*, Ov.; custodia, *surveillance, confinement to a single house or town*, Cic.; fenus, *unlimited by law*, Liv.; liberum habere aliquid, *to have in complete possession*, Liv.; liberum est mihi, foll. by infin., *I am free to do*, Cic.; **b**, *free in thought* or *expression;* animus, Cic.; liberiores litterae, Cic.; **3**, *morally free;* **a**, *in the philosophical sense*, Cic.: **b**, in a bad sense, = *profligate, unbridled, unrestrained;* turba temulentorum, Cic.

2. lĭber -bri, m. **I.** *the inner bark of a tree*, Verg. **II.** And, as this was used by the ancients as a material upon which to write, *a book, writing, treatise;* **a**, librum inchoare, conficere, Cic.; libri Sibyllini, Cic.; nos autem in libris (*account books*) habemus, Cic.; **b**, *a book, a division into which a work is divided;* tres libri de Natura Deorum, Cic.; **c**, *a register, catalogue*, Cic.; **d**, *a letter*, Nep.

3. Lĭber -ĕri, m. **1**, *an old Italian deity, presiding over agriculture, and in later times identified with the Greek Bacchus;* **2**, meton., *wine*, Hor.

4. lĭber -ĕri, v. liberi -ōrum.

Lĭbĕra -ae, f. (3. Liber), **1**, *Proserpina, daughter of Ceres, sister of Liber;* **2**, *Ariadne, wife of Bacchus.*

Lĭbĕrālĭa -ium, n. (3. Liber), *the festival of Liber on the 17th of March, at which youths received the toga virilis*, Cic.

lĭbĕrālis -e (1. liber). **I.** *relating to freedom; causa, a lawsuit in which the freedom of some person is the matter in dispute*, Cic. **II.** *becoming* or *suitable to a freedman, noble;* **1**, mens, Cic.; artes liberales, *liberal arts, such as a freedman ought to be versed in*, Cic.; sumptus, *expenses to keep up station and appearances* (cpp. necessarii), Cic.; **2**, **a**, *kind;* responsum, Cic.; **b**, *liberal, generous, giving freely*, Cic.; laudis avidi, pecuniae liberales erant, Sall.

lĭbĕrālĭtas -ātis, f. (liberalis), **1**, *a noble disposition* or *character, kind, friendly disposition*, Cic.; **2**, *liberality, generosity*, Cic.

lĭbĕrālĭtĕr, adv. (liberalis), *in a manner becoming a freedman.* **I.** *nobly, becomingly;* vivere, Cic. **II.** Esp., **a**, *in a friendly manner, kindly, liberally;* liberalissime erat pollicitus omnibus, Cic.; **b**, *richly, bountifully*, Cic.

lĭbĕrātĭo -ōnis, f. (libero), **1**, *a setting free, releasing from;* culpae, Cic.; **2**, *a legal acquittal*, Cic.

lĭbĕrātor -ōris, m. (libero), *one who sets free, a liberator;* patriae, Cic.; attrib., liberator populus, Liv.

lĭbĕrē, adv. (1. liber). **I.** *like a freeman, liberally*, Ter. **II. 1**, *freely, without restraint, without hindrance;* vivere, Cic.; respirare, Cic.; **2**, **a**, *spontaneously;* tellus omnia liberius ferebat, Verg.; **b**, *frankly, openly, boldly;* loqui, Cic.

lĭbĕri -ērōrum and -ērum, m. (1. liber), **1**, *children;* liberos procreare, liberis operam dare, *to beget children*, Cic.; **2**, *the young of animals*, Plaut.

lĭbĕro, **1**. (1. liber), *to set free, liberate.* **I.** From slavery, *to manumit;* aliquem, Cic. **II.** *to set free from something that fetters.* **A.** *to set free, liberate, deliver, release;* te ab eo vindico ac libero, Cic.; divinus animus liberatus a corpore, Cic.; aliquem culpā, Cic.; aliquem periculo, Caes.; obsidionem urbis, *to raise*, Liv. **B. 1**, *to set free from a debt* or *engagement;* aliquem, Cic.; aliquem eodem illo crimine, Cic.; with genit. of the debt or fault, aliquem culpae, Liv.; **2**, templa liberata, *having a free prospect, free from buildings which obstruct the view*, Cic.

lĭbĕrta -ae, f., v. libertus.

lībertas -ātis, f. (1. liber). **I.** *freedom, liberty* (opp. slavery). **A.** Lit., **1**, se in libertatem vindicare, Cic.; **2**, **a**, *civil liberty, as containing certain rights;* ad usurpandam libertatem vocare, *to summon to the voting*, Cic.; libertatem eripere, *to take away political privileges*, Liv.; **b**, *national freedom, independence;* libertatem capessere, Cic.; perdere, Cic.; recipere, Cic. **B.** Transf., **1**, *freedom, liberty of action, freedom from restraint;* **a**, vivendi, loquendi, Cic.; dat populo libertatem ut quod velint faciant, Cic.; **b**, *licence*, Cic.; **2**, *freedom of speech, frankness, candour;* multa cum libertate dicere, Cic. **II.** Libertas, *personified as the goddess of Freedom, having a temple on the Aventine Hill*, Cic.

lībertīnus -a -um (libertus), *of* or *relating to the class of freedmen*, Cic.; hence, subst., **lībertīnus** -i, m. *a freedman*, Cic.; **lībertīna** -ae, f. *a freedwoman*, Hor.

lībertus -a -um (for liberatus), *placed in freedom;* subst., **a**, **lībertus** -i, m. *a freedman*, Cic.; **b**, **lïberta** -ae, f. *a freedwoman*, Cic.

lĭbet (lŭbet) -bŭit or -bĭtum est, **3**. impers., *it pleases, is agreeable;* mihi, tibi, etc., or absol., facite quod libet, Cic.; non libet plura scribere, Cic.

Lĭbēthra (Λείβηθρα) -ōrum, n. and **Lībēthrus** -i, m. (Λειβηθρός), *a Thessalian spring, sacred to the Muses;* hence, adj., **Lĭbēthrĭs** -ĭdis, f. nymphae Libethrides, *the Muses*, Verg.

lĭbīdĭnōsē, adv. (libidinosus), *lustfully, wilfully, wantonly*, Cic.

lĭbīdĭnōsus -a -um (libido), *full of desire, wilful, wanton, lustful;* homo, Cic.; caper, Hor.; applied to abstract things, libidinosissimae liberationes, Cic.; sententia, Cic.

lĭbīdo (lŭbīdo) -ĭnis, f. (libet), *violent desire, appetite, longing.* **I.** ad libidinem, *according to inclination*, Cic.; ex libidine, Sall.; libidine, *wantonly, out of mere caprice*, Cic.; libidinem habere in armis, *to take pleasure in*, Sall. **II. 1**, *immoderate* or *unrestrained desire, self-will, wilfulness, wantonness;* alicuius libidini adversari, obsistere, Cic.; libidines refrenare, Cic.; **2**, *sensual desire, lust, lewdness;* meton., libidines, *obscenities in painting and sculpture*, Cic.

Lĭbītĭna -ae, f. **I.** *the goddess of corpses, in whose temple the requisites for a funeral were kept for hire, and the register of deaths was preserved.* **II.** Meton., **1**, *the requisites for a funeral;* pestiientia tanta erat, ut Libitina **vix** sufficeret, Liv.; 2, *death;* multaque pars mei vitabit Libitinam, Hor.

lībo, 1. (λείβω). **I.** *to take away from.* **A.** a natura deorum libatos animos habemus, Cic. **B.** 1, *to taste;* jecur, Liv.; hence a, *to touch;* cibos digitis, Ov.; b, oscula natae, *to kiss,* Verg.; 2, *to pour a libation in honour of a god;* in mensam, Verg.; 3, *to sacrifice, offer, consecrate;* diis dapes, Liv.; frugem Cereri, Ov. **II.** *to diminish or injure by taking away;* vires, Liv.

lībra -ae, f. (λίτρα). **I.** *a balance, pair of scales;* 1, a, lit., librae lanx, Cic.; per aes et libram, aere et librā, *a fictitious form of sale used in making wills, adopting sons,* etc.; mercari aliquid aere et librā, *in due form,* Hor.; b, meton., *the Roman pound of 12 oz.;* 2, *the constellation called the Balance,* Verg. **II.** *a level, a plummet level;* ad libram fecisse turres, Caes.

lībrāmen -ĭnis, n. (libro), *balance, poise,* Liv.

lībrāmentum -i, n. (libro). **I.** *that which gives a thing a downward motion;* a, *weight,* Liv.; b, *that which gives a missile its impetus;* tormentorum, *the thong,* Tac. **II.** Transf., *a horizontal plane, flat superficies,* Cic.

lībrārĭa -ae, f. (libra), *a female who weighed out the wool to the slaves,* Juv.

lībrārĭŏlus -i, m. (dim. of librarius), 1, *a transcriber, copyist, secretary,* Cic.; 2, *a bookseller,* Cic.

lībrārĭum -ĭi, n., v. librarius.

lībrārĭus -a -um (2. liber), *of or relating to books.* **I.** Adj., taberna, *a bookshop,* Cic. **II.** Subst., 1, **lībrārĭus** -ĭi, m. *a transcriber of books, a copyist,* Cic.; 2, **lībrārĭum** -ĭi, n. *a place to keep books in, a bookcase,* Cic.

lībrātor -ōris, m. (libro) 1, *a leveller or surveyor,* Plin.; 2, *one who hurls missiles by means of a machine,* Tac.

lībrātus -a -um, p. adj. (from libro), *well-poised, swung, hurled with force;* glans, Liv.; ictus, Liv.

lībrīlis -e (libra), *of a pound weight;* fundae libriles, *slings, the stones of which weighed a pound,* Caes.

lībro, 1. (libra), a, *to poise, keep in equilibrium;* terra librata ponderibus, Cic.; b, *to swing, hurl, launch, brandish;* glandem, Liv.; se, *to poise oneself in the air* (of bees), Verg.; poet., corpus in herba, *to stretch out,* Ov.; c, *to keep suspended, keep in its place;* vela librantur ab aura, Ov.

lībs, lībis, m. (λίψ), *a west-south-west wind,* Plin.

lībum -i, n. *a cake offered to the gods, especially on a birthday,* Ov., Verg.

Lĭburni -ōrum, m. *the Liburnians, a people inhabiting the modern Croatia;* sing., Liburnus, *a Liburnian slave,* Juv. Hence, adj., a, **Lĭburnus** -a -um, *Liburnian;* subst., **Lĭburna** -ae, f. *a light vessel of war, schooner, brigantine,* Caes.; b, **Lĭburnĭcus** -a -um, *Liburnian.*

Lĭbÿa -ae, f. and **Lĭbÿē** -ēs, f. (Λιβύη), *Libya, the Northern part of Africa.* Hence, 1, **Lĭbÿcus** -a -um, *Libyan;* fera, *lioness,* Ov.; 2, **Lĭbÿs** -ÿos, *Libyan;* subst., Libys, *a Libyan,* Ov.; 3, **Lĭbÿssa** -ae, f. *Libyan;* arenae, Cat.; 4, **Lĭbÿstis** -ĭdis, f. *Libyan;* ursa, Verg.; 5, **Lĭbÿus** -a -um, *Libyan;* 6, **Lĭbÿstīnus** -a -um, *Libyan.*

Lĭbÿphoenīces -um, m. (Λιβυφοίνικες), *a Libyan people, descended from the Phoenicians, in Byzacium.*

lĭcens -centis. **I.** Partic. of liceor (q.v.). **II.** P. adj. (licet), *free, unrestrained, unbridled;* Lupercus, Prop., of things, licentior dithyrambus, Cic.

lĭcentĕr, adv. (licens), *freely, according to one's own pleasure;* and in a bad sense, *boldly, impudently, unrestrainedly,* Cic.; of discourse, errare, *to wander on without rule or order,* Cic.

lĭcentĭa -ae, f. (licet), *freedom or permission to do what one pleases, leave, licence, liberty.* **I.** pueris non omnem ludendi damus licentiam, Cic.; tantum licentiae dabat gloria, Cic. **II.** Esp., a, *freedom from restraint, licence;* poetarum, Cic.; verborum, Ov.; b, *dissoluteness, licentiousness;* comprimere hominum licentiam, Cic.; personif., Licentia, as a goddess, *Licence,* Cic.

lĭcĕo -ŭi -ĭtum, 2. *to be on sale, to be valued at, to be estimated at a price;* quanti licuisse tu scribis hortos, *at what sum they were valued,* Cic.

lĭcĕor -cĭtus sum, 2. (liceo) *to bid for, offer a price for;* liciti sunt usque eo, Cic.; followed by acc., hortos, Cic.

lĭcet -cŭit or -cĭtum est, 2., impers. and intransit. **I.** *it is allowed, allowable, one can or may, one is at liberty;* with dat. of pers. or absol., a, with infin., as subject, licet rogare? *may I ask?* Cic.; licet intelligi, *one can understand,* Cic.; with acc. and infin., nos frui liceret, Cic.; with dat. of predicate, Themistocli licet esse otioso, Cic.; with acc. of predicate, civi Romano licet esse Gaditanum, Cic.; b, with a neuter pronoun or adj. as subject, quid deceat vos, non quantum liceat vobis, spectare debetis, Cic.; c, with subj., fremant omnes licet, Cic.; sequatur licebit, *he may follow,* Cic.; with per ac dat., per me licet, *as far as I am concerned,* Cic. **II.** Transf., *granted that, allowed that;* foll. by the subj., omnia licet concurrant, Cic.

Lĭchās -ae, m. (Λίχας), *a servant of Hercules.*

līchēn -ēnis, m. (λειχήν), *moss or lichen,* Plin.

Lĭcĭnĭus -a -um, *name of a Roman gens, the most celebrated members of which were:* 1, C. Licinius Crassus, *tribune of the people;* 2, L. Licinius Crassus, *a celebrated orator;* 3, M. Licinius Crassus, *the triumvir.*

lĭcĭtātĭo -ōnis, f. (licitor), *a bidding, bid, at a sale or auction,* Cic.

lĭcĭtor, 1. dep. (intens. of liceor), *to bid for,* Plaut.

lĭcĭtus -a -um (licet), *allowed, permitted;* sermo, Verg.; neut. plur. subst., *things permitted,* Tac.

lĭcĭum -ĭi, n. *the thrum, or remnant of old web to which the weaver attaches the new fabric;* telae licia addere, Verg.; in general, *a thread,* Ov.

lictor -ōris, m. *a lictor,* plur. lictores, *the lictors, the public attendants of the principal Roman magistrates, who bore before them the fasces as emblem of their criminal jurisdiction, and executed the sentences which they pronounced.* Of these lictors, the dictator was attended by twenty-four, a consul by twelve, and a praetor by six; lictor proximus, *the one nearest to the consul,* Cic.

lĭen -ēnis, m. or **lĭēnis** -is, m. *the milt, or spleen,* Plaut.

lĭēnōsus -a -um (lien), *splenetic,* Plaut.

lĭgāmen -ĭnis, n. (1. ligo), *a string, tie, bandage,* Ov.

lĭgāmentum -i, n. (1. ligo), *a bandage,* Tac.

Lĭgārĭus -a -um, *the name of a Roman gens, the most famous member of which was* Q. Ligarius, *a member of the Pompeian party, taken prisoner after the battle of Thapsus, and banished by Caesar,* *afterwards pardoned, defended by Cicero.* Hence, adj., **Lĭgārĭānus** -a -um, *relating to Ligarius;* oratio, Cic.; and subst., **Lĭgārĭāna** -ae, f. *Cicero's speech on behalf of Ligarius,* Cic.

Lĭgĕa -ae, f. (Λίγεια, *the clear-voiced*), *name of a wood-nymph.*

Lĭgĕr -gĕris, m. *a river on the borders of Aquitania and Gallia Lugdunensis,* now the Loire (acc. Ligerem and Ligerim; abl. Ligere and Ligeri, Caes).

lignārĭus -ĭī, m. (lignum), *a carpenter;* inter lignarios, *in the wood-market,* Liv.

lignātĭo -ōnis, f. (lignor), *a felling of timber, wood-cutting,* Caes.

lignātor -ōris, m. (lignor), *a wood-cutter,* Caes.

lignĕŏlus -a -um (dim. of ligneus), *wooden,* Cic.

lignĕus -a -um (lignum), **1,** *made of wood, wooden;* ponticulus, Cic.; **2,** transf., *like wood, dry;* conjux, Cat.

lignor, 1. dep. (lignum), *to fetch wood;* lignari pabularique, Caes.

lignum -i, n. **I.** *wood,* esp., *firewood* (opp. materia, *wood used for building*); ignem ex lignis viridibus in loco angusto fieri jubere, Cic; prov., in silvam ligna ferre, *to carry coals to Newcastle,* Hor. **II.** Meton., **1,** *a writing-table of wood,* Juv.; **2,** = *a tree,* Verg.

1. lĭgo, 1. **I.** *to bind, tie;* aliquem vinculo, Tac.; manus post terga, Ov.; pisces in glacie ligati, *frozen fast,* Ov.; *to bind up, bandage;* vulnera veste, Ov. **II.** 1, a, *to harness;* mulam, Hor.; b, laqueo guttura, *to tie up, to bind around,* Ov.; **2,** transf., *to bind together, connect, unite;* dissociata locis concordi pace ligavit, Ov.

2. lĭgo -ōnis, m. **1,** *a hoe,* Hor.; **2,** meton., *tillage,* Juv.

lĭgŭla (lingŭla) -ae, f. (dim. of lingua). **I.** *a little tongue,* and hence, *a tongue of land, promontory,* Caes. **II.** *a shoe-strap,* Juv.

Lĭgŭres -um, m. *the Ligurians, a people in modern Piedmont;* sing., **Lĭgŭs (Lĭgŭr)**-gŭris, c. *a Ligurian;* adj. = *Ligurian.* Hence, **1, Lĭgŭria** -æ, f. *the country of the Ligures;* **2, Lĭgustĭcus** -a -um, *Ligurian;* **3, Lĭgustīnus** -a -um, *Ligurian.*

lĭgŭrĭo (lĭgurrĭo), 4. (lingo), **1,** *to lick, lick up;* jus, Hor.; furta, *to feed upon, gloat over stealthily,* Hor.; **2,** *to lust after, long for;* lucra, Cic.

lĭgurrītĭo -ōnis, f. (ligurrio), *daintiness,* Cic.

Lĭgus -gŭris, m., v. Ligures.

Lĭgusticus -stīnus, v. Ligures.

lĭgustrum -i, n. *privet,* Verg.

līlĭum -ĭi, n. (λείριον), *a lily;* **1,** lit., Verg.; **2,** transf., milit. t. t., *a kind of fortification consisting of low palisades,* Caes.

Lĭlybaeŏn (-baeum) -i, n. (Λιλύβαιον), *a promontory in the west of Sicily,* now *Capo di Boco,* with a town of the same name. Adj., a, **Lĭlybaeus** -a -um, b, **Lĭlybēïus** -a -um, and c, **Lĭlybaetānus** -a -um, *Lilybaean.*

līma -ae, f. (limo), *a file,* Plaut.; fig., of style, *polishing, revision, correction;* defuit et scriptis ultima lima meis, Ov.

līmātē, adv. (limatus), *elaborately, elegantly,* Cic.

līmātŭlus -a -um (dim. of limatus), *polished, refined;* opus est huc limatulo et polito tuo judicio, Cic.

līmātus -a -um, p. adj. (limo), *polished, refined, elegant;* genus librorum limatius, Cic.

limbus -i, m. *a border, hem, selvage, fringe round the edge of a robe,* Verg.

līmen -ĭnis, n. (connected with 1. limus and ob-liquus), *the threshold.* **I. A.** Lit., intrare limen, Cic. **B.** Meton., **1** = *house, dwelling;* limine contineri, Liv.; limine pelli, Verg.; **2,** *entrance;* in limine portus, Verg.; **3,** a, *the starting-point of a chariot-race in the circus;* limen relinquunt, Verg.; **b,** *border, boundary;* extra limen Apuliae, Hor. **II.** Fig., *a beginning;* belli, Tac.

līmes -ĭtis, m. (1. limus), *a cross path or by-way.* **I. A.** Lit., *the boundary between two fields indicated by a path or stone,* Verg. **B.** Meton., **1,** *a boundary-line;* partiri limite campum, Verg.; fig., *a distinction, difference;* judicium brevi limite falle tuum, Ov.; **2,** *a fortified boundary-line,* Tac. **II.** *a pathway, road;* Appiae, Liv.; acclivis, Ov.; transversus, Liv.; solitus limes fluminis, *river-bed,* Ov.; sectus, *the zodiac,* Ov.; quasi limes ad caeli aditum patet, Ov.

Limnaeum -i, n. (Λιμναία), *a town in Acarnania.*

Limnātĭs -tĭdis, f. (Λιμνᾶτις), *a surname of Diana, as the patroness of fishermen.*

līmo, 1. (lima), **I.** *to file;* **1,** lit., gemmas, Plin.; **2,** *to whet, sharpen,* Plaut.; **3,** fig., a, *to polish, finish;* quaedam institui, quae limantur a me politius, Cic.; b, *to investigate accurately;* veritatem, Cic. **II.** *to file off;* fig., *to take away from, to diminish;* alteri affinxit, de altero limavit, Cic.

līmōsus -a -um (2. limus), *slimy, miry, muddy;* lacus, Verg.; planities, Sall.

limpĭdus -a -um (connected with liquidus), *clear, limpid, pellucid;* lacus, Cat.

1. līmus -a -um (connected with limen and obliquus), *of the eyes, sidelong, looking sideways;* ocelli, Ov.

2. līmus -i, m. (lino), **1,** *slime, mud, mire,* Cic.; fig., malorum, Ov.; **2,** *dirt, filth,* Hor.

3. līmus -i, m. (1. ligo), *an apron trimmed with purple, worn by a priest when offering sacrifice,* Verg.

Līmyra -ōrum, n. (Λίμυρα, τὰ), and **Līmyra** -ae, f. or **Līmyrē** -ēs, f. (Αἰμύρα, ἡ), *a town in the south of Lycia on the river Limyrus or Limyra.*

1. linctus, partic. of lingo.

2. linctus -ū, m. (lingo), *a licking, taste,* Lucr.

Lindŏs and **-dus** -i, f. (Λίνδος), *a town in Rhodes.*

linĕa -ae, f. (linum), *a linen thread.* **I.** Lit., **A.** Plin.; linea dives, *a string of pearls,* Mart. **B.** *a carpenter's plumb-line,* Cic.; lineā discere uti, Cic.; ad lineam, *exactly straight* or *perpendicular,* Cic. **II.** Transf., *a line made with a pen* or *pencil, geometrical line.* **A.** Gen., lineam scribere, Cic. **B.** 1, *a boundary-line in the circus, a starting-point* or *goal;* fig., si quidem est peccare tanquam transilire lineas, Cic.; mors ultima linea rerum est, *the final goal,* Hor.; **2,** *the line in the theatre by which the seats were separated;* cogit nos linea jungi, Ov.

linĕāmentum -i, n. (linea), *a line drawn with pen* or *pencil, a geometrical line.* **I.** Lit., in geometria lineamenta, Cic. **II.** Transf., **1,** pl., *a drawing, delineation, sketch, outline;* tu operum lineamenta sollertissime perspicis, Cic.; **2,** *a feature, lineament;* corporis, Cic.

linĕus -a -um (linum), *made of linen, linen;* vincula, Verg.; lanterna, Cic.

lingo, linxi, linctum, 3. (λείχω), *to lick,* Cat.

Lingŏnes -um, m. *a people in Gaul,* whence the modern *Langres.*

lingua -ae, f. *a tongue.* **I. A.** Lit., linguam ab irrisu exserere, Liv.; linguam ejicere, Cic. **B.** Meton., 1, *speech, language;* linguam diligentissime continere, *to restrain,* Cic.; Aetolorum linguas retundere, *to silence,* Liv.; transf., of the sounds of animals, linguae volucrum,Verg.; 2, a, *a language, tongue;* Latina, Cic.; Gallica, Caes.; utraque lingua, *Greek and Latin;* b, *a dialect;* disciplinis linguāque divisa, Cic.; 3, *readiness of speech, eloquence;* est animus tibi, sunt mores et lingua fidesque, Hor.; in a bad sense, *loquacity;* poenam lingua commeruisse, Ov.; or *boasting,* Ov.; or *bold talk,* Ov. **II.** Transf., of tongue-shaped objects, *a tongue of land, promontory,* Liv.; tribus haec (Sicilia) excurrit in aequora linguis, Ov.

līnĭa, v. linea.

līnĭāmentum, v. lineamentum.

līnĭgĕr -gĕra gĕrum (linum and gero), *clothed in linen,* applied to Isis and her priests, Ov.

līno, līvi and lēvi, lĭtum, 3. **I.** *to smear upon, spread over;* medicamenta per corpora, Ov. **II.** *to besmear, anoint;* 1, spiramenta cerā, Verg.; 2, a, *to cover;* labra alicui, *to cheat, cozen,* Mart.; tecta auro, Ov.; b, *to rub over with the blunt end of the stylus what has been written on waxen tablets;* digna lini, *worthy of being erased,* Ov.; c, *to besmear, dirty;* ora luto, Ov.; fig., splendida facta carmine foedo, Hor.

linquo, līqui, 3. (λείπω), *to leave.* **I.** Gen., **A.** Lit , socios ignotae terrae, Verg. **B.** Transf., 1, *to leave, give up, abandon;* haec, Cic.; severa, Hor.; 2, with double acc., nil intentatum, Hor. **II.** *to leave, depart from;* urbem, Cic.; linqui, *to faint,* Ov.; linquere dulces animas, *to die,* Verg.

lintĕātus -a -um (linteum), *clothed in linen;* legio, *a Samnite legion, so called from the canvas covering of the place where they took the military oath,* Liv.

lintĕŏlum -i, n. (dim. of linteum), *a small linen cloth,* Plaut.

linter -tris, f. **I.** *a boat, skiff, wherry;* prov., loqui e lintre (of an orator who sways his body up and down in speaking), ap. Cic. **II.** Transf., *a trough, tray, tub, vat,* used in the vintage, Verg.

lintĕus -a -um (linum), *linen, made of linen;* vestis, Cic.; libri, *written on linen,* Liv. Subst., **lintĕum** -i, n. *linen cloth, linen;* merces linteis delatae, Cic.; esp., *a sail:* dare lintea ventis, Ov.

lintrĭcŭlus -i, m. (dim. of linter), *a small boat,* Cic.

līnum -i, n. (λίνον), *flax, linen.* **I.** Lit., linum tenuissimum, Cic. **II.** Meton., 1, *a thread, line;* a, *the thread with which letters were tied up;* nos linum incīdimus, legimus, Cic.; b, *a fishing-line,* Ov.; 2, *a linen-cloth or garment,* Hor.; 3, *a rope, cable,* Ov.; 4, *a net for hunting or fishing,* Ov., Verg.

Līnus (-ŏs) -i, m. (Λίνος), *Linus.* **I.** *son of Apollo and Psamathe, daughter of the Argive king, Crotopus, torn in pieces by dogs.* **II.** *son of Apollo and the Muse Terpsichore, celebrated singer and poet, the teacher of Orpheus and Hercules, the latter of whom killed him with a blow of the lyre.*

Lĭpăra -ae, f. and **Lĭpărē** -ēs, f. (Λιπάρα), *the largest of the Aeolian islands, north of Sicily,* now *Lipari;* plur., Liparae, *the Aeolian islands.* Adj., a, **Lĭpăraeus** -a -um; b, **Lĭpărensis** -e, *Liparean.*

lippĭo, 4. *to have sore eyes, be blear-eyed;* quum leviter lippirem, Cic.

lippĭtūdo -ĭnis, f. (lippus), *inflammation in the eyes,* Cic.

lippus -a -um, *having inflamed or watery eyes, blear-eyed,* Hor.; *sand-blind, half-blind,* Juv.

lĭquĕfăcĭo -fēci -factum, 3., pass., lĭquĕfĭo -factus sum -fĭĕri (liqueo and facio), *to melt, dissolve, make liquid.* **I.** Lit., 1, glacies liquefacta, Cic.; 2, *to putrefy;* viscera liquefacta, Verg. **II.** Transf., *to make weak, enervate;* aliquem languidis voluptatibus, Cic.

lĭquĕo, līqui or līcŭi, 2. (λείβω). **I.** *to be fluid, liquid;* concrescendi, liquendi, Cic.; hence partic., liquens, *fluid, liquid;* vina, Verg.; campi, *the sea,* Verg. **II.** Transf., *to be clear, to be evident, apparent;* a, dixit sibi liquere, Cic.; with accus. and infin., cui neutrum licuerit, nec esse deos nec non esse, Cic.; b, legal t. t., non liquet, *a phrase used by the jury when they declined to pronounce the accused person either innocent or guilty,* Cic.

lĭquesco, līcŭi, 3. (inchoat. of liqueo), *to become fluid, to melt.* **I.** Lit., 1, cera liquescit, Verg.; 2, *to putrefy;* liquescunt corpora, Ov. **II.** Transf., 1, *to become effeminate;* voluptate, Cic.; 2, *to melt or waste away;* liquescit fortuna, Ov.

lĭquĭdē, adv., with compar. and superl. (liquidus), *clearly, plainly, positively;* liquidĭ·s negare, Cic.

lĭquĭdo, v. liquidus.

lĭquĭdus -a -um (liqueo), *fluid, flowing, liquid.* **I.** **A.** Lit., odores, Hor.; Nymphae, *nymphs of springs,* Ov. **B.** Transf., genus sermonis, Cic. **II.** *clear, bright,* **A.** Lit., fontes, Verg.; aër, Verg.; vox, Verg. **B.** Transf., 1, *pure, clear;* liquida voluptas et libera, Cic.; 2, *calm;* mens, Cat.; 3, *clear, certain,* Plaut. Subst., **lĭquĭdum** -i, n. *certainty,* Liv.; adv., liquido, *clearly, plainly:* dicere, Cic.

lĭquo, 1. *to make liquid, melt, liquefy.* **I.** Lit., Cic. poet. **II.** *to strain, percolate, clarify;* vinum, Hor.

1. **lĭquor,** 3. dep. *to be fluid, be liquid, flow, melt:* toto corpore sudor liquitur, Verg.; transf., *to melt away, pass away;* in partem pejorem liquitur aetas, Lucr.

2. **lĭquor** -ōris, m. (liqueo), *liquidity, fluidity.* **I.** Lit., Cic. **II.** Meton., *a liquid, fluid, liquor;* perlucidi amnium liquores, Cic.; absol., *the sea,* Hor.

Lĭrĭŏpē -ēs, f. (Λειριόπη), *a sea-nymph, mother of Narcissus.*

Līris -is, acc. -em and -im, abl. -i, m. (Λείρις), *a river of Latium, flowing into the Sinus Cajetanus,* now *the Garigliano.*

līs (old form, stlis), lītis, f. *a contention, strife, controversy, quarrel.* **I.** Gen., aetatem in litibus conterere, Cic.; lites eorum sedare, Cic., componere, *to settle,* Verg.; discernere, *to decide,* Verg. **II.** *a legal contention or controversy, an action, suit;* 1, lit., litem alicui intendere, in aliquem inferre, *to bring an action against,* Cic.; litem habere cum aliquo, Cic.; litem suam facere, said of an advocate who neglects his client's business to defend himself, Cic.; 2, meton., *the subject or cause of a suit;* litem in rem suam vertere, Liv.; litem lite resolvere, *to illustrate one obscure point by another,* Hor.

Lissus -i, f. *town in the south of Dalmatia,* now *Alessio,* or *Lesch.*

Lītăna silva -ae, f. *a forest in Cisalpine Gaul, where the Romans were defeated by the Gauls,* 216 A.C.

lītātĭo -ōnis, f. (lito), *an auspicious offering, successful sacrifice;* hostiae majores sine litatione caesae, Liv.

lĭtĕra (lĭttĕra) -ae, f. (1. lino), *a letter of the alphabet.* **I.** Lit., literarum notae, Cic.; homo trium literarum =fur, *a thief,* Plaut.; literae grandes, *uncial characters,* Cic.; tristis (C), which stood upon the balloting tickets for Condemno, salutaris (A), for Absolvo, Cic.; literas discere, *to learn to read,* Cic.; ad me literam nunquam misit, *not a line,* Cic.; literis parcere, *to be sparing with paper,* Cic. **II.** Meton., **A.** Sing., litera; **1,** *handwriting;* ad similitudinem literae tuae, Cic.; **2,** poet. for plur. literae, a, *a letter,* Ov.; **b,** *an epitaph,* Ov.; **c,** *a bond,* Ov. **B.** Plur. literae, *that which is written;* **1,** *written records;* quod parvae et rarae per eadem tempora literae fuere, Liv.; **2,** a, *writing, document, deed, contract;* litteras conquirere, Cic.; **b,** *a letter, private or official despatch, edict, decree, epistle;* dare alicui literas ad aliquem, *to give to a messenger a letter for a third person,* Cic.; liber literarum missarum et allatarum, *a book of letters despatched and received,* Cic.; **c,** *literature, letters, science, culture;* literis omnibus a pueritia deditus, Cic.; literis tinctus, Cic.

lĭtĕrārĭus -a -um (litera), *relating to reading and writing;* ludus, *an elementary school,* Tac.

lĭtĕrātē, adv. (literatus). **I.** *distinctly, clearly, legibly;* literate et scite perscriptae rationes, Cic. **II. 1,** *literally, word for word;* respondere, Cic.; **2,** *learnedly, scientifically;* dicta, Cic.

lĭtĕrātor -ōris, m. (litera), *a philologist, grammarian, critic.*

lĭtĕrātūra -ae, f. (literae). **I.** *a writing composed of letters;* **a,** *that which is written,* Cic.; **b,** *the alphabet,* Tac. **II.** *culture, learning, scholarship,* Sen.

lĭtĕrātus -a -um (literae). **I.** *lettered, inscribed with letters;* servus, *branded,* Plaut. **II.** *learned, liberally educated;* Canius nec infacetus et satis literatus, Cic.; transf., otium, *learned leisure,* Cic.

Līternum -i, n. *a town in Campania, north of the mouth of the river Liternus,* now *Patria.* Adj., a, **Līternus** -a -um; b, **Līternīnus** -a -um, *Liternian.* Subst., **Līternīnum** -i, n. *an estate near Liternum.*

lĭtĕrŭla -ae, f. (dim. of litera). **I.** *a little letter* (of the alphabet), literulae minutae, Cic. **II.** Plur., literulae, **1,** *a little letter, note,* Cic.; **2,** *letters, literature, literary and scientific culture,* Cic.

lĭtĭcen -cĭnis, m. (lituus and cano), *a trumpeter, clarion-blower,* Cic.

lĭtĭgātor -ōris, m. (litigo), *a party in a lawsuit, litigant,* Cic.

lĭtĭgĭōsus -a -um (litigium), *full of strife, contentious.* **I.** With comp. and superl., *fond of dispute, litigious;* homo minime litigiosus, Cic. **II.** Of things, a, *full of dispute, quarrelsome;* disputatio, Cic.; **b,** *contested at law;* praediolum, Cic.

lĭtĭgĭum -ĭi, n. (litigo), *a quarrel, contention,* Plaut.

lītĭgo, 1. (for litem ago), *to quarrel, dispute, brawl.* **I.** Gen., acerrime cum aliquo pro aliquo, Cic. **II.** Esp., *to go to law;* noli pati fratres litigare, Cic.

līto, 1. **I.** Intransit., **A.** *to bring an acceptable offering, to make an auspicious or accepted sacrifice, to obtain favourable omens;* alicui deo, Cic.; litemus Lentulo, *to appease, make an atonement to,* Cic.; with abl. of the sacrifice, proximā hostiā litatur saepe pulcherrime, Cic.; litato (abl. absol.), non auspicato nec litato aciem instruunt, *without having offered an auspicious sacrifice.* Liv. **B.** Of the victim, *to give*

a favourable omen, promise success; victima nullā litat, Ov. **II.** Transit., *to sacrifice successfully;* sacris litatis, Verg.

lĭtŏrālis -e (litus), *of or relating to the shore;* dii, *gods of the shore,* Cat.

lĭtŏrĕus -a -um (litus), *of or belonging to the shore;* arena, Ov.; aves, Verg.

littĕra, etc., v. litera, etc.

lītūra -ae, f. (lino). **1,** *the drawing of the blunt end of the stylus over the waxen tablet to erase what has been written, an erasure, correction;* flagitiosa litura tabularum, Cic.; **2,** meton., *the passage erased;* nomen esse in litura, Cic.; poet. transf., *a blot,* Ov.

littus, etc., v. litus, etc.

lītus (littus) -tŏris, n. (lino). **I. 1,** *the seashore, beach, strand, coast;* litus insulae, Cic.; naves agere in litus, Liv.; prov., litus arare, *to plough the shore, to labour in vain,* Ov.; in litus arenas fundere, *to carry coals to Newcastle,* Ov.; **2,** *the sea-coast, territory near the coast;* cui litus arandum dedimus, Verg. **II.** Transf., *the shore of a lake,* Ov.; *of a river,* Cic.

lĭtŭus -i, m. (lito). **I.** *the curved staff or wand of an augur,* Cic. **II.** Transf., *a curved trumpet, clarion,* Cic.

līvēns -entis, p. adj. (from liveo), **1,** *lead-coloured, bluish-grey;* plumbum, Verg.; crura compedibus, *livid, black and blue,* Ov.; **2,** *envious,* Mart.

līvĕo, 2. **1,** *to be of a bluish colour,* Ov.; **2,** transf., *to be envious, to envy;* alicui, Tac.

līvesco, 3. (liveo), *to become bluish, grow livid,* Lucr.

līvĭdŭlus -a -um (dim. of lividus) *somewhat envious,* Juv.

līvĭdus -a -um (liveo), *bluish, blue.* **I.** Lit., racemi, Hor.; vada (of the Styx), Verg.; esp. from blows, *livid, black and blue;* brachia, Hor. **II.** Transf., *envious, malicious, spiteful;* differ opus, livida lingua, tuum, Ov.; oblivio, Hor.

Līvĭus -a -um, *name of a Roman gens, the most celebrated members of which were:* 1, C. or M. Livius, *surnamed Salinator, because of the salt-tax which he introduced when censor;* 2, Livius Andronicus, *of Tarentum, slave of Livius Salinator, Roman tragic and comic poet;* 3, T. Livius Patavinus, *of Padua, the great Roman historian, born* 59 A.C., *died* 16 A.D.; 4, Livia Drusilla, *the second wife of the Emperor Augustus;* 5, Livia Orestilla, *wife of the Emperor Caligula.* Adj., *Livian;* lex, Cic.; hence, **Līvĭānus** -a -um, *Livian;* fabulae, *of Livius Andronicus,* Cic.; exercitus, *of the consul M. Livius,* Liv.

līvor -ōris, m. (liveo), **1,** *a bluish colour, livid spot on the body;* niger livor in pectore, Ov.; **2,** *envy, spite, malice;* ap. Cic.

lixa -ae, m. *a sutler,* Liv.; plur., **lixae** -ārum, m. *camp-followers of every kind,* Sall.

lŏcātĭo -ōnis, f. (loco), *a letting out to hire, leasing;* a, lit., Cic.; **b,** meton., *a contract of letting and hiring, a lease,* Cic.

lŏcellus -i, m. (dim. of loculus), *a compartment in a chest,* Caes.

lŏcĭto, 1. (intens. of loco), *to let out to hire,* Ter.

lŏco, 1. (locus), *to place, lay, put, set.* **I.** Gen., **1,** lit., castra, Cic.; milites super vallum, Sall.; fundamenta urbis, Verg.; **2,** transf., *to place;* homines in amplissimo gradu dignitatis, Cic. **II.** Esp., **A.** *to give in marriage, bestow in marriage;* virginem in matrimonio, Plaut. **B.** a, *to let out to hire, to farm out taxes;* vectigalia, portorium, fundum, Cic.; agrum campanum fruendum, Liv.; with abl. of the price, agrum frumento, *for a tenth part of the produce,* Liv.; subst.,

11

lŏcātum -i, n. *that which is let out to hire,* Cic.; **b,** hence, *to give out on contract;* statuam faciendam, Cic.; **c,** *to hire out, let one's services on hire;* **se,** Plaut. **C.** *to lend money at interest,* Plaut.; se locare, *to yield an interest, profit;* disciplina quae erat ab hoc tradita locabat se non minus, etc., *produced no less than,* etc., Cic.; fig., beneficia apud gratos, Liv. (locassint for locaverint, Cic.).

Lŏcri -ōrum, m. (Λοκροί), **1,** *the inhabitants of Locris, in Greece.* Hence, **a, Lŏcrenses** -ium, m. *the Locrians;* **b, Lŏcris** -idis and -idos, f. *a Locrian woman,* Cat.; *the country Locris,* Liv.; **2,** *the name of a town in Lower Italy, in Bruttium, with the name Epizephyrii, and also of its inhabitants, the Locrians.*

lŏcŭlus -i, m. (dim. of locus), *a little place.* Esp., **1,** *a coffin,* Plin.; **2,** plur., loculi, *a box or chest containing many divisions, a coffer, casket;* nummum in loculos demittere, Hor.

lŏcŭplēs -plētis (locus and *pleo). **I.** *possessing large landed property,* Cic. **II.** *rich, wealthy, opulent;* **1,** lit., **a,** of persons, mulier copiosa plane et locuples, Cic.; with abl., copiis rei familiaris locupletes et pecuniosi, Cic.; **b,** of things, villa tota locuples est, Cic.; annus locuples frugibus, Hor.; aquila, *the lucrative post of centurion,* Juv.; **2,** transf., **a,** *rich, abounding in;* Lysias oratione locuples, *of copious eloquence,* Cic.; **b,** *credible, trusty, sufficient, satisfactory;* auctor, Cic.; testis, Cic.; tabellarius, Cic. (abl. sing. locuplete and gen. (in Cic. always) locupleti, genit. plur. locupletium, Cic.; locupletum, Caes.).

lŏcŭplēto, **1.** (locuples), *to enrich;* homines fortunis, Cic.; templum picturis, Cic.; transf., sapientem locupletat ipsa natura, Cic.

lŏcus -i, m. (plur. loci, *single places;* loca, *places connected with one another, neighbourhood, region*). **I.** *a place.* **A.** Gen., **1,** lit., omnes copias in unum locum convenire, Cic.; ex loco superiore agere, of a speaker from the rostra or of a judge who gives judgment from the bench; ex aequo loco, of a speaker in the senate, Cic.; ex inferiore loco, of a pleader in a court of justice, Cic.; **2,** fig., locum dare, *to give occasion;* consilio, suspicioni, Cic.; often with partic. genit., quo loci, Cic.; eo loci, Cic.; so, **a,** *the right* or *proper place* or *occasion;* nec vero hic locus est, ut multa dicantur, Cic.; dulce est desipere in loco, *in the right place,* Hor.; **b,** *place in the order of succession;* secundo loco, *secondly,* Cic.; loco dicere, *in his turn,* Cic.; **c,** *position, degree, rank;* esse ex equestri loco, Cic.; infimo loco natus, Cic.; loco, with the genit., *in the place of;* alicui parentis loco esse, Cic. **B.** Esp., **1,** t. t., of military or pugilistic language, *place, ground, post;* locum tenere, relinquere, Cic.; fig., loco movere, *drive from one's position,* Cic.; **2,** *place, part of a book;* aliquot locis significavit, Cic.; **3,** loci, *means of proof;* locos nosse, Cic.; **4,** *a piece of ground, an estate,* Cic.; **5,** **a,** *a dwelling, house;* loca et lautia, Liv.; **b,** *place = town;* opportunitas loci, Cic.; **c,** *neighbourhood;* ea loca incolere, Caes. **II.** Transf., **1,** *time;* **a,** ad id locorum, *up to that time,* Sall.; **b,** *opportunity, occasion;* si est ullus gaudendi locus, Cic.; **2,** *condition, situation;* meliore loco erant res nostrae, Cic.

1. lŏcusta (lūcusta) -ae, f. **1,** *a locust;* lucustarum examina, Liv.; **2,** *a kind of lobster or crab,* Plin.

2. Lŏcusta -ae, f. *a woman in Rome, notorious for her skill in poisoning the contemporary and accomplice of Nero.*

lŏcūtĭo (lŏquūtĭo) -ōnis, f. (loquor), **1,** *a speaking, speech,* Cic.; **2,** *pronunciation,* Cic.

lōdix -dīcis, f. *a rough blanket, rug, counterpane,* Juv.

lŏgēum -ēi, n. and **lŏgĭum** -ĭi, n. (λογεῖοι and λόγιον), *archives,* Cic.

lŏgĭca -ae, f. and **lŏgĭcē** -ēs, f. (λογική, sc. τέχνη), *logic,* Cic.

lŏgĭcus -a -um (λογικός), *logical;* subst., **lŏgĭca** -ōrum, n. *logic,* Cic.

lŏgos (-us) -i, m. (λόγος), **1,** *a word,* Plaut.; **2,** *a joke, jest, bon mot,* Cic.

lōlĭgo, v. lolligo.

lōlĭum -ĭi, n. *darnel, cockle, tares,* Verg.

lollīgo -ginis, f. *a cuttle-fish,* Cic.

Lollīus -a -um, *name of a Roman gens;* hence, **Lollĭānus** -a -um, *Lollian.*

lōmentum -i, n. (lavo), *an unguent for the purpose of smoothing the skin, made of bean-meal and rice,*Mart.; *a means of cleansing,* ap. Cic.

Londinĭum (Lundinĭum) -ĭi, n. *London.*

longaevus -a -um (longus and aevum), *aged, old;* parens, Verg.; manus, Ov.

longē, adv. (longus), *long.* **I.** In space. **A.** *a long way off, far off, at a distance;* **1,** lit., longe absum, Cic.; longe videre, Cic.; discedere, Cic.; longe lateque, *far and wide,* Cic.; **2,** fig., **a,** *far off;* longissime abesse a vero, Cic.; ab aliquo longe abesse, *not to help,* Caes.; **b,** *far;* longe dissimilis contentio, Cic.; longe dissentire, with compar. and superl., *by far;* longe melior, Verg.; longe maximus, Cic. **B.** *from afar;* agnoscere regem, Verg.; fig., tam longe repetita principia, *far-fetched,* Cic. **II.** Transf., of time, *long, for a long time, far;* aetate longius provectus, Cic.

longinquĭtas -ātis, f. (longinquus). **I.** Lit., *length;* **1,** itineris, Tac.; **2,** *distance, remoteness,* Cic. **II.** Transf., of time, *length, duration;* temporum, Cic.; morbi, Cic.; bellorum, Liv.

longinquus -a -um (longus), *long.* **I.** Lit., **1,** amnes, Tac.; **2,** **a,** *distant, far, remote;* hostis, Cic.; Lacedaemon, Cic.; e (ex) loginquo, *from a distance,* Tac.; **b,** *living at a distance, foreign;* homo alienigena et longinquus, Cic.; **c,** *standing at a distance,* Cic. **II.** Transf., of time; **1,** *long in duration, long;* observatio, Cic.; morbus, Cic.; **2,** *distant;* in longinquum tempus aliquid differre, Cic.

Longīnus -i, m. *the name of a family of the gens Cassia,* v. Cassius.

longĭtĕr, adv. (longus), *far;* ab leto errare, Lucr.

longĭtūdo -ĭnis, f. (longus), *length.* **I.** Lit., itineris, Cic. **II.** Transf., *length of time;* noctis, Cic.; orationis, Cic.

longĭuscŭlus -a -um (dim. of compar. longior), *somewhat long;* versus, Cic.

Longŭla -ae, f. *a Volscian town not far from Corioli.*

longŭlē, adv. (longulus), *somewhat far off, at a little distance;* ex hoc loco, Plaut.

longŭlus -a -um (dim. of longus), *somewhat long;* iter, Cic.

longŭrĭus -ĭi, m. (longus), *a long pole, rod, rail,* Caes

longus -a -um, *long.* **I.** Lit. **1,** gen., **a,** of things, epistola, Cic.; spatium, Caes.; navis, *a man-of-war,* Liv.; versus, *the hexameter,* ap. Cic.; with acc. of length, ratis longa pedes centum, Liv.; **b,** of persons, Cic.; longus homo est, Cat.; **2,** esp. poet., *vast, spacious;* freta, Ov.; pontus, Hor. **II.** Transf., of time; **1,** gen., *long, of long duration, tedious;* horae quibus expectabam longae videbantur, Cic.; longa mora, Cic.;

with acc., mensis XLV dies longus, Cic.; longum est dicere, *it is tedious to relate,* Cic.; ne longum sit, ne longum faciam, *to make a long story short, in brief,* Cic.; nihil est mihi longius, *I can hardly wait,* Cic.; in longum, *for a long time,* Verg.; ex longo, *for a long time back,* Verg.; as applied to persons, *prolix, tedious;* nolo esse longus, Cic.; **2,** esp., a, of syllables, *long;* syllaba, Cic.; b, *far-seeing, looking far into the future;* spes, Hor.; poet. transf., of persons, longus spe, *hoping to live long,* Hor.

lŏquācĭtas -ātis, f. (loquax), *talkativeness, loquacity;* mea, Cic.

lŏquācĭtĕr, adv. (loquax), *loquaciously, talkatively;* respondere, Cic.

lŏquācŭlus -a -um (dim. of loquax), *somewhat talkative,* Lucr.

lŏquax -quācis (loquor), *talkative, garrulous, loquacious;* **1,** of persons, homo omnium loquacissimus, Cic.; **2,** of animals, ranae, *croaking,* Verg.; **3,** transf., of things, nidus, *full of nestlings,* Verg.; stagna, *full of frogs,* Verg.; lymphae, *babbling,* Hor.; epistola, *gossiping,* Cic.; vultus, *expressive,* Ov.

lŏquēla (lŏquella) -ae, f. (loquor). **I.** *a speaking, speech, discourse,* Plaut. **II.** Transf., **1,** *a word;* fundit has ore loquelas, Verg.; **2,** *a speech, language;* Graja, Ov.

lŏquĭtor, l. dep. (intens. of loquor), *to speak,* Plaut.

lŏquor, lŏcūtus (lŏquūtus) sum, 3. dep. (connected with λέγω), *to speak.* **I.** Intransit., *to speak* (of conversation; dicere, of an orator); **1,** lit., bene loqui de aliqua re, de aliquo, Cic.; cum aliquo, Cic.; pro aliquo (either = *in defence of* or *in the name of some one*), Cic.; apud (*before*) aliquem, Cic.; **2,** transf., ut consuetudo loquitur, Cic. **II.** Transit., **1,** *to say;* quid loquar de militari ratione, Cic.; loquuntur, *they say,* with acc. and infin., Cic.; **2,** *to talk of, speak of constantly;* classes, Cic.; proelia, Hor.; **3,** *to tell, mention;* pugnantia, Cic. (archaic locuntur = loquuntur, Cic.).

lōrātus -a -um (lorum), *bound with thongs,* Verg.

lōrĕus -a -um (lorum), *made of thongs,* Plaut.

lōrīca -ae, f. (lorum). **I.** *a leather cuirass, corselet,* Cic.; transf., libros mutare loricis, to *exchange study for war,* Hor. **II.** Milit. t.t., *a breastwork, parapet,* Caes.

lōrīco, l. (lorica), *to arm with a corselet or cuirass;* gen. partic., **lōrīcātus** -a -um, *armed with a cuirass,* Liv.

lōrum -i, n. *a strap or thong of leather.* **I.** Lit., esp. for binding, quum apparitor Postumium laxe vinciret, 'Quin tu,' inquit, 'adducis lorum,' Liv. **II.** Meton., **1,** *the girdle of Venus,* Mart.; **2,** *a rein;* loris ducere equos, Liv.; lora dare, *to relax the reins,* Verg.; **3,** *a scourge, whip;* loris uri, Hor.; loris caedere aliquem, Cic.; **4,** *a leathern bulla* (v. bulla), Juv.

Lōtŏphăgi, genit. -phăgōn, m. (Λωτοφάγοι), myth., *the Lotus-eaters, a people in Africa.*

lōtŏs (-us) -i, f. (λωτός). **I.** *the Egyptian lotus,* Plin. **II.** *a tree growing in North Africa,* said to have been *the food of the Lotus-eaters;* transf., *the fruit of the lotus,* Ov.; meton., *a flute made of the lotus-tree wood,* Ov. **III.** m. and f. *an Italian plant* (Diospyros Lotos, Linn.), Cic. **IV.** *a plant used for fodder,* Verg.

1. **lōtus** -a -um, v. lavo.

2. **lōtus** -i, f., v. lotos.

Lŭa -ae, f. *a goddess to whom arms captured in war were dedicated.*

lŭbet, lubido, etc. = libet, libido, etc. (q.v.).

lūbrĭco, l. (lubricus), *to make smooth or slippery,* Juv.

lūbrĭcus -a -um, *slippery.* **I.** Gen., **A.** Lit., glacies, Liv.; neut. subst., **lūbrĭcum** -i, n. *a slippery place,* Tac. **B.** Transf., *slippery, uncertain, insecure, tottering, perilous;* aetas puerilis maxime lubrica atque incerta, Cic.; lubrica defensionis ratio, Cic.; poet. with infin., vultus nimium lubricus aspici, *dangerous to look upon,* Hor.; in lubrico versari, Cic. **II.** Transf., **A.** *smooth, slimy;* anguis, Verg. **B.** *quickly moving, fleeting;* **1,** lit., amnis, Hor.; **2,** transf., annus, *quickly passing,* Ov.

1. **Lūca** -ae, f. *town in Etruria* (now *Lucca*). Hence, adj., **Lūcensis** -e, *of Luca.*

2. **Lūca,** v. Lucani.

Lūcāni -ōrum, m. (Λευκανοί), *an Italian people in Lower Italy,* and meton. = *the country of the Lucani,* Caes.; sing., Lucanus, collective, Liv. Hence, **1,** adj., **Lūcānus** -a -um, *Lucanian;* **2, Lūcānia** -ae, f. *the country of the Lucani;* **3, Lūcānĭcus** -a -um, *Lucanian;* subst., **Lūcānĭca** -ae, f. *a kind of sausage,* Cic.; **4, Lūca** -ae, m. *Lucanian;* Luca bos, *a Lucanian ox,* i.e., *an elephant,* because the Romans first saw elephants in Lucania with the army of Pyrrhus.

1. **Lūcānus** -a -um, v. Lucani.

2. **Lūcānus** -i, m., M. Annaeus, *a poet, native of Corduba in Spain, contemporary of the Emperor Nero, author of the still extant Pharsalia.*

lūcar -āris, n. (lucus), *the money paid to actors from the treasury, stipend, salary,* Tac.

lūcellum -i, n. (dim. of lucrum), *a little profit, a small gain;* Apronio aliquid lucelli jussi sunt dare, Cic.

Lūcensis, v. Luca.

lūcĕo, luxi, 2. (lux), *to be bright, shine, glitter.* **I.** stella lucet, Cic.; lucent oculi, Ov.; impers., lucet, *it is light, it is daylight, it is day;* nondum lucebat, *it was not yet light,* Cic. **II.** *to shine forth, be plain, evident;* nunc imperii nostri splendor illis gentibus lucet, Cic.; quum res ipsa tot, tam claris argumentis luceat, Cic.

Lūcĕres -um, m. *one of the three tribes into which the Romans of the age of Romulus are said to have been divided.*

Lūcĕrĭa -ae, f. *a town in Apulia* (now *Lucera*). Hence, **Lūcĕrīnus** -a -um, *of Luceria.*

lūcerna -ae, f. (luceo), *a lamp, oil-lamp;* lumen lucernae, Cic.

lūcesco (lūcisco), luxi, 3. (inchoat. of luceo), *to begin to shine;* a, pers., novus sol lucescit, Verg.; cras lucescere Nonas, *appear,* Ov.; b, impers., lucescit, *it grows light, day is breaking,* Cic.

lūci = luce, v. lux.

lūcĭdē, adv. (lucidus), *clearly, plainly, lucidly;* definire verbum, Cic.

lūcĭdus -a -um (lux), *full of light, clear, bright, lucid.* **I.** Lit., **1,** amnis, Ov.; sidera, Hor.; adv., lucidum fulgentes oculi, Hor.; **2,** bright, shining white; ovis, Tib. **II.** Transf., *clear, plain, lucid;* ordo, Hor.

lūcĭfĕr -fĕra -fĕrum (lux and fero), *light-bearing, light-bringing.* **I.** Adj., **1,** gen., equi, *the horses of the moon,* Ov.; **2,** *bringing to light;* manus (of Lucina), Ov. **II.** Subst., **Lūcĭfĕr** -fĕri, m. *Lucifer, the morning star, the planet Venus,* Cic.; myth., *the son of Aurora, and father of Ceyx;* hence, Lucifero genitus (= *Ceyx*), Ov.; meton., *the day;* tot Luciferi, Ov.

lūcĭfŭgus -a -um (lux and fugio), *shunning the light;* blatta, Verg.; transf., homines, Cic.

Lūcīlĭus -a -um, *name of a Roman gens, the most celebrated members of which were :* 1, Qu. Lucilius Balbus, *a Stoic philosopher ;* 2, C. Lucilius, *born at Suessa Aurunca,* B.C. 148, *died* B.C. 103, *a Roman knight, founder of Roman satiric poetry.*

Lūcīna -ae, f. (lux), *"she that brings to light," the goddess of births, a surname of Juno or of Diana ;* meton., *a bearing of children, birth ;* Lucinam pati (of the cow), *to calve,* Verg.

lūcisco = lucesco (q.v.).

Lūcĭus -ĭi, m. *a common Roman praenomen* (gen. abbreviated to L.).

lūcrātīvus -a -um (lucror), *attended with gain, profitable ;* sol, Cic.

Lūcrētīlis -is, m. *a mountain in the Sabine country, part of the modern Monte Gennaro.*

Lūcrētĭus -a -um, *name of a Roman gens, the most famous members of which were :* 1, Sp. Lucretius Tricipitinus, *successor of* L. Junius Brutus *in the consulate ;* 2, *his daughter* Lucretia, *who, being ravished by Sextus, the son of Tarquinius Superbus, stabbed herself, and thereby led to the expulsion of the kings from Rome ;* 3, T. Lucretius Carus, *a Roman poet, contemporary of Cicero, author of the still extant poem* De rerum natura.

lūcrĭfăcĭo -fēci -factum, 3. (sometimes written separately lucri facio), *to gain, receive as profit ;* pecuniam, Cic.; tritici modios centum, Cic.

lūcrĭfĭcābĭlis -e, *gainful, profitable, lucrative,* Plaut.

lūcrĭfĭcus -a -um (lucrum and facio), *gainful, profitable,* Plaut.

lūcrĭfŭga -ae, c. (lucrum and fugio), *one who shuns gain,* Plaut.

Lūcrīnus -i, m. (with or without lacus), *a lake on the coast of Campania, near Baiae.* Hence, adj., a, **Lūcrīnus** -a -um, *Lucrine ;* conchylia, Hor., and subst., **Lūcrīna** -ōrum, n. Mart., *Lucrine oysters,* celebrated for their flavour ; b, **Lūcrīnensis** -e, *Lucrine ;* res, *oysters,* Cic.

lūcror, 1. dep. (lucrum), *to get gain, to gain, profit* (opp. perdere). **I.** Lit., auri pondo decem, Cic.; stipendium, Cic. **II.** Transf., nomen ab Africa, *to win,* Hor.; lucretur indicia veteris infamiae, *I will make him a present of,* i.e., *I will say nothing about,* Cic.

lūcrōsus -a -um (lucrum), *full of gain, profitable, lucrative,* Ov.

lūcrum -i, n. (cf λαύω), *gain, profit, advantage* (opp. damnum). **I.** Lit., lucri causā, Cic.; ad praedam lucrumque revocare, *to turn to one's profit,* Cic.; ponere in lucro or in lucris, *to reckon a gain,* Cic.; lucra facere ex vectigalibus, Cic.; lucri with dare, facere, addere, conferre, numerare, auferre, *as gain,* Cic.; de lucro vivere, *to have to thank some one else for being alive,* Cic. **II.** Meton., 1, *the love of gain, avarice,* Hor. ; 2, *lucre, riches,* Ov.

luctāmen -ĭnis, n. (luctor), *effort, exertion, struggling, toil,* Verg.

luctātĭo -ōnis, f. (luctor). **I.** *a wrestling,* Cic. **II.** Transf., **A.** *a struggle, contest,* Liv. **B.** *a contention in words, dispute, contest ;* magna cum aliquo, Cic.

luctātor -ōris, m. (luctor), *a wrestler,* Ov.

luctĭfĭcus -a -um (luctus and facio), *causing grief, mournful, baleful ;* Alecto, Verg.

luctĭsŏnus -a -um (luctus and sono), *sorrowfully sounding ;* mugitus, Ov.

luctor, 1. dep. *to wrestle.* **I.** Lit., fulvā arenā, Verg.; luctabitur Olympiis Milo, Cic. **II. A.** Physically, *to struggle, strive, contend*

with ; in arido solo, Liv. ; in turba, Hor. ; with abl., Africus luctatur fluctibus, Hor. ; foll. by infin., telum eripere, Verg. **B.** Intellectually, *to strive, struggle ;* cum aliquo, Cic.

luctŭōsē, adv. (luctuosus), *mournfully, sorrowfully,* Liv.

luctŭōsus -a -um (luctus), *mournful, sorrowful, lamentable, doleful, baleful ;* o diem illum reipublicae luctuosum, Cic.; luctuosissimum bellum, Cic. ; misera tempora et luctuosa, Cic.

luctus -ūs, m. (lugeo). **I.** *mourning, lamentation,* especially for a *bereavement ;* 1, lit., a, luctus domesticus, Cic.; luctus publicus, privatus, Liv.; luctum minuere or levare, Cic.; luctum ex aliqua re percipere or haurire, Cic.; plur., *expressions of sorrow ;* in maximos luctus incidere, Cic. ; b, *mourning apparel, mourning ;* erat in luctu senatus, Cic. ; 2, meton., *the cause of sorrow ;* tu . . . luctus eras levior, Ov. **II.** personif., Luctus, *the god of mourning,* Verg.

lūcŭbrātĭo -ōnis, f. (lucubro), 1, *working by night or lamp-light, nocturnal study ;* vix digna lucubratione anicularum, *to be told by old wives while spinning at night,* Cic.; plur., lucubrationes detraxi et meridiationes addidi, Cic. ; 2, meton., *that which is produced by lamp-light, a lucubration ;* lucubrationem meam perire, Cic.

lūcŭbro, 1. (lux). **I.** Intransit., *to work by night ;* inter lucubrantes ancillas sedere, Liv. **II.** Transit., *to produce by night, to compose at night ;* parvum opusculum, Cic.

lūcŭlentē, adv. (luculentus), *excellently, admirably, splendidly ;* a, opus texere, Cic.; ironic., calefacere, Cic. ; b, of style, *excellently ;* scribere, dicere, Cic.

lūcŭlentĕr, adv. (luculentus), *excellently, well ;* Graece luculenter scire, Cic.

lūcŭlentus -a -um (lux). **I.** *full of light, bright ;* caminus, Cic. **II.** Transf., *distinguished, splendid, excellent ;* a, *of outward appearance,* forma, Ter. ; b, of importance, extent, plaga, Cic. ; patrimonium, Cic. ; c, of reputation, auctor, Cic. ; d, of style, oratio, Sall. ; verbis luculentioribus, Cic.

Lūcullus -i, m. *the name of a family of the gens* Licinia. *The most distinguished of the* Luculli *was* L. Licinius Lucullus, *general against* Mithridates, *notorious for his riches and lavish expenditure.* Adj., 1, **Lūcullānus** -a -um ; 2, **Lūcullēus** -a -um ; 3, **Lūcullĭānus** -a -um, *Lucullan.*

lūcŭlus -i, m. (dim. of lucus), *a little grove,* Suet.

Lŭcŭmo and syncop., **Lucmo** or **Lucmōn** -ōnis, m. (Etruscan Lauchme); plur., **Lŭcŭmōnes**, *the magnates of Etruria, who were also priests, an Etrurian prince and priest ;* galeritus Lucmon =*an Etrurian,* Prop.

1. **lūcus** -i, m. *a sacred grove, consecrated wood,* Cic. ; poet., *a wood,* Verg.

2. **lūcus** -ū, m. (= lux), *light,* Ter

lūdĭa -ae, f. (ludius), 1, *an actress or female dancer,* Mart. ; 2, *a gladiator's wife,* Juv.

lūdĭbrĭum -ĭi, n. (ludo), *derision, mockery, sport, jest.* **I.** Lit., alicui esse ludibrio, Cic. ; per ludibrium auditi dimissique, *heard and dismissed with scorn,* Hor. **II.** *a laughing-stock, plaything ;* is ludibrium verius quam comes, Liv.; fortunae, Cic. ; ludibria ventis, Verg.

lūdĭbundus -a -um (ludo), 1, *playful, sportive,* Liv. ; 2, transf., *playing,* i.e., *with ease, without difficulty* or *danger ;* coelo sereno in Italiam ludibundi pervenimus, Cic.

lūdĭcer and **lūdĭcrus** -cra- crum (ludus), *done for sport* or *recreation, serving as sport* or *recreation, playful, sportive.* **I.** Adj., **1,** gen., sermo, Cic. ; ars ludicra armorum, Cic. ; **2,** esp., *relating to the stage ;* ars, *acting,* Cic. **II.** Subst., **lŭdĭcrum** -i, n. **1,** gen., *a plaything,* Cat. ; **2,** esp., *a theatrical performance, public spectacle,* Liv.

lŭdĭfĭcātĭo -ōnis, f. (ludifico), *a making game of, deriding, deceiving ;* quum omni morā, ludificatione, calumniā, senatus auctoritas impediretur, Cic.

lŭdĭfĭcātor -ōris, m. (ludifico). *one who makes game of another, a derider,* Plaut.

lŭdĭfĭco, **1.** (ludus and facio), *to make game of, make a mock of, deride, cheat, cozen ;* aliquem, Sall. ; absol., Cic.

lŭdĭfĭcor, **1.** dep. (ludus and facio). **I.** *to make game of, make a mock of, deride, delude, cheat ;* aliquem, Liv. ; absol., Cic. **II.** Transf., *to make vain, frustrate by cunning ;* ea quae hostes agerent, Liv.

lŭdĭmăgister -tri, m. *a schoolmaster,* Cic.

lŭdĭo -ōnis, m. *a pantomimic actor,* Liv.

lŭdĭus -ĭi, m. **1,** *a pantomimic actor or dancer,* Cic. ; **2,** *a gladiator,* Juv.

lŭdo, lūsi, lūsum, 3. *to play.* **I.** Intransit., **A.** Lit., aleā, Cic. ; trocho, Hor. **B.** Transf., **1,** *to play, sport, toy ;* exempla honesta ludendi, Cic. ; in numerum, *to dance,* Verg. ; **2,** *to sport, amuse oneself ;* lusisti satis, Hor. **II.** Transit., *to play.* **A.** Gen., proelia latronum, *chess,* Ov. ; ludum insolentem ludere, Hor. **B. 1,** *to do for amusement, amuse oneself with doing,* *to play with ;* opus, Hor. ; causam illam disputationemque, Cic. ; **2,** a, *to rally, banter ;* aliquem, Cic. ; b, *to deceive, delude,* Cic.

lŭdus -i, m. *a game, sport, pastime.* **I.** Lit., **1,** ludus campestris, Cic. ; novum sibi aliquem excogitant in otio ludum, Cic. ; dare ludum alicui, Cic. ; **2,** esp., a, ludi, *public games or spectacles celebrated in honour of the gods ;* ludos facere, *to give, celebrate,* Cic. ; ludis, *at the time of the games,* Cic. ; ludos committere, *to begin the games,* Cic. ; b, *a satire ;* in Naevii ludo, Cic. **II.** Transf., **A.** *a game, a child's game, a trifle ;* illa perdiscere ludus esset, Cic. **B.** *a sport, jest, joke ;* per ludum et jocum, Cic. **C.** *a place where the body or mind is exercised, a school ;* gladiatorius, *for training gladiators ;* esp., *a school for learning the elements of knowledge,* Cic. ; ludus literarum, Liv. ; ludum habere, *to keep a school,* Cic. (archaic form loedus, Cic.).

lŭēla (lŭella) -ae, f. (luo), *punishment, expiation,* Lucr.

lŭēs -is, f. (luo), *a plague, pestilence, contagious disease,* Verg. ; transf., a, *a word of reproach for criminals, pest, plague,* Cic. ; b, *any wide-spreading or universal calamity, destruction, war,* Tac. ; *earthquake, tempest,* Tac.

Lugdūnum -i, n. *town on the north border of Gallia Narbonensis and Gallia Lugdunensis* (now *Lyons*). Adj., **Lugdūnensis** -e.

lūgĕo, luxi, luctum, 2. **I.** Intransit., *to mourn, be in mourning* (as shown by cries and outward signs, while maereo = *to be dejected) ;* luget senatus, Cic. ; lugere pro aliquo, Cic.; campi lugentes, *places of mourning* (of the lower world), Verg. **II.** Transit., *to bewail, lament, deplore, to wear mourning for ;* matronae annum, ut parentem, eum luxerunt, Liv. ; aliquem, Cic. ; mortem alicuius, Cic.

lūgūbrĕ, adv. (lugubris), *mournfully, plaintively,* Verg.

lūgūbris -e (lugeo), *relating to mourning, nourtful.* **I.** Lit., lamentatio, *for the dead,* Cic.; domus, *a house of mourning,* Liv. Subst., **lūgūbrĭa** -ĭum, n. *mourning attire,* Ov. **II. 1,**

causing mourning ; bellum, Hor. ; **2,** *doleful, plaintive ;* verba, Ov.

lumbus -i, m. *the loin,* Cic.

lūmen -ĭnis, n. (for lucmen, from luceo), *light.* **I.** Lit., **A.** Gen., tabulas collocare in bono lumine, *in a good light,* Cic. ; lumen solis, Cic. ; **B.** Esp. **1,** *a light, lamp, taper ;* lumini oleum in stillare, Cic. ; sub lumina prima, *at twilight,* Cic. ; **2,** *the light of day, day ;* lumine quarto, Verg.; **3,** *the light of life, life ;* relinquere, Verg. ; **4,** *the light of the eye, the eye ;* luminibus amissis, *being blind,* Cic. ; caecitas luminis, Cic.; lumina defixa tenere in aliqua re, Ov. ; **5,** *light in a house ;* luminibus obstruere, *to block up light by building,* Cic. **C.** Meton., *an opening through which light can enter ;* **1,** duo lumina ab animo ad oculos perforata nos habere, Cic. ; **2,** *a window,* Cic. **II.** Fig., **1,** *light, clearness, insight ;* ordo maxime est, qui memoriae lumen affert, Cic. ; **2,** *a light, a remarkable excellence, glory, ornament ;* Corinthus totius Graeciae lumen, Cic. ; lumina civitatis, Cic.

lūmĭnārĕ -āris, n. (lumen), *a window-shutter, window ;* plur. Cic.

lūmĭnōsus -a -um (lumen), *full of light ;* of discourse, *bright, luminous,* Cic.

1. lūna -ae, f. (for lucna, from luceo). **I.** *the moon.* **A.** Lit., plena, *full moon,* Caes. ; ortus aut obitus lunae, Cic. ; lunae defectus, Cic. ; laborans, *the moon in eclipse,* Juv. ; quarta luna, *the fourth day after new moon,* Cic.; luna crescit, Cic. **B.** Meton., **1,** *the night ;* roscida, Verg. ; **2,** *a half-moon, an ivory ornament in the shape of a half-moon, worn by Roman senators on their shoes,* Juv. **II.** Personif., Luna, *the goddess of the Moon,* afterwards identified with Diana.

2. Lūna -ae, f. *town on the borders of Liguria and Etruria.* Hence, adj., **Lūnensis** -e, *of Luna.*

lūnaris -e (luna), **1,** *relating to the moon, lunar ;* cursus, Cic.; **2,** *like the moon ;* cornua, Ov.

lūno, **1.** (luna), *to bend into a crescent or half-moon ;* arcum, Ov. Partic., **lūnātus** -a -um, *bent into a crescent, half-moon or sickle-shaped ;* peltae Amazonidum, Verg.

1. lŭo, lŭi, 3. (λούω), *to wash.*

2. lŭo, lŭi, lŭĭtūrus, 3. (λύω), *to loose ;* transf., **1,** *to expiate, atone for ;* stuprum voluntariā morte, Cic. ; **2,** *to pay ;* luere poenam or poenas, *to suffer punishment, pay a penalty for ;* itaque mei peccati luo poenas, Cic. ; poenam pro caede, Ov.

lŭpa -ae, f. (lupus), **1,** *a she-wolf,* Liv. ; **2,** *a prostitute,* Cic.

lŭpānar -āris, n. (lupa), *a brothel,* Juv.

lŭpātus -a -um (lupa), *provided with wolf's teeth*—i.e., *iron spikes ;* frena, Hor. Hence, **lŭpāti** -ōrum, m. and **lŭpāta** -ōrum, n. *a curb with jagged spikes,* Verg.

Lŭpercal -cālis, n. (Lupercus). **I.** *a grotto on the Palatine Hill, sacred to Pan or Lupercus,* Verg. **II.** Plur., **Lŭpercālĭa** -ĭum, *the festival of Pan or Lupercus, celebrated in February.*

Lŭpercus -i, m. (lupus and arceo), "*the keeper off of wolves,*" **1,** *an old Italian deity, protector of flocks against wolves, sometimes identified with the Arcadian Pan ;* **2,** *a priest of Lupercus,* Cic.

Lupĭa -ae, m. *a river in North-west Ger many,* now *the Lippe.*

lŭpīnus -a -um (lupus), *of or relating to a wolf, wolfish.* **I.** Adj., ubera, Cic. **II.** Subst., **lŭpīnus** -i, n. and **lŭpīnus** -i, m. *the lupine* (Lupinus albus, Linn.), *used on the stage instead of coin ;* nec tamen ignorat quid distent aera lupinis, Hor.

lŭpus -i, m. (λύκος), *a wolf.* **I.** Lit., genus acre luporum atque canum, Verg.; prov., lupus in fabula, *talk of the devil, and he'll appear,* Cic.; hac urget lupus, hac canis angit, *to be between two fires,* Hor. **II.** Transf., **1,** *a voracious fish, the pike,* Hor.; **2,** a, *a horse's bit with jagged points,* Ov.; b, *a hook;* ferrei, Liv.

lurco -ōnis, m. *a glutton, gormandiser,* Plaut.

lūridus -a -um, *pale yellow, livid, lurid, ghastly, deadly pale.* **I.** Lit., pallor, Ov.; dentes, Hor.; sulfur, Ov. **II.** Transf., *producing paleness;* horror, Ov.; aconita, Ov.

lŭror -ōris, m. *ghastliness, deathly paleness,* Lucr.

luscĭnĭa -ae, f. *the nightingale,* Hor.

luscĭnĭŏla -ae, f. (dim. of luscinia), *a little nightingale,* Plaut.

1. luscīnus -a -um (luscus), *one-eyed,* Plin.

2. Luscīnus, C. Fabricius, v. Fabricius.

lusciōsus and **luscĭtiōsus** -a -um (luscus), *purblind, dim-sighted,* Plaut.

luscus -a -um, **1,** *hollow-eyed, blind;* statua, Juv.; **2,** *one-eyed,* Cic.; dux, Hannibal, Juv.

lūsĭo -ōnis, f. (ludo), *a playing, sport;* lusio pilae, Cic.

Lūsĭtānĭa -ae, f. *the country of the Lusitani, between the Durius and the Tagus; the modern Portugal, with a part of the modern Spain.* Hence, adj., **Lūsĭtānus** -a -um, *Lusitanian.*

lūsĭto, **1.** (intens. of ludo), *to play, sport,* Plaut.

Lūsĭus -ĭi, m. *a river of Arcadia.*

lūsor -ōris, m. (ludo). **I.** *one that plays, a player,* Ov. **II.** a, *a playful or wanton writer;* tenerorum lusor amorum, Ov.; b, *a mocker,* Plaut.

lūsōrĭus -a -um (lusor), *relating to play,* Plin.

lustrālis -e (2. lustrum). **I.** *relating to expiation or atonement, expiatory, atoning;* sacrificium, Liv.; exta, Verg. **II.** *relating to a period of five years* (because of the quinquennial expiatory sacrifice at Rome), Tac.

lustrātĭo -ōnis, f. (lustro), **1,** *a purification by sacrifice, expiation;* lustrationis sacro peracto, Liv.; **2,** *a going round, going over, traversing, wandering;* municipiorum, Cic.; solis, Cic.

lustro, **1.** (connected with luceo). **I.** *to make bright, illumine.* **A.** sol cuncta suā luce lustrat et complet, Cic. **B.** 1, *to look at, regard, observe, examine;* quae sit me circum copia, lustro, Verg.; alicuius vestigia, Verg.; 2, *to wander over, traverse, pass through;* Aegyptum, Cic.; aequor navibus, Verg. **II.** *to purify, cleanse* by sacrifices. **A.** Lit., populum, exercitum, Cic. **B.** Meton. 1, *to review, muster an army* (when a sacrifice was offered); exercitum, Cic.; 2, *to go round, dance round, encircle;* aliquem choreis, Verg.

1. lustrum -i, n. (luo or lavo). **I.** *a bog, morass,* Varr. **II.** Transf., **1,** *the den or lair of a wild beast;* ferarum, Verg.; **2,** *a wood, forest,* Verg.; **3,** *a brothel,* Cic.

2. lustrum -i, n. (connected with 2. luo). **I.** *an expiatory sacrifice, offered every five years* by the censors at the close of the census on behalf of the Roman people, at which an ox, sheep, and sow were sacrificed; lustrum condere, *to offer the expiatory sacrifices,* Cic.; sub lustrum censeri, *to be enrolled near the end of the census,* Cic. **II.** Meton., *a period of five years, a lustre;* octavum claudere lustrum, Hor.

lūsus -ū, m. (ludo). **I.** *a playing, game, sport;* trigon, Hor. **II.** Transf., *sport, amusement, trifling;* **1,** per lusum atque lasciviam, Liv.; **2,** *dalliance,* Ov.

Lūtātĭus -a -um, *name of a Roman gens,* v. Catulus.

lūtĕŏlus -a -um (dim. of luteus), *yellowish;* caltha, Verg.

Lūtētĭa (Pārĭsĭōrum) -ae, f. *town in Gallia Lugdunensis* (now Paris).

1. lūtĕus -a -um (lūtum); a, *of the colour of the plant lutum, yellow, saffron-yellow;* Aurora, Verg.; b, *rose-coloured;* soccus, Cat.

2. lūtĕus -a -um (lŭtum), **1,** *of mud or clay,* Ov.; transf., *worthless;* negotium, *a trifle,* Cic.; **2,** *dirty, covered with dirt;* Vulcanus, Juv.

lŭto, **1.** (lŭtum), *to besmear with mud or dirt,* Mart.

lŭtŭlentus -a -um (lŭtum), **1,** *muddy, dirty;* sus, Hor.; humus erat lutulenta vino, Cic.; amnis, Ov.; **2,** fig., *filthy, dirty;* homo, Cic.; vitia, Cic.; esp., of style, *turbid, impure,* Hor.

1. lūtum -i, n. **I.** *a plant used for dyeing yellow, dyers' weed, weld,* Verg. **II.** Meton., *yellow colour,* Verg.

2. lŭtum -i, n. (λύω). **I.** *mud, mire dirt;* volutari in luto, Cic.; crates luto contegere, Caes.; prov., in luto esse, haerere, *to stick in the mud, be in great perplexity,* Plaut., Ter.; used as a term of reproach, *filthy fellow, scum of the earth,* Cic. **II.** *loam, clay;* caementa interlita luto, Liv.

lux, lūcis, f. *light* (root LUC, Gk. λύκ-η). **I.** **A.** Lit., **1,** gen., solis, Cic.; lunae, Verg.; lychnorum, Cic.; **2,** esp., *daylight, day;* cum prima luce, primā luce, *as soon as it was day,* Cic.; ante lucem, Cic.; ad lucem, *in the morning,* Cic.; luce or luci, *by day, by daylight,* Cic.; meton., *a day;* centesima lux ab interitu P. Clodii, Cic. **B.** Transf., **1,** *a heavenly body,* Cic.; **2,** *the light* (of life); a, *in lucem edi,* Cic.; b, meton., *life;* corpora luce carentum, Verg.; **3,** *the eye, eyesight,* Ov. **II.** Transf., *the light;* **1,** *publicity, the public view, the sight of men;* res occultas in lucem proferre, Cic.; Isocrates luce forensi caruit, Cic.; **2,** *light, illustration, elucidation;* historia testis temporum, lux veritatis, Cic.; **3,** *light, help, succour;* lucem afferre reipublicae, Cic.; **4,** *light, ornament;* haec urbs, lux orbis terrarum, Cic.

luxor, **1.** dep. (luxus), *to riot, revel,* Plaut.

luxŭrĭa -ae, f. and **luxŭrĭes** -ēi, f. (luxus). **I.** Lit., of plants, *rankness, exuberant or luxuriant growth;* segetum, Verg.; fig., Cic. **II.** Transf., *excess, prodigality, dissipation, riotous living, luxury;* a, odit populus Romanus privatam luxuriam, publicam magnificentiam diligit, Cic.; b, *unbridled insolence,* Liv.

luxŭrĭo, **1.** and **luxŭrĭor,** **1.** dep. **I.** *to be luxuriant, rank, abundant in growth;* humus, seges, Ov.; transf., a, of animals, *to be playful, sportive, wanton;* ludit et in pratis luxuriatque pecus, Ov.; b, *to be exuberant, abound in;* faciem decet deliciis luxuriare novis, Ov.; *to swell, increase;* membra, Ov. **II.** Transf., *to be luxurious, run riot, be dissolute;* ne luxuriarent otio animi, Liv.; Capua luxurians felicitate, Cic.

luxŭriōsē, adv. (luxuriosus), *luxuriously, voluptuously;* vivere, Cic.

luxŭriōsus -a -um (luxuria). **I.** *luxuriant in growth;* frumenta, Cic. **II.** Fig., a, *immoderate, excessive;* laetitia, Liv.; amor, Ov.; b, *luxurious, dissolute, prodigal;* nihil luxuriosius (homine illo), Cic.

1. luxus -a -um (λοξός), *dislocated;* pes, Sall.

2. luxus -ūs, m. **1,** *luxury, debauchery, sensual excess, revelling,* Cic.; **2,** *splendour,* Verg.

Lyaeus -i, m. (Λυαῖος), *the releaser from care surname of Bacchus;* pater Lyaeus. Verg.; meton *wine;* uda Lyaei tempora, Hor.; attrib., latex Lyaeus, Verg.

Lўcaeus -i, m. (Λύκαιον), *a mountain in Arcadia, sacred to Jupiter and Pan.* Adj., **Lўcaeus** -a -um, *Lycaean.*

Lўcambes -ae, m. (Λυκάμβης), *a Theban who, for refusing his daughter in marriage to Archilochus, was attacked by the poet in such sarcastic verses that he and his daughter hanged themselves.* Hence, adj., **Lўcambeus** -a -um, *Lycambean.*

Lўcāon -ŏnis, m. (Λυκάων), *king of Arcadia, transformed by Jupiter into a wolf, father of Callisto.* Hence, a, adj., **Lўcāŏnĭus** -a -um; Arctos, *Callisto, as a constellation,* Ov.; *whence* axis, *the northern sky,* Ov.; b, **Lўcāŏnĭs** -ĭdis, f. *Callisto, daughter of Lycaon,* Ov.

Lўcāŏnes -um, m. (Λυκάονες), *the Lycaonians, a people in Asia Minor between Cappadocia, Cilicia, and Pisidia.* Hence, adj., **Lўcāŏnĭus** -a -um, *Lycaonian.* Subst., **Lўcāŏnĭa** -ae, f. *the country of the Lycaones.*

Lўcēum -i, n. and **Lўcīum** -ii, n. (Λύκειον), 1, *a gymnasium at Athens, at which Aristotle taught;* 2, *a gymnasium with a library in Cicero's Tusculan villa.*

lychnūcus -i, m. (λυχνοῦχος), *a lamp-stand, candelabrum,* Cic.

lychnus -i, m. (λύχνος), *a lamp,* Cic.

Lўcĭa -ae, f. (Λυκία), *a country of Asia Minor between Caria and Pamphylia;* hence, adj., **Lўcĭus** -a -um, *Lycian;* deus, *Apollo,* Prop.; sortes, *the oracle of Apollo at Patara,* Verg.; hasta, *of the Lycian king Sarpedon,* Ov.; subst., **Lўcĭi** -ōrum, m. *the Lycians.*

Lўcĭum = Lyceum (q.v.).

Lўcŏmēdēs -is, m. (Λυκομήδης), *king of the island of Scyros, where Achilles hid himself in female attire.*

Lўcŏphrōn -phrŏnis, m. (Λυκόφρων), *a Greek tragic poet of Chalcis in Euboea.*

Lўcōrĭās -ădis, f. (Λυκωριάς), *daughter of Nereus and Doris, a sea-nymph.*

Lўcōrĭs -ĭdis, f. *a freedwoman of Volumnius Eutrapelus, the mistress of the triumvir Antonius and of the poet L. Cornelius Gallus.*

Lўcormăs -ae, m. (Λυκόρμας), *a river in Aetolia.*

Lyctus (-ŏs) -i, f. (Λύκτος), *a town in Crete.* Adj., **Lyctĭus** -a -um = *Cretan,* Verg.

Lўcurgus -i, m. (Λυκοῦργος). **I.** Myth., *son of Dryas, king of the Edoni in Thrace, who prohibited the worship of Bacchus among his subjects.* **II.** Myth., *son of Aleus and Neaera, father of Ancaeus, king in Arcadia;* hence, **Lўcurg-ĭdēs** -ae, m. = *Ancaeus,* Ov. **III.** Hist., *an Athenian orator, famed for his severity;* hence **Lўcurgēi** -ōrum, m. (Λυκούργειοι) = *strict, inflexible citizens.* **IV.** Hist., *the celebrated Spartan legislator.*

Lўcus (-ŏs) -i, m. (Λύκος), *name of several rivers;* 1, *a river in Paphlagonia, flowing into the Pontus Euxinus, near Heraclea (now Turak);* 2, *a river in Phrygia, flowing into the Maeander.*

Lўdĭa -ae, f. (Λυδία), *a country of Asia Minor, from which according to the legend the Etruscans originally came;* hence, adj., **A. Lўdĭus** -a -um, a, *Lydian;* aurifer amnis, *Pactolus,* Tib.; b, *Etruscan;* fluvius, *the Tiber,* Verg. **B. Lўdus** -a -um; a, *Lydian;* puella, *Omphale,* Verg.; b, *Etruscan;* plur., Lydi, *the Etruscans,* Cic.

lympha (limpha) -ae, f. *clear spring or*

river water, Verg.; personif., **Lymphae** = *Nymphs of the springs,* Hor.

lymphātĭcus -a -um (lymϼha), *raving, raging, insane, mad, frantic;* pavor, *a panic terror,* Liv.

lympho, 1. (lympha), *to make mad, strike with frenzy,* Plin.; partic., **lymphātus** -a -um, *mad, frantic, insane;* lymphata mens, Hor.; lymphati, *struck with panic,* Liv.

Lyncestae -ārum, m. (Λυγκεσταί), *a people in the south-west of Macedonia near whom was a fountain, the waters of which caused drunkenness.* Adj, **Lyncestĭus** -a -um, *Lyncestian.*

Lynceus -ĕi, m. (Λυγκεύς). **I.** *a Messenian hero, one of the Argonauts, renowned for the sharpness of his sight;* hence, 1, adj., **Lynceūs** -a -um, a, *belonging to Lynceus,* Ov.; b, *sharp-sighted,* Cic.; 2, **Lyncĭdēs** -ae, m. *a descendant of Lynceus.* **II.** *a companion of Aeneas.*

Lyncus -i (Λύγκος) **I.** m. *a king in Scythia, changed into a lynx.* **II.** f. *the capital of the Lyncestae.*

lynx -cis, c. (λύγξ), *a lynx,* Verg.

lўra -ae, f. (λύρα). **I.** *the lyre, a stringed instrument;* quum (Themistocles) in epulis recusaret lyram, Cic. **II.** Transf., 1, *lyric poetry, song;* Aeoliae lyrae amica, Ov.; 2, *the constellation Lyra,* Ov.

Lyrcēïus (Lyrcēus) -a -um, *belonging to the mountain Lyrceum between Arcadia and Argolis.*

lўrĭcus -a -um (λυρικός), *of or relating to the lyre, lyric;* vates, *a lyric poet,* Hor.

Lyrnēsos -i, f. (Λυρνησός), *town in the Troad, birthplace of Briseis.* Hence, 1, **Lyrnēsis** -ĭdis, subst., f. *Briseis;* 2, **Lyrnēsĭus** -a -um, *Lyrnesian.*

Lȳsander -dri, m. (Λύσανδρος), 1, *a celebrated Spartan general, conqueror of the Athenians;* 2, *an ephor of Sparta, friend of the king Agis.*

Lȳsĭas -ae, m. (Λυσίας), *a celebrated Athenian orator, contemporary with Socrates.*

Lȳsĭmăchĭa -ae, f. (Λυσιμάχεια), *a town in Thrace, founded by Lysimachus.* Hence, **Lȳsĭmăchienses** -ĭum, m. *the inhabitants of Lysimachia.*

Lȳsĭmăchus -i, m. (Λυσίμαχος), *one of the generals of Alexander the Great, ruling after A.'s death in Thrace and Pontus.*

Lȳsippus -i, m. (Λύσιππος), *a celebrated worker in metal of Sicyon.*

Lȳsĭs -ĭdis, m. (Λῦσις), 1, *a Pythagorean philosopher of Tarentum, teacher of Epaminondas;* 2, *a river in Asia.*

Lȳsĭthŏē -ēs, f. (Λυσιθόη), *daughter of Oceanus.*

M.

M m, *the twelfth letter of the Latin Alphabet, corresponding in form and sound with the Greek M, μ. For M. as an abbreviation, see Table of Abbreviations.*

Măcăreus -ĕi and -ĕos, m. (Μακαρεύς), *son of Aeolus, brother of Canace.* Hence, **Măcărēïs** -ĭdis, f. (Μακαρηίς), *the daughter of Macareus (Isse).*

Măcĕdō (-ōn) -dŏnis, m. (Μακεδών), *a Macedonian;* plur., **Măcĕdŏnes** -um, m. *the Macedonians.* Hence, 1, **Măcĕdŏnĭa** -ae, f. (Μακεδονία), *a country between Thessaly and Thra-*

2, Măcĕdŏnĭcus -a -um, *Macedonian;* **3, Măcĕdŏnĭus** -a -um, *Macedonian.*

măcellārĭus -a -um (macellum), *of or relating to the provision market.* Subst., **măcellārĭus** -ĭi, m. *a victualler, provision-dealer,* Suet.

măcellum -i, n. *a provision-market, meat-market;* annonam in macello cariorem fore, Cic.

măcĕo, 2. *to be lean,* Plaut.

1. măcĕr -cra -crum, *lean;* taurus, Verg.; transf., of soil, *poor;* solum, Cic.; fig., me macrum reducĭt, Hor.

2. Măcĕr -cri, m. *a Roman family name;* **1,** C. Licinius Macer, *a Roman historian;* **2,** Aemilius Macer, *a poet, friend of Vergil and Ovid.*

măcĕrĭa -ae, f. (μάκελος, or μάκελλον, *an enclosure*), *a wall enclosing a garden, vineyard, or park,* Cic.

măcĕro, 1. **I.** *to soak, steep in water,* Ter. **II.** Transf., **1,** *to make weak, bring down, reduce;* aliquem fame, Liv.; **2,** *to torment, tease, vex;* quae vos, quum reliqueritis, macerent desiderio, Liv.

măcesco, 3. (maceo), *to grow thin, become lean,* Plaut.

măchaera -ae, f. (μάχαιρα), *a sword, knife,* Plaut.

măchaerŏphŏrus -i, m. (μαχαιροφόρος), *armed with a sabre or machaera,* Cic.

Măchāōn -ŏnis, m. (Μαχάων), myth., *son of Aesculapius, celebrated physician.* Hence, adj., **Măchāōnĭus** -a -um, *of or belonging to Machaon.*

măchĭna -ae, f. (μηχανή), **1,** *a machine, any artificial contrivance for performing work,* especially a machine for moving heavy weights, Cic., pulling down columns, Cic., drawing ships down to the sea, Hor.; fig., ut omnes adhibeam machinas ad tenendum adulescentulum, Cic.; **2,** *a military engine, a catapult, balista,* etc., Sall.; **3,** *a platform on which slaves were exposed for sale,* Q. Cic.; **4,** *a device, contrivance, trick, stratagem,* Cic.

măchĭnāmentum -i, n. (machinor), *a machine, instrument,* Liv.

măchĭnātĭo -ōnis, f. (machinor), **1,** *contrivance, machinery, mechanism;* cum machinatione quâdam moveri aliquid videmus, Cic.; transf. *a cunning device, machination,* Cic.; **2,** meton., *a mechanical contrivance, a machine;* navalis, Caes.

măchĭnātor -ōris, m. (machinor), **1,** *a maker of machines, architect;* tormentorum, Liv.; **2,** transf., in a bad sense, *a deviser, contriver,* originator; horum omnium scelerum, Cic.; huius belli, Liv.

măchĭnor, 1. dep. (machina), **1,** *to contrive, invent, devise;* opera, Cic.; versum, Cic.; **2,** *to plot some evil, contrive;* pestem in aliquem, Cic.

măcĭes -ēi, f. (maceo), **1,** *leanness, thinness;* **a,** of men, corpus macie intabuit, Cic.; **b,** of soil or crops, *poverty, barrenness,* Ov.; **2,** transf., *meagreness of expression,* Tac.

măcĭlentus -a -um (macies), *thin, lean,* Plaut.

Măcra -ae, **1,** *a river in Italy, between Liguria and Etruria,* now *Magra;* **2,** Măcra cōmē (Μακρὰ κώμη), *a place in Locris on the borders of Thessaly.*

măcresco, măcrŭi, 3. (macer), *to grow lean, become thin,* Hor.

Măcri Campi and **Campi Măcri** -ōrum, m. *a valley in Gallia Cispadana.*

Măcrŏbĭus -ĭi, m., Aurelius Ambrosius Theodosius, *a grammarian of the fifth century,* A.D.

măcrŏcollum -i, n. (μακρόκωλον), *paper of the largest size, royal paper,* Cic.

mactābĭlis -e (macto), *deadly,* Lucr.

mactātus -ū, m. (macto), *a slaying, killing,* Lucr.

macte, macti, v. mactus.

macto, 1. (intens. of * mago, akin to mactus), *to honour, glorify.* **I.** *to honour a god with a sacrifice;* puerorum extis deos manes, Cic.; transf., **a,** *to reward, honour with anything;* aliquem honoribus, Cic.; **b,** in a bad sense, *to afflict, punish with;* aliquem summo supplicio, Cic. **II.** *to sacrifice, offer;* hostiam, Hor.; transf., *to devote;* aliquem Orco, Liv.

mactus -a -um (from * mago, maxi, **mactum** = augeo), **1,** *found only in the forms* macte, macti, joined with an abl. and generally with the imper. of the verb esse, *well done! bravo!* all hail! *good luck attend thee!* macte virtute! Cic.; macte esto virtute! Hor.; macte virtute diligentiâque esto! Liv.; macti virtute, milites Romani, este! Liv.; with genit., macte animi, Mart.; **2,** = mactatus, *sacrificed,* Lucr.

măcŭla -ae, f. (connected with maceo, macies, macer), **1,** *a spot, mark;* equus albis maculis, Verg.; **2,** *the mesh of a net,* Cic.; **3,** transf., *a blot, stain, blemish, fault;* hunc tu vitae splendorem maculis aspergis tuis? Cic.; familiae, Cic.

măcŭlo, 1. (macula), *to cover with spots, to make spotted, stain, pollute;* **1,** lit., terram tabo maculant, Verg.; candor corporum magis sanguine atro maculabatur, Liv.; **2,** transf., *to stain, defile, pollute;* rex ille optimi regis caede maculatus, Cic.; partus suos parricidio, Liv.

măcŭlōsus -a -um (macula), *full of spots, spotted, speckled;* **1,** lynx, Verg.; **2,** *stained, polluted, defiled;* vestis Pompeii, Cic.; fig., *defiled, polluted;* senatores, Cic.; nefas, Hor.

mădĕfăcĭo -fēci -factum, 3., pass. **mădĕfĭo** -factus sum -fĭeri (madeo and facio), *to make wet, moisten, soak;* gladii sanguine madefacti, Cic.; sanguis madefecerat herbas, Verg.

mădĕo -ŭi, 2. (μαδάω), *to be wet, moist, to drip, flow.* **I.** Lit. **A.** Gen., natabant pavimenta vino, madebant parietes, Cic.; sanguine terra madet, Verg.; partic., madens, moist, Cic. **B.** Esp., **1,** *to melt* (of snow); nix sole madens, Ov.; **2,** *to be drunk,* Plaut.; **3,** *to be boiled, to be made soft by boiling,* Verg. **II.** Transf., *to be full of, abound in, overflow with;* pocula madent Baccho, Tib.; Socraticis madet sermonibus, *steeped in,* Hor.

mădesco, mădŭi, 3. (madeo), *to become moist or wet;* semusta madescunt robora, Verg.

mădĭdus -a -um (madeo), *moist,wet.* **I.** Gen., fasciculus epistolarum totus aquâ madidus, Cic.; genae, *wet with tears,* Ov.; vestis cocco madida, *dyed with,* Mart. **II.** Esp., *drunk,* Plaut.

mădor -ōris, m. (madeo), *moisture, wetness,* Sall.

Maeandĕr -dri, m. and **Maeandrŏs (-us)** -dri, m. (Μαίανδρος). **I.** *a river of Asia Minor, proverbial for its winding course,* now *Meinder;* *in the legend, father of Cyane, the mother of Caunus and Byblis.* **II.** Appellat., *a winding, turning;* **a,** of a road, Cic.; **b,** *a winding border of a dress,* Verg. Hence, adj., **Maeandrĭus** -a -um, *of or belonging to Maeander;* juvenis, *Caunus,* Ov.

Maecēnās -ātis, m., C. Cilnius, *a Roman knight, the friend of Augustus, and the patron of Horace and Vergil.*

Maecĭus -a -um, *Maecian.* **I.** *name of a place in Latium, not far from Lanuvium.* **II.** *name of a Roman gens, of which the most celebrated member was* Sp. Maecius Tarpa, *a celebrated Roman critic.*

Maedi -ōrum, m. (Μαῖδοι), *a Thracian people.*
Adj., **Maedĭcus** -a -um, *belonging to the Maedi;* subst., **Maedĭca** -ae, f. *the country of the Maedi.*

Maelĭus -a -um, *name of a Roman gens, of which the most celebrated member was* Sp. Maelius, *slain, on suspicion of aiming at kingly power, by* C. *Servilius Ahala, master of the horse to the dictator Cincinnatus.*

maena (mēna) -ae, f. (μαίνη), *a kind of small sea-fish,* often salted, Cic.

Maenălus (-ŏs) -i, m. and **Maenăla** -ōrum, n. (Μαίναλον), *a mountain in Arcadia, sacred to Pan.* Hence, 1, **Maenălĭus** -a -um, *Maenalian, Arcadian;* deus, Pan, Ov.; versus, *pastoral poetry,* Verg.; 2, **Maenălis** -ĭdis, f. *belonging* or *relating to Maenalus;* ursa, Callisto, Ov.; ora, *Arcadia,* Ov.

Maenăs -ădis, f. (μαινάς), 1, *a bacchante,* Ov.; transf., a, *a priestess of Priapus,* Juv.; b, *a priestess of Cybele,* Cat.; 2, *a prophetess (Cassandra),* Prop.

Maenădes, v. Maenas.

Maenĭus -a -um, *name of a Roman gens;* columna Maenia, v. columna. Hence, **Maenĭānus** -a -um, *Maenian.* Subst., **Maenĭānum** -i, n. *a projecting balcony,* first introduced by C. Maenius, Cic.

Maeŏnes -um, m. (Μαίονες), *the inhabitants of Maeonia, the Maeonians;* hence, a, **Maeŏnĭa** -ae, f. (Μαιονία), *Maeonia, a part of Lydia,* and, as the Etruscans were said to derive their origin from Lydia = *Etruria,* Verg.; b, **Maeŏnĭdēs** -ae, m., (a) *Homer,* as a native, according to some, of Colophon or Smyrna, Ov.; (β) *an Etruscan,* Verg.; c, **Maeŏnis** -ĭdis, f. *a Lydian woman,* Arachne, Ov.; *Omphale,* Ov.; d, **Maeŏnĭus** -a -um, (a) *Maeonian, Lydian;* ripa (of the river Pactolus), Ov.; esp., senex or vates, *Homer,* Ov.; so *Homeric* or *heroic;* carmen, pes, chartae, Ov.; (β) *Etruscan;* nautae, Ov.

Maeōtae -ārum, m. (Μαιῶται), *a Scythian people on Lake Maeotis.* Hence, a, **Maeōtĭcus** -a -um, *Maeotic;* palus, *the Lake Maeotis,* Plin.; b, **Maeōtĭdae** -ārum, m. *the persons living on Lake Maeotis;* c, **Maeōtis** -ĭdis, f. *relating to the Maeotae* or *to Lake Maeotis;* esp., Maeotis palus or lacus, *now the Sea of Azov;* d, **Maeōtĭus** -a -um, *Maeotian.*

maerĕo, 2. I. Intransit., *to be sad, mournful, to grieve, mourn, lament;* maeret Menelaus, Cic.; with abl. of cause, suo incommodo, Cic.; with abl. of instr., sono tenui, *in a gentle tone,* Ov.; maeret, foll. by quod, *he is pained that,* etc., Ov.; partic., maerens, *mournful, sorrowful;* quis Sullam nisi maerentem vidit? Cic. II. Transit., *to lament, mourn over, bewail;* casum, Cic.; filii mortem graviter, Cic.; with acc. and infin., Cic.; talia maerens, *uttering lamentations,* Ov.

maeror -ōris, m. (maereo), *mourning, grief, sorrow, sadness;* in maerore jacere, Cic.; maerorem minuere, Cic.

maestĭtĭa -ae, f. (maestus). I. *sadness, sorrowfulness, dejection, grief;* esse in maestitia, Cic. II. Transf., *gloominess;* orationis quasi maestitiam sequi, Cic.

maestĭtūdo -ĭnis, f. (maestus), *sadness,* Plaut.

maestus -a -um (maereo), *sad, sorrowful, dejected, cast down, melancholy.* I. Ulixes, Cic.; senex, Cic.; manus, Ov. II. Transf., 1, *gloomy;* neci maestum dimittit, Verg.; 2, *causing* or *indicating sorrow;* vestes, Prop.; funera, Ov.

Maevĭus -ĭi, m. *a bad poet of the time of Vergil.*

măga -ae, f. (magus), *the enchantress,* Ov. (?)

11*

măgālĭa -ĭum, n. (a Punic word), *huts, cottages, hovels,* Verg.

măgĕ = magis (q.v.).

măgĭcus -a -um (μαγικός), *relating to magic* or *enchantment, magical;* artes, Verg.; dii, *gods invoked in enchantments* (as Pluto, Hecate, Proserpina), Tib.

măgis, adv. with compar. (from root MAC, with adverbial ending -is), *more.* I. Of degree, *more = in a higher degree.* A. Gen., 1, with adj. and adv., to form the comp. of adj. and adv. not inflected in the comp., magis necessarius, Cic.; 2, with verbs; a, foll. by quam, *more, rather . . . than;* sed praeterita magis reprehendi possunt quam corrigi, Cic.; b, sometimes without comparison, magis aedilis esse non potuisset, Cic. B. Particular combinations, a, non (neque) magis . . . quam, *not more . . . than, just as much . . . as,* Cic.; b, quo magis . . . eo magis, *the more . . . the more,* Cic.; quo magis . . . eo minus, Cic.; c, eo magis, *so much the more, all the more,* Cic.; d, with abl., impendio magis, *considerably more,* Cic.; multo magis, *much more, more by far,* Cic.; nihilo magis, *just as little,* Cic.; solito magis, *more than usual,* Liv.; e, magis etiam, *even more,* Cic.; f, magis magisque, magis et magis, *more and more,* Cic. II.= potius, *rather, more willingly.* A. Gen., magis id diceres, si, etc., Cic. B. Particular phrases, magis malle = potius malle, Cic.; magis est quod . . . quam quod, or magis est ut . . . quam ut, *it is more the cause that . . . than,* etc., Cic. Superl., **maxĭmē (maxŭmē,** adv. (for magissime, from old magus = magnus), *in the highest degree, most of all, especially, exceedingly, very.* I. Of degree, A. Gen., 1, with adj., a, maxime fidus, Cic.; b, to form the superl. of adjectives which are not inflected in the superl., maxime necessarius, Cic.; c, to add force to a superl., aberratio maxime liberalissima, Cic.; 2, with verbs, a, cupere, velle, Cic.; b, where the meaning must in part be supplied, alicui confidere maxime, *implicitly,* Caes. B. Particular combinations, a, with unus, omnium, multo, *most of all, far before all the rest;* unus omnium maxime, Nep.; multo maxime, Cic.; b, quam maxime, *as much as possible,* Cic.; ut quisque . . . ita maxime, *the more . . . the more,* Cic.; hoc maxime officii est, ut quisque maxime opis indigeat, ita ea potissimum opitulari, Cic.; quum maxime, *just, precisely,* Liv.; quum maxime, *just now,* Cic.; c, quam or ut qui maxime, *in the highest possible degree,* Cic.; d, non maxime, *not altogether;* ingenium non maxime defuit, Cic. II.= potissimum, *principally, particularly, especially;* 1, quae ratio poëtas, maximeque Homerum impulit, *and most of all Homer,* Cic.; quum . . . tunc maxime, *both . . . and especially,* Cic.; 2, *just, exactly;* nunc quum maxime, Cic.; 3, in colloquial language maxime is used to express emphatic assent, and with immo, emphatic dissent; vos non timetis eam? Immo vero maxume, Sall.

măgister -tri, m. (root MAC, whence magnus), *master, ruler, president, chief, head, director, leader, superintendent.* I. Lit., 1, populi, *dictator,* Cic.; equitum, *master of the horse, the dictator's lieutenant,* Liv.; morum, *the censor,* Cic.; societatis, *the director of a company formed for farming the revenue,* Cic.; scripturae or in scriptura and portus (of a company that farmed the rents, tolls, etc.), Cic.; P. Terentius operas in portu et scriptura Asiae pro magistro dedit, *exercised the functions of vice-director,* Cic.; elephanti, *driver,* Liv.; auctionis, *director* or *conductor of a sale by auction,* Cic.; cenandi, *the president of a feast;* navis, a, *master, captain.*

Liv.; **b,** *helmsman,* Verg.; ludi, *schoolmaster,* Cic.; **2, a,** *the trustee of a bankrupt's estate,* Cic.; **b,** *a teacher;* artium, religionis, virtutis, Cic.; usus est magister optimus, Cic.; gladiatorum, *a fencing-master,* Cic. **II.** Transf., *an instigator, inciter;* magister ad despoliandum Dianae templum, Cic.

măgistĕrĭum -ĭi, n. (magister), *the office or power of a master, president, chief, director;* morum, *the censorship,* Cic.; sacerdotii, *priesthood,* Liv.; me magisteria (conviviorum) delectant, Cic.

măgistra -ae, f. (magister), *a mistress, directress, leader;* transf., lex aeterna quae quasi dux et magistra studiorum, Cic.; arte magistrā, *by the help of art,* Verg.

măgistrātus -ūs, m. (magister). **I.** *the office or dignity of a magister, a magistracy, official dignity, office;* magistratum gerere, Cic.; inire, ingredi, Sall.; deponere, Caes.; magistratu abire, Cic. **II.** Meton., *a magistrate, high official.* Magistrates in Rome were either ordinarii—e.g., the praetors, consuls, etc.; or extraordinarii— e.g., dictator, master of the horse; curules or non curules, according to the seat on which they sat; patricii or plebeii, according as they were taken from the patricians or plebeians; majores or minores, the elections to the former taking place in the comitia centuriata, to the latter in the comitia tributa; est proprium munus magistratus intelligere se gerere personam civitatis, Cic.; creare magistratus, Liv.

magnănĭmĭtas -ātis, f. (magnanimus), *greatness of soul, magnanimity,* Cic.

magnănĭmus -a -um (magnus and animus), *high-minded, courageous, high-spirited, magnanimous,* Cic. (genit. plur., magnanimûm, Verg.).

Magnês -nêtis, v. Magnesia.

Magnēsĭa -ae, f. (Μαγνησία). **I.** *a district of Thessaly.* **II.** *a town in Caria on the Maeander* (now *Inek-bazar*). **III.** *a town in Lydia on Mount Sipylus* (now *Manissa*). Hence, **1, Magnēs** -nētis, m. (Μάγνης), *Magnesian;* esp., lapis Magnes or simply Magnes, *a loadstone, magnet;* plur. subst., **Magnētes** -um, m. *the Magnesians;* **2, Magnēsĭus** -a -um, *Magnesian;* saxum, *the magnet,* Lucr.; **3, Magnessa** -ae, f. *a Magnesian woman,* Hor.; **4, Magnētarchēs** -ae, m. *the chief magistrate of the Magnesians,* Liv.; **5, Magnētis** -ĭdis, f. *Magnesian;* Argo, *built at Pagasae in Magnesia,* Ov.

Magni Campi -ōrum, m. *a place in Africa not far from Utica.*

magnĭdĭcus -a -um (magnus and dico), *boastful,* Plaut.

magnĭfĭcē, compar., **magnĭfĭcentĭus;** superl., **magnĭfĭcentissĭmē,** adv. (magnificus), **a,** *splendidly, nobly, grandly, pompously, magnificently;* habitare, vivere, Cic.; **b,** *gloriously;* vincere, Cic.; **c,** *eloquently, in a lofty strain;* collaudare aliquem, Liv.; in a bad sense, *haughtily, proudly;* loqui de bello, Sall.

magnĭfĭcentĭa -ae, f. (magnificus). **I.** Of persons, **1,** *loftiness of thought and action, high-mindedness, magnanimity,* Cic.; and in a bad sense, *boasting, pomposity of language,* Cic.; **2,** *magnificence, splendour;* odit populus Romanus privatam luxuriam, publicam magnificentiam diligit, Cic. **II.** Transf., of inanimate objects, *splendour, grandeur, magnificence;* epularum, villarum, Cic.

magnĭfĭco, 1. (magnificus), *to prize highly, esteem greatly,* Plaut.

magnĭfĭcus -a -um, compar., **magnĭfĭcentĭor;** superl., **magnĭfĭcentissĭmus**

(magnus and facio). **I.** Of persons, **a,** *mag nificent, fond of display;* in suppliciis deorum magnifici, domi parci, Sall.; **b,** *glorious, distinguished;* vir factis magnificus, Liv.; **c,** *imposing, dignified;* adhortator, Liv.; **d,** *high-souled, lofty;* animo excelso magnificoque, Cic. **II.** Transf., of things, **a,** *splendid, magnificent;* villa, Cic.; **b,** *glorious;* aedilitas, Cic.; **c,** *dignified, lofty* (of language); dicendi genus, Cic.; and in a bad sense, *boastful, pompous;* alia magnifica pro se et illis dolentia, Sall.; **d,** *famous, eminent, distinguished;* magnificentissimum decretum, Cic.

magnĭlŏquentĭa -ae, f. (magniloquus), **1,** *lofty or elevated language;* Homeri, Cic.; **2,** *pompous, boastful language, magniloquence;* alicuius, Liv.

magnĭlŏquus -a -um (magnus and loquor), *pompous or boastful in talk, magniloquent;* os, Ov.

magnĭtūdo -ĭnis, f. (magnus), *greatness, size, magnitude.* **I.** Lit., **A. 1,** of space, mundi, Cic.; fluminis, Caes.; **2,** of number, *great quantity;* fructuum, Cic.; pecuniae, Cic. **II.** Transf., **1,** *size, importance;* **a,** beneficii, Cic.; **b,** *power;* reipublicae, Sall.; **2,** *greatness, high degree;* amoris, Cic.; animi, *magnanimity,* Cic.

magnŏpĕrĕ, and separately **magno ŏpĕrĕ,** adv. (magnus and opus), *greatly, exceedingly, very much;* nihil mirari, Cic.; magnopere delectare, Cic.; non magno opere laboro quorsum, etc., Cic.; in the superl., maximopere, Cic.; maximo opere, *very greatly,* Cic.

magnus -a -um, compar., **mājor** -us; superl., **maxĭmus (maxŭmus)** -a -um (from root MAC, whence magis, mactus, macto = μέγας), *great, large.* **I.** Lit., **1,** of size, *large, great tall, long, broad;* domus, Cic.; montes, Cat.; lit terae maximae, Cic.; magnae aquae, *an inunda tion,* Liv.; **2,** a, applied to number, *bulk, mass,* maximum pondus auri, magnum numerum frumenti, vim mellis maximam exportasse, Cic.; multitudo peditatūs, Caes.; **b,** of value, *high, great, considerable;* ornatus muliebris pretii majoris, Cic.; thus abl. magno and genit. magni, *at a high value, dear;* magni aestimare, *to esteem highly,* Cic.; magni, maximi facere, Cic.; magno emere, Cic.; **3,** of sound, *loud;* vox, Cic.; exclamare majus, *in a louder tone,* Cic. **II. A.** Of time, **1,** *long;* annus, Verg.; **2,** magno natu, *of great age,* Liv.; and esp. in compar. and superl., with or without natu or annis, *older;* natu major frater, Cic.; annos natus major quadraginta, Cic.; Fabii Ambusti filiae duae nuptae, Ser. Sulpicio major, minor Licinio Stoloni erat, *the elder to Sulpicius, the younger to Licinius,* Liv.; majores natu, *the older people,* Cic.; esp. = *the senate,* Cic.; majores, *ancestors, forefathers,* Cic.; maxima virgo, *the oldest of the Vestals,* Ov. **B.** Of importance, **1,** *great, important, significant;* magna et ampla negotia, Cic.; reipublicae magnum aliquod tempus, Cic.; **2, a,** *great, powerful, mighty;* propter summam nobilitatem et singularem potentiam magnus erat, Cic.; **b,** of talents, ability, *distinguished, eminent, able;* nemo vir magnus sine aliquo afflatu divino umquam fuit, Cic.; **3,** *serious, heavy, severe;* periculum, Caes.; infamia, Cic.; **4, a,** *strong, high, noble;* magno animo, Cic.; **b,** *proud;* magna verba, Verg.

Māgo (-ōn) -ōnis, m. *brother of Hannibal.*

1. **măgus** -i, m. (μάγος), *a learned man or magician among the Persians,* Cic.

2. **măgus** -a -um, *magical;* artes, Ov.

Māja -ae, f. (Μαῖα), *the daughter of Atlas, who bore Mercury to Jupiter, one of the Pleiades;* Majā genitus, Verg., Majā natus, Hor., Majā creatus, Ov., *Mercury* (acc. Majan, Ov.).

mājālis -is, m. *a gelded boar*, Varr.; used as a term of reproach, Cic.

mājestas -ātis, f. (majus = magnus). **I.** *grandeur, dignity, majesty;* applied to the gods, to all persons in high office, and frequently to the Roman people, dii non censent esse suae majestatis, *to be consistent with their majesty*, Cic.; consulis, Cic.; patria, *the paternal authority*, Liv.; populi Romani, Cic.; majestatem minuere, *to offend against the sovereignty of the people*, Cic.; crimen majestatis, *treason*, Cic.; lex majestatis, Cic. **II.** *honour, excellence, splendour;* matronarum, Liv.

mājor, majores, v. magnus.

Mājus -i, m. mensis Majus or simply Majus, *the month of May*, Cic.; used adj., Calendae Majae, Cic.

mājuscŭlus -a -um (dim. of major), *somewhat larger, somewhat greater;* in aliqua majuscula cura, Cic.

māla -ae, f. (contracted for mandela from mando, as scala for scandela from scando), **1**, *the cheek-bone, jaw-bone*, both in men and animals, Verg.; **2**, *the cheek;* malae decentes, Hor.

mālăcĭa -ae, f. (μαλακία), *a calm at sea;* tanta subito malacia ac tranquillitas exstitit ut, etc., Caes.

mălăcisso, 1. (μαλακίζω), *to soften, render pliable*, Plaut.

mălăcus -a -um (μαλακός), *soft, pliable,* Plaut.; fig., *effeminate, delicate*, Plaut.

mălē, adv., compar., **pējus;** superl., **pessĭme** (malus), *badly, ill.* **I.** Lit., **1**, male olere, Cic.; male vestitus, Cic.; L. Antonio male sit, *evil be to L. Antonius*, Cic.; male audire, *to be ill spoken of*, Cic.; **2, a,** *wrongly, improperly, badly;* male agere, Cic.; alicui male facere, Cic.; **b,** *unsuccessfully, unfortunately;* suos labores et apparatus male cecidisse, Cic.; **c,** *inopportunely, in the wrong place;* male salsus, Hor.; **d,** *dishonestly, wickedly;* male agere, Cic.; Carthago jam diu male cogitans, Cic. **II.** Transf., **1,** *bitterly;* male odisse, Caes.; **2, a,** *too much, excessively;* male superbus, Caes., **b,** with adj. and partic., to give a directly opposite meaning, male sanus, Cic.; male gratus, *unthankful*, Ov.

Mălĕa -ae, acc. -an, f. (Μαλέα, Μάλεια), *promontory in Laconia* (now *Malio di S. Angelo*).

mălĕdĭcē, adv. (maledicus), *calumniously, abusively, scurrilously;* dicere, Cic.

mălĕdīcens -entis, p. adj. (from maledico), *evil-speaking, abusive, scurrilous;* maledicentissima civitas, Cic.

mălĕdīco -dixi -dictum, 3. *to speak ill, slander, asperse, abuse, revile;* alicui, Cic.

mălĕdictĭo -ōnis, f. (maledico), *a reviling, abusing*, Cic.

mălĕdictum -i, n. (maledico), *a railing accusation, foul, abusive language;* maledicta in vitam alicuius conjicere, Cic.; maledicta in aliquem dicere or conferre or congerere, Cic.

mălĕdĭcus -a -um (maledico), *abusive, scurrilous;* conviciator, Cic.

mălĕfăcĭo -fēci -factum, 3. *to do an injury, to injure;* alicui, Plaut.

mălĕfactor -ōris, m. (malefacio), *an evil-doer, malefactor*, Plaut.

mălĕfactum -i, n. (malefacio), *an ill deed, injury*, Cic.

mălĕfĭcē, adv. (maleficus), *maliciously, mischievously*, Plaut.

mălĕfĭcĭum -ii, n. (maleficus), **1,** *an evil deed, crime, mischief;* maleficium committere, admittere, Cic.; se non maleficii causā (with

hostile intent) ex provincia egressum, Caes.; sine ullo maleficio, *without doing any harm*, Caes.; **2,** *sorcery*, Tac.

mălĕfĭcus -a -um (malefacio), *wicked, malicious, mischievous;* homo, Cic.

mălēsuādus -a -um (male and suadeo), *ill advising, seductive, persuading to evil*, Verg.

Mălĕventum -i, n. *an old town of the Hirpini in Samnium, the name of which the Romans changed to Beneventum.*

mălĕvŏlens -entis (male and volo), *envious, malevolent*, Plaut.; superl., malevolentissimae obtrectationes, Cic.

mălĕvŏlentĭa -ae, f. (malevolens), *ill-will, malice, hatred, malevolence;* malevolentia est voluptas ex malo alterius sine emolumento suo, Cic.

mălĕvŏlus -a -um (male and volo), *ill-disposed, wishing evil, malicious, envious, spiteful, malevolent;* alicui, Cic.; in aliquem, Cic.; malevoli de me sermones, Cic. Superl., v. malevolens. Subst., **mălĕvŏli** -ōrum, m. *envious, ill-disposed persons*, Cic.

Mălĭăcus sinus (κόλπος Μαλιακός), *a gulf in Thessaly, opposite Euboea.* Hence, **Mălĭensis** -e, *Malian.*

mālĭfĕr -fĕra -fĕrum (malum and fero), *apple-bearing*, Verg.

mălignē, adv. (malignus), **1,** *maliciously, malignantly, enviously;* loqui, Cic.; **2,** *stingily, sparingly;* dividere, Liv.; laudare, Hor.

mălignĭtas -ātis, f.(malignus), **1,** *maliciousness, ill-nature, malignity, spite*, Liv.; **2,** *stinginess, niggardliness;* malignitas praedae partitae, Liv.

mălignus -a -um (opp. benignus, malus and' gigno). **I.** *of bad disposition, ill-disposed, malicious, malignant, wicked;* vulgus, Hor.; oculis malignis spectare, Verg.; leges, Ov. **II. A. 1,** *stingy, niggardly;* caupo, Hor.; **2,** transf., **a,** *barren, unfruitful;* collis, Verg.; **b,** *small, little, scanty;* lux, Verg.; aditus, Verg. **B.** *coy, shy*, Ov.

mălĭtĭa -ae, f. (malus), *badness of quality.* **I.** *wickedness, vice*, Sall. **II.** *craft, cunning, malice;* malitia est versuta et fallax nocendi ratio, Cic.; sometimes used in a playful sense like our *"roguery;"* tamen a malitia non discedis, Cic.

mălĭtĭōsē, adv. with compar. (malitiosus), *wickedly, knavishly, perfidiously;* facere aliquid, Cic.

mălĭtĭōsus -a -um (malitia), *crafty, roguish, knavish, wicked;* homo, Cic.; juris interpretatio, Cic.

mallĕŏlus -i, m. (dim. of malleus), *a little hammer;* **1,** *a hammer-shaped slip* (of a vine), *a mallet-shoot for planting*, Cic.; **2,** *a kind of fire-dart*, Cic.

mallĕus -i, m. *a hammer, mallet;* **a,** gen., Liv.; **b,** esp., *the axe used for slaying animals offered in sacrifice*, Ov.

Malloea -ae, f. *town in Thessaly* (near modern *Mologhusta*).

mālo, mālŭi, malle (for mavolo, from magis volo), *to choose rather, prefer.* **I.** Gen., **a,** with acc., hunc animum, Cic.; **b,** with infin., servire quam pugnare, Cic.; **c,** with acc. and infin., malo me vinci quam vincere, Cic.; with potius, Uticae potius quam Romae esse maluisset, Cic.; with magis, Liv.; **d,** with nom. and infin., esse quam videri bonus malebat, Sall.; **e,** with subj., mallem cognoscerem, Cic. **II.** Esp., *to be more favourable to;* in hac re malo universae Asiae et negotiatoribus, Cic.

mālŏbăthron (-um) -i, n. (μαλόβαθρον);

1, an Indian or Syrian plant, from which a costly ointment was prepared, Plin.; **2,** meton., the oil of the plant, Hor.

1. mălum -i, n., v. malus.

2. mălum -i, n. (μῆλον), an apple, and generally any similar fruit, as the quince, peach, pomegranate, etc., Verg.; prov., ab ovo usque ad mala, from beginning to end (as the Roman dinner began with eggs and ended with fruit), Hor.

1. mălus -a -um; comp., **pējor** -us; superl., **pessĭmus** -a -um; bad. **I.** Subjective, **A.** bad, physically and intellectually, **1,** mali versus, Cic.; loquendi consuetudo, Cic.; **2,** a, incapable; poeta, Cic.; b, cowardly, weak; juxta boni malique, strenui et imbelles inulti obtruncari, Sall. **B.** Morally bad, wicked; **1,** mala consuetudo, Cic.; subst., malus, a villain, Cic.; **2,** in politics, evil-disposed, disloyal, demagogic; cives, Sall. **II.** Objective, **1,** adj., a, bad, as regards condition, position, etc.; mala valetudo, ill health, Cic.; mala copia (excess) stomachum sollicitat, Hor.; carmen, a libel, Hor.; malam opinionem habere de aliquo, Cic.; fama, ill repute, Sall.; b, unfavourable, unsuccessful, disadvantageous; pugna, Cic.; in pejus ruere, to become worse, Verg.; auspicium, ill-omened, Cic.; **2,** subst., **mălum** -i, n. an evil; a, bona aut mala, good qualities or faults, Sall.; b, harm, disaster, evil; ne malum habeat, Cic.; mala civilia, Cic.; malo esse alicui, Cic.; as an interjection to express aversion or dislike, quae, malum, est ista tanta audacia atque amentia, what in the world, Cic.

2. mălus -i, f. (2. malum), an apple-tree, Verg.

3. mălus -i, m. (prob. from root MAC, whence magnus), **1,** the mast of a ship; malum erigere, Cic.; **2,** in the circus, the pole to which the awnings were fastened, Liv.

malva -ae, f. (μαλάχη, from μαλακός), the mallow, Cic.

Māmers -mertis, m. the Oscan and Sabine name of Mars; hence **Māmertīni** -ōrum, m. (sons of Mars), the name assumed by certain mercenary troops who seized Messana. Adj., **Māmertīnus** -a -um, Mamertine; civitas, Messana, Cic.

Māmīlĭus -a -um, name of a Roman gens.

mămilla -ae, f. (dim. of mamma), a breast, teat, pap, Juv.; used as a term of endearment, Plaut.

mamma -ae, f. (μάμμα). **I.** a breast, teat; a, of men, mamma et barba, Cic.; b, of women, mammam matris appetere, Cic.; c, of the females of animals, suibus mammarum data est multitudo, Cic. **II.** mother, mamma, Mart.

mammōsus -a -um (mamma), full-breasted, having large breasts, Lucr.

Māmurra -ae, m. a Roman knight of Formiae, praefectus fabrum in Caesar's army in Gaul, where he amassed great wealth; urbs Mamurrarum, Formiae, Hor.

mānābĭlis -e (mano), flowing, penetrating; frigus, Lucr.

manceps -cĭpis, m. (manus and capio). **I.** a person who bought anything at a public legal auction, and esp., one who publicly contracted farm state property; a purchaser, farmer, contractor; praedae, Cic; manceps fit Chrysogonus, Cic. **II.** Transf., **1,** a tenant, lessee, Plin.; **2,** a surety, Plaut.

Mancīnus -i, m., C. Hostilius, consul at Rome, delivered up to the Numantines in consequence of a dishonourable peace made by him with them, which the senate refused to ratify.

mancĭpātĭo -ōnis, f. (mancipo), a formal transfer of property; also purchase, Plin.

mancĭpātus -ūs, m. (mancipo), a sale, Plin.

mancĭpĭum (mancŭpĭum) -ĭi (manus and capio), a taking by the hand, an old form of purchase in Rome in the presence of five witnesses. Hence, **I.** Lit., in Roman law, a formal, legal purchase of anything; lex mancipi (mancipii), the contract of sale, Cic.; mancipio dare, to sell formally, Cic.; mancipio accipere, to buy, Cic.; res mancipi, property which could be acquired by the ceremony of mancipium, Cic. **II.** Meton., a slave acquired by the process of mancipium, Cic.

mancĭpo (mancŭpo), **1.** (manus and capio), **1.** to transfer by mancipium or formal sale, to sell formally; alienos, Plaut.; quaedam mancipat usus, gives a title to, Hor.; transf., to give up to; saginae mancipatus, Tac.

mancus -a -um, **1,** maimed, crippled, lame; mancus et omnibus membris captus ac debilis, Cic.; **2,** transf., imperfect, incomplete, defective; virtus, Cic.; praetura, Cic.

mandātor -ōris, m. (mando), one who suborns accusers or informers, Suet.

mandātum -i, n. (mando), a commission, charge, injunction, order; and esp., a verbal commission, message; a, dare alicui mandata ut, etc., Cic.; mandata efficere, Cic., perficere, Liv.; to execute a commission; negligere, fallere, fail to execute, Ov.; mandato meo, by my command, Cic.; b, mandati judicium, an action for the non-performance of a commission, Cic.

mandātus, abl. -ū, m. found only in abl. sing. (mando), a commission, order, injunction; mandatu meo, Cic.

Mandēla -ae, f. a town in the Sabine country.

1. mando, **1.** (perhaps for manui or in manum do). **I.** to commit to the charge of, entrust, deliver; alicui magistratum, Cic.; aliquem aeternis tenebris, Cic.; corpus humo, to bury, Verg.; se fugae, to take to flight, Caes.; aliquid memoriae, to commit to memory, Cic.; litteris, scriptis, to commit to writing. **II.** to enjoin, order, command, commission; a, with acc., typos tibi mando (sc. comparandos, emendos), Cic.; Rhodiaca vasa mandavi, ordered, Cic.; b, with ut or ne and the subj., or simply the subj., tibi mandavit ut, etc., Cic.; Trebonio mandaverat ne, etc., Cic.; huic mandat, Remos adeat, Cic.

2. mando, mandi, mansum, **3.** (μάω, μάσσω); to chew, masticate. **I.** animalia alia sugunt, alia carpunt, alia vorant, alia mandunt, Cic.; equi fulvum mandunt sub dentibus aurum, champ the bit, Verg.; humum, to bite the ground (cf. mordere humum), of those who fall in battle, Verg. **II.** to eat, devour, consume; lora, Liv.

mandra -ae, f. (μάνδρα), **1,** a stall, cattle-pen, Mart.; **2,** a herd of cattle, Juv.; **3,** a row of pawns, on a draught-board, Mart.

Mandŭbĭi -ōrum, m. a people in Gallia Celtica, with a capital Alesia (now Alise).

mandūcus -i, m. (2. mando), a mask to represent a glutton, Plaut.

Mandŭrĭa -ae, f. a town in Lower Italy, between Aletium and Tarentum.

māne, subst. indecl. n. the early morning, dawn of morning; ad ipsum mane, Hor.; multo mane, very early in the morning, Cic. Adv., in the morning, at early morning; hodie mane, early this morning, Cic.; bene mane, very early in the morning, Cic.

mănĕo, mansi, mansum, **2.** (μένω). **I.** Intransit. to remain, stay in any place. **A**

seu maneant, seu proficiscantur, **Caes.** ; in patria, Cic. ; ad exercitum, Caes. **B.** 1, *to stay the night;* apud me, Cic. ; sub Jove frigido, Hor. ; 2, **a**, *to remain, endure, last;* nihil suo statu manet, Cic. ; **b**, *to remain fast, continue steadfast in;* in amicitia, Cic.; in voluntate, Cic.; in conditione, *to abide by,* Cic. ; 3, *to wait,* Plaut. ; transf., *to wait for, await;* cuius fatum tibi manet, Cic. **II.** Transit., **a,** *to wait for;* hostium adventum, Liv. ; **b,** *to await as fate or destiny;* quis me manet exitus ? Ov.

mānes -ium, m. (lit.= boni, *the good*). **I.** *the shades of the departed, the spirits of the dead;* dii manes, Cic. ; *of the shade of a single person,* patris Anchisae, Verg. **II.** Transf., 1, poet., *the lower world, infernal regions,* Verg. ; 2, *the punishment of the lower world;* quisque suos patimur manes, Verg.; 3, *corpse, ashes, remains;* accipiet manes parvula testa meos, Prop. ; omnium nudatos manes, Liv.

mango -ōnis, m. (μάγγανον), 1, *a dealer in articles, which he seeks to sell by rubbing up, furbishing,* etc. ; *a roguish dealer,* Plin., Quint. ; 2, esp., *a slave-dealer,* Suet.

mănĭca -ae, f. (manus). **I.** *the long sleeve of the tunic reaching to the hand, and serving as a glove,* Cic. **II.** Transf., *handcuff, manacle,* Hor., Verg.

mănĭcātus -a -um (manica), *having long sleeves;* tunicae, Cic.

mănĭcŭla -ae, f. (dim. of manus), *a little hand,* Plaut.

mănĭfestārĭus -a -um (manifestus), *plain, visible, evident, manifest,* Plaut.

mănĭfestē, adv. (manifestus), *plainly, visibly, evidently, manifestly,* Verg.

1. mănĭfestō, adv., v. manifestus.

2. mănĭfesto, 1. (manifestus), *to manifest, show clearly, reveal, discover;* aliquem, Ov.

mănĭfestus -a -um (manus and * fendo, lit. *struck with the hand*), *clear, visible, evident, manifest.* **I.** manifestae et apertae res, Cic. ; manifestum atque deprehensum scelus, Cic. ; adv., manifesto, *clearly, plainly;* manifesto deprehendere, comprehendere, comperisse, Cic. **II.** *caught in, manifestly betraying;* uti eos maxime manifestos habeant, *caught in the act,* Sall. ; with genit. of crime, rerum capitalium, Sall. ; vitae, *giving evident signs of life,* Tac.

Mănīlĭus -a -um, *name of a Roman gens.* **C.** Manilius, *tribune of the people,* B.C. 67, *the author of the Lex Manilia, which gave to Pompeius the sole command in the Mithridatic War.*

mănĭprĕtĭum = manupretium (q.v.).

mănĭpŭlāris (mănĭplāris) -e (manipulus), *belonging to a maniple;* judex, *chosen from a maniple* (from the common soldiers), Cic. Subst., **mănĭpŭlāris** -is, m. *a common soldier,* Cic

mănĭpŭlārĭus -a -um (manipulus), *belonging or relating to a private soldier,* Suet.

mănĭpŭlātim, adv. (manipulus), 1, *in bundles* or *handfuls,* Plin. ; 2, milit. t. t., *in maniples;* manipulatim structa acies, Liv.

mănĭpŭlus (poet. **mănĭplus**) -i, m. (manus and * pleo), *a handful.* **I.** Lit., *a small bundle* or *handful;* filicum manipli, Verg. **II.** Transf., *a company of foot soldiers, a division of the Roman army, three maniples forming a cohort* (so called because in early times the standard was a pole with a bundle of hay at the top), Caes.

Manlĭus -a -um, *name of a Roman gens.* **I.** M. Manlius Capitolinus, *who repulsed the attack of the Gauls upon the Capitol, afterwards thrown from the Tarpeian rock, on suspicion of aiming at kingly power.* **II. L.** Manlius and

his son T. Manlius, *who received the surname of Imperiosus from their severity.* Hence, adj., **Manlĭānus** -a -um, *Manlian, relating to Manlius;* turba, seditio, Liv. ; Manliana imperia, *severe commands,* Liv. Subst., **Manlĭānum** -i, n. *an estate of Cicero's.*

1. mannus -i, m. (a Celtic word), *a small horse of Gaulish breed, highly prized by the Romans for its swiftness,* Liv.

2. Mannus -i, m. *a god of the Germans, son of Tuisco,* Tac.

māno, 1. **I.** Intransit., *to flow, run.* **A.** Of fluids, fons nigra sub ilice manat, Ov. ; aliquā re, *to flow, run, drip with anything,* Cic. ; Herculis simulacrum multo sudore manavit, Cic. **B.** Of the air and other things, *to flow, spread;* 1, aër, qui per maria manat, *diffuses itself,* Cic. ; 2, transf., *to proceed, come from;* peccata ex vitiis manant, Cic. ; 3, *to spread abroad, spread, be diffused;* malum manavit per Italiam, Cic. **II.** Transit., *to exude, give out;* lacrimas (of a statue), Ov. ; fig., mella poëtica, Hor.

mansĭo -ōnis, f. (maneo). **I.** *a remaining, stay, sojourn;* in vita, Cic. **II.** *a station, halting-place, night-quarters,* Plin.

mansĭto, 1. (intens. of maneo), *to abide, stay, sojourn, remain;* sub eodem tecto, Tac.

mansuēfăcĭo -fēci -factum, 3., pass. **mansuēfīo** -factus sum -fĭeri (mansues and facio). **I.** Lit., of animals, *to tame;* uri mansuefieri non possunt, Caes. **II.** Of men, **a,** *to soften, pacify;* plebem, Liv. ; **b,** *to civilise;* a quibus mansuefacti et exculti, Cic.

mansuēs -is or -ētis (manus and sueo), *tame,* Plaut.

mansuesco -suēvi -suētum, 3. (manus and suesco). **I.** Transit., *to tame,* Verg. **II.** Intransit., *to become tame, grow tame, to become mild, softened;* nesciaque humanis precibus mansuescere corda, Verg.

mansuētē, adv. (mansuetus), *mildly, gently, quietly,* Cic.

mansuētūdo -ĭnis, f. (mansuetus). **I.** *tameness,* Plin. **II.** Transf., *mildness, clemency, gentleness;* imperii, Cic. ; uti clementiā et mansuetudine in aliquem, Caes.

mansuētus -a -um, p. adj. (from mansuesco), *tame.* **I.** Lit., of animals, sus, Liv. **II.** Transf., *mild, soft, gentle, quiet;* mansuetus in senatu, Cic. ; ut mansuetissimus viderer, Cic.; Musae mansuetiores (of philosophy, rhetoric, etc., as opposed to contentious and political eloquence), Cic.

mantēlē (mantīlē) -is, n. and **mantēlium** -ĭi, n. (manus), *a towel, napkin,* Verg.

mantēlĭum (mantēlium) -ĭi, n. = mantele (q.v.).

mantēlum (mantellum) -i, n. *a covering, veil, concealment,* Plaut.

mantĭca -ae, f. *a wallet, knapsack, saddlebag,* Hor.

Mantīnēa -ae, f. (Μαντίνεια), *a town in Arcadia, scene of the victory and death of Epaminondas.*

1. manto, 1. (freq. of maneo), *to remain, wait, wait for,* Plaut.

2. Mantō -ūs, f. (Μαντώ). **I.** *daughter of the Theban seer Tiresias, mother of the seer Mopsus.* **II.** *an Italian prophetess, mother of Ocnus, the founder of Mantua.*

Mantŭa -ae, f. *a town in north Italy, on the river Mincius, near to the birthplace of Vergil.*

mănŭālis -e (manus), *adapted, fitted to the hand, fitting the hand, relating to the hand;* saxa, *thrown by hand,* Tac.

mănŭbĭae -ārum, f. (manus), **1**, *the money obtained from the sale of booty*, esp. *the general's share, who usually spent it in erecting some public building ;* porticum de manubiis Cimbricis fecit, Cic. ; transf., *the profits of an office ;* manubias alicui concedere, Cic. ; *plunder, booty*, Suet. ; **2**, in augury, *a flash of lightning*, Sen.

mănŭbĭālis -e (manubiae), *of or relating to booty*, Suet.

mănŭbĭārĭus -a -um (manubiae), *of or relating to booty*, Plaut.

mănūbrĭum -ĭi, n. (manus), *a haft, handle ;* aureum vasis, Cic.

mănŭf . . . v. manif . . .

mănŭlĕus -i, m. (manus), *the long sleeve of a tunic*, Plaut.

mănŭmissĭo -ōnis, f. (manumitto), *the emancipation or manumission of a slave*, Cic.

mănŭmitto -mīsi -missum (manus and mitto), **3**. *to manumit, emancipate a slave ;* aliquem, Cic.

mănŭprětĭum (mănĭprětĭum) -ĭi, n. (often found in two words, manus pretium), *wages, hire, pay*, Cic.; transf., *a reward ;* perditae civitatis, Cic.

mănus -ūs, f. (connected with μάω, *to touch*), *the hand*. **I.** Lit. and fig. **A.** Gen., manus dextera, laeva, Cic. ; accipere aliquid manibus, Cic. ; manus adhibere vectigalibus, *lay hands on, rob*, Cic. ; conferre ferrum et manus, Cic. ; manus dare, *to surrender*, Cic. ; deponere aliquid de manibus, Cic. ; elabi de manibus, Cic. ; esse in manibus, **1**, *to be in our hands ;* oratio est in manibus, *can be read, is well known*, Cic. ; **2**, *to be in preparation ;* liber mihi est in manibus, Cic. ; **3**, *to be near, to be present*, Caes.; sed ecce in manibus vir et praestantissimo ingenio, etc., Cic. ; fugere *ie* manibus, Cic.; lavare manus, Cic. ; prehendere alicuius manum, Cic., aliquem manu, Cic. ; ne manum quidem vertere alicuius rei causā, *not to move a finger, not to take any trouble*, Cic. Particular phrases : victoriam in manibus videre, *at hand*, Cic. ; ad manum esse, *to be near at hand*, Liv. ; servum sibi habere ad manum, *as a private secretary*, Cic. ; de manu, *with one's own hand ;* facere, Cic. ; de manu in manum tradere, *to give from one's hand into the hand of another*, Cic. ; plenā manu, *liberally ;* plenā manu alicuius laudes in astra tollere, Cic.; per manus, *with the hands ;* trahere, Caes. : *from hand to hand ;* traditae per manus religiones, Liv.; manibus aequis (*with equal advantage, after a drawn battle*) dirimere pugnam, Liv. **B.** Esp. **1**, *the fist*, used for courage, force, violence ; manu capere urbes, Sall. ; **2**, *hand to hand fight ;* res venit ad manus atque ad pugnam, Cic. ; **3**, abl. manu, *by manual labour, by art, artificially ;* manu sata, *sown by hand*, Caes. ; urbs manu munitissima, Cic. ; **4**, *power, jurisdiction ;* haec non sunt in manu nostra, Cic. **II.** Meton., **1**, *the hand*, i.e., *the work of the artist or craftsman ;* extrema, *the finishing touch*, Cic.; extrema manus non accessit eius operibus, Cic. ; **2**, *handwriting ;* redeo ad meam manum, *I have begun again to write with my own hand*, Cic. **III.** Transf., **1**, *the trunk of an elephant*, Cic.; **2**, manus ferrea, *a grappling-iron used in naval warfare*, Caes. ; **3**, **a.** *a band or body of men ;* conjuratorum, Cic. ; **b**, *an armed band ;* manum facere, Cic., conducere, Caes., cogere, Caes.

măpālĭa -ĭum, n. (a Punic word), *huts, hovels, the movable habitations of the African Nomads*, Sall.

mappa -ae, f. **1**, *a table-napkin*, Hor. ; **2**, *a cloth* or *napkin thrown down in the circus as a signal for the races to begin*, Juv.

Mărăthōn -ōnis, m. and f. (Μαραθών), *a plain in Attica, where the Persian army was defeated by the Athenians*. Adj., **Marathonĭus** -a -um, *Marathonian*.

Mărăthos -i, f. (Μάραθος), *a Phoenician town opposite to the island of Aradus*. Adj., **Mărăthēnus** -a -um, *belonging to Marathos*.

mărăthrum -i, n. (μάραθρον), *fennel*, Ov.

Marcellus -i, m. *the cognomen of an illustrious family of the gens Claudia*. **I. M.** Claudius Marcellus, *the conqueror of Syracuse, defeated Hannibal at Nola, slew Viridomarus king of the Insubres with his own hand*. **II. M.** Claudius Marcellus, *an enemy of Caesar's, but afterwards pardoned by him*. **III. M.** Claudius Marcellus, *nephew, adopted son, and son-in-law of the Emperor Augustus*. Hence, **Marcellĭa** -ōrum, n. *the festival of Marcellus, a festival of the family of Marcellus in Sicily*, Liv.

marcĕo, **2. I.** *to wither, to droop*, Mart. **II.** Transf., *to be faint, languid, feeble, lazy*, either from old age or indulgence ; marcent luxuriā, Liv.

marcesco, **3.** (marceo). **I.** *to begin to droop*, Plin. **II.** Transf., *to languish, grow weak, feeble ;* vino, Ov. ; desidiā, Liv.

marcĭdus -a -um (marceo), **1**, *faded, withering, drooping ;* lilia, Ov. ; **2**, transf., *enfeebled, languid, heavy, besotted from immoderate indulgence in eating, drinking*, or *sleeping ;* somno aut libidinosis vigiliis, Tac.

Marcĭus -a -um, *name of a Roman gens, the most celebrated members of which were :* **1**, Ancus Marcius, *fourth king of Rome ;* **2**, L. Marcius, *a Roman knight, who commanded in Spain on the death of Scipio*. Adj., *Marcian ;* aqua, *an aqueduct commenced by Ancus Marcius, restored by Q. Marcius Rex ;* saltus (in Liguria, so called from the defeat of Q. Marcius, 188 B.C.), Liv. Hence, **Marcĭānus** -a -um, *Marcian ;* foedus, *made by L. Marcius with the inhabitants of Cadiz*.

Marcŏmāni and **Marcŏmanni** -ōrum, m. *a powerful German tribe*.

marcor -ōris, m. (marceo), *rottenness, decay, putrefaction*, Plin.

Marcus -i, m. *a common Roman praenomen*, gen. abbreviated M.

măre -is, n. *the sea*. **I.** Lit., mare Aegaeum, Cic. ; mare oceanus, Caes. ; nostrum mare, *the Mediterranean Sea*, Caes. ; superum, *the Adriatic*, Cic. ; inferum, *the Tuscan Sea*, Cic. ; conclusum, *inland sea*, Caes. ; clausum, *not navigable*, Cic. ; mare ingredi, *to go to sea*, Cic. ; mare infestum habere, *to infest the sea* (of pirates), Cic. ; terrā marique, *by sea and land*, Cic.; polliceri maria et montes, *to make boundless promises*, Sall. **II.** Meton., *sea-water ;* Chium maris expers, *unmixed with sea-water*, Hor.

Mărĕa -ae, f. or **Mărĕōta** -ae, f. (Μαρέα), *a lake and city of Lower Egypt, famous for its wine ;* hence, adj., **1**, **Mărĕōtĭcus** -a -um, *Mareotic, Egyptian ;* subst., **Mărĕōtĭcum** -i, n. *Mareotic wine ;* **2**, **Mărĕōtis** -ĭdis, f. poet. = *Egyptian ;* vites, Verg.

margărīta -ae, f. (μαργαρίτης) and **margărītum** -i, n. *a pearl*, Cic.

margĭno, **1**. (margo), *to make a border to, to border*, Liv.

margo -ĭnis, m. and f. **I.** *a border, edge ;* scuti, Liv. ; fontis, Ov. **II.** Transf., *boundary ;* imperii, Ov.

Mărīca -ae, f. *a nymph to whom a grove near Minturnae was sacred ;* poet , *a lake near Minturnae named after her*, Hor.

mărīnus -a -um (mare), *of or relating to the sea, marine;* marini terrenique humores, Cic.; ros, *rosemary,* Hor.

mărisca -ae, f. **I,** *a large fig,* Mart.; **2,** *the piles,* Juv.

mărīta, v. maritus.

mărītālis -e (maritus), *relating to marriage* or *a married pair, conjugal, matrimonial, marital;* vestis, Ov.

mărītĭmus (mărītŭmus) -a -um (mare), **1,** *of or relating to the sea, marine, maritime;* praedo, *a pirate,* Cic.; imperium, *a naval command,* Cic.; **2,** *on the sea* or *on the sea-coast;* civitas, Caes.; silva, Cic. Subst., **mărītĭma** -ōrum, n. *maritime regions, places on the sea-coast,* Cic.

mărīto, l. (maritus). **I.** *to wed, marry, give in marriage;* principem, Tac. **II.** Transf., of plants, *to bind one to another, to train one on another,* Hor.

mărītus -a -um (mas). **I.** Adj., **1,** lit., *of or relating to marriage, matrimonial, nuptial;* foedus, Ov.; Venus, *conjugal love,* Ov.; domus, *houses of married people,* Liv.; **2,** transf., of plants, *tied* or *trained together;* ulmus, Cat. **II.** Subst., **1, mărītus** -i, m. a, *a husband,* Cic.; b, *a lover, suitor,* Prop.; c, transf., of animals, maritus olens, *the he-goat,* Hor.; **2, mărīta** -ae, f. *a wife,* Hor.

Mărĭus -a -um, *the name of a Roman gens, the most distinguished member of which was C.* Marius, *seven times consul, conqueror of Jugurtha and the Cimbri, rival of Sulla, leader of the popular party at Rome.* Adj., *Marian.* Hence, **Mărĭānus** -a -um, *Marian.*

Marmărĭca -ae, f. *a district in Africa between Egypt and the Syrtes,* now *Barka.* Hence, **Marmărĭdēs** -ae, m. *a man of Marmarica.*

marmor -ŏris, n. (μάρμαρος). **I.** *marble.* **A.** Lit., Cic. **B.** Meton., **1,** *a marble statue,* Ov.; duo marmora, Ov.; in plur., *public monuments,* Hor.; **2,** *the white foamy surface of the sea;* marmor infidum, Verg. **II.** Transf., *stone generally,* Ov.

marmŏrĕus -a -um (marmor). **I.** *marble, made of marble;* signum, Cic.; aliquem marmoreum facere or ponere, *to make a marble statue of,* Verg. **II.** Transf., *like marble in smoothness* or *colour;* cervix, Verg.; gelu, Ov.; aequor, Verg.

Māro -ōnis, m. *the cognomen of the poet P. Vergilius,* v. Vergilius.

Marobŏdŭus -i, m. *king of the Suevi, who was defeated by Arminius, fled to Italy, and was kindly received by the Romans.*

Mărōnēa (-ĭa) -ae, f. (Μαρώνεια). **I.** *a town of Italy in the Samnite country,* now *Mcrano.* **II.** *a town in Thrace,* now *Marogna.* Hence, **Mărōnītēs** -ae, m. *a Maronite.*

Marpessus (Marpēsus) -i, m. *a mountain in the Island of Paros.* Adj., **Marpessĭus (Marpēsius)** -a -um, *Marpessian.*

marra -ae, f. *a hoe for rooting up weeds,* Juv.

Marrŭbĭum -ĭi, n., v. Marruvium.

Marrŭcīni -ōrum, m. *a people on the coast of Latium, between the Frentani and the river Aternus.* Hence, adj., **Marrŭcīnus** -a -um, *of or belonging to the Marrucini.*

Marrŭvĭum (Marrŭbĭum) -ĭi, n. *capital of the Marsi, on the banks of the Lacus Fucinus,* now *S. Benedetto.* Adj., **Marrŭvĭus** -a -um, *of or belonging to Marruvium.*

Mars, Martis, m. (poet. form, Māvors). **I.** *Mars, the god of war.* **A.** Lit., Mars Gradivus, Liv. **B.** Meton., **1,** *war, battle, fight;* a, lit.,

Hectoreus, *with Hector,* Ov.; invadunt martem, *begin the fray,* Verg.; suo marte cadunt, *in fight with one another,* Ov.; femineo marte cadere, *in fight with a woman,* Ov.; prov., suo marte, *by one's own resources;* rex suo marte res suas recuperavit, Cic.; esp., *manner of fighting;* equitem suo alienoque marte pugnare—i.e., *both on horse and on foot,* Liv.; b, transf., of legal disputes, forensis, Ov.; **2,** *the fortune* or *issue of war;* aequo marte, Liv.; mars belli communis, Cic.; **3,** *bravery, warlike spirit;* si patrii quid martis habes, Verg. **II.** Transf., *the planet Mars,* Cic. Adj., **Martius, Martĭālis** (q.v.).

Marsi -ōrum, m. **I.** *the Marsians, a people of Latium, notorious as sorcerers and snake-charmers.* Adj., a, **Marsĭcus** -a -um, *Marsic;* bellum, *the Social War,* Cic.; b, **Marsus** -a -um, *Marsian;* nenia, *enchantments,* Hor. **II.** *a people in Germany, between the Rhine, the Lippe, and the Ems.*

marsūpium -ĭi, n. (μαρσύπιον), *a money-bag, purse, pouch,* Plaut.

Marsyās -ae, m. and **Marsўa** -ae, m. (Μαρσύας). **I.** *a satyr, beaten in a musical contest with Apollo, who flayed him alive. A statue of Marsyas stood in the Roman forum, at the spot where lawyers transacted their business.* **II.** *a river in Phrygia Major, flowing into the Maeander.*

1. Martĭālis -e (Mars), **1,** *of or relating to Mars, consecrated to Mars;* flamen, Cic.; lupi, *sacred to Mars,* Hor.; plur. subst., **Martĭāles,** m. *the priests of Mars,* Cic.; **2,** *relating to the Legio Martia;* milites, Cic.

2. Martĭālis -is, m. M. Valerius, *the celebrated Roman epigrammatist of Bilbilis in Spain, who flourished under the emperors Domitian, Nerva, and Trajan.*

Martĭcŏla -ae, c. (Mars and colo), *a worshipper of Mars,* Ov.

Martĭgĕna -ae, c. (Mars and geno = gigno), *begotten of Mars, offspring of Mars,* Ov.

Martĭus -a -um (Mars). **I.** *of or relating to the god Mars, sacred to Mars;* a, lit., mensis, *the month of March,* Plin.; Calendae Martiae, *the 1st of March,* Cic.; proles, *Romulus and Remus,* Ov.; miles, *Roman* (as Mars was considered to be the ancestor of the Roman people), Ov.; Campus Martius, *the plain of Mars at Rome,* Cic.; gramine Martio, *on the Campus Martius,* Hor.; Martia legio, *name of a Roman legion,* Cic.; b, meton., *warlike;* Penthesilea, Verg.; Thebe, *scene of many wars,* Ov. **II.** Transf., *belonging to the planet Mars;* fulgor rutilus horribilisque terris quem Martium dicitis, Cic.

Marus -i, m. *a river in Dacia,* now *the Marosch.*

mas, māris, m. *the male* (opp. femina), applied to men, animals, and plants. **I.** Lit., a prima congressione maris et feminae, Cic.; mas vitellus, *a male yolk,* i.e., *that would produce a male chick,* Hor.; applied to plants, ure mares oleas, Ov. **II.** *manly, vigorous;* animi mares, Hor.; male mas, *unmanly, effeminate,* Cat.

Masaesŭli and **Masaesўli** -ōrum and -ûm, m. *a people in Numidia.*

mascŭlīnus -a -um (masculus), *of the male sex, masculine,* Phaedr.

mascŭlus -a -um (dim. of mas), *of the male sex, male.* **I.** Lit., tura, Verg.; libido, Hor. Subst., **mascŭlus** -i, m. *a male,* Liv. **II.** Transf., *masculine, manly, bold, courageous;* proles, Hor.

Măsĭnissa -ae, m. *king of Numidia, father of Micipsa, grandfather of Jugurtha, ally of the Romans.*

massa -ae, f. (μάζα), *a lump, mass;* picis, Verg.; esp., a, lactis coacti, *of cheese,* Ov.; b, of metals, Plin.; absol., *a mass of gold,* Ov.; *copper,* Verg.; c, *chaos,* Ov.

Massăgĕtēs -ae, m. (Μασσαγέτης), plur., Massagētae, *a Scythian people on the east coast of the Caspian Sea.*

Massīcus -i, m. *a mountain in Campania, famous for its wine,* now *Monte Masso* or *Massico;* hence, Massicum vinum, or subst., **Massĭcum** -i, n. *Massic wine,* Hor.; so, humor Massicus, Verg.

Massīlĭa -ae, f. *a celebrated town in Gallia Narbonensis, colonised from Phocaea in Asia Minor,* now *Marseilles.* Adj., **Massĭlĭensis** -e, *of or belonging to Massilia.*

Massўli -ōrum, m. and (poet.) -ûm, *a people in Numidia.* Adj., **Massўlus** -a -um, poet. = *African;* equites, Verg.

mastīgĭa -ae, m. (μαστιγίας), *a worthless fellow, scoundrel,* lit., *one who deserves a whipping,* Plaut.

mastrūca (mastrūga) -ae, f. (a Sardinian word), *a rough garment of sheep-skin, used as a term of reproach,* Plaut.

mastrūcātus -a -um (mastruca), *clothed in the* mastruca, Cic.

matăra -ae, f. and **matăris (matĕris)** -is, f. (a Celtic word), *a Gallic pike,* Caes.

mătellĭo -ōnis, m. (dim. of matula), *a small pot, vessel,* Cic.

māter, mātris, f. (μήτηρ), *a mother.* **I.** Lit., 1, of men, a, de pietate in matrem, Cic.; matrem fieri de Jove, *to become pregnant by,* Ov.; b, esp., (α) = *woman, wife,* Liv.; (β) applied to a nurse, Verg.; (γ) to goddesses, Mater Terra, Liv.; magna mater, Cic., or simply, mater (sc. deorum), *Cybele,* Verg.; Amorum, *Venus,* Ov.; 2, of animals, *dam, parent,* Verg.; 3, a, of plants, *the parent stem,* Verg.; b, of towns, *mother-city;* Populonia mater, Verg.; c, of countries, haec terra quam matrem appellamus, Liv. **II.** Meton., *motherly love;* simul matrem labare sensit, Ov. **III.** Fig., *source, origin;* mater omnium bonarum artium est sapientia, Cic.; utilitas justi prope mater et aequi, Hor.

mātercŭla -ae, f. (dim. of mater), *a little mother,* Cic.

mătĕrĭa -ae, f. and **mătĕrĭes** -ēi, f. (mater), *matter, material, stuff of which anything is composed.* **I.** Lit., **A.** Gen., materia rerum, Cic.; materiam praebet seges arida, *fuel,* Ov.; materiam superabat opus, Ov.; esp., *building materials;* delata materia omnis infra Veliam, Liv. **B.** Esp., 1, *wood;* a, *green wood;* materies vitis, *the stem,* Cic.; b, *wood for building, timber,* Cic.; materiam caedere, Liv.; 2, *provisions,* Ov. **II.** Transf., 1, *matter, stuff, materials;* ad jocandum, Cic.; artis, Cic.; 2, *incitement, occasion, cause;* seditionis, Cic.; aurum summi materies mali, Hor.; materiam dare invidiae, Cic.; 3, *natural disposition, abilities;* Catonis, Cic.

mătĕrĭārĭus -a -um (materia), *of or relating to timber,* Plin. Subst., **mătĕrĭārĭus** -ĭi, m. *a timber merchant,* Plaut.

mătĕrĭes -ēi, f. = materia (q.v.).

mătĕrĭo, 1, (materies), *to build, construct of wood;* aedes male materiatae, *of bad wood-work,* Cic.

mătĕrĭor, 1., dep. (materia), *to fell wood, procure wood,* Caes.

mătĕris = matara (q.v.).

māternus -a -um (mater), *of or relating to a mother, maternal;* sanguis, Cic.; tempora, *period of pregnancy,* Ov.; nobilitas, *on the*

mother's side, Verg.; Caesar cingens materna tempora myrto (i.e., of Venus, mother of Aeneas and myth. ancestress of the Julian gens), Verg.

mātertĕra -ae, f. (mater), *a mother's sister, maternal aunt,* Cic.

măthēmătĭcus -a -um (μαθηματικός). **I.** Adj., *mathematical,* Plin. **II.** 1, subst., **măthēmătĭcus** -i, m., a, *a mathematician,* Cic.; b, *an astrologer,* Tac.; 2, **măthēmătĭca** -ae, f., a, *mathematics,* Sen.; b, *astrology,* Suet.

Mātīnus -i, m. *a mountain in Apulia, famous for its honey.* Hence, adj., **Mătīnus** -a -um, *Matine.*

Matisco -ōnis, f. *town of the Aedui in Gaul,* now *Mâçon.*

Mātĭus -a -um, *name of a Roman gens.*

Mātrālĭa -ĭum, n. (mater), *the annual festival of the Mater Matuta, celebrated on the 11th of June,* Ov.

mātrīcīda -ae, c. (mater and caedo), *a person who murders his mother, a matricide,* Cic.

mātrīcīdĭum -ĭi, n. (matricida), *the slaying of a mother by her son, matricide,* Cic.

mātrĭmōnĭum -ĭi, n. (mater). **I.** *marriage, matrimony;* aliquam in matrimonium ducere, *to marry,* Cic.; dare alicui filiam in matrimonium, Cic.; habere aliquam in matrimonio, Cic.; aliquam ex matrimonio expellere, Cic. **II.** Meton., matrimonia, *married women,* Tac.

mātrĭmus -a -um (mater), *having a mother still living,* Cic.

1. **mātrōna** -ae, f. (mater), *a married woman, matron;* esp., *an honourable, noble, respectable lady,* Cic.; *an epithet of Juno,* Hor.; more rarely = *wife,* Cic.

2. **Mātrōna** -ae, m. *a river in Gallia Lugdunensis,* now the *Marne.*

mātrōnālis -e (matrona), *of or relating to a married woman, fit for a matron, matronly;* decus, Liv.; feriae Matronales, *a festival of the Roman matrons held in honour of Juno Lucina on the 1st of March* (hence called femineae calendae), Juv.

matta -ae, f. *a mat of rushes,* Ov.

mattĕa -ae, f. (ματτύα), *a dainty dish, a dainty,* Mart.

Mattĭăcum -i, n. *a town near the modern Wiesbaden;* hence, **Mattĭăcus** -a -um, *relating to Mattiacum.*

mătŭla -ae, f. *a vessel, pot;* as a term of reproach, *simpleton!* Plaut.

mātūrātē, adv. (maturatus from maturo), *quickly,* Plaut.

mātūrē, adv. (maturus). **I.** *at the right time, seasonably, opportunely;* sentire, Cic.; satis mature occurrere, Caes. **II.** 1, *in good time, betimes, soon, early;* senem fieri, Cic.; maturius proficisci, Caes.; maturissime rem vindicare, Cic.; 2, *too soon, prematurely;* mature decessit, Nep.

mātūresco, mātūrŭi, 3. (maturus). **I.** *to ripen, become ripe;* quum maturescere frumenta inciperent, Caes. **II.** *to come to maturity;* partus maturescunt, Ov.; nubilibus maturuit annis, Ov.

mātūrĭtas -ātis, f. (maturus), *ripeness.* **I.** Lit., of fruits, frugum, Cic. **II.** Transf., a, *full development, ripeness, maturity;* scelerum maturitas in nostri consulatūs tempus erupit, Cic.; of the development of the mind; aetatis ad prudentiam, Cic.; b, *the right moment of time, fulness of time;* eius rei maturitas nequedum venit, Cic.

mātūro, 1. (maturus). **I.** Transit., **A.** Lit. *to make fruits ripe, to ripen;* uvas, Tib.; maturata uva, *ripe*, Cic. **B**. Transf., **1**, *to do early, betimes;* multa . . . quae matŭrare datur, Verg.; **2**, *to quicken, hasten, accelerate;* huic mortem, Cic.; insidias consuli. Sall.; iter, Caes.; fugam, Verg.; with infin., *to hasten, make haste to do anything;* flumen exercitum transducere maturavit, Caes.; oro ut matures venire, Cic.; ni Catilina maturasset signum dare, *had been too hasty in giving the signal*, Sall. **II**. Intransit., *to hasten, make haste;* successor tuus non potest ita maturare, Cic.

mātūrus -a -um. **I**. *ripe*, **A**. Of fruits, poma, Cic.; uva, Verg. **B**. *ripe, mature, perfect, seasonable;* **1**, lit., physically, a, maturi soles, *powerful*, Verg.; b, *ripe in point of age, grown up, marriageable;* virgo, Hor.; with dat., virgo matura viro, Verg.; progenies matura militiae, *ripe for*, Liv.; also *aged*, *of ripe years;* senex, Hor.; maturus aevi, Verg.; aetas, Hor.; **2**, transf., a, intellectually and morally, *ripe in understanding and character;* annis gravis atque animi maturus Aletes, Verg.; b, *ripe, developed, mature, timely;* gloria, Liv.; maturum videbatur (*it seemed the proper time*) repeti patriam, Liv. **II**. **1**, *early;* hiems, Caes.; decessio, Cic.; **2**, transf., *quick, speedy;* judicium, Cic.

Mātūta -ae, f. *the goddess of the early morn;* gen., Matuta Mater, *an ancient Italian goddess, identified with Ino or Leucothea.*

mātūtīnus -a -um, *early in the morning, pertaining to the morning;* tempora, Cic.; equi, *horses of Aurora*, Ov.; pater, *Janus invoked in the morning*, Hor.

Mauri -ōrum, m. (Μαῦροι), *the Moors, inhabitants of Mauritania;* hence, **1**, **Maurus** -a -um, *Moorish;* poet., *African, Carthaginian;* **2**, **Maurĭtānĭa** -ae, f. *Mauritania, a district in Africa, between Numidia and the Atlantic Ocean.*

Maurūsĭa -ae, f. (Μαυρουσία), *Mauritania.* Adj., **Maurūsĭus** -a -um, *Mauritanian, also* poet. for *African.*

Mausōlus -i, m. (Μαύσωλος), *king of Caria, husband of Artemisia, who erected a splendid monument to his memory.* Adj., **Mausōlēus** -a -um, *belonging to Mausolus;* sepulchrum, or gen. subst., **Mausōlēum** -i, n. *the tomb of Mausolus;* or, in general, *any splendid sepulchre*, Suet.

māvŏlo = malo (q.v.).

Māvors -vortis, m., archaic and poet. for Mars. Adj., **Māvortĭus** -a -um, *belonging to Mars, Martial;* moenia, *Rome*, Ov.; tellus, *Thrace*, Verg.; proles, *the Thebans*, Ov.; subst., Mavortius, *Meleager, the son of Mars*, Ov.

maxilla -ae, f. (dim. of mala), *the jaw-bone, jaw*, Cic.

maxĭmē, superl. of magis (q.v.).

maxĭmĭtas -ātis, f. (maximus), *greatness, size*, Lucr.

maxĭmŏpĕrĕ, v. magnopere.

1. maxĭmus, superl. of magnus (q.v.).

2. Maxĭmus, v. Fabius.

māzŏnŏmus -i, m. (μαζονόμος), *a charger, large dish*, Hor.

mĕāmet, meapte, v. meus.

mĕātus -ūs, m. (meo), **1**, *a going, passing motion;* aquilae, *flight*, Tac.; **2**, *a way, path, passage;* Danubius in Ponticum mare sex meatibus (*mouths*) erumpit, Tac.

Mēcastor, v. Castor.

meddix -ĭcis, m. (Oscan metideicos, *giver of counsel*), *the name of a magistrate among the Oscans:* with the addition, tuticus, meddix tuticus, *chief magistrate*, Liv.

Mēdēa -ae, f. (Μήδεια), *an enchantress,*

daughter of king Aeetes in Colchis; helped Jason, the Argonaut, to obtain the golden fleece, fled away with him, afterwards deserted by him.

Mēdēis -ĭdis, f. (Medea), *magical*, Ov.

mĕdens -entis, m. (partic. of medeor), subst., *a physician*, Ov.

mĕdĕor, 2. dep. *to heal, to cure:* **1**, lit., a, of persons, with dat., morbo, Cic.; b, prov., quum capiti mederi debeam, reduviam curo, *to neglect a great evil while taking care of a small one*, Cic.; of things, *to do good to, be good for*, Liv.; **2**, transf., *to heal, assist, alleviate;* incommodis omnium, Cic.; afflictae et perditae reipublicae, Cic.

Mēdi -ōrum, m. (Μῆδοι), *the Medes;* poet. = *the Persians, Assyrians, Parthians;* sing., Medus, *the Mede*, poet. = *Persian.* Hence, a, **Mēdĭa** -ae, f. (Μηδία), *Media, a district of Asia;* flumen, *Euphrates*, Hor.; b, **Mēdĭcus** -a -um, *Median;* transf., *Assyrian, Persian;* c, **Mēdus** -a -um, *Median*, poet. = *Persian, Assyrian.*

mĕdĭastīnus -i, m. (medius), *a slave who performed menial offices, a drudge*, Cic.

mĕdĭca -ae, f. (Μηδική), *lucerne, clover*, Verg.

mĕdĭcābĭlis -e (medicor), *curable;* nullis amor est medicabilis herbis, Ov.

mĕdĭcāmen -ĭnis, n. (medicor), *a drug, medicine, medical substance.* **I**. Lit., **A**. In a good sense, Cic.; fig., iratae medicamina fortia praebe, Ov. **B**. In a bad sense, *poison, poisonous draught*, Tac. **II**. Transf., **1**, *colouring matter, dye*, and esp., *rouge, paint*, Cic.; **2**, *an artificial means of improving a natural product*, Plin.

mĕdĭcāmentum -i, n. (medicor), *a drug, medicine, remedy.* **I**. Lit., **A**. salutare, Cic.; fig., *remedy, cure;* doloris, Cic. **B**. *a poisonous drug, poison*, Cic.; coquere medicamenta, Liv. **II**. Transf., *a colouring substance, dye*, Cic.; fig., fucati medicamenta ruboris et candoris, Cic.

1. mĕdĭcātus -a -um, p. adj. (from medico), *healing, medicinal*, Plin.

2. mĕdĭcātus -ūs, m. (medicor), *a means of enchantment, charm*, Ov.

mĕdĭcīna -ae, f., v. medicinus.

mĕdĭcīnus -a -um (medicus), *relating or belonging to the art of healing.* **I**. Adj., Varr. **II**. Subst. **mĕdĭcīna** -ae, f. **A**. (sc. ars), *the art of healing;* medicinam exercere, *to practise medicine*, Cic.; medicinam facere alicui, *to heal*, Cic. **B**. (sc. res), *means of healing, medicine;* medicinam adhibere, Cic.; fig., *cure;* laboris, Cic.

mĕdĭco, 1. (medicus), *to heal, cure;* **1**, *to sprinkle with medicinal juices, to medicate, drug;* semina, Verg.; partic., medicatus, e.g., medicatae sedes, *medicated, sprinkled with a preparation*, Verg.; somnus, *procured by drugs or magic*, Ov.; **2**, *to dye;* capillos, Ov.

mĕdĭcor, 1. dep. (medicus), *to heal, cure;* alicui, Verg.; aliquid, Verg.

1. mĕdĭcus -a -um (medeor), *healing, wholesome, medicinal.* **I**. Adj., ars, Ov. **II**. Subst., **mĕdĭcus** -i, m. *a doctor, physician;* medicum ad aegrum adducere, Cic.

2. Mēdĭcus, v. Medi.

mĕdĭē, adv. (medius), *moderately*, Tac.

mĕdĭĕtas -ātis, f. (medius), *the middle, midst, that which is in the middle*, translation of the Greek μεσότης, Cic.

mĕdĭmnum -i, n. and **mĕdĭmnus** -i, m. (μέδιμνος), *a Greek measure of capacity, containing six Roman modii*, Cic. (genit. plur., gen. medimnûm).

mĕdĭŏcris -e (medius), *moderate, middling,*

f. Lit., spatium, Caes. **II.** Transf., 1, *middling, mediocre, tolerable, indifferent;* orator, vir, Cic.; eloquentia, Cic.; **2,** *moderate, calm;* animus, Caes.

mĕdĭŏcrĭtas -ātis, f. (mediocris), 1, *moderation, medium, the mean between excess and defect;* mediocritatem illam tenere quae est inter nimium et parum, Cic.; auream mediocritatem diligere, *the golden mean,* Hor.; plur., mediocritates probabant, *moderation in passion,* Cic.; **2,** *mediocrity, inferiority, insignificance;* ingenii, Cic.

mĕdĭŏcrĭtĕr, adv. (mediocris), 1, *moderately, tolerably, not extraordinarily;* nemo mediocriter doctus, Cic.; in aliqua re mediocriter versatum esse, Cic.; **2,** *with moderation;* aliquid non mediocriter ferre, Cic.

Mĕdĭōlānum -i, n. and **-lānĭum** -ĭi, n. *town in Cisalpine Gaul* (now *Milan*). Hence, adj., **Mĕdĭōlānensis** -e, *belonging to Mediolanum.*

Mĕdĭōmatrĭci -ōrum, m. *a people in Gaul, on the Moselle.*

Mĕdĭōn -ōnis, m. (Μεδίων or Μεδέων), *town in Acarnania.* Hence **Mĕdĭōnii** -ōrum, m. *the inhabitants of Medion.*

mĕdĭoxĭmus (mĕdĭoxŭmus) -a -um (medius), *that which is in the middle, the midmost;* dii superi atque inferi et medioxumi, *between the celestial and infernal deities,* Plaut.

mĕdĭtāmentum -i, n. (meditor), *a thinking upon anything, preparation;* in plur., belli meditamenta, Tac.

mĕdĭtātē, adv. (meditatus, from meditor), *with meditation, designedly, thoroughly,* Plaut.

mĕdĭtātĭo -ōnis, f. (meditor). **I.** *a thinking over anything, contemplation, meditation;* **1,** gen., futuri mali, Cic.; **2,** esp., *a preparation for anything;* obeundi muneris, Cic. **II.** *practice, exercise;* locos multā commentatione atque meditatione paratos atque expeditos habere, Cic.

mĕdĭtātus -a -um, partic. of meditor.

mĕdĭterrānĕus -a -um (medius and terra), *inland, far from the sea* (opp. maritimus); regiones, Caes.; urbs, Cic.; iter, Liv. Subst., **mĕdĭterrānĕum** -i, n., gen. plur., mediterranea, *inland country;* mediterranea Galliae petit, Liv.

mĕdĭtor, 1. dep. (connected with μελετάω, as lacrima with δάκρυον). **I.** *to think over, consider, meditate;* 1, gen., a, with acc., haec multa, Cic.; b, with de and the abl., de sua ratione, Cic.; c, with rel. sent., mecum, quid dicerem, Cic.; 2, esp., *to think upon anything in preparation, study, prepare oneself for, meditate, intend;* a, with acc., alicui pestem, Cic.; accusationem, Cic.; b, with ad and the acc., ad praedam, Cic.; c, with in and the acc., in proelia, Verg.; d, with infin., multos annos regnare, Cic. **II.** Transf., *to practise, exercise oneself;* Demosthenes perfecit meditando, ut, etc., Cic.; partic. **mĕdĭtātus** -a -um, pass., *meditated, considered, reflected, prepared, devised;* meditatum et cogitatum scelus, Cic.

mĕdĭum -ĭi, n. *the middle,* v. medius.

mĕdĭus -a -um (connected with μέσος -η -ον), *the middle, midmost, midst.* **I.** Lit., 1, of space; a, gen., medius mundi locus, Cic.; b, partitive, = *the middle of;* in foro medio, *the midst of the forum,* Cic.; c, subst., **mĕdĭum** -ĭi, n. *the midst, the middle point;* medium ferire, Cic.; aliquem in medium accipere, *into their midst,* Liv.; obscoenas voluptates faciles, communes, in medio sitas, *available to all,* Cic.; tabulae sunt in medio, *in every one's view,* Cic.; rem in medium vocare, *to bring before a court of law,* Cic.; aliquem tollere de medio, *to remove out of the way, to murder,*

Cic.; **2,** of time, a, gen., ultimum, proximum medium tempus, Cic.; mediis diebus, *in the intervening days,* Liv.; of age, media aetas, *middle age,* Cic.; b, partitive = *the middle of;* medius dies, *the middle of the day,* Ov.; c, subst., **mĕdĭum** -ĭi, n. *the middle;* jam diei medium erat, Liv. **II.** Fig., 1, *that which stands between two extremities;* a, gen., quum inter bellum et pacem medium nihil sit, *no middle thing, no mean,* Cic.; b, *standing between two views or parties, neutral, intermediate;* medium quendam cursum tenebant, Cic.; medium se gerere, *to keep oneself neutral,* Cic.; medios esse jam non licebit, Cic.; c, *ordinary, common, usual, middling;* gratia non media, Liv.; **2,** a, *containing a mixture of two opposites;* medium erat in Anco ingenium, et Numae et Romuli memor, Liv.; b, *acting as mediator;* medium se offert, Verg.; mediis diis, Ov.; **3,** *coming between two persons to disturb or separate;* quos inter medius venit furor, Verg.

mĕdĭus fĭdĭus, v. fidius.

medix, medixtuticus, v. meddix.

mĕdulla -ae, f. (medius), *marrow of bones;* 1, lit., cum albis ossa medullis, Ov.; 2, transf., *the inmost part;* mihi haeres in medullis, *I love you from the bottom of my heart,* Cic.

Mĕdullĭa -ae, f. *a town in Latium, colony of Alba* (now *St. Angelo*). Hence, adj., **Mĕdullīnus** -a -um, *of or belonging to Medullia.*

mĕdullĭtŭs, adv. (medulla), *in the very marrow;* fig., *inwardly, cordially,* Plaut.

mĕdullŭla -ae, f. (dim. of medulla), *marrow,* Cat.

1. **Mēdus** -i, m., v. Medi.

2. **Mēdus** -i, m. (Μῆδος). **I.** *a river in Persia,* now *Polwar;* poet. adj., Medum flumen, Hor. **II.** *son of Medea, title of a tragedy by Pacuvius.*

Mĕdūsa -ae, f. (Μέδουσα), *the daughter of Phorcus, mother of the horse Pegasus by Neptune, one of the Gorgons, slain by Perseus.* Hence, adj., **Mĕdūsaeus** -a -um, *Medusean;* equus, *Pegasus,* Ov.; fons, *Hippocrene,* Ov.

Mĕgăbocchus (Mĕgăboccus) -i, m. *Caius, fellow-conspirator with Catiline.*

Mĕgaera -ae, f. (Μέγαιρα), *one of the Furies.*

Mĕgălē -ēs, f. (Μεγάλη), *the Great One,* name of Cybele. Hence, a, **Mĕgălensis** -e, *belonging to the Magna Mater* (Cybele); gen. subst., **Mĕgălensĭa** -ĭum, n. and **Mĕgălēsĭa** -ĭum, n. *the festival annually celebrated on the 4th of April, in honour of Cybele, the Magna Mater;* b, **Mĕgălēsĭăcus** -a -um, *relating to this festival.*

Mĕgălŏpŏlis, acc. -im, f. and **Mĕgălŏpŏlis,** acc. -in, f.(Μεγαλόπολις and Μεγάλη πόλις), *a town in Arcadia, birthplace of Polybius.* Hence, a, **Mĕgălŏpŏlītae** -ārum, m. *the inhabitants of Megalopolis;* b, adj., **Mĕgălŏpŏlītānus** -a -um, *of or belonging to Megalopolis.*

Mĕgăra -ae, f. and **Mĕgăra** -ōrum, n. (Μέγαρα, τά). **I.** *a town in Megaris* (now *Magara*). **II.** *a town in Sicily* (now *Cattaro*). Hence, a, adj., **Mĕgărensis** -e, *Megarian;* b, **Mĕgăreus** -a -um, *Megarian;* c, **Mĕgărĭcus** -a -um, *Megarian.* Subst., **Mĕgărĭci** -ōrum, *philosophers of the Megaric school, disciples of Euclides;* e, **Mĕgărus** -a -um, *Megarian.*

1. **Mĕgăreus** v. Megara.

2. **Mĕgăreus** -ĕos, m. (Μεγαρεύς), *son of Neptune, father of Hippomenes.* Hence, **Mĕgărēĭus** -a -um, *relating to Megareus;* heros, *Hippomenes,* Ov.

Měgărǐs -ǐdis, f. (Μεγαρίς). **I.** *a district in Greece.* **II.** *a town in Sicily,* also called *Megara.*

měgistānes -um, m. (μεγιστᾶνες), *grandees, magnates, nobles,* Tac.

měhercle, mehercule, mehercules, **v.** Hercules.

mejo, 3. *to make water,* Hor.

měl, mellis, n. (μέλι), *honey.* **I.** Lit., stilla mellis, Cic. ; plur., roscida mella, Verg. ; prov., of a vain attempt, mella petere in medio flumine, Ov. **II.** Transf., *sweetness, pleasantness ;* poetica mella, Hor. ; hoc juvat et melli est, *is pleasant,* Hor. ; as a term of endearment, Sempronius, mel ac deliciae tuae, ap. Cic.

Měla -ae, m., Pomponius, *a Roman writer on geography under the Emperor Claudius.*

Mělampūs -pŏdis, m. (Μελάμπους), *a celebrated physician and soothsayer, son of Amythaon.*

mělanchŏlǐcus -a -um (μελαγχολικός), *having black bile, melancholy,* Cic.

Mělanthǐus -ǐi, m. (Μελάνθιος), *the goatherd of Ulysses.*

Mělanthō -ūs, f. (Μελανθώ), *a sea-nymph, daughter of Deucalion.*

Mělanthus -i, m. (Μέλανθος). **I.** *a river of Sarmatia.* **II.** *king in Athens, father of Codrus.* Hence, adj., **Mělanthěus** -a -um, *of or relating to Melanthus.*

mělănūrus -i, m. (μελάνουρος), *a kind of sea-fish,* Ov.

Mělas, acc. -āna and -an, m. (Μέλας). **I.** *a river of Sicily,* now Mela. **II.** *a river of Thessaly,* now Mavra-neria. **III.** *a river in Thrace,* now Kavatch.

melcŭlum -i, n. and **melcŭlus** -i, m. (mel), *little honey* (a term of endearment), Plaut.

Meldi -ōrum, m. *a people in Gallia Celtica.*

Mělěăgěr and **Mělěăgrus (-ŏs)** -i, m. (Μελέαγρος), *son of Oeneus, king in Calydon, and of Althaea ; his life depended on the preservation of an extinguished fire-brand, which was burnt by his mother in anger at the death of her brother by the hand of Meleager.* Hence, **Mělěăgrǐs** -ǐdis, f., plur., **Mělěăgrǐdes, a,** sc. aves or gallinae, *guinea-fowls,* Plin. ; b, *the sisters of Meleager, who, according to the legend, were changed to guinea-fowls on his death.*

1. Mělēs -ētis, m. (Μέλης), *a river near Smyrna, where Homer is said to have been born.* Hence, adj., a, **Mělētěus** -a -um, *belonging to Meles,* poet., *Homeric ;* b, **Mělētīnus** -a -um, *belonging to Meles.*

2. Meles -ǐum, f. *a place in Samnium.*

Mělǐboea -ae, f. (Μελίβοια), *a town in Thessaly on Mount Ossa, birthplace of Philoctetes.* Hence, adj., **Mělǐboeus** -a -um, *Meliboean ;* dux, *Philoctetes,* Verg.

Mělǐcerta (-ēs) -ae, m. (Μελικέρτης), *son of Athamas and Ino ; Ino plunged with him into the sea to escape the fury of her husband, and thereupon Melicerta was changed into a sea-god, called Palaemon by the Greeks and Portumnus by the Romans.*

mělǐcus -a -um (μελικός), *musical,* Lucr. ; esp., *lyrical, lyric ;* poema, Cic.

Mělǐē -ēs, f. (Μελία), *a nymph beloved by the river-god Inachus.*

mělǐlōtos -i, f. (μελίλωτος), *a species of clover,* Ov.

mělǐmēlum -i, n. (μελίμηλον), *a honeyapple, a kind of sweet apple,* Hor.

mělǐor -us, comp. of bonus (q.v.).

mělisphyllum and **mělissŏphyllŏn** -i, n. (μελισσόφυλλον), *balm, a plant of which bees are very fond,* Verg.

Mělissus -i, m. (Μέλισσος). **I.** *a Greek philosopher of Samos.* **II.** C. Maecenas Melissus, *the freedman of Maecenas, and librarian to Augustus.*

Mělīta -ae, f. and **Mělītē** -ēs, f. (Μελίτη). **I.** *the island of Malta.* **II.** *an island near Dalmatia,* now *Meleda.* **III.** (form -ē) *a sea-nymph.* Adj., **Mělītensis** -e, *of or belonging to the island of Malta ;* vestis, Cic.; and subst., **Mělītensǐa** -ǐum, n. *Maltese garments,* Cic.

mělǐuscŭlē, adv. (meliusculus), *somewhat better, pretty well* (in health) ; alicui est, Cic.

mělǐuscŭlus -a -um (dim. of compar. melior), *somewhat better in health,* Plaut.

Mella -ae, m. *a river in Upper Italy,* now Mela.

mellǐcŭlum -i, n. = melculum (q.v.).

mellǐfěr -fěra -fěrum (mel and fero), *producing honey ;* apes, Ov.

mellītus -a -um (mel), *sweetened with honey ;* placenta, Hor. ; transf., *as sweet as honey, pleasant, agreeable, delightful,* Cat.

1. mělos, n. (μέλος), *a tune, song, melody,* Hor.

2. Mēlos -i, f. (Μῆλος), *an island of the Aegaean Sea.* Hence, adj., **Mēlǐus** -a -um, *Melian.*

Melpŏměnē -ēs, f. (Μελπομένη), *the muse of tragic and lyric poetry.*

membrāna -ae, f. (membrum). **I.** *a skin, membrane, in the human or any animal body ;* natura oculos membranis tenuissimis vestivit, Cic. **II.** Transf., **1,** *the skin or slough of a snake,* Ov.; **2,** esp., *skin prepared to write on, parchment,* Hor. ; **3,** *surface of anything,* Lucr.

membrānŭla -ae, f. (dim. of membrana), *a little membrane ;* transf., *parchment,* Cic.

membrātim, adv. (membrum), **1,** *limb by limb ;* deperdere sensum, Lucr. ; **2,** transf., *piecemeal, singly ;* quasi membratim gestum negotium, Cic. ; of discourse, *in short, detached sentences ;* dicere, Cic.

membrum -i, n. **I.** *a limb or member of the body,* Cic. ; captus (crippled) omnibus membris, Liv. **II.** Transf., a, *a limb, member, part, portion of anything ;* omnes eius (philosophiae) partes atque omnia membra, Cic. ; b, *an apartment of a house ;* cubicula et eiusmodi membra, Cic. ; c, *a clause in a sentence,* Cic.

měmǐni -nisse (connected with moneo, mens, Gr. μέμνω, μνάω). **I.** *to remember, recollect, be mindful, bear in mind ;* (α) with genit., vivorum memini, Cic. ; (β) with acc., dicta, Cic. ; (γ) with de, de Herode et Mettio meminero, Cic.; (δ) with rel. sent., meministi quanta esset, etc., Cic. ; (ε) with acc. and infin., memini te narrare, Cic. ; (ζ) with infin., Hor.; (η) absol., ut ego meminisse videor, Cic. **II.** Transf., *to make mention of, to mention ;* de exsulibus, Cic.

Memmǐus -a -um, *name of a Roman gens, to which belonged C.* Memmius, *the friend of Cicero and Lucretius, who was condemned for bribery and went into exile at Athens.* Hence, a, **Memmǐădēs** -ae, m. *one of the Memmian gens, a Memmius ;* b, **Memmǐānus** -a -um, *belonging to Memmius.*

Memnōn -ŏnis, m. (Μέμνων), *king in Aethiopia, son of Tithonus and Aurora, killed before Troy by Achilles ;* mater lutea Memnonis, *Aurora,* Ov.; Memnonis saxa offspring = *a statue of Memnon near Thebes, which gave forth a note on being struck by the first rays of the sun,* Tac. Hence

a, adj., **Memnŏnĭs** -ĭdis, f. *of or relating to Memnon*; subst., **Memnŏnĭdes** -um, f. *the birds of Memnon, birds which arose from his ashes*; **b, Memnŏnĭus** -a -um, *Memnonian*; transf., *eastern, Moorish, black*.

mĕmor -ŏris (memini). **I.** *mindful, not forgetful.* **A.** Gen., **1,** of persons, (a) with genit., beneficii, Cic.; (β) with rel. sent., memor quae essent dicta, Cic.; (γ) absol., memori animo notavi, Ov.; **2,** transf., of things, memor libertatis vox, Liv. **B.** Esp., **1,** a, *remembering, thankful, grateful;* nimium memor nimiumque gratus, Cic.; **b,** *unappeasable, relentless;* memorem Junonis ob iram, Cic.; **2,** *thoughtful,* Verg.; **3,** *with a good memory, retentive;* memor an obliviosus sit, Cic. **II.** Act., *reminding of, calling to mind;* indicii memor poema, Ov. (abl. sing., memori always).

mĕmŏrābĭlis -e, adj. with compar. (memoro), *remarkable, worthy of mention, memorable;* vir, Liv.; virtus, Cic.

mĕmŏrandus -a -um (memoro), *worthy of being remembered, memorable;* of persons, juvenis memorande, Verg.; of things, proelium, Liv.

mĕmŏrātor -ōris, m. (memoro), *a narrator, relater,* Prop.

1. mĕmŏrātus -a -um, p. adj.(from memoro), *celebrated, well known;* inter paucas memorata populi Romani clades, Liv.

2. mĕmŏrātus -ūs, m. (memoro), *a mention, mentioning,* Plaut.

mĕmŏrĭa -ae, f. (memor). **I.** Gen. **A.** Lit., **1,** of the past, *remembrance, memory;* primam sacramenti memoriam, Caes.; Pompeii memoriam amisisse, Cic.; deponere, *to forget,* Caes.; memoriaalicuius(rei)excĭdit, orabiit, orabolevit, *it has fallen into oblivion, it has been forgotten,* Liv.; memoriae prodere, Cic. and Nep., or tradere, Liv., *to commit to writing, to leave on record* (of historians); viri digni memoriā, *worthy of remembrance,* Cic.; **2,** of the future, *thinking, thought;* periculi, Liv.; **3,** meton., *recollection;* nostrā memoriā, *in our recollection,* Cic. **B.** Transf., *handing down by word of mouth or by writing, tradition, history, information;* de hominum memoria (*oral evidence*) tacere; litterarum memoriam (*written evidence*) flagitare, Cic.; aliquid prodere memoriā, *by word of mouth,* Caes.; memoriā ac litteris, *by word of mouth and by writing,* Cic. **II.** *capacity for remembering, memory;* memoria bona, melior, Cic.; aliquid memoriae mandare, Cic.; memoriā comprehendere or complecti aliquid, *to remember,* Cic.

mĕmŏrĭālis -e (memoria), *of or relating to memory or remembrance,* Suet.

mĕmŏrĭŏla -ae, f. (dim. of memoria), *memory,* Cic.

mĕmŏrĭtĕr, adv. (memor), *by heart, from memory;* orationem memoriter habere, Cic.

mĕmŏro, 1. (memor), *to mention, call to mind, recount, relate;* (a) with acc., artibus quas supra memoravi, Sall.; (β) with de and the abl., de magna virtute, Sall.; (γ) with acc. and infin., id factum per ambitionem consulis memorabant, Sall.; in pass. with nom. and infin., ubi ea gesta esse memorantur, Cic.

Memphĭs -ĭdis, f. (Μέμφις), *a celebrated city of Egypt.* Hence, **a, Memphītes** -ae, m *belonging to Memphis;* bos, *Apis,* Tib.; **b, Memphĭticus** -a -um, *belonging to Memphis;* **c, Memphītĭs** -ĭdis, f. *belonging to Memphis,* and poet. = *Egyptian;* vacca (of Io), Ov.

Mēnae -ārum, f. (Μέναι), *town in Sicily,* now *Meneo.* Adj., **Mēnaenus** -a -um, *of Menae.*

Mĕnander -dri, m. (Μένανδρος), *a famous Greek comic poet, imitated by Terence.* **Adj., Mĕnandrēus** -a -um, *Menandrian.*

Mĕnăpĭi -ōrum, m. *a people in Gallia Celtica, between the Meuse and the Scheldt.*

menda -ae, f., v. mendum.

mendācĭum -ĭi, n. (mendax). **I.** *a lie, falsehood, untruth;* impudens, Cic.; mendacium alicuius refellere et redarguere, Cic. **II.** *deceit, deception;* oculorum reliquorumque sensuum mendacia, Cic.

mendācĭuncŭlum -i, n. (dim. of mendacium), *a little lie,* Cic.

mendax -ācis (mentior). **I.** *lying, mendacious;* homo, Cic. Subst., **mendax** -ācis, m. *a liar,* Cic. **II.** Of inanimate objects, *deceitful, counterfeit, false, untrue;* visa, Cic.; speculum, Ov.; fundus, *bearing less than the expected crop,* Hor.

Mendēs -ētis, f. (Μένδης), *a town in Egypt on the Nile.* Hence, adj., **Mendēsĭus** -a -um, *Mendesian.*

mendīcābŭlum -i, n. (mendico), *a beggar,* Plaut.

mendīcĭtas -ātis, f. (mendicus), *the condition of a beggar, indigence, poverty,* Cic.

mendīco, 1. and **mendīcor, 1.** dep. (mendicus). **I.** Intransit., *to beg, go begging,* Plaut. **II.** Transit., *to beg for;* mendicatus cibus, Ov.

mendīcŭlus -a -um (dim. of mendicus), *belonging to a beggar,* Plaut.

mendīcus -a -um, *poor as a beggar, beggarly, indigent.* **I.** Lit., of persons, solos sapientes esse, si mendicissimi (sint), divites, Cic. Subst., **mendīcus** -i, m. *a beggar,* Cic.; plur., mendici, *the begging priests of Cybele,* Hor. **II.** Transf., of things, *paltry, pitiful, beggarly;* instrumentum, Cic..

mendōsē, adv. (mendosus), *faultily, erroneously, incorrectly;* scribere, Cic.; mendosissime scriptum esse, Cic.

mendōsus -a -um (mendum). **I.** Pass., *full of faults;* **a,** *full of physical blemishes;* nec equi mendosa sub illo deteriorque viro facies, Ov.; **b,** *full of inaccuracies;* historia rerum nostrarum est facta mendosa, Cic.; **c,** poet., *full of moral blemishes;* mendosi mores, Ov. **II.** Act., *making a mistake;* car servus semper in Verrucii nomine mendosus esset, Cic.

mendum -i, n. and **menda** -ae, f. **I.** a *bodily defect, blemish,* Ov. **II.** a, *an error, mistake in writing;* quod mendum ista litura correxit? Cic.; **b,** *a mistake in reasoning or calculation,* Cic.

Mĕneclēs -is, m. (Μενεκλῆς), *an Asiatic rhetorician of Alabanda.* Hence, adj., **Mĕnĕclīus** -a -um, *of or relating to Menecles.*

Mĕnĕlāus (-ŏs) -i, m. (Μενέλαος), *son of Atreus, brother of Agamemnon, husband of Helen.* Hence, adj., **Mĕnĕlāēus** -a -um, *of or relating to Menelaus.*

Mĕnĕnĭus -a -um, *name of a Roman gens,* to which belonged Menenius Agrippa, *consul, said to have composed the differences between the patricians and the plebeians on the secession of the latter.*

Mēninx (Mēnix) -ingis, f. (Μήνιγξ), *an island near Africa,* now *Jerbi.*

Mĕnippus -i, m. (Μένιππος). **I.** *a Cynic philosopher.* **II.** *the greatest of the Asiatic orators of the time of Cicero.*

Mĕnoeceus -ĕi and -ĕos, m. (Μενοικεύς), *son of the Theban king Creon, who sacrificed his life for his country in obedience to an oracle.*

Měnoetĭădēs -ae, m. (Μενοιτιάδης), *the son of Menoetius*, i.e., *Patroclus*, Ov.

mens, mentis, f. (root MEN, whence memini), *the mind.* **I. A.** *the mind, opinion, way of thinking, character;* vestrae mentes atque sententiae, Cic. **B.** *the mind as the seat of feeling;* 1, gen., mens mollis ad perferendas calamitates, Cic.; 2, esp., *the conscience,* Cic. **II.** *the mind, understanding, reason, intellect, judgment.* **A.** Gen., mens cui regnum totius anini a natura tributum est, Cic.; mente complecti aliquid, *to comprehend,* Cic.; mentis suae esse, mentis compotem esse, *to be in possession of one's faculties,* Cic.; captus mente, *insane,* Cic. **B.** Esp., 1, *reflection, insight;* sine ulla mente, Cic.; 2, *courage;* addere mentem, *to inspire courage,* Hor.; demittere mentem, *to lose courage,* Verg.; 3, *passion,* Hor.; 4, *the thoughts;* a, venit (mihi) in mentem, *it occurs to me, I remember,* Cic.; temporis, Cic.; non venit in mentem pugna? Liv.; classem eā mente comparavit, ut, *with that intention,* Cic.; b, esp., *opinion, plan, resolve;* muta jam istam mentem, Cic. **C.** Person., Mens, *as goddess of understanding,* Cic.

mensa -ae f. (perhaps from root MEN, whence eminere, *anything raised up*), *a table,* 1, esp., *a table for eating upon;* a, lit., mensas cibis exstruere, Cic.; mensam ponere, *to bring in dinner,* Ov.; tollere, Cic., removere, Verg., *to take dinner away;* b, meton., *a course;* mensa secunda, *dessert,* Cic.; 2, a, *the table or counter of a money-changer, banker;* publica, *a public bank,* Cic.; b, *a sacrificial table, altar,* Verg.

mensārĭus -ĭi, m. (mensa), *a money-changer, banker,* esp., *a public banker who regulated the payments out of the treasury,* Cic.; mensarii tresviri, quinqueviri, Liv.

mensĭo -ōnis, f. (metior), *a measuring;* vocum, Cic.

mensis -is, m. (root MEN, whence μήν, μήνη, English *month*), *a month;* intercalarius, Cic.

mensor -ōris, m. (metior). **I.** *a measurer;* maris et terrae, Hor. **II.** *a measurer of land,* Ov.

menstrŭālis -e (menstruus), *monthly,* Plaut.

menstrŭus -a -um (mensis). **I.** *monthly;* usura, Cic. **II.** *lasting for a month;* spatium, Cic.; subst., **menstrŭum** -i, n. (sc. frumentum), *victuals, rations for a month,* Liv.

mensŭla -ae, f. (dim. of mensa), *a little table,* Plaut.

mensūra -ae, f. (metior), *a measuring.* **I.** Lit., mensuram alicuius rei facere, *to measure,* Ov. **II.** Meton., *a measure;* 1, *length, thickness, size, circumference,* etc.; a, of space, nosse mensuras itinerum, Caes.; b, of time, alicui mensuram bibendi dare, Ov.; 2, *a measure, that by which anything is measured;* majore mensurā reddere, Cic.; qui modus mensurae medimnus appellatur, *which species of measure,* Nep.; 3, *measure = size, nature, character;* mensuram nominis implere, *to be worthy of one's name, character, capacity,* Ov.; legati, Tac.

menta (mentha) -ae, f. (μίνθη), *the herb mint,* Ov.

mentĭens -entis, m., partic. of mentior, as subst., *a fallacy, sophism,* Cic.

mentĭo -ōnis, f. (memini), *a speaking of, mention;* mentionem facere alicuius rei, or de aliqua re, or de aliquo, *to make mention of, to mention;* esp., *to bring before the senate,* Cic.; casu in eorum mentionem incidi, *I mentioned them accidentally,* Cic.; alicuius rei mentionem movere, *to mention,* Liv.

mentĭor, 4. dep. (mens), *to lie, utter that which is not true, whether intentionally or not.* **I.**

Intransit., **A.** Gen., 1, of persons, si te mentiri dicis, verumque dicis, mentiris, Cic.; aperte, Cic.; in aliqua re, de aliqua re, Cic.; 2, transf., of inanimate objects, *to deceive, mislead;* frons, oculi, vultus persaepe mentiuntur, Cic. **B.** 1, of poets, *to feign, invent;* ita mentitur (Homerus), Hor.; 2, *to fail in a promise, break one's word;* quod promisisti mihi, quod mentita, inimica es, Cat.; mentiri honestius, Cic. **II.** Transit., **A.** *to say something falsely, to invent;* 1, gen., a, lit., Cic.; tantam rem, Sall.; res quas mentiris, Ov.; b, transf., of things, in quibus nihil umquam immensa et infinita vetustas mentita sit, Cic.; 2, *to deceive, disappoint;* seges mentita spem, Hor. **B.** 1, *to allege falsely, speak falsely about;* auspicium, Cic.; 2, *to counterfeit, put on, assume;* centum figuras, Ov.; partic., **mentītus** -a -um, as pass., *invented, feigned,* Verg.

Mentōr -ōris, m. (Μέντωρ), *a celebrated artist in metal work.* Hence, adj., **Mentŏrĕus** -a -um, *of or relating to Mentor.*

mentum -i, n. *the chin,* Cic.

mĕo, 1. (connected with eo), *to go, pass;* 1, of persons, domus Plutonia, quo simul mearis, Hor.; 2, of inanimate objects, quum triremes huc illuc mearent, Tac.; meantia sidera, Ov.

mĕopte, v. meus.

mĕphītis -is, f. 1, *a noxious exhalation from the earth, malaria,* Verg.; 2, personif., Mephitis, *the goddess who protects against malaria,* Tac.

mĕrācŭlus -a -um (dim. of meracus), *tolerably pure, unmixed,* Plaut.

mĕrācus -a -um (merus), *pure, unmixed.* **I.** Lit., vinum meracius, Cic.; helleborum, Hor. **II.** Transf., *undiminished; libertas,* Cic.

mercābĭlis -e (mercor), *that can be bought,* Ov.

mercātor -ōris, m. (mercor). **I.** *a merchant, wholesale trader* (opp. caupo, *a shopkeeper, retailer*), Cic. **II.** Transf., *a buyer;* signorum, Cic.; transf., provinciarum, Cic.

mercātōrĭus -a -um (mercator), *relating to a trader;* navis, *a merchant-ship,* Plaut.

mercātūra -ae, f. (mercor), *trade, traffic;* mercaturas facere, *to carry on trade,* Cic.; transf., non erit ista amicitia, sed mercatura quaedam utilitatum suarum, Cic.

mercātus -ūs, m. (mercor). **I.** *trade, traffic, business,* Cic. **II.** *a market, fair, public place of business;* mercatum indicere, habere, Cic.; ad mercatum proficisci, Cic.; frequens, *a full market,* Liv.

mercēdŭla -ae, f. (dim. of merces), 1, *a small reward, low wages;* mercedulā adducti, Cic.; 2, *low rent;* praediorum, Cic.

mercennārĭus (mercēnārĭus) -a -um (orig. mercedinarius, then mercednarius, then assimilated mercennarius, from merces), *hired, paid, mercenary;* miles, Liv.; testes, suborned, Cic.; of things, arma, Liv.; liberalitas, Cic. Subst., **mercennārĭus** -ĭi, m. *a hired servant, hireling,* Cic.

mercēs -ēdis, f. (mereo). **I.** *hire, pay, wages, reward, fee, salary;* 1, gen., a, in a good sense, operae, Cic.; conducere aliquem mercede, Cic.; b, in a bad sense, *hire, bribe;* lingua astricta mercede, Cic.; 2, esp., a, *the fee of a teacher;* mercede docere, Cic.; b, *the pay of soldiers;* mercede milites conducere, Liv.; 3, transf., euphem., a, *pay = punishment;* temeritatis, Cic.; b, *= harm, loss;* istuc nihil dolere non sine magna mercede contingit, Cic. **II.** *interest, rent. income;* praediorum, Cic.: insul-

rum, *rent,* Cic.; quinas hic capiti mercedes exsecat, 5 *per cent.,* Hor.

mercĭmōnĭum -ii, n. (merx), *goods, merchandise,* Plaut.

mercor, 1. dep. (merx). **I.** Intransit., *to carry on trade, to traffic,* Plaut. **II.** Transit., *to buy;* a, lit., fundum de pupillo, Cic.; aliquid ab aliquo, Cic.; aliquid tanto pretio, Cic.; b, transf., officia vitā, *with life,* Cic.; hoc magno mercentur Atridae, *would give a high price for,* Verg.

Mercŭrĭus -ii, m. **1,** Mercury, *identified with the Greek Hermes, son of Jupiter and Maia, the messenger of the gods, inventor of the lyre, god of oratory, conductor of the souls of the dead to the lower world, patron of merchants and thieves;* **2,** *the planet Mercury.* Hence, adj., **Mercŭrĭālis** -e, of or *relating to Mercury;* viri, *lyric poets,* Hor. Subst., **Mercŭrĭāles** -ium, m. *a corporation of traders at Rome,* Cic.

merda -ae, f. *excrement,* Hor.

mĕrē, adv. (merus), *purely, without mixture,* Plaut.

mĕrenda -ae, f. *an afternoon meal, taken between 4 and 5 P.M.*

mĕrens -entis, partic. of mereo.

mĕrĕo -ui -itum, 2. and **mĕrĕor** -itus sum, 2. dep. **I. A.** *to earn, obtain;* **1,** lit., mereri non amplius duodecim aeris, Cic.; nardo vina, *to exchange,* Hor.; **2,** transf., *to earn, win;* nullam gratiam hoc bello, Liv. **B.** *to earn pay as a soldier* = *to serve as a soldier;* gen., merere or mereri stipendia, Cic.; sub aliquo imperatore, Liv.; equo, equis, *in the cavalry,* Cic.; pedibus, *in the infantry,* Liv. **II. A.** *to deserve, merit,* be *worthy of;* **1,** in a good sense, praemia, laudem, Caes.; ut honoribus decoraretur, Cic.; **2,** in a bad sense, *to merit* (punishment, etc.); odium, Caes.; poenam, Ov.; fustuarium, Liv.; meruisse mori, Ov.; partic., a, merens, *deserving;* in a good sense *worthy,* in a bad sense *guilty,* Sall.; b, meritus; (*a*) act., *deserving;* meriti juvenci,Verg.; (β) pass., *deserved, merited;* dona, Liv.; iracundia, Cic. **B.** mereri de, *to deserve of;* in a good and bad sense, bene, optime de republica, Cic.; male de civibus suis, Cic.; ita se de populo Romano meritos esse ut, etc., Caes.

mĕrĕtrĭcĭē, adv. (meretricius), *after the manner of a harlot,* Plaut.

mĕrĕtrĭcĭus -a -um (meretrix), *of or relating to a harlot or prostitute;* amores, Cic.

mĕrĕtrĭcŭla -ae, f. (dim. of meretrix), *a public prostitute,* Cic.

mĕrĕtrix -icis, f. (mereo), *a public prostitute, harlot,* Cic.

mergae -ārum, f. (mergo), *a two-pronged fork,* Plaut.

mergĕs -gitis, f. *a sheaf of corn,* Verg.

mergo, mersi, mersum, 3. **I.** *to dip, plunge into water, immerse.* **A.** aves quae se in mari mergunt, Cic.; nec me deus aequore mersit, Verg. **B.** *to sink;* naves in alto, Liv. **II.** Transf., **A.** 1, *to sink down, plunge in, fix in;* canes mersis in corpora rostris dilacerant dominum, Ov.; caput in terram, Liv.; middle, mergi, of stars, *to sink,* Ov.; 2, transf., *to sink, overwhelm, immerse;* me his malis, Verg.; funere acerbo, *to destroy by a bitter death,* Verg.; se in voluptates, Liv.; vino somnoque mersi jacent, *sunk in wine and sleep,* Liv. **B.** *to hide, conceal;* suos in cortice vultus, Ov.

mergus -i, m. (mergo), *a diver, gull,* Verg.

mĕrĭdĭānus -a -um (meridies). **I.** *of or relating to midday, meridian;* tempus, Cic.; sol, Liv. **II.** *southern;* regio, Liv.; vallis, Liv.

mĕrĭdĭātĭo -ōnis, f. (meridio), *a noontide repose, midday sleep, siesta,* Cic.

mĕrĭdĭes -ēi, m. (for medidies, from medius and dies), 1, *midday, noon,* Cic.; 2, *the south;* inflectens sol cursum tum ad septentriones, tum ad meridiem, Cic.

mĕrĭdĭo, 1. and **mĕrĭdĭor,** 1. dep. (meridies), *to take a siesta* or *midday sleep,* Cat.

Mĕrĭōnēs -ae, m. (Μηριόνης), *a Cretan, friend and charioteer of Idomeneus.*

1. mĕrĭto, 1. (intens. of mereo), *to earn;* fundus qui sestertia dena meritasset, *brought in,* Cic.

2. mĕrĭto, adv. (meritus), *deservedly, with reason, rightly;* merito sum iratus Metello, Cic.; merito ac jure laudari, Cic. Superl., meritissimo, Cic.

mĕrĭtōrĭus -a -um (mereo). **I.** *that for which hire is paid* or *by which money is made;* rheda, *a hackney-coach,* Suet. Subst., **mĕrĭtōria** -ōrum, n. *lodgings,* Juv. **II.** *gaining money by prostitution,* Cic.

mĕrĭtum -i, n. (mereo). **I.** *desert,* and hence, *reward, punishment;* merita invenire, Sall. **II.** *desert, merit, any action which deserves thanks* or *reward.* **A.** magnitudo tuorum in me meritorum, Cic. **B. 1,** *a good action, benefit;* dare et recipere merita, Cic.; **2,** *demerit, blame, fault;* non meo merito, Cic.; nullo meo in se merito, *though I am guilty of no offence against him,* Liv.; **3,** *worth, value, importance of a thing;* quo sit merito quaeque notata dies, Ov.

mĕrĭtus -a -um, partic. of mereo (q.v.).

mĕrōbĭbus -a -um (merum and bibo), *drinking wine unmixed,* Plaut.

Mĕrŏē -ēs, f. (Μερόη), *a large island in the Nile.*

Mĕrŏpē -ēs, f. (Μερόπη), *daughter of Atlas, wife of Sisyphus, one of the Pleiades, whose star is dimmer than the others because she married a mortal.*

1. Mĕrops -ŏpis, m. (Μέροψ), *king of Aethiopia, husband of Clymene, who bore Phaëthon to Apollo.*

2. mĕrops -ŏpis, f. (μέροψ), *a bird, the bee-eater,* Verg.

merso, 1. (intens. of mergo), *to dip in, immerse;* gregem fluvio, Verg.; transf., mersari civilibus undis, Hor.

mĕrŭla -ae, f. **1,** *a blackbird,* Cic.; **2,** *a fish, the sea-carp,* Ov.

mĕrum -i, n., v. merus.

mĕrus -a -um. **I.** *pure, unmixed,* esp. applied to wine; vinum, Ov.; and subst., **mĕrum** -i, n. *wine unmixed with water* (only drunk by the intemperate), Hor.; undae, *water not mixed with wine,* Ov.; fig., meram haurientes libertatem, *unrestrained,* Liv. **II. A.** *naked, uncovered;* pes, Juv. **B.** 1, *mere, only, nothing but,* Cic.; merum bellum loqui, *to talk of nothing but war,* Cic.; 2, *real, genuine;* meri principes, Cic.; libertas, Hor.

merx, mercis, f. *merchandise, goods, wares;* fallaces et fucosae, Cic.; femineae, *for women,* Ov.

Mĕsembrĭa -ae, f. (Μεσημβρία), *a town in Thrace at the foot of Mount Haemus.* Hence, adj., **Mĕsembrĭācus** -a -um, *of or relating to Mesembria.*

Mĕsŏpŏtămĭa -ae, f. (Μεσοποταμία), *a country of Asia between the Euphrates and the Tigris.*

Messalla (Messāla) -ae, m. *a cognomen of the gens Valeria, the most celebrated members of which were:* **1,** M. Valerius Messalla Corvinus, *he patron of Tibullus, a skilled orator ;* and **2,** Messalina, *the wife of the Emperor Claudius.*

Messāna -ae, f. *a town in Sicily, on the straits between Italy and Sicily, now Messina.* Hence, **Messēnius** -a -um, *Messenian.*

Messāpĭa -ae, f. *old name of a part of Lower Italy, Calabria.* Hence, **Messāpĭus** -a -um, *Messapian.*

Messēnē -ēs, f. (Μεσσήνη), *the chief town in the district of Messenia in the Peloponnese.* Hence, **Messēnius** -a -um, *Messenian.*

messis -is, f. (meto -ĕre), *harvest.* **I. A.** Lit., messem amittere, Cic.; *the gathering of honey,* Verg. **B.** Meton., **1, a,** *the grain gathered in, harvest ;* illius immensae ruperunt horrea messes, Verg. ; **b,** *the crop, standing crop,* Ov. ; **2,** *the time of harvest, harvest-tide,* Verg; and poet., *the year ;* sexagesima messis, Mart. **II.** Fig., illa Sullani temporis messis, Cic.

messor -ōris, m. (meto -ĕre), *a reaper, mower,* Cic.

messōrĭus -a -um (messor), *of or relating to a reaper ;* corbis, Cic.

mēta -ae, f. *a conical or pyramid-shaped figure.* **I.** Gen., collis in modum metae in acutum cacumen fastigatus, Liv. **II.** Esp., **1,** *the pyramidal columns at the extremities of the Roman circus* (the race consisted in making the circuit seven times); metaque fervidis evitata rotis, Hor.; fig., in flexu aetatis haesit ad metas, *he was unfortunate,* Cic.; hence, **2, a,** *a place round which one has to go ;* metas lustrare Pachyni, Verg.; **b,** *the goal, end, term, boundary ;* mortis, aevi, Verg.; vitae metam tangere, Ov.

mĕtallum -i, n. (μέταλλον). **I.** *a metal, gold, silver, iron,* etc.; potior metallis libertas, *gold and silver,* Hor. **II.** Meton., *a mine, quarry ;* reditus metallorum, *income,* Liv.; metalla instituit, Liv.

mĕtămorphōsis -is, f. (μεταμόρφωσις), *a transformation, metamorphosis;* plur., **Mĕtămorphōses** -ĕōn, *the title of a poem by Ovid.*

Mĕtăpontum -i, n. (Μεταπόντιον), *a Greek colony in Lucania.* Hence, adj. **Mĕtăpontīnus** -a -um, *Metapontine.*

mētātor -ōris, m. (metor), *a measurer, one who marks ;* castrorum, Cic. ; urbis, Cic.

Mĕtaurus -i, m. (Μέταυρος), *a river in Umbria, where Hasdrubal was defeated and slain* 207 A.C. Adj., poet., Metaurum flumen, Hor.

Mĕtellus -i, m. *a cognomen in the Caecilian gens, the most remarkable members of which were :* **1,** Qu. Metellus Macedonicus, *who made Macedonia a Roman province, proverbial for the success of his private and public life ;* **2,** Qu. Caecilius Metellus Numidicus, *general in the war against Jugurtha ;* **3,** C. Caecilius Metellus Celer, *a contemporary of Cicero, husband of Clodia ;* **4,** Qu. Caecilius Metellus Pius (Scipio), *son of Scipio Nasica, adoptive son of Qu. Metellus Pius, father-in-law of Pompeius.* Hence, adj., **Mĕtellinus** -a -um, *relating to Metellus ;* oratio, *against Metellus Nepos, brother of Celer,* Cic.

Mĕtĕreus -a -um, *Meterean ;* turba, *a people near the Danube on the Black Sea,* Ov.

Mēthymna -ae, f. (Μήθυμνα), *a town in Lesbos.* Hence, adj., a, **Mĕthymnaeus** -a -um ; **b, Mĕthymnĭăs** -ădis, f. *of or relating to Methymna.*

mētĭcŭlōsus -a -um (metus), **1,** *full of fear, fearful,* Plaut.; **2,** *exciting fear, fearful,* Plaut.

mētĭor, mensus sum, 4. dep. *to measure.* **I.** Lit., **A.** agrum, Cic.; pedes syllabis, Cic. **B. 1,** *to measure out, distribute ;* frumentum rm exer-

citus, Cic. ; **2,** *to measure, traverse, pass over ;* aequor curru, Verg. ; iter amnium, Cat. **II.** Transf., *to measure according to a certain standard, to measure, estimate, judge of ;* sonantia auribus, Cic. ; oculo latus alicuius, Hor. ; omnia quaestu, *estimate everything with reference to gain,* Cic. odium aliorum suo odio, Liv. ; fidelitatem ex mea conscientia, Cic.

Mētĭosēdum -i, n. *town in Gallia Lugdunensis, in the country of the Senones.*

1. mēto, messŭi, messum, 3. **I.** Intransit., *to reap, mow, gather harvest ;* in metendo occupati, Caes. ; applied to the vintage, Verg. ; prov., ut sementem feceris, ita et metes, *as a man sows, so shall he reap,* Cic. **II.** Transit., **A.** *to mow, reap ;* arva, Prop. ; farra, Ov. ; transf., *of bees,* apes metunt flores, Verg. **B. 1,** *to crop off, pluck off, cut off ;* virgā lilia summa metit, Ov.; barbam forfice, Mart. ; **2,** in battle, *to hew down, mow down ;* proxima quaeque metit gladio, Verg.

2. Mēto (-ōn) -ōnis, m. (Μέτων), *a celebrated Athenian astronomer.*

3. mēto -āre = metor.

mētor, 1. dep. (meta). **I.** *to measure ;* caelum, Ov. **II.** *to measure off, lay out, define the boundaries of any spot ;* regiones, Liv. ; castra, Sall. ; frontem castrorum, Liv.

mētrēta -ae, f. (μετρητής), **1,** *a Greek liquid measure, containing about nine English gallons ;* **2,** *a large tub, cask,* Juv.

Mētrŏdōrus -i, m. (Μητρόδωρος). **I.** *a disciple of Epicurus.* **II.** *a rhetorician and philosopher of Skepsis in Mysia, disciple of Carneades.*

Mētrŏpŏlis, acc. -im, f. (Μητρόπολις), *town in Thessaly, between Pharsalus and Gomphi.* Hence, a, **Mētrŏpŏlītae** -ārum, m. (Μητροπολῖται), *inhabitants of Metropolis ;* **b, Mētrŏpŏlītānus** -a -um, *belonging to Metropolis.*

mētrum -i, n. (μέτρον), *a measure ;* and esp., *the measure of verses, metre,* Mart.

Mettĭus (Mētĭus) -ii, m. *a magistrate of the Albani.*

mĕtŭendus -a -um, p. adj. (from metuo), *fearful ;* multae metuendaeque res, Cic.

mĕtŭens -entis, p. adj. (from metuo), *fearing, standing in awe of ;* legum, Cic.

mĕtŭo -ŭi -ūtum, 3. (metus). **I.** Intransit., *to fear, be afraid* (esp. of some threatening evil, while timere is rather of fear of an object actually present); de sua vita, *for his life,* Cic. ; ab Hannibale, Liv. ; senectae, Verg. **II.** Transit., *to fear.* **A.** aliquem, Cic. ; insidias ab aliquo, Cic. ; metuit tangi, *he is afraid of being touched,* Hor.; metuo ne . . . *I fear that something will happen ;* metuo ut . . . *I fear that something will not happen,* Cic. **B.** *to shun, seek to avoid ;* nocentem corporibus Austrum, Hor.

mĕtus -ūs, m. *fear, apprehension, dread.* **I.** Lit., **1,** in metu esse, Cic. ; adducere aliquem in eum metum ut, etc., Cic. ; metum facere, *to cause fear,* Ov. ; deponere metum, Cic. ; with genit., existimationis, Cic. ; with ab or ex, a Romanis, Liv.; with ne and the subj., Cic.; metus hostilis, Cic. ; **2,** *reverence, awe ;* laurus multos metu servata per annos, Verg. **II.** Meton., **1,** *the object of fear,* Tac. ; **2,** *danger, crisis ;* metus maximi belli, Cic. (dat., metu, Verg., Tac.).

mĕus -a -um (root ME, MI), poss. pron. *my, mine, my own.* **I.** Adj., **1,** meum dictum consulis, Liv. ; meum est with infin., *it is my duty, falls to my lot,* Cic. ; meus hic est, *he is in my power,* Plaut.; nisi plane esse vellem meus, *except I wished to be quite original,* Cic. ; Nero meus, *my friend Nero,* Cic. ; **2,** *against me ;* crimina mea.

charges against me, Liv. **II.** Subst , **1, měa** -ae, f. *my love*, Ov. ; **2, měum** -i, n. *mine own* ; plur., **měa** -ōrum, n. *my possession*, Cic. ; **3, měi** -ōrum, m. *my attendants, slaves, my people*, Cic. (voc., sing. masc., **mí**, but also poet., meus, Verg. ; genit. plur., meûm, Plaut. The cases of meus are frequently strengthened by the enclitic additions, met, pte ; meopte, meâpte, meâmet, Plaut.).

Mēvānĭa -ae, f. *a town in Umbria*, now *Bevagna*.

Mezentĭus -ĭi, m. (lit., *a prince, ruler*), *name of a tyrant of Caere or Agylla*.

mica -ae, f. *a crumb, morsel, grain ;* mica saliens (sc. salis), Hor.

Mĭcipsa -ae, m. *son of Masinissa, king of Numidia*.

micans -antis (partic. of mico), *shining, glittering, sparkling*, Ov.

mīco -ŭi, 1. *to move rapidly up and down, tremble, beat like the pulse.* **I. 1,** venae et arteriae micare non desinunt, Cic. ; micat (equus) auribus, Verg. ; corda timore micant, Ov. ; auribus, Verg. : **2,** micare digitis, *to play at a game which consisted in holding out the fingers suddenly that another might guess their number* (the Italian game of *alla mora*) ; quid enim sors est? Idem propemodun quod micare, Cic. ; prov., of a thoroughly honourable man ; dignus quicum in tenebris mices, Cic. **II.** *to shine, glitter, sparkle ;* ignibus aether, Verg. ; micant gladii, Liv.

Mīdās (Mīda) -ae, m. (Μίδας), *a king of Phrygia, who received from Bacchus the gift of turning to gold everything that he touched ; as judge in a musical contest between Apollo and Pan he decided in favour of Pan, and Apollo punished him by changing his ears into those of an ass.*

Migdĭlybs -lўbis, m. (μίγδα and λίψ), *one of mixed African and Tyrian race, as the Carthaginians*, Plaut.

mĭgrātĭo -ōnis, f. (migro), *a removal from one place of abode to another, migration*, Cic. ; transf., verbi migrationes (sunt) in alienum multae, *metaphorical uses*, Cic.

mĭgro, 1. **I.** Intransit., *to remove from one place to another, quit a place, depart.* **A.** Lit., etiam mures migrârunt, Cic. ; ab Tarquiniis, Liv. **B.** Transf., **1,** gen., de vita, ex vita, *to die*, Cic. ; **2,** esp., *to change;* omnia migrant, all things change, Lucr. ; in colorem marmoreum, *to be changed into*, Lucr. **II.** Transit., **1,** *to remove from one place to another, transport ;* migratu difficilia, *difficult of transportation*, Liv. ; **2,** *to transgress ;* jus civile, Cic. (archaist., migrassit = migraverit, Cic.).

mil . . . v. mill . . .

Mīlănĭōn -ōnis, m. (Μειλανίων), *husband of Atalanta*.

mīles -ĭtis, c. (mille), *a soldier.* **I.** Gen., **a,** lit., *a soldier ;* scribere milites, *to enrol*, Liv.; ordinare, *to draw up in order*, Liv. ; mercede conducere, *to take into pay*, Liv. ; dimittere milites, Cic. ; *a common soldier*, Liv. ; **b,** poet. transf., (a) of persons, nova miles eram, Ov. ; (β) *a piece on a draught-board*, Ov. **II.** milites = *infantry*, as opposed to cavalry, Caes. ; miles, used collectively, Liv.

Mīlētus -i (Μίλητος). **I.** m., myth., *father of Caunus and Byblis, mythical founder of Miletus.* **II.** f. *a town in Caria.* Hence, adj., **1, Mīlēsĭus** -a -um, *Milesian* ; **2, Mīlētĭs** -ĭdis, f., a, *daughter of Miletus = Byblis*, Ov. ; **b,** *belonging to the town Miletus ;* urbs, *Tomi, a colony of the Milesians*, Ov.

mīlĭtāris -e (miles), *of or relating to a soldier*

or *to war, military ;* tribuni, Cic. ; signa, Cic. ; aetas, *the legal period of military service, from the seventeenth*, namely, *to the forty-sixth year*, Tac. Subst., **mīlĭtāris** -is, m. *a soldier, warrior*, Tac.

mīlĭtārĭtěr, adv. (militaris), *in a military* or *warlike manner ;* tecta sibi militariter aedificare, Liv.

mīlĭtĭa -ae, f. (miles), *military service, warfare.* **I.** Lit., munus militiae sustinere, Caes. ; discere, Sall. ; militiae vacatio, *exemption from military service*, Caes. ; domi militiaeque, domi et militiae, *at home and abroad, at peace and in war*, Cic. **II.** Meton., *the military, soldiery ;* cogere militiam, Liv.

mīlĭto, 1. (miles), *to serve as a soldier, be a soldier ;* in exercitu alicuius, Cic. ; sub signis alicuius, *under any one's command*, Liv. ; transf., *to serve under the banners of love ;* militavi non sine gloria, Hor.

mīlĭum -ĭi, n. (μελίνη), *millet*, Verg.

mīllě, numeral, *a thousand.* **I.** Adj., mille passibus, Caes. **II.** Subst., *a thousand.* **A.** Lit., sing., mille with genit., mille hominum versabatur ; plur., millia or milia, viginti millibus peditum, quatuor equitum, Liv. ; esp., mille passuum, *a thousand paces, a mile* (among the Romans, less by 142 yards than the English mile), Cic. **B.** Transf., *innumerable, countless ;* mille pro uno Caesones exstitisse, Liv. ; temptat mille modis, Hor.

millēsĭmus -a -um (mille), *the thousandth ;* pars, Cic. ; adv., millesimum, *for the thousandth time*, Cic.

millĭārĭus (mīlĭārĭus) -a -um (mille), *containing a thousand.* **I.** Gen., Plin. **II.** Esp., *containing a thousand paces.* Subst., **millĭārĭum** -ĭi, n. *a mile-stone*, Cic. ; aureum, *the central stone erected by Augustus in the forum, from which the miles were measured*, Tac.

millĭēs (mīlĭēs, mīlĭens), adv. (mille), **1,** *a thousand times ;* plus millies audivi, Ter. ; **2,** *innumerable times, countless times ;* millies melius, *a thousand times better*, Cic.

1. **Mīlo (-ōn)** -ōnis, m. (Μίλων), *of Crotona, a celebrated athlete.*

2. **Mīlo** -ōnis, m., T. Annius Milo Papianus, *tribune of the people with Clodius* (57 B.C.), *whose adversary he was, and whom he slew in a street brawl on the Appian Way ; on his trial for the murder he was defended by Cicero.* Hence, **Mīlōnĭānus** -a -um, *relating to Milo ;* subst., **Mīlōnĭāna** -ae, f. (sc. oratio), *the speech of Cicero in defence of Milo.*

Mīltĭădēs -is and -i, m. (Μιλτιάδης), *a celebrated Athenian general who conquered the Persians at Marathon.*

mīlŭīnus (milvīnus) -a -um (milvus), *of* or *relating to a kite ;* pullus, *a young kite* (fig. of the son of an avaricious man), Cic.

mīlŭus (milvus) -i, m. **I.** *a kite, hawk*, Cic. **II.** Transf., **1,** *a fish, the gurnard*, Ov. ; **2,** *a star*, Ov.

Mĭlyās -ădis, f. (Μιλυάς), *a district of Phrygia Major.*

mīma -ae, f. (mimus), *a female mime*, Cic.

Mĭmallŏnĭs -ĭdis, f. *a Bacchante.* Adj., **Mĭmallŏněus** -a -um, *Bacchanalian.*

Mĭmās -antis, m. (Μίμας). **I.** *a mountain in Ionia, opposite Chios.* **II.** *a giant.*

mīmĭcē, adv. (mimicus), *like a mime* or *buffoon*, Cat.

mīmĭcus -a -um (μιμικός), **1,** *mimic, farcical ;* jocus, Cic. ; **2,** *counterfeit, unreal*, Plin.

Mimnermus -i, m. (Μίμνερμος), *a Greek elegiac poet of Colophon.*

mimŭla -ae, f. (dim. of mima), *a female mime,* Cic.

mimus -i, m. (μῖμος). **I.** *a mime, mimic actor, pantomimist,* Cic. **II.** *a dramatic piece so called, broad farce;* persona de mimo, Cic.; fig., *a farce;* famam mimum facere, Cic.

min' = mihine, Pers.

mina -ae, f. (μνᾶ), 1, *a Greek weight* = 100 *trachmae,* Plin.; 2, *a Greek silver coin* = 100 *drachmae* or *Roman denarii,* Cic.

mĭnācĭae -ārum, f. (minax), *threats, menaces,* Plaut.

mĭnācĭtĕr, adv. (minax), *threateningly,* Cic.

mĭnae -ārum, f. (connected with mineo). **I.** *the battlements, parapets of a wall;* murorum, Verg. **II.** Transf., *threats, menaces;* minas jactare, *to threaten,* Cic.; of animals, Ov., Verg.; or of the wind, etc., Ov.

mĭnantĕr, adv. (1. minor), *threateningly,* Ov.

mĭnātĭo -ōnis, f. (1. minor), *a threatening, threat, menace* (plur.), Cic.

mĭnax -ācis, f. (1. minor). **I.** *overhanging;* scopulus, Verg. **II.** *threatening, full of threats;* homo, Cic.; vituli, Ov.; litterae, Cic.; fluvius, Verg.

Mincĭus -ĭi, m. *a river near Mantua, now Mincio.*

mĭnĕo, 2. *to project, overhang,* Lucr. (?)

Mĭnerva-ae, f.(Etruscan Menerfa or Meurfa), *the goddess Minerva, daughter of Jupiter, goddess of wisdom, and patroness of all the arts and sciences, identified with the Greek Athene;* prov., crassâ (pingui) Minervâ, *with homely mother-wit,* Cic.; sus Minervam (sc. docet), *when a foolish person begins to teach a wise one,* Cic.; invitâ Minervâ, *without ability,* Cic.; meton. = *working in wool,* Verg.

Mĭnervĭum -ĭi, n. (arx Minervae, Verg.), *a castle and temple of Minerva in Calabria.*

Mĭnervae prōmontōrĭum, *a promontory in Campania, south-east of Surrentum, the seat of the Sirens.*

mingo, minxi, minctum and mictum, 3. *to make water,* Hor.

mĭnĭātŭlus -a -um (dim. of miniatus), *somewhat coloured or tinged with cinnabar,* Cic.

mĭnĭātus -a -um, v. minio.

mĭnĭmē, v. parum.

mĭnĭmus, v. parvus.

1. **mĭnĭo,** 1. (minium), *to colour with cinnabar or red-lead,* Plin. Partic., **mĭnĭātus** -a -um, *coloured with cinnabar or red-lead, painted red,* Cic.

2. **Mĭnĭo (Mŭnĭo)** -ōnis, m. *a river in Etruria, now Mignone.*

mĭnister -tri, m. and **mĭnistra** -ae, f. (root MIN, whence also minus), *a servant, attendant, assistant;* **a,** in a house, minister cubiculi, Liv.; transf., virtutes voluptatum ministrae, Cic.; **b,** *a servant in a temple, the servant of a god;* Martis, Cic.; **c,** in a public office, ministri imperii tui, Cic.; **d,** *an assistant, supporter, aider, helper;* libidinis, Cic.; ministros se praebent in judiciis oratoribus, Cic.; ales minister fulminis, *Jupiter's eagle,* Hor.

mĭnistĕrĭum -ĭi, n. (minister). **I.** *service, assistance, attendance, office, employment, occupation,* Liv.; ministerio fungi, Liv. **II.** Meton., **a,** *servants,* Tac.; **b,** *retinue, personnel;* scribarum, Liv.

mĭnistra -ae, f., v. minister.

mĭnistrātor -ōris, m. (ministro), **1,** *a ser-vant, attendant, assistant,* Suet.; 2, esp., *one who supplied an advocate with the facts needed in his oration,* Cic.

mĭnistro, 1. (minister). **I.** *to serve, wait upon;* 1, alicui, Cic.; 2, esp., *to wait at table, to hand;* servi ministrant, Cic.; cibos, Tac.; pocula, Cic.; coenam, Hor. **II.** Transf., 1, *to attend to, take care of, govern, direct;* velis, *to attend to the sails,* Verg.; jussa medicorum, Ov.; 2, *to afford, procure, provide;* faces furiis Clodianis, Cic.; prolem, Tib.; furor arma ministrat, Verg.; vinum quod verba ministrat, Hor.

mĭnĭtābundus -a -um (minitor), *threatening, menacing,* Liv.

mĭnĭtor, 1. dep. (1. minor), *to threaten;* alicui mortem, Cic.; huic orbi ferro ignique, Cic.; minitans per litteras se omnia quae conarentur prohibiturum, Cic.

mĭnĭum -ĭi, n. (a Spanish word), *native cinnabar, red-lead, vermilion,* Verg.

1. **mĭnor,** 1. dep. (connected with minae and mineo). **I.** *to jut out, project, hang over;* gemini minantur in caelum scopuli, Verg. **II.** 1, *to threaten, menace;* alicui, Cic.; alicui crucem, Cic.; 2, *to promise boastfully;* multa, Hor.

2. **mĭnor** -ōris, compar., parvus (q.v.).

Mĭnōs -ōis, acc. -ōem and -ōa, m. (Μίνως). **I.** *a mythical king and lawgiver in Crete, son of Zeus, and, after death, judge in Tartarus.* **II.** *Minos II., king of Crete, grandson of the preceding, husband of Pasiphaë, father of Ariadne, Phaedra, and Deucalion.* Hence, **a, Mĭnōĭs** -ĭdis, f. *a daughter of Minos, Ariadne,* Ov.; **b,** adj., **Mĭnōĭus** -a -um, *relating to Minos, Cretan;* virgo, Ariadne, Ov.; **c, Mĭnōus** -a -um, *relating to Minos;* poet.= *Cretan;* Thoas, *son of Ariadne,* Ov.; arenae, *shore of Crete,* Ov.

Mĭnōtaurus -i, m. (Μινώταυρος), *a monster, half-bull, half-man, the offspring of Pasiphaë and a bull, slain by Theseus.*

mintha -ae, f. (μίνθα), *mint,* Plin.

Minturnae -ārum, f. *town in Latium, on the borders of Campania.* Hence, adj., **Minturnensis** -e, *relating to Minturnae.*

Mĭnŭcĭus -a -um, *name of a Roman gens, the most noted member of which was M. Minucius Rufus, magister equitum to the dictator Fabius Maximus Cunctator.*

mĭnŭme = minime (q.v.).

mĭnŭmus = minumus (q.v.).

mĭnŭo -ŭi -ūtum, 3. (root MIN, whence 2. minor, μινύω, μινύθω), *to make smaller.* **I.** *to cut up into small pieces, to chop up;* ligna, Ov. **II.** *to lessen, diminish;* 1, lit., sumptus civitatum, Cic.; minuente aestu, *at the ebbing of the tide,* Caes.; 2, transf., *to lessen, diminish, lower, reduce, limit;* gloriam alicuius, Cic.; molestias vitae, Cic.; ut controversiam minuam, *limit, confine to the point,* Cic.; majestatem P. R. per vim, *to offend against,* Cic.

mĭnus, compar. **I.** Adj., v. parvus. **II.** Adv., v. parum.

mĭnuscŭlus -a -um (dim. of compar. minor), *somewhat less, somewhat small,* Cic.

mĭnūtal -ālis, n. (minutus), *a dish of mince-meat,* Juv.

mĭnūtātim, adv. (minutus), *in small pieces, bit by bit, piecemeal, gradually;* aliquid addere, Cic.; interrogare, Cic.

mĭnūtē, adv. (minutus), *in small portions, meanly, pettily, paltrily;* res minutius tractare Cic.

mĭnūtĭa -ae, f. (minutus), *smallness, little-ness, minuteness,* Sen.

mĭnūtus -a -um, p. adj. (from minuo), *small, little, minute, unimportant, trifling;* res minutae, *trifles,* Cic. ; philosophi, *petty, insignificant,* Cic.

Mĭnўās -ae, m. (Μινύας), *a rich king of Orchomenus, the fabulous ancestor of the Minyae.* Hence, a, **Mĭnўae** -ārum, m. (Μινύαι), *the Argonauts, companions of Jason;* b, **Mĭnўēïās** -ădis, f. *daughter of Minyas;* c, **Mĭnўēïus** -a -um, *belonging to Minyas.*

mīrābĭlis -e (miror). I. *wonderful, astonishing;* mirabile est, followed by quam and the subj., Cic. ; by quomodo, Cic. ; with 2. supine, auditu, Cic. ; dictu, Cic. II. *extraordinary, unusual;* mirabilem in modum, Cic.

mīrābĭlĭtĕr, adv. (mirabilis), *wonderfully, marvellously, singularly, extraordinarily;* cupere, laetari, Cic. ; mirabiliter moratus est, *is of an extraordinary disposition,* Cic.

mīrābundus -a -um (miror), *full of wonder, wondering;* mirabundi quidnam esset, Liv.

mīrācŭlum -i, n. (miror), *a wonderful thing, wonder, prodigy, miracle, marvellousness;* miracula philosophorum somniantium, *the wonderful opinions,* Cic. ; adjiciunt miracula huic pugnae, *wonders,* Liv. ; magnitudinis, *a wonder for size,* Liv.

mirandus -a -um, p. adj. (from miror), *wonderful, singular;* mirandum in modum, Cic.

mīrātĭo -ōnis f. (miror), *a wondering, wonder, astonishment,* Cic.

mīrātor -ōris, m. (miror), *an admirer,* Ov.

mīrē, adv. (mirus), *wonderfully, extraordinarily, astonishingly;* favere, Cic. ; mire quam, *in a wonderful manner,* Cic.

mīrĭfĭcē, adv. (mirificus), *wonderfully, extraordinarily;* dolere, Cic.

mīrĭfĭcus -a -um (mirus and facio), *causing wonder, wonderful, astonishing;* homo, Cic. ; turris mirificis operibus exstructa, Caes. ; convicium, voluptas, Cic.

mirmillo (murmillo) -ōnis, m. *a kind of gladiator, generally matched with the Thraces or retiarii,* Cic.

mīror, 1 dep. I. *to wonder, be astonished at;* negligentiam hominis, Cic. ; foll. by acc. and infin., me ad accusandum descendere, Cic. ; foll. by quod, mirari quod non rideret haruspex, Cic.; with rel. sent utrius rei quae causa esset miratus, Caes. ; foll. by si, miror illā superbiā si quemquam amicum habere potuit, Cic. ; miror, *I wonder, I cannot understand, I am curious to know;* mirantes quid rei esset, Liv. II. *to admire, look on with admiration;* puerorum formas et corpora magno opere, Cic. ; with genit. of cause, Verg.

mīrus -a -um, *wonderful, astonishing, extraordinary, very great;* desiderium urbis, Cic. ; mirum quam inimicus erat, *it is wonderful how hostile,* i.e., *exceedingly hostile,* Cic. ; se mirum quantum profuit, Liv. ; mirum est ut, with subj., Cic. ; quid mirum? *what wonder?* Ov.

Mĭsargўrĭdēs -ae, m. (μισαργυρία, *hatred of money*), *a hater of money* (a name invented by Plautus and applied to a usurer), Plaut.

miscellānĕa -ōrum, n. (misceo), *a hash of different meats, hotchpotch, the food of gladiators,* Juv.

miscĕo, miscŭi, mixtum, and (later) mistum, 2. (μίσγω = μίγνυμι). I. Gen., *to mix, mingle;* 1, lit., mella Falerno, Hor. ; 2, transf., a, *to blend, mingle;* gravitate modestiae, Cic.; mixta metu spes, Liv. ; b, *to unite;* sanguinem et genus cum aliquo, *to marry,* Liv. ; se miscere viris, Verg. ; corpus cum aliqua, Cic. ; of battle,

miscere certamina, Liv. II. 1, *to mix a beverage, prepare by mixing;* a, lit., mulsum, Cic. pocula alicui, Ov. ; b, *to stir up, excite;* incendia, Verg. ; motus animorum, Cic. ; 2, *to confuse, confound;* a, caelum terramque, *to raise a storm,* Verg. ; b, of moral and political events, malis contionibus rempublicam, *to disturb,* Cic. ; 3, *to fill;* domum gemitu, Verg.

mĭsellus -a -um (dim. of miser), *miserable, wretched, unhappy;* homo, Cic. ; spes, Lucr.

Mĭsēnus -i, m. *the trumpeter of Aeneas.* Hence, **Mĭsēnum** -i, n. *a promontory and town in Campania,* now *Capdi Miseno;* mons Misenus, Verg. Adj., **Mĭsēnensis** -e, *relating to Misenum.*

mĭser -ĕra -ĕrum. I. *miserable, wretched, unhappy, pitiable, unfortunate, deplorable;* 1, of persons, hic miser atque infelix, Cic. ; miserrimum habere aliquem, *to torment greatly,* Cic. ; O me miserum! Cic.; 2, transf., of things, misera fortuna, Cic. ; as parenthetical exclamation, miserum ! *how wretched!* Verg. II. *suffering, ill;* miserum latus caputve, Hor.

mĭsĕrābĭlis -e, (miseror). I. *miserable, wretched, lamentable, deplorable;* aspectus, Cic. ; squalor, Cic. II. *mournful, sad, plaintive;* vox, Cic. ; elegi, Hor.

mĭsĕrābĭlĭtĕr, adv. (miserabilis). I. *miserably, lamentably, pitiably;* mori, Cic. II. *in a mournful* or *plaintive manner;* epistola miserabiliter scripta, Cic.

mĭsĕrandus -a -um (miseror), *pitiable, deplorable;* miserandum in modum, Cic.

mĭsĕrātĭo -ōnis, f. (miseror). I. *pity, compassion;* cum quadam miseratione, Cic. II. *pathetic* or *moving speech* or *tone;* uti miserationibus, Cic.

mĭsĕrē, adv. (miser). I. *wretchedly, pitiably, miserably;* vivere, Cic. II. *violently, exceedingly;* amare, Ter. ; deprimere emere, Plaut.

mĭsĕrĕo -sĕrŭi -sĕritum and -sertum, 2. and **mĭsĕrĕor** -sĕritus and -sertus sum, 2. dep. (miser). I. *to pity, have compassion on, commiserate;* sociorum, Cic. ; laborum tantorum, Verg. II. Impers., miseret or miseretur me, *I pity, I am sorry for, I have compassion on;* me miseret tui, Cic.; cave, te fratrum pro fratris salute obsecrantium misereatur, Cic.

mĭsĕresco, 3. (misereo), 1, *to pity, have compassion on, commiserate;* regis, Verg. ; 2, impers., me miserescit alicuius, *I am sorry for, have compassion on,* Plaut.

mĭsĕrĭa -ae, f. (miser). I. *wretchedness, unhappiness, misery, sorrow, grief, affliction, distress;* ubi virtus est, ibi esse miseria non potest, Cic. ; in miseriis versari, Cic. II. Personif., Miseria, *the daughter of Erebus and Nox.*

mĭsĕrĭcordĭa -ae, f. (misericors), *pity, compassion, tenderness of heart, mercy;* populi, on *the part of the people,* Cic. ; puerorum, *for boys,* Cic. ; adhibere misericordiam, *to show,* Cic. ; ad misericordiam inducere, Cic. ; alicui suam misericordiam tribuere, Cic.

mĭsĕrĭcors -cordis (misereo and cor), *pitiful, compassionate, tender-hearted;* in aliquem, Cic. ; quis misericordior inventus est? Cic.

mĭsĕrĭtus, v. misereor.

mĭsĕrĭtĕr, adv. (miser), *wretchedly, lamentably,* Cat.

mĭsĕror, 1. dep. (miser), *to pity, have compassion on, bewail, lament, deplore;* fortunam, Cic. ; casum, Sall.

mĭsertus, v. misereor.

missĭcĭus (-tĭus) -a -um (mitto), *discharged from military service,* Suet.

missĭle -is, v. missilis.

missĭlis -e (mitto), *that can be thrown, missile;* lapides, Liv.; ferrum, *a javelin,* Verg. Subst., gen. plur., **missĭlĭa** -ōrum, n. *missiles,* Liv.; res missiles, or subst., missilia, *gifts thrown among the people, donatives,* Suet.

missĭo -ōnis, f. (mitto). **I.** *a sending off, sending away;* legatorum, litterarum, Cic. **II.** *a letting go, releasing;* 1, a, of a prisoner, Cic.; b, *a discharge* or *dismission from military service;* nondum justa, injusta, Liv.; honesta, *honourable discharge,* gratiosa, *out of favour,* Liv.; c, *a permission given to gladiators to cease fighting;* sine missione munus gladiatorium dare, *to exhibit gladiators who fought till death,* Liv.; 2, *cessation, termination;* ludorum, Cic.

missĭto, 1. (freq. of mitto), *to send repeatedly;* auxilia, Liv.

missor -ōris, m. (mitto), *one who shoots, an archer,* Cic.

1. **missus** -ūs, m. (mitto). **I.** *a sending;* 1, missu Caesaris ventitare, *having been sent by Caesar,* Caes.; 2, *a throwing, shooting;* pili, Liv. **II.** 1, *a shot, the distance shot;* missus bis mille sagittae, Lucr.; 2, in the public races, *a course, heat,* Suet.

2. **missus** -a -um, v. mitto.

mistim (mixtim), adv. (mistus or mixtus), *confusedly,* Lucr.

mistūra (mixtūra) -ae, f. (misceo), *a mixing, mixture;* rerum, Lucr.

mĭtē, adv. (mitis), *mildly, softly, gently;* mitius ferre, perire, Ov.

mĭtella -ae, f. (dim. of mitra), *a bandage for the head, head-dress, turban,* Cic.

mĭtesco, 3. (mitis), *to become mild.* **I.** Of fruits, *to ripen, become ripe,* Plin. **II.** 1, of the weather, *to become mild;* hiems, Liv.; frigora, Hor.; of abstract things, *to be allayed, to subside;* seditio, Tac.; discordiae, Liv.; ira, Ov.; 2, *to become tame;* ferae quaedam nunquam mitescunt, Liv.

Mithrĭdātēs -is, m. (Μιθριδάτης), *king in Pontus* (135–63 B.C.), *who waged a long war with the Romans, and was conquered by Pompeius.* Adj., **Mithrĭdātĭcus** -a -um, *Mithridatic.*

mītĭfĭco, 1. (mitificus), *to make mild, soft;* cibus mitificatus, *well digested,* Cic.

mĭtĭgātĭo -ōnis, f. (mitigo), *an assuaging, alleviating, appeasing,* Cic.

mītĭgo, 1. (= mitem ago), *to make mild, soft.* **I.** Lit., fruges, *to make ripe,* Cic.; cibum, *to make soft by cooking,* Cic.; agros, *to break up, loosen, till,* Cic. **II.** a, of character, *to soothe, make gentle, pacify;* animum alicuius, *to soothe,* Cic.; Lampsacenos in istum, Cic.; b, of things, *to soothe, assuage, alleviate, charm, enchant;* tristitiam et severitatem, Cic.; dolorem, Cic.

mītis -e, *mild, gentle, ripe.* **I.** Of fruits, poma, uva, Verg.; fig., of style, Thucydides fuisset maturior et mitior, Cic.; of climate, caelo mitissimo, Liv.; of water, wind, etc., fluvius, Verg. **II.** Transf., of character; a, of persons, *mild, gentle, free from harshness;* homo mitissimus atque lenissimus, Cic.; of animals, taurus, Ov.; b, of things, *mild, gentle;* dolor, Cic.; aliquid mitiorem in partem interpretari, *put a lenient interpretation upon,* Cic.; c, of speech, *mild;* mitis et compta oratio, Cic.

mitra -ae, f. (μίτρα), *a head-dress, in general use among Asiatic nations, but in Greece and Rome worn only by women and effeminate men,* Cic.

mitrātus -a -um (mitra), *wearing the mitra,* Prop.

mitto, mīsi, missum, 3. *to send, let go.* **I.** *to send, despatch.* **A.** Gen., 1, lit., *to send away;* filium ad propinquum suum, Cic.; legatos de deditione ad eum, Caes.; misi, qui hoc diceret, Cic.; Deiotarus legatos ad me misit, se esse venturum, *with the intelligence that he was about to come,* Cic.; Curio misi, ut medico honos haberetur, *I sent word to Curius,* etc., Cic.; ad mortem, *to put to death,* Cic.; litteras ad aliquem or alicui, Cic.; 2, transf., aliquem in possessionem, *to put in possession,* Cic.; funera Teucris, *to prepare,* Verg. **B.** 1, *to dedicate a book to a person;* librum ad aliquem, Cic.; 2, *to conduct;* alias (animas) sub Tartara mittit (of Mercury), Verg.; 3, *to send forth from oneself, give forth;* luna mittit lucem in terras, Cic.; vocem pro aliquo, *to speak for,* Cic.; 4, *to push, throw;* pueros in profluentem aquam, Liv.; telum ex aliquo loco, Caes.; 5, medic. t. t., *to let blood,* Sen.; fig., missus est sanguis invidiae sine dolore, Cic. **II. A.** *to let go, release, give up;* 1, lit., Cat.; 2, transf., mittere ac finire odium, Liv.; maestum timorem, Verg.; of orators, *to cease speaking, not to speak, to avoid, pass over;* mitto illud dicere, *I pass over that,* Cic.; mitto de amissa parte exercitūs, Cic. **B.** 1, in the race-course, *to start the competitors;* quadrigas, Liv.; 2, *to dismiss an assembly;* senatum, Caes.; 3, a, *to dismiss, discharge, send away;* esp. of soldiers, legiones missas fieri jubere, Cic.; b, *to release from imprisonment;* mitti eum jubere, Liv.

mĭtŭlus (mūtŭlus) -i, m. (μίτυλος), *a species of edible mussel,* Hor.

mixtūra, etc. = mistura (q.v.).

mna = mina (q.v.).

Mnēmŏnĭdes -um, f. *the Muses, daughters of Mnemosyne,* Ov.

Mnēmŏsynē -ēs, f. (Μνημοσύνη), *Mnemosyne, mother of the Muses.*

mnēmŏsynum -i, n. (μνημόσυνον), *a memorial,* Cat.

mōbĭlis -e (for movibilis, from moveo). **I.** *moveable, easy to be moved; not firm, not fixed;* 1, lit., oculi, Cic.; 2, transf., a, *excitable, pliable, flexible;* mobilis aetas, Verg.; gens ad omnem auram spei mobilis, Liv.; b, *changeable, inconstant;* animus, Cic.; Galli sunt in capiendis consiliis mobiles, Caes. **II.** *rapid;* rivi, Hor.

mōbĭlĭtas -ātis, f. (mobilis). **I.** *moveableness, mobility;* animal mobilitate celerrimā, Cic.; linguae, Cic.; transf., *inconstancy, changeableness;* alicuius, Cic. **II.** *rapidity;* equitum, Caes.

mōbĭlĭter, adv. (mobilis), *rapidly, with quick motion;* palpitare, Cic.; ad bellum mobiliter excitari, *easily, quickly,* Caes.

mōbĭlĭto, 1. (mobilis), *to make moveable, put into motion,* Lucr.

mŏdĕrābĭlis -e (moderor), *moderate;* nihil moderabile suadere, Ov.

mŏdĕrāmen -ĭnis, n. (moderor), *a means of governing* or *guiding* (e.g., *a helm, rudder*); navis, Ov.; transf., rerum, *the management, government of the State,* Ov.

mŏdĕrantĕr, adv. (moderans from moderor), *moderately, with moderation,* Lucr.

mŏdĕrātē, adv. (moderatus), *moderately, with moderation;* moderatius id volunt fieri, Cic.

mŏdĕrātim, adv. (moderatus), *moderately, gradually,* Lucr.

mŏdĕrātĭo -ōnis, f. (moderor), *moderating.* **I. A.** *moderating, restraining;* effrenati populi, Cic. **B.** *government;* mundi, Cic. **II.** *moderation, temperance;* temperantia et moderatio naturae tuae, Cic.; vocis, *articulation,* Cic.

mŏdĕrātor -ōris, m. (moderor), *a governor, guide, manager, ruler;* equorum, *a driver,* Ov.; arundinis, *a fisher,* Ov.; reipublicae, Cic.

mŏdĕrātrix -īcis, f. (moderator), *she that rules* or *governs;* respublica moderatrix omnium factorum, Cic.

mŏdĕrātus -a -um (modero), *moderate, temperate, keeping within due measure;* of persons, frugi homo et in omnibus vitae partibus moderatus ac temperans, Cic.; of things, convivium, Cic.; ventus, Ov.; otium, Cic.; oratio, Cic.

mŏdĕro, 1. *to moderate, keep within bounds;* voci meae, Plaut.

mŏdĕror, 1. dep. (modus). **I.** *to set bounds to, keep within bounds; to regulate, moderate, restrain;* (a) with dat., alicui, Cic.; animo et orationi, Cic.; irae, odio, Liv.; (β) with acc., animos, Cic. **II.** *to direct, guide.* **A.** Lit., (a) with dat., navi funiculo, Cic.; (β) with acc., habenas, Ov. **B.** Transf., *to govern, rule, regulate;* (a) with dat., quibus totis moderatur oratio, Cic.; (β) with acc., Deus qui regit et moderatur et movet id corpus, Cic.; cantus numerosque, Cic.

mŏdestē, adv. (modestus), *moderately, temperately, discreetly, modestly;* Romam venire, Cic.

mŏdestĭa -ae, f. (modestus). **I. A.** *moderation, temperance;* neque modum neque modestiam victores habere, Sall. **B. 1,** applied to behaviour, *modesty, unassuming conduct;* in dicando, Cic.; **2,** *respect, obedience to authority;* in milite modestiam et continentiam desiderare, Caes.; **3,** as translation of the Stoic phrase εὐταξία, *good, practical judgment,* Cic. **II.** *mildness;* hiemis, Tac.

mŏdestus -a -um (modus), *moderate, keeping within bounds; moderate in desires* or *passions, temperate.* **A.** modestum ordinem, Cic. **B. 1,** *modest, unassuming, unpretending;* adolescentuli modestissimi pudor, Cic.; **2,** *modest, chaste, virtuous;* videas dolere flagitiosis modestos, Cic.

mŏdĭālis -e (modius), *containing a modius,* Plaut.

mŏdĭcē, adv. (modicus), *meterately;* **1,** *tolerably;* modice locuples, *tolerably well off,* Liv.; modice vinosus, *no great wine-bibber,* Liv.; **2,** *moderately, with moderation, temperately;* facere, agere, Cic.

mŏdĭcus -a -um (modus). **I.** *moderate, not very large, middling, ordinary;* convivia, potiones, *not excessive,* Cic.; fossa, *not very deep,* Liv.; acervus, Hor.; laus, Tac.; equites, senatores, *possessing moderate wealth,* Tac. **II.** *moderate, keeping within bounds, temperate, modest, unpretending;* severitas, Cic.; modicus voluptatum, *temperate in enjoyment,* Tac.; animus belli ingens, domi modicus, Sall.

mŏdĭfĭco, 1. (modus and facio), *to measure off, measure, moderate;* verba ab oratore modificata, Cic.

mŏdĭus -ĭi, m. (modus), *a dry measure among the Romans =* 16 *sextarii, and containing somewhat less than two imperial gallons, a peck,* Cic.; pleno modio, *in full measure, abundantly,* Cic. (genit. plur., modiûm, Cic.).

mŏdŏ, adv. (modus), *only, alone, but.* **I. A.** Gen., quod dixerit *solere* modo, non etiam *oportere,* Cic.; nemo eorum progredi modo extra agmen audeat, *only to go, so much as to go,* Caes.; ut ea modo exercitui satis superque foret, *that it alone was more than enough for the army,* Sall. **B.** Esp., **1,** with wishes, commands, etc., *only, just;* veniat modo, Cic.; vide modo, *only see,* Cic.; **2, a,** in conditional sentences, modo ut, or modo alone with subj., *provided that, if only;* quos, valetudo modo bona sit, tenuitas ipsa delectat, *if the health be only good,* Cic.; modo ne,

if only not, provided that not; tertia aderit, **modo** ne Publius rogatus sit, Cic.; **b,** with relatives, servus nemo, qui modo tolerabili conditione sit servitutis, *if he only be, provided only that he is,* Cic.; **c,** si modo, *if only;* tu scis, si modo meministi, me tibi dixisse, Cic.; **3,** in negative sentences, **a,** non modo . . . **sed** (verum), *not only* . . *but;* non modo . . . sed (verum) etiam, *not only* . . . *but also;* non modo . . . sed (verum) ne quidem, *not only* . . . *but not even,* Cic.; **b,** non modo non . . . sed, sed potius, sed etiam, *not only not* . . . *but rather;* non modo non . . . sed ne quidem, *not only not* . . . *but not even,* Cic. **II.** Transf., of time, **A. a,** *now, but now, just now, just; advenis modo?* **are you just come?** Ter.; **b,** used also of a remoter past, *lately, some time ago;* modo hoc malum in rempublicam invasit (i.e., *seventy years previously*), Cic. **B.** modo . . . modo, *sometimes . . . sometimes, now . . . now, at one time . . . at another;* modo ait, modo negat, Cic.; in place of the second modo is found nunc, Liv.; interdum, Sall.; aliquando, Tac.; saepe, Sall.; modo . . . tum (deinde, paullo post, postremum, vicissim), *now . . . then, in the first place . . . in the second place, first . . . afterwards,* Cic.

mŏdŭlātē, adv. with compar. (modulatus), *in good time, in time* (of music); modulate canentes tibiae, Cic.

mŏdŭlātor -ōris, m. (modulor), *one who observes a regular rhythm, a musician,* Hor.

mŏdŭlātus -a -um, p. adj. (from modulor), *properly measured* or *modulated, in good time, rhythmical, melodious;* verba, Ov.

mŏdŭlor, 1. dep. (modus). **I.** *to measure, measure off, measure regularly,* Plin. **II. 1, t. t.** of music, *to measure rhythmically, to modulate, to mark time;* vocem, Cic.; virgines sonum vocis pulsu pedum modulantes, Liv.; **2, a,** *to sing;* carmina, Verg.; **b,** *to play;* lyram, Tib.

mŏdŭlus -i, m. (dim. of modus). **I.** *a measure, standard of measurement;* metiri quendam suo modulo, Hor. **II.** *rhythm, musical time, measure, melody,* Plin.

mŏdus -i, m. *a measure, standard of measurement.* **I.** Lit., Varr. **II.** Transf., **A.** *size, quantity, length,* etc.; **1,** gen., agri certus modus, Caes.; **2,** esp. as musical t.t., *rhythm, melody, time;* vertere modum, Hor.; esp. in plur., flebilibus modis concinere, Cic. **B.** *a measure, bound, limit, boundary;* **1,** gen., modum imponere magistratui, Liv.; modum lugendi aliquando facere, *to make an end of bewailing,* Cic.; **2,** esp. in action, *moderation, control;* imitari caelestium ordinem vitae modo et constantiā, Cic.; sine modo ac modestia, Sall. **C.** *order, rule;* aliis modum pacis ac belli facere, Liv. **D.** *manner, mode, fashion, way, method;* concludendi, Cic.; servorum modo, *after the manner of slaves,* Liv.; hostilem in modum, *in a hostile manner,* Cic.; mirum in modum, Caes.; quonam modo? Cic.; eius modi, *in that manner, of that kind,* Cic.; huius modi, Cic.

moecha -ae, f. (moechus), *an adulteress,* Hor.

moechor, 1. dep. (moechus), *to commit adultery,* Cat.

moechus -i, m. (μοιχός), *a fornicator, adulterer,* Plaut., Ter.

moenĕra = munera (q.v.).

1. moenĭa -ĭum, n. (connected with munio). **I.** *the walls* or *fortifications of a city;* sub ipsis Numantiae moenibus, Cic.; transf., **a,** poet., *the walls, external compass, enclosure;* navis, Ov.; theatri, Lucr.; caeli, Ov.; **b,** *defence, protection, bulwarks;* alpes moenia Italiae, Ov. **II.** Meton., **1,** *the city enclosed within the walls;* Syracusarum moenia ac portus, Cic. ; moenia triplici circumdata muro, Verg. ; 2, *mansion, dwelling;* Ditis, Verg.

2. moenĭa -ĭum, n. = munia (q. v.).

moenio = munio (q. v.).

1. Moenus -i, m. *the river Main.*

2. moenus = munus (q. v.).

moerus = murus (q. v.).

Moesi -ōrum, m. *a people in the modern Servia and Bulgaria;* hence a, **Moesĭa (Maesĭa)** -ae, f. *the country of the Moesi;* b, **Moesĭăcus** -a -um, *belonging to the Moesi.*

moerĕo, moeror, moestus = maereo, maeror, maestus (q. v.).

mōla -ae, f. (molo), lit., *a mill-stone.* **A.** Hence, sing. and gen. plur., *the mill-stone = the mill* for grinding corn, olives, etc.; molis operam dare, Cic. **B.** Meton., *grits, coarse meal,* or *flour,* usually of spelt, which, mixed with salt, was sprinkled on victims before sacrifice; mola et vinum, Cic.

mōlāris -e (mola). **I.** *of* or *relating to a mill;* 1, lit., subst., **mōlāris** -is m. *a mill-stone,* Verg. ; **2,** transf., *as big as a mill-stone;* saxa, Sen.; subst., **mōlāris** -is, m. *a huge block of stone,* Verg. **II.** *belonging to grinding;* subst., **mōlāris** -is, m. *a molar tooth, grinder,* Juv.

mōles -is, f. *a mass, a heap.* **I.** Abstr. = *something heavy, weighty.* **A.** Lit., opposui molem clipei, *weighty shield,* Ov. ; ingenti mole Latinus, Verg. **B.** Transf., 1, *mass, heap = greatness, might, power;* tanti imperii, Liv. ; pugnae, Liv. ; 2, *trouble, difficulty;* majore mole pugnare, Liv. **II.** Concr., **A.** *a heavy, shapeless mass;* chaos, rudis indigestaque moles, Ov. **B.** Esp., 1, *a massive construction;* a, *a dam, mole;* oppositae fluctibus, Cic. ; b, *a large building;* insanae substructionum moles, Cic. ; c, moles belli, *large military machines, preparations for war, military works;* refectis vineis aliāque mole belli, Liv. ; 2, a, *a mass of men, large number;* hostes majorem molem haud facile sustinentes, Liv. ; b, *a mass of clouds, storm,* Verg.

mōlestē, adv. (molestus), 1, *unwillingly, with vexation, with annoyance;* moleste fero, *I take it ill, I am annoyed, I am sorry;* with acc. and infin., te de praedio aviae exerceri moleste fero, Cic. ; foll. by si, Cic. ; by quod, Cic. ; by acc., Cic. ; 2, *in a troublesome* or *disagreeable manner;* of discourse, gait, etc., *affectedly,* Cat.

mōlestĭa -ae, f. (molestus), *annoyance, dissatisfaction, chagrin, disgust, dislike;* 1, gen., fasces habent molestiam, *are attended with annoyance,* Cic. ; sine molestia tua, *without trouble to yourself,* Cic.; ex pernicie reipublicae molestiam trahere, *to be chagrined at,* Cic. ; molestiam alicui aspergere, *to cause annoyance to,* Cic. ; 2, *affectation, stiffness* (of style); Latine loquendi accurata et sine molestia diligens elegantia, Cic.

mōlestus -a -um (moles), *burdensome, troublesome, annoying, irksome;* 1, gen., labor, Cic. ; nisi molestum est, exsurge, *if it be not inconvenient,* Cic.; tunica, *a dress of inflammable materials put on condemned criminals and set alight,* Juv. ; 2, of discourse, *affected, laboured;* veritas, Cic.

mōlīmen -ĭnis, n. (molĭor), *a great effort, exertion, undertaking;* res suo ipsa molimine gravis, Liv. ; meton., *building;* molimine vasto, Ov.

mōlīmentum -i, n. (molior), *a great effort, exertion, endeavour;* sine magno commeatu atque molimento, Caes. ; motam sede suā parvi molimenti adminiculis, *by machines of small power,* Liv.

mōlĭor, 4. dep. (moles). **I.** Transit., **A.** Gen., *to set in motion, remove, displace;* ancoras, *to weigh anchor,* Liv. ; naves ab terra, *to unmoor,* Liv. ; montes sede suā, Liv. ; fulmina dextrā, *to hurl,* Verg. ; habenas, *to guide, direct,* Verg. **B.** 1, *to cause to totter, undermine;* portam, Liv.; transf., fidem, *to undermine credit,* Liv. ; 2, *to work, cultivate the earth;* terram, Liv.; arva ferro, Lucr. ; 3, a, *to build, erect, rear, raise;* muros, arcem, Verg. ; classem, Verg. ; b, *of abstract objects, to undertake;* nulla opera, Cic. ; 4, *to cause, produce;* morbos, Verg. ; sibi opem, Verg.; struere et moliri alicui aliquid calamitatis, *to plot, devise,* Cic.; alicui insidias, *to lay snares,* Cic. ; peregrinum regnum, *to strive after, endeavour to obtain,* Liv. **II.** Reflex., *to toil, struggle, exert oneself.* **A.** Lit., in demoliendo signo permulti homines moliebantur, Cic. **B.** Transf., agam per me ipse et moliar, Cic.

mōlītĭo -ōnis, f. (molior), 1, *a demolition, demolishing;* valli, Liv. ; 2, *an effort, laborious undertaking, preparation;* rerum, Cic.

mōlītor -ōris, m. (molior), *a builder, erector, producer, contriver, author;* mundi, Cic.

mollesco, 3. (mollio), 1, *to become soft,* Ov. ; 2, transf., *to become soft, effeminate;* tum genus humanum primum mollescere coepit, Lucr.

mollĭcellus -a -um (dim. of mollis), *somewhat soft, somewhat tender,* Cat.

mollĭcŭlus -a -um (dim. of mollis), 1, *somewhat soft* or *tender,* Plaut. ; 2, transf., *somewhat effeminate,* Cat.

mollĭo, 4. (mollis), *to make pliable, flexible, soft, supple.* **I. A.** Lit., lanam trahendo, *to spin,* Ov. ; artus oleo, Liv. ; ceram pollice, Ov. ; cibum vapore, Lucr. ; frigoribus durescit humor, et idem mollitur tepefactus, Cic. ; glebas, *to loosen, soften,* Ov. **B.** Transf., 1, clivum anfractibus modicis, *to diminish the steepness of the ascent,* Caes. ; 2, fructus feros colendo, *to render less harsh,* Verg. **II.** Fig., **A.** lacrimae meorum me interdum molliunt, Cic. **B.** 1, *to soften, to make milder, make gentle;* poetae molliunt animos nostros, Cic. ; feroces militum animos, Sall. ; vocem, *make womanish,* Cic.; ferro mollita juventus, *emasculated, castrated,* Lucr. ; 2, a, *to make milder, less disagreeable, render bearable;* verba usu, Cic.; poenam, Ov. ; b, *to tame, restrain, keep within bounds;* Hannibalem exsultantem patientiā suā molliebat, Cic. ; sedare motus et animos eorum mollire, Cic. (syncop. imperf., mollibat, Ov.).

mollĭpes -pēdis (mollis and pes), *soft-footed,* i.e., *having a trailing walk* (Gr. εἰλίπους), Cic.

mollis -e (= movilis, from moveo), *soft, tender, pliant, supple, flexible, yielding.* **I. A.** 1, lit., juncus, acanthus, Verg. ; crura, colla, Verg. ; brachia, Ov. ; arcus, unstrung, Ov. ; zephyri, gentle, Ov. ; 2, transf., a, of works of art, *soft, not stiff, graceful;* signa, Cic. ; of orators and poetry, oratio mollis et tenera, Cic. ; b, of places, *with a gentle ascent;* fastigium, Caes. **B.** *soft to the touch;* 1, lit., cervix, manus, Ov. ; of the ground, mollis humus, Ov.; 2, transf., mild; aestas, Verg. ; vina, Verg. **II.** Fig. **A.** *gentle, sensitive, tender;* 1, mollis animus ad accipiendam et ad deponendam offensionem, Cic. ; homo mollissimo animo, Cic. ; 2, *effeminate, unmanly, weak;* philosophus, Cic. ; disciplina, Cic. ; vita, Ov. **B.** *gentle, mild, pleasant;* Cic. ; 2, a, *compassionate, gentle, mild, complaisant, easy;* oratio, Cic. ; jussa, Verg. ; b, *tender, moving;* verbis mollibus lenire aliquem, Hor. ; illud mollissimum carmen, Cic.

mollĭtĕr, adv. (mollis), 1, *softly, easily, gently;* quis membra movere mollius possit.

Hor. ; excudent spirantia mollius aera, *with more grace* or *skill*, Verg. ; **2**, fig., a, *gently, easily ;* quod ferendum est molliter sapienti, Cic. ; 'n a bad sense, *weakly, without energy ;* nimis molliter aegritudinem pati, Sall. ; b, *effeminately ;* delicate et molliter vivere, Cic. ; c, *mildly, compassionately ;* feci parce et molliter, Cic.

mollĭtĭa -ae, f. and **mollĭtĭes** -ēi, f. (mollis). **I.** Lit., *softness, tenderness, flexibility, pliancy ;* cervicum, Cic. **II.** Fig., **A.** Gen., *tenderness, gentleness, mildness, sensibility ;* animi, Cic. ; naturae, Cic. **B.** Esp., *effeminacy, weakness;* civitatum mores lapsi ad mollitiam, Cic.

mollĭtūdo -ĭnis, f. (mollis). **I.** *softness, pliability, flexibility ;* assimilis spongiis mollitudo, Cic. **II.** Fig., *tenderness, softness, sensitiveness ;* humanitatis, Cic.

mŏlo -ŭi -ĭtum, 3. (mola), *to grind in a mill.* Partic., **mŏlĭtus** -a -um, *ground ;* cibaria molita, *meal*, Caes.

Mŏlorchus -i, m. (Μόλορχος), *a poor vinedresser near Nemea, who hospitably received Hercules when about to slay the Nemean lion ;* Molorchi luci, poet. = *the Nemean woods*, Verg.

Mŏlossi -ōrum, m. (Μολοσσοί), *the inhabitants of Mɔlossia, a district of Eastern Epirus.* Hence, adj., a, **Mŏlossus** -a -um, *Molossian ;* canis, Hor. ; subst., **Mŏlossus** -i, m. *a Molossian hound, in great request as a sporting dog,* Hor. ; b, **Mŏlossĭcus** -a -um, *Molossian.*

mŏly -ўos, n. (μῶλυ), *the herb moly, given by Mercury to Ulysses as a counter charm against the enchantments of Circe*, Ov.

mōmen -ĭnis, n. (= movimen, from moveo), **1**, *movement, motion ;* e salso consurgere momine ponti, Lucr. ; **2**, *momentum, impulse*, Lucr.

mōmentum -i, n. (= movimentum, from moveo). **I.** *movement, motion.* **A. 1**, lit., astra formā ipsā figurāque suā momenta sustentant, Cic. ; **2**, of time, *a small portion of time, minute, moment ;* parvo momento, Caes. ; momento temporis, Liv. ; momento horae, *in the short space of an hour*, Liv. ; or simply momento, Liv. **B.** Fig., **1**, *oscillation ;* sine momento rerum, Lucr. ; **2**, *change, alteration ;* momentum facere annonae, Liv. **II.** *that which puts in motion, impulse.* **A.** Lit., ut (arbores) levi momento impulsae occiderent, Liv. **B.** Fig., **1**, *influence, cause ;* parva momenta in spem metumque animum impellere, Liv. ; **2**, *turning-point, influencing cause ;* a, parvo momento si adjuvassent, *with slight help*, Liv. ; b, *weight, importance, influence ;* si quid habeat momenti commendatio mea, Cic. ; esse maximi momenti et ponderis, Cic. ; argumentorum momenta, *decisive proofs*, Cic. ; juvenis egregius maximum momentum rerum eius civitatis, *a man of commanding influence*, Liv.

Mōna -ae, f. *an island off the coast of Britain* (*Anglesea* or *the Isle of Man*).

Mŏnaesēs -is, m. (Μοναίσης), *a general of the Parthians, who defeated the Romans.*

mŏnēdŭla -ae, f. *a daw, jackdaw*, Cic.

mŏnĕo -ŭi -ĭtum, 2. (from root MEN, whence mens), *to remind, admonish.* **I.** Terentiam de ʒestamento, Cic. **II. A.** Lit., **1**, a, *to warn, teach, admonish ;* with de and the abl., aliquem de retinenda Sestii gratia, Cic. ; with acc. of person and neut. acc., id ipsum quod me mones, Cic. ; with acc. and infin., magis idoneum tempus te esse ullum umquam reperturum, Cic. ; with rel. sent., monet quo statu sit res, Liv. ; b, *to advise, recommend ;* with ut and the subj., ut magnam infamiam fugiat, Cic. ; with subj. alone, eos hoc moneo desinant furere, Cic. ; with ne and the subj., ne id faceret. Cic. ; with infin.,

officium conservare, Cic. ; **2**, *to instruct, prompt, suggest ;* tu vatem, tu, diva, mone, Verg. ; de aliqua re, Cic. **B. 1**, *to admonish by punishment,* Tac. ; **2**, *to urge on ;* canes, Prop.

mŏnēris -is, f. (μονήρης), *a vessel having only one bank of oars*, Liv.

Mŏnēta -ae, f. (moneo). **I. A.** *the mother of the Muses* (= Μνημοσύνη). **B.** *a surname of Juno,* and, as the Roman money was coined in the temple of Juno Moneta, hence, **II. A.** *the mint, the place where money was coined*, Cic. **B.** Meton., **1**, *coined metal, money*, Ov. ; **2**, *the die* or *stamp with which money was coined*, Mart. ; transf., communi feriat carmen triviale moneta, Juv.

mŏnētālis -is, m. (moneta), *relating to the mint ;* in jest, *one who asks for money*, Cic.

mŏnīle -is, n. *a necklace, a collar*, Cic.

mŏnĭmentum = monumentum (q.v.).

mŏnĭta -ōrum, n. (moneo), **1**, *warning*, Cic., **2**, *prophecies ;* deorum, Cic.

mŏnĭtĭo -ōnis, f. (moneo), *a reminding, warning, admonishing, admonition*, Cic.

mŏnĭtor -ōris, m. (moneo). **I.** *one who reminds.* **A.** officii, Sall. **B.** a, *one who supplies an orator with facts, an assistant, prompter,* Cic. ; b, *a nomenclator, who reminds one of persons' names*, Cic. **II.** *an adviser, instructor ;* fatuus, Cic.

mŏnĭtus -ūs, m. (moneo), **1**, *a reminding, warning, admonition*, Ov. ; **2**, *an intimation of the will of the gods by oracles, augury, portents, omens*, etc.; monitus Fortunae, Cic.

Mŏnoecus -i, m. (Μόνοικος, *he that dwells alone*), *surname of Hercules ;* Monoeci Arx et Portus, *promontory and harbour on the coast of Liguria*, now *Monaco.*

mŏnogrammos -on (μονόγραμμος), *of pictures, consisting only of outlines, sketched ;* Epicurus monogrammos deos et nihil agentes commentus est, *incorporeal, shadowy*, Cic.

mŏnŏpŏdĭum -ĭi, n. (μονοπόδιον), *a table with one foot*, Liv.

mŏnŏpōlĭum -ĭi, n.(μονοπώλιον), *a monopoly, sole right of sale*, Suet.

mons, montis, m. *a mountain.* **I. A.** Lit., mons impendens, Cic. ; prov. of large promises followed by small performance, parturiunt montes, nascetur ridiculus mus, Hor. **B.** Meton., *a rock ;* improbus, Verg. **II.** Transf., *a large mass, great quantity ;* mons aquarum, Verg. ; maria montesque polliceri, *to make large promises*, Sall.

monstrātor -ōris, m. (monstro), *a discoverer, teacher ;* aratri, Triptolemus, Verg.

monstrĭfĕr -fĕra -fĕrum (monstrum and fero), *producing monsters, horrible, monstrous,* Plin.

monstro, 1. (= monestro, from moneo), *to show, point out.* **I.** By signs or gestures, digito indice ad hoc, Hor. ; proceram palmam Deli monstrant, Cic. **II.** By words, **A.** *to show, point out, teach, inform ;* tu istic si quid librarii mea manu non intelligent monstrabis, Cic. **B. 1**, *to ordain, institute, appoint ;* piacula, Verg. ; **2**, *to inform against, denounce ;* alii ab amicis monstrabantur, Tac. ; **3**, *to advise, urge ;* conferre manum pudor iraque monstrat, Verg.

monstrum -i, n. (= monestrum, from moneo). **I.** *a supernatural event, a prodigy, portent*, Cic. **II.** *a monster, monstrosity ;* a, of persons, monstrum horrendum, Polyphemus, Verg. ; inmanissimum ac foedissimum monstrum, Clodius, Cic. ; b, of things, non mihi jam furtum, sed monstrum ac prodigium **vide**

batur, Cic.; esp., *wonders* or *marvels;* monstra 'auntiare, Cic.

monstrŭōsē, adv. (monstruosus), *strangely, wonderfully, monstrously,* Cic.

monstrŭōsus -a -um (monstrum), *strange, singular, wonderful, monstrous;* monstruosissima bestia, Cic.

montānus -a -um (mons). **I.** *of or relating to a mountain, dwelling on mountains, found on mountains;* loca montana et aspera, Liv.; Ligures, Liv.; subst., a, **montānus** -i, m. *a mountaineer,* Caes.; b, **montāna** -ōrum, n. *mountainous districts,* Liv. **II.** *rich in mountains, mountainous;* Dalmatia, Ov.

montĭcŏla -ae, c. (mons and colo), *a dweller among the mountains, mountaineer,* Ov.

montīvăgus -a -um (mons and vagus), *wandering over the mountains;* cursus, Cic.

montŭōsus -a -um (mons), *mountainous, full of mountains;* regio aspera et montuosa, Cic.; subst., **montŭōsa** -ōrum, n. *mountainous districts,* Plin.

mŏnŭmentum (mŏnĭmentum) -i, n. (moneo), *that which is intended to preserve the recollection of anything; a memorial, monument.* **I.** Lit., monumenti causā, Cic.; esp., a, *a building, statue, temple, gallery,* etc.; monumenta Africani, *statues,* Cic.; b, *a sepulchre,* Cic.; c, *written memorials, annals, memoirs;* monumenta rerum gestarum, Cic.; *commendare aliquid monumentis,* Cic. **II.** Transf., laudis, clementiae, furtorum, Cic.

Mopsĭi -ōrum, m. *a noble family in Compsa.* Hence, **Mopsĭāni** -ōrum, m. *the dependants of the Mopsii.*

Mopsŏpĭus -a -um (from Μοψοπία, *an ancient name of Attica*), *Attic, Athenian;* juvenis, *Triptolemus,* Ov.; muri, urbs, *Athens,* Ov.

Mopsuhestĭa (Mobsuëstĭa) -ae, f. *a town in Cilicia.*

Mopsus -i, m. (Μόψος). **I.** *the seer of the Argonauts.* **II.** *son of Apollo and Manto.* **III.** *name of a shepherd in Vergil.*

1. **mŏra** -ae, f. **I.** *delay.* **A.** Gen., moram alicui rei inferre, afferre, Cic.; creditoribus facere, *to put off the day of payment,* Cic.; trahere, Verg.; res habet (*suffers*) moram, Cic.; non (or nulla) mora est with quin or quominus and the subj., Cic.; sine mora, *without delay,* Cic. **B.** 1, *pause on a march,* Liv.; 2, *a pause in discourse,* Cic. **II.** Transf., 1, *space of time,* Ov.; 2, *a hindrance,* Liv.

2. **mŏra** -ae, f. (μόρα), *a division of the Spartan army, of* 400, 500, 700, *or* 900 *men,* Nep.

mōrālis -e (mores), *moral, ethical;* philosophiae pars, Cic.

mŏrātor -ōris, m. (moror). **I.** *a loiterer or lagger oehind,* Liv. **II.** *a delayer, retarder.* **A.** Gen., publici commodi, Liv. **B.** *an advocate who talked against time,* Cic.

1. **mŏrātus**, partic. of moror.

2. **mōrātus** -a -um (mores). **I.** *having certain manners or morals;* bene, melius, optime moratus, Cic. **II.** *adapted to manners or character, characteristic;* poema, Cic.; recte morata fabula, *in which the characters are correctly drawn,* Hor.

morbĭdus -a -um (morbus), 1, *sickly, diseased, morbid,* Plin.; 2, *unwholesome, causing disease,* Lucr.

morbōsus -a -um (morbus), *sickly, diseased, worn out,* Cat.

morbus -i, m. *disease, sickness.* **I.** Physical; a, *mortifer,* Cic.; in morbo esse, *to be sick,*

Cic.; **morbo laborare, opprimi, Cic.; conflictari,** Nep.; morbus ingravescit, *grows worse, increases in violence,* Cic.; ex morbo convalescere, *to get well,* Cic.; morbum simulare, Cic.; b, *personif.,* as a goddess, Verg. **II.** Of mental diseases, animi morbi sunt cupiditates immensae et inanes divitiarum gloriae, Cic.

mordācĭtĕr, adv. (mordax), *bitingly, sharply;* limā mordacius uti, Ov.

mordax -ācis (mordeo), *biting, given to biting, snappish.* **I. A.** Lit., canis, Plaut. **B.** Fig., a, *biting, satirical;* Cynicus, Hor.; carmen, Ov.; b, *wearing, corroding;* sollicitudines, "*eating cares,*" Hor. **II.** a, *stinging;* urtica, Ov.; b, *sharp;* ferrum, Hor.; c, *pungent, biting in taste;* fel, Ov.

mordĕo, mŏmordi, morsum, 2. *to bite.* **I. A.** Lit., 1, canes mordent, Cic.; 2, *to bite, eat;* pabula dente, Ov. **B.** Transf., *to bite. sting, hurt, pain;* aliquem dictis, Ov.; conscientiā mordeor, Cic.; valde me momorderunt epistolae tuae, Cic. **II.** *to bite into, cut into, take fast hold of;* a, fibula mordet vestem, Ov.; b, *of rivers, to indent, wear away;* rura quae Liris quietā mordet aquā, Hor.; c, *to nip, bite, sting;* matutina parum cautos jam frigora mordent, Hor.

mordĭcĭtus = mordicus (q.v.).

mordĭcus, adv. (mordeo). **I.** Lit., *with the teeth, by biting;* auferre mordicus auriculam, Cic. **II.** Transf., tenere aliquid mordicus, *to keep fast hold of;* perspicuitatem, Cic.

mŏrētum -i, n. *a rustic salad made of garlic, parsley, vinegar, oil,* etc., Ov.

mŏrĭbundus -a -um (morior). **I.** Middle, 1, *dying, expiring;* jacentem moribundumque vidisti, Cic.; 2, *subject to death, mortal;* membra, Verg. **II.** Act., *causing death, deadly,* Cat.

mŏrĭgĕror, 1. dep. (mos and gero), *to accommodate oneself to, comply with, gratify, subserve;* voluptati aurium morigerari debet oratio, Cic.

mŏrĭgĕrus -a -um (mos and gero), *compliant, obedient, accommodating, obsequious,* Lucr.

Mŏrīni -ōrum, m. *a people in Gallia Belgica.*

mŏrĭor, mortŭus sum, mŏrĭtūrus, 3. dep. *to die.* **I.** Lit., ex vulnere, Liv.; ferro, Liv.; hoc morbo, Cic.; fame, Cic.; frigore, Hor.; in suo lectulo, Cic.; voces morientes, *of a dying man,* Cic.; moriar si, *may I die if,* Cic. **II.** Transf. **A.** *to perish with love,* Ov. **B.** Of things and abstr. subjects, *to die away, wither away, decay;* a, segetes moriuntur in herbis, Ov.; b, of fire, *to be extinguished;* flammas et vidi nullo concutiente mori, Ov.; of parts of the body, *to lose strength;* at hi (lacerti) mortui jam sunt, Cic.; c, *of abstractions, to come to an end, perish;* suavissimi hominis memoria moritur, Cic.; p. adj., **mortŭus** -a -um, *dead;* subst., **mor tŭus** -i, m. *a dead man,* Cic.

mormyr -yris, f. (μορμύρος), *a sea-fish,* Ov

mōrŏlŏgus -a -um (μωρολόγος), *talking like a fool, foolish;* subst., *a fool,* Plaut.

1. **mŏror,** 1. dep. (mora), *to linger, loiter, tarry, delay.* **I. A.** Lucceius narravit Brutum valde morari, Cic.; with infin., alicui bellum inferre, Cic.; nihil moror, foll. by quominus and subj., Liv. **B.** *to stay, tarry in a place;* Brundisii, Cic.; in provincia, Cic. **II.** 1, *to cause delay to another, to delay, retard, keep back, detain, hinder;* impetum sustinere atque morari, Caes.; aliquem ab itinere, Liv.; 2, a, esp. of the judge in acquitting and dismissing a person, C. Sempronium nihil moror, Liv.; b, as a formula, in breaking off a discourse; ne te morer, Hor.; c, nihil morari, (a) *to care nothing for;* nec

dona moror, Verg.; (β) *to have nothing to say against;* nihil moror, eos salvos esse, ap. Cic.; 3, *to detain the attention of, fetter;* novitate morandus spectator, Hor.

2. **mōror**, 1. dep. (μωρός), *to be foolish, to be a fool,* Suet.

mōrōsē, adv. (morosus), *peevishly, captiously,* Cic.

mōrōsĭtas -ātis, f. (morosus), *peevishness, fretfulness, moroseness,* Cic.; *pedantry, excessive fastidiousness in style,* Suet.

mōrōsus -a -um (mos), *peevish, morose, capricious, captious, fretful;* senes, Cic.; canities, Hor.; morbus, *obstinate,* Ov.

Morpheus -ĕos, m. (Μορφεύς), *god of dreams.*

mors, mortis, f. (root MOR, whence morior, connected with βροτός, μαραίνω), *death.* **I. A.** Lit., omnium rerum mors est extremum, Cic.; mortem sibi consciscere, *to commit suicide,* Cic.; mortem alicui inferre, *to slay, kill,* Cic.; alicui morti esse, *cause a person's death,* Cic.; aliquem ex media morte eripere, Cic.; plur., mortes, *kinds of death;* clarae mortes pro patria oppetitae, Cic. **B.** Personified as a goddess, *daughter of Erebus and Nox.* **II.** Meton., 1, *a corpse,* Plin.; 2, *life-blood;* ensem multā morte recepit, Verg.; 3, *one who brings death or destruction;* mors terrorque sociorum lictor Sextius, Cic.

morsus -ūs, m. (mordeo), *a bite, biting.* **I. A.** Lit., 1, serpentis, Cic.; morsu dividere escas, Cic.; 2, *eating;* mensarum, Verg. **B.** Transf., 1, *a seizing, laying hold of,* like the bite of an anchor, Verg.; and meton., *that which seizes,* morsus uncus, *the fluke of an anchor,* Verg.; roboris, *the cleft of a tree holding fast a javelin,* Verg.; 2, *a biting taste, pungency,* Mart. **II.** Fig., 1, *a carping or malicious attack with words,* Hor.; 2, *mental pain, vexation;* curarum, Ov.; doloris, Cic.

mortālis -e (mors), *subject to death, mortal.* **I.** Lit., 1, omne animal esse mortale, Cic. Subst., a, **mortālis** -is, m. *a mortal man, a man;* and esp., plur., *mortals, men,* Cic.; b, **mortāle** -is, n. *that which is mortal or perishable,* Cic.; 2, transf., *transitory, temporary, passing away;* leges, inimicitiae, Cic. **II.** Transf., *relating or belonging to mortal men, mortal, human, earthly;* conditio vitae, Cic. Subst., **mortālĭa** -ium, n. *mortal things, mortal affairs,* and esp., *human sufferings;* et mentem mortalia tangunt, Verg.

mortālĭtas -ātis, f. (mortalis). **I.** *the being subject to death,* Cic. **II.** *human nature, the nature of man regarded as mortal;* mortalitatem explere, *to die,* Tac.

mortārĭum -ĭi, n. *a mortar,* Plin.

mortĭcīnus -a -um (mors), *dead,* Plin.

mortĭfer -fĕra -fĕrum (mors and fero), *causing death, fatal, deadly, mortal;* vulnus, morbus, Cic.

mortŭālĭa -ĭum, n.(mortuus), *funeral songs, dirges,* Plaut.

mortŭus -a -um, partic. of morior (q.v.).

mōrum -i, n. (μῶρον, μόρον), 1, *a mulberry,* Verg.; 2, *a blackberry,* Ov.

1. **mōrus** -i, f. *a mulberry-tree,* Ov.

2. **mōrus** -a -um (μωρός), *silly, foolish,* Plaut.

mos, mōris, m. *the will of a person.* **I.** *self-will, caprice;* morem alicui gerere, *to comply with a person's wishes,* Cic. **II. A.** Lit., *custom;* 1, a, *custom, usage, wont;* de more suo decedere, Cic.; esse in more majorum, *traditional line of conduct,* Cic.; mos est with genit. gerund, mos est ita rogandi, Cic.; with infin., magorum mos est non humare corpora, Cic.; with acc. and infin.. mos est Athenis laudari in contione eos,

etc., Cic.; mos est or moris est with ut and the subj., mos est hominum ut nolint eundem pluribus rebus excellere, Cic.; eum morem tenere, *to observe,* Cic.; abl. as adv., more majorum, *after the way of the ancestors,* Cic.; meo, tuo, suo more, Cic.; b, *fashion, mode;* quoniam ita se mores habent, Sall.; 2, gen. plur., *manners, character, disposition, morals;* suavissimi, justi, feri, Cic.; totam vitam, naturam, moresque alicuius cognoscere, Cic.; describere hominum sermones moresque, Cic. **B.** Transf., 1, *quality, nature, manner, use and wont;* siderum, Verg.; more, ad morem or in morem, *after the fashion of,* foll. by genit., Cic.; 2, *rule, law;* mores viris ponere, Verg.; sine more, *without rule or control,* Verg.; quid ferri duritiā pugnacius? sed cedit et patitur mores, Plin.

Mōsa -ae, f. *a river in Gallia Belgica, now the Meuse.*

Moschus -i, m. (Μόσχος), *a rhetorician of Pergamus, accused of poisoning.*

Mōsella -ae, f. *a river in Gallia Belgica, now the Moselle.*

Mostēni -ōrum, m. *the inhabitants of the Lydian town Mostena or -en.*

mōtĭo -ōnis, f. (moveo). **I.** *movement, motion;* corporum, Cic. **II.** Transf., *emotion, feeling;* motiones animi, Cic.

mōto, 1. (intens. of moveo), *to move up and down, move frequently;* lacertos, Ov.; zephyris motantibus, Verg.

1. **mōtus** -a -um, partic. of moveo.

2. **mōtus** -ūs, m. (moveo). **I.** *a motion, movement.* **A.** Lit., a, natura omnia ciens motibus suis, Cic.; b, terrae, *an earthquake,* Cic.; c, *motion of the body, movement, gesture;* esp. of an orator, manuum motus teneant illud decorum, Cic.; ex motus mei mediocritate, Cic.; *the gestures of actors or pantomimic dancers;* haud indecoros motus more Tusco dare, Liv.; dare motus Cereri, *to lead dances,* Verg. **B.** Transf., 1, *motion of the mind;* a, of the senses, dulcem motum afferent, Cic.; b, of the mind, *activity;* motus animorum duplices sunt, alteri cogitationis, alteri appetitūs, Cic.; esp., (a) *movement of the passions;* motus animi nimii, Cic.; (β) *motion of the will, impulse;* sine motu animi et cogitatione, Cic.; 2, *political movement, insurrection, riot, commotion;* omnes Catilinae motus prohibere, Cic.; motum afferre reipublicae, Cic. **II.** *revolution in a state,* Cic.

mŏvĕo, mōvi, mōtum, 2. (connected with mutare, ἀμείβειν, etc.). **I.** *to move, set in motion, stir.* **A.** Lit., a, caelum, Cic.; reflex., terra movet, Liv.; b, *to move the body;* se movere and moveri, *to dance,* Cic.; c, milit. t. t., movere arma, *to take up arms;* adversus aliquem, Liv. **B.** Transf., 1, *to produce a bad effect on the body, to attack, affect;* intoleranda vis aestus corpora movit, Liv.; 2, *to move mentally;* a, se ad motum fortunae, Caes.; b, (a) *to influence, work upon, affect;* pulchritudo corporis movet oculos, Cic.; moveri aliquā re, *to be disturbed, made anxious by,* Verg.; (β) *to move compassion, move, affect;* Roscii morte moveri, Cic.; (γ) *to work upon, induce;* with ut and the subj., Cic.; 3, politically, *to cause a commotion, arouse, excite;* omnia, Sall.; 4, *to change, shake, shatter;* alicuius sententiam, Cic.; fidem, Ov. **II.** *to move from a place.* **A.** a, limum e gurgite, Ov.; b, *to cause, produce, excite;* risum, Cic.; misericordiam, Cic.; c, *to bring to notice, bring before;* historias, Hor.; d, *to begin;* bellum, Cic. **B.** *to remove, put out of its place;* a, fundamenta loco, Cic.; se de Cumano, Cic.; b, milit. t. t., movere signa, castra, or simply movere or moveri, *to march away, move from a place;* castra ex eo loco,

Caes.; c, *to dispossess; aliquem* ex agro, Cic.; **d,** *to cause to move from one's position, dislodge;* hostem statu, Liv.; **e,** *to expel;* aliquem de senatu, Cic.; **f,** *to make a person change his opinion;* aliquem de sententia, Liv.

mox, adv. (moveo). **I.** Of *future time, soon, presently;* jussit mihi nunciari mox se venturum, Cic. **II.** *then, thereupon;* mox rediit Cremonam reliquus populus, Tac.; mox . . . postremo, Liv.

Mōȳsēs -is or -i, m. *Moses.*

mūcĭdus -a -um (mucus), *mouldy, musty,* Juv.

Mūcĭus -a -um, *name of a Roman gens, the most celebrated members of which were:* 1, C. Mucius Cordus (Scaevola), *a Roman who came to Porsena's camp to kill him, and being detected, thrust his right hand into the fire, and received the name of Scaevola (left-handed);* 2, P. Mucius Scaevola, *friend of the Gracchi, enemy of the younger Scipio Africanus;* 3, Qu. Mucius Scaevola, *augur, husband of Laelia;* 4, Qu. Mucius Scaevola, *jurist and statesman, Pontifex Maximus, whose administration of the province of Asia was so upright that the Asiatics celebrated a festival in honour of him, called Mucia;* 5, Mucia, *the wife of Cn. Pompeius.* Adj., *Mucian;* subst., **Mūcĭa** -ōrum, n. *the festival instituted in honour of Mucius Scaevola* (IV). Hence, adj., **Mūcĭānus** -a -um, *relating to Mucius;* exitus, *death of Qu. Mucius Scaevola* (IV), murdered by Damasippus in the temple of Vesta.

mūcro -ōnis, m. *a sharp point or edge.* **A.** Lit., a, cultri, Juv.; b, esp., *a sword's point or edge;* transf., *the sword;* mucrones militum tremere, Cic. **B.** Transf., *sharpness, point;* tribunicius, Cic.; defensionis tuae, Cic.

mūcus -i, m. (mungo), *the mucous matter of the nose,* Cat.

mūgil (mūgĭlis) -is, m. (μύξος), *a fish,* perhaps *the mullet,* Plin.

mūgĭnor, 1. dep. (mugio), *to loiter, trifle away time, dally;* dum tu muginaris, Cic.

mūgĭo -īvi and -ĭi -ītum, 4. (from sound mu, whence μυκάω), *to bellow as an ox, low.* **I.** Lit., of cattle, Liv.; subst., mugientes = *oxen,* Hor. **II.** Transf., *to roar, bray, rumble, groan;* mugit tubae clangor,Verg.; sub pedibus mugire solum, Verg.; si mugiat Africis malus procellis, Hor.

mūgītus -ūs, m. (mugio). **I.** *the lowing, bellowing of cattle;* boum, Verg. **II.** Transf., *a rumbling, groaning, creaking;* terrae, Cic.

mūla -ae, f. (mulus), *a female mule,* Cic.

mulcĕo, mulsi, mulsum, 2. *to stroke.* **I. A.** Lit., manu mulcens barbam, Ov. **B.** Transf., *to touch lightly;* virgā capillos, Ov. **II.** Fig., 1, *to charm, delight, enchant;* aliquem fistulā, Hor.; 2, *to soothe, appease;* tigres, Verg.; et ipso mulcente et increpante Marcio, Liv.; aliquem dictis, Ov.; fluctus, iras, Verg.; vulnera, *to allay pain,* Ov.

Mulcĭbĕr -ĕris and -ĕri, m. (mulceo, lit., *the melter*), 1, *a surname of Vulcan,* Cic., Ov.; 2, meton., *fire,* Ov. (genit. syncop., Mulcibri).

mulco, 1. (MULC, whence also mulc-eo, mulg-eo), *to thrash, maltreat, cudgel, handle roughly;* male mulcati clavis ac fustibus repelluntur, Cic.

mulcta, mulcto, = multa, multo (q.v.).

mulctra -ae, f. (mulgeo), *a milk-pail,* Verg.

mulctrārĭum -ĭi, n. (mulgeo), *a milk-pail,* Hor.

mulctrum -i, n. (mulgeo), *a milk-pail,* Hor.

mulgĕo, mulsi, mulctum, 2. (root MULC, whence also mulceo), *to milk,* Verg.; prov.,

mulgere hircos, *of an impossible undertaking,* Verg.

mŭlĭēbris -e (mulier). **I.** *of or relating to a woman, womanly, feminine;* vox, Cic.; vestis, Nep.; bellum, Cic.; certamen, *on account of a woman,* Liv.; Fortuna Muliebris, *revered in memory of the women who had appeased the anger of Coriolanus,* Liv. **II.** Transf., *womanish, effeminate, unmanly;* sententia, Cic.

mŭlĭēbrĭtĕr, adv. (muliebris), *after the manner of a woman, effeminately, womanishly;* se lamentis muliebriter lacrimisque dedere, Cic.

mŭlĭer -ēris, f. **I.** *a woman,* Cic. **II.** *a wife, matron;* virgo aut mulier, Cic.; cras mulier erit, Cic.

mŭlĭĕrārĭus -a -um (mulier), *womanish;* manus, *a troop of soldiers sent by a woman,* Cic.

mŭlĭercŭla -ae, f. (dim. of mulier), *a little woman,* used contemptuously, suas secum mulierculas in castra ducere, Cic.

mŭlĭĕrōsĭtas -ātis, f. (mulierosus), *excessive love of women,* Cic.

mŭlĭĕrōsus -a -um (mulier), *fond of women,* Cic.

mūlīnus -a -um (mulus), *of or relating to a mule,* Juv.

mūlĭo -ōnis, m. (mulus), *a mule-keeper, mule-driver, muleteer, one who lets mules to hire,* Cic.

mūlĭōnĭus -a -um and (later) **mūlĭōnĭcus** -a -um (mulio), *of or relating to a muleteer,* Cic.

mullus -i, m. *the red mullet,* Cic.

mulsus -a -um (mel), 1, *mixed with honey, sweetened with honey,* Plin.; subst., **mulsum** -i, n. *wine sweetened with honey;* calix mulsi, Cic.; 2, transf., *as sweet as honey;* dicta mulsa, *sweet words,* Plaut.

multa (mulcta) -ae, f. *a punishment consisting in loss of property* (originally a fine in cattle); usually *a money-fine, fine, mulct;* multam dicere, *to fix a fine,* Cic.; multam petere, irrogare, *to propose that an accused person should be fined to a certain amount,* Cic.; multam certare, *to discuss on both sides the amount of a fine,* Cic.; aliquem multā multare, *to punish by a fine,* Cic.; multam committere, *to incur a fine,* Cic.

multangŭlus -a -um (multus and angulus), *many-cornered, multangular,* Lucr.

multātĭcĭus -a -um (multa), *belonging or relating to a fine;* pecunia, Liv.

multātĭo -ōnis, f. (1. multo), *a penalty, fine, mulct;* bonorum, Cic.

multēsĭmus -a -um (multus), *very small;* pars, Lucr.

multĭcāvus -a -um (multus and cavus), *having many holes, porous;* pumex, Ov.

multĭcĭa -ōrum, n. (multus and ico), *soft, finely-woven garments,* Juv.

multĭfārĭam,adv.(multifarius from multus), *on many sides, in many places,* Cic.

multĭfĭdus -a -um (multus and findo), *cloven into many parts;* faces, Ov.; transf., Ister, *having many branches,* Mart.

multĭformis -e (multus and forma), *having many shapes, multiform, manifold, of many kinds;* qualitates, Cic.

multĭfŏrus -a -um (multus and foris), *having many openings, pierced with many holes;* multifori tibia buxi, Ov.

multĭgĕnĕris -e (multus and genus), *of many kinds, of many sorts,* Plaut.

multĭgĕnus -a -um = multigeneris (q.v.).

multĭjŭgus -a -um and **multĭjŭgis** -e (multus and jugum), *many-yoked, yoked many* *together.* **I.** Lit., equi, Liv. **II.** Transf., *manifold, of many sorts;* literae, Cic.

multĭmŏdis, adv. (for multis modis), *in many ways, variously,* Lucr.

multĭmŏdus -a -um (multus and modus), *various, manifold,* Liv. (?)

multĭplex -plĭcis (multus and plex, from plico), *having many folds.* **I.** Lit., a, alvus est multiplex et tortuosa, Cic.; b, *with many winds and turnings;* vitis serpens multiplici lapsu, Cic.; c, *with many layers;* lorica, Verg.; d, *having many parts;* corona, Cic.; e, *manifold, many, numerous;* multiplices fetus, *numerous offspring,* Cic.; f, *many times as large;* multiplex quam pro numero damnum est, Liv. **II.** Transf., **A.** Of things, *of many different kinds, many-sided, manifold;* multiplex ratio disputandi, Cic. **B.** Of persons, *many-sided;* varius et multiplex et copiosus, Cic.; multiplices naturae, Cic.; ingenium, *versatile, changeable,* Cic.

multĭplĭcābĭlis -e (multiplico), *having many folds,* Cic.

multĭplĭco, 1. (multiplex), *to increase many times, multiply;* aes alienum, Caes.; flumina collectis multiplicantur aquis, Ov.; domus multiplicata, *enlarged,* Cic.

multĭtūdo -ĭnis, f. (multus), *a large number, multitude.* **I.** Gen., litterarum, Cic. **II.** Esp., of men; **1,** *a large number of men, crowd, multitude;* tanta multitudo lapides ac tela jaciebat, Caes.; **2,** in a contemptuous sense, *the common people, mob, multitude;* famā et multitudinis judicio moveri, Cic.

multĭvŏlus -a -um (multus and volo), *having many wishes or desires,* Cat.

1. multo (mulcto), 1. (multa), *to punish;* aliquem morte, Cic.; exsilio, Liv.; vitia hominum damnis, ignominiis, vinculis, Cic.; aliquem pecuniā, *to punish with a fine,* Nep.; Veneri esse multatum, *punished with a fine paid to Venus,* Cic.

2. **multo,** multum, used adv., v. multus.

multus -a -um; comp., **plūs,** plūris; superl., **plūrĭmus** -a -um, *much.* **I.** Lit., **A.** Of number, *many, numerous;* multis verbis, Cic.; viri, Cic.; multi, *many persons,* Cic.; minime multi, *exceedingly few,* Cic.; quam minime multa vestigia, *as few as possible,* Nep.; multis verbis, *diffusely, copiously,* Cic.; elliptically, ne multa, ne multis, *briefly, in brief,* Cic.; multi (= οἱ πολλοί), *the many, the multitude, the common herd;* unus de multis, Cic.; orator e multis, Cic.; compar., plures, genit. plurium, *several, more than one,* Cic.; quid plura? *in short,* Cic.; pluribus verbis rogare, Cic.; superl., plurimi, *very many, the most;* plurimis verbis, Cic.; mons, *very large,* Verg.; Aetna, *the greatest part of,* Ov. **B.** Of strength or fulness, *much, great, strong, considerable;* **1,** multo labore, Cic.; superl., plurimus sol, *very hot,* Ov.; 2, of time, ad multum diem, *till late in the day,* Cic.; multā nocte, *late at night,* Cic.; multo mane, *very early,* Cic. **C.** Of space, *great;* multa pars Europae, Liv. **II.** Transf., **A.** Of discourse, *copious, diffuse, prolix;* ne in re nota multus et insolens sim, Cic. **B.** Of an action, *busy, vigorous, zealous;* in eodem genere causarum multus erat T. Juventius, Cic. **C.** *obtrusive, troublesome;* qui in aliquo genere aut inconcinnus aut multus est, Cic. Hence, **multum,** compar., **plūs,** superl., **plūrĭmum,** *much, a great part.* **I.** Subst., **A.** In nom. or acc., with genit., ad multum diei, *till far in the day,* Liv.; multum diei, *a large part of the day,* Sall.; compar., plus posse, plus facere, Cic.; plus pecuniae, Cic.; plurimum posse, Cic.; plurimum gravitatis, Cic. **B.** In genit., *of price* or value, pluris emere, vendere, *dearer, at*

a higher price, Cic.; mea mihi conscientia **plūris** est quam omnium sermo, *is of more value to me,* Cic.; aliquem pluris aestimare, *to think more highly of,* Cic.; superl., plurimi, *very dear;* esse, Cic. **II.** Adv., **A. multo,** *by far,* with comparatives or words of similar force; multo pauciores, Cic.; multo anteponere, Cic.; non multo post, *not long after,* Cic. **B. multum;** 1, of degree, *much, very;* longe multumque superare, Cic.; vir multum bonus, Cic.; non multum est majus, Cic.; 2, of time, *often;* multum mecum loquuntur, Cic. **C.** plus; 1, of number, *more;* non plus quam semel, Cic.; without quam plus mille capti, Liv.; with abl., nec esse plus uno, Cic.; 2, of degree, *more;* quem plus plusque in dies diligo, *more and more,* Cic. **D** plurimum, *most;* ut te plurimum diligam, Cic.

Mŭluccha (Mŭlucha) -ae, m. *a river in Mauritania,* now *Maluia* or *Moluya.*

mūlus -i, m. *a mule,* Cic.

Mulvĭus -a -um, *Mulvian;* pons, *a bridge above Rome on the via Flaminia,* now *Ponte Molle.*

Mummĭus -a -um, *name of a Roman gens, the most famous member of which was* L. Mummius Achaicus, *the destroyer of Corinth.*

Mūnātĭus -a -um, *name of a Roman gens, the most famous member of which was* L. Munatius Plancus, *one of the legates of Caesar.*

Munda -ae, f. *town in Hispania Baetica, scene of a victory of Julius Caesar over the sons of Pompeius,* 45 B.C.

mundānus -a -um (mundus), *of* or *relating to the world, mundane.* Subst., **mundānus** -i, m. *a citizen of the world,* Cic.

mundĭtĭa -ae, f. and (not in Cic.) **mundĭties** -ēi, f. (mundus), *cleanness.* **I.** Lit., Plaut. **II.** *neatness, spruceness, elegance;* 1, non odiosa neque exquisita nimis, Cic.; munditiis capimur, Ov.; simplex munditiis, Hor.; 2, *neatness, elegance of style,* quā munditiā, homines quā elegantiā, Cic.

mundo, 1. (mundus), *to cleanse, purify,* Verg.

1. **mundus** -a -um, *clean, neat, elegant.* **I.** supellex, coena, Hor. **II.** 1, of manner of life, *elegant, refined;* homo, Cic.; cultus justo mundior, *too elegant apparel,* Liv.; 2, of discourse, *neat, elegant;* verba, Ov.

2. **mundus** -i, m. (1. mundus, like Gr. κόσμος). **I.** *ornament;* muliebris, Liv. **II.** *the universe, the world, and the heavenly bodies.* **A.** hic ornatus mundi, *harmony of the universe,* Cic.; mundi innumerabiles, Cic. **B.** 1, *the heavens;* lucens, Cic.; 2, *the world, the earth;* a, lit., quicumque mundo terminus obstitit, Hor.; b, meton., *the inhabitants of the world, mankind;* fastos evolvere mundi, Hor.

mūnĕro, 1. (munus), *to give, present;* aliquem aliquā re, Cic.

mūnĕror, 1. dep. *to present;* natura aliud alii muneratur, Cic.

mūnĭa -īum, n. *duties, functions, official duties, official business;* candidatorum, Cic.

mūnĭceps -cĭpis, c. (munia and capio). **I.** *the citizen of a municipium;* municeps Cosanus, *of Cosa,* Cic. **II.** *a fellow-citizen, countryman, fellow-countryman;* meus, Cic.; municipes Jovis advexisse lagoenas, *countrymen of Jupiter,* i.e., *Cretan,* Juv.

mūnĭcĭpālis -e (municipium), *relating or belonging to a municipium, municipal;* homines, Cic.; sometimes in a contemptuous sense, *provincial;* eques, Juv.

mūnĭcĭpĭum -ĭi, n. (municeps), *a town, usually in Italy, the inhabitants of which had the Roman citizenship, but were governed by their* *own magistrates and laws; a free town, municipal town*, Cic.

mūnĭfĭcē, adv. (munificus), *munificently, bountifully*, Cic.

mūnĭfĭcentĭa -ae, f. (munificus), *munificence, bountifulness*, Sall.

mūnĭfĭco, 1. (munificus), *to present, to give*, Lucr.

mūnĭfĭcus -a -um (munus and facio), *munificent, liberal;* in dando, Cic. (compar., munificentior, superl., munificentissimus).

mūnīmen -ĭnis, n. (munio), *a protection, defence, fortification;* munimine cingere fossas, Ov.; ad imbres, *against the rains*, Verg.

mūnīmentum -i, n. (munio). **I.** *a fortification, bulwark, defence, protection;* ut instar muri hae sepes munimenta praeberent, Caes.; tenere se munimentis, *entrenchments*, Tac. **II.** Fig., *protection;* rati noctem sibi munimento fore, Sall.

mūnĭo (moenĭo) -īvi and -ĭi -ītum, 4. (moenia). **I.** *to build, build with walls;* oppidum, Hor.; absol., *to build a wall*, Nep. **II. A.** *to surround with a wall, fortify;* 1, a, lit., palatium, Nep.; montem, Caes.; castra vallo fossaque, Caes.; b, transf., *to protect, defend;* Alpibus Italiam munierat natura, Cic.; domum praesidiis, Cic.; quae (herbescens viriditas) contra avium morsus munitur vallo aristarum, Cic.; 2, fig., *to secure, make sure;* munio me ad haec tempora, Cic. **B.** *to make or build a road, to pave a road;* viam, Cic.; itinera, Nep.; fig., munire alicui viam accusandi, *to prepare a way for*, Cic.

mūnītĭo -ōnis, f. (munio). **I.** *fortifying, entrenching;* 1, lit., milites munitione prohibere, Caes.; 2, meton., *a fortification, entrenchment;* urbem operibus munitionibusque saepire, Cic. **II.** *a making passable, paving of roads;* ex viarum munitione quaestum facere, Cic.; munitio fluminum, *bridging over*, Tac.

mūnĭto, 1. (intens. of munio), *to pave, make passable;* viam, Cic.

mūnĭtor -ōris, m. (munio), *a builder of fortifications, a sapper and miner, military engineer*, Liv.

mūnītus -a -um, p. adj. (from munio), *fortified, made safe, secured;* oppidum munitissimum, Cic.

mūnus -ĕris, n. (moenus). **I.** *an office, function, employment, duty;* reipublicae, *a public office*, Cic.; officii, *the performance of a duty*, Cic.; tuum est hoc munus, Cic.; consulare munus sustinere, Cic.; belli munera inter se partiri, Liv. **II. A.** *an affectionate service, favour;* neque vero verbis auget suum munus, Cic.; munere alicuius rei (poet.), *by the help of*, Verg.; esp., *the last services to the dead, funeral honours, interment;* munere inani fungi, Verg. **B.** *a gift, present;* 1, alicui munus mittere, Cic.; mittere alicui aliquid muneri, *to send or give as a present*, Caes.; munera Liberi, *wine*, Hor.; Cereris, *bread*, Ov.; transf., opusculum majorum vigiliarum munus, *the fruit of*, Cic.; 2, a, *a sacrifice;* munera ferre templis, Verg.; b, *a public show, especially of gladiators, generally given by the aediles to the people;* munus magnificum dare, praebere, Cic.; munus gladiatorium, Cic.; hence, *a building or theatre erected for the people*, Ov.

mūnuscŭlum -i, n. (dim. of munus), *a small gift, little present;* alicui mittere munusculum levidense crasso filo, Cic.

Mūnўchĭa -ae, f. (Μουνυχία), *one of the ports of Athens.* Adj., **Mūnўchĭus** -a -um = *Athenian*, Ov.

1. **mūraena** = murena (q.v.).
2. **Mūraena** = Murena (q.v.).

mūrālis -e (murus), *of or relating to a wall, mural;* pila muralia, *used by those who defend a wall*, Caes.; falces, *hooks or grappling-irons for pulling down walls*, Caes.; corona, *the crown given to the one who first ascended the wall of a besieged city*, Liv.; also corona, *the diadem of Cybele, adorned with walls and towers*, Lucr.

Murcĭa (Murtĭa, Myrtĕa) -ae, f. *a surname of Venus;* ad Murciae (sc. aedem), or ad Murciam, *a valley separating the Palatine from the Aventine at Rome*, Liv.

1. **mūrēna (mūraena)** -ae, f. (μύραινα), *a sea-fish highly prized by the Romans.*

2. **Mūrēna** -ae, m. (1. murena), *a cognomen belonging to the gens Licinia, the most celebrated members of which were:* 1, L. Licinius Murena, *defended by Cicero, in the extant oration* "Pro Murena," *on a charge of bribery;* 2, L. Licinius Varro Murena, *friend of Cicero, executed for suspected complicity in a plot against Augustus.*

mūrex -ĭcis, m. **I.** *the purple-fish, a shell-fish from which the Tyrian dye was obtained;* the shell in poets is represented as the trumpet of Triton, Ov.; it was also used to adorn grottos, Ov.; meton., 1, *the purple dye itself*, Tyrioque ardebat murice laena, Verg.; 2, *a sharp stone, projecting rock*, resembling the murex in shape; acutus, Verg. **II.** *an edible shell-fish;* Baianus, Hor.

Murgantĭa -ae, f. **I.** *a town in Samnium*, now Croce di Morcone. **II.** *town in Sicily*, now Mandri Bianchi. Adj., **Murgantīnus** -a -um, *relating to Murgantia.*

murmillo = mirmillo (q.v.).

mūrĭa -ae, f. (ἁλμυρίς), *brine, pickle*, Hor.

murmur -ŭris, n. (onomatop.), *a murmur, a humming, buzzing, roaring, growling noise.* **I.** of men and animals, populi, Liv.; of indistinct supplication, placare deos precibus et murmure longo, Ov.; *the humming of bees*, Verg.; *the roar of a lion*, Mart. **II.** Of things, of the sea, Cic.; of the wind, Verg.; of the sound of wind-instruments, cornuum, Hor.; inflati buxi, Ov.

murmŭro, 1. (murmur). **I.** *to murmur, make a humming, growling noise;* with acc., flebile lingua murmurat exanimis, Ov. **II.** Of things, *to roar;* mare murmurans, Cic.

1. **murra (murra)** = 1. myrrha (q.v.).

2. **murrha (murra, myrrha)** -ae, f. *a mineral, perhaps fluor spar, out of which costly vases and goblets were made;* hence, poet., *the goblets themselves*, Mart.

1. **murrhĕus (murrĕus)** = 1. myrrheus (q.v.).

2. **murrhĕus (murrĕus, myrrhĕus)** -a -um (2. murrha), *made of fluor spar*, pocula, Prop.

1. **murrhĭnus (murrĭnus)** = 1. myrrhinus (q.v.).

2. **murrhĭnus (murrĭnus, myrrhĭnus)** -a -um (murrha), *made of or relating to the mineral called myrrha*, Plaut.

murt ... v. **myrt** ...

Murtĭa = Murcia (q.v.).

mūrus -i, m. *a wall.* **I. A.** Lit. a, *a wall round a city;* urbis, Cic.; muro lapideo urbem cingere, Cic.; b, *the wall of a private building*, Cic. **B.** Transf., 1, *the wall of a building*, Cic.; 2, *a bank or dyke of earth*, Varr.; 3, *the rim or edge of a vessel*, Juv. **II.** *protection, defence;* lex Aelia et Fufia propugnacula murique tranquillitatis, Cic.; Graium murus Achilles, Ov.

1. **mūs**, mūris, c. (μῦς), *a mouse;* rusticus or agrestis, *field-mouse*, Hor.; non solum inquilini sed etiam mures migrarunt, Cic.; under

the word mus the Romans comprehended *the rat, marten, sable, ermine,* etc.

2. **Mūs**, Mūris, m. *the name of a family of the gens Decia, two members of which,* P. *Decius Mus and his son of the same name, devoted themselves to death to gain victory for their country.*

Mūsa -ae, f. (Μοῦσα). **I.** *a muse, goddess of music, poetry, and generally of the fine arts.* The Muses, usually said to be the daughters of Zeus and Mnemosyne, were nine in number, namely, Clio, Melpomene, Thalia, Euterpe, Terpsichore, Calliope, Erato, Urania, Polyhymnia. **II.** Meton., 1, *song, poetry ;* pedestris, *poetry bordering on prose,* Hor. ; 2, musae, *learning, studies ;* agrestiores, Cic.

1. **Mūsaeus** -i, m. (Μουσαῖος), *a fabulous Greek poet.*

2. **mūsaeus** -a -um (Musa), *poetical, musical,* Lucr.

musca -ae, f. (μυῖσκα, dim. of μυῖα), *a fly,* Cic. ; transf., *a troublesome, inquisitive person,* Plaut.

muscārīus -a -um (musca), 1, *of* or *relating to flies,* Plin. ; 2, subst., **muscārīum** -ii, n. *a fly-flap, made of peacocks' feathers* or *an ox's* or *horse's tail,* Mart.

muscǐpǔla -ae, f. and **muscǐpǔlum** -i, n. (mus and capio), *a mouse-trap,* Phaedr.

muscōsus -a -um (muscus), *covered with moss, full of moss, mossy ;* fontes, Virg. ; nihil muscosius, Cic.

muscǔlus -i, m. (dim. of mus). **I.** *a little mouse,* Cic. **II.** Transf., 1, milit. t. t., *a shed, mantelet,* Caes. ; 2, *a species of whale,* Plin.

muscus -i, m. *moss,* Hor.

mūsēus -a -um = 2. musaeus (q.v.).

mūsǐca -ae, f. and **mūsǐcē** -ēs, f. (μουσική), *music ;* musicam tractare, Cic.

1. **mūsǐcē** -ēs, f. = musica (q.v.).

2. **mūsǐcē**, adv. (μουσικῶς), *splendidly, pleasantly, finely ;* musice hercle aetatem agitis, Plaut.

mūsǐcus -a -um (μουσικός). **I.** *belonging* or *relating to music, musical ;* leges, *rules of music,* Cic. Subst., a, **mūsǐcus** -i, m. *a musician,* Cic. ; b, **mūsǐca** -ōrum, n. *music,* Cic. **II.** Esp., *relating to poetry, poetical,* Ter.

mussǐto, 1. (intens. of musso), *to murmur to oneself, to mutter to oneself,* Liv. ; clam mussito, Liv.

musso, 1. (like mutio, from sound mu). **I.** a, *to murmur, mutter, whisper to oneself ;* mussantes inter se rogitabant, Liv. ; b, *to hum, buzz ;* of bees, mussant oras et limina circum, Verg. **II.** *to be in fear and uncertainty ;* mussat rex ipse Latinus, quos generos vocet, Verg.

mustācĕum (mustācĭum) -i, n. and **mustācĕus (mustācĭus)** -i, m. (mustum), *a must-cake, a laurel-cake, a sort of wedding-cake, mixed with must and baked on bay-leaves ;* prov., laureolam in mustaceo quaerere, *to look for fame in trifles,* Cic.

mustēla (mustella) -ae, f. (dim. of mus), *a weasel,* Cic.

mustēlīnus (mustellīnus) -a -um (mustela), *of* or *relating to a weasel,* Ter.

mustum -i, n., v. mustus.

mustus -a -um, *young, new, fresh.* **I.** Adj., agna, Cato ; vinum, *must,* Cato. **II.** Subst., **mustum** -i, n. *new wine, must,* Verg. ; fig., nova ista quasi de musto ac lacu fervida oratio, Cic.; meton., ter centum musta videre, *vintages,* Ov.

Musulāmi (Musulāmii) -ōrum, m. *a warlike people of Numidia.*

Mūta -ae, f. (mutus), *a nymph, whom Jupiter made dumb because of her loquacity.*

mūtābǐlis -e (muto), *changeable, variable, inconstant ;* ea forma reipublicae mutabilis est, Cic.

mūtābǐlǐtas -ātis, f. (mutabilis), *changeableness, mutability ;* mentis, Cic.

mūtātǐo -ōnis (muto). **I.** *a changing, change, mutation ;* facere mutationem alicuius rei, Cic. **II.** *a mutual change, exchange ;* officiorum, Cic.

mūtǐlo, 1. (mutilus). **I.** *to maim, mutilate, cut off ;* nasoauribusque mutilatis, Liv. ; caudam colubrae, Ov. **II.** Transf., *to curtail, diminish ;* exercitum, Cic.

mūtǐlus -a -um (μίτυλος, μύτιλος). **I.** *maimed, mutilated ;* esp. of animals which have lost one or both horns ; alces mutilae sunt cornibus, Caes. ; so transf. in jest, sic mutilus militaris, Hor. **II.** Fig., of speech, mutila loqui, *briefly,* Cic.

Mūtǐna -ae, f. *town in Cispadane Gaul,* now *Modena.* Hence, adj., **Mǔtǐnensis** -e, *relating to Mutina.*

mūtǐo (muttǐo), 4. (from sound mu), *to mutter, mumble, murmur,* Plaut., Ter.

mūtǐtǐo (muttǐtǐo) -ōnis, f. *a muttering,* Plaut.

mūto, 1. (for movito), *to move.* **I.** *to move away, remove ;* ne quis invitus civitate mutetur, *should be removed from the state,* Cic. **II.** Transf. **A.** *to change, alter ;* 1, a, transit., sententiam, consilium, voluntatem, Cic. ; mutari alite, *to be changed into a bird,* Ov. ; b, reflex. mutare, and pass. mutari, *to be changed ;* annona nihil mutavit, Liv. ; 2, a, *to dye ;* vellera luto, Verg. ; b, vinum mutatum, *spoiled, soured,* Hor. **B.** *to change, exchange ;* 1, jumenta, *to change horses,* Caes. ; but, mutare calceos et vestimenta, *to undress,* Cic. ; esp., mutare vestem, *to put on mourning,* Liv. ; mutare terram, *to go into another country,* Liv. ; mutata verba, *used metaphorically,* Cic. ; 2, *to exchange, barter ;* merces, Verg. ; res inter se, Sall.

mūtŭātǐo -ōnis, f. (mutuor), *a borrowing,* Cic.

mūtŭē, adv. (mutuus), *mutually, reciprocally, in return ;* respondere, Cic.

mūtŭō, adv. (mutuus), *mutually, reciprocally ;* aestus maritimi mutuo accedentes et recedentes, Cic.

mūtŭor, 1. dep. (mutuum), *to borrow.* **I.** Lit., a, *money, money ;* pecunias, Caes. ; without acc., ab aliquo, Cic. ; b, *other things,* auxilia ad bellum, Auct. bell. Gall. **II.** Transf., orator subtilitatem ab Academicis mutuatur, Cic. ; verbum a simili, *to speak metaphorically,* Cic.

mūtus -a -um. **I.** *unable to speak, not possessing the power of articulate speech, dumb ;* bestia, Cic. **II.** Transf. **A.** muta dolore lyra est, Ov. **B.** *uttering no sound, mute, silent ;* imago, Cic. ; artes quasi mutae, *the fine arts as opposed to rhetoric,* Cic. **C.** a, of places whence no sound is heard, *still, quiet ;* forum, Cic. ; b, of time, tempus mutum litteris, *when nothing is written,* Cic.

mūtŭus -a -um (muto), lit., *given in exchange.* **I.** *borrowed, lent ;* pecuniam dare mutuam, *to lend,* Cic. ; sumere ab aliquo pecunias mutuas, *to borrow,* Cic. Subst., **mūtŭum** -i, n. *a loan,* Cic. **II.** *mutual, reciprocal ;* nox omnia erroris mutui implevit, *on both sides,* Liv. ; benevolentia, Cic. Subst., **mūtŭum** -i, n. *reciprocity ;* mutuum in amicitia, Cic. ; pedibus per mutua nexis, *fastened on each other,* Verg.

Mǔtўcē -ēs, f. *town in Sicily,* now *Modica.* Hence, adj., **Mǔtўcensis** -e, *relating to Mutyce.*

Mўcălē -ēs, f. (Μυκάλη), *a promontory of Ionia, opposite the island of Samos.*

Mўcēnae -ārum, f., and **Mўcēna** -ae, f., and **Mўcēnē** -ēs, f. (Μυκῆναι, Μυκήνη), *a city in Argolis of which Agamemnon was king;* hence, **1**, adj., **Mўcēnaeus** -a -um, *relating to Mycene or to Agamemnon;* **2**, **Mўcēnenses** -ium, m. *inhabitants of Mycenae;* **3**, **Mўcēnis** -ĭdis, f. *a Mycenian woman,* e.g., *Iphigeneia,* Ov.

Mўcōnus (-ŏs) -i, f. (Μύκονος), *one of the Cyclades Islands in the Aegean Sea.*

Mygdŏnĕs -um, m. (Μυγδόνες), *a Thracian people who settled in Phrygia, Bithynia, and Mesopotamia.* Hence, **1**, **Mygdŏnis** -ĭdis, f. = *Lydian,* Ov.; **2**, **Mygdŏnĭus** -a -um = *Phrygian,* Hor.

Mygdŏnĭdēs -ae, m. *son of Mygdon, king of Phrygia.*

Mўlăsa -ōrum, n. (Μύλασα), *a town in Caria.* Hence, **A. Mўlăsēni** -ōrum, m. and **B. Mўlăsenses** -ium, m. *the inhabitants of Mylasa.* **C. Mўlăseus** -ĕi, m. *an inhabitant of Mylasa.* **D. Mўlăsĭus** -a -um, *Mylasian.*

Myndus (-ŏs) -i, f. (Μύνδος), *sea-town in Caria.* Hence, **Myndĭi** -ōrum, m. *the inhabitants of Myndus.*

mўŏpăro -ōnis, m. (μυοπάρων), *a small piratical skiff,* Cic.

mўrīcē -ēs, f., and **mўrīca** -ae, f. (μυρίκη), *the tamarisk,* Verg.

Myrīna -ae, f. (Μυρίνα), *fortified sea-port of the Aeolians in Mysia.*

Myrmēcĭdēs -ae, m. (Μυρμηκίδης), *a celebrated sculptor.*

Myrmĭdŏnes -um, m. (Μυρμιδόνες), *the Myrmidons, a people in Thessalia Phthiotis under the rule of Achilles.*

myrmillo = mirmillo (q.v.).

Mўrō -ōnis, m. (Μύρων), *a celebrated Greek sculptor.*

mўrŏpōla -ae, m. (μυροπώλης), *a seller of unguents,* Plaut.

mўrŏpōlĭum -ĭi, n. (μυροπώλιον), *a shop where unguents are sold,* Plaut.

1. myrrha (murrha, murra) -ae, f. (μύρρα), **1**, *the myrrh-tree,* Plin.; **2**, *myrrh, a gum obtained from the myrrh-tree.*

2. myrrha = 2. murrha (q.v.).

3. Myrrha -ae, f. (Μύρρα), *the daughter of Cinyras, changed into a myrrh-tree.*

1. myrrhĕus (murrhĕus, murrĕus) a -um (myrrha), **1**, *perfumed or anointed with myrrh,* Hor.; **2**, *myrrh-coloured, yellow,* Prop.

2. myrrhĕus = 2. murrheus (q.v.).

1. myrrhĭnus (murrhĭnus, murrĭnus) -a -um (1. myrrha), *of myrrh,* Plaut.

2. myrrhĭnus = 2. murrhinus (q.v.).

myrtētum (murtētum) -i, n. (myrtus), *a grove* or *thicket of myrtle-trees,* Sall.

myrtĕus (murtĕus) -a -um, **1**, *of or relating to the myrtle,* Verg.; **2**, *myrtle-coloured,* Tib.

myrtum -i, n. (μύρτον), *the myrtle-berry,* Verg.

myrtus -i and -us, f. (μύρτος), *the myrtle, myrtle-tree,* Verg.

Myrtĭlus -i, m. (Μυρτίλος), *the son of Mercury, who threw himself into the sea, hence according to some called* mare Myrtoum (*but see under* Myrtos).

Myrtos -i, f. (Μύρτος), *a small island near Euboea;* hence, adj., **Myrtōus** -a -um, *mare* Myrtoum, *a part of the Aegean sea between Crete, the Peloponnese, and Euboea.*

Myscĕlus -i, m. (Μύσκελος), *an Achaean, founder of Crotona.*

Mўsi -ōrum, m. (Μύσοι), *the people of Mysia in Asia Minor;* hence, **1**, **Mўsia** -ae, f. *their country;* **2**, **Mўsus** -a -um, *Mysian.*

mystăgōgus -i, m. (μυσταγωγός), *a priest or attendant who showed the temple to strangers;* *a cicerone,* Cic.

mystērĭum -ĭi, n. (μυστήριον). **I.** Sing., *a secret, secret science;* aliquid tacitum tamquam mysterium tenere, Cic. **II.** Plur., **mystēria** -ōrum, n. (μυστήρια). **A.** *mysteries or secret rites with which some gods of antiquity were worshipped;* *especially the Eleusinian worship of Ceres,* Cic. **B.** *secrets, mysteries* (of an art); mysteria rhetorum aperire, Cic.

mystēs -ae, m. (μύστης), *a priest at the mysteries,* Ov.

mystĭcus -a -um (μυστικός), *relating to the mysteries, secret, mystic,* Verg.

Mўtĭlēnae -ārum, f. and **Mўtĭlēnē** -ēs, f. (Μυτιλήνη), *capital of the island of Lesbos.* Hence, adj., **Mўtĭlēnaeus** -a -um, *Mytilenean.*

Mўūs -untis, f. (Μυοῦς), *a town in Caria.*

mўtĭlus = mitulus (q.v.).

N.

N, n, the thirteenth letter of the Latin alphabet, corresponds in sound to the Greek nu (N, ν). For the uses of N. as an abbreviation, see Table of Abbreviations.

Nābătaei (Nābăthaei) -ōrum, m. (Ναβαταῖοι, Ναβαθαῖοι), *the Nabataeans in Arabia Petraea.* Hence, **Nābătaeus** -a -um, *Nabataean,* poet. = *Arabian, Eastern;* subst., **Nābătaea** -ae, f. (Ναβαταία), *a country of Arabia Petraea.*

Nābis -bĭdis, m. (Νάβις), *king of Sparta about* 200 A.C.

nablĭum (naulĭum) -ĭi and **nablum** -i, n. *a stringed instrument of uncertain form; a kind of harp or lyre,* Ov.

nae = 1. ne (q.v.).

naenĭa = nenia (q.v.).

Naevĭus -a -um, *name of a Roman gens, of which the most notable member was* Cn. Naevius, *Roman dramatic and epic poet, born about* 274 A.C. Hence, **Naevĭānus** -a -um, *Naevian.*

naevus -i, m. *a mole on the body,* Cic.

Nahanarvali -ōrum, m. *a German tribe.*

Nāĭăs -ădis and **Nāĭs** -ĭdis (-ĭdos), acc. plur. -ĭdas, f. (Ναϊάς, Ναΐς, *a swimmer*), **1**, *a water-nymph, Naiad;* used attrib., puellae Naiades, Verg.; **2**, *a nymph, hamadryad, Nereid,* Ov. Hence, **Nāĭcus** -a -um, *belonging to the Naiads.*

nam, conj. *for* (differs from enim in standing at the beginning of a clause or proposition). **I.** Introducing an explanation, is pagus appellabatur Tigurinus; nam omnis civitas Helvetia in quatuor pagos divisa est, Caes.; hence, esp., a, sometimes introducing a parenthesis, in insula quae est in Tiberino (nam opinor illud alteri flumini nomen esse) sermoni demus operam, Cic.; b, or taking up the thought interrupted by a parenthesis, duplex inde Hannibali gaudium fuit (neque enim quidquam eorum, quae apud hostes agerentur, eum fallebat); nam et liberam Minucii temeritatem, etc., Liv.; also c, introducing examples in illustration of a previous general assertion, vivo Catone minores natu multi uno tempore oratores floruerunt; nam et A. Albinus et literatus et disertus fuit, Cic. **II.** Introducing a reason, argument, fact, in justification of a preceding statement, celebratote illos dies cum conjugibus ac liberis vestris; nam multi saepe honores dis immortalibus justi habiti sunt, sed profecto justiores numquam, Cic. ; also used in rhetorical questions to express a climax, numquam illum ne minimā quidem re offendi . . . una domus erat, idem victus isque communis ; nam quid ego de studiis dicam? Cic.; often found in connexion with hercle, mehercle, edepol, Cic. **III.** Used to add emphasis to an interrogation, and in this application often enclitic, quis est nam ludus in undis ! Verg.

Namnĕtes -um, m *a people in Gallia Celtica near the modern Nantes.*

namquĕ, conj., a more emphatic form of nam (q.v.), standing like it at the beginning of a sentence or clause, though sometimes after the first or second word : prodigium extemplo dedicationem secutum ; namque lapidibus pluit, Liv. ; Alcibiades ad omnes res aptus consiliique plenus ; namque imperator fuit summus mari et terrā, Nep.

nanciscor, nactus and nanctus sum, 3. dep. *to get, obtain, meet.* **I.** Lit., *to find, fall on;* anulum, Ter.; morbum, Nep.; spem, Cic.; fidem, Ov. **II.** Transf., **A.** = *to reach;* vitis claviculis suis, quicquid est nacta, complectitur, Cic. **B.** *to find, meet with;* aliquem, Cic. ; turbidam tempestatem, Caes.

Nantŭātes -ĭum, m *a Celtic Alpine people.*

nānus -i, m. (νάννος, νᾶνος), *a dwarf,* Juv.

nāpaeus -a -um (ναπαῖος), *of or relating to the forest;* subst., **nāpaeae** -ārum, f. *wood-nymphs,* Verg.

Nār, Nāris, m. *a river of Italy, that flows into the Tiber, now Nera.*

Narbo -ōnis, m. *town in Gallia Narbonensis,* now Narbonne. Hence, adj., **Narbōnensis** -e, *of or belonging to Narbo.*

narcissus -i, m. (νάρκισσος). **I.** *the narcissus, daffodil,* Verg. **II.** Proper name, *Narcissus, son of Cephisus and Liriope, a youth of remarkable beauty, who fell in love with his own reflection in a fountain, and wasted away till he was changed into the flower of the same name.*

nardus -i, f. and **nardum** -i, n. (νάρδος), 1, *nard, a name given by the ancients to various aromatic plants,* Plin. ; 2, *the unguent or balsam of nard,* Hor.

Narnĭa -ae, f. *a town in Umbria on the Nar,* now Narni. Hence, adj., **Narnĭensis** -e, *relating to Narnia.*

narrābĭlis -e (narro), *that can be told or narrated,* Ov.

narrātĭo -ōnis, f. (narro), *a telling, narrating, relating, narration;* rem narrare ita ut verisimilis narratio sit, Cic.

narrātŏr -ōris, m. (narro), *a relater, narrator,* Cic.

narrātus -ūs, m. (narro), *a narration, narrative,* Ov.

narro, 1. (for gnaro = gnarum facio), *to make known.* **I.** *to relate, tell, narrate ;* ego tibi ea narro, quae tu melius scis quam ipse qui narro, Cic. ; de mea solicitudine, Cic. ; male bene, narrare, *to bring good* or *bad tidings,* Cic. ; with acc. and infin., Cic.; with rel. sent, Cic.; pass., narratur, with nom. and infin., *it is narrated, it is told,* Liv. **II.** *to say, speak, tell ;* narro tibi (a form of asseveration), *I assure you,* Cic.

narthēcĭum -ĭi, n. (ναρθήκιον), *a case for keeping perfumes and medicines,* Cic.

narus = gnarus (q.v.).

Nărўcum -i, n. and **Nārўx** -rўcis, f. (Νάρυξ), *a town of the Ozolian Locrians, whence the town of Locri in Bruttium was founded.* Adj., **Nărўcĭus** -a -um, *Narycian;* urbs, *Locri in Italy,* Ov.

Năsămōnes -um, *a people in the south-west of Cyrenaica.* Hence, adj., **Năsămōnĭăcus** -a -um, *Nasamonian.*

nascor (gnascor), nātus sum, 3. dep. **I.** Lit., **A.** *to be born,* nasci patre certo, Cic. ; non nobis solum nati sumus, Cic. ; post hominum genus natum, *since the beginning of the world,* Cic. **B.** *to descend from, spring from ;* natus summo loco, *of a good family,* Cic. **II.** Transf. *to arise, be produced, spring forth ;* nascitur ibi plumbum, Caes. ; ab eo flumine collis nascebatur, *began to rise,* Cic. ; nulla tam detestabilis pestis est, quae non homini ab homine nascatur, Cic.

Nāsĭca -ae, m. *name of a family of the Scipios, the most famous member of which, was* P. Cornel. Scipio Nasica, *famous for his integrity.*

Nāso -ōnis, m. *the cognomen of the poet* P. Ovidius ; v. Ovidius.

Nāsos -i, f. (νᾶσος = νῆσος, *island*), *a part of the city of Syracuse.*

nassa (naxa) -ae, f. *a narrow-necked basket for catching fish,* Plaut. ; fig., *a trap, net, snare,* ex hac naxa exire constitui, Cic.

nasturcĭum (nasturtĭum) -ĭi, n. *a kind of cress,* Cic.

nāsus -i, m. *the nose.* **I.** Lit., **A.** nasus ita locatus est, ut quasi murus oculis interjectus esse videatur, Cic. **B.** *the nose;* a, as the seat of smell, nasus illis nullus erat, Hor. ; b, as expressing anger, scorn, etc., aliquem or aliquid naso suspendere adunco, *to turn up the nose at,* *ridicule, mock,* Hor. **II.** Transf., *the nose, nozzle, spout of a vessel,* Juv.

nāsūtus -a -um (nasus) 1, *having a large nose,* Hor.; 2, *acute, sagacious, satirical,* Mart.

nāta -ae, f. (nascor), *a daughter,* Verg.

nātālĭcĭus -a -um (natalis), *of or relating to birth,* and esp. *to the time of birth;* praedicta, *of a horoscope,* Cic. Subst., **nātālĭcĭa** -ōrum, n. *a birthday festival,* Cic.

nātālis -e (2. natus), *of or relating to birth, natal.* **I.** Adj., dies, Cic. ; lux, Ov. ; hora, Hor. ; diem natalem suum agere, *celebrate,* Cic. ; **II.** Subst. **nātālis** -is, m., a, *a birth-place,* Delos natalis Apollinis, Hor. ; b, *a birth-day,* Cic. ; natalis Romae, *festival of Palilia in honour of the founding of Rome,* Ov. ; plur. **nātāles** -ĭum, m. *birth, origin, condition ;* Cornelius Fuscus, claris natalibus, *of illustrious origin* Tac.

nătans -antis (partic. of nato), *swimming ;* poet. subst. f., natantes, *fishes,* Verg.

nătātĭo -ōnis, f. (nato), *swimming,* ap. Cic.

nătātŏr -ōris, m. (nato), *a swimmer,* Ov.

nătes, v. natis.

nātĭo -ōnis, f. (nascor). **I.** Abstr., *a being born, birth ;* natione Numidā, Tac. ; hence, personif., Natio, *the goddess of birth.* Cic. **II.**

Concr., **A.** Lit., *a nation, people;* externae nationes **ot** gentes, Cic. **B.** Transf., *a breed, race, species, stock, class;* candidatorum, Cic.; Epicur**sorum,** Cic.; vestra natio (of the Stoics), Cic.

nătis -is, f., usually plur., **nătes** -ium, f. *the rump, buttocks,* Hor.

nătīvus -a -um (2. natus). **I.** *born, that which* **has** *come into existence by birth;* Anaximandri opinio est, nativos esse deos, Cic. **II.** *inborn, innate, native, natural, not artificial;* beluae nativis testis inhaerentes, Cic.

năto, 1. (from no, nare), *to swim.* **I.** Lit., studiosissimus homo natandi, Cic.; in oceano, Cic.; natant aequore pisces, Ov.; natat uncta carina, *floats,* Verg.; poet., followed by acc., caeca freta, Verg. **II.** Transf., **A.** *to stream, spread abroad;* qua se Tiberinus in altum dividit et campo liberiore natat, Ov.; fig., *to totter = to be insecure;* tu mihi natare visus es, Cic. **B.** 1, *to swim with anything, be full of, overflow;* natabant pavimenta vino, Cic.; omnia plenis rura natant fossis, Verg.; 2, of the eyes, *to swim, to be glassy;* vinis oculique animique natabant, Ov.

nātrix -īcis, f. *a water-snake,* Cic.

nātūra -ae, f. (nascor). **I.** *birth,* Cic.; naturā frater, adoptione filius, Cic. **II.** *nature.* **A.** 1, *natural qualities of anything;* a, of things, haec est natura propria animae et vis, Cic.; montis, Caes.; loci, Caes.; b, of men, *nature, natural disposition, character;* quae tua natura est, Cic.; versare suam naturam, Cic.; naturam expellas furcā, tamen usque recurret, Hor.; 2, *nature,* a, *the laws of nature, the order and constitution of the world;* quod rerum natura non patitur, Cic.; naturae satisfacere, *to pay the debt of nature, to die,* Cic.; naturae concedere, Sall.; b, *nature, possibility;* in rerum natura fuisse, *to be possible,* Cic. **B.** 1, a, *the world, creation;* in full, rerum natura, Cic.; b, *nature as the soul of the universe,* Cic.; 2, *an element, substance, essence;* ex duabus naturis conflata, Cic.

nātūrālis -e (natura). **I.** *that which has arisen or been produced by birth, natural;* pater, *own father* (opp. *adoptive father*), Cic. **II.** 1, *natural;* societas, lex, Cic.; neut. plur. subst., naturalia anteponantur non naturalibus, *that which is natural to that which is not natural,* Cic.; 2, *relating to nature;* quaestiones, Cic.

nātūrālĭtĕr, adv. (naturalis), *naturally, by nature, according to nature;* divinare, Cic.

1. **nātus** -a -um, p. adj. (from nascor). **I.** Adj., *born;* 1, *born for, fitted by nature for;* with ad or in and the acc., or with dat., Judaei et Syrae nationes natae servituti, Cic.; poet. with inf., animal natum tolerare labores, Ov.; 2, *naturally constituted;* ita natus locus est, Liv.; pro re nata, *under present circumstances, as things are now,* Cic.; 3, with a date, expresses age, eques Romanus annos prope XC natus, *almost ninety years old,* Cic. **II.** Subst., 1, **nātus** -i, m. *a son,* Cic.; 2, **nāta** -ae, f. *a daughter,* Verg.

2. **nātus** -ū, m. (found only in the abl. sing., {nascor), *birth* (particularly applied to denote *age*); magnus natu, grandis natu, *of considerable age,* Cic.; qui fuit major natu quam Plautus et Naevius, *older,* Cic.; ex his omnibus natu minimus, *the youngest,* Cic.

nauarchus -i, m. (ναύαρχος), *a captain of a ship,* Cic.

nauci, v. naucum.

Naucrătes, acc. -em, m. (Ναυκράτης), *a Greek orator, pupil of Isocrates.*

naucum -i, n., lit., *a nut-shell,* fig., *a trifle, something very small;* only used in such expressions as non nauci habere, *to esteem lightly,* Cic.

naufrăgĭum -ii, n. (for navifragium, from navis and frango), *a shipwreck.* **I.** Lit., naufragium (naufragia) facere, *to suffer shipwreck,* Cic.; naufragio interire, Caes.; perire, Cic.; prov., naufragia alicuius ex terra intueri, *to behold danger from a place of safety,* Cic.; fig., *misfortune, ruin, loss;* fortunarum, Cic.; patrimonii, Cic.; tabula ex naufragio, literally, *a plank from a shipwreck, a means of safety, way of deliverance,* Cic. **II.** Meton., *the remains of a shipwreck, wreckage;* fig., colligere naufragium reīpublicae, Cic.

naufrăgus -a -um (for navifragus, from navis and frango). **I.** Pass., *that suffers or has suffered shipwreck;* Marium Africā devictā ex pulsum et naufragum vidit, Cic.; corpora, Verg.; puppis, Ov.; fig., patrimonio naufragus, Cic. **II.** Act., poet., *causing shipwreck;* mare, Hor.; unda, Tib.

naulĭum = nablium (q.v.).

naulum -i, n. (ναῦλον), *fare, passage-money,* Juv.

naumăchĭa -ae, f. (ναυμαχία), 1, *a naval battle exhibited as a spectacle,* Suet.; 2, *the place in which the spectacle was exhibited,* Suet.

naumăchĭārĭus -a -um (naumachia), *of or relating to a mock sea-fight,* Plin.; subst., **naumăchĭārĭus** -i, m. *one who fought in a mock sea-fight,* Suet.

Naupactus (-ŏs) -i, f. (Ναύπακτος), *a seaport on the Gulf of Corinth in Locri Ozolae,* now *Nepactos or Lepanto.* Hence, adj., **Naupactĭus** -a -um, *of or relating to Naupactus.*

Nauportus -i, f. *a town in Pannonia,* now *Ober-Laibach.*

nausĕa (nausĭa) -ae, f. (ναυσία), *sea-sickness;* navigamus sine timore et nausea, Cic.; transf., *sickness, nausea,* Hor.

nausĕo (nausĭo), 1. (nausea). **I.** *to be seasick;* epistola quam dedisti nauseans Buthroto, Cic.; transf., *to vomit, be sick;* quidlibet, modo ne nauseet, faciat, Cic. **II.** Transf., *ista effutientem nauseare, to belch out nonsense,* Cic.

nausĕŏla (nausĭŏla) -ae, f. (dim. of nausea), *a slight squeamishness,* Cic.

nauta -ae, m. (for navita, from navis), *a sailor, seaman, mariner,* Cic.

nautĭcus -a -um (ναυτικός), *of or relating to a sailor, nautical, naval;* verbum, Cic.; scientia atque usus nauticarum rerum, Caes.; subst., **nautĭci** -ōrum, m. *sailors,* Liv.

nāvālis -e (navis), 1, adj., *of or relating to ships, naval, nautical;* bellum, pugna, Cic.; castra, *for the protection of ships when drawn upon shore,* Caes.; socii navales, *sailors* (chosen from the freedmen of the colonists and allies), Liv.; pedes navales, *galley-slaves,* Plaut.; 2, subst., a, **nāvāle** -is, n. [a *station for ships,* Ov.; b, **nāvālĭa** -ium, n., (a) *a dockyard,* and esp. *a place in Rome so called,* Liv.; (β) *materials for ship-building,* Liv.

nāvarchus = nauarchus (q.v.).

nāvē = naviter (q.v.).

nāvĭcŭla -ae, f. (dim. of navis), *a little ship, skiff, boat,* Cic.

nāvĭcŭlārĭus -a -um (navicula), *relating to small ships, boats.* **A.** **nāvĭcŭlārĭa** -ae, f. (sc. res), *the business of one who lets out ships for transport, the business of a ship-owner;* naviculariam facere, Cic. **B.** **nāvĭcŭlārĭus** -ii, m. *one who lets out ships for transport, a ship-owner,* Cic.

nāvĭfrăgus -a -um (navis and frango), *causing shipwreck, ship-destroying*, Verg.

nāvĭgābĭlis -e (navigo), *navigable;* mare, Liv.

nāvĭgātĭo -ōnis, f. (navigo), *a sailing, voyage, navigation;* bona, Cic.; primam navigationem (*chance of sailing*) ne omiseris, Cic.

nāvĭger -gĕra -gĕrum (navis and gero), *ship-bearing, navigable;* mare, Lucr.

nāvĭgĭŏlum -i, n. (dim. of navigium), *a little ship, a bark*, ap. Cic.

nāvĭgĭum -ĭi, n. (navigo), 1, *a sailing, navigating*, Lucr.; 2, *a vessel, ship;* navigium facere, Cic.

nāvĭgo, 1. (navis). **I.** Intransit., *to sail, voyage.* **A. ex** Asia in Macedoniam, Cic.; of ships, decrevimus, ut classis in Italiam navigaret, Cic. **B.** Transf., of a naval war, *to proceed, go;* quam celeriter, Cn. Pompeio duce, belli impetus navigavit, Cic. **II.** Transit., 1, *to sail over, sail through, navigate;* terram, Cic.; aequor, Verg.; 2, *to get or earn by navigation;* quae homines arant, navigant, aedificant, Sall.

nāvis -is, f. (ναῦς), *a ship, vessel.* **I.** Lit., navis longa, *a man-of-war*, Liv.; oneraria, *a ship of burden, transport-ship*, Liv.; praetoria, *admiral's ship, flag-ship*, Liv.; tecta, Liv.; constrata, *decked*, Cic.; aperta, *undecked*, Cic.; navis auri, *laden with gold*, Cic.; navem deducere in aquam, *to launch*, Liv.; subducere, *to drag on shore*, Caes.; conscendere in navem, *to embark*, Cic.; prov., navibus et quadrigis, *with all one's might*, Hor. **II.** Fig., of the state, una navis bonorum omnium, Cic.; esse in eadem navi, *to be in the same boat with any one, to share a common lot*, Cic.

nāvĭta = nauta (q.v.).

nāvĭtas (gnāvĭtas) -ātis, f. (navus), *assiduity, zeal*, Cic.

nāvĭtĕr, adv. (navus), 1, *assiduously, zealously, actively*, Liv.; 2, *entirely, quite;* impudens, Cic.

nāvo, 1. (navus), *to do anything zealously, actively, assiduously, diligently;* navare operam alicui, *to come to help, render assistance*, Cic.; fortiter in acie navare operam, Liv.; quam vellem Bruto studium tuum navare potuisses, Cic.; bellum, *to carry on war with energy*, Tac.; rempublicam, *to serve the state*, Cic.

nāvus (gnāvus) -a -um, *active, diligent, energetic, assiduous;* homo navus et industrius, Cic.

naxa -ae, f.= nassa (q.v.).

Naxus (-ŏs) -i, f. (Νάξος), *an island of the Aegean Sea, the largest of the Cyclades*, now *Naxia* or *Axia.* Hence, **Naxius** -a -um, *Naxian.*

1. **nē (nae)**, adv. (νή), *yes, verily, truly;* ne illi multa saecula exspectanda fuerunt, Cic.

2. **nē**, the original Latin particle of negation. **I.** Adv., **A.** *not;* obsolete and rare in this sense, which however appears in compounds such as nemo (= ne-hemo), ne-scio, etc., and in such phrases as : **B.** 1, ne . . . quidem, *not even;* ne in oppidis quidem, Cic.; 2, ne . . . quoque = ne . . . quidem, ne quis, etc. **C. a**, with the imper. to express a prohibition, ne timete, Liv.; **b**, with the subj., to express a prohibition, nobis nostras ne ademeris, Cic.; **c**, with subj., si certum est facere, facias, verum ne post conferas culpam in me, Tac.; with a negative wish, ne id Juppiter Opt. Max. sirit, Liv.; illud utinam ne vere scriberem, Cic.; ne vivam, si scio, *may I die if I know*, Cic. **D.** 1, with compar., *not;* ut hoc desiderium ne plus sit annuum, Cic.; 2, in concessive and restrictive clauses, sint sane liberales ex sociorum fortunis,

sint misericordes in furibus aerarii, **ne** illis sanguinem nostram largiantur, *only let them not lavish our blood*, Sall. **II.** Conj.= *that not.* **A.** to express purpose; gallinae pennis fovent pullos, ne frigore laedantur, Cic.; ne multa dicam, *in short*, Cic. **B.** to express consequence; hoc te rogo ne demittas animum, Cic. **C.** 1, ut ne, *that not;* quam plurimis de rebus ad me velim scribas, ut prorsus ne quid ignorem, Cic.; 2, ne non, *that not;* timeo ne non impetrem, Cic.

3. **nĕ**, interrog. and enclitic particle. **I.** In simple questions; 1, in direct questions, mitto alios; etiamne nobis expedit? Cic.; 2, in indirect questions, ut videamus, satisne ista sit defectio, Cic. **II.** In compound questions; 1, in direct questions, satisne ergo pudori consulat, si quis sine teste libidini pareat, an est aliquid per se ipsum flagitiosum? Cic.; 2, in indirect questions, nescio gratulerne tibi an timeam, Cic.

Nĕāpŏlĭs -pŏlis, acc. -pŏlim, f. (Νεάπολις). **I.** *a part of Syracuse.* **II.** *a sea-port in Campania*, now *Naples.* Adj., **Nĕāpŏlĭtānus** -a -um, *Neapolitan.*

nĕbŭla -ae, f. (νεφέλη). **I.** Lit., 1, *exhalation, fog, mist;* matutina, Liv.; 2, *poet., cloud*, Hor.; pulveris, *a cloud of dust*, Lucr.; 3, *smoke*, Ov. **II.** Transf., *anything soft and transparent;* vellera nebulas aequantia tactu, Ov.

nĕbŭlo -ōnis, m. (nebula), *a good-for-nothing fellow, idle rascal, worthless wretch*, Cic.

nĕbŭlōsus -a -um (nebula), *misty, foggy, cloudy, dark;* nebulosum et caliginosum caelum, Cic.

nĕc and **nĕquĕ**, negative particles. **I. A.** *and not;* quia non viderunt nec sciunt, Cic.; neque vero, *and indeed not*, Cic.; nec tamen, *and yet not*, Cic.; neque etiam, *and indeed not*, Cic.; nec enim, neque enim, *for not*, Cic.; neque non, *and;* necnon, *and also, and indeed*, Cic. **B.** 1, *and also not;* Stoicum est nec admodum credibile, Cic.; 2, *and indeed not;* nuntii nobis tristes nec varii venerunt, Cic.; 3, *and yet not;* conscripsi epistolam noctu; nec ille ad me rediit, Cic. **II.** Joined with other particles; 1, nec . . . nec, or neque . . . neque, *neither . . . nor;* 2, neque . . . et, *not only not . . . but also;* nec miror et gaudeo, Cic.

necdum, adv. *and not yet*, Cic.

nĕcessārĭē, adv. (necessarius), *necessarily, unavoidably*, Cic.

nĕcessārĭō, adv. (necessarius), *necessarily, unavoidably*, Cic.

nĕcessārĭus -a -um (necesse), *necessary, unavoidable, inevitable.* **I.** Adj., lex, Cic.; mors, Cic.; res, *necessity*, Caes.; omnia quae sint ad vivendum necessaria, Cic.; quod mihi maxime necessarium, Cic.; necessarium est, with infin.; senatori necessarium est, nosse rempublicam, *it is necessary, indispensable*, Cic. **II.** Transf., *closely connected or related;* esp., subst., **nĕcessārĭus** -ĭi, m., **-a** -ae, f., *an intimate friend, connexion, near relation;* meus familiaris ac necessarius, Cic.

nĕcessĕ, adj. n. (ne and cedo), found only in connexion with esse and habere, *necessary, fated, unavoidable, inevitable, indispensable;* nihil fit, quod necesse non fuerit, Cic.; homini necesse est mori, Cic.; necesse habere, *to consider necessary, be obliged;* eo minus habeo necesse scribere, Cic.

nĕcessĭtas -ātis, f. (necesse). **I.** Lit., **A.** necessitati parere, Cic.; necessitatem alicui imponere alicuius rei or aliquid faciendi, Cic. **1, a**, *that which is inevitable, fate;* mors est necessitas naturae, Cic.; **b**, *want, need, poverty,*

Tac.; 2, plur., necessitates, *necessaries, necessary expenses*, Caes. **II.** Transf., *intimate connexion, friendship, relationship;* si nostram necessitatem familiaritatemque violasset, Cic.

nĕcessĭtūdo -ĭnis, f. (necesse), *necessity, inevitableness.* **I.** Lit., puto hanc esse necessitudinem, cui nullā vi resisti potest, Cic. **II.** Transf., 1, *of things, close connexion;* rerum, Cic.; 2, *close connexion or relationship, intimate friendship;* liberorum necessitudo, Cic.; sunt mihi cum illo omnes amicitiae necessitudines, Cic.; familiaritatis et necessitudinis oblitus, Cic.; 3, plur., *intimate friends, near relations,* Suet.

nĕcessum and **nĕcessus** est = necesse est, *it is necessary;* with infin., Liv.; or acc. and infin., Liv.

necnĕ, *or not.* **I.** Generally in the second half of indirect questions, sintne dii necne, Cic. **II.** More rarely in direct questions, sunt haec tua verba necne? Cic.

necnon (neque non), v. nec.

nĕco, 1. (nex), *to kill, slay* (usually by hunger, poison, etc., rather than by a weapon); plebem fame, Cic.; aliquem igni, Caes.; aliquem verberibus, Cic.

nĕcŏpīnans -antis, *not expecting, unaware;* aliquem necopinantem liberare, Cic.

nĕcŏpīnāto, adv. (necopinatus), *unexpectedly;* si necopinato quid evenerit, Cic.

nĕcŏpīnātus -a -um, *unexpected;* bona, Cic.; ex necopinato, *unexpectedly,* Liv.

nĕcŏpīnus -a -um, 1, pass., *unexpected;* mors, Ov.; 2, act., *not expecting, careless,* Phaedr.

nectar -ăris, n. (νέκταρ). **I.** *nectar, the drink of the gods,* Cic. **II.** Applied to anything very sweet or pleasant; *honey,* Verg.; *milk,* Ov.

nectărĕus -a -um (νεκτάρεος), *sweet as nectar;* aqua, Ov.

necto, nexŭi and nexi, nexum, 3. **I.** Lit., **A.** *to tie, bind, fasten, connect, weave or fasten together;* catenas, coronam, Hor.; comam myrto, Ov. **B.** *to bind, fetter, enslave,* especially for debt; nexus, *a person enslaved in consequence of debt,* Liv.; eo anno plebi Romanae velut aliud initium libertatis factum est, quod necti desierunt, Liv. **II.** Transf., **A.** *to affix, attach;* ex hoc genere causarum ex aeternitate pendentium fatum a Stoicis nectitur, Cic. **B.** *to connect;* omnes virtutes inter se nexae et jugatae sunt, Cic.; dolum, *to plot,* Liv.; causas inanes, *bring forward,* Verg.; numeris verba, Ov.

nēcŭbi, adv. *lest anywhere, that nowhere,* Caes.

nēcundĕ, adv. *lest from any quarter, that from no direction,* Liv.

nēdum, adv. (lit. *while not*), 1, *much less, still less, to say nothing of;* foll. by subj., optimis temporibus nec P. Popillius nec Q. Metellus vim tribuniciam sustinere potuerunt, nedum his temporibus sine vestra sapientia salvi esse possimus, *much less at present,* Cic.; with ut and the subj., ne voce quidem incommodi, nedum ut ulla vis fieret, Liv.; 2, *much more;* consules bellicosi qui vel in pace tranquilla bellum excitare possent, nedum in bello respirare civitatem forent passuri, Liv.

nĕfandus -a -um (ne and fari), *not to be spoken of, impious, execrable, abominable;* scelus, Cic.; neut. subst., dii memores fandi atque nefandi, *of right and wrong,* Verg.

nĕfārĭē, adv. (nefarius), *impiously, abominably, execrably;* aliquid nefarie facere or committere, Cic.

nĕfārĭus -a -um (nefas), *impious, abominable, execrable, nefarious;* homo, Cic.; bellum, Cic.; subst., a, **nĕfārĭus** -ĭi, m. *a wicked person,* Cic.; b, **nĕfārĭum** -ĭi, n. *an abominable, execrable action,* Liv.

nĕfas, n. indecl., *that which is sinful, contrary to divine command, unlawful, wrong, an impious deed, a sin, crime;* 1, quicquid non licet, nefas putare debemus, Cic.; Mercurius, quem Aegyptii nefas habent nominare, Cic.; per fas et nefas, *by fair means or foul,* Liv.; in omne nefas se parare, Ov.; nefas est, *it is a sin;* with infin., indicare in vulgus nefas (est), Cic.; sometimes used as an interjection, *shocking, dreadful!* heu nefas! Hor.; 2, *a horrible thing;* exstinxisse nefas laudabor (Helen as the cause of the ruin of Troy), Verg.

nĕfastus -a -um, *forbidden, unholy.* **I.** Of time, a, religious t. t., dies nefasti, *on which no legal or public business could be transacted,* Liv.; b, *unlucky, inauspicious;* ille et nefasto te posuit die, Hor.; ne qua terra sit nefasta victoriae suae, Liv. **II.** Of action, *forbidden, sinful;* a, as religious t. t., quae augur injusta, nefasta defixerit, Cic.; b, transf., quid intactum nefasti liquimus? Hor.

nĕgantĭa -ae, f. (nego), *a denying,* Cic.

nĕgātĭo -ōnis, f. (nego), *a denying;* negatio instiatioque facti, Cic.

nĕgĭto, 1. (intens. of nego), *to deny frequently, persist in denying;* quam multos annos esse negativisset, Cic.

neglectĭo -ōnis, f. (negligo), *neglect;* amicorum, Cic.

1. **neglectus** -a -um, p. adj. (from negligo), *neglected, disregarded;* quum inter nos abjecti neglectique simus, Cic.

2. **neglectus** -ūs, m. (negligo), *a neglecting, neglect, disregard,* Ter.

neglĕg . . . v. neglig . . .

neglĭgens -entis, p. adj. (from negligo), 1, *negligent, careless, indifferent, unconcerned;* in amicis eligendis, Cic.; with genit., amicorum, Cic.; 2, esp. in regard to property, *careless, prodigal, extravagant;* adolescentia negligens luxuriosaque, Liv.

neglĭgentĕr, adv. (negligens), *carelessly, unconcernedly, negligently;* scribere, Cic.

neglĭgentĭa -ae, f. (negligens). **I.** *carelessness, negligence;* in accusando, Cic.; accusare aliquem de literarum negligentia, *of omitting to write a letter,* Cic. **II.** *neglect shown towards persons;* deûm, Liv.

neglĭgo (neglĕgo, neclĕgo) -lexi -lectum, 3. (nec and lego), *to neglect, disregard.* **I.** Unintentionally; mandatum, Cic.; with de and the abl., de Theopompo, summo homine, neglex-imus, Cic.; with infin., obire diem edicti, Cic. **II.** Intentionally, 1, *to make light of, despise, pay no heed to;* periculum fortunarum et capitis sui, Cic.; 2, *to overlook, pass over;* injurias Aeduorum, Caes.

nĕgo, 1. (perhaps from ne and aio). **I.** Intransit., *to say no* (opp. aio, *to say yes);* Diogenes ait, Antipater negat, Cic.; with dat., saepius idem roganti, Cic. **II.** Transf., **A.** *to deny, to maintain or assert that a thing is not;* crimen, Cic.; with acc. and infin., Stoici negant, quicquam esse bonum nisi quod honestum sit, Cic.; pass., with nom. and infin., ibi vis facta (esse) negabitur, Cic.; non negare (foll. by quin and the subj.), negare non posse quin rectius sit exercitum mitti, Liv. **B.** *to deny a request, to refuse;* nunquam reo cuiquam tam praecise negavi, quam hic mihi, Cic.; of inanimate objects, poma negat regio, *refuses to produce apples,* Ov.

12*

nĕgōtĭālis -e (negotium), *of* or *relating to business*, Cic.

nĕgōtĭans -antis, m. (partic. of negotior as subst.), *a wholesale dealer, merchant, banker*, Cic.

nĕgōtĭātĭo -ōnis, f. (negotior), *wholesale business, extensive trade, bankers' business ;* reliquiae negotiationis vestrae, Cic.

nĕgōtĭātor -ōris, m. (negotior), *a large wholesale dealer, extensive merchant, banker*, Cic.

nĕgōtĭŏlum -i, n. (dim. of negotium), *a small transaction, little business ;* tua negotiola Ephesi curae mihi fuerunt, Cic.

nĕgōtĭor, 1. dep. (negotium). **I.** *to carry on business,* especially on a large scale, as e.g., *a banker ;* Patris, *at Patrae*, Cic. **II.** *to trade,* Liv.

nĕgōtĭōsus -a -um (negotium), *full of business, busy ;* provincia, Cic. ; homo, Sall. ; dies, *working days*, Tac.

nĕgōtĭum -ĭi, n. (nec and otium), *absence of leisure, business, occupation, employment.* **I.** satis negotii habui in sanandis vulneribus, Cic. ; neque esse quidquam negotii (*any difficulty*) hanc sub sarcinis adoriri, Caes. ; negotium alicui exhibere or facere, *to cause trouble to a person,* Cic. **II.** Transf., **A.** *some single employment or occupation ;* 1, negotia privata, domestica, Cic. ; negotium suscipere, Cic. ; conficere, Caes. ; 2, **a,** *public business ;* negotia forensia, Cic. ; b, of a battle, *affair ;* facies negotii, Sall. ; c, *money-transactions ;* habere negotia vetera in Sicilia, Cic. ; d, *management of a household ;* negotium male gerere, Cic. **B.** Meton., of men, Callisthenis quidem vulgare et notum negotium, Cic.

Nēleus -ěi, m. (Νηλεύς), *a mythical king of Pylos, father of Nestor ;* hence, 1, adj., **Nēlēïus** -a -um, and 2, **Nēlēus** -a -um, *of* or *relating to Neleus* or *Nestor ;* 3, subst., **Nēlĭdēs** -ae, m. *a male descendant of Neleus, Nestor*, Ov.

Nĕmĕa -ae, f. (Νεμέα), and **Nĕmĕē** -ēs, f. (Νεμέη), *a city of Argolis, near which Hercules killed the Nemean lion, and founded the Nemean games.* Hence, 1, adj., **Nĕmĕaeus** -a -um, *Nemean ;* leo, Ov. ; 2, subst., **Nĕmĕa** -ōrum, n. *the Nemean games*, Liv.

Nĕmĕsis -sěos, f. (Νέμεσις), *the goddess of justice and equity who punished pride and arrogance,* also called *Adrastea* and *Rhamnusia.*

Nĕmētes -um, *a people in Gallia Belgica.*

nēmo -ĭnis c. (for nehemo, from ne and hemo = homo), *no man, no one, nobody.* **I.** Subst., nemo omnium mortalium, Cic. ; nemo unus, Cic. ; nemo alius, *no one else*, Cic. ; nemo nec deus nec homo, *no god* or *mortal*, Cic. ; nemo est quin (with subj.), *there is no one who does not,* etc., Cic. ; nemo non, *every one*, Cic. ; non nemo, *many a one*, Cic. **II.** Adj. = *no* ; homo, Cic. ; civis Cic. ; Romanus, Liv. (of the oblique cases only nemini and neminem are usually found).

nĕmŏrālis -e (nemus), *of* or *relating to woods* or *groves, sylvan ;* umbrae, antrum, Ov.

nĕmŏrensis -e (nemus), *belonging to a grove* or *wood ;* esp., *of* or *relating to the grove of Diana at Aricia*, Suet.

nĕmŏrĭcultrix -īcis, f. (nemus and cultrix), *an inhabitant of the woods*, Phaedr.

nĕmŏrĭvăgus -a -um (nemus and vagus), *wandering in the woods*, Cat.

nĕmŏrōsus -a -um (nemus), 1, *woody, full of groves ;* Zacynthos, Verg. ; 2, *thickly leaved, full of foliage ;* silvae, Ov.

nempĕ, conj. (from nam and demonstrative suff. -pe), *forsooth, truly, certainly, to be sure, namely ;* nempe incomposito dixi pede currere versus Lucili, Hor. ; si dat tantam pecuniam Flacco, nempe idcirco dat, ut rata sit emptio, *of course*, Cic. ; nempe negas ? Cic.

nēmus -ŏris, n. (νέμος), *a wood with glades and pasture land for cattle, grove, forest ;* 1, agri et nemora, Cic. ; 2, esp., *the grove at Aricia sacred to Diana*, Cic.

nēnĭa (naenĭa) -ae, f. *a funeral song, dirge,* 1, lit., Cic. ; 2, *any mournful song*, Hor. ; 3, *a song of incantation, an incantation*, Hor. ; 4, *a popular song, nursery song, lullaby*, Hor. (nēniā (abl.), dissyll., Ov. Fast. 6.[142.).

nĕo, nēvi, nētum, 2. (νέω). **I.** *to spin ;* stamina, fila, esp. of the Parcae, Ov. **II.** *to weave, interweave ;* tunicam quam molli neverat auro, Verg. (syncop. perf., nerunt, Ov.).

Nĕŏcles -is and -i, m. (Νεοκλῆς), *father of Themistocles.* Hence, **Nĕŏclĭdēs** -ae, m. *son of Neocles,* i.e., *Themistocles.*

nĕpa -ae, f. 1, *a scorpion*, Cic. ; *the constellation so called*, Cic. poet. ; 2, *the crab*, Plaut. ; *the constellation so called*, Cic. poet.

Nĕpĕtē -is, n. *a town of Etruria, now Nepi.* Hence, adj. **Nĕpĕtīnus** -a -um, *of* or *relating to Nepete.*

Nĕphĕlē -ēs, f. (Νεφέλη), *wife of Athamas, mother of Phrixus and Helle.* Hence, **Nĕphĕlēïs** -ēïdos, f. *a daughter of Nephele, Helle*, Ov.

1. **nĕpos** -ōtis, m. and f. *a grandchild.* **I.** **A.** Lit., Q. Pompeii ex filia nepos, Cic. **B.** Transf., 1, *a brother's* or *sister's child, nephew,* Suet. ; 2, *a descendant*, Verg., Hor. **II.** Meton., *a spendthrift, prodigal* (opp. patruus), Cic.

2. **Nĕpos** -pōtis, m., C. Cornelius, *a Roman historian, friend of Atticus, Cicero, and Catullus, living probably between 94 and 24 A.C., of whose works a part the book De viris illustribus is extant.*

nĕpōtŭlus -i, m. (dim. of nepos), *a little grandson*, Plaut.

neptis -is, f. (nepos), *a grand-daughter*, Cic. ; neptis Veneris, *Ino*, Ov. ; doctae neptes, *the Muses*, Ov.

Neptūnīnē -ēs, f. *a daughter* or *grand-daughter of Neptune*, Cat.

Neptūnus -i, m. *Neptune, god of the sea, brother of Jupiter, husband of Amphitrite, identified with the Greek Poseidon ;* meton., *the sea,* Verg. ; hence, adj., **Neptūnĭus** -a -um, *Neptunian ;* Troja, *built by Neptune*, Verg. ; heros, *Theseus*, Ov. ; dux, *Sext. Pompeius*, Hor. ; aquae, *a well at Tarracina*, Liv.

nēquam, adj. indecl., compar. **nēquĭor**, superl. **nēquissĭmus** (for ne-aequam, from aequus), *worthless, good for nothing, useless, bad, wicked ;* quid est nequius effeminato viro ! Cic. ; liberti nequam et improbi, Cic.

nēquāquam, adv. *by no means, in no wise*, Cic.

nēquĕ = nec (q.v.).

nēquĕdum (necdum), adv. *and not yet*, Cic.

nēquĕo -īvi and -ĭi -ĭtum, 4. *to be unable ;* actam aetatem meminisse nequimus, Lucr. ; cum Demosthenes rho dicere nequiret, Cic. ; pass., quicquid sine sanguine civium ulcisci nequitur, jure factum sit, Sall. (imperf., nequibat, Sall. ; partic., nequiens, Sall.).

nēquiquam (nēquicquam, nēquidquam), adv. (ne and abl. quiquam), *in vain, fruitlessly, to no purpose ;* et sero et nequidquam pudet, Cic. ; alicuius auxilium implorare, Caes.

nēquĭtĕr, adv. (nequam), *worthlessly, wretchedly, badly, miserably ;* ille porro male, prave nequiter, turpiter coenabat, Cic.

nĕquĭtĭa -ae, f. and **nĕquĭtĭes** -ēī, f. (nequam), 1, *worthlessness, laziness, idleness, inactivity;* inertissimi homines nescio qua singulari nequitiā praediti, Cic.; 2, *extravagance, prodigality,* Cic.; 3, *wantonness, profligacy;* uxor pauperis Ibyci, tandem nequitiae pone modum tuae, Hor.; 4, *wickedness, villainy,* Cic.

Nĕrētum -i, n. *a town in Calabria,* now *Nardo.*

Nēreus -ĕos and -ĕi, m. (Νηρεύς), *a sea-god, son of Oceanus and Tethys, father, by Doris, of the Nereids;* meton., *the sea,* Tib.; hence, 1, **Nērēïs** -ĭdis, f. *a daughter of Nereus, a Nereid,* Ov.; 2, **Nērīnē** -ēs, f. *a Nereid,* Verg.; 3, adj., **Nērēïus** -a -um, *of or belonging to Nereus;* genitrix, *Thetis, mother of Achilles,* Ov.; nepos, *Achilles,* Ov.

Nērĭtus (-ŏs) -i, m. (Νήριτος), *a mountain of Ithaca,* also *the name of a small island near Ithaca;* hence, **Nērĭtius** -a -um, *Neritian;* ratis, *the ship of Ulysses,* Ov.; dux, *Ulysses,* Ov.

Nēro -ōnis, m. *a family name of the gens Claudia, the most celebrated of which were:* 1, C. Claudius Nero, *consul* 207 B.C., *who defeated Hasdrubal at the battle of the Metaurus;* 2, C. Claudius Nero, *the fifth Roman emperor* (54–68 A.D.). Hence, adj., 1, **Nērōnēus** -a -um, and 2, **Nērōnĭānus** -a -um, *Neronian.*

Nersae -ārum, f. *a town in Italy, probably in Latium.*

Nĕrŭlum -i, n. *a fortified place in Lucania.*

Nervĭi -ōrum, m. *a warlike people in the north of Gallia Belgica.* Hence, adj., **Nervĭcus** -a -um, *Nervian.*

nervōsē, adv. (nervosus), *strongly, vigorously, energetically;* nervosius dicere, Cic.

nervōsus -a -um (nervus), *sinewy, nervous.* I. Lit., poples, Ov. II. Fig., *of discourse, vigorous, nervous in style;* quis Aristotele nervosior? Cic.

nervŭlus -i, m. (dim. of nervus), *nerve, strength;* in plur., nervulos adhibere, Cic.

nervus -i, m. (νεῦρον), *a sinew, tendon, nerve;* gen. plur., nervi, *the sinews, nerves.* I. A. Lit., nervi a quibus artus continentur, Cic. B. Transf., 1, *the string of a musical instrument;* quotidiano cantu vocum et nervorum et tibiarum tota vicinitas personat, Cic.; 2, *a bowstring;* nervo aptare sagittas, Verg.; 3, *the leather with which shields are covered,* Tac.; 4, *a strap or thong with which the limbs are bound, bonds, fetters,* and hence, *prison, imprisonment;* in nervis teneri, Liv. II. Fig., A. 1, *nerve, strength, vigour, effort;* in quo omnes nervos aetatis industriaeque meae contenderim, Cic.; 2, esp., *of discourse, vigour, energy;* nervi oratorii, Cic. B. *the chief strength;* nervi belli pecunia, *money the sinews of war,* Cic.; nervi conjurationis, Liv.

nescĭo -īvi and -ĭi -ītum, 4. *not to know, to be ignorant of.* I. Gen., de Oropo opinor, sed certum nescio, *I do not certainly know,* Cic.; with rel. sent., nescis quanta cum expectatione sim te auditurus, Cic.; quid nobis agendum sit, nescio, Cic.; nescio qui, quae, quod (interrog.), nescio quis, quid, *I know not who or what, somebody or something;* casu nescio quod, Cic.; in oppidum, nescio quod, Cic.; nescio quid exsculpserunt, Cic.; nescio quomodo, *I know not how, somehow or other,* Cic. II. Esp., A. *not to know or recognise a person or thing;* non nescire hiemem, Verg. B. *not to understand anything, to be unable to do anything, not to have learnt;* non tam praeclarum est scire Latine quam turpe nescire, Cic.; Stoici omnino irasci nesciunt, Cic.

nescĭus -a -um (ne and scio). I. Act., A.

not knowing, ignorant, unaware, unconscious; nescia mens hominum fati sortisque futurae, Verg.; non sum nescius, ista inter Graecos dici, Cic. B. *not knowing how to do anything, unable to do anything;* pueri fari nescii, Hor.; cedere nescius, Hor. II. Pass., *unknown;* nescia tributa, Tac.; causa, Ov.

Nēsĭs -ĭdis, f. *an island in the Gulf of Puteoli,* now *Nisita.*

Nessus -i, m. (Νέσσος). I. *a river in Thrace.* II. *a Centaur killed by Hercules with a poisoned arrow.*

Nestōr -ŏris, m. (Νέστωρ), *son of Neleus, king of Pylus, the oldest and most experienced of the Greek heroes before Troy.*

Nētum -i, n. *a town of Sicily, south-west of Syracuse.*

neu = neve (q.v.).

neuter -tra -trum (ne and uter), *neither of two.* I. Lit., quid bonum sit, quid malum, quid neutrum, Cic.; neutram in partem moveri, Cic.; neuter consulum, Liv. II. In grammar, nomina neutra, or simply neutra, *neuter nouns,* Cic.

neutĭquam, adv. *by no means, not at all;* monebas de Q. Cicerone ut eum quidem neutiquam relinquerem, Cic.

neutrō, adv. (neuter), *in neither direction, towards neither side;* neutro inclinata res, spes, Liv.

neutrŭbĭ, adv. (neuter and ubi), *in neither place,* Plaut.

nēvĕ or **neu,** adv. *and not, or not, nor* (follows ut or ne); rogo te, ne contrabas, neve sinas, Cic.; cohortatus est, uti suae pristinae virtutis memoriam retinerent, neu perturbarentur animo, Caes.; sometimes follows the subj. only, hic ames dici pater atque princeps, neu sinas Medos equitare inultos, Hor.; sometimes repeated, *neither . . . nor;* ut id neve in hoc, neve in alio requiras, Cic.

nēvis, nevult = nonvis, nonvult, v. nolo.

nex, nĕcis, f. (cf. Gr. νέκυς). I. *violent death, murder;* necem sibi consciscere, *to commit suicide,* Cic.; vitae necisque potestatem habere in aliquem, Caes.; alicui necem inferre or offerre, Cic. II. Meton., *blood of the person slain;* manus nece Phrygiā imbutae, Ov.

nexĭlis -e (necto), *tied together, bound together;* sinus, Ov.

nexo, 1. (intens. of necto), *to tie together, bind together,* Lucr.

nexum -i, n. (necto), *a formal transaction between debtor and creditor, by which the debtor pledged his liberty as security for his debt,* Liv.; meton., *the obligation created by nexum,* Cic.; quum sunt propter unius libidinem, omnia nexa civium liberata nectierque postea desitum, Cic.

nexus -ūs, m. (necto). I. *a binding, tying together, entwining, connecting;* atomorum, Cic.; serpens, baculum qui nexibus ambit, Ov. II. Fig., A. legis nexus, Tac. B. *the relation or obligation arising from* nexum; nexu vincti, Liv.; se nexu obligare, Cic.

nī, adv. and conj. I. = ne in sentences with the subj., ni teneant cursus, Verg.; hence, quid ni? *why not?* Cic. II. = si non, *if not, except, unless;* moriar, ni puto, *I wish I may die if I don't think,* Cic.; plures cecidissent, ni nox praelio intervenisset, Liv.; excidium minitans, ni causam suam dissociarent, Tac.

Nĭcaea -ae, f. (Νίκαια). I. *a town in Bithynia,* now *Isnik.* II. *a town in Locris, not far from Thermopylae.*

nĭcaeus -a -um (νικαῖος, *victorious*), *epithet of Jupiter.*

Nīcander -dri, m. (Νίκανδρος), *poet, grammarian, and physician of Colophon.*

nĭcātor -ōris, acc. plur. -ōras, m. (νικάτωρ), *the conqueror; soldier of a body-guard of Perseus, king of Macedonia.*

Nīcĕphŏrĭum (-ŏn) -ĭi, n. (Νικηφορίον), 1, *a grove near Pergamum;* 2, *a town in Mesopotamia.*

Nīcĕphŏrĭus -ĭi, m. *a river in Armenia.*

nĭcētērĭum -ĭi, n. (νικητήριον), *the reward of victory, prize,* Juv.

Nīcŏmēdēs -is, n. (Νικομήδης), *name of several kings of Bithynia.*

Nīcŏpŏlis, acc. -lin, f. (Νικόπολις), *a town in Acarnania, founded by Augustus to commemorate his victory at Actium.*

nicto, 1. and **nictor**, 1. dep. (* nico, *to beckon*), 1, *to move the eyelid up and down, to wink,* Plin.; 2, *to wink with the eye, as a signal;* alicui, Plaut.

nictus -ūs, m. (* nico), *a winking with the eye,* Ov. (?)

nīdāmentum -i, n. (nidus), *the materials of a nest,* Plaut.

nīdĭfĭco, 1. (nidus and facio), *to build a nest,* Plin.

nīdor -ōris, m. (connected with κνίσσα), *a vapour, odour, steam arising from anything which is cooked;* ganearum, Cic.

nīdŭlus -i, m. (dim. of nidus), *a little nest;* Ithaca illa in asperrimis saxulis tamquam nidulus affixa, Cic.

nīdus -i, m. *a nest.* **I.** 1, lit., effingere et constituere nidos, Cic.; nidum tignis suspendit hirundo, Verg.; fig., me majores pennas nido extendisse, *to raise oneself above the condition in which one is born,* Hor.; 2, meton., *the young birds in the nest, nestlings;* nidi loquaces, Verg. **II.** Transf., *a dwelling on a height;* celsae Acherontiae, Hor.

nĭger -gra -grum, *black, dark-coloured.* **I. A.** Lit., hederae, Verg.; silvae, Hor.; coelum pice nigrius, Ov.; subst., **nĭgrum** -i, n. *a black spot,* Ov. **B.** Meton., *making black, blackening;* Auster, Verg. **II.** Transf., 1, *of or relating to death;* ignes, *the funeral pile,* Hor.; dies, *the day of death,* Prop.; 2, a, *unlucky, unpropitious;* b, of character, *black = wicked,* Cic.

nĭgrans -antis, p. adj. (from nigro), *black, dark-coloured,* Verg.

nĭgresco -grŭi, 3. (* nigreo), *to become black, grow dark in colour, grow dark;* tenebris nigrescunt omnia circum, Verg.

nĭgro, 1. (niger), *to be black,* Lucr.

nĭgror -ōris, m. (niger), *blackness; mortis,* Lucr.

nĭhil and contr. **nīl**, n. indecl. *nothing.* **I.** Subst., **A.** *nothing;* nihil agere, Cic.; with genit. of subst. or neut. adj., nihil rerum humanarum, Cic.; nihil mali, Cic.; nihil est cur, quamobrem, quod, *there is no reason why;* nihil est cur gestias, Cic.; nihil ad rem, *it has nothing to do with the business,* Cic.; nihil non, *everything;* nihil mali non inest, Cic.; non nihil, *something,* Cic.; nihil nisi, *nothing but,* Cic.; nihil aliud nisi, *nothing else but,* Cic.; nihil . . . quin, e.g., nihil agis quin ego audiam, *you do nothing that I do not hear of,* Cic. **B.** *a nothing;* nihil esse, *to be good for nothing,* Cic.; aliquem nihil putare, *to think nothing of,* Cic. **II.** Adj. in the phrases, nihil quidquam, nihil unum, Cic. **III.** Adv., *not at all, in nothing;* de fratre nihil ego te accusavi, Cic.; Thebani nihil moti sunt, Liv.

nĭhildum, conj. *nothing as yet,* Cic.

nĭhĭlōmĭnus, v. nihilum.

nĭhĭlum -i, n. (nihil), *nothing.* **I.** Subst., ex nihilo oriatur, Cic.; ad nihilum venire ot recĭdere, Cic.; pro nihilo est, *it is as good as nothing,* Cic.; nihili, the genit. of price; facere, aestimare, *to think nothing of,* Cic.; de nihilo, *without ground or reason,* Liv.; abl., nihilo, with compar., *by nothing, no;* nihilo benevolentior, Cic.; nihilo magis, Cic.; nihilominus = *no less, nevertheless, notwithstanding;* nihilominus eloquentiae studendum est, etsi eā quidam perverse abutuntur, Cic. **II.** Adv.. *in no way,* Hor., Liv.

nīl = nihil (q. v.).

nīlum = nihilum (q. v.).

Nīlus -i, m. (Νεῖλος), *the river Nile;* hence, 1, adj., **Nīlĭăcus** -a -um, *belonging to the Nile;* fera, *a crocodile,* Mart.; modi, *Egyptian,* Ov.; 2, **Nīlĭgĕna** -ae, m. (Nilus and gigno), *one born on the Nile, an Egyptian;* 3, transf.= *a canal, aqueduct,* Cic.

nimbātus -a -um (nimbus), *shrouded in cloud or mist,* Plaut.

nimbĭfĕr -fĕra -fĕrum (nimbus and fero), *storm-bringing, stormy,* Ov.

nimbōsus -a -um (nimbus), *rainy, stormy;* ventus, Ov.

nimbus -i, m. (connected with nubo). **I.** *a storm of rain, violent shower of rain;* 1, lit., nimbus effusus, Liv.; 2, transf., ferreus, *shower of missiles,* Verg. **II.** *a storm;* 1, lit., a, Cic.; b, *a storm-wind;* toto sonuerunt aethere nimbi, Verg.; 2, fig., hunc quidem nimbum cito transisse laetor, Cic. **III.** *a cloud;* 1, a, *a black rain-cloud;* involvere diem nimbi, Verg.; 2, *a cloud, mist,* Liv., Verg.; 3, transf., a, fulvae nimbus arenae, Verg.; b, of a large number of persons or things, *a cloud;* peditum, Verg.

nīmĭo, v. nimius.

nīmĭrum, adv. (ni = ne and mirum), *undoubtedly, doubtless, truly, certainly;* nimirum Themistocles est auctor adhibendus, Cic.; often ironically, *doubtless, forsooth;* uni nimirum tibi recte semper erunt res, Hor.

nĭmĭs, adv. *too much, overmuch, excessively;* valde, saepe, Cic.; foll. by genit., insidiarum, Cic.; non nimis, *not particularly, not very much;* praesidium non nimis firmum, Cic.

nĭmĭum, v. nimius.

nĭmĭus -a -um (nimis), *too great, too much, excessive.* **I.** Adj., **A.** Lit., 1, gen., a, of things, celeritas, Cic.; b, of persons, *intemperate, immoderate;* nimius in honoribus decernendis, Cic.; with genit., imperii, Liv.; 2, *too powerful, too great;* (legio) consularibus nimia, Tac. **B.** Transf., *very large, excessively large;* nimium quantum, *to an extraordinary degree;* sales in dicendo nimium quantum valent, Cic. **II.** Subst., *excess, too much;* nimium dixisse, Cic.; nimium hostium, Liv. **III.** Adv., **A.** nimio, *by far, very much, exceedingly;* esp. with compar., Albi, ne doleas plus nimio, Hor. **B.** nimium, *too, too much;* nimium diu, *too long,* Cic.; non nimium, *not particularly,* Cic.

ningo (**ningŭo**), ninxi, 3. (nix), *to snow,* 1, usually impers., ningit, *it snows,* Verg.; 2, transf., ningunt floribus rosarum, Lucr.

ninguis -is, f. *snow,* Lucr.

Nīnus -i, m. (Νίνος). **I.** m. *king of Assyria, husband of Semiramis.* **II.** f. *Nineveh, the capital of Assyria.*

Nĭŏbē -ēs, f. and **Nĭŏba** -ae, f. (Νιόβη), *daughter of Tantalus, wife of Amphion.* Hence, adj., **Nĭŏbēus** -a -um, *of Niobe.*

Nĭphātes -ae, m. (Νιφάτης, *the snow-mountain*), *a mountain of the Taurus range in Armenia.*

Nīreus, acc. Nīrĕa, m. (Νιρεύς), *son of Charopus, next to Achilles the most beautiful of all the Greek heroes at the siege of Troy.*

Nīsaeus, Niseis, Niseius, v. 1. Nisus.

nĭsĭ, conj. (for nĭ-sĭ). **I.** *if not;* quod nisi esset, certe postea non discessisset, Cic. **II. A.** After negatives and questions, *except, unless;* hoc sentio, nisi in bonis, amicitiam non posse, Cic.; Labienus juravit se, nisi victorem, in castra non reversurum, Cic.; *after nihil aliud, quid aliud,* etc., nisi = *than, but;* erat historia nihil aliud nisi annalium confectio, Cic. **B.** nisi si, *except if, except in case that;* nisi si qui ad me plura scripsit, Cic.; nisi quod, *except that;* praedia me valde delectant, nisi quod illum aere alieno obruerunt, Cic.

Nĭsībis, acc. -in, f. (Νίσιβις), *capital of the province of Mygdonia in Mesopotamia.*

1. Nīsus -i, m. **I.** *king in Megara, father of Scylla, changed into a sparrow-hawk.* Hence, adj., **A. Nīsaeus** -a -um, *of Nisus;* canes (of Scylla, the daughter of Phorcus, confused with Scylla, daughter of Nisus), Ov. **B. Nĭsĭăs** -ădis, f. = *Megarian,* Ov. **C. Nīsēis** -ĭdis, f. *Scylla, daughter of Nisus.* **D. Nīsēius** -a -um, *of or relating to Nisus;* virgo, *Scylla,* Ov. **II.** *the friend of Euryalus (in Vergil's Aeneid).*

2. nīsus (nixus) -ūs, m. (1. nitor). **I.** *a step, tread;* stat gravis Entellus nisuque immotus eodem, *in the same posture,* Verg. **II.** 1, *an ascent;* nisus per saxa, Sall.; 2, *flight,* Verg.; **3**, *the course of the stars,* Cic.; 4, *the pains of labour, a giving birth,* Cic.

3. nīsus -a -um, v. 1. nitor.

nĭtēdŭla -ae, f. *a field-mouse, shrew-mouse,* Cic.

nĭtella = nitedula (q.v.).

1. nĭtens -entis, p. adj. (from niteo). **I.** 1, *shining, bright, glittering;* lacrimis oculos suffusa nitentes, Verg.; **2**, *of animals, taurus, sleek,* Verg.; **3**, *of men, bright, beautiful,* Cat.; **4**, *of plants, blooming;* nitentia culta, Verg. **II.** Fig., *brilliant;* oratio, Cic.

2. nĭtens -entis, partic. of nitor.

nĭtĕo -ŭi, 2. (nix), *to shine, glitter, be bright.* **I. A.** Lit., luna nitet, Lucr.; qui nitent unguentis, fulgent purpurā, Cic. **B.** Fig., *to be brilliant;* illorum vides quam niteat oratio, Cic. **II.** Transf., 1, *of men and animals, to be sleek, appear in good condition, look bright or beautiful,* Hor.; **2**, *of things, to abound, to flourish;* vectigal in pace niteat, Cic.

nĭtesco, 3. (niteo), *to begin to shine, to be bright.* **I.** juventus nudatos humeros oleo perfusa nitescit, Verg. **II.** Of animals, *to be sleek, in good condition,* Plin.

nĭtĭdē, adv. (nitidus), *brilliantly, splendidly;* cenare, Plaut.

nĭtĭdiuscŭlē, adv. (nitidiusculus), *somewhat splendidly, with moderate brilliance,* Plaut.

nĭtĭdiuscŭlus -a -um (dim. of compar. nitidior), *somewhat splendid, somewhat brilliant,* Plaut.

nĭtĭdus -a -um (niteo), *bright, brilliant, shining, glittering.* **I. A.** Lit., ebur, Ov. **B.** Transf., a, *of animals, sleek, fat, in good condition;* vacca, Ov.; b, *of men,* (a) *sleek, healthy-looking;* me pinguem et nitidum bene curatā cute vises, Hor.; robur, Liv.; (β) *handsome, spruce, trim, elegant;* quos pexo capillo nitidos videtis, Cic.; ex nitido fit rusticus, Hor.; c, *of fields and plants, flourishing, blooming, luxuriant;* campi,

Cic. **II.** Fig., *elegant, refined, polished, cultivated;* nitidum quoddam genus verborum et laetum, Cic.

Nĭtiobrĭges -um, m. *a Celtic people in Aquitania.*

1. nītor, nīsus or nixus sum, 3. dep. *to rest, lean, support oneself upon anything.* **I.** Gen., **A.** Lit., stirpibus suis, Cic.; hastili, Cic.; baculo, Ov.; in hastam, Verg. **B.** Transf., 1, *to rest upon, depend upon;* in te nititur civitatis salus, Cic.; **2**, *to confide in, put one's trust in, lean upon;* consilio alicuius, Cic. **II. A.** Lit., 1, *to tread, move;* simul ac primum niti possunt, Cic.; **2**, *to give birth to, bring forth,* Ov.; **3**, *to make an effort,* Caes.; **4**, *of birds or winged creatures, to fly,* Verg.; **5**, *to climb, ascend, push up towards a height;* gradibus, Verg. **B.** Transf., *to strain, strive, exert oneself, endeavour;* tantum, quantum potest, quisque nitatur, Cic.; *pro libertate,* Sall.; ad immortalitatem gloriae, Cic.; *with* acc. and infin., nitamur igitur nihil posse percipi, Cic.; *with* ut or ne and the subj., Nep., Sall.

2. nĭtor -ōris, m. (niteo), *brilliance, brightness, splendour.* **I.** Lit., diurnus, *daylight,* Ov.; argenti et auri, Ov.; *elegance, charm, beauty,* Cic.; urit me Glycerae nitor, Hor. **II.** Fig., *splendour, elegance of style;* orationis, Cic.; nitor et cultus descriptionum, Tac.

nītrum -i, n. (νίτρον), *natron, natural soda,* used for washing, ap. Cic.

nĭvālis -e (nix), *of or relating to snow, snowy.* **I. A.** Lit., dies, Liv. **B.** Meton., *snow-white;* equi candore nivali, Verg. **II.** *covered with snow;* Othrys, Verg.

nĭvātus -a -um (nix), *cooled with snow, iced,* Suet.

1. nĭvĕ = ni (q.v.).

2. nĭvĕ = neve (q.v.).

nĭvĕus -a -um (nix), *of or relating to snow, snowy.* **I.** Lit., agger, Verg.; mons, *covered with snow,* Cat. **II.** Meton., *white as snow, snowy;* lacerti, Verg.; lac, Verg.

nĭvōsus -a -um (nix), *abounding in snow, snowy;* grando, Liv.; hiems, Liv.

nix, nĭvis, f. (* νίψ, acc. νίφα). **I.** Lit., *snow,* Cic. **II.** = *grey hair;* nives capitis, Hor.

Nixi dii, *three images of gods in a kneeling position in the Capitol at Rome, invoked as the deities of child-birth.*

nixor, 1. dep. (intens. of nitor), *to lean upon, rest upon, to strive, strain,* Lucr., Verg.

1. nixus = 2. nisus (q.v.).

2. nixus, v. 1. nitor.

no, nāvi, nāre (νέω), *to swim.* **I.** Lit., bestiae nantes, Cic.; prov., nare sine cortice, *to be able to do without a guardian,* Hor. **II.** Transf., *to sail, float, flow, fly,* Verg., Cat.

nōbĭlis -e (nosco), *noticeable, well-known.* **I.** Gen., inimicitiae nobiles inter eos erant, Liv. **II. A.** *celebrated, renowned, well-known;* ex doctrina, Cic.; ut arcendis sceleribus exemplum nobile esset, Liv.; in a bad sense, *infamous, notorious;* nobilis clade Romanā Caudina pax, Liv. **B.** *of noble birth, noble, belonging to a family some members of which had held curule magistracies* (opp. novus or ignobilis), Cic.; nobili genere nati, Cic.; homo, Cic. **C.** *excellent, noble;* tres nobilissimi fundi, Cic.

nōbĭlĭtas -ātis, f. (nobilis). **I.** *fame, celebrity,* Cic. **II.** *noble birth, nobility;* genere et nobilitate sui municipii facile primus, Cic.; meton., *the aristocrats, the nobility;* omnis nostra nobilitas interiit, Caes. **III.** *excellence, worth, superiority;* signa summā nobilitate, Cic.

nōbĭlĭtĕr, adv. (nobilis), *excellently, admirably, nobly*, Plin.

nōbĭlĭto, 1. (nobilis), *to make known.* **I.** Gen., rem, Liv. **II.** *to make famous, renowned;* **a**, in a good sense, poëtae post mortem nobilitari volunt, Cic.; **b**, in a bad sense, *to make infamous, notorious;* Phalaris, cuius est praeter ceteros nobilitata crudelitas, Cic.

nŏcens -entis, p. adj. (from noceo). **I.** Gen., *hurtful, injurious, noxious;* caules, Cic. **II.** Esp., *culpable, criminal, guilty, wicked;* homo, Cic.; subst. nocens, *a guilty person*, Cic.

nŏcĕo -ŭi -ĭtum, 2. *to hurt, injure, harm;* with dat., alteri, Cic.; with dat. and neut. acc., nihil iis, Caes.; with acc. and infin., nocet esse deum, Ov.; pass. impers., ne quid eis noceatur, Cic.

nŏcīvus -a -um (noceo), *hurtful, injurious*, Phaedr.

noctĭfĕr -fĕri, m. (nox and fero), *the nightbringer*, i.e., *the Evening Star*, Cat.

noctĭlūca -ae, f. (nox and luceo, *something that shines by night*), *the moon*, Hor.

noctĭvăgus -a -um (nox and vagus), *wandering by night;* currus (of the moon), Verg.

noctū (another form of nocte), **a**, abl., hac noctu, Plaut.; **b**, adv. *by night, in the night* (opp. interdiu, *by day*), Cic.

noctŭa -ae, f. (*noctuus from nox), *the owl*, Verg.

noctŭābundus -a -um (*noctuor from nox), *travelling by night;* tabellarius, Cic.

noctŭīnus -a -um (noctua), *of or relating to the owl*, Plaut.

nocturnus -a -um (noctu), *by night, nightly, nocturnal;* labores diurnos nocturnosque suscipere, Cic.; fur, Cic.; lupus, *preying by night*, Verg.; Bacchus, *worshipped at night*, Verg.; subst., **Nocturnus** -i, m. *the god of night*, Plaut.

nŏcŭus -a -um (noceo), *hurtful, injurious*, Ov.

nōdo, 1. (nodus), *to knot, tie in a knot.* **I.** Lit., crines in aurum, Verg. **II.** Transf., *to fetter;* collum laqueo nodatus amator, Ov.

nōdōsus -a -um (nodus), *full of knots, knotty.* **I.** Lit., lina, nets, Ov. **II.** Fig., *knotty, full of difficulties*, Sen.; transf., Cicuta, *a usurer, cunning in ensnaring debtors*, Hor.

nōdus -i, m. *a knot.* **I. A.** Lit., Cic. **B.** Meton., **a,** *a girdle*, Verg.; anni, *the equator*, Lucr.; **b**, *the knot into which the hair was sometimes collected*, Ov. **C.** Fig., **1,** *a tie, bond, connexion;* amicitiae, Cic.; **2, a,** *a bond, obligation, fetter;* exsolvere animos nodis religionum, Lucr.; **b,** *a difficulty, entanglement, perplexity;* dum hic nodus expediatur, Cic. **II.** Transf., **1,** *a knot or knob on the joint of an animal;* crura sine nodis articulisque habere, Caes.; **2,** *a knot in the wood of plants*, Verg., Liv.; **3,** *a star in the constellation Pisces*, Cic. poet.

Nōla -ae, f. *a town in Campania*, now *Nola.* Hence, adj., **Nōlānus** -a -um, *belonging to Nola;* subst., **Nōlāni** -ōrum, m. *the inhabitants of Nola;* subst., in Nolano, *in the territory of Nola*, Cic.

nōlo, nōlŭi, nolle (ne and volo). **I.** *to be unwilling, not to wish;* with acc., quae etiamsi nolunt, Cic.; with acc. and infin., nolo enim, eundem populum imperatorem esse et portitorem terrarum, Cic.; pluribus praesentibus eas res jactari nolebat, Caes.; with infin., alienare nolui, Cic.; with subj., nolo accusator in judicium potentiam afferat, Cic.; the imper., noli, nolite, nolito, is frequently used with the infin. of another verb to form a periphrastic

imper.; noli putare, *don't imagine*, Cic.; velle, Liv.; nollem, *I could wish not;* Carthaginem et Numantiam funditus sustulerunt; nollem Corinthum, Cic. **II.** *to wish evil, to be unfavourable to;* alicui, Cic.

Nŏmăs -ădis, c. (νομάς), *pasturing;* hence, 1, plur., Nomades, *nomads, nations who lead a migratory, pastoral life*, Plin.; 2, *the Numidians*, Verg.

nōmen -ĭnis, n. (from root GNO, whence nosco), *a name.* **I. A.** Lit., gen., 1, nomen est quod unicuique personae datur, quo suo quaeque proprio et certo vocabulo appellatur, Cic.; imponere nova rebus nomina, Cic.; appellare aliquem nomine, Cic.; cantus cui nomen neniae, Cic.; nomen dare, Cic., edere, profiteri, Liv., *to give in one's name as a soldier, enlist*, Liv., 2, esp., *the gentile name of a Roman*, as e.g., Cornelius in P. Cornelius Scipio, though sometimes used for the praenomen (Publius) or the cognomen (Scipio); Cic.; 3, meton., a, nomina tanta (like our *great names = great men*), Ov.; b, nomen Romanum, *the Roman power.* **B.** Fig., 1, *name, fame, glory;* nomen habere, Cic.; 2, a, *name, cause;* nomine meo, tuo, *in my name, on my behalf*, Cic.; nomine lucri, *for the sake of*, Cic.; uno nomine, *at once;* accusati sunt uno nomine consulares, Cic.; b, *ground, pretext;* nomen inductum fictae religionis, Cic.; 3, *the name* (as opposed to the thing); legionum, *the mere name*, Cic. **II.** Transf., polit. t. t., 1, nomen alicuius deferre, *to give information against, accuse judicially*, Cic.; nomen recipere, *to receive an information*, Cic.; 2, *a security for a debt;* certis nominibus, *on good security*, Cic; nomina solvere, exsolvere, expedire, *to pay a debt*, Cic.; nomina sua exigere, *to collect one's debts*, Cic.; nomen facere, *to set down a debt in the account-book, to lend money*, Cic.; meton., *a debtor;* bonum nomen, *a good payer*, Cic.

nōmenclātĭo -ōnis, f. (*nomenclo, from nomen and calo = voco), *a calling by name, naming*, Qu. Cic.

nōmenclātor -ōris, m. (*nomenclo), *a slave who told his master the names of his clients at his reception, or of the persons whom he met in the streets*, Cic.

Nōmentum -i, n. *a town fourteen miles north-east of Rome.* Hence, adj., **Nōmentānus** -a -um, *of or belonging to Nomentum.*

nōmĭnātim, adv. (nomino), *by name, expressly, particularly;* centuriones nominatim appellare, Caes.; de aliquo nominatim decernere ut, etc., Cic.

nōmĭnātĭo -ōnis, f. (nomino), *a naming, nomination to a priesthood or other public office*, Cic.

nōmĭnātus -a -um, p. adj. (from nomino), *well-known, noted, celebrated*, Cic.

nōmĭnĭto, 1. (intens. of nomino), *to name, call by name*, Lucr.

nōmĭno, 1. (nomen). **I.** *to name, give a name to;* amore quo amicitia est nominata, Cic. **II.** *to mention, speak about;* ad flumen Sabim quod supra nominavimus, Cic.; Sulla quem honoris causā nomino, *whom I mention to do him honour*, Cic. **III. A.** *to make famous, make renowned;* praedicari de est nominari volunt omnes, Cic. **B.** Polit. t. t., a, *to name, appoint, nominate to a priesthood or other office;* me augurem nominaverunt, Cic.; b, *to accuse judicially, give information against;* aliquem apud dictatorem, Liv.

Nōmĭus (-ŏs) -ĭi, m. (Νόμιος), *the pasturer, a name of Apollo (from his having fed the flocks of Admetus).*

nŏmisma (**nŭmisma**) -mătis, n. (νόμισμα) *a coin, a piece of money*, Hor.

nōn, adv. (from old Latin noenum = ne unum). **I.** *not.* **A.** non est ita, judices, non est profecto, Cic. ; before negatives, non forms a weak affirmative, e.g., non nihil, non nemo, non nullus, Cic. ; after negatives the affirmative thus formed is emphatic, nihil non ad rationem dirigebat, Cic. ; with affirmative adjectives the negative formed by non is emphatic, *by no means;* Cethegus homo non probatissimus, Cic. ; homo non aptissimus ad jocandum, Cic. ; non quod, non quo, *not that, not as if;* non quod sola ornent, sed quod excellant, Cic. ; non nisi, *only;* non modum (solum) *not only,* Cic. ; non ita, non tam, *not very, not particularly;* simulacra perampla, sed non ita antiqua, Cic. **B. 1,** non in questions = nonne? non idem fecit? Cic. ; **2,** poet. = ne, non petito, Ov. **II.** Used in answers, *no;* aut etiam aut non respondere, Cic.

Nōnācris -is, f. (Νώνακρις), *a mountain in Arcadia.* Hence, adj., **1, Nōnācrīnus** -a -um, *Arcadian;* virgo, *Callisto,* Ov. ; **2, Nōnācrius** -a -um, *Arcadian;* heros, *Evander,* Ov. ; subst., **Nōnācrĭa** -ae, f. = *Atalanta,* Ov.

nōnae -ārum, f. (nonus), *the nones, the fifth day in all the months* (except March, May, and July, when it was the seventh), *so called from being the ninth day before the Ides.*

nōnāgēnārĭus -a -um (nonageni), *containing ninety,* Plin.

nōnāgēni -ae -a (nonaginta), *ninety each,* Plin.

nōnāgēsĭmus -a -um (nonaginta), *the ninetieth,* Cic.

nōnāgĭēs, adv. (nonaginta), *ninety times,* Cic.

nōnāginta, numer. *ninety,* Cic.

nōnānus -a -um (nona, sc. legio), *belonging to the ninth legion;* miles, Tac. ; or subst., **nōnānus** -i, m. *a soldier of the ninth legion,* Tac.

nondum, adv. *not yet,* Cic.

nongenti -ae -a, *nine hundred,* Cic.

nonnĕ, interrog. adv., asks a question to which an affirmative answer is expected ; **1,** in direct questions, nonne animadvertis? *do you not perceive?* Cic. ; **2,** in indirect questions, quaero nonne id effecerit, Cic.

nonnēmo, nonnĭhil, v. nemo, nihil.

nonnullus (non nullus) -a -um, *some, several;* nonnulla in re, *in some respects,* Cic. ; nonnulla pars militum, Caes. ; non nullae cohortes, Caes. ; subst., **nonnulli,** *some,* Cic.

nonnumquam (non numquam), adv. *sometimes,* Cic.

nonnusquam, adv. *in some places, in several places,* Plin.

nōnus -a -um (= novenus, from novem), *the ninth,* Cic. ; subst., **nōna** -ae, f. *the ninth hour* (about three o'clock p.m.), when the chief meal (cena) was taken at Rome, Hor.

nōnusdēcĭmus, nonadecima, nonumdecimum, *the nineteenth,* Tac.

Nōra -ōrum, n. **I.** *a town in Sardinia;* hence, **Nōrenses** -ĭum, *the inhabitants of Nora.* **II.** *a fort in Cappadocia.*

Norba -ae, f. *a town in Latium,* now *Alcantara.* Hence, adj., **Norbānus** -a -um, *of or belonging to Norba.*

Nōrēja -ae, f. *a town in Noricum,* now *Neumarkt.*

Nōrĭcum -i, n. *Noricum, a country south of the Danube.* Hence, adj., **Nōrĭcus** -a -um, *Noric.*

norma -ae, f. (nosco), **1,** *a carpenter's square for measuring right angles,* Plin. ; **2,** *a rule, precept, model, pattern;* dirigere vitam ad certam rationis normam, Cic.

nōs, plur. of ego (q.v.).

Nortĭa -ae, f. (for Nevortia, from ne and vorto, Gk. Ἄτροπος, *the Unchangeable*), *an Etruscan goddess of fate, worshipped at Volsinii.*

noscĭto, l. (intens. of nosco), *to get to know.* **I.** Lit., **A.** Gen., *to observe, perceive,* Liv. **B.** Esp., *to investigate, explore;* aedes, vestigia, Plaut. **II.** Transf., *to recognise again;* aliquem facie, Liv.

nosco, nōvi, nōtum, 3. (root NO, archaic GNO, whence gnosco ; Gr. ΓΝΟ -Ω, whence γιγνώσκω). **I.** Lit., *to become acquainted with, get knowledge of;* and hence, in the perfect tenses, *to be acquainted with, to know;* (a) present tenses, studeo cursos istos mutationum noscere, Cic. ; (β) perfect tenses, quam (virtutem) tu ne de facie quidem nosti, Cic. ; si Caesarem bene novi, Cic. **II. A.** *to recognise;* ad res suas noscendas recipiendasque, Liv. **B.** Of a judge, *to investigate a case;* quae olim a praetoribus noscebantur, Tac. **C.** *to allow, admit, acknowledge a reason or excuse;* illam partem excusationis nec nosco, nec probo, Cic. (contracted perfect tenses, nosti, nostis, noram, noras, nosse).

noster -tra -trum (nos), *our, ours.* **I.** Gen., a, subject., provincia nostra, Caes. ; b, object. (= *towards us*) amor noster, Cic. **II.** Esp., **A.** *our, our adherent* or *friend, on our side, one of us;* a, Furnius noster, *our friend Furnius,* Cic. ; nostri, *our people,* Cic. ; b, noster in jest = ego, Plaut. **B.** *favourable to us;* nostra loca, Liv. ; noster Mars, Verg.

nostras -ātis (noster), *of our country, native;* mirifice capior facetiis, maxime nostratibus, Cic. ; philosophi, Cic.

nŏta -ae, f. (nosco), *a mark, token, note, sign.* **I.** Gen., **1,** lit., signa et notae locorum, Cic. ; **2,** fig., *distinguishing mark, sign;* notae argumentorum, Cic. **II. A.** *marks in writing;* **1,** *letters of the alphabet, numbers;* notae litterarum, Cic. ; poet., mento, notae, *a writing, letter,* Hor., Ov. ; **2,** notae librariorum, *marks of punctuation,* Cic. **B.** *marks on an object;* **1,** *marks on the body,* Hor.; **2,** *a branded mark, brand;* barbarus compunctus notis Thraeciis, tattooed, Cic.; fig., *disgrace, shame, ignominy;* quae nota domesticae turpitudinis non inusta vitae tuae est? Cic. ; **3,** *a mark on a cask of wine* or *honey* (to mark the quality) ; a, interior nota Falerni, (a better kind, Hor. ; b, transf., *sort, quality;* aliquem de meliore nota commendare, Cic. ; **4,** *a mark in a book* (to express approval or disapproval), Cic. ; **5,** *the official censure of the senate;* motise senatu notas ascribere, Liv. ; **6,** *a distinguishing name, mark of honour;* ille Numantina traxit ab urbe notam, Ov.

nŏtābĭlis -e (noto), *notable, remarkable, striking noteworthy;* exitus, Cic.

nŏtābĭlĭtěr, adv. (notabilis), *notably, remarkably, extraordinarily,* Tac.

nŏtārĭus -ii, m. (nota), *a rapid writer, shorthand writer,* Quint.

nŏtātĭo -ōnis, f. (noto), *a marking.* **I.** Lit., tabellarum, *a marking of the voting-tickets with different coloured wax,* Cic. **II.** **1,** *the stigma of the censor;* censoria, Cic. ; **2,** *a choice; judicium,* Cic. ; **3,** *the etymology of a word,* Cic. ; **4,** *observing, noting, taking notice of;* naturae, Cic.

nŏtātus -a -um, p. adj. (from noto), *known, marked;* homo omnium scelerum libidinumque notis notatissimus, Cic.

nōtesco, nōtŭi, 3. (1. notus), *to become known,* Cat.

nŏthus -a -um (νόθος). **I.** Lit., **1,** of men, *illegitimate, bastard,* Verg. ; **2,** of animals, *of mixed breed, hybrid, mongrel,* Verg. **II.** Transf., *not genuine, spurious.* Lucr., Cat.

nōtĭo -ōnis, f. (nosco), *a making oneself acquainted with anything.* **I.** 1, lit., Plaut.; 2, transf., *an idea, notion of anything, image, mental conception;* deorum, Cic.; rerum, Cic. **II. A.** *an investigation;* pontificum, Cic. **B.** *the investigation of the censor;* 1, judicium et notio censoria, Cic.; 2, *the blame, animadversion of the censor;* notiones animadversionesque censorum, Cic.

nōtĭtĭa -ae, f. (1. notus), *a being known.* **I.** Pass., 1, hi propter notitiam sunt intromissi, Nep.; 2, *fame, celebrity,* Tac. **II.** Act., 1, *knowing, becoming acquainted with;* notitia nova mulieris, Cic.; 2, a, *knowledge;* corporis sui, Cic.; b, *an idea, notion, conception;* dei, Cic.

nōtĭtĭes -ēi, f. = notitia (q.v.).

nŏto, 1. (nota). **I.** *to mark.* **A.** Lit., 1, tabellam cerā, Cic.; 2, a, *to mark out;* notat et designat oculis ad caedem unumquemque nostrum, Cic.; b, polit. **t. t.,** *of the censor, to place a mark against a Roman citizen's name in the burgess-list, to censure publicly, blame, reprimand;* quos censores furti et captarum pecuniarum nomine notaverunt, Cic. **B.** Transf., 1, *to mark, denote;* res nominibus, Cic.; aliquid verbis Latinis, *to express,* Cic.; 2, *to mark out, make noticeable;* aliquem decore, Cic.; 3, *to blame, censure;* verbis aliquem, Cic. **II.** *to express by signs.* **A.** 1, lit., *to unite;* litteram, Ov.; 2, a, *to point out shortly;* caput, Cic.; b, *to observe;* cantus avium, Cic. **B.** Fig., *to impress;* dicta memori pectore, Ov.

nŏtŏs = 2. notus (q.v.).

1. **nŏtus** -a -um, p. adj. (from nosco), *known.* **I.** 1, lit, res nota, Cic.; noti atque insignes latrones, Cic.; aliquid notum habere, *to know,* Cic.; subst., noti, *friends, acquaintances;* 2, transf., a, = *friendly;* notis compellat vocibus, Verg.; b, *customary;* ulmus nota quae sedes fuerat columbis, Hor. **II.** 1, *distinguished, celebrated;* scriptor, Hor.; 2, *notorious;* mulier, Cic.

2. **nŏtus** (-ŏs) -i, m. (νότος), *the south wind;* 1, lit., Verg.; 2, transf., *the wind,* Verg.

nŏvācŭla -ae, f. (novo), *a sharp knife or razor;* cotem novaculā praecidere, Cic.

nŏvālis -is, f. and **nŏvāle** -is, n. 1, *fallow land,* Verg.; 2, *a cultivated field;* novalia culta, Verg.

nŏvātrix -īcis, f. (novator), *she that renews;* rerum, Ov.

nŏvē, adv. (novus). **I.** *newly, in a new and unusual manner,* Plaut. **II.** novissime; a, *lately, recently,* Sall.; b, *lastly, in the last place,* Sall.

nŏvellus -a -um (dim. of novus), a, *new, young;* arbor, Cic.; b, oppida, *lately conquered,* Liv.

nŏvem, numer. *nine,* Cic.; decem novem, *nineteen,* Caes.

November -bris, m. (novem and suffix -ber), *relating to the number nine;* a, mensis November, *the ninth month of the Roman year, November,* Cic.; b, *belonging to the month of November;* kalendae Novembres, Cic.

nŏvemdĕcim, numer. (novem and decem) *nineteen,* Liv.

nŏvendĭālis -e (novem and dies), 1, *that which happens on the ninth day;* coena, *a funeral banquet held on the ninth day after death,* Tac.; pulveres = *new, fresh,* Hor.; 2, *that which lasts nine days;* feriae, *a nine days' festival celebrated on the occasion of any portent* (such as a shower of stones), Cic.

Nŏvensĭles dii (novus and suffix -ensilis), *gods whose worship had been introduced from foreign countries* (opp. indigetes, *native divinities*), Liv.

nŏvēnus -a -um (novem), *nine each, nine,* Liv.

nŏverca -ae, f. *a step-mother,* Cic.; saeva, Verg.; prov., apud novercam queri, i.e., *in vain,* Plaut.

nŏvercālis -e (noverca), *of or relating to a step-mother,* Juv., Tac.

Nŏvesĭum -ĭi, n. *fort of the Ubii on the Rhine,* now *Neuss.*

nŏvĭcĭus -a -um (novus), *new, fresh,* Plaut.; esp. of *persons who have not long been enslaved;* subst., novicii; Syrum nescio quem de grege noviciorum factum esse consulem, Cic.

nŏvĭes, adv. numer. (novem), *nine times,* Verg.

Nŏvĭŏdūnum -i, n., 1, *a town of the Suessiones,* now *Soissons;* 2, *a town of the Bituriges Cubi,* now *Nouan.*

nŏvĭtas -ātis, f. (novus), *newness.* **I.** Lit. **A.** anni, *the spring,* Ov.; plur., novitates = *new acquaintances,* Cic. **B.** *the condition of a* homo novus (v. novus), *newness of nobility,* Cic. **II.** *novelty, unusualness, strangeness;* terror quem tibi rei novitas attulerit, Cic.

nŏvo, 1. (novus). **I.** *to make new, renew.* **A.** transtra, Verg.; membra, *to revive,* Ov.; ager novatus, *a field reploughed,* Cic. **B.** Transf., a, *to revive, refresh;* (animus) risu novatur, Cic.; b, *to change, alter;* aliquid in legibus, Cic.; novare res, *to alter the constitution of a state, make a revolution,* Liv. **II.** *to invent something new;* verba, *invent new words,* Cic.

nŏvus -a -um (νέος), superl., novissimus, *new, fresh, young* (opp. vetus). **I.** Lit., **A.** Gen., miles, *a recruit,* Liv.; novae res, *novelties,* Cic.; and esp., *political changes, revolutions;* rebus novis studere, Cic.; lac, *new milk,* Verg. Subst., **nŏvum** -i, n. *a new thing, novelty;* num quidnam novi? Cic. **B.** Esp., a, novus homo or homo novus, *the first of a family who held a curule office in Rome,* e.g., M. T. Cicero, Cic.; b, novae tabulae, *new account-books* (that is, *a total extinction of debts*), Cic.; c, novae tabernae, or novae, *certain money-changers' shops in the forum which had been burnt down* A.U.C. 543, *and rebuilt;* sub Novis, Cic.; d, Nova via, *a road in Rome leading down to the forum,* Liv. **II.** Transf., 1, *fresh, inexperienced;* equus, Cic.; novus delictis, *inexperienced in crime,* Tac.; 2, *new, novel, unusual, extraordinary;* genus dicendi, Cic.; 3, = alter, *a second;* Camillus, *a second Camillus,* Liv.; novus Hannibal, Cic.; 4, *of succession,* the superl., **nŏvissĭmus** -a -um = (a) *the latest, last;* agmen, *the rear,* Caes.; (β) *the extremest, severest;* exempla, Tac.

nox, noctis, f. (νύξ), *night.* **I. A.** Lit., 1, gen., nocte, or de nocte, *by night,* Cic.; multā nocte, *de multa nocte, deep in the night, late at night,* Cic.; nocte mediā, de nocte media, *at midnight,* Cic.; noctes et dies urgeri, *night and day,* Cic.; se conjicere in noctem, *to hasten away under shelter of night,* Cic.; eam noctem pervigilare, Cic.; 2, personif., Nox, *the goddess Night, sister of Erebus,* Verg. **B.** Transf., 1, meton., *sleep,* Verg.; 2, a, *the darkness of a storm,* Verg.; b, *the lower world,* Verg.; c, *death,* Verg.; d, *blindness,* Ov. **II.** Fig., 1, *obscurity;* mei versus aliquantum noctis habebunt, Ov.; 2, *confusion, darkness, peril;* haec reipublicae nox, Cic.

noxa -ae, f. (noceo). **I.** *harm, injury, damage;* sine ullius urbis noxa, Liv. **II.** Meton., 1, *a crime, fault, offence;* in noxa esse, Liv.; 2. *punishment;* noxā liberari, Liv.

noxĭa -ae, f. (sc. causa, from noxius), *a fault, offence, crime;* alicui noxiae esse, *to be accounted a fault,* Liv.

noxĭus -a -um (noxa). **I.** *noxious, hurtful, injurious;* tela, Ov. **II.** *criminal, culpable, guilty;* aliquem noxium judicare, Liv.

nūbēcŭla -ae, f. (dim. of nubes). **I.** *a little cloud,* Plin. **II.** Fig., *a troubled, dark expression;* frontis, Cic.

nūbes -is, f. (cf. nubo), *a cloud.* **I. A.** Lit., aer concretus in nubes cogitur, Cic. **B.** Transf., 1, *a cloud,* e.g., of dust, pulveris, Liv.; 2, *a great number, dense mass of any objects;* locustarum, Liv.; volucrum, Verg. **II.** Fig., 1, *a cloud, or dark expression on the countenance;* deme supercilio nubem, Hor.; 2, *veil, concealment;* fraudibus objice nubem, Hor.; 3, *a cloud,* i.e., *threatening* or *impending misfortune;* belli, Verg.; 4, *a sad, miserable condition;* reipublicae, Cic.; 5, *a cloud* (as emblem of something unsubstantial), *a phantom;* nubes et inania captare, Hor.

nūbĭfĕr -fĕra -fĕrum (nubes and fero), *cloud-bearing, cloud-bringing,* Ov.

nūbĭgĕna -ae, c. (nubes and gigno), *born of a cloud, produced from a cloud;* esp., of the Centaurs, *offspring of Ixion and a cloud;* Nubigenae alone = *Centaurs,* Verg.

nūbĭlis -e (nubo), *marriageable;* filia, Cic.

nūbĭlus -a -um (nubes), *covered with clouds, cloudy, overcast.* **I. A.** Lit., plur. subst., **nūbĭla** -ōrum, n. clouds, Hor. **B.** Transf., 1, act., *cloud-bringing;* Auster, Ov.; 2, *dark;* via nubila taxo, Ov. **II.** Fig., 1, of expression, *dark, gloomy;* toto nubila vultu, Ov.; 2, *unfavourable;* nubila nascenti non mihi Parca fuit, Ov.; 3, *dark, unhappy;* tempora, Ov.

nūbo, nupsi, nuptum, 3. (stem NUB, whence nubes), *to cover, veil;* and especially, of a bride, *to be married to, to marry any one;* virgo nupsit ei, cui Caecilia nupta fuerat, Cic.; nuptam esse cum aliquo, Cic.; nubere in familiam, *to marry into a family,* Cic.; aliquam nuptum collocare, *to give in marriage,* Caes.; partic., **nuptus** -a -um, *married;* filia, Cic.; subst., **nupta** -ae, f. *a wife,* Liv.

Nūcĕrĭa -ae, f. *a town in Campania,* now *Nocera.* Hence, adj., **Nūcĕrīnus** -a -um, *relating to Nuceria.*

nūcĭfrangĭbŭlum -i, n. (nux and frango), *a nut-cracker* (in jest = *a tooth*), Plaut.

nuclĕus -i, m. (nux). **I.** Lit., 1, *the kernel of a nut,* or *any nut-like fruit,* Plin.; 2, *the stone* or *uneatable kernel of fruits,* Plin. **II.** Transf., *the kernel* or *inside of anything;* conchae, Plin.

nūdĭus = nunc dius (= dies), *it is now the ... day since;* always with the ordinal numerals; nudius tertius, *the day before yesterday,* Cic.; nudius tertius decimus, *thirteen days ago,* Cic.

nūdo, 1. (nudus), *to make naked, to make bare, strip.* **I. A.** Lit., 1, aliquem, Cic.; 2, a, *to lay bare, uncover;* gladium, *to draw,* Liv.; murus nudatus defensoribus, Caes.; b, milit. t. t., *to lay bare, leave undefended;* castra nudentur, Caes. **B.** Transf., 1, *to strip, make bare by robbery, to spoil, plunder;* spoliavit nudavitque omnia, Cic.; quem praeceps alea nudat, Hor.; 2, *to deprive;* aliquem praesidio, Cic. **II.** Fig., 1, *to strip, lay bare, expose;* nudata omnibus rebus tribunicia potestas, Caes.; vis ingenii scientiā juris nudata, Cic.; 2, *to uncover, expose, make visible, reveal;* animos, Liv.

nūdus -a -um, *naked, unclothed, nude, bare.* **I. A.** Lit., 1, Cic.; nudo capite, *bare-headed,* Sall.; 2, *uncovered;* vertex, Verg.; subsellia, vacant, Cic.; terga, Liv. **B.** Transf., 1, *deprived of;* with abl., praesidio, Cic.; with genit., loca nuda gignentium, Sall.; 2, *without;* republica nuda a magistratibus, Cic. **II.** Fig., 1, *simple,*

unadorned, plain; commentarii Caesaris, Cic.; 2, *bare, mere, alone, only;* nuda ista, si ponas, Cic.; hoc nudum relinquitur, Cic.

nūgae -ārum, f. (naucum), *trifles, nonsense, stuff, trumpery.* **I.** Lit., hunccine hominem tantis delectatum esse nugis? Cic.; applied also to verses, nescio quid meditans nugarum, Hor. **II.** Transf., of persons, *a foolish, trifling fellow;* amicos habet meras nugas, Cic.

nūgātor -ōris, m. (nugor), *a trifler, foolish fellow, a jester,* Cic.

nūgātōrius -a -um (nugator), *trifling, good for nothing, frivolous, futile, nugatory;* mala nugatoriaque accusatio, Cic.

nūgax -ācis (nugor), *trifling, frivolous,* ap. Cic.

nūgor, 1. dep. (nugae), 1, *to trifle, be frivolous, talk nonsense;* non inscite, Cic.; cum aliquo, Hor.; 2, *to trick, cajole, make game of,* Plaut.

nullus -a -um (ne and ullus), *no, none, nobody, no one.* **I. A.** Lit., 1, adj., nullā unā re, Cic.; nullo modo, nullo pacto, *by no means,* Cic.; nullo certo ordine neque imperio, Caes.; 2, subst., a, **nullus** = *nobody, no one,* Cic.; b, **nullum** -i, n. = *nothing,* Hor. **II.** Fig., 1, nullus sum; a, *I am ruined, it is all over with me;* nullus repente fui, Liv.; b, of persons and things, *I am no longer in existence;* de mortuis loquor, qui nulli sunt, Cic.; nullus = mortuus, Ov.; vellem nulla, Ov.; 2, *insignificant, of no importance, trifling, poor;* nullos judices habemus, Cic.; nullum argumentum est, Cic.

num, interrog. particle, asking a question to which a negative answer is expected. **A.** In direct questions, num censes etiam eosdem fuisse? Cic.; compounded with ne, deum ipsum numne vidisti? Cic.; num quid vis? *is there anything else which you want?* (a common form in leave-taking), Hor. **B.** In indirect questions, *whether;* quaero, num aliter ac nunc eveniunt evenirent? Cic.

Nūma -ae, m., Pompilius, *the second king of Rome.*

Nūmantĭa -ae, f. *a town in Hispania Tarraconensis, taken and destroyed by Scipio Africanus the younger.* Hence, adj., **Nūmantīnus** -a -um, *Numantine.*

nūmārĭus = nummarius (q.v.).

nūmātus = nummatus (q.v.).

nūmen -ĭnis, n. (= nuimen, from nuo), *a nodding, beckoning with the head; a nod,* as sign of a command, *a command.* **I.** Gen., numen vestrum, Cic.; magnum numen senatūs, Cic. **II.** Esp., of a deity, a, *the divine will, divine command;* numen interdictumque deorum immortalium, Cic.; mundum censent regi numine deorum, Cic.; Jovis numina, Phoebi numina, Verg.; b, (a) *the might of a deity, majesty, divinity;* qui nullam vim esse dicit numenve divinum, Cic.; of deities themselves, conversa numina, pia numina, Verg.; (β) of the Roman emperors, violatum numen Augusti, Tac.

nŭmĕrābĭlis -e (numero), *that can be counted, enumerated,* Ov.

nŭmĕrātus -a -um, p. adj. (from numero), *counted, in hard cash, in ready money;* dos, pecunia, Cic.; subst., **nŭmĕrātum** -i, n. *hard cash, money down;* numerato solvere, Cic.

1. **nŭmĕro,** 1. (numerus), *to count.* **I.** Lit., **A.** aliquem a se primum, Cic.; aliquid per digitos, *on the fingers,* Ov.; consule et numera (senatum), *count the house* (with a view to determine whether a sufficient number to transact business were present), Cic. **B.** *to count,* i.e.,

to pay money; militibus stipendium, Cic. **II.**
Transf., 1, *to count up, reckon, enumerate;* dies
deficiat, si velim numerare, quibus bonis male
evenerit, Cic.; 2, *to reckon under, class under;*
inter suos, Cic.; inter honestos homines, Cic.;
mortem in beneficii loco, Cic.; 3, with double
acc., in pass. with double nom., *to count, esteem,
hold, consider;* Sulpicium accusatorem suum
numerabat, non competitorem, Cic.; sapientes
cives, qualem me et esse, et numerari volo, Cic.
2. **nŭmĕrō**, adv. (lit., abl. of numerus), 1,
just, exactly, at the right time, Plaut.; 2, *quickly,
soon, too quickly, too soon,* Plaut.

nŭmĕrōsē, adv. (numerosus), 1, *numerously,*
Plin.; 2, *rhythmically, harmoniously;* circumscripte numeroseque dicere, Cic.

nŭmĕrōsus -a -um (numerus). **I.** *numerous, in great number;* numerosissima civitas,
populous, Tac. **II.** *rhythmical, harmonious;*
oratio, Cic.

nŭmĕrus -i, m. (connected with nummus),
a number. **I. A.** Lit., 1, numerum inire, *to
count,* Caes.; 2, a, *a certain number, a number of
persons* or *things, considered as a whole;* ad
pristinum numerum duo augures addidit, Cic.;
haec enim sunt tria numero, *are three in number,*
Cic.; numero quadraginta, *forty in number,* Sall.;
referre in deorum numero, *to count as a god,*
Cic.; b, *an uncertain number, a heap, mass;*
hominum, Cic.; innumerabilis frumenti numerus,
an enormous quantity, Cic.; c, *a division of the
army, company;* sparsi per provinciam numeri,
Tac.; d, *a cipher,* i.e., *of no consequence;* nos
numerus sumus, Hor. **B.** Meton., plur., numeri = 1, *dice* (as being marked with numbers);
numerosque manu jactabit eburnos, Ov.; 2,
mathematics, Cic. **II.** Transf., 1, *the part of a
whole;* elegans omni numero poema, *in every
respect,* Cic.; 2, a, *melody, music,* Verg., Ov.;
b, *dance,* Cic.; c, *a metrical foot, number;* numeri ac modi, Cic.; poet., numeri graves, *heroic
verse,* Ov.; d, in oratory, *harmony;* oratorius,
Cic.; 3, *rank, place, position;* obtinere aliquem
numerum, Cic.; numero or in numero, *in the
post of, as;* parentis numero esse, Cic.; 4, *order,
rule;* in numerum or numero, *according to rule,*
Verg.

Nŭmīcus (Nŭmīcĭus) -i, m. *a small river
in Latium, flowing into the Tyrrhene sea near
Ardea,* now *Numico.*

Nŭmīda -ae, m. (nomas, νομάς), *a Numidian;*
plur., **Nŭmīdae** -ārum, *the Numidians,* attrib.
= *Numidian;* Numidae jaculatores, Liv. Hence,
1, **Nŭmīdĭa** -ae, f. *a country in North Africa;*
2, **Nŭmīdĭcus** -a -um, *Numidian.*

nŭmisma = nomisma (q.v.).

Nŭmistro -ōnis, f. *town in Lucania, on the
borders of Apulia.*

Nŭmĭtor -ōris, m. *king of Alba, father of
Ilia, grandfather of Romulus and Remus.*

nummārĭus -a -um (nummus). **I.** *belonging to money;* theca, Cic.; difficultas nummaria
or rei nummariae, *scarcity of money,* Cic. **II.**
bribed with money, venal; judex, Cic.

nummātus -a -um (nummus), *provided with
money, rich;* adolescens non minus bene nummatus quam capillatus, Cic.

nummŭlus -i, m. (dim. of nummus), *a little
money, some money;* nummulis acceptis jus ac fas
cmne delere, *for a paltry sum,* Cic.

nummus (nūmus) -i, m. (νοῦμμος, Tarentine
and Sicilian = νόμος, *the regular silver currency).*
I. *money, coin;* adulterini nummi, *bad money,*
Cic.; habere in nummis, *to have in cash,* Cic.
II. Esp., *the sesterce, a Roman coin* worth about
2¼d.; quinque millia nummûm, Cic.; transf.,

like the English *penny, farthing* (to express a very
small sum); ad numum convenit, *it comes right to
a farthing,* Cic. (genit plur., gen. nummûm).

numquam, adv. (ne and unquam), *never*
Cic.; numquam adhuc, numquam ante, numquam
alias, Cic.; numquam non, *always,* Cic.; non
numquam, *sometimes,* Cic.

nūmus = nummus (q.v.).

nunc, adv. (νῦν). **I.** *now, at present, at this
moment;* ut nunc est, *as things are now,* Cic.;
nunc ipsum, *at this very moment,* Cic.; qui nunc
sunt, *the present generation,* Cic.; nunc . . .
nunc, *now* . . . *now, at one time* . . . *at another,*
Liv. **II.** *but now, now however,* Cic.

nunccīne = nuncne?

nuncĭa = nuntia, v. nuntius.

nuncĭātĭo = nuntiatio (q.v.).

nuncĭo = nuntio.

nuncĭus = nuntius (q.v.).

nuncŭpātĭo -ōnis, f. (nuncupo), *a naming,
the public offering* or *pronouncing of a vow;* sollemnis nuncupatio votorum, Liv.

nuncŭpo, 1. (nomine capio), *to name, call by
name.* **I.** aliquid nomine dei, Cic. **II. A.** *to
pronounce solemnly and openly;* a, vows; vota
pro republica, Cic.; b, an adoption, Tac. **B.**
to nominate as heir; heredem, Tac.

nundĭnae, v. nundinus.

nundĭnātĭo -ōnis, f. (nundinor), *the holding
of a market, trafficking, trade, business;* fuit
nundinatio aliqua, Cic.

nundĭnor, 1. dep. (nundinae). **I.** *to transact business, trade, traffic.* **A.** Intransit., sedere
nundinantem, Liv. **B.** Transit., *to buy;* jus
ab aliquo, Cic.; totum imperium P. R., Cic.
II. Transf., *to be present in great numbers* (as
at a market); ubi ad focum angues nundinari
solent, Cic.

nundĭnus -a -um (lit., nouendinus = noven-
dinus, from novem and dies), *belonging to the
ninth day.* Subst., **I. nundĭnae** -ārum, f. *the
market-day, held every ninth day,* Cic.; transf.,
a, *the market-place;* illi Capuam nundinas rustic-
orum, horreum Campani agri esse voluerunt,
Cic.; b, *traffic, trade, business;* vectigalium
flagitiosissimae nundinae, Cic. **II. nundĭnum**
-i, n. (sc. tempus), *the market-time;* trinum nundinum, *the interval between one market-day and
the next but one after* (17–24 *days*); se praesentem
trinum nundinum (*on the three market-days*),
petiturum, Cic.; comitia in trinum nundinum
indicere, Liv.

nuntĭātĭo -ōnis, f. (nuntio), *religious t. t.,
a declaration, announcement made by the augur
of his observations,* Cic.

nuntĭo, 1. (nuntius), *to announce;* vera, Cic.;
qui nuntiarent prope omnes naves afflictas esse,
Caes.; oppugnata domus C. Caesaris per multas
noctis horas nuntiabatur, Cic.; with ut and the
subj., paulo post ferunt nuntiatum Simonidi
ut prodiret, Cic.; absol., nuntiato, *this being
announced,* Liv.

nuntĭus -a -um (contr. from noventius),
announcing, bringing news. **I.** Adj., *rumor,*
Cic. **II.** Subst., **A. nuntĭus** -ĭi, m. 1, *messenger, announcer;* facere aliquem certiorem
per nuntium, Cic.; a, *message, news;* nuntium
afferre, Cic.; b, nuntium alicui remittere, *to
send one's wife* or *a letter of divorce,* Cic.; transf.,
nuntium remittere virtuti, *to renounce,* Cic. **B.**
nuntĭa -ae, f. *she that announces;* historia
nuntia veritatis, Cic. **C. nuntĭum** -ĭi, n.
message, news, Cat.

nūpĕr, superl. **nūperrĭmē,** adv. (for

ñovper, from novus, *lately, not long ago;* qui nuper Romae fuit, Cic. ; sometimes employed ωo denote a more distant period, nuper, id est, paucis ante seculis, Cic.

nupta -ae, f. (nubo), *a wife, spouse, bride,* Ov.

nuptiae -ārum, f. (nubo), *marriage, nuptials;* Cornilicia multarum nuptiarum, *often married,* Cic. ; celebrare nuptias, Liv. ; cenare apud aliquem in eius nuptiis, Cic.

nuptiālis -e (nuptiae), *of or relating to a marriage;* cena, Liv. ; donum, Cic.

nuptus -a -um (partic. of nubo), *married;* filia, mulier, Cic.

Nursia -ae, f. *a town in the west of the Sabine country,* now *Norcia.* Hence, adj., **Nursinus** -a -um, *belonging to Nursia.*

ñũrus -ūs, f. (νυός), **1**, *a daughter-in-law, son's wife,* Cic. ; **2**, poet., *a young matron, young married woman,* Ov.

nusquam, adv. (ne and usquam), *nowhere.* **I.** Lit., nusquam alibi, Cic. **II.** Transf., **1**, *in nothing, on no occasion;* praestabo sumptum nusquam melius poni posse, Cic. ; **2**, *to nothing;* ut ad id omnia referri oporteat, ipsum autem nusquam, Cic.

nūto, 1. (*nuo). **I.** Gen., **1**, *to move up and down, totter, waver, nod;* ornus nutat, Verg.; nutant galeae, Liv. ; **2**, transf., **a**, *to waver;* nutans acies, Tac. ; **b**, *to waver, be uncertain in opinion;* etiam Democritus nutare videtur in natura deorum, Cic. ; **c**, *to waver in fidelity;* Galliae nutantes, Tac. **II.** *to move the head up and down, to nod,* Plaut. ; *of persons, sleeping,* Hor.

nūtrīcius -ĭi, m. (nutrix), *a foster-father, guardian,* Caes.

nūtrīco, 1. and **nūtrīcor**, 1. dep. (nutrix), *to suckle, nourish;* transf., *to support, sustain;* mundus omnia, sicut membra et partes suas, nutricatur, Cic.

nūtrīcŭla -ae, f. (dim. of nutrix), *nurse,* Hor.; transf., Gallia nutricula seditiosorum, Cic.

nūtrīmen -ĭnis, n. (nutrio), *nourishment,* Ov.

nūtrīmentum -i, n. (nutrio), *nourishment, nutriment;* transf., **a**, *of fuel,* arida nutrimenta, Verg. ; **b**, *support, training;* educata huius nutrimentis eloquentia, Cic.

nūtrĭo -ivi and -ĭi -ĭtum, 4. (**nūtrĭor**, 4. dep., Verg.), *to give suck, suckle, nourish.* **I.** Lit., **A.** a, of animals, nutritus lacte ferino, Ov.; **b**, of plants, terra herbas nutrit, Ov. ; **c**, of fire, ignes foliis, Ov. **B.** *to tend, wait upon;* corpora, Liv. ; damnum naturae, *remove,* Liv. **II.** Transf., *to nourish, support, sustain;* amorem, Ov. ; mens rite nutrita, *educated,* Hor.

nūtrix -īcis, f. (nutrio), *a nurse, foster-mother.* **I.** Lit., ut paene cum lacte nutricis errorem suxisse videamur, Cic. ; meton., nutrices, *the breasts,* Cat. **II.** Transf., oratoris, Cic.; curarum maxima nutrix nox, Ov.

nūtus -ūs, m. (*nuo). **I.** *inclination, downward tendency, gravity,* Cic. **II.** *a nod, a signal, or beckoning of the head.* **A.** Lit., Liv. **B.** Transf., **1**, *command, will;* deorum nutu, Cic. ; auctoritate nutuque deorum, Cic. ; **2**, *assent;* annuite nutum numenque vestrum invictum Campanis, Liv.

nux, nŭcis, f. **I.** *a nut.* **A.** Lit., Liv. ; prov., nux cassa, *something entirely worthless,* Hor. **B.** Transf., of similar fruit, castaneae nuces, *chestnuts,* Verg. **II. 1**, *the nut-tree,* Verg.; **2**, *an almond-tree,* Verg.

Nÿctēlĭus -i, m. (Νυκτέλιος), *nightly, a sur-* *name of Bacchus* (so called because his mysteries were celebrated by night), Ov.

nympha -ae, f. and **nymphē** -ēs, f. (νύμφη). **I.** *a bride, woman lately married,* Ov. **II.** Nymphae, *the Nymphs, beings of half-divine nature, believed to inhabit the seas, streams, woods,* etc., Verg.

Nymphaeum -i, n. (Νυμφαῖον), *a promontory and sea-port in Illyria.*

Nÿsa (**Nyssa**) -ae, f. (Νῦσα). **I.** *a town in Caria.* **II.** *a town in Palestine.* **III.** *a city in India, where Bacchus was said to have been brought up.* Hence, adj., **A.** **Nÿsaeus** -a -um, *Nysean.* **B.** **Nÿsēis** -ĭdis, f. *Nysean.* **C.** **Nÿsĭās** -ādis, f. *of or relating to Bacchus.* **D.** **Nÿsĭgĕna** -ae, m. *born in Nysa.* **E.** **Nÿseus** -ĕi, *a surname of Bacchus.*

O.

1. **O**, o, the fourteenth letter of the Latin alphabet, corresponding to the two Greek letters Omicron and Omega (O, o; Ω, ω). For the use of O. in abbreviations, see Table of Abbreviations.

2. **ō**! and **ōh**! interj. *an exclamation of joy, astonishment, derision, sorrow, pain,* etc., generally followed by voc. or acc. : o paterni generis oblite! Cic. ; o me miserum! Cic. ; in wishes, o si, *if only!* Verg. ; poet., put the second word of the clause, spes o fidissima Teucrum! Ov.

Ōărīŏn -ōnis, m. (Ὠαρίων) = Orion (q.v.).

Ōaxes -is, m. (Ὄαξις), *a river in Crete.*

ob, prep. with acc. **I.** Of space, a, with verbs of motion, *towards, to;* ignis qui est ob os effusus, Cic. ; **b**, with verbs not denoting motion, *at, before;* ob oculis versari, Cic. **II. 1**, *on account of;* ob rem judicandam pecuniam accipere, Cic. ; unius ob iram prodimur, Verg. ; ob eam rem, *on that account,* Cic. ; quam ob rem, *on which account,* Caes. ; ob id, ob id ipsum, ob hoc, ob haec, *on this account, therefore,* Liv. ; ob metum, *out of fear,* Tac. ; **2**, *in consideration of, for, as recompense for;* ager oppositus est pignori ob decem minas, Ter. ; **3**, ob rem, *to the purpose, with advantage;* verum id frustra an ob rem faciam, in vestra manu situm est, Sall.

ŏbaerātus -a -um, adj. with compar. (ob and aes), *in debt,* Liv. ; plur. subst., **ŏbaerāti** -ōrum, m. *debtors,* Cic.

ŏbambŭlo, 1. *to walk up and down, backwards and forwards;* with dat., muris, Liv. ; with acc., Aetnam, Ov.; with prep., ante vallum, Liv. ; in herbis, Ov.

ŏbarmo, 1. *to arm;* dextras securi, Hor.

ŏbăro, 1. *to plough up,* Liv.

1. **obba** -ae, f. *a species of drinking-cup,* Pers.

2. **Obba** -ae, f. *a town in Africa, near Carthage.*

obbrūtesco -tŭi, 3. *to become brutish, stupid,* Lucr.

obc . . . v. occ . . .

obdo -dĭdi -dĭtum, 3. *to set, put, place before, put against;* pessulum ostio, *to bolt the door,* Ter. ; fores, *to shut the door,* Ov. ; nullique malo latus obdit apertum, *offers an unprotected side to no evil,* Hor.

obdormĭo -ivi and -ĭi -ĭtum. 4. *to go to sleep,* Cic.

obdormisco, 3. (obdormio), *to go to sleep,* Cic.

obdūco -duxi -ductum, 3. **I. A.** *to draw over, draw in front ;* 1, fossam, Caes.; fig., callum dolori, Cic. ; 2, *to cover ;* trunci obducuntur libro aut cortice, Cic. ; transf., obducta cicatrix reipublicae, *closed wound,* Cic. **B.** 1, *to drink,* venenum, Cic.; 2, *to wrinkle ;* frontem, Hor. **II.** *to lead against ;* Curium, *to bring forward, produce,* Cic. ; transl., *to pass, spend ;* diem posterum, Cic.

obductĭo -ōnis, f. (obduco), *a covering ;* capitis, Cic.

obdūresco -dūrŭi, 3. *to become hard, grow hard.* **I.** Lit., Plaut. **II.** Fig., *to become hardhearted, to lose one's natural feeling, become obdurate ;* ipse obdurui, Cic.; ad dolorem novum, Cic.

obdūro, 1. *to be hard ;* fig., *to stand out, hold out, persist ;* perfer et obdura, Ov.; impers., obduretur hoc triduum, Cic.

ŏbēdĭens (ŏboedĭens) -entis, p. adj. (from obedio), *obedient, compliant ;* with dat., nulli est naturae obediens aut subjectus deus, Cic.; with ad and the acc., ad nova consilia, Liv. Subst., **ŏbēdĭens,** *one who obeys, a dependant,* Cic.

ŏbēdĭentĕr (ŏboedĭentĕr), adv. (obediens), *obediently ;* obedienter imperata facere, Liv.

ŏbēdĭentĭa (ŏboedĭentĭa) -ae, f. (obediens), *obedience, compliance,* Cic.

ŏbēdĭo (ŏboedĭo) -ĭvi -ĭtum, 4. (ob and audio). **I.** *to give ear to, listen to, follow a person's advice ;* alicui, Nep. **II.** *to obey ;* praecepto, Cic. ; magistratibus, Cic.; alicui ad verba, Cic.

ŏbēliscus -i, m. (ὀβελίσκος), *a pointed column, obelisk,* Plin.

ŏbĕo -ĭvi and -ĭi -ĭtum, 4. **I.** Intransit., **A.** *to go to, come to, go to meet, go against ;* ad omnes hostium conatus, *to oppose,* Liv. ; in infera loca, Cic. **B.** a, of the heavenly bodies, *to set ;* in reliquis orientis aut obeuntis solis partibus, Cic. ; b, *to die ;* tecum vivere amem, tecum obeam libens, Hor. **II.** Transit., **A.** a, *to go to, reach ;* quantum flamma obire non potuisset, Cic. ; b, *to go to, engage in, apply oneself to any business ; to perform, execute, accomplish an object ;* negotium, Cic. ; hereditatem, *to take possession of,* Cic. ; vadimonium, *to discharge one's bail, to appear at the fixed time,* Cic. ; diem supremum, *to die,* Nep. ; so obire mortem, Cic. **B.** 1, *to visit, travel through ;* provinciam, Cic. ; 2, *to take part in ;* comitia, Cic. ; 3, *to surround ;* clipeum obit pellis circumdata, Verg.

ŏbĕquĭto, 1. *to ride up to ;* castris Liv.

ŏberro, 1. *to wander about ;* tentoriis, Tac. ; transf., chordā eādem, *to blunder,* Hor.

ŏbēsĭtas -ātis, f. (obesus), *fatness, corpulence, obesity,* Suet.

ŏbēsus -a -um (ob and edo), 1, *fat, plump ;* turdus, Hor.; transf., *swollen ;* fauces, Verg.; 2, *coarse, not delicate, unrefined, rude ;* juvenis naris obesae, Hor.

ŏbex -ĭcis, and objĭcis, m. and f. (objicio), 1, *the fastening of a door, bolt, bar, barrier, barricade ;* fultosque emuniit objice postes, Verg. ; 2, *an obstacle, hindrance,* Plin.

obf . . . v. off . . .

obg . . . v. ogg . . .

ŏbhaerĕo, 2. *to stick to, cleave to,* Suet.

ŏbhaeresco -haesi -haesum, 3. *to stick fast, adhere to,* Lucr.

ŏbĭcĭo = objicio (q.v.).

ŏbīrascor -īrātus sum, 3. dep. *to be angry ;* fortunae, *with fortune,* Liv.

ŏbīrātĭo -ōnis, f. (obirascor), *a being angry,* anger, Cic.

ŏbīrātus -a -um, p. adj. (from obirascor), *angry, wrathful ;* with dat., fortunae, Liv.

ŏbĭtĕr, adv. (ob), 1, *on the way, in passing, on the journey,* Juv.; 2, *by the way, incidentally,* Juv.

ŏbĭtus -ūs, m. (obeo), 1, *an approaching, going to,* Ter. ; 2, *a going down* (esp. of the heavenly bodies), *setting ;* siderum, Cic. ; 3, *a downfall, ruin, destruction, death ;* post obitum vel potius excessum Romuli, Cic.

objăcĕo -jăcŭi, 2. *to lie at, against, in the way ;* saxa objacentia pedibus, Liv.

objectātĭo -ōnis, f. (objecto), *a reproach,* Caes.

objecto, 1. (intens. of objicio). **I.** *to put in the way, set against.* **A.** Lit. (of birds), caput fretis, *to dip, dive into,* Verg. **B.** Transf., *to expose ;* aliquem periculis, Sall. ; se hostium telis, Liv. ; moras, *to cause, interpose delay,* Ov. **II.** Transf., *to reproach with anything, object anything to a person, throw in a person's teeth ;* alicui probrum, Cic. ; with acc. and infin., nobilitas objectaŋo Fabio fugisse eum Ap. Claudium collegam, Liv.

1. **objectus** -a -um, p. adj. (from objicio), 1, *lying at, near, opposite to ;* insula objecta Alexandriae, Caes. ; 2, *exposed to ;* fortunae, Cic. ; ad omnes casus, Cic.

2. **objectus** -ūs, m. (objicio), *a placing at, before, opposite, a lying against, lying opposite ;* insula portum efficit objectu laterum, Verg.

objex = obex (q.v.).

objĭcĭo -jēci -jectum, 3. (ob and jacio). **I.** *to throw in the way of.* **A.** Lit., se telis hostium, Cic. **B.** Transf., 1, *to oppose,* Cic. ; 2, *to expose ;* consulem morti, Cic. ; se in dimicationes, Cic. ; 3, *to cause, produce ;* alicui errorem, Cic.; metum et dolorem, Cic. ; objicitur animo metus, *the heart is seized with fear,* Cic. ; hic aliud majus miseris objicitur, *presents itself,* Verg. **II.** *to place before, throw before.* **A.** Lit., 1, *corpus* feris, Cic. ; 2, *to put before, hold before as a defence, protection ;* Aŋpium vallum contra transgressionem Gallorum, *to oppose,* Cic. ; carros pro vallo, Caes. **B.** 1, *to offer ;* delenimentum animis, Liv. ; 2, *to hold out as an example ;* unum ex judicibus selectis, Hor. ; 3, *to object to, reproach with, charge with ;* alicui furta, Cic. ; with acc. and infin., objicit mihi, me ad Baias fuisse, Cic. ; with quod, non tibi objicio quod spoliasti, Cic.

objurgātĭo -ōnis, f. (objurgo), *a blaming, chiding, reproving,* Cic.

objurgātor -ōris, m. (objurgo), *a scolder, chider, reprover, blamer,* Cic.

objurgātōrĭus -a -um (objurgator), *scolding, chiding ;* epistola, Cic.

objurgo, 1. and **objurgor,** 1. dep. *to scold chide, reprove, reprimand, blame ;* aliquem molli brachio de Pompeii familiaritate, Cic. ; verecundiam alicuius, Cic. ; quum objurgarer me, quod nimiā laetitiā paene desiperem, Cic.

oblanguesco -gŭi, 3. *to become languid,* Cic.

oblātro, 1. *to bark at or against, to rail at, scold,* Suet.

oblectāmen -ĭnis, n. (oblecto), *a delight, pleasure,* Ov.

oblectāmentum -i, n. (oblecto), *a delight, amusement, solace ;* meae senectutis requies oblectamentumque, Cic.

oblectātĭo -ōnis, f. (oblecto), *a delighting, pleasing ;* animi, vitae, Cic.

oblecto, 1. (ob and lacto). **I.** *to delight, please, amuse ;* quum eorum inventis scriptisque

se oblectent, Cic.; senectutem, Cic.; legentium animos fictis, Tac.; me cum aliqua re, Cic.; se cum aliquo, Cic. **II.** *to pass time pleasantly, while away time;* lacrimabile tempus studio, Ov.

oblīcus, v. obliquus.

oblīdo -līsi -līsum, 3. (ob and laedo), *to squeeze together;* collum digitulis duobus, *to throttle,* Cic.; oblisis faucibus, *strangled,* Tac.

oblĭgātĭo -ōnis, f. (obligo), *a being bound, a legal obligation;* obligatio pecuniae, Cic.

oblĭgātus -a -um, p. adj. (from obligo), *bound, under an obligation to any one;* obligatus ei nihil eram, Cic.

oblĭgo, 1. *to bind, fasten to.* **I. A.** Lit., *to tie, bind up, bandage a wound;* vulnus, Cic.; medicum requirens a quo obligetur, Cic.; venas, Tac. **B.** Transf., *to bind, fetter by an oath, law, benefit, to bind, fetter, oblige, lay under an obligation, make liable;* **a,** se nexu, Cic.; aliquem sibi liberalitate, Cic.; poet., obligatam redde Jovi dapem, *that is due,* Hor.; **b,** *to pledge;* praedia obligata, *mortgaged,* Cic. **II.** *to make liable to punishment, make guilty;* aliquem scelere, Cic.; pass., obligari, *to commit an offence, be guilty;* obligari fraude impiā, Cic.

oblīmo, 1. (ob and limus). **I.** *to cover with slime* or *mud;* agros, Cic. **II.** *to lavish, squander,* Hor.

oblīno -lēvi -lītum, 3. **I.** *to smear, daub, besmear.* **A.** Lit., obliti unguentis, Cic.; oblitus faciem suo cruore, Cic. **B.** Transf., *to cover, load;* actor oblitus divitiis, Hor.; facetiae oblitae Latio, Cic. **II.** *to stain, pollute, defile;* oblitus parricidio, Cic.; sunt omnia summo dedecore oblita, Cic.; aliquem versibus atris, *to satirise, lampoon,* Hor.

oblīquē, adv. (obliquus), 1, *sideways, athwart, aslant, obliquely;* ferri, Cic.; 2, *indirectly, covertly, by implication,* Tac.

oblīquo, 1. (obliquus), *to make oblique, turn sideways, turn aside, slant, crook;* oculos, Ov.; ensem in latus, Ov.

oblīquus (oblīcus) -a -um (ob and liquis), *slanting, oblique, sideways, aslant, on one side.* **I.** Lit., hos partim obliquos, partim aversos, partim etiam adversos stare vobis, Cic.; amnis cursibus obliquis fluens, Ov.; ab obliquo, Ov., per obliquum, Hor., *sideways, obliquely.* **II.** Transf., **a,** *of discourse, indirect, covert;* insectatio, Tac.; **b,** *looking askance, envious;* invidia, Verg.

oblĭtĕrātĭo -ōnis, f. (oblitero), *a blotting out, obliteration;* and **adj.,** *a blotting out from memory, total forgetfulness,* Plin.

oblĭtĕro, 1. (oblino), *to blot out, obliterate, to blot out of memory, bring to forgetfulness;* famam rei, Liv.; publici mei beneficii memoriā privatam offensionem obliterarunt, Cic.

oblītesco -tŭi, 3. (ob and latesco), *to hide, conceal oneself;* a nostro aspectu, Cic.

oblīvĭo -ōnis, f. (obliviscor), *forgetfulness, oblivion;* laudem alicuius ab oblivione atque a silentio vindicare, Cic.; dare aliquid oblivioni, *to bury in oblivion,* Liv.; in oblivionem negotii venire, *to forget,* Cic.

oblīvĭōsus -a -um (oblivio), 1, *oblivious, forgetful,* Cic.; 2, *causing forgetfulness;* Massicum, Hor.

oblīviscor, oblītus sum, 3. dep. (perhaps from oblino), *to forget.* **I.** Lit., with genit., temporum suorum, Cic.; with acc. of thing, injurias, Cic.; with infin., ne oblivoscar vigilare, Cic.; with acc. and infin., obliviscor Roscium et Cluvium viros esse primarios, Cic. **II.** Transf., *to forget, lose sight of;* consuetudinis suae, Cic.; oblivisci sui, *to forget oneself,* Cic.

oblīvĭum -ĭi, n. (obliviscor), usually plur., *forgetfulness;* agere oblivia laudis, *to forget,* Ov.

oblongus -a -um, *rather long, oblong,* Liv.

oblŏquor -quūtus (-cūtus) sum, 3. dep. **I.** *to speak against, gainsay, contradict, interrupt;* 1, gen., alicui, Cic.; 2, esp., **a,** *to blame,* Tac.; **b,** *to chide,* Cat. **II.** *to join in singing, to accompany;* non avis obloquitur, Ov.

obluctor, 1. dep. *to struggle against, strive against;* genibus adversae arenae, Verg.

obmōlĭor, 4. dep. **I.** *to build* or *pile against* (as a defence); nec in promptu erat quod obmolirentur, Liv. **II.** *to obstruct, block up,* Liv.

obmurmŭro, 1. *to murmur against* or *at;* precibus, Ov.

obmūtesco -mūtŭi, 3. **I.** Lit., **A.** *to become dumb, become speechless* with astonishment, etc.; vocem mittenti non et linguam obmutuisse et manum obtorpuisse, Cic. **B.** = *to be silent;* ego neque Antonium verbum facere patiar et ipse obmutescam, Cic. **II.** Transf., *to cease;* dolor animi obmutuit, Cic.

obnātus -a -um (*obnascor), *growing on;* obnata ripis salicta, *growing on the bank,* Liv.

obnītor -nixus (-nisus) sum, 3. dep. *to push against, press against.* **I.** Lit., taurus arboris obnixus trunco, Verg.; scutis corporibusque ipsis obnixi, Liv. **II.** Transf., *to strive against, oppose;* consilio or manu hostibus, Tac.

obnīxē, adv. (obnixus, from obnitor), *with all one's might, with all one's strength,* Ter.

obnīxus -a -um, p. adj. (from obnitor), *steadfast, firm, unyielding,* Liv.

obnoxĭē (obnoxius). **I.** *culpably,* Plaut. **II.** *slavishly, servilely, submissively;* sententias dicere, Liv.

obnoxĭōsus -a -um (obnoxius), *submissive, compliant,* Plaut.

obnoxĭus -a -um (ob and noxa). **I.** *liable to punishment;* hence, *guilty of any crime, vice,* etc.; animus neque delicto neque lubidini obnoxius, Sall.; pecuniae debitae, *indebted,* Liv. **II. A.** *subject, obedient, compliant;* 1, lit., subjecti atque obnoxii vobis, Cic.; 2, **a,** *dependent upon;* luna radiis fratris obnoxia, Verg.; **b,** *slavish, servile, submissive;* pax obnoxia, Liv. **B.** *subject to, exposed to, obnoxious to;* arbores quae frigoribus obnoxiae sunt, Liv.; **B.** obnoxium est, *it is dangerous,* Tac.

obnūbo -nupsi -nuptum, 3. *to cover;* comas amictu, Verg.; caput, ap. Cic.

obnuntĭātĭo -ōnis, f. (obnuntio), in the language of augurs, *the announcement of an evil omen,* Cic.

obnuntĭo, 1. in the language of augurs, *to announce, report an unfavourable omen;* consuli, Cic.

oboed . . . v. obed . . .

ŏbŏlĕo -ŭi, 2. *to smell of anything, emit an odour,* Plaut.

ŏbŏlus -i, m. (ὀβολός), *a Greek coin, in value one-sixth of a drachma,* rather more than 1½d. English, Ter.

ŏbŏrĭor -ortus sum -ŏrīri, 4. *to arise, appear;* bellum, Liv.; vide quanta lux liberalitatis et sapientiae tuae mihi apud te dicenti oboriatur, Cic.

obp . . . v. opp . . .

obrēpo -repsi -reptum, 3. *to creep, to crawl to.* **I.** Lit., ap. Cic. **II.** Transf., *to come up silently and unexpectedly, steal on imperceptibly, come on by surprise;* senectus adolescentiae obrepit, Cic.; ad honores, Cic.; imagines obrepunt in animos dormientium, Cic.

obreptus (partic. of obripio), *surreptitious.*

obrētĭo, 4. (ob and rete), *to catch in a net,* Lucr.

obrĭgesco -rĭgŭi, 3. *to become stiff* or *frozen, to freeze ;* nive pruināque, Cic.

Obrĭmas -ae, m. *a river in Phrygia.*

obrŏgo, 1. *to amend* or *repeal a law by another ;* obrogare legibus Caesaris, Cic.

obrŭo -rŭi -rŭtum, fut. partic. -rŭtūrus, 3. *to cover over, cover with earth, clothes,* etc., *to bury.* **I.** Lit., **A.** se arenā, Cic. ; thesaurum, Cic. ; obruere aliquem vivum, Sall. **B.** *to overload ;* se vino, Cic. **II.** Transf., **A.** testem omnium risus obruit, *overwhelmed,* Cic. ; obrui aere alieno, *plunged in debt,* Cic. ; obrutus criminibus, Cic. **B.** 1, *to overwhelm, bury, ruin, consign to oblivion ;* ut adversa quasi perpetuā oblivione obruamus, Cic. ; Marius talis viri interitu sex suos obruit consulatus, *obscured the fame of his six consulships,* Cic. ; 2, *to surpass, eclipse ;* famam alicuius, Tac.

obrussa -ae, f. (ὄβρυζον), *the essaying of gold by fire,* Suet. ; fig., adhibenda tamquam obrussa ratio, *as a test,* Cic.

obsaepĭo -saepsi -saeptum, 4. *to fence round, inclose, to block up, render access impossible.* **I.** Lit., hostium agmina obsaepiunt iter, Liv. **II.** Fig., plebi iter ad curules magistratus, Liv.

obsātŭro, 1. *to satisfy,* Ter.

obscoenē (obscēnē), adv. (obscoenus), *impurely, lewdly, immodestly, obscenely,* Cic.

obscoenĭtas (obscēnĭtas) -atis, f. (obscoenus), *impurity, foulness, lewdness, obscenity ;* verborum, Cic.

obscoenus (obscēnus) -a -um (ob and coenum). **I.** *repulsive, filthy, disgusting, offensive ;* volucres, *the Harpies,* Verg. ; risus, Ov. **II.** Transf., **A.** *morally disgusting, impure, lewd, foul, obscene ;* voluptates, Cic. ; adulterium, Ov. ; jocandi genus, Cic. **B.** *ill-omened, unpropitious ;* volucres, *owls,* Verg.

obscūrātĭo -ōnis, f. (obscuro), *an obscuring, darkening ;* solis, Cic. ; fig., Cic.

obscūrē, adv. (obscurus). **I.** *darkly,* Cic. **II.** a, *of discourse, obscurely, unintelligibly ;* disserere, Cic.; b, *covertly, secretly, unobservedly ;* aliquid non obscure ferre, Cic.

obscūrĭtas -ātis, f. (obscurus). **I.** *darkness, obscurity ;* latebrarum, Tac.; lucis, Liv. **II.** Fig., **a,** of discourse, *obscurity, unintelligibleness, want of perspicuity ;* oratio quae lumen adhibere rebus debet, ea obscuritatem affert, Cic. ; verborum, Cic. ; ǀin ea obscuritate et dubitatione omnium, Cic.. b, of condition, *obscurity, low birth and station,* Cic.

obscūro, 1. (obscurus). **I.** *to make dark, darken, obscure.* **A.** Lit., obscuratur luce solis lumen lucernae, Cic. ; caelum nocte atque nubibus obscuratum, Sall. **B.** a, of discourse, *to make dark, indistinct, unintelligible ;* aliquid dicendo, *to pronounce indistinctly,* Cic. ; b, *to make obscure, keep in obscurity, cause to be forgotten ;* fortuna res celebrat obscuratque, Sall. ; eorum memoria obscurata est, Cic. **II.** Transf., *to conceal, hide ;* magnitudinem periculi, Cic.

obscūrus -a -um (perhaps for obsculsus connected with occultus). **I.** *dark, obscure ;* 1, lit., lucus, Verg. ; nox, Verg. ; subst., **obscūrum** -i, n. *darkness ;* sub obscurum noctis, Verg. ; applied to persons, ibant obscuri, *in the dark,* Verg. ; 2, fig., a, of discourse or a writer, *obscure, unintelligible, indistinct ;* Heraclitus obscurus, Cic. ; brevis esse laboro, obscurus fio, Hor. ; b, *unknown, obscure, not celebrated ;* Pompeius humili atque obscuro loco natus, *of humble*

origin, Cic. **II.** Transf., **A.** *dark, insecure ;* obscurā spe et caecā exspectatione, Cic. **B.** *concealed, hidden ;* 1, lit., locus, Liv. ; 2, fig., of character, *secret, reserved, close ;* homo, Cic. ; odium, Cic.

obsēcrātĭo -ōnis, f. (obsecro). **I.** *an earnest entreaty, supplication, adjuration ;* obsecratione humili ac supplici uti, Cic. **II.** *a public prayer* or *supplication ;* obsecratio a populo duumviris praeuntibus facta, Liv.

obsēcro, 1. (ob and sacro), *to beseech earnestly, implore, adjure, entreat ;* aliquem multis lacrimis, Cic. ; obsecro te, ut id facias, Cic. ; te hoc uti, etc., Cic. ; esp., as a polite phrase, *pray ;* Attica, obsecro te, quid agit, Cic.

obsĕcundo, 1. *to be subservient to, compliant with, fall in with ;* voluntatibus alicuius, Cic.

obsēpĭo = obsaepio (q.v.).

obsĕquēla -ae, f. (obsequor), *compliance, yielding,* Plaut.

obsĕquens -entis, p. adj. (from obsequor), 1, *compliant, yielding, obedient ;* patri, Ter. ; 2, esp., an epithet applied to the gods, *favourable, gracious,* Plaut.

obsĕquentĕr, adv. (obsequens), *compliantly, obediently ;* haec facere, Liv.

obsĕquentĭa -ae, f. (obsequens) *yielding, compliance, complaisance,* Caes.

obsĕquĭōsus -a -um (obsequium), *compliant, yielding, obsequious,* Plaut.

obsĕquĭum -ĭi, n. (obsequor), *compliance, complaisance, deference to others, submission, obsequiousness.* **I.** Gen., Cic. ; ventris, *gluttony,* Hor. ; transf., of inanimate objects, flectitur obsequio curvatus ab arbore ramus, Ov. **II.** *obedience ;* obsequium erga aliquem exuere, Tac.

obsĕquor -cūtus (-quūtus) sum, 3. dep. **I.** *to comply with, humour, gratify, obey ;* tibi roganti, Cic.; neque, uti de M. Pompilio referrent, senatui obsequebantur, Liv. **II.** Transf., *to give oneself up to anything ;* tempestati, Cic.; alicuius voluntati, Cic.

1. **obsēro,** 1. *to bolt, bar, fasten ;* plebis aedificiis obseratis, Liv. ; transf., aures, Hor.

2. **obsēro** -sēvi -situm, 3. *to sow, plant ;* terram frugibus, Cic. Partic., **obsĭtus** -a -um, *sown with,* i.e., *full of, covered with ;* obsita pomis rura, Ov. ; vestis obsita squalore, Liv.; legati obsiti squalore et sordibus, Liv.

observans -antis, p. adj., *with* compar. and superl. (observo), *attentive, respectful ;* observantissimus mei, Cic.

observantĭa -ae, f. (observans), *respect, esteem, attention ;* observantia est, per quam aetate, aut sapientiā, aut honore, aut aliquā dignitate antecedentes veremur et colimus, Cic. · in regem, Liv.

observātĭo -ōnis, f. (observo), 1, *an observing, observation ;* siderum, Cic. ; 2, *care, accuracy, exactness, circumspection ;* summa erat observatio in bello movendo, Cic.

observātor -ōris, m. (observo), *an observer, watcher,* Plin.

observĭto, 1. (intens. of observo), *to watch, observe diligently ;* motus stellarum, Cic.

observo, 1. *to watch, observe, regard, attend to.* **I.** occupationem alicuius, Cic. ; tempus epistolae alicui reddendae, *to watch for,* Cic. **II. A.** *to watch, guard, keep ;* greges, Ov. **B.** *to keep, obey, regard, observe a law, rule, precept ;* leges, Cic. ; praeceptum, Caes. ; observare ne, with the subj., quod ne accidat observare nec potest nec necesse est, Cic. **C.** *to respect, esteem, prize, honour ;* me ut alterum patrem, Cic.

obsĕs -sĭdis, c. (ob and sedeo). **I.** *a hostage ;* obsides accipere, dare, Caes. **II.** *a surety, security, pledge ;* seque eius rei obsidem fore, pollicitus est, *that he would be surety for that thing,* Nep. ; obsides dare, *to give security,* with acc. and infin., Cic.

obsessĭo -ōnis, f. (obsideo), *a blockade, siege, encompassing ;* viae, Cic.

obsessor -ōris, m. (obsideo), *one who sits or remains a long time in a place ;* 1, gen., vivarum obsessor aquarum (of the water-snake), Ov. ; 2, esp., *one who besieges or blockades ;* curiae, Cic. ; Luceriae, Liv.

obsĭdĕo -sēdi -sessum, 2. (ob and sedeo). **I.** Intransit., *to sit down, remain anywhere,* Ter. **II.** Transit., **A.** *to sit, remain in or on, haunt, frequent a place,* Plin. **B.** 1, lit., *to blockade, besiege, beset ;* omnes aditus, Cic. ; totam Italiam, Cic. ; 2, transf., **a**, *to occupy, fill ;* corporibus omnis obsidetur locus, *every place is filled,* Cic. ; **b**, *to be on the look-out for, watch for an opportunity ;* jacere humi ad obsidendum stuprum, Cic.

obsĭdĭo -ōnis, f. (obsideo), *a blockade, siege.* **A.** Lit., obsidione urbes capere, Cic. ; obsidione solvere or eximere, *to raise the siege of a place,* Liv. **B.** Transf., *pressing danger ;* rempublicam liberare obsidione, Cic.

obsĭdĭōnālis -e (1. obsidium), *of or relating to a blockade, siege ;* corona, *the honorary crown of grass given to the commander who had raised a siege,* Liv.

1. obsĭdĭum -ĭi, n. (obsideo), *a blockade, siege, besetting.* **I.** Lit., occupare obsidio Lacedaemonis exercitum, Liv. **II.** Fig., *danger,* Plaut.

2. obsĭdĭum -ĭi, n. (obses), *the condition of a hostage,* Tac.

obsĭdo -sēdi -sessum, 3. *to blockade, besiege, invest, environ ;* pontem, Sall. ; milite campos, Verg.

obsignātor -ōris, m. (obsigno), *one who seals, a sealer ;* literarum, Cic. ; esp., *a witness who puts his seal to a will ;* testamenti, Cic.

obsigno, 1. **I.** *to seal.* **A.** Gen., epistolam, Cic. **B.** Esp., 1, of a witness, *to sign and seal a document ;* prov., agere cum aliquo tabellis obsignatis, *to deal with any one in strict form of law,* Cic. ; 2, *to seal an accusation against any one ;* contra Scaurum patrem suum, Cic. **II.** *to stamp, impress ;* formam verbis, Lucr.

obsisto -stĭti, 3. 1, *to stand, place oneself before or in the way of ;* alicui abeunti, Liv. ; 2, *to oppose, withstand, resist ;* omnibus eius consiliis, Cic. ; alicui obsistere, foll. by quominus and the subj., Cic. Partic., **obstĭtus** -a -um (in the language of the augurs) = *struck with lightning,* Cic.

obsĭtus -a -um, partic. of 2. obsero (q.v.).

obsŏlĕfăcĭo -fēci -factum, 3. (obsoleo and facio), *to wear out, degrade, corrupt, make common ;* obsolefiebant dignitatis insignia, Cic.

obsŏlesco -lēvi -lētum, 3. (obs and oleo), *to pass away by degrees, decay, wear out, fall into disuse, lose value ;* oratio, Cic. ; vectigal, Cic.

obsŏlētē, adv. (obsoletus), *poorly, meanly ;* obsoletius vestitus, *shabbily dressed,* Cic.

obsŏlētus -a -um (partic. of obsolesco), *worn out, decayed ;* 1, lit., vestitu obsoletiore, Cic. ; obsoletus Thessalonicam venisti, *dressed in old clothes,* Cic. ; verba, obsolete, Cic. ; 2, *common, everyday ;* crimina, Cic. ; oratio, *ordinary,* Cic.

obsōnĭum -ĭi, n. (ὀψώνιον), *that which is eaten with bread,* e.g., *vegetables, fruit,* and esp. *fish,* Hor.

1. obsōno and **obsōnor,** 1. dep. (ὀψωνέω),

to buy for the kitchen, purvey ; 1, lit., Plaut. ; **fig.,** ambulando famem, *to buy the sauce of hunger,* Cic. ; 2, *to give a feast,* Ter.

2. obsŏno, 1. *to interrupt a person speaking,* Plaut.

obsorbĕo -bŭi, 2. *to swallow, gulp down,* Plaut.

obstĕtrix -īcis, f. (obsto), *a midwife,* Hor.

obstĭnātē, adv. with compar. and superl. (obstinatus), *resolutely, persistently, obstinately,* negare, Caes. ; credere, Liv.

obstĭnātĭo -ōnis, f. (obstino), *resolution, persistence, firmness, obstinacy ;* sententiae, Cic.

obstĭnātus -a -um, p. adj. (from obstino), *firmly resolved, persistent, firm, obstinate ;* obstinatior voluntas, Cic. ; adversus obstinatior lacrimas muliebres, Liv. ; ad decertandum obstinati mori, Liv.

obstĭno, 1. (ob and sto), *to persist in, be resolved on anything ;* with infin., obstinaverant animis aut vincere aut mori, Liv.

obstĭpesco = obstupesco (q.v.).

obstĭpus -a -um, *leaning to either side* (opp. rectus) ; caput, Cic. ; cervix, *thrown back* (said of a haughty person), Suet. ; caput, *bent or bowed down,* Hor.

obsto -stĭti -stātūrus, 1. **I.** *to stand at, before, against,* Plaut. **II.** *to stand in opposition to, to oppose, resist, hinder, obstruct ;* with dat., alicui, Cic. ; vita cetera eorum huic sceleri obstat, *stands in opposition to, is inconsistent with,* Sall. ; with quin, quominus, ne and the subj., quid obstat, quominus sit beatus? Cic. ; ea ne impedirent tribuni, dictatoris obstitit metus, Liv. Partic. subst., **obstantĭa,** neut. plur., *hindrances, obstacles, impediments,* Tac.

obstrĕpo -strĕpŭi -strĕpĭtum, 3. **I.** *to make a noise, clamour at or against ;* nihil sensere Poeni obstrepente pluviā, Liv. ; with dat., fontesque lymphis obstrepunt manantibus, Hor. ; obstrepunt portis, Liv. **II.** 1, *to disturb, interrupt a speaker by clamour ;* alicui, Cic. ; impers., decemviro obstrepitur, Liv. ; 2, *to disturb, molest ;* tibi literis, Cic.

obstringo -strinxi -strictum, 3. *to bind to, fasten to, tie to, to bind up, tie fast, keep bound.* **A.** ventos, Hor. **B.** Fig., 1, *to bind, fetter, entangle, put under an obligation ;* jurejurando, *to bind by an oath,* Caes. ; aliquem legibus, Cic. ; beneficio obstrictus, Cic. ; 2, *to entangle, involve ;* aliquem aere alieno, *to entangle in debt,* Cic. ; se parricidio, se scelere, *to be guilty of,* Cic.

obstructĭo -ōnis, f. (obstruo), *a hindrance, obstruction,* Cic.

obstrūdo = obtrudo (q.v.).

obstrŭo -struxi -structum, 3. **I.** *to build against, build before ;* pro diruto novum murum, Liv. ; luminibus alicuius, *to block up the light, build before the windows,* Cic. **II.** *to build up, block up, close ;* **a,** portas, Caes. ; aditus, Cic. ; iter Poenis (to the Carthaginians) vel corporibus suis, Cic. ; **b,** fig., obstruere perfugia improborum, Cic.

obstŭpĕfăcĭo -fēci -factum, *to bewilder, astound, stupefy, to render senseless, benumb ;* pass., **obstŭpĕfĭo** -factus sum -fĭĕri, *to be bewildered, amazed ;* ipso miraculo audaciae obstupefactis hostes, Liv. ; obstupefactis hominibus ipsā admiratione, Cic.

obstŭpesco -stŭpŭi (-stĭpŭi), 3. *to become senseless, be stupefied, to be astounded, amazed ;* quum eorum aspectu obstupuisset bubulcus, Cic.

obsum, obfŭi (offŭi) -esse, *to be in the way, hinder, impede, injure, be prejudicial to ;* with dat., obsunt auctoribus artes, Ov. ; obest Clodii mors Miloni, Cic. ; non or nihil obest with infin., nihil obest dicere, Cic.

obsŭo -sŭi -sūtum, 3. **1,** *to sew on ;* caput, Ov. ; **2,** *to close up, stop up ;* spiritus oris obsuitur, Verg.

obsurdesco -dŭi, 3. *to become deaf, to be deaf ;* **1,** lit., hoc sonitu oppletae aures hominum obsurduerunt, Cic. ; **2,** *to be deaf to warnings,* etc., *not to give ear to,* Cic.

obtĕgo -texi -tectum, 3. **1,** *to cover, protect ;* se servorum et libertorum corporibus, Cic. ; eam partem castrorum vineis, Caes. ; **2,** *to cover, conceal, hide, keep secret ;* vitia multis virtutibus obtecta, Cic.

obtempĕrātĭo -ōnis, f. (obtempero), *compliance, obedience ;* legibus, Cic.

obtempĕro, 1. *to obey, comply with, conform to, submit to :* alicui, Cic. ; imperio populi Romani, Caes. ; ut ad verba nobis obediant, ad id, quod ex verbis intelligi possit, obtemperent, Cic.

obtendo -tendi -tentum, 3. **I.** *to stretch before, spread before ;* **1,** pro viro nebulam, Verg. ; poet., obtentā nocte, *under the shelter of night,* Verg. ; obtendi = *to lie before, be over against ;* Britannia Germaniae obtenditur, Tac. ; **2,** *to put forward as an excuse, plead, allege ;* matris preces, Tac. ; valetudinem corporis, Tac. **II.** *to cover, conceal, hide ;* diem nube atrā, Tac. ; fig., quasi velis quibusdam obtenditur unius cuiusque natura, Cic.

1. obtentus -ūs, m. (obtendo), **1,** lit., *a stretching* or *spreading before ;* frondis, Verg.; **2,** fig., *a pretext, pretence, excuse ;* tempora reipublicae obtentui sumpta, *taken as an excuse,* Tac. ; sub eius obtentu cognominis, Liv.

2. obtentus -a -um, **1,** partic. of obtineo ; **2,** partic. of obtendo.

obtĕro -trīvi -trītum, 3. *to trample, crush ;* **1,** lit., Cic. ; obtriti sunt plures quam ferro necati, Liv. ; **2,** transf., *to crush, annihilate, destroy ;* calumniam, Cic. ; jura populi, *trample under foot,* Liv. (syncop. pluperf., obtrisset, Liv.).

obtestātĭo -ōnis, f. (obtestor), **1,** *a solemn calling of God to witness, an adjuring in the name of the gods ;* obtestatio et consecratio legis, Cic. ; tua obtestatio tibicinis, Cic. ; **2,** *an earnest supplication, vehement entreaty,* Liv.

obtestor, 1. dep. **I.** *to call to witness, protest before some person* or *thing ;* deum hominumque fidem, Liv. **II.** 1, *to adjure, implore, entreat, supplicate in the name of the gods ;* per omnes deos te obtestor ut, etc., Cic. ; qua re oro obtestorque vos, judices, ne, etc., Cic. ; **2,** *to assert solemnly ;* summam rempublicam agi obtestans, Tac.

obtexo -texŭi -textum, 3. **1,** *to weave on, weave over,* Plin. ; **2,** *to cover ;* coelumque obtexitur umbrā, Verg.

obtĭcĕo, 2. (ob and taceo), *to be silent,* Ter.

obtĭcesco -cŭi, 3. (obticeo), *to become quiet, grow silent,* Hor.

obtĭgo = obtego (q.v.).

obtĭneo -tinŭi -tentum, 4. (ob and teneo). **I.** *to hold with the hands ;* obtine aures, Plaut. **II.** *to hold, possess, keep possession of, occupy.* **A.** suam domum, Cic. ; vada custodiis, Cic. ; citeriorem ripam armis, Liv. **B.** Transf., *to hold, occupy ;* principem locum, *to hold the chief place,* Caes. ; secundum dignitatis locum, Caes. ; numerum deorum, *to be among the number of the gods,* Cic. **III. A.** *to maintain, hold firmly ;* pontem, Liv. ; hereditatem, Cic. **B.** Transf., a, jus suum contra aliquem, Cic. ; causam, *to carry one's point,* Cic. ; absol., obtinuit, with

ut and the subj., *he carried his point that,* etc., Liv. ; b, *to maintain an assertion ;* duas contrarias sententias, Cic. **IV.** a, *to keep, observe ;* silentium, Cic. ; vitam, Cic. ; lex quae in conviviis Graecorum obtinebatur, Cic. ; b, reflex., *to obtain, be held ;* pro vero, Sall.

obtingo -tīgi, 3. (ob and tango), *to fall to the lot of any one, to happen, befall ;* a, quod cuique obtigit, is quisque teneat, Cic. ; si quid mihi obtigerit, *if anything should happen to me, if I should die,* Cic. ; b, esp. as polit. t.t., of the casting of lots for public offices, alicui sorte obtingit provincia aquaria, Cic.

obtorpesco -torpŭi, 3. *to become stiff, numb, torpid, insensible ;* et linguam obmutuisse et manum obtorpuisse, Cic. ; manus prae metu, Liv. ; obtorpuerunt animi, Liv.

obtorquĕo -torsi -tortum, 2. *to turn* or *twist towards, to turn round, wrench, twist round* (usually found in partic. perf.) ; obtortā gulā in vincula abripi jussit, Cic.

obtrectātĭo -ōnis, f. (obtrecto), *envious disparagement, detraction ;* obtrectatio est aegritudo ex eo, quod alter quoque potiatur eo, quod ipse concupiverit, Cic. ; laudis, Caes.

obtrectātor -ōris, m. (obtrecto), *an envious detractor, disparager ;* obtrectatores et invidi Scipionis, Cic.

obtrecto, 1. (ob and tracto), *to disparage, detract from, enviously decry, to oppose, thwart, injure any one ;* with dat., alicui, Cic. ; gloriae alicuius, Liv. ; inter se, Nep. ; legi alicuius, Cic. ; with acc., eius laudes, Liv.

obtrūdo (obstrūdo) -trūsi -trūsum, 1, a, *to gulp down, swallow down,* Plaut. ; **2,** a, *to thrust, force, obtrude anything upon one ;* virginem alicui, Ter. ; b, *to cover ;* obstrusa carbasa pullo, *edged with,* Ov.

obtrunco, 1. *to cut down, cut in pieces, slay ;* regem, Liv.

obtŭĕor 2. dep. *to look at, gaze at, see, behold,* Plaut.

obtundo -tŭdi -tūsum, 3. **I.** *to beat upon, thump ;* os mihi, Plaut. **II.** *to make dull by striking.* **A.** Lit., telum, Lucr. **B.** Transf., 1, *to make blunt, dull, render obtuse, weaken ;* obtundere aures, *to din into a person's ears ;* obtuderunt eius aures te socium praetoris fuisse, Cic. ; obtundere vocem, of orators, *to speak hoarsely,* Cic. ; ingenia, *to make dull,* Cic. ; 2, *to weary ;* aliquem longis epistolis, Cic.

obturbo, 1. **I. A.** *to disturb, make turbid ;* aquam, Plin. **B.** *to disturb, put into confusion, perturb ;* hostes, Tac. **II.** Transf., **A.** *to deafen, stun ;* a, with shouts, obturbabatur militum vocibus, Tac. ; b, mentally, me scriptio et literae non leniunt sed obturbant, *distract,* Cic. **B.** *to disturb, break in upon ;* solitudinem, Cic.

obturgesco -tursi, 3. *to swell up,* Lucr.

obtūro, 1. *to stop up.* **I.** Lit., eas partes (corporis) obstructas et obturatas esse dicebat, Cic. **II.** Transf., alicui aures, *to refuse to listen,* Hor.

obtūsus -a -um, p. adj. (from obtundo), *blunt.* **I.** Lit., pugio, Tac. **II.** Transf., a, *darkened, dulled ;* neque tum stellis acies obtusa videtur, Verg. ; b, of the intellect, *dulled, blunted ;* cuius animis obtusior sit acies, Cic. ; c, of feeling, *insensible ;* pectora, Verg. ; d, *weak powerless,* Verg.

obtūtus -ūs, m. (obtueor), *a looking at, beholding, look, gaze ;* oculorum, Cic. ; dum stupet obtutuque haeret defixus in uno, Verg.

ŏbumbro, 1. *to overshadow.* **I.** Lit., humum, *to darken ;* aethera telis, Verg. **II.** Fig., **1,** *to obscure, overcloud ;* numquam obscura nomina, etsi aliquando obumbrentur, Tac.; **2,** *to conceal, protect, cover;* erroris sub imagine crimen, Ov.

ŏbuncus -a -um, *bent inwards, hooked inwards;* rostrum, Verg.

ŏbustus -a -um (ob and uro), *burnt, hardened in the fire;* sudes, Verg.; transf., gleba obusta (*pinched*) gelu, Ov.

obvallo, 1. *to surround with a wall, wall round;* fig., locus omni ratione obvallatus, Cic.

obvĕnĭo -vēni -ventum, 4. **I.** *to come in the way of, to meet;* se in tempore pugnae obventurum, Liv. **II.** Transf., a, *to fall in the way of, occur to, happen;* vitium obvenit consuli, Liv.; id obvenit vitium quod, etc., Liv.; **b,** *to fall to, fall to the lot of;* ei sorte provincia obvenit, Cic.

obversor, 1. dep. *to move up and down before; appear before, be before, go about, show oneself.* **A.** Lit., castris, Liv.; Appio in somnis eadem obversata species, *appeared,* Liv. **B.** Transf., sed mihi ante oculos obversatur reipublicae dignitas, *hovers before my eyes,* Cic.

obversus -a -um (partic. of obverto), *turned towards;* in agmen utrumque, Ov.

obverto (-vorto) -verti (-vorti) -versum (-vorsum), 3. *to turn towards, twist towards, direct towards.* **I.** Act., arcus in aliquem, Ov.; proras pelago, Verg. **II.** Middle, obverti, *to turn towards.* **A.** Lit., a, gen., in hostem, Liv.; **b,** esp., *to oppose;* profligatis obversis, *the opponents being scattered,* Tac. **B.** Transf., milite ad sanguinem et caedes obverso, Tac.

obvĭam, adv. *in the way, on the way;* hence, *towards, against, to meet* in a friendly or hostile manner; obviam alicui ire or prodire or procedere, Cic.; obviam alicui fieri, Cic.; obviam venire, *to come to meet,* Cic.; obviam ire alicui rei, *to oppose,* Cic.; cupiditati hominum, Cic.

obvĭus -a -um (ob and via), *in the way, meeting.* **I.** Lit., obvius esse alicui, Cic.; dare se obvium alicui, *to meet,* Liv.; obvias mihi literas mittas, Cic.; subst., obvios percunctari, Cic. **II.** Transf., 1, *exposed to;* furiis ventorum, Verg.; 2, *ready at hand;* testes, Tac.; 3, *affable, courteous, easy of access;* comitas, Tac.

obvolvo -volvi -vŏlūtum, 3. *to roll up, wrap up, cover all round;* capite obvoluto, *with head muffled up,* Cic.; transf., verbisque decoris obvolvas vitium, Hor.

occaeco, 1. (ob and caeco). **I.** Lit., *to make blind, to blind;* a, lit., occaecatus pulvere effuso hostis, Liv.; **b,** transf., occaecati cupiditate, Cic. **II.** *to darken, overcloud;* a, lit., densa caligo occaecaverat diem, *to hide from sight;* **b,** transf., *to make obscure, unintelligible;* obscura narratio totam occaecat orationem, Cic. **III.** *to conceal, make invisible;* semen, Cic.

occallesco -callŭi, 3. (ob and calleo), *to become thick-skinned;* 1, lit., Ov.; 2, transf., *to become insensible, unfeeling,* Cic.

occāno -cănŭi, 3. (ob and cano), *to blow, sound;* cornua tubasque, Tac.

occāsĭo -ōnis, f. (from occasum, supine of occido), *a favourable moment, opportunity, occasion.* **I.** Gen., occasionem nancisci, Cic.; arripere, Liv.; amittere, Cic.; dimittere, Caes.; occasione datā, *when an opportunity is offered,* Cic.; ut primum occasio data est, *as soon as an opportunity offered,* Cic.; per occasionem, *on a favourable opportunity,* Liv.; quaerere criminandorum patrum occasiones, Liv. **II.** *an opportunity to make a coup-de-main;* occasionis esse rem, non proelii, Caes.

1. occāsus -a -um, partic. of occido.

2. occāsus -ūs, m. (occido), *the setting of the*

heavenly bodies. **A.** Lit., **1,** solis, Caes.; **2,** the west; ab occasu, Verg. **B.** Transf., *fall, destruction, end, death;* occasus interitusque reipublicae, Cic.; occasus noster, *exile,* Cic.

occātĭo -ōnis, f. (occo), *a harrowing,* Cic.

occēdo -cessi -cessum, 3. (ob and cedo), *to go to, go towards, meet;* in conspectum alicuius, Plaut.

occento, 1. (ob and canto), 1, *to sing to, sing a serenade to,* Plaut.; 2, *to sing a lampoon or pasquinade against any one,* Cic.

occĭdens -entis, m. (lit., partic. of occĭdo, sc. sol), *the evening, the west,* Cic.

occĭdĭo -ōnis, f. (occido), *complete slaughter, extermination, utter destruction;* occidione occidere, *to destroy utterly, slay to the last man,* Cic.; occidione occumbere, *to be slain to the last man,* Tac.

1. occĭdo -cĭdi -cīsum, 3. (ob and caedo). **I.** *to knock down, beat to the ground;* Ctesipho me pugnis occidit, Ter. **II.** *to kill, slay.* **A.** Lit., L. Virginius filiam suā manu occidit, Cic.; ipse fortissime pugnans occiditur, Caes. **B.** *to plague to death, to torture, annoy, torment;* rogando, legendo, Hor.

2. occĭdo -cĭdi -cāsum, 3. (ob and cado). **I.** *to fall, fall down;* alia signa de coelo ad terram occidunt, Plaut. **II. A.** Of the heavenly bodies, *to set;* sol occidit, Liv.; ab orto usque ad occidentem solem, *from the east to the west,* Liv. **B.** *to die, perish;* 1, lit., in bello, Cic.; suā dextrā, *to die by one's own hand,* Verg.; 2, transf., *to perish, be ruined;* sin plane occidimus, Cic.; ornatus mundi occidat, Cic.; spes occidit, Hor.

occĭdŭus -a -um (occido). **I.** *setting;* a, lit., sol, Ov.; **b,** meton., *western, westerly,* Ov. **II.** Transf., *approaching death, near to dissolution,* Ov.

occĭno -cĕcĭni and -cĭnŭi, 3. (ob and cano), *to sing or chirp inauspiciously, to croak;* si occinuerit avis, Liv.

occĭpĭo -cēpi -ceptum, 3. (ob and capio). **I.** Intransit., *to begin;* a meridie nebula occepit, Liv. **II.** Transit. **A.** *to begin, commence;* quaestum, Ter.; with infin., regnare occepit, Liv. **B.** *to enter on;* magistratum, Liv.

occĭpĭtĭum -ĭi, n. (occiput), *the back of the head, occiput,* Plaut.

occĭput -ĭtis, n. (ob and caput), *the back of the head,* Pers.

occīsĭo -ōnis, f. (occido), *a slaying, killing, murdering, slaughter;* parentis, Cic.

occīsor -ōris, m. (occido), *a slayer, murderer,* Plaut.

occīsus -a -um, p. adj. (from occido), *ruined, unfortunate;* occisissimus sum omnium qui vivunt, Plaut.

occlūdo -clūsi -clūsum, 3. (ob and claudo). **I.** *to shut up, close up;* tabernas, Cic. **II.** *to restrain, keep in;* furax servus, cui nihil sit obsignatum nec occlusum, Cic.

occlūsus -a -um, partic. of occludo.

occo, 1. *to harrow;* poet., segetem, *to till,* Hor.

occoepi -isse = occipio (q.v.).

occŭbo, 1. (ob and cubo), *to lie down,* esp., *to rest in the grave;* ad tumulum, quo maximus occubat Hector, Verg.

occulco, 1. (ob and calco), *to trample, tread in, trample down;* occulcare signa ordinesque (of elephants), Liv.

occŭlo -cŭlŭi -cultum, 3. (ob and root CUL, whence also cucullus), *to cover* (esp. for the purpose of hiding), *to hide, conceal:* aliquem.

Liv.; vulnera, Cic.; transf., puncta argument-**orum**, Cic.

occultātĭo -ōnis, f. (occulto), *a hiding, concealing, concealment;* occultatione se tutari, Cic.

occultātor -ōris, m. (occulto), *a hider, concealer;* latronum, Cic.

occultē, adv. (occultus), *secretly, in secret, privately;* latēre, Cic.; dicere, *obscurely,* Cic.

occulto, 1. (intens. of occulo), *to hide, conceal;* se latebris, Cic.; transf., flagitia, Cic.

occultus -a -um, p. adj. (from occulo), *secret, hidden, concealed, private.* **I.** Adj., **A.** Lit., occultissimus exitus, Liv. **B.** Transf., occultior cupiditas, Cic.; of persons, *secret, close, reserved;* si me astutum et occultum lubet fingere, Cic. **II.** Subst., a, **occulta** -ōrum, m. *secret things, secrets,* Cic.; b, in adv. expressions, in occulto, Cic., per occultum, Tac., ex occulto, *secretly,* Cic.

occumbo -cŭbŭi -cŭbĭtum, 3. (ob and cumbo), *to fall down, sink down;* usually, *to fall down in death, to die;* mortem, *to die,* Cic.; poet., morti, Verg.; or simply occumbere, aut occubuissem honeste, aut victores hodie viveremus, Cic.

occŭpātĭo -ōnis, f. (occupo). **I.** *a seizing, taking possession of, occupation;* fori, Cic. **II.** *a business, employment, occupation;* occupationes reipublicae, Caes.; maximis occupationibus impediri, distineri, Cic.

occŭpātus -a -um, p. adj. (from occupo), *busy, engaged, occupied;* in apparando bello, Cic.

occŭpo, 1. (ob and capio), *to take possession of, occupy, lay hold of, seize.* **I.** Lit., 1, totam Italiam suis praesidiis, Cic.; tyrannidem, Cic.; poet., aliquem amplexu, *to embrace,* Ov.; **2**, *to fill, occupy with anything;* Tyrrhenum mare caementis, Hor.; aream fundamentis, Liv. **II.** Transf., 1, *to fall upon, attack;* aliquem gladio, Verg.; **2**, *to anticipate, to do anything first;* with infin., occupant bellum facere, *first begin the war,* Liv.; **3**, *to occupy, master;* pavor occupat animos, Liv.; mentes Siculorum occupat superstitio, Cic.; **4**, *to make busy, engage, occupy,* Liv.; **5**, *to employ, occupy, to put out, invest money;* pecuniam grandi fenore, Cic.

occurro -curri -cursum, 3. (ob and curro). **I.** *to run to meet, hasten to meet.* **A.** 1, lit., a, gen., Caesari venienti, Caes.; b, esp., *to fall upon, attack;* duabus legionibus, Caes.; **2**, transf., *of things, to come in the way of;* in asperis locis silex saepe impenetrabilis ferro occurrebat, Liv. **B.** Fig., a, *to work against, oppose, counteract;* omnibus eius consiliis, Cic.; b, *to come to the help of, assist;* vestrae sapientiae, Cic. **II. A.** *to be present at, engage in;* neutri proelio, Liv.; negotiis, Cic. **B.** Fig., *to meet the eye, to come into the thoughts, to occur to any one, to present itself, occur, happen;* animo, cogitationi, Cic.; in mentem, Cic.

occursātĭo -ōnis, f. (occurso), *a going to meet a person, attention, officiousness;* facilis est illa occursatio et blanditia popularis, Cic.

occurso, 1. (intens. of occurro). **I.** *to go to meet, to meet.* **A.** Lit., fugientibus, Tac. **B.** *to oppose;* invidi, occursantes, factiosi, Sall. **II.** *to rush upon, fall upon, attack;* occursat ocius gladio, Caes.

occursus -ūs, m. (occurro), *a meeting, a falling in with;* vacuae occursus hominum viae, Liv.; alicuius occursum vitare, *to avoid meeting with any one,* Tac.

Ōcĕănus -i, m. ('Ωκεανός), 1, *the ocean, the sea which encompasses the earth;* mare Oceanus, Caes.; 2, personified as a god, *the husband of Tethys and father of the Nymphs;* hence **Ōcĕănītĭs** -ĭdis, f. *a daughter of Oceanus,* Verg.

ŏcellus -i, m. (dim. of oculus), *a little eye,* Ov.; fig., of something excellent, ocelli Italiae, villulae nostrae, Cic.

ōcĭor, ōcĭus, adj. compar. (ὠκίων), superl. **ōcissĭmus** (ὠκιστος), *swifter, quicker, more rapid;* ocior cervis, Hor.; ocior Euro, Hor.

ōcĭus, adv. (= ὠκέως), superl. **ōcissĭmē**, *more quickly, swiftly, rapidly;* facere, Cic.; recreari, Cic.; serius, ocius, sors exitura, *sooner or later,* Hor.

Ocnus -i, m. ("Οκνος), *the founder of Mantua.*

ōcrĕa -ae, f. *a metal greave,* Verg.

ōcrĕātus -a -um (ocrea), *wearing the ocrea,* Hor.

Ocrēsĭa -ae, f. *mother of Servius Tullius.*

Ocrĭcŭlum -i, n. *a town in Umbria, on the Tiber,* now *Otricoli.* Hence, adj., **Ocrĭcŭlānus** -a -um, *of or belonging to Ocriculum.*

octăphŏros = octophoros (q.v.).

Octāvĭus -a -um, *name of a Roman gens.* Hence, adj., **Octāvĭānus** -a -um, *Octavian;* bellum, *of Cn. Octavius with Cinna,* Cic.; subst., **Octāvĭānus** -i, m. *name of the Emperor Augustus after his adoption into the gens Julia.*

octāvus -a -um (octo), *the eighth;* ager efficit cum octavo, *bears eight-fold,* Cic.; adv., octavum, *for the eighth time,* Liv.; subst., **octāva** -ae, f. (sc. hora), *the eighth hour,* Juv.

octāvusdĕcĭmus -a -um, *the eighteenth,* Tac.

octĭēs, adv. (octo), *eight times,* Cic.

octingēnārĭus -a -um (octingeni), *consisting of eight hundred,* Varr.

octingentēsĭmus -a -um (octingenti), *the eight hundredth,* Cic.

octingenti -ae -a (octo and centum), *eight hundred,* Cic.

octĭpes -pĕdis (octo and pes), *having eight feet,* Ov.

octō (ὀκτώ), *eight,* Cic.

Octōber -bris -bre, m. (octo and suff. -ber), *belonging to the number eight;* a, mensis October, *the eighth month of the Roman year,* reckoning from March, *October;* b, *belonging to the month of October;* Idus, Calendae, Cic.

octōdĕcim, numer. (octo and decem), *eighteen,* Liv.

octōgēnārĭus -a -um (octogeni), *containing eighty, consisting of eighty,* Plin.

octōgēni -ae -a, *eighty each,* Liv.

octōgēsĭmus -a -um (octoginta), *the eightieth,* Cic.

octōgĭēs, adv. *eighty times,* Cic.

octōginta, numer. *eighty,* Cic.

octōjŭgis -e (octo and jugum), *yoked eight together;* transf., octojuges ad imperia obtinenda ire, *eight together,* Liv.

octōnārĭus -a -um (octoni), *consisting of eight, containing eight,* Plin.

octōni -ae -a (octo), *eight each,* Caes.

octŏphŏros -on (* ὀκτώφορος), *borne by four;* lectica octophoro ferri, Cic. Subst., **octŏphŏron** -i, n. (ὀκτώφορον), *a litter carried by eight bearers,* Cic.

octŭāgĭes, octuaginta = octogies, octoginta (q.v.).

octŭplĭcātus -a -um (octuplus), *increased eight-fold,* Liv.

octŭplus -a -um (ὀκταπλοῦς), *eight-fold;* pars, Cic. Subst., **octŭplum** -i, n. *an eight-fold penalty;* damnari octupli, Cic.

octussis -is, m. (octo and as), *eight asses,* Hor.

ŏcŭlātus -a -um (oculus), *having eyes;* hence, 1, testis, *an eye-witness,* Plaut. ; 2, *catching the eye,* Cic. (?)

ŏcŭlěus -a -um (oculus), *having many eyes, sharp-sighted;* Argus, Plaut.

ŏcŭlus -i, m. (dim. of OC -us, connected with ὄσσομαι, ὄσσε), *the eye.* **I.** Lit., oculos amittere, *to lose one's sight,* Caes. ; cadere sub oculis, Cic.; esse in oculis, *to be visible,* Cic.; ante oculos ponere, proponere oculis, *to set before one's eyes,* Cic. ; res posita in oculis, *visible,* Cic. ; in oculis, *before one's eyes, in one's presence,* Cic. ; in oculis esse alicuius (alicui), *to be loved by,* Cic.; so also aliquem in oculis ferre, *to esteem highly,* Cic. ; esse ante oculos, *to be visible,* Cic. **II.** Transf., a, of something highly prized or excellent, illos oculos orae maritimae (Corinth and Carthage) effodere, Cic. ; **b,** *the spot upon a panther's skin or a peacock's tail,* Plin. ; **c,** *a bud* or *eye of a plant,* Verg.

ōdi, ōdisse, partic. fut., ōsūrus. **I.** *to hate, detest;* aliquem acerbe, Cic. **II.** *to dislike, be displeased with;* Persicos apparatus, Hor. (perf.), odivi, ap. Cic.).

ŏdĭōsē, adv. (odiosus), *hatefully, odiously,* Cic.

ŏdĭōsus -a -um (odium), *hateful, odious, troublesome, irksome, vexatious, burdensome;* orator, *tedious,* Cic. ; verbum, Cic. ; cupidis rerum talium odiosum et molestum est carere, *it is annoying, unpleasant,* Cic.

ŏdĭum -ii, n. (odi), *hatred.* **I.** Subject., **a,** odium in omnes, Cic.; odium mulierum, *towards women,* Cic. ; vestrum, *towards you,* Liv.; in odium alicuius irruere, *to become hated by any one,* Cic. ; odium est mihi cum aliquo, *I am at enmity with,* Cic. ; esse odio alicui, *to be hated by,* Cic.; in odio esse alicui or apud aliquem, *to be hated by,* Cic. ; odium saturare, *to satisfy one's hatred,* Cic. ; **b,** meton., *the object of hatred;* Antonius insigne odium omnium hominum, Cic. **II.** Object., *offensive conduct, expression of hatred;* odio et strepitu senatus coactus est perorare, Cic.

ŏdor and **ŏdōs** -ōris, m. (ὄζω, ὀδμή), *a smell, odour.* **I.** 1, lit., Cic.; esp., **a,** *an unpleasant smell, stench, stink;* camera incultu, tenebris, odore foeda, Sall. ; **b,** *a sweet smell,* Verg.; **c,** *steam, vapour;* insolitus, Liv.; 2, transf., *a scent, suspicion, inkling, presentiment;* dictaturae, Cic.; urbanitatis, Cic.; suspicionis, Cic. **II.** Meton., *perfume, incense;* and in plur., *perfumery, unguents, spices;* incendere odores, Cic.

ŏdōrātĭo -ōnis, f. (odoror), *a smelling, smell,* Cic.

1. **ŏdōrātus** -ūs, m. (odor), 1, *a smell, smelling,* Cic. ; 2, transf., **a,** *the sense of smell,* Cic. ; **b,** *an odour,* Plin.

2. **ŏdōrātus** -a -um (odor), *odorous, sweet-smelling;* cedrus, Verg.; capilli, Hor.

3. **ŏdōrātus** -a -um, partic. of odoror.

ŏdōrĭfer -fěra -fěrum (odor and fero), 1, *odoriferous, having a pleasant smell;* panacea, Verg.; 2, *producing perfumes;* gens, Ov.

ŏdōro, 1. (odor), *to make odorous;* odorant aëra fumis, Ov.

ŏdōror, 1. dep. (odor). **I.** *to smell;* **a,** *to examine by smell;* aliquid, Plaut. ; **b,** *to scent, smell;* cibum, Hor. **II.** Transf., **a,** *to snuff at,* nose (as a dog); *to aim at, aspire to;* quos odorari hunc decemviratum suspicamini, Cic. ; **b,** *to search into, track out, investigate;* quid sentiant, Cic. ; **c,** *only to smell of, to have the slightest smattering of;* philosophiam, Tac.

ŏdōrus -a -um (odor), 1, *having a pleasant smell, sweet-smelling, odorous;* flos, Ov. ; 2, *keen-scented, tracking by smell;* odora canum vis, Verg.

ŏdōs = odor (q.v.).

Ŏdrȳsae -ārum, m. (Ὀδρύσαι), *a people of Thrace;* hence, adj., **Ŏdrȳsĭus** -a -um, poet. = *Thracian.*

Ŏdyssěa -ae, f. (Ὀδύσσεια), 1, *the Odyssey, a poem by Homer;* 2, Odysseae portus, *a promontory in the south of Sicily.*

Oea -ae, f. *a town in Africa,* now *Tripoli.* Hence, adj., **Oeensis** -e, *of or belonging to Oea.*

Oeägrus -i, m. (Οἴαγρος), *a mythical king of Thrace, father of Orpheus;* hence, adj., **Oeägrĭus** -a -um, poet. = *Thracian.*

Oebälus -i, m. (Οἴβαλος), *a king of Sparta, father of Tyndarus, grandfather of Helen.* Hence, **A. Oebălĭdēs** -ae, m. *a descendant of Oebalus* = *a Spartan;* puer, Hyacinthus, Ov. ; plur., Oebalidae, Castor and Pollux, Ov. **B. Oebălĭs** -ĭdis, f. *relating to Oebalus;* nympha, Helen, Ov.; matres, Sabine, as the Sabines were supposed to be descended from the Spartans, Ov. **C. Oebălĭus** -a -um, *relating to Oebalus;* vulnus, *of Hyacinthus,* Ov. ; **Oebălĭa** -ae, f. *Tarentum* (colonised from Sparta), Verg.

Oechālĭa -ae, f. (Οἰχαλία), *town in Euboea, residence of Eurytus, father of Iole.* Hence, **Oechālĭs** -ĭdis, f. *Oechalian.*

Oecleus -ěi, m. (Οἰκλεύς), *father of Amphiaraus.* Hence, **Oeclīdēs** -ae, m. *son of Oecleus* = *Amphiaraus.*

oecŏnŏmĭcus -a -um (οἰκονομικός), *relating to domestic economy.* Subst., **Oecŏnŏmĭcus** -i, m. *title of a book by Xenophon,* Cic.

Oedĭpūs -pŏdis, m. (Οἰδίπους), *king of Thebes, son of Laius and Jocasta, fated to kill his father and to espouse his mother; known as having solved the riddle of the Theban Sphinx:* prov., Davus sum, non Oedipus, *I am no Oedipus to unriddle riddles,* Ter. Hence, **Oedĭpŏdīŏnĭus** -a -um, *Oedipodean,* Ov.

Oeneus -ěi or -ěos, m. (Οἰνεύς), *king of Aetolia or Calydon, father of Meleager, Tydeus and Deianira;* hence, **A. Oenēĭus** -a -um and **Oenēus** -a -um, *relating to Oeneus;* agri, Aetolia, Ov. **B. Oenĭdēs** -ae, m. *son of Oeneus, Meleager;* also *Diomedes, son of Tydeus, grandson of Oeneus,* Ov.

Oenŏmäus -i, m. (Οἰνόμαος), *king in Elis, father of Hippodamia, grandfather of Atreus and Thyestes.*

Oenōnē -ēs, f. (Οἰνώνη), *a Phrygian nymph, daughter of the river-god Cebrenus, beloved and afterwards deserted by Paris.*

oenŏphŏrum -i, n. (οἰνοφόρον), *a basket* or *hamper for wine,* Hor.

Oenōpĭa -ae, f. (Οἰνοπία), *the island afterwards called Aegina.* Hence, adj., **Oenōpĭus** -a -um, *relating to Oenopia.*

Oenŏpĭōn -ōnis, m. (Οἰνοπίων), *king in Chios, father of Merope.*

oenŏpōlĭum -i, n. (οἰνοπωλεῖον), *a wine-shop, tavern,* Plaut.

Oenōtrĭa -ae, f. (Οἰνωτρία), *old name of the south-east part of Italy;* hence, adj., **Oenōtrĭus** -a -um and **Oenōtrus** -a -um, *Oenotrian* meton., *Italian, Roman.*

1. **oenus** = unus (q.v.).

2. **Oenūs,** acc. -unta, m. *a river in Laconia, falling into the Eurotas.*

oestrus -i, m. (οἶστρος), *the gadfly, horsefly, breeze,* Verg.

oesus = usus (q.v.).

oesўpum -i, n. (οἶσυπος), *the fat and dirt of unwashed wool,* Plin. ; hence, *a cosmetic, used by Roman ladies, prepared from it,* Ov.

Oeta -ae, f. and **Oetē** -ēs, f. (Οἴτη), *the mountain-chain between Thessaly and Macedonia, where Hercules burnt himself;* hence, adj., **Oetaeus** -a -um, *Oetean;* deus, Prop., and simply, Oetaeus, *Hercules,* Ov.

ŏfella -ae, f. (dim. of offa as mamilla of mamma), *a bit, morsel,* Juv.

offa -ae, f. **I.** *a bit, morsel,* esp., *a ball or pellet of flour;* pultis, Cic. **II.** Transf., a, *a piece, lump;* gummi in offas convolutum, Plin.; hence, *a swelling,* Juv. ; b, *an untimely birth, abortion,* Juv.

offendo -fendi -fensum, 3. (ob and *fendo). **I.** Intransit., *to strike, knock, dash against.* **A.** Lit., 1, qui in tantis tenebris nihil offendat, Cic. ; 2, *to suffer damage;* naves in redeundo offenderunt, Caes. **B.** Transf., a, *to make a mistake;* si quid offenderit, Cic. ; b, *to offend against a person;* si in me aliquid offenditis, Cic. ; c, *to come into danger, suffer reverse;* apud judices, *to be condemned,* Cic. **II.** Transit., *to strike, knock against something.* **A.** Lit., 1, caput, Liv. ; 2, a, *to hit upon a person, fall in with, come upon;* aliquem imparatum, *to come upon unawares, surprise,* Cic. ; b, *to injure;* latus vehementer, Cic. **B.** Transf., *to offend, displease;* aliquem or alicuius animum, Cic.; animum in aliquo, *to feel hurt by some one,* Cic. ; eos splendor offendit, Cic. ; partic., **offensus** -a -um, a, *injured, hurt;* offensus animus, Cic.; b, *repulsive;* civibus, Cic. ; subst., **offensum** -i, n. *something causing offence,* Cic.

offensa -ae, f. (offendo). **I.** Lit., *a striking against, knocking against,* Plin. **II.** *dislike, hatred, enmity, affront, injury;* magna in offensa sum apud Pompeium, Cic.; offensas vindicet ense suas, Ov.

offensio -ōnis, f. (offendo), *a striking against, hitting against.* **I.** a, lit., pedis, *a stumbling,* Cic. ; b, meton., *that against which one stumbles, a stumbling-block,* Cic. **II.** 1, *indisposition, complaint;* corporum, Cic. ; 2, a, *hatred, enmity, disfavour, aversion;* in alicuius offensionem cadere, Cic. ; effugere alicuius offensionem, Cic.; b, *defeat, loss, misfortune;* offensionem timere, Cic.

offensiuncŭla -ae, f. (dim. of offensio), 1, *a slight offence, displeasure,* Cic. ; 2, *a slight failure,* Cic.

offenso, 1. (intens. of offendo), *to strike, dash against;* capita, Liv.

1. **offensus** -a -um, partic. of offensus.

2. **offensus** -ūs, m. (offendo), 1, *a dashing against, a shock,* Lucr. ; 2, *offence, dislike,* Lucr.

offĕro, obtŭli, oblātum, offerre (ob and fero), *to carry or bring to, place before, present, produce, offer.* **I.** Lit., aciem strictam venientibus, Verg.; os suum non modo ostendere, sed etiam offerre, Cic. ; reflex., se offerre, *to present oneself, appear;* pass., offerri, *to present oneself, offer oneself, appear;* multis in difficillimis rebus praesens auxilium eius numinis oblatum est, Cic. **II.** Transf., a, *to offer, expose;* nos periculis sine causa, Cic. ; se morti, Caes. ; se ad mortem pro patria, Cic. ; vitam in discrimen, Cic. ; b, *to adduce, bring forward;* crimina, Cic. ; c, *to offer, proffer;* alicui operam suam, Liv. ; d, *to cause, occasion;* alicui beneficium, Cic.; stuprum alicui, Cic. ; mortem alicui, Cic.

offīcīna -ae, f. (= opificina, from opifex), *a*

workshop, manufactory, in which any handicraft is carried on; armorum, *a manufactory of arms,* Caes. ; fig., *a workshop, laboratory;* falsorum commentariorum et chirographorum officina, Cic. ; discendi, Cic. ; nequitiae, sapientiae, Cic.

offīcĭo -fēci -fectum, 3. (ob and facio), *to be in the way of, impede, hinder.* **A.** Lit., with dat., alicui apricanti, *to stand between any one and the sun,* Cic. ; ipsa umbra terrae soli officiens, *coming before the sun,* Cic. **B.** Transf., *to hinder, obstruct, be in the way of, to injure;* meis commodis, Cic. ; consiliis alicuius, Sall. ; officiunt laetis frugibus herbae, Verg.

offīcĭōsē, adv. (officiosus), *obligingly, courteously;* hoc facere, Cic. ; sed illa officiosius, Cic.

offīcĭōsus -a -um (officium), *obliging, courteous, attentive, kind, respectful* (especially used of the behaviour of inferiors to superiors); 1, homo, Cic. ; in aliquem, Cic. ; 2, *dutiful, conformable to duty;* dolor, Cic. ; labores, Cic.

offīcĭum -ĭi, n. (perhaps for opificium). **I.** *duty, obligation, service, part.* **A.** esse in officio, Cic. ; officio fungi, *to do one's duty,* Cic. ; officium praestare, Caes. ; officio suo deesse, *to fail in one's duty,* Cic. **B.** *subjection, allegiance;* in officio continere, Cic. **II.** *dutiful action.* **A.** meorum officiorum conscientia, Cic. **B.** 1, *respect, courtesy, deference;* homo summo officio praeditus, Cic. ; 2, *attention, complaisance, friendly service;* a, illius in ullum ordinem officia, Cic. ; b, *ceremony, attendance on some solemn occasion, service of honour;* urbana officia alicui praestare, ap. Cic. ; officio togae virilis interfui, *I was present at the ceremony of taking the toga virilis,* Plin.; suprema in aliquem officia, *the last offices, the ceremony of interment,* Tac.; so officium triste, Ov.; 3, *service, business, official employment;* toti officio maritimo M. Bibulus praepositus, *over the whole naval service,* Cic. ; confecto legationis officio, Cic.

offīgo -fixi -fixum, 3. (ob and figo), *to fix in, fasten;* ita densos offigunt implicantque ramos, Liv.

offīrmātē, adv. (offirmatus), *firmly, obstinately,* Suet.

offīrmātus -a -um (offirmo), *firm, steadfast, obstinate,* Cic.

offīrmo, 1. (ob and firmo), *to make firm, to fasten;* transf., *to make resolute, steadfast;* ne tam offirma te, *don't be so obstinate,* Ter.

offūcia -ae, f. (ob and fucus), 1, *paint, rouge,* Plaut. ; 2, transf., *deceit, deception,* Plaut.

offulgĕo -fulsi, 2. (ob and fulgeo), *to shine upon, appear;* nova lux oculis offulsit, Verg.

offundo -fūdi -fūsum, 3. (ob and fundo). **I.** *to pour before, pour around, pour out.* **A.** Lit., Plaut. **B.** Transf., pass., offundi, *to be poured out, to be poured round, to be spread around;* nobis aër crassus offunditur, *surrounds us,* Cic. ; fig., si quid tenebrarum offudit exsilium, Cic.; ne nimium terroris offundam, Liv. ; omnium rerum terrorem oculis auribusque est offusus, Liv. **II.** *to spread over, to cover, conceal;* obscuratur et offunditur luce solis lumen lucernae, Cic. ; fig., civitus pavore, Tac.

oggannĭo -īvi and -ĭi -ītum, 4. (ob and gannio), *to yelp, growl at,* Plaut.

Ōgўgēs -is, m. (Ὠγύγης), *a mythical king of Thebes.* Hence, **Ōgўgĭus** -a -um, *Theban;* deus, Bacchus, Ov.

oh, interj. *oh! ah!* Plaut.

ōhē, interj. *ho! holloa!* Plaut.

ōho, interj. *oho! aha!* Plaut.

oi, interj. *oh!* an exclamation of pain, Ter.

Oīleus -ĕi and -ĕos, m. ('Οϊλεύς), *king of Locris, father of Ajax* (who was also called *Ajax Oileus*).

Olbĭa -ae, f. ('Ολβία), *a town on the east coast of Sardinia.* Hence, adj., **Olbĭensis** -e, *Olbian.*

ŏlĕa -ae, f. (ἐλαία), 1, *the olive, the fruit of the olive-tree,* Varr. ; 2, *the olive-tree,* Cic.

ŏlĕăgĭnĕus (**ŏlĕăgĭnus**) -a -um (olea), *of or relating to the olive-tree,* Nep.

ŏlĕārĭus -a -um (oleum), *of or belonging to oil ;* cella, Cic.

Ŏlĕărus (-ŏs) and **Ŏlĭăros** -i, f. ('Ωλέαρος), *one of the islands of the Sporades,* now *Anti-paros.*

ŏlĕaster -tri, m. (olea), *the wild olive-tree,* Verg.

ŏlens -entis, p. adj. (from oleo), *smelling ;* hence, a, *fragrant, sweet-smelling,* Ov. ; b, *bad-smelling, stinking, fetid,* Verg.

Ŏlĕnus (-ŏs) -i, f. ('Ωλενος). **I.** *a town in Achaia.* **II.** *a town in Aetolia.* Hence, **Ŏlĕnius** -a -um = *Achaian ;* capella or pecus, *the goat of Amalthea,* Ov.

ŏlĕo, ŏlŭi, 2. (cf. ὄζω, *odor*). **I.** *to emit an odour, smell.* **A.** bene, Cic. ; with abl., sulfure, Ov. ; with acc., crocum, *to smell of,* Cic. ; nihil, Cic. **B.** Fig., *to smell of, to savour of, to smack of ;* nihil ex Academia, Cic. ; malitiam, Cic. **II.** *to be revealed or be betrayed by smell ;* quid, illud non olet, unde sit, quod dicitur "cum illis?" Cic.

ŏlĕum -i, n. (ἔλαιον) *olive-oil, oil ;* instillare oleum lumini, Cic. ; prov., oleum et operam perdere, *to lose time and trouble,* Cic. ; nitidum quoddam genus est verborum et laetum sed palaestrae magis et olei, etc., *shows signs of too much effort* (from the oil used in the palaestra by wrestlers), Cic.

olfăcĭo -fēci -factum, 3. (oleo and facio), *to smell.* **A.** Lit., ea quae stamus, Cic. **B.** Fig., *to scent out, trace by smell, detect ;* nummum, Cic.

olfacto, 1. (intens. of olfacio), *to smell at, smell,* Plaut.

ŏlĭdus -a -um (oleo), *smelling, emitting an odour ;* capra, *stinking, fetid,* Hor.

ŏlim, adv. (from ollus, old Lat. for ille). **I. A.** Of the past, *formerly, once upon a time, in times past ;* qui mihi dixit olim, Cic. **B.** Of the future, *hereafter, at a future time ;* non, si male nunc, et olim sic erit, Hor. ; utinam coram tecum olim potius quam per epistolas, Cic. **II.** *at times, often ;* ut pueris olim dant crustula blandi doctores, Hor.

ŏlĭtor -ōris, m. (olus), *cultivator of pot-herbs, kitchen-gardener,* Cic.

ŏlĭtōrĭus -a -um (olitor), *of or relating to culinary herbs ;* forum, *vegetable market,* Liv.

ŏlīva -ae, f. **I.** *the olive,* Hor. **II.** *the olive-tree.* **A.** Lit., Cic. **B.** Meton., 1, *an olive-branch,* Hor.; 2, *a staff of olive-tree wood,* Ov.

ŏlīvētum -i, n. (oliva), *a place planted with olives, olive-garden,* Cic.

ŏlīvĭfĕr -fĕra -fĕrum (oliva and fero), *olive-bearing,* Verg., Ov.

ŏlīvum -i, n. (oliva), 1, *olive-oil, oil,* Verg. ; 2, *oil for anointing, unguent,* Cat.

olla -ae, f. (orig. ola = aula), *an earthenware jar or pot,* Cic.

ollus, olle, obsolete form of ille -a -ud (q.v.).

ŏlo, 3. = oleo (q.v.).

ŏlor -ōris, m. *a swan,* Hor.

ŏlōrīnus -a -um (olor), *of or relating to a swan,* Verg.

ŏlus (**hŏlus**) -ĕris, n. *any kind of culinary vegetable, pot-herb,* Hor.

ŏluscŭlum -i, n. (dim. of olus), *a herb, vegetable,* Cic.

Ŏlympĭa -ae, f. ('Ολυμπία), *a holy city and territory in Elis, where stood the temple of Jupiter Olympius, and where the Olympic games were celebrated.* Hence, adj., **A. Ŏlympĭăcus** -a -um, *Olympian.* **B. Ŏlympĭcus** -a -um, *Olympian.* **C. Ŏlympĭus** -a -um, *Olympian.* Subst., **Ŏlympĭum** -ii, n. *the temple of Jupiter Olympius,* Liv. ; **Ŏlympĭa** -ōrum, n. *the Olympic games,* Cic. **D. Ŏlympĭăs** -ădis, f. *an Olympiad or period of four years, elapsing between each celebration of the Olympic games,* Cic. **E.**

Ŏlympĭŏnīces -ae, m. (Ολυμπιονίκης), *a victor at Olympia,* Cic.

1. **Ŏlympĭăs,** v. Olympia.

2. **Ŏlympĭăs** -ădis, f. ('Ολυμπιάς), *daughter of Neoptolemus, king in Epirus, mother of Alexander the Great.*

Ŏlympus (-ŏs) -i, m. ('Ολυμπος). **I.** m. **A.** *a mountain on the borders of Macedonia and Thessaly, supposed to be the habitation of the gods ;* poet. = *heaven,* Verg. **B.** *a celebrated flute-player, the pupil of Marsyas.* **II.** f. *a town of Lycia on the Mount Olympus there.* Hence, **Ŏlympēni** -ōrum, m. *the inhabitants of Olympus.*

Ŏlynthus (-ŏs) -i, f. ("Ολυνθος), *town in Chalcidice, on the borders of Macedonia.* Hence, adj., **Ŏlynthĭus** -a -um, *Olynthian.*

ōmāsum -i, n. *bullocks' tripe ;* transf., pingui tentus omaso, *with fat paunch,* Hor.

ōmĕn -Inis, n. *an omen, sign, augury, prognostication.* **I.** Lit., **A.** hisce ominibus proficiscere, Cic. ; ire secundo omine, *in God's name,* Hor. ; omen avertere, *to avert an omen,* Cic. ; accipere, *to accept,* Cic. **B.** *a wish,* as a good omen ; optima omina, Cic. **II.** Meton., *that which is accompanied by auspices ;* 1, prima omina = nuptiae, Verg. ; 2, *a solemn usage,* Verg.

ōmentum -i, n. (= ob-mentum, connected with opimus), *the entrails, bowels,* Juv.

ōmĭnor, 1. dep. (omen). **I.** *to augur, presage, prophesy, predict ;* malo alienae quam nostrae reipublicae ominari, Cic. **II.** *to speak words of* (good or bad) *omen ;* ominari horreo, Liv.

ōmĭnōsus -a -um (omen), *foreboding, ominous,* Plin.

ōmissus -a -um, p. adj. (from omitto), *neglectful, remiss,* Ter.

ōmitto -mīsi -missum, 3. (= ommitto, from ob and mitto), *to let go, let alone, let fall.* **I.** Lit., arma, Liv. ; habenas, Tac. **II.** Transf., **A.** *to give up, lay aside, leave off ;* pietatem et humanitatem, *to put on one side,* Cic. ; timorem, Cic. ; with infin., *to cease ;* omittat urgere, Cic. **B.** *of discourse, to leave unmentioned, to omit ;* ut haec omittam, Cic. ; de reditu, Cic.

omnĭfĕr -fĕra -fĕrum (omnis and fero), *bearing everything, all-bearing,* Ov.

omnĭgĕna -ae, genit. plur., -ûm, c. (omnis and genus), *of all sorts ;* omnigenûm deum monstra, Verg.

omnĭgĕnus -a -um (= omne genus), *of all kinds,* Lucr.

omnĭmŏdīs, adv. (omnis and modus), *in every way, wholly, entirely,* Lucr.

omnīnō, adv. (omnis), *altogether, entirely, wholly, totally.* **I.** quum senatoriis muneribus aut omnino aut magna ex parte essem liberatus, Cic.; esp., **a,** *in general, especially;* de hominum genere aut omnino de animalibus loquor, Cic.; **b,** *in all, in the total;* quinque omnino fuerunt, Cic. **II.** *utterly, entirely, at all;* fieri omnino neges, Cic.; esp., a, with superl., miserrima est omnino ambitio, Cic.; **b,** with negatives, is omnino servus in familia erat, Cic. **III.** In concessive clauses foll. by sed = *certainly . . . but;* pugnas omnino sed cum adversario facili, Cic.

omnĭpărens -entis (omnis and parens), *all-producing, all-bearing;* terra, Verg.

omnĭpŏtens -entis (omnis and potens), *almighty, all-powerful, omnipotent,* Verg.

omnis -e, *all.* **I.** Of number, **A.** omnis fortuna, Cic.; leges aliae omnes, Cic.; subst., omnes, *all men,* Cic.; omne, *everything,* Cic.; so omnia, Cic.; omnia facere, *to do whatever is possible,* Cic.; omnia mihi sunt cum aliquo, *I am quite in agreement with,* Cic.; sic in eo sunt omnia, *everything depends upon that,* Cic.; per omnia, *in every respect,* Liv.; ante omnia, *especially,* Liv. **B.** a, *each, every, all;* omnis amans, *every lover,* Ov.; omnibus mensibus, Cic.; **b,** *of all kinds;* olus omne, Hor.; omnibus precibus petere, Cic. **II.** *the whole;* Gallia omnis, Caes.; non omnis moriar, *not entirely,* Hor.; sanguinem suum omnem effundere, Cic.

omnĭtŭens -entis (omnis and tueor), *all-seeing, all-beholding,* Lucr.

omnĭvăgus -a -um (omnis and vagus), *wandering everywhere,* Cic.

omnĭvŏlus -a -um (omnis and volo), *all-willing, all-wishing,* Cat.

Omphălē -ēs, f. ('Ομφάλη), *a queen of Lydia, whom Hercules served in woman's dress.*

ŏnăger and **ŏnăgrus** -i, m. *the wild ass,* Verg.

ŏnĕrārĭus -a -um (onus), *of or relating to freight, burden,* etc.; jumenta, *beasts of burden,* Liv. Subst., **ŏnĕrārĭa** -ae, f. *a merchant or transport ship,* Cic.

ŏnĕro, 1. (onus). **I.** *to load, pack, freight, burden with anything.* **A.** Lit., 1, naves, Caes.; 2, a, *to burden, trouble, tire, oppress, weigh down;* aures lapillis, Ov.; hostes (saxis), Liv.; b, *to cover;* ossa aggere terrae, Verg.; c, *to load, fill;* mensas dapibus, *to load the tables with victuals,* Verg.; manus jaculis, Verg. **B.** Fig., 1, *to load, burden, oppress, overwhelm;* aliquem mendaciis, Cic.; judicem argumentis, Cic.; 2, a, *to weary, tire;* aethera votis, Verg.; b, *to overwhelm;* aliquem contumeliis, Cic.; in a good sense, aliquem laudibus, Liv.; c, *to make more burdensome, to aggravate;* curas, Tac.; inopiam alicuius, Liv. **II.** *to put into a cask, vessel,* etc.; vina cadis, Verg.

ŏnĕrōsus -a -um (onus). **I.** *heavy, burdensome;* praeda, Verg. **II.** Fig., *troublesome;* onerosior altera sors est, Ov.

ŏnus -ĕris, n. *a load, burden, freight.* **I. A.** Lit., merces atque onera, Cic. **B.** Transf., *any kind of burden, weight;* tanti oneris turrim in muros collocare, Caes. **II.** Fig., **A.** *weight, burden, trouble, charge;* oneri esse, *to be burdensome,* Sall., Liv.; plus oneris sustuli quam ferre me posse intelligo, Cic. **B.** Esp., *a public burden, tax, charge;* his temporibus hoc municipium maximis oneribus pressum, Cic.; haec omnia in dites a pauperibus inclinata onera, Liv.

ŏnustus -a -um (onus), *laden, loaded, freighted.* **I.** Lit., asellus onustus auro, Cic.; naves onustae frumento, Cic. **II.** *full, filled;* onusti cibo et vino, Cic.; pharetra onusta telis, Tac.

ŏnyx -ўchis (ὄνυξ). **I.** m. **A.** *a kind of*

yellowish marble, onyx, from which many articles of luxury were made, Plin. **B.** Meton., *a box* or *casket of onyx,* Hor. **II.** f. *a precious stone of a yellowish colour, onyx,* Plin. **III.** *a shell-fish,* Plin.

ŏpācĭtas -ātis, f. (opacus), *a shade, shadiness;* arborum, Tac.

ŏpāco, 1. (opacus), *to shade, overshadow;* locum, Cic.

ŏpācus -a -um. **I.** Pass., *shaded, shady.* **A.** Lit., ripa, Cic.; neut. subst., per opaca locorum, *shady places,* Verg. **B.** Transf., *dark, shadowy, obscure;* nox, Verg.; mater, *the earth,* Verg. **II.** Act., *casting a shade, shading, shady;* arbor, Verg.

ŏpălus -i, m. *a precious stone, the opal,* Plin.

ŏpella -ae, f. (dim. of opera), *a little work, little labour, trouble, service,* Lucr., Hor.

ŏpĕra -ae, f. (1. opus), *trouble, pains, effort, exertion.* **I.** Lit., **A.** Gen., laborem et operam in aliqua re consumere, Cic.; operam tribuere reipublicae, *devote oneself to,* Cic.; operam dare alicui rei, *to work hard at,* Cic.; operam dare, with ut or ne and the subj., *to do one's best to,* etc., Cic.; non operae est, with infin., *it is not worth the while,* Liv. **B.** Esp., *a service, doing service;* Cn. Pompeius, qui est in operis eius societatis, *who is in the service of that company,* Cic.; Musis operas reddere, *to serve the Muses,* Cic. **II.** 1, *time for work;* deest mihi opera, Cic.; 2, *a day-labourer, workman,* gen. in plur.; operae fabrorum, Cic.; sometimes in a contemptuous sense, *mercenaries, hired assistants,* Cic.; operae theatrales, *the claqueurs,* Tac.

ŏpĕrārĭus -a -um (opera), *of or relating to work;* homo, *a day-labourer,* Cic. Subst., **ŏpĕrārĭus** -ĭi, m. *a day-labourer, workman;* transf., quidam operarii linguā celeri et exercitatā (of bad orators), Cic.

ŏpercŭlum -i, n. (operio), *a lid, cover,* Cic.; operculum dolii ferreum, Liv.

ŏpĕrīmentum -i, n. (operio), *a cover, covering,* Cic.

ŏpĕrĭo -pĕrŭi -pertum, 4. (ob and pario). **I.** *to cover.* **A.** 1, gen., amphoras auro, Nep.; 2, esp., a, *to cover with a garment,* esp. with a toga; capite operto esse, Cic.; b, *to cover with earth, to bury;* reliquias malae pugnae, Tac. **B.** Fig., 1, *to cover, load;* judicia operta dedecore, Cic.; 2, *to cover, conceal;* res opertae, Cic. **II.** *to close, shut up;* opertā lecticā latus est, Cic.

ŏpĕror, 1. dep. (opus), *to work, labour, be busied, occupied with;* followed by dat. of the occupation, 1, connubiis arvisque novis, Verg.; materiis caedendis, Tac.; 2, esp., *to be engaged in worship;* sacris, Liv.; with dat. of deity, *to worship, sacrifice;* deo, Tib.; absol., *to worship, sacrifice;* laetis operatus in arvis, Verg.

ŏpĕrōsē, adv. (operosus), *laboriously, carefully,* Cic.

ŏpĕrōsus -a -um (opera), *laborious, painstaking, industrious.* **I.** Lit., a, senectus, Cic.; colonus, Ov.; b, of medicines, *active, powerful;* herba, Ov. **II.** *that which causes much labour or trouble, laborious, toilsome, difficult;* artes, Cic.; moles mundi, Ov.; carmina, Hor.

ŏpertum -i, n. (operio), *a secret place.* **I.** Bonae Deae, Cic. **II.** *a secret;* operta Apollinis, *the mysterious oracles of Apollo,* Cic.

ŏpes v. ops.

Ophĭon -ŏnis, m. ('Οφίων), *father of Amycus;* hence, **Ophĭōnĭdēs** -ae, m. *son of Ophion =* Amycus.

Ophĭūchus -i, m. ('Οφιοῦχος), *the snake holder, a constellation,* Cic.

Ŏphĭūsa -ae, f. ('Οφίουσα), *old name of the island of Cyprus.* Hence, **Ŏphĭūsĭus** -a -um, *Ophiusian = Cypriote.*

Ŏpĭcus -a -um, *Oscan;* transf., *stupid, foolish, silly, clownish,* Juv.

ŏpĭfĕr -fĕra -fĕrum (ops and fero), *helpful, rendering help;* deus (of Aesculapius), Ov.

ŏpĭfex -fĭcis, c. (opus and facio), 1, *a worker, framer, fabricator;* mundi, Cic.; verborum, Cic.; 2, *a workman, artificer, artizan,* Cic.; opifices atque servitia, Sall.

ŏpĭfĭcīna = officina (q.v.).

ŏpīlĭo and **ūpīlĭo** -ōnis, m. (for ovilio, from ovis), *a shepherd,* Verg.

ŏpīmē, adv. (opimus), *richly, splendidly,* Plaut.

ŏpīmĭtas -ātis, f. (opimus), *sumptuousness, splendour,* Plaut.

ŏpīmus -a -um (ops). **I.** Act., *fruitful, fertile;* ager, regio, Cic. **II.** Pass., *well-fed, fat.* **A.** a, lit., bos, Cic.; habitus corporis, Cic.; b, fig., of speech, *overloaded;* genus dictionis, Cic. **B.** Transf., a, *enriched, wealthy;* b, *splendid, sumptuous, abundant, rich, copious,* Verg.; praeda, Cic.; dapes, Verg.; esp., spolia opima, *the spoils taken from the enemy's general when slain by the commander of the army himself,* Liv.

ŏpīnābĭlis -e (opinor), *founded upon conjecture, conjectural,* Cic.

ŏpīnātĭo -ōnis, f. (opinor), *a supposing, supposition, conjecture,* Cic.

ŏpīnātor -ōris, m. (opinor), *one who supposes or conjectures,* Cic.

1. **ŏpīnātus** -a um, p. adj. (from opin *» conjectured, supposed, fancied;* bonum, Cic.

2. **ŏpīnātus** -ūs, m (opinor), *a con' t, supposition,* Lucr.

ŏpīnĭo -onis, f. (opinor), *an opinion, conjecture, supposition, belief, imagination.* **I.** Gen., with subj. genit., opinione vulgi, Cic.; with obj. genit., opinio eius diei, Cic.; with de, opinio de dis immortalibus, Cic.; adducere aliquem in opinionem ut putet, etc., Cic.; magna nobis pueris opinio fuit, with acc. and infin., Cic.; ut opinio nostra est (fert), *in my opinion,* Cic.; praeter opinionem, *contrary to expectation,* Cic.; celerius opinione, *quicker than was expected,* Cic. **II. A.** 1, *good opinion, favourable judgment;* opinione nonnullā, quam de meis moribus habebat, Cic.; 2, a, *a good name, reputation;* propter eximiam opinionem virtutis, Caes.; b, a *bad name, notoriety,* Liv. **B.** *fame, report;* quae opinio erat edita in vulgus, Liv.

ŏpīnĭōsus -a -um (opinio), *full of conjectures or suppositions,* Cic.

ŏpīnor, 1. dep. (from opinus in nec-opinus, from root OP, connected with ὀφθῆναι, ὄπωπα), *to be of opinion, opine, believe, think, suppose;* me in provinciam exiturum, Cic.; de vobis non secus ac de teterrimis hostibus opinatur, Cic.; ut opinor (in a parenthesis), *as I hold,* Cic.

ŏpīpărē, adv. (opiparus), *splendidly, sumptuously;* opipare apparatum convivium, Cic.

ŏpīpărus -a -um (opes and paro), *splendid, sumptuous,* Plaut.

1. **Ŏpis** -is, acc. -im, f. ("Ωπις), *a nymph in the train of Diana.*

2. **Ŏpis**, v. 1. Ops.

ŏpĭtŭlor, 1. dep. (ops and tulo = fero), *to help, aid, assist;* sontibus, Cic.

ŏpĭum -ĭi, n. (ὄπιον), *opium,* Plin.

ŏportet -tŭit, 2. impers. *it behoves, is needful, proper, it must he ought to be;* foll. by the subj. alone, by the acc. and infin., by the infin., hoc fieri et oportet et opus est, Cic.; exstent oportet vestigia, Cic.; absol., quidquid veto non licet, certe non oportet, Cic.

oppēdo, 3. (op and pedo), *to mock, insult;* Judaeis, Hor.

oppĕrĭor -pertus and (more rarely) -pĕrītūs sum, 4. (root PER, whence experior), *to wait.* **I.** Intransit., *to wait;* ibidem, Cic. **II.** Transit., *to expect;* agmen peditum, Liv.; abi intro, ibi me opperire, Ter.

oppĕto -īvi and -ĭi -ītum, 3. (ob and peto), *to go to meet, encounter (especially an evil);* pestem, Plaut.; mortem, *to die,* Cic.; or simply oppetere, Verg.

oppĭdānus -a -um (oppidum), *of or belonging to a town (except Rome, of which urbanus was used), belonging to a small town;* in a contemptuous sense, *provincial;* senex, Cic.; genus dicendi, Cic.; subst., **oppĭdāni** -ōrum, m. *the inhabitants of a town,* Caes.

oppĭdātim, adv. (oppidum), *in the towns, in all the towns,* Suet.

oppĭdo, adv. *very, very much, exceedingly;* ridiculus, Cic.; pauci, Cic.; in answers, *certainly,* P ut.

ŏppĭdŭlum -i, n. (dim. of oppidum), *a little town,* Cic.

oppĭdum -i, n. (perhaps from ob and PED, whence Gr. πέδον, im-ped-ire, etc.), *a town* (urbs generally used for Rome); a, oppidum pervetus in Sicilia, Cic.; sanguine per triduum in oppido (*in town = in Rome*), pluisse, Liv.; with genit. of the name of the town, in oppido Antiochiae, Cic.; b, *a fortified wood in Britain,* Caes.

oppignĕro, 1. (ob and pignero), *to pledge, pawn, give in pledge;* libellos pro vino, Cic.

oppĭlo, 1. (ob and pilo), *to stop up, close up, block up;* scalas tabernae librariae, Cic.

opplĕo -plēvi -plētum, 2. (ob and pleo), *to fill, fill up,* Liv.; nives omnia oppleverant, Liv. **II.** Transf., nam vetus haec opinio Graeciam oppressit, Cic.

oppōno -pŏsŭi -pŏsĭtum (-postum, Lucr.), 3. (ob and pono), *to put or place opposite, before.* **I.** Lit., **A.** oculis manus, Ov.; luna subjecta atque opposita soli, Cic. **B.** *to place against o: in the way of for protection;* a, omnes corpora nostra opponimus, Cic.; b, moles oppositae fluctibus, Cic.; se alicui, Caes. **II.** Transf., 1, *to pledge against, mortgage for;* ager oppositus est pignori ob decem minas, Ter.; 2, *to expose;* se periculis, Cic.; 3, *to allege as an objection, to oppose, oppose in argument;* a, alicui nomen, valetudinem alicuius, Cic.; b, *to place one thing against another in the way of comparison, to contrast;* nunc omni virtuti vitium contrario nomine opponitur, Cic.

opportūnē, adv. (opportunus), *opportunely, seasonably, fitly, conveniently;* opportune adesse, Cic.

opportūnĭtas -ātis, f. (opportunus), *convenience, fitness, appropriateness, suitableness.* **I.** loci, Caes. **II.** a, *a fit time, right season, opportunity;* divina, Cic.; opportunitates ad cultum hominum, Cic.; b, *a fit state of the body or mind;* corporis, Cic.; c, *an advantage,* Cic.; opportunitate aliquā datā, Cic.

opportūnus -a -um (ob and POR-o, PORT-o, whence also portus, porta), *opportune, fit, suitable, appropriate, favourable.* **I. A.** Lit., loca, Sall. **B.** Transf., a, of time, *suitable, favourable;* tempus, Cic.; b, of nature, *serviceable, useful;* (a) of things, with dat. of object, ceterae res opportunae sunt singulae rebus fere singulis

Cic.; (β) of persons, *suitable;* homines, Sall. **II.** *exposed to, liable to;* huic eruptioni, Liv.; injuriae, Sall.

oppŏsĭtĭo -ōnis, f. (oppono), *opposing, opposition,* Cic.

1. **oppŏsĭtus** -a -um, p. adj. (from oppono), *opposed, opposite, standing against;* Buthrotum oppositum Corcyrae, Caes.

2. **oppŏsĭtus** -ūs, m. (oppono), *a placing, setting against* or *opposite, interposition,* Cic.

oppressĭo -ōnis, f. (opprimo). **I.** *a pressing down, oppression;* legum et libertatis, Cic. **II.** *a forcible taking possession of;* curiae, Cic.

oppressor -ōris, m. (opprimo), *a suppresser, crusher;* dominationis, ap. Cic.

1. **oppressus** -ū, m. (opprimo), *a pressing down, pressure,* Lucr.

2. **oppressus** -a -um, partic. of opprimo.

opprĭmo -pressi -pressum, 3. (ob and premo). **I. A.** Lit., 1, *to press down, press together;* ora loquentis, Ov.; 2, a, *to crush;* opprimi ruinā conclavis, *to be crushed,* Cic.; senem injectu multae vestis, *to stifle, smother,* Tac.; b, of a flame, *to extinguish;* cum aquae multitudine vis flammae opprimitur, Cic.; c, of a letter, *to slur over in pronunciation;* litterae neque expressae neque oppressae, Cic. **B.** Transf., 1, *to suppress;* a, dolorem, Cic.; b, *to conceal;* insigne veri, Cic.; 2, *to crush, bear hard upon, weigh down;* opprimi aere alieno, Cic.; 3, *to crush an evil, suppress, stamp out;* perniciosam potentiam, Cic.; 4, *to crush, subdue an adversary;* a, in war, nationem Allobrogum, Cic.; b, in politics, aliquem, Cic.; 5, *to hold firm, not to let go;* institit, oppressit, non remisit, Cic. **II.** *to seize upon, fall upon, surprise.* **A.** Antonium mors oppressit, Cic.; improvidos incautosque hostes, Liv. **B.** Transf., numquam ille me opprimet consilio, Cic.

opprōbrāmentum -i, n. (opprobro), *a reproach, disgrace,* Plaut.

opprōbrĭum -ĭi, n. (ob and probrum), *a reproach, scandal, disgrace, opprobrium;* 1, majoris fugiens opprobria culpae, Hor.; 2, meton., a, *a verbal reproach, taunt;* morderi opprobriis falsis, Hor.; b, of persons, *shame, disgrace;* majorum, Tac.

opprobro, 1. (ob and probrum), *to taunt, upbraid, reproach,* Plaut.

oppugnātĭo -ōnis, f. (oppugno), *a storming, taking by storm;* oppidorum, Caes.; oppugnationem sustinere, Caes.; relinquere, Tac.; judicium sine oppugnatione, *without opposition,* Cic.

oppugnātor -ōris, m. (oppugno), *one who storms, attacks, assaults;* fig., hostis et oppugnator patriae Antonius, Cic.

1. **oppugno**, 1. (ob and pugno), *to attack, assault, storm, besiege.* **I.** Lit., oppidum, Cic.; castra, Caes. **II.** Transf., *to attack, lay siege to;* fig., aliquem clandestinis consiliis, Cic.

2. **oppugno**, 1, (ob and pugnus), *to buffet with the fists,* Plaut.

1. **Ops**, Opis, f. = *the Earth, the goddess of abundance, wife of Saturn,* and *protectress of agriculture.*

2. **ops**, ŏpis, f., plur., **ŏpes** -um (sing. only in genit., acc., and abl.). **I.** *might, power;* a, *resources;* opibus, armis, potentiā valere, Cic.; b, *forces, troops;* tantas opes prostravit, Cic.; c, *political power, influence;* alicuius opes evertere, Cic. **II.** *physical power, might, strength;* omni ope atque operā enitar, Cic.; grates persolvere dignas non opis est nostrae, *is not in our power,* Verg. **III.** *help, assistance, support;* opem petere ab aliquo, Cic.; opem afferre, *to help,* Ov.

ops ... v. obs ...

optābĭlis -e (opto), *desirable, to be wished for;* mihi pax in primis fuit optabilis, Cic.

optandus -a um, p. adj. (from opto), *to be wished for, desirable;* maxime fuit optandum Caecinae ut, etc., Cic.

optātĭo -ōnis, f. (opto), *a wish:* alicui tres optationes dare, Cic.

optātō, adv. (optatus), *according to one's wish,* Cic.

optātus -a -um, p. adj. (from opto), *wished for, desired, pleasant, dear;* rumores, Cic.; frater, Cic. Subst., **optātum** -i, n. *a wish;* optatum impetrare, Cic.

optĭmās -ātis (optimus), *one of the best, aristocratic;* genus, Cic. Subst., **optĭmās** -ātis, m. *an aristocrat;* ap. Cic.; gen. plur., **optĭmātes** -ĭum and -um, m. *the aristocratic party, the aristocrats,* Cic.

optĭmē, superl. of bene (q.v.).

optĭmus (optŭmus) -a -um, superl. of bonus (q.v.).

1. **optĭo** -ōnis, f. (* opo), *choice, free choice, option;* utro frui malis optio sit tua, Cic.; si mihi optio daretur, utrum malim defendere, an, etc., Cic.

2. **optĭo** -ōnis, m. in military language, *an adjutant,* Tac.

optĭvus -a -um (opto), *chosen;* cognomen, Hor.

opto, 1. (stem OP, Gr. OΠ, whence ΟΠΤΩ, ὄψομαι). **I.** *to choose, elect, select;* utrum vis, opta, dum licet, Plaut.; locum tecto, Verg.; ut optet utrum malit an, etc., Cic. **II.** *to wish for, desire;* illam fortunam, Cic.; with infin., finem accusandi facere, Cic.; with acc. and infin., redargui me, Cic.; with ut and the subj., optavit, ut in currum tolleretur, Cic.; with subj. alone, crescat tua civibus opto urbs, Ov.; with acc. and dat., alicui furorem et insaniam, Cic.

ŏpŭlens -entis (opes), **1,** *rich,* Nep.; **2,** *powerful;* civitas, Sall.

ŏpŭlentē and **ŏpŭlentēr**, adv. (opulentus and opulens), *richly, splendidly, sumptuously;* ludos opulentius facere, Liv.

ŏpŭlentĭa -ae, f. (opulens), **1,** *wealth, riches, opulence,* Sall.; **2,** *the power, greatness of a state,* Sall.

ŏpŭlentĭtas -ātis, f. (opulens), *riches, opulence,* Plaut.

ŏpŭlento, 1. (opulens), *to make opulent, enrich,* Hor.

ŏpŭlentus -a -um (ops). **I.** *rich, wealthy, opulent.* **A.** civitas, Cic.; oppidum, Caes.; Numidia agro virisque opulentior, Sall. **B.** *rich, splendid, sumptuous;* res haud opulenta, Liv. **II.** *powerful, mighty;* reges, Sall.; factio, Liv.

Ŏpuntĭus, v. 3. Opus.

1. **ŏpus** -ĕris, n. *a work, labour.* **I. A.** Lit., 1, *onus nostrarum artium,* Cic.; opus quaerere, *to seek for work,* Cic.; 2, a, *work in the fields;* facere patrio rure opus, Ov.; b, *building;* lex operi faciundo, *building-contract,* Cic.; c, milit. t. t., *a military work, fortification, entrenchment;* operibus oppugnare urbem, Liv.; Mutinam operibus munitionibusque sepsit, Cic.; d, *work as opposed to nature, art;* nihil est opere aut manu factum, quod non aliquando consumat vetustas, Cic.; e, *the work of an artist;* hydria Boëthi manu facta praeclaro opere, *of admirable workmanship,* Cic. **B.** Meton., 1, a, *finished work;* opera magnifica atque praeclara, Cic.; b, *a work of art;* Silanionis opus (of a statue), Cic.; c, *a literary work;* opus habeo in manibus, Cic. **II.** a, *action, work, business;* censorium

Cic.; certatim ad hoc opus curretur, Cic.; b, *in undertaking*, Liv.; c, *trouble;* magno opere, Cic.; nimio opere, Cic.

2. ŏpus, n. indecl., found in the phrases opus est, *there is need, it is needful, it is necessary;* with nom., dux nobis, et auctor opus est, Cic.; with abl. of the thing needed, opus est auctoritate tuā, Cic.; maturato opus est, *there is need of haste,* Liv.; with genit., quanti argenti opus fuit, Liv.; with acc., Plaut.; with infin., quid opus est affirmare, Cic.; with 2. supine, quod scitu opus est, Cic.

3. Ŏpūs -puntis, f. ('Οποῦς), *town in Locris,* now *Talanta.* Adj., **Ŏpuntĭŭs** -a -um, *Opuntian.*

ŏpuscŭlum -i, n. (dim. of 1. opus), *a little work,* Cic.

1. ōra -ae, f. (1. os), *the edge, border, rim, boundary.* **I.** poculi, Lucr.; regionum, Cic.; clipei, Verg. **II. A.** *the coast, sea-coast;* Italiae, Cic. **B.** *a region, clime, country;* quācumque in ora ac parte terrarum, Cic.; Acheruntis orae, *the lower world,* Lucr.; luminis orae, *the upper world,* Verg. **C.** *a zone, belt of the earth,* Cic.

2. ōra -ae, f. *a cable or hawser by which a ship was made fast to the shore,* Liv.

ōrācŭlum (ōrāclum) -i, n. (oro). **I.** *a place where an oracle is given, an oracle;* illud oraculum Delphis, Cic.; transf., domus jureconsulti oraculum civitatis, Cic. **II.** *an oracle, divine response;* **1,** oraculum edere, Cic.; petere a Dodona, Cic.; **2,** a, *a prophecy;* oracula fundere, Cic.; b, *a wise speech, oracular declaration;* physicorum, Cic.

ōrātĭo -ōnis, f. (oro). **I.** *speaking, speech, language.* **A.** Gen., quae (ferae) sunt rationis et orationis expertes. **B.** *eloquence;* satis in eo fuit orationis, Cic. **II.** Meton., **A.** *speech, utterance;* orationem bonorum imitavi, Cic. **B.** *a set speech;* comparare ad id longam orationem, Cic.; habere orationem in senatu, Cic.; in extrema oratione nostra, *at the end of our speech,* Cic.; b, *prose* (as opp. to poetry); saepissime et in poematis et in oratione peccatur, Cic.

ōrātĭuncŭla -ae, f. (dim. of oratio), *a little speech, short oration,* Cic.

ōrātor -ōris, m. (oro), *speaker.* **I.** *the spokesman of an embassy,* Cic. **II.** *an orator,* Cic.

ōrātōrĭē, adv. (oratorius), *oratorically, like an orator,* Cic.

ōrātōrĭus -a -um (orator), *relating to an orator, oratorical;* ingenium, Cic.; ornamenta, Cic.

ōrātrix -īcis, f. (orator), *a female suppliant;* virgines oratrices pacis, Cic.

ōrātus -ūs, m. (oro), *a request, entreaty;* oratu tuo, Cic.

orbātor -ōris, m. (orbo), *one who deprives another of children or parents,* Ov.

orbĭcŭlātus -a -um (orbiculus), *circular, round;* ap. Cic.

orbĭcŭlus -i, m. (dim. of orbis), *a little circle or disk,* Plin.

orbis -is, m. *a circle, ring, anything round.* **I. A.** Gen., torquere in orbem, Cic. **B.** Esp., **1,** milit. t. t., *a circle of soldiers;* in orbem consistere, Caes.; **2,** of the heavens, orbis signifer, *the zodiac,* Cic.; lacteus, *the Milky Way,* Cic.; **3,** *a circular motion, serpentine fold, winding;* immensis orbibus angues incumbunt pelago, Verg.; of the rounding off or period of a speech, orationis or verborum, Cic.; orbis terrarum, *the circle of the world, the world,* Cic. **II.** *a disk.* **A.** Gen., orbis mensae, *a round table,* Ov. **B.** Esp., **1, a,** *the disk of the sun or moon,* Liv.; **b,** *the heavens;* **c,** orbis terrae, *the earth,* (α) Cic.; (β) poet. = *land;* Eous, *the East,* Ov.; (γ) meton., *mankind;* orbis terrae judicio ac testimonio comprobari, Cic.; **2, a,** *a shield,* Verg.; **b,** *a wheel,* Verg.; *the wheel of fortune,* Ov.; **c,** *the hollow of the eye,* Ov. (locat., orbi terrarum, Cic.).

orbĭta -ae, f. (orbis), *a wheel-rut, mark of a wheel,* Cic.; fig., orbita veteris culpae, *bad example,* Juv.

orbĭtas -ātis, f. (orbus), *a bereaving, bereavement, loss of children or parents;* orbitates liberûm, Cic.; fig., orbitas reipublicae virorum talium, Cic.

orbo, 1. (orbus), *to bereave.* **I.** Gen., Italiam juventute, Cic. **II.** *to deprive of parents or children;* filio orbatus, Cic.

Orbōna -ae, f. (orbus), *the goddess invoked by bereaved parents,* Cic.

orbus -a -um (root ORB, Gk. 'ΟΡΦ-ανός), *deprived of.* **I.** Gen., *bereft, destitute;* with abl., rebus omnibus, Cic.; with genit., luminis, Ov. **II.** Esp., *deprived of parents or children, bereft, without parents or children;* orbus senex, Cic.; with abl., liberis, Liv.; with genit., Memnonis orba mei venio, Ov.; subst., **orbus** -i, m. and **orba** -ae, f. *an orphan,* Liv.; fig., respublica, Cic.; Sulpicius legationem orbam reliquit, Cic.

orca -ae, f. **1,** *a kind of whale,* Plin.; **2,** *an earthenware pot or jar with a large belly,* Hor.

Orcădes -um, f. *islands near Scotland,* now *the Orkneys.*

orchăs -ădis, f. (ὀρχάς), *a species of olive,* Verg.

orchestra -ae, f. (ὀρχήστρα), *the part of a Roman theatre reserved for the senators;* meton., *the senate,* Juv.

Orchŏmĕnus (-ŏs) -i, m. and **Orchŏmĕnum** -i, n. ('Ορχομενός). **I.** *town in Boeotia.* **II.** *town in Arcadia.*

orcīnus -a -um (Orcus), *of or relating to Orcus or the dead;* senatores, *those who became senators by the will of Caesar,* Suet

Orcus -i, m. (connected with ἕρκος and urgeo). **I.** *Orcus, the infernal regions.* **II. A.** *the god of the lower world, Pluto,* Cic. **B.** *death,* Hor.

ordĕum = hordeum (q.v.).

ordĭa prīma = primordia (q.v.).

ordĭnārĭus -a -um (ordo), *according to order, regular, ordinary;* consules, *elected in the regular manner* (opp. to suffecti), Liv.; ordinarii reipublicae usus, Liv.

ordĭnātim, adv. (ordinatus), **1,** *in order, in good order,* Caes.; **2,** *regularly, properly,* Caes.

ordĭnātĭo -ōnis, f. (ordino), *a setting in order, arrangement,* Plin.

ordĭnātus -a -um, p. adj. (from ordino), *set in order, arranged, orderly,* Cic.

ordĭno, 1. (ordo), *to set in order.* **I. a,** *to plant in rows;* latius arbusta sulcis, Hor.; b, *to arrange in rank* (of soldiers); agmina, Hor. **II.** Transf., **1,** *to settle;* aliter apud alios ordinatis magistratibus, Liv.; **2,** *to arrange, appoint, settle, dispose, classify;* partes orationis, Cic.; res publicas, *to narrate the history of the state,* Hor.

ordĭor, orsus sum, 4. dep. (connected with ordo), *to begin, commence.* **A.** Gen., alterius vitae quoddam initium, Cic. **B.** Esp., in speaking, *to begin;* with acc., sermonem, Cic.; with infin., de aliqua re disputare, Cic.; absol., de aliquo paulo altius, Cic.; sic orsus Apollo, *began to speak,* Verg.

ordo -ĭnis, m. (orior). **I.** *series, line, row, order.* **A.** Lit., olivarum, Cic.; ordine, (a) *in* *detail*, Cic.; (β) *in due order*, Cic.; *ex ordine, in succession*, Cic.; *in ordinem, in order*, Cic.; *nullo ordine, without order, in a disorderly manner*, Caes.; *extra ordinem*, (a) *in an unusual, irregular manner*; *alicui provinciam decernere*, Cic.; (β) *extraordinarily, very greatly*, Cic. **B.** Meton., 1, *a row of seats in a theatre*, Cic.; *a row or bank of oars in a vessel*, Verg.; 2, milit. t. t., *rank, file*; ordines explicare, Liv.; ordine egredi, Sall.; *a company*; ordinem ducere, *to be a centurion*, Caes.; ordines primi, *commanders*, Caes.; 3, a, politically, *an order, rank, class*; senatorius or amplissimus, *the senatorial body*, Cic.; equester, *the body of knights*, Cic.; b, *a class, body of men*; publicanorum, Cic. **II.** *order, arrangement*; nomina in ordinem referre, Cic.; res in ordinem adducere, *to put into order*, Cic.

Ordŏvīces -um, m. *a people in Britain, opposite to the island of Mona*, now *Anglesea.*

Ŏrĕās -ādis, f. (Ὀρειάς), *a mountain-nymph, Oread*, Verg.

Ŏrestēs -ae and -is, m. (Ὀρέστης), *son of Agamemnon and Clytaemnestra, brother of Iphigenia and Electra, who killed his mother, the murderess of his father, and with his friend Pylades and his sister Iphigenia (priestess of Diana in the Tauric Chersonese), carried away the image of Diana to Italy, near Aricia.* Hence, adj., **Ŏrestēus** -a -um, *Orestean.*

ŏrexis -is, f. (ὄρεξις), *desire, appetite*, Juv.

orgănĭcus -a -um (ὀργανικός), *musical, relating to musical instruments*, Lucr.; subst., **orgănĭcus** -i, m. *a musician*, Lucr.

orgănum -i, n. (ὄργανον), *any implement or instrument*, Plin.; *a musical instrument, a water-organ*, Suet.

Orgĕtŏrix -rīgis, m. *a celebrated Helvetian.*

orgĭa -ōrum, n. (ὄργια), *nocturnal festivals in honour of Bacchus*, Verg.; and hence, *any secret festival, orgies*, Juv.

ŏrĭchalcum -i, n. (ὀρείχαλκος), *yellow copper ore*; hence, *brass made from it*, Cic.

ŏrĭcilla -ae, f. (= auricilla), *an ear-lap*, Cat.

Ŏrĭcŏs -i, f. and **Ŏrĭcum** -i, n. *a town in Epirus*, now *Erico.* Hence, 1, adj., **Ŏrĭcĭus** -a -um, *Orician*; and 2, **Ŏrĭcĭni** -ōrum, m. *the inhabitants of Oricum.*

ŏrĭcŭla = auricula (q.v.).

ŏrĭens -entis, m. (lit., partic. of orior, sc. sol). **I.** *the rising sun*; personif., *the sun-god, day-god*, Verg., Ov. **II.** Meton., 1, *the east*, as a part of the sky, Cic.; 2, *the east*, as a part of the world, Cic.

ŏrīgo -ĭnis, f. (orior). **I.** *origin, source*; principii nulla est origo, Cic. **II.** *birth, descent.* **A.** Lit., Ov. **B.** Transf., a, *race*, Verg.; b, *ancestor, founder of a race*; pater Aeneas Romanae stirpis origo, Verg.

Ŏrīon -ōnis, m. (Ὠρίων), *the constellation Orion.*

ŏrĭor, ortus sum, ŏrītūrus, ŏrīri, 4. dep. (root OR, Gk. OP, whence ὄρνυμι), *to rise.* **I.** Of persons, quum consul oriens de nocte silentio diceret dictatorem, Liv. **II.** Transf., *to arise = to become visible.* **A.** Of the heavenly bodies; ortā luce, *in the morning*, Caes.; oriens sol, *the East*, Cic. **B.** *to arise, spring from, proceed from, come forth*; Rhenus oritur ex Lepontiis, *takes its rise*, Caes.; clamor, Caes.; hence, a, *to be born*; equestri loco ortus, Cic.; b, *to grow*; uva oriens, Cic.; c, *to begin*; ab his sermo oritur, Cic. (indic. pres. acc. to 3rd conjug., orior, orĕris, orĭtur, orĭmur, orĭmini; so imperf. subj., orĕretur).

Ŏrīthyia -ae, f. (Ὠρείθυια), *daughter of Erechtheus, king of Athens, mother of Zethes and Calais by Boreas.*

1. **ŏrĭundus** -a -um (orior), *arising from, springing from, born of*; ab ingenuis, Cic.; ex Etruscis, Liv.

2. **Ŏrĭundus** -i, m. *a river in Illyria.*

Ormĕnis -ĭdis, voc. -i, f. (Ὀρμενίς), *the Ormenid (granddaughter of Ormenus) = Astydamia.*

ornāmentum -i, n. (orno). **I.** *equipment, accoutrement, trappings, furniture*; certas copias et ornamenta vestra, Cic. **II. A.** *ornament, decoration, embellishment*; omnia ornamenta ex fano Herculis in oppidum contulit, Caes.; fig., senectutis, Cic.; esp., *rhetorical ornament*; oratoria ornamenta dicendi, Cic. **B.** *honour, ornament, distinction*; omnia ornamenta congerere ad aliquem, Cic.

ornātē, adv. with compar. and superl. (ornatus), *ornately, splendidly, elegantly*; comparare convivium, Cic.; loqui, Cic.

ornātrix -īcis, f. (ornator), *a female adorner, a tire-woman*, Ov.

1. **ornātus** -ūs, m. (orno). **I.** *dress, attire, equipment*; militaris, Cic.; regalis, Cic. **II.** *embellishment, decoration*; 1, lit., urbis, Cic.; 2, fig., verborum, Cic.; meton., of discourse, *embellishment, ornament*; ornatum afferre orationi, Cic.; 3, as a translation of the Greek κόσμος, *the world*, Cic.

2. **ornātus** -a -um, p. adj. (from orno). **I.** *furnished, equipped, accoutred, provided*; scutis telisque parati ornatique sunt, Cic. **II.** a, *adorned, decorated, embellished, beautiful*; oratio, Cic.; so of persons, *adorned with all noble qualities, admirable, illustrious*; adolescens, Cic.; b *honoured*; honoribus, Cic.

orno, 1. **I.** *to equip, accoutre, provide with necessaries, fit out*; aliquem armis, Verg.; decemviros apparitoribus, Cic.; classem, consules, Cic.; provinciam, *to provide troops, money*, etc., *for the government of a province*, Cic. **II.** *to adorn, decorate, embellish.* **A.** Lit., 1, domum suam, Cic.; cornua sertis, Verg.; 2, *to praise, honour, show honour to*; fuit ornandus in Manilia lege Pompeius, Cic. **B.** Transf., *to adorn, decorate, honour, distinguish*; civitatem omnibus rebus, Caes.; aliquem laudibus, Cic.

ornus -i, f. *the mountain-ash*, Verg.

ōro, 1. (1. os). **I.** *to speak*; a, talibus orabat Juno, Verg.; b, *to speak as an orator*; vestra in nos promerita complecti orando, Cic.; ipse pro se oravit, *defended himself*, Liv.; c, *to treat or handle in speech, to argue, plead*; capitis causam, Cic.; litem, Cic. **II.** *to beg, pray, entreat, beseech*; with acc. of the person entreated, principem, Tac.; oro te (parenthetic), *I pray*, Cic.; with acc. of the thing, auxilium ad bellum, Liv.; with acc. of pers. and acc. of thing, auxilia regem, Liv.; with ut or ne and the subj., or subj. alone, oro ut homines conserves, Cic.; with infin., Verg.

Ŏrōdēs -is and -i, m. *king of the Parthians, who took Crassus prisoner.*

Ŏrontēs -is, m. (Ὀρόντης), *the chief river of Syria.* Hence, adj., **Ŏrontēus** -a -um, poet. = *Syrian.*

Orpheus -ĕi and -ĕos, acc. -ĕum and -ĕa, abl. -ĕo, m. (Ὀρφεύς), *a celebrated mythical minstrel of Thrace, husband of Eurydice.* Hence, adj., 1, **Orphēus** -a -um; and 2, **Orphĭcus** -a -um, *Orphic, of or relating to Orpheus.*

orphus -i, m. (ὀρφός), *a sea-fish*, Ov.

orsa -ōrum, n. (ordior), 1, *a beginning, com-*

nencement, undertaking, Liv.; **2,** poet., *speech, words,* Verg.

1. **orsus** -ūs, m. (ordior), *a beginning, undertaking,* Cic.

2. **orsus** -a -um, partic. of ordior.

orthŏgrăphĭa -ae, f. (ὀρθογραφία), *orthography,* Suet.

Ortōna -ae, f. *town of the Frentani in Latium,* now *Ortona.*

1. **ortus** -ūs, m. (orior). **I.** *a rising of the heavenly bodies;* **1,** lit., solis et lunae reliquorumque siderum ortus, Cic.; **2,** meton., solis, *the east,* Cic. **II. a,** *birth;* primo ortu, *immediately after birth,* Cic.; ortu Tusculanus, Cic.; ortum ducere ab Elide, Cic.; **b,** *origin, source;* tribuniciae potestatis, Cic.

2. **ortus** -a -um, partic. of orior.

Ortўgĭa -ae, f. and **Ortўgĭē** -ēs, f. (Ὀρτυγία). **I.** *an island forming part of Syracuse.* **II.** *the old name of the island of Delos.* Hence, adj., **Ortўgĭus** -a -um, *Ortygian.*

ŏryx -ўgis, m. (ὄρυξ), *a species of wild goat or gazelle,* Juv.

ŏrўza -ae, f. (ὄρυζα), *rice,* Hor.

1. **ōs,** ōris, n. **I.** *the mouth;* **1,** lit., cadit frustum ex ore pulli, Cic.; aliquem semper in ore habere, *to be always talking about,* Cic.; in ore vulgi esse, Cic.; alicui esse ante os, *before one's eyes,* Cic.; uno ore, *unanimously,* Cic.; in ora vulgi (hominum) abire (pervenire), Cat.; **2,** transf., *mouth, opening;* portus, Cic.; dolii, Liv.; *source,* ora novem Tinavi, Verg. **II.** *the face, countenance.* **A. 1,** lit., in ore hominum, in the *presence of men,* Cic.; **2,** meton., used for *impudence, shamelessness;* nostis os hominis, nostis audaciam, Cic. **B.** *a mask;* Gorgonis, Cic.

2. **ŏs,** ossis, n. *a bone;* dolorem cineri eius atque ossibus inussisti, Cic.; ossa legere, *to gather up the ashes of the bones after the burning of a corpse,* Cic.; tum vero exarsit juveni dolor ossibus ingens, *in his heart,* Verg.; fig., of orators, imitari non ossa solum sed etiam sanguinem, Cic.; of a meagre style, ossa nudare, Cic.

Osca -ae, f. *town in Hispania Tarraconensis,* now *Huesca.* Hence, adj., **Oscensis** -e, *belonging to Osca.*

oscen -ĭnis, m. (= obscen from obs and cano), t. t. of augural language, *a bird from whose note auguries were taken* (e.g., the raven, owl, crow), Hor.

Osci -ōrum, *an ancient people of Italy;* hence, adj., **Oscus** -a -um, *Oscan.*

oscillum -i, n. (dim. of 1. os), *a little mask,* Verg.

oscĭtantĕr, adv. (oscito), *yawningly, carelessly, negligently,* Cic.

oscĭtātĭo -ōnis, f. (oscito), *the opening of the mouth, a gaping,* Plin.

oscĭto. 1. (perhaps from os and cieo = moveo), *to open the mouth, gape, yawn,* Cic.; fig., *to be lazy, idle, inactive;* oscitat Epicurus, Cic.

oscŭlābundus -a -um (osculor), *kissing,* Suet.

oscŭlātĭo -ōnis, f. (osculor), *a kissing,* Cic.

oscŭlor, 1. dep. (osculum), *to kiss;* consulem filium, Cic.; fig., *to caress, make much of, make a pet of;* scientiam juris tamquam filiolam osculari suam, Cic.

oscŭlum -i, n. (dim. of 1. os). **I.** *a little mouth;* oscula summa delibare, Verg. **II.** Meton., *a kiss;* oscula ferre, Cic.

Ŏsīris -ris, -rĭdis and -rĭdos, m. (Ὄσιρις),

husband of Isis, god of Egypt, the genius of the Nile.

Ossa -ae, m. (Ὄσσα), *a high mountain in Thessaly,* now *Kissavo.* Adj., **Ossaeus** -a -um, *belonging to Ossa.*

ossĕus -a -um (2. os), *made of bone, like bone, bony,* Juv.

ossĭfrăgus -i, m. and **ossĭfrăga** -ae, f. (2. os and frango), *the sea-eagle, osprey,* Lucr.

ostendo -tendi -tentum and (later) -tensum, 3. (obs and tendo), *to show, display, exhibit, expose to view.* **I.** Lit., **a,** os suum populo Romano, Cic.; equites sese ostendunt, *come in sight,* Caes.; **b,** *to expose, lay open;* supinatas Aquiloni glebas, Verg. **II.** Fig., **1,** *to show, display;* spem, metum, Cic.; **2,** esp. of discourse, *to show, make plain, declare;* nihil sibi gratius ostendit futurum esse, Cic.; quid sui consilii sit ostendit, Caes.

ostentātĭo -ōnis, f. (ostento). **I.** *a showing, displaying, revealing;* ostentationis causā latius vagari, Caes. **II.** Transf., **a,** *a boasting, display, ostentation;* ingenii, Cic.; **b,** *false, deceitful show, pretence;* consul veritate, non ostentatione popularis, Cic.

ostentātor -ōris, m. (ostento) *one who shows boastingly, a boaster, vaunter, parader;* factorum, Liv.

ostento, 1. (intens. of ostendo), *to hold out, offer.* **I.** Lit., **A.** alicui jugula sua pro capite alicuius, Cic. **B. a,** *to show publicly, display, exhibit;* passum capillum, Caes.; **b,** *to show boastingly;* equum armaque capta, Liv. **II.** Fig., **A.** *to hold before a person's eyes, to show boastingly, to proffer, promise;* agrum, Cic. **B. 1,** *to show off, display;* prudentiam, Cic.; **2,** *to hold out with a menace, threaten;* caedem, Cic.; **3,** *to show, reveal;* **a,** se in aliis rebus, Cic.; **b,** of discourse, *to show, declare, make known;* et simul ostentavi tibi me istis esse familiarem, Cic.

ostentum (ostendo) -i, n. *a prodigy, portent;* magnorum periculorum metus ex ostentis portenditur, Cic.

ostentus, dat. -ŭi, abl. -ū, m. (ostendo). **I.** *a showing, displaying;* corpora abjecta ostentui, *for a show,* Tac. **II. 1,** *outward show, parade;* illa deditionis signa ostentui esse, Tac.; **2,** *a sign, indication, proof;* ut Jugurthae scelerum ostentui essem, Sall.

Ostĭa -ae, f. and **Ostĭa** -ōrum, n. (ostium), *the harbour and port of Rome, situate at the mouth of the Tiber.* Hence, adj., **Ostiensis** -e, *relating to Ostia;* incommodum, *the destruction of the Roman fleet by the pirates,* Cic.; provincia, *the office of the quaestor, who superintended the aqueducts and the supply of corn to the city,* Cic.

ostĭārĭus -a -um (ostium), *belonging to a door;* subst., **1, ostĭārĭus** -ĭi, m. *a doorkeeper, porter,* Varr.; **2, ostĭārĭum** -ĭi, n. (sc. tributum), *a tax upon doors, a door-tax,* Caes.

ostĭātim, adv. (ostium), *from door to door, from house to house;* compilare totum oppidum, Cic.

ostĭum -ĭi, n. (1. os), *the entrance.* **I.** portus, Cic.; fluminis Cydni, *mouth,* Cic.; Oceani, *Straits of Gibraltar,* Cic. **II.** *the door of a house;* ex actio ostiorum, *the door-tax,* Cic.; aperto ostio dormire, Cic.

ostrĕa -ae, f. and **ostrĕum** -i, n. (ὄστρεον), *an oyster,* Hor.

ostrĕātus -a -um (ostrea), *rough like an oyster-shell,* Plaut.

ostrĕōsus -a -um (ostrea), *abounding in oysters,* Cat.

ostrĭfĕr -fĕra -fĕrum (ostreum and fero), *producing oysters*, Verg.

ostrīnus -a -um (ostrum), *purple;* colores, Prop.

ostrum -i, n. (ὄστρεον), **1,** *the purple dye prepared from a shell-fish;* vestes ostro perfusae, Veig.; **2,** *stuff dyed with purple, a purple dress,* Verg.

ōsus -a -um, partic. of ōdi (q.v.).

Ōtho -ōnis, m. *a Roman name;* **1,** L. Roscius Otho, *author of a law giving special seats in the theatre to the knights;* **2,** M. Salvius Otho, *a Roman emperor who succeeded Galba.* Hence, **Ŏthōnĭānus** -a -um, *relating to Otho.*

Othrŷădēs -ae, m. (Ὀθρυάδης). **I.** *son of Othrys = Panthus.* **II.** *a Spartan general, the sole survivor in a battle with the Argives.*

Othrŷs -ўos, m. (Ὄθρυς), *a high mountain in Thessaly.*

ōtĭŏlum -i, n. (dim. of otium), *a little leisure;* ap. Cic.

ōtĭor, 1. dep. (otium), *to be idle, to be at leisure;* quum se Syracusas otiandi non negotiandi causâ contulisset, Cic.

ōtĭōsē, adv. (otiosus). **I.** *idly, without occupation,* Cic. **II.** *leisurely, lazily, gently, quietly,* Cic.

ōtĭōsus -a -um (otium), *idle, at leisure, without occupation.* **I.** Lit., **a,** homo, Cic.; tempus, Cic.; **b,** *free from public duties, occupied in literary work only;* numquam se minus otiosum esse quam quum otiosus, Cic.; **c,** *politically indifferent, neutral, quiet;* istos otiosos reddam, Cic. **II.** Transf., *quiet, calm, undisturbed,* Cic.

ōtĭum -ĭi, n. (opp. negotium), *idleness, leisure, ease;* **a,** otium inertissimum et desidiosissimum, Cic.; hebescere et languescere in otio, Cic.; **b,** *leisure, time for anything;* otium suum consumere in historia scribenda, Cic.; otium litteratum, Cic.; si modo tibi est otium, *if only thou hast time,* Cic.; **c,** *peace, repose, quietness;* multitudo insolens belli diuturnitate otii, Caes.; otium domesticum, Cic.; valde me ad otium pacemque converto, Cic.; ab hoste otium fuit, Liv.

ŏvātĭo -ōnis, f. (ovo), *an ovation, a kind of lesser triumph in which the victorious general proceeded to the Capitol on horseback or on foot,* Plin.

Ŏvĭdĭus -ĭi, m., P. Ovidius Naso, *the celebrated Roman poet, born at Sulmo,* B.C. 43, *died* A.D. 17.

ŏvīle -is, n. (ovis), **1,** *a sheepfold,* Verg.; **2,** *an enclosed place in the Campus Martius, where votes were given at the Comitia,* Liv.

ŏvillus -a -um (ovis), *of or relating to sheep;* ap. Liv.

ŏvis -is, f. (ὄις), *a sheep.* **I. a,** lit., pascere oves, Verg.; **b,** transf., as a term of reproach, *simple, foolish fellow,* Plaut. **II.** Meton., poet. *= wool,* Tib.

ŏvo, 1. (euoe, like Gr. εὐάζω). **I.** *to rejoice, exult;* ovans victoriâ, Liv. **II.** *to celebrate an ovation;* ovantem in Capitolium ascendisse, Cic.

ōvum -i, n. (ὠόν), **1,** *an egg;* ovum gignere, or parere, *to lay an egg,* Cic.; prov., integram famem ad ovum afferre, *to the beginning of the meal* (as Roman dinners often began with eggs), Cic.; ab ovo usque ad mala, *from beginning to end,* Hor.; **2,** transf., *one of the seven egg-shaped balls by which the heats in the circus were counted;* ova curriculis numerandis, Liv.

P.

P p, *the fifteenth letter of the Latin alphabet,* corresponds with the Greek pi (Π, π). For the use of P. in abbreviations, see Table of Abbreviations.

pābŭlātĭo -ōnis, f. (pabulor), *procuring of fodder, foraging;* pabulatione intercludi, Caes.

pābŭlātor -ōris, m. (pabulor), *a forager,* Caes.

pābŭlor, 1. dep. (pabulum), *to forage, seek fodder,* Caes.

pābŭlum -i, n. (pasco). **I.** Lit., **1,** *food,* nutrimtut; pabula caelestia, ambrosia, Ov.; **2,** *the food of animals, fodder;* pabulum secare, convehere, Caes. **II.** Transf., *food, nourishment;* studii atque doctrinae, Cic.

pācālis -e (pax), *belonging or relating to peace, peaceful;* laurus, Ov.

pācātus -a -um, p. adj. (from paco), *pacified, made peaceful;* and hence, *peaceful, quiet;* **a,** lit., pacatae tranquillaeque civitates, Cic.; mare, Hor.; subst., **pācātum** -i, n. *a peaceful, friendly country;* ex pacatis praedas agere, Sall.; **b,** transf., illorum oratio pacatior, Cic.

Păchŷnum -i, n. and **Păchŷnus (-ŏs)** -i, f. (Πάχυνος), *the south-east promontory of Sicily,* now *Capo di Passaro.*

pācĭfer -fĕra -fĕrum (pax and fero), *peace-bringing, establishing or announcing peace;* oliva, Verg.; frequently used as an epithet of the gods, e.g., of Mercury, Ov.

pācĭfĭcātĭo -ōnis (pacifico), f. *an establishing of peace, pacification,* Cic.

pācĭfĭcātor -ōris (pacifico), m. *one who establishes peace, a pacificator,* Cic.

pācĭfĭcātōrĭus -a -um (pacifico), *establishing peace, pacificatory;* legatio, Cic.

pācĭfĭco, 1. (pax and facio), *to reconcile, appease, pacify;* caelestes heros, Cat.

pācĭfĭcor, 1. dep. (pax and facio), *to make peace;* pacificatum legati veniunt, Liv.

pācĭfĭcus -a -um (pax and facio), *peace-making, pacific;* persona, Cic.

păcīscor, pactus sum, 3. dep. (root PAC, whence pac-s, * pago, pango), *to make a bargain, contract, agreement with any one, to agree, stipulate about anything;* **a,** intransit., cum illo, Plaut.; paciscitur magnâ mercede cum Celtiberorum principibus, ut copias inde abducant, Liv.; pacisci cum decumano, Cic.; **b,** transit., provinciam, Cic.; pretium, Cic.; ex qua domo pactus esset (feminam), *betrothed himself,* Liv.; with infin., *to bind oneself;* stipendium populo Romano dare, Liv. Partic., **pactus** -a um, pass. = *agreed upon, promised, appointed, settled;* pactam esse diem, Cic.

pāco, 1. (pax), *to reduce to peace, pacify, make peaceful,* Cic.; **a,** Amanum, Cic.; omnem Galliam, Caes.; **b,** poet., *to make fruitful;* incultae pacantur vomere silvae, Hor.

Păcōrus -i, m. (Πάκορος), *son of Orodes, king of Parthia, enemy of the Romans, born about 68 B.C.*

pacta -ae, f. (paciscor), *a betrothed spouse,* Verg.

pactĭo -ōnis, f. (paciscor), *a bargain, contract, covenant, agreement, treaty.* **I.** Gen., facere pactionem de aliqua re, Cic.; arma per factionem dare, *to capitulate,* Liv. **II. A.** *a contract between the farmers of the taxes of a province and its inhabitants;* pactiones conficere

Cic. B. *a fraudulent* or *collusive agreement;* pactionis suspicio, Cic.

Pactōlus -i, m. (Πακτωλός), *a river in Lydia, said to bring down golden sands,* now *Sarabat.* Adj., **Pactōlis** -idis, f. *of Pactolus;* Nymphae, Ov.

pactor -ōris, m. (paciscor), *one who makes a contract* or *treaty, negotiator;* societatis, Cic.

pactum -i, n. (paciscor), *a bargain, contract, agreement, covenant, treaty, pact;* manere in pacto, Cic. ; transf., nullo pacto, *by no means,* Cic. ; alio pacto, *in another way,* Cic. ; isto pacto, *in that way,* Cic.

pactus -a -um, partic. of paciscor.

Pācŭvĭus -ĭi, m., M. Pacuvius, *a Roman tragic poet of Brundisium, nephew of Ennius, flourishing about the time of the Second Punic War; died at Tarentum, about* 132 B.C.

Pădus -i, m. *the largest river in Italy,* now *the Po.*

Pădūsa -ae, f. *a canal running from the Po to Ravenna,* now *Canali di S. Alberti.*

Paean -ānis, m. (Παιάν). **I.** Lit., *the Healer, a surname of Apollo,* Cic. **II.** Meton., *a hymn, paean,* originally *addressed to Apollo only, but afterwards to other deities;* conclamant socii laetum paeana secuti, Verg.

paedăgōgus -i, m. (παιδαγωγός), *a slave who accompanied children to and from school and had charge of them at home,* Cic.

paedor -ōris, m. *dirt, filth,* Cic.

paelex = pelex (q.v.)

Paeligni -ōrum, m. *an Italian tribe in Samnium,* in modern *Abruzzo Citeriore.* Hence, **Paelignus** -a -um, *Pelignian;* anus, *a witch,* Hor.

paene, adv. *nearly, almost;* paene amicus, Cic.

paeninsŭla -ae, f. (paene and insula), *a peninsula,* Liv.

paenŭla -ae, f. (φαινόλης), *a species of overcoat, without sleeves, and close to the body, worn on a journey,* or *in wet, cold weather,* Cic. ; prov., paenulam alicui scindere, *to beg a guest very earnestly to remain,* Cic.

paenŭlātus -a -um (paenula), *clothed in the paenula,* Cic.

paeōn -ōnis , m. (παιών), *a metrical foot, consisting of three short syllables and one long,* Cic.

Paeŏnes -um, m. (Παίονες), *the Paeonians, the people of Paeonia;* sing., **Paeon** -ŏnis, m. Hence, **A. Paeŏnĭa** -ae, f. (Παιονία), *Paeonia, a district of Macedonia,* afterwards *Emathia.* **B. Paeŏnis,** f. *a Paeonian woman.*

Paeŏnĭus -a -um (Παιώνιος), *relating to the god of healing, Apollo, medicinal;* herbae, Verg.

Paestum -i, n. *a town in Lucania, famous for its roses,* now *Pesto.* Hence, **Paestānus** -a -um, *of Paestum.*

paetŭlus -a -um (dim. of paetus), *having a slight cast in the eye,* Cic.

paetus -a -um, *having a cast in the eyes, blink-eyed;* and, as an epithet of Venus, *having an engaging leer, leering prettily,* Hor.

pāgānus -a -um (pagus), *belonging* or *relating to a village, rural;* focus, Ov. ; and hence, **pāgānus** -i, m., subst., 1, *a villager, countryman,* Cic. ; 2, *a person in civil life, a civilian,* (opp. miles), Tac.

Păgăsa -ae, f. and **Păgăsē** -ēs, f. and **Păgăsae** -ārum, f. (Παγασαί), *a seaport of Thessaly, where the ship Argo was built;* hence, adj., **Păgăsaeus** -a -um, *Pagasean;* puppis, carina, *the Argo,* Ov. ; conjux, Alcestis, *daughter*

of the Thessalian king Pelias, Ov. ; **Pagaseus,** *Jason, leader of the Argonauts,* Ov.

pāgātim, adv. (pagus), *in villages, by village,* Liv.

pāgella -ae, f. (dim. of pagina), *a little page,* Cic.

pāgĭna -ae, f. (* pago, pango). **I.** *a page* or *leaf of paper,* or *of a book;* complere paginam, Cic. **II.** Transf., *a leaf, slab, tablet;* pagina honorum, *a list of titles and honours on a statue,* Juv.

pāgĭnŭla -ae, f. (dim. of pagina), *a little page,* Cic.

pāgur -i, m. *a fish of unknown species,* Ov.

pāgus -i, m. (pango). **I.** *a village;* a, *as a place,* Liv. ; b, collectively, *the inhabitants of a village;* pagus agat festum, Ov. **II.** *a district, canton, province* (esp. of the Germans and Gauls); omnis civitas Helvetia in quatuor pagos divisa, Caes.

pāla -ae, f. (for pagela from pango). **I.** *a spade,* Liv. **II.** *the socket of a ring in which the jewel is set, the bezel of a ring,* Cic.

Pălaemōn -mŏnis, m. (Παλαίμων). **I.** *a sea-god, formerly called Melicerta.* **II.** *a shepherd,* Verg.

Pălaepharsālus -i, f. *Old Pharsalus, a town in Thessaly, near Pharsalus,* now *Farsa.*

Pălaeŏpŏlis, acc. -pŏlim, f. (Παλαιόπολις), *the older part of the town of Neapolis in Campania.* Hence, **Pălaeŏpōlītāni** -ōrum, m. *the inhabitants of Palaeopolis.*

Pălaestē -ēs, f. (Παλαιστή), *a town of the province Chaonia in Epirus,* now *Palasa.* Hence, adj., **Pălaestīnus** -a -um, *relating to Palaeste.*

Pălaestīna -ae, f. and **Pălaestīnē** -ēs, f. (Παλαιστίνη), *Palestine;* hence, adj., **Pălaestīnus** -a -um, *relating to Palestine;* aqua, *the Euphrates,* Ov. ; subst., **Pălaestīni** -ōrum, m. = *the Syrians,* Ov.

pălaestra -ae, f. (παλαίστρα). **I.** *a gymnasium* or *wrestling school;* a, lit., Cic. ; b, transf., *a school of rhetoric,* Cic. **II.** Meton., a, *wrestling;* discere palaestram, Cic.; b, *exercise in the schools of rhetoric, rhetorical exercises, rhetorical practice;* quasi quandam palaestram et extrema lineamenta orationi attulit, Cic. ; c, *art;* utemur eā palaestrā, Cic.

pălaestrĭcē, adv. (palaestricus), *after the manner of the palaestra;* spatiari in xysto, Cic.

pălaestrĭcus -a -um (παλαιστρικός), *of* or *relating to the palaestra;* motus, Cic.

pălaestrīta -ae, m. (παλαιστρίτης), *the superintendent of a palaestra,* Cic.

pălam (from same root as planus, πλατύς, pellis, etc.). **I.** Adv., *openly, publicly.* **A.** Lit., rem gerit, Cic. **B.** 1, *openly, without concealment;* palam agere et aperte dicere, Cic. ; 2, *openly, apparently, evidently;* palam proferre, Cic.; 3, palam factum est (with acc. and infin.), *it is well known,* Cic. **II.** Prep. (= coram), with abl., *in the presence of;* populo, Liv. ; me, Ov.

Pălămēdēs -is, m. (Παλαμήδης), *son of the Euboean king Nauplius, the mythical inventor of the balance, of dice, and of some of the Greek letters, one of the Greek heroes in the Trojan war, put to death through a false accusation by Ulysses.*

Pălātĭum -ĭi, n. **I.** *the Palatine Hill in Rome, on which Augustus had his house.* Hence, **II.** *a palace;* Palatia fulgent, Ov. Hence, adj., **Pălātīnus** -a -um, *Palatine;* a, *of* or *relating to the Palatine Hill;* Apollo, *whose temple was on the Palatine,* Hor. ; Palatina tribus or subst., **Pălātīna** -ae, f. *the Palatine tribe,* Cic. ; b, *relating to the imperial palace, imperial,* Ov.

pălātum -ı, n. and **pălātus** -i, m. **I.** *the palate as the organ of taste;* quae voluptas palato percipiatur, Cic.; fig., *taste, critical judgment, the palate as the organ of taste and judgment;* Epicurus dum palato quid sit optimum judicat, Cic.; *the palate as the organ of speech;* ferire balba verba palato, Hor. **II.** Transf., palatum caeli, *the vault of the heavens;* ap. Cic.

pălĕa -ae, f. *chaff,* Cic.

pălĕar -āris, n. *the dewlap of an ox;* gen. plur., Verg.

Păles -is, f. (PA, ΠΑ-ω, pasco), *the tutelary goddess of herds and shepherds.* Hence, adj., **Pălīlis** -e, *belonging to Pales;* flamma, *a fire of straw, part of the ceremonies at the feast of Pales;* subst., **Pălīlĭa** -ium, n. *the feast of Pales on the 21st of April.*

Pălĭci -ōrum, m. (sing., Palicus, Verg., Ov.), *twin sons of Jupiter by the nymph Aetna, worshipped as heroes in Sicily.*

Pălīlis -e, v. Pales.

pălimpsestos -i, m. (παλίμψηστος), *parchment, from which old writing has been erased for the purpose of using the parchment again, a palimpsest,* Cic.

Pălīnŭrus -i, m. (Παλινοῦρος). **I.** *the pilot of Aeneas who fell into the sea off the coast of Lucania.* **II.** *a promontory on the west coast of Lucania,* now *Cap Palinuro.*

pălĭūrus -i, m. (παλίουρος), *a plant, Christ's thorn* (Rhamnus Paliurus, Linn.), Verg.

palla -ae, f. *a long and wide outer garment worn by Roman women, also by tragic actors,* Hor.

pallăca -ae, f. (παλλακή), *a concubine,* Suet.

Pallacinē -ēs, f. *a place in Rome.* Hence, **Pallacinus** -a -um, *relating to Pallacine.*

1. **Pallăs** -ădis and -ădos, f. (Παλλάς), *the Greek name of Minerva, goddess of wisdom, and discoverer of the olive;* Palladis ales, *the owl,* Ov.; arbor, *the olive-tree,* Ov.; meton., a, *the olive-tree,* Ov.; b, *olive-oil,* Ov.; c, *the image of Pallas, the Palladium,* Ov.; hence, adj., **Pallădĭus** -a -um, *of or relating to Pallas;* rami, *olive branches,* Verg.; latices, *oil,* Ov.; ratis, *the ship Argo,* Ov.; arces, *Athens,* Ov.; subst., **Pallădĭum** -ĭi, n. *the image of Pallas in Troy, which fell from heaven.*

2. **Pallas** -antis, m. (Πάλλας). **I.** *son of Pandion, father* (according to one legend) *of Minerva.* **II.** *grandfather* or *great-grandfather of Evander.* **III.** *son of Evander.* **IV.** *one of the giants.* Hence, **A. Pallantēus** -a -um, *belonging to Pallas;* subst., **Pallantēum** -i (sc. oppidum); a, *a town in Arcadia;* b, *a town in Italy on the site of Rome.* **B. Pallantĭăs** -ădis, f. *Aurora, a descendant of Pallas* (IV.). **C. Pallantĭs** -ĭdos = Pallantias. **D. Pallantĭus** -a -um, *relating to Pallas* (II. or III.), *heros, Evander,* Ov.

pallens -entis, p. adj. (from palleo). **I. A.** *pale, wan;* umbrae Erebi, Verg. **B.** *pale* or *wan in colour, pale-yellow, pale-green;* violae, Verg.; hedera, Verg. **II.** *making pale, causing paleness;* morbi, Verg.

pallĕo -ŭi, 2. *to be pale.* **I.** Gen., **A.** 1, lit., sudat, pallet, Cic.; 2, meton., a, *to be pale* or *sick with desire, to long for;* argenti pallet amore, Hor.; b, *to be pale with fear* or *anxiety;* ad omnia fulgura, Juv.; pontum, *to pale at the sight of,* Hor. **B.** Transf., *to lose one's natural colour,* Ov. **II.** *to be yellow,* Ov.

pallesco, pallŭi, 3. *to grow pale, turn pale, lose colour.* **I.** Lit., nullā culpā, Hor. **II.** Transf., *to grow yellow;* pallescunt frondes, Ov.

pallĭātus -a -um (pallium), *clad in a pallium,* i.e., *as a Greek* (opp. togatus, *clad as a Roman*); Graeculus, Cic.

pallĭdŭlus -a -um (dim. of pallidus), *somewhat pale,* Cat.

pallĭdus -a -um (palleo), *pale, wan, pallid* **I.** Gen. 1, lit., pallida sedi, *pale with fright,* Ov.; 2, meton., pass., *causing paleness;* mors, Hor. **II.** *yellow, olive-green,* Cat.

pallĭŏlātus -a -um (palliolum), *wearing a cloak, cape,* or *hood,* Suet.

pallĭŏlum -i, n. (dim. of pallium), 1, *a little Greek cloak* or *mantle,* Plaut.; 2, *a hood,* Ov.

pallĭum -i, n. **I.** *a coverlet,* Ov. **II.** *a long Greek mantle,* Cic.

pallor -ōris, m. (palleo), *paleness, pallor;* 1, lit., *terrorem pallor consequitur,* Cic.; amant ium, Hor.; 2, meton., *anxiety, fright;* personif. as a goddess, Liv.; 3, *unsightliness, unpleasant colour,* Ov.

palma -ae, f. (παλάμη). **I.** *the palm of the hand;* 1, lit., Cic.; 2, meton., a, *the whole hand, the hand,* Cic.; b, *the blade of an oar,* Cat. **II.** *the palm-tree;* 1, lit., Plin.; 2, meton., a, *the fruit of the palm, a date,* Ov.; b, *a palm-branch, a besom* or *broom made of palm-branches,* Hor.; *the palm-branch* as a token of victory, Liv.; hence, (a) *the reward of victory;* palmam dare, accipere, Cic.; fig., palmam ferre, Cic.; *fame,* Liv.; (β) *victory;* alicui hanc palmam reservare, Cic. **III.** *a shoot, twig;* palma stipitis, Liv.

palmāris -e (palma), *deserving the palm* or *prize, excellent, admirable;* statua, Cic.; sententia, Cic.

palmārĭum -ĭi, n. (palma), *a masterpiece,* Ter.

palmātus -a -um (palma), *worked* or *embroidered with palm-branches;* tunica (worn by triumphing generals), Liv.

palmes -itis, m. (palma), *a young branch* or *shoot of a vine, a vine-sprout,* Verg.

palmētum -i, n. (palma), *a palm-grove,* Hor.

palmĭfĕr -fĕra -fĕrum (palma and fero), *producing palm-trees, abounding in palm-trees,* Ov.

palmōsus -a -um (palma), *full of palms,* Verg.

palmŭla -ae, f. (dim. of palma), *the blade of an oar, an oar,* Verg.

palmus -i, m. (palma), *the palm of the hand,* Plin.; *as a measure, a span* (¼ of a Roman foot), Plin.

pālor, 1. dep. *to wander about, stray about;* agmen palatur per agros, Liv.; palantia sidera, Lucr.

palpēbra -ae, f. (palpo), *the eyelid;* gen. plur., palpebrae, *the eyelids,* Cic.

palpĭto, 1. *to move quickly, tremble, palpitate, throb;* cor palpitat, Cic.; esp. of persons in death-agony, Ov.

1. **palpo,** 1. and **palpor,** 1. dep. **I.** *to stroke* or *touch gently,* Ov. **II.** Fig., *to coax, wheedle, caress;* with dat., scribenti palparer, ap. Cic.; with acc., quem munere palpat, Juv.

2. **palpo** -ōnis, m. (1. palpo), *a coaxer, wheedler, flatterer,* Pers.

pălūdāmentum -i, n. *the military cloak, a soldier's cloak,* esp., *a general's cloak,* Liv.

pălūdātus -a -um, *clad in the military cloak, dressed in a general's cloak;* Pansa noster paludatus profectus est, Cic.

pălūdōsus -a -um (2. palus), *marshy, boggy,* Ov.

pălumbes (pălumbis) -is, m. and f. *a wood-pigeon, ring-dove*, Verg.

1. pālus -i, m. (for paglus, from *pago, pango), *a pale or stake*. **I.** Gen., aliquem ad palum alligare or deligare, Cic. **II.** Milit. t. t., *a stake on which Roman recruits exercised their weapons;* aut quis non vidit vulnera pali? Juv.

2. pālus -ūdis, f. *stagnant water, a swamp, marsh, morass, bog, fen,* Cic.; tarda palus, the Styx, Verg.

păluster -tris -tre (2. palus). **I.** *marshy,* boggy, fenny; limus paluster, Liv.; plur., **pălustria** -ium, n. *marshy places,* Plin. **II.** *found or living in marshes;* ranae, Hor.

Pamphylia -ae, f. (Παμφυλία), *a district in Asia Minor, between Cilicia and Lycia.* Adj., **Pamphylius** -a -um, *Pamphylian.*

pampineus -a -um (pampinus), *pertaining to or consisting of vine-tendrils or leaves;* hastae, garlanded with vine-leaves, Verg.; corona, of vine-leaves, Tac.

pampinus -i, m. and f. *a vine-tendril, vine-leaf;* uva vestita pampinis, Cic.

Pān, Pānis and Pānos, m. (Πάν), *the god of woods and shepherds;* plur., **Pānes**, *rural deities resembling Pan.*

pănăcea -ae, f. and **pănăcēs** -is, n. and **pănax** -ācis, m. (πανάκεια, πανάκες, πάναξ, lit., all-healing), *a fabulous plant, to which was attributed the power of healing all diseases, panacea, heal-all,* Verg.

Pănaetius -ii, m. (Παναίτιος), *a Stoic philosopher of Rhodes, teacher and friend of the younger Scipio Africanus,* 185–112 B.C.

Pănaetōlicus -a -um (Παναιτωλικός), *relating to the whole of Aetolia;* consilium, Liv.

Pănaetōlius -a -um (Παναιτώλιος), *relating to the whole of Aetolia;* consilium, Liv.

pānārium -ii, n. (panis), *a bread-basket,* Plin.

Pănăthēnāicus -a -um (Παναθηναϊκός), of or relating to the Athenian festival of the Panathenaea; hence, subst., **Pănăthēnāicus** -i, m. *an oration of Isocrates delivered at the Panathenaea,* Cic.

pănax = panacea (q.v.).

Panchāia -ae, f. (Παγχαῖα), *a fabulous island in the Indian Ocean, near Arabia, famous for its incense;* hence, adj., **Panchāius** and **Panchaeus** -a -um, *Panchean.*

panchrestus -a -um (πάγχρηστος), *good or useful for everything;* medicamentum, *sovereign remedy,* i.e., *gold,* Cic.

pancrātium (-ŏn) -ii, n. (παγκράτιον), *a gymnastic contest, including both boxing and wrestling,* Prop.

Pandātăria (Pandātĕria) -ae, f. (Πανδαταρία), *an island in the bay of Naples, a place of exile under the Emperors, now Vandotina.*

Pandīōn -ōnis, m. (Πανδίων), *a king of Athens, father of Progne and Philomela;* Pandionis populus, *the Athenians,* Lucr.; Pandione nata, Progne or Philomela, Ov.; hence, adj., **Pandīōnius** -a -um, poet. = *Athenian.*

1. pando, 1. (pandus), *to bend, bow, curve,* Plin.

2. pando, pandi, pansum and passum, 3. **I.** *to stretch out, extend, expand;* a, lit., vela, Cic.; pennas ad solem, Verg.; crines passi, capillus passus, dishevelled hair, Caes.; passis manibus or palmis, with outstretched hands, Caes.; b, fig., alia divina bona longe lateque se pandunt. Cic. **II.** Transf., **A.** *to throw open;*

and in pass., *to open itself, open;* a, lit., januam, Plaut.; moenia urbis, Verg.; panduntur inter ordines viae, Liv.; b, fig., (a) *to open, throw open;* viam alicui ad dominationem, Liv.; (β) *to lay open in speech, tell, announce, explain;* nomen, Ov.; res, Verg. **B.** *to spread out to dry in the sun;* racemi passi, Verg.; lac passum, *curdled,* Ov.

Pandrŏsos -i, f. (Πάνδροσος), *daughter of Cecrops.*

pandus -a -um, *bent, curved, bowed, crooked,* Verg.

pănēgўrĭcus -i, m. (πανηγυρικός), *an oration of Isocrates, celebrating the glories of Athens,* Cic.

Pangaeus mons, m. and poet., **Pangaea** -ōrum, n. (τὸ Πάγγαιον), *a mountain of Macedonia on the Thracian borders.*

pango, panxi, panctum, and pēgi and pēpigi, pactum, 3. (stem PAG, whence pac-s, paciscor, Gr. ΠΑΓ, whence πήγνυμι, *to fasten,* fix, drive in. **I.** Lit., clavum, Liv. **II.** Transf., **A.** 1, *to make, undertake;* neque prima per artem temptamenta tui pepigi, Verg.; 2, *to compose, write;* versus de rerum natura, Lucr.; poëmata, Hor.; aliquid Sophocleum, Cic. **B.** *to fix;* 1, terminos, fines, Cic.; 2, *to agree upon, stipulate, contract;* a, pacem, Liv.; with genit. or abl. of price, tanti pepigerat, Liv.; pretium quo pepigerant, Liv.; with ut and the subj., ut vobis mitterem ad bellum auxilia pepigistis, Liv.; with infin., obsides dare pepigerant, Liv.; b, esp., used frequently of a contract of marriage, haec mihi se pepigit, pater hanc tibi, has betrothed, Ov.

pănĭcum -i, n. *the Italian panic grass, or wild millet* (panicum Italicum, Linn.), Caes.

pānis -is, m. (root PA, Gr. ΠΑ, whence pa-sco, πά-ομαι), *bread;* panis cibarius, *common bread,* Cic.; secundus, *black bread,* Hor.; plur., ex hoc (genere radicis) effecti panes, Caes.

Pāniscus -i, m. (Πανίσκος), *a sylvan deity, a little Pan,* Cic.

pannĭcŭlus -i, m. (dim. of pannus), *a little rag;* bombycinus, *a thin and scanty garment,* Juv.

Pannŏnii -ōrum, m. *the Pannonians, inhabitants of Pannonia.* Hence, **Pannŏnia** -ae, f. *Pannonia, a district between Dacia, Noricum, and Illyria, part of modern Hungary, Slavonia and Bosnia.*

pannōsus -a -um (pannus), *ragged, tattered,* Cic.

pannūcĕus (-ĭus) -a -um (pannus), *wrinkled, shrivelled,* Pers.

pannus -i, m. (πῆνος). **I.** *a piece of cloth, garment;* assuitur pannus, Hor.; *a bandage for the head,* Ov.; in sing. or plur., used contemptuously, *shabby clothes, rags,* Hor. **II.** *a rag,* shred, Hor.

Pănomphaeus -i, m. (Πανομφαῖος), *the founder of oracles, surname of Jupiter.*

1. Pănŏpē -ēs, f. (Πανόπη), *an old town in Phocis, on the Cephisus.*

2. Pănŏpē -ēs, f. and **Pănŏpēa** -ae, f. *a sea-nymph.*

Pănormus -i, f. and **Pănormum** -i, n. *a town on the north coast of Sicily, colony of the Phoenicians, near modern Palermo.* Hence, adj., **Pănormitānus** -a -um, *belonging to Panormus.*

pansa -ae (pando), *splay-footed, having broad feet,* Plaut.

pansus -a -um, partic. of pando.

Pantăgiēs (-ās) -ae, m. (Πανταγίης), *a small river on the east coast of Sicily.*

panthēra -ae, f. (πάνθηρα), *a panther*, Cic.

Panthēum -i, n. (Πάνθειον), *a temple of Jupiter at Rome, built by Agrippa.*

Panthŏus (-ŏŏs) (Πάνθοος), and **Panthus** -i, m. (Πάνθους), *son of Othrys, father of Euphorbus.* Hence, **Panthŏïdēs** -ae, m. *a descendant of Panthus;* a, *Euphorbus*, Ov.; b, *Pythagoras* (who pretended that the soul of Euphorbus had passed into his), Hor.

pantŏlăbus -i, m. (παντολάβος, *taking everything), name of a parasite.*

pantŏmīmus -i, m. (παντόμιμος), 1, *a male dancer, mime*, Suet.; 2, *a ballet, pantomime*, Plin.

păpae (παπαί), interj. *wonderful! indeed!* Ter.

păpāver -ĕris, n. *the poppy*, Verg.

păpāvĕrĕus -a -um (papaver), *of or relating to the poppy;* comae, *the stamens of a poppy*, Ov.

Paphlăgō -ōnis, m. (Παφλαγών), *a Paphlagonian.* Hence, **Paphlăgŏnĭa** -ae, f. (Παφλαγονία), *a district in Asia Minor, between Pontus and Bithynia.*

Păphus (-ŏs) -i (Πάφος). **I.** m. *son of Pygmalion, founder of the town of the same name.* **II.** f. *a town of Cyprus, sacred to Venus;* hence, adj., **Păphĭus** -a -um, *Paphian;* heros, *Pygmalion, father of Paphos;* myrtus, *sacred to Venus*, Ov.

păpĭlĭo -ōnis, m. *a butterfly*, Ov.

păpilla -ae, f. *a nipple, teat*, used of both human beings and animals, Plin.; meton.= *the breast*, Verg.

Păpĭrĭus -a -um, *name of a Roman gens;* hence, **Păpĭrĭānus** -a -um, *Papirian.*

Papĭus -a -um, *name of a Roman gens.*

păpŭla -ae, f. *a pimple, pustule*, Verg.

păpyrĭfĕr -fĕra -fĕrum (papyrus and fero), *producing the papyrus;* Nilus, Ov.

păpyrum -i, f. and **păpyrum** -i, n. (πάπυρος). **I.** *the plant papyrus*, Sen. **II.** Meton., **A.** *a garment made of the bark*, Juv. **B.** *paper made of the papyrus bark*, Juv.

păr, păris, *equal, like.* **I.** *like* or *equal to another thing or person.* **A.** Gen., 1, adj., pari intervallo, Caes.; est finitimus oratori poetae ac paene par, Cic.; with in and the abl., ut sint pares in amore, Cic.; with abl., libertate esse parem ceteris, Cic.; with genit., cuius paucos pares tulit, *like to him*, Cic.; with dat., hominem cuivis parem, Cic.; with cum, quaedam ex eis paria cum Crasso, Cic.; with inter se, inter se aequales et pares, Cic.; followed by conj., par atque, Cic.; et, Cic.; quam, Liv.; 2, subst., a. c., *a mate*, Ov.; b, neut., (a), *the like;* par pari respondere, Cic.; par impar ludere, *to play at odd and even*, Hor.; (β) *a pair;* tria aut quatuor paria amicorum, Cic. **B.** Esp., 1, *equally strong as;* a, adj., alicui, Caes.; b, subst., *an adversary*, Liv.; 2, fig., *suitable, appropriate;* par est, with acc. and infin., Cic. **II.** *like to oneself, equal to oneself;* ut par sis in utriusque orationis facultate, Cic.

părābĭlis -e (paro), *that can be easily procured, procurable;* divitiae, Cic.

Păraetăcēnē -ēs, f. (Παραιτακηνή), *a district on the borders of Media and Persia;* hence, **Păraetăcae** -ārum, m. *the inhabitants of Paraetacene.*

Păraetŏnĭum -iī, n. (Παραιτόνιον), *a frontier town of Egypt, on the sea.*

părăsita -ae, f. (parasitus), *a toady, parasite*, Hor.

părăsītaster -tri, m. (parasitus), *a poor, contemptible parasite*, Ter.

părăsītĭcus -a -um (παρασιτικός), *like a parasite, parasitic*, Plaut.

părăsītor, 1. dep. (parasitus), *to play the parasite*, Plaut.

părăsītus -i, m. (παράσιτος, *eating with another), a toady, parasite*, Cic.

părātē, adv. (paratus), *with preparation, readily;* ad dicendum venire magis audacter quam parate, Cic.

părātĭo -ōnis, f. (paro), *a preparation, preparing for;* paratio regni, *a striving after sovereignty*, Sall.

1. **părātus** -a -um, p. adj. (from 1. paro). **I.** *prepared, ready;* 1, victoria, *easily won*, Liv.; parata in agendo et in respondendo celeritas, Cic.; 2, *ready for something;* a, of things, omnia sibi esse ad bellum apta ac parata, Caes.; b, of persons, *ready for, inclined to;* animo paratus, Caes.; ad omnia mulieris negotia paratus, Cic.; acies parata neci, Verg.; with infin., id quod parati sunt facere, Cic. **II.** a, *well prepared* or *provided with anything, equipped;* adolescens et equitatu et peditatu et pecuniā paratus, Cic.; b, *instructed, prepared;* ad permovendos animos instructi et parati, Cic.

2. **părātus** -ūs, m. (1. paro), *preparation, fitting out, provision, equipment;* necessarius vitae cultus aut paratus, Cic.

Parca -ae, f. (connected with plec-to, amplec-tor, Gr. πλέκ-ω, etc.), *the goddess that allots the fate to each, the goddess of fate*, Hor. Plur., Parcae, *the three Fates*, Clotho, Lachesis, and Atropos, Cic.

parcē, adv. (parcus). **I.** *sparingly, frugally, economically;* frumentum parce metiri, Caes. **II.** 1, *sparingly, moderately;* parcius dicere de laude alicuius, Cic.; 2, *rarely, seldom;* parcius quatiunt fenestras, Hor.

parco, péperci and parsi, parsum, 3. (parcus). **I.** *to spare, to be sparing, moderate, frugal with anything;* with dat., impensae, Liv.; sumptu, Cic.; with acc., talenta guatis parce tuis, Verg. **II.** Transf., **A.** *to spare, refrain from injuring;* aedificiis, Cic.; sibi, Caes. **B.** a, *to leave off, desist from, cease;* labori, Cic.; with infin., parce fidem ac jura societatis jactare, Liv.; b, *to refrain from, keep oneself from;* with dat., auxilio, *to make no use of proffered aid*, Cic.; metu, Verg.; with ab and the abl., ab incendiis, Liv.

parcus -a -um (connected with parum and παῦρος). **I.** *sparing* (esp. in expenditure), *frugal, thrifty, economical;* a, colonus, Cic.; with genit., donanli, Hor.; b, *moderate, sparing;* in largienda civitate, Cic. **II.** *scanty, small, little, slight;* parco sale contingere, Verg.; lucerna, Prop.

pardus -i, m. (πάρδος), *a panther, pard*, Juv.

1. **pārens** -entis, p. adj. (from pareo), *obedient;* parentiores exercitus, Cic.; subst., **pārentes** -ium, m. *subjects*, Sall.

2. **pārens** -entis, c. (pario). **I.** *a parent, father, mother;* a, lit., Cic.; usually plur., *the parents;* quae caritas est inter natos et parentes, Cic.; alma parens Idaea deûm, Hor.; b, transf., (a) *author, cause, origin;* operum, Cic.; parens lyrae, Mercury, Hor.; (β) *a mother-city*, Liv. **II.** *a grandfather*, Ov.; plur., *ancestors*, Verg.

părentālis -e (2. parens). **I.** *parental, of* or *relating to parents;* umbra, Ov. **II.** *of* or *relating to the funeral of parents* or *other relations;* a, adj., dies, Ov.; b, subst., **părentālĭa** -ium, n. *a festival in honour of deceased parents* or *other relations*, Cic.

părento, 1. (2. parens). **I.** *to celebrate the parentalia in honour of the dead;* Februario mense mortuis parentari voluerunt, Cic. **II.** Transf., *to bring an offering to the dead* = *to avenge the death of a person by that of another* ; Cethego, Cic.

păreo -ŭi -ĭtum, 2. (akin to pario). **I.** *to appear, become visible.* **A.** Lit., Mart. **B.** Transf., *to be clear, evident* ; impers. paret, a legal formula, *it is proved*, Cic. **II.** 1, *to obey, be obedient to* ; **a**, voluntati, legibus, Cic. ; ducibus, Liv. ; **b**, *to be compliant, yield, give way to* ; necessitati, Cic. ; promissis, *to perform one's promises*, Ov. ; **2**, *to be subject to, to serve* ; neque uni neque paucis, Cic.

păries -ĕtis, m. *the wall of a house* (opp. murus, *the wall of a city*) ; nullo modo posse iisdem parietibus tuto esse tecum, *within the same house*, Cic. ; prov., duo parietes de eadem fidelia dealbare, *to kill two birds with one stone*, ap. Cic.

părĭĕtinae -ārum, **f.** (paries), *old walls, ruined walls, ruins*, Cic.

Părīlia = Palilia (v. under Pales).

părīlis -e (par), *similar, like, equal* ; aetas, Ov. ; vox, Ov.

părĭo, pĕpĕri, partum, fut. partic., părĭtūrus, 3. (root PAR, whence 1. paro), *to bring forth.* **I.** Lit., quintum, *for the fifth time*, Cic. ; of birds, ova, *to lay eggs*, Cic. **II.** Transf., **A.** *to bring forth, produce* ; fruges et reliqua quae terra pariat, Cic. **B.** *to invent, compose*, verba, Cic. **C.** *to produce, occasion, bring forth, invent, devise, obtain* ; **a**, in a good sense, sibi laudem, Cic. ; consulatum, Cic. ; parta bona, *acquired*, Cic. ; plur. subst., **parta** -ōrum, n. *property that has been acquired* ; **b**, in a bad sense, *to occasion, procure, cause* ; suspicionem, Cic.

Păris -ĭdis, m. (Πάρις), *son of the Trojan king, Priam, the judge in the contest of beauty for the golden apple between Juno, Minerva, and Venus* ; *carried away Helen from her husband Menelaus to Troy, and thus caused the Trojan war.*

Părisĭi -ōrum, m. *a people in Gallia Celtica, whose capital was Lutetia (Parisiorum), now Paris.*

părĭtĕr, adv. (par). **I.** *in like manner, alike* ; caritate non pariter omnes egemus, Cic. ; followed by ut, atque, ac, et, Cic. ; qualis, Sall. ; by dat., Liv. **II.** Transf., **A.** *together with, at the same time as* ; pariter cum luna crescere, Cic. **B.** *likewise, also*, Ov.

părĭto, 1. (intens. of 1. paro), *to prepare, to get ready to do anything*, Plaut.

1. **parma** - ae, f. (πάρμη), *the small round shield or buckler worn by light-armed troops and cavalry*, Liv. ; poet., *any kind of shield*, Verg.

2. **Parma** -ae, f. *town in Gallia Cispadana, colony of the Etruscans, now Parma.* Hence, adj., **Parmensis** -e, *of or belonging to Parma.*

Parmĕnĭdēs -is, m. (Παρμενίδης), *a famous Greek philosopher of the Eleatic School.*

parmātus -a -um (parma), *armed with the parma*, Liv.

parmŭla -ae, f. (dim. of parma), *a small round shield, buckler*, Hor.

Parnāsus (ŏs) and **Parnassus** (ŏs) -i, m. (Παρνασός), *a mountain in Phocis, sacred to Apollo and the Muses* ; hence, adj., **Parnāsius** (**Parnassius**) -a -um, *Parnassian, Delphian, relating to Apollo* ; laurus, Verg.

1. **păro**, 1. (root PAR, whence paro). **I.** *to prepare, make ready, provide, furnish, equip* ; convivium, Cic. ; bellum, Caes. ; alicui necem, Liv. ; with infin., *to prepare to do something* ; publicas litteras Romam mittere parabam, Cic. ; foll. by ut with the subj., si ita naturā paratum esset, ut ea dormientes agerent, Cic. **II.**

13*

Transf., *to procure, get, obtain.* **A.** exercitum, copias, Sall. ; non modo pacem sed etiam societatem, Liv. ; praesidium senectuti, Cic. **B.** Esp., *to procure with money, buy* ; hortos, Cic.

2. **păro**, 1. (par), 1, *to prize or esteem equally* ; eodem vos pono et paro, Plaut. ; **2**, *to agree, arrange with* ; se paraturum cum collega, Cic.

3. **păro** -ōnis, m. (παρών), *a small, light vessel, skiff*, Cic.

părŏchus -i, m. (πάροχος), 1, *an officer in Italy or in the provinces who provided with necessaries ambassadors and magistrates when on a journey*, Cic. ; **2**, transf., *one who gives an entertainment, a host*, Hor.

părŏpsis -ĭdis, f. (παροψίς), *a small dish, dessert-dish*, Juv.

Părus (-ŏs) -i, f. (Πάρος), *an island in the Aegean Sea, famous for its white marble.* Hence, **Părius** -a -um (Πάριος), *Parian* ; lapis, *Parian marble*, Verg. ; iambi, *of Archilochus, who was born at Paros*, Verg.

parra -ae, f. *a bird of ill omen*, according to some, *the owl*, to others, *the woodpecker*, Hor.

Parrhăsia -ae, f. (Παρρασία), *a district and city in Arcadia* ; hence, adj., 1, **Parrhăsis** -ĭdis, f. *Arcadian* ; Arctos or ursa = *ursa major* or *Callisto* ; subst., Parrhasis = *Callisto*, Ov.; 2, **Parrhăsius** -a -um ; **a**, *Arcadian* ; virgo, *Callisto*, Ov. ; dea, *Carmenta*, Ov. ; **b**, *relating to the Palatine Hill, imperial* (because the Arcadian Evander was said to have settled upon the Palatine), Mart.

1. **Parrhăsius**, v. Parrhasia.

2. **Parrhăsius** -ĭi, m. (Παρράσιος), *a celebrated Greek painter of Ephesus, rival of Zeuxis, flourishing about 400 B.C.*

parrĭcīda -ae, c. (perhaps from pater and caedo), *a parricide* ; **a**, *one who murders his father or parents*, Cic. ; **b**, *one who slays near relations* ; parricida liberûm, *Virginius*, Liv. ; **c**, *murderer of a free citizen* ; parricida civium, Cic. ; **d**, *murderer of the head of the state*, Cic. ; **e**, *a traitor, betrayer of one's country, rebel* ; parricidae reipublicae, Cic.

parrĭcīdĭum -ĭi, n. (parricida), 1, *the murder of a father or parents, parricide* ; *the murder of any near relation* ; fratris, Liv. ; patris et patrui, Cic. ; **2**, *the murder of a free citizen*, Cic. ; **3**, *high treason, the betraying of one's country* ; parricidium patriae, Cic.

pars, partis, acc. partim and partem, f. **a** *part, portion, piece.* **I.** Gen., urbis, Cic. ; partes facere, *to divide*, Cic. ; partem habere in aliqua re, *to have a share in*, Cic. Especial phrases, **a**, pars . . . pars, *some . . . others*, Liv. ; **b**, parte . . . parte, *partly . . . partly*, Ov. ; pro parte or pro sua, mea, etc., parte, *for his part*, Cic. ; **c**, ex aliqua parte, *in some degree*, Cic. ; magna ex parte, *to a great extent*, Cic. ; omni ex parte, *altogether*, Cic. ; **d**, magnam partem, *to a great extent*, Cic. ; **e**, acc. partim, *in part*, Cic. ; **f**, multis partibus = *many times, much* ; plures, Cic. ; **g**, in eam partem, *in such a manner*, Cic., or *with a view to*, Cic. ; in utramque partem (*on both sides, pro and contra*) disputare, Cic., or *in both cases*, Cic. ; **h**, in omnes partes, *altogether, completely*, Cic. ; **i**, in partem venire alicuius rei, *to take a share in*, Cic. ; **j**, in parte, *in part*, Liv. ; **k**, pro parte, *to the best of his ability*, Liv. **II. A.** *species*, Cic. **B.** *a party, faction* ; nullius partis esse, *neutral*, Cic. **C.** *the part or rôle of an actor* ; **a**, lit., primas partes agere, *the leading part*, Cic. ; **b**, transf., *a part, office, function, duty* ; tuum est hoc munus, tuae partes, Cic. **D.** *a part, portion, district of the earth* ; partes orientis, Cic.

parsĭmōnĭa -ae, f. (parco), *thriftiness, parsimony*, Cic.

Parthāon -ŏnis, m. (Παρθάων), *son of Agenor, king in Calydon, father of Oeneus;* Parthaone natus, *Oeneus*, Ov. Adj., **Parthāŏnĭus** -a -um, *of Parthaon;* domus, *of Oeneus*, Ov.

Parthĕni (Parthīni) -ōrum, m. *an Illyrian people near Dyrrhachium.*

parthĕnĭcē -ēs, f. (παρθενική), *the plant parthenium*, Cat.

Parthĕnĭus -ĭi, m. *a mountain on the borders of Argolis and Arcadia.*

Parthĕnŏpaeus -i, m. (Παρθενοπαῖος), *one of the seven princes who fought against Thebes.*

Parthĕnŏpē -ēs, f. (Παρθενόπη), *old name of the town of Neapolis, so called from the Siren Parthenope, who was said to have been buried there.* Adj., **Parthĕnŏpēïus** -a -um, *Parthenopean;* poet. = *Neapolitan.*

Parthi -ōrum, m.(Πάρθοι),*a Scythian nomadic people, famous for their archery; savage enemies of the Romans.* Hence, **Parthĭcus** and **Parthus** -a -um, *Parthian.*

partĭceps -cĭpis (pars and capio), *sharing, participating in;* animus rationis compos et particeps, Cic.; praedae ac praemiorum, Caes.; with dat., alicui ad omne secretum, Tac. Subst., *a sharer, partaker, comrade;* huius belli ego particeps et socius et adjutor esse cogor, Cic.

partĭcĭpo, 1. (particeps), *to cause to share, share with any one;* laudes cum aliquo, Liv.; ad participandum alium alio communicandumque inter omnes jus, Cic.

partĭcŭla -ae, f. (dim. of pars), *a small part, portion, particle;* caeli, Cic.

partim, adv. (acc. of pars), *partly, in part,* Cic.

partĭo, 4. and **partĭor**, 4. dep. (pars), *to divide, sub-divide.* **I.** genus universum in species certas partietur ac dividet, Cic. **II.** *to divide, distribute, share;* consules designati provincias inter se partiverant, Sall.; nonne aerarium cum eo partitus es? Cic.

partītē, adv. (partitus, from partior), *with proper divisions;* dicere, Cic.

partītĭo -ōnis, f. (partio). **I.** *a division;* 1, Graecus partitionem quandam artium fecisse video, Cic.; 2, esp., *a logical or rhetorical division of a subject*, Cic. **II.** *a division, distribution, partition;* aequabilis praedae partitio, Cic.

partītus -a um, partic. of partior.

partŭrĭo, 4. (desider. of pario). **I.** *to desire to bring forth, have the pains of labour;* 1, lit., prov., parturiunt montes, nascetur ridiculus mus, Hor.; 2, fig., a, *to be pregnant with anything, to meditate, intend;* ut aliquando dolor P. R. pariat, quod jamdiu parturit! Cic.; b, *to be anxious, troubled;* si tamquam parturiat unus pro pluribus, Cic. **II.** *to bear, bring forth, produce;* nunc omnis parturit arbos, Verg.

partus -ūs, m. (pario). **I.** *a bearing, bringing forth young, a birth;* quum jam appropinquare partus putaretur, Cic.; fig., Graeciae ●ratorum partus atque fontes, *beginnings*, Cic. **II.** Meton., **A.** *the time of bearing*, Cic. **B.** *that which is brought forth, the fruit of the womb;* partum edere, *to give birth to*, Cic.; partus terrae, *the giants*, Hor.

părum, adv. (from same root as parvus and παῦρος), compar., **mĭnŭs**, superl., **mĭnĭmē**; *too little, not enough* (opp. satis, nimium). **I.** Posit., parum id facio, *I make little account of that*, Sall.; parum est, foll. by quod, *it is not enough that*, etc., Cic.; parum habere, *to think too little, be*

dissatisfied with; foll. by infin., Liv.; parum diu, *too short*, Cic.; non parum saepe, *often enough*, Cic. **II.** Compar., minus. **A.** *less;* minus ac minus, Plin.; minus minusque, *less and less*, Liv.; nihil minus, *nothing less, not at all, by no means*, Cic.; foll. by quam, ac, atque, Liv.; with quam omitted, haud minus duo millia, *not less than two thousand*, Liv.; foll. by abl., minus triginta diebus, *in less than thirty days*, Cic.; uno minus teste haberet, *one witness the less*, Cic.; multo minus, *much less*, Cic.; bis sex ceciderunt, me minus uno, *except me alone*, Ov. **B.** *not particularly;* minus multi, Cic. **C.** *not;* a, after quo, *that*, prohibuisse, quo minus, etc., Cic.; b, in the formulae, si minus, *if not;* sin minus, *but if not*, Cic. **D.**= parum, *too little;* dicere, Cic. **III.** Superl., minime, *in the least degree, very little, least of all;* quod minime apparet et valet plurimum, Cic.; with adjectives = *not at all, by no means;* homo minime ambitiosus, Cic.; in answers, *by no means, not at all*, Cic.; minime vero, Cic.

părumpĕr, adv. (παῦρόν περ), *for a little while, a little space;* abduco parumper animum a molestiis, Cic.

părun@cŭlus -i, m. (dim. of 3. paro), *a little skiff or vessel*, Cic.

Părus = Paros (q.v.).

parvĭtās -ātis, f. (parvus), *littleness, smallness*, Cic.

parvŭlus -a -um (dim. of parvus). **I.** *very small, very little, minute;* res, pecunia, Cic. **II.** Of age, *young, little;* filius, Cic.; ab parvulis, *from childhood*, Caes.

parvus -a -um (pavrus, by change of consonants, from same root as παῦρος), compar., **minor**, superl., **minimus**; *little, small.* **I.** Lit., **A.** Of size or extent, locus, Cic.; navicula, Cic.; minor capitis = capite deminutus (see deminuo), Hor. **B.** Of number or quantity, a, adj., minimus numerus, Liv.; b, subst., **parvum** -i, n. *a little;* contentus parvo, Cic.; minus praedae, Liv.; c, adv., **mĭnĭmum**, *very little;* valere, Cic. **II.** Transf., **A.** Of value, *slight, unimportant;* a, adj., parvo vendere pretio, Cic.; b, subst., **parvum** -i, n. *something little or slight;* parvi aestimo or duco, *I think little of*, Cic.; minoris vendere, *cheaper*, Cic. **B.** Of strength or degree, *slight, weak;* a, of the voice, etc., (a) *weak;* parvae murmura vocis, Ov.; (β) *abject;* verbis minoribus uti, Ov.; b, of the intellect, *poor, unproductive;* ingenium, Hor.; c, of thought, will, etc., *little, abject, mean;* parvi animi, Cic.; d, of circumstances, *trifling, unimportant, slight;* commodum, Cic.; prov., minima de malis, *we must choose the least evil*, Cic.; e, of persons, *poor in position, unimportant, low, insignificant;* domus, Ov. Compar., minor, with abl., *inferior to, dependent on;* te minor, Hor. **C.** Of time, 1, *short;* dies, Ov.; 2, = *young;* minor natu, *younger*, Cic. Subst., **parvus** -i, m. *a little boy*, Cic.; **parva** -ae, f. *a little girl*, Cic.; a parvo, *from boyhood*, Cic.; minores, *young people*, Hor., Ov.

pasco, pāvi, pastum, 3. (root PA, whence panis, Gr. ΠΑ, whence πάομαι). **I.** *to feed cattle, lead cattle to pasture.* **A.** Lit., 1, sues, Cic.; 2, hence, gen., *to feed, nourish, support;* of animals, ubi bestiae pastae sunt, Cic.; of human beings, olusculis nos soles pascere, Cic.; quot pascit servos, Juv. **B.** Transf., 1, *to feed, increase, enlarge, let grow;* barbam, Hor.; crinem, Verg.; 2, *to feed, feast, gratify;* oculos in aliqua re, Cic. **II.**= depascere. **A.** *to feed on;* asperrima (collium), Verg. **B.** *to consume*, Ov. Hence, **pascor**, pastus sum, pasci, 3. dep. **I.** 1, *to feed, eat, graze on;* boves pa@scuntur frondĭbus, Verg.; **2**, of the sacred chickens, to eat; quum pulli non pascerentur, refused to eat, Cic. **II**. With acc., to feed on; pascuntur silvas, Verg.

pascŭus -a -um (pasco), fit for pasture or grazing; ager, Cic.; hence, subst., **pascŭum** -i, n. a pasture; plur., **pascŭa** -ōrum, n. pastures, Cic.

Pāsĭphăë -ēs, f. and **Pāsĭphăa** -ae, f. (Πασιφάη), daughter of Helios (Sol), sister of Circe, mother of the Minotaur, Androgeus, Phaedra, and Ariadne. Adj., **Pāsĭphăēĭus** -a -um, relating to Pasiphaë; subst., **Pāsĭphăēĭa** -ae, f.= Phaedra, Ov.

Pāsĭthĕa -ae, f. and **Pāsĭthĕë** -ēs, f. (Πασιθέα, Πασιθέη), one of the three Graces.

passer -ĕris, m. (for panser, from pando), **1**, a sparrow, Cic., Cat.; **2**, a sea-fish, a turbot or plaice, Ov.

passercŭlus -i, m. (dim. of passer), a little sparrow, Cic.

passim, adv. (passus from pando). **I**. here and there, up and down, far and wide, in a disorderly manner, confusedly; Numidae nullis ordinibus passim consederant, Caes. **II**. without distinction, indiscriminately, promiscuously; scribimus indocti doctique poëmata passim, Hor.

passum -i, n. (pando, sc. vinum), wine made of dried grapes, raisin-wine, Verg.

1. **passus** -a -um, partic. of pando.

2. **passus** -a -um, partic. of patior.

3. **passus** -ūs, m. **I**. a step, stride, pace. **A**. a, lit., passus perpauculi, Cic.; b, fig., passibus ambiguis Fortuna errat, Ov. **B**. a footstep, track; passu stare tenaci, Ov. **II**. the pace (a Roman measure of length) = five feet; mille passus, a mile, Cic.

pastillus -i, m. (dim. of panis), a lozenge used to give an agreeable smell to the breath, Hor.

pastĭo -ōnis, f. (pasco), a pasture, Cic.

pastor -ōris, m. (pasco), a herd; esp., a shepherd, Cic.; pastorum domina, Pales, Ov.; pastorum dux geminus, Romulus and Remus, Cic.

pastōrālis -e (pastor), of or relating to a shepherd, pastoral, Cic.

pastōrĭcĭus -a -um (pastor), relating to shepherds, Cic.

pastōrĭus -a -um (pastor), relating to shepherds, Ov.

pastus -ūs, m. (pasco). **I**. feeding. **A**. Lit., ad pastum accedunt, Cic. **B**. Meton., fodder, food; pastum capessere et conficere, Cic. **II**. pasture, Verg.

Pătăra -ōrum, n. (Πάταρα), a city in Lycia, with a celebrated oracle of Apollo; hence, **1**, **Pătărōüs** -ĕi and -ĕos, m. a surname of Apollo; **2**, **Pătăraeus** -a -um, Patarean; **3**, **Pătărăni** -ōrum, m. the inhabitants of Patara.

Pătăvĭum -ĭi, n. a town in Venetia, on the banks of the Medoacus, birth-place of the historian Livy, now Padua. Adj., **Pătăvīnus** -a -um, Patavinian.

pătĕfăcĭo -fēci -factum, 3., pass., **pătĕfīo** -factus sum -fieri (pateo and facio), to open, make open, lay open. **I**. Lit. **A**. aures assentatoribus, Cic. **B**. **1**. to make accessible, to open; vias, iter, Caes.; to open up a place, patefactum nostris legionibus esse Pontum, Cic.; **2**, to make visible, Cic.; **3**, to open (by digging, etc.); presso sulcum aratro, Ov. **II**. Transf., to bring to light, disclose, display, reveal; odium suum in me, Cic.; comparationem, Cic.; rem, Cic.

pătĕfactĭo -ōnis, f. (patefacio), a throwing open, disclosing; rerum opertarum, Cic.

pătella -ae, f. (dim. of patera), **1**, a dish, platter, plate (used both in the cookery and serving up of food), Hor.; **2**, a dish in which offerings were presented to the gods, a sacrificial dish, Cic.

pătens -entis, p. adj. (from pateo). **I**. open, unobstructed, accessible; caelum, Cic.; loca, Caes. **II**. open, exposed to; domus patens cupiditati et voluptatibus, Cic.

pătentĕr, adv. (patens), openly, evidently, clearly; compar., patentius, Cic.

pătĕo -tŭi, 2. (perhaps connected with πετάννυμι), to be open, stand open, lie open. **I**. nares semper propter necessarias utilitates patent, Cic. **II**. **A**. to be open, accessible; a, lit., aditus patuit, Cic.; b, to stand open, to be at the service of, to be in the power of; honores patent alicui, Cic. **B**. to lie open to, to be exposed to; vulneri, Liv **C**. to lie open before the eyes, to be visible; a, lit., nomen in adversariis patet, Cic.; b, transf., to be revealed, disclosed, clear; res patent, Cic. **D**. Geograph. t. t., a, lit., to stretch out, extend; Helvetiorum fines in longitudinem millia passuum CXL patebant, Cic.; b, transf., to spread, extend itself; in quo vitio latissime patet avaritia, Cic.

păter -tris, m. (πατήρ), a father. **I. A**. Lit., aliquem patris loco colere, Cic.; plur., patres, parents, Ov. **B**. Poet., meton., **1**, fatherly love; rex patrem vicit, Ov.; **2**, the author or source of anything, Verg. **II**. Transf., **A**. father-in-law, Tac. **B**. a, pater familias or familiae, the head of a household, Cic.; b, pater cenae, the host, Hor. **C**. patres, fathers, ancestors; aetas patrum nostrorum, Cic. **D**. Used as a title of honour; a, of the gods, Lemnius, Vulcan, Cic.; Lenaeus, Bacchus, Verg.; b, esp. the title by which the senators were addressed, patres conscripti, Cic.; c, pater patriae, father of his country, a name sometimes given to distinguished statesmen, Ov.; d, pater patratus, the chief of the fetiales, Cic.; e, used as a title of respect towards an old man, Verg.

pătĕra -ae, f. (pateo), a shallow dish or saucer from which a libation was poured, Cic.

Pătercŭlus -i, m., C. Velleius, a Roman historian under Augustus and Tiberius.

păternus -a -um (pater), **1**, of or relating to a father, fatherly, paternal; horti, Cic.; **2**, of or relating to one's native country, native; flumen, Hor.

pătesco, pătŭi, 3. (pateo), to be opened, lie open. **I**. Gen., a, lit., atria longa patescunt, Verg.; b, to be revealed, disclosed; Danaum patescunt invidiae, Verg. **II**. to extend, stretch out; deinde paulo latior patescit campus, Liv.

pătĭbĭlis -e (patior). **I**. Pass., endurable, bearable; dolores, Cic. **II**. Act., sensitive; natura, Cic.

pătĭbŭlum -i, n. a fork-shaped yoke, an instrument of punishment fastened on the neck of slaves and criminals, Cic.

pătĭens -entis, p. adj. (from patior). **I**. bearing, enduring, capable of enduring. **A**. Lit., with genit., patiens laborum, Sall.; amnis navium patiens, navigable, Liv.; animum patientem incommodorum, Cic. **B**. Poet., firm, hard, unyielding; aratrum, Ov. **II**. enduring, patient; ut ne offendam tuas patientissimas aures, Cic.

pătĭentĕr, adv. (patiens), patiently; ferre, Cic.

pătĭentĭa -ae, f. (patiens), endurance. **I**. famis, frigoris, Cic. **II. A**. patience, long-suffer-

ing; in carendo, Cic. **B.** *indolence, faint-heartedness,* Tac. **C.** *subjection,* Tac.

pătīna -ae, f. (πατάνη), *a dish,* Cic.

pătĭor, passus sum, 3. dep. (root PAT, connected with πάσχω, aor. ἔ-παθ-ον), *to suffer, bear, endure.* **I.** Lit., **A.** Gen., a, of persons, toleranter dolores, Cic.; gravissimum supplicium, Caes.; id damnum haud aegerrime pati, Liv.; **b,** of things, tunc patitur cultus ager, Ov. **B.** *to last, endure;* novem saecula (of the crow), Ov. **II.** Transf., 1, *to suffer, experience;* multam repulsam, Ov.; 2, *to suffer, permit, allow;* ista, Cic.; with acc. and infin., nullo se implicari negotio passus est, Cic.; with ut and the subj., quod si in turpi reo patiendum non esset ut arbitrarentur, Cic.; non patior, foll. by quin, nullam patiebatur esse diem quin in foro diceret, *he allowed no day to pass without speaking,* Cic.; with adv., facile, libenter, aequo animo, indigne pati, with acc. and infin., Cic.; with things as subjects, quantum patiebatur pudor, Cic.

Patrae -ārum, f. (Πάτραι), *a sea-port in Achaia,* now *Patras.* Adj., **Patrensis** -e, *relating to Patrae.*

pătrātor -ōris, m. (patro), *an accomplisher, achiever, effector;* necis, Tac.

pătrĭa -ae, f. *father-land,* v. patrius.

pătrĭcĭātus -ūs, m. *the rank or condition of a patrician,* Suet.

pătrĭcīda (pater and caedo), *one who murders his father,* Cic.

pătrĭcĭus -a -um (patres, v. pater, II. D. b), *patrician, noble;* 1, adj., familia, Cic.; 2, subst., patricius, *a patrician,* and plur., patricii, *the Roman patricians or nobility,* Cic.; exire e patriciis, *to be adopted into a plebeian family,* Cic.

pătrĭmōnĭum -ĭi, n. (pater), *property inherited from a father, patrimony;* accipere duo lauta et copiosa patrimonia, Cic.; fig., filio meo satis amplum patrimonium relinquam, memoriam nominis mei, Cic.

pătrĭmus -a -um (pater), *having a father still living,* Cic.

pătrītus -a -um (pater), *paternal;* patrita illa atque avita philosophia, Cic.

pătrĭus -a -um (pater), *of or relating to a father, fatherly, paternal.* **I.** Adj., animus, Cic.; amor, Ov.; res, *property inherited from one's father,* Cic.; mos, *ancestral, ancient,* Cic. **II.** Subst., **pătrĭa** -ae, f. (sc. terra), *father-land, native land;* aliquem restituere in patriam, Cic.; hence, **pătrĭus** -a -um, *relating to one's native country;* ritus, Cic.

pătro, 1. *to accomplish, perform, execute, achieve;* promissa, Cic.; bellum, *to bring to an end,* Sall.; pacem, Liv.; jusjurandum, *to pronounce a solemn oath at the conclusion of a treaty,* Liv.

pătrōcĭnĭum -ĭi, n. (= patronocinium, from patronus). **I.** *protection, defence in a court of law;* controversiarum patrocinia suscipere, Cic.; meton., patrocinia = *clients,* ap. Cic. **II.** Transf., *defence, protection;* patrocinium voluptatis repudiare, Cic.

pătrōcĭnor, 1. dep. (patronus), *to protect, defend;* alicui, Ter.

Pătrŏclus -i, m. (Πάτροκλος), *son of Menoetius, friend and cousin of Achilles, slain by Hector before Troy.*

pătrōna -ae, f. (patronus), *a protectress, patroness,* Ter.; esp., *the mistress or protectress of a freedman,* Plin.; fig., *a protectress;* provocatio patrona illa civitatis et vindex libertatis, Cic.

pătrōnus -i, m. (pater). **I.** *the protector, defender, patron of a body of clients; the patron or powerful friend at Rome of a state or city; a defender, advocate before a court of justice;* patronus, defensor, custos coloniae, Cic.; huic causae patronum exsistere, Cic.; esp., *the protector of a freedman,* i.e., *his master before he was freed,* Cic. **II.** Transf., *a defender, protector;* plebis, Liv.; foederum, Cic.

pătrŭēlis -e (patruus). **I.** *descended from a father's brother;* frater patruelis, *cousin on the father's side,* Cic.; transf., *the son of a paternal aunt,* Cic. **II.** *of or relating to a cousin, cousinly,* Ov.

1. **pătrŭus** -i, m. (pater), *a father's brother, paternal uncle;* a, lit., Cic.; b, fig., *a severe reprover,* Cic.

2. **pătrŭus** -a -um (pater), *of or relating to an uncle,* Hor.

Pătulcĭus -ĭi, m. (pateo), *a surname of Janus, whose temple was always open in time of war,* Ov.

pătŭlus -a -um (pateo). **I.** *open, standing open;* pinna, Cic.; fenestrae, Ov. **II.** *widespreading, extended;* rami, Cic.; loca urbis, Tac.

paucĭtas -ātis, f. (paucus), *fewness, scarcity, paucity;* oratorum, Cic.; militum, Caes.

paucŭlus -a -um (dim. of paucus), *very small;* gen. in plur., *very few;* dies, Cic.

paucus -a -um, oftener plur., **pauci** -ae -a (connected with paulus and pauper, and Gr. παῦρος). **I.** *few, little;* pauco foramine (= paucis foraminibus), Hor.; paucis rebus, Cic.; pauciores viri, Cic. Plur. subst., a, **pauci** -ōrum, m. *a few;* esp., (α) (like οἱ ὀλίγοι), *the oligarchs;* (β) *the select few* (opp. populus), Cic.; b, **pauca** -ōrum, n. *a few words;* ut in pauca conferam, Cic. **II.** *a few;* paucis diebus, Cic.

paulātim (paullātim), adv. **I.** *gradually, little by little;* a, of place, paulatim ab imo acclivis, Caes.; b, of time, si paulatim haec consuetudo serpere ac prodire coeperit, Caes. **II.** *singly, one after another;* ex castris discedere coeperunt, Caes.

paulispĕr (paullispĕr), adv. *a little while, a short time;* partes alicuius suscipere, Cic.; foll. by dum, Cic.; donec, Liv.

paulo (paullo), v. paulus.

paulŭlo (paullŭlo), v. paululus.

paulŭlus (paullŭlus) -a -um (dim. of paulus), *very little, very small;* via, Liv.; neut., **paulŭlum** -i, n., a, subst., *a very little;* morae, Cic.; b, adv., *a little;* paululum respirare, Cic.; paululo with compar., paululo deterius, *a little worse,* ap. Cic.

1. **paulus (paullus)** -a -um (connected with paucus and pauper, and Gr. παῦρος), *little, small;* sumptus, Ter.; neut., paulum; a, subst., *a little;* paulum aliquid damni, Cic.; paulo, *by a little, a little;* with compar., paulo melior, Cic.; with adv., paulo secus, Cic.; b, adv., *a little;* paulum commorari, Cic.

2. **Paulus (Paullus)** -i, m. *the name of a family of the gens Aemilia, of which the most famous were:* 1, L. Aemilius Paulus, *who commanded, with C. Terentius Varro, at Cannae, and was there slain;* 2, L. Aemilius Paulus Macedonicus, *son of the preceding, the conqueror of Perseus, king of Macedonia.*

pauper -ĕris (contracted for pauci-per = πένης), *poor, not wealthy;* a, of persons, homo, Cic.; vir, Cic.; with genit., argenti, Hor.; subst., pauper, *a poor man,* Ov.; b, transf., of things, *poor, scanty, meagre;* domus, Verg.

paupercŭlus -a -um (dim. of pauper), *poor,* Hor.

paupĕrĭes -ēi, f. (pauper), *poverty, indigence,* Hor.

paupĕro, 1. (pauper). **I.** *to make poor,* Plaut. **II.** Transf., *aliquem aliquā re, to rob or deprive of anything,* Hor.

paupertas -ātis, f. (pauper), *poverty.* **A.** Lit., *humble circumstances* (opp. divitiae); paupertas vel potius egestas ac mendicitas, Cic. **B.** Transf. (= egestas, inopia), *need, want, indigence,* Cic.

pausa -ae, f. (παῦσις), *a pause, cessation, stoppage, end;* vitae, Lucr.

Pausănĭās -ae, m. (Παυσανίας), *son of Cleombrotus, commander of the Spartans at Plataea.*

pausĕa (pausia) and **pōsĕa** -ae, f. *a species of olive, which produced an excellent oil,* Verg.

Pausĭās -ae, acc. -an, m. (Παυσίας), *a Greek painter of Sicyon, contemporary with Apelles.* Adj., **Pausĭācus** -a -um, *of or relating to Pausias;* tabella, Hor.

pausillŭlum = pauxillulum, v. under pauxillulus.

pauxillātim, adv. (pauxillus), *gradually, by degrees,* Plaut.

pauxillispĕr, adv. (pauxillus), *a little while,* Plaut.

pauxillŭlus -a -um (dim. of pauxillus), *very little, very small,* Plaut.; subst., **pauxillŭlum** -i, n. *a little,* Plaut.

pauxillus -a -um (dim. of paucus), *small, little,* Lucr.; subst., **pauxillum** -i, n. *a little,* Plaut.

păvĕfăcĭo, 3. (paveo and facio), *to frighten, terrify;* found only in partic., pavefactus, *terrified,* Ov.

păvĕo, pāvi, 2. *to fear, be afraid of, to quake with fear;* inde admiratione paventibus cunctis, Liv.; with acc., lupos, Hor.; varia miracula, Liv.; with ad and the acc., ad omnia, Liv.; with infin., Ov.

păvesco, 3. (paveo), *to fear, be afraid of, be terrified;* with abl. of cause, omni strepitu, Sall.; with acc., bellum, Tac.

păvĭdē, adv. (pavidus), *fearfully, in a state of terror;* fugere, Liv.

păvĭdus -a -um (paveo). **I.** *trembling, quaking, fearful, terrified;* castris se pavidus tenebat, Liv.; with ne and the subj., pavidi ne jam facta in urbem via esset, Liv.; with genit., offensionum, Tac. **II.** *causing terror, producing fear;* religiones, Lucr.; metus, Ov.

păvimento, 1. (pavimentum), *to pave,* ap. Cic.

păvimentum -i, n. (pavio), *a pavement of tiles, brick, stone,* etc., *laid in a bed of strong cement;* pavimentum facere, Cic.

păvĭo, 4. (παϝίω), *to beat;* terram, Cic.

păvĭto, 1. (intens. of paveo), 1, *to tremble, quake with fear,* Verg.; 2, *to quake, shiver with ague,* Ter.

pāvo -ōnis, m. (onomatop., root PA, cf. Gr. ταώς), *a peacock,* Cic.

păvor -ōris, m. (paveo). **I.** *a trembling or trepidation produced by fear, expectation, joy,* etc., Cic.; alicui pavorem injicere, incutere, *to cause fear,* Liv.; pavor est, pavor aliquem capit, foll. by ne and the subj., Liv. **II.** Personif., Pavor, *as a deity,* Liv.

pax, pācis, f. (root PAC, whence paciscor, pango, πήγνυμι), *peace.* **I.** Lit., pacem conciliare, conficere, facere cum aliquo, *to make peace,* Cic.; servare pacem cum aliquo, *to keep peace,* Cic.; uti pace, *to be at peace,* Cic.; turbare pacem, Liv. Plur., paces, *conditions or pro-*

posals of peace; bella atque paces, Sall. Personif., Pax, *the goddess of Peace,* Ov. **II.** Transf., 1, *peace, quiet;* a, of things, flumen cum pace delabens, *quietly,* Hor.; b, of looks or of feelings, semper in animo sapientis est placidissima pax, Cic.; pace tuā dixerim, *with your good leave,* Cic.; 2, *favour or approval of the gods;* ab Jove ceterisque dis pacem ac veniam peto, Cic.

peccātum -i, n. (pecco), *a sin, crime, offence, fault;* peccatum suum confiteri, Cic.

peccātus -ū, m. (pecco), *a fault;* manifesto peccatu teneri, Cic.

pecco, 1. **I.** *to commit a fault or crime, to sin;* Empedocles multa alia peccat, Cic.; in se, Cic.; in servo necando, Cic. **II.** *to fail, to err, to go wrong;* in homine, Caes.; ne peccet equus, Hor.

pecten -ĭnis, m. (pecto), *a comb.* **I.** Lit., *for combing the hair;* deducere pectine crines, Ov. **II.** Transf., a, *a weaver's comb,* Verg.; b, *a rake,* Ov.; c, *the clasping of the hands in trouble;* digiti inter se pectine juncti, Ov.; d, *an instrument with which the strings of the lyre were struck,* Verg.; meton., *song;* alterno pectine, *in elegiac verse* (first a hexameter, then a pentameter), Ov.; e, *a shell-fish, the scallop,* Hor.

pecto, pexi; pexum and pectĭtum, 3. (πεκτέω). **I.** *to comb;* comas, Ov. **II.** *to comb, card;* stuppam, Plin. Partic., **pexus** -a -um, *with the nap on, woolly;* tunica, *new,* Hor.

pectus -ŏris, n. *the breast in men and animals, the breast-bone.* **I.** Lit., Verg. **II.** Fig., 1, *the breast as the seat of the affections, the heart, soul;* toto pectore amare, *to love with the whole heart,* Cic.; forti pectore, *courage,* Hor.; puro pectore, *with good conscience,* Hor.; 2, *the breast, as the seat of reason, understanding;* toto pectore cogitare, Cic.; excidere pectore alicuius, *to be forgotten,* Ov.

pĕcu, dat. -ū, abl. -ū, nom. and acc. plur. pecŭa, n., genit. plur. pecŭum (connected with pecus), *cattle,* Cic.

pĕcŭārĭus -a -um (pecu), *of or relating to cattle.* **I.** Adj., res, *the breeding of cattle,* Cic. **II.** Subst., **A. pĕcŭārĭus** -ĭi, m. *a breeder of cattle, grazier,* Cic. Plur., pecuarii, *the farmers of the public pastures* (in the provinces), Cic., Liv. **B. pĕcŭārĭa** -ōrum, n. *herds of cattle,* Verg.

pĕcŭlātor -ōris, m. (peculor), *one who embezzles the public money,* Cic.

pĕcŭlātus -ūs, m. (peculor), *the embezzlement of the public money, peculation;* peculatum facere, Cic.

pĕcŭlĭāris -e (peculium). **I.** *belonging to one's private property;* oves, Plaut. **II.** Transf., a, *proper, special, peculiar;* testis, Cic.; hoc mihi peculiare fuerit, Cic.; b, *peculiar, extraordinary, singular;* edictum, Cic.

pĕcŭlĭo, 1. (peculium), *to provide with private property.* Partic., **pĕcŭlĭātus** -a -um, *provided with property,* ap. Cic.

pĕcŭlĭum -ĭi, n. (pecus), *property* (orig., *property in cattle).* **I.** Gen., cura peculi, Verg.; cupiditas peculii, Cic. **II.** Esp., *the private property possessed by a son or slave independent of the father or master;* peculium castrense, *earnings of the son on military service;* quasi castrense, *in other occupations;* profecticium, *property possessed by grant from the father;* adventicium, *by inheritance from the mother,* Cic., Liv.

pĕcūnĭa -ae, f. (pecus, orig. *property in cattle).* **I.** *property;* pecuniam facere, *to gain property,* Cic. **II.** Esp., *money, cash, sums of* *money*; accipere pecuniam, *to allow oneself to be bribed*, Cic.; coacervare pecuniam, *to heap money together*, Cic.; flare et conflare pecuniam, *to make money, to become rich*, Cic.; pecuniam mutuam sumere ab aliquo, *to borrow*, Cic.

pĕcūnĭārĭus -a -um (pecunia), *of or relating to money, pecuniary*; res pecuniaria, *a money-matter, business*, Cic., or simply = *money*, Cic.

pĕcūnĭōsus -a -um (pecunia), *wealthy, rich;* homo pecuniosissimus, Cic.

1. **pĕcus** -ŏris, n. *cattle, a herd, flock* (collectively, while pecus -ūdis = *single head of cattle*). **I.** Lit., **A.** setigerum, *swine*, Ov.; lanigerum, *sheep*, Ov.; applied also to *bees*, Verg., *fish*, Hor. **B.** Esp., **1**, *a flock of sheep;* balatus pecorum, Ov.; **2**, poet., pecus magnae parentis (of young lions), Ov. **II.** Transf., applied contemptuously to human beings, imitatorum servum pecus, *a servile herd*, Hor.

2. **pĕcus** -ūdis, f. (pecu, 1. pecus), *a single head of cattle, a beast, animal*. **I.** Lit., **A.** quā pecude (sc. sue) nihil genuit natura fecundius, Cic.; solertia pecudum (of bees), Verg.; pecudes et bestiae, *wild and domestic animals*, Cic. **B.** Esp., a, *sheep;* pecus Helles, the ram, Ov.; b, in plur., *land animals;* genus aequoreum, pecudes pictaeque volucres, Verg. **II.** Transf., contemptuously applied to a human being, stupor hominis, vel dicam pecudis? Cic.

pĕdālis -e (pes), *of the length of a foot*, Caes.; or *of the breadth* (in diameter) *of a foot*, Cic.

pĕdārĭus -a -um (pes), *relating to a foot;* senatores pedarii, *senators of inferior rank, who held no curule office*, Tac. Subst., **pĕdārĭī** -ōrum, m., Cic.

pĕdes -itis, m. (pes). **I.** *one who goes on foot;* quum pedes iret, on *foot*, Verg.; etiamsi pedes incedat, Liv. **II.** Esp., *a foot-soldier;* a, lit., Caes.; collect., *infantry*, Liv.; b, transf., equites peditesque, *the whole people*, Cic.

pĕdester -tris -tre (pes), *on foot, pedestrian*. **I.** Lit., **A.** (opp. equester), statua pedestris, Cic.; esp. as milit. t. t., copiae, *infantry*, Caes.; scutum, *infantry shield*, Liv. **B.** *relating to land* (opp. maritimus, navalis); iter, Caes., pugna, Cic. **II.** Fig., **A.** Of style, *written in prose;* historiae, Hor. **B.** *simple, ordinary, prosaic;* sermo, Hor.; musa, Hor.

pĕdĕtemptim, adv. (pes and tendo), *slowly, gradually, carefully, cautiously;* timide et pedetemptim, Cic.

pĕdĭca -ae, f. (pes), *a trap, snare, a fetter*, Liv.

pĕdĭsĕquus -i, m. and **pĕdĭsĕqua** -ae, f. (pes and sequor), *a servant whose business it was to attend upon the master or mistress*, m. *lackey, footman*, and f. *a waiting-woman*, Cic.; fig., juris scientiam eloquentiae tamquam ancillulam pedisequamque adjunxisti, Cic.; transf., clamore pedisequorum nostrorum, *followers*, Cic.

pĕdĭtātus -ūs, m. (pedes), *infantry*, Caes.

pĕdo, pĕpēdi, pēdĭtum, 3. *to break wind*, Hor.

1. **pĕdum** -i, n. *a shepherd's crook*, Verg.

2. **Pĕdum** -i, n. *a town in Latium, ten miles south of Rome*. Adj., **Pĕdānus** -a -um, *of or relating to Pedum;* subst., a, **Pĕdānum** -i, n. *an estate near Pedum;* b, **Pĕdāni** -ōrum, m. *the inhabitants of Pedum*.

1. **Pĕgăsis**, v. Pegasus.

2. **Pĕgăsĭs** -ĭdis, f. (πηγή), *a water-nymph.*

Pĕgăsus (-ŏs) -i, m. (Πήγασος), *the winged horse which sprang from the blood of Medusa, and produced the fountain Hippocrene by a blow from his hoof.* Hence, adj., **A. Pĕgăsēĭus**

-a -um. **B. Pĕgăsēus** -a -um. **C. Pĕgăsĭs** -ĭdis, f. *Pegasean ;* undae, *fountains sacred to the Muses, Hippocrene, Aganippe.* Plur. subst., Pegasides, *the Muses*, Ov.

pegma -ătis, n. (πῆγμα), **1**, *a bookcase, shelf*, Cic.; **2**, *a theatrical machine*, Suet.

pējĕro (perjĕro) and **perjūro**, 1. *to commit perjury, forswear oneself;* verbis conceptis, Cic.; jus perjeratum, *a false oath*, Hor.; dii, *falsely sworn by*, Ov.

pejor, comp. of malus (q.v.).

pējūrus = perjurus (q.v.).

pĕlăgē, v. pelagus.

pĕlăgĭus -a -um (πελάγιος), *of or relating to the sea, marine ;* conchae, Plin.; cursus, Phaedr.

Pĕlăgŏnes -um, m. (Πελαγόνες), *the Pelagonians, a people in the north of Macedonia.* Hence, **Pĕlăgŏnĭa** -ae, f., a, *the country of the Pelagones ;* b, *a town in Pelagonia*, now Bitoglia.

pĕlăgus -i, n. (πέλαγος). **I.** *the sea, ocean*, Verg. **II.** Poet., transf., *a mass of water like the sea, a flood ;* pelago premit arva, *with its flood*, Verg. (Greek plur., pelage, πελάγη, Lucr.).

pĕlămys -ydis, f. (πηλαμύς), *the young tunny-fish* (before it is a year old), Juv.

Pĕlasgi -ōrum and (poet.) -ûm, m. (Πελασγοί), *the oldest inhabitants of Greece*, and hence, poet., *the Greeks*, Verg. Hence, **A. Pĕlasgĭas** -ădis, f. **B. Pĕlasgĭs** -ĭdis, f. **C. Pĕlasgus** -a -um, *Pelasgian, Greek*.

Pĕlēthrŏnĭus -a -um, *of or belonging to the district of Thessaly, where the Lapithae lived, Pelethronian.*

Pēleus -ĕi and -ĕos, m. (Πηλεύς), *a mythical king of Thessaly, husband of Thetis, father of Achilles ;* hence, **Pĕlīdēs** -ae, m. *son of Peleus* = *Achilles.*

pĕlex (pellex) and **paelex** -lĭcis, f. (πάλλαξ), *a mistress of a married man, a concubine*, Cic.; Oebalia, *Helen ;* Tyria, *Europa ;* barbara, Medea, Ov.

1. **Pĕlĭăs**, v. Pelion.

2. **Pĕlĭăs** -ae, m. (Πελίας), *king in Thessaly, half-brother of Aeson, whose son Jason he sent to fetch the golden fleece. On Jason's return Pelias, at the instigation of Medea, was slain by his own daughters.*

pĕlĭcātus (paelĭcātus) -us, m. (pelex), *concubinage*, Cic.

Pĕlīdēs, v. Peleus.

Pĕlĭgni = Paeligni (q.v.).

Pēlĭon -ĭi, n. (Πήλιον), and **Pēlĭus** -ĭi, m. *a lofty mountain of Thessaly.* Hence, adj., **A. Pēlĭăcus** -a -um, *of or belonging to Pelion;* trabs, *the ship Argo* (the wood of which was cut from Mount Pelion), Prop.; cuspis, *the shield of Achilles*, Ov. **B. Pēlĭăs** -ădis, *belonging to Pelion.*

Pella -ae, f. and **Pellē** -ēs, f. (Πέλλα), *the chief city of Macedonia, birth-place of Alexander the Great ;* hence, **Pellaeus** -a -um, *relating to Pella ;* a, *Macedonian;* juvenis, *Alexander*, Juv.; b, *relating to Alexandria in Egypt*, and hence, *Egyptian*, Verg.

pellācĭa -ae, f. (pellax), *an enticing, alluring*, Lucr.

pellax -ācis (pellicio), *deceitful, seductive*, Verg.

pellectĭo (perlectĭo) -ōnis, f. (pellego), *a reading through, perusing*, Cic.

pellĕgo = perlego (q.v.).

Pellēnē -ēs, f. (Πελλήνη), *a town in Achaia.* Hence, adj., **Pellēnensis** -e, *Pellenian.*

pellex = pelex (q.v.).

pellĭcātus = pelicatus (q.v.).

pellĭcĭo -lexi -lectum, 3. (per and lacĭo), *to entice, decoy, seduce.* **I.** Lit., mulierem ad se, Cic.; animum adolescentis, Cic.; populum in servitutem, Liv. **II.** Transf., multo majorem partem sententiarum suo lepore, *bring over to one's side,* Cic.

pellĭcŭla -ae, f. (dim. of pellis), *a little skin or hide;* haedina, Cic.; pelliculam curare, *to take care of one's skin,* Hor.

pellis -is, f. *a hide, skin.* **I.** Lit., caprina, Cic.; pelles pro velis tenuiter confectae, Caes.; fig., detrahere alicui pellem, *to disclose a person's faults,* Hor. **II.** Transf., 1, *hide, leather;* a, as a covering for tents, sub pellibus, *in camp;* Caesar sub pellibus hiemare constituit, Caes.; b, as used for clothing, pellibus tecta tempora, *hood,* Ov.; 2, meton., a, *a shoe-latchet,* Hor.; b, *a shoe,* Ov.

pellītus -a -um (pellis), *clothed in hides or skins;* Sardi, Liv.; testes, *from Sardinia,* Liv.; oves pellitae, *sheep with fine wool, covered with skins to protect the wool,* Hor.

pello, pĕpŭli, pulsum, 3. *to strike, knock, beat against.* **I.** a, lit., terram pede, Hor.; humum pedibus, Cat.; fores, *to knock at the door,* Cic.; puer pulsus, *beaten,* Cic.; b, transf., *to touch, move, make an impression upon;* quemadmodum visa non pellerent, Cic. **II.** Esp., **A.** *to put in motion by pushing or striking, to impel, propel, move;* sagittam, Verg.; nervos in fidibus, Cic. **B.** *to drive out, drive away, expel;* 1, a, lit., quum viri boni lapidibus e foro pellerentur, Cic., uti omnes ex Galliae finibus pellerentur, Caes.; aliquem possessionibus, Cic.; aliquem civitate, Cic.; b, transf., maestitiam ex animis, *banish,* Cic.; curas vino, Hor.; 2, transf., a, milit. t. t., *to repel, drive back an enemy;* hostes pelluntur, Caes.; b, legal t. t., *to banish, exile;* exsules pulsi, Liv.

pellŭcĕo = perluceo (q.v.).

pellŭcĭdŭlus = perlucidulus (q.v.).

pellŭcĭdus = perlucidus (q.v.).

pellŭo = perluo (q.v.).

Pĕlŏponnēsus -i, f. (Πελοπόννησος), *the Peloponnesus,* now *the Morea;* hence, adj., **A. Pĕlŏponnēsĭus** -a -um. **B. Pĕlŏponnēsĭăcus** -a -um, *Peloponnesian.*

Pĕlops -ŏpis, m. (Πέλοψ), *a mythical king of Phrygia, son of Tantalus, father of Atreus and Thyestes, grandfather of Agamemnon and Menelaus; when a child he was killed by his father and served up as food to the gods; he was restored to life through the agency of Hermes (Mercury), and his shoulder, which had been eaten by Demeter (Ceres), was replaced by an ivory one.* Hence, **A. Pĕlŏpēĭăs** -ădis, f. *Pelopean, Peloponnesian;* Mycenae, Ov. **B. Pĕlŏpēĭus** -a -um, *relating to Pelops* or *his descendants;* virgo, *Iphigenia,* Ov.; arva, *Phrygia,* Ov. **C. Pĕlŏpēus** -a -um, *relating to Pelops;* moenia, *Argos,* Verg. **D.** subst., **Pĕlŏpĭdae** -ārum, m. *descendants of Pelops.*

pĕlŏrĭs -ĭdis, f. (πελωρίς), *a large species of mussel,* Hor.

Pĕlōrus (-ŏs) -i, m. (Πέλωρος), and **Pĕlōrum** -i, n. *the north-east promontory of Sicily,* now *Capo di Faro* or *Faro di Messina.* Hence, adj., 1, **Pĕlōrĭăs** -ădis, f.; and 2, **Pĕlōrĭs** -ĭdis, f. *Pelorian.*

pelta -ae, f. (πέλτη), *a small, light, crescent-shaped shield,* Liv.

peltastae -ārum, m. (πελτασταί), *soldiers armed with the pelta,* Liv.

peltātus -a -um (pelta), *armed with the pelta,* Mart.

Pēlūsĭum -ĭi, n. (Πηλούσιον), *a town in Egypt on the Mediterranean Sea,* now *Castle of Tineh.* Hence, **Pēlūsĭăcus** -a -um, *Pelusian.*

pelvis -is, f. *a basin,* Plin.

pĕnārĭus (**pĕnŭārĭus**) -a -um (penus), *of* or *relating to provisions;* cella, *store-room,* Cic.

pĕnātes -ĭum, m., with or without dii (connected with pen-itus, pen-etro). **I.** *the household* or *family deities among the Romans;* publici or majores, *the guardian deities of the state,* Cic.; minores, familiares, privati, *of the family,* Cic. **II.** Meton., *the house, dwelling;* penates relinquere, Liv.; poet., *the cells of bees,* Verg.

pĕnātĭgĕr -gĕra -gĕrum (penates and gero), *carrying the Penates,* Ov.

pendĕo, pĕpendi, 2. (pendo), *to hang, hang down.* **I.** Lit., **A.** Gen., *ab humero,* Cic.; *ex arbore,* Cic.; *de collo,* Ov.; *in arbore,* Cic.; *with abl. alone,* tigno, Ov. **B.** Esp., 1, *to be hung up;* pendebit fistula pinu, Verg.; 2, *of clothes, to hang down, flow down; ut pendeat apte* (chlamys), Ov.; 3, *to overhang;* a, *to hover;* dum nubila pendent, Verg.; b, *to hang in the air;* capellae pendent de rupe, Verg.; c, *of birds, to hover;* olor niveis pendebat in aere pennis, Ov.; 4, transf., a, *to hang about a place, be continually there;* nostroque in limine pendes, Verg.; b, *to hang down* (from weakness); fluidos pendere lacertos, Ov. **II.** Fig., **A.** *to hang upon the lips of any one, listen* or *gaze attentively,* Verg.; narrantis conjux pendet ab ore viri, Ov. **B.** 1, *to be suspended, discontinued;* pendent opera interrupta, Verg.; 2, *to be in suspense, be uncertain, undecided;* ne diutius pendeas, Cic.; frequently with animi, pendere animi exspectatione, Cic.; also with animo, Cic.; and animis, Cic.; 3, *to depend upon;* a, spes pendet ex fortuna, Cic.; b, *to be a follower of a person, to imitate;* hinc omnis pendet Lucilius, Hor.

pendo, pĕpendi, pensum, 3. lit., *to cause to hang down;* hence, *to weigh.* **I.** Lit., **A.** 1, herbae pensae, Ov.; 2, fig., a, *to weigh, consider, judge;* res, non verba, Cic.; b, *to value, esteem;* with genit., magni, *at a high price,* Hor. **B.** Esp., *to pay* (since money was originally paid by weight); 1, lit., Achaei ingentem pecuniam pendunt L. Pisoni quotannis, Cic.; vectigal, Cic.; 2, fig., poenas, supplicia, *to pay a penalty, suffer punishment,* Cic., Liv.; maximas poenas pendo temeritatis meae, Cic.; poenas capitis, Ov. **II.** Transf., intransit., *to weigh,* Liv.

pendŭlus -a -um (pendeo), 1, *hanging, hanging down;* collum, Hor.; 2, fig., *uncertain, undecided;* spe pendulus, Hor.

pēne = paene (q.v.).

Pēnēis, Peneius, v. Peneus.

Pēnēlŏpa -ae, f. and **Pēnēlŏpē** -ēs, f. (Πηνελόπεια, Πηνελόπη), *the wife of Ulysses, mother of Telemachus, famous for her chastity and constancy.* Hence, adj., **Pēnēlŏpēus** -a -um. *of Penelope.*

pĕnēs, prep. with acc. (from root PEN, whence penus, penates), *with, in possession of, in the power of;* 1, penes quem est potestas, Cic.; penes se esse, *to be in one's senses,* Hor.; penes quos laus fuit, Cic.; 2, *with;* penes Aetolos culpam belli esse, Liv.

Pĕnestae -ārum, m. (Πενέσται), *a people in Illyria.* Hence, **Pĕnestia** -ae, f. *the country of the Penestae.*

pĕnĕtrābĭlis -e (penetro). **I.** *that can be passed through, penetrable;* corpus nullo pene-

trabĭle telo, Ov. **II.** Act., *easily penetrating, piercing;* frigus, Verg.; fulmen, Ov.

pĕnētrālis -e (penetro). **I.** *passing through, penetrating;* frigus, ignis, Lucr. **II.** *inward, inside, internal, interior;* focus, Cic. Subst.,

pĕnētrāle and **pĕnētrăl** -ālis, n., gen. plur.,

pĕnētrālĭa -ĭum, n. 1, *the inner chambers, interior of a house or city;* penetrale urbis, Liv.; penetralia regum, Verg.; 2, esp., *the inmost part or shrine of a temple;* conditum in penetrali fatale pignus, Liv.

pĕnĕtro, 1. (penitus). **I.** Transit., *to set, place, put in.* **A.** intra aedes penetravi pedem, Plaut. **B.** *to pass through* or *into,* *to penetrate;* a, lit., Illyricos sinus, Verg.; b, fig., id Tiberii animum altius penetravit, *sank deep into,* Tac. **II.** Intransit., *to make one's way into, to enter, penetrate into;* sub terras, Cic.; intra vallum, Liv.; in urbem, Liv.; transf., nulla res magis penetrat in animos, Cic.

Pēnēus (-ēŏs) -i, m. (Πηνειός), *the chief river of Thessaly, rising in Mount Pindus,* now *Salembria;* as a river-god, *father of Cyrene.* Hence, adj., 1, **Pēnēis** -ĭdis, f. *of Peneus;* nympha, *Daphne,* Ov.; 2, **Pēnēïus** -a -um, *of* or *relating to Peneus.*

pēnĭcillum -i, n. and **pēnĭcillus** -i, m. (dim. of peniculus), *a painter's brush* or *pencil,* Cic.; meton., *painting,* Plin.; and transf., *style of painting,* Cic.

pēnĭcŭlus -i, m. (dim. of penis), *a brush,* Plaut.

pēnis -is, m. 1, *a tail,* Cic.; 2,= membrum virile, Cic.

pēnītē, adv. (penitus), *inwardly, internally,* Cat.

1. **pēnĭtus** -a -um, *inward, interior, internal,* Plaut.

2. **pēnĭtus**, adv. (root PEN), *internally.* **I.** *in the inmost part, deep within;* 1, lit., periculum inclusum penitus in venis reipublicae, Cic.; argentum penitus abditum, Cic.; 2, transf., a, ea penitus animis vestris mandate, *impress deeply in your minds,* Cic.; b, *accurately;* perspicere, Cic.; nosse, Cic.; c, *through and through, thoroughly, entirely, wholly;* diffidere reipublicae, Cic.; perdere se ipsos, Cic. **II.** Transf., *far away, far removed;* penitus repostas gentes, Verg.

Pēnĭus -ĭi, m. (Πηνιός), *a river in Colchis, flowing into the Black Sea.*

penna -ae, f. (old Lat. pesna, root PET, whence peto, impetus, praepes), *a feather.* **I.** Gen., 1, lit., Plin.; 2, meton., a, *wing,* gen. in plur., *wings* (of birds or insects); aves pullos pennis fovent, Cic.; b, *a flying, flight,* Ov. **II.** Poet., *the feathers on an arrow,* Ov., and hence, meton., *arrow,* Ov.

pennātus -a -um (penna), *feathered, winged;* fama, Verg.

pennĭgĕr -gĕra -gĕrum (penna and gero), *feathered, winged,* Cic.

pennĭpes -pĕdis (penna and pes), *wing-footed,* Cat.

pennĭpŏtens -entis (penna and potens), *able to fly, winged,* Lucr.; subst., **pennĭpŏtentes** -ĭum, f. = *birds,* Lucr.

pennŭla -ae, f. (dim. of penna), *a little wing,* Cic.

pensĭlis -e (pendeo), *hanging, hanging down, pendent,* Plaut.; uva, *hung up to dry,* Hor.

pensĭo -ōnis, f. (pendo), *a paying, payment, day of payment;* 1, nihil debetur ei nisi ex tertia pensione, Cic.; 2, *rent,* Juv.

pensĭto, 1. (intens. of penso), *to weigh.* **I.** Transf., *to weigh, ponder, consider;* imperatoria consilia, Liv. **II.** *to pay;* vectigalia, Cic.; praedia quae pensitant, *are liable to taxes,* Cic.

penso, 1. (intens. of pendo). **I.** *to weigh.* **A.** Lit., aurum, Liv.; fig., Romanos scriptores eādem trutinā, Hor. **B.** Transf., 1, *to weigh =* *to judge;* amicos ex factis, Liv.; 2, a, *to ponder, consider, reflect upon;* consilium, Liv.; b, *to weigh one thing against another, to compare;* adversa secundis, Liv. **II.** *to counterbalance, repay, compensate, recompense, make good, requite;* a, lit., vulnus vulnere, Ov.; transmarinae res quādam vice pensatae, Liv.; b, transf., *to pay for, purchase with;* nece pudorem, Ov.

pensum -i, n. (pendo). **I.** *a portion of wool weighed out to a spinner as a day's work;* hence, a *day's work, task;* nocturna carpentes pensa puellae, Verg.; mollia pensa, Verg. **II.** Transf., *a task, a duty, engagement;* me ad meum munus pensumque revocabo, Cic.

pensus -a -um, p. adj. (from pendo), *weighty, esteemed, valued, prized;* nihil pensi habere aliquid, *to put no value upon, be indifferent about,* Sall.; alicui nec quicquam pensi est, Sall.; illis nec quid dicerent nec quid facerent quicquam pensi fuisse, *they cared nothing what they did or said,* Cic.

pentămĕter -tri, m. (πεντάμετρος), *a pentameter verse,* Quint.

Pentĕlĭcus mons (Πεντελικὸν ὄρος), *a mountain near Athens, celebrated for its marble quarries.* Hence, **Pentĕlĭcus** -a -um, *belonging to Pentelicus;* Hermae Pentelici, *made of Pentelic marble,* Cic.

Penthĕsĭlēa -ae, f. (Πενθεσίλεια), *queen of the Amazons, ally of Priam against the Greeks in the Trojan War, slain by Achilles.*

Pentheus -ēi and -ĕos, acc. -ĕum and -ĕa (Πενθεύς), *king of Thebes, grandson of Cadmus, who treated with contempt the worship of Bacchus, and was torn to pieces by his mother and her sisters in a Bacchic fury.* Hence, **A. Penthēus** -a -um, *of Pentheus.* **B. Penthĭdes** -ae, m. *a descendant of Pentheus = Lycurgus,* Ov.

Pentri -ōrum, m. *a people in Samnium, with a capital city Bovianum.*

pēnūrĭa -ae, f. (πεῖνα), *want, need of anything,* esp., *want of the necessaries of life, penury;* cibi, Lucr.; victūs, Hor.; sapientium civium bonorumque, Cic.; liberorum, Sall.

pĕnus -ūs and -i, c., **pĕnum** -i, n., and **pĕnus** -ŏris, n. (root PEN, whence penetro, penates, penitus, lit., *that which is kept within), provisions, store of food, victuals;* est enim omne, quo vescuntur homines, penus, Cic.

Pĕpărēthus (-ŏs) -i, f. (Πεπάρηθος), *an island of the Aegean Sea,* now *Scopelo.*

peplum -i and **peplus** -i, m. (πέπλον, πέπλος), *the robe with which the statue of Athene at Athens was clad at the Panathenaea,* Cic.

per, prep. with acc. **I.** Of space, *through;* a, *through* (of passage through); alterum iter per provinciam nostram multo facilius, Caes.; b, *through, along, over;* coronam auream per forum ferre, Cic.; per mare pauperiem fugiens, per saxa, per ignes, Hor.; c, *before, in the presence of;* incedunt per ora vestra magnifici, Sall.; d, *over, about, all over;* equites per oram maritimam erant dispositi, Caes.; qui per imperii tui provincias ei credidissent, Cic. **II.** Transf., **A.** Of time, 1, *through, during;* ludi decem per dies facti sunt, Cic.; 2, *in the course of;* per somnum, *in sleep,* Cic.; 3, *during, under the influence of;* quod fecisset per iram, Cic. **B.** Of the means or instrument by which

anything is done, *through by, by means of;* **1,**
a, statuerunt istius injurias per vos ulcisci,
Cic. ; per se (te, etc.), *by oneself, alone, without
help,* Cic. ; per litteras, *by letter,* Cic. ; **b,** *under
pretence of, under shelter of;* fraudare aliquem
per tutelam aut societatem, Cic. ; **2,** *from motives
of, on account of;* per avaritiam decipere, Cic. ;
per metum, *from fear,* Liv. ; quum antea per
aetatem nondum huius auctoritatem loci attingere auderem, *on account of age,* Cic. ; **3,** *on
account of, for the sake of, regarding;* per me
vel stertas licet, *as far as I am concerned,* Cic. ;
cum per valetudinem posses, venire tamen
noluisti, Cic. ; hence, in entreaties, oaths, etc.
= *by;* oro te per deos, Cic. ; per tuam fidem
perque huius solitudinem te obtestor ; in this
sense per is often separated from the noun
which it governs, per ego te, fili, precor quaes-
oque, Liv. ; per deos atque homines ! *by gods
and men !* Cic.

pēra -ae (πήρα), *a scrip or wallet,* Mart.

pĕrabsurdus -a -um, *excessively absurd,*
Cic.

pĕraccommŏdātus -a -um, *very convenient;* (in tmesis) per fore accommodatum, Cic.

pĕrācer -cris -cre, *very sharp;* judicium,
Cic.

pĕrăcerbus -a -um, *very sour, harsh;* uva
peracerba gustatu, Cic.

pĕrăcesco -ācŭi, 3. *to become thoroughly sour;*
transf., *to be exceedingly vexed,* Plaut.

pĕractĭo -ōnis, f. (perago), *a finishing, completion;* peractio fabulae, Cic.

pĕrăcūtē, adv. (peracutus), *very sharply,
very acutely;* queri quod, etc., Cic.

pĕrăcūtus -a -um, *very sharp.* **I.** *very
shrill, piercing;* vox, Cic. **II.** Transf., *sharp-
witted, acute;* ad excogitandum, Cic.

pĕrădŏlescens -entis, *a very young man,*
Cic.

pĕrădŏlescentŭlus -i, m. *a very young
man,* Nep.

Pĕraea -ae, f. **I.** *a strip of land on the
south coast of Caria, opposite Rhodes.* **II.** *a district in the south of Palestine.* **III.** *a town in
Argolis.*

pĕraequē, adv. *quite alike, quite equally,*
Cic.

pĕrăgĭto, 1. *to drive about violently, harass;*
vehementius peragitati ab equitatu, Caes.

pĕrăgo -ēgi -actum, 3. **I.** *to pierce through,
thrust through, transfix;* Theseus latus ense
peregit, Ov. **II. A.** *to drive about, harass, disquiet;* **1,** agili freta remo, Ov. ; agrum, *to till,*
Ov. ; **2,** fig., totum Sempronium usque eo
perago ut, etc., ap. Cic. **B. 1,** *to bring to an
end, complete, finish, accomplish;* navigationem,
Cic. ; inceptum, Liv. ; concilium, Caes. ; fabulam, *to play a drama through,* Cic. ; transf., fabulam vitae, Cic. ; as legal t. t., *to conduct a suit
to the end;* causam rei, Hor. ; reum, Liv. ; **2,**
to go through, relate, go over, mention; verbis
auspicia, Liv. ; postulata, Liv. ; sententiam,
Liv.

pĕrăgrātĭo -ōnis, f. (peragro), *a wandering
through;* itinerum, Cic.

pĕrăgro, 1. (per and ager). **I.** *to wander
through, pass through, travel through;* omnes
provincias, Cic. **II.** Fig., *to search out, penetrate, examine;* omnes latebras suspicionum
dicendo, Cic.

pĕrămans -antis, *very loving;* homo per-
amans semper nostri fuit, Cic.

pĕrămantĕr, adv. *very lovingly;* observare,
Cic.

pĕrambŭlo, 1. *to walk through, pass through,*

travel through, perambulate; rura, Hor. ; transf,
frigus perambulat artus, Ov.

pĕrămoenus -a -um, *very pleasant,* Tac.

pĕramplus -a -um, *very large,* Cic.

pĕrangustē, adv. *very narrowly,* Cic.

pĕrangustus -a -um, *very narrow, strait,
confined;* fretum, Cic. ; aditus, Caes.

pĕranno, 1. *to live through a year,* Suet.

pĕrantīquus -a -um, *very old;* sacrarium,
Cic.

pĕrappŏsĭtus -a -um, *very fit, suitable;*
alicui, Cic.

perardŭus -a -um, *very difficult;* mihi hoc
perarduum est demonstrare, Cic.

pĕrargūtus -a -um, *very acute, clever, witty,*
Cic.

pĕrăro, 1. *to plough through;* **1,** *to cover
with wrinkles;* ora, Ov. ; **2,** *to scratch letters
with the stylus, to write on waxen tablets, to write;*
litteram, Ov.

pĕrattentē, adv. *very attentively;* ab aliquo
audiri, Cic.

pĕrattentus -a -um, *very attentive;* per-
attentos vestros animos habuimus, Cic.

perbacchor, 1. *to revel throughout or during;*
multos dies, Cic.

perbĕātus -a -um, *very happy,* Cic.

perbellē, adv. *very prettily, very finely;*
simulare, Cic.

perbĕnē, adv. *very well;* loqui Latine, Cic.

perbĕnĕvŏlus -a -um, *very well wishing,
very well disposed to;* alicui, Cic.

perbĕnignē, adv. *very kindly;* (in tmesis)
per mihi benigne respondit, Cic.

perbĭbo -bĭbi, 3. *to drink in, drink up.* **I.**
Lit., lacrimas, Ov. **II.** Fig., *to imbibe, take in
mentally;* rabiem, Ov.

perblandus -a -um, *very charming, very
engaging;* successor, Cic.

perbŏnus -a -um, *very good,* Cic.

perbrĕvis -e, *very short;* perbrevi tempore,
or simply perbrevi, in *a very short time,* Cic.

perbrĕvĭtĕr, adv. *very shortly, very briefly,*
Cic.

perca -ae, f. (πέρκη), *a fish, the perch,* Ov.

percălĕfăcio -fēci -factum, 3. *to make very
warm;* pass., **percălĕfīo** -factus sum -fĭĕri,
to become very warm, to be thoroughly heated, Lucr.

percălesco -călŭi, 3. *to become very warm,* Ov.

percallesco -callŭi, 3. **I.** Intransit., *to lose
all sensibility, become quite callous,* Cic. **II.** *to
become experienced;* usu rerum, Cic.

percārus -a -um, **1,** *very dear, very costly,*
Ter. ; **2,** *very dear, much beloved,* Cic.

percautus -a -um, *very cautious,* Cic.

percĕlĕbro, 1. *to speak of very frequently, to
talk of often;* in pass. = *to be in the mouths of
people;* percelebrantur versus de, etc., Cic.

percĕlĕr -is -e, *very swift, very rapid;* alicuius
interitus, Cic.

percĕlĕrĭtĕr, adv. (perceler), *very swiftly,
very rapidly;* auferre diploma, Cic.

percello -cŭli -culsum, 3. (per and * cello).
I. *to beat down, strike down, overturn, shatter.*
A. a, lit., aliquem, Verg. ; fig., quod duo fulmina domum meam per hos dies perculerint, Liv.;
b, transf., eos vis Martis perculit, Cic. **B.**
Fig., *to shatter;* **a,** *to ruin;* rempublicam, Tac.;
b, *to cast down the courage of, dispirit, daunt;*
aliquem, Liv. ; timore perculsa civitas, Cic. ;
quos pavor perculerat in silvas, *driven to,* Liv.
II. *to strike, push;* aliquem genu, Liv.

percensĕo -censŭi, 2. **I.** *to count through,* *count, reckon;* a, promerita numerando, Cic.; locos inveniendi, Cic.; gentes, Liv.; b, *to survey, review;* captivos, Liv.; fig., *to judge, criticise;* orationes, Liv. **II.** *to travel through;* Thessaliam, Liv.

perceptus -a -um, partic. of percipio. Subst., **percepta** -ōrum, n. *principles, rules;* artis, Cic.

perceptĭo -ōnis, f. (percipio). **I.** *a collecting, gathering together;* frugum fructuumque, Cic. **II.** *perception, apprehension, comprehension;* perceptiones animi, Cic.

percīdo -cīdi -cīsum, 3. (per and caedo), *to beat, cut to pieces,* Plaut.

percĭo -cīvi -cītum, 4. and **percĭĕo** -cĭēre, 2. **I.** *to stir up, set in motion;* se, Lucr.; hence, **percĭtus** -a -um, a, *aroused, mad, excited,* Cic.; b, *excitable, irritable;* ingenium, Liv. **II.** *to call, name;* aliquem impudicum, Plaut.

percĭpĭo -cēpi -ceptum, 3. (per and capio). **I.** *to lay hold of, take possession of, seize;* percipit me voluptas atque horror, Lucr. **II.** *to take to oneself.* **A.** 1, sensus percipit rem in se, Lucr.; 2, *to get, receive, collect, gather;* fructus, Cic.; praemia, Caes. **B.** Transf., 1, *to perceive, be sensible of, feel;* voluptatem, Cic.; sonum, Cic.; 2, *to receive mentally;* a, *to learn,* and in perf. tenses, *to know;* praecepta artis, Cic.; omnia civium nomina perceperat, *he knew,* Cic.; b, *to comprehend, understand;* aliquid animo, Cic.

percĭtus -a -um, partic. of percio.

percīvīlis -e, *very condescending, very gracious, courteous,* Suet.

1. **percōlo,** 1. **I.** *to strain through a sieve,* Cato. **II.** *to allow to drain or pass through;* humor per terras percolatur, *percolates through,* Lucr.

2. **percŏlo** -cŏlŭi -cultum, 3. **I.** *to adorn, decorate;* quae priores nondum comperta eloquentiā percoluere, Tac. **II.** *to honour, reverence exceedingly;* patrem, Plaut.

percōmis -e, *very friendly, courteous,* Cic.

percommŏdē, adv. *very conveniently, very appropriately;* percommode cadit, or accidit, or factum est quod, etc., Cic.

percommŏdus -a -um, *very convenient, fit, appropriate, opportune;* with dat., ipsis castris percommodum fuit, Liv.

percontātĭo (percunctātĭo) -ōnis, f. (percontor), *an inquiry, interrogation, question,* Cic.; percontationem facere, Liv.

percontātor (percunctātor) -ōris, m. (percontor), *an inquirer, asker of questions,* Hor.

percontor (percunctor), 1. dep. (per and contus), *to ask, inquire, interrogate, question, investigate;* aliquem de aliqua re, Cic.; aliquid ab or ex aliquo, Cic.; aliquem aliquid, Liv.; percontantes, quid praetor edixisset, ubi cenaret, quo denuntiasset, Cic.

percontŭmax -ācis, *very obstinate,* Ter.

percŏquo -coxi -coctum, 3. *to boil thoroughly.* **I.** Lit., carnes, Plin. **II.** Transf., **A.** *to heat, make hot;* humorem, Lucr. **B.** *to ripen, make ripe;* uvas, Ov.; *to burn, blacken;* nigra virum percocto saecla colore, Lucr.

percrēbresco -brŭi, and **percrēbesco** -bŭi, 3. *to become very frequent, be spread abroad, become prevalent, be well known;* res percrebuit, Cic.; fama percrebruit, with acc. and infin., Caes.

percrēpo -crĕpŭi -crĕpĭtum, 3. *to resound, ring with;* lucum illum percrepare mulierum vocibus, Cic.

pereunctor, percunctatio, etc. = percontor, percontatio, etc. (q.v.).

percŭpĭdus -a -um, *very fond of;* tui, Cic.

percŭpĭo, 3. *to wish, desire exceedingly,* Plaut., Ter.

percūrĭōsus -a -um, *very inquisitive,* Cic.

percūro, 1. *to cure, heal thoroughly;* vixdum satis percurato vulnere, Liv.

percurro -cŭcurri or -curri -cursum, 3. **I.** Intransit., **A.** *to run along or over;* per temonem, Caes. **B.** *to hasten to;* citato equo Cales, Liv. **II.** Transit., *to run through, hasten through, travel through.* **A.** Lit., omnem agrum Picenum, Caes. **B.** Transf., a, of discourse, *to run through, discuss cursorily, mention in passing;* multas res oratione, Cic.; b, *to run over in the mind or with the eye;* veloci percurrere oculo, Hor.; multa animo et cogitatione, multa etiam legendo, Cic.

percursātĭo -ōnis, f. (percurso), *a running through, travelling through;* Italiae, Cic.

percursĭo -ōnis, f. (percurro). **I.** *a rapid consideration or reflection upon anything;* propter animi multarum rerum brevi tempore percursionem, Cic. **II.** Rhet. t. t., *a rapid or hasty passing over a subject;* huic (commorationi) contraria saepe percursio est, Cic.

percurso, 1. (percurro). **I.** Transit., *to ramble over or about;* ripas, Plin. **II.** Intransit., *to rove about;* totis finibus nostris, Cic.

percussĭo -ōnis, f. (percutio). **I.** *a striking, knocking against;* digitorum, *a snapping of the fingers,* Cic. **II.** T. t. of music and rhet., *a beating time,* hence *time, rhythm;* numerorum percussiones, Cic.

percussor -ōris, m. (percutio), 1, *a striker,* Plin.; 2, *a murderer, assassin,* Cic.

percussus -ūs, m. (percutio), *a beating, knocking, striking;* percussu crebro, Ov.

percŭtĭo -cussi -cussum, 3. (per and quatio). **I.** *to strike through, pierce, transfix;* rostro navem, Liv. **II.** *to strike, beat, hit.* **A.** Lit., 1, aliquem lapide, Cic.; forem virgā, Liv.; turres de caelo percussae, *struck by lightning,* Cic.; 2, a, *to kill, slay;* aliquem securi, Cic.; aliquem fulmine (of Jupiter), Cic.; fulmine percussus, Cic.; b, *to strike, play upon;* lyram, Ov.; pennas, *to soar,* Ov. **B.** Fig., 1, non percussit locum, *he has missed the point,* Cic.; 2, a, *to affect, move, astound, strike, shock;* percussus atrocissimis litteris, Cic.; suspicione sum percussus, Cic.; b, *to deceive;* aliquem strategemate, Cic.; c, *to wound mentally, afflict;* percussus calamitate, Cic. (syncop. perf., percusti, Hor.).

perdēlīrus -a -um, *very silly, senseless,* Lucr.

perdiffĭcĭlis -e, *very difficult;* navigatio, quaestio, Cic.

perdiffĭcĭlĭtĕr, adv. *with very great difficulty,* Cic.

perdignus -a -um, *quite worthy of;* tuā amicitiā, Cic.

perdīlĭgens -entis, *very careful, very diligent,* Cic.

perdīlĭgentĕr, adv. *very carefully, very diligently,* Cic.

perdisco -dĭdĭci, 3. *to learn thoroughly;* dictata, Cic.; perf., perdidici, *to understand thoroughly;* with infin., hominis speciem pingere, Cic.

perdīsertē, adv. *very eloquently,* Cic.

perdītē, adv. (perditus), 1, *exceedingly, immoderately;* filiam amare, Ter.; 2, *in an abandoned manner, very badly;* se gerere, Cic.

perdĭtor -ōris, m. (perdo), *a destroyer;* rei-publicae, Cic.

perditus -a -um, p. adj. (from perdo). **I.** *wretched, miserable, ruined;* valetudo, Cic.; res, Cic.; judicia, Cic. **II. A.** *immoderate;* amor, Cat.; perditus luctu, *sunk in grief,* Cic.; aere, Cic. **B.** *morally lost, abandoned, profligate;* adolescens perditus ac dissolutus, Cic.; homo perditissimus, Cic.

perdĭū, adv. *a very long time, for a very long time,* Cic.

perdĭūturnus -a -um, *lasting a very long time, very tedious,* Cic.

perdīvĕs -vĭtis, *very rich,* Cic.

perdix -dīcis, c. (πέρδιξ), *a partridge,* Plin.

perdo -dĭdi -dĭtum, 3. (in pass., gen., pereo, perditus, perire). **I.** *to destroy, ruin.* **A.** funditus civitatem, Cic.; aliquem, Cic.; poet., perdere serpentem, *to kill,* Ov. **B.** *to waste, squander, spend uselessly;* operam, or oleum et operam, Cic.; tempus, Cic. **II.** Transf., **A.** *to lose;* liberos, Cic.; litem, *to lose a lawsuit,* Cic.; oculos, Cic.; vocem, Cic. **B.** *to lose money in gambling;* quod in alea perdiderat, Cic. (old subj. pres., perdŭim -is -it -int, esp. in the execration, di te perduint! Cic.).

perdŏcĕo -dŏcŭi -doctum, 2. *to teach, instruct thoroughly;* aliquem, Ov.; absol., res difficilis ad perdocendum, Cic.

perdoctē, adv. *very learnedly, very skilfully,* Plaut.

perdoctus -a -um (perdoceo), *very learned, very skilful,* Cic.

perdŏlĕo -dŏlŭi -dŏlĭtum, 2. *to suffer great pain or grief,* Ter.

perdŏlesco -dŏlŭi, 3. *to suffer violent pain or grief;* suam virtutem irrisui fore perdoluerunt, Cic.

perdŏmo -dŏmŭi -dŏmĭtum, 1. *to tame thoroughly;* a, tauros feroces, Ov.; b, *to subdue thoroughly, to conquer;* Latium, Liv.

perdūco -duxi -ductum, 3. **I.** *to lead or bring to any place.* **A.** 1, aliquem Romam, Liv.; aliquem ad Caesarem, Caes.; bovem ad stabula, Verg.; 2, a, *to seduce a woman,* Cic.; b, *to carry or construct buildings, aqueducts,* etc., from one point to another; murum a lacu Lemano ad montem Juram, Caes.; viam a Bononia Arretium, Liv. **B.** Transf., *to bring to;* 1, ad dignitatem, Caes.; aliquem ad furorem, Cic.; ad exitum, Cic.; 2, a, *to bring over to one's opinion, induce to do anything;* aliquem ad suam sententiam, Cic.; aliquem ad ducenta (talenta), *to induce to pay,* Cic.; b, *to continue, prolong;* agri colendi studia ad centesimum annum, Cic. **II.** *to spread over, smear over;* totum nati corpus ambrosiae odore, Verg.

perductor -ōris, m. (perduco), *a pimp, pander,* Cic.

perdŭellĭo -ōnis, f. (perduellis), *a hostile attempt against the state, treason,* Cic.

perdŭellis -is, m. (per and duellum, archaic for bellum). **I.** *a public enemy, an enemy actually carrying on hostilities,* Cic. **II.** Transf., *a private or personal enemy,* Plaut.

perdŭim -is -it, etc., v. perdo.

perdulcis -e, *very sweet,* Lucr.

perdūro, 1. *to last a long time, endure;* probitas longum perdurat in aevum, Ov.

pĕrĕdo -ēdi -ēsum, 3. *to eat up, devour entirely;* a, cibum, Plaut.; b, *of things, to consume, destroy;* vellera morbo illuvieque peresa, Verg.; transf., quos durus amor crudeli tabe peredit, Verg.

pĕrĕgrē, adv. (per and ager), *in a foreign country, abroad;* a, habitare, Liv.; depugnare, Cic.; fig., animus est peregre, Hor.; b, *from abroad;* nuntiare, Liv.; c, *to a foreign country, abroad;* exire, Hor.

pĕrĕgrīnābundus -a -um (peregrinor), *travelling about,* Liv.

pĕrĕgrīnātĭo -ōnis, f. (peregrinor), *a travelling or sojourning in foreign countries;* omne tempus in peregrinatione consumere, Cic.

pĕrĕgrīnātor -ōris, m. (peregrinor), *one who travels about,* Cic.

pĕrĕgrīnĭtas -ātis, f. (peregrinus). **I.** *the condition of a foreigner or alien,* Suet. **II.** *foreign manners, customs;* quum in urbem nostram infusa est peregrinitas, Cic.

pĕrĕgrīnor, 1. dep. (peregrinus), *to sojourn or to travel in foreign countries.* **I.** Lit., totā Asiā, Cic.; in aliena civitate, Cic. **II.** Transf., **A.** a, of things, haec studia pernoctant nobiscum, peregrinantur, rusticantur, Cic.; b, of persons, *to stray, wander, ramble* (mentally); in infinitatem omnem, Cic. **B.** *to be strange, foreign;* philosophiam quae quidem peregrinari Romae videbatur, Cic.

pĕrĕgrīnus -a -um (peregre). **I.** *foreign, strange;* amores, *foreign sweethearts,* Ov.; terror, *caused by foreign enemies,* Liv.; subst., **pĕrĕgrīnus** -i, m. and **pĕrĕgrīna** -ae, f.: a, *a foreigner, stranger,* Cic.; b, esp., *a foreigner resident in Rome, an alien;* neque civis neque peregrinus, Cic. **II.** *strange to, inexperienced in;* in agendo, Cic.

pĕrēlĕgans -antis, *very pretty, neat, elegant;* oratio, Cic.

pĕrēlĕgantĕr, adv. *very prettily, elegantly;* dicere, Cic.

pĕrēlŏquens -entis, *very eloquent,* Cic.

pĕremnis -e (per and amnis), *relating to the crossing of a river;* auspicia, *the auspices taken on crossing a river or any running water,* Cic.

pĕremptus -a -um, partic. of perimo.

pĕrendĭē, adv. *the day after to-morrow; scies igitur fortasse cras, summum perendie,* Cic.

pĕrendĭnus -a -um (perendie), *relating to the day after to-morrow;* dies, *the day after to-morrow,* Cic.

pĕrennis -e (per and annus). **I.** *lasting or remaining throughout the year;* militia, Liv. **II.** *lasting, durable, perennial;* aquae, Cic.; cursus stellarum, Cic.; monumentum aere perennius, Hor.; virtus, Cic.; loquacitas, Cic.

pĕrennĭtas -ātis, f. (perennis), *duration, durableness, perpetuity;* fontium, Cic.

pĕrenno, 1. (perennis), *to last many years, be durable;* arte perennat amor, Ov.

pĕrĕo -ĭi and - īvi -ĭtum, 4. (*to go through*). **I.** *to pass away, vanish, disappear;* pereunt victae sole tepente nives, Ov.; dolum lymphae pereuntis, *passing through, moving away,* Hor. **II.** *to be lost, to perish.* **A.** Lit., a, of persons, *to perish, die;* foede, praeclare, Cic.; naufragio, Cic.; summo cruciatu supplicioque, Cic.; eodem leto, Cic.; b, of things, urbes pereunt funditus, Hor.; peritura regna, Verg. **B.** Transf., 1, *to pine away, vaste away with love;* amore, Verg.; 2, *to be ruined politically;* meo vitio pereo, Cic.; perii I *I am undone!* Plaut., Ter.; peream si (nisi), etc., a common form of imprecation, *may I die if (if not),* Ov.; 3, *to be lost;* a, *to be wasted, spent in vain;* ne oleum et opera philologiae nostrae perierit, Cic.; b, legal t. t., *to be extinguished, to be lost, to expire;* quia multis actiones et res peribant, Liv. (syncop. perf. infin., perisse, Ov., Liv.).

pĕrĕquĭto, 1. **I.** Intransit., *to ride through, ride round;* per omnes partes, Caes. **II.** Transit., *to ride round;* aciem, Liv.

pĕrerro, 1. *to wander, ramble, stray through;* totum Latium, Liv.; forum, Hor.; pass., pererr- ato ponto, Verg.

pĕrērŭdītus -a -um, *very learned,* Cic.

pĕrexĭgŭē, adv. *very scantily, very sparingly,* Cic.

pĕrexĭgŭus -a -um, *very small, very little, very scanty.* **I.** Lit., 1, of space, loci spatium, Caes.; 2, of number, quantity, etc., bona corporis, Cic. **II.** Transf., of time, *very short;* dies, Cic.

pĕrexpĕdītus -a -um, *very easy,* Cic.

perfăcētē, adv. *very wittily;* perfacete dicta sunt, Cic.

perfăcētus -a -um, *very witty, facetious;* aliquid perfacetum dicere, Cic.

perfăcĭlĕ, adv. *very easily;* perfacile ap- paret, Cic.

perfăcĭlis -e. **I.** *very easy;* erat perfacilis cognitu, Cic. **II.** *very courteous;* in audiendo, Cic.

perfămĭlĭāris -e, *very intimate, familiar;* alicui, Cic.; subst., m. *a very intimate friend;* meus, Cic.

perfectē, adv. (perfectus), *perfectly, com- pletely;* eruditus, Cic.

perfectĭo -ōnis, f. (perficio), *perfection, com- pleteness, completion;* perfectio maximorum operum, Cic.; hanc perfectionem absolutionem- que in oratore desiderans, Cic.

perfector -ōris, m. (perficio), *a perfecter, completer, finisher;* dicendi, Cic.

perfectus -a -um, p. adj. (from perficio), *perfect, complete, finished;* homo, orator, Cic.; in dicendo, in arte, Cic.; C. Memmius perfectus litteris, Cic.; eloquentia, Cic.; valvas perfectiores nullas ullo unquam tempore fuisse, Cic.; quod ego summum et perfectissimum judico, Cic.

perfĕrens -entis, p. adj. (from perfero), *patient;* injuriarum, Cic.

perfĕro -tŭli -lātum -ferre, *to carry through, bear, bring to a certain place or end.* **I.** Lit., **A.** nec pertulit ictum, *did not reach the mark,* Verg.; alveus fluminis non pertulit gravissimas naves, *did not admit of,* Liv.; reflex., se perferre hinc, *to betake oneself,* Verg. **B.** a, *to carry, bring, bear, convey;* literas ad aliquem, Cic.; alicui nuntium, Cic.; pass., *to be brought, to reach;* quum ad eum fama perlata esset, Liv.; b, esp., *to bring news;* equites pertulere consulem ob- sideri, Liv. **II.** Transf., **A.** *to maintain, pre- serve;* intrepidos ad fata novissima vultus, Ov. **B.** 1, *to bring to an end, carry through, com- plete;* mandata, Liv.; id quod suscepi, quoad potero, perferam, Cic.; 2, *to carry through;* legem, rogationem, Cic.; 3, *to bear, suffer, endure;* perfero et perpetior omnes, Cic.; omnes indignitates contumeliasque, Caes.

perfĭca -ae, f. (perficio), *she that accomplishes;* natura, Lucr.

perfĭcĭo -fēci -fectum, 3. (per and facio). **I.** *to bring to an end, complete, finish;* 1, *to make ready, finish;* pontem, Caes.; candelabrum, Cic.; 2, *to accomplish a period of time, to live through;* centum qui perficit annos, Hor. **II.** 1, a, *to accomplish, achieve;* cogitata, Cic.; conata, Caes.; scelus, Cic.; b, *to bring to an end, to conduct to a close;* comitia, Liv.; bellum, Liv.; c, *to bring about, accomplish, effect;* perficiam ut, etc., Cic.; omnia perficit ne, etc., Cic.; non perficio, foll. by quominus, Cic.; 2, *to make perfect;* Achillem citharā, Ov.

perfĭdēlis -e, *very faithful,* Cic.

perfĭdĭa -ae, f. (perfidus), *faithlessness, per- fidy, treachery, falsehood;* fraude et perfidiā aliquem fallere, Cic.

perfĭdĭōsē, adv. (perfidiosus), *perfidiously, faithlessly, treacherously;* multa perfidiose facta, Cic.

perfĭdĭōsus -a -um (perfidia), *perfidious, faithless, treacherous,* Cic.

perfĭdus -a -um (per and fides), *perfidious, faithless, treacherous, false;* a, of persons, ami- cus, Cic.; b, of inanimate objects, arma, verba, Ov.; sacramentum, Hor.

perfixus -a -um, *pierced through, transfixed,* Lucr.

perflābĭlis -e (perflo), *that can be blown through;* dii, Cic.

perflāgĭtĭōsus -a -um, *very shameful, very flagitious,* Cic.

perflo, 1. *to blow through, blow over;* venti terras turbine perflant, Verg.

perfluctŭo, 1. *to swarm all over,* Lucr.

perflŭo -fluxi -fluxum, 3. *to flow, stream through,* Lucr.

perfŏdĭo -fōdi -fossum, 3. *to dig through, pierce through;* a, parietes, Cic.; b, *to pierce through with the sword;* thoraca, Verg.

perfŏro, 1. **I.** *to pierce through, perforate;* a, navem, Cic.; operculum ferreum, Liv.; b, *to pierce (with the sword);* latus ense, Ov. **II.** *to form by boring;* duo lumina ab animo ad oculos perforata, Cic.

perfortĭtĕr, adv. *very bravely,* Ter.

perfrĕquens -entis, *much visited, much fre- quented;* emporium, Liv.

perfrĭco -frĭcŭi -frĭcātum and -frictum, 1 **I.** *to rub over, to scratch;* caput sinistrā manu, Cic. **II.** *to rub the face to hide the sign of blush- ing;* os, Cic.; hence, *to lay aside shame or modesty,* Cic.

perfrĭgĭdus -a -um, *very cold;* tempestas perfrigida, Cic.

perfringo -frēgi -fractum, 3. (per and frango). **I.** *to break through, break in pieces, shatter.* **A.** Lit., saxum, Cic.; naves perfregerant proras, Liv. **B.** Fig., *to break through, set at nought, disregard, violate;* decreta senatus, Cic.; leges, Cic. **II.** *to break through, bear down.* **A.** Lit., phalangem hostium, Caes. **B.** Fig., omnes alti- tudines, Cic.; animos, *to overpower,* Cic.

perfrŭor -fructus sum, 3. dep. **I.** *to enjoy thoroughly;* laetitiā, Cic.; regali otio, Cic. **II.** *to execute completely;* mandatis patris, Ov.

perfŭga -ae, m. (perfugio), *a deserter,* Cic.

perfŭgĭo -fūgi -fŭgĭtum, 3. *to flee away;* a, *to fly to any place, take refuge in any place;* ad ali- quem, Liv.; transf., ad otium, Cic.; b, *to de- sert to the enemy;* quum paene quotidie a Pompeio ad Caesarem perfugerent, Caes.

perfŭgĭum -ii, n. (perfugio), *a place of refuge, refuge, asylum;* perfugium et praesidium salutis, Cic.; plur., intercludere perfugia fortunae, Cic.

perfunctĭo -ōnis, f. (perfungor), *a perform- ing, discharging;* honorum, Cic.

perfundo -fūdi -fūsum, 3. *to pour over.* **I.** Lit., 1, *to moisten, wet;* a, aliquem sanguine, besprinkle, Tac.; perfundi, *to be moistened with,* and in middle, *to bathe in, swim in;* aquā fer- venti a Rubrio, Cic.; vivo flumine, Liv.; per- fusus fletu, Liv.; b, *to dye, stain;* ostro per- fusae vestes, Verg.; 2, *to sprinkle, bestrew;* Lethaeo perfusa papavera somno, Verg. **II.** Fig., *to imbue or fill with anything;* qui me horror perfudit! Cic.; sensus jucunditate quādam per- funditur, Cic.; timore, Liv.

perfungor -functus sum, 3. dep., **a**, *to accomplish, perform, execute, discharge;* reipublicae muneribus, Cic.; rebus amplissimis, Cic.; **b**, *to go through, endure;* molestiā, Cic.; bello, Cic.; partic. pass., memoria perfuncti periculi, Cic.; absol., perfunctus sum, *I have endured,* Cic.; **c**, *to enjoy;* epulis, Ov.

perfŭro, 3. *to rage furiously,* Verg.

Pergămum -i, n. and **Pergămus (-ŏs)** -i, f. (Πέργαμος -ον). **I.** *The citadel of Troy;* gen. plur., **Pergăma** -ōrum, n. **II.** *a town in Mysia, on the river Caicus, capital of the kingdom of Pergamus, residence of the Attalian kings,* now *Bergamo.* Hence, **A. Pergămēnus** -a -um, *relating to Pergamum* (in Mysia). **B. Pergămĕus** -a -um, *relating to the citadel of Troy,* and hence, *Trojan.*

pergaudĕo, 2. *to rejoice exceedingly,* Cic.

pergo, perrexi, perrectum, 3. (per and rego). **I.** Lit., *to continue, proceed with, prosecute anything;* with acc., iter, Sall., Liv.; with infin., ad eum ire, Cic.; absol., perge porro, Cic.; in Macedoniam, Cic. **II.** Transf., **A.** Of abstract subjects, ut ad eas (virtutes) cursim perrectura beata vita videatur, Cic. **B.** Of persons, *to continue;* id agere perrexi, Cic.; perge quatuor mihi istas partes explicare, Cic.; absol., perge ut coeperas, Cic.

pergrandis -e, *very large, very great;* **a**, of size, gemma, Cic.; **b**, of value, pecuniae summa, Cic.; **c**, of time, pergrandis natu, *very old,* Liv.

pergrātus -a -um, *very pleasant, very delightful;* pergratum mihi feceris si, etc., *you would give me great pleasure if,* etc., Cic.

pergrăvis -e, *very weighty, very important;* oratio, Cic.

pergrăvĭtĕr, adv. *very seriously;* aliquem reprehendere, Cic.

pergŭla -ae, f. (pergo), **a**, *a shed or outhouse used for various purposes, a shop, workshop,* Plin.; **b**, *a school,* Juv.

pĕrhĭbĕo -ŭi -ĭtum, 2. (per and habeo). **I.** *to bring forward, propose;* quem Caecilius suo nomine perhiberet, Cic. **II.** a, *to speak, say;* ut Graii perhibent, *as the Greeks say,* Verg.; in pass., with nom. and infin., nuntii fuisse perhibentur; **b**, *to call, consider;* vatem hunc perhibebo optimum, Cic.

pĕrhĭlum, *very little,* Lucr.

pĕrhŏnōrĭfĭcē, adv. *very respectfully,* Cic.

pĕrhŏnōrĭfĭcus -a -um, 1, *very honourable;* discessus, Cic.; 2, *very respectful;* collega in me perhonorificus, Cic.

pĕrhorrĕo, 2. *to shudder at, to dread,* Ov.

pĕrhorresco -horrŭi, 3. *to become rough.* **I.** Of water, *to be agitated;* aequor perhorruit, Ov. **II.** *to be filled with dread, to shudder.* **A.** Lit., a, intransit., recordatione consulatus vestri perhorrescere, Cic.; b, transit., *to shudder at;* tantam religionem, fugam virginum, Cic. **B.** Transf., *to tremble, quake;* clamore perhorruit Aetne, Ov.

pĕrhorrĭdus -a -um, *very dreadful;* silvae, Liv.

pĕrhūmānĭtĕr, adv. *very civilly, very kindly,* Cic.

pĕrhūmānus -a -um, *very friendly, kind, civil;* epistola, Cic.

Pĕrĭclēs -is, m. (Περικλῆς), *a celebrated Athenian statesman* (d. 429 B.C.).

pĕrĭclĭtātĭo -ōnis, f. (periclitor), *a trial, experiment,* Cic.

pĕrĭclĭtor, 1. dep. (periculum). **I.** Intransit., **A.** *to try, make a trial;* periclitemur in exemplis, Cic. **B.** *to be in danger, to be imperilled;*

ut potius Gallorum vita quam legionariorum periclitaretur, Caes.; with abl., rebus suis, Liv. **II.** Transit., **A.** *to try, test, prove, put to the proof;* fortunam, Cic.; vires ingenii, Cic. **B.** *to risk;* non est salus periclitanda reipublicae, Cic.

Pĕrĭclymĕnus -i, m. (Περικλύμενος), *son of Neleus, an Argonaut.*

pĕrĭcŭlōsē, adv. (periculosus), *dangerously;* aegrotare, Cic.

pĕrĭcŭlōsus -a -um (periculum), *full of danger, threatening danger, dangerous, perilous;* vulnus, Cic.; with dat., periculosae libertati opes, Liv.

pĕrĭcŭlum (contr. **pĕrĭclum**) -i, n. (root PER, whence experior), *a trial, proof, test.* **I.** Gen., 1, periculum facere, *to make a trial,* Caes.; with genit., fidei, Cic.; 2, *an attempt in authorship* Cic. **II.** *danger, peril.* **A.** Gen., periculum facere alicuius rei, *to risk,* Liv.; salutem sociorum summum in periculum ac discrimen vocare, Cic.; capitis periculum adire, *danger of life,* Cic.; periculum subire pro amico, Cic.; periculum alicui creare, or conflare, or inferre, or injicere, or facessere, Cic.; periculum est, with ne and the subj., *there is danger that,* etc., Cic. **B.** Esp., a *trial, action, suit;* a, lit., Cic.; b, *a legal record* or *register;* pericula magis tratuum, Cic.

pĕrĭdōnĕus -a -um, *very fit, suitable, appropriate;* locus peridoneus castris, Caes.

Pĕrillus -i, m. (Πέριλλος), *an artist in metal at Athens, who made for Phalaris of Agrigentum a brazen bull, in which criminals were to be shut up and roasted, and who was the first to suffer death by it.*

pĕrillustris -e, 1, *very plain, very evident,* Nep.; 2, *very distinguished,* Cic.

pĕrimbēcillus -a -um, *very weak,* Cic.

pĕrĭmo -ēmi -emptum, 3. (per and emo), *to destroy, ruin, annihilate.* **I.** Lit., **A.** sensu perempto, Cic.; Troja perempta, Verg.; corpus pallore et macie peremptum, Liv. **B.** Esp., *to kill a person;* aliquem, Ov.; partic. perf. = *slain,* Verg., Liv. **II.** Fig., *to hinder, thwart, frustrate;* reditum, consilium, Cic.; causam publicam, Cic.

pĕrincertus -a -um, *very uncertain,* Sall.

pĕrincommŏdē, adv. *very inconveniently, very inopportunely;* accidit incommode, Cic.

pĕrincommŏdus -a -um, *very inconvenient, very troublesome,* Liv.

pĕrindē, adv. *as, like as, just as, in a like manner;* foll. by ac si, Cic.; atque, Cic.; quasi, Cic.; tamquam, Cic.; ut, Cic.; perinde ut . . . ita, Liv.; perinde utcumque . . . ita, Cic.

pĕrindignē, adv. *very indignantly,* Suet.

pĕrindulgens -entis, *very indulgent, very tender,* Cic.

pĕrinfāmis -e, *very infamous,* Suet.

pĕrinfirmus -a -um, *very weak,* Cic.

pĕringĕnĭōsus -a -um, *very clever,* Cic.

pĕrinīquus -a -um, 1, *very unfair,* Cic.; 2, *very discontented, very unwilling;* periniquo animo pati, with acc. and infin., Cic.

pĕrinsignis -e, *very conspicuous, very remarkable,* Cic.

Pĕrinthus (-ŏs) -i, f. (Πέρινθος), *a city in Thrace, afterwards called Heraclea,* now *Erekli.*

pĕrinvīsus -a -um, *much hated;* homo, Cic.

pĕrinvītus -a -um, *very unwilling,* Cic.

pĕrĭor, pĕrītus sum, 4. *to experience, make a trial of,* Plaut.

Pĕrĭpătētĭcus -a -um (Περιπατητικός), *Peripatetic, belonging to the Peripatetic or Aristotelian* *school of philosophy;* subst., **Pĕrĭpătētĭcī** -ōrum, m. *Peripatetic philosophers.*

pĕrĭpĕtasma -ătis, n. (περιπέτασμα), *a curtain, hanging, covering,* Cic.

pĕrīrātus -a -um, *very angry,* Cic.

pĕriscĕlĭs -ĭdis, f. (περισκελίς), *a garter or an anklet,* Hor.

pĕristrōma -ătis, n. (περίστρωμα), *a curtain, carpet, hanging,* Cic. (abl. plur. heterocl., peristromatis).

pĕristўlum -i, n. (περίστυλον), *a peristyle or court surrounded by a colonnade,* Cic.

pĕrītē, adv. (peritus), *skilfully, cleverly;* perite dicere, Cic.; nihil (peritius) de foederibus, Cic.; peritissime venditare, Cic.

pĕrītĭa -ae, f. (peritus), *knowledge derived from experience, skill;* locorum ac militiae, Sall.

pĕrīto, 1. *to perish utterly,* Lucr.

pĕrītus -a -um (perior), *experienced, skilful, practised, expert;* absol., peritissimi duces, Caes.; with genit., rerum, Cic.; with abl., quis jure peritior? Cic.; with ad and the acc., ad usum et disciplinam, Cic.; with infin., cantare, Verg.

perjĕro = pejero (q.v.).

perjūcundē, adv. *very pleasantly, very delightfully;* in aliqua re versari, Cic.

perjūcun ıs -a -um, *very pleasant, very delightful;* litterae, disputatio, Cic.

perjūrĭōsus -a -um (perjurium), *full of perjury, perjured,* Plaut.

perjūrĭum -ĭi, n. (perjurus), *false swearing, perjury,* Cic.

perjūro = pejero (q.v.).

perjūrus (pējūrus) -a -um (per and jus), *perjured;* perjurus et mendax, Cic.; leno perjurissimus, Cic.; subst., *a perjured person,* Cic.

perlābor -lapsus sum, 3. *to glide through, penetrate;* rotis summas levibus perlabitur undas, glides along, Verg.; with ad and the acc., *to reach to;* inde perlapsus ad nos et usque ad Oceanum Hercules, Cic.

perlaetus -a -um, *very joyful,* Liv.

perlātē, adv. *very widely, very extensively,* Cic.

perlĕcĕbra (pellĕcĕbra) -ae, f. (pellicio), *an enticing, alluring,* Plaut.

perlectĭo = pellectio (q.v.).

perlĕgo (pellĕgo) -lēgi -lectum, 3. **I.** *to survey thoroughly, scan, examine accurately;* omnia oculis, Verg. **II. A.** *to read through;* librum, Cic. **B.** *to read through, call over;* senatum, *to call over the roll of senators,* Liv.

perlĕvis -e, *very light, very slight;* perlevi momento, Cic.

perlĕvĭtĕr, adv. *very slightly;* pungit animi dolor, Cic.

perlĭbens (perlŭbens) -entis, *very willing,* Cic.

perlĭbentĕr, adv. *very willingly,* Cic.

perlībĕrālis -e, *well brought up, well-bred,* Ter.

perlībĕrālĭtĕr, adv. *very liberally, very bountifully,* Cic.

perlĭbet (perlŭbet) -bŭit, 3. *it is pleasing, very pleasant,* Plaut.

perlĭcĭo = pellicio (q.v.).

perlīto, 1. *to offer an auspicious sacrifice, to sacrifice with favourable omens;* primis hostiis, Liv.

perlongē, adv. *very far,* Ter.

perlongus -a -um, 1, *very long;* via, Cic.; 2, *lasting a long time, tedious,* Plaut.

perlŭbet, etc. = perlibet, etc. (q.v.).

perlūcĕo (pellūcĕo) -luxi, 2. **I.** *to shine through, gleam through;* 1, lit., lux perlucens, Liv.; 2, fig., *to shine through, be visible;* perlucet ex eis virtutibus, Cic. **II.** *to be transparent;* pellucens, *transparent;* aether, Cic.; fig., oratio, Cic.

perlūcĭdŭlus (pellūcĭdŭlus) -a -um (dim. of perlucidus), *somewhat transparent;* lapis, *pearl,* Cat.

perlūcĭdus (pellūcĭdus) -a -um, *transparent;* membranae, Cic.; transf., illustris et perlucida stella, *bright,* Cic.

perluctŭōsus -a -um, *very mournful,* Cic.

perlŭo -lŭi -lūtum, 3. *to wash, bathe;* manus undā, Ov.; pass., perlui, as middle, *to bathe;* in fluminibus perluuntur, Caes.; undā, Hor.

perlustro, 1. **I.** *to pass, wander, range through;* agros, Liv. **II.** *to regard, consider, examine;* omnia oculis, Liv.; aliquid animo, Cic.

permagnus -a -um, *very great, very large;* hereditas, Cic.; permagnum est, with infin., Cic.; subst., **permagnum** -i, n. *a very great thing;* quod permagni interest, Cic.

permălĕ, adv. *very badly or unsuccessfully;* pugnare, Cic.

permănantĕr, adv. (permano), *by flowing through,* Lucr.

permănĕo -mansi -mansum, 2. *to remain, stay, abide.* **I.** Lit., Seleucus in maritima ora permanens, Liv. **II.** 1, *to last, continue;* ut quam maxime permaneant diuturna corpora, Cic.; 2, *to abide, remain;* in mea pristina sententia, Cic.

permăno, 1. **I.** *to flow through.* **A.** Lit., in saxis ac speluncis permanat aquarum liquidus humor, Lucr. **B.** Transf., *to penetrate;* permanat frigus ad ossa, Lucr. **II.** *to flow to.* **A.** Lit., succus permanat ad jecur, Cic. **B.** Transf., *to reach, penetrate, extend;* doctrina in civitatem, Cic.; ad aures alicuius, Cic.; conclusiunculae ad sensum non permanantes, Cic.

permansĭo -ōnis, f. (permaneo). **I.** *a remaining, abiding in a place;* quodvis enim supplicium levius est hac permansione, Cic. **II.** *abiding in an opinion;* in una sententia, Cic.

permărīnus -a -um, *relating to the sea;* Lares, *guardian deities of those who travel by sea,* Liv.

permātūresco -mātūrŭi, 3. *to become thoroughly ripe,* Ov.

permĕdĭŏcris -e, *very moderate,* Cic.

permĕo, 1. **I.** *to go through, pass through, traverse;* maria ac terras, Ov. **II.** *to penetrate or reach;* 1, longius in hostes, Tac.; 2, *to pervade,* Cic.

Permessus -i, n. (Περμησσός), *a river in Boeotia, rising in the spring on Helicon, sacred to the Muses, and flowing into the Copaic lake.*

permētĭor -mensus sum, 4. dep. **I.** *to measure through, measure out;* solis magnitudinem, Cic. **II.** *to traverse;* aequor, Verg.

permĕtŭens -entis, *greatly fearing,* Verg.

permingo -minxi, 3. *to defile,* Hor.

permĭnūtus -a -um, *very small, very trifling,* Cic.

permīrus -a -um, *very wonderful;* illud mini permirum accĭdit, with acc. and infin., Cic.

permiscĕo -miscŭi -mixtum or -mistum, 2. *to mix, mingle thoroughly.* **I.** Lit., naturam cum materia, Cic.; permixti cum suis fugientibus, Caes. **II.** Fig., **A.** fructus acerbitate permixti, Cic. **B.** *to confound, confuse, bring into disorder;* omnia jura divina et humana, Caes.; Graeciam, Cic.

permissĭo -ōnis, f. (permitto). **I.** *yielding, surrender,* Liv. **II.** *permission, leave;* mea permissio mansionis tuae, Cic.

permissus -ū, m. (permitto), *leave, permission;* only in abl., permissu legis, Cic.

permitto -mīsi -missum, 3. *to let go, let loose.* **A.** Lit., **1,** equos permittunt in hostem, Liv.; **2,** *to throw, hurl at a mark;* saxum in hostem, Ov. **B.** Fig., **1,** permittere tribunatum, *to make use of,* Liv.; **2,** a, *to give up, yield, cede, surrender;* alicui potestatem, Cic.; consulibus rempublicam, Cic.; se in fidem ac potestatem populi, Caes.; b, *to give up, sacrifice;* inimicitias patribus conscriptis, Cic.; permitto aliquid iracundiae tuae, *make some allowances for,* Cic.; c, *to allow, permit;* with infin., Liv.; with ut and the subj., Cic.; partic. subst., **permissum** -i, n. *permission,* Hor.

permixtē, adv. (permixtus, from permisceo), *in a mixed manner, confusedly,* Cic.

permixtĭo -ōnis, f. (permisceo), *a mixing, mixture,* Cic.

permŏdestus -a -um, *very modest, very moderate,* Cic.

permŏdĭcus -a -um, *very moderate, very small, very slight,* Suet.

permŏlestē, adv. (permolestus), *very hardly, with much difficulty;* permoleste tuli, *I was much vexed,* Cic.; with acc. and infin., Cic.

permŏlestus -a -um, *very troublesome, very burdensome,* Cic.

permōtĭo -ōnis, f. (permoveo). **I.** *a movement, motion, agitation;* animi, Cic. **II.** *an emotion,* Cic.

permŏvĕo -mōvi -mōtum, 2. *to move or stir up thoroughly.* **I.** Lit., mare permotum, *agitated,* Lucr. **II.** Transf., **A.** *to move, excite, agitate mentally;* a, *to persuade, induce, influence;* aliquem pollicitationibus, Caes.; nihil te curulis aedilitas permovit quominus ludos flagitio pollueres, Cic.; permotus auctoritate, injuriis, Cic.; b, *to move, affect;* mentem judicum, Cic.; permotus metu, dolore, iracundiā, odio, Cic. **B.** *to excite any particular passion or emotion;* invidiam, misericordiam, metum et iras, Tac.

permulcĕo -mulsi -mulsum and (rarely) -mulctum, 2. *to stroke.* **I. A.** Lit., aliquem manu, Ov.; barbam alicuius, Liv. **B.** Fig., a, *to charm, delight;* sensum voluptate, Cic.; b, *to soothe, tranquillise, soften;* senectutem, Cic.; iram alicuius, Cic. **II.** Transf., *to touch gently;* lumina virgā, Ov.

permultus -a -um, *very much, very many;* a, adj., viri, Cic.; b, subst.. **permultum** -i, n. *much,* Cic.; hence, permulto o, b *ur, by much;* with compar., permulto cla ora, Cic.; c, adv., permulti m, *very much;* permultum ante, *long before,* Cic.

permunĭo -ivi -itum, 4. *to fortify completely, to finish fortifying;* quae munimenta inchoaverat, permunit, Liv.

permūtātĭo -ōnis, f. (permuto). **I.** *change, alteration;* coloris, Cic.; magna permutatio rerum, Cic. **II.** *an exchange, barter;* **1,** permutatio mercium, Tac.; plur., partim emptiones, partim permutationes, Cic.; **2,** *exchange of money;* publica, Cic.

permūto, 1. **I.** *to change completely;* sententiam, Cic.; dominos, Hor. **II.** *to exchange, barter;* **1,** nomina inter se, Plaut.; **2,** a, *to exchange money;* ut cum quaestu populi pecunia permutaretur, Cic.; b, *to exchange prisoners;* captivos, Liv.

perna -ae, f. (πέρνα), *a leg of pork, a ham, or gammon,* Hor.

pernĕcessārĭus -a -um. **I.** *very necessary,* tempus, Cic. **II.** *very intimate;* homo intimus ac mihi pernecessarius, Cic.

pernĕcessĕ, adv. *very necessary;* esse, Cic.

pernĕgo, 1. **I.** *to deny obstinately, persist in denying;* with acc. and infin., Cic. **II.** *to persist in refusing,* Plaut.

pernĭcĭābĭlis -e (pernicies), *deadly, destructive, fatal;* morbi, Liv.; id perniciabile reo, Tac.

pernĭcĭālis -e (pernicies), *deadly, fatal,* Lucr.

pernĭcĭes -ēi, f. (per and nex). **I.** *destruction, disaster, calamity, ruin;* perniciem afferre vitae alicuius, Cic.; incumbere ad alicuius perniciem, Cic.; moliri alicuius perniciem, Cic. **II.** Meton., *a dangerous person* or *thing;* pernicies provinciae Siciliae, Cic. (old genit., pernicii and dat., pernicie).

pernĭcĭōsē, adv. (perniciosus), *destructively, ruinously, calamitously, perniciously;* multa perniciose sciscuntur in populis, Cic.; quo perniciosius de republica merentur vitiosi homines, Cic.

pernĭcĭōsus -a -um (pernicies), *calamitous, pernicious, dangerous;* esp., *dangerous to the state;* exemplum, Cic.; lex, Cic.; morbi, Cic.

pernīcĭtas -ātis, f. (pernix), *swiftness, fleetness, agility,* Cic.

pernĭcĭtĕr, adv. (pernix), *swiftly, actively, nimbly;* equo desilire, Liv.

pernĭmĭum, adv. *far too much,* Ter.

pernix -nīcis (* pernitor), *swift, nimble, agile, active;* corpus, Liv.

pernōbĭlis -e, *very celebrated;* epigramma Graecum, Cic.

pernocto, 1. (pernox), *to pass the night, spend the night;* ad ostium carceris, Cic.; in nive, Cic.; extra moenia, Liv.; fig., haec studia pernoctant nobiscum, Cic.

pernosco -nōvi -nōtum, 3. *to investigate thoroughly, to become thoroughly acquainted with;* hominum mores ex oculis, vultu, etc., Cic.

pernōtesco -nōtŭi, 3. *to become generally well known,* Tac.

pernox -nocte (only in nom. and abl.), *lasting all night;* luna pernox erat, Liv.

pernŭmĕro, 1. *to count out, reckon completely;* imperatam pecuniam, Liv.

1. **pēro** -ōnis, m. *a boot of rough leather or untanned hide,* Verg.

2. **Pērō** -ūs, f. (Πηρώ), *daughter of Neleus, sister of Nestor.*

pĕrobscūrus -a -um, *very obscure;* quaestio, Cic.

pĕrōdi -ōsus sum -ōdisse, *to hate exceedingly;* only in partic. perf., **pĕrōsus** -a -um, *hating, detesting;* decem virorum scelera, Liv.; lucem, *shunning the light,* Ov.; perosum esse, *to hate, detest;* plebs consulum nomen perosa erat, Liv.

pĕrōdĭōsus -a -um, *much hated, very troublesome,* Cic.

pĕroffĭcĭōsē, adv. *very obligingly, very attentively;* qui me perofficiose observant, Cic.

pĕrŏlĕo, 2. *to emit a bad smell,* Lucr.

pĕrōnātus -a -um (1. pero), *wearing boots of untanned leather,* Pers.

pĕropportūnē, adv. *very opportunely, very seasonably;* venire, Cic.

pĕropportūnus -a -um, *very opportune, very seasonable, very convenient;* deversorium, Cic.

pĕroptātō, adv. *according to one's desire,* Cic.

pĕrŏpŭs, adv. *very necessary,* Ter.

pĕrōrātĭo -ōnis, f. (peroro), a, *the conclusion of a speech, peruration*, Cic. ; b, *the closing speech*, Cic.

perornātus -a -um, *very ornate* (of an orator), Cic.

perorno, 1. *to adorn greatly ;* senatum, Tac.

pĕrōro, 1. **I.** *to speak from beginning to end, to plead a cause throughout, explain or state thoroughly ;* totam causam, Cic. **II.** *to end, close ;* a, with accus., totum hoc crimen decumanum perorabo, Cic. ; res illä die non peroratur, Cic. ; b, absol., *to conclude a speech, to wind up ;* quoniam satis multa dixi est mihi perorandum, Cic. ; also *to close a case* (of the last speaker at a trial), Cic.

pĕrōsus -a -um, v. perodi.

perpāco, 1. *to pacify thoroughly, tranquillise ;* necdum omnia in Graecia perpacata erant, Liv.

perparcē, adv. *very sparingly, very frugally,* Ter.

perparvŭlus -a -um, *very little ;* sigilla, Cic.

perparvus -a -um, *very little, very small ;* perparva et tenuis civitas, Cic.

perpastus -a -um (per and pasco), *well fed, fat ;* canis, Phaedr.

perpaucŭlus -a -um, *very few, very little ;* passus, Cic.

perpaucus -a -um, *very few, very little ;* a, adj., advocati, Cic. ; b, plur. subst., (α) m., perpauci, *very few*, Cic. ; (β) n., perpauca dicere, Cic.

perpaulŭlum (perpaullŭlum) -i, n. dim. *a very, very little*, Cic.

perpaulum (perpaullum), adv. *a very little*, Cic.

perpauper -ĕris, *very poor*, Cic.

perpauxillum -i, n. *a very little*, Plaut.

perpăvĕfăcĭo, 3. *to terrify exceedingly,* Plaut.

perpello -pŭli -pulsum, 3. 1, *to drive, to urge, compel, prevail upon, constrain ;* urbem eo metu ad deditionem, Liv. ; gen. with ut or ne and the subj., Sall., Liv. ; 2, *to make a deep impression on ;* candor huius te et proceritas, vultus oculique perpulerunt, Cic.

perpendĭcŭlum -i, n. (perpendo), *a plumb-line, plummet ;* ad perpendiculum columnas exigere, Cic. ; ad perpendiculum, *in a straight line*, Cic., Caes.

perpendo -pendi -pensum, 3. *to weigh carefully, to consider, examine, investigate ;* transf., aliquid ad disciplinae praecepta Cic. ; perpenditur amicitia veritate, Cic.

perpĕram, adv. *wrongly, falsely, untruly ;* judicare, Cic. ; facere, Cic.

perpĕs -pĕtis (= perpetuus), *continuous, unbroken, perpetual ;* noctem perpetem, *throughout the night*, Plaut.

perpessĭo -ōnis, f. (perpetior), *suffering, endurance ;* laborum, Cic. ; dolorum, Cic.

perpĕtĭor -pessus, 3. dep. (per and patior), *to bear, endure, suffer steadfastly ;* dolorem, Cic.; with acc. and infin., Verg.

perpĕtro, 1. (per and patro), *to complete, accomplish, perform, commit, effect, bring about, finish ;* caedem, sacrificium, Liv.

perpĕtŭĭtas -ātis, f. (perpetuus), *uninterrupted continuance, perpetuity, continuity ;* vitae, Cic. ; orationis, Cic. ; ad perpetuitatem, *for ever*, Cic.

1. perpĕtŭō, adv. (perpetuus), *perpetually, for ever, uninterruptedly*, Cic.

2. perpĕtŭo, 1. (perpetuus), *to make continual* or *perpetual, continue, perpetuate ;* verba,

to pronounce in unbroken succession, Cic. ; potestatem judicum, *to maintain unbroken*, Cic.

perpĕtŭus -a -um (peto), *continuous, uninterrupted, continual.* **I.** a, of space, munitiones, Caes. ; oratio, Cic. ; carmen, Hor. ; b, of time, *unbroken, continuing, lasting, perpetual ;* ignis Vestae perpetuus ac sempiternus, Cic. ; quaestiones, *composed of a standing body of judges*, Cic. ; in perpetuum, *for ever*, Cic. **II.** *universal, general ;* jus, Cic.

perplăcĕo, 2. *to please exceedingly ;* ea (lex) mihi perplacet, Cic.

perplexē, adv. (perplexus), *confusedly, obscurely ;* indicare, Liv.

perplexus -a -um (partic. of * perplecto), *confused, intricate, entangled.* **I.** Lit., iter, Verg. **II.** Transf., *confused, intricate, obscure, perplexed, dark, ambiguous ;* sermones, Liv. ; perplexum Punico astu responsum, Liv.

perplicātus -a -um (per and plico), *entangled, involved*, Lucr.

perplŭo, 3. *to let the rain through ;* perpluunt tigna, Plaut.; hence, *to rain into ;* amor in pectus perpluit meum, Plaut.

perpŏlĭo, 4. **I.** *to smooth, polish thoroughly,* Plin. **II.** *to polish, perfect, complete ;* illam superiorem partem perpolire atque conficere, Cic.

perpŏlītus -a -um, p. adj. (from perpolio), *polished, accomplished, refined ;* perfecti in dicendo et perpoliti homines, Cic. ; vita perpolita humanitate, Cic.

perpŏpŭlor, 1. dep. *to lay waste, devastate completely ;* Italiam, Liv.

perporto, 1. *to carry, transport to any place,* Liv.

perpōtātĭo -ōnis, f. (perpoto), *a continued drinking, drunken debauch ;* plur., intemperantissimae potationes, Cic.

perpōto, 1. **I.** *to continue drinking, to keep up a drunken debauch ;* totos dies, Cic. ; potant ad vesperum, Cic. **II.** *to drink up,* Lucr.

perprĕmo = perprimo (q.v.).

perprimo -pressi -pressum, 3. (per and premo), *to press hard ;* cubilia, *to lie upon*, Hor.

perprŏpinquus -a -um, *very nearly related ;* M. illius Aurii perpropinquus, Cic.

perprosper -ĕra -ĕrum, *very prosperous ;* valetudo, *very good*, Suet.

perprūrisco, 3. *to itch all over*, Plaut.

perpugnax -ācis, *very pugnacious ;* in disputando, Cic.

perpulcher -chra -chrum, *very beautiful,* Ter.

perpurgo, 1. **I.** *to make thoroughly clean ;* se quädam herbulä, Cic. **II.** Fig., 1, *to explain thoroughly, to clear up ;* locum orationis, Cic. ; 2, *to confute, refute ;* crimina, Cic.

perpŭsillus -a -um, *very small, very little ;* in double sense, perpusillus testis processit . . . non accusabis, perpusillum rogabo, i.e., *I will ask a little question, I will question the little man*, Cic.

perquam, adv. (per and quam), *very much, extremely ;* perquam grave est dictu, Cic. ; perquam breviter, Cic.

perquīro -sīvi -sītum, 3. (per and quaero), *to inquire earnestly, make accurate inquiries, search for eagerly ;* vias, Caes. ; vasa, Cic. ; ilia ab accusatore, Cic.

perquīsītē, adv. (perquisitus, from perquiro), *accurately ;* in compar., perquisitius et diligentius conscribere, Cic.

perrāro, adv. (perrarus), *very rarely, very seldom,* Cic.

perrārus -a -um, *very uncommon, very rare,* Liv.

perrĕcondĭtus -a -um, *very abstruse, very recondite,* Cic.

perrēpo -repsi -reptum, 3. *to crawl through, creep over,* Tib.

perrepto, 1. (intens. of perrepo), *to crawl about, to crawl through,* Plaut.

Perrhaebia -ae, f. (Περραιβία), *a district in Thessaly.* Adj., **Perrhaebus** -a -um, *Perrhaebian,* poet. = *Thessalian.*

perrĭdĭcŭlē, adv. (perridiculus), *very laughably,* Cic.

perrĭdĭcŭlus -a -um, *very laughable, very ridiculous,* Cic.

perrŏgo, 1. *to ask a number of persons in succession, to ask one after another;* sententiam, sententias, Liv.

perrumpo -rūpi -ruptum, 3. **I.** Intransit., *to break through, burst a way through;* per medios hostes, Caes.; per aciem, Liv. **II.** Transit., *to break through, burst through.* **A.** Lit., 1, rates, Caes.; 2, *to make a way through;* paludem, Caes.; cuneos hostium, Liv. **B.** Fig., *to break through, subdue, overpower, annihilate;* periculum, Cic.; quaestiones, Cic.

1. **Persa** -ae, f. (Πέρση). **I.** *a nymph, mother of Aeetes, Circe, and Hecate by Sol.* Hence, adj., **Persēis** -ĭdis, f. (Περσηίς), = *magical;* herbae, Ov.; sc. Musa, *a poem,* Ov. **II.** *name of a little dog,* Cic.

2. **Persa,** v. **Persae.**

Persae -ārum, m. (Πέρσαι), *the Persians;* sing., **Persa** -ae, m. and **Persēs** -ae, m.; hence, **A. Persĭa** -ae, f. *Persia.* **B. Persĭs** -ĭdis, f. 1, adj., *Persian,* Ov.; 2, subst., *Persia in a narrower sense, Persis, the district between Carmania, Media, and Susiana,* now *Fars* or *Farsistan.* **C.** Adj., **Persĭcus** -a -um, *Persian;* arbor, or simply **Persĭcus** -i, f. *the peach-tree;* **Persĭca** -ōrum, n. *Persian history.*

persaepĕ, adv. *very often,* Cic.

persalsē, adv. (persalsus), *very wittily;* per-salse et humaniter gratias mihi agit, Cic.

persalsus -a -um, *very witty,* Cic.

persălūtātĭo -ōnis, f. (persaluto), *a greeting, salutation,* Cic.

persălūto, 1. *to greet a number in succession, greet all round;* omnes, Cic.

persanctē, adv. *very sacredly,* Ter.

persăpĭens -entis, *very wise;* homo, Cic.

persăpĭentĕr, adv. (persapiens), *very wisely,* Cic.

perscĭentĕr, adv. (per and scio), *very knowingly, very discreetly,* Cic.

perscindo -scĭdi -scissum, 3. *to tear to pieces;* omnia perscindente vento, Liv.

perscītus -a -um, *very fine, very clever, very pretty;* (in tmesis) per mihi scitum videtur, Cic.

perscrībo -scripsi -scriptum, 3. *to write down accurately, explicitly.* **A.** Gen., rationes sunt perscriptae scite et litterate, Cic. **B.** Esp., 1, officially, *to note down, enter in a memorandum-book* or *register;* a, omnia judicum dicta, interrogata, responsa, Cic.; b, *to enter in an account-book;* falsum nomen, Cic.; 2, *to notify, announce, relate in writing;* alicui mitissimam alicuius orationem, Cic.; de suis rebus ad Lollium. Cic.; **3,** *to make over or assign to in writing;* illam pecuniam in aedem sacram reficiendam perscribere, **Cic.**

perscriptĭo -ōnis, f. (perscribo). **I. a,** *an entering in a register,* Cic.; b, *an entering in an account-book,* Cic. **II.** *a making over or assigning by a written document,* Cic.

perscriptor -ōris, m. (perscribo), *one who writes down* or *makes an entry,* Cic.

perscrūtor, 1. dep. **I.** *to search through, look through, seek through;* arculas muliebres, Cic. **II.** Transf., *to examine into, to investigate;* naturam rationemque criminum, Cic.

persĕco -sĕcŭi -sectum, 1. *to cut off entirely, cut through, cut out;* 1, id ne serperet iterum latius, Liv.; 2, *to dissect, lay bare;* rerum naturas, Cic.

persector, 1. dep. **I.** *to follow, pursue eagerly;* accipitres persectantes, Lucr. **II.** Transf., *to investigate :* primordia, Lucr.

persĕcūtĭo -ōnis, f. (persequor), *a prosecution,* Cic.

persĕdĕo -sēdi -sessum, 2. *to remain sitting;* in equo dies noctesque persedendo, Liv.

persegnis -e, *very sluggish, very languid :* proelium, Liv.

persĕnex -is, *very old,* Suet.

persentĭo -sensi -sensum, 4. 1, *to perceive distinctly;* eam tali peste teneri, Verg.; 2, *to feel deeply;* magno pectore curas, Verg.

persentisco, 3. 1, *to perceive distinctly,* Ter.; 2, *to feel deeply,* Lucr.

Persĕphŏnē -ēs, f. (Περσεφόνη), *the Greek name of Proserpina* (q.v.).; meton. = *death,* Ov.

persĕquor -sĕcūtus and -sĕquūtus sum, -sĕqui, 3. dep. **I.** *to follow constantly, pursue earnestly.* **A.** Lit., 1, gen., vestigia alicuius, Cic.; 2, esp., a, *to follow with hostile intent, pursue;* fugientes usque ad flumen, Caes.; b, *to search through a place;* omnes solitudines, Cic. **B.** Transf., 1, omnes vias, *to use every method,* Cic.; 2, a, *to strive after, seek to attain;* voluptates, Cic.; b, *to follow after, busy oneself with;* artes, Cic.; c, *to imitate;* ironiam, Cic.; aliquem, Cic.; d, *to belong to a sect, to be a follower of;* sectam et instituta alicuius, Cic.; Academiam veterem, Cic.; e, *to pursue hostilely, avenge, punish;* civitatem bello, Caes.; injurias, Cic.; mortem alicuius, *to avenge,* Cic.; f, *to prosecute judicially;* (a) a person, aliquem judicio, Cic.; (β) *to strive to obtain;* jus suum, Cic.; bona sua lite atque judicio, Cic.; g, *to follow up an act, bring about, accomplish, perform, execute;* mea mandata, Cic.; incepta, Liv.; h, *to treat of verbally or in writing;* set forth, expound, describe; quae versibus persecutus est Ennius, Cic.; Brutus philosophiam Latinis literis persequitur, Cic. **II.** *to reach to, attain to.* **A.** Lit., aliquem ne persequi quidem posse triginta diebus, Cic. **B.** Transf., 1, *to collect, call in;* hereditates aut syngraphas, Cic.; 2, *to write down, register;* quae dicuntur, Cic.

1. **Persēs** -ae and **Perseus** -ĕi, m. (Πέρσης), *the last king of Macedonia, defeated by the Roman general Aemilius Paulus* (168 B.C.). Hence, **1, Persĭcus** -a -um, *relating to Perseus;* 2, **Persēis,** acc. -ĭda, f. *a town in Macedonia.*

2. **Persēs** -ae, m. *a Persian,* v. **Persae.**

Perseus -ĕi and -ĕos, m. (Περσεύς), *son of Jupiter and Danaë, slayer of the Medusa and the monster to whom Andromeda was exposed;* hence, adj., 1, **Persēus** -a -um ; 2, **Persēïus** -a -um, *relating to Perseus.*

persĕvērans -antis, p. adj. (from persevero), *holding out, enduring, persevering,* Liv.

persĕvērantĕr, adv. (perseverans), *perseveringly, persistently;* bene coeptam rem tueri, Liv.

persĕvērantĭa -ae, f. (persevero), *perseverance, endurance, persistence,* Cic.

persĕvēro, 1. (perseverus). **I.** Intransit., *to persist, remain constant, persevere in anything;* a, in sua sententia, Cic.; pass. used also impers., non est ab isto perseveratum, Cic.; **b,** *to continue* or *finish a voyage* or *journey;* una navis perseveravit, Caes. **II.** Transit., *to proceed with, persist in;* id, Cic.; with infin., injuriam facere fortissime, Cic.; with acc. and infin., *to maintain that;* perseverabat se esse Orestem, Cic.

persĕvērus -a -um, *very strict;* imperium, Tac.

Persĭa, v. Persae.

Persĭcus, v. Persae and Perses.

persĭdĕo -sēdi -sessum, 2. = persedeo (q.v.).

persĭdo -sēdi -sessum, 3. *to settle down,* Verg.

persigno, 1. *to note down, record;* dona, Liv.

persĭmĭlis -e, *very like, very similar;* statua istius persimilis, Cic.

persimplex -lcis, *very simple,* Tac.

persisto, 3. *to remain constant, persist in anything;* in eadem impudentia, Liv. (for perfect form v. persto).

Persĭus -ii, m. **I.** *an orator, contemporary with Lucilius.* **II.** *a celebrated Roman satirist in the reign of Nero.*

persolla -ae, f. (dim. of persona), *a little mask;* hence, as a term of reproach, *a little fright,* Plaut.

persolvo -solvi -sŏlūtum, 3. **I.** *to unloose;* fig., = *to explain, expound,* Cic. **II.** *to pay, pay off;* a, lit., stipendium militibus, Cic.; aes alienum alienis nominibus suis copiis, *to pay the debts of others with one's own money,* Sall.; b, transf., *to pay, give, render to any one his due, discharge an obligation;* grates, Verg.; meritam diis immortalibus gratiam, Cic.; poenas, *to suffer punishment,* Cic.; epistolae, *to answer a letter,* Cic.

persōna -ae, f. *the mask worn by the actors in the Greek and Roman drama.* **I.** Lit., ut ex persona mihi ardere oculi hominis histrionis viderentur, Cic. **II.** Meton., 1, *the part, character, person represented by the actor;* persona de mimo, Cic.; 2, transf., a, *the part which any one plays; the character which he sustains in the world;* accusatoris, Cic.; petitoris personam capere, Cic.; personam in republica tueri principis, *to be a leading man in the state,* Cic.; b, *a person in the abstract* = *a personality, individuality, character;* huius Staleni persona, Cic.

persōnātus -a -um (persona), 1, *clad in a mask, masked;* Roscius, Cic.; 2, *fictitious, not genuine, counterfeited;* quid est, cur ego personatus ambulem, Cic.

persōno -sŏnŭi -sŏnĭtum, 1. **I.** Intransit., **A.** *to sound through, resound thoroughly;* domus cantu personabat, Cic.; aures personant huiusmodi vocibus, Cic.; id totis personabat castris, Liv.; of persons, *to shout,* Tac. **B.** *to perform upon a musical instrument;* cithara Iopas personat, Verg. **II.** Transit., **A.** *to fill with sound, cause to resound;* aequora conchā, Verg. **B.** a, *to cry loudly,* with acc. and infin., Cic.; b, *to proclaim loudly;* quas (res) isti in angulis personant, Cic.

perspecto, 1. (intens. of perspicio), 1, *to look at to the end,* Suet.; 2, *to look all about,* Plaut.

perspectus -a -um, p. adj. (from perspicio), *well known, fully known;* virtus, Cic.; (superl.), benevolentia perspectissima, Cic.

perspĕcŭlor, 1. dep. *to investigate, explore thoroughly,* Suet.

perspergo, 3. (per and spargo), *to sprinkle,*

---

moisten; fig., quo tamquam sale perspergatur omnis oratio, Cic.

perspĭcācĭtas -ātis, f. (perspicax), *sharp-sightedness,* Cic. (?)

perspĭcax -ācis (perspicio), *sharp-sighted, acute;* id quod acutum ac perspicax natura est, Cic.

perspĭcientĭa -ae, f. (perspicio), *a perfect acquaintance with* or *knowledge of;* veri, Cic.

perspĭcĭo -spexi -spectum, 3. (per and specio). **I.** Intransit., *to look into, to penetrate by the look;* quo non modo non intrari, sed ne perspici quidem posset, Cic. **II.** Transit., **A.** *to see through, look through, behold;* ut prae densitate arborum perspici caelum vix posset, Liv. **B.** a, *to look at attentively, survey, examine;* domum tuam, Cic.; b, *to read through something written;* eas (epistolas) ego oportet perspiciam, Cic.; c, *to regard mentally, note, observe, investigate, ascertain;* alicuius fidem, Cic.; animos regum, Cic.; with acc. and infin., Cic.; or pass., with nom. and infin., Cic.; with rel. sent., ista veritas quae sit, non satis perspicio, Cic.

perspĭcŭē, adv. (perspicuus), *clearly, plainly, evidently;* plane et perspicue expedire aliquid, Cic.

perspĭcŭĭtas -ātis, f. (perspicuus), 1, *clearness, brightness, transparency,* Plin.; 2, transf., *clearness, perspicuity,* Cic.

perspĭcŭus -a -um (perspicio). **I.** *transparent, bright, clear;* aquae, Ov. **II.** Transf., *clear, evident, perspicuous;* utilitatis ratio aut perspicua nobis aut obscura, Cic.

persterno -strāvi -strātum, 3. *to make quite level, pave thoroughly;* viam silice, Liv.

pĕrstĭmŭlo, 1. *to goad on violently,* Tac.

persto -stĭti -stātūrus, 1. *to stand firm, remain standing.* **I.** Lit., armati omnes diem totum perstant, Liv. **II.** Transf., **A.** *to remain unchanged, to last, endure;* nihil est quod toto perstet in orbe, Ov. **B.** *to stand firm, persist, persevere;* in incepto, Liv.; in sententia, Cic.; with infin., si perstiteris corpus ad ea quae dixi referre, Cic.

perstrĕpo -ŭi, 3. *to make a great noise,* Ter.

perstringo -strinxi -strictum, 3. *to graze, graze against.* **I.** Lit., a, portam aratro, Cic.; solum aratro, *to plough,* Cic.; b, esp., *to wound slightly;* femur, Cic. **II.** Transf., a, *to touch, seize, lay hold of;* horror ingens spectantes perstringit, Lit.; consulatus meus eum perstrinxerat, *had moved,* Cic.; b, *to scold, blame, reproach;* voluntatem facetiis, Cic.; aliquem suspicione, Cic.; c, *to touch upon in discourse, relate briefly;* tantummodo perstringere unamquamque rem, Cic.

perstŭdĭōsē, adv. (perstudiosus), *very eagerly, very willingly,* Cic.

perstŭdĭōsus -a -um, *very eager, very desirous, very fond;* litterarum, Cic.

persŭādĕo -suāsi -suāsum, 2. **I.** *to convince;* with or without dat. of pers., with accus. and infin., or rel. sent., or with de and the abl., velim tibi ita persuadeas me tuis consiliis nullo loco defuturum, Cic.; imprimis hoc volunt persuadere, non interire animas, Caes.; pass. impers., hoc ipsis Siculis ita persuasum est, Cic. **II.** *to persuade, prevail upon a person to adopt any course of action;* with or without dat. of pers. and with ut and the subj., or the subj. alone, or with rel. sent., or with the infin., huic persuadet uti ad hostes transeat, Caes.; with accus. of thing, quorum si utrumvis (Pompeio) persuasissem, Cic.; pass. impers., quibus persuasum est hostem persequi, Cic.

persŭāsĭo -ōnis, f. (persuadeo), 1, *a con-*

vincing, persuasion, Cic. ; **2,** *a conviction, belief, opinion ;* superstitionum persuasione, Tac.

persuāsus -ū, m. (persuadeo), *persuasion ;* huius persuasu, Cic.

persubtīlis -e, 1, *very fine, very subtle,* Lucr. ; 2, *very subtle, very refined ;* oratio, Cic.

persulto, 1. (salto). **I.** Intransit., *to leap, skip about a place ;* in agro, Liv. **II.** Transit., *to range through ;* captam Italiam, Tac.

pertaedet -taesum est, 2. impers. *to be weary of, disgusted with anything ;* pertaesum est levitatis, Cic.; vos injuriae pertaesum est, Sall.

pertendo -tendi -tensum and -tentum, 3. **I.** *to continue, carry through ;* aliquid, Ter. **II.** *to direct one's steps anywhere, to go ;* pars maxima Romam pertenderunt, Liv.

pertento, 1. **I.** *to prove, test, try.* **A.** Lit., pugionem utrumque, Tac. **B.** Transf., a, *to put to the test ;* adolescentium animos, Liv. ; b, *to consider, to examine ;* perspice rem et pertenta, Cic. **II.** *to seize, lay hold of, affect ;* tremor pertentat corpora, Verg.

pertĕnŭis -e, 1, *very fine, very small,* Plin. ; 2, *very small, very slight ;* **s**pes salutis, Cic. ; suspicio, Cic.

pertĕrĕbro, 1. *to bore through ;* columnam, Cic.

pertergĕo -tersi -tersum, 2. *to wipe off, wipe up.* **I.** Lit., gausape mensam, Hor. **II.** Transf., *to touch gently,* Lucr.

perterrĕfăcĭo (-fēci) -factum, 3. (perterreo and facio), *to frighten, terrify exceedingly,* Ter.

perterrĕo -terrŭi -terrĭtum, 2. *to frighten, terrify exceedingly ;* maleficii conscientiā perterritus, Cic.

perterrĭcrĕpus -a -um, *sounding, rattling terribly,* Lucr.

pertexo -texŭi -textum, 3. *to weave entirely ;* transf., *to complete, accomplish ;* pertexe modo quod exorsus es, Cic.

pertĭca -ae, f. *a long pole or rod,* Ov.

pertĭmĕfactus -a -um (pertimeo and facio), *frightened exceedingly,* ap. Cic.

pertĭmesco -tĭmŭi, 3. (pertimeo), *to fear exceedingly, be very much afraid of ;* nullius potentiam, Cic. ; de suis periculis, Cic.

pertĭnācĭa -ae, f. (pertinax), *firmness, obstinacy, pertinacity ;* hominum nimia pertinacia et arrogantia, Caes. ; in pertinacia perstare, Liv. ; frangere pertinaciam, Liv.

pertĭnācĭtĕr, adv. (pertinax), *firmly, obstinately, pertinaciously ;* fusos insequi, Liv.

pertĭnax -ācis (per and tenax). **I.** *having a firm hold, tenacious ;* digito male pertinaci, Hor. **II.** *firm, persistent, persevering, pertinacious, obstinate ;* virtus, Liv. ; concertatio, Cic. ; pertinax ad obtinendam injuriam, Liv.

pertĭnĕo -tĭnŭi, 2. (per and teneo), *to reach to, extend to.* **I.** Lit., venae in omnes partes corporis pertinentes, Cic. ; Belgae pertinent ad inferiorem partem fluminis Rheni, Caes. **II.** Transf., 1, *to reach, extend, spread ;* eadem bonitas ad multitudinem pertinet, Cic. ; 2, *to tend towards, to have as an object or result ;* ea quae ad effeminandos animos pertinent, Caes. ; quorsum pertinet? *of what service is it ? of what good is it ?* Hor. ; 3, *to relate, pertain, belong to ;* a, illa res at officium meum pertinet, Cic. ; interpretando, quorsum quidque pertineat, Cic. ; b, *to attach to, to fall upon ;* ad quem suspicio maleficii pertineat, Cic. ; 4, *to have an influence upon, affect ;* si quid hoc ad rem pertinet, Cic. ; 5, *to relate to ;* quod or quantum pertinet ad, with

acc., *in relation to ;* quod ad populum pertinet, Cic.

pertingo, 3. (per and tango), *to stretch out, extend to ;* collis in immensum pertingens, Sall.

pertŏlĕro, 1. *to endure to the end, bear completely,* Lucr.

pertorquĕo, 2. *to twist, distort,* Lucr.

pertractātĭo -ōnis, f. (pertracto), *an occupying or busying oneself with, application to anything ;* rerum publicarum, Cic.

pertracto (pertrecto), 1. **I.** *to touch with the hands, lay hold of, handle, feel ;* barbatulos mullos exceptare de piscina et pertractare, Cic. **II.** Transf., a, *to busy oneself with, treat, study ;* philosophiam, Cic.; b, *to influence, work upon ;* sensus mentesque hominum, Cic.

pertrăho -traxi -tractum, 3. *to drag to a place ;* a, *to forcibly conduct ;* aliquem in castra, Liv. ; b, *to entice or allure to a place ;* hostem ad insidiarum locum, Liv.

pertrecto = pertracto (q.v.).

pertristis -e, 1, *very sorrowful,* ap. Cic. ; 2, *very austere ;* quidam patruus, Cic.

pertŭmultŭōsē, adv. *in an agitated or tumultuous manner ;* nuntiare, Cic.

pertundo -tŭdi -tūsum (-tussum) and -tunsum, 3. *to bore through, thrust through, push through,* Cat.

perturbātē, adv. (perturbatus), *confusedly, in a disorderly manner ;* dicere, Cic.

perturbātĭo -ōnis, f. (perturbo), *confusion, disorder, disquiet.* **I.** Lit., caeli, *stormy weather,* Cic. **II.** Transf., **A.** *confusion, disorder ;* rationis atque ordinis, Cic. ; animorum, Cic. ; vitae, Cic. **B.** 1, *political disorder, disquiet, disturbance ;* magnā rerum perturbatione impendente, Cic. ; 2, *passion, emotion ;* perturbationes sunt genere quatuor, aegritudo, formido, libido, laetitia, Cic.

perturbātrix -īcis, f. (perturbo), *she that disturbs,* Cic.

perturbātus -a -um, p. adj. (from perturbo), *confused, disquieted, disturbed ;* numquam vidi hominem perturbatiorem metu, Cic.

perturbo, 1. *to disturb greatly, bring into complete confusion.* **I.** Lit., aciem, Sall. ; ordines, Caes. **II.** Transf., **A.** *to disturb, confuse ;* conditiones factionesque bellicas perjurio, *to break,* Cic. **B.** 1, *to disturb politically ;* provinciam, Cic. ; 2, *to disturb the feelings, to disquiet, alarm ;* de reipublicae salute perturbari, Cic.; perturbari animo, Caes.

perturpis -e, *very base, very disgraceful,* Cic.

pertūsus -a -um, p. adj. (from pertundo) *bored through, perforated ;* dolium a fundo pertusum, Liv.

pĕrungo -unxi -unctum, 3. *to anoint thoroughly, besmear ;* corpora oleo, Cic.

pĕrurbānus -a -um, 1, *very polite, refined, witty,* Cic. ; 2, in a bad sense, *over-polite,* Cic.

pĕrurgĕo -ursi, 2. *to urge greatly, earnestly press upon,* Suet.

pĕruro -ussi -ustum, 3. **I.** *to burn thoroughly, to burn up ;* agrum, Liv. **II. A.** *to inflame* (with love, etc.) ; perurimur aestu, Ov. ; perustus inani gloriā, Cic. **B.** 1, *to gall, chafe, inflame ;* subducant oneri colla perusta boves, Ov. ; 2, *to pinch, nip with cold ;* terra perusta gelu, Ov.

Pĕrŭsĭa -ae, f. *one of the twelve allied Etruscan towns,* now *Perugia.* Hence, **Pĕrŭsīnus** -a -um, *belonging to Perusia.*

pĕrūtĭlis -e, *very useful,* Cic.

pervādo -vāsi -vāsum, 3. **I.** *to go through, come through, pass through.* **A.** Lit., incendium per agros pervasit, Cic.; per aequa et iniqua loca, Liv. **B.** Transf., *pervade;* opinio quae per animos gentium barbararum pervaserat, Cic. **II.** *to attain, to reach to, to arrive at.* **A.** Lit., in Italiam, Cic.; ad castra, Liv. **B.** Transf., *to reach to;* locus nullus est quo non hominum libido pervaserit, Cic.

pervăgātus -a -um, p. adj. (from pervagor). **I.** *spread abroad, well known;* sermo, Cic.; pervagatissimus versus, Cic.; neut. plur. subst., ista communia et pervagata, *those well-known rules,* Cic. **II.** *common, general;* pars est pervagatior, Cic.

pervăgor -ātus sum, 1. **I.** Intransit., *to wander, to rove about.* **A.** Lit., omnibus in locis, Caes. **B.** Transf., *to be widely spread;* a, = *to become known everywhere;* quod in exteris nationibus usque ad ultimas terras pervagatum est, Cic.; b, *to become common;* ne is honos nimium pervagetur, Cic. **II.** Transit., *to wander through.* **A.** Lit., bello prope orbem terrarum, Liv. **B.** Transf., cupiditates, timores omnium mentes pervagantur, Cic.

pervăgus -a -um, *wandering everywhere;* puer, Ov.

pervălĕo -ŭi, 2. *to be very strong,* Lucr.

pervărĭē, adv. *very variously,* Cic.

pervasto, 1. *to devastate, lay waste completely;* omnia ferro flammāque, Liv.

peī věho -vexi -vectum, 3. **I.** *to carry through, conduct through;* commeatus, Liv.; pass., pervehi, as middle, *to travel, sail, pass through,* Tac. **II.** *to carry, lead, conduct, bring to a place;* virgines Caere, Liv.; pass., pervehi, as middle = *to travel to;* Chalcidem, Liv.; in portum (fig.), Cic.

pervello -velli, 3. *to pluck, pull, twitch violently.* **I.** Lit., aurem, Phaedr.; stomachum, *to excite,* Hor. **II.** Fig., *to pinch, hurt, pain;* si te forte dolor aliquis pervellerit, Cic.; hence, *to disparage, revile;* jus civile, Cic.

pervĕnĭo -vēni -ventum, 4. *to arrive at, come to, reach.* **I.** Lit., Germani in fines Eburonum pervenerunt, Caes.; ad portam, Cic. **II.** Transf., a, of persons, *to attain to, to arrive at, reach;* in maximam invidiam, Cic.; in senatum, *to become a senator,* Cic.; in scripta alicuius, *to be mentioned by an author,* Cic.; ad suum, *to obtain one's own,* Cic.; ad primos comoedos, *to attain to the rank of,* Cic.; b, of things, *to come to;* pecunia ad Verrem pervenit, Cic.

perversē, adv. (perversus), *wrongly, perversely;* interpretari, Cic.; uti deorum beneficio, Cic.

perversĭtas -ātis, f. (perversus), *perversity;* hominum, Cic.; opinionum, Cic.

perversus -a -um, p. adj. (from perverto), *crooked, awry, askew.* **I.** Lit., perversissimi oculi, *squinting dreadfully,* Cic. **II.** *perverse, froward, wrong;* sapientia Tuberonis, Cic.

perverto (pervorto) -verti (-vorti) -versum (-vorsum), 3. *to turn upside down, overturn, overthrow.* **I.** Lit., tecta, Cic. **II.** Transf., **A.** *to invert, pervert;* perverso more, *against tradition, custom,* etc., Cic.; perverso numine, *against the will of the gods,* Verg. **B.** Meton., *to overthrow, destroy, pervert;* amicitiam aut justitiam, Cic.; omnia jura divina atque humana, Cic. **C.** *to trip up, put down;* numquam (ille me) ullo artificio pervertet, Cic.

pervespĕri, adv *very late in the evening,* Cic.

pervestīgātĭo -ōnis, f. (pervestigo), *a tracking out, investigation,* Cic.

pervestīgo, 1. *to track out.* **I.** Lit., of hunting dogs, Cic. **II.** Fig., *to investigate, search into;* pervestigare et cognoscere, Cic.

pervĕtus -ĕris, *very old;* rex, Cic.; amicitia, Cic.

pervĕtustus -a -um, *very old;* verba, Cic.

pervĭcācĭa -ae, f. (pervicax), *persistency;* usually in a bad sense, *obstinacy, stubbornness;* mulierositas, pervicacia, ligurritio, Cic.; pervi cacia tua et superbia, Liv.; pervicacia in hostem. *firmness,* Tac.

pervĭcācĭtĕr, adv. (pervicax), *firmly, obstinately, stubbornly;* compar., pervicacius, Liv.

pervĭcax -ācis (*pervico for pervinco), *firm, unyielding;* in a bad sense, *stubborn, obstinate;* virtus, Liv.; with genit., pervicax irae, Tac.; with adversus, adversus peritos pervicax, Tac.

pervĭdĕo -vīdi -visum, 2. **I.** *to overlook, look at, regard, behold;* 1, lit., sol qui pervidet omnia, Ov.; 2, transf., a, cunctaque mens oculis pervidet usa suis, Ov.; b, *to look over = to review;* quum tua pervideas oculis mala lippus inunctis, Hor. **II.** *to look through and through;* 1, lit., *to distinguish;* ut neque . . . quae cuiusque stipitis palma sit pervideri possit, Liv.; 2, transf., a, *to examine;* quid ea postulat pervidendum, Cic.; b, *to look at, perceive, discern;* animi mei firmitatem, Cic.; meton., *to consider, examine;* videbo te et pervidebo, Cic.

pervĭgĕo -gŭi, 2. *to flourish, bloom continually;* opibus atque honoribus perviguere, *remained long in possession of,* Tac. [*ing,* Ov.

pervĭgil -ilis, *very watchful, always watch-*

pervĭgĭlātĭo -ōnis, f. (pervigilo), *a vigil, a religious watching,* Cic.

pervĭgĭlĭum -ii, n. 1, *a watching throughout the night,* Plin.; 2, *a religious watching, vigil;* castra pervigilio neglecta, Liv.; pervigilium celebrare, Tac.

pervĭgĭlo, 1. *to watch, remain awake throughout the night;* noctem, Cic.

pervīlis -e, *very cheap;* annona, Liv.

pervinco -vici -victum, 3. **I.** Intransit., *to gain a complete victory.* **A.** Lit., pervicit Vardanes, Tac. **B.** Transf., *to carry one's point;* pervicit Cato, Cic. **II.** Transit., *to conquer completely, subdue utterly.* **A.** Lit., Plaut. **B.** Transf., 1, *to surpass, outdo;* voces pervincunt sonum, Hor.; 2, *to induce, prevail upon, succeed in prevailing;* with ut and the subj., multis rationibus pervicerat Rhodios ut Romanam societatem retinerent, Liv.; *to bring about with difficulty;* pervicerunt remis ut tenerent terram, Liv.; 3, *to prove, demonstrate;* aliquid dictis, Lucr.

pervĭus -a -um (per and via), *passable, accessible, having a road through;* pervius usus, Verg. Æn. II. **I.** Lit., loca equo pervia, Ov.; transitiones, Cic. Subst., **pervĭum** -ii, n. *a passage,* Tac. **II.** Fig., *accessible;* nihil ambitioni pervium, Tac.

pervolgo = pervulgo (q.v.).

pervŏlĭto, 1. (intens. of 1. pervolo), *to fly through or round, to flit about;* omnia late loca, Verg.

1. **pervŏlo,** 1. **I.** *to fly through, fly round;* 1, lit., aedes, Verg.; iter aërium, Ov.; 2, transf., of any rapid motion, sex milia passuum cisiis, Cic. **II.** *to fly to a place;* in hanc sedem, Cic.

2. **pervŏlo** -vŏlŭi -velle, *to wish greatly, to be very desirous;* pervelim scire, Cic.

pervŏlūto, 1. (intens. of pervolvo), *to roll round;* esp., *to unroll, read a book;* libros, Cic.

pervŏlvo -volvi -vŏlūtum, 3. *to roll about.* **I.** Gen., 1, lit., aliquem in luto, Ter.; 2, fig., ut in iis locis pervolvatur animus, *may be en-*

vaged in, Cic. **II.** *to turn over a book, to read.*

pervorsē, pervorsio, pervorto, etc. = per-verse, perversio, perverto, etc. (q.v.).

pervulgātus -a -um, p. adj. (from pervulgo), 1, *very usual, very common;* consolatio, Cic. ; 2, *well known;* ista maledicta pervulgata in omnes, Cic.

pervulgo (pervolgo), 1. **I.** *to publish, make publicly known;* 1, res in vulgus pervulgata, Cic. ; illas tabulas pervulgari atque edi P. R. imperavi, Cic. ; 2, of a woman, see *to prostitute herself*, Cic. **II.** *to visit or sojourn often in a place*, Lucr.

pēs, pĕdis, m. (πούς), *the foot* (used both of men and animals). **I.** Lit., 1, calcei apti ad pedem, Cic. ; pedem ferre, *to go*, Verg. ; pedem portā non efferre, Cic. ; pedem referre, Cic., revocare, *to go back, return*, Verg. ; pedibus, *on foot*, also *by land*, Cic. ; servus a pedibus, *an attendant, lackey*, Cic. ; accidere ad pedes alicuius, Cic. ; prohibiti estis in provincia vestra pedem ponere, Cic. ; pede pulsare terram, *to dance*, Hor. ; 2, esp., a, milit. t. t., pedibus merere, *to serve in the infantry*, Liv. ; descendere ad pedes (of cavalry), *to dismount*, Liv. ; pedem conferre, *to fight hand to hand*, Liv. ; b, as polit. t. t. (of senators), pedibus ire in sententiam alicuius, *to agree with, support some one's proposal*, Liv. ; ne (quis) pedibus iret, *should vote*, Cic. ; 3, fig., sub pedibus, *under the power of*, Liv. ; sub pedibus esse or jacere, *to be thought little of*, Ov. ; so sub pede ponere, Hor. ; pedem opponere, *to withstand*, Ov. ; pedem trahere, *to limp* (of iambic verse), Ov. ; per me ista trahantur pedibus, *may as far as I am concerned be turned topsy-turvy, may go to the dogs*, Cic. ; ante pedes positum esse, *to be before one's feet* or *eyes*, Cic. ; circum pedes = circum se, Cic. ; ante pedes Manilii, *before Manilius*, Cic. ; pes secundus, felix, dexter, *happy* or *fortunate arrival*, Verg., Ov. **II. A.** Transf., 1, poet., of water, crepante lympha desilit pede, Hor. ; of time, tacito pede lapsa vetustas, Ov. ; 2, a, *the foot of a chair, table*, or *other article of furniture*, Tac. ; b, pes veli, *the rope* or *sheet attached to the lower edge of a sail, by which it was tightened or relaxed;* hence, pede aequo, *with fair wind*, Ov. ; facere pedem, *to veer out the sheet to catch a side wind*, Verg. ; c, *the pole on which a litter is carried*, Cat. **B.** Meton., 1, pedibus vincere, *in a foot-race*, Ov. ; 2, esp., a, t. t. of poetry, *a metrical foot*, Cic. ; b, *a metre, species of verse ;* Lesbius, Hor. ; c, *a foot*, as a measure of length ; pedem non egressi sumus, Cic. ; citus pes, the iamb.

pessĭmus, pessime, v. malus.

Pessĭnūs (Pěsĭnūs) -untis, f. (Πεσσινοῦς, Πεσινοῦς -οῦντος), *one of the most celebrated towns of Galatia, near Mount Dindymus, chief seat of the worship of Cybele*, now *Balahazar* or *Bala-hissar*. Adj., **Pessinuntĭus** -a -um, *relating to Pessinus*.

pessŭlus -i, m. (πάσσαλος), *a bolt;* pessulum ostio obdere, Ter.

pessum, adv. (for pedis versum), *to the ground, to the bottom, downwards ;* pessum ire, *to sink to the ground*, Cic. ; *to be ruined, to perish*, Tac. Esp., **pessum do** (or pessumdo, or pessundo) dēdi, dătum, dăre, *to let fall to the ground, to destroy, ruin, put an end to*, Sall. ; ad inertiam pessum datus est, *sunk into*, Sall.

pestĭfĕr -fĕra -fĕrum and **pestĭfĕrus** -a um (pestis and fero), 1, *pestiferous, pestilential ;* odor corporum, Liv. ; 2, transf., *deadly, fatal, destructive, injurious;* vipera, Cic. ; civis, Cic.

pestĭfĕrē, adv. (pestifer), *balefully, injuriously*, Cic.

pestĭlens -entis (pestis). **I.** *pestilential, unhealthy ;* aedes, Cic. ; annus pestilentissimus, Cic. **II.** Transf., *deadly, fatal, noxious ;* homo pestilentior, Cic.

pestĭlentĭa -ae, f. (pestilens), *pestilence, plague, infectious disease.* **I.** Lit., and meton., 1, lit., causa pestilentiae, Cic. ; pestilentiā laborare, Liv. ; 2, meton., *unhealthy air, weather, place ;* pestilentiae possessores (of unhealthy places), Cic. ; autumni, Caes. **II.** Transf. (moral), *plague, pest*, Cat.

pestĭlĭtas -ātis, f. = pestilentia (q.v.).

pestis -is, f. **I.** *a pest, pestilence, plague, infectious disease, malaria*, Gk. ΠΕΤ, pestem ab Aegypto avertere, Cic. **II.** Transf., **A.** *destruction, ruin, death ;* pestem in aliquem machinari, Cic. ; illam a republica pestem depellere, Cic. **B.** Meton., *an injurious thing or person, a pest, curse, bane;* illae inclusae in republica pestes, Cic.

pĕtăsātus -a -um (petasus), *wearing the petasus* (q.v.) = *equipped for a journey*, Cic.

pĕtăsĭo (pĕtăso) -ōnis, m. (πετασών), *a fore-quarter of pork*, Varr.

pĕtăsuncŭlus -i, m. (dim. of petaso), *a little fore-quarter of pork*, Juv.

pĕtăsus -i, m. (πέτασος), *a broad-brimmed felt hat, used by travellers*, Plaut.

pĕtaurum -i, n. (πέταυρον), *a spring-board used by tumblers and rope-dancers*, Juv.

Pĕtēlĭa (Pĕtīlĭa) -ae, f. *a town in the Bruttian territory colonised by the Lucanians*, now *Strongoli*. Hence, adj., **Pĕtēlīnus** -a -um, Petelian.

pĕtesso (pĕtisso), 3. (peto), *to desire, long for, strive after eagerly ;* aliquid, Cic.

pĕtītĭo -ōnis, f. (peto). **I.** *an attack, thrust, blow ;* tuas petitiones effugi, Cic. ; *an attack in words;* novi omnes hominis petitiones rationesque dicendi, Cic. **II.** Transf., 1, *a requesting ;* a, petitio indutiarum, Liv. ; b, *an application for office, candidature;* consulatūs, Caes. ; dare se petitioni, Cic. ; 2, a, *a suit, legal claim*, Cic. ; b, *a right of claim, a right to bring an action ;* cuius sit petitio, Cic.

pĕtītor -ōris, m. (peto), *one who strives after anything.* **I.** *a candidate*, Hor. **II.** *the plaintiff in a civil or private suit*, Cic.

pĕtītŭrĭo, 4. (desider. of peto), *to desire to become a candidate ;* video hominem valde petiturire, Cic.

pĕtītus -ūs, m. (peto), *an inclining towards*, Lucr.

pĕto -īvi and -ĭi -ītum, 3. (root PET, whence impet-o, impes, impetus, Gk. ΠΕΤ, whence πέτο-μαι, πίπτω), *to reach towards.* **I.** Gen., **A.** Lit., a, with the hand, *to grasp;* Ilionea petit dextrā, Verg. ; b, with a weapon, *to fall upon, attack, assail, aim at, thrust at ;* caput et colluum, Cic. ; aliquem telis, Liv. ; c, with the feet or with other kinds of motion, (a) *to make for, go to, hasten to;* Dyrrhachium, Cic. ; loca calidiora, Cic. ; caelum pennis, *to fly to*, Ov. ; transf., of inanimate objects, mons petit astra, rears its head towards, Ov. ; (β) *to go to a person, to approach;* ut te supplex peterem, Verg. ; (γ) *to take a certain direction, to take a road;* alium cursum petere, Cic. **B.** Transf., 1, *to attack, assail;* qui me epistolā petivit, Cic. ; aliquem fraude, Liv. ; 2, *to ask, require, claim, beg, beseech, request, entreat;* a, alicuius vitam, Cic. ; pacem a Romanis, Caes. ; with ut and the subj., peto a te ut, etc., Cic. ; with subj. alone, abs te peto, efficias ut, etc., Cic. ; with ne and the subj., peto a te ne me putes, etc., Cic. ; transf., of inanimate objects, quantum res petit, *needs or demands*, Cic. ; b, *to make a claim at* *law*, *to bring an action*, *to sue for*; hereditatis possessionem, Cic. ; c, *to sue for*, *to solicit*; (α) *to become a candidate for public office*; consulatum, Cic. ; (β) *to woo a maiden*; virginem petiere juvenes, Liv. ; 3, *to seek for*; a, sedes apibus statioque petenda, Verg. ; b, *to seek*, *strive after*, *endeavour to obtain*; praedam pedibus, Ov. ; sapientiam, Cic. ; mortem, Cic. ; *with* infin., Verg. **II.** *to fetch*, *derive*; 1, lit., a, *to fetch*; cibum e flamma, Ter. ; b, *to fetch*, *to bring forth*; gemitus alte de corde, Ov. ; 2, transf., a litteris oblivionem, Cic. (petit = petiit, Verg.).

pĕtorrĭtum (pĕtōrĭtum) -i, n. *an open*, *four-wheeled Gallic carriage*.

1. **pĕtra** -ae, f. (πέτρα), *a stone, rock*, Plin.

2. **Petra** -ae, f. (Πέτρα). **I.** *a town in Arabia Petraea*, now *ruins of Wady Musa*. **II.** *a town in Sicily*. Hence, **Petrīni** -ōrum, m. *the inhabitants of Petra*.

Pĕtrējus -ii, m., M., *a Roman general, legate of Pompey in the Civil War*.

Pĕtrīnum -i, n. *an estate near Sinuessa in Campania*.

Pĕtrŏcŏrĭi -ōrum, m. *a Gallic tribe in Aquitania*, in modern *Perigord*.

Pĕtrōnĭus -ii, m., T. (or C.) Arbiter, *a Roman satirist under Nero*.

pĕtŭlans -antis (*petulo, from peto), *freakish, capricious, pert, wanton, froward, petulant*; and esp., *wanton, lustful*; homo, Cic. ; genus dicendi, Cic.

pĕtŭlantĕr, adv. (petulans), *freakishly, capriciously, petulantly, frowardly, wantonly*; petulanter vivere, Cic. ; petulantius jactari, Cic. ; petulantissime fieri, Cic.

pĕtŭlantĭa -ae, f. (petulans), *capriciousness, freakishness, wantonness, petulance* (opp. pudor, modestia), Cic.

pĕtulcus -a -um (peto), *butting with the head*; agni, Lucr. ; haedi, Verg.

Peucĕtia -ae, f. *a district of Apulia*. Adj., **Peucĕtĭus** -a -um, *Peucetian*.

pexus -a -um (partic. of pecto), *hairy, woolly, having a nap*, and hence (of a garment), *new*, Hor.

Phacus -i, m. (Φάκος), *stronghold of the Macedonian kings, near Pella*.

Phaeāces -ācum, m. (Φαίακες), *the Phaeacians, mythical inhabitants of the island of Scheria* (identified with *Corcyra), famed for their prosperity*. Sing., **Phaeax** -ācis, m. *a Phaeacian*; pinguis Phaeaxque, *a comfortable, luxurious person*, Hor. Hence, **A. Phaeācius** -a -um, *Phaeacian*. **B. Phaeācis** -idis, f. *a poem on the stay of Ulysses among the Phaeacians*.

Phaedōn -ōnis, m. (Φαίδων), *disciple of Socrates and friend of Plato, who gave his name to a dialogue on the immortality of the soul*.

Phaedra -ae, f. (Φαίδρα), *daughter of Minos, sister of Ariadne and wife of Theseus; she fell in love with, and was (by a false accusation) the cause of the death of, her step-son Hippolytus*.

Phaedrus -i, m. (Φαῖδρος). **I.** *an Epicurean philosopher at Athens, teacher of Cicero*. **II.** *a disciple of Socrates*. **III.** *a freedman of Augustus, Thracian by birth, author of Latin fables*.

Phaestum -i, n. (Φαιστός). **I.** *a town on the south coast of Crete*. Hence, **Phaestĭas** -ādis, f. *a dweller in Phaestum*. **II.** *a town in Thessaly*.

Phăĕthon -ōntis, m. (Φαέθων), *the shining one*. **I.** Epithet of Helios, *the sun*. **II.** *the son of Helios and Clymene, who, attempting to drive the chariot of his father, set the world on fire, and*

was killed by a thunderbolt of Jupiter. Hence, **A.** Adj., **Phăĕthontēus** -a -um, *relating to Phaethon*. **B.** Subst., **Phăĕthontĭas** -ādis, f. ; plur., **Phăĕthontĭădes** -um, f. *the sisters of Phaethon, who were turned into poplars*.

Phăĕthūsa -ae, f. (Φαέθουσα), *a sister of Phaethon*.

phăgĕr -gri, m. (φάγρος), *a fish*, Ov.

Phălaecus -i, m. (Φάλαικος), *a tyrant of the Phocaeans*. Hence, adj., **Phălaeceus** -a -um, *of Phalaecus*.

phălangae (pălangae) -ārum, f. (φάλαγγες), *rollers on which heavy bodies were moved*, Caes.

phălangītae -ārum, m. (φαλαγγῖται), *soldiers belonging to a phalanx*, Liv.

Phălantus -i, m. (Φάλαντος), *a Spartan who emigrated to Italy and founded Tarentum*; regnata Laconi rura Phalanto, *the Tarentine territory*, Hor.

phălanx -angis, f. (φάλαγξ). **I.** Gen., *a closely-serried array of soldiers*, Verg. **II.** Esp., a, *a division of the Athenian and Spartan army drawn up in battle array, a phalanx*, Nep. ; b, *the Macedonian phalanx, a body of men* (from eight to sixteen thousand strong) *drawn up in a close parallelogram, fifty men abreast and sixteen deep*; c, transf., *the order of battle array among the Gauls and Germans drawn up in a parallelogram*; phalange factā, *in close formation*, Cic.

Phălăra -ōrum, n. (Φάλαρα), *a port in Thessaly on the Sinus Maliacus*, now *Stylidha*.

Phălărĭs -idis, m. (Φαλαρίς), *a tyrant of Agrigentum, notorious for his cruelty* (v. Perillus).

Phălăsarna -ae, f. (Φαλάσαρνα), *a town in Crete*. Adj., **Phălăsarnēus** -a -um, *of Phalasarna*.

phălērae (fălērae) -ārum, f. (φάλαρα). **I.** *a metal ornament worn on the breast as a military decoration*, Cic. **II.** *a trapping on a horse's head and breast*, Liv., Verg.

phălĕrātus -a -um (phalerae), *adorned with the phalerae*; equi, Liv.

Phălērum -i, n. (Φαληρόν), *the oldest port of Athens, connected with the city by a long wall*. Hence, **A. Phălēreus** -ĕi and -ĕos, m. *belonging to Phalerum*; Demetrius Phalereus, or simply Phalereus, *regent of Athens* (about 300 B.C.). **B. Phălērĭus** -a-um, *belonging to Phalerum*; subst., **Phălērĭcus** -i, m. (sc. portus), *the harbour of Phalerum*.

Phānae -ārum, f. (Φαναί), *harbour and promontory in the south of Chios*, now *Cap Mastico, the country near which was famous for its wine*; adj., **Phānaeus** -a -um, *Phanean*; rex Phanaeus, poet. for *Phanaean wine* (as the king among wines), Verg.

Phantăsos -i, m. (Φάντασος), *a son of Somnus*.

Phāon -ōnis, m. (Φάων), *a youth of Lesbos, beloved by Sappho*.

phăretra -ae, f. (φαρέτρα), *a quiver*, Verg.

phărĕtrātus -a -um (phaetra), *furnished with a quiver, wearing a quiver*; virgo, Diana, Ov. ; puer, Cupid, Ov.

pharmăceutrĭa -ae, f. (φαρμακευτρία), *the sorceress* (title of Vergil's Eighth Eclogue).

pharmăcŏpōla (-ēs) -ae, m. (φαρμακοπώλης), *a seller of drugs, a quack*, Cic.

Pharnăces -is, m. (Φαρνάκης), *king in Pontus, son of Mithridates, conquered by Caesar*.

Pharsālus (-ŏs) -i, f. (Φάρσαλος), *a town in Thessaly, near which Pompeius was defeated by Caesar,* 48 B.C., *now Pharsa.* Hence, adj., **Pharsālīcus** -a -um and **Pharsālīus** -a -um, *Pharsalian.*

Phărus (-ŏs) -i, f. (Φάρος), *an island off Alexandria, where Ptolemy Philadelphus built a light-house;* adj., **Phărīus** -a -um, a, *relating to Pharus;* b, *Egyptian;* juvenca, *Io,* Ov.; turba, *the priests of Isis,* Tib.; conjux, *Cleopatra,* Mart.

Phăsēlis -ĭdis, f. (Φασηλίς), *a town in Lycia, on the border of Pamphylia.* Hence, **Phăsēlītae** -ārum, m. *the inhabitants of Phaselis.*

phăsēlus (-ŏs) -i, m. and f. (φάσηλος), 1, *an edible bean, the kidney-bean,* Verg.; 2, *a kind of light skiff formed of osiers or papyrus, or burnt and painted clay,* Cic.

Phăsis -ĭdis and -ĭdos, m. (Φᾶσις), *a river in Colchis, falling into the Black Sea, now Rion or Rioni.* Hence, **A. Phăsis** -ĭdis, f. adj. *Phasian,* poet. = *Colchian;* volucres, *pheasants,* Mart.; subst., *Phasis* (sc. femina), *the Colchian woman* = *Medea,* Ov. **B. Phăsĭăcus** -a -um (Φασιακός), *Phasian,* poet. = *Colchian.* **C. Phăsĭānus** (**Făsĭānus**) -a -um, avis, and simply *Phasiana,* Plin., or *Phasianus,* Suet., *a pheasant.* **D. Phăsĭăs** -ădis, f. (Φασιάς), *Phasian,* poet. = *Colchian;* puella, and simply *Phasias,* = *Medea,* Ov.

phasma -ătis, n. (φάσμα), *a ghost, spectre* (title of a comedy of Meander, and of a poem by Catullus), Ter., Juv.

phatnē -ēs, f. (φάτναι), *the Crib, a space between two stars of the constellation Cancer,* Cic.

Phēgeus -ĕi and -ĕos, m. (Φηγεύς), *king of Psophis.* Hence, **A.** Adj., **Phēgēius** -a -um, *belonging to Phegeus.* **B.** Subst., **Phēgĭs** -ĭdis, f. *the daughter of Phegeus.*

Phēmĭus -ii, m. (Φήμιος), *a celebrated harp-player in Ithaca;* hence, appell., *a good harp-player,* Ov.

Phĕnĕus (-ŏs) -i, f. (Φένεος), *a town in Arcadia.* Hence, **Phĕnĕātae** -ārum, m. *the inhabitants of Pheneos.*

phengītēs -ae, m. (φεγγίτης), *selenite or crystallised gypsum* (used for window panes), Suet.

Phĕrae -ārum, f. (Φέραι). **I.** *a town in Messenia, near modern Kalamata.* **II.** *a city in Thessaly, the residence of Admetus and of the tyrant Alexander, now Valestino;* hence, adj., **Phĕraeus** -a -um, *Pherean,* or *Thessalian;* vaccae, *of Admetus,* Ov.; gens, *a cruel race, like that of the tyrant Alexander of Pherae,* Ov.

Phĕrēclus -i, m. (Φέρεκλος), *a ship-builder who built the ship in which Paris carried off Helen.* Hence, adj., **Phĕrēclēus** -a -um, *of Phereclus.*

Phĕrĕcȳdēs -is, m. (Φερεκύδης). **I.** *a philosopher of Scyros, teacher of Pythagoras.* Hence, adj., **Phĕrĕcȳdēus** -a -um, *of Pherecydes.* **II.** *an Athenian chronicler,* flor. 480 B.C.

Phĕrēs -ētis, m. (Φέρης), *prince in Thessaly, father of Admetus.* Hence, **Phĕrētĭădēs** -ae, m. *son of Pheres* = *Admetus.*

phiăla -ae, f. (φιάλη), *a drinking-vessel,* broad at the bottom, *bowl, saucer,* Juv.

Phĭdĭās -ae, m. (Φειδίας), *a celebrated sculptor of Athens, contemporary of Pericles.* Hence, **Phĭdĭăcus** -a -um, *of Phidias.*

Phĭlădelphēni (**Phĭlădelphīni**) -ōrum, m. *the inhabitants of Philadelphia in Asia Minor.*

Phīlaeni -ōrum, and Gr. -ōn, m. (Φίλαινοι), *two Carthaginian brothers who submitted to be buried alive for the sake of their country;* arae *Philaenorum* and *Philaenon, a port on the borders of Cyrene.*

Phīlammōn -ōnis, m. (Φιλάμμων), *son of Apollo and Chione, a celebrated singer.*

Phĭlippi -ōrum, m. (Φίλιπποι), *a city in Macedonia, where Octavianus and Antony defeated Brutus and Cassius,* now *Filibah* or *Filibejik;* hence, adj., **A. Phĭlippensis** -e. **B. Phĭlippĭcus** -a -um, *relating to Philippi.*

Phĭlippŏpŏlis -ĕos, f. (Φιλιππόπολις), *a town in Thrace on the right bank of the Hebrus, now Philippopoli.*

Phĭlippus -i, m. (Φίλιππος). **I.** *the names of several kings of Macedon, the most celebrated of whom was the father of Alexander the Great;* meton., *a gold coin coined by Philip,* Hor.; hence, adj., **A. Phĭlippēus** -a -um, *belonging to Philip;* nummus, *a gold coin of King Philip, worth twenty drachmae.* **B. Phĭlippĭcus** -a -um, *relating to Philip;* orationes, *the speeches of Demosthenes against Philip;* subst., **Phĭlippĭcae** -ārum, f. *the speeches of Demosthenes against Philip, and of Cicero against Antonius.* **II.** *a Roman name, cognomen of the gens Marcia.*

Phĭlistus -i, m. (Φίλιστος), *a Greek historian of Syracuse, imitator of Thucydides.*

phĭlĭtĭa -ōrum, n. (φιλίτια), *the public meals of the Lacedaemonians,* Cic.

Phĭlo -ōnis, m. (Φίλων). **I.** *an academic philosopher, flourishing at Athens,* 91 B.C. **II.** *a celebrated Athenian architect.*

Phĭloctēta (-ēs) -ae, m. (Φιλοκτήτης), *son of Poeas, the companion of Hercules, whose bow and poisoned arrows he received after Hercules' death; joined in the expedition against Troy, but was left behind in the island of Lemnos wounded by a snake; brought to Troy in the tenth year of the war* (as Troy could not be taken without his arrows); *healed by Machaon; slew Paris.* Adj., **Phĭloctētaeus** -a -um, *belonging to Philoctetes.*

phĭlŏlŏgĭa -ae, f. (φιλολογία), *love of learning, study of letters,* Cic.

phĭlŏlŏgus -i, m. (φιλόλογος), *a learned man, a student of literature, a scholar,* Cic.

Phĭlŏmēla -ae, f. (Φιλομήλα). **I.** *the daughter of Pandion, king of Athens, turned into a nightingale.* **II.** Meton., *a nightingale,* Verg.

Phĭlŏmēlĭum -ii, n. (Φιλομήλιον), *a small town in the south-east of Phrygia, not far from the borders of Lycaonia, now Ak-cher.* Hence, **Phĭlŏmēlienses** -ium, m. *the inhabitants of Philomelium.*

Phĭlŏpoemēn -ĕnis, m. (Φιλοποίμην), *general of the Achaean League, born* 253 B.C.

phĭlŏsŏphĭa -ae, f. (φιλοσοφία). **I.** *philosophy,* Cic. **II.** Meton., **A.** *a philosophical subject,* Nep. **B.** Plur., *philosophiae, philosophical sects or systems,* Cic.

phĭlŏsŏphor, 1. dep. *to philosophise, to apply oneself to philosophy,* Cic.

phĭlŏsŏphus -a -um (φιλόσοφος), *philosophic.* **I.** Adj., Cic. **II.** Subst., **A.** **phĭlŏsŏphus** -i, m. *a philosopher,* Cic. **B.** **phĭlŏsŏpha** -ae, f. *a female philosopher,* Cic.

philtrum -i, n. (φίλτρον), *a love-potion, philtre,* Ov.

1. **phĭlȳra** -ae, f. (φιλύρα), *the inner bark of the linden-tree, of which bands for chaplets were made,* Hor.

2. **Phĭlўra** -ae, f. (Φίλυρα), a nymph, daughter of Oceanus, and mother of Chiron, changed into a linden-tree. Hence, **A. Phĭlўrēĭus** -a -um, relating to Philyra; heros, Chiron, Ov.; tecta, of Chiron, Ov. **B. Phĭlўrĭdēs** -ae, m. son of Philyra = Chiron, Ov.

phīmus -i, m. (φιμός), a dice-box, Hor.

Phīneus -ĕi and -ĕos, m. (Φινεύς). **I.** a king of Salmydessus in Thrace, who was deprived of sight and tormented by the Harpies for having put his sons to death on a false accusation. Hence, **A. Phīnēĭus** and **Phīnēus** -a -um, of or relating to Phineus. **B. Phīnĭdēs** -ae, m. a male descendant of Phineus. **II.** brother of Cepheus, fought with Perseus about Andromeda.

Phintĭa -ae, f. a town in Sicily.

Phintĭās -ae, m. (Φιντίας), a Pythagorean, famous for his friendship with Damon.

Phlĕgĕthōn -ontis, m. (Φλεγέθων, burning), a river in the infernal regions, in which fire flowed instead of water; adj., **Phlĕgĕthontĭs** -ĭdis, f. of Phlegethon; lympha, Ov.

Phlĕgra -ae, f. (Φλέγρα = φλεγυρά, burning), a district in Macedonia, afterwards called Pallene, where the gods were said to have killed the giants with lightning. Hence, adj., **Phlĕgraeus** -a -um, relating to Phlegra; campi, Ov.; transf., campus, the field of Pharsalia (because of the fierce battle fought there), Prop.

Phlĕgўās -ae, m. (Φλεγύας). **I.** king of the Lapithae, father of Ixion and Coronis. **II.** Plur., **Phlĕgўae** -ārum, m. a robber tribe in Thessaly.

Phlīus -untis, f. (Φλιοῦς), a city in the Peloponnese between Sicyon and Argos. Hence, adj., **Phliāsĭus** -a -um, of Phlius.

Phŏbētŏr -ŏris, m. (Φοβήτωρ), a son of Morpheus.

phōca -ae, f. and **phōcē** -ēs, f. (φώκη), a seal, sea-dog, sea-calf, Verg.

Phōcaea -ae, f. (Φώκαια), a sea-port in Ionia, mother-city of Massilia, now Fouges. Hence, **A. Phōcaeensis** -e, Phocaean. **B. Phōcaei** -ōrum, m. the Phocaeans. **C. Phōcăĭcus** -a -um, Phocaean.

Phōcĭs -ĭdis and -ĭdos, f. (Φωκίς), Phocis, a district in the north of Greece, between Boeotia and Aetolia. Hence, 1, **Phōcăĭcus** -a -um, Phocian; 2, **Phōcenses** -ĭum, m. the inhabitants of Phocis; 3, **Phōceus** -a -um, Phocian; juvenis Phoceus, or simply Phoceus, the Phocian = Pylades, son of Strophius, king of Phocis, Ov.; 4, **Phōcĭi** -ōrum, m. the Phocians.

Phōcus -i, m. (Φῶκος), son of Aeacus, brother of Peleus and Telamon.

Phoebē -ēs, f. (Φοίβη). **I.** a, the sister of Phoebus, the Moon-goddess, Diana; b, meton., Night, Ov. **II.** daughter of Leucippus. **III.** daughter of Leda and sister of Helena.

Phoebĭgĕna -ae, m. (Phoebus and geno = gigno), the son of Phoebus, Aesculapius, Verg.

Phoebus -i, m. (Φοῖβος), Apollo, the Sungod; poet. = sun; fugat astra Phoebus, Hor.; and = quarter of the heavens; sub utroque Phoebo, in the east and west, Ov. Hence, **A. Phoebās** -ādis, f. (Φοιβάς), priestess of Phoebus, a prophetess. **B. Phoebēĭus** -a -um and **Phoebēus** -a -um (Φοιβήϊος, Φοιβεῖος), of Phoebus; juvenis, Aesculapius, Ov.; ales, the raven, Ov.; virgo, Daphne, and poet. = laurel brown, Ov.

Phoenīcē, v. Phoenices.

Phoenīces -um, m. (Φοίνικες), the Phoe-

nicians, inhabitants of the district of Phoenicia, famous for their skill in navigation and commerce, founders of several colonies, Carthage, Hippo, etc. Hence, **A. Phoenīcē** -ēs, f. and **Phoenīca** -ae, f. (Φοινίκη), Phoenicia, a small strip of the coast of Syria, with the chief towns Tyre and Sidon. **B. Phoenissa** -ae, f. (Φοίνισσα), Phoenician; exsul, Anna, sister of Dido, Ov.

phoenīcoptĕros -i, m. (φοινικόπτερος), the flamingo, Juv.

Phoenix -īcis, m. (Φοῖνιξ). **I.** son of Amyntor, companion of Achilles at the Trojan War. **II.** a fabulous bird of Arabia, said to live 500 years, and then to be burnt to death; from the ashes of the dying bird a new phoenix was said to spring.

Phŏlŏē -ēs, f. (Φολόη), a woody mountain in Arcadia, on the border of Elis, now Olona.

Phŏlus -i, m. (Φόλος), a centaur.

Phorcus -i, m. (Φόρκος), **Phorcўs** -cўis, m. (Φόρκυς), and **Phorcyn** -cўnis, m. (Φόρκυν), a sea-god, son of Neptune, father of Medusa and her sisters. Hence, **A. Phorcĭs** -ĭdos, f. daughter of Phorcys; sorores Phorcides = Graeae Ov. **B. Phorcўnis** -ĭdis, f. the daughter of Phorcus, Medusa.

Phŏrōneus -ĕi and -ĕos, m. (Φορωνεύς), king of Argos, son of Inachus, brother of Io. Hence, **Phŏrōnis** -ĭdis, f. = Io, Ov.

Phrāātēs (Phrăhātēs) -is, m. name of several Parthian kings.

phrēnētĭcus -a -um (φρενητικός) and **phrĕnĭtĭcus** -a -um (φρενιτικός), mad, frantic, Cic.

Phrixus -i, m. (Φρίξος), son of Athamas and Nephele, brother of Helle, with whom he fled to Colchis on a ram with a golden fleece. Hence, adj., **Phrixēus** -a -um, belonging to Phrixus; stagna sororis Phrixeae, the Hellespont, Ov.

Phrўges -um, m. (Φρύγες), the Phrygians, the inhabitants of Phrygia, famous for their embroidery, but despised for their sloth and stupidity. Sing., **Phryx** -ўgis, adj. = Phrygian; subst., a Phrygian; esp., a, = Aeneas, Ov.; b, = a priest of Cybele, Prop. Hence, **A. Phrўgĭa** -ae, f. the country of Phrygia, in Asia Minor. **B. Phrўgĭus** -a -um (Φρύγιος), Phrygian, and poet. = Trojan; maritus, Aeneas, Ov., Pelops, Prop.; pastor, Paris, Verg.; tyrannus, Aeneas, Verg., Ov., Laomedon, Ov.; mater, Cybele, Verg.; vestes, embroidered, Verg.; buxum, the Phrygian flute, Ov.; lapis, Phrygian marble, Ov.

1. **Phryx** -ўgis, m. (Φρύξ), a river in Lydia, now Ocletschak-Su.

2. **Phryx**, v. Phryges.

Phryxeus, v. Phrixus.

Phthĭa -ae, f. (Φθία), a town in Thessaly, birth-place of Achilles. Hence, **A. Phthĭās** -ădis, f. (Φθιάς), a woman of Phthia. **B. Phthĭōtēs** -ae, m. (Φθιώτης), an inhabitant of Phthia. **C. Phthĭōtĭs** -ĭdis, f. (Φθιῶτις), Phthiotis, the district of Thessaly in which Phthia is. **D. Phthĭōtĭcus** -a -um (Φθιωτικός), meton. = Thessalian. **E. Phthĭus** -i, m. (Φθῖος), belonging to Phthia; rex, Peleus, Ov.; meton. = Thessalian, Liv.

Phўlăcē -ēs, f. (Φυλακή). **I.** a city in Thessaly, where Protesilaus reigned. Hence, **A. Phўlăceĭs** -ĭdis, f. belonging to Phylace; matres, Thessalian, Ov. **B. Phўlăceĭus** -a -um; conjux, Laodamia, Ov. **II.** a town in Molossis in Epirus.

Phўlăcus -i, m. (Φύλακος). **I.** founder of Phylace. **II.** grandfather of Protesilaus. Hence,

Phўlăcĭdēs -ae, m. (Φυλακίδης), *a descendant of Phylacus = Protesilaus,* Ov.

phўlarchus -i, m. (φύλαρχος), *the head of a tribe, an emir ;* Arabum, Cic.

Phyllŏs -i, f. (Φύλλος), *town in Thessaliotis.* Hence, **Phyllēïus** -a -um (Φυλλήϊος), poet. = *Thessalian ;* juvenis, Caeneus, Ov.

phўsĭca -ae, f. and **phўsĭcē** -ēs, f. (φυσική), *physics, natural science,* Cic.

phўsĭcē, adv. *in the manner of the natural philosophers ;* dicere, Cic.

phўsĭcus -a -um, *relating to physics or natural philosophy, physical.* **A.** Adj., ratio, Cic. **B.** Subst., 1, **phўsĭcus** -i, m. *a natural philosopher,* Cic.; 2, **phўsĭca** -ōrum, n. *natural philosophy, physics,* Cic.

phўsĭognōmōn -ŏnis, m. (φυσιογνώμων), *a physiognomist, one who judges men's characters by their features,* Cic.

phўsĭŏlŏgĭa -ae, f. (φυσιολογία), *natural philosophy,* Cic.

pĭābĭlis -e (pio), *expiable, that can be atoned for ;* fulmen, Ov.

pĭācŭlāris -e (piaculum), *atoning, expiating ;* sacrificia, and subst., **pĭācŭlāria** -ium, n. *expiatory sacrifices,* Liv.

pĭācŭlum -i, n. (pio). **I.** *any means of expiating sin or appeasing a deity.* **A.** *an expiatory sacrifice, a sin-offering,* Cic.; porco feminā piaculum pati, Cic.; transf., ut luendis periculis publicis piacula simus, Liv.; hence, *any means of healing, remedy,* Hor. **B.** *punishment ;* gravia piacula exigere, Liv. **II.** *that which renders an offering necessary, a sin, crime, evil deed ;* piaculum committere, Liv.

pĭāmen -ĭnis. n. (pio), *a means of atonement or expiation,* Ov.

pīca -ae, f. *a pie, magpie,* Ov.

pĭcārĭa -ae, f. (pix), *a place where pitch is made, a pitch-hut,* Cic.

pĭcĕa -ae, f. (pix), *the pitch-pine* (pinus silvestris, Linn.), Verg.

Pĭcēnum -i, n. *a district in the east of Italy on the Adriatic, famed for its oil.* Hence, **A. Pĭcens** -entis, *belonging to Picenum ;* **Pĭcentes** -ium, m. *the people of Picenum.* **B. Pĭcēnus** -a -um, *belonging to Picenum.*

pĭcĕus -a -um (pix), *pitchy, pitch-black ;* caligo, Verg.

pĭco, 1. (pix), *to pitch, smear, cover with pitch ;* cadus picatus, Verg.

Pictŏnes -um, m. *a people in Gallia Aquitania,* whence *Poitou.*

1. **pictor** -ōris, m. (pingo), *a painter,* Cic.

2. **Pictor** -ōris, m. *a surname in the gens Fabia,* v. Fabius.

pictūra -ae, f. (pingo). **I. A.** Lit., *painting, the art of painting ;* ars ratioque picturae, Cic. **B.** Meton., *a painting, picture ;* pictura textilis, *embroidery,* Cic. **II.** Fig., *a painting in words, picture, description,* Cic.

pictūrātus -a -um (pictura), *painted ;* vestes, *embroidered,* Verg.

pictus -a -um, p. adj. (from pingo). **I.** Of style, *ornamental, ornate, artistic ;* genus orationis, Cic. **II.** *unreal, vain ;* metus, Prop.

1. **pīcus** -i, m. *a woodpecker,* Ov.

2. **Pīcus** -i, m. (Πῖκος), *an Italian deity, husband of Canens, father of Faunus ; according to a later legend, changed by Circe into a woodpecker.*

pĭē, adv. (pius), *viously, dutifully* (opp. scelerate), Cic.

14

Pĭĕrĭa -ae, f. (Πιερία), *a district of Macedonia on the coast.*

Pĭĕrus (-ŏs) -i, m. (Πίερος). **I.** *king of Emathia, who gave his nine daughters the name of the nine Muses.* **II.** *a Macedonian, father of the nine Muses.* Hence, **A. Pĭĕris** -ĭdis, f. (Πιερίς), *a Muse.* Plur., Pierides, *the Muses.* **B. Pĭĕrius** -a -um, *Pierian ;* subst., Pieriae, *the Muses,* Cic.; hence, poet., via, *the study of poetry,* Ov.; modi, *poems,* Hor.

pĭĕtas -ātis, f. (pius), *dutifulness.* **I.** Lit., a, *towards the gods, piety ;* est pietas justitia adversus deos, Cic.; b, *dutifulness towards parents, native country, benefactors ; filial piety, gratitude, patriotism ;* quid est pietas nisi voluntas grata in parentes ? Cic.; in patrem patriamque, Liv.; c, *justice, equity,* Verg.; d, *kindness, compassion,* Verg. **II.** Pietas, personif. *as a goddess with two temples in Rome.*

pĭger -gra -grum (root PIG, whence piget), *disinclined, unwilling, lazy, slothful.* **I.** Lit., serpens frigore pigra, Ov.; with in and the abl., in labore militari, Cic.; with ad and the acc., gens pigerrima ad militaria opera, Liv.; with genit., militiae, Hor.; with infin., ferre laborem scribendi. **II.** Transf., **A.** *inactive, slow ;* bellum, *tedious,* Ov.; campus, *unfruitful,* Hor.; pectora, *insensible,* Ov. **B.** Of waters, *flowing slowly, sluggish, stagnant ;* palus, Ov.

pĭget -gŭit -gĭtum est, 2. impers. **I.** Lit., *it causes annoyance, it disgusts ;* with acc. of pers. and genit. of thing, me pigeat stultitiae meae, Cic.; with infin., referre piget, Liv.; absol., oratione multitudo inducitur ad pigendum, Cic. **II.** Transf., 1, *it repents ;* illa me compousisse piget, *I repent that I,* etc., Ov.; 2, *it causes shame ;* with infin., fateri pigebat, Liv.

pigmentārĭus -ĭi, m. (pigmentum), *a seller of paints and unguents,* Cic.

pigmentum -i, n. (pingo), *a paint, colour,* pigment. **I.** Lit., aspersa temere pigmenta in tabula, Cic. **II.** Transf., of discourse, *ornament, decoration ;* pigmenta Aristotelia, Cic.

pignĕro, 1. (pignus), *to give as a pledge, put in pledge, mortgage ;* bona, Liv.; transf., quum velut obsidibus datis pigneratos haberent animos, Liv.

pignĕror, 1. dep. (pignus). **I.** *to take in pledge, appropriate as one's own ;* Mars fortissimum quemque pignerari solet, Cic. **II.** *to accept as a pledge of certainty ;* quod das mihi pigneror omen, *I take as a pledge of the fulfilment of my prayer,* Ov.

pignus -nŏris and -nĕris, n. (root PAG, pango, perf. pe-pig-i), *a pledge, pawn, security.* **I.** Lit., **A.** Gen., se pignori opponere, Plaut.; rem alicuius pignori accipere, Tac.; esp., *a security to enforce attendance of senators in the senate ;* senatores pignoribus cogere, Cic. **B.** Esp., 1, *a wager, bet, stake ;* pignore certare cum aliquo, Verg.; 2, *a pledge of love,* used of children and parents ; pignora conjugum ac liberorum, Liv. **II.** Fig., *a pledge, token, assurance, proof ;* voluntatis, injuriae, Cic.

pĭgrĭtĭa -ae, f. and **pĭgrĭtĭes** -ēi, f. (piger), *sluggishness, sloth, indolence,* Cic.; militandi, Liv.; ad sequendum, Cic.

pĭgro, 1. (piger), *to be sluggish, slothful, lazy,* Lucr.

pĭgror, 1. dep. (piger), *to be slow, sluggish ;* with infin., scribere ne pigrere, Cic.

1. **pīla** -ae, f. (for pisula, from piso), *a mortar,* Ov.

2. **pīla** -ae, f. (for pigula, from pango), *a pillar ;* nulla meos habeat pila libellos = *a bookstall,* books being sold in Rome round pillars or

buildings, Hor.; collect., **saxea pila**, *a pier or mole in the sea*, Verg.

3. **pĭla** -ae, f. *a ball.* **I.** Lit., *a ball to play with ;* pilā ludere, Cic.; prov., claudus pilam, *one who cannot make a right use of a thing*, Cic.; meton., *a game at ball ;* quantum alii tribuunt alveolo, quantum pilae, Cic. **II.** Transf., *any ball* or *sphere-shaped substance, a balloting-ball*, Prop.

pĭlānus -i, m. (pilum) = triarius (q.v.).

pĭlātus -a -um (pilum), *armed with the* pilum *or javelin*, Verg.

pĭlĕātus -a -um (pileus), *wearing the* pileus *or felt cap ;* fratres, *Castor and Pollux*, Cat.; pileati epulati sunt, Liv.; *used of freedmen* (slaves at their emancipation receiving the pileus), coloni, Liv.; rex, Liv.

pĭlentum -i, n. *a carriage, coach,* esp. used by Roman ladies, Liv.

pĭlĕŏlus -i, m. and **pĭlĕŏlum** -i, n. (dim. of pileus), *a little cap, skull-cap*, Hor.

pĭlĕus -i, m. and **pĭlĕum** -i, n. (πῖλος), *a felt cap, fitting close to the head, worn at feasts, especially the Saturnalia, and by slaves in token of manumission*, Liv.; servos ad pileos vocare, *to summon the slaves to freedom*, Liv.

pĭlo, 1. (1. pilus), *to deprive of hair, make bald*, Mart.

pĭlōsus -a -um (1. pilus), *covered with hair, hairy ;* genae, Cic.

pĭlum -i, n. (piso, pinso), 1, *a pestle*, Plin.; 2, *the short pike or javelin of the Roman infantry, used as a missile*, Cic., Liv.; pila Horatia, *a place in Rome on the forum*, Liv.

Pĭlumnus -i, m. *husband of Danaë, father of Daunus, ancestor of Turnus*.

1. **pĭlus** -i, m. *a single hair ;* munitae sunt palpebrae vallo pilorum, Cic.; fig., *a trifle* (usually with a negative); ego ne pilo quidem minus me amabo, *not a hair less*, Cic.; non facit pili cohortem, Cat.

2. **pīlus** -i, m. (pilum). **I.** *a maniple of the* triarii *in the Roman army ;* primi pili centurio, Caes.; aliquem ad primum pilum transducere, *to promote to be chief centurion*, Caes.; primum pilum ducere, *to be the centurion of the first maniple of the* triarii, Caes. **II.** Meton. = *the centurion of the* triarii ; primus pilus, *the centurion of the first maniple of the* triarii (the first of the sixty centurions of the legion), Liv.

Pimpla -ae, f. (Πίμπλα), *a place in Pieria, with a mountain and spring, sacred to the Muses.* Hence, **A. Pimplēis (Piplēis)** -idis, f. *a Muse*, Hor. **B. Pimplēus** -a -um, *sacred to the Muses ;* mons, Cat. Subst., **Pimplēa** -ae, f. *a Muse*, Hor.

pīnă = 2. pinna (q.v.).

Pĭnārĭus -a -um, *name of a Roman gens. The Pinarii and Potitii were the priests of Hercules at Rome.*

Pindărus -i, m. (Πίνδαρος), *a celebrated lyric poet of Thebes in Boeotia, contemporary with Aeschylus.* Adj., **Pindărĭcus** -a -um, *of Pindar, Pindaric.*

Pindĕnissus -i, f. (Πινδένισσος), *a town in Sicily ;* hence, **Pindĕnissĭtae** -ārum, m. *the inhabitants of Pindenissus.*

Pindus -i, m. (Πίνδος), *a mountain in Thessaly,* now Mezzara.

pīnētum -i, n. (pinus), *a pine-wood*, Ov.

pīnĕus -a -um (pinus), *made of pine-wood* or *deal ;* claustra, *the wooden horse of Troy*, Verg.; plaga, *places where pines grow*, Verg.; pineus ardor, *a fire of pine-wood*, Verg.

pingo, pinxi, pictum, 3. *to paint.* **I.** Lit., **A.** 1, *to paint ;* hominis speciem, Cic.; 2, esp., *to embroider*, with or without acu, Cic.; toga picta, *the embroidered robe of the triumphing general*, Liv.; picti reges, *clad in embroidered garments*, Mart. **B.** Transf., 1, *to stain, dye, colour ;* frontem moris, Verg.; 2, *to decorate, adorn ;* bibliothecam, Cic. **II.** Fig., *of speech, to embellish, depict eloquently ;* Britanniam pingam coloribus tuis penicillo meo, Cic.

pinguesco, 3. (pinguis), *to become fat, grow fertile ;* sanguine pinguescere campos, Verg.

pinguis -e (πίων), *fat.* **I.** Lit., a, *of animals,* Thebani, Cic.; pinguior agnus, Plaut. Subst., **pingue** -is, n. *fatness, fat*, Verg.; b, *of things,* merum or vinum, *oily*, Hor.; ara, *covered with fat of victims*, Verg.; oî soil, *rich ;* pinguior campus, Hor. **II.** Transf., 1, *be-smeared ;* crura luto, Juv.; 2, *thick, gross ;* caelum, air, Cic.; 3, *without understanding, heavy, stupid ;* ingenium, Ov.; 4, *of speech, bombastic ;* poetae pingue quiddam sonantes, Cic.; 5, *quiet, undisturbed ;* somnus, Ov.; amor, Ov.

pĭnĭfer -fĕra -fĕrum (pinus and fero), *producing pines*, Verg.

pĭnĭgĕr -gĕra -gĕrum (pinus and gero), *producing pines*, Ov.

1. **pinna** -ae, f. (another form of penna), *a feather.* **I. A.** Lit., *a feather*, and plur., *feathers,* esp., *the feathers in the wings and tail*, Tac. **B.** Meton., 1, = *the wing ;* praepetibus pennis, Cic.; prov., alicui incidere pinnas, Cic.; 2, poet.= *flight*, Ov.; 3, *an arrow*, Ov. **II.** Transf., 1, *the fin of a fish*, Ov.; 2, *the battlement along the top of a wall*, Caes.

2. **pinna (pīna)** -ae, f. (πίννα), *a species oj mussel*, Cic.

pinnātus -a -um (pinna), *feathered, winged,* Cic.

pinnĭgĕr -gĕra -gĕrum (pinna and gero), *having feathers, feathered, winged*, Lucr.; transf., piscis, *having fins*, Ov.

pinnĭrăpus -i, m. (pinna and rapio), *a gladiator who fought against a Samnite having a peak to his helmet*, Juv.

pinnŭla -ae, f. (dim. of pinna), lit., *a small feather ;* plur., meton., *small wings*, Cic.

pīnōtērēs (pīnŏthērās) -ae, m. (πινοτήρης), *the pinna-guard, a small crab found in the shell of the pinna.*

pinso, pinsi and pinsŭi, pinsum, pinsĭtum, pistum and pisum 3. (root PIS, whence piso, Gk. πίσσω, πτίσσω), *to stamp, pound, crush*, Plaut.

pinus -i and -ûs, f. (for pic-nus from pix, picis), *the pine, fir* (pinus silvestris, Linn.). **A.** Lit., Verg. **B.** Meton. = *something made of pine-wood ;* a, *a ship*, Verg.; b, *a torch*, Verg.; c, *a garland of pine-leaves*, Ov.

pĭo, 1. (pius). **I.** *to seek to appease by an offering, to appease, propitiate ;* Silvanum lacte, Hor. **II.** Transf., **A.** *to pay religious honours to, venerate*, Prop. **B.** *to cleanse, purify*, Cic. **C.** *to make good, atone for ;* damna, Ov.; fulmen, *to avert the misfortune portended by lightning*, Ov.; nefas triste, Verg.; culpam morte, Verg.

pĭper, pĭpĕris, n. (πέπερι), *pepper*, Hor.

pīpŭlus -i, m. and **pīpŭlum** -i, n. *a chirping ;* hence, *an out-cry, upbraiding*, Plaut.

Pīraeus -ĕi, m. (Πειραιεύς) and **Pīraeus** -i, m. *the Piraeus, a port of Athens, connected with the city by long walls ;* poet. form in neut. plur., Piraea tuta, Ov. Adj., **Pīraeus** -a -um, *belonging to the Piraeus.*

pīrāta -ae, m. (πειρατής), *a pirate, corsair,* Cic.

pīrātĭcus -a -um (πειρατικός), *piratical;* myoparo, Cic. ; subst., **pīrātĭca** -ae, f. *piracy;* piraticam facere, Cic.

Pīrēnē -ēs, f. (Πειρήνη), *a spring in Corinth, sacred to the Muses.* Hence, **Pīrēnis** -ĭdis, f. (Πειρηνίς), *Pirenian;* Pirenis Ephyre, *Corinth,* Ov.

Pīrĭthŏus -i, m. (Πειρίθοος), *son of Ixion, king of the Lapithae, husband of Hippodamia, friend of Theseus, with whom he went down to the lower world to carry off Proserpina.*

pĭrum -i, n. *a pear,* Verg.

pĭrus -i, f. *a pear-tree,* Verg.

Pīrustae -ārum, m. (Πιρούσται), *an Illyrian robber-tribe.*

Pīsa -ae, f. (Πίσα), and **Pīsae** -ārum, f. **I.** *a town in Elis on the river Alpheus, where the Olympian games were held.* Hence, **Pīsaeus** -a -um, *Pisaean;* Arethusa, *because she came originally from Elis,* Ov. ; hasta, *of Oenomaus,* Ov. ; subst., **Pīsaea** -ae, f. = *Hippodamia,* Ov. **II. Pīsae** -ārum, f. *a town in Etruria, famous for its baths* (now Pisa), *said to be a colony of Pisa in Elis.* Hence, **Pīsānus** -a -um, *Pisan.*

Pīsandrus (-ŏs) -i, m. (Πείσανδρος), *son of Polyctor, one of the suitors of Penelope.*

Pīsaurum -i, n. *a town in Umbria,* now *Pesaro.* Hence, adj., **Pīsaurensis** -e, *Pisaurian.*

Pīsaurus -i, m. *a river in Umbria, near Pisaurum,* now *Foglia.*

piscārĭus -a -um (piscis), *of or belonging to fish;* forum, *the fish-market,* Plaut.

piscātor -ōris, m. (piscor), *a fisherman, angler,* Cic.

piscātōrĭus -a -um (piscator), *of or relating to fishermen and fishing;* navis, *a fishing-smack,* Caes. ; forum, *fish-market,* Liv.

piscātus -ūs, m. (piscor). **I.** *a fishing, catching of fish,* Cic. **II.** Meton., *fish,* Plaut.

piscĭcŭlus -i, m. (dim. of piscis), *a little fish,* Cic.

piscīna -ae, f. (piscis). **I.** *a tank for keeping fish, fish-pond;* mullos except re de piscina, Cic. **II.** Transf., 1, *a tank for bathing, swimming-bath,* Plin. ; 2, *a reservoir,* Plin.

piscīnārĭus -ĭi, m. (piscina), *one fond of fish-ponds,* Cic.

piscis -is, m. *a fish.* **I.** Lit., pisces capere, Cic. ; sing., used collectively, Ov. **II.** Transf., Pisces, *the sign of the zodiac so called,* Ov. ; pisces gemini or gemelli, Ov. ; piscis aquosus, Verg.

piscor, 1. dep. (piscis), *to fish;* ante hortulos alicuius, Cic.

piscōsus -a -um (piscis), *abounding in fish;* amnis, Ov.

piscŭlentus = piscosus (q.v.).

Pĭsīda -ae, m. (Πισίδης), *a Pisidian;* plur., Pisidae, *the Pisidians, inhabitants of Pisidia.* Hence, **Pĭsīdĭa** -ae, f. (Πισιδία), *a district in Asia Minor bordering on the east on Cilicia, on the north and west on Phrygia, Caria, and Lycia, on the south on Pamphylia.*

Pīsistrătus -i, m. (Πεισίστρατος), *tyrant at Athens, contemporary of Servius Tullius.* Hence, **Pisistrătĭdae** -ārum, m. (Πεισιστρατίδαι), *the sons of Pisistratus.*

1. **pīso**, v. pinso.

2. **Pīso** -ōnis, m. *a surname in the gens Calpurnia,* v. *Calpurnius.*

pistillum -i, n. or **pistillus** -i, m. (pinso), *a pestle,* Plaut.

pistor -ōris, m. (pinso). **I.** *a grinder, miller,* Plaut. **II.** *a baker,* Cic. ; Pistor, *surname of Jupiter.*

Pistōrĭum -ĭi, n. *a town in Etruria,* now *Pistoja.* Hence, **Pistōrĭensis** -e, *relating to Pistorium.*

pistrilla -ae, f. (dim. of pistrina), *a small mortar or mill,* Ter.

pistrīna -ae, f. (pinso), *a bakehouse,* Plin.

pistrīnum -i, n. (pinso), *a mill* (usually worked by horses and asses, though sometimes by slaves as a punishment); homo pistrino dignus, Ter. ; transf., tibi mecum in eodem est pistrino vivendum, *in the same drudgery,* Cic.

pistris = pristis (q.v.).

pīsum -i, n. (πίσον), *the pea, pease,* Plin.

Pĭtănē -ēs, f. (Πιτάνη), *a town in Asia Minor,* now *Sandarlik.*

Pĭthēcūsa -ae, f. and **Pĭthēcūsae** -ārum, f. (Πιθηκοῦσα, Πιθηκοῦσαι), *an island in the Tyrrhene Sea, near Cumae,* now *Ischia.*

Pittăcus (-ŏs) -i, m. (Πίττακος), *a philosopher of Mitylene, one of the Seven Wise Men.*

Pittheus -ĕi and -ĕos, m. (Πιτθεύς), *king in Troezen, father of Aethra, who was the wife of Aegeus and mother of Theseus.* Hence, **A. Pitthēis** -ĭdos, f. (Πιτθηίς), *a daughter of Pittheus* = *Aethra,* Ov. **B. Pitthēīus** and **Pitthēus** -a -um, *belonging to Pittheus.*

pītūīta -ae, f. *phlegm, rheum;* quum pituita redundat, Cic.

pītūītōsus -a -um (pituita), *full of phlegm;* homo, Cic.

pĭtysma = pytisma (q.v.).

pĭus -a -um (superl. piissimus, condemned by Cicero). **I.** *acting dutifully, dutiful, pious;* a, *upright, God-fearing, virtuous;* homo, Cic. ; pii, *"the blessed dead,"* Cic. ; transf., of things or actions, *upright;* pax, Cic. ; subst., justum piumque, *justice and equity,* Ov. ; pium est, with infin., Ov. ; b, *affectionate towards one's parents, benefactors, relations, native country, etc., grateful, patriotic, obedient;* in parentes, Cic. ; adversus sororem, Liv. **II.** Esp. (like φίλος), *kind, gentle;* pia testa (of wine), Hor.

pix, pĭcis, f. (πίσσα), *pitch;* aliquid pice linere, Liv.

plācābĭlis -e (placo), *easy to be appeased, easy of propitiation, placable;* homines, Cic. ; with ad and the acc., placabile ad justas preces ingenium, Liv. ; poet., transf., ara Dianae, Verg.

plācābĭlĭtas -ātis, f. (placabilis), *placability,* Cic.

plācāmen -ĭnis, n. (placo), *a means of appeasing, propitiating;* placamina irae, Liv.

plācāmentum -i, n. (placo), *a means of appeasing,* Tac.

plācātē, adv. (placatus), *calmly, composedly;* omnia humana placate et moderate ferre, Cic.

plācātĭo -ōnis, f. (placo), *a soothing, appeasing, propitiating;* deorum, Cic.

plācātus -a -um, p. adj. (from placo). **I.** *soothed, appeased, placable;* placatiore eo et suā et regis spe invento, Liv. **II.** *calm, gentle, quiet;* vita, Cic. ; quies placatissima, Cic. ; transf., mare, Verg.

plăcenta -ae, f. (πλακοῦς), *a cake,* Hor.

Plăcentĭa -ae, f. *a town in Gallia Cispadana,* now *Piacenza.* Hence, **Plăcentīnus** -a -um, *Placentine.*

plăcĕo -ŭi -ĭtum, 2. (root PLAC, cf. placo), *to please, be agreeable, acceptable to.* **I.** Gen., a, of persons, velle placere alicui, Cic.; placere sibi, *to please, be satisfied with oneself,* Cic.; middle perf., placitus sum, *I am pleased,* Ov.; b, of things, placet hoc tibi? *does this please you?* Cic.; foll. by quod, sibi non placere quod tam cupide elaborasset, Nep. **II.** Esp., **A.** Of actors and artists, *to please, to win applause;* admodum placere in tragoediis, Cic. **B.** placet, *with or without dat.* of pers., *it pleases, it seems good, it is the opinion of, I hold* : a, ut doctissimis placuit, Cic.; with ut and the subj., his placuit ut tu in Cumanum venires, Cic.; with infin., nec mihi ipsi placebat diutius abesse, Cic.; with acc. and infin., placet Stoicis homines hominum causâ esse generatos, Cic.; as a parenthesis, si placet, Cic.; si diis placet, Liv.; b, as legal t. t., *to seem good, resolve, order, command;* with ut and the subj., senatui placere ut, etc., Cic.; with acc. and infin., suggestum adornari placuit, Liv.

plăcĭdē, adv. (placidus), *quietly, gently, composedly, placidly;* ferre dolorem, Cic.

plăcĭdus -a -um (placeo), *quiet, still, placid, gentle;* reddere aliquem placidum, Cic.; senatus, Cic.; amnis, Ov.; placidior civitas, Liv.; placidissima pax, Cic.

plăcĭtum, v. placitus.

plăcĭtus -a -um, p. adj. (from placeo). **I.** Adj., *pleasing, pleasant, agreeable;* amor, Verg.; locus, Sall. **II.** Subst., **plăcĭtum** -i, n. **A.** *that which pleases one;* ultra placitum, *more than is agreeable,* Verg. **B.** *opinion, teaching;* placita majorum, Tac.

plāco, 1. (causat. of placeo, as sedo of sedeo, connected with pla-nus), *to soothe, appease, calm.* **I.** Lit., aequora tumida, Verg. **II.** Transf., *to assuage, reconcile, appease;* animum, animos, Cic.; aliquem, Cic.; aliquem alicui, Cic.: homo sibi ipse placatus, *of a quiet mind,* Cic.; transf., ventrem, Hor.

1. plāga -ae, f. (πληγή), *a blow, stroke.* **I.** Gen., Cic.; plagam ferre, Verg. **II.** Esp., *a stroke that wounds,* and meton. = *the wound itself;* plagam accipere, Cic.; infligere, imponere, Cic.; fig., oratio parem plagam facit, Cic.; levior est plaga ab amico, Cic.

2. plāga -ae, f. (root PLAC, whence placentum, Gr. ΠΛΑΚ, πλάξ), *a flat surface.* **I.** *a net for hunting boars and similar animals;* 1, lit., plagas tendere, Cic.; in plagam cadere, Ov.; 2, fig., *a net, snare, toil;* quas plagas ipsi contra se Stoici texuerunt, Cic.; Antonium conjeci in Octaviani plagas, Cic. **II.** *a district, zone, tract, region;* caeli, Cic.; aetheria, *the air,* Verg.; quatuor plagae, *the four zones,* Verg.

plăgĭārĭus -ĭi, m. *a man-stealer, kidnapper,* Cic.; hence, in jest, *a literary thief, plagiarist,* Mart.

plăgōsus -a -um (1. plaga), *fond of flogging;* Orbilius, Hor.

plăgŭla -ae, f. (dim. of 2. plaga), *a curtain, bed-curtain,* Liv.

Planasĭa -ae, f. (Πλανασία), *an island south of Elba in the Ligurian Sea,* now Pianosa, *place of banishment under the emperors.*

Plancĭus -a -um, *name of a Roman gens, the most celebrated member of which was Cn. Plancius, whom Cicero defended when tried for bribery.*

planctus -ūs, m. (plango), *a loud noise as of beating, esp., beating the breast, wailing, lamentation;* planctus et lamenta, Tac.

Plancus -i, m. (= πλατύπους, *broad-footed*), *a family of the gens Munatia.*

plānē, adv. (planus). **I.** *plainly, simply,*

intelligibly; loqui, Cic.; planius dicere, Cic.; planissime explicare, Cic. **II.** *wholly, entirely, quite, thoroughly;* plane eruditus, Cic.; si plane occidimus, Cic.; plane nihil sapit, Cic.

plango, planxi, planctum, 3. (root PLAC, Gk. ΠΛΑΓ, whence πλήσσω), *to beat, strike with a loud noise.* **I.** tympana palmis, Cat.; litora planguntur fluctu, Ov. **II.** Esp., *to strike the breast, head,* etc., as a sign of grief; pectora, Ov.; femur, Ov.; lacertos, Ov. **B.** Transf., as κόπτεσθαι, refl. plangere, middle plangi, *to bewail loudly;* planguntur matres, Ov.; agmina plangentia, Verg.

plangor -ōris, m. (plango), *a striking or beating accompanied by noise.* **I.** Gen., Ov. **II.** Esp., *the beating of the head and breast in token of grief, loud lamentation;* plangore et lamentatione implere, complere forum, Cic.; plangorem dare, Ov.

plangunculă -ae, f. (dim. of πλαγγών), *a wax doll,* Cic.

plānĭpes -pēdis, m. (planus and pes), *a mime who played the part of slaves,* etc., *and wore no shoes,* Juv.

plānĭtas -ātis, f. (planus), *plainness, distinctness,* Tac.

plānĭtĭa -ae, f. and **plānĭtĭes** -ēi, f. (planus), *level surface, a plain,* Cic.

planta -ae, f. **I.** *a green twig, cutting, graft;* a, of the vine, Cic.; of trees, Verg.; b, *a slip for transplanting,* Ov. **II.** *the sole of the foot, with or without pedis,* Verg.

plāntārĭa -ĭum, n. (planta), *young trees, slips,* Verg.

1. plānus -a -um (root PLA, whence placo), *level, flat.* **I.** Lit., locus, Cic.; filum, *thick,* Ov. Subst., **plānum** -i, n. *a plain, level ground,* Sall., Liv.; fig., via vitae plana et stabilis, Cic.; de plano, *easily, without trouble,* Lucr. **II.** Transf., *plain, clear, intelligible;* narratio, Cic.; planum facere, *to explain;* foll. by acc. and infin., Cic.

2. plănus -i, m. (πλάνος), *a vagrant, juggler, charlatan,* Cic.

Plătaeae -ārum, f. (Πλαταιαί), *a town in Boeotia, famed for a victory of the Greeks over the Persians* (479 B.C.), now *Palaeo - Castro.* Hence, **Plătaeenses** -ĭum, m. *the inhabitants of Plataea.*

plătălĕa -ae, f. *a water-bird, the spoonbill,* Cic.

plătănus -i, f. (πλάτανος), *the plane-tree,* Cic.; caelebs, *not used to train the vine on* (like the elm), Hor.

plătēa -ae, f. (πλατεῖα), *a street,* Caes.

Plăto (**-ōn**) -ōnis, m. (Πλάτων). **I.** *a celebrated Greek philosopher, disciple of Socrates, founder of the Academic philosophy.* Hence, **Plătōnĭcus** -a -um, *Platonic;* homo, transf. = *a deep thinker,* Cic. Plur. subst., **Plătōnĭci** -ōrum, m. *the Platonists,* Cic. **II.** *an Epicurean of Sardis, living at Athens, in* 59 B.C.

plaudo (**plōdo**), plausi (plōsi), plausum (plōsum), 3. **I.** Intransit., *to clap, strike, beat.* **A.** Gen., alis, Verg.; pennis, Ov.; rostro, Ov. **B.** Esp., *to clap the hands in token of applause;* a, lit., manus in plaudendo consumere, Cic.; impers., huic ita plausum est ut, etc., Cic.; esp. in the theatre, plaudite (said at the end of a piece), Hor.; b, transf., *to give signs of approval, applaud, to approve;* ingeniis sepultis, Hor.; diis hominibusque plaudentibus, Cic.; hence plur., sibi, Hor. **II.** Transit. **A.** *to beat, clap;* pectora manu, Ov.; plausa colla equorum, Verg.; pedibus choreas, *to dance, stamping with* *the feet,* Verg. **B.** *to strike together;* plausis alis, Ov.

plausĭbĭlĭs -e (plaudo), *worthy of applause,* Cic.

plausor -ōris, m (plaudo), *an applauder at the theatre,* Hor.

plaustrum (plostrum) -i, n. **I.** *a wagon, cart;* omnia ex locis publicis plaustris coacta, Cic. **II.** Transf., *Charles's Wain, the constellation of the Great Bear,* Ov.

plausus -ūs, m. (plaudo), *the noise made by the striking together of two bodies.* **I.** Gen., plausum dare pennis, Verg.; ingenti sonuerunt omnia plausu, Verg. **II.** Esp., *the clapping of the hands in sign of approval, applause;* accipere plausum, Cic.; captare plausus, Cic.; comprimitur plausus ipsā admiratione, Cic.

Plautĭus (Plōtĭus) -a -um, *name of a Roman gens;* hence, adj., **Plautiānus (Plotiānus)** -a -um, *Plautian.*

Plautus -i, m. (lit. *flat-footed*), M. Accius (or T. Maccius), *a celebrated Roman comic poet, who died about eighty years before Cicero's birth;* hence, **Plautīnus** -a -um, *relating to Plautus;* Plautinus pater, *in a comedy of Plautus.*

plēbēcŭla -ae, f. (dim. of plebs), *the common people, mob, rabble,* Cic.

plēbēïus -a -um (plebs). **I.** *relating or belonging to the plebs or people* (opp. patricius), plebeïan; familia, Cic.; ludi, *games celebrated in honour of the driving out of the kings or of the return of the plebeians from their secession to the Aventine Hill,* Cic. Subst., **plēbēïus** -i, m. *a plebeian,* and **plēbēïa** -ae, f. *a plebeian woman,* Liv. Plur., **plēbēïi** or **plēbēï**, Cic. **II.** plebeïan = *common, vulgar, low, mean, inferior;* sermo, *of the lower classes,* Cic.; purpura, Cic.; philosophi, Cic.

plēbes -ēi, f. = plebs (q.v.).

plēbĭcŏla -ae, m. (plebs and colo), *a friend of the common people,* Cic.

plēbiscītum -i, n. (plebs and scisco), *a decree or ordinance of the people,* Cic.

plebs, plēbis, f. (root PLE, whence ple-o, ple-nus, Gr. ΠΛΕ, ΠΛΗ, whence πλῆθω, πλῆθος), *the multitude.* Hence, **I.** As a political division, *the plebeians, the people* (opp. patricii, patres, senatus, while populus includes both these and the plebeians); consulem de plebe non accipiebat, Cic. **II.** Transf., *the common people, the multitude, mass of the people, the lower orders, rabble, mob;* plebs et infima multitudo, Cic.; plebs eris, Hor.; plebs deorum, *the lower order of deities,* Ov.

1. **plecto**, plexi and plexŭi, plexum, 3. (root PLEC, Gr. ΠΛΕΚ, πλέκω), *to plait, braid;* more frequently in partic., **plexus** -a -um, *braided, plaited;* corollae, Lucr.; flores, Cat.

2. **plecto**, 3. (πλήττω), *to punish;* usually in pass., *to be punished with blows.* **A.** Lit., tergo, Hor. **B.** Transf., 1, *to be punished,* with abl. of crime; negligentiā, Cic.; **2**, *to be blamed, censured,* Nep.

plectrum -i, n. (πλῆκτρον), *a short stick or quill with which the strings of a stringed instrument were struck.* **A.** Lit., Cic. **B.** Poet., meton., 1, *the lyre,* Hor.; 2, *lyrical poetry,* Hor.

Plēïăs (Πληϊάς), **Plējăs**, and **Plĭăs** (Πλειάς) -ădis, f. *a Pleiad;* gen. plur., **Plēïădēs (Plĭădēs)** and **Plejădēs** -ădum, f. *the Pleiads, the Seven Stars, according to the legend, the seven daughters of Atlas by Pleione* (Electra, Halcyone, Celaeno, Maia, Sterope, Taygete, Merope).

Plēïŏnē -ēs, f. (Πληϊόνη), *the wife of Atlas,*

mother of the Pleiads; Pleiones nepos, *Mercury, son of Maia,* Ov.

Plēmўrĭum (Plēmŭrĭum) -ĭi, n. (Πλημμύριον), *a promontory of Sicily, near Syracuse,* now *Punta di Gigante.*

plēnē, adv. (plenus), *fully;* fig., *fully, completely, wholly, abundantly;* plene perfectae munitiones, Caes.; plene sapientes homines, Cic.

plēnĭtūdo -ĭnis, f. (plenus), *fulness, completeness,* Plin.

plēnus -a -um (root PLE, whence ple-o, Gr. ΠΛΕ, πλέος), *full.* **I.** Lit., **A.** Gen., a, lit., with genit., argenti, Cic.; with abl., plena domus ornamentis, Cic.; absol., plenissimis velis navigare, Cic.; calcari ad plenum, *completely,* Verg.; b, fig., plenus timoris, Caes.; plenus expectatione, Cic.; absol., plenā manu alicuius laudes in astra tollere, Cic. **B.** Esp., 1, *plump, portly, stout;* homo, Cic.; velamina filo pleno, *thick,* Ov.; 2, *pregnant,* Cic.; 3, *full, satiated;* plenus eras minimo, Ov.; 4, *full of, richly provided with, rich in;* exercitus plenissimus praedā, Cic.; fig., plenus inimicorum, Cic.; negotiis, *occupied,* Cic.; hence, absol.= *well-stocked, rich;* urbs, Cic.; homo, Cic.; epistola plenior, *full of matter,* Cic. **II.** Transf., **A.** *full,* of quantity and number; 1, *numerous;* agmen, Ov.; 2,= *complete, entire;* a, lit., annus, Cic.; legio, Caes.; b, fig., *complete, perfect;* gaudium, Cic.; pleno gradu, *at quick step,* Liv. **B.** Of strength, *strong, loud;* vox, Cic.; pleniore voce, Cic.

plērumquĕ, v. plerusque.

plērus = plerusque (q.v.).

plērusquĕ -rāquĕ -rumquĕ, gen. plur., **plērĭquĕ** -raequĕ -rāquĕ, *very many, a large part, the most, the greatest part, the majority* (opp. unus, pauci). **I.** Plur., 1, absol., multi nihil prodesse philosophiam, plerique etiam obesse arbitrantur, Cic.; plerique Belgae, Caes.; in plerisque, *in the majority of cases,* Cic.; 2, with genit., plerique Poenorum, Cic.; 3, with the abl., plerique ex factione, Sall. **II.** Sing., juventus, Sall.; nobilitas, Sall.; Africa, Sall. Neut., plerumque; a, subst., *the greater part;* noctis, Sall.; per Europae plerumque, Liv.; b, adv., *for the most part, mostly, generally, commonly,* Cic.

Pleumoxĭi -ōrum, m. *a people in Gallia Belgica.*

Pleurōn -ōnis, f. (Πλευρών), *a town in Aetolia.* Hence, adj., **Pleurōnĭus** -a -um, *Pleuronian.*

plĭco -ŭi -ātus, 1. (πλέκω), *to fold, double up, fold together;* se in sua membra, Verg.

Plīnĭus -a -um, *name of a Roman gens, the most famous members of which were:* **1**, C. Plinius Secundus (Major, *the Elder*), *probably of Como, author of a Natural History in thirty-seven books, killed 79 A.D., at the eruption of Mount Vesuvius;* **2**, C. Plinius Caecilius Secundus (Junior, *the Younger*), *governor under Trajan in Bithynia, author of letters and of a panegyric on Trajan.*

Plisthĕnēs -is, m. (Πλεισθένης). **I.** *son of Pelops, brother of Atreus and Thyestes, father of Agamemnon and Menelaus, who was brought up by his brother Atreus.* Hence, **Plisthĕnīcus** -a -um, torus, *of Agamemnon,* Ov.

plōdo = plaudo (q.v.).

plōrābĭlĭs -e (ploro), *deplorable, lamentable,* Pers.

plōrātor -ōris, m. (ploro), *a wailer, howler, lamenter,* Mart.

plōrātus -ūs, m. (ploro), *a crying, weeping, lamenting;* gen. in plur., audivi civitatum gemitus, ploratus, Cic.

plōro, 1. I. Intransit., *to lament, wail, cry aloud for grief;* plorando fessus sum, Cic.; jubeo te plorare (= οἰμώζειν λέγω σοι, *bad luck to you!*), Hor. **II.** Transit., *to weep over, to lament, deplore;* turpe commissum, Hor.

plostellum -i, n. (dim. of plostrum). *a little wagon,* Hor.

plostrum = plaustrum (q.v.).

ploxĕmum (ploxĭmum, ploxĭnum) -i, n. *a wagon-box,* Cat.

plŭit, v. pluo.

plūma -ae, f. *the downy part of a feather, a small, soft feather;* plur. = *down.* **I.** Lit., plumae versicolores columbarum, Cic.; in plumis delituisse Jovem, *to have been disguised in the form of a bird,* Ov.; in plumam, *after the fashion of feathers,* Verg.; *used to stuff pillows, bolsters,* etc., with; hence, meton.= *bolster, feather-bed, pillow,* Juv.; as an emblem of lightness, fickleness, etc., plumā aut folio facilius moventur, Cic. **II.** Transf., *the first down on the chin,* Hor.

plūmātus -a -um (pluma), *covered with feathers,* Cic. poet.

plumbĕus -a -um (plumbum), *leaden, made of lead.* **I.** Lit., glans, Lucr. **II.** Transf., *leaden;* 1, = *blunt;* gladius, Cic.; pugio, Cic.; 2, = *bad;* vina, Mart.; 3, *dull, stupid;* plumbeus in physicis, Cic.; 4, *heavy, oppressive, burdensome;* auster, Hor.

plumbum -i, n. (akin to μόλυβδος), *lead.* **I.** Lit., plumbum album, *tin,* Caes. **II.** Meton., 1, *a bullet,* Verg.; 2, *a leaden-pipe,* Hor.

plūmĕus -a -um (pluma), *downy, consisting of, covered with fine feathers;* culcita, Cic.; torus, Ov.

plūmĭpes -pĕdis (pluma and pes), *feather-footed,* Cat.

plūmōsus -a -um (pluma), *feathered, covered with down, downy,* Prop.

plŭo, plŭi, 3. (root PLU, connected with FLU-o, Gr. ΠΛΥ, whence πλύνω), *to rain.* **I.** Lit., impers., pluit, *it rains;* dum pluit, Verg.; aqua, quae pluendo crevisset, Cic.; with acc. and abl. of what falls, sanguine pluisse, Cic.; lapides pluere, Liv. **II.** Transf., *to fall down in a great mass or number;* tantum glandis pluit, Verg.

plūrĭēs, adv. (plus), *often, frequently,* Caes.

plūrĭfārĭam (plus), *on many sides, in many places,* Suet.

plūrĭmus, plurimum, v. multus.

plūs, pluris, v. multus.

pluscŭlus -a -um (dim. of plus), *somewhat more, rather many;* **pluscŭlum** -i, n. used subst., causae in quibus plusculum negotii est, Cic.

plŭtĕus -i, m. and **plŭtĕum** -i, n. **I. A.** a, *a moveable penthouse, shed,* or *mantlet* (made of hurdles covered with hides to protect the besiegers of a town), Caes.; b, *a breastwork, battlement on a tower,* Caes. **II. A.** *the back board of a bed* or *sofa,* Mart. **B.** *the board on which a corpse is laid out,* Mart. **C.** *a book-shelf, book-case,* Juv.

Plūto (-ōn) -ōnis, m. (Πλούτων), *the king of the lower world, brother of Jupiter and Neptune, husband of Proserpina.* Hence, **Plūtōnĭus** -a -um, *belonging to Pluto;* domus, *the grave,* Hor.; plur. subst., **Plūtōnĭa** -ōrum, n. (sc. loca), *a place in Asia Minor, perhaps in Lydia, where there was a temple to Pluto.*

plŭvĭa -ae, f. (pluvius), *rain;* pluvias metuo, Cic.

plŭvĭālis -e (pluvia), *of* or *relating to rain,*

rainy; aquae, Ov.; fungi, *growing after rain,* Ov.; auster, Verg.

plŭvĭus -a -um (pluo), *of* or *relating to rain, rainy, rain-bringing;* aquae, Cic.; Hyades, Verg.; venti, Hor.; arcus, *a rainbow,* Hor.

pōcillum -i, n. (dim. of poculum), *a little drinking-cup, goblet;* Jovi Victori pocillum mulsi facere, *to offer,* Liv.

pōcŭlum -i, n (root PO, whence potus, poto), *a drinking-cup, goblet.* **I.** poculum impavide haurire, Liv.; poculum mortis exhaurire, Cic.; poscunt majoribus poculis (sc. bibere), *to drink out of goblets,* Cic. **II.** Meton., **A.** *a drink, draught;* ad pocula venire, Verg.; amoris poculum, *a love-philtre,* Hor.; in ipsis tuis immanibus poculis, *in thy cups, in the midst of thy revels,* Cic. **B.** Esp., *a poisonous draught,* Cic.

pŏdăgra -ae, f. (ποδάγρα), *the gout in the feet;* podagrae doloribus cruciari, Cic.

Pŏdălīrĭus -ĭi, m. (Ποδαλείριος). **I.** *son of Aesculapius, a celebrated physician.* **II.** *a Trojan.*

pōdex -ĭcis, m. *the fundament,* Hor.

pŏdĭum -ĭi, n (πόδιον), *a basement* or *balcony immediately above the arena in the amphitheatre, where the emperor and other distinguished persons sat,* Juv.

Poeās (Paeās) -antis, m. (Ποίας), *the father of Philoctetes;* Poeante satus, *son of Poeas = Philoctetes,* Ov. Hence, **A.** adj., **Poeantĭus** -a -um, *proles* or *heros,* or *simply* Poeantius = *Philoctetes,* Ov. **B.** **Poeantĭădēs** -ae, m. *son of Poeas = Philoctetes,* Ov.

pŏēma -ătis, n. (ποίημα), *a poem;* poema facere, or componere, or condere, Cic.; plur., poemata = *poetry* (opp. oratio, *prose*), Cic.

poena -ae, f. (ποινή), *the fine paid for murder;* hence, *punishment, penalty, expiation, compensation.* **I.** poena dupli, octupli, Cic.; vitae, Cic.; capitis, Caes.; mortis, Cic.; oculorum, *loss of eyesight,* Cic.; votorum, *payment of one's vows,* Verg.; poenas justas et debitas solvere, Cic.; poenas expetere ab aliquo, Cic.; poenas domestici sanguinis expetere, *to avenge the murder of a blood-relation,* Cic.; poenas parentium a filiis expetere, *to visit the sins of the fathers on the children,* Cic.; poenas capere pro aliquo, *to avenge some one,* Sall.; poenam habere, *to be punished,* Liv.; poenas habere ab aliquo, *to obtain vengeance from some one,* Liv.; poenas dare, *to be punished,* Cic.; poenā aliquam afficere or multare, Cic.; poenas subire, ferre, perferre, luere, Cic.; extra poenam esse, *to get off scot-free,* Liv. **II.** Personif., Poena, *the goddess of revenge* or *punishment,* Cic.; plur., a liberûm Poenis actum esse praecipitem, Cic.

Poeni -ōrum, m. *the Phoenicians = the Carthaginians* (colonists from Phoenicia), proverbial among the Romans for faithlessness and breach of treaties; Poeni foedifragi, Cic.; sing., **Poenus** -i, m. *a Phoenician, a Carthaginian;* used for *Hannibal,* Cic.; collective, Poenus advena, Liv.; Poenus uterque, *the Carthaginians in Africa and Spain,* Hor. Hence, **A. Poenus** -a -um, *Phoenician, Punic, Carthaginian;* navita, Hor.; leones, Verg. **B. Pūnĭcus (Poenĭcus)** -a -um, *Phoenician, Punic, Carthaginian;* a, lit., Punicum bellum, Cic.; fides = *faithlessness,* Sall.; so ars, Liv.; b, poet., transf. = *purple-red;* sagum, Hor. **C. Pūnĭcĕus (Poenĭcĕus)** and **Pūnĭcĭus (Poenĭcĭus)** -a -um, a, *Punic, Carthaginian;* b, *purple-red.*

Poenīnus -a -um, *Pennine;* Alpes or juga, *the Pennine Alps.* Poeninus mons, *the Great St Bernard;* or simply Poeninus, Liv.

poenĭo, poenĭor = punio (q.v.).

poenĭtens -entis (partic. of poeniteo).

poenĭtentĭa (paenĭtĕntĭa) -ae, f. (poeniteo), repen*'ance, penitence*, Liv.

poenĭtĕo (paenĭtĕo) -ŭi, 2. (from poenire = punire; lit., *to punish*). **I.** *to displease*, Plaut. **II.** *to feel displeasure, to repent, to regret, to be sorry*. **A.** Pers., *to rue*; poenitens consilii, Sall. ; si poenitere possint, Liv. ; poenitens, Cic.; poeniturus, Sall. ; poenitendo, *by repentance*, Cic. **B.** Impers., poenitet aliquem alicuius rei, etc., *it repents one, one is displeased, vexed*, etc. ; (α) with acc. of pers. and genit. of thing, suae quemque fortunae poenitet, Cic. ; me poenitet consilii, Cic.; without acc. of pers., tamquam poeniteat laboris, Liv.; (β) with acc. of pers. and nom. pron. neuter, nihil sane esset quod nos poeniteret, Cic. ; with only nom. pron., nihil quod poenitere possit, *of which one could repent*, Cic.; (γ) with acc. of pers. and infin., non poenitet me vixisse, Cic.; or, (δ) simple infin., ut fortiter fecisse poeniteat, Cic. ; or with acc. and infin., in posterum diem dilatum (esse) certamen, Liv. ; (ε) with acc. of pers. and rel. sent., Quintum poenitet quod animum tuum offendit, Cic. ; (ζ) or with rel. sent. alone, poenitet quod deduxisti, Liv. ; (η) absol., poenitet et torqueor, Ov.

pŏēsis -is, acc. -in, f. (ποίησις), *poetry*, Cic.

pŏēta -ae, m. (ποιητής), *a poet* ; poeta comicus, tragicus, Cic.

pŏētĭca -ae, f. and **pŏētĭcē** -ēs, f. (ποιητικὴ, sc. τέχνη), *the art of poetry*, Cic.

pŏētĭcē, adv. (poeticus), *poetically, after the manner of a poet* ; ut poetice loquar, Cic.

pŏētĭcus -a -um (ποιητικός), *poetical*; verbum, Cic. ; facultas, Cic.

Poetovĭo -ōnis, f. *a town in Pannonia, now Pettau.*

pŏētrĭa -ae, f. (ποιήτρια), *a poetess*, Cic.

pol! interj. *by Pollux! truly! really!* Cic.

Pŏlĕmo (-ōn) -ōnis, m. (Πολέμων). **I.** *a Greek philosopher at Athens, pupil of Xenocrates, teacher of Zeno and Arcesilaus.* Hence, **Pŏlĕmōnēus** -a -um, *of Polemo.* **II.** *a king in Pontus.*

pŏlenta -ae, f. (root POL, POLL, whence pollen, Gr. ΠΑΛ, πάλη), *pearl-barley, barley-groats*, Ov.

pŏlĭo, 4. *to polish, file, make smooth.* **I.** **A.** 1, rogum asciā, Cic. ; 2, esp., *to cover with white mortar* or *gypsum, to whiten* ; columnas albo, Liv. **II.** Fig., *to adorn, embellish, to polish, finish* ; orationem, Cic.

pŏlītē, adv. (politus), *in a polished manner, elegantly*, Cic.; politius limare, Cic.

pŏlītĭa -ae, acc. -an, f. (πολιτεία), 1, *the state*; 2, *the Republic* (title of a work by Plato), Cic.

pŏlītĭcus -a -um (πολιτικός), *of* or *relating to the state, political* ; philosophi, Cic.

Pŏlītōrĭum -ĭi, n. *a town in Latium, south of the Tiber, according to the legend founded by the Trojan Polites, son of Priam.*

pŏlītus -a -um, p. adj. (from polio), *polished, refined, accomplished* ; homo, Cic.; politior humanitas, Cic.; vir omni liberali doctrinā politissimus, Cic.

pollen -ĭnis, n. and **pollis** -ĭnis, c. (cf. polenta), *fine flour, meal*, Ter.

pollens -entis, p. adj. (from polleo), *strong, powerful, mighty*; matrona, Ov. ; herbae, Ov.; with abl., viribus, Sall.

1. **pollentĭa** -ae, f. (polleo). **I.** *power, strength, might*, Plaut. **II.** Personif., *the goddess of might*, Pollentia, Liv.

2. **Pollentĭa** -ae, f. *a town in Liguria, famous for its wool, now Polenza.*

pollĕo, 2. (potis and valeo), *to be strong, mighty, powerful, able*; qui in republica plurimum pollebant, *had the most power*, Cic.; plurimum pollet oratio, Cic.; with abl., scientiā, Cic.

pollex -ĭcis, m. (polleo), lit., *that which is strong.* **A.** *the thumb* ; Aeginetis pollices praecidere, Cic. ; as a measure, clavi ferrei digiti pollicis crassitudine, Caes. **B.** *the great toe*, Plin.

pollĭcĕor -cĭtus sum, 2. dep. (pro and liceor), *to offer, promise, proffer.* **I.** Gen., a, with acc. of thing, pecuniam, Cic.; b, with acc. of thing, and dat. of person, senatui frumentum, Cic. ; maria montesque, *to make boundless promises*, Sall.; c, with double acc., sese itineris periculique ducem, Sall. ; d, with de and the abl., with or without the acc., nihil ego tum de meis opibus pollicebar, Cic. ; e, with infin., obsides dare, Caes. ; f, with acc. and infin., gen. future, me tibi satisfacturum, Cic. ; g, with rel. sent., quae meum tempus postularet, Cic. ; h, with adv., ultro polliceri, Cic. ; bene, Sall. ; benigne, Liv. ; liberaliter, Caes. **II.** Esp., *of an orator at the beginning of his speech, to promise, declare* ; docui quod primum pollicitus sum, Cic. (partic. perf. pass., pollicita fides, Ov.).

pollĭcĭtātĭo -ōnis, f. (pollicitor), *an offer, proffer, promise* ; magnis praemiis pollicitationibusque polliceri, Caes.

pollĭcĭtor, 1. dep. (intens. of polliceor), *to promise, proffer*, Sall.

pollĭcĭtum -i, n. (polliceor), *that which is promised, a promise*, Ov.

Pollĭo (Pōlĭo) -ōnis, m., C. Asinius, *the patron of Vergil.*

pollis = pollen -ĭnis (q.v.).

pollŭcĕo -luxi -luctum, 2. **I.** *to place something upon the altar as a sacrifice, to offer* ; decumam partem Herculi, Plaut. **II.** *to put on the table as a dish*, Plaut.

pollŭo -ŭi -ūtum, 3. (pro and luo), *to befoul, defile, pollute.* **I.** Lit., ora cruore, Ov. **II.** Transf., *to defile morally, pollute, dishonour* ; jura scelere, Cic. ; caerimonias stupro, Cic.

pollŭtus -a -um, p. adj. (from polluo), *morally defiled, polluted* ; hence (of women), *unchaste* ; femina, Liv.

Pollux -ūcis, m.(Πολυδεύκης), *the twin-brother of Castor, son of Tyndarus* (or *Jupiter*) *and Leda, renowned for his skill in boxing*, Cic. ; Pollux uterque, *Castor and Pollux*, Hor.

pŏlus -i, m. (πόλος). **I.** *the pole of the earth* ; polus gelidus, glacialis, and simply polus, *the north pole*, Ov. ; polus australis, *the south pole*, Ov. **II.** Transf., *the sky, the heavens*, Verg., Hor.

Pŏlўbĭus -ĭi, m. (Πολύβιος), *a Greek historian, contemporary and friend of Scipio Africanus Minor.*

Pŏlўclītus (Pŏlўclētus) -i, m. (Πολύκλειτος), *a celebrated Greek sculptor of Sicyon, contemporary of Pericles.*

Pŏlўcrātes -is, m. (Πολυκράτης), *tyrant of Samos, famed for his prosperity, but crucified by the Persian satrap Orontes.*

Pŏlўdāmas -mantis, m. (Πολυδάμας), *a Trojan, friend of Hector.*

Pŏlўdectēs -ae, m. (Πολυδέκτης), *king in Seriphos, who brought up Perseus.*

Pŏlўdōrus -i, m. (Πολύδωρος), *son of Priam, entrusted to the care of Polymnestor, king in Thrace, but slain by him.*

Pŏlўgnōtus -i, m. (Πολύγνωτος), *a celebrated Greek painter of Thasos, contemporary with Socrates.*

Pŏlўhymnĭa -ae, f. (Πολύμνια), *one of the Muses.*

Pŏlўmestōr (Pŏlymnestōr) -ŏris, m. (Πολυμήστωρ), *king in Thrace, husband of Ilione, daughter of Priam; the murderer of Polydorus.*

Pŏlўphēmus (-ŏs) -i, m. (Πολύφημος), *the one-eyed Cyclops in Sicily, son of Neptune, blinded by Ulysses.*

pŏlўpus -i, m. (πολύπους, Dor. and Aeol., πωλύπος, hence with long ō in Horace). **I.** *the polypus, a marine animal,* Ov. **II.** *a polypus in the nose,* Hor.

Pŏlyxĕna -ae, f. (Πολυξένη), *daughter of Priam, sacrificed at the tomb of Achilles.*

pōmārĭus -a -um (pomum), *of or relating to fruit;* subst., **A. pōmārĭus** -ii, m. *a fruiterer,* Hor. **B. pōmārĭum** -ii, n. *a fruit-garden, orchard,* Cic.

pōmĕrīdĭānus = postmeridianus (q.v.).

pōmērĭum -ii, n. (orig. pomoerium, post and moerus = murus), *a space left free from buildings for a certain breadth on each side the walls of a town, bounded by stones* (cippi or termini); pomerium intrare, transire, Cic.

Pōmētĭa -ae, f. and **Pōmētĭi** -ōrum, m. *old town of the Volsci in Latium.* Hence, **Pōmētīnus** -a -um, *Pometine.*

pōmĭfĕr -fĕra -fĕrum (pomum and fero), *fruit-bearing, fruit-bringing,* Hor.

Pōmōna -ae, f. (pomum), *the goddess of fruit and fruit-trees.*

pōmōsus -a -um (pomum), *full of fruit, abounding in fruit,* Prop.

pompa -ae, f. (πομπή), *a solemn procession.* **I. A.** Lit., 1, gen., *of funerals,* Cic.; pompam funeris ire, Ov.; *of a wedding,* pompam ducit, Ov.; *of a triumph,* Ov.; pomparum ferculis similes esse, *to resemble in gait the bearers at a procession,* Cic.; 2, esp., *the procession at the Circensian Games at which the images of the gods were carried.* **B.** Transf., *a train, suite, retinue;* lictorum, Cic. **II.** Fig., *display, parade, ostentation;* genus (orationis) pompae quam pugnae aptius, Cic.

Pompēji -ōrum, m. *town in the south of Campania, destroyed by an eruption of Vesuvius,* 79 A.D. Hence, adj., **Pompējānus** -a -um, *belonging to Pompeji;* subst., a, **Pompējānum** -i, n. (sc. praedium), *an estate of Cicero, near Pompeji;* b, **Pompējāni** -ōrum, m. *the inhabitants of Pompeji.*

Pompējŏpŏlis -is, f. (Πομπηϊούπολις), *later name of the town Soli, destroyed by Tigranes, rebuilt by Pompejus.*

Pompējus (Pompēïus) -a -um, *name of a Roman gens, the most famous members of which were:* 1, Cn. Pompejus, *triumvir with Caesar and Crassus, conqueror of Mithridates and the pirates, defeated by Caesar at Pharsalia and slain off Egypt;* 2, Pompeja, *wife of P. Vatinius;* adj., *Pompeian;* domus, Cic.; lex, *proposed by Cn. Pompey.* Hence, **Pompējānus** -a -um, *belonging to Pompey;* subst., **Pompējānus** -i, m. *a member of the Pompeian party.*

Pompīlius -a -um, *name of a Roman gens, to which belonged Numa Pompilius, second king of Rome, legendary founder of many religious rites at Rome.* Adj., *Pompilian;* sanguis, *descendants of Numa Pompilius,* Hor.

pompĭlus -i, m. (πομπίλος), *the pilot-fish; according to some, the nautilus,* Ov.

Pompōnĭus -a -um, *the name of a Roman gens, the most famous member of which was* T. Pomponius Atticus, *friend of Cicero.*

Pomptīnus (Pomtīnus) -a -um, *Pomptine or Pontine;* palus and paludes, *a marshy district, thirty miles long and twelve to thirteen miles wide, exposed to the inundation of the river Amasenus and Ufens, on the Appian road.* Subst., a, **Pomptīnum** -i, n. *the neighbourhood of the Pontine marsh;* b, **Pomptīna** -ae, f. *the upper end of the Pontine marsh.*

pōmum -i, n. **I.** *any kind of fruit, a mulberry,* Ov.; plur., poma, *fruit,* Verg., Hor. **II.** Transf., *a fruit-tree,* Verg.

pondĕro, 1. (pondus). **I.** *to weigh,* Plaut. **II.** Transf., *to weigh mentally, to consider, deliberate upon;* verborum delectum, Cic.; causas, Cic.

pondĕrōsus -a -um (pondus), *heavy, weighty, ponderous.* **I.** Lit., Plin. **II.** Transf., *weighty, significant;* epistola, Cic.

pondo (abl. of obsolete pondus -i), *in weight, heavy;* corona libram pondo, *a pound in weight,* Liv.; used as an indecl. subst., *a pound, pounds;* argenti pondo viginti milia, Caes.; auri quinque pondo, Cic.

pondus -ĕris, n. (pendo), *a weight.* **I. A.** Lit., 1, *a weight used in a pair of scales; pondera ab Gallis allata,* Liv.; 2, *a pound weight, a pound,* Liv. **B.** Transf., 1, abstr., a, *the weight of any body;* moveri gravitate et pondere, Cic.; b, *balance, equilibrium;* tertius motus oritur extra pondus et plagam, Cic.; 2, concr., a, *a heavy body, weight, load, burden;* in terram feruntur omnia pondera, Cic.; b, *a mass = a quantity, sum;* auri pondus ingens, Liv. **II.** Fig., **A.** In a good sense, 1, *weight, gravity, authority, influence;* commendationem magnum apud te pondus habuisse, Cic.; 2, *weight of words or thoughts;* omnium verborum ponderibus est utendum, Cic. **B.** In a bad sense, *an oppressive weight, burden;* pondera amara senectae, Ov.

pŏnĕ (perhaps from posne, connected with ποτί, πρός). **I.** Adv. *behind, at the back;* moveri et ante et pone, Cic. **II.** Prep. with acc., *behind;* pone quos aut ante labantur, Cic.

pōno, pŏsŭi (pŏsīvi), pŏsĭtum, 3. (for pō-sĭno), 1, *to lay down, put, place,* lay. Constr. with adv. of place; with in and abl.; with ad, ante, sub, super; poet. with abl. alone. **I.** Gen., **A.** Lit., 1, a, *of things,* vestigium, Cic.; fig., pedem ubi ponat in suo (regno) non habet, Cic.; ponere genu, *to kneel,* Ov.; ponere scalas, *to put up ladders,* Caes.; b, *of persons,* positi vernae circa Lares, Hor.; 2, *of furniture or tools, to lay out, prepare;* mensam, Hor.; casses, Ov.; 3, *to lay, stretch out;* artus in litore, Verg.; somno positae, Verg.; positae det oscula frater, laid out, i.e., *dead,* Ov.; 4, *to erect a statue in honour of some one;* alicui statuam, Nep., esp., *to consecrate a gift to the gods;* coronam auream in Capitolio, Liv.; 5, *to wager in play;* pocula fagina, Verg.; 6, t. t. *of calculators, ponere calculum, to calculate,* Juv.; 7, milit. t. t., *to station men, to place;* praesidium ibi, Caes.; 8, *to remove away to a distant place;* pone sub curru solis, Hor.; 9, *to publish;* edictum, Tac.; 10, *to put down in writing;* signa novis praeceptis, Hor.; 11, partic. perf., **pŏsĭtus** -a -um, a, *of snow, etc., fallen;* posita nix, Hor.; b, *of places, situated;* Roma in montibus posita, Cic. **B.** Transf., 1, *to place, put, present;* aliquid sub uno aspectu, Cic.; 2, *to bring, put;* aliquem ponere in gratia apud aliquem, Cic.; in laude positum esse, *to be famed,* Cic.; 3, *to place, build, rest;* omnem spem salutis in virtute, Cic.; 4, *to* *pass time in some occupation;* totum diem in consideranda causa, Cic.; **5,** *to reckon, count;* mortem in malis, Cic.; aliquid in beneficii loco, Cic.; haud in magno discrimine ponere, *to attach no great importance to,* Liv.; with double acc., *to hold, regard;* aliquem principem, Cic.; **6,** *to put down in writing, to remark, observe, mention;* cuius pauca exempla posui, Cic. **II. A.** *to lay, place by way of building, making,* etc.; **1,** lit. **a,** of building, *to erect;* urbem, Verg.; milit. t.t., castra in proximo colle, *to pitch one's camp,* Caes.; **b,** of an artist, *to represent, picture;* Orphea in medio silvasque sequentes, Verg.; ponere totum, *to present a whole,* Hor.; **2,** transf., **a,** *to found, place;* ponere initia male, Cic.; **b,** *to fix, settle;* leges in conviviis, Cic.; ponere praemium, *to promise a reward,* Cic.; **c,** *to maintain, lay down;* nosmet ipsos commendatos esse nobis, Cic.; **d,** *to put, ask;* quaestiunculam, Cic.; **e,** *to put a person in some position or office;* alicui custodem, Caes.; aliquem custodem in frumento publico, Cic. **B.** *to put food, dainties,* etc., *before one;* pavonem, merulas, Hor. **C.** *to plant;* piros, Verg. **D.** *to deposit;* tabulas testamenti in aerario, Caes. **E.** *to lay out money, to invest, lend;* pecuniam apud aliquem, Cic.; in praedio, Cic. **F.** *to arrange the hair;* comas, Ov. **G.** Of the winds, etc., *to lay, to soothe;* tollere seu ponere vult freta, Hor.; refl., ponere, of the winds, *to lull,* Verg. **H.** *to lay aside;* **1,** lit., librum de manibus, Cic.; arma, *to lay down,* Caes.; and hence, *to submit,* Caes.; **2,** transf., *to lay aside, remove, give up;* vitam, Cic.; vitia, Cic.; dolorem, Cic.; moras, Verg.; **3,** naut. t.t., *to throw out anchor;* ancoris positis, Liv. (syncop. perf. partic., postus, Lucr.).

1. pons, pontis, m. *a bridge,* Cic. **I.** facere pontem in flumine, *to bridge over a river,* Caes.; pontem facere in Tiberi, Liv.; pontem interscindere, *to cut down,* Cic. **II.** Esp., **A.** *a plank between a ship and the shore,* Verg. **B.** *a drawbridge,* Verg. **C.** *the bridge at the comitia over which the voters passed singly, to pass into the* saepta, Cic. **D. a,** *the deck of a ship,* Tac.; **b,** *the floor of a tower,* Verg.

2. Pons, Pontis, *as a geographical name.* **I.** Pons Argenteus, *a place and bridge over the river Argenteus in Gallia Narbonensis.* **II.** Pons Campanus, *a bridge on the Via Appia.*

Pontia -ae, f. *an Island off the coast of Latium,* now *Isola di Ponza.* Hence, **Pontiāni** -ōrum, m. *the inhabitants of Pontia.*

ponticulus -i, m. (dim. of pons) *a little bridge,* Cic.

1. Ponticus -a -um, v. Pontus.

2. Ponticus -i, m. *a Roman poet, contemporary and friend of Propertius and Ovid.*

pontifex -fĭcis, m. (from pons and facio, or = pompifex, from pompa and facio), *a pontiff, a high priest, pontifex;* plur., pontifices, *a guild of priests at Rome, containing at first four, then eight, then fifteen members, the president of which was called* pontifex maximus; pontifices minores, *a lower class of pontiffs, assistants to the guild of* pontifices, Cic. Hence, **A. pontĭficālis** -e, *pontifical;* auctoritas, Cic. **B. pontĭficātus** -ūs, m. *the office of pontiff, the pontificate,* Cic. **C. pontĭficĭus** -a -um, *relating to the pontificate;* libri, Cic; jus, Cic.

pontĭficālis, v. **pontifex.**

pontĭficātus, v. **pontifex.**

pontĭficĭus, v. **pontifex.**

Pontĭus -a -um, *name of a gens, originally* Samnite, *afterwards Roman, the most famous members of which were:* **1,** C. Pontius, *commander of the Samnites at Caudium;* **2,** L. Pontius Aquila,

14*

one of the murderers of Caesar; **3,** Pontius Pilatus, *procurator of Judaea at the time of the crucifixion of Christ.*

ponto -ōnis, m. (pons), *a flat-bottomed boat,* punt, Caes.

1. pontus -i, n. (πόντος). **I.** *the deep, depth;* maris, Verg. **II.** Meton., **A.** *the deep sea,* Verg. **B.** *a wave of the sea,* Verg.

2. Pontus -i, m. (Πόντος). **I.** *the Black Sea.* **II.** Meton., **A.** *the country on the shores of the Black Sea.* **B.** Esp., *a district of Asia Minor between Bithynia and Armenia, the realm of Mithridates, later a Roman province, Pontus.* Hence, **Pontĭcus** -a -um (Ποντικός), *belonging to Pontus, Pontic;* mare, *the Black Sea,* Liv.; serpens, *the dragon that guarded the golden fleece at Colchis,* Juv.

pŏpa -ae, m. *the inferior priest or temple-servant who slew the victims,* Cic.

pŏpānum -i, n. (πόπανον), *a sacrificial cake,* Juv.

pŏpellus -i, m. (dim. of populus), *the common people, rabble,* Hor.

pŏpīna -ae, f. (πέπω, πέπτω, *to cook*). **I.** *a cook-shop, eating-house,* Cic. **II.** Meton., *the food sold at an eating-house,* Cic.

pŏpīno -ōnis, m. (popina), *the frequenter of eating-houses, glutton,* Hor.

pŏplĕs -ĭtis, m. **I.** *the ham, hough;* succidere poplitem, Verg.; femina poplitesque, Liv. **II.** Meton., *the knee;* duplicato poplite, *with bent knee,* Verg.; contento poplite, *with stiff knee,* Hor.

Poplĭcŏla = Publicola (q.v.).

poppysma -ătis, n. (πόππυσμα), and **poppysmus** -i, m. (ποππυσμός), *a clucking of the tongue as a sign of approbation,* Juv.

pŏpŭlābĭlis -e (populor), *that can be laid waste, devastated,* Ov.

pŏpŭlābundus -a -um (populor), *laying waste, devastating,* Liv.

pŏpŭlāris -e (1. populus), *belonging to the same people or country, native;* **1,** adj., flumina, Ov.; **2,** subst., a, lit. *a fellow-countryman;* Solon popularis tuus, Cic.; b, transf., *participator;* conjurationis, Sall. **II.** *belonging to the people, relating to the whole state, proceeding from the state;* **1,** gen., leges, Cic.; admiratio, Cic.; oratio, *to the people,* Cic.; **2,** esp., a, *popular, agreeable to the people, beloved by the people;* b, *of or relating to the people* (as opposed to the aristocracy), *popular, democratic;* popularis vir, *a friend of the people,* Liv.; homo, Cic. Subst., **pŏpŭlāres** -ĭum, m. *the popular party, the democracy,* Cic.

pŏpŭlārĭtas -ātis, f. (popularis), *desire to please the people, popular behaviour,* Tac.

pŏpŭlārĭtĕr, adv. (popularis). **I.** *after the manner of the people, commonly, vulgarly;* loqui, scribere, Cic. **II.** *after the fashion of a friend of the people, in a popular manner,* or, *in a bad sense, like a demagogue;* agere, Cic.

pŏpŭlātĭo -ōnis, f. (populor), *a laying waste, devastating, plundering;* populatio agrorum ceterorum, Liv.; ita libera populatio a tergo erat, Liv.; plur., Vejentes pleni jam populationum, *who had had their fill of plundering,* Liv.; hostem populationibus prohibere, Caes.

pŏpŭlātor -ōris, m. (populor), *a devastator, plunderer,* Liv.

pŏpŭlĕus -a -um (2. populus), *of or relating to the poplar;* frondes, Verg.

pŏpŭlĭfer -fĕra -fĕrum (2. populus and fero) *producing poplars,* Ov.

pŏpŭliscĭtum -i, n. *a decree of the people,* Liv.

Pŏpŭlōnĭa -ae, f., **Pŏpŭlōnĭum** -ĭi, n., and **Pŏpŭlōnĭi** -ōrum, m. *a town in Etruria,* now *ruins of Poplonia;* hence, **Pŏpŭlōnĭenses** -ĭum, m. *the inhabitants of Populonia.*

pŏpŭlo, 1. and **pŏpŭlor,** 1. dep. (1. populus), *to lay waste, devastate, plunder.* **I.** Lit., agros, Caes.; provinciae populatae, Cic. **II.** Poet., transf., *to destroy, ruin, spoil, rob;* populat acervum curculio, Verg.; populatus hamus, *robbed of the bait,* Ov.

1. **pŏpŭlus** -i, m. (connected with πλῆθος, plenus, etc., redupl. populus, syncop. poplus), *the people as forming a political community, a state.* **I.** Lit., 1, *the union of the inhabitants of a district, a state, a free state;* populi liberi . . . reges, Cic.; reges et populi liberi, Sall.; hence, meton., *a district, canton;* frequens cultoribus alius populus, Liv.; 2, transf., *a crowd, host, multitude;* fratrum, Ov. **II.** In narrower sense, 1, *the sovereign body in a free state, the sovereign people;* a, civitas popularis in qua in populo sunt omnia, Cic.; b, esp. in Rome, originally *the patricians,* afterwards *the whole people,* as opp. to the senate; often in the phrase, senatus populusque Romanus, Cic.; et patres in populi potestate fore, Liv.; as opp. to the plebs, non populi sed plebis judicium esse, Liv.; often, esp. with historians, *the people as a party, the democratical party;* populum a senatu disjunctum, Cic.; 2, *the people, multitude;* malus poeta de populo, Cic.

2. **pŏpŭlus** -i, f. *the poplar-tree,* Verg.

porca -ae, f. (porcus), *a sow;* sometimes poet., *a pig, hog,* Verg.

porcīna -ae, f. (sc. caro), *pork,* Plaut.

porcīnus -a -um, *of or relating to swine,* Plaut.

Porcĭus -a -um, *name of a Roman gens, the most famous members of which were:* 1, M. Porcius Cato Censorinus or Major, *a severe Censor, after whom Cicero named his work on old age;* 2, M. Porcius Cato, *the Younger, a contemporary of Cicero, called* Uticensis, *from his suicide at Utica;* 3, Porcia, *sister of the younger Cato, wife of Domitius Ahenobarbus.* Adj., *Porcian;* lex, *forbidding corporal punishment of a Roman citizen,* Cic.

porcŭlus -i, m. (dim. of porcus), *a young pig, porker,* Plaut.

porcus -i, m. *a pig, hog;* porcus femina, *a sow;* used as a term of reproach against a glutton, Epicuri de grege porcus, Hor.

porgo = porrigo (q.v.).

Porphyrĭo (-ōn) -ōnis, m. *one of the giants.*

porrectĭo -ōnis, f. (porrigo), *a stretching out, extension.*

porrectus -a -um, p. adj. (from porrigo). **I.** *stretched out, extended, long;* porrectior acies, Tac. **II.** Transf., poet. of time, *long;* mora, Ov.

porrĭcĭo -rēci and -rexi -rectum, 3. *to offer sacrifice to the gods;* prov., inter caesa et porrecta, *between the slaying and the offering of the victim*—i.e., *at the eleventh hour,* Cic.

1. **porrĭgo** -rexi -rectum, 3. (pro and rego), *to stretch out, reach out, extend.* **I.** A. 1, lit., a, membra, Cic.; manum, Cic.; middle, porrigi, *to be stretched out, to lie stretched out;* corpus porrigitur in novem jugera, Verg.; b, milit. t. t., *to extend;* aciem, Sall.; c, porrigere manum, *to hold up the hand in voting;* 2, transf., of position, scopulus frontem porrigit in aequor, Ov.: porrecta in dorso urbs, Liv. B. Fig., a,

vectigalia, *to increase,* Hor.; se porrigere, *to extend, reach;* quo se tua porrigat ira, Ov.; b, syllabam, *to lengthen the quantity of a syllable,* Ov. **II.** A. *to lay at full length, to lay low;* hostem, Liv.; hence, partic., porrectus = *dead;* senex, Cat. **B.** Meton., *to hold out to, reach to, offer to;* 1, lit., dextram regi Deiotaro, Cic.; gladium nobis, Cic.; 2, fig., *to afford, supply;* praesidium clientibus, Cic.

2. **porrīgo** -gĭnis, f. (= prurigo), *scurf, dandriff,* Hor.

porro, adv. (πόρρω), *forward, further.* **I.** Of space, *at a distance, afar off;* a, with verbs of motion, ire, Liv.; agere armentum, Liv.; b, with verbs of rest, inscius Aeneas quae sint ea flumina porro, Verg. **II.** Transf., A. Of time, *formerly,* Cat. **B.** To express advances from one thought to another, *then, next, further, again, in succession, in turn;* saepe audivi a senioribus natu, qui se porro pueros a sensibus audisse dicebant, Cic.; sequitur porro, nihil deos ignorare, Cic.

porrus -i, m. and **porrum** -i, n. (πράσον), *a leek,* Juv.

Porsĕna (Porsenna) and **Porsĭna (Porsina)** -ae, m. (Πορσήνας, Πορσίνας), *king of Etruria, who attacked Rome in order to bring back Tarquinius Superbus;* as a formula on the sale of booty, bona Porsinae regis veneunt, Liv.

porta -ae, f. (connected with περάω, πορθμός, experior, etc.), *a gate, city-gate.* **I.** A. Lit., with or without urbis, Cic.; portas claudere, Caes.; portā introire, Cic.; pedem portā non extulisse, Cic. **B.** Transf., *any place of ingress or egress, door, gate of a camp;* porta decumana, Caes.; porta Taenaria (where Hercules entered the lower world), Ov.; portae jecoris, Cic. **II.** Fig., quibus e portis occurri cuique deceret, *by what ways or means,* Lucr.

portātĭo -ōnis, f. (porto), *a carrying, conveying;* armorum, Sall.

portendo -tendi -tentum, 3. (pro-tendo), *to indicate, predict, presage, forbode, portend;* magnitudinem imperii portendens prodigium, Liv.; dii periculum portendunt, Liv.

portentĭfĕr -fĕra -fĕrum (portentum and fero), *bringing prodigies,* Ov.

portentĭfĭcus -a -um (portentum and facio), *extraordinary, supernatural, marvellous, miraculous;* venena, Ov.

portentōsus -a -um (portentum), *extraordinary, prodigious, portentous, monstrous, unnatural;* nata, *abortions,* Cic.

portentum -i, n. (portendo). **I.** *a prodigy, portent,* Cic. **II.** Transf., A. *a wonderful story, extravagant tale;* poëtarum et pictorum, Cic. **B.** *a monster, monstrosity;* hominum pecudumque portenta, Cic.; so of "*a monster of depravity;*" portentum reipublicae (of Piso), Cic.

porthmeus -ěi and -ěos, m. (πορθμεύς), *a ferryman* (of Charon), Juv.

portĭcŭla -ae, f. (dim. of porticus), *a little gallery or portico,* Cic.

portĭcus -ūs, f. (porta), *a portico, colonnade, arcade, gallery.* **I.** 1, lit., a, quum paullulum inambulavisset in porticu, Cic.; b, *the hall of justice, tribunal of the praetor,* Cic.; 2, meton., *the Stoic school* (so named from στοά, *a porch*), the Stoics; clamat Zeno et tota illa porticus tumultuatur. **II.** Transf., plur. porticus, *galleries to protect the besiegers of a place,* Caes.

portĭo -ōnis, f. (root POR, Gr. ΠΟΡ-ω), *a part, portion, section, division.* **I.** Lit., Plin. **II.** Transf., *proportion, ratio;* pro portione, *in proportion, proportionally,* Cic.

1. portĭtor -ōris, m. (portus), *a custom-house officer, collector of customs*, Cic.

2. portĭtor -ōris, m. (root POR-o, whence porto), *a carrier ;* and usually, *a boatman, ferryman ; Charon*, Verg.

porto, 1. (root POR-o, ΠΟΡ-ω, whence fero, portus), *to bear, carry, convey, bring.* **I.** Lit., concrete objects, **1**, gen., a, things, (α) onera, Caes. ; omnia mecum porto mea, Cic. ; with abl. or abl. and prep., in triumpho Massiliam, *a representation of Massilia*, Cic. ; with adv., or prep., or acc., multa undique portari, Caes. ; Romae domum ad Antonium frumentum, Cic. ; viaticum ad hostem, Cic. ; (β) of things as subjects, portans in corpore virus lolligo, Ov. ; b, persons, lecticā portari, Cic. **II.** Transf., with abstract objects, sociis atque amicis auxilia portabant, Sall.; has spes cogitationesque secum portantes, Liv.

portōrĭum -ĭi, n. (POR-o, porto), *customs, tax on imported and exported goods ;* portorium vini instituere, Cic. ; exigere portorium, Cic. ; portorium locare, *to let out the duties to farm,* Cic.

portŭla -ae, f. (dim. of porta), *a little gate, postern,* Liv.

Portūnus -i, m. (portus), *the god of harbours* (identified with the Greek Palaemon); hence, **Portūnālĭa** -ĭum, n. *the festival of Portunus, on the 17th of August.*

portŭōsus -a -um (portus), *having many harbours, abounding in ports ;* superum mare, Cic. ; navigatio minime portuosa, *without harbours,* Cic.

portus -ūs, m. (POR-o, whence porto), *a harbour, port, haven.* **I.** 1, lit., portus Caietae celeberrimus, Cic. ; e portu solvere, Cic. ; in portum pervehi, Cic. ; as a place for levying duties, in portu operam dare, *to be a customhouse officer,* Cic. ; prov., in portu esse, navigare, *to be out of danger,* Cic. ; 2, transf., *the estuary of a river,* Ov. **II.** Fig., *a place of refuge, harbour, haven ;* nationum portus et refugium senatus, Cic. ; se in philosophiae portum conferre, Cic.

poscaenĭum -ĭi, n. (post and scaena), *the theatre behind the scenes ;* fig., poscaenia vitae, *the secret actions of men,* Lucr.

posco, pŏposci, 3. (pet-sco, from peto), *to ask earnestly, request strongly, demand.* **I.** Gen., **A.** Of persons, pugnam, Liv. ; argentum, Cic. ; with eth. dat., audaciae partes sibi, Cic. ; with acc. and ab with abl., munus ab aliquo, Cic. ; with double acc., magistratum Sicyonium nummos poposcit, Cic. ; absol., poscimur, *we are asked for a song,* Hor. ; with ut and the subj., Tac. ; with acc. and infin., Ov. **B.** Transf., of things, *to demand, require;* quod res poscere videbatur, Caes. **II.** Esp., **A.** *to demand for judgment, require to be given up;* accusant ii, quos populus jussit, Cic. **B.** *to challenge to fight;* aliquem in proelia, Verg. ; so absol., transf., poscunt majoribus poculis, *challenge one another,* Cic. **C.** *to inquire;* causas, Verg. **D.** *to call ;* **1**, poscor Olympo, *heaven summons me to battle,* Verg. ; **2**, *to call upon;* tua numina posco, Verg.

Pŏsidōnĭus -ĭi, m. (Ποσειδώνιος), *a Stoic philosopher, pupil of Panaetius and teacher of Cicero.*

pŏsĭtĭo -ōnis, f. (pono), *a placing, putting;* caeli, *climate,* Tac.

pŏsĭtor -ōris, m. (pono), *a founder, builder,* Ov.

pŏsĭtūra -ae, f. (pono), *position, situation, place, posture,* Lucr.

pŏsĭtus -ūs, m. (pono). **I.** *position, place,* urbis, Ov. ; regionis, Tac. **II.** *arrangement of the hair,* Ov.

possessĭo -ōnis, f. (possideo). **I.** *possession ;* a, lit., fundi, Cic. ; possessionem hereditatis alicui dare, eripere, Cic. ; aliquem movere, demovere de possessione, Cic. ; b, fig., prudentiae doctrinaeque, Cic. **II.** Meton., *that which is possessed, a possession, property ;* paternae atque avitae possessiones, Cic.

possessĭuncŭla -ae, f. (dim. of possessio), *a little possession, small property,* Cic.

possessor -ōris, m. (possideo), *a possessor.* **I.** Gen., locorum, Cic. **II.** Esp., *a possessor of land ;* possessor agrorum, Liv. ; absol., Cic.

possĭdĕo -sēdi -sessum, 2. (potis and sedeo), *to possess, have, hold.* **I. A.** Lit., ex edicto bona, Cic. **B.** Fig., ingenium, Cic. **II.** Transf., *to occupy a place by force, beset ;* forum armatis catervis perditorum hominum, Cic.

possĭdo -sēdi -sessum, 3. (potis and sido), *to take possession of, occupy.* **I.** Lit., bona sine testamento, Cic. **II.** Fig., totum hominem totamque eius praeturam, Cic.

possum, pŏtŭi, posse (potis and sum), *to be able, I (thou, he, etc.) can.* **I.** Gen., facere ut possem, Cic.; potest fieri ut fallar, *I may be mistaken,* Cic.; fieri non potest ut non or quin, *it cannot but be that,* Cic. ; ut nihil ad te dem litterarum, facere non possum, *I cannot help writing to you,* Cic. ; si potest, *if it is possible,* Cic. ; quī potest? *how is it possible ?* Cic. ; with superl., Caesari commendavi ut gravissime potui, *as strongly as I could,* Cic. **II.** Esp., *to avail, be efficacious, have influence ;* a, of persons, apud Sequanos plurimum, Caes. ; quum omnia se posse censebat, *thought himself all-powerful,* Cic.; b, of things, plus potest apud te pecuniae cupiditas, Cic.

post (= ponst, from pone). **I.** Adv. *behind.* **A.** Of place, *behind, in the rear ;* qui post erant, Cic. **B.** Transf., 1, of time, *after, afterwards, subsequently;* multis post annis, *many years afterwards,* Cic. ; aliquanto post, *shortly afterwards,* Cic. ; multo post, *long after,* Cic. ; 2, of the order of succession, primo . . . post, Cic. **II.** Prep. with acc. **A.** Of place, *behind ;* post nostra castra, Caes. **B.** Transf., 1, of time, *after ;* post Brutum consulem, Cic. ; foll. by quam, post diem tertium . . . quam dixerat, Cic. ; 2, of order, *next to ;* erat Lydia post Chloen, Hor.

postĕă, adv. (post and abl. eā), *after, after that, afterwards ;* postea aliquanto, Cic. ; quid postea? *what then ? what next ?* Cic.

postĕāquam, conj. *after that ;* with indic.; (α) with perf., posteaquam victoria constituta est, Cic. ; (β) with pluperf., posteaquam bis consul fuerat, Cic. ; (γ) with imperf., posteaquam e scena explodebatur, Cic. ; (δ) with pres., posteaquam in Formiano sum, Cic.

postĕri, v. posterus.

postĕrĭus, v. posterus.

postĕrĭtas -ātis, f. (posterus). **I.** *the future ;* habere rationem posteritatis, Caes. ; posteritatis otio consulere, Cic. **II.** *future generations, after-ages, posterity ;* omnium seculorum, Cic.; posteritati servire, Cic.; invidia posteritatis, Cic.

postĕrus (poster) -a -um, compar., **postĕrĭor** -us ; superl., **postrēmus** and **postŭmus** -a -um (post). **I.** Posit., *subsequent, ensuing, following, next, future ;* lit., postero die, Cic. ; in posterum, *for the next day, and for the future,* Cic. ; subst., **postĕri** -ōrum, m. *posterity.* **II.** Compar., **postĕrĭor** -us, 1, *following after,* next in order, later, posterior; posteriores cogitationes, second thoughts, Cic.; paulo aetate posterior, Cic.; neut. adv., posterius = later, Cic.; **P**, transf., inferior, worse; nihil posterius, Cic. **III.** Superl., **postrēmus** and **postūmus** -a -um. **A.** postremus, the hindmost, last; **1**, lit., pagina, Cic.; acies, Sall.; hoc non in postremis, Cic.; abl., postremo, at last; primum . . . deinde . . . postremo, Cic.; postremum, for the last time, Cic.; **2**, transf., of position and value, the worst, most pitiable; homines, Cic. **B.** ad postremum, at last, lastly; meton., the last; **postūmus** -a -um, the last, last-born (esp. of children born after the father's will or death), posthumous; proles, Verg.; subst., **postūmus** -i, m., Cic.

postfĕro -ferre, to esteem less, consider of less account; libertati plebis suas opes, Liv.

postgĕnĭti -ōrum, m. (post and gigno), posterity, descendants, Hor.

posthăbĕo -ŭi -ĭtum, 2. to esteem less, make of less account; omnibus rebus posthabitis, Cic.

posthāc, adv. hereafter, after this, in future, Cic.

postīcus -a -um (post), hinder, back, behind. **I.** Adj., partes aedium, Liv. **II.** Subst., posticum aedium, a back-door, Liv.

postĭlĭo -ōnis, f. (postulo), the demand of a deity for a sacrifice, Cic.

postillā, adv. after, afterwards, Cat.

postis -is, m. a post, door-post. **I.** Lit., postem tenere (of a person who consecrated a temple), Cic. **II.** Plur., meton., poet., a door, gate, Verg.

postlīmĭnĭum -ĭi, n. (post and limen), a return home, postliminy; the resumption by a prisoner of war of his civil rights, which were in abeyance during his captivity; ei esse postliminium, Cic.; gen. abl., postliminio, by right of postliminy; redire, Cic.

postmĕrīdĭānus (pōmĕrīdĭānus) -a -um (post and meridianus), belonging to the afternoon, afternoon; tempus, Cic.

postmŏdŏ and **postmŏdum**, adv. after, afterwards, Liv.

postpōno -pŏsŭi -pŏsĭtum, 3. to esteem less, consider of less account, put after; omnia, Cic.; aliquem alicui, Ov.; omnibus rebus postpositis, Cic.

postquam, conj. after, after that, as soon as; a, with indic., (a) gen. with perf., postquam Caesar pervenit, Caes.; (β) with pluperf., undecimo die, postquam a te discesseram, Cic.; (γ) with pres., Hostilia curia minor mihi esse videtur, postquam est major, Cic.; (δ) with imperf., postquam amici non poterant vincere etc., Cic.; b, with historic infin., postquam exui aequalitas, Tac.

postrēmo, v. posterus.

postrēmum, v. posterus.

postrēmus -a -um, superl. of posterus (q.v.).

postrīdĭē, adv. (for posteri diei), the day after, the following day, on the next day; primā luce postridie, Caes.; foll. by quam, postridie quam a vobis discessi, Cic.; with acc., ludos, the day after the games, Cic.; with genit., postridie eius diei, Caes.

postrīdŭo = postridie (q.v.).

postscrībo -scripsi -scriptum, 3. to write after, Tac.

postŭlātĭo -ōnis, f. (postulo), a request, entreaty, demand. **I.** Gen., ignoscendi, for pardon, Cic.; concedere postulationi eius, Cic. **II.**

Legal t. t., an application to the praetor to allow a complaint or charge to be brought, Cic.

postŭlātum -i, n. (postulo), a demand, request, Cic.

postŭlātus -ūs, m. (postulo), a legal complaint, accusation, Liv.

postŭlĭo = postilio (q.v.).

postŭlo, 1. (= posculo, from posco), to demand, beg, entreat, ask, request. **I.** Gen., (a) with acc., auxilium, Cic.; (β) with double acc., haec quum praetorem postulabas, Cic.; (γ) with ut or ne or ut ne and the subj., postulat abs te ut Romam rem rejicias, Cic.; with subj. alone, qui postularent, eos sibi dederent, Caes.; (δ) with infin., or acc. and infin., dicendo vincere non postulo, Cic.; hic postulat Romae se absolvi, Cic.; with nom. and infin. pass., bona possideri postularentur, Cic.; (e) absol. and transf., of things or subjects, quum tempus necessitasque postulat, Cic. **II.** Esp., legal t. t., a, to demand from the praetor against some one; judicium, Cic.; b, to impeach, accuse; aliquem de ambitu, Cic.; aliquem majestatis, Cic.

Postŭmĭus -a -um, name of a Roman gens, the most celebrated members of which were: **1**, the consul P. Postumius Tubertus, conqueror of the Sabines; **2**, A. Postumius Tubertus, dictator, who ordered the execution of his own son for fighting against orders; poet. form, Postumus; adj., Postumian, and hence, **Postŭmĭānus** -a -um, Postumian.

1. postŭmus -a -um, superl. of posterus (q.v.).

2. Postŭmus, v. Postumius.

Postverta (Postvorta) -ae, f. (post and verto), the goddess of childbirth, invoked in case of an irregular presentation, Ov.

pōtātĭo -ōnis, f. (poto), a drinking-bout; hesterna ex potatione oscitantes, Cic.

pōtātor -ōris, m. (poto), a drinker, Plaut.

pŏtĕ, v. potis.

pŏtens -entis, p. adj. (from possum). **I.** powerful, having power over. **A.** neque jubendi neque vetandi, Tac. **B.** 1, capable of; armorum tenendorum, Liv.; **2**, mighty, influential; civis, civitas, Cic.; subst., a powerful person, Liv.; plur., Cic.; **3**, of things, powerful, efficacious; nihil est potentius auro, Ov.; **4**, master of, lord of; potentes rerum suarum et urbis, Liv.; dum mei potens sum, as long as I am my own master, Liv.; Diva potens Cypri, ruling over Cyprus, Hor.; fig., potens sui, having command over oneself, temperate, Hor.; potens irae, able to control one's anger, Liv. **II.** that which has obtained something; voti, Ov.; iussi, having fulfilled the command, Ov.

pŏtentātus -ūs, m. (potens), political power, supremacy, Cic.

pŏtentĕr, adv. (potens). **I.** powerfully, strongly, efficaciously, Hor. **II.** according to one's power, Hor.

1. pŏtentĭa -ae, f. (potens), power, might, ability. **I.** Physical, **1**, lit., solis, Verg.; **2**, transf., efficacy, potency; herbarum, Ov. **II.** political power; a, influence, authority; erant in magna potentia qui consulebantur, Cic.; b, supremacy, rule; rerum, Cic.

2. Pŏtentĭa -ae, f. a town in Picenum, on the river Floris, now, perhaps, Monte Santo.

pŏtestas -ātis, f. (possum), power. **I.** Gen., might, strength, efficacy; herbarum, Verg. **II.** power to do something, power over something. **A.** **1**, gen., habere potestatem vitae necisque in aliquem, Cic.; esse in potestate senatūs, Cic.;

exisse ex or de potestate (sc. mentis), *to lose the control of one's reason*, Cic. ; 2, esp., a, *political power, supremacy, dominion ;* esse in alicuius ditione ac potestate, Cic. ; b, *the power, authority of a magistrate, official authority, office ;* (α) lit., praetoria, Cic. ; dare alicui potestatem legati, Cic. ; (β) meton., *the magistracy itself ;* imperia et potestates, *military and civil commands*, Cic. B. *might, power, ability, opportunity, possibility, occasion ;* data est potestas augendae dignitatis, Cic. ; facere potestatem alicui, (α) *to give an opportunity of fighting,* Caes. ; (β) *to allow access to oneself, grant an interview,* Caes. ; potestas est, *it is possible,* with infin., non fugis hinc praeceps dum praecipitare potestas, Verg.

l. **pŏtĭo** -ōnis, f. (poto), *a drinking, draught, potion.* I. Gen., Cic. II. a, *a draught of poison,* Cic. ; b, *a love-draught, philtre,* Hor.

2. **pŏtĭo,** 4. (potis), *to put any one in the power of ;* aliquem servitutis, *to reduce to slavery,* Plaut.

l. **pŏtĭor,** 4. dep. (potis). I. *to get, get possession, become partaker of, obtain ;* with abl., urbe, Cic. ; victoriā, Caes. ; with genit., illius regni, Cic. ; with acc., urbem, Cic. II. *to possess, have, be master of ;* with abl., mari, Liv. ; with genit., rerum, Cic. (potior has some forms from the third conjug., potĭtur, Verg. ; potĕremur, Ov. ; potĕrentur, Liv.).

2. **pŏtĭor,** v. potis.

pŏtis, pŏtĕ (root POT, whence δεσ-πότης, compos, etc.). I. Adj., compar., **pŏtĭor** -us ; superl., **pŏtissĭmus** -a -um. A. Posit., *able, capable ;* usually in the phrase potis est, *he can, is able ;* potis est vis ulla tenere, Verg. ; nec potis est cerni, *nor is it possible to distinguish,* Lucr. ; neut., pote est, Cat. ; pote = pote esse, hoc quidquam pote impurius, Cic. B. Compar., **pŏtĭor** -us, *preferable, better ;* cives potiores quam peregrini, Cic. ; potior patre, Cic. ; mors servitute potior, Cic. C. Superl., **pŏtissĭmus** -a -um, *best of all, chief, principal ;* quid potissimum sit, Cic. II. Adv., only in compar., **pŏtĭus,** and superl., **pŏtissĭmum.** A. compar., potius, *rather, more, preferably ;* magnus (homo) vel potius summus, Cic. ; potius quam, foll. by ut and subj., or simply subj., Cic. ; with verbs expressing a comparison, emori potius ,uam servire praestaret, Cic. B. ɔuperl., **pŏtissĭmum** (**pŏtissĭme**), *chiefly, above all,* Cic.

pŏtissĭme, potissimum, v. potis.

pŏtĭto, l. (intens. of poto), *to drink frequently, drink hard,* Plaut.

pŏtĭus, v. potis.

Potnĭae -ārum, f. (Ποτνιαί), *a place in Boeotia on the river Asopus, the pastures of which were said to make animals that grazed them mad.* Hence, **Potnĭăs** -ădis, f. *belonging to Potniae ;* equae, Ov., quadrigae, Verg., *the team of horses which threw out and killed their master Glaucus.*

pōto, pōtāvi, pōtātum and pōtum, l. *to drink.* I. Lit., aquas, Ov.; absol., huc veniunt potum juvenci, Verg. ; 2, *to drink, revel ;* totos dies potabatur, Cic. II. Transf., *to absorb, suck in ;* potantia vellera fucum, Hor. ; partic., a, **ptŏus** -a -um, (α) pass., *drunk, drunk up, drained ;* sanguine poto, Cic.; poti faece tenus cadi, Hor. ; (β) act., *having drunk, drunken ;* anus, Hor. ; bene potus, Cic. ; b, **pōtūrus** -a -um, Prop.

pōtor -ōris, m. (poto), *a drinker.* I. aquae, Hor. ; Rhodani, *a dweller by the Rhone,* Hor. II. *a tippler, drunkard,* Hor.

pōtrix -īcis, f. (potor), *a female tippler,* Phaedr.

pōtŭlentus -a -um (poto), *drinkable, potable ;* hence, subst., **pōtŭlenta** -ōrum, *things that can be drunk, drinkables ;* esculenta et potulenta, Cic.

l. **pōtus,** v. poto.

2. **pōtus** -ūs, m. (poto). I. *a drinking ;* immoderatus, Cic. II. Meton., *a draught, that which is drunk, drink ;* cibi potusque, Ter.

prae, adv. and prep. (old dat. fem., like pro, dat. neut., from *prus -a -um, formed from per). I. Adv. *before, in front ;* i prae, Plaut., Ter. II. Prep. with abl., A. *before ;* prae se pugionem tulit, Cic. ; prae se armentum agens, Liv.; fig., prae se ferre, *to show, exhibit, betray, discover, manifest ;* scelus, Cic.; vocem, Cic. B. Transf., l, *in comparison with, compared with ;* Atticos prae se agrestes putat, Cic.; prae nobis beatus, Cic.; 2, *on account of, because of, in consequence of ;* nec loqui prae maerore potuit, Cic. ; prae metu, Cic. ; prae ira, Liv.

praeăcŭo (-ŭi) -ūtum, 3. *to sharpen to a point ;* gen. in partic., **praeăcūtus** -a -um, *sharpened to a point, pointed ;* sudes, Sall. ; stipites, Caes.

praealtus -a -um. I. *very high ;* rupes, Liv. II. *very deep ;* flumen, Liv.

praebĕo -bŭi -bĭtum (= praehibeo, from prae and habeo). I. *to offer, hold out ;* crus alterum, Cic. ; os ad contumeliam, Liv. ; manum verberibus, Ov. II. Transf., A. *to expose ;* se telis hostium, Liv. B. *to show, give ;* operam alicui, *to serve,* Liv. ; reflex., with or without se, *to show oneself, prove oneself ;* with acc. of predicate, misericordem se praebuit, Cic.; se virum, Cic. ; in eos se severum vehementemque, Cic. ; utrisque se aequum, Cic. C. *to furnish, supply, afford ;* alicui naves, Liv. ; rebus adversis perfugium ac solatium, Cic. ; hence, a, *to offer, present, cause, bring about ;* speciem horribilem, Caes. ; modum, *to make music,* Ov. ; b, *to allow ;* praebuit ipsa rapi, Ov.

praebĭbo -bĭbi, 3. *to drink before, to drink to ;* ei cui venenum praebiberat, Cic.

praebĭtor -ōris, m. (praebeo) = πάροχος, *a furnisher, supplier, one who in the provinces furnished officials with necessaries,* Cic.

praecălĭdus -a -um, *very hot,* Tac.

praecānus -a -um, *prematurely grey,* Hor.

praecăvĕo -cāvi -cautum, 2. I. Intransit., *to take precaution beforehand, to be on one's guard, to be careful ;* providens et praecavens, Cic. ; ab insidiis, Liv. ; with dat., *to take care for some person's safety ;* decemviris ab ira et impetu multitudinis, Liv. ; with ne and the subj., id ne accideret, sibi praecavendum existimabat, Caes. II. Transit., *to beware of, guard against beforehand, seek to avert ;* quod a me ita praecautum est, Cic.; peccata, quae difficillime praecaventur, Cic.

praecēdo -cessi -cessum, 3. *to go before, precede.* I. Lit., l, intransit., praecedens consulis filius, Liv.; cum equite, Liv. ; 2, transit., agmen, Verg. II. Transit., A. Of time, *to go before, precede ;* fama loquax praecessit ad aures tuas, Ov. B. Of rank, etc., *to surpass, be before ;* reliquos Gallos virtute, Caes. ; vestros honores rebus agendis, Liv.

praecellens -entis, p. adj. (from praecello), *excellent, admirable, distinguished, surpassing :* vir et animo et virtute praecellens, Cic. ; vir omnibus rebus praecellentissimus, Cic.

praecello, 3. (prae and *cello), *to surpass, excel, exceed ;* a, absol., gravitate morum, Tac. ; b, with acc. or dat., aliquam fecunditate, Tac. ; genti. *had the supremacy over,* Tac.

praecelsus -a -um, *very high, very lofty;* .rupes, Verg.

praecentĭo -ōnis, f. (praecino), *a musical prelude, playing before a sacrifice,* Cic.

praeceps -cĭpĭtis (prae and caput), *headlong, headforemost.* **I.** Adj., **A.** Of motion, 1, lit., **a,** of persons, (a) aliquem praecipitem dejicere, Cic.; praeceps in terram datus, Liv.; (β) *in haste, hasty, quick;* praecipites columbae, Verg.; praecipites se fugae mandabant, Caes.; praeceps fertur, Cic.; **b,** transf., (a) of things, *hasty, precipitate;* profectio, Cic.; celeritas dicendi, Cic.; (β) of time, *declining;* praeceps dies, Liv.; praeceps aetas, Sall.; 2, fig., **a,** of persons, *blind, rash, headlong;* agunt eum praecipitem poenae civium Romanorum, Cic.; homo in omnibus consiliis praeceps, Cic.; praeceps ingenio in iram, *inclined to,* Liv.; **b,** of things, circumstances, etc., *dangerous;* libertas, Liv.; lubricum genus orationis adulescenti non acriter intellegenti est saepe praeceps, Cic. **B.** Of rest, 1, adj., of places, *steep, precipitous;* locus, Caes.; saxa, Liv.; fig., iter ad finitimum malum praeceps ac lubricum, Cic.; 2, subst., **praeceps** -cĭpĭtis, n. *a steep place, precipice;* in praeceps deferri, Liv.; fig., *danger;* prope totam rempublicam in praeceps dederat, Liv. **II.** Adv., vim mortalium praeceps trahit, *drags headlong,* Tac.

praeceptĭo -ōnis, f. (praecipio), 1, *a preconception,* Cic.; 2, *a precept;* Stoicorum, Cic.

praeceptor -ōris, m. (praecipio), *a teacher, instructor, preceptor;* vivendi atque dicendi, Cic.

praeceptrix -trīcis, f. (praeceptor), *she that teaches;* quā (sapientiā) praeceptrice, Cic.

praeceptum -i, n. (praecipio), *a precept, command, rule, ordinance, injunction;* medicorum, philosophorum, rhetorum, Cic.; Latine loquendi, Cic.; praecepta dare, Cic.

praecerpo -cerpsi -cerptum, 3. (prae and carpo), *to pluck prematurely, gather before the time.* **I.** Lit., messes, Ov. **II.** Fig., *to lessen* or *take away;* fructum officii tui, Cic.

praecīdo -cīdi -cīsum, 3. (prae and caedo). **I.** *to cut off in front, cut off.* **A.** Lit., alicui caput, Liv.; fistulas (aquae), Cic.; ancoras, *to cut the cables,* Cic. **B.** Fig., 1, *to cut short, to cut, abbreviate, abridge;* brevi praecidam, *I will express myself briefly,* Cic.; praecide, *make it short,* Cic.; 2, *to take away, deprive of;* sibi reditum, Cic.; 3, *to refuse point blank;* plane sine exceptione, Cic. **II.** *to cut in pieces.* **A.** Lit., canem, Liv.; cotem novaculā, Cic. **B.** Fig., *to break off suddenly;* amicitias magis decere diluere quam repente praecidere, Cic.

praecinctus -a -um, partic. of praecingo.

praecingo -cinxi -cinctum, 3. *to gird, surround with a girdle;* middle, praecingi, *to gird oneself,* Cic. Partic., recte praecincti pueri, Hor.; altius ac nos praecincti, *girded higher up,* i.e., *more rapid travellers,* Hor.

praecino -cěcini and -cīnŭi -centum, 3. (prae and cano). **I.** Intransit., **A.** *to sing or play before;* **a,** of musical instruments (esp. the flute), epulis magistratuum fides praecinunt, Cic.; **b,** of flute-players, praecinere sacrificiis or sacris, Liv. **B.** *to sing an incantation,* Tib. **II.** Transit., *to prophesy, predict;* magnum aliquid deos populo Romano praecinere, Cic.

praecĭpes -is = praeceps (q.v.).

praecĭpĭo -cēpi -ceptum, 3. (prae and capio), *to take before, get before, receive in advance.* **I.** Lit., pecuniam mutuam, Cic.; iter, *to get the start,* Liv.; si lac praeceperit aestus, *if the heat dries the milk beforehand,* Verg.; praecipitur seges, *ripens too fast,* Ov. **II.** Transf., **A.** *to*

take beforehand, anticipate; **praecipio** gaudia suppliciorum vestrorum, *I enjoy in anticipation,* ap. Cic.; animo victoriam, Caes.; consilia hostium, *know beforehand,* Cic. **B.** Esp., *to tell beforehand, to write beforehand;* **a,** *to instruct, advise, warn, prescribe, admonish, charge, command;* hoc tibi praecipio, Cic.; with ut or ne and the subj., illud potius praecipiendum fuit ut, etc., Cic.; with subj. alone, Sall.; with infin., temporibus parēre, Cic.; absol., ut erat praeceptum, Caes.; **b,** *to teach;* artem, Ov.; alicui rationem tempestatum, Cic.; praecipe cantus, Hor.; absol., *to be a teacher, to give instruction;* de eloquentia, Cic.

praecĭpĭtantĕr, adv. (praecipito), *headlong, headforemost, precipitately,* Lucr.

praecĭpĭto, 1. (praeceps). **I.** Transit., *to cast down headlong.* **A.** 1, lit., sese Leucade, Cic.; sese in fossas, Caes.; pass., praecipitari, in middle sense, *to cast oneself down,* Sall.; poet., lux praecipitatur aquis, *sinks beneath the waves,* Ov.; 2, transf., partic., praecipitatus, *drawing to a close,* Ov.; nox praecipitata, Ov. **B.** Fig., **a,** *to cast down;* aliquem ex altissimo dignitatis gradu, Cic.; *to cast to the ground, destroy, ruin;* rempublicam, Liv.; **b,** pass., praecipitari, as middle, *to rush into;* in insidias, Liv.; hence, (a) *to hurry away;* furor iraque mentem praecipitant, Verg.; (β) *to hasten;* moras omnes, Verg.; (γ) *to press on;* with infin., dare tempus sociis humandis, Verg. **II.** Intransit., *to fall down, to sink violently.* **A.** 1, lit., Nilus praecipitat ex montibus, Cic.; in fossam, Liv.; 2, transf., *to draw to a close, hasten to the end;* sol praecipitans, *declining,* Cic.; hiems jam praecipitaverat, *was drawing to a close,* Caes. **B.** Fig., **a,** praecipitantem impellere, *to give a push to a falling man, to knock a man when he is down,* Cic.; praecipitare ad exitium, Cic.; respublica praecipitans, *hastening to its fall,* Cic.; **b,** *to fall into;* in amorem, *to fall in love,* Plaut.

praecĭpŭē, adv. (praecipuus), *especially, chiefly, particularly, principally,* Cic.

praecĭpŭus -a -um (prae and capio). **I.** *peculiar, especial;* mihi consuli praecipuum fuit praeter alios, Cic.; in communibus miseriis praecipuo quodam dolore angi, Cic. Subst., **praecĭpŭum** -i, n. *a special right, a prerogative,* Cic. **II.** *excellent, distinguished, extraordinary, especial;* **a,** quos praecipuo semper honore Caesar habuit, Caes.; natura ingenerat praecipuum quendam amorem, Cic.; praecipuus toro (*distinguished by a seat of honour*) Aeneas, Verg. Subst., **praecĭpŭum** -i, n. *pre-eminence, superiority;* homini praecipui a natura nihil datum esse, Cic.; plur., **praecĭpŭa** -ōrum, n. = προηγμένα, *things* (in the Stoic philosophy) *that come next to the greatest good;* **b,** *especially suited for;* praecipuus ad pericula, Tac.

praecīsē, adv. (praecisus). **I.** *briefly, in few words;* id praecise dicitur, Cic. **II.** *absolutely, decidedly;* negare, Cic.

praecīsus -a -um, p. adj. (from praecido). **I.** *steep, abrupt, precipitous;* saxa, Verg. **II.** Rhet. t. t., *short, brief, broken off,* Cic.

praeclārē, adv. (praeclarus). **I.** *very plainly, very clearly;* intelligere, Cic.; explicare, Cic. **II.** *admirably, excellently;* gerere negotium, Cic.; meminisse, Cic.; facere, *to do something remarkable,* Cic.

praeclārus -a -um, *very bright, very brilliant.* **I.** Lit., lux, Lucr. **II.** Fig., 1, *noble, illustrious, remarkable, distinguished, excellent, admirable, famous;* gens bello praeclara, Verg.; situs (urbis), Cic.; indoles, Cic.; praeclarissimi conatus, Cic.; subst., **praeclāra** -ōrum, n.

valuables, Cic.; **2,** in a bad sense, *notorious;* **scel**eribus ferox atque praeclarus, Sall.

praecludo -clūsi -clūsum, 3. (prae and claudo). **I.** Lit., *to close in front, to shut up, to close;* praecludere portas consuli, Caes. **II.** Transf., *to close to any one, deprive of access to;* sibi curiam, Cic. ; maritimos cursus, Cic.; vocem alicui, *to stop a person's mouth,* Liv.

praeco -ōnis, m. **I.** *a public crier, herald* (in a court of justice, at public assemblies, at auctions) ; per praeconem vendere aliquid, Cic. ; fundum subjicere praeconi, *bring to the hammer,* Liv. **II.** Transf., *a publisher, herald, one who praises;* virtutis, Cic.

praecōgĭto, 1. *to think meditate, consider carefully beforehand;* multo ante facinus, Liv.

praecognosco (-cognōvi) -cognĭtum, 3. *to learn beforehand;* praecognito nostro adventu, ap. Cic.

praecŏlo -cŏlŭi -cultum, 3. *to cultivate before,* fig. **I.** animi praeculti rectis studiis et artibus, Cic. **II.** *to honour highly, to revere;* nova et ancipitia, Tac.

praecompŏsĭtus -a -um (prae and compono), *composed beforehand, studied;* os, mien, Ov.

praecōnĭus -a -um, *belonging to a praeco* or *crier.* **I.** Adj., quaestus, Cic. **II.** Subst., **praecōnĭum** -ĭi, n. **A.** *the office or business of a public crier;* praeconium facere, Cic. **B.** Transf., 1, *a public crying, publishing, making known;* tibi praeconium deferam, Cic.; perago praeconia casus, Ov.; 2, *a public laudation, commendation;* laborum suorum, Cic.

praeconsūmo -consumptus, 3. *to consume, exhaust beforehand,* Ov.

praecontrecto, 1. *to handle beforehand,* Ov.

praecŏquis -e and **praecŏquus** -a -um = praecox (q.v.).

praecordĭa -ōrum, n. (prae and cor). **I.** *the muscle separating the heart and lungs from the abdomen, the midriff, the diaphragm,* Cic. **II.** Transf., **A.** *the bowels, stomach;* anulus in praecordiis piscis inventus, Cic.; quid veneni saevit in praecordiis, Hor. **B.** *the breast, heart* (as the seat of feelings and passions); reditin praecordia virʾus, Verg.; spiritus remanet in praecordiis, Liʾ

praecorrumpo -rūpi -ruptum, 3. *to corrupt, bribe beforehand;* me donis, Ov.

praecox -cŏcis, **praecŏquis** -e, and **praecŏquus** -a -um (prae and coquo), *ripe before the time, premature,* Plin.

praecultus -a -um, partic. of praecolo.

praecurro -cŭcurri and -curri -cursum, 3. **I. A.** Lit., *to run before, hasten before;* praecurrit ante omnes, Caes. ; ad aliquem, Caes.; aliquem equis albis, fig. = *to excel,* Hor. Partic. subst., **praecurrentĭa** -ium, n. *what goes before, antecedents,* Cic. **B.** Transf., 1, *to go on before;* eo fama jam praecurrerat de praelio Dyrrhachino ; 2, *of time, to precede;* aliquem aetate, Cic.; with dat., ut certis rebus certa signa praecurrerent. **II.** Esp., *to surpass, exceed;* aliquem celeritate, Caes.

praecursĭo -ōnis f. (praecurro), *a going before.* **I.** Gen., sine praecursione visorum, Cic. **II.** In rhet., *the previous preparation of the hearer,* Cic.

praecursor -ōris, m. (praecurro), *a goer before, precursor.* **I.** Lit., **A.** Milit. t. t., praecursores, *the vanguard, advanced guard,* Liv. **II.** Transf., *a spy, scout;* in omni calumnia praecursorem habere, Cic.

praecŭtĭo -cussi -cussum, 3. (prae and

quatio), *to shake before, brandish before;* taedas, Ov.

praeda -ae, f. (connected with praehendo), *spoils of war, plunder, booty.* **I.** Lit., praeda parta, Cic. ; ingentes praedas facere, Liv. **II.** Transf., **A.** *the spoils of the chase, quarry, prey;* cervi luporum praeda rapacium, Hor. **B.** *plunder, gain;* maximos quaestus praedasque facere, Cic.

praedābundus -a -um (praedor), *plundering,* Sall.

praedamno, 1. **I.** *to condemn before;* aliquem. **II.** *to give up;* spem, Liv.

praedātĭo -ōnis, f. (praedor), *a plundering, pillaging,* Tac.

praedātor -ōris, m. (praedor). **I.** Lit., *a plunderer, pillager, robber;* vexatores ac praedatores, Cic. **II.** Transf., **A.** *a hunter;* caprorum, Ov. **B.** *a gain-loving, greedy person,* Tib.

praedātōrĭus -a -um (praedator), *plundering, pillaging, predatory;* classis, Liv.

praedēlasso, 1. *to weary, weaken beforehand,* Ov.

praedestĭno, 1. *to appoint, ordain beforehand ;* sibi similes triumphos, Liv.

praedĭātor -ōris, m. (praedium), *a buyer of landed estates sold by auction, a dealer in estates,* Cic.

predĭātōrĭus -a -um (praediator), *of or relating to the sale of land by auction;* jus, Cic.

praedĭcābĭlis -e (1. praedico), *praiseworthy,* Cic.

praedĭcātĭo -ōnis, f. (1. praedico). **I.** *a making publicly known, the public announcement of the praeco,* Cic. **II.** Transf., 1, *a declaration, deposition;* nefariae societatis, *relating to,* Cic. ; 2, *a praising, commending, praise,* Cic.

praedĭcātor -ōris, m. (1. praedico), *a praiser, commender, public eulogist,* Cic.

1. **praedĭco,** 1. *to make publicly known, publish.* **I.** Lit., of the praeco, dimidias venire partes, Cic. **II.** Transf., 1, *to declare, speak out, relate, proclaim, say, tell ;* paucitatem nostrorum militum suis, Caes. ; with acc. and infin., praedicantem contumeliam illam sibi a Cicerone impositam esse, Sall. ; ea juventutis exercendae causā fieri praedicant, Caes. ; praedicat se servo imperasse, Cic. ; 2, *to mention with praise, to commend, eulogise, boast ;* virtutem, Cic. ; falsa de se, Cic. ; de suis laudibus, Cic.; with acc. and infin., Galli se omnes ab Dite patre prognatos praedicant, Caes.

2. **praedĭco** -dixi -dictum, 3. **I.** *to say beforehand, speak before ;* praedicta cornua quaerunt, Ov. ; esp. of writers and orators, haec mihi praedicenda fuerunt, Cic. **II.** Esp., **A.** *to predict, foretell, prophesy;* defectiones solis, Cic. ; futura, Cic. ; with acc. and infin., nihil Antonium facturum (esse), Cic. **B.** a, *to fix, appoint beforehand ;* diem (of the praetor), Tac. ; b, *to warn, admonish, instruct, charge, command;* Pompeius suis praedixerat, ut Caesaris impetum exciperent, Caes. ; Junonem praedicere, ne id faceret, Cic.

praedictĭo -ōnis, f. (2. praedico), *a prophesying, predicting,* Cic.

praedictum -i, n. (2. praedico), *a prophecy, prediction,* Cic. **II.** *an order, command,* Liv. **III.** *a concert, agreement,* Liv.

praedĭŏlum -i, n. (dim. of praedium), *a small landed estate, little farm,* Cic.

praedisco -dĭdĭci, 3. *to learn before;* ea quae agenda sunt in foro, Cic.

praedispŏsĭtus -a -um, *arranged beforehand;* nuntii, Liv.

praedĭtus -a -um (prae and do), *endowed, furnished, provided with*; -vith abl., sensibus, Cic.; virtute, Cic.; amentiā, Cic.; crudelitate, Cic.

praedĭum -ii, n. (praes), *a plot of land, landed estate*; rusticum, Cic.; praedium vendere, Cic.

praedīvĕs -ĭtis, *very rich*, Liv.

1. **praedo**, 1. = praedor (q.v.).

2. **praedo** -ōnis, m. (praeda), *a robber, pillager, plunderer*; urbis, Cic.; maritimi, *pirates*, Nep.; praedo maritus, *the husband that carried her off* (of Pluto), Ov.

praedŏcĕo -doctus, 2. *to teach before, instruct before*; praedocti ab duce, Sall.

praedŏmo -dŏmŭi, 1. *to tame before*, Sen.

praedor, 1. dep. (praeda). **I.** Intransit., **A.** Lit., praedatum exisse in agrum Latinum, Liv.; milites praedantes, Caes. **B.** Transf., *to rob, plunder, get gain*; in bonis alienis, Cic.; de aratorum bonis, Cic.; apud Mamertinos, Cic.; ex alterius inscitia, Cic. **II.** Transit., **A.** *to plunder, pillage, rob*; socios magis quam hostes, Tac. **B.** 1, lit., *to carry off as prey*; ovem unam, Ov.; 2, transf., amores alicuius, one's sweetheart, Ov.; singula de nobis anni praedantur, Hor.

praedūco -duxi -ductum, 3. *to lead forward, carry forward*; fossas viis, Caes.; murum, Caes.

praedulcis -e. **I.** Lit., *very sweet*, Plin. **II.** Transf., *very pleasant, very delightful*; decus, Verg.

praedūrus -a -um, *very hard, very strong*; homo praedurus viribus, Verg.; corpora, Verg.

praeēmĭnĕo (praemĭnĕo), 2. *to surpass, excel*; ceteros peritiā legum, Tac.

praeĕo -ivi and -ii -ĭtum, 4. *to go before, precede*. **I.** Lit., Laevinus Romam praeivit, Liv. **II.** Fig., **A.** Gen., naturā praeeunte, Cic. **B.** Esp., 1, *to say before, sing before, play before*; a, gen., ut vobis voce praeirent, quid judicaretis, Cic.; b, religious and legal t. t., *to dictate the words of an oath, or any solemn form of words*; verba praeire, Liv.; carmen, Liv.; praeire alicui, Cic.; 2, *to order, command*; omnia, ut decemviri praeierunt, facta, Liv.

praefātĭo -ōnis, f. (praefor), *a religious or legal form of words, formula*; sacrorum, Liv.; donationis, Cic.

praefectūra -ae, f. (praefectus), *the office of superintendent or overseer.* **I.** Gen., annonae, Tac.; vigilum, Tac. **II.** Esp., 1, *the command of auxiliary troops*, esp. of cavalry, Suet.; 2, *a subordinate provincial command*; praefecturam petere, Cic.; 3, meton., *an Italian town governed by a praefectus, a prefecture*, Cic.

1. **praefectus** -a -um, partic. of praeficio.

2. **praefectus** -i, m. (praeficio), *an overseer, superintendent.* **I.** In private life, his utitur quasi praefectis libidinum suarum, Cic. **II.** In political life, *a civil or military officer or superintendent.* **A.** Gen., annonae, Liv.; castrorum and castris, Tac.; praefectus urbis, *governor of the city* (Rome), *and commander of the five cohortes urbanae*, in the time of the republic only commanding in the place of the consul when absent, Liv.

praefĕro -tŭli -lātum -ferre. **I. A.** *to bear, carry before or in front*; ardentem facem, Cic.; fasces praetoribus, Cic. **B.** Fig., 1, gen., clarissimum lumen praetulistis menti meae, Cic.; 2, esp., a, *to bring to light, to show, manifest, display*; avaritiam, Cic.; judicium, *express one's judgment*, Liv.; haec eius diei praefertur opinio, Caes.; b, *to give the preference to, to prefer*; aliquem sibi, Cic.; otium labori, Sall.

II. *to carry by*; middle, praeferri = *to hasten by, to ride by*; praeter castra praelati, Liv. **III.** *to anticipate*; diem triumphi, Liv.

praefĕrox -ōcis, *very bold, impetuous*; legati, Liv.

praefervĭdus -a -um, *burning hot, very hot.* **I.** Lit., balneum, Tac. **II.** Fig., ira, Liv.

praefestīno, 1. **I.** *to hasten exceedingly, hasten too much*; ne deficere praefestinarent, Liv. **II.** *to hasten by*; sinum, Tac.

praeficīo -fēci -fectum, 3. (prae and facio), *to set over, appoint as superintendent, overseer*, etc.; aliquem pecori, Cic.; bello gerendo or simply bello, Cic.; legioni, Caes.; praeficere aliquem in eo exercitu, Cic.

praefidens -entis, *very confident, over confident*, Cic.

praefīgo -fixi -fixum, 3. *to fix in front, fasten before*; ripa sudibus praefixis munita, Caes.; arma puppibus, Verg. **II.** Transf., **A.** *to tip, point with*; jacula praefixa ferro, Liv. **B.** *to pierce through, transfix*, Tib.

praefīnĭo, 4. *to fix, prescribe, appoint beforehand*; diem, Cic.; sumptum funerum, Cic.; non praefinire, foll. by quominus, Cic.

praeflōro, 1. *to pluck the blossom prematurely*; fig., *to diminish, lessen*; gloriam eius victoriae praefloratam apud Thermopylas esse, Liv.

praeflŭo, 3. *to flow past*; infimā valle, Liv.; with acc. of place, Tibur fertile, Hor.; Noricam provinciam, Tac.

praefōco, 1. (prae and faux), *to choke, suffocate*; viam animae, Ov.

praefŏdĭo -fōdi -fossum, 3. **I.** *to dig in front of*; portas, Verg. **II.** *to bury previously*; aurum, Ov.

praefor -fātus sum -fāri, *to speak before.* **A.** a, *to utter beforehand*; majores nostri omnibus rebus agendis quod bonum, faustum, felix sit, praefabantur, Cic.; carmen, Liv.; so with acc. of deity, divos, Verg.; b, *to mention beforehand, to premise*; quae de deorum natura praefati sumus, Cic. **B.** *to prophesy, foretell*, Liv.

praefractē (praefractus), *sternly, resolutely*; nimis praefracte vectigalia defendere, Cic.

praefractus -a -um, p. adj. with compar. (from praefringo). **I.** Of written style, *abrupt, disconnected*; Thucydides praefractior, Cic. **II.** Of character, *stern, severe, harsh*; Aristo Chius praefractus, ferreus, Cic.

praefrīgĭdus -a -um, *very cold*, Ov.

praefringo -frēgi -fractum, 3. (prae and frango), *to break off in front, break in pieces*; hastas, Liv.

praefulcĭo -fulsi -fultum, 4. *to support, prop up*; fig., illud praefulci atque praemuni ut, etc., Cic.

praefulgĕo -fulsi, 2. *to gleam forth, shine forth.* **I.** Lit., equus praefulgens dentibus aureis, Verg. **II.** Fig., triumphali decore praefulgens, *conspicuous, distinguished*, Tac.

praegĕlĭdus -a -um, *very cold*; Alpes, Liv.

praegestĭo, 4. *to desire exceedingly*; praegestit animus videre, Cic.

praegnans (prae and root GNA, whence gnascor), *pregnant.* **I.** Lit., Cic. **II.** Fig., *full of*; fusus stamine, Juv.

praegrăcĭlis -e, *very slim, slender, lank*, Tac.

praegrăvis -e, *very heavy.* **I.** Lit., **A.** Of weight, onus, Ov. **B.** Of movement, praegravis corpore, Liv. **II.** Transf., of persons *wearisome*, Tac.

praegrăvo, 1. *to press heavily upon, weigh upon, oppress, to weigh down.* **I.** Lit., praegravata inhaerentibus scuta, Liv. **II.** Fig., *to overwhelm, oppress, weigh down;* dantem et accipientem, Liv.; animum, Hor.

praegrědĭor -gressus sum, 3. dep. (prae and gradior). **I.** *to go before, precede;* praegredientes amici, Cic.; with acc., signa, agmen, Liv.; nuntios, famam, *outstrip,* Liv. **II.** *to pass by, march by;* ea (castra), Liv.

praegressĭo -ōnis, f. (praegredior), *a going before, precedence;* causae, Cic.

praegressus -ūs, m. (praegredior), *a going on before,* Cic.

praegustātor -ōris, m. (praegusto), *one who tastes before, a taster, foretaster.* **I.** Lit., Suet. **II.** Fig., libidinum tuarum, Cic.

praegusto, 1. *to taste before;* cibos, Ov.

praehĭběo -ŭi -ĭtum, 2. (prae and habeo), *to offer, hold out, afford, supply, furnish,* Plaut.

praejăcěo, 2. *to lie before;* campus qui castra praejacet, Tac.

praejūdĭcātus -a -um, v. praejudico.

praejūdĭcĭum -ĭi, n. *a previous judgment, a preliminary decision or examination* (for the sake of investigating facts for subsequent proceedings). **I.** Lit., a, de quo non *praejudicium* sed plane *judicium* jam pactum putatur, Cic.; apud eosdem judices reus est factus, quum duobus jam praejudiciis damnatus esset, Cic.; b, transf., *a premature decision;* neminem praejudicium tantae rei afferre, Liv. **II.** Meton., *an example, precedent;* Pompeius vestri facti praejudicio demotus, *by your example,* Caes.

praejūdĭco, 1. *to decide beforehand, to give a preliminary judgment;* a, legal t. t., re semel atque iterum praejudicatā, Cic. Partic. perf. subst., **praejudĭcātum** -i, n. = praejudicium, (I.); b, transf., **in** partic., **praejūdĭcātus** -a -um, *previously decided;* opinio praejudicata, Cic.

praejŭvo -jūvi, 1. *to assist before,* Tac.

praelābor -lapsus sum, 3. dep. *to glide before, flow, swim before or along;* insula in quam Germani nando praelabebantur, Tac.; with acc., praelabi flumina rotis, Verg.

praelambo -lambi, 3. *to lick before, taste before,* Hor.

praelargus -a -um, *very abundant,* Juv.

praelěgo -lēgi -lectum, 3. *to sail past, coast along;* Campaniam, Tac.

praelĭgo, 1. **I.** *to bind in front;* sarmenta praeligantur cornibus boum, Liv. **II.** *to bind up;* os obvolutum est folliculo et praeligatum, Cic.

praelium, etc. = proelium, etc. (q.v.).

praelongus -a -um, *very long;* gladius, Liv.

praelūcěo -luxi, 2. *to carry a light before;* lit., *to light before.* **I.** Lit., Suet. **II.** Fig., 1, with acc. (amicitia) bonam spem praelucet in posterum, *sheds the kindly light of hope,* Cic.; 2, *to outshine, surpass;* nullus sinus Baiis praelucet, Hor.

praelum = prelum (q.v.).

praelustris -e (prae and lustro), *very illustrious;* praelustri ab arce, Ov.

praemando, 1. *to order beforehand;* ut conquireretur, ap. Cic.; hence, **praemāndāta** -ōrum, n. *a writ of arrest,* Cic.

praemātūrus -a -um, *too early, premature;* hiems, Tac.; canities, Tac.

praemědĭcātus -a -um, *protected by medicine or charms,* Ov.

praemědĭtātĭo -ōnis, f. (praemeditor), *considering beforehand;* futurorum malorum, Cic.

praemědĭtor, 1. dep. *to meditate upon, consider beforehand;* praemeditari quo animo accedam ad urbem, Cic.; with acc. and infin., id praemeditari ferundum modice esse, Cic.; partic. perf. pass., **praemědĭtātus** -a -um, *considered beforehand;* mala, Cic.

praemětŭens -entis, p. adj. (from praemetuo), *fearing beforehand,* Phaedr.

praemětŭentěr, adv. (praemetuens), *apprehensively, anxiously,* Lucr.

praemětŭo, 3. *to fear beforehand, be apprehensive.* **I.** Intransit., alicui, Caes. **II.** Transit., *to fear beforehand;* deserti conjugis iras, Verg.

praemitto -mīsi -missum, 3. *to send before, send on, despatch before.* **I.** Lit., (a) of persons, aliquem, Cic.; legiones in Hispaniam, Caes.; without acc., *to send before;* ad eos equites, Caes.; (β) of things, alicui odiosas literas, Cic. **II.** Transf., *to send before;* haec favorabili oratione praemisit, Tac.

praemĭum -ĭi, n. (prae and emo), *that which is taken first.* **I.** Gen., *advantage, gain, profit;* omnia praemia donaque fortunae, Cic. **II.** Esp., **A.** *an honourable reward, recompense;* praemia bene de republica meritorum, Cic.; alicui praemium dare pro aliqua re, Cic.; praemium praeponere or exponere, *to promise,* Cic.; ironically = *punishment;* cape praemia facti, Ov. **B.** Esp., *booty;* in war, pugnae, Verg.; in the chase, leporem et gruem jucunda captat praemia, Hor.

praemŏlestĭa -ae, f. *trouble beforehand,* Cic.

praemŏlĭor, 4. dep. *to prepare beforehand;* rem, Liv.

praemŏněo -ŭi -ĭtum, 2. *to warn, advise, admonish beforehand.* **I.** Gen., with acc., conatus hostis, *against hostile attempts,* Liv.; with ut and the subj., me, ut magnopere caverem, praemonebat, Cic. **II.** *to foretell, presage,* Ilion arsurum Ov.

praemŏnĭtus -ūs, m. (praemoneo), *a prediction, premonition,* Ov.

praemonstro, 1. **I.** *to show, point out before,* Lucr. **II.** *to prophesy, presage, predict;* magnum aliquid populo Romano, Cic.

praemorděo -mordi -morsum, 2. *to bite off;* fig., *to pilfer;* aliquid ex aliquo, Juv.

praemŏrĭor -mortŭus sum -mŏri, 3. dep. *to die prematurely,* Ov.; transf., praemortui jam est pudoris, *his modesty is dead,* Liv.

praemūnĭo (**praemoenĭo**), 4. **I.** *to fortify in front;* aditus duos magnis operibus, Caes. **II.** Fig., *to fortify, secure, make safe;* genus dicendi praemunitum, Cic.; quae praemuniuntur sermoni, *premised to meet objections,* Cic.

praemūnĭtĭo -ōnis, f. (praemunio), *a fortifying beforehand;* rhet., fig., of an orator, *a preparation of the minds of his hearers,* Cic.

praenăto, 1. *to swim before, swim past, flow by,* Verg.

Praeneste -is, n. (f. in Verg.), *a town in Latium, famous for its roses, its nuts, and for the temple and oracle of Fortuna,* now *Palestrina.* Hence, **Praenestīnus** -a -um, *belonging to Praeneste;* sortes, *the utterances of the oracle there,* Cic.

praenĭtěo -ŭi, 2. *to shine forth;* fig., cur tibi junior praeniteat, *outshines thee,* Hor.

praenōmen -ĭnis, n. *the name which stood before the gentile name, and distinguished the individual, the first name, the praenomen* (e.g., Caius, in C. J. Caesar; Marcus, in M. T Cicero), Cic.

praenosco -nōvi -nōtum, 3. *to become acquainted with beforehand, foreknow;* futura, Cic.

praenōtĭo -ōnis, f. (praenosco), *preconception, innate idea* (translation of πρόληψις), Cic.

praenūbĭlus -a -um, *very cloudy, very dark,* Ov.

praenuncĭa, etc. = praenuntia, etc. (q.v.).

praenuntĭa, v. praenuntius.

praenuntĭo, 1. *to announce, report, tell beforehand, foretell, predict;* futura, Cic.

praenuntĭus -a -um, *foretelling;* subst. (m. f. and n.), *that which announces beforehand, a harbinger, sign, token, omen;* stellae calamitatum praenuntiae, Cic.; ales praenuntius lucis, *the cock,* Ov.

praeoccŭpātĭo -ōnis, f. (praeoccupo), *a taking possession of before;* locorum, Nep.

praeoccŭpo, 1. **I.** *to take possession of before, seize before;* iter, Caes.; loca, Liv. **II.** Transf., 1, *to take possession of beforehand, to preoccupy;* animos timor praeoccupaverat, Caes.; 2, *to anticipate, to surprise;* ne adventu Caesaris praeoccuparetur, Caes.; with infin., legem ipsi praeoccupaverant ferre, Liv.

praeopto, 1. **I.** *to prefer, wish rather, desire more;* nemo non illos sibi, quam vos, dominos praeoptet, Liv.; with infin., nudo corpore pugnare, Caes. **II.** aliquid alicui rei, *to prefer;* otium urbanum militiae laboribus, Liv.

praepando, 3. *to open wide in front, stretch open in front, extend before,* Cic.

praepărātĭo -ōnis, f. (praeparo), *preparation;* ad minuendum dolorem, Cic.

praepăro, 1. *to make ready, provide, prepare;* naves, Cic.; res necessarias ad vitam degendam, Cic.; animos ad sapientiam, Cic.; aures (auditorum) praeparatae, Liv.

praepĕdĭo -īvi and -ĭi -ītum, 4. (prae and root PED). **I.** *to entangle by the feet, shackle, fetter;* praepeditis Numidarum equis, Tac. **II.** Transf., *to hinder, impede, obstruct;* quum lassitudo ac vulnera fugam praepedissent, Liv.; singultu medios praepediente sonos, Ov.; praepediri valetudine, *to be hindered by ill-health,* Tac.

praependĕo -pendi, 2. intransit., *to hang before, hang in front,* Caes.

praepĕs -pĕtis (prae and peto). **I.** Lit., t. t. of augury, *of birds from whose flight favourable omens were gathered, quick in flight, rapidly flying, swift;* praepes avis, and subst. simply praepes, Cic.; praepetibus pennis se credere caelo, Verg. **II.** Transf., *quick in flight and motion;* a, adj., deus, *the winged god*—i.e., Cupid, Ov.; b, subst., *a bird;* Jovis, *the eagle,* Ov.; Medusaeus (of Pegasus), Ov.

praepĭlātus -a -um, *having a ball or button in front* (applied to foils or blunt weapons); missilia, Liv.

praepinguis -e, *very fat, very rich;* solum, Verg.

praepollĕo -pollŭi, 2. *to be very powerful, to excel or surpass in power;* vir virtute praepollens, Liv.

praepondĕro, 1. *to outweigh;* fig., neque ea volunt praeponderari honestate, Cic.

praepōno -pōsŭi -pŏsĭtum, 3. *to put before, place before.* **I.** Lit., **A.** Gen., pauca (scribendo), Cic.; transf., praepositae causae, *antecedent,* Cic. **B.** Esp., *to put over, set over as overseer, commander,* etc.; aliquem bello, provinciae, navibus, Cic.; militibus, Caes. Partic. subst., **praepŏsĭtus** -i, m. *a commander,* Tac. **II.** Fig., *to prefer;* salutem reipublicae vitae suae, Cic. Partic. subst., **praepŏsĭtum** -i. (translation

of προηγμένον), *something to be preferred, something advantageous, but not* (in the Stoic philosophy) *absolutely good,* e.g., riches, etc., Cic.

praeporto, 1. *to carry before,* Lucr.

praepŏsĭtĭo -ōnis, f. (praepono), *a placing before.* **I.** 1, lit., negationis, Cic.; 2, meton., grammat. t. t., *a preposition,* Cic. **II.** *a preferring, preference,* Cic.

praepŏsĭtus, partic. of praepono.

praepossum -pŏtŭi -posse, *to be very powerful, have the chief power,* Tac.

praepostĕrē, adv. (praeposterus), *in a reversed order, perversely, absurdly,* Cic.

praepostĕrus -a -um. **I.** *having the last first, inverted, perverse, distorted, absurd;* gratulatio, Cic.; consilia, Cic. **II.** Transf., *of persons, perverse,* Cic.

praepŏtens -entis, *very powerful, very mighty;* a, of persons, viri, Cic.; Carthago praepotens terrā marique, Cic.; with abl. instr., praepotens armis Romanus, Liv.; with genit., Juppiter omnium rerum praepotens, *ruling over,* Cic.; b, transf., of things, philosophia, Cic.

praeprŏpĕrantĕr, adv. *very quickly, very hastily,* Lucr.

praeprŏpĕrē, adv. (praeproperus), *very hastily, too quickly;* festinare, Liv.; agere, Liv.

praeprŏpĕrus -a -um, *exceedingly quick, too quick, overhasty, precipitate.* **I.** Lit., festinatio, Cic.; celeritas, Liv. **II.** Transf., ingenium, Liv.

praepūtĭum -ĭi, n. *the foreskin,* Juv.

praequam, v. prae.

praequĕror -questus sum -quĕri, *to complain beforehand,* Ov.

praerădĭo, 1. *to outshine,* Ov.

praerăpĭdus -a -um, *very rapid;* gurges, Liv.

praerĭgesco -rigŭi, 3. *to grow very stiff,* Tac.

praerĭpĭo -rĭpŭi -reptum, 3. (prae and rapio), *to snatch away, pluck from, tear away, carry off.* **I.** Gen., alicui arma, Ov.; alicui laudem destinatam, Cic. **II.** Esp., a, *to carry off before the time;* deorum beneficium festinatione, Cic.; b, *to anticipate, forestall;* hostium consilia, Cic.

praerōdo -rōdi -rōsum, *to gnaw in front, to gnaw off, bite through,* Hor.

praerŏgātīvus -a -um (praerogo, *to ask beforehand), asked before others* (for vote, opinion, etc.). **I.** Lit., polit. t. t., *voting first, voting before others;* centuria praerogativa, and gen. subst., **praerŏgātīva** -ae, f. *the century to which the lot fell of voting first in the comitia,* Cic.; praerogativam referre, Cic.; hence, omen praerogativae, *the omen given by the name of the prerogative century,* Cic. **II.** Transf. **praerŏgātīva** -ae, f. **A.** *a previous choice,* Liv. **B.** *a sure sign, indication, presage;* triumphi, Cic.; voluntatis, Cic.

praerumpo -rūpi -ruptum, 3. *to break off, tear off in front;* funes, Caes.

praeruptus -a -um, p. adj. (from praerumpo), *broken off.* **I.** Lit., of places, *steep, precipitous, overhanging;* saxa, Cic.; mons, Verg. Plur. subst., **praerupta** -ōrum, n. *precipices,* Liv. **II.** Transf., *juvenis animo praeruptus, violent,* Tac.; dominatio, *stern, severe,* Tac.

praes, praedis, m. (praevideo). **I.** *a surety, security;* praedem esse pro aliquo, Cic.; praedes dare, Cic. **II.** Meton., *the property of the security;* L. Plancus praedes tuos venderet, Cic.

praesaepes (prasaepis) -is, f., **prae-saepe** -is, n., and **praesaepium** -ii, n.

(praesaepio), *an inclosure.* **I.** *a crib, manger,* Ov., transf., *certum* praesaepe, contemptuously= *table,* Hor. **II.** *a stall,* Verg.; transf., praesaepibus arcent, *from the hives,* Verg.; in praesaepibus, *in low houses,* Cic.

praesaepĭo -saepsi -saeptum, 4. *to block up in front;* omnem aditum, Cic.

praesāgĭo, 4. **I.** *to presage, forebode, have a presentiment of;* praesagire, id est, futura ante sentire, Cio.; quasi praesagiret, Cic.; de fine belli, Liv. **II.** Transf., *to foreshow, predict,* Lucr.

praesāgītĭo -ōnis, f. (praesagio), *a premonition, foreboding, presentiment,* Cic.

praesāgĭum -ĭi, n. (praesagio). **I.** *a presage, presentiment, foreboding;* malorum, Tac. **II.** Transf., *a prediction, prophesying;* Tiberii de Servio Galba, Tac.

praesāgus -a -um. **I.** *presaging, foreboding;* pectora, . . v.; with genit., mens praesaga mali, Verg. **II.** Transf., *predicting;* fulmen, Verg.; verba, Ov.

praescisco -scīvi, 3. *to learn, find out beforehand;* praescisccere quam quisque eorum provinciam, quem hostem haberet volebat, Liv.

praescĭus -a -um, *knowing beforehand, prescient;* corda, Verg.; with genit., periculorum, Tac.

praescrībo -scripsi -scriptum, 3. **I.** *to write before, set before in writing;* 1, lit., sibi nomen, Verg.; auctoritates praescriptae, *the names of senators contained in a decree of the senate,* Cic.; 2, transf., *to put forward or take as a pretext,* Tac. **II.** *to write down for imitation.* **A.** *to prescribe, ordain, define, direct beforehand;* jura civibus, Cic.; ne quid ageret, Cic. **B.** *to draw up an outline of,* Tac.

praescriptĭo -ōnis, f. (praescribo). **I.** Lit., *a writing before;* hence, meton., *a title, inscription, preamble, introduction;* legis, Cic. **II.** Transf., 1, *a precept, rule, order;* rationis, Cic.; 2, *limitation;* in hac praescriptione semihorae, Cic.; 3, *a pretext;* honesta, Cic.; hence, legal t. t., *an objection, demurrer,* Cic.

praescriptum -i, n. (praescribo), *that which is written down.* **I.** Lit., **A.** *a prescribed limit;* intra praescriptum equitare, Hor. **II.** Fig., *an order, a precept, rule;* legum, Cic.

praescco -sccŭi -scctum -sectum, 1. *to cut in front;* crines, Caes.; fig., carmen praesectum, *pruned down,* Hor.

praesens -entis (praesum). **I.** Gen., *present, in person, at hand;* quo praesente, *in whose presence,* Cic.; praesens tecum egi, *in person,* Cic.; in praesenti (sc. tempore), *now,* Cic.; in praesens tempus, *for the present time,* Cic. Subst., **praesentĭa** -ium, n. *the present,* Ov. **II.** 1, *on the spot, immediate, momentary, not delayed;* poena, *immediately following the offence,* Cic.; decretum, *passed instantly,* Liv.; 2, *immediately efficacious, effective, powerful;* auxilium, Cic.; memoria praesentior, *more vivid,* Liv.; with infin., praesens imo tollere de gradu, *with power to,* Hor.; 3, *open, visible;* ora, Verg.; transf., insidiae, *plain,* Cic.; 4, *pressing, urgent;* jam praesentior res erat, Liv.; 5, *of character, resolute, determined;* animus, Cic.; 6, *present, aiding, propitious;* deus, Cic.

praesensĭo -ōnis, f. (praesentio), *a presentiment, foreboding, premonition;* rerum futurarum, Cic.

praesentĭa -ae, f. (praesens). **I.** *presence;* alicuius, Cic.; animi, *presence of mind, determination, courage,* Caes., Cic.; in praesentia. *for the present, now, at present,* Cic. **II.** *impression, effect;* veri, Ov.

praesentĭo -sensi -sensum, 4. *to feel or perceive beforehand, to have a presentiment or premonition;* animo providere et praesentire, Caes.; futura, Cic.

praesēpes, etc. = praesaepes, etc. (q.v.).

praesēpĭo = praesaepio (q.v.).

praesertim, adv. *especially, chiefly;* praesertim quum and quum praesertim, Cic.; praesertim si, Cic.; praesertim quod, Cic.

praesĕs -sĭdis, c. (praesideo), *sitting before* (i.e., *to protect, take care of*); hence, **I.** *protecting;* usually subst., *a protector, protectress;* reipublicae, Cic.; templorum, Cic. **II.** *a chief, ruler, president;* praeses belli, *goddess of war* (of Minerva), Verg.; praeside pendet ab uno, Ov.

praesĭdens -entis, m. (praesideo), *a president, ruler,* Tac.

praesĭdĕo -sēdi -sessum, 2. (prae and sedeo). **A.** *to sit before, protect, guard;* with dat., huic imperio, Cic.; urbi, Liv.; foribus caeli (of Janus), Ov.; with acc., Galliae litus, Tac. **B.** *to preside over, manage, direct, govern;* rebus urbanis, Caes.; orbi terrarum, Cic.; with acc., exercitum, Tac.

praesĭdĭārĭus -a -um (praesidium), *serving as a guard or protection;* milites, Liv.

praesĭdĭum -ĭi, n. (praeses), *a sitting before;* hence, **I.** Lit., *protection, defence;* a, alicui esse praesidio, Cic.; b, milit. t. t., *a guard, patrol, escort;* legiones quae praesidio impedimentis erant, Caes. **II.** Meton., **A.** *that which defends, protection, help;* a, classis praesidium provinciae, Cic.; b, milit. t. t., *the soldiers who form the guard;* praesidium agitare, *to set guards,* Liv.; praesidia in urbes inducere, Cic.; fig., in praesidio collocatus, Cic. **B.** *a place occupied by a garrison or guard, post, camp, fortification;* quum legio praesidium occupavisset, Caes.; in praesidiis esse, Cic.; praesidium communire, Liv.; fig., de praesidio et statione vitae decedere, Cic. **C.** *help, assistance, support;* magnum sibi praesidium ad beatam vitam comparare, Cic.

praesignĭfĭco, 1. *to signify, announce beforehand;* hominibus futura, Cic.

praesignis -e (signum), *distinguished, remarkable before others,* Ov.

praesŏno -sŏnŭi, 1. *to sound forth, resound,* Ov.

praespargo, 3. *to scatter, strew before,* Lucr.

praestābĭlis -e (praesto), *distinguished, preeminent, remarkable;* res magnitudine praestabiles, Cic.; melius fuisse et praestabilius me civem in hac civitate nasci, Cic.; nullam dignitatem praestabiliorem, Cic.

praestans -antis, p. adj. (from praesto) *excellent, distinguished, preeminent;* a, of persons, gen. with abl., or in with the abl., homo prudentiā praestans, Cic.; Aristoteles longe omnibus praestans et ingenio et diligentiā, Cic.; virginibus praestantior omnibus, Ov.; in illis artibus praestantissimus, Cic.; b, of things, praestanti et singulari fide, Cic.; praestanti corpore Nymphae, Verg.

praestantĭa -ae, f. (praestans), *superiority, excellence;* si quam praestantiam virtutis, ingenii, fortunae consecuti sunt, Cic.; mentis, Cic.

praesterno, 3. *to strew, spread before,* Plaut.

praestĕs -stĭtis, c. (2. praesto) = praeses, *a tutelary, protecting deity;* Lares, Ov.

praestĭgĭa -ae, f., usually plur., **praestĭgĭae** -ārum, f. (praestringo), *deception, illusion, juggling;* verborum, Cic.

praestĭtŭo -stĭtŭi -stĭtūtum, 3. (statuo), *to prescribe, appoint beforehand;* tempus alicui, Cic. ; diem operi, Cic.

1. praestō, adv. (from praestus = praesitus, as repostus = repositus), *present, at hand, here, ready;* gen. with esse, *to be at hand, to show oneself, to appear,* with the notion of, *to attend* or *to wait upon, to be at one's service;* alicui, *to appear to help one at a court of law,* Cic. ; quaestores consulibus ad ministeria belli praesto essent, Liv. ; praesto esse virtutes ut ancillulas, Cic. ; fig., praesto esse, *to serve;* alicui, Cic. ; saluti tua , Cic.

2. praesto -stĭti -stĭtum and -stātum -stātūrus, 1. **I.** Intransit., *to stand before, excel, be distinguished;* inter suos, Cic. ; aliquā re, Cic. ; with dat. or acc. of person, *to surpass, excel;* alicui, Cic. ; alicui aliquā re, Cic. ; aliquem aliquā re, Liv. ; praestat used impers., *it is better, it is preferable;* with infin., praestat in eandem recidere fortunam, Cic. ; with quam, mori millies praestitit, quam haec pati, Cic. **II.** Transit., *to become surety* or *guarantee for, answer for, be responsible for.* **A.** Lit., Messallam Caesari, Cic. ; damnum emptori, Cic. ; a vi, *from violence,* Cic. ; de me, Cic. ; with acc. and infin., nullos (praedones) fore quis praestare poterat, Cic. **B.** Transf., a, *to perform, do, execute, fulfil;* suum munus, Cic. ; officium, Caes. ; b, *to keep, hold;* fidem, *to keep one's word,* Cic. ; c, *to preserve;* socios salvos, Cic. ; rempublicam, Cic. ; d, *to show, manifest, exhibit;* benevolentiam, Cic. ; se, with acc. of predicate, *to show oneself, behave oneself as;* se invictum, Ov. ; praesta te eum, Cic. ; e, *to give, evince;* honorem debitum patri, *to show proper respect,* Cic. ; sententiam, *to give one's opinion,* Cic.

praestōlor, 1. dep. (connected with 1. praesto), *to wait for, expect;* with dat., tibi ad forum Aurelium, Cic. ; with acc., huius adventum ad Clupeam, Cic.

praestringo -strinxi -strictum, 3. **I.** *to bind up, tie up;* faucem laqueo, Ov. ; pollices nodo, Tac. **II.** *to make blunt;* aciem oculorum, *to weaken, darken,* Liv. ; oculos, Cic. ; fig., aciem animi or mentis, Cic.

praestrŭo -struxi -structum, 3. **I.** *to build in front, construct before;* hence, *to block up, render impassable;* aditum montis, Ov. **II.** *to prepare, make ready for anything;* fraus fidem sibi in parvis praestruit, *procures for itself credibility in little things,* Liv.

praesŭl -sŭlis, c. *one who jumps* or *dances before others,* a dancer, Cic.

praesultātor -ōris, m. (praesulto), *one who dances before others,* a dancer, Liv.

praesulto, 1. (prae and salio), *to leap, spring before,* Liv.

praesum -fŭi -esse, *to be before.* **I.** *to be over, be placed over, preside over;* a, sacris, Cic. ; navi faciendae, Cic. ; b, *to be placed over, to govern;* populo, Cic. ; magistratui, *to preside as a magistrate,* Cic. ; c, milit. t. t., *to command;* exercitui, Caes. ; in Bruttiis, Liv. **II.** Transf., *to be the chief person, to take the lead in;* temeritati T. Gracchi, Cic. ; illi crudelitati, Cic.

praesūmo -sumpsi -sumptum, 3. *to take beforehand.* **I.** remedia, Tac. ; domi dapes, Ov. **II.** Transf., 1, *to enjoy beforehand, to anticipate;* fortunam principatūs, Tac. ; 2, a, *to imagine, represent to oneself beforehand;* spe praesumite bellum, Verg. ; praesumptum habere, *to suppose, take for granted,* Tac. ; b, *to assume, presume, suppose, conjecture, believe,* Tac.

praesumptus -a -um, p. adj. (from praesumo), *taken for granted, presumed;* suspicio, a *preconceived suspicion,* Tac.

praesŭo -sūtus, 3. *to sew up, to cover conceal;* praesuta foliis hasta, Ov.

praetempto = praetento (q.v.).

praetendo -tendi -tentum, 3. **I.** *to stretch out before, extend backwards;* hastas dextris, Verg. ; ramum olivae manu, Verg. ; poet., nec conjugis umquam praetendi taedas, i.e., *never laid claim to lawful wedlock,* Verg. **II.** *to place before, hold, spread before.* **A.** 1, lit., saepem segeti, Verg. ; 2, transf., *to place before;* sermonem decreto, Liv. ; hence, praetendi, of places, *to lie before* or *in front;* praetentaque Syrtibus arva, Verg. ; absol., tenue praetentum litus esse, Liv. **B.** Fig., *to hold before as a pretext, pretend;* hominis doctissimi nomen tuis immanibus et barbaris moribus, *allege in excuse for,* Cic. ; aliquid seditioni, Liv.

praetento (praetempto), 1. *to feel, try, test beforehand.* **A.** Lit., iter baculo, Ov. **B.** Fig., vires, Ov.

praetĕpesco -tĕpŭi, 3. *to glow beforehand* fig., si praetepuisset amor, Ov.

praeter (from prae and suffix -ter, like inter, propter). **I.** Adv., **A.** With negatives, *more than, except, with exception of;* nil praeter canna fuit, Ov. **B.** *more than;* foll. by quam, praeter sapit quam, etc., Plaut. **II.** Prep. with acc., **A.** Of space, *past, by, beyond;* praeter castra Caesaris suas copias transduxit, Caes. ; praeter oculos Lollii haec omnia ferebant, *before the eyes of,* Cic. **B.** Transf., 1, *beyond, beside, contrary to;* praeter spem, Liv. ; praeter modum, *beyond measure,* Cic. ; praeter opinionem, Cic. ; praeter naturam, Cic. ; 2, *beyond, more than;* praeter ceteros laborare, Cic. ; 3, *except, with the exception of;* omnes praeter Hortensium, Cic. ; with preceding negatives, nihil praeter suum negotium agere, Cic. ; hence, sometimes = *besides, in addition to, with;* num quid aliud ferret praeter arcam? Cic. ; ut praeter se denos adduceret, Caes.

praetĕrăgo, 3. *to drive past, drive by;* equum, Hor.

praetĕrĕā (praeter and abl. eā). **I.** *besides, beyond this, further,* Cic. **II.** *henceforth, hereafter,* Verg.

praetĕrĕo -ivi and oftener -ĭi -ĭtum -īre. **I.** Intransit., *to go by, pass by;* unda praeteriit, Ov. ; of time, *to pass, elapse;* hora, Ov. **II.** Transit., *to go by, pass by.* **A.** Gen., 1, hortos Cic. ; of time, in pass. partic., praetĕrĭtus -a -um, *past,* Cic. ; praetĕrĭta -ōrum, n. *the past,* Cic. ; 2, fig., a, *to escape the notice of, be unknown to;* non me praeterit, *I am not unaware,* Cic. ; b, (a) *to pass, omit;* nullum genus crudelitatis praeterire, *leave unpractised,* Cic. ; ut nulla fere pars orationis silentio praeteriretur, *was unapplauded,* Cic. ; (β) *to omit, not to mention;* caedes praetereo, libidines praetereo, Cic. ; esp., of the Censor, *not to read the name of a senator at the census* (*to publish his expulsion from the senate*); quatuor praeteriti sunt, Liv. ; (γ) *to forget to do;* foll. by quin and subj., praeterire non potui quin scriberem ad te, Cic. ; (δ) *to omit, leave out, take no notice of, pass over,* in presents, legacies, etc.; Philippus et Marcellus praetereuntur, *are passed by, get nothing,* Caes. ; filium fratris (in a will), Cic. **B.** Esp., 1, *to pass in a race, outstrip;* jamque hos cursu, jam praeterit illos, Verg. ; 2, fig., *to surpass;* virtus tua alios praeterit, Ov.

praetĕrĕquĭto, 1. *to ride past, ride by,* Liv.

praetĕrfĕro -tŭli -lātum -ferre, *to carry past;* pass., praeterferri, *to be carried past, to flow, drive, go past,* Liv.

praeterflŭo, 3. *to flow past, flow by;* moenia

Liv.; **fig., nec praeteritam (voluptatem) praeterfluere siuere,** *vanish from the recollection,* Cic.

praetergrĕdĭor -gressus sum, 3. dep. (praeter and gredior), *to pass by, go beyond;* castra, Cic.; primos suos, Sall.

praetĕrĭtus -a -um, partic. of praetereo.

praeterlābor -lapsus sum, 3. dep. **I.** *to glide by, flow by;* tumulum, Verg.; tellurem, *to sail by,* Lucr. **II.** Fig., *to slip away;* ante enim (definitio) praeterlabitur quam percepta est, Cic.

praetermĕo, 1. *to pass by, go by,* Lucr.

praetermissĭo -ōnis, f. (praetermitto). **I.** *a leaving out, omission;* sine ullius (formae) praetermissione, Cic. **II.** *a passing over, neglecting;* aedilitatis, Cic.

praetermitto -mīsi -missum, 3. *to let pass.* **A.** Lit., neminem, Cic. **B.** Transf., **1,** *to let pass time, opportunity,* etc.; diem, Cic.; occasiones, Caes.; **2,** *to neglect, omit;* gratulationem, Cic.; defensionem, Cic.; non or nihil praetermittere, foll. by quin, or nihil praetermittere, foll. by quominus, Cic.; **3,** in writing or speaking, *to pass over, omit;* quod dignum memoriā visum, praetermittendum non existimavimus, Caes.; verba, Cic.; tantam rem negligenter, Liv.; **4,** *to overlook, let pass unpunished,* Liv.

praeterquam, adv. *except,* Cic.; praeterquam quod, *except that,* Cic.; praeterquam . . . etiam, Liv.; nihil praeterquam, Liv.

praetervectĭo -ōnis, f. (praetervehor), *a passing by, travelling past;* in praetervectione omnium, Cic.

praetervĕhor -vectus sum, 3. dep. **I.** *to ride by, sail by, be carried past,* Cic.; naves Apolloniam praetervectae, Caes.; classis praetervehens, Liv.; praetervehens equo, Liv.; fig., locum cum silentio, *pass by in silence,* Cic.; oratio aures vestras praetervecta est, Cic. **II.** Of soldiers, *to march past,* Tac.

praetervŏlo, 1. *to fly past.* **I.** Lit., quem praetervolat ales, Cic. **II.** Fig., *to slip by, escape;* praetervolat numerus, Cic.; occasionis opportunitas praetervolat, Cic.

praetexo -texŭi -textum, 3. **I.** *to weave before, form an edge, border, fringe;* **1,** lit., purpura saepe tuos fulgens praetexit amictus, Ov.; toga or tunica purpurā praetexta, Liv.; or simply toga praetexta, Cic.; or subst., **praetexta** -ae, f. *an upper garment, bordered with purple,* worn by the magistrates at Rome and in the Italian municipia and coloniae, and by free-born children, till they assumed the toga virilis, Cic.; hence, meton., **praetexta** -ae, f. (sc. fabula), *a Roman national tragedy,* Hor.; **2,** transf., **a,** *to provide with a border, adorn; to provide, furnish with;* omnia lenioribus principiis natura praetexuit; **b,** *to fringe, cover;* puppes praetexunt litora, Verg.; fig., *to cover, conceal;* culpam nomine conjugii, Verg.; **c,** *to adorn;* Augusto praetextum nomine templum, Ov. **II.** *to put forward as a pretext;* cupiditatem triumphi, Cic.

praetexta, v. praetexo.

praetextātus -a -um (praetexta, from praetexo). **I.** *clad in the* praetexta, Cic. **II.** *licentious;* mores, Juv.

praetextum -i, n. (praextexo), *a pretence, pretext,* Tac.

praetextus -ū, m. (praetexo). **I.** *outward appearance, consideration, consequence,* Tac. **II.** *a pretext;* sub levi verborum praetextu, Liv.

praetingo -tinctus, 3. *to dip in or moisten beforehand,* Ov.

praetor -ōris, m. (for praeitor, from praeeo),

lit., *one who goes before;* hence, *a leader, chief.* Hence, **I.** In civil business, *the praetor;* used of the chief magistrate at Capua, Cic.; of the Suffetes at Carthage, Nep.; of the consul at Rome (also called praetor maximus), Liv.; at Rome, esp., *one of the praetors,* the Roman magistrates who administered justice (orig. two, the praetor urbanus and the praetor peregrinus, of whom the former was judge in disputes between Roman citizens, the latter in disputes between foreigners and between Roman citizens and foreigners); praetor is also used for propraetor, a magistrate who, after he had been praetor, was sent as a governor to a province; praetor primus, *the praetor who headed the poll,* Cic. **II.** To translate Gr. στρατηγός, *a commander of the army of a non-Roman nation,* Cic.

praetōrĭānus -a -um (praetorium), *belonging to the imperial body-guard, praetorian,* Tac.; plur. subst., **praetōrĭāni** -ōrum, m. *the praetorian guard,* Tac.

praetōrĭum, v. praetorius.

praetōrĭus -a -um (praetor). **I.** Adj., **A.** *relating to the praetor, praetorian;* **a,** of the praetor at Rome, comitia, *election of the praetor,* Liv.; jus, *administered by the praetor,* Cic.; potestas, *office of praetor,* Cic.; **b,** *relating to a praetor* or *propraetor in the provinces;* domus, *dwelling of a propraetor,* Cic. **B.** *relating to a general* or *commander,* Cic.; navis, *the admiral's ship,* Liv.; imperium, *command of the fleet,* Cic.; porta, *the gate of the camp near the general's tent,* Caes.; cohors praetoria; (a) *the general's body-guard,* Caes.; ironically, scortatorum praetoria cohors, Cic.; (b) (in imperial Rome) *the emperor's body-guard, the praetorian guard,* Tac. **II.** Subst., **A. praetōrĭum** -ii, n. **1,** *the official residence of the praetor* or *propraetor in a province,* Cic.; hence, transf., *a palace,* Juv.; **2,** *the chief place in a Roman camp, where the general's tent was, and where the ara, the augurale, and the tribunal were, to which the soldiers were summoned to hear speeches from the general, the officers to hold a council of war;* fit celeriter concursus in praetorium, Caes.; praetorium mittere, dimittere, *to dismiss the council of war,* Liv.; poet., *the cell of the queen-bee,* Verg.; **3,** *the imperial body-guard,* Tac. **B. praetōrĭus** -ii, m. (sc. vir), *a past praetor,* Cic.

praetrĕpĭdo, 1. *to tremble exceedingly, to be hasty* or *impatient;* praetrepidans, *hasty,* Cat.

praetūra -ae, f. (praetor). **I.** *the office, dignity of a praetor at Rome;* praeturā se abdicare, Cic. **II.** = στρατηγία, *the dignity of a general in Greece,* Cic.

Praetūtĭi -ōrum, m. *a people in Italy, in Picenum.* Adj., **Praetūtĭānus** -a -um, *Praetutian;* ager, Liv.

praeumbro, 1. *to overshadow;* fig., *to obscure,* Tac.

praevălens -entis, partic. of praevaleo (q.v.).

praeuro -ussi -ustum, 3. *to burn at the end or tip;* hasta praeusta, Liv.; stipites ab summo praeacuti et praeusti, Caes.

praevălĕo -vălŭi, 2. **I.** *to be physically strong;* praevalens juvenis Romanus, Liv. **II.** Transf., *to be very strong* or *powerful. to have great influence, to be stronger, to have more influence than others, to prevail, to get the upper hand;* praevalens populus, Liv.; praevalet pugnā equestri, *to be stronger in,* Tac.

praevălĭdus -a -um. **I.** Lit., *very strong, very powerful;* juvenis, Liv. **II.** Fig., **a,** of persons, etc., Blaesus, Tac.; urbs, Liv.; **b,** of things, terra, *too fertile, too productive,* Verg.

praevārĭcātĭo -ōnis, f. (praevaricor), *a violation of duty;* esp. of an advocate who has an understanding with the opposite party, *collusion,* Cic.

praevārĭcātor -ōris, m. (praevaricor), *one who violates his duty,* esp. of an advocate, *accuser,* etc., *one who has a secret understanding with the opposite party, a double dealer;* praevaricator significat eum qui in contrariis causis quasi varie esse positus videatur, Cic.

praevārĭcor, 1. dep. (varico). **I.** Lit., *to go crooked, walk crookedly,* Plin. **II.** Fig., *to play a false* or *double part;* esp. of an advocate or accuser who has a secret understanding with the other side, *to be guilty of collusion,* Cic.

praevārus -a -um, *very perverse,* Cic.

praevĕhor -vectus sum, 3. dep. *to ride* or *be carried before, in front, past;* praevectus equo, *riding past,* Verg., Liv.

praevĕnĭo -vēni -ventum, 4. *to come before, anticipate, get the start of;* hostis breviore viā praeventurus erat, Liv.; with acc., hostem, Liv.; morte praeventus, *overtaken by death,* Liv.

praeverro, 3. *to sweep* or *brush before;* veste vias, Ov.

praeverto (praevorto) -verti (-vorti) -versum (-vorsum), 3. and **praevertor** -verti, 3. dep. **I.** *to undertake before;* quod huic sermoni praevertendum, Cic. **II.** *to go before, run before, outstrip.* **A.** Lit., ventos, Verg. **B.** Fig., 1, *to anticipate;* with acc. = *to hinder, make of no avail;* quorum usum opportunitas praevertit, Liv.; 2, *to lay hold of before, preoccupy;* praevertere animos amore, Verg.; 3, *to be of more importance, to surpass, to be weightier;* nec posse bello praevertisse quidquam, Liv.; 4, (dep. praevertor only in present forms); a, *to turn to first, to take more notice of;* illuc praevertamur, Hor.; b, *to go to, make a visit to;* in Thessaliam, Liv.

praevĭdĕo -vīdi -vīsum, 2. *to see before, foresee.* **I.** Physically, ictum venientem, Verg. **II.** Transf., respublica quam praevideo in summis periculis, Cic.

praevĭtĭo, 1. *to corrupt* or *vitiate beforehand;* gurgitem, Ov.

praevĭus -a -um (prae and via), *going before, preceding,* Ov.

praevŏlo, 1. *to fly before;* praevolantes grues, Cic.

pragmătĭcus -a -um (πραγματικός), *skilled in civil affairs, state business,* etc.; pragmatici homines, Cic.; subst., **pragmătĭcus** -i, m. *a person who supplied orators and advocates with materials for their speeches,* Cic.

prandĕo, prandi, pransum, 2. (prandium), *to take breakfast, to breakfast,* Cic.; with acc., *to breakfast on;* olus, luscinias, Hor.

prandĭum -ĭi, n. (conn. with Dor. πράν = πρωήν), *a late breakfast* or *lunch, taken about noon, of bread, fish, cold meat,* etc.; prandium (alicui) dare, Cic.; aliquem ad prandium invitare, Cic.

pransus -a -um (prandeo), *having lunched;* curatus et pransus (of soldiers), *ready for action, prepared for battle,* Liv.; pransus, potus, *having eaten and drunk well,* Cic.

prātensis -e (pratum), *of* or *relating to a meadow, growing in a meadow;* fungus, Hor.

prātŭlum -i, n. (dim. of pratum), *a little meadow,* Cic.

prātum -i, n. **I.** *a meadow;* pratorum viriditas, Cic. **II.** Meton., *meadow-grass,* Cic.

prāvē, adv. (pravus), lit., *crookedly;* hence, *ill, wrongly,* Cic.

prāvĭtas -ātis, f. (pravus). **I.** *crookedness, irregularity, deformity;* membrorum, Cic.; oris, *a distortion of the mouth in speaking,* Cic. **II.** Transf., **A.** *irregularity, impropriety,* Cic. **B.** *moral irregularity, wickedness, perversity, pravity;* mentis, Cic.; consulum, Liv.

prāvus -a -um, *crooked, irregular, misshapen, deformed.* **I.** Lit., membra, Cic. **II.** Transf., *morally crooked, perverse, improper, wrong;* affectio, Cic.; pravissima regula, Cic.

Praxĭtĕlēs -is and -i, m. (Πραξιτέλης), *a sculptor of Athens, especially famous for his statues of Aphrodite at Cnidus and of Eros at Thespiae.* Hence, adj., **Praxĭtĕlĭus** -a -um, *of Praxiteles.*

prĕcārĭo, adv. (precarius), *by entreaty;* rogare, Cic.

prĕcārĭus -a -um (precor), *begged for, asked for, obtained by entreaty.* **I.** libertas, Liv.; orare precariam opem, Liv. **II.** Transf., *uncertain, insecure, precarious;* forma, Ov.; imperium, Tac.

prĕcātĭo -ōnis, f. (precor), *a begging, entreating, request, prayer;* illa sollemnis comitiorum precatio, Cic.

preces, v. prex.

prĕcĭae (prĕtĭae) -ārum, f. *a kind of vine,* Verg.

prĕcor (praecor), 1. dep. (prex), *to beg, entreat, request, pray, invoke.* **I.** Gen., (a) with acc. of pers., deos, Cic.; (β) with acc. of thing, opem, Liv.; haec precatus sum, Cic.; (γ) with ut or ne, or ut ne or non precor, foll. by quominus and subj., precor ab diis ut, etc., Cic.; (δ) absol., eum sororem dedisse Prusiae precanti atque oranti, Liv.; used also of things, dextra precans, Verg. **II.** *to wish good* or *evil;* bene precari, Liv.; male precari, Cic.; precari alicui, *to curse a person,* Cic. (partic., precantia, three syllables, Verg.).

prĕhendo, prĕhendi, prĕhensum, 3. and syncop., prendo, prendi, prensum (prae and HENDO, χανδάνω), *to lay hold of, seize hold of, catch.* **I.** aliquem manu, Cic.; of the soil, tellus prehendit stirpes, Cic. **II.** Esp., **A.** *to lay hold of, to catch, detain,* in order to speak to a person; aliquem, Cic. **B.** *to catch, detect in any act;* in furto, Plaut. **C.** *to seize violently, to take hasty possession of;* Pharum, Caes. **D.** Meton., *to reach;* oras Italiae, Verg.; quum ipsum ea moderantem et regentem paene prenderit, *observed,* Cic.

prĕhenso, and oftener **prenso** (intens. of prehendo), 1. *to lay hold of, seize.* **I.** manus, Liv. **II.** Esp., **A.** *to lay hold of a person in order to speak to him, to make a request,* etc.; genua, Tac.; veteranos, Liv. **B.** *to canvass for an office;* homines, Liv.; patres, Liv.; absol., prensat Galba, Cic.

prĕlum -i, n. (premo), *a wine-press, olive-press,* Verg.

prĕmo, pressi, pressum, 3. *to press.* **I.** Gen., 1, a, lit., ad pectora natos, Verg.; vestigia alicuius, *to follow in any one's footsteps,* Cic.; frena dente, *to champ,* Ov.; b, fig., *necessitas* eum premebat, Cic.; premi aere alieno, Cic.; 2, transf., a, *to touch;* litus, Hor.; insulam premit amnis, *surrounds,* Ov.; b, *to hold;* frena manu, Ov.; c, locum, *to be often, in a place, frequent;* forum, Cic.; so *to press with the body, lie on;* humum, Ov.; ebur, poet.= *the curule chair of ivory,* Ov.; d, *to cover, conceal;* canitiem galeā premimus, Verg.; ossa, *to bury,* Ov.; fig., (a) *to bury, wrap;* me pressit alta quies, Verg.; (β) *to conceal, suppress;* curam sub corde, Verg.; e, *to make something by pressing;* caseum, Verg.; lac, *to make cheese,* Verg.; f, *to press hard, to pursue closely, press upon;* hostes, Caes.; oppĭdum obsidione, Caes.; cervum ad retia, *to drive into the nets*, Verg.; fig., *to pursue with words*; aliquem Cic.; aliquem criminibus, Ov.; **g,** *to lade, to load*; carinae pressae, Verg. **II. A.** *to press in*; dentes in vite, Ov.; presso vestigio, Cic.; transf., *to mark*; rem notā, Ov. **B. a,** *to extinguish*; ignem, Verg.; **b,** *to press out*; oleum, Hor. **C.** *to press down*; **a,** lit., (a) currum, Ov.; aulaeum premitur, Hor.; (β) *to plant*; virgulta per agros, Verg.; (γ) *to strike to the ground*; tres famulos, Verg.; **b,** fig., (a) *to slander, depreciate*; aliquem, Liv.; humana omnia, *to despise*, Cic.; (β) *to surpass*; facta premant annos, Ov.; (γ) *to rule, keep within bounds*; populos ditione, Verg. **D.** *to press together*; **a,** alicui fauces, Ov.; collum laqueo, Hor.; **b,** *to draw in*; habenas, Verg.; equos currentes, *to check*, Verg.; **c,** *to pare down, prune*; umbram falce, Verg.; fig., *to shorten*; quae dilatantur a nobis, Zeno sic premebat, Cic. **E.** *to hold back*; cursum, *to check*, Cic.; vocem, *to be silent*, Verg.

prendo = prehendo (q.v.).

prensātĭo -ōnis, f. (prenso), *the canvassing for an office*, Cic.

prenso = prehenso (q.v.).

pressē, adv. (pressus), **a,** of pronunciation, *not broadly, neatly*; presse et aequabiliter et leniter, Cic.; **b,** of style, *briefly, concisely*; dicere, Cic.; **c,** *accurately, precisely*; pressius agere, Cic.

pressĭo -ōnis, f. (premo), in plur., *props, stays*, Caes.

presso, 1. (intens. of premo), *to press*; manu brachia, Hor.; ubera, *to milk*, Ov.

1. **pressus** -a -um, p. adj. (from premo). **I.** Lit., *slow, measured*; presso gradu, Liv. **II.** Transf., 1, *measured*; of pronunciation, *slow, controlled, moderate*; soni, Cic.; 2, *short, concise*; oratio. Cic.; orator, Cic.; 3, *accurate, precise*; Thucydides verbis pressus, Cic.

2. **pressus** -ūs, m. (premo), *a pressing, pressure*; ponderum, Cic.

prestēr -ēris, m. (πρηστήρ), *a fiery whirlwind*, Lucr.

prĕtĭōsē, adv. (pretiosus), *in a costly manner, splendidly, magnificently*; vasa pretiose caelata, Cic.

prĕtĭōsus -a -um (pretium). **I.** *costly, precious, of great value*; equus, Cic.; fulvo pretiosior aere, Ov.; res pretiosissimae, Cic. **II.** Transf., **A.** *costly, high-priced, dear*, Prop. **B.** *extravagant, giving a high price for a thing*; emptor, Hor.

prĕtĭum -ĭi, n. (root PRET, ΦΡΑΔ, φράζω), *worth, value, price.* **I.** Lit. and fig., 1, lit., pretium constituere, *to fix the price*, Cic.; pretium habere, *to be worth something*, Cic.; so esse in pretio, Liv.; parvi pretii esse, Cic.; 2, fig., operae eorum pretium facere, *to prize*, Liv. **II.** Transf., **A.** *money*; pretio emere, *for money*, Cic.; esp., *ransom-money*; pactum pro capite pretium, Cic. **B.** *wages, pay*; **a,** manus, Cic.; fig., operae pretium est, or videtur, with infin., *it is worth the while*, Cic.; **b,** *prize, reward*; certaminis, Ov.; nullo satis digno morae pretio tempus terunt, Liv.; **c,** *pay* = *punishment*; et peccare nefas, aut pretium est mori, Hor.; **d,** *bribe*; adduci pretio ad hominem condemnandum, Cic.

prex, precis, only in dat., acc., and abl., gen. plur., prĕces, prĕcum, f. *a request, entreaty.* **I.** Gen., preces adhibere, Cic.; prece humili, Cic.; omnibus precibus petere or orare ut, etc., Caes., Cic. **II.** Esp., **a,** *prayer*; eorum preces ac vota, Cic.; **b,** *a curse, execration*; omnibus precibus detestari aliquem, Caes.; **c,** *a wish*; damus alternas accipimusque preces, Ov.;

Prĭămus -i, m. (Πρίαμος). **I.** *the last king of Troy, husband of Hecuba, father of Paris, Hector, Cassandra, etc.* Hence, **A. Prĭămēïs** -ĭdis, f. *a daughter of Priam, Cassandra*, Ov. **B. Prĭămĭdēs** -ae, m. *a son of Priam*, Verg. **C.** Adj., **Prĭămēïus** -a -um, *belonging to Priam*; hospes, *Paris*, Ov.; conjux, *Hecuba*, Ov. **II.** *grandson of foregoing, son of Polites.*

Prĭāpus (-ōs) -i, m. (Πρίαπος), *the god of gardens and vineyards, the god of fertility*, orig. worshipped at Lampsacus.

prīdem, adv. (from old form pris, whence prior, pridie and -dem). **I.** *long ago, long since*; jam pridem, long ago, Cic.; non ita pridem, *not very long ago*, Cic. **II.** *formerly*, Cic.

prīdĭē, adv. (from old form pris, whence prior, pridem and dies), *on the day before yesterday*; with acc. or genit. of the day from which the reckoning is taken, or foll. by quam, pridie eum diem, Cic.; pridie eius diei, Cic.; pridie quam Athenas veni, Cic.

Prĭēnē -ēs, f. (Πριήνη), *a sea-port in Ionia, birthplace of Bias*, now *Samsun Kalesi.*

prīmaevus -a -um (primus and aevum), *young, youthful*; Helenor, Verg.

prīmānus -a -um (primus), *belonging to the first legion.* Subst., **prīmāni** -ōrum, m. *soldiers of the first legion*, Tac.

prīmārĭus -a -um (primus), *in the first rank, excellent, distinguished*; vir populi, Cic.

prīmĭgĕnĭus -a um (primus and geno = gigno), *original, primitive*, Varr. Subst., **Prīmĭgĕnĭa** -ae, f. *a surname of the goddess Fortune*, Cic.

prīmĭgĕnus -a -um (primus and geno = gigno), *original, primitive*, Lucr.

prīmĭpīlāris -is, m. (primipilus), *the centurion of the first maniple of the triarii.*

prīmĭpīlus, v. pilus.

prīmĭtĭae -ārum, f. (primus), *first-fruits*, Ov.; transf., metallorum, *the minerals first taken out of a mine*, Tac.; spolia et primitiae, *first-fruits of victory*, Verg.

prīmĭtŭs, adv. *first, for the first time*, Lucr.

prīmō, adv. (primus), *firstly, at first, in the beginning*; primo . . . dein or deinde, Cic.; primo . . . post, Liv.; quum primo, *as soon as*, Liv.

prīmor -ōris (primus), *the first.* **I.** *the foremost part, tip, end*; primori in acie versari, Tac.; sumere aliquid digitulis duobus primoribus, *with the tips of the fingers*, Plaut.; aliquid primoribus labris attingere, or gustare, *to touch with the lips*, i.e., *to treat superficially*, Cic. Subst., primores, *the foremost* (milit t. t.); quum primores caderent, Liv. **II.** Transf., *the first in rank, most distinguished*; juventus, Liv. Subst., **prīmōres** -um, m. *the most illustrious*; civitatis, Liv.

prīmordĭum -ĭi, n. (primus and ordior), *the first beginning, commencement, origin*; urbis, Liv. Plur., primordia rerum, Cic.

prīmum, adv. (primus). **I.** *first, firstly, at first*; foll. by deinde, tum, etc., Cic. **II.** *for the first time*; quo die primum convocati sumus, Cic. **III.** With ut, ubi, quam, simulac, *as soon as*, Cic.; quam primum, *as soon as possible*, Cic.

prīmus, v. prior.

princeps -cĭpis, c. (primus and capio), adj. and subst. **I.** Lit., princeps est in agendo, Cic.; principes inveniendi, *first to discover*, Cic.; princeps senatūs, *the senator whose name stood first on the Censor's list*, Liv. **II.** *the chief, the most distinguished.* **A.** Gen., with genit., principes civitatis, Cic.; principes conjurationis, *the heads*, Cic.; rerum publicarum principes, Cic.; esp., princeps juventutis, *one of the most distinguished of the patrician youth*, esp. *among the patrician knights*, Cic.; with in and the abl., in jure civili princeps, Cic.; plur., principes, *distinguished men*, Cic. **B.** Esp., 1, *chief, leader, founder;* Zeno princeps Stoicorum, Cic.; 2, *a ruler, prince*, esp. of the emperor at Rome, Ov.; 3, principes, orig. *the first rank in a Roman army, afterwards the second line, between the hastati and triarii;* hence, princeps, a, *a maniple of the* principes; signum primi principis, Liv.; b, *a centurion of the* principes; princeps prior, Caes.

principālis -e (princeps). **I.** *first, original; causae*, Cic. **II.** Transf., *relating to the chief place in a Roman camp* (principia); via, porta, *the broad alley which passed through the centre of a Roman camp*, Liv.; porta principalis, dextra, sinistra, *the gate on each side*, Liv.

principātus -ūs, m. (princeps), *the first place, preeminence.* **I.** Gen., tenere principatum sententiae, *to have the right to vote first*, Cic. **II.** Esp., **A.** *the first rank in the state or army*, and gen., *rule, dominion;* Cassio principatum dari, Cic.; principatum in civitate obtinere, Cic. **B.** In philosophy, *the governing principle of actions* (Gk. τὸ ἡγεμονικόν), Cic. **C.** *a beginning, origin*, Cic.

principiālis -e (principium), *original*, Lucr.

principium -ii, n. (princeps), *a beginning, origin.* **I.** Lit., principium dicendi, Cic.; principio belli, Liv.; ducere principium ab aliquo, *to make a beginning with*, Cic.; (in) principio, *in the beginning, at first*, Cic.; a principio, *from the beginning*, Cic. **II.** Meton., **A.** *the groundwork, foundation;* id est principium urbis, Cic.; plur., principia, *the elements, first principles;* juris, Cic. **B.** 1, *the tribe or curia which voted first, the prerogative tribe*, etc.; Faucia curia fuit principium, Liv.; 2, *the beginner, founder;* moris, Ov. **C.** Milit. t. t., **principia** -ōrum, 1, *the front ranks*, Sall.; 2, *the chief place, chief street in a camp, where stood the tents of the general, legates, and tribunes, and where speeches were delivered to the soldiers, the head-quarters;* in vestrorum castrorum principiis, Cic.

prior -us, genit. -ōris, superl., **primus** -a -um (from old form pris, whence pridem, pridie, pristinus). **I.** Compar., **A.** Lit., *the first, the first of two;* priores pedes, Nep. **B.** Transf., 1, *first in order of time, former, first of two;* comitia, Cic.; consul anni prioris, Liv.; priore aestate, *in the previous summer*, Cic.; subst., **priores** -um, m. *ancestors*, Verg.; 2, *better, preferable, more excellent;* res nulla prior potiorque visa est, Liv.; nihil prius nec potius est quam (foll. by infin.), Liv. **II.** Superl., **primus** -a -um, *the first.* **A.** Of place, *the first, foremost;* a, adj., Eburonum fines, Caes.; primis labris, *with the tips of the lips*, Cic.; b, subst., primi, *the foremost*, Cic. **B.** Transf., 1, *first in order or in time;* a, adj., primae litterae, Cic.; esp.,(a) in poets, primus for primum, vix prima inceperat aestas, Verg.; (β) partitive, primā nocte, *in the first part of the night*, Caes.; b, subst., a primo, *from the beginning*, Cic.; in primo, *at first*, Cic.; plur., prima, *the beginning*, Liv.; *the elements*, Lucr.; in primis, *at the beginning*, Liv.; 2, of rank, station, etc., *first, most excellent, most distinguished;* homines primi, *the most illustrious*, Cic.; comitia prima (i e., centuriata and tributa), Cic.; prima tenere, *to hold the first place*, Verg.; partes primae, or simply primae, *the leading part (on the stage)*, Cic.; primas agere, Cic.; primae, *the first prize;* primas ferre, deferre. Cic.: in primis, *especially*, Cic.

priscē, adv. (priscus), *after the manner of the ancients, sternly, severely;* agere, Cic.

priscus -a -um (from pris, cp. Gk. πρίν). **I.** *ancient, antique;* priscis viris, Cic.; hence Tarquinius Priscus, *the first of his line*, Liv.; esp. with the notion of *ancient, venerable, belonging to the good old times;* priscam imitari severitatem, Cic. **II.** Transf., **A.** *former, previous;* Venus, Hor. **B.** *severe, stern*, Cat.

pristīnus -a -um (from pris, cp. Gk. πρίν, as crastinus from cras), *former, previous, early, pristine.* **I.** Gen., dignitas, Cic.; suos, Cic.; in pristinum statum redire, Caes. **II.** *just past, of or relating to yesterday;* diei pristini, Caes.

pristis -is, f. and **pistrix** -tricis, f. (πρίστις). **I.** *any sea monster, a whale, shark, saw-fish*, Verg. **II.** Transf., a, *the constellation of the Whale*, Cic.; b, *a small, swift-sailing ship of war*, Liv.; *name of a ship*, Verg.

prīus, adv. (prior). **I.** *before, previously*, Cic.; foll. by quam, *before that, before*, Cic. **II.** *formerly*, Cat.

prīvātim, adv. (privatus), *privately, as a private person, in private life.* **I.** Lit., privatim aliquid gerere, Cic.; si privatim mandasset, Cic. **II.** Transf., *at home;* privatim se tenere, *to remain at home*, Cic.

prīvātio -ōnis, f. (privo), *a freeing from;* doloris, Cic.

prīvātus -a -um (privo), *private, of or relating to a private individual.* **I.** a, of things, privati et separati agri, Caes.; vita, Cic.; neut. subst., in privato, *at home*, Liv.; privato consilio, *without the authority of the state, on one's own account*, Caes.; in privatum vendere, *for private use*, Liv.; tributum ex privato conferre, *from one's private property*, Liv.; b, of persons, *as a private man*, Cic.; vir privatus, Cic.; and subst., privatus, *a private person*, Cic.; reges, augures, privati, Cic. **II.** Esp., in imperial times, *not belonging to the royal family*, Tac.

Prīvernum -i, n. *a town in Latium*, now Piperno. Hence, **Prīvernās** -ātis, *relating to Privernum*, Cic.; in Privernati, *in the county of Privernum*, Cic.

prīvigna -ae, f. (fem. of privignus), *a stepdaughter*, Cic.

prīvignus -i, m. (= privigenus, from privus and gigno, *one begotten separately*), *a step-son*, Cic.

prīvilēgium -ii, n. (privus and lex), *a law relating to one person only, a special law, private law;* privilegium ferre, irrogare, Cic.

prīvo, 1. (privus). **I.** In a bad sense, *to deprive of;* aliquem vitā, Cic. **II.** In a good sense, *to free from;* aliquem dolore, Cic.

prīvus -a -um. **I.** *single;* in dies privos, Lucr.; homines, Cic. **II.** Transf., **A.** *each, every*, Lucr.; used distributively, *one each;* bubus privis binisque tunicis donati, Liv. **B.** *particular, special, one's own;* priva triremis, Hor.

1. **pro** (old abl. neut. of * prus -a -um, cp. prae, connected with πρό), *before, far.* **I.** Adv., only in phrases proquam, prout. **II.** Prep. with abl. **A.** Lit., of space, 1, *before, in front of;* a, in answer to the question, where? sedens pro aede, Cic.; b, in answer to question, whither? Caesar pro castris suas copias produxit; 2, *before, on, in;* pro tribunali, Cic. **B.** Transf., 1, *for, in behalf of, in favour of;* hoc non modo non pro me, sed contra me est, Cic.; dimicare pro legibus, Cic.; 2, a, *in place of, for;* pro consule, Cic.; pro quaestore, Cic.; b, *as, as good as;* pro damnato esse, *as good as condemned*, Cic.; se pro cive gerere, *to behave as a citizen*, Cic.; 3, *for, as a reward, or as wages for;* (alicui) pro meritis gratiam referre, Cic.; pro

rectura solvere, Cic.; aliquem pro scelere suo ulcisci, Caes.; **4,** *in proportion to, according to, conformably with, in consideration of;* pro multitudine hominum et pro gloria belli atque fortitudinis, Cic.; pro caritate reipublicae, Cic.; agere pro viribus, Cic.; pro virili parte, *to the best of one's abilities,* Cic.; pro tempore et re, *as the time and circumstances demanded,* Caes.; pro mea parte, *for my part,* Cic.; pro se quisque, *each one according to his strength,* Cic.; pro eo, *just as, according as;* foll. by ac and atque, or quam, quantum, etc., pro eo quanti te facio, *according to my estimation of you;* **5,** *through;* ut pro suffragio renuntiaretur, Cic.

2. pro! (proh!), interj. *oh! ah!* pro dii immortales, Cic.; pro deûm atque hominum fidem! Cic.; pro sancte Juppiter, Cic.

prŏăgŏrus -i, m. (προήγορος), *the chief magistrate in certain Sicilian cities,* Cic.

prŏăvītus -a -um (proavus), *of or relating to a great-grandfather, ancestral;* regna, Ov.

prŏăvus -i, m. **I.** *a great-grandfather,* Cic. **II.** Transf., *an ancestor, forefather,* Cic.

prŏbăbĭlis -e (probo). **I.** *probable, credible, not impossible;* ratio, Cic. **II.** *pleasing, acceptable, worthy of approval, good;* probabilior populo orator, Cic.; vir ingenio sane probabili, Cic.

prŏbăbĭlĭtas -ātis, f. (probabilis), *probability, credibility;* captiosa, Cic.

prŏbăbĭlĭtĕr, adv. (probabilis), *probably, credibly;* dicere, Cic.; probabilius accusare, Cic.

prŏbātĭo -ōnis, f. (probo). **I.** *a proving, testing, test, trial, examination;* athletarum, Cic. **II.** *an approving, approval,* Cic.

prŏbātor -ōris, m. (probo), *one who approves, an approver;* facti, Cic.

prŏbātus -a -um, p. adj. (from probo). **A.** *approved, excellent;* ceterarum homines artium ×pectati et probati, Cic.; femina probatissima, Cic. **B.** *pleasant, agreeable;* ut nemo probatior primoribus patrum esset, Liv.; probatissimus alicui, Cic.

prŏbē, adv. (probus), *well, rightly, fitly, properly, excellently;* scire, nosse, meminisse, Cic.; de Servio probe dicis, Cic.; hoc probe stabilito et fixo, Cic.

prŏbĭtas -ātis, f. (probus), *honesty, uprightness, probity, worth, modesty,* Cic.

prŏbo, 1. (probus). **I. A.** *to try, test, prove, examine;* a, lit., munera, Tac.; opera quae locassent, Liv.; b, transf., amicitias utilitate, Ov. **B.** *to approve, be satisfied with, esteem good and serviceable;* (α) lit., domum tuam perspexi atque vehementer probavi, Cic.; (β) transf., *to approve of, morally or intellectually;* consilium, Cic.; causam et hominem, Caes.; aliquem judicem, Cic. **II.** *to recommend as good, represent as good, guarantee;* a, alicui libros oratorios, Cic.; obscurius vitium pro vero probatur, Cic.; se probare alicui, *to recommend oneself to some one, gain a person's approval;* se in legatione sociis, Cic.; in pass., probari alicui, *to appear worthy of approval,* Cic.; b, *to show, prove, demonstrate;* crimen, Cic.; causam, Cic.; with acc. and infin., probare judicibus Verrem pecunias cepisse, Cic.; absol., difficile est probatu, Cic.

prŏbrōsus -a -um (probrum), *shameful, disgraceful, infamous, ignominious;* crimen, Cic.; carmen, Tac.

prŏbrum -i, n. **I.** *a shameful, infamous deed;* 1, gen., alicui probrum objectare, Cic.; emergere ex paternis probris ac vitiis, Cic.; 2, esp., *unchastity;* probri insimulasti pudicissimam feminam, Cic. **II.** Transf., *shame, disgrace, infamy;* 1, gen., probro esse, Cic.; pro-

brum inferre alicui, Cic.; alicui ut probrum objicere quod, etc., Cic.; 2, esp., *abuse, insult, libel;* epistolae plenae omnium in me probrorum, Cic.; multa objicere probra, Cic.

prŏbus -a -um, *good, excellent, fine;* a, physically or intellectually, res, Cic.; navigium, Cic.; ingenium, Cic.; b, morally, *good, upright, virtuous, honourable;* filius, Cic.; homo probior, Cic.

Prŏca (Prŏcās) -ae, m. *an old king of Alba.*

prŏcācĭtas -ātis, f. (procax), *shamelessness, impudence,* Cic.

prŏcācĭtĕr, adv. (procax), *shamelessly, impudently,* Liv.

prŏcax -cācis (proco), *shameless, bold, impudent, importunate, insolent;* a, of persons, in lacessendo, Cic.; procacius stipendium flagitare, Liv.; b, of things, sermo, Sall.; scripta, Tac.; auster, *blustering,* Verg.

prŏcēdo -cessi -cessum, 3. *to go forth, go before, proceed.* **I.** Lit. and transf., **A.** Gen., 1, lit., a, e tabernaculo in solem, Cic.; alicui obviam procedere, *to go to meet,* Cic.; b, milit. t. t., *to advance;* lente atque paulatim, Caes.; ad dimicandum, Liv.; c, *to appear, show oneself, step forward;* procedere in medium, Cic.; esp., *to come forward to speak to an assembly;* procedere in contionem, Liv.; 2, transf., *to advance;* a, of ships, quantum naves processissent, Caes.; b, of stars, *to appear;* processit Vesper, Verg. **B.** Transf., *to advance, progress, of work, etc.,* magna pars operis Caesaris processerat, Caes. **II.** Fig., **A.** Gen., a, in dando et credendo longius procedere, *to go too far,* Cic.; eo processit vecordiae ut, etc., *he went to such a pitch of madness that,* etc., Sall.; esp., *to advance towards some good, go on, make progress;* in philosophia, Cic.; b, *to run on, continue, be counted up;* stipendia, aera alicui procedunt, Liv.; hence, transf., *to be of use to, do good to;* benefacta mea reipublicae procedunt, Sall.; c, of time, dies procedens, Cic.; si (puer) aetate processerit, Cic.; multum diei processerat, Sall. **B.** Of actions, etc., *to turn out in a certain way, to result;* si bene processit, Cic.; alicui bene, pulcherrime, Cic.; and absol., *to turn out well, to be prosperous;* si processit, Cic.

prŏcella -ae, f. (procello), *a storm, tempest, gale;* 1, lit., nimbi, procellae, turbines, Cic.; 2, transf., a, *a sudden charge of cavalry, onset, charge;* primam procellam eruptionis sustinere non posse, Liv.; b, procellae insidiarum, Cic.; procellam temporis devitare, Cic.

prŏcello, 3. (pro and cello), *to throw down, cast down,* Plaut.

prŏcellōsus -a -um (procella), *stormy, tempestuous,* Verg., Liv.

prŏcer -ēris, m. *an illustrious person;* usually plur., **prŏcĕres** -um, m. *chiefs, nobles, princes;* audiebam enim nostros proceres clamantes, Cic.

prŏcērē, adv. (procerus), *far outstretched;* compar., brachium procerius projectum, Cic.

prŏcērĭtas -ātis, f. (procerus), *height, slimness, slenderness.* **I.** Lit., cameli adjuvantur proceritate collorum, *by the length of their necks,* Cic.; arborum, Cic. **II.** Transf., *length* (of a syllable or foot in poetry); pedum, Cic.

prŏcērus -a -um (pro and cerus, from root CER, CRE, whence cresco), *tall, slender, long.* **I.** Lit., of bodies, etc., collum, rostrum, Cic.; of trees, procerissima populus, Cic. **II.** Transf., in rhythm and pronunciation, *long;* procerio: quidam numerus, Cic.

prŏcessĭo -ōnis, f. (procedo), *a military advance,* Cic.

prōcessus -ūs, m. (procedo), *a going forth, advance, course, progress;* gradus et quasi processus dicendi, Cic.; tantos progressus efficiebat ut, etc., Cic.

Prŏchўta -ae, f. and **Prŏchўtē** -ēs, f. (Προχύτη), *an island on the coast of Campania,* now *Procida.*

prōcĭdo -cĭdi (pro and cado), 3. *to fall down forward, fall forward;* preaceps procidit ante proram, Liv.

procinctus -ūs, m.(procingo), *a being girded;* hence, *a being equipped for battle, readiness for battle;* in procinctu ac castris habiti, Tac.; testamentum in procinctu facere, *on the battlefield,* Cic.

proclāmātor -ōris, m. (proclamo), *a bawler, vociferator* (of a bad advocate), Cic.

proclāmo, 1. *to call out, cry out;* absol., Cic.; with acc. and infin., se filiam jure caesam judicare, Liv.; pro aliquo (contemptuously of an advocate), *to defend a person,* Liv.

Prŏcles -is, m. (Προκλῆς), *son of Aristodemus, brother of Eurysthenes, king of Sparta, founder of the family of the Proclidae.*

prōclīno, 1. act. *to bend, incline forwards, to bend;* mare in litora, Ov.; transf., proclinatā jam re, *approaching consummation,* Caes.; adjuvare rem proclinatam, *tottering to its fall,* Caes.

prōclīvĕ (prōclīvĭ), compar., prōclīvĭus, adv. (proclivis), *downwards;* proclivi currere, labi, Cic.

prōclīvis -e and **prōclīvus** -a -um (pro and clivus), *inclined forwards, sloping downwards, steep.* **I.** Lit., via proclivis, Liv.; subst., per proclive, *downwards,* Liv. **II.** Fig., 1, meton., *going downwards;* proclivi cursu et facili delabi, Cic.; 2, *inclined to, ready for, prone to;* ad morbum, Cic.; ad comitatem, Cic.; 3, *easy to do;* illa facilia, proclivia, jucunda, Cic.; alicui est proclive, with infin., Caes.; dictu proclive est, *it is easy to say,* with acc. and infin., Cic.

prōclīvĭtas -ātis, f. (proclivis), *a slope;* fig., *inclination, tendency, proneness;* ad morbos, Cic.

prōclīvus = proclivis (q.v.).

Procnē (Prognē) -ēs, f. (Πρόκνη). **I.** *daughter of Pandion, sister of Philomela and wife of Tereus, changed into a swallow.* **II.** Meton., *a swallow,* Verg.

prŏco, 1. and **prŏcor,** 1. dep. *to ask, intreat,* Cic.

prōconsul -sŭlis, m. *a proconsul, one who after his consulship* (and sometimes without having been consul), *was governor of a province,* Cic.

prōconsŭlāris -e (proconsul), *of or relating to a proconsul, proconsular,* Liv.

prōconsŭlātus -ūs, m. (proconsul), *the office* or *dignity of a proconsul,* Tac.

prōcrastĭnātĭo -ōnis, f. (procrastino), *a putting off from day to day, procrastination,* Cic.

prōcrastĭno, 1. (pro and crastino), *to put off till to-morrow, procrastinate,* Cic.

prōcrĕātĭo -ōnis, f. (procreo), *begetting, procreation,* Cic.

prōcrĕātor -ōris, m. (procreo), *a begetter;* mundi, *Creator,* Cic.; procreatores = *parents,* Cic.

prōcrĕātrix -īcis, f. (procreator), *one that brings forth, mother;* transf., artium, Cic.

prōcrĕo, 1. **I.** *to beget, procreate;* of animals, *to bring forth;* multiplices fetus, Cic. **II.** Fig., *to bring forth, produce, cause, make;* inter arma civium (tribunatum) procreatum, Cic.

prōcresco, 3. **I.** *to grow forth, arise,* Lucr. **II.** Fig., *to increase,* Lucr.

Prŏcris -crĭdis, f. (Πρόκρις), *daughter of Erectheus, wife of Cephalus, who killed her in a forest, mistaking her for an animal.*

Prōcrustēs -ae, m. (Προκρούστης), *a robber in Attica, who tied his prisoners to a bed, stretching the limbs of those shorter than the bed, and cutting off the limbs of those who were taller; killed by Theseus.*

prōcŭbo, 1. *to lie stretched out, to lie along;* ubi saxea procubet umbra, Verg.

prōcūdo -cūsi -cūsum, 3. **I.** 1, *to thrust or drive forward,* Lucr.; 2, *to forge;* enses, Hor. **II.** Fig., linguam, *to form, train,* Cic.

prōcŭl, adv. (from procello). **I.** *afar off, at a distance, far away;* non procul, sed hic, Cic.; foll. by a, ab, *far from;* procul a terra abripi, Cic.; by abl. alone, procul coetu hominum, Liv. **II.** Transf., *far from, far away;* with abl., procul dubio, *without doubt,* Liv.; haud procul est, with quin and subj., *it is not far from,* Liv.; of time, haud procul occasu solis, *not long before,* Liv.

prōculco, 1. (pro and calco), *to tread, trample upon;* 1, things, is (aper) modo crescentes segetes proculcat in herba, Ov.; 2, persons, *to trample to the ground, to tread down;* aliquem, Tac.

Prōcŭlēius -i, m. *a Roman knight, friend of Augustus.*

prōcumbo -cŭbŭi -cŭbĭtum, 3. *to lean or bend forward.* **I.** Gen., **A.** 1, lit., of persons, olli certamine summo procumbunt (of rowers), Verg.; 2, transf., of things, *to incline forward;* secundum naturam fluminis, Caes. **II.** *to fall down, sink down, to fall prostrate.* **A.** 1, lit., of living beings, alces procumbunt, Caes.; of persons in prayer, entreaty, etc., procumbere alicui ad pedes, Caes.; ad genua alicuius, Liv.; of persons wounded, vulneribus confectum procumbere, Caes.; 2, transf., of things, frumenta imbribus procubuerant, *were laid low,* Caes. **B.** Fig., *to sink, fall;* res procubuere meae, Ov.

prōcūrātĭo -ōnis, f. (procuro), *a taking care of, management, administration.* **I.** Gen., reipublicae, Cic.; mearum rerum, Cic.; annonae, Cic. **II.** Esp., 1, under the empire, *the office of imperial procurator,* Tac.; 2, *a religious act for the propitiation of an offended deity;* ut sue plena procuratio fieret, Cic.

prōcūrātor -ōris, m. (procuro), *a manager, administrator, agent, factor, deputy.* **I.** Gen., regni, *a viceroy,* Caes.; with genit. of person, procurator P. Quinctii, Cic. **II.** Esp., 1, *a land steward, land agent,* Cic.; 2, in imperial times, *a functionary who collected the imperial revenue both in Rome and in the provinces;* procurator Caesaris, Tac.; procurator Judaeae, Tac.

procūrātrix -trīcis, f. (procurator), *she that governs;* fig., sapientia totius hominis procuratrix, Cic.

prōcūro, 1. *to take care of, look after, tend.* **I.** Gen., corpus, Verg.; sacrificia, Caes. **II.** Esp., 1, *to manage, administer any one's affairs;* alicuius negotia, Cic.; hereditatem, Cic.; 2, *to offer sacrifice in order to avert an evil omen;* monstra, Cic.; prodigia, Cic.

prōcurro -curri and -cŭcurri -cursum, 3. *to run forward, rush forward, charge.* **I.** Lit., of persons, ex castris, Caes.; in vias, Liv.; ad repellendum hostem, Caes. **II.** Transf., of places, *to project, jut out, run forward;* infelix saxis in procurrentibus haesit, Verg.; terra procurrit in aequor, Ov.

prōcursātĭo -ōnis, f. (procurso), *a running forward, charge;* velitum, Liv.

prōcursātor -ōris, m. (procurso). *one who runs forward;* milit. t. t., procursatores, *skirmishers,* Liv.

prōcurso, 1. (intens. of procurro), *to run forward, spring forward;* as milit. t. t., *to skirmish,* Liv.

prōcursus -ūs, m. (procurro), *a running forward;* and esp., in military language, *an advance, charge;* procursu militum, Liv.

prōcurvus -a -um, *bent forward, curved forward;* falx, Verg.; litora, *winding,* Verg.

prōcus -i, m. (proco), *a wooer, suitor;* transf., impudentes proci, *candidates,* Cic.

Prōcўōn -ōnis, m. (Προκύων), *a constellation which rises before the Dog-star,* Cic.

prōd = pro (q.v.)

prōdĕo -ii -ītum, 4. *to go, come forth.* **I.** **A.** 1, lit., obviam mihi est proditum, Cic.; prodire ex portu, Caes.; in publicum, *to appear in public,* Cic.; in proelium, Caes.; 2, esp., *to appear in some character, to come forth,* e.g., *as an actor;* in scenam, Cic. **B.** Fig., a, *to appear, show itself;* consuetudo prodire coepit, Cic.; b, *to go forth* = *to become;* prodis ex judice Dama turpis, Hor. **II.** *to advance, go forward.* **A.** 1, lit., longius, Caes.; 2, transf., *to project;* rupes prodit in aequor, Verg. **B.** Fig., sumptu extra modum, *to exceed the mark,* Cic.

prōdico -dixi -dictum, 3. **I.** *to say before,* Cic. (?) **II.** *to fix for a later time, put off;* diem in Quirinalia, Cic.

prōdictātor -ōris, m. *one who acts as dictator,* Liv.(?)

Prōdĭcus -i, m. *a Greek sophist of Ceos, contemporary of Socrates.*

prōdĭgē, adv. (prodigus), *prodigally, extravagantly;* vivere, Cic.

prōdĭgentĭa -ae, f. (prodigo), *profusion prodigality,* Tac.

prōdĭgĭālĭtĕr, adv. *strangely, wonderfully,* Hor.

prōdĭgĭōsus -a -um (prodigium), *unnatural, strange, wonderful, prodigious,* Ov.

prōdĭgĭum -ii, n. (prod and agere), *a prodigy, portent, omen, ominous sign.* **I.** Lit., multa prodigia eius vim declarant, Cic. **II.** Transf., a, *a monstrosity, something unnatural;* prodigium videbatur civitatum frumentum improbare, suum probare, Cic.; b, *a monster;* prodigium triplex, Cerberus, Ov.; fatali portentum prodigiumque reipublicae (of Clodius), Cic.

prōdĭgo -ēgi -actum, 3. (prod and ago), **I.** *to drive forth;* sues, Varr. **II.** Transf., *to spend, waste;* aliena, Sall.

prōdĭgus -a -um (prodigo), *prodigal, profuse, extravagant.* **I.** a, lit., Cic.; with genit., aeris, Hor.; b, fig., with genit., animae, *not sparing his own life,* Hor.; arcani, *revealing a secret,* Hor.; with in and the abl., in honoribus decernendis nimius et tamquam prodigus, Cic. **II.** Transf., *rich, abounding in;* locus prodigus herbae, Hor.

prōdĭtĭo -ōnis, f. (prodo), *a betraying, betrayal, treachery, treason;* amicitiarum proditiones et rerum publicarum, Cic.

prōdĭtor -ōris, m. (prodo), *a betrayer, traitor;* consulis, Cic.; transf., risus latentis puellae proditor, Hor.

prōdo -dĭdi -dĭtum, 3. **I.** *to put forth, bring forth.* **A.** Gen., *to bring forth;* fumoso condita vina cado, Ov.; suspiria pectore, Ov. **B.** Esp., 1, a, *to give, show, publish;* decretum, Cic.; exemplum, Liv.; b, *to proclaim elected, to appoint;* flaminem, interregem, Cic.; c, *to relate;*

quae scriptores prodiderunt, Cic.; d, *to reveal, betray something secret, to betray;* conscios, Cic.; crimen vultu, Ov.; 2, *to give up, discover, betray treacherously;* classem praedonibus, Cic.; aliquem ad mortem, Verg.; utilitatem communem, Cic. **II.** **A.** *to hand over, deliver, transmit;* sacra suis posteris, Cic.; esp. in writing, *to betray prodere, to commit to writing,* Cic.; memoriae prodiderunt, with acc. and infin., Cic. **B.** *to propagate;* genus, Verg.

prōdŏcĕo, 2. *to teach, inculcate,* Hor.

prōdrŏmus -i, m. (πρόδρομος), *a messenger, forerunner.* **I.** Lit., Cic. **II.** Transf., *a north north-east wind, said to blow for eight days before the rising of the Dog-star,* Cic.

prōdūco -duxi -ductum, 3. *to lead forth.* **I.** Gen., **A.** Lit., 1, equos, jumenta, Caes.; 2, milit. t. t., *to lead forth troops;* copias pro castris, Caes.; 3, a, polit. t. t., *to bring before the public assembly* or *before a court of justice;* harum rerum omnium auctores testesque, Cic.; b, *to bring out of prison;* aliquem capite involuto ad necem, Cic.; c, *to bring forward on the stage, on the arena,* etc.; aliquem, Cic.; 3, *to bring forth a corpse to the funeral pile;* aliquem funere, Verg.; 4, *to entice forth;* aliquem dolo in proelium, Nep. **B.** Fig., *to bring before some one, reveal;* occulta ad patres crimina, Juv. **II.** **A.** Lit., 1, *to advance;* unam navem longius, Caes.; *to draw out, stretch out, extend;* a, ferrum incude, Juv.; b, in pronunciation, *to lengthen out, make long;* litteram, Cic.; syllabam, Ov.; 2, a, *to beget, produce;* fig., nova (vocabula) quae genitor produxerit usus, Hor.; b, *to rear, bring up;* subolem, Hor.; of plants, arborem, Hor. **B.** Fig., 1, *to advance, promote;* aliquem ad dignitatem, Cic.; 2, *to prolong* (in duration of time); a, *to continue, keep on;* sermonem longius in multam noctem, Cic.; b, *to put off, postpone;* rem in hiemem, Caes.; c, *to put off, delay;* conditionibus hunc, quoad potest, producit, Cic.

prōductē, adv. (productus), *in a lengthened manner, long* (of pronunciation); producte dici, Cic.

prōductĭo -ōnis, f. (produco), *an extending, lengthening;* a, of a word by the addition of a syllable, Cic.; b, of a syllable in pronunciation, Cic.; c, of time, *prolonging;* temporis, Cic.

prōductus -a -um, p. adj. (from produco). **I.** Adj., *extended, lengthened, prolonged;* productiore cornu sinistro, Tac.; quinto productior actu fabula, Hor.; of words, nomen, *lengthened by addition of a syllable,* Cic.; of syllables, *long* (in pronunciation); (syllaba) producta atque longa, Cic.; of time, *prolonged, drawn out;* dolores, Cic. **II.** Subst., **producta** -ōrum, n. (τὰ προηγμένα), *preferable things* (in the Stoic philosophy, *things which,* while not absolutely good, were to be preferred, e.g., beauty, health), Cic.

proelĭātor -ōris, m. (proelior), *a warrior, combatant,* Tac.

proelĭor, 1. dep. (proelium), *to give battle, fight;* ad Syracusas, Cic.; pedibus, Caes.; transf., vehementer proeliatus sum, *striven,* Cic.

proelĭum -ii, n. *a battle, fight.* **I.** a, lit., proelium facere, Cic.; redintegrare, Caes.; inire, Liv.; proelio abstinere, Caes.; b, transf., of a fight in words, proelia meā causā sustinere, Cic. **II.** Meton., proelia = *fighters, combatants,* Prop.

Proetus -i, m. (Προῖτος), *king in Tiryns, brother of Acrisius.* Hence, **Proetis** -idis, f. *a daughter of Proetus;* plur., Proetides, *the daughters of Proetus, who were punished with madness, and imagined themselves to be cows.*

prŏfāno, 1. (profanus), *to profane, desecrate;* **sacra**, Liv.; festum, Ov.

prŏfānus -a -um (pro and fanum, lit., *lying before a temple,* i.e., *outside it*), *not sacred, not consecrated.* **I.** Gen., *common, profane;* 1, lit., locus, Cic.; bubo, avis, *of evil omen,* Ov.; subst., **prŏfānum** -i, n. *that which is profane, unconsecrated,* Tac.; 2, transf., *profane, godless, impious;* verba, Ov. **II.** Esp., 1, *not initiated, uninitiated;* procul este profani, Verg.; 2, transf., *not initiated in the service of the Muses;* profanum vulgus, Hor.

prŏfectĭo -ōnis, f. (proficiscor), 1, *a departure,* Cic.; 2, transf., *source, origin;* pecuniae, Cic.

prŏfecto, adv. (pro and factus), *truly, really, indeed,* Cic.

prŏfĕro -tŭli -lātum -ferre. **I.** *to carry forth, bring forth* (from a place); 1, lit., a, nummos ex arca, Cic.; pecuniam alicui, Cic.; b, milit. t. t., *to deliver up, bring forth;* arma tormentaque ex oppido, Caes.; c, *to raise a limb or part of the body;* caput, Ov.; digitum, Cic.; d, *to bring forth, show;* proferre in conspectum liberos, Caes.; of writings, *to publish, make known;* orationem, Cic.; 2, fig., a, *to bring to light, reveal;* (a) aliquid in medium, Cic.; (β) as a discoverer, *to bring to light, produce;* aliquid proferre in aspectum lucemque, Cic.; proferre artem, Cic.; b, *to bring forward, produce, cite, mention;* testes, Cic.; nominatim multos, Cic.; exempla omnium nota, Cic. **II.** 1, *to advance, move forward;* a, milit. t. t., signa, *to march on,* Liv.; inde castra, *to move from thence,* Liv.; b, *to extend;* fines agri publici paulatim, Liv.; fig., fines officiorum paulo longius, Cic.; 2, fig., a, of duration of time, *to extend, lengthen;* beatam vitam usque ad rogum, Cic.; b, *to put off, postpone;* diem auctionis, Cic.

prŏfessĭo -ōnis, f. (profiteor), *acknowledgment, declaration, profession.* **I.** Gen., bonae voluntatis, ap. Cic. **II.** Esp., **A.** Lit., *public declaration of one's name, property, occupation,* etc.; haec pecunia ex eo genere est, ut professione non egeat, Cic. **B.** Meton., 1, *the register of persons and their property,* Cic.; 2, *an occupation, art, profession;* bene dicendi, Cic.

prŏfessōrĭus -a -um, *of or relating to a professor, professorial,* Tac.

prŏfessus -a -um, partic. of profiteor (q.v.).

prŏfestus -a -um, *not kept as a festival, common;* dies, *work-days, ordinary days,* Liv.

prŏfĭcĭo -fēci -fectum, 3. (pro and facio). *to make progress, advance, gain ground, to get an advantage, to effect anything.* **I.** Of persons, nihil in oppugnatione, Caes.; aliquid in philosophia, Cic. **II.** Of things, a, *to be of use or advantage to, to assist, help;* nulla res tantum ad dicendum proficit, quantum scriptio, Cic.; b, of medical remedies, herbā proficiente nihil, Hor.

prŏfĭciscor -fectus sum -ficisci, 3. dep. (pro and facio, facesso, faciscor), *to set out, depart, go, travel, march, take a journey.* **I.** Lit., ex portu, Caes.; Aegyptum, Cic.; ad or contra hostem, Caes.; cum exercitus parte frumentatum, Liv. **II.** Fig., **A.** *to go towards;* ad reliqua, Cic. **B.** 1, *to set out from, begin with;* a lege, Cic.; ab hoc initio, Caes.; 2, meton., *to arise from, spring from, originate from;* a natura, Cic.; qui a Zenone profecti sunt, *Zeno's disciples,* Cic.

prŏfĭtĕor -fessus sum, 2. dep. (pro and fateor), *to acknowledge openly, confess, avow.* **I.** Gen., fateor atque etiam profiteor, Cic.; with acc. and infin., profiteor me relaturum, Cic. **II.** Esp., **A.** *to profess or declare oneself anything;* a, with double acc. of pers., se grammaticum, Cic.; b,

with acc. and infin., me defensorem esse profiteor, Cic.; c, with acc. of thing, *to profess any science, art,* etc.; philosophiam, Cic.; jus, Cic. **B.** indicium, *to turn king's evidence,* Sall., Tac.; *to offer, promise;* operam, Cic.; profitetur se venturum, Cic. **C.** *to make a public statement or return of property,* etc.; jugera, Cic.; frumentum, Liv.; nomen, Cic.; and simply profiteri, *to announce oneself as a candidate,* Sall. (Partic., **prŏfessus** -a -um, pass., *known, acknowledged, avowed;* culpa, Ov.)

prŏflīgātŏr -ōris, m. (profligo), *a spendthrift, prodigal,* Tac.

prŏflīgātus -a -um, p. adj. (from profligo), 1, *cast down, ruined, wretched,* Cic.; 2, *dissolute, profligate;* tu omnium mortalium profligatissime, Cic.

prŏflīgo, 1. (pro and fligere), *to strike to the ground.* **I.** Lit., *to overthrow, overcome;* copias hostium, Cic.; classem hostium, Caes. **II.** Fig., **A.** a, politically, *to ruin;* rempublicam, Cic.; b, *to lower, abase;* judicia senatoria, Cic.; c, *to bring almost to an end, nearly finish;* profligatum bellum et paene sublatum, Cic.; profligata jam haec, et paene ad exitum adducta quaestio est, Cic.

prŏflo, 1. *to blow forth, breathe forth;* flammas, Ov.; fig., toto proflabat pectore somnum, Verg.

prŏflŭens -entis, p. adj. (from profluo), *flowing.* **I.** Lit., aqua, Cic. Subst., **prŏflŭens** -entis, f. *running water,* Cic. **II.** Transf., of discourse, *flowing, fluent;* genus sermonis, Cic.

prŏflŭentĕr, adv. (profluens), *flowingly, easily,* Cic.

prŏflŭo -fluxi -fluxum, 3. *to flow, flow forth.* **I.** Lit., ex monte, Caes.; in mare, Cic. **II.** Fig., *to flow forth, proceed;* ab his fontibus profluxi ad hominum famam, Cic.

prŏflŭvĭum -ĭi, n. (profluo), *a flowing forth;* sanguinis, Lucr.

prŏfor -fātus sum, 1. dep. 1, *to say, speak,* Verg.; 2, *to foretell, predict,* Lucr.

prŏfŏre, v. prosum.

prŏfŭgĭo -fūgi -fŭgitum, 3. **I.** Intransit., *to flee away, escape;* ex oppido, Caes.; domo, Cic.; absol., Catilina ipse pertimuit, profugit, Cic. **II.** *to flee away from;* agros, Hor.

prŏfŭgus -a -um (profugio), *flying, fleeing, fugitive;* a, gen., (a) of persons, populus, Tac.; poet., Scythae, *wandering, migratory, flying from one's native country, banished,* Hor.; (β) of animals, taurus, Tac.; (γ) of things, currus, Ov.; b, of soldiers, *flying from battle,* Sall.; c, of exiles, with abl., patriā profugus, Liv.; at Thebis, Liv.; ex Peloponneso, Liv.; subst., **prŏfŭgus** -i, m. *a fugitive, exile,* Ov.

prŏfundo -fūdi -fūsum, 3. *to pour forth, shed abundantly, cause to flow.* **I. A.** Lit., sanguinem suum omnem, Cic.; vim lacrimarum, Cic.; reflex., se profundere, and middle, profundi, *to stream forth;* lacrimae se profuderunt, Cic. **B.** Transf., 1, *to stretch at full length;* somnus membra profudit, Lucr.; 2, a, reflex., se profundere, or middle, profundi, *to pour out, rush forth;* omnis multitudo sagittariorum se profudit, Caes.; of plants, quae (in vitibus) se nimium profuderunt, *have shot out,* Cic.; b, *to utter;* clamorem, Cic.; c, *to bring forth, produce;* ea quae frugibus atque bacis terrae fetu profunduntur, Cic.; 3, *to spend, sacrifice, give up;* pro patria vitam, Cic.; in a bad sense, *to spend, lavish, squander;* pecuniam, Cic.; patrimonia, Cic. **II.** Fig., a, *to pour, vent, expend upon;* omne odium in me, Cic.; b, reflex., se profundere, *to burst forth, to pour forth, rush forth;* voluptates subito se pro fundunt, Cic.

prŏfundus -a -um. **I.** *deep, profound;* 1, lit., mare, Cic.; subst., **prŏfundum** -i, n. *the bottomless depth;* aquae, Cic.; absol., poet. = *the sea,* Verg.; 2, fig., libidines, Cic.; avaritia, Sall. **II.** Transf., **A.** *high;* caelum, Verg. **B.** *deep, dense;* silvae, Lucr.

prŏfūsē, adv. (profusus). **I.** *in a disorderly manner;* profuse tendere in castra, Liv. **II.** Fig., *lavishly, extravagantly;* profusius sumptui deditus erat, Sall.

prŏfūsus -a -um, p. adj. (from profundo), *immoderate, extravagant;* 1, gen., hilaritas, Cic.; 2, esp., a, *immoderate in expenditure, extravagant,* Cic.; with genit., sui profusus, Sall.; b, transf., *costly;* epulae, Cic.

prōgĕner -i, *a grand-daughter's husband,* Tac.

prōgĕnĕro, 1. *to engender, produce,* Hor.

prōgĕnĭes -ēi, f. (progigno). **I.** *descent, race, lineage,* Cic. **II.** Meton., *progeny, offspring, descendants;* veteres, qui se deorum progeniem esse dicebant, Cic.

prōgĕnĭtor -ōris, m. (progigno), *the founder of a family, ancestor, progenitor,* Ov.

prōgigno -gĕnŭi -gĕnĭtum, 3. *to engender, bring forth, bear,* Cic.

prognātus - a -um (partic. of *prognoscor), *born, sprung from;* deo, Liv.; ex Cimbris, Caes.; ab Dite patre, Caes.

Prognē = Procne (q.v.).

prognostĭca -ōrum, n. (προγνωστικά), *signs of the weather,* a poem by Aratus, translated by Cicero, Cic.

prōgrĕdĭor -gressus sum -grĕdi, 3. dep. (pro and gradior). **I.** *to go forth, go out;* ex domo, Cic. **II.** *to go forwards, to advance.* **A.** Lit., of persons, regredi quam progredi mallent, Cic.; milit. t.t., *to advance;* longius a castris, Caes. **B.** Fig., *to proceed, advance;* a, quatenus amor in amicitia progredi debeat, Cic.; b, in a speech, etc., *to proceed to, go on;* ad reliqua, Cic.; c, of time, paulum aetate progressus, *advanced in years,* Cic.

prōgressĭo -ōnis, f. (progredior), *an advancing, progress, increase;* a, progressionem facere ad virtutem, Cic.; b, rhet. t. t., *a gradual strengthening of expression, climax,* Cic.

prōgressus -ūs, m. (progredior), *a going forwards, advance.* **I.** Lit., aliquem progressu arcere, Cic. **II.** Fig., a, *beginning of a speech;* primo progressu, Cic.; b, *progress, increase;* aetatis, Cic.; tantos progressus habebat in Stoicis, *progress in the Stoical philosophy,* Cic.; progressus facere in studiis, Cic.

proh! = pro! (q.v.).

prŏhĭbĕo -bŭi -bĭtum, 2. (pro and habeo). **I.** *to hold back, hold in, check, restrain, hinder.* **A.** Gen., praedones a Sicilia, Cic.; aliquem a familiaritate, Cic.; vim hostium ab oppidis, Caes.; se suosque ab injuria, Caes.; exercitum itinere, *to obstruct on the march,* Caes.; with infin., prohibeo aliquem exire domo, Cic.; with ne and the subj., potuisti prohibere ne fieret, Cic.; with quin and the subj., nec, quin erumperet, prohiberi poterat, Liv.; with quominus and the subj., prohibuisse, quominus de te certum haberemus, Cic.; with double acc., ideo ut prohiberet, Liv.; with simple acc., Caesarem, Caes.; conatus alicuius, Cic. **B.** *to hinder by words, forbid, prohibit;* lex recta imperans, prohibensque contraria, Cic. **II.** *to preserve, defend, protect;* a quo periculo prohibere rempublicam, Cic.

prŏhĭbĭtĭo -ōnis, f. (prohibeo), *a hindering, prohibition;* tollendi, Cic.

prŏĭcĭo = projicio (q.v.).

prŏin = proinde (q.v.)

prŏindĕ, adv. **I.** *just as, in the same manner, in like manner;* foll. by atque (ac), ut, quasi, quam, tamquam, Cic. **II.** *therefore, then, hence, accordingly;* esp. used in phrases of exhortation, encouragement, etc., Cic.

prōjectĭo -ōnis, f. (projicio), *a throwing forward, stretching out;* brachii, Cic.

1. **prōjectus** -ūs, m. (projicio), *a projecting, jutting out,* Lucr.

2. **prōjectus** -a -um, p. adj. (from projicio), *stretching out, jutting forward, projecting;* urbs, Cic.; saxa, Verg. **I.** Fig., a, *prominent;* audacia, Cic.; b, *addicted to;* homo ad audendum projectus, Cic. **II.** *stretched out, prostrate, lying.* **A.** Lit., ad terram, Caes.; in antro, Verg. **B.** Fig., a, *abject, base;* patientia, Tac.; b, *cast down;* vultus, Tac.

prōjĭcĭo -jēci -jectum, 3. (pro and jacio). **I.** *to throw, cast before, throw down.* **A.** Gen., cibum, Hor. **B.** Esp., 1, *to stretch forth, throw out;* a, of limbs, brachium, Cic.; b, of buildings, pass., projici, *to project;* tectum projiceretur, Cic.; c, *to throw or place a weapon before one;* clipeum prae se, Liv.; 2, *to push forth, drive forth;* a, aliquem foras, Cic.; aliquem ab urbe, Ov.; b, *to banish;* aliquem in insulam, Tac. **II.** *to throw out, throw in front.* **A.** Gen., crates, Caes.; se ad pedes alicuius, Cic.; projectā viliŏr algā, *cast upon the shore,* Verg. **B.** Esp. 1, *to throw away;* arma, Caes.; fig., a, se projicere, *to lower oneself to, to stoop to;* in muliebres fletus, Liv.; b, *to reject, abandon;* libertatem, Cic.; c, *to expose, betray;* ab aliquo projici et prodi, Cic.; 2, *to cast to the ground;* effigies, Tac.; 3, *to put off;* aliquem ultra quinquennium, Tac.

prōlābor -lapsus sum -lābi, 3. **I.** *to glide forward, slide forward, slip along.* **A.** Lit. (elephanti) clunibus subsistentes prolabebantur, Liv. **B.** Fig., 1, *to come to, fall into;* huc libido est prolapsa, Cic.; 2, *to slip out, escape;* verbum a cupiditate prolapsum, Liv. **II.** *to fall down.* **A.** Lit., ex equo, Liv.; prolapsa Pergama, Verg. **B.** Fig., 1, *to fail, to err;* cupiditate, timore, Cic.; 2, *to fall, go to ruin, sink;* ita prolapsa est juventus ut, etc., Cic.

prōlapsĭo -ōnis, f. (prolabor), *a slipping, sliding,* Cic.

prōlātĭo -ōnis, f. (profero). **I.** *a bringing forward in discourse, mentioning;* exemplorum, Cic. **II.** 1, *an extension;* finium, Liv.; 2, *a putting off, deferring;* judicii, Cic.

prōlāto, 1. (intens. of profero). **I.** *to extend, enlarge, lengthen;* agros, Tac. **II.** Transf., **A.** *to put off, delay, defer;* comitia, Liv.; malum, Cic. **B.** *to prolong;* vitam, Tac.

prōlecto, 1. (intens. of prolicio), *to entice, allure;* egentes spe largitionis, Cic.

prōles -is, f. (pro and *aleo, alesco). **I.** *offspring, descendants, posterity;* a, of gods and men, illa futurorum hominum, *future generations,* Cic.; Apollinea, Aesculapius, Ov.; Latonia, Apollo and Diana, Ov.; b, of animals, Verg.; c, of plants, *fruit,* Verg. **II.** Transf., *youth, young men;* equitum peditumque, Cic.

prōlētārĭus -ĭi, m. (proles), *a citizen of the lowest class who served the state only by being the father of children,* Cic.

prōlĭcĭo, 3. (pro and lacio), *to lure forth, entice,* Ov.

prōlixē, adv. (prolixus). **I.** *abundantly, copiously;* id prolixe cumulateque fecit, Cic. **II.** *freely, willingly;* in delectu parum prolixe respondere, Cic.

prōlixus -a -um (pro and laxus), *widely extended, wide, broad, long.* **I.** Lit., Lucr. **II.**

Fig., 1, *willing, obliging;* tua prolixa beneficaque natura, Cic.; **2,** *prosperous, fortunate;* cetera spero prolixa esse competitoribus, Cic.

prŏlŏgus -i, m. (πρόλογος), *a prologue,* Ter.

prŏlŏquor -lŏcūtus (-lŏqūutus) sum -lŏqui, 3. dep. *ιο̄ speak out, say out.* **I.** Gen., quod proloqui piget, Liv. **II.** Esp., *to prophesy, predict,* Prop.

prŏlūdo -lūsi -lūsum, 3. *to play beforehand, to prelude, to practise beforehand.* **I.** Lit., ad pugnam, Ov. **II.** Fig., ut ipsis sententiis, quibus proluserint, vel pugnare possint, Cic.

prŏlŭo -lŭi -lūtum, 3. **I.** *to wash forth or out.* **A.** *to cast up, to wash out;* genus omne natantum litore in extremo fluctus proluit, Verg. **B.** *to wash off;* tempestas ex omnibus montibus nives proluit, Caes. **II.** *to wash;* in vivo prolue rore manus, Ov.; leni praecordia mulso (of drinking), Hor.

prŏlūsĭo -ōnis, f. (proluo), *a prelude, preliminary exercise, essay,* Cic.

prŏlŭvĭes -ēi, f. (proluo). **I.** *an inundation,* Lucr. **II.** *excrement;* ventris, Verg.

prŏmĕrĕo -ŭi -ĭtum, and **prŏmĕrĕor** -ĭtus sum -ēri, 2. dep. *to deserve.* **I.** reus levius punitus quam sit ille promeritus, Cic.; suo beneficio promeruit, se ut ames, Cic.; partic. subst., **prŏmĕrĭtum** -i, n. *deserts, merit;* vestra in nos universa promerita, Cic. **II.** (Gen. in form promereor), *to deserve* (well) *of;* promereri bene de multis, Cic.

Prŏmētheus -ĕi and -ĕos, m. (Προμηθεύς, *the Forethinker*), *son of Iapetus, brother of Epimetheus and father of Deucalion, the mythical hero, who made man of clay, and stole fire to animate his creation from heaven; for which he was bound to a rock in the Caucasus, where a vulture devoured his liver.* Hence, **A.** Adj., **Prŏmēthēus** -a -um, *Promethean:* juga, Prop.; rupes, *the Caucasus,* Mart. **B.** Subst., **Prŏmēthĭădes** -ae, m. *son of Prometheus, Deucalion.*

prŏmĭnens -entis (promineo), *jutting out, projecting;* subst., **prŏmĭnens** -entis, n. *a projection;* in prominenti litoris, Tac.

prŏmĭnĕo -mĭnŭi, 2. *to stand out, jut out, project.* **I.** Lit., collis prominens, Liv.; prominet in altum, Liv.; pectore nudo prominentes, Caes. **II.** Fig. (justitia) foras tota promineat, *to step forth, be prominent,* Cic.; maxima pars (gloriae) in posteritatem prominet, *extends,* Liv.

prŏmiscē, adv. (promiscus) = promiscue, Cic.

prŏmiscŭē, adv. (promiscuus), *promiscuously, without distinction,* Caes.

prŏmiscus = promiscuus (q.v.).

prŏmiscŭus -a -um, *mixed, in common, indiscriminate, promiscuous.* **I.** Lit., comitia plebi et patribus promiscua, Liv.; connubia, *between patricians and plebeians,* Liv.; divina atque humana promiscua habere, *to make no distinction between,* Sall.; in promiscuo esse, *to be common,* Liv. **II.** Transf., *common, usual, general,* Tac.

prŏmissĭo -ōnis, f. (promitto), *a promise;* auxilii, Cic.

prŏmissor -ōris, m. (promitto), *a promise,* esp., *one who promises boastingly, a boaster,* Hor.

prŏmissum -i, n. (promitto), *a promise;* promissum facere, *to make a promise,* Hor.; promissa servare or promissis stare, *to keep promises,* Cic.; praemiorum promissa, Cic.

prŏmissus -a -um, p. adj. (from promitto). **I.** *long, hanging down;* of hair, capillus, Caes.; caesaries, Liv.; barba, Liv. **II.** *producing much expectation;* carmen, Hor.

prōmitto -mīsi -missum, 3. *to let go forward, send forth.* **I.** *to grow;* capillum et barbam, *to let grow,* Liv. **II. 1,** *to promise, cause to expect, assure;* **a,** with acc. of thing and with or without acc. of person, si Neptunus, quod Theseo promiserat, non fecisset, Cic.; with de and the abl., de horum erga me benevolentia promittebam, Cic.; with acc. and fut. infin., promitto tibi, si valebit, tegulam illum in Italia nullam relicturum, Cic.; **b,** *to vow, promise to a god;* donum Jovi dicatum et promissum, Cic.; **c,** promittere ad aliquem, ad cenam, *to accept an invitation to dine with;* ad fratrem promiserat, Cic.

prōmo, prompsi, promptum, 3. (for proimo, from pro and emo), *to bring forth, bring out, produce.* **I.** Lit., **1,** gen., medicamenta de narthecio, Cic.; **2,** esp., **a,** *to bring money out of a coffer, to produce;* aurum ex aerario, Cic.; esp. of the quaestor, alicui pecuniam ex aerario, Cic.; **b,** *to bring wine up out of the cellar;* vina, Hor.; **c,** *to bring weapons out;* tela e pharetra, Ov. **II.** Transf., **1,** gen., *to bring forth, draw forth;* animus eruditus, qui semper ex se aliquid promat, quod delectet, Cic.; **2,** *to bring forward, utter, express, mention;* plura adversus Cottam, Tac.

prōmŏnĕo, 2. *to warn;* t. t. of augury, de periculis promoveri, Cic.

prōmontōrĭum -ĭi, n. (promineo). **I.** *a mountain-peak,* Liv. **II.** *a promontory,* Cic.

prōmōta -ōrum, n. (promoveo), (translation of the Greek προηγμένα), *preferable things, next in degree to the absolute good,* Cic.

prōmŏvĕo -mōvi -mōtum, 2. *to move forwards, push onwards.* **I.** Lit., **A.** Gen., **a,** of things, saxa vectibus, Caes.; castra ad Carthaginem, Liv.; **b,** of persons, promovere legiones, *cause to advance,* Caes. **B.** Esp., **1,** *to advance a building in a certain direction, to push on;* aggerem in urbem, Liv.; assa in alterum angulum, *to remove,* Cic.; **2,** *to extend;* imperium, Ov. **II.** Fig., **A.** Gen., promovere arcana loco, *to bring to light,* Hor. **B.** *to increase, improve;* doctrina vim promovet insitam, Hor.

promptē, adv. (promptus). **I.** *promptly, quickly, readily,* Tac. **II.** *easily,* Juv. **III.** *frankly, freely;* dicam paulo promptius, Cic.

1. promptus -a -um, p. adj. (from promo). **I.** *visible, apparent, manifest;* aliud clausum in pectore, aliud promptum in lingua habere, Sall.; prompta et aperta, Cic. **II.** Transf., *ready, at hand, prepared.* **A.** Of things, **1,** gen., fidem suam populo Romano promptam, *at the disposition of,* Cic.; **2,** esp., *easy;* defensio, Cic. **B.** Of persons, *ready, prepared, resolute, quick, disposed for;* promptissimus homo et experiens, Cic.; with ad or in and the acc., ad vim promptus, Cic.; with abl., ingenio, linguā, Liv.; with genit. (of place), belli (*in war*) promptissimos, Sall.

2. promptus -ū, m. (promo). **I.** *a being visible, visibility,* only in the phrases: in promptu esse, *to be visible, manifest,* etc., Cic.; in promptu ponere, *to make manifest,* Cic.; in promptu habere, Sall. **II.** Transf., **A.** *readiness,* only in the phrases: in promptu esse, *to be ready at hand,* Cic.; in promptu habere, *to have ready at hand,* Cic. **B.** *easiness,* only in phrases in promptu esse, *to be easy,* Sall.

prōmulgātĭo -ōnis, f. (promulgo), *a making publicly known, proclamation, promulgation* (of a proposed law), Cic.

prōmulgo, 1. (pro and mulco), *to publish, promulgate.* **I.** Lit., legal t. t., *to publish a proposed law* (on three market-days); leges, promulgare de aliquo, Cic. **II.** Transf., *to publish, make known;* proelia, Cic.

prōmulsĭs -ĭdis, f. (pro and mulsum), *a dish taken as a relish before a meal (eggs, salt-fish, radishes, etc.), a whet.*

prōmuntŭrĭum = promontorium (q.v.).

prōmus -i, m. (promo), *the slave who had charge of the store-room and served out the daily supplies, steward, butler,* Hor.

prōmūtŭus -a -um, *advanced, paid before-hand,* Caes.

prōnē, adv. (pronus), *downwards, on an incline;* prone ac fastigate, Cic.

prōnĕpos -pōtis, m. *a great-grandson,* Cic.

prōneptis -is, f. *a great grand-daughter,* Pers.

prōnis = pronus, (q.v.).

prōnoea -ae, f. (πρόνοια), *providence,* Cic.

prōnŭba -ae, f. (pro and nubo), *a matron who attended on a bride at a Roman wedding;* Juno Pronuba, *the goddess who presided over marriage;* transf., of Bellona, *as presiding over an unlucky marriage* (leading to war), Verg.; so of the Furies, Ov.

prōnuntĭātĭo -ōnis, f. (pronuntio). *making known publicly, publication,* Caes.; esp., *the decision of a judge, a judgment,* Cic. **II.** In logic, *a proposition,* Cic.

prōnuntĭātor -ōris, m. (pronuntio), *a relater;* rerum gestarum, Cic.

prōnuntĭātum -i, n. (pronuntio), in logic, *a proposition,* Cic.

prōnuntĭo, 1. *to make publicly known, publish.* **I.** Gen., *to proclaim, announce;* pronuntiare quae gesta sunt, Caes. **II. A.** Esp., polit. and milit. t. t., *to publish, proclaim, make known by proclamation;* **a,** in public gatherings, by the herald or crier at the command of the magistrate; te illo honore affici pronuntiavit, Cic.; pronuntiare aliquem praetorem, Liv.; so of a command given to the soldiers in a camp; pronuntiatur primā luce ituros, Caes.; so, *publicly to promise something to the people;* nummos in tribus, Cic.; **b,** in the senate, of the consul, *to announce a resolution and the name of its proposer;* Lentulus sententiam Calidii pronuntiaturum se negavit, Cic. **B.** Legal t. t., a, of judges, etc., (a) *to express;* graviorem sententiam, Caes.; (β) *to decide, pronounce a judgment;* de tribunali pronuntiavit sese recepturum, Cic.; **b,** in an agreement for a sale, *to make a statement as to the defects of the thing sold;* quum in vendendo rem eam scisset et non pronuntiasset, Cic. **C.** Rhet. t. t., *to declaim, recite, deliver;* summā voce versus multos uno spiritu, Cic.

prōnŭrus -ūs, f. *a grandson's wife,* Ov.

prōnus -a -um, *inclined forward, stooping forward, hanging down.* **I. A.** Adj., **a,** of persons, pronus pendens in verbera, *leaning forward to the blow,* Verg.; so of persons, *swiftly running,* Ov.; **b,** of the position of parts of the body, motu prono, Cic.; **c,** of things, amnis, *rushing down,* Verg.; **d,** transf., (a) of places, *sloping;* Anxur fuit urbs prona in paludes, Liv.; poet., *precipitous, steep;* via, Ov.; (β) of stars, *setting;* Orion, Hor.; (γ) of time, *hastening away;* menses, Hor. **B.** Subst., **prōnum** -i, n., nihil proni habere, Cic. **II.** Fig. **A.** *inclined towards;* **1,** to something good or bad; ad novas res, Tac.; in obsequium, Hor.; in hoc consilium, Liv.; **2,** *inclined, well-disposed, favourable;* in aliquem, Tac. **B.** Meton., *easy;* omnia virtuti prona, Sall.; id pronius ad fidem est, *is more creditable,* Liv.

prōoemĭum -ĭi, n. (προοίμιον). **I.** *a preface, introduction, prelude,* Cic. **II.** *a beginning,* Juv.

prōpāgātĭo -ōnis, f. (1. propago). **I.** *an extension, enlargement.* **A.** In space, imperii nostri, Cic. **B.** In time, *prolonging, extending;* temporis, Cic.; vitae, Cic. **II.** *planting, propagation,* Cic.; transf., of a race, Cic.; nominis, Cic.

prōpāgātor -ōris, m. (1. propago), *an extender, enlarger;* provinciae, Cic.

1. **prōpāgo,** 1. (pro and PAG-o, pango). **I.** Gen., **A.** *to extend, enlarge;* fines provinciae, Cic. **B.** *to extend in point of time, prolong;* bellum, Cic.; laudem alicuius ad sempiternam gloriam, Cic.; imperium consuli in annum, Liv.; multa saecula reipublicae, *to prolong the existence of the state by many centuries,* Cic. **II.** Esp., *to propagate, plant;* transf., of a race, stirpem, Cic.

2. **prōpāgo** -ĭnis, f. (1. propago). **I.** *a sucker, layer, shoot;* esp., of the vine, Cic. **II.** Transf. of men and animals, *offspring, progeny, race, posterity;* Romana, Verg.; catulorum, Lucr.; plur., clarorum virorum propagines, *genealogies,* Nep.

prōpālam, adv. *publicly, in public;* dicere, Liv.; collocare, Cic.

prōpātŭlus -a -um, *open, uncovered.* **I.** Adj., in aperto ac propatulo loco, Cic. **II.** Subst., **prōpātŭlum** -i, n. *an open place, unroofed space;* hence, in propatulo; **a,** *openly,* Cic.; transf., *visibly, publicly,* Sall.; **b,** esp., in propatulo aedium, *in the open fore-court of a house,* Liv.

prōpĕ (from pro and pe, or else the neuter of an unused adj., propis). Compar., **prōpĭus;** superl., **proxĭmē. I.** Adv., **A.** *near;* **1,** of space, *near;* volebam prope alicubi esse, Cic.; propius, *nearer;* accedere, Cic.; proxime, *next;* proxime trans Padum, Caes.; **2,** of time, *near;* hence, proxime, *a short time ago, just now;* quem proxime nominavi, Cic.; **3,** of other relations; **a,** of approximation to; (a) *nearly;* prope erat ut pelleretur, *he was near being,* etc., Liv.; propius nihil est factum quam ut occideretur, Cic.; (β) *nearly, almost;* annis prope quadraginta, Liv.; prope desperatis rebus, Cic.; prope adesse, *to be close at hand,* Cic.; (γ) *more closely, more accurately;* propius res aspice nostras, Verg.; (δ) of similarity, proxime atque (ac) ille, Cic.; **b,** of order, *near;* proxime a Lacyde, Cic. **B.** *near by, close to, hard by;* gen. with a and the abl., prope a Sicilia, Cic. **II.** Prep. with acc. (sometimes with dat.), **1,** of space, *near to;* prope me, Cic.; proxime hostem, *next the enemy,* Caes.; propius grammatico accessi, Cic.; **2,** of time, *near to, close on;* prope calendas Sext., Cic.; **3,** of approximation or similarity, *not far from, near to;* propius, *nearer to;* proxime, *nearest to, very like to;* prope secessionem plebis res venit, Liv.; propius fidem est, *it deserves more credit,* Liv.; proxime morem Romanum, Liv.

prōpĕdĭem, adv. *at an early day, very soon,* Cic.

prōpello -pŭli -pulsum, 3. *to drive before one, drive forth, drive away.* **I.** Lit., **1,** of things, **a,** *to drive away, push away;* crates pro munitione objectas, Caes.; **b,** *to hurl down;* corpus alicuius e scopulo in profundum, Ov.; **c,** *to drive forward;* navem in altum, Ov.; **2,** **a,** of persons, *to drive away forcibly, repulse;* hostes, Caes.; **b,** of animals, *to drive away;* pecus extra portam, Liv. **II.** Fig., **a,** *to drive away;* vitae periculum ab aliquo, Liv.; **b,** *to drive forwards;* orationem dialecticorum remis, Cic.; **c,** *to drive, to compel;* aliquem ad voluntariam mortem, Tac.

prōpĕmŏdō, adv. (prope and modus), *almost, nearly,* Liv.

prōpĕmŏdum, adv. (prope and modus), *almost, nearly,* Cic.

prōpendĕo -pendi -pensum, 2. *to hang down.* **I.** Lit., tantum propendere illam boni lancem ut, etc., Cic. **II.** Fig., bona propendent, *to preponderate,* Cic.; inclinatione voluntatis ad aliquem, *to be inclined to, favourable towards,* Cic.

prōpensē, adv. (propensus), *readily, willingly;* gen. compar., propensius, Liv.

prōpensĭo -ōnis, f. (propendeo), *an inclination towards, propensity,* Cic.

prōpensus -a -um, p. adj. (from propendeo), **I.** *inclined to, disposed to;* ad misericordiam, Cic.; in alteram partem, Cic.; **2,** *coming near to;* ad veritatis similitudinem, Cic.

prŏpĕrantĕr, adv. (propero), *hastily, quickly,* Tac.; properantius, Sall., Ov.

prŏpĕrantĭa -ae, f. (propero), *haste, rapidity,* Sall.

prŏpĕrātĭo -ōnis, f. (propero), *haste,* Cic.

prŏpĕrātō, adv. (propero), *hastily, quickly,* Tac.

prŏpĕro, 1. (properus). **I.** Intransit., *to hasten* (from a particular point); **a,** of persons, Romam, Cic.; with in and acc., in patriam, Caes.; with ad and acc., ad aliquem, Caes.; with adv., alio, Sall.; with infin., redire, Cic.; absol., properantes arma currunt, Sall.; **b,** of things, properans aqua per agros, Hor. **II.** Transit., *to hasten something, to accelerate, complete quickly;* iter, Sall.; mortem, Verg.; opus, studium, Hor.

Prŏpertĭus -ĭi, m., Sex. Aurelius, *a Roman elegiac poet, born in Umbria, educated in Rome* (about 49–15 B.C.).

prŏpĕrus -a -um, *quick, rapid, hasty, bustling;* circumstant properi aurigae, Verg.

prōpexus -a -um (pro and pecto), *combed forwards, hanging down;* propexa in pectore barba, Verg.; propexam ad pectora barbam, Ov.

prōpīnātĭo -ōnis, f. (propino), *a drinking to one's health,* Sen.

prōpīno, 1. (προπίνω). **I.** *to drink to any one;* propino hoc pulchro Critiae, Cic. **II.** Transf., *to give drink to any one,* Mart.

prŏpinquē, adv. (propinquus), *near, close by,* Plaut.

prŏpinquĭtas -ātis, f. (propinquus). **I.** *nearness, proximity;* loci, Cic.; hostium, Caes. **II.** Transf., *relationship;* vinculis propinquitatis conjunctus, Cic.

prŏpinquo, 1. (propinquus). **I.** Intransit., *to come near, draw near, approach.* **A.** Lit., **a,** of persons, with dat., scopulo, Verg.; with acc., campos, Tac.; **b,** of things, ignis domui alicuius propinquat, Tac. **B.** Transf., of time, *to draw near;* Parcarum dies et vis inimica propinquat, Verg. **II.** Transit., *to bring near, hasten;* augurium, Verg.

prŏpinquus -a -um (prope), *near.* **I.** Of space or position, *neighbouring, bordering;* provincia, Cic.; with dat., propinquus cubiculo hortus, Liv.; subst. (in sing. only with a prep.), in propinquo esse, *to be near,* Liv.; oppido propinqua, *the neighbourhood of the town,* Sall. **II.** Transf., as regards time; reditus, Cic. **B.** Of other relations, **a,** *similar;* quae propinqua videntur et finitima, Cic.; **b,** *near in point of relationship, closely connected;* cognatio, Cic.; with dat., tibi genere propinqui, Sall.; subst., *a kinsman,* Cic.

prŏpĭor -us, genit. -ōris, superl., **proxĭmus** -a -um (prope). **I.** Compar., **prŏpĭor,** *nearer.* **A.** Lit., of place, portus, Verg.; pons, Caes.; with dat., propior patriae, Ov.; neut. plur. subst., propriora, *the nearer re-*

gions, Verg. **B.** Transf., **1,** of time, *nearer, more recent;* epistola, Cic.; with dat., propior leto, Ov.; **2, a,** of relationship, *nearer, more closely connected;* societas, Cic.; quibus propior P. Quinctio nemo est, Cic.; **b,** *nearer, more closely affecting;* sua sibi propriora esse pericula quam mea, Cic.; **c,** *nearer in point of likeness,* more similar; sceleri propriora, Cic.; propius est vero, Ov.; with acc. and infin., Liv.; **d,** *more suitable to;* portus propior huic aetati, Cic.; **e,** more inclined towards; proprior Saturnia Turno, Ov. **II.** Superl., **proxĭmus** -a -um, *very near, nearest.* **A.** Lit., of place, oppidum, Caes.; vicinus, Cic.; with dat., huic proximus locus, Cic.; with acc., proximus quisque hostem, Liv.; with ab and the abl., dactylus proximus a postremo, Cic.; subst., **a,** **proxĭmi,** *those standing next,* Caes., or *those standing nearest,* Caes.; **b,** **proxĭmum** -i, n. *the nearest, the neighbourhood;* e proximo, Nep.; proxima Illyrici, Liv. **B.** Transf., **1,** of time, **a,** of the future, *next, following;* nox, Caes.; annus, Cic.; **b,** of the past, *nearest, most recent;* quid proximā nocte egeris, Cic.; proximis superioribus diebus, Caes.; **2,** of succession, *next, following next;* proximus post Lysandrum, Cic.; proximus est, with infin., non nasci homini optimum est, proximum autem *(the next best thing)* quam primum mori, Cic.; proximum est, with ut and the subj., *the next thing is to,* etc.; proximum est ut doceam, Cic.; **3,** *next in succession, in rank, in worth;* proximus est huic dignitati ordo equester, Cic.; **4,** *nearest akin, most nearly related;* proximus cognatione, Cic.; subst., **proxĭmi** -ōrum, m. *near relations,* Cic.; **5,** *nearest in resemblance, most like;* deo proximum, Cic.

prŏpitĭo, 1. (propitius), *to soothe, propitiate, appease;* Venerem, Plaut.

prŏpitĭus -a -um (pro and peto, Gr. προπετής), *favourably inclined, favourable, gracious, propitious;* dii, Cic.; hunc propitium sperant, Cic.

prŏpĭus, comp. of prope (q.v.).

Prŏpoetĭdes -um, f. *maidens of Cyprus who denied the divinity of Venus and were changed into stone.*

prŏpōla -ae, m. (προπώλης), *a forestaller, retailer, huckster,* Cic.

prŏpollŭo, 3. *to pollute greatly,* Tac.

prŏpōno -pŏsŭi -pŏsĭtum, 3. **I.** *to put forth, place out, set in view, expose, display.* **A.** Lit., vexillum, Caes.; aliquid venale, *expose for sale,* Cic.; oculis and ante oculos, *to place before the eyes,* Cic. **B.** Fig., **1,** *to place before, set before;* aliquem sibi ad imitandum, Cic.; **2,** *to bring forward;* proposita sententia, Cic.; **3,** *to propose;* proponat quid dicturus sit, Cic.; **4,** *to report, relate, tell;* rem gestam, Caes.; **5,** *to make known;* epistolam in publico, Cic.; hence, **a,** *to propose, promise, offer as a reward;* praemia alicui, Cic.; **b,** *to threaten, menace;* poenam improbis, Cic.; **6,** *to propose a question for answer;* quaestionem, Nep.; **7,** *to propose to oneself, purpose, intend;* consecutus id, quod animo proposuerat, Caes.; with ut or ut ne and subj., quum mihi proposuissem ut commoverem, Cic.; with infin., quibus propositum est contra omnes philosophos dicere, Cic. **II.** *to state the premiss of a syllogism,* Cic.

Prŏpontis -ĭdis and -ĭdos, f. (Προποντίς), *the Propontis, now the Sea of Marmora;* hence, **Prŏpontĭăcus** -a -um, *of or relating to the Propontis.*

prŏporrō, adv. *further, moreover,* Lucr.

prŏportĭo -ōnis, f. *proportion, relation. analogy, similarity,* Cic.

prōpŏsĭtĭo -ōnis, f. (propono). **I.** *a setting before oneself;* 1, *the representation which a man forms in his own mind of something ;* animi, Cic.; vitae, Cic. ; 2, *the subject* or *theme of a discourse,* Cic. **II.** In logic, *the first proposition of a syllogism,* Cic.

prōpŏsĭtum -i, n, (propono). **I.** *that which is set before one ;* 1, *a design, plan, purpose, intention ;* propositum assequi, *to accomplish a design,* Cic. ; tenere, *to keep to a design,* Cic. ; 2, *the subject* or *theme of a discourse ;* ad propositum redeamus, Cic. **II.** *the premiss of a syllogism,* Cic.

prōpraetor -ōris, m. and **pro praetōre,** *a propraetor, a Roman who, after having been praetor at Rome, was sent as governor to a province without a military command,* Cic.

prōprĭē, adv. (proprius). **I.** Lit., *peculiarly, exclusively for onesself ;* proprie parvā parte frui, Cic. **II.** Transf., a, *peculiarly, characteristically, personally ;* quod tu ipse tum amandus es, id est proprie tuum, Cic. ; b, *specially, expressly ;* cuius causam neque senatus publice neque ullus ordo proprie susceperat, Cic. ; c, *accurately, in a proper sense ;* illud honestum quod proprie vereque dicitur, Cic.

prōprĭĕtas -ātis, f. (proprius), *a property, peculiarity ;* rerum, Cic. ; plur., frugum proprietates, Liv.

prōprĭtim (proprius), *properly, peculiarly,* Lucr.

prōprĭus -a -um, *one's own, special, particular, peculiar.* **I.** Lit., a, opp. to communis ; ista calamitas communis est utriusque nostrûm, sed culpa mea propria est, Cic ; often with possess. pron., proprius et suus, suus proprius, noster proprius, Cic. ; b, *one's own,* as opp. to alienus ; assumpto aliunde uti bono, non proprio, non suo, Cic. **II.** Transf., **A.** *peculiar to a person* or *thing ;* a, *characteristic of ;* proprium est senectutis vitium, Cic. ; proprium est alicuius, with acc. and infin., *it is the distinguishing mark of, it is peculiar to ;* fuit hoc proprium populi Romani longe a domo bellare, Cic. ; b, *special, exclusive ;* nulla est in republica causa mea propria, Cic. ; c, *of words, proper, peculiar ;* discedebat a verbis propriis rerum ac suis, Cic. **B.** Esp., *lasting, permanent ;* munera, Hor. ; illud de duobus consulibus perenne ac proprium manere potuisset, Cic.

proptĕr (for propiter from prope), adv. **I.** *near, hard by ;* quum duo reges cum maximis copiis prope assint, Cic. **II.** Prep. with acc. **A.** Lit., *of a place, near, hard by ;* insulae propter Siciliam, Cic. **B.** Transf., *on account of, by reason of, because of, for, from ;* metum, Cic. ; frigora, Caes. ; propter quos vivit, *by whose means he is alive, whom he has to thank for his life,* Cic. (propter sometimes put after its case, as quem propter, Cic.).

proptĕrĕā, adv. *on that account, therefore,* Cic. ; foll. by quia, Cic. ; quod, Cic. ; ut or ne and the subj., Cic.

prōpŭdĭōsus -a -um (propudium), *covered with infamy, full of shame, infamous,* Plaut.

prōpŭdĭum -ii, n. (= quasi porro pudendum). **I.** *a shameful action,* Plaut. **II.** Meton., *a wretch, villain, rascal ;* propudium illud et portentum L. Antonius, Cic.

prōpugnācŭlum -i, n. (propugno), *a fortification, rampart, fortress, defence.* **I.** Lit., moenium, Tac. ; propugnaculum. Siciliae, *of the fleet,* Cic. ; propugnacula imperii, *fleets and armies,* Cic. **II.** Fig., a, lex Aelia et Fufia propugnacula tranquillitatis, Cic. ; b, *grounds of defence ;* firmissimo propugnaculo uti, Liv.

15

prōpugnātĭo -ōnis, f. (propugno), *defence, defending ;* fig., nostra propugnatio et defensio dignitatis tuae, Cic.

prōpugnātŏr -ōris, m. (propugno), *a defender, combatant, soldier.* **I.** Lit., a, duplic' propugnatorum ordine defendi, Caes. ; b, *marine ;* dimissio propugnatorum, Cic. **II.** Fig., *a defender ;* patrimonii sui, Cic.

prōpugno, 1. *to skirmish to the front.* **I.** Intransit., *to fight in defence, to defend oneself ;* a, lit., uno tempore propugnare et munire, Caes. ; e loco, Caes. ; pro vallo, Liv. ; pro suo partu (of animals), Cic. ; partic. subst., propugnantes, *the defenders,* Caes. ; b, transf., *to fight for something, to fight in defence ;* pro fama alicuius, Cic. **II.** Transit., *to defend ;* munimenta, Tac.

prōpulso, 1. (intens. of propello), *to drive back, repel, ward off.* **I.** Lit., hostem, Caes.; populum ab ingressione fori, Cic. **II.** Transf., frigus, famem, Cic. ; suspicionem a se, Cic.

prōpȳlaeon -i, n. (προπύλαιον), *a gateway, entrance ;* plur., **Prōpȳlaea** -ōrum, n. (τὰ προπύλαια), *the celebrated entrance to the Parthenon at Athens, built by Pericles.*

prō-quaestōre, *a proquaestor, a quaestor in a Roman province, who attended to the finances and pay of the army,* Cic.

prōquam, conj. *according as,* Lucr.

prōra -ae, f. (πρώρα), *the prow, bow of a ship.* **I.** Lit., Caes. ; prorae tutela = proreta, Ov. **II.** Meton.= *a ship,* Verg., Ov.

prōrēpo -repsi -reptum, 3. *to creep forward, crawl forth,* Hor.

prōrēta -ae, m. (πρωράτης), *the look-out man at the prow of a ship,* Plaut.

Prōreus -ĕi, m. (Πρωρεύς), *a Tyrrhene sailor,* Ov.

prōrĭpĭo -rĭpŭi -reptum (pro and rapio), 3. *to snatch, tear, drag forth ;* hominem, Cic. ; se proripere, *to rush forward, hurry ;* se in publicum, Liv. ; se ex curia, Cic. ; se portā foras, Caes. ; quo proripis (sc. te)? Verg. ; fig., quae libido non se proripiet, Cic.

prōrŏgātĭo -ōnis, f. (prorogo), 1, *a prolongation of a term of office,* Liv. ; 2, *a deferring of a fixed time, prorogation,* Cic.

prōrŏgo, 1. 1, *to propose to the people an extension of something for some person, to prolong ;* imperium alicui, Cic. ; provinciam, Cic. ; 2, *to put off ;* dies ad solvendum, Cic.

prorsum, adv. (pro and versum), *forwards.* **I.** Lit., a, Plaut. ; b, *straightforwards, straight on,* Plaut. **II.** Transf., *at all,* Plaut., Ter.

prorsŭs, adv. (pro and versus), *turned forwards, forwards.* **I.** prorsus ibat res, Cic. **II.** Transf., a, *utterly, absolutely, wholly, entirely ;* ita prorsus existimo, Cic. ; prorsus assentior, Cic.; non prorsus, nullo modo prorsus, *not at all ;* nullo modo prorsus assentior, Cic. ; b, *in a word, to sum up,* Sall.

prōrumpo -rūpi -ruptum, 3. **I.** Transit., *to cause to break forth, thrust forth, send forth ;* 1, lit., nubem atram, Verg. ; mare proruptum, *the sea breaking in front,* Verg.; transf., prorupta audacia, *unbridled,* Cic. **II.** Intransit., *to burst forth, break forth.* **A.** Lit., per medios, Cic. **B.** Transf., *to break out ;* prorumpit pestis, Cic.; of persons, in scelera ac dedecora, Tac.

prōrŭo -rŭi -rŭtum, 3. **I.** Intransit., *to rush forth ;* qua proruebat, Caes. **II.** Transit., *to overthrow, throw down, cast to the ground, destroy ;* munitiones, Caes.; vallum, Liv.; Albam a fundamentis, Liv.; hostem profligare ac proruere, Tac.

prōsāpĭa -ae, f. *a family race, stock* (an archaic word), Sall.; eorum, ut utamur veteri verbo, prosapiam, Cic.

proscaenĭum (proscēnĭum) -ĭi, n. (προ-σκήνιον), *the part of a theatre before the scenes, stage*, Liv.

proscindo -scĭdi -scissum, 3. *to tear off in front, to rend.* **I.** Lit., *to break up fallow land, plough up;* poet., *to plough;* terram, Verg.; meton., aequor, *to plough the waters*, Cat. **II.** Transf., *to censure, defame, satirise*, Ov.

proscrībo -scripsi -scriptum, 3. **I.** *to make publicly known, publish*, Cic.; with acc. and infin., auctionem in Gallia Narbone se facturum esse, Cic. **II.** Esp., **A.** *to offer publicly for sale or hire, advertise;* insulam, bona, fundum, Cic. **B.** *to confiscate the property of any one;* possessiones, Cic.; Pompeium, *to confiscate the estates gained by Pompey*, Cic. **C.** *to proscribe, outlaw* (by publishing the person's name in a list); aliquem, Cic.; **proscripti** -ōrum, m. *the proscribed*, Sall.

proscriptĭo -ōnis, f. (proscribo), 1, *an advertisement of sale;* bonorum, Cic.; 2, *a proscription, outlawry*, Cic.

proscriptŭrĭo, 4. (desider. of proscribo), *to desire to declare any one an outlaw*, Cic.

prōsĕco -sĕcŭi -sectum, 1. *to cut off in front, cut off*, esp., *to cut off the portions of a victim to be sacrificed;* exta, Liv.

prōsectum -i, n. (proseco), *the part of a victim cut off to be offered to a god, the entrails*, Ov.

prōsēmĭno, 1. *to sow.* **I.** Lit., vel in tegulis proseminare ostreas, Cic. **II.** Fig., *to disseminate, propagate*, Cic.

prōsĕquor -cūtus (-quūtus) sum -sĕqui, 3. dep. *to follow, accompany.* **I.** In a friendly sense, **A.** *to accompany, attend*, esp. of friends who *"see off"* a person going on a journey; aliquem usque ad agri fines, Cic.; prosequi exsequias, Cic.; transf., of things, ventus prosequitur euntes, Verg.; eos honos, memoria, desiderium prosequitur amicorum, Cic. **B.** Fig., 1, *to accompany;* aliquem votis, ominibus, lacrimisque, Caes.; 2, a, *to honour, adorn, or present with, treat with;* aliquem verbis honorificis, Cic.; aliquem beneficiis, Cic.; misericordiā, Cic.; b, of a discourse, *to go on with, continue;* quod non longius prosequar, Cic. **II.** In a hostile sense, *to attack, pursue;* hostem, Caes.; longius fugientes, Caes.

Prōserpĭna -ae, f. (Περσεφόνη), *the daughter of Ceres and Jupiter, carried off by Pluto to be queen of the lower world;* hence, meton., *the lower world*, Hor. (in Verg. and Ov. Prōserpĭna, in Hor. Prōserpĭna).

prōseucha -ae, f. (προσευχή), *a place of prayer for the Jews*, Juv.

prōsĭlĭo -ŭi (-ĭvi or -ĭi), 4. (pro and salio). **I.** *to spring, leap forth.* **A.** 1, lit., ex tabernaculo, Liv.; ab sede, Liv.; repente, Cic.; finibus suis, Verg.; 2, of things, flumina prosiliunt, Ov. **B.** Fig., vaga prosiliet frenis natura remotis, Hor. **II.** *to spring forward to a place;* in contionem, Liv.

prōsŏcer -ĕri, m. *a wife's grandmother*, Ov.

prospecto, 1. (intens. of prospicio), *to look forward, look forth upon.* **I. A.** Lit., e puppi pontum, Ov.; euntem, Verg.; ex tectis fenestrisque, Liv. **B.** Transf., of places, *to look towards, be situate towards;* villa quae subjectos sinus prospectat, Tac. **II.** Fig., *to look for, hope, expect;* exsilium, Cic.; te quoque fata prospectant paria, *a like fate awaits*, Verg.

prospectus -ūs, m. (prospicio). **I.** *an out-*

look, *view, prospect;* unde longe ac late prospectus erat, Liv.; prospectum impedire, Caes.; meton., *the sight;* aequora prospectu metior alta meo, Ov. **II.** Pass., *view, sight;* cum jam extremi essent in prospectu, *were within sight*, Caes.

prospĕcŭlor, 1. dep. **I.** Intransit., *to look out to a distance;* hence, *to explore, reconnoitre*, Liv. **II.** Transit., *to look for, wait for;* adventum imperatoris, Liv.

prosper (prospĕrus) -a -um (pro and spero), *according to one's hope;* hence, **I.** *fortunate, favourable, lucky, prosperous;* fortuna, Cic.; exitus, Cic.; subst., **prospĕra** -ōrum, n. *prosperity, good fortune*, Ov. **II.** Transit., *bringing good fortune, propitious;* Bellona, Ov.; with genit., prospera frugum, Hor.

prospĕrē, adv. (prosper), *prosperously, fortunately, favourably;* procedere prospere, Cic.

prospergo -spersi -sparsum, 3. (pro and spargo), *to sprinkle*, Tac.

prospĕritas -ātis, f. (prosper), *prosperity, good fortune;* vitae, Cic.; plur., improborum prosperitates, Cic.

prospĕro, 1. (prosper), *to make fortunate or prosperous, to cause to succeed, to give a favourable issue to;* alicui victoriam, Liv.

prospĕrus = prosper (q.v.).

prospĭcĭentĭa -ae, f. (prospicio), *foresight, precaution*, Cic.

prospĭcĭo -spexi -spectum, 3. (pro and specio). **I.** Intransit., *to look forward, look into the distance.* **A.** Lit., 1, ex castris in urbem, Caes.; multum, *to have a wide prospect*, Cic.; 2, *to look out, be upon the watch*, Nep. **B.** Fig., *to exercise foresight, to take precaution;* with dat., consulite vobis, prospicite patriae, Cic.; with ut and the subj., Cic.; with ne and the subj., Caes. **II.** Transit., *to see, behold, gaze upon from afar.* **A.** Lit., 1, Italiam ab unda, Verg.; 2, transf., of places, *to look towards, be situate towards;* domus prospicit agros, Hor. **B.** Fig., a, *to foresee;* casus futuros, Cic.; b, *to look out for, provide, procure;* ferramenta, Cic.; commeatus, Liv.

prosterno -strāvi -strātum, 3. *to strew before, throw down in front, cast down.* **A.** Lit., a, circa viam corpora humi, Liv.; se ad pedes alicuius, Cic.; hence, **prostrātus** -a -um (sc. humi), *lying on the ground;* ad pedes, Cic.; b, *to throw down with violence;* hostem, Cic. **B.** Fig., 1, se abjicere et prosternare, *to debase oneself*, Cic.; 2, *to throw to the ground, overthrow, destroy, ruin;* omnia furore, Cic.; aliquem, Cic. (syncop. infin. perf., prostrasse = prostravisse, Ov.).

prostĭtŭo -stĭtŭi -stĭtūtum, 3. (pro and statuo), *to prostitute;* vocem ingrato foro, Ov.

prosto -stĭti, 1. *to stand before;* hence, **I.** *to stand forward, project*, Lucr. **II.** Of goods, *to be exposed for sale;* liber prostat, Hor.; vox prostitit, Cic.; *to sell one's person, prostitute oneself;* transf., illud amicitiae quondam venerabile nomen prostat, Hor.

prōsŭbĭgo, 3. *to dig up, throw up;* terram, Verg.

prōsum, prōfŭi, prōdesse, *to be useful, advantageous to;* illa quae prosunt aut quae nocent, Cic.; with dat., qui nec sibi nec alteri prosunt, dicere quod causae prosit, Cic.; with infin., multum prodest ea quae metuuntur ipsa contemnere, Cic.; quid mihi fingere prodest? Ov.

Prōtăgŏras -ae, m. (Πρωταγόρας), *a Greek philosopher, of Abdera, contemporary with Socrates, banished from Attica on a charge of atheism.*

prōtĕgo -texi -tectum, 3. **I.** *to cover in front.* **A.** Lit., tabernacula protecta hederā, Caes.; aliquem scuto, *protect*, Caes. **B.** Transf., *to cover, protect*; jacentem, Cic.; regem, Liv. **II.** *to furnish with a roof*; aedes, Cic.

prōtēlo, 1. (pro and telum), *to drive off, put to flight,* Ter.

prōtēlum -i, n. (protendo), *a yoke of oxen*; fig., *a series, succession,* Lucr.

prōtendo -tendi -tentum and -tensum, 3. *to stretch forward, stretch out*; brachia in mare, Ov.; cervicem, Tac.; temo protentus in octo pedes, *eight feet long,* Verg.

prōtĕnŭs (prōtĭnŭs), adv. *forward, further, further on.* **I.** Lit., protenus ago capellas, Verg.; quum ad alias angustias protenus pergerent, Liv. **II.** Transf., **A.** *without delay, straightway, on the spot*; Laodiceam protenus ire, Cic.; ut is ad te protenus mittat, Cic. **B.** *of unbroken extent, continuously*; quum protenus utraque tellus una foret, Verg. **C.** Of unbroken succession in time, **1,** *constantly, continuously*; quem (morem) protenus urbes Albanae coluere sacrum, Verg.; **2,** *immediately, at once*; **a,** prōtenus Carthaginem ituros, Liv.; protenus de via, Liv.; **b,** *immediately, at the beginning*; oratio protenus perficiens auditorem benevolum, Cic.

prōtĕro -trīvi -trītum, 3. **I.** *to trample under foot, tread down.* **A.** a, lit., equitatus aversos proterere incipit, Caes.; frumentum, Liv.; **b,** hence, *to overthrow in battle, rout, defeat*; Poenos, Hor. **B.** Fig., *to trample on, despise*; aliquem, Cic. **II.** *to drive away, push aside*; ver proterit aestas, Hor.

prōterrĕo -terrŭi -terrĭtum, 2. *to frighten away, scare away*; Themistoclem patriā pulsum atque proterritum, Cic.; aliquem verbis gravissimis, Cic.

prōtervē, adv. (protervus), *boldly, impudently, shamelessly,* Ov.

prōtervĭtas -ātis, f. (protervus), *boldness, impudence,* Cic.; and in a milder sense, *wantonness, pertness,* Hor.

prōtervus -a -um (protero), *trampling upon everything*; hence, **I.** *violent, vehement*; venti, Hor.; stella canis, Ov. **II.** *bold, impudent, shameless,* and in a milder sense, *wanton, pert*; homo, Cic.; juvenes, Hor.

Prōtĕsĭlāus -i, m. (Πρωτεσίλαος), *the husband of Laodamia, the first Greek who landed before Troy in the Trojan war, and the first of the Greeks to be slain.* Adj., **Prōtĕsĭlāĕus** -a -um, *belonging to Protesilaus.*

Prōteus -ĕi and -ĕos, m. (Πρωτεύς), *a god of the sea, the herdsman of Poseidon's sea-calves, a prophet who would not answer those who consulted him except when bound in chains, and who had the power of changing himself into different shapes; Protei columnae,* poet., *the borders of Egypt,* Verg.; appellat., *a changeable or a crafty man,* Hor.

prōtĭnam (prōtĕnam), adv. (protinus), *immediately, directly, at once,* Plaut.

prōtĭnus = protenus (q.v.).

Prōtŏgĕnēs -is, m. (Πρωτογένης), *a famous Greek painter of Caunos on the coast of Caria, flourishing about 300 B.C.*

prōtollo, 3. **I.** *to put forth, stretch forth,* Plaut. **II.** *to extend, lengthen, prolong,* Plaut.

prōtrāho -traxi -tractum, 3. *to draw, drag forth.* **I.** *to drag to a place.* **A.** Lit., aliquem hinc in convivium, Cic. **B.** Transf., **1,** *to draw forth*; **a,** aliquid in lucem, Lucr.; **b,** *to bring to light, to reveal, make known*; auctorem nefandi facinoris, Liv.; **2,** *to compel, force*; aliquem ad

indicium, Liv. **II.** Transf., *to extend in point of time, protract, defer,* Suet.

prōtrūdo -trūsi -trūsum, 3. *to push forward, thrust forth.* **I.** Lit., cylindrum, Cic. **II.** Fig., *to put off, defer*; comitia in Januarium mensem, Cic.

prōturbo, 1. *to drive forward, drive away, repel*; **a,** of persons, equites, Caes.; hostes telis missilibusque saxis, Liv.; **b,** of things, pectore silvas, *to throw down,* Ov.

prōŭt, conj. *according as*; prout res postulat, Cic.

prōvectus -a -um (p. adj. from proveho), *advanced in age*; longius aetate provectus, Cic.

prōvĕho -vexi -vectum, 3. *to carry forward, to lead forward.* **I.** Act., **A.** Lit., aër a tergo quasi provehit, Lucr. **B.** Fig., 1, *to carry away, carry too far, lead on*; pass., provehi = *to be carried away, to allow oneself to be carried away*; vestra benignitas provexit orationem meam, Cic.; gaudio provehente (me), Liv.; studio rerum rusticarum provectus sum, Cic.; **2,** *to bring forwards, to advance, raise, promote*; aliquem ad summos honores, Liv. **II.** Pass., provehi, in a middle sense, *to go forward, ride forward, ride, drive, sail to a place.* **A.** Lit., of persons, esp. of persons in a ship or of the ship itself, Nasidius cum classe freto Siciliae provehitur, Caes. **B.** Fig., *to go too far*; sentio me esse longius provectum quam, etc., Cic.; longius in amicitia provehi, Cic.; quid ultra provehor? *why do I continue?* Verg.

prōvĕnĭo -vēni -ventum, 4. *to come forth.* **I.** Lit., in scenam, *to appear upon the stage,* Plaut. **II.** Transf., **A.** *to come up, shoot forth, grow*; frumentum propter siccitates angustius provenerat, Caes. **B.** Fig., *to result, turn out*; ut initia belli provenissent, Tac.; and esp., *to turn out well, succeed, prosper*; carmina proveniunt animo deducta sereno, Ov.

prōventus -ūs, m. (provenio). **I.** *a coming forth, growing.* **A.** Lit., Plin. **B.** Meton., *growth, product, crop*; proventu oneret sulcos, Verg. **II.** Fig., *the result, issue*; pugnae, Caes.; secundi rerum proventus, Caes.; esp., *fortunate result, success,* Liv.; temporis superioris, Caes.

prōverbĭum -ĭi, n. (pro and verbum), *a proverb*; in proverbii consuetudinem venit, *has become a proverb,* Cic.; veteri proverbio, *after the old proverb,* Cic.; ut est in proverbio, *as is said in the proverb,* Cic.; quod est Graecis hominibus in proverbio, *is a proverb among,* Cic.

prōvĭdens -entis, p. adj. (from provideo), *provident, prudent,* Cic.; quod est providentius, Cic.

prōvĭdentĕr, adv. (providens), *providently, with forethought,* Sall.; providentissime constituere aliquid, Cic.

prōvĭdentĭa -ae, f. (provideo). **I.** *foresight, foreknowledge*; providentia est, per quam futurum aliquid videtur ante quam factum sit, Cic. **II.** *forethought, providence*; deorum, Cic.

prōvĭdĕo -vīdi -vīsum, 2. *to look forward to, see at a distance.* **I.** Lit., aliquem non providisse, Hor.; quid petatur provideri, Liv. **II.** Transf., 1, *to see beforehand, to foresee*; quod ego, priusquam loqui coepisti, sensi atque providi, Cic.; medicus morbum providet, Cic.; **2,** *to take precautions for or against something, to provide for, make preparation for, care for*; (α) with acc., rem frumentariam, Caes.; multa, Cic.; consilia in posterum, Cic.; (β) with dat., de Brundisio atque illa ora, Cic.; (γ) with dat., saluti hominum, Cic.; (δ) with ut or ne and the subj., ne quid ei desit, Cic.; ut res quam rectissime agantur, Cic.; (ε) absol., actum de te est, nisi provides, Cic.

prŏvĭdus -a -um (provideo). **I.** *foreseeing;* rerum futurarum, Cic. **II.** *caring beforehand;* **1,** *providing for, taking measures for;* natura provida utilitatum, Cic.; **2,** *cautious, provident, prudent;* orator, Cic.

prŏvincĭa -ae, f. (perhaps pro and VIC, root of *vices*). **I.** *employment, charge, sphere of duty, office;* illam officiosam provinciam ut me in lectulo trucidaret, Cic.; quasi provincias atomis dare, Cic. **II.** Polit. t.t., *the sphere of office assigned to a magistrate, a charge, office.* **A.** a, of Roman magistrates, sortiri provincias (inter se), Liv.; of the jurisdiction of the praetor urbanus and peregrinus, provincia urbana et peregrina, Liv.; of a military command, Sicinio Volsci, Aquilio Hernici (nam hi quoque in armis erant) provincia evenit, Cic.; of a command at sea, provincia classis, provincia maritima, Liv.; b, of non-Roman magistrates, Hannonis cis Iberum provincia erat, *had the command*, Liv. **B.** *the government of a province, a country outside the limits of Italy;* and meton., *the province itself;* primus annus provinciae erat, Cic.; dare alicui provinciam, Cic.; administrare provinciam, Cic.; hence, provincia, *the province,* esp., either a, *the east part of Gallia Narbonensis,* Caes., or b, *the Roman province of Asia,* Caes.

prŏvincĭālis -e, *of or relating to a province.* **I.** Adj., scientia, *how to govern a province,* Cic.; administratio, *government of a province,* Cic.; abstinentia, *moderation in governing,* Cic. **II.** Subst., **prŏvincĭāles** -ium, m. *inhabitants of the provinces, provincials,* Cic.

prŏvīsĭo -ōnis, f. (provideo), **1,** a, *a foreseeing, a foreknowledge;* animi, Cic.; b, *foresight;* animi, Cic.; **2,** *a providing, provision;* a, *for something;* temporis posteri, Cic.; b, *against something;* vitiorum atque incommodorum, Cic.

1. prŏvīso, 3. *to look out for, go to see,* Ter.

2. prŏvīsō, adv. *with forethought, circumspectly,* Tac.

prŏvīsor -ōris, m. (provideo), **1,** *one who foresees;* dominationum, Tac.; **2,** *a provider;* utilium, Hor.

prŏvīsus -ūs, m. (provideo). **I.** *a looking before, a looking into the distance,* Tac. **II.** Transf., **A.** *seeing beforehand, foreseeing;* periculi, Tac. **B.** *a providing, provision;* provisus rei frumentariae, Tac.

prŏvīvo -vixisse, 3. *to live on, continue to live,* Tac.

prŏvŏcātĭo -ōnis, f. (provoco), *a calling forth, an appeal to a higher court of law;* provocatio ad populum, Cic.; magistratus sine provocatione, *from whose decision there is no appeal,* Liv.; est provocatio, *an appeal is possible,* Liv.

prŏvŏcātor -ōris, m. (provoco), *one who challenges or summons to fight,* esp., *a kind of gladiator,* Cic.

prŏvŏco, 1. *to call forth, call out.* **I.** Gen., a, lit., herum, Plaut.; b, transf., of things, *to cause to come forth;* roseo ore diem (of Aurora), Ov. **II.** Esp., **A.** *to call forth, to excite, rouse,* and in a bad sense = *to provoke;* **1,** munificentiā nostrā provocemus plebem, Liv.; beneficio provocati, Cic.; **2,** *to challenge to a game, combat, drinking,* etc.; ad pugnam, Cic.; esp. in pass., provocatus maledictis, injuriis, Cic. **B.** Legal t. t., *to summon before a higher court, to appeal to a higher tribunal;* a, lit., ad populum, Cic.; ab omni judicio poenaque provocari licere, Cic.; b, transf., *to appeal to;* provocare ad Catonem, Cic.

prŏvŏlo, 1. *to fly forth;* transf., of men, *to rush forth, hasten forth;* subito, Caes.; ad primores, Liv.

prŏvolvo -volvi -vŏlūtum, 3. *to roll forward,* roll along, roll over and over. **I.** Lit., a, gen., congestas lapidum moles, Tac.; b, *to throw oneself down, fall down before;* se alicui ad pedes, Liv.; provolvi ad genua alicuius, Liv. **II.** Fig., a, multi fortunis provolvebantur, *were ruined,* Tac.; b, middle = *to abase oneself,* Tac.

prŏvŏmo, 2. *to vomit forth,* Lucr.

proxĭme, superl. of prope (q.v.).

proxĭmĭtas -ātis, f. (proximus). **I.** *nearness, vicinity, proximity,* Ov. **II.** Fig., **1,** *near relationship,* Ov.; **2,** *similarity,* Ov.

proxĭmo, adv. (abl. of proximus), *very lately,* Cic.

proxĭmus -a -um, superl. of propior (q.v.).

prūdens -entis (contr. from providens), *foreseeing.* **I.** Partic. = *knowing, with intention;* quos prudens praetereo, Hor.; prudens et sciens sum profectus, Cic. **II.** Adj., **A.** *versed, skilled, experienced, practised in anything;* rei militaris, Nep.; locorum, Liv.; with infin., prudens dissipare, Hor. **B.** *prudent, discreet, wise, sagacious, judicious;* vir naturā peracutus et prudens, Cic.; transf., of things, consilium, Cic.; with genit. ceterarum rerum prudens, *in all other matters,* Cic.; with de and the abl., in jure civili, Cic.; in existimando admodum prudens, Cic.

prūdentěr, adv. (prudens), *prudently, discreetly, sagaciously, wisely;* facere, Cic.; intelligere, Cic.

prūdentĭa -ae, f. (prudens). **I.** *knowledge of any subject;* juris publici, Cic.; physicorum, Cic. **II.** *prudence, sagacity, practical wisdom, discretion;* prudentia est rerum expetendarum fugiendarumque scientia, Cic.; prudentia cernitur in delectu bonorum et malorum, Cic.

prūīna -ae, f. **I.** *hoar-frost, rime,* Cic. **II.** Plur., pruinae, meton., a, = *winter,* Verg.; b, = *snow,* Verg.

prūīnōsus -a -um (pruina), *full of hoar-frost, covered with hoar-frost;* nox, Ov.; axis (Aurorae) pruinosus = matutinus, Ov.

prūna -ae, f. *a live coal,* Hor.

prūnĭcěus -a -um, *of plum-tree wood,* Ov.

prūnum -i, n. *a plum,* Hor.

prūnus -i, f. (προύνη), *a plum-tree,* Plin.

prūrīgo -ĭnis, f. (prurio), *the itch,* Mart.

prūrĭo, 4. *to itch,* Juv.

Prūsĭas -ae, m. *king in Bithynia, who received Hannibal, but afterwards betrayed him to the Romans.*

prytănēum -i, n. (πρυτανεῖον), *the town-hall in certain Greek cities where the prytanes assembled and where persons who had done distinguished services to the state were entertained,* Cic.

prytănis, acc. -in, m. (πρύτανις), *a chief magistrate in certain of the Greek states,* Liv.

psallo, psalli, 3. (ψάλλω), *to play on, sing to a stringed instrument, especially the cithara;* psallere docta, *skilled in singing,* Hor.

psaltērĭum -ĭi, n. (ψαλτήριον), *a stringed instrument, the psaltery,* Cic.

psaltrĭa -ae, f. (ψάλτρια), *a female player on, or singer to the cithara,* Cic.

Psămăthē -ēs, f. **I.** *daughter of the Argive king Crotopus,* Ov. **II.** *a sea-nymph, mother of Phocus,* Ov.

1. psēcăs -ădis, f. (ψεκάς), *the female slave who anointed her mistress's hair,* Juv.

2. Psēcăs -ădis, f. *name of a nymph among the attendants of Diana.*

psēphisma -ătis, n. (ψήφισμα), *a decree of the people among the Greeks,* Cic.

Pseudŏcăto -ōnis, m. *a sham Cato*, Cic.

Pseudŏdămăsippus -i, m. *a sham Damasippus*, Cic.

Pseudŏlus -i, m. *The Liar* (title of a comedy by Plautus), Cic.

pseudŏmĕnos -i, m. (ψευδόμενος), *a sophistical syllogism*, Cic.

Pseudŏphĭlippus -i, m. (Ψευδοφίλιππος), *a sham Philip*, i.e., Andriscus, *who gave himself out to be Philip, son of Perseus, king of Macedonia.*

pseudŏthўrum -i, n. (ψευδόθυρον), *a secret door;* fig., per pseudothyrum revertantur (nummi), *in a secret way*, Cic.

psithĭus (**psýthĭus**) -a -um, *psithian, name of a kind of Greek vine;* vitis, Verg.; subst., **psithĭa** ae, f. (sc. vitis), Verg.

psittăcus -i, m. (ψίττακος), *a parrot;* loquax, Ov.

Psŏphĭs -ĭdis, f. (Ψωφίς), *a town in Arcadia.*

psŏra -ae, f. (ψώρα), *the mange, itch*, Plin.

psўchŏmantīum -ii, n. (ψυχομαντεῖον), *the place where the souls of the dead were invoked, a place where necromancy is practised*, Cic.

psýthĭus = psithius (q.v.).

-ptĕ, enclit. particle appended to pers. and poss. pronouns in the abl., *self, our;* suopte pondere, Cic.; suāpte manu, Cic.

Ptĕlĕon (**-um**) -i, n. (Πτελεόν), *a town in Thessaly, over against Euboea,* now *Ftelia*, Liv.

ptĭsănărĭum -ii, n. *a decoction of crushed barley or rice*, Hor.

Ptŏlĕmaeus (**Ptŏlŏmaeus**) -i, m. (Πτολεμαῖος), *the first king of Egypt after Alexander's death with the surname Lagi* (sc. filius, i.e., *son of Lagus);* after him each king of his line was called Ptolemaeus. Hence, 1, **Ptŏlĕmaeus** -a -um, *belonging to Ptolemy, Ptol.* = *Egyptian;* 2, **Ptŏlĕmaïs** -ĭdis, f. *name of several towns, one in Egypt, another in Phoenicia, another in Cyrene.*

pūbens -entis (* pubeo), *arrived at puberty;* transf., of plants, *in full growth, luxuriant*, Verg.

pūber -bĕris = 2. pubes (q.v.).

pūbertas -ātis, f. (puber), *puberty, the age of maturity.* **I.** Lit., nondum pubertatem ingressus, Tac. **II.** Meton., **A.** *the signs of puberty, the hair on the chin*, Cic. **B.** *virility*, Tac.

1. **pūbes** -is, f. **I.** *the signs of puberty, the hair on the chin*, Plin. **II.** Meton., **A.** *the pudenda*, Verg. **B.** a, *the youth, adult population;* omnis Italiae pubes, Verg.; b, transf., *people, folk;* agrestis, Verg.

2. **pūbes** -ĕris, *arrived at the age of puberty, adult.* **I.** Lit., prope puberem aetatem, Liv.; subst., **pūbĕres** -um, m. *the men, the adult population*, Caes. **II.** Transf., *downy, ripe;* folia, Verg.

pūbesco -bŭi, 3. (inchoat. of pubeo). **I.** *to become pubescent, arrive at the age of puberty.* **A.** Lit., Hercules, quum primum pubesceret, Cic. **B.** Transf., *to grow up, arrive at maturity;* quae terra gignit, maturata pubescunt, Cic. **II.** Esp., *to be covered with the signs of puberty;* transf., *to be covered or clothed with something;* prata pubescunt variorum flore colorum, Ov.

publĭcānus -a -um (publicum), *relating to the farming of the public taxes*, Cic.; gen. subst., **publĭcānus** -i, m. *a farmer of the Roman taxes* (generally of the equestrian order), Cic.

publĭcātĭo -ōnis, f. (publico), *a confiscation;* bonorum, Cic.

publĭcē, adv. (publicus). **I.** *publicly* (opp. privatim); **a,** *in the name or at the command of* the state; dicere, Cic.; venire, Cic.; **b,** *in the interest of the state, to the good of the state, for the state;* publice esse laudem, *it is an honour to the state,* Caes.; publice scribere or litteras mittere, Cic.; **c,** *at the cost of the state;* vesci, Liv. **II.** *generally, all together, without distinction;* publice ire exsulatum, Liv.

publĭcĭtŭs, adv. (publicus). **I.** *at the public expense, in the public service*, Plaut. **II.** Transf., *publicly, before all the world*, Plaut.

Publĭcĭus -a -um, *name of a Roman gens, the most famous members of which were the two brothers* L. and M. Publicii Malleoli, *both Aediles, who laid out and paved the Clivus Publicius, the chief entrance to the Aventine.* Hence, adj., **Publĭcĭānus** -a -um, *Publician.*

publĭco, 1. (publicus). **I.** *to appropriate to the public use, confiscate;* regnum, Caes.; privata, Cic. **II.** *to give over to the public use.* **A.** Gen., Aventinum, Liv. **B.** Esp., *to make public, publish*, Tac.

Publĭcŏla -ae, m. (also written Poplicola and Popicula, from poplus (= populus) and colo), *the honourer of the people, the people's friend,* a surname of P. Valerius Publicola, *the first consul of the Roman republic.*

publĭcus -a -um (so poblicus and poplicus from poplus for populus), *belonging to the people, public.* **I.** *of or belonging to the commonwealth, in the name of* or *on account of the people, at the public expense.* **A.** Adj., loca, Cic.; sumptu publico, *at the cost of the state,* Cic.; bonum publicum, *the commonweal*, Liv. **B.** Subst., **publĭcum** -i, n., a, *the property of the state, public territory;* Campanum, Cic.; b, *the public revenue, the treasury;* convivari de publico, *at the cost of the state,* Cic.; in publicum emere, Liv.; dum in eo publico essent, *farming of the taxes,* Liv.; plur., societates publicorum, companies of the farmers of the taxes, Cic.; c, *the public stores;* in publicum conferre frumenti quod inventum est, Cic.; d, *publicity, an open place, the open street;* prodire in publicum, Cic.; blandiores in publico quam in privato, Liv.; publico carere, *to remain at home*, Cic.; legem proponere in publicum or in publico, *openly,* Liv., Cic. **II.** *universal, common, general, ordinary;* a, lit., verba, Cic.; lux publica mundi, *the sun*, Ov.; publica cura juvenum prodis, *general object of the care of,* etc., Hor.; b, poet., *common, bad, ordinary;* structura carminis, Ov.

Publĭlĭus -a -um, *name of a Roman gens, the most famous of which were:* Publilia, *the second wife of Cicero;* Publilius, *her father;* and Publius Publilius Lochius Syrus, *a celebrated mime and writer of mimes towards the end of the republic;* adj., *relating to the Publilian gens*, Liv.

Publĭus -ii, m. *a common Roman praenomen,* abbreviated P.

pŭdendus -a -um (partic. of pudeo), *of which one ought to be ashamed, shameful, disgraceful;* vita, Ov.; vulnera, Verg.

pŭdens -entis, p. adj. (from pudeo), *modest, shamefaced;* pudentes ac boni viri, Cic.; te videri pudentiorem fuisse, Cic.; femina pudentissima, Cic.

pŭdentĕr, adv. (pudens), *modestly, bashfully,* Cic.; pudentius ad hoc genus sermonis accedere, Cic.; pudentissime hoc Cicero petierat, Cic.

pŭdĕo -ŭi -ĭtum, 2. **I.** *to be ashamed;* induci ad pudendum, Cic.; partic. subst., pudentes, *modest persons*, Caes. **II.** *to cause shame, fill with shame.* **A.** Pers., me autem quid pudeat, qui, etc., Cic. **B.** Impers., *I (you, he,* etc.) *am ashamed,* with acc. of the pers.; ceteros pudeat, Cic.; and with genit. of the thing causing the shame; te huius templi pudet, Cic.; with genit. alone, pudet deorum hominumque, *it is a disgrace before God and men*, Liv.; with infin., pudet dicere, Cic.; dep., puditum est, nonne esset puditum si, etc.? *ought they not to be ashamed that*, etc.? Cic.

pŭdĭbundus -a -um (pudeo), *shamefaced, modest, bashful;* matrona, Hor.

pŭdīcē, adv. (pudicus), *modestly, virtuously, chastely*, Cat.

pŭdīcĭtĭa -ae, f. (pudicus), *bashfulness, modesty, chastity, virtue*, Cic.; Pudicitia, personif. as a goddess (patrician and plebeian), Liv.

pŭdīcus -a -um (pudeo), *modest, bashful, chaste, virtuous;* **a**, of persons, Cic.; **b**, transf., of things, mores, preces, Ov.

pŭdor -ōris, m. (pudeo), *the feeling of shame, shyness, bashfulness, modesty, decency.* **I.** Lit., **a**, natura pudorque meus, *my natural modesty*, Cic.; paupertatis, *on account of poverty*, Cic.; famae, Cic.; pudor est or pudori est with infin., *I am ashamed*, Ov.; **b**, *chastity, purity;* pudorem projicere, Ov.; Pudor, personif. as a deity, Verg. **II.** Meton., **A.** *that which causes shame, a disgrace;* pudori esse, Liv. **B.** *the blush of shame;* famosus, Ov.

pŭella -ae, f. (puellus), *a girl, maiden.* **I.** Lit., **A.** Gen., *a maiden*, Cic. **B.** Esp., 1, *a sweetheart*, Ov.; 2, *a daughter;* Danai puellae, Hor. **II.** Transf., *a young woman, a young wife*, used of Penelope, Ov.; of Lucretia, Ov.; puella Phasias, *Medea*, Ov.; Lesbis, *Sappho*, Ov.; Lyda, Omphale, Ov.; Cressa, *Phaedra*, Ov.

pŭellāris -e (puella), *of or belonging to a maiden or young woman, girlish, maidenly*, Ov.

pŭellŭla -ae, f. (dim. of puella), *a little girl*, Cat.

pŭellus -i, m. (dim. of puer, for puerulus), *a little boy*, Lucr.

pŭer -i, m. (root PU, whence Laconian πόῖρ = παῖς). **I.** *a child;* plur., pueri = *children*, Cic. **II.** Esp., *a male child, boy, lad.* **A.** Lit., **a**, properly *a boy under seventeen*, Cic.; but used also of Octavianus in his nineteenth year, Cic.; and of Pallas, who commanded a company of soldiers, Verg.; puer sive jam adolescens, Cic.; *a puero*, a pueris, *from boyhood*, Cic.; ex pueris excedere, *to pass out of boyhood*, Cic.; **b**, *boy = son;* Ascanius puer, Verg.; Latonae, *Apollo*, Hor.; Ledae pueri, *Castor and Pollux*, Hor. **B.** Transf., 1, (like παῖς), *a waiter, serving-lad, a servant, slave;* tuus, Cic.; pueri regii, *royal pages*, Liv.; 2, *an unmarried man, a bachelor*, Ov.

pŭerīlis -e (puer), *youthful, boyish.* **I.** Lit., aetas, Cic. **II.** Transf., *puerile, childish, silly;* consilium, Cic.; si puerilius his ratio esse evincet amare, Hor.

pŭerīlĭter, adv. (puerilis). **I.** *boyishly, like a boy;* blandiri, Liv. **II.** Transf., *childishly, foolishly;* facere, Cic.

pŭerĭtĭa -ae, f. (puer), *boyhood;* a pueritia, *from boyhood*, Cic.

pŭerpĕrus -a -um (puer and pario), *relating to child-birth;* verba, *words supposed to assist labour*, Ov.

pŭerpĕrĭum -ĭi, n. (puerperus), *a lying-in, labour, confinement*, Tac.

pŭertĭa = pueritia (q.v.).

pŭerŭlus -i, m. (dim. of puer), *a little boy, a young slave*, Cic.

pūga (pȳga) -ae, f. (πυγή), *the rump, buttocks*, Hor.

pūgil -ĭlis, m. (connected with pugnus), *a boxer, fighter with the cestus, pugilist*, Cic.

pŭgĭlātĭo -ōnis, f. (pugil), *a fight with the cestus*, Cic.

pŭgĭlātus -ūs, m. (pugil), *a fighting with the cestus*, Plaut.

pŭgillāris -e (pugillus), *that can be grasped with the fist*, Juv.; subst., **pŭgillāres** -ium, m. (sc. libelli or codicilli), *writing-tablets, waxen tablets*, Cat.

pŭgillus -i, m. (dim. of pugnus), *a handful*, Plin.

pūgĭo -ōnis, m. (pungo), *a dagger, dirk, poniard.* **I.** Lit., cruentum pugionem tenens, Cic. **II.** Fig., plumbeus pugio, *a weak argument*, Cic.

pūgiuncŭlus -i, m. (dim. of pugio), *a little dagger*, Cic.

pugna -ae, f. (connected with pugnus), *a fight, either of one man against another*, or *of several* (proelium, *a fight between armies*, cp. diurtinitate pugnae defessi praelio excedebant, Caes.). **I. A.** Lit., **a**, gen., equestris, *cavalry engagement*, Cic.; navalis, Cic.; pugnam committere, Cic., cum aliquo, Cic.; pugnā decertare, Caes.; **b**, esp., *athletic games;* pugna quinquennis Graia Elide, Ov. **B.** Meton., **a**, *the line or array of battle;* pugnam mediam tueri, Liv. **II.** Transf., *contest, contention;* doctissimorum hominum, Cic.

pugnācĭtas -ātis, f. (pugnax), *desire of fighting, pugnacity*, Tac.

pugnācĭter (pugnax), *pugnaciously, obstinately;* certare cum aliquo, Cic.; pugnacissime defendere sententiam, Cic.

pugnātor -ōris, m. (pugno), *a fighter, combatant, soldier*, Liv.

pugnax -ācis (pugno), *fond of fighting, combative, contentious, martial.* **I.** Lit., pugnax Minerva, Ov.; centurio, Cic. **II.** Transf., **A.** *combative, contentious, polemical;* exordium dicendi, Cic.; oratio pugnacior, Cic. **B.** Of discourse, *obstinate, refractory;* contra senatorem, Cic.

pugno, 1. (pugna), *to fight, combat, give battle.* **I.** Lit., both of single combatants and of whole armies, cum aliquo, Caes.; ex equo, Cic.; pro commodis patriae, Cic.; pugna summā contentione pugnata, Cic.; impers., pugnatur uno tempore omnibus locis, Caes.; partic. subst., pugnantes, *the combatants*, Caes. **II.** Transf., **A.** *to struggle, to contend, fight;* pugnant Stoici cum Peripateticis, Cic.; sed ego tecum in eo non pugnabo, quominus utrum velis eligas, Cic.; with acc. and infin., *to maintain in dispute*, Cic.; transf., of things, pugnat diu sententia secum, Ov. **B.** Esp., **a**, *to contradict;* ut tota in oratione tua tecum ipse pugnares, Cic.; **b**, *to strive, struggle, exert oneself;* followed by ut or ne or quominus with the subj., illud pugna et enitere ut, etc., Cic.

pugnus -i, m. (root PUG, Gr. ΠΥΓ, whence πυξ), *the fist;* pugnum facere, Cic.; aliquem pugnis concidere, Cic.

pulchellus -a -um (dim. of pulcher), *very pretty;* Bacchae, Cic.; used ironically of Clodius, with a pun on his surname Pulcher, Cic.

1. **pulcher** -chra -chrum and **pulcer** -cra -crum (connected with pol-ire, parēre, etc.), *beautiful, fair, lovely.* **I.** Lit., puer, Cic.; quid aspectu pulchrius? Cic.; urbs pulcherrima, Caes. **II.** Transf., **a**, *excellent, admirable, fine, glorious;* exemplum, Caes.; facinus, Sall.; factum pulcherrimum, Sall.; pulchrum est, *it is noble, glorious, fine;* with acc. and infin., illis pulcherrimum fuit tantam vobis imperii gloriam tradere, Cic.; **b**, *lucky, happy;* dies, Hor.; ne pulchrum se ac beatum putaret, Cic.

2. Pulcher -chri, m. **I.** *a Roman surname*, e.g., P. Claudius Pulcher. **II.** Pulchri Promontorium, *a promontory in Africa, now Cap Bono.*

pulchrē (pulcrē), adv. (pulcher), *beautifully, admirably, excellently, nobly ;* dicere, Cic. ; hostia litatur pulcherrime, *very favourably,* Cic.; pulchre est mihi, *all's well with me,* Cic. ; used as an exclamation of approval, *bravo ! well done !* Hor.

pulchrĭtūdo (pulcrĭtūdo) -ĭnis, f. (pulcher), *beauty, excellence.* **I.** Lit., corporis. **II.** Fig., *excellence ;* virtutis, Cic. ; verborum, Cic.

pūlējum (pūlēgĭum) -ĭi, n. *fleabane, pennyroyal,* Cic. ; fig., ad cuius rutam pulejo mihi tui sermonis utendum est, *sweetness,* Cic.

pūlex -ĭcis, m. *a flea,* Plaut.

pullārĭus -ĭi, m. (pullus), *the feeder of the sacred chickens,* Cic.

pullātus -a -um (2. pullus), *clad in dirty or black garments* (of mourners) ; proceres, Juv.

pullŭlo, 1. *to shoot up, sprout out.* **A.** a, of plants, etc., Verg. ; b, poet., transf., tot pullulat atra columbis, *burgeons with,* Verg. **B.** Fig., quae (luxuria) incipiebat pullulare, *luxuriate,* Nep.

1. pullus -i, m. (root PU, whence puer, Gr. πῶλος, etc.), *a young animal.* **I.** Lit., a, gen., columbinus, Cic. ; pulli ex ovis orti, Cic. ; b, esp., *a young cock* (whence Fr. poulet), Hor. ; of the sacred chickens, Cic., Liv. **II.** Transf., of men ; a, as a term of endearment, *chicken,* Hor. ; b, pullus milvinus, *a young kite,* Cic.

2. pullus -a -um (connected with πελλός), *dark-coloured, blackish, greyish black ;* capilli, Ov. ; myrtus, *dark-green,* Hor. ; esp., pulla vestis, *a garment of undyed wool, worn as mourning,* Cic. ; poet., pulla stamina (of the threads of the Parcae), *sad, gloomy,* Ov. ; subst., **pullum** -i, n. *a dark-coloured garment,* Ov.

pulmentārĭum -ĭi, n. (pulmentum), *a relish, anything eaten with bread;* pulmentaria quaere sudando, *get an appetite by hard work,* Hor.

pulmentum -i, n. (= pulpamentum, from pulpa), *a relish,* Hor. ; in general, *food, victuals ;* mullum in singula pulmenta minuere, *into small portions,* Hor.

pulmo -ōnis, m. (from πλεύμων = πνεύμων), *the lung ;* usually pl., pulmones, *the lungs,* Cic.

pulmōnĕus -a -um, *of or relating to the lungs, pulmonary,* Plaut.

pulpa -ae, f. *flesh ;* a, lit., Mart.; b, meton., pulpa scelerata, *the flesh as sign of sensuality,* Pers.

pulpāmentum -i, n. (pulpa). **I.** *flesh,* esp. of fish, Plin. **II.** *a relish ;* mihi est pulpamentum fama, Cic.

pulpĭtum -i, n. *a platform, tribune for public readings, debates,* etc., Hor. ; for actors, *"the boards" of a theatre,* Ov.

puls, pultis, f. (πόλτος), *a porridge or pottage of flour, pulse, used as food for the sacred chickens,* Cic.

pulsātĭo -ōnis, f. (pulso), *a knocking, striking, beating,* Cic. ; scutorum, Liv.

pulso, 1. (intens. of pello), *to strike, beat, knock.* **I.** Gen., 1, lit., a, of stamping the ground, dancing, etc., pede libero tellurem, Hor.; of horses, pedibus spatium Olympi, poet. = *to hasten over,* Ov. ; b, of knocking at the door, fores, Ov. ; c, *to beat, ill-treat ;* pulsare et verberare aliquem, Cic. ; transf., of the wind, storms, etc., piniferum caput et vento pulsatur et imbri, Verg. ; d, *to knock against, reach to ;* ipse ar duus alta pulsat sidera, Verg. ; e, *to*

strike, touch, of a musical instrument ; septem discrimina vocum, Verg. ; 2, fig., a, *to move, affect ;* dormientium animos externā et adventiciā visione pulsari, Cic. ; b, *to alarm, agitate ;* pavor pulsans, Verg. **II.** *to drive away ;* sagittam, Verg. ; divi pulsati, Verg.

pulsus -ūs, m. (pello), **[**a *pushing, beating, striking, blow, push, stroke.* **I.** Gen., remorum, Cic. ; pedum, *a footstep,* Verg. ; lyrae, *a playing on the lyre,* Ov. ; pulsum venarum attingere, *to feel the pulse,* Tac. **II.** *influence, impulse ;* ex ternus pulsus animos commovet, Cic.

pulto, 1. (= pulso), *to knock, beat, strike ;* januam, Plaut.

pulvĕrĕus -a -um (pulvis). **I.** *full of dust, dusty ;* nubes, *dust-clouds,* Verg. ; solum, Ov **II.** Act., *raising dust ;* palla (Boreae), Ov.

pulvĕrŭlentus -a -um (pulvis), *full of dust, dusty.* **I.** Lit., via, Cic. **II.** Fig., *won by hard work ;* praemia militiae, Ov.

pulvillus -i, m. (dim. of pulvinus), *a little pillow,* Hor.

pulvīnar -āris, n. (pulvinus). **I.** *a couch covered with cushions placed for the images of the gods at the Lectisternium* (q.v.)*, a cushioned seat ;* pulvinar suscipere, Liv.; dedicare, Cic.; meton., ad omnia pulvinaria supplicatio decreta est, *at all the temples,* Cic. **II.** Transf., *a state couch for any distinguished person,* Cic.

pulvīnārĭum -ĭi, n. (pulvinus), *a cushioned seat for the gods,* Liv.

pulvīnus -i, m. *a pillow, cushion,* Cic.

pulvis -ĕris, m. and rarely f. *dust.* **I.** Lit., **A.** multus erat in calceis pulvis, Cic. ; pulvis eruditus, or simply pulvis, *the sand or dust in which the old mathematicians drew their diagrams,* Cic. ; numquam eruditum illum pulverem attigistis, *you have never learnt mathematics,* Cic.; pulvis exiguus, *a handful of dust thrown on the dead,* Hor. ; poet., pulvis hibernus, *dry winter,* Verg. ; plur., novendiales pulveres, *dust nine days old* (= *fresh ashes of the dead*)*,* Hor. ; prov., sulcos in pulvere ducere, *to labour in vain,* Juv. **B.** Esp., *the dust of the circus or wrestling-place ;* pulvis Olympicus, Hor. ; hence, meton., *place of exercise, arena ;* domitant in pulvere currus, Verg. ; and fig., *scene of action ;* doctrinam in solem atque pulverem produxit, *into public,* Cic. ; sine pulvere palmae, *without effort,* Hor. **II.** Transf., *the earth,* Prop.

pūmex -ĭcis, m. (f. Cat.), *pumice-stone.* **I.** Lit., esp. as used for polishing marble, books, etc., Cat., Ov. **II.** Transf., *any kind of soft, porous stone ;* pumices cavi, Verg.

pūmĭcĕus -a -um (pumex), *made of pumice-stone,* Ov.

pūmĭco, 1. (pumex), *to polish with pumice-stone,* Cat.

pūmĭlĭo -ōnis, c. *a dwarf,* Lucr.

punctim, adv. (pungo), *by stabbing, by thrusting* (opp. caesim) ; petere hostem, Liv.

punctum -i, n. (pungo). **I.** *a little hole, small puncture,* Mart. **II.** 1, lit., a, *a point,* and meton., *a division of a discourse, a short clause, section ;* puncta argumentorum, Cic. ; b, in the comitia, *the point made on a tablet as often as one of the candidates was voted for,* hence *a vote ;* quot in ea tribu puncta tuleris, Cic. ; hence, transf., *approval, applause ;* discedo Alcaeus puncto illius, Hor. ; omne tulit punctum qui miscuit utile dulci, Hor. ; 2, transf., *a mathematical point, the smallest quantity ;* hence, a, *a very small space ;* quasi punctum terrae, Cic. ; b, *a small portion of time, a moment ;* ad punctum temporis, *in a moment,* Cic.

pungo, pŭpŭgi, punctum, 3. *to prick, puncture, stab.* **I.** 1, lit., a, neminem, Cic.; b, *to make by piercing;* vulnus quod acu punctum videretur, Cic.; 2, transf., a, *to penetrate, enter;* corpus, Lucr.; b, *to touch, move;* sensum, Lucr.; c, *to point off;* hence, puncto tempore, *in a moment,* Lucr. **II.** Fig., *to sting, vex, annoy, mortify;* epistola illa ita me pupugit, ut somnum mihi ademerit, Cic.; si paupertas momordit, si ignominia pupugit, Cic.

Pūnĭcĕus, v. Poeni.

Pūnĭcus, Punice, v. Poeni.

pūnĭo (poenĭo) -ivi and -ĭi -ītum -īre, and ƌep. **pūnĭor (poenĭor)** -ītus sum -īri (poena). **I.** *to punish;* sontes, Cic.; maleficia, Cic.; aliquem supplicio, Cic.; dep., peccatum, Cic. **II.** *to avenge;* dolorem, Cic.; dep., necem, Cic.

pūnītor -ōris, m. (punio), *a punisher, avenger;* doloris, Cic.

pūpa -ae, f. (pupus). **I.** *a little girl,* Mart. **II.** *a doll,* Pers.

pūpilla -ae, f. (dim. of pupa). **I.** *an orphan girl, ward, minor,* Cic. **II.** Transf. (like Gr. κόρη), *the pupil of the eye,* Cic.

pūpillāris -e (pupillus), *of or relating to a ward;* pecuniae, Liv.

pūpillus -i, m. (dim. of pupulus), *an orphan, ward,* Cic.

Pupinĭa -ae, f. *the Pupinian country in Latium, a sterile tract of country;* hence, Pupiniensis ager, Liv.

Pūpĭus -a -um, *name of a Roman gens;* adj., lex Pupia, *proposed by Pupius, a tribune, that the senate should not hold a meeting on the day of the Comitia.*

puppis -is, f. *the poop or stern of a vessel.* **I.** Lit., navem convertere ad puppim, Cic.; ventus surgens a puppi, *from behind,* Verg.; fig., sedebamus in puppi, *I sat at the helm of the state,* Cic. **II.** Meton., *the whole ship,* Verg.; *the constellation of the Ship,* Cic. (abl. sing., puppi, acc., puppim).

pūpŭla -ae, f. (dim. of pupa), *the pupil of the eye,* Cic.; meton., *the eye,* Hor.

pūpŭlus -i, m. (dim. of pupus), *a little boy,* Cat.

pūpus -i, m. *a boy, child,* used as a term of endearment, Suet.

pūrē and poet. **pūrĭtĕr,** adv. (purus). **I. A.** Lit., a, *purely, cleanly;* pure lauta corpora, Liv.; b, *brightly;* splendens Pario marmore purius, Hor. **B.** Transf., *clearly, naturally;* pure apparere, Hor. **II.** Fig., 1, gen., a, *uprightly, purely;* pure et eleganter acta vita, Cic.; pure et caste deos venerari, Cic.; b, of style, *purely, faultlessly;* pure et emendate loqui, Cic.; 2, esp., *finely, perfectly, entirely;* quid pure tranquillet, Hor.

purgāmen -ĭnis, n. (purgo). **I.** *filth, dirt, sweepings;* Vestae, *that which was annually swept from the temple of Vesta,* Ov. **II.** *a means of purgation or expiation;* mali, Ov.; caedis, Ov.

purgāmentum -i, n. (purgo), *that which is cleaned out, swept away, sweepings, rubbish, filth;* urbis, Liv.

purgātĭo -ōnis, f. (purgo), *a cleaning out, cleansing.* **I.** 1, lit., alvi, *purging,* Cic.; 2, meton., plur., purgationes, *purgatives,* Cic. **II.** Transf., *excusing, justification,* Cic.

purgo, 1. (purigo, from purus), *to clean, cleanse.* **I.** Lit., 1, locum, *to clean out, make ready for ploughing,* Cic.; arva longis ligonibus, Ov.; 2, *to purge the body;* purgor bilem, *I free myself from gall,* Hor.; purgatum te illius morbi,

healed, Hor. **II.** Transf., 1, *to purge, cleanse, purify;* educ tecum omnes tuos, purga urbem, Cic.; 2, *to cleanse morally;* a, *to excuse, defend, justify;* aliquem de luxuria, Cic.; civitatem facti dictique, Liv.; crimen, *to confute,* Cic.; with acc. and infin., *to allege in defence,* Liv.; b, *to purge, purify religiously;* populos, Ov.; c, *to make good;* malum facinus forti facinore, Liv.

pūrĭtĕr = pure (q.v.).

purpŭra -ae, f. (πορφύρα). **I.** *the purplefish,* Plin. **II.** Meton., **A.** *the purple dye, purple,* Verg. **B.** *any stuff or texture dyed purple, purple cloth,* Cic.

purpŭrasco, 3. *to become purple or dark,* Cic.

purpŭrātus -a -um (purpura), *clad in purple.* **I.** Adj., mulier, Plaut. **II.** Subst., *a high dignitary among eastern princes (clad in purple);* plur., *courtiers;* purpuratis tuis ista minitare, Cic.

purpŭrĕus -a -um (πορφύρεος). **I.** *purple,* and so of shades resembling purple, *blackish, dark-red, dark-brown, dark-violet;* vestitus, Cic.; rubor, *blush,* Ov.; capillus, crinis, Verg.; mare, Cic. **II.** Meton., **A.** *clad in purple;* rex, Ov.; tyrannus, Hor.; transf., *adorned with purple;* torus, Ov.; purpureis pennis, *with purple plumes,* Verg. **B.** *bright, beautiful;* olores, Hor.; ver, Verg.

pūrus -a -um, *clean, pure.* **I. A.** Lit., a, unda, Verg.; fons, Plaut.; aëre purior ignis, Ov.; terra, *cleared of stones, stubble,* etc., Cic.; b, of the air, sun, etc., *bright, clear,* Cic.; neut. subst., per purum, *the clear sky,* Verg. **B.** Transf., *without addition, simple, plain;* a, hasta, *without a head,* Verg.; b, *unadorned, plain;* parma, Verg.; argentum, *without reliefs,* Cic.; of dress, *without ornament;* esp., among the Romans, *without a purple stripe;* vestis, Verg.; toga, Phaedr.; c, *clear, unmixed, unadulterated;* nardum, Tib.; d, *clear (gain, profit);* quid possit ad dominos puri ac reliqui pervenire, Cic. **II.** Fig., **A.** Gen., 1, *spotless;* a, *holy, upright;* purus et integer, Cic.; b, *free from crime,* esp., *murder;* pura manus, Verg.; with genit., sceleris, Hor.; c, *free from sensuality, chaste, pure;* animam puram conservare, Cic.; d, of discourse, *pure, faultless;* pura et incorrupta consuetudo, Cic.; 2, a, religious t. t., (α) *unconsecrated,* Cic.; (β) *untrodden, undefiled;* locus, Liv.; (γ) *free from mourning* (by completion of funeral rites); familia, Cic.; (δ) act., *purifying;* arbor, Ov.; b, rhet. t. t., *unadorned, natural, simple;* purum genus dicendi, Cic.; c, *legal* t. t., *without conditions, absolute, unconditional;* judicium, Cic.

pūs, pūris, n. *corrupt matter;* fig., *gall, venom,* Hor.

pŭsillus -a -um, dim. *very small, tiny, puny.* **I.** Lit., testis, Cic.; Roma, Cic.; epistola, Cic. Subst., **pŭsillum** -i, n. *a trifle, a little,* ap. Cic. **II.** Transf., a, of ability, *very insignificant;* ingenium, Mart.; b, of courage, animus, *timid,* Hor.; c, *petty, mean;* animus, Cic.; d, *little, insignificant;* causa, Ov.

pūsĭo -ōnis, m. *a little boy,* Cic.

pŭtā (imper. 2. puto), *for example, suppose, for instance,* Hor.

pŭtāmen -ĭnis, n. (1. puto), *a cutting, paring, shred, shell,* Cic.

pŭtĕal -ālis, n. (puteus). **I.** *a stone curb round the mouth of a well.* **II.** Transf., *a similar enclosure around a sacred place*—e.g., the Puteal Libonis or Scribonianum at Rome, where the usurers carried on business, in the Comitium, Cic.

pŭtĕālis -e (puteus), *of or relating to a well;* undae, Ov.; lymphae, Lucr.

pŭtĕārĭus -ĭi, m. (puteus), *a well-sinker,* Liv.

pŭtĕo, 2. (root PUT, Gr. ΠΥΘ, whence πύθω, πύθομαι), *to stink,* Cic.

Pŭtĕŏli (**Pŏtĕŏli**) -ōrum, m. *a town in Campania on the coast, with many mineral springs, favourite resort of the Romans, now Pozzuolo.* Hence, **Pŭtĕŏlānus** -a -um, *belonging to Puteoli.* Subst., a, **Pŭtĕŏlānum** -i, n. *an estate of Cicero, near Puteoli;* b, **Pŭtĕŏlāni** -ōrum, m. *the people of Puteoli.*

pŭter -tris -tre and **putris** -e. **I.** *rotten,* putrid, stinking; poma, Ov.; fervent examina putri de bove, Ov. **II.** Transf., *loose, flabby,* crumbling, friable; gleba, Verg.; campus, Verg.; mammae, Hor.; oculi, languishing, Hor.

pŭtesco (pŭtisco) -tŭi, 3. (puteo), *to decay, become rotten, grow putrid,* Cic.

pŭtĕus -i, m. (root PUT, connected with ΒΟΘ, whence βόθρος), *a pit;* a, in agriculture, *a pit, trench,* Verg.; b, *a well, spring,* Cic.

pŭtĭdē, adv. (putidus), *of discourse, affectedly, disgustingly;* dicere, Cic.; putidius litteras exprimere, Cic.

pŭtĭdĭuscŭlus -a -um (dim. of putidus), *somewhat affected, nauseous,* Cic.

pŭtĭdus -a -um (puteo), *rotten, stinking,* putrid. **A.** Lit., caro, Cic. **B.** Transf., 1, cerebrum putidius, addled, Hor.; 2, *nauseous,* troublesome, pedantic, affected; haec satis spero vobis molesta et putida videri, Cic.; putidum est, with infin., *it is pedantic,* etc., Cic.; of orators, affected, ornate; Demosthenes, Cic.

1. **pŭto**, 1. (root PU, whence purus, putus), *to cleanse;* hence, *to lop, to prune trees;* vites, Verg.

2. **pŭto**, 1. (root PUT, Gr. ΠΥΘ, πυθέσθαι, aor. of πυνθάνομαι), *to reckon.* **I.** Gen., a, *to reckon, calculate, compute, to estimate, value at;* with genit. of value, magni putare honores, Cic.; with pro and the abl., aliquem pro nihilo, Cic.; with in and the abl., in hominum numero putabat, Cic.; with acc. of predicate, se solum beatum, Cic.; b, *to consider, hold, believe, suppose;* with acc., putare deos, *to believe in the gods,* Cic.; with acc. and infin., noli putare me maluisse, Cic.; absol., non putaram, Cic.; parenthet., puto or ut puto, *I suppose,* Cic. **II. a**, *to count over;* rationes cum publicanis, *settle accounts with,* Cic.; b, *to weigh, reflect;* debes putare comitiis studium esse populi, non judicium, Cic.

pŭtor -ōris, m. (puteo), *bad smell, stink,* Lucr.

pŭtrĕfăcĭo -fēci -factum, 3., pass., **pŭtrĕfĭo** -factus sum -fĭĕri (putreo and facio). **I.** *to make rotten,* and pass., *to become rotten, decay;* nudatum tectum patere imbribus putrefaciendum, Liv. **II.** *to make pliable, to soften;* ardentia saxa infuso aceto, Liv.

pŭtresco -trŭi, 3. (putreo), *to become rotten* or *decayed,* Hor.

pŭtrĭdus -a -um (putreo), 1, *rotten, decayed,* putrid; dentes, Cic.; 2, *loose, flabby,* Cat.

pŭtror -ōris, m. *rottenness, putridity,* Lucr.

pŭtus -a -um (root PU, whence puto, purus), *pure, unmixed, unadulterated;* usually found in connexion with purus, Plaut.; without purus, meae putissimae orationes, *brilliant,* Cic.

pycta (-es) -ae, m. (πύκτης), *a boxer, pugilist,* Phaedr.

15*

Pydna -ae, f. (Πύδνα), *a town in Macedonia, where Aemilius Paulus defeated Perseus, king of Macedonia,* 168 B.C., *perhaps modern Ayan.* Hence, **Pydnaei** -ōrum, m. *the inhabitants of Pydna.*

pȳga = puga (q.v.).

pȳgargus -i, m. (πύγαργος), 1, *the fish-eagle,* Plin.; 2, *a species of antelope,* Juv.

Pygmaei -ōrum, m. (Πυγμαῖοι), *the Pygmies, a race of dwarfs supposed to inhabit Africa, and to engage in war with cranes.* Hence, adj., **Pygmaeus** -a -um, *Pygmaean;* quae Pygmaeo sanguine gaudet avis, *the crane,* Ov.

Pygmălĭon -ōnis, m. (Πυγμαλίων), 1, *grandson of Agenor, who fell in love with a beautiful statue which he had made, and which Venus at his prayer endowed with life.* **II.** *king in Tyre, brother of Dido, whose husband he slew.*

Pyládēs -ae and -is, m. (Πυλάδης), *son of Strophius, and the faithful friend of Orestes;* hence, prov. for *a faithful friend,* Ov. Hence, adj., **Pyládēus** -a -um, *Pyladean;* amicitia, i.e., *faithful, tender,* Cic.

pylae -ārum, f. (πύλαι, *gates*), *passes between mountains, defiles.* **I.** Gen., Tauri, *separating Cappadocia from Cilicia,* Cic. **II.** Esp., Pylae = *Thermopylae,* Liv. Hence, **Pylăĭcus** -a -um, *relating to Thermopylae;* concilium, *convention, congress held at Thermopylae,* Liv.

Pylaemĕnēs -is, m. *an old king of the Heneti in Paphlagonia, killed before Troy.*

Pylĭus, Pylus.

Pylus (**-ŏs**) -i, f. (Πύλος), *name of two cities in the Peloponnesus, one in Messenia, the residence of Neleus, now Alt-Navarino; the other in Triphylia, the residence of Nestor, hence called Nestorea,* Ov.; subst., **Pylĭus** -a -um, a, *relating to Pylus;* subst., **Pylĭus** -ĭi, m. *the Pylian,* i.e., *Nestor;* b, poet. = *of Nestor;* dies, Ov.

pȳra -ae, f. (πυρά). **I.** *a funeral pyre,* Verg. **II.** As a proper name, **Pyra** -ae, f. *a place on Mount Oeta, where Hercules burnt himself.*

Pȳracmōn -ōnis, m. (Πυράκμων), *one of the Cyclopes of Vulcan.*

Pȳracmŏs -i, m. *one of the Centaurs at the wedding of Pirithous.*

pȳrămĭdātus -a -um, *pyramidal,* Cic.

pȳrămĭs -ĭdis, f. (πυραμίς), *a pyramid,* Cic.

1. **Pȳrămus** -i, m. (Πύραμος), *the lover of Thisbe, who stabbed herself in the belief that he was dead.*

2. **Pȳrămus** -i, m. (Πύραμος), *a river in Cilicia, now Geihun.*

Pyrēne -ēs, f. (Πυρήνη), *daughter of Bebryx, beloved by Hercules, buried in the mountain called after her;* hence, **Pyrēnaeus** -a -um, *belonging to Pyrene;* Pyrenaei Montes, *the Pyrenees, the mountains between Gaul and Spain;* so simply, **Pyrēnaeus** -i, m., Liv. (Pyrēnē, in Tib.).

pȳrĕthrum -i, n. (πύρεθρον), *a plant, pellitory,* Ov.

Pyrgi -ōrum, m. (Πύργοι = turres), *a town in Etruria, now the village of St. Severo.* Hence, **Pyrgensis** -e, *belonging to Pyrgi.*

Pyrgo -ūs, f. *the nurse of Priam's children.*

Pȳrĭphlĕgĕthōn -ontis, m. (Πυριφλεγέθων), *the fire-stream, a river in the lower world;* gen. simply *Phlegethon.*

Pȳrŏis (**-eis**) -entos, m. (πυρόεις), *fiery, one of the horses of the Sun,* Ov.

pȳrōpus -i, m. (πυρωπός), *a kind of mixed metal, bronze,* Ov.

Pyrrha -ae, f. (Πύρρα). **I.** *daughter of Epimetheus, wife of Deucalion.* **II.** *a town in Lesbos, now Caloxi.* Adj., **Pyrrhĭăs** -ădis, f. *relating to the town of Pyrrha.*

Pyrrho (Pyrro) -ōnis, m. (Πύρρων), *a Greek philosopher of Elis, founder of the so-called Sceptical School, contemporary of Alexander the Great.* Hence, **Pyrrhōnēi** -ōrum, m. *the followers of Pyrrho.*

Pyrrhus -i, m. (Πύρρος). **I.** *son of Achilles and Deidamia of Scyrus (also called Neoptolemos), founder of a monarchy in Epirus, killed at Delphi by Orestes.* **II.** *king in Epirus, enemy of the Romans.* Hence, **Pyrrhēum** -i, n. *the royal castle of Pyrrhus.*

Pȳthăgŏrās -ae, m. (Πυθαγόρας), *Greek philosopher of Samos* (about 550 B.C.), *who afterwards settled in Lower Italy* (in Crotona and Metapontum), *and founded the school named after him.* Hence, **Pȳthăgŏrēus** -a -um, *Pythagorean,* and subst., *a Pythagorean.*

Pȳtho -ūs, f. (Πυθώ), *the old name of the part of Phocis at the foot of Parnassus where Delphi lay.* Hence, **A. Pȳthĭcus** -a -um, *Pythian, Delphic, relating to Apollo.* **B. Pȳthĭus** -a -um, *relating to Apollo, Delphic;* subst., **a, Pȳthĭa** -ae, f. *the priestess who delivered the oracles at Delphi;* **b, Pȳthĭa** -ōrum, n. (τὰ Πύθια), *the Pythian games, celebrated every five years in the Cumaean plains near Delphi in honour af Apollo, who slew the Python.*

Pȳthōn -ōnis, m. (Πύθων), *a great snake killed by Apollo, near Delphi.*

pȳtisma, m. (πύτισμα), *the wine which is spit out or spurted through the lips* (in tasting), Juv.

pȳtisso, 1. (πυτίζω), *to spit out wine* (in tasting), Ter.

pyxĭs -ĭdis, f. (πυξίς), *a little box, casket, used for drugs,* etc.; veneni, Cic.

Q.

Q, q, *the sixteenth letter of the Roman alphabet, only used before u followed by a vowel.* It not unfrequently represents the Greek π; e.g., quinque πέντε, equus ἵππος, sequor ἕπω. For abbreviations in which Q. is used, see Table of Abbreviations.

quā, adv. (from qui, quae, quod). **I.** *on which side, where;* ad omnes introitus qua adiri poterat, Cic.; corresp., ea . . . qua, Caes. **II.** Transf., **A.** partitive, qua . . . qua, *partly . . . partly; both . . . as well as,* qua dominus qua advocatus, Cic. **B.** *in so far as, in as much as;* effuge qua potes, Ov., Cic. **C.** *in what manner, how;* illuc qua veniam? Cic.

quācumque, adv. (sc. parte, from quicumque). **I.** *wherever, wheresoever;* quacumque iter fecit, Cic. **II.** *by all means, in every manner,* Verg.

quădamtĕnŭs, adv. *to a certain point, so far;* found in the tmesis, est quadam prodire tenus, Hor.

Quădi -ōrum, m. *a people in the south-east of Germany in modern Moravia.*

quădra, v. quadrus.

quădrāgēni -ae -a, num. distrib. (quadra-ginta), *forty each,* Cic.

quădrāgēsĭmus -a -um (quadraginta), *the*

---

fortieth; subst., **quădrāgēsĭma** -ae, f. *the fortieth part ;* esp., *as a tax,* Tac.

quădrāgĭes, adv. *forty times,* Cic.

quădrāginta, *forty,* Cic.

quădrans -antis, m. (quadro), *a fourth part, quarter.* **I.** heres ex quadrante, *to the fourth part of the property,* Suet. **II.** As a coin, *the fourth part of an as, three unciae,* Liv.; *the ordinary price of a bath;* dum tu quadrante lavatum rex ibis, Hor.

quădrantal -ālis, n. *a liquid measure containing* 8 congii, Plaut.

quădrantārĭus -a -um (quadrans), *pertaining to a quarter.* **I.** Gen., tabulae quadrantariae, *reduction of debts by a quarter in consequence of the lex Valeria feneratoria,* Cic. **II.** Esp., *costing a quarter of an as,* Cic.

quădrātus -a -um (quadro), *quadrangular, square.* **A.** Adj., saxum, Liv.; agmen, *a square of soldiers,* Cic. **B.** Subst., **quădrātum** -i, n. a, *a square,* Cic.; b, t. t. of astronomy, *quadrature,* Cic.

quădrīdŭum (quătrīdŭum, quattrīdŭum) -i, n. (quatuor and dies), *a space of four days ;* quadriduo quo haec gesta sunt, Cic.

quădriennĭum -ĭi, n. (quatuor and annus), *a period of four years,* Cic.

quădrĭfārĭam, adv. (quatuor), *fourfold, in four parts,* Liv.

quădrĭfĭdus -a -um (quatuor and findo), *split into four portions,* Verg.

quădrīgae -ārum, f. (= quadrijugae, from quatuor and jugum), *a team of four horses abreast,* used of the animals alone, of the animals and the chariot, and of the chariot alone. **I.** Lit., alborum equorum, Liv.; esp., of racing chariots, curru quadrigarum vehi, Cic. **II.** Fig., equis aut quadrigis poeticis, Cic.

quădrīgārĭus -ĭi, m. (quadriga), *the driver of four horses, a racing charioteer,* Cic.

quădrīgātus -a -um (quadriga), *stamped with the figure of a quadriga ;* nummi, *silver denarii,* Cic.

quădrĭgŭlae -ārum, f. (dim. of quadriga), *a little team of four horses,* Cic.

quădrījŭgis -e (quatuor and jugum), *yoked four together ;* equi, Verg.

quădrījŭgus -ā -um (quatuor and jugum), *yoked four together ;* equi, Ov.; currus, Verg · subst., **quădrījŭgi** -ōrum, m. *a team of four horses,* Ov.

quădrīmus -a -um (quatuor), *four years old,* Cic.

quădringēnārĭus -a -um (quadringeni), *of four hundred each,* Cic.

quădringēni -ae -a (quadringenti), num. distrib., *four hundred each,* Liv.

quădringentēni -ae -a, *four hundred each,* Liv.

quădringentēsĭmus -a -um (quadringenti), *the four hundredth,* Liv.

quădringenti -ae -a (quatuor and centum), *four hundred,* Cic.

quădringentĭes, *four hundred times,* Cic.

quădrĭpartītō, *in four parts,* Co.

quădrĭpartītus (quădrĭpertītus) -a -um (quatuor and partior), *divided into four parts, fourfold ;* distributio, Cic.

quădrĭrēmis -e (quatuor and remis), *with four banks of oars ;* quadriremis navis, and subst., **quădrĭrēmis** -is, f. *a ship with four banks of oars*, Cic.

quădrĭvĭum -ĭi, n. (quatuor and via), *a place where four roads meet*, Cat.

quădro, 1. (quadrus). **I.** Transit., *to make square, to square;* transf., *to join properly together, complete rhythmically;* quadrandae orationis industria, Cic. **II.** Intransit., *to be square;* a, *to fit exactly, to suit;* omnia in istam quadrant, *correspond with*, Cic.; b, esp., *of accounts, to agree;* quo modo sexcenta eodem modo quadrarint, Cic.

quădrum, v. quadrus.

quădrŭpĕdans -antis (quatuor and pes), *going on four feet, galloping;* a, adj., Echetlus, *a Centaur,* Ov.; transf., sonitus (of a galloping horse), Verg.; b, subst., *a horse*, Verg.

quădrŭpes -pĕdis (quatuor and pes), *four-footed;* usually subst., **quădrŭpes** -pĕdis, c. *a fourfooted animal, quadruped;* (a) masc., saucius quadrupes, Verg.; (β) fem., quadrupes nulla, Verg.

quădrŭplātor -ōris, m. (quadruplor), *an informer who received a fourth part of the penalty,* Cic.

quădrŭplex -plĭcis (quatuor and plico), *fourfold, quadruple,* Liv.

quădrŭplor, 1. dep. *to be an informer,* Plaut. (cf. quadruplator).

quădrŭplus -a -um (quatuor and plus = πλοῦς = τετραπλοῦς), *fourfold.* Subst., **quădrŭplum** -i, n. *four times the amount, four times as much;* judicium dare in quadruplum, Cic.

quădrus -a -um (quatuor), *square.* Subst., **A. quădra** -ae, f. *a square;* 1, *a square dining-table;* hence, *a piece of bread used as a plate,* Verg.; aliena vivere quadrā, *to live at another person's table,* Juv.; 2, *a square piece or morsel,* Hor. **B. quădrum** -i, n. *a square;* transf., redigere omnes in quadrum numerumque sententias, *proper order,* Cic.

quaerĭto, 1. (intens. of quaero). **I.** *to seek eagerly,* Plaut. **II.** *to inquire eagerly,* Plaut.

quaero, quaesīvi, quaesītum, 3. **I.** *to seek, search for;* 1, lit., (a) of persons, suos, Caes.; liberos ad necem, Cic.; portum, Caes.; (β) of things, te decisa suum dextera quaerit, Verg.; 2, transf., (a) *to seek to obtain, strive to get;* alicui or sibi honores, Cic.; gloriam bello, Cic.; (β) *to prepare, make ready for;* fugam ex Italia, Cic.; (γ) *to seek with longing, to miss, want;* Caesarem, Hor.; eas balneas, Cic.; with ut and the subj., quaeris ut suscipiam cogitationem, Cic.; (δ) *to look round about for, think of;* omisso veteri consilio novum, Sall.; (e) with infin., *to seek to, wish to;* abrumpere lucem, Verg.; 3, *to investigate, make an examination of;* reliquorum sententiam, Cic.; with de and the abl., de vita et de moribus, Cic.; 4, *to wish to know, to ask, to inquire;* aliquem a janua, *to ask after some one at the door of his house,* Cic.; aliquid ex or de aliquo, gen. with rel. sent., de te quaero utrum . . . an, Cic.; quaesivit si (*whether*) incolumis evasisset, Liv.; partic. subst., **quaesitum** -i, n. *the question,* Ov.; 5, *to ask judicially, hold a judicial investigation, inquire into;* de morte alicuius, Cic.; de servo in dominum, *to interrogate the slave under torture about his master,* Cic. **II.** a, *to seek* = *to obtain* (by work, etc.), *to win, gain;* nummos aratro et manu, Cic.; jam diu nihil quaesivisse, Cic.; partic. subst., **quae-sĭtum** -i, n. and plur., **quaesĭta** -ōrum, n. *that which is gained, acquisition,* Ov.; b, *to look round for in vain, to miss;* Siciliam in Sicilia,

Cic.; quaerit Boeotia Dircen, Ov.; c, *to demand, make necessary;* dictatoriam majestate.n, Liv.

quaesītĭo -ōnis, f. (quaero), *an interrogation by torture,* Tac.

quaesītor -ōris, m. (quaero), *an investigator, inquirer,* esp., *a judicial investigator,* Cic.; criminum, Liv.

quaesītum, v. quaero.

quaesītus -a -um, p. adj. (from quaero). **I.** *sought out, uncommon, select, extraordinary;* leges quaesitiores (opp. simplices), Tac. **II.** *unnatural, affected;* comitas, Tac.

quaeso -īvi, 3. (another form of quaero). **I.** *to seek for, strive to obtain,* Plaut. **II.** *to beg, beseech, entreat;* with acc., ventorum paces, Lucr.; with ut or ne and the subj., a vobis quaeso ut, etc., Cic.; absol., *I beg, I entreat;* tu, quaeso, scribe, Cic.

quaestĭcŭlus -i, m. (dim. of quaestus), *a small gain, slight profit,* Cic.

quaestĭo -ōnis, f. (quaero), *a seeking, searching.* **A.** *an asking, questioning;* captivorum, Caes. **B.** 1, *an inquiring, investigating, inquiry;* tota fere quaestio tractata videtur, Cic.; in quaestionem vocare, *to investigate,* Cic.; 2, meton., a, *the subject of inquiry;* de natura deorum, Cic.; b, esp., rhet. t. t., (a) *the subject of debate in a speech,* Cic.; (β) *the main point, the issue,* Cic. **C.** 1, *a public judicial inquiry, investigation,* often with torture, hae quaestiones in senatu habitae, Cic.; quaestionem habere de viri morte, Cic.; quaestionem habere de servis in filium, Liv.; quaestionem inter sicarios exercere, *on an assassination,* Cic.; quaestiones perpetuae, *standing courts of justice at Rome for the investigation of crime* (instituted 149 B.C.); 2, meton., *record* (of such a court), fictam quaestionem conscribere, Cic.

quaestiuncŭla -ae, f. (dim. of quaestio), *a little question;* ponere alicui quaestiunculam, Cic.

quaestor -ōris, m. (for quaesitor, from quaero), *the quaestor,* in plur., *the quaestors, magistrats in Rome, originally two in number, who inquired into and punished capital crimes;* in full, quaestores parricidii; gen., simply quaestores, Cic.; in later times there were other quaestors, quaestores aerarii and urbani, *the magistrats who took charge of the public treasury and expenditure;* other quaestors accompanied the consuls and praetors on military expeditions and to provincial commands, and acted as paymasters; the number of quaestors, originally two, was in the end raised to eighteen.

quaestōrĭus -a -um (quaestor), *belonging or relating to a quaestor.* **I.** Gen., **A.** Adj., comitia, *for choice of a quaestor,* Cic.; officium, *duty of quaestor,* Cic.; scelus, *committed by a quaestor,* or *investigated by a quaestor,* Cic.; porta, *gate in the camp near the quaestor's tent,* Liv. **B.** Subst., **quaestōrĭum** -ĭi, n. 1, (sc. tentorium), *the quaestor's tent in camp,* Liv.; 2, (sc. aedificium), *the quaestor's dwelling in a province,* Cic. **II.** Esp., *having the rank of a quaestor.* **A.** Adj., legatus, Cic. **B.** Subst., **quaestōrĭus** -ĭi, m. *one who had been quaestor,* Cic.

quaestŭōsus -a -um (quaestus), *gainful, profitable.* **I.** mercatura, Cic. **II.** Of persons, 1, *fond of gain, eager after profit;* homo, Cic.; 2, *having gained much, rich,* Tac.

quaestūra -ae f. (quaestor), *the office or dignity of the quaestor, quaestorship,* Cic.

quaestus -ūs, m. (quaero), *a gaining, getting, profit, gain, advantage;* quaestus ac lucrum unius agri et unius anni, Cic.; quaestui deditum esse, *to be devoted to money-getting,* Sall.; quaestui habere rempublicam, *to make the administra-*

tion of the state an occasion of profit, Cic.; furtis quaestum facere, Cic.; quaestu judiciario pasci, *to live on the pay of a judge,* Cic.

quālĭbĕt (quālŭbĕt), adv. (abl. of quilibet). **I.** *wherever you like, everywhere,* Plaut. **II.** *in any way you please,* Cat.

quālis -e (from quam, as talis from tam) = ποῖος, *of what sort, what kind of.* **I.** Interrog., qualis est istorum oratio? Cic. **II.** Rel., with corresponding talis, as; *without* talis, *of such a kind, such as;* qualem te praebuisti, talem te impertias, Cic.; ut res non tales, quales ante habitae sint, habendae videantur, Cic.; in hoc bello, quale bellum nulla barbaria gessit, *such a war as,* Caes.; doce me quales sint, Cic. **III.** Indef. subst., quale, *having some quality or other;* illa quae appellant qualia, Cic.

quāliscumquĕ, quālĕcumquĕ. **I.** Rel., *of whatever kind, of whatever sort;* homines qualescumque sunt, Cic. **II.** Indef., *any, without exception, any whatever;* sin qualemcumque locum sequimur, Cic.

quālislĭbĕt, quālĕlĭbĕt, *of what sort you will;* formae litterarum vel aureae vel qualeslibet, Cic.

quālĭtas -ātis, f. (qualis), *a quality, property,* Cic.

quālĭtĕr, adv. (qualis), *as, just as,* Ov.

quālus -i, m. and **quālum** -i, n. *a wicker-basket,* Verg.

quam (acc. of quae, analogous to tam), *how, in what way;* and emphatic, *how much.* **I.** In correlation. **A.** In comparison, a, with tam, v. tam; with tam left out, homo non, quam isti sunt, gloriosus, Liv.; quam si = tamquam si, *as if,* Cic.; often with superl., quam maximā possum voce dico, *with as loud a voice as possible,* Cic.; quam celerrime potuit, Caes.; elliptically, without possum, *as much as possible, very;* with adj. and adv. in posit. and superl., quam magnis itineribus, Caes.; quam plurimo vendere, *as dear as possible,* Cic.; quam saepissime, *as often as possible,* Cic.; quam primum, *as soon as possible,* Cic.; nocte quam longa est, *the whole long night through,* Verg.; b, with tantus, v. tantus; c, with sic, Verg.; d, with comparatives or words implying comparison, *than, as;* nihil est magis timendum quam, etc., Cic.; major sum quam cui possit, etc., *too great to be,* etc., Ov.; with a second comparative following, longior quam latior, *more long than wide,* Cic.; with a superl., to express an emphatic comparative, cum tyranno, quam qui umquam, saevissimo, Liv.; with verbs implying a comparison, such as malle, potius malle, praestat, etc., Caes.; and other words of similar meaning, as aeque, supra, ultra, secus, alius, aliter, alibi, dissimilis, diversus, etc.; quam pro, foll. by abl., after a comparison; proelium atrocius quam pro numero pugnantium editur, *fiercer than you would expect from the number of the combatants,* Liv. **B.** In phrases relating to time, *after that, that;* postero die or postridie quam, Cic. **II.** To express degree, *how, how great, how little;* a, in indirect speech, (a) with adv. and adj., memoriā tenetis quam valde admurmurarint, Cic.; (β) with verbs, attende jam, quam defugiam auctoritatem consulatus mei, Cic.; b, in direct speech, in questions and exclamations; (a) with adj. and adv., quam multis, quam paucis, Cic.; (β) with verbs, quam hoc non curo, Cic.

quamdīū, *so long as, as long as, until;* quamdiu potuit tacuit, Caes.; disces quamdiu voles, Cic.

quamlĭbĕt, adv. **I.** *as you please, as you will,* Lucr. **II.** *howsoever, ever so much;* manus quamlibet infirmae Ov.

quamobrem (quam ob rem), *on which account, for which reason, wherefore, why.* **I.** Interrog., Cic. **II.** Rel., si res reperietur quam ob rem videantur, Cic.

quamprīmum, adv. *as soon as possible,* forthwith, Cic.

quamquam, conj. *although, though,* and sometimes at the beginning of a sentence, *nevertheless, notwithstanding, and yet, yet;* gen. with indic., only in classical prose with subj. when the thought would require the subj. even without quamquam; medici quamquam intelligunt saepe, tamen numquam aegris dicunt, Cic.; at the beginning of a sentence, quamquam quis ignorat, Cic.; with a partic., omnia illa quae sunt extra, quamquam expetenda, summo bono continerentur, Cic.

quamvis, **I.** Adv. **A.** Gen., *as you will, as much as you please, ever so much;* quamvis multos nominatim proferre, Cic.; et praeter eos quamvis enumeres multos licet, Cic. **B.** *as much as possible, very much, exceedingly;* quamvis copiose, Cic. **II.** Conj. *however much, although, albeit,* gen. with subj.; quamvis prudens sis, tamen, etc., Cic.; with an adj. or partic. without a verb, quamvis iniqua passi, Cic.

quānam (abl. of quinam), *where indeed, where,* Liv.

quando, adv. and conj. **I.** Adv., *when.* **A.** *when = at what time;* a, interrog., quando enim me ista curasse arbitramini? Cic.; b, rel., non intelligitur, quando obrepat senectus, Cic.; c, indef., *at any time, ever;* quaestio num quando amici novi veteribus sint anteponendi, Cic. **B.** *when = in what circumstances,* Cic. **II.** Conj., a, temporal = *when;* tum quando legatos Tyrum misimus, Cic.; b, causal, *since, because;* quando ad majores quaedam nati sumus, Cic.

quandŏcumquĕ, adv. **I.** Rel., *whenever, as often as;* quandocumque trahunt invisa negotia Romam, Hor. **II.** Indef., *at some time or other;* quandocumque mihi poenas dabis, Ov.

quandŏquĕ, adv. **I.** Rel., *whenever, as often as,* Cic. **II.** Indef., *at some time or other,* Cic.

quandŏquĭdem, conj. *since, because,* Cic.

quantillus -a -um (dim. of quantulus), *how little! how small! how insignificant!* Plaut.

quanto, v. quantus.

quantŏpĕrĕ (quanto ŏpĕrĕ), adv. (quantus and opus), *with what great trouble.* **I.** Lit., *with what care, how much;* quanto se opere custodiant bestiae, Cic. **II.** Transf., *to what an extent, how much;* dici non potest, quanto opere gaudeant, Cic.

quantŭlus -a -um (dim. of quantus), *how little, how small, how unimportant;* quantulus sol nobis videtur! Cic.; quantulum judicare possemus, Cic.

quantŭluscumquĕ -ācumquĕ -umcumquĕ, *how little soever, however small;* de hac mea, quantulacumque est, facultate, Cic.; neut. subst., *how little soever;* quantulumcumque dicebamus, Cic.

quantum, v. quantus.

quantumvis. **I.** Adv. *as much as you please, ever so much, very much,* Suet. **II.** Conj. *although;* ille catus, quantumvis rusticus, Hor.

quantus -a -um (from quam and adj. ending tus), *of what size, how great.* **I.** Rel. = ὅσος. **A.** Gen. of size, number, etc., *how great;* and (without corresponding tantus) *as great as;* of time, *how long, so long as;* of other relations *how important, as important as;* 1, adj., (a) with tantus or tam, v. tantus, tam; (β) with correl left out, ut acciperent pecuniam quantam vellent, Cic.; nox acta, quanta fuit, *as long as it lasted, the whole long night*, Ov.; quantā maximā celeritate potui, *with the greatest possible speed*, Liv.; **2,** neut. subst., quantum ; **a,** with genit. or absol., quantum est ex Sicilia frumenti, Cic.; quantum ego sentio, Cic.; quantum in me est, *as far as in me lies*, Cic.; in quantum, *in so far*, Ov.; **b,** genit. of price, *how dear, at what price;* quanti locaverint, tantam pecuniam solvendam, Cic.; quanti quanti, *at whatever price*, Cic.; **c,** abl., quanto in comparatives, *the more;* quanto longius discederent, eo, etc., Liv.; **so,** quanto ante, Cic.; **3,** neut., quantum, adv., **a,** *as far as;* nisi quantum usus necessario cogeret, Liv.; **b,** = quam, to strengthen a superl., quantum maxime accelerare poterat, Liv.; **c,** parenthet., ea, quantum potui, feci, *to the best of my power*, Cic. **II.** Interrog. = πόσος, *how great?* **A.** Gen., **1,** adj., (α) in direct questions, in exclamations, quanta notitia antiquitatis? Cic.; (β) in direct speech, quum ipsa pecunia numero et summa sua, quanta fuerit, ostendat, Cic.; **2,** neut. subst., genit. quanti, *at what a price? how dear?* in indirect questions, cum scias, quanti Tulliam faciam, *how highly I esteem*, Cic.; **3,** neut., quantum, adv., *how much;* quantum mutatus ab illo Hectore, Verg.; **B.** Emphatic, *how little!* **1,** adj., in indirect speech, me ipsum poenitet, quanta sint, Cic; **2,** subst., **a,** quantum, (α) in direct question, Ov.; (β) in indirect speech, quantum tu speres perspicio, Cic.; **b,** genit., quanti est ista hominum gloria quae, etc., Cic.

quantuscumquĕ -ācumquĕ -umcumquĕ, **I.** *how great soever;* bona, quantacumque erant, Cic.; emphat., quantacunque victoria, Cic. **II.** *as much soever as;* quantumcumque possum, Cic.

quantuslĭbet -tālĭbet -tumlĭbet, *as great as you will, however great, however much ;* ordo, Ov.; magnitudo hominis, Liv.

quantusvis -āvis -umvis, *as great as you please, how great or how much soever ;* quantasvis magnas copias sustineri posse, Caes.; portum satis amplum quantaevis classi, Liv.

quāpropter, *on which account, wherefore,* Cic.

quāquā (abl. of quisquis), *wherever, whithersoever,* Plaut.

quārē, adv. (qui and res). **I.** *by which means, whereby ;* permulta sunt quae dici possunt, quare intelligatur, Cic. **II.** *wherefore, on which account.* **A.** Interrog., quare negasti, etc., Cic. **B.** Rel., utendum est excusatione, quare id necesse fuerit, Cic.

quartădĕcŭmāni -ōrum, m. (quartus decimus), *soldiers of the fourteenth legion,* Tac.

quartāna, v. quartanus.

quartānus -a -um (quartus), *relating to the fourth.* **I.** *relating to the fourth day ;* febris quartana, Cic.; and subst. simply, **quartāna** -ae, f. *a quartan fever;* quartana ab aliquo discessit, Cic. **II.** *relating to the fourth legion;* **quartāni** -ōrum, m. *the soldiers of the fourth legion,* Tac.

quartārĭus -ĭi, m. (quartus), *the fourth part of a sextarius,* Liv.

quarto, v. quartus.

quartum, v quartus.

quartus -a -um, *the fourth.* **I.** Adj., pars, Caes. **II.** Subst., **1, quartus** -i, m., (α) (sc. liber), *the fourth book ;* in quarto accusationis, Cic.; (β) (sc. lapis), *the fourth milestone,* Tac.; **2, quarta** -ae, f. (sc. hora), *the fourth hour,* Hor. **III.** Adv., **1,** quartum, *for the fourth time,* Cic.; **2,** quarto, *for the fourth time,* Ov.

quartusdĕcĭmus -a -um, *the fourteenth,* Tac.

quăsĭ, adv. *as if.* **I.** Of the comparison of whole sentences ; **1,** in hypothetical comparisons, *as if ;* **a,** corresponding to ni, ita, tam, perinde, proinde, and idem, with subj., sensu amisso fit idem quasi natus non esset omnino, Cic.; with partic., quas ni avide arripui quasi sitim explere cupiens, Cic.; **b,** without any corresponding partic. in the subj., quid ego his testibus utor, quasi res dubia autobscura sit, Cic.; often ironical, *as if, just as if ;* medico tria millia jugerum (dedisti) quasi te sanasset, Cic.; with partic., hostes maximo clamore insecuti quasi partā jam atque exploratā victoriā, Cic. ; **2,** in pure comparison, *as, like as ;* with the indic., quasi poma ex arboribus, cruda si sunt, vix evelluntur ni, etc., Cic. **II.** To compare clauses or words ; **1,** to soften an unusual expression, *as it were, a sort of ;* philosophia procreatrix quaedam et quasi parens, Cic. ; **2,** transf., *as it were, almost, all but ;* quasi in extrema pagina, Cic.

quăsillus -i, m. and **quăsillum** -i, n. (dim. of qualus), *a little wicker-basket,* esp. for holding wool, Cic.

quassātĭo -ōnis, f. (quasso), *a shaking,* Liv.

quasso, **1.** (intens. of quatio). **I.** Transf., *to shake violently.* **A.** Lit., **1,** gen., hastam, Verg.; **2,** esp., *to shatter, break in pieces, dash to pieces ;* classis ventis quassata, Verg. ; naves quassatae, Liv. **B.** Transf., *to shake, shatter ;* rempublicam, Cic. **II.** Reflex., *to shake oneself, shake ;* siliquā quassante, Verg.

quassus -a -um, partic. of quatio.

quătĕnŭs, adv. *how far.* **I.** Lit., quatenus progredi debeat, Cic. ; ut nulla in re statuere possimus quatenus, Cic. **II.** Transf., **A.** Of time, *how long.* **B.** Of other relations, **1,** *in so far as,* Cic. ; **2,** *since, seeing that,* Hor.

quătĕr, adv. numer. (quatuor), *four times,* Verg.; ter et quater, *again and again, often,* Hor., Verg.

quăterni -ae -a, num. distrib. (quatuor). *four each ;* quaternae centesimae, *interest at four per cent. monthly,* Cic.

quătĭo, quassi, quassum, **3.** *to shake.* **I.** Lit., **1,** gen., caput, Liv.; alas Verg.; hastam, *to brandish,* Verg.; **2,** esp., **a,** *o convulse ;* risu populum, *make their sides shake with laughing,* Hor.; **b,** *to strike, beat ;* cymbala, Verg.; **c,** *to crash, shatter ;* muros arietibus, Liv.; esp. partic., quassus ; quassae naves, *leaky, shattered,* Liv. **II.** Transf., **a,** *to shake, agitate, trouble;* quod aegritudine quatiatur, Cic.; **b,** *to harass;* oppida bello, Verg.

quătrĭdŭum = quadriduum (q.v.).

quătŭor (quăttŭor), adj. num. (τέσσαρες or τέτταρες), *four,* Cic.

quătŭordĕcim, adj. num. (quatuor and decem), *fourteen;* quatuordecim ordines, or simply quatuordecim, *the fourteen rows of seats reserved in the circus for the equites,* or *knights, at Rome ;* in quatuordecim ordinibus sedere, *to be a knight,* Cic.

quătŭorvĭrātus -ūs, m. (quatuorviri), *the office of the quatuorviri ;* ap. Cic.

quătŭorvĭri -ōrum, m. *a college of four magistrates ;* e.g., in Rome, for the care of the streets ; in municipia and coloniae, the *chief magistrates,* Cic.

-quĕ (Gr. τε) (an enclitic conj. always affixed to a word), *and ;* teque hortor, Cic. ; que . . . que, *both* . . . *and, and* . . . *and ;* quique Romae quique in exercitu erant, Liv.; special uses of que, **a,** *and above all ;* largitiones temeritatisque invitamenta, Liv.; **b,** *and in-deed,* Caes.; **c,** *and accordingly,* Cic.; **d,** *and rather;* non nobis solum nati sumus ortusque nostri partem patria vindicat, Cic.; **e,** *also, moreover;* Trebatioque mandavi, Cic.; **f,** *or,* uxores habent deni duodenique inter se com-munes, Caes.

queis, quis = quibus, v. qui.

quĕmadmŏdum (quem ad mŏdum), *in what manner, how.* **I.** Interrog., quemad-modum est asservatus? Cic. **II.** Rel., **A.** Gen., semper vigilavi et providi, quemadmodum salvi esse possemus, Cic. **B.** Esp., corresponding with sic, ita, item, etc., *as, just as;* quemad-modum socius in societate habet partem, sic heres in hereditate habet partem, Cic.

quĕo, quīvi and quĭi, quĭtum, quire, *to be able, I* (*thou, he,* etc.) *can;* often with the negative non queo, esp. with Cicero, who never uses the 1st pers. nequeo ; non queo reliqua scribere, Cic.

quercētum -i, n. (quercus), *an oak-wood,* Hor.

quercĕus -a-um (quercus), *oaken ;* coronae, *of oakleaves,* Tac.

quercus -ūs, f. **I.** *the oak,* Cic. **II.** Poet., meton., 1, *that which is made of oak;* quercus civilis, *a crown of oak-leaves for saving the life of a citizen in war,* Cic.; 2, *an acorn,* Juv.

quĕrēla (quĕrella) -ae, f. (queror), *a com-plaint.* **I.** *as an expression of pain ;* **a,** *wailing, cry;* maestis implere juga querelis, Ov.; **b,** *a cry* or *plaintive sound of animals,* Verg. **II.** *as an expression of sadness,* complaint, *complaining ;* epistola plena querelarum, Cic.; vestrum bene-ficium nonnullam habet querelam, *gives some occasion of complaint,* Cic.

quĕrĭbundus -a -um (queror), *complaining, plaintive;* vox, Cic.

quĕrĭmōnĭa -ae, f. (queror), *a complaining, complaint ;* de tuis injuriis, Cic.

quĕrĭtor, 1. dep. (intens. of queror), *to com-plain excessively,* Tac.

quernĕus -a -um (for querceneus from quer-cus), *of* or *relating to the oak, oaken;* frondes, Prop.

quernus = querneus (q.v.).

quĕror, questus sum, 3. dep. *to complain, bewail.* **I.** Gen., **a,** of birds, Hor.; **b,** of musical instruments, flebile nescio quid queritur lyra, Ov. **II.** *to lament* or *bewail something;* suum fatum, Caes.; injurias, Cic.; de Milone, Cic.; cum patribus conscriptis, *to have a cause of complaint of, to complain of,* Liv. ; with acc. and infin., se tum exstingui, Cic.; with dat. of pers. and acc. of thing, Oceano furta mariti, Ov.

querquētŭlānus -a -um (querquetum), *of* or *belonging to an oak-wood ;* Querquetulanus mons, *old name of the Caelius mons at Rome,* Tac.

querquētum = quercetum (q.v.).

quĕrŭlus -a -um (queror). **I.** *complaining, plaintive,* cicada, Verg.; vox, Ov. **II.** *com-plaining, querulous ;* senex, Hor.

questus -ūs, m. (queror), *a complaining, complaint, lament ;* **a,** of human beings, qui questus, qui maeror dignus inveniri in tanta calamitate potest, Cic.; **b,** *of the nightingale's song,* Verg.

1. **quī,** quae, quŏd. **I.** Pron. rel., *who, which, what, that.* **A.** Agreement: agrees in gender and number with its antecedent, but for case depends on its own verb, luna eam lucem, quam a sole accipit, mittit in terras, Cic. Pe-culiarities : **a,** qui sometimes has the same noun as the antecedent in its own clause, quas res violentissimas natura genuit, earum moderat-

ionem nos soli habemus, Cic.; **b,** qui takes a subst. as an attribute, ab Romanis cui uni fidebant auxilio, Liv.; often used paren-thetically with esse, spero, quae tua prudentia et temperantia est, te valere, *such is your tem-perance,* Cic.; **c,** with an adj. as attribute, ad suas res revocet, quas aut tulerit acerbas aut timeat, Cic.; **d,** qui often introduces a new sentence, *and this;* res loquitur ipsa; quae semper valet plurimum, Cic. Irregularities : **a,** qui in a different gender from its antecedent, (*a*) with a verb of calling, when it agrees with an attrib. subst. in its own clause, agrum, quae postea sunt Mucia prata appellata, Liv.; (β) quod with neut., referring to the whole previous sentence, Lacedaemonii regem, quod numquam antea apud eos acciderat, necaverunt, Cic.; **b,** when qui is in a different number from its antecedent, (*a*) with a collective noun as ante-cedent, equitatum praemittit qui videant, Cic.; (β) when the rel. sent. is more general than the antecedent clause, si tempus est ullum jure hominis necandi, quae multa sunt, Cic.; **c,** qui is sometimes attracted into the case of its antecedent, illo augurio quo diximus, Cic. **B.** Mood : 1, foll. by the indic. when a simple statement is made, moris qua natură debita est, Cic. ; 2, by the subj, **a,** to express purpose, *that;* eripiunt aliis quod aliis largiantur, Cic.; **b,** to express reason, *as;* recte Socrates exsecrari eum solebat, qui primus utilitatem a natura sejunxisset, Cic.; **c,** with such words as is, talis, eiusmodi, tam and with adj., aptus, idoneus, dignus, ego is sum qui nihil fecerim, *the kind of man to,* etc., Cic. ; and with verbs such as habere, reperire, esse, and in the phrase, nemo est qui, nullus est qui, quotusquisque est qui, etc., qui est qui dicere audeat, Cic.; also after a comparative, Liv. **II.** Pron. interrog., *who? which? what? what manner of? what kind of?* **A.** In direct speech, **a,** adj., qui cantus dulcior inveniri potest? Cic.; **b,** subst., qui primus Ameriam nuntiat, Cic. **B.** In indirect speech, **a,** adj., scribis te velle scire, qui sit reipublicae status, Cic.; **b,** subst., tu te collige, et qui sis considera, Cic. **III.** Pron. indef., qui, quae and qua, quod; **a,** adj., *any, some;* nisi qui deus subvenerit, Cic.; **b,** subst., *any one; si* qui Romae esset demortuus, Cic. (old form, abl. qui with cum, quicum = quocum, Cic.; plur. dat., queis, Verg. ; quis, Sall., Hor.).

2. **qui** (old abl. of qui). **I.** Rel., *where-with, wherefrom ;* in tanta paupertate decessit, ut qui efferretur, vix reliquerit, Nep. ; habeo qui utar, Cic. **II.** Interrog., **A.** In direct questions, *in what manner? how then?* deum nisi sempiternum intelligere qui possumus? Cic. **B.** In indirect questions, Plaut.

quĭă, conj. (old neut. plur. of qui), *because* (used only of a reason that is certain); often with particles, ideo, idcirco, propterea, etc., quia mutari natura non potest, idcirco verae amicitiae sempiternae sunt, Cic.; under the phrases, **a,** quiane, in questions, *is it because?* quiane juvat ante levatos, Verg.; **b,** quianam = cur, *why,* Verg.

quīcumquĕ, quaecumquĕ, quodcumquĕ, *whoever, whichever, whatever.* **I.** Gen., qui-cumque is est, ei, etc., Cic.; quācumque potui ratione, *in every possible way,* Cic.; ut quod-cumque vellet, liceret facere *every thing that he chose,* Nep. ; neut., quodcumque, *however much;* hoc quodcumque est or vides, *the whole,* Verg. **II.** = qualiscumque, *of whatever kind;* quae-cumque mens illa fuit, Gabinii fuit, Cic.; separ-ated, quā re cumque possemus, Cic.

quidam, quaedam, quoddam, and subst., quiddam, *a certain person* or *thing.* **I.** Lit., **a,** quaedam vox, Cic.; quodam tempore, *at a certain* *time;* subst., quidam de collegis nostris, Cic.; neut., quiddam divinum, *something divine,* Cic.; with genit., quiddam mali, Cic.; **b,** quidam or quasi quidam, tamquam quidam, velut quidam, *a kind of, so to speak;* incredibilis quaedam magnitudo ingenii, Cic. **II.** Plur., quidam, quaedam, *some;* quidam dies, Cic.

quidem, conj. *indeed, even.* **I.** To strengthen an assertion, est illum quidem vel maximum animo ipso animum videre, Cic. **II.** Uniting an assertion, *at least, for certain;* non video causam, cur ita sit, hoc quidem tempore, Cic.; ne . . . quidem, *not even,* Caes. **III.** In explanation, *indeed, truly;* doleo ac mirifice quidem, Cic.

quidni? *why not?* Cic.

quies -ētis, f. *rest.* **I.** Gen., *repose, quiet;* 1, lit., mors laborum ac miseriarum quies est, Cic.; quietem capere, *to enjoy,* Caes.; quies ab armis, Liv.; plur., somno et quietibus ceteris, *kinds of rest,* Cic.; 2, meton., *a place of rest,* Lucr. **II.** Esp., **A.** *rest at night, sleep;* 1, lit., a, gen., ire ad quietem, *to go to sleep,* Cic.; datur hora quieti, Verg.; **b,** *the sleep of death;* dura quies, Verg.; 2, meton., a, *dream,* Tac.; **b,** *time of sleep, night,* Verg. **B.** *silence,* Tac. **C.** *keeping quiet;* 1, lit., a, *peace,* Sall.; **b,** *neutrality,* Tac.; **c,** *quiet of the mind,* Ov.; 2, transf., of things, *calm,* Verg.

quiesco -ēvi -ētum, 3. (quies), *to rest, repose.* **I.** Gen., *to rest from work,* etc.; a, of living beings, ipse dux (gruum) revolat, ut ipse quoque quiescat, Cic.; **b,** transf., of things, prato gravia arma quiescunt, Verg. **II.** Esp., **A.** *to rest, to lie down,* Cic. **B.** *to rest* = *to sleep;* a, of the living, cenatus quiescebat, Cic.; **b,** of the dead, *to rest in the grave;* placidā compostus pace quiescit, Verg. **C.** *to keep quiet;* 1, lit., a, *to be silent;* quiescebant voces hominum canumque, Ov.; **b,** *to remain quiet, to do nothing;* esp. in politics, (a) *to be inactive;* quiescere viginti dies, Cic.; (β) *to undertake no war,* etc., *to be at peace;* urbs illa non potest quiescere, Cic.; (γ) *not to mix in politics, to hold aloof, to be neutral;* quiescere in republica, Cic.; 2, transf., of things; a, *to be still, calm;* alta quierunt aequora, Verg.; **b,** of the soil, *to remain fallow;* ager qui multos annos quiescit, Cic. **D.** *to remain free from trouble, to be peaceful, undisturbed;* numquamne quiescit civitas nostra a suppliciis? Liv. **E.** *to rest;* a, *to cease from some action, to leave off doing something,* Hor.; **b,** *to cease to be of any weight;* potentia quiescit, Cic. **F.** *to be quiet in mind,* Ter. (syncop. form, quierunt, quierim, quierint, quiessem, quiesse).

quiete, adv. (quietus), *quietly, peaceably;* vivere, Cic.; apte est quiete ferre aliquid, Cic.

quietus -a -um (quies), *quiet, peaceful.* **I.** Lit., *resting from activity.* **A.** Gen., aër, Verg. **B.** Esp., 1, *resting, sleeping,* Tac.; 2, *resting from tumult, uproar, combat,* etc.; a, *quiet, inactive;* (a) of persons, quieto sedente rege ad Enipeum, Liv.; (β) of places, *free from tumult, quiet, at peace;* quieta Gallia, Caes.; with ab and the abl., a seditione et a bello quietis rebus, Liv.; neut. plur. subst., quieta movere, Sall.; **b,** *neutral, quiet,* Liv.; 3, *keeping aloof from politics, retired, living in peace;* (a) of persons, major cura efficiendi rempublicam gerentibus quam quietis, Cic.; (β) of situations, vita privata et quieta, Cic. **II.** Transf., of character, 1, *quiet, peaceful, mild;* homo quietissimus, Cic.; animus quietus et solutus, Cic.; 2, *deliberate, slow,* in a bad sense (opp. acer); quietus, imbellis, placido animo, Sall.

quilibet, quaelibet, quodlibet and subst., quidlibet, *any you will, any one, anything.* **I.** Gen., quaelibet minima res, *any the least thing,* Cic.; quibuslibet temporibus, *at all times,* Liv.;

subst., quidlibet, *anything and everything,* Hor. **II.** Esp., with a contemptuous meaning, *the first that comes, any;* certo genere, non quolibet, Cic.

quin (for quine, from quî and ne). **I.** In dependent sentence with a preceding negative. **A.** *that not, so that not, without;* numquam tam male est Siculis quin aliquid facete et commode dicant, Cic.; esp., with phrases nemo est, nihil est, quis est, quid est, nemo fuit quin illud viderit, Cic.; non quin ipse dissentiam, *not as if I did not disagree,* Cic. **B.** a, with verbs of hindering, neglecting, etc., to be translated into English by *without* and the present participle, nullum adhuc intermisi diem, quin aliquid ad te litterarum darem, Cic.; nihil abest quin sim miserrimus, Cic.; **b,** after verbs of doubting, ignorance, etc., *that, but that;* non dubitari debet quin fuerint ante Homerum poetae, Cic.; quis ignorat, quin tria Graecorum genera sint? who *does not know that?* Cic. **II.** In principal sentences. **A.** To express encouragement, exhortation, etc., *why not?* quin conscendimus equos, Liv. **B.** To add emphasis, *rather, yea rather;* quin contra si, etc., Liv.; quin etiam, quin immo, Cic.

quinam, quaenam, quodnam, pron. interrog., *who, which, what then?* **I.** In direct questions, sed quinam est ille epilogus, Cic. **II.** In indirect questions, quaesivit quasnam formosas virgines haberet, Cic.

Quinctius (Quintius) -a um, *name of a Roman gens, the most famous members of which were:* 1, L. Quinctius Cincinnatus, *summoned from the plough to be dictator;* 2, T. Quinctius Flamininus, *the conqueror of the Macedonian king Philip.* Adj. = *Quinctian;* gens, Liv. Hence, adj., **Quinctiānus** -a -um, *Quinctian.*

quincunx -cuncis (quinque and uncia), *five-twelfths of a whole.* **I.** Lit., *five-twelfths of an as;* as a coin = *five unciae,* Hor. **II.** Transf., *the form of the five * * spots on dice;* and hence applied to *a plantation in which rows of trees were so planted;* directi in quincuncem ordines, Cic.

quindeciēs, adv. (quinque and decies), *fifteen times,* Cic.

quindecim, num. (quinque and decem), *fifteen,* Caes.

quindecimprimi -ōrum, m. *the fifteen chief senators of a municipium,* Caes.

quindecimvir -i, m. and **quindecimviri** -ōrum and (gen.) -ûm, *a college of fifteen magistrates;* esp., quindecimviri sacris faciundis or quindecimviri sacrorum, or simply quindecimviri, *one of the three great priestly colleges, having the superintendence of the Sibylline books;* separated, quindecim Diana preces virorum curet, Hor.

quindecimvirālis -e, *of or relating to the quindecimviri,* Tac.

quingēni -ae -a, num. distrib. (quingenti), *five hundred each,* Cic.

quingentēsimus -a -um (quingenti), *the five hundredth,* Cic.

quingenti -ae -a, num. (quinque and centum), *five hundred,* Cic.

quingentiēs, adv. (quingenti), *five hundred times,* Cic.

quini -ae -a, num. distrib. (quinque). **I.** *five each,* Cic. **II.** *five,* Liv.

quinidēni -ae -a, num. distrib. *fifteen each,* Liv.

quinivicēni -ae -a, num. distrib. *twenty-five each,* Liv.

quinquāgēni -ae -a, num. distrib. (quinquaginta), *fifty each*, Cic.

quinquāgēsĭmus -a -um, num. (quinquaginta), *the fiftieth*, Cic.; subst., **quinquāgēsima** -ae, f. (sc. pars), *a fiftieth part*, as a tax, Cic.

quinquāgĭēs, adv. *fifty times*, Plin.

quinquāginta, num. (πεντήκοντα), *fifty*, Cic.

quinquātrus -ŭum, f. and **quinquātrĭa** -ĭum, n. *a festival of Minerva;* majores (celebrated from the 19th to the 23rd of March); minores, minusculae (on the 13th of July), Cic.

quinquĕ, num. (πέντε), *five*, Cic.

Quinquĕgentiāni -ōrum, m. *a people in Cyrenaica* (Pentapolitani).

quinquennālis -e (quinquennis). I. *happening every five years, quinquennial;* celebritas ludorum, Cic. II. *lasting for five years;* censura, Liv.

quinquennis -e (quinque and annus). I. *five years old;* vinum, Hor. II. Transf., poet., *celebrated every five years;* Olympias, *the Olympic games*, Ov.

quinquennĭum -ĭi, n. (quinque and annus), *a period of five years;* quinquennii imperium, Cic.; filius quinquennio major, *more than five years old*, Liv.

quinquĕpertītus (quinquĕpartītus) -a -um, *divided into five portions, fivefold*, Cic.

quinquĕprīmi -ōrum, m. *the five chief senators in a municipium*, Cic.

quinquĕrēmis -e (quinque and remus), *having five banks of oars;* navis, Liv.; oftener as subst., **quinquĕrēmis** -is, f. *a ship with five banks of oars*, a quinquereme, Cic.

quinquĕvir -i, m., plur. quinqueviri, *a commission or college of five persons*, e.g., the agrarian commission for distributing the public land, Cic.; for repairing fortifications, Liv.; for helping the tresviri in the night-police, Liv.

quinquĕvīrātus -ūs, m. *the office or dignity of a quinquevir*, Cic.

quinquĭēs, adv. *five times*, Cic.

quinquĭplĭco, 1. *to make fivefold*, Tac.

quintădĕcĭmāni -ōrum, m. *the soldiers of the fifteenth legion*, Tac.

quintānus -a -um (quintus), *of or relating to the fifth*. I. Subst., **quintāna** -ae, f. *a road in a Roman camp which intersected the tents of the legionary soldiers, dividing the fifth maniple and the fifth turma from the sixth*, Liv. II. *belonging to the fifth legion;* subst., **quintāni** -ōrum, m. *soldiers of the fifth legion*, Tac.

Quintīliānus -i, m. *a Roman name, the most celebrated bearer of which was* M. Fabius Quintilianus, *the famous rhetorician, born at Calagurris in Spain, head of a school of rhetoric at Rome, teacher of Pliny the Younger and of Juvenal*.

Quintīlis (Quinctīlis) -is, m. (with or without mensis), *the fifth month* (reckoning from March as the first), *afterwards called Julius, in honour of Julius Caesar*, Cic.

Quintīlius Vārus, *of Cremona, a friend of Horace and Vergil*.

1. **quintus** -a -um (quinque), adv. *the fifth*, Cic.; quintum, quinto, *for the fifth time*, Liv.

2 **Quintus**, fem., **Quinta**, *a common Roman praenomen*, the masc. usually abbreviated Q.

quintusdĕcĭmus -a -um, *the fifteenth*, Liv.

quippĕ, conj. (quia-pe, as nempe from nampe), *certainly, indeed, by all means, to be sure.*

I. Gen., **a te** quidem apte et rotunde (dicta sunt), *quippe* habes enim **a** rhetoribus, Cic.; used with quod, Cic., quum, Cic.; qui, quae, quod (and subj. in Cic.); quippe etiam, quippe et, Verg. II. Esp., ironically, *forsooth;* quippe homini erudito, Cic.

quippīnī (quippĕnī), adv. *why not?* Plaut.

Quĭrīnus -i, m. (from Sabine curis, *a spear, the wielder of the spear, the warlike one*). I. *the name of Romulus after his apotheosis;* populus Quirini, *the Romans*, Hor.; gemini Quirini, *Romulus and Remus*, Juv. II. *Janus*, Suet. III. *Augustus*, Verg. IV. *Antonius*, Prop.; hence, **A. Quĭrīnus** -a -um, *of or relating to Romulus;* collis, *the Quirinal*, Ov. **B. Quĭrīnālis** -e, *relating to Quirinus or Romulus;* trabea, Verg.; collis, *the Quirinal Hill* (now Monte Cavallo), Cic.; sub., **Quĭrīnālia** -ĭum, n. *a festival in honour of Quirinus, celebrated on the 17th of February*, Cic.

1. **Quĭris**, v. Quirites.

2. **quĭris** -is, f. (curis) (a Sabine word), *a spear*, Ov.

quĭrītātĭo -ōnis, f. (quirito), *a shriek, scream, cry of distress*, Liv.

Quĭrītes -ĭum and -um, m. (Cures), *the inhabitants of the Sabine town Cures*, Verg.; after the union of the Romans and Sabines the name Quirites was used of the citizens of Rome considered in their civic character, Romani of them in their political and military character : found in the expressions, Populus Romanus Quiritium, Populus Romanus Quiritesque, Quirites Romani, Liv.; for a general to address his soldiers by the term *Quirites* was equivalent to a discharge, Tac.; jus Quiritium, *full Roman citizenship;* sing., **Quĭris** -itis, m. *a Roman citizen*, Cic.; plur., **Quĭrites**, poet., transf., *of the bees in a hive*, Verg.

quĭrīto, 1. and **quĭrītor** -āri, 1. dep. (Quirites), orig., *to call the Quirites to help;* hence, gen., *to utter a cry of distress, to shriek, scream, cry out;* vox quiritantium, Liv.

1. **quĭs**, quĭd, pron. interrog. I. In direct questions, *who? what?* quis clarior Themistocle? Cic.; quis tu? Cic.; esp., quid, a, subst., *what?* quid tum? *what follows?* Cic.; quid igitur est? *how stands it, then?* Cic.; with genit. = *how much? how many?* quid pictarum tabularum, Cic.; b, adv., (a) to express surprise, quid! *what! how!* quid! eundem nonne destituisti? Cic.; (β) *why? wherefore?* sed quid argumentor? Cic.; quid ita? *why so? how so?* Cic.; quidni? *why not?* Cic. II. In indirect questions. A. Subst., considera quis quem fraudasse dicatur, Cic. B. Adj., rogitat. quis vir esset, Liv.

2. **quĭs**, quĭd, pron. indef., *any one, anybody, anything;* potest quis errare aliquando, Cic.

3. **quis** = quibus, v. qui.

quisnam, quidnam, pron. interrog. *who then? what then?* quisnam igitur tuebitur P. Scipionis memoriam mortui? Cic.; frequently joined with num, num quidnam novi (sc. accidit)? Cic.; sometimes separated with nam placed first or afterwards, quid se nam facturum arbitratus est? Cic.; nam quis te nostras jussit adire domos? Verg.

quispiam, quaepiam, quodpiam and subst., quidpiam or quippiam. I. *any, any one, anything, some one, something;* quaepiam cohors, Caes.; si cuipiam pecuniam ademit, Cic. II. *many a one;* innocens est quispiam, Cic.

quisquam, quaequam, quidquam (quicquam), *any person, anybody, any one, anything;* used chiefly in negative sentences, or in questions ; esne quisquam qui, etc. ? Cic. ; nec quisquam, *and no one,* Cic. ; with genit., vestrûm quisquam, Liv.

quisquĕ, quaequĕ, quidquĕ and adj., quodquĕ, *each, every, every one, everybody, everything ;* often used with the plur. of verbs ; pro se quisque nostrûm debemus, Cic. ; *generally used* with sui, sibi, se, suus ; suo cuique judicio est utendum, *every one must use his own judgment,* Cic. ; suum quisque flagitium aliis objectantes, Tac. ; with comp., quo quisque est sollertior, hoc docet laboriosius, *the more . . . the more,* Cic. ; with superl., doctissimus quisque, *all the most learned,* Cic. ; optimum quidque rarissimum est, Cic. ; so with numerals, quinto quoque anno, *every five years,* Cic. ; esp., primus quisque, (*a*), *the first possible, the very first ;* primo quoque tempore, *on the very first occasion,* Cic. ; (*β*) *one after the other,* Cic.

quisquĭlĭae -ārum, f. (perhaps from quisque, *any sort of thing*), *rubbish, sweepings, refuse, offscourings ;* applied to persons, quisquiliae seditionis Clodianae, Cic.

quisquis, quaequae, quidquid (quicquid), and adj. quodquod. **I.** *whoever, whichever, whatever ;* quisquis ille est, *whoever he may be,* Cic. ; quoquo modo res se habeat, *however the affair may stand,* Cic. ; with genit., (*a*) masc., deorum quisquis amicior Afris, Hor. ; (*β*) neut., deorum quidquid regit terras, *all the gods who,* etc., Cic. ; acc., quidquid, adv., *how much soever ;* quidquid progredior, Liv. ; abl., quoquo, adv., *whithersoever,* Cic. **II.** *any one, anything, any ;* quocumque in loco quisquis est, Cic.

quīvīs, quaevis, quidvis and adj., quodvis, *whoever, whatever you will, any one, anything whatever ;* quivis ut perspicere possit, Cic. ; quodvis genus, Cic. ; quivis unus, *any one you please,* Cic. ; quidvis, *anything whatever, everything ;* quidvis perpeti, *all possible evil,* Cic.

quīvīscumquĕ, quaeviscumquĕ, quodviscumquĕ, *who or whatsoever you will,* Lucr.

quō, adv. (orig. quoi, dat. and abl. of neut. of rel. pron., qui). **I.** Indef., **A.** *any whither ;* si quo erat prodeundum, Cic. **B.** *anyhow,* Liv. **II.** Rel., **A.** 1, lit., *whither ;* ad partem provinciae venturum, quo te velle arbitrarer, Cic. ; eos quo se contulit (= ad quos), Cic. ; with genit., quo terrarum possent, Liv. ; 2, transf., a, *how far, to what extent ;* scire quo amentiae progressi sitis, Liv. ; b, *to what end ;* quo tantam pecuniam, Cic. **B.** Causal, 1, *because, as if ;* non quo ipse audieris, Cic. ; 2, with compar., *to the end that, that the (more),* Cic. ; 3, *wherefore, on which account ;* in causa esse, quo serius, etc., Liv. ; quominus, *that not,* after verbs of hindering, such as impedire, deterrere, recusare, Liv.; stetit per Trebonium quominus, etc., *it was owing to Trebonius that not,* Cic. **C.** *how,* Ov.

quŏăd, adv. **I.** Of space, *how far, as far as ;* videte nunc quoad fecerit iter, Cic. ; quoad possem, Cic. ; quoad possunt ab homine cognosci, *as far as men can know them,* Cic. ; with genit. of the object or limit ; quoad eius facere possum, Cic. **II.** Of time, a, *as long as ;* quoad potui, Cic. ; b, *until, up to the time that ;* (*a*) with indic., quoad senatus dimissus est, Cic. ; (*β*) with subj., quoad te videam, Cic. (quoad one syllable, in Hor.).

quŏcircā, conj. *therefore, on that account* Cic. ; in tmesis, quo, bone, circa, Hor.

quŏcumquĕ, adv. *whithersoever,* Cic.; in tmesis, num eam rationem, quo ea me cumque ducet, sequar ? Cic.

quod, orig. neut. of rel. pron., qui. **I.** Rel. adv., 1, *in which relation, wherein ;* quod

continens memoria sit, Liv. ; 2, *why, on which account ;* esp., est quod, *there is reason for,* etc. ; est magis quod gratuler, Cic. ; *at the beginning of a new sentence, therefore, thereby ;* quod vobis venire in mentem necesse est, Cic. ; with other conjunctions, quod si, *but if,* Cic.; quod utinam, *might it be so,* Cic. ; *so also,* quod ubi, Cic.; quod quum, Caes. **II.** Conj., **A.** 1, *because ;* nocte ambulabat, quod somnium capere non posset, Cic. ; 2, after verbs of rejoicing, praising, blaming, *that, because ;* tibi agam gratias, quod me vivere coegisti, Cic. **B.** 1, bene facis, quod me adjuvas, Cic. ; 2, *as respects that, as to that ;* quod scribis, Cic. ; 3, *although,* Ov.

quŏdammŏdŏ, adv. *in a certain way, in a certain measure,* Cic.

quōlĭbĕt, adv (orig. quoilibet, dat. of quilibet), *whithersoever you please,* Ov.

quōmĭnus, v. quo.

quōmŏdŏ, adv. *in what manner, how.* **I.** Interrog., a, in questions, quomodo ? Cic. ; b, in exclamations, quomodo mortem filii tulit l Cic. **II.** Rel., haec negotia quomodo se habeant ne epistolâ quidem narrare audeo, Cic. ; corresponding with sic or ita, Cic.

quōmŏdŏcumquĕ, adv. *in what way soever howsoever,* Cic.

quōmŏdŏnam, adv. *how then ?* Cic.

quōnam, *whither then, whither pray,* Cic.; quonam haec omnia nisi ad suam perniciem pertinere ? *what end tend they to ?* Caes.

quondam, adv. (= quumdam). **I.** *at a certain time ;* a, *once,* Cic. ; b, *at times,* Cic. **II.** Esp., a, of past time, *once,* Cic. ; b, of the future, *at some future time, sometime,* Verg.

quŏnĭam, conj. (quom = quum and jam), *since, seeing that, whereas, because,* Cic.

quŏquam, adv. *to any place, any whither,* Lucr.

1. **quŏquĕ**, adv. (never at the beginning of a clause, but placed after the word to which it immediately refers), *also,* Cic. ; ne . . . quoque = ne . . . quidem, Liv.

2. **quŏquĕ**, a, from quisque (q.v.); **b,**= et quo, Liv.

quōquō, v. quisquis.

quŏquŏversŭs (**quŏquŏvorsŭs**) and **quŏquŏversum** (**quŏquŏvorsum**), adv *in every direction,* Cic.

quorsum (**quorsŭs**), adv. (= quo versus), *whither, to what place ?* transf., a, quorsum haec pertinent? Cic. ; b, *to what purpose ? with what view ? to what end ?* quorsum igitur haec disputo, Cic.

quŏt, adj. plur. indecl. **I.** *how many ;* a, interrog., *how many ?* quot calamitates? Cic. ; b, rel., quot dies erimus in Tusculano, *as long as I shall be,* etc., Cic. ; in correlation with tot, *as many, so many ;* quot homines, tot causae. Cic. **II.** *all, every ;* quot annis, *yearly,* Cic

quŏtannis, v. quot.

quŏtcumquĕ, *as many as, how many soever,* Cic.

quŏtēni -ae -a (quot), *how many each,* Cic.

quŏtīdĭānus (**cŏtīdĭānus, cottīdĭānus**) -a -um (quotidie). **I.** *every day, daily,* aspectus, Cic. ; exercitatio, Caes. ; vita, Cic.; adv., quotidiano, *daily,* Cic. **II.** Transf., *every-day, common, ordinary ;* verba, Cic. ; vis, Cic.

quŏtīdĭē (**cŏtīdĭē, cottīdĭē**), adv. *daily every day,* Cic.

quŏtīēs (**quŏtīens**), adv. (quot). **I.** Interrog., *how often ?* Cic. **II.** Rel., in correlation, *as often . . . so often ;* toties . . . quoties, Cic. ;

and with toties omitted, quoties mihi potestas erit, non praetermittam, Cic.

quŏtĭescumquĕ, adv. *how often soever*, Cic.

quotquŏt, num. indecl. *however many, as many soever as*, Cic.

quŏtus -a -um (quot), *what in number? of what number? how many?* quotus erit iste denarius qui non sit ferendus? Cic. ; hora quota est? *what o'clock is it?* Hor. ; tu, quotus esse velis, rescribe, *how many guests you would like to be invited with you*, Hor. ; quotusquisque, *how many*, ironically = *how few* ; quotus enim quisque disertus, Cic.

quŏtuscumquĕ -ācumquĕ -umcumquĕ, *whatever in number, how great or how small soever*, Tib.

quŏtusquisque, v. quotus.

quŏusquĕ, adv. *until when, how long, how far ;* quousque tandem abutere, Catilina, patientiā nostrā? Cic. (separated, quo enim usque, Cic.)

quum (cum), conj. (an old acc. neut. from quus = qui). **I.** Of time, **A.** Gen., 1, *when ;* qui non defendit injuriam quum potest, injuste facit, Cic. ; esp. with tunc, tum, num, jam ; quum primum, *as soon as*, Cic. ; with historic present or aorist perf. or imperf., or with the historic infin., Liv., Cic. ; 2, *as often as, whenever ;* quum ad aliquod oppidum venerat, in cubiculum deferebatur, Cic. ; 3, *since ;* multi anni sunt, quum Fabius in aere meo est, Cic. **B.** 1, used in a relative sense after a subst., *when, at which ;* fuit quoddam tempus, quum homines vagabantur, Cic. ; with the subj., fuit quum arbitrarer, Cic. ; 2, used in a causal sense, *when ;* praeclare facis quum puerum diligis, Cic.; quum . . . tum, *when . . . so also, both . . . and*, not only . . . but also; volvendi sunt libri, quum aliorum tum inprimis Catonis, Cic. ; quum maxime, *particularly, above all ;* nunc quum maxime, Cic. **II.** To express cause with subj., **A.** *as ;* quum vita metus plena sit, Cic. **B.** 1, with a mixture of connexion in time and in cause, esp. in narrative, with imperf. and pluperf., *as when ;* Epaminondas quum vicisset Lacedaemonios, quaesivit, Cic. ; 2, *although ;* quum ipse litteram Socrates nullam reliquisset, Cic.

R.

R r, the seventeenth letter of the Latin alphabet, corresponds with the Greek rho ('P, ρ). On account of the aspirate which always accompanies the Greek letter, we find it represented by *rh* in some words derived from that language. The letters *r* and *s* seem to have been interchangeable to a great extent, as in arbor, arbos ; honor, honos ; quaeso for quaero ; hesternus, from heri, etc. ; *r* is also assimilated with *l*, as in the diminutive libellus from liber, in intelligo from inter-lego, etc. For abbreviations in which R. is used, see Table of Abbreviations.

răbĭdē, adv. (rabidus), *madly, savagely, fiercely ;* omnia appetere, Cic.

răbĭdus -a -um (rabies), *raging, mad.* **I.** In a narrow sense, Plin. **II.** In a wider sense, *fierce, raving, savage.* **A.** 1, lit., of animals, canes, Ov. ; leones, Hor. ; 2, transf., of things, personal characteristics, *wild, savage ;* mores, Ov. ; fames, Verg. **B.** Of inspired madness, *raging ;* os, ora, Verg.

răbĭes -ēi, f. (rabio), *madness.* **I.** In a narrow sense, as a disease, Ov.; contacto eo scelere velut injectā rabie ad arma ituros, Liv. **II.** In a wider sense. **A.** *raging, fierceness, fury, rage ;* a, of persons, animi acerbitas quaedam et rabies, Cic. ; ira et rabies Latinorum, Liv. ; b, transf., of things, *fury, rage ;* fatalis temporis, Liv. ; caeli marisque, Verg. **B.** Esp., of the inspired madness of the Sibyl, Verg.

răbĭo, 3. *to be mad*, Varr.

răbĭōsē, adv. (rabiosus), *madly, furiously*, Cic.

răbĭōsŭlus -a -um (dim. of rabiosus), *somewhat raging, furious*, Cic.

răbĭōsus -a -um (rabies), *raging, mad.* **I.** In a narrow sense, of madness as a disease, Plaut. **II.** In a wider sense, *furious, savage ;* canis, Hor.; transf., of things, vide ne fortitudo minime sit rabiosa, Cic.

Răbīrĭus -a -um, *name of a Roman gens*, the most famous members of which were: 1, C. Rabirius Postumus, *accused of treason, and defended by Cicero ;* 2, Rabirius, *a poet, contemporary of Vergil.* Adj., **Răbīrĭānus** -a -um, *relating to Rabirius.*

răbo = arrhabo (q.v.).

răbŭla -ae, m. (rabio), *a bawling advocate, pettifogger*, Cic.

răcēmĭfer -fĕra -fĕrum (racemus and fero). 1, *bearing berries ;* uva, Ov. ; 2, *crowned with grapes ;* capilli, Ov.

răcēmus -i, m. **I.** *the stalk of a cluster of grapes ;* uva lentis racemis, Verg. **II.** Meton., **A.** *a cluster of grapes*, Verg. **B.** *the juice of the grape*, Ov.

Răcĭlĭus -a -um, *name of a Roman gens*, the most famous member of which was L. Racilius, *a tribune of the people in the time of Cicero.* **Răcĭlĭa** -ae, f. *wife of the dictator* L. Q. Cincinnatus.

rădĭātus (radius), *provided with rays, beaming ;* sol, Cic. ; lumina, Ov.

rādīcĭtŭs, adv. (radix), *with the root.* **I.** Lit., Plin. **II.** Fig., *roots and all, utterly ;* extrahere cupiditatem, Cic.

rādīcŭla -ae, f. (dim. of radix), *a little root*, Cic.

rădĭo, 1. and **rădĭor**, 1. dep. (radius, beam), *to gleam, glitter, emit rays* or *beams, radiate ;* argenti radiabant lumine valvae, Ov. ; partic., radians, *gleaming ;* luna, Verg.

rădĭus -ii, m. *a staff, rod.* **I.** Lit., **A.** Gen., acuti atque alius per alium immissi radii, Liv. **B.** Esp., 1, *the spoke of a wheel*, Verg. ; 2, mathem. t. t., *the staff that mathematicians used for drawing figures on the abacus ;* 3, t. t. of weaving, *a shuttle*, Verg. ; 4, t. t. of zoology, a, *the sting of the fish* pastinaca, Plin. ; b, radii, *the spurs of birds*, Plin. ; 5, t. t. of botany, *a kind of long olive*, Verg. **II.** Transf., 1, mathem. t. t., *the radius* or *semi-diameter of a circle*, Cic.; 2, *a ray, beam of light ;* radii solis, Cic.

rādix -īcis, f. (perh. connected with ρίζα), *a root.* **I.** Gen., **A.** 1, lit., *the root of a tree* or *plant ;* cortices et radices, Cic.; arbores ab radicibus subruere, Caes. ; 2, transf., a, *the root* or *lowest part of anything* (of the tongue), Ov. ; of a feather, Ov.; b, *the foot of a mountain ;* in radicibus Caucasi natus, Cic. **B.** Fig., a, *origin, source ;* patientiae, Cic. ; ex iisdem, quibus nos, radicibus natum, *a native of the same place*, Cic. ; b, *firm foundation ;* Pompejus, eo robore vir, iis radicibus, Cic. **II.** Esp., *an edible root ;* a, genus radicis quod appellatur chara, Caes. ; b, *a radish*, Hor.

rādo, rāsi, rāsum, 3. *to scrape, scratch, shave.*
I. *to make smooth by scraping, shaving,* etc.;
lapides palmā, Hor. **II.** *to graze, brush along,*
touch; litora, Verg.; terras, Hor. **III.** *to*
scratch or scrape away, erase; a, nomen fastis,
Tac.; b, *to shave the hair with a razor* (tondere,
to cut it with scissors); caput et supercilia, Cic.;
radere caput, as a sign of slavery, Liv., in pursuance of a vow, Juv.

Raeti (Rhaeti) -ōrum, m. *a people between*
the Danube, the Rhine, and the Lech, north of the
Po. Hence, **A. Raetia** -ae, f. *Raetia, their*
country. **B. Raetĭcus** -a -um, *Raetian.* **C.**
Raetus -a -um, *Raetian.*

rāja -ae, f. *a fish, the ray,* Plin.

rallum -i, n. (rado), *a scraper for cleaning a*
ploughshare, Plin.

rallus -a -um (rad-lus, from rado), *thin, of*
fine texture, Plaut.

rāmāle -is, n. (ramus), usually plur., *twigs,*
branches, brushwood, Ov.

rāmentum -i, n. (for radmentum, from
rado, as caementum from caedo). **I.** *a shaving,*
splinter, chip, Lucr. **II.** Transf., *a bit, morsel;*
aurum cum ramento, *every halfpenny,* Plaut.

rāmĕus -a -um (ramus), *of or relating to*
branches; fragmenta, *brushwood,* Verg.

rāmex -icis, m. **I.** *a rupture,* Plin. **II.**
ramices, *the blood-vessels of the lungs, the lungs,*
Plaut.

Ramnes -ium, m. (from ROM -us, Romulus),
and **Ramnenses** -ium, m. **I.** *one of the*
three tribes into which the early Roman citizens
were divided by Romulus according to their nation-
ality (Ramnes, the Latin stem; Tatian, the
Sabine; Luceres, the Etruscan), *and hence the*
name of one of the three centuries of cavalry in-
stituted by Romulus. **II.** Poet., transf. = *nobles,*
Hor.

rāmōsus -a -um (ramus), *full of boughs,*
branching, branchy. **I.** Lit., arbor, Liv. **II.**
Poet., transf., hydra ramosa natis e caede colubris, *the hydra, from whose trunk, as from a tree,*
grew young serpents, Ov.

rāmŭlus -i, m. (dim. of ramus), *a little*
branch, twig, Cic.

rāmus -i, m. **I.** *a bough, branch, twig.* **A.**
Lit., in quibus non truncus, non rami, non folia,
Cic. **B.** Meton., a, *the fruit growing on a*
bough; rami atque venatus alebat, Verg.; b,
a branch of a stag's antlers, Caes. **II.** Transf., 1,
branch of a mountain range, Plin.; 2, rami, *the*
arms of the Greek letter Y, *regarded by the Pytha-*
goreans as symbolical of the two paths of life;
Samii rami, Pers.

rāna -ae, f. *a frog.* **I.** Lit., Verg.; rana
turpis, *a toad,* Hor. **II.** Transf., rana marina,
a *sea-fish* (Lophius piscatorius, Linn.), Cic.

rancĕo, *to stink,* only in partic., **rancens**
-entis, *stinking, putrid,* Lucr.

rancĭdŭlus -a -um (dim. of rancidus). **I.**
somewhat stinking, putrid, Juv. **II.** Transf.,
loathsome, Pers.

rancĭdus -a -um (ranceo), *stinking, rank.* **I.**
Lit., aper, Hor. **II.** Transf., *disgusting, offensive,*
Juv.

rānuncŭlus -i, m. (dim. of rana). **I.** *a little*
frog, a tadpole, Cic.; in jest, used of the inhabitants of Ulubrae, which was near the Pomptine
Marshes, Cic. **II.** *a plant, perhaps crowfoot,* Plin.

rāpa -ae, f. = rapum (q.v.).

răpācĭda -ae, m. (rapax), *a robber,* Plaut.

răpācĭtas -ātis, f. (rapax), *greediness, ra-*
pacity; quis in rapacitate avarior? Cic.

răpax -ācis (rapio). **I.** *seizing to oneself,*
bearing or snatching away, furious, violent. **A.**
Lit., ventus, Ov.; fluvius, Lucr. **B.** Transf.,
grasping, prone to grasp; nihil est appetentius,
similius sui, nec rapacius quam natura, Cic. **II.**
plundering, greedy of plunder. Subst., *a robber;*
a, of persons, Cic.; b, of animals, lupus, Hor;
c, of abstr. personif., mors, Tib.; Orcus, Hor.

rāphănīnus -a -um (ῥαφάνινος), *of radishes,*
made from radishes, Plin.

rāphănītĭs -idis, f. (ῥαφανῖτις), *a sword-lily,*
Plaut.

rāphănus -i, m. and f. (ῥάφανος), *a radish,*
Cat.

răpĭdē, adv. (rapidus), *hurriedly, quickly,*
rapidly. **I.** Lit., rapide dilapsus fluvius, Cic.
II. Transf., quod quum rapide fertur, Cic.

răpĭdĭtas -ātis, f. (rapidus), *rapid flow,*
rapidity; fluminis, Caes.

răpĭdus -a -um (rapio), *tearing, seizing.* **I.**
a, of living beings, *violent, savage;* ferae, Ov.;
b, of things, *consuming, devouring;* sol, Verg.
II. of motion, *hurried, hasty, quick, rapid;* 1,
a, of living beings, Achates, Verg.; equus, Ov.;
b, of things, amnis, Hor.; torrens, Verg.; 2,
transf., oratio, Cic.

răpīna -ae, f. (rapio). **I.** Lit., *robbery, plun-*
dering, pillage; gen. in plur., Cic. **II.** Meton.,
booty, plunder, Verg.

răpĭo -răpŭi -raptum, 3. (stem RAP, Gk.
ΑΡΠ in ἁρπάζω), *to snatch.* **I.** Gen., **A.** Lit., a,
to snatch to oneself, seize hastily; bipennem
dextrā, Verg.; b, *to drag away hastily;* corpus
consulis, Liv.; c, *to hurry away, lead away with*
haste, hurry off; aliquem hinc, Liv.; manipulos
aliquot in primam aciem secum rapit, Verg.;
reflex., se rapere hinc ocius, *to hasten away,* Hor.;
inde se ad urbem, id est ad caedem optimi cuiusque, Cic.; d, (a) *to conquer hastily, overpower;*
castra urbesque primo impetu, Liv.; (β) *to*
hasten through; densa ferarum tecta, Verg. **B.**
Transf., a, *to snatch, to enjoy or use in haste;*
occasionem de die, Hor.; b, *to accomplish in*
haste, to hasten; viam, Ov.; nuptias, Liv. **II.**
to take or snatch away by force. **A.** Lit., a, *to*
snatch away, carry off; pilam, Cic.; b, *to drag*
away by force, lead away; in jus ad regem, Liv.;
e carcere ad palum et ad necem, Cic.; c, *to*
carry off as plunder, to seize, rob; quantum rapere
potuisset, Cic.; virgines, Cic. Subst., (a) **rapta**
-ae, f. *she that is carried off,* Ov.; (β) **raptum**
-i, n. *that which is carried off, plunder, booty;*
rapto gaudere, Liv.; d, = diripere, *to plunder;*
Armeniam, Tac.; e, *to carry off prematurely,* of
death or disease, improvisa leti vis rapuit gentes,
Hor. **B.** Transf., a, *to seize for oneself;* commoda
ad se, Cic.; b, *to carry off, take away;* almum quae
rapit hora diem, Hor.; c, *to carry away, lead*
astray; ipsae res verba rapiunt, Cic.; rapi in
invidiam, Cic.; d, *to transport, carry away;*
in a bad sense, animus cupidine caecus ad inceptum scelus rapiebat, Sall.; in a good sense,
ad divinarum rerum cognitionem curā omni
studioque rapi, Cic. (archaic fut. perf., rapsit,
ap. Cic.).

raptim, adv. (raptus, from rapio), *violently,*
hastily, quickly, hurriedly; haec scripsi raptim,
Cic.

raptĭo -ōnis f. (rapio), *a carrying off, ab-*
duction, Ter.

rapto, 1. (intens. of rapio). **I.** *to carry away*
in haste, hurry away; huc illuc vexilla, Tac.;
transf., of things, me Parnasi deserta per ardua
raptat amor, Verg. **II.** *to carry off from, drag*
away violently. **A.** Lit., a, conjugem, Cic.;
Hectora circa muros, Verg.; nubila caeli, Lucr.;
b, *to rob, plunder,* Tac. **B.** Fig., a, *to drag along;*

quid raptem in crimina divos, *accuse*, Prop. ; b, *to hurry along with passion*, Plaut.

raptor -ōris, m. (rapio). **A.** Lit., a, *a robber, plunderer*, Tac. ; attrib., lupi raptores, *ravenous*, Verg. ; b, *an abductor, ravisher*, Ov. **B.** Transf., raptores alieni honoris, Ov.

raptus -ūs, m. (rapio). **I.** *a tearing off, rending away*, Ov. **II.** 1, *a carrying off, abduction, rape*, Cic. ; 2, *plundering*, Tac.

rāpŭlum -i, n. (dim. of rapum), *a little turnip*, Hor.

rāpum -i, n. (ῥάπυς), *a turnip*, Liv.

rārē, adv. (rarus), *rarely, seldom*, Plaut.

rārĕfăcĭo -fēci -factum 3. (rarus and facio), *to make thin, rarefy*, Lucr.

rāresco, 3. (rarus). **I.** *to become thin, to lose density*; humor aquai ab aestu, Lucr. ; ubi angusti rarescunt claustra Pelori, *open themselves, expand*, Verg. **II.** Transf., *to become rarer, to diminish, to lessen*; paulatim rarescunt montes, Tac.

rārĭtas -ātis, f. (rarus). **I.** *want of density, thinness, looseness of texture, distance apart*, Cic. **II.** Transf., *fewness, rarity*; dictorum, Cic.

rārō, adv. (rarus), *seldom, rarely*; ita raro, Cic. ; quod si rarius fiet, Cic.

rārus -a -um, *loose in texture, loose, wide apart, thin* (opp. densus). **I.** Lit., retia, Verg. ; cribrum, Ov. **II.** Transf., **A.** a, *scattered, scanty, far apart*; vides habitari in terra raris et angustis in locis, Cic. ; b, milit. t. t., *scattered, wide apart, dispersed* (opp. confertus) ; ipsi ex silvis rari propugnabant, Caes. **B.** 1, gen., a, *few in number, rare*; raris ac prope nullis portibus, Caes. ; in omni arte optimum quidque rarissimum, Cic. ; Oceanus raris navibus aditur, Tac. ; neut. plur. subst., rara (anteponantur) vulgaribus, Cic. ; b, of a man that does something rarely, nec Iliacos coetus nisi rarus adibat, *seldom*, Ov. ; 2, esp., *rare, extraordinary, distinguished in its kind*; rara quidem facie sed rarior arte canendi, Ov.

rāsĭlis -e (rado), *scraped, having a smooth surface, polished*; torno rasile buxum, Verg.

raster -tri, m. and **rastrum** -i, n. (rado), plur., gen. **rastri** -ōrum, m. *an instrument for scraping, a toothed hoe, a rake, a mattock*, Verg.

rătĭo -ōnis, f. (reor), *a reckoning, account, computation, calculation.* **I. A.** Lit., (a) sing., eius pecuniae, cuius ratio in aede Opis confecta est, Cic. ; auri ratio constat, *comes right, is correct*, Cic. ; rationem ducere, *to compute, calculate*, Cic. ; rationem referre, *give in an account*, Cic. ; (β) plur., rationes cum aliquo putare, Cic.; rationes subducere, *to close*, Cic. **B.** Transf., 1, *a roll, register, a list, catalogue, account*; rationem carceris, quae diligentissime conficitur, Cic. ; 2, *a sum, number*, Plaut. ; 3, *a business transaction, matter, affair*; de tota illa ratione atque re Gallicana, Cic. ; haec res non solum ex domestica est ratione, attingit etiam bellicam, Cic. ; fori judiciique rationem Messala suscepit, *public and legal business*, Cic. ; meae (tuae, etc.) rationes, *my* (*thy*, etc.) *interest, advantage*; rationes meas vestrae saluti anteposuissem, Cic. **II.** Fig., **A.** *an account, reckoning, calculation*; rationem habere, *to make a calculation*, Cic. ; semper ita vivamus ut rationem reddendam nobis arbitremur, Cic. **B.** Transf., 1, a, *a relation with, reference to*; rationem habere, aliquid rationis habere cum aliquo, *to have relations with*, Cic. ; quae ratio tibi cum eo intercesserat? Cic. ; b, *respect, consideration, regard for anything*; vel dignitatis vel commodi rationem habere, Cic. ; suam rationem ducere, *to consider his own advantage*, Cic. ; c, *plan, mode*

of procedure, method, manner, fashion, nature kind, way; ita fiet ut tua ista ratio existimetur astuta, Cic. ; scribendi consilium ratioque, Cic. ; meae vitae rationes ab ineunte aetate susceptae, Cic. ; rationes belli gerendi, *principles*, Caes. ; 2, esp., *the faculty of mind which calculates and plans, the reason*; homo rationis particeps, Cic. ; mens et ratio et consilium, Cic. ; consilio et ratione, Cic. ; ratio est, *it seems reasonable*, with infin., Cic. ; hence, a, *reason, motive, ground*; (a) nostra confirmare argumentis ac rationibus, Cic. ; consilii causa ratioque, Cic. ; (β) rhet. t. t., *ground or reason brought forward to support a proposition*, Cic.; b, meton., *reasonableness, propriety, method, order, rule*; modo et ratione omnia facere, *moderately and reasonably*, Cic. ; c, *principle, view, tendency*; florens homo in populari ratione, *the most distinguished representative of the democratic view*, Cic. ; d, *theory, doctrine, system, knowledge*; Epicuri ratio, *philosophical system*, Cic. ; de ratione vivendi, *the art of living*, Cic.; e, meton., *a view, opinion*; quum in eam rationem quisque loqueretur, Cic. ; f, *an adducing of proof, reasoning*; concludatur igitur ratio, Cic.

rătĭŏcĭnātĭo -ōnis, f. (ratiocinor). **I.** *a careful and deliberate consideration and conclusion*, Cic. **II.** *a reasoning, ratiocination, argument, syllogism*, Cic.

rătĭŏcĭnātīvus -a -um (ratiocinor), *argumentative, syllogistic*, Cic.

rătĭŏcĭnātŏr -ōris, m. (ratiocinor), *a calculator, accountant*, Cic.

rătĭŏcĭnor, 1. dep. (ratio), 1, *to compute, calculate*, Cic. ; 2, *to argue, infer, conclude*; inter se, with acc. and infin., Cic.

rătĭōnālis -e (ratio), *reasonable, rational*, Quint.

rătĭōnārĭum -ĭi, n. (ratio), *a statistical account*; imperii, Suet.

rătis -is, f. **I.** *a raft*, Cic., Caes. ; ratibus, quibus junxerat flumen, resolutis, Liv. ; sing., collect.= *a bridge of boats*, Liv. **II.** Poet., transf., *a ship, boat, vessel*, Verg.

rătĭuncŭla -ae, f. (dim. of ratio). **I.** *a little reckoning, account*, Plaut. **II.** Transf. **A.** *a poor, insufficient reason*; huic incredibili sententiae ratiunculas suggerit, Cic. **B.** *a petty syllogism*; concludunt ratiunculas Stoici, Cic.

rătus -a -um, p. adj. (from reor). **I.** *reckoned, calculated*; pro rata parte, or simply pro rata, *according to a fixed proportion, in proportion, proportionally*, Cic. **II.** Transf., *determined, fixed, settled*; a, rati astrorum ordines, Cic ; b, *valid, fixed, legal*; id jussum ratum ac firmum futurum, Cic. ; ratum facere, *to ratify, confirm, make valid*, Cic. ; ratum habere, ducere, *to consider valid*, Cic. ; aliquid mihi ratum est, *I approve*, Cic.

raucĭsŏnus -a -um (raucus and sonus), *hoarse, hoarsely sounding*, Lucr.

raucĭtas -ātis, f. (raucus), *hoarseness*, Plin.

raucus -a -um (for ravicus, connected with ravis), *hoarse*. **I.** Lit. **A.** *hoarse through illness*; fauces, Lucr. **B.** a, *hoarse through shouting*; nos raucos saepe attentissime audiri video, Cic. ; of birds, *screaming*; cornix, Lucr.; palumbes, *cooing*, Verg.; b, of sound, vox ranarum, Ov. **II.** Poet., transf., *hoarse, hollow-sounding, deep or dull-sounding*; cornu, Plaut.; murmur undae, Verg.

Raudĭus -a -um, *Raudian*; Raudius Campus, and Raudii Campi, *a plain in Upper Italy, where Marius defeated the Cimbri.*

raudus (rōdus, rūdus) -ĕris, n. *a rough*

mass or lump; esp., *a piece of brass used as a coin*, Liv.

rauduscŭlum -i, n. (dim. of raudus), *a small sum of money;* transf., *de rausdusculo* Numeriano, *the little debt of Numerius*, Cic.

Raurĭci -ōrum, m. *a Celtic people in Gaul, near modern Basle.*

Răvenna -ae, f. *a town in Gallia Cispadana, near the Adriatic, made a naval station by Augustus*, now *Ravenna*. Hence, **Răvennās** -ātis, m. *belonging to Ravenna.*

răvĭo, 4. (ravis), *to talk oneself hoarse*, Plaut.

răvis -is, f. (connected with raucus), *hoarseness*, Plaut.

răvus -a -um, *grey, greyish*, Hor.

rĕ- prep. insepar., *meaning sometimes back*, as in recurro; sometimes *against*, as in reluctor; sometimes *again*, as restituo (orig. form red, which appears before vowels, e.g., redeo, sometimes lengthened, as redi-vivus).

1. **rĕa**, v. reus.

2. **Rĕa** = Rhea (q.v.).

rĕapsĕ, adv. (re and eapse, i.e., eā and suff. -pse), *indeed, in truth, really*, Cic.

Rĕātĕ, n. (defect., with same form for nom., acc., and abl.), *an old town in the Sabine country*, now *Rieti*. Adj., **Rĕātinus** -a -um, *Reatine;* subst., **Rĕātini** -ōrum, m. *the people of Reate.*

rĕātus -ūs, m. (reus), *the state or condition of an accused person*, Mart.

rĕbellātĭo, = rebellio (q.v.).

rĕbellātrix -īcis, f. (rebello), *renewing war, rising again;* Germania, Ov.

rĕbellĭo -ōnis, f. (rebellis), *a renewal of war by a conquered people;* rebellionem facere, Caes. Plur., Carthaginiensium rebelliones, Cic.

rĕbellis -e (re and bellum), *renewing a war, insurgent;* 1, lit., colonia, Tac.; 2, fig., amor, Ov.

rĕbellĭum = rebellio (q.v.).

rĕbello, 1. *to renew a war;* a, lit., septies rebellare, Liv.; b, poet., transf., *to renew the fight*, Ov.

rĕbīto, 3. *to go back, return*, Plaut.

rĕbŏo, 1. *to echo, resound*, Verg.

rĕcalcĭtro, 1. of a horse, *to kick backwards;* fig., *to deny access*, Hor.

rĕcălĕfăcĭo = recalfacio (q.v.).

rĕcălĕo, 2. *to be warm again;* recalent nostro Tiberina fluenta sanguine, Verg.

rĕcălesco -călŭi, 3. (recaleo), *to become warm again;* quum motu atque exercitatione recalescunt corpora, Cic.; fig., mens recalescit, Ov.

rĕcalfăcĭo (rĕcălĕfăcĭo) -fēci -factum, 3. *to make warm again*, Ov.

rĕcandesco -candŭi, 3. **I.** *to grow white;* recanduit unda, Ov. **II.** Transf., *to become hot, to begin to glow.* **A.** Lit., (tellus) recanduit aestu, Ov. **B.** Fig., recanduit ira, Ov.

rĕcanto, 1. **I.** Intransit., *to resound, echo*, Mart. **II.** Transit., **A.** *to recall, recant;* recantata opprobria, Hor. **B.** *to charm away;* curas, Ov.

rĕcēdo -cessi -cessum, 3. **I.** *to go back, draw back, recede, retreat, retire.* **A.** 1, lit., of persons, ex eo loco, Caes.; non modo e Gallia non discessisse, sed ne a Mutina quidem recessisse, Cic.; 2, transf., of things, a, ut illae undae ad alios accedant, ab aliis autem recedant, Cic.; b, of places, *to retire, stand back;* Anchisae domus recessit, Verg.; c, *to recede in the distance, disappear from the view;* proveh-

imur portu, terraeque urbesque recedunt, Verg. **B.** Fig., 1, of persons, in otia tuta, Hor.; 2, of things, anni recedentes, Hor. **II.** *to go away, depart, go to a distance.* **A.** 1, lit., of living beings, nec vero a stabulis recedunt longius (apes), Verg.; 2, transf., of inanimate things, a, *to separate from;* recedit caput e cervice, Ov.; b, *to vanish, disappear;* in ventos vita or anima exhalata recessit, Verg., Ov. **B.** Fig., 1, of persons, a, *to depart from, abandon;* ab officio, Cic.; b, *to depart from, give up, renounce;* ab armis, *to lay down arms*, Cic.; a vita, Cic.; 2, transf., of things, a, *to depart from, lose;* res ab usitata consuetudine recessit, Cic.; b, *to vanish, disappear, cease;* et pariter Phoebes pariter maris ira recessit, Ov.; c, recedere ab aliquo, *to pass away from, be lost;* quum res (*property*) ab eo quicum contraxisset, recessisset et ad heredem pervenisset, Cic.

rĕcello, 3. *to spring back, fly back, bend back;* quum (ferrea) manus gravi libramento recelleret ad solum, Liv.

rĕcens -entis, *new, fresh, young, recent.* **I.** Adj., **A.** Lit., (α) absol., caespes, Caes.; his recentibus viris, *men of modern times*, Cic. Subst., recentiores, *later authors*, Cic.; recenti re, recenti negotio, *while the business is still fresh*, Cic.; injuriarum memoria, Caes.; (β) with ab and the abl., *fresh from, soon after, a little subsequent to;* Homerus, qui recens ab illorum aetate fuit, Cic.; (γ) with ex and the abl., quum e provincia recens esset, Cic.; (δ) with abl. alone, praeturā, Tac.; with abl. of name of town, Regini quidam eo venerunt, Romā sane recentes, *direct from Rome*, Cic. **B.** Transf., of strength, *fresh, vigorous;* of soldiers, integri et recentes, Caes.; of horses, Liv.; of things, animus (consulis), Liv. (abl. sing., gen. recenti, in poets sometimes recente; genit. plur., gen. recentium, in poets sometimes recentum). **II.** Adv., *lately, recently;* sole recens orto, Verg.; recens ad Regillum lacum accepta clades, Liv.

rĕcensĕo -censŭi -censĭtum and -censum, 2. *to review, muster, examine.* **I.** Lit., milit. t. t., exercitum, legiones, Liv.; polit. t. t., of the censor, equites, Liv. **II.** Transf., **A.** *to go through, pass through;* signa (of the sun), Ov. **B.** Esp., 1, *to go over in thought, review;* fataque fortunasque virûm, Ov.; 2, *to go over in words, recount;* fortia facta, Ov.

rĕcensĭo -ōnis, f. (recenseo), *a reviewing, mustering, enumeration by the censor*, Cic.

rĕcensus -ūs, m. (recenseo) = recensio, *a reviewing, mustering;* equitum recensum habere, *of the censor*, Liv.

rĕceptācŭlum -i, n. (recepto). **I.** *a magazine, reservoir, receptacle;* cibi et potionis (of the stomach), Cic.; cloaca maxima receptaculum omnium purgamentorum urbis, Liv. **II.** Esp., *a place of refuge, shelter, retreat;* militum Catilinae, Cic.; receptaculum esse classibus nostris, Cic.; fugientibus, Liv.

rĕceptĭo -ōnis, f. (recipio), *a receiving, reception*, Plaut.

rĕcepto, 1. (intens. of recipio). **I. A.** *to draw back;* 1, transit., hastam, Verg., 2, reflex., se receptare, *to retire;* Saturni sese quo stella receptet, Verg. **B.** *to receive back*, Lucr. **II.** *to receive frequently;* mercatores, Liv.

rĕceptor -ōris, m. (recipio), *one who receives or harbours, a harbourer;* praedarum, Tac.; transf., ipse ille latronum occultator et receptor locus, Cic.

rĕceptrix -trīcis, f. (receptor), *a receiver* (of stolen goods); furtorum, Cic.

rĕceptus -ūs, m. (recipio). **I.** *a drawing back.* **A.** Lit., spiritus, Quint. **B.** Fig., retractation, recantation; nimis pertinacis sententiae, Liv. **II. A. a,** *a retreat;* non tutissimus a malis consiliis receptus, Liv.; **b,**. esp., *recourse to;* receptus ad Caesaris gratiam atque amicitiam, Caes. **B.** Milit. t. t., *a retreat, falling back;* ut expeditum ad suos receptum habeant, Caes.; Caesar receptui cani jussit, *ordered the signal of retreat,* Caes.; fig., canere receptui a miseriis, Cic.

rĕcessim, adv. (recedo), *backwards,* Plaut.

rĕcessus -ūs, m. (recedo). **I.** *a going back, receding, retreating;* **1,** lit., lunae accessus et recessus, Cic.; (aestuum maritimorum) accessus et recessus, *ebb and flow,* Cic.; recessum primis ultimi non dabant, *chance of retreating,* Caes.; **2,** fig., accessum ad res salutares, a pestiferis recessum, *disinclination for,* Cic.; ut metus recessum quendam animi et fugam efficiat, Cic. **II.** Meton., **1,** lit., **a,** *a hollow, recess,* Verg.; **b,** *a place of retreat, quiet, retired place;* mihi solitudo et recessus provinciae est, Cic.; **2,** fig., in animis hominum tanti sunt recessus, *corners, intricacies,* Cic.

rĕcĭdīvus -a -um (recĭdo), *returning, repeated;* poet., Pergama, *rebuilt,* Verg.

1. rĕcĭdo -cĭdi -cāsūrus, 3. (re and cado). **I.** *to fall back.* **A.** Lit., recidunt omnia in terras, Cic. **B.** Transf., **1, a,** *to relapse, sink;* in graviorem morbum, *to relapse,* Cic.; in eandem fortunam, Cic.; **b,** *to fall to;* cum ad eum potentatus omnis recidisset, Cic.; **c,** *to fall upon, reach;* hunc casum ad ipsos recidere posse, Cic.; esp., *to fall on the head of;* ut amentiae poena in ipsum eiusque familiam recidat, Cic.; **2,** *to come to, fall to, sink to,* Cic.; **3,** *to fall, happen, occur, light upon;* illa omnia ex laetitia ad lacrimas reciderunt, Cic.; ad nihilum, *to come to naught,* Cic. **II.** **1,** *to fall into, to become;* quorsum recidat responsum tuum non magno opere laboro, Cic.; **2,** *to fall within a certain time;* in nostrum annum, Cic.

2. rĕcīdo -cīdi -cīsum, 3. (re and caedo). **I.** *to cut off, cut away;* **1,** caput, Ov.; ceras inanes, Verg.; **2,** transf., *to extirpate;* nationes, Cic. **II.** *to cut away;* **1,** lit., barbam falce, Ov.; **2,** transf., *to cut away, lop off, abbreviate, retrench;* ambitiosa ornamenta, Hor.

rĕcingo -cinxi -cinctum, 3. *to ungird;* tunicas, Ov.; pass. as middle, recingor, *I ungird myself,* Ov.

rĕcĭno, 3. (re and cano), *to resound, echo.* **I.** Intransit., in vocibus nostrorum oratorum recinit quiddam et resonat urbanius, Cic.; parra recinens, *shrieking,* Hor. **II.** Transit., *to cause to resound;* **a,** of echo, cuius recinet jocosa nomen imago, *re-echo,* Hor.; **b,** of a poet, *to praise loudly on the lyre;* curvâ lyrâ Latonam, Hor.

rĕcĭpĭo -cēpi -ceptum, 3. (re and capio). **I.** *to take back.* **A.** *to draw back, fetch back;* **1,** lit., **a,** of things, ensem, *to draw back, draw out,* Verg.; **b,** of pers., aliquem medio ex hoste, Verg.; esp. as milit. t. t., *to draw back, cause to retreat;* milites defessos, Caes.; reflex., se recipere, *to withdraw, retire, retreat, betake oneself to any place;* se ex hisce locis, Cic.; se ad nos, Cic.; esp. as milit. t. t., se hinc, se inde, se ex aliquo loco, se ad or in aliquem locum, se aliquo ad aliquem, Caes.; **2,** transf., **a,** vocem ab acutissimo sono usque ad gravissimum sonum, Cic.; reflex., se recipere, *to turn to, to have recourse to;* se ad bonam frugem, Cic.; se ad reliquam cogitationem belli, Caes.; **b,** business t. t., *to keep back, retain, reserve a portion;* ruta caesa, Cic.; sibi aliquid, Cic.; **c,** *to seize out of the hands of the enemy;* aliquem ex hostibus, Liv. **B.** *to take back, receive again, receive;* **1,** lit., merita, Cic.; arma, Liv.; obsides, Caes.; so *to reduce again by conquest, to recover;* Tarentum, Cic.;

suas res amissas, Liv.; **2,** transf., *to recover;* antiquam frequentiam, Liv.; vitam herbis fortibus, Ov.; animos ex pavore, *to regain courage,* Liv. **II.** *to receive, accept, take to oneself;* **1,** lit., **a,** *to take in to oneself;* ferrum, gladium, *to receive the death-wound,* Cic.; necesse erat ab latere aperto tela recipi, Caes.; of animals, frenum, Hor.; of rivers, Mosa, parte quadam ex Rheno accepta quae, etc., Caes.; **b,** *to receive into a place;* (a) with acc. alone, of persons, Xerxen, Cic.; aliquem libentissimo animo, Caes.; of places, hos tutissimus portus recipiebat, Caes.; (β) with ad and the acc., aliquem ad epulas, Cic.; (γ) with in and the acc., Tarquinium in civitatem, Cic.; (δ) with abl. alone, exercitum tectis ac sedibus suis, Cic.; (ε) with acc. of place, aliquem domum suam, Cic.; (ζ) with supine, senem sessum, Cic.; (η) absol., qui receperant, Caes.; **c,** *to take possession of, conquer;* oppidum, civitatem, Caes.; **d,** *to receive money;* pecuniam ex novis vectigalibus, Cic.; **2,** transf., **a,** *to receive into a certain rank or position;* aliquem in ordinem senatorium, Cic.; aliquem in fidem, Cic.; **b,** *to receive, accept, admit, allow;* fabulas, *to believe,* Cic.; nec inconstantiam virtus recipit, *admits, allows of,* Cic.; **c,** *to accept a task, undertake, take upon oneself;* causam Siculorum, Cic.; officium, Cic.; **d,** hence, *to accept an obligation, guarantee, promise, be responsible for;* pro Cassio et te, si quid me velitis recipere, recipiam, Cic.; ea quae tibi promitto ac recipio, Cic.; partic. subst., **rĕceptum** -i, n. *an engagement, guarantee;* **e,** legal t. t., of the praetor, recipere nomen, *to entertain, receive an accusation against any one,* Cic.

rĕcĭprŏcātĭo -ōnis, f. (reciproco), *a returning by the same path,* Plin.

rĕcĭprŏco, 1. (reciprocus). **I.** Transit., *to move backwards, to move backwards and forwards;* animam, *to draw in and breathe out the air, to breathe,* Liv.; quinqueremem in adversum aestum reciprocari non posse, *turned round and moved back,* Liv.; esp. of the ebb tide, in motu reciprocando, *on the ebb,* Cic.; fig., si quidem ista reciprocantur, *if the proposition is converted or reversed,* Cic. **II.** Intransit., *to move backwards and forwards;* fretum Euripi non septies die temporibus statis reciprocat, *ebbs and flows,* Liv.

rĕcĭprŏcus -a -um, *returning, going back in the same path.* **I.** Lit., mare, *ebbing,* Tac.; vox, *echoing,* Plin. **II.** Fig., ars, *alternating,* Plin.

rĕcīsāmentum -i. n. (recīdo), *a chip, shaving,* Plin.

rĕcīsĭo -ōnis, f. (recīdo), *a cutting off,* Plin.

rĕcīsus -a -um, partic. of recīdo.

rĕcĭtātĭo -ōnis, f. (recito), *a reading aloud;* **a,** of documents in legal proceedings, Cic.; **b,** of literary works, Plin.

rĕcĭtātor -ōris, m. (recito), *a reader aloud;* **a,** of documents in legal proceedings, Cic.; **b,** of literary works, *a reciter,* Hor.

rĕcĭto, 1. *to read, read aloud, read publicly;* **a,** legal t. t., (a) *to read a document;* litteras in senatu, in contione, Cic.; aliquid ex codice, Cic.; (β) *to read out the name of a person;* testamento heredem aliquem, Cic.; aliquem praeterire in recitando senatu, *in reading the list of senators,* Cic.; (γ) *to read the words of an oath, to dictate,* Tac.; **b,** *to read* or *recite one's literary works before friends,* Hor.

rĕclāmātĭo -ōnis, f. (reclamo), *a crying out against, loud disapprobation,* Cic.

rĕclāmĭto, 1. (intens. of reclamo), *to cry out against loudly, violently contradict,* Cic.

rĕclāmo, 1. *to cry out against, shout in disapprobation, contradict loudly.* **I. A.** Lit., (a)

absol , Cic. ; (β) with dat. of pers., alicui, Cic. ;
of things, orationi, Cic. ; alicuius promissis,
Cic. ; (γ) with ne and the subj., unā voce omnes
judices, ne is juraret, reclamasse, Cic. **B.** Fig.,
quoniam ratio reclamat vera, Lucr. **II.** Poet.,
transf., *to reverberate, re-echo, resound ;* with dat.,
scopulis reclamant aequora, Verg.

rĕclīnis -e (reclino), *leaning backwards,*
bent backwards, reclining, Ov.

rĕclīno, 1. (re and * clino), *to bend back,*
cause to lean back. **I.** Lit., se, Caes. ; scuta,
Verg. ; **rĕclīnātus** -a -um, *bent back, reclined,*
Caes. **II.** Transf., nullum ab labore me reclinat
otium, *releases me from labour,* Hor.

rĕclūdo -clūsi -clūsum, 3. (re and claudo),
to unclose, to open. **I. A.** Lit., portas hosti,
Ov. **B.** Transf., 1, *to bring to light, to disclose,*
reveal ; viam, Ov. ; tellurem unco dente, *to*
turn over, cultivate, Verg. ; ensem, *to draw from*
the scabbard, Verg. ; 2, *to open with a weapon*
= *to pierce ;* pectus mucrone, Verg. **II.** Fig.,
ebrietas operta recludit, *reveals,* Hor. ; fata, *to*
relax, Hor.

rĕcōgĭto, 1. *to think over again, consider,*
deliberate upon ; de re, Cic.

rĕcognĭtĭo -ōnis, f. (recognosco). **I.** *re-*
collection ; scelerum suorum, Cic. **II.** *investi-*
gation, inspection, examining ; agri Campani, Liv.

rĕcognosco -nōvi -nĭtum, 3. **I. A.** *to re-*
cognise, to know again ; res, *as one's property,*
Liv.; illa reminiscendo, Cic. **B.** *to recall, to go*
over again ; recognosce mecum noctem illam,
Cic. **II. a,** *to inspect, examine, investigate ;*
agros, Liv. ; **b,** *to examine critically, to revise,*
authenticate, certify ; decretum populi, Cic. ;
codicem, Cic.

rĕcollĭgo -lēgi -lectum, 3. *to collect again,*
gather together again ; fig., se, *to regain courage,*
Ov.; primos annos, *to become young again,* Ov. ;
animum alicuius, *to reconcile,* Cic.

rĕcŏlo -cŏlŭi -cultum, 3. *to cultivate again.*
I. Lit., desertam terram, Liv. **II.** Fig., **A.**
Gen., 1, *to practise again, resume ;* artes, Cic. ;
studia, Cic. ; 2, *to set up again, renew, repair ;*
imagines subversas, Tac. ; dignitatem, Cic. ; 3,
to honour again ; aliquem sacerdotiis, Tac. **B.**
Esp., 1, *to reflect upon again ;* inclusas animas
lustrabat studio recolens, Verg. ; 2, *to recollect,*
think over again ; quae si tecum ipse recolis,
Cic. ; 3, *to call to mind, remember again,* Ov.

rĕcommĭniscor, 3. dep. *to recollect,* Plaut.

rĕcompōno (-pŏsŭi) -pŏsĭtum, 3. *to re-*
adjust, re-arrange ; comas, Ov.

rĕconcĭlĭātĭo -ōnis, f. (reconcilio). **I.** *a*
restoration, re-establishment ; concordiae, Cic.
II. *reconciliation ;* irridebatur haec illius reconciliatio, Cic.

rĕconcĭlĭātor -ōris, m. (reconcilio), *a re-*
storer, re-establisher ; pacis, Liv.

rĕconcĭlĭo, 1. **I. A.** *to make good again,*
restore, repair ; diuturni laboris detrimentum
sollertiā et virtute militum brevi reconciliatur,
Caes. **B.** *to re-unite, bring together again ;* **a,**
inimicos in gratiam, Cic.; **b,** *to appease, to recon-*
cile ; aliquem alicui, Cic **II.** *to restore, re-*
establish ; existimationem judiciorum, Cic.

rĕconcinno, 1. *to restore, renovate, repair ;*
tribus locis aedifico, reliqua reconcinno, Cic.

rĕcondĭtus -a -um, p. adj. (from recondo),
far removed, secret, concealed. **I.** Lit., locus,
Cic.; neut. plur., occulta et recondita templi,
secret recesses, Caes. **II.** Fig., **a,** *abstruse, pro-*
found ; reconditae abstrusaeque res, Cic. ; **b,** of
character, *reserved, mysterious ;* naturā tristi ac
reconditā fuit, Cic.

rĕcondo -dĭdi -dĭtum, 3. **I.** *to lay back, put*
back ; gladium in vaginam, Cic. ; poet., oculos,
to close again, Ov. **II.** *to lay aside.* **A.** Gen.,
1, lit., a, tamquam in vagina reconditum, Cic. ;
b, of provisions, treasure, etc., *to lay up in*
store, keep ; prome reconditum Caecubum, Hor.;
recondita alia (medicamenta), Liv. ; 2, fig.,
mens alia recondit, e quibus memoria oritur, *lays*
up in store, Cic. **B.** *to conceal, hide ;* 1, lit., a,
quod celari opus erat habebant sepositum ac
reconditum, Cic. ; Ascanium curvā valle, Verg. ;
b, *to thrust,* etc. ; ensem in pulmone, Verg. ; c,
to devour ; volucres avidā alvo, Verg. ; 2, fig.,
to conceal ; voluptates, Tac.

rĕcondūco -duxi -ductum, 3. *to bargain,*
contract for again, Plin.

rĕconflo, 1. *to rekindle,* Lucr.

rĕcŏquo -coxi -coctum, 3. **I.** *to boil again ;*
Peliam (*in order to make young again*), Cic. **II.**
to melt, smelt, forge again. **A.** Lit., enses, Verg.
B. Fig., recoctus scriba ex quinqueviro, *new-*
moulded, Hor.

rĕcordātĭo -ōnis, f. (recordor), *a recollection,*
remembrance ; ultimi temporis recordatio, Cic. ;
plur., recordationes fugio, Cic.

rĕcordor, 1. dep. (re and cor). **I.** *to re-*
member, recollect ; (a) with genit., flagitiorum
suorum, Cic.;(β) with acc., majorum diligentiam,
Cic.; (γ) with acc. and infin., hoc genus poenae
saepe in improbos cives esse usurpatum, Cic.;
(δ) with rel. sent., non recordor, unde ceciderim, Cic. ; (ε) with de and the abl., de ceteris,
Cic. ; (ζ) absol., si recordari volumus, Cic. **II.**
to think of something in the future, to ponder over ;
quae sum passura recordor, Ov.

rĕcrastĭno, 1. (re and crastinus), *to put off*
from day to day, Plin.

rĕcrĕātĭo -ōnis, f. (recreo), *a restoration, a*
recovery, Plin.

rĕcrēmentum -i, n. (cerno), *dross, slag,*
refuse, Plin.

rĕcrĕo, 1. **I.** *to create again,* Lucr. **II.** *to*
restore to a sound condition, to refresh, invigorate,
revive ; reflex., se recreare and middle, recreari,
to revive, to recover, to be refreshed ; **a,** physically,
voculae recreandae causā, Cic. ; recreari ex
vulnere, Cic.; ex vulneribus, Liv.; **b,** politically,
provinciam afflictam et perditam erigere atque
recreare, Cic. ; middle, civitas recreatur, Cic. ;
c, mentally, afflictos animos, Cic.; recreare se ex
magno timore, *to recover from,* Cic.

rĕcrĕpo, 1. *to echo, resound,* Cat.

rĕcresco -crēvi -crētum, 3. *to grow again,*
Liv.

rĕcrūdesco -crūdŭi, 3. *to become raw again.*
I. Of wounds, *to open afresh ;* quae consanuisse
videbantur, recrudescunt, Cic. **II.** Fig., tc
break out again ; recrudescente Manlianā seditione, Liv.

rectā, adv. (sc. viā), *straightway, straight-*
forward, right on, directly, Cic.

rectē, adv. (rectus). **I.** *in a straight line,*
in a straight (horizontal) direction ; recte ferri,
Cic. **II.** Fig., *rightly, properly, well, duly, suit-*
ably. **A. a,** of conduct, behaviour, recte atque
ordine facere, judicare, Cic. ; recte et vere respondere, Cic.; **b,** of condition, *well ;* apud
matrem recte est, *it is all right with,* Cic.; **c,** of
consequence, *well, favourably, safely ;* se alicui
recte committere, Caes. ; quicum quidvis reet-
issime facere posset, Cic.; recte vendere, *at a*
high price, Cic. **B.** Of degree, recte ambulare,
Cic.

rectĭo -ōnis, f. (rego), *a ruling, governing ;*
rerum publicarum, Cic.

rector -ōris, m. (rego), *a ruler, governor, director, guide, leader.* **I.** Lit., navis, *steersman,* Cic. **II.** Fig., rector et gubernator civitatis, Cic.; of deities, *ruler;* Olympi, or superûm, or deûm, *Jupiter,* Ov.; maris, *Neptune,* Ov.

rectrix -īcis, f. (rector), *she that leads or guides,* Plin.

rectus -a -um, p. adj. (from rego), *straight* (whether horizontally or vertically), *upright.* **I.** 1, lit., a, *in a horizontal direction, straight;* recto itinere ad Iberum contendere, Caes.; rectus cursus hinc ad Africam, Liv.; recti oculi, *straight, steadfast look,* Cic.; b, of vertical direction, *upright;* ita jacēre talum, ut rectus assistat, Cic.; 2, transf., grammat. t. t., casus rectus, the nom. (opp. casus obliquus), Quint. **II.** Fig., *right, correct, proper, suitable, due;* a, physically and intellectually, (α) rectum et justum proelium, Liv.; (β) *simple, natural, plain, straightforward;* commentarii Caesaris, Cic.; (γ) *right, free from mistakes;* quae sint in artibus ac rationibus recta ac prava, Cic.; neut. subst., rectum pravumque, Cic.; b, morally, (α) *straightforward, honest, upright;* consilia recta, Liv.; conscientia recta, Cic.; praetor populi Romani rectissimus, Cic.; (β) *right, virtuous, dutiful;* in neut. subst., *right, virtue, good;* neque quidquam nisi honestum et rectum alter ab altero postulabit, Cic.; rectum est, *it is right,* with acc. and infin., Cic.

rĕcŭbĭtus -ūs, m. (recumbo), *a falling down,* Plin.

rĕcŭbo, 1. *to lie back, to lie on the back, recline;* in hortulis suis, Cic.

rĕcumbo -cŭbŭi, 3. *to lie backwards, recline.* **I.** Of persons. **A.** Gen., in cubiculo, Cic.; in herba, Cic. **B.** Esp., *to recline at table;* in triclinio, Cic. **II.** Transf., of inanimate things, *to sink down, fall down;* cervix in humeros, Verg.

rĕcŭpĕrātĭo -ōnis, f. (recupero), *a recovery;* libertatis, Cic.

rĕcŭpĕrātor -ōris, m. (recupero). **I.** *a recoverer;* urbis, Tac. **II.** Esp., recuperatores, *a college of three or five magistrates appointed by the praetor to decide causes which required speedy settlement,* Cic.

rĕcŭpĕrātōrĭus -a -um (recuperator), *of or relating to the recuperatores;* judicium, Cic.

rĕcŭpĕro, 1. (recipio), *to get again, regain, recover.* **I.** Lit., a, of things, villam suam ab aliquo, Cic.; urbem, Liv.; amissa, Caes.; rempublicam, *supremacy in the state,* Cic.; b, of persons, obsides, Caes., Cic.; si vos et me ipsum recuperaro, Cic. **II.** Transf., *to win again, recover again (a person's favour);* voluntatem alicuius, Cic.

rĕcūro, 1. *to restore, refresh,* Cat.

rĕcurro -curri -cursum, 3. *to run back, hasten back.* **I.** a, lit., of persons, ad aliquem, Cic.; ad redam, Cic.; in Tusculanum, Cic.; rure, Hor.; b, transf., of things, luna tum crescendo, tum defectionibus in initia recurrendo, Cic.; bruma recurrit iners, Hor.; esp., of the course of the sun and the year, *to roll round;* sol recurrens, Verg.; (α) *to run in a circle;* naturam expellas furcâ, tamen usque recurret, Hor. **B.** *to come back to, return to;* ad easdem deditionis conditiones, Caes.

rĕcurso, 1. (intens. of recurro), *to run back, hasten back, return.* **I.** Lit., Lucr. **II.** Fig., cura recursat, Verg.

rĕcursus -ūs, m. (recurro), *a return, coming back, retreat;* a, of persons, Liv.; b, of water, etc., Ov.

rĕcurvo, 1. (recurvus), *to bend or curve back-*

wards; colla equi, Ov.; aquas in caput, *mʌki to flow back,* Ov.; undae recurvatae, *winding,* Ov.

rĕcurvus -a -um, *bent or curved backwards;* cornu, Verg.; tectum, *labyrinth,* Ov.; aera, *hooks,* Ov.; nexus hederae, *winding,* Ov.

rĕcūsātĭo -ōnis, f. (recuso). **I.** *a refusal,* Cic.; adimere alicui omnem recusationem, *possibility of refusing,* Cic. **II.** Legal t. t., *a protest,* Cic.

rĕcūso, 1. (re and causa), *to refuse, decline, reject, be unwilling to do.* **I.** Gen., (α) with acc.; laborem, Caes.; molestias non recusare, Cic.; with double acc., populum Romanum disceptatorem, Cic.; transf., of things, genua cursum recusant, Verg.; (β) with infin., gen. with preceding negative, non recusare mori, Caes.; (γ) with ne and the subj., sententiam ne diceret recusavit, Cic.; (δ) when a negative precedes, with quin or quominus and the subj., non possumus quin alii a nobis dissentiant recusare, Cic.; non recusabo quominus omnes mea legant, Cic.; (ε) with de and the abl., de judiciis transferendis, Cic.; (ζ) absol., non recuso, non abnuo, Cic. **II.** Esp., legal t. t., *to object, take exception, plead in defence;* quoniam satis recusavi, Cic.

rĕcussus -ū, m. (recutio), *a striking back, rebound, recoil,* Plin.

rĕcūtĭo -cussi -cussum, 3. (re and quatio), *to strike back, cause to rebound,* Verg.

rĕcūtītus -a -um (re and cutis). **I.** *circumcised;* Judaei, Mart. **II.** *smooth-shorn,* Mart.

rēda (rhēda) and **raeda** -ae, f. (a Gallic word), *a travelling carriage with four wheels;* vehi in reda, Cic.

rĕdambŭlo, 1. *to walk back,* Plaut.

rĕdămo, 1. *to love again, return love for love,* Cic.

rĕdardesco, 3. *to break out again* (into flames), Ov.

rĕdargŭo -gŭi -gūtum, 3. *to confute, refute, disprove, contradict;* a, of persons, redargue me, si mentior, Cic.; b, of things as objects, referre et redarguere mendacium alicuius, Cic.; with things as subjects, improborum prosperitates redarguunt vires deorum, Cic.

rēdārius -ĭi, m. (reda), *the driver of a reda, coachman,* Cic.

rĕdauspĭco, 1. *to take fresh auspices;* jestingly = *to return,* Plaut.

reddĭtĭo -ōnis, f. (reddo), *the consequent clause of a sentence, apodosis,* Quint.

reddo -dĭdi -dĭtum, 3. **I.** *to give back, restore;* 1, *to restore (the same object);* (α) of concr. obj., obsides, captivos, Caes.; equos, Cic.; alicui pecuniam, Cic.; reflex., se reddere convivio, *to return to,* Liv.; se terris, Verg.; so pass., reddi as middle, reddar tenebris, *I shall return to,* Verg.; (β) of abstr. obj., alicui patriam, Liv.; 2, *to give back something as an equivalent, to give back, requite, repay;* a, gen., (α) of concr. obj., oscula, Ov.; (β) of abstr. obj., beneficium, Cic.; pro vita hominis hominis vitam, Caes.; b, esp., (α) *to give back in another language* = *to translate, render, interpret;* quum ea quae legeram Graece, Latine redderem, Cic.; (β) *to give back in utterances, to imitate;* verba bene (of a parrot), Ov.; *to answer,* veras audire et reddere voces, Verg.; 3, *to represent, imitate, reflect, resemble;* qui te nomine reddet Sylvius Aeneas, Verg.; 4, *to make, render, cause to be,* with double acc. aliquid or aliquem, foll. by an adj., aliquem iratum, Cic.; itinera infesta, Caes.; with a subst., aliquem avem, Ov. **II.** *to give forth from oneself, to give out;* 1, *to give what is due or asked for* or *settled;* a, suum cuique, Cic.;

honorem, Cic.; caute vota, *to fulfil*, Cic.; rationem alicui, *to render an account*, Cic.; so also (α) of the dying, eum spiritum, quem naturae debeo, patriae reddere, Cic.; vitam naturae, Cic.; (β) of persons sacrificing, *to offer*; liba deae, Ov.; (γ) of persons writing or speaking, *to communicate;* sed perge, Pomponi, de Caesare et redde quae restant, Cic.; **b,** (a) *to give, bestow, grant;* responsa, Verg.; peccatis veniam, Hor.; legal t. t., reddere judicium, *to grant* or *appoint a judicial inquiry;* in aliquem, Caes.; reddere jus, *to administer justice, pronounce sentence;* alicui petenti, Caes.; (β) *to grant, allow, leave;* Thermitanis urbem, agros legesque suas, Cic.; **2,** *to give forth from the body;* **a,** *to give out, give forth* (animam) a pulmonibus, Cic.; sonum, *to sing* or *play*, Hor.; **b,** *to repeat, recite, narrate;* ea sine scripto verbis iisdem, Cic.; carmina, Hor.

rĕdemptĭo -ōnis, f. (redimo). **I.** *a buying up;* **a,** *bribing;* judicii, *a corrupting by bribery*, Cic.; **b,** *a farming of taxes*, Cic. **II.** *ransoming, redemption;* captivorum, Liv.

rĕdempto, 1. (freq. of redimo), *to ransom, redeem;* captivos, Tac.

rĕdemptor -ōris, m. (redimo), *a buyer, contractor, farmer* (of taxes), Cic.; frumenti, Liv.

rĕdemptūra -ae, f. (redimo), *a contracting, farming* (of taxes, etc.); redempturis auxisse patrimonia, Liv.

rĕdĕo -ĭi (-īvi) -ĭtum, 4. *to go back, come back, return.* **I. A.** Lit., **a,** of persons, e provincia, Cic.; a Caesare, Cic.; Romam, Cic.; domum, Caes.; in proelium, Liv.; ad suos, Caes.; with predic. nom., victor ex hac pugna redit, Liv.; with l. sup., spectatum e senatu, Cic.; **b,** of things as subjects, redeunt humerique manusque, Ov.; of water, flumen in eandem partem, ex qua venerat, redit, Caes.; of the stars, day and night, etc., quum ad idem, unde profecta sunt, astra redierint, Cic.; of places, collis paulatim ad planitiem redibat, *sloped down to*, Caes.; poet., of plants, redeunt jam gramina campis, Cic.; of physical qualities, forma prior rediit, Ov. **B.** Transf., 1, gen., **a,** of persons, in pristinum statum, Caes.; cum aliquo in gratiam, *to be reconciled with*, Cic.; redire ad se, *to return to one's senses*, physically, Liv., and mentally, Cic.; redire ad se atque ad mores suos, Cic.; ad sanitatem, Cic.; Caesar ad duas legiones redierat, *was reduced to*, Caes.; **b,** of things, res redit, *the matter comes up again*, Cic.; 2, esp., of discourse, *to return to the previous subject;* sed de hoc alias, nunc redeo ad augurem, Cic. **II. A.** Of revenue, income, *to come in;* pecunia publica, quae ex metallis redibat, Nep. **B.** *to come to, be brought to, fall to;* **a,** pilis omissis, ad gladios redierunt, *they betook themselves to their swords*, Caes.; **b,** of things, bona in tabulas publicas redierunt, *have been registered in*, Cic.; summa imperii, summa rerum redit ad aliquem, Caes.; mortuo Tullo res (*government of the state*) ad patres redierat, Liv.

rĕdhālo, 1. *to breathe out again*, Lucr.

rĕdhĭbĕo -ŭi -ĭtum, 2. (re and habeo). **I.** *to give back, return*, Plaut. **II.** In business, *to give back, return a damaged article;* mancipium, Cic.

rĕdĭgo -ēgi -actum, 3. (re and ago). **I.** *to drive back, bring back, lead back.* **A.** Lit., hostium equitatum in castra. **B.** Fig., rem in pristinam belli rationem, Caes.; in memoriam alicuius, *to a person's recollection* (foll. by acc. and infin.), Cic. **II.** *to bring* or *carry to.* **A.** Lit., *to draw in, call in, collect;* quantam (pecuniam) ex bonis patriis redegisset, Cic.; omnem pecuniam Idibus, Hor.; magnam pecuniam in aerarium, Liv.; esp., aliquid in publicum redigere, *to deliver into the public treasury, to confiscate*, Liv., or simply redigere; Heraclii bona verbo redigere, re dis-

sipare, Cic. **B.** Fig., **a,** *to bring* or *reduce to a state* or *condition;* *to make, render such;* Aeduos in servitutem, Caes.; civitatem in ditionem potestatemque populi Romani, Cic.; ad certum, *to make certain*, Liv.; victoriam ad vanum et irritum, *make fruitless*, Liv.; aliquem or aliquid eo ut, etc., *to bring to such a point that*, etc., Liv.; with double acc., quae facilia ex difficillimis animi magnitudo redegerat, *had made difficulties easy*, Caes.; in ordinem redigere, *reduce to order*, Liv.; **b,** *to reduce in compass, number, value*, etc.; *to lessen, bring down;* ex hominum millibus LX. vix ad D., Caes.; nobilissima familia jam ad paucos redacta, Cic.; vilem ad assem redigi, Cic.

rĕdĭmĭcŭlum -i, n. (redimio), *a lappet* or *fillet, frontlet, necklace*, Cic.

rĕdĭmĭo -ĭi -ĭtum, 4. *to bind round, tie round, wreathe round, crown;* sertis redimiri et rosâ, Cic.; tempora vittâ, Verg.; partic. perf., **rĕdĭmītus** -a -um, silvis redimita loca, Cat. (syncop. imperf., redimibat, Verg.).

rĕdĭmo -ēmi -emptum (-emtum), 3. (re and emo). **I.** *to buy back;* domum, Cic.; fundum, Cic. **II.** *to buy;* **A.** Gen., 1, lit., necessaria ad cultum, Liv.; vitam alicuius pretio, Cic.; 2, transf., *to buy,* i.e., *to procure, obtain for a price;* pacem parte fructuum, Cic.; pacem obsidibus, Caes. **B.** Esp., polit. and legal t. t., 1, *to farm, hire;* vectigalia, Caes.; picarias, Cic.; 2, *to contract for;* opus, Cic. **III.** *to ransom.* **A.** *to set free by payment of money;* 1, lit., captivos e servitute, Cic.; 2, transf., *to set free, deliver;* se pecuniâ a judicibus, Cic.; se a Gallis auro, Liv. **B.** *to buy off, avert, remove;* acerbitatem a republica, Cic.; litem, *to compromise*, Cic.

rĕdintĕgro, 1. *to restore, renew, repair;* **a,** of persons, deminutas copias, Caes.; proelium, Caes.; memoriam auditoris, Cic.; spem, Caes.; pacem, Liv.; **b,** of things as subjects, redintegravit luctum in castris consulum adventus, Liv.

rĕdĭpiscor, 3. dep. (re and apiscor), *to get, obtain again*, Plaut.

rĕdĭtĭo -ōnis, f. (redeo), *a going back, coming back, returning, return;* celeritas reditionis, Cic.

rĕdĭtus -ūs, m. (redeo). **I.** *a coming back, going back, return.* **A.** Lit., **a,** of persons, domum, Cic.; in urbem, Cic.; ad aliquem, Cic.; est hominibus reditus in curiam, *may return to*, Cic.; intercludere alicuius reditum, Cic.; plur., sanguine quaerendi reditus, Verg.; **b,** transf., of the stars, Cic. **B.** Fig., ad rem, ad propositum, Cic.; reditus in gratiam, *reconciliation*, Cic. **II.** *returns, income, revenue;* sing., Nep.; plur., reditus metallorum, Liv.

rĕdīvia = reduvia (q.v.).

rĕdīvīvus -a -um (redi = re and vivus), *renewed, renovated;* applied to old building materials used a second time; lapis, Cic.; subst., **rĕdīvīvum** -i, n. and **rĕdīvīva** -ōrum, n. *old building materials used again*, Cic.

rĕdŏlĕo -ŭi, 2. *to emit an odour, diffuse an odour.* **I.** Lit., redolent murrae, Ov.; with abl., redolere thymo, *smell of thyme*, Verg.; with acc., vinum, *to smell of wine*, Cic. **II.** Fig., ita domus ipsa fumabat, ut multa eius sermonis indicia redolerent, Cic.; mihi quidem ex illius orationibus redolere ipsae Athenae videntur, Cic.; with acc., doctrinam, Cic.; antiquitatem, Cic.

rĕdŏmĭtus -a -um, *tamed again, subdued again*, Cic.

rĕdŏno, 1. **I.** *to give back*, Hor. **II.** *to pardon;* graves iras et invisum nepotem Marti redonabo, Hor.

rĕdordĭor, 4. dep. *to unravel, unweave,* Plin.

rĕdormĭo, 4. *to sleep again,* Plin.

rĕdormītĭo -ōnis, f. (redormio), *a going to sleep again,* Plin.

rĕdūco -duxi -ductum, 3. **I.** *to bring back, lead back.* **A.** *to draw back, to draw backwards, draw towards oneself ;* 1, lit., a, gen., falces tormentis internis, Caes. ; remos ad pectora, Ov. ; b, esp., (a) *to draw in ;* auras naribus, Lucr. ; (β) *to extend a fortification ;* reliquas omnes munitiones ab ea fossa pedes CCC. reduxit, Caes.; 2, fig., a, *to rescue ;* socios a morte reduxi, Verg. ; b, *to keep back from ;* meque ipse reduco a contemplatu dimoveoque mali, Ov. **B.** *to lead back,* often with rursus or rursum ; 1, lit., a, gen., (a) of persons as obj., aliquem domum, Cic.; (β) of things, diem or lucem, Verg. ; b, esp., (a) *to accompany, to escort,* as a mark of respect ; aliquem domum, Cic. ; (β) *to restore an exile ;* aliquem de exsilio, Cic. ; regem, Cic. ; (γ) milit. t. t., *to draw back forces, withdraw, cause to retire, take back ;* legiones ex Britannia, Caes.; copias a munitionibus, Caes. ; victorem exercitum Romam, Liv. ; 2, fig., a, aliquem in gratiam cum aliquo, Cic. ; aliquem ad officium sanitatemque, Cic. ; in memoriam, *to recall to recollection,* Cic. ; b, *to re-introduce ;* legem majestatis, Tac. **II.** *to bring or reduce to a certain state or condition ;* (carnem) lambendo mater in artus fingit et in formam reducit (of the she-bear), Ov.

rĕductĭo -ōnis, f. (reduco), *a bringing back ;* regis Alexandrini, *restoration,* Cic.

rĕductor -ōris (reduco), *one who brings back ;* plebis Romanae in urbem, Liv.

rĕductus -a -um, p. adj. (from reduco), *withdrawn, retired.* **I.** Lit., of places, *retired, sequestered ;* vallis, Verg. **II.** Fig., virtus est medium vitiorum et utrinque reductum, *distant from both extremes,* Hor. ; applied to a painting, reductiora, *the background,* Quint. ; subst., **rĕducta** -ōrum, n. (translation of ἀποπροηγμένα), in the language of the Stoics, *things which though not evils were to be regarded as inferior* (opp. producta), Cic.

rĕduncus -a -um, *bent, bowed, curved ;* rostrum (aquilae), Ov.

rĕdundantĭa -ae, f. (redundo), *an overflowing ;* fig., of style, *redundancy,* Cic.

rĕdundo, 1. (re and unda), *to overflow, stream over.* **I.** 1, lit., of water, etc., lacus, Cic. ; pituita, Cic. ; partic. perf., redundatus poet. = redundans, *overflowing ;* aquae, Ov. ; 2, transf., *to overflow with ;* foll. by abl., Asia, quae eorum ipsorum sanguine redundat, Cic. **II.** Fig., 1, *to overflow, abound, flow forth freely ;* a, nationes in provincias redundare poterant, Cic.; infamia ad amicos redundat, Cic. ; b, of orators, Asiatici oratores nimis redundantes, *copious, diffuse,* Cic. ; 2, *to be very abundant, abound ;* ut neque in Antonio deesset hic ornatus orationis, neque in Crasso redundaret, Cic. ; with abl., *to abound in ;* splendidissimorum hominum multitudine, Cic.

rĕdŭvĭa (rĕdĭvĭa) -ae, f. (from *reduo, as exuviae from exuo), *a hangnail, whitlow, a loosening of the skin round the nails ;* prov., quum capiti mederi debeam, reduviam curem, *attend to a trifle,* Cic.

rĕdux -dŭcis (reduco). **I.** Act., *bringing back, restoring ;* epithet of Jupiter, Ov. **II.** Pass., *brought back, returned ;* reduces socii, Verg.; me reducem esse voluistis, *returned from exile,* Cic. (abl. sing., reduci in poets, Ov.).

rĕfectĭo -ōnis, f. (reficio), *a repairing, restoration,* Suet.

rĕféctor -ōris, m. (reficio), *a repairer, restorer,* Suet.

rĕfello -felli, 3. (re and fallo), *to refute, confute, disprove ;* aliquem, Cic. ; refellere et redarguere mendacium alicuius, Cic. ; crimen commune ferro, Verg.

rĕfercĭo -fersi -fertum, 4. (re and farcio), *to stuff quite full, fill full.* **I.** Lit., cloacas coriporibus civium, Cic. **II.** Fig., **A.** Gen., complures aures istis sermonibus, Cic. ; libros puerilibus fabulis, Cic. **B.** *to crowd together ;* quae Crassus peranguste refersit in oratione sua, Cic.

rĕfērĭo, 4. **I.** *to strike back, strike again,* Plaut. **II.** *to reflect ;* speculi referitur imagine Phoebus, Ov.

rĕfĕro -tŭli -lātum -ferre. **I.** *to carry back, bring back, bear back.* **A.** 1, to a place, a, *to bring back, carry back ;* candelabrum, Cic. ; pecunias in templum, Caes.; esp., of the wounded, aliquem in castra, Liv. ; b, *to take back, restore what has been lent or stolen, give back ;* pateram, Cic. ; fig., ad equestrem ordinem judicia, Cic. ; c, *to give back from oneself ;* (a) *to spit out ;* cum sanguine mixta vina, Verg. ; (β) *to cause to sound back, to cause to echo ;* in pass. = *to echo, to resound ;* theatri natura ita resonans, ut usque Romam significationes vocesque referantur, Cic.; d, *to carry back* = *to make to return ;* (a) of return, me referunt pedes in Tusculanum, Cic. ; esp., referre pedem, or referre se, or pass., referri, as middle, *to return, to turn back again, to return home ;* se iterum Romam, Cic. ; classem relatam nuntio, Verg. : esp., (aa) *to bring back time that is past ;* o mihi praeteritos referat si Juppiter annos, Verg. ; (ββ) *to direct again one's look, energy,* etc. ; oculos animumque ad aliquem, Cic. ; animum ad studia, Cic. ; se ad philosophiam, Cic. ; (γγ) *to restore to a condition ;* consilia in melius, Verg. ; (δδ) legal t. t., *to bring again before a court of justice ;* rem judicatam, Cic. ; (εε) *to refer to, to judge by, measure according to a certain standard ;* omnia ad voluptatem, Cic. ; omnia consilia atque facta ad dignitatem et ad virtutem, Cic.; (β) of retreat, *to move back ;* castra, Liv.; esp., referre pedem or vestigia, or gradum (gradus), or reflex., se referre and pass., referri, as middle, *to retreat, move back, yield ;* esp. as milit. t. t., paulatim cedere ac pedem referre, Caes.; (γ) naut. t. t., *to drive back ;* auster aliquem in Italiam refert, Cic. ; 2, *to bring back from a place, as a trophy, present, discovery ;* a, tabulas repertas ad Caesarem, Caes. ; pro re certa falsam spem domum, Cic.; esp., milit. t. t., signa militaria sex, Caes. ; b, *to bring back a message, report,* etc. ; responsum, Cic. ; rumores, Cic. ; with acc. and infin., imminere Volscum bellum, Liv. ; 3, *to bring back as equivalent, return, requite ;* a, vicem, Ov. ; alicui plurimam salutem, Cic. ; b, gratiam, *to return thanks, to recompense,* Cic. ; 4, *to turn back* (parts of the body) ; oculos ad terram identidem, Cic. ; os in se, Ov. ; 5, *to repeat, renew, restore ;* a, eandem totius caeli descriptionem, Cic. ; b, *to represent, be the image of, recall ;* aliquem ore, Verg. **II.** *to give away from oneself.* **A.** *to give up, present, deliver ;* frumentum omne ad se referri jubet, Caes. ; polit. t. t., hanc ex fenore pecuniam populo, *deliver into the public treasury,* Cic. ; rationes ad aerarium, Cic. ; esp., a, *to pay off ;* octonis idibus aera, Hor. ; b, *to offer as a sacrifice ;* sollemnia ludis, Verg. ; c, *to procure, confer upon ;* consulatum ad patrem, Cic. ; d, *to report, relate by word of mouth or by writing ;* certorum hominum sermones ad aliquem, Cic. ; haec mandata Caesari. Caes.; aliquem in numero deorum, *to raise to,* Cic. ; with acc. and infin., referunt Suebos ad extremos fines se recepisse, Caes. ; e, *to place before for advice, apply to, refer to ;* de signo Concordiae dedicando ad pontificum collegium, Cic.; esp., **1**, referre ad senatum, *to bring a question before the senate*; ad senatum de legibus abrogandis, Cic.; **2**, *to register, record, enter*; judicium in tabulas publicas, Cic.; aliquid in commentarium, in libellum, Cic.; aliquem in proscriptos, *in the list of proscribed*, Cic.; esp., *to write in an account-book*; pecuniam operi publico, *under the head of a public work*, Cic.; aliquid in acceptum referre or acceptum referre, *to enter as paid*, Cic. (perf. and sup., rettuli and rellatum sometimes in poets to make the first syllable long).

rĕfert, rĕtŭlit, rĕferre, impers. (from re, for ex re and fert), *it matters, it concerns, is of use, is advantageous, is one's interest*; with meā, tuā, nostrā, vestrā, cujā; more rarely with ad and the acc., or only acc., or with genit.; a, with possess. pron., non ascripsi id, quod tuā nihil referebat, Cic.; non plus sua referre, quam si, etc., Cic.: b, without poss. pron., refert magno opere id ipsum; with infin. as subj., neque refert videre quid dicendum sit, Cic.; with depend. interrog. sent., quid refert, qua me ratione cogatis? Cic.; quid refert, utrum voluerim fieri, an gaudeam factum? Cic.; c, with dat., quid referat intra naturae fines viventi, jugera centum an mille aret? Hor.; d, with genit., faciendum aliquid, quod illorum magis, quam suā retulisse videretur, Sall.; e, absol., tamquam referret, as *if it were of any consequence*, Tac.

rĕfertus -a -um, p. adj. (from refercio), *stuffed, crammed, filled, full*; (α) with abl., insula referta divitiis, Cic.; (β) with genit., mare refertum praedonum, Cic.; (γ) with de and the abl., cur de prooemiis referti essent eorum libri, Cic.; (δ) absol., aerarium refertius, Cic.; theatrum refertissimum, Cic.

rĕfervĕo, 2. *to boil over*; fig., refervens falsum crimen, Cic.

rĕfervesco, 3. (referveo), *to boil up, bubble up*; sanguis refervescit, Cic.

rĕfĭcĭo -fēci -fectum, 3. (re and facio). **I.** *to make again.* **A.** *to make afresh, prepare again*; arma, Sall.; ea quae sunt omissa, Cic. **B.** *to choose again*; tribunos, Cic. **II.** *to re-establish, restore a thing to its previous condition*; salutem, Cic.; esp., a, *to build again*; pontem, Caes.; fana, Cic.; b, *to refit, repair*; naves, classem, Caes.; aedes, Cic.; c, *to light again, kindle again*; flammam, Ov.; d, *to restore in point of number, to fill up, complete*; exercitum, Liv.; copias, Caes.; e, *to restore health, heal, cure*; Tironis reficiendi spes, Cic.; f, *to restore* (physically, politically, mentally), *to refresh, revive*; reficere se et curare, Cic.; fessum viā ac vigiliis militem, Liv.; me recreat et reficit Pompeii consilium, *gives me strength*, Cic.; of things, herbas, Ov. **III.** *to get back again, receive, get*; plus mercedis ex fundo, Cic.

rĕfigo -fixi -fixum, 3. *to tear, loose, pluck off, pluck apart, unfasten.* **I.** Lit., tabulas, Cic.; signa templis, Hor. **II.** Meton., a, *to take down the tables of the law*, i.e., *to repeal, abrogate*; leges, aera, Cic. **B.** *to pack up*, ap. Cic.

rĕfingo, 3. *to form anew*; cerea regna, Verg.

rĕflāgĭto, 1. *to ask back, demand again*, Cat.

rĕflātus -ū, m. (reflo). **I.** *a blowing against*, Plin. **II.** Meton., *a contrary wind*; naves delatas Uticam reflatu hoc, Cic.

rĕflecto -flexi -flexum, 3. *to turn back, bend back.* **I.** Lit., cervicem, Ov.; oculos, Ov.; pass., reflecti, as middle, tereti cervice reflexa, Verg.; longos reflectitur ungues, *bends his nails into long talons*, Ov. **II.** Fig., *to turn back, turn, divert*; animum, Cic.; mentes, Cic.; orsa in melius, Verg.

rĕflo, 1. **I.** Intransit., *to blow back, blow against, blow contrary*; etsi etesine valde reflant, Cic. **II.** Transit., *to blow out, breathe out*, Lucr.

rĕflōresco -flōrŭi, 3. *to begin to bloom again*, Plin.

rĕflŭo -fluxi -fluxum, 3. *to flow back, to overflow*; Nilus refluit campis, Verg.

rĕflŭus -a -um (refluo), *flowing back*; mare, Ov.

rĕfŏdĭo -fōdi -fossum, 3. *to dig out, dig up*, Plin.

rĕformātor -ōris, m. (reformo), *one who forms again, a reviver, improver*, Plin.

rĕformīdātĭo -ōnis, f. (reformido), *excessive dread, fear, terror*, Cic.

rĕformīdo, 1. *to dread, fear, be afraid of, shun, avoid*; a, of persons, (α) with acc., aliquem, Cic; bellum, Cic.; (β) with infin., refugit animus eaque dicere reformidat, Cic.; (γ) with rel. sent., nec, quid occurrat, reformidat, Cic.; (δ) absol., vide, quam non reformidem, Cic.; b, of things, ante (vites) reformidant ferrum, Verg.

rĕformo, 1. *to form again, mould anew, alter in form*; Iolcus reformatus in annos primos, Ov.

rĕfŏvĕo -fōvi -fōtum, 2. *to warm again, cherish again, revive, restore, refresh.* **I.** Lit., corpus, Ov.; vires, Tac.; ignes tepidos, Ov. **II.** Fig., provincias internis certaminibus fessas, Tac.

ĕrfractārĭŏlus-a-um (dim. of refractarius), *somewhat contentious, stubborn*; hoc judiciale dicendi genus, Cic.

rĕfractārĭus -a -um (refragor), *stubborn, refractory, contentious*, Sen.

rĕfrăgor, 1. dep. (opp. to suffragor), *to oppose, withstand, thwart*; petenti, Cic.; honori eius, Liv.; illa lex petitioni tuae refragrata est, *is opposed to*, Cic.

rĕfrēno, 1. *to hold back, rein in*; transf., *to hold back, restrain, curb*; fluvios, Lucr.; aquas, Ov.; fig., animum, Cic.; juventutem, Cic.; adolescentes a gloria, Cic.

rĕfrĭco -frĭcŭi -frĭcātūrus, 1. *to rub again, scratch again, gall.* **I.** Lit., alicuius vulnera, *to tear open*, Cic.; cicatricem, Cic. **II.** Transf., *to excite again, renew*; pulcherrimi facti memoriam, Cic.; tuis sceleribus reipublicae praeterita fata refricabis, Cic.; dolorem, Cic.; crebro refricatur lippitudo, *breaks out afresh, appears again*, Cic.

rĕfrĭgĕrātĭo -ōnis, f. (refrigero), *a cooling, coolness*; me delectant et refrigeratio et vicissim aut sol aut ignis hibernus, Cic.

rĕfrĭgĕrātōrĭus -a -um (refrigero), *cooling*, Plin.

rĕfrĭgĕrātrix -īcis, f. *cooling*, Plin.

rĕfrĭgĕro, 1. *to make cool.* **I.** Lit., a, physically, stella Saturni refrigerat, Cic.; b, of animal heat, membra undā, Ov.; dei membra partim ardentia partim refrigerata dicenda sunt, Cic.; pass., refrigerari, as middle, *to cool oneself, grow cool*; umbris aquisve, Cic. **II.** Transf., *to cool, to deprive of warmth or zeal*; and hence, pass., *to be cold, exhausted, languid, to grow cool or languid*; refrigerata accusatio, Cic.; sermone refrigerato, Cic.

rĕfrĭgesco -frixi, 3. *to grow cold, cool down, become cool.* **I.** Lit., cor corpore cum toto refrixit, Ov. **II.** Transf., *to lose warmth, vigour, zeal, grow cool, to flag, to fail, to abate, to grow stale*; illud crimen de nummis caluit re recenti, nunc in causa refrixit, Cic.; vereor ne hasta (the public auction) refrixerit, Cic.; of persons, Scaurus refrixerat, Cic.

rĕfringo -frēgi -fractum, 3. (re and frango), *o break up, break open.* **I.** Lit., claustra, Cic.; carcerem, Liv. **II.** Transf., *to break in pieces, to break, destroy;* vim fluminis, Caes.; vim fortunae, Liv.

rĕfŭgĭo -fūgi -fŭgĭtum, 3. **I.** Intransit., *to flee away, take to flight, escape.* **A.** Lit., velocissime, Caes.; ad suos, Caes.; Syracusas, Cic.; ex castris in montem, Caes. **B.** Transf., a, *to turn away from, avoid;* vites a caulibus refugere dicuntur, Cic.; b, of places, *to retire from,* recede *from;* refugit ab litore templum, Verg.; c, *to take refuge with, have recourse to;* ad legatos, Cic. **II.** Transit., *to fly from, avoid, run away from.* **A.** Lit., impetum, Cic. **B.** Fig., *to avoid, shun;* judicem, Cic.; ministeria, Verg.

rĕfŭgĭum -ĭi, n. (refugio), *a place of refuge, a refuge;* silvae dedere refugium, Liv.; refugium populorum erat senatus, Cic.

rĕfŭgus -a -um (refugio). **I.** *flying, fugitive, receding;* quidam in castra refugi, Tac. Subst., refugi, *fugitives,* Tac. **II.** Poet., transf., *receding, recoiling;* unda, Ov.

rĕfulgĕo -fulsi, 2. *to gleam or glitter back, to shine brightly, to glitter.* **I.** Lit. arma refulgentia, Liv.; Jovis tutela refulgens (of Jupiter, as an auspicious birth-star), Hor. **II.** Fig., splendidaque a docto fama refulget avo, Prop.

rĕfundo -fūdi -fūsum, 3. **I.** *to pour back;* vapores eādem, Cic.; aequor in aequor, Ov.; refusus Oceanus, *ebbing and flowing,* Verg. **II.** *to cause to flow forth;* pass., refundi, as middle, *to overflow;* stagna refusa vadis, Verg.

rĕfūtātĭo -ōnis, f. (refuto), *a refutation, confutation,* Cic.

rĕfūtātus, abl. -ū = refutatio (q.v.).

rĕfūto, 1. **I.** *to drive back, press back;* nationes bello, Cic. **II.** Fig., *to resist, oppose, repel, repress.* **A.** Gen., clamorem, Cic; cupiditatem, Cic.; virtutem aspernari ac refutare, Cic. **B.** Esp., *to confute, refute, disprove;* sceleratorum perjuria testimoniis, Cic.; aliquos domesticis testibus, Cic.; Fors dicta refutet! *may fate avert!* Verg.

rēgālĭŏlus -i, m. (dim. of regalis), *a small bird,* perhaps *the wren,* Suet.

rēgālis -e (rex), *royal, regal, kingly.* **I.** Lit., genus civitatis, *monarchical,* Cic.; nomen, Cic.; carmen, *celebrating deeds of kings,* Ov. **II.** Transf., *kingly, princely, worthy of a king;* ornatus, Cic.; regalem animum in se esse, Liv.

rēgālĭtĕr, adv. (regalis), *royally, regally;* a, in good sense, centum hostiis sacrificium regaliter Minervae conficere, Liv.; b, in a bad sense, *despotically, tyrannically;* precibus minas regaliter addere, Ov.

rĕgĕlo, 1. *to thaw, warm,* Mart.

rĕgĕnĕro, 1. *to bring forth again, to generate again, reproduce,* Plin.

rĕgermĭnātĭo -ōnis, f. (regermino), *a budding again, putting forth of buds again,* Plin.

rĕgermĭno, 1. *to put forth buds again, germinate again,* Plin.

rĕgĕro -gessi -gestum, 3. *to carry back, bear back, bring back.* **I.** Lit., quo regesta e fossa terra foret, Liv.; tellurem, *to throw back again,* Ov. **II.** Transf., *to throw back, return, retort;* convicia, Hor.

rēgĭa, v. regius.

rēgĭē, adv. (regius), *royally;* a, in a good sense, Plaut.; b, in a bad sense, *arbitrarily, despotically, tyrannically;* crudeliter et regie fieri, Cic.; ea quae regie seu potius tyrannice statuit in aratores, Cic.

rēgĭfĭcus -a um (rex and facio), *royal, princely, splendid;* luxus, Verg.

rēgigno, 3. *to bring forth again, beget again,* Lucr.

Rēgillus -i, m. **I.** *a town in the country of the Sabines, from which Appius Claudius came to Rome.* Hence, **Rēgillensis** -e and **Rēgillānus** -a -um, *belonging to Regillus.* **II.** *a small lake in Latium on the via Lavicana, scene of a victory of the Romans over the Latins,* 496 B.C. Hence, **Rēgillensis** -e, *surname of the Postumii, as the Roman commander was the dictator Postumius.* **III.** *surname of the gens Aemilia.*

rĕgĭmen -ĭnis, n. (rego). **I.** *guiding, leading.* **A.** Lit., equorum, Tac.; navis, Tac.; cohortium, Tac. **B.** Fig., *guidance, rule, government, direction;* totius magistratūs, Liv.; absol., *the government of a state,* Tac. **II.** *that which guides.* **A.** Poet., *the rudder,* Ov. **B.** Fig., *a ruler, governor;* rerum, *of a state,* Liv.

rēgīna -ae, f. (rex), *a queen.* **I. A.** Lit., 1, gen., Plaut.; 2, esp., of Cleopatra, Cic.; of Dido, Verg. **B.** Transf., a, of goddesses, regina, Juno, Cic.; b, *a king's daughter, a princess* (of Ariadne), Verg.; of Medea, Ov. **II.** Fig., *queen, mistress, sovereign;* haec una virtus (justitia) omnium est domina et regina virtutum, Cic.; regina pecunia, Hor.

Rēgīnus, v. Regium.

rēgĭo -ōnis, f. (rego). **I.** *a direction, line.* **A.** Gen., si qui tantulum de recta regione de flexerit, Cic.; haec eadem est nostra regio et via, Cic.; oppidi murus rectā regione, si nullus anfractus intercederet, MCC passus aberat, Caes.; rectā regione, in *a straight line,* Liv. **B.** Esp., e regione, adv., a, *in a straight line;* alterum e regione movetur, alterum declinat, Cic.; b, in *the opposite direction, over, against;* (a) with genit., e regione solis, Cic.; (β) with dat., esse e regione nobis e contraria parte terrae, Cic. **II.** Transf., **A.** *a boundary line, boundary;* 1, gen., a, lit., usually plur., res ea orbis terrae regionibus definiuntur, Cic.; b, fig., sese regionibus officii continet, Cic.; 2, esp., a, t. t. of augurs' language, *the line of sight;* per lituum regionum facta descriptio, Cic.; b, *a region of the heavens* or *earth;* regio aquilonia, australis, Cic.; c, *geographical position,* eam esse naturam et regionem provinciae tuae, Cic. **B.** 1, *a region, country, territory, district;* a, lit., locus in regione pestilenti saluber, Cic.; b, fig., *sphere, department, territory;* bene dicere non habet definitam aliquam regionem, Cic.; 2, esp., a, *an administrative division, province, district;* principes regionum atque pagorum inter suos jus dicunt, Caes.; b, *a division, quarter, ward, district of Rome,* Tac.

rĕgĭōnātim, adv. (regio), *according to districts, provinces;* tribus describere, Liv.

Rēgĭum -ii, n. **I.** *a town of the Boii in Gallia Cispadana,* now *Reggio.* Hence, **Rēgienses** -ium, m. *the inhabitants of Regium.* **II.** *a town of the Bruttii, at the south of Italy, near Sicily,* now *Reggio.* Hence, **Rēgīnus** -a -um, *belonging to Regium.*

rēgĭus -a -um (rex), *royal, regal, kingly.* **I. A.** Lit., anni, *the period of monarchy at Rome,* Cic.; ales, *the eagle,* Cic.; causa (of the installation of Ptolemaeus Auletes), Cic. **B.** Transf., *royal, splendid, magnificent;* moles, Hor.; morbus, *jaundice,* Hor. **II.** Subst., **A. rēgii** -ōrum, m. 1, *the troops of the king,* Liv.; 2, *the satraps of the king,* Nep. **B. rēgia** -ae, f. 1, *the royal dwelling, the palace;* a, gen., Cic.; b, esp., *a building in Rome on the Via Sacra, the palace of Numa, afterwards used by the priests,*

Cic.; so **atrium regium**, Liv.; **c**, meton., *the court, the royal family*, Liv.; **2**,= basilica, *a public hall*, Suet.

rēglūtĭno, 1. *to unglue, separate*, Cat.

regnātor -ōris, m. (regno), *a ruler, governor, king;* Olympi, *Jupiter*, Verg.; Asiae, Verg.

regnātrix -trīcis, f. (regnator), *ruling;* domus, Tac.

regno, 1. (regnum). **I.** Intransit., *to exercise royal authority, be a king, reign.* **A.** Lit., septem et triginta regnavisse annos, Cic.; imnpers., post Tatii mortem ab sua parte non erat regnatum, Liv. **B.** Transf., *to rule as a king;* a, of persons, *to be master, to have absolute sway, to play the lord;* partly in a good sense, Graeciā jam regnante, Cic.; partly in a bad sense, *to be a tyrant;* regnavit is quidem (Gracchus) paucos menses, Cic.; b, of things, *to rule, get the mastery;* ignis per alta cacumina regnat, Verg.; ardor edendi per viscera regnat, **rages**, Ov.; of abstractions, in quo uno regnat oratio, Cic. **II.** Transit., *to rule;* only in pass., regnandam accipere Albam, Verg.; with abl. of pers., terra regnata Lycurgo, Verg.; gentes quae regnantur, *which are ruled by kings,* Tac.

regnum -i, n. (rex), *royal power* or *authority, royalty, monarchy, the throne.* **I. A.** Lit., superbi regni initium, Cic.; regnum affectare, Liv. **B.** Transf., 1, in a good sense, *authority, rule, unrestrained power;* alicui regnum deferre, Caes.; abuti ad omnia atomorum regno et licentiā, Cic.; **2**, in a bad sense, under the republic at Rome, *tyranny, despotism;* regnum appetere, Cic.; crimen regni, Ov.; regnum judiciorum, regnum forense, Cic. **II.** Meton., **A.** *a country ruled by a king, a kingdom;* fines regni, Caes. **B.** Transf., 1, *the kingdom of the dead,* Verg.; **2**, *any possession, estate;* in tuo regno, Cic.; mea regna, Verg.

rĕgo, rexi, rectum, 3. *to guide, direct.* **I.** Lit., **A.** equum, Liv.; regit beluam quocumque vult, Cic. **B.** Legal t. t., regere fines, *to mark out boundaries*, Cic. **II.** Fig., **A.** *to guide, direct;* **a**, motum mundi, Cic.; juvenem, Cic.; b, esp., as a ruler, *to guide, direct, rule, govern, administer;* rempublicam, Cic.; Massilienses summā justitiā, Cic.; transf., of abstract objects, omnes animi partes, Cic.; suorum libidines, Cic. **B.** *to show the right way to, to set right;* errantem, Caes.; te regere possum, Cic.

rĕgrĕdĭor -gressus sum, 3. (re and gradior), *to go back, retreat, step back.* **I.** Lit., a, ut regredi quam progredi mallent, Cic.; b, as milit. t. t., *to retreat*, Caes. **II.** Fig., in illum annum, Cic.

rĕgressĭo -ōnis, f. (regredior), *a going back, repetition*, as a rhetorical figure, Quint.

rĕgressus -ūs, m. (regredior), *a going back, return.* **I.** Lit., a, Cic.; dare alicui regressum, Ov. Plur., conservare progressus et regressus, Cic.; b, milit. t. t., *a retreat*, Liv. **II.** Fig., **a**, *a return;* ab ira, Liv.; b, *refuge, recourse;* ad principem, Tac.

rēgŭla -ae, f. (rego), *a rule, a bar, staff, lath, stick.* **I.** Gen., Caes. **II.** Esp., **A.** Lit., *a rule*, Cic. **B.** Fig., *a rule, pattern, model;* juris, Cic.; regula ad quam omnia judicia rerum dirigentur, Cic.

1. **rēgŭlus** -i, m. (dim. of rex). **I.** *a petty king, prince*, Sall. **II.** *a king's son, prince*, Liv.

2. **Rēgŭlus**, *surname of the gens Atilia, the most famous member of which was the consul M. Atilius Regulus, famous for his devoted return into captivity in the First Punic War.*

rĕgusto, 1. *to taste again or repeatedly.* **I.** Lit., Pers. **II.** Fig., crebro litteras alicuius, *to*

take pleasure in reading over again, Cic.; **laudationem Lollii**, Cic.

rēĭcĭo = rejicio (q.v.).

rējectānĕus -a -um (rejicio), *to be rejected;* subst., **rējectānĕa** -ōrum, transl. of the Stoic ἀποπροηγμένα, *things which, though not evil, are to be rejected*, Cic.

rējectĭo -ōnis, f. (rejicio). **I.** Lit., *a throwing out, throwing back, throwing up;* sanguinis, *a spitting of blood*, Plin. **II.** Fig., **A.** *a casting out, rejection, despising;* a, huius civitatis, Cic.; b, esp., legal t. t., *the refusal to accept a particular judex, challenging a juryman;* judicum, Cic. **B.** In rhet., in alium, *a shifting off from oneself to another*, Cic.

rējecto, 1. (intens. of rejicio), *to cast back,* throw back, Lucr.

rējĭcĭo -jēci -jectum, 3. (re and jacio), *to throw back.* **I.** Gen., **A.** In a narrow sense, *to cast behind, throw behind;* a, scutum (to protect oneself), Cic.; esp., of a garment, *to throw behind;* togam ab humero, Liv.; paenulam, *to throw back on the shoulders* (to leave the hands free), Cic.; b, esp., (a) rejicere or pass., rejici, as middle, *to sink back;* se in alicuius gremium, Lucr.; (β) *to place behind;* accensos in postremam aciem, Liv.; rejecta mater, Cic. **B.** In a wider sense, *to cast back from oneself, throw away, repel, drive back;* 1, lit., a, colubras ab ore, Ov.; oculos Rutulorum arvis, *turn from*, Verg.; esp., (a) *to throw away a garment;* vestem ex humeris, Ov.; sagulum, Cic.; (β) *to throw back, cause to echo;* gen., in pass., *to echo back;* imago rejecta, Lucr.; b, esp., (a) *to drive off* living beings; capellas a flumine, Verg.; esp., as milit. t. t., *to drive back;* equitatum, Caes.; hostes ab An tiochea, Cic.; fig., alicuius ferrum et audaciam in foro, Cic.; (β) as naut. t. t., of a storm, *to drive back, cast up;* naves tempestate rejectae, Caes.; rejici austro ad Leucopetram, Cic.; **2**, fig., a, *to drive off from oneself, remove, repulse;* hanc proscriptionem hoc judicio a se rejicere et aspernari, Cic.; b, esp., (a) *to reject with scorn, disdain, spurn;* bona diligere et rejicere contraria, Cic.; omnem istam disputationem, Cic.; as legal t. t., *to challenge the judices or jury;* judices, Cic.; recuperatores, Cic.; (β) *to refer to;* aliquem ad ipsam epistolam, Cic.; (γ) *to bring a matter before the senate*, or *a magistrate;* rem ad senatum, Liv.; (δ) *to put off;* totam rem in mensem Januarium, Cic. **II.** *to throw back at some one;* telum in hostem, Caes. (imper., reice, dissyll., Verg.).

rēlābor -lapsus sum, 3. dep. *to slide, glide, flow, fall back.* **I.** Lit., prenso rudente relabi, Ov.; relabi montibus, Hor. **II.** Fig., tunc mens et sonus relapsus, Hor.; nunc in Aristippi furtim praecepta relabor, *come back to*, Hor.

rēlanguesco -langui, 3. *to become faint, languid.* **I.** Physically, Ov. **II.** Morally or intellectually, a, *to be weakened, be made effeminate;* iis rebus relanguescere animos, Caes.; b, *to become relaxed, to abate;* taedio impetus relanguescit regis, Liv.; relanguisse se dicit, *his animosity had abated*, Liv.

rēlātĭo -ōnis, f. (refero), *a carrying back, bringing back.* **I.** Lit., Quint. **II.** Fig., **A.** Legal t. t., criminis, *a retorting of the accusation upon the accuser*, Cic. **B.** 1, polit. t. t., *a motion, proposal, proposition of a magistrate in the senate*, Cic.; **2**, grammat. t. t., *relation, reference, respect*, Cic.

rēlātor -ōris, m. (refero), *a mover, proposer in the senate*, ap. Cic.

rēlātus -ūs, m. (refero), *a bringing before.* **I.** *a narrative, recital;* quorum (carminum) relatus, Tac. **II.** *a proposal, report in the senate*, Tac.

rĕlaxātĭo -ōnis, f. (relaxo), *a relaxation, easing*; animi, Cic.

rĕlaxo, 1. **I.** *to loosen, widen, enlarge, relax*; alvus tum astringitur, tum relaxatur, Cic.; ora fontibus, Ov. **II.** *to make slack, to ease, to open, unfasten.* **A.** Lit., claustra, Ov.; vias et caeca spiramenta, Verg. **B.** Fig., *to ease, lighten, alleviate, assuage, relax*; a, gen., (*a*) transit., continuationem verborum modo relaxet, Cic.; pater nimis indulgens quidquid astrinxi relaxat, *loosens the reins which I drew tight*, Cic.; (risus) tristitiam ac severitatem mitigat et relaxat, Cic.; (*β*) reflex. and middle, animi cum se plane corporis vinculis relaxaverint, *shall have freed themselves*, Cic.; simply relaxare and middle, relaxari = *to slacken*; (dolor) levis dat intervalla et relaxat, Cic.; insani quum relaxentur, *when they have a lucid interval*, Cic.; b, esp., *to relax by way of recreation, to lighten, enliven, cheer up*; (*a*) transit., animum, Cic.; (*β*) reflex. and middle, se istā occupatione, Cic.; relaxari animo, Cic.

rĕlēgātĭo -ōnis, f. (1. relego), *a banishing, banishment, the mildest form of exile from Rome, by which the exile preserved his civil rights*, Cic.

1. rĕlēgo, 1. *to send away.* **I.** Lit., 1, tauros procul atque in sola pascua, Verg.; 2, as a punishment, *to remove, banish*; filium ab hominibus, Cic.; aliquem in exsilium, Liv.; relegatus, non exsul dicor (the relegatio being the mildest form of banishment), Ov. **II.** Transf., a, *to remove far away*; terris gens relegata ultimis, Cic.; b, *to reject*; Samnitium dona, Cic.

2. rĕlēgo -lēgi -lectum, 3. **I.** *to gather up, collect again.* **A.** Lit., filo relecto, Ov. **B.** Transf., *to travel, sail through, traverse again*; Hellespontiacas aquas, Ov. **II.** *to go over again*; a, *to read over again*; Trojani belli scriptorem, Hor.; scripta, Ov.; b, *to talk over*; suos sermone labores, Ov.

rĕlentesco, 3. *to become languid, feeble again*; amor, Ov.

rĕlĕvo, 1. **I.** *to lift, raise up again*; e terra corpus, Ov. **II.** *to make light again, to lighten.* **A.** Lit., epistolam graviorem pellectione, Cic.; relevari longā catenā, *to be freed from*, Ov. **B.** Fig., 1, *to relieve, free from an evil, to lessen, diminish*; communem casum misericordiā hominum, Cic.; morbum, Cic.; 2, *to lighten, alleviate, refresh*; pectora mero, Ov.; potius relevare quam castigare, Cic.; relevari, *to be relieved, refreshed*; relevata respublica, Cic.

rĕlictĭo -ōnis, f. (relinquo), *a leaving, deserting*; reipublicae, Cic.

rĕlĭcŭus and **rĕlĭcus** = reliquus (q.v.).

rĕlĭgātĭo -ōnis, f. (religo), *a tying up, training*; vitium, Cic.

rĕlĭgĭo (rellĭgĭo) -ōnis, f. (perhaps from re-ligo). **I.** Gen., *conscientiousness, scrupulousness, conscientious exactness*; hac ego religione non sum ab hoc conatu repulsus, Cic.; nulla in judiciis severitas, nulla religio, Cic.; with object. genit., non nullius officii, privati officii, Cic.; with subject. genit., fides et religio judicis, Cic. **II.** Esp., *respect for what is sacred.* **A.** *conscientious scruples, respect for conscience*; perturbari religione et metu, Cic.; res in religionem alicui venit, *is a matter of conscience to*, Cic.; religio alicui non est, quominus, etc., a *man is not prevented by conscience from*, etc., Cic.; in plur., quas religiones, Cic. **B.** *religious feeling, religious awe*; 1, lit., a, in a good sense, inclita justitia religioque Numae Pompilii, Liv.; in plur., hostis omnium religionum, Cic.; b, in a bad sense, *superstition*; animos multiplex religio et pleraque externa incessit, Liv.; 2, meton., *that which is holy or sacred*; a, gen., (*a*) in a good sense, in sacerdotibus tanta offusa oculis animoque religio, Liv.; (*β*) in a bad sense, *an insult to religion, sin, curse*; religio Clodiana, Cic.; b, esp., (*a*) act., *religious obligation*; tantā religione obstricta tota provincia est, Cic.; so of an oath, religio jurisjurandi, Cic.; (*β*) *holiness, sanctity*; deorum, Cic.; magistratus religione inviolati, Cic.; of a place, fani, sacrarii, Cic. **C.** *religious worship, the worship of the gods, external religion*; 1, lit., religio, id est, cultus deorum, Cic.; plur., religiones, *religious observances*; diligentissimus religionum cultor, Liv.; 2, meton., *an object of worship, holy thing*; religio domestica (of a statue), Cic.; hence, the *sacred dwelling of a god*; a deorum religionibus demigrare, Cic. (in poets the first syllable is long, hence written relligio).

rĕlĭgĭōsē (rellĭgĭōsē), adv. (religiosus). **I.** *conscientiously, scrupulously*; testimonium dicere, Cic. **II.** *piously, religiously*; deos colere, Liv.; religiosissime templum colere, Cic.

rĕlĭgĭōsus (rellĭgĭōsus) -a -um (religio). **I.** *conscientious, scrupulous*; testis, Cic. **II. A.** *religiously scrupulous*; civitas, Liv.; dies, *a day of evil omen*, as the dies Alliensis, Cic. **B.** a, in a good sense, *religious, god-fearing, pious*; (*a*) lit., qui omnia, quae ad cultum deorum pertinerent, diligenter retractarent et tamquam relegerent sunt dicti religiosi, Cic.; (*β*) meton., *holy, sacred*; templum sanctum et religiosum, Cic.; b, in a bad sense, *superstitious*, Ter.

rĕlĭgo, 1. **I.** *to tie, fasten behind.* **A.** Lit., 1, virginem, Ov.; rite equos, Verg.; trabes axibus, Caes.; aliquem ad currum, Cic.; funera in stipite, Ov.; funiculum a puppi, Cic.; 2, *to bind up the hair*; alicui, *for the sake of some one*; flavam comam, Hor.; 3, *to fasten a boat or ship to the bank, to moor*; naves ad terram, Caes.; religata in litore pinus, Ov. **B.** Transf., quae (prudentia) si extrinsecus religata pendeat, *connected with*, Cic. **II.** *to unbind, unfasten*, Cat.

rĕlīno -lēvi -lītum, 3. *to unseal, open anything fastened by pitch*, etc., Verg., Ter.

rĕlinquo -līqui -lictum, 3. **I.** *to leave behind, leave.* **A.** Gen., 1, lit., aliquem in Gallia, Caes.; 2, fig., *to leave behind*; aculeos in animo aliculus, Cic. **B.** Esp., 1, of a deceased person, *to leave, leave behind*; a, lit., heredem testamento reliquit hunc, Cic.; so of posthumous work, scriptum in Originibus, Cic.; b, fig., memoriam, Cic.; nomen, Hor.; 2, *to leave over, leave to, to let remain*; a, alicui ne paleas quidem ex omni fructu, Cic.; equitatus partem alicui, Caes.; relinquebatur una per Sequanos via, *there remained*, Caes.; b, fig., populari reipublicae laudem, Cic.; spes relinquitur, *remains*, Cic., Caes.; urbem direptioni ac incendiis, Cic.; relinquitur with ut and the subj., Cic., Caes.; 3, *to leave behind in a certain state, to let lie, leave*; a, lit., aliquem insepultum, Cic.; b, fig., rem integram, Cic.; sine imperio tantas copias, Caes. **II.** *to abandon, forsake, separate oneself from some one or something.* **A.** Gen., 1, lit., domum propinquosque, Caes.; 2, fig., a quartana aliquis relinquitur, Cic.; vitam, Verg.; relinquit aliquem animus, Caes.; ab omni honestate relictus, Cic. **B.** *to desert, abandon, leave in the lurch*; 1, lit., equos, Caes.; signa, desert, Liv.; 2, fig., a, *to neglect, abandon, let go, take no thought for*; rem et causam et utilitatem communem, Cic.; agrorum et armorum cultum, Cic.; b, esp., (*a*) *to pass over, not to notice*; caedes relinquo, libidines praetereo, Cic.; (*β*) *to leave unfinished*; artem inveniendi totam, Cic.; (*γ*) *to leave unavenged, unpunished*; injurias suas, Cic.

rĕlĭquiae (rellĭquiae) -ārum, f. (reliquus), *remains, relics, remainder, remnant.* **I.** Lit. **A.** Gen., conjurationis, Cic.; Tioas

Danaum reliquias, *remnant left by the Greeks*, Verg. **B.** Esp., a, *the fragments of food, remnants of a feast*, Plaut.; fig., vellem me ad cenam *(the murder of Caesar)* invitasses, reliquiarum nihil haberes (*had not left Antonius alive*), Cic.; b, *the remains of some one dead, carcass;* humauorum corporum, Tac.; c, *the remains, ashes of a corpse burnt on the funeral pyre;* Marii, Cic. **II.** Fig., pristinae fortunae reliquiae miserae, Cic. (in poets, to lengthen the first syllable, also written relliquiae).

rĕlĭquus (rĕlĭcus) -a -um (relinquo), *that which is left behind, remaining, left.* **I.** Lit., **A.** Gen., spes, Cic.; subst., (a) plur., **rĕlĭqui** -ōrum, m. *the rest* ; with genit., reliqui peditum, Liv.; (β) **rĕlĭquum** -i, n. and **rĕlĭqua** -ōrum, n. *the rest, the remainder ;* de reliquo, Cic.; reliqua belli perficere, Liv.; esp., reliquum est ut, foll. by subj. only, *it remains that*, Cic.; reliquum est with infin., Cic.; nihil est reliqui, *nothing remains*, Cic.; reliquum facere, *to leave remaining ;* nullum munus cuique reliquum fecisti, *thou hast left no duty unperformed,* Cic.; nihil reliqui facere, *to leave nothing remaining,* Cic. **B.** Esp., 1, t. t. of business language, *outstanding* (of a debt), *remaining ;* pecuniam reliquam ad diem solvere, Cic.; subst., **rĕlĭquum** -i, n. and plur., **rĕlĭqua** -ōrum, n. *what is outstanding, remaining ;* quum tanta reliqua sunt, Cic.; 2, of time, *remaining, future ;* gloria, Cic.; in reliquum tempus, Cic. **II.** Transf., *that which is left of a whole when the part is taken away, remaining ;* reliqua pars exercitus, Caes.; reliqui omnes, *all the rest,* Cic.

rellĭgĭo, relligiosus, etc. = religio, etc. (q.v.).

rellĭquĭae = reliquiae (q.v.).

rĕlūcĕo -luxi, 2. *to gleam back, to glitter, shine,* Cic.

rĕlūcesco -luxi, 3. (inchoat. of reluceo), *to become bright again, begin to shine again ;* imago solis reluxit, Ov.

rĕluctor, 1. dep. *to strive against, struggle against ;* draco, Hor.

rĕmācresco -crŭi, 3. *to grow thin again,* Suet.

rĕmălĕdīco, 3. *to revile again,* Suet.

rĕmando, 3. *to chew the cud, ruminate,* Plin.

rĕmănĕo -mansi -mansum, 2. *to remain behind, remain.* **I.** Gen., Romae, Cic.; in exercitu, Cic.; ad urbem, Caes.; domi, Cic.; apud aliquem, Caes. **II.** Esp., *to remain, abide, continue ;* 1, lit., animi remanent post mortem, Cic.; 2, *to remain in a certain condition ;* pars integra remanebat, Cic.

rĕmāno, 1. *to flow back,* Lucr.

rĕmansĭo -ōnis, f. (remaneo), *a remaining, continuing in one place,* Cic.

rĕmĕdĭum -ii, n. (re and medeor). **I.** *a means of healing, a cure, remedy, medicine ;* remedium quoddam habere, Cic.; remedio quodam uti, Cic.; remedio esse, Cic. **II.** Transf., *a means of assistance or relief, a remedy ;* injuriae tuae, Cic.; remedia incommodorum, Cic.; ad magnitudinem frigorum hoc sibi remedium comparare, Cic.

rĕmĕo, 1. *to go back, come back, return ;* remeat victor, Verg.; aër, Cic.; with acc., urbes, Verg.; aevum peractum, *to live over again,* Hor.

rĕmētĭor -mensus sum, 4. *to measure over again, measure back.* **I.** Gen., astra rite, *to observe carefully,* Verg. **II.** *to go back,* Plin.; in pass. meaning, iter retro pari ratione remensum est, *has been traversed,* Lucr.

rēmex -mĭgis, m. (remus and ago), *a rower,* Cic.; collectively = remiges, *the crew of rowers,* Verg.

Rēmi (Rhēmi) -ōrum, m. *a people of N. Gaul, between the Matrona* (Marne) *and the Axona* (Aisne), *whence* modern *Rheims;* sing., Iccius Remus, Caes.

rēmĭgātĭo -ōnis, f. (remigo), *a rowing,* Cic.

rēmĭgĭum -ii, n. (remex). **I.** *rowing.* **A.** Lit., Ov. **II.** Meton., **A.** *the oars;* a, lit., Verg.; b, transf., of the oar-like motion of wings, remigio alarum, Verg. **B.** *the crew of rowers, the oarsmen,* Liv.

rēmĭgo, 1. (remex), *to row,* Cic.

rēmĭgro, 1. *to wander back, come back, return.* **I.** Lit., in domum suam, Cic.; Romam, Cic. **II.** Fig., ei ne integrum quidem erat, ut ad justitiam remigraret, Cic.

rēmĭniscor, 3. dep. *to call to mind, recollect, remember ;* absol., de quaestoribus reminiscentem recordari, Cic.; with genit., veteris incommodi populi Romani, Caes.; with acc., eas res, Cic.; with rel. sent., quae tradantur mysteriis, Cic.

rēmiscĕo -miscŭi -mistum (-mixtum), 2. *to mix, mix up, mingle;* Lydis remixtum carmen tibiis, Hor.

rēmissē, adv. (remissus). **I.** *loosely ;* orationem non astricte, sed remissius numerosam esse oportere, Cic. **II.** *gently, mildly ;* remissius disputare, Cic.

rēmissĭo -ōnis, f. (remitto). **I.** *sending back;* obsidum captivorumque, Liv. **II.** *a letting down.* **A.** Lit., 1, *a letting fall, lowering ;* superciliorum, Cic.; 2, *letting fall, lowering, sinking ;* vocis contentiones et remissiones, Cic. **B.** Transf., 1, *breaking off, interrupting, ceasing ;* morbi, Cic.; usūs, Cic.; 2, *a remitting ;* tributi in triennium, Tac.; 3, remissio animi; a, *relaxation, recreation,* Cic.; b, *quiet, tranquillity ;* in acerbissima injuria remissio animi ac dissolutio, Cic.; c, *mildness,* Cic.

rēmissus -a -um, p. adj. (from remitto), *relaxed, languid.* **I.** Lit., corpora, Cic. **II.** Fig., **A.** In a bad sense, *negligent, remiss, inactive;* animus, Cic.; te remissiorem in petendo, Cic **B.** In a good sense; 1, *less severe ;* ventus re missior, Caes.; frigora remissiora, Caes.; 2, *mild, gentle,* Cic.; 3, *cheerful, merry, lively ;* homo, Cic.; jocus, Cic.

rēmitto -mīsi -missum, 3. **I.** *to send back, send ;* mulieres Romam, Cic.; obsides alicui, Caes.; nuntium, *to send a divorce to,* Cic.; so 1, *to throw back ;* pila, Caes.; 2, *to give back, return ;* alicui beneficium, Caes.; 3, *to give back from oneself ;* a, vocem nemora reinittunt, echo, Verg.; b, *to cause, produce ;* atramenta remittunt labem, Hor. **II.** *to let go back, relax ;* habenas, Cic.; frena equo, Ov.; arcum, Hor.; so 1, *to let sink down ;* brachia, Verg.; tunica remissa, Ov.; 2, *to loosen ;* vincula, Ov.; esp., a, *to make liquid (again);* calor mella liquefacta remittit, Verg.; b, *to free ;* vere remissus ager, *freed from ice and snow,* Ov.; c, *to cause to relax, to relieve, release, abate ;* spes animos a certamine remisit, Liv.; se remittere, *to leave off work, refresh oneself,* Nep.; cantus remittunt animum, *relieve, enliven the mind,* Cic.; reflex., se remittere, or simply remittere, *to abate, become milder, cease ;* quum remiserant dolores, Cic.; ventus remisit, Caes.; 3, *to give free scope to ;* animi appetitus, qui tum remitterentur, tum continerentur, Cic.; 4, *to give up, to allow, forego, concede, grant ;* a, omnia ista concedam ac remittam, Cic. · provinciam remitto, exercitum depono, Cic.; b, *to renounce some work, punishment,* etc., *to remit, forego, give up ;* navem in triennium, Cic.; Erycis tibi terga remitto, *make no use of,* Verg.;

inimicitias suas reipublicae, Liv.; c, to abate, stop; de celeritate, Cic.; aliquantum, Cic.; aliquid de severitate cogendi, Cic.

rĕmōlĭor, 4. dep. to press back, push back, move back; pondera terrae, Ov.

rĕmollesco, 3. to become soft again. I. Lit., cera remollescit sole, Ov. II. Fig., a, to be moved by; precibus, Ov.; b, to become effeminate; eā re ad laborem ferendum remollescere homines, Caes.

rĕmollĭo, 4. to make soft again; fig., to make effeminate, to weaken; artus, Ov.

rĕmōra -ae, f. a delay, hindrance, Plaut.

rĕmōrāmen -ĭnis, n. (remoror), a delay, Ov.

rĕmordĕo -mordi -morsum, 2. to bite again; fig., to annoy, disquiet, harass; te cura remordet, Verg.

rĕmŏror, 1. dep. I. Intransit., to remain behind, delay, dally, linger, loiter; in Italia, Liv. II. Transit., to delay, obstruct, hinder; aliquem, Cic.; iter alicuius, Sall.

rĕmōtē, adv. (remotus), afar off, at a distance; aliae (stellae) propius a terris, aliae remotius eadem spatia conficiunt, Cic.

rĕmōtĭo -ōnis, f. (removeo), a putting away, removing; criminis, repelling, Cic.

rĕmōtus -a -um, p. adj. (from removeo). I. Lit., distant, afar off, remote; locus ab arbitris remotus, Cic.; loci remoti a mari, Cic. II. Fig., removed from; a, free from; ab suspicione remotissimus, Cic.; a vulgari scientia remotiora, Cic.; b, disinclined to, averse from; ab inani laude remotus, Cic.; c, subst., rĕmōta -ōrum, n. = ἀπόπροηγμένα, of the Stoics, things to be rejected, Cic.

rĕmŏvĕo -mōvi -mōtum, 2. to move back, remove, take away, put away; pecora, Caes.; arbitros, Cic.; aliquid ex oratione, Cic.; aliquid de medio, Cic.; aliquid ab oculis, Cic.; equos ex conspectu, Caes.; aliquem a republica, to deprive of political rights, Cic.; aliquem senatu, Liv.; removere se artibus, Cic.

rĕmūgĭo, 4. I. to bellow again, bellow back; ad verba alicuius, Ov. II. Transf., to roar back, resound, echo; vox assensu nemorum ingeminata remugit, Verg.

rĕmulcĕo -mulsi -mulsum, 2. to stroke back; caudam, Verg.

rĕmulcum -i, n. (ῥυμουλκέω, for ῥυμὸν ἕλκω), a tow-rope, towing cable; navem remulco adducere, Caes.

Rĕmŭlus -i, m. I. a king in Alba, Ov. II. the name of a hero, Verg.

rĕmūnĕrātĭo -ōnis, f. (remuneror), a recompense, repaying, return; benevolentiae, Cic.; officiorum, Cic.

rĕmūnĕror, 1. dep. to recompense, repay, reward; (α) with acc. of pers., aliquem simillimo munere, Cic.; aliquem magno praemio, Caes. (β) with acc. of thing, beneficia alicuius officiis, Cic.; (γ) absol., in accipiendo remunerandoque, Cic.

Rĕmŭrĭa = Lemuria, v. Lemures.

rĕmurmŭro, 1. to murmur against, murmur back; nec fracta remurmurat unda, Verg.

1. rēmus -i, m. (ἐρετμός), an oar. I. A. Lit., navigium remis incitare, Caes.; prov., remis ventisque, or ventis remis, by oars and sails, by all means in our power; res velis, ut aiunt, remisque fugienda, Cic. B. Fig., orationem dialecticorum remis propellere, Cic. II. Transf., remi, the hands and feet of a person swimming, Ov.; of the wings of a bird, alarum remis, Ov.

2. Rēmus -i, m. the twin brother of Romulus, first king of Rome, who slew him in a dispute respecting the foundation of the city.

3. Rēmus, v. Remi.

rĕnarro, 1. to relate again; fata divum, Verg.

rĕnascor -nātus sum, 3. dep. to be born again, arise, grow again. I. Lit., pinnae renascuntur, Cic. II. Transf., a, of concr., ab secunda origine velut ab stirpibus laetius feraciusque renata urbs, Liv.; b, of abstr., bellum istuc renatum, Cic.

rĕnāvĭgo, 1. to sail back; in haec regna, Cic.

rĕnĕo, 2. to unspin, unravel that which has been spun; dolent fila reneri, that the destiny is reversed, Ov.

rēnes -um and -ĭum, m. the kidneys, Cic.

rĕnīdĕo, 2. I. to shine, gleam back, to glitter, be bright, to shimmer; pura nocturno renidet luna mari, Hor.; non ebur neque aureum mea renidet in domo lacunar, Hor. II. Meton., to beam with joy, be joyful, cheerful, to laugh, and in a bad sense to laugh scornfully, to grin; homo renidens, Liv.; adjecisse praedam torquibus exiguis renidet, Hor.

rĕnīdesco, 3. (renideo), to glitter, Lucr.

rĕnītor, 3. dep. to oppose, withstand, resist, Liv.

1. rĕno, 1. to swim back, Hor.

2. rēno (rhēno) -ōnis, m. an animal of northern Europe, perhaps the reindeer, Caes.

rĕnōdo, 1. to unbind, untie; comam, Hor.

rĕnōvāmen -ĭnis, n. (renovo), a renewal, new condition, Ov.

rĕnŏvātĭo -ōnis, f. (renovo), a renewing, renewal, renovation. I. Lit., mundi, Cic.; esp., renovatio singulorum annorum, compound interest, Cic. II. Transf., renovatio timoris, Cic.

rĕnŏvo, 1. to renew, renovate, restore. I. Lit., templum, Cic.; agrum aratro, to plough land that has been left fallow for some time, Ov.; esp., fenus in singulos annos, to reckon compound interest, Cic.; centesimae quotannis renovatae, Cic. II. Transf., a, to renew; scelus suum illud pristinum, Cic.; bellum, Caes.; ex morbo velut renovatus flos juventae, Liv.; animos ad odium renovare, to inflame afresh to, Cic.; b, to renew in thought or words, to repeat, recall; renovabo illud quod initio dixi, Cic.; c, to refresh, restore, renew in strength; reficere et renovare rempublicam, Cic.

rĕnŭmĕro, 1. to count over, pay, pay back, repay, Plaut.

rĕnuntĭātĭo -ōnis, f. (renuntio), a proclamation, declaration, public announcement; with subject. genit., eius, Cic.; with object. genit., suffragiorum, Cic.

rĕnuntĭo (rĕnuncĭo), 1. I. to bring back word, report, announce; a, gen. with acc., with de and the abl., with acc. and infin., with a depend. rel. sent., assentior renuntioque vobis nihil esse quod, etc., Cic.; renuntiatum est de obitu Tulliae filiae tuae, I was informed, ap. Cic.; b, to make an official announcement or declaration, to report; aliquid ad senatum, Cic.; c, to make a thing publicly known, to announce, e.g., the election of a consul, etc., to proclaim; with double acc., L. Murenam consulem, Cic.; in comit. pass. with double nom., sacerdos Climachias renuntiatus est, Cic. II. to disclaim, refuse, renounce; amicitiam alicui, Liv.; hospitium alicui, Cic.; decisionem tutoribus, Cic.

rĕnuntĭus -ĭi, m. one who brings back word, a reporter, Plaut.

rĕnŭo -nŭi, 3. *to deny by a motion of the head, to refuse, deny, disapprove, reject;* renuit negitatque Sabellus, Hor.; with dat., huic decem millium crimini, *to deny,* Cic.; with acc., nullum convivium, *to decline,* Cic.

rĕnūto, 1. (intens. of renuo), *to refuse, deny, decline,* Lucr.

rĕnūtus, abl. -ū, m. (renuo), *a denial, refusal,* Plin.

rĕor, rătus sum, 2. dep. (root RE, Gr. PE-ω, *I say*), *to think, be of opinion, suppose, judge;* (a), with acc. and infin. or with infin. alone, rentur eos esse, quales se ipsi velint, Cic.; rebantur enim fore ut, etc., Cic.; (β) with double acc., alii rem incredibilem rati, Sall.; (γ) absol., reor in parenthesis, nam, reor, nullus posset esse jucundior, Cic.

rĕpāgŭla -ōrum, n. (repango). **I.** *the barrier in a circus or racecourse to keep in the horses,* Ov. **II.** *the bars* or *bolts fastening a door;* convulsis repagulis, Cic.; fig., omnia repagula pudoris officiique perfringere, *restraints, limits,* Cic.

rĕpandus -a -um, *bent backwards, turned up;* calceoli, Cic.

rĕpărābĭlis -e (reparo), *that can be repaired or restored;* damnum, Ov.

rĕparco (rĕperco), 3. *to spare, refrain from, abstain from;* id facere, Lucr.

rĕpăro, 1. **I.** *to prepare anew, repair, restore, renew.* **A.** Gen., perdere videbatur, quod reparare posset, Cic.; vires, Ov.; tribuniciam potestatem, Liv. **B.** Esp., *to fill up, complete;* exercitum, Liv.; damna caelestia lunae, Hor.; cornua (of the moon), Ov. **II.** *to barter for, purchase with;* vina Syrā reparata merce, Hor.

rĕpastĭnātĭo -ōnis, f. (repastino), *a digging up again,* Cic.

rĕpastĭno, 1. *to dig, trench, delve again,* Plin.

rĕpecto -pexus, 3. *to comb again;* coma repexa, Ov.

rĕpĕdo, 1. (pes), *to go back, retreat,* Lucr.

rĕpello, rĕpŭli (reppŭli) -pulsum, 3. **I.** *to drive back, drive away.* **A.** Lit., homines a templi aditu, Cic.; aliquem ex urbe, Cic.; hostes in silvas, Caes. **B.** Fig., *to drive away, banish, repel;* vim vi, Cic.; dolorem a se, Cic.; aliquem a spe, *deprive of hope,* Caes. **II.** *to push back, repulse.* **A.** Lit., repagula, Ov.; aliquem a genibus, Cic.; tellurem (sc. a mari), *to sail away from,* Ov.; amnes Oceani pede repellere, *to spurn* (of a star rising from the sea), Verg. **B.** Fig., **1,** criminationes, *to refute,* Cic.; **2,** *to spurn, scorn, repel;* connubia, Verg.; preces, Ov.; repulsi sunt ii, quos, etc., Cic.

rĕpendo -pendi -pensum, 3. **I.** *to weigh back again;* pensa, *to return an equal weight of,* Ov. **II.** *to weigh against.* **A.** Lit., **1,** aurum pro capite, Cic.; **2,** *to ransom;* miles auro repensus, Hor. **B.** Transf., *to repay, recompense, requite;* gratiam, Ov.; si magna rependam, Verg.; pretium vitae, Prop.; damna formae ingenio, *make up for,* Ov.

rĕpens -entis (ῥέπω, i.e., vergo). **I.** *sudden, unexpected;* adventus, Cic.; adv., repens alia nuntiatur clades, Liv. **II.** (In Tacitus only), *new, fresh, recent;* perfidia, Tac.

rĕpenso, 1. (intens. of rependo), *to repay, requite, recompense, make up for,* Sen.

rĕpentĕ, adv. (repens), *suddenly, unexpectedly,* Cic.

rĕpentīnus -a -um (repens), *sudden, unlooked for, unexpected;* amor, Cic.; adventus, Caes.; venenum, *quick-working,* Tac.; ignoti

homines et repentini, *upstarts,* Cic. Hence, adv., **rĕpentīno,** *suddenly, unexpectedly,* Cic.

rĕpercussĭo -ōnis, f. (repercutio), *a rebounding,* Sen.

rĕpercussus -ūs, m. (repercutio), *a rebounding, reverberation* (of sound, etc.), *echo, reflection;* quo plenior et gravior vox repercussu intumescat, Tac.

rĕpercŭtĭo -cussi -cussum, 3. *to strike back, drive back, cause to rebound* (of sound, etc.); discus repercussus in aëra, Ov.; esp., pass., repercuti, *to bound back,* and repercussus, *bounding back;* **a,** of sound, *to re-echo;* valles repercussae (clamoribus), Liv.; **b,** of light, *to be reflected;* lumen aquae sole repercussum, Verg.

rĕpĕrĭo, rĕpĕri (reppĕri) -pertum (re and PER-io, cf. comperio), 4. *to find, meet again.* **I.** Lit., mortui sunt reperti, Cic. **II.** Fig., **A.** 1, *to reveal, discover, ascertain, find out;* causas duas, Cic.; neque reperire poterat quanta esset, etc., Caes.; in pass. with double nom., *to be found out* = *to appear;* Stoici inopes reperiuntur, Cic.; improbus reperiebare, Cic.; with acc. and infin. = *to find out,* as stated in history; quem Tarentum venisse L. Camillo Appio Claudio consulibus reperio, Liv; in pass. with nom. and infin., in Italiae partes Pythagoras venisse reperitur, Cic.; **2,** *to find, acquire, gain;* sibi salutem, Caes.; nomen ex inventore, Cic. **B.** *to find out something new, discover, invent;* nihil novi, Cic.; viam quā, etc., Cic.

rĕpertor -ōris, m. (reperio), *a discoverer, inventor;* medicinae, Verg.; hominum rerumque, *Jupiter,* Verg.

rĕpertus -a -um, partic. of reperio.

rĕpĕtentĭa -ae, f. (repeto), *a recollection, remembrance,* Lucr. (?)

rĕpĕtītĭo -ōnis, f. (repeto), *repetition;* **a,** eiusdem verbi crebra repetitio, Cic.; **b,** as a figure of speech = ἀναφορά, *the repetition of the same word at the beginning of several sentences,* Cic.

rĕpĕtītor -ōris, m. (repeto), *one who reclaims* or *demands back again;* nuptae ademptae, Cic.

rĕpĕto -īvi and -ii -ītum, 3. **I.** *to strive after again.* **A.** *to attack again, fall upon again;* regem repetitum saepius cuspide, Liv. **B.** *to go to again, turn to again, return to;* castra, Cic.; retro in Asiam, Liv. **II.** Transf., **A.** *to ask back* or *again;* **1,** *to ask again* or *anew, ask for;* Gallum ab eodem repetit, Caes.; **2,** *to ask back, demand back;* promissa, Cic.; Salaminii Homerum repetunt, *claim as their countryman,* Cic.; pecunias ereptas, Cic.; esp., **a,** res repetere, *to demand satisfaction of an enemy* (used of the Fetiales), Cic.; **b,** *to demand back again;* res, *to demand one's own property from a legal tribunal,* Cic.; pecuniae repetundae, or simply repetundae, *money extorted from the provinces by their governors;* meton., *extortion;* lex repetundarum pecuniarum, de pecuniis repetundis, *law against extortion,* Cic.; **3,** *to demand as one's right;* jus suum, Cic.; rationem ab aliquo, Cic. **B.** *to fetch back;* **1,** **a,** *to fetch afresh;* alii (elephanti) repetiti ac trajecti sunt, Liv.; **b,** *to renew, begin again;* pugnam, Liv.; studia, Caes.; partic., repetitus, poet., as an adv. = *anew, afresh;* repetita robora caedit, Ov.; **c,** *to think over again, recall, remember;* rei memoriam, Cic.; **2,** *to repeat by words or writing;* repete quae coepisti, Cic.; **3,** *to trace back from antiquity, deduce, fetch;* originem domūs, Verg.; aliquid alte, et a capite, Cic.; haec tam longe repetita principia, Cic.; **4,** *to regain, recover;* libertatem, Liv.; **5,** *to reckon again;* repetitis et enumeratis diebus, Caes.

rĕpĕtundae, v. **repeto.**

16

rĕplĕo -plēvı -plētum, 2. *to fill again, fill up.* **I.** Lit., exhaustas domos, *complete, make good,* Cic.; consumpta, Cic.; exercitum, Liv. **II.** *to make full, fill, satisfy.* **A.** corpora carne, Ov.; exercitum frumento, *supply with,* Caes.; fig., repleri scientiâ juris, Cic.; hence, **rĕplētus** -a -um, *filled, full;* lit. and fig., templa, Cic. **B.** *to infect;* ut curantes eâdem vi morbi repletos secum traherent, Liv.

rĕplētus -a -um, partic. of repleo (q.v.).

rĕplĭcātĭo -ōnis, f. (replico), *a rolling again, rolling round;* ut replicatione quâdam mundi motum regat atque tueatur, Cic.

rĕplĭco, 1. *to fold back, unroll;* fig., *to unfold, unroll, turn over;* memoriam temporum, Cic.; memoriam annalium, Cic.; temporis primum quidque replicans, Cic.

rēpo, repsi, reptum, 3. (root REP, Gr. ΕΡΠ-ω), *to creep, crawl;* 1, lit., cochleae inter saxa repentes, Sall.; 2, transf., of slow travellers, Hor.; of clouds, Lucr.; fire, Lucr.; 3, fig., sermones repentes per humum, *a vulgar, prosaic style,* Hor.

rĕpōno -pŏsŭi -pŏsĭtum (-postum), 3. **I.** *to place back, put behind;* 1, cervicem, *to bend back,* Lucr.; 2, *to lay up in store, lay by, preserve;* pecuniam in thesauris, Liv.; arma, Caes.; fig., haec sensibus imis reponas, *impress deep in,* Verg.; 3, *to lay aside, put on one side;* tela, Ov.; faciemque deae vestemque, Verg.; falcem arbusta reponunt, *make unnecessary,* Verg.; transf., to *give up;* caestum artemque, Verg.; 4, *to bury, lay in the earth;* tellure repostos, Verg. **II.** *to place a thing back in its former place, put back, restore;* 1, columnas, Cic.; lapidem suo loco, Cic.; se in cubitum, *recline at table again, begin to eat,* Hor.; 2, *to place on the table again;* plena pocula, Verg.; 3, *to restore a thing to its former condition;* robora flammis ambesa, Verg.; hence, *to restore a person;* aliquem in sceptra, Verg.; 4, *to bring on the boards again, represent again;* fabulam, Hor. **III.** *to place one thing against another, in the place of another;* 1, *to put in the place of;* te meas epistolas delere, ut reponas tuas, Cic.; 2, *to answer again;* ne tibi ego idem reponam, Cic.; 3, *to requite, return;* haec pro virginitate reponit, Verg. **IV.** *to place in or on;* 1, lit., quae sacra quaedam more Atheniensium virginum reposita in capitibus sustinebant, Cic.; 2, transf., a, sidera in numero deorum, Cic.; b, *to place, cause to rest;* spem in virtute, Caes.; causam totam in judicum humanitate, Cic.

rĕporto, 1. *to bear back, bring back, carry back.* **I.** Lit., **A.** exercitum Britanniâ, Cic.; milites navibus in Siciliam, Caes. **B.** *to bring back, to bring back home,* as victor, nihil ex praeda domum, Cic.; victoriam, non pacem domum, Liv. **II.** Transf., 1, *to bring back, deliver;* adytis haec tristia dicta, Verg.; 2, *to bring to a person;* alicui solatium aliquod, Cic.

rĕposco, 3. **I.** *to ask back again, demand back;* arma, Ov.; alter a me Catilinam, alter Cethegum reposcebat, Cic.; with double acc., *to ask back something from a person;* aliquem simulacrum, Cic.; Parthos signa, Verg. **II.** *to demand as a right, claim:* regem ad supplicium, Verg.; ab aliquo rationem vitae, Cic.; with double acc., quos illi poenas (*as a punishment*) reposcent, Verg.

rĕpŏsĭtōrĭum -ĭi, n. (repono), *a tray, waiter, stand,* Plin.

rĕpŏsĭtus (rĕpostus) -a -um. **I.** Partic. of repono. **II.** P. adj., *remote, distant;* terrae repostae, Verg.

rĕpostor -ōris, m. (repono), *a restorer;* templorum, Ov.

rĕpōtĭa -ōrum, n. (re and poto), *a drinking, revelling the day after an entertainment,* Hor.

rĕpraesentātĭo -ōnis, f. (repraesento). **I.** *a representation, a lively description,* Plin. **II.** *payment in cash,* Cic.

rĕpraesento. 1. **I.** *to represent, make present to the imagination, bring before the mind, show, make manifest;* a, quod ipsum templum repraesentabat memoriam consulatus mei, Cic.; b, *to express, imitate;* virtutem moresque Catonis, Hor. **II.** *to perform immediately, hasten;* a, se repraesentaturum id, etc., Caes.; medicinam, *use directly,* Cic.; diem promissorum, Cic.; si repraesentari morte mea libertas civitatis posset, *brought about at once,* Cic.; b, esp. t. t. of commercial language, *to pay cash, pay ready money;* pecuniam, Cic.

rĕprĕhendo -prĕhendi -prĕhensum, 3. and **rĕprendo** -prendi -prensum, 3. *to catch, to hold back, to seize, hold fast, detain.* **I.** Lit., quosdam manu, Liv., fig., revocat virtus vel potius reprehendit manu, Cic. **II.** Fig. **A.** Gen., genus pecuniae, Cic. **B.** Esp., 1, *to blame, censure, reprove, reprehend;* aliquem, Cic.; aliquem in eo quod, etc., Cic.; id in me reprehendis, Cic.; 2, rhet. t. t., *to refute,* Cic.

rĕprĕhensĭo -ōnis, f. (reprehendo). **I.** *a holding back;* fig., *a stopping or check in speaking, sine reprehensione,* Cic. **II.** Esp., 1, *blame, censure, reprehension;* culpae, vitae, Cic.; plur., Cic.; 2, rhet. t. t., *a refuting, refutation,* Cic.

rĕprĕhenso, 1. (freq. of reprehendo), *to hold back eagerly, to hold fast;* singulos, Liv.

rĕprĕhensor -ōris, m. (reprehendo). **I.** *a censurer, reprover,* Cic. **II.** *an improver, reformer;* comitiorum, Cic.

rĕpressor -ōris, m. (reprimo), *a represser, restrainer;* caedis quotidianae, Cic.

rĕprĭmo -pressi -pressum, 3. (re and premo), *to hold back, restrain, hinder, repress.* **I.** Lit., lacum Albanum, Cic.; dextram, Verg.; retro pedem, Verg.; represso jam Lucterio ac remoto (in battle), Caes.; (Mithridatem) repressum magna ex parte, non oppressum, Cic. **II.** Fig., *to keep under, check, curb, restrain, repress;* a, of things, furorem exsultantem, Cic.; animi incitationem atque alacritatem, Caes.; conatus alicuius, Cic.; b, of persons as objects, se, *to restrain oneself,* Cic.; concitatam multitudinem, Cic.

rĕprŏbo, 1. *to disapprove,* Cic.(?)

rĕprōmissĭo -ōnis, f. (repromitto), *a counter-promise,* Cic.

rĕprōmitto -mīsi -missum, 3. *to make a counter-promise, to promise in return,* Cic.

reptātĭo -ōnis, f. (repto), *a creeping, crawling,* Quint.

reptātus -ūs, m. (repto), *a creeping (of plants),* Plin.

rĕpto, 1. (intens. of repo), *to creep, crawl,* applied to slow walkers or travellers, Hor.

rĕpŭdĭātĭo -ōnis, f. (repudio), *a refusal, rejecting, disdaining;* supplicum, Cic.

rĕpŭdĭo, 1. (repudium). **I.** *to refuse, reject, disdain;* cuius vota et preces a vestris mentibus repudiare debetis, Cic.; pacem, Cic.; conditionem aequissimam, Cic. **II.** Esp. of married or betrothed persons, *to repudiate, divorce, separate oneself from;* uxorem, Suet.

rĕpŭdĭum -ĭi, n. (re and pes, as tripudium from terra and pes), *a separation between married or betrothed persons, repudiation, divorce;* alicui repudium renuntiare, or remittere, *to send a divorce to,* Plaut.; repudium dicere. Tac.

rĕpŭĕrasco, 3. *to become a boy again, to sport, frolic like a child*, Cic.

rĕpugnans, p. adj. (from repugno), *contrary, opposed*; subst., **rĕpugnantĭa** -ium, n. *contradictory things*, Cic.

rĕpugnantĕr, adv.(repugnans),*unwillingly, with repugnance*, Cic.

rĕpugnantĭa -ae, f. (repugno). **I.** *resistance, means of resistance*; natura hanc dedit repugnantiam apibus, Plin. **II.** Fig., *a contrariety, discordance* (opp. concordia); rerum, Cic.

rĕpugno, 1. *to oppose, resist, withstand.* **I.** Lit., nostri primo fortiter repugnare, Caes. **II.** Transf., **A.** Gen., *to be opposed to, to oppose, resist*; contra veritatem, Caes.; quum huic (cupiditati) obsecutus sis, illi est repugnandum, Cic.; non repugno, foll. by quominus and subj., Cic. **B.** Esp., *to be naturally opposed or repugnant to, to be inconsistent with, incompatible with*; simulatio amicitiae repugnat maxime, Cic.; haec inter se quam repugnent, plerique non vident, Cic.

rĕpullŭlo, 1. *to sprout out again*, Plin.

rĕpulsa -ae, f. (repello). **I.** *a repulse in soliciting an office, a rejection*; repulsa consulatus, Cic.; aediiicia, Cic.; a populo repulsam ferre, or accipere, Cic. **II.** Transf., *a denial, refusal*; amor crescit dolore repulsae, Ov.

rĕpulso, 1. (intens. of repello), *to beat back.* **I.** colles verba repulsantes, *echoing*, Lucr. **II.** *to repel again and again*; vera repulsans pectus verba, Lucr.

1. **rĕpulsus** -a -um, p. adj. with compar. (repello), *removed*; quod procul a vera nimis est ratione repulsum, Lucr.

2. **rĕpulsus** -ūs, m. (repello), *a striking back*, hence, *the reflection of light, echoing of sound*; durioris materiae, *resistance*, Cic.

rĕpūmĭcātĭo -ōnis, f. (re and pumico), *a rubbing down again, repolishing*, Plin.

rĕpungo, 3. *to prick again, goad again*; fig., leviter illorum animos, Cic.

rĕpurgo, 1. *to cleanse again.* **I. A.** Lit., iter, Liv.; humum saxis, Ov. **B.** Transf., caelum, Ov. **II.** Meton., *to clear away, purge out*; quicquid in Aenea fuerat mortale repurgat, Ov.

rĕpūtātĭo -ōnis, f. (reputo), *a consideration, reflecting upon, pondering*, Tac.

rĕpūto, 1. **I.** *to reckon, count, compute*; ex hoc die superiores solis defectiones usque ad illam quae, etc., Cic. **II.** Transf., *to think over, consider, ponder*; horum nihil umquam, Cic.; with acc. and infin., cum tibi nihil inerito accidisse reputabis, Cic.; with depend. interrog. sent., quid ille vellet, Cic.

rĕquĭes -ētis, f. *rest, repose.* **I.** Lit., non labor meus, non requies, Cic.; curarum, Cic.; animi et corporis, Cic. **II.** Meton., *a resting-place*, Hor. (dat. not used, acc., requietem and requiem, Oic.; abl., requiete, Cic. poet.; requie, Ov.).

rĕquĭesco -quĭēvi -quĭētum, 3. *to rest, repose.* **I.** Lit., **A.** Gen., 1, of persons, in sella, Cic.; sub umbra, Verg.; a muneribus reipublicae, Cic.; 2, of things, vixdum requiesse aures a strepitu et tumultu hostili, Liv.; requiescit vitis in ulmo, *rests upon, is supported by*, Cic. **B.** Esp., 1, *to rest, to sleep*; lecto, Prop.; 2, *to rest in the grave*; in sepulchro requiescere mortuum, Cic. **II.** Transf., *to repose, find rest*; animus ex multis miseriis atque periculis requievit, Sall.; in spe huius, Cic. (syncop. perf. form, requierunt, Verg.; requiesse, Cic.).

rĕquĭētus -a -um, p. adj. (from requiesco), *rested, refreshed*; miles, Liv.; ager, *fallow*, Ov.

rĕquīrĭto, 1. (intens. of requiro), *to inquire after*, Plaut.

rĕquīro -quīsīvi -quīsītum, 3. (re and quaero). **I.** *to seek, search for again.* **A.** Lit., libros, Cic. **B.** Transf., 1, *to miss, need, feel the want of*; majorum prudentiam in aliqua re, Cic.; subsidia belli, Cic.; 2, *to demand, to desire, consider necessary*; virtus nullam voluptatem requirit, Cic.; in hoc bello virtutes multae requiruntur, Cic. **II.** *to ask for, inquire after.* **A.** Gen., domum alicuius, Cic.; quae a me de Vatinio requiris, Cic.; quoniam nihil ex te hi majores natu requirunt, Cic.; with depend. interrog., illud quoque requirit, qua ratione fecerit, Cic. **B.** *to investigate*; rationes, Cic.

rĕquīsītum -i, n. (requiro), *need, necessity*, Sall.

rēs, rĕi, f. (connected with PE -ω, whence ῥῆμα), *a thing, object, matter, affair, circumstance.* **I.** Gen., *divinae humanaeque res, natura rerum, the world*, Cic.; genit., rerum, *pleonastic, ficta rerum*, Hor.; abdita rerum, Hor.; rerum, used to strengthen a superl., rerum pulcherrima, Roma, Verg.; si res postulabit, *if the position oj affairs shall require*, Cic.; homines nullā re bonā digni, *good for nothing*, Cic.; re natā, Cic.; pro re, *according to circumstances*, Liv.; res populi Romani perscribere, *to narrate the affairs of the Roman people, write the history of Rome*, Liv. **II.** Esp., **A.** Emphatic, *the thing itself, the real thing, the reality*; rem opinor spectari oportere, non verba, Cic.; hos deos non re, sed opinione esse, Cic.; quantum distet argumentatio ab re ipsa atque a veritate, Cic.; et re vera, *and in truth*, Cic. **B.** *possessions, property, wealth*; rem facere, Hor.; augere, Cic.; plur., privatae res, Cic. **C.** *interest, advantage, benefit*; consulere suis rebus, Nep.; in rem suam convertere, Cic.; e or ex re publica (*to the advantage of the state*) fecisse, Cic.; ducere, Liv.; ex or e re publica est, with acc. and infin., *it is for the public benefit*, Cic.; ex re mea, *to my advantage*, Cic. **D.** *ground, reason*, only in the phrases, eā (hāc) re, ob eam (hanc) rem, *on this account, on that account*, Cic. **E.** *a matter of business, an affair*; rem cum aliquo transigere, Cic.; transf., res (alicui) est cum aliquo, *to have to do with*; tecum mihi res est, T. Rosci, quoniam, etc., Cic. **F.** *a lawsuit, cause, action*; utrum rem an litem dici oporteret, Cic. **G.** res publica, (and in histor.) simply res; a, res publica, *the republic, the state, commonwealth, government*; rem publicam sustinere, Cic.; b, simply res, res Romana, *the Roman state*, Liv.

rĕsăcro, 1. *to free from a curse*, Nep

rĕsaevĭo, 4. *to rage again*, Ov.

rĕsălūtātĭo -ōnis, f. (resaluto), *a greeting in return*, Suet.

rĕsălūto, 1. *to salute again, return a greeting to*; aliquem, Cic.

rĕsānesco -sānŭi, 3. *to become sound again*; to heal again, Ov.

rĕsarcĭo -sarsi -sartum, 4. *to patch again, mend again, repair.* **I.** Lit., tecta, Liv. **II.** Fig., *to repair, restore*; detrimentum, Caes.

rescindo -scĭdi -scissum, 3. *to tear off again, tear away again, cut off, cut away.* **I. A.** Lit., vallum ac loricam falcibus, Caes.; pontem, *to break away*, Caes.; latebram teli, *to cut open*, Verg.; vulnus, *to open again*, Ov.; and fig., luctus obductos, *to renew*, Ov. **B.** Meton., hence, *to open*; locum firmatum, Cic. **II.** Transf., *to rescind, repeal, abrogate a law, decree, etc.*; acta M. Antonii, Cic.; totam triennii praeturam, Cic.

rescisco -scīvi and -scĭi -scītum, 3. *to find out, ascertain*; quum id rescierit, Cic.

rescrībo -scripsi -scriptum, 3. **I.** *to write again, to write anew; ex eodem milite novas legiones, to enrol again*, Liv. **II.** *to write back, answer in writing;* 1, ad aliquem, Cic.; alicui, Cic.; 2, litteris, ad litteras, or ad epistolam, Cic.; *of the emperor, to answer a petition or inquiry in writing*, Suet.; hence, **rescriptum** -i, n. *an imperial rescript*, Tac. **III.** a, in book-keeping, *to enter to the credit of an account, to pay, repay;* reliqua rescribamus, Cic.; quod tu numquam rescribere (*pay again*) possis, Hor.; b, *to transfer from one class of soldiers to another;* ad equum, jestingly, with a double meaning, *to make cavalry* and *to place in the order of knights*, Caes.

rĕsĕco -sĕcŭi -sectum, 1. *to cut off.* **I.** Lit., linguam, Cic.; partem de tergore, Ov. **II.** Transf., *to cut off, put away, remove;* libidinem, Cic.; spem longam, Hor.

rĕsĕcro, 1. (re and sacro), *to adjure repeatedly, implore again and again*, Plaut. (another form resacro, q.v.).

rĕsēdo, 1. *to heal, assuage*, Plin.

rĕsegmĭna -um, n. (reseco), *cuttings, parings*, Plin.

rĕsēmĭno, 1. *to beget, produce again*, Ov.

rĕsĕquor -sĕcūtus (-sĕquūtus), 3. dep. *to follow, pursue;* aliquem dictis, *to answer*, Ov.

1. **rĕsĕro** -sēvi, 3. *to sow again, set again, plant again*, Plin.

2. **rĕsĕro**, 1. *to unclose, open.* **I.** Lit., **A.** In a narrow sense, *to open a door;* fores, januam, Ov. **B.** In a wider sense, *to open;* pectus, *to tear open*, Ov. **II.** Transf., **A.** *to open, make accessible;* Italiam exteris gentibus, Cic.; aures, Liv. **B.** *to reveal;* augustae oracula mentis, Ov. **C.** *to open* = *to begin;* annum, Ov.

rĕservo, 1. **I.** *to lay up, keep back, reserve, keep;* hoc consilium ad extremum, Caes.; in aliud tempus, Caes.; cetera praesenti sermoni, Cic. **II.** a, *to save;* omnes, Cic.; b, *to retain, preserve;* nihil ad similitudinem hominis, *nothing human*, Cic.

rĕses -sĭdis (resideo). **I.** *remaining, sitting, staying behind;* reses in urbe plebs, Liv. **II.** *motionless, inactive, inert;* eum residem tempus terere, Liv.; animus, Verg.

rĕsĭdĕo -sēdi -sessum, 2. (re and sedeo), *to remain sitting, to abide, stay.* **I.** Lit., a, *to re-sideamus, let us sit down*, Cic.; in equo, Ov.; in republica, Cic.; b, *to celebrate a festival or holiday;* denicales, quae a nece appellatae sunt, quia residentur mortuis, *kept in honour of the dead*, Cic. **II.** Transf., in corpore nullum residere sensum, Cic.; residet spes in tua virtute, *depends upon*, Cic.; cuius culpa non magis in te residit, Cic.

rĕsĭdo -sēdi -sessum, 3. **I.** *to sit down, place oneself;* a, *to sit down to rest*, Cic.; mediis aedibus, Verg.; b, *to settle;* Siculis arvis, Verg.; c, *to stay in a place, remain;* in villa, Cic.; in oppido aliquo, Cic. **II.** Of inanimate things, *to sink down, settle.* **A.** Gen., 1, lit., si montes resedissent, Cic.; 2, fig., a, *to sink, to settle down, abate, grow quiet;* mens resedit, Caes.; cum tumor animi resedisset, Cic.; b, *to become tired, to be weary, exhausted;* longiore certamine sensim residere Samnitium animos, Liv. **B.** *to sink down* = *to draw back, withdraw;* a, lit., maria ʼn se ipsa resldant, Verg.; b, fig., sex mihi surgat opus numeris, in quinque residat, *interchange hexameter and pentameter*, Ov.

rĕsĭdŭus -a -um (resideo), *remaining, left behind, outstanding;* odium, Cic.; simulatio, Liv.; pecuniae, Cic.; subst., **rĕsĭdŭum** -i, n. *that which remains, the remainder, residue, rest*, Cic.

rĕsigno, 1. **I.** *to unseal, open.* **A.** Lit., literas, Cic.; testamenta, Hor. **B.** Fig., 1, *to open* = *to reveal;* venientia fata, Ov.; 2, *to cancel, annul, destroy;* omnem tabularum fidem, Cic.; 3, *to release, free;* lumina morte resignat (Mercurius), *releases from death*, Verg. **II.** *to enter from one account-book into another, to give back, resign;* cuncta, Hor.; quae dedit, Hor.

rĕsĭlĭo -sĭlŭi -sultum, 4. (re and salio), *to leap back, spring back;* in gelidos lacus, Ov.; ad manipulos, Liv. **I.** Of inanimate things, *to spring back, rebound;* resilit grando a culmine tecti, Ov.; fig., ubi scopulum offendis eiusmodi, ut non modo ab hoc crimen resilire videas, verum etiam, etc., Cic. **II.** Transf., *to contract, diminish;* in spatium breve, Ov.

rĕsĭmus -a -um, *bent backwards, turned up;* nares, Ov.

rēsīna -ae, f. (ῥητίνη), *resin*, Plin.

rēsīnācĕus -a -um (resina), *resinous*, Plin.

rēsīnātus -a -um (resina). **I.** *flavoured with resin;* vinum, Mart. **II.** *smeared with resin;* juventus (to take hairs off the skin), Juv.

rēsīnōsus -a -um (resina), *full of resin, resinous*, Plin.

rĕsĭpĭo, 3. (re and sapio), *to have a smack, taste, flavour of anything.* **I.** Lit., Plin. **II.** Fig., Epicurus minime resipiens patriam, *with no trace of the wit of his country*, i.e., *Athens*, Cic.

rĕsĭpisco -sĭpŭi and -sĭpĭi, also -sĭpīvi, 3. (resipio). **I.** *to recover one's senses, come to oneself again* (from fainting, etc.), Cic. **II.** *to become rational again, come to one's right mind*, Cic. (syncop. perf., resipisset, Cic.).

rĕsisto -stĭti, 3. **I.** *to remain standing.* **A.** a, in a position of rest, *to remain, continue;* ibi, Caes.; Romae, Cic.; b, *after motion, to stand still, halt*, Caes.; virtus resistet extra fores carceris, Cic.; negabat se umquam cum Curione restitisse, *had stopped to talk*, Cic. **B.** Transf., a, of discourse, sed ego in hoc resisto, *stop here*, Cic.; b, *to recover a footing, get to one's feet again;* ubi lapsi resistamus, Cic. **II.** *to resist, oppose, withstand.* **A.** Physically, a, of persons, hostibus, Caes.; vi contra vim, Liv.; b, of things, quae nunc immotae perstant ventisque resistunt, Ov.; c, morally, dolori fortiter, Cic.; lacrimis et precibus, Cic.; resistere et pugnare contra veritatem, Cic.; impers., omnibus huis resistitur, Caes.; foll. by ne and the subj., ne sibi statua poneretur, restitit, Nep.; foll. by quin and the subj., vix deorum opibus, quin obruatur Romana res, resisti potest, Liv.; cui nullâ vi resisti potest, foll. by quo secius and subj., Cic.; absol., restitit et pervicit Cato, Cic.

rĕsŏlūtus -a -um, p. adj. (from resolvo), *relaxed, effeminate*, Mart.

rĕsolvo -solvi -sŏlūtum, 3. *to unbind, untie, loose, loosen, open.* **I. A.** vestes, Ov.; equos, *to unyoke*, Ov.; puella resoluta capillos, *with di-shevelled hair*, Ov. **B.** Transf., 1, gleba se resolvit, *becomes loose*, Verg.; Cerberus immania terga resolvit fusus humi, *stretches out in sleep*, Verg.; 2, *to open;* litteras, Liv.; fauces in verba, Ov.; 3, *to melt;* ignis aurum resolvit, Lucr.; nivem, Ov.; 4, *to drive away, dissipate;* tenebras, Verg.; nebulas, Ov. **II.** Fig., 1, *to end;* curas, Verg.; litem lite, Hor.; 2, *to dissolve, to relax physically, weaken, make languid;* ut jacui totis resoluta medullis, Ov.; 3, *to abolish, destroy;* jura pudoris, Verg.; 4, *to free;* te piacula nulla resolvent, Hor.; 5, *to unravel, reveal;* dolos tecti (Labyrinthi) ambagesque, Verg.; 6, *to pay*, Plaut., Cic.

rĕsŏnābĭlis -e (resono), *resounding, echoing,* Ov.

rĕsŏno -sŏnŭi and -sŏnāvi, 1. **I.** Intransit., **A.** *to give back an echo, to resound, echo;* aedes plangoribus resonant, Verg.; resonans theatrum, Cic.; gloria virtuti resonat, *is an echo of*, Cic. **B.** *to sound again and again, to resound;* nervos resonare, Cic.; resonant avibus virgulta, Verg. **II.** Transf., **A.** *to re-echo, repeat;* doces silvas resonare Amaryllida, Verg.; umbrae resonarent triste et acutum, Hor.; in pass., in fidibus testudine resonatur (sonus), Cic. **B.** *to fill with sound;* lucos cantu, Verg.

rĕsŏnus -a -um (resono), *resounding, echoing;* voces, Ov.

rĕsorbĕo, 2. *to swallow, suck in, absorb again;* fluctus, Ov.

respecto, 1. (intens. of respicio). **I.** *to look eagerly back, look about for.* **A.** Lit., respectare ad tribunal, Liv.; with acc., arcem Romanam, Liv. **B.** Transf., verum haec ita praetereamus, ut tamen intuentes et respectantes relinquamus, Cic.; with acc., si qua pios respectant numina, *have regard for*, Cic. **II.** Meton., *to look for, expect;* par munus ab aliquo, Cic.

respectus -ūs, m. (respicio). **I.** *a looking back, looking around one.* **A.** Lit., sine respectu fugere, Liv.; incendiorum, *looking back upon*, Cic. **B.** Transf., *care, regard, respect, consideration towards;* Romanorum maxime respectus civitates movit, Liv.; sine respectu majestatis, Liv. **II.** Meton., *a place of refuge, a retreat;* quum respectum ad senatum non haberet, Cic.

respergo -spersi -spersum, 3. (re and spargo), *to besprinkle, sprinkle over;* manus sanguine, Cic.; aliquem cruore, Liv.; fig., servili probro respergi, Tac.

respersĭo -ōnis, f. (respergo), *a sprinkling over, besprinkling;* pigmentorum, Cic.; sumptuosa respersio, *sprinkling of the grave with incense and wine*, Cic.

respersus, abl. -ū, m. (respergo), *a sprinkling, besprinkling,* Plin.

respĭcĭo -spexi -spectum, 3. (re and specio), transit. and intransit., *to look behind, to look back.* **I.** Lit., Cic.; nusquam circumspiciens aut respiciens, Liv.; with acc., a, *to look back upon;* tribunal, Liv.; Eurydicen suam, Ov.; amicum, Verg.; b, *to see behind one, to observe;* quos ubi rex respexit, Liv.; angues a tergo, Verg.; with acc. and infin., respiciunt atram in nimbo volitare favillam, Verg. **II.** Transf., **A.** *to look back upon, reflect upon;* spatium praeteriti temporis, Cic.; b, *to have respect to;* (a) *to think upon, provide for;* ut respiciam generum meum, Caes.; (β) *to care for, consider;* rempublicam, Cic.; commoda populi, Cic.; c, *to belong to, fall to the care of;* ad hunc summa imperii respiciebat, Caes.; d, *to look towards with desire, to hope, expect;* spem ab Romanis, Liv.

respīrāmen -ĭnis, n. (respiro), *the windpipe,* Ov.

respīrātĭo -ōnis, f. (respiro). **I.** *a taking breath, respiration;* 1, lit., Cic.; 2, meton., *a pause in a speech where the speaker takes breath,* Cic. **II.** *an exhalation;* aquarum, Cic.

respīrātus -ū, m. (respiro), *a taking breath,* Cic.

respīro, 1. **I.** *to blow back, blow in a contrary direction;* of winds, Lucr. **II.** Esp., *to breathe back.* **A.** *to take breath, breathe, breathe out;* animam, Cic.; ex ea pars redditur respirando, Cic. **B.** *to take breath, recover oneself after any violent exertion;* 1, lit., Cic.; 2, fig., *to be relieved from fear, anxiety,* etc.; paulum a metu, Cic.; of abstractions, *to abate, decline;* cupiditas atque avaritia respiravit paulum, Cic.; oppugnatio respiravit, *took breath, declined in*

violence, Cic.; pass. impers., ita respiratum est, Cic.

resplendĕo -ŭi, 2. *to glitter back, be bright,* resplendent, Verg.

respondĕo -spondi -sponsum, 2. **I.** *to promise in return,* Plaut. **II.** *to answer.* **A.** Lit., *to answer* (prop., *by word of mouth*); tibi non rescribam, sed respondeam, Sen.; *to answer by word of mouth or by writing;* epistolae, Cic.; ad haec, Cic.; alicui ad rogatum, Cic.; videat quid respondeat, Cic.; respondent "cui," Cic.; esp., a, of judges, *to give decisions;* de jure, Cic.; criminibus respondere, *to defend oneself against,* Cic.; of oracles and soothsayers, *to answer,* Cic.; transf., saxa respondent voci, *give an echo,* Cic.; b, *to answer to one's name,* hence, *to appear, be present;* quum ad nomen nemo responderet, Liv.; Verrem non responsurum, Cic.; so of soldiers, *to answer to one's name, take one's place;* ad nomina non respondere, Liv.; fig., pedes respondere non vocatos, *be in readiness,* Cic. **B.** Transf., a, *to correspond to, to answer to, to agree or accord with;* verba verbis respondeant, Cic.; tua virtus opinioni hominum respondet, Cic.; b, *to requite, return;* amori amore, Liv.; c, *to lie over against;* contra respondet tellus, Verg.; d, *to be punctual in paying;* ad tempus, Cic.; e, *to balance, correspond to in strength,* etc.; orationi illorum, Cic.

responsĭo -ōnis, f. (respondeo). **I.** *a reply,* *answer;* responsionem elicere, Cic. **II.** Rhet. t., sibi ipsi responsio, *a replying to one's own argument* (= ἀπόκρισις), Cic.

responsĭto, 1. (intens. of responso), *to give an answer, opinion* (of legal advisers), Cic.

responso, 1. (intens. of respondeo), *to answer, reply, respond.* **I. A.** Lit., Plaut. **B.** Transf., *to re-echo;* lucus ripaeque responsant circa, Verg. **II.** Fig., responsare cupidinibus, *to withstand,* Hor.; cenis, *to scorn,* Hor.; palato, *to defy,* Hor.

responsor -ōris, m. (respondeo), *one who answers,* Plaut.

responsum -i, n. (respondeo), *an answer.* **I.** Gen., responsum dare alicui, Cic.; reddere, Cic.; ferre, auferre, obtain, Cic. **II.** Esp., a, *the answer of an oracle or soothsayer;* haruspicum, Cic.; Sibyllae, Verg.; b, *the answer or opinion of a lawyer,* Cic.

respublĭca, v. res.

respŭo -ŭi, 3. **I.** Lit., *to spit back or out, to reject;* reliquiae cibi, quas natura respuit, Cic. **II.** Fig., *to reject, refuse, repel, disapprove of;* quum id dicat, quod omnium mentes aspernentur ac respuant, Cic.; defensionem, Cic.; poëtas, Hor.; conditionem, Caes.

restagnātĭo -ōnis, f. (restagno), *an overflowing;* Euphratis, Plin.

restagno, 1. *to overflow;* quas (paludes) restagnantes faciunt lacus, Liv.; restagnans mare, Ov.; transf., of places, *to be overflowed;* late is locus restagnat, Caes.

restauro, 1. (re and *stauro, from sto, whence instauro), *to restore, replace, repair, rebuild;* aedem, Tac.

restĭcŭla -ae, f. (dim. of restis), *a thin rope* or *cord,* Cic.

restillo, 1. *to drop back again;* fig., quae (litterae) mihi quiddam quasi animulae restillarunt, *have instilled,* Cic.

restinctĭo -ōnis, f. (restinguo), *a slaking, quenching;* sitis, Cic.

restinguo -stinxi -stinctum, 3. *to extinguish, quench.* **I.** Lit., ignem, Cic. **II.** Transf., a, *to quench, master, subdue, control;* sitim, Cic.; ardorem cupiditatum, Cic.; odium alicuius, Cic.;

b, *to extinguish, destroy, put an end to;* studia, Cic.; animos hominum sensusque morte restingui, Cic.

restĭo -ōnis, m. (restis), *a rope-maker,* Suet.; in jest, *one who is scourged with ropes,* Plaut.

restĭpŭlātĭo -ōnis, f. (restipulor), *a counter-engagement,* Cic.

restĭpŭlor, 1. *to promise, engage in return,* Cic.

restis -is, acc. -im and -em, abl. -e, f. *a rope, cord;* per manus reste datā, *in a kind of dance, where the rope ran through the hands of the dancers,* Liv.

restĭto, 1. (freq. of resto), *to remain behind, loiter, linger,* Liv.

restĭtrix -trīcis, f. (resisto or resto), *she that remains behind,* Plaut.

restĭtŭo -ŭi -ūtum, 3. (re and statuo). **I.** *to put in its former place, replace, restore.* **A.** Gen., statuam, Cic. **B.** a, *to bring back again, restore;* causa restituendi mei, Cic.; b, *to give back, give up again, restore;* agrum alicui, Liv.; fig., se alicui, *to become friends again,* Cic. **II.** *to restore, build again, bring a thing back to its previous condition;* oppida, Caes.; provinciam in antiquum statum, Cic.; aliquid in pristinam dignitatem, Cic.; aliquem in amicitiam, Cic.; aliquem, *to restore a person's property to him,* Cic.; aliquem in integrum, *to place a man in his former condition,* Cic.; rem, aciem, proelium, Liv.; damna Romano bello accepta, *to repair,* Liv.

restĭtūtĭo -ōnis, f. (restituo). **I.** *a restoration;* Capitolii, Suet. **II.** *a calling back again;* a, from banishment, *restoration of a person to his previous condition,* Cic.; b, *a pardoning;* damnatorum, Cic.

restĭtūtor -ōris, m. (restituo), *a restorer;* templorum, Liv.; salutis, Cic.

resto -stĭti, 1. **I.** *to remain behind, remain standing, stand still.* **A.** Gen., Prop. **B.** *to resist, oppose, withstand,* Liv.; pass. impers., quā minimā vi restatur, *where the least resistance is,* Liv. **II.** *to remain, remain over.* **A.** Gen., 1, of things, hic restat actus, Cic.; dona pelago et flammis restantia, *saved from,* Verg.; restat ut, etc., *it remains that,* etc., Cic.; non or nihil aliud restat nisi or quam, foll. by infin., Liv.; 2, of persons, *to remain, be left;* (a) restabam solus de viginti, Ov.; (β) *to remain alive;* qui pauci admodum restant, Cic. **B.** With reference to the future, *to remain for, await;* placet (vobis) socios sic tractari, quod restat, ut per haec tempora tractatos videtis, *for the future,* Cic.; hoc Latio restare canunt, with acc. and infin., Verg.

restrictē, adv. (restrictus). **I.** *sparingly;* tam restricte facere id, Cic. **II.** *accurately, strictly;* praecipere, Cic.; observare, Cic.

restrictus -a -um, p. adj. (from restringo). **I.** *close, tight;* toga, Suet. **II.** Transf., 1, *close, stingy;* homo, Cic.; quum naturā semper ad largiendum ex alieno fuerim restrictior, Cic.; 2, *strict, severe;* imperium, Tac.

restringo -strinxi -strictum, 3. **I.** *to bind back, bind fast, bind tight;* restrictis lacertis, Hor. **II.** 1, *to draw back, confine, restrict, restrain,* Tac.; 2, *to draw back, to open;* dentes, Plaut.

resulto, 1. (intens. of resilio), *to spring back, rebound.* **I.** tela resultant galeā, Verg. **II.** Of sound, *to echo, resound;* imago vocis resultat, Verg.; transf., of places, *to resound;* pulsati colles clamore resultant, Verg.

resūmo -sumpsi -sumptum, 3. *to take again, take back.* **I.** Lit., tabellas, Ov. **II.** Transf.,

l, *to renew, repeat;* pugnam, Tac.; **2,** *to obtain again, to recover;* vires, Ov.

resŭpīno, 1. **I.** *to bend, turn backwards, assurgentem umbone, to strike back to the ground,* Liv.; middle, resupinari, *to bend back;* resupinati Galli, *prostrate from intoxication,* Juv. **II.** Meton., *to break open;* valvas, Prop.

resŭpīnus -a -um, *bent backwards.* **I. A.** Gen., collum, Ov.; resupinus haeret curru, Verg.; resupinum aliquem fundere, *to lay low on the ground,* Ov. **B.** Esp., *lying on one's back;* jacuit resupinus, Ov.; resupini natant, *on their backs,* Ov. **II.** Meton., *throwing back the head, with the nose high in the air* (of the proud), Ov.

resurgo -surrexi -surrectum, 3. *to rise up again, appear again.* **I. A.** Lit., herba resurgens, Ov.; resurgam (from bed), Ov. **B.** Fig., 1, *to rise up again;* in ultionem, Tac.; 2, *to come up again, reappear;* amor, re-awakens, Verg.; 3, *to come forth again;* quum res Romana contra spem votaque eius velut resurgeret, Liv. **II.** Meton., *to stand up again = to be built again;* resurgens urbs, Tac.

resuscĭto, 1. *to revive, resuscitate;* fig., veterem iram, Ov.

resūtus -a -um, *ripped open,* Suet.

rĕtardātĭo -ōnis, f. (retardo), *a retarding, protracting, delay,* Cic.

rĕtardo, 1. *to delay, protract, retard, impede, detain.* **I.** Lit., aliquem in via, Cic.; in middle signification, motus stellarum retardantur, *move slowly,* Cic. **II.** Fig., *to hinder, prevent; aliquem* a scribendo, Cic.

rĕtaxo, 1. *to censure in return,* Suet.

rētĕ -is, n. *a net* (both for fishes and for hunting animals with); retia ponere cervis, Verg.; retia tendere, Ov.; ex araneolis aliae quasi rete texunt, Cic.

rētĕgo -texi -tectum, 3. *to uncover, reveal, lay bare, to open.* **I.** Lit., A. thecam numariam, Cic.; homo retectus, *not covered by a shield,* Verg. **B.** Poet., *to make visible, to illuminate;* orbem radiis, Verg.; jam rebus luce retectis, Verg. **II.** Transf., *to reveal, discover; arcanum* consilium, Hor.; scelus, Verg.

rētendo -tendi -tensum and -tentum, 3. *to slacken, unbend;* arcum, Ov.

rĕtentĭo -ōnis, f. (retineo), *a keeping back, holding in.* **I.** Lit., aurigae, Cic. **II.** Transf., *a withholding;* assensionis, Cic.

l. rĕtento, 1. (intens. of retineo), *to hold firmly back, hold fast.* **I.** Lit., Liv.; caelum a terris, *to keep apart,* Lucr. **II.** Transf., *to preserve, maintain;* sensus hominum vitasque, Cic. poet.

2. rĕtento (rĕtempto), 1. (re and tento), *to try, attempt again;* fila lyrae, Ov.; foll. by infin., Ov.

rĕtentus -a -um. **I.** Partic. of retendo. **II.** Partic. of retineo.

rĕtexo -texŭi -textum, 3. **I.** *to unweave, unravel.* **A.** Lit., quasi Penelope telam retexens, Cic. **B.** Transf., 1, gen., dum luna quater plenum tenuata retexuit orbem, *diminished again,* Ov.; 2, esp., *to dissolve, cancel, annul, reverse;* praeturam, Cic.; orationem, *retract,* Cic.; scriptorum quaeque, *to revise, correct,* Hor. **II.** *to weave again;* poet., transf., *to renew, repeat;* properata retexite fata, Ov.

rētĭārĭus -ĭi, m. (rete), *a fighter with a net, a gladiator furnished with a net, with which he strove to entangle his adversary,* Suet.

rĕtĭcentĭa -ae, f. (reticeo), *a keeping silent, silence* (opp. locutio). **I.** Gen., Cic.; vestræ virtus neque oblivione eorum qui nunc sunt, neque *reticentiā posterorum* sepulta esse poterit, Cic. ; *poena reticentiae*, i.e., *for keeping silent about a defect in an object offered for sale*, Cic. **II.** As a figure of speech, *a sudden pause* (Gr. ἀποσιώπησις), Cic.

rĕtĭcĕo -cŭi, 2. (re and taceo). **I.** Intransit., *to be silent, keep silence;* (a) absol., quum Sulpicius reticuisset, Cic. ; de injuriis, Cic. ; (β) with dat., *to give no answer to*, Liv. **II.** Transit., *to keep secret, conceal;* cogitationes suas, Cic. ; quod ii, qui ea patefacere possent, reticuissent, Cic.

rētĭcŭlātus -a -um (reticulum), *net-like*, *reticulated*, Plin.

rētĭcŭlus -i, m. and **rētĭcŭlum** -i, n. (dim. of rete), *a little net;* **a,** *for catching fish*, Plaut. ; **b,** *a bag of net-work used for carrying certain articles;* reticulum plenum rosae, Cic. ; reticulum panis, Hor. ; **c,** *a net for the hair*, Juv. ; **d,** *a racket for striking a ball*, Ov.

rētĭnācŭlum -i, n. (retineo), *a rope, a cable, cord*, Verg., Ov.

rĕtĭnens -entis, p. adj. (from retineo), *tenacious of anything;* sui juris dignitatisque, Cic.

rĕtĭnentĭa -ae, f. (retineo), *a retaining in the memory, recollection*, Lucr.

rĕtĭnĕo -tĭnŭi -tentum, 3. (re and teneo). **I.** *to hold back, hold fast, detain.* **A.** Lit., **1,** *to keep back;* **a,** of persons, concilium dimittit, Liscum retinet, Caes. ; nisi jam profecti sunt, retinebis homines, Cic. ; **b,** of things, lacrimas, Ov. ; manus ab ore, Ov. ; **2,** *to keep back, preserve, hold back;* armorum parte tertiā celatā atque in oppido retentā, Caes. ; **3,** *to retain a conquest;* oppidum, Caes. **B.** Transf., **1,** *to keep within bounds, restrain;* moderari cursum atque in sua potestate retinere, Cic. ; retinere in officio, Cic. ; foll. by quin, aegre sunt retenti, quin oppidum irruperent, Caes. ; **2,** *to keep, preserve, hold fast;* ut amicos observantiā, rem parsimoniā retineret, Cic. ; statum suum, Cic. ; memoriam suae pristinae virtutis, Caes. ; aliquid memoriā, Cic. **II.** *to hold fast.* **A.** Lit., arcum manu, Cic. **B.** Transf., ordo ipse annalium mediocriter nos retinet quasi enumeratione fastorum, Cic.

rĕtinnĭo, 4. *to resound, to ring again;* in vocibus nostrorum oratorum retinnit et resonat quiddam urbanius, Cic.

rētis -is, f. = rete (q.v.).

rĕtondĕo -tonsus, 2. *to reap, mow again*, Plin.

rĕtŏno, 1. *to thunder back, to resound*, Cat.

rĕtorquĕo -torsi -tortum, 2. *to twist back, bend back, turn back.* **I.** Lit., oculos saepe ad hanc urbem, Cic. ; caput in sua terga, Ov. ; brachia tergo, *to bind behind the back*, Hor. **II.** Transf., *to change;* mentem, Verg.

rĕtorrĭdus -a -um, *parched up, dried up*, Plin.

rĕtostus -a -um, *roasted*, Plin.

rĕtractātĭo -ōnis, f. (retracto), *refusal, denial;* sine ulla retractatione, Cic.

rĕtractātus -a -um, p. adj. (from retracto), *revised;* idem σύνταγμα misi ad te retractatius, Cic.

rĕtracto (rĕtrecto), 1. **I.** *to lay hold of, handle again, undertake anew.* **A.** Lit., ferrum, Verg. ; arma, Liv. ; cruda vulnera, *to open the old wounds*, Ov. **B.** Transf., **a,** *to take in hand again, retouch, use again;* verba desueta, Ov. ; **b,** *to renew;* augere dolorem retractando, Cic. ; **c,** *to think of again;* aliquid diligenter, Cic. ; fata, Ov. **II.** *to draw back;* transf., **a,** *to recall, retract;* dicta, Verg. ; **b,** *to refuse, be unwilling, be reluctant, decline*, Cic. ; quid retractas, Verg.

rĕtractus -a -um, p. adj. (from retraho), *afar off, distant, remote;* retractior a mari murus, Liv.

rĕtrăho -trāxi -tractum, 3. **I.** *to draw back.* **A.** *to draw backwards;* **1,** lit., **a,** manum, Cic.; Hannibalem in Africam, Cic. ; se ab ictu, Ov. ; **b,** *to fetch back a fugitive, bring back*, Cic. ; aliquem ex fuga, Sall. ; **2,** transf., **a,** *to keep back, prevent;* consules a foedere, Cic. ; **b,** *to hold back, not to give out;* quos occulere aut retrahere aliquid suspicio fuit, Liv. ; **c,** se, *to withdraw oneself;* quum se retraxit, ne pyxidem traderet, Cic. **B.** *to drag forth again, draw forth again;* Treveros in arma, Tac. **II.** *to draw towards;* fig., in odium judicis, Cic.

rĕtrĭbŭo -trĭbŭi -trĭbūtum, 3. **I.** *to give again.* **A.** *to give back, restore;* pro Siculo frumento acceptam pecuniam populo, Liv. **B.** *to give again, afresh*, Lucr. **II.** *to give back a man his due;* alicui fructum quem meruit, Cic.

rĕtrō (from re and pron. suff. ter, as citro, intro), adv. **I.** Lit., *backwards, back, behind;* redire, retro repetere, Liv. ; retro respicere, Cic. ; quod retro atque a tergo fieret, ne laboraret, Cic. **II.** Transf., **A.** Of time, *in times past, formerly, back;* et deinceps retro usque ad Romulum, Cic. **B.** Of other relations, **1,** *back, backwards;* retro ponere, *to postpone*, Cic. ; **2,** *again, on the contrary, on the other hand*, Cic.

rĕtrŏăgo -ēgi -actum, 3. *to drive back, lead back, turn back*, Plin.

rĕtrŏĕo, 4. *to go back, return*, Plin.

rĕtrōgrădĭor -gressus sum, 3. dep. *to go backwards, move backwards*, Plin.

rĕtrōgrădus -a -um (retrogradior), *retrograde, going backwards*, Sen.

rĕtrorsum and **rĕtrorsŭs**, adv. (= retroversum [-vorsum] and retroversus [-vorsus]), *backwards, behind.* **I.** Lit., retrorsum vela dare, Hor. **II.** Transf., *in return, in reversed order;* deinde retrorsum vicissim, etc., Cic.

rĕtrorsus = retrorsum (q.v.).

rĕtrōversus -a -um (verto), *turned backwards, back*, Ov.

rĕtrūdo -trūsus, 3. *to push back, thrust back*, Plaut. Partic., **rĕtrūsus** -a -um, *remote, distant, sequestered, obscure;* simulacra deorum jacent in tenebris ab isto retrusa atque abdita, Cic.; voluntas abdita et retrusa, Cic.

rĕtundo, rĕtŭdi (rettŭdi) -tūsum (-tunsum), 3. *to beat back, to drive back.* **I. A.** Lit., Lucan. **B.** Transf., *to check, keep within bounds;* linguas Aetolorum, Liv. **II.** *to hammer back something sharp, to blunt, make dull.* **A.** Lit., tela, Ov. ; fig., ferrum alicuius, *to frustrate a murderous attempt*, Cic. **B.** Transf., impetum, Liv. ; mucronem stili, Cic.

rĕtūsus (rĕtunsus) -a -um, p. adj. (from retundo), *dull, blunt.* **I.** Lit., ferrum, Verg. **II.** Transf., *dull;* ingenium, Cic.

Reudigni -ōrum, m. *a people in the north of Germany.*

rĕus -i, m. and **rĕa** -ae, f. (res). **I.** *an accused person, prisoner, culprit, defendant;* gen. with acc. of the charge, more rarely with de and the abl., reum facere aliquem, *to accuse*, Cic. ; reum fieri, *to be accused*, Cic. ; referre in reos (of the praetor), *to enter a name on the list of accused persons*, Cic.; aliquem ex reis eximere, *to strike out the name of an accused person*, Cic. ; Sextius qui est de vi reus, Cic. ; used without reference to a court of justice, reus fortunae, *accused as responsible for ill fortune*, Liv. ; reus sine te criminis huius agor, Ov. ; plur., rei, *the parties to a suit, both plaintiff and defendant;*

reos appello quorum res est, Cic. **II.** *bound by, answerable for;* voti, *bound to fulfil my vow* (i.e., *having obtained the object of my wishes),* Verg.; suae partis tutandae, *answerable for,* Liv.

rĕvălesco -vălŭi, 3. *to become well again, be restored to health.* **I.** Lit., ope qua revalescere possis, Ov. **II.** Transf., *to be restored;* Laodicea revaluit propriis opibus, Tac.

rĕvĕho -vexi -vectum, 3. *to carry, bear, bring back.* **I.** Lit., a, act. and pass., tela ad Grajos, Ov.; praeda revecta, *brought back,* Liv.; b, middle, revehi, *to drive back, ride back, sail back;* (with or without equo, curru, nave, etc.) in castra, Liv.; Ithacam, Hor. **II.** Fig., ad superiorem aetatem revecti sumus (in discourse), *have gone back,* Cic.

rĕvello -velli -vulsum, 3. **I.** *to tear, pull, pluck away.* **A.** Lit., tela de corpore, Cic.; caput a cervice, Verg.; saxum e monte, Ov.; morte ab aliquo revelli, *to be separated from,* Ov. **B.** Fig., *to tear away, destroy, banish;* consulatum ex omni memoria, Cic.; omnes injurias, Cic. **II.** *to tear up, to open;* humum dente curvo, *to plough,* Ov.; cinerem manesque, *to disturb, violate a tomb,* Verg.

rĕvēlo, 1. *to unveil, uncover, lay bare;* frontem, Tac.; os, Ov.; sacra, Ov.

rĕvĕnĭo -vēni -ventum, 4. *to come back, return;* domum, Cic.; in urbem, Tac.

rēvērā, adv. (re and vera), *indeed, in truth, truly,* Cic.

rĕverbĕro, 1. *to beat back, drive back,* Sen.

rĕvĕrendus -a -um, p. adj. (from revereor), *inspiring awe, venerable;* nox, Ov.; facies, Juv.

rĕvĕrens -entis, p. adj. (from revereor), *respectful, reverent;* erga patrem, Tac.

rĕvĕrentĕr, adv. (reverens), *reverently, respectfully,* Plin.; reverentius, Tac.; reverentissime, Suet.

rĕvĕrentĭa -ae, f. (revereor), *reverence, respect, fear, awe;* adversus homines, Cic.; legum, *before the laws,* Juv. Personif., **Rĕvĕrentĭa** -ae, f. *a goddess, mother of Majestas by Honor.*

rĕvĕrĕor -vĕrĭtus sum, 2. dep. *to feel awe or respect or shame before, to revere, reverence, respect, to fear;* suspicionem, Cic.; multa adversa, Cic.; coetum virorum, Liv.

rĕverro, 3. *to sweep again,* Plaut.

rĕversĭo (rĕvorsĭo) -ōnis, f. (revertor). **I.** *a turning back on the way before a man has reached the end of his journey* (while reditus = *return after a man has reached his journey's end),* Cic.; reditu vel potius reversione, Cic.; consilium profectionis et reversionis meae, Cic. **II.** Transf., *a return, recurrence;* tertianae febris et quartanae reversio, Cic.; plur., sol binas in singulis annis reversiones ab extremo contrarias facit, Cic.

rĕverto (rĕvorto) -verti (-vorti) -versum (-vorsum) -ĕre and **rĕvertor (rĕvortor)** -versus (-vorsus) sum -verti (-vorti), dep. **I.** *to turn back, return.* **A.** Lit., ex itinere, Cic.; ad aliquem, Caes.; Laodiceam, Cic.; with double nom., quum victor a Mithridatico bello revertisset, Cic.; poet., of things, Tiberim reverti, Hor. **B.** Transf., *to return, come back;* ad sanitatem, *to a better frame of mind,* Cic.; in gratiam cum aliquo, *to be reconciled with,* Liv.; poena reversura est in caput tuum, *doomed to fall,* Ov.; esp., in discourse, *to return, revert;* rursus igitur eadem revertamur, Cic.; ad propositum revertar, Cic.; ad id, unde digressi sumus, revertamur, Cic. **II.** reverti, *to turn to;* revertitur ad commodum, Cic. (act. not used in present tenses in prose).

rĕvĭdĕo, 2. *to see again,* Plaut.

rĕvincĭo -vinxi -vinctum, 4. **I.** *to tie back, tie behind;* juvenem manus post terga revinctum, Verg. **II. A.** Lit., *bind fast, bind round;* trabes, Caes.; zona de poste revincta, Ov. **B.** Transf., mentem amore, Cat.

rĕvinco -vīci -victum, 3. *to reconquer, subdue again.* **I.** Lit., catervae consiliis juvenis revictae, Hor. **II.** Transf., **A.** Gen., revictam conjurationem, *suppressed,* Tac. **B.** Esp., *to confute, convict;* aliquem, Cic.

rĕvĭresco -vĭrŭi, 3. (inchoat. of revireo), *to grow green again, to grow strong, flourish again, revive;* senatum ad auctoritatis pristinae spem revirescere, Cic.

rĕvĭsĭto, 1. *to visit repeatedly,* Plin.

rĕvīso -vīsi -vīsum, 3. *to look back at, come again to see, revisit.* **I.** Intransit., furor revisit, returns, Lucr. **II.** Transit., revise nos aliquando, Cic.; domos, Liv.

rĕvīvisco -vixi, 3. *to come to life again, revive.* **I.** Lit., Cic. **II.** Transf., reviviscere memoriam ac desiderium mei, Cic.

rĕvŏcābĭlis -e (revoco), *that can be revoked* or *called back,* Ov.

rĕvŏcāmen -ĭnis, n. (revoco), *a calling back, recall,* Ov.

rĕvŏcātĭo -ōnis, f. (revoco). **I.** *a calling back.* **A.** Lit., a bello, Cic. **B.** Fig., avocatio a cogitanda molestia et revocatio ad contemplandas voluptates, Cic. **II.** In rhetoric, *a withdrawal, withdrawing, revocation;* verbi, Cic.

rĕvŏco, 1. **I.** *to call again.* **A.** 1, in suffragium, Liv.; 2, legal t. t., *to summon again before a court of justice, to bring a fresh charge against;* hominem revocat populus, Cic.; **3,** theatrical t. t., *to call again for a repetition of a speech,* etc., *to encore;* quum saepius revocatus vocem obtudisset, Cic.; with acc. of thing to be repeated, *to call for again;* primos tres versus, Cic.; impers., millies revocatum est, Cic.; **4,** milit. t. t., *to summon again soldiers who had been discharged;* milites, Cic. **B.** 1, *to call again, in turn;* unde tu me vocasti, unde te ego revoco, Cic.; 2, *to invite back* or *again;* qui non revocaturus esset, Cic. **II.** *to call back.* **A.** In a narrow sense, 1, lit., a, *aliquem ex itinere,* Cic.; qui me revocastis, *out of exile,* Cic.; with things as objects, oculos, Ov., pedem, Verg., gradum, Verg., *to turn away;* b, esp., milit. t. t., *to recall soldiers from a march, expedition,* etc.; legiones ab opere, Caes.; 2, transf., a, *to call back, bring back again, recover, renew;* studia longo intervallo intermissa, *to take up again,* Cic.; b, *to call back, apply again;* se ad industriam, Cic.; se ad se revocare, or *simply se* revocare, *to recover oneself, collect oneself,* Cic.; hence, (a) *to keep back;* aliquem a tanto scelere, Cic.; (β) *to confine;* comitia in unam domum, Cic.; (γ) *to recall, revoke;* facta, Ov. **B.** In a wider sense, *to call to;* 1, lit., abi, quo blandae juvenium te revocant preces, Hor.; 2, transf., a, *to apply to, refer to;* illam rem ad illam rationem conjecturamque revocabant, Cic.; b, *to bring to;* in dubium, Cic.; omnia ad suam potestatem, Cic.; c, *to judge according to;* omnia ad gloriam, Cic.

rĕvŏlo, 1. *to fly back.* **I.** Lit., dux gruum revolat, Cic. **II.** Transf., revolat telum, Ov.

rĕvŏlūbĭlis -e (revolvo), *that can be rolled back;* pondus, Ov.

rĕvolvo -volvi -vŏlūtum, 3. *to roll back, unroll.* **I. A.** Gen., 1, transit., Tac.; poet., rursus iter omne, *measure back again, traverse again,* Verg.; 2, reflex. and middle, draco revolvens sese, Cic.; revolutus equo, *falling down from,*

Verg.; **ter revoluta toro est**, *sank back*, Verg.; revoluta dies, *returning*, Verg. **B.** Esp., *to unroll or open a book;* Origines (a work of Cato's), Liv. **II.** Fig., **A.** Gen., 1, act. and pass., omnia ad communes rerum atque generum summas revolventur, *will be brought back to, reduced to*, Cic.; poet., iterum casus, *to undergo again*, Verg.; 2, middle, revolvi, a, *to return to, in speaking or writing;* ut ad illa elementa revolvar, Cic.; b, *to come to (something bad);* revolutus ad dispensationem inopiae, Liv. **B.** Esp., *to read again;* loca jam recitata, Hor.; *to think of again;* visa, Ov.; *to tell again;* haec, Verg.

rĕvŏmo -vŏmŭi, 3. *to vomit up, disgorge;* fluctus, Verg.

rĕvorsĭo = reversio (q.v.).

rĕvorsus, etc. = reversus, etc. (q.v.).

rĕvulsĭo -ōnis, f. (revello), *a tearing away*, Plin.

rex, rēgis, m. (rego), *ruler, prince.* **I.** Lit., rex Dejotarus, Cic.; rex regum (of Agamemnon), Liv.; simply rex, used of the Parthian king, Suet.; of the Persian king (like Gr. βασιλεύς), Nep.; regem deligere, creare, constituere, Cic.; poet. attrib., populus late rex, *ruling far*, Verg. **II.** Transf., 1, of some of the gods, rex divum atque hominum, or deorum, *Jupiter*, Verg.; rex aquarum, *Neptune*, Ov.; rex Stygius, *Pluto*, Verg.; 2, *the king and his consort;* reges excitos, Liv.; *the royal family;* direptis bonis regum, Liv.; 3, during the republic at Rome, rex = *a despot, an absolute monarch, tyrant;* rex populi Romani, i.e., *Caesar*, Cic.; decem reges aerarii, Cic.; 4, in the religious language, rex sacrorum, sacrificiorum, Cic., sacrificus, Liv., sacrificulus, Liv., *a priest who under the republic performed the sacrifices which formerly the kings performed;* 5, gen. = *head, chief, leader;* a, of animals, rex apum, Verg.; b, of rivers, rex Eridanus (the chief stream in Italy), Verg.; c, of the patron of a parasite, Hor.; d, *the guide, tutor of a young man;* rex pueritiae, Hor.

rhācōma (rhēcŏma) -ae, f. *a root*, perhaps rhubarb, Plin.

Rhădămanthus (-ŏs) -i, m. (Ῥαδάμανθυς), *son of Jupiter, brother of Minos, judge in the lower world.*

Rhaeti = Raeti (q.v.).

rhăgădes -um, f. and **rhăgădĭa** -ōrum, n. (ῥαγάδες, ῥαγάδια) *a kind of sores or ulcers*, Plin.

rhăgĭon -ĭi, n. (ῥάγιον), *a kind of small spider*, Plin.

Rhamnes = Ramnes (q.v.).

rhamnos -i, f. (ῥάμνος), *buckthorn*, Plin.

Rhamnus -nuntis, f. (Ῥαμνοῦς), *a village of Attica, where the goddess Nemesis was worshipped;* hence, **A.** Adj., **Rhamnūsĭus** -a -um, virgo, Cat., or simply Rhamnusia, *Nemesis*, Ov. **B.** **Rhamnūsis** -ĭdis, f. *Nemesis*, Ov.

Rhamses -sesis, m. *an old king of Egypt.*

rhapsōdĭa -ae, f. (ῥαψῳδία), *a rhapsody;* secunda, *the second book of the Iliad*, Nep.

1. **Rhēa (Rēa)** -ae, f. Rhea Silvia, *daughter of King Numitor of Alba, mother of Romulus and Remus by Mars.*

2. **Rhēa** -ae, f. (Ῥέα), *an old name of Cybele.*

rhēcōma = rhacoma (q.v.).

rhēda = reda (q.v.).

rhēdārĭus = redarius (q.v.).

Rhēgĭum = Regium (q.v.).

Rhēmi = Remi (q.v.).

Rhēnus -i, m. *the Rhine;* poet. adj., flumen Rhenum, Hor.: in poets, meton. = *the people*

16*

dwelling on the banks of the Rhine. Adj., **Rhēnānus** -a -um, *belonging to the Rhine.*

Rhēsus -i, m. (Ῥῆσος), *king in Thrace, who came to the help of Troy; according to an oracle, the Greeks could not capture Troy if the horses of Rhesus tasted of Trojan pastures, so Diomedes and Ulysses stole the horses and killed Rhesus.*

rhētor -ŏris, m. (ῥήτωρ). **I.** *a teacher of rhetoric, a rhetorician*, Cic. **II.** *an orator*, Nep.

rhētŏrīca v. rhetoricus.

1. **rhētŏrīcē**, v. rhetoricus.

2. **rhētŏrīcē**, adv. (rhetoricus), *rhetorically, oratorically*, Cic.

rhētŏrīcus -a -um (ῥητορικός). **I.** *of or relating to a rhetorician, rhetorical;* mos, Cic.; ars, Cic.; whence subst., **rhētŏrīca** -ae, f. and **rhētŏrīcē** -ēs, f. (ῥητορική), Cic. **II.** *relating to rhetoric;* doctores, *teachers of rhetoric*, Cic.; libri rhetorici, *text-books of rhetoric*, Cic.; subst., **rhētŏrīca** -ōrum, n. *rhetoric*, Cic.

rheumătismus -i, m. (ῥευματισμός), *rheum, catarrh*, Plin.

rhīna -ae, f. (ῥίνη), *a kind of shark*, Plin.

rhīnŏcĕrōs -ōtis, m. (ῥινόκερως). **I.** *a rhinoceros*, Plin.; prov., nasum rhinocerotis habere, *to turn up the nose, sneer at everything*, Mart. **II.** Meton., *a vessel made of the horn of the rhinoceros*, Juv.

Rhīnŏcŏlūra -ae, f. (Ῥινοκόλουρα), *a town on the coast of the Mediterranean between Egypt and Syria, now El-Arish (Arisch).*

Rhintōn -ōnis, m. (Ῥίνθων), *a tragic poet of Tarentum.*

Rhĭōn (-um) -ĭi, n. (Ῥίον), *a promontory in Achaia, opposite Antirrhium.*

Rhīphaeus = Riphaeus (q.v.).

Rhīzōn -ōnis, m. (Ῥίζων), *a town in Illyria, now Risano;* hence, **Rhīzōnītae** -ārum, m. *the inhabitants of Rhizon.*

rhō, n. indecl. (ῥῶ), *the Greek name of the letter R*, Cic.

Rhŏda -ae, f. *a town of the Indigetes in Hispania Tarraconensis, now Rosas.*

Rhŏdănus -i, m. (Ῥοδανός), *a river in Gaul, now the Rhone;* Rhodani potor, *a dweller on the banks of the Rhone*, Hor.

rhŏdīnus -a -um (ῥόδινος), *made of roses*, Plin.

Rhŏdĭus, v. Rhodus.

rhŏdŏdaphnē -ēs, f. (ῥοδοδάφνη), *the oleander*, Plin.

rhŏdŏdendrŏs -i, f. and **rhŏdŏdendrŏn** -i, n. (ῥοδόδενδρον) = rhododaphne (q.v.).

Rhŏdŏpē -ēs, f. (Ῥοδόπη), *a mountain in Thrace, now Despoto or Despoti Dag;* meton. = *Thrace*, Verg.; hence, adj., **Rhŏdŏpēïus** -a -um, *Thracian;* vates, heros, *Orpheus*, Ov.

Rhŏdus (-ŏs) -i, f. (Ῥόδος), *Rhodes, an island in the Carpathian Sea, off the coast of Asia Minor, famous for its trade, its school of rhetoric, and its colossus.* Hence, adj., **Rhŏdĭus** -a -um, *Rhodian;* plur. subst., **Rhŏdĭi** -ōrum, m. *the Rhodians*, Cic.

Rhoetēum (Ῥοίτειον), *a promontory in the Troad;* hence, **Rhoetēus** -a -um, *Rhoetean*, a, lit., *profundum;* and subst., **Rhoetēum** -i, n. *the sea near Rhoeteum*, Ov.; b, poet., transf. = *Trojan;* ductor, *Aeneas*, Verg.

Rhoetus (Rhoecus) -i, m. (Ῥοῖκος). **I.** *a giant*, Hor. **II.** *a centaur*, Verg.

rhombus (-ŏs) -i, m. (ῥόμβος). **I.** *a magician's circle*, Ov. **II.** *the turbot*, Hor.

rhomphaea -ae, f. *a long missile weapon.*

Rhōsus (-ŏs) -i, f. (ʿΡῶσος), *a sea-port in Cilicia, famous for its pottery.* Hence, **Rhōsĭăcus** -a -um, *Rhosian;* vasa, Cic.

Rhoxŏlānī (**Roxŏlānī**) -ōrum, m. *a Scythian people in modern European Tartary.*

rhythmĭcus -i, m. (ῥυθμικός), *one who teaches the art of preserving rhythm in composition,* Cic.

rhythmus -i, m. (ῥυθμός), *rhythm, time* (either in music or discourse), Quint.

rhȳtium -ii, n. (ῥύτιον), *a drinking-horn,* Mart.

rīca -ae, f. *a veil,* Plaut.

rīcĭnĭum -ii, n. (rica), *a small veil worn especially as an article of mourning,* Cic.

rictum = rictus (q.v.).

rictus -ūs, m. and **rictum** -i, n. (ringor), *the opening of the mouth, the open mouth;* a, of man, risu diducere rictum, Hor.; b, of animals, *the expanded jaws;* rictus Cerberei, Ov.

rīdĕo, rīsi, rīsum, 2. **I.** Intransit., *to laugh.* **A.** Gen., *ridere* convivae, *cachinnare* ipse Apronius, Cic.; in stomacho ridere, *to laugh grimly,* Cic.; pass. impers., ridetur, *there is laughter,* Hor. **B.** Esp., 1, *to laugh* or *smile in a friendly manner;* alicui or ad aliquem, *to smile upon;* cui non risere parentes, Verg.; so transf., (α) *to laugh, to look cheerful, to look bright;* omnia nunc rident, Verg.; domus ridet argento, Hor.; (β) *to please;* ille terrarum mihi praeter omnes angulus ridet, Hor.; 2, *to laugh triumphantly, to triumph over;* muneribus aemuli, Hor. **II.** Transit., *to laugh at.* **A.** Gen., joca tua de haeresi Vestoriana risisse me, Cic.; haec ego non rideo, *I do not jest,* Cic.; pass., non sal sed natura ridetur, Cic. **B.** Esp., *to ridicule;* aliquem, Cic.; pass., Pyrrhi ridetur largitas a consule, Cic.

rīdĭbundus -a -um (rideo), *laughing,* Plaut.

rīdĭcŭlārĭus -a -um (ridiculus), *laughable, droll;* subst., **rīdĭcŭlārĭa** -ōrum, n. *drolleries,* Plaut.

rīdĭcŭlē, adv. (ridiculus). **I.** In a good sense, *jokingly, humorously,* Cic. **II.** In a bad sense, *ridiculously, absurdly;* homo ridicule insanus, Cic.

rīdĭcŭlōsus -a -um (ridiculus), *laughable, facetious,* Pers.

rīdĭcŭlus (rideo), *exciting laughter.* **I.** In a good sense, *droll, humorous, funny, facetious.* **A.** Adj., cavillator facie magis quam facetiis ridiculus, Cic.; poet. with infin., (Porcius) ridiculus totas simul absorbere placentas, Hor. **B.** Subst., a, **rīdĭcŭlus** -i, m. *a joker, jester,* Plaut., Ter.; b, **rīdĭcŭlum** -i, n. *a thing to laugh at, joke, jest;* per ridiculum dicere, Cic.; plur., sententiose ridicula dicere, Cic. **II.** In a bad sense, *laughable, absurd, ridiculous;* insania quae ridicula aliis, Cic.; ridiculum poema, Hor.; ridiculum est with infin., Cic.

rĭgens -entis, p. adj. (from rigeo), *stiff, unbending;* aqua, *frozen,* Mart.

rĭgĕo, 2. (root RIG, Gr. ΠΙΓ, connected with FRIG-eo), *to be stiff, to stiffen.* **I. A.** Lit., 1, with cold, frost, etc.; rigere frigore, Cic.; 2, poet., *to be stiff, bend, unbending;* terga boum plumbo insuto ferroque rigebant, Verg.; 3, poet., *to be stiffened;* auro or ex auro, Verg. **B.** Transf., 1, *to be stiff = to be immovable;* nervi rigent, Hor.; 2, *to stand stiff* or *upright;* cervix riget horrida, Ov.; of hair, *to stand on end;* gelido comae terrore rigebant, Ov. **II.** Fig., feritas immota riget, Mart.

rĭgesco, rĭgŭi (inchoat. of rigeo), 3. *to grow stiff, become stiff.* **I.** Lit., with cold; vestes rigescunt, Verg. **II.** Transf., of hair, *to stand on end* (from terror); metu capillos riguisse, Ov.

rĭgĭdē, adv. (rigidus), *stiffly;* fig., *rigorously, severely,* Ov.

rĭgĭdus -a -um (rigeo), *stiff, unbending, rigid.* **I. A.** Lit., from cold; tellurem Boreā rigidam movere, Verg.; or by nature, *hard;* silex, Ov.; ensis, Verg. **B.** Transf., 1, *stiff = standing upright;* columna, Ov.; capilli, Ov.; 2, *stiff, stretched out;* crura, Cic.; cervix, Liv. **II.** Fig., 1, *immovable, inflexible;* innocentia, Liv.; vultus, Ov.; 2, *stiff, rough, unpolished;* mores, Ov.; signa rigidiora, *not elaborated,* Cic.; 3, *stern, inflexible;* satelles, Hor.; censor, Ov.; 4, *wild, savage;* ferae, Ov.

rĭgo, 1. **I.** *to lead* or *conduct water to any place.* **A.** Lit., aquam per agros, ap. Liv. **B.** Fig., hinc motus per membra rigantur, Lucr. **II.** *to wet, moisten, bedew.* **A.** 1, lit., lucum fons perenni rigabat aquā, Liv.; 2, poet., transf., *to bedew;* ora lacrimis, fletibus, Verg., Ov.; 3, fig., Prop.

Rĭgŏdūlum -i, n. *a town in the country of the Treveri, now Ricol* or *Reol.*

rĭgor -ōris, m. (rigeo), *stiffness, rigidity, hardness.* **I.** Gen., **A.** Lit., of gold, Lucr.; of wood or iron, Verg. **B.** Fig., 1, *severity, harshness, sternness,* Tac.; 2, *roughness, rudeness, harshness of manner,* Ov. **II.** Esp., *rigidity* or *numbness produced by cold;* torpentibus rigore membra, Liv.

rĭgŭus -a -um (rigo). **I.** Act., *watering, irrigating;* amnes, Verg. **II.** Pass., *well-watered, irrigated;* hortus, Ov.

rīma -ae, f. *a crack, cleft, fissure;* rimas agere, Cic.; naves rimis dehiscunt, *spring a leak,* Verg.; poet., ignea rima micans, *the lightning,* Verg.

rīmor, 1. dep. (rima), *to cleave.* **I.** Gen., *to turn up;* terram rastris, Verg. **II.** Esp., *to grub up, burrow through, root up.* **A.** Lit., of birds and other animals, Verg. **B.** Transf., *to turn over, pry into, search, examine;* id quoque rimatur quantum potest, Cic.; secreta, Tac.

rīmōsus -a -um (rima), *full of cracks, chinks, fissures;* cymba, Verg.; fig., quae rimosa bene deponuntur in aure, *that cannot keep a secret,* Hor.

ringor, 3. dep. *to show the teeth;* fig., *to snarl, growl, be angry at,* Hor.

rīpa -ae, f. *a bank.* **I.** Lit., *the bank of a river* (litus, *the shore of the sea,* ora, *the sea-coast*); ripa magni fluminis, Cic.; plur., ripae, of one of the banks of a river, Liv. **II.** Poet. and post-classical, *the shore of the sea,* Hor.

Rīpaeus = Rhiphaeus (q.v.).

rīpārĭus -a -um (ripa), *frequenting river-banks;* hirundo, Plin.

Rīphaeus (**Rhīphaeus, Rhipaeus, Rĭpaeus**) -a -um (ʿΡιπαῖος), *name of a country in Sarmatia* or *Scythia;* arces, *the Riphaean mountains;* pruina, Verg.

rīpŭla -ae, f. (dim. of ripa), *a little bank* (of a river), Cic.

riscus -i, m. (ῥίσκος), *a box, chest, trunk,* Ter.

rīsĭo -ōnis, f. (rideo), *laughing, laughter,* Plaut.

rīsor -ōris, m. (rideo), *a laugher, mocker,* Hor.

rīsus -ūs, m. (rideo), *laughing, laughter;* in a bad sense, *jeering, ridicule.* **I.** Lit., hominum de te, Cic.; risus consecutus est, non in te, sed in errorem tuum, Cic.; miros risus edere,

Cic.; risum movere, commovere, excitare, *to cause laughter*, Cic.; risus captare, *to try to raise a laugh*, Cic.; risum tenere, continere, *to check*, Cic. **II.** Meton., *an object of laughter;* deus omnibus risus erat, Ov.

rītĕ, adv. (root RI, Gr. PE-ω, whence ritus; prop. abl., instead of ritu). **I.** *with suitable religious ceremonies;* deos colere, Cic. **II.** Transf., **A.** *properly, duly, fitly, rightly;* deum rite beatum dicere, Cic.; rebus rite paratis, Verg.; poet., *fortunately, luckily;* propinquare augurium, Verg.; **2,** *usually, in the ordinary manner;* quorum plaustra vagas rite trahunt domos, Hor.

rītŭālis -e (ritus), *relating to religious usage;* libri, Cic.

rītus -ūs, m. (root RI, Gr. PE-ω, lit., *course*). **I.** *religious custom, usage, ceremony, rite,* Cic. **II.** Gen., *a custom, usage, observance;* ritus Cyclopum, Ov.; esp. abl., ritu, *after the manner of, as;* mulierum ritu, Liv.; pecudum ritu, latronum ritu, Cic.

rīvālis -e (rivus), *of or relating to a brook or canal.* **I.** Adj., Col. **II.** Subst., **A.** Lit., *one who uses a brook or canal in common with another.* **B.** Transf., *a rival in love, rival suitor,* Ov.; prov., se amare sine rivali, *to have no rival to fear,* Cic.

rīvālītas -ātis, f. (rivalis), *rivalry (in love),* Cic.

rīvŭlus -i, m. (dim. of rivus), *a small brook, rivulet;* fig., Cic.

rīvus -i, m. (root RI, Gr. PE-ω, whence ῥεῦσαι), *a stream.* **I. 1,** lit., **a,** *a brook;* rivorum a fonte deductio, Cic.; **b,** *an artificial water-course, channel, dyke;* rivos ducere, Ov.; **2,** transf., *a stream,* of other fluids, such as blood, milk, etc.; lacrimarum, Ov.; rivis currentia vina, Verg. **II.** Fig., *a stream, course;* fortunae, Hor.

rixa -ae, f. (connected with ἔρις, ἐρίζω), *a quarrel, brawl, strife, dispute,* (a) *between men;* Academiae nostrae cum Zenone magna rixa est, Cic.; (β) *between animals,* Ov.

rixātor -ōris, m. (rixor), *a brawler,* Quint.

rixor, 1. dep. (rixa), *to quarrel, brawl;* cum aliquo de amicula, Cic.

rōbīgĭnōsus -a -um (robigo), *rusty,* Plaut.; robiginosis dentibus cuncta rodit, *with envious teeth,* Mart.

1. **rōbīgo (rūbīgo)** -ĭnis, f. (1. robus, ruber), *rust.* **I.** Lit., scabra robigine pila, Verg.; ferrum robigine roditur, Ov.; poet., *of the dark deposit on the teeth,* Ov. **II.** Fig., *the rust of inactivity* or *oblivion;* ingenium longā robigine laesum torpet, Ov.

2. **Rōbīgo (Rūbīgo)** -ĭnis, f. and **Rōbīgus (Rūbigus)** -i, m. (1. robigo), *the deity invoked by the Romans to preserve their grain from mildew.* Hence, **Rōbīgālĭa** -ium, n. *the festival of the deity Robigo, celebrated annually on the 25th of April.*

rōbŏr = robur (q.v.).

rōbŏrĕus -a -um (robur), *oaken,* Ov.

rōbŏro, 1. (robur), *to strengthen, make firm.* **I.** Lit., artus, Lucr. **II.** Fig., pectora, Hor.; gravitatem (animi), Cic.

rōbur (rōbus, archaic) -ŏris, n. (root RO, Gr. ΄ΡΩ-ννυμι, ΄ΡΩ-μη), *strength.* **I.** Lit., *hard wood;* esp., *oak, oak-wood;* **a,** gen., quercus antiquo robore, Verg.; sapiens non est e saxo sculptus aut e robore dolatus, Cic.; **b,** poet., *of other hard wood,* morsus roboris (of the oleaster), Verg. **II.** Meton., **A.** *Of things made of oak or other hard wood;* **a,** in robore accumbunt, *on oaken benches,* Cic.; robur sacrum, *the Trojan* horse, Verg.; robur praefixum ferro, *a lance,* Verg.; **b,** esp., *the underground cellar in the prison of Servius Tullius at Rome,* also called the Tullianum, Liv. **B.** *hardness, strength, firmness;* **1, a,** *of physical strength,* robur juventae, Liv.; **b,** *of political power,* neque his ipsis tantum umquam virium aut roboris fuit, Liv.; **c,** *of intellectual or moral strength, firmness, constancy;* alter virtutis robore firmior quam aetatis, Cic.; robur incredibile animi, Cic.; **2,** concr., *the strength, pith of anything;* **a,** versaris in optimorum civium vel flore vel robore, Cic.; **b,** *of soldiers, the flower of the army;* quod fuit roboris duobus proeliis interiit, Caes.

1. **rōbus** -a -um, archaic = rufus, *red,* Juv.

2. **rōbus** -ŏris, n. = robur (q.v.).

rōbustus -a -um (robur). **I.** *of hard wood, of oak, oaken;* stipites, Liv. **II.** Transf., **1,** *strong, powerful, hard, firm, solid, robust;* si esses usu atque aetate robustior, Cic.; **2,** *intellectually strong, powerful;* animus, Cic.; malum fit robustius, Cic.

rōdo, rōsi, rōsum, 3. *to gnaw, nibble at.* **I.** Lit., **1,** vivos ungues, Hor.; **2,** fig., *to calumniate, disparage, backbite, slander;* absentem amicum, Hor.; absol., in conviviis rodunt, Cic. **II.** Transf., *to eat away, corrode, consume;* ferrum robigine roditur, Cic.

1. **rōdus** = raudus (q.v.).

2. **rōdus** = rudus (q.v.).

rōduscŭlum = rausculum (q.v.).

rŏgālis -e (rogus), *of or relating to the funeral pile,* Ov.

rŏgātĭo -ōnis, f. (rogo). **I.** *asking, question.* **A.** Act., *asking,* Cic. **B.** Pass., *that which is asked, a question;* **a,** *as a figure of speech,* Cic.; **b,** polit. t. t., *a proposal, proposition, project of law, bill laid before the people;* Caecilia, *proposed by Caecilius,* Cic.; rogationem ad populum ferre, Caes.; rogationem perferre, Cic. **II.** *a request, entreaty,* Cic.

rŏgātiuncŭla -ae, f. (dim. of rogatio). **I.** *a little question,* Cic. **II.** *an unimportant proposal or bill,* Cic.

rŏgātor -ōris, m. (rogo), *one who asks.* **I.** *the proposer of a bill,* Cic. **II.** *an officer who took the votes in the comitia, a polling-clerk;* rogator primus, *the one who took the votes of the prerogative century,* Cic.

rŏgātus -ū, m. (rogo), *a request, entreaty;* rogatu tuo, Cic.; eius rogatu, Cic.

rŏgĭtātĭo -ōnis, f. (rogito), *a proposition, project of law,* Plaut.

rŏgĭto, 1. (freq. of rogo), *to ask, inquire frequently* or *eagerly;* rogitantes alii alios, Liv.; quid rei sint, rogitant, Liv.

rŏgo, 1. (root ROG, Gr. ΟΡΓ, whence ὀρέγω, ὀρέγομαι), *to stretch after something, to fetch.* **I.** Lit., Plaut. **II.** Transf., **A.** *to ask, inquire, question;* **1,** gen., **a,** aliquem aliquid : quid me istud rogas? Cic.; **b,** with de and the abl., quae de te ipso rogaro, Cic.; **c,** with dep. interrog. sent., rogatus de cybaea, quid responderit, Cic.; **2,** esp., **a,** polit. t. t., (a) aliquem sententiam or aliquem, *to ask a person his opinion;* quos priores sententiam rogabat, Cic.; (β) rogare populum or legem or *to ask the people about a law,* hence, *to make a proposal, proposition, project of law,* etc., *to the people, to propose a bill;* rogare populum, Cic.; rogare plebem, Cic.; rogare legem, Cic.; (γ) rogare (populum) magistratum, *to propose a magistrate to the choice of the people, offer a person for election;* ut consules roget praetor vel dictatorem dicat, Cic.; **b,** milit. t. t., rogare milites sacramento, *to administer an oath to the troops,* Caes. **B.** *to ask,* *entreat, beseech, request ;* 1, gen., a, aliquem aliquid, Cic. ; b, aliquem : Taurum de aqua per fundum eius ducenda, Cic. ; c, with ut or ne and the subj., or the subj. alone, id ut facias, te etiam atque etiam rogo, Cic. ; Caesar consolatus rogat finem orandi faciat, Caes. ; d, absol., Cic. ; 2, esp., *to invite ;* aliquem, Cic. (archaic. subj. perf., rogassit, rogassint, Cic.).

rŏgus -i, m. *a funeral pile ;* rogum exstruere, Cic. ; aliquem in rogum imponere, Cic.; poet., carmina diffugiunt rogos, *escape destruction,* Ov.

Rōma -ae, f. (Ῥώμη), *Rome, the chief city of Latium and the Roman empire, founded* 753 or 754 B.C.; *honoured as a goddess in a separate temple.* Hence, **A. Rōmānus** -a -um, 1, *Roman ;* ludi, *the oldest games at Rome* (also called ludi magni and maximi), Cic. ; Romano more, *straightforwardly, candidly,* Cic.; Romanum est, *it is the Roman custom ;* foll. by acc. and infin., Liv. ; subst., a, **Rōmānus** -i, m., (α) sing., collect. = *the Romans,* Liv. ; (β) plur., Romani, *the Romans,* Cic. ; b, **Rōmāna** -ae, f. *a Roman woman ;* 2, = *Latin ;* lingua, Ov.

Rōmŭlus -i, m. *son of Ilia or Rhea Silvia and Mars, twin brother of Remus, the founder and first king of Rome, worshipped after his death under the name of Quirinus.* Hence, **A.** Adj., **Rōmŭlěus** -a -um, *of Romulus ;* fera, *the she-wolf which suckled Romulus,* Juv. **B. Rŏmŭlus** -a -um, a, *belonging to Romulus ;* ficus = Ruminalis, Ov. ; b, *Roman,* Verg. **C. Rōmŭlĭdēs** -ae, *a descendant of Romulus ;* plur., **Rōmŭlĭdae** -ārum and -um, poet., *the Romans,* Verg.

rōrāriĭ -ōrum, m. (sc. milites), *a kind of light-armed troops, skirmishers,* Liv.

rōrĭdus -a -um (ros), *bedewed,* Prop.

rōrĭfěr -fěra -fěrum (ros and fero), *dew-bringing,* Lucr.

rōro, 1. (ros). **I.** Intransit., *to cause dew, to drop* or *distil dew.* **A.** Lit., quum rorare Tithonia conjux coeperit, Ov. **B.** Transf., *to drip, drop, be moist ;* rorant pennae, Ov.; capilli rorantes, Ov. ; rorabant sanguine vepres, Verg. **II.** Transit., *to bedew, cover with dew.* **A.** Lit., roratae rosae, Ov. **B.** Transf., 1, *to moisten, water ;* ora lacrimis, Lucr. ; 2, *to drip, let fall in drops ;* roratae aquae, Ov. ; pocula rorantia, *which let fall the wine drop by drop,* Cic.

rōrŭlentus -a -um (ros), *bedewed, dewy,* Plaut.

rōs, rōris, m. (connected with δρόσος), *dewy.* **I.** Lit., ros nocturnus, Caes. **II.** Transf., 1, poet., *any dripping moisture ;* rores pluvii, *rain-clouds,* Hor. ; of tears, stillare ex oculis rorem, Hor. ; stillans, *blood,* Ov. ; of perfume, Arabus, Ov. ; 2, ros marinus, Ov. or in one word rosmarinus, *rosemary,* Hor. ; poet., ros maris, Ov. ; or simply ros, Verg.

rŏsa -ae, f. *a rose.* **I. A.** As a flower, a, Cic.; plena rosarum atria, Ov. ; b, collect. = *roses, a garland of roses ;* reticulum plenum rosae, Cic.; in rosa, *crowned with roses,* Cic. **B.** As a plant, flores rosae, Hor., Verg. **II.** As term of endearment, mea rosa, *my rosebud,* Plaut.

rŏsācěus -a -um (rosa), *made of roses,* Plin.; rosaceum oleum, or subst., **rŏsācěum** -i, n. *oil of roses,* Plin.

rŏsārĭus -a -um (rosa), *made of roses,* Plin.; subst., **rŏsārĭum** -i, n. *a rose-garden, rosary,* Verg.

rŏscĭdus -a -um (ros), *bedewed, dewy.* **I.** Lit., mala, Verg. ; mella, *dripping like dew,* Verg. ; dea, *Aurora,* Ov. **II.** Poet., transf., *moistened, watered ;* Hernica saxa rivis, Verg.

Rŏscĭus -a -um, *name of a Roman gens, the most celebrated members of which were:* 1, Sex.

Roscius, *of Ameria, accused of the murder of hi. father, and defended by Cicero ;* 2, Q. Roscius, *of Lanuvium, a celebrated Roman actor, the contemporary and friend of Cicero ;* appellat., *a Roscius* = *a master in his art ;* hence, adj., **Roscĭānus** -a -um, *Roscian ;* imitatio, Cic.; 3, L. Roscius Otho, *friend of Cicero, tribune of the people, proposer of the lex Roscia ;* adj., **Roscĭus** -a -um, *Roscian ;* lex Roscia, *a law giving the equites special seats in the theatre.*

Rŏsěa (Rōsĭa) -ae, f. *a district in the Sabine country, famous for the rearing of horses.* Hence, adj., **Rŏsěus** -a -um, *Rosean.*

rŏsētum -i, n. (rosa), *a garden of roses,* Varr.

1. **rŏsěus** -a -um (rosa). **I.** *made of roses, full of roses ;* strophium, Verg. **II.** Meton., *rose-coloured, rosy ;* rubor, Ov. ; poet., epithet of the deities of the morning and of light ; dea, *Aurora,* Ov. ; Phoebus, Verg.; so of anything young or fresh, *blooming ;* esp., of parts of the body, cervix, os (of Venus), Verg.

2. **Rŏsěus** -a -um, v. Rosea.

rŏsĭdus = roscidus (q.v.).

rōsĭo -ōnis, f. (rodo), *corrosion,* Plin.

rosmărīnus, v. ros.

rostellum -i, n. (dim. of rostrum), *a little beak or snout,* Plin.

rostra -ōrum, n., v. rostrum.

rostrātus -a -um (rostrum), *having a beak or hook, beaked ;* esp., of the beaked ornament of ships, *curved ;* navis, Cic. ; corona, *a crown ornamented with small figures of the beaks of ships, given to the person who first boarded an enemy's ship,* Plin.; hence, poet., transf., cui tempora navali fulgent rostrata coronā, *with the crown of honour on his brow,* Verg. ; columna rostrata, *the pillar adorned with ships' prows, erected in the forum to commemorate the naval victory of Duilius,* Liv.

rostrum -i, n. (rodo), *that which gnaws.* **I.** Lit., in birds, *the beak ;* in other animals, *the snout,* Cic. **II.** Transf., of things resembling a beak or snout ; esp., **A.** *the curved end of a ship's prow, a ship's beak* (used for ramming other ships), Caes. **B.** Meton., 1, poet., *the prow of a ship,* Verg. ; 2, **rostra** -ōrum, n. *the speaker's platform* or *tribune in the forum* (so called because ornamented with the prows of the ships taken from the Antiates, 338 B.C.) ; escendere in rostra, Cic. ; descendere de rostris, Cic.; a rostris, Hor.

rŏta -ae, f. *a wheel.* **I.** Lit., **A.** Gen., *the wheel of a carriage,* Lucr.; *of a machine,* ne currente rotā funis eat retro, Hor. **B.** Esp., 1, *a wheel for torture* (Gr. τροχός), in rotam ascendere, Cic. ; used often of the wheel of Ixion, rota orbis Ixionii, Verg. ; 2, *a potter's wheel ;* currente rotā cur urceus exit? Hor. ; 3, *a wheel* or *roller for moving heavy weights,* Tac. **II.** Transf., 1, *the wheel of a chariot :* meton., poet., *the chariot itself ;* pedibusve rotāve, Ov. ; plur., rotae, Verg. ; 2, *the sun's disk,* Lucr. ; 3, *the course in a circus, Prop.* **III.** Fig., 1, fortunae rota, *the wheel, vicissitudes of fortune,* Cic. ; 2, poet., imparibus vecta Thalia rotis, *in the unequal alternation of hexameter and pentameter,* i.e., *in elegiac verse,* Ov.

rŏto, 1. (rota). **I.** Transit., *to cause to turn round like a wheel, to whirl round, swing round.* **A.** Lit., ensem fulmineum, *to brandish,* Verg. ; middle, rotari, *to revolve, to turn* or *roll round ;* circum caput igne rotato, Ov. **B.** Fig., Juv. **II.** Intransit., *to turn* or *wheel round ;* saxa rotantia, Verg.

rŏtŭla -ae, f. (dim. of rota), *a little wheel,* Plaut.

rŏtundē, adv. (rotundus), *roundly; fig., of expression, elegantly, smoothly,* Cic.

rŏtundĭtas -ātis, f. (rotundus), *roundness, rotundity,* Plin.

rŏtundo, 1. (rotundus), *to round, make round.* **I.** Lit., Cic. **II.** Transf., *to make up a round sum of money;* mille talenta rotundentur, Hor.

rŏtundus -a -um (rota), *round, circular, spherical.* **I.** Lit., caelum, Hor.; nihil rotundius, Cic.; prov., mutat quadrata rotundis, *turn everything upside down,* Hor. **II.** Transf., 1, *round, perfect, complete, self-contained;* teres atque rotundus, Hor.; 2, of style, *well-rounded, elegant, smooth, well-turned;* verborum apta et quasi rotunda constructio, Cic.

rŭbĕfăcĭo -fēci -factum, 3. (rubeo and facio), *to redden, make red,* Ov.

rŭbellus -a -um (dim. of ruber), *reddish, somewhat red,* Plin.

rŭbens -entis, p. adj. (from rubeo), *red, reddish;* 1, gen., uva, Verg.; 2, esp., *red with shame, blushing,* Tib.

rŭbĕo, 2. (v. ruber), 1, *to be red;* sol rubere solitus, Liv.; 2, *to be red with shame, blush,* Cic.

rŭber -bra -brum (root RU, whence rufus and rutilus), *red, ruddy.* **I.** Gen., flamma, Ov.; sanguis, Hor.; aequor rubrum oceani, *reddened by the setting sun,* Verg. **II.** Adj. proper, **A.** Rubrum Mare, *the Red Sea, the Arabian and Persian Gulfs,* Cic. **B.** Saxa Rubra, *a place in Etruria, not far from Cremera,* Cic.

rŭbesco -bŭi, 3. (rubeo), *to grow red, become red;* mare rubescebat radiis, Verg.

1. **rŭbēta** -ae, f. (rubus), *a species of toad found in bramble-bushes,* Juv.

2. **rŭbēta** -ōrum, n. (rubus), *bramble-bushes,* Ov.

1. **rŭbĕus (rŏbĕus)** -a -um (ruber), *red, reddish,* Varr.

2. **rŭbĕus** -a -um (rubus), *made of bramble, twigs;* virga, Verg.

Rŭbi -ōrum, m. *a town in Apulia, now Ruvo.*

rŭbĭa -ae, f. *madder,* Plin.

Rŭbĭco -ōnis, m. *a small river in Italy, south of Ravenna, which before the time of Augustus marked the boundary between Italia and Gallia Cisalpina, the crossing of which by Caesar was an act of war against the senate; now Pisatello, also called Rukon.*

rŭbĭcundŭlus -a -um (dim. of rubicundus), *somewhat red* (for shame), Juv.

rŭbĭcundus -a -um (rubeo), *red, reddish, ruddy, rubicund;* Priapus, *painted red,* Ov.; matrona, *browned by the sun,* Ov.; Ceres, *golden-red,* Verg.

rŭbĭdus -a -um (ruber), *red, reddish, ruddy,* Plaut.

Rŭbĭgālĭa, v. 2. Robigo.

rŭbigo = robigo (q.v.).

Rŭbĭgus, v. 2. Robigo.

rŭbor -ōris, m. (rubeo), *redness.* **I. a,** *red paint, rouge;* fucati medicamenta candoris et ruboris, Cic.; **b,** *purple;* Tyrii rubores, Verg. **II.** As a quality, 1, *lasting,* **a,** gen., Ov.; **b,** *the red tint of the skin, glow;* ille fusus et candore mixtus rubor, Cic.; 2, *momentary,* **a,** *redness of the skin;* flammae latentis indicium rubor est, Ov.; **b,** *glow of the eyes in anger;* saepe suum fervens oculis dabat ira ruborem, Ov.; **c,** *reddening from shame, blush;* Masinissae rubor suffusus, Liv.; alicui non rubor est, with infin., *one need not blush that,* etc., Ov.; hence, meton., (a) *modesty,* Cic.; (β) *the cause of shame, disgrace,* Cic.

Rŭbra Saxa, v. ruber.

rŭbrĭca -ae, f. **I.** *red earth, and esp., red ochre,* Hor. **II.** Meton., *the title of a law which was written in red, the rubric;* and hence, *the law itself,* Pers.

rŭbrĭcōsus -a -um (rubrica), *full of red earth,* Plin.

rŭbus -i, m. (root RU, whence ruber), 1, *a bramble-bush,* Caes.; 2, *a blackberry,* Prop.

ructo, 1. and **ructor**, 1. dep. (root RUC, whence ructus, erugo, eructo), 1, *to belch, eructate,* Cic.; 2, *to belch out, vomit forth;* fig., versus, Hor.

ructor = ructo (q.v.).

ructus -ūs, m. (conn. with ructo), *belching, eructation,* Cic.

rŭdens -entis, m. (f. Plaut.), *a strong rope, cable;* rudentis explicatio, Cic.; stridor rudentum, Verg.

rŭdĕra -um, n., v. 1. rudus.

Rŭdĭae -ārum, f. *a town in Calabria, birth-place of Ennius,* now Rotigliano or *Ruge.* Hence, **Rŭdĭnus** -a -um, *of Rudiae;* Rudinus homo, i.e., *Ennius,* Cic.

rŭdĭārĭus -ĭi, m. (2. rudis), *a gladiator who had been presented with a rudis, i.e., one who had served his time, a discharged gladiator,* Suet.

rŭdĭcŭla -ae, f. (dim. of 2. rudis), *a small wooden spoon, used in cooking,* Plin.

rŭdĭmentum -i, n. (rudis), *the first trial or beginning in anything, an attempt, essay;* **a,** gen., primum regni puerilis, Liv.; **b,** in warfare, militare, Liv.; belli, Verg.; rudimentum adolescentiae ponere, Liv.

Rŭdĭnus, v. Rudiae.

1. **rŭdis** -e, *rough, raw, rude, unwrought, uncultivated.* **I.** Lit., **a,** of things, rudis campus, Verg.; rudis indigestaque moles, *chaos,* Ov.; lana, *unspun,* Ov.; **b,** poet., of living creatures, *young, fresh,* Cat. **II.** Transf., *rude, uncultivated, unrefined, ignorant, unskilled, inexperienced;* (a) absol., forma quaedam ingenii admodum impolita et plane rudis, Cic.; rudis et integer discipulus, Cic.; (β) with in and the abl. or the abl. alone, in disserendo, Cic.; arte, Ov.; (γ) with ad and the acc., rudis ad pedestria bella gens, Ov.; (δ) with genit., Graecarum literarum, Cic.

2. **rŭdis** -is, f. *a small stick.* **I.** *a ladle, scoop,* used for stirring and mixing in cooking, Plin. **II.** *a staff used for soldiers and gladiators in fencing exercises, a foil,* Liv.; *a staff of this kind was given to a gladiator on his discharge from service;* tam bonus gladiator rudem tam cito accepisti? Cic.; hence, transf., rude donari, *to be discharged,* Ov.

rŭdo, rŭdĭvi, 3. *to bellow, roar.* **I.** Lit., of lions, Verg.; of asses, *to bray,* Ov. **II.** Transf., **a,** of men, Verg.; **b,** of things, prora rudens, *rattling,* Verg.

1. **rŭdus (rōdus)** -ĕris, n. 1, *broken frag-ments of stone used for making floors,* Plin.; 2, *rubbish from ruined buildings,* Tac.

2. **rŭdus** = raudus (q.v.).

rŭduscŭlum = raudusculum (q.v.).

rūfesco, 3. (rufus), *to grow reddish,* Plin.

rūfo, 1. (rufus), *to make reddish,* Plin.

Rufrae -ārum, f. *a town in Campania, on the borders of Samnium.*

Rufrĭum -ĭi, n. *a town of the Hirpini, now Ruvo.*

rūfŭlus -a -um (dim. of rufus). **I.** *reddish, somewhat red,* Plaut. **II.** Rufuli, *those tribuni militum who were chosen by the army or general himself* (opp. comitiati), Liv.

rŭfus -a -um (root RU, whence ruber and rutilus), *red, ruddy, reddish,* Plaut., Ter.

rūga -ae, f. *a wrinkle in the face.* **I.** Lit., Hor.; sulcare rugis cutem, Ov.; as a sign of age, non rugae auctoritatem arripere possunt, Cic.; of sadness, nunc ruga tristis abit, Ov.; of anger, *a frown*; rugas coegit, Ov.; populum rugis supercilioque decepit, Cic. **II.** Transf., 1, nitidis rebus maculam ac rugam figere, *to disgrace, mar,* Juv.; 2, *a crease, fold, plait of any kind,* Plin.

Rŭgĭi -ōrum, m. *a German people between the Elbe and the Weichsel, and on the island of Rügen.*

rūgo, 1. (ruga). **I.** Transit., *to fold, wrinkle,* Plin. **II.** Intransit., *to be wrinkled,* Plaut.

rūgōsus -a -um (ruga), *full of wrinkles, wrinkled*; genae, Ov.; cortex, Ov.; rugosus frigore pagus, *villagers,* Hor.

rŭīna -ae, f. (ruo), *a falling down, fall.* **I.** **A.** Lit., 1, jumentorum sarcinarumque, Liv.; 2, esp., *the falling down of a building*; turris, Caes.; eā ruinā oppressum interire, Cic.; ruinam dare, *to fall down,* Verg. **B.** Transf., *fall, ruin, disaster, calamity, catastrophe, destruction*; urbis, Liv.; ruinae fortunarum tuarum, Cic.; ille dies utramque ducet ruinam, *death,* Hor. **II.** Meton., **A.** *that which falls down*; 1, caeli ruina, *a rain-storm,* Verg.; 2, *the ruins of a building, rubbish*; gen. in plur., ruinae templorum, Liv. **B.** Of persons, *a destroyer, overthrower, bane*; reipublicae, Cic.; ruinae publicanorum, *Piso and Gabinius,* Cic.

rŭīnōsus -a -um (ruina), *going to ruin*; 1, *ruinous*; aedes, Cic.; 2, *ruined, fallen*; domus, Ov.

Rullus -i, m., P. Servilius, *tribune of the people, against whom Cicero delivered three speeches.*

rūma = rumis (q.v.).

rūmen -ĭnis, n. *the gullet.*

rŭmex -ĭcis, c. *sorrel,* Plin.

rūmĭfĭco, 1. (rumor and facio), *to report,* Plaut.

Rŭmĭna -ae, f. (ruma), *a Roman goddess, whose temple stood near the fig-tree under which, according to the legend, the she-wolf had suckled Romulus and Remus.* Hence, **Rŭmĭnālis** ficus, Liv., also called Rūmĭna ficus, *the fig-tree above-mentioned,* Ov.

rūmĭnātĭo -ōnis, f. (rumino), *a chewing the cud.* **I. A.** Lit., Plin. **B.** *a repetition, return,* Plin. **II.** *turning over in the mind, ruminating upon,* Cic.

rūmĭno, 1. and **rūmĭnor,** 1. dep. (rumen), *to chew the cud, ruminate, chew over again*; pallentes herbas, Verg.

rūmis -is, f. and **rūma** -ae, f. *the breast, teat,* Plin.

rūmor -ōris, m. *a dull noise.* **I.** Gen., a, of things, *the noise of the oars,* Verg.!; b, *murmuring, murmur, confused cry*; rumore secundo = *clamore secundo, with favouring shout,* Hor. **II. A.** *a report, rumour, common talk, hearsay*; rumores incerti, Caes.; rumor multa fingit, Caes.; rumor multa perfert, Cic.; with genit. of the cause, uno rumore periculi, Cic.; with de and the abl., graves de te rumores, Cic.; rumor est, with acc. and infin., Cic.; rumor vulgatur, Liv.; crebri rumores afferebantur, Caes.; increbrescit rumor, Liv. **B.** *common or general opinion, popular judgment*; 1, gen., parvā aura rumoris, Cic.; 2, esp., *good opinion*; rumorem quendam et plausum popularem esse quaesitum, Cic.

rumpo, rūpi, ruptum, 3. *to break, break in pieces, burst, rend, tear asunder.* **I.** Lit., **A.** Gen., 1, vincula, Cic.; pontem, *to break down,* Liv.; pass., rumpi = *to be burst*; inflatas rumpi vesiculas, Cic.; 2, *to burst, split, injure, damage*; jecur, Juv.; pass., rumpi, as middle = *to burst*; ut licentiā audacium, quā ante rumpebar (*burst with anger*), nunc ne movear quidem, Cic.; 3, milit. t. t., *to break through*; ordines, mediam aciem, Liv.; 4, poet., transf., unde tibi reditum certo subtemine Parcae rupere, *cut off,* Hor. **B.** 1, *to break through, to force, make open*; ferro per hostes viam, Verg.; eo cuneo viam, Liv.; 2, *to cause to break forth*; a, fontem, Ov.; often reflex., se rumpere, and middle, rumpi, *to break forth*; tantus se nubibus imber ruperat, Verg.; b, *to cause a sound to burst forth, to utter*; questus, Verg. **II.** Fig., *to break*; a, *to destroy, violate, annul, make void*; foedera, Cic.; jus gentium, Liv.; testamentum, Cic.; b, *to break off, interrupt, disturb*; visum, Cic.; somnum, Verg.; silentia, Ov.; rumpe moras, Verg.

rūmuscŭlus -i, m. (dim. of rumor), *a trifling rumour, idle talk, gossip*; imperitorum hominum rumusculos aucupari, Cic.

rūna -ae, f. *a species of missile, a dart or javelin,* Cic. (?)

runcĭno, 1. *to plane, plane off,* Plaut.

runco, 1. *to weed, thin out,* Plin.

rŭo, rŭi, rŭtum, but partic. fut., rŭĭtūrus, 3. (connected with ῥέω, *to flow*), *to run, to rush, to hasten.* **I.** Intransit., **A.** Gen., 1, lit., a, of persons, (Pompejum) ruere nuntiant et jam jamque adesse, Cic.; in aquam caeci ruebant, Liv.; b, of rivers, de montibus, Verg.; c, of sounds, unde ruunt, *rush forth,* Verg.; d, of night and day, ruit oceano nox, *hastens over,* Verg.; (but) nox ruit, *hastens away,* Verg.; 2, fig., a, in arma ac dimicationem, Liv.; ad interitum, Cic.; b, esp. of over hasty actions, *to be hasty, precipitate*; ruere in agendo, in dicendo, Cic. **B.** *to fall down, sink, fall to the ground*; 1, lit., a, poet., of persons, ruebant victores victique, Verg.; b, of things, ruere illa non possunt, ut haec non eodem labefacta motu non concidant, Cic.; 2, transf., *to fall, be ruined*; ruere illam rempublicam, Cic. **II.** Transf., **A.** 1, *to snatch up, pick up*; a, cinerem et confusa ossa focis, Verg.; b, *to collect together, scrape together*; unde divitias aerisque ruam acervos, Hor.; 2, *to cast up from below*; a, ruere spumas salis aere (of ships), Verg.; b, legal. t. t., rūta et caesa, and by asyndeton, rūta caesa, *everything on an estate dug up* (ruta), *and fallen down* (caesa), *minerals and timber,* Cic. **B.** *to cast down*; immanem molem volvuntque ruuntque, Verg.

rūpes -is, f. (rumpo), *a rock, cliff,* Caes., Liv.

rūpĭcapra -ae, f. (rupes and capra), *a chamois,* Plin.

ruptor -ōris, m. (rumpo), *a breaker, violator*; foederis, Liv.

rūrĭcŏla -ae, c. (rus and colo), *inhabiting, cultivating the country*; boves, Ov.; deus, *Priapus,* Ov. Subst., **rūrĭcŏla** -ae, m. *a countryman, a tiller of the field*; poet., of an ox, Ov.

rūrĭgĕna -ae, m. (rus and gigno), *born in the country, rustic.* Subst., **rūrĭgĕnae** -ārum, c. *the countryfolk,* Ov.

rūro, 1. and **rūror,** 1. dep. (rus), *to live in the country,* Plaut.

rūrsūs and **rursum,** adv. (contr. for revorsus, revorsum, i.e., reversus, reversum). **I.** *backward, back*; rursum traduct, Cic. **II.** Transf., **A.** *on the other hand, on the contrary, in return*; rursus repudiaret, Cic. **B.** To express repetition of a previous action, *again, once more, afresh*; rursus sevocanda videatur Cic.; rursus resistens, Caes.

rūs, rūris, n. *the country* (in opposition to the town), *lands, a country-seat, villa, farm.* **I.** Lit., habes rus amoenum, Cic.; acc., rus, *to the country*, Plaut.; plur., in sua rura venire, Cic.; abl., rure, and locat., ruri, *in the country; ruri vivere*, Cic. **II.** Meton., manent vestigia ruris, *traces of boorish nature*, Hor.

Ruscīno -ōnis, f. *a town in Gallia Narbonensis, on a river of the same name, now Tour de Rousillon.*

ruscum -i, n. and **ruscus** -i, f. *butcher's broom*, Verg.

Rūsellae -ārum, f. *one of the twelve confederate towns of Etruria*, now ruins near *Roselle*; hence, adj., **Rūsellānus** -a -um, *belonging to Rusellae.*

russus -a -um, *red, russet*, Cat.

rustĭcānus -a -um (rusticus), *of or relating to the country, rustic;* vita rusticana, Cic.; homines rusticani, Cic.

rustĭcātĭo -ōnis, f. (rusticor). **I.** *a living in the country*, Cic. **II.** *agriculture*, Cic.

rustĭcē, adv. (rusticus). **I.** *like a rustic, in a countrified manner;* loqui, Cic. **II.** Meton., *clownishly, awkwardly;* facere, Cic.

rustĭcĭtas -ātis, f. (rusticus), **a,** *rustic manners, rusticity, awkwardness*, Ov.; **b,** *bashfulness, timidity*, Ov.

rustĭcor, 1. dep. (rusticus), *to live in the country, to rusticate;* absol., Cic.; cum aliquo, Cic.

rustĭcŭlus -a -um (dim. of rusticus), *somewhat rustic, boorish.* Subst., **rustĭcŭlus** -i, m. *a little countryman, a little rustic*, Cic.

rustĭcus -a -um (rus), *of or belonging to the country, rural, rustic.* **I.** Lit., **A.** Adj., praedium, Cic.; vita, Cic.; homo, *a countryman*, Cic. **B.** Subst., **rustĭcus** -i, m. *a countryman, a rustic*, Cic. **II.** Meton., *country-like.* **A.** In a good sense, *plain, simple, homely;* mores, Cic. **B.** In a bad sense, *clownish, countrified, awkward, boorish;* rustica vox et agrestis, Cic. Subst., **rustĭcus** -i, m. *a boor, clown;* **rustĭca** -ae, f. *a country-girl*, Ov.

1. **rūta** -ae, f. (ῥυτή), *the herb rue.* **I.** Lit., Cic.; plur., Ov. **II.** Fig., *bitterness, unpleasantness*, Cic.

2. **rūta** caesa, v. ruo.

rūtābŭlum -i, n. (ruo), *a fire-shovel*, Suet.

rūtātus -a -um (1. ruta), *flavoured with rue*, Mart.

Rūtēni (**Rūthēni**) -ōrum, m. *a Celtic people in Gallia Aquitania*, in modern *Rovergue*, with capital Segodunum, now *Rhodez.*

rŭtĭlesco, 3. (rutilo), *to become reddish*, Plin.

Rŭtīlĭus -a -um (orig. appellat. = red), *name of a Roman gens, the most celebrated member of which was* P. Rutilius Rufus, *an orator and historian, consul in the time of Marius.*

rūtĭ͞o, 1. (rutilus). **I.** Intransit., *to shine with a reddish gleam, to glitter like gold;* arma rutilare vident, Verg. **II.** Transit., *to make reddish, to dye red;* comae rutilatae, Liv.

rŭtĭlus -a -um (root RU, whence ruber and rufus), *red, gold-red, golden, yellow, auburn;* capilli, Ov.; ignis, Verg.; cruor, Ov.; fulgor, Cic.

rūtrum -i, n. (ruo), *a spade, shovel*, Liv.

rŭtŭla -ae, f. (dim. of ruta), *a little bit of rue*, Cic.

Rŭtŭli -ōrum and (poet.) -ûm, m. *the Rutuli, an ancient people of Latium, whose capital was Ardea;* sing., **Rŭtŭlus** -i, m. *a Rutulian,*

Verg.; Rutulus audax, *Turnus, king of the Rutuli*, Verg. Hence, adj., **Rŭtŭlus** -a -um, *Rutulian;* rex, *Turnus*, Verg.

Rŭtŭpĭae -ārum, f. *a town of the Caverni in Britain*, perhaps the modern *Richborough.* Hence, adj., **Rŭtŭpīnus** -a -um, *belonging to Rutupiae.*

S.

S, the eighteenth letter of the Latin alphabet, corresponding to the Greek sigma (Σ, σ, ς), sometimes representing the Greek aspirate, e.g., sex = ἕξ, sal = ἅλς, serpo = ἕρπω, ὑπέρ = super. It is occasionally interchanged with *t* (as mersare, pulsare, mertare, pultare), and *r* (as honor and honos). The poets of the older period often elided *s* before a consonant, e.g., vitā illā dignu' locoque; by assimilation, *s* before *f* becomes *f*, as difficilis; it often represents another consonant which has been assimilated to it, as jubeo, jussi (for jubsi), cedo, cessi (for cedsi), premo, pressi (for premsi), pando, passum (for pandsum). For abbreviations in which S. is used, v. Table of Abbreviations.

Sāba -ae, f. (Σάβη), *a district in Arabia Felix, famous for its perfumes.* Hence, **Sābaeus** -a -um (Σαβαῖος), *Sabaean;* poet. = *Arabian.* Subst., **a,** **Sābaea** -ae, f. (sc. terra), *the country of Sabaea* (= *Arabia Felix*); **b,** **Sābaei** -ōrum, m. *the Sabaeans.*

Sābātē -ēs, f. *a town in Etruria, on a lake of the same name*, now *Lago di Bracciano.* Hence, adj., **Sābātīnus** -a -um, *of or relating to Sabate;* tribus, Liv.

Sābāzĭus (**Sābādĭus, Sěbādĭus**) -ĭi, m. (Σαβάζιος), *a surname of Bacchus*, Cic. Hence, **Sābāzĭa** -ōrum, n. *a festival in honour of Bacchus.*

Sabbāta -ōrum, n. (Σάββατα), *the Sabbath, Jewish day of rest;* tricesima sabbata, either *the great Sabbath* (a Jewish festival in October), or else *the new moon*, Hor. Hence, **Sabbātārĭus** -a -um, *relating to the Sabbath.* Subst., **Sabbātārĭi** -ōrum, m. *the observers of the Sabbath, the Jews*, Mart.

Sābelli -ōrum, m. (dim. of Sabini), *a poetic name of the Sabines;* sing., Sabellus, *the Sabine* (i.e., Horace, as owner of an estate in the Sabine country), Hor. Hence, **A.** Adj., **Sābellus** -a -um, *Sabine.* **B.** **Sābellĭcus** -a -um, *Sabine.*

Sābīni -ōrum, m. *an ancient people of Italy, neighbours of the Latins;* meton. = *the country of the Sabines*, Liv.; sing., **Sābīnus** -i, m. *a Sabine*, Liv.; **Sābīna** -ae, f. *a Sabine woman*, Juv. Hence, adj., **Sābīnus** -a -um, *a Sabine.* Subst., **Sābīnum** -i, n. (sc. vinum), *Sabine wine*, Hor.

Sabis -is, acc. -im, m. *a river in Gallia Belgica*, now the *Sambre.*

sābŭlēta -ōrum, n. (sabulum), *sandy places*, Plin.

sābŭlo -ōnis, m. *gravel, sand*, Plin.

sābŭlōsus -a -um (sabulum), *abounding in sand, sandy, gravelly*, Plin.

sābŭlum -i, n. *gravel, sand*, Plin.

1. **sāburra** -ae, f. *sand used as ballast*, Verg.

2. **Sāburra** -ae, m. *a general of king Juba.*

săburro, 1. (saburra). **I.** *to load with ballast*, Plin. **II.** Transf., *to cram full* (with food), Plaut.

sacal, indecl. (an Egyptian word), *Egyptian amber*, Plin.

saccārius -a -um (saccus), *relating to sacks;* navis, *laden with sacks*, Quint.

saccharon -i, n. (σάκχαρον), *a saccharine juice exuding from the joints of the bamboo*, Plin.

saccīpērium -ii, n. (saccus and pera), *a pocket or fob for a purse*, Plaut.

sacco, 1. (saccus), *to strain* or *filter through a bag*, Plin.; transf., Lucr.

saccūlus -i, m. (dim. of saccus), *a small bag*, Cic.

saccus -i, m. (σάκκος), *a sack, bag*, Cic.; esp., *a purse, money-bag*, Hor.; also *a bag* (for straining wine through), Plin.

săcellum -i, n. (dim. of sacrum), *a small shrine or chapel*, Cic.

săcer -cra -crum (root SA, whence sancio, sanus, Gr. σάος), *sacred, holy, consecrated.* **I.** Adj., **A.** Gen., a, with dat. and genit., sacrum deae pecus, Liv.; illa insula eorum deorum sacra putatur, Cic.; b, absol., sacra aedes, Cic.; vates, *sacred to Apollo*, Hor.; poet., of deities themselves, Vesta, Prop.; *name of certain places*, as sacer mons, *the holy hill, a hill in the Sabine country, three Roman miles from Rome, on the right bank of the Anio*, Liv.; sacra via, *the holy street, a street in Rome beginning at the Sacellum Streniae and ending at the Capitol;* also sacer clivus, Hor. **B.** Esp., *consecrated to one of the infernal deities, hence accursed, devoted to destruction;* a, relig. t. t., eius caput Jovi (Stygio) sacrum esset, ap. Liv.; eum qui eorum cuiquam nocuerit sacrum sanciri, Liv.; b, transf., *detestable, accursed, horrible;* is intestabilis et sacer esto, Hor.; auri sacra fames, Verg. **II.** Subst., **săcrum** -i, n, *that which is holy.* **A.** *a holy thing;* a, lit., sacrum rapere, Cic.; b, poet., transf., of poems, sacra caelestia, Ov. **B.** *some holy observance, a festival, sacrifice;* a, lit., sacra Cereris, Cic.; sacra facere Graeco Herculi, Liv.; so of the private religious rites peculiar to each Roman gens, sacra gentilicia, Liv.; sacra interire majores noluerunt, Cic.; eisdem uti sacris, Cic.; b, transf., *a secret, mystery*, Ov.

săcerdos -dōtis, c. (sacer), *a priest, priestess;* sacerdotes populi Romani, Cic.; in apposition, regina sacerdos, *Rhea, a vestal*, Verg.

săcerdōtālis -e (sacerdos), *of or relating to a priest, priestly, sacerdotal*, Plin.

săcerdōtĭum -ii, n. (sacerdos), *the office or dignity of a priest, priesthood;* sacerdotium inire, Cic.

săcŏpēnĭum -ii, n. (σαγόπηνον), *the gum of an umbelliferous plant*, Plin.

săcrāmentum -i, n. (sacro), *that which binds or obliges a person.* **I.** Legal t. t., *the money deposited with the tresviri capitales by the parties in a suit, which the defeated party lost;* multae sacramenta, Cic.; meton., *a kind of legal challenge or wager, a civil suit, process;* justo sacramento contendere cum aliquo, Cic. **II.** Milit. t. t., *the engagement entered into by newly-enlisted soldiers, the military oath of allegiance;* 1, a, lit., aliquem militiae sacramento obligare, Cic.; milites sacramento rogare, Caes., Liv., or adigere, Liv.; dicere sacramentum, Caes., or sacramento, Liv.; alicui sacramento or sacramentum dicere, *to swear allegiance to*, Caes.; b, meton., *military service*, Tac.; 2, transf., *an oath;* perfidum sacramentum dicere, Hor.

Săcrāni -ōrum, m. *a people in Latium;* hence, **Săcrānus** -a -um, *of the Sacrani;* acies, Verg.

săcrārium -ii, n. (sacrum). **I.** *a place where sacred things are kept, the sacristy of a temple*, Ov.; Caere sacrarium populi Romani (as the Roman religious vessels, etc., were said to have once been taken to Caere), Liv. **II.** *a place of worship, a chapel, temple;* Bonae Deae, Cic.; *the chapel in a private house;* in tuo sacrario, Cic.

săcrātus -a -um, p. adj. (from sacro), *sacred, holy, consecrated;* templum, Verg.; used esp. of the Roman emperor, whose genius was worshipped, dux (i.e., Augustus), Ov.

săcrĭcŏla -ae c. (sacrum and colo), *a sacrificing priest or priestess*, Tac.

săcrĭfer -fera -ferum (sacrum and fero), *carrying sacred things;* rates, Ov.

săcrĭfĭcālis (**săcrĭfĭciālis**) -e (sacrificium), *of or relating to the sacrifices*, Tac.

săcrĭfĭcātĭo -ōnis, f. (sacrifico), *a sacrificing*, Cic.

săcrĭfĭcĭum -ii, n. (sacrifico), *a sacrifice;* facere sacrificia and sacrificia, Cic.

săcrĭfĭco, 1. and **săcrĭfĭcor**, 1. dep. (sacrificus). **I.** Intransit., *to offer sacrifice, to sacrifice;* alicui majoribus hostiis, Liv.; in sacrificando, Cic. **II.** Transit., *to offer in sacrifice, to sacrifice;* suem, Ov.; pecora, Liv.

săcrĭfĭcŭlus -i, m. (dim. of sacrificus), *a sacrificing priest*, Liv.; rex sacrificus, *the priest in Rome under the Republic who offered the sacrifices previously offered by the kings*, Liv.

săcrĭfĭcus -a -um (sacrum and facio). **I.** *sacrificing;* Ancus, Ov.; rex (v. sacrificulus), Liv. **II.** *of or relating to a sacrifice;* ritus, Ov.

săcrĭlĕgĭum -ii, n. (sacrilegus). **I.** *robbery of a temple, stealing of sacred things, sucrilege;* sacrilegium prohibere, Liv. **II.** *profanation of religious rites*, Nep.

săcrĭlĕgus -a -um (sacra and lego). **I.** *stealing sacred things, sacrilegious;* subst., *a temple-robber*, Cic. **II.** *violating or profaning sacred things, irreligious, impious;* a, lit., used of Pentheus, who despised the worship of Bacchus, Ov.; b, transf., *godless, impious, wicked;* linguae, manus, Ov.

Săcrĭportus -ûs, m. (sacer and portus). **I.** *a town not far from Rome in the Volscian country between Signia and Praeneste.* **II.** *a town on the Tarentine Gulf.*

săcrĭum -ii, n. *Scythian amber*, Plin.

săcro, 1. (sacer). **I.** *to dedicate to a god, consecrate.* **A.** Lit., caput, Liv.; aras, Verg. **B.** Transf., 1, *to devote, give, allot;* honorem alicui, Verg.; 2, meton., *to consecrate, make holy, make inviolable;* foedus, Liv.; lex sacrata, *a law, the violation of which was punished by a curse*, Cic. **II.** *to make imperishable, to immortalise;* aliquem Lesbio plectro, Hor.; vivit eloquentia Catonis sacrata scriptis omnis generis, Liv.

săcrōsanctus -a -um (sacer and sanctus), *consecrated with religious ceremonies;* hence, *holy, sacred, inviolable* (of the tribunes of the people); ut plebi sui magistratus essent sacrosancti, Liv.; possessiones, Cic.; potestas (of the tribune), Liv.; alicuius memoria, Cic.

săcrum, v. sacer.

Sădāla and **Sădălēs** -ae, m. *a Thracian prince, son of Cotys III.*

saeculum = saeculum (q.v.).

saeculāris (**sēcŭlāris**) -e (saeculum), *relating to a saeculum or age;* ludi, *secular games* (celebrated at intervals of 110 years), Suet.; carmen, *a hymn sung at the secular games*, Suet.

saecŭlum (sēcŭlum, syncop. **saeclum, sēclum)** -i, n. (perhaps connected with 1. secus and with sexus). **I.** *race, sex, generation ;* muliebre, Lucr. **II.** Transf., **A.** In a restricted sense, like γενεά, *the average duration of a man's life* (33⅓ years), *a generation, age ;* 1, lit., multa saecula hominum, Cic.; 2, meton., a, *the human race living at any particular generation, the age, the times ;* ipse fortasse in huius saeculi errore versor, Cic.; b, *the spirit of the age, the prevailing tone of manners ;* mitescent saecula, Verg. **B.** In a wider sense, *the longest duration of a man's life, a hundred years, a century ;* 1, a, lit., duobus prope saecula ante, Cic.; b, transf., *an indefinitely long time, an age ;* aliquot saeculis post, Cic.; saeclis effeta senectus, Verg.; 2, meton., *the men living in a particular century, the century ;* saeculorum reliquorum judicium, Cic.

saepĕ, adv., comp. saepĭus, superl. saepissĭme, *often, oftentimes, frequently*, Cic.; bene saepe, Cic.; saepe et multum, Cic.; saepe multi, Cic.; saepenumero, *repeatedly, again and again*, Cic.

saepes (sēpes) -is, f. (σηκός), *a hedge, fence*.

saepĭa = sepia (q.v.).

saepĭcŭlē, adv. (dim. of saepe), *pretty often*, Plaut.

saepīmentum (sēpīmentum) -i, n. (saepio), *an inclosure*, Cic.

Saepīnum -i, n. *a small town in Samnium*, now *Sepino*.

saepĭo (sēpĭo), saepsi, saeptum, 4. (saepes), *to surround with a hedge, to hedge in, to inclose*. **I.** a, lit., vallum arboribus, Liv.; b, fig., locum cogitatione, Cic. **II.** Transf., 1, *to shut in, to confine, to surround ;* urbes moenibus, Cic.; se tectis, *to shut oneself up at home*, Verg.; 2, a, *to beset, to occupy ;* vias, Liv.; b, *to guard, to secure, protect ;* natura oculos membranis vestivit et saepsit, Cic.

saepta -ōrum, n., v. saeptum.

saeptum (septum) -i, n. (saepio), *an inclosure, barrier.* **I.** Gen., quibus saeptis beluas continebimus, Cic. **II.** Esp., **saepta** -ōrum, n. *the inclosure where the Romans voted at the comitia, sometimes erected in the forum, sometimes in the Campus Martius*, Cic.

saet . . . v. set . . .

Saetăbis -bis. **I.** m. *a river in Spain*, now *Mijares* or *Myares*, or else *Cenia* or *Senia*. **II.** f. *a town in Hispania Tarraconensis, famous for its flax.* Adj., **Saetăbus** -a -um, *relating to Saetabis*.

saetĭger and **saetōsus** = setiger, setosus (q.v.).

saevē, adv. with compar. and superl. (saevus), *cruelly, barbarously, ferociously*, Hor.

saevĭdĭcus -a -um (saevus and dico), *angrily spoken ;* dicta, Ter.

saevĭo -ii -ītum, 4. (saevus), *to rage, be fierce, furious.* **I.** Lit., of animals, saevit lupus, Ov.; anguis, Verg.; saevire coepisse (of elephants), Liv.; in aliquem, Ov. **II.** Transf., a, of men, *to be furious, angry ;* saevire in obsides, Liv.; impers., in ceteros saevitum esse, Liv.; b, of things and of abstractions, *to rage ;* saevit pontus, Hor.; saevit venenum in praecordiis, Hor.; saevit amor ferri, Verg.

saevĭter = saeve (q.v.).

saevĭtĭa -ae, f. (saevus), *ferocity.* **I.** Lit., of animals, canum, Plin. **II.** Transf., *fierceness, rage, cruelty, harshness, severity ;* a, of men, judic's, Cic.; creditorum, Tac.; hostium, Sall.;

b, of inanimate and abstract things ; annonae *high price of provisions*, Tac.

saevum = sebum (q.v.).

saevus -a -um, *raging, wild, violent, fierce.* **I.** Lit., of animals, leones, Lucr.; saevior leaena, Verg. **II.** Transf., *raging, fierce, cruel, savage, harsh ;* a, of persons, Juno, Verg.; Aeneas saevus in armis, *terrible*, Verg.; poet. with the infin., quaelibet in quemvis opprobria fingere saevus, Hor.; b, of inanimate and abstract things, aequora, Verg.; ventus, Cic.; scopulus, Verg.; funera, Verg.

sāga -ae, f. (root SAC, whence sagio), *a female soothsayer, prophetess, fortune-teller*, Cic.

săgācĭtas -ātis, f. (sagax), **I.** *keenness, acuteness of the senses ;* esp., *keenness of scent in dogs ;* canum ad investigandum sagacitas narium, Cic. **II.** Transf., *mental acuteness, sagacity, shrewdness ;* hominis, Cic.

săgācĭtěr, adv. (sagax), *sharply, keenly.* **I.** Of the senses, *with keen scent*, Plin. **II.** Transf., of the mind, *acutely, sagaciously, shrewdly ;* pervestigare, Cic.; tu sagacius odorabere, Cic.; ut odorer, quam sagacissime possim, quid sentiant, etc., Cic.

Săgăris, acc. -im, abl. -i, m. and **Sangărĭus** -ii, m. (Σαγγάριος), *a river in Phrygia and Bithynia, flowing into the Propontis*, now *Sakarja, Sakari.* Hence, **Săgărītis** -ĭdis, f. *of or relating to Sagaris ;* nympha, Ov.

săgātus -a -um (sagum), *clothed with a sagum ;* esp., of a soldier in a military cloak, Cic.

săgax -ācis (sagio), *having keen senses.* **I.** *keen-scented ;* canes, Cic.; *of quick hearing ;* sagacior anser, Ov. **II.** Transf., of mental acuteness, *acute, clever ;* mens, Cic.; sagacissimus ad suspicandum, Cic.; with infin., sagax quondam ventura videre, Ov.

săgīna -ae, f. (σάττω, *to fill*). **I.** *fattening, feeding, nourishing, stuffing, cramming*, Cic. **II.** Transf., *food, fodder, nourishment*, Tac.

săgīno, 1. (sagina), *to fatten, feed up, cram.* **I.** Lit., porcum, Prop.; quae copia rerum omnium (illos Gallos) saginaret, Liv. **II.** Transf., sanguine reipublicae saginari, Cic.

săgĭo, 4. (root SAC, whence sagax, sagus), *to perceive quickly, feel keenly ;* sagire sentire acute est, Cic.

săgitta -ae, f. *an arrow.* **I.** Lit., Cic. **II.** Transf., *the Arrow, a constellation*, Cic.

săgittārĭus -a -um (sagitta), *of or relating to arrows ;* subst., **săgittārĭus** -ii, m. *an archer ;* a, lit., Cic.; b, transf., *the constellation Sagittarius*, also called *Arcitenens*, Cic.

săgittĭfěr -fěra -fěrum (sagitta and fero). **I.** *carrying arrows ;* pharetra, Ov. **II.** *armed with arrows ;* Geloni, Verg.

Săgittĭpŏtens -entis, m. (sagitta and potens), *the constellation Sagittarius*, Cic.

sagmen -ĭnis, n. (SAC, sacer, sancio), *a bunch of sacred herbs plucked in the citadel, by bearing which the persons of the Roman fetiales and ambassadors became inviolable*, Liv.

Sagra -ae, c. *a river in the country of the Bruttii, on the banks of which a battle was fought* 580 B.C., *between Croton and Locri*, now *Sacriano*.

săgŭlum -i, n. (dim. of sagum), *a small military cloak*, Cic.

săgum -i, n. (σάγος, a Celtic word), *a mantle made of coarse wool worn by slaves, also the plaid of the Celts ;* esp., of soldiers, *a military cloak*, Caes.; hence, symbolical of war, as the toga of peace ; hence, saga sumere, ad saga ire, *to take up arms, prepare for war*, Cic.; in sagis esse, *u* be in arms, Cic.; saga ponere, to lay down arms, Liv.

Saguntĭa, v. Segontia.

Săguntum -i, n. and **Săguntus** (-ŏs) -i, f. a town in Spain, south of the Ebro, now Murviedro, the besieging of which by Hannibal led to the outbreak of the Second Punic War. Hence, **A. Săguntinus** -a -um, Saguntine. **B. Săguntii** -ûm, m. the people of Saguntum.

săgus -a -um (root SAC, whence sagio), prophetical, soothsaying; subst., **săga** -ae, f. a fortune-teller, Cic.

Săis -is, f. (Σάϊς), the old capital of Lower Egypt, now ruins near Sâ el Haggar. Hence, **Săĭtae** -ārum, m. the inhabitants of Sais.

săl, sălis, m. and n., and plur., sāles, m. (root 'ΑΛ, ἅλς), salt. **I. 1**, lit., multi modii salis, Cic.; **2**, fig., salt, i.e., wit, facetiousness; epistolae humanitatis sparsae sale, Cic.; sale et facetiis Caesar vicit omnes, Cic. **II.** Meton., **1**, the salt sea; campi salis, Verg.; **2**, plur., sales, salt taste, Ov.

Sălācĭa -ae, f. (salum and cieo), a sea-goddess, corresponding to the Greek Tethys, wife of Oceanus.

sălāco -ōnis, m. (σαλάκων), a swaggerer, boaster, braggart, Cic.

Sălămis -mīnis, acc. -mīna, f. (Σαλαμίς). **I.** an island and town in the Saronic Gulf, over against Eleusis, scene of a naval victory of the Greeks over the Persians, now Koluri. **II.** a town in Cyprus, built by Teucer. Hence, **Sălămĭnĭus** -a -um, a, relating to the island Salamis; **Sălămĭnĭi** -ōrum, m. the Salaminians, inhabitants of Salamis; b, relating to the town of Salamis in Cyprus; subst., **Sălămĭnĭi** -ōrum, m. the inhabitants of Salamis in Cyprus.

Sălăpĭa -ae, f. a town in Apulia, now the village of Sapi. Hence, **Sălăpĭtāni** -ōrum, m. and **Sălăpĭni** (**Salpini**) -ōrum, m. the inhabitants of Salapia.

sălăputtĭum (**sălăpūtĭum**) -ĭi, n. a little dwarf, manikin, Cat.

sălārĭus -a -um (sal), of or relating to salt. **I.** Adj., annona, yearly revenue from salt, Liv.; adj. prop., Salaria via, or simply Salaria, a road beginning at the Porta Capena and leading into the Sabine country, the Salt Road, so called because the Sabines used it for conveying their salt from the sea, Cic. **II.** Subst., **sălārĭum** -ĭi, n. salt rations, money given to soldiers and officers for salt, and hence, allowance, pay, wages, salary, Suet.

Salassi -ōrum, m. the Salassi, an Alpine people in modern Savoy.

sălax -ācis (1. salio). **I.** Of male animals, lustful, lecherous; aries, Ov. **II.** Transf., exciting lust; eruca, Ov.

sălĕbra -ae, f. (1. salio), a rough, uneven road. **I.** Lit., Hor. **II.** Fig., applied to discourse, roughness, ruggedness; oratio haeret in salebra, sticks fast, Cic.

sălĕbrōsus -a -um (salebra), rugged, rough; saxa, Ov.

Sălentini (**Sallentini**) -ōrum, m. a people of Calabria on the coast; meton., the country of the Salentini. Adj., **Sălentinus** -a -um, Salentinian.

Sălernum -i, n. a town on the Adriatic Sea, in the Picentine country, now Salerno.

Sălĭāris, v. Salii.

Sălĭātus -ūs, m. (Salii), the office or dignity of a priest of Mars.

sălĭcastrum -i, n. (salix), a kind of vine growing wild among the willows, Plin.

sălictārĭus -a -um (salix), of or relating to willows, Plin.

sălĭctum -i, n. (syncop. for salicetum, from salix), a plantation of willows, Cic.

sălĭentes -ĭum, m., v. 2. salio.

sălignus -a -um (salix), made of willow-wood; fustis, Hor.

Sălĭi -ōrum, m. (salio, i.e., the leapers, jumpers), a college of priests of Mars, instituted by Numa, whose sacred processions, accompanied by singers and armed dancers, took place annually in the beginning of March. Hence, **Sălĭāris** -e, a, lit., relating to the Salii; carmen Numae, Hor.; b, transf., splendid, magnificent (from the sumptuous feasts that followed the procession of the Salii); epulari Saliarem in modum, Cic.

sălillum -i, n. (dim. of salinum), a little salt-cellar, Cat.

sălinae -ārum, f. (sal), salt-works, brine-pits. **I.** Gen., Cic., Caes.; in jesting reference to sal (wit), possessio salinarum mearum, Cic. **II.** Esp., **A.** salt-works on the banks of the Tiber; in full, salinae Romanae, Liv. **B.** Salinae, a place in Rome, near the Porta Trigemina, Liv.

sălīnum -i, n. (sal), a salt-cellar, Hor.

1. sălĭo (**sallĭo**), 4. (sal), to salt, pickle, Varr.

2. sălĭo, sălŭi (sălĭi rare), saltum, 4. (root SAL, Gr. 'ΑΛ, whence ἅλλομαι). **I.** Intransit., to spring, leap, jump, bound. **A.** Lit., of living beings, de muro, Liv.; in aquas, Ov.; super vallum, Liv.; saliunt in gurgite ranae, Ov. **B.** Transf., of things, a, salit grando, Verg.; sal or mica (salis) saliens, sacrificial salt, which (as a good omen) leapt up when thrown into the fire; farre pio et saliente micâ, Hor.; pectora trepido salientia motu, Ov.; b, of water, to spring, leap, flow; dulcis aquae saliens rivus, Verg. Partic. subst., **sălĭentes** -ĭum, m. (sc. fontes), fountains, Cic. **II.** Transit., of animals, to leap, to cover, Ov.

Sălĭsubsĭlus -i, m. (= Salius subsiliens), one of the Salii, Cat.

sălĭunca -ae, f. wild or Celtic nard, Verg.

sălīva -ae, f. (connected with σίαλος), spittle, saliva. **I. A.** Lit., Cat. **B.** Meton., **1**, appetite, desire, Pers.; **2**, taste, Prop. **II.** Transf., any similar moisture, e.g., tears, Plin., honey, Plin.

sălīvārĭus -a -um (saliva), slimy, Plin.

sălīvo, 1. (saliva), to spit out, Plin.

sălīvōsus -a -um (saliva), slimy, Plin.

sălix -icis, f. a willow, Verg.

Sallentini = Salentini (q.v.).

sallĭo = 1. salio (q.v.).

Sallustĭus (**Sălustĭus**) -ĭi, m. a Roman name, the most celebrated bearers of which were: **1**, C. Sallustius Crispus, of Amiternum, the celebrated Latin historian, contemporary and opponent of Cicero; **2**, Sallustius Crispus, great nephew of the historian, friend of Augustus, famous for his great riches, the owner of splendid gardens at Rome. Hence, adj., **Sallustĭānus** (**Sălustĭānus**) -a -um, Sallustian.

salmăcĭdus -a -um, salt, Plin.

Salmăcis -ĭdis, f. (Σαλμακίς), a fountain in Caria, fabled to make those who drank of it effeminate. Personif., the nymph of this fountain, Ov.

salmo -ōnis, m. a salmon, Plin.

Salmōneus -ĕi and -ĕos, m. (Σαλμωνεύς), son of Aeolus, brother of Sisyphus, king in Elis, founder of the town Salmone; he imitated the thunder and lightning of Zeus, who on that account struck him with a thunderbolt, and hurled *him down to Tartarus.* Hence, **Salmōnĭs** -ĭdis, f. (Σαλμωνίς), *the daughter of Salmoneus,* i.e., *Tyro, mother of Neleus and Pelias by Neptune, who took the form of the Enipeus.*

Sălōna -ae, f. and **Sălōnae** -ārum, f. *a seaport in Dalmatia.*

salpa -ae, f. *a kind of stock-fish,* Ov.

Salpĭa = Salapia (q.v.).

Salpīnātes -um, m. *a people of Etruria, near Volsinii.* Hence, adj., **Salpīnās** -ātis, *belonging to the Salpinates;* ager, Liv.

Salpīnī = Salapini, v. Salapia.

salsāmentārĭus -a -um (salsamentum), *of* or *relating to salt-fish.* Subst., **salsāmentārĭus** -ĭi, m. *a dealer in salt-fish,* Suet.

salsāmentum -i, n. (* salso -āre), 1, *fish-pickle, brine,* Cic. ; 2, *salted* or *pickled fish,* gen. in plur., Ter.

salsē, adv. with compar. and superl. (salsus), *wittily, humorously, facetiously;* dicere, Cic.

salsĭtūdo -ĭnis, f. (salsus), *saltness,* Plin.

salsūgo -ĭnis, f. (salsus), *saltness,* Plin.

salsūra -ae, f. (sal), *a salting, pickling,*Varr.; fig., meae animae salsura evenit, *I am in an ill-humour,* Plaut.

salsus -a -um, p. adj. (from sallo), *salted, salt.* **I. A.** Lit., fluctus salsi, *the sea,* Verg. **B.** Transf., *tasting like salt, sharp, biting;* lacrimae, Lucr. ; robigo, *corrosive,* Verg. **II.** Fig., *witty, humorous, facetious, satirical;* inveni ridicula et salsa multa Graecorum, Cic. ; male salsus, *with poor wit,* Hor.

saltātĭo -ōnis, f. (salto), *a dancing, pantomimic dance,* Cic.

saltātor -ōris, m. (salto), *a (pantomimic) dancer,* Cic.

saltātōrĭus -a -um (saltator), *of* or *relating to dancing;* orbis, Cic.

saltātrix -trīcis, f. (saltator), *a female dancer, a dancing-girl,* Cic.

saltātus -ūs, m. (salto), *a dancing, dance,* Liv.

saltem, adv. (orig. salutim, from salus, as viritim, from vir), *at least, at all events.* **I.** Affirmative, **a,** with an antithetical sentence, eripe mihi hunc dolorem aut minue saltem, Cic.; **b,** without an antithetical sentence, nunc saltem ad illos calculos revertamur, Cic. **II.** With negatives, non, neque, *not even, nor even,* Liv.

salto, 1. (intens. of salio). **I.** Intransit., *to dance with pantomimic gestures.* **A.** Lit., ad tibicinis modos, Liv. ; saltare in convivio, Cic. ; discere saltare, *to learn to dance,* Cic. **B.** Transf., of orators, Hegesias saltat incidens particulas (of a jerking, hopping style), Cic. **II.** Transit., *to represent in pantomimic dancing;* Cyclopa, Hor.; carmina, poemata, *sing with gestures,* Ov.

saltŭōsus -a -um (saltus), *wooded, well wooded,* Sall.

1. **saltus** -ūs, m. (salio), *a spring, leap, bound,* Cic.; saltum and saltus dare, Ov.

2. **saltus** -ūs, m. (connected with ἄλσος, ἄλτις). **I.** *a pass through a mountain* or *forest, a dale, ravine, glade;* Thermopylarum, Liv. ; saltus Pyrenaei, Caes. **II.** *a forest* or *mountain pasture, cattle-run;* saltibus in vacuis pascant, Verg. ; sometimes, *an estate including a cattle-run;* de saltu agroque dejicitur, Cic.

sălūbris -e and **sălūber** -bris -bre (salus), *healthy.* **I.** *conducive to health, healthful, healthy, salubrious, wholesome.* **A.** Lit., natura loci, Cic. ; annus salubris, Cic. ; somnus, Verg. **B.** Transf., *sound, serviceable, useful;* consilia,

Cic. ; res salubrior, Liv ; sententia reipublicae saluberrima, Cic. **II.** *healthy, strong, sound, vigorous.* **A.** Lit., corpora salubriora, Liv. **B.** Transf., *good, fit, suitable;* quidquid est salsum aut salubre in oratione, Cic.

sălūbrĭtas -ātis, f. (saluber). **I.** *wholesomeness, salubrity.* **A.** Lit., loci, Cic. ; tum salubritatis tum pestilentiae signa, Cic. **B.** Fig., omnis illa salubritas Atticae dictionis et quasi sanitas, Cic. **II.** *soundness, healthiness, health;* corporum, Tac.

sălūbrĭtĕr, adv. (saluber). **I.** *healthfully, wholesomely;* salubrius refrigerari, Cic. **II.** *serviceably, advantageously;* bellum trahere, Liv.

sălum -i, n. (σάλος). **I. a,** *the open sea,* esp., *a place where ships lie anchored, a roadstead;* propter vim tempestatis stare ad ancoram in salo non posse, Liv.; **b,** poet., *the sea* generally ; altum, Hor. **II.** *the rolling of a ship at sea, motion of a ship;* salo nauseāque confecti, Caes.

sălus -ūtis, f. (salvus), *health.* **I.** Gen., **1,** medicinā aliquem ad salutem reducere, Cic.; **2,** *welfare, well-being, weal, good fortune;* utilitati salutique servire, Cic. ; spes salutis, Cic. ; also *the civil well-being of a Roman citizen* (not in exile); restitutio salutis meae, *my recall from exile,* Cic. ; hence, **a,** *a term of endearment,* Plaut.; **b,** personif., Salus, *the goddess of the public safety of Rome, whose temple was on the Quirinal,* Liv.; **c,** *deliverance from death, danger,* etc., ad salutem vocare, *to save,* Cic. ; salutem afferre reipublicae, *to save,* Cic. ; also *a means of deliverance;* nulla salus reipublicae reperiri potest, Cic. ; una est salus, *there is one means of deliverance,* foll. by infin., Cic. ; **d,** *security, safety;* fortunarum suarum salus in istius damnatione consistit, Cic. **II.** Esp., *a wish for a person's welfare* (spoken or written), *salutation, greeting;* salutem nuntiare, Cic. ; ascribere, Cic.; alicui salutem dicere jubere, *to send a greeting to,* Plaut. ; and ellipt., Anacharsis Hannoni salutem (sc. dicit), Cic. ; fig., salutem dicere foro et curiae, *to bid farewell to, renounce,* Cic.

sălūtāris -e (salus), *healthful, beneficial, salutary, serviceable, wholesome, advantageous.* **I.** Gen., **a,** absol., (α) of things, ut quae mala perniciosaque sunt, habeantur pro bonis ac salutaribus, Cic. ; herba salutaris, Ov. ; salutares litterae, Cic. Subst., **sălūtārĭa** -ĭum, n. *remedies, medicines;* pro salutaribus mortifera conscribere, Cic. ; (β) of persons, agri ipsi tam beneficum, tam salutarem, tam mansuetum civem desiderant, Cic. ; **b,** with dat., and ad and acc., and contra and acc., consilium salutare utrique, Cic. **II.** Esp., **A.** Appell., salutaris littera— i.e., *the letter A,* abbreviation of absolvo (littera tristis, C = condemno, Cic). **B.** Adj. proper, **Sălūtāris,** as a surname of Jupiter (Gr. Σωτήρ, as a surname of Zeus).

sălūtārĭtĕr, adv. (salutaris), *beneficially, advantageously;* uti armis, Cic. ; se recipere, Cic.

sălūtātĭo -ōnis, f. (saluto). **I.** *greeting, salutation,* Cic. **II.** Esp., *a greeting, salutation, a call, visit of ceremony, waiting upon a person;* dare se salutationi amicorum, Cic. ; ubi salutatio defluxit, Cic.

sălūtātor -ōris, m. (saluto), *one who pays complimentary visits, a visitor, caller,* ap. Cic.

sălūtātōrĭus -a -um (salutator), *relating to greeting* or *visits;* cubicula, *hall of audience,* Plin.

sălūtātrix -trīcis, f. (salutator). **I.** *greeting, saluting,* Mart. **II.** Esp., *paying a visit calling, waiting upon;* turba, Juv.

sălūtĭfĕr -fĕra -fĕrum (salus and fero), *health-bringing, salubrious;* puer, Aesculapius, Ov.; opem salutiferam dare, Ov.

sălūtĭgĕrŭlus -a -um (salus and gero), *carrying complimentary messages*, Plaut.

sălūto, 1. (salveo), *to say salve to a person, to greet, salute.* **I.** Gen., aliquem, Cic.; sternutamentis, *to say "God bless you," when a person sneezes*, Plin.; deos, *to pay respect to, to worship*, Cic.; with double acc., *to greet as, to name*; aliquem imperatorem, Tac. **II.** Esp., **1,** *to call upon, to pay court to, wait upon*; venit salutandi causā, Cic.; **2,** *to greet a person*; a, *on his arrival*, Cic.; **b,** *on his departure*, Plaut.

Sălūvĭi (Sallūvĭi) -ōrum and -ûm, m. *a Ligurian people in modern Provence.*

salvē, v. salveo.

salvĕo, 2. (salvus), *to be well in health*, found chiefly in the forms salve, salvete, salveto, salvebis, salvere (jubeo), used by the Romans as a greeting, *Good day! I hope you are well? How are you?* a, in welcoming a person, *Good day! good morning!* jubeo te salvere, *I greet you*, Cic.; Dionysium velim salvere jubeas, *greet Dionysius for me*, Cic.; salvebis a meo Cicerone, *my son Cicero sends you greeting*, Cic.; so of greetings addressed to a distinguished person, or of respect paid to a deity, *hail!* salve vera Jovis proles, Verg.; **b,** in taking farewell, *good-bye! God be with you!* vale, salve, Cic.

salvĭa -ae, f. (salvus), *the herb sage*, Plin.

salvus -a -um (root SAL, whence salus, connected with σαόω), *safe, unhurt, uninjured, well, sound.* **I.** Gen., a, of persons, salvus atque incolumis, Caes.; salvus revertor, Cic.; se salvo, *while he is alive*, Cic.; **b,** of things, clipeus, Cic.; with abl. absol., *saving, without infraction of*, Cic.; salvo jure nostrae veteris amicitiae, Cic.; salvo officio, Cic. **I°.** Esp. formulae (of conversation); a, of persons, ne salvus sim, si, etc., *may I die if*, etc., Cic.; salvus sis = salve! Plaut.; **b,** of things, salva res est, *it is all right*; often in questions, satine or satin' salvae? *Is all right (with you)?* Liv.

Sămăria -ae, f. (Σαμάρεια), *a district of Palestine.* Hence, **Sămărītes** -ae, m. *a Samaritan.*

Sămărŏbrīva -ae, f. *a town in Gallia Belgica, chief town of the Ambiani*, now *Amiens.*

sambūca -ae, f. (σαμβύκη), *a species of harp*, Plaut.

sambūcĕus -a -um (sambucus), *made of elder-wood*, Plin.

sambūcĭna -ae, f. (sambuca and cano), *a female harp-player*, Plaut.

sambūcistria -ae, f. (σαμβυκίστρια), *a woman that plays on the sambuca*, Liv.

sambūcus (săbūcus) -i, f. *an elder-tree*, Plin.

Sămē -ēs, f. (Σάμη), *older name of the island Cephallenia*, now *Cefalonia.* Another form, **Sămŏs** -i, f. Hence, **Sămaei** -ōrum, m. *the inhabitants of Same.*

sāmĕra (sămāra) -ae, f. *the seed of the elm*, Plin.

Sămĭŏlus, v. Samos.

Samnis, Samnites v. Samnium.

Sămĭus, v. Samos.

Samnĭum -ii, n. (syncop. from Sabinium), *a mountainous region of central Italy between Campania and the Adriatic Sea.* Hence, **A.** Adj., **Samnis** -itis, *Samnite*; subst., a, *a Samnite*; used collectively, *the Samnites*, Liv.; **Samnītes** -ium, m. *the Samnites*; **b,** *a gladiator armed with Samnite weapons*, Cic. **B.** **Samnītĭcus** -a -um, *Samnite.*

1. Sāmŏs (-us) -i, f. (Σάμος), *an island in the Aegean Sea, off the coast of Asia Minor, opposite Ephesus, the birth-place of Pythagoras, chief seat of the worship of Hera, famous for its clay and the vessels made from it*, now *Sussam* or *Sussam-Adassi*; Threicia Samus = *Samothrace*, Verg., Ov. Hence, **A. Sămius** -a -um, *Samian*; vir, senex, Pythagoras, Ov.; capedines, *made of Samian earthenware*, Cic.; terra, *a part of the main-land of Asia Minor or belonging to Samos*, Liv.; subst., a, **Sămius** -ii, m. *the Samian* = Pythagoras, Ov.; plur., **Sămii** -ōrum, m. *the inhabitants of Samos, Samians*, Cic.; **b, Sămia** -ōrum, n. (sc. vasa), *Samian ware.* **B. Sămiŏlus** -a um, adj. dim., *Samian*, Plaut.

2. Sămŏs = Same (q.v.).

Sămŏthrācē (Sămŏthrēcē) -ēs, f. and **Sămŏthrāca** -ae, f. (Σαμοθράκη), and **Sămŏthrācĭa** -ae, f. *an island of the Aegean Sea on the coast of Thrace opposite the mouth of the Hebrus, famous for the mystic rites of the Cabiri*, now *Samothraki.* Hence, **A. Sămŏthrāces** -um, m. a, *the inhabitants of the island of Samothrace*, Ov.; b, *the Cabiri*, Juv. **B. Sămŏthrācĭus** -a -um, *Samothracian.*

Sampsĭcĕrāmus -i, m. *an Arab prince of Emesa in Libanus, whom Pompejus overcame*; hence, in jest, *a name for Pompejus himself*, Cic.

sampsūchĭnus -a -um (σαμψύχινος), *made of marjoram*, Plin.

sampsūchum -i, n. (σάμψυχον), *marjoram*, Plin.

sānābĭlis -e (sano), *that can be healed, curable*; a, physically, vulnus, Ov.; b, of the mind, iracundi sanabiles, Cic.

sānātĭo -ōnis, f. (sano), *a healing, curing*; corporum, Cic.; fig., malorum, Cic.

sancĭo, sanxi, sanctum, 4. (root SA, whence sacer, sanus, Gr. σάος, σῶς, etc.), *to make sacred or inviolable by a religious act.* **I.** Lit., a, *to make irrevocable, to appoint, order* (of a law, league, etc.); legem, Cic.; foedus sanguine alicuius, Liv.; Solon capite sanxit, si qui, etc., *Solon ordered, on pain of death*, Cic.; b, *to sanction, render valid by law*; acta Caesaris, Cic. **II.** Transf., *to forbid on pain of punishment, lay under a penalty*; incestum supplicio, Cic. (partic. sancitus, Lucr.).

sanctē, adv. (sanctus), *piously, conscientiously, scrupulously*; pie sancteque colere naturam, Cic.; multa sunt severius scripta et sanctius, Cic.; se sanctissime gerere, Cic.; sanctissime observare promissa, *sacredly*, Cic.

sanctĭmōnĭa -ae, f. (sanctus). **I.** *sanctity, sacredness*; ad deorum religionem et sanctimoniam demigrasse, Cic. **II.** *purity, chastity, virtue*; domum habere clausam pudori et sanctimoniae, Cic.

sanctĭo -ōnis, f. (sancio). **I.** *the article or clause in a law which recites the penalty*; legum sanctionem poenamque recitare, Cic. **II.** In treaties, *a clause, proviso*; foederis, Cic.

sanctĭtas -ātis, f. (sanctus). **I.** *inviolability, sanctity*; tribunatus, Cic.; templi insulaeque, *right of asylum*, Tac. **II.** *piety, virtue, chastity*; a, matronarum, Cic.; b, *piety towards the gods*; deos placatos pietas efficiet et sanctitas, Cic.

sanctĭtūdo -ĭnis, f. = sanctitas (q.v.).

sanctor -ōris, m. (sancio), *an ordainer*; legum, Tac.

sanctŭārĭum -ii, n. (sanctus), *the private cabinet of a prince*, Plin.

sanctus -a -um, p. adj. (from sancio). **I.** *sacred, inviolable*; tribuni plebis, Cic.; officium, Cic.

II. *venerable, holy, divine;* **a,** of deities or distinguished men, stella Mercurii, Cic.; sancte deorum, Verg.; so, of the senate, sanctissimum orbis terrae consilium, Cic.; vates, *the Sibyl,* Verg.; **b,** *pious, virtuous, holy, blameless;* nemo sanctior illo (viro), Cic.; homo sanctissimus, Cic.; virgo, *a Vestal virgin,* Hor.; conjux, *chaste,* Verg.

Sancus -i and -ūs, m., also **Semo, Semo Sancus** or **Fidius Sancus,** *an Umbrian and Sabine deity,* probably=Ζεὺς Πίστιος *afterwards identified with Hercules.*

sandălĭārĭus -a -um (sandalium), *of or relating to sandals;* Apollo, *who had a statue in the Street of the Sandal-makers,* Suet.

sandălĭgĕrŭlae -ārum, f. (sandalium and gero), *female slaves who carried their mistresses' sandals,* Plaut.

sandălĭs -ĭdis, f. *a kind of palm-tree,* Plin.

sandálĭum -ii, n. (σανδάλιον), *a slipper, sandal,* Ter.

sandăpĭla -ae, f. *a kind of bier used by poor persons,* Juv.

sandărăca -ae, f. (σανδαράκη), *sandarach, a kind of red dye,* Plin.

sandărăcătus -a -um (sandaraca), *mixed with sandarach,* Plin.

sandarēsos -i, f. *an oriental precious stone, perhaps a kind of cat's-eye,* Plin.

sandyx -dўcis, c. (σάνδυξ), *vermilion, or a similar colour,* Verg.

sānē, adv. (sanus). **I.** *soberly, rationally, sensibly;* non ego sanius bacchabor Edonis, Hor. **II.** Transf., **A.** *really, indeed* (used emphatically), sane vellem, *I could indeed wish,* Cic.; hence, **a,** in answers, *surely, to be sure;* sane hercle or sane hercule, Cic.; **b,** in concessions, *to be sure, certainly;* sint falsa sane, Cic.; **c,** with imperatives, *then, if you will;* age sane, Cic. **B.** *exceedingly;* bene sane or sane bene, Cic.; sane quam, *exceedingly, extremely;* with verbs and adj., Cic.

Sangărĭus, v. Sagaris.

sanguĭnārĭus -a -um (sanguis), *of or relating to blood;* fig., *bloody, blood-thirsty, sanguinary;* juventus, Cic.

sanguĭnĕus -a -um (sanguis), *relating to blood.* **I. A.** Lit., **1,** *of blood, bloody;* imber, Cic.; guttae, Ov.; **2,** *stained with blood;* caput, Ov.; manus, Ov. **B.** Transf., **1,** *stained with blood-shed, bloody;* rixa, Hor.; **2,** *blood-red;* sagulum, Cic. **II.** Fig., *bloody, blood-thirsty;* Mavors, Verg.

sanguĭno, **1.** (sanguis), *to be blood-thirsty,* Tac.

sanguĭnŏlentus (sanguĭnŭlentus) -a -um (sanguis), *bloody.* **I.** *stained with blood, bloody;* **1,** lit., conjugis imago, Ov.; **2,** *stained, wounding, injuring;* nulla exstat littera Nasonis sanguinolenta legi, Ov. **II.** *blood-red;* color, Ov.

sanguis (sanguen) -ĭnis, m. *blood, blood flowing in the veins of a living being,* while cruor = *blood of the dead* or *blood from wounds.* **I. 1,** lit., tauri sanguis, Cic.; sanguinem mittere, *to let blood,* Cic.; sanguinem effundere, *to shed one's blood,* Cic.; **2,** fig., **a,** *vigour, strength, force;* amisimus sucum et sanguinem, Cic.; so of orators, verum sanguinem deperdebat, Cic.; **b,** *property, money;* de sanguine aerarii detrahere, Cic. **II.** Meton., **1,** *shedding of blood, murder;* odio civilis sanguinis, Cic.; **2,** *blood-relationship, race, blood, family;* **a,** abstr., magnam possidet religionem paternus maternusque sanguis, Cic.; **b,** concr., *a descendant, progeny;* regius sanguis, Europa, Hor.; saevire in suum sanguinem, Liv.

sănĭes -ēi, f. (connected with sanguis). **I.** *diseased blood, bloody matter,* Verg. **II.** Transf., *venom, poison, slaver;* perfusus sanie atroque veneno, Verg.; sanies manat ore trilingui, Ov.

sānĭtas -ātis, f. (sanus), *health.* **I.** Lit., *physical health,* Cic. **II.** Transf., **1,** *a sound state of mind, reasonableness, good sense, sanity;* ad sanitatem se convertere or redire, Cic.; **2,** of style, *soundness or correctness, purity;* orationis, Cic.

sanna -ae, f. (σάννας), *a mocking grimace,* Juv.

sannĭo -ōnis, m. (sanna), *one who makes grimaces, a buffoon,* Cic.

sāno, **1.** (sanus), *to heal, cure, restore to health.* **I.** Lit., tumorem oculorum, Cic. **II.** Transf., *physically and morally, to heal, restore, repair, quiet;* partes aegras reipublicae, Cic.; vulnera avaritiae, Liv.: mentes eorum, *to change to right views,* Caes.

Sanquālis (Sanguālis) -e (Sancus), *oelonging to Sancus;* avis, *the bird sacred to Sancus, the osprey.*

Santŏnes -um, m. and **Santŏni** -ōrum, m. *a people in Aquitanian Gaul,* whence *Saintonge.* Hence, adj., **Santŏnĭcus** -a -um, *belonging to the Santones.*

sānus -a -um, *sound, healthy.* **I.** Lit., pars corporis, Cic.; aliquem sanum facere, Cic. **II.** Transf., **a,** *sound, uninjured;* respublica, Cic.; **b,** of sound mind, *rational, sane;* mens, homo, Cic.; **c,** of discourse, *sound, sensible, natural;* genus dicendi, Cic.

săpa -ae, f. *must or new wine boiled to one-third of its bulk,* Ov.

Săpaei -ōrum, m. *a Thracian people on the Propontis,* Ov.

săperda -ae, m. (σαπέρδης), *a small fish caught in the Palus Maeotis, a kind of herring,* Pers.

săpĭens -entis, p. adj. (from sapio), *wise, sensible, prudent, judicious.* **I.** Gen., rex aequus ac sapiens, Cic.; quis sapientior ad conjecturam rerum futurarum, Cic.; Cyrus ille Perses justissimus fuit sapientissimusque rex, Cic.; of things, vera et sapiens animi magnitudo, Cic.; subst., *a sensible, judicious person;* insani sapiens nomen ferat, Hor.; used as a surname of the jurists, L. Atilius, M. Cato, etc., Cic. **II.** Like the Greek σοφός, *wise;* subst., *a wise man, a practical philosopher, a sage;* septem sapientes, *The Seven Wise Men of Greece;* sometimes simply septem, Cic.

săpĭentĕr, adv. (sapiens), *wisely, discreetly, judiciously;* facere, Cic.

săpĭentĭa -ae, f. (sapiens). **I.** *good sense, discernment, prudence;* pro vestra sapientia, Cic. **II.** (like σοφία) *wisdom,* esp., *practical wisdom, knowledge of the world, knowledge of the art of government,* Cic.; with genit., constituendae civitatis, Cic.; plur., virtutes ebullire et sapientias, *rules of wisdom,* Cic.

săpĭo -ĭi. 3. **I.** *to taste, have a flavour or taste;* **a,** lit., Plin.; **b,** *to smell of something;* crocum, Cic. **II.** *to taste, to have taste;* **a,** lit., ut, cui cor sapiat, ei non sapiat palatus, Cic.; **b,** fig., *to discern, perceive, to be sensible, discreet, wise;* sapere eum plus quam ceteros, Cic.; with acc., *to understand;* recta, Cic.

săpo -ōnis, m. (a Celtic word), *soap used by the Gauls as a pomade for the hair,* Plin.

săpor -ōris, m. (sapio), *taste.* **A.** *the taste of a thing;* **1,** a, lit., qui non sapore capiatur, Cic.; **b,** fig., *elegance in discourse;* vernaculus, Cic.; **2,** meton., *a delicacy, a titbit;* gallae admiscere saporem, Verg.; **3,** transf.,

went, Plin.; meton., sapores, *pleasant odours*, Verg. **B.** *the taste which a person has;* **1**, lit., Lucr.; **2**, fig., *good taste in behaviour or discourse;* homo sine sapore, *without taste*, Cic.

Sapphĭcus -a -um, v. Sappho.

sapphīrus (sappīrus) -i, f. (σάπφειρος), *the sapphire*, Plin.

Sapphō -ūs, f. (Σαπφώ), *a lyrical poetess of Mytilene in Lesbos, who threw herself into the sea on account of her unrequitted love for Phaon.* Hence, adj., **Sapphĭcus** -a -um, *Sapphic.*

sappīrus = sapphirus (q.v.).

saprus -a -um (σαπρός), *putrid, rotten*, Plin.

sarcĭna -ae, f. (sarcio), *a bundle, pack, package, portable luggage of a person.* **I. A.** Lit., a, sing., Plaut.; b, plur., sarcinas conferre, Cic.; legionem sub sarcinis adoriri, Caes. **B.** Fig., *burden, load;* publica rerum, *burden of government*, Ov. **II.** Transf., *the fruit of the womb*, Ov.

sarcĭnārĭus -a -um (sarcina), *pertaining to burdens* or *baggage;* jumenta, *pack-horses, beasts of burden*, Caes.

sarcĭnātor -ōris, m. (sarcio), *a patcher, mender, cobbler*, Plaut.

sarcĭnātus -a -um (sarcina) *loaded, burdened*, Plaut.

sarcĭnŭla -ae, f. (dim. of sarcina), *a little bundle* or *package*, gen. plur., Cat., Juv.

sarcĭo, sarsi, sartum, **4**. *to mend, patch, repair.* **I.** Lit., tunicam, Juv. **II.** Fig., *to make good, repair;* damna, Cic.; detrimentum, Caes.; injuriam, Caes.; gratia male sarta, *not completely restored*, Hor. Partic., **sartus** -a -um, with special phrase sartus et tectus or sartus tectus, *in good condition;* a, lit., of buildings, *in good repair, in good condition, well repaired* or *built;* aedem Castoris sartam tectam tradere, Cic.; omnia sarta tecta exigere, Cic.; b, fig., *in a good condition, well preserved, safe;* M. Curium sartum et tectum, ut aiunt, ab omni incommodo conserves, Cic.

sarcĭon -ĭi, m. (σαρκίον), *a flaw in an emerald*, Plin.

sarcŏcolla -ae, f. (σαρκοκόλλα), *a kind of Persian gum*, Plin.

sarcŏphăgus -a -um (σαρκοφάγος), lit., *flesh-eating;* lapis, *a kind of stone used for coffins, which was believed to consume the body;* hence, subst., **sarcŏphăgus** -i, m. *a coffin, sarcophagus*, Juv.

sarcŭlātĭo -ōnis, f.(sarculum), *a hoeing*, Plin.

sarcŭlum -i, n. (sarrio), *a light hoe*, Hor.

sarda -ae, f. **I.** *a small fish which was pickled*, perhaps *a sardine*, Plin. **II.** *a precious stone*, perhaps *cornelian*, Plin.

Sardănăpālus (Sardănăpallus) -i, m. (Σαρδανάπαλος, Σαρδανάπαλλος), *the last king of the Assyrians, who, on a revolt against him, burnt himself with his seraglio and all his treasures.*

1. Sardi, v. Sardis.

2. Sardi -ōrum, m. (Σαρδώ = Sardinia) *the inhabitants of the island of Sardinia, the Sardinians, notorious for their perfidy*, Cic. Hence, **A. Sardus** -a -um, *Sardinian.* **B. Sardōnĭus** -a -um, *Sardinian;* herba, v. Sardous. **C. Sardōus** (Σαρδῷος), *Sardinian;* herba, *a kind of poisonous crow's-foot.* **D. Sardĭnĭa** -ae, f. *the island of Sardinia*, Cic.; hence, **Sardĭniensis** -e, *Sardinian.*

Sardis -ium, acc. -is, f. (Σάρδεις), *Sardis, the old capital of Lydia on the Pactolus, residence of King Croesus, now Sart.* Hence, **A. Sardi** -ōrum, m. *the Sardians, Lydians.* **B. Sardi-**

ānus -a -um, *Sardian;* plur., **Sardĭānī** -ōrum, m. *the Sardians.*

sardŏnyx -nўchis, (σαρδόνυξ) *a precious stone, the sardonyx*, Juv.

Sardōus, v. Sardi.

Sardus -a -um, v. 2. Sardi.

sargus -i, m. *a salt-water fish much esteemed by the Romans*, Ov.

sărĭo = sarrio (q.v.).

sărīsa (sărissa) -ae, f. (σάρισσα), *the long Macedonian pike*, Liv.

sărīsŏphŏrus (sarissŏphŏrus) -i, m. (σαρισσοφόρος), *a Macedonian pikeman*, Liv.

Sarmăta -ae, m. (Σαρμάτης), *a Sarmatian;* plur., Sarmatae, *the Sarmatians, a nation in modern Poland, Little Tartary and adjoining countries.* Hence, **A. Sarmătĭa** -ae, f. (Σαρματία), *Sarmatia, the country of the Sarmatae.* **B. Sarmătĭcus** -a -um (Σαρματικός), *Sarmatic;* mare, *the Black Sea*, Ov.; adv., **Sarmăticē**, *after the Sarmatian manner;* loqui, Ov. **C. Sarmătis** -ĭdis, f. *Sarmatian;* tellus, Ov.

sarmen -ĭnis, n. = sarmentum (q.v.).

sarmentōsus -a -um (sarmentum), *full of twigs* or *small branches*, Plin.

sarmentum -i, n. *twigs, loppings, small branches, brushwood;* a, green, of the vine, Cic.; b, dry = brushwood, *loppings, faggots;* fasces sarmentorum, *fascines*, Liv.; ligna et sarmenta circumdare, Cic.

Sarnus -i, m. *a river in Campania, on which was Pompeii*, now *Sarno.*

Sarpēdōn -ŏnis, m. (Σαρπηδών). **I.** *son of Jupiter, king in Lycia, who came to the help of the Trojans, and was slain by Patroclus.* **II.** *a promontory in Cilicia, now Lissan el Kahpe.*

Sarra -ae, f. *the Hebrew Zor, old name of the city of Tyre;* hence, adj., **Sarrānus** -a -um, *Tyrian, Phoenician;* ostrum, Verg.

sarrācum -i, n. = serracum (q.v.).

Sarrānus -a -um, v. Sarra.

Sarrastes -um, m. *a people in Campania, living on the Sarnus.*

sarrĭo (sărĭo) -ŭi and -ĭvi -ĭtum, **4.** *to hoe,* and thence, *to weed*, Plin.

sarrītor -ōris, m. (sarrio), *one who hoes up weeds, a hoer, weeder*, Varr.; syncop., sartor, fig., Plaut.

sartāgo -ĭnis, f. *a frying-pan*, Juv.; sartago loquendi, *medley, hotch-potch*, Plin.

sartor = sarritor (q.v.).

sartus -a -um, partic. of sarcio (q.v.).

săt = satis, *enough, sufficient.* **I.** Adj., *enough, sufficient;* tantum, quantum sat est, Cic.; foll. by genit., nec sat rationis in armis, Verg.; by infin., nonne id sat erat, accipere ab illo injuriam, Tac. **II.** Adv., a, with verbs, bibere, Verg.; b, with adj., bonus, Cic.; c, with another adv., sat diu, Cic.

sătăgĭto, **1.** *to have enough to do, have one's hands full*, Plaut.

sătăgo, **3.** **I.** *to satisfy* or *pay a creditor*, Plaut. **II.** *to be very busy, have enough to do, have one's hands full, be in trouble*, Petr.

sătellĕs -ĭtis, c. **I.** *a guard, attendant*, and plur., *guards, escort, suite, train*, Cic. **II.** Transf., **1**, *a companion, attendant;* Aurorae, *Lucifer*, Cic.; Orci, *Charon*, Hor.; **2**, esp., in a bad sense *lackey, aider, accomplice, abettor;* audaciae, Cic.; scelerum, Cic.

sătĭas -ātis, f. (satis) = satietas. **I.** *a sufficiency, abundance;* cibi, Lucr. **II.** *satiety, satis-*

ĭed desire, loathing; quo de die epulatis jam vini satias esset, Liv.

Sătīcŭla -ae, f. *a town of Samnium,* near *modern Caserta Vecchia.* Hence, **A. Sătīcŭlānus** -a -um, *relating to Saticula.* **B. Sătīcŭlus** -i, m. *an inhabitant of Saticula.*

sătĭětas -ātis, f. (satis). **I.** *a sufficiency, abundance,* Plaut. **II.** *satiety, loathing;* cibi, Cic.; tig., satietas provinciae, Cic.; studiorum omnium satietas vitae facit satietatem, Cic.

sătĭnĕ, satin' = satisne, v. satis.

1. **sătĭo,** 1. (satis), *to satisfy, satiate.* **I.** 1, lit., with food and drink, Ov.; 2, transf., a, of natural desires, *to satisfy, appease;* desideria naturae, Cic.; sitim, Plaut.; b, of other things, ignes odoribus, Ov. **II.** Fig., 1, *to satisfy, sate;* aviditatem legendi, Cic.; 2, *to overfill, to cloy, to disgust, satiate;* numerus agnoscitur, deinde satiat, Cic.

2. **sătĭo** -ōnis, f. (sero). **I.** *a sowing;* plur., sationes, concr., *the sown fields,* Cic. **II.** *planting,* Verg., Liv.

sătĭra (sătŭra) -ae, f. (satur), *satirical poetry, satire,* Hor

sătĭs, compar., **sătĭus,** *enough, sufficient.* **I.** In posit., **A.** Gen., 1, adj., satis est alicui aliquid, Cic.; satis est foll. by si, Cic.; satis superque habere, *enough* and *more than enough,* Cic.; foll. by genit., ea amicitia non satis habet firmitatis, Cic.; ad dicendum temporis satis habere, Cic.; (non) satis est, foll. by infin., Cic.; satis habeo, with infin., Sall.; with quod, Liv.; 2, adv. (often satine or satin'=satisne); a, with verbs, consequi, Cic.; satin' est id ad, etc., Cic.; b, with adj., satis multa restant, Cic.; c, with adv., honeste, Cic.; absol., de hoc satis, *enough of this,* Cic. **B.** Particular phrases; a, satis ago, *to have enough to do;* impers., agitur tamen satis, Cic. (cf. satagito and satago); b, legal t. t., satis accipere, *to take bail, security,* Cic. **II.** Compar., satius, *better, more advantageous;* satius est, or satius (esse) existimo, or satius puto; with infin., mori satius esse, Cic.

sătisdătĭo -ōnis, f. (satisdo), *a giving bail* or *security,* Cic.

sătisdo -dĕdi -dătum -dăre, 1. *to give bail or security;* with genit., damni infecti, Cic.; hence, satisdato, *by bail, by security;* debere, Cic.

sătisfăcĭo -fēci -factum, 3. *to satisfy, give satisfaction.* **I.** Gen., officio suo, Cic.; vitae satisfeci, *I have lived long enough,* Cic.; alicui aliquid petenti, Cic.; histriones satisfaciebant, Cic. **II.** Esp., **A.** *to satisfy, pay a creditor;* ipse Fufiis satisfacit, Cic. **B.** a, *to give satisfaction, make amends, make reparation;* alicui, Caes., Cic.; omnibus rationibus de injuriis, Caes.; b, *to prove sufficiently;* alicui with acc. and infin., Cic.

sătisfactĭo -ōnis, f. (satisfacio). **I.** *satisfaction, amends, reparation, excuse, apology;* satisfactionem alicuius accipere, Cic., Caes. **II.** *satisfaction by punishment,* Tac.; Caesar Ubiorum satisfactionem accepit, Cic.

sătĭus, comp. of satis (q.v.).

sătīvus -a -um (sero, sevi), *sown* or *planted,* Plin.

sător -ōris, m. (sero, sevi). **I.** *a sower, planter;* omnium rerum seminator et sator est mundus, Cic. **II.** Transf., *begetter, father, producer, causer;* sator hominum atque deorum, i.e., *Jupiter,* Verg.; *so* also litis, Liv.

sătrăpes -ae and -is, m., **sătrăpa** -ae, m., and **sătraps** -ăpis, m. (σατράπης, a Persian word), *the governor of a Persian province, satrap,* Nep.

sătrăpīa (sătrăpēa) -ae, f. (σατραπεία), *a province governed by a satrap, satrapy,* Plin.

Satrĭcum -i, n. *a Latin town on the Appian Road,* now *Casale di Conca.* Hence, **Satricāni** -ōrum, m. *the inhabitants of Satricum.*

sătur -tūra -tūrum (satis), *full, sated, satiated.* **I. A.** Lit., pullus, Cic. **B.** Transf., 1, *satisfied;* expleti atque saturi, Cic.; 2, *rich, fertile;* Tarentum, Verg.; 3, of colours, *deeply dyed, full, dark;* color, Verg. **II.** Fig., *rich, copious;* nec satura jejune (dicet), Cic.

sătŭra -ae, f. (sc. lanx), *a dish of various fruits annually offered to the gods;* hence, transf., *a mixture, medley;* per saturam, *indiscriminately, confusedly, pell-mell;* quasi per saturam sententias exquirere, Sall. Hence, satira (q.v.).

Sătŭrae palus, *a lake in Latium.*

sătŭrēja -ae, f. *the herb savory,* Plin.; heteroclite plur., **sătŭrēja** -ōrum, n. Ov.

Sătŭrējānus -a -um, *belonging to a district of Apulia,* hence, poet. = *Apulian,* Hor.

sătŭrĭtas -ātis, f. (satur). **I.** *satiety, repletion,* Plaut. **II.** Transf., *abundance;* saturitas copiaque rerum omnium, Cic.

Sāturnālĭa, etc., v. Saturnus.

Sāturnīnus -i, m., L. Apulejus, *tribune of the people, killed in a riot,* 100 B.C.

Sāturnus -i, m. (sero, sevi), *an old Latin god, honoured as the god of planting* (a satu or satione frugum); in later times identified with the Κρόνος of the Greeks; Saturni sacra dies, *Saturday,* Tib.; Saturni stella, Cic., or simply Saturnus, Hor., *the planet Saturn.* Hence, adj., **A. Sāturnĭus** -a -um, *Saturnian;* stella, *the planet Saturn,* Cic.; tellus, or arva, *Italy* (because Saturn was said to have reigned there), Verg.; gens, *the Italians,* Ov.; numerus, *the old Italian poetry,* Hor.; proles, *Picus, son of Saturn,* Ov.; domitor maris, *Neptune,* Verg.; virgo, *Vesta, daughter of Saturn,* Ov.; Saturnus pater, *Jupiter,* Verg.; and subst., 1, **Sāturnĭus** -ii, m., (a) *Jupiter,* Ov.; (β) *Pluto;* 2, **Sāturnĭa** -ae, f., (a) *Juno,* Verg.; (β), *an old mythical town on the Capitoline Hill,* Verg. **B. Sāturnālis** -e, *belonging to Saturn;* gen. subst. plur., **Sāturnālĭa** -ium, n. *the festival beginning with the 17th of December, at which there were public spectacles and banquets, presents were exchanged, slaves were waited upon by their masters;* the festival lasted several days, the first of which was called Saturnalia prima, the next Saturnalia secunda, and the third, Saturnalia tertia, Cic. Hence, adj., **Sāturnālĭcĭus** -a -um, *of* or *relating to the Saturnalia,* Mart.

sătŭro, 1. (satur), *to satisfy, satiate.* **I. A.** Lit., *animalia ubertate mammarum,* Cic. **B.** Transf., *to satisfy = to fill;* sola fimo, *to manure,* Verg. **II.** Fig., *to satiate, glut, appease, satisfy;* crudelitatem suam odiumque, Cic.; homines saturati honoribus, Cic.

1. **sătus** -a -um, partic. of 2. sero (q.v.).

2. **sătus** -ūs, m. (2. sero). **I.** *a sowing, setting, planting,* Cic.; fig., *seed;* haec preparat animos ad satus accipiendos, Cic. **II.** Transf., *begetting, origin, stock, race;* Hercules Jovis satu editus, Cic.; a primo satu, Cic.

Sătўrĭcus -a -um, v. Satyrus.

Sătўrĭon -ii, n. (σατύριον), *the plant ragwort,* Plin.

Sătўrĭscus -i, m. (σατυρίσκος), *a little Satyr,* Cic.

Sătўrus -i, m. (Σάτυρος). **I.** *a Satyr, a companion of Bacchus, represented with long pointed ears, behind which were the stumps of horns, with the tail of a goat, bristly hair, and a* *flat nose;* in later times identified with the fauns of the Roman mythology, deities of the woods with horns and the feet of goats; Satyrus Phryx, *Marsyas,* Ov. **II.** Transf., *Greek Satyric drama,* in which Satyrs formed the chorus; Satyrorum scriptor, Hor.

sauciātĭo -ōnis, f. (saucio), *a wounding,* Cic.

saucĭo 1. (saucius), *to wound, hurt.* **I.** Lit., **a,** aliquem telis, Cic.; **b,** *to let blood;* euphem., *to wound mortally,* Cic. **II.** Transf., *to tear up the ground with the plough;* duram humum, Ov.

saucĭus -a -um, *wounded, injured, hurt.* **I.** Lit., graviter saucius, Cic.; paucis sauciis, Caes.; plur. subst., **saucĭi** -ōrum, m. *the wounded,* Cic. **II.** Transf., **a,** of inanimate objects, *injured;* malus saucius Africo, Hor.; glacies saucia sole, Ov.; **b,** *attacked by illness,* Prop.; **c,** *drunken,* Mart.; **d,** of accused persons, *half condemned;* de repetundis saucius, ap. Cic.; **e,** *wounded, injured in mind;* (*a*) *troubled, distressed;* animus eius, Cic.; (*β*) esp., *wounded by love;* regina saucia curā, Verg.

saurĭon -i, n. (σαυρίον), *mustard,* Plin.

Sauroctŏnos -i, m. (σαυροκτόνος), *the lizard-killer* (the name of a statue of Apollo by Praxiteles), Plin.

Saurŏmātēs -ae, m. (Σαυρομάτης), *a Sarmatian;* plur., **Saurŏmātae** -ārum, *the Sarmatians,* Ov.

sāvĭŏlum -i, n. (dim. of savium), *a little kiss,* Cat.

sāvĭor, 1. dep. (savium), *to kiss;* aliquem, Cic.

sāvĭum -ĭi, n. **I.** *the mouth formed for kissing,* Plaut. **II.** Meton., *a kiss;* Atticae meis verbis savium des volo, Cic.

saxātĭlis -e (saxum), *frequenting rocks, to be found among rocks,* Plin.

saxētum -i, n. (saxum), *a rocky place,* Cic.

saxĕus -a -um (saxum), *made of rock or stone, rocky, stony;* scopulum, Ov.; umbra, *cast by a rock,* Verg.; Niobe saxea facta, *turned to stone,* Ov.

saxĭfĭcus -a -um (saxum and facio), *turning into stone, petrifying;* Medusa, Ov.

saxĭfrăgus -a -um (saxum and frango), *stone-breaking, stone-crushing,* Plin.

saxōsus -a -um (saxum). **I.** *full of rocks, rocky;* valles, Verg. Subst., **saxōsa** -ōrum, n. *rocky places,* Plin. **II.** Transf., *stony, flowing between rocks;* saxosus sonans Hypanis, Verg.

saxŭlum -i, n. (dim. of saxum), *a little rock,* Cic.

saxum -i, n. *a rock or large stone, a detached fragment of rock* (rupes, *a cliff, precipitous rock*). **I.** Lit., **A.** *a rock;* **1,** gen., saxo undique absciso rupes, Liv.; saxa latentia, *reefs,* Verg.; **2,** esp., **a,** Saxum sacrum, *the holy rock, the place on the Aventine where Remus took the auspices,* Cic.; **b,** *the Tarpeian rock,* Cic.; **c,** Saxa rubra, v. ruber. **B.** *a stone;* **a,** *a (large) stone;* saxa jacere, Cic.; **b,** *a stone for building;* saxum quadratum, Liv.; or for statues, non e saxo sculptus, Cic. **II.** Meton., **a,** *a stone wall;* saxo lucum circumdedit alto, Ov.; **b,** *a stone building;* perrumpere amat saxa, Hor.

scăbellum -i, n. (dim. of scamnum). **I.** *a small stool, footstool,* Varr. **II.** *a musical instrument played with the foot, used to accompany dancing,* Cic.

scăber -bra -brum (scabo), *rough, scurvy.* **I.** Gen., unguis, Ov.; robigo, Verg.; of persons, *rough, untidy,* Hor. **II.** Esp., *scabby, mangy;* oves, Plaut.

scăbĭes -ēi, f. (scabo), *roughness.* **I.** ferri, Verg. **II.** *the scab, mange, the itch.* **A.** Lit., Verg. **B.** Fig., *an itch, itching desire for anything,* Cic.; lucri, Hor.

scăbĭōsus -a -um (scabies). **I.** *rough,* Plin. **II.** *scabby, mangy,* Pers.

scăbo, scābi, 3. (root SCAB, Gk. ΣΚΑΠ-τω), *to scratch, rub;* caput, Hor.

scăbrĭtĭa -ae, f. and **scăbrĭtĭes** -ēi, f. (scaber), *roughness,* Plin.

Scaea porta -ae, f. and **Scaeae portae** (Σκαιαὶ πύλαι), *the west gate of Troy.*

scaena (scēna) -ae f. (σκηνή), *the boards of the theatre, the stage, the scene, the theatre.* **I.** **A.** Lit., de scaena decedere, *to go off the stage,* Cic.; sphaeram in scenam afferre, Cic.; Agamemnonius scaenis agitatus Orestes, *on the stage,* i.e., *in the tragedies,* Verg. **B.** Transf., of nature, *a background;* tum silvis scaena coruscis, Verg. **II.** Fig., **A.** *the stage, the boards of any public action;* **a,** of the forum, etc., *publicity, the world;* in scaena, id est, in contione, Cic.; minus in scena esse, *to be less before the eyes of the world,* Cic.; scaenae servire, Cic.; **b,** of schools of rhetoric, Tac.; **c,** gen., *scene, sphere;* scaena manet dotes grandis tuas, Ov. **B.** *anything presented for outward display;* **a,** *parade, outward show;* (verba) ad scaenam pompamque sumuntur, Cic.; **b,** *deception, fraud,* scena rei totius haec, ap. Cic.

scaenālis -e (scena), *belonging to the theatre, theatrical,* Lucr. (?)

scaenĭcus -a -um (σκηνικός), *belonging to the boards, scenic, theatrical.* **A.** Adj., ludi, Liv.; voluptas, Cic. **B.** Subst., **scaenĭcus** -i, m. *a stage-hero, an actor,* Cic.

Scaevŏla -ae, m. (dim. of scaevus, *the left-handed*), *a surname of the gens Mucia,* v. Mucius.

scaeva -ae, f. (scaevus), *an omen, portent,* Plaut.

scaevus -a -um (σκαιός). **I.** *left, on the left hand,* Varr. **II.** *awkward,* Cic.

scālae -ārum, f. (from scando, as ala from ago), *a flight of stairs, staircase, ladder;* se in scalas tabernae librariae conjicere, Cic.; scalas admovere (muris or moenibus), *scaling-ladders,* Caes., Liv.; muros scalis aggredi, Sall.

Scaldis -is, m. *a river in Gallia Belgica,* now *the Scheldt.*

scalmus -i, m. (σκαλμός), *a thole or tholepin, on which an oar works, a row-lock;* navicula duorum scalmorum, *two-oared,* Cic.; scalmum nullum videt, *no trace of boats,* Cic.

scalpellum -i, n. (dim. of scalprum), and **scalpellus** -i, m. *a small surgical knife, lancet, scalpel,* Cic.

scalpo, scalpsi, scalptum, 3. (root SCALP, Gk. ΓΛΑΦ-ω), *to scrape, scratch, tear.* **I.** Gen., **a,** lit., terram unguibus, Hor.; **b,** fig., *to tickle,* Pers. **II.** Esp. t.t. of art, *to scratch with a sharp tool, to engrave on wood, gems, etc.;* apta manus est ad fingendum, ad scalpendum, Cic.

scalprum -i, n. (scalpo), *a sharp, cutting instrument;* **a,** *a cobbler's awl,* Hor.; **b,** *a chisel,* Liv.; **c,** *a pen-knife,* Tac.

scalptor -ōris, m. (scalpo), *a cutter, engraver,* Plin.

scalptūra -ae, f. (scalpo). **I.** *a cutting, engraving;* gemmarum, Plin. **II.** Meton., *a figure engraved, an engraving,* Suet.

Scămander -dri, m. (Σκάμανδρος), *a river in Troas, rising on Mount Ida and joining the Simois, called Xanthus, on account of its red colour.*

scambus -a -um (σκαμβός), *crooked-legged,* Suet.

scammōnĭa (scāmōnĭa) and **scammōnĕa** -ae, f. (σκαμμωνία. σκαμωνία), *scammony,* Cic.

scammōnītes -ae, m. *scammony-wine,* Plin.

scamnum -i, n. (root SCAP (cf. scabellum and scapus), Gr. ΣΚΗΠ, whence σκήπτω, σκῆπτρον, Doric, σκᾶπτρον), *a prop, bench, stool, step, footstool;* scamnum facere, Hor.; cava sub tenerum scamna dare pedem, Ov.; ante focos scamnis considere longis, Ov.

scandix -ĭcis, f. (σκάνδιξ), *chervil,* Plin.

scando, scandi, scansum, 3. **I.** Intransit., *to climb;* a, lit., in aggerem, Liv.; in domos superas, Ov.; b, transf., *to raise oneself, to rise;* supra principem, Tac. **II.** Transit., *to ascend, to climb up;* malos, Cic.; muros, Liv.; Capitolium, Hor.; fig., scandit aeratas vitiosa naves cura, Hor.

scansĭlis -e (scando), *that can be climbed;* ficus, Plin.

scansĭo -ōnis, 1. (scando), *a climbing up, ascending,* Varr.

Scantĭus -a -um, *name of a Roman gens,* Cic.; adj., Scantia silva, *a wood in Campania,* Cic.

scăpha -ae, f. (σκάφη), *a small boat, skiff,* Cic.

scăphĭum -ĭi, n. (σκαφίον), *a bowl in the shape of a boat;* esp., *a drinking-vessel,* Cic.

Scaptensŭla -ae, f. (Σκαπτὴ ὕλη), *a small town in Thrace near Abdera, famous for its gold and silver mines, and as the place of exile of Thucydides.*

Scaptĭa -ae, f. *a town in Latium;* hence, adj., **Scaptĭus** -a -um, *Scaptian;* tribus, Liv.

Scăpŭla -ae, m. *a surname of the Cornelian gens;* adj., **Scăpŭlānus** -a -um, *belonging to Scapula;* horti, Cic.

scăpŭlae -ārum, f. *the shoulder-blades, the shoulders, the back,* Plaut.

scăpus -i, m. (v. scamnum), *anything that supports,* e.g., **I.** *the stalk of plants,* Plin. **II.** *a weaver's beam,* Lucr. **III.** *the shaft or stem of a candelabrum,* Plin.

scărăbaeus -i, m. (*σκαράβαιος, from σκάραβος = κάραβος), *a beetle,* Plin.

scărĭfātĭo (scărĭfĭcātĭo) -ōnis, f. (scarifo), *a scratching up, scarifying,* Plin.

scărĭfo (scărĭfĭco), 1. (σκαριφάομαι), *to scratch up with any sharp-pointed instrument, scarify,* Plin.

scărus -i, m. (σκάρος), *a salt-water fish, much liked by the Romans, the parrot-fish,* Hor.

scătĕbra -ae, f. (scateo), *a spouting up, bubbling up of water,* Verg.

scătĕo, 2. and (archaic) **scăto,** 3. *to gush forth, spout out, bubble out.* **I.** Lit., Lucr. **II.** Meton., *to swarm, abound;* with abl., arx scatens fontibus, Liv.; with genit., terra ferarum scatet, Lucr.

scătūrĭgo (scătŭrrĭgo) -gĭnis, f. (scaturio), *a spring of bubbling water;* plur., scaturigines turbidae, Liv.

scătūrĭo (scătŭrrĭo), 4. (scateo), *to gush forth;* meton., Curio totus hoc scaturit, *is full of* (love for this party), ap. Cic.

scăturrex = scaturigo (q.v.).

scaurus -a -um (connected with σκάζειν). **I.** *having projecting or swollen ankles,* Hor. **II.** Scaurus, *a Roman surname of the gens Aemilia and Aurelia, the most famous bearer of the name being* M. Aemilius Scaurus, *whom Cicero defended.*

scazon -ontis, m. (σκάζων, *limping,* **an** iambic trimeter with a spondee or trochee in the last foot, Plin.

scĕlĕrātē, adv. (sceleratus), *impiously, wickedly;* facere, Cic.; dicere in aliquem, Cic.; domus sceleratius aedificata quam eversa, Cic.; sceleratissime machinari omnes insidias, Cic.

scĕlĕrātus -a -um, p. adj. (from scelero). **I.** *polluted, profaned by guilt;* terra, Verg.; limina Thracum, Ov.; esp., sceleratus vicus, *the accursed street, the highest point of the vicus Cyprius on the Esquiline, where Tullia, the daughter of Servius Tullius, drove over the corpse of her father;* sceleratus campus, *the accursed field, on the porta Collina, where unchaste Vestal virgins were buried alive,* Liv.; scelerata sedes, *the lower world,* Ov. **II.** Transf., **A.** *impious, wicked, profane, infamous, accursed;* hasta sceleratior, Cic.; homo sceleratissimus, Cic.; subst., **scĕlĕrāti** -ōrum, m. *villains, miscreants,* Cic.; poet., sceleratas sumere poenas, *for impiety, wickedness,* Verg. **B.** *wretched, unlucky, calamitous, noxious;* frigus, Verg.

scĕlĕro, 1. (scelus), *to pollute, profane with guilt;* manus, Verg.

scĕlĕrōsus -a -um (scelus), *full of guilt, wicked, impious, accursed;* facta, Lucr.

scĕlestē, adv. (scelestus), *wickedly, impiously;* facere, Liv.; suspicari, Cic.

scĕlestus -a -um (scelus). **I.** *wicked, accursed, infamous;* a, facinus, Cic.; sermo scelestior, Liv.; scelestissimum te arbitror, Plaut.; b, *knavish, roguish,* Plaut. **II.** Transf., *unlucky, wretched, pernicious,* Plaut.

scĕlus -ĕris, n. *wickedness.* **I.** Lit., *subject., impiety, wickedness,* Cic. **II.** Meton., *object.,* **A.** *a crime, evil deed, impious action, heinous offence;* 1, lit., scelus facere, admittere, committere, edere, concipere, in sese concipere or suscipere, Cic.; minister sceleris, Liv.; scelus est (civem Romanum) verberare, Cic.; 2, transf., *misfortune, calamity,* Plaut. **B.** *a villain, scoundrel, rascal;* ne bestiis, quae tantum scelus attigissent, immanioribus uteremur, Cic.; scelus viri, *a rogue of a man,* Plaut.; so scelus artificis, Verg.

scēna = scaena (q.v.).

scēnālis = scaenalis (q.v.).

scēnĭcus = scaenicus (q.v.).

Scepsis -is, f. (Σκῆψις), *a town in Mysia,* now Eskiupschi or Eski-Schupsche. Hence, **Scepsius** -a -um, *of Scepsis;* Metrodorus, Cic.

sceptrĭfĕr -fĕra -fĕrum (sceptrum and fero), *sceptre-bearing,* Ov.

sceptrĭgĕr = sceptrifer (q.v.).

sceptrum -i, n. (σκῆπτρον), *a sceptre, royal wand or staff.* **I.** Lit., Cic.; so jestingly, paedagogorum, Mart. **II.** Transf., *dominion, kingdom, royal authority;* sceptra petit Evandri, Verg.

sceptūchus -i, m. (σκηπτοῦχος), *the wand-bearer, a high official in Eastern courts,* Tac.

schĕda (schĭda) and **scĭda** -ae, f. (σχίδη). **I.** *a strip of papyrus bark,* Plin. **II.** Transf., *a leaf of paper;* ut scida ne qua depereat, Cic.

schēma -ae, f. and **schēma** -ătis, n. (σχῆμα), *shape, figure, form, fashion,* Quint.

schĭda = scheda (q.v.).

schistos -a -on (σχιστός), *cleft, cloven, split,* Plin.

Schoeneus -ĕi and -ĕos, m. (Σχοινεύς), *a king of Boeotia, father of Atalanta;* hence, **A.** Adj., **Schoenēĭus** -a -um, *belonging to Schoeneus;*

Schoeneia virgo or simply Schoeneia, *Atalanta*, Ov. **B. Schoeneïs** -ĭdis, f. *Atalanta*, Ov.

schoenŏbătes -ae, m. (σχοινοβάτης), *a rope-walker, rope-dancer*, Juv.

schoenus -i, m. (σχοῖνος). **I.** *an aromatic reed used by the Romans to flavour wine, and as an ingredient in an unguent*, Cato. **II.** Meton., **A.** *an ointment*, Plaut. **B.** *a Persian measure of distance* (between 30 and 60 stadia), Plin.

schŏla (scŏla) -ae, f. (σχολή), *leisure, rest from work;* hence, **I.** *learned leisure, learned conversation, debate, dispute, lecture, dissertation;* certae scholae sunt de exsilio, de interitu patriae, etc., Cic.; scholas Graecorum more habere, Cic.; vertes te ad alteram scholam, *matter*, Cic. **II.** Meton., 1, a, *a place where learned disputations are carried on, a school*, Cic.; b, transf., (a) *a gallery of works of art, used for such disputations and conferences*, Plin.; (β) *a waiting-room, room in a bath*, Vitr.; 2, *the disciples of a philosopher, a school, sect;* clamabant omnes philosophorum scholae, Cic.

schŏlastĭcus -a -um (σχολαστικός), *of or relating to a school;* esp., *to a school of rhetoric or to rhetoric, rhetorical.* **I.** Adj., controversia, Quint. **II.** Subst., **A. schŏlastĭca** -ōrum, n. *rhetorical exercises*, Quint. **B. schŏlastĭcus** -i, m. 1, *a student of rhetoric*, Quint.; 2, *a teacher of rhetoric, a professor*, Suet.

sciădeus -ĕi, m. and **sciaena** -ae, f. (σκιαδεύς, σκίαινα), *the male and female of a saltwater fish*, perhaps Salmo Thymallus, Linn., Plin.

Sciăthus (-ŏs) -i, f. (Σκίαθος), *an island in the Aegean Sea, north of Euboea.*

scida = schida (q.v.).

sciens -entis (scio). **I.** Partic., *knowing something*, Ter. **II.** Adj., with compar. and superl., **A.** = *purposely, knowingly;* ut offenderet sciens neminem, Cic. **B.** *acquainted with a matter, knowing, understanding, versed in, acquainted with;* with genit., belli, Sall.; citharae, Hor.; scientissimo reipublicae gerendae, Cic.; with infin., flectere equum sciens, Hor.; absol., quis hoc homine scientior, Cic.; scientissimus gubernator, Cic.

scientĕr, adv. (sciens), *skilfully, expertly;* dicere, Cic.

scientĭa -ae, f. (sciens), *a knowing, knowledge of, acquaintance with.* **I.** Gen., regionum, Cic.; futurorum malorum, Cic.; memoriā et scientiā comprehendisse, Cic. **II.** Esp., *theoretical, philosophical knowledge, theory, science;* an, quum eā non utare, scientiā tamen ipsā teneri potest, Cic.; scientia dialecticorum, juris, Cic.; rei militaris, Cic.; plur., tot artes, tantae scientiae, Cic.

scīlĭcĕt, adv. (contr. from scire licet). **I.** *actually, just think!* (to call attention to something strange); rogat et prece cogit, scilicet ut tibi se laudare et tradere cogar, etc., Hor.; ter sunt conati Olympum scilicet atque Ossae frondosum involvere Olympum, Verg. **II.** *of course, naturally, evidently.* **A.** Gen., a, with acc. and infin., Lucr.; b, as a simple particle, cur igitur eos manumisit? metuebat scilicet, Cic. **B.** Esp., a, *naturally, of course, undoubtedly;* with an adversative sent. (gen. with tamen, sed tamen, or sed), nihil scilicet novi, ea tamen, quae te ipsum probaturum confidam, Cic.; b, *ironically, of course, to be sure, forsooth;* id populus curat scilicet, *much the people trouble themselves about that!* Ter.; ego istius pecudis consilio scilicet aut praesidio uti volebam, Cic.; c, *doubtless alas!* unda scilicet omnibus enaviganda, Hor. **III.** *to wit, namely*, Suet.

scilla (squilla) -ae, f. (σκίλλα), 1, *a sea leek, squill*, Plin.; 2, *a small sea-crab*, Cic.

scillīnus -a -um (scillus), *made of squills*, Plin

scillītes -ae, m. (σκιλλίτης), *flavoured with* or *made of squills*, Plin.

scillītĭcus = scillinus (q.v.).

scin' = scisne (q.v.).

scincos -i, m. (σκίγκος), *an Egyptian species of lizard*, Plin.

scindo, scĭdi, scissum, 3. (connected with σχίζω), *to tear, rend, tear asunder, break, split.* **I.** Lit., crines, Verg.; mater scissa comam, *with torn hair*, Verg.; epistolam, Cic.; vestem de corpore, Prop.; lignum cuneis, *split, cleave*, Verg.; prov., paenulam alicui, *to tear* (off a person's travelling cloak), i.e., *to urge a person to stay*, Cic. **II.** Transf., 1, *to part, divide, separate;* genus amborum scindit se sanguine ab uno, Verg.; pass., scindi, as middle, *to separate, part;* in contraria studia scinditur vulgus, Verg.; 2, esp., a, *to break off, interrupt;* verba fletu, Ov.; b, *to destroy*, Plaut.; c, (= rescindo) *to renew;* ne scindam ipse dolorem meum (from the metaphor of tearing open a wound), Cic.

scintilla -ae, f. *a spark.* **I.** Lit., Liv.; silici scintillam excudere, Verg. **II.** Fig., *a spark, glimmer, faint trace;* belli, Cic.; ingenii, Cic.

scintillātĭo -ōnis, f. (scintillo), *a sparkling*, Plin.

scintillo, 1. (scintilla), *to sparkle, glitter;* scintillat oleum testā ardente, Verg.

scintillŭla -ae, f. (dim. of scintilla), *a little spark;* fig., virtutum quasi scintillulae, Cic.

scĭo -īvi and -ĭi -ītum, 4. *to know, to have knowledge of, to experience.* **I.** Gen. (opp. opinari, arbitrari), (α) with acc., istarum rerum nihil, Cic.; quod sciam, *as far as I know*, Cic.; (β) with infin., scio tibi ita placere, Cic.; scimus Atilium appellatum esse sapientem, Cic.; (γ) with dep. rel. or interrog. sent., cum sciatis, quo quaeque res inclinet, Cic.; (δ) absol., statim fac ut sciam, Cic.; with de and the abl., cum is, qui de omnibus scierit, de Sulla se scire negavit, Cic. **II.** Esp., a, *to know, have learned, be acquainted with;* (α) with acc., literas, Cic.; (β) with infin., qui tractare et uti sciat, Cic.; (γ) absol., scire Graece, Latine, *to understand Greek, Latin;* b, *to perceive, to mark*, Plaut. (syncop. perf., scisti, Ov.; infin., scisse, Cic.).

sciŏthērĭcŏn -i, n. (σκιοθηρικόν), *a sun-dial*, Plin.

Scīpĭădas and **Scīpĭădes**, v. 2. Scipio.

1. **scĭpĭo** -ōnis, m. (σκίπων, σκήπων), *a staff, wand*, Plaut.; eburneus, carried by *viri triumphales*, Liv.

2. **Scīpĭo** -ōnis, m. (Σκιπίων, Σκηπίων), *a family name of the gens* Cornelia, v. Cornelius. Hence, **Scīpĭădas (-ēs)** -ae, m. (Σκιπιάδης), *one of the family of the Scipios, a Scipio.*

Scīron -ōnis, m. (Σκίρων, Σκείρων). **I.** *a noted robber on the coast between Megaris and Attica, killed by Theseus.* **II.** (Sciron, Scyron, Siron, Syron), *an Epicurean philosopher, contemporary with Cicero and Vergil.*

scirpĕus (sirpĕus) -a -um (scirpus), *made of rushes.* **I.** Adj., imago or simulacrum (v. Argei), Ov. **II.** Subst., scirpea or sirpea (sirpia) -ae, f. *basket-work made of rushes* (to form the body of a waggon), Ov.

scirpĭcŭlus (sirpĭcŭlus) -a -um (scirpus), *made of rushes.* Subst., **scirpĭcŭlus** -i, m. *a rush-basket*, Prop.

scirpus (sirpus) -i, m. *a rush, bulrush*, Plin.; prov., nodum in scirpo quaerere, *to find a difficulty where there is none*, Plin.

scirros -i, m. (σκίρρος), *a hard swelling,* Plin.

sciscitātor -ōris, m. (sciscitor), *an inquirer, examiner,* Mart.

sciscitor, 1. dep. *to investigate, inquire into, examine into, ask, interrogate ;* (a) with acc. of thing, consulis voluntatem, Liv. ; (β) with acc. and ex and the abl., ex eo eius sententiam, Cic.; (γ) with de and the abl., sciscitari de victoria, Cic. ; (δ) with acc. of person, *to consult ;* deos, Liv. ; (ε) with dep. interrog. sent., sciscitari, uter Porsena esset, Liv. ; (ζ) absol., elicuit comiter sciscitando ut, etc., Liv.

scisco, scīvi, scītum, 3. (scio). **I.** *to seek to find out, investigate, inquire,* Plaut. **II.** Polit. **t. t.,** *to approve of by voting, to vote, assent to ;* **a,** of the people, *to ordain, resolve :* quae scisceret plebes, Cic.; with ut and the subj., Athenienses sciverunt ut, etc., Cic. ; of an individual, *to vote for ;* legem, Cic.

scissūra -ae, f. (scindo), *a splitting, cleaving, rending, separating, parting,* Plin.

scissus -a -um, p. adj. (from scindo), *torn, rent ;* transf., genus vocum, *harsh, grating,* Cic.

scītāmenta -ōrum, n. (1. scitus), *dainties, titbits,* Plaut.

scītē, adv. (1. scitus), *cleverly, skilfully, tastefully, nicely, elegantly ;* scite loqui, Liv. ; capella scite facta, Cic.

scītor, 1. (scio), *to wish to know, inquire, ask ;* aliquid, Verg. ; aliquem de aliqua re, Ov. ; oracula, *to consult,* Verg. ; with dep. interrog., quid veniat, scitatur, Ov.

scītŭlus -a -um (dim. of scitus), *neat, pretty, elegant ;* facies, Plaut.

scītum -i, n. (scisco). **I.** *a decree, statute, ordinance ;* plebis scitum, populi scitum, Cic. ; plebei and plebi scitum, Liv. ; scita pontificis, Liv. ; Ctesiphon scitum fecit ut, etc., Cic. **II.** *a philosophical tenet* or *maxim* (δόγμα), Sen.

1. **scītus** -a -um, p. adj. (from scisco). **I.** *clever, wise, shrewd, skilful, adroit ;* sermo, Cic. ; with genit., scitus vadorum, *acquainted with,* Ov. ; lyrae, Ov. ; hence, scitum est, *it is a clever saying,* Cic. ; vetus illud Catonis admodum scitum est, Cic. **II.** Transf., *pretty, fine,* Plaut.

2. **scītus** -ū, m. (scisco), *a statute, decree ;* plebi scitu, Cic.

sciūrus -i, m. (σκίουρος), *a squirrel,* Plin.

scius -a -um (scio), *knowing,* Petr.

scŏbīna -ae, f. (scobis), *a rasp, file,* Plin.

scŏbis -is, f. (scabo), *that which is scratched or scraped off, filings, cuttings, chips, shavings, sawdust,* Hor.

Scodra -ae, f. *a town in Macedonian Illyria,* now *Scodar* or *Scutari.* Hence, **Scodrenses** -ium, m. *the inhabitants of Scodra.*

Scodrus -i, m. mons, *the easterly continuation of the Dalmatian and Illyrian mountains,* now *Argentaro.*

scŏla, etc.= schola, etc. (q.v.).

scŏlŏpendra -ae, f. (σκολόπενδρα), *a kind of multipede, scolopendra,* Plin.

scŏlўmus -i, m. (σκόλυμος), *a species of artichoke,* Plin.

scomber -bri, m. (σκόμβρος), *a sea-fish, a mackerel,* Plin.

scōpa -ae, f. **I.** *a thin twig, a sprig,* gen. in plur., Plin. **II.** Meton., plur., **scopae** -ārum, f. *a besom* or *broom, made of a number of twigs* or *branches ;* scopae viles, Hor. ; hence, prov., scopas dissolvere, *to untie a broom,* i.e., *throw anything into confusion,* Cic.; scopae solutae = *a muddled, foolish man,* Cic.

Scŏpās -ae, m. (Σκόπας), *a famous sculptor of Paros.*

scōpes -um, f. (σκῶπες), *a kind of owl,* Plin.

scōpĭo -ōnis, f. *the stalk of a bunch of grapes,* Plin.

scŏpŭlōsus -a -um (scopulus), *rocky, full of cliffs, craggy.* **I.** Lit., mare, Cic. **II.** Fig., intelligo quam scopuloso difficilique in loco verser, Cic.

scŏpŭlus -i, m. (σκόπελος). **I.** *a rock, crag, cliff ;* esp., *a rock in the sea ;* ad scopulos allidi, Caes.; affligi, Cic.; poet., of a promontory, infames scopuli, Acroceraunia, Hor. ; in comparisons, o scopulis undāque ferocior, Ov. **II.** Fig., **A.** Gen., ad scopulum ire, *to be ruined,* Lucr. **B.** Esp., *a rock, cliff* (as symbolical of danger, difficulty, peril) ; in hos scopulos incidere vitae, Cic. ; of persons, vos geminae voragines scopulique reipublicae (of Piso and Gabinius), Cic.

scōpus -i, m. (σκοπός), *a mark set up to shoot at,* Suet.

scordĭon -ĭi, n. (σκόρδιον), *a plant having an odour of garlic* (Teucrion scordium, Linn.), Plin.

Scordus -i, m. (τὸ Σκάρδον ὄρος), *a mountain in Illyria barbara* or *Romana, on the borders of Moesia and Macedonia.*

scōrĭa -ae, f. (σκωρία), *dross* or *slag* (of metals), Plin.

scorpaena -ae, f. (σκόρπαινα), *a sea-scorpion,* Plin.

scorpĭo -ōnis, m. and **scorpĭus** (-ŏs) -i, m. (σκορπίων). **I.** *a scorpion,* Ov. **II.** Transf., **a,** *the Scorpion, as one of the signs of the Zodiac,* **b,** *a military engine for throwing missiles,* Caes. ; **c,** *a prickly salt-water fish* (Cottus scorpio, Linn.), Plaut. ; **d,** *a prickly plant* (Spartium scorpius, Linn.), Plin.

scorpĭōnĭus -a -um (scorpio), *of* or *relating to a scorpion,* Plin.

scorpĭūron -i, n. (σκορπίουρον), *a plant, scorpion's tail, heliotrope,* Plin.

scortātor -ōris, m. (scortor), *a fornicator,* Hor.

scortĕus -a -um (scortum), *of* or *relating to hides, leathern, made of leather,* Mart. ; subst., **scortĕa** -ae, f. *a leathern garment,* Mart.

scortillum -i, m. (dim. of scortum), *a little harlot,* Cat.

scortor, 1. dep. (scortum), *to whore,* Plaut.

scortum -i, n. **I.** *a skin, hide,* Varr. **II.** *a prostitute,* Cic.

scrĕātor -ōris, m. (screo), *one who hawks* or *hems,* Plaut.

scrĕātus -ūs, m. (screo), *a hawking, hemming,* Terr.

scrĕo, 1. *to hawk, hem,* Plaut.

scrība -ae, m. (scribo), *a clerk* or *secretary ;* **a,** in a public capacity, *a clerk in the service of the senate* or *the higher magistrates ;* scriba aedilicius, Cic. ; **b,** of private persons, *private secretary ;* scriba meus, Cic.

scriblīta -ae, f. *a kind of tart,* Plaut.

scrībo, scripsi, scriptum, 3. (root SCRIB, SCRIP, connected with ΓΡΑΦ-ω, as sculpo with γλύφω), *to engrave with a sharp-pointed pencil, draw lines.* **I.** 1, gen., lineam, Cic. ; **2,** *to draw, sketch, make an outline of ;* scribetur tibi forma et situs agri, Hor. **II.** *to write* **A.** Gen., literam, Cic. ; meā manu scriptae literae, Cic. **B.** Esp., **1,** *to write a letter to ;* alicui, Cic. ; ad aliquem, Cic. ; ad aliquem de aliquo (*to command a person in writing to some one else*) accuratissime, Cic. ; pass., with acc. and infin., scribitur nobis multinudinem

convenisse, Cic.; **2**, *to beg, entreat, command by letter;* with ut or ne and the subj., velim domum ad te scribas ut mihi tui libri pateant, Cic.; Scipioni scribendum, ne bellum remitteret, Liv.; with subj. alone, scribit Labieno, veniat, Caes.; **3**, *to write, put down in writing, compose, prepare;* libros, Cic.; leges, Cic.; senatus consultum, Cic.; absol., (*a*) like the English, *to write,* i.e., *to compose a literary work;* se ad scribendi studium contulit, Cic.; (β) *to treat of in writing;* hac super re scribam ad te, Cic.; (γ) *to compose a legal instrument, to draw up, write drafts;* haec urbana militia respondendi, scribendi, cavendi, Cic.; **4**, with double acc., *to appoint in writing;* aliquem heredem, Cic.; **5**, commercial t. t., *to give an order for the payment of money;* scribe decem a Nerio, *let the debtor pay* 10,000 *sesterces through* (the money-changer) *Nerius,* Hor.; **6**, *to write about, describe, celebrate in writing;* Marium, Cic.; scriberis Vario fortis, Hor.; **7**, polit. t. t., *to enrol soldiers, colonists,* etc., supplementum legionibus, Cic.; quinque milia colonorum Capuam, Liv.; transf., scribe tui gregis hunc, *enrol him as one of your friends,* Hor.

scrīnium -ĭi, n. *a cylindrical case, casket, or box for books, papers, unguents,* etc., Sall., Hor.

Scrībōnĭus -a -um, *name of a Roman gens.*

scriptĭo -ōnis, f. (scribo). **I.** *writing, the art of writing,* Cic. **II.** Esp., *writing, written composition;* nulla res tantum ad dicendum proficit, quantum scriptio, Cic.

scriptĭto, 1. (intens. of scribo). **I.** *to write frequently;* et haec et si quid aliud ad me scribas velim vel potius scriptites, Cic. **II.** *to write, compose;* orationes multas, Cic.

scriptor -ōris, m. (scribo). **I.** *a writer, clerk, secretary,* Cic. **II.** *a writer, author, composer, narrator;* **1**, a, with genit., rerum suarum domestici scriptores et nuntii, Cic.; scriptor rerum, *a historian,* Liv.; b, absol., *an author, writer;* of orators, subtilis scriptor (Lysias), Cic.; of historians, Sall.; of poets, Hor.; **2**, polit. t. t., *a composer, one who draws up;* legis, Cic.

scriptŭla -ōrum, n. (dim. of scriptum), *the lines on a draught-board,* Ov.

scriptum -i, n. (scribo). **I.** *a line drawn on a draught-board;* ludere duodecim scriptis, *to play at draughts,* Cic. **II.** *anything written, a writing;* **1**, gen., Latina scripta, Cic.; mandare scriptis, Cic.; **2**, esp., a, *a written decree, a law,* Cic.; b, *the text or letter of a work;* quum videtur scriptoris voluntas cum scripto ipso dissentire, Cic.

scriptūra -ae, f. (scribo), *a writing.* **I.** Gen., Plin. **II.** Esp., *a composing in writing, written composition.* **A.** Lit., scriptura assidua ac diligens, Cic.; scripturā aliquid persequi, Cic. **B.** Meton., **1**, *the writing* or *work itself,* Tac.; **2**, *testamentary disposition;* deinde ex superiore et ex inferiore scriptura docendum id, quod quaeratur, Cic.; **3**, *a tax* or *rent paid for the public pastures;* vectigal ex scriptura, Cic.; magistri scripturae, Cic.

scrīpŭlum (scrūpŭlum) -i, n. (another form of scrupulus), *a scruple, the smallest part of a weight* or *mass.* **I.** Lit., ¹⁄₂₄ *part of an uncia;* argenti scripulum, Cic. **II.** Transf., *the smallest portion of a degree* (in astronomy), *a minute,* Plin.

scrōbĭcŭlus -i, m. (dim. of scrobis), *a little ditch,* Plin.

scrōbis -is, c. *a ditch,* Verg.; *a grave,* Tac.

scrōfa -ae, f. (γρομφάς), *a breeding sow,* Varr.

scrōfĭpascus -i, m. (scrofa and pasco), *a keeper of pigs,* Plaut.

scrupěda and **scrūpĭpěda** -ae, f. *hobbling, limping,* Plaut.

scrūpěus -a -um (scrupus), *consisting of sharp stones, rugged, rough;* spelunca, Verg.

scrūpōsus -a -um (scrupus), *rough, rugged,* Lucr.

scrūpŭlōsē, adv. (scrupulosus), *accurately, exactly, scrupulously,* Quint.

scrūpŭlōsus -a -um (scrupulus). **I.** Lit., *full of sharp stones, rough, rugged;* cotes, Cic. **II.** Fig., *exact, accurate, scrupulous, precise,* Plin.

scrūpŭlum = scripulum (q.v.).

scrūpŭlus -i, m. (dim. of scrupus), lit., *a small stone;* fig., *uneasiness, care, disquiet, anxiety, doubt, scruple;* scrupulum alicui injicere, Cic.; scrupulus tenuissimus residet, Cic.; scrupulum ex animo evellere, Cic.

scrūpus -i, m. **I.** *a sharp stone,* Petr. **II.** Fig., *anxiety, disquiet, care,* Cic.

scrūta -ōrum, n. (γρύτη), *frippery, trash, trumpery,* Hor.

scrūtātĭo -ōnis, m. (scrutor), *a searching, investigating,* Quint.

scrūtātor -ōris, m. (scrutor), *one who searches, investigates, examines,* Suet.

scrūtor, 1. dep. (scruta). **I.** *to search into, search through, investigate accurately, examine, inspect.* **A.** Lit., domos, naves, Cic.; Alpes, Cic.; abdita loca, Sall. **B.** Fig., *to examine thoroughly, to seek for;* locos ex quibus argumenta eruamus, Cic. **II.** *to search into, find out;* arcanum, Hor.; mentes deûm, Ov.

sculpo, sculpsi, sculptum, 3. (root SCULP, Gr. ΓΛΥΦ, γλύφω), *to carve, hew, grave, cut, chisel;* ebur, *a statue of ivory,* Ov.

sculpōnĕae -ārum, f. *wooden shoes,* Plaut.

sculptĭlis -e (sculpo), *carved, hewn, cut;* opus dentis Numidae, *work in ivory,* Ov.

sculptūra -ae, f. (sculpo), *raised work in wood, ivory, marble, gems, sculpture,* Quint.

scurra -ae, m. **I.** *a dandy, beau, man about town, a fine gentleman;* scurrae locupletes, Cic. **II.** *a jester, buffoon, a parasite who earned his dinner at the tables of the great by witty conversation;* Zeno Socratem scurram Atticum fuisse dicebat, Cic.; scurra vagus, non qui certum praesepe teneret, Hor.

scurrīlis -e (scurra), *like a buffoon, mocking, jeering;* jocus, Cic.; dicacitas, Cic.

scurrīlĭtas -ātis, f. (scurrilis), *buffoonery,* Tac.

scurrīlĭtěr, adv. (scurrilis), *like a buffoon,* Plin.

scurror, 1. dep. (scurra), *to play the buffoon;* scurrantis speciem praebere, Hor.

scŭtāle -is, n. (scutum), *the thong of a sling,* Liv.

scŭtārĭus -ĭi, m. (scutum), *a shield-maker,* Plaut.

scŭtātus -a -um (scutum), *armed with a shield;* cohortes, Caes.

scŭtella -ae, f. (dim. of scutra), *a little flat dish* or *salver;* dulciculae potionis, Cic.

scŭtĭca (scўtĭca) -ae, f. (σκυτική, from σκῦτος, *leather*), *a whip, lash,* Hor.

scŭtĭgěrŭlus -i, m. (scutum and gero), *a shield-bearer, armour-bearer,* Plaut.

scŭtra -ae, f. *a tray, dish, salver,* Plaut.

scŭtŭla -ae, f. (σκυτάλη). **I.** *a roller for moving heavy weights,* Caes. **II.** *a small tray* or *dish,* Mart. **III.** *a diamond* or *lozenge-shaped figure,* Tac.

scŭtŭlātus -a -um (scutula), *lozenge or diamond-shaped fabrics woven in checks*, Juv. Plur. subst., **scŭtŭlāta** -ōrum, n. (sc. vestimenta), *clothes made of such fabrics*, Juv.

scŭtŭlum -i, n. (dim. of scutum), *a little shield*, Cic.

scŭtum -i, n. (σκῦτος, *leather*), *a large quadrangular shield, made of wood covered with hides* (clipeus, *a smaller oval shield of metal*); pedestre (of a foot-soldier), Liv.; scutum abjicere, Cic.; scuto vobis magis quam gladio opus est, Liv.

Scȳlācēum -i, n. *a town in Lower Italy*, now *Squillace*; navifragum, Verg.; hence, **Scȳlācēus** -a -um, *relating to Scylaceum*; litora, Ov.

Scylla -ae, f. (Σκύλλα). **I.** *a lofty rock at the entrance to the straits between Sicily and Italy, opposite to the whirlpool Charybdis, dangerous for sailors*; personif., *daughter of Phorcus, changed by Circe into a monster, with dogs about the lower part of her body*. **II.** *daughter of Nisus, king in Megara, who cut off her father's hair, on which his happiness depended, and was turned into the bird Ciris*. Hence, **Scyllaeus** -a -um (Σκυλλαῖος), *belonging to Scylla* I. Subst., Scyllaeum = Scylla I., *a rock*; transf., Scyllaeum illud aeris alieni, Cic.

scymnus -i, m. (σκύμνος), *a young animal, whelp*; leonum, Lucr.

scȳphus -i, m. (σκύφος), *a drinking-cup, goblet*; inter scyphos, *over our wine, in our cups*, Cic.; vadit in eundem carcerem atque in eundem paucis post annis scyphum (*cup of poison*) Socrates, Cic.

Scȳrĭăs, v. Scyros.

Scȳrōn = II. Sciron (q.v.).

Scȳrus (-ŏs) -i, f. (Σκῦρος), *an island in the Aegean Sea, near Euboea*, now *Sciro, where Achilles concealed himself in woman's clothes, the residence of Lycomedes, whose daughter Deidamia was the mother of Pyrrhus by Achilles*. Hence, **A. Scȳrĭăs** -ădis, f. *of Scyrus*; puella, Deidamia, Ov. **B. Scȳrĭus** -a -um, *of Scyrus*; pubes, Verg.; membra (of Pyrrhus), Ov.

scȳtăla -ae, f. and **scȳtălē** -ēs, f. (σκυτάλη), *a roller*; hence, *the roller used by the Spartans*, around which they bound strips, and thus wrote their despatches, so that the despatches which were unwound could only be read by being rolled round a similar stick; hence, meton., *a secret despatch*, Nep.

Scȳthēs (Scȳtha) -ae, m. (Σκύθης), *a Scythian*. Plur., Scythae, *the Scythians, a name of various meaning, sometimes including all the nomadic tribes to the north of the Black and the Caspian Seas*. Hence, **A. Scȳthĭa** -ae, f. (Σκυθία), *Scythia*. **B. Scȳthĭcus** -a -um (Σκυθικός), *Scythian*; amnis, *the Tanais*, Hor. **C. Scȳthĭs** -ĭdis, f. *a Scythian woman*. **D. Scȳthissa** -ae, f. *a Scythian woman*.

1. sē (sēd), prep. = *without*. **I.** With abl., se fraude esto, ap. Cic. **II.** Prep. insepar., a, = *without*, as securus (= sine curā); b, = *apart*, e.g., sepono.

2. **sē** = semi, *half*, as semodius.

3. **sē** = sex, *six*, as semestris.

4. **sē**, acc. and abl. of sui (q.v.).

Sēbēthos (Sēbētos) -i, m. *a river in Campania, near Neapolis*. Hence, **Sēbēthĭs (Sēbētis)** -ĭdis, f. *of Sebethos*; nympha, Verg.

sēbōsus -a -um (sebum), *full of tallow, tallowy*, Plin.

sēbum (sēvum) and **saevum** -i, n. *tallow, suet, fat, grease*, Caes.

sēcāle -is, n. *a species of grain, perhaps rye*, Plin.

sēcāmenta -ōrum, n. (seco), *carved work*, Plin.

sēcēdo -cessi -cessum, 3. *to go apart, go away, withdraw*. **I.** Gen., a, of persons, secedant improbi, Cic.; b, of things, *to be distant*; tantum secessit ab imis terra, Cic. **II.** Esp., a, *to withdraw, retire, go aside*; in abditam partem aedium, Sall.; ad deliberandum, Liv.; b, *to withdraw, secede*; plebs a patribus secessit, Sall.; in sacrum montem, Liv.

sēcerno -crēvi -crētum, 3. *to separate, sever, part, sunder, set apart*. **I.** Lit., nihil praedae in publicum, Liv.; with ab and the abl., se a bonis, Cic.; inermes ab armatis, Liv.; with ex and the abl., aliquem e grege imperatorem velut inaestimabilem, Liv. **II.** Fig., **A.** Gen., animum a corpore, Cic. **B.** Esp., 1, *to distinguish*; blandum amicum a vero, Cic.; poet., with abl. alone, honestum turpi, Hor.; 2, *to set aside, to reject*; frugalissimum quemque, Cic.; contraria non fugere, sed quasi secernere, Cic.

sēcespĭta -ae, f. (seco), *a sacrificial knife*, Suet.

sēcessĭo -ōnis, f. (secedo). **I.** *a going on one side*; secessione factā, Liv.; esp. for a conference or parley, secessiones subscriptorum, Cic.; milites vesperi secessionem faciunt, *collect together*, Caes. **II.** *a political withdrawal, secession*; populi, Caes.; in Aventinum montem, Liv. Plur., secessiones plebei, Cic.

sēcessus -ūs, m. (secedo). **I.** *a going away*; avium, migration, Plin. **II.** *retirement, retreat*, Ov.; hence, meton., (a) *a place of retirement, a retreat*, esp., *a summer place of residence*, Verg.; (β) *a recess*; longus, *a bay running far into the land*, Verg.

sēclūdo -clūsi -clūsum, 3. (cludo, i.e., claudo), *to shut off*. **I.** *to shut away, shut up apart*; antro seclusa, Verg.; transf., inclusum supplicium atque a conspectu parentium ac liberûm seclusum, Cic. **II.** *to sever, separate, sunder*, Cic.; munitione flumen a monte. Caes.; transf., curas, *to banish*, Verg.

sēcĭus, v. secus.

sēclūsus -a -um, partic. of secludo.

sēco, sĕcŭi, sectum, but sĕcātūrus, 1. (root SEC, connected with German sägen, English *to saw*), *to cut, cut off, cut in pieces*. **I.** Lit., **A.** Gen., pabula, Caes.; unguis sectus, Hor. **B.** Esp., 1, medical t. t., *to cut off, amputate, to cut surgically*; varices Mario, Cic.; 2, *to cut, geld, castrate*, Mart. **II.** Transf., 1, *to tear, wound, scratch, injure, hurt*; securunt corpora vepres, Verg.; si quem podagra secat, *torments*, Cat.; 2, *to cut through, run through, sail through, traverse*; avis secat aethera pennis, Verg.; aequor puppe, Ov. **III.** Fig., 1, *to lash in words, satirise*; urbem, Pers.; 2, *to divide*; causas in plura genera, Cic.; hence, a, *to settle, decide*; lites, Hor.; b, *to pursue, follow up*; spem secare, Verg.

sēcrētō, adv. (secretus), *separately*; consilia secreto ab aliis coquebant, Liv.; eadem secreto ab aliis quaerit, Caes.; secreto hoc audi, tecum habeto, Cic.

sēcrētus -a -um, p. adj. (from secerno), *separate, apart*. **I.** Adj., **A.** Lit., 1, gen., arva, Verg.; imperium, Liv.; 2, esp., *separate, solitary*; colles, Tac.; secreta petere loca, Hor. **B.** Fig., a, *deprived of*; with abl., secreta cibo natura, Lucr.; with genit., corpora secreta teporis, Lucr.; b, *secret*; artes, Ov.; nec quic quam secretum alter ab altero habent, Liv. **II.** Subst., **sēcrētum** -i, n. 1, *retirement, solitude, a solitary place*; secreta Sibyllae, Verg.; abducere aliquem in secretum, Liv.; in secreto, Liv.; **2,** *a secret, mystery; omnium secreta rimari,* Tac.; in secretis eius, *in his private papers,* Suet.

secta -ae, f. (sequor), *a mode of life, procedure, conduct, plan.* **I.** Gen., nos qui hanc sectam rationemque vitae secuti sumus, Cic. **II.** Esp., 1, *political method, party; sequi eius auctoritatem cuius sectam atque imperium secutus est, Cic.; 2, a philosophical school, sect;* philosophorum sectam secutus es, Cic.

sectārius -a -um (seco), *cut, gelded,* Plaut.

sectātor -ōris, m. (sector), *a follower, hanger on; plur., a suite of attendants, train, retinue.* **A.** Gen., lex Fabia quae est de numero sectatorum, *dependents, clients,* Cic. **B.** *a member of a sect or school,* Tac.

sectĭlis -e (seco). **I.** *cut, cloven;* ebur, Ov.; pavimenta, *made up of small pieces, mosaic,* Suet. **II.** *that can be cut or cloven,* Mart.

sectĭo -ōnis, f. (seco). **I.** *a cutting, cutting up,* Plin. **II.** *the buying up of confiscated property, both of the goods of proscribed persons and of booty taken in war, and of inheritances which lapsed to the state;* ad illud sectionis scelus accedere, Cic.; exercendis apud aerarium sectionibus famosus, Cic.; concr. = *property of this kind put up to auction;* cuius praedae sectio non venierit, Cic.; sectionem eius oppidi universam Caesar vendidit, Caes.

sectīvus -a -um (seco), *that can be cut or chopped up,* Plin.

1. **sector** -ōris, m. (seco), 1, *a cutter;* collorum, *a cut-throat,* Cic.; 2, *a buyer of confiscated or other public property;* bonorum, Cic.; Pompeji, *of the property of Pompey,* Cic.

2. **sector,** 1. dep. (intens. of sequor), *to follow eagerly, continually.* **I.** Lit., 1, in a friendly way, *to accompany constantly, run after;* a, aliquem totos dies, Cic.; b, as a servant, *to be in the train of;* ii servi ubi sunt? Chrysogonum sectantur, Cic.; 2, in a hostile manner, *to run after in order to ridicule, to harass;* a, ut pueri eum sectentur, Cic.; b, *to follow animals in the chase, to hunt, pursue;* leporem, Hor.; apros, Verg. **II.** Transf., 1, *to strive after, pursue eagerly;* praedam, Caes.; virtutes, Tac.; 2, *to try to find out;* mitte sectari quo, etc., Hor.

sectrix -trīcis, f. (sector), *she that purchases the confiscated property of the proscribed,* Plin.

sectūra -ae, f. (seco). **I.** *a cutting,* Plin. **II.** Meton., *a place where something is cut or dug out;* aerariae secturae, *copper-mines,* Caes.

sēcŭbĭtus -ūs, m. (secumbo), *a sleeping alone,* Ov.

sēcŭbo -ŭi, 1. *to sleep alone, sleep by one's self.* **I.** Lit., Ov., Liv. **II.** *to live a solitary life,* Prop.

sēcŭlāris = saecularis (q.v.).

sēcŭlum = saeculum (q.v.).

sēcum = cum se, v. sui and cum.

sēcundāni -ōrum, m. (secundus), *soldiers of the second legion,* Liv.

sēcundārius -a -um (secundus), *belonging to the second rank or class, of second-rate quality;* panis, Suet.; of abstr., status de tribus secundarius, Cic.; subst., **sēcundārium** -ĭi, n. *secondary matter of discussion,* Cic.

1. **sēcundō,** adv. (secundus). **I.** *in the second place,* Cic. **II.** *for the second time,* Lucr.

2. **sēcundo,** 1. (secundus), *to make favourable, to favour, bless, assist, second;* dii incepta secundent, Verg.; secundante vento, Tac.

sēcundum, adv. and prep. (secundus). **I.** Adv., 1, *afterwards, behind;* ite hac secundum,

Plaut.; 2, *secondly, in the next place,* Cic. **II.** Prep. with acc., *after.* **A.** In space, 1, *close behind;* aram, Plaut.; 2, *along, close along, by, near to;* secundum mare, Cic. **B.** In time and order of events, 1, lit., a, of time, *after;* secundum comitia, Cic.; secundum haec, *after this,* Liv.; secundum quietem, *in a dream,* Cic.; b, of order, *after, next to;* secundum te, nihil mihi amicius est solitudine, Cic.; heres secundum filiam, *next after the daughter,* Cic.; 2, transf., a, *according to, in accordance with;* secundum naturam vivere, Cic.; b, legal t. t., *in favour of, to the advantage of;* decernere secundum aliquem, Cic.

sēcundus -a -um (sequor), *following.* **I.** Gen., 1, of time, lumine secundo, *on the following day,* Enn.; mensa, *the dessert,* Cic.; 2, in succession, *following the first, second;* a, lit., id secundum erat de tribus, Cic.; heres, *a person to inherit in case the first heir dies,* Cic.; partes secundae, *the second rôle,* Cic.; hence, subst., (a) **sēcundae** -ārum, f. *the second rôle;* agere, Sen.; fuit M. Crassi quasi secundarum, *was second fiddle to Crassus, followed after him,* Cic.; (β) **sēcunda** -ae, f. (sc. hora), *the second hour;* ad secundam, Hor.; b, fig., (a) *second in rank, next, following;* secundus ad principatum, Cic.; (β) *second in value, second-rate, inferior;* panis, Hor.; nulli Campanorum secundus, Liv. **II.** Esp., *following easily or willingly.* **A.** Lit., 1, of persons, dum ridetur fictis Balatrone secundo, Hor.; 2, of wind or tide, *following* (i.e., *favourable*); a, of water, secundo flumine, *with the stream,* Caes.; b, of wind, navem secundis ventis cursum tenentem, Cic.; vento secundissimo, Cic.; c, of sails filled with a favourable wind, secunda vela dato, Ov.; 3, of things, curruque (dat.) volans dat lora secundo, Verg. **B.** Fig., a, *favourable, favouring;* voluntas contionis, Cic.; secundo populo, *with the goodwill of the people,* Cic.; secundo Marte, *with success in battle,* Verg.; leges secundissimae plebi, Liv.; b, *fortunate, successful;* secundissimum proelium, Caes.; res secundae, *prosperity,* Cic.; subst., **sēcundum** -i, n. *prosperity,* Nep.; plur., secunda, Hor.

sēcūrē, adv. (securus). **I.** *composedly, tranquilly, unconcernedly,* Suet. **II.** *securely, safely,* Plin.

sēcūrĭcŭla -ae, f. (dim. of securis), *a little axe,* Plaut.

sēcūrĭfĕr -fĕra -fĕrum (securis and fero), *carrying an axe,* Ov.

sēcūrĭgĕr -gĕra -gĕrum (securis and gero), *carrying an axe;* puellae, *the Amazons,* Ov.

sēcūris -is, acc. -im, abl. -i, f. (seco). *an axe, hatchet.* **I. A.** Lit., for felling trees, Verg.; as a weapon of war, *a battle-axe,* Verg.; for killing victims at a sacrifice, Verg.; esp., for executing criminals, *the headsman's axe;* securi ferire, percutere, Cic.; saevus securi Torquatus (who had his own son beheaded), Verg.; prov., securi Tenediā (Τενεδίᾳ πελέκει), *with the extremest severity* (from king Tenes of Tenedos, who executed every person who accused an innocent man), Cic. **B.** Fig., *wound, injury, disaster;* graviorem infligere securim reipublicae, Cic. **II.** Meton., (as secures, fasces and virgae were carried by the lictors of the highest magistrates at Rome), *supreme power, Roman supremacy;* a, plur., Gallia securibus subjecta, *completely subdued,* Caes.; b, sing., Germania colla Romanae praebens animosa securi, Ov.

sēcūrĭtas -ātis, f. (securus). **I.** *freedom from care.* **A.** In a good sense, *peace of mind, quiet,* Cic. **B.** In a bad sense, *carelessness, indifference,* Tac. **II.** Transf., *freedom from danger, security,* Tac.

sĕcūrus -a -um (1. se and cura), *free from care.* **I.** Lit., *unconcerned, fearless, tranquil;* **a,** of persons, animus securus de aliqua re, Cic.; securior ab aliquo, Liv.; with genit., amorum, Verg.; famae, Ov.; with dep. interrog. sent., quid Tiridaten terreat, unice securus, Hor.; non securus, followed by ne and the subj., ne quis etiam errore labatur vestrûm quoque non sum securus, Liv.; **b,** of inanimate things, (*a*) *untroubled, cheerful;* quies, Ov.; olus, *simple, plain meal,* Hor.; with genit., sint tua vota licet secura repulsae, *safe against,* Ov.; (*β*) in a bad sense, *negligent, careless;* castrensis jurisdictio, Tac. **II.** Transf., *safe, secure;* tempus, locus, Liv.

1. **sĕcus,** n. indecl. = sexus, *sex;* virile et muliebre secus, Liv.

2. **sĕcŭs,** adv. (root SEC, SEQ, whence sequor). **I.** Posit., **A.** Adv., a, *otherwise, not so;* secus est, non (haud) secus, *just as,* foll. by atque (ac) quam, etc.; longe secus, *far otherwise,* Cic.; **b,** *not right, not well, badly* (opposed to preceding recte, bene, beate, etc.); recte an secus, *rightly or wrongly,* Cic.; aut beate aut secus vivere, *happily or the reverse,* Cic.; secus existimare de aliquo, Cic.; **c,** *less;* neque multo secus in iis virium, Tac. **B.** Prep. with acc. = secundum, Cato. **II.** Compar., **sĕquĭŭs** (**sĕcĭŭs**) and **sectĭŭs** (**sētĭŭs**), 1, *otherwise, not so;* non setius ut, *not otherwise than, just as,* Verg.; non setius uritur quam, Ov.; 2,= minus, *less;* nilo and nihilo setius (sequius), *none the less,* Cic.; haud setius and non setius, Verg.; 3, *less well, badly;* invitus quod sequius sit de meis civibus loquor, Liv.

sĕcūtor -ōris, m. (sequor), *a gladiator armed with a sword and shield who fought with a* retiarius, Juv.

1. **sĕd,** v. 1. se.

2. **sĕd** (old Latin sĕt), conj. (connected with sĕd = se, *without*). **I.** *but, yet;* **1,** to limit or qualify a person's statement, Cic.; sed enim, Cic.; sed enimvero, Liv.; sed autem, Verg.; **2,** esp., **a,** to express an ascending climax, sed etiam, *but also, nay rather;* avarissimae sed etiam crudelissimae, Cic.; consilium defuit, sed etiam obfuit, Cic.; **b,** in transitions, *but, yet;* (*a*) in returning to a previous subject, sed redeamus ad Hortensium, Cic.; (*β*) in resuming a discourse after a parenthesis, ut peroravit (nam . . . peregerat) sed ut peroravit, etc., Cic.; **c,** in breaking off discourse, *but, yet;* sed haec hactenus, Cic. **II.** To limit or qualify a previous negative sent., *but;* esp., in the phrases non modo (non solum, non tantum), sed etiam (quoque), *not only . . . but also;* non modo (solum) . . . sed, *not only . . . but even;* negotiis non interfuit solum, sed praefuit, Cic.

sĕdāmen -ĭnis, n. (sedo), *a sedative,* Sen.

sĕdātē, adv. (sedatus), *quietly, composedly, tranquilly;* placide atque sedate, constanter et sedate dolorem ferre, Cic.; of discourse, sedate placideque labi, Cic.

sĕdātĭo -ōnis, f. (sedo), *an allaying, soothing, assuaging of violent emotion or passion;* animi, Cic.; maerendi, Cic.; plur., sedationes (animi), Cic.

sĕdātus -a -um, p. adj. (from sedo), *quiet, composed, tranquil;* homo, Cic.; sedato gradu abire, Liv.; animus sedatior, Cic.

sĕdēcĭēs, adv. (sedecim), *sixteen times,* Plin.

sĕdĕcĭm and **sexdĕcĭm** (sex and decem), *sixteen,* Caes.

sĕdēcŭla -ae, f. (dim. of sedes), *a low seat or stool,* Cic

sĕdentārĭus -a -um (sedens), *sitting, sedentary;* sutor. Plaut

sĕdĕo, sēdi, 2. *to sit.* **I.** Gen., **A.** Lit., 1, a, of persons, with in and the abl., in sella, in solio, in equo, Cic.; with abl. alone, carpento, sede regiā, Liv.; absol., quum tot summi oratores sedeant, Cic.; **b,** of animals, *to settle;* cornix sedet in humo, Ov.; **2,** esp., of magistrates, *to sit in council, sit in judgment;* Scaevolā (tribuno) in rostris sedente, Cic.; pro tribunali, Cic.; in tribunali, Cic. **B.** Transf., of things, *to settle, sink down;* sedet nebula densior campo, Liv.; sedisse montes, Tac.; of food, *to settle, be digested;* esca quae tibi sederit, Hor. **II.** With a notion of endurance. **A.** Lit., 1, *to remain in one place, settle, stay;* also with the notion of *to be inactive, idle;* in villa totos dies, Cic.; Corcyrae, Cic.; desidens domi, Liv.; sedit qui timuit, *remained at home,* Hor.; consulibus sedentibus, Cic.; prov., compressis manibus sedere, *to sit with folded hands,* Liv.; 2, esp., a, *to sit as a suppliant at the altar of some god;* meliora deos sedet omnia poscens, Verg.; b, milit. t. t., *to remain encamped, to sit down before a place, to remain inactive;* Arretii ante moenia, Liv. **B.** Transf., 1, lit., a, *to be firmly settled;* in liquido sederunt ossa cerebro, Ov.; b, of weapons, *to be fixed, be fastened, to stick;* clava sedet in ore viri, Ov.; 2, fig., a, *to remain fast, unchanged;* pallor in ore sedet, Ov.; b, of resolves, *to be firmly determined, to remain fixed;* idque pio sedet Aeneae, Verg.

sēdes -is, f. (sedeo), *a seat.* **I.** Lit., *a stool, chair, throne;* sedes honoris, sella curulis, Cic.; sedes ponere, Liv.; priores sedes tenere, *the first rank,* Hor. **II.** Transf., a, *an abode, habitation, place of settlement, home;* sedes fundatur Veneri, *a temple,* Verg.; sceleratorum, *the infernal regions,* Cic.; eam sibi domum sedesque deligere, Cic.; plur., sedes sanctae penatium deorumque, Cic.; his sedibus sese continere, Cic.; esp., (*a*) *the grave;* sedibus hunc refer ante suis et conde sepulchro, Verg.; (*β*) *the dwelling-place of the soul, the body;* anima misera de sede volens exire, Ov.; b, of things, *place, seat, spot, base, foundation;* turrim convellimus altis sedibus, Verg.; suis sedibus convulsa Roma, Cic.; montes moliri sede suā, Liv.

sĕdīle -is, n. (sedeo), *a seat;* (*a*) sing., Verg.; (*β*) plur., sedīlia, *a row of seats* or *benches in the theatre* or *elsewhere,* Hor.; *benches for rowers,* Verg.

sēdīmentum -i, n. (sedeo), *a settling, sediment,* Plin.

sēdĭtĭo -ōnis, f. (from sed = se, *apart,* and itio), *a dissension.* **I.** Between individuals, *dissension, quarrel;* domestica (of brothers), Liv.; crescit favore turbida seditio, Ov. **II.** Between members of a political union, esp., citizens and soldiers, *a civil* or *military revolt, insurrection, sedition, rising, mutiny.* **A.** 1, lit., militaris, Liv.; seditionem ac discordiam concitare, Cic.; seditionem concire, Liv.; conflare, Cic.; facere, Caes.; restinguere, Cic.; personif. *as an attendant of Fama;* Seditio repens, Ov.; 2, meton., *the rebels,* Liv. **B.** Transf., *rising, tumult;* intestina corporis, Liv.; iracundia dissidens a ratione seditio quaedam, Cic.

sēdĭtĭōsē, adv. with compar. and superl (seditiosus), *seditiously,* Cic.

sēdĭtĭōsus -a -um (seditio). **I.** *seditious, turbulent;* civis, Cic.; triumviri seditiosissimi, Cic. **II.** *restless;* seditiosa ac tumultuosa vita, Cic.

sēdo, 1. (causat. of sedeo). **I.** Lit., tc cause *to settle;* pulverem, Phaedr. **II.** *to settle, soothe, still, calm, allay, assuage, put an end to, extinguish;* bellum, pugnam, Cic.; incendia, Liv.; invidiam, Cic.; impetum populi, Cic.; iram. Plin.: seditionem. Cic.; lites eorum, Cic.

sēdūco -duxi -ductum, 3. *to take or lead a part.* **I.** Lit., a, in order to speak secretly to a person ; aliquem, Cic.; aliquem a debita peste, *to lead aside and so rescue from danger,* Cic. ; b, of things, vacuos ocellos, *to turn aside,* Prop.; stipitem, *to push aside,* Ov.; vina paulum seducta, *placed aside,* Ov. **II.** Transf., a, poet., *to separate, sever;* seducit terras unda duas, Ov.; seducunt castra, *divide into two,* Ov.; b, *to exclude;* consilia seducta plurium conscientiâ, Liv.

sēductĭo -ōnis, f. (seduco), *a leading or drawing aside;* testium, Cic.

sēductus -a -um, p. adj. (from seduco), *remote, distant;* recessus gurgitis, Ov.

sēdŭlē = sedulo (q.v.).

sēdŭlĭtas -ātis, f. (sedulus), *assiduity, zeal, application,* Cic.

sēdŭlō, adv. (sedulus), a, *busily, zealously ;* sedulo argumentaris, Cic.; b, *purposely, designedly,* Liv.

sēdŭlus -a -um (from sedeo, as credulus from credo), *busy, diligent, assiduous, sedulous, earnest, zealous;* homo, Cic.; apis, Cic.; brachia, Ov.

sēdum -i, n. *the plant houseleek,* Plin.

Sēdūni -ōrum, m. *a Helvetian people, near modern Sion.*

sĕgĕs -ĕtis, f. (perhaps from root SEC, Gr. TEK-ω, *that which is produced.* **I.** *the seed in a field, from its being sown to the crop being reaped;* a, lit., laetae segetes, Cic.; seges farris est matura messi, Liv.; used of the vine, Verg.; b, fig., *advantage;* quae inde seges, Juv.; 2, transf., *a thickly-packed mass or number;* seges clipeata virorum, Ov.; telorum, Verg. **II.** Meton., *a sown field;* 1, a, lit., Cic.; b, fig., *field, soil;* quid odisset Clodium Milo segetem ac materiem suae gloriae? Cic. ; 2, poet., transf., *fruitful plains, fields;* fert casiam non culta seges, Tib.; ubi prima paretur arboribus seges, Cic.

Sĕgesta -ae, f. *Roman name of the old town Acesta* (Ἀκέστη), *on the north coast of Sicily, near Mount Eryx, now Castel a mare di Golfo.* Hence, **A. Sĕgestāni** -ōrum, m. *the inhabitants of Segesta.* **B. Sĕgestenses** -ĭum, m. *the inhabitants of Segesta.*

sĕgestre -is, n. (στέγαστρον), *a covering, wrapper of straw matting or skins,* Plin.

segmentātus -a -um (segmentum), *ornamented with a purple or gold border, bordered ;* cunae, Juv.

segmentum -i, n. (root SEC, whence seco). **I.** *a piece cut off, cutting, shred ;* 1, lit., Plin. ; 2, transf., *a zone or region of the earth,* Plin. **II.** Plur., segmenta, *pieces of purple or cloth of gold sewn on the skirt of women's dresses, gold or purple border,* Ov.

segnĕ, adv., v. segniter.

segnĭpēs -pĕdis (segnis and pes), *slow-footed,* Juv.

segnis -e (root SEC, sequor), *slow, slothful, tardy, sluggish, dilatory;* a, absol., segniores castigat, Caes. ; bellum, *sluggishly prosecuted,* Liv.; mors, *a lingering death by poison,* Liv.; b, with ad and acc., segnior ad respondendum, Cic.; nec ad citharam segnis nec ad arcum, Ov.; c, with in and the acc., non in Venerem segnes Verg. ; d, with genit., laborum, Tac. ; e, with infin., solvere nodum, Hor.

segnĭtas -ātis, f. (segnis), *sluggishness, tardiness, dilatoriness,* Cic.

segnĭtĕr and **segnĕ** (segnis), *sluggishly, slothfully, slowly ;* a, posit., Liv. ; b, compar., segnius, Liv.; esp. with preceding negative, nihilo segnius, Sall.

segnĭtĭa -ae, f. and **segnĭtĭēs** -ēi, f. (segnis), *sluggishness, slothfulness, slowness, tardiness ;* a, lit., Cic.; b, transf., segnitia maris, *calmness,* Tac.

Sĕgŏdūnum -i, n. *the chief town of the Ruteni, on the northern border of Gallia Narbonensis,* now *Rodez,* Cic.

Segontĭa (Saguntĭa) and **Secontĭa** -ae, f. *a town in Hispania Baetica, near modern Siguenza.*

Segontĭāci -ōrum, m. *a people in the south of Britain.*

Segovax -actis, m. *one of the British chiefs in Kent at the time of Caesar's invasion.*

sēgrĕgo, 1. (grex). **I.** *to separate from the flock, segregate;* oves, Phaedr. **II.** Transf., *to separate, sever, remove;* aliquem a numero civium, Cic.; aliquem a se, Cic.; virtutem a summo bono, Cic.

Sēgūsĭāvi (Sēgūsĭāni) -ōrum, m. *a people in Gallia Lugdunensis, in modern Feurs* (Dép. de la Loire).

segutilum -i, n. *the external indication of a gold-mine,* Plin.

Sējānus, v. Sejus.

sējŭgātus -a -um, *disjointed, separated;* animi partem ab actione corporis sejugatam, Cic.

sējŭges -ĭum, m. (sex and jugum), *a chariot drawn by six horses abreast,* Liv.

sējunctim, adv. (sejunctus), *separately,* Tib.

sējunctĭo -ōnis, f. (sejungo), *a separation, severance,* Cic.

sējungo -junxi -junctum, 3. *to separate, sever, disjoin.* **I.** Lit., Alpes Italiam a Gallia sejungunt, Nep. ; se ab aliquo, Cic. **II.** Transf., 1, gen., se a libertate verborum, *to refrain from,* Cic. ; bonum quod non possit ab honestate sejungi, Cic.; 2, esp., *to distinguish;* liberalitatem ac benignitatem ab ambitu atque largitione, Cic.

Sējus -i, m. *a Roman name, the most celebrated bearer of which was M. Sejus, a friend of Atticus and Cicero.* Hence, **Sējānus** -a -um, *relating to Sejus;* subst., as name, L. Aelius Sejanus, *son of Sejus Strabo, the praefectus praetorii of Tiberius.*

sēlas, n. (σέλας), *a species of fiery meteor,* Sen.

sēlectĭo -ōnis, f. (seligo), *a choosing out, selection ;* si selectio nulla sit ab iis rebus quae, etc., Cic.

Sēleucēa (Sēleucīa) -ae, f. (Σελεύκεια), *name of several towns.* **I.** S. Babylonia : *a town near the Tigris, on the canal connecting it with the Euphrates, built by Seleucus Nicator,* now *El-Madaien.* **II.** S. Pieria : *a town in Syria, not far from the Orontes,* now ruins near *Kepse.* **III.** S. Trachēa : *a town in Cilicia,* now *Selefkieh.*

Sēleucus -i, m. (Σέλευκος), Nicator, *a famous general of Alexander the Great, king of Syria.*

sēlibra -ae, f. (for semilibra), *half a pound,* Liv.

sēlĭgo -lēgi -lectum, 3. (se and lego), *to choose, choose out, select.* **I.** Gen., exempla, Cic. **II.** Esp., judices selecti, *the judges appointed by the praetor in a criminal case,* Cic.

Sēlĭnūs -nuntis, f. (Σελινοῦς). **I.** *a sea-port in Sicilia,* now *Selinonto.* **II.** *a town in Cilicia, afterwards called Trajanopolis,* now *Selenti,* Liv. Hence, adj., **Sēlĭnūsĭus** -a -um, *belonging to Selinus.*

sella -ae, f. (for sedla, from sedeo), *a seat, stool, settle.* **I.** Gen., in sella sedere, Cic. **II.** Esp., 1, *a work-stool, a stool or bench on which handicraftsmen sit ;* in foro sellam ponere, Cic. ;

2, the stool of a teacher, Cic.; **3**, the curule stool, in full, sella curulis, on which the higher magistrates sat at Rome, Cic.; **4**, a throne, Nep.; **5**, a sedan-chair; gestatoria, Suet.

sellārĭus -a -um (sella), relating to a seat or stool; subst., **sellārĭa** -ae, f. a room furnished with seats, a sitting-room, Plin.

sellisternĭum -ĭi, n. (sella and sterno), a religious banquet in honour of goddesses, at which their images were placed on seats and food put before them, Tac.

sellŭla -ae, f. (dim. of sella), a little sedan-chair, Tac.

sellŭlārĭus -a -um (sellula), of or relating to a seat; artifex, a handicraftsman who sat at his work; hence, subst., **sellŭlārĭus** -ĭi, m. a handicraftsman, Cic.

sĕmĕl, adv. numer. **I**. once, a single time; semel atque iterum, semel iterumque, once and again, twice, Cic.; semel atque iterum ac saepius, Cic.; plus quam semel, Cic.; non semel, Cic. **II**. Transf., **A**. the first time, firstly; foll. by iterum, deinde, item, etc., Cic. **B**. once; a, quoniam semel ita vobis placuit, Cic.; b, once (of things which cannot be altered); qui semel verecundiae fines transierit, eum bene et naviter oportet esse impudentem, Cic. **C**. once, once for all; a, semel exorari soles, Cic.; vitam semel finirent, Liv.; b, in discourse, once for all, in a word, briefly; ut fundus semel indicaretur, Cic.

Sĕmĕla -ae, f. and **Sĕmĕlē** -ēs, f. (Σεμέλη), daughter of Cadmus, mother of Bacchus by Jupiter; she asked Jupiter to appear to her in his person as a god, and was consumed by the blaze of his majesty; Semeles puer, Bacchus, Hor. Hence, **Sĕmĕlēïus** and **Sĕmĕlēus** -a -um, of Semele; Semeleia proles, Bacchus, Hor.

sēmen -ĭnis, n. (root SE, whence se-ro, se-vi), the seed. **I**. **A**. Lit., a, of plants, semen manu spargere, Cic.; b, (a) of animals, creatae semine Saturni, Ov.; (β) of the elements of water, fire, stone, etc., Verg., Lucr. **B**. Meton., the seed; **1**, the race; Romanum, Cic.; regio semine orta, Liv.; **2**, descendant, child, offspring; caelestia semina, Ov.; semina Phoebi, Aesculapius, son of Phoebus, Ov. **II**. Fig., seed = cause, origin, author, instigator; stirps ac semen malorum omnium, Cic.

sēmentĭfĕr -fĕra -fĕrum (sementis and fero), seed-bearing, fruitful, Verg.

sēmentis -is, acc. -em and -ĭm, f. (semen), a sowing. **I**, a, lit., sementes maximas facere, Cic.; prov., ut sementem feceris, ita metes, Cic.; b, fig., malorum sementim or proscriptionis sementem facere, Cic. **II**. Meton., sementes, the young growing corn, Ov.

sēmentīvus -a -um (sementis), of or relating to seed or seed-time; dies, Ov.

sēmento, 1. (sementis), to bear seed, Plin.

sēmestris (**sēmenstris**) -e (sex and mensis), of six months, six-monthly; a, = six months old; infans, Liv.; b, = limited to six months; regnum, Liv.; semestri vatum digitos circumligat auro, the ring of the tribunes of the soldiers worn for six months, Juv.

sēmēsus -a -um (semi and esus), half-eaten, half-consumed; praeda, ossa, Verg.

sēmĭădăpertus -a -um (semi and adaperio), half-open, Ov.

sēmĭambustus -a -um (semi and amburo), half-burnt, Suet.

sēmĭănĭmis -e and **sēmĭănĭmus** -a -um (semi and anima), half-alive, half-dead; corpora semianima, Liv.

sēmĭăpertus -a -um (semi and aperio), half-open; portarum fores, Liv.

sēmĭbarbărus -a -um, semi-barbarous, Suet.

sēmĭbos -bŏvis. m. half-ox; vir, the Minotaur, Ov.

sēmĭcăper -pri, m. half-goat, Ov.

sēmĭcinctĭum -ĭi, n. (semi and cinctus), a narrow girdle or apron, Mart.

sēmĭcircŭlus -i, m. a semicircle, Col.

sēmĭcoctus -a -um (semi and coquo), half cooked, Plin.

sēmĭcrĕmātus -a -um (semi and cremo), half-burnt, Ov.

sēmĭcrĕmus (semi and cremo), half-burnt, Ov.

sēmĭcrūdus -a -um, half-raw, Suet.

sēmĭcŭbĭtālis -e, half a cubit in length, Liv.

sēmĭdĕus -a -um, half-divine; subst., a demigod, demigoddess; semideum genus, the Nereids, Ov.

sēmĭdoctus -a -um (semi and doceo), half-taught, half-learned; haec ut apud doctos et semi doctos ipse percurro, Cic.

sēmĭermis (**sēmermis**) -e and **sēmĭermus** (**sēmermus**) -a -um (semi and arma), half-armed, half-equipped, Liv.

sēmĭēsus = semesus (q.v.).

sēmĭfactus -a -um (semi and facio), half-done, half-finished, Tac.

sēmĭfĕr -fĕra -fĕrum (semi and ferus), half-animal, half-bestial, half-man and half-animal. **I**. Lit., pectus Tritonis, Verg.; subst., of the Centaurs, Ov. **II**. Transf., half-wild, half-savage. Subst., **sēmĭfĕr** -fĕri, m. half a savage, Verg.

sēmĭfultus -a -um (semi and fulcio)), half propped, Mart.

sēmĭgermānus -a -um, half-German, Liv.

sēmĭgraecus -a -um, half-Greek, Suet.

sēmĭgrăvis -e, half-intoxicated, Liv.

sēmĭgro, 1. to go away, depart, remove from; a patre, Cic.

sēmĭhĭans -antis (semi and hio), half-open; labellum, Cat.

sēmĭhŏmo -hŏmĭnis, m. half a man. **I**. half a man and half an animal; Centauri, Ov. **II**. Transf., half-wild; Cacus, Verg.

sēmĭhōra -ae, f. half an hour, Cic.

sēmĭlăcer -cĕra -cĕrum, half-torn, half-mangled, Cic.

sēmĭlautus -a -um, half-washed, Cat.

sēmĭlīber -bĕra -bĕrum, half-free, Cic.

sēmĭlixa -ae, m. half a sutler, used as a term of reproach, Liv.

sēmĭmărīnus -a -um, half-marine, half in the sea; corpora (Scyllarum), Lucr.

sēmĭmas -măris, m. **I**. half-male, hermaphrodite, Liv. **II**. castrated; oves, Ov.

sēmĭmortŭus -a -um, half-dead, Cat.

sēmĭnārĭus -a -um (semen), of or relating to seed; subst., **sēmĭnārĭum** -ĭi, n. a plantation, nursery; fig., equites seminarium senatus, Liv.; Catilinarum, Cic.; triumphorum, Cic.

sēmĭnātor -ōris, m. (semino), a producer, begetter, author; qui est verus omnium seminator malorum, Cic.

sēmĭnex -nĕcis, half-dead, Liv.

sēmĭnĭum -ĭi, n. (semen), a race or breed of animals, Lucr.

sēmĭno, 1. (semen). **I.** *to sow,* Col. **II.** *to beget, produce,* Plaut. ; *of plants, viscum, quod* non *sua seminat arbos,* Verg.

sēmĭnūdus -a -um, *half-naked,* Liv. ; *pedes prope seminudus, nearly defenceless, without arms,* Liv.

sēmĭpāgānus -i, m. *half a rustic,* Pers.

sēmĭpĕdālis -e, *half a foot in dimension,* Plin.

sēmĭpĕdānĕus = semipedalis (q.v.).

sēmĭperfectus -a -um (semi and perficio), *half-finished,* Suet.

sēmĭpes -pĕdis, m. *a half-foot,* Plin.

sēmĭplēnus -a -um, *half-full; naves, half-manned,* Cic. ; stationes, Liv.

sēmĭpŭtātus -a -um (semi and puto), *half-pruned; vitis,* Verg.

Sĕmĭrămĭs (Sāmĭrămĭs, Sămērămĭs) -midis and -midos, f. (Σεμίραμις), *wife and successor of Ninus, king of Assyria.*

sēmĭrāsus -a -um (semi and rado), *half-shaven, half-shorn,* Cat.

sēmĭrĕductus -a -um (semi and reduco), *half bent back,* Ov.

sēmĭrĕfectus -a -um (semi and reficio), *half-repaired,* Ov.

sēmĭrŭtus -a -um (semi and ruo), *half-ruined, half pulled down, half-destroyed;* urbs, Liv. ; castella, Tac. ; plur. subst., **sēmĭrŭta** ōrum, n. *half-demolished places,* Liv.

sēmis -issis, m. and sometimes indecl. (semis, *half,* and as), *the half of anything;* esp., **1,** *half an as,* Cic. ; **2,** as a rate of interest, = 6 *per cent. per annum;* semissibus magna copia, etc., *there is plenty of money to be had at 6 per cent.,* Cic. ; **3,** as a measure of land, *half a juger,* Liv.

sēmĭsĕpultus -a -um (semi and sepelio), *half-buried,* Ov.

sēmĭsomnus -a -um, *half-asleep, drowsy,* Cic.

sēmĭsŭpīnus -a -um, *half-inclined backwards,* Ov.

sēmĭta -ae, f. *a narrow path, footpath, footway.* **I.** Lit., angustissimae semitae, Cic. ; omnibus viis semitisque essedarios ex silvis emittebat, Cic. **II.** Fig., Aesopi semitā feci viam, *I have amplified the materials in Aesop,* Phaedr. ; pecuniam, quae viā visa est exire ab isto, eandem semitā revertisse, Cic.

sēmĭtactus -a -um (semi and tango), *half-touched,* Mart.

sēmĭtārĭus -a -um (semita), *frequenting lanes or by-paths,* Cat.

sēmĭtectus -a -um (semi and tego), *half-covered,* Sen.

sēmĭustŭlatus = semustulatus (q.v.).

sēmĭustus (sēmustus) -a -um (semi and uro), *half-burnt;* Enceladi semustum fulmine corpus, Verg. ; in fig., se populare incendium priore consulatu semiustum effugisse, Liv.

sēmĭvir -vĭri, m. *half-man.* **I.** Lit., **1,** *half-man, half-animal;* Chiron, *the centaur,* Ov. ; bos, *the Minotaur,* Ov. ; **2,** *a hermaphrodite,* Ov. **II.** Transf., **1,** *castrated, gelded,* Juv. ; **2,** *effeminate, unmanly,* Verg.

sēmĭvīvus -a -um, *half-dead, almost dead.* **I.** Lit., Cic. **II.** Fig., voces, *faint,* Cic.

sēmĭvōcālis -e, *half-sounding;* in grammar, subst., **sēmĭvōcāles** -ium, f. (sc. litterae), *semivowels,* Quint.

Semnōnes -um, m. *a German people between the Elbe and the Weichsel,* Tac

sēmŏdĭus -ĭi, m. (semi and modius), *a half-modius,* Mart.

sēmōtus -a -um, p. adj. (from semoveo), *remote, distant.* **I.** Lit., locus a militibus semotus, Caes. ; neut. plur. subst., quae terris semota ridet, Hor. **II.** Transf., a, *far from,* semotus a curis, Lucr. ; **b,** *distinct from, different from,* Lucr. ; **c,** *confidential;* arcana semotae dictionis, Tac.

sēmŏvĕo -mōvi -mōtum, 2. *to move away sever, separate.* **I.** Lit., qui voce praeconis s liberis semovebantur, Cic. **II.** Transf., *to lay aside, exclude;* voluptatem, Cic. ; Strato ab ea disciplina omnino semovendus est, *is not to be reckoned under that school,* Cic.

sempĕr, adv. (sem (= semel) and per, *as* nu (= novi) and per), *always, at all times,* Cic. ; with subst., used almost as an adj., heri semper lenitas, *the constant mildness,* Ter. ; Hasdrudal pacis semper auctor, Liv.

sempĭternus -a -um (semper), *continual, perpetual, everlasting;* tempus, Cic. ; ignes Vestae, Cic. ; adv., **sempĭternum,** *for ever,* Plaut.

Semprōnĭus -a -um, *name of a gens at Rome, the most famous members of which were the brother.* Tib. Sempronius Gracchus, and C. Sempronius Gracchus, *tribunes of the people, who introduced agrarian laws and other reforms, but were both killed in riots provoked by the senatorial party.* Adj., *Sempronian;* lex, Cic. Hence, **Semprōnĭānus** -a -um, *relating to Sempronius;* senatus consultum, *proposed by C. Sempronius Rufus,* Cic. ; clades, *the defeat of the consul, C. Sempronius Atratinus.*

sēmuncĭa -ae, f. (semi and uncia), *half an uncia,* $\frac{1}{24}$ *of an as;* **1,** as a weight = $\frac{1}{24}$ *of a pound,* Cic. ; **2,** to express the share of an inheritance; facit heredem ex deunce et semuncia Caecinam, Cic.

sēmuncĭārĭus -a -um (semuncia), *relating to half an ounce;* fenus, $\frac{1}{24}$ *per cent. monthly,* i.e., *one-half per cent. per annum,* Liv.

sēmustĭlātus (sēmĭustŭlātus) and **sēmustĭlātus (sēmĭustĭlātus)** -a -um (semi and ustulo, ustilo), *half-burnt,* Cic.

Sēna -ae, f. *a town in Umbria on the Adriatic Sea, where Livius Salinator defeated Hasdrubal,* now Senigaglia. Hence, **Sēnensis** -e, *relating to Sena;* proelium, Cic.

sēnācŭlum -i, n. (senatus), *a senate-house, hall of council,* Liv.

sēnārĭŏlus -i, m. (dim. of senarius), *a little trifling senarius,* Cic.

sēnārĭus -a -um (seni), *composed of six;* senarius versus and subst. **sēnārĭus** -ĭi, m. *a verse of six feet* (generally iambic), Cic.

sĕnātor -ōris, m. (senex), *a member of the Roman senate, senator,* Cic. ; transf., of the governing or deliberative bodies of other states ; of the Nervii, Caes. ; of the Rhodians, Cic. ; of the Macedonians, Liv.

sĕnātōrĭus -a -um (senator), *of or relating to a senator, senatorial;* ordo, *the rank of senator,* Cic. ; consilium, *the panel of senators from which judges were chosen,* Cic.

sĕnātus -i and -ūs, m. **I.** *the Roman senate,* Cic. ; princeps senatus, *the senator whose name stood at the head of the censor's list,* Liv. ; in senatum venire, *to become a senator,* Cic. ; senatu movere, *to expel from the senate,* Cic. ; senatum legere, *to call over the senate,* Liv. ; so senatum recitare, Cic. ; senatum vocare, Liv. ; convocare, Cic. ; senatus (senati) consultum, *a formal resolution of the senate,* Cic. ; used also of similar bodies in other nations, Carthaginiensis, Liv.; Aeduos omnem senatum amisisse, Caes. **II.** Meton., *a meeting, assembly of the senate; senatum habere*, dimittere, Cic.; frequens, *a full house*, Cic.; datur alicui senatus, *obtains an audience of the senate*, Cic.

sĕnātusconsultum, v. senatus.

Sĕnĕca -ae, m. *a family name of the Annaean gens, the most celebrated members of which were:* 1, M. Annaeus Seneca, *a rhetorician of Corduba in Spain;* 2, L. Annaeus Seneca, *son of the foregoing, a celebrated philosopher, author of many works in prose and verse* (tragedies and epigrams), *the tutor of Nero, who compelled him to commit suicide.*

sĕnecta, v. l. senectus.

1. **sĕnectus** -a -um (senex), *old, aged.* **I.** Adj., aetas, *old age*, Sall. **II.** Subst., **sĕnecta** -ae, f. *old age.* **A.** Lit., Liv.; of animals, Verg., Ov. **B.** *the slough of a serpent*, Plin.

2. **sĕnectus** -ūtis, f. (senex), *age, old age.* **I. A.** Lit., vivere ad summam senectutem, Cic.; of animals, Verg.; in fig., of discourse, plena litteratae senectutis oratio, Cic. **B.** Meton., 1, *gloom, moroseness*, Hor.; 2, concr., a, *grey hair*, Verg.; b, *old age = the old men;* senectus semper agens aliquid, Cic.; c, *the slough of a serpent*, Plin. **II.** Transf., of a thing, *old age*, age; vini, Juv.; cariosa (tabellarum), Ov.

sĕnĕo, 2. (senex), *to be old*, Cat.

sĕnesco, sĕnŭi, 3. (seneo). **I.** *to grow old in years, become old;* tacitis senescimus annis, Ov. **II.** *to grow old in strength.* **A.** 1, of living beings, *to lose strength, become weak, waste away;* senescens equus, Hor.; otio tam diutino, Liv.; 2, of things, *to become old, to decay;* arbor hiemali tempore cum luna simul senescens, Cic. **B.** Transf., a, *to wane, come to an end, flag, be relaxed;* luna senescens, Cic.; hiems senescens, Cic.; of abstractions, senescit laus, morbus, Cic.; b, of polit. power, *to wane, fade, lose power;* prope senescente Graeciā, Cic.; senescit Hannibalis vis, Liv.

sĕnex, sĕnis, compar., **sĕnĭor**, neut. sĕnĭus, genit. sĕnĭōris, *old, aged.* **I.** Adj., a, of persons, miles, Ov.; senem fieri, *to age*, Cic.; of animals, cervus, Ov.; of things, vis est senior quam, etc., Cic.; b, fig., *ripe;* senior, ut ita dicam, quam illa aetas ferebat, oratio, Cic. **II.** Subst., a, m. *an old man, a man over sixty*, while senior = *a man between forty-five and sixty* (for which Hor. and Liv. sometimes use senex), Cic.; b, f. *an old woman*, Tib.

sēni -ae -a (sex). **I.** *six each*, Cic. **II.** *six*, Ov.

sĕnīlis -e (senex), *of or relating to an old man, senile;* prudentia, Cic.; stultitia, Cic.; statua incurva, Cic.; animus, Liv.; amor, Ov.

sĕnīlĭtĕr, adv. (senilis), *like an old man*, Quint.

sĕnĭo -ōnis, m. (seni), *the number six upon dice*, Mart.

sĕnĭor, compar. of senex (q.v.).

sĕnĭum -ĭi, n. (senex), *old age, the weakness, decay of old age.* **I. A.** Lit., omni morbo senioque carere, Cic. **B.** Transf., *decline, decay;* lentae velut tabis, Liv.; mundus se ipse consumptione et senio alebat sui, Cic. **II.** Meton., **A.** Abstr., 1, *gloom, moroseness*, Hor.; 2, *chagrin, vexation, sadness;* tota civitas confecta senio, Cic. **B.** Concr., *an old man;* with m. pron., illum senium, Ter.

Sĕnŏnes -um, m. **I.** *a people in Gallia Lugdunensis, with chief town Agendicum, now Sens.* **II.** *a kindred people in northern Italy.*

sensĭbĭlis -e (sentio), *that can be perceived by the senses*, Suet.

sensĭcŭlus -i, m. (dim. of sensus), *a little sentence*, Quint.

sensĭfĕr -fĕra -fĕrum (sensus and fero), *producing sensation*, Lucr.

sensĭlis -e (sentio), *endowed with sensation*, Lucr.

sensim, adv. (root SENS, whence sentio, sensi, sensus), *scarcely observably, gradually, by degrees, slowly;* sensim sine sensu, Cic.; amicitias sensim dissuere, Cic.

sensus -ūs, m. (sentio). **I.** *perception, observation;* utere igitur argumento tute ipse sensus tui, Cic. **II.** *the power of perceiving.* **A.** Physically, a, *feeling, consciousness;* sensus moriendi, Cic.; voluptatis sensum capere, Cic.; b, *a sense;* sensus videndi, audiendi, Cic.; c, *feeling, consciousness*, in plur., *senses;* a mero redeunt in pectora sensus, Ov. **B.** Morally, a, *emotion, sense, feeling;* amoris, amandi, diligendi, Cic.; b, *a manner of thinking, the sense, signification of a word, sentence, discourse, meaning;* verbi, Ov.; testamenti, Hor.

sententĭa -ae, f. (sentio). **I.** *an opinion, thought, sentiment, meaning, purpose* (opp. to expression). **A.** Gen., abundans sententiis, *rich in ideas*, Cic.; sententiam fronte tegere, Cic.; in sententia manere, Cic.; ex sententia, *to one's mind*, Cic.; meā sententiā, *in my opinion*, Cic. **B.** Esp., a, *an expressed opinion, vote of senators;* sententiam dicere, ferre, Cic.; dare, Liv.; in sententiam alicuius discedere, *to support a proposition*, Liv.; so (pedibus) ire in sententiam, Liv.; of judges, *decision, judgment;* sententiam dicere, Cic.; sententiam ferre, Cic.; b, as formula for an oath, ex animi mei sententia jurare, *to the best of my knowledge and belief*, Cic. **II.** Transf. **A.** Abstr., a, *the meaning, signification of a word or sentence;* id habet hanc sententiam, Cic.; b, *the purport of a speech;* contionis, Cic. **B.** Concr., a, *a thought expressed in words, a sentence;* b, esp., *a maxim, aphorism;* acuta, Cic.

sententĭŏla -ae, f. (dim. of sententia), *a short sentence, maxim, aphorism*, Cic.

sententĭōsē, adv. (sententiosus), *sententiously;* dicere, Cic.

sententĭōsus -a -um (sententia), *pithy, sententious*, Cic.

sentĭcētum -i, n. (sentis), *a thorn-bush*, Plaut.

sentīna -ae, f. *bilge-water in the hold of a ship.* **I.** Lit., sentinae vitiis conflictari, Caes. **II.** Fig., 1, gen., sedebamus in puppi et clavum tenebamus; nunc autem vix est in sentina locus, *we can scarcely find room in the lowest part of the ship*, i.e., *we are of next to no importance*, Cic.; 2, esp., *the lowest of the people, rabble, dregs of the population;* reipublicae, Cic.; urbis, Cic.

Sentīnum -i, n. *a town in Umbria.* Hence, adj., **Sentīnās** -ātis, *belonging to Sentinum.*

sentĭo, sensi, sensum, 4. *to feel, perceive, have a sensation of.* **I.** With the outward sense, **A.** Gen., suavitatem cibi, Cic.; dolorem, Lucr.; colorem, *to see*, Lucr.; pass., posse prius ad angustias veniri quam sentirentur, Caes.; with nom. of partic., sensit medios delapsus in hostes, Verg. **B.** *to feel, experience, learn;* (a) of persons, quod ipse sensisset ad Avaricum, Caes.; (β) of things, ora senserat vastationem, Liv. **II.** Mentally, *to feel.* **A.** Lit., *to perceive, remark, observe, notice;* plus sentire, *have more insight*, Caes.; quod quidem senserim, *as far as I have observed*, Cic.; with acc. and infin., sentit animus se moveri, Cic.; with rel. sent., quod sentio, quam sit exiguum, Cic.; nec aliter sentire, foll. by

quin and the subj., *to be convinced that*, Caes. ;
ex nocturno fremitu de profectione eorum sen-
serunt, *observed their departure*, Caes. ; impers.,
non ut dictum est in eo genere intelligitur, sed
ut sensum est, Cic. **B.** Transf., *to judge, think ;*
a, idem, Cic. ; recte, Cic. ; humiliter, Cic. ; cum
aliquo, Cic. ; with double acc., *to consider or
think a person something ;* aliquem bonum civem,
Cic. ; partic. subst., **sensa** -ōrum, n. *thoughts ;*
mentis, Cic. ; b, legal t. t., *to give one's opinion,
to vote ;* sentire lenissime, Cic.

sentis -is, c. *a thorn-bush, briar ;* usually
plur., rubi sentesque, Caes.

sentisco, 3. (inchoat. of sentio), *to perceive,
observe,* Lucr.

sentus -a -um (sentis), *thorny, rough ;* loca,
Verg.

sēnus -a -um, sing. of seni (q. v.).

sĕorsum (**sĕorsŭs**) and **sēvorsŭs** (from se
and vorto or verto), *especially, particularly ;* omnibus gratiam habeo et seorsum tibi, Ter. ; foll.
by ab, *apart from, separately from ;* seorsum ab
rege exercitum ductare, Sall. ; abs te seorsum
sentio, *I am of a different opinion,* Plaut. ; with
abl. alone, seorsus corpore, *without a body,* Lucr.

sēpărātē, adv. only in compar. (separatus),
apart, particularly, Cic.

sēpărātim, adv. (separatus), *apart, separately, distinctly, differently ;* separatim semel,
iterum cum universis, Cic. ; nihil accidet ei
separatim a reliquis civibus, Cic. ; castra separatim habebant, Liv. ; with ab and the abl., dii
separatim ab universis singulos diligunt, Cic.

sēpărātio -ōnis, f. (separo), *separation,
severance.* **I.** Lit., distributio partium ac separatio, Cic. **II.** Transf., sui facti ab illa defin-
itione, Cic.

sēpărătus -a -um, p. adj. (from separo),
*separated, severed, sundered, separate, apart,
distinct ;* volumen, Cic. ; exordium, Cic. ; separ-
atis temporibus, *at different times,* Nep.

sēpăro, 1. *to disjoin, sever, separate.* **I.** Lit.,
(α) aliquem or aliquid ab, etc.. Cic. ; (β) aliquid
aliquā re ; Seston Abydenā separat urbe fretum,
Ov ; (γ) aliquid ex aliqua re or in aliquid, equitum
magno numero ex omni populi summa separato,
Cic. ; (δ) with acc. alone, nec nos mare separat
ingens, Ov. **II.** Fig., *to separate, treat separately ;* (α) with ab and the abl., a perpetuis
suis historiis bella ea, Cic. ; (β) with acc. alone,
utilitatem, Cic.

sĕpĕlībĭlis -e (sepelio), *that can be buried ;*
fig., *that can be concealed,* Plaut.

sĕpĕlĭo -pēlīvi and -pēlĭi -pultum, 4. (root
SEP, connected with sop-or, sop-io), *to lay to rest
the remains of the dead, to bury.* **I.** Lit., a, *to
bury ;* ossa, Ov. ; b, *to burn,* Liv. **II.** Fig., 1,
to bury, put an end to, ruin, destroy ; patriam,
Cic. ; dolorem, Cic. ; 2, poet. partic., sepultus,
buried, sunk, immersed in anything ; somno
vinoque sepultus, Verg. ; inertia sepulta, Hor.

sēpes = saepes (q. v.).

sēpĭa -ae, f. (σηπία), *the cuttle-fish,* Cic.

sēpīmentum = saepimentum (q. v.).

sēpĭo = saepio (q. v.).

sēpĭŏla -ae, f. (dim. of sepia), *a small cuttle-
fish,* Plaut.

Sēplăsĭa -ae, f. *a street in Capua, where unguents were sold.*

sēpōno -pŏsŭi -pŏsĭtum, 3. *to put, lay on one
side, place apart.* **I.** Gen., **A.** Lit., aliquid ad
fanum, Cic. ; captivam pecuniam in aedificationem templi, Liv. ; primitias magno Jovi, Ov.
B. Transf., *to keep back, reserve ;* ut alius aliam
sibi partem, in qua elaboraret, seponeret, Cic.

II. Esp., **A.** *to separate ;* 1, lit., de mille sagittis
unam, *to select,* Ov. ; 2, transf., a, *to separate,
divide ;* a ceteris dictionibus eam partem dicendi,
Cic. ; b, *to distinguish ;* inurbanum lepido dicto,
Hor. **B.** *to keep far off ;* 1, lit., a, interesse
pugnae imperatorem an seponi melius foret
dubitavere, Tac. ; b, *to remove out of the way,
banish ;* aliquem in insulam, Tac. ; 2, transf.,
graves curas, *to banish,* Ov.

sēpŏsĭtus -a -um, p. adj. (from sepono). **I.**
distant, remote ; fons, Prop. **II.** *choice, select ;*
vestis, Tib.

1. **seps,** sēpis, c. (σήψ). **I.** *a species of venomous lizard,* Plin. **II.** *an insect,* perhaps *the wood-
louse,* Plin.

2. **seps** = saepes (q. v.)

sepsē = se ipse.

septa, v. saeptum.

septem, numer. (ἑπτά), *seven.* **I.** Gen., Cic.
II. Esp., **A.** septem (οἱ ἑπτά), *the Seven Wise
Men of Greece,* Cic. **B.** Septem Aquae, *the meet-
ing of streams near Reate,* now *Lake Sta. Susanna.*

September -bris -bre, abl. -bri (septem and
suffix -ber), *belonging to September ;* a, mensis
September, *the seventh month of the Roman
year* (reckoning from March), *September ;* b,
kalendae, nonae, idus (*the* 1st, 5th, 13th *of September*) ; horae, *the unhealthy time of September,*
Hor.

septemdĕcim, numer. *seventeen,* Cic.

septemflŭus -a -um (fluo), *having a sevenfold flood, with seven mouths ;* Nilus, Ov.

septemgĕmĭnus -a -um, *sevenfold, with
seven mouths ;* Nilus, Verg.

septempĕdālis -e, *seven feet high,* Plaut.

septemplex -plicis (septem and plico), *sevenfold ;* clipeus, *with seven layers of hides,* Verg. ;
Nilus, *with seven mouths,* Verg. ; so Ister, Ov.

**septemtrĭo (septemptrio, septen-
trio)** -ōnis, m., gen. plur., septemtriones, *the
seven plough-oxen.* **I.** As a constellation, *the
Great Bear, the Wain ;* septemtrio minor, *the Little
Bear,* Cic. **II.** Meton., a, *the north ;* (a) sing.,
septemtrio a Macedonia obicitur, Liv. ; in tmesis,
septem subjecta trioni, Verg. ; (β) plur., inflectens sol cursum tum ad meridiem, tum ad
septemtriones, Cic. ; b, *the north wind,* Cic.

septemtrĭōnālis -e (septemtrio), *northern ;*
subst., **septemtrĭōnālia** -ium, m. *the northern regions,* Tac.

septemvir -vīri, m., plur., **septemvĭri**
-ōrum and -ûm, m. *the seven men, a college or
guild of seven persons.* **I.** Of the Epulones, v.
epulo. **II.** *to divide public land among colonists,*
Cic.

septemvĭrālis -e, *of or relating to the septemviri ;* auctoritas, Cic. ; subst., **septemvĭr-
āles** -ium, m. = septemviri (q. v.).

septemvĭrātus -ūs, m. *the office or dignity
of a septemvir,* Cic.

septēnārĭus -a -um (septeni), *containing
the number seven ;* numerus, Plin. ; plur. subst.,
septēnārĭi, m. (sc. versus), *verses containing
seven feet,* Cic.

septendĕcim = septemdecim (q. v.).

septēni -ae -a (septem). **I.** *seven each ;* duo
fana septenos habere libros, Liv. ; genit. plur.,
septenûm, e.g., pueri annorum senûm septe-
nûmque denûm, Liv. **II.** *seven ;* septena fila
lyrae, Ov. ; sing., Lucr.

septentrĭo = septemtrio (q. v.).

septentrĭōnālis = septemtrionalis (q. v.).

septĭcus -a -um (σηπτικός), *causing putrefaction,* Plin.

septĭēs (septĭens), adv. (septem), *seven times;* septies milliens sestertium or simply **septiens** milliens, 700 *millions of sesterces,* Cic.

septĭmānus (septĭmānus) -a -um, *relating to the number seven.* **I.** Adj., nonae, *falling on the seventh day of the month,* Varr. **II.** Subst., **septĭmāni** -ōrum, m. *soldiers of the seventh legion,* Tac.

Septĭmontĭālis -e, *of or relating to the festival Septimontium,* Suet.

Septĭmontĭum -ĭi, n. (septem and mons). **I.** *the circuit of seven small hills round the Palatine, which became the germ of the city of Rome.* **II.** *a festival at Rome in December to celebrate the walling-in of these small hills and the formation of a city.*

septĭmus (septŭmus) -a -um (septem), *the seventh;* adv., **septĭmum,** *for the seventh time,* Cic.

septingēnārĭus -a -um (septingeni), *containing seven hundred,* Varr.

septingēni -ae -a (septingenti), *seven hundred each,* Plin.

septingentēsĭmus -a -um (septingenti), *the seven hundredth,* Liv.

septingenti -ae -a (septem and centum), *seven hundred,* Liv.

septingentĭēs, adv. (septingenti), *seven hundred times,* Plin.

Septizōnĭum -ĭi, n. (septem and zona), *a lofty building in Rome,* Suet.

septŭāgēni -ae -a (septuaginta), *seventy each,* Plin.

septŭāgēsĭmus -a -um (septuaginta), *the seventieth,* Cic.

septŭāgĭēs, adv. (septuaginta), *seventy times,* Col.

septŭāginta, numer. (ἑβδομήκοντα), *seventy,* Cic.

septŭennis -e (septem and annus), *of seven years, seven years old;* puer, Plaut.

septum = saeptum (q.v.)

septunx -uncis, m. (septem and uncia), *seven-twelfths of the as, or of any unity with twelve parts;* jugeri, Liv.; auri, *seven ounces,* Liv.

sepulch ... v. sepulc ...

sĕpulcrālis (sĕpulchrālis)-e(sepulcrum, sepulchrum), *of or belonging to a tomb, sepulchral;* arae, Ov.; fax, *funeral torch,* Ov.

sĕpulcrētum -i, n. *a burial-place, cemetery,* Cat.

sĕpulcrum (sĕpulchrum) -i, n. (from sepelio, as fulcrum from fulcio), *the resting-place.* **I. A.** Lit., *a place of burial;* 1, a, *a grave, sepulchre;* monumenta sepulcrorum, Cic.; b, *the mound over a grave;* onerare membra sepulcro, Verg.; 2, *the place where a corpse is burnt;* ara sepulcri, Verg. **B.** Transf., sepulcrum vetus, *of an old man,* Plaut. **II.** Meton. **A.** *the tomb,* including grave, monument, and inscription; sepulcrum facere, Cic.; legere sepulcra, *to read the epitaph on a grave-stone,* Cic. **B.** *the dead person;* placatis sepulcris, Ov.

sĕpultūra -ae, f. (sepelio), *the laying the body of a dead person to rest;* a, *a burying, burial, interment, sepulture;* sepulturā aliquem afficere, *to bury,* Cic.; b, *the burning of the body of the dead,* Tac.

Sēquăna -ae, m. *a river of Gaul, forming, with the Matrona, the boundary between the Celts and the Belgae,* now the Seine.

Sēquăni -ōrum, m. *a Gallic people in modern Burgundy and Franche-Comté.*

sĕquax -ācis (sequor). **I.** *following easily or quickly;* equus, Ov.; undae, *following each other rapidly,* Verg.; hederae, *quickly spreading itself,* Pers.; fumus, *penetrating,* Verg.; Latio (= Latinis) dant terga sequaci, *pursuing,* Verg. **II.** Transf., *easily worked, pliable, ductile;* materia sequacior, Plin.

sĕquester -tra -trum and **sĕquester** -tris -tre (from 2. secus, as magister from magis), *mediating.* **I.** Adj., pace sequestrā, *by the medium of peace,* Verg. **II.** Subst., **A. sĕquester** -tri or -tris, m. a, *a go-between or agent* (in cases of bribery); quo sequestre in illo judice corrumpendo dicebatur esse usus, Cic.; b, *a stake-holder, depositary, a person in whose hands the matter in dispute is deposited till the dispute is settled,* Plaut. **B. sĕquestrum** -i, n. and **sĕquestre** -is, n. *the deposit of the matter in dispute in the hands of a third person;* sequestro deponere, *by way of deposit,* Plaut.

sĕquĭus = secius, compar. of secus (q.v.).

sĕquor, sĕcūtus (sĕquūtus) sum, sĕqui, 3. dep. (root SEC, connected with Ἑπ-ομαι), *to follow, accompany.* **I. A.** Lit., 1, gen., a, of persons, qui ex urbe amicitiae causā Caesarem secuti, Caes.; vestigia alicuius, Ov.; b, of things, zonā bene te secutā, Hor.; 2, esp., a, *to follow with hostile intent, pursue;* hostes, Caes.; feras, Ov.; b, *to follow a person to a place;* Formias, Cic.; secutae sunt nares vicinitatem oris, *have sought for,* Cic. **B.** Transf., a, of time or order, *to follow, ensue;* sequitur hunc annum nobilis clade Caudina pax, Liv.; sequenti anno, Liv.; sequenti die, Liv.; et quae sequentia, *and so on,* Cic.; b, *to fall to any one as an inheritance or possession, to fall to the share of;* urbes captae Aetolos sequerentur, Liv.; heredes monumentum ne sequeretur, Hor.; c, *to follow,* i.e., *to yield, to give way;* ipse (ramus) facilis sequetur, Verg. **II.** Fig., **A.** Gen., *to follow, follow after;* gloria virtutem tamquam umbra sequitur, Cic.; edictum, *the words of the edict,* Cic. **B.** Esp., 1, *to follow a person's authority, example, opinion, to tread in the steps of, to agree to;* leges, Cic.; amicum, Cic.; liberi sequuntur patrem, *follow the rank of their father,* Liv.; 2, *to strive after, aim at, seek to gain;* amicitiam fidemque populi Romani, Cic.; 3, *to follow in discourse, ensue;* sequitur illa divisio, Cic.; sequitur ut doceam, Cic.; 4, *to follow as a consequence, be the consequence of, be caused by;* moneo ne summa turpitudo sequatur, Cic.; poena quae illud scelus sequeretur, Cic.; esp., *to follow logically, be the logical consequence of,* gen. with ut and the subj.; si hoc enuntiatum verum non est, sequitur, ut falsum sit, Cic.; 5, *to follow easily, come of itself;* non quaesitum esse numerum, sed secutum, Caes.

sēra -ae, f. (root SER, whence 2. sero, series), *a moveable bar or bolt for fastening doors;* centum postibus addere seras, Ov.

Sĕrāpis (Sărāpis) -pis and -pĭdis, m. (Σεράπις, Σάραπις), *a deity of the Egyptians, in later times worshipped at Greece and at Rome.*

sĕrēnĭtas -ātis, f. (serenus), *clearness, serenity,* esp., *clear, bright, fair weather.* **I.** Lit., caeli, Cic. **II.** Fig., fortunae, Liv.

sĕrēno -a, 1. (serenus). **I.** *to make clear, serene, bright;* caelum, Verg. **II.** Fig., spem fronte, Verg.

sĕrēnus -a -um, *clear, bright, fair, serene.* **I. A.** Lit., caelum, Cic.; nox, Verg.; pelagus, Verg.; subst., **sĕrēnum** -i, n. *fair weather,* Plin.; aperta serena, Verg. **B.** Transf., 1, *clear;* aqua, Mart.; vox, Pers.; 2, act., *making bright, bringing fair weather;* Favonius, Plaut. **II.** Fig., *cheerful, tranquil, serene;* frons, Cic.

Sēres -um, m. (Σῆρες), *a people in eastern*

Asia, famous for their silken stuffs, the Chinese; hence, adj., **Sērĭcus** -a -um, *Chinese; pulvillus, silken,* Hor. Subst., **Sērĭca** -ōrum, n. *silken garments,* Prop.

1. **sēresco**, 3. (serenus), *to become dry,* Lucr.

2. **sēresco**, 3. (serum), *to turn to whey,* Plin.

Sergĭus -a -um, *name of a Roman gens, the most celebrated member of which was* L. Sergius Catilina, *the head of a conspiracy suppressed in the consulship of Cicero.*

1. **sērĭa** -ae, f. *a large earthen jar for holding wine and oil,* Liv.

2. **sērĭa,** v. 1. serius.

sērĭcātus -a -um (Seres), *clothed in silken garments,* Suet.

Sērĭcus, v. Seres.

sērĭes, acc. -em, abl. -e, genit. and dat. not found, f. (root SER, whence 2. sero), *a row, succession, chain, series.* **I.** Gen., **A.** Lit., *juvenum, dancing hand in hand,* Tib. **B.** Fig., *a succession, series;* rerum, Cic.; innumerabilis annorum, Hor. **II.** Esp., *a line of descent, lineage;* digne vir hāc serie, Ov.

sērĭo, v. 1. **sērĭus.**

sērĭŏla -ae, f. (dim. of seria), *a small jar,* Pers.

Sērĭphus (-ŏs) -i, f. (Σέριφος), *an island in the Aegean Sea,* now *Serfo* or *Serfanto.* Adj., **Sērĭphĭus** -a -um, *Seriphian;* subst., **Sērĭphĭus** -ii, m. *a Seriphian.*

sēris -ĭdis, f. (σέρις), *a species of endive,* Plin.

1. **sērĭus** -a -um, *serious, earnest* (used gen. only of things, not of persons); res, Cic.; with 2. supine, verba seria dictu, Hor. Subst., **sērĭum** -ii, n. *earnestness, seriousness,* Plaut.; hence, abl. serio, *in earnest, earnestly, seriously;* serio audire, Liv.; plur., seria, *serious things;* seria ac jocos celebrare, Liv.; quam joca, seria, ut dicitur (sc. agimus or aguntur), Cic.

2. **sērĭus,** adv., v. sero under serus.

sermo -ōnis, m. (2. sero), *talk, conversation, discourse.* **I.** Lit., **A.** Gen., 1, sermonem conferre cum aliquo, Cic.; esse in sermone omnium, *the subject of every one's conversation,* Cic.; jucundus mihi est sermo litterarum tuarum, Cic.; 2, meton., *the subject of conversation;* Cataplus ille Puteolanus, sermo illius temporis, Cic. **B.** Esp., 1, *learned conversation, discussion, dialogue;* sermonem cum aliquo habere de amicitia, Cic.; 2, in writing or speaking, *a familiar, conversational style;* sermonis plenus orator, Cic.; scribere sermoni propiora, Hor.; hence, meton., a, in Horace, his *Letters* and *Satires* as opposed to his more ambitious poems; b, *spoken words, utterance;* multi et illustres et ex superiore et ex aequo loco sermones habiti, *utterances on the bench and in ordinary conversation,* Cic.; 3, *the talk of the multitude about something, common talk, report, rumour;* vulgi, hominum, Cic. **II.** Transf., 1, *manner of speaking, language, style, expression, diction;* sermo rusticus, urbanus, Liv.; plebeius, Cic.; sermonis error, Cic.; 2, *language, dialect;* sermone debemus uti, qui natus est nobis, *our mother-tongue,* Cic.; quae philosophi Graeco sermone tractavissent, *in the Greek language,* Cic.

sermōcĭnātĭo -ōnis, f. (sermocinor), *a discussion, disputation, dialogue,* Quint.

sermōcĭnātrix -īcis, f. (sermocinor), *the art of conversation,* Quint.

sermōcĭnor, 1. dep. (sermo), *to converse, talk, discuss with any one.* **I.** Gen., sermocinari cum isto diligenter, Cic. **II.** Esp., *to hold a learned discourse or discussion,* Suet.

sermuncŭlus -i, m. (dim. of sermo), *a report, rumour, tittle-tattle;* urbani malevolorum sermunculi, Cic.

1. **sēro, sēvi, sătum,** 3. (root SE-o, whence semen). **I.** *to sow, set, plant.* **A.** 1, lit., oleam et vitem, Cic.; frumenta, Caes.; partic. subst., **sāta** -ōrum, n. *the sown fields, standing corn,* Verg., Liv.; 2, transf., *to beget, engender, bring forth;* genus humanum, Cic.; partic., **sātus** -a -um, *sprung from, born of;* sate sanguine divûm, Verg.; matre satus terrā, Ov.; Anchisā satus, *son of Anchises,* Verg.; satus Nereide, *son of Thetis,* Ov.; satae Peliā, *daughters of Pelias* Ov. **B.** Fig., *to plant, sow, spread abroad, disseminate, cause, occasion;* cum patribus certamina, Liv.; discordias, Liv.; crimina, Liv.; mentionem, *to make mention of,* Liv.; mores, Cic.; diuturnam rempublicam, Cic. **II.** *to plant, sow, sow over;* agrum, Ov.; jugera sunt sata, Cic.

2. **sēro** (sērŭi), sertum, 3. (root SER, Gr. EP-ω, εἴρω), *to join together, weave together, entwine.* **I.** Lit., only in the partic. perf., **sertus** -a -um; loricae, *linked,* Nep. **II.** Fig., *to join together, connect, combine;* ex aeternitate causa causam serens, Cic.; fati lege immobilis rerum humanarum ordo seritur, Liv.; fabulam argumento, Liv.; colloquia cum hoste, Liv.; multa inter sese vario sermone serebant, Verg.

3. **sēro,** v. serus.

sērōtĭnus -a -um (3. sero), *late;* hiems, Plin.

serpens -entis, c. (serpo), *an animal that crawls.* **I.** *a snake, serpent.* **A.** Lit., Cic. **B.** *a constellation in the northern hemisphere* (also called Draco and Anguis), Ov. **II.** *a creeping insect on the human body, louse,* Plin.

serpentĭgĕna -ae, c. (serpens and gigno), *offspring of a serpent,* Ov.

serpentĭpes -pĕdis (serpens and pes), *snake-footed,* Ov.

serpĕrastra -ōrum, n. (sirpo, *to bind*), *bandages or knee-splints for straightening the crooked legs of children,* Varr.; in jest, of officers who keep their soldiers in order, Cic.

serpillum = serpyllum (q.v.).

serpo, serpsi, serptum, 3. (ἕρπω), *to creep, crawl.* **I. A.** Lit., of animals, quaedam bestiae serpentes, quaedam gradientes, Cic.; serpere per humum, Ov. **B.** Transf., of any slow and imperceptible motion, vitis serpens multiplici lapsu et erratico, Cic.; flamma per continua serpens, Liv.; et (Ister) tectis in mare serpit aquis, Ov. **II.** Fig., **A.** Gen., of prosaic poetry, serpit humi tutus, Hor. **B.** Esp., *to spread abroad, increase, extend imperceptibly;* serpit hoc malum longius quam putatis, Cic.; si paullatim haec consuetudo serpere ac prodire coeperit, Cic.; serpit hic rumor, foll. by acc. and infin., Cic.

serpyllum (serpillum) and **serpullum** -i, n. (ἕρπυλλον), *wild thyme* (Thymus serpyllum, Linn.), Verg.

serra -ae, f. (sec-ra, from seco = *that which cuts*), *a saw.* **I.** Gen., Cic. **II.** Transf., *a kind of saw-fish,* Plin.

serrācum (sarrācum) -i, n. **I.** *a kind of waggon used by the Roman peasants to carry their goods and families in,* Juv. **II.** Transf., *a constellation, the Wain,* Juv.

serrātŭla -ae, f. *betony,* Plin.

serrātus -a -um (serra), *toothed like a saw, serrated;* dentes, Plin. Subst., **serrāti** -ōrum, m. (sc. nummi), *silver denarii notched on the edge,* Tac.

serrŭla -ae, f. (dim. of serra), *a little saw,* Cic.

serta, v. sertum.

Sertōrĭus -ĭi, m., Q., *a celebrated Roman general of the Marian faction, who, on Sulla gaining the upper hand in Rome, fled to Spain, and resisted there bravely and successfully till he was treacherously killed by Perperna.* Adj., **Sertōrĭānus** -a -um, *Sertorian.*

sertŭm -i, n., gen. plur., **serta** -ōrum, n., and **serta** -ae, f. (sero), *a garland of flowers;* sertis redimiri, Cic.; serta Campanica, and simply serta, *a plant* = melilotos, Cato.

1. **sĕrum** -i, n. I. *the watery part of curdled milk, whey,* Verg. II. *the watery part or serum of other things,* Plin.

2. **sērum**, v. serus.

sērus -a -um. I. *late.* A. Gen., gratulatio, Cic.; hora serior, Ov.; si hiems magis sera (= serior), Liv.; subst., **sērum** -i, n., rem in serum trahere, *to retard,* Liv.; serum diei, *late in the day, evening,* Liv.; abl., sero, adv. = *late,* Cic.; esp., late = *in the evening,* Cic.; compar., serius, *later;* biduo serius, Cic.; spe omnium serius (id bellum fuit), Liv.; serius ocius, *sooner or later,* Hor. B. Esp., 1, *late in being fulfilled;* spes, Liv.; portenta, Cic.; 2, *doing something late;* serus abi, *go late away,* Ov.; with genit., o seri studiorum ! *late learned* (ὀψιμαθεῖς), Hor.; 3, *aged, old;* platanus, Ov.; ulmus, Verg.; 4, *lasting a long time;* bellum, Ov. II. *too late;* kalendae, Cic.; bellum, Sall.; sera assurgis, Verg.; abl., sero, adv. = *too late,* Cic.; prov., sero sapiunt (sc. Phryges, i.e., Trojani), Cic.; compar., serius, *somewhat too late;* venire, Cic.

serva, v. servus.

servābĭlis -e (servo), *that can be saved,* Ov.

servans -antis, p. adj. only in superl. (servo), *observing;* servantissimus aequi, Verg.

servātor -ōris, m. (servo), *a preserver, saviour;* reipublicae, Cic.; salutis, Ov.

servātrix -ĭcis, f. (servator), *she that preserves, a preserver, saviour,* Cic.

servīlis -e (servus), *of or relating to a slave, slavish, servile;* vestis, Cic.; tumultus, *a servile insurrection,* Cic.; terror, *dread of an insurrection of slaves,* Liv.

servīlĭtĕr, adv. (servilis), *slavishly, servilely;* ne quid serviliter muliebriterve faciamus, Cic.

Servīlĭus -a -um, *name of a Roman gens, the most celebrated members of which were:* 1, C. Servilius Ahala, *who as magister equitum killed Maelius;* 2, P. Servilius Rullus, *composer of the lex Servilia concerning the selling of the Italian public lands, against which Cicero delivered his agrarian speeches;* 3, Servilia, *mother of Brutus, mistress of Caesar.* Adj., *Servilian;* lex, Cic.; lacus, *a piece of artificial water near the Capitol, where the heads of the proscribed were put up,* Cic.

servĭo -ivi and -ĭi -ĭtum, 4. (servus), *to serve, be a servant or slave.* I. A. Lit., alicui, Ter.; apud aliquem, Cic.; with cognate acc., servitutem, Cic. B. Transf., of things, a, of land, buildings, etc., *to be subject to certain rights of other persons than the owner, to be subject to an easement,* Caes.; (aedes) serviebant, Cic.; b, *to serve, be useful, serviceable for;* chartis serviunt calami, Plin. II. Fig., 1, *to subserve, assist, comply with, accommodate, gratify;* alicui, Cic.; amori aliorum, Cic.; iracundiae, Cic.; 2, a, *to care for, have regard to, devote one's attention to;* brevitati, Cic.; b, *to adapt oneself to, to allow oneself to be governed by;* incertis rumoribus, Caes.; tempori, Cic.

servītĭum -ĭi, n. (servus). I. *slavery, service, servitude, subjection;* ducere aliquem in servitium, Liv., civitatem a servitio abstrahere, Cic.; animi imperio, corporis servitio magis utimur, *the mind is the master, the body the slave,* Sall. II. Meton., *slaves, servants, a household or slaves;* used both sing. and plur., servitia sileant, Cic.; servitia concitare, Cic.; servitium in scaenam immissum, Cic.

servītrīcĭus -a -um (servus), *belonging to a slave,* Plaut.

servītūdo -ĭnis, f. (servus), *slavery, servitude,* Liv.

servītus -ūtis, f. (servus), *the condition of a slave, slavery, servitude.* I. A. Lit., both of individuals and states, diutina, Cic.; perpetua, Caes.; aliquem in servitutem abducere, Cic.; addicere aliquem in servitutem, Cic., perpetuae servituti, Caes.; anteponere mortem servituti, Cic.; esse in servitute, *to be a slave,* Cic. B. Transf., 1, *subjection, obedience;* of the wife towards the husband, muliebris, Liv.; officii, Cic.; 2, of houses, lands, etc., *liability to certain burdens, easements,* e.g., a right of way, fundo servitutem imponere, Cic. II. Meton., *slaves;* servitus crescit nova (of the lovers of a maiden), Hor.

Servĭus -ĭi, n. (servus, *son of a slave*), *a Roman praenomen occurring in the name of the king Servius Tullius and in the Sulpician gens,* v. Sulpicius.

servo, 1. (root SERV, connected with 'ΕΡΥ-ω, ἐρύομαι). I. *to keep, preserve, save, rescue, deliver.* A. Gen., 1, of concrete objects, populum, Cic.; aliquem ex judicio, Cic.; with double acc., se integros castosque, Cic.; 2, of abstract objects, *to observe, pay heed to, keep;* ordinem, Liv.; ordines, Caes.; concentum, Cic.; amicitiam, Cic.; legem, Cic.; pacem cum aliquo, Cic.; fidem juris jurandi cum hoste, Cic.; foll. by ut or ne and the subj., quum ita priores decemviri servassent, ut unus fasces haberet, Liv. B. Esp., *to keep for the future, to lay up, keep, preserve, reserve;* Caecuba centum clavibus, Hor.; se ad tempora, Cic.; se ad majora, Liv.; eo me servavi, Cic.; with dat., res judicio voluntatique alicuius, Cic. II. Transf., A. *to give regard to, pay attention to, watch;* 1, gen., me omnibus servat modis ne, etc., Plaut.; sidera, *to observe,* Verg.; ortum Caniculae, Cic.; servare de caelo, *to observe lightning* (the duty of the augurs), Cic.; *to keep watch;* cetera servabant atque in statione manebant, Ov.; 2, esp., a, *to take care, take precautions;* servarent ne qui nocturni coetus fierent, Liv.; serva, *take care,* Hor.; b, *to watch, keep, detain, preserve;* (a) aliquem liberā custodiā, Cic.; limen, *stay at home,* Verg.; (β) *to dwell, remain in a place, inhabit;* silvas et flumina, Verg. B. *to keep, preserve;* quum populus suum servaret, Cic.

servŭlus (servŏlus) -i, m. (dim. of servus), *a young slave,* Cic.

servus -i, m. and **serva** -ae, f. *a slave, servant;* servi publici, *slaves of the state,* Cic.; Transf., servi cupiditatum, Cic.; legum, Cic. Hence, adj., **servus** -a -um, *servile, slavish;* a, gen., aqua, *drunk by slaves,* Cic.; civitas, Liv.; imitatorum servum pecus, Hor.; b, legal t. t., of lands or buildings, *subject to right of other persons than the owner, subject to a servitude or easement;* praedia serva, Cic.

sēsămĭnus -a -um (σησάμινος), *made of sesame,* Plin.

sēsămŏīdes -is, n. (σησαμοειδές), *a plant like sesame,* Plin.

sēsămum (-on) -i, n., **sīsămum** -i, n. and **sēsăma** -ae, f. (σήσαμον), *an oily plant, sesame,* Plaut.

sescennāris -e (sesqui and annus), *a year and a half old;* bos, Liv.

sescŭplĕx -a -um (sesqui), *one and a half times as much,* Quint.

sĕsĕlis -is, f. (σέσελις), *a plant, hartwort,* Cic.

Sĕsostrĭs -trĭdis and **Sĕsōsĭs** -sĭdis, m. (Σέσωστρις), a mythical king of Egypt.

sesquī, adv. num. (semis and qui), one half more, half as much again; sesqui major, Cic.

sesquĭalter and syncop. **sesqualter** altera -alterum (Gr. ἐπιδεύτερος), one and a half, Cic.

sesquĭhōra -ae, f. an hour and a half, Plin.

sesquĭjūgĕrum -i, n. an acre and a half, Plin.

sesquĭlībra -ae, f. a pound and a half, Cato.

sesquĭmensis -is, m. a month and a half, Varr.

sesquĭmŏdĭus -ĭi, m. a modius and a half, Cic.

sesquĭŏbŏlus -i, m. an obolus and a half, Plin.

sesquĭoctāvus -a -um, containing ⅛ of a thing, Cic.

sesquĭŏpus -ĕris, n. the work of a day and a half, Plaut.

sesquĭpĕdālis -e, a foot and a half long; tigna, Caes.; hence, poet., very long; dentes, Cat.; verba, Hor.

sesquĭpĕdānĕus = sesquipedalis (q.v.)

sesquĭpēs -pĕdis, m. a foot and a half, Plaut.

sesquĭplāga -ae, f. a blow and a half, Tac.

sesquĭplex -plĭcis, taken one and a half times, Cic.

sesquĭtertĭus -a -um, containing ⅓ of anything, Cic.

sessībŭlum -i, n. (sedeo), a seat, stool, chair, Plaut.

sessĭlis -e (sedeo), fit for sitting upon. **I.** Pass., tergum (equi), Ov. **II.** Act., of plants, low, dwarf, spreading, Plin.

sessĭo -ōnis, f. (sedeo). **I.** 1, sitting, the act of sitting; status, incessio, sessio, Cic.; sessiones quaedam (postures in sitting) contra naturam sunt, Cic.; 2, esp., a, a sitting idle, loitering in a place; Capitolina, Cic.; b, a sitting, session for discussion; pomeridiana, Cic. **II.** Meton., a place for sitting, seat, Cic.

sessĭto, 1. (intens. of sedeo), to sit much, sit always; quam deam (Suadam) in Pericli labris scripsit Eupolis sessitavisse, Cic.

sessĭuncŭla -ae, f. (dim. of sessio), a little company or assembly for conversation, Cic.

sessor -ōris, m. (sedeo). **I.** one who sits, a sitter, Hor. **II.** an inhabitant, dweller; urbis, Nep.

sestertĭus -a -um (semis-tertius), two and a half; sestertĭus -ĭi, m., and in full, sestertius nummus, genit. plur. sestertiûm nummûm, and simply sestertiûm and sestertiorum, a sesterce. **A.** a silver coin, in the time of the Republic = ¼ denarius = 2½ asses (= about 2d.), Cic.; 1, lit., sestertii duodeni, Cic.; genit. plur., sestertiûm (sc. mille), treated as a neut. noun, and so declined, = 1,000 sesterces; decies sestertiûm (sc. centena millia) = a million sesterces; centies sestertiûm = ten million sesterces, Cic.; millies sestertiûm = 100 millions, Cic.; 2, transf., nummo sestertio or sestertio nummo, for a mere trifle; nummo sestertio or sestertio nummo alicui addici, Cic. **B.** In Imperial times, a copper coin of the value of 4 asses, Plin.

Sestus (Sestōs) -i, f. (Σηστός), a town in Thrace on the Hellespont, residence of Hero, now, perhaps, Jalova. Adj., **Sestus** -a -um. Sestian; puella, Hero, Ov.

set = sed (q.v.).

sēta (saeta) -ae, f. **I.** a bristle, stiff hair; of pigs, Ov.; seta equina, horsehair, Cic.; of goats, cows, lions, Verg.; of coarse, bristly, human hair Verg. **II.** Meton., part of an angler's line, Ov.

sētānĭa -ae, f. and **sētănĭon** -ĭi, n. (σητανία) **I.** a species of medlar, Plin. **II.** a kind of onion, Plin.

sētĭgĕr (saetĭgĕr) -gĕra -gĕrum (seta and gero), having bristles, bristly; sus, Verg.; subst., sētĭgĕr -gĕri, m. a boar, Ov.

sētōsus (saetōsus) -a -um (seta), full of bristles, bristly; aper, Verg.

seu = sive (q.v.).

sĕvērē, adv. with compar. and superi. (severus), seriously, gravely, austerely, severely, Cic.

sĕvērĭtas -ātis, f. (severus), gravity, seriousness, severity, austerity, sternness, strictness; censorum, censoria, Cic.; severitatem in filio adhibere, Cic.; severitatem adhibere reipublicae causā, Cic.

sĕvērĭtūdo -ĭnis, f. = severitas (q.v.).

1. sĕvērus -a -um, grave, serious, strict, rigid, stern, austere, severe. **I.** A good sense. **A.** Lit., 1, of persons, Tubero vitā severus, Cic.; familia quum ad ceteras res tum ad judicandum severissima, Cic.; 2, of things, frons, Ov.; congressio, Cic.; subst., a, **sĕvērus** -i, m. a grave, serious man, Hor.; b, **sĕvēra** -ōrum, n. serious things, Hor. **B.** Transf., Falernum (vinum), harsh, Hor.; amnis Eumenidum or Cocyti, awful, Hor. **II.** In a bad sense, hard, cruel; a, lit., Neptunus saevus severusque, Plaut.; turba Eumenidum, Prop.; b, transf., uncus, Hor.

2. Sĕvērus -i, m. a Roman family name, the most celebrated persons bearing which were: **1,** Cornelius Severus, epic poet in the time of Augustus, friend of Ovid; **2,** L. Septimius Severus, emperor 193-211 A.D.; **3,** Aurelius Alexander Severus, emperor 222-234 A.D.

3. Sĕvērus mons, a mountain in the Sabine country, a branch of the Apennines, now Vissa.

sĕvŏco, 1. to call aside, call away. **I.** Lit., singulos, Caes.; plebem in Aventinum, Cic. **II.** Fig., to call off, call away, separate; animum a voluptate, Cic.

sēvum, etc. = sebum, etc. (q.v.).

sex, numer. (ἕξ), six, Cic.; sex septem, six or seven, Hor.

sexāgēnārĭus -a -um (sexageni), containing the number sixty; and esp., sixty years old, Quint.

sexāgēni -ae -a, genit. -ēnûm (sexaginta), sixty each, Cic.

sexāgēsĭmus -a -um (sexaginta), the sixtieth, Cic.

sexāgĭēs (sexāgĭens), adv. (sexaginta), sixty times; sestertiûm sexagies, six millions of sesterces, Cic.; so simply sexagiens, Cic.

sexāginta, num. (ἑξήκοντα). **I.** sixty, Cic. **II.** = very many, Mart.

sexangŭlus -a -um, hexagonal, Ov.

sexcēnārĭus -a -um (sexceni), consisting of six hundred; cohortes, Caes.

sexcēni (sescēni) -ae -a (sexcenti), six hundred each, Cic.

sexcentēni = sexceni (q.v.).

sexcentēsĭmus -a -um (sexcenti), the six hundredth, Cic.

sexcenti -ae -a (sex and centum). **I.** six hundred, Cic. **II.** To denote an indefinite round number = countless; epistolae, Cic.

sexcentĭēs (sexcentĭens), adv. (sexcenti), six hundred times, Cic.

sexcentŏplāgus -i, m. (sexcenti and plaga), *one who receives innumerable stripes*, Plaut.

sexdĕcim = sedecim (q.v.).

sexennis -e (sex and annis), *six years old*, Plaut.

sexennĭum -ĭi, n. (sexennis), *a period of six years*, Cic.

sexĭēs (**sexĭens**), adv. (sex), *six times*, Cic.

sexprĭmi -ōrum, m. *the six highest magistrates in colonies and municipia*, Cic.

sextādĕcĭmāni -ōrum, m. (sextusdecimus), *soldiers of the 16th legion*, Tac.

sextans -antis, m. (sex), *the sixth part of an as*, Varr.; esp., **a**, *as a coin, two unciae*, Liv.; **b**, *the sixth part of an inheritance*; in sextante sunt ii, quorum pars, etc., Cic.; **c**, *the sixth part of a pound*, Ov., **d**, *of an acre*, Varr., **e**, *of a sextarius*, Mart.

sextantārĭus -a -um (sextans), *containing a sixth part; asses sextantario pondere, weighing only one-sixth of the former asses*, Plin.

sextārĭŏlus -i, m. (dim. of sextarius), *a small liquid measure*, Suet.

sextārĭus -ĭi, m. (sextus), *the sixth part*. **I.** In liquid measure, *the sixth part of a congius* (about a pint), Cic. **II.** As a dry measure, *the sixteenth part of a modius*, Plin.

Sextĭlis -is, m. (sextus), mensis, or simply Sextilis, *the sixth month of the Roman year* (reckoning from March), afterwards called *August; kalendae* Sextiles, *the 1st of August*, Cic.

Sextĭus (**Sestĭus**) -a -um, *name of a Roman gens, the most famous members of which were*: 1, L. Sextius, *tribune of the people, the author of a law enacting that one of the consuls should always be a plebeian*; 2, P. Sextius, *tribune of the people, who proposed the recall of Cicero from exile.* Adj., *Sextian*; lex, *the above-mentioned law of L. Sextius*; tabula, *of a banker named Sextius*, Cic.; esp., Aquae Sextiae, *Roman colony near Manilia, founded by C. Sextius Calvinus*, 123 B.C., now *Aix*. Hence, adj., **Sextiānus** (**Sestiānus**) -a -um, *Sextian*.

sextŭla -ae, f. (sc. pars, from sextulus, dim. of sextus), *the sixth part of an uncia, therefore* 1-72nd of an as, Varr.; 1-72nd part of an inheritance, Cic.

sextus -a -um (sex). **I.** *the sixth*, Cic.; adv., **sextum**, *for the sixth time*; sextum consul, Cic. **II.** Sextus, *a Roman name*.

sextusdĕcĭmus -a -um, *sixteenth*, Cic.

sexus -ūs, m. (another form of secus), *the male or female sex*; **a**, of men, hominum genus et in sexu consideratur, virile an muliebre sit, Cic.; **b**, of animals, Plin.; **c**, of plants, minerals, etc., Plin.

sī, conj. (*ei*). **I.** A particle expressing condition, *if, in case that*; foll. by both indic. and subj. **A.** Gen., numquam labere, si te audies, Cic.; si minus, *if not*, Cic.; quod si, *and if, but if*, Cic. **B.** Esp., **a**, to confirm or explain or justify what has gone before, *if only, provided that*; delectus habetur, si hic delectus appellandus, Cic.; bellum vobis indictum est, magno eorum malo, qui indixere, si viri estis, Liv.; **b**, in wishes, *if only*; si nunc se ostendat, Verg.; **c**, in comparisons, *as if, just as if*; with subj., Cic., Liv.; **d**, to express a concession, *even if*; si omnes deos hominesque celare possumus, Cic. **II.** In indirect questions and dependent clauses, *whether, if*; conati, si possent, etc., Cic.; dicito, si etc., Cic.; castra movet, si . . . posset, *to try whether*, etc., Liv.

sībīlo, 1. (sibilus). **I.** Intransit., *to hiss;*

17*

of snakes, Verg.; anguis sibilat, Ov.; transf., of red-hot iron plunged into water; in tepida submersum sibilat unda, Ov. **II.** Transf., *to hiss at, hiss down*; aliquem, Cic.

1. **sībĭlus** -i, m. (plur., sibili, and in poets, sibila), *a hissing, whistling, rustling*; austri, Verg.; of persons, *whistling*; sibilo signum dare, Liv.; esp., *a contemptuous hissing*; sibilum metuis? Cic.; sibilis conscindi, Cic.; sibilis aliquem explodere, Cic.

2. **sībĭlus** -a -um, *hissing*; colla (of a snake) Verg.; ora, Verg.

Sĭbylla -ae, f. (Σίβυλλα, from Σιὸς (= Διὸς βουλή, *God's counsel*), *a prophetess and priestess of Apollo, a Sibyl; in the Roman mythol.*, esp., *the Sibyl of Cumae whom Aeneas consulted; another Sibyl of Cumae was said to have composed the Sibylline books, which were bought by Tarquin from an old woman, and kept in the Capitol, and consulted in time of danger.*

Sĭbyllīnus -a -um, *of or relating to the Sibyl, Sibylline*; libri, Cic.; vaticinatio, Cic.

sīc (from root i (whence is and ita), with the spirant prefixed and the demonstrative suffix -ce added, si-ce, which became sic), *so, thus, in this manner*. **I.** Gen., **a**, sive enim sic est, sive illo modo, Cic.; illa civitas popularis (sic enim appellant) in qua in populo sunt omnia, Cic.; **b**, to introduce something that follows, *thus, as follows*; ingressus est sic loqui Scipio, Cic.; esp., with acc. and infin., sic velim existimes, te nihil gratius facere posse, Cic.; **c**, in affirmative answers, sic est, etc.; sic plane judico, Cic. **II.** Esp., **A.** In comparisons, *so, as*; gen. corresponding to ut, more rarely to quemadmodum, tamquam, quasi, etc., Atticum sic amo, ut alterum fratrem, Cic.; quemadmodum . . . sic, Cic.; sic . . . tanquam, Cic.; sic . . . quasi, Cic.; in wishes, *so*; sic tua Cyrneas fugiant examina taxos, Verg. **B.** *of such a kind, of such a nature*; sic est vulgus; ex veritate pauca, ex opinione multa, existimant, Cic. **C.** **a**, *in such circumstances, in such a manner, so, and thus*; sic ad supplicium Numitori Remus deditur, Liv.; **b**, *consequently, in consequence*; quia non est obscura tua in me benevolentia, sic fit ut, etc., Cic. **D.** To express limitation or condition, *so = on condition that, in so far as*; gen. corresp. with ut, recordatione amicitiae sic fruor, ut beate vixisse videar, Cic.; sic . . . si, *then* . . . *if, only if*; decreverunt, id sic ratum esset, si patres auctores fierent, Liv. **E.** To express degree, *so much, to such a degree*; often foll. by ut, Caecinam a puero semper sic dilexi ut non ullo cum homine conjunctus viverem, Cic. **F.** To express carelessness, indifference, *thus, simply*; sic nudos (*naked as they are*) in flumen projicere, Cic.

sīca -ae, f. (seco). **I.** *a dagger, dirk, poniard;* maximus sicarum numerus et gladiorum, Cic. **II.** Meton., *assassination, murder*; hinc sicae, venena, falsa testamenta nascuntur, Cic.

Sĭcāni -ōrum, m. *a people of Celtic origin who originally inhabited the banks of the Tiber, and thence migrated to Sicily.* Hence, **A.** Adj., **Sĭcānus** -a -um, *Sicanian*, poet.= *Sicilian.* **B.** **Sĭcānĭus** -a -um, *Sicanian*, poet.= *Sicilian.* **C.** **Sĭcānis** -ĭdis, f. adj., *Sicanian*, poet.= *Sicilian.* **D.** Subst., **Sĭcānĭa** -ae, f. *Sicania* = *Sicily.*

sĭcārĭus -ĭi, m. (sica), *an assassin, murderer;* accusare aliquem inter sicarios, *of murder*, Cic.

Sicca -ae, f., Veneria, *an important town in Numidia, on the Bagradas, with a temple to Venus*, now *Keff*. Hence, **Siccenses** -ium, m. *the inhabitants of Sicca.*

siccānus -a -um (siccus), *dry*, Plin.

siccātĭo -ōnis, f. (sicco), *a drying*, Plin.

siccē, adv. (siccus), *dryly*; fig., of discourse; dicere, *plainly, vigorously*, Cic.

siccesco, 3. (siccus), *to become dry*, Plin.

siccĭnĕ (**sīcĭnĕ** or **sīcĭn'**), adv. (sic-ce), taterrog. particle, *is it thus? thus? so?* Cat.

siccĭtas -ātis, f. (siccus). **I.** *dryness*; **a,** lit., paludum, Caes.; **b,** meton., *dryness of weather, drought*, Cic. **II.** Transf., *freedom from humours, firm health*; **a,** lit., Cic.; **b,** fig., of discourse, *plainness, simplicity, dryness*; orationis, Cic.

sicco, 1. (siccus), *to make dry, to dry.* **I.** Transf., **A.** Gen., vellera, Verg.; herbas, Ov.; esp., *to dry up water or soil*; paludes, Cic. **B.** **a,** *to drain dry, to drink up, empty*; calices, Hor.; **b,** *to milk*; ovem, Ov.; **c,** *to suck dry*; ubera, Verg. **II.** Intransit. and impers., siccat, *it dries up*, Cat.

siccŏcŭlus -a -um (siccus and oculus), *having dry eyes*, Plaut.

siccus -a -um, *dry.* **I. A.** Lit., **1,** gen., lignum, Verg.; subst., **siccum** -i, n. *the dry land*; in sicco hibernare, Liv.; **2,** esp., **a,** *without tears, tearless*; oculi, Hor.; **b,** *dry, thirsty*; siccus, inanis, Hor.; poet., dies = *hot, thirsty*, Hor.; meton., *temperate, abstinent*, Cic.; **c,** *fasting, a poor starving wretch*; accedes siccus ad unctum, Hor.; **d,** *bright, cloudless*, Prop.; **e,** *bright, rainless*; fervores, Ov. **B.** Fig., *dry, cold, impassive*; puella, Ov. **II.** Transf., **A.** Of the body, *free from humours, in sound, vigorous health*; corpora, Plin. **B.** Of discourse, *plain, simple*; oratio, Cic.

sicĕlĭcon -i, n. (Σικελικόν), *the plant flea-wort*, Plin.

Sĭcĭlĭa -ae, f. (Σικελία), *the island of Sicily.* Hence, **A. Sĭcĕlĭs** -ĭdis, f. *Sicilian.* **B. Sĭcĭliensis** -e, *Sicilian.*

sĭcĭlĭcŭla -ae, f. (dim. of sicilis), *a small sickle*, Plaut.

sĭcĭlĭcus -i, m. (sicilis), **a,** *the 4th part of an un uncia, and therefore* 1-48th *of an as*; **b,** *a quarter of an inch*, Plin.; **c,** 1-48th *of an hour*, Plin.

sĭcĭlĭo, 4. (sicilis), *to cut or mow with the sickle*, Plin.

sĭcĭlis -is, f. (seco), *a sickle*, Plin.

Sĭcŏris -is, m. *a tributary of the Hiberus in Spain*, now *Segre.*

sīcŭbĭ, adv.(= si alicubi), *if anywhere*, Cic.

Sĭcŭli -ōrum, m. *a people of Celtic origin, akin to the Sicani, who settled on the coast of Italy, but were afterwards compelled to migrate to Sicily*; hence, transf., *the inhabitants of Sicily, the Sicilians*, Cic.; sing., **Sĭcŭlus** -i, m. *a Sicilian*, Cic.; hence, **Sĭcŭlus** -a -um, *Sicilian*; tyrannus, *Phalaris*, Ov.

sĭcundĕ, adv. (= si alicunde), *if from anywhere*, Cic.

sīcŭt and **sīcŭtĭ**, adv. *as, just as.* **I.** Gen., **a,** with a verb, sicut sapiens poeta dixit, Cic.; foll. by ita, itidem, sic; sicuti . . . ita, Liv.; sicuti . . . sic, Caes.; sicuti . . . ita, Caes.; **b,** without a verb, sicut apud nos, Cic.; viri in uxoi es, sicut in liberos potestatem, Caes.; foll. by ita, sicuti in foro, item in theatro, Cic. **II.** Esp., **1,** *inasmuch as*; sicuti cras aderit, hodie non venerit, Plaut.; **2,** sicut est, sicut erat, *as the case really is, in fact*; quamvis felix sit, sicuti est, Cic.; **3,** in a comparison, **a,** *as it were*; hic locus sicut aliquod fundamentum est huius constitutionis, Cic.; **b,** *just as if*; sicuti foret 'acessitus, Sall.; **4.** to add an example, *as, as*

for example; quibus in causis omnibus, sicuti in ipsa M. Curii, Cic.; **5,** *to express a state or condition, just as*; sicut eram, fugio, Ov.

Sĭcўōn -ōnis, m. and f. (Σικυών), *a city of Peloponnesus*; hence, adj., **Sĭcўōnius** -a -um, *Sicyonian*; calcei, Cic.; and subst., **Sĭcўōnia** -ōrum, n. *a kind of soft shoes from Sicyon*, Lucr.

Sĭda -ae, f. (Σίδη), *a town in Pamphylia, west of the river Meles*, now *Eski-Adalia.* Hence, **Sĭdētae** -ārum, m. *the inhabitants of Sida.*

sīdĕrālis -e (sidus), *of or relating to the stars*, Plin.

sīdĕrātĭo -ōnis, f. (sideror), *a blast, blight upon plants, supposed to be produced by the influence of the stars*, Plin.

sīdĕrĕus -a -um (sidus), *of or belonging to the stars, starry.* **I.** Lit., **a,** caelum, starry, Ov.; ignes, *the stars*, Ov.; Canis, *the Dog-star*, Ov.; dea = Nox, Prop.; conjux, *Ceyx* (as son of Lucifer), Ov.; **b,** esp., *of or relating to the sun, solar*; ignes, Ov.; lux, Ov. **II.** Transf., *gleaming, glittering*; clipeus, Verg.

sĭdĕrĭon -ĭi, n. (σιδήριον), *the plant vervain*, Plin.

sĭdĕrītes -ae, m. (σιδηρίτης) = sideritis(q.v.).

sĭdĕrītis -is, f. (σιδηρῖτις). **I.** *a stone*; **a,** *a magnet*, Plin.; **b,** *a kind of diamond*, Plin. **II.** *a plant, vervain*, Plin.

sīdĕror, 1. (sidus) = sidere afflari, *to suffer from a sun-stroke, be planet-struck*, Plin.

Sīdĭcīni -ōrum, m. *a people of Campania, whose chief town was Teanum.* Hence, adj., **Sīdĭcīnus** -a -um, *Sidicine.*

sīdo, sīdi and sēdi, sessum, 3. (ἵζω), *to sit down, settle, alight.* **I.** Lit., of living creatures, columbae super arbore sidunt, Verg.; imusne sessum? Cic. **II.** Transf., of inanimate things. **A.** Gen., *to sink down, settle*; orta ex lacu nebula campo quam montibus densior sederat, Liv. **B.** Esp., **1,** *to remain lying or fixed, to settle*; **a,** quum sederit glans, Liv.; **b,** naut. t. t., *to stick fast, to be stranded*; ubi cymbae siderent, Liv.; **2,** *to sink* = *to vanish, disappear*, Prop., Tac.

Sīdon -ōnis, f. (Σιδών), *a city of Phoenicia.* Hence, adj., **A. Sīdōnius** -a -um, *Phoenician*; *Sidonian*; amor, *of Jupiter for Europa*, Mart.; esp., of purple, ostrum, Ov.; subst., **Sīdōnĭi** -ōrum, m. *the Sidonians or Tyrians.* **B. Sīdōnĭcus** -a -um, *Sidonian.* **C. Sīdōnis** -ĭdis, f. *Sidonian, Tyrian*; concha, *Tyrian purple*, Ov.; tellus, *Phoenicia*, Ov.; subst. = *the Sidonian woman*; Europa, Ov.; Dido, Ov.; Anna, *sister of Dido*, Ov.

sīdus -ĕris, n. *a group of stars, constellation*, sometimes used of a single star. **I. A.** Lit., **a,** (α) sing., sidus Vergiliarum, Liv.; sidus aetherium, Ov.; (β) plur., illi sempiterni ignes, quae sidera et stellas vocatis, Cic.; **b,** poet., sidera solis (of the sun itself), Ov. **B.** Meton., **1,** sing., **a,** *the time of year*; hiberno sidere, *in winter*, Verg.; mutato sidere, *at another time of the year*, Verg.; **b,** *the day*; brumale, *the shortest day*, Ov.; **c,** *climate, regions*; tot sidera emensae, Verg.; **d,** *weather*; grave sidus et imber, Ov.; Minervae, *storm raised by Minerva*, Verg.; **e,** *a star, as bringing disaster* (cf. sideratio), haud secus quam pestifero sidere icti, Liv.; **2,** plur., *the heavens*; ad sidera missus, Juv.; ad sidera ferre, *to praise to the skies*, Verg.; poma ad sidera nituntur, *grow up*, Verg.; sub sidera lapsae, Verg.; vertice sideri tangere, Ov., or ferire, Hor., *to touch the stars, to be elevated in happiness or prosperity beyond measure*; sub pedibus videt nubes et sidera, *ü raised to heaven*, Verg. **II.** Transf., **1,** of beautiful eyes, geminum, sua lumina, sidus, Ov.; 2, *pride, glory;* O sidus Fabiae, Maxime, gentis, Ov.

Sĭgambri = Sugambri (q.v.).

Sĭgēum -i, n. (Σίγειον), *a promontory and port in Troas, where was the grave of Achilles,* now *Jenischer.* Hence, **A. Sĭgēus** -a -um, *Sigean.* **B. Sĭgēĭus** -a -um, *Sigean.*

sĭgilla -ōrum, n. (dim. of signum), *small figures, images;* patella in qua sigilla erant egregia, Cic.; *statuettes,* Cic.; *figures cut upon a signet-ring,* Cic., and hence, *a seal,* Hor.

Sĭgillāria -ōrum, abl. -iis and -ibus, n. (sigilla). **I.** *a festival in Rome, at which little figures were exchanged as presents,* Suet. **II.** *the little images thus used,* Sen. **III.** *a place in Rome where such images were sold,* Suet.

sĭgillātus -a -um (sigilla), *ornamented with small figures;* scyphi, Cic.

sĭgillum, v. sigilla.

sigma -ātis, n. (σίγμα), *the Greek letter sigma,* and hence, *a semicircular dining-couch in the original shape of a capital sigma* (C), Mart.

signātor -ōris, m. (signo), *one who seals a document as a witness;* a, *the witness to a will,* Suet.; signatores falsi, *forgers of wills,* Sall.; b, *the witness to a marriage-contract,* Juv.

Signĭa -ae, f. *a city in Latium,* now *Segni.* Hence, adj., **Signīnus** -a -um, *of or belonging to Signia;* opus, or simply subst., **Signīnum** -i, n. *a kind of plaster for walls and pavements;* plur. subst., **Signīni** -ōrum, m. *the inhabitants of Signia.*

signĭfĕr -fĕra -fĕrum (signum and fero), *bearing figures, adorned with figures.* **I.** Gen., puppis, Lucan. **II.** Esp., **A.** *bearing stars, covered with constellations;* aether, Lucr.; orbis, *the zodiac,* Cic. **B.** Subst., **signĭfĕr** -fĕri m., milit. t. t., *a standard-bearer,* Caes., Cic.; transf., *a leader, head;* calamitosorum, Cic.; juventutis, Cic.

signĭfĭcābĭlis -e (significo), *significant, conveying a meaning;* vox, Varr.

signĭfĭcans -antis, p. adj. (from significo), *graphic, distinct, clear,* Quint.

signĭfĭcantĕr, adv. (significans), *plainly, distinctly, clearly;* acrius, apertius, significantius dignitatem alicuius defendere, Cic.

signĭfĭcantĭa -ae, f. (significo), *expressiveness, energy, distinctness,* Quint.

signĭfĭcātĭo -ōnis, f. (significo). **I.** *a showing, pointing out, indicating, sign, token, indication;* a, absol., declarare aliquid significatione, Cic.; b, with subject. genit., litterarum, Cic.; c, with object. genit., virtutis, Cic.; d, with acc. and infin., significatio fit non adesse constantiam, Cic. **II.** Esp., 1, *a sign of assent, approbation, applause;* significatio omnium, Cic.; significatione florere, Cic.; 2, *a sign, prognostic of a change of weather,* Plin.; 3, *emphasis,* Cic.; 4, *the meaning, signification of a word;* scripti, Cic.

signĭfĭcātus -ūs, m. (significo), *a sign, prognostic of a change of weather,* Plin.

signĭfĭco, 1. (signum and facio), *to give a sign, indication, to indicate, notify.* **I.** Gen., a, with acc., hoc mihi significasse et annuisse visus est, Cic.; b, with acc. and infin., omnes significabant ab eo se esse admodum delectatos, Cic.; c, with ut and the subj., ut statim dimitterentur, Caes.; d, with rel. sent., litterae neque unde neque quo die datae essent significabant, Cic.; e, with de and the abl., de fuga, Caes. **II.** Esp., **A.** *to indicate that which is to come;* a, futura, Cic.; b, *to give signs of, indicate a change*

of weather, Plin. **B.** Of words, *to mean, signify,* uno verbo significari res duas, Cic.

Signīnus, v. Signia.

signo, 1. (signum), *to put a mark upon, mark, designate.* **I.** Lit., **A.** Gen., humum limite, Ov.; caeli regionem in cortice signant, *cut in,* inscribe, Verg.; sonos vocis, Cic.; humum pede certo, *to tread on,* Hor. **B.** Esp., 1, *to mark with a seal, seal, seal up;* libellum, Cic.; volumina, Hor.; arcanas tabellas, Ov.; 2, *to coin,* stamp money; argentum signatum, Cic.; 3, *to adorn;* honore, Verg. **II.** Fig., **A.** Gen., signatum memori pectore nomen habe, Ov. **B.** Esp., 1, *to signify, express;* ossa nomen (Cajeta) signat, Verg.; 2, *to observe, notice;* ora sono discordia, Verg.

signum -i, n. (perhaps connected with εἰκών, εἰκός, a sign, mark, token.* **I.** Gen., signa et notae locorum, Cic.; signum imprimere pecori, Verg.; signa pedum sequi, *to follow the footsteps,* Ov.; signa doloris ostendere, Cic. **II.** Esp., **A.** Milit. t. t., 1, *a standard, flag, banner;* a, of large divisions of an army, *the legion,* etc.; signa relinquere, *to desert,* Sall.; signa ferre, *to march away,* Caes.; signa convelli jubere, *to give the signal for marching away,* Liv.; signa inferre, *to attack,* Caes.; signa conferre, (a) *to bring the standards together,* Caes., (β) *to fight;* cum Alexandrinis, Cic.; b, of small divisions, of cohorts and maniples, Cic.; hence, transf. = *a small division of the army, company;* signa et ordines, Liv.; 2, a, *the signal, order, command given by the general;* signum pugnae proponere, Liv.; signum tubâ dare, Caes.; b, *a watchword, pass-word;* it bello tessera signum, Verg. **B.** *the sign* or *signal in the circus given by the praetor* or *consul for the races to begin;* signum mittendis quadrigis dare, Liv. **C.** *a sign, token, indication of the future;* signum se objicit, Cic.; medici signa habent ex venis, Cic. **D.** *a sign = a proof;* hoc signi est, id signi est, or signum est with acc. and infin., Cic. **E.** *a figure, image, statue;* signum aëneum, marmoreum, Cic.; hence, a, *a seal, signet,* Cic.; b, *a group of stars, constellation,* Cic.

sil, sĭlis, f. *a kind of yellow earth, ochre,* Plin.

Sĭla ae, f. *a forest in Bruttii.*

sĭlācĕus -a -um (sil), *like ochre;* color, Plin.

sĭlānus -i, m. (Σιληνός), *a fountain* (frequently made to issue from the head of Silenus), Lucr.

Sĭlārus -i, m. *a river in Lucania,* now *Sele.*

sĭlaus -i, m. *a species of parsley,* Plin.

sĭlens, v. sileo.

sĭlentĭum -ĭi, n. (sileo), *silence, stillness, quietness.* **I.** Lit., **A.** Gen., audire aliquid magno silentio, Cic.; silentium fieri jubere, Cic.; animadvertere cum silentio, *to notice in silence,* Ter.; silentio praeterire, Cic.; silentium noctis, *the stillness of night,* Caes.; ruris, Ov. **B.** Esp., a, *freedom from disturbance,* and hence, *completeness, perfectness in taking the auspices;* id silentium dicimus in auspiciis, quod omni vitio caret, Cic.; b, *obscurity, ingloriousness;* laudem eorum a silentio vindicare, Cic. **II.** Transf., *quiet, repose, inactivity;* judiciorum ac fori, Cic.; vitam silentio transire, Cic.

Sĭlēnus -i, m. (Σεληνός), *the tutor and attendant of Bacchus, represented with a bald head, as always drunk, and riding on an ass.*

sĭlĕo -ŭi, 2. *to be still, noiseless, silent.* **I.** Lit., 1, of persons, a, absol., or with de and the abl., optimum quemque silere, Liv.; ceteri de nobis silent, Cic.; partic., silens, *silent;* umbrae silentes (of the dead), Verg.; subst., **sĭlentes,** *the silent;* (a) = *the dead;* rex silentum (Pluto), Ov.; (β) *the Pythagoreans;*

coetus silentum, Ov.; **b**, with acc., *to be silent about;* tu hoc silebis, Cic.; neque te silebo, Hor.; in pass., res siletur, Cic.; partic. subst., **sĭlenda** -ōrum, n. *things to be silent about, secrets, mysteries,* Liv.; **2,** of things, silet aer, Ov.; aequor, Verg.; nox, Verg.; with foll. rel. sent., si chartae sileant quod bene feceris, Hor.; partic., **sĭlens,** *quiet, still;* nox, Verg.; agmen, Liv. **II.** Transf., *to rest, to be inactive;* **a,** of persons, silent diutius Musae quam solebant, Cic.; **b,** of things, si quando ambitus sileat, Cic. (partic. pres. in abl., gen. silente; syncop. genit. plur., silentum, Verg., Ov.).

sĭler -ĕris, n. *a species of willow, the brook-willow,* Verg.

sĭlesco, 3. (inchoat. of sileo), *to become silent, grow still,* Verg.

sĭlex -ĭcis, m. (rarely f.), *any hard stone, flint, granite, basalt,* esp. *as material for pavement.* **I.** Lit., certo in loco silicem caedere, Cic.; vias in urbe silice sternere, Liv.; as fig. of cruelty or hardheartedness, dicam silices pectus habere tuum, Ov. **II.** Poet., transf., = *scopulus, rock, cliff;* acuta silex praecisis undique saxis, Verg.

Sĭlĭānus, v. Silius.

sĭlĭcernĭum -ĭi, n. *a funeral feast,* Varr.; hence, transf., as a term of abuse applied to an infirm old man, Ter.

sĭlĭcĭa -ae, f. *the plant fenugreek,* Plin.

sĭlĭcŭla -ae, f. (dim. of siliqua), *a little pod or husk,* Varr.

sĭlĭgĭnĕus -a -um (siligo), *made of wheat, wheaten,* Plin.

sĭlĭgo -ĭnis, f. **1,** *a kind of very white wheat* (Triticum hibernum, Linn.), Plin.; **2,** meton., *wheaten flour,* Juv.

sĭlĭqua -ae, f. *a husk, pod, shell,* Verg.; plur., **sĭlĭquae** -ārum, *pulse,* Hor.

sĭlĭquor, 1. dep. (siliqua), *to put forth or get pods,* Plin.

Sĭlĭus -a -um, *name of a Roman gens:* **1,** A. Silius, *a friend of Cicero;* **2,** P. Silius Nerva, *propraetor in Bithynia and Pontus,* 51 B.C.; **3,** C. Silius Italicus, *an epic poet of the first century* A.D., *author of an epic poem on the Punic War in seventeen books.* Hence, **Sĭlĭānus** -a -um, *relating to Silius.*

sillȳbus = sittybos (q.v.).

silphĭum -ĭi, n. (σίλφιον) = laserpitium (q.v.).

Sĭlūres -um, acc. -as, *a people in Britain, to the west of the Severn and the Avon.*

sĭlūrus -i, m. (σίλουρος), *a species of river-fish,* prob. *the sheat-fish,* Juv.

sĭlus -a -um (σιλλός and σιλός) = simus, *flat-nosed, snub-nosed, pug-nosed,* Cic.

silva (sylva) -ae, f. (connected with ὕλη), *a wood, forest.* **I.** Lit., **a,** silva densa, Cic.; silvarum dea, *Diana,* Ov.; **b,** *a plantation, a grove, a park;* signa in silva disposita, Cic.; **2,** meton., **a,** *a quantity of shrubs or plants, underwood,* Verg; **b,** poet., *a tree or trees,* Verg., Ov. **II.** Transf., **1,** *a dense mass or quantity;* immanem aerato circumfert tegmine silvam, *a dense mass of spears,* Verg.; **2,** *plentiful supply, abundance;* virtutum et vitiorum, Cic.; esp., of materials for speaking and writing, silva rerum, Cic.; omnis ubertas et quasi silva dicendi, Cic. (silvae, trisyll. in Hor.).

Silvānus -i, m. (silva), *a Latin god of forests and the country;* plur., Silvani, *gods of the forests and the country.*

silvātĭcus -a -um (silva), **1,** *of or relating to*

a forest or wood, Varr.; **2,** of plants and animals, *wild,* Plin.

silvesco, 3. (silva), (of a vine), *to run wild, to run to wood,* Cic.

silvester -tris -tre and gen. **silvestris** -e (silva). **I.** *belonging to a wood or forest;* **a,** *covered with trees, wooded, woody;* collis, Caes.; locus, Cic.; subst., **silvestria** -ĭum, n. *woody places;* **b,** *living or being in the woods;* belua, Cic.; homines, Hor.; cursus, Cic. **II.** Transf., **A.** *growing wild, wild;* oliva, Ov. **B.** *rural, pastoral;* Musa, Verg.

Silvĭa, v. 1. Rhea.

silvĭcŏla -ae, c. (silva and colo), *an inhabitant of the woods,* Verg.

silvĭcultrix -trīcis, f. (silva and colo), *inhabiting the woods,* Cat.

silvĭfrăgus -a -um (silva and frango), *shattering the woods,* Lucr.

silvĭgĕr -gĕra -gĕrum (silva and gero), *wooded, covered with forests;* montes, Plin.

silvōsus -a -um (silva), *well wooded, abounding in forests;* saltus, Liv.

Simbrŭvĭum -ĭi, n. *a district in the country of the Aequi.* Hence, **Simbrŭīnus** -a -um, *relating to Simbruvium.*

sĭmĭa -ae, f. and **sĭmĭus** -i, m. (simus), *an ape, monkey,* Cic.; used as a term of abuse of men, simius iste, Hor.

sĭmĭla -ae, f. *the finest wheaten flour,* Mart.

sĭmĭlāgo = simila (q.v.).

sĭmĭlis -e (connected with simul, simulare), *like, resembling, similar;* **a,** with genit. (nearly always so in Cicero when used of persons) fratris, hominis, Cic.; simile veri, Cic.; non est veri simile ut occiderit, Cic.; mihi minus simile veri visum est, with acc. and infin., Liv.; compar., veri similius, Liv.; similiores Atticorum, Cic.; superl., simillimum veri, Cic.; **b,** with dat., si similes Icilio tribunos haberet, Liv.; quid simile habet epistola aut judicio aut contioni, Cic.; compar., similius id vero fecit, Liv.; superl., simillimus deo, Cic.; **c,** with dat. and genit. together, similis illi . . . similis deorum, Cic.; **d,** with inter se, homines inter se quum formā tum moribus similes, Cic.; **e,** foll. by atque, ut si, tamquam si, Cic.; **f,** absol., animus, Cic. Subst., **simĭle** -is, n. *a resemblance,* Cic.

sĭmĭlĭtĕr, adv. (similis), *in like manner, similarly;* foll. by atque, ut si, Cic.

sĭmĭlĭtūdo -ĭnis, f. (similis), *likeness, similitude, resemblance.* **I.** **1,** gen., est inter ipsos similitudo, Cic.; est homini cum deo similitudo, Cic.; veri similitudo, *probability,* Cic.; plur., similitudines, concr., *similar things,* Cic.; **2,** esp., **a,** *likeness in a portrait,* Cic.; **b,** *a metaphor, simile,* Cic. **II.** Transf., **1,** *a comparison, similitude,* Cic.; **2,** *uniformity,* Cic.

sĭmĭlo = simulo (q.v.).

sĭmĭŏlus -i, m. (dim. of simius), *a little ape* (of a man), Cic.

sĭmĭtū, adv., old form of simul (q.v.).

Sĭmŏis -mŏentis, m. (Σιμόεις), *a small stream in Troas, falling into the Scamander.*

Sĭmōnĭdes -is, m. (Σιμωνίδης), *a lyric poet of Cos.* Adj., **Sĭmōnĭdēus** -a -um, *Simonidean.*

simplex -plĭcis (sim = *simple,* cf. sincerus, and plex, from plico), *simple, uncompounded, unmixed.* **I.** Lit., **a,** natura animantis, Cic.; aqua, *pure,* Ov.; jus, Hor.; **b,** *single,* one; simplici ordine urbem intrare, Liv.; plus vice simplici, *more than once,* Hor. **II.** Transf., **A. a,** *plain, simple, not complicated;* causa, Cic.; genus

mortis, *without torture,* Liv.; necessitudo, *unconditional,* Cic.; **b,** *natural, simple;* ratio veritatis, Cic. **B.** Esp., *morally simple, straightforward, upright, guileless;* animus apertus ac simplex, Cic.

simplĭcĭtas -ātis, f. (simplex). **I.** *simplicity, simpleness,* Lucr. **II.** *moral simplicity, straightforwardness, guilelessness, honesty, candour;* puerilis, Liv.; sermo antiquae simplicitatis, Liv.

simplĭcĭtĕr, adv. (simplex). **I. a,** *plainly, straightforwardly, directly;* defendere, Cic.; sententiam referre, Cic.; **b,** *simply, without art, artlessly;* loqui, Cic. **II.** Esp., *frankly, candidly, honestly,* Tac.

simplus -a -um (ἁπλοῦς), *simple.* Subst., **simplum** -i, n. *that which is single* (opp. duplum), Cic.

simpŭlum -i, n. *a ladle;* prov., excitare fluctus in simpulo, *to make a storm in a tea-cup, to make much ado about nothing,* Cic.

simpŭvĭum -ĭi, n. *a sacrificial vessel,* Cic.

sĭmŭl (archaic **sémŭl**), adv. (connected with ἅμα), *at once, at the same time as.* **I.** Gen., **a,** absol., venire, Cic.; simul commonefacere, Caes.; **b,** with cum, testamentum simul obsignavi cum Clodio, Cic.; **c,** with et, que, atque, simul et ostendi, Cic.; simul inflatus exacerbatusque, Liv.; simul honoribus atque virtutibus, Liv.; **d,** with abl., simul septemviris, Tac.; simul his dictis, Verg. **II.** Special phrases. **A.** simul . . . simul, *not only . . . but at the same time, partly . . . partly* (ἅμα μὲν . . . ἅμα δὲ); increpando simul temeritatem, simul ignaviam, Liv.; foll. by ut or ne and subj., by quod and indic. or subj., simul sui purgandi causā, simul ut, etc., Caes. **B.** simulatque (simulac), *as soon as;* **a,** simulatque cognitum est, Cic.; **b,** with ut, simul ut experrecti sumus, Cic.; **c,** simul alone (as a conj.), simul inflavit tibicen, Cic. **C.** (Like Gr. ἅμα) with partic. pres., simul hoc dicens, *while saying this,* Verg.

sĭmŭlācrum -i, n. (from simulo, as lavacrum from lavo), *an image, likeness, portrait, effigy.* **I.** Lit., **1, a,** oppidorum, Cic.; Helenae, Cic.; **b,** *a doll;* simulacra cerea, Ov.; **2,** *a reflection in a mirror, a shadow, vision in a dream or seen in fancy;* **a,** *a reflection in a mirror or in water,* Lucr.; **b,** *a shade, ghost,* Ov.; **c,** *a vision in a dream;* vana (noctis), Ov.; **d,** t. t. of the Epicurean philosophy, *a conception of an object in the mind,* Lucr.; **e,** *the recollection of a thing,* Cic.; **3,** transf., in a discourse, *a character-picture,* Liv. **II.** Fig., as opposed to what is real, **1,** *a mere image, imitation;* simulacra virtutis, Cic.; **2,** esp., **a,** *a phantom, appearance;* religionis, Cic.; **b,** *a shade, ghost* (of something lost); auspiciorum, Cic.

sĭmŭlāmen -ĭnis, n. (simulo), *an imitation,* Ov.

sĭmŭlans -antis, p. adj. (from simulo), only in compar., *imitating, imitative;* simulantior vocum ales, *the parrot,* Ov.

sĭmŭlātē, adv. (simulatus), *in appearance, feignedly,* Cic.

sĭmŭlātĭo -ōnis, f. (simulo), *the assumed appearance of anything, pretence, feint, simulation, false show;* imitatio simulatioque virtutis, Cic.; agere cum simulatione timoris, Cic.; absol., simulatio ficta, Cic.

sĭmŭlātor -ōris, m. (simulo). **I.** *an imitator;* figurae, Ov. **II.** Transf., *a hypocritical imitator, hypocrite, counterfeiter, feigner;* segnitiae, Tac.; cuius rei libet simulator ac dissimulator, Cic.; simulator in omni oratione; *a master in irony,* Cic.

sĭmŭlo, **1.** (similis), *to make like.* **I.** Lit., **A.** Gen., Minerva simulata Mentori, Cic. **B.** Esp., **1,** *to present, represent;* cupressum, Hor.; **2,** *to imitate;* nimbos, Verg.; Catonem, Hor. **II.** Transf., *to put on the appearance of, simulate, feign, counterfeit;* simulare gaudia vultu, Ov.; lacrimas, Ov.; negotia, Sall.; aegrum, *to play the part of a sick man,* Liv.; aliud agentes, aliud simulantes, Cic.; with acc. and infin., se furere, Cic.; poet., with infin. alone, simulat Jove natus abire, Ov.; absol., non sui commodi causā simulare, Cic. Esp., partic., **sĭmŭlātus** -a -um, *feigned, counterfeit;* nec simulatum quidquam potest esse diurnum, *nothing counterfeit can be lasting,* Cic.

sĭmultas -ātis, f. (= similitas, as facultas = facilitas), *enmity towards some one who is like us, rivalry, jealousy, feud, animosity, dissension, hatred;* **a,** sing., simultatem deponere, Cic.; **b,** plur., simultates exercere cum aliquo, Cic.; simultates dirimere, Cic.

sĭmŭlus -a -um (dim. of simus), *a little pug-nosed, somewhat snub-nosed,* Lucr.

sīmus -a -um (σιμός), *flat-nosed, pug-nosed, snub-nosed,* Verg.

sin, conj. *but if, if however.* **I.** With preceding particle, si, nisi, *if* . . . *but if,* Cic.; si . . . sin aliter, Cic.; si . . . sin autem, Cic.; sin minus, sin aliter, sin secus, ellipt., *but if not, if on the contrary,* Cic. **II.** Without preceding particle, Cic.; strengthened, sin autem, Cic.

sĭnāpi, indecl. n. and **sĭnāpis** -is, acc. -im, abl. -e and gen. -i, f. (σίναπι), *mustard,* Plin.

sincērē, adv. (sincerus), *honestly, frankly, sincerely;* loqui, Cic.; pronuntiare, Caes.

sincērĭtas -ātis, f. (sincerus). **I.** *purity, freedom from adulteration, clearness,* Plin. **II.** *uprightness, integrity,* Phaedr.

sincērus -a -um (from sin = simple and cerus, connected with cresco, cf. procerus = simply grown). **I.** *pure, unmixed, unadulterated, genuine;* **a,** lit., secernere fucata et simulata a sinceris atque veris, Cic.; genae, Ov.; **b,** transf., *upright, honourable, sincere;* nihil sinceri, Cic.; fides, Liv. **II.** *pure;* **1,** *sound, healthy;* **a,** lit., corpus, Ov.; sincerum integrumque conserva, Cic.; **b,** transf., *uninjured, undestroyed;* Minerva, Ov.; judicium, Cic.; **2,** *unmixed, pure, mere;* **a,** lit., proelium equestre, Liv.; **b,** fig., voluptas, Cic.; gaudium, Liv.

sinciput -pĭtis, n. (for semi caput). **I.** *half a head;* esp., *the smoked chap of a pig,* Juv. **II.** Meton., *the brain,* Plaut.

sindon -ōnis, f. (σινδών), *fine cotton cloth, muslin,* Mart.

sĭnē, prep. with abl., *without* (opp. cum), semper ille ante cum uxore, tum sine ea, Cic.; sine dubio, Cic.; sine ulla dubitatione, *without doubt,* Cic.; sometimes placed after its case, vitiis nemo sine nascitur, Hor.

singŭlārĭtĕr, adv. (singulus), *singly,* Lucr.

singillātim (singŭlātim), adv. (singulus), *singly, one by one,* Cic.

singŭlāris -e (singuli), *belonging to single persons or things.* **I.** Lit., **A.** gen., **a,** *single, individual;* ubi aliquos singulares ex nave egredi conspexerant, Caes.; non est singulare nec solivagum genus hoc, Cic.; **b,** *relating to an individual;* imperium, potentia, *absolute rule,* Cic. Esp., **1,** grammat. t. t., *singular, belonging to the singular number,* Quint.; **2,** subst., **singŭlāres** -ium, m. *a select body of life-guards in the imperial service,* Tac. **II.** Fig., *single in its kind, distinguished, eminent, singular, unique, extra-*

ordinary; **a**, in a good sense, ingenio atque animo singulares, Cic.; Pompeii singularis eximiaque virtus, Cic.; **b**, in a bad sense, *exceptional*; nequitia, Cic.

singŭlărĭtĕr, adv. (singularis). **I.** *singly*; **a**, Lucr.; **b**, *in the singular number*, Quint. **II.** Transf., *particularly, singularly, extraordinarily*; aliquem diligere, Cic.

singŭlārĭus -a -um (singularis), *single*; catenae, *once twisted* (or *one pound in weight*), Plaut.

singŭlātim = singillatim (q.v.).

singŭli, v. singulus.

singultim, adv. (singultus), *in sobs*; transf. = *stammeringly*; pauca loqui, Hor.

singultĭo, 4. (singultus). **I.** *to hiccough*, Plin. **II.** *to throb*, Pers.

singulto, 1. (singultus). **I.** Intransit., *to hiccough, to sob*, Quint.; of dying persons, *to rattle in the throat*, Verg. **II.** Transit., *to sob out, gasp out*; animam, Ov.

singultus -ūs, m. (singuli). **I.** *weeping, sobbing*; **a**, of persons, singultuque pias interrumpente querellas, Ov.; multas lacrimas et fletum cum singultu videre potuisti, Cic.; **b**, of persons dying, *rattling in the throat*, Verg. **II.** Of similar sounds, *the croaking of a raven, the gurgling of water*, Plin.

singŭlus -a -um, more freq. in plur., **singŭli** -ae -a (from sim = semel, *singly*, as simplex). **I.** *single, a single person* or *thing, one alone*; **a**, sing., singulum-vestigitam, Plaut.; **b**, plur., frequentes an pauci an singuli, Cic. **II.** Distributive, *one each*; legiones singulas posuit Brundisii, Tarenti, etc., *one legion at Brundisium, one at Tarentum*, Cic.; filiae singulos filios habentes, Liv.

Sĭnis -is, m. (Σίνις, i.e., *he that injures*), *a robber on the isthmus of Corinth, killed by Theseus.*

sĭnister -tra -trum, *left, on the left hand*. **I.** Lit., **A.** Adj., manus, Nep.; ripa, Hor.; compar., **sĭnistĕrĭor** -us, rota, Ov. **B.** Subst., 1, **sĭnistra** -ae, f. **a**, *the left hand*, Caes.; used in stealing, natae ad furta sinistrae, Ov.; **b**, *the left side*; dextrā sinistrā, Cic.; sub sinistra, Caes.; 2, **sĭnistri** -ōrum, m. *the left wing of a line of battle*, Liv. **II.** 1, *awkward, wrong, perverse*; mores, Verg.; 2, *unfavourable, adverse*; signa, Ov.; notus pecori sinister, Verg.; 3, t.t. of augury, **a**, amongst the Romans, who, turning towards the south, had the east on the left, *favourable*; tonitrus, Ov.; **b**, among the Greeks, who, turning towards the north, had the east on the right, *unfavourable*; omen, Ov.

sĭnistĕrĭtas -ātis, f. (sinister), *left-handedness, awkwardness*, Plin.

sĭnistrē, adv. (sinister), *unfavourably, unpropitiously*; excipere, Hor.; rescribere, Tac.

sĭnistrorsus (**sĭnistrorsum**), adv. (for sinistroversus, sinistroversum), *on the left hand*, Caes., Hor.

sĭno, sīvi, sĭtum, 3. lit., *to place, put down, to set down*; only used in this sense in the partic. situs, and in the compound pono (= posino); in the finite verb only transf., *to permit, allow, suffer*. **I.** Gen., **a**, with acc. and infin., vinum ad se importari omnino non sinunt, Caes.; non transalpinas gentes oleam et vitem serere non sinimus, Cic.; in pass., with nom. and infin., hic accusare eum moderate per senatus auctoritatem non est situs, Cic.; **b**, with subj. alone, sire pascat aretque, Hor.; **c**, with acc., sinite arma viris, Verg.; **d**, absol., non feram, non patiar, non sinam, Cic. **II.** Esp., **A.** In conversation, sine, *let* = *may*; feriant sine litora

fluctus, Verg.; or simply sine, *good, be it so*, Plaut. **B.** ne di sinant (sirint), ne Juppiter sirit, *God forbid*, Liv. (perf. tenses syncop., sisti, sistis, siris, sirit, siritis; pluperf., sisset and sissent). Hence, **sĭtus** -a -um. **I.** Partic., *placed, laid down*; 1, gen., Plaut.; 2, esp., **a**, *built*; Philippopolis a Philippo sita, Liv.; **b**, *buried*; C. Marii sitae reliquiae apud Anienem, Cic. **II.** P. Adj. = *lying, situate*. **A.** Lit., 1, gen., lingua in ore sita est, Cic.; 2, esp., of places, *situate*; locus situs in media insula, Cic. **B.** Fig., 1, gen., voluptates in medio sitas esse dicunt, Cic.; 2, esp., situm esse in aliqua re or in aliquo, *to rest upon, depend upon*; assensio quae est in nostra potestate sita, Cic.

Sĭnōpa -ae, f. and **Sĭnōpē** -ēs, f. (Σινώπη). **I.** *a town in Paphlagonia on the Black Sea, a colony from Miletus, birth-place of the cynic Diogenes*, now *Sinap, Sinabe, Sinub*. Hence, **A. Sĭnōpensis** -e, *belonging to Sinope*. **B. Sĭnōpeus** -ěi, m. (Σινωπεύς), *the Sinopian*; Cynicus, Diogenes, Ov. **C. Sĭnōpis** -ĭdis, f. *a kind of red ochre, found near Sinope*. **II.** *a Greek town in Latium, afterwards called Sinuessa* (q.v.).

Sĭnŭessa -ae, f. (Σινόεσσα or Σινύεσσα), *a town in Latium, formerly called Sinope, colonised by Romans, the neighbourhood of which was famous for its wine and warm baths*. Adj., **Sĭnŭessānus** -a -um, *of* or *belonging to Sinuessa*.

sĭnum, v. 1. sinus.

sĭnŭo, 1. (2. sinus), *to bend, curve*; terga, Verg.; arcum, Ov.; pass. as middle, muri introrsus sinuati, *bent inwards*. Tac.; serpens sinuatur in arcus, Ov.

sĭnŭōsus -a -um (2. sinus). **I.** *full of windings, bendings, curves, sinuous*; vestis, Ov.; flexus (anguis), Verg. **II.** Fig., of discourse, *diffuse, digressive*, Quint.

1. **sĭnus** -i, m. and **sĭnum** -i. n. *a large bowl, a basin*, Verg.

2. **sĭnus** -ūs, m. *a bending, curve, fold*. **I.** Gen., of the windings of a snake, Cic.; of the curls of hair, Ov.; *the fold of a garment*, sinu ex toga facto, Liv.; *the belly of a sail swollen by the wind*; sinus implere secundos, Verg.; pleno pandere vela sinu, Ov.; cedendo sinum in medio dedit, *formed a curve*, Liv. **II.** Esp., **A.** *the lap*; 1, lit., a, a sinum implere floribus, Ov.; **b**, *the hanging fold of the toga, the bosom, lap*; litteras in sinu ponere, Liv.; optatum negotium sibi in sinum delatum esse dicebat, Cic.; in sinu gaudere, *to rejoice in secret*, Cic.; 2, meton., *a garment*; indue regales sinus, Ov.; 3, a, *the bosom*; hence, *love, affection, affectionate protection*; in sinu est meo, *is my darling*, Cic.; in sinu gestare, *to hold dear*, Cic.; **b**, *the inmost part of anything, the heart*; in sinu urbis sunt hostes, Sall. **B.** *a bay, gulf*; a, lit., maritimus, Cic.; **b**, meton., *land on a bay* or *gulf*, Liv. **C.** *a chasm in the earth*, Liv. (dat. and abl. plur., always sinibus).

sĭpārĭum -ĭi, n. (dim. of siparum = supparum). **I.** *a drop-scene at a theatre*; a, lit., Cic.; **b**, meton. = *comedy*, Juv. **II.** *a curtain to exclude the sun*, Quint.

sĭpho (**sĭpo**) -ōnis, m. (σίφων), *a siphon*, Juv.

Sĭpontum -i, n. (Σιποῦς), *an important harbour in Apulia*, now *Maria di Siponto*. Adj., **Sĭpontīnus** -a -um, *Sipontine*.

siptachŏras -ae, m. *an Indian tree, supposed to yield amber*, Plin.

Sĭpỹlus -i, m. (Σίπυλος), *a mountain in Lydia, where, according to the legend, Niobe was turned into stone.*

sīquandŏ, adv. *if ever*, Cic.

sīquĭdem, conj. **I.** *if indeed*, Cic. **II.** *since, because*, Cic.

sīraeum -i, n. (σίραιον) = sapa (q.v.).

sīremps and **sīrempse** (similis re ipsā), *the same;* sirempse legem, Plaut.

Sīrēn -ēnis, f., usually plur., **Sīrēnes** -um, f. (Σειρῆνες), *the Sirens, birds with the faces of women, on the coast of Southern Italy, who by their song lured mariners to destruction.* **Sīrēnum** scopuli, *three small rocky islands on the south-west coast of Campania, between Surrentum and Cupreae;* transf., vitanda est improba Siren, desidia, Hor.

sīrĭăsis -is, f. (σειρίασις), *a disease in children, caused by excessive heat*, Plin.

sīrĭus -ii, m. (σείριος), *the dogstar*, Verg.; poet. attrib., sirius ardor, *of the dogstar*, Verg.

sirpĕa and **sirpĭa**, v. scirpeus.

sirpĭcŭlus = scirpiculus (q.v.).

sirpus = scirpus (q.v.).

sīrus -i, m. (σειρός), *a pit or cellar for keeping corn, a silo*, Plin.

sis = si vis, v. 1. volo.

Sīsăpo -ōnis, f. *a town in Hispania Baetica, near which were gold-mines*, now *Guadalcanal.*

Sīsenna -ae, m. **I.** *L. Cornelius, a famous Roman orator and historian, contemporary of Cicero.* **II.** *a notorious slanderer in Rome in the time of Horace.*

sīser -ĕris, n. (σίσαρον), *a plant with an edible root* (Sium sisarum, Linn.), Plin.

sisto, stĭti and stĕti, stătum, 3. (reduplication of sto). **I.** Transit., **A.** *to cause to stand, put, place;* 1, aciem in litore, Verg.; alicui jaculum in ore, *to hit on the mouth*, Verg.; 2, esp., a, legal t. t., sistere se or aliquem, *to produce, cause to appear before a court of justice*, Cic.; vadimonium sistere, *to appear on the appointed day*, Cic.; b, *to erect;* effigiem, Tac. **B.** 1, *to stop, bring to a stand, check;* a, lit., legiones, Liv.; equos, Verg.; pedem or gradum, Verg.; b, fig., querelas, lacrimas, Ov.; fugam, Liv.; 2, *to make firm, settle firmly, establish;* rem Romanam, Verg. **II.** Intransit., **A.** *to stand;* 1, gen., Plaut.; 2, esp., *to appear, present oneself in court*, Cic. **B.** *to stand still, to halt;* 1, lit., ubi sistere detur, Verg.; 2, *to stand firm;* rempublican sistere negat posse, Cic.; impers., vix concordiā sisti posse, *one cannot hold out, one can stand it no longer*, Liv.; partic., **stătus** -a -um, *fixed, determined, recurring periodically;* dies, Liv.; sacrificium, Cic.

sistrātus -a -um (sistrum), *furnished with a sistrum*, Mart.

sistrum -i, n. (σεῖστρον), *a sort of rattle used in the worship of Isis*, Ov.

sĭsymbrĭum -ii, n. (σισύμβριον), *an aromatic herb sacred to Venus;* perhaps, *mint*, Ov.

Sīsyphus (**-ŏs**) -i, m. (Σίσυφος), *a son of Aeolus, brother of Salmoneus, a king of Corinth, a cunning robber, killed by Theseus, condemned in the lower world to roll up hill a great stone which constantly fell back.* Hence, **A.** Adj., **Sīsyphĭus** -a -um, a, *of or relating to Sisyphus*, Prop.; sanguine cretus Sisyphio, *Ulysses*, Ov.; b, *Corinthian*, Ov. **B.** Subst., **Sīsyphĭdēs** -ae, m. *Ulysses, said to be the son of Sisyphus.*

sĭtānĭus -a -um (σητάνιος), *of this year, this year's*, Plin.

sĭtella -ae, f. (dim. of situla), *an urn, used for drawing lots*, Liv., Ov.

Sĭthōn -ŏnis, m. (Σίθων), *son of Neptune,*

king in the Thracian Chersonese. Hence, **A.** **Sīthōn** -ŏnis, *Sithonian;* poet. = *Thracian.* **B.** **Sīthōnĭs** -ĭdis, f., subst., *a Thracian woman*, Ov. **C.** **Sīthōnĭus** -a -um, *Sithonian, Thracian;* subst., **Sīthōnĭi** -ōrum, m. *the Thracians*, Hor.

sĭtĭcŭlōsus -a -um (sitis), *very dry, parched*, Hor.

sĭtĭens, v. sitio.

sĭtĭentĕr, adv. (sitiens), *thirstily, greedily, eagerly;* expetere, Cic.

sĭtĭo -īvi and -ii -ītum, 4. (sitis), *to thirst, be thirsty.* **I.** Intransit., **A.** 1, lit., Cic.; prov., sitire mediis in undis, *to starve in the midst of plenty*, Ov.; 2, transf., a, of plants, the soil, etc., *to be dry, parched;* sitiunt agri, Cic.; tellus, Ov.; b, *to suffer from heat, to be situated in a hot climate;* Afri sitientes, Verg. **B.** Fig., *to be eager;* partic., **sĭtĭens**, *thirsting, eager;* eo gravius avidiusque sitiens, Cic.; fac venias ad sitientes aures, *languishing for news*, Cic. **II.** Transit., *to thirst for something.* **A.** Lit., Tagum, Mart.; pass., aquae sitiuntur, Ov. **B.** Fig., *to thirst after, eagerly desire;* sanguinem, Cic.; honores, Cic.; partic., sitiens, with genit., virtutis, Cic.

sĭtis -is, f. *thirst.* **I.** 1, lit., arentibus siti faucibus, Liv.; sitim colligere, *to feel thirst*, Ov., *to cause thirst*, Verg.; sitim explere, Cic., exstinguere, Ov., restinguere, Cic., depellere, Cic.; 2, transf., of the earth or of plants, *dryness, drought;* deserta siti regio, Verg. **II.** Fig., *thirst, eager desire;* libertatis, Cic.; argenti, Hor.

sĭtĭtor -ōris, m. (sitio), *one who thirsts, a thirster*, Mart.

sittybos (**sittŭbos**) -i, plur., **sittyboe**, m. (σίττυβος = σίττυβον), *a strip of parchment on which the title of a book was written*, Cic.

sĭtŭla -ae, f. and **sĭtŭlus** -i, m. a, *a small urn for drawing water*, Plaut.; b, *an urn used in drawing lots*, Plaut.

1. sĭtus -a -um, v. sino.

2. sĭtus -ūs, m. (sino). **I.** *the place, site, situation of anything;* 1, lit., loci, urbis, Cic.; plur., situs oppidorum, castrorum, Caes.; terrarum, Cic.; 2, meton., a, *situation = building;* monumentum regali situ pyramidum altius, Hor.; b, *a region of the earth, zone, quarter*, Plin. **II. A.** 1, lit., situ durescere campum, *rest*, Verg.; 2, meton., a, *want of cultivation;* cessat terra situ, Ov.; b, *rust, mould, dirt caused by remaining in one place;* occupat arma situs, Tib.; canescunt tecta situ, Ov.; c, *filthiness of the body*, Ov. **B.** Fig., of the mind, *rusting, dulness, weakness;* marcescere otio situque civitatem, Liv.; senectus victa situ, Ov.

sīvĕ and **seu**, conj. **I.** *or if;* si omnes declinabunt, sive aliae declinabunt, Cic.; me, seu corpus spoliatum lumine mavis, redde meis, Verg. **II.** With a disjunctive sense; a, doubled, sive... sive, seu... seu, *whether... or, if... or if;* sive tu medicum adhibueris (fut. perf.) sive non adhibueris (fut. perf.), Cic.; sive fecisset sive voluisset, Cic.; sive deus sive natura ademerat, Cic.; sive casu, sive consilio deorum, Caes.; in the same sense, sive... seu, Verg., Liv.; seu ... sive, Verg.; repeated several times, sive ... sive ... sive, Cic.; with other disjunct. particles, sive ... aut, Verg.; with interrog. particles, -ne ... seu, Verg.; sive ... an, Tac.; b, or; regis Philippi sive Persae, Cic.

smăragdus -i, m. and f. (σμάραγδος), *an emerald*, Lucr.

smectĭcus -a -um (σμηκτικός), *cleansing, cleaning;* vis, Plin.

smegma -ătis, n. (σμῆγμα), *a means of cleaning, detergent*, Plin.

smĭlax -ăcis, f. (σμῖλαξ). **I.** *bindweed*, Plin. **II.** Smilax, *a maiden changed into the plant of the same name*, Ov.

Smintheus -ĕi, m. (Σμινθεύς), *a surname of Apollo*, either from σμίνθος (in Cretan = *mouse*), *the mouse-killer*, or from Smintha (Σμίνθη), a town in the Trojan country.

1. **smyrna** -ae, f. (σμύρνα), *myrrh*, Lucr.

2. **Smyrna** -ae, f. (Σμύρνα), *a famous trading town in Ionia, one of the places where Homer was said to have been born*. Hence, **Smyrnaeus** -a -um, *of or belonging to Smyrna*.

smyrrhiza = myrrha, myrrhis (q.v.).

sŏbŏles, sobolesco = suboles, subolesco (q.v.).

sōbrĭē, adv. (sobrius). **I.** *moderately, frugally, soberly;* vivere, Cic. **II.** *prudently, carefully*, Plaut.

sōbrĭĕtas -ātis, f. (sobrius), *moderation in drinking. sobriety*, Sen.

sōbrīna -ae, f. (sobrinus), *a cousin on the mother's side*, Tac.

sōbrīnus -i, m. (for sororinus, from **soror**), *a cousin on the mother's side*, Cic.

sōbrĭus -a -um (perhaps =se-ebrius, as socors = secors), *sober, not intoxicated*. **I.** a, lit., of persons, Cic.; b, meton., of inanimate things, lympha, Tib.; nox, Prop. **II.** 1, transf., *moderate, frugal, continent;* homines plane frugi ac sobrii, Cic.; **2**, fig., *sober-minded, prudent, reasonable, cautious;* orator, homo, Cic.

soccātus -a -um (soccus), *wearing the soccus*, Sen.

soccŭlus -i, m. (dim. of soccus), *a little soccus*, Plin.

soccus -i, m. (συκχίς, συγχίς), *a light shoe or slipper in use among the Greeks*, Cic.; esp., *the soccus or low shoe worn by comic actors* (as the cothurnus was worn by tragic actors); hence, meton., a, *comedy*, Hor.; b, *comic style*, Hor.

sŏcer -ĕri, m. (ἑκυρός), *a father-in-law*, Cic.; plur., soceri, *the father- and mother-in-law*, Liv.

sŏcĕra = socrus (q.v.).

sŏcĭa -ae, f., v. socius.

sŏcĭābĭlis -e (socio), *sociable, easily united or joined together;* consortio inter reges, Liv.

sŏcĭālis -e (socius). **I.** *social, sociable;* homo sociale animal, Sen. **II.** Esp., **A.** *conjugal;* amor, Ov. **B.** *of or relating to allies, allied;* exercitus, Liv.; bellum, *the Social War*, Nep.; lex, Cic.

sŏcĭālĭtĕr, adv. (socialis), *sociably*, Hor.

sŏcĭennus -i, m. (socius), *a companion, comrade*, Plaut.

sŏcĭĕtas -ātis, f. (socius). **I.** *society, company, companionship, fellowship, association;* hominum inter ipsos, Cic.; vitae, Cic.; regni, Liv.; sceleris, Cic.; societatem coire, statuere, inire, conflare, Cic.; venire in societatem laudum alicuius, Cic. **II.** Esp., **1**, *commercial partnership;* a, societatem facere, Cic., gerere, Cic.; judicium societatis, *relating to partnership*, Cic.; b, *the partnership or company of the publicani to farm the taxes of the provinces;* Bithynica, Cic.; **2**, *a political alliance between states;* societatem belli facere, Cic.

sŏcĭo, 1. (socius). **I.** *to unite, combine, associate, share;* vim rerum cum dicendi exercitatione, Cic.; vitae suae periculum cum aliquo, *to risk one's life with any one*, Cic.; sanguinem (of relationship), Liv.; of things, omne genus hominum sociatum inter se esse, Cic.; nos urbe, domo

socias, *givest us a share in*, Verg. **II.** Esp., *to accomplish in company with others;* sociati parte laboris fungi, Ov.

sŏcĭŏfraudus -i, m. (socius and fraudo), *one who cheats a comrade*, Plaut.

sŏcĭus -a -um (from sequor, or else connected with sodalis). **I.** *taking part, sharing in;* subst. =*a companion, comrade, associate, partner, sharer;* socii penates, Ov.; socius regni, *fellow regent*, Cic.; socius periculorum, Cic.; belli, Cic.; amentiae, Cic.; nocte sociā, *under the shelter of night*, Cic. **II.** Esp., **1**, of relationship, socius sanguinis, *a brother*, Ov.; **2**, of marriage, socius tori, *a husband*, Ov.; socia tori, Ov., and simply socia, Sall., *a wife;* **3**, *allied, confederate;* socii Carthaginiensium populi, Liv.; classis socia, Ov.; subst., **sŏcĭus** -ĭi, m. *an ally;* huic populo socii fuerunt, Cic.; Socii, *the Italian nations beyond the boundaries of Latium in alliance with the Romans, the allies;* Socii et Latini, Cic.; Socii Latini nominis, *the Latin allies*, Liv.; **4**, in relation to trade, a, *a partner;* judicium pro socio, *a judgment in a partnership suit*, Cic.; pro socio damnari, *to be condemned for defrauding a partner*, Cic.; b, socii = *the company of* publicani *for the purpose of farming the taxes*, Cic. (genit. plur., sociûm, Liv., Verg.).

sŏcordĭa -ae, f. (socors). **I.** *stupidity, folly, weakness of intellect*, Tac. **II.** *carelessness, negligence, indolence, inactivity*, Liv.

sŏcordĭtĕr, adv. only in compar. (socors), *lazily, slothfully, carelessly;* ab Albanis socordius res acta, Liv.

sŏcors -cordis (se and cor). **I.** *weak-minded, stupid, silly*, Cic. **II.** *negligent, careless, slothful, inactive*, Sall.

sŏcra = socrus (q.v.).

Sŏcrătēs -is, m. (Σωκράτης), *the famous Athenian philosopher, contemporary of Xenophon and Alcibiades, put to death on a charge of impiety and of corrupting the youth by his teaching.* Adj., **Sŏcrătĭcus** -a -um, *Socratic; chartae, philosophy*, Hor. Plur. subst., **Sŏcrătĭci** -ōrum, m. *the pupils and followers of Socrates*.

sŏcrus -ūs, f. (ἑκυρά), *a mother-in-law*, Cic.

sŏdālĭcĭus -a -um (sodalis), *of or relating to companionship.* **I.** Adj., jure sodalicio, Ov. **II.** Subst., **sŏdālĭcĭum** -ĭi, m. **A.** *comradeship, intimacy*, Cat. **B.** In a bad sense, *a secret society;* lex Licinia quae est de sodaliciis, Cic.

sŏdālis -e, *relating to comradeship.* **I.** Adj., turba, Ov. **II.** Subst., **sŏdālis** -is, m. **A.** *a comrade, intimate associate, companion, mate, friend;* 1, lit., Cic.; 2, transf., a, of things, *a companion, attendant on;* sodalis hiemis (of the Hebrus), Hor.; b, *a sharer with = resembling;* sodalis istius erat in hoc morbo, Cic. **B.** Esp., 1, *a table companion, a boon-companion*, Cic.; 2, *a member of a club, association, corporation;* a, in a good sense, of a college of priests, sibi in Lupercis sodalem esse, Cic.; esp. of the priests of the deified emperor, sodales Augustales, Tac.; b, in a bad sense, *a member of a secret and illegal society*, Cic. (abl., sodali, Cic.).

sŏdālĭtas -ātis, f. (sodalis). **I.** *companionship, intimate association;* officia sodalitatis familiaritatisque, Cic.; homo summā sodalitate, Cic. **II.** Esp., 1, *a club for feasting*, Plin., Cic.; 2, *a club, association;* a, in a good sense, *a religious brotherhood;* quaedam sodalitas Lupercorum, Cic.; b, in a bad sense, *a secret, illegal society*, Cic.

sŏdēs (for si audes), *pray, if you please, with your leave, prithee;* jube sodes numinos curari Cic.; me, sodes (sc. relinque), Hor.

sōl, sōlis, m. *the sun.* **I. A.** Lit., 1, sol praecipitans, *inclining towards evening,* Cic.; supremo sole, *at evening,* Hor.; sol mihi excidisse e mundo videtur, Cic.; prov., nondum omnium dierum sol occidit, *the sun has not yet set for ever,* Liv.; 2, as a proper name, Sol, *the sun-god, the Phoebus of the Greeks, father of Phaethon, Pasiphae, Circe;* filia Solis, *Pasiphae,* Ov. **B.** Meton., 1, *the light, warmth, heat of the sun;* plur., soles often = *sunny days;* sol nimius, Ov.; ambulare in sole, Cic.; hence, of work done in the sun (opp. to umbra), a, *military service;* cedat umbra (i.e., jurisprudentia) soli, Cic.; b, *appearance in public;* procedere in solem et publicum, Cic.; 2, *the day;* tres soles erramus, Verg. **II.** Fig., *the sun,* of distinguished persons, P. Africanus sol alter, Cic.; solem Asiae Brutum appellat, Hor.

sōlācĭum = solatium (q.v.).

sōlāmen -ĭnis, n. (solor), *a means of consolation, comfort,* Verg.

sōlānum -i, n. *the plant nightshade,* Plin.

sōlāris -e (sol), *of or relating to the sun, solar;* lumen, Ov.

sōlārĭum -ĭi, n. (sol). **A.** *a sundial,* Plaut.; *a much frequented place in the forum, where a sundial stood;* non ad solarium versatus est, Cic. **B.** *a balcony, terrace exposed to the sun,* Plaut.

sōlātĭŏlum -i, n. (dim. of solatium), *a small consolation,* Cat.

sōlātĭum (sōlācĭum) -ĭi, n. (solor), *a consolation, comfort, solace, relief.* **I.** 1, lit., servitutis, Cic.; solatium afferre or praebere, Cic.; absenti magna solatia dedisse, Cic.; 2, transf., a, *a means of help, refuge in need;* annonae, Cic.; b, *amends, compensation,* Tac. **II.** Meton., = *a consoler;* aves, solatia ruris, Ov.

sōlātor -ōris, m. (solor), *a consoler, comforter,* Tib.

sōlātus -a -um (sol), *sun-struck,* Plin.

soldurĭi -ōrum, m. (a Celtic word), *retainers, vassals,* Caes.

soldus = solidus (q.v.).

sŏlĕa -ae, f. (solum). **I.** *a leather sole strapped on the foot, a sandal;* soleas poscere (after dinner), Hor. **II.** Transf., a, *a species of clog or fetter,* Cic.; b, *a kind of shoe for animals, not nailed on, like our horse-shoes, but tied on,* Cat.; c, *a fish, the sole,* Ov.

sŏlĕārĭus -ĭi, m. (solea), *a sandal-maker,* Plaut.

sŏlĕātus -a -um (solea), *wearing sandals,* Cic.

sŏlēn -ēnis, m. (σωλήν), *a species of mussel, the razor-fish,* Plin.

sŏlennis, solennitas = sollemnis, etc. (q.v.).

sŏlĕo, sŏlĭtus sum, 2. *to be accustomed, be used, be wont;* with infin., mentiri, Cic.; ut soleo, ut solet (sc. facere), *as is my custom,* Cic.; ut solet (sc. fieri), *as is the custom,* Cic.

sŏlers, solertia = sollers, sollertia (q.v.).

Sŏli (Sŏloe) -ōrum, m. (Σόλοι), *a town in Cilicia, a Greek colony, native place of the Stoic Chrysippus, of Menander, and of the astronomer Aratus.*

sŏlĭdē, adv. (solidus). **I.** *firmly, densely, solidly,* Col. **II.** *surely, certainly;* aliquid scire, Plaut.

sŏlĭdĭpes -pĕdis (solidus and pes), *not dividing the hoofs, having undivided hoofs,* Plin.

sŏlĭdĭtas -ātis, f. (solidus), *solidity;* nec dii habent ullam soliditatem nec eminentiam, Cic.

sŏlĭdo, 1. (solidus). **I.** a, *to make dense, solid;* aream cretâ, Verg.; b, *to make firm;*

muros, Tac. **II.** Transf., *to join together, to make whole,* Plin.

sŏlĭdus -a -um (Gr. ὅλος), *dense, firm, solid.* **I.** Lit., gen., a, paries, Cic.; subst., **sŏlĭdum** -i, n., (a) *firm ground,* Ov.; (β) *a thick body,* Verg.; b, of metals, *massive, solid;* crateres auro solidi of *massive gold,* Verg.; c, *firm, hard;* ripa Ov.; adamas, Verg.; subst., **sŏlĭdum** -i, n something *firm,* Hor.; solido carere, Cic.; in solido, fig., *in safety;* aliquem in solido locare, Verg. d, *thick, strong;* tori Herculis, Ov. **II.** Transf. 1, *whole, complete, entire;* usura, Cic.; partem solido demere de die, Hor.; subst., **sŏlĭdum** -i, n. *the whole sum,* Cic.; 2, *firm, enduring real, substantial, solid;* laus, Cic.; utilitas, Cic.; subst., *that which is real* or *genuine,* Hor.; **3,** *firm, immovable;* mens, Hor.

sōlĭfĕr -fĕra -fĕrum (sol and fero), *sun-bringing,* Sen.

sōlĭfūga -ae, f. (sol and fugio), *a kind of poisonous ant,* Plin.

sōlistĭmum (sollistŭmum) and **sollistŭmum tripudium,** *the good omen afforded when the sacred chickens ate so eagerly that the food fell out of their beaks,* Cic.

sōlĭtārĭus -a -um (solus), *standing alone;* a, *solitary, alone, lonely;* solitarius homo atque in agro vitam agens, Cic.; b, *single, alone, by itself;* quoniam solitaria non posset virtus ad ea pervenire, Cic.

sōlĭtūdo -ĭnis, f. (solus). **I.** *solitude, loneliness* (opp. frequentia, celebritas); loci, Cic.; in solitudine secum loqui, Cic.; plur., in animi doloribus solitudines captare, Cic. **II.** *a state of desertion, deprivation, want,* liberorum, Cic.

sōlĭtus -a -um, p. adj. (from soleo), *usual, customary, wonted, habitual;* a, adj., locus, Ov.; solito matrum de more, Verg.; b, subst., **sōlĭtum** -i, n. *that which is usual or customary, custom;* often with prep., praeter solitum, Hor.; in abl. with compar., major solito, Liv.; plus solito, Liv.

sŏlĭum -ĭi, n. **I.** *a chair of state, royal seat, throne;* a, for kings, regale, Liv.; meton. = *throne, regal power;* in paterno solio locare, Liv.; b, for the gods in the temples; deorum solio, Cic.; c, of jurists, *an arm-chair, seated in which they gave their opinion;* quo minus more patrio sedens in solio consulentibus responderem, Cic. **II.** *a bathing-tub of stone or wood,* Suet. **III.** *a stone coffin, sarcophagus,* Suet.

sōlĭvāgus -a -um (solus and vagus), *wandering alone.* **I.** Lit., bestiae, Cic. **II.** Fig., *solitary, lonely, single;* cognitio, Cic.

sollemnis (sŏlemnis, sŏlennis) -e (from sollus = totus and annus). **I.** *yearly, annual* (applied to annually recurring festivals); sacra, sacrificia, Cic. **II.** Transf., **A.** *solemn, festive, religious;* epulae, ludi, Cic.; subst., **sollenne** -is, n. *a solemn feast, sacrifice, a religious rite;* sollemne clavi tigendi, Liv.; esp., plur. = the *sacrificial victims;* extis sollemnibus vesci, Liv. **B.** *usual, customary, wonted, common;* lascivia militum, Liv.; officium, Cic.; subst., **sollemne** -is, n. *a custom;* nostrum illud solemne servemus, Cic.

sollemnĭtĕr (sŏlemnĭtĕr, sŏlennĭtĕr), adv. (sollemnis). **I.** *solemnly, religiously;* omnia peragere, Liv. **II.** *according to use, custom,* Plin.

sollers (sŏlers)-ertis (sollus=totus and ars), lit., *possessed entirely of an art* (opp. iners), hence, *clever, skilful, adroit;* a, of persons, agricola, Cic.; Ulysses, Ov.; quo quisque est sollertior et ingeniosior, hoc, etc., Cic.; sollertissimus omnium, Sall.; with infin., Hor.; with genit., Musa lyrae sollers, Hor.; **b,** of things, *ingenious, intelligent;* natura, Cic.; descriptio, Cic. (abl. sing., gen. sollerti; sollerte, Ov.).

sollertĕr (sōlertĕr), adv. with compar. and superl., *cleverly, skilfully, adroitly,* Cic.

sollertĭa (sōlertĭa) -ae, f. (sollers), *cleverness, skilfulness, inventiveness, adroitness, ingenuity;* naturae, Cic.; ingenii, Sall.; with object. genit., cogitandi, judicandi, Cic.; in hac re tanta inest ratio atque sollertia ut, etc., Cic.

sollĭcĭtātĭo -ōnis, f. (sollicito), *an inciting, instigating, instigation, solicitation,* Cic.

sollĭcĭtē, adv. (sollicitus),*anxiously, solicitously, carefully,* Plin.

sollĭcĭto, 1. (sollicitus), *to move violently, shake, stir, agitate.* **I. 1,** lit., tellurem, *to plough,* Verg.; freta remis, Verg.; spicula, Verg.; stamina docto pollice, *to touch the strings,* Ov.; **2,** transf., *to weaken, disturb;* malā copiā aegrum stomachum, Hor. **II. Fig., 1,** *to disturb, trouble;* pacem, Liv.; **2, a,** *to agitate, vex, disquiet, annoy;* haec cura me sollicitat, Cic.; sollicitatus Juppiter, Liv.; **b,** *to stir up, incite, instigate to any action, solicit, tamper with;* (a) in a bad sense, civitates, Caes.; sollicitatus ab Arvernis pecuniā, Caes.; poet., with a thing as object, sollicitare judicium donis, *seek to obtain by bribery,* Ov.; to express the object, with ad and the acc., causa and the genit., ut or ne and the subj., poet. infin., servos ad hospitem necandum, Cic.; dixit se sollicitatum esse, ut regnare vellet, Cic.; (β) in a good sense, *to persuade, solicit, influence,* Lucr.

sollĭcĭtūdo -ĭnis, f. (sollicitus), *uneasiness, mental disturbance, anxiety, solicitude, care, trouble;* **a,** sing., cura et sollicitudo, Cic.; with object. genit., provinciae, *about the province,* Cic.; abstrahere se ab omni sollicitudine, Cic.; demere sollicitudinem, Cic.; sollicitudinis aliquid habere, Cic.; **b,** plur., sollicitudines domesticae, Cic.; habere aliquem sollicitudinum socium, Cic.

sollĭcĭtus -a -um (sollus = totus and cio), *strongly moved, stirred up, agitated.* **I. Lit.,** physically, mare, Verg. **II. Transf., A.** *politically disturbed,* Sall. **B.** *mentally disturbed, anxious, uneasy, disturbed, solicitous;* **a,** of the mind, anxius animus aut sollicitus, Cic.; **b,** of living beings; (a) of persons, vehementer sollicitum esse, Cic.; aliquem sollicitum habere, *to trouble,* Cic.; with prep. or with vicem, sollicitum esse de alicuius valetudine, Cic.; pro Aetolis sollicitus, Liv.; sollicitus propter difficultatem locorum, Liv.; meam vicem sollicitus, Liv.; with abl., sollicitus morte Tigelli, Hor.; with ne and the subj., quae cruciatur et sollicita est, ne eundem paulo post spoliatum omni dignitate conspiciat, Cic.; (β) of animals, canes, *watchful,* Ov.; **c,** of things, (a) pass., *troubled;* in vita omnia semper suspecta atque sollicita, Cic.; (β) act., *disquieting, causing trouble;* amores, Verg.

sollĭferrĕum (sōlĭferrĕum) -i, n. (sollus = totus and ferrum), *a javelin entirely of iron,* Liv.

sollistĭmus = solistimus (q.v.).

sollus -a -um (Oscan) = totus (q.v.).

1. **sōlo,** 1. (solus), *to make solitary, make desert,* Sen.

2. **Sōlo** = Solon (q.v.).

Sōloe = Soli (q.v.).

sōloecismus -i, m. (σολοικισμός), *a grammatical error, solecism,* Quint.

Sōlon (Sōlo) -ōnis, m. (Σόλων), *one of the Seven Wise Men of Greece, a famous Athenian legislator, living about 600 B.C.*

Solonĭus -a -um, *name of a district in Latium.*

sōlor, 1. *to comfort, console.* **I. Lit.,** inopem, Hor. **II. Transf., a,** *to assuage, soothe, relieve, mitigate;* famem, Verg.; laborem cantu, Verg.; aestum fluviis, Hor.; **b,** *to indemnify, to compensate,* Tac.

solstĭtĭālis -e (solstitium). **I.** *of or relating to the summer solstice;* dies, *the longest day,* Cic.; nox, *the shortest night,* Ov.; orbis, *the tropic of Cancer,* Cic. **II. Meton., A.** *relating to summer or to the warmth of summer;* solstitiali tempore, Liv. **B.** *of or relating to the sun, solar;* orbis, Liv.

solstĭtĭum -ii, n. (sol and sisto). **I.** *a solstice,* Plin. **II. Esp.,** *the summer solstice, the longest day.* **A. Lit.,** Cic. **B. Meton.,** *summer, summer-heat;* solstitium pecori defendite, Verg.

1. **sōlum** -i, n. *the bottom or lowest part of anything.* **I. Gen., a,** lit., fossae, Caes.; clivus ad solum exustus est, Liv.; **b,** fig., *ground, foundation;* solum et quasi fundamentum oratoris, locutionem emendatam et Latinam, Cic. **II. Esp., 1,** *the floor of a room,* Cic.; **2,** *the sole of a foot,* Cic.; **3,** of a shoe, Plin.; **4,** *soil, ground, earth, land;* **a,** macrum, Cic.; prov., quodcunque in solum venit, *whatever falls on the ground* (i.e., *whatever comes into one's head*), Cic.; ellipt., ibi loquor, quod in solum, ut dicitur, Cic.; **b,** *soil, country;* solum patriae, *the soil of one's native country,* Cic.; solum vertere, mutare, *to leave one's country, go into exile,* Cic.; **5,** *soil = that which is underneath;* Cereale, *a layer of biscuit underneath other food,* Verg.; substratiturque solum (sc. navi), *sea,* Verg.; astra tenent caeleste solum, *= heaven,* Ov.

2. **sōlum,** adv. (solus), *alone, only;* **a,** una de re solum est dissensio, Cic.; **b,** in negat. sent., non solum . . . verum etiam, *not only . . . but also,* Cic.; non solum . . . sed etiam, Cic.; non solum . . . sed ne quidem, *not only . . . but not even,* Cic.; non solum . . . sed vix, Cic.

Sŏluntīnus, v. 2. Solus.

1. **sōlus** -a -um, genit. sōlīus, dat. sōli (from se), *alone, only, sole.* **I. Gen.,** solum regnare, Cic.; solos novem menses, *only nine months,* Cic. **II.** Of places, *solitary, desert, uninhabited;* quum in locis solis moestus errares, Cic.

2. **Sŏlūs** -untis, f. (Σολοῦς), *a town on the north coast of Sicily, east of Panormus, now Castello di Solanto.* Hence, **Sŏluntīnus** -i, m. *an inhabitant of Solus.*

sōlūtē, adv. (solutus). **I. a,** *without impediment, freely;* moveri, Cic.; **b,** *without difficulty, easily,* Cic. **II.** *carelessly, negligently,* Cic.

sōlūtĭlis -e (solutus), *easily coming to pieces,* Suet.

sōlūtĭo -ōnis, f. (solvo). **I.** *a loosening.* **A. Lit.,** linguae, *a loose, ready tongue,* Cic. **B. Fig., 1,** *a paying, payment;* legatorum, Cic.; **2,** solutio rerum creditarum, Cic. **II.** *dissolution;* **a,** totius hominis, Cic.; **b,** *explanation,* Sen.

sōlūtus -a -um, p. adj. (from solvo), *loosened.* **I.** *loosened, unbound, free.* **A. Lit.,** tunica, Quint. **B. Fig.,** *unbound, free from fetters, free, independent;* **1,** in a good sense, **a,** solutus liberque animus, Cic.; soluta optio eligendi *unhindered,* Cic.; with ab and the abl., soluti a cupiditatibus, Cic.; with abl. alone, ambitione, Hor.; with genit., famuli operum soluti, Hor.; **b,** *free from debt or mortgage, unencumbered;* praedia, Cic.; **c,** of orators, *fluent, ready;* solutus atque expeditus ad dicendum, Cic.; **d,** of discourse, *unbound;* (a) *free from the fetters of metre, prose;* soluta oratio (opp. poemata), Cic.;

(β) *loose, flowing, not carefully constructed;* verba, Cic.; numeri, of Pindaric poetry, Hor.; **2,** in a **bad** sense, a, *unrestrained, unbridled, unchecked, dissolute, licentious;* libido solutior, Liv.; praetura, Cic.; risus, Verg.; b, *lazy, sluggish;* Titius tam solutus et mollis in gestu, Cic.; **c,** *negligent,* Cic. **II.** Of soil, *loose, loosened;* terra, Plin.

solvo, solvi, sŏlūtum, 3. (1. se and luo), *to loosen.* **I.** *to loosen, untie, unbind.* **A.** 1, lit., funem a stipite, Ov.; corollas de nostra fronte, Prop.; crines, capillos, Hor.; nodum, Tib.; **2,** transf., a, *to unbind, release, set free;* canem, Phaedr.; equum senescentem, *to unyoke,* Hor.; b, transf., *to untie, loosen, open;* epistolam, Cic.; ora, *open the mouth,* Ov.; c, naut. t. t., ancoram, navem, *to weigh anchor, set sail;* so solvere funem, Verg.; absol., naves a terra solverunt, Caes. **B.** Fig., 1, commercial t. t., *to pay or discharge a debt;* a, lit. (α) aliquid; pecuniam debitam, Cic.; pro frumento nihil, Cic.; solvendo non erat, *he was insolvent,* Cic.; (β) aliquem, *to pay any one,* Plaut.; b, transf., *to perform a promise or duty, fulfil an engagement;* si solveris ea quae polliceris, Cic.; justa paterno funeri, Cic.; suprema alicui, Tac.; capite poenas, *to suffer capital punishment,* Sall.; **2,** *to set free, release;* aliquem curā et negotio, Cic.; civitatem, rempublicam religione, Cic.; per aes et libram heredes testamenti, Cic.; ut si solvas (*if you release from the fetter of verse,* i.e., *turn into prose*) "postquam Discordia," etc., Hor. **II.** *to break up, to loosen, break in pieces.* **A.** 1, lit., a, gen., *to break to pieces;* navem, *to dash to pieces,* Ov.; pontem, Tac.; b, *to melt, dissolve;* nivem, Ov.; solvuntur viscera, *putrefy,* Verg.; **2,** transf., a, *to part, separate;* agmina diductis choris, Verg.; b, *to weaken, relax;* homines solverat alta quies, Ov.; solvuntur frigore membra, Verg.; solvi morte, or solvi alone, *to die,* Ov. **B.** Fig., 1, *to remove by breaking up;* a, *to bring to an end, terminate;* injuriam, Sall.; pass., hiems solvitur, *is broken up, disappears,* Hor.; b, *to break, to violate;* Hor.; traditum a prioribus morem, Liv.; solventur risu tabulae (perhaps = *the laws will lose their force,* but see under tabulae, II. 1.), Hor.; c, *to banish, get rid of;* pudorem, Verg.; metum corde, Verg.; **2,** *to solve, explain;* juris nodos et legum aenigmata, Juv.; captiosa, Cic.

Sŏlўmi -ōrum, m. (Σόλυμοι), *the earliest inhabitants of Lycia, from whom, according to some, the Jews were descended, whence the name Hierosolyma, Jerusalem.* Hence, adj., **Sŏlўmus** -a -um, *belonging to Jerusalem or the Jews.*

somnĭātor -ōris, m. (somnio), *a dreamer,* Sen.

somnĭcŭlōsē, adv. (somniculosus), *sleepily, lazily,* Plaut.

somnĭcŭlōsus -a -um (somnus), *sleepy, drowsy, sluggish;* senectus, Cic.

somnĭfĕr -fĕra -fĕrum (somnus and fero). **I.** *sleep-bringing, sleep-causing;* virga (Mercurii), Ov. **II.** *narcotic, deadly;* venenum, Ov.

somnĭfĭcus -a -um (somnus and facio), *bringing or causing sleep,* Plin.

somnĭo, 1. (somnium), *to dream.* **I.** Lit., totas noctes, Cic.; de aliquo, Cic.; with acc., *to dream of;* ovum, Cic.; with accus. and infin., ovum pendēre ex fascia lecti, Cic. **II.** Transf., *to dream, think,* or *imagine foolishly; portenta non disserentium philosophorum sed somniantium, Cic.; with acc. (=of, etc.), Trojanum, Cic.

somnĭum -ĭi, n. (somnus), *a dream;* 1, lit., per somnia (*in a dream*) loqui, Cic.; **2,** transf., *vain imagination, foolishness, nonsense,* Ter.

somnus -i, m. (for sop -nus, root SOP, whence sopor and sopio), *sleep, slumber.* **I.**

A. Lit., 1, gen., Endymionis, *everlasting,* Cic.; somnum capere non posse, *not to be able to sleep,* Cic.; somnum tenere, *to keep oneself from sleeping,* Cic.; somnum alicui afferre, Cic.; somno consopiri sempiterno, Cic.; dare se somno, Cic.; aliquem ex somno excitare, Cic.; in somnis videre, Cic.; **2,** esp., *drowsiness, laziness, inactivity;* somno nati, Cic.; dediti somno, Sall. **B.** Transf., *the sleep of death;* longus, Hor. **II.** Meton., *night;* libra die (= diei) somnique pares ubi fecerit horas, Verg.

sŏnābĭlis -e (sono), *sounding, resounding;* sistrum, Ov.

sŏnans -antis, p. adj. (from sono) *sounding;* concha, Ov.; of words, ut sint alia (verba) sonantiora, *full-sounding, sonorous,* Cic.

sŏnax -ācis (sono), *sounding, resounding,* Ov.

sonchos -i, m. (σόγχος), *the plant sow-thistle,* Plin.

sŏnĭpēs -pĕdis (sonus and pes), *sounding with the feet;* usually subst., m. *the horse,* Verg.

sŏnĭtus -ūs, m. (sono), *a sound, noise;* Olympi, *thunder,* Verg.; sonitum reddere, Cic.

sŏnīvĭus -a -um (sono), *sounding,* only used in augury in the phrase sonivium tripudium, *the noise of the food falling from the beaks of the sacred chickens,* Cic.

sŏno, sŏnŭi, sŏnĭtum, 1. (sonus). **I.** Intransit., 1, *to sound, resound, make a noise;* a, sonuerunt tympana, Caes.; classica sonant, Verg.; sonare inani voce, *to produce an empty jingle of words,* Cic.; with acc. neut., amnis rauca sonans, *sounding harshly,* Verg.; b, esp., of discourse, *to sound;* bene, melius, optime sonare, Cic.; **2,** *to re-echo;* ripae sonant, Verg. **II.** Transit., *to sound;* 1, a, *to produce a sound;* inconditis vocibus inchoatum quiddam atque peregrinum sonantes, Cic.; nec vox hominem sonat, *sounds human,* Verg.; b, *to betray by a sound;* furem sonuere juvenci, Prop.; **2,** *to mean;* quid sonet haec vox, Cic.; **3,** a, *to shout, cry, sing;* euhoë Bacche, Ov.; b, *to sing of;* bella, Ov.; c, *to celebrate;* atavos et atavorum antiqua nomina, Verg. (fut. partic., sonaturum, Hor.).

sŏnor -ōris, m. (sono), *sound, noise, din;* sonorem dant silvae, Verg.

sŏnōrus -a -um (sonor), *sounding, resonant, ringing, loud, sonorous;* cithara, Tib.; tempestas, Verg.

sons, sontis, *guilty, deserving of punishment;* anima, Verg.; sanguis, Ov.; subst., punire sontes, *the guilty,* Cic.

Sontĭātes -um, m. *a people in Gallia Aquitania, on the borders of Gallia Celtica.*

sontĭcus -a -um (sons), *dangerous;* morous, dangerous (such a disease as forms an excuse for not appearing in a court of law); hence, causa, *a weighty, serious, important excuse,* Tib.

sŏnus -i, m. *a noise, sound, din.* **I.** 1, lit., a, dulcis, Cic.; ab acutissimo sono usque ad gravissimum sonum, *from the highest treble to the deepest bass,* Cic.; inanes sonos fundere, Cic.; b, esp., *a word;* ficti soni, Ov.; 2, meton., *voice, speech;* tunc mens et sonus relapsus, Hor. **II.** Transf., *tone,* Cic.

sŏphĭa -ae, f. (σοφία), *wisdom,* Mart.

sŏphisma -ătis, n. (σόφισμα), *a sophism,* Sen.

sŏphistēs -ae, m. and **sŏphistes** -ae, m. (σοφιστής), *a sophist, a philosopher who taught for money eloquence, practical wisdom, the art of disputing,* etc.; hence often = *a quibbler, charlatan,* Cic.

Sŏphŏcles -is, m., voc. Sophocle (Σοφοκλῆς), *the famous Greek tragic poet.* Hence, adj.,

Sŏphŏclēus -a -um, *Sophoclean, relating to Sophocles*, Cic.

Sŏphŏnība -ae, f. (Σοφονίβα), *daughter of Hasdrubal, wife of the Numidian king, Syphax.*

1. **sŏphus** (-ŏs) -i, m. (σοφός), *wise*, Phaedr.; subst., *a wise man*, Mart.

2. **sŏphōs** (σοφῶς), adv. *bravo, well done*, Mart.

sōpĭo -īvi and -ĭi -ītum, 4. I. *to put to sleep, lull to sleep;* 1, gen., a, of living beings, vino oneratos, Liv.; pervigilem draconem herbis, Ov.; partic., sopitus, *lulled to sleep;* vigiles, Liv.; b, transf., of things, *to lull, quiet;* in pass., sopiri, sopitum esse = *to slumber, rest;* virtus sopita sit, Cic.; ignis sopitus, *slumbering under the ashes*, Verg.; 2, *to lull to an eternal sleep, kill;* quiete sopitus, Lucr. II. Meton., *to stun, render senseless;* impactus ita est saxo, ut sopiretur, Liv.

sōpor -ōris, m. (root SOP, whence sopio and somnus), *deep sleep*. I. Lit., 1, gen., sopor aliquem opprimit, Liv.; personif., Sopor, *the god of sleep*, Verg.; 2, *the sleep of death;* perpetuus sopor, Hor. II. Meton., 1, *sleepiness, laziness, inactivity*, Tac.; 2, *a sleeping draught;* patri soporem dare, Nep.

sŏpōrātus -a -um, p. adj. (from soporo). I. *sleeping;* hostes, Ov. II. *provided with sleep-giving power, stupefying;* ramus vi soporatus Stygiā, Verg.

sŏpōrĭfĕr -fĕra -fĕrum (sopor and fero), *causing deep sleep, soporific*, Verg.

sŏpōro -1, (sopor), *to put to sleep, cast into a deep sleep*, Plin.

sŏpōrus -a -um (sopor), *sleep-bringing;* Nox, Verg.

Sōra -ae, f. *the most northerly town of the Volsci, in Latium, on the right bank of the Liris,* still called *Sora.* Hence, **Sōrānus** -a -um, *belonging to Sora.*

Sōractĕ (**Sauractĕ**) -is, n. *a mountain in Etruria, near Rome, on which stood a famous temple of Apollo,* now *Monte di S. Silvestro.*

Sōrānus -a -um, v. Sora.

sōrācum -i, n. (σώρακος), *a pannier, hamper*, Plaut.

sorbĕo, sorbŭi, 2. (root SORB, Gk. POB, whence ροφέω), *to suck up, suck in, drink down, to swallow.* I. Lit., a, of persons, sanguinem, Plin.; b, of things, Charybdis vastos sorbet in abruptum fluctus, Verg.; sorbent avidae praecordia flammae, Ov. II. Fig., odia, *to swallow, put up with*, Cic.

1. **sorbĭlo** (**sorbillo**), 1. (dim. of sorbeo), *to suck in, sip*, Ter.

2. **sorbĭlo**, adv. (sorbeo), *drop by drop*, Plaut.

sorbĭtĭo -ōnis, f. (sorbeo), *a draught, potion*, Pers.

sorbum -i, n. *the fruit of the sorbus, a service-berry*, Verg.

sorbus -i, f. *the service-tree*, Plin.

sordĕo, sordŭi, 2. (sordes). I. *to be dirty, filthy;* cunctae prae campo sordent? Hor. II. Fig., 1, *to be mean, sordid in appearance*, Plaut.; 2, *to be contemptible, be despised;* adeo se suis etiam sordere, Liv.

sordes -is, f. and gen. plur., **sordes** -ium, f. *dirt, filth.* I. 1, lit., a, sine sordibus ungues, Hor.; in sordibus aurium inhaerescere, Cic.; b, esp., *soiled* or *dirty garments, used by mourners and persons accused;* sordes lugubres, Cic.; 2, meton., of persons, O tenebrae, lutum, sordes, Cic.; apud sordem urbis et faecem, *the dregs of the people*, Cic. II. Transf. 1. *meanness, baseness;* hom-

inis, Cic.; fortunae et vitae, Cic.; 2, *sordid frugality, stinginess, niggardliness;* a, rarely in sing., nulla in re familiari sordes, Cic.; b, gen. in plur., mens oppleta sordibus, Cic.

sordesco, sordŭi, 3. (sordeo), *to become dirty*, Hor.

sordĭdātus -a -um (sordidus), *wearing dirty clothes;* a, gen., Cic.; b, (v. sordes, I. b.), *clad in mourning*, Cic.

sordĭdē, adv. (sordidus). I. *meanly, in a low station;* nasci, Tac. II. Transf., a, *vulgarly;* meanly; dicere, Cic.; b, *sordidly, stingily*, Cic.

sordĭdŭlus -a -um (dim. of sordidus), *somewhat dirty*, Juv.

sordĭdus -a -um (sordeo), *dirty, filthy, unclean.* I. Lit., 1, gen., amictus, Verg.; mappa, Hor.; 2, *in soiled* or *dirty clothes, as a sign of mourning;* squalore sordidus, Cic. II. Transf., 1, *poor, mean, base* (in rank or condition), *humble, small, paltry;* loco sordido ortus, Liv.; reus, Cic.; oratores sordidiores, artes sordidiores, Cic.; ut quisque sordidissimus videbitur, Cic.; 2, *mean, base, vile, disgraceful;* iste omnium turpissimus et sordidissimus, Cic.; esp., *stingy, sordid;* homo, Cic.; cupido, Hor.

sordĭtūdo -inis, f. (sordes), *dirt, filth*, Plaut.

sōrex -icis, m. (ὕραξ), *a shrew-mouse*, Plin.

sōricīnus -a -um (sorex), *of* or *relating to o shrew-mouse*, Plaut.

sōrites -ae, m. (σωρείτης), *a sorites, a sophism formed by accumulation of arguments*, Cic. (dat., soriti, Cic.; acc. sing., soritam, Cic.).

sŏror (= sosor, connected with English *sister*, and German *schwester*), *a sister.* I. Lit., 1, gen., Cic.; Phoebi, Luna, Ov.; magna soror matris Eumenidum, *the earth as sister of night*, Verg.; plur., Sorores, *the Parcae*, Ov.; so tres sorores, Hor.; *the Furies*, Ov.; 2, esp. = soror patruelis, *aunt*, Cic., Ov. II. Transf., a, as a term of endearment, *friend, playmate;* sorores meae, Verg.; b, of things alike or connected, e.g., the hair, Cat.

sŏrōrĭcīda -ae, m. (soror and caedo), *one who murders a sister*, Cic.

sŏrōrĭo, 1. (soror), *applied to the female breasts, to grow up* or *swell together*, Plin.

sŏrōrĭus -a -um (soror), *of* or *relating to a sister, sisterly;* stupra, *incest*, Cic.

sors, sortis, f. (from 1. sero, as *fors* from *fero*), *a lot.* I. A. Lit., a, conjicere sortes in hydriam, Cic.; or simply, conjicere sortes, Cic.; dejicere sortes, Cic.; sors mea exit, *comes out*, Cic.; ut sors exciderat, Liv.; b, esp., *sortes*, used as oracles, verses (from Vergil, etc.), written on leaves and drawn by persons; sortes ducere, Juv. B. Transf., res revocatur ad sortem, Cic.; conjicere in sortem provincias, *to cast lots for*, Liv. II. Meton., 1, *an oracular response, prophecy;* sors oraculi, Liv.; sors ad sortes referenda, Cic.; 2, *official duty;* nunquam afuit nisi sorte, Cic.; 3, a, = *part;* in nullam sortem bonorum nati, Liv.; Saturni sors prima, *first child*, Ov.; b, *lot, fate, fortune, destiny;* nescia mens hominum fati sortisque futurae, Verg.; illacrimare sorti humanae, Liv.; hence, esp., (a) *rank* or *station of a person;* prima, secunda, Liv.; (β) *sex;* altera, *female*, Ov.; (γ) *kind;* nova pugnae sors, Verg.; 4, *money, capital out at interest;* sorte caret, usurā nec eā solidā contentus est, Cic. (archaic abl., sorti, Verg.).

sortĭcŭla -ae, f. (dim. of sors), *a little lot* or *ticket*, Suet.

sortīlĕgus -a -um (sors and lego), *prophetic, oracular*, Hor. Subst., **sortīlĕgus** -i. m. *a soothsayer, fortune-teller*, Cic.

sortĭor, 4. dep. (sors). **I.** Intransit., *to cast lots;* inter se, Cic. **II.** Transit., **A.** *to decide by lot, cast lots for;* 1, lit., provinciam, Cic.; consules sortiti, uter dedicaret, Liv.; quasi sortiri, quid loquare, Cic.; 2, transf., **a,** *to choose, select;* subolem, Verg.; **b,** *to share, divide;* regnum in plebem, Liv. **B.** *to gain by lot;* 1, lit., peregrinam (provinciam), Liv.; 2, transf., *to gain by fate, to get, receive, obtain;* mediterranea Asiae, Liv.; amicum casu, Hor.; **sortītus** -a -um, pass., *gained by lot,* Cic.

sortītĭo -ōnis, f. (sortior), *a casting lots, deciding by casting lots;* judicum sortitio fit, Cic.

sortītō, adv. (abl. of sortitus, from sortior), *by lot,* Cic.

sortĭtor -ōris, m. (sortior), *one who draws lots,* Sen.

1. **sortītus** -ūs, m. (sortior), *a casting of lots, deciding by lot,* Cic., Verg.

2. **sortītus** -a -um, partic. of sortior.

sōry (sōri) -rĕŏs, n. (σῶρυ), *inkstone, sory,* Plin.

sospĕs -ĭtis (root SOS, σῶς), *safe, unhurt, uninjured.* **I.** a, of persons, sospites brevi in patriam ad parentes restituunt, Liv.; **b,** of things, navis sospes ab ignibus, Hor. **II.** Transf. = *lucky, favourable;* cursus, Hor.

Sospĭta -ae, f. (sospes), *the Saviour;* Juno Sospita, *a goddess worshipped originally in Lanuvium, afterwards at Rome;* illa vestra Sospita, Cic.

sospĭtālis -e (sospes), *salutary,* Plaut.

sospĭto, 1. (sospes), *to keep safe, preserve;* suam progeniem, Liv.

sōtēr -tēris, acc. -tēra, m. (σωτήρ), *a saviour,* Cic.

sōtērĭa -ōrum, n. (σωτήρια), *presents given in celebration of a recovery from sickness,* Mart.

spādix -dīcis (σπάδιξ), *of the colour of a palm-branch with its fruit, chestnut-coloured;* equi, Verg.

spādo -ōnis, m. (σπάδων), *a eunuch,* Liv.

spādōnĭus -a -um (spado), *unfruitful, producing no seed,* Plin.

spargănĭon -ĭi, n. (σπαργάνιον), *the plant burweed,* Plin.

spargo, sparsi, sparsum, 3. (root SPAR, Gr. ΣΠΑΡ, whence σπείρω). **I.** *to scatter, strew, sprinkle.* **A.** Gen., nummos populo, Cic.; nuces, Verg. **B.** Esp., **1,** *to scatter seeds, to sow;* semina humo, Ov.; fig., animos in corpora, Cic.; **2,** *to throw, hurl, cast;* tela, Verg.; **3,** *to scatter, disperse, dissipate;* **a,** (*a*) of things, arma (*war*) per agros, Liv.; hence, *to scatter, spread abroad, circulate a report;* spargere voces in vulgum ambiguas, Verg.; Argolicas nomen per urbes Theseos, Ov.; (*β*) of things, *to divide, distribute;* per vias speculatores, Liv.; also, *to disperse, scatter in flight;* spargere se in fugam, Liv.; **b,** *to dissipate property;* spargas tua prodigus, Hor.; **c,** *to tear in pieces;* corpora, Ov. **II.** *to besprinkle, bestrew;* **1,** lit., humum foliis, Verg.; 2, transf., **a,** *to besprinkle;* aurora spargebat lumine terras, Verg.; fig., litterae humanitatis sale sparsae, Cic.; **b,** *to bedew, moisten;* lacrimā favillam amici, Hor.; **c,** *to dash, speckle;* alas coloribus, Verg.

sparsĭo -ōnis, f. (spargo), *a sprinkling of perfumed waters in the theatre,* Sen.

sparsus -a -um, p. adj. (spargo). **I.** *spread out, scattered;* crines, dishevelled, Liv. **II.** *speckled, coloured, spotted;* anguis maculis sparsus, Liv.

Sparta -ae, f. and **Spartē** -ēs, f. (Σπάρτη), *Sparta, the capital of Laconia, now Misitra.* Hence, adj., **A. Spartānus** -a -um, *Spartan;*

subst., **Spartānus** -i, m. *a Spartan.* **B. Spartĭcus** -a -um, *Spartan.* **C.** Subst., **Spartĭātes** -ae, m. *a Spartan.*

Spartăcus -i, m. *a gladiator, by birth a Thracian, head of the Gladiatorial War against the Romans,* 73–71 B.C., *defeated by Crassus.*

spartārĭus -a -um (spartum), *bearing esparto grass,* Plin.; plur. subst., **spartārĭa** -ōrum, n. (sc. loca), *places where esparto grass grows,* Plin.

spartum (-on) -i, n. (σπάρτον), **1,** *a kind of grass, esparto grass,* Liv., Plin.; **2,** *rope made of esparto grass,* Plin.

spărŭlus -i, m. (dim. of sparus), *a kind of fish, a bream,* Ov.

spărus -i, m. and **spărum** -i, n. *a small curved spear or javelin, a hunting-spear,* Verg., Sall.

spasmus -i, m. (σπασμός), and **spasma** -ătis, n. (σπάσμα), *a cramp, spasm,* Plin.

spastĭcus -a -um (σπαστικός), *seized with cramp or spasm,* Plin.

spătha -ae, f. (σπάθη). **I.** *a wooden instrument for stirring or mixing, a spatula,* Plin. **II.** *an instrument of like shape used by weavers,* Sen. **III.** *a broad two-edged sword without point,* Tac. **IV.** *the pedicle of the leaf or flower of a palm-tree,* Plin. **V.** *a kind of pine or fir,* also called elate, Plin.

spătĭor, 1. dep. (spatium), *to walk, walk about, to take a walk, to promenade;* in xysto, Cic.; in sicca arena, Verg.; transf., of things, *to spread out, expand;* alae spatiantes, Ov.

spătĭōsē, adv. (spatiosus). **I. a,** *widely, extensively,* Plin.; **b,** *greatly;* spatiosius increvit flumen, Ov. **II.** Fig., of time, *long,* Prop.

spătĭōsus -a -um (spatium). **I.** *occupying much space, wide, spacious, large;* taurus, Ov. **II.** Fig., of time, *long;* nox, Ov.

spătĭum -ĭi, n. (σπάδιον Dorian = σταδιον), *space, distance, or extension in length and breadth.* **I. A.** Gen., spatia locorum, Caes.; caeli spatium, Verg. **B.** Esp., *space or distance between two points;* **1,** **a,** *distance, interval;* paribus spatiis intermissae trabes, Caes.; **b,** *circumference, size, length;* oris et colli, Ov.; **2, a,** *tract, extent, course;* longum spatium itineris, Caes.; eadem spatia quinque stellae conficiunt, Cic.; **b,** *the course in a race;* spatia corripere, Verg.; fig., quasi decurso spatio, Cic.; **c,** *a walk;* 2 a) duobus spatiis tribusve factis, Cic.; (*β*) *a place for walking in, walk, promenade;* spatia silvestria, Cic. **II.** Transf., of time, **A.** Gen., **a,** *a division or space of time, time;* spatium preteriti temporis, Cic.; hoc interim spatio, Cic.; **b,** *duration of time, length of time;* spatio pugnae defatigati, Caes. **B.** Esp., **1,** *the time fixed for any action, time, leisure, opportunity;* nisi tempus et spatium datum sit, Cic.; irae spatium dare, *give the reins to,* Liv.; si mihi aliquid spatii ad scribendum darent, Cic.; **2,** *metrical time, measure, quantity,* Cic.

spĕcĭālis -e (species), *individual, particular, special,* Quint.

spĕcĭēs -ēi, f. (specio). **I.** Act., *a seeing, sight, view, look;* speciem aliquo vertere, Lucr. **II.** Pass. = 1, *sight, look, appearance,* speciem boni viri prae se ferre, Cic.; speciem ridentis praebere, Liv.; 2, *form, figure,* esp. of imposing appearance; humana, Cic.; divina, Liv.; 3, *beautiful form, beauty;* vaccae, Ov.; esp. of outward ornament, *glitter, splendour;* triumpho maximam speciem captiva arma praebuere, Liv.; 4, *that which a man sees mentally;* **a,** *model, ideal;* eloquentiae, Cic.; **b,** *idea, conception, notion;* boni viri, Cic.; **c,** *a vision seen in a dream. a dream. vhantom;* consuli visa species

viri, Liv. ; **d,** *appearance, show;* speciem utilitatis habere, Cic.; specie, *in appearance,* Cic.; ad speciem, *for the sake of outward show* (to deceive), Cic.; **5,** *a statue, representation, image,* Cic.; **6,** *a kind, species, division of a genus,* Cic. (genit. and dat. plur. not used by classical authors).

spĕcillum -i, n. (specio), *a surgeon's probe,* Cic.

spĕcĭmen -ĭnis, n. (specio), *that by which a thing is known, mark, token, sample, specimen.* **I.** Lit., ingenii, Cic.; justitiae, Liv. **II.** Transf., *a pattern, example, ideal;* prudentiae, Cic.; num dubitas quin specimen naturae capi debeat ex optima quaque natura, Cic. (only used in the sing.).

spĕcĭo (spĭcĭo), spexi, spectum (σκέπτω), *to look at, behold, see,* Plaut.

spĕcĭōsē, adv. (speciosus), *beautifully, splendidly, handsomely, showily;* speciosius instratus equus quam uxor vestita, Liv.

spĕcĭōsus -a -um (species). **I.** *beautiful, splendid, handsome;* mulier, Ov.; hence, **a,** *dazzling, well-sounding;* nomina, Tac.; **b,** *imposing, distinguished;* opes, Tac.; exemplum, Liv. **II.** *plausible, specious;* vocabula, Hor.; titulus, Liv.; with 2. supine, si vera potius quam dictu speciosa dicenda sunt, Liv.

spectābĭlis -e (specto), **1,** *visible;* corpus, Cic.; **2,** *worth seeing, notable, remarkable;* heros, Ov.

spectācŭlum -i, n. (specto), *a sight, show, spectacle.* **I.** Gen., luctuosum, Cic.; rerum caelestium, Cic.; alicui spectaculum praebere, Cic.; spectaculo esse, Cic. **II.** Esp., *a spectacle in the theatre* or *circus;* **1,** lit., spectaculum apparatissimum, Cic.; gladiatorum, Liv.; **2,** meton., *a place from which* or *where one can see a spectacle;* gen. plur., spectacula; **a,** *the stage, the seats;* spectacula sunt tributim data, Cic.; **b,** *the theatre,* Suet.

spectāmen -ĭnis, n. (specto), *a sign, token, pooof,* Plaut.

spectātē, adv., but only in superl. (spectatus), *admirably, excellently,* Plin.

spectātĭo -ōnis, f. (specto), *a looking at, beholding, viewing.* **I.** Gen., apparatus, Cic.; animum spectatione levari, Cic. **II.** *the inspection, testing of money,* Cic.

spectātīvus -a -um (specto), *contemplative* (opp. activus), *theoretical,* Quint.

spectātor -ōris, m. (specto). **I.** *one who beholds, contemplates, a spectator, observer;* **a,** quasi spectatores superarum rerum atque caelestium, Cic.; **b,** *a spectator at the theatre* or *public games,* Cic. **II.** *an inspector, examiner;* formarum, *connoisseur,* Ter.; acrior virtutis spectator ac judex, Liv.

spectātrix -trīcis, f. (spectator), *a female spectator, beholder, observer,* Ov.

spectātus -a -um, p. adj. (from specto). **I.** *proved, approved, tried;* homo, Cic.; castitas, Liv. **II.** Esp., *of tried abilities, excellent, respected, renowned;* vir spectatissimus, Cic.

spectĭo -ōnis, f. (specio), *the right of observing the auspices appertaining to certain of the higher magistrates;* nos (augures) nuntiationem solum habemus, consules et reliqui magistratus etiam spectionem, Cic.

specto, 1. (intens. of specio), *to look at carefully, contemplate, observe.* **I.** Lit., **A.** Gen., aliquid, Cic.; tota domus quae spectat in nos solos, Cic.; spectatumne huc venimus? Liv. **B.** Esp., **1,** *to be a spectator of a spectacle* or *play, to look at, look on at;* fabulam, ludos, Hor.; Megalesia. Cic.; **2, a,** *to look at with*

wonder; gaude quod spectant oculi te mille loquentem, Hor.; **b,** *to look at for the purpose of examining* or *testing, to test, to examine;* spectatur in ignibus aurum, Ov.; fig., hunc igni spectatum arbitrantur, *tried by fire,* Cic.; **3,** of places, *to look towards, lie towards, be situate towards;* collis ad orientem solem spectabat, Caes.; spectare in Etruriam, Liv.; spectare inter occasum solis et septentriones, Caes. **II.** Fig., **A.** *to look at, contemplate, observe;* voluptates procul specto, Cic. **B.** Esp., **1,** *to look to as an aim* or *object, bear in mind, have a regard to, strive after;* **a,** of persons, magna, Cic.; ea quae sunt in usu vitaque communi, Cic.; fugam, Cic.; with ut and the subj., spectavi semper ut possem, etc., Cic.; with ad and the acc., ad imperatorias laudes, Cic.; **b,** transf., *to tend to, incline to;* ad perniciem, Cic.; ad bene beateque vivendum, Cic.; quo igitur haec spectat oratio? *what is the aim* (or *tendency) of this speech?* Cic.; **2,** *to judge, test;* aliquem ex trunco corporis, Cic.; non ex singulis vocibus philosophi spect andi sunt, Cic.

spectrum -i, n. (specio), *the appearance, image of anything, spectre, apparition,* Cic.

1. spĕcŭla -ae, f. (specio). **I.** *a watch-tower;* speculas per promunturia omnia ponere, Liv.; multo ante tamquam ex specula prospexi tempestatem futuram, Cic.; fig., homines in speculis sunt, *on the watch,* Cic. **II.** Transf., in speculis, *any lofty place,* Verg.

2. spēcŭla -ae, f. (dim. of spes), *a little hope;* qui aliquid ex eius sermone speculae degustarat, Cic.

spĕcŭlābundus -a -um (speculor), *watching, on the watch,* Tac.

spĕcŭlāris -e (speculum), *of* or *relating to a mirror,* Sen.; lapis, *a species of transparent stone, talc,* Plin. Subst., **spĕcŭlāria** -ium and -ōrum, n. *window-panes made of talc,* Plin.

spĕcŭlātor -ōris, m. (speculor). **I.** *a looker-out, scout, spy,* Caes., Cic. **II.** Transf., *an observer, investigator;* naturae, Cic.

spĕcŭlātōrĭus -a -um (speculator), *of* or *relating to a looker-out* or *scout;* navigia, Caes.; naves, Liv., and subst., speculatoriae, *vessels on the look-out, spy-boats,* Liv.

spĕcŭlātrix -īcis, f. (speculator), *she that observes, a looker-out, observer, watcher;* Furiae sunt speculatrices et vindices facinorum et scelerum, Cic.

spĕcŭlor, 1. dep. (specio). **I.** Intransit., *to spy, to look about;* unde sedens partes speculatur in omnes, Ov. **II.** Transit., *to look out, spy out, watch, observe, explore;* omnia, Cic.; loca, Cic.; alicuius consilia, Sall.; with rel. sent., quae fortuna esset, Liv.

spĕcŭlum -i, n. (specio), *a mirror* (made of glittering plates of metal). **I.** Lit., speculorum levitas, Cic.; speculo placere, *to be brilliantly adorned,* Ov.; speculum suum consulere, Ov.; se speculo videre alterum, Hor. **II.** Fig. = *an image, copy;* quae (parvos et bestias) putat esse specula naturae, Cic.

spĕcus -ūs, m. f. and n. (σπέος), *a cave.* **I.** Lit., **a,** *a natural cave,* Hor., Liv.; horrendum, Verg.; **b,** *an artificial cave, excavation;* (α) in defossis specubus, Verg.; (β) *a covered watercourse, culvert;* subterranei, Cic. **II.** Transf., *a hole, hollow;* vulneris, Verg.

spēlaeum -i, n. (σπήλαιον), *a cave, grotto, hole, den;* ferarum, Verg.

spēlunca -ae, f. (σπήλυγξ), *a cave, grotto,* Cic., Verg.

spērābĭlis -e (spero), *that may be hoped for,* Plaut.

Sperchĕŏs (-chĕus) and **Sperchĭos (-chĭus)** -i, m. (Σπερχειός), *a river in Thessaly.* Hence, **A. Spercheïs** -ēïdis, f. *of Spercheus.* **B. Sperchĭŏnĭdes** -ae, m. *a person who lives near the Spercheus.* **C. Sperchīae** -ārum, f. *a town in the valley of the Spercheus.*

sperno, sprēvi, sprētum, 3. **I.** *to separate, remove,* Plaut. **II.** Transf., *to reject, to despise, contemn, scorn, spurn;* nos sprevit et pro nihilo putavit, Cic.; voluptatem, Hor.; poet. with infin., nec partem solido demere de die spernit, Hor.; partic., **sprētus** -a -um, *despised,* Cic., Liv.

spēro, 1. *to look for, to expect.* **I.** *to expect something favourable, to hope, hope for, promise oneself, flatter oneself;* bene or recte, *to have good hopes,* Cic.; ut spero (in a parenthesis), Cic.; de aliqua re, Cic.; pacem, Cic.; in pass., sperata gloria, Cic.; with acc. and fut. infin., sperant se maximum fructum esse capturos, Cic.; more rarely with pres. or perf. infin. (when there is no reference to the future), spero ex hoc ipso non esse obscurum, Cic.; de nostra Tullia spero cum Crassipede nos confecisse, Cic.; with ut and the subj., Liv.; partic. as subst., **spērāta** -ōrum, n. *one's hopes;* potiri speratis, *to realise one's hopes,* Liv. **II.** Like ἐλπίζω, *to expect something unfavourable, to forebode, fear;* id quod non spero, Cic.; with acc. and infin., haec spero vobis molesta videri, Cic.

spēs -ĕi, f. (root SPE, whence spero). **I.** *hope;* 1, lit., a, spes est exspectatio boni, Cic.; spes emptionis, Cic.; summae spei adulescentes, *of great promise,* Caes.; spes est in vobis, *rests on you,* Cic.; communem spem salutis in virtute ponere, Caes.; spem habere, in spem venire, ingredi, adduci, spes me tenet, *I hope,* foll. by acc. and infin., Cic.; si spem afferunt ut, etc., Cic.; spe duci, with acc. and infin., Cic.; spem alicui dare, *to infuse,* Cic.; pax fuit in spe, *was hoped for,* Cic.; spem abscidere, Liv., praecidere, Cic., fallere, Cic., eripere, Cic., adimere, Cic., perdere, Cic.; praeter spem, Cic.; contra spem, Liv.; plur., spes, Liv.; b, personif., Spes, *Hope as a goddess,* with several temples in Rome, and a festival on the 1st of August; 2, meton., *that which is hoped for, hope;* spe potitur, *realises his hope,* Ov.; castra Achivom, vestras spes, uritis, Verg.; of living beings, spes gregis, Verg.; spes nostra reliqua, Cicero, Cic. **II.** *expectation of, fear of, foreboding;* mala res, spe multo asperior, Sall.

speustĭcus -a -um (σπευστικός), *made in haste,* Plin.

sphaera -ae, f. (σφαῖρα), *a globe, sphere.* **I.** Gen., Cic. **II.** a, *an astronomical globe or sphere,* Cic.; b, *the orbit of planets,* Cic.

sphaeristērĭum -ĭi, n. (σφαιριστήριον), *a place for playing ball,* Plin.

sphaerŏmăchĭa -ae, f. (σφαιρομαχία), *a kind of boxing in which the combatants had iron balls strapped to their hands,* Sen.

sphagnos -i, m. (σφάγνος), *a kind of aromatic moss,* Plin.

sphingĭon -ĭi, n. (σφίγγιον), *a species of ape,* Plin.

Sphinx, Sphingis, f. (Σφίγξ), *a female monster at Thebes, who proposed riddles to all the passers-by, and destroyed them if they could not answer the riddles;* represented among the Egyptians as a winged lion with a human head, among the Greeks and Romans as an unwinged lion with the head and breast of a maiden.

sphrăgis -ĭdis, f. (σφραγίς). **I.** *a species of stone used for seals,* Plin. **II.** *Lemnian earth, so called because sold with a seal on it,* Plin.

spīca -ae, f., **spīcus** -i, m., and **spīcum** -i, n. (from same root as spi-na); lit., *a spike;* hence, *an ear of corn.* **I.** Lit., ad spicam perducere fruges, Cic. **II.** Transf., a, *the brightest star in the constellation Virgo,* Cic.; b, *the tuft or head of other plants resembling the shape of an ear of corn,* Ov.

spīcĕus -a -um (spica), *consisting of ears of corn;* corona, Tib.; serta, Ov.

spīcĭfer -fĕra- fĕrum (spica and fero), *wearing or carrying ears of corn,* Mart.

spīcĭlĕgĭum -ĭi, n. (spica and lego), *a gleaning,* Varr.

spīco, 1. (spica), *to furnish with spikes or ears,* Plin.; partic., **spīcātus** -a -um, *having spikes or ears;* herbae spicatae, Plin.

spīcŭlo, 1. (spiculum), *to make pointed, sharpen to a point,* Plin.

spīcŭlum -i, n. (spicum), *a sharp point, sting;* a, lit., of bees, Verg.; of the scorpion, Ov.; *the point of a spear, arrow, javelin,* Cic., Liv., Hor.; b, poet., meton. = *a spear, javelin,* Verg., Ov.

spīcum, spicus = spica (q.v.).

spīna -ae, f. (from same root as spica). **I.** a *thorn.* **A.** Lit., Verg. **B.** Fig., a, spinae = *cares, anxieties;* spinas animo evellere, Hor.; b, *difficulties, subtleties, perplexities;* disserendi, Cic. **II.** Transf., 1, *the prickle or spine of certain animals, the hedgehog, sea-urchin,* etc., Cic.; 2, *the backbone,* Varr.; 3, *a fish-bone,* Ov.

spīnĕa -ae, f. = spionia (q.v.).

spīnētum -i, n. (spina), *a thorn-hedge, thorn-bush* (only used in plur.), Verg.

spīnĕus -a -um (spina), *made of thorns,* thorny, Ov.

spīnĭger -gĕra -gĕrum (spina and gero), *thorn-bearing,* Cic. poet.

spīnōsus -a -um (spina). **I.** *full of thorns, thorny, prickly,* Ov. **II.** Fig., a, *of discourse, thorny, crabbed, obscure;* disserendi genus, Cic.; b, *full of cares, anxiety,* Cat.

spinter -ēris, n. (σφιγκτήρ), *a bracelet, armlet,* Plaut.

spīnus -i, m. (spina), *the blackthorn,* Verg.

spĭonĭa -ae, f. *a kind of vine,* Plin.

spīra -ae, f. (σπεῖρα), *anything coiled, wreathed, twisted.* **I.** Gen., *the winding of a snake,* Verg. **II.** Esp., 1, *the base of a column,* Plin.; 2, *a string for fastening a hat or cap under the chin,* Juv.

spīrābĭlis -e (spiro). **I.** *that may be breathed;* a, natura, cui nomen est aër, Cic.; b, *sustaining life, vital;* lumen caeli, Verg. **II.** *fitted for breathing;* viscera, Plin.

spīrācŭlum -i, n. (spiro), *an air-hole, breathing-place,* Verg.

spīraea -ae, f. (σπειραία), *the plant meadow-sweet,* Plin.

spīrāmen -ĭnis, n. (spiro), *a breathing-hole, air-hole,* Lucan.

spīrāmentum -i, n. (spiro). **I.** *a breathing-hole, air-hole,* Verg. **II.** *breathing;* meton., a *breathing-time, short pause, interval;* temporum, Tac.

spīrĭtus -ūs, m. (spiro), *breathing.* **I.** 1, a *gentle blowing, breath of air, air in gentle motion;* spiritus Boreae, Verg.; 2, *the breathing in of the air, breath;* spiritum ducere, *to draw breath,* Cic.; 3, *breath;* angustior, *short breath,* Cic.; esp., *the breath of life, life;* spiritum auferre, Cic.; extremum spiritum effundere in victoria, Cic.; hence, a, a *sigh,* Hor.; Prŏp.; b, *the hissing of a snake,* Verg.; c, *the voice,* Quint.;

d, *the air,* Lucr. **II.** *the spirit, soul.* **A.** dum spiritus hos regit artus, Verg. **B.** Fig., 1, *a haughty spirit, pride, arrogance, high spirit, courage;* filia Hieronis, inflata muliebri spiritu, Liv.; spiritus tribuuicii, Cic.; remittere spiritus, Cic.; 2, *opinion, feeling,* Liv.; 3, *irritation, animosity,* Tac.; 4, *divine* or *poetic inspiration;* divinus, Liv.; carent libri spiritu illo, etc., Cic.

spīro, 1. **I.** Intransit., 1, *to blow gently, blow, breathe;* zephyri spirant, Verg.; 2, *to breathe;* poet. = *to rush, to foam, ferment, roar;* freta spirantia, Verg.; spirat e pectore flamma, Verg.; with abl., spirare ignibus, *to breathe out flame,* Verg.; 3, *to breathe, to draw in breath;* dum spirare potero, Cic.; hence transf., **a,** *to live, be alive;* ab eo spirante defendi, Cic.; videtur Laelii mens spirare in scriptis, Cic.; **b,** *to seem to live;* of works of art, *to be depicted to the life, to breathe;* spirantia signa, Verg.; **c,** *to have poetic inspiration, to be inspired;* quod spiro et placeo tuum est, Hor.; 4, *to breathe, to smell;* thymbra graviter spirans, Verg. **II.** Transit., 1, *to breathe, exhale;* Diomedis equi spirantes naribus ignem, Lucr.; flammas spirantes, *breathing forth flames,* Liv.; spirare ignem naribus, Verg.; tunc immensa cavi spirant mendacia folles, Juv.; transf., homo tribunatum etiamnunc spirans, *inspired with the spirit of a tribune,* Liv.; tragicum satis, *to have tragic genius,* Hor.; 2, *to exhale, give forth;* divinum vertice odorem, Verg.

spissāmentum -i, n. (spisso), *a stopper, plug,* Sen.

spissē, adv. (spissus). **I.** *densely, closely,* Plin. **II.** *slowly;* spisse atque vix ad aliquem pervenire, Cic.

spissesco, 3. (spissus), *to become thick, thicken,* Lucr.

spissigrădus -a -um (spisse and gradior), *walking slowly,* Plaut.

spissĭtas -ātis, f. (spissus), *closeness, density,* Plin.

spissĭtūdo -ĭnis, f. (spissus), *closeness, density,* Sen.

spisso, 1. (spissus), *to make thick, thicken,* Ov.

spissus -a -um, *close, dense, thick.* **I.** Lit., nubes, Ov.; theatrum, *full,* Hor.; arena, Verg.; with abl., corona spissa viris, Verg. **II.** Transf., *slow, tardy, difficult;* opus spissum et operosum, Cic.; exitus spissi et producti, Cic.

spĭthăma -ae, f. (σπιθαμή), *a span,* Plin.

splēn, splēnis, m. (σπλήν), *the spleen, milt,* Plin.

splendĕo, 2. *to shine, glitter, be bright.* **I.** Lit., splendet tremulo sub lumine pontus, Verg. **II.** Fig., *to be bright, illustrious;* virtus splendet per sese semper, Cic.

splendesco -dŭi, 3. (splendeo), *to become bright.* **I.** Lit., Verg. **II.** Fig., nihil est tam incultum, quod non splendescat oratione, Cic.

splendĭdē, adv. (splendidus). **I.** *splendidly, magnificently;* ornare convivium, Cic.; acta aetas honeste ac splendide, Cic. **II.** *clearly, plainly;* loqui, Cic.

splendĭdus -a -um (splendeo), *shining, bright, brilliant, splendid.* **I. A.** Lit., fons splendidior vitro, Hor.; brachia, Ov.; splendidissimus candor, Cic. **B.** Fig., **a,** *well-sounding;* nomen, Cic.; **b,** *brilliant, fine;* oratio, Cic.; **c,** *illustrious, distinguished, renowned;* eques, Cic. **II.** Transf., *clear;* vox, Cic.

splendor -ōris, m. (splendeo), *brilliance, brightness, lustre.* **I. A.** Lit., flammae, Ov.; argenti, Hor. **B.** Fig., **a,** *splendour, magnificence;* omnia ad gloriam splendoremque revocare, Cic.; **b.** *splendour. lustre. honour, distinc-*

---

tion; animi et vitae, Cic.; summorum hominum, Cic.; eo negotio M. Catonis splendorem maculare, Cic.; **c,** *ornament, honour;* ordinis, Cic. **II.** Transf., *clearness;* vocis, Cic.

splēniātus -a -um (splenium), *plastered,* Mart.

splēnĭcus -a -um (σπληνικός), *splenetic,* Plin.

splēnĭum -ĭi, n. (σπλήνιον). **I.** *spleenwort,* Plin. **II.** *an adhesive plaster,* Mart.

spŏdĭum -ĭi, n. (σπόδιον). **I.** *the dross of metals, slag,* Plin. **II.** *ashes,* Plin.

spŏdos -i, f. (σποδός), *the dross of metals, slag,* Plin.

Spŏlētĭum -ĭi, n. *one of the most important towns of Umbria,* now *Spoleto.* Hence, **Spŏlētīnus** -a -um, *of* or *belonging to Spoletium, Spoletian.*

spŏlĭārĭum -ĭi, n. (spolium). **I.** *the place in the amphitheatre where the slain gladiators were stripped of their arms and clothing,* Sen. **II.** Transf., *a den of robbers,* Sen.

spŏlĭātĭo -ōnis, f. (spolio), *a plundering, spoliation;* omnium rerum, Cic.; sacrorum, Cic.; transf., *violent taking away;* consulatus, Cic.; dignitatis, Cic.

spŏlĭātor -ōris, m. (spolio), *a plunderer;* monumentorum, Cic.; templorum, Liv.

spŏlĭātrix -trīcis, f. (spoliator), *plundering, she that plunders;* Venus, Cic.

spŏlĭātus -a -um, p. adj. with compar. (from spolio), *plundered,* Cic.

spŏlĭo, 1. (spolium). **I.** *to rob a man of his clothes, strip, despoil;* aliquem, Cic.; corpus caesi hostis, Liv. **II.** *to plunder, rob, despoil;* fana sociorum, Cic.; hominem, Cic.; with abl., aliquem argento, Cic.; poet., with acc. of respect, hiems spoliata suos capillos, Ov.

spŏlĭum -ĭi, n. **I.** *the skin* or *hide stripped from an animal;* leonis, Ov. **II.** Transf., gen. plur., 1, *arms taken from an enemy, booty* (opp. praeda = *cattle,* etc.), spolia caesorum legere, Liv.; spolia opima (v. opimus); meton. = *victory;* spolia ampla referre, Verg.; 2, transf., *booty;* **a,** *booty* or *plunder taken from an enemy, spoil;* spolia classium, Cic.; **b,** *any kind of plunder* or *booty;* aliorum spoliis nostras facultates augeamus, Cic.; sceleris, *the golden hair which Scylla robbed from her father,* Ov.

sponda -ae, f. **I.** *the frame of a bed* or *sofa, bedstead,* Ov. **II.** Meton., **a,** *a bed,* Hor.; **b,** *a sofa,* Verg.; **c,** *a bier,* Mart.

spondālĭum (spondaulĭum) -ĭi, n. *a sacrificial hymn, accompanied on the flute,* Cic.

spondĕo, spŏpondi, sponsum, 2. (root SPOND, Gr. ΣΠΕΝΔ, σπένδω), *to pledge oneself, promise solemnly, engage;* **a,** political and legal t.t. of alliances, contracts, etc., quis spopondisse me dicit? Cic.; with acc., quod spopondit, Cic.; illis spondere pacem, Liv.; with acc. and infin., si spopondissemus urbem hanc relicturum populum Romanum, Liv.; **b,** *to be a security* or *guarantee for any one;* se quisque paratum ad spondendum Icilio ostendere, Liv.; hic sponsum (supine) vocat, Hor.; with pro and the abl., pro multis, Cic.; **c,** *to promise, betroth a daughter,* Ter., Plaut.; partic. subst., **sponsus** -i, m. *a bridegroom,* and **sponsa** -ae, f. *a bride,* Cic.; **d,** *to promise, vow;* (a) of persons, with acc. iis honores et praemia, Cic.; with neut. acc. and de with the abl., quod de me tibi spondere possum, Cic.; with acc. and infin., promitto, recipio, spondeo C. Caesarem talem semper fore civem qualis, etc., Cic.; (β), transf., of things, quod propediem futurum spondet et virtus et fortuna vestra, Liv.

spondēus (spondīus) -i, m. (σπονδεῖος), *a spondee; a metrical foot consisting of two long syllables* (- -), Cic.

spondȳlē -ēs, f. (σπονδύλη), *an insect that lives upon roots*, Plin.

spondȳlium -ii, n. (σπονδύλιον), *bear's-foot*, Plin.

spondȳlus -i, m. (σπόνδυλος). **I.** *one of the upper vertebrae of the back*, Plin. **II.** *the fleshy part of the oyster or mussel*, Plin. **III.** *a kind of mussel*, Plin.

spongïa (spongĕa) -ae, f. (σπογγιά), *a sponge*. **I.** Lit., *raritas quaedam et assimilis* spongiis mollitudo, Cic. **II.** Transf., 1, *an open-worked cuirass*, Liv.; 2, *the roots of the asparagus*, Plin.; 3, *spongiae, pieces of iron melted together*, Plin.

spongïŏla -ae, f. (spongia), *the gall-apple which grows upon rose-trees*, Plin.

spongïōsus -a -um (spongia), *porous, spongy*, Plin.

spongītis -ĭdis, f. (σπογγῖτις), *a kind of precious stone*, Plin.

spons, spontis, f. (from spondeo, as fors from fero), *free-will; only found in genit. and abl.* **I.** Abl., sponte alicuius, *with the free-will of some one;* sponte Antonii, Tac.; gen., sponte meā, tuā, suā, etc., or simply sponte; a, *of my, thy, his,* etc., *free-will, voluntarily, of one's own accord, willingly, freely;* meā sponte feceram, Cic.; b, *of oneself, of one's own knowledge;* neque id meā sponte (prospexi), Cic.; c, *of oneself alone, without assistance;* nec suā sponte sed eorum auxilio, Cic.; d, *of itself, merely, alone;* an est aliquid, quod te suā sponte delectet, Cic.; e, *first, without an example or precedent;* suā sponte instituisset, Cic. **II.** Genit., homo suae spontis, *one's own master*, Col.

sponsa, v. spondeo.

sponsālis -e (sponsa), *of or relating to a betrothal*. **I.** Adj., Varr. **II.** Subst., **sponsālïa** -um or -ōrum, n. *a betrothal; sponsalia facere*, Cic.; b, *a betrothal feast*, Cic.

sponsïo -ōnis, f. (spondeo), *a solemn promise, engagement.* **I.** Of a vow, voti, Cic. **II.** *a solemn engagement between two parties.* **A.** In alliances, contracts, etc., *a solemn promise, pledge, surety, guarantee;* non foedere sed per sponsionem pax facta est, Liv. **B.** In civil process, *a solemn promise or engagement between the two parties that the loser shall forfeit a certain sum, a kind of legal wager;* quum sponsionem fecisset NI VIR BONUS ESSET, *he agreed to pay the stipulated sum if he was not,* etc., Cic.; vincere sponsionem or sponsione, Cic.

sponsor -ōris, m. (spondeo), *a surety, bail, guarantee*, Cic.

sponsum -i, n. (spondeo). **I.** *that which is promised* or *guaranteed, a covenant;* sponsum negare, Hor. **II.** = sponsio No. II., ex sponso agere, Cic.

1. **sponsus** -a -um, v. spondeo.

2. **ꞟponsus** -ūs, m. (spondeo), *an engagement, suretyship*, Cic.

spontānĕus -a -um (spons), *voluntary, spontaneous;* Sen.

spontĕ, spontis, v. spons.

sporta -ae, f. (σπυρίς), *a basket, hamper*, Plin.

sportella -ae, f. (dim. of sporta), *a little basket, cake,* or *fruit-basket*, Cic.

sportŭla -ae, f. (dim. of sporta). **I.** *a little basket*, Plaut. **II.** *a provision-basket.* **A.** *the basket in which clients and dependents provisions or an equivalent in money* (gen. *ten sesterces*), Juv.;

hence, *a gift, present*, Plin. **B.** = δεῖπνον ἀπὸ σπυρίδος, *a picnic*, Juv.

sprētïo -ōnis, f. (sperno), *a despising, contemning*, Liv.

sprētor -ōris, m. (sperno), *a despiser;* deorum, Ov.

spūma -ae, f. (spuo), *foam, froth, scum;* cum spumas ageret in ore, Cic.; Venus spuma procreata, *from the foam of the sea*, Cic.; spuma argenti, *litharge of silver*, Verg.; spuma caustica, *a soap used by the Germans and Gauls for the purpose of giving a red tinge to the hair*, Mart.

spūmesco, 3. (spuma), *to begin to foam*, Ov.

spūmĕus -a -um (spuma), *foaming, frothy,* Verg.

spūmĭfĕr -fĕra -fĕrum (spuma and fero), *foam-bearing, foaming;* amnis, Ov.

spūmĭgĕr -gĕra -gĕrum (spuma and gero), *foaming*, Lucr.

spūmo, 1. (spuma). **I.** Intransit., *to foam, froth;* spumans aper, Verg. **II.** Transit., *to cover with foam;* partic., **spūmātus** -a -um, *covered with foam;* saxa, Cic. poet.

spūmōsus -a -um (spuma), *foaming, full of foam*, Ov.

spŭo, spŭi, spūtum, 3. (πτύω), *to spit out;* terram, Verg.

spurcē, adv. (spurcus), *filthily, dirtily;* fig., basely, impurely; quin in illam miseram tam spurce, tam impie dixeris, Cic.

spurcĭdĭcus -a -um (spurce and dico), *talking filthily, obscenely*, Plaut.

spurcĭfĭcus -a -um (spurce and facio), *making filthy, polluting*, Plaut.

spurcĭtïa -ae, f. and **spurcĭtïes** -ēi f. (spurcus), *dirt, filth*, Lucr.

spurco, 1. (spurcus), *to defile, pollute*, Cat.; partic. adj. in superl., helluo spurcatissimus, Cic.

spurcus -a -um (perhaps connected with spargo), *swinish, dirty, filthy, unclean, impure.* **I.** Lit., Cat. **II.** Fig., *of character or position, mean, base, low, foul, impure;* homo spurcissimus, Cic.

spūtātĭlĭcĭus -a -um (sputo) = κατάπτυστος, *abominable, detestable*, ap. Cic.

spūtātor -ōris, m. (sputo), *one who spits much, a spitter*, Cic.

spūto, 1. (intens. of spuo), *to spit, spit out;* cum atro mixtos sanguine dentes, Ov.

spūtum -i, n. (spuo), *spittle.* **I.** Lit., Lucr. **II.** Meton., *a very thin plate of metal*, Mart.

squālĕo, 2. *to be rough, stiff.* **I.** Gen., squaleutes conchae, Verg.; with abl., *to be rough with, to be stiff with* = *to be thickly covered with;* tunica or lorica squalens auro, Verg. **II.** Esp., 1, *to be rough from neglect, dirty, squalid, slovenly;* barba squalens, Verg.; coma squalens, Ov.; hence, meton., *to wear dirty apparel as a sign of mourning, to mourn;* squalent municipia, Cic.; 2, *of places, to be uncultivated, untilled;* squalent abductis arva colonis, Verg.

squālēs -is, f. (squaleo), *dirt, filth*, Varr.

squālĭdē, adv. (squalidus), *roughly, in a slovenly manner;* dicere, Cic.

squālĭdus -a -um (squaleo). **I.** *rough, stiff;* membra, Lucr.; fig., of discourse, *rough, unpolished;* quoniam suā sponte squalidiora sunt, Cic. **II.** Esp., *rough from want of attention, cultivation, squalid, dirty:* 1, lit., corpora, Liv.; 2, transf., a, *in mourning attire;* reus, Ov.; b, *waste, desert;* humus, Ov.

squālor -ōris, m. (squaleo). **I.** *roughness,* Lucr. **II.** *roughness arising from dirt and* *neglect, filthiness, squalor;* **1**, lit., squaloris plenus ac pulveris, Cic.; **2**, transf., *dirty clothing worn as a sign of mourning;* squalor et maeror, Cic.

squălus -i, m. *a kind of salt-water fish,* Ov.

squāma -ae, f. (squaleo), *a scale.* **I.** Lit., of a fish, serpent, bee, etc., Cic. **II.** Transf., a, of things like scales, e.g., *scale armour,* Verg.; b, meton., *a fish,* Juv.

squāmātim, adv. (squama), *like scales,* Plin.

squāmĕus -a -um (squama), *scaly,* Verg.

squāmĭfĕr -fĕra -fĕrum (squama and fero), *scale-bearing, scaly,* Sen.

squāmĭgĕr -gĕra -gĕrum (squama and gero), *scale-bearing, scaly,* Ov.; subst., **squāmĭgĕri** -ōrum, m. *fishes,* Lucr.

squāmōsus -a -um (squama), *covered with scales, scaly,* Verg.

squatīna -ae, f. *a salt-water fish, a species of shark,* Plin.

st! interj. *hush! hist!* Ter., Plaut.

Stăbĭae -ārum, f. *a town in Campania, between Pompeii and Surrentum, destroyed with Pompeii and Herculanum on the eruption of Mount Vesuvius.* Hence, adj., **Stăbĭānus** -a -um, *belonging to Stabiae;* subst., **Stăbĭānum** -i, n. *an estate at Stabiae.*

stăbĭlīmen -ĭnis, n. (stabilio), *a stay, support,* Cic.

stăbĭlīmentum = stabilimen (q.v.).

stăbĭlĭo, 4. (stabilis), *to make firm.* **I.** Lit., stipites, Caes. **II.** Fig., *to make stable, to establish;* leges, rempublicam, Cic.

stăbĭlis -e (sto), *firm, steadfast, stable.* **I.** Lit., via, Cic.; solum, Liv. **II.** Fig., *firm, steadfast, stable, lasting, unwavering;* amici, Cic.; matrimonium, Cic.; oratio, Cic.; with ad and the acc., nihil est tam ad dinturnitatem memoriae stabile, Cic.; subst., **stăbĭlĭa** -ĭum, n. *things that are stable,* Cic.

stăbĭlĭtas -ātis, f. (stabilis), *firmness, stability, steadfastness.* **I.** Lit., peditum in proeliis, Caes.; stirpes stabilitatem dant iis, quae sustinent, Cic. **II.** Fig., *durability, steadfastness;* amicitiae, Cic.; fortunae, Cic.

stăbĭlĭtĕr, adv. (stabilis), *firmly, durably,* Suet.

stăbĭlĭtor -ōris, m. (stabilio), *one who makes firm, establishes,* Sen.

stăbŭlārĭus -ĭi, m. (stabulum), *a low inn-keeper,* Sen.

stăbŭlo, 1. (stabulum), *to have a stall or abode, to stall;* in foribus (Orci), Verg.

stăbŭlor, 1. dep. (stabulum) of animals, *to stand, be stabled, abide,* Ov.

stăbŭlum -i, n. (sto). **I.** *a place of abode, habitation,* Plaut. **II.** *a place of abode for animals and men of the poorer class.* **A.** Of animals; **1**, of wild animals, *den, lair;* ferarum stabula alta, Verg.; **2**, of tame animals, *a stall, stable;* poet., of pasture, Verg.; plur., stabula, *the stalls, cattle-yard,* as a place of abode for shepherds; pastorum stabula, Cic. **B.** Of men of the lower classes, *inn, tavern, pot-house,* Cic.

stăchys -yos, f. (στάχυς), *horse-mint,* Plin.

stacta -ae, f. and **stactē** -ēs, f. (στακτή), *oil of myrrh,* Lucr.

stădĭum -ĭi, n. (στάδιον). **I.** *a Greek measure of length, being* 625 *feet* = 606 *English feet, and rather less than a furlong,* Cic. **II.** Meton., *a race-course;* qui stadium currit, Cic.; fig., *contest, emulation;* me adolescentem multos annos in stadio eiusdem laudis exercuit, Cic.

Stăgīra -ōrum, m. (Στάγειρος), *a town in Macedonia, birth-place of Aristotle,* now *Libanora.* Hence, **Stăgīrītēs** -ae, m. (Σταγειρίτης), *the Stagirite,* i.e., *Aristotle.*

stagnātĭlis -e (stagnum), *found in ponds or pools;* pisces, Plin.

stagno, 1. (stagnum). **I.** Intransit., **1**, of water, *to overflow;* stagnans flumine Nilus, Verg.; **2**, transf., of places, *to be overflowed, to stand under water;* orbis stagnat paludibus, Ov. **II.** Transit., *to overflow, inundate;* Tiberis plana urbis stagnaverat, Tac.

stagnum -i, n. (root STAC, Gr. ΣΤΑΓ, whence στάζω, σταγών, στάγες), *water that overflows.* **I.** Lit., *standing water, left by the overflow of the sea* or *of a river, a pool, pond, marsh, swamp;* fontes et stagna, Cic. **II.** Transf., **A.** (poet.), *a sluggish stream of water;* Phrixeae stagna sororis, *the Hellespont,* Ov. **B.** *an artificial lake;* stagna et euripi, Ov.

stăgŏnĭas -ae, m. (σταγονίας), *a species of frankincense,* Plin.

stăgŏnītis -ĭdis, f. (σταγονῖτις), *the gum called galbanum,* Plin.

stălagmĭas -ae, m. (σταλαγμίας), *natural vitriol,* Plin.

stălagmĭum -ĭi, n. (στάλαγμα), *an ear-drop, pendant,* Plin.

stāmen -ĭnis, n. (from STA, root of sisto, as στήμων from ἵστημι). **I.** *the warp, which in the upright looms of the ancients was stretched in a vertical direction;* stamen secernit arundo, Ov. **II.** Transf., **1**, *the thread;* a, *the thread on the spindle;* stamina ducere or torquere, *to spin,* Ov.; *the thread spun by the Parcae,* Ov.; hence, de nimio stamine queri, *of too long a life,* Juv.; b, *a thread of another kind,* e.g., *that by which Ariadne guided Theseus through the labyrinth,* Prop.; of a spider, Ov.; *the string of a lyre,* Ov.; **2**, meton., *cloth woven of thread;* hence, *the fillet worn by priests,* Prop.

stāmĭnĕus -a -um (stamen), *full of threads,* Prop.

stannĕus -a -um, *made of stannum,* Plin.

stannum -i, n. *an alloy of silver and lead,* Plin.

Stăta mater = Vesta; or simply Stata, Cic.

stătārĭus -a -um (status), *standing firm, steady, stable, stationary;* miles, Liv.; esp., stataria comoedia, *a quiet kind of comedy* (opp. comoedia motoria), Ter.; subst., **stătārĭi** -ōrum, m. *the actors in the comoedia stataria,* Cic.; transf., C. Piso, statarius et sermonis plenus orator, *quiet, composed,* Cic.

Statelli and Statielli -ōrum, m. *a people in Liguria, whose chief town was* Aquae Statiellorum or Aquae Statiellae, now *Acqui;* hence, **A.** **Statellās** -ātis, *belonging to the Statelli.* **B.** **Statiellenses** -ĭum, m. *the inhabitants of* Aquae Statiellorum.

stătēra -ae, f. (στατήρ), *a steelyard, a balance;* aurificis, Cic.

stătĭcŭlum -i, n. (statua), *a small statue,* Plin.

stătĭcŭlus -i, m. (dim. of 2. status), *a kind of slow dance,* Plin.

stătim, adv. (sto). **I.** *without yielding, firmly, steadfastly;* rem gerere, Plaut. **II.** Transf., *on the spot, immediately, at once;* ut statim alienatio disjunctioque facienda sit, Cic.; foll. by ac, atque, ut, quam, quum, simulac, *as soon as,* Cic.

stătĭo, ōnis, f. (sto). **I.** *a standing, standing still;* manere in statione, *to stand still,* Lucr. **II.** Transf., *a place of abode or sojourn;* **1**, gen., alternā fratrem statione redemit, Ov.; 2, esp., **a**, of soldiers, (a) post, watch, picket, guard; equites ex statione, Caes.; stationem portis disposuit, Liv.; in statione and (of several cohorts) in stationibus esse, Caes.; stationem relinquere, Verg.; (β) quarters; fig., imperii, Ov.; de praesidio et statione vitae decedere, Cic.; **b**, a place of abode, resting-place; sedes apibus statioque petenda, Verg.; in arce Athenis statio (post) mea nunc placet, Cic.; **c**, a roadstead, anchorage, bay, Cic.; fig., fluctibus ejectum tutā statione recepi, haven, Ov.; **d**, the proper place, order (of things), comas ponere in statione, Ov.

stătĭōnālis -e (statio), standing still, stationary, Plin.

Stătĭus -ĭi, m.: **1**, Caecilius Statius, of Insubria, a Roman comic poet, born 168 B.C.; **2**, P. Papinius Statius, an Epic poet, under Domitian, composer of Silvae, a Thebais, and an unfinished Achilleis.

stătīvus -a -um (sto), standing, standing still. **I**. Adj., praesidium, picket, Cic.; castra, fixed quarters, Liv. **II**. Subst., **stătīva** -ōrum, n. (sc. castra), permanent camp, Liv.

1. stător -ōris, m. (sto), a magistrate's servant or attendant, Cic.

2. Stător -ōris, m. (sisto), the supporter, establisher, the stayer of flight; a surname of Jupiter, Cic.

stătŭa -ae, f. (statuo), a statue, image (of a man, while simulacrum = statue of a god); simulacra deorum, statuae veterum hominum, Cic.; statuam alicui ponere or statuere, Cic.

stătŭārĭus -a -um (statua), of or relating to statues. **I**. Adj., Plin. **II**. Subst., **1**, **stătŭārĭa** -ae, f. (sc. ars), the art of casting statues, Plin.; **2**, **stătŭārĭus** -ĭi, m. a maker or caster of statues, a statuary, Quint.

stătūmen -ĭnis, n. (statuo), a stay, support, prop; plur., the ribs of a ship, Caes.

stătūmĭno, **1**. (statumen), to underprop, Plin.

stătŭo -ŭi -ūtum, **3**. (from statum, the supine of sisto), to cause to stand, put, place, set, set up. **I**. Lit., 1, gen., captivos in medio, Liv.; crateras, Verg.; 2, esp., to set up, erect, build; statuam, Cic.; tropaeum, Cic.; tabernacula, to pitch, Caes.; urbem, Verg.; regnum, Cic. **II**. Transf., **1**, to establish in one's mind, to consider, believe; ut mihi statuo, Cic.; laudem statuo esse maximam, Cic.; **2**, to resolve, determine, decide; with de and the abl., de aliquo, Caes.; de capite civis, Cic.; with in and the acc., in aliquem aliquid gravius, Caes.; with acc. alone, stipendium alicui de publico, Liv.; with rel. sent., utrum diem tertium an perendinum dici oporteret, Cic.; with infin., judices rejicere, Cic.; with ut and the subj., ut naves conscenderent, Cic.

stătūra -ae, f. (sto), stature, height, size of a man; homines tantulae staturae, of so small stature, Caes.; quā facie fuerit, quā staturā, Cic.

1. stătŭs -a -um, v. sisto.

2. stătŭs -ūs, m. (sto), a standing, standing position. **I**. Lit., **1**, gen., status, incessus, sessio, Cic.; erectus, Cic.; **2**, esp., posture, position; minax, Hor.; statu movere hostem, Liv. **II**. Fig., **1**, gen., position, condition, state; adversarios de omni statu dejicere, Cic.; restituere aliquem in pristinum statum, Cic.; omnes vitae status, Cic.; **2**, esp., **a**, one's position in life as determined by birth; agnationibus familiarum distinguuntur status, Cic.; **b**, a firm position, stability, prosperity; civitatis, Cic.; **c**, rhet. t. t., status causae, or simply status, the status of the question, state of the case = στάσις, Cic.

stĕătōma -ătis, n. (στεάτωμα), a kind of fatty swelling, Plin.

stĕga -ae, f. (στέγη), a ship's deck, Plaut.

stegnus -a -um (στεγνός), causing costiveness, Plin.

stēla -ae, f. (στήλη), a pillar, column, Plin.

stēlis -ĭdis, f. (στελίς), mistletoe growing on firs and larches, Plin.

stella -ae, f. (= sterula, connected with ἀστήρ), a star. **I**. Lit., 1, a star, planet, comet; stella Saturni, stella Jovis, the planet Saturn, planet Jupiter, Cic.; stellae inerrantes, fixed stars, Cic.; vagae, planets, Cic.; stella comans, a comet, Ov.; **2**, transf., **a**, a figure in the form of a star, Plin.; **b**, a star-fish, Plin. **II**. In poets, **1**, = sidus, constellation, Verg., Ov.; **2**, = sun; auget geminos stella serena polos, Ov.

stellans -antis (stella), **1**, starry, set with stars; caelum, Lucr.; **2**, bright, shining, glittering; gemma, Ov.

Stellātis campus or ager, a very fruitful district in Campania. Hence, adj., **Stellātīnus** -a -um, Stellatian.

stellātus -a -um (stella), set with stars, starry; **a**, lit., Cepheus, Cic.; **b**, transf., Argus, having many eyes, Ov.; ensis, bright, glittering, Verg.

stellĭfer -fĕra -fĕrum (stella and fero), starbearing, starry; stellifer cursus, Cic.

stellĭgĕr -gĕra -gĕrum (stella and gero), star-bearing, starry, Varr.

stellĭo (stēlĭo) -ōnis, m. a lizard with spots on its back (Lacerta gecko, Linn.), Verg.

stello, **1**. (stella), to set with stars, Plin.

stemma -ătis, n. (στέμμα). **I**. a crown, chaplet, Sen. **II**. Meton., a genealogical tree, Suet.; transf., nobility, high antiquity, Mart.

Stentor -ōris, m. (Στέντωρ), one of the Greeks before Troy, famed for his loud voice and the strength of his lungs.

stĕphănĕplŏcos -i, f. (στεφανηπλόκος), the weaver of chaplets, the name of a painting by Pausias, Plin.

stĕphănītis -ĭdis, f. (στεφανῖτις), a kind of vine, Plin.

stĕphănŏmĕlis -is, f. a plant which stops a bleeding at the nose, Plin.

stĕphănŏpōlis -is, f. (στεφανόπωλις), the seller of chaplets; the name of a picture by Pausias, also called stephaneplocos, Plin.

stĕphănos -i, m. (στέφανος), lit., a garland, chaplet; the name of several plants, Plin.

stercŏrārĭus -a -um (stercus), of or relating to dung, Varr.

stercŏrātĭo -ōnis, f. (stercoro), a manuring, Varr.

stercŏrĕus -a -um (stercus), filthy, stinking; miles, Plaut.

stercŏro, **1**. (stercus), to dung, manure; agrum, Cic.

stercus -ŏris, n. dung, muck, manure, Cic.; as a term of reproach, stercus curiae, Cic.

stergēthron -i, n. (στέργηθρον), a plant, great houseleek, Plin.

stĕrĭlesco, **3**. (sterilis), to become barren, Plin.

stĕrĭlis -e (connected with Gr. στερεός, στερρός). **I**. barren, unfruitful, sterile (applied to animals and plants). **A**. **a**, lit., ager, Verg.; vacca, Verg.; **b**, transf. = empty; corpora sonito sterila (= sterilia), Lucr. **B**. Fig., unfruitful empty, vain; amor, unrequited, Ov. **II**. (Poet.) act., making unfruitful; robigo, Hor.

stĕrĭlĭtas -ātis, f. (sterilis), *unfruitfulness, sterility, barrenness;* agrorum, Cic.; mulierum, Plin.

stĕrĭlus = sterilis (q.v.).

sternax -ācis (sterno), *throwing to the ground;* equus, *throwing his rider,* Verg.

sterno, strāvi, strātum, 3. (root STER, Gr. ΣΤΟΡ, whence στορέννυμι). **I.** *to stretch out, spread out.* **A.** Gen., vellus in duro solo, Ov.; arenam, Ov.; strata jacent passim sua quaque sub arbore poma, Verg. **B.** Esp., 1, a, *to stretch on the ground, lay down, throw down;* corpora passim, Liv.; reflex., se sternere, *to lie down;* se somno in litore, Verg.; so pass. as middle, sterni passim ferarum ritu, Liv.; partic., **strātus** -a -um, *stretched out, prostrate;* humi, Cic.; b, *to throw down violently, to strike to the ground, lay low;* (a) lit., caede viros, Verg.; ingenti caede sterni, Liv.; poet., ventos, *to calm,* Hor.; (β) fig., *to overthrow, lay prostrate;* afflictos se et stratos esse, Cic.; 2, *to make smooth, level;* a, of the sea, (a) placidi straverunt aequora venti, Verg.; (β) fig., *to calm, allay;* odia militum, Tac.; b, *to make a rough road smooth, to level;* viam, Lucr.; esp., *to pave;* semitam saxo quadrato, Liv. **II.** Meton., *to cover, overlay with;* a, solum telis, Verg.; b, esp., (a) *to cover with carpets, etc.:* triclinium, Cic.; (β) *to saddle a horse;* equum, Liv.

sternūmentum -i, n. (sternuo), *a sneezing, sneeze,* Cic.

sternŭo -ŭi, 3. (connected with πτάρνυμαι). **I.** Intransit., *to sneeze;* a, lit., Plin.; b, transf., of a light, *to crackle, sputter,* Ov. **II.** Transit., *to give by sneezing;* omen, Prop.

sternŭtāmentum -i, n. (sternuo), *a sneezing, sneeze,* Sen.

sterquĭlĭnĭum -ĭi, n. (stercus), *a dung-pit,* Plaut.

Stertĭnĭus -ĭi, m. *a Stoic philosopher.* Hence, **Stertĭnĭus** -a -um, *of Stertinius.*

sterto, 3. (connected with δέρθω, δαρθάνω), *to snore,* Cic.

Stēsĭchŏrus -i, m. (Στησίχορος), *a Greek lyric poet of Himera* (632-553 B.C.), *contemporary of Sappho.*

Sthĕnĕlus -i, m. (Σθένελος). **I.** *son of Capaneus and Euadne, one of the Epigoni, leader of the Argives against Troy under Diomedes.* **II.** *king in Liguria, whose son Cycnus was changed into a swan.* Hence, **A. Sthĕnĕlēĭus** -a -um, *Sthenelean;* hostis, *Eurystheus,* Ov.; proles, *Cycnus,* Ov. **B. Sthĕnĕlēĭs** -ĭdis, f. *Sthenelean;* volucris, *the swan,* Ov.

stĭbădĭum -ĭi, n. (στιβάδιον), *a semicircular sofa,* Plin.

stĭbĭum -ĭi, n. (stĭbi and stimmi -is, n.), *antimony, used for dyeing the eyebrows black, and as an eye-salve,* Plin.

stigma -ātis, n. (στίγμα). **I.** *a mark or brand put upon slaves;* 1, lit., Sen.; 2, fig., *infamy, stigma,* Mart. **II.** *a cut inflicted by an unskilful barber,* Mart.

stigmātĭas -ae, m. (στιγματίας), *a branded slave,* Cic.

stilla -ae, f. (dim. of stiria), *a drop,* Cic.

stillātĭcĭus -a -um (stillo), *dropping, dripping,* Plin.

stillĭcĭdĭum -ĭi, n. (stilla and cado). **I.** *a dripping* or *dropping moisture,* Lucr. **II.** Esp., *rain-water falling from the eaves of houses,* Cic.

stillo, 1. (stilla). **I.** Intransit., *to drip, drop;* de ilice stillabant mella, Ov.; pugio stillans, *dripping with blood,* Cic. **II.** Transit., *to drop, let drop;* a, lit., ex oculis rorem, Hor.; b, fig.,

tuae litterae, quae mihi quiddam quasi animulae stillarunt, Cic.

stilus (not **stylus**) -i, m. (for stig-lus; cf. Gr. στίζω, στίγ-μα). **I.** *a stake, pale,* Auct. b. Afr. **II.** 1, *the pointed iron* or *bone instrument with which the Romans wrote on their waxen tablets,* Plin.; as one end was flat, in order to erase the impression made by the other, vertere stilum = *to rub out, erase writing,* Hor.; vertit stilum in tabulis suis, Cic.; 2, meton., *writing, composing, written composition,* and hence, *mode of writing, speaking, style;* stilus exercitatus, *a practised pen,* Cic.; unus sonus est totius orationis et idem stilus, Cic.

stĭmŭlātĭo -ōnis, f. (stimulo), *a spurring on, stimulating,* Tac.

stĭmŭlātrix -īcis, f. (stimulator), *she that goads on, stimulates,* Plaut.

stĭmŭlĕus -a -um (stimulus), *relating to the goad;* supplicium, *punishment* (of slaves) *with the goad,* Plaut.

stĭmŭlo, 1. (stimulus). **I.** *to goad, prick,* Lucan. **II.** Fig., 1, *to goad, disquiet, vex, annoy;* te conscientiae stimulant maleticiorum tuorum, Cic.; 2, *to goad, incite, stir up, stimulate to any action;* (a) with acc., aliquem incitare et stimulare, Verg.; (β) with ad and the acc., ad huius salutem defendendam stimulari, Cic.; (γ) with ut and the subj., ut caverem, Cic.; (δ) poet., with infin., Verg.

stĭmŭlus -i, m. (root STIG, whence in-stig-o and 1. stinguo; Gr. ΣΤΙΓ, whence στίζω, στίγμή). **I.** Milit. t. t., stimuli, *pointed stakes to repel the advance of troops,* Caes. **II.** *a goad used for driving cattle, slaves,* etc. **A.** Lit., Plaut.; used contemptuously, dum te stimulis fodiam, Cic. **B.** Fig., a, *a sting, torment;* doloris, Cic.; amoris, Liv.; b, *a goad, spur, incentive, stimulus;* gloriae, Cic.; alicui stimulos admovere, Cic.

1. * **stinguo,** 3. *to goad,* a word only found in compounds, such as distinguo, instinguo, interstinguo (interstinctus).

2. **stinguo,** 3. *to extinguish, put out,* Lucr.

stĭpātĭo -ōnis, f. (stipo), *a crowd of attendants round any one, numerous suite, retinue,* Cic.

stĭpātor -ōris, m. (stipo), *an attendant, follower;* plur., *a suite, train, retinue,* Cic.

stĭpātus -a -um, p. adj. (from stipo).

stĭpendĭārĭus -a -um (stipendium). **I.** *liable to taxes* or *tribute, tributary;* Aeduos sibi stipendiarios factos, Cic.; vectigal, *a yearly contribution,* Cic.; subst., **stĭpendĭārĭi** -ōrum, m. *tributaries;* socii stipendiariique populi Romani, Cic. **II.** *Of soldiers, serving for pay, mercenary,* Liv.

stĭpendĭor, 1. dep. (stipendium), *to serve, serve for hire,* Plin.

stĭpendĭum -ĭi, n. (= stipipendium, from stips and pendo). **I.** *a tax, tribute, contribution;* a, lit., stipendium imponere alicui, Caes.; pacisci annuum stipendium, Liv.; b, transf., *punishment; quod me manet stipendium?* Hor. **II.** *pay of a soldier;* a, lit. (in full, stipendium militare), stipendium alicui decernere, Cic.; persolvere, Cic.; flagitare, Caes.; stipendia merere and mereri, *to serve in the army,* Cic.; b, meton., *military service;* finis stipendiorum, Cic.; esp., *a year's service, campaign;* septem et viginti enumerare stipendia, Liv.; fig., tam quam emeritis stipendiis libidinis, ambitionis, etc., Cic.

stĭpes -ĭtis, m. (στύπος), *a log, stump, trunk of a tree;* a, in a rough state, Verg.; poet., *a tree,* Ov.; b, worked into something, *a stake, post,* Caes.; poet., *a club,* Ov.; as a term of reproach, *blockhead,* Ter.

stipo, 1. (connected with Gr. στέφ-ω, στέφ-ανος, etc.), *to press closely together, compress.* **I.** Gen., mella (of bees), Verg.; ita in arte stipatae erant naves ut, etc., Liv.; Graeci stipati, quini in lectulis, saepe plures, Cic. **II. A.** *to crowd a place;* curia quum patribus fuerit stipata, Ov. **B.** *to press round, accompany, surround, attend;* senatum armatis, Cic.; qui *stipatus* semper sicariis, *saeptus* armatis, *munitus* judicibus fuit, Cic.; senectus stipata studiis juventutis, Cic.

stips, stipis, f. *an offering, gift, donation in money, a religious offering, alms;* stipem conferre, Liv.; stipem cogere, Cic.; stipem aut stipes dare, Ov., Tac.; stipem tollere, *to put an end to begging,* Cic.

stĭpŭla -ae, f. *the stalk, haulm;* **a,** of corn; plur. = *straw,* Ov.; **b,** of a reed, contemptuously of a flute made of a reed, a *reed-pipe,* Verg.; **c,** of the bean, Ov.

stĭpŭlātĭo -ōnis, f. (stipulor), *a verbal agreement, covenant, stipulation,* Cic.

stĭpŭlātiuncŭla -ae, f. (dim. of stipulatio), *an unimportant engagement* or *stipulation,* Cic.

stĭpŭlātor -ōris, m. (stipulor), *one who stipulates for* or *demands a formal agreement,* Suet.

stĭpŭlor, 1. dep. *to demand, stipulate for by a formal agreement,* Cic.

stiria -ae, f. *an icicle,* Verg.

stirpesco, 3. (stirps), *to run to stalk,* Plin.

stirpĭtŭs, adv. (stirps), *root and branch, thoroughly, entirely,* Cic.

stirps (stirpes, stirpis), stirpis, f. **I.** *the stock* or *stem of a tree.* **A.** Lit., **a,** *the trunk with the root,* Cic.; **b,** *the trunk,* Verg.; **c,** *a branch, a young shoot* or *sprout,* Verg. **B.** Transf., 1, of plants, **a,** *a plant, stalk, root;* stirpes et herbae, Cic.; **b,** *a twig,* Lucr.; **2,** of hair, *the root,* Prop.; **3,** of men, **a,** abstr., *the stem* = *the source, origin;* divina, Verg.; ne Italicae quidem stirpis, Liv.; a stirpe par, Verg.; **b,** concr., (*a*) *male offspring;* unum prope puberem aetate relictum stirpem genti Fabiae, Liv.; (β) *family, race;* Herculis, Cic.; (γ) *offspring;* stirpem ex se relinquere, Liv. **II.** Fig., *the root;* 1, gen., ex hac nimia licentia ut ex stirpe quadam exsistere et quasi nasci tyrannum, Cic.; Carthago ab stirpe interiit, *root and branch,* Sall.; 2, esp., **a,** *foundation, origin;* virtutis, Cic.; **b,** *original nature,* Cic. (stirps masc. once in Verg.).

stĭva -ae, f. *a plough-handle,* Verg.

stlātārius -a -um (from stlata, *a kind of ship*), *brought by sea,* and therefore, *costly,* Juv.

stlis, archaic = lis (q.v.).

stloppus -i, m. *the noise of a slap on the inflated cheeks,* Pers.

sto, stĕti, stătum, stătūrus, stāre (STA, root of i-στη-μι), *to stand.* **I.** As opposed to sitting, *to remain standing.* **A.** Lit., 1, gen., **a,** of persons, quum virgo staret, et Caecilia in sella sederet, Cic.; ad januam, Cic.; **b,** of things, quorum statuae steterunt in rostris, Cic.; 2, esp., **a,** milit. t. t., *to stand, to be stationed;* pro porta, Liv.; **b,** of buildings, *to stand, to be built;* jam stabant Thebae, Ov.; **c,** of ships, *to be at anchor;* stant litore puppes, Verg.; stare ad ancoram in salo Romana classis non poterat, Liv.; **d,** *to stand upright, stand on end;* steterunt-que comae, Verg.; **e,** with abl., *to stand stiff with, to be full of, loaded with;* stat nive candidum Soracte, Hor. **B.** Fig., 1, gen., pericula stant circum aliquem, Verg.; 2, *to stand at the side of, to support,* or *to stand opposite to as an enemy, to range oneself;* **a,** with ab and the abl., *stare a se* potius quam ab adversariis, Cic.; **b,** with cum and the abl., vobiscum me stet-

isse dicebat, Cic.; **c,** with pro and the abl., pro nobis, Ov.; **d,** with in or contra or adversus and acc., quum saepe a mendacio contra verum stare homines consuescerent, Cic.; 3, *to rest upon;* omnis in Ascanio cari stat cura parentis, Verg.; 4, = *to cost* (like English *stand*); centum talentis, Liv.; transf., multo sanguine ac vulneribus ea Poenis victoria stetit, Liv. **II. A.** Lit., 1, as opposed to motion, *to stand still, not to move;* **a,** lit., (*a*) of animals, equus stare nescit, Ov.; (β) of things, e.g., of ships, videsne navem illam? stare nobis videtur, at iis qui in navi sunt *moveri* haec villa, Cic.; **b,** transf., of time, *to stop, stand still;* veluti stet volucris dies, Hor.; 2, with the notion of steadfastness; **a,** milit. t. t., (*a*) *to stand, hold one's ground;* qui (miles) steterit, Cic.; stare in pugna, Liv.; (β) transf., of a battle, *to remain in a certain position, to waver, not to be decided;* diu pugna neutro inclinata stetit, Cic.; **b,** of buildings, rocks, etc., *to stand firm, last, endure, remain;* nec domus ulla nec urbs stare poterit, Cic.; **c,** of missiles, *to stick fast, remain;* hasta stetit medio tergo, Ov. **B.** Fig., 1, gen., *to remain still, remain, continue;* utinam respublica stetisset quo coeperat statu, Cic.; 2, stare per aliquem, *to happen through some one's fault,* Ter.; often stat or non (nihil) stat per aliquem, foll. by quominus and subj., *it is owing to some one that not,* etc., Cic., Liv.; stat per aliquem, foll. by quin or ne and subj., Liv.; 3, with the notion of steadfastness or duration; **a,** *to remain steadfast, firm, immovable, to stand one's ground, hold out;* si stare non possunt, corruant, Cic.; stas animo, Hor.; stamus animis, Cic.; **b,** *to remain firm in something;* (*a*) *to remain in, continue in;* with in and the abl., in fide, Cic.; with abl. alone, suis stare judiciis, Cic.; (β) transf., *to be fixed* or *determined;* stat sua cuique dies, Verg.; tempus agendae rei nondum stare, Liv.; stat alicui sententia, with infin., *to be resolved* or *determined to,* Liv.; so stat alicui, or simply stat, Cic.; **c,** of a play or an actor, *to please, gain applause, keep the stage,* Hor. (perf., stētērunt, Verg., *Aen.* II. 774; III. 48).

Stŏĭcē, adv. (Stoicus), *like a Stoic, stoically,* Cic.

Stŏĭcĭda -ae, m. *a satirical name given to a voluptuary who pretended to be a Stoic,* Juv.

Stŏĭcus -a -um (Στωϊκός), *of* or *relating to Stoic philosophy, Stoic;* schola, Cic. Subst., **a, Stŏĭcus** -i, m. *a Stoic philosopher,* Cic.; **b, Stoica** -ōrum, n. *the Stoic philosophy,* Cic.

stŏla -ae, f. (στολή), *a long outer garment.* **I.** *the long outer garment worn by Roman ladies, robe,* Cic. **II.** Of men, *the robe of a flute-player at the festival of Minerva,* Ov.

stŏlātus -a -um (stola), *clad in a stola,* Suet.

stŏlĭdē, adv. (stolidus), *stupidly, foolishly, stolidly;* stolide laetus, Liv.; stolide ferox, Liv.

stŏlĭdus -a -um (connected with stultus). **I.** *stupid, foolish, dull, obtuse;* **a.** of persons, o vatum stolidissime, Ov.; **b,** of things, fiducia, superbia, Liv. **II.** *inactive, indolent,* Cic.

stŏlo -ōnis, m. *a useless sucker, superfluous shoot on a tree,* Plin.

stŏmăcăcē -ēs, f. (στομακάκη), *a disease of the mouth* or *gums,* Plin.

stŏmăchĭcus -a -um (στομαχικός), *suffering from disease in the stomach,* Plin.

stŏmăchor, 1. dep. (stomachus), *to be angry, pettish, irritated, vexed;* **a,** absol., stomachari coepit, Cic.; **b,** with cum and the abl., cum Metello, Cic.; **c,** with abl., jucundissimis tuis litteris, Cic.; **d,** with quod, quod de eadem re again saepius, Cic.; **e,** with si, si quid asperius dixeram, Cic.; **f.** with neut. acc., omnia. Cic

stŏmăchōsē, adv. (stomachosus), *peevishly, pettishly, angrily;* rescripsi ei stomachosius, Cic.

stŏmăchōsus -a -um (stomachus), *peevish, pettish, irritable, cross, angry,* Cic.

stŏmăchus -i, m. (στόμαχος). **I.** *the gullet, the oesophagus,* Cic. **II.** Transf. = ventriculus, *the stomach.* **A.** Lit., stomachi calor, Cic.; stomachus aeger, Hor. **B.** Fig., 1, stomachus bonus, *a good digestion* = *good humour,* Mart.; 2, **a,** *taste, liking;* ludi apparatissimi, sed non tui stomachi, Cic.; **b,** *dislike, distaste, vexation, chagrin, anger;* stomachum facere or movere alicui, Cic.

stŏmătĭcē -ēs, f. (στοματική), *a remedy for diseases of the mouth,* Plin.

stŏmōma -ātis, n. (στόμωμα), *thin scales of metal,* Plin.

stŏrĕa (stŏrĭa) -ae, f. (connected with στορέννυμι), *a rush mat,* Caes.

străbo -ōnis, m. (στραβών). **I.** *a squinter,* Cic. **II.** Fig., *an envious person,* Varr.

străges -is, f. **I.** *a throwing to the ground, overthrow, downfall;* **a,** aedificiorum, Tac.; tectorum, Liv.; **b,** *a sinking down, dying away through illness;* canum, Ov.; **c,** *a defeat, a slaughter, butchery, massacre, carnage;* quas strages ille edidit, Cic. **II.** Meton., *a fallen mass;* hominum armorumque, Liv.

străgŭlum, v. stragulus.

străgŭlus -a -um (sterno), *covering, serving as a rug,* carpet, mattress, etc., *to lie upon.* **I.** Adj., vestis stragula, Cic. **II.** Subst., **străgŭlum** -i, n. *a covering, rug, carpet, mattress,* etc.; textile, Cic.

strāmen -ĭnis, n. (sterno), *straw, litter, spread under anything,* Verg., Ov.

strāmentārius -a -um (stramentum), *relating to straw;* falces, *for cutting straw,* Cato.

strāmentĭcĭus -a -um (stramentum), *made of straw;* casa, Auct. b. Hisp.

strāmentum -i, n. (sterno). **I.** *the stalk of corn, straw, litter;* casae, quae more Gallico stramentis erant tectae, Caes. **II.** *a saddle, housing* (for mules), Caes.

strāmĭnĕus -a -um (stramen), *made of straw;* casa, Ov.; Quirites, *figures of straw thrown every year into the Tiber,* Ov.

strangĭas -ae, m. (στραγγίας), *a kind of wheat in Greece,* Plin.

strangŭlātĭo -ōnis, f. (strangulo), *a choking, strangulation,* Plin.

strangŭlātus = strangulatio (q.v.).

strangŭlo, 1. (στραγγαλόω), *to choke, strangle.* **I. a,** lit., patrem, Caes.; **b,** transf., vocem, Quint.; arborem, Plin. **II.** Fig., *to torment, torture;* strangulat inclusus dolor, Ov.

strangūrĭa -ae, f. (στραγγουρία), *a painful discharge of urine, strangury,* Cic.

strătēgēma -ătis, n. (στρατήγημα), *a piece of generalship, a stratagem;* transf., strategemate hominem percussit, Cic.

strătēgĭa -ae, f. (στρατηγία), *a province, district, canton,* Plin.

strătēgus -i, m. (στρατηγός), *a general,* Plaut.

strătĭōtes -ae, m. (στρατιώτης), *an aquatic plant,* Plin.

strătĭōtĭcus -a -um (στρατιωτικός), *soldierly, soldierlike;* homo, *a soldier,* Plaut.

Străto (-ōn) -ōnis, m. (Στράτων). **I.** *a Peripatetic philosopher of Lampsacus.* **II.** (Strato), *a physician of the time of Cicero.*

Strătŏnīcēa -ae, f. (Στρατονίκεια), *an important town in Caria,* now *Eski Hissar.* Hence, **Strătŏnīcensis** -e, *belonging to Stratonicea.*

strātum -i, n. (sterno), *that which is spread out.* **I.** *a covering;* 1, *the covering of a rug, bed, blanket,* and meton., *a bed;* molle stratum, Liv.; strato surgere, Verg.; 2, *a horse-cloth, saddle-cloth, saddle,* Liv. **II.** *a pavement;* strata viarum, Lucr.

strātūra -ae, f. (sterno), *a paving, pavement,* Suet.

1. **strātus** -a -um, partic. of sterno.

2. **Strātus** -i, f. (Στράτος), *a town in Acarnania on the Achelous.*

strēna -ae, f. **I.** *a portent, omen,* Plaut. **II.** *a new year's gift* (Fr. étrenne), Suet.

strēnŭē, adv. (strenuus), *briskly, promptly, actively, strenuously;* arma capere, Cic.

strēnŭĭtas -ātis, f. (strenuus), *briskness, promptness, activity,* Ov.

strēnŭo, 1. (strenuus), *to be brisk, prompt, active,* Plaut.

strēnŭus -a -um, *brisk, prompt, active, strenuous, vigorous;* **a,** lit., of persons, fortis ac strenuus socius, Liv.; gens linguā strenua magis quam factis, Liv.; compar., strenuior, Plaut.; superl., strenuissimus quisque ut occiderat in proelio, Sall.; in a bad sense, *turbulent, restless,* Tac.; **b,** transf., navis, *fast,* Ov.; inertia, *masterly inactivity,* Hor.

strĕpĭto, 1. (intens. of strepo), *to make a loud noise, to rustle, rattle, clatter,* Verg.

strĕpĭtus -ūs, m. (strepo). **I.** *a loud noise, clattering, crashing, creaking, rumbling;* rotarum, Caes.; fluminum, Cic.; valvarum, Hor.; inter strepitum tot bellorum, Liv.; plur., strepitus nocturni, Liv. **II.** Poet., transf., *a measured, regular sound;* testudinis aureae, Hor.

strĕpo -ŭi -ĭtum, 3. **I.** *to make a loud noise, creak, rattle, clash, rumble, clatter.* **A.** Intransit., **a,** of living beings, mixti strepentium paventiumque clamores, Liv.; strepere vocibus, Sall.; **b,** of things, arma et scuta offensa quo levius streperent, *make less noise,* Sall.; fluvii strepunt hibernā nive turgidi, Hor.; esp., of places, *to resound;* ludos litterarum strepere discentium vocibus, Liv. **B.** Transit., haec quum streperent, *cried out,* Liv. **II.** Poet., transf., of musical instruments, *to crash, bray;* strepunt litui, Hor.

strepsĭcĕros -ōtis, m. (στρεψικέρως), *an African animal with twisted horns,* Plin.

strĭa -ae, f. *a furrow, ridge,* Plin.

strictim, adv. (strictus). **I.** *closely,* Plaut. **II.** Fig., *superficially, slightly, briefly, summarily,* dicere, Cic.; librum attingere, Cic.

strictīvus -a -um (stringo), *plucked, gathered, stripped off,* Cato.

strictor -ōris, m. (stringo), *one who plucks,* Cato.

strictūra -ae, f. (stringo), *a bar of iron,* Verg.

strictus -a -um, p. adj. (from stringo), *drawn together;* hence, **I.** Lit., *close, tight;* janua strictissima, Ov. **II.** Fig., 1, *brief, concise,* Quint.; 2, of character, *rigid, severe, strict,* Sen.

strīdĕo (strīdo), strīdi -ēre and -ēre (connected with τρίζω), *to make a harsh noise, to creak, grate, hiss,* etc.; of snakes, Verg.; of a missile, Verg.; of the wind, Verg.; of the rope of a ship, Ov.; of a waggon, Verg.; of the sea, Verg.; of men, inamabile stridet, lisps, Ov.; of bees, *to hum,* Verg.

strīdor -ōris, m. (strido), *a creaking, grating, hissing, whistling cry or noise, of the wind*, Cic. ; of the hinge of a door, Cic. ; of a saw, Cic.; of animals, as a snake, Ov. ; of a pig, *grunting*, Ov. ; of asses, *braying*, Ov. ; of bees, *humming*, Ov. ; of men, tribuni, *whispering*, Cic.

strīdŭlus -a -um (strido), *creaking, hissing, whistling, grating;* cornus (of a spear), Verg ; claustra, Ov.

strīges -um, f., v. **strix.**

strīgĭlis -is, abl. -i, genit. plur. -ĭum, f. (stringo), *a scraper used by bathers for scraping the skin*, Cic.

strigmentum -i, n. (stringo), *that which is scraped or rubbed off*, Plin.

strīgo, 1. *to halt in ploughing*, Plin.

strīgōsus -a -um, *lean, thin.* **I.** Lit., equi strigosiores, Liv. **II.** Fig., of an orator, *dry, meagre, jejune*, Cic.

stringo, strinxi, strictum, 3. (root STRIC, connected with στράγγω). **I.** *to draw together.* **A.** *to draw tight together, to bind, tie together;* 1, lit., tamquam laxaret elatum pedem ab stricto nodo, Liv. ; stringebant magnos vincula parva pedes, Ov. ; 2, transf., of cold, stricta matutino frigore vulnera, Liv. **B.** *to draw off;* 1, *to strip off, pluck, gather, clip, prune;* folia ex arboribus, Caes. ; frondes, Verg. ; rubos, Liv.; 2, *to draw a weapon from its sheath, to unsheathe;* a, lit., gladium, Caes. ; ferrum, Liv. ; cultrum, Liv.; b, fig., stringitur iambus in hostes, *attacks an enemy with satirical verses*, Ov. **II.** *to graze* = *to touch lightly;* 1, gen., metas interiore rotā, Ov. ; 2, esp., *to wound slightly;* tela stringentia corpus, Verg. ; poet., transf., (a) *to injure;* nomen, Ov. ; (β) *to touch;* animum strinxit patriae pietatis imago, Verg.

stringor -ōris, m. (stringo), *a drawing together, power of drawing together*, Lucr.

strix, strĭgis, f. (στρίγξ), *a screech-owl*, Ov.

strombus -i, m. (στρομβός), *a species of spiral snail*, Plin.

strongȳlē -es, f. (στρογγύλη), *a kind of alum*, Plin.

strŏpha -ae, f. and **strŏphē** -ēs, f (στροφή), *a trick, device, artifice*, Sen.

Strŏphădes -um, f. (Στροφάδες), *two islands in the Ionian Sea, between Zakynthos and the Peloponnesus, the mythical abode of the Harpies,* now *Strofadia* or *Strivali*.

strŏphĭārĭus -ĭi, m. (strophium), *one who makes or sells strophia*, Plaut.

strŏphĭŏlum -i, n. (dim. of strophium), *a small chaplet*, Plin.

strŏphĭum -ĭi, n. (στρόφιον). **I.** *a breast-band, stay, stomacher*, Cic. **II.** *a chaplet*, Verg.

Strŏphĭus -ĭi, m. (Στρόφιος), *king in Phocis, father of Pylades* ; Strophio natus, *Pylades*, Ov.

structĭlis -e (struo), *of or relating to building, used in building*, Mart.

structor -ōris, m. (struo). **I.** *a builder, mason, carpenter*, Cic. **II.** *an arranger* = τραπεζοποιός, *a slave who arranged the table and superintended the waiting*, Juv.

structūra -ae, f. (struo). **I.** *a putting together;* 1, *a building, erecting, constructing;* parietum, Caes. ; 2, meton., *that which is built, a building;* aerariae structurae, *mines, mining-works*, Caes. **II.** Transf., *of discourse, an arrangement, putting together of words;* verborum, Cic.

strŭes -is, f. (struo), *a heap.* **I.** Gen., pontes et moles ex humanorum corporum strue facere, Liv. **II.** Esp., a, *a heap of wood;* lig-

norum, Liv. ; b, *a heap of small sacrificial cakes*, Ov. ; c, *a thick or dense mass*, as of the phalanx, Liv.

strŭix -ĭcis, f. (struo), *a heap*, Plaut.

strūma -ae, f. (struo), *a scrofulous tumour*, Cic.

strūmōsus -a -um (struma), *afflicted with struma, strumous*, Juv.

strūmus -i, m. (struma), *a herb that cures the struma*, Plin.

strŭo, struxi, structum, 3. (connected with στορέννυμι, sterno). **I.** *to place one thing upon another, to join together, pile up;* arbores in pyram, Ov. ; lateres, Caes. **II. A.** *to build, erect, construct;* a, lit., pyram, Verg. ; aggerem, Tac. ; fornices, Liv. ; b, transf., *to prepare* (something bad), *to devise, contrive;* alicui aliquid calamitatis, Cic. ; periculosas libertati opes, Liv. ; dices me ipsum mihi sollicitudinem struere, Cic. **B.** *to arrange, order, set up;* aciem, Liv.; transf., compositi oratoris bene structa collocatio, Cic. **C.** *to heap up, load with;* altaria donis, Verg.

struppus (stroppus) -i, m. (στρόφος), *a strap, thong, rope*, Plin.

strūthĕus (strūthĭus) -a -um (στρούθιος), *of or relating to a sparrow;* mala, *sparrow-apples, quinces*, Cato.

strūthĭŏcămēlīnus -a -um, *of or relating to an ostrich*, Plin.

strūthĭŏcămēlus -i, m. (στρυθιοκάμηλος), *an ostrich*, Plin.

strūthŏpus -pŏdis (στρουθόπους), *sparrow-footed*, Plin.

strychnos -i, m. (στρύχνος), *a kind of nightshade*, Plin.

Strymo (-ōn) -mōnis and -mŏnos, m. (Στρυμών), *one of the most important rivers of Thrace, rising in Mt. Haemus and flowing into the Strymonic Gulf*, now *Karasu* or *Struma* (*Strumo*). Hence, **A. Strȳmŏnĭs** -ĭdis, f. (Στρυμονίς), *a Thracian woman, an Amazon*, Prop. **B. Strȳmŏnĭus** -a -um, *Strymonian*, poet. = *Thracian* or *northern*, Ov.

stŭdĕo -ŭi, 2. (perhaps connected with σπεύδω, σπουδή, σπουδάζω), *to be eager, zealous, earnest, take pains about anything, strive after, be busy with, seek after, aim at.* **I.** Gen., a, with dat., praeturae, Cic. ; novis rebus, *political change*, Caes. ; litteris, Cic. ; laudi, Cic. ; b, with acc., unum, hoc unum, Cic. ; c, with infin., or acc. and infin., studeo scire quid egeris, *I should like to know*, Cic. ; d, with ut or ne and the subj., id studere, ne super impunitatem etiam praemio sceleris frueretur, Liv. **II.** Esp., *to take sides with, to support, favour;* alicui, Cic.

stŭdĭōsē, adv. (studiosus), a, *eagerly, zealously, diligently;* qui haec caelestia vel studiosissime solet quaerere, Cic. ; b, *intentionally, designedly;* quum studiose de absentibus detrahendi causā malitiose dicitur, Cic.

stŭdĭōsus -a -um (studium), *eager, zealous, diligent, anxious for, striving after anything, fond of.* **I.** Gen., with genit., venandi, Cic. ; dicendi, Cic. ; studiosissimus homo natandi, Cic. ; with in and the abl., hoc te studiosiorem in me colendo fore, Cic. **II.** Esp., **A.** *favourable to a person, attached to, devoted to;* mei, Cic. ; studiosissimus existimationis meae, Cic. **B.** *devoted to learning, studious;* cohors, Hor. Plur. subst., **stŭdĭōsi** -ōrum, m. *students*, Cic.

stŭdĭum -ĭi, n. (studeo), *zeal, eagerness, eager application, assiduity, fondness, desire, striving after.* **I.** Gen., with subject. genit. amici, Cic. ; with object. genit., veri reperiendi,

Cic. ; pugnandi, Caes. ; studium quaestūs, Cic. ; absol., incensi sunt studio, Cic.; omne studium ad aliquid conferre, Cic. ; studio accusare, *passionately*, Cic. **II.** Esp., *particular inclination towards a person or a thing.* **A.** Towards a person, *attachment to, zeal for, devotion to, goodwill towards;* studia competitorum, Cic.; studia Numidarum in Jugurtham accensa, Sall. **B.** Towards a thing, **1,** *fondness for, partiality, inclination;* suo quisque studio maxime ducitur, Cic. ; **2,** *application to learning, study;* juris, Cic. ; studiis illis se dare, Cic.

stultē, adv. with compar. and superl. (stultus), *foolishly, sillily,* Cic.

stultĭlŏquentĭa -ae, f. (stulte and loquor), *foolish talk,* Plaut.

stultĭlŏquus -a -um (stulte and loquor), *talking foolishly,* Plaut.

stultĭtĭa -ae, f. (stultus), *foolishness, folly, silliness, stupidity;* multorum stultitiam perpessum esse, Cic.; plur., hominum ineptias ac stultitias non ferebat, Cic.

stultĭvĭdus -a -um (stulte and video), *seeing things foolishly, in a foolish light,* Plaut.

stultus -a -um (connected with stolidus), *foolish, silly, fatuous;* **a,** of persons, reddere aliquem stultiorem, Cic. ; stultissima persona, Cic. Subst., **stultus** -i, m. *a simpleton, a fool,* Cic.; **b,** transf., of things, loquacitas, Cic. ; consilium, Cic.

stūpa = stuppa (q.v.).

stŭpĕfăcĭo -fēci -factum, 3., pass., **stŭpĕfīo** -factus sum -fĭĕri (stupeo and facio), *to make senseless, benumb, stun, stupefy;* privatos luctus stupefecit publicus pavor, Liv.; partic., **stŭpĕfáctus** -a -um, *astounded,* Cic.

stŭpĕo -ŭi, 2. (connected with ΤΥΠ-ω, τύπτω, *to strike and stun by a blow*). **I.** *to be stunned.* **A.** Physically, *to be struck senseless, to be stunned ;* partic., stupens, *stunned, stupefied ;* quum semisomnus stuperet, Cic. **B.** Mentally, *to be astounded, amazed ;* haec quum loqueris nos stupemus, Cic. ; with abl. (*at* or *by*), carminibus, Hor.; with in and the abl., in Turno,Verg.; with ad and the acc., ad auditas voces, Verg. ; with acc., donum exitiale Minervae, *is astonished at,* Verg. ; with acc. and infin., Verg. ; partic., stupens, *astonished, amazed ;* quae quum tuerer stupens, Cic. **II.** Transf., of inanimate things, *to stand still, to rest;* stupuit Ixionis orbis, Ov.; stupente seditione, Liv.; stupuerunt verba palato, *died away,* Ov.

stŭpesco, 3. (stupeo), *to begin to be amazed, astounded,* Cic.

stŭpĭdĭtas -ātis, f. (stupidus), *dulness, stupidity, senselessness,* Cic.

stŭpĭdus -a -um (stupeo), **1,** *senseless, stunned,* Cic. ; **2,** *senseless, stupid, dull;* stupidum esse Socratem dixit, Cic.

stŭpor -ōris, m. (stupeo). **I. a,** *senselessness, insensibility ;* sensus, Cic.; in corpore, Cic. ; **b,** *astonishment, amazement ;* stupor patres defixit, Liv.; meton., *a startled man,* Cat. **II.** *senselessness, stupidity,* Cic.

stuppa (stūpa) -ae, f. (στύππη), *tow, oakum,* Caes., Liv.

stuppārĭus -a -um (stuppa), *of or relating to tow,* Plin.

stuppĕus (stūpĕus) -a -um (stuppa), *made of tow* or *oakum ;* vincula, Verg.

stŭprātor -ōris, m. (stupro), *a ravisher, defiler,* Quint.

stŭpro, 1. (stuprum), *to defile.* **I.** Gen., pulvinar, Cic. **II.** Esp., *to defile, pollute by lust, ravish,* Cic.

stŭprum -i, n. *pollution by lust, a debauching, ravishing, violation,* Cic.

sturnus -i, m. *a starling, a stare,* Plin.

Stўgĭālis, Stygius v. Styx.

stўlŏbātes -ae and -is, m. (στυλοβάτης), *the pedestal of a row of columns,* Varr.

stymma -ātis, n. (στύμμα), *the main ingredient of a salve* or *ointment,* Plin.

Stymphālus (-ŏs) -i, m. and **Stymphālum** -i, n. (Στύμφαλος), *a lake with a river and town of the same name in Arcadia, famous in legend as the abode of birds of prey with iron feathers, which fed on human flesh, and were destroyed by Hercules.* Hence, **A.** **Stymphālĭcus** -a -um, *Stymphalian.* **B.** **Stymphālĭs** -ĭdis, f. *Stymphalian.* **C.** **Stymphālĭus** -a -um, *Stymphalian.*

styptĭcus -a -um (στυπτικός), *astringent, styptic,* Plin.

styrax -ăcis, m. (στύραξ), *storax, a resinous fragrant gum,* Plin.

Styx, Stўgis and Stўgos, acc. Stygem and Styga, f. (Στύξ). **I.** *a river in the infernal regions by which the gods swore.* **II.** Poet., meton., *the lower world,* Verg. Hence, **A.** **Stўgĭālis** -e, *belonging to the Styx, Stygian.* **B.** **Stўgĭus** -a -um, *Stygian, infernal ;* cymba or carina, *the boat of Charon,* Verg. ; Juppiter, or pater, or rex, *Pluto,* Verg.; hence, *hellish* = *fatal, deadly, sad ;* bubo, Ov. ; vis, Verg.

suādēla -ae, f. (suadeo). **I.** *persuasion,* Plaut. **II.** Personif., Suadela = Πειθώ, *the goddess of persuasion,* Hor.

suādĕo, suāsi, suāsum, 2. (root SUAD, Gr. ᾽Αδ-έω, ἀνδάνω), lit., *to present in a pleasing manner.* Hence, **I.** Intransit., *to advise, give advice ;* an C. Trebonio persuasi cui ne suadere quidem ausus essem ? Cic. ; in suadendo et dissuadendo, Cic.; of things as subjects, suadet enim vesana fames, Verg. **II.** Transit., **A.** *to advise something, recommend something, recommend to ;* **a,** pacem, Cic.; legem, Cic. ; quod ipse tibi suaseris, Cic. ; with acc. of pers., non desino tamen per litteras rogare, suadere, accusare regem, Cic.; **b,** with infin., mori, Cic. ; **c,** with acc. and infin., nullam esse rationem amittere eiusmodi occasionem, Cic.; **d,** with ut or ne and the subj., postea me, ut sibi essem legatus, non solum suasit, verum etiam rogavit, Cic. ; **e,** with subj. alone, se suadere, Pharnabazo id negotium daret, Nep. **B.** *to convince, persuade,* Plaut.

suārĭus -a -um (sus), *of or relating to swine,* Plin. Subst., **suārĭus** -ĭi, m. *a swineherd,* Plin.

suāsĭo -ōnis, f. (suadeo). **I.** *advice,* Sen. **II.** Esp., **a,** polit. t. t., *the advocacy, recommendation of a proposed law;* legis Serviliae, Cic.; **b,** rhet. t. t., *eloquence of the persuasive kind,* Cic.

suāsor -ōris, m. (suadeo), *an adviser, counsellor;* facti, Cic. ; deditionis, Cic. ; esp., *one who advocates a proposed law;* legis, Liv.

suāsōrĭus -a -um (suadeo), *relating to persuasion,* Quint. Hence, subst., **suāsōrĭa** -ae, f. *persuasive discourse* or *eloquence,* Quint.

suāsus -ūs, m. (suadeo), *a persuading, exhorting, persuasion,* Plaut., Ter.

suāvē, adv. (suavis) = suaviter, *sweetly, pleasantly ;* suave rubens, Verg.

suāvĕŏlens -entis, and **suāvĕ ŏlens** -entis (suave and oleo), *sweet-smelling,* Cat.

suāvĭdĭcus -a -um (suave and dico), *sweetly speaking,* Lucr.

suāvillum (sāvillum) -i, n. (suavis), *a kind of sweet cake,* Cato.

suāvĭlŏquens -entis (suave and loquor), *sweetly speaking, agreeable,* Lucr.

suāvĭlŏquentĭa -ae, f. (suaviloquens), *a sweet, agreeable manner of speaking,* Cic.

suāvĭlŏquus = suaviloquens (q.v.).

suāvĭŏlum = saviolum (q.v.).

suāvĭor = savior (q.v.).

suāvis -e (connected with ἡδύς), *sweet, pleasant, agreeable, delightful.* **I.** As regards the senses, odor, Cic.; flores, Lucr. **II.** As regards the mind, litterae tuae, Cic.

suāvĭtas -ātis, f. (suavis), *sweetness, agreeableness, pleasantness.* **I.** For the senses, cibi, Cic.; odorum, Cic.; coloris, Cic. **II.** As regards the mind, vitae, Cic.; cuius eximia suavitas, Cic.

suāvĭtĕr, adv. (suavis), *sweetly, agreeably, pleasantly, delightfully.* **I.** As regards the senses, quam suaviter voluptas sensibus blandiatur, Cic. **II.** As regards the mind, loqui, meminisse, Cic.; suavissime scriptae litterae, Cic.

suāvĭtūdo = suavitas (q.v.).

suāvĭum = savium (q.v.).

sŭb, prep. with abl. and acc. (connected with ὑπό). **I.** With abl., **A.** Of place, 1, to express staying under, *under;* a, with verbs implying rest, *under;* sub terra habitare, Cic.; sub pellibus hiemare, Cic.; vitam sub divo agere, Hor.; transf., sub armis esse, *to be under arms,* Caes.; sub corona, sub hasta vendere, Cic.; b, with verbs of motion, sub hoc jugo dictator Aequos misit, Liv.; 2, to express nearness to, *beneath, under, at the bottom of, at the foot of;* castra sub monte consedit, Caes.; sub ipsis Numantiae moenibus, Cic.; transf., sub oculis domini, Liv.; sub manu esse, Caes.; 3, *down in, within;* silvis inventa sub altis, Ov.; 4, *just behind;* quo deinde sub ipso ecce volat, Verg. **B.** Of time, 1, *during, at the time of, within;* primis spectata sub annis, Ov.; 2, *at, near to;* sub luce urbem ingressus, Liv.; sub adventu Romanorum, Liv. **C.** Of condition, 1, to express subjection, *under, beneath;* sub imperio alicuius, Caes.; sub regno alicuius, Cic.; sub rege, *under the rule of a king,* Cic.; sub judice lis est, *before the judge,* Hor.; 2, *at, on, under;* Bacchi sub nomine risit, Ov.; multa vana sub nomine celebri vulgabantur, Tac. **II.** With acc., **A.** Of place, 1, to express motion, *under;* manum sub vestimenta deferre, Plaut.; exercitum sub jugum mittere, Caes.; transf., sub sensum cadere non possunt, Cic.; 2, to express motion near to, *under, beneath, at the bottom of, very near to;* sub montem succedunt milites, Caes. **B.** Of time, 1, *about, towards, just before;* Pompeius sub noctem naves solvit, *about night, towards night,* Caes.; sub galli cantum, *about cockcrow,* Hor.; 2, *immediately after;* sub eas litteras statim recitatae sunt tuae, Cic. **C.** To express subjection, *under;* matrimonium vos sub legis superbissimae vincula conjicitis, Liv. (sub in composition, = a, *under;* b, *somewhat, a little;* c, *secretly*).

sŭbabsurdē, adv. (subabsurdus), *somewhat absurdly,* Cic.

sŭbabsurdus -a -um, *somewhat absurd, somewhat foolish,* Cic.

sŭbaccūso, 1. *to accuse, blame, find fault with a little;* aliquem, Cic.

sŭbācĭdus -a -um, *somewhat sour, acid,* Cato.

sŭbactĭo -ōnis, f. (subigo), *a working up, preparing;* fig., *preparation, discipline,* Cic.

sŭbactus = subactio (q.v.).

sŭbaerātus -a -um, *having copper inside or underneath,* Pers.

sŭbāgrestis -e, *somewhat rustic, somewhat boorish;* consilium, Cic.

sŭbālāris -e, *under the arms, under the arm pits,* Nep.

sŭbalbĭcans -antis, *somewhat white, whitish,* Varr.

sŭbalbĭdus -a -um, *whitish,* Plin.

sŭbalpīnus -a -um, *beneath or near the Alps,* Plin.

sŭbămārus -a -um, *somewhat bitter;* sub amara aliqua res, Cic. Plur. subst., **sŭbămāra** -ōrum, n. *things somewhat bitter,* Cic.

sŭbăquĭlus -a -um, *somewhat dark-coloured brownish,* Plaut.

sŭbărātor -ōris, m. (subaro), *one who ploughs near anything,* Plin.

sŭbăro, 1. *to plough close to anything,* Plin.

sŭbarrŏgantĕr, adv. *somewhat arrogantly or proudly,* Cic.

sŭbausculto, 1. *to listen secretly,* Cic.

subbāsĭlĭcānus -i, m. (sub and basilica), *one who lounges about a basilica,* Plaut.

subbĭbo -bĭbi, 3. *to drink a little,* Suet.

subblandĭor, 4. *to flatter, coax, caress a little,* Plaut.

subbrĕvis -e, *somewhat short,* Plin.

subcăvus -a -um, *somewhat hollow,* Lucr.

subcentŭrĭo = succenturio (q.v.).

subcingo = succingo (q.v.).

subcontŭmĕliōsē, adv. *somewhat insolently;* aliquem tractare, Cic.

subcresco = succresco (q.v.).

subcrispus -a -um, *somewhat curled;* capillus, Cic.

subcumbo = succumbo (q.v.).

subdēbilis -e, *somewhat lame,* Suet.

subdēbĭlĭtātus -a -um, *somewhat discouraged, wanting in spirit,* Cic.

subdĭālis -e (sub dio), *in the open air,* Plin. Subst., **subdĭālĭa** -ĭum, n. *open galleries, balconies,* Plin.

subdĭffĭcĭlis -e, *somewhat difficult;* quaestio subdifficilis, Cic.

subdĭffīdo, 3. *to be somewhat mistrustful,* Cic.

subdĭtīvus -a -um (subdo), *suppositious, not genuine, false;* archipirata, Cic.

subdĭto, 1. (intens. of subdo), *to supply, apply,* Lucr. (?)

subdo -dĭdi -dĭtum, 3. **I.** *to put, place, lay, set under;* 1, lit., a, ignes, Cic.; se aquis, se dive under, Ov.; b, partic., subditus, of places, *lying under or near;* subdita templo Appia, Ov.; 2, fig., a, irae facem, Lucr.; alieni acriores ad studia dicendi faces, Cic.; alicui spiritus, *to infuse,* Liv.; b, esp., *to subject, subdue;* ne feminae imperio subderentur, Tac. **II.** *to put in the place of another, substitute.* **A.** Gen., me in Hirtii locum, Cic. **B.** *to substitute falsely, counterfeit, suborn;* testamenta, Tac.

subdŏcĕo, 2. *to teach as an assistant, to assist in teaching,* Cic.

subdŏlē, adv. (subdolus), *somewhat slyly, craftily,* Cic.

subdŏlus -a -um, *somewhat sly, crafty, cunning, deceitful;* oratio, Caes.

subdŏmo, 1. *to tame, subject by taming,* Plaut.

18

subdŭbĭto, 1. *to doubt* or *hesitate a little, be undecided;* subdubitare te, quā essem erga illum voluntate, Cic.

subdūco -duxi -ductum, 3. **I.** *to draw from under, to withdraw, take away,* esp., *secretly.* **A.** Lit., **1**, gen., ensem capiti, Verg.; lapides ex turri, Caes..; transf., se subducere colles incipiunt, *to withdraw themselves gradually,* i.e., *slope down to,* Verg.; **2**, esp., **a**, *to take away to some place, lead away, draw off;* aliquem in contionem, Liv.; esp., as milit. t.t., cohortes e dextro cornu, Liv.; copias in proximum collem, Caes.; **b**, *to take away secretly, to steal;* furto obsides, Liv.; se subducere, *to withdraw secretly, go away quietly, to steal away;* de circulo se subduxit, Cic.; **c**, *to take away;* cibum athletae, Cic.; pugnae Turnum, Verg. **B.** Transf., subducere rationem, or ratiunculam, *to balance an account, cast up, reckon,* Cic.; so also calculos, Cic.; summam, Cic. **II.** *to draw up on high, lift up;* **1**, gen., cataractam in tantum altitudinis, Liv.; **2**, esp., naut. t.t., *to draw* or *haul up a ship on shore;* classem, Liv.; naves, Caes.

subductārĭus -a -um (subduco), *useful for drawing up;* funis, Cato.

subductĭo -ōnis, f. (subduco). **I.** *the drawing up of a ship on dry land,* Caes. **II.** *a reckoning, computing,* Cic.

subdulcis -e, *somewhat sweet,* Plin.

subdūrus -a -um, *somewhat hard,* Q. Cic.

sŭbĕdo -ēdi -ēsum, 3. *to eat under, wear away;* scopulos, quem rauca subederat unda, Ov.

sŭbĕo -ĭi -ĭtum -īre, *to go under, come under, pass under, dive under, crawl under.* **I. A.** Lit., **a**, with a prep., subit oras hasta per imas clipei, Verg.; **b**, with dat., luco, Verg.; as a bearer (under a burden), ingenti feretro, Verg.; **c**, with acc., aquas, Ov.; tectum non subisse, Caes.; mucronem, *to run under,* Verg.; as a bearer, onus dorso gravius, Hor.; **d**, absol., ille astu subit, Verg. **B.** Fig. *to go under* (as a burden), *to submit to, to take upon oneself;* quamvis carnificinam, Cic.; quemque casum, Cic.; pro amico periculum aut invidiam, Cic.; minus sermonis subissem, Cic. **II.** *to approach to.* **A.** *to come near a point, advance to, mount to, climb to;* **1**, lit., **a**, (a) with prep., sub orbem solis (of the moon), Liv.; in latebras, Ov.; ad urbem, Liv.; (β) with dat., muro, Verg.; (γ) with acc., muros, Liv.; (δ) absol., pone subit conjux, Verg.; **b**, *to approach secretly* or *gradually, to steal into;* (a) with acc., lumina fessa (of sleep), Ov.; (β) absol., an subit (amor), Ov.; **c**, of water, *to approach near, to wash;* ubi maxime montes Crotonenses Trasumenus subit, Liv.; **2**, fig.; **a**, *to come under;* (a) with sub and the acc., sub acumen stili, Cic.; (β) with acc., clarum subit Alba Latinum, *comes under the rule of,* Ov.; **b**, *to approach some action, to undertake, take upon oneself;* with acc., invicem proelium, Liv..; **c**, of situations or conditions, *to come upon one, happen to, befall;* (a) with dat., subeunt mihi fastidia cunctarum, Ov.; (β) with acc., horror animum subit, Tac.; (γ) with infin., subit ira cadentem ulcisci patriam, Verg.; (δ) absol., *to draw near, come;* subeunt morbi tristisque senectus et labor, Verg.; **d**, of thoughts, *to occur, come into the mind, creep in;* (a) with dat., subeant animo Latmia saxa tuo, Ov.; (β) with acc., mentem patriae subiit pietatis imago, Verg.; with acc. and infin., cogitatio animum subit indignum esse, etc., Liv.; (γ) absol., subiit cari genitoris imago, Ov. **B.** *to come immediately after, to take the place of, to follow;* **1**, lit., **a**, with dat., primae legioni tertia, dexterae alae sinistra subiit, Liv.; **b**, with acc., furcas subiere columnae, Ov.; **2**, fig., **a**, with in and

the acc., in eorum locum subiere fraudes, Ov.; **b**, absol., pulchra subit facies, Ov. (perf., subivit, Ov.).

sŭber -ĕris, n. *the cork-tree,* Verg.

subf . . . v. suff. . . .

subg . . . v. sugg. . . .

sŭbhorrĭdus -a -um, *somewhat rough,* Cic.

sŭbĭcĭo, v. subjicio.

sŭbĭgo -ēgi -actum, 3. (sub and ago), *to drive under.* **I.** *to drive under or to a place;* **1**, lit., sues in umbrosum locum, Varr.,; naves ad castellum, Liv.; adverso flumine lembum remigio, *to row,* Verg.; ratem conto, *to push,* Verg.; **2**, transf., *to drive a person to do something against his will, to force, compel;* gen., with ad or in and the acc., Volscos ad deditionem, Liv.; with infin. or acc. and infin., Tarquinienses metu subegerat frumentum exercitui praebere, Liv.; with ut and the subj., ut relinquant patriam atque cives, Liv. **II.** **1**, *to work through, to work thoroughly;* in cote secures, *to sharpen,* Verg.; digitis opus, *to make smooth,* Ov.; so esp., *to work the earth, to break up, plough, cultivate;* terras fissione glebarum, Cic.; **2**, transf., **a**, *to tame;* (a) of animals, belua facilis ad subigendum, Cic.; (β) of men, *to practise, train, inure;* tot subacti atque durati bellis, Liv.; **b**, *to subdue, conquer;* subacti bello, Liv.; populos armis, Cic.; partic. subst., victi ac subacti, Cic.

sŭbimpŭdens -entis, *somewhat impudent,* Cic.

sŭbĭnānis -e, *somewhat vain,* Cic.

sŭbindĕ, adv. **I.** *immediately upon, immediately after,* Hor., Liv. **II.** *repeatedly, from time to time, continually,* Liv.

sŭbinsulsus -a -um, *somewhat insipid,* Cic.

sŭbinvĭdĕo, 2. **I.** *to envy somewhat;* subinvideo tibi, Cic. **II.** Partic., **sŭbinvīsus** -a -um, *somewhat hated,* Cic.

sŭbinvīto, 1. *to invite secretly;* with ut and the subj., Cic.

sŭbīrascor -īrasci, dep. *to be a little angry;* interdum soleo subirasci, Cic.; foll. by dat., brevitati litterarum, Cic.; by quod, quod me non invitas, Cic.

sŭbīrātus -a -um, *somewhat angry,* Cic.

sŭbĭtārĭus -a -um (subitus), *sudden, hasty;* exercitus, milites, legiones, *gathered in haste,* Liv.

sŭbĭto, adv. (subitus), *suddenly, unexpectedly, on a sudden,* Cic.; dicere, *to speak extempore,* Cic.

sŭbĭtus -a -um, p. adj (from subeo), *sudden, unexpected.* **I.** Adj., res, Cic.; bellum, Caes. **II.** Subst., **sŭbĭtum** -i, n. *a sudden occurrence, unexpected chance;* ad subita rerum, Liv.

subjăcĕo -jăcŭi, 2. **I.** *to lie under or beneath,* Plin. **II.** *to be subject to, belong to, to be connected with,* Quint.

subjectē, adv., only used in superl. (subjectus), *submissively,* Caes.

subjectĭo -ōnis, f. (subjicio). **I.** *a laying under, placing under;* rerum, quasi gerantur, sub aspectum paene subjectio, Cic. **II.** *a counterfeiting, forging;* testamenti, Liv. **III.** Rhet. t.t. = ἀνθυποφορά, *the answer given by an orator to a question which he has himself asked,* Quint.

subjecto, 1. (intens. of subjicio). **I.** *to place, lay, put under;* stimulos alicui, Hor. **II.** *to throw up from below,* Verg.

subjector -ōris, m. (subjicio), *a forger, counterfeiter;* testamentorum, Cic.

1. subjectus -ū, m. (subjicio), *a placing, laying under,* Plin.

2. subjectus -a -um, p. adj. (from subjicio). **I.** Of places, *lying near, adjacent;* Heraclea, quae est subjecta Candaviae, Caes.; alter (circulus terrae) subjectus aquiloni, Cic. **II.** Transf., a, *subjected, subject to;* nulli est naturae oboediens aut subjectus deus, Cic. Subst., **subjecti** -ōrum, m. *subjects, dependents,* Tac.; b, *exposed to;* subjectior invidiae, Hor.

subjĭcĭo (sŭbĭcĭo) -jēci -jectum, 3. (sub and jacio). **I.** *to throw, cast, place, set, put under.* **A.** Lit., 1, gen., ignem, Cic.; aliquid oculis, Cic.; aedes colli, *to build under,* Liv.; castra urbi, *to pitch under the walls of,* Liv.; 2, esp., a, milit. t.t., *to advance near;* aciem collibus, or castris, legiones castris, Caes.; b, *to present;* libellum alicui, Cic. **B.** Fig., 1, gen., ea quae sub sensus subjecta sunt, Cic.; res, quae subjectae sunt sensibus, Cic.; 2, esp., a, *to subdue,* subjugate, *subject;* Gallia securibus subjecta, Caes.; se alicui, Cic.; or se imperio alicuius, Cic.; b, *to expose;* fortunas innocentium fictis auditionibus, Caes.; aliquid praeconi, Liv., or voci praeconis, Cic., or sub praeconem, Cic., *to bring to the hammer, have sold by auction;* c, *to subordinate;* partes generibus, Cic.; d, in discourse and writing, *to place after, append, subjoin;* rationem, Cic.; e, *to whisper to, to suggest, to remind;* subjiciens quid dicerem, Cic.; consilia, Liv.; spem alicui, *to infuse,* Liv. **II.** *to throw from under;* 1, *to throw up on high, to raise, lift;* regem in equum, Liv.; reflex., alnus se subjicit, *shoots up,* Verg.; 2, *to haul from under;* tragulas inter carros, Caes. **III.** *to substitute;* 1, gen., potiorem, Liv.; pro verbo proprio subjicitur aliud, quod idem significet, Cic.; 2, a, *to forge, counterfeit;* testamenta, Cic.; b, *to suborn;* Metellum, Caes.

subjŭgĭus -a -um (sub and jugum), *attached to the yoke,* Cato.

subjungo -junxi -junctum, 3. **I.** *to join with, unite to;* 1, lit., puppis rostro Phrygios subjuncta leones, *having affixed,* Verg.; 2, fig., omnes artes oratori, Cic.; carmina percussis nervis, *with playing on the lyre,* Ov. **II.** *to yoke, harness;* 1, lit., tigres curru, Verg.; 2, fig., *to subdue, subjugate;* urbes sub imperium, Cic.; sibi res, Hor.

sublābor -lapsus sum -lābi, 3. dep. **I.** *to glide in, slide in,* Verg. **II.** *to glide away;* fig., retro sublapsa spes, Verg.

sublāmĭna -ae, f. *an under-plate,* Cato.

sublātē, adv. (sublatus, from tollo), *highly;* fig., a, *loftily, sublimely;* dicere, Cic.; b, *proudly, haughtily;* de se sublatius dicere, Cic.

sublātĭo -ōnis, f. (tollo), *a lifting up, elevation;* fig., animi, Cic.

sublātus -a -um, p. adj. (from tollo), *raised aloft, proud, haughty;* with abl., hāc victoriā, Caes.; rebus secundis, Verg.; absol., leo fidens magis et sublatior ardet, Ov.

sublecto, 1. (from *sublicio, as allecto from allicio), *to flatter, wheedle,* Plaut.

sublĕgo -lēgi -lectum, 3. **I.** *to gather below, pick up,* Hor. **II.** *to carry off, catch up secretly;* liberos parentibus, *to kidnap,* Plaut.; fig., nostrum sermonem, *to listen to secretly,* Plaut. **III.** *to choose in the place of another person;* in demortuorum locum, Liv.; e postremo in tertium locum esse sublectum, Cic.

sublestus -a -um, *slight, weak, trivial,* Plaut.

sublĕvātĭo -ōnis, f. (sublevo), *a relieving, assuaging,* Cic.

sublĕvo, 1. **I.** *to lift up, hold up; ab iis sublevatus murum ascendit, Caes.; aliquem stratum ad pedes, Cic. **II.** Transf., *to lessen, diminish;* pericula, Cic.; offensionem, Cic.;

---

esp., a, *to lessen* or *relieve by consoling;* res adversas, Cic.; b, *to support; causam inimici, Cic.

sublĭca -ae, f. (ὑποβλής), *a pile driven into the ground, palisade,* Caes., Liv.; esp. of the piles of a bridge, Caes.

sublĭcĭus -a -um (sublica), *resting upon piles;* pons, *a wooden bridge across the Tiber, said to have been built by Ancus Martius,* Liv.

sublĭgācŭlum -i, n. (subligo), *a cloth worn round the loins, drawers,* Cic.

sublĭgar -āris, n. = subligaculum (q.v.).

sublĭgo, 1. *to bind below, bind on;* clipeum sinistrae, Verg.

sublīmē, adv., v. sublimis.

sublīmis -e (sublevo), *high.* **I.** Adj., **A.** Lit., *high, lofty, exalted, lifted up;* a, cacumen montis, Ov.; b, *in the air, aloft;* sublimis abiit, *went away on high,* Liv.; c, *raised on high;* iret consul sublimis curru multijugis equis, Liv. **B.** Transf., *sublime, elevated, lofty;* a, mens, Ov.; b, of style, *lofty, sublime;* carmina, Juv. **II.** Subst., **sublīme** -is, n. *height,* Suet. **III.** Adv., **sublīme,** *on high, aloft;* aer sublime fertur, Cic.; sublime elatus, Liv. (Other forms: sublimus -a -um, Lucr.; sublimen = sublime, adv., Enn. ap. Cic.)

sublīmĭtas -ātis, f. (sublimis), *loftiness, height;* a, lit., Plin.; b, transf., *loftiness, sublimity,* Plin.

sublīmĭtĕr, adv. (sublimis), *aloft, on high;* sublimius attollere altum caput, Ov.

sublīmus, v. sublimis.

sublingĭo -ōnis, m. (sub and lingo), *a scullion,* Plaut.

sublĭno -lēvi -lītum, 3. **I.** *to smear below, to lay on colour as a ground,* Plin. **II.** Transf., 1, *to line, overlay, veneer with anything,* Plin.; 2, fig., os alicui, *to deceive, cozen, cajole, delude,* Plaut.

sublūcānus -a -um (sub and lux), *about daybreak, towards morning,* Plin.

sublūcĕo -luxi, 2. *to gleam forth, glimmer,* Verg., Ov.

sublŭo -lŭi -lūtum, 3. **I.** *to wash from below, bathe underneath,* Mart. **II.** Transf., of rivers, *to flow beneath, flow at the foot of;* hunc montem flumen subluebat, Caes.

sublustris -e (sub and lux), *somewhat light, having a glimmering light;* nox, Hor.

sublŭvĭes -ēi, f. (subluo), *a disease in the feet of sheep,* Plin.

submergo -mersi -mersum, 3. *to plunge under; to sink;* pass., submergi = *to dive* or *plunge under;* of persons, *to be drowned;* navem, Tac.; with abl., classem Argivûm ponto, Verg.; often in pass., submersae beluae, *living under the water,* Cic.; submersus equus voraginibus, Cic.; with in and the abl., ferrum submersum in unda, Ov.

submĭnistro, 1. *to aid, give, furnish, supply.* **I.** Lit., tela clam, Cic.; alicui pecuniam, Cic. **II.** Fig., huic arti plurima adjumenta, Cic.

submissē (summissē), adv. (submissus). **I.** Of speech, *softly, calmly;* dicere, Cic.; Demosthenes submissius a primo, Cic. **II.** Of character, *modestly, humbly, submissively;* supplicare, Cic.; submissius nos geramus, Cic.

submissim (summissim), adv. (submissus), *gently, softly, quietly,* Suet.

submissĭo (summissĭo) -ōnis, f. (submitto), *a letting down, sinking, lowering;* contentio vocis et submissio, Cic.; orationis, Cic.

submissus (summissus) -a -um, p. adj. (from submitto). **I.** *lowered, low;* vertex, Ov.;

submissiores, *in a lower position*, Liv. **II.** Transf., **A.** Applied to the voice, *low, soft, gentle;* used of discourse, *quiet, mild, gentle;* **a**, vox, Cic.; **b**, *quiet, unpretentious;* submissa dicere, Cic.; orator, Cic. **B.** Of character, **a**, in a bad sense, *mean, abject;* submissum vivere, Cic.; ne quid humile, submissum faciamus, Cic.; **b**, in a good sense, *humble;* submissi petimus terram, Verg.

submitto (summitto) -mīsi -missum, 3. **I.** *to let down.* **A.** Lit., 1, gen., fasces, *to lower*, Liv.; alicui se ad pedes, *to fall at the feet of*, Liv.; 2, esp., of places, in pass., submitti, as middle = *to sink, slope down;* submissa fastigio planities, Liv. **B.** Fig., 1, gen., animos, *cause to sink*, Liv.; se, *to abase oneself*, Cic.; 2, esp., **a**, *to diminish, lessen;* multum (in discourse), *not to speak strongly*, Cic.; **b**, *to give over;* alicui imperium, Liv.; **c**, *to subject to, subordinate to;* citharae cannas, Ov.; **d**, *to slacken, relax;* furorem, Verg. **II.** *to place under;* fig., *to submit;* animos amori, Verg. **III.** *to send up from below, to raise;* 1, gen., oculos, Ov.; 2, esp., **a**, *to cause to spring up;* flores, Lucr.; transf., *to produce;* non monstrum summisere Colchi majus, Hor.; **b**, *to let grow;* capillum, Plin.; **c**, *to rear;* vitulos, Verg. **IV.** *to send secretly;* aliquem, Cic.; subsidia alicui, Caes.

submŏlestē (summŏlestē), adv. (submolestus), *with some vexation;* te non esse Romae submoleste fero, Cic.

submŏlestus (summŏlestus) -a -um, *somewhat vexatious;* illud est mihi submolestum quod parum properare Brutus videtur, Cic.

submŏnĕo (summŏnĕo) -mŏnŭi, 2. *to remind secretly*, Ter.

submŏrōsus (summŏrōsus)-a-um, *somewhat morose, somewhat peevish*, Cic.

submōtor (summōtor) -ōris, m. (submoveo), *one who clears a space in a crowd*, Liv.

submŏvĕo (summŏvĕo) -mōvi -mōtum, 2. *to move away, drive away, remove.* **I.** Lit., **A.** Gen., **a**, of persons, aliquem, Ov.; strictis gladiis inertes, Liv.; populum aris, Ov.; **b**, of things, silva suis frondibus Phoebeos submovet ictus, *keeps off*, Ov.; submotis nubibus, Verg. **B.** Esp., 1, of living beings, **a**, *to remove, cause to withdraw;* arbitros, Liv.; recusantes nostros advocatos, Cic.; **b**, of the lictor, *to clear a way for a magistrate, to keep off, move back;* turbam, Liv.; submoveri jubet, Liv.; abl. absol., submoto, *when a way had been cleared*, Liv.; **c**, *to banish, expel;* aliquem patriā, Ov.; **d**, *to drive off in a hostile manner, drive away, force back;* cohortes sub murum, Caes.; victorem hostem a vallo, Liv.; hostes ex muro ac turribus, Caes.; 2, of things, **a**, *to remove, move back;* maris litora, Hor.; **b**, pass. partic., submotus, *lying out of the way, remote;* spelunca vasto submota recessu, Verg. **II.** Transf., 1, of persons, *to keep away from, force from, compel to give up;* a bello Antiochum et Ptolemaeum reges, Liv.; aliquem magnitudine poenae a maleficio, Cic.; 2, of things, *to remove, banish;* tumultus mentis et curas, Hor.

submūto (summūto), 1. *to exchange;* verba pro verbis, Cic.

subnascor -nātus sum, 3. dep. *to grow up under, grow up out of or after*, Ov.

subnecto -nexŭi -nexum, 3. **I.** *to bind, tie, bind on beneath;* antennis totum subnectite velum, Ov. **II.** *to join or tie together;* aurea purpuream subnectit fibula vestem, Verg.

subnĕgo, 1. *to deny a little, partly deny*, Cic.

subnĭger -gra -grum, *somewhat black, blackish*, Plaut.

subnixus (subnĭsus) -a -um (sub and nitor). **I.** *propped under;* mitrā mentum et crinem subnixus, *bound under*, Verg. **II.** *supported by, resting upon;* **a**, lit., circuli vertĭcĭbus subnixi, Cic.; **b**, fig., *trusting, relying upon, depending upon;* with abl., auxiliis, Liv.; victoriā, Liv.; qui artis arrogantiā ita subnixi ambulant, Cic.

subnŏto, 1. **I.** *to mark beneath, write underneath*, Plin. **II.** *to observe, notice secretly*, Mart.

subnūba -ae, f. (sub and nubo), *a rival*, Ov.

subnūbĭlus -a -um, *somewhat cloudy; nox*, Caes.

sŭbo, 1. *to be in heat*, Lucr., Hor.

sŭbobscoenus (sŭbobscēnus) -a -um, *somewhat obscene*, Cic.

sŭbobscūrus -a -um, *somewhat obscure*, Cic.

sŭbŏdiōsus -a -um, *somewhat odious, unpleasant*, Cic.

sŭboffendo, 3. *to give some offence;* apud aliquem, Cic.

sŭbŏlĕo, 2. lit., *to emit a smell;* hence, fig., hoc subolet mihi, or subolet mihi, *I smell, perceive, scent*, Plaut.

sŭbŏles (sŏbŏles) -is, genit. plur., -um (subolesco). **I.** Of things, *a sprout, shoot, offshoot, sucker*, Plin. **II.** Of living beings, of men and animals, *race, offspring, progeny, issue;* **a**, of men, stirpis, Liv.; juventutis, Cic.; of one person, suboles imperatorum (of Scipio), Liv.; **b**, of animals, haedus, suboles lascivi gregis, Hor.

sŭbŏlesco, 3. (sub and olesco = alesco), *to grow up*, Liv.

sŭbŏrĭor, 4. dep. *to arise, come forth, spring up*, Lucr.

sŭborno, 1. **I.** *to furnish, equip, provide;* a natura subornatus, Cic.; fig., legati subornati criminibus, Liv. **II.** *to incite, instigate secretly*, suborn; fictum testem, Cic.; aliquem ad caedem regis, Liv.

sŭbortus -ūs, m. (suborior), *a coming forth, arising*, Lucr.

subp . . . v. supp. . . .

subrādo (surrādo) -rāsi -rasum, 3. *to scrape below*, Cato.

subrancĭdus (surrancĭdus) -a -um, *somewhat putrid;* caro, Cic.

subraucus (surraucus) -a -um, *somewhat hoarse;* vox, Cic.

subrectus (surrectus), v. subrigo.

subrēmĭgo (surrēmĭgo), 1. *to row underneath, row along*, Verg.

subrēpo (surrēpo) -repsi -reptum, 3. *to creep or crawl from below, creep to, approach imperceptibly;* **a**, lit., sub tabulas, Cic., moenia, Hor.; **b**, transf., somnus in oculos subrepit, Ov.; subrepet iners aetas, Tib.

subreptĭcĭus (surreptĭcĭus) -a -um (surripio), 1, *stolen, kidnapped*, Plaut.; 2, *secret, surreptitious*, Plaut.

subrīdĕo (surrīdĕo) -rīsi -rīsum, 2. *to smile*, Cic.

snbrīdĭcŭlē (surrīdĭcŭlē), adv. *somewhat laughably*, Cic.

subrīgo (surrīgo) and contr., **surgo**, surrexi, surrectum, 3. (sub and rego). **I. subrĭgo** (surrigo) -rexi, etc., *to raise on high, lift up;* pass., subrigi, *to rise up;* partic., subrectus, *rising up;* aures, Verg.; subrecto mucrone, Liv. **II. surgo**, surrexi, surrectum. **A.** Transit., *to raise up, lift*, Plaut. **B.** Intransit., *to rise, rise*

up erect, stand up; 1, gen., **e** lectulo, Cic.; de sella, Cic.; humo, Ov.; poet., surgit ab Arpis Tydides, *comes from*, Verg.; **2,** esp., a, of orators, *to rise up to speak, to come forward;* ad dicendum, Cic.; **b,** *to rise up from bed or sleep;* ante lucem, Cic.; **3,** transf., a, *to arise, appear, become visible;* surgit dies, Verg.; ventus, Verg.; fig., discordia, Verg.; **b,** *to grow up, become larger;* (a) of things, as seed, Hor.; of the sea, Ov.; of buildings, surgens novae Carthaginis urbs, Verg.; (β) of living beings, *to grow up;* surgens Iulus, Verg. (syncop. perf. infin., surrexe, Hor.).

subrĭgŭus (surrĭgŭus) -a -um, *watered, irrigated,* Plin.

subringor (surringor), 3. dep. *to make a somewhat wry face, to be a little put out,* Cic.

subrĭpĭo = surripio (q.v.).

subrŏgo (surrŏgo), 1. *to cause a person to be chosen in place of or as substitute for another* (used of the magistrate presiding at the comitia, sufficere of the people choosing); in annum proximum decemviros alios, Cic.; collegam in locum Bruti, Liv.; with double acc., sibi Sp. Lucretium collegam, Cic.

subrostrāni (surrostrāni) -ōrum, m. (sub and rostra), *loungers about the rostra, idlers;* ap. Cic.

subrŭbĕo (surrŭbĕo), 2. *to be somewhat red;* part., subrubens = reddish, Ov.

subrŭbĭcundus (surrŭbĭcundus) -a -um, *somewhat red, reddish,* Plin.

subrūfus (surrūfus) -a -um, *reddish,* Plin.

subrūmus (surrūmus) -a -um (sub and ruma), *sucking;* agnus, Varr.

subrŭo (surrŭo) -rŭi -rŭtum, 3. *to tear down below, dig under, undermine, overthrow, destroy.* **I.** Lit., arbores, Caes.; murum, Liv. **II.** Fig., *to destroy, undermine;* nostram libertatem, Liv.

subrustĭcus (surrustĭcus) -a -um, *somewhat clownish;* pudor, Cic.

subrŭtĭlus (surrŭtĭlus) -a -um, *reddish,* color, Plin.

subsalsus -a -um, *somewhat salt,* Plin.

subscrībo -scripsi -scriptum, 3. I. *to write under, write beneath.* **A.** Gen., statuis subscripsit reges esse exactos, Cic.; causam parricidii, Cic.; haec subscribe libello, Hor. **B.** Esp., **1,** *to sign a document;* a, lit., Suet.; b, transf., *to support, assent to, approve of;* odiis accusatorum, Liv.; irae Caesaris, Ov.; **2,** of the censor, *to write the ground of his censure beneath the name of the person censured;* istam causam, Cic.; **3,** of an accuser or joint-accuser, *to write their names under the accusation;* a, of the accuser, *to sign a charge;* hence, *to prosecute;* subscripsit quod is pecuniam accepisset, accused him of having, etc., Cic.; in aliquem, *to accuse,* Cic.; b, of a joint-accuser = *to join in the accusation;* Gabinium de ambitu reum fecit subscribente privigno, Cic. **II.** *to note down, make a note of;* numerum, Cic.

subscriptĭo -ōnis, f. (subscribo), *a writing beneath, inscription.* **I.** Gen., Cic. **II.** Esp., a, censoria, *the noting down of the offence censured;* subscriptiones censorum, Cic.; b, *the signing of one's name to an accusation;* (a) of the accuser, Cic.; (β) of a joint-accuser, *a joining in an accusation,* Cic.; c, *the signing, subscription of a document,* Suet.; d, *a register,* Cic.

subscriptor -ōris, m. (subscribo), *the signer of an indictment, a joint-accuser,* Cic.

subsĕcīvus = subsicivus (q.v.).

subsĕco -sĕcŭi -sectum, 1. *to cut away below;* ungues ferro, Ov.

subsellĭum -ĭi, n. (sub and sella). **I.** *a low bench or form,* Varr. **II.** *any ordinary or usual bench used for sitting on,* Sen.; a bench in a theatre, Cic.; of the senators in the senate-house, Cic.; longi subsellii judicatio et mora, *a long sitting to decide,* Cic.; of the tribunes in the market, Liv.; esp., of the benches of the judges, accusers, advocates, etc., Cic.; meton., subsellia = judicia, *courts;* habitare in subselliis, Cic.; versari in utrisque subselliis (*both as an advocate and judge*) optimā et fide et famā, Cic.

subsentĭo -sensi, 4. *to notice, perceive secretly,* Ter.

subsĕquor -sĕcūtus (-sĕquūtus) sum, 3. dep. *to follow, follow after.* **I.** a, lit., of persons, signa, Caes.; b, transf., of things, stella subsequitur, Cic.; hos motus subsequi debet gestus, Cic. **II.** Fig., *to follow, follow in opinion, comply with, imitate any one;* Platonem avunculum, Cic.; suo sermone humanitatem litterarum, Cic.

subservĭo, 4. *to be subject to, serve, subserve, comply with,* Plaut., Ter.

subsicīvus (subsĕcīvus) -a -um (sub and seco), *cut off.* **I.** Lit., t. t. of land-measuring; subst., **subsĕcīvum -i,** n. *a remainder or small parcel of land,* Varr. **II.** Transf., of time, superfluous, spare; tempora, *leisure hours,* Cic.; transf., of what is done in the leisure hours, quae (arripui) subsicivis operis, ut aiunt, Cic.

subsĭdĭārĭus -a -um (subsidium), *of or relating to a reserve, reserve;* cohortes, Caes., Liv.; subst., **subsĭdĭārĭi -ōrum, m.** *reserve troops,* Liv.

subsĭdĭor, 1. dep. (subsidium), *to serve as a reserve,* Hirt.

subsĭdĭum -ĭi, n. I. Concr., milit. t. t., *the troops stationed in the rear, reserved troops, a reserve, auxiliary forces;* subsidia et secundam aciem adortus, Liv.; subsidium and subsidia submittere, Caes. **II.** Abstr., **1,** milit. t. t., *help, assistance* (of such troops), subsidium ferre, Caes.; subsidio proficisci, Caes.; **2,** transf., a, *aid, means of aid, help, succour;* subsidium bellissimum existimo esse senectuti otium, Cic.; subsidio esse, of persons, *to be a help to,* Ov.; of things, *to serve as a help;* his difficultatibus, Caes.; or oblivioni, Cic.; b, *a place of refuge, an asylum,* Tac.

subsīdo -sēdi and -sīdi -sessum, 3. I. *to sit down, squat, crouch down, settle down, sink down.* **A.** Lit., **1,** of living beings, a, subsidunt Hispani, Liv.; elephanti clunibus subsidentes, Liv.; b, *to lie in wait for, lurk in ambush;* in insidiis, Liv.; in loco, Cic.; with acc., Asiam devictam, Verg.; c, of females, *to submit to the male,* Lucr., Hor.; **2,** transf., of things, *to sink down, subside;* subsidunt undae, Verg.; jussit subsidere valles, Ov. **B.** Fig., *to abate,* Plin. **II.** *to remain sitting, to stay, remain, settle;* subsedi in via, Cic.; multitudo calonum in castris subsederant, Caes.

subsignānus -a -um (sub and signum), *serving beneath the standard;* milites, *legionary soldiers kept as a reserve,* Tac.

subsigno, 1. I. *to write beneath, sign, subscribe,* Plin. **II.** Transf., **1,** *to enter on a list, to register;* praedia apud aerarium, Cic.; **2,** *to pledge,* Plin.

subsĭlĭo (sussĭlĭo) -sĭlŭi, 4. *to leap up, spring up,* Lucr.

subsĭmus -a -um, *somewhat snub-nosed,* Varr.

subsisto -stĭti, 3. I. Transit., *to make a stand against, to withstand;* feras, Liv.; Romanum nec acies subsistere ullae poterant, Liv.

II. Intransit., **A.** *to stand still, come to a stand,* kalt; 1, lit., a, of persons, in itinere, Caes.; b, of things, *to stay, stop;* substitit unda, Verg.; 2, fig., *to cease;* substitit clamor, Ov. **B.** *to tarry, remain, abide;* 1, lit., in Samnio adversus Caudinas legiones, Liv.; 2, fig., intra priorem paupertatem, *to remain, continue,* Tac. **C.** *to withstand, oppose, hold out;* 1, lit., a, of persons, Hannibali atque eius armis, Liv.; b, of things, quod neque ancorae funesque subsisterent neque, etc., Caes.; 2, fig., *to withstand, support;* sumptui, ap. Cic.

subsŏlānus -a -um, *eastern, oriental,* Plin.; subst., **subsŏlānus** -i, m. *the east wind,* Plin.

subsortĭor -sortitus sum, 4. dep. *to choose by lot, to substitute;* judices, *to choose fresh jurymen for those challenged by either party,* Cic.

subsortītĭo -ōnis, f. (subsortior), *the choosing of a judicial substitute by lot;* judicum, Cic.

substantĭa -ae, f. (substo). **I.** *substance, essence,* Quint. **II.** *property, means of subsistence;* facultatum, Tac.

substerno -strāvi -strātum, 3. **I.** *to strew or spread beneath, lay under;* 1, lit., cinnama, Ov.; 2, fig., *to offer, give up;* omne corporeum animo, Cic. **II.** Transf., *to cover;* gallinae nidos quam possunt mollissime substernunt, Cic.

substĭtŭo -ŭi -ūtum, 3. (sub and statuo). **I.** *to put under, place beneath;* 1, lit., Auct. b. Afr.; 2, fig., substituerat animo speciem corporis, Liv. **II.** *to put in the place of, substitute;* a, in locum eorum cives Romanos, Cic.; aliquem pro aliquo, Cic.; aliquid pro aliqua re, Cic.; b, heredem, *to name a second heir in case of the death of the first,* Suet.

substo, 1. *to stand firm,* Ter.

substrāmen -ĭnis, n. (substerno), *that which is strewed beneath, straw, litter,* Varr.

substrātus -ūs, m. (substerno), *a strewing, laying, scattering beneath,* Plin.

substrictus -a -um, p. adj. (from substringo), *narrow, tight, contracted, small;* crura, Ov.

substringo -strinxi -strictum, 3. *to draw together, to bind, tie beneath, bind up;* crinem nodo, Tac.; aurem alicui, *to prick up the ear* (in order to listen to some one), Hor.

substructĭo -ōnis, f. (substruo), *that which is built below, base, foundation;* substructionum moles, Caes.

substrŭo -struxi -structum, 3. *to build, construct beneath, lay a foundation;* Capitolium saxo quadrato substructum est, *built with a foundation of hewn stone,* Liv.

subsultim, adv. (subsilio), *springing up, leaping up,* Suet.

subsulto (sussulto), 1. (intens. of subsilio), *to spring up, leap up, jump up,* Plaut.

subsum -fŭi -esse, *to be under.* **I.** Lit., 1, *to be behind;* suberat Pan ilicis umbrae, Tib.; nigra subest lingua palato, Verg.; 2, *to be near at hand;* suberat mons, Caes.; dies, Cic.; templa mari subsunt, Ov. **II.** Fig., 1, *to be subjected to,* Ov.; 2, *to be there, to exist, to be in question;* subest nulla periculi suspicio, Cic.; tamquam spes subesset, Cic.

subsūtus -a -um, *sewed beneath;* vestis, *fringed, edged below,* Hor.

subtĕgŭlānĕus -a -um (sub and tegula), *beneath the tiles, under the roof, in-doors,* Plin.

subtēmen (subtegmen) -mĭnis, n. (contracted from subteximen), *that which is worked in;* hence, **I.** *the weft or woof in weaving,* Ov.; fert picturatas auri subtemine vestes, Verg. **II.** Meton., *that which is woven or spun, thread, yarn.* Tib

---

subtendo -tendi -tentum (-tensum), 3. *to stretch underneath,* Cato.

subtĕnĕo, 2. *to hold underneath,* Cato (syncop. imper., subtento).

subtĕnŭis -e, *somewhat thin,* Varr.

subtĕr (sub). **I.** Adv., *beneath, below, underneath;* omnia haec, quae supra et subter, Cic. **II.** Prep., *beneath, below, underneath;* a, with acc., cupiditatem subter praecordia locavit, Cic.; b, with abl., subter se, Cic. (in composition subter means *under, beneath,* as in subterfluo, or *underhand, in secret,* as subterduco).

subterdūco, 3. *to lead away secretly, carry off secretly,* Plaut.

subterflŭo, 3. *to flow beneath,* Plin.

subterfŭgĭo -fūgi, 3. **I.** Intransit., *to flee in secret,* Plaut. **II.** Transit., *to escape by stealth, evade, shun;* poenam, Cic.; periculum, Cic.

subterlābor -lapsus sum, 3. dep. **I.** *to glide, flow under;* fluctus Sicanos, Verg. **II.** *to slip away underneath, to escape,* Liv.

subterlīno, 3. *to smear underneath,* Plin.

subtĕro -trīvi -trītum, 3. *to rub off, wear underneath, to grind, pound,* Plin.

subterrānĕus -a -um (sub and terra), *underground, subterranean;* specus in fundo, Cic.

subtervăcans -antis, *empty below,* Sen.

subtexo -texŭi -textum, 3. **I.** *to weave beneath;* transf., a, *to draw together under;* patrio capiti (the sun) bibulas nubes, Ov.; b, *to cover, darken;* caelum fumo, Verg. **II.** *to weave on to:* 1, transf., *to join to;* lunam alutae, Juv.; 2, fig., in speech, *to connect, subjoin;* subtexit deinde fabulae huic legatos in senatu interrogatos esse, Liv.

subtīlis -e (contracted from subtexilis, as tela from texela and exilis from exiglis), lit., *finely woven;* hence, **I.** *thin, fine, slender;* 1, lit., filum, Lucr.; 2, transf., a, gen., *fine, accurate, exact;* descriptio, Cic.; venustas, *elegant,* Cic.; b, esp., of expression, *plain, simple, unadorned;* oratio, Cic.; subtilis scriptor atque elegans, Cic. **II.** Of the senses, *fine, acute;* 1, lit., palatum, Hor.; 2, transf., of taste and discernment, *fine, acute, subtle;* judicium, Cic.

subtīlĭtas -ātis, f. (subtilis), *thinness, fineness, minuteness.* **I.** Lit., linearum, Cic. **II.** Transf., a, *accuracy, fineness, subtlety, exactness;* sententiarum, Cic.; sermonis, Cic.; b, of discourse, *plainness, simplicity;* orationis, Cic.

subtīlĭtĕr, adv. (subtilis), *finely, minutely.* **I.** Lit., res subtiliter connexae, Lucr. **II.** Transf., a, *finely, accurately, exactly, subtly;* judicare, Cic.; subtilius haec disserere, Cic.; subtilissime perpolita, Cic.; b, of expression, *plainly, simply, without ornament;* dicere, Cic.

subtīmĕo, 2. *to be a little afraid,* with ne and the subj., Cic.

subtrăho -traxi -tractum, 3. **I.** *to draw away from under;* subtractus Numida mortuo superincubanti Romano vivus, Liv. **II.** *to draw away secretly, withdraw, remove, take away.* **A.** Lit., cibum alicui, Cic.; hastatos ex acie, Liv.; se, *to withdraw oneself;* se aspectui, Verg.; middle, subtrahitur solum, *withdraws itself from under the ship,* Verg. **B.** Fig., materiem furori tuo, Cic.; reflex., se subtrahente, *withdrawing himself* (as surety), Liv.; cui judicio eum mors subtraxit, Liv.; me a curia et ab omni parte reipublicae, Cic.; aliquem irae militum, Tac.

subtristis -e, *somewhat sad,* Ter.

subturpĭcŭlus -a -um, *somewhat disgraceful,* Cic.

subturpis -e. *somewhat disgraceful,* Cic.

subtŭs, adv. (sub),*beneath, below, underneath,* Liv.

subtūsus -a -um (sub and tundo), *somewhat bruised,* Tib.

sŭbūcŭla -ae,' f. (perhaps from * sub-uo, whence ex-uo), *an inner tunic, shirt,* Hor.

sŭbŭla -ae, f. *a shoemaker's awl,* Mart.

sŭbulcus -i, m. (sus), *a swineherd,* Varr.

sŭbŭlo -ōnis, m. (connected with sibilus). **I.** *a Tuscan name for* tibicen, *a flute-player,* Enn. **II.** *a kind of stag,* Plin.

Sŭbūra -ae, f. *a street in the noisiest quarter of Rome;* hence, adj., **Sŭbūrānus** -a -um, *belonging to the Subura.*

sŭburbānĭtas-ātis, f. (suburbanus), *vicinity to the city,* Cic.

sŭburbānus -a -um, *near the city* (Rome), *suburban.* **I.** Adj., ager, gymnasium, Cic. **II.** Subst., **A. sŭburbānum** -i, n. (sc. praedium), *an estate near Rome, a suburban estate,* Cic. **B. sŭburbāni** -ōrum, m. *inhabitants of the suburbs,* Ov.

sŭburbĭum -Ii, n. (sub and urbs), *a suburb.* Cic.

sŭburgŭĕo, 2. *to drive close to;* proram ad saxa, Verg.

sŭbūro (-ussi) -ustum, 3. *to burn a little, to singe,* Suet.

Sŭburra = Subura (q.v.).

subvectĭo -ōnis, f. (subveho), *a carrying, conveyance, transport;* frumenti, Liv.; plur., ne ab re frumentaria duris subvectionibus laboraret, *lest he should have difficulties to contend with in the transport of provisions,* Caes.

subvecto, 1. (intens. of subveho), *to carry, convey, transport, bring;* saxa humeris, Verg.

subvectus = subvectio (q.v.).

subvĕho -vexi -vectum, 3. *to bring up from below, bring up stream, carry, convey, transport;* frumentum flumine Arari, Caes.; subvecta utensilia ab Ostia, Tac.; commeatus ex Samnio, Liv.; pass. as middle, ad arces subvehitur matrum caterva, *is borne up,* Verg.

subvĕnĭo -vēni -ventum, 4. *to come up to aid, to help, assist, succour.* **I.** Lit., milit. t. t., circumvento filio subvenit, Caes.; absol., nisi Romani subvenissent, Liv. **II.** Transf., *to help, aid, to remedy* or *relieve an evil;* alicui, Cic.; patriae, Cic.; gravedini, Cic.; impers., reipublicae difficillimo tempore esse subventum, Cic.

subvento, 1. (intens. of subvenio), *to come to the help of,* Plaut.

subvĕrĕor, 2. *to fear a little, be a little anxious,* Cic.

subversor -ōris, m. (subverto), *an overturner, overthrower;* fig., suarum legum, Tac.

subverto (subvorto) -verti (-vorti) -versum (-vorsum), 3. *to overthrow, overturn.* **I.** Lit., mensam, Suet.; montes, Sall.; absol., Hor. **II.** Fig., *to overthrow, ruin, subvert, destroy;* probitatem ceterasque artes bonas, Sall.; jura, Tac.

subvexus -a -um (subveho), *sloping upward,* Liv.

subvĭrĭdis -e, *somewhat green, greenish,* Plin.

subvŏlo, 1. *to fly up, fly forth;* utque novas humeris assumpserat alas, subvolat, Ov.; with in and the acc., rectis lineis in caelestem locum, Cic.

subvolvo, 3. *to roll up;* manibus saxa, Verg.

subvultŭrĭus -a -um, *somewhat vulture-like,* = *somewhat brown,* Plaut.

succăvus = subcavus (q.v.).

succēdānĕus (succīdānĕus) -a -um (suc cedo), *following, succeeding, ensuing, supplying the place of,* Plaut.

succēdo -cessi -cessum, 3. (sub and cedo). **I.** *to go under, go from under, ascend, mount.* **A.** Lit., tectum, Cic.; tumulo terrae, Verg.; tectis, Verg.; transf., fons, quo mare succedit, Caes. **B.** Fig., a, *to come under;* sub acumen stili, Cic.; b, *to submit to;* oneri, Verg. **II.** *to approach.* **A.** Lit., 1, milit. t. t., *to march forward, advance;* sub aciem, Caes.; ad castra, Liv.; moenibus, Liv.; 2, *to come after, take the place of;* ut integri et recentes defatigatis suc cederent, Caes.; in pugnam, Liv. **B.** Transf., 1, *to follow, succeed to;* a, in locum alicuius, Cic.; in paternas opes, Cic.; b, of position, *to come next to;* ad alteram partem succedunt Ubii, Caes.; 2, of time, *to follow, succeed;* alicui, Cic.; aetas aetati succedit, Cic.; orationi, Cic.; 3, of things, *to turn out well, to prosper, succeed;* haec prospere succedebant, Cic.; res nulla success erat, Caes.; absol., succedit, *it is successful;* si ex sententia successerit, Cic.; coeptis suc cedebat, Liv.; pass., nolle successum patribus, Liv.

succendo -cendi -censum, 3. (sub and * cando, from candeo), 3. *to kindle, set on fire from below.* **I.** Lit., pontem, Liv.; aggerem, Caes. **II.** Fig., *to kindle, set on fire, inflame;* Deucalion Pyrrhae successus amore, Ov.

succensĕo = suscenseo (q.v.).

succentivus -a -um (succino), *accompanying, played as an accompaniment,* Varr.

1. succentŭrĭo -ōnis, f. (sub and centurio -are), *to receive in a century as a substitute;* hence, *to put in the place of another, to substitute,* Ter.

2. succentŭrĭo -ōnis, f. (sub and centurio -onis), *an under-centurion,* Liv.

successĭo -ōnis, f. (succedo), *a succeeding, taking place of some person* or *thing, succession;* a, voluptatis, Cic.; b, *succession in an office;* in locum Antonii, ap. Cic.

successor -ōris, m. (succedo), *a successor, follower in office, possession, inheritance,* etc., Cic.; sagittae, *heir to,* Ov.; transf., Junius successor Maii, Ov.; novus, *a new shield,* Ov.

successus -ūs, m. (succedo). **I.** *an advance, approach;* hostium, Caes.; equorum, Verg. **II.** *happy issue;* prosperos successus dare orsis, Liv.; successum artes non habuere meae, Ov.

succidĭa -ae, f. (succido), *a flitch of bacon;* hortum ipsi agricolae succidiam alteram appellant, *their second flitch,* Cic.

1. succĭdo -cĭdi, 3. (sub and cado), *to fall under, sink, sink down;* aegri succidimus, Verg.

2. succīdo -cīdi -cīsum, 3. (sub and caedo), *to cut under, cut below, cut off, cut down;* femina poplitesque, Liv.; frumenta, Caes.

succĭdŭus -a -um (sub and cado), *falling down, sinking;* genu, Ov.

succinctus -a -um, p. adj. (from succingo), 1, *ready, equipped, prepared;* praedae, Ov.; 2, *short,* Mart.

succingo -cinxi -cinctum, 3. (sub and cingo). **I.** *to gird below, gird up, tuck up the clothes in the girdle;* tunicas, Juv.; oftener partic., **succinctus** -a -um, *with the clothes tucked up;* Diana, Ov.; poet., transf., succincta comas pinus, *with bare trunk,* Ov. **II.** *to girdle, surround;* a, lit., Scylla feris atram canibus suc cingitur alvum, Ov.; gen. partic., **succinctus** -a -um, *girded with something, armed with;* ferro, Liv.; pharetrā, Verg.; b, transf., *to surround,* arm, *prepare, provide ;* se canibus, Cic.; partic., Carthago succincta portubus, Cic. ; succinctus armis legionibusque, Liv.

succingŭlum -i, n. (succingo), *a girdle,* Plaut.

succĭno, 3. 1, *to sing to, to accompany,* Petr.; 2, transf., *to agree, chime in with ;* succinit alter, Hor.

succlāmātĭo -ōnis, f. (succlamo), *a shouting, acclamation,* Liv.

succlāmo (subclāmo), 1. *to shout at or after anything, call out ;* haec Virginio vociferanti succlamabat multitudo, Liv.; impers., succlamatum est, Liv. ; with acc. and infin., quum succlamasset nihil se mutare sententiae, Liv.

succollo, 1. (sub and collum), *to take upon the shoulders, to shoulder,* Suet.

succontŭmēlĭōsē = subcontumeliose (q.v.).

succresco (subcresco) -crēvi -crētum, 3. *to grow beneath, grow from beneath, grow up, increase ;* a, lit., succrescit ab imo cortex, Ov.; b, transf., per seque vident succrescere vina, Ov.; c, fig., non enim ille mediocris orator vestrae quasi succrescit aetati, Cic. ; se gloriae seniorum succrevisse, Liv.

succrispus = subcrispus (q.v.).

succumbo -cŭbŭi -cŭbĭtum, 3. (sub and *cumbo, as decumbo, accumbo, etc.), to lie down under, fall down, sink down.* I. Lit., succumbens victima ferro, Cat. ; omnes succubuisse oculos, *had sunk in sleep,* Ov. II. Fig., *to yield, give way, succumb, surrender ;* arrogantiae divitum, Cic. ; senectuti, Cic. ; tempori, Liv.; absol., non esse viri debilitari, dolore frangi, succumbere, Cic.

succurro -curri -cursum, 3. (sub and curro). I. *to run or go under ;* 1, transf., nequeat succurrere lunae corpus, Lucr. ; 2, fig., a, gen., licet undique omnes in me terrores impendeant, succurram, *undergo them,* Cic.; b, esp., *to come into the thoughts of, to occur to ;* ut quidque succurrit, libet scribere, Cic.; alicui succurrit, with acc. and infin., sed mihi succurrit numen non esse severum, Ov. II. *to hasten to help, to aid ;* 1, lit., milit. t. t., alicui (with or without auxilio), Caes., Cic.; impers., si celeriter succurratur, Caes. ; 2, transf., *to help, succour, assist ;* saluti fortunisque communibus, Cic. ; alicui, Cic.; foll. by quominus and subj., hic tantis malis haec subsidia succurrebant, quominus omnis deleretur exercitus, Caes.

succussĭo -ōnis, f. (succutio), *a shaking from beneath, earthquake,* Sen.

succussus -ūs, m. (succutio), *a shaking,* ap. Cic.

succŭtĭo -cussi -cussum, 3. (sub and quatio), *to shake from beneath, shake up, fling aloft,* Ov.

sūcĭdus -a -um (sucus), *juicy, full of sap,* Plin.

sūcĭnum -i, n. (sucus), *amber,* Plin.

sūcĭnus -a -um (sucus), *of amber ;* gutta, Mart.

sūco -ōnis, m. *a sucker* (a term applied to a usurer) ; Oppios de Velia sucones dicis (a pun, because ὅπός in Greek = sucus, and the Oppii were rich usurers), Cic.

sūcōsus (succōsus) -a -um (sucus), *full of sap, juicy, succulent,* Plin.

Sucro -ōnis, m. *a river in Hispania Tarraconensis,* now *Xucar ;* at its mouth was a town of the same name, now *Cullera.* Hence, **Sucrōnensis** -e, *of or near Sucro ;* sinus, now *Gulf of Valencia.*

suctus -ūs, m. (sugo), *a sucking, suction* Plin.

sūcŭla -ae, f. (dim. of sus). I. *a little sow,* Plaut. II. Transf., A. *a winch, windlass, capstan,* Plaut. B. Suculae, wrong translation of Gr. ὑάδες, *a constellation, the Hyades,* Cic.

sūcus (succus) i, m. (connected with Gr. ὁπός), *juice, sap.* I. 1, lit., stirpes ex terra succum trahunt, Cic. ; sucus is quo utimur, Cic. ; 2, meton., like χυμός, *taste ;* piscis suco ingratus, Ov. ; 3, fig., a, *vigour ;* amisimus sucum et sanguinem, Cic. ; b, esp., *of orators and speeches, vigour, energy ;* orationis, Cic. II. *any thick fluid ;* a, olivi, unguent, Ov.; nectaris sucos ducere, *juice of nectar,* Hor.; b, esp., in medicine, *a draught, potion ;* amarus, Ov.

sūdārĭum -ĭi, n. (sudo), *a handkerchief* (to wipe off perspiration from the face), Mart.

sūdātĭo -ōnis, f. (sudo), *a sweating,* Sen.

sūdātor -ōris, m. (sudo), *one who perspires easily or copiously,* Plin.

sūdātōrĭus -a -um (sudo), *of or relating to sweating, producing perspiration.* I. Adj., unctio, Plaut. II. Subst., **sūdātōrĭum** -ĭi, n. *a sweating-room, sweating-bath,* Sen.

sūdātrix -trīcis, f. (sudator), toga, *causing perspiration,* Mart.

sūdis -is, f. I. *a stake, pile ;* ripa erat acutis sudibus praefixis munita, Caes. II. Transf., *a point,* Juv.

sūdo, 1. I. Intransit., *to sweat, perspire ;* 1, lit., puer sudavit et alsit, Hor. ; quum Cumis Apollo (i.e., *the statue of Apollo*) sudavit, Cic.; 2, transf., a, *to drip with any moisture ;* scuta duo sanguine sudasse, Liv.; cavae tepido sudant humore lacunae, Verg. ; b, *to drip, distil ;* balsama odorato sudantia ligno, Verg. ; 3, fig., *to toil, make a great effort, work hard ;* vides, sudare me jamdudum laborantem, ut ea tuear quae, etc., Cic. ; se sine causa sudare, Cic. II. Transit., *to throw off by sweating, to sweat out, to exude ;* durae quercūs sudabunt roscida mella, Verg.; ubi tura balsamaque sudantur, Tac.

sūdor -ōris, m. *sweat, perspiration.* I. a, lit., sudor a capite et a fronte defluens, Cic. ; simulacrum multo sudore manavit, Cic. ; b, fig., *great exertion, labour, fatigue, effort ;* stilus ille tuus multi sudoris est, Cic. ; multo eius sudore ac labore sub populi Romani imperium ditionemque ceciderunt, Cic. II. Transf., *any kind of moisture ;* veneni, Ov.

sūdus -a -um (se and udus), *dry, without moisture ;* and (applied to weather), *bright, cloudless ;* ver, Verg. Subst., **sūdum** -i, n. a, *the bright cloudless sky,* Verg.; b, *clear, bright weather,* Cic.

Suēbi -ōrum, m. *the Suebi, an important German nation.* Hence, A. **Suēbĭa** -ae, f. *the country of the Suebi.* B. **Suēbĭcus** -a -um, *belonging to the Suebi.*

sŭeo, 2. *to be wont, be accustomed,* Lucr.

suesco, suēvi, suētum, 3. (inchoat. of sueo), *to become accustomed, inured to ;* militiae, Tac. ; hence, suevi, *I am accustomed, I am wont ;* mittere suevit, Lucr.; and syncop. perf., quod suesti, *as you are wont,* Cic.

Suessa -ae, f. I. *an old town of the Aurunci, in Campania, birthplace of the poet Lucilius,* now *Sessa ;* hence, **Suessānus** -a -um, *relating to Suessa.* II. *a town of the Volsci, in Latium, near the Pontine marshes,* gen. in full Suessa Pometia.

Suessĭōnes -um, m. *a Gallic people, near modern Soissons.*

Suessŭla -ae, f. *a small town in Samnium, near Mons Tifata, now Castel di Sessola.* Hence, **Suessŭlānus** -a -um, *of or belonging to Suessula.*

Suētōnĭus -ĭi, m., C. Suetonius Tranquillus, *author of the Lives of the Caesars, a contemporary of the younger Pliny.*

suētus -a -um, p. adj. (from suesco). **I.** *accustomed to;* latrociniis, Tac.; foll. by infin., Verg., Liv. **II.** *that to which a person is accustomed, usual;* sueta apud paludes proelia, Tac.

Suēvi = Suebi (q.v.).

sūfes (suffes) -fĕtis, m. (from a Phoenician word = *judge*), *the name of the highest magistrate in Carthage,* Liv.

suffarcĭno, 1. (sub and farcino), *to stuff full, fill full,* cram; Plaut., Ter.

suffarrānĕus -a -um (far), *carrying corn;* mulio, Cic.

suffĕro, sufferre (sub and fero). **I.** *to carry under, put under,* Plaut. **II.** *to hold up, support;* 1, lit., reflex., se sufferre, *to carry oneself upright, stand upright,* Suet.; 2, fig., *to bear, endure, suffer;* poenam sui sceleris, Cic.; eam multam, Cic.

suffertus -a -um (sub and farcio), *stuffed full,* crammed full, Suet.

suffervĕfăcĭo, 3. (sub and fervefacio), *to heat, make somewhat hot,* Plin.; pass., suffervefio -factus sum -fĭĕri, *to become somewhat hot,* Plin.

suffes = sufes (q.v.).

suffĭbŭlum -i, n. (sub and fibula), *a white oblong veil worn by priests and vestals,* Varr.

sufficĭo -fēci -fectum, 3. (sub and facio). **I.** Transit., **A.** *to put under;* hence, *to imbue, impregnate, suffuse;* lanam medicamentis, Cic.; angues ardentes oculos suffecti sanguine, Verg. **B.** *to add, cause to grow up after;* 1, lit., aliam ex alia generando suffice prolem, Verg.; 2, transf., *to choose in the place of* or *as a substitute for any one;* consul in sufficiendo collega occupatus, Cic.; collegam suffici censori, Liv.; of bees, regem parvosque Quirites sufficiunt, Verg.; esp., suffectus consul, *a consul chosen in the place of another,* Liv. **C.** *to provide, supply;* 1, lit., ipsa satis tellus sufficit humorem et gravidas fruges, Verg.; 2, fig., *to give;* Danais animos viresque secundas, Verg. **II.** Intransit., neut., *to be sufficient, enough, adequate, to suffice;* **a,** absol., nec scribae sufficere, nec tabulae nomina eorum capere poterant, Cic.; **b,** with dat., nec vires sufficere cuiquam nec, etc., Caes.; **c,** with ad and the acc., quomodo nos ad patiendum sufficiamus, Liv.; **d,** with adversus and the acc., non suffecturum ducem unum et exercitum unum adversus quatuor populos, Liv.; **e,** with in and the acc., nec locus in tumulos nec sufficit arbor in ignes, Ov.; **f,** with infin. = *to be in a position to, to be able;* nec nos obniti contra nec tendere tantum sufficimus, Verg.; **g,** with ut or ne and the subj., Tac.

suffīgo -fixi -fixum, 3. (sub and figo), *to fasten, fix beneath;* aliquem cruci, Cic.

suffīmen = suffimentum (q.v.).

suffīmentum -i, n. (suffio), *incense,* Cic.

suffĭo -īvi and -ĭi -ītum (sub and *fio, fire, connected with θύω). **I.** Intransit., *to burn incense, fumigate;* thymo, Verg. **II.** Transit., *to fumigate, perfume;* **a,** lit., locum, Prop.; **b,** fig., *to warm,* Lucr.

suffītĭo -ōnis, f. (suffio), *a fumigation,* Plin.

suffītor -ōris, m. (suffio), *a fumigator,* Plin.

suffītus -ūs, m. (suffio), *a fumigating, fumigation,* Plin.

18*

sufflāmen -ĭnis, n. *a break, drag, clog.* **I.** Lit., Juv. **II.** Fig., *a hindrance, obstacle,* Juv.

sufflāmĭno, 1. (sufflamen), *to stop by a drag,* Suet.

sufflātĭo -ōnis, f. (sufflo), *a blowing up, puffing up,* Plin.

sufflāvus -a -um (sub-flavus), *somewhat yellow,* Suet.

sufflo, 1. (sub and flo). **I.** Intransit., *to blow upon,* Mart. **II.** Transit., *to blow up, to puff up, inflate;* **a,** lit., Plaut.; **b,** fig., se uxori, *to be angry with,* Plaut.

suffōcātĭo -ōnis, f. (suffoco), *a choking strangling, suffocation,* Plin.

suffŏco, 1. (sub and faux), *to strangle, choke, suffocate.* **I.** Lit., patrem, Cic. **II.** Fig., urbem et Italiam fame, *to starve out,* Cic.

suffŏdĭo -fōdi -fossum, 3. (sub and fodio), *to pierce underneath, pierce, dig into, excavate, undermine;* **a,** of things, murum, Sall.; sacella suffossa, Caes.; **b,** of animals or parts of the body, *to stab from below;* equos, Caes.

suffrāgātĭo -ōnis, f. (suffragor), *a voting in favour of, favourable vote, support;* urbana, *of the city;* militaris, *of the soldiers,* Cic.; illi honestissimā suffragatione consulatus petebatur, Sall.; plur., exstinctae (sunt) suffragationes, Cic.

suffrāgātor -ōris, m. (suffragor), *a voter in favour of any one, a political supporter,* Cic.

suffrāgātōrĭus -a -um (suffragor), *of or relating to the support of a candidate,* Q. Cic.

suffrāgĭum -ĭi, n. (sub and frango), *something broken off, a potsherd, used by the ancients for voting;* hence, meton., **I.** *the vote of a citizen at the comitia and of a juror in giving his verdict;* **a,** lit., ferre suffragium, *to vote,* Cic.; suffragium it per omnes, *all vote,* Liv.; non proliberi jure suffragii, Cic.; **b,** transf., *vote, judgment, approval, support;* tuum, Cic.; populi, Hor. **II.** *the right or permission to vote, suffrage, franchise;* alicui suffragium impertire, Liv.; sine suffragio habere civitatem, *citizenship without the franchise,* Liv.

suffrāgo -ĭnis, f. (sub and frango), *the ham* or *hough on the hind leg of a quadruped,* Plin.

suffrāgor, 1. dep. (suffragium). **I.** *to vote in any one's favour;* suffragandi libido, Cic. **II.** Transf., *to be favourable to, to approve, recommend, support;* cupiditati alicuius, Cic.; sibi, Cic.; suffragante fortunā, Cic.

suffrēnātĭo -ōnis, f. (sub and freno), *a bridling;* transf., *a cementing, fastening;* lapidis, Plin.

suffringo -frēgi -fractum, 3. (sub and frango), *to break underneath, break in pieces;* crura canibus, Cic.

suffŭgĭo -fūgi -fŭgĭtum, 3. (sub and fugio). **I.** Intransit., *to fly to any place;* in tecta, Liv. **II.** Transit., *to fly from, evade, shun;* tactum, Lucr.

suffŭgĭum -ĭi, n. (sub and fugio), *a place of refuge.* **I.** Lit., propinqua suffugia, Tac. **II.** Transf., *a refuge, resort, remedy;* urgentium malorum suffugium, Tac.

suffulcĭo -fulsi -fultum, 4. (sub and fulcio), *to support beneath, underprop,* Lucr.

suffūmĭgo, 1. (sub and fumigo), *to fumigate from below,* Plin.

suffundo -fūdi -fūsum, 3. (sub and fundo). **I.** 1, *to pour beneath, spread through, suffuse;* **a,** of fluids, animum esse cordi suffusum sanguinem, Cic.; intumuit suffusa venter ab unda, *dropsy,* Ov.; **b,** of blushing, virgineum ore ruborem, Ov.; rubor Masinissae suffusus est, *blushed,* Liv.; **2,**

:o bedew, colour, fill with; aether calore suffusus, Cic.; lacrimis oculos suffusa nitentes, Verg.; fig., animus nullā in ceteros malevolentiā suffusus, Cic. **II.** *to pour out, pour into;* merum, Ov.

suffūror, 1. (sub and furor), *to abstract secretly, steal away,* Plaut.

suffuscus -a -um (sub and fuscus), *brownish, dark brown,* Tac.

suffūsĭo -ōnis, f. (suffundo), *a suffusion;* fellis, *jaundice,* Plin.

Sŭgambri (Sўgambri, Sĭgambri) -ōrum, m, *a powerful German tribe.* Adj., **Sŭgāmbĕr** -bra -brum, *Sugambrian.*

suggĕro -gessi -gestum, 3. (sub and gero). **I.** *to carry, bring, lay, put, place under.* **A.** Lit., flammam costis aëni, Verg. **B.** Fig., *to add, subjoin, annex;* a, huic incredibili sententiae ratiunculas, Cic.; b, *to cause to follow* (in order of time), *to place next;* Bruto statim Horatium, Liv.; c, *to put upon secretly;* Druso ludus est suggerendus, Cic. **II.** *to furnish, supply, afford;* 1, lit., alicui tela, Verg.; 2, fig., *to supply, give opportunity for;* prodiga divitias alimentaque mitia tellus suggerit, Ov.

suggestĭo -ōnis, f. (suggero), *a rhetorical figure in which an orator answers a question which he has asked himself,* Quint.

suggestum -i, n. (suggero). **I.** *anything heaped up, a heap, raised place, height, elevation,* Varr. **II.** Esp., *a platform from which an orator spoke to the people, soldiers,* etc.; illud suggestum ascendens, Cic.; in suggestis consistere, Cic.

suggestus -ūs, m. (suggero). **I.** *an elevation, height,* Cato. **II.** Esp., *a platform for addressing the people, soldiers,* etc., *a tribune,* Cic., Caes.

suggill ... v. sugill ...

suggrandis -e (sub and grandis), *somewhat large,* Cic.

suggrĕdĭor -gressus sum, 3. dep. (sub and gradior), *to go to, approach, to attack,* Tac.

suggrunda -ae, f. *the eaves of a house,* Varr.

sŭgillātĭo -ōnis, f. (sugillo). **I.** *a livid or black spot on the skin, weal, bruise,* Plin. **II.** Fig., *a mocking, insulting,* Liv.

sŭgillo, 1. *to beat black and blue.* **I.** Lit., Plin. **II.** Fig., *to insult, affront;* aliquem, Liv.

sūgo, sūxi, suctum, 3. *to suck.* **I.** Lit., Cic. **II.** Fig., *to suck in;* cum lacte nutricis errorem, Cic.

sŭi (genit.), *of himself, herself, itself, themselves;* dat., sibi, *to himself,* etc.; se, *himself,* etc.; pron. reflex., referring to the next preceding subject. **I.** Gen., se ipsum amat, Cic.; sui conservandi causā profugerunt, Cic.; qui hoc sibi nomen arrogaverunt, Cic. **II.** Esp., **A.** sibi, ethic dat., quidnam sibi clamor vellet, Liv. **B.** ad se, apud se = *at his house,* Cic. (strengthened form, sepse = se ipse, Cic.; semet, Hor., Liv.).

sŭĭle -is, n. (sus), *a pigsty,* Varr.

sŭillus -a -um (sus), *of or relating to swine, swinish.* **I.** Adj., caro, Juv.; caput, Liv. **II.** Subst., **sŭilla** -ae, f. (sc. caro), *pork,* Plin.

sulco, 1. (sulcus), *to furrow, plough, cut through.* **I.** Lit., humum vomere, Ov. **II.** Transf., a, *to furrow;* serpens sulcat arenam, Ov.; cutem rugis, *to wrinkle,* Ov.; b, *to furrow* = *to sail over, pass through;* vada carinā, Verg.; undas rate, Ov.

sulcus -i, m. (connected with ὁλκός), *a furrow.* **I.** Lit., sulcum imprimere, Cic. **II.** Transf., a, *a cutting like a furrow, the furrow cut*

in the sea by a ship, Verg.; b, *a long, narrow trench,* Verg.

sulfur (sulphur) -ŭris, n. **I.** *sulphur,* Liv., Hor., Verg. **II.** Meton., *lightning,* Pers.

sulfūrātĭo -ōnis, f. (sulfur), *a vein of sulphur in the earth,* Sen.

sulfūrātus -a -um (sulfur), *full of sulphur, containing sulphur, sulphureous,* Plin. Subst., **sulfūrāta** -ōrum, a, *brimstone matches,* Mart.; b, *veins of sulphur,* Plin.

sulfūrĕus -a -um (sulfur), *sulphureous;* aqua, Verg.

Sulla (Sylla) -ae, m. *a name of a family in the gens Cornelia, the most celebrated member of which was* L. Cornelius Sulla, *the dictator, rival of Marius.* Hence, **A. Sullānus (Syllānus)** -a -um, *Sullan;* subst., **Sullāni** -ōrum, m. *the partisans of Sulla.* **B. Sullātūrĭo** -ire, *to wish to imitate Sulla,* Cic.

Sulmo -ōnis, m. *a town in the country of the Peligni, birthplace of Ovid, now Sulmona;* hence, adj., **Sulmonensis** -e, *belonging to Sulmo.*

sulphur = sulfur (q.v.).

Sulpĭcĭus -a -um, *name of a Roman gens, the most distinguished member of which was* Serv. Sulpicius Rufus, *a celebrated jurist in the time of Cicero, consul with M. Marcellus;* hence, **Sulpĭcĭānus** -a -um, *Sulpician.*

sultis = si vultis, v. volo.

sum, fŭi, esse (an irregular verb, derived from two different roots, sum shortened for esum, root ES, Gr. ΕΣ, whence εἰμί; fui from an old verb fuo, Gr. φύω). **I.** *to be, to exist.* **A.** Gen., 1, a, *of the existence of an object, to be, to exist, to be in life;* esse ea dico, quae cerni tangive possunt, Cic.; adhuc sumus, Cic.; omnium qui sunt, qui fuerunt, qui futuri sunt, Cic.; fuit, *he has lived,* Tib.; fuimus Troes, fuit Ilium, Verg.; nullus sum, *I exist no longer, I am lost,* Cic.; b, *of the presence of a condition, to be, to exist;* non est periculum, Cic.; quid tibi est? *what is the matter with you?* Cic.; c, *to be at a place, to live at;* quum Athenis fuissem, Cic.; d, *to be in a certain state or condition;* in servitute, Cic.; in spe, Cic.; e, *to rest, to depend upon;* totum in eo est, ut, etc., Cic.; 2, especial phrases, a, sunt qui, *there are some people or things who or which;* (a) with indic. when certain definite persons or things are meant, sunt qui audent, Cic.; (β) with the subj. when the persons or things are indefinite, sunt qui dicant, Cic.; b, mihi est (res), *I have (something);* cui nomen Arethusa est, Cic.; c, esse ad or apud aliquem, *to be at the house of, to visit;* apud te est, ut volumus, Cic.; d, esse cum aliquo (aliqua); (a) *to be in the house of, to be in a room with;* esset ne quis intus cum Caesare, Cic.; (β) *to be with, go about with;* erat nemo quicum essem libentius, Cic.; e, esse alicui cum aliquo, *to have to do with;* sibi cum illa nihil futurum, Cic.; f, esse ab aliquo, *to belong to or be related to;* erat ab Aristotele, *he was an Aristotelian,* Cic.; vide, ne hoc totum sit a me, *speaks for me,* Cic.; g, esse pro aliquo, *to be in the place of,* Cic.; h, esse in, with abl., *to be in some writing;* quid fuit in litteris? Cic. **B.** *to be the fact, to be really so;* sunt ista, *that is so, good,* Cic.; so also, esto, Cic.; est ut or with infin., *it is the case that;* est, ut id deceat, Cic.; b, est ubi = *at times,* Cic.; c, est quod, with indic. or subj. or ut and the subj., *there is reason for, I (you, etc.) have reason to, cause to; magis* est quod gratuler, Cic.; nihil est quod or cur, *there is no reason for;* nihil est, quod gestias, Cic. **II.** As copulative verb = *to be something* *ir in some way;* **a,** with an adj., subst., or pron., praeclara res est et sumus *otiosi,* Cic. ; **b,** with adv., (*a*) of manner, sic est, Cic.; *mihi pulchre est* or *pulchre est mihi,* Cic. ; (β) of place or time, sunt procul ab huius aetatis memoria, Cic. ; **c,** with genit. or abl., *to be of a certain nature or kind;* (*a*) with genit., summi ut sint laboris, Cic.; esp., magni, tanti, etc., esse (pretii), *to be of high or of such value,* etc., Cic. ; frumentum fuit tanti, Cic. ; (β) with abl., aegro corpore esse, *to be ill,* Cic. ; simus eā mente, *so disposed,* Cic. ; **d,** with genit. to express belonging to, (*a*) *to be one's own, to belong to;* Gallia est Ariovisti, Caes.; (β) *to be devoted to;* me Pompeii totum esse, Cic. ; (γ) *to be a mark of, to be the nature of, to be characteristic of;* cuiusvis hominis est errare, Cic. ; so with poss. pron., est tuum videre, Cic.; **e,** with genit. of gerund., *to serve for, have for its object;* quod conservandae libertatis fuerat, Sall. ; **f,** with dat. to express object, (*a*) *to be in the place of, to be;* Romam caput Latio esse, Liv.; (β) *to be capable of;* non esse solvendo, Cic. ; (γ) *to be, to prove;* impedimento esse alicui, Cic. ; **g,** with ad and the acc., *to be serviceable for;* res quae sunt ad incendia, Caes.; **h,** with de and the abl., *to treat of, be about;* is liber, qui est de animo, Cic. ; id est, hoc est, *that is,* or sometimes *which is as much as to say,* Cic. (archaic forms, escunt = erunt, ap. Cic.; fuat = sit, Verg.; fuvimus = fuimus, ap. Cic.).

sūmen -ĭnis, n. (= sugmen, from sugo). **I.** *a teat, pap,* Lucil. **II.** Esp., *the udder of a sow* (esteemed a delicacy by the Romans); **1,** lit., Plaut. ; **2,** meton., *a sow, pig,* Juv.

summa -ae, f. (summus), *the highest.* **I.** *the highest place;* qui vobis summam ordinis consiliique concedunt, Cic. **II.** *the chief matter, main thing, most important point.* **A.** Gen., ipsae summae rerum atque sententiae, Cic. **B.** Esp., **1,** *the whole, totality;* exercitus, Caes.; belli, *supreme command,* Caes.; rerum or omnium rerum, *the highest power,* Cic.; ad summam, adv. *in a word, in short,* Cic.; so in summa, *on the whole,* Cic.; **2,** *the sum total of an amount;* equitum magnum numerum ex omni summa separare, Cic.; so esp., **a,** *a sum of money;* hāc summā redempti, Cic. ; **b,** *a mass, quantity;* praedae, Cic.

Summānus -i, m. *an old Roman deity, to whom lightnings by night were ascribed,* Cic.

summārĭum -ĭi, n. (summa), *an epitome, abridgment, summary,* Sen.

summas -ātis, c. (summus), *of high birth, noble, illustrious,* Plaut.

summātim, adv. (summa), *slightly, summarily, briefly;* quae longiorem orationem desiderant summatim perscribere, Cic.

summātus -ūs, m. (summus), *the chief authority,* Lucr.

summē, adv. (summus), *in the highest degree, extremely;* officiosus, Cic.; contendere, Cic.

summergo = submergo (q.v.).

summĭnistro = subministro (q.v.).

summissē = submisse (q.v.).

summissim = submissim (q.v.).

summissĭo = submissio (q.v.).

summissus = submissus (q.v.).

summitto = submitto (q.v.).

Summoenĭum -ĭi, n. (sub and moenia), *a place in Rome frequented by common prostitutes;* hence, adj., **Summoenĭānus** -a -um, *relating to the Summoenium.*

summŏlestē = submoleste (q.v.).

summŏlestus = submolestus (q.v.).

summŏnĕo = submoneo (q.v.).

summŏpĕre, adv. (= summo opere), *very much, exceedingly,* Cic.

summŏrōsus = submorosus (q.v.).

summōtor = submotor (q.v.).

summŏvĕo = submoveo (q.v.).

summŭla -ae, f. (dim. of summa), *a little sum,* Sen.

summus -a -um, superl. of superus (q.v.).

summūto = submuto (q.v.).

sūmo, sumpsi, sumptum, 3. (sub and emo), *to take, lay hold of.* **I.** Lit. **A.** Gen., fustem, Plaut.; legem in manus, Cic.; pecuniam mutuam, *to borrow,* Cic. **B.** Esp., **a,** *to take for use, to put on;* calceos et vestimenta, Cic.; **b,** *to buy;* genus signorum, Cic.; or, *to hire;* navem, Cic.; **c,** *to take, apply, employ;* operam, Ter. **II.** Fig., **A.** Gen., tempus cibi, Liv.; supplicium, *to punish,* Liv. **B.** Esp., **a,** *to choose, pick out, select;* sibi studium philosophiae, Cic.; diem ad deliberandum, Caes.; **b,** *to take in hand, to begin;* bellum, Sall.; inimicitias, Cic.; **c,** in discourse, (*a*) *to mention;* homines notos, Cic.; (β) *to assume, assert, maintain;* beatos esse deos sumpsisti, Cic.; **d,** *to assume;* arrogantiam sibi, Cic.; **e,** *to arrogate to oneself, take upon oneself;* sibi partes imperatorias, Cic.; mihi non tantum sumo, Cic.

sumptĭo -ōnis, f. (sumo), *the premiss of a syllogism,* Cic.

sumptĭto, 1. (intens. of sumo), *to take in large quantities,* Plin.

sumptŭārĭus -a -um (sumptus), *of or relating to expense, sumptuary;* lex, Cic.; rationes, Cic.

sumptŭōsē, adv. with compar. (sumptuosus), *in a costly, expensive manner, sumptuously,* Cic.

sumptŭōsus -a -um (sumptus). **I.** Of things, *costly, expensive, dear, sumptuous;* cena, Cic.; ludi sumptuosiores, Cic. **II.** Of persons, *extravagant, prodigal;* homo, Cic.

sumptus -ūs, m. (sumo), *cost, expense;* sumptum facere in rem, or impendere, or insumere, or ponere, Cic.; sumptu ne parcas, Cic.; suo sumptu fungi officio, Cic.; plur., minuendi sunt sumptus, Cic. (dat., often sumptu, Cic.).

Sūnĭŏn (-ĭum) -ĭi, n. (Σούνιον), *a promontory forming the most southerly point of Attica, now Capo Colonni, with a temple of Athena and a town of the same name.*

sŭo, sŭi, sūtum, 3. *to sew, sew together, stitch together, join together;* tegumenta corporum vel texta vel suta, Cic.

sŭopte, v. suus.

sŭŏvĕtaurīlĭa (sŭŏvĭtaurīlĭa) -ĭum, n. (sus, ovis and taurus), *a purificatory sacrifice of a pig, a sheep, and a bull,* Liv.

sŭpellex -lectĭlis, abl. -lectĭle and -lectĭli, f. *furniture.* **I.** Lit., *household furniture;* multa et lauta supellex, Cic. **II.** Fig., *ornament, equipment;* amicos parare, optimam vitae supellectilem, Cic. ; *oratoria quasi supellex,* Cic.

1. sŭper -a -um, v. superus.

2. sŭper (ὑπέρ). **I.** Adv., **1,** of place; **a,** *over, above, on the top of;* eo super tigna bipedalia injiciunt, Caes. ; **b,** = ἄνωθεν, *from above;* superque immane barathrum cernatur, Verg. ; **2,** of other relations ; **a,** *besides;* super quam, *moreover,* Liv.; dederatque super, Ov.; **b,** *thereupon;* super tales effundit voces, Verg. ; **c,** *beyond, more;* super quam, *more than,* Hor.; satis superque dixi, *enough and more than enough,* Cic.; **d,** *over and above;* quid super sanguinis (esse), Liv. **II.** Prep. with abl. and acc. **A.** With abl. **1,** of place. *over above;* ensis

super cervice pendet, Hor. ; 2, **of time,** *during ;* nŏcte super media, Verg. ; 3, of relation, *concerning, about ;* hae super re scribam ad te, Cic. ; 4, of measure, *beyond ;* super his, Hor. **B.** With acc., 1, of place, *over, above ;* a, to express remaining over an object, super aspidem assidēre, Cic. ; aqua super montium juga concreta erat, Liv. ; b, of position, (a) *over, above ;* super templum circaque, Liv. ; (β) *beyond ;* super Numidiam Gaetulos accepimus, Sall. ; c, of motion, *over or beyond a place ;* super Sunium navigans, Liv. ; 2, of degree, *beyond, over, above ;* a, lit., super ceteros honores, Liv. ; super cetera, Liv. ; vulnus super vulnus, *wound on wound, one wound after another,* Liv. ; b, transf., of superiority, *beyond, more than ;* aetas et forma et super omnia Romanorum nomen te ferociorem facit, *above all,* Liv. (super sometimes put after its case in Lucr., Verg., and Tac.).

sŭpĕrā (sc. parte) = supra. **I.** Adv. = *over,* Lucr. **II.** Prep. with acc., *over,* Lucr.

sŭpĕrābĭlis -e (supero). **I.** *that can be ascended ;* murus, Liv. **II.** *that can be conquered ;* non est per vim superabilis ulli, Ov. ; nullis casibus superabilis Romani, Tac.

sŭpĕraddo -addĭdi -addĭtum, 3. *to add over and above,* superadd, Verg.

sŭpĕrādornātus -a -um (super and adorno), *adorned on the surface,* Sen.

sŭpĕrans -āntis, p. adj., only in compar. and superl., *prevailing ;* superantior ignis, Lucr.

sŭpĕrātor -ōris, m. (supero), *one who overcomes, a conqueror,* Ov.

sŭperbē, adv. (superbus), *proudly, haughtily ;* superbe et crudeliter imperare, Caes. ; legatos appellare superbius, Cic. ; preces superbissime repudiare, Cic.

sŭperbĭa -ae, f. (superbus), *pride.* **I.** In a bad sense, *pride, haughtiness ;* often with arrogantia and insolentia, Cic. ; superbiam ponere, *lay aside,* Hor. **II.** In a good sense, *lofty spirit, honourable pride ;* sume superbiam, Hor.

sŭperbĭbo, 3. *to drink upon,* Plin.

sŭperbĭfĭcus -a -um (superbus and facio), *making proud, making haughty,* Sen.

sŭperbĭo, 4. (superbus). **I.** *to be proud, haughty, to pride oneself on ;* with abl., formā, Ov. ; foll. by quod, Tac. **II.** Transf., of things, *to be splendid, superb,* Prop.

sŭperbus -a -um (super) = ὑπερήφανος, *raising oneself above others, proud.* **I.** In a bad sense, 1, lit., of persons, *proud, haughty ;* a, absol., superbum se praebuit in fortuna, Cic. ; superbiorem te pecunia facit, Cic. ; superbissima familia, Cic. ; surname of the younger Tarquinius, last king of Rome, Cic. ; b, with abl., *proud of ;* pecuniā, Hor. ; 2, transf., of things or abstract subjects, oculi, Ov. ; aures, Liv. ; virtus, Cic. ; judicium aurium superbissimum, Cic. **II.** In a good sense, 1, of persons, *distinguished, remarkable ;* Atridae, Hor. ; 2, of things, *brilliant, magnificent, splendid ;* triumphus, Hor.

sŭpercĭlĭōsus -a -um (supercilium), *severe, gloomy,* Sen.

sŭpercĭlĭum -ĭi, n. *the eyebrow ;* plur. (and often sing. in collective sense), *the eyebrows.* **I. A.** Lit., a, sing., altero ad mentum depresso supercilio, Cic. ; b, plur., superciliorum aut remissio aut contractio, Cic. ; capite et superciliis rasis, Cic. **B.** Meton., a, *the eyebrows contracted = gloom, severity, sternness ;* supercilii severi matrona, Ov. ; quid de supercilio dicam, quod tum hominibus non supercilium sed pignus reipublicae videbatur, Cic. ; b, *pride, arrogance ;* hunc Capuae Campano supercilio ac regio spiritu videremus, Cic. **II.** Transf. (like ὀφρύς,

and English *brow*), *the projecting part of any object, ridge, summit ;* tramitis, Verg. ; tumuli, **Liv.**

sŭpercurro, 3. *to run beyond, surpass,* Plin.

sŭpērĕdo, 3. *to eat upon or after,* Plin.

sŭpĕrēmĭnĕo, 2. *to project over, overtop ;* omnes viros, Verg.

sŭpĕrēmŏrĭor, 3. dep. *to die upon,* Plin.

sŭperférŏ -tŭli -lātum -ferre, *to carry over, bear over,* Plin.

sŭperfĭcĭes -ēi, f. (super and facies), *the top, surface, superficies of anything.* **I.** Gen., testudinum, Plin. **II.** Esp., legal t.t., *something (e.g., a building) placed on the ground so as to become attached to it,* Cic.

sŭperfīo -fĭĕri, *to be over and above,* Plaut.

sŭperfixus -a -um, *fixed on the top,* Liv.

sŭperflōrescens -entis, *blooming all over,* Plin.

sŭperflŭĭtas -ātis, f. (superfluus), *superfluity,* Plin.

sŭperflŭo -fluxi, 3. *to flow over, overflow.* **I.** Lit., of water, superfluentis Nili receptacula, Tac. **II.** Transf., a, ut nos superfluentes juvenili quādam dicendi impunitate et licentiā reprimeret, Cic. ; b, *to be in superfluity, be superfluous,* Tac.

sŭperflŭus -a -um (superfluo), *overflowing, superfluous,* Sen.

sŭperfundo -fūdi -fūsum, 3. **I.** *to pour over, pour upon ;* 1, lit., a, of water, superfundi, middle, *to overflow, spread itself over ;* circus Tiberi superfuso irrigatus, Liv. ; b, of other things, *to spread about, throw about ;* magnam vim telorum, Tac. ; pass., superfundi, as middle, *to be poured on, to run on ;* hostes superfusi, *rushing in numbers,* Liv. ; 2, transf., superfundere se, *to spread itself out, spread ;* superfudit se (regnum Macedoniae) in Asiam, Liv. **II.** *to cover with anything,* Tac.

sŭpergrĕdĭor -gressus sum -grĕdi, 3. dep. (super and gradior), *to go over or beyond, overstep ;* fig., *to exceed, surpass ;* aetatis suae feminas pulchritudine, Tac.

sŭpĕri, v. superus.

sŭpĕrillĭgo, 1. *to bind on, bind over,* Plin.

sŭpĕrimmĭnĕo, 2. *to overhang,* Verg.

sŭpĕrimpendens -entis (super and impendeo), *overhanging,* Cat.

sŭpĕrimplĕo, 2. *to fill quite full,* Verg.

sŭpĕrimpōno -(pŏsŭi) -pŏsĭtum, 3. *to lay over, place upon ;* saxum ingens machinā, *by means of a machine,* Liv. ; monumento (dat.), statuam, Liv.

sŭpĕrincĭdens -entis, *falling from above,* Liv.

sŭpĕrincŭbans -antis, *lying over or upon ;* superincubans Romanus, Liv.

sŭpĕrincumbo -cŭbŭi, 3. *to lie on, lie over,* Ov.

sŭpĕrindŭo -ŭi -ūtum, 3. *to put on over,* Suet.

sŭpĕringĕro -(gessi) -gestum, 3. *to throw upon, heap upon,* Plin.

sŭpĕrinjĭcĭo -jēci -jectum, 3. *to throw over, throw upon ;* raras frondes, Verg.

sŭpĕrinl . . . v. superill . . .

sŭpĕrinm . . . v. superimm . . .

sŭpĕrinp . . . v. superimp . . .

sŭpĕrinsterno -strāvi -strātum, 3. *to spread over, lay over ;* tabulas, Verg.

sŭpĕrintĕgo, 3. *to cover over,* Plin.

sŭpĕrĭor -ōris, comp. of sŭpĕrus (q.v.).

sŭperjăcĭo -jēci -jectum (-jactum), 3. **I.** to throw over, throw upon; membra superjecta cum tua veste fovet, Ov. **II.** to throw over, flow over; scopulos superjacit undā pontus, Verg. **III.** to exceed, go beyond; fidem augendo, Liv. (partic. also superjactus, Sall., Tac.).

sŭperjacto, 1. to spring over, leap over, Plin.

sŭperjectĭo -ōnis, f. (superjacio), a throwing over; fig., exaggeration, hyperbole, Quint.

sŭperjūmentārĭus -ĭi, m. the chief groom, head of the drivers of beasts of burden, Suet.

sŭperlābor, 3. to glide, slide over, Liv.

sŭperlātĭo -ōnis, f. (superfero), rhet. t.t., exaggeration, hyperbole; veritatis, Cic.

sŭperlātus -a -um, p. adj. (from superfero), exaggerated, hyperbolical; verba, Cic.

sŭperlĭno -lēvi -lĭtum, 3. to smear over. besmear, Plin.

sŭpermando, 3. to chew upon or after anything, Plin.

sŭpermĕo, 1. to go over, pass over, Plin.

sŭpernas -ātis (supernus), belonging to the upper country, esp. to the upper (i.e. the Adriatic) sea, Plin.

sŭpernăto, 1. to swim upon, swim over, Sen.

sŭpernātus -a -um, growing over, Plin.

sŭpernĕ, adv. (supernus), upwards; a, from above, Liv.; b, on the upper side, above, Hor.

sŭpernus -a -um (super), above, over, on the upper side, on the top; Tusculum, lying high, Hor.; numen, celestial, Ov.

sŭpĕro, 1. (super). **I.** Intransit., to be above; hence, 1, to over-top, project; a, lit., superant capite et cervicibus altis, Verg.; b, transf., (a) milit. t.t., to have the upper hand, to be conqueror, to conquer; virtute facile, Caes.; per biduum equestri proelio, Caes.; (β) in other relations, to have the upper hand, have the preference, be superior, overcome, surpass; superat sententia, Caes.; tantum superantibus malis, Liv.; totidem formā superante juvencae, of surpassing beauty, Verg.; 2, to be remaining; a, to abound, be in abundance; partem superare mendosum est, Cic.; superante multitudine, Liv.; b, to remain, to be over; si quod superaret pecuniae retulisses, Cic.; esp. (with, or poet. without vitā), to remain in life, to survive, live; uter eorum vitā superavit, Caes.; superatne et vescitur aurā? Verg.; c, to be too much; quae Jugurthae fesso et majoribus astricto superaverant, Sall.; d, to flow over with, overflow with; victor superans animis, Verg. **II.** Transit., 1, to rise above, surmount, overtop, mount, ascend; montes, Verg.; summas ripas fluminis, Caes.; hence, transf., to overtop; turris superat fontis fastigium, Caes.; 2, a, to sail by, to round; promontorium, Liv.; b, transf., (a) to penetrate to; clamor superat inde castra hostium, Liv.; (β) met., to surpass, excel, exceed; aliquem doctrinā, Cic.; omnes in re, Cic.; (γ) to overcome, conquer; bello superatos esse Arvernos a Q. Fabio Maximo, Caes.; fig., injurias fortunae facile veterum philosophorum praeceptis, Cic.

sŭpĕrobrŭo -ŭi -ŭtum, 3. to cover over, Prop.

sŭperpendens -entis, overhanging; saxum, Liv.

sŭperpōno -pŏsŭi -pŏsĭtum, 3. **I.** to lay, place, put over, or upon; superpositum capiti decus, Liv. **II.** to set over, put in a station of authority; in maritimam regionem superpositus, Liv.

sŭperrāsus -a -um, shaved, scraped above, Plin.

sŭperscando (**sŭperscendo**), 3. to climb up, climb over; superscandens vigilum strata somno corpora, Liv.

sŭperscrībo -scripsi -scriptum, 3. to write over or upon, Suet.

sŭpersēdĕo -sēdi -sessum, 3. **I.** to sit above, sit upon, Suet. **II.** Fig., to be above anything, refrain from doing anything, omit, leave off; with abl., hoc labore, Cic.; proelio, Caes.; with infin., loqui apud vos, Liv.

sŭperstagno, 1. to spread out into a lake, Tac.

sŭpersterno -strāvi -strātum, 3. to strew, spread over or upon; superstratis Gallorum cumulis, Liv.

sŭperstĕs -stĭtis (super and sto). **I.** standing near, present, witnessing; suis utrisque superstitibus praesentibus (old legal formula), ap. Cic. **II.** surviving, living beyond another; (a) with dat., ut sui sibi liberi superstites essent, Cic.; (β) with genit., alterius vestrûm superstes, Liv.; aliquem non solum vitae, sed etiam dignitatis suae superstitem relinquere, Cic.

sŭperstĭtĭo -ōnis, f. (super and sisto). **I.** superstition, superstitious fear, fanaticism; 1, lit., anilis, Cic.; capti quādam superstitione animi, Cic.; superstitionem tollere, Cic.; 2, meton., a binding, awe-inspiring oath; una superstitio superis quae reddita divis, Verg. **II.** external religious observance; quaenam illa superstitio, quod numen, interrogat, Tac.; in plur. = religious observances or ceremonies; hostes operati superstitionibus, Liv.

sŭperstĭtĭōsē, adv. (superstitiosus), superstitiously, Cic.

sŭperstĭtĭōsus -a -um (superstitio). **I.** superstitious; philosophi, Cic. **II.** prophetical, Plaut.

sŭperstĭto, 1. (superstes). **I.** Transit., to preserve alive, Enn. **II.** Intransit., to be over and above, remain, Plaut.

sŭpersto -stĕti, 1. to stand over or upon; with dat., corporibus, Liv.; with acc., aliquem, Verg.; absol., Liv.

sŭperstrŭo -struxi -structum, 3. to build over or upon, Tac.

sŭpersum -fŭi -esse, to be over and above, either as remnant or as superfluity. **A.** As remnant, to be left, remain; a, of things, duae partes, quae mihi supersunt illustrandae, Cic.; biduum supererat, Cic.; quod superest, the rest, Verg.; quod superest, as for the rest, Cic.; superest, foll. by infin., Liv., Ov.; b, of persons, (a) to be left, to remain; et superesse videt de tot modo millibus unum, Ov.; perexigua pars illius exercitus superest, Caes.; (β) to survive; alicui, Liv.; pugnae, Liv. **B.** to be superfluous, abound; vereor ne jam superesse mihi verba putes, quae dixeram defutura, Cic.; in a bad sense, to be superfluous, to be redundant; ut neque desit aliquid quidquam neque supersit, Cic.

sŭpertĕgo -texi -tectum, 3. to cover over, Tib.

sŭpĕrurgĕo, 2. to press from above, Tac.

sŭpĕrus (rarely **sŭpĕr**) -a -um (from adv. super), compar., **sŭpĕrĭor**; superl., **sŭpĕrrĭmus**, **sŭprēmus** and **summus**. **I.** Posit., **sŭpĕrus** -a -um, upper, the upper, higher; 1, gen., res superae, Cic.; mare superum, the upper sea, i.e. the Adriatic Sea, Cic.; 2, esp., of things on or above the earth, superis ab oris, from the upper world, Verg.; hence, subst., a, **sŭpĕri** -ōrum, m.; (a) the gods above, Verg.; (β) the men on the earth; ad superos fleti, Verg.; b, **sŭpĕra** -ōrum, n. the heights; supera alta, the heights of heaven, Verg. **II.** Compar., **sŭpĕrĭor** -ōris,

m. and f., **sŭpĕrĭus** -ōris, n. *higher, upper, and* partit., *the upper or higher part of anything;* **1**, lit., a, of place, pars collis, Caes.; domus, Cic.; *ex loco superiore, from a higher place,* Caes.; de loco superiore dicere, *from the tribunal,* as praetor, Cic.; de loco superiore agere, *from the speaker's tribune,* Cic.; et ex superiore et ex aequo loco sermones, *utterances on the tribunal and in private life,* Cic.; b, in writing, scriptura superior, *preceding,* Cic.; **2**, transf., a, of time, *earlier, prior, former, past;* and, as applied to human life, *older;* annus, Cic.; nox, *night before last,* Cic.; omnes aetatis superioris, *of advanced age,* Caes.; b, of rank, *higher;* superioris ordinis nonnulli, Caes.; c, of power, importance, etc., *higher, more distinguished;* (a) absol., aliquis superior, *a distinguished person,* Cic.; milit. t. t., discessit superior, *gained the advantage,* Nep.; (β) with abl., loco, fortunā, famā, Cic.; facilitate et humanitate superior, Cic. **III.** Superl., **A. sŭprēmus** -a -um, *the highest, uppermost;* **1**, lit., of place, montes, Verg.; **2**, transf., a, in time or succession, *the last;* (a) nox, Verg.; sole supremo, *on the setting of the sun,* Hor.; adv., supremum, *for the last time,* Ov.; (β) *of or relating to the end of life;* dies, *the day of death,* Cic.; honor, *the last rites,* Verg.; subst., **sŭprēma** -ōrum, n., (aa) *death,* Ov., Tac.; (ββ) *funeral rites,* Tac.; b, *highest, greatest, most extreme;* supplicium, Cic.; ventum est ad supremum, *the end is reached,* Verg. **B. summus** -a -um (for sup -mus), *the highest, uppermost,* and partit. = *the highest part of, the top;* **1**, lit., of place, summum jugum montis, Caes.; partit., summa urbs, *the highest part of the city,* Cic.; in summa sacra via, *at the top of the sacra via,* Cic.; subst., **summum** -i, n. *the highest point;* a summo, Cic.; summum tecti, Verg.; **2**, transf. a, of the voice, *the highest, loudest;* vox summa, Hor.; b, of time or succession, *the last;* dies, Verg.; senectus, *extreme old age,* Cic.; c, in rank, value, estimation, *the highest, most distinguished, most valuable, most important, greatest, best;* (a) of things, deorum summus erga vos amor, Cic.; summo studio, *with the greatest zeal,* Cic.; summa salus reipublicae, Cic.; quo res summa loco, *how is it with the state?* Verg.; adv., summum, *at the most;* quatuor aut summum quinque, Cic.; (β) of persons, *highest, most elevated, most distinguished;* optimus et supremus vir, Cic.; poet. neut. plur., summa ducum Atrides, *the chief person,* Ov.

sŭpervācănĕus -a -um, *superfluous, unnecessary, useless;* litterae, Cic.; opus, *done at leisure hours,* Cic.

sŭpervācŭus -a -um, *superfluous, unnecessary, useless, needless;* metus, Ov.

sŭpervādo, 3. *to go over surmount;* ruinas, Liv.

sŭpervĕhor -vectus sum, 3. dep. *to ride, sail, pass over, sail by;* promunturium Calabriae, Liv.

sŭpervĕnĭo -vēni -ventum, 4. **I.** *to come over;* unda supervenit undam, Hor. **II.** *to come up;* a, legati superveniunt, Liv.; b, *to come upon unexpectedly;* with dat., huic laetitiae, Liv.

sŭperventus -ūs, m. (supervenio), *a coming up, arrival,* Tac.

sŭpervīvo -vixi, 3. *to survive,* Suet.

sŭpervŏlĭto, 1. *to fly over;* sua tecta alis, Verg.

sŭpervŏlo, 1. *to fly over, fly above,* Verg.; totum orbem, Ov

sŭpīnĭtas -ātis, f. (supinus), *a bending backwards, a lying with the body bent back,* Quint.

sŭpīno, 1. (supinus), *to bend, stretch backwards, to throw back;* nasum nidore supinor,

I sniff up, Hor.; poet., glebas, *to turn over* Verg.

sŭpīnus -a -um (root SUP, Gr. ὕπ-τιος), *bent backwards, inclined backwards, lying on the back.* **I.** Lit., **A.** Gen., motus corporis pronus, obliquus, supinus, Cic.; manus supinas ad caelum tendere, *spread out with the palm upwards,* Verg. **B.** Esp., **1**, *going backwards, returning;* nec redit in fontes unda supina suos, Ov.; **2**, of localities, *sloping, spread out, outstretched;* collis, Verg.; vallis, Liv. **II.** Fig., **1**, of character, *careless, heedless, negligent, supine,* Juv.; **2**, *proud, arrogant,* Mart.

suppalpor, 1. dep. *to stroke, caress, flatter a little,* Plaut.

suppar -păris (sub and par), *almost equal, nearly contemporary with;* huic aetati suppares Alcibiades, Critias, Cic.

suppărăsītor, 1. dep. (sub and parasitor), *to flatter a little like a parasite,* Plaut.

suppărum (**sĭpărum** and **sĭphărum**) -i, n. and **suppărus** (**sĭphărus**) -i, m. (σίφαρος). **I.** *a linen garment usually worn by women,* Plaut. **II.** *a topsail,* Sen.

suppĕdĭtātĭo -ōnis, f. (suppedito), *an abundant provision, superfluity;* bonorum, Cic.

suppĕdĭto, 1. **I.** Intransit., **1**, *to abound, be in abundance, be at hand, be in store;* ne chartam quidem suppeditare, Cic.; cui si vita suppeditavisset, *had lasted longer,* Cic.; **2**, *to be in sufficient quantity, suffice;* ad cultum, Cic. **II.** Transit., **1**, *to provide, supply, offer, give abundantly;* (a) with acc., alicui frumentum, Cic.; cibos, Cic.; (β) with dat., *to support, stand by;* alicui, Cic.; **2**, suppeditari aliquā re, *to be provided with,* Cic.

suppernātus -a -um (sub and perna), *lamed in the hip;* transf., alnus suppernata securi, *hewn down,* Cat.

suppĕtiae -ārum, f. (suppeto), *help, aid, assistance,* only in nom. and acc., Plaut.

suppĕtĭor, 1. dep. (suppetiae), *to come to help, assist,* Cic. (?)

suppĕto -īvi and -ĭi -ītum, 3. (sub and peto). **A.** *to be in store, be in hand;* ne pabuli quidem satis magna copia suppetebat, Caes.; ut mihi ad remunerandum nihil suppetat praeter voluntatem, Cic.; si vita suppetet, *if I live so long,* Cic.; of materials for a speech, vererer ne mihi crimina non suppeterent, Cic. **B.** Transf., *to suffice, be enough, correspond with;* ut quotidianis sumptibus copiae suppetant, Cic.

suppĭlo, 1. (sub and * pilo, whence compilo), *to steal secretly, filch;* and, with personal object, *to pluck, fleece,* Plaut.

suppingo -pēgi -pactum, 3.(sub and pango), *to fasten underneath,* Plaut.

supplanto, 1. (sub and planta), *to throw down a person by tripping up his heels;* aliquem, Cic.

supplaudo = supplodo (q.v.).

supplēmentum -i, n. (suppleo), *a filling up, supply, supplement;* milit. t. t., *a recruiting of troops, supply of recruits, reinforcements;* exercitūs, Liv.; supplementum scribere legionibus, Cic.; supplementa distribuere, Liv.

supplĕo -plēvi -plētum, 2. (sub and pleo), *to fill up, make full, complete, supply.* **I.** Lit., sanguine venas, Ov.; inania mittola *to people,* Ov. **II.** Transf., *to fill up something that is wanting, make good, repair;* bibliothecam, Cic.; milit. t. t., *to recruit, fill up the number of;* legiones, Liv.

supplex -plĭcis, abl. -plĭce and -plĭci, genit. plur. -plĭcum and (rarely) -plĭcĭum (sub and plico

thus lit., *bending the knee*), hence, *humbly entreating, supplicating, suppliant;* supplex te ad pedes **abjiciebas**, Cic.; transf., of things, multis et supplicibus verbis, Cic.; with dat., alicui fieri or esse supplicem, Cic.; with possess. pron. or genit. of person besought, vester est supplex, Cic.; misericordiae vestrae, Cic.

supplĭcātĭo -ōnis, f. (supplico), *a solemn public thanksgiving, a religious festival or fast on some public success or misfortune;* ad omnia pulvinaria supplicatĭonem decernere, Cic.; prodigiorum averruncandorum causā supplicationes in biduum decernere, Liv.

supplĭcĭtĕr, adv. (supplex), *suppliantly, humbly;* respondere, Cic.

supplĭcĭum -ĭi, n. (supplex), *a kneeling down, either for entreaty or to receive punishment.* Hence, **I.** *a humble entreaty;* a, of the gods, *prayer;* precibus suppliciisque deos placare, Liv.; b, *humble entreaty* of men ; fatigati suppliciis regis, Sall. **II.** *punishment, penalty, torture,* esp., *capital punishment;* 1, lit., sumere supplicium de aliquo, *to inflict upon,* Cic.; ad ultimum supplicium progredi, Caes.; hence, transf., *torture, pain;* satis supplicii tulisse, Caes.; 2, meton., *wounds, marks of mutilation;* dira tegens supplicia, Verg.

supplĭco, 1. (supplex), *to fall down on the knees before.* **I.** Gen., *to beseech humbly, entreat suppliantly;* alicui publice, Cic.; Caesari or senatui pro aliquo, Cic. **II.** *to pray to the gods, supplicate, worship;* per hostias diis, Sall.

supplōdo (supplaudo) -plōsi -plōsum, 3. (sub and plaudo), *to stamp;* pedem, Cic.

supplōsĭo -ōnis, f. (supplodo), *a stamping;* pedis, Cic.

suppoenĭtet, 2. impers. (sub and poenitet), *it repents somewhat;* with acc. of pers. and genit. of thing, illum furoris, Cic.

suppōno -pŏsŭi (-pŏsīvi, Plaut.) -pŏsĭtum (syncop. partic., suppostus, Verg.), 3. **I.** *to put, place, lay under;* 1, lit., ova gallinis, Cic.; aliquem tumulo or terrae, *to bury,* Ov.; terrae dentes vipereos, *to sow,* Ov.; 2, fig., *to subject;* se criminibus, Cic. **II.** *to put under something;* 1, lit., falcem maturis aristis, Verg.; 2, fig., a, *to add, annex;* generi partes, Cic.; b, *to place after, to esteem less;* Latio Samon, Ov. **III.** *to put in the place of a person or thing;* 1, gen., aliquem in alicuius locum, Cic.; 2, *to substitute that which is not genuine, to counterfeit, forge;* testamenta falsa, Cic.

supporto, 1. (sub and porto), *to bring, bear, carry, convey to;* frumentum, Caes.; omnia inde in castra, Liv.

suppŏsĭtīcĭus -a -um (suppono), 1, *put in the place of another, substituted,* Mart.; 2, *supposititious, not genuine,* Varr.

suppŏsĭtĭo -ōnis, f. (suppono), *the substitution* of one child for another, Plaut.

suppŏsĭtrix -trīcis, f. (suppono), *she that substitutes;* puerorum, Plaut.

suppostus, v. suppono.

suppressĭo -ōnis, f. (supprimo), *embezzlement;* judiciales (sc. pecuniae), Cic.

suppressus -a -um, p. adj. (from supprimo), of the voice, *low, subdued;* vox, Cic.; orator suppressior ut vocae, sic etiam oratione, Cic.

supprĭmo -pressi -pressum, 3. (sub and premo), *to press down, press under.* **I.** navem, *to sink,* Liv. **II.** a, *to hold back, check, restrain;* hostem nostros insequentem, Caes.; vocem, Ov.; iram, *to check,* suppressus, Liv.; b, *to keep from publicity, keep back, suppress, conceal;* famam decreti, Liv.; pecuniam, nummos, *to embezzle,* Cic.

supprōmus -i, m. (sub and promus), *an under-butler,* Plaut.

suppŭdet, 2. impers. (sub and pudet), *to be somewhat ashamed;* me alicuius, *I am somewhat ashamed of;* eorum (librorum) me suppudebat, Cic.

suppūrātĭo -ōnis, f. (suppuro), *a purulent ulcer, suppuration,* Plin.

suppūrātōrĭus -a -um (suppuro), *of or relating to an ulcer,* Plin.

suppūro, 1. (sub and pus). **I.** Intransit., *to form matter, suppurate.* **II.** Transit., *to cause to suppurate;* hence, **suppūrātus** -a -um, *suppurated, full of ulcerous sores,* Plin. Subst., **suppūrāta** -ōrum, n. *sores,* Plin.

suppŭto, 1. (sub and puto), 1, *to cut, prune beneath,* Cato; 2, *to count up, compute;* with rel. sent., et sibi quid sit utile sollicitis supputat articulis, Ov.

sūprā, adv. and prep. (for superā, sc. parte, from superus). **I.** Adv., with compar., 1, of place, a, *above, over, on the top;* omnia haec, quae supra et subter, unum esse, Cic.; et mare quod supra teneant, quodque alluit infra, Verg.; toto vertice supra est, *is taller,* Verg.; b, in writing or discourse, *before, above;* ut supra dixi, Cic.; uti supra demonstravimus, Caes.; 2, of time, *before, previously;* pauca supra repetere, Sall.; 3, of degree, a, lit., *more, beyond;* supra adjicere, *to offer more,* Cic.; b, transf., *beyond, further;* ita accurate ut nihil possit supra, Cic.; supra deos lacessere, Hor.; supra quam, *more than;* rem supra feret quam fieri potest, Cic. **II.** Prep. with acc., 1, of place, a, with verbs of rest, *above, over;* supra subterque terram per dies quindecim pugnatum est, Liv.; of position at table, accumbere supra aliquem, Cic.; fig., supra caput esse, *to be over a person's head, to be a burden, to be vexatious;* ecce supra caput homo levis, Cic.; b, with verbs of motion, (a) *over, beyond;* fera saltu supra venabula fertur, Verg.; (β) *up to;* nec exissent unquam supra terram, Verg.; (γ) *above;* supra aliquem transire, *to surpass,* Verg.; 2, of time, *before;* supra hanc memoriam, Caes.; 3, of degree, a, lit., *more than, above;* supra millia viginti, Liv.; b, transf., (a) *above, beyond;* supra modum, Liv.; supra vires, Hor.; (β) *besides;* supra belli Latini metum id quoque accesserat quod, etc., Liv.

sūprascando, 3. *to climb over, surmount;* fines, Liv.

sūprēmus, etc., v. superus.

1. **sūra** -ae, f. *the calf of the leg,* Ov.

2. **Sūra** -ae, m., P. Cornelius Lentulus, *fellow-conspirator with Catiline.*

surcŭlācěus -a -um (surculus), *woody,* Plin.

surcŭlārĭus -a -um (surculus), *of or relating to young shoots,* Varr.

surcŭlōsus -a -um (surculus), *woody, like wood,* Plin.

surcŭlus -i, m. (dim. of surus), *a young shoot, sprout, sucker.* **I.** Gen., Verg.; surculum defringere (as a sign of taking possession), Cic. **II.** Esp., *a sap for planting,* Cic.

surdaster -tra -trum (surdus), *somewhat deaf,* Cic.

surdĭtas -ātis, f. (surdus), *deafness,* Cic.

surdus -a -um, *deaf.* **I.** Lit., Cic.; prov., surdis canere, *to sing to deaf ears,* Verg.; haud surdis auribus dicta, Liv. **II.** Transf., **A.** Act., 1, *deaf = not willing to hear, insensible;* per numquam surdos in tua vota deos, Ov.; **surdae** ad omnia solatia aures, Liv.; leges rem surdam

esse, Liv.; 2, *deaf = not understanding;* in horum sermone surdi, Cic. **B.** Pass., *not heard, still, silent;* lyra, Prop.; gratia, Ov.

Surēna -ae, m. *a grand vizier, prime minister among the Parthians,* Tac.

surgo = subrigo (q.v.).

surpŭit, surpuerat, surpere, surpite, v. surripio.

surrādo = subrado (q.v.).

surrancĭdus = subrancidus (q.v.).

surraucus = subraucus (q.v.).

surrēmĭgo = subremigo (q.v.).

Surrentum -i, n. *a town in Campania,* now *Sorrento.* Hence, **Surrentīnus** -a -um, *Surrentine.*

surrēpo = subrepo (q.v.).

surreptīcĭus = subrepticius (q.v.).

surrīdĕo = subrideo (q.v.).

surrīdĭcŭlē = subridicule (q.v.).

surrĭgŭus = subriguus (q.v.).

surringor = subringor (q.v.).

surrĭpĭo -rĭpŭi -reptum, 3. (sub and rapio), *to take away secretly, to steal, filch, pilfer.* **I.** Lit., vasa ex privato sacro, Cic.; filium ex custodia, Liv.; Parmam, *conquer by cunning,* Cic.; of plagiarism, a Naevio vel sumpsisti multa, si fateris, vel, si negas, surripuisti, Cic. **II.** Fig., **a,** aliquid spatii, Cic.; virtus nec eripi nec surripi potest, Cic.; **b,** surripi of an accused person, *to be rescued from punishment by underhand means,* such as bribery, Cic. (syncop. forms, surpite, Hor.; surpuit, Plaut.; surpuerat, Hor.; surpere, Lucr.).

surrŏgo = subrogo (q.v.).

surrostrāni = subrostrani (q.v.).

surrŭbĕo = subrubeo (q.v.).

surrŭbĭcundus = subrubicundus (q.v.).

surrūfus = subrufus (q.v.).

surrŭo = subruo (q.v.).

surrustĭcus = subrusticus (q.v.).

surrŭtĭlus = subrutilus (q.v.).

sursum, adv. (sub and versum). **I.** *upwards, on high;* sursum deorsum, *up and down, backwards and forwards,* Cic. **II.** *high up, above;* nares recte sursum sunt, Cic. (susque deque = sursum deorsum, *up and down;* prov., de Octavio susque deque (sc. fero or habeo), *I do not trouble myself about,* Cic.).

sūrus -i, m. *a shoot, twig,* Varr.

sūs, sŭis, c. (ὖς), 1, *a sow, swine, pig, hog,* Cic.; 2, *a kind of fish,* Ov.

suscensĕo -censŭi -censum, 2. *to be angry with, to be enraged;* **a,** with dat., alicui vehementer, Cic.; **b,** with neut. acc., illud vereor ne tibi illum suscensere aliquid suspicēre, Cic.; **c,** with propter and the acc., Cic.; **d,** with quia or quod, Cic.; **e,** with acc. and infin., Liv.

susceptĭo -ōnis, f. (suscipio), *an undertaking;* causae, Cic.

suscĭpĭo -cēpi -ceptum, 3. (subs = sub and capio), *to take up or on oneself.* **I.** As a bearer. **A.** Lit., *to carry, hold upright,* Plin. **B.** Fig., 1, *to support, defend;* aliquem, ap. Cic.; 2, *to take upon oneself;* **a,** *to undertake a business, begin, take up;* res., of something undertaken voluntarily; negotium, Cic.; personam viri boni, Cic.; sacra peregrina, *to adopt,* Cic.; **b,** *to suffer,* submit to, endure; invidiam, Cic.; dolorem, Cic.; magnam molestiam, Cic. **II.** As a receiver, *to take, receive, catch up.* **A.** Lit., dominam

ruentem, Verg.; esp., **a,** aliquem, *to take up a new-born child from the ground and so acknowledge it;* in lucem editi et suscepti sumus, Cic.; hence, filium, etc., suscepisse ex aliqua, *to have, to beget a child;* liberos ex filia libertini suscepisse, Cic.; **b,** *to receive as a citizen, as a scholar,* etc.; aliquem in civitatem, Cic. **B.** Fig., **a,** *to receive as true, maintain;* quae si suscipimus, Cic.; **b,** *to admit of;* consolationem, Cic.; **c,** *to answer, take up the speech,* Verg.

suscĭto, 1. **I.** *to lift up.* **A.** *to raise on high, lift up,* Verg.; lintea, Ov. **B.** *to cause to rise, to rouse up, awake, cause to stand up;* **te** ab tuis subselliis contra te testem suscitabo, Cic.; of persons sleeping, *to arouse;* aliquem **e** somno, Cic.; transf., ignes sopitos, Verg. **II.** *to stir up;* **a,** *to put in motion, arouse;* viros in arma, Verg.; **b,** *to stir up, bring about;* Romanum cum Saguntino bellum, Liv.

sūsĭnus -a -um (σούσινος), *made of lilies,* Plin.

suspecto, 1. (intens. of suspicio). **I.** *to look at, regard, gaze upon carefully,* Ter. **II.** *to look upon with suspicion, suspect;* aliquem, Tac.

1. **suspectus** -a -um, p. adj. (from 1. suspicio), *suspected, awakening suspicion;* suspectum meis civibus, Cic.; aliquem suspectum habere, *to suspect,* Caes.; with de and the abl., quum filius patri suspectus esset de noverca, Cic.; with genit., suspectus cupiditatis imperii, Liv.; with infin., suspectus eius consilia fovisse, Tac.

2. **suspectus** -ūs, m. (1. suspicio). **I.** *a looking upwards;* **a,** lit., aetherium ad Olympum, Verg.; **b,** meton., *height;* turris vasto suspectu, Verg. **II.** Fig., *looking up to, honour, respect, esteem,* Ov.

suspendĭōsus -a -um (suspendium), *one who has hanged himself,* Plin.

suspendĭum -ii, n. (suspendo), *a hanging of oneself,* Cic.; suspendio perire, Cic.; plur., praebuit illa arbor misero suspendia collo, *has served for hanging,* Ov.

suspendo -pendi -pensum, 3. *to hang up.* **I.** Lit., **a,** nidum tigno, Verg.; aliquem arbori infelici, Cic.; aliquem in oleastro, Cic.; se de ficu, Cic.; simply se, *to hang oneself,* Cic.; partic., esp., *to suspend as an offering in a temple, consecrate;* vestimenta deo maris, Hor. **II.** Transf., **A.** *to raise up, make high;* tectum turris, Caes.; tellurem sulco tenui, *to plough up,* Verg. **B.** Transf., *to cause to waver, or be uncertain;* 1, lit., **a,** ferre suspensos gradus, uncertain, Ov.; **b,** esp., *to build upon arches, to vault;* balneola, Cic.; 2, transf., *to support, prop up;* ita aedificatum, ut suspendi non posset, Cic.; 3, fig., **a,** *to check, stop, break off;* fletum, Ov.; **b,** *to leave undecided;* rem medio responso, Liv.; **c,** *to leave in uncertainty;* animos fictā gravitate, Ov.

suspensus -a -um, p. adj. (from suspendo). **I.** *hovering, hanging, suspended;* currus in aqua, Cic.; aquila suspensis demissa leniter alis, Liv. **II.** Fig., **a,** *resting upon, dependent upon;* ex bono casu omnia suspensa sunt, Cic.; **b,** *uncertain, doubtful, in suspense, wavering;* animus, Cic.; aliquem suspensum tenere, Cic.; **c,** *fearful, anxious, restless;* timor, Ov.

suspĭcax -ācis (suspicor), *suspicious, awakening suspicion,* Tac.

1. **suspĭcĭo** -spexi -spectum, 3. **I.** Intransit., *to look at from below, to look upwards;* in caelum, Cic. **II.** Transit., **A.** *to look at from below, regard, contemplate;* **a,** lit., caelum, Cic.; **b,** fig., *to look up to, to esteem, respect, honour;*

viros, Cic. **B.** Esp., *to suspect*; with infin., suspectus regi, et ipse eum suspiciens, novas res cupere, Sall.

2. **suspĭcĭo** -ōnis, f. **I.** *mistrust, suspicion*; in qua nulla subest suspicio, Cic.; suspicionem habere, *to suspect*, Cic., and, *to be suspicious*, Cic.; suspicio cadit in aliquem or pertinet ad aliquem, Cic.; est suspicio, foll. by acc and infin., Cic.; suspicionem alicui dare, Cic.; or afferre, Cic.; or inferre, Cic.; in suspicionem alicui venire, foll. by acc. and infin., Cic. **II.** Transf., *a notion, idea, conception*; deorum, Cic.

suspĭcĭōsē, adv. (suspiciosus), *in a suspicious manner, suspiciously*; aliquid dicere, Cic.; suspiciosius dicere, Cic.

suspĭcĭōsus -a -um (2. suspicio). **I.** *cherishing suspicion, suspecting, suspicious*; in aliquem, Cic. **II.** *exciting suspicion, suspicious*, Cic.

suspĭcor, 1. dep. (1. suspicio). **I.** *to suspect*; with acc. of thing, res nefarias, Cic.; with acc. and infin., ea quae fore suspicatus erat, Caes. **II.** Transf., *to conjecture, form an opinion, surmise*; licet aliquid etiam de Popilii ingenio suspicari, Cic.; quantum ex monumentis suspicari licet, Cic.; with rel. sent., quid sibi impenderet coepit suspicari, Cic.; with acc. and infin., quod valde suspicor fore, Cic.

suspīrātĭo -ōnis, f. (suspiro), *a drawing a deep breath*, Plin.

suspīrātus -ūs, m. (suspiro), *a deep breath, sigh*, Ov.

suspīrĭōsus -a -um (suspirium), *breathing with difficulty, asthmatic*, Plin.

suspīrĭtus -ūs, m. (suspiro), *a breathing deeply, a sigh*, Cic.

suspīrĭum -ĭi, n. (suspiro). **I.** *a deep breath, a sigh*, Cic. **II.** *asthma, difficulty of breathing*, Mart.

suspīro, 1. (sub and spiro). **I.** Intransit., *to breathe deeply, to sigh*; a, occulte, Cic.; b, in aliquo, in aliqua, in aliquam, *to sigh for, long for*, Ov. **II.** Transit., *to breathe forth, sigh forth, long for*; amores, Tib.; Chloen, Hor.

susque dēque, v. sursum.

sustentācŭlum -i, n. (sustento), *a prop, support*, Tac.

sustentātĭo -ōnis, f. (sustento), **1**, *a delay, deferring*; habere aliquam moram et sustentationem, Cic.; **2**, as a figure of speech, *keeping in suspense*, Quint.

sustento, 1. (intens. of sustineo), *to hold up, support, sustain.* **I.** Lit., fratrem ruentem dextrā, Verg. **II.** Transf., **1**, *to sustain, support, strengthen, maintain*; rempublicam, Cic.; imbecillitatem valetudinis tuae, Cic.; **2**, *to sustain with food or money, maintain, support*; se amicorum liberalitate, Cic.; aër spiritu ductus alit et sustentat animantes, Cic.; **3**, *to bear, sustain*; maerorem tuum, Cic.; absol., in battle, *to hold out*; aegre sustentatum est, Caes.; **4**, *to put off, hinder, delay*; rem, Cic.; consilio bellum, Cic.

sustĭnĕo -tĭnŭi -tentum, 2. (subs = sub and teneo), *to hold up, support, sustain.* **I.** Lit., **1**, aër volatus alitum sustinet, Cic.; se a lapsu, *to keep oneself from falling, to keep oneself upright*, Liv.; so simply se, Cic.; **2**, *to carry*; bovem, Cic.; of trees, (arbores) sustineant poma, Ov.; **3**, *to hold back, check, restrain*; equum incitatum, Cic.; remos, Cic.; impetum, Cic.; se, *to hold oneself back from, refrain from*; se ab assensu, Cic. **II.** Fig., **1**, a, causam, Cic.; munus in republica, Cic.; sustines non parvam expectationem, Cic.; eos querentes non sustinuit, *could not withstand*, Cic.; sustineo, *I have the heart to, I can induce myself to*; with acc. and infin.,

sustinebunt tales viri se tot senatoribus, tot populorum privatorumque litteris non credidisse, Cic.; b, absol., milit. t. t., *to stand one's ground*; Brutus Mutinae vix sustinebat, Cic.; **2**, *to support, maintain, nourish, sustain*; ager non amplius hominum quinque millia sustinere potest, Cic.; **3**, *to put off, delay*; solutionem, Cic.; rem in noctem, Liv.; **4**, *to sustain, support, maintain, preserve*; civitatis dignitatem ac decus, Cic.

sustollo, 3. **1**, *to lift up, raise up, elevate*, Ov.; **2**, *to take off, carry off*; filiam, Plaut.

sustringo = substringo (q.v.).

sŭsurrātor -ōris, m. (susurro), *a murmurer, mutterer*, ap. Cic.

sŭsurro, 1. (susurrus), *to murmur, mutter, whisper*; of men, Ov.; of bees, *to hum*, Verg.; of water, Verg.; of the wind, Verg.

1. **sŭsurrus** -i, m. (reduplicated from the root of συρίζειν, σύριγξ), *a murmuring, muttering, whispering, humming, buzzing*, Cic.

2. **sŭsurrus** -a -um (1. susurrus), *whispering, muttering*; lingua, Ov.

sūtēla -ae, f. (suo), *a sewing together*; fig., *a cunning trick, artifice*, Plaut.

Suthul -ūlis, n. *a fort in Numidia*, perhaps ruins of Guelma.

sūtĭlis -e (suo), *stitched together, fastened together*; cymba, Verg.

sūtor -ōris, m. (suo), *a shoemaker, cobbler*, Cic.; prov., ne sutor supra crepidam (sc. judicet), *let the cobbler stick to his last*, Plin.

sūtōrĭus -a -um (sutor), *of or relating to a shoemaker*; atramentum, *blacking*, Cic.

sūtrīnus -a -um (sutor), *of or relating to a shoemaker.* **I.** Adj., taberna, *cobbler's stall*, Tac. **II.** Subst., **sūtrīna** -ae, f. a, (sc. ars), *a shoemaker's trade*, Varr.; b, (sc. taberna), *a shoemaker's stall or shop*, Plin.

Sūtrĭum -ĭi, n. *a town in Etruria*, now Sutri. Hence, **Sūtrīnus** -a -um, *of or belonging to Sutrium*; plur. subst., **Sūtrīni** -ōrum, m. *the inhabitants of Sutrium*.

sūtūra -ae, f. (suo), *a seam, suture*, Liv.

sŭus -a -um, pron. poss., *his, her, its, own.* **I.** Lit., **A.** Gen., **1**, adj., a, suus cuique erat locus definitus, Cic.; aliquem suum facere, *make one's own*, Liv.; b, (a) with quisque in a different case, quo sua quemque natura maxime ferre videatur, Cic.; or in the same case, quas tamen inter omnes est suo quoque in genere mediocres, Cic.; (β) with proprius, sua cuique laus propria debetur, Cic.; (γ) with the ethic dat., factus (consul) est bis, primum ante tempus, iterum sibi suo tempore, Cic.; (δ) with ipse, sua ipsam peremptam (esse) mercede, Liv.; (ε) strengthened by -pte or -met, Crassum suāpte interfectum manu, Cic.; capti suismet ipsi praesidiis, Liv.; **2**, subst., a, sui, *his men, dependents, countrymen*, etc.; quem sui Caesarem salutabant, Cic.; b, **sŭum** -i, n. *one's own property*; ad suum pervenire, Cic. **B.** 1, *his, its*, etc. = *proper, suitable*; suum numerum habere, Cic.; **2**, = *favourable, propitious*; utebatur populo suo, Cic.; **3**, *his or their own* = *not strange*; sui dei aut novi, Cic.; **4**, *independent, in one's own power*; is poterit semper esse in disputando suus, Cic. **II.** Transf., rarely used for sui, injuria sua, *against himself*, Sall.

sȳăgrus -i, f. (σύαγρος), *a species of palm-tree*, Plin.

Sȳbăris -ris, f. (Σύβαρις). **I.** *a river in Lucania*, now Sibari. **II.** *a Greek town in Lucania, on the river of the same name, destroyed 510 B.C., and afterwards rebuilt under the name of*

Thurii, famous for its luxury. Hence, **A. Sўb-ărītae** -ārum, m. *the people of Sybaris.* **B. Sўbārītis** -ĭdis, f. *name of a wanton poem.*

sўcē -ēs, f. (συκῆ), 1, *a plant also called peplis,* Plin. ; 2, *a species of resin,* Plin. ; 3, *a running sore in the eye,* Plin.

Sўchaeus -i, m. *husband of Dido,* Hence, adj., **Sўchaeus** -a -um, *belonging to Sychaeus.*

sўcites -a -um (συκίτης), *fig-wine,* Plin.

sўcŏphanta -ae, f. (συκοφάντης). **I.** *an in-former, trickster, deceiver,* Plaut., Ter. **II.** *a cunning flatterer, sycophant,* Plaut.

sўcŏphantia -ae, f. (συκοφαντία), *craft, de-ception,* Plaut.

sўcŏphantiōsē, adv. (sycophanta), *roguish-ly, craftily,* Plaut.

sўcŏphantor, 1. dep. (συκοφαντέω), *to play tricks, act craftily,* Plaut.

Sўēnē -ēs, f. (Συήνη), *a town in Upper Egypt, famous for its red granite.* Hence, **Sўēnītēs** -ae, m. (Συηνίτης), *of or belonging to Syene, Syenitic.*

Syla = Sila (q.v.).

Sўlēum (Syllēum) -i, n. (Συλειον), *a moun-tain-town in Pamphylia.*

Sylla = Sulla (q.v.).

syllăba -ae, f. (συλλαβή), 1, *a syllable;* syl-laba brevis, longa, Cic. ; 2, meton., syllabae, *verses, poems,* Mart.

syllăbātim, adv. (syllaba), *syllable by syl-labie,* Cic.

syllĭbus = sittybos (q.v.).

syllŏgismus -i, m. (συλλογισμός), *a syllog-ism,* Sen.

syllŏgistĭcus -a -um (συλλογιστικός), *syl-logistic,* Quint.

Sўmaethus -i, m. (Σύμαιθος), *the largest river in Sicily, on the east of the island, receiving a number of smaller streams, now Giaretta.* Hence, **A. Sўmaethēus** -a -um, *belonging to the Symae-thus.* **B. Sўmaethis** -ĭdis, f., nympha, *the nymph of the river Symaethus.* **C. Sўmae-thius** -a- um, *Symaethian;* flumina, *which fall into the Symaethus,* Verg. ; heros, Acis, *son of the nymph of the Symaethus,* Ov.

symbŏla -ae, f. (συμβολή), *a contribution of money to a common feast,* Plaut., Ter.

symbŏlus -i, m. and **symbŏlum** -i, n. (σύμβολος), *a sign, token, signal, symbol,* Plaut.

symmetrĭa -ae, f. (συμμετρία), *symmetry,* Plin.

sympăthĭa -ae, f. (συμπάθεια), *sympathy, natural inclination or agreement of two things,* Plin.

symphōnĭa -ae, f. (συμφωνία), *a concert, musical performance,* Cic.

symphōnĭăcus -a -um (συμφωνιακός), *of or relating to a concert;* pueri, *singing boys,* Cic.

Symplēgădes -um, f. (Συμπληγάδες), *the Symplegades, rocks in the entrance to the Euxine, which, according to the fable, dashed against one another till they were fixed after the passage of the Argo between them.*

symplegma -ătis, n. (σύμπλεγμα), *a group of wrestlers, closely embracing each other,* Plin.

Sўnăpothnescontĕs (συναποθνῄσκοντες), *Those Dying Together* (the title of a comedy of Diphilus).

Sўnăristōsae -ārum, f. (συναριστῶσαι), *the Women Breakfasting Together* (the title of a comedy of Menander), Plin.

syncĕrastum -i, n. (συγκεραστόν), *a dish of hotch-potch, hash,* Varr.

sўnecdŏchē -ēs, f. (συνεκδοχή), *a figure of speech by which a part is put for the whole,* or *the cause for the result, synecdoche,* Quint.

sўnēdrus -i, m. (σύνεδρος), *among the Macedonians* = senator, Liv.

Sўnĕphēbi -ōrum, n. (συνέφηβοι), *The Fellow-Youths* (a comedy by Statius Caecilius), Cic.

syngrăpha -ae, f. (συγγραφή), *a bond, pro-missory note, agreement to pay;* cedere alicui aliquid per syngrapham, Cic.; facere syngraphas cum aliquo, Cic. ; jus dicere ex syngrapha, Cic.

syngrăphus -i, m. (σύγγραφος), 1, *a written contract,* Plaut. ; 2, *a passport,* Plaut.

synl . . . v. syll . . .

Synnăda -ōrum, n. (τὰ Σύνναδα), and **Syn-nās** -ădis and -ădos, f. *a small town in Phrygia, famous for its marble, now Eski-karahissar.* Hence, **Synnădensis** -e, *of or belonging to Synnada.*

sўnŏdontītis -ĭdis, f. (συνοδοντῖτις), *a pre-cious stone found in the brain of the fish synodus,* Plin.

sўnŏdūs -ontis, m. (συνόδους), *a fish,* per-haps *a kind of bream,* Ov.

syntectĭcus -a -um (συντηκτικός), *wasting away, consumptive,* Plin.

syntexis -is, f. (σύντηξις), *wasting away, consumption,* Plin.

synthĕsĭna = synthesis, II. b.

synthĕsis -is, f. (σύνθεσις, *a putting together*). **I.** *a service of plate, set of dishes,* Mart. **II.** *a suit of clothes;* a, Mart. ; b, *a light upper gar-ment, dressing-gown,* Mart.

syntŏnum -i, n. (σύντονον), *a musical in-strument,* Quint.

Sўphax -phācis, m. (Σύφαξ), *king of the Massaesyli, in Numidia, at the time of the Second Punic War, son-in-law of Hasdrubal.*

Sўrācūsae -ārum, f. (Συρακοῦσαι), *the chief town of Sicily, a Corinthian colony founded 758 B.C., birthplace of Archimedes and Theocritus.* Hence, **A. Sўrācūsānus** -a -um, *Syracusan.* **B. Sўrācūsius** -a -um, *Syracusan.* **C. Sўrā-cōsius** -a -um, *Syracusan.*

Sўri (Sūri) -ōrum, m. (Σύροι), *the Syrians, the inhabitants of Syria.* Hence, **A. Sўrus** -a -um, *Syrian.* **B. Sўria** -ae, f. (Συρία), *Syria, a country in Asia, on the Mediterranean Sea, in a wider sense including the country east of Syria as far as the Tigris;* Syria = Assyria, Cic. **C. Sўriăcus** -a -um, *Syrian.* **D. Sўrius** -a -um, *Syrian.*

sўringias -ae, m. (συριγγίας), *a kind of reed, adapted for making pipes,* Plin.

sўrites -ae, m. (συρίτης), *a stone found in a wolf's bladder,* Plin.

1. **Sўrius,** v. Syri.

2. **Sўrius,** v. Syros.

syrma -ātis, n. (σύρμα). **I.** *a long, trailing robe, frequently worn by tragic actors,* Juv. **II.** Meton. = *tragedy,* Juv.

Sўrŏphoenix -nīcis, m. (Συροφοίνιξ), *a Syro-phoenician,* i.e., *of Phoenicia on the border of Syria.*

Sўrŏs -i, f. (Σύρος), *an island in the Aegean Sea,* now Sira. Hence, **Sўrius** -a -um (Σύριος), *of Syros, born at Syros.*

Syrtis -is and -ĭdos, f. (Σύρτις), *a sand-bank,* esp., *those sandbanks on the coast of Northern Africa, including Syrtis Major,* now Sidra, *and Syrtis Minor,* now Cabes; a, lit., Liv.; b, transf., *the coast opposite the Syrtis,* Hor. ; **c,** meton., Syrtis patrimonii, Cic.

Sўrus -a -um, v. Syri.

tab 563 tac

T.

T t, the nineteenth letter of the Latin alphabet, corresponding with the Greek tau (T, τ). It is interchanged with *d*, *c*, and *s*, and assimilated with *s*, as quatio, quassi, mitto, missus. For the use of T. as an abbreviation, see Table of Abbreviations.

tăbānus -i, m. *a gadfly, horsefly*, Varr.

tăbella -ae, f. (dim. of tabula). **I.** *a small flat board* or *tablet; liminis, the threshold*, Cat. **II.** Meton., 1, *the tray* or *trough in which Romulus and Remus were exposed*, Ov.; 2, *a draught-board*, Ov.; 3, *a picture*, Cic.; 4, *a writing-tablet;* cerata, *covered with wax*, Cic.; meton., in plur., a, *a letter, note;* tabellas proferri jussimus, Cic.; b, *a record, proctocol, register*, etc.; tabellae quaestionis, Cic.; tabellis obsignatis agis mecum, *you take note of what I said*, Cic.; 5, *a votive tablet hung up in a temple*, Ov.; 6, *a voting-ticket, ballot;* a, in the comitia, b, in the courts of law, Cic.

tăbellārĭus -a -um (tabella). **I.** *of* or *relating to letters;* naves, *mail-boats*, Sen.; gen. subst., **tăbellārĭus** -ii, m. *a letter-carrier*, Cic. **II.** *of* or *relating to voting;* lex, Cic.

tābĕo, 2. (connected with τήκω, ἐ-τάκ-ην). **I.** *to waste away, fall away, melt, be consumed;* corpora tabent, Cic. **II.** Transf., *to drip with;* artus sale (*sea-water*) tabentes, Verg.

tăberna -ae, f. (root TAB, whence tabula), *a booth, hut.* **I.** As a dwelling-place, pauperum tabernae, Hor. **II.** As a place of business, *a stall, shop;* libraria, *a bookseller's shop*, Cic.; in tabernam devertere, *a tavern*, Cic. **III.** *an arcade in the circus*, Cic. **IV.** As proper name, Tres Tabernae, *a place on the Appian Road.*

tăbernācŭlum -i, n. (taberna). **I.** *a hut, a tent;* tabernaculum in campo Martio sibi collocare, Cic. **II.** Esp., in religious language, *a place outside the city chosen by the augurs for taking the auspices previous to the comitia*, Cic.; capere tabernaculum, Cic.

tăbernārĭus -ii, m. (taberna), *a shopkeeper*, Cic.

tăbernŭla -ae, f. (dim. of taberna), *a little shop, small tavern*, Suet.

tābes -is, f. (tabeo). **I.** *wasting away, putrefaction, melting;* 1, gen., liquescentis nivis, Liv.; 2, esp., a, *a wasting away, decline, consumption*, Cic.; b, *a plague, pestilence;* tanta vis morbi, uti tabes, plerosque civium animos invaserat, Sall. **II.** Meton., *moisture arising from melting* or *decay, corruption;* sanguinis, Liv.

tābesco, tābŭi, 3. *to melt, waste away, be gradually consumed*, **I.** Of things, a, lit., with abl., corpora calore, Ov., b, transf., nolite pati regnum Numidiae per scelus et sanguinem familiae nostrae tabescere, *be ruined*, Sall. **II.** Of men, *to waste away, languish, perish, be ruined;* a, with abl., dolore, Cic.; absol., perspicio nobis in hac calamitate pertabescendum esse, Cic.; b, of love, *to pine away*, Ov.; c, *to pine away with envy*, Hor.

tābĭdŭlus -a -um (dim. of tabidus), *wasting, consuming;* mors, Verg.

tābĭdus -a -um (tabes). **I.** *melting, consuming, wasting, decaying, pining away, dissolving;* nix, Liv. **II.** Act., *consuming, causing to waste away;* lues, Verg.

tābĭfĭcus -a -um (tabes and facio), *melting, dissolving, consuming, causing to waste away;* mentis perturbationes. Ov.

tābĭtūdo -ĭnis, f. (tabes), *decline, consumption*, Plin.

tăbŭla -ae, f. (root TAB, whence taberna), *a board, plank.* **I.** Lit., tabulam arripere de naufragio, Cic. **II.** Meton., 1, *a bench* (for sitting); solventur risu tabulae (perhaps = *the benches will burst with laughter*, but v. solvo II. B. 1, b), Hor.; 2, *a gaming-board, draught-board*, Ov.; 3, *a painted panel; a, a painting, picture;* tabula picta or simply tabula, Cic.; prov., manum de tabula, *hold! enough!* Cic.; b, *a votive tablet*, Hor.; 4, *a tablet for writing;* a, *writing-tablet*, Liv.; b, *a tablet on which a law was engraved;* XII tabulae, *the Twelve Tables*, Cic.; c, *a tablet used at an auction;* adest ad tabulam, *at the auction*, Cic.; d, *the tablet on which a list of the proscribed was drawn up*, Cic.; e, *a vote in the comitia*, Cic.; f, *a map, chart.* Cic.; g, *a contract, register, record*, Cic.; esp., *the lists of the censor*, Cic.; h, tabulae, *account-books;* conficere tabulas, Cic.; tabulae novae, *new account-books, by which old debts were cancelled*, Cic.; i, tabulae, *state papers, public records, archives;* tabulas corrumpere, Cic.; j, *a will*, Hor.; k, *a money-changer's table*, Cic.

tăbŭlāris -e (tabula), *of* or *relating to boards, plates of wood*, or *metal*, Plin.

tăbŭlārĭus -a -um (tabula), *of* or *relating to written documents.* Subst., 1, **tăbŭlārĭus** -ii, m. *a keeper of records*, Sen.; 2, **tăbŭlārĭum** -ii, n. (sc. aedificium), *archives*, Cic.

tăbŭlātĭo -ōnis, f. (tabula), *a flooring, planking, boarding, story*, Caes.

tăbŭlātum -i, n. (tabula). **I.** *a flooring, boarding, floor, story;* turris quatuor tabulatorum, Caes. **II.** Transf., *a row* or *layer of vines*, Verg.

tăbŭlīnum -i, n. and (syncop.) **tablīnum** -i, n. (tabula), *a record-room, muniment-room, archives*, Plin.

tābum -i, n. (= tabes). **I.** *a plague, pestilence;* corpora affecta tabo, Liv. **II.** Meton., *a corrupt moisture, clotted blood, matter;* terram tabo maculant, Verg.

Tăburnus -i, m. *a range of mountains in Campania.*

tăcĕo, tăcŭi, tăcĭtum, 2. **I.** Intransit., *to be silent.* **A.** Lit. = *not to speak;* an me taciturum tantis de rebus existimavistis? Cic. **B.** Transf., = silere, *to be noiseless, still, quiet;* tacet omnis ager, Verg.; Ister tacens, *frozen*, Ov.; loca, noiseless, *the lower world*, Verg. **II.** Transit., *to be silent about anything, pass over in silence;* quod adhuc semper tacui, et tacendum putavi, Cic.; ut alios taceam, *to say nothing about others*, Ov.; pass., aureus in medio Marte tacetur amor, Ov.

Tăcĭta (dea) -ae, f. (taceo), *the goddess of silence.*

tăcĭtē, adv. (tacitus). **I.** *silently, in silence;* tacite rogare, Cic. **II.** *quietly, secretly;* perire, Cic.

tăcĭturnĭtas -ātis, f. (taciturnus). **I.** *silence;* taciturnity; testium, Cic. **II.** *silence*, as a virtue, opus est fide ac taciturnitate, Ter.; nosti hominis taciturnitatem, Cic.

tăcĭturnus -a -um (tacitus). **I.** *silent, taciturn* (opp. loquax); homo, Cic.; ingenium statuā taciturnius, Hor.; tineas pasces taciturnas (of a book), Hor. **II.** Transf., *still, quiet;* amnis, Hor.

1. **tăcĭtus** -a -um, p. adj. (from taceo). **I.** Pass., **A.** *that which is passed over in silence, unmentioned;* aliquid tacitum relinquere, Cic.; aliquid (e.g. dolorem, gaudium) tacitum continere,

Liv.; non feres tacitum, *I will not be silent about it,* Cic.; subst., **tăcĭtum** -i, n. *a secret,* Ov. **B.** Transf., 1, *silently assumed, implied, tacit;* induciae, Liv.; assensio, Cic.; 2, *done silently or secretly, secret, concealed;* judicium, Cic.; vulnus, Verg. **II.** Act., **A.** *not speaking, silent, quiet, mute;* me tacito, *I being silent,* Cic.; hoc tacitus praeterire non possum, Cic.; tacita lumina, *eyes in a fixed stare,* Verg.; often in the place of the adv., tacita tecum loquitur patria, *silently,* Cic. **B.** Transf., *making no noise, still, quiet;* nox, Ov.; exspectatio, Cic.

2. **Tăcĭtus** -i, m., Cornelius, *the celebrated historian of the early empire, contemporary and friend of the younger Pliny, born between 50 and 60 A.D.*

tactĭlis -e (tango), *that can be touched,* Lucr.

tactĭo -ōnis, f. (tango). **I.** *a touching,* Plaut. **II.** *the sense of touch;* voluptates oculorum et tactionum, Cic.

tactus -ūs, m. (tango). **I.** *a touch, touching.* **A.** Lit., chordae ad quemque tactum respondent, Cic. **B.** Transf., 1, *influence, operation;* solis, Cic.; 2, *the sense of touch;* res sub tactum cadit, Cic. **II.** *tangibility,* Lucr.

taeda -ae, f. (connected with δαίς or δάς, acc. δαῖδα or δᾷδα). **I.** *the pine-tree,* Plin.; plur., *pine-wood,* Hor. **II.** Meton., **A.** *a board of pine,* Juv. **B.** Esp., a, *a torch of pine-wood;* taedae ardentes, Cic.; esp., as used at weddings, taeda jugalis, Ov.; meton. = *marriage,* Verg., Ov., and = *love,* Prop.; b, *an instrument of torture,* Juv.

taedet, taedŭit and taesum est, 2. impers. *to be disgusted with,* with acc. of pers. and genit. of thing; sunt homines quos libidinis infamiaeque suae neque pudeat neque taedeat, Cic.

taedĭfer -fēra -fērum (taeda and fero), *torch-bearing;* dea, Ceres, *who kindled a pine-torch on Mount Aetna when searching for Proserpine,* Ov.

taedĭum -ĭi, n. (taedet). **I.** *disgust, weariness, loathing;* longinquae obsidionis, Liv.; taedio curarum fessus, Tac. **II.** In an objective sense, *that which causes disgust, loathsomeness,* Plin.

Taenărus (-ŏs) -i, c. and **Taenărum (-on)** -i, n. (Ταίναρος and -ον), and **Taenăra** -ōrum, n. *a promontory and town in Laconia, where was a temple of Neptune, and whence there was supposed to be a descent into Tartarus, now Cape Matapan;* hence, **A.** Adj., **Taenārĭus** -a -um, *Laconian, Spartan;* marita, Helen, Ov.; fauces, *entrance into hell,* Verg.; so porta, Ov.; hence, meton. = *infernal;* valles, *the lower world,* Ov. **B.** **Taenārĭs** -ĭdis, f. *Taenarian;* poet, *Spartan, Laconian;* soror, Helena, Ov. **C.** Subst., **Taenărĭdes** -ae, m. poet. = *the Laconian,* i.e. *Hyacinthus,* Ov.

taenĭa -ae, f. (ταινία). **I.** *a fillet, the ribbon of a chaplet,* Verg. **II.** Meton., **A.** *the tape-worm,* Plin. **B.** *a reef of rocks under water,* Plin. (abl. plur., contr. taenis, Verg.).

taeter = teter (q.v.).

tăgax -ācis (tago), *thievish, given to pilfering,* Cic.

Tăges -gētis and -gae, m. *an Etruscan deity, grandson of Jupiter, said to have sprung from the earth, as it was being ploughed, in the form of a boy, and to have taught the Etruscans soothsaying.*

tăgo = tango (q.v.).

Tăgus -i, m. *a river in Lusitania, now Tejo, celebrated for its golden sands.*

tălārĭa, v. talaris.

tălārĭs -e (talus), *of or relating to the ankles,* tunica, *reaching to the ankles,* Cic.; subst., **tălārĭa** -ĭum, n. 1, *wings on the ankles, winged sandals,* assigned to Mercurius, Verg., Perseus, Ov., Minerva, Cic.; prov., talaria videamus, *let us think of flight,* Cic.; 2, *a long robe reaching to the ankles,* Ov.

tălārĭus -a -um (talus), *of or relating to the ankles;* ludus, *a game accompanied with gestures, noisy instruments* (such as the crotala, cymbala), *so called because the persons engaged in it wore the tunica talaris,* Cic.

Tălassĭo -ōnis, m., **Tălassĭus** -ĭi, m., and **Tălassus** -i, m. *a cry usual at Roman weddings.*

Tălāus -i, m. (Ταλαός), *one of the Argonauts, father of Adrastus, Eriphyle, etc.;* Talai gener, *Amphiaraus, husband of Eriphyle,* Ov. Hence, **Tălāĭōnĭus** -a -um, *of or belonging to Talaus.*

tălĕa -ae, f. (root TAG, whence talus, taxillus). **I.** *a cutting, slip for planting,* Plin. **II.** a, *a short stake, with an iron hook, thrown on the ground to prevent the attack of cavalry,* Caes.; b, talea ferrea, *a bar of iron used as money in Britain,* Caes.

tălentum -i, n. (τάλαντον). **I.** *a Greek weight, which varied in different states,* the Italian =100 Roman pounds; aurique eborisque talenta, Verg. **II.** *a sum of money,* also varying in amount, but in Attica probably about £243 15s., Cic. (genit. pl., gen. talentûm).

tălĭo -ōnis, f. (talis), *retaliation or recompense,* Cic.

tălis -e, *of such a kind, such.* **I.** Gen., **a,** aliquid tale, Cic.; foll. by qualis, ut, atque, etc., ut facillime, quales simus tales esse videamur, Cic.; tales esse ut laudemur, Cic.; talis qualem te esse video, Cic.; b, *the following, as follows;* talia fatus, Verg. **II.** Like τοιοῦτος; a, *of such a distinguished, remarkable, special kind;* judices tali dignitate praediti, Cic.; b, *so exceptional, blamable;* facinus, Nep.

tălĭter, adv. (talis), *in such a manner, so,* Plin.

tălĭtrum -i, n. *a snap of the finger, fillip,* Suet.

talpa -ae, f. (m. Verg.), *a mole,* Cic.

Talthȳbĭus (Talthŭbĭus) -ĭi, m. (Ταλθύβιος), *a herald and messenger of Agamemnon.*

tălus -i, m. (root TAG, whence talea, taxillus). **I.** Lit., a, *the ankle, ankle-bone,* Plin.; b, *the heel;* purpura usque ad talos demissa, Cic. **II.** Meton., *a die* (made originally out of the ankle-bones of the hind feet of certain animals), which, as used among the Romans, had only four flat sides, the other two being left round; talis ludere, Cic.

tam, adv. (orig. an accusative, like quam, jam, clam, palam). **I.** Correl. demonstr. particle, *to express comparison, so far, to such a degree;* a, with quam; (a) before adj. and adv., tam esse clemens tyrannus, quam rex importunus potest, Cic.; tam . . . quam, *both . . . and,* Suet.; quam . . . tam before comparatives and superlatives, quam magis . . . tam magis, *the more . . . the more,* Verg.; (β) before verbs, e.g., esse = talis, haec tam esse quam audio, non puto, Cic.; and before subst., tam . . . quam, *not so much . . . as;* utinam non tam fratri pietatem quam patriae praestare voluisset, Cic.; with qui, quae, quod, quis est tam lynceus, qui nihil offendat, Cic.; b, with ut and the subj., non essem tam inurbanus, uti ego graverer, Cic. **II.** Demonstr. particle, without a correl. = so, *so very, so much, of such high degree;* quid tu tam mane? Cic.; before a subst., cur tam tempore exclamarit occisum? Cic.

tămărix -ĭcis, f. *the tamarisk*, Plin.

Tāmăsos -i, f. (Ταμασός), *a town in Cyprus*. Hence, **Tāmăsēus** -a -um, *belonging to Tamasos;* ager, Ov.

tamdĭū, adv. **I.** *so long;* foll. by quamdiu, quoad, dum, quam, donec, tamdiu requiesco, quamdiu scribo, Cic. **II.** *so long*, i.e., *so very long*, Cic.

tămĕn, adv. an adversative particle, used— **I.** In the apodosis; 1, with quamquam, quamvis, etsi, etiamsi, tametsi, licet, quum = *however, yet, nevertheless, notwithstanding, for all that;* quamquam abest a culpa, suspicione tamen non caret, Cic.; 2, in the apodosis of a conditional sentence, *yet, yet at least, still;* si Massilienses per delectos cives reguntur, inest tamen in ea conditione, etc., Cic. **II.** To begin a fresh clause, *still, however, yet;* hi non sunt permolesti; sed tamen insident et urgent, Cic.; joined with si = *but if, if only*, Ov.

tămĕn-etsi, conj. *although*, Cic.

Tămēsis -is, m. and **Tămēsa** -ae, m. *a river in Britain*, now *the Thames*.

tămetsi, conj. (tamen and etsi). **I.** *although, though, nevertheless;* fo'l. by indic., Cic. **II.** *however;* tametsi quae est ista laudatio, Cic.

tamquam (tanquam), adv. **I.** Introducing a comparison, *as, just as, like as, as if, as it were;* quod video tibi etiam novum accidisse tamquam mihi, Cic.; gloria virtutem tamquam umbra sequitur, Cic.; foll. by sic or ita, tamquam bona valetudo jucundior est, sic, etc., Cic.; tamquam si, *just as if;* t~mquam si tua res agatur, Cic.; so with tamquam alone, tamquam clausa sit Asia, *as if*, Cic.).I. Causal, *as though;* classis, tamquam eo diu pugnatura, e portu movit, Liv.

Tănăger -gri, m. *a river in Lucania*, now *Negro*.

Tănāgra -ae, f. (Τάναγρα) *a town in the east of Boeotia;* adj., **Tănăgraeus** -a -um, *of or belonging to Tanagra*.

Tănăis -ĭdis and -is, m. (Τάναϊς). **I.** *a river in Sarmatia*, now *the Don*. **II.** *a river in Numidia*.

Tănăum -i, n. *a bay in Britain*, now *Firth of Tay*.

Tănăquil -quīlis, f. *wife of Tarquinius Priscus*.

tandem, adv. (tam and demonstr. suffix dem). **I.** *at length, at last;* tandem vulneribus defessi pedem referre coeperunt, Caes.; strengthened by jam, aliquando, Cic. **II.** In interrogations, *pray, then;* quid tandem agebatis? Cic.; quod genus est tandem ostentationis et gloriae? Cic.

Tanfăna -ae, f. *a German deity*.

tango, tětĭgi, tactum, 3. and (archaic) **tăgo**, taxi, 3. (root TAC), *to touch*. **I.** Bodily; 1, gen., terram gero, Cic.; 2, *to touch a place*, i.e., a, *to border on;* villa tangit viam, Cic.; b, *to enter, reach a place;* provinciam, Cic.; 3, *to touch, seize, strike, push, hit;* a, chordas, Ov.; fulmine tactus, Cic., or de caelo tactus, *struck by lightning*, Cic.; b, *to touch = to kill;* quemquam oportuisse tangi, Cic.; 4, *to sprinkle;* corpus aquā, Ov.; 5, a, = *to take;* non teruncium de praeda, Cic.; b, *to touch, take part of, taste, eat;* cibos dente, Hor. **II.** Of the mind, 1, gen., *to touch, move, affect, impress;* minae Clodii modice me tangunt, Cic.; 2, *to touch upon in discourse, mention;* ubi Aristoteles ista tetigit? Cic.; 3, *to cheat, cozen*, Plaut.; 4, *to undertake, prepare;* carmina, Ov.

tanĭăcae -ārum, f. *long strips of pork*, Varr.

Tantălus (-ŏs) -i, m. (Τάνταλος) *a king of Phrygia, father of Pelops and Niobe, who set his own child as food before the gods, and was punished in Hades by being placed near fruit and water,*

which drew back whenever he attempted to satisfy his everlasting hunger and thirst. Hence, **A.** adj., **Tantălěus** -a -um, *of or belonging to Tantalus.* **B.** Subst., **Tantălĭdēs** -ae, m. *a son or descendant of Tantalus, Pelops,* Ov.; *Agamemnon,* Ov.; Tantalidae fratres, *Atreus* and *Thyestes*, Ov. **C.** **Tantălĭs** -ĭdis, f. *a daughter or other female descendant of Tantalus, Niobe, Hermione,* Ov.

tantillus -a -um **(tantulus)** = *tantulus, so little, so small*, Plaut. Subst., **tantillum** -i, n. *so small a thing, such a trifle*, Plaut.

tantispě adv. (tantus). **I.** *so long*, foll. by dum; ut ibi esset *tant~* ~ dum culeus compararetur, Cic. **II.** *meanwhile*, Cic.

tantŏpěrě, or sep. **tanto ŏpěrě**, adv. *so greatly, so much;* discere, Cic.

tantŭlus -a -um (dim. of tantus), *so small, so little;* causa, Cic. Subst., **tantŭlum** -i, n. *so small a thing, such a trifle;* tantulo venierint, *at so small a price*, Cic.

tantum, v. tantus.

tantummŏdo, adv. *only;* ut tantummodo per stirpes alantur suas, Cic.

tantundem, v. tantusdem.

tantus -a -um, correl. adjectival pron. **I.** *of such size, so great;* a, foll. by quantus, nullam unquam vidi tantam (contionem), quanta nunc vestrûm est, Cic.; b, foll. by qui, quae, quod, gen. with subj., nulla est tanta vis, quae non frangi possit, Cic.; c, foll. by quam, Liv., Verg.; d, foll. by ut and the subj., non fuit tantus homo in civitate, ut de eo potissimum conqueramur, Cic.; e, without a correl., in tantis mutationibus, Cic.; tot tantaque vitia, Cic. **II.** *so much;* tanta pecunia, Cic.; 1, neut., tantum, subst., a, in nom. and acc., *so much;* (a) ut tantum nobis, quantum ipsi superesse posset, remitteret, Cic.; (β) with genit., auctoritatis, Cic.; b, in genit. of actual or moral value, *at such a price, so dear;* hortos emit tanti, quanti Pythius voluit, Cic.; esp., (a) aliquid or aliquis est tanti, *is worth so much;* tanti eius apud se gratiam esse, uti, etc., Caes.; (β) aliquid tanti est, *it is worth the while;* est mihi tanti, huius invidiae crimen subire, dummodo, etc., Cic.; c, abl. tanto; (a) before comparatives, *the more;* tanto nos submissius geramus, Cic.; (β) with adv. of time, tanto ante, *so long before,* Cic.; (γ) with verbs expressing a comparison, as praestare, Ov.; d, in tantum, *so far, so much;* in tantum suam felicitatem virtutemque enituisse, Liv.; 2, neut., tantum, as adv. = *so much, so far;* (a) with verbs, de quo tantum, quantum me amas, velim cogites, Cic.; (β) with adj., instead of tam, tantum magna, Hor. **III.** *of such a kind, so little, so small;* ceterarum provinciarum vectigalia tanta sunt, ut iis ad provincias tutandas vix contenti esse possimus, Cic.; neut., tantum, as subst. = *so little;* praesidii, Caes.; as adv. = *only;* nomen tantum virtutis usurpas, Cic.; tantum non, *all but*, Liv.; tantum quod; (a) *just*, Cic.; (β) *only;* tantum quod hominem non nominat, Cic.; non tantum . . . sed etiam, *not only . . . but also*, Liv.

tantusdem, tantādem, tantumdem and tantundem, *just so much, just so great;* neut. tantumdem or tantundem, *just so much;* a, in nom. and acc., magistratibus tantumdem detur in cellam, quantum semper datum est, Cic.; b, genit. of price, tantidem, Cic.

tăpētě -is, n. and **tăpētum** -i, n. (τάπης), *drapery, tapestry*, used for covering walls, floors, couches, etc., Verg. (abl. plur., tapetibus, Verg., Liv., Ov; tapetis, Verg.; acc. plur.. tapetas from unused nom. tapes, Verg.).

Tāprŏbănē -ēs, f. (Ταπροβάνη), *an island south of India, now Ceylon.*

tărandrus -i, m. *a rein-deer*, Plin.

Tarbelli -ōrum, m. *a people in Aquitania.*

tardē, adv. (tardus). **I.** *slowly ;* navigare, Cic. ; tardius moveri, Cic. : judicare, Cic. **II.** *late, not in tim* ; triennio tardius (*later*) triumphare, Cic. ; t. ssime perferri, Cic.

tardesco, 3. (tardus), *to become slow*, Lucr.

tardigrădus -a -um (tarde and gradior), *slowly stepping*, ap. Cic.

tardĭlŏquus -a -um (tarde and loquor), *slowly speaking*, Sen.

tardĭpes -pĕdis (tardus and pes), *slow footed ;* deus, *limping*, i.e., *Vulcan*, Cat.

tardĭtas -ātis, f. (tardus). **I.** *slowness, tardiness ;* a, of persons, plerisque in rebus gerendis tarditas et procrastinatio odiosa est, Cic. ; b, of things, *slowness, inactivity :* pedum, Cic. ; navium, Caes. ; esp., *slowness in speaking ;* cursum contentiones magis requirunt, expositiones rerum tarditatem, Cic. **II.** Transf., *mental and moral slowness, slothfulness, inertness, dulness, stupidity ;* ingenii, Cic.

tardĭtūdo -ĭnis, f. (tardus), *slowness*, Plaut.

tardĭuscŭlus -a -um (tardus), *somewhat slow, tardy*, Plaut.

tardo, 1. (tardus). **I.** Intransit., *to loiter, to be slow ;* num quid putes reipublicae nomine tardandum esse nobis, Cic. **II.** Transit., *to make slow, tardy, to hinder, delay, retard ;* cursum, Cic. ; with ab and the abl., aliquem a laude alicuius, Cic. ; with infin., ut reliqui hoc timore propius adire tardarentur, Caes.

tardus -a -um, *slow, tardy.* **I.** Lit., **1,** gen., **a**, of living creatures, pecus, Cic. ; homo, Cic. ; with in and the abl., in decedendo tardior, Cic. ; with ad and the acc., tardior ad discedendum, Cic. ; **b,** of things, tibicinis modi, Cic. ; vox, Cic. ; esp., (*a*) *coming late ;* poena, Cic. ; (*β*) *lasting a long time, lingering ;* menses, Verg. ; **2**, poet., *making slow ;* podagra, Hor. **II.** Transf., **a**, of persons, *slow of comprehension, dull, stupid ;* nimis indociles quidam tardique sunt, Cic. ; **b**, of things, *dull ;* ingenium, Cic. ; **c**, of speech or a speaker, *slow, measured, deliberate ;* in utroque genere dicendi principia tarda sunt, Cic.

Tărentum -i, n. and **Tărentus** -i, f. (Τάρας), *a wealthy town on the coast of Magna Graecia, founded by Spartan exiles,* 707 B.C., *famous for its purple dyes, now Taranto.* Hence, adj., **Tărentīnus** -a -um, *Tarentine ;* plur. subst., **Tărentīni** -ōrum, m. *inhabitants of Tarentum.*

tarmes -ĭtis, m. *a wood-worm*, Plaut.

Tarpējus -a -um, *name of a Roman family, the most celebrated member of which was Sp. Tarpejus, commander of the citadel at Rome, whose daughter Tarpeja was said to have admitted the Sabines into the citadel, and to have been crushed beneath their shields in reward.* Adj., *Tarpeian ;* lex, Cic. ; mons Tarpejus or saxum Tarpejum, *the Tarpeian rock, a peak of the Capitoline Hill, from which criminals were thrown ;* arx, *the Capitol*, Verg.

Tarquĭnĭi -ōrum, m. *an old town in Etruria, whence came the Tarquin family.* Hence, **A.** **Tarquĭnĭus** -a -um, **a,** *of Tarquinii*, name of two kings of Rome, Tarquinius Priscus and the last king of Rome, Tarquinius Superbus ; **b,** *belonging to the Tarquin family ;* nomen, Liv. **B.** **Tarquĭnĭensis** -e, *of Tarquinii.*

Tarrăcīna -ae, f. and **Tarrăcīnae** -ārum, f. *a town in Latium. formerly called Anxur. now*

Terracina ; flumen Terracinae = **Amasenus**, Liv. Hence, adj., **Tarrăcīnensis** -e, *of Tarracina.*

Tarrăco -ōnis, f. *a town in Spain, now Tarragona.* Hence, **Tarrăcōnensis** -e, *of Tarraco ;* Hispania Tarraconensis, *name of the north-east division of Spain.*

Tarsus -i, f. (Ταρσός), *the chief town of Cilicia, now Tarso.* Hence, adj., **Tarsensis** -e, *of or belonging to Tarsus.*

Tartărus (-ŏs) -i, m., plur., **Tartăra** ōrum, n. (Τάρταρος, plur., Τάρταρα), *the infernal regions.* Hence, adj., **Tartărĕus** -a -um, *Tartarean ;* custos, *Cerberus*, Verg. ; sorores, *the Furies*, Verg.

Tartessus (-ŏs) -i, f. (Ταρτησσός), *a town in Hispania Baetica, on the Baetis.* Hence, **Tartessĭus** -a -um, *Tartessian ;* litora, *on the Atlantic*, Ov.

tarum -i, n. *aloe-wood*, Plin.

Tarusātes -ĭum, m. *a people in Aquitania.*

tasconĭum -ĭi, n. *a white, clayey earth*, Plin.

tăt ! interj. *an exclamation of astonishment, what !* Plaut.

tăta -ae, m. *father*, in the lisping speech of children, Varr.

tătae = tat (q.v.).

Tătĭus -ĭi, m., Titus Tatius, *king of the Sabines, co-regent with Romulus.* Adj., **Tătĭus** -a -um, *of Tatius.*

Taulantĭi -ōrum, m. *a people of Illyria.*

taura -ae, f. (ταῦρα), *a barren cow*, Varr.

taurĕus -a -um (taurus), *of or relating to an ox ;* terga, *ox-hides*, Verg. ; meton., *a drum*, Ov. ; subst., **taurĕa** -ae, f. *a whip of bull's hide*, Juv.

Tauri -ōrum, m. *a people of Scythian descent, near the Crimea.* Adj., **Tauricus** -a -um, *Tauric.*

taurĭformis -e (taurus and forma), *shaped like a bull* (of the river Aufidus), *because rivergods were represented with the heads of oxen,* Hor.

Tauri ludi -ōrum, m. *games celebrated in the Circus Flaminius at Rome, in honour of the infernal deities*, Liv.

Taurīni -ōrum, m. *a people of Ligurian race in Gallia Cisalpina, with capital Augusta Taurinorum, whence Turin.* Hence, adj., **Taurīnus** -a -um, *of or relating to the Taurini.*

1. **taurīnus** -a -um (taurus), *of or relating to a bull ;* tergum, Verg. ; frons, Ov.

2. **Taurīnus** -a -um, v. Taurini.

Taurŏis -ŏentis, f. *a fort in Gallia Narbonensis, belonging to Massilia.*

Taurŏmĕnĭum (**Taurŏmĭnĭum**) -ĭi, n. *a town on the east coast of Sicily, now Taormina.* Hence, **Taurŏmĕnĭtānus** -a -um, *of or belonging to Tauromenium.*

Taurŏpŏlos, f. (Ταυροπόλος), *surname of Artemis (Diana).*

1. **taurus** -i, m. (ταῦρος), *a bull.* **I.** Lit., Cic. **II.** Transf., **1**, *the sign of the zodiac so called*, Verg. ; **2**, *the bull of Phalaris*, Cic. ; **3**, *a bird, perhaps a bittern*, Plin. ; **4**, *a kind of beetle*, Plin. ; **5**, *the root of a tree*, Quint.

2. **Taurus** -i, m. (Ταῦρος), *a high mountain-range in Asia, now Ala-Dagh or Al-Kurun.* Tauri Pylae, *a narrow pass between Cappadocia and Cilicia*, Cic.

tax = tuxtax (q.v.).

taxa -ae, f. *a species of laurel*, Plin.

taxātĭo -ōnis, f. (taxo), *a rating, valuing, appraising ;* eius rei taxationem facere, Cic.

taxĭcus -a -um (taxus), *of or relating to the yew-tree*, Plin.

taxillus -i, m. (root TAG, whence talus), *a small die*, Cic.

taxo, 1. (tago, tango), *to touch, to handle.* Fig., **A.** *to reproach, tax with a fault;* aliquem, Suet. **B.** *to estimate, rate, appraise the value of anything*, Suet.

taxus -i, f. *a yew-tree*, Caes.

Tāy̆gĕtē (Tāŭgĕtē) -ēs, f. (Ταϋγέτη), *daughter of Atlas, one of the Pleiads.*

Tāy̆gĕtus -i, m. (Ταϋγετον), and **Tāy̆gĕta** -ōrum, n. *a mountain between Laconia and Messenia.*

1. **tē**, v. tu.

2. **-tĕ**, pronominal suffix added to tu (v. tu).

Tĕānum -i, n. (Τέανον). **I.** Teanum Sidicinum, *a town in Campania*, now *Teano.* **II.** Teanum Apulum or Apulorum, *town in Apulia*, now *Ponte Rotto.* Hence, **Tĕānenses** -ium, m. *the inhabitants of Teanum.*

Tĕātes -um, m. *a people in Apulia.*

teba -ae, f. *a hill*, Varr.

techna -ae, f. (τέχνη), *a cunning trick, artifice*, Plaut.

technĭcus -i, m. (τεχνικός), *a teacher of any art*, Quint.

Tecmessa -ae, f. (Τέκμησσα), *daughter of Teuthras, mistress of the Telamonian Ajax.*

Tecmōn -ōnis, m. *a town in Cyprus.*

Tecta via, *a street in Rome, leading to the porta Capena.*

tectē, adv. with compar. (tectus), 1, *cautiously, securely*, Cic.; 2, *covertly, secretly*, Cic.

tector -ōris, m. (tego), *one who covers walls with plaster, stucco*, etc., *a plasterer*, Varr.

tectōrĭŏlum -i, n. (dim. of tectorium), *plaster or stucco work*, Cic.

tectōrĭus -a -um (tector), *used for covering.* **I.** Gen., paniculus, *straw for thatching*, Plaut. **II.** Esp., *relating to the plastering, stuccoing of walls;* hence, opus tectorium, and subst., **tectōrĭum** -ii, n. *plaster, stucco, fresco-painting;* concinnum, Cic.; transf., *of paste put on the face to preserve the complexion*, Juv.

Tectōsāges -um, m. and **Tectŏsāgi** -ōrum, m. *a people in Gallia Narbonensis, a branch of whom settled in Galatia, in Asia Minor.*

tectum -i, n. (tego), *a roof.* **I.** Lit., sub tectum congerere, Cic. **II.** Meton., *a roof, shelter, quarters, abode, dwelling;* ager sine tecto, Cic.; aliquem tecto ac domo invitare, Cic.; inter annos XIV tectum non subire, *had not come under a roof*, Caes.; Triviae tecta, *temple*, Verg.; Sibyllae, *grotto*, Verg.; doli tecti, *of the labyrinth*, Verg.

tectus -a -um, p. adj. (from tego), *covered.* **I.** Lit., naves, Liv.; scaphae, Caes. **II.** Fig., **A.** *concealed or concealing oneself, close, reserved, cautious;* quis tectior, Cic. **B.** *concealed;* a, *secret;* cupiditas, Cic.; b, *of speech, disguised, obscure;* verba, Cic.

Tĕgĕa -ae, f. (Τεγέα), *a city of Arcadia.* Hence, **A. Tĕgĕaeus (Tĕgĕēus)** -a -um, *Tegean*, and poet. = *Arcadian;* virgo, *Callisto, daughter of the Arcadian king Lycaon*, Ov.; aper, *the wild boar of Erymanthus*, Ov.; parens, *Carmenta, mother of Evander*, who is also called Tegeaea sacerdos, Ov.; domus, *of Evander*, Ov.; subst., **Tĕgĕaea** -ae, f. *Atalanta*, Ov. **B. Tĕgĕātes** -ae, m. *an inhabitant of Tegea.*

tĕges -ētis, f. (tego), *a mat, rug, covering*, Varr.

tĕgĕtĭcŭla -ae, f. (dim. of teges), *a little mat or rug*, Mart.

tĕgillum -i, n. (dim. of tegulum), *a small hood or cowl*, Plin.

tĕgĭmen (tĕgŭmen) and **tegmen** -ĭnis, n. (tego), *a cover, covering;* mihi amictui est Scythicum tegumen, Cic.; transf., *a shield;* quod tegumen modo omnis exercitus fuerat, Liv.

tĕgĭmentum (tĕgŭmentum) and **tegmentum** -i, n. (tego), *a covering;* tegimenta corporum vel texta vel suta, Cic.

tegmen = tegimen (q.v.).

tĕgo, texi, tectum, 3. (στέγω), *to cover.* **I.** Gen., amica corpus eius texit suo pallio, Cic.; casas stramentis, Caes. **II.** Esp., 1, *to bury, cover with earth;* ossa tegebat humus, Ov.; 2, *to cover, conceal, hide;* a, lit., ferae latibulis se tegunt, Cic.; b, transf., *to conceal, keep secret;* ut sententiam tegeremus, Cic.; 3, *to cover so as to protect, to shield;* a, lit., aliquem, Caes.; patriam, Cic.; b, fig., *to protect;* legatos ab ira, Liv.

tĕgŭla -ae, f. (tego), *a roofing-tile*, Cic.; plur., tegulae, frequently used for *roof;* per tegulas demitti, Cic.

tĕgŭlum -i, n. (tego), *a covering, roof*, Plin.

tĕgŭmentum = tegimentum (q.v.).

tĕgŭmen = tegimen (q.v.).

tēla -ae, f. (for texla, from texo). **I.** *a web, that which is woven;* Penelope telam retexens, Cic.; *a spider's web*, Cat.; fig., *a device;* ea tela texitur, Cic. **II.** Meton., 1, *the warp*, Verg.; 2, *the loom*, Ov.

Tĕlămo (-ōn) -ōnis, m. (Τελαμών), *one of the Argonauts, father of Ajax and Teucer.* Hence, **A. Tĕlămōnĭus** -a -um, *Telamonian;* subst., = *Ajax*, Ov. **B. Tĕlămōnĭădēs** -ae, m. *the son of Telamon*, i.e., *Ajax*, Ov.

Telchīnes -um, m. (Τελχῖνες), *a priestly family of Rhodes, famous for metal work, and notorious for their sorceries.*

Tĕlĕbŏae -ārum, m. (Τηλεβόαι), *a people in Acarnania, notorious for brigandage, a colony of whom settled in the island of Capreae.*

Tĕlĕgŏnos -i, m. (Τηλέγονος), *son of Ulysses and Circe, builder of Tusculum;* Telegoni moenia, *Tusculum*, Ov.; appell., **Tĕlĕgŏni** -ōrum, m. *of the love poems of Ovid* (which were destructive to him their author, just as Telegonus killed his father Ulysses).

Tĕlĕmăchus -i, m. (Τηλέμαχος), *son of Ulysses and Penelope.*

Tĕlĕphus -i, m. (Τήλεφος), *son of Hercules, king in Mysia, wounded by the spear of Achilles, but healed by its rust.*

Tĕlĕthūsa -ae, f. *mother of Iphis.*

tēlīnum -i, n. (τήλινον), *a costly salve made of the herb fenugreek*, Plin.

tēlis -is, f. (τῆλις), *the herb fenugreek*, Plin.

Tellēna -ōrum, n. *a town in Latium.*

tellus -ūris, f. **I.** *the earth;* 1, lit., Cic.; esp., *the earth, soil, as bearing fruits*, humida, Ov.; 2, transf., poet., a, *land, district, country;* Gnossia, Verg.; b, *land, possessions;* propria, Hor.; c, *land = people;* Pontica tellus, Ov. **II.** Personif., Tellus, *the Earth, as the all-nourishing goddess*, Cic.

Telmessus (-ŏs) -i, f. (Τελμησσός), *an old town in Lycia on the borders of Caria.* Hence, **A. Telmesses** -ium, m. *the inhabitants of Telmessus.* **B. Telmessĭcus** -a -um, *of or relating to Telmessus.* **C. Telmessĭus** -a -um, *Telmessian.*

tēlum -i, n. *a missile, dart, javelin, spear.* **I.** 1, lit., a, arma atque tela militaria, Sall. ; tela intendere, excipere, Cic. ; **b**, *a sword, dagger,* etc., *weapon;* stare cum telo, Cic. ; used of the cestus, Verg. ; of the horns of a bull, Ov. ; 2, transf., *the beams of the sun;* tela diei, Lucr. ; *lightning;* arbitrium est in sua tela Jovi, Ov. **II.** Fig., *weapon, arrow, dart, arms;* tela fortunae, Cic. ; isto telo tutabimur plebem, Liv.

Tĕmĕnos (τέμενος, τό), *a place at Syracuse, where was a grave sacred to Apollo.* Hence, **Tĕmĕnītēs** -ae, m. (Τεμενίτης), *of Temenos;* Apollo, *a statue of Apollo,* Cic.

tĕmĕrārĭus -a -um (temere). **I.** *by chance, fortuitous, casual,* Plaut. **II.** *inconsiderate, thoughtless, indiscreet, rash, imprudent;* homo, Caes.; consilium, Liv.; bella, Ov.; cupiditas, Cic.

tĕmĕrē, adv. *by chance, accidentally, casually, fortuitously, rashly, heedlessly, without purpose.* **I.** Gen., equo temere acto, Liv. ; domus quae temere et nullo consilio administratur, Cic.; nihil temere, nihil imprudenter factum, Caes. **II.** Esp., **A.** non temere est, *it is not for nothing that, it is not without importance or meaning,* Verg. **B.** non temere, *not easily;* qui hoc non temere nisi libertis suis deferebant, Cic.

tĕmĕrĭtas -ātis, f. (temere). **I.** *chance, accident;* temeritas et casus, non ratio nec consilium valet, Cic. **II.** *rashness, inconsiderateness, temerity* in action ; *an inconsiderate, unfounded opinion,* in judgment ; temeritas cupiditasque militum, Caes.; numquam temeritas cum sapientia commiscetur, Cic.

tĕmĕro, 1. (temere), *to defile, dishonour, pollute;* templa, Verg. ; thalamos, Ov.

Tĕmēsa -ae, f., **Tĕmēsē** -ēs, f., and **Tempsa (Temsa)** -ae, f. (Τεμέση, Τέμψα), *an old town in Bruttium, famous for its copper mines.* Hence, **A. Tĕmēsaeus** -a -um, *Temesean.* **B. Tĕmēsēĭus** -a -um, *Temesean.* **C. Tempsānus** -a -um, *Tempsan.*

tēmētum -i, n. (root temum, whence temulentus), *any intoxicating drink, wine,* Cic.

temno, tempsi, 3. *to despise, contemn;* vulgaria, Hor.

Temnŏs -i, f. (Τῆμνος), *a town in Aeolia,* now *Menimen.* Hence, **A. Temnĭtēs** -ae, m. *of Temnos.* **B. Temnĭī** -ōrum, m. *the inhabitants of Temnos.*

tēmo -ōnis, m. (tendo), *a pole;* **1**, lit., a, of a waggon, Verg. ; **b**, of a plough, *a plough-beam,* Verg. ; 2, meton., a, *a waggon;* **b**, *the constellation of Charles's Wain,* Cic. poet.

Tempē, neut. plur. (Τέμπη, τά). **I.** *a valley in Thessaly, famous for its beauty, through which the river Peneus flowed.* **II.** Transf., *any beautiful valley,* Ov., Verg.

tĕmpĕrāmentum -i, n. (tempero). **I.** *a right proportion of things mixed together ;* eadem est materia, sed distat temperamento, Plin. **II.** *a middle way, mean, moderation;* inventum est temperamentum, quo tenuiores cum principibus aequari se putarent, Cic.

tĕmpĕrans -antis, p. adj. (from tempero), *moderate, temperate, continent, self-denying;* homo, Cic. ; homo temperantissimus, Cic. ; with ab and the abl., temperantior a cupidine imperii, Liv.

tĕmpĕrantĕr, adv. with compar. (temperans), *temperately, moderately ;* temperantius agere, Cic.

tĕmpĕrantĭa -ae, f. (temperans), *temperance, moderation, sobriety, continence;* temperantia in praetermittendis voluptatibus cernitur, Cic.

tĕmpĕrātē, adv. (temperatus), *moderately, temperately ;* agere, Cic. ; temperatius scribere, Cic.

tĕmpĕrātĭo -ōnis, f. (tempero). **I.** *temperateness, moderation, just proportion, proper mixture of ingredients, constitution, organisation;* caeli, Cic. ; caloris, Cic. ; corporum, Cic.; civitatis, reipublicae, Cic. **II.** Concr., *the organising principle;* sol mens mundi et temperatio, Cic.

tĕmpĕrātor -ōris, m. (tempero), *one who arranges or governs;* varietatis, Cic.

tĕmpĕrātūra -ae, f. (tempero), *proper mixture, temperature, organisation,* Plin.

tĕmpĕrātus -a -um, p. adj. (from tempero). **I.** *properly arranged ;* prela, Cato. **II.** *ordered, moderate ;* a, esca, Cic. ; loca temperatiora, Caes.; b, fig., *moderate, mild, quiet, temperate ;* homo temperatissimus, Cic.; oratio temperatior, Cic.

tĕmpĕrī, temperius, v. tempus.

tĕmpĕrĭēs -ēi, f. (tempero), *a proper mixture, preparation, organisation, tempering ;* temperiem sumpsere humorque calorque, Ov.

tĕmpĕro, 1. (tempus, *a section*), *to set bounds to a thing, keep within limits.* **I.** Intransit., *to observe proper limits, be temperate;* 1, gen., in multa, Liv. ; with dat., *to control, keep back, use with moderation ;* victoriae, Sall. ; linguae, Liv. ; with abl., risu, Liv. ; with ab and the abl., *to keep from, refrain from ;* ab injuria, Caes. ; sibi non temperare and simply non or vix temperare, foll. by quominus or quin and subj., *not to refrain from ;* neque sibi temperaturos existimabat, quin in provinciam exirent, Caes. ; 2, esp., *to spare,* with dat.; hostibus superatis, Cic. **II.** Transit., 1, a, *to distribute or mix properly,* to *temper ;* acuta cum gravibus, Cic. ; b, esp., *to mix a drink, prepare ;* poculum, Hor. ; 2, a, *to regulate;* rempublicam legibus, Cic.; b, *to rule;* res hominum ac deorum, Hor.; 3, *to temper, make mild ;* calores solis, Cic. ; aequor, Verg.

tempestas -ātis, f. (tempus). **I.** *a space or period of time, season;* eā tempestate, *at that time,* Sall. ; eādem tempestate, Cic. ; multis ante tempestatibus, Liv. **II.** *weather.* **A.** Gen., bona, certa, Cic. ; clara, Verg. ; turbulenta, Cic.; perfrigida, Cic. ; tempestates, *kind of weather,* Cic. **B.** *bad weather, storm, tempest ;* 1, lit., immoderatae tempestates, Cic.; 2, fig., *storm, tempest, attack, fury ;* invidiae, Cic.; querelarum, Cic. ; telorum, Cic. ; *of persons,* Siculorum tempestas (of Verres), Cic. ; turbo ac tempestas pacis (of Clodius), Cic.

tempestīvē, adv. with compar. (tempestivus), *at the right time, seasonably ;* tempestive caedi (of trees), Cic. ; tempestivius in domum Pauli comissabere, Hor.

tempestīvĭtas -ātis, f. (tempestivus), *the fit time, proper season ;* sua cuique parti aetatis tempestivitas est data, Cic.

tempestīvō = tempestive (q. v.).

tempestīvus -a -um (tempus). **I.** *happening at the right time, opportune, seasonable, fit, appropriate.* **A.** nondum tempestivo ad navigandum mari, Cic. ; oratio, Liv. ; multa mihi ad mortem tempestiva fuere, *convenient opportunities for,* Cic. **B.** *early ;* cena, convivium, Cic. **II.** a, *of fruit, in season, ripe ;* fructus, Cic.; b, *of persons, ripe, mature;* puella tempestiva viro, *ripe for marriage,* Hor.

templum -i, n. (= tempulum, dim. of tempus), lit., *a section, a part cut off.* **I.** *a space in the sky or on the earth marked out by the augur for the purpose of taking auspices,* Liv. **II.** Transf., **A.** *a place from which one can survey ;*

a, *a prospect, range of vision ;* deus, cuius hoc templum est omne quod conspicis, Cic. ; **b**, *a height ;* templa Parnassia, *the Mount Parnassus,* Ov. **B.** *a consecrated piece of ground ;* **a**, gen., *any consecrated spot, a sanctuary, asylum,* Liv. ; of a chapel dedicated to the dead, Verg. ; of the curia, because consecrated by an augur ; curia, templum publici consilii, Cic.; *the tribunal,* Cic.; transf., of any clear, open space ; mundi, Lucr.; fig., = *the interior ;* templa mentis, Cic. ; **b**, esp., *a place dedicated to a particular deity, a temple ;* Jovis, Cic.

tempŏrālis -e (tempus), *temporary, lasting for a time ;* laudes, Tac.

tempŏrārĭus -a -um (tempus). **I.** *temporary,* Plin. **II.** *seasonable, adapted to time and circumstances,* Nep.

tempŏri, v. tempus.

Tempsa, Tempsanus, v. Temesa.

tempus -ŏris, n. (τέμνω, *to cut off*), *a division, section ;* hence, **I.** *a division of time, section of time, period of time.* **A.** Lit., extremum tempus diei, Cic. ; matutina tempora, *the morning hours,* Cic. ; hibernum tempus anni, Cic. ; hoc tempore, Cic. ; omni tempore, Cic.; in tempus praesens, *for the present,* Cic. ; ex tempore, *without preparation,* Cic. ; ad tempus, *for a time,* Cic. **B.** Transf., **1**, *a distinct point of time ;* abiit illud tempus, Cic.; ad tuum tempus, *up to your consulship,* Cic. ; tempus est, with infin., *it is high time to ;* tempus est dicere, Cic.; with acc. and infin., tempus est jam hinc abire me, Ov.; **2**, *time as a whole ;* tempus ponere in re, *to spend,* Cic. ; in omne tempus, *for all time,* Cic. ; **3**, *a proper, fit time, occasion, opportunity ;* tempus amittere, Cic. ; tempus habere, Cic. ; ad tempus, *at the right time,* Cic. ; old abl., tempori or temperi, *at the right time, seasonably,* Cic. ; compar., temperius, Cic. ; **4**, **a**, *the state, condition of things ;* freq. plur., *the times ;* temporibus servire, Cic. ; **b**, *the circumstances of a thing* or *person ;* reipublicae, Cic. ; esp., *calamitous circumstances, misfortune, calamity ;* scripsi de temporibus meis, Cic. ; **5**, *time in pronouncing a syllable, quantity,* Cic. ; **6**, *time in grammar, tense of a verb,* Varr. **II.** *the temple on the forehead,* Verg. ; plur., *the temples,* Verg. ; poet., *the face,* Prop. ; *the head,* Prop.

Tempȳra -ōrum, n. *a town in Thrace, between Mt. Rhodope and the coast.*

Temsa = Temesa (q.v.).

tēmŭlentĭa -ae, f. (temulentus), *drunkenness, intoxication,* Plin.

tēmŭlentus -a -um (temum, whence temetum), *drunken, intoxicated, tipsy ;* of persons, Cic. ; of things, vox, Cic.

tĕnācĭtas -ātis, f. (tenax). **I.** *a firm holding, tenacity ;* unguium tenacitate arripiunt, Cic. **II.** *frugality, stinginess,* Liv.

tĕnācĭtĕr, adv. (tenax). **I.** *firmly, tenaciously ;* premere, Ov. **II.** Transf., *constantly, firmly ;* miseros urgere, Ov.

tĕnax -ācis (teneo), *holding fast, griping, tenacious.* **I.** Lit., **A.** Gen., forceps, Verg. ; dens (of an anchor), Verg. **B.** Esp., **a**, *holding fast to possessions, money,* etc., *sparing, frugal, stingy ;* pater parcus et tenax, Cic.; with genit., quaesiti tenax, Ov.; **b**, *holding firmly together, sticky, gluey ;* gramen, *matted,* Hor. ; cerae, Verg. **II.** Transf., **A.** Gen., *firm, steadfast ;* longa tenaxque fides, Ov. **B.** Esp., of character, **a**, in a good sense, *firm, resolute, steadfast, holding to ;* with genit., propositi, Hor.; **b**, in a bad sense, *obstinate ;* equus, Liv. ; ira, Ov.

Tenctĕri -ōrum and -ûm, m. *a German people on the Rhine.*

tendĭcŭla -ae, f. (tendo), *a gin, noose, snare ;* fig., aucupia verborum et litterarum tendiculae, Cic.

tendo, tĕtendi, tentum and tensum, 3. (root TEN, whence τείνω, *to stretch*), *to stretch, stretch out, extend.* **I.** Act., **A.** 1, lit., plagas, Cic. ; arcum, Verg.; **2**, meton., **a**, *to pitch (a tent) ;* praetorium, Caes.; **b**, *to string ;* barbiton, Hor.; **c**, *to direct ;* iter ad naves, Verg.; sagittas arcu, *to shoot,* Hor. ; **d**, *to reach, present ;* parvum patri Iulum, Verg. **B.** Fig., **1**, gen., alicui insidias, *to lay snares for,* Cic. ; **2**, *to present, give ;* spem amicis porrigere atque tendere, Cic. **II.** Reflex. (with or without se) and middle, **A.** Lit., 1 (without se), *to stretch out ;* milit. t. t., *to pitch one's tent,* encamp, Caes., Verg. ; in iisdem castris, Liv.; 2 (without se), *to direct one's course to, tend towards, go towards, march towards ;* **a**, of persons, Venusiam, Cic. ; ad aedes, Hor. ; unde venis? et quo tendis? Hor.; **b**, of inanimate things, simulacra viis de rectis omnia tendunt, Lucr.; **3**, of places, reflex. (with and gen. without se), or middle, *to stretch towards, extend to ;* via tendit sub moenia, Verg. **B.** Transf. (reflex without se), 1, **a**, *to have recourse to ;* ad alienam opem quisque inops tendere, Liv.; **b**, *to be inclined, tend in any direction, aim at, strive after ;* ad reliqua alacri tendebamus animo, Cic. ; foll. by infin., *to try, attempt ;* manibus divellere nodos, Verg. ; praevenire, Liv. ; **2**, *to strive, contend against ;* **a**, with arms, summa vi, Sall.; **b**, with words, etc., *to contend for, strive for ;* quod summa vi ut tenderent, amicis mandaverat, Liv.; with ut and the subj., ut delectum haberet, Liv. ; with acc. of pron., quid tendit? *what is he striving for?* Cic.

tĕnēbrae -ārum, f. *darkness.* **I.** Lit., **a**, Cic. ; tetris tenebris, Cic. ; **b**, esp., *the darkness of the night, night ;* quomodo redissem luce, non tenebris, Cic. ; **2**, **a**, *darkness = blindness ;* tenebras et cladem lucis ademptae objicit, Ov. ; **b**, *the darkness before the eyes in fainting ;* tenebris nigrescunt omnia circum, Verg. ; **c**, *the darkness of death,* Plaut. ; **3**, meton., *a dark place ;* of the lower world, Stygiae, Verg. ; absol., Verg., Ov. ; of a prison, clausi in tenebris, Sall. ; of a hiding-place, quum illa conjuratio ex latebris atque ex tenebris erupisset, Cic. **II.** Transf., 1, *obscurity, inglorious condition ;* vestram familiam obscuram e tenebris in lucem evocavit, Cic.; 2, *darkness, gloom, obscurity ;* latent ista omnia crassis occultata in tenebris, Cic.

tĕnēbricōsus -a -um (tenebricus), *dark, gloomy, shrouded in darkness, obscure ;* illud tenebricosissimum tempus ineuntis aetatis tuae, Cic.

tĕnēbrĭcus -a -um (tenebrae), *dark, gloomy,* Cic. poet.

tĕnēbrōsus -a -um (tenebrae), *dark, gloomy ;* palus, Verg.

Tĕnēdus (-ŏs) -i, f. (Τένεδος), *an island in the Aegean Sea, near Troy,* now *Tenedo.* Hence, **Tĕnēdĭus** -a -um, *belonging to Tenedos.*

tĕnellŭlus -a -um (dim. of tenellus), *exceedingly tender, delicate,* Cat.

tĕnellus -a -um (dim. of tener), *very tender, delicate,* Plaut.

tĕnĕo, tĕnŭi, tentum, 2. (root TEN, whence tendo, τείνω, *to hold.* **I.** Gen., **A.** 1, lit., pyxidem in manu, Cic. ; pateram dexterā manu, Cic. ; cibum ore, Cic. ; 2, transf., **a**, gen., res oculis et manibus tenetur, *is visible and tangible,* Cic. ; rem manu tenere, *to have al one's fingers' ends, to understand thoroughly,* Cic.; **b**, *to hold in the mind, to understand, grasp, know ;* quae et saepe audistis et tenetis animis, Cic. ; quibus rebus capiatur Caesar, tenes, Cic.

B. Meton., **1,** *to reach a place, arrive at, land on;* regionem, Liv. ; transf., per cursum rectum regnum, Cic. ; **2,** *to direct;* **a,** oculos sub astra, Verg. ; **b,** *to direct one's course;* quo tenetis iter? Verg. ; intransit., of ships, *to sail to;* ad Mendaeum, Liv. **II.** With the notion of property, *to hold in one's possession, have, possess;* **1,** lit., **a,** multa hereditatibus, multa emptionibus tenebantur sine injuria, Cic. ; **b,** milit. t. t., *to occupy, garrison;* locum praesidiis, montem, portum, Caes. ; **2,** transf., of persons as objects, te jam tenet altera conjux, Ov. ; *to possess as a ruler,* terras, Hor.; imperium, Caes.; qui tenent (sc. rempublicam), *the rulers of the state,* Cic. **III.** With the notion of firmness, *to hold fast;* **1,** lit., **a,** ut quo major se vis aquae incitavisset, hoc artius illigata tenerentur, Caes.; **b,** as milit. **t. t.,** *to defend, keep;* suum locum, tumulum, Caes. ; **2,** transf., **a,** *to hold fast in the mind;* memoriam alicuius, Cic. ; memoriâ tenere = *to remember,* foll. by acc. and infin., Cic. ; **b,** *to catch, detect;* teneo te, Cic. ; teneri in manifesto peccato, Cic. ; **c,** of passions, *to possess, master;* misericordia me tenet, Cic. ; magna spes me tenet, with acc. and infin., Cic.; **d,** *to charm, amuse;* varias mentes carmine, Verg.; pueri ludis tenentur, oculi picturā tenentur, Cic. ; **e,** *to bind;* leges eum tenent, Cic. ; lege, foedere, promisso teneri, Cic. ; **f,** *to hold fast, preserve;* auctoritatem, imperium in suos, Cic.; causam apud centum viros, *to gain,* Cic. ; **g,** *to maintain a proposition;* illud arte tenent accurateque defendunt, voluptatem esse summum bonum, Cic. **IV.** With the notion of endurance or quiet, *to preserve, keep.* **A.** Gen., **a,** lit., terra tenetur nutu suo, Cic. ; **b,** transf., aliquem in officio, Cic. **B.** Esp., **1,** transit., *to keep to, not to swerve from;* **a,** lit., cursum, Caes., Cic.; absol., medio tutissimus ibis, inter utrumque tene, *hold your course,* Ov.; **b,** transf., *to observe, remain true to;* ordinem, fidem, Cic. ; **2,** intransit., *to last, endure, keep on;* imber per totam noctem tenuit, Liv. ; fama tenet, *the report holds,* with acc. and infin., Liv. **V.** With the notion of motion checked, *to hold fast.* **A.** *to keep in, hold back;* **1,** lit., manus ab aliquo, Ov. ; aliquem or se domi, *to keep at home,* Liv. ; se castris, Caes. ; se oppido, Cic. ; **2,** transf., *to restrain, suppress, check, hold back;* risum, dolorem, iracundiam, Cic. ; lacrimas, Cic. ; se ab accusando, *to refrain from,* Cic. ; se non tenere, or se tenere non posse quin, etc., *not to be able to refrain from,* Cic. **B.** *to detain;* **1,** lit., septimum jam diem Corcyrae teneri, Cic. ; **2,** transf., non teneo te pluribus, Cic. **VI.** With the notion of containing, *to contain, comprise;* in pass., teneri aliquā re, *to be contained in, to belong to;* si Asia hoc imperio non teneretur, Cic.

tĕner -ĕra -ĕrum, *tender, delicate, soft.* **I.** Lit., **1,** gen., caules, Hor. ; uva, Verg. ; **2,** esp., *tender, youthful, young;* saltator, Cic. ; a teneris, ut Graeci dicunt, unguiculis, *from childhood,* Cic. ; subst., in teneris, *in childhood,* Verg. **II.** Transf., *tender, soft, effeminate;* tenerum quiddam atque molle in animis, Cic. ; tenerior animus, Cic.

tĕnĕrasco, 3. (tener), *to grow tender, delicate, soft,* Plin.

tĕnĕrē, adv. with compar. and superl. (tener), *tenderly, delicately, softly,* Plin.

tĕnĕrĭtas -ātis, f. (tener), *tenderness, softness;* in primo ortu inest teneritas et mollities, Cic.

tĕnĕrĭtūdo = teneritas (q.v.).

tēnesmos -i, m. (τειρεσμός), *a straining at stool,* Nep.

tĕnor -ōris, m. (teneo), *course, continued*

course, Cic. **I.** Lit., hasta servat tenorem, Verg. **II.** Transf., *uninterrupted course, duration,* tenor, career; tenorem pugnae servabant, Liv. ; fati, Ov.; vitae, Liv. ; adv., uno tenore, *in an uninterrupted course, uniformly,* Cic.

Tēnus (-ŏs) -i, f. (Τῆνος), *one of the Cyclades Islands,* now *Tino.* Hence, **Tēnĭi** -ōrum, m. *the inhabitants of Tenos.*

tensa -ae, f. *a car on which the images of the gods were carried at the Circensian games,* Cic.

tensĭo -ōnis, f. (tendo), *a stretching, tension,* Plin.

tensus -a -um, partic. of tendo (q.v.).

tentābundus (temptābundus) -a -um (tento), *trying, attempting,* Liv.

tentāmen (temptāmen) -ĭnis, n. (tento), *a trial, attempt,* Ov.

tentāmentum (temptāmentum) -i, n. (tento), *a trial, attempt, test, essay,* Verg., Ov.

tentātĭo (temptātĭo) -ōnis, f. (tento). **I.** *an attack;* novae tentationes, *new attacks of disease,* Cic. **II.** *a trial, test,* Liv.

tentātor (temptātor) -ōris, m. (tento), *a tempter,* Hor.

tentĭgo -ĭnis, f. (tendo), *lecherousness,* Hor.

tento (tempto), **1.** (intens. of tendo), *to touch, feel, handle.* **I.** Gen., **1,** lit., pectora manibus, Ov.; flumen pede, Cic. ; venas, *to feel the pulse,* Quint. ; **2,** transf., **a,** *to try, prove, test;* alicuius patientiam, Cic. ; se, Cic. ; **b,** *to try, attempt;* oppugnationem eius castelli, Liv. ; belli fortunam, Cic. ; Thetim ratibus, Verg.; with rel. sent., tentavi, quid in eo genere possem, Cic.; with ut and the subj., quum ille Romuli senatus tentaret, ut ipse gereret rempublicam, Cic.; with infin., irasci, Verg. **II.** *to attack, assail;* **1,** lit., Achaiam, Caes.; castra, Liv.; of diseases, morbo tentari, Cic. ; **2,** transf., *to work upon, tamper with a person, tempt, excite, disturb;* animos spe et metu, Cic. ; judicium pecuniā, *to try to bribe,* Cic.

tentōrĭŏlum -i, n. (dim. of tentorium), *a little tent,* Auct. b. Afr.

tentōrĭum -ĭi, n. (tendo), *a tent,* Liv.

tentus -a -um, partic. of tendo and teneo.

Tentȳra -ōrum, n. (Τέντυρα), *a town in Upper Egypt,* now *Denderah.*

tĕnŭĭcŭlus -a -um (dim. of tenuis), *very poor, mean, miserable;* apparatus, Cic.

tĕnŭis -e (root TEN). **I.** *thin, fine, slight, slender.* **A.** Lit., **1,** gen., collum, Cic. ; acus, Ov. ; **2,** esp., **a,** *small, narrow;* litus, Liv. ; **b,** *shallow;* unda, Ov.; sulcus, Verg.; **c,** *bright, clear;* aqua, Ov. **B.** Fig., **a,** *thin, plain, simple;* argumentandi genus, Cic. ; **b,** *fine, subtle;* distinctio, Cic. **II.** Transf., *weak, poor, miserable, unimportant, little, slight.* **A.** Lit., oppidum, Cic.; opes, Cic.; praeda, Caes.; transf., of persons, *poor, needy,* Cic. **B.** Fig., **a,** *poor, weak, feeble;* valetudo tenuissima, Caes. ; causa tenuis et inops, Cic. ; spes, Cic. ; **b,** of birth or position, *low, mean;* qui tenuioris ordinis essent, Cic. ; transf., of persons, tenues homines, Cic. ; Subst., tenuiores, *persons of lower rank,* Cic.

tĕnŭĭtas -ātis, f. (tenuis). **I.** *thinness, fineness.* **A.** Lit., **1,** gen., animi, Cic. ; **2,** esp., *leanness;* tenuitas ipsa delectat, Cic. **B.** Fig., *simplicity, plainness;* rerum et verborum, Cic. **II.** Transf., *miserable condition, poverty;* aerarii, Cic. ; hominis, Cic.

tĕnŭĭter, adv. (tenuis). **I.** *thinly.* **A.** Lit., alutae tenuiter confectae, Caes. **B.** Fig., *plainly, simply;* disserere, Cic. **II.** Transf., *sparingly.* **A.** Lit., Ter. **B.** Fig., *lightly;* tenuissime aestimare, Cic.

tĕnŭo, 1. (tenuis). **I.** *to make thin, fine, slender, meagre, to attenuate;* 1, lit., assiduo vomer tenuatur ab usu, Ov.; 2, esp., a, *to make thin;* armenta macie, Verg.; b, *to contract;* vocis via est tenuata, Ov. **II.** Fig., *to weaken, lessen, diminish, enfeeble;* iram, Ov.; vires, Ov.

1. **tĕnŭs -ŏris,** n. (root TEN, whence tendo), *a noose, gin, springe,* Plaut.

2. **tĕnŭs,** prep. with abl. and genit. (connected with teneo, tendo, τείνω), *up to, as far as.* **I.** Of place, a, with genit., crurum tenus, Verg.; Corcyrae tenus, Liv.; b, with abl., Tauro tenus regnare, Cic.; cadi faece tenus poti, Hor. **II.** Transf., est quadam prodire tenus, si non datur ultra, *up to a certain point,* Hor.; vulneribus tenus, Liv.; verbo tenus, *in name, nominally,* Cic.

Tĕŏs -i, f. (Τέως), *a town on the coast of Ionia, birthplace of Anacreon;* hence, **Tējus -a -um,** and **Tēïus -a -um,** *Teian,* poet. = *Anacreontic,* Ov.

tĕpĕfăcĭo -fēci -factum, 3., pass., **tĕpĕfīo** factus sum -fĭĕri (tepeo and facio), *to make warm, to warm, heat;* sol tepefaciat solum, Cic.

tĕpĕo, 2. *to be lukewarm, tepid.* **I.** Lit., hiems tepet, Hor.; partic., tepens, *warm; aurae,* Verg. **II.** Fig. 1, *to be warm with love;* aliquo, *for some one,* Hor.; 2, *to be only lukewarm in love;* seu tepet, sive amat, Ov.

tĕpesco, tĕpŭi, 3. (tepeo). **A.** *to grow warm;* maria agitata ventis ita tepescunt, ut, etc., Cic. **B.** *to lose warmth, grow cool,* Mart.

tephrĭas -ae, m. (τεφρίας), *a species of ashcoloured stone,* Plin.

tĕpĭdē, adv. (tepidus), *lukewarmly,* Plin.

tĕpĭdo, 1. (tepidus), *to make lukewarm,* Plin.

tĕpĭdus -a -um (tepeo). **I.** *lukewarm, tepid;* bruma, Hor. **II.** *lukewarm, cooling;* 1, lit., focus, Ov.; 2, fig., *wanting in ardour;* ignes, mens, Ov.

tĕpor -ŏris, m. (tepeo). **I.** *lukewarmness, a moderate heat;* solis, Liv.; maris, Cic. **II.** Fig., of discourse, *want of fire,* Tac.

Tĕpŭla ăqua, *a stream of water which was brought to the Capitol at Rome,* Plin.

tĕr, adv. num. (tres), *three times, thrice.* **I.** Lit., ter in anno, Cic. **II.** Meton., a, *often, repeatedly;* Aeneam magnā ter voce vocavit, Verg.; b, = *very;* ter felix, Ov.

terdĕcĭēs (terdĕcĭens), adv. *thirteen times,* Cic.

tĕrĕbinthĭnus -a -um (τερεβίνθινος), *of the terebinth-tree,* Plin.

tĕrĕbinthus -i, f. (τερέβινθος), *the terebinth-tree,* Verg.

tĕrĕbra -ae, f. (tero), *a gimlet, borer,* Cato.

tĕrĕbro, 1. (terebra), *to bore through, pierce, perforate;* latebras uteri, Verg.

tĕrēdo -ĭnis, f. (τερηδών), *a worm that gnaws wood,* Ov.

Tĕrentĭus -a -um, *the name of a Roman gens, of which the most celebrated were:* 1, C. Terentius Varro, *consul* 216 B.C., *defeated by Hannibal at Cannae;* 2, M. Terentius Varro, *born* 116 B.C., *a celebrated grammarian, contemporary of Cicero;* 3, P. Terentius Afer, *freedman of P. Terentius Lucanus, the celebrated Roman comic dramatist, contemporary of Laelius and Scipio Africanus;* 4, Terentia, *the wife of Cicero.* Adj., **Tĕrentĭus -a -um,** *Terentian;* lex, *law proposed by the consuls Cassius and M. Terentius.* Hence, **Tĕrentĭānus -a -um,** *Terentian;* exercitus, *of C. Terentius Varro,* Liv.; Chremes, *appearing in the comedies of Terence,* Cic.

Tĕrentum (Tărentum) -i, n., **Tĕrentŏs (-us),** and **Tărentŏs (-us) -i,** m. *a place in the Campus Martius, where the ludi saeculares were held.* Hence, **Tĕrentīnus -a -um,** *Terentine.*

tĕrĕs -rĕtis, abl. -rĕti (root TER, Gr. TEP, τείρω), *rounded, polished, well-turned.* **I.** stipes, Caes.; gemma, Verg.; hence, fig., sapiens in se ipso totus teres atque rotundus, Hor. **II.** *firmly-woven;* plagae, Hor. **III.** Of the parts of the body, *well-turned, slender, graceful;* 1, lit., cervix, Lucr.; sura, Hor.; 2, fig., *polished, refined elegant;* aures, oratio, Cic.

Tēreus -ĕi and **-ĕos,** m. (Τηρεύς), *king in Thrace, husband of Procne, sister of Philomela, father of Itys, who outraged Philomela, and for punishment was changed into a hoopoe.* Hence, **Tēreïdēs -ae,** m. (Τηρείδης), *the son of Tereus* i.e., *Itys.*

tergĕmĭnus = trigeminus (q.v.).

tergĕo and **tergo,** tersi, tersum -ēre and -ēre (root TER, whence tero), *to wipe, wipe off, dry, clean,* Cic.; lumina lacrimantia tersit, Ov.; specula, *to polish,* Verg.; arma, Liv.

Tergestē -is, n. *a town in Istria,* now *Trieste.* Hence, **Tergestīnus -a -um,** *Tergestine.*

tergĭnum -i, n. (tergum), *a whip of leather, thong for scourging,* Plaut.

tergĭversātĭo -ōnis, f. (tergiversor), *backwardness, reluctance, delay;* mora et tergiversatio, Cic.

tergĭversor, 1. dep. (tergum and verto), *to turn the back,* hence, *to be reluctant, shuffle, find excuses, to delay;* quid taces? quid dissimules? quid tergiversaris? Cic.

tergŏro, 1. (tergus), *to cover,* Plin.

tergo = tergeo (q.v.).

tergum -i, n. *the back.* **I.** Lit., Cic.; terga dare, Liv., vertere, Caes., *to turn one's back, flee;* a tergo, *from behind,* Cic.; praebere terga Phoebo, *to sun oneself,* Ov.; plur., terga, meton. = *flight;* terga Parthorum dicam, Ov. **II.** Transf. 1, *the hindmost part of a thing;* castris ab tergo vallum objectum, *from behind,* Liv.; 2, *the surface of anything;* e.g., of a field, *the earth ploughed up between the furrows,* Verg.; of a river, Ov.; 3, *a covering;* clipei, Verg.; 4, *a body;* centum terga suum, *a hundred swine,* Verg.; 5, *the hide, skin;* a, lit., taurinum, Verg.; b, meton., *things made out of hide;* Sulmonis, *shield,* Verg.; duro intendere brachia tergo, *the cestus,* Verg.

tergus -ŏris, n. *the back.* **I.** Lit., Prop. **II.** Transf., 1, *the body of an animal,* Ov.; 2, *skin, hide, leather,* Verg.

Tĕrina -ae, f. *a town in Bruttii, near modern Eufemia.* Hence, **Tĕrīnaeus -a -um,** *of or belonging to Terina.*

termes -ĭtis, m. *a branch cut off a tree;* olivae, Hor.

Termessus -i, f. (Τερμησσός), *a town in Pisidia.* Hence, **Termessenses -ĭum,** m. *the inhabitants of Termessus.*

Termĭnālĭa -ĭum and **-ĭōrum** (Terminus), n. *the Festival of Terminus, on the 23rd of February.*

termĭnātĭo -ōnis. f. (termino), *a limiting, bounding.* **I.** Lit., Liv. **II.** Transf., 1, *a fixing, ordaining, determining;* versus inventus est terminatio aurium, Cic.; 2, rhet. t.t., *the end, termination of a period;* ordo verborum alias aliā terminatione concluditur, Cic.

termĭno, 1. (terminus), *to bound, limit, set bounds to.* **I.** Lit., finem loci quem oleae terminabant, Cic. **II.** Transf., 1, *to limit;* a, *to restrain, restrict;* sonos vocis paucis litterarum notis, Cic.; b, *to define, determine;* bona volupᵗate, mala dolore, Cic.; **2,** *to close, end, terminate;* ᵣrationem, Cic.

termĭnus -i, m. (root TER, whence termen, termo, Gr. TEP, whence τέρμα), *a boundary-mark, limit, boundary.* **I.** Lit., a, nulli possessionum termini, Cic.; b, personif., Terminus, *the god of boundaries,* Ov. **II.** Transf., 1, *limit, bound, object;* certos mihi fines terminosque constituam, extra quos egredi non possim, Cic.; **2,** *end, conclusion;* contentionum, Cic.

ternĭ -ae -a (ter). **I.** *three each,* Cic.; sing., terno ordine, Verg. **II.** *three together,* Verg.

tĕro, trivi, tritum, 3. (root TER, whence τείρω), *to rub.* **I.** Gen., **A.** Lit., 1, dentes in stipite, Ov.; calcem = *to overtake in running,* Verg.; calamo labellum = *to play the flute,* Verg.; 2, esp., a, *to rub for the sake of cleaning* or *ornamenting, to smoothe, adorn;* crura pumice, Ov.; b, *to turn* (at a lathe); radios rotis, Verg.; c, *to thresh out* corn; milia frumenti, Hor.; d, of places, *to visit, frequent;* iter, Verg. **B.** Transf., 1, *to read often, have often in the hands, use often;* quod legeret tereretque viritim publicus usus, Hor.; 2, fig., *to use often in discourse;* verbum, Cic. **II. A.** *to rub, bruise, grind;* bacam, Verg. **B.** *to rub off, wear away;* 1, lit., silices, Ov.; 2, fig., a, *to tire oneself;* se in opere longinquo, Liv.; b, *to pass away time;* interea tempus, Cic. (syncop. perf., tristi, Cat.).

Terpsĭchŏrē -ēs, f. (Τερψιχόρη), *the muse of dancing;* hence = *muse, poetry,* Juv.

terra -ae, f. (root TER, whence torreo), lit., *that which is dry;* hence, *the earth* (as opp. to heavens, sea, air), *land, ground, soil.* **I.** a, *the earth;* terrae motus, *earthquake,* Cic.; terrā, *by land,* Cic.; terrā marique, *by land and sea,* Cic.; in terris, *on the earth,* Hor.; sub terras ire, *to visit the lower world,* Verg.; b, *the earth = the ground, the soil;* gleba terrae, Liv.; mihi terram injice, Verg.; terrae filius, *a son of the earth, an unknown person,* Cic.; ea quae gignuntur e terra, Cic.; c, *the earth = the surface of the earth, ground;* de terra saxa tollere, Cic.; d, *a particular country, land, region;* abire in alias terras, Cic.; plur., terrae, *the world;* has terras incolentes, Cic.; orbis terrarum, *the world,* Cic.; genit. plur. often partitive, with adv. of place, ubi terrarum sumus? *where in the world are we?* Cic. **II.** Personif., Terra, *the earth as a goddess;* gen., Tellus, Cic.

Terracīna, Terracinensis = Tarracina, Tarracinensis (q.v.).

terrēnus -a -um (terra). **I.** *earthy, earthen;* tumulus, Caes.; genus, Cic. Subst., **terrēnum** -i, n. *land, ground;* herbidum, Liv. **II.** 1, *belonging to the earth, terrene, terrestrial;* bestiae, *land-animals,* Cic.; humor, *moisture of the earth,* Cic.; poet., numina, *of the lower world,* Ov.; 2, *earthy* (opp. caelestis); eques, *mortal,* Hor.

terrĕo, terrŭi, terrĭtum, 2. *to frighten, terrify.* **I.** Gen., aliquem, Cic.; with ne and the subj., Liv. **II.** 1, *to frighten away, scare away;* profugam per totum orbem, Ov.; 2, *to frighten, deter;* a repetunda libertate, Sall.; with ne and the subj., Liv.; with quominus and the subj., Caes.

terrestĕr -tris -tre, gen., **terrestris** -e (terra), 1, *terrestrial* (opp. marinus), animantium genus terrestre, Cic.; terrestres navalesque pugnae, Cic.; 2, *found on the earth, earthly* (opp. caelestis), res caelestes atque terrestres, Cic.; Capitolium terrestre domicilium Jovis, Cic.

terrĕus -a -um (terra), *made of earth, earthly;* progenies, Verg.

terrĭbĭlis -e (terreo), *terrible, frightful, fearful, dreadful;* a, of things, sonus, Liv.; mors est terribilis iis, etc., Cic.; with 2. supine, ter-

ribiles visu formae, Verg.; neut. plur. subst., majora ac terribiliora afferre, Liv.; b, of persons, jam ipsi urbi terribilis erat, Liv.; with 2. supine, quam terribilis aspectu, Cic.

terrĭcŭla -ae, f. and **terrĭcŭlum** -i, n. (terreo), *something that causes fright;* abl. plur., terriculis, Liv.

terrĭfĭco, 1. (terrificus), *to frighten, terrify,* Verg.

terrĭfĭcus -a -um (terreo and facio), *causing terror, frightful, terrible,* Verg.

terrĭgĕna -ae, c. (terra and gigno), *earth-born, sprung from the earth,* Lucr., Ov.

terripavium, terripudium = tripudium (q.v.).

terrĭto, 1. (intens. of terreo), *to frighten, scare, terrify;* a, of persons, aliquem metu, Caes.; b, of things, tribunicium domi bellum patres territat, Liv.

terrĭtōrĭum -ĭi, n. (terra), *the land belonging to a town, district, territory;* coloniae, Cic.

terror -ōris, m. (terreo), *fright, fear, terror, dread, panic.* **I.** Lit., with subject. genit., exercitus, Caes.; with object. genit. (*on account of*), belli, Cic.; minis et terrore commoveri, Cic.; attulit terrorem hostibus, Caes.; alicui terrori esse, Caes.; facere terrorem et militibus et ipsi Appio, Liv.; incutere alicui terrorem, Liv.; inferre terrorem alicui, Cic.; injicere alicui terrorem, Caes. **II.** Meton. a, *the object which causes terror;* terra repleta est trepido terrore, Lucr.; plur., huius urbis terrores (Carthage and Numantia), Cic.; b, *news causing terror;* Romam tanti terrores erant allati, Liv.; also *threatening* or *frightening expressions;* non mediocres terrores jacēre atque denuntiare, Cic.; or, *events causing terror;* caeiestes maritimique terrores, Liv. **III.** Personif., Terror, Ov.

tersus -a -um, p. adj. (from tergeo), *wiped,* **I.** Lit., *clean, neat;* mulier, Plaut.; plantae, Ov. **II.** Fig., *free from mistakes, neat;* judicium, Quint.

tertĭădĕcŭmāni -ōrum, m. (tertius decimus), *soldiers of the thirteenth legion,* Tac.

tertĭānus -a -um (tertius), *belonging to the third.* **I.** *to the third day;* febris, *tertian fever,* i.e., *recurring every third day,* Cic.; subst., **tertĭāna** -ae, f. *a tertian fever,* Plin. **II.** *belonging to the third legion;* subst., **tertĭāni** -ōrum, m. *soldiers of the third legion,* Tac.

tertĭārĭus -a -um (tertius), *containing one-third;* stannum, *containing one-third tin with two-thirds lead,* Plin.

tertĭō, adv. (tertius). **I.** *for the third time;* tertio pecuniam dedit, Cic. **II.** *thirdly,* Caes.

tertĭum, adv. (tertius), *for the third time,* Cic.

tertĭus -a -um (ter), *the third.* **I.** Adj., pars, Caes.; tertio quoque verbo, *always at the third word,* Cic.; tertius e nobis, *one of us three,* Ov.; tertia regna, *the lower world,* Ov.; tertia Saturnalia, *the third day of the Saturnalia,* Cic.; ab Jove tertius Ajax, *of the third generation, great-grandson,* Ov. **II.** Subst. **tertĭae** -ārum, f. a, *one-third,* Plin.; b, *the third* or *inferior part in a play,* Plin.

tertĭusdĕcĭmus -a -um, *the thirteenth,* Cic.

tĕruncĭus -ĭi, m. (ter or tres and uncia), *three twelfth parts.* **I.** *the fourth part of an as,* Cic.; prov., ne teruncius quidem, *not a farthing,* Cic. **II.** *the fourth part of an inheritance;* heres ex teruncio, *heir to one-fourth of the property,* Cic.

tervĕnēfĭcus -i, m. *an arch-poisoner, a double-dyed rogue,* Plaut.

tesca (**tesqua**) -ōrum, n. (with or without loca), *wastes, deserts,* Hor.

tessella -ae, f. (dim. of tessera), *a small cube of marble or other substance used for pavements,* or *for playing dice,* Juv.

tessellātus -a -um (tessella), *set with small cubes;* pavimentum, mosaic, Suet.

tessĕra -ae, f. (τέσσαρα), *a cube of wood, stone,* or *other substance used for various purposes.* **I.** *a piece of mosaic for paving,* Plin. **II.** *a die for playing;* tesseras jacĕre, Cic. **III.** *a token;* 1, *a square tablet on which the military watchword was written;* hence, meton. = *the watchword;* omnibus tesseram dare, Liv.; 2, *a tablet or token which entitled the holder to receive money or provisions,* Juv.; 3, hospitalis, *a token of hospitality* (a small die, which friends broke into two parts), Plaut.

tessĕrārĭus -ĭi, m. (tessera), *the officer who received from the general the ticket* (tessera) *on which the watchword was written, and communicated it to the army,* Tac.

tessĕrŭla -ae, f. (dim. of tessera), 1, *a little cube of stone for paving,* ap. Cic.; 2, *a little voting-ticket,* Varr.; 3, *a ticket for the distribution of food,* Pers.

testa -ae, f. (perhaps = tosta), *burnt clay.* **I.** Lit., 1, *an earthen vessel, pot, pitcher, jug, urn;* vinum Graecā testā conditum, Hor.; 2, *a brick, a tile,* Cic.; 3, *a potsherd,* Ov.; esp., *the potsherd used in voting by the Greeks;* testarum suffragia, ostracism, Nep. **II.** Transf., 1, *the shell of shell-fish,* Cic.; 2, meton., *a shell-fish,* Hor.; 3, poet., transf., *shell, covering* = *ice;* lubrica testa, Ov.

testācĕus -a -um (testa). **I.** 1, *made of bricks or tiles,* Plin.; subst., **testācĕum** -i, n. *brick-work,* Plin.; 2, *brick-coloured,* Plin. **II.** Of animals, *covered with a shell, testaceous,* Plin.

testāmentārĭus -a -um (testamentum), *of or relating to a will, testamentary;* subst., **testāmentārĭus** -ĭi, m. *a forger of wills,* Cic.

testāmentum -i, n. (testor), *a last will, testament;* id testamento cavere, *to provide,* Cic.; conscribere testamentum, Cic.; testamentum facere, Cic.; irritum facere testamentum, *to annul,* Cic.; obsignare testamentum, Caes.; relinquere alicui testamento sestertiûm milies, Cic.

testātĭo -ōnis, f. (testor). **I.** *a calling to witness;* ruptorum foederum, Liv. **II.** *a bearing witness,* Quint.

testātor -ōris, m. (testor), *one that makes a will, a testator,* Suet.

testātus -a -um, p. adj. (from testor), *attested, proved, clear;* res, Cic.; quo notior testatiorque virtus eius esset, Caes.

testĭcŭlus -i, m. (dim. of 2. testis), *a testicle,* Pers.

testĭfĭcātĭo -ōnis, f. (testificor). **I.** *a bearing witness, testifying;* hāc testificatione uti, Cic. **II.** Transf., *attestation, evidence, proof;* officiorum, Cic.

testĭfĭcor, 1. dep. (testis and facio). **I.** *to call to witness;* deos hominesque, ap. Cic. **II.** *to bear witness, testify;* 1, lit., testificor me esse rogatum, Cic.; 2, transf., *to show, publish, bring to light;* partic. pass., abs te testificata voluntas, Cic.

testĭmōnĭum -ĭi, n. (1. testis), *witness, evidence, testimony.* **I.** Lit., testimonium in aliquem dicere, Cic.; *of a written attestation,* testimonium componere, obsignare, Cic. **II.** Transf., in general, *a proof, evidence, indication;* dedisti judicii tui testimonium, Cic.

1. **testis** -is, c. *one who gives evidence, a witness.* **I.** Lit., testis falsus, Cic.; testes dare in singulas res, Cic.; testes adhibere, Cic. **II.** Transf. = arbiter, *an eye-witness, spectator,* Ov.

2. **testis** -is, m. *a testicle,* Hor.

testor, 1. dep. (1. testis). **I.** *to bear witness, to give evidence of, to make known, publish, declare, assert, testify;* utraeque vim testantur, Cic.; pass., *to be attested, declared;* testata est voce praeconis libertas Argivorum, Liv. **II.** *to call to witness;* 1, gen., omnes deos, Cic.; 2, esp., *to make a will;* de filii pupilli re, Cic.

testū, indecl. and **testum** -i, n. (perhaps= tostu, tostum, as testa = tosta), *an earthen pot, a pot,* Ov.

testŭātĭum -ĭi, n. (testu), *a cake baked in an earthen pan,* Varr.

testūdĭnĕus -a -um (testudo). **I.** *like a tortoise;* gradus, Plaut. **II.** *adorned with or made of tortoise-shell;* lyra, Prop.

testūdo -ĭnis, f. (testa), *a tortoise.* **I.** Lit., Liv. **II.** Meton., **A.** *the shell of the tortoise,* used for ornamenting furniture; varii testudine postes, Verg. **B.** 1, *a curved string-instrument, the lyre, cithara,* etc., Hor.; transf., *a way of dressing the hair of similar form,* Ov.; 2, *a room with a vaulted roof,* Cic.; 3, milit. t.t., a, *a shed to protect soldiers while attacking fortifications,* Caes.; b, *a formation in which soldiers charged, holding their shields over their heads,* Caes.

testŭla -ae, f. (dim. of testa), *a potsherd, an Athenian voting-ticket;* meton., *ostracism;* a Themistocle collabefactus testulā illā, Nep.

tĕtănĭcus -a -um (τετανικός), *suffering from lockjaw,* Plin.

tĕtănus -i, m. (τέτανος), *lockjaw,* Plin.

tĕtartēmŏrĭon -ĭi, n. (τεταρτημόριον), *the fourth part of the zodiac,* Plin.

tēter (**taeter**) -tra -trum, *foul, noisome, hideous, offensive.* **I.** Lit., *to the senses, odor,* Cic.; tenebrae, Cic.; with 2. supine, illud teterrimum non modo aspectu, sed etiam auditu, Cic. **II.** Transf., *hateful, hideous, disgraceful, shameful, abominable;* homo, Cic.; quis tetrior hostis huic civitati? Cic.; sententia teterrima, Cic.

tĕthălassōmĕnos -i, m. (τεθαλασσωμένος οἶνος), *wine mixed with sea-water,* Plin.

Tēthys -thўos, acc. -thyn, f. (Τηθύς). **I.** *a marine goddess, wife of Oceanus, mother of the river-gods and sea-nymphs.* **II.** Poet., appell. = *the sea,* Cat.

tĕtrachmum -i, genit. plur. -ōrum and -ûm, n. (τέτραχμον), *a Greek coin of four drachmae,* Liv.

tĕtrăchordos -on (τετράχορδος), *having four notes;* subst., **tĕtrăchordon** -i, n. *harmony of four notes, a tetrachord,* Varr.

tĕtrăcōlon -i, n. (τετράκωλον), *a period having four clauses,* Sen.

tĕtrădrachmum = tetrachmum (q.v.).

tĕtragnăthĭus -ĭi, m. (τετράγναθος), *a poisonous spider,* Plin.

tĕtrălix -ĭcis, f. (τετράλιξ), *the plant heath,* Plin.

tĕtrăo -ōnis, m. (τετράων), *a heathcock,* Plin.

tĕtrarches and **tĕtrarcha** -ae, m. (τετράρχης), *the ruler over one-fourth of a country, a tetrarch,* Cic.

tĕtrarchĭa -ae, f. (τετραρχία), *the country governed by a tetrarch, tetrarchy,* Cic.

tĕtrastĭchă -ōn, n. plur. (τετράστιχα), *a poem consisting of four lines,* Quint.

tĕtrē (taetrē), adv. (teter), *foully, hideously, noisomely, offensively;* multa facere impure atque tetre, Cic.; religionem impurissime teterrimeque violasse, Cic.

1. **tētrĭcus** -a -um, *harsh, gloomy, severe, forbidding;* puella, Ov.; deae, *the Parcae,* Mart.

2. **Tētrĭcus** mons, *a mountain in the Sabine country,* now *Monte S. Giovanni;* poet. subst., **Tētrĭca** -ae, f. (sc. rupes), Verg.

tettĭgŏmētra -ae, f. (τεττιγομήτρα), *the larva of the cicada,* Plin.

tettĭgŏnĭa -ae, f. (τεττιγονία), *a species of small cicada,* Plin.

tĕtŭli = tuli, v. tulo.

Teucer -cri, m. and **Teucrus** -i, m. (Τεῦκρος). I. (Teucer and Teucrus) *son of Telamon, king of Salamis, brother of Ajax, who, after his return from Troy, sailed away to Cyprus.* II. (Teucrus) *son of Scamander, first king of Troy;* hence, a, **Teucrus** -a -um, *Teucrian,* poet. = *Trojan;* b, **Teucrius** -a -um, *Teucrian,* poet. =*Trojan.* Subst., **Teucri** -ōrum, m. *the Trojans.*

teuchītis -ĭdis, f. (τευχῖτις), *a species of aromatic rush,* Plin.

teucrĭon -ĭi, n. (τεύκριον), *the plant called germander,* Plin.

Teucrius, Teucrus, v. Teucer.

Teuthrās -thrantis, m. (Τεύθρας). I. *a river in Campania.* II. *a king in Mysia, father of Thespius.* Hence, A. **Teuthrānĭa** -ae, f. *a district in Mysia.* B. **Teuthrantēus** -a -um, *Mysian.* C. **Teuthrantius** -a -um, *of or belonging to Teuthras;* turba, *the fifty sisters and daughters of Thespius,* Ov. III. *a soldier of Turnus.*

Teutŏni -ōrum, m. and **Teutŏnes** -um, m. *a collective name of the German peoples, a branch of which invaded the Roman Empire with the Cimbri, and were defeated by C. Marius.* Hence, **Teutŏnĭcus** -a -um, *Teuton,* and poet.= *German.*

texo, texŭi, textum, 3. *to weave.* I. tegumenta corporum vel texta vel suta, Cic. II. *to weave, twine together, intertwine, plait, construct, build;* casas ex arundine, Liv.; basilicam in medio foro, Cic.; fig., epistolas quotidianis verbis, *to compose,* Cic.

textĭlis -e (texo). I. *woven, textile;* stragulum, Cic. Subst., **textĭle** -is, n. (sc. opus), *a woven fabric, a piece of cloth.* II. *plaited, braided,* Mart.

textor -ōris, m. (texo), *a weaver,* Hor.

textōrĭus -a -um (textor), *of or relating to weaving,* Sen.

textrīnus -a -um (for textorinus, from textor), *relating to weaving.* Subst., **textrīnum** -i, n. *weaving,* Cic.

textrix -trīcis, f. (f. of textor), *a female weaver,* Mart.

textum -i, n. (texo). I. *that which is woven, a web;* a, lit., Ov.; b, *that which is plaited, woven, fitted, put together in any way, a fabric;* pinea (navis), Ov.; clipei, Verg. II. Fig., of written composition, *texture, style,* Quint.

textūra -ae, f. (texo). I. *a web, texture,* Plaut. II. Transf., *a putting together, connexion,* Lucr.

textus -ūs, m. (texo). I. *a web,* and transf., *texture, structure,* Lucr. II. Fig., *of discourse, mode of putting together, connexion,* Quint.

Thāis -ĭdos, f. (Θαΐς), *a celebrated hetaira of Athens, afterwards wife of Ptolemaeus I. of Egypt.*

Thala -ae, f. *a town in Numidia,* now *Ferreanah.*

thălămēgus -i, f. (θαλαμηγός), *a barge or gondola provided with cabins,* Suet.

thălămus -i, m. (θάλαμος), *a room in the interior of a house.* I. *a living-room,* Ov.; hence, *a place of abode, dwelling;* Eumenidum, Verg.; of the cells of bees, Verg. II. *a bed-room; a,* lit., Ov.; b, *a marriage-bed,* Verg.; hence, meton., *marriage;* vita expers thalami, *unmarried,* Verg.; thalamos ne desere pactos, *the promised bride,* Verg.

thalassĭcus -a -um (θαλασσικός), *sea-green,* Plaut.

thalassĭnus -a -um (θαλάσσινος), *sea-green,* Lucr.

Thălassĭo, Thalassius, etc., v. Talassio.

thălassĭtes -ae, m. (θαλασσίτης), *wine which has been sunk in the sea to be ripened,* Plin.

thălassŏmĕli, n.(θαλασσόμελι), *honey mixed with sea-water,* Plin.

Thălēa = Thalia (q.v.).

Thāles -lis and -lētis, m. (Θαλῆς), *a philosopher of Miletus, one of the Seven Wise Men of Greece.*

Thālīa -ae, f. (Θάλεια). I. *the Muse of comic poetry.* II. *one of the sea-nymphs.*

thallus -i, m. (θαλλός), *a green branch,* Verg.

Thămỹras -ae, m. and **Thămỹris** -ĭdis, m. (Θάμυρις), *a Thracian poet, who entered into a contest with the Muses, and being conquered was deprived of his lyre and eyes.*

Thapsus (-ŏs) -i, f. (Θάψος). I. *a peninsula and town in Sicily.* II. *a town in Africa Propria, where Caesar conquered the Pompeians.*

Thāsus (-ŏs) -i, f. (Θάσος), *an island in the Aegean Sea.* Adj., **Thāsius** -a -um, *Thasian.*

Thaumās -antis, m. (Θαύμας), *father of Iris.* Hence, A. **Thaumantēus** -a -um, *of Thaumas;* virgo, *Iris,* Ov. B. **Thaumantĭās** -ădis, f. *daughter of Thaumas,* i.e., *Iris.* C. **Thaumantis** -ĭdos, f.= Thaumantias.

theamēdes, acc. -en, m. *an Ethiopian stone,* perhaps *tourmaline,* Plin.

thĕātrālis -e (theatrum), *of or relating to a theatre, theatrical;* consessus, Cic.

thĕātrum -i, n. (θέατρον). I. *a theatre;* 1, lit., a, gen., *for dramatic performances,* Cic.; b, *an open place for the exhibition of games,* Verg.; 2, meton., a, *the people assembled in the theatre, the audience;* theatra tota reclamant, Cic.; b, transf., *spectators, assemblage;* senatus consultum frequentissimo theatro (populi) comprobatum, Cic. II. Fig., *the sphere, theatre for any action;* forum populi Romani quasi theatrum illius ingenii, Cic.

Thēbae -ārum, f. (Θῆβαι). I. *a city of Upper Egypt.* II. *a city of Boeotia, founded by Cadmus, the birthplace of Pindar.* III. Thebae Phthioticae or Phthiae, *a town in Thessalia Phthiotis,* now *Armiro.* IV. *a town in Mysia, residence of Aetion, father-in-law of Hector, destroyed by Achilles.* Hence, A. **Thēbāis** -ĭdis and -ĭdos, f. 1, *belonging to Thebes in Egypt;* 2, *belonging to Thebes in Boeotia;* Thebaides, *Theban women,* Ov.; 3, *belonging to Thebes in Mysia.* B. **Thēbānus** -a -um, 1, *belonging to Thebes in Boeotia;* modi, Pindaric, Ov.; dea, Ino (Leukothea, Matuta), Ov.; mater, Agave, Ov.; soror, Antigone, Ov.; semina, *the dragon's teeth sown by Cadmus,* Ov.; duces, Eteocles and Polynices, Prop.; deus, Hercules, Ov.; subst., **Thēbānus** -i, m. *a Theban;* 2, *belonging to Thebes in Mysia;* subst., Thebana, Andromache, Ov.

Thēbē -ēs, f. (Θήβη). I.= Thebae. II. *a nymph, beloved by the river-god Asopus.* III. *wife of the tyrant Alexander of Pherae.*

thĕca -ae, f. (θήκη), *a case, sheath, envelope, covering;* vasa sine theca, Cic.

Thelxinŏē -ēs, f. *one of the first four Muses.*

thĕlўphŏnon = aconitum (q.v.).

thĕlyptĕris -ĭdis, f. (θηλυπτερίς), *the female fern plant,* Plin.

thĕma -ătis, n. (θέμα). **I.** *the theme, topic, subject of discourse.* Sen. **II.** *the position of the heavenly bodies at the moment of a birth,* Suet.

Thĕmis -ĭdis, f. (Θέμις), *the goddess of justice, also regarded as the goddess of prophecy.*

Thĕ.nista -ae, f. and **Thĕmistē** -ēs, f. *an Epicurean philosopher of Lampsacus.*

Thĕ.iistŏclēs -is and -i, m. (Θεμιστοκλῆς), *the celebrated general of the Athenians in the Persian War.* Hence, **Thĕmistŏclēus** -a -um, *Themistoclean.*

Thĕŏcrĭtus -i, m. (Θεόκριτος), *the famous Greek bucolic poet, born at Syracuse, flourished* 281–250 B.C.

Thĕŏdectēs -is and -i, m. (Θεοδέκτης), *Greek orator of Cilicia, teacher of Isocrates and Aristotle.*

Thĕŏdōrus -i, m. (Θεόδωρος). **I.** *Of Byzantium, a Greek sophist.* **II.** *Of Cyrene, a Greek sophist.* **III.** *a famous rhetorician of Gadara, teacher of Tiberius.*

Thĕŏgŏnĭa -ae, f. (Θεογονία), *the Theogony, or Generation of the Gods, a poem by Hesiod,* Cic.

thĕ.lŏgus -i, m. (θεολόγος), *a theologian, one who treats of the descent and existence of the gods,* Cic.

Thĕŏphănē -ēs. f. (Θεοφάνη), *daughter of Bisaltes, mother by Poseidon of the ram which bore Phrixus to Colchis.*

Thĕŏphănēs -is and -i, m. (Θεοφάνης), *a historian, friend of Pompeius.*

Thĕŏphrastus -i, m. (Θεόφραστος), *a celebrated Greek philosopher of the town of Cresos in Lesbos, pupil of Plato and Aristotle.*

Thĕŏpompus -i, m. (Θεόπομπος). **I.** *a celebrated Greek historian of Chios, pupil of Isocrates.* **II.** *a dependent of Caesar's.* **III.** *a dependent of Cicero's in Asia.*

Thēra -ae, f. (Θήρα), *an island in the Cretan Sea, now Santorin.* Hence, **Thēraeus** -a -um, *Theraean.*

Thērămēnēs -ae, m. (Θηραμένης), *of Chios or Ceos, adopted son of the Athenian Hagnon, one of the thirty tyrants at Athens, but put to death for opposing the oppressions of his colleagues Critias and Charicles.*

Thĕrapnē (Thĕramnē) -ēs, f. and **Thĕrapnae** -ārum, f. (Θεράπναι), *a town of Laconia, the birthplace of Helen;* hence, adj., **Thĕrapnaeus** -a -um, *Therapnean;* poet., *Spartan;* marita, or nata rure Therapnaeo, *Helen,* Ov.; sanguis Therapnaeus (of the boy Hyacinthus of Amyclae), Ov.

Thēriăcus -a -um (θηριακος), *serviceable against animal poison, esp., the bite of serpents,* Plin. Subst., **thēriăca** -ae, f. and **thēriăcē** -ēs, f. *an antidote against the bite of poisonous serpents,* Plin.

Thērĭclēs -is, m. (Θηρικλῆς), *a celebrated artist, maker of pottery and wooden vessels at Corinth.* Hence, **Thērĭclius** -a -um (Θηρίκλειος), *Thericlean;* pocula, *drinking-cups of clay or wood,* Cic.

thermae -ārum, f. (θερμός, *warm*). **I.** *warm baths,* Plin. **II.** Proper name, **Thermae** -ārum, f. *a town with warm springs on the north coast of Sicily, now Sciacca.* Hence, **Thermĭtānus** -a -um, *of or belonging to Thermae.*

Thermē -es, f. (Θέρμη), *a town in Maced. nia, afterwards called Thessalonica.* Hence, **Thermaeus** -a -um, *Thermaean;* sinus, now *il Golfo di Salonichi.*

therminus -a -um (θέρμινος), *made of lupines,* Plin.

Thermōdŏn -ontis, m. (Θερμώδων), *a river in Pontus, on which the Amazons lived, now Terma.* Hence, **Thermōdontēus** (-tĭăcus) -a -um, poet.= *Amazonian.*

thermŏpōlĭum -ĭi, n. (θερμοπώλιον), *a place where warm drinks are sold,* Plaut.

thermŏpōto, l. *to refresh with warm drinks,* Plaut.

Thermŏpўlae -ārum, f. (Θερμοπύλαι), *a pass in Locris, on the borders of Thessaly, where Leonidas and a small body of Spartans fell fighting against the whole Persian army.*

thermŭlae -ārum, f. (dim. of thermae), *warm baths,* Mart.

Thērŏdămās -antis, m. and **Thērŏmĕdōn** -ontis, m. (Θηρομέδων), *a Scythian king, who fed lions with human flesh.* Adj., **Thērŏdămantēus** -a -um, *of Therodamas.*

Thersītēs -ae, m. (Θηρσίτης), *son of Agrius, one of the Greeks before Troy, notorious for his ugliness and scurrilous tongue.*

thēsaurārĭus -a -um (thesaurus), *of or relating to the treasury,* Plaut.

thēsaurus -i, m. (θησαυρός). **I.** *a treasury, store, hoard;* 1, lit., thesaurum obruere, Cic.; defodere, Cic.; 2, fig., *a treasure* (of persons, etc.), Plaut. **II.** *the place where a treasure is kept;* 1, lit., a, servata mella thesauris, Verg.; b, esp., *the treasury of a temple or state;* thesauros Proserpinae spoliare, Liv.; 2, fig., *a storehouse, magazine, repertory;* thesaurus rerum omnium memoria, Cic.

Thēseūs -ĕi and -ĕos, m. (Θησεύς), *a king of Athens, son of Aegeus, husband of Ariadne and Phaedra, conqueror of the Minotaur.* Hence, **A.** adj., **Thēseūs** -a -um, *of or belonging to Theseus;* crimen, *the desertion of Ariadne,* Ov.; poet., *Athenian,* Pr-p. **B.** **Thēseïus** -a -um, *of or belonging to Theseus;* heros, *Hippolytus,* Ov. **C.** Subst., **Thēsīdēs** -ae, m. *a son of Theseus, Hippolytus,* Ov. **D.** **Thēseïs** -ĭdis, f. *a poem on Theseus,* Juv.

thēsīon (-um) -ĭi, n. (θήσειον), *a species of flax* (Thesium linophyllum, Linn.), Plin.

thĕsis -is, f. (θέσις), *a proposition, thesis,* Quint.

thesmŏphŏrĭa -ōrum, n. (θεσμοφόρια), *the great Greek festival in honour of Demeter,* Plin.

Thespĭae -ārum, f. (Θεσπιαί), *a town in Boeotia, at the foot of Mount Helicon.* Hence, **A.** **Thespĭās** -ădis, f. (Θεσπιάς), *Thespian;* deae Thespiades, Ov., and simply, Thespiades, Cic., *the Muses.* **B.** **Thespĭenses** -ĭum, m. *the inhabitants of Thespiae.*

Thespis -ĭdis, m. (Θέσπις), *the founder of the Greek drama, contemporary of Solon and Pisistratus.*

Thespĭus -ĭi, n. (Θέσπιος), *son of Erechtheus, founder of Thespiae, father of fifty daughters.*

Thesprōtĭa -ae, f. (Θεσπρωτία), *a district in Epirus.* Hence, **Thesprōtĭus** -a -um, *Thesprotian.*

Thessălĭa -ae, f. (Θεσσαλία), *Thessaly, a country of northern Greece.* Hence, adj., **A.** **Thessălĭcus** -a -um, *Thessalian;* juga (of Mount Pelion), Ov. **B.** **Thessălus** -a -um, *Thessalian;* tela (of Achilles), Hor.; ignes, *in the camp of Achilles.* Hor.; pinus, *the ship Argo,*

Ov. **C. Thessālīus** -a -um, *Thessalian.* **D.**
Thessālis -idis, f. adj., *Thessalian;* umbra, *of*
Protesilaus, Prop.; ara, *of Laodamia, husband of*
Protesilaus, Ov.; subst., *a Thessalian woman.*

Thessălŏnĭca -ae, f. and **Thessălŏnīcē**
-ēs, f. (Θεσσαλονίκη), *Thessalonica, a town in*
Macedonia, now *Salonichi.* Hence, **Thessăl-**
ŏnicenses -ium, m. *the inhabitants of Thes-*
salonica.

Thessālus, v. Thessalia.

Thestīus -ii, m. (Θέστιος). **I.** *a king in*
Aetolia, father of Leda and Althaea, of Plexippus
and Toxeus. Hence, **A. Thestĭădēs** -ae, m.
(Θεστιάδης), *a descendant of Thestius;* Thestiadae
duo, *Plexippus and Toxeus;* respice Thestiaden,
Meleager, son of Althaea, Ov. **B. Thestĭăs**
-ădis, f. *a daughter of Thestius,* i.e., *Althaea.*
II.= Thespius.

Thestor -ŏris, m. (Θέστωρ), *father of the sooth-*
sayer Calchas. Hence, **Thestŏrĭdēs** -ae, m.
(Θεστορίδης), *the son of Thestor,* i.e., *Calchas.*

thēta, n. (θῆτα), *the Greek letter theta* (Θ, θ),
used by the Greeks in voting tickets as a symbol
of condemnation, because beginning the word
θάνατος; nigrum, Pers.

Thĕtĭs -idis, f. (Θέτις), *a sea-nymph, wife of*
Peleus, mother of Achilles; hence, poet., *the sea,*
Verg.

Theudŏrĭa -ae, f. *a town in Athamania,*
now *Todoriana.*

Theuma -mātis, n. *a place in Macedonia.*

thĭăsus -i, m. (θίασος), *a dance in honour of*
Bacchus, Verg.

thieldones -um, m. *a kind of Spanish horses,*
Plin.

Thirmĭda -ae, f. *a town in Numidia.*

Thisbē -ēs, f. (Θίσβη). **I.** *a beautiful Baby-*
lonian maiden, beloved by Pyramus. **II.** *a town*
in Boeotia. Hence, **Thisbēus** -a -um, *Thisbean*
= *Babylonian.*

thlaspi, n. (θλάσπι), *a kind of cress,* Plin.

Thŏas -antis, m. (Θόας). **I.** *a king of*
Lemnos, father of Hypsipyle; whence, **Thŏ-**
antĭăs -ădis, f. *a daughter of Thoas,* i.e., *Hyp-*
sipyle. **II.** *a king of the Tauric Chersonese, slain*
by Orestes. Hence, **Thŏanteus** -a -um, poet.=
Tauric.

thŏlus -i, m. (θόλος), *a cupola, dome,* Verg.

thōrācātus -a -um (thorax), *armed with a*
breast-late, Plin.

thŏrax -ācis, m. (θώραξ), 1, *the breast, chest,*
Plin.; 2, meton., *a breastplate, cuirass,* Liv.

thōs, thōis, m. (θώς), *a kind of wolf,* Plin.

Thot, *the Egyptian name of Mercury.*

Thrāces -um, acc. -es and -as, m. (Θρᾷκες),
the Thracians, the inhabitants of Thrace in south-
east Europe; sing., **Thrāx** -ācis, m. (Θρᾷξ), a, *a*
Thracian; poet. adj. = *Thracian;* b, esp. Thrax,
or Thraex, *a gladiator with Thracian armour.*
Hence, **A. Thrācĭa** -ae, f. *the country of Thrace;*
Greek form, **Thrācē** -ēs, f., or latinised
Thrāca -ae, f. **B. Thrācĭus** (Thrēcĭus)
-a um, *Thracian.* **C.** (Poet.), **Thrēicĭus** -a
-um (Θρηΐκιος), *Thracian;* sacerdos, Verg., or
vates, Ov. = *Orpheus;* Samus, Samothracia, Verg.;
penates, *of Diomedes, king of Thrace,* Ov. **D.**
Thraeissa, and contr., **Thraessa** -ae, f. *in or*
from Thrace; subst., *a Thracian woman.*

thranis -is, m. (θράνις), *a fish,* also called
xiphias, Plin.

thrascĭas -ae, m. (θρασκίας), *a north north-*
west wind, Plin.

Thrăsўbūlus -i, m. (Θρασύβουλοι), *an*
Athenian who freed Athens from the Thirty
Tyrants.

Thrăsўmennus, v. Trasumenus.

Thrax, v. Thraces.

Threïssa, Thressa, v. Thraces.

Threx = Thrax, v. Thraces.

thrips -ipis, m. (θρίψ), *a wood-worm,* Plin.

thrŏnus -i, m. (θρόνος), *a lofty seat, throne,*
Plin.

Thūcўdĭdēs -is and -i, m. (Θουκυδίδης), *an*
Athenian, general in and historian of the Pelopon-
nesian war. Hence, **Thūcўdīdius** -a -um,
Thucydidean.

Thūlē (**Thȳlē**) -ēs, f. (Θούλη), *an island*
in the extreme north of Europe, perhaps one of the
Shetland Islands, perhaps *Iceland.*

thunnus (**thynnus**) -i, m. (θύννος), *a tunny-*
fish, Ov.

Thūrĭi -ōrum, m. (Θούριοι), and **Thūrīae**
-ārum, f. *a town built on the site of the destroyed*
Sybaris, on the Tarentine Gulf. Hence, **Thūr-**
ĭnus -a -um, *of or belonging to Thurii.*

thūs, thūrārĭus, etc. = tus, turarius, etc.
(q.v.).

Thuys, dat. Thuyni, acc. Thuynem, and
Thuyn, m. *a prince of Paphlagonia at the time of*
Artaxerxes Memnon.

thȳa -ae, f. (θύα) and **thȳŏn** -i, n. (θυόν), *the*
Greek name of the citrus-tree, Plin.; hence, **thȳĭus**
-a -um, *of the wood of the citrus-tree,* Prop.

Thȳāmĭs -ĭdis, m. (Θύαμις), *the most nor-*
therly river in Epirus, now *Callama.*

Tĭyatira -ae, f. and **Thyatīra** -ōrum, n.
(Θιάτειρα), *a town in Lydia, rebuilt by Seleucus*
Nicator, now *Akhissar.*

Thȳbris = Tiberis (q.v.).

Thȳēnē -ēs, f. *a nymph, nurse of Jupiter.*

Thȳestēs -ae and -is, m. (Θυέστης), *son of*
Pelops, father of Aegisthus, brother of Atreus,
who placed before Thyestes for food Thyestes' own
son.

Thyĭăs (dissyll.) -ădis, f. (Θυιάς), *a Bacchante,*
Verg.

thȳĭus, v. thya.

Thȳlē = Thule (q.v.).

1. **thymbra** -ae, f. (θύμβρα), *the herb savory,*
Verg.

2. **Thymbra** -ae, f. (Θύμβρη), *a town in*
Troas, on the river Thymbrios, with a temple to
Apollo. Hence, **Thymbraeus** -a -um, *Thym-*
braean, surname of Apollo.

thȳmĭon (-**um**) -ii, n. (θύμιον), *a kind of*
wart, Plin.

thȳmōsus -a -um (thymum), *full of thyme;*
mel, Plin.

thȳmum -i, n. (θύμον), and **thȳmus** -i, m.
(θύμον and θύμος), *the herb thyme,* Verg.

Thȳni -ōrum, m. (Θυνοι), *a Thracian people,*
dwelling originally on the Black Sea. Hence, **A.**
Thȳnia -ae, f. (Θυνία), *Thynia, the northern*
part of Bithynia. **B. Thȳnĭăcus** -a -um,
Thynian; sinus, *on the Black Sea,* Ov. **C.**
Thȳnus -a -um, *Thynian.* **D. Thȳnĭăs** -ădis,
f. *Thynian.*

Thȳnus, v. Thyni.

thynnus = thunnus (q.v.).

Thȳŏnē -ēs, f. (Θυώνη). **I.** *mother of Bacchus*
(acc. to one legend), *identified by some with Semele.*
Hence, **A. Thȳŏneus** -ĕi, m. (Θυωνεύς), *son of*

Thyōne, i.e. Bacchus. B. Thўōnĭānus -i, m., meton. = wine, Cat. **II.** a nymph, nurse of Jupiter.

Thўrē -ēs, f. and **Thўrĕa** -ae, f. (Θυρέα), a town and district in Argolis. Hence, **Thўrĕātĭs** -ĭdis, f. (Θυρεᾶτις), of or belonging to Thyrea.

Thўrĕum -i, n. and **Thyrĭum** -ĭi, n. a town in Acarnania, near Leucas. Hence, **Thyrĭenses** -ĭum, m. inhabitants of Thyreum.

thyrsĭgĕr -gĕra -gĕrum (thyrsus and gero), bearing a thyrsus, Sen.

thyrsus -i, m. (θύρσος). **I.** the stalk or stem of a plant, Plin. **II.** a wand, wound round with ivy and vine-leaves, carried by Bacchus and his attendants, Hor.

tĭāra -ae, f. and **tĭāras** -ae, m. (τιάρα), a turban, Verg.

Tĭbĕris -bĕris, acc. -bĕrim, abl. -bĕri, m. and poet., **Thўbris** -brĭdis, acc. -brin or -brim, m. the river Tiber; personif., Thybris, the river-god of the Tiber. Hence, **A.** Adj., **Tĭbĕrinus** -a -um, belonging to the river Tiber; amnis, Liv., or flumen, Verg., the river Tiber; pater, or deus, the river-god, Verg. Subst., **Tĭbĕrinus** -i, m. a, the Tiber, Cic., Verg.; b, a king of Alba, Liv. **B. Tĭbĕrĭnĭs** -ĭdis, f. belonging to the river Tiber; Tiberinides Nymphae, Ov.

Tĭbĕrĭus -ĭi, m. **I.** a common Roman praenomen, abbreviated Ti. or Tib. **II.** Esp., the second emperor of Rome, Tiberius Claudius Nero Caesar. Hence, **Tĭbĕrĭŏlus** -i, m. dim. little (= dear) Tiberius, Tac.

tibĭa -ae, f. the shin-bone, tibia; meton., a pipe, fife, flute, originally made of a hollow bone; tibiis canere, Cic.

tibĭālis -e (tibia), of or relating to a flute, Plin.

tibĭcen -ĭnis, m. (for tibiicen, from tibia and cano). **I.** a flute-player, piper, fifer, Cic. **II.** a pillar, prop, Ov.

tibĭcĭna -ae, f. (tibicen), a female flute-player, piper, Hor.

tibĭcĭnĭum -ĭi, n. (tibicen), playing on the flute, Cic.

Tĭbris = Tiberis (q.v.).

Tĭbullus -i, m., Albius, a Roman elegiac poet, friend of Horace and Ovid, born 54 B.C., died about 19 B.C.

tĭbŭlus -i, f. a kind of pine or fir-tree, Plin.

Tĭbŭr -būris, abl. -būre, loc., būri, n. an old town in Latium, on both sides of the Anio, on a rocky hill (whence called supinum and pronum, Hor.), famous for its romantic position, a famous summer resort for the rich Romans, now Tivoli. Hence, **A.** Tiburs -burtis, Tiburtine. Subst., **Tiburtes** -um and -ĭum, m. the inhabitants of Tibur; esse in Tiburti, in the Tiburtine district, Cic. **B.** Tĭburtinus -a -um, Tiburtine. C. **Tiburnus** -a -um, Tiburnian. Subst., **Tĭburnus** -i, m. the builder of Tibur.

Tĭburtus -i, m. the builder of Tibur.

Tĭcĭnum -i, n. a town in Cisalpine Gaul on the river Ticinus, now Pavia.

Tĭcĭnus -i, m. one of the tributaries of the Padus in Cisalpine Gaul, now Tessino.

Tĭfāta -ōrum, n. a mountain north of Capua in Campania, on which was a temple to Diana, now Torre di Sessola.

Tĭfernum -i, n. a town in Samnium on the river Tifernus.

Tĭfernus -i, m. **1,** a mountain in Samnium; **2,** a river in Samnium.

Tĭgellĭus -ĭi, m. name of two musicians at Rome in Horace's time.

---

tĭgillum -i, n. (dim. of tignum), a small beam, Liv.

tignārĭus -a -um (tignum), of or relating to beams; faber, a carpenter, Cic.

tignum -i, n. (tego), a beam of wood, a log of timber, Caes.

Tĭgrānes -is, m. (Τιγράης). **I.** king in Great Armenia, son-in-law and ally of Mithridates, conquered by Lucullus. **II.** his son.

Tĭgrānŏcerta -ae, f. and **Tĭgrānŏcerta** -ōrum, n. the chief town of Armenia, founded by Tigranes.

tĭgrinus -a -um (tigris), spotted like a tiger, Plin.

tĭgris -ĭdis and -is, acc. -ĭdem and -im or -in, abl. -ĭde or -i, acc. plur., poet., -ĭdas (τίγρις, in Persian = an arrow). **I.** c. (masc. gen. in prose, fem. gen. in poetry), a tiger; 1, lit., Verg.; 2, transf., a, a name of one of the dogs of Actaeon, Ov.; b, name of a ship decorated with the figure of a tiger, Verg. **II.** m. **Tigris** -ĭdis and -is, acc. -ĭdem and -im, abl. -ĭde and -ĕ or -ĭ, the river Tigris in Asia.

Tigurini -ōrum, m. a Helvetian people. Adj., **Tigurinus** -a -um, Tigurine; pagus, the modern canton Vaud.

tĭlĭa -ae, f. **I.** a linden or lime-tree, Verg. **II.** the inner bark of the lime-tree, Plin.

Tĭmaeus -i, m. (Τίμαιος). **I.** a Greek historian in Sicily under Agathocles. **II.** a Pythagorean philosopher of Locri, after whom one of Plato's dialogues was named.

Tĭmăgĕnēs -is, m. (Τιμαγένης), a rhetorician of the time of Augustus.

Tĭmanthēs -is, m. (Τιμάνθης), a famous Greek painter, contemporary of Parrhasius.

Tĭmāvus -i, m. a river in the Venetian country between Aquileia and Trieste, now Timavo.

tĭmĕfactus -a -um (timeo and facio), made fearful, frightened, alarmed, Cic.

tĭmendus -a -um, p. adj. (from timeo), to be feared, fearful, dread; reges, Hor.

tĭmens -entis, p. adj. (from timeo), fearing, fearful; a, with genit., mortis, Lucr.; b, absol., hortatus timentem, Ov.; plur. subst., the fearful; timentes confirmant, Caes.

tĭmĕo -ŭi, 2. to be afraid, fear, dread, apprehend; with acc., aliquem, Cic.; with ne, ne non, or ut and the subj., timeo, ne non impetrem, Cic.; with infin., to be afraid to; nomen referre in tabulas, Cic.; with interrog. clause, quid possem, timebam, Cic.; with dat. (of the object on whose account fear is felt), sibi, Caes.; with de, de republica, Cic.; with a and the abl., a quo quidem genere ego numquam timui, Cic.

tĭmĭdē, adv. with compar. and superl. (timidus), timidly, fearfully, Cic.

tĭmĭdĭtas -ātis, f. (timidus), fearfulness, timidity, Cic.

tĭmĭdus -a -um (timeo), fearful, timid, faint-hearted, Cic.; with ad and the acc., timidus ad mortem, Cic.; with in and the abl., timidus in labore militari, Cic.; with genit., timidus procellae, Hor.; non timidus, foll. by the infin., non timidus pro patria mori, Hor.

Tĭmŏcrātes -is, m. (Τιμοκράτης), an Epicurean philosopher, flourishing about 260 B.C.

Tĭmŏlĕōn -ontis, m. (Τιμολέων), a Corinthian general, contemporary of Philip of Macedon. Hence, **Tĭmŏlĕonteus** -a -um, of or belonging to Timoleon.

Tĭmōn -ōnis, m. (Τίμων), a citizen of Athens, notorious for his misanthropy.

tĭmor -ōris, m. (timeo), fear, dread, apprehen-

19

sion. **I.** Lit., **a,** gen., definiunt timorem metum mali appropinquantis, Cic. ; timorem deponite, Cic. ; injicere timorem Parthis, Cic. ; percelli timore, Cic. ; foll. by ne and the subj., Liv. ; by infin., Ov. ; by acc. and infin., Liv. ; personif., Timor, son of Aether and Tellus, Hor., Verg., Ov.; **b,** *religious fear, superstition,* Hor. **II.** Meton., *an object exciting fear;* Cacus Aventinae timor atque infamia silvae, Ov.

Tïmöthëus -i, m. (Τιμόθεος). **I.** *son of Conon, the rebuilder of the long walls of Athens.* **II.** *a musician of Miletus.*

tinctïlis -e (tingo), *in which something is dipped,* Ov.

tinctörïus -a -um (tingo), *of or relating to dyeing;* fig., mens, bloodthirsty, Plin.

tinctūra -ae, f. (tingo), *a dyeing,* Plin.

tinctus -ū, m. (tingo), *a dipping, dyeing,* Plin.

tïnĕa (tïnĭa) -ae, f. *a moth, bookworm,* Ov., Hor. ; *a worm in beehives,* Verg.

tingo (tinguo), tinxi, tinctum, 3. (root TING, Gk. ΤΕΓΓ, τέγγω), *to wet, moisten, imbue with any fluid.* **I.** Gen., a, lit., tunica sanguine tincta, Cic. ; b, fig., *to tinge, imbue;* orator sit mihi tinctus literis, Cic. **II.** Esp., *to dye, colour,* Cic.

tinnīmentum -i, n. (tinnio), *a tinkling,* ringing, Plaut.

tinnĭo -īvi and -ĭi -ītum, 4. *to ring, tinkle, tingle, jingle.* **I.** Lit., Varr. **II.** Transf., 1, *to sing, to scream,* Plaut. ; 2, *to chink, to make to chink;* of money = *to pay;* ecquid Dollabella tinniat, Cic.

tinnītus -ūs, m. (tinnio), *a ringing, tinkling, jingling,* Verg. **I.** Lit., Ov. **II.** Transf., of discourse, *a jingle of words,* Tac.

tinnŭlus -a -um (tinnio), *ringing, clinking, tinkling, jingling,* Ov.

tinnuncŭlus -i, m. *a kind of falcon* (Falco tinnunculus, Linn.), Plin.

tintinnābŭlum -i, n. (tintinno), *a bell,* Juv.

tintinnācŭlus -a -um (tintinno), *ringing, jingling,* Plaut.

tintinno (tintĭno), 1. *to ring, jingle, tinkle,* Cat.

tinus -i, f. *a shrub* (ViburnumTinus, Linn.),Ov.

tïphē -ēs, f. (τίφη), *a species of grain* (Triticum monococcon, Linn.), Plin.

Tïphÿs, acc. -phyn, voc. -phy, m. (Τῖφυς), *the helmsman of the Argo.*

tippŭla -ae, f. *a water-spider* (which runs swiftly over the water), Varr. ; used to express something very light, Plaut.

Tïrēsĭās -ae, m. (Τειρεσίας), *the famous blind soothsayer of Thebes.*

Tïrïdātēs -dātis, m. (Τιριδάτης), *name of several kings in Armenia.*

tïro (tÿro) -ōnis, m. **I.** *a young soldier, a recruit;* 1, lit., Cic. ; adj., exercitus tiro, Cic.; 2, transf., a, *a beginner, a learner;* in aliqua re, Cic. ; tiro esset scientiâ, Cic. ; b, *a youth who assumes the toga virilis,* Ov. **II.** Proper name, M. Tullius Tiro, *the freedman of Cicero.*

tïrōcinĭum -ĭi, n. (tiro). **I.** *military ignorance and inexperience;* a, lit., juvenis, Liv.; b, meton., *recruits,* Liv. **II.** Transf., *of the entry of a young man on any career;* in L. Paulo accusando tirocinium ponere, *come before the public,* Liv.

tïruncŭlus -i, m. (dim. of tiro), *a young beginner,* Plin.

Tïryns, acc. -ryntha, f. (Τίρυνς), *an Argive town where Hercules was brought up.* Hence, adj., **Tïrynthĭus** -a -um, poet., *Herculean, relating to Hercules;* so simply, **Tïrynthĭus**

-ĭi, m. *Hercules;* **Tïrynthia**, *Alcmena, the mother of Hercules.*

Tïsĭās -ae, m. (Τισίας), *of Sicily, the first founder of a rhetorical system.*

Tïsïphönē -ēs, f. (Τισιφόνη), *one of the Furies;* hence, adj., **Tïsïphönēus** -a -um, *hellish, impious;* tempora, Ov.

Tïssäphernēs -ae, m. (Τισσαφέρνης), *a satrap under Xerxes II. and Artaxerxes II.*

Tïssē -ēs, f. *a town in Sicily, now Randazzo* Hence, **Tïssenses** -ĭum, m. *the inhabitants of Tisse.*

Tïtan -tānis, m. (Τιτάν), and **Tïtānus** -i, m. **I.** Gen., plur., *Titanes* and *Titani, the sons of Uranus and Gaea* (lat. Tellus), *who warred against Jupiter for supremacy in heaven, and were by him cast down into Tartarus.* **II.** *one of the Titans;* a, *the Sun-god, son of Hyperion;* b, *Prometheus.* Hence, **A. Tïtānĭus** -a -um, *of or relating to the Titans;* subst., **Tïtänĭa** -ae, f. a, *Latona,* Ov.; b, *Pyrrha,* Ov.; c, *Diana,* Ov.; d, *Circe,* Ov. **B. Tïtānĭäcus** -a -um, *Titanian.* **C. Tïtānis** -ĭdis -ĭdos, f. *Titanian;* subst. a, *Circe,* Ov.; b, *Tethys,* Ov.

Tïthōnus -i, m. (Τιθωνός), *the husband of Aurora, who obtained from his wife the gift of immortality, but without perpetual youth, and was at last changed into a grasshopper.* Hence, adj., **Tïthōnĭus** -a -um, *Tithonian;* Tithonia conjux, *Aurora,* Ov.

Tïtĭes -ĭum, m. and **Tïtĭenses** -ĭum, m. *one of the three tribes* (Ramnes, Tities, and Luceres) *into which the Roman burgesses were at first divided, and out of which three centuries of knights are said to have been formed by Romulus.*

tïtillätĭo -ōnis, f. (titillo), *a tickling, titillation,* Cic.

tïtillätus -ūs, m. = titillatio (q.v.).

tïtillo, 1. *to tickle;* sensus, Cic. ; fig., ne vos titillet gloria, Hor.

tïtĭo -ōnis, m. *a firebrand,* Varr.

tïtïvillïcĭum -ĭi, n. *a trifle,* Plaut.

tïtŭbantĕr, adv. (titubo), *hesitatingly, uncertainly,* Cic.

tïtŭbantĭa -ae, f. (titubo), *a wavering, staggering;* linguae, oris, *stammering,* Suet.

tïtŭbätĭo -ōnis, f. (titubo), *a staggering, reeling,* Sen. ; fig., *uncertainty, hesitancy,* Cic.

tïtŭbo, 1. *to totter, stagger.* **I.** Lit., 1, of persons, Silenus titubans annisque meroque,Ov.; vestigia titubata, *tottering,* Verg. ; 2, transf., *to stammer;* Licinius titubans, Cic.; lingua titubat, Ov. **II.** Fig., 1, *to waver, to hesitate,* Plaut. ; 2, *to blunder, err;* si verbo titubarint (testes), Cic.

tïtŭlus -i, m. *an inscription, label, title.* **I.** Lit., 1, gen., titulum inscribere lamnae, Liv.; 2, esp., a, *a notice on a house that is to let;* sub titulum nostros misit avara lares, Ov. ; b, *an epitaph;* sepulchri, Juv. **II.** Transf., 1, a, *a title of honour, honourable designation;* consulatus, Cic. ; b, *glory, honour;* par titulo tantae gloriae fuit, Liv. ; 2, *a pretence, pretext, reason;* quem titulum praetenderis, Liv.

Tïtŭrĭus -ĭi, m. *a legate of Caesar's in the Gallic war.* Hence, **Tïtŭrĭänus** -a -um, *of or belonging to Titurius.*

Tïtus -i, m. **I.** *a common Roman praenomen,* usually abbreviated T. **II.** *the emperor Titus Flavius Sabinus Vespasianus, son and successor of the Emperor Vespasian.*

Tïtÿos -i, m. (Τιτυός), *son of Jupiter, punished for an insult to Latona by being stretched out in Tartarus, and having his liver devoured by vultures.*

Tītўrus -i, m. (Τίτυρος, Doric = Σάτυρος). I. *the name of a shepherd in Vergil's Eclogues;* poet., meton., a, = *the Eclogues of Vergil,* Ov.; b, *Vergil himself,* Prop. II. Transf., *a shepherd ;* sit Tityrus Orpheus, Verg.

Tlēpŏlĕmus -i, m. (Τληπόλεμος), *son of Hercules*

Tmārus (-ŏs) -i, m. (Τμάρος), syncop. from

Tŏmārus -i, m. (Τόμαρος), *a mountain in Epirus on which was Dodona and the temple of Zeus.*

Tmōlus -i, m. (Τμῶλος), *a mountain in Lydia, famous for its wine.* Hence, **A. Tmōlĭus** -a -um, *Tmolian ;* subst., Tmolius, *Tmolian wine,* Verg. **B. Tmōlītēs** -ae, m. *a dweller on Mount Tmolus.*

tŏcullĭo -ōnis, m. (from τόκος, *interest*), *a usurer,* Cic.

tŏfācĕus (tŏfācĭus) -a -um (tofus), *made of tufa, like tufa,* Plin.

tŏfīnus -a -um (tofus), *made of tufa,* Suet.

tŏfus (tōphus) -i, m. *tufa,* Verg.

tŏga -ae, f. (tego), *a covering ;* esp., *the white woollen upper garment worn by the Romans in time of peace, when they appeared in their public capacity as citizens;* it was also worn by freedwomen and prostitutes (while the stola was worn by honourable women); especial kinds of the toga were : purpurea, *the kingly,* Liv. ; pura, *worn by young men on coming of age,* also called virilis, Cic.; candida, *of a candidate for office,* Cic.; meton., a, = *peace,* Cic. : b, = togatus, (α) togata, *a prostitute,* Tib. ; (β) plur., = *clients,* Mart.

tŏgātārĭus -ĭi, m. (toga), *an actor in the Fabula togata,* v. togatus, Suet.

tŏgātŭlus -i, m. (dim. of togatus), *a client,* Mart.

tŏgātus -a -um (toga), *wearing the toga.* I. Lit., gen., as a sign of a Roman citizen, as opp. to a foreigner or a soldier ; gens, *the Roman people,* Verg. II. Transf., 1, **togāta** -ae, f. (sc. fabula), *the national drama of the Romans, treating of Roman subjects* (opp. fabula palliata), Cic. ; 2, Gallia togata, *the Romanised part of Gallia Cisalpina,* Cic. ; 3, togata, *a freedwoman, a prostitute,* Hor. ; 4, *a client,* Juv.

tŏgŭla -ae, f. (dim. of toga), *a little toga,* Cic.

Tŏlēnus -i, m. *a river in the country of the Sabines,* now *Turano.*

tŏlĕrābĭlis -e (tolero), *that can be borne, bearable, tolerable;* conditio, Cic. ; poena, Cic.

tŏlĕrābĭlĭtĕr, adv. (tolerabilis), *patiently ;* aliquid tolerabilius ferre, Cic.

tŏlĕrandus -a -um (tolero), *endurable,* Liv.

tŏlĕrans -antis, p. adj. (from tolero), *bearing, enduring, patient, tolerant;* with genit., laborum, Tac.

tŏlĕrantĕr, adv. (tolerans), *patiently ;* illa ferre, Cic.

tŏlĕrantĭa -ae, f. (tolero), *a bearing, enduring, supporting ;* rerum humanarum, Cic.

tŏlĕrātĭo -ōnis, f. (tolero), *capacity for endurance,* Cic.

tŏlĕro, 1. (lengthened form of root TOL, whence tollo, tuli, τλάω, τλῆμι), to *bear, endure, sustain, tolerate;* fig., 1, hiemem, Cic. ; inopiam, Sall. ; with acc. and infin., Sall. ; 2, *to support, sustain, nourish, feed, keep;* equitatum, Caes. ; vitam aliquā re, Caes.

Tŏlētum -i, n. *a town of the Carpetani in Hispania Tarraconensis,* now *Toledo.* Hence, **Tŏlētāni** -ōrum, m. *the inhabitants of Toletum.*

tollēno -ōnis, m. (tollo), *a machine for raising water, a swing-beam or swipe,* Plin. ; *a military engine,* Liv.

tollo, sustŭli, sublātum, 3. **L** *to lift up, raise, elevate.* **A.** Lit., 1, gen., saxa de terra, Cic. ; oculos, Cic. ; aliquem in crucem, *to crucify,* Cic. ; 2, esp., a, naut. t. t., tollere ancoras, *to weigh anchor,* Caes.; b, milit. t. t., tollere signa, *to break up camp,* Caes. ; c, *to take up, take with one;* aliquem in currum, in equum, Cic. ; of ships, *to have on board;* naves quae equites sustulerant, Caes. **B.** Fig., 1, *to raise, elevate :* aliquem humeris suis in caelum, Cic.; laudes alicuius in astra, Cic. ; clamorem, Cic.; animos, *to assume a proud demeanour,* Sall. ; 2, esp., a, *to extol, magnify;* aliquem honoribus, Hor. ; tollere aliquem, *to help to honour,* Cic. ; aliquem laudibus, *to extol,* Cic. ; b, *to raise up;* animum, *regain one's spirits,* Liv.; amicum, *to comfort,* Hor. ; c, *to take on oneself;* quid oneris in praesentia tollant, Cic. ; d, *to bring up a child,* Plaut. ; transf., *to get, have a child;* liberos ex Fabia, Cic. **II.** *to take away, carry off.* **A.** 1, gen., praedam, Caes.; frumentum de area, Cic.; solem mundo, Cic. ; 2, esp., a, *to remove the food from the table ;* cibos, Hor. ; b, *to reserve for one's own use;* omnes chlamydes, Hor. ; c, *to destroy, get rid of;* aliquem e or de medio, or simply aliquem, Cic. ; Carthaginem, Cic. **B.** Fig., *to remove ;* 1, gen., amicitiam e mundo, Cic. ; 2, esp., a, *to consume;* tempus, diem, Cic. ; b, *to annul, bring to naught;* legem, Cic.; dictaturam funditus a republica, Cic.

Tŏlōsa -ae, f. *a rich town in Gallia Narbonensis,* now *Toulouse.* Hence, **A. Tŏlōsānus** -a -um, *of or belonging to Tolosa;* aurum, *taken by the consul Q. Servilius Caepio from Tolosa,* Cic. **B. Tŏlōsās** -ātis, *Tolosan;* subst., **Tŏlōsātes** -ĭum, m. *the inhabitants of Tolosa.*

Tŏlostobŏgĭi -ōrum, m. *one of the three races of the Galatians in Asia Minor.*

Tŏlumnĭus -ĭi, m. 1, *a king of the Veientines ;* 2, *a soothsayer of the Rutuli.*

tŏlūtārĭus -a -um (tolutim), *trotting ;* equus, Sen.

tŏlūtim, adv. (tollo), *trotting, on the trot,* Plin.

tŏmācīna -ae, f. (tomaculum), *a kind of sausage,* Varr.

tŏmācŭlum (tŏmaclum) -i, n. (τομή), *a kind of sausage,* Juv.

Tŏmārus, v. Tmarus.

tōmentum -i, n. *the stuffing of a pillow, mattress, cushion,* etc., Tac.

Tŏmi -ōrum, m. (Τόμοι), and **Tŏmis** -ĭdis, f. (Τόμις), *a town in Lower Moesia, on the Black Sea, the place of exile of Ovid, near modern Anadolkioi.* Hence, **A. Tŏmītae** -ārum, m. *the inhabitants of Tomi.* **B. Tŏmītānus** -a -um, *of Tomi.*

tŏmus -i, m. (τόμος), *a cutting, chip, shred,* Mart.

tondĕo, tŏtondi, tonsum, 2. *to shave, shear, clip.* I. Lit., a, transit., barbam et capillum, Cic. ; oves, Hor. ; b, intransit., *to shave the beard ;* tondere filius docuit, Cic. ; c, reflex., tondere and middle tonderi, *to shave oneself, have oneself shaved ;* candidior postquam tondenti barba cadebat, Verg. ; eum tonderi et squalorem deponere coegerunt, Liv. **II.** Transf., 1, *to cut off, shear, make smooth ;* ilex tonsa bipennibus, Hor. ; 2, *to mow, cut down ;* prata, Verg. ; 3, *to pluck off, crop off, browse upon ;* campum, Verg.

tŏnĭtrus -ūs, m. and **tŏnĭtrŭum** -i, n. (tono), *thunder,* Verg., Ov.

tŏno -ŭi, 1. *to sound, resound.* **I.** Gen., caelum tonat fragore, Verg. **II.** Esp., **ⓑ**

thunder; **1,** lit., Juppiter tonabat, Prop.; impers., **tonat,** *it thunders,* Cic.; tonans, as a surname of Juppiter, Cic.; **2,** transf., like βροντᾶν, of the powerful voice of an orator; a, absol., Pericles tonare dictus est, Cic.; **b,** *to thunder out something;* verba foro, Prop.

tonsa -ae, f. *an oar,* Verg.

tonsĭlis -e (tondeo), **1,** *that can be shorn or cut,* Plin.; **2,** *shorn, clipped, cut,* Plin.

tonsillae -ārum, f. *the tonsils in the throat,* Cic.

tonsĭto, 1. (intens. of tondeo), *to shear, clip,* Plaut.

tonsor -ōris, m. (tondeo), *a hair-cutter, barber,* Cic.

tonsōrĭus -a -um (tonsor), *of or for clipping, cutting;* culter, Cic.

tonstrĭcŭla -ae, f. (dim. of tonstrix), *a little female barber,* Cic.

tonstrīna -ae, f. (tondeo), *a barber's shop,* Plaut.

tonstrix -īcis, f. (tonsor), *a female barber,* Plaut.

tonsūra -ae, f. (tondeo), *a clipping, shearing, shaving;* capillorum, Plaut.

tonsus -ūs, m. (tondeo), *the mode of cutting or wearing the hair,* Plaut.

tŏnus - i, m. (τόνος), *the tone or sound* of an instrument; applied to painting, *tone,* Plin.

tŏparchĭa -ae, f. (τοπαρχία), *a territory, district, province,* Plin.

tŏpāzus (-ŏs) -i, f. (τόπαζος), *the topaz,* chrysolith, or *green jasper,* Plin.

tŏphus, etc. = tofus, etc. (q.v.).

tŏpĭa -ōrum, n. (sc. opera, from τόπος), *ornamental gardening;* hence, **tŏpĭārĭus** -a -um, *of or relating to ornamental gardening;* subst., **a, tŏpĭārĭus** -ĭi, m. *a landscape gardener,* Cic.; **b, tŏpĭārĭa** -ae, f. *the art of landscape gardening;* topiariam facere, *to be a landscape gardener,* Cic.; **c, tŏpĭārĭum** -ĭi, n. (sc. opus), *landscape gardening,* Plin.

tŏppĕr, [adv. *speedily, directly, forthwith,* Quint.

tŏral -ālis, n. (torus), *the valance of a couch* or *sofa,* Hor.

torcŭlar -āris, n. (torqueo), *a wine or oil press,* Plin.

torcŭlārĭus -e (torcular), *of or relating to a press;* subst., **torcŭlārĭum** -ĭi, n. *a press,* Cato.

torcŭlus -a -um (torqueo), *of or relating to a press.* **I.** Adj., vasa, Cato. **II.** Subst., torculum -i, n. *a press.*

tordȳlon -i, n. (τόρδυλον), *the seed of the plant seselis;* or, according to others, *the plant* Tordylium officinale, Plin.

tŏreuma -ătis, n. (τόρευμα), *carved* or *embossed work,* Cic., Sall.

tŏreutes -ae, m. (τορευτής), *an engraver, chaser, embosser,* Plin.

tŏreutĭcē -ēs, f. (τορευτική, sc. τέχνη), *the art of chasing, engraving, embossing,* Plin.

tormentum -i, n. (torqueo). **I.** *an instrument for twisting, winding, pressing;* **1,** *a windlass, pulley;* praesectis omnium mulierum crinibus tormenta effecerunt, Caes.; **2,** *an instrument of torture, the rack;* **a,** lit., tormenta adhibere, Cic.; dare se in tormenta, Cic.; de servo in dominum ne tormentis quidem quaeri licet, Cic.; **b,** transf., (a) *compulsion;* lene tormentum admovere ingenio, Hor.; (β) *torture, torment;* tormenta suspicionis, Cic. **II.** *a military engine*

for discharging missiles; **1,** ibi tormenta collocavit, Caes.; **2,** meton., *the missile so discharged;* telum tormentumve missum, Caes.

tormĭna -um, n. (torqueo). **I.** *the colic,* gripes, Cic. **II.** Transf., urinae, *a strangury,* Plin.

tormĭnālis -e (tormina), *of or relating to the colic,* Plin.

tormĭnōsus -a -um (tormina), *suffering from the colic,* Cic.

torno, 1. (τορνεύω), *to turn in a lathe, make round.* **I.** Lit., sphaeram, Cic. **II.** Fig., versus male tornati, *badly-turned, awkward,* Hor.

tornus -i, m. (τόρνος), *a lathe.* **I.** Lit., Verg. **II.** Fig., angusto versus includere torno, Prop.

Tŏrōnē -ēs, f. (Τορώνη), *a town on the Aegean Sea,* now *Toron;* Toronae promunturium, *the promontory Derris, near Torone,* Liv. Hence, **Tŏrōnăĭcus** -a -um, *of or belonging to Torone.*

tŏrōsus -a -um (torus), *muscular, fleshy, brawny;* colla boum, Ov.

torpēdo -īnis, f. (torpeo). **I.** *torpor, torpidity, sluggishness, inertness,* Sall., Tac. **II.** *the fish called the torpedo,* Cic.

torpĕo, 2. *to be stiff, immovable, sluggish, inert, torpid, numb.* **I.** Lit., physically, **a,** corpora rigentia gelu torpebant, Liv.; **b,** *to be inactive, continue inactive;* deum sic feriatum volumus cessatione torpere, Cic.; **c,** *to be immoveable from fear;* adeo torpentibus metu qui aderant, ut ne gemitus quidem exaudiretur, Liv. **II.** Transf., *to be mentally benumbed, torpid;* si tua re subitá consilia torpent, Liv.

torpesco -pŭi, 3. (torpeo), *to become stiff, grow stiff, become torpid;* **a,** from inactivity, ne per otium torpescerent manus aut animus, Sall.; **b,** from mental agitation, torpuerat lingua metu, Ov.

torpĭdus -a -um (torpeo), *stiff, numb, torpid,* Liv.

torpor -ōris, m. (torpeo), *stiffness, numbness, stupefaction, torpor;* **1,** physical, Cic.; **2,** mental, *dulness, inertness, inactivity;* sordes omnium ac torpor, Tac.

torquātus -a -um (torques), *wearing a twisted collar or necklace;* esp., as the surname of T. Manlius, *who killed a gigantic Gaul in single combat, and took from him the torques or necklace which he wore;* Alecto torquata colubris, *with a necklace of snakes,* Ov.; palumbus torquatus, *the ring-dove,* Mart.

torqueo, torsi, tortum, 2. (connected with τρέπω). **I.** *to twist, bend, wind, turn round;* **1,** gen., **a,** lit., cervices oculosque, Cic.; terra circum axem se torquet, Cic.; capillos ferro, *to curl,* Ov.; **b,** fig., *to guide, direct, turn;* omnia ad commodum suae causae, Cic.; **2,** esp., **a,** *to roll;* saxa, Verg.; **b,** *to turn round in a circle, to wind;* anguis tortus, Verg.; hence, **c,** *to hurl violently, whirl;* jaculum in hostem, Verg.; hastas, Cic.; **3,** transf., *to turn up;* spumas, Verg.; torquet medios nox humida cursus, *has finished the half of her journey,* Verg. **II. A.** *to throw round oneself;* tegumen immane, Verg. **B.** *to distort, sprain;* **1,** gen., **a,** lit., vultus mutantur, ora torquentur, Cic.; **b,** fig., *to distort;* verbo ac litterā jus omne torqueri, Cic.; **2,** esp., *to rack, torture, torment;* **a,** lit., Cic.; **b,** fig., (a) aliquem mero, *to make a person drink in order to test him,* Hor.; torqueatur vita Sullae, *be accurately examined,* Cic.; (β) *to torment, plague;* aliquem, Cic.; libidines te torquent, Cic.; expectatione torqueor, Cic.

torquis (torques) -is, m. and (in prose rarely) f. (torqueo), *that which is twisted or curved.* **I.** *a twisted collar or necklace;* torque

detracto, Cic. **II.** *the collar of draught oxen,* Verg. **III.** *a ring, wreath, chaplet;* ornatae torquibus arae, Verg.

torrens -entis, p. adj. (from torreo). **I.** *burning, hot, parched;* miles sole torrens, Liv. **II.** Transf., of water, *steaming, rushing, boiling.* **A.** Adj., aqua, Verg. **B.** Subst., **torrens** -entis, m. *a torrent,* Liv.; quam fertur quasi torrens oratio, Cic.

torrĕo, torrŭi, tostum, 2. *to burn, parch, dry up with heat or thirst;* aristas sole novo, Verg.; solis ardore torreri, Cic.; tosti crines, *singed,* Ov.; of fever, mihi torrentur febribus artus, Ov.; of thirst, Tib.; of love, torret amor pectora, Ov.

torresco, 3. (inchoat. of torreo), *to become parched, be dried up,* Lucr.

torrĭdus -a -um (torreo). **I.** Pass., *parched, burnt;* 1, *dry, arid;* **a,** lit., campi siccitate torridi, Liv.; **b,** transf., *meagre, lean;* homo vegrandi macie torridus, Cic.; 2, *pinched, nipped with cold;* membra torrida gelu, Liv. **II.** Act., *burning, hot;* aestas, Verg.; locus ab incendiis torridus, Liv.

torris -is, m. (torreo), *a firebrand,* Ov., Verg.

tortē, adv. (tortus), *crookedly, awry,* Lucr.

tortĭlis -e (torqueo), *twisted, twined;* aurum, *a golden chain,* Verg.

torto, 1. (intens. of torqueo), *to torture, torment,* Lucr.

tortor -ōris, m. (torqueo), *a torturer, tormentor, executioner,* Cic.

tortŭōsus -a -um (2. tortus). **I.** *full of turns and windings, tortuous.* **A.** Lit., alvus, Cic.; amnis, Liv.; loci, Cic. **B.** Fig., *perplexed, intricate, involved;* genus disputandi, Cic. **II.** *painful, tormenting,* Plin.

1. **tortus** -a -um, p. adj. (from torqueo), *twisted, crooked;* via, *the labyrinth,* Prop.; quercus, *an oak garland,* Verg.; vimen, *a beehive,* Ov.; fig., conditiones tortae, *intricate, perplexed,* Plaut.

2. **tortus** -ūs, m. (torqueo), *a twisting, winding, curve;* serpens longos dat corpore tortus, Verg.

tŏrŭlus -i, m. (dim. of torus), *a tuft,* Plaut.

tŏrus -i, m. (connected with sterno, στορέννυμι), *any round swelling protuberance.* Hence, **I.** *a knot in a rope,* Plin. **II.** *a knot or loop in a garland* (fig.), Cic. **III.** *a fleshy, projecting part of the body, muscle;* tori lacertorum, Cic. poet.; colla tument toris, Ov. **IV.** *a bed, sofa, mattress, cushion, couch,* Verg., Ov.; esp., (a) *the marriage couch,* Verg., Ov.; (β) *the bier;* toro componat, Ov. **V.** *a mound* or *elevation of earth;* tori riparum, Verg.

torvĭtas -ātis, f. (torvus), *savageness, wildness* (of appearance or character); vultus, Tac.

torvus -a -um (tero), *wild, savage, gloomy, severe, grim, fierce;* esp. of the eyes or the look, oculi, Ov.; forma minantis, Ov.; draco, Cic. poet.; proelia, Cat.

tŏt, num. indecl. (τόσα), *so many;* tot viri, Cic.; foll. by ut and the subj., Cic.; with quot, *as,* Cic.; by quoties, Cic.; with a prep. without a subst., ex tot, Ov.

tŏtĭdem, num. indecl. (= tot itidem), *just as many;* totidem annos vixerunt, Cic.; foll. by quot (as), totidem verbis, quot dixit, Cic.

tŏtĭens = toties (q.v.).

tŏtĭes, adv. (tot). **I.** *so often, so many times, as many times;* followed by quoties (as), quotiescumque, Cic.; quot, Liv. **II.** *just as many times,* Hor.

tōtus -a -um, genit. tōtīus, dat. tōti, *the whole, all, entire.* **I.** Of an object which is not divided, **a,** terra, Cic.; mons, Caes.; respublica, Cic.; **b,** *whole* = *with body and soul;* sum vester totus, *entirely yours,* Cic.; in prece totus eram, Ov.; **c,** *whole, complete, full;* sex menses totos, Ter.; subst., **tōtum** -i, n. *the whole,* Cic.; in toto, *on the whole,* Cic. **II.** Of an object opposed to its parts, *all, all together;* totis copiis, Caes.; totis viribus, Liv. (dat., toto, Caes., *B. G.,* 7, 89, 5).

toxĭcon (-um) -i, n. (τοξικόν), *poison for arrows,* Ov.

trăbālis -e (trabs). **I.** *of* or *relating to beams of wood;* clavus, *a spike,* Hor. **II.** *as strong* or *as large as a beam;* telum, Verg.

trăbĕa -ae, f. *the trabea, a white robe with scarlet horizontal stripes and a purple seam,* worn, **a,** by kings, Verg., Liv.; **b,** by knights on solemn processions, who were thence called trabeati; hence, meton. = *the equestrian order,* Mart.; **c,** by the augurs, Ov.

trăbĕātus -a -um (trabea), *clad in the* trabea; Quirinus, Ov.

trăbĕcŭla (**trăbĭcŭla**) -ae, f. (dim. of trabs), *a little beam,* Cato.

trabs, trăbis, f. (root TRAB, Gr. ΤΡΑΠ, whence τράπηξ). **I.** *a beam of wood,* Caes. **II.** Transf., 1, *the trunk of a tree, a tree;* trabes acernae, Verg.; 2, meton., *anything made out of beams;* **a,** *a ship;* Cypria, Hor.; **b,** *a roof, house;* sub isdem trabibus, Hor.; **c,** *a table,* Mart.

Trăchās -chantis, f. *a town in Italy* = Tarracina.

Trăchin -chīnis, f. (Τραχίν), *an old town in the Thessalian district of Phthiotis, residence of Ceyx, scene of the death of Hercules, afterwards called Heraclea.* Hence, **Trăchinius** -a -um (Τραχίνιος), *Trachinian;* heros, *Ceyx,* Ov.; so simply Trachinius, Ov.; plur. subst., Trachiniae, *the Trachinian women, name of a tragedy of Sophocles.*

tracta = tractum (q.v.).

tractābĭlis -e (tracto), *that can be handled* or *wrought, manageable.* **I.** Lit., tractabile onme necesse est esse, quod natum est, Cic.; caelum, *not stormy,* Verg. **II.** Transf., *yielding, compliant, tractable;* virtus, Cic.; nihil est eo (filio) tractabilius, Cic.

tractātĭo -ōnis, f. (tracto), *a handling, management.* **I.** Lit., beluarum, Cic.; armorum, Cic. **II.** Transf., 1, *a treating of, handling;* philosophiae, Cic.; 2, rhet. t. t., *a particular use of a word,* Cic.

tractātor -ōris, m. (tracto), *a slave who rubbed a bather's limbs, a shampooer,* Sen.

tractātrix -īcis, f. (tractator), *a female shampooer,* Mart.

tractātus -ūs, m. (tracto), *a handling, working, management.* **I.** Lit., Plin. **II.** Fig., *treatment, management;* 1, gen., ipsarum artium tractatu delectari, Cic.; 2, esp., *the treatment of a subject by an orator* or *writer,* Tac.

tractim, adv. (traho). **I.** *gradually, by degrees,* Lucr. **II.** *slowly, drawlingly;* susurrare, Verg.

tracto, 1. (traho). **I.** *to drag along, haul;* tractata comis antistita, Ov.; persona, quae propter otium ac studium minime in judiciis periculisque tractata est, Cic. **II.** *to touch;* 1, lit., **a,** manu or manibus aliquid, Cic.; vulnera, Cic.; fila lyrae, Ov.; **b,** *to handle, busy oneself with, work, manage;* terram, Lucr.; gubernacula, *to steer,* Cic.; arma, *to carry,* Cic.; pecuniam publicam, *to manage the public finances,* Cic.; 2, fig., **a,** gen., *to treat, handle, manage;* causas amicorum, Cic.; bellum, *conduct a war,* Liv.; tractare conditiones, *to treat about terms*

Caes.; partes secundas, *to act, play*, Hor.; in-transit., *to treat*; de conditionibus, Nep.; **b**, esp., (*a*) *to treat, behave oneself towards*; aspere, Cic.; honorificentius, Cic.; (*β*) *se, to behave oneself*; ita se tractare ut, etc., Cic.; (*γ*) *of speech or writing, to treat, discuss, handle a subject*; partem philosophiae, Cic.

tractum -i, n. (traho). **I.** *a flock of wool when carded or combed out*, Tib. **II.** *a cake*, Cato.

1. **tractus** -a -um, p. adj. (from traho). **I.** *drawn from, proceeding from*; venae a corde tractae, Cic. **II.** *fluent, flowing*; oratio tracta et fluens, Cic.

2. **tractus** -ūs, m. (traho), *a dragging.* **I.** 1, *drawing, draught, course*; **a**, lit., tractu gementem ferre rotam, Verg.; **b**, transf., (*a*) *the extent, space occupied by anything, position*; castrorum, Liv.; tractus ductusque muri, Caes.; (*β*) meton., *a tract of country, district*; totus, Cic.; hoc tractu oppidi erat regia, Caes.; corruptus caeli tractus, Verg.; 2, *a drawing away*; Syrtes ab tractu nominatae, Sall. **II.** Fig., 1, *course, motion*; **a**, *calm movement, composed style*; tractus orationis lenis et aequabilis, Cic.; **b**, of time, *course*, Lucr.; 2, esp., **a**, *drawling in pronunciation*; tractus verborum, Cic.; **b**, of time, *delay*; belli, Tac.

trāditĭo -ōnis, f. (trado). **I.** *a giving up, transferring, surrender*; rei, Cic.; oppidorum, Liv. **II.** *giving over by means of words*; **a**, of a teacher, *instruction*, Quint.; **b**, of a writer, *relation*, Tac.

trādĭtor -ōris, m. (trado), *a traitor*, Tac.

trādo -dĭdi -dĭtum, 3. *to give up.* **I.** In a narrow sense, *to give up, hand over*; alicui poculum, Cic.; equum comiti, Verg.; alicui testamentum legendum, Hor.; regnum or imperium alicui per manus, Liv. **II.** In a wider sense, *to give up, deliver over, consign to*; 1, gen., pecuniam regiam quaestoribus, Liv.; possessiones et res creditoribus, Caes.; 2, esp., **a**, *to hand over to a person's care, protection, management, to entrust*; alicui custodiam navium, Caes.; alicui turrim tuendam, Caes.; **b**, *to give to a person to lead*; alicui legionem, Caes.; **c**, *to give in marriage*; alicui neptem Agrippinam, Tac.; **d**, *to entrust to a person for instruction*; pueros magistris, Cic.; **e**, *to give by way of protection*; equites Romanos satellites alicui, Sall.; **f**, *to give over to the enemy, to hand over, deliver up*; arma, Caes.; alicui Galliae possessionem, Caes.; se alicui, Caes.; **g**, *to give over by way of sale, to sell*; aliquem dominis, Ov.; **h**, *to give up for punishment*; aliquem in custodiam, Cic.; aliquem ad supplicium, Caes.; **i**, *to expose*; feris populandas terras, Ov.; **j**, se, *to devote oneself to some thing or person, to give oneself over to*; se totum alicui, Cic.; se quieti, Cic.; totos se voluptatibus, Cic.; **k**, *to give over by words*; (*a*) *to entrust*; quae dicam trade memoriae, Cic.; (*β*) *to recommend*; aliquem alicui, Cic.; 1, *to hand down as a kind of inheritance to posterity*; (*a*) inimicitias posteris, Cic.; haec consuetudo a majoribus tradita, Cic.; (*β*) *to hand down in writing, report, relate*; qualia multa historia tradidit, Cic.; annales tradunt, foll. by acc. and infin., Liv.; so, tradunt (*they narrate*), tradi-tur, etc., with acc. and infin., Liv.; with nom. and infin., Lycurgi temporibus Homerus etiam fuisse traditur, Cic.; traditum est, with acc. and infin., Liv.; **m**, *to communicate by word of mouth*; (*a*) clamorem proximis, Caes.; (*β*) *to communicate in teaching, to teach*; elementa loquendi, Cic.; haec subtilius, Cic.

trādūco (transdūco) -duxi -ductum, 3. **I.** *to carry over, lead over, bring over or across.* **A.** Lit., 1, hominum multitudinem trans

Rhenum in Galliam, Caes.; **2**, esp., *to bring or lead on*, with acc. of object over which the thing is brought; flumen, pontem, Caes. **B.** Fig., 1, *to bring to, transpose, change*; **a**, Clodium ad plebem, Cic.; centuriones ex inferioribus ordinibus in superiores, Caes.; **b**, *to bring to a certain condition, alter, bring over*; animos a severitate ad hilaritatem risumque, Cic.; aliquem a disputando ad dicendum, Cic.; aliquem ad suam sententiam, Cic.; **2**, *to pass time, spend, lead*; otiosam aetatem, Cic.; **3**, *to direct*; curam in vitulos, Verg.; orationem traduxi et converti in increpandam fugam, Cic. **II.** *to lead, conduct through*; Helvetios per fines Sequanorum, Caes. **III.** *to lead by, lead past.* **A.** Lit., 1, copias praeter castra, Caes.; 2, esp., traducere equum (of a knight when he passed muster at the censor's inspection); quum esset censor et in equitum censu C. Licinius Sacerdos prodisset . . . jussit equum traducere, Cic. **B.** Fig., 1, *to show, let be seen*; se, Juv.; 2, *to expose to ridicule*; aliquem per ora hominum, Liv.

trāductĭo -ōnis, f. (traduco), *a leading on*; fig., 1, *a transferring of a man from a patrician family to a plebeian*; hominis ad plebem, Cic.; 2, *a bringing to public disgrace*, Sen.; 3, *a figure of speech, metonymy*, Cic.; 4, *temporis, passage, course or lapse of time*, Cic.

trāductor -ōris, m. (traduco), *a transferrer*; ad plebem (of Pompeius, who procured the transference of Clodius from a patrician to a plebeian family), Cic.

trādux -ŭcis, m. (traduco), *a vine-layer, prepared for transplanting*, Plin.

trăgăcantha -ae, f. (τραγακάνθα), *a plant*, goat's-thorn, tragacanth, Plin.

trăgēmăta -um, n. (τραγήματα), *dessert*, Plin.

trăgĭcē, adv. (tragicus), *tragically, after the manner of a tragedy*, Cic.

trăgĭcŏcōmoedĭa -ae, f. (*τραγικοκωμῳδία), tragi-comedy*, Plaut.

trăgĭcus -a -um (τραγικός). **I.** *of or relating to tragedy, tragic*; poema, tragedy, Cic.; poeta, a tragic poet, Cic.; actor, Liv.; Orestes, *appearing in a tragedy*, Cic.; subst., **trăgĭcus** -i, m. a tragic poet, Sen. **II.** Transf., *tragic*; **a**, *in tragic style, lofty, sublime*; orator, Cic.; **b**, *tragic, fearful, terrible, horrible*; scelus, Liv.

trăgĭon -ii, n. (τράγιον), *a plant with a smell like a goat*, Plin.

trăgoedĭa -ae, f. (τραγῳδία). **I.** *a tragedy*, Cic.; tragoedias facere, Cic.; tragoediam agere, Cic. **II.** Transf., *a tragic scene*; Appiae nomen quantas tragoedias excitat, Cic.; 2, *tragic pathos*; istis tragoediis tuis perturbor, Cic.

trăgoedus -i, m. (τραγῳδός), *a tragic actor*, tragedian, Cic.

trăgōnis = tragion (q.v.).

trăgŏpan -is, f. (τραγόπαν), *a bird* (perhaps vultur barbatus, Linn.), Plin.

trăgŏpōgon -ōnis, m. (τραγοπώγων), *the plant goat's-beard*, Plin.

trăgŏrīgănum -i, n. (τραγορίγανον), *a plant*, goat's-thyme, Plin.

trăgos -i, m. (τράγος), 1, *a thorny plant*, Plin.; 2, *a kind of sponge*, Plin.

trăgŭla -ae, f. (traho). **I.** *a species of javelin used by the Gauls and Spaniards*, Caes., Liv.; fig., tragulam injicere in aliquem, *to use artifice*, Plaut. **II.** *a kind of dragnet*, Plin. **III.** *a kind of sledge*, Varr.

trăgus -i, m. (τράγος), 1, *the smell under the armpits*, Mart.; 2, *a kind of fish*, Ov.

trăhĕa (trăha) -ae, f. (traho), *a sledge, drag,* Verg.

trăhax -ācis (traho), *drawing everything to oneself, greedy,* Plaut.

trăho, traxi, tractum, 3. *to draw, drag along.* **I.** Gen., **A.** Lit., *aliquem pedibus, Cic. ;* ad supplicium trahi, Sall., Tac., *or* trahi alone, Sall. **B.** Fig., 1, *to lead, draw away ;* trahit sua quemque voluptas, Verg. ; quid est quod me in aliam partem trahere possit? Cic. ; 2, *to bring upon ;* decus ad consulem, Liv. ; crimen in se, Ov. ; 3, *to ascribe, interpret, refer to ;* aliquid ad religionem, Liv. ; in diversa, Liv. **II.** Esp., **A.** *to draw after oneself, drag along ;* 1, a, lit., vestem, Hor. ; esp. from fatigue, corpus fessum, Liv. ; b, *to lead, conduct with oneself ;* exercitum, Liv. ; turbam prosequentium, Liv. ; 2, fig., tantum trahit ille timoris, Ov. **B.** *to draw to oneself, draw to, attract ;* 1, a, lit., auras ore, Ov. ; animam, *to breathe,* Liv. : esp., of persons drinking, *to quaff ;* pocula, Hor. ; b, transf., *to put on oneself ;* squamas, Ov. ; ruborem, Ov. ; 2, fig., a, *to assume ;* multum ex moribus (Sarmatarum) traxisse, Tac. ; b, *to take to oneself, appropriate ;* decumas, Cic. ; c, *to receive, gain ;* cognomen ex aliqua re, Cic. ; majorem ex pernicie et peste reipublicae molestiam, *to feel,* Cic.; d, *to take ;* in exemplum, Ov. **C.** *to draw together ;* vultus, Ov. ; vela, *to furl,* Verg. **D.** *to draw away, drag off ;* 1, lit., aliquem a templo, Verg.; praedas ex agris, Liv. ; hence, *to plunder ;* Aeduorum pagos, Tac. ; 2, fig., a, *to draw away from ;* ab incepto, Sall.; b, *to take away ;* partem doloris trahebat publica clades, Liv. ; c, *to borrow ;* consilium ex aliqua re, Sall. ; d, *to deduce, derive ;* sermonem ab initio, Cic. **E.** *to draw out, bring out, get out ;* 1, lit., aquam e puteis, Cic. ; ferrum e vulnere *or* a vulnere, Ov. ; 2, transf., vocem uno a pectore, Verg. **F.** *to draw down ;* lunam (de caelo), Ov. **G.** *to draw or drag hither and thither ;* 1, lit., corpus tractum, Cic. ; 2, fig., a, *to distract,* Tac.; b, *to squander ;* pecuniam, Sall. ; c, *to divide ;* sorte laborem, Verg. ; d, *to reflect on ;* rationes belli, Sall. **H.** *to draw out in length ;* 1, lit., a, *to lengthen ;* in spatium aures, Ov. ; b, *to spin out ;* data pensa, Ov. ; c, *to card ;* lanam mollem trahendo, Ov. ; 2, fig., of time, a, *to prolong, delay, put off ;* pugnam, Liv. ; comitia, Cic. ; rem in serum, Liv. ; b, *to drag along ;* vitam in tenebris, Verg.

trăĭcĭo = trajicio (q.v.).

trăjectĭo -ōnis, f. (trajicio). **I.** *a passing over, crossing over ;* a, of a person over the sea, *passage,* Cic. ; b, of things, stellarum, Cic. **II.** Fig., **A.** Gen., trajectio in alium, *a putting off upon,* Cic. **B.** Esp., 1, *the transposition of words ;* verborum, Cic. ; 2, *hyperbole ;* veritatis superlatio atque trajectio, Cic.

trăjectus -ūs, m. (trajicio), *a crossing over, passing over, passage ;* fluminis, Liv. ; commodissimus in Britanniam, Caes.

trăjĭcĭo (trāĭcĭo) -jēci -jectum, 3. (trans and jacio). **I.** *to throw over or across, to shoot across, convey over.* **A.** Gen., telum, Caes. ; vexillum trans vallum, Liv. **B.** Esp., 1, *to lead over or around, to remove, throw across ;* malos antennasque de nave in navem, Liv. ; trajecto in fune, *a rope slung round the mast,* Verg. ; 2, *to bring over ;* a, membra super acervum levi pede, *to leap over,* Ov. ; fig., aliquid ex illius invidia in te, Cic. ; b, *to transport over the sea, a river, a mountain, etc. ;* legiones in Siciliam, Liv.; copias trans fluvium, Liv.; Marius trajectus in Africam, *having crossed,* Cic. ; with acc. of the place, equitum magnam partem flumen, Caes.; reflex., with or without se, *to cross over, go over ;* sese ex regia ad aliquem, Caes. ; sese duabus navibus in Africam, Liv. ; trajicere

Trebiam navibus, Liv. ; with abl. of the water crossed, Aegaeo mari trajecit, Liv. **II.** *to throw over, hurl beyond ;* 1, murum jaculo, Cic. ; 2, a, *to pierce through, stab, transfix ;* aliquem venabulo, Liv. ; alicui femur tragulā, Caes. ; b, *to ride through, break through ;* pars magna equitum mediam trajecit aciem, Liv.

trālātīcĭus = translaticius (q.v.).

trālātĭo = translatio (q.v.).

trālātus, v. transfero.

trālŏquor (translŏquor), 3. dep. *to relate,* Plaut.

1. **Tralles** -ĭum, m. (Τράλλες), *an Illyrian people,* Liv. (acc. Trallis).

2. **Trallēs** = Trallis (q.v.).

Trallis -ĭum, f. (αἱ Τράλλεις), *a town in Caria, near Mount Mesogis.* Hence, **Trallĭānus** -a -um, *of or relating to Tralles*

trālūcĕo = transluceo (q.v.).

trāma -ae, f. (traho), *the woof* in weaving ; transf., *the spider's web,* Plin. ; trama figurae, *a lanky, lean person,* Pers. ; tramae putridae, *trifles,* Plaut.

trāmĕo = transmeo (q.v.).

trāmes -ĭtis, m. (trameo), *a by-way, cross-road.* **I.** Lit., Apennini tramites, Cic. ; transversis tramitibus transgredi, Liv. **II.** Transf., poet., *a way, course, road, path ;* cito decurrit tramite virgo, Verg.

trāmigro = transmigro (q.v.).

trāmitto = transmitto (q.v.).

trānāto (transnăto), 1. *to swim across,* Tac.; with acc. of place, Gangem, Cic.

trāno (transno), 1. **I.** *to swim over, swim across ;* ad suos, Liv.; with acc. of place, flumen, Caes. ; pass., tranantur aquae, Ov. **II.** Transf., *to swim through, to sail through, go through, fly through, pass through ;* nubila, Verg. ; genus igneum quod tranat omnia, *pervades,* Cic.

tranquillē, adv. with compar. and superl. (tranquillus), *quietly, tranquilly,* Cic.

tranquillĭtās -ātis, f. (tranquillus), *calmness, tranquillity.* **I.** Lit., *a calm, freedom from wind, calm sea, weather ;* maris, Cic. ; summā tranquillitate consecutā, Caes. ; tanta subito malacia et tranquillitas exstitit, Caes. **II.** Transf., *rest, peace ;* a, polit., summa tranquillitas pacis atque otii, Cic.; b, *mental ;* animi, Cic.

1. **tranquillō**, adv. (tranquillus), *quietly,* Liv.

2. **tranquillo**, 1. (tranquillus), *to make tranquil, tranquillise.* **I.** Lit., mare oleo, Plin. **II.** Fig., animos, Cic.

tranquillus -a -um (trans and quies), *tranquil.* **I.** Lit., *calm ; esp., free from wind ;* mare, Cic. ; serenitas, Liv. ; subst., **tranquillum** -i, n. *a calm ;* in tranquillo tempestatem adversam optare dementis est, Cic. **II.** Transf., *peaceful, tranquil, undisturbed, serene ;* tranquilla et serena frons, Cic. ; subst., **tranquillum** -i, n. *quiet ;* rempublicam in tranquillum redigere, Liv.

trans, prep. with acc. **I.** *on the other side of ;* trans montem, Cic.; trans Rhenum, Caes. **II.** *over, across ;* trans Alpes transfertur, Cic. ; trans mare currunt, Hor.

transăbĕo -ĭi -ĭtum, 4. *to go through, penetrate ;* ensis transabiit costas, Verg.

transactor -ōris, m. (transigo), *a manager, accomplisher ;* rerum huiuscemodi omnium transactor et administer, Cic.

transădĭgo -ēgi -actum, 3. **I.** *to drive through, thrust through ;* crudum ensem trans-

adigit costas, Verg. **II.** *to pierce, penetrate;* hasta horum unum transadigit costas, Verg.

transalpīnus -a -um, *beyond the Alps, transalpine;* Gallia, Caes.

transcendo (transscendo) -scendi -scensum, 3. (trans and scando). **I.** Intransit. *to climb over, step over, pass over;* 1, lit., in hostium naves, Caes.; 2, fig., ad ea (of discourse), Tac. **II.** Transit., *to climb over, step over;* 1, lit., muros, Liv.; Caucasum, Cic.; 2, fig., *to step over, transgress;* fines juris, Lucr.; ordinem aetatis, Liv.

transcīdo -cīdi -cīsum, 3. (trans and caedo), *to cut through,* Plaut.

transcrībo (transscrībo) -scripsi -scriptum, 3. *to copy, transcribe.* **I.** Gen., testamentum in alias tabulas, Cic. **II.** Esp., 1, *to transfer, assign;* a, lit., nomina in socios, Liv.; b, transf., alicui spatium vitae, Ov.; sceptra colonis, Ov.; 2, *to transfer;* matres urbi, Verg.

transcurro -cŭcurri and -curri -cursum, 3. **I.** 1, *to run over, hasten over;* ad forum, Ter.; in castra, Liv.; 2, fig., *to pass over;* ad melius, Hor. **II. A.** *to run* or *hasten through;* 1, lit., per spatium, Lucr.; with acc., caelum transcurrit nimbus, Verg.; 2, fig., cursum suum, Cic. **B.** *to sail* or *travel past;* 1, lit., Caes.; praeter oculos, Ov.; 2, fig., of time, *to pass by,* Plin.

transcursus -ūs, m. (transcurro), 1, a *running past, hastening through,* Sen.; 2, of discourse, *a brief mention,* Plin.

transdānŭvĭānus -a -um, *beyond the Danube,* Liv.

transdo = trado (q.v.).

transdūco = traduco (q.v.).

transenna -ae, f. (for transepna from trans and apo). **I.** *a number of ropes* or *wooden bars, transposed crosswise;* hence, *a net for catching birds;* 1, lit., Plaut.; 2, fig., *a net, trap, noose,* Plaut. **II.** *a lattice over a window,* Cic.

transĕo -ii -ĭtum, 4. **I.** Intransit., **A.** *to go over to, go to;* 1, a, ad uxorem, Ter.; in Helvetiorum fines, Caes.; b, *to go over as a deserter;* ad aliquem, Cic.; c, *to go over from one political party to another,* Tac.; d, *to pass from one rank to another;* a patribus ad plebem, Liv.; e, transf., *to be changed into, to be transformed into;* in saxum, Ov.; 2, fig., a, transitum est ad honestatem dictorum et factorum, Cic.; b, of discourse, *to pass over, make a transition;* ad partitionem, Cic.; c, *to go over to an opinion;* in alicuius sententiam, *to be converted to the opinion of,* Liv. **B.** *to go through;* 1, lit., per media castra, Sall.; 2, fig., *to penetrate;* quaedam animalis intelligentia per omnia permanat et transit, Cic. **C.** *to pass by;* transf., of time, *to pass by, pass away;* transiit aetas quam cito I Tib.; dies legis transiit, Cic. **II.** Transit. **A.** *to go over, pass over;* 1, lit., a, Euphratem, Cic.; pass., Rhodanus transitur, Caes.; b, esp., *to overtake;* equum cursu, Verg.; 2, fig., a, *to pass beyond, to transgress;* fines verecundiae, Cic.; b, *to surpass;* facile, Cic.; c, *to despatch;* magna, Tac. **B.** *to go through, pass through;* 1, lit., Formias, Cic.; vim flammae, Nep.; 2, fig., a, *to pass over cursorily, to touch lightly on;* leviter transire et tantummodo perstringere unamquamque rem, Cic.; b, of time, *to pass, spend;* annum quiete, Tac.; vitam, Sall. **C.** *to pass by;* 1, lit., omnes mensas, Plaut.; 2, fig., *to pass by;* aliquid silentio, Cic. (perf., transiit, Verg.).

transĕro (transsĕro) -sĕrŭi -sertum, 3. *to put, thrust through,* Cato.

transfĕro (trāfĕro), transtŭli, translātum, and trālātum, transferre, 3. *to carry over* or *across, transfer, transport, convey.* **A.** Lit., 1,

gen., Caesar paullo ultra eum locum **castra** transtulit, Caes.; aliquem trans Alpes, Cic.; reflex., se transferre Glycerae decoram in aedem, Hor.; 2, esp., *to write down;* in tabulas, Cic. **B.** Fig., 1, gen., *to bring over, remove, transpose;* regnum ab sede Lavini, Verg.; omnia Argos, *give the victory to Argos,* Verg.; in Celtiberiam bellum, Caes.; sermonem alio, *turn to another subject,* Cic.; 2, esp., a, *to put off, defer;* causam in proximum annum, ap. Cic.; b, *to change to;* definitionem in aliam rem, Cic.; c, *to translate into another language;* istum ego locum totidem verbis a Dicaearcho transtuli, Cic.; d, *to use figuratively* or *metaphorically;* verba, quae transferuntur, Cic.

transfīgo -fixi -fixum, 3. **I.** *to pierce through, transfix;* puellam gladio, Liv.; transfixus hastā, Cic. **II.** *to thrust through;* hasta transfixa, Verg.

transfīgūrātĭo -ōnis, f. (transfiguro), *a transformation, transfiguration,* Plin.

transfīgūro, 1. *to transform, transfigure,* Suet., Plin.

transflŭo -fluxi, 3. *to flow out, flow through,* Plin.

transfŏdĭo -fōdi -fossum, 3. *to stab through, transpierce, transfix;* alicui latus, Liv.; aliquem, Caes.; partic., with acc. of respect, pectora duro transfossi ligno, Verg.

transformis -e (trans and forma), *changed, transformed,* Ov.

transformo, 1. *to change, transfigure, transform;* se in vultus aniles, Verg.

transfŏro, 1. *to pierce, thrust through,* Sen.

transfrēto, 1. (trans and fretum), *to cross the sea,* Suet.

transfŭga -ae, c. (transfugio), *a deserter,* Cic.; specie transfugarum ad Flaccum venire, Liv.; transf., transfuga divitum partes linquere gestio, Hor.

transfŭgĭo -fūgi -fŭgĭtum, 3. *to desert to the enemy.* **I.** Lit., Gabios, Romam, Liv.; absol., quod in obsidione et fame servitia infida transfugerent, Liv. **II.** Fig., ab afflicta amicitia transfugere et ad florentem aliam devolare, Cic. *desert unhappy friends,* Cic.

transfŭgĭum -ĭi, n. (transfugio), *a going over to the enemy, deserting,* Liv.

transfundo -fūdi -fūsum, 3. *to pour from one vessel into another.* **I.** Lit., Plin. **II.** Transf., *to transfer;* omnem amorem in aliquem, Cic.

transfūsĭo -ōnis, f. (transfundo), *a pouring out, pouring off.* **I.** Lit., Plin. **II.** Transf., *the migration of a people,* Cic.

transgrĕdĭor -gressus sum, 3. dep. (trans and gradior). **I.** Intransit., *to go across* or *over, pass over.* **A.** Lit., 1, gen., in Europam, Liv.; per montes, Liv.; 2, esp., *to pass over to any one's side* or *party;* in partes alicuius, Tac. **B.** Transf., *to pass over to some action, advance;* tarde ad sacramentum, Tac. **II.** Transit., *to pass over, pass through.* **A.** Lit., Taurum, Cic.; flumen, Caes. **B.** Transf., a, *to pass beyond some measure* or *time,* Plin.; b, *to pass over in silence;* mentionem viri, Vell.; c, *to surpass,* Plin. (partic. perf. pass., transgresso Apennino, Liv. 10.27.1).

transgressĭo -ōnis, f. (transgredior). **I.** Intransit., *a going over, passage;* ascensus et transgressio Gallorum (over the Alps), Cic. **II.** Transit., *a transposition of words;* verborum, Cic.

transgressus -ūs, m. (transgredior), *a going over, passage;* auspicium prosperi transgressus, Tac.; with object. genit., amnis, Tac.

transĭgo -ēgi -actum, 3. (trans and ago), to drive through. **I.** Lit., to stab, pierce through; se ipsum gladio, Tac. **II.** Fig., 1, to pass time, spend, lead; tempus per ostentationem, Tac.; 2, to finish, complete, accomplish, transact any piece of business; a, gen., negotium, Cic.; aliquid cum aliquo, aliquid per aliquem, Cic.; impers., si transactum est, if it is done, Cic.; b, esp., to settle a difference or dispute, come to an understanding; cum aliquo H.S. ducentis milibus, Cic.; transf., to put an end to, have done with; transigite cum expeditionibus, Tac.

transĭlĭo (transsĭlĭo) -ŭi and (rarely) -ĭi and -ivi, 4. (trans and salio). **I.** Intransit., to spring over, leap across; 1, lit., de muro in navem, Liv.; 2, fig., ab illo consilio ad aliud, to go over to, Liv. **II.** Transit., to spring over something; 1, a, lit., to spring over; muros, Liv.; b, transf., to hasten over; rates transiliunt vada, Hor.; 2, fig., a, to pass by, pass over; rem, Cic.: b, to overstep, transgress; lineas, Cic.; munera Liberi, be immoderate with, Hor.

transĭlis -e (transilio), leaping across, going across; palmes, Plin.

transĭtĭo -ōnis, f. (transeo). **I.** a going across, passing over. **A.** Lit., 1, gen., imagines similitudine et transitione perceptae, Cic.; 2, esp., a going over from one party or faction to another; a, ad plebem transitiones, Cic.; b, a passing over to the enemy; sociorum, Liv.; exercitus transitionibus imminutus, Liv. **B.** Fig., infection, contagion, Ov. **II.** a passage (meton., as a place); transitiones perviae Jani nominantur, Cic.

transĭtōrĭus -a -um (transeo), having a passage through; domus, Suet.

transĭtus -ūs, m. (transeo). **I.** a passing over or across, transit. **A.** Lit., 1, gen., transitus fossae, Cic.; transitum claudere, Liv.; 2, esp., a passing over from one party or faction to another; facili transitu ad proximos et validiores, Tac. **B.** Fig., a, the transition (in painting) from shade to light, Plin., Ov.; b, transition in discourse, Quint. **II.** a passing through. **A.** Lit., per agros urbesque, Liv. **B.** Meton., the place through which one passes; transitus insidere, Liv. **III.** a passing by; tempestatis, Cic.; in transitu capta urbs, Tac.

transjectĭo, etc. = trajectio, etc. (q.v.).

translātĭcĭus (trālātĭcĭus) -a -um (translatus, from transfero), handed down as customary, prescriptive; a, edictum, received by a magistrate from his predecessor, Cic.; b, common, usual; haec tralaticia, ordinary course of things, ap. Cic.

translātĭo (trālātĭo) -ōnis, f. (translatus, from transfero), a transferring, handing over. **I.** Lit., 1, pecuniarum a justis dominis ad alienos, Cic.; 2, a grafting of plants, Plin. **II.** Fig., 1, a transferring; a, of a judge, accuser, place, etc., Cic.; b, of an accusation, criminis, Cic.; 2, a metaphor, trope, figure; verecunda, Cic.

translātīvus -a -um (transfero), of or relating to a transference; constitutio, Cic.

translātor -ōris, m. (transfero), a transferrer; quaesturae (of Verres, who, being quaestor to the consul Cn. Papirius Carbo, deserted to Sulla), Cic.

translūcĕo (trālūcĕo), 2. **I.** to shine across, Lucr. **II.** to shine through, be visible through, Ov.

translūcĭdus (trālūcĭdus) -a -um, transparent, translucent, Plin.

transmārīnus -a -um, from beyond sea, foreign, transmarine; artes, Cic.; legationes, Liv.

transmĕo (trāmĕo), 1. to go over, across, through, Plin.

19*

transmĭgro, 1. to migrate from one place to another; Veios, Liv.: transf. of plants, to be transplanted, Plin.

transmissĭo -ōnis, f. (transmitto), a passage; ab eā urbe in Graeciam, Cic.

transmissus -ūs, m. (transmitto), a passage; pari spatio transmissus atque ex Gallia in Britanniam, Caes.

transmitto (trāmitto) -mīsi -missum, 3. **I.** to send across, send over, convey across, transmit from one place to another. **A.** 1, lit., equitatum celeriter, Caes.; classem in Euboeam ad urbem Oreum, Liv.; 2, fig., a, bellum in Italiam, Liv.; b, to give over; (a) to entrust; huic hoc tantum bellum, Cic.; (β) to resign, yield; munia imperii, Tac.; (γ) to devote; suum tempus temporibus amicorum, Cic. **B.** to let pass, let through; 1, gen., exercitum per fines, Liv.; 2, to lead from one point to another; transmissum per viam tigillum, placed across the road, Liv. **C.** to let pass; Junium mensem transmisimus, Tac. **II.** to place oneself, to go, run, swim, pass through or over something; 1, lit., a, gen., (a) with acc. of place, maria, Cic.; (β) absol., sin ante transmisisset, Cic.; b, esp., to hurl, or throw over or through, Ov.; 2, fig., to leave unnoticed, take no heed to, take no notice of, not to mind; Scaurum silentio transmisit, Tac.

transmontāni -ōrum, m. dwellers beyond the mountains, Liv.

transmŏvĕo -mōvi -mōtum, 2. to remove from one place to another. **I.** Lit., Syriā legiones, Tac. **II.** Fig., to transfer, Ter.

transmūtātĭo -ōnis, f. (transmuto), the transmutation of letters, Quint.

transmūto, 1. to change, transmute; dextera laevis, Lucr.; incertos honores, Hor.

transnăto = tranato (q.v.).

transnōmĭno, 1. to change the name of a person or thing, Suet.

transpădānus -a -um, beyond (i.e., on the north side of) the Po, transpadane; colonia, Caes.; clientes, Cic. Subst., **transpădānus** -i, m. a person living on the north side of the Po, Cat.; plur., Cic.

transpectus -ūs, m. (transpicio), a looking through, seeing through, Lucr.

transpĭcĭo (transspĭcĭo), 3. (trans and specio), to look through, see through, Lucr.

transpōno -pŏsŭi -pŏsĭtum, 3. **I.** to put over, across, remove, transfer, Plin. **II.** (= trajicere), to put across (a river); militem dextras in terras iturum, Tac.

transportātĭo -ōnis, f. (transporto), a migration, Sen.

transporto, 1. to convey from one place to another, transport; exercitum in Graeciam, Cic.; milites his navibus flumen transportat, Caes.

transrhēnānus -a -um (trans and Rhenus), beyond (i.e., on the east side of) the Rhine; Germani, Caes.

transs . . . v. trans . . .

transtĭbĕrīnus -a -um (trans and Tiberis), beyond the Tiber. Subst., **transtĭbĕrini** -ōrum, m. the people living beyond the Tiber, Cic.

transtĭnĕo, 2. (teneo), to go through, pass through, Plaut.

transtrum -i, m. (from trans). **I.** a cross-bench in a ship on which the rowers sat, gen. plur., Caes. **II.** a cross-beam, Caes.

transulto (transsulto), 1. (intens. of transilio), to spring over or across, Liv.

transŭo (transsŭo) -sŭi -sūtum, 3. to sew

through, stitch through, pierce through; exta transuta verubus, Ov.

transvectĭo (trāvectĭo) -ōnis, f. (transveho). **I.** *a carrying over or across;* Acherontis, Cic. **II.** *the riding of a Roman knight past the censor at the periodical muster,* Suet.

transvĕho (trāvĕho) -vexi -vectum, **3. I.** *to carry over, convey across, transport.* **A.** Act., milites, Caes.; naves plaustris, Liv. **B.** Middle, transvehi, *to ride, sail, pass over or across;* in Africam, Sall.; Corcyram, Liv. **II.** *to carry through or by.* **A.** Act., *to bear along in triumph;* arma spoliaque carpentis, Liv. **B.** Middle, transvehi = *to go, ride, pass by;* **1,** lit., a, gen., transvectae a fronte pugnantium alae, Tac.; b, esp., at a public procession, *to ride by;* (α) of the Caesars at the games in the circus, Tac.; (β) of a knight, *to ride past the censor at a muster,* Liv.; **2,** fig., of time, *to pass, pass by;* abiit jam et transvectum est tempus, Tac.

transverbĕro, l. *to pierce through, transfix, perforate;* bestiam venabulo, Cic.; pectus alicuius abiete, Verg.

transversārĭus -a -um (transversus), *lying across, transverse;* tigna, Caes.

transversus (trāversus), and transvorsus -a -um, p. adj. (from transverto), *transverse, oblique, athwart.* **I.** Adj., **A.** Lit., fossa, Caes.; transverso ambulare foro, *across the forum,* Cic.; transverso itinere, *in an oblique direction,* Liv.; fig., transversum digitum, *a finger's breadth,* Cic.; transversum digitum, *the breadth of a nail,* Cic. **B.** Fig., cuius in adulescentiam transversa incurrit misera reipublicae fortuna, *crossed, thwarted,* Cic. **II.** Subst., **transversum** -i, n. *a cross-direction,* Plin.; de or ex transverso, *unexpectedly;* ecce tibi e transverso Lampsacenus Strabo qui, etc., Cic. **III.** Adv., transversum and plur., transversa, *across, sideways;* venti transversa fremunt, Verg.

transvŏlĭto, l. *to fly across,* Lucr.

transvŏlo (trāvŏlo), l. **I.** *to fly over or across;* **1,** lit., of birds, Plin.; **2,** transf., *to hasten over, hasten across, pass over hastily;* Alpes, ap. Cic.; eques transvolat in alteram partem, Liv. **II.** l, *to fly through or to, to fly through;* transf. = *to hasten through;* dum (vox) transvolat aures, Lucr.; **2,** *to fly past;* a, transf., *to hasten past;* aridas quercus, Hor.; b, fig., transvolat in medio posita, *passes by,* Hor.

trăpētus -i, m., **trăpētum** -i, n., and plur., **trăpētes** -um, m. (τραπέω, *to tread grapes), an oil-press,* Verg.

trăpezĭta -ae, m. (τραπεζίτης), *a money-changer,* Plaut.

Trăpezūs -untis, f. (Τραπεζοῦς), *a town in Pontus, colony of Sinope, now Trebizond, Tarabosan.*

Trăsūmēnus (Trăsŭmennus, Trăsĭmēnus, Trăsўmēnus) -i, m. (with or without lacus), *the Trasimene lake, on the banks of which Hannibal conquered the Romans under Flaminius* (217 B.C.), *now Lago di Perugia.* Hence, adj., **Trăsūmēnus** -a -um, *Trasimenian.*

trav . . . v. transv . . .

trăvĭo, l. *to go through, penetrate,* Lucr.

Trēbĭa -ae, m. *a river in Cisalpine Gaul, where Hannibal conquered the Romans,* 217 B.C., now *Trebbia.*

Trĕbŭla -ae, f. *three towns in Italy.* **I.** In the Sabine country. **A.** Trebula Mutusca. Hence, **Trĕbŭlānus** -a -um, *belonging to Trebula.* **B.** Trebula Suffena. **II.** In Campania, near Suessula and Saticula. now *Maddaloni.*

Hence, **Trĕbŭlānus** -a -um, *belonging to Trebula.*

trĕcēnārĭus -a -um (trecenti), *three-hundred-fold,* Varr.

trĕcēni -ae -a (tres and centum). **I.** *three hundred each,* Liv. **II.** *three hundred,* Plin.

trĕcentēsĭmus -a -um (trecenti), *the three-hundredth,* Cic.

trĕcenti -ae -a (tres and centum), *three hundred,* Cic.

trĕcentĭēs (trĕcentĭens), adv. (trecenti), *three hundred times,* Cat.

trĕchĕdipnum -i, n. (τρεχέδειπνος -ον, *hastening to dinner), a light garment worn by parasites at table,* Juv.

trĕdĕcim (tres and decem), *thirteen,* Liv.

trĕmĕbundus (trĕmĭbundus) -a -um (tremo), *trembling;* manus, Cic.

trĕmĕfăcĭo -fēci -factum, **3.** (tremo and facio), *to cause to tremble;* pass., **trĕmĕfīo** -factus sum -fĭeri *to tremble,* Verg., Ov.

trĕmendus -a -um (tremo), *fearful, dreadful, terrible, dread,* Hor.; rex, Pluto, Verg.

trĕmesco (trĕmisco), **3.** (inchoat. of tremo). **I.** Intransit., *to tremble, quake;* a, of things, tonitru tremescunt ardua terrarum et campi, Verg.; b, of persons, omnem tremescens ad strepitum, Ov. **II.** Transit., *to tremble at;* sonitum pedum vocemque, Verg.; with infin., telum instare tremescit, Verg.

trĕmĭbundus = tremebundus (q.v.).

trĕmisco = tremesco (q.v.).

trĕmo -ŭi, **3.** (τρέμω), *to tremble, quake.* **I.** Intransit., **a,** of things, tremit hasta, Verg.; b, of persons, toto pectore tremens, Cic.; with acc. of respect, tremis ossa pavore, Hor. **II.** Transit., *to tremble, quake at;* offensam Junonem, Ov.; te, Verg.; virgas ac secures dictatoris, Liv.

trĕmor -ōris, m. (tremo). **I.** *a trembling, quaking, tremor;* of the limbs, pallor et tremor et dentium crepitus, Liv.; of fire, tremor ignium clarus, Lucr.; of the earth, Verg.; plur., Lucr., Ov. **II.** Meton., *an object which causes fear and trembling,* Mart.

trĕmŭlus -a -um (tremo). **I.** *trembling, quaking, quivering, tremulous;* a, of things, lumen, Verg.; mare, Ov.; b, of persons, accurrit ad me tremulus, Ter. **II.** Act., *causing trembling,* Prop.

trĕpĭdantĕr, adv. (trepido), *anxiously, with trepidation;* omnia trepidantius timidiusque agere, Caes.

trĕpĭdātĭo -ōnis, f. (trepido), *agitation, anxiety, disquiet, alarm, trepidation,* Cic.; tantam trepidationem injecit ut, etc., Liv.

trĕpĭdē, adv. (trepidus), *tremblingly, anxiously, with trepidation;* castra relinquere Liv.

trĕpĭdo, l. (trepidus), *to be in anxious, confused motion, be agitated, be in alarm, be busy, bustle about anything;* a, lit., of living beings, totis trepidatur castris, *the whole camp is in confusion,* Caes.; circa advenam, *swarm confusedly around,* Liv.; circa signa, *give way in front,* Liv.; of anxious haste, ad arma, Liv.; with inter and the acc., *to be undecided between,* *to waver between;* inter fugae pugnaeque consilium, Liv.; with acc.= *to fear anxiously;* occursum amici, Juv.; with infin., ne trepidate meas defendere naves, Verg.; b, transf., of things, aqua per pronum trepidat rivum, *ripples,* Hor.; trepidant flammae, *flicker* Hor.; with infin., cuius octavum trepidavit (*is hastening on*) aetas claudere lustrum, Hor.

trĕpĭdus -a -um (τρέω), *unquiet, anxious, alarmed, restless, disturbed;* **a,** lit., of living beings and the situation of living beings, trepida Dido, Verg.; of undecided or rash haste, civitas, Liv.; with genit., *on account of;* rerum suarum, Liv.; metus, Ov.; cursus, Verg.; in re trepida, in rebus trepidis, *in an alarming state of things,* Liv.; **b,** transf., of things, unda, *boiling, bubbling,* Ov.; ahenum, *boiling,* Verg.

trēs (archaic, **trīs**), **trĭa** (τρεῖς, τρία), *three,* Cic.

tressis -is, m. (tres and as), *three asses,* Varr.

tresvĭri = triumviri (q.v.).

Trēvĕri (Trēvĭri) -ōrum, m. *a powerful German nation from the Rhine to the Maas, whose capital Augusta or Colonia Treverorum is now Trèves or Trier.* Sing., **Trēvir** -vĭri, *one of the Treveri.* Hence, adj., **Trēvĕrĭcus (Trēvĭrĭcus)** -a -um, *of or belonging to the Treveri.*

trĭangŭlus -a -um (tres and angulus), *three-cornered, triangular.* Subst., **triangŭlum** -i, n. *a triangle,* Cic.

triārĭi -ōrum, m. (tres), *the oldest and most experienced Roman soldiers, who were drawn up in the third rank, kneeling behind the* hastati *and* principes, *ready to help these in need;* hence, prov., res ad triarios rediit, *the matter has come to the extremest need,* Liv.

tribas -ădis, f. (τριβάς), *an unchaste woman,* Phaedr.

Trĭbŏces -um, m. and **Trĭbŏci** -ōrum, m. *a Gallic people on the left bank of the Rhine, in modern Alsace.*

trĭbrăchys, acc. -chyn, m. (τρίβραχυς), sc. pes, *a metrical foot, consisting of three short syllables* (∪ ∪ ∪), Quint.

trĭbŭārĭus -a -um (tribus), *of or relating to a tribe,* Cic.

trĭbŭla = tribulum (q.v.).

trĭbŭlis -is, m. (tribus), *one who belongs to the same tribe, a fellow tribesman;* tribulis tuus, Cic.; esp., *a fellow tribesman of the lower classes, one of the common people,* Hor.

trĭbŭlo, 1. (tribulum), *to press,* Cato.

trĭbŭlum -i, n. (tero), *a threshing machine,* Varr.

trĭbŭlus -i, m. 1, *a thorny plant* (Tribulus terrestris, Linn.), Ov.; 2, *an aquatic plant* (Trapa natans, Linn.), Plin.

trĭbŭnal -ālis, n. (= tribunaie, from tribunus), *the tribunal.* **I.** Lit., *a raised platform for magistrates,* e.g., for the consul when he directed the comitia, the praetor when he administered justice; in tribunali Pompeii praetoris urbani sedentes, Cic.; of the raised seat of a general in the camp, Liv.; of the praetor in the theatre, Suet.; meton., of the magistrate sitting on the tribunal, omne forum (*the people*) quem spectat et omne tribunal, *the magistrates, distinguished persons,* Hor. **II.** Transf., **A.** *a monument erected in honour of the dead,* Tac. **B.** *a mound, embankment of earth,* Plin.

trĭbūnātus -ūs, m. (tribunus), *the office or dignity of a tribune, tribuneship;* **a,** of the people, with or without plebis, Cic.; **b,** of a military tribune, militaris, Cic.

trĭbūnĭcĭus -a -um (tribunus), *of or relating to a tribune, tribunicial;* **a,** *belonging to a tribune of the people;* potestas, Cic.; subst., **trĭbūnĭcĭus** -ii, m. *a person who has been tribune;* **b,** *relating to the tribunes of the soldiers;* honos, Caes.

trĭbūnus -i, m. (tribus). **I.** tribuni, *the presidents of the three old tribes, representative of the tribules, at the head of whom was the tribunus* Celerum, Liv. **II. A.** tribuni aerarii, *pay-*

masters who assisted the quaestors, and who were afterwards made judges, Cic. **B.** Milit. t. t., tribuni militum or militares, *military tribunes, six to every legion, who commanded it each for two months in the year,* Caes. **C.** tribuni militum consulari potestate (also called tribuni consulares), *chosen to govern in the place of consuls,* from 444–366 B.C., Liv. **D.** tribuni plebis (plebi) and (more frequently) simply tribuni, *the tribunes of the people, the magistrates who protected the plebeians,* Cic., Liv.

trĭbŭo -ŭi -ūtum, 3. **I.** *to allot to any one as a share, bestow, assign, give.* **A.** Lit., praemia alicui, Caes.; suum cuique, Cic. **B.** Fig., 1, gen., *to give, show;* alicui misericordiam suam, Cic.; alicui magnam gratiam, Cic.; 2, esp., **a,** *to give up, concede, yield to;* valetudini aliquid, Cic.; alicui priores partes, Cic.; **b,** *to ascribe; attribute to;* id virtuti hostium, Caes.; **c,** *to devote time to a particular purpose;* his rebus tantum temporis, Caes. **II.**= distribuo, *to divide;* rem in partes, Caes.

trĭbus -ūs, f. (from root tri, *three,* and the root fu in φυλή), originally, *a third part of the Roman people.* Hence, **I.** *a tribe, one of the three tribes of the Roman people* (Ramnes, Tities, Luceres); from the time of Servius Tullius a new division was made, viz., of four tribes for the city (tribus urbanae), and twenty-six, and later thirty-one, for the ager Romanus (tribus rusticae); populum in tribus convocare, Cic. **II.** Meton., plur., tribus = *the lower classes, the mob,* Plin.

trĭbūtārĭus -a -um (tributum), *of or relating to tribute;* tabellae, Cic.

trĭbūtim, adv. (tribus), *according to tribes, tribe by tribe;* nummos dividere, Cic.

trĭbūtĭo -ōnis, f. (tribuo), *a distribution, dividing,* Cic.

trĭbūtum -i, n. (tribuo). **I.** *tax, contribution, tribute;* tributum conferre, facere, pendĕre, Cic. **II.** Transf., *a gift, present,* Ov..

1. **trĭbūtus** -a -um (tribus), *arranged according to tribes;* comitia, *in which the people voted by tribes,* Liv.

2. **trĭbūtus,** v. tribuo.

trīcae -ārum, f. 1, *trifles, trumpery, nonsense,* Mart.; 2, *vexations, troubles, perplexities;* quomodo domesticas tricas (fert)? Cic.

Trĭcastīni -ōrum, m. *a Gallic people, near modern Aouste.*

Tricca -ae, f. (Τρίκκη), *an old town in Thessaly on the Peneus, now Trikkala.*

trĭcēnārĭus -a -um (triceni), *containing the number thirty;* filius, *thirty years old,* Sen.

trĭcēni -ae -a, genit. tricenûm (triginta), 1, *thirty each,* Cic.; 2, *thirty,* Plin.

trĭceps -cĭpĭtis (tres and caput), 1, *three-headed,* Cic.; 2, *three-fold,* Varr.

trĭcēsĭmus -a -um (triginta), *the thirtieth,* Cic.

trĭcessis -is, m. (triginta and as), *thirty asses,* Varr.

trĭchĭas -ae, m. (τριχίας), *a species of sardine,* Plin.

trĭchĭla -ae, f. *a summer-house, arbour,* Caes.

trĭchītis -ĭdis, f. (τριχῖτις), *a kind of alum,* Plin.

trĭcĭēs (trĭcĭens), adv. (triginta), *thirty times,* Cic.

trĭclīnĭāris -e (triclinium), *of or relating to a dining-couch,* Plin. Subst., **trĭclīnĭāria** -ium, n. a, *a dining-room,* Plin.; **b,** *drapery for a dining-couch,* Plin.

trĭclīnĭum -ĭ, n. (τρικλίνιον). **I.** *a dining-couch, a couch on which the Romans reclined at meals* (generally three on each, sometimes four and five), Cic. **II.** *a dining-room;* exornat ample et magnifice triclinium, Cic.

trĭcōlum (-on) -i, n. (τρίκωλον), *a period consisting of three parts or clauses,* Sen.

trĭcor, 1. dep. (tricae), *to make difficulties, to shuffle, trifle;* cum aliquo, Cic.

trĭcornis -e (tres and cornu), *having three horns,* Plin.

trĭcorpor -pŏris (tres and corpus), *having three bodies;* forma tricorporis umbrae, *of Geryon,* Verg.

trĭcuspis -ĭdis (tres and cuspis), *having three points,* Ov.

trīdacna -ōrum, n. (τρί = ter, and δάκνω = mordeo), *a kind of oyster,* Plin.

trĭdens -entis (tres and dens), *having three teeth or prongs.* **I.** Adj., rostra, Verg. **II.** Subst., **trĭdens** -entis, m. *a trident, a three-pronged spear for piercing large fish,* Plin.; an attribute of Neptune, Verg.

trĭdentĭfĕr -fĕri, m. (tridens and fero), *the trident-bearer,* epithet of Neptune, Ov.

trĭdentĭgĕr -gĕri, m. (tridens and gero), *the trident-bearer,* epithet of Neptune, Ov.

trĭdŭum -ĭi, n. *a space of three days;* quum tridui viam processisset, Caes.; triduo illum aut summum quadriduo periturum, Cic.

trĭennĭa -ĭum, n. (tres and annus), *a festival celebrated every three years,* Ov.

trĭennĭum -ĭi, n. (tres and annus), *a space of three years;* biennium aut triennium est quum nuntium remisisti, Cic.; multis locis Germaniae triennium vagati, Cic.

trĭens -entis, m. (tres), *a third part, one-third.* **A.** Gen., Cic. **B.** Esp., 1, *the third part of an as,* Hor.; 2, *of a sextarius,* Prop.; 3, in inheritances, *a third part of a whole;* cum duobus coheredibus esse in triente, Cic.

trĭentābŭlum -i, n. (triens), *the equivalent in land for the third part of a sum of money,* Liv.

trĭentālis -e (triens), *containing one-third of a foot,* Plin.

trĭērarchus -i, m. (τριήραρχος), *the commander of a trireme,* Cic.

trĭēris -e (τριήρης), *having three banks of oars.* Subst., **trĭēris** -is, f. *a trireme,* Nep.

trĭĕtērĭcus -a -um (τριετηρικός), *recurring every three years, triennial;* trieterica sacra or orgia, Verg., Ov.

trĭĕtēris -ĭdis, f. (τριετηρίς), 1, *a space of three years,* Mart.; 2, *a triennial festival,* Cic.

trĭfārĭam, adv. (trifarius, three-fold, sc. partem), *in a three-fold manner = in three places, on three sides;* adoriri, munire, Liv.

trĭfaux -faucis (tres and faux), *having three throats, triple-throated;* latratus (Cerberi), Verg.

trĭfĕr -fĕra -fĕrum (ter and fero), *bearing fruit thrice a year,* Plin.

trĭfĭdus -a -um (ter and findo), *split in three parts, three-forked;* flamma (of lightning), Ov.

trĭfĭlis -e (tres and filum), *having three hairs,* Mart.

trĭfŏlĭum -ĭi, n. (tres and folium), *trefoil,* Plin.

trĭformis -e (tres and forma). **I.** *three-formed, having three forms;* Chimaera, Hor.; dea, Hecate, Ov. **II.** *three-fold;* mundus (because composed of air, sea, and earth), Ov.

trĭfur -fūris, m. (ter and fur), *a three-fold thief, arch-thief,* Plaut.

trĭfurcĭfĕr -fĕri, m. **(ter and furcifer), *an arch-rogue,* Plaut.

trĭgārĭus -a -um, subst. (triga, *a team of three horses), relating to a team of three horses;* subst., 1, **trĭgārĭus** -ĭi, m. *a driver of a team of three horses,* Plin.; 2, **trĭgārĭum** -ĭi, n. *a circus or training-ground where teams of three horses are driven,* Plin.

trĭgĕmĭnus (tergĕmĭnus) -a -um, *three-fold;* vir, Geryon, Hor.; canis, Cerberus, Ov.; tergemini honores, *the aedileship, praetorship and consulship,* Hor.; of children, *three born at a birth;* fratres, the Horatii and the Curiatii, Liv.; Trigemina Porta, *a gate in the old city-wall of Rome, opposite the northern corner of the Aventine,* Plin.

trĭgemmis -e (tres and gemma), *having three buds,* Plin.

trĭgĭnta, num. (τριάκοντα), *thirty,* Cic.

trĭgon -ōnis, m. (τρίγων). **I.** *a ball for playing,* Mart. **II.** Meton., *a game at ball,* Hor.

trĭgōnālis -e (trigonum), *three-cornered;* pila (= trigon), Mart.

trĭgōnum -i, n. (τρίγωνον), *a triangle,* Varr.

trĭgōnus -i, m. *a kind of fish, the sting-ray,* Plaut.

trĭlibris -e (tres and libra), *of three pounds' weight,* Hor.

trĭlinguis -e (tres and lingua), *having three tongues;* os Cerberi, Hor.

trĭlix -īcis (tres and licium), *having three threads;* loricam consertam hamis auroque trilicem, Verg.

trīmātus -ūs, m. (trimus), *the age of three years,* Plin.

trĭmestris, 3. (tres and mensis), *three-monthly.* **I.** Adj., haedi, *three months old,* Varr. **II.** Subst., **trĭmestrĭa** -ĭum, n. *crops which ripen three months after sowing,* Plin.

trĭmĕtĕr = trimetros (q.v.).

trĭmĕtrŏs (-us) -a -um, *containing three metra,* i.e., *three double feet,* Quint.; subst. **trĭmĕtrŏs (-us)**, and (Latinised form), **trĭmĕtĕr** -tri, *a trimeter,* Hor.

trĭmŏdĭa -ae, f. and **trĭmŏdĭum** -ĭi, n (tres and modius), *a vessel containing thre emodii or bushels,* Plaut.

trĭmus -a -um (tres), *three years old;* equa, Hor.

Trīnăcrĭa -ae, f. (Τρινακρία), *the oldest name of Sicily, so called from its triangular shape.* Hence, **A.** **Trīnăcrĭus** -a -um (Τρινάκριος), *Trinacrian,* and **B.** **Trīnăcris** -ĭdis, f. (Τρινακρίς), *Trinacrian;* Trinacris alone = Sicily, Ov.

trīni -ae -a (tres). **I.** *three each,* Plin. **II.** *three together* (found with subst. only used in plur.), trinae litterae, Cic.; trina castra, Caes.

Trĭnobantes -um, m. *a people in the east of Britain.*

trĭnōdis -e (tres and nodus), *having three knots,* Ov.

trĭŏbŏlus (-ŏs) -i, m. (τριόβολος), *a coin of the value of three oboli,* Plaut.

Trĭōcăla -ōrum, n. *a mountain fastness in Sicily.* Hence, **Trĭōcălĭnus** -a -um, *relating to Triocala.*

trĭōnes -um, m. (= teriones, from tero), *the ploughing oxen;* transf., *the constellations known as the Great Bear and Little Bear* (as the stars resembled the shape of a waggon and the oxen attached to it), Verg.

Trĭŏpās -ae, m. (Τριόπας), *a king in Thessaly, father of Erysichthon.* Hence, **A.** **Trĭŏpēĭos**

II_ m. (Τριόπειος)= *Erysichthon*, Ov. **B. Triö-pěïs** -ïdis, f. = *Mestra, daughter of Erysicthon.*

trïorchis, acc. -chem, f. (τριορχίς). **I.** *a buzzard,* Plin. **II.** *a kind of centaury,* Plin.

trïparcus -a -um (ter and parcus), *very stingy,* Plaut.

trïpartīto (and gen.) **trïpertītō**, adv. (tripartitus), *in three parts;* bona dividere, Cic.

trïpartïtus (and gen.) **trïpertītus** -a -um (ter and partior), *divided into three parts, threefold, triple, tripartite;* divisio, Cic.

trïpectŏrus -a -um (tres and pectus), *having three breasts,* Lucr.

trïpĕdālis -e (ter and pedalis), *of three feet in measure;* parma, Liv.

trïpĕdānĕus = tripedalis (q.v.).

trïpert . . . v. tripart . . .

trïpes -pĕdis (ter and pes), *having three feet;* mulus, Liv.

Trïphȳlïa -ae, f. (Τριφυλία), *the south part of Elis in the Peloponnesus.*

trïplex -plĭcis (tres and plico), *three-fold, triple.* **I.** Adj., acies, Caes. ; Plato triplicem finxit animum, Cic. ; deae, *the three Parcae,* Ov. ; Minyeides, *the three daughters of Minyas,* Ov. **II.** Subst., 1, **trïplĭces** -um, m. (sc. codicilli), *a writing tablet with three leaves,* Cic.; 2, **trïplex** -plĭcis, n. = triplum, *three times as much ;* pediti in singulos centeni dati . . . triplex equiti, Liv.

trïplĭco, 1. (triplex), *to triple, make threefold,* Plin.

trïplus -a -um (τριπλοῦς), *three-fold, triple;* pars, Cic.

Trïpōlis -is, f. (Τρίπολις), *the name of several towns and places.* **I.** *a mountainous district in Thessaly south of the Cambunian mountains.* Hence, **Trïpōlĭtānus** ager, *the district of Tripolis,* Liv. **II.** *a town in Thessalia Hestiaeotis.* **III.** *a district of Arcadia, near Tegea.* **IV.** *a district in Africa, now Tripoli.* **V.** *a town in Phoenicia, now Trapoli.* **VI.** *a town in Pontus.* **VII.** *a town in Phrygia.*

Trïptŏlĕmus -i, m. (Τριπτόλεμος), *son of Celeus, king of Eleusis, and of Metaneira, the inventor of agriculture, a judge in the lower world;* prov., Triptolemo dare fruges, *to carry coals to Newcastle,* Ov.

trïpŭdĭo, 1. (tripudium), *to beat the ground with the feet, to dance;* e.g., a savage war dance, tripudiantes more suo (of the Spaniards), Liv.; of an old Roman dance on festive and religious occasions, Sen. ; hence, transf., tot in funeribus reipublicae exsultans ac tripudians, *dancing for joy,* Cic.

trïpŭdĭum -ïi, n. (ter and pes). **I.** *a religious dance;* e.g., of the Salian priests, Salios per urbem ire canentes carmina cum tripudiis sollemnique saltatu, Liv.; so of a savage war dance, cantus (Gallorum) ineuntium proelium et ululatus et tripudia, Liv.; of the wild Bacchic dance, Cat. **II.** T. t. of augury, *a favourable omen when the sacred chickens eat so fast that the food fell out of their beaks,* Cic.

trïpūs -pŏdis, m. (τρίπους), *a three-legged seat, tripod.* **I.** Gen., Verg., Hor. **II.** Esp., *the tripod of the Delphic priestess,* Cic., Verg. ; hence, meton., *the Delphic oracle,* Ov.

trïquĕtrus -a -um. **I.** *three-cornered, triangular;* insula (of Britain), Caes. **II.** (Because Sicily from its triangular shape was called Triquetra, hence =) *Sicilian,* Lucr., Hor.

trïrēmis -e (tres and remus), *having three banks of oars,* Caes. ; subst., **trïrēmis** -is, f. *a trireme,* Caes., Cic.

trïschoenus -a -um (τρίσχοινος), *containing three schoeni,* Plin.

trïscurrïa -ōrum, n. (tres and scurra), *gross buffooneries,* Juv.

tristě, adv. (tristis). **I.** *sadly, sorrowfully, mournfully;* adolescentes gravius aegrotant, tristius curantur, Cic. **II.** *harshly, severely;* tristius respondere, Cic.

tristi = trivisti, v. tero.

tristĭcŭlus -a -um (dim. of tristis), *somewhat sorrowful; filiola,* Cic.

tristĭfĭcus -a -um (tristis and facio), *causing sadness,* Cic. poet.

tristĭmōnĭa -ae, f. (tristis), *sadness, melancholy,* Auct. b. Afr.

tristis -e, *sad, sorrowful, mournful, melancholy.* **I.** Gen., **A.** Lit., of persons, tristis et conturbatus, Cic.; quos quum tristiores vidisset, Cic. **B.** Transf., a, *sad, gloomy;* of the lower world, Tartara, Verg.; poet., *harsh of taste;* suci, Verg.; b, object., *troubled, unfortunate, disastrous;* tempora, Cic.; ira, *with disastrous consequences,* Hor.; sors, Cic.; tristia ad recordationem exempla, Cic.; neut. subst., triste lupus stabulis, *a disastrous thing,* Verg. ; tristia miscentur laetis, Ov. **II.** Esp., 1, of humour, gloomy; **a**, = *unfriendly, surly, morose,* Cic.; natura, Cic.; vultus tristior, Cic.; b, = *angry;* dicta, Ov.; 2, *harsh, severe, rough;* judex, Cic.; triste et severum dicendi genus, Cic.

tristĭtĭa -ae, f. (tristis). **I.** *sadness, sorrowfulness, melancholy.* **A.** Lit., Cic. **B.** Transf. of things, sermonis, Cic. **II.** Esp., 1, *ill-humour, moroseness,* Ov. ; 2, *severity, sternness;* quod ille vos tristitiā vultuque deceperit, Cic.

trïsulcus -a -um (tres and sulcus), *three-fold, three-pointed, three-pronged;* lingua serpentis, *forked,* Verg.; telum Jovis, *lightning,* Ov.; ignes, *lightning,* Ov.

trïsyllăbus -a -um (τρισύλλαβος), *trisyllabic,* Varr.

trĭtăvus -i, m. (tres and avus). **I.** *the father of the atavus or atava,* Plaut. **II.** Transf., *remote ancestors,* Varr.

trītĭcĕus (**trītĭcēïus**) -a -um (triticum), *of wheat, wheaten;* messis, Verg.

trītĭcum -i, n. *wheat;* granum tritici, Cic.

Trītōn -ōnis, m. (Τρίτων). **I.** *Triton, son of Neptune and the nymph Salacia, a deity of the sea, represented with a horn made of a shell, which he blew at the bidding of Neptune to raise or appease the waves.* **II. A.** *a lake in Africa, on the smaller Syrtis, according to tradition the birthplace of several deities, particularly of Pallas.* Hence a, **Trītōnĭăcus** -a -um, = *belonging to Pallas;* arundo, *the tibia discovered by Pallas,* Ov.; b, **Trītōnis** -ĭdis, f. *Tritonian;* subst., = Pallas, Verg.; arx = *the city of Pallas, Athens,* Ov.; pinus, *the Argo, built at the order of Pallas,* Ov.; c, **Trītōnius** -a -um, *Tritonian;* subst., Tritonia = Pallas, Verg. **B.** *a lake in Thrace which had the power of changing into a bird any one who bathed nine times in its waters;* also called **Trītōnĭăca** palus, Ov.

trītor -ōris, m. (tero), *a rubber,* Plaut.

trītūra -ae, f. (tero), *a treading out of corn, threshing,* Verg.

1. **trītus** -a -um, p. adj. (from tero). **I. A.** *much trodden, much frequented;* 1, lit., iter, Cic.; 2, fig., of discourse, *in common use, common, trite, well-known;* faciamus hoc proverbium tritius, Cic. **B.** *practised;* aures, Cic. **II.** *worn-out;* vestis, Hor.

2. **trītus** -ūs, m. (tero), *a rubbing,* Cic.

trĭumphālis -e (triumphus), *of or relating to a triumph, triumphal;* corona, *of a triumphing general,* Liv.; provincia, *the conquest of which has gained a triumph,* Cic.; porta, *the gate through which the triumphing general entered Rome,* Cic.; imagines, *busts of ancestors who had triumphed,* Hor.; triumphalia ornamenta, *and* subst., **trĭumphālĭa** -ĭum, n. *the decorations of a triumphing general* (corona aurea, toga picta, tunica palmata, scipio eburneus, etc.), Tac.; senex, *an old man who had had a triumph,* Liv.

trĭumpho, 1. (triumphus). **I.** Intransit., *to triumph, to have a triumph.* **A.** Lit., de Numantinis, Cic.; ex Macedonia, Cic. **B.** Transf., 1, *to triumph, gain a victory;* amor de vate triumphat, Ov.; 2, *to triumph, exult;* gaudio, Cic.; laetaris in omnium gemitu et triumphas, Cic. **II.** *to triumph over, to conquer completely;* pass., ne triumpharetur Mithridates, Tac.; triumphati Medi, Hor.; aurum triumphatum, *captured,* Hor.

trĭumphus -i, m., old form, **trĭumpus** -i, m. (ter and pes), lit., *a solemn dance* (like tripudium); hence, **A.** Lit., *a triumphal procession, a triumph,* granted by the senate to a general and his army after an important victory, when the general entered Rome in a car drawn by white horses, clothed in a toga picta and tunica palmata, with a crown of laurel on his head, preceded by waggons carrying captives and booty, and followed by the soldiers shouting "Io triumphe!" and singing jocular songs; alicui triumphum decernere, Cic.; triumphum tertium deportare, Cic.; triumphum agere, *to triumph,* with genit. or de or ex and abl. of persons or country over which the triumph was held, Bojorum, Liv.; ex Aequis, Liv.; Pharsalicae pugnae, Cic.; de Liguribus, Liv. **B.** Transf., *triumph, victory;* ut repulsam suam triumphum suum duxerint, Cic.

trĭumvir -vĭri, m. (tres and vir), *a triumvir;* plur., triumviri (also tresviri, written III. viri). **I.** coloniae deducendae, or agro dando, or agro dividendo, or agris dividendis, or agro assignando (or agrarii), *commissioners for the formation of a colonia and the division of land amongst the colonists;* quum triumvir coloniam deduxisset, Cic. **II.** triumviri capitales or carceris lautumiarum, *superintendents of prisons, who also looked after the execution of punishments and watched over the public peace,* Cic. **III.** triumviri epulones, v. epulones. **IV.** triumviri mensarii, *commissioners for the regulation of payments from the exchequer,* Liv. **V.** triumviri monetales (auro, argento, aeri flando, feriundo), *the masters of the mint,* Cic. **VI.** triumviri (tresviri) reipublicae constituendae, Antonius, Lepidus, Octavianus, *who joined together to settle the state,* Suet. **VII.** commissioners for raising recruits, Liv. **VIII.** triumviri sacris conquirendis donisque persignandis, *commissioners for making an inventory of votive gifts,* Liv. **IX.** commissioners for repairing or rebuilding temples, Liv. **X.** magistrates in the municipia, Cic.

trĭumvĭrālis -e (triumvir), *of or relating to a triumvir;* flagella (of the triumviri capitales), Hor.

trĭumvĭrātus -ūs, m. (triumvir), *the office of a triumvir;* in trumviratu (sc. agrario), Cic.

trĭvĕnēfĭca -ae, f. (ter and venefica), *an arch-poisoner or sorceress,* Plaut.

Trĭvĭa, v. trivius.

trĭvĭālis -e (trivium), *common, ordinary, trivial;* carmen, Juv.

trĭvĭum -ĭi, n. (ter and via), *a place where three roads meet,* Cic.; meton., *an open street, public place,* Cic.

trĭvĭus -a -um (trivium), *honoured at three cross-roads,* name of deities who had chapels at cross-roads; dea, Prop., or virgo, Lucr., *Diana* or *Hecate;* so absol., **Trĭvĭa** -ae, f., Verg.; lacus Triviae, *a lake in Latium, near Aricia,* now *Lago di Nemi.*

trĭxāgo (**trĭssāgo**) -ĭnis, f. *a plant called germander,* Plin.

Trŏās -ădis, v. Tros.

trŏchaeus -i, m. (τροχαῖος), 1, *a trochee, a metrical foot* (-◡), Cic.; 2, = tribrachys (q.v.).

trŏchăĭcus -a -um (τροχαϊκός), *trochaic,* Quint.

trŏchĭlus -i, m. (τρόχιλος), *the golden-crested wren,* Plin.

trochlĕa (**troclĕa**) -ae, f. *a set of blocks and pulleys for raising weights,* Lucr.

trŏchus -i, m. (τροχός), *a boy's hoop,* Hor.

Trocmi -ōrum, m. *one of the three main stocks of the Galatians in Asia Minor.*

Trōes, v. Tros.

Troezĕn -zēnis, acc. -zēna, f. (Τροιζήν), *an old town in Argolis, residence of Pittheus, grandfather of Theseus.* Hence, **Troezēnĭus** -a -um (Τροιζήνιος), *Troezenian;* heros, Lelex, *son of Pittheus.*

Trōglŏdy̆tae -ārum, m. (Τρωγλοδύται), *cavedwellers, name of the old inhabitants of the west coast of the Arabian Gulf in Aethiopia.*

Trōĭădes, v. Tros.

Trōĭcus, v. Tros.

Trōĭlus (-ŏs) -i, m. (Τρώϊλος), *son of Priam, taken prisoner before Troy, and strangled by order of Achilles.*

Trōja, Trojanus, v. Tros.

Trōjŭgĕna -ae, c. (Troja and gigno), *born in Troy, Trojan.* Subst., **Trōjŭgĕna** -ae, m. *a Trojan.* Plur.= *the Trojans* (genit. Trōjŭgĕnûm), Verg., and = *the Romans* (descended from Aeneas), Juv.

Tromentīna tribus, *one of the tribus rusticae.*

trŏpaeum -i, n. (τρόπαιον), *a trophy, a monument of victory,* originally consisting of arms taken from the enemy hung on the stem of a tree. **I. A.** Lit., tropaeum statuere or ponere, to erect, Cic. **B.** Meton.= *the victory;* Salaminium, Cic. **II.** Fig.= *a memorial;* necessitudinis atque hospitii, Cic.

trŏpaeus -a -um (τροπαῖος), *turning back;* venti, *blowing from the sea to the land,* Plin.

Trŏphōnĭus -ĭi, m. (Τροφώνιος). **I.** *brother of Agamedes, with whom he built the Delphic oracle.* **II.** *a deity who gave prophetic answers to those who slept in his cave* (near Lebadia, in Boeotia). Hence, **Trŏphōnĭānus** -a -um, *of or belonging to Trophonius.*

trŏpis -is, f. (τρόπις), *the lees of wine,* Mart.

trŏpus -i, m. (τρόπος), *a metaphor, trope, figure of speech,* Quint.

Trōs, Trōis, m. (Τρώς), *son of Erichthonius, king of Phrygia, after whom Troy was named.* Hence, **Trōja** or **Trōĭa** -ae, f. (Τροία), *the town of Troy;* 1, lit., Liv., Verg.; 2, transf., a, *the town built by Aeneas in the Laurentine country,* Liv.; b, *the town built by Helenus in Epirus,* Ov.; c, *a Roman game played on horseback,* Verg. Hence, **A. Trōĭus** -a -um, *Trojan.* **B. Trōjānus** -a -um, *Trojan;* judex, i.e., *Paris,* Hor.; prov., equus Trojanus, *a hidden danger,* Cic. **C. Trōĭcus** -a -um, *Trojan.* **D. Trōs**, Trōis, m. *a Trojan;* plur., **Trōes** -um, m. *the Trojans.*

E. Trŏās -ădos, adj. fem., *Trojan; subst., a Trojan woman*, Verg. **F. Trŏïădes** -um, f. *Trojan women.*

Trosmis, acc. -min, f. *a town in Moesia*, Ov.

trossŭli -ōrum, m. (perhaps an Etruscan word for equites). **I.** *a name given to the Roman knights in active service*, Varr. **II.** Transf., *fops, coxcombs, dandies*, Sen.

troxallis -ĭdis, f. (τροξαλλίς), *an animal resembling a grasshopper*, Plin.

trŭcīdātĭo -ōnis, f. (trucido). **I.** *a slaughtering, massacre; civium*, Cic.; *non pugna sed trucidatio velut pecorum*, Liv. **II.** *a cutting off, cutting to pieces*, Plin.

trŭcīdo, 1. *to cut to pieces, slaughter, massacre.* **I. A.** Lit., *cives Romanos*, Cic. **B.** Transf., a, *to chew; seu pisces, seu porrum, seu cepe*, Hor.; b, poet. = *to extinguish; ignem*, Lucr. **II.** Fig., 1, *to demolish* (in words); a Servilio trucidatus, Cic.; 2, *to ruin, destroy; ne fenore trucidetur*, Cic.

trŭcŭlentĕr, adv. (truculentus), *fiercely, ferociously; quod truculentius se ferebat quam caeteri*, Cic.

trŭcŭlentĭa -ae, f. (truculentus), 1, *roughness, savageness, ferocity*, Plaut.; 2, *severity of climate*, Tac.

trŭcŭlentus -a -um (trux), *rough, ferocious, savage, cruel.* **I. A.** Lit., Cic. **B.** Transf., of the voice, *wild*, Tac. **II.** Fig., **A.** Of character or behaviour, *unfriendly, wild, angry, furious; fetā truculentior ursā*, Ov. **B.** Transf., of the sea, *wild, disturbed*, Cat.

trŭdis -is, f. *a sharp stake*, Verg.

trŭdo, trūsi, trūsum, 3. *to push, shove, press.* **I.** Lit., **A.** Gen., apros in plagas, Hor. **B.** Esp., *to push forth, to put forth buds; gemmas*, Verg. **II.** Fig., *to press, urge, force;* ad mortem trudi, Cic.; truditur dies die, *one day presses hard on another*, Hor.

Trŭentum -i, n. *a town in Picenum.* Hence, **Trŭentīnus** -a -um, *Truentine;* Castrum = Truentum, ap. Cic.

trulla -ae, f. (= truella, dim. of trua, *a ladle*). **I.** *a ladle for transferring wine from the bowl to the cup*, Cic. **II.** Transf., 1, *a pan for carrying live coals*, Liv.; 2, *a washing-basin*, Juv.

trullĕum -i, n. and **trullĕus** -i, m. *a basin, washing-basin*, Varr.

trunco, 1. (truncus), *to shorten by cutting off, maim, mutilate;* simulacra, statuas, Liv.

1. **truncus** -i, m. *the stem or trunk of a tree.* **I.** Lit., meton. and fig. **A.** Lit. and meton., 1, lit., Cic., Caes.; trunci induti hostilibus armis, i.e., tropaea, Verg.; 2, meton. = *the tree*, Hor. **B.** Fig., *the stem, the main part;* ipso trunco (aegritudinis) everso, Cic. **II.** Transf., 1, *the trunk of the human body*, Cic.; 2, as a term of reproach, *blockhead*, Cic.

2. **truncus** -a -um, *maimed, mutilated, cut short, dismembered.* **I.** Lit., corpus, Liv.; truncae inhonesto vulnere nares, Verg.; frons (Acheloi amnis), *deprived of its horns*, Ov.; tela, *broken off*, Verg.; with genit., animalia trunca pedum, *without feet*, Verg. **II.** Transf., urbs trunca, sine senatu, etc., Liv.

trūsātĭlis -e (truso), *of or relating to pushing; mola, a handmill*, Cato.

trūso, 1. (intens. of trudo), *to push violently*, Cat.

trŭtīna -ae, f. (τρυτάνη), *a balance, pair of scales;* iu fig., ad ea probanda, quae non aurificis staterā, sed quādam populari trutinā examinatur, Cic.

trŭtīnor, 1. dep. (trutina), *to weigh*, Pers.

trux, trŭcis (connected with tor-vus), *rough, savage, fierce, ferocious, grim.* **I.** Of look, oculi, Cic. **II.** Transf., 1, of tones, *wild, rough;* cantus, Ov.; classicum, Hor.; 2, *rough;* a, eurus, Ov.; pelagus, Hor.; b, *harsh, violent;* orator, Liv.; sententia, Liv.; 3, of character or manner, *wild, furious, threatening;* tribunus plebis, Cic.

tryblĭum -ĭi, n. (τρύβλιον), *a dish*, Plaut.

trȳgĭnon -i, n. (τρύγινον), *a black pigment made from wine-lees*, Plin.

trȳgon -ōnis, m. (τρυγών), *a fish, the sting-ray*, Plin.

tū, pron. pers. (genit. tŭi, dat. tĭbĭ, acc. tc, abl. te; plur. nom., vos; genit., vestrum or vostrum and vestri or vostri, dat. vobis, acc. vos, abl. vobis), *thou;* plur., *you.* **I.** Gen., Cic.; strengthened, a, by te, tute, Cic.; b, in oblique cases by met, vosmet, Liv. **II.** Esp., **A.** Used in the ethic dat., ecce tibi exortus est Isocrates, Cic. **B.** Often with singular collective names, vos, Romanus exercitus, Liv.; vos, o Calliope (= Muses), Verg.

tŭātim, adv. (tuus), *in thine own way, after thine own fashion*, Plaut.

tŭba -ae, f. (connected with tubus), *the straight war-trumpet of the Romans, used for giving military signals.* **I. A.** Lit., tubae sonus, Caes.; cornua ac tubae, Liv.; tubā signum dandum, Caes.; used also in religious festivities, games, funeral processions, Hor., Verg. Ov. **B.** Fig. = *provoker;* belli civilis tubam quam illi appellant, Cic. **II.** Meton., **A.** *war*, Mart. **B.** *lofty epic poetry*, Mart.

1. **tŭber** -ĕris, n. (tumeo), *a swelling, protuberance, hump.* **I.** a, lit., cameli, Plin.; b, fig., tubera = *great mistakes* (opp. verrucae, *little blunders*), Hor. **II.** Transf., 1, *a knot in wood*, Plin.; 2, *a round, swelling root*, Plin.; 3, *a truffle*, Mart.; 4, tuber terrae; a, *the root of the cyclamen*, Plin.; b, *molehill*, as a term of abuse, Petr.

2. **tŭber** -ĕris, a, m. *a kind of apple-tree.* Plin.; b, f. *the fruit of this tree*, Mart.

tŭbercŭlum -i, n. (dim. of 1. tuber), *a little swelling, boil, tubercle*, Plin.

tŭbĕrōsus -a -um (tuber), *full of swellings or protuberances*, Varr.

tŭbĭcen -ĭnis, m. (tuba and cano), *a trumpeter*, Liv.

tŭbĭlustrĭum -ĭi, n. (tuba and lustrum), *a feast of trumpets held March 23rd and May 23rd*, plur., Ov.

tŭbŭlātus -a -um (tubulus), *tubular*, Plin.

tŭbŭlus -i, m. (dim. of tubus), *a little pipe.*

tŭburcĭnābundus -a -um (tuburcinor), *eating greedily, gobbling*, Cato.

tŭburcĭnor, 1. dep. *to eat greedily, to gobble*, Plaut.

tŭbus -i, m. *a pipe, tube, water-pipe*, Plin.

tuccētum (not tūcētum) -i, n. *a kind of sausage common in Cisalpine Gaul*, Pers.

tŭdĭto, 1. (intens. of tudo = tundo), *to strike violently, strike often*, Lucr.

tŭĕo, 2. = tueor (q.v.).

tŭĕor, tŭĭtus and tūtus sum, tŭēri, 2. dep. *to look at, behold, regard, see.* **I.** Lit., naturam, Cic.; poet. with neut. plur. of adj. used adverbially, acerba, *to look wild*, Verg. **II.** Fig., **A.** *to regard;* quod ego perinde tuebar, ac si usus essem, Cic. **B.** *to look at with care or for the purpose of protection;* 1, *to care for, protect, guard, support;* concordiam, Cic.; dignitatem suam,

Cic.; personam principis civis facile dicendo, Cic.; 2, esp., a, *to defend, protect* (with arms); fines suos ab excursionibus, Cic.; turrim militibus complevit tuendamque ad omnes repentinos casus tradidit, Caes.; b, with words, etc., armis prudentiae causas tueri et defendere, Cic.; c, t. t. of business, *to keep a house in good repair;* sarta tecta aedium tueri, Cic.; d, *to keep, support, maintain;* se, vitam corpusque, Cic.; se ac suos, Liv.; sex legiones (re suâ), Cic.

tŭgŭrĭum -ĭi, n. (for tegurium, from tego), *a peasant's hut, cottage;* tugurium ut jam videatur esse illa villa, Cic.

tŭĭtĭo -ōnis, f. (tueor), *a protecting, preserving;* sui, Cic.

Tullĭŏla -ae, f. (dim. of Tullia), *the pet name of Tullia, Cicero's daughter.*

Tullĭus -a -um, *the name of a Roman family;* 1, Servius Tullius, *the sixth king of Rome;* 2, a, M. Tullius Cicero, *the celebrated Roman orator and statesman;* b, *his daughter,* Tullia; c, *his brother,* Qu. Tullius Cicero. Hence, **Tullĭānus** -a -um, *Tullian;* subst., **Tullĭānum** -i, n. *the underground part of a Roman state prison, said to have been built by Servius Tullius.*

tŭlo, tŭli and tĕtŭli, 3. *to bear, bring,* Plaut.

tum, adv. of time. **I.** Expressing a point of time which coincides with some other, gen., *then, at that time;* quum ... tum, Cic.; ubi ... tum, Ter.; postquam ... tum, Sall.; made emphatic by the addition of demum, Liv., denique, Cic., vero, Cic.; absol., Cic. **II.** Expressing a point of time which is subsequent to some other, *then, thereupon;* 1, lit., in ripa ambulantes, tum autem residentes, Cic.; introducing the words of a subsequent speaker, tum Scipio, Cic.; 2, transf., a, in numeral or logical succession, *then, afterwards, in the next place;* gigni autem terram, aquam, ignem, tum ex his omnia, Cic.; primum ... tum, Caes.; primum ... deinde ... tum ... tum, Cic.; b, as a correl. conj., (a) tum ... tum, at one time ... at one time, Cic.; (β) quum ... tum, *if* ... *then, surely; as well ... as; both ... and especially; not only ... but also,* Cic., Caes.

tŭmĕfăcĭo -fēci -factum, 3., pass., **tŭmĕfĭo** -factus sum -fĭĕri (tumeo and facio), *to cause to swell.* **I.** Lit., humum, Ov.; tumefactus pontus, swollen, Ov. **II.** Fig., *to puff up with pride,* Prop.

tŭmĕo, 2. *to swell, be swollen, be puffed up.* **I.** Lit., corpus omne veneno, Ov.; vere tument terrae, Verg. **II.** Fig., 1, *to swell, glow, boil with passion* or *excitement;* a, *with anger;* sapientis animus nunquam tumet, Cic.; b, *with pride;* laudis amore, Hor.; c, *to be in a ferment;* tument negotia, *are in disorder,* Cic.; 2, of discourse, *to be pompous, tumid,* Tac.

tŭmesco, tŭmŭi, 3. (inchoat. of tumeo), *to begin to swell, to swell.* **I.** Lit., tumescit mare, Verg. **II.** Fig., a, *to swell with anger;* ora tumescunt, Ov.; b, poet., transf., *to begin to break out;* tumescunt bella, Verg.

tŭmĭdē, adv. (tumidus), *pompously, bombastically,* Sen.

tŭmĭdus -a -um (tumeo). **I.** *swollen, puffed up, tumid.* **A.** Lit., membrum, Cic.; mare, Verg. **B.** Transf., 1, a, *swollen, boiling, raging with passion* or *excitement;* tumida ex ira tum corda residunt, Verg.; b, *swollen, puffed up with pride;* tumidus successu, Ov.; quum tumidum est (cor), *puffed up with ambition,* Hor.; 2, of discourse, *pompous, tumid, bombastic;* sermones, Hor.; sermo tumidior, Liv. **II.** Act.= *causing to swell;* auster, Verg.; euri, Ov.; fig., honor, *making rain,* Prop.

tŭmor -ōris, m. (tumeo), *a swelling, tumour.* **I.** Lit., oculorum, Cic. **II.** Transf., 1, *a swelling, commotion, excitement of the mind;* animi, Cic.; esp., a, *anger;* tumor et ira deûm, Verg.; b, *pride;* intempestivos compesce tumores, Ov.; c, *ferment, commotion;* rerum, Cic.; 2, of discourse, *bombast,* Quint.

tŭmŭlo, 1. (tumulus), *to cover with a mound, to bury,* Ov.

tŭmŭlōsus -a -um (tumulus), *full of mounds, hilly,* Sall.

tŭmultŭārĭus -a -um (tumultus). **I.** *hastily brought together, suddenly levied;* miles, Liv. **II.** Transf., *that which is done in a hurry or on the spur of the moment, sudden, hasty, disorderly;* pugna (opp. justa), Liv.; opus, Quint.; dux, *chosen on the spur of the moment,* Liv.; castra, Liv.

tŭmultŭātĭo -ōnis, f. (tumultuor), *a confusion, bustle, tumult,* Liv.

tŭmultŭor, 1. dep. and **tŭmultŭo,** 1. (tumultus), *to be tumultuous, confused, in an uproar,* Cic.; pass. impers., in castris Romanorum praeter consuetudinem tumultuari, Caes.

tŭmultŭōsē, adv. (tumultuosus), *confusedly, tumultuously;* tumultuose excepta est (res) clamoribus, Liv.; senatus tumultuosius consulitur, Liv.; ut hominem quam tumultuosissime adoriantur, Cic.

tŭmultŭōsus -a -um (tumultus). **I.** *alarmed, disquieted, turbulent, tumultuous;* contio, Cic.; vita, Cic.; mare, Hor.; quod tumultuosissimum pugnae erat parumper sustinuit, Liv. **II.** *causing alarm or confusion;* nuntius, Liv.; in otio tumultuosi, *restless,* Liv.

tŭmultus -ūs, m. (tumeo), *a noise, confusion, uproar, bustle, tumult.* **I.** Lit., 1, tantum tumultum injicere civitati, Cic.; tumultum praebere, Liv.; sedare, Liv.; 2, esp., a, *the sudden breaking out of war, insurrection, rebellion;* Italicus, Cic.; Gallicus Cic., Liv.; tumultum decernere, *to order a levy en masse,* Cic.; b, in the air, *crash, roar, thunder, storm;* Juppiter ruens tumultu, Hor.; c, *rumbling in the body,* Hor. **II.** Fig., *mental disturbance, commotion, excitement;* mentis, Hor.

tŭmŭlus -i, m. (tumeo), *a mound of earth, hill.* **I.** Gen., tumuli silvestres, Cic. **II.** Esp., *a mound of earth as a monument for the dead;* tumulus Achillis, Cic.; inanis, *a cenotaph,* Cic.

tunc, adv., denoting a point of time which corresponds with another. **I.** Gen., *then;* tunc ... quum, Cic. **II.** Esp., a fixed point of past time, *at that time, then,* Cic.

tundo, tŭtŭdi, tunsum and tūsum, 3. *to beat, strike repeatedly.* **I.** Lit., **A.** Gen., converso bacillo alicui oculos vehementissime, Cic.; pectora manu, Ov.; tunsae pectora (acc. of respect) palmis, Verg.; prov., tundere eandem incudem, *to be always treating of the same subject,* Cic. **B.** Esp. *to break to pieces in a mortar,* Plin. **II.** Transf., *to deafen, importune;* aures, Plaut.; assiduis hinc atque illinc vocibus heros tunditur, Verg.

Tunēs -nētis, m. *a town on the coast of Africa Propria,* now *Tunis.*

Tungri -ōrum, m. *a German people in modern Lüttich.*

tŭnĭca -ae, f. **I.** *the under garment worn by both men and women, a tunic,* Cic. **II.** Transf., *a skin, coating, covering, peel;* gemmae tenues rumpunt tunicas, Verg.

tŭnĭcātus -a -um (tunica), *clothed in a tunic,* Cic.; esp., of the poorer classes, who wore only a tunic (without a toga over it), tunicatus populus, Tac., or popellus, Hor. Subst. plur., tunicati, Cic.

tŭnĭcŭla (**tŭnicla**) -ae, f. (dim. of tunica). **I.** *a little tunic*, Cic.   **II.** Transf., *a little membrane;* oculorum, Plin.

tŭor = tueor (q.v.).

tūrārĭus -a -um (tus), *of or relating to incense*, Plin.

turba -ae, f. (τύρβη). **I.** *the tumult, uproar, disturbance, commotion caused by a crowd of people;* quanta in turba viveremus, Cic. ; maximas in castris effecisse turbas dicitur, Cic. **II.** Meton., *a disorderly crowd, heap, swarm;* 1, a, aliquem videre in turba, Cic. ; b, esp. = vulgus (contemptuously), *the mob;* admiratio vulgi atque turbae, Cic. ; 2, *of deities, animals, and things,* Chrysippus magnam congregat turbam ignotorum deorum, Cic. ; rerum, Ov.

turbāmentum -i, n. (turbo), *a means of disturbance*, Tac.

turbātē, adv. (turbatus), *confusedly;* aguntur omnia raptim atque turbate, Caes.

turbātĭo -ōnis, f. (1. turbo), *disturbance, disorder, confusion*, Liv.

turbātor -ōris, m. (1. turbo), *a disturber, stirrer-up, troubler;* plebis, Liv.

turbātus -a -um, p. adj. (from 1. turbo). **I.** *disturbed, perturbed, disordered;* mare, Liv. **II.** Transf., a, *disquieted, restless, troubled;* voluntates populi, Cic. ; b, *angered, exasperated;* Pallas, Verg.

turbellae -ārum, f. (dim. of turba), *tumult, disorder, confusion*, Plaut.

turben -ĭnis, n. (2. turbo), *a whirlwind*, Cat.

turbĭdē, adv. (turbidus), *confusedly, in disorder*, Cic.

turbĭdus -a -um (turba), *confused, disordered, unquiet, wild.* **I.** Lit., a, *of weather,* tempestas, Cic. ; b, *of water, turbid, troubled;* aqua, Cic. ; c, *of hair, disordered;* coma, Ov. **II.** Transf., 1, *mentally disturbed, disordered, disquieted;* Aruns, Verg. ; pectora turbidiora mari, Ov. ; turbidum laetari, *with confused fear,* Hor. ; 2, *excited, vehement, angry;* a, *of persons,* sic turbidus infit, Verg. ; b, *of things, unquiet, agitated;* res, Cic. Subst., **turbĭdum** -i, n. *a troubled time, disquiet;* in turbido, Liv.; si turbidiora sapienter ferebas, tranquilliora laete feras, Cic. ; 3, *causing disturbance;* homo, milites, Tac.

turbĭnātĭo -ōnis, f. (turbinatus), *a pointing in the form of a cone*, Plin.

turbĭnātus -a -um (2. turbo), *cone-shaped, conical*, Plin.

turbĭnĕus -a -um (2. turbo), *shaped like a top*, Ov.

1. **turbo**, 1. (turba), *to disturb, throw into disorder or confusion.* **I.** Lit., **A.** Gen., mare, aequora, Cic. ; transf., with Gr. acc., turbatus capillos, *with disordered hair*, Ov. **B.** Esp., a, *to bring a mass of men into disorder, to throw into disorder;* esp., milit. t.t., ordines, aciem peditum, Liv. ; absol. = *to cause disorder;* ferae ita ruunt atque turbant ut, etc., Cic. ; milit. t.t. (equites) modice primo impetu turbavere, Liv. ; b, *to trouble water, etc., make turbid;* pedibus manibusque lacus, Ov. **II.** Transf., *to bring into confusion, to disturb.* **A.** Gen., contiones, Liv. ; delectum atque ordinem, Cic. ; ne quid ille turbet, vide, Liv. **B.** Esp., 1, *to bring one's affairs into confusion, become bankrupt*, Juv. ; 2, *to make restless, disturb, alarm, confuse;* mentem dolore, Verg. ; 3, *to cause a political disturbance, to unsettle, stir up;* Macer in Africa haud dubie turbans, Tac. ; impers., si in Hispania turbatum esset, Cic. (archaic fut. perf. pass., turbassitur, ap. Cic.).

2. **turbo** -ĭnis, m. **I.** *anything that turns round in a circle, an eddy.* **A.** Of the wind, c *whirlwind, hurricane;* 1, lit., a, Cic. ; b, *the eddy made by a whirlwind*, Verg. ; 2, fig., *storm;* in turbinibus reipublicae, Cic. ; mentis turbine agar, Ov. ; tu procella patriae, turbo ac tempestas pacis atque otii, Cic. **B.** *a top, a plaything for boys;* 1, lit., Cic. ; 2, transf., *an object of the shape of a top;* turbine crescit (bucina) ab imo, *in a circular form*, Ov. ; esp., a, *a reel,* Hor. ; b, *a spindle*, Cat. **II.** *motion in the shape of an eddy;* of smoke, Verg. ; *circular course of a missile;* celeri ad terram turbine fertur, Verg. ; fig., non modo militiae turbine factus eques, *by going through the different grades*, Ov.

turbŭlentē and **turbŭlentĕr**, adv. with compar. and superl. (turbulentus), *turbulently, tumultuously;* nos nihil turbulenter, nihil temere faciamus, Cic. ; egit de Caepione turbulentius, Cic.

turbŭlentus -a -um (turba), *restless, stormy, boisterous.* **I.** Lit., tempestas, Cic. ; concursio, Cic. **II.** Fig., **A.** Pass. = *stormy, disturbed;* respublica, Cic. ; animus, Cic. **B.** Fig., a, *causing disturbance, restless;* civis, Cic. ; b, *confusing;* errores, Cic.

turda, v. turdus.

turdārĭum -ĭi, n. (turdus), *a place where thrushes are kept*, Varr.

Turdetāni -ōrum, m. *a people in Hispania Baetica, near modern Seville.* Hence, **Turdetānĭa** -ae, f. *the country of the Turdetani.*

Turdŭli -ōrum, m. *a people in Hispania Baetica.* Hence, **Turdŭlus** -a -um, *Turdulian.*

turdus -i, m. and **turda** -ae, f. **I.** *a thrush,* Hor. **II.** *a kind of fish*, Plin.

tūrĕus -a -um (tus), *of or relating to incense;* dona, Verg.

turgĕo, 2. **I.** *to swell up, be swollen;* frumenta turgent, Verg. **II.** Fig., *of discourse, to be pompous, turgid;* professus grandia turget, Hor.

turgesco (inchoat. of turgeo), 3. *to begin to swell, swell up.* **I.** Lit., semen turgescit in agris, Ov. **II.** Transf., *to swell, be excited with passion;* sapientis animus nunquam turgescit, Cic.

turgĭdŭlus -a -um (dim. of turgidus), *somewhat swollen;* flendo turgiduli ocelli, Cat.

turgĭdus -a -um (turgeo), *swollen, turgid.* **I.** Lit., membrum, Cic. **II.** Fig., *turgid, bombastic;* Alpinus (a poet), Hor.

Tūrĭa -ae, f. *a river in Hispania Tarraconensis, now Guadalaviar.* Hence, **Tūriensis** -e, *Turian;* proelium (in the Sertorian war), Cic.

tūrĭbŭlum -i, n. (tus), *a censer for burning incense*, Cic.

tūrĭcrĕmus -a -um (tus and cremo), *burning with incense;* arae, Verg.

tūrĭfĕr -fĕra -fĕrum (tus and fero), *producing incense;* Indus, Ov.

tūrĭlĕgus -a -um (tus and lego), *collecting incense*, Ov.

turma -ae, f. (connected with **turba**). **I.** *a troop of cavalry containing thirty men, the tenth part of an ala, a squadron*, Cic. **II.** Transf., *a troop, throng;* in turma inauratarum equestrium (sc. statuarum), Cic. ; Gallica (of the priests of Isis), Ov.

turmālis -e (turma), *of or relating to a troop or squadron.* Subst., **turmāles** -ium, m. *the men of a squadron*, Liv.

turmātim, adv. (turma), *troop by troop, in troops*, Caes., Sall.

Turnus -i, m. *king of the Rutuli, killed by Aeneas.*

Tŭrōnes -um, m. and **Tŭrŏni** -ōrum, m. *a people in Gallia Lugdunensis, near modern Tours.*

turpĭcŭlus -a -um (dim. of turpis), *somewhat ugly or deformed.* **I.** Lit., nasus, Cat. **II.** Fig., res turpiculae et quasi deformes, Cic.

turpĭfĭcātus -a -um (turpis and facio), *made foul, corrupted;* animus, Cic.

turpĭlŭcrĭcŭpĭdus -a -um (= turpis lucri cupidus) = αἰσχροκερδής, *greedy after base gain,* Plaut.

turpis -e, *ugly, foul, unsightly, filthy.* **I.** Lit., aspectus, Cic.; turpia membra fimo, Verg.; pes, Hor. **II.** Fig., in a moral sense, *disgraceful, shameful, base, dishonourable, infamous;* fuga, Cic.; quid turpius? Cic.; homo turpissimus, Cic.; with 2. supine, turpe factu, Cic. Subst., **turpe** -is, n. *a disgrace;* habere quaestui rempublicam turpe est, Cic.

turpĭtĕr, adv. (turpis), *foully, in an ugly, unsightly manner.* **I.** Lit., claudicare, Ov.; desinere in piscem, Hor. **II.** Fig., *disgracefully, scandalously, basely, dishonourably, infamously;* facere, Cic.; fugere, Caes.; turpius ejicitur, quam non admittitur hospes, Ov.; in deorum opinione turpissime labitur, Cic.

turpĭtūdo -inis, f. (turpis), *ugliness, unsightliness.* **I.** Lit., Cic. **II.** Fig., *turpitude, baseness, disgrace, infamy, dishonour;* maximam turpitudinem suscipere vitae cupiditate, Cic.; nullā conditione hanc turpitudinem subire, Cic.; plur., flagitiorum ac turpitudinum societas, Cic.

turpo, 1. (turpis), *to make ugly, befoul, defile.* **I.** Lit., capillos sanguine, Verg. **II.** Fig., *to disgrace, dishonour;* ornamenta, Cic.; castra urbanae seditionis contagione, Liv.

turrĭcŭla -ae, f. (dim. of turris), *a little tower, turret;* transf., *a dice-box,* Mart.

turrĭgĕr -gĕra -gĕrum (turris and gero), *tower-bearing;* urbes, Verg.; hence an epithet of Cybele, who was represented with a crown of towers (the earth with its towers personified); Cybele, Ov.; dea, Cybele, Ov.; Ops, Ov.

turris -is, f. (τύῤῥις, τύρσις), *a tower.* **A.** Gen., Cic. **B.** Esp., 1, in war, *a tower with which walls and camps were strengthened;* turris latericia, Caes.; or, *a tower of wood for attacking towns,* Cic.; or, *a tower full of armed soldiers,* borne by elephants, Liv.; 2, *a dove-cote,* Ov.

turrītus -a -um (turris). **I.** *furnished with towers;* moenia, Ov.; turrita, as an epithet of Cybele, Prop.; Berecyntia mater, Verg. **II.** Poet. transf., *tower-like, towering high;* scopuli, Verg.

tursĭo -ōnis, m. *a species of dolphin or porpoise,* Plin.

turtur -ūris, m. *a turtle-dove,* Verg.

turtŭrilla -ae, f. (dim. of turtur), *a little turtle-dove,* Sen.

turunda -ae, f. (perhaps = terenda, from tero). **I.** *a pellet for fattening poultry,* Varr. **II.** *a roll of lint,* Cato.

tūs (**thūs**), tūris, n. (θύος), *incense, frankincense;* tus incendere, Cic.

Tusci -ōrum, m. *the Tuscans, Etruscans, inhabitants of Etruria.* Hence, adj., **Tuscus** -a -um, *Etruscan;* amnis, *the Tiber,* Verg.; dux, Mezentius, Ov.; eques, Maecenas, Verg.; vicus, *a street in Rome,* Liv.; semen, spelt, Ov.

Tuscŭlānus, v. Tusculum.

1. **tusculum** -i, n. (dim. of tus), *a little incense,* Plaut.

2. **Tuscŭlum** -i. n. *an old town in Latium.*

now *Frascati.* Hence, **A. Tuscŭlus** -a -um, *Tusculan.* **B. Tuscŭlānus** -a -um, *Tusculan;* plur. subst., **Tuscŭlāni** -ōrum, m. *the inhabitants of Tusculum.* **Tuscŭlānum** -i, n. (sc. rus or praedium), *an estate of Cicero's near Tusculum.*

tussĭlāgo -ĭnis, f. *the plant coltsfoot,* Plin.

tussĭo, 4. (tussis), *to have a cough, to cough;* male, Hor.

tussis -is, acc. -im, f. *a cough,* Verg.

tūtāmen -ĭnis, n. (tutor), *a defence, protection,* Verg.

tūtāmentum -i, n. (tutor), *defence, protection,* Liv.

tūtē, adv. (tutus), *safely, securely;* in vadis consistere tutius, Caes.

tūtēla -ae, f. (tueor). **I.** *protection, guard, charge.* **A.** Gen., 1, lit., tutelam januae gerere, Plaut.; cuius in tutela Athenas esse voluerunt, Cic.; 2, meton., a, act., *protector, guardian,* templi, Ov.; b, pass., *the person or thing protected;* virginum primae puerique claris patribus orti, Deliae tutela deae, Hor. **B.** Esp., a, *guardianship, tutelage;* in alicuius tutelam venire, Cic.; judicium tutelae, Cic.; b, *the property of the ward;* legitima, Cic. **II.** *a keeping, care, management;* villarum, Plin.

tūtēlārius -ii, m. (tutela), *a keeper;* tutelarii, *the keepers of a temple,* Plin.

tūtĭcus, v. meddix.

tūtō, adv. (tutus), *safely, securely;* esse, Cic.; dimicare, Caes.; with ab and the abl., ab incursu, Caes.; superl., tutissimo, *at the safest;* non quaerere, ubi tutissimo essem, Cic.

1. **tūtor** -ōris, m. (for tuitor, from tueor). **I.** *a protector;* finium, Hor.; religionum, Cic. **II.** *the guardian of a woman, a minor, or imbecile person;* a, lit., aliquem tutorem instituere, Cic.; tutorem esse alicuius or alicui, Cic.; b, fig., eloquentiae quasi tutores, Cic.

2. **tūto**, 1. and **tūtor**, 1. dep. (intens. of tueor). **I.** *to protect, preserve, watch, keep;* domum, Verg.; oculos ab inferiore parte, Cic.; urbem muris, Liv.; se adversus injusta arma, Liv. **II.** *to ward off;* pericula, Sall.; inopiam, Caes.

tūtŭlus -i, m. *a particular mode of dressing the hair, by gathering it into a high knot at the back of the head;* esp. used by the flamen and his wife, Varr.

tūtus -a -um, p. adj. (from tueor). **I.** *safe, secure, out of danger;* res, Cic.; tutiorem vitam hominum reddere, Cic.; medio tutissimus ibis, Ov.; tutus ab hostibus, Caes.; subst., **tūtum** -i, n. *a safe place, safety;* esse in tuto, Cic.; aliquem (aliquid) in tuto collocare; tutum est, with infin., Caes. **II.** *watchful, cautious;* consilia, Liv.

tŭus -a -um, pron. poss. (tu), *thy, thine.* **I.** Subject., **A.** Gen., tua bona, Cic.; subst., tui, *thy friends, people, party,* Cic.; tuum est, *it is thy custom, it is thy duty,* Plaut., Ter. **B.** *favourable to thee;* tempore tuo pugnasti, Liv. **II.** Object. = *to thee, towards thee;* desiderio tuo, *for you,* Cic.

tuxtax, *whack, whack,* onomatop. imitation of the sound of blows, Plaut.

Tўăna -ōrum, n. (Τύανα), *a town in Cappadocia, at the foot of Mount Taurus.* Hence, **Tўănēĭus** -a -um, *of or belonging to Tyana.*

Tўba -ae, f. *a town on the borders of Syria.* now *Taibe.*

Tўbris = Tiberis (q.v.).

Tўbur = Tibur (q.v.).

Tўcha -ae, f. (Τύχη), *a part of the town of Syracuse, in Sicily, with a temple to Fortune, whence the name.*

Tўchius -ii, m. (Τυχίος), *a celebrated Boeotian worker in leather.*

Tўdeus -ĕi and -ĕos, m. (Τυδεύς), *son of Oeneus, father of Diomedes.* Hence, **Tўdidēs** ae, m. (Τυδείδης), *the son of Tydeus,* i.e., *Diomedes.*

tympănīticus -i, m. (τυμπανιτικός), *one who has the dropsy,* Plin.

tympănĭum -ii, n. (τυμπάνιον), *a drum-shaped pearl,* Plin.

tympănizo, l. (τυμπανίζω), *to play the tambourine* or *kettle-drum,* Suet.

tympănōtrĭba -ae, m. (τυμπανοτρίβης), *a tambourine-player,* Plaut.

tympănum -i, n. (τύμπανον), *a tambourine, kettle-drum* (esp. used by the priests of Cybele). **I.** Lit., Verg. **II.** Transf., *a drum* or *wheel for raising weights,* Verg., Lucr.

Tyndărĕus -ĕi, m. (Τυνδάρεος), *king of Sparta, husband of Leda, father of Castor and Pollux, Helen and Clytemnestra.* Hence, **A.** Subst., **Tyndărīdēs** -ae, m. *a male descendant of Tyndareus;* Tyndaridae, *Castor and Pollux,* Cic. **B. Tyndăris** -ĭdis, f. *a female descendant of Tyndareus,* Helen, Verg., Ov., Clytemnestra, Ov.

1. **Tyndăris,** v. Tyndareus.

2. **Tyndăris** -ĭdis, f. (Τυνδαρίς), *a town on the north coast of Sicily, possessing a celebrated statue of Mercury, which was taken by the Carthaginians and restored by Scipio Africanus the Younger.* Hence, **Tyndărītānus** -a -um, *of Tyndaris.*

Tỹnes -ētis, m. (Τύνης), *a town in Zengitana,* now *Tunis.*

Tўphoeus -ĕos, m. (Τυφωεύς), *a giant who tried to force Jupiter from heaven, and was for punishment buried beneath Aetna.* Hence, **A. Tўphoïus** -a -um, *of or belonging to Typhoeus.* **B. Tўphoïs** -ĭdos, *of or belonging to Typhoeus;* Ætna, Ov.

1. **Tўphōn** -ōnis, m. (Τυφών), *another name of the giant Typhoeus.*

2. **tўphon** -ōnis, m. (τυφών), *a whirlwind, hurricane, typhoon,* Plin.

tўpus -i, m. (τύπος), *a figure on a wall,* Cic.

tўrannĭcē, adv. (tyrannicus), *tyrannically, despotically;* ea quae regie seu potius tyrannice statuit in aratores, Cic.

tўrannĭcīda -ae, c. (tyrannus and caedo), *the slayer of a tyrant, a tyrannicide,* Plin.

tўrannĭcīdĭum -ii, n. (tyrannicida), *the slaying of a tyrant,* Sen.

tўrannĭcus -a -um (τυραννικός), *tyrannical;* leges, facinus, Cic.

Tўrannĭo -ōnis, m. *a Greek grammarian and geographer, who came to Rome as a captive in the Mithridatic War, and taught the children and arranged the library of Cicero.*

tўrannis -ĭdis, f. (τυραννίς), *the supremacy of a tyrant, tyranny;* vivit tyrannis, tyrannus occidit, Cic.; tyrannidem delere, Cic.

tўrannoctŏnus -i, m. (τυραννοκτόνος), *the slayer of a tyrant,* Cic.

tўrannus -i, m. (τύραννος, Dor. for κοίρανος), *lord, master.* **I.** Gen., *an absolute ruler, prince, lord;* of Aeneas, Verg.; Phrygius, Laomedon, Ov.; of Neptune, as ruler of the sea, Ov. **II.** Esp., *of one who in a free state gains supreme power and overthrows the constitution of the state, a usurper, despot, tyrant;* clemens tyrannus, Cic.

Tўrās -ae, m. (Τύρας), *a river in Sarmatia,* now *the Dniester.*

tўrianthĭna -ōrum, n. (τυριάνθινος), *violet-coloured garments,* Mart.

Tўrĭus, v. Tyrus.

tўrŏtărĭchum -i, m. (τυροτάριχος), *a dish of cheese and salt-fish,* Cic.

Tyrrhēni -ōrum, m. (Τύρρηνοι), *the Etruscans, the people who inhabited the country north of Latium.* Hence, **A. Tyrrhēnĭa** -ae, f. *Etruria.* **B. Tyrrhēnus** -a -um, *Etruscan;* corpora, *the sailors whom Bacchus turned into dolphins,* Ov.; so monstra, Ov.; rex, *Mezentius,* Ov.; mare, aequor, *the part of the Mediterranean between Italy and Corsica and Sardinia,* Verg., Liv.; subst., **Tyrrhēnus** -i, m. *an Etruscan.*

Tyrrhīdae -ārum, m. *the sons of Tyrrhus, the herdsmen of king Latinus.*

Tўrus (-ŏs) -i, f. (Τύρος), *Tyre, a city of Phoenicia, famous for its purple;* hence, adj., **Tўrĭus** -a -um, *a, Tyrian;* puella, *Europa, daughter of the Tyrian king Agenor,* Ov.; subst., **Tўrĭi** -ōrum, m. *the inhabitants of Tyre;* b, meton. = *purple;* vestes, Hor.; colores, Ov.; c, transf. = *Carthaginian;* urbs, *Carthage,* Verg.; subst., **Tўrĭi** -ōrum, m. *the Tyrians.*

U.

U u, *originally written V, v, the 20th letter of the Latin alphabet, corresponds with the Greek upsilon* (Υ, υ). *It is frequently interchanged with i,* as optimus, optumus, satira, satura, etc.

1. **ūber** -ĕris, n. (οὖθαρ). **I.** *an udder, pap, teat, breast;* ubera praebere, Ov.; admovere, Verg. **II.** Transf., a, *richness, abundance, fertility;* fertilis ubere ager, Ov.; b, poet., *a fruitful field,* Verg.

2. **ūber** -ĕris, *rich, abounding in anything, fertile, fruitful, productive, abundant, copious.* **I.** Lit., a, seges spicis uberibus, Lucr.; uberior solito (of a river), *fuller than usual,* Ov.; arbor niveis uberrima pomis, Ov.; b, *full of matter;* uberiores litterae, Cic. **II.** Fig., quis uberior in dicendo Platone? Cic.; uberrima supplicationibus triumphisque provincia, Cic.; uberrimae artes, Cic.

ūbĕrĭus, superl., **ūberrĭmē,** adv. (2. uber). **I.** *more abundantly, more copiously;* provenit seges, Ov. **II.** Fig., *more copiously, more at length;* disputare, Cic.

ūbertas -ātis, f. (2. uber), *fruitfulness, fertility, copiousness, abundance.* **I.** Subject., *productiveness;* a, lit., agrorum, Cic.; b, fig., utilitatis, Cic. **II.** Object., *abundance, plenty;* a, lit., frugum, Cic.; b, fig., improborum, Cic.; plur., ubertates virtutis et copiae, Cic.

ūbertim, adv. (2. uber), *abundantly, copiously;* fundere lacrimas, Cat.

ūberto, l. (ubertas), *to make fruitful,* Plin.

ŭbi (old archaic form cubi), *where.* **I.** Lit., a, omnes, qui tum eos agros, ubi hodie est haec urbs, incolebant, Cic.; ubi tyrannus est, ibi, etc., Cic.; with particle nam, in qua non video ubinam mens constans et vita beata possit insistere, Cic.; with genit., terrarum, loci, e.g., quid ageres, ubi terrarum esses, Cic.; b, in direct questions, *where?* ubi sunt qui Antonium Graece negant scire? Cic. **II.** Transf., **A.** Of time, *when, as soon as;* quem ubi vidi, equidem ṽim lacrimarum profudi, Cic.; ubi de eius adventu Helvetii certiores facti sunt, legatos ad eum mittunt, Caes.; with primum, at hostes, ubi primum nostros equites conspexerunt, Caes. **B.** *wherein, whereby, in which, by which,* etc.; est, ubi id isto modo valeat, Cic. **C.** ubi ubi = ubicumque, *wherever;* facile ubi ubi essent se conversuros aciem, Liv.

ŭbĭcumquĕ (ŭbĭcunquĕ), adv. *wherever, wheresoever.* **I.** Relat., ubicumque erimus, Cic.; with genit., ubicumque gentium or terrarum, Cic. **II.** Indef., *anywhere, everywhere;* malum est ubicumque, Hor.

Ubĭi -ōrum, m. *a German people who, in Caesar's time, dwelt on the east bank of the Rhine near Cologne.* Adj., **Ubĭus** -a -um, *Ubian.*

ŭbĭlĭbĕt, adv. *anywhere you please, everywhere,* Sen.

ŭbĭnam, v. ubi.

ŭbĭquāquĕ (sc. parte), *wherever,* Ov.

ŭbĭquĕ, adv. *wherever, wheresoever, everywhere;* omnes qui ubique sunt, or sunt nati, *all in the world,* Cic.

ŭbĭvis, *wherever you will, anywhere, everywhere,* Cic.

Ūcălĕgŏn -ōnis, m. *name of a Trojan;* jam proximus ardet Ucalegon, *the house of Ucalegon,* Verg.

ūdo -ōnis, m. *a fur shoe or sock,* Mart.

ūdus -a -um (contr. from uvidus). **I.** Lit., *wet, moist;* paludes, Ov.; oculi, *tearful,* Ov.; aleator, *drunken,* Hor. **II.** Transf., *soft, bending, yielding;* argilla, Hor.

Ūfens -tis, m. **I.** *a small river in Latium;* hence, **Ūfentīnus** -a -um, *Ufentine.* **II.** *a commander of the Aequi.*

ulcĕrātĭo -ōnis, f. (ulcero), *a sore, ulcer, ulceration,* Plin.

ulcĕro, 1. (ulcus), *to make sore, to ulcerate.* **I.** Lit., mantica cui lumbos onere ulceret, Hor.; nondum ulcerato Philoctetā morsu serpentis, Cic. **II.** Fig., jecur, *to wound the heart,* Hor.

ulcĕrōsus -a -um (ulcus), *full of sores, ulcerated, ulcerous.* **I.** a, lit., facies, Tac.; b, transf., of trees, *full of knots.* **II.** Fig., jecur, *wounded by love,* Hor.

ulciscor, ultus sum, ulcisci, 3. dep. **I.** *to take vengeance for some one, to avenge;* patrem, Cic.; se, Cic. **II.** *to take vengeance on some one, to punish;* a, with acc. of person, aliquem, Cic., Caes.; b, with acc. of thing, scelus, Cic.; injuriam, Cic. (ulcisci, ultus, pass., quidquid sine sanguine civium ulcisci nequitur, Sall.; quae defendi repetique et ulcisci fas sit, Liv.).

ulcus -ĕris, n. (ἕλκος), *a sore, ulcer.* **I.** a, lit., Verg.; b, transf., *an excrescence on trees,* Plin. **II.** Fig., ulcus (of love) enim vivescit et inveterascit alendo, Lucr.; quidquid horum attigeris, ulcus est, Cic.

ulcuscŭlum -i, n. (dim. of ulcus), *a little ulcer,* Sen.

ulex -ĭcis, m. *a shrub resembling rosemary,* Plin.

ūlĭgĭnōsus -a -um (uligo), *wet, damp, moist, marshy,* Varr.

ūlĭgo -ĭnis, f. (for uviligo, from *uveo), *moisture of the soil, wetness of the earth;* uligines paludum, Tac.

Ūlixēs -is, m. Latin name (after Etruscan Uluxe or Sicilian Οὐλίξης) for 'Οδυσσεύς, *son of Laertes, husband of Penelope, father of Telemachus, king of Ithaca, famed for his cunning and for his* wanderings after the siege of Troy (genit., Ulixĕi, Hor., Ov.; acc., Ulixen, Hor., Ov.).

ullus -a -um, genit. ullīus, dat. ulli (dim. of unus, for unulus), *any,* gen. used in negative and hypothetical sentences. **I.** Adj., sine ulla dubitatione, Cic.; neque ullam in partem disputo, *for or against,* Cic.; neque ullam picturam fuisse, quin conquisierit, Cic. **II.** Subst., a, m. *any one,* Cic.; b, n. *anything;* nemo ullius nisi fugae memor, Liv. (ullīus, Cat., Verg., Ov.).

ulmārĭum -ĭi, n. (ulmus), *a nursery or plantation of elms,* Plin.

ulmĕus -a -um (ulmus), *of or relating to the elm, made of elm-wood,* Plaut.

ulmĭtrĭba -ae, m. (ulmus and τρίβω, tero), lit., *an elm-rubber;* in jest, *one who has often been beaten with elm-rods,* Plaut.

ulmus -i, f. *the elm,* Verg.

ulna -ae, f. (ὠλένη), *the elbow.* **I.** 1, lit., Plin.; 2, meton., *the arm;* ulnis aliquem tollere, Ov. **II.** Transf., a, as a measure of length, *an ell,* Verg.; b, *as much as a man can span with both arms,* Plin.

ulpĭcum -i, n. *a kind of leek,* Cato.

uls (archaic ouls) and **ultis**, *on the other side of, beyond,* Varr.

ultĕr -tra -trum, compar., **ultĕrĭor;** superl., **ultĭmus. I.** Posit., **ulter** -tra -trum, not found except in the adverbial forms ultra, ultro. **II.** Compar., **ultĕrĭor** -ius, genit. -ōris, *on the other side, further, beyond, ulterior.* **A.** Lit., Gallia, *Gaul on the other,* i.e., *the north side of the Alps,* Cic.; equitatus, *placed at a greater distance,* Caes. **B.** Transf., a, *distant, past, farther;* ulteriora mirari, Tac.; ulteriora pudet docuisse, Cic.; b, *farther, worse;* quo quid ulterius privato timendum foret? Liv. **III.** Superl., **ultĭmus** -a -um, *the most distant, furthest, extremest, last.* **A.** Lit., of space, 1, luna, quae ultima a caelo est, Cic.; subst., a, m., recessum primi ultimis non dabant, Caes.; b, n., caelum, quod extremum atque ultimum mundi est, Cic.; ultima signant, *the goal,* Verg.; 2, partitive for ultima pars, in ultimam provinciam, *into the most distant part of the province,* Cic. **B.** Transf., 1, in time or succession, *the most distant, remotest, the last, final;* tempus, antiquitas, Cic.; principium, Cic.; lapis, *a gravestone,* Prop.; adv., ad ultimum, *to the last,* Liv.; or (oftener), *lastly, finally,* Liv.; ultimum, *for the last time,* Liv.; 2, in rank or degree; a, *the highest, greatest;* natura, Cic.; supplicium, *capital punishment,* Caes.; subst., **ultĭmum** -i, n. *the greatest, the extremest,* and, in a bad sense, *the worst;* ultima audere, Liv.; ultimum bonorum, *the highest good,* Cic.; adv., ad ultimum, *utterly, entirely;* ad ultimum demens, Liv.; b, *the meanest, lowest;* laus, Hor.; subst., (a) m., in ultimis militum, Liv.; (β) n., in ultimis laudum esse, Liv.

ultĕrĭus. I. Neut. of ulterior, v. ulter. **II.** Adv., v. ultra.

ultĭmus, v. ulter.

ultĭo -ōnis, f. (ulciscor), *an avenging, punishing, revenging, revenge;* ultionem petere, Liv.; with object. genit., violatae per vim pudicitiae, Liv.

ultis = uls (q.v.).

ultor -ōris, m. (ulciscor), *an avenger, punisher;* injuriarum, Cic.; attrib., deus ultor = Anteros, Ov.; as a surname of Mars, Ov.

ultrā, sc. parte (from ulter). **I.** Adv., posit., *on the other side of;* 1, lit., cis Padum ultraque, Liv.; 2, transf., of that which is beyond a certain limit, *beyond, further;* a, in space, (a) lit., ultra ueque curae neque gaudic locum esse, Sall.; (β) fig., *farther, beyond;* estne aliquid ultra, quo progredi crudelitas possit? Cic.; foll. by quam, quod ultra quam satis est, Cic.; **b,** of time, *farther;* nec ultra bellum dilatum est, Liv.; compar., ulterius, *further;* (α) lit., ulterius abit, Ov.; (β) fig., ulterius ne tende odiis, Verg. **II.** Prep. with acc., **1,** of space, *beyond, on the further side of;* ultra Silianam villam, Cic.; **2,** transf., **a,** of time, *beyond;* ultra biennium, Tac.; **b,** of number or measure, *beyond, more than;* modum, quem ultra progredi non oportet, Cic.; ultra vires, Verg. (ultra sometimes put after its case, quem ultra, Cic.).

ultrix -īcis, f. (ultor), *avenging;* Dirae, *the Furies,* Verg.

ultrō (sc. loco, from ulter), adv. *on the other side.* **I.** Lit., *on the other side, beyond;* gen., with citro, *up and down, on both sides;* ultro et citro cursare, Cic. **II.** Transf., **a,** *away, off;* ultro istum a me! Plaut.; **b,** *besides, moreover;* ultroque iis sumptum intulit, Cic.; **c,** *of one's own accord, spontaneously, voluntarily;* ultro se offerre, Cic.; improbos ultro lacessere, Cic.; hence, ultro tributa, *money which the treasury had to expend every year on public buildings,* Liv.

ultrōnĕus -a -um (ultro), *of one's own accord, voluntarily,* Sen.

ultrōtrĭbūta, v. ultro.

Ŭlŭbrae -ārum, *a place in Latium, near the Pontine Marshes.* Hence, **Ŭlŭbrānus** -a -um, *Ulubran.*

ŭlŭla -ae, f. (lit., *the screeching one* (sc. **avis),** from ululo), *a screech-owl,* Verg.

ŭlŭlātus -ūs, m. (ululo), *a howling, wailing, shrieking, yelling;* ululatus nocturni, Liv.

ŭlŭlo, 1. (connected with ὀλολύζω). **I.** In-transit., *to howl, yell;* **a,** lit., of living beings, Tisiphone ululavit, Ov.; ululanti voce, Cic.; **b,** transf., of places, *to resound with howling;* cavae plangoribus aedes femineis ululant, Verg. **II.** Transit., *to call upon with howling;* nocturnis Hecate triviis ululata per urbem, Verg.

ulva -ae, f. *sedge,* Verg.

Ŭlysses = Ulixes (q.v.).

umbella -ae, f. (dim. of umbra), *a parasol,* Juv.

Umber, v. Umbri.

umbĭlĭcātus -a -um (umbilicus), *shaped like a navel,* Plin.

umbĭlĭcus -i, m. (ὀμφαλός), *the navel.* **I.** Lit., Liv., Ov. **II.** Meton., *the middle, centre of anything;* **1,** gen., Siciliae, Cic.; terrarum, Delphi, Cic.; **2,** esp., **a,** *the end of a roller on which a MS. was rolled,* Cat.; fig., inceptos iambos ad umbilicum adducere, *bring to the end,* Hor.; **b,** transf., *the index of a sun-dial,* Cic.; **c,** *a kind of sea-snail,* Cic.

umbo -ōnis, m. (ἄμβων). **I.** *the boss in the centre of a shield;* summus clipei umbo, Verg.; hence, meton., *a shield;* salignae umbonum crates, Verg. **II.** *the elbow,* Mart. **III.** *the full part or swelling of a garment;* meton., *a toga,* Pers.

umbra -ae, f. *a shade, shadow.* **I. A.** Lit., arboris, Cic.; prov., umbras timere, *to be frightened at shadows,* Cic. **B.** Transf., *shade;* **a,** *protection, help;* auxilii, Liv.; sub umbra Romanae amicitiae latēre, Cic.; **b,** *idleness, pleasant rest;* veneris cessamus in umbra, Ov.; cedat umbra soli, Cic.; **c,** *appearance* (as opposed to reality), *shadow, semblance;* gloriae, Cic. **II. A.** Transf., **1,** *a shade, shadow in painting;* transf., in discourse, Cic.; **2,** *the shadow = that which accompanies;* luxuriae, Cic.; *an uninvited guest,*

brought *by one who has been invited* (σκιά), Hor. **B.** Meton., **1,** *that which is shady;* **a, as** trees, houses, etc., umbras falce premere, Verg.; inducite montibus umbras (i.e., arbores), Verg.; **b,** *any shady place;* Pompeja, Ov.; tonsoris, barber's shop, Hor.; **2,** *the shade of a dead person, ghost;* tricorpor, Verg.; plur., umbrae, Verg.; **3,** *a fish, the grayling,* Ov.

umbrācŭlum -i, n. (umbra). **I.** *a shady place, arbour,* Verg.; in plur., *a quiet place* (as opp. to public life); Theophrasti, Cic.; doctrinam ex umbraculis eruditorum (*schools*) otioque in solem produxerat, Cic. **II.** *a parasol,* Ov.

umbrātĭcŏla -ae, m. (umbra and colo), *a lounger in the shade,* Plaut.

umbrātĭcus -a -um (umbra), *belonging to the shade;* homo, *an idler, lounger,* Plaut.

umbrātĭlis -e (umbra), *remaining in the shade.* **I.** *retired, contemplative;* vita, Cic. **II.** Of discourse, in the schools, *rhetorical* (opp. to public, political), domestica exercitatio et umbratilis, Cic.; oratio, *only meant for perusal, not for speaking,* Cic.

Umbri -ōrum, m. *a people in Italy between the Padus, the Tiber, and the Adriatic Sea, who in later times descended farther into Italy, and inhabited a country between the Rubicon, the Nar, and the Tiber.* Hence, **A. Umber** -bra -brum, *Umbrian;* subst., **Umber** -bri, m. *an Umbrian.* **B. Umbrĭa** -ae, f. *Umbria, the country of the Umbri.*

umbrĭfĕr -fĕra -fĕrum (umbra and fero), *shady, umbrageous;* nemus, Verg.; platanus, Cic.

umbro, 1. (umbra), *to cover with shade, shade, overshadow;* umbrata tempora quercu, Verg.

umbrōsus -a -um (umbra), *shady, umbrageous.* **I.** Pass., *shaded;* ripa, Cic.; locus umbrosior, Cic. **II.** Act., *affording shade;* cacumina, Verg.; salix, Ov.

ūmecto = humecto (q.v.).

ūmĕrus = humerus (q.v.).

ūmesco, umidus = humesco, humidus (q.v.).

ūmor = humor (q.v.).

umquam (unquam), adv. (orig. cum-quam), *at any time, ever* (used chiefly in negative, interrog., and conditional sentences), Cic.; non umquam, Liv.; haud umquam, Verg.; si umquam, Liv.

ūnā, adv. (unus), *at the same place, at the same time, together;* **a,** absol., qui una venerant, Cic.; **b,** with cum and the abl., amores una cum praetexta ponere, Cic.

ūnănĭmans = unanimus (q.v.).

ūnănĭmĭtas -ātis, f. (unanimus), *concord, unanimity,* Liv.

ūnănĭmus -a -um (unus and animus), *of one mind, concordant, agreeing, unanimous;* sodales, Cat.; fratres, Verg.

uncĭa -ae, f. (Sicilian οὐγκία, from unus), *an ounce, the twelfth part of any whole.* **I.** Lit., **1,** as a coin, *one-twelfth of an as,* Varr.; **2,** as a weight or measure, **a,** *an ounce, one-twelfth of a pound,* Plaut.; **b,** as a measure, *one-twelfth of a foot, an inch,* Plin.; **3,** in inheritances, *a twelfth part;* Caesar ex uncia, *heir to one-twelfth,* Cic. **II.** Transf., *a trifle, bit;* eboris, Juv.

uncĭālis -e (uncia), *of or relating to a twelfth part;* asses, *weighing an ounce each,* Plin.

uncĭārĭus -a -um (uncia), *of or relating to a twelfth part;* fenus, *one-twelfth of the capital yearly, i.e.,* 8½ *per cent. for the year of ten months,* 10 *per cent. for the year of twelve months,* Tac.

uncĭātim, adv. (uncia), *by ounces,* Plin.; Transf., *little by little,* Ter.

uncĭnātus -a -um (uncinus), *shaped like a hook, hooked;* uncinata corpora, Cic.

uncĭŏla -ae, f. (dim. of uncia), *a little ounce, a little twelfth part* (of an inheritance), Juv.

unctĭo -ōnis, f. (ungo). **I.** *an anointing,* Plaut.; philosophum unctionis causâ reliquerunt, *to wrestle in the palaestra,* Cic. **II.** Meton., *ointment, salve,* Plin.

unctĭto, 1. (intens. of ungo), *to salve, anoint,* Plaut.

unctĭuscŭlus -a -um (dim. of unctus), *somewhat unctuous,* Plaut.

unctor -ōris, m. (ungo), *an anointer,* Cic.

unctōrĭum -Ii, n. (ungo), *an anointing-room in the bath,* Plin.

unctūra -ae, f. (ungo), *the anointing of the dead,* ap. Cic.

1. **unctus** -a -um, p. adj. (from ungo). **I.** Adj., *smeared, anointed;* 1, lit., manus, Hor.; sol, *basking in the sun after being anointed,* Cic.; poet., palaestra, *where one is anointed,* Ov.; 2, transf., accedes siccus ad unctum, *to a rich and luxurious person,* Hor.; unctior quaedam consuetudo loquendi, *rich, copious,* Cic. **II.** Subst., **unctum** -i, n. *a sumptuous repast,* Hor.

2. **unctus** -ūs, m. (ungo), *an anointing,* Plin.

1. **uncus** -i, m. (ὄγκος), *a hook;* uncus ferreus, Liv.; nec severus uncus abest, *as typical of Necessitas,* Hor.; esp., *the hook with which the executioner dragged the bodies of the dead malefactors to throw them into the Tiber;* alicui uncum impingere, Cic.

2. **uncus** -a -um, *bent like a hook, hooked, curved;* manus, Verg.; aratrum, Verg.

unda -ae, f. *a wave of the sea,* and collective, *the waves.* **I.** Lit., maris unda, Cic. **II. A.** Transf., *wave, storm, surge;* undae comitiorum, *disorder,* Cic.; unda salutantum, *crowd,* Verg. **B.** Meton., 1, *moisture;* a, *flowing water, water;* fontis, Ov.; faciunt justos ignis et unda viros (fire and water being used at the ceremony of marriage), Ov.; b, of other liquids, e.g., oil, Plin., 2, *stream* (of objects which are not liquid), qua plurimus undam fumus agit, *eddies,* Verg.

undātim, adv. (unda), *like waves,* Plin.

undĕ, adv. (orig. cunde), *whence, from where.* **I.** Lit., of place, 1, correlative, nec enim inde venit, unde mallem, Cic.; ut aliae eodem, unde erant profectae, referrentur, Caes.; 2, absol., a, in direct questions, unde dejectus est Cinna? Cic.; b, in indirect questions, non recordor unde ceciderim, Cic. **II.** Transf., **A.** Of origin, ground, cause, means, etc., *whence, from what person or thing, from what origin;* 1, correlative; a, unde necesse est, inde initium sumatur, Cic.; b, qui eum necasset, unde ipse natus esset, Cic.; 2, esp., legal t. t., unde petitur = *the accused person* or *defendant;* ego omnibus, unde petitur, hoc consilium dederim, Cic. **III.** unde unde = undecumque, *whencesoever,* Hor.

undēcentum (unus, de, and centum), *ninety-nine,* Plin.

undēcĭēs (**undēcĭens**), adv. (undecim), *eleven times,* Mart.

undēcim (unus and decem), *eleven,* Cic.

undēcĭmus -a -um (undecim), *the eleventh;* legio, Liv.; annus, Verg.

undēcĭrēmis -is, f. sc. navis (undecim and remus), *a ship with eleven banks of oars,* Plin.

undēcŭmāni -ōrum, m. (undecimus or undecumus), *soldiers of the eleventh legion,* Plin.

undēcumquĕ (**undēcunquĕ**), adv. *whencesoever,* Quint.

undēni -ae -a (for undeceni, from undecim), *eleven each;* Musa per undenos emodulanda pedes,

i.e., of hexameter and pentameter, Ov.; quater undenos implevisse Decembres, *i.e., forty-four years,* Hor.

undēnōnāginta (unus, de, and nonaginta), *eighty-nine,* Liv.

undēoctōginta (unus, de, and octoginta) *seventy-nine,* Hor.

undēquădrāgĭēs, adv. (undequadraginta), *thirty-nine times,* Plin.

undēquădrāginta (unus, de, and quadraginta), *thirty-nine,* Cic.

undēquinquāgēsĭmus -a -um (undequinquaginta), *the forty-ninth,* Cic.

undēquinquāginta (unus, de, and quinquaginta), *forty-nine,* Liv.

undēsexāginta (unus, de, and sexaginta) *fifty-nine,* Liv.

undētrīcēsĭmus -a -um (undetriginta), *the twenty-ninth,* Liv.

undētrīginta (unus, de, and triginta), *twenty-nine,* Vitr.

undēvīcēni -ae -a (undeviginti), *nineteen each,* Quint.

undēvīcēsĭmus (**undēvīgēsĭmus**) (undeviginti), *the nineteenth,* Cic.

undēvīginti (unus, de, and viginti), *nineteen,* Cic., Liv.

undĭquĕ, adv. (unde and que). **I.** *on all sides, from everywhere, everywhere;* concurrere, Cic.; colligere, Cic.; amens undique dicatur, *by all people,* Hor. **II.** *on all sides, in every respect;* partes undique aequales, Cic.; undique religionem tolle, Cic.

undĭsŏnus -a -um (unda and sono), *resounding with waves;* dii, *sea-gods,* Prop.

undo, 1. (unda), *to rise in waves, surge.* **A.** Lit., flammis inter tabulata volutus ad caelum undabat vortex, Verg. **B.** Transf., *to have a wave-like motion, to wave, to undulate;* fumus Verg.; habenae, *hanging loosely,* Verg.

undōsus -a -um (unda), *full of waves, surging, billowy,* Verg.

ūnēdo -ōnis, m. *the arbutus-tree, and its fruit,* Plin.

ūnetvīcēsĭmāni -ōrum, m. (unetvicesimus), *soldiers of the twenty-first legion,* Tac.

ūnetvīcēsĭmus -a -um (unus-et-vicesimus), *the twenty-first,* Tac.

ungo (**unguo**), unxi, unctum, 3. *to anoint, smear, salve.* **I.** Lit., aliquem unguentis, Cic.; gloria quem supra vires ungit, *adorns,* Hor.; (with reference to the anointing after a bath), unctus est, accubuit, Cic.; of the anointing of a corpse, corpus, Ov.; of the dressing of pro visions, *to dress;* caules oleo, Hor. **II.** Transf., *to besmear;* tela manu, *with poison,* Verg.; uncta aqua, *dirty,* Hor.; uncta carina, *pitched,* Verg.

unguen -Inis, n. (ungo), *a fatty substance, salve,* Verg.

unguentārĭus -a -um (ungentum), *of* or *relating to salve* or *ointment.* **I.** Adj., Suet. **II.** Subst., **A.** **unguentārĭus** -Ii, m. *a dealer in unguents,* Cic. **B.** **unguentārĭa** -ae, f. a, *a female dealer in unguents,* Plin.; b, *the art of preparing unguents,* Plaut. **C.** **unguentārĭum** -Ii, n. *money for unguents,* Plin.

unguentātus -a -um (unguentum), *anointed,* Cat.

unguentum -i, n. (ungo), *a salve, ointment, unguent,* Cic.

unguĭcŭlus -i, m. (dim. of unguis), *the finger-nail, the toe-nail;* integritas unguiculorum omnium, Cic.; prov., qui mihi a teneris, ut

Graeci dicunt, unguiculis (Gr. ἐξ ἁπαλῶν ὀνύχων) cognitus est, *from childhood*, Cic.

unguïnōsus -a -um (unguen), *fatty, unctuous*, Plin.

unguis -is, m. (ὄνυξ), *a finger or toe-nail.* **I.** Lit., of men, ungues ponere, Hor. ; rodere, Hor. ; prov., ab imis unguibus usque ad verticem summum, *from top to toe*, Cic. ; a recta conscientia transversum unguem non discedere, *to depart a finger's breadth* (Engl. *a hair's breadth*) *from*, etc., Cic. ; de tenero ungui, *from childhood*, Hor. ; ad (in) unguem, *to a hair, nicely, perfectly* (an expression borrowed from sculptors who tested the smoothness of their work with the nail), ad unguem factus homo, Hor. ; carmen decies castigare ad unguem, Hor. ; omnis in unguem secto via limite quadret, Verg. **II.** Transf., **A.** Of plants, *a nail-like spot, tip*, Plin. **B.** *a kind of mussel*, Varr. (abl., gen. ungue, in poets also ungui).

ungŭla -ae, f. (unguis), *a hoof, claw, talon.* **I.** Lit., vestigium ungulae (equi), Cic. **II.** Meton., *a horse;* ungula rapit currus, Hor.

ungŭlus -i, m. (dim. of unguis). **I.** *a toe-nail*, Plaut. **II.** *a finger-ring*, Plin.

ūnĭcălămus -a -um (unus and calamus), *having one haulm*, Plin.

unguo = ungo (q.v.).

ūnĭcaulis -e (unus and caulis), *having one stalk*, Plin.

ūnĭcē, adv. (unicus), *singly, especially, particularly;* diligere, Cic. ; unice securus, *altogether free from care*, Hor.

ūnĭcŏlor -ōris (unus and color), *uniform in colour, of one colour;* torus, Ov.

ūnĭcornis -e (unus and cornu), *having one horn*, Plin.

ūnĭcus -a -um (unus), *only, sole.* **I.** Lit., filius, Cic. **II.** Transf., *singular, unparalleled, unique, alone in its kind;* liberalitas, Cic. ; fides, Liv.

ūnĭformis -e (unus and forma), *having one form, simple*, Tac.

ūnĭgĕna -ae (unus and gigno). **I.** *born at one birth, of the same race;* unigena Memnonis, Zephyrus, *brother of Memnon*, Cat. **II.** *only-born, only-made;* singularis hic mundus atque unigena, Cic.

ūnĭjŭgus -a -um (unus and jugum), *having only one yoke;* vinea, *fastened to the same cross-beam*, Plin.

ūnĭmănus -a -um (unus and manus), *having but one hand;* puer, Liv.

1. **ūnĭo**, 4. (unus), *to unite*, Sen.

2. **ūnĭo** -ōnis, m. (unus), *a single, large pearl*, Sen.

ūnĭstirpis -e (unus and stirps), *having one stock or stem*, Plin.

ūnĭtas -ātis, f. (unus), *unity, oneness.* **I.** Lit., Plin. **II.** Fig., **A.** *likeness, similarity*, Plin. **B.** *agreement, unanimity*, Sen.

ūnĭtĕr, adv. (unus), *in one, together;* aptus, Lucr.

ūnĭusmŏdi, adv. (unus and modus), *of one kind*, Cic.

ūnĭversālis -e (universus), *general, universal*, Quint.

ūnĭversē, adv. (universus), *in general;* generatim atque universe loquar, Cic.

ūnĭversĭtas -ātis, f. (universus), *the whole, total.* **I.** Lit., generis humani, Cic. ; rerum, *the universe*, Cic. **II.** Transf., *the world*, Cic.

ūnĭversus (archaic, **ūnĭvorsus**) -a -um (unus and versus), lit., *turned into one, combined into one.* **I.** *whole. entire.* **A.** Adj., mundus,

Cic. ; de re universa tractare, Cic. ; plur , **ūnĭversi** -ae -a, *all together;* universi (homines), Cic. ; natura universa atque omnia continens, *all things in entirety and in detail*, Cic. **B.** Subst., **universum** -i, n. *the whole;* hence, *the whole world, the universe*, Cic. **II.** Transf., *relating to all or to the whole, general;* pugna, *a general engagement*, Liv. ; in universum, *in general*, Liv.

ūnŏcŭlus -i, m. (unus and oculus), *a one-eyed man*, Plaut.

ūnus (old Latin, **oenus**) -a -um, genit. ūnīus, dat. ūni, *one.* **I.** Lit., **A.** Gen., unus de magistratibus, Cic. ; foll. by alter, una ex parte . . . altera ex parte, Caes. ; plur. (esp., with words used only in the plur.), unae decumae . . . alterae, Cic. ; ad unum (unam) omnes, *all to a man*, Cic. ; in unum (Gr. εἰς ἕν) = *into one place;* confluere, Cic. **B.** Esp., 1, *one, only one, alone;* Demosthenes unus eminet, Cic. ; uni ex omnibus Sequani, Caes. ; strengthened by the superl., or by omnium, summus vir unus omnis Graeciae, Cic. ; 2, *one, one and the same;* uno tempore, *at the same time*, Cic. ; id unis aedibus, Cic. **II.** Transf., indefinite, *a, an, one, some one, any one;* unus paterfamilias, Cic. ; without subst., tradidit uni, Cic. ; unus quidam, Cic. ; nemo unus, nullus unus, Cic. ; unus et alter, *one and another*, Cic. (genit., ūnīus, Verg., Ov., Lucr., Cat. ; ūni, Cat.).

ūpĭlio (**ōpĭlio**) -ōnis, m. *a shepherd*, Verg.

ūpŭpa -ae, f. (ἔποψ), *a hoopoe*, Varr. ; (with a play on the word), *a kind of hoe*, Plaut.

Ūrănĭa -ae, f. and **Ūrănĭē** -ēs, f. (Οὐρανία, Οὐρανίη, *the heavenly one*), *one of the nine Muses, the Muse of Astronomy.*

urbānē, adv. (urbanus). **I.** *politely, civilly, urbanely;* urbane, urbanius agere, Cic. **II.** Of discourse, *wittily, acutely, elegantly;* ridere Stoicos, Cic. ; vexare, Cic.

urbānĭtas -ātis, f. (urbanus), *city life.* **I.** Esp., *life in Rome;* desideria and desiderium urbanitatis, Cic. **II.** Meton., *the city manner;* 1, in a good sense, a, *politeness, urbanity, refinement of manner*, Cic. ; plur., deponendae tibi sunt urbanitates, rusticus Romanus factus es, Cic.; b, *elegance, refinement in speaking, both in pronunciation and in expression*, Cic. ; c, *elegance in wit, fine wit, pleasantry;* vetus, Cic. ; 2, in a bad sense, *city roguery*, Tac.

urbānus -a -um (urbs), *of or belonging to a city* (esp. to Rome), *urban.* **I.** Lit., tribus, Cic.; praetor, Cic. ; exercitus (of Roman citizens), Liv. ; suffragatio (of the city population), Cic. ; subst., **urbāni** -ōrum, m. *the inhabitants of the city, the townsfolk*, Cic. **II.** Meton., *after the city fashion;* 1, in a good sense, a, *refined in manner, elegant;* homo, *a man of the world*, Cic.; b, *of discourse, choice, elegant, refined;* quiddam resonat urbanius, Cic. ; c, *fine, witty, pleasant, humorous;* homo urbanissimus, Cic. ; sales, Cic. ; subst., *a wit*, Hor. ; 2, in a bad sense, *bold, impudent;* frons, Hor.

urbĭcăpus -i, m. (urbs and capio), *a taker of cities*, Plaut.

Urbĭcua -ae, f. *a town in Hispania Tarraconensis.*

urbĭcus -a -um (urbs), *of or belonging to a city, civic, urban*, Suet.

Urbīnum -i, n. *a town in Umbria, now Urbino.* Hence, **Urbīnās** -ātis, *belonging to Urbinum.*

Urbĭus clivus, *a place in Rome between the Esquiline and vicus Cyprius.*

urbs -bis, f. *the town surrounded by a ring wall, the city.* **I.** Lit., **A.** Gen., urbem condere, aedificare, Cic.; capere, Cic.; evertere, Cic. **B.** *the city of Rome* (like Gr. ἄστυ, of Athens), ad urbem, *near Rome* or *at Rome*, Cic.; ad urbem esse, of Roman generals waiting outside Rome till a triumph was granted them, or of magistrates waiting to proceed to their provinces, Sall. **II.** Meton., *the city* = *the dwellers in the city*; urbs somno vinoque sepulta, Verg.

urcĕŏlāris -e (urceolus), *of* or *relating to a jug* or *pitcher;* herba, *pellitory, a plant used for polishing glass pitchers,* Plin.

urcĕŏlus -i, m. (dim. of urceus), *a small jug* or *pitcher,* Juv.

urcĕus -i, m. (connected with orca), *an earthenware jug, pitcher,* Hor.

ūrēdo -ĭnis, f. (uro), 1, *a blight upon plants,* Cic.; 2, *an inflammatory itch,* Plin.

urgĕo (urguĕo), ursi, 2. *to push, press, drive, urge.* **I.** Lit., **A.** Transit., pedem (alicuius) pede (suo), Verg.; naves in Syrtes, *drive on the sand-banks,* Verg. **B.** Intransit., *to press;* longique urguent ad litora fluctus, Verg. **II.** Transf., 1, *to press upon, beset, oppress, burden, bear hard upon;* urgens malum, *urgent, pressing,* Cic.; mortifero morbo urgeor, Cic.; urgeri, with genit., *to be pressed hard on account of something;* male administratae provinciae aliorumque criminum, Tac.; 2, a, *to hem in a place;* urbem urbe aliā premere atque urgere, Verg.; b, of time, *to press upon;* urget diem nox et dies noctem, Hor.; 3, of discourse, *to urge, press hard upon;* interrogando, Cic.; 4, *to apply oneself to diligently, ply hard, urge on, follow up;* occasionem, Cic.; propositum, Hor.; iter, Ov.

ūrĭca -ae, f. *a caterpillar,* Plin.

ūrīna -ae, f. (οὖρον), *urine,* Cic.

ūrīnātor -ōris, m. (urinor), *a diver,* Liv.

ūrīnor, 1. dep. *to dive,* Cic.

Ūrĭos -ĭi, m. (Οὔριος), *the giver of a favourable wind* (of Jupiter), Cic.

urna -ae, f. **I.** *a pitcher for drawing water,* Hor.; attribute of the constellation Aquarius, Ov., and of the rivers personified as deities, Verg. **II.** Transf., **A.** *a jug, pitcher, urn;* a, *for holding money;* argenti, Hor.; b, *for holding the ashes of the dead,* Ov.; c, *for throwing lots into;* nomina in urnam conjicere, Liv.; educere ex urna tres (judices), Cic.; hence, of the urn of fate, assigned to Jupiter and the Parcae, omne nomen movet urna, Hor. **B.** As a measure of capacity, *half an amphora,* Plin.

urnālis -e (urna), *containing half an amphora,* Cato.

urnārĭum -ĭi, n. (urna), *a table on which water-cans were placed,* Varr.

urnŭla -ae, f. (dim. of urna), *a little pitcher,* Cic.

uro, ussi, ustum, 3. (connected with εὔω), *to burn.* **I. A.** Lit., 1, gen., calore, Cic.; 2, esp., a, medical t. t., *to burn* = *to treat by burning, to burn out;* in corpore si quid eiusmodi est quod reliquo corpori noceat, id uri secarique patimur, Cic.; b, t. t. of painting, *to burn in;* picta ustis coloribus puppis, Ov.; c, *to burn, destroy by fire;* (a) hominem mortuum, Cic.; agros, Liv.; domos, Hor.; (β) *to burn lights;* odoratam nocturna in lumina cedrum, Verg. **B.** Transf., 1, *to burn, dry up, parch, pain acutely;* fauces urit sitis, Ov.; 2, *to pinch, chafe, gall;* calceus urit, Hor.; urit lorica lacertos, Prop.; 3, *to pinch with cold;* ustus ab assiduo frigore Pontus, Ov. **II.** Fig., **A.** *to burn with passion,* and pass., *to be on fire, glow with passion;* me tamen urit amor, Verg.; uritur infelix Dido, Verg. **B.** *to disquiet, disturb, harass;* eos bellum Romanum urebat, Liv.

urruncum -i, n. *the lowest part of an ear of corn,* Varr.

ursa -ae, f. (ursus). **I.** *a female bear;* poet. = *bear* generally, Verg., Ov. **II.** Meton., *the constellations of the Great and Little Bear;* ursa major, or Erymanthis, or Maenalis, or Parrhasis, *the Great Bear,* ursa minor or ursa Cynosuris, *the Little Bear,* Ov.

ursīnus -a -um (ursus), *of* or *relating to a bear,* Plin.

ursus -i, m. *a bear.* **I.** Lit., ursi informes, Verg. **II.** Meton., poscunt ursum, *a bear hunt in the circus,* Hor.

urtīca -ae, f. (uro). **I.** *a nettle;* 1, lit., Plin.; 2, transf., *a sea-nettle,* Plin. **II.** Fig., *lustfulness, lewd desire,* Juv.

ūrus -i, m. *the urus, a kind of wild ox,* Caes.

urvum (urbum) -i, n. *a plough-tail,* Varr.

Uscāna -ae, f. *a town in Illyria on the borders of Macedonia,* now *Voscopoli.* Hence, **Uscānenses** -ĭum, m. *the inhabitants of Uscana.*

ūsĭo -ōnis, f. (utor), *use, using,* Cato.

Ūsĭpĕtes -um, m. and **Ūsĭpĭi** -ōrum, m. *a powerful German tribe near the Tencteri, on the Lippe and the Rhine, conquered by Caesar.*

ūsĭtātē, adv. (usitatus), *in the usual manner;* loqui, Cic.

ūsĭtātus -a -um, p. adj. (* usito, *customary, usual, wonted, accustomed;* vocabula, Cic.; facimus usitatius hoc verbum, Cic.; utatur verbis quam usitatissimis, Cic.; usitatum est, foll. by acc. and infin., *it is usual, customary,* ap. Cic.

uspĭam, adv. (orig. cuspiam), *anywhere,* Cic.

usquam, adv. (orig. cusquam). **I.** *anywhere* (gen. used in negative and conditional sentences). **A.** Lit., iste cui nullus esset usquam consistendi locus, Cic.; with genit., usquam gentium, Cic. **B.** *in any case,* Cic., Sall. **II.** *any whither, in any direction;* nec vero usquam discedebam, Cic.

usquĕ, adv. (orig. cusque), *at every point, through and through, from . . . to, all the way, continuously.* **I.** Of space, a, with prep., usque a mare supero Romam proficisci, Cic.; usque ad castra hostium accessit, Caes.; b, with adv. of place, quod eos usque istim (istinc) exauditos putem, Cic.; usque quaque, *everywhere,* Cic.; c, with acc. of the object or place reached (with names of towns), ut usque Romam significationes vocesque referantur, *as far as Rome,* Cic. **II.** Of time, a, with prep., usque a Romulo, *from the time of Romulus,* Cic.; b, with adv. of time, inde usque repetens, Cic.; usque quaque, *always,* Cat.; usque eo se tenuit, Cic.; c, absol., *always, constantly;* juvat usque morari, Verg. **III.** In other relations, hoc malum usque ad bestias perveniat, Cic.

usquĕquāquĕ, v. usque I. and II.

usta -ae, f. (uro), *a red pigment, burnt cinnabar,* Plin.

Ustīca -ae, f. **I.** *a valley in the Sabine country, near Horace's estate.* **II.** *a small island opposite the west coast of Sicily.*

ustil . . . v. ustul . . .

ustĭo -ōnis, f. (uro), *a burning,* Plin.

ustor -ōris, m. (uro), *a burner of corpses,* Cic.

ustŭlo (ustĭlo), 1. (dim. of uro), *to burn a little, to singe,* Cat.

1. **ūsūcăpĭo** -cēpi -captum, 3. (usu, abl. of usus, and capio), *to acquire ownership by length of possession* or *prescription,* Cic.; velut usucepisse Italiam, Liv.

2. ūsūcăpǐo -ōnis, f. (usū, abl. of usus, and ̯apio), *ownership acquired by length of possession or prescription;* usucapio fundi, Cic.

ūsūra -ae, f. (utor). **I.** *the use, enjoyment of anything;* a, natura dedit usuram vitae, Cic.; unius horae, Cic.; b, *the use of borrowed capital,* Cic. **II.** Meton., *interest paid for money borrowed;* usura menstrua, Cic.; usurae gravissimae, Caes.; alicui usuram pendĕre, *to pay,* Cic.; transf., terra nec umquam sine usura reddit, Cic.

ūsūrārǐus -a -um (usura). **I.** *relating to* (temporary) *use,* Plaut. **II.** *out at interest, paying interest,* Plaut.

usurpātǐo -ōnis, f. (usurpo), *a using, use, making use;* doctrinae, Cic.; vocis, Liv.; ad usurpationem vetustatis, *to practise an old custom,* Cic.; itineris, *undertaking,* Liv.

ūsurpo, 1. (contr. from usu and rapio), *to draw to oneself by use.* **I.** Gen., *to make use of, to use, to bring into use;* genus poenae, Cic. **II.** Esp., **A.** *to lay claim to, to assert one's right to;* nomen civitatis, Cic. **B.** Legal t. t., *to take possession of, acquire;* a, lawfully, amissam possessionem, Cic.; b, unlawfully, *to appropriate, to usurp;* alienam possessionem, Liv. **C.** *to make use of by the senses, to perceive, to notice;* sensibus, Lucr. **D.** *to make use of by the voice;* a, *to use, to mention;* nomen tantum virtutis usurpas, Cic.; b, *to call by any name habitually;* C. Laelius, is qui Sapiens usurpatur, Cic.

ūsus -ūs, m. (utor), *use, using, making use of, application, practice, exercise.* **I.** Lit., **A.** Gen., usus privatus, Cic.; quia ea pecunia non posset in bellum usui esse, Liv.; scientia atque usus rerum nauticarum, *theory and practice,* Caes.; usus magister est optimus, Cic. **B.** Esp., **1,** *intercourse with men;* a, *social intercourse, familiarity;* domesticus usus et consuetudo, Cic.; b, *carnal intercourse,* Ov.; **2,** legal t. t., usus et fructus, usus fructusque, ususfructus, *the use and enjoyment of property not one's own,* Cic.; usus fructus omnium bonorum, Cic. **II.** Transf., **1,** *practice = practical experience;* usus atque exercitatio, Cic.; amicitia quam nec usu (*by experience*) nec ratione (*by theory*) habent cognitam, Cic.; habere magnum in re militari or in castris usum, Caes.; **2,** *the usefulness, useful quality of anything;* magnos usus affert ad navigia facienda, Cic.; usui and ex usu esse, *to be useful, of use,* Cic.; **3,** *occasion, need, want;* a, usus provinciae supplere, Cic.; b, usus est, usus venit, usus adest, *it is necessary, requisite,* (a) usus est; (aa) absol., si quando usus esset, Cic.; (ββ) with abl., si quid erit quod extra magistratus curatore usus sit, Cic.; (β) usus adest; absol., ut equites Pompeianorum impetum, quum adesset usus, sustinere auderent, Caes.; (γ) usus venit, si usus veniat, Caes.; c, usu venit, *it happens;* quid homini potest turpius usu venire? Cic.

ūsusfructus, v. usus, III.

ŭt (orig. form **ŭtī**), adv. and conj. **I.** Adv., **A.** (Like *ιναι*) adv. of place, *where,* Verg. Aen. 5, 329, Ov. Met. 1, 15. **B.** Adv. of manner, *in what way, as;* **1,** a, absol., perge ut instituisti, Cic.; esp. in a parenthesis, facilius est currentem, ut aiunt, incitare, Cic.; b, with correspond. sic, ita, item, omnia sic constitueram mihi agenda, ut tu admonebas, Cic.; ut optasti, ita est, Cic.; c, ut ut or utut, *however,* Plaut.; **2,** in comparisons, a, with sic, ita, item, itidem, *so . . . as,* sic, ut avus hic tuus, ut ego, justitiam ̯ole, Cic.; b, *as . . . so also, as well . . . as also;* ut cum Titanis, ita cum Gigantibus, Cic.; c, *indeed, it is true . . . but;* Saguntini ut a proeliis quietem habuerant . . . ita non nocte, non die

umquam cessaverant **ab** opere, Liv.; **d,** ut quisque, with superl. . . . sic or ita, with superl., *the more . . . the more;* ut quisque est vir optimus, ita difficillime esse alios improbos suspicatur, Cic.; with ita preceding, colendum esse ita quemque maxime, ut quisque maxime virtutibus erit ornatus, Cic.; with ita to be supplied, ut quisque maxime perspicit, quid, etc. . . . is prudentissimus haberi solet, Cic.; e, in oaths, protestations, etc., ita vivam, ut maximos sumptus facio, Cic.; **3,** to introduce an explanation, *as, as being;* homo acutus ut Poenus, Cic.; aiunt hominem, ut erat furiosus, respondisse, Cic.; permulta alia colligit Chrysippus, ut est in omni historia curiosus, Cic.; **4,** to introduce a reason, a, in a rel. clause, *inasmuch as;* magna pars Fidenatium, ut qui coloni additi Romanis essent, Latine sciebant, Liv.; b, in a hypothetical clause, *as if;* ut si esset res mea, Cic.; **5,** *as well as;* ut potui, tuli, Cic.; esp. with a superl., ut blandissime potest, *in the most flattering manner possible,* Cic.; with the superl., strengthened by quum, domus celebratus, ut quum maxime, Cic.; **6,** to introduce examples, *as, as for example;* quae tactu intimo sentiant, ut dolorem, ut voluptatem, Cic.; **7,** in exclamations, *how! how much!* ut ille tum humilis, ut demissus erat! Cic.; **8,** to introduce a question, *how;* a, direct, ut valet? ut meminit nostri? Hor.; b, indirect, videte, ut hoc iste correxerit, Cic.; **9,** to express time, a, gen. with the perf., *when, as soon as;* ut haec audivit, Cic.; strengthened by primum, ut primum loqui posse coepi, Cic.; b, *since;* ut Brundisio profectus es, nullae mihi abs te sunt redditae litterae, Cic. **II.** Conj., with the subj., *that, so that.* **A.** To express something effected or happening; **1,** of something actually resulting; a, with expressions denoting to happen, to cause, to bring about, to come to pass, *that;* sol efficit, ut omnia floreant, Cic.; evenit ut, contigit ut, est ut, ex hoc nascitur ut, etc., Cic.; b, with expressions denoting a peculiarity, a necessity, an appearance, mos est hominum, ut, etc., Cic.; hic locus est, ut de moribus majorum loquamur, Cic.; certum,verum, falsum, verisimile, rectum, justum, usitatum est ut, etc., Cic.; **2,** of something supposed or imagined to result; a, with verbs of wishing, commanding, asking, resolving, taking care, agreeing, suffering, etc., equidem vellem, ut aliquando redires, Cic.; praecipitur ut nobis ipsis imperemus, Cic.; petunt atque orant ut, etc., Caes.; placuit his ut, etc., Cic.; illud natura non patitur ut, etc., Cic.; assentior, ut, quod est rectum, verum quoque sit, Cic.; b, with verbs of demanding, persuading, compelling, postulant ut, etc., Liv.; hortor ut, etc., Cic.; suasit ut, etc., Cic.; impellimur naturâ ut, etc., Cic.; Lentulum, ut se abdicaret praeturâ, coegistis, Cic.; c, with verbs of fearing = *that not;* timeo ut sustineas, Cic.; d, ellipt. for fac ut, *provided that, granted that, even if;* ut quaeras omnia, non reperies, Cic.; e, ellipt. to express anger in a rhetorical question, tu ut umquam te corrigas? Cic.; f, ellipt. to express a wish, *oh that!* ut dolor pariat, quod jam diu parturit, Cic. **B.** To express a consequence, *that, so that;* **1,** with correspond. ita, sic, tam, eo, adeo, usque eo; talis, tantus, is, hic, etc.; Tarquinius sic Servium diligebat, ut is eius vulgo haberetur filius, Cic.; **2,** without a correl., ruere illa non possunt, ut haec non eodem labefacta motu concidant, Cic. **C.** To express a purpose, *that, in order that;* **1,** with a demonstr., ideo, idcirco, ad eam rem, etc., idcirco omnes servi sumus, ut liberi esse possimus, Cic.; **2,** mostly without a demonstr., Romani ab aratro abduxerunt Cincinnatum, ut dictator esset, Cic.

utcumquĕ (utcunquĕ), adv. **I.** *in what manner soever, however ;* utcumque se videri volet, Cic. **II.** *whenever ;* utcumque mecum eritis, Hor.

1. **ūtens** -entis, p. adj. (from utor), *using, possessing ;* utentior sit, Cic.

2. **Utens** -entis, m. *a river in Cisalpine Gaul,* now *Montone.*

ūtensĭlis -e (utor), *that can be used, fit for use, useful.* **I.** Adj., Varr. **II.** Subst., **ūtensĭlĭa** -ĭum, n. *useful things, necessaries, utensils,* Liv.

1. **ūter**, ūtris, m. (connected with uterus), *the skin of an animal used as a bag or bottle ;* Aeolios Ithacis inclusimus utribus euros, Ov. ; used (like a bladder) for crossing rivers, Caes., Liv. ; poet., tumidis infla sermonibus utrem, *of a puffed-up, arrogant man,* Hor.

2. **ŭter**, ūtra, ūtrum, genit. ūtrīus, dat. ūtri. **I.** *which of two, which ;* uter nostrum popularis est ? tune an ego ? Cic. ; neque dijudicare posset, uter utri virtute anteferendus videretur, Caes. ; utros eius habueris libros an utrosque nescio, Cic. **II.** Indefinite, *one of the two, either of the two ;* si uter volet, Cic. (genit., utrīus, Hor.).

ŭtercumquĕ (-cunquĕ), ūtrăcumquĕ, ūtrumcumquĕ, *whichever of the two, whichever ;* utercumque vicerit, Cic.

ŭterlĭbĕt, ūtrălĭbĕt, ūtrumlĭbĕt, *whichever of the two you please, either of the two ;* utrumlibet elige, Cic.

ŭterquĕ, ūtrăquĕ, ūtrumquĕ, genit. ūtrīusquĕ, dat. ūtrĭquĕ, *each of two, both* (considered separately), **a,** sing., uterque cum exercitu veniret, Caes. ; sermones utriusque linguae, Cic. ; uterque alio quodam modo, Cic. ; uterque Phoebus, *the rising and the setting sun, morning and evening,* Ov. ; uterque polus, *the North and South Pole,* Ov. ; Oceanus, *the east and west,* Ov. ; solis utraque domus, *east and west,* Ov. ; parens, *father and mother,* Ov. ; in utramque partem, *on both sides, in both cases,* Cic. ; hic qui utrumque probat, ambobus debuit uti, Cic. ; with partit. genit., uterque nostrum, Cic. ; with predicate in the plur., uterque eorum ex castris exercitum educunt, Caes. ; **b,** in plur. prop., to express two pluralities, quoniam utrique Socratici et Platonici volumus esse, Cic. ; then to express two individuals together, duae fuerunt Ariovisti uxores ; utraeque in ea fuga perierunt, Caes. ; (utrīusque, Lucr., Hor., Cic.).

ŭtĕrus -i, m. and **ŭtĕrum** -i, n. (ούθαρ). **I.** *the belly, paunch ;* 1, gen., Verg. ; 2, esp., *the womb,* Cic., Ov., Hor. ; meton., a, *birth,* Plin. ; **b,** *the cavities of the earth, out of which the first creatures are said to have been born,* Lucr. **II.** Transf., *the belly = the inside of a ship,* Tac. ; of the Trojan horse, Verg.

ŭtervis, ūtrăvis, ūtrumvis, genit. ūtrīusvis, dat. ūtrĭvis. **I.** *which of the two you will, either of the two ;* utrumvis facere potes, Cic. **II.** *both,* Ter., Plaut.

ūtī = ut (q.v.).

ūtĭbĭlis -e (utor), *that can be used, useful,* Ter., Plaut.

Ŭtĭca -ae, f. *a town in Africa Propria, north of Carthage, colony from Tyre, the place where the senatorial party made the last stand against Caesar, and where M. Porcius Cato the younger killed himself.* Adj., **Ŭtĭcensis** -e, *of or belonging to Utica.*

ūtĭlis -e (= utibilis from utor), *useful, profitable, serviceable, beneficial, advantageous ;* **a,** absol., utiles et salutares res, Cic. ; **b,** with ad and the acc., homo ad eam rem, or ad ullam rem

utilis, Cic. ; **c,** with in (*in relation to, for*) and acc., res maxime in hoc tempus utilis, Liv. ; **d,** with dat., equi utiles bello, Ov. ; non mihi est vita mea utilior, Cic. ; **e,** (poet.), with genit., radix medendi utilis, Ov. ; **f,** with infin., tibia adesse choris erat utilis, Hor. ; **g,** utile est, with infin., numquam utile est peccare, Cic. ; with acc. and infin., eos utile est praeesse vobis, Liv.

ūtĭlĭtas -ātis, f. (utilis), *usefulness, utility, advantageousness, profitableness, use, profit, advantage ;* **a,** sing., utilitas parta per amicum, Cic. ; **b,** plur., utilitates ex amicitia maxime capientur, Cic.

ūtĭlĭtĕr, adv. (utilis), *usefully, serviceably, advantageously, profitably ;* utiliter a natura datum esse, Cic.

ŭtĭnam, adv. *would that ! oh that !* utinam incumbat in causam ! Cic. ; utinam haberetis ! Cic. ; with quod, quod utinam minus vitae cupidi fuissemus ! Cic. ; with negative, utinam ne or utinam non, *would that not !* illud utinam ne vere scriberem ! Cic.

ŭtĭquĕ, adv. **a,** *in any case, at any rate, certainly, at least ;* utique apud me sis, Cic. ; **b,** *yet, at least, certainly ;* utique postridie, Cic. ; **c,** *especially ;* commota est plebs, utique postquam etc., Liv.

ūtor, ūsus sum, ūti, 3. dep. *to use, make use of employ, enjoy.* **I.** Lit., **A.** Gen., **a,** with abl., armis, Cic. ; oratione, *to speak,* Cic. ; male uti lege, *to make a bad use of the law,* Cic. ; uti eā criminatione in aliquem, Cic. ; with double abl., vel imperatore vel milite me utimini, Sall. ; **b,** with neut. acc., ne filius quidem quidquam utitur, Cic. ; huic omnia utenda ac possidenda tradiderat, Cic. ; **c,** absol., divitiae (expetuntur) ut utare, *that you may make use of them,* Cic. **B.** Esp., 1, *to associate with, be intimate with ;* Trebonio multos annos utor, Cic. ; 2, *to live on ; habere qui* utar, Cic. ; 3, *to enjoy ;* lacte et herbis, Ov. **II.** Transf., 1, *to be in possession of, to possess ;* valetudine bonā, Caes. ; honore, Cic. ; 2, *to stand in need of, have occasion for ;* ambitione nihil uteris, Cic. ; ea nihil hoc loco utimur, Cic.

utpŏtĕ, adv. *seeing that, inasmuch as, since ;* utpote qui nihil contemnere solemus, Cic. ; utpote lecti utrimque, Liv.

ūtrālĭbĕt, adv. (sc. parte, from uterlibet), *on either side, on whichever side,* Plin.

ūtrārĭus -ĭi, m. (1. uter), *one who carries water in skins, a water-carrier,* Liv.

ūtrĭcŭlārĭus -ĭi, m. *a bagpiper,* Suet.

ūtrĭcŭlus -i, m. (dim. of uterus). **I.** *the belly ;* 1, gen., Plin. ; 2, esp., *the womb,* Plin. **II.** *the bud or envelope of a flower,* Plin.

ūtrĭmquĕ (ūtrinquĕ), adv. (2. uter), *from both sides, on both sides.* **I.** Lit., Cic. **II.** Transf., *in both parties ;* utrimque anxii, Tac.

ūtro (sc. loco, from 2. uter), adv. *to which of two places, to which side, whither,* Cic., Liv.

ūtrŏbi (ūtrŭbi), adv. (uter and ubi), *at which of two places, where,* Plaut.

ūtrŏbĭdem, adv. (utrobi and suffix -dem), *on both sides,* Plaut.

ūtrŏbīquĕ (ūtrŭbīquĕ), adv. *on each of two sides, on both sides,* Liv. ; sequitur ut eadem veritas utrobique sit, *among the gods and men,* Cic. ; Eumenes utrobique plus valebat, *both by land and sea,* Nep.

ūtrŏlĭbĕt, adv. (uterlibet), *to either of two sides, to either side,* Quint.

ūtrŏquĕ, adv. (uterque), *to both sides ;* lit., of place, utroque citius quam vellemus cursum confecimus, Cic. ; **b,** transf., *in both directions ;* si natura utroque adjuncta est, Liv.

ŭtrŭbĭ, etc. = utrobi, etc. (q.v.).

ŭtrum, adv. (2. uter), *whether*, used in disjunctive questions. **I.** In direct questions, a, with a second clause; (α) foll. by an, utrum ea vestra an nostra culpa est? (β) foll. by annon, utrum cetera nomina in codicem accepti et expensi digesta habes, annon? Cic. ; b, without a second clause, utrum hoc bellum non est? Cic. **II.** In indirect questions, a, with corresponding an, anne, necne, (α) with an, multum interest, utrum laus diminuatur an salus deseratur, Cic. ; (β) foll. by anne, utrum illi sentiant, anne simulent, tu intelliges, Cic. ; (γ) by necne, jam dudum ego erro, qui quaeram, utrum emeris necne, Cic. ; b, without an, hoc dicere audebis, utrum de te aratores, utrum denique Siculi universi bene existiment, ad rem id non pertinere, Cic.

ŭtŭt, adv. *however*, Ter.

ūva -ae, f. *a cluster, bunch.* **I.** Lit., **A.** Gen., Plin. **B.** Esp., *a bunch of grapes;* 1, lit., uva colorem ducit, Verg. ; 2, meton., *the vine*, Verg. **II.** Transf., *a cluster, like a bunch of grapes, which bees form when they swarm and settle on trees*, Verg.

ūvens -entis (partic. of *uveo), *moist, wet*, Petr.

ūvesco, 3. (*uveo), *to become moist, be wet*, Lucr. ; of persons drinking, *to moisten or refresh oneself*, Hor.

ūvĭdŭlus -a -um (dim. of uvidus), *somewhat moist, wet*, Cat.

ūvĭdus -a -um (*uveo), *moist, damp, wet, humid.* **I.** Lit., vestimenta, Hor. ; Menalcas, *wet with dew*, Verg. ; Juppiter uvidus austris (Ζεὺς ἱκμαῖος), Verg. **II.** Meton., = *drunken;* Bacchus, Hor. ; dicimus integro sicci mane die, dicimus uvidi, Hor.

ūvor -ōris, m. (*uveo), *moistness, dampness, humidity*, Varr.

uxor -ōris, f. *a wife, spouse.* **I.** Lit., uxor justa, Cic. ; duas uxores habere, Cic. ; uxorem ducere, *to marry a wife;* uxori nuntium remittere, *to divorce a wife*, Cic. **II.** Transf., of animals, olentis uxores mariti, *she-goats*, Hor.

uxorcŭla -ae, f. (dim. of uxor), *a little wife* (used as a term of endearment), Plaut.

uxōrĭus -a -um (uxor). **I.** *of or relating to a wife;* res uxoria, Cic. ; arbitrium rei uxoriae, *relating to the property of a (divorced) wife*, Cic. **II.** *too devoted to one's wife, a slave to a wife, uxorious;* of Aeneas as the slave to Dido, Verg.; amnis, *the Tiber, as the husband of Ilia*, Hor.

V.

V, v, the twenty-first letter of the Latin alphabet, corresponding partly with the Greek digamma (F), partly with the Greek υ. V frequently passes into u, e.g., solvo, solutum, navita, nauta ; and between two vowels is often elided, e.g., deleverunt, delerunt, providens, prudens ; ne volo, nolo. For the use of V. in abbreviations, see Table of Abbreviations.

Văcālus = Vahalis (q.v.).

văcātĭo -ōnis, f. (vaco). **I.** *a freedom from, immunity, exemption from anything, a being without;* a, the thing from which one is freed is put in the genit., or in the abl. with ab, vacatio militiae, Cic. ; alicui dare vacationem a causis, Cic. ; b, the person who is freed is put in the genit., or the cause for which one is

freed, adolescentiae, Cic. ; rerum gestarum, Cic.; vacationes militum, Liv. ; c, absol., pretium ob vacationem datum, Cic. **II.** Meton., *money paid for exemption from military service*, Tac.

1. **vacca** -ae, f. *a cow*, Cic.
2. **Vacca** = Vaga (q.v.).

Vaccaei -ōrum, m. *a people in Hispania Tarraconensis.*

vaccĭnĭum -ĭi, n. *the blueberry, whortleberry*, Verg., Ov.

vaccĭnus -a -um (vacca), *of or relating to a cow*, Plin.

văcēfĭo, v. vacuefacio.

văcerrōsus -a -um, *mad, crazy*, Suet.

Văchălis = Vahalis (q.v.).

văcillātĭo -ōnis, f. (vacillo), *a rocking, reeling motion*, Suet.

văcillo, 1. *to totter, reel, stagger, wave to and fro.* **I.** Lit., litterulae vacillantes, *written with unsteady hand*, Cic. ; of persons, ex vino, Cic.; in utramque partem toto corpore, Cic. **II.** Fig., tota res vacillat et claudicat, Cic. ; of persons, in aere alieno, *to be deep in debt*, Cic. ; legio vacillans, *wavering in its fidelity*, Cic.

văcīvē, adv. (vacivus), *idly, at leisure*, Phaedr.

văcīvĭtas -ātis, f. (vacivus), *emptiness, want of anything;* cibi, Plaut.

văcīvus -a -um (vaco), *empty;* aedes, Plaut.; with genit., virium, *powerless*, Plaut.

văco, 1. *to be empty, void of anything, be free from, without anything.* **I.** Lit., **A.** Gen., a, absol., tota domus superior vacat, Cic.; b, with abl., natura caelestis et terra vacat humore, Cic. **B.** Esp., of property, *to be vacant, to have no master;* ut populus vacantia teneret, Tac. **II.** Transf., **A.** Gen., *to be free from something, to be without;* a, with abl., curā et negotio, Cic. ; populo, *to keep oneself far from the people*, Cic. ; b, with ab and the abl., ab opere, Caes. ; ab omni concitatione animi semper, Cic. ; a metu et periculis, Liv. ; of things, haec a custodiis classium loca maxime vacabant, Caes. ; of time, tantum quantum vacabit a publico officio et munere, Cic. **B.** Esp., 1, *to be free from duties;* with abl., muneribus, Cic. ; 2, *to be free from work, idle, at leisure, unoccupied, to have time;* a, of persons, (α) absol., scribes aliquid, si vacabis, Cic. ; (β) with dat., *to have time for, to have leisure for;* ego vero, inquam, philosophiae semper vaco, Cic. ; (γ) poet., with in and the acc., in grande opus, Ov. ; b, impers., vacat and vacat alicui, *there is leisure for, there is time for;* (α) with infin., hactenus indulsisse vacat, Verg. ; (β) absol., quum vacat, Ov.

văcŭĕfăcĭo -fēci -factum, 3. (vacuus and facio), and pass., **văcŭĕfīo** (**văcēfīo**) -factus sum -fĭĕri (vacuus and fio), *to make empty;* in pass. = *to be empty;* morte superioris uxoris domum novis nuptiis, Cic. ; adventu tuo ista subsellia vacuefacta sunt, Cic.

văcŭĭtas -ātis, f. (vacuus), *emptiness, vacuity, freedom, exemption, immunity from, a being without anything.* **I.** Gen., a, with genit., doloris, Cic. ; b, with ab and abl., ab angoribus, Cic. **II.** Esp., *the vacancy of a public office*, e.g., of the consulship, ap. Cic.

Văcūna -ae, f. *the beneficent goddess of the plain worshipped at Reate, goddess of the Sabines.* Adj., **Văcūnālis** -e, *of or belonging to Vacuna.*

văcŭo, 1. (vacuus), *to make empty, void, to empty*, Lucr.

văcŭus -a -um, *empty, void, free from, exempt, without.* **I.** Lit., **A.** Gen., 1, adj., a, absol., castra, Caes. ; theatrum, Hor. ; b, with abl.

nihil igni vacuum, Cic.; c, with ab and the abl., ab his rebus, Cic.; vacuum oppidum ab defensoribus, Caes.; 2, subst., **văcŭum** -i, n. *an empty place, vacuum*; per vacuum incurrere, Hor., or irrumpere, Liv. **B.** Esp., 1, *free, vacant, without a master*; praeda, Cic.; possessio regni, Caes.; venire in vacuum or vacua, Hor., Cic.; 2, of women, *free, unmarried*, Ov. **II.** Transf., **A.** Gen., *free from something, without, keeping oneself free from*; a, with abl., animus sensibus et curis vacuus, Cic.; b, with ab and the abl., animus a talibus factis vacuus et integer, Cic.; c, with genit., vacuus operum, Hor. **B.** Esp., 1, *free from duties, freed*; a, with abl., tributo, Tac.; b, with ab and the abl., ab omni sumptu, Cic.; 2, a, *free from work, unoccupied, at leisure, idle*; (a) of persons, quoniam vacui sumus, dicam, Cic.; transf., of places, *where one is idle*; Tibur, Hor.; (β) of time, vacua nox operi, Liv.; quum vacui temporis nihil habebam, *leisure*, Cic.; b, *free from anxiety or love*; animus vacuus ac solutus, Cic.; 3, *free from hindrances*, Tac.; 4, of places, a, *free* = *open, accessible*; porticus, Verg.; aures vacuae, Hor.; b, *open, exposed*; mare, Tac.; 5, *empty* = *worthless, useless, vain*; vacua nomina, Tac.

1. **Vada** -ae, f. *a castle in the country of the Batavi.*

2. **Vada** -ōrum, n. *a town in Liguria, now Savona.*

3. **Vada Volaterrāna** -ōrum, n. *a port in Etruria, south of Pisa*, now *Torre di Vado.*

Vadimōnis lacus, *a lake in Etruria*, now *Lago di Bassano.*

vădĭmōnĭum -ĭi, n. (1. vas), *bail, security, recognizance* (for appearance before a court of law); sine vadimonio disceditur, Cic.; vadimonium constituere, Cic.; vadimonium obire or ad vadimonium venire, *to appear on bail* (opp. vadimonium deserere, *to forfeit recognizances*), Cic.

vādo, 3. (root VA, Gr. BA-ω, whence βαίνω), *to go, walk, hasten, rush*; haud dubiam in mortem, Verg.; ad aliquem postridie mane, Cic.; in eundem carcerem (of Socrates), Cic.

vădor, 1. dep. (1. vas), *to bind over by bail*; hominem in praesentia non vadatur, Cic.; tot vadibus accusator vadatus est reum, Liv.; partic. pass., vadato, *after bail had been fixed*, Hor.

vădōsus -a -um (vadum), *full of shallows, shallow*; mare, Caes.

vădum -i, n. (root VA, Gr. BA-ω, whence βατός -ή -όν, pervius), *a shallow, shoal, ford.* **I. A.** Lit., exercitum vado transducere, Verg. **B.** Fig., cera tentet vadum, Ov. **II.** Transf., **A.** Gen. = *water, river, sea*, Verg., Hor. **B.** *the bottom of the water*, Plin.

vae, interj. (οὐαί), to express pain or anger, *alas! woe!* a, absol., Verg., Hor.; b, with dat., vae victis, Liv.

vaecors = vecors (q.v.).

vaesanus = vesanus (q.v.).

văfer, văfra, văfrum, *artful, cunning, subtle, sly, crafty*; in disputando, Cic.; somniorum vaferrimus interpres, Cic.

văfrē, adv. (vafer), *artfully, cunningly, craftily*, Cic.

văfrĭtĭa -ae, f. (vafer), *artfulness, slyness, subtlety, cunning*, Sen.

Văga -ae, f. *a town in Numidia*, now *Begia.* Hence, **Văgenses** -ĭum, m. *the inhabitants of Vaga.*

văgē, adv. (vagus), *scattered far and wide, dispersedly*; vage effusi per agros, Liv.

văgīna -ae, f. (connected with vas, *a vessel*) *the sheath of a sword, scabbard.* **I.** Lit., gladius vaginā vacuus, Cic.; gladium e vagina educere, Cic. **II.** Transf., *a sheath, case*; esp., *the hull or husk of grain*, Cic.

văgīnŭla -ae, f. (dim. of vagina), *a little sheath or husk of grain*, Plin.

văgĭo -īvi and -ĭi -ītum, 4. *to cry, whimper like a child*; repuerascere et in cunis vagire, Cic.

văgītus -ūs, m. (vagio), *the crying of young children*; dare vagitus, Ov.; *of the bleating of goats*, Ov.

1. **văgo,** 1. and **văgor,** 1. dep. (vagus), *to wander about, ramble, rove.* **I.** Lit., **A.** Gen., a, of living creatures, in agris passim bestiarum more, Cic.; of birds, volucres huc illuc passim vagantes, Cic.; b, of things, luna iisdem spatiis vagatur quibus sol, Cic. **B.** Esp., of ships and sailors, *to cruise*; cum lembis circa Lesbum, Liv. **II.** Fig., vagabitur tuum nomen longe atque late, *will be spread far and wide*, Cic.; animus vagatus errore, Cic.; vagabimur nostro instituto, *digress*, Cic.

2. **văgor** = vagitus (q.v.).

văgus -a -um, *wandering, roaming, roving, unsettled, vagrant.* **I.** Lit., a, of living creatures, multitudo dispersa atque vaga, Cic.; matronae vagae per vias, Liv.; plur. subst., vagi quidam, *wanderers*, Liv.; b, of things, luna, Cic.; venti, Hor. **II.** Transf., a, *inconstant, fickle*; puella, Ov.; sententia, Cic.; b, *general*; pars quaestionum, Cic.; c, *diffuse, aimless*; orationis genus, Cic.

văh (**văhă**), interj. *ah! oh!* Plaut.

Văhălis (**Vālis**) -is, m. *the Waal, the west arm of the Rhine.*

valdē, adv. (syncop. for valide from validus), *very, very much, greatly, exceedingly*; a, with verbs, alicui arridere, Cic.; valdius oblectare, Hor.; b, with adj., valde magnus, Cic.; valde lenis, Cic.; c, with adv., valde bene, valde vehementer, valde graviter, Cic.

vălēdĭco, 3., v. valeo, I. B. 2. b.

vălens -entis, p. adj. (from valeo), *strong, powerful.* **I.** Lit., **A.** Gen., robusti et valentes satellites, Cic.; valentissimi homines, Cic.; trunci, Verg. **B.** *well, healthy*; medicus confirmat propediem te valentem fore, Cic. **II.** Transf., *powerful, mighty*; a, politically, by armies, etc., viribus cum valentiore pugnare, Cic.; b, intellectually, *powerful, energetic, effective*; valens dialecticus, Cic.; fraus valentior quam consilium meum, Cic.

vălentĕr, adv. (valens), *strongly, powerfully*; valentius spirare, Ov.

vălentŭlus -a -um (dim. of valens), *strong*, Plaut.

vălĕo -ŭi -ĭtum, 2. *to be strong.* **I.** Lit., **A.** Gen., 1, puer ille ut magnus est et multum valet, Plaut.; 2, *to be strong* (bodily) *for a particular purpose*; a, with prep., alios velocitate ad cursum, alios viribus ad luctandum valere, Cic.; b, with infin., valeo stare aut, etc., Hor.; valet ima summis mutare deus, Hor. **B.** *to be well, healthy, strong*; 1, a, with adv., optime valeo, Cic.; bene, melius, Cic.; minus valeo, Cic.; b, with the abl., corpore, Cic.; c, with ab and abl. of disease, a morbo, Plaut.; d, absol., valeo et salvus sum, Plaut.; hence the phrase at the commencement of a letter, si vales, bene est (S. V. B. E.), Cic.; also with the addition, ego or ego quoque valeo (E. V. or E. Q. V.), Cic.; 2, as a farewell greeting, a, vale, valeas, *adieu, farewell, good-bye*; esp., as the usual ending of letters, Cic.; ut valeas, Cic.; also as a farewell greeting to the dead, Verg.; as an expression of scorn.

refusal, rejection, **si talis est deus**, valeat, *let me have nothing to do with him*, Cic.; **quare valeant ista**, *away with them !* Cic.; **b**, valere jubere or dicere, *to say good-bye;* illum salutavi, post ,tiam jussi valere, Cic.; supremum vale dicere, Ov.; vale dicere (or in one word, valedicere), *to say farewell*, Sen. **II.** Transf., **A.** *to avail, have force, to be strong, prevail;* **1**, multum equitatu, Caes.; plurimum proficere et valere, Cic.; longe plurimum valere ingenio, Cic.; *of things, sine* veritate nomen amicitiae valere non potest, Cic.; **2**, with reference to a certain object, a, with ad and the acc., or in and the acc., or infin., *to have force for, to be able to, to be strong enough for;* tu non solum ad negligendas leges, verum etiam ad evertendas valuisti, Cic.; *of things,* illud perficiam, ut invidia mihi valeat ad gloriam, Cic.; nec continere suos ab direptione castrorum valuit, Liv.; **b**, with in and the acc., *to be of avail against, to be designed for or against;* in se, in Romanos, in ipsum, Cic.; definitio in omnes valet, *avails for all*, Cic. **B.** Esp., **1**, *to be worth;* dum pro argenteis decem aureus unus valeret, Liv.; **2**, of words, *to mean, signify;* verbum, quod idem valeat, Cic.

Vălĕrĭus -a -um, *name of a Roman gens, the most famous members of which were:* **1**, P. Valerius Volesus Publicola (Popl.), *who took part in the driving out of the Roman kings;* **2**, Qu. Valerius Antias, *a Roman chronicler, living about* 140 B.C., *used by Livy.* Adj., *Valerian;* tabula, *a place in the Forum, near the Curia Hostilia, where the money-changers' stalls were.* Hence, **Vălĕrĭā-nus** -a -um, *of or belonging to a Valerius.*

vălesco -ŭi, **2**. (inchoat. of valeo), *to grow strong.* **I.** Lit., Lucr. **II.** Fig., superstitiones, Tac. ; tantum spe conatuque valuit, Cic.

vălētūdĭnārĭus -a -um (valetudo), *sickly,* Varr.

vălētūdo -ĭnis, f. (valeo), *state of health, physical condition, health.* **I.** Lit., **A.** Gen., prosperitas valetudinis, Cic.; incommoda, Cic.; adversa, Cic.; infirmā atque aegrā valetudine usus, Cic.; quasi mala valetudo animi, Cic. **B.** Esp., **1**, in a bad sense, *ill-health, weakness;* oculorum, Cic.; affectus valetudine, *ill*, Caes.; plur., subsidia valetudinum, Cic. ; **2**, in a good sense, *good health;* valetudinem amiseram, Cic. **II.** Transf., of discourse, Cic.

Valgĭus -a -um, *name of a Roman gens, the most famous members of which were:* **1**, Valgius, *the father-in-law of Rullus;* **2**, T. Valgius Rufus, *a distinguished poet.*

valgus -a -um, *bow-legged, bandy-legged,* Plaut.; transf., suavia, *wry mouths*, Plaut.

vălĭdē, adv. (validus). **I.** *strongly, powerfully, mightily;* validissime favere alicui, ap. Cic. **II.** Used in answers, *certainly, to be sure,* Plaut.

vălĭdus -a -um (valeo), *strong, powerful.* **I.** Lit., **A.** Gen., **1**, tauri, Ov.; vires, Verg.; **2**, milit. t. t., of posts or stations, *strong;* valida urbs et potens, Cic. ; valida urbs praesidiis, muris, Liv.; **3**, of medicines, *powerful, efficacious;* sucus, Ov.; **4**, of persons, *superior, having the advantage* (in age); aetate et viribus validior, Liv. **B.** *healthy, well;* si, ut spero, te validum videro, Cic.; nondum ex morbo satis validus, Liv. **II.** Transf., *strong, powerful, mighty, influential;* hostis validior, Liv.; with abl., ingenium sapientiā validum, Sall.; with dat., ludibrium illud vix feminis puerisve morandis satis validum, Liv.; with adversus and the acc., adversus consentientes nec regem quemquam satis validum nec tyrannum fore, Liv.

Vālis = Vahalis (q.v.).

vallāris -e (vallus or vallum), *of or relating to the vallum; corona, given to the soldier who first mounted the fortifications of the hostile camp,* Liv.

valles (vallis) -is, f. *a vale, valley.* **I.** Lit., vicus positus in valle, Caes. **II.** Poet., transf., *a hollow;* alarum, Cat.

vallo, **1**. (vallus or vallum), *to surround, fortify with a mound and palisade.* **I.** Lit., castra, Tac. **II.** Transf., *to fortify, protect, strengthen;* Catilina vallatus sicariis, Cic.; sol radiis frontem vallatus, Ov.

vallum -i, n. (vallus). **I.** *a mound or wall defended with palisades, a stockade;* oppidum vallo et fossā cingere, Cic.; vallum scindere, Caes. **II.** Transf., *a wall, fortification, defence;* spica munitur vallo aristarum, Cic.

1. vallus -i, m. *a post, stake.* **I.** Gen., used as a prop for vines, Verg. **II.** Esp., to form a palisade; ferre vallum, Cic.; collective (for vallum), *the palisade, stockade;* duplex vallus, Caes. ; poet., transf., vallus pectinis, *the teeth of a comb*, Ov.

2. vallus -i, f. (dim. of vannus), *a small winnowing-fan*, Varr.

valvae -ārum, f. *folding-doors;* effractis valvis (fani), Cic.

valvātus -a -um (valvae), *provided with folding-doors*, Varr.

Vandăli -ōrum, m. *the Vandals, in the time of Tacitus a tribe in North Germany, who, in the fifth century, invaded the south of Europe, and settled in Spain and Africa.*

vănesco, **3**. (vanus), *to pass away, disappear, vanish.* **I.** Lit., nubes, Ov. **II.** Transf., amor, Ov.

Vangĭōnes -um, m. *a German people on the Rhine, near modern Worms.*

vānĭdĭcus -a -um (vanus and dico), *talking vainly, lying*, Plaut.

vānĭlŏquentĭa -ae, f. (vanus and loquor), *idle talking, vaunting*, Liv.

vānĭlŏquus -a -um (vanus and loquor). **I.** *lying*, Plaut. **II.** *boasting, vaunting*, Liv.

vānĭtas -ātis, f. (vanus), *emptiness.* **I.** Gen., **a**, *unreality, superficiality, untruth;* opinionum, Cic.; **b**, *failure, fruitlessness;* itineris, Liv. **II.** Esp., *idle talk, lying, boasting, ostentation;* orationis, Cic. ; nihil turpius est vanitate, Cic.

vānĭtūdo -ĭnis, f. (vanus), *idle, lying talk,* Plaut.

vannus -i, f. *a winnowing-fan;* vannus mystica Iacchi (borne at the Bacchic festival), Verg.

vānus -a -um (connected with vastus), *empty, void.* **I.** Lit., arista, Verg. ; imago, *shade, spirit* (as being bodiless), Hor. ; vanior acies hostium, Liv. **II.** Fig., *vain, meaningless, lying, fruitless, idle, groundless.* **A.** Of things, **1**, adj., oratio, Cic.; spes, Ov.; gaudia, Hor.; *of missiles, ictus, Liv.; **2**, neut. subst., *that which is empty* or *vain;* haustum ex vano, *from a false source*, Liv.; poet., vana tumens, *with empty show*, Verg.; with genit., vana rerum, Hor. **B.** Of persons, **1**, *one whose action is without consequence;* ne vanus iisdem castris assideret, *in vain*, Liv.; **2**, esp. in moral sense, *lying, vain, ostentatious, fickle, inconstant, boastful;* harus-pex, Cic. ; vanum se esse et perfidiosum fateri, Cic. ; vanus auctor est, *deserves no credence*, Liv.

văpĭdē, adv. (vapidus), *mouldily;* vapide se habere, *to be "seedy,"* Aug. ap. Suet.

văpĭdus -a -um (root VAP, whence vappa), *spoiled, flat, vapid*, Pers.

văpor (văpos) -ōris, m. *vapour, steam.* **I.** Gen., aquarum, Cic. ; poet. = *heat,* Verg. **II.** Esp., *warm exhalation, warmth;* semen tepefactum vapore, Cic. ; *locus vaporis plenus,* Liv.; poet. = *fire;* vapor est (= edit) carinas, Verg.

văpōrārĭum -ĭi, n. (vapor), *a flue for conveying hot air,* Cic.

văpōrātĭo -ōnis, f. (vaporo), *an exhalation, steaming, steam, vapour,* Plin.

văpōro, 1. (vapor). **I.** Intransit., *to steam, reek,* fig., Lucr. **II.** Transit., *to fill with warm vapour, to fumigate, heat, to warm;* a, laevum latus, Hor. ; b, *to incense, fumigate;* templum ture, Verg.

vappa -ae, f. (root, VAP, whence vapidus), *spoiled, flat wine.* **I.** Lit., Hor. **II.** Transf., *a good-for-nothing, worthless fellow,* Hor.

văpŭlāris -e (vapulo), *well whipped,* Plaut.

văpŭlo -āvi -ātūrus, 1. *to cry out like one that is beaten ;* meton. = *to be flogged, whipped, beaten.* **I.** Lit., Lucr., Plaut. **II.** Transf., a, of troops, *to be beaten ;* ap. Cic. ; b, *to be attacked by words;* omnium sermonibus, Cic.

Varguntējus -i, m., Lucius, *a Roman senator and accomplice of Catiline.*

1. **vărĭa** -ae, f. (varius). **I.** *a panther,* Plin. **II.** *a kind of magpie,* Plin.

2. **Vărĭa** -ae, f. *a town in Italy, on the right bank of the Anio,* now *Vico-Varo.*

vărĭantĭa -ae, f. (vario), *difference, variation,* Lucr.

vărĭānus -a -um (varius), *many-coloured, varicoloured,* Plin.

vărĭātĭo-ōnis, f. (vario), *difference, variation;* eosdem consules sine ulla variatione dicere, Liv.

vărĭco, 1. (varicus), *to stand with feet apart, to straddle,* Varr.

vărĭcōsus -a -um (varix), *having varicose veins,* Juv.

vărĭcus -a -um (varus), *straddling,* Ov.

vărĭē, adv. (varius). **I.** *with various colours,* Plin. **II.** *variously, in different ways ;* numerus varie diffusus, Cic.; varie bellatum, *with varying success,* Liv.

vărĭĕtas -ātis, f. (1. varius), *variety, difference, diversity.* **I.** Lit., of colours, florum, Cic. **II.** Transf., **A.** Gen., *variety, difference, diversity;* pomorum, Cic. ; plur., varietates temporum, Cic. **B.** Esp., 1, *variety, manysidedness;* of ideas, knowledge, etc., multiplex ratio disputandi rerumque varietas, Cic. ; 2, *difference in opinion;* in disputationibus, Cic. ; 3, *fickleness, inconstancy, changeable humour;* venditorum, Cic.

vărĭo, 1. (1. varius). **I.** Transit., *to vary, diversify, variegate, make various, to change, alter, vary.* **A.** Lit., 1, vocem, Cic. ; capillos, Ov. ; 2, *to make particoloured, to colour, spot;* (sol) variat ortum maculis, Verg. **B.** Transf., *to change a thing in its nature, to alter, interchange with ;* a, caloresque frigoraque, Liv. ; voluptatem, Cic. ; b, *to vary in writing or speaking, to give a different account of ;* quae de Marcelli morte va·iant auctores, *relate differently,* Liv. ; c, *to change the issue of ;* variante fortunā eventum, Liv. ; d, *to change an opinion cause to waver;* quum timor atque ira in vicem sententias variassent, Liv.; in pass., variari, *to waver, be divided, to vary ;* variatis hominum sententiis, Liv. **II.** Intransit., *to be different, to vary.* **A.** Lit. variantes formae, Lucr. **B.** Transf., *to change, vary, alter, waver;* 1, of things, a, sic mei variant timores, Ov. ; dissidet et variat sententia, Ov. ; b, *to vary* (in an account or relation), quamquam et opinionibus et monumentis

litterarum variarent, Liv. ; 2, of persons, *to vary, be of different opinions, waver;* fremitus variantis multitudinis, Liv.

1. **vărĭus** -a -um, *manifold.* **I.** Of colour, *diversified, variegated, various ;* columnae, Hor. ; caelum, Ov. ; lynces, Verg. **II.** Transf., of nature, *various, manifold, changeable, diverse.* **A.** Of things, a, varium poema, varia oratio, varii mores, varia fortuna, voluptas etiam varia dici solet, Cic. ; b, of opinion, *varying ;* quales sint (dii) varium est, *different opinions are held,* Cic. ; c, of success, *changing, varying, uncertain ;* fortunae varii eventus, Caes. **B.** Of persons, a, *many-sided, of various information ;* varius et multiplex et copiosus fuit, Cic. ; b, of character, *fickle, changeable ;* animus, Sall. ; varium et mutabile semper femina, Verg.

2. **Vărĭus** -a -um, *name of a Roman gens, the most famous members of which were:* 1, Q. Varius Hybrida, of Sucro, in Spain, *tribune of the people,* 91 B.C., *author of a* lex de majestate; 2, L. Varius, *a poet, the friend of Horace and Vergil.*

vărix -ĭcis, c. *a varicose vein,* esp. in the leg, Cic.

Varro -ōnis, m. *a surname in the Gens Terentia, the most famous members of which were :* 1, C. Terentius Varro, and 2, M. TerentiusVarro, v. Terentius ; 3, P. Terentius Varro Atacinus, a poet, born 82 B.C., *died* 37 B.C. Hence, **Varrōnĭānus** -a -um, *Varronian;* milites, *who served under C. Terentius Varro,* Liv.

1. **vărus** -a -um, *deviating from the right line.* **I.** Lit., *bent outwards ;* a, cornua, Ov. ; manus, Ov. ; b, *bandy-legged ;* subst., a *bandy-legged man,* Hor. **II.** Transf., *diverse, different;* alterum (genus) huic varum, Hor.

2. **vărus** -i, m. *a pimple or boil on the face,* Plin.

3. **Vărus** -i, m. *a name of several Roman families, the most famous members of which were :* 1, Q. Attius Varus, *a leader in the Civil War ;* 2, P. Alfenus Varus, *consul and celebrated lawyer ;* 3, P. Quintilius Varus, *the celebrated general of Augustus, defeated and killed with his army by Arminius,* 9 B.C.

4. **Vărus** -i, m. *a river in Gallia Narbonensis,* now the *Var.*

1. **văs,** vădis, m. (vado), *a bail, surety ;* vades poscere, Cic. ; vades deserere, Liv. ; vas factus est alter (Damon) eius sistendi, Cic.

2. **vās,** vāsis, n. (plur., **vāsa** -ōrum), *a vessel, utensil of any kind.* **I.** Gen., vas vinarium, Cic. **II.** Esp., plur., *war materials, baggage;* vasa colligere, *to pack up one's baggage,* Cic. ; vasa conclamare, *to give the signal for packing up,* Caes.

vāsārĭum -ĭi, n. (2. vas). **I.** *money given to the governor of a province for his outfit,* Cic. **II.** *the hire of an oil-press,* Cato.

Vascōnes -um, m. *a people in Hispania Tarraconensis.*

vascŭlārĭus -ĭi, m. (vasculum), *a maker of metal vessels and dishes, goldsmith,* Cic.

vascŭlum -i, n. (dim. of 2. vas). **I.** *a small vessel or dish,* Cato. **II.** *the seed capsule of certain fruits,* Plin.

vastātĭo -ōnis, f. (vasto), *a devastating, laying waste ;* agri, Liv. ; omnium, Cic. ; plur., depopulationes, vastationes, caedes, rapinae, Cic.

vastātor -ōris, m. (vasto), *devastator, ravager;* Arcadiae (of a boar), Ov. ; ferarum, a hunter, Verg.

vastē, adv. (vastus). **I.** *widely, vastly, extensively ;* vastius insurgens, Ov. **II.** *rudely, roughly ;* loqui, Cic.

vastĭfĭcus -a -um (vastus and facio), *laying waste, devastating, ravaging,* Cic. poet.

vastĭtas -ātis, f. (vastus), *an empty space, waste, emptiness.* **I.** Lit., **A.** Gen., *judiciorum* vastitas et fori, Cic. **B.** Esp., *emptiness through laying waste, devastation, desolation;* Italiam totam ad exitium et vastitatem vocare, Cic. **II.** Meton., **1,** *vastness, vast size,* Plin.; **2,** plur., vastitates, *the devastators;* provinciarum vastitates, Cic.

vastĭtĭes -ēi, f. (vastus), *devastation, destruction,* Plaut.

vasto, 1. (vastus), *to empty, make empty.* **I.** Gen., forum, Cic.; with abl., agros cultoribus, Verg. **II.** Esp., **1, a,** *to waste, lay waste, ravage, devastate;* agros, Caes., Cic.; omnia ferro ignique, Liv.; **b,** *to plunder;* cultores, Tac.; **2,** fig., *to prey upon;* ita conscientia mentem excitam vastabat, Sall.

vastus -a -um (root VA, whence vanus), *empty, waste, deserted, desolate.* **I.** Lit., **A.** Gen., a, absol., loci coaedificati an vasti, Cic.; b, with ab and the abl., urbs a defensoribus vasta, Liv. **B.** Esp., *made empty by ravages, devastated;* solum, Liv.; poet., haec ego vasta dabo, *will ravage,* Verg. **II.** Meton., **1,** *vast, fearful in size, enormous, frightful, horrible;* vasta et immanis belua, Caes.; mare, Caes.; **2,** *rough, rude, unrefined;* vastus homo atque foedus, Cic.; littera vastior, *rougher,* Cic.

vātes -is, c. *a prophet, soothsayer, seer.* **I.** Lit., **A.** Liv., Cicero quae nunc usu veniunt cecinit ut vates, Cic. **B.** Esp., *the inspired prophetic singer, bard, poet;* cothurnatus, *a tragic poet,* Ov.; Maeonius, *Homer,* Ov.; Lesbia, *Sappho,* Ov.; vates Aeneidos, *Vergil,* Ov. **II.** Transf., *a teacher, master,* Plin. (genit. plur., gen. vatum, also vatium).

Vātĭcānus -a -um, *Vatican;* mons, collis, *the Vatican Hill on the west side of the Tiber,* Hor.; plur., Vaticani colles, *the hill with its surroundings,* Cic.; ager Vaticanus, *the country round the Vatican, notorious for its bad soil, which produced poor wine,* Cic.

vātĭcĭnātĭo -ōnis, f. (vaticinor), *a soothsaying, prophesying;* earum litterarum vaticinationem falsam esse cupio, Cic.; plur., sortes et vaticinationes, Caes.

vātĭcĭnātor -ōris, m. (vaticinor), *a soothsayer, prophet,* Ov.

vātĭcĭnĭum -ĭi, n. (vates), *a prophecy,* Plin.

vātĭcĭnor, 1. dep. (vates), *to prophesy.* **I.** Lit., **A.** Gen., vaticinari furor vera solet, Cic.; with acc. and infin., saevam laesi fore numinis iram, Ov. **B.** Esp., **1,** *to warn as a seer,* Ov.; **2,** *to teach as a seer;* doctum quendam virum carminibus Graecis vaticinatum ferunt, Cic. **II.** Transf., *to talk nonsense, to rave;* sed ego fortasse vaticinor, Cic.

vātĭcĭnus -a -um (vates), *soothsaying, prophetic,* Liv., Ov.

vātillum (bătillum) -i, n. *a chafing-dish,* Hor.

Vătīnĭus -a -um, *the name of a Roman family,* the most notorious member of *which was* P. Vatinius, *a dependent of Caesar, so often attacked by Cicero that odium Vatinianum and crimina Vatiniana* became proverbial. Hence, **Vātīnĭānus** -a -um, *Vatinian.*

vātis = vates (q.v).

vātĭus -a -um, *bent inwards* (applied to knock-kneed persons), Varr.

1. -vĕ (shortened form of vel), enclitic, *or, or perhaps;* duabus tribusve horis, Cic.; poet., ve . . . ve, Ov., ve . . . aut, Prop., *either* . . . *or.*

2. vē- (vae), an inseparable particle, *expressing excess or deficiency;* e.g., vecors, vegrandis, vesanus.

Vecĭlĭus mons, *a mountain in Latium.*

vēcordĭa (vaecordĭa) -ae, f. (vecors), *senselessness, foolishness, madness,* Sall., Ter.

vēcors (vaecors) -cordis, abl. -cordi, genit. plur. -cordium (2. ve and cor), *silly, senseless, foolish, mad, insane;* a, of persons, vecordes sine colore, Cic.; vecors de tribunali decurrit, Liv.; iste vecordissimus, Cic.; b, of things, impetus, Liv.

vectābĭlis -e (vecto), *that can be carried, portable,* Sen.

vectātĭo -ōnis, f. (vecto), *a riding, driving, sailing,* etc.; equi, Suet.

vectĭgal -gālis, abl. -gāli, n. (for vectigale, from vectigalis), *revenue.* **I.** Of the state, or of individual magistrates; a, of the state, *a tax, impost, duty;* portorium, *dues on merchandise;* ex scriptura, *a rent paid for the state pasture land;* decuma, *a tithe on grain;* portoria reliquaque vectigalia, Caes.; vectigal pergrande *imponere* agro, Cic.; vectigalia pendère, *to pay,* Cic.; b, of magistrates, praetorium, *presents to governors,* Cic.; aedilicium, *contribution through the governors of provinces to the aediles for the games at Rome,* Cic. **II.** *private income, revenue;* ex meo tenui vectigali, Cic.

vectĭgālis -e (veho). **I.** *of or relating to taxes;* a, *paid in taxes;* pecunia, *taxes,* Cic.; b, *liable to taxes, tributary;* civitas, Cic.; Ubios sibi vectigales facere, Cic. **II.** *bringing in income for private persons;* equi, Cic.

vectĭo -ōnis, f. (veho), *a carrying, conveyance;* quadripedum vectiones, Cic.

vectis -is, m. (veho), *a lever.* **I.** Gen., for lifting or for breaking something, *a crow-bar;* signum vectibus labefacere, Cic.; biremes impellere vectibus, Caes. **II.** Esp. = κλείς, *a large bar for fastening a door, a bar, bolt,* Cic., Verg.

vecto, 1. (intens. of veho), *to carry, convey;* plaustris ornos, Verg.; fructus ex agris, Liv.; pass., *to ride;* equis, Ov.; or *to be driven;* carpentis per urbem, Liv.

Vectŏnes = Vettones (q.v.).

vector -ōris, m. (veho). **I.** *one who carries, a carrier, bearer,* Ov. **II.** Pass., *one who is carried;* 1, on a ship, *a passenger, a seafaring man,* Verg.; 2, on a horse, *a rider,* Ov.

vectōrĭus -a -um (vector), *of or relating to carrying;* navigia, *transports,* Caes.

vectūra -ae, f. (veho). **I.** *a conveying, carrying by ship or carriage;* frumenti, Caes.; sine vecturae periculo, *of a sea-passage,* Cic. **II.** Meton. *passsage-money, fare,* Plaut.

vĕgĕo, 2. (connected with vigeo), *to stir up quicken, excite to rapid motion,* Enn.

vĕgĕtus -a -um (vegeo), *lively, vigorous active;* homo, Cic.; mens, Cic.; ingenium, Liv

vēgrandis -e. **I.** *small, tiny, diminutive;* farra, Ov. **II.** *of huge size, very great;* homo vegrandi macie torridus, Cic.

vĕhĕmens -entis. **I.** *violent, vehement, furious, impetuous;* a, of living beings, nimis es vehemens feroxque naturā, Cic.; in agendo, Cic.; se vehementem praebere in aliquem, Cic.; lupus, Hor.; b, of abstractions, vehemens et pugnax exordium dicendi, Cic. **II.** Transf., *strong, powerful, vigorous;* vehementius telum, Liv.; vehementior somnus, Liv. (also vēmens Lucr., Cat., Hor.).

vĕhĕmentĕr, adv. (vehemens). **I.** *vehemently, violently;* agere, Cic.; ingemuisse vehementius, Cic.; se vehementissime exercere in

aliqua re, Caes. **II**. Transf., *strongly, power-*
*fully, forcibly, exceedingly ; * hoc te vehementer
etiam atque etiam rogo, Cic. ; vehementer delectari, Cic.; vehementissime displicet, Cic. ;
vehementer utilis, Cic.

věhěmentia -ae, f. (vehemens). **I**. *vehe-*
mence, violence, passionateness, Plin. **II.** Transf.,
strength, power, Plin.

věhes -is, f. (veho), *a cartload*, Cato.

věhicǔlum -i, n. (veho), *a vehicle, convey-*
*ance ; * a, *by water, a boat, skiff*, Cic. ; b, *by*
*land, a waggon, carriage ; * vehiculum frumento
onustum, Liv.

věho, vexi, vectum (root VE, whence vea,
old Lat. = via), *to carry, bear, convey*. **I**. Transit.,
A. Act., a, *of men, on the shoulders or the*
back, in the arms, etc.; reticulum humero, Hor.;
of animals, taurus qui vexit Europam, Cic. ; b,
on water, quos vehit unda, Verg. ; c, on horseback, in a carriage, triumphantem (Camillum)
albi vexerant equi, Liv. ; d, in other manners,
formica vehit ore cibum, Ov.; transf., quod fugiens hora vexit, Hor. **B.** Pass., vehi, as middle ;
a, *to ride, drive ; * curru vehi, Cic. ; in navi, Cic.;
vehi post se, Liv. ; b, *to advance; * sex motibus
vehitur, Cic. ; c, *to fly; * apes trans aethera
vectae, Verg. **II.** Intransit., *to be borne, to ride ; *
only in partic. pres. and gerund, vehens quadrigis, Cic.

Veïus, v. Veji.

Vejens, v. Veji.

Vějento -ōnis, m. *a surname of the Fabricii,*
one of whom, a contemporary of Cicero, was left
governor of Syria by Bibulus.

Věji -ōrum, m. *an old town in Etruria, for a*
long time the rival of Rome, detroyed by Camillus,
near modern Isola. Hence, **A. Vějens** -entis,
m. *Veientine; * subst., **Vejens** -entis, m. *a*
*Veientine; * plur., **Vējentes** -um, m. *the Veien-*
tines. **B. Vějentanus** -a -um, *Veientine ; *
subst., **Vějentanum** -i, n. *a kind of poor wine,*
Hor. **C. Veïus** -a -um, *Veian.*

Vějǒvis (Vēdiǒvis) -is, m. (ve and Jovis),
an old Roman avenging deity identified with
Jupiter of the lower world, and with Apollo.

věl (lit., imper. of volo = *take what you will,*
the one or the other. **A**. Gen., 1, when alone,
*or; * oppidum vel urbem appellaverunt, Cic. ;
used with potius to correct a previous statement, ex hoc populo indomito vel potius immani, Cic.; 2, doubled (sometimes repeated
three or four times), *either . . or; * cur non
adsum vel spectator laudum tuarum vel particeps vel socius vel minister consiliorum? Cic. ;
the last statement is sometimes emphasised by
joining to vel etiam or vero or omnino ; quae
vel ad usum vitae vel etiam ad ipsam rempublicam conferre possumus, Cic. **B.** Esp., 1,
*and also; * pariter pietate vel armis, Verg. ; 2,
in a climax, *or even, actually ; * per me vel stertas
licet, Cic. ; often used with the superl., vel
maxime, *especially*, Cic. ; 3, a, *especially ; * est
tibi ex his ipsis, qui adsunt, bella copia, vel ut
a te ipso ordiare, Cic. ; b, *for example ; * raras
tuas quidem, sed suaves accipio litteras ; vel
quas proxime acceperam, quam prudentes, Cic.

Vēlābrum -i, n. *a district in Rome between*
the vicus Tuscus and the forum boarium.

vēlāmen -inis, n. (velo) *a covering, clothing,*
garment, Verg.

vēlāmentum -i, n. (velo). **L** *a covering*,
Sen. **II.** Esp., velamenta, *the olive-branches*
*wound round with wool, carried by suppliants; *
ramos oleae ac velamenta alia supplicum por-
rigentes, Liv.

vēlāris -e (velum), *belonging to a curtain; *
anulus, *a curtain-ring*, Plin.

vēlārium -ii, n. (velum), *the awning spread*
over the uncovered part of a theatre, Juv.

vēlāti -ōrum, m., milit. t. t., *the reserve,*
supernumerary troops who took the place of those
*who fell in battle; * used always in the phrase,
accensi velati, Cic.

vēles -itis, m., usually plur., velites, *light-*
armed infantry, skirmishers, Liv. ; transf., scurra
veles, Cic.

Vělia -ae, f. **I**. *a district on the Palatine*
Hill in Rome. **II.** *the Latin name of the Lucanian*
town Elea (Ἐλέα), *now Castell' a Mare della*
Bruca. Hence, **A. Věliensis** -e, *Velian.* **B.**
Vělinus -a -um, *Veline.*

vēlifěr -fěra -fěrum (velum and fero), *carry-*
ing sail, Ov.

vēlificātio -ōnis, f. (velifico), *a sailing*, Cic.

vēlifīco, 1. (velificus), *to sail.* **I**. Intransit.,
Prop. **II.** Transit., partic., **vēlifīcatus** -a
-um, *sailed through; * Athos, Juv.

vēlifīcor, 1. dep. (velificus), *to spread the*
*sails, sail; * hence, **I.** *to sail*, Prop. **II.** Fig.,
to work with full sails, to strive for earnestly, be
*zealous for; * alicui, ap. Cic. ; honori suo, Cic.

vēlifīcus -a -um (velum and facio), *sailing,*
Plin.

1. **Vělinus**, v. Velia.

2. **Vělinus** -i, m. *a lake in the Sabine country,*
drained by the consul M'. Curius Dentatus, now
Pie di Lugo or Lago delle Marmore. Hence,
Vělina tribus, *the tribe in the valley of the*
Velinus, Cic.

Veliocasses -ium, m. and **Veliocassi**
-ōrum, m. *a Gallic people on the right bank of the*
Seine, whose capital was Rodomagus, now Rouen.

vēlitāris -e (veles), *of or relating to the velites*
or *light-armed troops ; * arma, Sall. ; hastae, Liv.

vēlitātio -ōnis, f. (velitor), *skirmishing; *
transf., *a wrangling, bickering*, Plaut.

vēlitor, 1. dep. (veles), *to skirmish; * transf.
to wrangle, dispute, Plaut.

Vēlitrae -ārum, f. *a town of the Volsci in*
Latium, now Veletri. Hence, **Vēliternus** -a
-um, *of Velitrae.*

vēlivǒlans = velivolus (q.v.).

vēlivǒlus -a -um (velum and volo), *flying*
*with sails; * of ships, rates, Ov. ; of the sea,
traversed by sails, Verg.

Vellaunodūnum -i, n. *a town in Gallia*
Lugdunensis, now Chateau-Landon or Montargis.

Vellāvi -ōrum, m. *a Celtic people in modern*
Velay in the Cevennes.

Vellějus -a -um, *a Roman gens, the most*
*celebrated members of which were : * 1, **C.** Vellejus
Paterculus, *a famous Roman historian under*
*Augustus and Tiberius ; * 2, **C.** Vellejus, *friend*
of the orator Crassus, tribune of the people, 91 B.C.

vellicātio -ōnis, f. (vellico), *a plucking ·*
fig., *twitting, taunting*, Sen.

vellico, 1. (intens. of vello), *to pluck, twitch*
I. Lit., Plaut. **II.** *to taunt, criticise, censure,*
*rail at; * in circulis, Cic. ; absentem, Hor.

vello, vulsi (volsi) and velli, vulsum (vol-
sum), 3. *to pluck, pull, twitch.* **I.** Gen., alicui
barbam, Hor. ; latus digitis (to arrest a person's
attention), Ov.; aurem, Verg. **II.** Esp., *to pluck*
*off, pluck out ; * a, spinas, Cic.; postes a cardine,
Verg. ; b, milit. t. t., vallum, *to pull up the pali-*
sade, and so tear down the rampart, Liv. ; signa,
to take the standards out of the ground, to march
away, Liv.; transf., of bees, castris signa, Verg.

Vellocasses = Vellocasses (q.v.).

vellus -ĕris, n. (root VELL, whence villus, connected with pellis), *wool when shorn off, a fleece.* **I. A.** Lit., vellera motis trahere dignis, *to spin,* Ov. **B.** Meton., *the whole skin with the wool,* either on or off the animal ; Phrixea vellera, Ov. ; poet., transf., *any hide,* e.g., of a lion or stag, Ov. **II.** Transf. *of that which is like wool,* lanae vellera, per caelum ferri, *fleecy clouds,* Verg.

vēlo, 1. (velum), *to cover, veil, envelop.* **I. A.** Lit., capita amictu, Verg. ; togā velatus, Liv. **B.** Transf., *to crown, adorn;* tempora myrto, Verg. ; caput velatum filo, Liv. **II.** Fig., *to hide, conceal, veil;* odium fallacibus blanditiis, Tac.

vēlōcĭtas -ātis, f. (velox), *quickness, rapidity, velocity.* **I.** Lit., velocitas corporis celeritas vocatur, Cic. **II.** Transf., mali, Plin.

vēlōcĭtĕr, adv. (velox), *quickly, rapidly, swiftly;* aliquid velociter auferre, Ov. ; velocius pervolare in hanc sedem, Cic. ; velocissime moveri, Cic.

vēlox -ōcis (from 2. volo, as ferox from fero), *swift, rapid, quick, fleet.* **I.** Lit., pedites velocissimi, Caes. ; cervi, Verg. ; jaculum, Verg. ; toxicum, *quick in operation,* Hor. ; poet. for adv., ille velox desilit in latices, Ov. **II.** Transf., animus, Hor. ; nihil est animo velocius, Cic.

1. vēlum -i, n. (from veho, as prelum from premo), *a sail.* **I.** Lit., antennis subnectere totum velum, Ov. ; sing. collect., velo et remige portus intrat, Ov. ; gen. plur., vela dare, *to sail away,* Verg., Ov. ; vela facere, *to have all the sails set,* Verg. ; fig., dare vela ad id, unde aliquis status ostenditur, Cic. ; pandere vela orationis, *to follow the current of one's speech,* Cic. ; vela contrahere, Cic. ; prov., remis velisque, *with all one's might,* Cic. **II.** Meton., *a ship;* reditura vela tenebat eurus, Ov.

2. vēlum (root VE, whence vestis), *a covering, curtain;* tabernacula carbaseis intenta velis, Cic.; velis amicti, non togis, *wrapped up like women,* Cic.

vēlūmen = vellus (q.v.).

vēlŭt (**vēlŭtī**), adv. *as, even as, just as.* **I.** Correl. with sic foll. **A.** Gen., velut in cantu et fidibus, sic ex corporis totius natura et figura varios modos ciere, Cic. **B.** Esp., to introduce a simile, ac veluti magno in populo quum saepe coorta est seditio, sic, etc., Verg. **II.** Absol., **A.** Gen., velut hesterno die, Cic. ; veluti pecora, Sall. **B.** Esp., **1,** to introduce an example, *as, as for instance;* in bestiis aquatilibus iis, quae gignuntur in terra, velut crocodili, etc., Cic. ; **2,** to introduce a comparison, *as, just as;* frena dabat Sipylus, veluti quum praescius imbris, etc., Ov. ; **3,** velut si, or simply velut, to introduce a hypothetical comparison, *as if, just as if, just as though;* a, velut si ; absentis Ariovisti crudelitatem, velut si coram adesset, horrerent, Caes. ; b, velut or veluti alone ; velut ea res nihil ad religionem pertinuisset, Liv.

vēmens = vehemens (q.v.).

vēna -ae, f. *a blood-vessel, vein.* **I. A.** Lit., 1, venae et arteriae a corde tractae, Cic. ; 2, = arteria, *an artery;* plur.= *the pulse;* si cui venae sic moventur, is habet febrem, Cic. **B.** Transf., a, *a water-course;* venas et flumina fontis elicuere sui, Ov. ; b, *a vein of metal;* aeris, argenti, auri, Cic. ; meton. = *metal;* venae pejoris aevum, Ov. ; c, *a vein or streak in wood or stone,* Ov. **II.** Fig., 1, met., *the inmost, vital part;* periculum inclusum in venis et visceribus reipublicae, Cic. ; 2, *a vein of talent, disposition, natural inclination;* benigna ingenii vena, Hor.

vēnābŭlum -i, n. (venor), *a hunting-spear;* aprum venabulo percutere, Cic.

Vĕnăfrum -i, n. *a very old town of the Samnites in Campania, famous for its oil, near modern Venafro.* Hence, **Vĕnăfrānus** -a -um, *of Venafran.*

vēnālĭcĭus -a -um (venalis). **I.** *of or relating to sale;* subst., **vēnālĭcĭa** -ĭum, n. *import and export wares;* portoria venalicium, Liv. **II.** Esp., *relating to the sale of slaves;* subst., **vēnālĭcĭus** -ĭi, m. *a slave-dealer,* Cic.

vēnālis -e (2. venus). **I.** *on sale, to be sold;* horti, Cic. ; subst., venales, *slaves put up for sale,* Cic. **II.** Transf., *that can be bought with bribes* or *gifts, venal;* vox, Cic. ; habere venalem in Sicilia jurisdictionem, Cic.

vēnātĭcus -a -um (venatus), *of or relating to the chase;* canis, Hor.

vēnātĭo -ōnis, f. (venor). **I.** *the chase, hunting.* **A.** Lit., aucupium atque venatio, Cic. **B.** Meton., *game;* venatio capta, Liv. **II.** *a wild-beast hunt in the circus or amphitheatre;* ludorum venationumque apparatus, Cic.

vēnātor -ōris, m. (venor), *a hunter, sportsman,* Cic. ; fig., physicus id est speculator venatorque naturae, Cic.

vēnātōrius -a -um (venator), *of or relating to hunting or the chase;* galea, Nep.

vēnātrix -ĭcis, f. (venator), *a huntress,* Ov., Verg. ; attrib., puella, *Diana,* Juv.

vēnātūra -ae, f. (venor), *a hunting,* Plaut.

vēnātus -ūs, m. (venor), *the chase, hunting;* labor in venatu, Cic.

vendax -ācis, (vendo), *fond of selling,* Cato.

vendĭbĭlis -e (vendo). **I.** *on sale, saleable;* illa via Herculanea, Cic. **II.** Transf., *pleasant, acceptable;* oratio, Cic. ; sint illa vendibiliora, Cic.

venditārius -a -um (vendo), *on sale, saleable,* Plaut.

venditātĭo -ōnis, f. (vendito), *a putting up for sale;* hence, fig.= *a boasting, vaunting display;* venditatio atque ostentatio, Cic. ; sine venditatione, Cic.

venditātor -ōris, m. (vendito), *a vaunter, boaster,* Tac.

venditĭo -ōnis, f. (vendo), *a selling, sale.* **I.** Gen., venditioni exponere, *to expose for sale,* Tac. **II.** Esp., *sale by auction;* bonorum, Cic. ; plur., quam ad diem proscriptiones venditionesque fiant, Cic.

vendĭto, 1. (intens. of vendo), *to offer for sale repeatedly, try to sell.* **I.** Lit., Tusculanum, Cic. **II.** Transf., **1,** *to sell (corruptly);* decreta, Cic. ; pacem pretio, Liv. ; **2,** *to cry up, praise, recommend;* operam suam alicui, Liv. ; se alicui, Cic. ; se existimationi hominum, Cic.

vendĭtor -ōris, m. (vendo), *a seller, vendor,* Cic.

vendo -dĭdi -dĭtum, 3. (contr. from venum do), *to sell, vend.* **I. A.** Lit., **1,** gen., aliquid pecuniā grandi, Cic. ; male, *cheap,* Cic. ; partic. subst., **vendĭtum** -i, n. *sale;* ex empto aut vendito, Cic. ; 2, esp., a, *to sell by auction;* bona civium, Cic. ; b, *to let out to the highest bidder;* decumas, Cic. **B.** Transf., a, *to sell, betray for money;* auro patriam, Verg. ; b, *to give oneself up to, to devote to* (for money or some advantage), se regi, Cic. **II.** Fig., *to cry up, recommend;* Ligarianam, Cic. (the passive of vendo is veneo, as in classical Latin venditus and vendendus are the only passive forms of vendo used).

vĕnēfĭcĭum -ĭi, n. (veneficus). **I.** *a poisoning;* meton. = *poison,* Liv. **II.** *the preparation of magical draughts, magic, sorcery,* Cic.

vĕnēfĭcus -a -um (venenum and facio), *poisoning, poisonous, magical.* **I.** Adj., artes,

Plin. ; verba, Ov. **II.** Subst., **A. věněfĭcus** -i, m. *a poisoner, an enchanter,* Cic. **B. věně-fĭca** -ae, f. *a poisoner, a witch,* Hor.

Venelli -ōrum, m. *a Gallic tribe in modern North-west Normandy.*

věněnārĭus -ĭi m. (venenum), *a poisoner,* Suet.

věněnātus -a -um (venenum). **I.** *poisonous, poisoned ;* a, lit., vipera, Cic. ; telum, Cic. ; b, fig., jocus, Ov. **II.** *enchanted ;* virga, Ov.

věněnĭfěr -fěra -fěrum (venenum and fero), *poisonous,* Ov.

věněno, l. (venenum), *to poison ;* carnem, Cic.

věněnum -i, n. **I. A.** *poison ;* 1, lit., venenum alicui dare, Cic. ; aliquem veneno necare, Cic. ; dare venenum in poculo Cic. ; 2, fig.= *ruin, destruction, bane ;* discordia est venenum urbis, Liv. ; pus atque venenum (of envenomed language), Hor. **B.** *a magic draught, a philtre ;* quasi veneno perficere ut, etc., Cic. **II.** *colouring matter, dye ;* Assyrium, Verg. ; Tarentinum, Hor. ; *rouge,* Ov.

věněo (vaeněo), věnĭi, věnum, 4. (for venum eo, from venus, *sale), to go to sale, to be sold* (pass. of vendo). **I.** Gen., mancipia venibant, Cic. ; venire sub corona a consule et praetore, Liv. ; with abl. of price, auro, Hor. ; with genit. of price, minoris, Cic. **II.** Esp., *to be let to the highest bidder ;* quanti venierant, Cic.

věněrābĭlis -e (veneror), *venerable, reverend ;* venerabilis vir miraculo litterarum, venerabilior divinitate, Liv. ; of things, donum, Verg.

věněrābundus -a -um (veneror), *reverent, respectful,* Liv.

věněrandus -a -um, p. adj. (from veneror), *worthy of reverence, to be revered ;* amicus, Hor.

věněrātĭo -ōnis, f. (veneror). **I.** Act., *reverence, respect, veneration ;* habet venerationem justam quidquid excellit, Cic. **II.** Pass., *venerableness ;* feminae, Tac.

věněrātor -ōris, m. (veneror), *a venerator, reverer ;* domus vestrae, Ov.

Věněrĭus, v. 1. venus.

věněro = veneror (q.v.).

věněror, l. dep. **I.** *to reverence, venerate, regard with religious awe, honour ;* deos sancte, Cic. ; Larem farre pio, Verg. **II.** Meton., *to ask reverently, beseech with awe ;* nihil horum veneror, Hor. (partic., veneratus, pass. = *honoured ;* venerata Ceres, Hor.).

Věněti -ōrum, m. **I.** *a people originally of Thracian origin, who settled on the north-west coast of the Adriatic.* Hence, **Věnětĭa** -ae, f. *the land of the Veneti.* **II.** *a people in Gallia Lugdunensis, near modern Vannes.* Hence, **A. Věnětĭa** -ae, f. *the land of the Veneti.* **B. Věnětĭcus** -a -um, *Venetian.*

věnětus -a -um, *bluish, sea-coloured,* Juv. ; factio, *the party of charioteers who were clad in blue,* Suet.

věnĭa -ae, f. (root VEN, whence 1. venus), *grace, indulgence, favour.* **I.** Gen., a, petere veniam legatis mittendis, Liv. ; dedi veniam homini impudenter petenti, Cic. ; dare veniam excusationis, Cic. ; b, in the phrase, bonā veniā or bona cum venia, *with your permission, by your leave ;* bona venia me audies, Cic. ; vos oro atque obsecro, judices, ut attente bonaque cum venia verba mea audiatis, Cic. ; bonā veniā huius optimi viri dixerim, Cic. **II.** *indulgence to faults, grace, pardon, forgiveness ;* veniam impetrare errati, Cic. ; dare veniam et impunitatem, Cic.

Věnĭlĭa -ae, f. **I.** *a nymph, mother of Turnus.* **II.** *wife of Janus.*

věnĭo, věni, ventum, 4. *to come.* **I.** Lit., **A.** Gen., 1, of persons, a, istinc, Cic.; huc, Cic.; ad aliquem, Cic.; ad urbem, Cic.; sub aspectum, Cic. ; with acc. of place, domum ad aliquem, Cic.; sexto die Delum Athenis, Cic.; with dat. of object, venire auxilio, subsidio, Caes. ; with infin., speculari, Liv. ; impers., ad quos ventum erat, Caes.; b, *to come with hostile intent ;* veniens hostis, Verg. ; impers., veniri ad se existimantes, Caes.; 2, of things, frumentum Tiberi venit, Liv.; dum tibi litterae meae veniant, Cic. **B.** Esp., 1, *to come = to return ;* Romam, Liv.; quum venies, Ov.; 2, *to come = to come forth ;* a, veniens sol, Hor.; b, = *to grow ;* veniunt felicius uvae, Verg. **II.** Transf., **A.** Gen., 1, o persons, a, ut ad id aliquando, quod cupiebat veniret, Cic. ; b, *to come hostilely ;* contra sum mam amici existimationem, Cic. ; 2, of things, a, venire in mentem, *to come into one's head,* Cic.; b, of time, *to happen, to come, arrive ;* ubi ea dies quam constituerat venit, Caes. ; venientis anni, *of the coming year,* Cic. **B.** Esp., 1, venio in aliquid, *to come to* or *fall into any state* or *condition ;* in calamitatem, Cic. ; in consuetudinem, Cic.; alicui in amicitiam, Caes. ; 2, of speech, *to come to, arrive at a part of a subject ;* venio ad recentiores litteras, Caes. ; 3, a, = *to be derived from ;* Bebrycia de gente, Verg. ; b, *to arise from ;* majus commodum ex otio meo quam ex aliorum negotiis reipublicae venturum, Sall. ; 4, *to happen ;* haec ubi veniunt, Cic. ; 5, *to come to the lot of, fall to ;* hereditates mihi negasti venire, Cic. ; 6, *to turn out,* Tac.

vennūcŭla (vennuncŭla) uva -ae, f. *a kind of grape,* Hor.

vēnor, l. dep. *to hunt.* **I.** Intransit., ii qui venari solent, Cic. **II.** Transit., *to hunt, chase ;* 1, lit., leporem, Verg. ; 2, fig., *to pursue, strive after ;* suffragia ventosae plebis, Hor.

vēnōsus -a -um (vena), *full of veins, veiny,* Plin.

venter -tris, m. (connected with ἔντερον), *the belly.* **I.** Lit., a, fabā venter inflatur, Cic. b, *the belly as the organ and emblem of gluttony ;* ventrem fame domare, Liv. ; ventri oboedire, Sall. ; c, *the womb,* Juv. ; meton., *the fruit of the womb,* Hor. **II.** Transf., *a curving, protuberance, belly ;* cresceret in ventrem cucumis, Verg.

ventĭlābrum -i, n. (ventilo), *a winnowing-fork,* Varr.

ventĭlātĭo -ōnis, f. (ventilo), *an airing,* Plin.

ventĭlo, 1. (for ventulo from ventulus), *to toss to and fro in the air, fan, brandish in the air.* **I.** Lit., 1, ventilat aura comas, Ov. ; 2, *to winnow grain,* Varr. **II.** Transf., *to fan, to blow = to excite, provoke ;* illius linguā, quasi flabello seditionis, illa tum est egentium contio ventilata, Cic.

ventĭo -ōnis, f. (venio), *a coming,* Plaut.

ventĭto, 1. (intens. of venio), *to come often, be wont to come ;* domum, Cic. ; in castra, Caes.

ventōsus -a -um (ventus), *full of wind, windy.* **I.** a, lit., folles, Verg. ; Germania ventosior, Tac. ; ventosissima regio, Liv. ; b, meton., *swift* or *light as the wind ;* equi, Ov.; alae, Verg. **II.** Fig., 1, *windy, blown out = empty, vain ;* lingua, Verg. ; 2, *changeable, unstable, inconstant ;* homo ventosissimus, ap. Cic.; imperium, Cic.

ventrāle -is, n. (venter), *a belly-band,* Plin.

ventrĭcŭlus -i, m. (dim. of venter), *the belly.* **I.** Gen., Juv. **II.** Esp., *the stomach,* Plin. ; cordis, *a ventricle,* Cic.

ventrĭōsus -a -um (venter), *large-bellied, pot-bellied,* Plaut.

ventŭlus -i, m. (dim. of ventus), *a slight wind, gentle breeze,* Plaut., Ter.

ventus -i, m. *wind.* **I.** Lit., ventus increbrescit, Cic.; ventus intermittitur, Caes.; quum saevire ventus coepisset, Caes.; prov., in vento et aqua scribere, *to labour in vain,* Cat.; profundere verba ventis, Lucr.; dare verba in ventos, Ov.; *to talk in vain;* dare verba ventis, *not to keep one's word,* Ov.; ventis tradere rem, *to oblivion,* Hor.; ferre videre sua gaudia ventos, *to come to nothing,* Verg. **II.** Fig., a, *the wind* as a sign of good or ill success; venti secundi, *good fortune,* Cic.; **b,** as a means of raising a disturbance; omnes rumorum et contionum ventos colligere, *rumours,* Cic.; **c,** in the state; quicumque venti erunt, *whichever way the wind blows, whatever the circumstances may be,* Cic.; **d,** *favour of the people;* ventum popularem esse quaesitum, Cic.

vēnŭcŭla = vennucula (q.v.).

vēnundo -dēdi -dătum, 1. (for venundo, from 2. venus and do), *to sell;* esp., *captives taken in war;* captivos sub corona, Liv.

1. **vēnus** -ĕris, f. (root VEN, whence venia), *that which is pleasing.* **I.** Appellat., *beauty, charm, loveliness, attractiveness;* a, quo fugit venus? Hor.; **b,** in works of art; fabula nullius veneris, Hor. **II.** Proper name, **Vĕnus. A.** *the goddess of love and grace, wife of Vulcan, mother of Cupid;* Veneris puer, Cupid, Ov.; so Veneris filius, Cupid, Ov., or Aeneas (son of Anchises and Venus), Ov.; mensis Veneris, *April,* Ov. **B.** Meton., 1, *love,* Ov.; 2, *the beloved object,* Verg.; 3, *the planet Venus,* Cic.; 4, *the Venus throw, the highest throw of the dice,* Prop. Hence, **A. Vĕnĕrĭus** -a -um, 1, *of or relating to Venus;* Venerii servi and simply Venerii, *the slaves in the temple of the Erycinian Venus,* Cic.; subst., a, **Vĕnĕrĭus** -i, m. (sc. jactus), *the Venus throw, the highest throw of the dice,* Cic.; **b, Vĕnĕreae** -ārum, f. *a kind of mussel,* Plin.; 2, *relating to sensual love;* res, Cic.

2. **vēnus** -ūs and -i, m. only found in dat. and acc., *sale;* a, dat., venui and veno, veno dare aliquid alicui, Tac.; b, gen. acc., venum dare, *to sell,* Sall.; venum ire, *to be sold,* Liv.

Vĕnūsĭa -ae, f. *an old town of the Samnites in Apulia,* now *Venosa.* Hence, **Vĕnŭsīnus** -a -um, *Venusine.*

vĕnustas -ātis, f. (venus), *loveliness, beauty, charm, attractiveness;* a, of the body, corporis, Cic.; b, of discourse, *grace, wit;* hominum, Cic.; c, of manner, *charm, attractiveness;* homo affluens omni venustate, Cic.

vĕnustē, adv. (venustus), *beautifully, charmingly;* alicui venustissime respondere, ap. Cic.

vĕnustŭlus -a -um (dim. of venustus), *charming, beautiful,* Plaut.

vĕnustus -a -um (venus), *charming, lovely, beautiful, graceful;* a, of the body, gestus et motus corporis, Cic.; b, of discourse, *charming, attractive, delightful;* sermo, Cic.; sententiae, Cic.

vēpallĭdus -a -um, *very pale,* Hor.

vēprēcŭla -ae, f. (dim. of vepres), *a thorn-bush, bramble-bush,* Cic.

vēpres -is, m. (f. Lucr.), gen. plur., vepres, *a thorn-bush, briar-bush, bramble-bush;* sepulcrum saeptum undique et vestitum vepribus et dumetis, Liv.

vēr, vēris, n. (ἦρ), *spring.* **I.** a, lit., primo vere, *in the beginning of spring,* Liv.; quum ver esse coeperat, Cic.; b, transf., *spring-time of life, spring;* aetatis, Ov. **II.** Meton., *that which is brought by spring;* ver sacrum, *an offer-*

ing *of the firstlings,* originally *of men and of cattle,* afterwards *of cattle alone, made on extraordinary occasions;* ver sacrum vovere, Liv.

Vēragri -ōrum, m. *an Alpine people in Gallia Narbonensis.*

vērātrum -i, n. *hellebore,* Plin.

vērax -ācis (verus), *speaking the truth, truthful, veracious;* oraculum, Cic.; Herodotum cui veraciorem ducam Ennio, Cic.; with infin. vosque veraces cecinisse Parcae, Hor.

verbascum -i, n. *the plant mullein,* Plin.

verbēnāca -ae, f. *the plant vervain,* Plin.

verbēnae -ārum, f. *boughs of olive, laurel, myrtle, cypress and tamarisk, sacred boughs,* carried by the Fetiales, Liv., and by certain priests, Cic.

verbēnārĭus -ĭi, m. (verbenae), *one who carries sacred boughs, applied to the Fetiales,* Plin.

verbēnātus -a -um (verbenae), *crowned with sacred boughs,* Suet.

verber -ĕris, n. in sing. only in genit. and abl. (reduplicated form of root FER, whence ferire). **I.** *a blow, stroke, lash;* 1, gen., a, sing., virgae, Ov.; trementes verbere ripae, Hor.; **b,** plur., verbera caudae, Hor.; dare verbera ponto, of swimmers, Ov.; 2, esp. only plur., verbera, *blows with a whip* or *scourge, a thrashing, flogging, whipping;* a, lit., castigare aliquem verberibus, Cic.; verberibus lacerari, Liv.; b, fig., patruae verbera linguae, *invectives,* Hor.; contumeliarum verbera, Cic. **II.** *the instrument that inflicts the blow.* **A.** *a cudgel,* or gen., *a whip, scourge;* a, sing., verber tortus, Verg.; ictus verberis, Ov.; b, plur., jubet verbera afferri, Liv. **B.** *the thong of a sling* or *other missile weapon,* Verg.

verbĕrābĭlis -e (verbero), *deserving to be flogged,* Plaut.

verbĕrātĭo -ōnis, f. (verbero), *punishment, chastisement;* transf., ap. Cic.

verbĕrātus -ū, m. (verbero), *a beating,* Plin.

verbĕrĕus -a -um (verber), *deserving to be flogged,* Plaut.

1. **verbĕro,** 1. (verber), *to beat, strike.* **I.** Gen., aethera alis, Verg.; Mutinam tormentis, *to fire upon,* Cic.; vineae grandine verberatae, *beaten down,* Hor. **II.** Esp., *to beat with a whip, scourge,* etc.; *to flog, thrash, scourge;* aliquem pulsare et verberare, Cic.; alicuius oculos virgis, Cic.; 2, fig., *to lash with words, to attack, assail;* orator istos verberabit, Cic.

2. **verbĕro** -ōnis, m. (verber), *one who deserves a flogging, a rascal,* Cic.

Verbĭgēnus pagus, *one of the cantons of the Helvetii.*

verbōsē, adv. (verbosus), *diffusely, verbosely;* satis verbose, Cic.; haec ad te scripsi verbosius, Cic.

verbōsus -a -um (verbum), *copious, diffuse, verbose;* a, of persons, Cic.; b, of things, simulatio, Cic.; epistola verbosior, Cic.

verbum -i, n. (root VER, Gr. EP, whence εἴρω, ῥῆμα), *a word, expression; plur., talk, discourse.* **I.** Gen., a, verbum nunquam in publico facere, *to speak in public,* Cic.; videtis hoc uno verbo *unde* significari res duas, et *ex quo* et *a quo loco,* Cic.; verba facere, *to speak,* absol., Cic.; pro aliquo, de aliquo, Cic.; ille dies nefastus erit, per quem tria verba silentur, *when the praetor does not use the formula,* Do, Dico, Addico, i.e., *when he does not administer justice,* Ov.; b, esp. phrases, (a) verbo, *by a word;* verbo de sententia destitisti, Cic.; (β) uno verbo, *in a word, briefly;* ut uno verbo complectar, diligentia, Cic.; (γ) verbis, *by words alone* (opp. *opere*), Cic.; (δ) ad verbum, ‖ verbo, *de* verbo, *pro* verbo, *word for word, accurately*; fabellae Latinae ad verbum de Graecis expressae, Cic.; reddere verbum pro verbo, Cic.; (ε) verbi causā or gratiā, *for example*; si quis, verbi causā, oriente Caniculā ortus est, Cic.; (ζ) meis (tuis, suis) verbis, *in my (thy, his) name*; si uxori tuae meis verbis eris gratulatus, Cic. **II. A.** *mere words, mere talk* (opp. *reality*); existimatio, decus, infamia, verba sunt atque ineptiae, Cic.; in quibus (civitatibus) verbo sunt liberi omnes, *nominally*, Cic.; verba dare alicui, *to cheat, cozen, deceive*, Cic. **B.** Collect., *an expression, saying*; quod verbum in pectus Jugurthae altius, quam quisquam ratus erat, descendit, Sall. **C.** Grammat. **t. t.,** *a verb*; ut sententiae verbis finiantur, Cic.

Vercellae -ārum, f. *a town in Gallia Cisalpina*, now *Vercelli.*

Vercingĕtŏrix -rĭgis, m. *a chief of the Gauls in the time of Caesar.*

vercŭlum -i, n. (dim. of ver), *little spring*, used as a term of endearment, Plaut.

vērē, adv. (verus), *truly, in truth, rightly, aright*; dicere, Cic.; ne libentius haec in ullum evomere videar quam verius, Cic.; verissime loqui, Cic.

vĕrēcundē, adv. (verecundus), *modestly, shyly, bashfully*; tum ille timide vel potius verecunde inquit, Cic.; verecundius hac de re jam dudum loquor, Cic.

vĕrēcundĭa -ae, f. (verecundus), a, *modesty, shame, bashfulness, shyness*; (a) absol., meam stultam verecundiam! Cic.; (β) with subject. genit., Tironis, Cic.; (γ) with object. genit., turpitudinis, *on account of disgrace*, Cic.; b, *propriety, respect*; harum rerum commemorationem verecundia saepe impedivit utriusque nostrum, Cic.; c, *religious reverence, awe, respect*; with object. genit., deorum, Liv.; d, *a feeling of shame, a sense of shame*, Liv.; verecundiae est, with infin., *one is ashamed, hesitates*; privatis dictatorem poscere reum verecundiae non fuit, Liv.

vĕrēcundor, 1. dep. (verecundus), *to be bashful, ashamed, shy*; with infin., in publicum prodire, Cic.

vĕrēcundus -a -um (vereor), *feeling shame, bashful, shamefaced, modest, shy, diffident, coy*; 1, of persons, a, absol., homo non nimis verecundus, Cic.; b, with in and the abl., nec in faciendis verbis audax et in transferendis verecundus et parcus, Cic.; 2, of things, vultus, Ov.; color, *blush*, Hor.; oratio, Cic.; translatio, *not forced, natural*, Cic.

vĕrēdus -i, m. *a swift horse, hunter*, Mart.

vĕrendus -a -um, p. adj. (from vereor), *venerable, reverend*; majestas, Ov.; patres, Ov.

vĕrĕor -ĭtus sum, 2. dep. **I.** *to stand in awe of*; 1, *to fear*; a, with acc., hostem, Caes.; bella Gallica, Cic.; b, with acc. and infin., vereor committere ut, etc., Cic.; quos interficere vereretur, Cic.; 2, *to feel reverence, to be reverent towards, to revere*; a, with acc., metuebant eum servi, verebantur liberi, Cic.; quem et amabat ut fratrem et ut majorem fratrem verebatur, Cic.; b, with genit., ne tui quidem testimonii veritus, Cic. **II.** *to fear* = *to have to fear, to be afraid, to be anxious about, to suspect*; a, with acc., periculum, Caes.; b, with *ne* (*that*), or *ut*, or *ne non* (*that not*), vereor ne turpe sit timere, Cic.; et tamen veremur ut hoc natura patiatur, Cic.; c, absol., eo minus veritus navibus quod, etc., Caes.

vĕrētrum -i, n. (vereor) = αἰδοῖον.

Vergĭlĭus -ĭi, m., P. Vergilius Maro, *the great Roman poet, born at Andes in the Mantuan*

country, contemporary of Augustus, Horace, and Ovid, author of the Aeneid, the Georgics, and the Eclogues.

Verginĭus -a -um, *the name of a Roman family, the most celebrated of which was* Verginia, *the daughter of the centurion* L. Verginius, *who killed her in the market-place, to deliver her from the designs of the decemvir Appius Claudius.*

vergo, versi, 3. (connected with verto). **I.** Intransit., *to bend, to be inclined.* **A.** Lit., omnibus eius (terrae) partibus in medium vergentibus, Cic. **B.** Transf., 1, *to be inclined, to be directed*; a, of persons and objects connected with persons, nisi Bruti auxilium ad Italiam vergere quam ad Asiam maluissemus, Cic.; b, of places, *to lie towards, be situated towards*; ad flumen, Caes.; ad septemtriones, Caes.; 2, *to approach, come near*; a, of time, vergente autumno, Tac.; b, of disposition, etc., *to tend to*, Tac. **II.** Transit., *to bend, turn, incline*; 1, gen., middle, vergi, *to incline*, Lucr.; 2, esp., *to pour in*; amoma in sinus, Ov.

vergŏbrĕtus (from Celtic guerg = *efficax*, and breth or breath = *judicium*, thus = *judicium exsequens*), *the executor of judgment, name of the highest magistrate of the Aedui*, Caes.

vērĭdĭcus -a -um (verus and dico). **I.** *truth-speaking, truthful*; vox, Cic.; veridica interpres deûm, Liv. **II.** *truly spoken, true*, Plin.

vērĭlŏquĭum -ĭi, n. (verus and loquor) translation of ἐτυμολογία, *etymology*, Cic.

vērĭsĭmĭlis -e, *probable, likely*, Cic.

vērĭsĭmĭlĭtūdo -ĭnis, f. (verisimilis), *probability*, Cic.

vērĭtas -ātis, f. (verus), *truth.* **I.** Gen., *the true, actual nature of a thing, reality*; in omni re vincit imitationem veritas, Cic.; imitari veritatem (of works of art), *to be true to nature*, Cic.; quum in veritate dicemus, *in reality* (i.e., in the forum, not simply for practice), Cic. **II.** Esp. (as opp. to falsehood), *truth*; 1, lit., cuius aures veritati clausae sunt, Cic.; 2, meton., *truthfulness, honesty*; in tuam fidem, veritatem confugit, Cic.

vērĭverbĭum -ĭi, n. (verus and verbum), *speaking the truth*, Plaut.

vermĭcŭlātĭo -ōnis, f. (vermiculor), *a worm-hole in plants*, Plin.

vermĭcŭlātus -a -um (vermiculus), *vermiculated*; pavimentum, *inlaid with very small stones*, Plin.

vermĭcŭlor, 1. dep. (vermiculus), *to be full of worms, to be worm-eaten*, Plin.

vermĭcŭlus -i, m. (dim. of vermis), *a little worm*, Lucr.

vermĭnātĭo -ōnis, f. (vermino), 1, *the worms, a disease of animals*, Plin.; 2, *a pain in the limbs*, Sen.

vermĭno, 1. (vermis), 1, *to have worms*, Sen.; 2, *to have a crawling, itching pain in the limbs*, Sen.

vermĭnōsus -a -um (vermis), *full of worms*, Plin.

vermis -is, m. (verto), *a worm*, Lucr.

verna -ae, c. *a slave born in the house.* **I.** Lit., Hor. **II.** Transf., *a native*, Mart.

vernācŭla -a -um (verna). **I.** *of or relating to a slave born in the house*; subst., **vernācŭlus** -i, m. *a jester, buffoon*, Suet. **II.** Transf., *native, domestic*, i.e., *Roman*; crimen domesticum et vernaculum, Cic.

vernātĭo -ōnis, f. (verno). **I.** *the shedding of the skin by snakes*, Plin. **II.** Meton. *the slough or cast-off skin*, Plin.

vernīlis -e (verna), 1, *slavish, mean, abject;* blanditiae, Tac.; 2, *pert, froward;* verbum, Tac.

vernīlĭtas -ātis, f. (vernilis), 1, *mean servility,* Sen.; 2, *pertness, frowardness,* Plin.

vernīlĭtĕr, adv. (vernilis), *like a house-slave;* fungi officiis, Hor.

verno, 1. (ver), *to be spring-like, flourish, grow green.* I. Lit., vernat humus, Ov.; avis, *to begin to sing,* Ov. II. Transf., dum vernat sanguis, *is lively,* Prop.

vernŭla -ae, c. (dim. of verna), 1, *a slave born in the house,* Juv.; 2, transf., *native, indigenous,* Juv.

vernus -a -um (ver), *of or relating to spring, spring-like, vernal;* aequinoctium, Liv.; flores, Hor.; tempus, Cic.

vērō, adv. (verus), *in truth, truly, really, indeed, in fact.* I. Adv., a, Cic.; at the beginning of a letter, ego vero cupio, te ad me venire, *I wish really,* Cic.; b, often placed before affirmative answers, *certainly, to be sure;* vero, mea puella, Cic.; in negative answers, minime vero, Cic.; c, in addresses, invitations, demands, *then, pray;* tu vero me ascribe talem in numerum, Cic.; d, in a climax, *even, indeed;* in mediocribus vel studiis vel officiis, vel vero etiam negotiis contemnendum, Cic. II. Transf., as an adversative particle, *but indeed, but in fact;* illud vero plane non est ferendum, Cic.; so in transitions in speech, nec vero tibi de versibus respondebo, Cic.

Vērōna -ae, f. *one of the most flourishing towns of North Italy, birthplace of Catullus.* Hence, **Vērōnensis** -e, *of Verona;* subst., **Vērōnenses** -ium, m. *the inhabitants of Verona.*

verpa -ae, f. *the penis,* Cat.

verpus -i, m. (verpa), *a circumcised man,* Juv.

1. **verres** -is, m. *a boar,* Hor.

2. **Verres** -is, m., C. Cornelius, *praetor in Sicily, prosecuted and driven into exile by Cicero on a charge of extortion.* Hence, **A. Verrīus** -a -um, *of or belonging to Verres.* **B. Verrīnus** -a -um, *of or belonging to Verres;* jus (with a pun on 1. verres and on the double meaning of jus, *law* and *broth*), Cic.

1. **verrīnus** -a -um (1. verres), *of or relating to a boar,* Plin.

2. **Verrīnus,** v. 2. Verres.

verro, versum, 3. *to drag, trail on the ground.* I. Gen., A. Lit., a, versā pulvis inscribitur hastā, Verg.; b, of the winds, *to sweep, drag away;* maria et terras ferre secum et verrere per auras, Verg. B. *to sweep, to brush against;* a, of mourners, crinibus templa, crinibus passis aras, Liv.; b, of persons with long dresses, *to sweep the ground;* verrit humum pallā, Ov.; c, of animals swimming, *to pass over, sweep along;* aequora caudis, Verg.; so of ships, remis vada livida, Verg.; d, of a harp-player, duplici genialia nablia palmā, Ov. II. A. *to sweep with the broom;* a, Plaut.; b, on the thrashing-floor, *to sweep together, collect together;* quidquid de Libycis verritur areis, Hor. B. *to sweep clean, to clean;* absol., qui tergunt, qui verrunt, Cic.

verrūca -ae, f. *a wart, excrescence,* Plin.; fig., *a small fault* (opp. tuber, *a serious fault*), Hor.

verrūcārĭa herba -ae, f. (verruca), *a plant that removes warts, heliotropion,* Plin.

Verrūgo -gĭnis, f. *a town of the Volsci.*

verrunco, 1. (verto), *to turn out,* esp. as religious t.t., bene verruncare, *to turn out well,* have a happy issue; populo, Liv.

versābĭlis -e (verso), *movable, 'changeable,* Sen.

versābundus -a -um (verso), *turning round, revolving;* turbo, Lucr.

versātĭlis -e (verso), *turning round, revolving.* I. Lit., templum caeli, Lucr. II. Fig., *versatile;* ingenium, Liv.

versātĭo -ōnis, f. (verso), *a turning round, revolving.* I. Lit., Plin. II. Fig., *a changing, mutation,* Sen.

versĭcŏlor -ōris (verso and color), *changing in colour, of various colours, parti-coloured;* vestimentum, Liv.; arma, Verg.; plumae, Cic.

versĭcŭlus -i, m. (dim. of versus), 1, *a little line;* a, epistolae, Cic.; b, uno versiculo (i.e., the formula, Videant consules ne quid detrimenti respublica capiat), Cic.; 2, *little verse, versicle,* Cic.

versĭfĭcātĭo -ōnis, f. (versifico), *a making of verses, versification,* Quint.

versĭfĭcātor -ōris, m. (versifico), *a verse-maker, versifier,* Quint.

versĭfĭco, 1. (versus and facio), *to write in verse, versify,* Quint.

versĭpellis (vorsĭpellis) -e (verto and pellis), *changing one's skin;* hence, *changing one's form.* I. Lit., versipellem se facit (of Jupiter), Plaut. Subst., *one who can change himself into a wolf at pleasure, a werewolf,* Plin. II. *sly, subtle, crafty,* Plaut.

verso (vorso), 1. (verto). I. Freq.= *to turn about often, to turn hither and thither, to turn round.* A. 1, lit., a, ferrum or massam forcipe, Verg.; lumina suprema, *cast a last look,* Ov.; sortem urnā, *shake,* Hor.; exemplaria Graeca nocturnā versate manu, versate diurnā, *read night and day,* Hor.; reflex. and middle, *to turn oneself round;* se in utramque partem, non solum mente, sed etiam corpore, Cic.; middle, qui (orbes) versantur retro, Cic.; b, of spinning, *to turn the spindle;* levi teretem versare pollice fusum, Ov.; 2, transf., *to move hither and thither, to drive round;* a, act., (a,) oves, *to pasture,* Verg.; (β) *to torment, beat, harass;* Dareta, Verg.; b, middle, versari, (a) of persons = *to stay, live, dwell;* cum aliquo, Cic.; in fundo, Cic.; intra vallum, Caes.; (β) of things, *to have place;* partes eae, in quibus aegritudines, irae libidinesque versentur, Cic. B. Fig., 1, *to direct, turn hither and thither;* a, mentem ad omnem malitiam et fraudem, Cic.; b, of fate, *to turn upside down, change;* Fortuna omnia versat, Verg.; c, *to explain, to twist;* verba, Cic.; d, *to turn, influence in a certain direction;* muliebrem animum in omnes partes, Liv.; e, *to reflect, meditate upon;* in animis secum unamquamque rem, Liv.; 2, transf., *to put in motion;* a, *to disquiet, disturb;* nunc indignatio nunc pudor pectora versabat, Liv.; odiis domos, Verg.; b, middle, versari, (a) *to stay, to hover, to rest;* alicui ante oculos dies noctesque, Cic.; (β) esp., *tc be engaged in, take part in, be employed in, be occupied with;* in sordida arte, Cic.; of things, jura civilia quae jam pridem in nostra familia versantur, *are native,* Cic. II. Intens., *to turn round and round, to turn up;* gramen, Ov.; terram, Ov. (infin., versarier, ap. Cic.).

versōrĭa -ae, f. (verto), *a turning round;* versoriam capere, *to leave off, desist from anything,* Plaut.

versum = 1. versus (q.v.).

versūra -ae, f. (verto), *a turning;* fig., *the borrowing of money to pay a debt;* versuram facere, Cic.; versurā solvere or dissolvere, Cic.

1. versus (vorsus), versum (vorsum).
I. Adv., *towards, in the direction of;* ad oceanum versus, Caes.; in forum versus, Cic.
II. Prep. with acc., *towards;* Romam versus, Cic.
2. **versus** -a -um, partic. **I.** of verro (q.v.)., **II.** of verto (q.v.).
3. **versus (vorsus)** -ūs, m. (verto). **I.** *the turning of a plough;* hence, *a furrow,* Plin. **II.** *a row, line;* 1, gen., in versum distulit ulmos, Verg.; 2, in writing, **a,** in prose, primus (legis), Cic.; **b,** in poetry, *a verse,* plur., *verses, poetry;* versus Graeci, Latini, Cic.; *facere* versum, Cic. **III.** *a step in a dance,* Plaut.

versūtē, adv.with superl. (versutus), *craftily, adroitly, cunningly,* Cic.

versūtia -ae, f. (versutus), *cunning, craftiness,* Liv.

versūtilŏquus -a -um (versutus and loquor), *slyly speaking,* ap. Cic.

versūtus -a -um (verto), fig., *dexterous, adroit, cunning, crafty, sly;* acutus atque versutus animus, Cic.; versutissimus Lysander, Cic.; hoc si versutius videbitur, Cic.

vertăgus = vertragus (q.v.).

vertĕbra -ae, f. (verto), *a joint,* esp., *a joint of the back, vertebra,* Plin.

vertĕbrātus -a -um (vertebra), *jointed, movable, flexible,* Plin.

vertex (vortex) -ĭcis, m. (verto), *that which turns or is turned,* hence, *a whirl.* **I.** *a whirlpool of water, an eddy;* **a,** lit., Liv., Verg.; **b,** fig., amoris, Cat. **II.** *an eddy of wind or flame;* **a,** of wind, *a whirlwind,* Liv.; **b,** of fire, flammis volutus, Verg. **III.** *the crown of the head.* **A.** Lit., ab imis unguibus usque ad verticem summum, Cic. **B.** Meton., 1, *the head,* Cat.; 2, *the pole of the heavens,* Cic., Verg.; 3, *any height, elevation;* Aetnae, Cic.; hence, a vertice, *from above,* Verg.

vertĭcillus -i, n. (verto), *the whirl* or *whorl of a spindle,* Plin.

vertĭcōsus (vortĭcōsus) -a -um (vertex), *full of whirlpools;* mare, Liv.

vertĭgĭnōsus -a -um (vertigo), *suffering from giddiness,* Plin.

vertīgo -ĭnis, f. (verto), *a turning round, whirling round, revolution.* **I.** Lit., assidua caeli, Ov. **II.** Transf., *giddiness, vertigo;* vertigo quaedam simul oculorum animique, Liv.

verto (vorto), verti (vorti), versum (vorsum), 3. *to turn, turn round,* reflex., vertere se and simply vertere, and pass., verti, as middle, *to turn oneself.* **I.** Gen., **A.** Lit., **a,** equos ad moenia, Verg.; reflex., verti me a Minturnis Arpinum versus, Cic.; without se, alterius ramos videmus vertere in alterius, Verg.; **b,** milit. t. t., aliquem (hostes, equites, etc.) in fugam, *to put to flight, rout,* Liv.; Philippis versa acies retro, *the defeat at Philippi,* Hor.; terga, *to flee,* Caes.; reflex., se, Caes.; without se, versuros omnes in fugam exemplo ratus, Liv.; **c,** of position, middle, versus with in or ad and the acc., *turned, lying towards;* Epirus in septentrionem versa, Liv. **B.** Fig., 1, gen., **a,** in nos vertite iras, Liv.; middle, pater totus in Persea versus, *devoted to,* Liv.; reflex., without se, verterat periculum in Romanos, Liv.; **b,** of money, etc., *to devote, turn to;* ex illa pecunia magnam partem ad se, *to appropriate,* Cic.; **c,** *to turn to* (in a bad or good direction), construe as, *impute;* ne sibi vitio verterent, quod, etc., Cic.; auspicia in bonum verterunt, Liv.; 2, esp., **a,** *to alter, change;* auster in Africum se vertit, Caes.; quae sententia te vertit,

Verg.; fortuna jam verterat, Liv.; middle, verso Marte, Liv.; **b,** *to change to, cause to pass into;* aliquid in lapidem, Ov.; reflex. and middle, *to change to, to become;* terra in aquam se vertit, Cic.; **c,** *to translate;* verterunt nostri poetae fabulas, Cic.; **d,** polit. t. t., vertere solum, *to go into exile,* Cic. **II. A.** = versare, *to turn round and round;* 1, **a,** lit., lumina, *to roll,* Verg.; vertitur interea caelum, Verg.; **b,** transf., (a) *to move about;* inter primos, Verg.; (β) of time, *to roll round;* septima post Trojae excidium jam vertitur aestas, Verg.; esp. in partic., anno vertente, *in the course of a year,* Cic.; 2, fig., **a,** stimulos sub pectore, Verg.; **b,** esp., middle, verti, *to move in a certain sphere* or *element;* in jure in quo causa illa vertebatur paratissimus, Cic. **B.** = invertere, convertere, *to turn round* or *over;* 1, lit., **a,** gen., (a) stilum, Hor.; (β) as t. t. of agriculture, *to turn up with the plough* or *hoe;* terram aratro, Verg.; poet., transf. of ships, freta versa lacertis, Verg.; (γ) *to empty;* crateras, Verg.; **b,** esp., *to overthrow;* moenia ab imo, Verg.; 2, fig., **a,** Callicratidas quum multa fecisset egregie, vertit ad extremum omnia, *destroyed,* Cic.; **b,** *to destroy politically;* res Phrygias fundo, Verg.

vertrăgus -i, m. and **vertrăha** -ae, f. *a greyhound,* Mart.

Vertumnus (Vortumnus) -i, m. (verto), *the changing one), the god of exchange;* orig., *the god of the changing nature of the seasons, then of all transactions of sale, whose image stood at the end of the vicus Tuscus;* near his statue the booksellers had their shops.

vĕru -ūs, n. 1, *a spit,* Verg.; 2, *a javelin,* Verg.

vĕrūina -ae, f. (veru), *a small javelin,* Plaut.

Vĕrŭlae -ārum, f. *a town of the Hernici, in Latium,* now *Veroli.* Hence, **Vĕrŭlānus** -a -um, *Verulan.*

1. **vērum,** adv. (verus). **I.** *in truth, truly, really,* Plaut. **II.** *but, but yet, nevertheless, still;* verum haec civitas isti praedoni ac piratae Siciliensi Phaselis fuit, Cic.; non modo (tantum, solum) . . . verum etiam, Cic.; hence, **a,** in passing over to another subject in discourse, verum veniat sane, Cic.; **b,** in breaking off a discourse, verum quidem haec hactenus, Cic.

2. **vērum,** v. verus.

vērumtămen (vērumtāmen), conj. *but yet, notwithstanding, nevertheless ; consilium* capit primo stultum, verumtamen clemens, Cic.

vērus -a -um. **I.** *true, real, genuine;* dena ius, Cic.; timor, *well-grounded,* Cic.; res veriot causa verissima, Cic. Subst., **vērum** -i, n. *the truth;* verum scire, Cic. **II. A.** *right, fitting, reasonable;* lex, Cic.; verum est, with acc. and infin., negat verum esse allici beneficio benevolentiam, Cic. **B.** *truth-telling, truthful;* judex, Cic.

vērūtum -i, n. (veru), *a javelin,* Caes.

vērūtus -a -um (veru), *armed with a javelin,* Verg.

vervactum -i, n. *fallow ground,* Plin.

vervăgo, 3. *to plough up fallow ground,* Plin.

vervex -vēcis, m. *a wether,* Cic.; as a term of ridicule, *a sheepish, silly person,* Plaut.

vēsānia -ae, f. (vesanus), *madness, insanity,* Hor.

vēsānĭens -entis (vesanus), *raging,* Cat.

vēsānus (vaesānus) -a -um, *mad, insane;* **a,** of persons, remex, Cic.; poeta, Hor.; **b,** of inanimate and abstract things, *fierce, furious, wild;* vires, Ov.; famœs, Verg.

Vescĭa -ae, f. *a small town in Latium, on the Liris.* Hence, **Vescīnus** -a -um, *of or belonging to Vescia.*

vescor, 3. dep. (connected with esca). **I.** *to eat, feed on;* gen. with abl., rarely with acc., dii nec cibis nec potionibus vescuntur, Cic. ; lacte et ferinā carne, Sall. ; humanis corporibus, Liv. ; sacros lauros, Tib. ; absol., vescentes sub umbra, Liv. **II.** Transf., *to use, enjoy;* vitalibus auris, Lucr. ; paratissimis voluptatibus, Cic. ; aurā aetheriā, *to breathe, live,* Verg.

vescus -a -um (connected with vescor). **I.** Act. =*devouring, consuming;* sal, Lucr. ; papaver, *exhausting the land,* Verg. **II.** Pass., *wasted, thin;* hence = *containing little nutrition;* salicum frondes, Verg. ; farra, Ov.

Vesĕris -is, m. *a river in Campania, at the foot of Mount Vesuvius, where the consul T. Manlius Torquatus defeated the Latins, 340 B.C.*

vēsīca -ae, f. *the bladder.* **I.** *the urinary bladder.* **A.** Lit., Cic. **B.** Meton., *anything made from a bladder, a purse, a lantern, etc.,* Mart., Varr. **II. A.** *a bladder-like swelling, a blister,* Plin. **B.** Of discourse, *bombast, tumidity,* Mart.

vēsīcŭla -ae, f. (dim. of vesica), *a vesicle, a little bladder on plants,* Cic.

Vesontĭo -ōnis, m. *a town in Gaul, now Besançon.*

vespa -ae, f. *a wasp,* Cic.

Vespāsĭānus -i, m., T. Flavius Vespasianus Sabinus, *Roman emperor from 69–79 A.D.*

vesper -ĕris or -ĕri, m. (ἕσπερος). **I.** *the evening star,* Verg. **II.** Meton., **A.** *the evening;* iiei vesper erat, Sall. ; primā vesperis (sc. horā), Caes. ; ante vesperum, Cic. ; sub vesperum, Caes. ; primo vespere, Caes. ; abl., vespere and vesperi, *in the evening, late;* heri vesperi, Cic. ; prov., quid vesper ferat, incertum est, Liv. ; de vesperi suo vivere, *to be one's own master,* Plaut. **B.** *the west,* Ov., Verg.

vespĕra -ae, f. (ἑσπέρα), *the evening;* ad vesperam, *towards evening,* Cic. ; primā vesperā, Liv. ; abl., vesperā, *in the evening,* Plin.

vespĕrasco, 3. (vespera), *to become evening;* vesperascente jam die, *drawing towards night,* Tac.

vespĕrĕ, vesperi, v. vesper.

vespertīlĭo -ōnis, m. (vesper), *a bat,* Plin.

vespertīnus -a -um (vesper). **I.** Lit., *of or relating to evening;* litterae, *received at evening,* Cic. ; vespertinis temporibus, Cic. **II.** *lying towards the west, western;* regio, Hor.

vespĕrūgo -ĭnis, f. (vesper), *the evening star,* Plaut.

vespillo -ōnis, m. (vesper), *a corpse-bearer for the poor, who were buried in the evening,* Suet.

Vesta -ae, f. (Ἑστία), *the daughter of Saturn and Ops, goddess of the hearth and domestic life;* ad Vestae (sc. aedem), Hor. ; a Vestiae (sc. aede), Cic. ; in her temple at Rome burnt the sacred fire, the extinction of which was thought to involve the ruin of the state; the Vestal virgins were consecrated to her service; Vestae sacerdos = pontifex maximus, *who had control over the Vestal virgins,* Ov. ; meton., a, = *the temple of Vesta;* Vesta arsit, Ov.; b, *the hearth,* Verg. Hence, adj., **Vestālis** -e, *Vestal;* sacra, *the festival of Vesta, on the 9th of June,* Ov. ; virgo Vestalis, and subst., **Vestālis** -is, f. *a Vestal virgin, one of the priestesses of Vesta, of whom there were first four and then six, chosen between their sixth and tenth years, obliged to remain*

virgins in the service of Vesta for thirty years. Hence again, adj., **Vestālis** -e, *relating to the Vestal virgins, Vestal;* oculi, *chaste,* Ov.

vester (voster) -tra -trum (vos), *your;* yours. **I.** Subject., majores vestri, Cic. **II.** Object. = *against you;* odio vestro, Liv.

vestĭārĭus -a -um (vestis), *of or relating to clothes;* subst., **vestĭārĭum** -i, n. a, *a clothes-chest,* Plin. ; b, *a stock of clothes, wardrobe,* Sen.

vestĭbŭlum -i, n. *an entrance-court, court-yard.* **I. A.** Lit., templi, Cic. **B.** Transf., *the entrance to a place;* sepulcri, Cic. ; urbis, Liv. ; in vestibulo Siciliae, Cic. **II.** Fig., *a beginning,* Cic.

vestīgātor (vestigiātor) -ōris, m. (vestigo), *a tracker, investigator,* Varr.

vestīgĭum -ii, n. **I.** Act. = *the part of the foot that treads, the sole of the foot.* **A.** Lit., qui adversis vestigiis stant contra nostra vestigia, Cic. **B.** Meton., 1, *a foot-step, track, foot-mark;* a, lit., vestigia in omnes ferentia partes, Liv. ; vestigium facere in foro, Cic. ; vestigiis aliquem sequi, Liv. ; consequi, Cic. ; b, transf., *a trace, mark;* frons non calamistri notata vestigiis, Cic.; c, fig., (a) vestigiis ingredi patris, *to tread in his father's steps,* i.e., *to imitate him,* Cic. ; (β) *a mark, sign;* vestigia sceleris, avaritiae, Cic. ; 2, poet., *the whole of the lower part of the foot;* vestigia nuda sinistri pedis, Ov. **II.** Pass., *that which is trodden upon, a position, post, station;* 1, lit., a, in suo vestigio mori malle quam fugere, Liv.; b, *the position of a destroyed town, ruins;* in vestigiis huius urbis, Cic. ; 2, fig., *of time, a moment;* in illo vestigio temporis, Caes. ; eodem et loci vestigio et temporis, Caes. ; adv., e vestigio, *immediately, on the spot,* Cic.

vestīgo, 1. (vestigium), *to track, follow the trace of, investigate.* **I.** Of animals, Plin. **II.** Of men, 1, lit., a, virum, Verg. ; b, causas rerum, Cic. ; 2, meton., *to come upon the track of;* perfugas et fugitivos inquirendo, Liv. .

vestīmentum -i, n. (vestio), *clothing, covering, garment, vestment,* Cic.

Vestīni -ōrum, m. *a people in Italy, on the Adriatic, famous for their cheese.* Hence, **Vestīnus** -a -um, *of or belonging to the Vestini.*

vestĭo -īvi and -ĭi -ītum, 4. (vestis), *to cover with a garment, clothe.* **I. A.** Lit., animantes villis vestitae, Cic. **B.** Transf., *to cover as with a garment, to adorn;* oculos membranis, Cic.; campos lumine purpureo, Verg.; sepulcrum vestitum vepribus et dumetis, Cic. ; trabes aggere, Caes.; se gramine, Verg. **II.** Fig, in- venta vestire oratione, Cic.

vestis -is, f. (connected with ἐσθής), *a cover- ing.* **I.** Lit., **A.** Of men, *a garment,* and a, sing. collective, *clothing;* vestis lintea, Cic. ; ves- tem mutare, *to put on other clothes,* esp., *to put on mourning,* Cic. ; b, plur., vestes, *clothes;* vestibus hunc velant, Ov. **B.** *a carpet, tapestry;* pretiosa vestis multa et lauta supellex, Cic. **II.** Poet., transf., a, *the clothing of the chin, the beard,* Lucr. ; b, *the skin of a snake,* Lucr. ; c, *the spider's web,* Lucr.

vestispĭca -ae, f. (vestis and specio), *the mistress of the robes, keeper of the wardrobe,* Plaut.

vestītus -ūs, m. (vestio), *clothing, clothes, garments, apparel, attire, raiment.* **I. A.** Lit., color vestitus, Caes. ; vestis muliebris, Cic. ; vestitum mutare, *to go into mourning,* Cic. ; ad suum vestitum redire, *to go out of mourning,* Cic. **B.** Transf., *a covering;* riparum, Cic.; vestitus densissimi montium, Cic. **II.** Fig., ea vesti- tu illo orationis, quo consueverat, ornata non erat, Cic.

Vēsŭlus -i, m. *a mountain in the Cottian Alps*, now *Viso*.

Vēsŭvĭus -ĭi, m. *Vesuvius, the celebrated volcano in Campania, at the first eruption of which, under Titus, the towns of Herculaneum, Pompeii, and Stabiae were destroyed.*

vĕtĕrāmentārĭus -a -um (vetus), *of or relating to old things*; sutor, *a cobbler*, Suet.

vĕtĕrānus -a -um (vetus), *old*; boves, Varr.; hostis, Liv.; esp., of soldiers, *veteran*; plur., milites veterani, or subst. simply veterani, *old soldiers*, veterans, Cic.; legio veterana, Cic.

vĕtĕrasco -āvi, 3. (vetus), *to become old, grow old*, Cic. (?)

vĕtĕrātor -ōris, m. (vetus), *one who has grown old in* or *become experienced in anything*; a, in causis, Cic.; b, in a bad sense, *subtle, tricky*; non sunt in disputando vafri, non veteratores, non malitiosi, Cic.; absol. = *a cunning fellow*, old fox, Cic.

vĕtĕrātōrĭē, adv. (veteratorius), *cunningly, craftily*; dicere, Cic.

vĕtĕrātōrĭus -a -um (veterator), *cunning, crafty*, Cic.

vĕtĕrīnārĭus -a -um (veterinus), *of or relating to draught-animals*; subst., **vĕtĕrīnārĭus** -ĭi, m. *a veterinary surgeon*, Col.

vĕtĕrīnus -a -um (perhaps contr. from vehiterinus, from veho), *of or relating to draught.* **I.** Adj., bestia, *a beast of burden*, Cato. **II.** Subst., **vĕtĕrīnae** -ārum, f. *draught-animals*, Varr.

vĕternōsus -a -um, adj. with superl. (veternus). **I.** *lethargic*, Cato. **II.** Transf., a, *sleepy, dreamy*, Ter.; b, *dull, without energy*; animus, lethargic, Sen.

vĕternus -i, m. (vetus), *age*; hence, *lethargy, sleepiness*; a, Plaut.; b, *inactivity, lethargy, sloth*; veternus civitatem occupavit, Cic.

vĕtĭtum -i, n. (veto). **I.** *that which is forbidden*; nitimur in vetitum semper cupimusque negata, Ov. **II.** *a prohibition*; quae contra vetitum discordia? Verg.; in Cic. only in the phrases jussa ac vetita and jussa vetita.

vĕto (**vŏto**), vĕtŭi (vŏtŭi), vĕtĭtum (vŏtĭtum), 1. *not to allow to happen, to forbid, prohibit, hinder, prevent*; used of the tribunes, praetor, magistrates, etc., or of the law, or as t. t. of augury, a, with object. clause, (α) with acc. and infin., rationes vetabant me ·eipublicae penitus diffidere, Cic.; lex peregrinum vetat in murum ascendere, Cic.; (β) with infin. alone, lex vetat delinquere, Cic.; b, with ut or ne, or (with preceding negative) quominus, or quin and the subj., or with subj. alone, edicto vetuit ne quis se praeter Apellem pingeret, Hor.; c, with acc. alone, bella, Verg.; pass., quod vetamur, Cic.; d, absol., lex jubet aut vetat, Cic.

Vettōnes (**Vectōnes**) -um, m. *a people in Lusitania, in modern Salamanca and Estremadura.*

vĕtŭlus -a -um (dim. of vetus), *somewhat old, oldish.* **I.** Adj., equus, Cic.; filia, Cic. **II.** Subst., **A.** **vĕtŭlus** -i, m. *an old man*, Plaut.; in jest, mi vetule, "*old boy*," Cic. **B.** **vĕtŭla** -ae, f. *an old woman*, Juv.

vĕtus -ĕris, abl. sing. -ĕre, compar., **vĕtĕrĭor** (archaic, the classical compar. is vetustior), superl., **vĕterrĭmus** (root VET, Gr. ET, whence ἔτος), *old, ancient.* **I.** Adj., a, as opposed to young, senatores, Liv.; b, as opposed to new, navis, Caes.; necessitudines, Cic.; with genit. = *grown grey in, experienced in*; operis ac laboris, Tac.; c, as opposed to the present, old =*former*,

ancient; res, Cic.; innocentia, Cic.; poetae veterrimi, Cic.; in Tac. gen., *of the time before the battle of Actium*; aetas, Tac. **II.** Subst., **A.** **vĕtĕres** -um, m. *the old = ancestors*, Cic. **B.** **Vĕtĕres** -um, f. (sc. tabernae), *the old booths on the south side of the Roman Forum.* **C.** **vĕtĕra** -um, n. *that which is old, the remote past*; illa vetera omittere, *the old stories*, Cic.

vĕtustas -ātis, f. (vetustus), *age.* **I.** Lit., **A.** Gen., vetustas possessionis, Cic.; verborum vetustas prisca, Cic. **B.** Esp., *antiquity*; historia nuntia vetustatis, Cic. **II.** Transf., **A.** *long duration, length of time*; vetustati condita, Cic.; plur., vetustates familiarum, Cic.; habitura vetustatem, *likely to endure for a long time*, Cic.; conjuncti vetustate, *a friendship of long standing*, Cic.; ingenio, vetustate (*experience*), artificio tu facile vicisti, Cic. **B.** *late posterity*; de me nulla umquam obmutescet vetustas, Cic.

vĕtustus -a -um (vetus), *old, ancient.* **I.** Gen., a, vinum, Plaut.; hospitium, *of long standing*, Cic.; b, *old in years*; vetustissimus ex censoribus, Liv. **II.** Esp., *old-fashioned, antiquated*; vetustior et horridior ille, Cic.

vexāmen -ĭnis, n. (vexo), *a shaking*; mundi, Lucr.

vexātĭo -ōnis, f. (vexo). **I.** *a shaking*, Plin. **II.** a, *trouble, annoyance, hardship*; corporis, Cic.; b, *ill-treatment*; sociorum, Cic.

vexātor -ōris, m. (vexo), *one who annoys, harasses, disturbs*; direptor et vexator urbis, Cic.

vexillārĭus -ĭi, m. (vexillum). **A.** *a standard-bearer*, Liv. **B.** Plur., **vexillārĭi** -ōrum, m. a, *under the empire, veterans who had served twenty years and were enrolled in special battalions, a reserve corps*, Tac.; b, *a detachment, a division of a larger body*, Tac.

vexillātĭo -ōnis, f. (vexillum), *a detachment*, Suet.

vexillum -i, n. (dim. of velum), *the standard of the maniples*, and esp., *of the cavalry, the veterans and the allies.* **I.** Lit., a, *a flag, standard*; vexillum tollere, Cic.; esp., *the red flag displayed on the general's tent* or *the admiral's ship as the signal of battle*; vexillum proponere, Caes. **II.** Meton., *the men who fought under one flag, a company, troop*, Liv.

vexo, 1. (intens. of veho), *to move violently, shake, shatter.* **I.** Lit., venti vexant nubila, Ov.; rates, Verg. **II.** Transf., *to harass, disquiet, molest, misuse, damage, annoy, vex*; agros, Caes.; hostes, Cic.; vexari difficultate viae, Liv.

vĭa -ae, f. (old Lat. vea, connected with veho), *a way.* **I.** Lit., **A.** *the way along which one goes*; a, *a highway, road*; militaris, main-road, Cic.; declinare de via ad dexteram, Cic.; viā ire, *to go straight on*, Liv.; dare alicui viam, *to give place*, Liv.; dare alicui viam per fundum, *to allow a passage through*, Cic.; b, *a street in a town*; transversa, Cic.; c, *a passage*, (a) *the gullet*, Cic.; the wind-pipe, Ov.; (β) *a cleft*, Verg.; (γ) *a stripe in a garment*, Tib. **B.** Abstr., *way = course, march, journey*; de via languere, Cic.; unam tibi viam et perpetuam esse vellent, *wished that you should never return*, Cic.; mare et (atque) viae, viae ac mare, *travels by land and sea*, Hor. **II.** Fig., **A.** Gen., vitae via, Cic.; de via (*from the straight road, from virtue*); decedere, Cic. **B.** Esp., 1, *means, way, method*) viam optimarum artium tradere, Cic.; 2, *manner, rule, kind*; per omes vias leti, Liv.; viā, *methodically, by rule*; dicere, Cic.

vĭālis -e (via), *of or relating to the highways*; Lares, Plaut.

vĭārĭus -a -um (via), *of or relating to highways*; lex, *for repairing the highways*, ap. Cic.

viātĭcātus -a -um (viaticum), *provided with money for a journey*, Plaut.

viātĭcus -a -um (via), *of or relating to a journey*. **I.** Adj., cena, *a farewell repast*, Plaut. **II.** Subst., **viātĭcum** -i, n. **A.** *money for a journey;* viaticum congerere, Cic. **B.** Esp., *prize-money of a soldier*, Hor.

viātor -ōris, m. (via). **I.** *a traveller, wayfarer*, Cic. **II.** *a runner* or *messenger attached to a magistrate's service*, Cic.

viātōrĭus -a -um (viator), *of or relating to a journey*, Plin.

vĭbix (**vībex**) -īcis, f. *a weal, mark of a stripe*, Plaut.

Vĭbo -ōnis, f. *a town in Bruttii*, now *Monte Leone*, in full *Vibo Valentia*. Hence, **A.** **Vĭbōnensis** -e, *belonging to Vibo*. **B.** **Valentīni** -ōrum, m. *the inhabitants of Vibo Valentia*.

vĭbro, 1. **I.** Transit., *to cause to vibrate, move rapidly to and fro; brandish, shake;* a, vibrabant flamina vestes, Ov.; b, *to brandish a missile;* poet., *to brandish and hurl;* hastam, Cic.; spicula per auras, Ov.; fig., truces iambos, Cat.; c, *to curl, frizzle;* crines vibrati, Verg. **II.** Reflex., *to shake, tremble, move to and fro, vibrate;* a, Plin.; b, *of limbs* or *parts of the body, to quiver;* tres vibrant linguae, Ov.; c, *to glimmer, glitter;* vibrat mare, Cic.; d, *of lightning, missiles*, etc., *to flash, glitter;* fig., of discourse, oratio incitata et vibrans, Cic.

viburnum -i, n. *a tree* (Viburnum Lantana, Linn.), Verg.

vĭcānus -a -um (vicus), *dwelling in a village;* vicani haruspices, Cic.; subst., **vĭcāni** -ōrum, m. *villagers*, Liv.

vĭcārĭus -a -um (vicis), *taking the place of a person* or *thing, substituted, vicarious*. **I.** Adj., operae nostrae vicaria fides amicorum supponitur, Cic. **II.** Subst., **vĭcārĭus** -ii, m. *one who takes another's place, a substitute;* a, diligentiae meae, *successor in the consulship*, Cic.; b, *a soldier substitute;* dare vicarios, Cic.; c, *an under-servant, under-slave*, Cic.

vĭcātim, adv. (vicus). **I.** *from street to street;* servorum omnium vicatim celebratur totā urbe descriptio, Cic. **II.** *in villages;* in montibus vicatim habitare, Liv.

vĭcĕ, vicem, v. vicis.

vĭcēnārĭus -a -um (viceni), *containing the number twenty*, Plaut.

vĭcēni -ae -a (viginti). **I.** *twenty each*, Caes. **II.** *twenty*, Plin.

vĭces, v. vicis.

vĭcēsĭma, v. vicesimus.

vĭcēsĭmāni -ōrum, m. (vicesimus), *soldiers of the twentieth legion*, Liv.

vĭcēsĭmārĭus -a -um (vicesimus), *of or relating to the twentieth part of anything;* aurum, *a tax of one twentieth*, or *five per cent., on the value of manumitted slaves*, Liv.

vĭcēsĭmus (**vīgēsĭmus**) -a -um (viginti), *the twentieth*. **I.** Adj., dies vicesimus, Cic. **II.** Subst., **vĭcēsĭma** -ae, f. (sc. pars), *the twentieth part;* a, gen., e.g., of the harvest, Liv.; b, esp., *the twentieth part as a toll* or *tax;* portorii, Cic.; *a tax of five per cent. on the value of manumitted slaves*, Cic.

Vīcĕtĭa -ae, f. *a town in North Italy*, now *Vicenza*. Hence, **Vīcĕtīni** -ōrum, m. *the people of Vicetia*.

vĭcĭa -ae, f. *a vetch;* plur., Ov

vĭcĭēs (**vĭcĭens**), adv. (viginti), *twenty times;* H.S. vicies, 2,000,000 *sesterces*, Cic.

20*

Vīcĭlīnus -i, m. (perhaps from vigil), *the watchful one;* Juppiter Vicilinus, Liv.

vīcīnālis -e (vicinus), *neighbouring, near;* ad vicinalem usum, *after the manner of neighbours*, Liv.

vīcīnĭa -ae, f. (vicinus), *neighbourhood, nearness, vicinity*. **I. A.** Lit., Persidis, Verg.; in nostra vicinia, Cic. **B.** Meton., *the neighbourhood = the neighbours;* Hispala ex Aventino libertina non ignota viciniae, Liv.; funus laudet vicinia, Hor. **II.** Fig., 1, *nearness*, Petr.; 2, *likeness, similarity, affinity*, Quint.

vīcīnĭtas -ātis, f. (vicinus), *neighbourhood, vicinity, nearness*. **I. A.** Lit., in ea vicinitate, Cic.; plur., *neighbourly connections*, Cic. **B.** Meton., *neighbourhood = neighbours;* signum quod erat notum vicinitati, Cic. **II.** Fig., *likeness, affinity*, Quint.

vīcīnus -a -um (vicus), *near, neighbouring*. **I.** Lit., **A.** Adj., bellum, Liv.; with dat., sedes vicina astris, Verg.; Thessalia quae est vicina Macedoniae, **Liv. B.** Subst., 1, **vīcīnus** -i, m., **vīcīna** -ae, f. *a neighbour;* vicini mei, Cic.; 2, **vīcīnum** -i, n. *the neighbourhood, vicinity;* plur., sonitu plus quam vicina fatigat, Ov. **II.** Fig., *similar, like, kindred;* in the dat., dialecticorum scientia vicina et finitima eloquentiae, Cic.

vĭcis (genit.; nom. not found), vicem, **vĭcĕ**, plur., vices, vicibus, *change, interchange, alternation, vicissitude*. **I.** Lit., **A.** Gen., a, hāc vice sermonum, *interchange of discourse*, Verg.; vice humanarum fortunarum, Liv.; solvitur acris hiems gratā vice veris et Favoni, Hor.; b, adv., (a) *per vices, alternately;* clamare, Ov.; (β) in vicem (invicem), *more rarely* vicem, in vices, *alternately, reciprocally, by turns;* simul eramus invicem, Cic.; hi rursus in vicem anno post in armis sunt, Caes. **B.** Esp., 1, *requital, recompense, compensation, retaliation;* recito vicem officii praesentis, Cic.; redde vicem meritis, Ov.; 2, *the vicissitude of fate, fate, lot, destiny;* tacite gementes tristem fortunae vicem, Phaedr.; convertere humanam vicem, Hor. **II.** Transf., *a place, office, post, duty;* a, nulla est enim persona, quae ad vicem eius, qui e vita emigrarit, propius accedat, Cic.; vestramque meamque vicem explete, Tac.; b, adv., vicem, vice, in vicem, ad vicem, *in place of, instead of, like, as;* in qua re tuam vicem saepe doleo, Cic.; Sardanapali vicem in suo lectulo mori, *like Sardanapalus*, Cic.; defatigatis invicem integri succedunt, Caes.

vĭcissātim = vicissim (q.v.).

vĭcissim, adv. (vicis). **I.** *in turn;* terra florere, deinde vicissim horrere potest, Cic. **II.** *on the other hand;* considera nunc vicissim tuum factum, Cic.

vĭcissĭtūdo -ĭnis, f. (vicis), *change, alteration, vicissitude;* imperitandi, Liv.; vicissitudo in sermone communi, *interchange of discourse;* plur., fortunae, Cic.

victĭma -ae, f. *an animal offered in sacrifice, a victim*, Caes.; fig., se victimam reipublicae praebuisset (Decius), Cic.

victĭmārĭus -ii, m. (victima), *an assistant* or *servant at a sacrifice*, Liv.

victĭto (intens. of vivo), 1. *to live upon, feed upon;* ficis, Plaut.

victor -ōris, m. (vinco), *a conqueror, victor*. **I.** Lit., a, absol., parere victori, Liv.; in apposition, *as a conqueror, victorious;* victores Sequani, Caes.; victor exercitus, Cic.; currus, Ov.; b, with genit., omnium gentium, Cic.; victor trium simul bellorum, Liv.; c, with abl., bello civili victor, Cic. **II.** Fig., animus libidinis et divitiarum victor, Sall.

victōrĭa -ae, f. (victor), *victory, conquest.*
I. Lit., **A.** victoria Cannensis, Liv.; clarissima, Cic.; with de and the abl., victoria de Vejentibus, Liv.; with ad and the acc., nuntius victoriae ad Cannas, Liv.; adipisci victoriam, Caes.; consecutum esse sibi gloriosam victoriam, Cic.; dare alicui victoriam, Liv. **B.** Proper name, Victoria, *the goddess of Victory, represented with wings and with a laurel crown or palm branch in the hand.* **II.** Transf., a, certaminis, Liv.; b, in a court of justice, nocentissima victoria, Cic.

victōrĭātus -i, m., genit. plur., victoriatûm (Victoria), *a silver coin stamped with a figure of Victory, worth half a denarius,* Cic.

victōrĭŏla -ae, f. (dim. of Victoria), *a small statue of Victory,* Cic.

victrix -tricis, f. neut. plur. -tricia (f. of victor), *she that conquers;* attrib. = *victorious, conquering.* **I.** Lit., Athenae, Cic.; literae, *bringing news of victory,* Cic. **II.** Fig., mater victrix filiae, non libidinis, Cic.

Victumŭlae -ārum, f. *a town in Gallia Cispadana.*

victus -ūs, m. (vivo). **I.** *manner of life, way of living;* Persarum, Cic.; in omni vita atque victu excultus, Cic. **II.** *support, nourishment, food;* alicui victum quotidianum in Prytaneo publice praebere, Cic.; parare ea, quae suppeditent ad victum, Cic.; plur., persequi animantium ortus, victus, figuras, Cic.

vīcŭlus -i, m. (dim. of vicus) *a little village, a hamlet,* Cic.

vīcus -i, m. (connected with οἶκος). **I.** *a quarter or district of a town, street;* nullum in urbe vicum esse, in quo non, etc., Cic.; vicos plateasque inaedificat, Caes. **II.** In the country, **A.** *a village, hamlet,* Cic., Caes. **B.** *an estate, country-seat;* scribis te vicum venditurum, Cic.

vĭdēlĭcĕt, adv. (videre licet, *one can see*). **I.** Lit., a, *clearly, plainly, manifestly, evidently;* quae videlicet ille non ex agri consitura, sed ex doctrinae indiciis interpretabatur, Cic.; elliptically, in answers, quid metuebant? vim videlicet, *evidently violence,* Cic.; b, *ironically, forsooth, of course, to be sure;* homo videlicet timidus et permodestus (of Catiline), Cic. **II.** Transf., *namely;* venisse tempus iis qui in timore fuissent, conjuratos videlicet dicebat, ulciscendi se, Cic.

vĭdēn' = videsne? v. video.

vĭdĕo, vĭdi, vīsum, 2. (root VID, Gr. ΙΔ, ΕΙΔ, εἶδον), *to see.* **I. A.** *to have the power of seeing, to be able to see;* a, absol., quam longe videmus? Cic.; b, with acc., at ille nescio qui mille et octoginta stadia quod abesset videbat, Cic. **B.** *to see* = *to have the eyes open, to be awake,* Verg. **II. A.** *to see, perceive something.* **AA.** Lit. and transf., 1, lit., a, Pompejanum non cerno, Cic.; with acc. and infin., quum suos interfici viderent, Caes.; b, = *to live to see;* utinam eum diem videam, quum, etc., Cic.; 2, transf., *to perceive with the senses;* mugire videbis sub pedibus terram, Verg. **BB.** Fig., of the mind, 1, *to perceive, notice, observe;* aliquem or aliquid in somnis, Cic.; quem virum P. Crassum vidimus, Cic.; 2, in pass., as εἴδομαι, *to have the appearance, seem, appear, be thought;* a, (α) with nom., ut imbelles timidique videamur, Cic.; (β) with infin., ut beate vixisse videar, Cic.; (γ) with nom. and infin., ut exstinctae potius amicitiae quam oppressae esse videantur, Cic.; with acc. and infin., *it appears;* non mihi videtur, ad beate vivendum satis posse virtutem, Cic.; b, of cautious expressions in official statements instead of decided utterances, majores nostri voluerunt, quae jurati judices cognovissent, ea non ut esse facta, set ut videri pronun-

tiarent, Cic.; c, videtur (alicui), *it seems good, it is the opinion of;* eam quoque, si videtur, correctionem explicabo, Cic. **B.** *to look at, to look upon, behold.* **AA.** Lit., a, *aliquem videre* non posse, Cic.; b, *to see* = *to find out and speak to;* Othonem vide, Cic.; c, *to look after with care, to provide for;* alicui prandium, Cic.; d, *to look to as a model,* Cic. **BB.** Fig., a, *to reflect upon, consider;* videas et considres quid agas, Cic.; b, *to trouble oneself about, see to;* viderunt ista officia viri boni, Cic.; foll. by ut or ne and the subj., videant consules ne quid respublica detrimenti capiat, Cic.; c, *to have in view, to aim at;* majus quiddam, Cic.; videt aliud, *he has other views,* Cic.

vĭdŭertas -ātis, f. (viduus), *failure of crops,* Cato.

vĭdŭĭtas -ātis, f. (viduus), *want.* **I.** Gen., omnium copiarum, Plaut. **II.** *widowhood,* Cic.

vĭdŭlus -i, m. (vieo), *a wicker trunk covered with leather,* Plaut.

vĭdŭo, 1. (viduus), *to deprive of.* **I.** Gen., urbem civibus, Verg.; arva numquam viduata pruinis, Verg. **II.** Esp., partic., **vĭdŭāta** -ae, f. *widowed,* Tac.

vĭdŭus -a -um (root VID. seen in divido), *separated from something.* **I.** Gen., *deprived of, bereaved of, destitute of;* with genit. or abl. or a with abl., pectus viduum amoris, Ov.; lacus vidui a lumine Phoebi, Verg. **II.** Esp., 1, *deprived of a husband, widowed;* domus, Ov.; so of an unmarried woman, se rectius viduam (*unmarried*) et illum caelibem futurum fuisse, Liv.; hence, mulier vidua and subst., **vĭdŭa** -ae, f. *a widow,* Cic.; hence, transf., a, of animals, Plin.; b, of trees, *to which no vine is trained,* arbor, Hor.; 2, *deprived of a lover;* puella, Ov.

Vĭenna -ae, f. *a town in Gallia Narbonensis, on the Rhone, now Vienne.* Hence, **Vĭennensis** -e, *of Vienne.*

vĭēo -ētum, 2. *to bind, weave together,* Varr.

vĭētus -a -um (vieo), *shrivelled, shrunken, withered;* cor, Cic.

vĭgĕo, 2. *to be vigorous, thrive, flourish, to be active.* **I.** Lit., quod viget, caeleste est, Cic., animus in rerum cognitione viget, Cic.; viget memoria, Cic. **II.** Transf., *to flourish, to be prosperous, to be in high repute or great power, to be at the height;* vigent studia, Cic.; quem (Philonem) in Academia maxime vigere audio, Cic.

vĭgesco (inchoat. of vigeo), 3. *to become vigorous, to begin to flourish or thrive.* Lucr.

vĭgesĭmus = vicesimus (q.v.).

vĭgĭl -ilis, abl. -ili, genit. plur. -um, *wakeful, watchful.* **I.** Lit., canes, Hor.; ales, *the cock,* Ov.; subst., *a watchman,* Liv.; plur., vigiles fanique custodes, Cic. **II.** Transf., vigiles oculi, Verg.; ignis, *ever-burning,* Verg., Ov.

vĭgĭlans -antis, p. adj. (from vigilo), *watchful, vigilant;* oculi, Verg.; consul, Cic.; ut nemo vigilantior ad judicium venisse videatur, Cic.

vĭgĭlantĕr, adv. (vigilans), *wakefully, vigilantly;* se tueri, Cic.; enitar vigilantius, Cic.; vehementius vigilantissimeque vexatus, Cic.

vĭgĭlantĭa -ae, f. (vigilo), *watchfulness, vigilance, wakefulness,* Cic.

vĭgĭlax -ācis (vigilo), *watchful, wakeful;* curae, *disturbing,* Ov.

vĭgĭlĭa -ae, f. (vigil). **I.** Gen., *wakefulness, sleeplessness,* also = *night spent in watching;* Demosthenis vigiliae, Cic. **II.** Esp., a *watching for the security of a place,* esp., *for a city or camp, watch, guard.* **A.** 1, lit., vigil as agere ad aedes

sacras, Cic.; vestra tecta custodiis vigiliisque defendite, Cic.; **2**, meton., **a**, *a watch, one of the four divisions into which the Romans divided the night;* prima vigilia, Liv.; **b**, *the soldiers keeping watch, sentinels;* si excubiae, si vigiliae, si delecta juventus, Cic. **B.** Fig., *watchfulness, vigilance, care;* ut vacuum metu populum Romanum nostrā vigiliā et prospicientiā redderemus, Cic.

vĭgĭlĭārĭum -ĭi, n. (vigilia), *a watch-house,* Sen.

vĭgĭlo, 1. (vigil). **I.** Intransit., *to be awake, keep awake, watch.* **A.** 1, lit., ad multam noctem, Cic.; **2**, transf., vigilantes curae, Cic.; lumina vigilantia, *on a lighthouse,* Ov. **B.** Fig., *to be vigilant, watchful, careful;* vigilabo pro vobis, Cic. **II.** Transit., 1, *to watch through, pass in watching;* vigilata nox, Ov.; **2**, *to care for by watching, provide for;* quae vigilanda viris, Verg.

vĭginti, num. (connected with εἴκοσι), *twenty,* Cic.

vĭgintĭvĭrātus -ūs, m. (vigintiviri), *the office of the vigintiviri;* **a**, for the division of the public land, Cic.; **b**, of an inferior civil court, Tac.

vĭgintĭvĭri -ōrum, m. *a commission of twenty members, appointed by Caesar for the division of lands in Campania,* Cic.

vĭgor -ōris, m. (vigeo), *vigour, force, energy;* aetatis, Liv.; animi, Liv.

vīla = villa (q.v.).

vīlĭcus = villicus (q.v.).

vīlĭpendo, 3. (vilis and pendo), *to think meanly of, hold cheap,* Plaut.

vīlis -e, *cheap, low-priced.* **I.** Lit., servulus, Cic.; frumentum vilius, Cic.; res vilissimae, Cic. **II.** Transf., **a**, *worthless, common, of little value;* honor vilior fuisset, Cic.; **b**, *found in quantities, abundant, common;* phaselus, Verg.

vīlĭtas -ātis, f. (vilis), *cheapness, low price.* **I.** Lit., annonae, Cic.; annus est in vilitate, *it is a cheap year,* Cic.; num in vilitate nummum dedit, *at the lowest price,* Cic. **II.** Transf., *trifling value, worthlessness, meanness,* Plin.

vīlĭtĕr, adv. (vilis), *cheaply,* Plaut.

villa -ae, f. (perhaps connected with vicus), *a country-house, an estate, country seat, farm.* **I.** Gen., qui ager neque villam habuit neque ex ulla parte fuit cultus, Cic. **II.** Esp., Villa Publica, *a public building at Rome in the Campus Martius, used by the magistrates when they held the census or the levy for the army, and by foreign ambassadors,* Liv.

villāris -e (villa), *of or relating to a country-house,* Plin.

villātĭcus -a -um (villa), *of or relating to a country-house,* Varr.

villĭca, v. villicus.

villĭco, 1. (villicus), *to manage an estate;* ut quasi dispensare rempublicam et in ea quodam modo villicare possit, Cic.

villĭcus -a -um (villa), *of or belonging to a country-seat.* Subst., **A. villĭcus** -i, m. *a bailiff, steward, overseer of an estate,* Cic. **B. villĭca** -ae, f. *a bailiff's wife,* Cat.

villōsus -a -um (villus), *shaggy, rough-haired, hairy;* leo, Verg., Ov.

villŭla -ae, f. (dim. of villa), *a small country-house, little farm,* Cic.

villum -i, n. (dim. of vinum, for vinulum), *a little drop of wine,* Ter.

villus -i, m. (connected with pilus), *shaggy hair;* animantium aliae villis vestitae, Cic.

vīmen -ĭnis, n. (vieo), *an osier, withe, twig;* 1, lit., scuta ex cortice facta aut viminibus intextis, Caes.; **2**, meton. = *a basket or vessel made of twigs,* etc.; curvum, *a bee-hive,* Ov.

vīmentum = vimen (q.v.).

vīmĭnālis -e (vimen), *of or relating to osiers.* **I.** Gen., Plin. **II.** Esp., as a proper name, Viminalis collis, *one of the hills of Rome, so called from an osier plantation there, where Jupiter Viminius was worshipped.*

vīmĭnētum -i, n. (vimen), *an osier-bed,* Varr.

vīmĭnĕus -a -um (vimen), *made of osiers, wicker;* tegumenta, Caes.

Vīmĭnĭus, v. viminalis.

vīn' = visne, v. 1. volo.

vīnācĕus -a -um (vinum), *belonging to wine.* Subst., **vīnācĕus** -i, m. *a grape-stone.*

vīnālĭa -ium, n. (vinum), *the wine festival, held twice a year on the 22nd of April and the 19th of August,* Ov.

vīnārĭus -a -um (vinum), *of or relating to wine.* **I.** Adj., vas, *a wine-cask,* Cic.; crimen, *relating to the duties on wine,* Cic. **II.** Subst., **A. vīnārĭus** -ĭi, m. *a vintner.* **B. vīnārĭum** -ĭi, n. *a wine-jar, wine-flask,* Plaut.

vincapervinca -ae, f. *a plant, periwinkle,* Plin.

vincĭbĭlis -e (vinco), *that can be easily gained;* causa, Ter.

vincĭo, vinxi, vinctum, 4. **I.** *to bind, to tie round;* 1, lit., **a**, suras cothurno alte, Verg.; tempora floribus, Hor.; boves vincti cornua vittis, Ov.; **b**, esp., *to bind, fetter;* manus lace, Liv.; aliquem trinis catenis, Caes.; **2**, fig., *to fetter;* **a**, *to bind, pledge;* eius religioni te vinctum astrictumque dedamus, Cic.; **b**, *to limit, confine, restrain;* si turpissime se illa pars animi geret, vinciatur, Cic. **II.** Transf., **A.** *to bind, confine;* membra orationis numeris, Cic. **B.** *to strengthen, protect;* oppida praesidiis, Cic. **C.** *to embrace closely,* Prop. **D.** *to fetter by enchantments;* linguas et ora, Ov.

vinco, vīci, victum, 3. (perhaps connected with per-vicax), *to conquer, overcome, defeat, subdue, vanquish.* **I. A.** Lit., **a**, milit. t. t., jus esse belli ut qui vicissent iis quos vicissent quemadmodum vellent imperarent, Caes.; Carthaginienses, Cic.; **b**, in a contest of skill, neque vincere certo, Verg.; **c**, in any kind of contention; (α) in play, Quint.; (β) in law, judicio (of the prosecutor), Cic.; judicium (of the accused), Cic.; (γ) at an auction, *to out-bid;* Othonem, Cic.; (δ) in debate, vicit ea pars senatus, etc., Sall. **B.** Transf., *to master, to get the mastery over;* **a**, non viribus ullis vincere posse ramum, Verg.; victus somno, Liv.; vincere noctem flammis (of lights), Verg.; multa saecula durando, *to last,* Verg.; **b**, of a place, aëra summum arboris jactu vincere, *to fly over,* Verg. **II.** Fig., **A.** *to master, control;* **a**, vincit ipsa rerum publicarum natura saepe rationem, Cic.; **b**, *to overcome by working on one's feelings, will,* etc.; vinci a voluptate, Cic.; victus animi respexit, Verg. **B.** 1, *to pass beyond, surpass;* opinionem vicit omnium, Cic.; **2**, *to prove victoriously;* vinco deinde bonum virum fuisse Oppianicum, hominem integrum, etc., Cic.; **3**, in colloquial language, **a**, vincimus, vicimus, *we have won, we have attained our object;* cui si esse in urbe tuto licebit, vicimus, Cic.; **b**, vicisti, *you are right;* viceris, *you shall have your way;* vincite, vincerent, *have your way, let them have their way;* vincite, si ita vultis, Caes.

vinctūra -ae, f. (vincio), *a bandage,* Varr.

vinctus -ū, m. (vincio), *a binding,* Varr.

vincŭlum (vinclum) -i, n. (vincio), *a band, cord, noose.* **I.** Lit., **A.** Gen., corpora constricta vinculis, Cic.; aptare vincula collo, Ov. **B.** Esp., vincula, *bonds, fetters of a prisoner*, and meton., *imprisonment;* conjicere aliquem in vincula, Caes.; rumpere alicuius vincula, Cic.; esse in vinculis et catenis, Liv. **II.** Transf., **A.** *a bond, fetter, chain;* a, concr., ex corporum vinculis tanquam e carcere evolaverunt, Cic.; b, abstr., vinculum ingens immodicae cupiditatis injectum est, Liv. **B.** *a band, bond;* a, concr., mollit pennarum vincula, ceras, Ov.; b, abstr., numerorum, Cic.; conjunctionis, Cic.; fidei, Liv.; vinclis propinquitatis conjunctus, Cic.; vincula judiciorum, Cic.

Vindĕlĭcī -ōrum, m. *a German people north of Rhaetia, south of the Danube, with a capital Augusta Vindelicorum, now Augsburg.*

vindēmĭa -ae, f. (vinum and demo), *the vintage.* **I. A.** Lit., Plin. **B.** Meton., *grapes, wine,* Verg. **II.** Transf., *harvest, ingathering;* olearum, Plin.

vindēmĭātor -ōris, m.(vindemio),*a vintager.* **I.** Lit., Hor. **II.** Transf., *a star in the constellation Virgo,* Ov.

vindēmĭo, 1. (vindemia), *to gather the vintage,* Plin.

vindēmĭŏla -ae, f. (dim. of vindemia), *a little vintage;* meton., omnes meas vindemiolas reservo, *income,* Cic.

vindex -ĭcis, c. (vindico). **I.** *one who lays claim to or protects, a surety, guarantee, protector, defender, deliverer, vindicator;* a, of a surety, Cic.; b, *a protector;* aeris alieni, *a protector of creditors,* Cic.; injuriae, *against wrong,* Liv. **II.** *an avenger, revenger, punisher;* conjurationis, Cic.

vindĭcātĭo -ōnis, f. (vindico), *a defending, protecting, avenging,* Cic.

vindĭcĭae -ārum, f. (vindico), *a making a legal claim to a thing in presence of the praetor;* injustis vindiciis ac sacramentis petere aliquid, Cic.; ni Appius vindicias ab libertate in servitutem dederit, *has adjudged a free person to be a slave,* Liv.

vindĭco, 1. (vim dico, *to threaten force*). **I.** *to make a legal claim for something, to claim.* **A.** Lit., sponsam in libertatem, Liv. **B.** Transf., 1, *to lay claim to, to claim, arrogate, assume, appropriate;* Chii suum (Homerum) aliquam sibi quisque vindicat, Cic.; 2, a, *to set free, liberate, deliver;* vindicare rem populi in libertatem, Cic.; te ab eo vindico et libero, Cic.; b, *to protect, preserve;* libertatem, Caes.; aliquem a verberibus, Cic. **II.** *to avenge, punish, take vengeance on.* **A.** Lit., acerrime maleficia, Cic.; in cives militesque nostros, Cic. **B.** Transf., Gracchi conatus perditos, Cic.

vindicta -ae, f. (vindico). **I.** *the rod with which the praetor touched the slave who was to be manumitted, a manumission staff;* si neque censu neque vindictā neque testamento liber factus est, Cic. **II.** Meton., **A.** *deliverance;* vindicta invisae huius vitae, Liv. **B.** *vengeance, punishment;* legis severae, Ov.

vīnĕa, v. vineus.

vīnĕātĭcus -a -um (vinea), *belonging to or relating to vines,* Cato.

vīnētum -i, n. (vinum), *a vineyard,* Cic.

vīnĕus -a -um (vinum), *of or belonging to wine.* Subst., **vīnĕa** -ae, f. **A.** *a vineyard,* Cic. **B.** Milit. t. t., *a shed built* (like an arbour) *for sheltering besiegers, a mantlet, penthouse,* Caes.

vīnĭtor -ōris, m. (vinum), *a vinedresser,* Cic.

vinnŭlus -a -um, *sweet, charming, pleasant,* Plaut.

vīnŏlentĭa -ae, f. (vinolentus), *wine-drinking, intoxication,* Cic.

vīnŏlentus -a -um (vinum). **I.** Gen., *mixed with wine;* medicamina, Cic. **II.** Esp., of persons, *drunk with wine, intoxicated,* Cic.; subst., vinolenti = *drunkards,* Cic.

vīnōsus -a -um (vinum), *full of wine, drinking much wine, wine-bibbing;* senex, Anacreon, Ov.; vinosior aetas, Ov.

vīnŭlent . . . v. vinolent.

vīnum -i, n. (connected with οἶνος), *wine.* **I. A.** Lit., leve, Cic.; mutatum, *sour,* Cic.; vini plenus, Cic.; obruere se vino, Cic.; plur., vina = *kinds of wine,* Cic. **B.** Meton., a, *the grape;* b, *wine = wine-drinking;* vino lustrisque confectus, Cic.; in vino ridere, Cic. **II.** Transf. *wine made from fruit,* Plin.

vĭŏcūrus -i, m. (via and curo), *an overseer of roads,* Varr.

vĭŏla -ae, f. (ἴον). **I.** *a violet;* pallens,Verg.; collect., an tu me in viola putabas aut in rosa dicere? *on beds of violets or roses?* Cic. **II.** Meton., *the colour of the violet, violet;* tinctus violā pallor amantium, Hor

vĭŏlābĭlis -e (violo), *that may or can be injured;* cor, Ov.; numen, Verg.

vĭŏlācĕus -a -um (viola), *violet-coloured,* Nep.

vĭŏlārĭum -ĭi, n. (viola), *a bed of violets,* Verg.

vĭŏlārĭus -ĭi, m. (viola), *one who dyes violet,* Plaut.

vĭŏlātĭo -ōnis, f. (violo), *an injury, violation, profanation;* templi, Liv.

vĭŏlātor -ōris, m. (violo), *an injurer, violator, profaner;* templi, Ov.; gentium juris, Liv.

vĭŏlens -entis (vis), *vehement,violent, furious,* Aufidus, Hor.

vĭŏlentĕr, adv. (violens), *violently, impetuously, vehemently;* aliquem accusare, Liv.

vĭŏlentĭa -ae, f. (violentus), *violence, vehemence, impetuosity;* hominis, Cic.; fortunae, Sall.

vĭŏlentus -a -um (vis), *violent, vehement, furious, impetuous;* ingenium, Cic.; ira, Ov.; violentior eurus, Verg.; violentissimae tempestates, Cic.

vĭŏlo, 1. (vis), *to treat with violence, violate, injure;* a, urbem, *to plunder,* Liv.; fines, *to lay waste,* Cic.; ebur sanguineo ostro, *to dye blood-red,* Verg.; b, morally, *to profane, dishonour;* loca religiosa, Cic.; jus, Cic.; amicitiam, Cic.

vīpĕra -ae, f. (perhaps for vivipara, from vivus and pario, *bearing the young alive*). **I.** *a viper,* Plin.; prov., in sinu atque deliciis viperam illam venenatam et pestiferam habere, *to nourish a snake in one's bosom,* Cic.; as a word of abuse, viper, Juv. **II.** Transf., in general, *a snake, serpent, adder,* Verg.

vīpĕrĕus -a -um (vipera). **I.** *of a viper or a snake;* dentes, Ov.; anima, *poisonous breath,* Verg. **II.** *having snakes;* monstrum, *the snaky-haired Medusa head,* Ov.; canis, *Cerberus,* Ov.; sorores, *the Furies, with snakes on their heads,* Ov.

vīpĕrīnus -a -um (vipera), *of or relating to a viper or snake;* sanguis, Hor.

vīpĭo -ōnis, m. *a kind of small crane,* Plin.

vĭr, vĭri, m. *a man, male person.* **I.** Gen., de viro factus femina, Ov. **II.** Esp., **A.** *a full-grown man, a man of mature age* (opp. puer), Ov. **B.** *a husband;* in viro suo Socrate, Cic.; transf., of animals, vir gregis ipse caper, Verg. **C.** Emphat., *a man of character, courage, spirit;* tulit dolorem

ut vir, Cic. **D.** Milit. t. t.= *soldier*, gen. plur., *soldiers*, or opp. to cavalry = *foot-soldiers*; equites virique, Liv. **E.** Used for is or ille, auctoritas viri moverat, Liv. **F.** *a single man, an individual*; in such a phrase as vir virum legit, *each singles out his opponent*, Verg. **G.** Plur., viri, poet. transf.= homines, *men, mortals*, as opp. to gods. **H.** Meton., *virility*, Cat. (genit. plur., often virûm).

vǐrāgo -ǐnis, f. (virgo), *a man-like woman, female warrior, heroine*; of Pallas, bello metu-ĕnda virago, Ov.; Juturna virago, Verg.

Virbǐus -ǐi, m. (said to be from vir and bis), *the name of Hippolytus after he was restored to life*; also *of his son*, Verg.

vǐrectum (vǐrētum) -i, n. (* virex from vireo), *greensward, turf*; plur., virecta nemorum, *glades*, Verg.

vǐrens, p. adj. (from vireo). **I.** *green*; agellus, Hor. **II.** Fig., *blooming, youthful*; puella, Hor.

1. **vǐrěo**, 2. *to be green*. **I.** Lit., arbores et vita virent, Cic. **II.** Fig., *to be blooming, vigorous, healthy, fresh, youthful*; virebat integris sensibus, Liv.

2. **vǐrěo** -ōnis, m. *a kind of bird*, perhaps *the green-finch*, Plin.

vǐres -ǐum, f., v. vis.

vǐresco, 3. (inchoat. of vireo), *to grow green, become green*; injussa virescunt gramina, Verg.

vǐrētum = virectum (q.v.).

virga -ae, f. (vireo). **I.** *a thin green twig, bough*; turea, Verg.; viscata, *a limed twig*, Ov. **II.** Meton., **A.** 1, *a slip for planting*, Ov.; 2, *a rod for inflicting stripes*, Plaut.; esp., plur., virgae, *the rods of which the lictors' fasces were formed*; aliquem virgis caedere, Cic.; sing. collect., *for the fasces*, Ov.; 3, *a broom*, Ov.; 4, *a magic wand*; esp. of Mercury, Ov., Verg. **B.** Of things resembling a rod or twig, 1, virgae, *the stalks of the flax plant*, Plin.; 2, *a streak, stripe of colour on clothes*; purpureis tingit sua corpora virgis, Ov.

virgātor -ōris, m. (virga), *one who beats with rods*, Plaut.

virgātus -a -um (virga), 1, *made of twigs or osiers*, Cat.; 2, *striped*; sagula, Verg.

virgētum -i, n. (virga), *an osier-bed, thicket of brushwood*, Cic.

virgěus -a -um (virga), *made of twigs or rods*; flamma, *of burning twigs*, Verg.

virgǐdēmǐa -ae, f. (formed in jest from analogy with vindemia), *a rod-harvest*, i.e., *a good beating*, Plaut.

Virgǐlǐus = Vergilius (q.v.).

virgǐnālis -e (virgo), *of or belonging to a virgin, maidenly*; habitus, vestitus, Cic.

virgǐnārǐus = virginalis (q.v.).

virgǐněus -a -um (virgo), *of or belonging to a virgin, maidenly*; favilla, *ashes of a dead maiden*, Ov.; rubor, Verg.; aqua or liquor, *the stream Virgo*, v. Virgo, Ov.

virgǐnǐtas -ātis, f. (virgo), *virginity*, Cic.

Virgǐnǐus = Verginius (q.v.).

virgo -ǐnis, f. (root VARG, whence ὀργή). **I.** *a maiden, virgin*; 1, lit., Cic.; Saturnia, *Vesta*, Ov.; Phoebea, *the laurel-tree into which Daphne was turned*, Ov.; virgo = *Astraea*, Verg.; dea, Diana, Ov.; virginis aequor, *the Hellespont*, Ov.; virgo vestalis or simply virgo, Cic.; 2, transf., of animals, Plin.; 3, meton., a, *the constellation Virgo*, Cic. poet.; b, Aqua Virgo, or simply Virgo, *a stream of water brought to Rome in an aqueduct by M. Agrippa, the source of which was said to* —

---

have been discovered by a maiden. **II.** *a young woman*; a, *unmarried*, Ov.; b, *married*, *a young wife*, Verg.

virgǔla -ae, f. (dim. of virga). **I.** *a little twig, a little bough*, Nep. **II.** Meton., *a rod, staff*; 1, gen., virgulā stantem circumscribere, Cic.; 2, esp., virga divina, *a magic staff*, Cic.; b, censoria, *a critical mark that the passage marked is not genuine*, Quint.

virgǔlātus -a -um (virgula), *striped*, Plin.

virgultum -i, n. (for virguletum from virgula). **I.** *a thicket, copse, brushwood*; gen. plur., Liv., Caes. **II.** *a slip for planting*, Lucr., Verg.

virguncǔla -ae, f. (dim. of virgo), *a young virgin, little girl*, Sen.

vǐrǐae -ārum, f. (vir), *armlets, bracelets*, Plin.

Vǐrǐāthus (Vǐrǐātus) -i, m. *a brave Lusitanian, who commanded his countrymen in their war against the Romans*.

vǐrǐdārǐum (vǐrǐdǐārǐum) -ǐi, n. (viridis), *a pleasure-garden*; plur., viridaria, Cic.

vǐrǐdǐcātus -a -um (viridis), *made green*, green, Cic. (?)

vǐrǐdis -e (vireo), *green* (in all its shades), grass-green, pea-green, sea-green. **I.** Lit., **A.** Adj., ripa, Cic.; Venafrum, *rich in olive-trees*, Hor.; esp., of the colour of the sea, or of water, or of what is found in it, of the nymphs, etc.; Mincius, Verg.; comae Nereidum, Ov. **B.** Subst., **vǐrǐde** -is, n. 1, *green, the colour green*, Plin.; 2, *a green growth, the green of grass or trees*; esp., of young corn, Liv.; plur., **vǐrǐdǐa** -ǐum, n. *green trees or herbs*, Sen. **II.** Transf., of age, *fresh, young, blooming, vigorous*; juventa, Verg.

vǐrǐdǐtas -ātis, f. (viridis). **I.** *greenness*; pratorum, Cic. **II.** Fig., *the freshness, bloom of youth*; senectus aufert viriditatem, Cic.

vǐrǐdo, 1. (viridis). **I.** Intransit., *to be green*; partic., viridans, green; laurus, Verg. **II.** Transit., *to make green*; hence, viridari, *to become green*, Ov.

Vǐrǐdǒmărus (Vǐrdǒmărus) -i, m. *a Gallic name*; a, *a leader of the Aedui*, Caes.; b, *a commander of the Insubres, killed by M. Claudius Marcellus*, 222 B.C.

vǐrīlis -e (vir), *manly, male, virile*. **I.** In relation to sex; 1, a, stirps, Liv.; secus, *male sex*, Liv.; b, in grammar, *masculine*, Varr.; 2, of age, *adult*; toga, *assumed by the Roman youths in their fifteenth or sixteenth year*, Cic.; 3, in relation to the person, pars virilis, *part, lot, share, duty*; est aliqua pars mea virilis, Cic.; pro virili parte, *to the utmost of one's ability*, Liv., Cic. **II.** *manly, courageous, spirited, vigorous, bold*; animus, Cic.; ingenium, Sall.

vǐrīlǐtas -ātis, f. (virilis), *manly age, manhood*; 1, lit., Tac.; 2, meton., *virility*, Tac.

vǐrīlǐtěr, adv. (virilis), *manfully, courageously, vigorously*; aegrotare, Cic.; facere, Hor.

vǐrǐǒlae -ārum, f. (dim. of viriae), *a small armlet, bracelet*, Plin.

vǐrǐpǒtens -entis (vires and potens), *mighty* (epithet of Jupiter), Plaut.

vǐrītim, adv. (vir). **I.** *man by man, individually*; agros viritim dividere civibus, Cic. **II.** Transf., *singly, separately, especially*; viritim commonefacere beneficii sui, Sall.

Vǐrǒmandǔi (Vērǒmandi) -ōrum, m. *a people in Gallia Belgica, east of the Atrebates, south of the Nervii*.

vǐrōsus -a -um (virus), *stinking, fetid*; castorea, Verg.

virtus -ūtis, f. (vir), *manly excellence.* **I. A.** Gen., 1, lit., *excellence, capacity, worth, virtue;* animi, corporis, Cic.; 2, transf., of animals, inanimate or abstract things, *characteristic excellence, goodness, worth, excellence;* equi, Cic.; herbarum, Ov.; oratoriae virtutes, Cic. **B.** Esp., 1, *moral excellence, virtue;* honesta in virtute ponuntur, Cic.; 2, *valour, bravery, courage,* Cic., Caes., Liv.; rei militaris, Cic.; bellandi, Cic.; plur., virtutes, *deeds of bravery,* Tac.; 3, *courage, resolution in difficulties;* nisi virtute et animo restitissem, Cic.

vīrus -i, n. **I.** *a slimy liquid, slime,* Verg. **II. A.** *poison;* of snakes, Lucr., Verg.; fig., aliquis apud quem evomat virus acerbitatis suae, Cic. **B.** *a harsh, bitter taste;* tetrum, of salt water, Lucr.

vīs (genit. sing., vis rare), acc. vim, abl. vi, plur., **vīres** -ium, f. *force, power, strength.* **I. A.** Lit., 1, a, sing., celeritas et vis equorum, Cic.; fluminis, Caes.; b, plur., vires, usually applied to physical strength, vires nervique, sanguis viresque, Cic.; 2, esp., *hostile force, violence;* cum vi vis allata defenditur, Cic.; alicui vim afferre, Cic.; per vim, *by force,* Caes. **B.** Meton., 1, *a large number* or *quantity;* magna vis auri argentique, Cic.; 2, plur., vires, *troops, forces;* satis virium ad certamen, Liv. **II.** Transf., 1, gen., *intellectual and moral strength, might, power, influence;* vis illa divina et virtus orationis, Cic.; 2, esp., *force, nature, meaning, essence;* a, in quo est omnis vis amicitiae, Cic.; b, esp., *the meaning of a word;* verbi, nominis, Cic.

viscātus -a -um (viscum), *smeared with birdlime;* virga, Ov.

viscĕra, v. viscus.

viscĕrātĭo -ōnis, f. (viscera), *a public distribution of meat to the people,* Cic.

visco, 1. (viscum), *to make sticky,* Juv.

viscum -i, n. (ἰξός). **I.** *mistletoe,* Verg. **II.** Meton., *bird-lime,* Cic.

viscus -ĕris, n. usually plur. **viscĕra** -um, n. *the inside of the body, entrails, viscera.* **I. A.** Lit., haerentia viscere tela, Ov. **B.** Transf., *the flesh;* e visceribus sanguis exeat, Cic. **II.** Meton., plur., a, of persons, *flesh and blood, one's own flesh = one's own child* or *children;* diripiunt avidae viscera nostra ferae, Ov.; b, of things, (a) *the inmost part of anything;* viscera montis, Verg.; reipublicae, Cic.; (β) *heartblood = wealth, means;* aerarii, Cic.

vīsendus -a -um, p. adj. (from viso), *worthy to be seen;* ornatus, Cic.; subst., **visenda** -ōrum, n. *things worth seeing,* Liv.

vīsĭo -ōnis, f. (video), *a seeing, view.* **I.** Lit., eamque esse dei visionem, ut similitudine cernatur, Cic. **II.** Meton., a, *an appearance;* adventicia, Cic.; b, *a notion, idea;* doloris, Cic.; veri et falsi, Cic.

vīsĭto, 1. (intens. of viso). **I.** *to see often,* Plaut. **II.** *to visit;* aliquem, Cic.

vīso -si -sum, 3. (intens of video), *to look at carefully, behold attentively, contemplate.* **I.** Lit., agros, Liv.; visendi causâ venire, Cic. **II.** Transf., **A.** Gen., *to come to see, go to see, look to, see after;* aedem Minervae, Plaut.; si domi est, Ter. **B.** Esp., a, *to visit, call upon;* esp., a sick person, ut viderem te et viserem, Cic.; b, *to visit a place;* Thespias, Cic.; domum alicuius, Cic.

vĭsulla -ae, f. *a kind of vine,* Plin.

vīsum -i, n. (video), *that which is seen, an appearance, vision.* **I.** Gen., Prop. **II.** Esp., **A.** *an appearance in a dream, a dream;* visa somniorum, Cic. **B.** As translation of Gr.

φαντασία of the Stoics, *an image of an external object received through the senses,* Cic.

Vīsurgis -is, m. *a river in North Germany,* the Weser.

vīsus -ūs, m. (video). **I.** *a seeing, sight, vision, look;* visu nocere, Cic.; obire omnia visu, Verg.; plur., visus effugiet tuos, Ov. **II.** Meton., *a sight, appearance;* hoc visu laetus, Liv.; of abstractions, visum habere quendam insignem et illustrem, Cic.

vīta -ae, f. (vivo), *life.* **I.** a, lit., in vita esse, *to live,* Cic.; vitam amittere, Cic.; vitam profundere pro aliquo, Cic.; vitam miserrimam degere, Cic.; vitam alicui adimere or auferre, Cic.; deûm vitam accipere, Verg.; in vita, *during my whole life,* Cic.; plur., serpit per omnium vitas amicitia, Cic.; b, transf., of trees, etc., *life, duration,* Plin. **II.** Meton., 1, *life, way of living;* rustica, Cic.; 2, *life = biography,* Nep.; 3, *life,* as a term of endearment; mea vita, Cic.; 4, *a soul, shade in the lower world;* tenues sine corpore vitae, Verg.; 5, *men living, the world,* Tib.

vĭtābĭlis -e (vito), *that may* or *ought to be shunned,* Ov.

vĭtābundus -a -um (vito), *trying to avoid, avoiding, shunning;* vitabundus erumpit, Sall.; with acc., vitabundus castra hostium, Liv.

vĭtālis -e (vita), *of* or *relating to life, vital,* Cic.; viae, *the windpipe,* Ov.; subst., **Ivtālĭa** -ium, n. *vital parts,* Plin.

vĭtālĭtas -ātis, f. (vitalis), *life, vitality,* Plin.

vĭtālĭtĕr, adv. (vitalis), *vitally,* Lucr.

vĭtātĭo -ōnis, f. (vito), *an avoiding, shunning;* oculorum, lucis, urbis, fori, Cic.; doloris, Cic.

Vĭtellĭa -ae, f. *a town of the Aequi in Latium,* now *Civitella.*

Vĭtellĭus -Ii, m., Aulus, *the Roman emperor who succeeded Otho, notorious for his gluttony and idleness.* Hence, **A.** **Vĭtellĭus** -a -um, *belonging to Vitellius.* **B.** **Vĭtellĭānus** -a -um, *Vitellian.*

vĭtellus -i, m. (dim. of vitulus). **I.** *a little calf,* as a term of endearment, Plaut. **II.** *the yolk of an egg,* Cic.

vītĕus -a -um (vitis), *of* or *relating to a vine;* pocula, vinea, Verg.

vītĭārĭum -ĭi, n. (vitis), *a nursery of young vines,* Var.

vĭtĭātĭo -ōnis, f. (vitio), *a defiling, ravishing,* Sen.

vĭtĭātor -ōris, m. (vitio), *a violator, ravisher,* Sen.

vītĭcŭla -ae, f. (dim. of vitis), *a little vine,* Cic.

vītĭfer -fĕra -fĕrum (vitis and fero), *vine-bearing,* Plin.

vītĭgĕnus -a -um (vitis and gigno), *produced from the vine;* liquor, Lucr.

vītĭgĭnĕus -a -um (vitis), *of* or *relating to the vine,* Plin.

vītīlĭgo -ĭnis, f. (vitium), *a kind of cutaneous eruption,* Plin.

vītĭlis -e (vieo), *plaited, intertwined,* Plin. Subst., **vītĭlia** -ium, n. *wicker-work,* Plin.

vĭtĭo, 1. (vitium), *to injure, damage, corrupt, spoil, mar, vitiate.* **I.** Lit., a, vitiatus aper, high, Hor.; omnem salibus amaris, Ov.; b, esp., *to defile, debauch a maiden,* Ter. **II.** Transf., **A.** Gen., *to forge, falsify;* senatus consulta, Liv.; comitiorum et contionum significationes, Cic. **B.** Esp. religious t.t., vitiare diem, *to declare a day unfit for the holding of the census,* Cic.

vĭtĭōsē, adv. (vitiosus), *faulty, defective.* **I.** Lit., vitiose se habere, Cic. **II.** Transf., **A.** *perversely, wrongly;* illud vero idem Caecilius vitiosius, Cic. **B.** Esp., *against the auguries;* ferre leges, Cic.

vĭtĭōsĭtas -ātis, f. (vitiosus), *viciousness, wickedness,* Cic.

vĭtĭōsus -a -um (vitium), *faulty, defective, corrupt, bad.* **I.** Lit., Varr.; in fig., vitiosas partes (*unsound limbs*) reipublicae exsecare, sanare, Cic. **II.** Transf., **A.** *defective, faulty, wrong;* suffragium, Cic.; lex, Cic.; vitiosissimus orator, Cic. **B.** Esp., **1,** *defective* = against the auguries, Cic.; consul, dictator, *elected informally,* Cic., Liv.; **2,** *morally corrupt, wicked;* non sunt vitiosiores, quam plerique qui, etc., Cic.; vitiosa et flagitiosa vita, Cic.

vītis -is, f. **I.** *a vine;* **1,** lit., Cic.; **2,** meton., *the centurion's staff, made of a vine-branch,* Tac.; meton., *the post of centurion,* Juv. **II.** Transf., vitis alba, *a plant, also called* ampeloleuce, Ov.

vītĭsător -ōris, m. (vitis and sator), *one who plants vines,* Verg.

vĭtĭum -ĭi, n. *a fault, defect, blemish, imperfection.* **I.** Lit., **a,** corporis, Cic.; si nihil est in parietibus aut in tecto vitii, Cic.; **b,** *dross,* in metal; ignis vitium metallis excoquit, Ov. **II.** Transf., **A.** Gen., *a fault, imperfection, defect;* adversum vitium castrorum, *defective position,* Cic.; vitia in dicente acutius quam recta videre, Cic.; omnia fere vitia vitare, Cic. **B.** Esp., **1,** religious t.t., *a defect in the auguries;* tabernaculum vitio(*against the auguries*) captum, Cic.; **2, a,** *a moral fault, crime, vice;* vitium fugere, Hor.; nullum ob totius vitae non dicam vitium, sed erratum, Cic.; in vitio esse, *to deserve blame,* Cic.; or of persons, *to be to blame,* Cic.; **b,** *a defiling, debauching a woman,* Plaut.

vīto, 1. *to avoid, shun.* **I.** Lit., tela, Caes.; hastas, Ov.; aspectum or oculos hominum, Cic. **II.** Fig., **A. a,** with acc., stultitiam, Cic.; suspiciones, Caes.; **b,** with ne and the subj., vitandum est oratori utrumque, ne aut scurrilis jocus ait mimicus, Cic.; **c,** with the infin., tangere vitet scripta, Hor. **B.** *to escape;* casum Cic.; fugâ mortem, Caes.

vitrĕus -a -um (vitrum), *made of glass.* **I.** Lit., hostis, *a glass draughtsman,* Ov. **B.** Meton., *like glass, glassy, transparent, glittering;* unda, Verg.; ros, Ov.; Circe, Hor. **II.** Fig., fama, *glittering,* Hor.

vĭtrīcus -i, m. *a stepfather,* Cic.

vitrum -i, n. **I.** *glass;* merces in chartis et linteis et vitro delatae, Cic. **II.** *woad, a plant producing a blue dye,* Caes.

Vĭtrūvĭus -ĭi, m., M. Vitruvius Pollio, of Verona, *whose work,* De Architectura Libri X, *composed probably about* 14 B.C., *we still possess.*

vitta -ae, f. *a ribbon, band, fillet;* **1,** as a binding for the head; **a,** for sacrificial victims, Verg.; **b,** of priests and priestesses, Verg.; **c,** of free-born women, Ov.; **2,** *a band round the altar,* Verg.; **3,** *the fillets round the branches carried by supplicants,* Verg.

vittātus -a -um (vitta), *decorated with a fillet;* capilli, Ov.

vĭtŭla -ae, f. (vitulus), *a calf, heifer,* Verg.

vĭtŭlīnus -a -um (vitulus), *of or relating to a calf;* caruncula, Cic.; assum, *roast veal,* Cic. Subst., **vĭtŭlīna** -ae, f. *veal,* Plaut.

vĭtŭlor, 1. dep. *to celebrate a festival, be joyful,* Plaut.

vĭtŭlus -i, m. (ἰταλός). **I.** *a bull-calf,* Cic. **II.** Applied to the young of other animals, e.g.,

of a horse, Verg.; vitulus marinus, or *simply* vitulus, *a sea-calf,* Plin.

vĭtŭpĕrābĭlis -e (vitupero), *blamable,* Cic.

vĭtŭpĕrātĭo -ōnis, f. (vitupero), *a blaming, scolding, vituperation;* in vituperationem venire, or adduci, or cadere, or subire vituperationem, Cic.; meton., *that which is blamable, blamable conduct,* Cic.

vĭtŭpĕrātor -ōris, m. (vitupero), *a blamer, vituperator;* mei, Cic.; philosophiae, Cic.

vĭtŭpĕro, 1. (vitium and paro), *to blame, scold, censure, vituperate;* consilium, Cic.; aliquem, Cic.

vīvācĭtas -ātis, f. (vivax), *length of life, longevity,* Plin.

vīvārĭum -ĭi, n. (vivus), *a place where living animals are kept, a park, warren, preserve, a fishpond,* Plin.; fig., excipiant senes, quos in vivaria mittant, *allure by presents,* Hor.

vīvātus -a -um (vivus), *lively, vivid,* Lucr.

vīvax -ācis (vivo). **I. a,** *long-lived;* phoenix, Ov.; **b,** *lasting, enduring;* oliva, Verg. **II. a,** *lively, vigorous;* sulfura, *inflammable,* Ov.; **b,** *brisk, vivacious,* Quint.

viverra -ae, f. *a ferret,* Plin.

vivesco (vivisco), vixi, 3. (vivo). **I.** *to begin to live,* Plin. **II.** *to be lively, vigorous,* Lucr.

vīvĭdus -a -um (vivo). **I.** *showing signs of life, animated;* **a,** lit., gemma, Ov.; **b,** transf., of pictures and statues, *life-like, true to life;* signa, Prop. **II.** *full of life, lively, vigorous;* senectus, Tac.; virtus, Verg.

vīvĭrādix -īcis, f. (vivus and radix), *a cutting which has a root, a layer,* Cic.

vīvisco = vivesco (q.v.).

vīvo, vixi, victum, 3. (βιόω), *to live, be alive.* **I.** Lit., **A.** Gen., **a,** of persons, ad summam senectutem, Cic.; annum, *a year,* Ov.; with cognate acc., vitam tutiorem, Cic.; vivere de lucro, *to owe one's life to the favour of another,* Cic.; si vivo, or si vivam, *if I live* (in threats), Ter.; ita vivam, as true as I live, Cic.; ne vivam, *may I die if,* etc., Cic.; **b,** transf., (*a*) of plants, *to live;* vivit vitis, Cic.; (*β*) of fire, *to burn;* cinis vivet, Ov. **B.** 1, *to live* = *to enjoy life;* vivamus, mea Lesbia, Cat.; quando vivemus, *have leisure,* Cic.; so vive, vivite, in saying good-bye, *farewell,* Hor., Verg.; **2,** *to last, continue;* vivunt scripta, Ov.; eius mihi vivit auctoritas, Cic. **II.** Meton., 1, **a,** *to live on anything;* lacte atque pecore, Caes.; **b,** *to pass one's life, live;* vivere cum timore, Cic.; in litteris, Cic.; in paupertate, Cic.; with double nom., vivo miserrimus, Cic.; **2,** *to live with some one* or *at some place;* **a,** *to live, to find oneself, to stay;* vixit Syracusis, Cic.; **b,** *to live with some one, to live in the company of;* cum aliquo valde familiariter, Cic.

vīvus -a -um (vivo), *alive, living.* **I.** Adj., **A.** Lit., aliquem vivum capere, Liv.; patrem et filium vivos comburere, Cic.; frangetis impetum vivi, *while he is alive,* Cic. **B.** Transf., **1,** *living, belonging to a living person;* vox, Cic.; calor, Ov.; **2,** *seeming to live, true to life, life-like;* vivos ducent de marmore vultus, Verg.; **3,** of plants, *living;* arundo, Ov.; **4,** *living, lasting, natural, lively;* flumen, *running water,* Verg., Liv.; lucerna, *burning,* Hor.; ros, *fresh,* Ov.; sulfur, *natural,* Liv. **II.** Subst., **vivum** -i, n. *that which is alive, the flesh with life and feeling;* calor ad vivum advenieus, Liv.; neque id ad vivum reseco, *cut to the quick,* i.e., *not take it in too literal a sense,* Cic.; de vivo detrahere (resecare), *to take away from the capital,* Cic.

vix, adv. (connected with **vis,** as Gr. μόγις with μόγος, thus orig. *with effort*). **I.** Gen., *with effort, scarcely;* vix teneor quin accurram, Cic. **II.** Esp. a, with quum or (poet.) et, and (poet.) without quum, *scarcely* . . . *when;* vix erat hoc plane imperatum, quum illum spoliatum stipatumque lictoribus videres, Cic.; vix in- opina quies laxaverat artus, et, etc., Verg.; b, without quum or et, vix proram attigerat, rumpit Saturnia funem, Verg.; c, strengthened with dum, gen., vixdum (in one word), *hardly, yet;* vixdum coetu nostro dimisso, Cic.; d, strengthened by tandem, *only just;* vix tandem legi literas, Cic.

vixdum, v. vix, II. c.

vŏcābŭlum -i, n. (voco), *the name, appella- tion of anything.* **I.** Lit., a, res suum nomen et proprium vocabulum non habet, Cic.; b, *a name peculiar to any person or thing;* cui (oppido) nomen inditum e vocabulo ipsius, Tac.; c, grammat. t.t., *a noun substantive,* Varr. **II.** *a pretext,* Tac.

vōcālis -e (vox), *uttering sounds, vocal, re- sounding, singing.* **I.** Adj., carmen, Ov.; Or- pheus, Hor.; ne quem vocalem praeterisse vide- amur, *any one with a good voice,* Cic. **II.** Subst., **vōcālis** -is, f. (sc. littera), *a vowel,* Cic.

vōcālĭtas -ātis, f. (vocalis), *harmony, eu- phony,* Quint.

vŏcāmen -ĭnis, n. (voco), *a name, appellation,* Lucr.

Vŏcātes -ĭum, m. *a people in Aquitanian Gaul,* now *Bazadois.*

vŏcātĭo -ōnis, f. (voco), 1, *a summoning before a court of law,* Varr.; 2, *an invitation to dinner,* Cat.

vŏcātor -ōris, m. (voco), *an inviter,* Plin.

vŏcātus -ūs, m. (voco). **I.** *a calling, sum- moning, invocation;* plur., vocatus mei, Verg. **II.** *an inviting, invitation,* e.g., to a sitting of the senate, Cic.

vōcĭfĕrātĭo -ōnis, f. (vociferor), *a loud shouting, vociferation,* Cic.

vōcĭfĕrātus -ūs, m. = vociferatio (q.v.).

vōcĭfĕro, 1. = vociferor; pass. impers., vociferatum fortiter, Liv.

vōcĭfĕror, 1. dep. (vox and fero), *to cry loudly, shout, vociferate;* palam, Cic.; talia, Verg.; with acc. and infin., quod vociferabare decem milia talentûm Gabinio esse promissa, Cic.; with interrog. sent., vociferari Decius, quo fugerent, Liv.; with de and the abl., de superbia patrum, Liv.

vōcĭfĭco, 1. (vox and facio), *to shout aloud,* Varr.

vōcĭto, 1. (intens. of voco). **I.** *to be accus- tomed to name, to be wont to call;* has Graeci stellas Hyadas vocitare suerunt, Cic. **II.** *to shout loudly,* Tac.

vŏco, 1. (vox), *to call, summon.* **I.** Lit., **A.** Gen., 1, Dumnorigem ad se, Caes.; aliquem in contionem, Cic.; 2, *to call upon, invoke;* deos, Hor. **B.** Esp.,1, *to summon before a court of law;* aliquem in jus, Cic.; 2, *to invite to dinner,* etc.; ad cenam, Cic.; 3, *to call forth, to provoke;* hostem, Verg., Tac.; 4, *to call, name, designate;* aliquid alio nomine, Cic.; patrioque vocat de nomine mensem, Ov. **II.** Transf., *to bring, put, place in any state or condition;* ne me apud milites in invidiam voces, Cic.; ad calculos amicitiam, Cic.; in dubium, *to call in question,* Cic.; aliquem in partem, Cic.

Vŏcontĭi -ōrum, m. *a people in Gallia Nar- bonensis, on the left bank of the Rhone.*

vōcŭla -ae, f. (dim. of vox). **I.** *a low, weak*

voice, Cic. **II.** Transf., 1, *a low tone in singing* or *speaking;* falsae voculae, Cic.; 2, contemptu- ously, *a little petty speech;* incurrere in voculas malevolorum, Cic.; *a petty speech,* Cic.

vŏla -ae, f. *the hollow of the hand* or *foot,* Plin.

vŏlaema, v. volemum.

Vŏlāterrae -ārum f. *an old town in Etruria,* now *Volterra.* Hence, **Vŏlāterrānus** -a -um, *of Volaterrae;* Vada, *a port in the district of Volaterrae,* now *Torre di Vado;* plur. subst., **Vŏlāterrāni** -ōrum, m. *the inhabitants of Volaterrae.*

vŏlātĭcus -a -um (2. volo). **I.** *having wings, winged;* a, *flying,* Plaut.; b, *flying here and there;* illius furentes ac volatici impetus, Cic. **II.** Fig., *fleeting, flighty, inconstant;* Academia, Cic.

vŏlātĭlis -e (2. volo). **I.** *having wings, winged;* bestiae, Cic.; puer, *Cupid,* Ov. **II.** Transf., 1, *swift, rapid;* ferrum, Verg.; 2, *fleeting, transitory;* aetas, Ov.

vŏlātūra -ae, f. (2. volo), *a flight,* Varr.

vŏlātus -ūs, m. (2. volo), *a flying, flight,* Cic.

Volcae -ārum, m. *a people in Gallia Narbon- ensis.*

vŏlēmum pirum, gen. plur., volema pira, *a kind of pears, large enough to fill the hollow of the hand* (vola), Verg.

vŏlens -entis, p. adj. (from 1. volo). **I.** *willing, voluntary,* Sall., Verg. **II.** *favourable, inclined to,* Liv., Sall.; dis volentibus, *by the help of the gods,* Sall.; volentia alicui, *favourable tidings* or *events,* Sall.

volgĭŏlus -i, m. *a garden tool for smoothing beds,* Plin.

volgo, volgus = vulgo, vulgus (q.v.).

vŏlĭto, 1. (intens. of volo). **I.** *to fly about, to fly to and fro, to flit, to flutter.* **A.** Lit., a, of birds, Cic., Liv.; b, of things, hic aliae (stellae) volitant, Cic. **B.** Fig., *to fly round;* a, of the soul, Cic.; b, of men with immoderate wishes, *to soar;* homo volitans gloriae cupiditate, Cic. **II.** Transf., *to fly round about, hasten about;* 1, lit., cum gladiis toto foro, Cic.; 2, fig., *to show oneself* or *itself;* quum illa conjuratio palam volitaret, Cic.

volnĕro = vulnero (q.v.).

1. **vŏlo,** vĕlle, vŏlŭi, velle (root VOL, Gr. ΒΟΛ, whence βούλομαι), *to be willing, to wish.* **I.** Gen., 1, a, with acc. and infin., volui id quidem efficere, Cic.; volo scire, velim scire, *I should like to know,* Cic.; b, with acc. and infin., ju- dicem me esse, non doctorem volo, Cic.; c, with nom. and infin., Ov.; d, with neut. acc., faciam, quod vultis, Cic.; num quid vellet, Liv.; e, with ut and the subj., volo, uti respondeas, Cic.; f, with the subj. alone, visne hoc primum videamus? Cic.; g, absol., velit nolit scire diffi- cile est, *whether he wishes or does not,* Cic.; si vis, and contracted sis, sultis, parenthet., refer anim- um, sis, ad veritatem, Cic.; 2, velle aliquem, *to wish to speak with;* centuriones trium cohortium me velle postridie, Cic.; 3, bene (male) alicui, *to wish well* or *ill to,* Plaut.; 4, aliquid alicuius causâ, *to wish something good to some one;* valde eius causâ volo, Cic.; 5, quid sibi vult (res), *what is the meaning of;* quid ergo illae sibi statuae equestres inauratae volunt, Cic. **II.** 1, Polit. t. t., *to will, choose, ordain;* majores de singulis magistratibus bis vos sententiam ferre voluerunt, Cic.; 2, *to think, be of opinion, mean;* vultis omnia evenire fato, Cic.; 3, foll. by quam (like Gr. βούλομαι ἤ, *to prefer*), malae rei se quam nullius, turbarum ac seditionum duces esse volunt, Liv. (contr., vin = visne, sis = si vis sultis = si vultis).

2. vŏlo, 1. *to fly.* **I.** Lit., Cic. ; partic. subst., volantes -ium, f. (sc. bestiae), *flying creatures, birds,* Verg. **II.** Transf., *to move rapidly, to fly ;* **currus,** Verg. ; fulmina, Lucr. ; aetas, Cic.

3. vŏlo -ōnis, m. (1. volo), *a volunteer ;* plur., **volones,** *the slaves who were bought at the public expense to serve as soldiers after the battle of Cannae, each of them being asked* " velletne militare," Liv.

Volsci (Vulsci) -ōrum, m. *a people in Latium, on both banks of the Liris, in modern Campagna di Roma and Terra di Lavoro.* Hence, **Volscus** -a -um, *Volscian.*

volsella -ae, f. *a pair of tweezers or pincers,* Mart.

Volsĭnĭi (Vulsĭnĭi) -ōrum, m. *a town in Etruria,* now *Bolsena.* Hence, **Volsĭnĭensis** -e, *Volsinian ;* plur. subst., **Volsĭnĭenses** -ium, m. *the Volsinians.*

volsus -a -um, v. vello.

Voltĭnĭus -a -um, *Voltinian ;* tribus, *a Roman tribe.* Hence, **Voltĭnĭenses** -ium, m. *citizens of the Voltinian tribe.*

Voltumna -ae, f. *the goddess of the twelve allied Etruscan states.*

voltur = vultur (q.v.).

Voltumus = Vulturnus (q.v.).

voltus = vultus (q.v.).

vŏlūbĭlis -e (volvo), *rolling, revolving, turning round, twisting round.* **I.** Lit., buxum, a top, Verg. ; caelum, Cic. **II.** Fig., a, *of fortune, changeable, inconstant ;* fortuna, Cic. ; b, *of discourse, rapid, fluent ;* Appii Claudii volubilis erat oratio, Cic.

vŏlūbĭlĭtas -ātis, f. (volubilis), *revolving motion, revolution.* **I.** Lit., mundi, Cic. **II.** Fig., a, *vicissitude, inconstancy ;* fortunae, Cic. ; b, *flow of discourse, fluency ;* verborum, Cic. ; linguae, Cic.

vŏlūbĭlĭtĕr, adv. (volubilis), *fluently ;* funditur numerose et volubiliter oratio, Cic.

vŏlŭcer, vŏlŭcris, vŏlŭcre (2. volo), *flying, winged.* **I. A.** Lit., 1, adj., angues, Cic. ; deus or puer, *Cupid,* Ov. ; bestiae volucres, *birds,* Cic. ; 2, subst., **vŏlŭcris** -is, f. (sc. bestia), *a bird,* Cic. **B.** Transf., applied to an object in rapid motion, *swift ;* lumen, Lucr.; fumi, Verg.; sagitta, Verg.; nuntius, Cic. **II.** Fig., 1, gen., *quick, fleet ;* nihil est tam volucre quam maledictum, Cic. ; 2, *fleeting, transitory ;* fortuna, Cic. (genit. plur., gen. volŭcrum).

vŏlŭcra -ae, f. and **vŏlŭcre** -is, n. (volvo), *a caterpillar found on vine-leaves,* Plin.

vŏlŭcris -is, f., v. volucer.

vŏlūmen -ĭnis, n. (volvo), *anything rolled up.* **I.** 1, *a book, roll, writing ;* volumen plenum querelae, Cic. ; plur., volumina selectarum epistolarum, Cic. ; 2, esp., *a part of a larger work, a book,* Nep.; mutatae ter quinque volumina formae, *the fifteen books of the Metamorphoses,* Ov. **II.** *a roll, wreath, whirl, fold ;* anguis sinuat immensa volumine terga, Verg.

vŏluntārĭus -a -um (voluntas), *voluntary.* **A.** Subject., *a person who does something of his own accord ;* procurator, Cic. ; auxilia sociorum, Cic. ; milites, *volunteers,* Caes. ; plur. subst., **vŏluntārĭi** -ōrum, m. *volunteers,* Caes. **B.** Object., *that which happens of one's own free will ;* mors, *suicide,* Cic. ; deditio, Liv.

vŏluntas -ātis, f. (1. volo), *will, wish, inclination.* **I.** Lit., **A.** Gen., 1, me conformo ad eius voluntatem, Cic. ; 2, *free will ;* ego voluntatem tibi profecto emetiar, Cic. ; voluntate, *of one's own free will ;* meā voluntate concedam,

willingly, Cic. ; **3,** *good disposition ;* confisus municipiorum voluntatibus, Caes. ; **4,** *desire, wish ;* ambitiosis voluntatibus cedere, Cic.; **5,** *aim, purpose ;* hanc mentem voluntatemque suscepi, Cic. **B.** 1, *inclination, wishing well to ;* mutua, Cic.; **2,** *a last will, testament ;* testamenta et voluntas mortuorum, Cic. **II.** Transf., *meaning, sense, signification of words,* Quint.

vŏlup, adv. (shortened from volupe, from 1. volo), *agreeably, delightfully, pleasantly,* Plaut.

vŏluptābĭlis -e (voluptas), *giving pleasure, pleasant,* Plaut.

vŏluptārĭus -a -um (voluptas), *relating to pleasure, esp., to sensual pleasure.* **I.** Act., a, *causing pleasure ;* possessiones, *simply for pleasure,* Cic. ; b, *relating to pleasure ;* disputatio, Cic. **II.** Pass., a, *devoted or given to pleasure, sensual ;* esp. of the Epicureans as opp. to the Stoics, homo (of Epicurus), Cic. ; b, *capable of pleasure ;* gustatus est sensus ex omnibus maxime voluptarius, Cic.

vŏluptas -ātis, f. (volup), *pleasure, delight,* in a good or bad sense. **I.** Lit., voluptate capi, Cic. ; alicui voluptati esse, Cic. ; voluptatibus frui, Cic. ; in a bad sense, voluptates corporis, *sensual pleasures,* Cic.; voluptate liquescere, Cic. **II.** Meton., 1, voluptates, *public shows,* Cic.; 2, of persons, as a term of endearment, care puer, mea sera et sola voluptas, Verg. ; (genit. plur., gen. voluptatum, but also voluptatium).

vŏluptŭōsus -a -um (voluptas), *full of pleasure, delightful,* Quint.

vŏlūtābrum -i, n. (voluto), *a place where pigs roll, slough,* Verg.

vŏlūtābundus -a -um (voluto), *rolling, wallowing ;* in voluptatibus, Cic.

vŏlūtātĭo -ōnis, f. (voluto). **I.** *a rolling about, wallowing,* Cic. **II.** Fig., 1, *disquiet ;* animi, Sen. ; 2, *vicissitude, inconstancy ;* rerum humanarum, Sen.

vŏlūtātus -ūs, m. (voluto), *a wallowing,* Plin.

vŏlūto, 1. (intens. of volvo), *to roll round, tumble about.* **I.** Lit., se in pulvere, Plin. ; ne fluxā habenā voluŭetur in jactu glans, Liv.; partic., volutans, reflex., *rolling oneself ;* volutans pedibus, *throwing himself at the feet of,* etc., Verg. **II.** Fig., 1, gen., middle, volutari, *to roll,* i.e., *to be in ;* in omni genere flagitiorum, Cic. ; 2, esp., a, *to spread abroad, give forth ;* vocem per atria, Verg. ; vocem volutant littora, echo back, Verg. ; b, *to turn over in the mind, revolve, consider ;* conditiones cum amicis, Liv.; nihil umquam nisi sempiternum et divinum animo, Cic. ; c, *to busy, occupy ;* animum saepe iis tacitis cogitationibus, Liv. ; in veteribus scriptis studiose et multum volutatum esse, Cic.

volva -ae, f. (volvo). **I.** *a covering, husk, shell,* Plin. **II.** *the womb, esp., a sow's womb, a favourite delicacy among the Romans,* Hor.

volvo, volvi, vŏlūtum, 3. *to roll, revolve, turn round, twist round.* **I.** Lit., **A.** Gen., a, of living beings, molem, Verg. ; oculos huc illuc, Verg. ; pass., volvi, as middle, *to roll ;* curru, *from a chariot,* Verg. ; esp., *to roll to the ground,* of those fallen in battle, humi, arvis, Verg.; b, of things, such as rivers, saxa glareosa, Liv.; of the wind, ignem ad fastigia summa, Verg.; reflex., se volvere, or simply volvere or middle, volvi, *to roll round, eddy, turn round ;* ii qui volvuntur stellarum cursus sempiterni, Cic. ; of tears, lacrimae volvuntur inanes, Verg. **B.** Esp., 1, *to unroll a roll, to read ;* libros Catonis, Cic. ; 2, *to roll along, roll away ;* flumen pecus et domos volvens unā, Hor. ; 3, meton., orbem, *to form a circle* (of men), Liv. **II.** Fig., **A.** Gen., a, of orators whose words flow without stopping, celeriter verba, Cic.; b, of time, to make to roll round; pronos volvere menses (of the moon-goddess), Hor.; tot casus = to experience, Verg.; middle, of time or of events, to roll round; ut idem in singulos annos orbis volveretur, Liv.; partic. volvens, reflex., rolling round; volvens annus, Ov.; volventibus annis, in the course of years, Verg.; c, to fix or determine fate; volvit vices (of Jupiter), Verg.; sic volvere Parcas, Verg. **B.** Esp., 1, a, to toss about in the mind, to have, entertain; ingentes jam diu iras eum in pectore volvere, Liv.; b, to busy oneself with a thought, reflect on, consider, ponder over; bellum in animo, Liv.; 2, = revolvere, to go over again; veterum monumenta virorum, Verg.

vŏmer -ĕris, m. a ploughshare, Cic.

vŏmĭca -ae, f. an ulcer, sore, boil. **I.** Lit., Cic. **II.** Fig, a plague, curse (of men), ap. Liv.

vŏmis -ĕris, m. = vomer (q.v.).

vŏmĭtĭo -ōnis, f. (vomo). **I.** a vomiting, throwing up; vomitione alvos curare, Cic. **II.** Meton., that which is thrown up, a vomit, Plin.

vŏmĭto, 1. (intens. of vomo), to vomit, Sen.

vŏmĭtor -ōris, m. (vomo), one who vomits, Sen.

vŏmĭtōrĭus -a -um (vomitor), provoking vomiting, Plin.

vŏmĭtus -ūs, m. (vomo). **I.** a vomiting, Plin. **II.** Meton., that which is vomited, a vomit, Plin.

vŏmo -ŭi -ĭtum, 1. (connected with ἐμέω). **I.** Intransit., to vomit, Cic. **II.** Transit., to vomit forth, throw up, give forth; animam, Verg.; flammas, Verg.; pass. impers., ab hora tertia bibebatur, ludebatur, vomebatur, Cic.

vŏrācĭtas -ātis, f. (vorax), voracity, gluttony, Plin.

vŏrāgĭnōsus -a -um (vorago), full of chasms, pits, Auct. b. Hisp.

vŏrāgo -ĭnis, f. (voro), a pit, chasm, abyss. **I.** Lit., in the earth, Liv.; in water, an abyss, eddy, gulf, whirlpool; summersus equus voraginibus, Cic. **II.** Transf., ventris, Ov.; gurges et vorago patrimonii, spendthrift, Cic.

vŏrax -ācis (voro), gluttonous, voracious; Charybdis, Cic.; ignis voracior, Ov.

vŏro, 1. (connected with βρόω, whence βιβρώσκω and βορά), to eat greedily, swallow whole, devour, consume. **I.** Lit., Cic. **II.** Transf., **A.** Gen., to devour, suck in; Charybdis vorat carinas, Ov.; illam (puppim = navem) rapidus vorat aequore vortex, Verg. **B.** Esp., 1, of property, to squander, dissipate, Plin.; 2, to read eagerly, devour; litteras, literature, Cic.

vors . . . v. vers . . .

vort . . . v. vert . . .

vōs, ye, v. tu.

vōtīvus -a -um (votum), of or relating to a vow, votive, vowed; ludi, Cic.; juvenca, Hor.

vōtum -i, n. (voveo). **I.** a vow. **A.** Gen., 1, lit., vota debere diis, Cic.; vota nuncupare or suscipere or concipere, Cic.; vota facere, Cic.; 2, meton., a, a prayer, Ov.; b, that which is vowed; spolia hostium, Vulcano votum, Liv. **B.** Esp., the vows made on the 3rd of January every year by the chief magistrates for the good health of the emperor, Tac. **II.** a wish, desire; vota facere, to wish, Cic.; hoc erat in votis, this was what I wished, Hor.; voti potens, having gained his wish, Ov.

vŏvĕo, vōvi, vōtum, 2. **I.** to vow, promise to a god; decumam Herculi, Cic.; aedem, Liv.;

with fut. infin., vovisse dicitur uvam se dec daturum, Cic. **II.** to wish; elige, quid voveas,Ov

vox, vōcis, f. (root VOC, perhaps connected with ὄψ), the voice of a person speaking, calling, or singing. **I.** Lit., 1, vocis contentio et remissio, Cic.; vocem attenuare, to make one's voice like a woman's, Cic.; of the cry of animals, boum, Verg.; 2, = pronunciation; rustica vox et agrestis quosdam delectat, Cic. **II.** Meton., **A.** sound, tone, of the voice or of a musical instrument, vocum gravitate et cantibus pelli vehementius, Cic.; septem discrimina vocum = the lyre with seven strings, Verg. **B.** a word, utterance, discourse; a, haec te vox non perculit? Cic.; carpi nostrorum militum vocibus, Caes.; b, a command; consulum voci atque imperio non oboedire, Cic.; c, a formula, decision, sentence; extremi ac difficillimi temporis vocem illam consulem mittere coegistis, Cic.; d, a formula, a magic incantation; voces Marsae, Hor. **C.** = sermo, language; Grajā scierit sive Latinā voce loqui, Cic. **D.** accent, tone; in omni verbo posuit acutam vocem, Cic.

Vulcānus (Volcānus) -i, m. (root VULC, VOLC = FULC, lit. the shining one), Vulcan, the god of fire, son of Jupiter and Juno, husband of Venus, who made the weapons, thunder-bolts, etc., of the gods, Cic.; insula Vulcani (Ἡφαίστου νῆσος), the island of Vulcan, the most southern of the Lipari islands, now Vulcanello; plur., insulae Vulcani, the Lipari islands; appell., fire; Vulcanum navibus efflant, Ov. Hence, **A.** **Vulcānius** -a -um, Vulcanian; acies, fire, Verg.; Lemnos, sacred to Vulcan, Ov.; Vulcaniis armis, with irresistible weapons, Cic. **B.** **Vulcānālis** -e, belonging to Vulcan; subst., **Vulcānālia** -ōrum, n. the annual festival of Vulcan, on the 23rd of August.

vulgāris -e (vulgus), common, ordinary, usual, vulgar; hominum consuetudo, Cic.; opinio, Cic.; subst., **vulgāria** -ĭum, n. that which is common; anteponantur rara vulgaribus, Cic.

vulgārĭtĕr, adv. (vulgaris), commonly, vulgarly, Plin.

vulgātus -a -um, p. adj. (from 1. vulgo). **I.** common, prostituted, Liv. **II.** Esp., generally known, well known; vulgatior fama est, with acc. and infin., Liv.

vulgĭvăgus -a -um (vulgus and vagor), wandering, vagrant, Lucr.

1. **vulgo (volgo),** 1. (vulgus), to make common to all, to communicate, make accessible to all. **I.** a, quum consulatum vulgari viderent, Liv.; munus vulgatum ab civibus esse in socios, Liv.; quae navis in flumine publico tam vulgata omnibus quam istius aetas, Cic.; b, to communicate a disease; vulgati contactu hi homines morbi, Liv.; c, to publish a book; carmina, Tac. **II.** to spread abroad by discourse, to divulge, make generally known; famam interfecti regis, Liv.

2. **vulgō (volgō),** adv. (lit. abl. of vulgus), commonly, generally, before the public, in public, openly; vulgo totis castris testamenta obsignabantur, Caes.; quas (litteras) vulgo ad te mitto, Cic.

vulgus (volgus) -i, n., rarely m., the people = the great multitude, the public. **I.** Gen., **A.** Lit., a, in the town; non est consilium in vulgo, non ratio, etc., Cic.; disciplinam in vulgum efferre, Cic.; b, in the army, vulgus militum, armatorum, Liv. **B.** Transf., the people = a mass, crowd; vulgus incautum mob. **A.** Lit., sapientis judicium a judicic vulgi discrepat, Cic.; odi profanum vulgus, Hor. **B.** Transf., the mass, the ordinary run; patron orum, Cic.

vulnĕrārĭus (volnĕrārĭus) -a -um (vulnus), *of or relating to wounds*, Plin.; subst., **vulnĕrārĭus** -ĭi, m. *a surgeon*, Plin.

vulnĕrātĭo -ōnis, f. (vulnero), *wounding*, Cic.; fig., major haec est vitae, famae, salutis suae vulneratio, Cic.

vulnĕro (volnĕro), 1, (vulnus), *to wound*, *injure*. **I.** Lit., aliquem, Cic.; corpus, Cic. **II.** Fig., *to wound, injure, harm, assail;* eos nondum voce vulnero, Cic.

vulnĭfĭcus (volnĭfĭcus) -a -um (vulnus and facio), *inflicting wounds;* telum, Ov.; chalybs, Verg.

vulnus (volnus) -ĕris, n. *a wound.* **I. A.** Lit., a, of living beings, vulnus inferre, Caes.; infligere, Cic.; vulnus accipere, excipere, Cic.; mori ex vulnere, Liv.; b, poet., transf., of injuries to things, falcis, Ov.; ornus vulneribus evicta, Verg. **B.** Fig., *wound = injury, disease, damage, loss;* vulnera reipublicae imponere, Cic.; poet., *wounds to the feelings.* esp., from love; vulnus alit venis, Verg. **II.** Meton., 1, *a blow;* mortifero vulnere ictus, Liv.; 2, *the instrument or weapon which causes the blow;* haesit sub gutture vulnus, Verg.

vulpēcŭla -ae, f. (dim. of vulpes), *a little fox*, Cic.

vulpes (volpes) -is, f. (ἀλώπηξ), *a fox.* **I.** Lit., Hor.; prov., vulpes jungere, *of something impossible*, Verg.; *the fox as an emblem of cunning, slyness;* animi sub vulpe latentes, Hor. **II.** Transf., vulpes marina, *a kind of shark*, Plin.

vulpīnus -a -um (vulpes), *of or relating to a fox, vulpine*, Plin.

Vulsci = Volsci (q.v.).

vulsūra -ae, f. (vello), *a plucking, pulling*, Varr.

vulsus -a -um, p. adj. (from vello), *having the hairs plucked out, smooth, effeminate*, Plaut., Mart.

vultĭcŭlus -i, m. (dim. of vultus), *the countenance, look, aspect;* non te Bruti nostri vulticulus ab ista oratione deterret? Cic.

vultŭōsus -a -um (vultus), *making faces, grimacing, full of airs, affected*, Cic.

1. **vultur (voltur)** -ŭris, m. *a vulture*, Liv., Verg.; applied to a *rapacious man*, Sen.

2. **Vultur (Voltur)** -ŭris, m. *a mountain in Apulia*, now *Voltore*.

vultŭrīnus (voltŭrīnus) -a -um (vultur), *of or relating to a vulture*, Plin.

vultŭrĭus (voltŭrĭus) -i, m. *a vulture.* **I.** Lit., Liv. **II.** Transf., **A.** *a rapacious man*, Cic. **B.** *an unlucky throw at dice*, Plaut.

Vulturnum (Volturnum) -i, n. *a town in Campania on the river Volturnus*, now *Castel Volturno*, Liv.

1. **Vulturnus (Volturnus)** -i, m. *a river in Campania*, now *Volturno*.

2. **vulturnus (volturnus)** -i, m. (2. Vultur), *with or without ventus, a wind named after the mountain Vultur, a south-east wind*, Liv.

vultus (voltus) -ūs, m. *the countenance, expression of the face, the look, mien, aspect.* **I.** Lit., a, Gen., hilaris atque laetus, Cic.; plur., vultus ficti simulatique, Cic.; vultus avortite vestros, Cic.; b, emphat., *a scornful, angry look;* vultus instantis tyranni, Hor. **II.** Transf. *the face;* 1, lit., a, cadere in vultus, Ov.; b, a *portrait*, Plin.; 2, meton., *look, appearance;* ‌alis (of the sea), Verg.; naturae, Ov.

X.

X, x, the twenty-first letter of the Latin alphabet, corresponds with the Greek Ξ, ξ. It arises out of the combination of c and s (dico, dixi), g and s (lego, lexi).

Xanthippē -ēs, f. (Ξανθίππη), *the shrewish wife of Socrates.*

Xanthippus -i, m. (Ξάνθιππος). **I.** *father of Pericles, conqueror over the Persians at Mycale.* **II.** *a general of the Lacedaemonians in the First Punic War, who took Regulus prisoner.*

Xanthus (-ŏs) -i, m. (Ξάνθος). **I.** = *Scamander.* **II.** *a river in Lycia.* **III.** *a river in Epirus.*

xĕnium -ĭi, n. (ξένιον), *a present given to a guest*, Plin.; in general, *a gift, present*, Plin.

Xĕno -ōnis, m. (Ξένων), *an Epicurean philosopher of Athens.*

Xĕnŏcrătes -is, m. (Ξενοκράτης), *a philosopher of Chalcedon, pupil of Plato, the head of the Academy after the death of Speusippus.*

Xĕnŏphănes -is, m. (Ξενοφάνης), *a celebrated Greek philosopher of Colophon, founder of the Eleatic school.*

Xĕnŏphōn -ontis, m. (Ξενοφῶν), *an Athenian, pupil of Socrates, a distinguished historian and general.* Hence, **Xĕnŏphontēus (-tīus)** -a -um, *of or belonging to Xenophon.*

xērampĕlīnae -ārum, f. (ξηραμπέλιναι), *dark-red garments*, Juv.

Xerxēs -is, m. (Ξέρξης), *the king of the Persians who invaded Greece and was defeated at Salamis.*

xĭphĭas -ae, m. (ξιφίας). **I.** *a sword-fish*, Plin. **II.** *a sword-shaped comet*, Plin.

xĭphĭon -ĭi, n. (ξιφίον), *a sword-flag*, Plin.

xўlŏbalsămum -i, n. (ξυλοβάλσαμον), *wood of the balsam-tree*, Plin.

xўlŏcinnămōmum -i, n. (ξυλοκιννάμωμον), *the wood of the cinnamon plant*, Plin.

xўlon -i, n. (ξύλον), *the cotton-tree*, Plin.

Xynĭae -ārum, f. (Ξυνία), *a town in Thessaly, on the lake Xynias.*

xўris -ĭdis, f. (ξυρίς), *the wild iris*, Plin.

xystus -i, m. (ξυστός), and **xystum** -i, n. *an open colonnade, a walk planted with trees, a promenade*, Cic.

Y.

Y, y, a letter borrowed from the Greek in order to represent the Greek ‌ psilon (Υ).

Z.

Z, z, represents the Greek zeta (Z, ς), and is only used in foreign words.

Zăcynthus (-ŏs) -i, f. (Ζάκυνθος), *an island in the Ionian Sea*, now *Zante*.

Zăleucus (Ζάλευκος), *a celebrated lawgiver of the Locrians in Italy, living about 650 B.C.*

Zăma -ae, f. (Ζάμα), *a town in Numidia, scene of the victory of Scipio over Hannibal.*

zāmĭa -ae, f. (ζημία), damage, injury, loss, Plaut.

Zanclē -ēs, f. (Ζάγκλη), old name of the town Messana (now Messina) in Italy, so called from its sickle-like form. Hence, adj., **A. Zanclaeus** -a -um, of or relating to Zancle. **B. Zancleïus** -a -um, of Zancle.

zĕa -ae, f. (ζέα), a kind of spelt, Plin.

zēlŏtўpĭa -ae, f. (ζηλοτυπία), jealousy, Cic.

zēlŏtўpus -a -um (ζηλότυπος), jealous, Juv.

Zēno (-ōn) -ōnis, m. (Ζήνων). **I.** a Greek philosopher of Citium in Cyprus, founder of the Stoic School. **II.** a Greek philosopher of the Eleatic School, teacher of Pericles. **III.** a later Greek philosopher of the Epicurean School, teacher of Cicero and Atticus.

Zēnŏbĭa -ae, f. **I.** daughter of Mithridates, king of Armenia. **II.** wife of Odenathus, king of Palmyra, which she ruled after her husband's death; conquered by the Emperor Aurelian.

Zĕphўrĭum -ĭi, n. (Ζεφύριον), a fort on the coast of Cilicia.

zĕphўrus -i, m. (ζέφυρος), a warm west wind, zephyr, Hor.; poet.= wind, Verg.

Zĕrynthus -i, f. (Ζήρυνθος), a town in Thracia, near Aenos. Hence, **Zĕrynthĭus** -a -um, Zerynthian.

Zētēs -ae, m. (Ζήτης), the brother of Calais, son of Boreas, one of the Argonauts.

Zēthus -i, m. (Ζήθος), son of Jupiter, brother of Amphion.

zeugītes -ae, m. (ζευγίτης), a kind of reed, Plin.

zĕus -i, m. (ζαιός), a fish, the dory, Plin.

Zeuxĭs -ĭdis, m. (Ζεῦξις), a celebrated Greek painter.

zingĭber -ĕris, n. (ζιγγίβερις), and **zingĭbĕri**, n. indecl. ginger, Plin.

zĭzĭphum -i, n. (ζίζυφον), the jujube, Plin.

zĭzĭphus -i, f. the jujube-tree, Plin.

zm ... v. sm ...

zōdĭăcus -i, m. (ζωδιακός), the zodiac, Cic. poet.

Zŏïlus -i, m. (Ζώιλος), a severe critic of Homer; appell., a petty critic, Ov.

zōna -ae, f. (ζώνη), a girdle. **I.** Lit., a, a maiden's girdle, Cat.; b, a girdle or money-belt, Liv. **II.** Transf., 1, the three stars called Orion's Belt, Ov.; 2, zonae, terrestrial zones, Verg., Ov.

zōnārĭus -a -um (zona), of or relating to a girdle, Plaut.; subst., **zōnārĭus** -ĭi, m. a girdle-maker, Cic.

zōnŭla -ae, f. (dim. of zona) a little girdle, Cat.

zōophthalmos -i, f. and zōophthalmon -i, n. (ζωόφθαλμος), the great houseleek, Plin.

zōpissa -ae, f. (ζώπισσα), pitch mixed with wax, which was scraped off ships, Plin.

1. zoster -ĕris, m. (ζωστήρ), a cutaneous eruption, the shingles, Plin.

2. Zōster -ĕris, m. (Ζωστήρ), a promontory in Attica.

zōthēca -ae, f. (ζωθήκη), a private cabinet, Plin.

zōthēcŭla -ae, f. (dim. of zotheca), a small private cabinet, Plin.

zўgĭa -ae, f. (ζυγία), a tree, the horn-bean, Plin.

zўthum -i, n. (ζύθος), a kind of Egyptian malt liquor. Plin.

ENGLISH-LATIN.

ENGLISH-LATIN DICTIONARY.

A

A, an, adj. not translated; — day, — month, *singulis diebus, mensibus;* to — man, *ad unum.*

abaft, aft, adv. *a puppi, a tergo.*

abandon, v.tr. *alqm (de)relinquĕre, destituĕre, deserĕre, (de)alqá re desistĕre;* — hope, *spem omittĕre.* **abandoned,** adj. =wicked, *nefarius;* see WICKED. **abandonment,** n. *relictio,* or infin. of abandon used substantively (e.g. *deserĕre amicum,* the — of a friend).

abase, v.tr. 1, = lessen, *alqd (de)minuĕre, (im)minuĕre;* 2, = humble, *frangĕre* (e.g. *animum, audaciam), comprimĕre, coercĕre, alcjs auctoritatem imminuĕre.* **abasement,** n. 1, *deminutio;* 2, legal, = loss of civil and social rights, *capitis* or *libertatis deminutio.*

abash, v.tr. *alqm percellĕre, perturbare, conturbare, animum alcjs affligĕre, debilitare, frangĕre.*

abate, I. v.tr. *(de)minuĕre, imminuĕre;* — a charge, *alqd de summá detrahĕre, sumptum* or *impensam circumcidĕre.* **II.** v.intr. 1, (de)*minui, imminui, decrescĕre;* 2, fig. of passion, *defervescĕre* (e.g. *ira,* etc.). **abatement,** n. *deminutio;* in taxation, *vectigaiium deminutio.*

abbat, abbot, n. **abbas, -ätis,* nearest equivalent in Class. Lat. *pontifex.* **abbess,** n. **abbatissa,* in Class. Lat. *antistes* or *antistita.* **abbey,** n. **abbatia* (= cloister), **ecclesia* (= church), Class. *templum.*

abbreviate, v.tr. 1, = shorten, *(de)curtare, praecidĕre, circumcidĕre;* 2, = compress (e.g. *orationem), contrahĕre, verba ad compendium,* or *compendii facĕre.* **abbreviation,** n. 1, = shortening, *compendium, contractio* (e.g. *orationis,* opp. to *longitudo);* mark of —, *sigla, -orum* (Jct.); 2, see EPITOME.

abdicate, v.tr. *magistratu, dictaturá,* etc., *se abdicare, magistratum,* etc., *ejurare.* **abdication,** n., legal, *abdicatio, ejuratio.*

abdomen, n. *abdomen.*

abduction, n. 1, = theft, *furtum;* 2, = forcible carrying away, *raptus, -ús, raptio;* to commit —, *rapĕre.*

abed, adv. *in lecto;* to lie —, *(in lecto) cubare.*

aberration, n. 1, = a wandering from the right path, lit. or fig. *error;* 2, = mental —, *mentis error;* 3, = a fault, *erratum.*

abet, v.tr. 1, = incite, *ad alqd instigare, impellĕre;* 2, = aid, *ab* or *cum algo,* or *alqá re,* or *e parte alcjs stare, auxilio alci esse;* — in a crime or fault, *sceleris* or *culpae participem* or *socium esse.* **abettor,** n. *socius, adjutor;* = — in anything, *alcjs rei,* or with abl. *conscius* (adj.).

abeyance, n. 1, in gen. to be in —, *in dubio, incertum, integrum esse, intermitti;* to leave in —, *rem integram relinquĕre;* 2, legal, *vacare;* the property is in — (i.e. without a proprietor), *fundus vacat;* conferred the priestly offices as in — on others, *sacerdotia ut vacua in alios contulit.*

abhor, v.tr. *abominari, detestari* (lit. = call a god to witness a curse), *odisse, alqm odio habēre.* **abhorrence,** n. *detestatio, odium.* **abhorrent,** adj. 1, = inconsistent with, *ab alquá re abhorrens, alci rei,* or *(ab) alqá re alienus, alci rei contrarius;* 2, see HATEFUL.

abide, v.intr. 1, = linger in, *(com)morari, in alqo loco esse,* or *versari;* 2, = last, *durare.* **abiding,** adj. *diuturnus, stabilis.*

abject, adj. = contemptible, *abjectus, contemptus, humilis.*

abjure, v.tr. 1, legal, *abjurare, ejurare;* 2, fig. =disown, *ejurare, recusare.*

ability, n. 1, = physical strength, *vires, -ium;* 2, = mental power, *facultas, ingenium, vires;* according to one's —, *pro facultate, pro viribus;* a man of —, *vir summi ingenii.* **able,** adj. 1, = having power, *alcjs rei potens,* 2, = fit for, *habilis, aptus, ad alqd idoneus;* 3, = mentally strong, *sagax, sol(l)ers;* 4, to be —, *posse, valēre* (= to have strength for); to be — in anything, *alqá re pollēre;* as well as I am —, *pro viribus (meis), pro virili parte.* **able-bodied,** adj. *firmus, robustus, validus.*

ablative, n. *(casus) ablativus* (Gram.).

ablution, n. *ablutio;* to make an —, *(aquá) abluĕre.*

abnegation, n. *animi moderatio, temperantia;* self —, *temperantia.*

abnormal, adj. 1, lit. =not according to rule, *enormis* (e.g. *vicus* (Tac.) = irregularly built; *toga* (Quint.) = irregularly cut), *abnormis* (= rare); 2, = out of the common, *novus, inusitatus, mirus, mirificus, incredibilis, singularis;* 3, = very great, *maximus;* 4, = rare, *infrequens*. Adv. *praeter morem.*

aboard, adv. to go —, *(in navem,* or *navem) conscendĕre;* to be —, *in nave esse;* to put —, *in navem imponĕre;* to have —, *vehĕre.*

abode, n. 1, = sojourn, *habitatio;* if in a foreign country, *peregrinatio;* 2, see HOUSE.

abolish, v.tr. 1, in gen. *abolēre* (not in Cic.), *tollĕre, subvertĕre, delēre, ex(s)tinguĕre;* 2, legal, *abrogare;* to — part of a law by a new one, *obrogare.* **abolition,** n. 1, in gen. = destruction, *dissolutio;* 2, legal, *abrogatio;* — of debts, *tabulae novae.*

abominable, adj. *foedus, teter, detestabilis, immanis, nefarius* (= **wicked**). **abominate,** v.tr. see ABHOR.

aboriginal, adj. *priscus; prisci Latini =* the Latins who lived before the foundation of Rome. **aborigines,** n. *indigenae.*

abortion, n. 1, = miscarriage, *abortio, abortus, -ūs;* to cause an —, *alci abortum facĕre,* or *inferre;* 2, = a monstrous birth, *abortus, portentum;* a drug to procure —, *abortivum* (Juv.). **abortive,** adj. 1, lit. = belonging to premature birth, *abortivus;* 2, fig. = unsuccessful, *irritus.* Adv. *incassum, ad irritum.*

abound, v.intr. *alqā re abundare, affluĕre, alci superesse,* or *suppeditare* (e.g. he —s in words, *oratio ei suppeditat).* **abundance,** n. *rerum,* i.e. *divitiarum,* etc., *abundantia, suppeditatio, affluentia, ubertas, copia.* **abundant,** adj. *affluens* (*ab*) *alqā re* = rich, *copiosus, dives, locuples.* Adv. *abunde, satis superque, abundanter, cumulate.*

about, I. adv. 1, of place, *circa, circum,* or abl. with or without *in;* 2, of time or number, *fere, ferme, circiter;* with fut. part. (e.g. he is about to go, *iturus est).* **II.** prep. with acc., 1, of place, both motion to and rest in, *circa, circum;* the people — one, *qui circum alqm sunt;* 2, of time, *circa;* 3, of respect, *de;* with abl. (e.g. he spoke — these things, *de his rebus dixit);* what are you — ? *quid agis?*

above, I. adv. 1, of place, *super, supra;* the — mentioned, *quod supra scriptum est;* 2, of degree. *super, supra;* over and —, *satis superque.* **II.** prep. 1, of place, *super,* acc. or abl. *supra, ante,* acc. ; to sit — anyone at table, *supra alqm accumbĕre;* 2, of degree, *super, supra;* — measure, *supra modum;* = more than, *plus* or *amplius* (e.g. he had — 200 soldiers, *plus ducentos milites habuit).*

abreast, adv. *pariter;* two horses —, *equi bijuges.*

abridge, see ABBREVIATE.

abroad, adv. *foras,* with verbs of motion; *foris,* with those of rest; to sup —, *foris cenare;* to spread —, v.tr. = publish, *divulgare;* = scatter, *diffundĕre;* v.intr. = to be spread, *percrebescĕre;* nations —, *gentes externae* or *exterae;* to travel —, *peregrinari.*

abrogate, see ABOLISH.

abrupt, adj. 1, lit. = steep, *abruptus, arduus, praeruptus;* 2, fig., of speech, *rudis, incompositus;* 3, = sudden, *subitus, repentinus, improvisus.* Adv. 1, *abrupte, praerupte;* 2, *incomposite;* 3, *subito, de improviso, repente.*

abscess, n. *ulcus, -eris,* n. *suppuratio* (Cels.), *fistula, apostema, -ātis,* n. (Plin.), *abscessus, -ūs* (Cels.), *cancer, carcinoma, -ātis,* n.

abscond, v.intr. 1, = to lie hidden, *delitescĕre, latēre, occultari;* 2, = to run away, *se in occultum abdĕre, se occultare* or *celare.*

absence, n. *absentia;* — abroad, *peregrinatio;* in my —, *me absente;* — of mind, *alcjs rei oblivio.* **absent, I.** adj. *absens;* to be — from, *ab alqo abesse;* to be — in mind, *animo excurrĕre et vagari;* — minded, *inscius,* or *oblitus alcjs rei.* **II.** v.tr. — oneself, *se removēre.*

absolute, I. adj. 1, = complete, *perfectus, absolutus, expletus;* 2, = unconditioned, *absolutus, simplex;* 3, = unlimited, *infinitus;* — power, *summum imperium;* = ruler, *imperator, qui summum imperium obtinet.* **II.** n. philosoph. t.t., opp. to relative, *alqd perfectum et absolutum, quod semper simplex et idem est.* **absolutely.** adv. 1, = entirely, *plane, prorsus, omnino;* 2, opp. to relatively, *per se, simpliciter.*

absolution, n., in gen. *venia;* to grant —, *alcjs rei veniam dare.* **absolve,** v.tr. 1, in gen. *alqm alqā re solvĕre* (e.g. soldiers from

military service); see EXCUSE; 2, legal t.t. *alqm alcjs rei* or *(de) alquā re* (*ab*)*solvĕre, alqm alqā re liberare;* 3, see PARDON.

absorb, v.tr. 1, lit. *sugĕre, bibĕre, absorbēre, exhaurire;* 2, fig. to be absorbed in anything, *alqā re occupatissimum esse.*

abstain, v.intr. *(se)* (*ab*) *alqā re abstinēre* or *continēre,* (*ab* or *in*) *alqā re, alci rei,* or with infin. (e.g. *alqd facĕre), temperare, sibi temperare quominus* (not in Cic.); to — from appearing in public, *publico carēre.* **abstinence,** n. *abstinentia, continentia, modestia, moderatio, temperantia;* days of —, fast days, *jejunium.* **abstinent,** adj. *abstinens, continens, sobrius, moderatus, temperatus;* — in drink, *sobrius.*

abstract, I. adj. 1, = removed from the sphere of the senses, *quod nullo sensu percipi potest;* an — idea, *notio nulli sensui subjecta, notio mente solā concepta;* an — discussion, *disputatio paul(l)o abstrusior;* 2, = deep or acute in thought, *subtilis* (*et acutus*); an — thinker, *subtilis philosophus;* see ABSTRUSE. **II.** v.tr. 1, to think —ly, *animum a corpore abstrahĕre, mentem ab oculis sevocare;* — the mind from pleasure, *animum a voluptate sevocare;* 2, = to make an abridgment, *epitomen facĕre;* 3, see STEAL. **III.** n. *epitome, -es,* f., or *epitoma.* **abstractly,** adv. to think —, see ABSTRACT, II. 1.; *subtiliter, acute.* **abstracted,** adj. 1, see ABSTRUSE; 2, = lost in thought, *omnium rerum* or *sui oblitus.* **abstraction.** n. 1, = forgetfulness, *oblivio;* 2, = a mere name or idea, *appellatio* (Suet.).

abstruse, adj. *obscurus, abditus, reconditus.* **abstruseness,** n. *obscuritas, res occulta,* or *involuta.* Adv. *obscure, abdite, recondite.*

absurd, adj. 1, = silly, *absurdus, ineptus, inscitus;* 2, = ridiculous, *ridiculus.* Adv. 1, *absurde, inepte, inscite;* 2, *ridicule.* **absurdity,** n. 1, as a quality, *insulsitas;* 2, = a joke, *ridiculum;* 3, = an act, *res inepta, ineptiae, nugae.*

abundance, abundant(ly), see ABOUND.

abuse, I. n. 1, = the wrong use of a thing, *immoderatio* (= excess), *usus, -ūs perversus* (= misapplication); 2, rhetor. t.t. *abusio* (= misuse of a word); 3, = bad language, *convicium, maledictum;* 4, = an evil custom, *res mali* or *pessimi exempli, malum, pestis, mos pravus, quod contra jus fasque est.* **II.** v.t. 1, = misuse, *alqā re perverse uti, abuti* (in bad sense may from context, lit. = to use up); 2, rhetor. t.t. (e.g. a term) *abuti;* 3, = to rail at, *alci maledicĕre.* **abuser,** n. 1, = one who misuses anything, *homo immoderatus qui alqā re abutitur;* 2, = a railer, *conviciator, homo maledicus* or *maledicens.* **abusive,** adj. *maledicus* or *maledicens contumeliosus.* Adv. *maledice, contumeliose.*

abut. v.tr. *alci loco adjacēre, finitimum, vicinum, confinem, continentem, conjunctum esse, locum tangĕre, attingĕre. alci loco imminēre* (= to hang over).

abyss, n. 1, lit. = a great depth, *profundum, altitudo* (= depth merely); *gurges, -itis,* m. (= a whirlpool); *locus praeceps* (= precipice); fig. *exitium;* see DESTRUCTION. He plunged in an — of pleasure, *se voluptatibus (prorsus) dedit;* ho plunged in an — of ruin, *semet ipse praecipitavit.*

academy, n. 1, = the Platonic school, *Academia;* 2, = a learned body, *collegium.* **academical,** adj. 1, = belonging to a university, *academicus;* 2, = an — (i.e. theoretical) question, *res ad cognitionem modo pertinens.*

accede, v.intr. 1, = to be added to, *accedĕre ad alqd* or dat.; 2, see AGREE.

accelerate, v.tr. *accelerare;* see HASTEN.

accent, n. 1, in pronunciation, *vox, accentus, ъis, (vocis) sonus, -ūs, tenor;* sharp —, *vox acuta;* **acute,** grave, circumflex —, *accentus* or *sonus acutus, gravis, circumflexus* or *inflexus;* 2, in writing, *apex, -icis,* m. (= the long or short mark over a vowel); a syllable with short, long, or circumflex —, *syllaba brevis, longa, circumflexa.*

accept, v.tr. 1, = to take, *accipēre;* 2, = to undertake, *suscipēre* (of one's own accord); *recipēre* (what is offered); not to — an office, *munus deprecari.* **acceptable,** adj. *jucundus, accipiendus, gratus.* Adv. *jucunde, grate.* **acceptance.** n. 1, *acceptio* (e.g. *frumenti*), *assumptio* (e.g. *argumenti*); better by infin., e.g. he intimated his —, *dixit se accipēre;* 2, = approbation, *comprobatio.* **acceptation,** = significance, *significatio.*

access, n. 1,= approach, *aditus, -ūs, accessio, accessus, -ūs;* difficult of —, *rari est accessūs;* 2, = addition, *accessio, cumulus;* 3, med. t.t. (e.g. of a fe·er), *accessio* (Cels.); 4, = an entrance, *aditus, -ūs, accessus, -ūs.* **accessary. I.** adj.1, see ADDITIONAL; 2, = privy to, *conscius alcjs rei,* dat., *in or de* with abl., or rel. clause (e.g. *conscius quae gererentur,* — to what was being done). **II.** n. = accomplice, *conscius, unus ex consciis, sceleri affinis,* (*culpae*) *socius.* **accessible,** adj. *patens, facilis aditu* or *accessu;* not — to any advice, *consilii non patiens;* he is little —, *difficilis est aditu.* **accession,** n. 1, = increase, *accessio;* 2, = — to the throne, *initium regnandi.*

accidence, n. = the rudiments, *elementa, -orum, rudimenta, -orum.*

accident, 1, = a chance event, *casu₋, -ūs, eventus, -ūs, eventum;* 2, = a misfortune, *casus, calamitas.* **accidental,** adj. *fortuitus* (e.g. *concursus atomorum*), *forte oblatus.* Adv. *forte, casu;* to mention —, *in mentionem alcjs rei incidēre.*

acclaim, acclamation, n. *acclamatio* (= shout of applause, in Cic. always of disapproval); with general —, *omnibus probantibus.* **acclaim,** v.tr. *alci acclamare.*

accommodate, v.tr. *accommodare alqd alci* or with *ad.* **accommodating,** adj. *obsequens, facilis;* to be — to, *alci morem gerēre, morigerari.* **accommodation,** n. 1, = adjustment of differences, *reconciliatio;* see AGREEMENT; 2, = entertainment or place of entertainment, *hospitium.*

accompany, v.tr. 1,= to go with, *comitem se alci adjungēre, dare, praebēre, alqm comitari, prosequi, deducēre* (as a mark of respect); *stipare* (of a crowd); accompanied by, *cum* (e.g. *tempestas cum grandine*); 2, in music, = to sing or play together, *alci concinēre;* — on an instrument, *vocem fidibus jungēre, cantum modis musicis excipēre.* **accompaniment,** n. 1, *comitatus, -ūs, stipatio;* 2, in music, *adjunctio fidium voci,* or *vocis fidibus.*

accomplice, n. *criminis conscius, socius, sceleri affinis.*

accomplish, v.tr. *conficēre, perficēre, absolvēre, consummare, perpolire;* to be —ed (of dreams, &c.), *exitum habēre.* **accomplished,** adj. (*per*)*politus, elegans, doctus, humanus.* **accomplishment,** n. 1, = fulfilment, *confectio, perfectio, absolutio;* = the end, *finis, exitus, -ūs;* 2, = — of the mind, *ars,* or by some term denoting the subject of the — (e.g. *musica,* music as an —).

accord, I. n. 1, = agreement of sounds (*sonorum*) *concentus, -ūs, nervorum* or *vocum concordia, harmonia;* 2, see AGREEMENT; of one's own —, *sponte, ultro.* **II.** v.intr. 1, lit. = to sound with, *concinēre;* 2, = agree with, *cum alqo congruēre.* **accordance,** see ACCORD, I. In — with, *ex;* in — with the agreement, *ex pacto, ex conventu;* — with my wishes, *ut volui;* — with his opinion, *ex ejus opinione.* **accordant,** adj. *congruens, consentiens, constans;* — together, *unanimus.* **according to,** see ACCORDANCE; *ad, secundum, ad alqd;* — you, *ex tuā sententiā;* — circumstances, *ex* or *pro re.* **accordingly,** adv. *itaque, quae cum ita sint.*

accost, I. n. *appellatio, salutatio.* **II.** v.tr. *alloqui* (rare in good Latin), *appellare, salutare.*

accouchement, n. *partus, -ūs;* a premature —, *abortio;* to be in —, *parēre, partum edēre.*

account, I. v.tr. 1, = to think, *habēre, aestimare;* to — highly, *magni facēre;* — lowly, *nihili facēre;* — nothing of, *non flocci facēre;* 2, = to — for, see EXPLAIN; 3,=to — to anyone, *rationem alci de alqā re reddēre.* **II.** n. 1, lit. = a reckoning, *ratio;* to take —, *rationem habēre;* to give —, *rationem alci de alqā re reddēre;* 2, fig. = to be of—, *magni* or *maximi haberi,* — with anyone, *multum apud alqm* (*auctoritate*) *valēre;* to be of no —, *nullā esse auctoritate;* 3, = — at a bank, *pecunia in argentariā* (*col*)*locata;* to open an —, *pecuniam in argentariam collocare;* to draw upon an —, *alqd de pecuniā suā detrahēre;* to pay upon —, *partem debiti* or *ex debito solvēre;* — book, *tabula;* 4, = pretext, reason; on my —, *meā de causā, meo nomine;* not on any —, *nullo modo;* on — of anything, *propter alqd;* 5, = narrative, *narratio;* give an — of, *alqd narrare.* **accountable,** see RESPONSIBLE. **accountant,** n. *scriba,* m., defined by context (e.g. *qui tabulas conficit*).

accoutre, v.tr. see EQUIP.

accredit, v.tr. 1,= add credit to, see CONFIRM; 2, = to — an ambassador, *alqm legatum* (*ad regem,* &c.) *facēre;* 3, see BELIEVE. **accredited,** adj. 1, = admitted, *probatus;* 2, = — envoy, *legatus publice missus.*

accretion, n. *accessio, incrementum, cumulus.*

accumulate, v.tr. (*co*)*acervare,* (*ac*)*cumulare, exaggerare.* **accumulation,** n. *cumulus, incrementum.*

accurate, adj. *accuratus, exactus, limatus, emendatus.* Adv. *accurate, exacte, pure, emendate.* **accuracy,** n. *accuratio* (a rare word), *diligentia;* with the greatest —, *accuratissime.*

accurse, v.tr. see CURSE.

accuse, v.tr. 1, legal t.t. *alqm alcjs rei* or *de alqā re accusare, postulare, compellare, citare, reum facēre, arguēre, alqm in jus vocare* or (*e*)*ducēre, in judicium adducēre, alci diem dicēre, nomen alcjs de alqā re deferre;* — of high treason, *alqm perduellionis,* or *majestatis* or *de majestate reum facēre;* — of assassination, *alqm inter sicarios accusare;* — of extortion, *de* (*pecuniis*) *repetundis accusare;* the accused, *reus;* 2, in gen. *accusare, incusare, criminari.* **accusation,** n. 1, legal t.t. *accusatio, criminatio, crimen,* esp. when unfounded; (= — of an informer, *secret —*) *delatio;* 2, in gen. *incusatio;* (= a speech against) *oratio in alqm.* **accusative,** n. *casus, -ūs. accusativus* (*casus*). **accuser,** n. *qui alqm accusat, accusator* (strictly of a public accuser, *petitor* being plaintiff in private case); an informer, *index;* a secret —, *delator.*

accustom, v.tr. *alqm assuefacēre alqā re, ad,* or dat. (abl. in Cic.), or with infin. ; to — oneself = be accustomed, *assuescēre, consuescēre,* with abl., *ad* or dat. or infin. **accustomed,** adj. *assuetus;* in the — way, *de more.*

ace, n. in cards, use terms from dice ; the side of the die marked 1, *canis* (= the dog-throw, i.e. worst) ; the best throw, the — of trumps, *Venus* (*jactus, -ūs*), *Venereus, basilicus* (because at a Roman symposium the king of the feast was chosen by this throw).

ache, I. n. *dolor.* **II.** v.intr. *dolēre.*

achieve, v.tr. 1, = to finish, *facĕre, conficĕre, efficĕre, perficĕre, consummare, finire* ; 2, = to gain, *assequi, consequi* ; to — something (i.e. make progress), *alqd* or *multum proficĕre.* **achievement,** n. 1, = the doing of anything, *confectio* ; 2, = a deed, *facinus, -ŏris,* n. (but more usual in bad sense) ; he has made an —, *magna confecit.*

acid, adj. 1, = sharp to the taste, *acidus, acerbus, acer* ; 2, = — in temper, *acer, acerbus, morosus.* **acidity,** n. 1, *sapor acidus* ; 2, *acerbitas, morositas.* **acerbity,** n. *acerbitas* (lit. and fig.).

acknowledge, v.tr. 1, = to accept as one's own, *a*(*d*)*gnoscĕre* (e.g. *alqm filium,* as a son) ; to — a child, *suscipĕre* (the father raised a new-born child from the ground) ; 2, = to admit, *confitēri* (= to confess, e.g. a fault) ; 3, = to — a kindness, *alci gratias agĕre* ; — a payment, (*in*) *acceptum referre* (i.e. to place to the credit side of an account-book) ; — a letter, *rescribĕre* with dat. or *ad.* **acknowledged,** adj. *cognitus, probatus, spectatus.* **acknowledgment,** n. 1, = approval, *approbatio, comprobatio* ; 2, = confession, *confessio* ; 3, gratitude (e.g. to make an —, *gratias alci agĕre, se gratum praebēre* ; 4, see RECEIPT.

acme, n. = height, *fastigium* ; to reach the — of glory, *summam gloriam assequi.*

acorn, n. *glans.*

acoustics, n. *ratio audiendi, quae ad auditum pertinent.*

acquaint, v.tr. see INFORM. **acquaintance,** n. 1, = knowledge of a thing, *peritia* (not in Cic.), *scientia, notitia, cognitio alcjs rei* ; with a person, *usus* or *familiaritas cum alqo* ; — with literature, *eruditio* ; to make — with, *alqm* or *alqd* (*cog*)*noscĕre* ; to seek — with, *appetĕre alcjs familiaritatem* ; 2, = a person slightly known, *amicus, familiaris, noti* (only used as n. in pl.). The distinction between friend and acquaintance was not marked in Latin, it can be rendered by *amicus* and *homo mihi amicissimus* = friend, or *homo mihi paene notus* = —. **acquainted,** adj. *notus, cognitus* ; — with, *alcjs familiaris* ; to make —, introduce, *alqm ad alqm deducĕre* ; to be — with, *alqm novisse* (*nosse*) ; to be familiarly — with, *alqo familiariter uti* ; — with anything, *alcjs rei peritus, gnarus, alqa re imbutus, doctus, institutus,* in *alqā re versatus* ; not — with, *alcjs rei ignarus, inscius, rudis.*

acquiesce, v.intr. (*in*) *alqā re acquiescĕre, alqd aequo animo* or *patienter ferre.* **acquiescence,** n. *assensus, -ūs* ; see ASSENT.

acquire, v.tr. see GAIN. **acquirement, acquisition.** n. 1, = anything gained, *res adepta* ; 2, = knowledge, *alcjs rei cognitio* ; a man of many —s, *vir perpolitus, multis artibus eruditus* ; 3, the process of —, *alcjs rei comparatio, adeptio.* **acquisitive,** adj. *aptus ad alqd impetrandum.*

acquit, v.tr. see ABSOLVE. **acquittal,** n. *absolutio alcjs rei.* **acquittance,** n. *apocha* (Jct.) ; to give or to enter an —, *in acceptum referre.*

acrid, adj. = hot and biting, both of physical taste and of temper, *acerbus, mordens, mordax.* **acridity,** n. *acerbitas.*

acrimonious, adj. *mordax, mordens, acer, bus, aculeatus.* Adv. *mordaciter, acerbe.* **acri- mony,** n. *acerbitas.*

across, prep. 1, = the other side of, *trans* ; 2, with verbs of motion, *trans, per* = right through ; something comes — my mind, *alqd mihi* (*de improvisu*) *ob*(*j*)*icitur.*

acrostic, n. = riddle, *aenigma, -ătis,* n.

act, I. v.intr. = to do, *agĕre, facĕre* (e.g. *bene, male,* well or ill) ; to — as a man, *se virum praebēre* ; so to — as to, *ita se gerĕre ut* ; the medicine —s, *efficax est.* **II.** v.tr. = to — a part 1, on the stage, *alcjs partes agĕre* ; to — the first part, *primas partes agĕre* or *tractare, personam tractare* ; to — a play, *fabulam agĕre* ; to forbid the players to —, *histrionibus scaenam interdicĕre* ; 2, in life, *personam sustinēre* or *tueri* ; 3, = to feign, *alqm simulare* ; 4, to — upon anyone, *multum, nihil,* etc., *apud alqm valēre* ; to be —ed upon, *alqā re affici.* **III.** n. of a play, *actus, -ūs* ; — of Parliament, *Senatusconsultum* ; — of amnesty, *oblivio sempiterna* ; the — of anyone, *factum* ; in pl. = achievements, *res gestae, gesta* or *acta, -orum,* n. ; in the very —, *in manifesto facinore.* **action,** n. 1, = the doing of anything, *actio* ; 2, = a deed, *factum* ; 3, in battle, *res gestae* ; = the battle itself, *praelium* ; 4, of a play, = the series of events, *actiones* ; = gesture, *actio, gestus, -ūs* ; 5, of a horse, *gradus, -ūs* ; 6, legal t.t. an — for anything, *lis, litis,* f., *actio alcjs rei,* or *de alqā re* (e.g. *furti, de repetundis*) ; to bring an — against, *actionem in alqm instituĕre, alci diem dicĕre.* **actionable.** adj. *cujus rei actio est, quod contra leges est.* **actor,** n. 1, = one who acts, *qui agit, facit, alcjs rei actor* ; 2, on the stage, *histrio, actor* ; comic —, *comoedus* ; tragic —, *tragoedus.* **actress,** n. only men acted in classical times, so use *quae partes agit.* **active,** adj. 1, = quick, *celer, acer, promptus* ; 2, = untiring, *industrius, impiger,* (*g*)*navus.* Adv. *acriter, impigre, industrie,* (*g*)*naviter.* **activity,** n. 1, = quickness, *celeritas* ; 2, = industry, *industria, impigritas.* **actual,** adj. *verus, manifestus.* Adv. *vere, re verā* ; actually? *itane vero?* **actuate,** v.tr. *excitare, impellĕre.*

acumen, n. *ingenii acies, acumen.*

acute, adj. 1, of pain, *acutus, gravis, vehemens acerbus* ; 2, of intellect, *acutus, subtilis, acer, perspicax, sagax* ; 3, see ANGLE, ACCENT. Adv. *acute, graviter, vehementer, subtiliter, sagaciter* **acuteness,** n. *sagacitas, perspicacitas, ingenii acies, acumen, subtilitas.*

adage, n. *proverbium.*

adamant, n. *adamas, -antis,* m. **adaman- tine,** adj. 1, lit. *adamantinus* ; 2, fig. = very strong, *validissimus* ; see STRONG.

adapt, v.tr. *alqd alci rei* or *ad alqd accommodare, aptare, efficĕre ut alqd cum alqā re con veniat.* **adapted,** adj. *aptus,* or *idoneus ad alqd* (*faciendum*), or *alci rei,* or *qui* with subj. **adaptation,** n. *accommodatio.*

add, v.tr. *alqd alci addĕre, adjungĕre, ad*(*j*)*icĕre* to — up, *summam facĕre, computare.* **addition,** n. 1, = adding to, *adjunctio* (esp. = an — that limits the meaning), *adjectio, accessio* ; 2, = a thing added, *alcjs rei accessio* or *additamentum* ; 3, in arith. *additio,* opp. to *subtractio* (= subtraction) (Quint.) ; by — and subtraction to find a total of various items, *addendo deducendoque summam facĕre.* **additional,** adj. *novus, additius, adjectus.*

adder, n. *vipera.*

addict, v.tr. *alci* or *alci rei se dare, dedĕre,* or *tradĕre* ; *se ad studium alcjs rei conferre, incum* *bĕre.* **addicted,** adj. *alci rei deditus, alcjs rei studiosus;* to be — to a person, *totum alcjs esse.*

addle, v.tr. *abortivum facĕre;* an addled egg, *ovum abortivum* (Mart.), *ovum irritum, zephyrium* (Plin.).

address, I. v.tr. 1, = apply oneself to anything, *se alci rei dedĕre, tradĕre, ad* or *in alqd incumbĕre;* 2, = to speak to, *alqm alloqui, affari, appellare* (both by speech and letter); 3, to — a letter to, *alci li(t)teras inscribĕre.* **II.** n. 1,=speech to anyone, *alloquium,* 2, = speech to a meeting, *contio* (in late Lat. also = a sermon), *oratio;* 3, of a letter, *inscriptio;* 4, = place, *locus* (e.g. to that —); 5, = adroitness, *sol(l)ertia;* 6, *—es* = courtship, to pay one's —es to, *alqam in matrimonium petĕre.*

adduce, v.tr. *adducĕre, producĕre, proferre,* (com)*memorare;* to — witnesses, testimony, *testes, testimonium proferre, testes citare, producĕre.*

adept, adj. *ad alqd callidus, alcjs rei* or *alqd re peritus.*

adequate, adj. *alci* or *alci rei proprius, alci, alci rei* or *ad alqd aptus, idoneus, alci rei* or *cum alqd re congruens, conveniens, consentaneus, ad alqd accommodatus;* — to the occasion, *ad tempus accommodatus.* Adv. *apte, convenienter, congruenter, pro ratā (parte).*

adhere, v. intr. *(in)alqd re* dat. or *ad alqd (in)-haerēre, adhaerēre;* to — to a person, *alci studēre, deditum esse, alcjs studiosum esse;* to — together, *cohaerēre;* — to a party, *e partibus esse, (alcjs) partibus favēre.* **adherence, adhesion,** n. 1, lit. by ADHERE; 2, = attachment, *amor, studium erga* or *in alqm.* **adherent,** n. *unus e sociis;* — of a school of thought, *discipulus;* = political —, *cum alqo consentiens;* his —s, *sui.* **adhesive,** adj. = sticky, *tenax;* — plaster, *cataplasma, -ătis,* n. (Cels.).

adieu! *vale!* pl. *valete;* to bid —, *alqm salvēre* or *valēre jubēre;* at the end of letters, *vale, valete, cura ut valeas, valeatis.*

adjacent, adj. *alci rei adjacens, adjectus, contiguus, vicinus, finitimus;* to be —, *adjacēre;* of a country, *contingĕre* (e.g. *fines Helvetiorum,* or *continentem esse* with dat. or abl. with *cum.*

adjective, n. *nomen adjectivum* (Gram.).

adjoin, see ADJACENT (to be).

adjourn, v.tr. *differre, proferre, prorogare;* to — the day of trial, *diem prodicĕre.* **adjournment,** n. *dilatio, prolatio.*

adjudge, v.tr. *alqd alci addicĕre, adjudicare;* to — a triumph, *alci triumphum decernĕre* (so of everything else awarded by the Senate, e.g. *honores, pecuniam.*)

adjunct, n. *accessio, alqd alci rei appositum, additum.*

adjure, v.tr. 1, = to impose an oath upon, *alqm jurejurando* or *sacramento, ad jusjurandum adigĕre, jurejurando obstringĕre;* 2, = to entreat, to — (by), *(per alqm* or *alqd) obsecrare, obtestari.* **adjuration,** n. = entreaty, *obsecratio, obtestatio.*

adjust, v.tr. 1, see ARRANGE; 2, see ADAPT. **adjustment,** n. *accommodatio.*

adjutant, n. *optio, -onis,* m.

administer, v.tr. *alqd administrare, gerĕre, procurare, alqā re fungi, alci rei praeesse;* to — an oath, to *alci jusjurandum deferre;* to — medicine, *medicinam alci dare;* — justice, *jus dicĕre.* **administration,** n. 1, = performance, *administratio, procuratio, functio;* 2, = the ministers of state, *qui reipublicae praesunt* or *praepositi sunt.*

admiral, n. *praefectus classis;* to appoint as —, *praeficĕre alqm classi;* to be an —, *classi praeesse.*

admire, v.tr. *(ad)mirari.* **admiration,** n. *(ad)miratio.* **admirable,** adj. 1, = worthy of admiration, *(ad)mirandus, (ad)mirabilis;* 2, = excellent, *optimus, egregius, eximius, praestans, praestabilis.* Adv. *mirum in modum, mirum quantum, (ad)mirabiliter, optime, egregie, eximie.*

admit, v.tr. 1, = to allow to enter, *alqm admittĕre, aditum alci dare, adeundi copiam* or *potestatem alci facĕre;* 2, = concede, *concedĕre, dare;* 3, = confess, *fatēri, confitēri;* 4, = to allow, *habēre* (e.g. *alqd excusationis,* = some excuse), *pati;* this —s of no doubt, *de hoc dubitari non potest.* **admission,** n. 1, = leave to enter, *admissio, aditus, adeundi copia;* 2, = concession, *concessio;* in a.gument, with this —, *hoc concesso.* **admissible,** 1, = to be received, *accipiendus;* 2, = fair, *aequus.*

admonish, v.tr. *alqm alqd, de alqd re* or *ut (ad)monēre, alqm ad alqd* or *ut (ad)hortari.* **admonition,** n. *(ad)monitio, (ad)hortatio.*

ado, n. with much —, *vix, aegre;* see FUSS.

adolescence, n. *adulescentia (adol.).*

adopt, v.tr. 1, legal t.t. *alqm adoptare, a(d)sciscĕre;* 2, = to accept, *accipĕre, recipĕre;* to — a resolution, *alqd constituĕre, consilium inire.* **adoption,** n. *adoptio.* **adoptive,** adj. *adoptivus* (mostly late, esp. Jct.).

adore, v.tr. 1, = to worship, *venerari, colĕre;* 2, = to admire, *colĕre, diligĕre, amare.* **adorable,** adj. *sanctus, venerandus.* **adoration,** n. *cultus, -ūs, veneratio.*

adorn, v.tr. *(ex)ornare, decorare;* an —ed style in speaking, *oratio ornata.* **adornment,** n. *ornatus, -ūs, ornamentum.*

adrift, adj. 1, lit. *fluctibus* or *vento jactatus;* 2, in mind, to be —, *(animo) vagari.*

adroit, adj. *callidus, sol(l)ers, habilis.* Adv. *callide.* **adroitness,** n. *habilitas, sol(l)ertia.*

adulation, n. *adulatio, assentatio, blanditia, ambitio.*

adult, I. adj. *adultus.* **II.** n. *pubes; —s, puberes.*

adulterate, v.tr. *adulterare, corrumpĕre, vitiare.*

adultery, n. *adulterium;* to commit —, *adulterium cum alqo* or *alqd facĕre, inire.* **adulterous,** adj. *adulteriis deditus.*

adumbrate. v.tr. *adumbrare.* **adumbration,** n. *adumbratio.*

advance, I. v.intr. 1, lit. *progredi, procedĕre;* 2, fig. *procedĕre, progredi, proficĕre;* to be advanced in years, *aetate provehi;* in rank, *ad ampliorem gradum* (e.g. *ad consulatum) provehi.* **II.** v.tr. 1, *alqm alqd in augēre, (ex)ornare;* to — anyone's interests, *alci* or *alcjs rei consulĕre;* 2, = to bring forward an opinion, *sententiam dicĕre, aperire;* 3, = to pay in advance, *in antecessum dare* (Sen.). **III.** n. 1, = a going forward, *progressus, -ūs, iter, -ineris,* n.; 2, = an increase, *progressus;* 3, = of money, *pecunia in antecessum data* (Sen.). **advance-guard,** n. *primum agmen.* **advancement,** n. 1, in rank, *gradus, -ūs amplior,* or by name of office to which — is made (e.g. to the consulship, *consulatus);* 2, in gen. = — of interests, etc., by infin. of verb to advance (e.g. the — of your interests, *tibi consulĕre).*

advantage, n. *commodum, lucrum, fructus, -ūs, emolumentum, utilitas, bonum* (esp. in pl. *bona, —s*); — of a position, *loci opportunitas;* to my

—, *e re meâ* or *in rem meam est* ; to gain — from, *fructum ex alqd re capere* ; with an eye to one's own —, *alqd ad fructum suum referre* ; it is for one's —, *expedit* (with acc. and infin.) ; to be of —, *utilem* or *utile esse, ex usu* or *usui esse, alci* or *alci rei prodesse.* **advantageous,** adj. *quaestuosus, utilis, fructuosus, opportunus.* Adv. *utiliter.*

advent, lit. *adventus, -ûs.* **adventitious,** adj. *adventicius, externus.*

adventure, I. n. 1, = daring deed, *facinus, -oris,* n., *audax inceptum* ; 2, =an unusual occurrence, *res nova* or *mira.* **II.** v.tr. *alqd audere, tentare, experiri, periclitari.* **adventurer,** n. *qui alqd tentat* ; a mere —, *fraudator.* **adventurous,** adj. *audax, temerarius.* Adv. *audacter, temere.*

adverb, n. *adverbium* (Gram.).

adversary, n. *adversarius* ; in trials, the —, *iste* ; see ENEMY.

adverse, adj. *alci* or *alci rei adversus, contrarius, oppositus* ; — winds, *venti adversi* ; — circumstances, *res adversae.* Adv. *contra* ; to act —, *alci* or *alci rei adversari, repugnare* ; to act — to one's own interest, *utilitati suae repugnare.* **adversity,** n. *adversa, res adversae, miseria.*

advert to, v.tr. *animum ad alqd intendere, alqd animadvertere.*

advertise, v.tr. 1, = to inform, *alqd alci nuntiare, alqm de alqa re certiorem facere* ; 2, = to make publicly known, *praedicare, pronuntiare* ; — in the papers, *in actis (diurnis* or *publicis) pronuntiare.* **advertisement,** n. 1, *indicium, significatio* ; 2, *praedicatio, proclamatio (in actis).*

advice, n. *consilium* ; by my —, *me auctore* ; a pretty piece of — ! *pulchre suades !* **advise,** v.tr. 1, = give advice, *consilium alci dare, alci suadere ut* or *alqd, alqm alqd* or *ut, monere, alqm alqd, ad* or *in alqd* or *ut, hortari* ; 2, = to inform, *alqm de alqâ re certiorem facere.* Adv. *consulte, considerate, de industriâ.* **adviser,** n. *suasor, consiliarius, (consilii) auctor.*

advocate, I. n. 1, legal t.t. *patronus, cognitor, procurator* ; to be an —, *caus(s)as dicere, agere* ; *in foro versari* ; 2, in gen. *alcjs rei auctor.* **II.** v.tr. = to defend, *defendere, tueri, tutari.*

adze, n. *ascia.*

aerial, adj. *aërius, aetherius.*

aeronaut, n. *qui se per aerem* (**curru**) *propellat.*

afar, adv. *procul, longe, e longinquo, eminus* (opp. *comminus*) ; to be —, *procul* or *longe abesse.*

affable, adj. *affabilis, blandus, comis, communis, mansuetus* (= gentle, opp. *ferus*), *commodus* (= obliging). **affability, affableness,** n. *mores commodi, affabilitas, mansuetudo, comitas, communitas* (Nep.).

affair, n. *res, opus, -eris,* n. (= work), *negotium, occupatio, ministerium, munus, -eris,* n., *cura* ; it is the — of a judge, *judicis (officium) est.* See BUSINESS.

affect, v.tr. 1, = to influence, *alqm tangere, (com)movere, alqm alqd re afficere* ; 2, = to injure, *alci nocere, noxium esse* ; 3, = to be fond of, *diligere, amare* ; 4, = to assume an appearance, *simulare, imitari, prae se ferre* ; to — constancy, etc., *constantiam, etc., simulare.* **affectation,** n. *simulatio, imitatio, ostentatio.* **affected,** 1, of persons, *mollis, ineptus* (= silly), *alqd ostentans* ; 2, of things, *quaesitus, simulatus, putidus, molestus* (of speech). Adv. *putide, inepte, molliter, moleste.*

affection, n. 1, = a state of the mind or feeling, the feelings, *animi motus, -ûs, (animi) affectus, -ûs, commotio, permotio, impetus, -ûs* ; 2, = loving

sentiment, *amor, caritas, benevolentia, studium, pietas* (= dutiful —) ; *indulgentia* (= indulgent —), *voluntas in* or *erga alqm.* **affectionate,** adj. *amoris plenus, alcjs amans* (e.g. *uxoris), pius* (= dutifully —), *indulgens.* Adv. *amanter, indulgenter, pie* ; — yours (at the end of a letter), *cura ut valeas* or *vale.*

affiance. I. n. 1, = trust, *fiducia, fides* ; in anything, *alcjs rei* ; with anything, see AFFINITY ; 2, = marriage contract, *sponsalia, -ium.* **II.** v.tr., see BETROTH.

affidavit, n. *testimonium per tabulas datum* (Quint.).

affinity, 1, = relationship, *propinquitas, propinquitatis vinculum, necessitudo* (= family ties), *cognatio* (on the side of the father or the mother), *a(d)gnatio* (on the side of the father), *affinitas, affinitatis vinculum* (by marriage) ; *consanguinitas, consanguinitatis vinculum, sanguinis vinculum* (by blood) ; 2, = close connection, similarity *cognatio, conjunctio* ; — of the sciences, *cognati studiorum.*

affirm, v.tr. 1, *aio* (defective = I say Yes, opp. *nego), affirmare, confirmare, annuere* (by nodding assent), *fateri, confiteri* (= to admit) ; 2, legal t.t. to — a contract, law, etc., *pactum, legem,* etc., *sancire, ratum esse jubere* (of the Senate). **affirmation,** n. 1, in gen. *affirmatio* ; 2, legal t.t. *confirmatio.* **affirmative,** adj. *aiens* (opp. *negans), affirmans* ; an — answer, *affirmatio.* Adv. to reply —, *aio, alqd confirmare.*

affix, v.tr. = to fasten or put to, *alqd alci rei (af)figere, alqd ad rem alligare, annectere, ad rem* or *alci rei alqd, alci rei agglutinare* (= to glue to).

afflict, v.tr. = to make sorrowful, *contristare, dolorem alci facere, efficere, afferre, commovere, dolore alqm afficere* ; *alqm torquere, angere, (ex)cruciare, vexare, mordere, pungere.* **affliction,** n. *aegritudo* (= sickness of mind), *dolor, maestitia* (= sadness, opp. *hilaritas, laetitia), molestia, maeror* (= dejection) ; — of body, *aegrotatio, morbus.* **afflicting,** adj. *tristis, miser, acerbus, luctuosus.*

affluence, n. *abundantia, affluentia* (more than you want), *ubertas* (= fulness), *copia* ; — of good things, *suppeditatio bonorum.* **affluent,** see ABUNDANT, under ABOUND.

afford, v.tr. 1, = to supply, *praestare, praebere, concedere, alcjs rei (facienda) potestatem facere* (e.g. to — an opportunity for an interview, *colloquendi secum pot. fac.*) ; 2, = to yield, *reddere, suppeditare* ; 3, = to have the means or to be able, *posse.*

affranchise, see FREE, v.tr.

affray, n. = disturbance or petty quarrel, *rixa, pugna, tumultus, -ûs* (of a mob).

affright, see FRIGHTEN.

affront, I. v.tr. 1, = to meet, *alci* or *ad* or *in alqd occurrere, alci obviam ire* ; 2, = to wound the feelings, *offendere, laedere, pungere* (= to sting), *mordere.* **II.** n. *opprobrium, contumelia, injuria.* **affronting,** adj. *injuriosus, contumeliosus.*

afield, adv. *in agros* (with verbs of motion), *in agris* (with verbs of rest).

afloat, adj. & adv., to be —, *navigare, navi vehi.*

afoot, adv. *pedibus* (e.g. *pedibus ire*).

aforesaid, adj. *quem* or *quod supra scripsi, commemoravi,* etc.

afraid, adj. *anxius, sol(l)icitus, timidus, pavidus, trepidus, ignavus, (per)territus* ; to be —, *alqm, alqd timere, metuere, reformidare* ; not to be —, *sine metu* or *securum esse.*

afresh, adv. see AGAIN.

after, I. prep. *post* (with accus.) 1, of place, *post eum* (= after or behind him); 2, of time, *post aliquot menses* (= after some months); or by abl. abs. (e.g. *Aegina relictā,* = — leaving Ægina); 3, of rank (*nemo est post te,* = no one is after or inferior to thee). As denoting sequence or order, rank, *secundus a* (e.g. *secundus a rege,* = next to the king); = according to, *secundum* (e.g. *secundum legem,* — *rationem,* etc.). If a model is intended, *ad* is used (e.g. *ad normam,* = after a set rule; *ad eorum arbitrium et nutum totos se fingunt,* = they form themselves wholly after their will and pleasure; *ad modum,* = moderately; *ad formam,* — *effigiem,* — *similitudinem,* denoting imitation). **II.** conj. 1, *postquam, ut, ubi;* three years after he had returned, *post tres annos* or *tertium annum quam redierat, tertio anno quam redierat;* the day — he came, *postridie quam venerat,* also *postridie ejus diei;* 2, by abl. abs., — he had done this, *quo facto.* **III.** adv., also **afterwards,** *post, postea, posthac* (denoting specially sequence in time); *dein(de), exin(de), inde* (denoting the sequence in time of two things, next); *deinceps* (an unbroken sequence in time), *mox* (= presently, shortly after, opp. *nunc*). When the "afterward" refers to the act in the foregoing member, the Romans liked to repeat the verb of that member in the form of a participle (e.g. the robbers took Remus prisoner, and afterwards gave him up to Amulius, *latrones Remum ceperunt et captum Amulio tradiderunt);* three years —, *post tres annos, tribus annis post, post tertium annum, tertio anno post, tertio anno;* first, afterward, lastly, *prius, deinde, extremo;* first, next, afterward, *principio, proximo, deinde.*

afternoon, I. n. *pomeridianum tempus;* in the —, *post meridiem.* **II.** adj. *pomeridianus.*

again, adv. 1, in gen. *iterum, denuo, rursus, rursum;* again and again, *iterum atque iterum, semel atque iterum;* in composition by *re-;* to rise —, *resurgēre;* 2, = hereafter, *posthac, postea;* 3, = in turn, *contra, vicissim;* 4, of the heads of a speech, *ad hoc* or *haec.*

against, prep. 1, = rest near, *ad* with accus. (e.g. *ad murum), contra* with accus. (e.g. *contra insulam);* 2, = motion towards, *adversus* or *ad alqm* or *alqd;* 3, = hostility towards, *adversus* or *in alqm, contra alqm* or *alqd;* a speech — Caecina, *oratio in Caecinam;* — expectation, *praeter* or *contra opinionem;* — the stream, wind, *adverso flumine, vento;* — one's will, *alqo invito;* for and —, *in utramque partem;* 4, of time, *ad* or *in* with accus.; *sub lucem,* — daylight (i.e. just before).

age, n. *aetas* (=the time of life, persons living at the same time); of the same —, *aequalis* (also = contemporaries); men of the same —, *ejusdem aetatis* or *temporis homines, ejusdem aetatis oratores* (= the orators of the same age, that is, the contemporaneous orators); next in —, *aetate proximus;* his — did not understand Socrates, *Socratem aetas sua parum intellexit, Socrates ab hominibus sui temporis parum intellegebatur;* *saeculum* (=a long indefinite period); *tempus, -ōris,* n., or in pl.; to be of —, *sui potentem, sui juris esse;* not of —, *nondum adultā aetate;* old —, *senectus, -ūtis,* f.; to be twenty years of —, *viginti annos natum esse.* **aged,** adj. *aetate provectior* or *grandior;* an — man, *senex, -is.*

agent, n. *actor, procurator;* a free —, *qui sui juris est.* **agency,** n. 1, = performance, *effectus, -ūs;* 2, = employment, *procuratio.*

aggrandize, v.tr. *amplificare, augēre.* **ag-**

grandizement, n. *amplificatio, dignitatis accessio* (= — in rank).

aggravate, v.tr. 1, = to increase, *augēre;* 2, = to exasperate, *exasperare, lacessēre, incitare.*

aggregate, I. n. *summa.* **II.** v.tr. *congregare.* **aggregation,** n. *congregatio.*

aggression, n. 1, in war, *impetus, -ūs, incursio, incursus, -ūs, excursio, oppugnatio* (= storming of a place); 2, in. gen. = encroachment, *injuria.* **aggressive,** adj. *hostilis, infensus.* Adv. *hostiliter, infense.* **aggressor,** 1, *qui bellum suscepit;* 2, in gen. *qui injuriam alci facit.*

aggrieve, v.tr., see GRIEVE.

aghast, adj. *(ex)territus, perturbatus;* to stand —, *stupēre.*

agile, adj. *agilis, velox, pernix.* **agility,** n. = nimbleness, *agilitas, pernicitas, velocitas.*

agitate, v.tr. 1, = to move hither and thither, to move greatly, *agitare, quatēre* (= to shake), *rotare, circumagēre* (= to drive round), *(com)movēre, (con)turbare;* 2, = to excite, *percutēre, perturbare, commovēre, percellēre;* 3, = to discuss, to — a question, *rem* or *de re agēre, disputare, disserēre; sol(l)icitare* (= to stir up), *alqm excitare* (by speech). **agitation,** 1, *agitatio, jactatus, -ūs, jactatio* (as of the sea), *concussus, -ūs, concussio;* — of the body, *corporis motus, -ūs,* comb. *agitatio motusque corporis;* to be in —, *moveri, agitari;* 2, — of mind, *animi motus, commotio, concitatio;* strong —, *animi perturbatio;* to be under —, *perturbatum esse;* 3, of a question, *disputatio.* **agitator,** n. *turbator plebis* or *vulgi;* to be an —, *rebus novis studēre.*

ago, adv. *abhinc;* thirty days —, *(jam) abhinc triginta diebus,* or *abhinc triginta dies, ante triginta dies;* long —, *jam pridem.*

agony, n. 1, of body, *dolor, aegrotatio;* 2, of mind, *aegritudo, dolor.* **agonize, I.** v.intr. *(ex)cruciari, torquēri.* **II.** v.tr. *(ex)cruciare, torquēre.*

agrarian, adj. *agrarius.*

agree, I. v.intr. = to be of one mind and voice, *concinēre, conspirare, consentire, congruēre;* not to —, *dissentire, discrepare de re;* **II.** v.tr. 1, to — upon, *alci rei assentiri, de alqā re congruēre, idem sentire;* to — upon terms, *conditiones accipēre;* 2, to — with, *saluhrem alci esse;* not to —, *gravem esse.* **agreement,** n. 1, *consensio, consensus, -ūs, concordia, unanimitas* (opp. *discordia);* 2, = a compact, *pactum;* to strike an —, *alqd cum alqo pacisci.* **agreeable,** adj. 1, = pleasant, *acceptus, gratus, dulcis, suavis;* 2, = witty, *lepidus, facetus;* 3, — to, *alci rei* or *ad alqd accommodatus, aptus, alci rei* or *cum alqa re conveniens.*

agriculture, n. *agri* (*agrorum*) *cultura* (or as one word, *agricultura),* or *agri cultio* (or as one word), or *agrorum cultus, -ūs.* **agricultural,** adj. *rusticis rebus deditus.* **agriculturist,** n. *arator, agricola,* m., *agri cultor* (oi as one word, *agricultor).*

aground, adv. 1, *in vado* (= on the shoal), *in litore, in scopulis* (= on the rocks), *in syrtibus* (= on the quicksands); 2, fig. *in luto esse, in difficultatibus versari.*

ague, n. *febris intermittens.*

ah! ah! aha! interj. *eu, euge.*

ahead, adv. = before, *ante;* to go —, *anteire, praeire;* to run —, *praecurrēre;* to swim —, *praenatare;* to sail —, *praevehi.*

aid, I. n. 1, = help, *auxilium, adjumentum, subsidium* (esp. = resource) *opem* (n. *ops* and dat. *opi* not used); 2, = a tax, *vectigal.* **II.** v.tr *auxilium alci afferre, alci adesse* or *praesto esse, alqm (ad)juvare.*

ailing, adj. *aeger;* see SICK.

aim, I. n. 1, *meta* (= the goal); *scopos, -i* (= mark. Suet.); to fix an —, *alqd petēre;* 2, fig. *propositum;* to propose an — to yourself, *finem sibi proponēre;* what is the — of this? *quorsum haec spectant?* **II.** v.tr. 1, *telum collineare, telum dirigēre* or *intendēre in alqm* or *alqd, telo petēre alqm* or *alqd;* 2, fig. *alqd (animo) intendēre, spectare, pertinēre ad alqd* (e.g. these things — at concord, *haec ad concordiam spectant*).

air, I. n. 1, *caelum*(=the whole atmosphere); *aër* (accus. sing. *aëra,* = ἀήρ, the atmosphere near the earth), *aether* (= αἰθήρ, the upper air). *aura* (= breeze), *ventus* (= the wind), *spiritus, -ūs* (= breath of air, or life), *anima* (= the breath of life); to take — (i.e. of a secret), *emanare;* 2, = appearance, *vultus, -ūs* (= the look of the face), *aspectus, -ūs, alcjs* or *alcjs rei species, forma, facies;* to have an — of any kind, *se gerēre* with adv. (e.g. *honeste*), *se praebēre* with adj. (e.g. *talem*); to give oneself —s, *se jactare* or *ostentare;* 3, = a tune, *modus :musicus), cantus, -ūs.* **II.** v.tr. *aeri exponēre, ventilare.* **airy,** adj. *aerius, aetherius, aëri expositus.* **airiness,** n. by adj. (e.g. the — of a place, *locus ventis expositus.*

aisle, n. *ala* (side), *spatium medium* (mid).

akin, adj. *propinquus, a(d)gnatus* (on the father's side), *cognatus* (on the mother's); to be near —, *arta propinquitate alci conjunctum esse, alci finitimum esse.*

alabaster, I. n. *alabastrites, -ae,* m. **II.** adj. *ex alabastritā factus;* an — box, *alabaster,* or *alabastra* (pl. neut.).

alack! alack-a-day! interj. *eheu, vae mihi.*

alacrity, n. 1, = quickness, *pernicitas, velocitas;* 2, = cheerfulness, *alacritas, hilaritas.*

alarm, I. n. 1, *strepitus, -ūs* (= a loud noise which calls out men and beast), *turba*(= confusion), *tumultus, -ūs* (= uprising and uproar, as in an insurrection) ; comb. *strepitus et tumultus;* to give — of fire, *incendium conclamare;* to sound the —, *classicum canēre;* from —, *prae strepitu;* to be in —, *trepidare;* 2, = fear, *terror, trepidatio;* see AFRAID, FEAR. **II.** v.tr. *conturbare, terrēre.*

alas! alas-a-day! see ALACK.

album, n. *über.*

alcove, n. *zotheca.*

alder, I. n. *alnus,* f. **II.** adj. *alneus.*

alderman, n. *magistratus, -ūs,* more definitely according to context (i.e. if the — is mentioned as a judge, *judex*).

ale, n. *cer(e)visia* (a Gallic word). **ale-house,** n. *caupona.*

alert, adj. *vigil, alacer;* to be on the —, *vigilem esse;* see ALACRITY.

algebra, n. * *algebra.*

alias, n. *nomen alienum;* to assume an —, *nomen sibi fingēre.*

alien, I. adj. *(ab) alqo, alqd re, alci* or *alci rei alienus;* see ABHORRENT. **II.** n. *aliegena,* m. (= born abroad), *advena,* m. and f. (= one who has come into a foreign land). **alienate,** v.tr. 1, legal t.t. *(ab) alienare* (= to make what is mine strange to me or to make it another's), *vendēre* (= to sell), *vendēre et (ab) alienare;* 2, = to estrange, *alqm ab alqo alienare.* **alienation,** n. 1, (of goods), *(ab) alienatio, venditio;* — of a part, *deminutio de alqa re;* 2, — of mind, *mentis alienatio* or *alienata mens, vesania* (= madness), *vecordia* (= folly), *delirium* (= wandering), *furor* ✓ (= rage).

alight, v.intr. *descendēre;* — from a horse, *ex equo descendēre.*

alike, I. adv. *pariter, aeque, eodem modo.* **II.** adj. *similis.*

alive, adj. *vivus;* to be —, *in vitā* or *in vivis esse, vivēre.* See LIFE.

all, adj. 1, = every, *omnis;* 2, = the whole, *totus, solidus;* — together, *cunctus, universus;* in — respects, *ex omne parte, plane, prorsus;* — the best men, *optimus quisque;* at —, *omnino, prorsus;* not much, if at —, *non multum, aut nihil omnino;* not at —, *minime;* in —, *in summā* (e.g. *absolvi in summā quat(t)uor sententiis,* = to be acquitted by four votes in —); taken together, *omnino* (e.g. there were five in —, *quinque omnino erant*).

allay, v.tr. *lenire, levare, sedare, mitigare.*

allege, v.tr. to — in excuse, *alqd alci excusare;* see ASSERT. **allegation,** n. 1, *affirmatio;* 2, = a charge, *indicium, accusatio.*

allegiance, n. *fides;* to swear —, *in verba alcjs jurare;* to keep in one's —, *alqm in officio suo retinēre.*

allegory, n. *allegoria* (Quint.).

alleviate, v.tr. see ALLAY. **alleviation, n.** *levatio, mitigatio, levamen(tum).*

alley, n. 1, of a house, *ambulatio;* 2, of a street, *angiportus, -ūs.*

allot, v.tr. = to assign by lot, *sortiri* (= to cast lots for), *sorte legēre.* **allotting,** n. *sortitio;* = to assign, *(at)tribuēre, assignare, addicēre, adjudicare.* **allotment,** n. 1, = act of allotting, *assignatio;* 2, = ground, *ager, possessio.*

allow, v.tr. 1, = permit, *sinēre* (subj. with or without *ut*), *pati* (with acc. and inf.), *permittēre alci* (with *ut* or inf.), *concedēre* (= to yield to a request); to — to go, *sinēre abeat;* 2, = concede, *concedēre, confiteri* (= acknowledged, *spectatus, cognitus;* 3, = to give, *dare;* for a public object, *decernēre.* **allowable,** adj. *concessus, licitus.* **allowance,** n. 1, = permission, *concessio, permissio;* 2, = indulgence, *indulgentia;* to make — for, *alqd condonare;* 3, = money, *pecunia in alqd data.*

alloy, I. n. = a spoiling, *corruptio, depravatio;* without —, *sincerus, purus.* **II.** v.tr. *corrumpēre, vitiare.*

allude to, v.tr. = to refer to, *significare alqm* or *alqd, designare, describēre.* **allusion,** n. *significatio, mentio alcjs rei.*

allure, v.tr. *in* or *ad alqd allicēre, invitare; inescare* (by a bait). **alluring,** adj. *blandus, dulcis.* **allurement,** n. *invitamentum* (=something inviting), *incitamentum* (= something impelling); —s, *illecebrae.*

ally, I. n. *socius, foederatus; foedere sociatus,* (= united by treaty); relating to an —, *socialis.* **II.** v.tr. *foedus facēre, alqm* or *alqd cum alqd re conjungēre, societatem cum alqo inire;* to — oneself, *se cum alqo (con)jungēre, foedus cum alqo sancire.* **alliance,** n. *societas, foedus -eris,* n., matrimonial —, *matrimonium.*

almanack, n. *fasti, -orum, ephemeris, -idis,* f.

almighty, adj. *omnipotens.*

almond, n. *amygdala, amygdalum;* — tree, *amygdalus,* f.

almost, adv. *prope, paene, fere, ferme, tantum non* (e.g. *tantum non bellum ante portas et murum erat,* = war was all but at the gates), *ad* (with accus. = close to), *circiter* (about), *haud multum* or *non longe abfuit quin.*

alms, n. *stips, -is,* f. (nom. not used), *beneficium* (= a kindness). **almoner,** n. *qui largitionibus praeest.* **alms-house, n.** *ptochotropheum* (Jct.).

aloe, n. *aloë, -es,* f.

aloft, adv. *sublime.*

alone, I. adj. *solus, unus, unus solus;* also by *unus omnium* or *ex omnibus; sine arbitris, remotis arbitris* (= without witness). **II.** adv. See ONLY.

along, I. adv. *porro, protinus;* get — with you, *abi, apage* (*ie*). **II.** prep. *secundum,* **praeter;** to sail —, *litus* or *oram praetervehi;* — with, *una cum.*

aloof, adv. *procul;* to stand — from, *se ab alqâ re removêre.*

aloud, adv. *clare, clarâ voce, magnâ voce, summâ voce.* See LOUD.

alphabet, n. *lit(t)erarum nomina et contextus, -ûs,* (Quint.). See LETTER. **alphabetical,** adj. *in lit(t)eras digestus.* Adv. *lit(t)erarum ordine.*

already, adv. *jam, jam tum, jam tunc, jam dix, jamdudum, jampridem* (= a long while ago).

also, conj. *etiam, praeterea* (= besides), *insuper* (= moreover), *quoque* (always after the word to which it refers), *necnon* (= moreover, joins sentences), *item, itidem* (= again, in the same way), *et ipse,* (e.g. *Vespasiano Titus filius successit, qui et ipse Vespasianus dictus est* = Vespasian was succeeded by his son Titus, who also received the name of Vespasian). If two or more different qualities are ascribed to the same subject or object, and the force of the sentence lies in the difference, use *idem* for "also," (e.g. *musici quondam iidem poëtae* = of old, musicians were also poets). See AND.

altar, n. *ara* (= every slight elevation of stone, &c.), *altaria, -ium* (= a high altar); to raise an —, *aram statuêre, Deo facêre aram.*

alter, I. v.tr. *(com)mutare alqd in* and *de alqâ re; immutare, (con)vertêre, novare* (= to give a new form), *emendare, corrigêre* (= to take away faults), *variare* (= to change often), *invertêre* (= to turn upside down), *corrumpêre* (= to falsify, as *tabulas publicas*); what is done cannot be altered, *factum fieri infectum non potest.* **II.** v.intr. *converti.* To be altered, *(com)mutari, immutari;* both minds and facts are much —, *magna facta est rerum et animorum commutatio;* he has not —, *non alius est ac fuit, est idem qui semper fuit.* **alterable,** adj. *mutabilis;* adv. *mutabiliter.* **altering, alteration,** n. *(com)mutatio, immutatio, conversio; varietas, vicissitudo;* — of the weather, *caeli varietas;* — of fortune, *fortunae vicissitudines;* — of your opinion, *mutatio sententiae.*

altercation, n. *altercatio, jurgium, rixa* (= a brawl, fight); see QUARREL.

alternate, I. v.tr. 1, *alqd cum alqo alternare, variare;* to — rest and labour, *otium labore variare;* 2, v.intr. *variari, variare.* **II.** adj. *alternus, mutuus;* adv. *in vicem, vicissim, mutuo.* **alternation,** n. *(per)mutatio, vicissitudo.* **alternative, I.** adj. see ALTERNATE. **II.** n. *consilium contrarium, ratio alci rei contraria* or *opposita;* peace or war is our only —, *inter pacem et bellum nihil est medium.*

although, conj. *tametsi, quanquam (quamq.)* (gen. with the indic. as presupposing a fact), *etsi* (presupposing a fact, use the indic.; a supposition, the subj.), *licet* (with subj., with or without *ut*), *quamvis* (= however much), *cum (quom, quum),* = since, seeing, that, with subj.

altitude, n. *altitudo.*

altogether, adv. 1, = at the same time, *una simul, eodem tempore, conjunctim* (= in common, e.g. *auxilia petêre*); 2, = all together, *ad unum omnes, cuncti, universi;* 3, = wholly, *prorsus.*

plane, *omnino, penitus, funditus* (esp. with verbs of destroying); he is — made up of, *totus ex alqâ re factus est.*

alum, n. *alūmen.*

always, adv. *semper, omni tempore, numquam (nunq.) non;* the best is — the last, *optimum quidque est ultimum;* I — do it, *hoc facêre soleo.*

amalgamate, v.tr. *alqd (cum) alqâ re* (com)-*miscêre.* **amalgamation,** n. *conjunctio.*

amanuensis, n. *a manu (servus,* Jct.), *ab epistulis (servus,* Jct.)*, qui pro alqo scribit.*

amass, v.tr. *(co)acervare, aggerare, accumulare.* See ACCUMULATE, HEAP.

amatory, adj. *amatorius;* see LOVE.

amaze, v.tr. *obstupefacêre, percutêre.* **amazed,** adj. *obstupefactus;* to be —, *stupêre,* (*ob*)*stupescêre.* **amazing,** adj. *mirus, immanis;* an — quantity of money, *immanes pecuniae.* Adv. *vehementer, mirum in modum.* **amazement,** n. *stupor;* see ASTONISH, ASTOUND, WONDERFUL.

amazon, n. 1, lit. *Amazon;* 2, fig. *mulier bellicosa.*

ambassador, n. *legatus* (as a deputy in state affairs), *orator* (as a political deputy to deliver a verbal message).

amber, n. *electrum, sucinum* (Plin.).

ambiguous, adj. *anceps, ambiguus, dubius.* Adv. *ambigue* (e.g. *dicêre*). **ambiguity,** n. *ambiguitas* (e.g. *verborum*); see DOUBT.

ambition, n. *ambitio, laudis studium, studium cupiditasque honorum, contentio honorum, cupido honoris* or *famae, aviditas* or *avaritia gloriae, aestus quidam gloriae* (sometimes merely gloria, e.g. *alcjs gloriae favêre* and *gloriâ duci*). **ambitious,** adj. *ambitiosus, avidus gloriae* or *laudis, cupidus honorum, laudis et honoris cupidus, appetens gloriae;* to be —, *laudis studio trahi, gloriâ duci;* adv. *cupide,* or by adj.

amble, v.tr. *lente procedêre.*

ambrosia, n. *ambrosia.* **ambrosial,** adj. *ambrosius.*

ambush, n. *insidiae* (= the place and the men); to lay in —, *in insidiis (col)locare* or *disponêre;* to lie in —, *in insidiis esse.*

ameliorate, v.tr. *corrigêre* (= to make right), *emendare* (= to free from errors); to — your condition, *amplificare fortunam, augêre opes.*

amen! interj. *ita fiat! ratum esto!* eccl. *amen*

amenable, adj. 1, *alci rei obaediens;* 2, legal t.t. *sub alcjs jus et jurisdictionem subjunctus.*

amend, I. v.tr. *emendare, corrigêre.* **II.** v.intr. *mores mutare* (of morals), *convalescêre* (of health). **amendment,** n. *correctio, emendatio.* **amends,** n. *satisfactio, expiatio;* to make — for, *alqd expiare* (of a crime), *damnum restituêre* or *rescarire* (of a loss).

amethyst, n. *amethystus* (Plin.).

amiable, adj. *suavis, dulcis, venustus, jucundus.* Adv. *suaviter, jucunde.* **amiability,** n. *suavitas, venustas, jucunditas.*

amicable, adj. see FRIENDLY.

amidst, prep. *vn medio* (*loco*), *in media* (*parte*) *alcjs rei;* sometimes by *ipse* (e.g. in the midst of the preparations for war, *in ipso apparatu belli*).

amiss, adv. *male;* there is something — with me, *male mecum agitur;* to use —, *alqa re perverse* (*ab*)*uti;* to take —, *aegre* or *moleste ferre, in malam partem accipêre.*

ammunition, n. (*instrumenta et*) *apparatus,* *ūs belli, arma, -orum, tela, -orum.*

amnesty, n. *venia praeteritorum, impunitas, incolumitas, fides publica* (= the public safeguard), *amnestia ;* to pass a general —, *omnium factorum dictorumque veniam et oblivionem in perpetuum sancire.*

among, prep. *inter, in* (with abl.) ; from —, *ex, de ;* — men, *inter homines, in hominibus.*

amorous, adj. 1, in good sense, *amans, amore incensus ;* 2, in bad sense, *libidinosus.* Adv. *maximo cum amore, libidinose.* **amorousness,** n. *amor, libido.*

amount, I. n. *summa, vivum* (= the capital) ; the whole —, *solidum ;* a not inconsiderable —, *nummi non mediocris summae ;* a great — of gold, *pecunia magna* or *grandis ;* a very great —, *incredibilis pecuniae summa.* **II.** v.intr. *alqd efficĕre ;* what does it — to, *quae summa est ;* it —s to the same thing, *idem* or *par est, nihil interest utrum.*

amphibious, adj. *animal cujus et in terrâ et in aquâ vita est.*

amphitheatre, n. *amphitheatrum.*

ample, adj. *amplus.* Adv. *ample, abunde.* **amplitude,** n. *amplitudo.* **amplify,** v.tr. *amplificare.*

amputate, v.tr. *praecidĕre* (e.g. *membra, aurem, manum, caput* or *cervices alci), amputare* (*caput alci*). **amputation,** n. by the verb ; i.e. to perform an —, (*membrum*) *praecidĕre.*

amuse, v.tr. *delectare, oblectare.* **amusing,** adj. *jucundus.* Adv. *jucunde.* **amusement,** n. *delectatio, oblectatio, oblectamentum.*

anachronism, n. *error de temporibus factus.*

analogy, n. *analogia* (ἀναλογία, translated by Cicero *comparatio proportioque), similitudo.* **analogous,** adj. *analogus, similis.*

analysis, n. *explicatio, explicatio et enodatio, expositio.* **analyze,** v.tr. *explicare, expedire, quasi in membra discerpĕre.*

anapaest, n. *anapaestus.*

anarchy, n. *licentia, perturbatio omnium rerum, turba et confusio ;* — (as a social state), *civitas in quâ libido multitudinis pro legibus est.* **anarchical,** adj. *legibus carens.* Adv. *sine legibus.*

anathema, n. in civil affairs, to put a person under —, *aquâ et igni interdicĕre alci ; devotio, anathēma, -ătis.*

anatomy, n. *anatomia ;* to practise —, *insecare aperireque humana corpora.* **anatomical,** adj. *anatomicus.* **anatomize,** v.tr. *incidĕre corpus mortui, rescindĕre artus cadaveris.* **anatomist,** n. *qui incidit,* etc.

ancestor, n. *auctor generis* or *gentis* (= founder of a clan or family), *unus e majoribus* (= a forefather). **ancestors, ancestry,** n. *priores, majores, patres.* **ancestral,** adj. *avitus, proavitus.*

anchor, I. n. *ancora ;* to cast —, *ancoram jacĕre ;* the — holds, *ancora subsistit ;* to lie at —, *consistĕre in ancoris* or *ad ancoras ;* to raise —, *ancoram* or *ancoras tollĕre* or *solvĕre ;* fig. *spes, auxilium* (e.g. *curia summum auxilium omnium gentium,* = the senate was the chief — of all nations). **II.** v. tr. *navem ad ancoras deligare.* **III.** v.intr. see LIE AT —. **anchorage,** n. *statio.*

ancient, adj. *antiquus* (= that which has been of old), *vetus* (= that which has existed long), *priscus* (= primitive), *inveteratus* (= grown old), *obsoletus* (= obsolete) ; the —s, *veteres*

antiqui, prisci, majores (= forefathers). Ad *olim, antea, antiquitus, patrum memoriâ.*

and, conj. *et, que* (enclit. unites things that are alike at least in aim and tendency, e.g. *exploratores centurionesque), atque, ac* (only before consonants). Sometimes "and" does not appear (e.g. horse and man, *equi viri ;* men and women, *viri mulieres ;* also *patri a laboribus, consiliis, periculis meis servata est* = my native land has been saved by my labours, counsels, and dangers). Sometimes you must use the relative instead of the copula (e.g. *venit nuntius qui nuntiabat) ;* also the participle (e.g. *prodiens haec locutus est,* he went forward and said these things) ; so *urbe relictâ in villam se recepit* = he left the city and betook himself to his countryseat. Also a conjunction (e.g. *Xanthippus cum Carthaginiensibus auxilio missus esset, fortiter se defendit* = Xan. was sent to assist the C. and bravely defended himself). And also, *et quoque, nec non, idemque* or *et idem* (e.g. *musicus idemque philosophus*) ; and so, *itaque ;* and yet, *et tamen ;* and not, *neque, nec, et non* (the former to negative a sentence ; the latter, a word) ; and yet, *nec* (e.g. *quidam se simulant scire, nec quidquam sciunt,* some pretend to know, and yet know nothing) ; and no one or nothing, *nec quisquam, quidquam ;* and never, *nec unquam (umq.) ;* = but, *autem* (e.g. I do this, and you that, *ego hoc facio, tu autem,* etc.).

anecdote, n. *dictum, fabula, fabella.*

anemone, n. *anemone, -es,* f.

anew, adv. *denuo, de* or *ab integro.*

angel, n. *angelus.*

anger, I. n. *ira, iracundia, bilis* (= the gall), *stomachus* (= temper), *indignatio ;* outbreaks of —, *irae, iracundiae ;* from —, *prae irâ ;* in or through —, *per iracundiam, iratus, cum irâ.* **II.** v.tr. *lacessĕre, iram, bilem* or *stomachum alci movēre.* **angry,** adj. *iratus, irâ incensus, accensus,* or *inflammatus, iracundus ;* to make angry, *iram* or *bilem* or *stomachum alci movēre.* Adv *irate, iracunde.*

angle, I. n. 1, *angulus ;* 2, = an instrument for fishing, *hamus.* **II.** v.tr. 1, *piscari, hamo pisces capĕre, arundine pisces captare ;* 2, fig. to — after, *alqd captare, aucupari ;* see FISH. **angler,** n. *piscator.*

anglican, adj. use *Britannicus.*

anguish, n. *cruciatus, -ūs, tormentum, dolor ;* see ACHE.

angular, adj. *angularis, angulatus.*

animadvert, v.tr. 1, = to observe or consider, *animadvertĕre, cognoscĕre, sentire, vidēre, perspicĕre,* (ob)*servare ;* 2, = to punish, *punire, in alqm animadvertĕre ;* 3, = to criticize, *judicare.*

animal, I. n. *animal, bestia* (opp. *homo), belua* (= one of the larger animals), *pecus, pecudis,* f. (= a head of cattle, opp. to *pecus, pecoris,* n. = a flock) ; (*belua) fera* (= wild —) ; a little—, *bestiola.* **II.** adj. by circumloc. (e.g. — life, *vita quae corpore et spiritu continetur*) or merely *corpus,* opp. *animus,* (e.g. animal pleasures, *corporis voluptates*) : = peculiar to animals, *beluarum* or *pecudum* (e.g. *hoc est beluarum*). **animalcule,** n. by circumloc. *animal exigui corporis,* etc.

animate, I. v.tr. 1, = to give life to, *animare ;* 2, fig. = to make lively, *excitare, incitare ;* — his courage, *animum erigĕre.* **II.** adj. *animalis, animatus.* **animated,** adj. 1, lit. *animatus ;* 2, fig. = lively, *vegetus, alacer ;* — by anything, *alqâ re incensus.* **animation,** n. *alacritas, vehementia.*

animosity, n. *odium, invidia, ira, simultas.*

ankle, ankle-bone, n. *talus.* **anklet,** n. *periscelis, -idis,* f.

annals, n. *annales, -ium,* m., *monumenta rerum gestarum.*

annex, v.tr. **1,** = to add to, *alqd alci rei* or *ad alqd (ad)jungere, addere.* **2,** = to conquer, *alqd alci rei sub(j)icere;* to — a country, *in ditionem suam redigere.* **annexation,** n. **1,** *adjunctio, accessio, appositio;* **2,** of a town, *expugnatio* (by storm).

annihilate, v.tr. *delēre, ex(s)tinguēre* (as a light, e.g. *alcjs salutem*), *excidēre, tollēre, funditus tollēre.* **annihilation,** n. *ex(s)tinctio, interitus, -ūs, excidium.*

anniversary, n. *sacra, -orum, anniversaria* (= festival), *festi dies anniversarii.*

annotate, v.tr. *annotare* (Plin.). **annotation,** n. *annotatio.*

announce, v.tr. *(re)nuntiare, indicare.* **announcement,** n. *(re)nuntiatio.*

annoy, v.tr. *molestiam alci afferre* or *exhibēre, vexare, torquēre;* — with requests, *alqm precibus fatigare.* **annoyance,** n. **1,** *molestia, vexatio, cruciatus, -ūs;* **2,** = a trouble, *onus, -eris,* n., *incommodum.*

annual, adj. *annuus, anniversarius* (= taking place every year). Adv. *quotannis.* **annuity,** n. *annua pecunia.* **annuitant,** n. *qui annuam pecuniam accipit.*

annul, v.tr. **1,** legal t.t. *legem tollēre, abrogare abolēre;* to — a contract *(dis)solvēre.* **2,** in gen. *tollēre, delēre.*

annular, adj. *in orbem circumactus.*

anodyne, n. *quod dolorem mitigat.*

anoint, v.tr. *unguēre.* **anointing,** n. *v actio.*

anomaly, n. *anŏmalia* (Varr.). **anomalous,** adj. *anŏmalus* (Gram.).

anon, adv. *brevi (tempore), mox;* ever and —, *interdum.*

anonymous, adj. *sine nomine;* — poems, *carmina incertis auctoribus vulgata.*

another, pron. *alius;* at — time, *alio tempore;* — Cato (= a new), *novus Cato;* one says one thing, another —, *alius aliud dicit;* one —, *alius alium, inter se* (e.g. they fear one —, *inter se timent*), or (of two persons) *alter—alterum.*

answer, I. n. **1,** in gen. *responsum;* **2,** to a charge, *defensio, excusatio;* **3,** a written—, *rescriptum;* **4,** of an oracle, *oraculum, sors, sortis,* f.; **5,** — to prayer, *alqd precibus impetratum.* **II.** v.tr. **1,** in gen. *alqd alci* or *ad alqd respondēre;* **2,** by letter, *alqd alci rescribēre;* **3,** to a charge, *se defendēre, excusare;* **4,** of an oracle, *responsum dare;* to be answered, *mihi respondetur;* to — to one's name, *ad nomen respondēre;* to — an objection, *alqd refutare;* to — for, *alqd praestare,* see SURETY; to — to, *alci rei respondēre;* see AGREE. **III.** v.intr. = succeed, *res alci succedit, bene evenire.* **answerable,** adj. **1,** = agreeing with, *alci rei conveniens, congruens, consentaneus.* **2,** = accountable, *alcjs rei auctor, alqd praestans;* — to anyone, *qui alci de alqd re rationem reddit.*

ant, n. *formica.* **anthill,** *formicarum cuniculus.*

antagonist, n. *adversarius* (in every relation), *qui contra dicit, qui contra disputat, qui alci adversatur; iste* (= the opponent in a law-suit); see ADVERSARY.

antarctic, adj. **1,** lit. *antarcticus* (late); **2,** fig. *gelidissimus.*

21

antecedent, adj. *antecedens, praecedens, prior;* antecedents, *antecedentia, -ium,* pl., *praeterita, -orum,* pl. (= past events). Adv. *antea, prius.*

antechamber, n. *vestibulum* (= the open place in front of a Roman house where visitors assembled).

antechapel, n. *pronaus.*

antediluvian, adj. **1,** = old, *priscus, antiquus;* **2,** = old-fashioned, *obsoletus.*

antelope, n. see DEER.

antenna, n. *corniculum* (Plin.).

anterior, adj. *antecedens, praecedens, prior, superior, proximus.*

anthem, n. *cantus, -ūs.*

anthropoid, adj. *homini similis.*

anthropomorphic, adj. *Deum humanum corpus habēre fingens.*

anticipate, v.tr. **1,** *anticipare* (= to do before), *praecipēre;* **2,** *ex(s)pectare* (= expect). **anticipation,** n. **1,** = expectation, *ex(s)pectatio, spes;* **2,** = a doing beforehand, by verb, ANTICIPATE.

antics, n. *ludi, joca, -orum, ridicula, -orum, nugae.*

antidote, n. *antidotus, antidotum* (Cels.), *remedium;* against anything, *alcjs rei* or *ad.*

antipathy, n. **1,** of things, *rerum discordia, repugnantia;* **2,** of persons, *odium.*

antipodes, n. **1,** lit. *antipodes, -um* (late); **2,** fig. = the opposite, by adj. *adversus, contrarius.*

antiquary, antiquarian, n. *rerum antiquarum studiosus.* **antiquated,** adj. *obsoletus.* **antique, I.** adj. *antiquus.* **II.** n. *opus antiquum, res antiqua, monumentum antiquum.* **antiquity,** n. *antiquitas.*

antithesis, n. **1,** rhet. t.t. *contentio;* **2,** fig. = the opposite, *contrarium.*

antler, n. *cornu.*

anvil, n. *incus, -ūdis,* f.

anxiety, n. *angor, anxietas, pavor, sol(l)icitudo, trepidatio, timor.* **anxious,** adj. *anxius, sol(l)icitus;* to be —, *de alqā re anxium esse, angi.* Adv. *anxie, sol(l)icite.*

any, I. pron. *quisquam* (in neg. sentences and questions); *quilibet, quivis* (= any you please); *quis* (only after *si, ne, num, quo, quanto, nisi*); *ecquis* (in impassioned questions). **II.** adj. *ullus* (in neg. sentences and questions), *quilibet, quivis* (= any you please), *ecqui* (in impassioned questions); — one, *aliquis, quispiam;* at — turn, *aliquando, quando* (after *si, ne, num*); *unquam* (in neg. questions and sentences); — where, *alicubi, ubivis, usquam* (in neg. questions and sentences).

apace, adv. *celeriter.*

apart, adv. by prefix *se* (e.g. *se—cernēre*), *separatim.* **apartment,** n. see ROOM.

apathy, n. *socordia* (not in Cic. or Caes.), *nequitia.* **apathetic,** adj. *hebes;* see LAZY.

ape, n. *simia;* a little —, *simiolus.* **II.** v.tr. *alqm imitari;* see IMITATE.

aperient, n. and adj. by *alvi dejectionem (alvi) purgationem (petēre, etc.).*

aperture, n. see OPENING.

apex, n. *apex.*

aphorism, n. *sententia, dictum, elogium.*

apiary, n. *alvearium, mellarium.*

apiece. adv. by distrib. numeral (e.g. *deni,* ten —).

apologist, n. *defensor.* **apology,** n. 1, = defence, *defensio ;* 2, = excuse, *excusatio.* **apologize,** v.intr. *alqd excusare.* **apologetical,** adj. by verb, *qui se excusat,* etc. **⁓pologue,** n. *apologus.*

apophthegm, n. *elogium, sententia, dictum.* **apoplexy,** n. *apoplexis, apoplexia* (late). **apostle,** n. *apostolus.*

apostrophe, n. 1, rhet. t.t. *apostrophe ;* 2, grammat. t.t. *apostrophis* (late). **apostrophize,** v.tr. see ADDRESS.

apothecary, n. *medicus.*

appal, v.tr. *terrēre ;* see FRIGHTEN.

apparatus, n. *apparatus, -ūs.*

apparel, n. *vestis, vestimentum.*

apparent, adj. 1, = evident, *manifestus, apertus, clarus ;* to make —, *patefacĕre, aperire ;* 2, opp. to real, *opinatus, fictus, simulatus.* Adv. *aperto, manifeste, evidenter.* **apparition,** n. 1, = appearance, *adventus, -ūs ;* 2, = a spectre, *alcjs simulacrum, species.*

appeal, I. v.intr. 1, legal t.t. *alqm appellare, ad alqm provocare ;* 2, = to refer to, *alqm testari.* II. n. 1, *appellatio, provocatio ;* court of —, *judices penes quos provocatio est ;* 2, = entreaty, *preces, -um,* f., *deprecatio.* **appealing,** adj. *supplex ;* in an — voice, *suppliciter.*

appear, v.intr. 1, = become visible, *apparēre, in conspectum venire, conspici* (= to be seen), *se offerre ;* it —s to me, *mihi videtur ;* to — publicly, *in publicum prodire ;* to —, = to be present, *adesse ;* — to exist, *ex(s)istĕre ;* to — in court, *in judicium venire ;* 2, = to seem, *videri.* **appearance,** n. 1, = arrival, *adventus, -ūs ;* 2, legal t.t. = surety, *vadimonium ;* 3, = a thing shown, *res objecta, visum, species ;* 4, = personal —, *corporis habitus, -ūs ;* in —, = under pretext of, *sub specie ;* to put on an —, *simulare* (with acc. and infin.) ; in all —, *verisimillimum est* (with acc. and infin.).

appease, v.tr. 1, = — a deity, *placare ;* 2, = — a man, *placare,* (re)*conciliare ;* 3, =to — hunger, *famem explēre, depellēre.* **appeasable,** adj. *placabilis ;* — in character, *ingenium placabile.* **appeasement,** n. *placatio, reconciliatio.*

appellant, n. *qui provocat.*

append, v.tr. *addĕre, adjungĕre, figĕre* (af)*figĕre alqd alci rei, alligare alqd ad rem.* **appendage, -ant,** n. *appendix, -icis,* f., *accessio, alqd alci rei additum.* **appendix,** n. *appendix, additamentum ;* — of a book, *quaedam libro addita.* See ADD, ATTACH.

appertain, v.tr. see BELONG.

appetite, 1, physical, *fames, -is ;* to have no —, *cibum fastidire ;* 2, = desire for, *alcjs cupiditas, aviditas, appetitus, -ūs.*

applaud, v.tr. (ap)*plaudĕre alci, plausu* or *plausibus alqm excipĕre.* **applause,** n. (ap)*plausus, -ūs ;* see PRAISE.

apple, n. *malum ;* — tree, *malus,* f.

apply, I. v.tr. 1, = to put or fit to, *alqd alci rei* or *ad alqd applicare, aptare, accommodare ;* 2, = to use for, *collocare in alqd re, conferre ad alqd, tribuere alqd alci rei, alqd ad alqd dirigĕre,* (con)*vertĕre.* II. v.intr. = to turn or go to, *se convertĕre, conferre ad alqm, adire* or *convenire alqm, appellare alqd, confugĕre ad alqm, se applicare ad alqm.* **appliance,** n. *apparatus, -ūs, instrumentum.* **application,** n. 1, = request, address, *appellatio, provocatio, petitio ;* 2, = putting to, *adjunctio, conjunctio* (fig.) ; 3, = of the mind, *animi intentio, diligentia ;* 4, = of a word, *significatio.* **applicable,** adj. *utilis ;* to be — to anything, *ad alqd pertinēre.*

appoint, v.tr. *constituĕre, destinare* (= to make fast), *designare* (= to order), *eligĕre* (= to choose) ; to — a day, *diem statuĕre, constituĕre, dicĕre.* **appointment,** n. 1, = designation, by verb ; e.g. — of consuls, *consules designare ;* 2, = an office, *munus, -ĕris,* n. ; 3, = command, *jussum, mandatum ;* 4, = agreement to meet, by verb, *cum alqo convenire ut.*

apportion, v.tr. *dispertire, distribuĕre, dispensare, disponĕre, assignare* (e.g. *militibus agros*)

apposite, adj. *conveniens, accommodatus* Adv. *convenienter, accommodate.*

appraise, v.tr. = to fix the value of, *aestimare, censēre* (the censor's act). See VALUE.

appreciate, v.tr. *aestimare ;* — highly *alqm magni facĕre.*

apprehend, v.tr. 1, = to lay hold on, *prehendĕre, apprehendĕre ;* 2, = to take in mentally, *comprehendĕre, complecti* (*animo* or *mente*), *cogitatione* (*mente*) *concipĕre, intellegĕre ;* 3 = fear ; see FEAR. **apprehension,** n. 1, = arrest, *comprehensio ;* 2, = mental —, *comprehensio, intellegentia* (*intellig.*) ; 3, = fear, *timor ;* see FEAR **apprehensive,** adj., see TIMID.

apprentice, I. n. *alci* (e.g. *sutori*) *addictus.* II. v.tr. *alqm alci addicĕre.*

approach, I. v.intr. *ad alqm* or *alqd accedĕre, alci* or *alci rei appropinquare ;* of time, *appropinquare ;* to — the truth, *prope ad veritatem accedĕre, a veritate non multum abesse.* II. n. *appropinquatio, adventus, -ūs, aditus, -ūs.*

appropriate, I. v.intr. 1, = to give, *alqd alci dedicare ;* 2, = to claim, *alqd sibi* or *alqd se vindicare, alqd sibi arrogare, alqd suum facĕre.* II. adj. *ad alqd* or *alci rei idoneus, aptus, accommodatus, cum alqd re conveniens, congruens.* Adv *accommodate, convenienter.* **appropriation,** n. 1, legal t.t. (*agrorum*) *assignatio,* (bonorum) *additio ;* 2, in gen. by verb APPROPRIATE.

approve, v.tr. 1, in gen. (com)*probare ;* 2, = legal t.t. *alqd ratum facĕre* or *ratum esse jubēre, sancire ;* 3, = to — oneself, *se* (*fidum,* etc.) *praebēre.* **approved,** adj. *probatus, spectatus.* **approver,** n., legal t.t. *index, -icis,* m. and f. **approval,** n. see APPROBATION. **approbation,** n. (com)*probatio ;* with someone's —, *alqo auctore, alcjs auctoritate, pace tua, sua,* etc. ; without —, *alcjs injussu, sine alcjs auctoritate.*

approximate, v.tr. & adj. see APPROACH, NEAR.

April, n. *Aprilis* (*mensis*) ; to make an — fool of, *alqm ludibrio habēre.*

apron, n. *subligaculum.*

apt, adj. 1, see APPROPRIATE ; 2, = ready, *habilis ;* — to learn, *docilis.* Adv. *convenienter ;* = cleverly, *perite, callide.* **aptitude,** n. *facultas* (with gen. or adj.).

aquatic, aqueous, adj. *aquatilis.* **aqueduct,** n. *aquae ductus, -ūs ;* also *aqua* alone ; to form an — for the city, *aquam in urbem ducĕre.*

aquiline, adj. *aduncus.*

arable, adj. *arabilis.* See PLOUGH.

arbiter, n. *arbiter, disceptator.*

arbitrate, v.tr. *alqd disceptare, dijudicare.* **arbitration,** n. *arbitrium.* **arbitrary,** adj. 1, = unbounded, *infinitus, summus ;* 2, = capricious, *inconstans ;* 3 = proud, *superbus.* Adv. *superbe.* **arbitrariness,** n. *superbia.*

arbour, n. *umbraculum, ramorum nexus, -ūs.*

arc, n. *arcus, -ūs.* **arcade,** n. *porticus, -ūs,* f

arch, I. n. *arcus, -ūs, fornix.* II. v.tr. *arcuare, conformicars.* III. v.intr. *arcuari ;* see CURVE. IV. adj. *petulans.* V. in comp. =

chief; — angel, *archangelus ; — bishop, *archiepiscopus (Eccl.).

archaeology, n. rerum antiquarum scientia. archais.n, n. verbum obsoletum.

archer, n. sagittarius. archery, n. by verb (e.g. sagittis alqd petĕre).

architect, n. = master builder, architectus. architecture, n. architectura.

archives, n. 1, (private) tab(u)linum = the place where papers are kept; 2, (public) tabulae publicae.

arctic, adj. septentrionalis (e.g. regio, occasus). ardent, adj. ardens, fervens, acer. Adv. ucriter, ardenter.

ardour, n. ardor, fervor, aestus, -ūs.

arduous, adj. arduus, difficilis.

area, n. superficies.

arena, n. arena (lit. and fig.).

argue, v.tr. 1, = to dispute, verbis contendĕre, concertare, disputare ; 2, = to give or draw a conclusion, arguĕre, concludĕre, colligĕre. argument, 1, in gen. argumentum ; 2, = subject-matter, sententia, argumentum.

arid, adj. aridus, siccus.

aright, adv. recte, bene. See RIGHT.

arise, v.intr. emergĕre (= to come up out of), exoriri, ex(s)istĕre (of distinguished men). See RISE.

aristocrat, n. 1, = a noble, unus e nobilibus or patriciis; 2, = defender of the aristocracy, optimatium fautor. aristocracy, n. 1, = the nobles, optimates, -(i)um, m. and f., patricii, nobiles ; 2, = a form of government, optimatium dominatus, -ūs. aristocratical, adj. quod ad optimates pertinet, or by gen. optimatium.

arithmetic, n. arithmetice, -es, f., or arithmetica, -ae, f., or arithmetica, -orum. arithmetical, adj. arithmeticus. arithmetician, n. arithmeticus.

ark, n. arca.

arm, I. n. 1, lit. brachium (from the elbow to the wrist); lacertus (from the elbow to the shoulder); bone of —, radius brachii ; to take into —s, alqm complecti ; to sink into anyone's —s, manibus alcjs excipi ; 2, fig. (of the sea), brachium; (of a hill), ramus; (of a harbour), cornu. II. v.tr. armare, lit. and fig. III. v.intr. armari, arma capĕre. armed, adj. armatus. arm-chair, n. use sella (= chair), or lectus, torus (= couch). armistice, n. indutiae. armour, n. arma, -orum, pl. ; — bearer, armiger. armourer, n. faber armorum. arm-pit, n. ala. armoury, n. armamentarium. arms, n. arma, -orum, tela, -orum (of missiles esp., but also of swords, etc.): without arms, inermis; to run to —, ire ad arma ; to — ! ad arma! to lay down —, arma deponĕre ; to be under —, in armis esse ; to bear — against, arma ferre contra alqm; to enter a country in —, arma inferre terrae. army, n. exercitus, -ūs, copiae, milites, -um, vires, -ium, f. ; — in marching array, agmen ; — in battle-array, acies.

aromatic, adj. odorus, odoratus, suavis.

around, I. adv. circa, circum ; in composition with a verb, circum (e.g. to look —, circumspicĕre). II. prep. circa, circum with accus. See ABOUT.

arouse, v.tr. 1, lit. (e somno) excitare ; 2, fig. excitare, (com)movēre.

arraign, v.tr., see ACCUSE.

arrange, v.tr. ordinare, componĕre, disponĕre; — in order of battle, aciem instruĕre, collo-

care, constituĕre, instruĕre ; to — troops, copias instruĕre. arrangement, n. 1, rhet. t.t. compositio, dispositio (of words or sentences) ; 2, in gen. constitutio, ratio; by part. (e.g. a good — of anything, res bene disposita, instructa, etc.).

arrant, adj. by superl. or summus. Adv. superl. of adv. or turpiter, foede.

array, I. n. 1, see ARRANGEMENT ; 2, battle —, acies; 3, = dress, vestis. II. v.tr. 1, see ARRANGE ; 2, = to dress, vestire ; fig. ornare, vestire.

arrears, n. pecuniae residuae ; to be in — with, legal t.t. alqd reliquare (Jct.).

arrest, v.tr. comprehendĕre, in vinculc con(j)icĕre ; to put under —, comprehendĕre, in custodiam dare.

arrive, v.intr. advenire, pervenire, adventare. arrival, n. adventus, -ūs, accessus, -ūs.

arrogant, adj. arrogans, insolens, superbus, elatus alqā re. arrogance, n. arrogantia, superbia. Adv. arroganter, superbe. arrogate, v.tr. sibi arrogare, (as)sumĕre.

arrow, n. sagitta.

arsenal, n. armamentarium ; naval —, navalia, -ium.

arsenic, n. arsenicum.

arsis, n. sublatio (Quint.), arsis (late).

art, n. 1, = skill, ars, artificium ; merely mental, scientia, peritia, studium alcjs rei ; 2, = an —, ars (e.g. pingendi),disciplina; the fine —s, artes ingenuae ; — and sciences, studia et artes ; 3, = a trick, ars ; by — or craft, per dolum et fraudem. artful, adj. callidus, versutus, vafer, astutus. Adv. astute, callide. artfulness, n. astutia, dolus. artificer, n. 1, in gen. artifex ; 2, = creator, auctor. artificial, adj. artificiosus. Adv. arte or per artem. artisan, n. opifex, faber. artist, n. poeta, pictor, etc., or opifex = artisan, as among the Romans art was not always included in the artes liberales. artistic, adj. (ingenuarum) artium amator or studiosus. artistically, adv. arte, summa arte. artless, adj. simplex, ingenuus. Adv. ingenue, simpliciter, sine arte. artlessness, n. simplicitas.

artichoke, n. cinara (Col.).

article, n. 1, in gen. res ; 2, = condition, condicio (e.g. pacis) ; 3, = law, lex (e.g. lex militaris). II. v.tr., see APPRENTICE.

articulate, I. v.tr. pronuntiare. II. adj. clarus. Adv. clare. articulation, n. 1, of words, pronuntiatio ; 2, of limbs, artus, -uum, articulus.

artillery, n. (=the larger offensive weapons) tormenta -orum, (comprising the ballistae and catapultae).

as, adv. and conj. 1, in gen. by double comparative (e.g. he is not — brave as he is good, melior est quam fortior); idem (he is — friendly as ever, idem est amicus qui, etc.), aeque cum alqo or et, atque ; et — et (= — well as); — far as I can, quoad ejus factĕre possum ; — quickly as possible, quam celerrime ; — much again, alterum tantum ; — many as, quotcumque ; — far as I know, quod sciam ; 2, = like, instar, alcjs rei, tanquam, ut or by adv. (e.g. to behave as a fool, stulte) ; by a noun in apposition (Caesar — consul, Caesar consul) ; 3, as to, de alqā re, ad alqd, quod ad alqd pertinet ; 4, of time, ubi, ut, cum (quom) ; — often —, quotie(n)s totie(n)s ; — long —, tam diu — quam ; — soon —, simul ac ; 5, causal, quoniam (indic.), cum (subj.) ; 6, = as if, tanquam (tamq.) si, non aliter quam si.

ascend, v.tr. in or ad alqd a(d)scendĕre.

ascension, n. a(d)scensus, -ūs. **ascent,** n. 1,= a hill, locus editus ; 2, a going up, a(d)scensus, -ūs.

ascendancy, n. praestantia.

ascendant, n. by adj. summus ; to be in the —, praevalēre, alci alqā re praestare ; his star is in the —, summam gloriam adeptus est.

ascertain, v.tr. explorare, rem exploratam habēre.

ascetic, n. qui cibo abstinet.

ascribe, v.tr. alqd alci or alci rei, a(d)scribēre, tribuēre, adjungēre ; — great value to, magnum pretium statuēre rei.

ash, I. n. fraxinus, f. **II.** adj. fraxineus.

ashamed, adj. pudore affectus ; to be —, pudet alqm alcjs rei or infin.

ashes, n. cinis, -ĕris, m., favilla ; to reduce to —, ad or in cinerem redigēre ; to lie in sack-cloth and —, sordidatum or atratum esse. **ashy,** adj. cinereus.

ashore, adv. 1, of rest, in litore ; 2, of motion, in litus or terram ; to go —, (e nave) exire ; to put men —, exponēre.

aside, adv. seorsum, ex obliquo ; to go —, secedēre ; to call —, alqm sevocare ; to lay —, alqd seponēre.

ask, v.tr. alqm rogare, ex alqo quaerēre, ex alqo sciscitari, alqm alqd orare, petēre, poscēre, flagitare (repeatedly) ; to — a price, indicare.

askance, adv. oblique ; to look — at, alqm limis oculis a(d)spicēre.

aslant, adv. oblique, ex transverso.

asleep, adj. dormiens, in somno, per somnum.

asp, n. aspis, -ĭdis, f., vipera.

aspect, n. 1, in gen. a(d)spectus, -ūs, conspec-tus, -ūs ; 2 (in astrology), aspectus siderum ; 3, = condition, status, -ūs, ratio, condicio.

asperity, n. asperitas, acerbitas.

asperse, v.tr. a(d)spergēre, both lit. and fig. **aspersion,** n. 1, lit. a(d)spersio ; 2, fig. calum-nia, opprobrium ; to cast an —, calumniari.

asphalt, n. bitumen.

aspirate, I. n. a(d)spiratio. **II.** v.tr. a(d)s-pirare.

aspire, v.intr. ad alqd a(d)spirare, alqd sequi or persequi, eniti, contendēre, operam dare ut. **aspiration,** n. after anything, alcjs rei ap-petitio, contentio.

ass, n. 1, asinus ; a little —, asellus ; a female —, asina ; 2, as a term of contempt, homo stul-tissimus. **ass-driver,** n. asinarius.

assail, v.tr. to — a town, oppugnare. **as-sailant,** n. qui alqm adoritur. **assault, I.** n. 1. in gen. impetus, -ūs, incursus, -ūs ; 2, = of a town, oppugnatio ; 3, legal t.t. to charge with —, alqm de vi reum facēre ; to commit an —, alci vim afferre. **II.** v.tr. see ATTACK.

assassin, n. sicarius. **assassination,** n. caedes facta ; to accuse of —, accusare inter sicarios. **assassinate,** v.tr. alqm ex insidiis interficēre.

assay, v.tr. see TRY, ATTEMPT.

assemble, I. v.tr. cogēre, congregare, con-vocare, contrahēre ; to — the people, contionem convocare ; t· — troops, copias in unum locum cogēre. **II.** .intr. cogi, congregari, convenire, coire, confluēre. **assembly,** n. congregatio, convocatio ; = the people assembled, conventus, -ūs, coetus, -ūs, contio.

assent, I. n. assensio, assensus, -ūs. **II.** v.intr. assentire ; — to anything, rei assentiri, assentari, alqd or de alqā re, cum alqo or inter se, convenire ; to nod —, annuēre.

assert, v.tr. (as an opinion) tenēre, conten-

dēre, affirmare, asseverare, dicĕre ; to — your right, jus tenēre. **assertion,** n. 1, sententia, opinio, affirmatio ; 2, = maintenance, defensio, vindicatio ; see AFFIRM.

assess, v.tr. tributum alci imponēre, censēre ; to be —ed at anything, alqd conferre. **assess-ment,** n. aestimatio (= act of —) tributum, vecti-gal (= tax). **assessor,** n. assessor ; — of taxes, censor. **assets,** n. by bona, -orum.

assever, v. see ASSERT.

assiduous, adj. assiduus, sedulus, industrius, acer, impiger, diligens. Adv. impigre, assidue, industrie, acriter, diligenter. **assiduity,** n. assiduitas, sedulitas.

assign, v.tr. alci alqd assignare, attribuēre. **assignation,** n. 1, assignatio, attributio ; 2, = appointment, constitutum ; to keep an —, ad constitutum venire.

assimilate, v.tr. 1, alqd cum alqā re (ad)ae-quare, alqd alci rei similem facēre ; 2, = to digest, concoquēre. **assimilation,** n. 1, aequalitas ; 2, concoctio.

assist, v.tr. auxilio alci esse, auxilium ferre, opitulari (= to bring aid), subvenire, adesse alci (= to stand by a person). **assistance,** n. auxilium or adjumentum ; to implore anyone's —, alcjs fidem implorare. **assistant,** n. adjutor, adju-trix ; — teacher, hypodidasculus, adjutor ; = colleague, collega, m. ; see HELP.

associate, I. v.tr. foedus facēre (= to make an alliance), comitem (socium) se alci adjungēre, se conjungēre. **II** v.intr. = to be associated, foedere conjungi, esse cum alqo ; like —s with like, pares cum paribus facillime congregantur. **III.** n. socius, sodalis, comes, -ĭtis, m. and f., conscius. **association,** n. societas, sodalitas, collegium ; see ASSEMBLY.

assort, v.tr. (in gen.) digerēre. **assortment,** n. apparatus, -ūs, numerus or by part. (e.g. res or merces collectae, digestae, etc.) ; see ALLOT, APPORTION.

assuage, v.tr. mitigare, lenire, sedare. **as-suagement,** n. mitigatio.

assume, v.tr. 1, = take to oneself, alqd sibi vindicare, sibi arrogare, sumēre, occupare ; 2, = to take for granted, ponĕre ; this being assumed, hoc posito or concesso. **assumption,** n. 1, = a taking, usurpatio ; 2, = arrogance, in-solentia, arrogantia, superbia ; 3, = postulate, by part. (e.g. hoc posito) ; this is a mere —, hoc non est confirmatum.

assure, v.tr. = to assert the certainty of, (pro certo) affirmare, asseverare ; be assured, crede mihi. **assurance,** n. see STATEMENT, IMPUDENCE. **assured,** adj. = fearless, securus ; = certain, certus, spectatus. Adv. certo, certe, haud dubie.

astern, adv. in or a puppe.

asthma, n. dyspnoea (Plin.). **asthmat-ic,** adj. asthmaticus (Plin.).

astonish, v.tr. perturbare, conturbare. **as-tonished,** adj. attonitus ; to be —, stupefactum esse. **astonishing,** adj. mirabilis, mirus, mirificus. Adv. mire, mirifice, miribiliter. **astonishment,** n. stupor, (ad)miratio.

astound, v.tr. see ASTONISH.

astray, adv. vage ; to be —, errare, vagari.

astringent, adj. a(d)strictorius. **astrin-gency,** n. a(d)strictio.

astrologer, n. astrologus, Chaldaeus. **as-trology,** n. astrologia.

astronomer, n. astrologus. **astronomy,** n. astrologia.

astute, adj. astutus, callidus.

asunder, adv. *seorsum;* in comp. by *dis* or *se* (e.g. *discurrēre, sevocare*).

asylum, n. *asylum.*

at, prep. 1, of place, *ad, apud, juxta* (with the accus. e.g. *ad ostium,* = at the door ; *ad portas,* = at the gate; *ad Cannas* = at Cannae); by the abl. with or without *in,* (*in*) *urbe,* = at the city ; (*in*) *initio,* = at the beginning ; or by the old locative case, *Romae,* = at Rome ; *Londini,* = at London; *Gadibus,* = at Cadiz ; so *domi, militiae,* = at home, at service, etc. ; 2, of time, abl. *eodem tempore,* = at the same time ; *ad meridiem,* = at midday ; by accus. with *apud,* at my house, *apud me;* = during, *inter;* at dinner, *inter cenam* (*coen.*); at once, *statim;* at first, *primo, primum;* at last, *postremo,* (*ad*) *postremum.*

atheist, n. *atheos* (or -*us*), *qui Deum esse negat.* **atheism,** n. * *atheismus, doctrina Deum esse negans;* to hold —, *Deum esse negare, nullum esse omnino Deum putare.*

athlete, n. *athleta,* m.

athwart, adv. *transverse, in obliquum;* see ACROSS, ASKANCE.

atlas, n. (in geography), use *tabulae geographicae.*

atmosphere, n. *caelum.* **atmospheric,** adj. by the genitive *aëris* or *caeli;* see AIR.

atom, n. 1, phil. t.t. *atŏmus* -*i,* f. ; 2, see PIECE.

atone, v.tr. *alqd luĕre, expiare, alqd* (*cum*) *alqā re compensare, poenas alcjs rei dare* or (*ex*)-*pendĕre.* **atonement,** n. *placatio, satisfactio, poena;* = reconciliation, *reditus, -ūs in gratiam.*

atrabilious, adj. *melancholicus.*

atrocious, adj. *nefandus, nefarius, atrox, immanis.* Adv. *atrociter, nefarie.* **atrocity,** n. 1, of mental quality, *immanitas, atrocitas;* 2, = an atrocious thing, *res atrox,* etc.

atrophy, n. *tabes, -is,* f.

attach, v.tr. 1, = fasten, *figĕre, affigĕre alqd alci rei, alligare alqd ad rem;* 2, = to make prisoner, *comprehendĕre, in vincula con(j)icĕre, in custodiam dare;* 3, = to make your friend, *conciliare, alqm sibi facĕre* or *reddĕre amicum;* to be —ed, *alcjs studiosum esse.* **attachment,** n. *studium alcjs, amor alcjs* or *in alqm observantia.*

attack, I. n. *petitio, impetus, -ūs, incursio, incursus, -ūs, excursus, -ūs, concursus, -ūs, congressus, -ūs, oppugnatio;* at the first —, *primo impetu, primo congressu;* to make an — on the enemy, *impetum facĕre in hostem.* **II.** v.tr. *petĕre, aggredi, adoriri* (= to fall on), *oppugnare* (= to storm), *procurrĕre in alqm* (= to rush out on a foe), *signa inferre in hostem, incurrĕre, invehi in hostem;* to — with words, *dicto* or *convicio, lacessĕre, alqm insectari; consectari, adoriri;* to be —ed by a disease, *morbo corripi.*

attain, v.tr. *alqd assequi, consequi, ad alqd pervenire.* **attainable,** adj. *facilis, quod alqs facile consequi potest.* **attainment,** n. 1, = the getting of anything, *adeptio, comparatio;* 2, = a piece of learning, *alcjs rei scientia; —s, doctrina, eruditio.* **attainder,** n. *accusatio.*

attempt, I. n. *conatus, -ūs, conata, -orum,* **II.** v.tr. *tentare, experiri, periclitari.*

attend, v.tr. 1, = to accompany, *alqm comitari, esse alcjs comitem;* 2, = to wait upon a dignitary, *alci apparēre;* as a servant, *alci famulari, alqd alci ministrare;* 3, = to frequent, of lectures, etc., *alqm audire;* 4, = pay attention to, *alqd curare;* = to hear, *audire, animadvertĕre;* Attend ! *attende;* 5, = be present at, *adesse* (e.g. *sacris,* public worship). **attendance.** n. 1, of servants, *ministerium;* 2, = pres-

ence at, by verb *adesse;* a great —, *frequentia.* **attendant,** n. 1, = companion, *comes, -itis,* m. and f., *socius;* 2, = servant, *servus, minister, famulus;* 3, = the —s of a great man, *comitatus, -ūs.* **attention,** n. 1, = — of the mind, *animi attentio, intentio, vigilantia;* 2, = diligence, *diligentia, studium;* to show — to, *alqm colĕre, observare.* **attentive,** adj. *assiduus, vigil, diligens, attentus, intentus, erectus;* to be —, *animo sequi alqd.* Adv. *attente, intente.*

attenuate, v.tr. *attenuare, extenuare, diluĕre.* **attenuation,** n. *extenuatio.*

attest, v.tr. 1, = prove, *alqd testificari,* (*at*)-*testari, testimonio confirmare, alci testimonio esse;* 2, = to call to witness, *alqm testari, testem facĕre.* **attestation,** n. 1, = giving evidence, *testificatio;* 2, = a piece of evidence, *testimonium.*

attire, I. v.tr. *induĕre alci vestem* or *alqm veste;* *vestire.* **II.** n. *vestis.*

attitude, n. 1, *corporis habitus, -ūs;* 2 = circumstances, *condicio, status, -ūs;* 3, = mental —, (*mentis*) *ratio.*

attorney, n. *procurator.*

attract, v.tr. *attrahĕre, ad se trahĕre, allicĕre.* **attraction,** n. 1, *vis attrahendi;* 2, = an attractive object, *oblectamentum.* **attractive,** adj. *jucundus, suavis.* Adv. *jucunde, suaviter.*

attribute, I. n. 1, *nota, insigne;* to bear the —s of royalty, *insignibus regiis uti;* 2, (in gram.) *attributio, attributum;* 3, = peculiarity, *proprium, natura, vis.* **II.** v.tr. *attribuĕre.*

attrition, n. by verb *terĕre.*

attune, v.tr. lit. and fig., *efficĕre ut alqd cum alqā re concinat.*

auburn, adj. *flavus.*

auction, n. *auctio;* to sell by —, *auctionari;* to sell by public —, *hastā positā auctionari;* to bid at an —, *licēri;* to be knocked down at an —, *alci addici.* **auctioneer,** n. *magister auctionis, praeco* (= the crier of bids, etc.).

audacious, adj. *procax, protervus, impudens.* Adv. *impudenter, proterve.* **audacity,** n. *procacitas, protervitas, impudentia.*

audience, n. 1, = hearing of anyone, *admissio, aditus, -ūs, ad alqm, colloquium;* 2, = hearers, *auditores, audientes, corona* (esp. of crowd round a public speaker); a large —, (*magna*) *audientium frequentia.* **audible,** adj. *quod audiri potest.* Adv. *clarā voce.* **audit,** v.tr. *rationem ducĕre, habēre, inire,* or *rationes cum alqo putare.* **auditor,** n. *qui rationes ducit.*

augment, v.tr. *alqd alqā re augēre, amplifi-care, addĕre alqd alci rei* or *ad alqd.* **augmentation,** n. *amplificatio, accessio.*

augur, I. n. *augur.* **II.** v.tr. *alqd prae. dicĕre, vaticinari, augurari.* **augury,** n. 1, = a predicting, *augurium, vaticinatio, praedictio.* 2, = a thing predicted, *omen* (= a natural —), *praedictum* (= a prophecy).

August, I. n. *Augustus,* (*mensis*) *Augustus, Sextilis.* **II.** adj. *augustus* (= sacred), *illustris, magnificus.*

aunt, n. *amita* (= a father's sister), *matertera* (= a mother's sister).

auriferous, adj. *aurifer.*

auspice, n. *auspicium.* **auspicious,** adj *prosper, secundus, faustus.* Adv. *fauste, prospere.*

austere, adj. *austerus, severus, tristis* Adv. *austere, severe.* **austerity,** n. *austeritas, severitas.*

authentic, adj. *certus, verus, sincerus.* Adv. *certo auctore.* **authenticity,** n. *fides, auctoritas.*

author, n. *auctor* (= originator); *inventor; scriptor* (= a writer). **authoritative,** adj. *imperiosus, arrogans.* Adv. *arroganter.*

authority, n. *auctoritas* (by birth, character, and office), *amplitudo* (by office), comb. *auctoritas atque amplitudo; dignitas, gravitas* (by personal worth); *gratia; dominatio* (= despotic authority); the —s = magistrates, *magistratus, -ūs.* **authorize,** v.tr. *alci mandare ut, alci permittĕre,* with infin.

autocrat, n. *dominus;* autocratical power, *summa potestas, imperium* (*summum*).

autograph, I. n. *alcjs manu scriptus.* **II.** adj. an— letter, *epistula meā ipsius manu scripta.*

autumn, n. *autumnus, tempus autumnale;* =— of life, *aetas grandior.* **autumnal,** adj. *autumnalis.*

auxiliary, I. n. as a city or state, *civitas foederata;* in the pl. *auxilia* (*milites*) *auxiliares* (= foreign soldiers who strengthen an army), *subsidia, -orum, subsidiarii* (= the reserve of an army). **II.** adj. *auxiliaris.*

avail, I. v.intr. *valēre, praevalēre, obtinēre.* **II.** n. *utilitas;* to be of much —, *multum apud alqm valēre;* to make of no —, *non flocci facĕre.*

avarice, n. *avaritia, cupiditas, pecunia.* **avaricious,** adj. *habendi cupidus, avidior ad rem, avarus.* Adv. *avare.*

avaunt! interj. *abi! apage!*

avenge, v.tr. *vindicare, ulcisci;* to — oneself on anyone, *alqm ulcisci pro alqā re.* **avenger,** n. *ultor, vindex.*

avenue, n. 1, = approach, *aditus, -ūs;* 2, = a shady walk, *xystus.*

aver, v.tr. see AFFIRM, ASSERT.

avert, v.tr. *alqd ab alqo avertĕre, aversari.* **aversion,** n. *fuga, odium, animus alienus* or *aversus.* **averse,** adj. *ab alqo or alqā re aversus, alienus.*

aviary, n. *aviarium.*

avoid, v.tr. *defugĕre, vitare, declinare.* **avoiding,** n. *devitatio, fuga.*

avow, v.tr. *profiteri, confiteri; prae se ferre.* **avowal,** n. *confessio.* **avowed,** adj. *apertus, permissus.* Adv. *aperte.*

await, v.tr. *alqm* or *alqd ex(s)pectare, opperiri.*

awake, I. v.tr. (e somno) *excitare, (ex)suscitare.* **II.** v.intr. *expergisci, excitari.* **III.** adj. *vigilans;* to be —, *vigilare.* **awakening,** n. by verb AWAKE.

award, I. v.tr. *alqd alci adjudicare.* **II.** n. *judicium, arbitrium, addictio.*

aware, adj. *alcjs rei gnarus;* to be —, *alqd scire, novisse.*

away, adv. *procul;* — with! *tolle! aufer!* — you! *apage te!* go —, *abire.* In comp. with *a* (e.g. *abesse,* to be —).

awe, I. n. *veneratio, religio;* to feel – towards, *vereri alqm.* **II.** v.tr. *terrēre;* see FRIGHTEN.

awful, adj. 1, = feeling awe, *verecundus* (= shy), *pius, religiosus;* 2, = terrible, *dirus, atrox, immanis.* Adv. 1, with fear, *verecunde* (= shyly), *pie, religiose;* 2, = terribly, *dire, atrociter.*

awhile, adv. *aliquamdiu, paul(l)isper; —ago, paul(l)o ante.*

awkward, adj. *agrestis, rusticus, rudis, inscitus.* Adv. *inscite, rustice.* **awkwardness,** n. *inscitia.*

awl, n. *subula* (Mart.).

awning, n. *velum.*

awry, I. adj. 1, lit. *obliquus;* 2, fig. *perversus.* **II.** adv. *oblique, perverse.*

axe, n. *securis, dolabra.*

axiom, n. *axioma, -ātis, pronuntiatum,*

axis, axle, n. *axis,* m.

ay, adv. *ita, ita est, recte, certe, vero, sane, sane quidem;* often by repeating the verb, e.g, will he come? yes! *venietne? veniet; I say ay. aio.*

azure, adj. *caeruleus.*

B

baa, I. v. intr. *balare.* **II.** n. *balatus, -ūs.*

babble, v. *blaterare, garrire, nugari.* **babbling,** n. *garrulitas, loquacitas.* **babbler,** n. *garrulus, loquax.*

babe, baby, n. *infans.*

baboon, n. *simia* (= ape).

bacchanal, n. *homo vinolentus ac dissolutus;* a female —, *baccha.*

bacchic, adj. *bacchicus.*

bachelor, n. *caelebs.*

back, I. n. 1, *tergum, dorsum;* to lie on the —, *supinum cubare;* to attack the enemy on the —, *hostes aversos aggredi;* (of soldiers) *terga dare;* behind a person's —, *clam;* 2, = the back part, *pars posterior;* the — of the head, *occipitium.* **II.** adv. **backwards,** *retro, retrorsum;* in comp. *rē* (e.g. *revocare,* to call —). **III.** adj. *posterior.* **IV.** v.tr. = to move backward, *retro movēre;* = to support, *alci favēre, fautorem esse; (ad)juvare, sustinēre* (= to help). **V.** v.intr. *se recipĕre, recedĕre;* to — water, *remos or remis inhibēre, navem retro inhibēre.*

backbite, v.tr. *alci absenti maledicĕre, alqm obtrectare.*

bacon, n. *lardum.*

bad, adj. 1 (in a physical sense), *malus;* bad weather, *tempestas mala, adversa, foeda* (= foul); — road, *iter difficile, incommodum;* — money, *nummi adulterini;* in — health, *aeger;* to go —, *corrumpi;* 2, (in a moral sense) *malus, adversus, pravus, turpis, depravatus, nequam;* — times, *tempora iniqua* (= unfavourable), *aspera* (= hard); = injurious, a — tongue, *lingua maledica.* Adv. *male, prave, nequiter, turpiter.*

badness, n. 1, = physical —, by adj., the — of anything, *res mala;* — of health, *aegritudo, aegrotatio;* 2, = moral —, *pravitas, turpitas, nequitia.*

badge, n. *signum, insigne, nota.*

badger, I. n. *meles, -is,* f. **II.** v.tr. *vexare, (ex)cruciare.*

baffle, v.tr. *eludĕre, ad vanum,* or *ad irritum redigĕre, disturbare, spem fallĕre.*

bag, n. *saccus.*

baggage, n. 1, *sarcinae, impedimenta, -orum;* 2, = a dissolute woman, *scortum.*

bail, I. n. 1, = money given, *sponsio, vadimonium, cautio;* to offer —, *vadimonium promittĕre;* to give —, *vadimonium facĕre;* 2, = one who gives —, *sponsor, vas, -dis,* m. **II.** v.tr. *alci sponsorem, vadem esse;* to accept —, *vades accipĕre.*

bailiff, n. 1, = on an estate, *procurator, villicus;* 2, = officer of a court of justice, *apparitor.*

bait, I. n. 1, for fish, *esca;* 2, fig. *illecebra;* 3, = food for horses, *cibus.* **II.** v.tr. 1, *escam (hamo) imponĕre;* 2, = to feed horses, *cibum praebēre;* 3, = to worry (bulls, etc.), *canibus (taurum) vexare, lacessĕre.* **III.** v.intr. = to rest on a journey, *(apud alqm) deversari.*

bake, I. v.tr. *coquĕre, torrēre.* **II.** v.intr. = to be prepared by 'fire, *coqui.* **baking,** n. *coctura;* bakehouse, *pistrina;* a baker, *pistor;* baker's business, *pistrina.*

balance, I. n. 1, = scales, *trutina, libra, lanx* (= the pan of the scales) ; 2, fig. *aequalĭtas;* to lose one's —, *labi;* — at the bank, *pecunia in argentariā deposita;* 3, = the remainder, by adj. *rel(l)iquus.* **II.** v.tr. 1, lit. *aequis ponderibus librare;* 2, fig. *alqd. perpendĕre.* **III.** v.intr. of accounts, *constare.*

balcony, n. *solarium.*

bald, adj. 1, lit. *glaber, calvus;* a — head, *calvitium;* — place, *glabreta, -orum;* 2, fig. of language, *inornatus, incultus, impolitus.* **baldness,** n. *calvitium.*

bale, n. *fascis, -is,* m. **baleful,** adj. *calamitosus, perniciosus, exitiosus.* **bale out,** v.tr. *exhaurīre.*

balk, I. n. 1, = a beam, *tignum, trabs;* 2, = boundary, *limes, -itis,* m. **II.** v.tr. *alci impedimento esse.*

ball, n. 1, *pila;* to play at —, *(datatim) pilā ludĕre;* 2, the — of the earth, *terrae globus;* the eye —, *pupilla;* a musket —, *lapis, -idis,* m. (as thrown by a balista) ; 3, = a dance, *saltatio.*

ballad, n. *carmen.*

ballast, n. *saburra.*

ballet, n. *pantomimus* (Plin.); — dancer, *pantomimus,* m. (Suet.) ; *pantomima,* f. (Sen.).

balloon, n. *machina aërobatica.*

ballot, n. *suffragium* (= a vote); to vote by —, *suffragia ferre;* — box, *cista.*

balm, n. 1, *balsamum;* 2, fig. *solatium.* **balmy,** adj. 1, *balsaminus;* 2, fig. *suavis, dulcis.*

balustrade, n. *cancelli, -orum.*

bamboo, n. *arundo Indica* (Plin.).

ban, n. *aquae et ignis interdictio.*

band, I. n. 1, = bandage, *fascia;* 2, = a fillet, *vitta, infula;* (of metal) *armilla;* 3, = a number of persons united together, *turba, grex, caterva.* **II.** v.tr. *(con)sociare, conjungĕre.*

bandage, I. n. *fascia, fasciola.* **II. v.tr.** *deligare.*

band-box, n. *capsa.*

bandit, n. *latro.* **banditti,** n. *latrones.*

bandy, v.tr. *ultro (et) citro agĕre;* to — words with, *cum alqo altercari.* **bandy-legged,** adj. *varus, cruribus distortis.*

bane, n. 1, lit. *venenum, virus, -i,* n. ; 2, fig. *pestis.* **baneful,** adj. *perniciosus, exitiosus.*

bang, n. 1, = a striking, *percussio;* 2, = a noise, *sonitus, -ūs.*

banish, v.tr. 1, lit. *alci aquā et igni interdicĕre, in ex(s)ilium e(j)icĕre, (ex)pellĕre* or *agĕre, exterminare, relegare, deportare* (to transport) ; 2, fig. *e(j)icĕre, (ex)pellĕre, amovēre.* **banishment,** n. *interdictio aquae et ignis, ejectio, relegatio, deportatio, ex(s)ilium.*

bank, n. 1, = a seat, *scamnum, scabellum, subsellium;* 2, = a river's side, *ripa;* 3, = a — of oars, *transtrum;* 4, = a — of earth, *agger, -ĕris,* m. ; 5, = a money-changer's table, or place for depositing money (the last, modern), *argentaria (mensa), mensa publica;* to put money in the —, *pecuniam apud mensam publicam occupare.* **banker,** n. *argentarius.* **banknote,** n. *as,* etc. or *perscriptio* (= assignment). **bankrupt,** n. *decoctor;* to become —, *foro cedĕre, (rationes) conturbare, decoquĕre.* **bankruptcy,** n. by verb (e.g. to suffer —, *foro*

cedĕre), or metaph. *fortunae naufragium* or *ruina;* a national —, *tabulae novae.*

banner, n. *vexillum;* see **Flag.**

bannock, n. *placenta (avenacea).*

banquet, n. *epulae, convivium.*

banter, I. n. *irrisio, derisio, cavillatio, ludibrium;* in —, *per ludibrium.* **II.** v.tr. *alqm ludibrio habēre, cavillari, deridēre, irridēre.*

baptize, v.tr. * *baptizare* (Eccl.). **baptism,** n. * *baptisma.*

bar, I. n. 1, = — of metal, etc., *later, -eris,* m. ; 2, = bolt, *claustrum, obex, repagula, -orum;* 3, = a stake, *pertica, sudes, -is,* f., *vectis, -is,* m. ; 4, = a limit or partition, *cancelli, carceres, -um, saepta, -orum;* 5, = a law court, *apud judices,* or *forum;* to be called to the —, *primum forum attingĕre;* to practise at the —, *caus(s)as agĕre;* the — (= advocates), *patroni.* **II.** v.tr. 1, = to bolt, *(claustro januam) occludĕre;* 2, fig. = to hinder, *alci impedimento esse, alqm impedire;* 3, = to except, *excipĕre.*

barbarous, barbaric, adj. *barbarus* (= foreign, strange), *rudis, inhumanus, immanis, crudelis, saevus.* Adv. *barbare, saeve, crudeliter.* **barbarity,** n. *immanitas, inhumanitas, crudelitas.*

barbed, adj. *hamatus.*

barber, n. *tonsor;* a —'s shop, *tonstrina.*

bard, n. *vates, -is,* m. and f.

bare, adj. 1, *nudus;* 2, = mere, *merus, tenuis, exiguus;* 3, = plain, *simplex;* a — room, *cubiculum nullo sumptu ornatum.* Adv. 1, = scarcely, *vix;* 2, = plainly, *simpliciter, nullo sumptu.* **bareness,** n. by adj. **Bare.** **barefaced,** *impudens.* **barefoot,** *pedibus nudis* or *intectis.*

bargain, I. n. *res, negotium, pactio, pactum;* to make a good —, *bene emĕre.* **II.** v.intr. *cum algo pacisci.*

barge, n. *actuariolum, lenunculus* (both = small vessel).

bark, I. n. *cortex, liber.* **II.** v.tr. *delibrare, decorticare.*

bark, I. v.intr. *latrare.* **II.** n. *latratus, -ūs.*

barley, I. n. *hordeum.* **II.** adj. *hordaceus.*

barn, n. *horreum;* — floor, *area.*

baron, n. **baronet,** n. see **Noble.**

barracks, n. *castra, -orum.*

barrel, n. *seria, dolium, orca;* of a gun, etc., *tubus.*

barren, adj. *sterilis, infecundus.* **barrenness,** n. *sterilitas.*

barricade, I. n. *munimentum.* **II.** v.tr *inaedificare, intersaepire, obstruĕre, oppilare.*

barrier, n. *limes, -itis,* m., *fines, -ium,* m. and f., *munimentum, murus.*

barrister, n. see **Advocate.**

barrow, n. *ferculum.*

barter, I. v.tr. *mutare res inter se, permutare merces.* **II.** n. *permutatio mercium.*

base, adj. = morally corrupt, *perditus, probrosus, ignominiosus, turpis;* — coin, *nummi adulterini;* — born, *ignobili loco natus.* Adv. *per ignominiam, cum ignominiā, contumeliose, turpiter.* **baseness,** n. *turpitudo, dedecus, -ĕris,* n., *nequitia.*

base, n. 1, *basis* (= pedestal), *fundamentum* (= ground-work, lit. and fig.) ; 2, = the lowest part, *radices* (= roots, e.g. *montis*) ; 3, of the voice, *vox* or *sonus gravis.*

bashful, adj. *pudens, pudicus, verecundus.* Adv. *pudenter, pudice, verecunde.* **bashfulness,** n. *pudor, pudicitia, verecundia.*

basin, n. **1,** = for washing, *pelvis;* **2.** = a pond, *piscina.*

basis, n. see BASE, n., 1 and 2.

bask, v.intr. *apricari.*

basket, n. *corbis, qualus, qualum, sporta.* **basket-work,** *opus vimineum.*

bas-relief, n. *opus caelatum, toreuma, -ătis,* n.

bass, n. = a mat of straw, *storea* or *storia.*

bastard, I. n. *nothus.* **II.** adj. see SPURI-OUS.

bastinado, n. *ictus, -ūs, fustis,* m.

bat, n. = an animal, *vespertilio.*

bat, n. for cricket, tennis, etc., *clava* (= *club*).

batch, n. *numerus.*

bate, I. v.tr. *(im)minuĕre.* **II.** v.intr. *(im)minui;* see ABATE.

bath, n. *balineum, balneum;* pl. *balneae, balnearia, -orum, aquae; lavatio; thermae* (=hot or mineral baths); *lavatum;* to take a cold bath, *frigidā lavari.* **bathe, I.** v.tr. *lavare, abluĕre* (sc. *se*); to — another, *demittĕre alqm in balneum;* to be bathed in tears, *effundi (effusum esse) in lacrimis;* bathing-rooms, *balnearia;* — for cold, hot baths, etc., *frigidarium, tepidarium, calidarium, sudatorium.* **II.** v.intr. *lavari.*

battalion, n. *cohors* (of cavalry), *legio* (= a regiment), *agmen primum, medium, extremum,* or *novissimum* (= the divisions of a marching army).

batter, v.tr. *percutĕre, verberare;* see BEAT; *pulsare;* to — down, *perfringĕre, evertĕre, dis-(j)icĕre.*

battering-ram, n. *aries, ĕtis,* m.

battery, n. *agger, -ĕris,* m. (= the mound), *tormenta, -orum* (= the weapons).

battle, n. *praelium, certamen, acies, dimicatio.* **battle-array,** n. *acies* (opp. to *agmen,* array on march). **battle-axe,** n. *bipennis* (only found in nom., dat., acc., and abl. sing., and nom. and abl. pl.), *securis.* **battle-cry,** n. *clamor.* **battle-field,** n. *locus pugnae* or *ubi pugnatur.*

battlement, n. *pinna.*

bawl, v.tr. *clamorem tollĕre, vociferari.*

bay, I. adj. *spadix, badius.* **II.** n. 1,= laurel, *laurus,* f. ; **2,** = a gulf, *sinus, -ūs;* **3,** = — window, *fenestra convexa* or *cava;* **4,** to stand at —, *adversus alqm se defendĕre.* **III.** v.intr. *latrare.*

bayonet, n. *gladius;* with fixed —s, *constrictis gladiis.*

be, v.intr. *esse, ex(s)istĕre;* to let —, *permittĕre.*

beach, n. *litus, -ōris,* n.

beacon, n. = lighthouse, *pharus,* f. ; = fire, *ignis.*

bead, n. *globulus.*

beak, n. *rostrum.*

beaker, n. *poculum, calix.*

beam, I. n. **1,** of wood, *lignum, trabs;* of a —, *trabalis;* **2,** — of light, *radius;* a — of hope shines out, *spes mihi affulget;* **3,** — of a balance, *scapus, jugum.* **II.** v. intr. *fulgēre.* **beaming, I.** n. *fulgor.* **II.** adj. *jucundus, hilaris.*

bean, n. *faba;* = kidney bean, *phaselus,* m. and f.

bear, I. n. **1,** *ursus, ursa* (=a she-bear) ; that which comes from —, *ursinus;* (as a constellation) *Arctos, Ursa;* the Great —, *Ursa Major;* the Lesser —, *Ursa Minor;* the two, *Septentriones, -um;* **2,** fig. = a rude fellow. *agrestis,*

incultus. **II.** v.tr. **1,** *ferre, gestare, portare;* — a sword, *cinctum esse gladio;* — (of trees) *ferre, efferre;* — the cost, *sumptus tolerare;* to — up against, *alqd sustinēre, pati;* **2,** = to show, to — affection towards, *alqm amare, diligēre;* **3,** to carry away, win, *auferre, consequi;* **4,** = to give birth to, *parēre.* **bearable,** adj. *quod tolerari potest;* to find anything —, *alcjs rei patientem esse.* **bearer,** n. *bajulus* (= a porter); *nuntius* (= — of news); *tabellarius* (= — of letters).

bearing, n. *portatio, gestatio, vectatio;* of children, *partus, -ūs.*

beard, I. n. *barba;* — of a goat, *aruncus* (Plin.). **II.** v.tr. *alqm provocare.*

beast, n. **1,** *bestia, jumentum* (= beast of burden) opp. to man, *belua;* wild —, *fera;* **2,** as a term of contempt, *belua, bestia.* **beastly,** adj. *spurcus, immundus.* **beastliness,** n. *spurcitia.*

beat, I. v.tr. **1,** = to strike, *ferire, caedĕre, percutĕre, pulsare, verberare;* to be beaten, *vapulare;* **2,** = to overcome, *vincĕre, superare;* — the enemy thoroughly, *hostem fundĕre et fugare;* **3,** = to beat down, *(pro)sternĕre, opprimĕre;* **4,** to — out, see THRASH ; **5,** to — up, *rudiculā peragitare.* **II.** v.intr. *palpitare.* **beating,** n. *verbera, -um.*

beatitude, n. *(summa) felicitas.*

beau, n. *homo bellus* or *elegans.*

beautiful, adj. *pulcher, formosus* (in form), *speciosus* (in appearance), *venustus* (= elegant); *bellus* (= fine). Adv. *pulchre, amoene, venuste, belle, eleganter.* **beautify,** v.tr. *(ex)ornare.* **beauty,** n. *pulchritudo, species, forma, venustas, amoenitas* (of places); beauty in the abstract, *pulchrum.*

beaver, n. *castor, fiber;* of a —, *castoreus;* — skin, *pellis fibrina.*

becalmed, adj. *ventis destitutus.*

because, conj. *quod, quia, quoniam, cum* (with subj.), *quandoquidem,* also with *qui, quippe qui,* as well as by a participle or abl. abs. ; — of, prep., *propter, ob* with accus.

beck, n. = a nod, *nutus, -ūs;* to be at anyone's — or call, ad *nutum alcjs esse.* **beckon,** v.tr. *digito innuĕre.*

become, I. v.intr. *fiĕri, evadĕre, nasci, oriri, ex(s)istĕre;* to become a perfect speaker, *perfectum oratorem evadĕre;* — a beggar, *ad mendicitatem redigi;* often by the inchoative verbs, as, to — warm, *calescĕre;* — rich, *ditescĕre;* **II.** v.tr. = to suit, *alqm convenit.*

bed, n. **1,** *lectus, lectus cubicularis;* to make a —, *lectum sternĕre;* to go to —, *cubitum ire;* a little —, *lectulus.* — **chamber,** n. *cubiculum.* **bedding,** n. *lodix* (= coverlet), *stragulum* (= mattress). — **post,** n. *fulcrum lecti.* **2,** — of a river, *alveus;* — of a garden, *area.*

bedabble, v.tr. *a(d)spergĕre.*

bedaub, v.tr. *(ob)linĕre, perungĕre.*

bedeck, v.tr. *(ex)ornare.*

bedew, v.tr. *irrorare.* **bedewed,** adj. *roscidus;* to be --, *humescĕre.*

bedim, v.tr. *obscurare.*

bedizen, v.tr. *(ex)ornare.*

bedlam, n. *domus quā continentur (homines) insani.*

bee, n. *apis;* — hive, *alvus, alveus;* a swarm of —, *examen apium;* queen —, *rex apium.*

beech, n. *fagus,* f. ; of —, *fageus, faginus.*

beef, n. *(caro) bubula.*

beer, n. *cer(e)visia.* **brewer,** n. *cerevisiae coctor.*

beetle, I. n. *scarabaeus.* **II. v.intr.** *im-uinēre.*

beeves, n. *boves, boum,* pl.

befall, v.intr. *accidĕre, contingĕre, evenire.*

befit, v.tr. *aptum, idoneum esse ad alqd;* it —s thee, *te decet;* does not —, *non convenit, dedecet.*

befool, v.tr. *infatuare, decipĕre.*

before, I. adv. *prius, citius, ante; prior,* e.g. *qui prior venit,* he comes before (the other); = rather, *prius, potius;* the year —, *superior annus;* = already, *jam(dudum);* the — mentioned, *qui supra dictus est.* **II.** prep. = in presence of, *coram,* with abl.; in front of, *ante,* with accus. ; of time, *ante;* — my consulship, *ante me consulem;* of worth, *ante* or *praeter,* with accus. ; to be —, *alci alqâ re praestare, antecellĕre;* the day — another day, *pridie ejus diei.* **III.** conj. *ante* or *prius, quam* (in one word), *antequam, priusquam).* **beforehand,** adv. *antea,* or *by prae* in comp. ; to be — with, *alqm alqâ re praevenire.* **beforetimes,** adv. *olim.*

befoul, v.tr. *inquinare.*

befriend, v.tr. *alqm (ad)juvare, alci favēre.*

beg, I. v. intr. *mendicare, stipem petĕre.* **II. v.tr.** *alqm alqd orare, rogare, flagitare,* or with *ut;* to — off, *deprecari.* **beggar, I.** n. *mendicus,* or adj. *egenus.* **II. v.tr.** *ad inopiam redigĕre.* **beggarly,** adj. *miser, vilis.* **beggary,** n. *egestas, paupertas, mendicitas.* **begging,** n. *mendicitas, stips* (= alms); a — off, *deprecatio.*

beget, v.tr. 1, lit. *gignĕre, generare, procreare;* 2, fig. *creare, alqd alci movēre.*

begin, I. v.intr. *incipĕre;* it — to be day, *dies appetit, lucescit;* — evening, *advesperascit.* **II.** v.tr. *incipĕre* (= to commence, e.g. *facinus*), *ordiri, inchoare, initium facĕre, aggredi* (= to enter on), *conari* (= to endeavour). **beginning,** n. *initium, principium, primordium, ortus, -ûs,* (= birth), *inceptio, inceptum;* — of a speech, *exordium;* the —s of a science, *elementa, rudimenta, incunabula* (all n. pl.). Often "beginning" is to be rendered by *primus,* e.g. *primâ fabulâ,* = in the — of the piece; so e.g. *vere novo, ineunte vere,* = in the — of spring; thus *primâ nocte, primo vespere;* from the —, *ab initio, repetĕre* (= to go back to the very —); without —, *aeternus;* to have neither — nor end, *nec principium nec finem habēre.* **beginner,** n. 1, = author, *auctor;* 2, = a novice, *tiro, rudis.*

begone! interj. *abi! apage te!*

begrime, v.tr. *inquinare, maculare.*

begrudge, v.tr. *invidēre alqd alci.*

beguile, v.tr. *decipĕre, circumvenire, fallĕre.*

behalf, n. in — of, *pro,* with abl., *propter,* with accus., *caus(s)â* (e.g. *meâ,* or with gen.).

behave, v.tr. *se gerĕre, exhibēre;* well behaved, *bene moratus.* **behaviour,** n. *vita, ratio, mores, -um.*

behead, v.tr. *caput alcjs praecidĕre.*

behind, I. adv. *pone, post, a tergo;* also by *extremus* and *ultimus* (e.g. *ultimus venit,* he came behind or last); with verbs by *rē-* (e.g. *oculos retorquēre,* to look behind); to attack a person behind, *aversum aggredi alqm.* **II.** prep. *pone, post,* with acc. **behindhand,** adv. *parum* (= too little).

behold, v.tr. *a(d)spicĕre, conspicĕre, intueri, contemplari, spectare alqd.* **behold!** interj. *en! ecce!* **beholden,** adj. *alcjs beneficio* (e.g. for one's life, *alcjs beneficio salvus*); to be — to, *alqd alci debēre, acceptum referre.*

behoof, n. see BEHALF.

behove, v.tr. impers., *decet, convenit, oportet.*

being, n. *natura* (= peculiar quality), *vis* (= active quality), comb. *natura atque vis; condicio* (= permanent state), *res* (= reality); the Supreme —, *Deus;* see LIFE.

belated, adj. *serus.*

belch, I. v.intr. *ructare.* **II. v.tr.** fig. *evomĕre.*

beldam, n. *anicula* (= an old woman).

beleaguer, v.tr. *obsidēre.*

belfry, n. *turris.*

belie, v.tr. *criminari, calumniari.*

belief, n. in gen., *opinio* (= view or conviction); of anything, *rei* or *de re), persuasio* (= assurance, *alcjs rei,* e.g. *veneni ab alqo accepti* = that someone has been poisoned), *fides* (= credibility, credence, trust); — in God, *opinio Dei;* — in immortality, *immortalitas* merely (e.g. *nemo me de immortalitate depellet,* = no one shall rob me of my belief in immortality); in my —, *ut ego existimo, meâ quidem opinione;* to have — in something, or hold it as a reality, *alqd esse credĕre.* **believe,** v.tr. *credĕre, putare, arbitrari* (= to think), *opinari, reri, existimare, ducĕre* (= account, to form a judgment), *censēre, sentire;* I firmly —, *mihi persuasum est, persuasum habeo* (with acc. and inf. ; *hoc mihi persuasit,* I am satisfied of this); I cannot —, *hoc quidem non adducor ut credam;* to — in something, *alqd esse arbitrari* or *credĕre* or *putare* (in the existence of, e.g. *Deum esse credĕre,* or merely *Deum putare* or *credĕre); credĕre de alqâ re* (e.g. *facilius de odio creditur* = people easily believe in hatred), *comprobare alqd* (= to approve); to — in an object, *alci rei credĕre,* or *fidem habēre,* or *fidem tribuĕre, alci rei* (never *alci) fidem adjungĕre;* — me (used parenthetically), *quod mihi credas velim, mihi crede, crede mihi;* I — (used parenthetically), *credo, opinor, puto;* as I —, *meâ quidem opinione, ut ego existimo.* **believer,** n. *qui credit.*

bell, n. *tintinnabulum, aes, aeris,* n.

belle, n. (*puella*) *pulchra, formosa.*

bellow, v.intr. *mugire.*

bellows, n. *follis, -is,* m.

belly, n. 1, *venter, -ris,* m. (= the hollow of the body containing the intestines), *uterus* (= the womb), *alvus* (= the passage or canal), *abdōmen* (= the protruding or fat part of the belly); 2, of a ship, *alveus.*

belong, v.intr. — to, *alci* or *alcjs esse.*

below, I. adv. *subter, infra.* **II.** prep. *sub;* acc. of motion towards (e.g. *ire sub muros*), abl. of rest; *infra* with acc. see UNDER.

belt, n. *cingulum, zona.*

bemire, v.tr. *inquinare.*

bemoan, v.tr. *deplorare.*

bench, n. *scamnum, scabellum; —* at which people work, *mensa;* of rowers, *transtrum;* of judges, *consessus, -ûs.*

bend, I. v.tr. 1, (*in)flectĕre; —* before a person, *submittĕre se alci;* 2, fig. = to move, *movēre, flectĕre;* 3, = to turn, *se* or *iter convertĕre, dirigĕre;* to — one's steps, *ire ad alqm* or *alqd;* to — one's mind to, *alqd animadvertĕre* (= to notice), *se ad alqd applicare.* **II.** v.intr. *flecti;* — beneath a weight, lit. *vacillare; —* fig. *gravari.* **III.** n. *bending,* n. *flexus, -ûs, (in)flexio.* **bent,** n. *animi inclinatio, voluntas. natura. ratio, studium.*

beneath, see BELOW.

benediction, n. to give a — to a person, *alqm bonis ominibus prosequi.*

benefit, I. n. *beneficium.* **II. v.tr.** *alqm (ad)juvare, alci utilem or usui or ex usu esse.*
beneficial, adj. *utilis, salutaris.* Adv. *utiliter, benefice, salubriter.* **beneficent,** adj. *liberalis, benignus, beneficus.* Adv. *benigne, liberaliter.*
beneficence, n. *beneficentia, benignitas, liberalitas.* **benefactor,** n. *beneficus, qui beneficia in alqm confert;* to be a — to mankind, *praeclare de genere humano meritum esse.*
benevolent, adj. *benevolus (beniv.).* **benevolence,** n. *benevolentia.*
benighted, adj. 1, lit. *nocte oppressus;* 2, fig. see IGNORANT.
benign, adj. *benignus erga alqm.* Adv. *benigne.* **benignity,** n. *benignitas.*
benumb, v.tr. *obstupefacēre;* to be —ed, *obtorpescēre, torpēre.*
bequeath, v.tr. *alqd alci legare.* **bequest,** n. *legatum.*
bereave, v.tr. *alqm alqā re orbare, privare.* **bereaved,** adj. *orbus.* **bereavement,** n. *orbitas, privatio.*
berry, n. *bac(c)a, bac(c)ula, acinus.*
beseech, v.tr. *alqm implorare, obtestari, alqm alqd or ut orare.*
beseem, v.tr. see BECOME (2).
beset, v.tr. *alqm urgēre, premēre, alci instare, obsidēre* (of a city).
beshrew, v.tr. *ex(s)ecrari; —* me, *di(i) me perdant.*
beside, prep. 1, = near, *prope, juxta,* acc.; 2, = except, *praeter,* acc.; 3, = away from, this is — the point, *nihil ad rem; —* oneself, *sui impotens.*
besides, I. adv. *praeterea, ultra, porro, ad hoc* or *haec, accedit quod* or *ut.* **II.** prep. *praeter* with acc.
besiege, v.tr. *obsidēre, obsidione claudēre* or *premēre, operibus cingēre, oppugnare.* **besieger,** n. *obsessor, obsidens.*
besmear, v.tr. *(ob)linēre.*
bespatter, v.tr. *a(d)spergēre, conspergēre, (com)maculare.*
bespeak, v.tr. *imperare.*
best, adj. *optimus;* see GOOD.
bestir, v.tr. *(se) (com)movēre, incitare, excitare.*
bestow, v.tr. see GIVE.
bet, I. n. *sponsio, pignus, -ĕris,* n. **II. v.tr.** *sponsionem cum alqo facēre.*
betake oneself, v.intr. *se conferre alqo, concedēre, ire, proficisci alqo, petēre locum;* see Go.
betimes, adv. *mox, brevi.*
betoken, v.tr. *notare, denotare, signare, designare.*
betray, v.tr. 1, = to make known, *prodēre, deferre, proferre; —* yourself, *se prodere;* when — is used in the sense of "it is the quality of," use the genitive (e.g. *est tardi ingenii,* it —s a dull wit); 2, = to make known treacherously, *prodēre, tradēre, destituēre;* **betrayal,** n. *proditio, perfidia* (= faithlessness), *delatio* (= an information in law). **betrayer,** n. *proditor, desertor, index* (the eyes are the —s of the mind, *animi indices sunt oculi*).
betroth, v.tr. *alci alqam (de)spondēre; —* to anyone, *sibi alqam despondēre* (male), *alci desponderi* (female). **betrothal,** n. *sponsalia, -ium.*
better, I. adj. *melior, potior* (= preferable), *praestantior* (= more excellent); is —, *melius* or *satius est, praestat;* to be — (morally), *alci alqā*

re praestare, antecellēre; I am —, *melius me habeo;* I am getting —, *convalesco.* **II.** adv. *melius.* **III.** v.tr. *corrigēre, meliorem (melius) facēre, augēre* (= increase).
between, prep. *inter* with acc.
beverage, n. *potio, potus, -ūs.*
bevy, n. *grex, grĕgis,* m.
bewail, v.tr. *deplorare, deflēre, (con)queri.*
beware, v.tr. to — of, *(sibi) ab alqo* or *alqā re,* or *ut* or *ne cavēre.*
bewilder, v.tr. *alqm (con)turbare.*
bewitch, v.tr. 1, *fascinare;* 2, fig. *capēre.*
beyond, I. adv. *ultra, supra,* in comp. *trans* (e.g. *transire).* **II.** prep. 1, = the other side of, *trans,* acc. of rest or motion; 2, of degree, *supra, plus, amplius (quam); —* ten thousand, *supra decem mil(l)ia; —* measure, *supra modum.*
bias, I. n. *inclinatio* or *propensio animi.* **II.** v.tr. *apud alqm plus, quam aequum est valēre;* to be —sed, *ad alqm (plus aequo) propensum esse.*
bible, n. *libri divini, lit(t)erae divinae* or *sacrae* or *sanctae,* * *biblia -orum,* n. **biblical,** adj. *quod ad lit(t)eras divinas pertinet.*
bibulous, adj. † *bibulus.*
bid, v.tr. 1, *jubēre, praecipēre;* see COMMAND; 2, = invite, *invitare;* 3, at a sale, *licēri;* 4, fig. — defiance to, *alqm provocare; —* welcome, *alqm salvēre jubēre; —* farewell, *valēre jubēre.* **bidding,** n. 1, see COMMAND; 2, = invitation, *invitatio;* 3, at a sale, *licitatio.* **bidder,** n. (at a sale) *illicitator.*
bide, v.tr. *manēre.*
biennial, adj. *biennis.*
bier, n. *feretrum, sandapila* (Juv.).
bifurcated, adj. *bifidus.*
big, adj. *magnus, grandis, vastus;* to be — with child, *gravidam esse;* see GREAT, LARGE.
bigamist, n. *qui duas uxores habet.*
bigot, n. *superstitiosus.* **bigotry,** n. *nimia et superstitiosa religio.*
bile, n. *bilis.* **bilious,** adj. *biliosus* (Cels.).
bilge-water, n. *sentina.*
bill, n. 1, = a tool, *falx;* 2, = — of a bird, *rostrum.*
bill, n. 1, = a proposed law, *rogatio;* to bring forward a —, *rogationem, legem ferre;* to adopt a —, *accipēre;* to refuse a —, *antiquare;* to carry a —, *perferre;* 2, of a tradesman, etc., *mercium emptarum index; —* of exchange, *syngrapha.*
billet, I. n. = a letter, *epistula; —* doux, *epistula amatoria.* **II.** v.tr. *milites per domos disponēre.*
billow, n. *fluctus, -ūs.* **billowy,** adj. *fluctuosus.*
bind, v.tr. 1, by tying, *(al)ligare, illigare, a(d)stringēre, revincire;* 2, = to restrain, *alqm circumscribēre* or *coercēre;* to — together, *colligare;* to — by an oath, *alqm sacramento a(d)stringēre;* to — books, *glutinare;* to — an apprentice, *alqm alci addicēre;* to — over, *vadari;* to be bound by something, *constrictum esse, teneri re; —* by business, *negotiis distentum esse.* **bindweed,** n. *convolvulus* (Plin.).
biography, n. *vitae alcjs descriptio.* **biographer,** n. *qui alcjs res gestas enarrat.*
biped, n. *bipes, -ĕdis,* adj.
birch, n. *betula* (Plin.).
bird, n. *avis, volucris, ales, -ĭtis,* m. and f.;

— **cage,** n. *cavea;* — **catcher,** n. *auceps, -cūptis,* m. ; — **lime,** n. *viscus.*

birth, n. *ortus, -ūs;* of noble —, *nobili genere* or *loco natus.* **birthday,** n. *dies natalis.* **birthright,** n. *patrimonium.*

biscuit, n. *panis, -is,* m.

bishop, n. *episcopus.*

bit, n. 1, of a horse, *frenum;* 2, see PIECE.

bitch, n. *canis (femina).*

bite, I. v.tr. *mordēre.* **II.** n. *morsus, -ūs.*

biting, adj. *mordens, mordax, acidus, aculeatus;* — words, *verborum aculei.*

bitter, adj. *amarus, acerbus, mordax.* Adv. *amare, aspere, acerbe.* **bitterness,** n. *amaritudo, amaritas, acerbitas.*

bitumen, n. *bitūmen.*

bivouac, I. v.intr. *in armis excubare.* **II.** n. *excubiae.*

black, I. adj. *ater, niger, pullus.* **II.** n. 1, color *niger;* 2, = mourning, *pulla vestis;* dressed in —, *sordidatus, pullatus, atratus;* 3, = a negro, *Aethiops.* **blacken,** v.tr. 1, = to make black, *nigrum facēre;* 2, fig. *conflare* or *conciliare alci invidiam.*

blackberry, n. *rubus.*

blackbird, n. *merula.*

blackguard, n. *nefarius (homo), sceleratus.*

blacklead, n. *plumbum nigrum* (Plin.).

blacksmith, n. *faber.*

bladder, n. *vesica.*

blade, n. 1, of grass, *herba;* 2, of an oar, *palma;* 3, of a knife, *lamina.*

blame. I. n. *reprehensio, vituperatio, objurgatio, convicium.* **II.** v.tr. *reprehendēre, culpare.* **blameable, blameworthy,** adj. *reprehensione* or *vituperatione dignus.* **blameless,** adj. *integer, sanctus.* **blamelessness,** n. *vitae integritas* or *sanctitas.*

bland, adj. *blandus, lenis, mitis.* Adv. *blande, leniter.* **blandness,** n. *lenitas.* **blandishment,** n. *adulatio, blanditiae.*

blank, I. adj. *vacuus;* — amazement, *stupor.* **II.** n. 1, in a lottery, *sors* or *tabella inanis;* 2, in life, *calamitas.*

blanket, n. *lodix.*

blaspheme, v.intr. *blasphemare.* **blasphemer,** n. *blasphemus.* **blasphemous,** adj. *blasphemus, impius erga Deum.*

blast, I. n. *venti impetus, -ūs.* **II.** v.tr. 1, see BLIGHT; 2, = blow up, *igne diruēre.*

blaze, I. n. *flamma, ardor;* to set in a —, *incendēre.* **II.** v.intr. *ardēre, flagrare.*

bleach, I. v.tr. *candidum reddēre.* **II.** v.intr. = to become white or pale, *albescēre.*

bleak, adj. see COLD.

blear-eyed, adj. *lippus.*

bleat, I. v.intr. *balare* (of sheep). **II.** n. *balatus, -ūs.*

bleed, I. v.intr. *sanguinem fundēre;* my heart —s, *vehementer* or *gravissime doleo, aegerrime fero;* — at something, *incredibilem dolorem ex re capio.* **II.** v.tr. to — a person (as a physician), *alci sanguinem mittēre;* to kill by — ing (as a punishment), *venam incīdēre.* **bleeding,** n. *sanguinis fluxio.*

blemish, I. n. *mendum, macula, labes, -is,* f. **II.** v.tr. *(com)maculare.*

blend, v.tr. *alqd cum alqâ re (com)miscēre;* see MIX.

bless, v.tr. *alqm bonis ominibus prosequi.*

blessed, adj. *beatus, fortunatus.* Adv. *beate, fortunate.* **blessedness,** n. *felicitas.*

blight, I. n. *robīgo (rub).* **II.** v.tr. *robigine afficēre.*

blind, I. adj. 1, *caecus, oculis* or *luminibus captus* or *orbatus;* — of one eye, *altero oculo captus;* 2, fig. *caecus, occaecatus, stultus.* Adv. 1, by *caecus;* 2, = rashly, *temere.* **II.** v.tr. 1, lit. *oculis privare, caecum reddēre;* 2, fig. see DAZZLE. **blindfold,** adj. *oculis opertis.* **blindness,** n. 1, lit. *caecitas;* 2, fig. *stultitia.* **blink,** v.intr. *con(n)ivēre, nictare.*

bliss, n. *summa felicitas.*

blister, I. n. *pustula.* **II.** v.tr. *pustulare.*

blithe, adj. *laetus, hilaris.* Adv. *laete, hilariter.* **blitheness,** n. *laetitia, hilaritas.*

bloated, adj. 1, lit. *turgidus;* 2, fig. *tumidus.*

block, I. n. *truncus, caudex.* **II.** v.tr. *claudēre, obstruēre, obsaepire (obsep.).* **block-ade, I.** n. *obsidio.* **II.** v.tr. *obsidēre.* **block-head,** n. *stolidus.*

blood, n. *sanguis, cruor;* to act in cold —, *consulto alqd facēre.* **bloodless,** adj. *exsanguis, incruentus* (= without bloodshed). **blood-relation,** n. *consanguineus.* **bloodshed,** n. *caedes, -is,* f. **bloodshot,** adj. *sanguine suffusus.* **blood-thirsty,** adj. *sanguinarius.* **blood-vessel,** n. *arteria, vena.* **bloody,** adj. *cruentus, cruentatus, sanguine respersus;* a — victory, *cruenta victoria;* — battle, *proelium cruentum, atrox.*

bloom, I. n. *flos;* to be in —, *florēre.* **II.** v.intr. *florēre, vigēre;* to begin to —, *florescēre.* **blooming,** adj. *florens, floridus.*

blossom, v.intr. see BLOOM.

blot, I. n. 1, on paper, *litura;* 2, = a stain, lit. & fig. *macula.* **II.** v.tr. 1, = to dry ink, *abstergēre;* 2, = to make a —, *lituram alci rei in(j)icēre;* 3, fig. *(com)maculare;* 4, to — out, *delēre, ex(s)tinguēre.*

blow, I. n. 1, *ictus, -ūs, plaga, verbera, -um;* 2, fig. *casus, -ūs, damnum.* **II.** v.intr. of the wind, *flare;* with the mouth, *flare.* **III.** v.tr. — the flute, *tibiâ (tibiis) canēre.* **blowing,** adj. *flatu figurare.*

blubber, n. *adeps balaenarum.*

bludgeon, n. *fustis, -is,* m.

blue, adj. *caeruleus, lividus* (= black-blue).

blunder, I. n. *error, erratum.* **II.** v.intr. *errare.*

blunt, I. adj. 1, lit. *hebes;* 2, fig. = dull, *hebes, obtusus;* 3, = rude, *agrestis, rusticus, inurbanus.* Adv. *rustice.* **II.** v.tr. *hebetare,* lit. and fig.; fig. *obtundēre.* **bluntness,** n. 1, lit. by adj. *hebes;* 2, fig. *rusticitas.*

blur, I. n. *macula.* **II.** v.tr. *obscurare.*

blush, I. n. *rubor.* **II.** v.intr. *erubescēre.*

bluster, I. n. 1, = self-assertion, *jactatio, ostentatio;* 2, = tumult, *fremitus, -ūs, strepitus, -ūs, tumultus, -ūs.* **II.** v.intr. 1, *se jactare, ostentare;* 2, *tumultum facēre, saevire.*

boar, n. *verres, -is,* m. ; a wild —, *aper.*

board, n. 1, *axis, -is,* m., *tabula;* 2. = food, *victus, -ūs, alimentum.* **board-wages,** n. *pecunia pro alimentis data.* **II.** v.tr. 1, *alci victum dare;* 2, — a ship, *navem conscendēre.* **III.** v.intr. to — with anyone, *apud alqm habitare.* **boarder,** n. *qui cum alqo habitat.*

boast, v.intr. *gloriari, se efferre, se jactare.* **boaster,** n. *jactator, ostentator, homo gloriosus.* **boasting,** n. *jactatio, ostentatio.* **boastful,** adj. *gloriosus.* Adv. *gloriose.*

boat, n. *scapha, navicula;* —man, *nauta,* m.

bodice, n. *thorax (linteus).*

body, n. 1, *corpus, -ŏris,* n.; a little —, *corpusculum;* a — guard, *cohors praetoria* or *regia;* —servant, *servus, mancipium, verna,* m. and f. 2, = company, *societas;* — of cavalry, *ala.*

bodily, adj. *corporeus;* —exercise, *exercitatio.*

bodiless, adj. *sine corpore.*

bog, n. *palus, -ŭdis,* f. **boggy,** adj. *uliginosus, paluster.*

boil, I. v.tr. *coquĕi* 2. **II.** v.intr. 1, *fervēre, effervescĕre, aestuare, bullare* or *bullire* (= bubble); 2, fig. *aestuare.* **boiler,** n. *vas, vasis,* n.; in a bath, *caldarium.*

boil, n. *vomica.*

boisterous, adj. *turbidus;* of the sea or wind, *procellosus, agitatus.*

bold, adj. *audens, audax, confidens;* to be —, *audēre* (with inf.). Adv. *audacter.* **boldness,** n. *audentia, audacia, confidentia.*

bole, n. *truncus, stirps.*

bolster, n. *culcita, pulvinus.*

bolt, I. n. 1, = a fastening, *obex, -icis,* m. and f., *claustrum;* 2, = a weapon, *sagitta.* **II.** v.tr. *claudēre, (obice) occludēre.*

bombard, v.tr. *urbem tormentis verberare.* **bomb,** n. * *pyrobolus.*

bombast, n. *verborum pompa* or *tumor, inflata oratio.* **bombastic,** adj. *inflatus.*

bond, n. 1, = a tie, *vinculum, ligamentum, compes, -pĕdis,* f. (= fetter); *catenae;* 2, fig. *societas, conjunctio;* 3, = surety, *chirographum, syngrapha.* **bondage,** n. *servitus, -utis,* f.

bone, n. *os, ossis,* n. **bony,** adj. *osseus.*

book, n. *liber, volumen, libellus.* **bookseller,** n. *bibliopōla, librorum venditor.*

boom, I. n. *obex, -icis,* m. and f. **II.** v.tr. *saevire.*

boon, I. n. *gratia, beneficium.* **II.** adj. *jucundus.*

boorish, adj. *agrestis, inurbanus.* Adv. *inurbane.*

boot, n. *calceamentum.*

boot, n. = gain, *commodum;* to —, *ultro.*

bootless, adj. *inutilis, irritus.* Adv. *frustra.*

booty, n. *praeda, spolia, exuviae.*

boozy, adj. *ebriosus.*

border, I. n. 1, of a river, *margo, -ĭnis,* m. and f., *ripa, ora;* 2, of a country, *fines, -ium,* m. **II.** v.tr. = to surround, *alqd alqā re cingĕre, circumdare.* **III.** v.intr. 1, of people, *confinem alci esse;* of lands, *adjacēre, attingĕre;* 2, = be near, *finitimum esse.*

bore, I. v.tr. 1, = perforate, *perterebrare;* 2, = to weary, *defatigare.* **II.** n. *homo importunus.*

born, v.intr. to be —, *nasci.*

borrow, v.tr. *mutuari, mutuum sumĕre.*

bosom, n. 1, *sinus, -ūs;* 2, fig. *pectus, -ŏris,* n. **bosom-friend,** *amicus conjunctissimus.* See BREAST.

boss, n. *umbo.*

botany, n. *herbaria (ars).* **botanical,** adj. *herbarius.* **botanize,** v.intr. *herbas quaerĕre* or *colligĕre.*

both, I. adj. *ambo.* **II.** pron. *uterque.* **III.** conj. *et — et, cum — tum.*

bother, I. n. *molestia, incommodum.* **II.** v.tr. *alqm alqā re defatigare, obtundĕre; molestiam alci afferre.*

bottle, I. n. *lagena, ampulla;* — of hay, *manipulus.* **II.** v.tr. *vinum,* etc., *diffundĕre.*

bottom, n. 1, *fundus, solum;* of a ship, *alveus;* to drain to the —, *faece tenus potare;* — of the sea, *mare imum;* 2, fig. to go to the —, *perire, interire;* get to the — of anything, *alqd perspicĕre;* he is at the — of this, *res ex eo pendet.*

bottomless, adj. *immensae altitudinis.*

bough, n. *ramus.*

bounce, v.intr. *resilire.*

bound, I. n. = a limit, *limes, -ĭtis,* m., *fines;* pl. (both lit. & fig.), to keep within —s, *intra fines se coercēre.* **II.** v.tr. = to limit, *finire, definire.* **III.** n. and v.intr. see LEAP.

bounden, adj. — duty, *officium.* **boundless,** adj. *infinitus, immensus.*

bounty, n. 1, *largitas, liberalitas, munificentia;* 2, = a reward, *praemium.* **bountiful,** adj. *largus, liberalis, beneficus;* to be —, *magnā esse liberalitate.* Adv. *large, liberaliter.*

bout, n. 1, a drinking —, *comissatio;* 2, of illness, *morbus;* 3, at one —, *uno impetu, simul.*

bow, I. v.tr. *flectĕre, demittĕre.* **II.** v.intr. *flecti, se demittĕre,* or *demitti;* to — to anything, *alci rei obtemperare.* **III.** n. 1, = a salutation, *corporis inclinatio, nutus, -ūs;* to make a —, *alqm salutare;* 2, = a weapon, *arcus, -ūs;* 3, of a ship, *prora.* **bowman,** n. *sagittarius.*

bowstring, n. *nervus.*

bowels, n. 1, *intestina* (= the inside), *viscera, -um* (= the entrails), *exta, -orum* (= the nobler parts, as the heart, lungs), etc.; 2, fig. *viscera.*

bower, n. *umbraculum.*

bowl, I. v.tr. *volvĕre.* **II.** n. 1, = a drinking-cup, *patera, phiala, poculum;* 2, = a ball, *pila.*

box, I. v.intr. *pugnis certare.* **II.** n. = — on the ear, *alapa.* **boxer,** n. *pugil.*

box, n. (tree), *buxus,* f., *buxum* (= boxwood); —, *buxeus;* = a small chest, *cista, arca, armarium, scrinium;* ballot —, *cista;* dice —, *fritillus.*

boy, n. *puer.* **boyhood,** n. *aetas puerilis, pueritia.* **boyish,** adj. *puerilis.* Adv. *pueriliter.*

brace, I. v.tr. 1, = to bind, *alligare;* 2, fig. (animum) erigĕre; of air, *sanare.* **II.** n. 1, *vinculum;* 2, of a ship, *funis quo antenna vertitur;* 3, = a pair, *par;* 4, braces, *fascia.*

bracelet, n. *armilla.*

brackish, adj. *amarus.*

brag, v. intr. *se jactare, gloriari;* see BOAST.

braid, I. v.tr. *texĕre, nectĕre.* **II.** n. *gradus, -ūs.*

brain, n. *cerebrum.*

bramble, n. *rubus.*

bran, n. *furfur.*

branch, n. 1, *ramus;* 2, fig. of a family, *familia.*

brand, n. 1, *fax* (lit. and fig.), *titio, torris, -is,* m.; 2, = a mark, *nota;* to —, *notam alci inurĕre.*

brandish, v.tr. *vibrare, jactare.*

brandy, n. *vinum.*

brasier, 1, = a place for fire, *foculus;* 2, = a worker in brass, *faber qui vasa ex orichalco facit.*

brass, n. *orichalcum, aes, aeris,* n.; of brass, *a(h)eneus.*

bravado, n. *jactatio, ostentatio.*

brave, adj. *fortis, acer, strenuus;* — titer, acrier, strenue. **bravery,** n. *fortis, fortitudo.* Adv. *for-*

bravo! interj. *euge! factum bene! laude!*

brawl, I. v.intr. *altercari.* **II.** n. *altercatio, jurgium.*

brawny, adj. *robustus.*

bray, I. v.tr. *contundĕre.* **II.** v.intr. *rudĕre.*

brazen, I. adj. 1, = of brass, *a(h)eneus* ; 2, ǎg. *impudens.* **II.** v.tr. to — anything out, *algd pertinacius asseverare, confirmare.*

breach, n. 1, lit. *via patefacta ;* to make a —, *muros perfringĕre ;* 2, fig. = violation, by partic. (e.g. — of treaty, *foedus ruptum*) ; to commit a — of duty, *officium neglegĕre (neglig.), ab officio discedĕre.*

bread, n. 1, *panis, -is,* m. ; 2, fig. — nutriment, *victus, -ūs, victus cot(t)idianus (quot.).*

breadth, n. *latitudo;* in —, *latus* (e.g. *fossa decem pedes lata*).

break, I. v.tr. *frangĕre, confringĕre, dirumpĕre ;* to — a treaty, *foedus violare ;* to — or subdue, *domare, frangĕre ;* to — off, *carpĕre, decerpere, avellĕre ;* to — up a camp, *castra movēre ;* to — a promise, *fidem fallĕre ;* to — silence, *silentium rumpĕre.* **II.** v.intr. *frangi, confringi, rumpi ;* the clouds —, *nubes discutiuntur ;* to — out from a place, *erumpĕre ;* of a war, *oriri ;* — in, *irrumpĕre ;* to — forth (as the sun), *sol inter nubes effulget ;* the day —s, *illucescit.* **III.** n. 1, *intervallum, rima* (= a chink) ; 2, — of day, *prima lux, diluculum.* **breaker,** n. *fluctus, -ūs.*

breakfast, I. n. *jentaculum* (on rising), *prandium* (about noon), *cibus meridianus.* **II.** v.intr. *jentare, prandĕre, cibum meridianum sumĕre.*

breakwater, n. *moles, -is,* f.

breast, I. n. *pectus, -ŏris,* n. (both lit. and fig.), *animus* (fig.); the —s, *mamillae.* **II.** v.tr. *alci rei obniti.* **breastbone,** n. *os pectoris* (Cels.). **breast-plate,** n. *thorax.* **breastwork,** n. *pluteus.*

breath, n. *spiritus, -ūs, anima, halitus, -ūs ;* to take —, *se colligĕre ;* of air, *aura ;* — of applause, *aura popularis.* **breathless,** adj. *exanimatus, exanimis.* **breathe,** v.intr. *spirare ;* to — upon, *algm* or *alci afflare ;* to — out, *exhalare.*

breeches, n. *bracae ;* wearing —, *bracatus.*

breed, I. v.tr. 1, *gignĕre, generare, parĕre, procreare ;* 2, = rear, *alĕre, colĕre ;* 3, fig. *efficĕre, fingĕre, creare.* **II.** n. *genus, -ĕris,* n. **breeding,** n. = education, *educatio, institutio, cultus, -ūs.*

breeze, n. *aura ;* favourable —, *aura secunda.*

brew, I. *coquĕre.* **II.** v. intr. *imminēre, impendĕre.* **brewing,** n. *coctura.* **brewer,** n. *coctor, coctor cerevisiae.*

bribe, I. n. *largitio, pecunia.* **II.** v.tr. *corrumpĕre (pecuniâ, donis,* etc.) ; to try to —, *sol(l)icitare algm pecuniâ ;* to be bribed, *largitionibus movēri.* **briber,** n. *corruptor, largitor ;* he that is bribed, *venalis.*

brick, n. *later, laterculus.*

bride, n. *sponsa.* **bridegroom,** *sponsus.* **bridal,** adj. *nuptialis ;* — procession, *pompa.*

bridge, n. *pons,* m. ; to make a —, *pontem facĕre in fluvio, amnem ponte jungĕre.*

bridle, I. n. *frenum,* pl. *freni* and *frena.* **II.** v.tr. 1, lit. *(in)frenare ;* 2, fig. *frenare, coërcēre, continēre, comprimĕre.*

brief, I. adj. *brevis ;* in —, *ne longus sim.* Adv. *breviter, paucis verbis, strictim.* **II.** n. a barrister's —, by verb *caus(s)am alĕjs agĕre, alci adesse.* **brevity,** n. *brevitas.*

brier, n. *frutex.* **briery,** adj. *fruticosus.*

brigade, n., see TROOP.

brigand, n. *latro.*

bright, adj. 1, in gen. *clarus, lucidus, splendidus, candidus, fulgens ;* to be —, *clarēre ;* to grow —, *clarescĕre ;* of the sky, *serenus ;* 2, = clever, *acutus, sol(l)ers.* Adv. *lucide, clare, splendide, candide.* **brightness,** n. *candor, splendor, nitor, fulgor ;* of the weather, *serenitas.* **brighten, I.** v.tr. 1, *illustrare, illuminare ;* 2, fig. = gladden, *oblectare.* **II.** v.intr. 1, *illustrari, illuminari ;* 2, fig. *oblectari, hilarem fieri.*

brilliant, I. adj. *splendidus, illustris, magnificus.* Adv. *splendide, magnifice.* **II.** n. *gemma, adamas, -antis,* m. **brilliancy,** n. *splendor, fulgor.*

brim, n. *ora, margo, labrum.*

brimstone, n. *sulfur (sulph.).*

brine, n. *aqua salsa.*

bring, v.tr. — to a place, *afferre, apportare, advehĕre ;* to — forth, *parĕre ;* to — forth fruit, *fructus edĕre ;* to — about, *efficĕre ut ;* to — before the senate, *rem ad senatum referre ;* to — to light, *in lucem proferre ;* to — over, *in partes suas trahĕre ;* to — to an end, *ad finem perducĕre ;* to — in = yield, *reddĕre ;* to — forward, *in medium proferre.*

brink, n. *margo, ripa ;* to be on the — of, by fut. partic. (e.g. on the — of death, *moriturus*).

brisk, adj. *alacer, vegetus, acer.* Adv. *acriter.* **briskness,** n. *alacritas.*

bristle, I. n. *seta.* **II.** v.intr. *algd re horrēre.* **bristly,** adj. *setosus.*

brittle, adj. *fragilis.* **brittleness,** n. *fragilitas.*

broach, I. n. *veru.* **II.** v.tr. 1, lit. *veru alci rei affigĕre, algd aperire ;* 2, fig. *aperire, divulgare.*

broad, adj. 1, *latus ;* — sea, *altum ;* — shouldered, *humeros latus ;* — day, *clarus* or *multus dies ;* 2, fig. = unrestrained of thought, etc., *liber,* = licentious, *impudicus.* Adv. *late.* **breadth,** n. 1, lit. *latitudo ;* a finger's —, *transversus digitus ;* 2, fig. — of mind, *humanitas.*

brogue, n. *barbara locutio.*

broil, I. v.tr. *torrēre.* **II.** v.intr. *torrēri.*

broker, n. *intercessor, interpres, -pretis,* m. *argentarius.*

bronze, adj. *a(h)eneus.*

brooch, n. *gemma.*

brood, I. v.intr. 1, lit. *ova incubare ;* = cover with wings, *pullos fovēre ;* 2, fig. *incubare ;* = ponder, *algd meditari, fovēre.* **II.** n. *foetus, suboles, -is,* f., *pulli.* **brooding,** 1, lit. *incubatio ;* 2, fig. *meditatio.*

brook, I. n. *rivulus.* **II.** v.tr. *ferre, tolerare ;* to — ill, *aegre ferre.*

broom, n. 1, = a plant, *genista ;* 2, = a besom, *scopae.*

broth, n. *jus, juris,* n.

brother, n. *frater.* **brotherhood,** n. = a bond of union or an association, *societas, sodalitas.* **brotherly,** adj. *fraternus.*

brow, n. 1, = eyebrow, *supercilium ;* 2, = the forehead, *frons ;* 3, of a hill, *summum collis.*

brown, n. *fuscus, fulvus* (=yellowish), *badius, spadix* (= red-brown, chestnut colour).

browse, v.intr. — upon, *algd depascĕre.*

bruise, I. v.tr. *contundĕre.* **II.** n. *contusio.*

bruit, v.tr. *divulgare.*

brunt, n. *impetus, -ūs.*

brush, I. n. *penicillus, peniculus,* or *peniculum.* **II.** v.tr. *verrĕre, tergĕre* (or *tergĕre*). **brush-wood,** n. *virgultum.*

brute, n. 1, = animal, *belua, bestia, animal;* 2, fig. *belua.* **brutish, brutal,** adj. *ferus* (= wild), *spurcus* (= foul), *immanis, atrox, crudelis.* Adv. *spurce, atrociter.* **brutalize,** v.tr. *ferum,* or *crudelem reddĕre.* **brutality,** n. *immanitas, crudelitas, atrocitas.*

bubble, I. n. *bulla, bullula.* **II.** v.intr. 1, lit. *bullare, bullire;* 2, fig. *effervescĕre.*

buccaneer, n. *pirata,* m., *praedo maritimus.*

bucket, n. *situla, situlus.*

buckle, I. n. *fibula.* **II.** v.tr. *alqd fibulā nectĕre;* see APPLY.

buckler, n. *scutum, clipeus.*

bud, I. n. *gemma;* (in flowers) *calyx.* **II.** v.intr. *gemmare.*

budge, v.intr. *loco cedĕre.*

budget, n. 1, *saccus;* 2, = statement of accounts, *ratio pecuniae publicae.*

buff, adj. *luteus.*

buffalo, n. *bos.*

buffet, I. n. 1, = a blow, *alapa, colaphus;* 2, = sideboard, *abaeus.* **II.** v.tr. *pugnis alqm xaedĕre.*

buffoon, n. *sannio, scurra.* **buffoonery,** n. *hilaritas, lascivia,* or *joca, -orum,* n.

bug, n. *cimex, -icis,* m. **bugbear,** n. *quod terret, monstrum, portentum.*

bugle, n. *cornu.*

build, v.tr. *aedificare, (ex)struĕre, construĕre; condĕre;* to — on, *alqa re (con)fidĕre, niti.* **building,** n. *aedificatio, ex(s)tructio* (= the act), *aedificium* (= the edifice). **builder,** n. 1, lit. *architectus;* 2, fig. *aedificator, auctor.*

bulb, n. *bulbus.*

bulk, n. *amplitudo, moles, -is,* f. **bulky,** adj. *amplus, ingens.*

bull, n. *bos, taurus.* **bullock,** n. *juvencus.*

bullet, n. *glans plumbea, lapis, -idis,* m., or *missile* (i.e. as hurled by *catapulta*).

bullion, n. *aurum, argentum.*

bully, I. v.tr. *jurgio adoriri alqm, alqm summā crudelitate tractare.* **II.** n. *homo crudelis, asper.*

bulrush, n. *juncus, scirpus.*

bulwark, n. *propugnaculum.*

bump, I. n. 1, *tumor, tuber, -ĕris,* n.; 2, = a knocking, *impetus, -ūs, concursus, -ūs.* **II.** v.tr. *alqd in or ad alqd or alci rei offendĕre.* **III.** v.intr. — against, *in alqd incidĕre.*

bumper, n. *calix plenus.*

bunch, n. 1, of berries, *racemus;* — of grapes, *uva;* 2, = bundle, *fascis,* m.

bundle, I. n. *fascis,* m., *fasciculus, mantĭpulus, sarcina.* **II.** v.tr. *colligĕre.*

bung, I. v.tr. *dolium obturare.* **II.** n. *obturamentum.*

bungling, adj., see AWKWARD.

buoy, I. n. *by signum* (e.g. *in mari positum*). **II.** v.tr. *sustinĕre.* **buoyant,** adj. 1, lit. *lĕvis;* 2, fig. *hilaris.* **buoyancy,** n. *lĕvitas, hilaritas.*

burden, I. n. 1, *onus, -eris,* n., *sarcina;* 2, fig. *molestia;* beast of —, *jumentum.* **II.** v.tr. *onerare.* **burdensome,** adj. *gravis, molestus.*

burgess, n. *civis,* m. and f.

burglar, n. *fur, latro* (= robber). **burg-**

lary, n. *furtum* (= theft); **to commit a** — *donum perfringĕre.*

burlesque, n. *alqd in ridiculum versum.*

burn, I. v.tr. *incendĕre, (comb)urĕre, igni consumĕre, cremare* (esp. of the dead). **II.** v.intr 1, lit. *(de)flagrare, incendi, igni consumi, cremari;* 2, fig. *ardĕre, flagrare.* **III.** n. 1, = a wound, *ambustum, ambustio;* 2, = a rivulet, *rivus, torrens.*

burnish, v.tr. *polire.*

burrow, I. n. *cuniculus.* **II.** v.tr. *cuniculos facĕre.*

burst, I. v.tr. *(di)rumpĕre.* **II.** v.intr. *(di)rumpi;* to — open, *effringĕre.*

bury, v.tr. 1, *humare, sepelire, efferre;* 2, fig. *obruĕre, opprimĕre.* **burial,** n. *sepultura, humatio.* **burial-ground,** n. *sepulturae locus, sepulc(h)rum, tumulus.*

bush, n. *frutex, dumus, vepres, -is,* m., *sentis,* m. **bushy,** adj. *fruticosus.*

bushel, n. *modius, medimnus.*

business, n. *mercatura, negotia, -orum, commercium.*

buskin, n. *cothurnus.*

bust, n. *effigies.*

bustle, I. n. *festinatio.* **II.** v.intr. *festinare.*

busy, I. adj. *occupatus, sedulus, strenuus, industrius, negotiosus.* Adv. *strenue, industrie.* **II.** v.tr. *alqm occupatum tenĕre;* to be busied with, *alqd agĕre.* **busy-body,** n. *homo importunus.*

but, I. conj. *autem, vero, at;* — yet, *sed, verum, vero, atqui* (*autem* and *vero* stand after a word, the rest at the beginning of a sentence); — yet, — however, *at, (at)tamen, sed tamen;* — otherwise, *ceterum;* — if, *sin (autem), si vero* (in a contrast); — if not, *si non, si minus, sin aliter;* — on the contrary, *at contra;* in contrasts — is omitted; e.g. *tu illum amas, ego odi,* you love, (—) I hate him; — yet (anticipating an objection), *at;* — rather, *immo (vero);* not only, — also, *non modo* or *solum* or *tantum, sed etiam;* — that, *quin,* with subj. *nisi.* **II.** prep. see EXCEPT. **III.** adv. = only, *modo, tantum, solum.*

butcher, I. n. *lanius, macellarius.* **II.** v.tr. 1, lit. *caedĕre, jugulare;* 2, fig. *trucidare.* **butchery,** n. *caedes, -is,* f.

butler, n. *cellarius.*

butt, I. n. *scopos, -i* (Suet.), *destinatum* (= an object to aim at); to make a — of, *alqm ludibrio habĕre;* *labrum* (= a large vessel), *sinum* (= a large wine-cask). **II.** v.tr. *cornu alqd ferire.*

butter, n. *butyrum* (Plin.).

butterfly, n. *papilio.*

buttocks, n. *clunes, -is,* m. and f., *nates, -ium,* f.

button, I. n. *fibula* (= clasp, buckle). **II.** v.tr. *fibulā nectĕre.*

buttress, I. n. *anterides, -um,* f. **II.** v.tr. *fulcire.*

buxom, adj. *hilaris.*

buy, v.tr. *(co)emĕre, mercari.* **buyer,** n. *emptor.*

buzz, v. *susurrare, bombum facĕre.* **buzzing,** n. *susurrus, bombus.*

by, prep. 1, of place, *ad, apud, juxta, prope* with acc.; to go —, *alqm praeterire;* to stand —, *alci adesse;* 2, of time, abl., — night, *nocte;* — moonlight, *ad lunam;* — this time, *jam;* — the year's end, *intra annum;* 3, of means, *per* with acc.; 4, an agent, *a(b);* 5,

= according to, *secundum* or *ad ;* — the authority of, *jussu* or *ex auctoritate;* **6,** in adjuration, *per ;* **7,** — oneself, *per se ;* — stealth, *furtim ;* — chance, *forte ;* — heart, *memoriter ;* — reason of, *propter,* with accus., or *propterea quod,* conj. ; one — one, *singillatim.* **by-way,** n. *trames, -itis,* m. (= footpath), *deverticulum.* **by-word,** n. to become a —, *contemptui esse.*

C

cab, n. see CARRIAGE.

cabal, I. n. = a plot, *conjuratio, conspiratio.* **II.** v.tr. *conjurationem inire ;* see PLOT.

cabbage, n. *brassica, caulis, -is,* m. (= — stalk).

cabin, n. *casa, tugurium ;* — in a ship, *cubiculum.* **cabinet,** n. **1,** *conclave ;* **2,** = a repository of precious things, *thesaurus ;* **3,** = ministry, *ii penes quos summa rerum est.*

cable, n. *ancorale, funis ancorarius.*

cackle, I. v.intr. *strepĕre.* **II.** n. *strepitus, -ūs.*

cadaverous, adj. *exsanguis* (= bloodless).

cadence, n, *numerus.*

cadet, n. *tiro.*

cage, I. n. *cavea.* **II.** v.tr. *in caveam includĕre.*

cairn, n. *(lapidum) acervus.*

cajolery, n. *blanditiae.*

cake, I. n. *placenta.* **II.** v.intr. = stick together, *concrescĕre.*

calamity, n. *calamitas, res adversae.* **calamitous,** adj. *calamitosus, tristis, luctuosus.* Adv. *calamitose, luctuose.*

calculate, v.tr. *computare.* **calculation,** n. *ratio.* **calculated,** adj. *ad alqd accommodatus, aptus, idoneus ;* he is — to do this, *is est qui hoc faciat.*

caldron, n. *a(h)enum, cortina.*

calendar, n. *ephemeris, -ĭdis,* f., *fasti.*

calf, n. *vitulus, vitula ;* of a —, *vitulinus ;* — of the leg, *sura.*

calico, n. *byssus, sindon.*

call, I. n. **1,** = a cry, *vox ;* **2,** = visit, *salutatio ;* **3,** = offer of an office, by *nominari.* **II.** v.tr. **1,** = to cry out, *clamare ;* **2,** = to name, *vocare, dicĕre, nominare, appellare ;* **3,** to — out troops, *evocare ;* to — out, = challenge, *provocare ;* to — back, *revocare ;* to — together, *convocare ;* to — for, *(de)poscĕre, flagitare.* **III.** v.intr. = to visit, *alqm salutare, visĕre.* **caller,** u. = visitor, *salutator.* **calling,** n. = vocation, *munus, -ēris,* n.

callous, adj. **1,** lit. *callosus :* **2,** fig. *durus.* Adv. *dure.*

callow, adj. *implumis, sine plumis.*

calm, I. n. *quies, -ētis,* f., *tranquillitas, otium, pax ;* — at sea, *malacia.* **II.** adj. *quietus, tranquillus, placidus.* Adv. *tranquille, placide.* **III.** v.tr. *sedare, lenire, permulcēre, tranquillare.*

calumny, n. *crimen, calumnia.* **calumniate,** v.tr. *calumniari, criminari.* **calumniator,** n. *obtrectator.*

camel, n. *camelus ;* of a —, *camelinus.*

cameo, n. *gemma ectypa.*

camp, n. *castra, -orum ;* to form a —, *castra ponĕre,* (*col*)*locare ;* to break up —, *castra movēre.*

campaign, n. *stipendium.*

can. n. see JUG.

can, v.intr. *posse.*

canal, n. *canalis, -is,* m., *fossa.*

cancel, v.tr. *delēre, eradēre, ex*(*s*)*tinguēre.*

cancer, n. *cancer* (Cels.).

candid, adj. *candidus, sincerus, verus, simplex.* Adv. *candide, sincere, vere, simpliciter.*

candour, n. *sinceritas, simplicitas, integritas.*

candidate, n. *candidatus.*

candle, n. *candela, lumen* (= light) ; to work by — light, *lucubrare.* **candlestick,** n. *candelabrum.*

cane, I. n. *arundo, calamus ;* of —, *arundineus ;* — stick or rod, *ferula ;* = walking-stick, *baculum.* **II.** v.tr. *verberare.*

canine, adj. *caninus.*

canker, v.tr. *corrumpēre.* **cankerworm,** n. *eruca.*

canister, n. *canistrum.*

cannibal, n. *qui hominibus vescitur.*

cannon, n. *tormentum ;* to be out of — shot *extra tormenti jactum esse.* **cannonade,** v.tr *tormentis verberare, tela tormentis (e)mittēre.* **cannon-ball,** n. *telum tormento missum.*

canoe, n. *cymba.*

canon, n. = a rule, *lex, regula, norma* (= standard). **canonize,** v.tr. *alqm in sanctorum numerum referre, sanctorum ordinibus a(d)scrībēre.*

canopy, n. *aulaeum.*

cant, n. *simulata* or *ficta pietas erga Deum.*

canton, n. *pagus.*

canvas, n. *pannus.*

canvass, I. n. **1,** = to examine, *explorare, disputare ;* **2,** = to seek for office, *ambire.* **II.** n. *ambitio, ambitus, -ūs.*

cap, n. *pileus, galerus ;* — for women, *mitra.*

capable, adj. *ad alqd so(l)lers, aptus, idoneus; alcjs rei capax.* **capability,** n. *ingenium, so(l)lertia, docilitas, facultas.*

capacious, adj. *capax.*

caparison, n. *phalerae.*

caper, n. *capparis* (Plin.).

capital, I. n. **1,** = chief city, *urbs opulentissima* or *potentissima ;* **2,** of a pillar, *capituium ;* **3,** = sum of money, *sors, caput.* **II.** adj. see Excellent ; = punishment, *poena capitalis.* **capitalist,** n. *homo pecuniosus, dives.*

capitulate, v.intr. see SURRENDER

caprice, n. *libido, licentia, voluntas.* **capricious,** adj. *inconstans.* Adv. *ad libidinem.*

captain, n. *centurio ;* to act as —, *ordinem ducēre ;* — of a ship, *navarchus, praefectus navis.*

captious, adj. *iracundus* (= angry), *insidiosus* (= deceitful). Adv. *iracunde, insidiose.* **captiousness,** n. *iracundia, fallacia, captio.*

captivate, v.tr. *capĕre, delenire, permulcēre.*

captive, n. *captus, captivus.* **captivity,** n. *captivitas* (Tac.) ; to be in —, *captivum esse.* **capture,** v.tr. *capĕre, comprehendĕre.*

car, n. *carrus, plaustrum, vehiculum.*

caravan, n. *comitatus, -ūs.*

caraway, n. *careum* (Plin.).

carbuncle, n. *carbunculus.*

carcase, n. *cadaver, -ĕris,* n. (of men and beasts).

card, I. n. *charta ;* to play at —s, see DICE. **II.** v.tr. *pectĕre.*

cardinal, I. adj. *princeps, eximius.* **II.** n. *Cardinalis.*

care, I. n. **1,** *cura, diligentia ;* **2,** = anxiety

sol(l)icitudo. **II.** v.intr. 1, = to take — of, *alqd curare*; what do I —? *quid mihi est?* 2, = to be interested in, *colēre, diligēre.* **careful,** adj. *diligens, accuratus.* Adv. *diligenter, accurate.*

careless, adj. *securus, imprudens, neglegens.*

carelessness, n. *securitas, imprudentia, neglegentia.*

career, I. n. *curriculum, cursus, -ūs* (lit. and fig.). **II.** v.intr. *currēre.*

caress, I. n. *blanditiae, blandimenta, -orum.* **II.** v.tr. *aici blandiri, alqm permulcēre.* **caressing,** adj. *blandus.*

cargo, n. *onus, -ēris, n.*

caricature, I. n. *vultus, -ūs, in pejus fictus.* **II.** v.tr. *vultum in pejus fingēre.*

carmine, n. *coccum;* of —, *coccineus.*

carnage, n. *caedes, -is,* f.

carnal, adj. *libidinosus.* Adv. *libidinose.*

carnival, n. *Saturnalia, -ium.*

carnivorous, adj. *qui carne vescitur.*

carousal, n. *convivium, comissatio.* **carouse,** v.intr. *comissare.*

carp, I. n. *cyprinus* (Plin.). **II.** v.intr. *to* — at, *alqm carpēre, perstringēre.*

carpenter, n. *faber (lignarius).* **carpentry,** n. *opera fabrilis, fabrica.*

carpet, n. *tapete, tapetum, peristroma, -ātis,* n.

carrion, n. *cadaver, -ēris* (or in pl.).

cart, I. n. *vehiculum, plaustrum.* **II.** v.tr. *plaustro vehēre.* **cart-load,** n. *onus, -ēris,* n.

carve, v.tr. *caelare, scalpēre, sculpēre, inscribēre;* — meat, *scindēre, secare.* **carver,** n. 1, of meat, *carptor;* 2, of works of art, *sculptor.* **carving,** n. 1, = act of, *caelatura, scalptura, sculptura;* 2, = thing carved, *signum, effigies.*

carry, v.tr. *portare, ferre, bajulare, vehēre, gerēre;* — a point, *alqd consequi;* — out, *conficēre;* — on, *alqd exercēre;* — too far, *modum excedēre;* — a town, *expugnare;* — a bill, *legem perferre.* **carriage,** n. 1, = carrying, *vectura, gestatio;* 2, = vehicle, *vehiculum, currus, -ūs, carpentum, cisium, raeda;* 3, = gait, *incessus, -ūs.* **carrier,** n. *gerulus;* letter —, *tabellarius.*

cascade, n. *aquae ex alto desilientes.*

case, n. 1, = a receptacle, *theca, involucrum;* 2, (in grammar), *casus, -ūs;* 3, = an incident, *.isus, -ūs, res;* 4, in medicine, *morbus;* 5, = judicial —, *cau(s)sa.*

casement, n. *fenestra.*

cash, I. n. = ready money, *pecunia.* **II.** v.tr. *praesenti pecuniâ solvēre.* **cashier, I.** n. *custos pecuniarum.* **II.** v.tr. = to discharge, *alqm dimittēre.*

cask, n. *dolium.* **casket,** n. *arcula, capsula, cistula.*

casque, n. *galea.*

cast, I. v.tr. 1, *jacēre, jactare, jaculari, mittēre;* 2, = to found, *fundēre;* 3, to be — in a suit, *caus(s)â cadēre;* 4, to be — down, *affligi;* 5, to — off, *(de)ponēre, exuēre;* to — out, *(ex)pellēre;* to — up (of accounts), *computare* (a mound, etc.), *exstruēre.* **II.** n. 1, *jactus, -ūs, ictus, -ūs;* 2, of dice, *alea;* 3, = image, *imago, effigies.* **castaway,** n. *perditus, profligatus;* — by shipwreck, *naufragus.*

caste, n. *societas, sodalitas.*

castigation, n. *castigatio, supplicium.*

castle, n. *arx, castellum;* to build —s in the air, *somnia sibi fingēre.*

castrate, v.tr. *castrare.*

casual, adj. *fortuitus, forte oblatus.* Adv. *forte, casu.* **casualty.** n. *fortuita -orum, res*

fortuitas. **casuistry,** n. *sophisma, -ātis, n., questio de moribus.* **casuist, n.** *sophistes, -æ,* m., *qui de moribus disputat.*

cat, n. *feles (felis), -is.*

catacomb, n. *puticuli.*

catalogue, n. *librorum index.*

catapult, n. *catapulta.*

cataract, n. 1, in the eye, *glaucoma* (Plin.); 2, see CASCADE.

catarrh, n. *destillatio, gravedo.*

catastrophe, n. *casus, -ūs (durus or acerbus).*

catch, I. v.tr. *capēre, excipēre, intercip're, deprehendēre, comprehendēre;* to — a dise.ise, *morbum contrahēre.* **II.** n. = gain, *lucrum, emolumentum.* **catching,** adj., of a disease, *pestilens.*

catechism, n. *＊catechismus.* **catechize,** v.tr. *＊catechizare* (Eccl.).

category, n. *genus, -ēris, numerus, ＊categoria.* **categorical,** adj. *simplex, definitus.*

cater, v.intr. *obsonare.*

caterpillar, n. *eruca.*

cathedral, n. *＊aedes cathedralis.*

Catholic, *＊homo Catholicus* (Eccl.). **Catholicism,** n. *＊fides Catholica* (Eccl.).

cattle, n. *pecus, -oris, armenta, -orum.*

caul, n. *omentum.*

cauldron, n. *a(h)enum, cortīna.*

cause, I. n. 1, *caus(s)a, auctor* (of a person); to have no —, *nihil est quod;* 2, = legal —, *caus(s)a,* see ACTION. **II.** v.tr. *alcjs rei auctorem esse, efficēre ut,* = excite, *excitare, (com)movēre.* **causal,** adj. *quod efficit ut.* **causeless,** adj. *vanus, futilis.* Adv. *temere, sine caus(s)â.*

causeway, n. *viae, agger, -ēris,* m.

caustic, I. n. *causticum* (Plin.). **II.** adj. *mordens, acerbus.* **cauterize,** v.tr. *adurēre.*

caution, I. n. *providentia, prudentia, cautio.* **II.** v.tr. *monēre.* **cautious,** adj. *providus, prudens, cautus.* Adv. *prudenter, caute.*

cavalcade, n. *equites, -um, comitatus, -ūs.*

cavalier, n. *eques, -ĭtis,* m. Adv. *arroganter, insolenter.*

cavalry, n. *equitatus, equites, -um, copiae equestres, ala;* to serve in —, *equo merēre.*

cave, n. *cavum, caverna, specus, spelunca.*

cavity, n. see HOLE.

cavil, v.intr. see CARP.

caw, v.intr. *crocire, crocitare.*

cease, v.intr. *alqd omittēre, intermittēre, ab alqâ re,* or infin. *desistēre, desinēre* with infin. **ceaseless,** adj. *perpetuus, assiduus, continuus.* Adv. *perpetue, assidue, continue.*

cedar, n. *cedrus,* f.

cede, v.tr. *alqd* or *ab alqâ re alci cedēre, alqd concedēre.*

ceiling, n. *lacunar, lacunar;* vaulted —, *camera.*

celebrate, v.tr. = solemnize, *celebrare, agēre.* **celebrated,** adj. *inclytus, clarus, illustris, nobilis.* **celebration,** n. *celebratio.* **celebrity,** n. *gloria, laus, claritas;* = a celebrated person, *vir insignis.*

celerity, n. *velocitas, celeritas.*

celestial, adj. 1, *caelestis, divinus;* 2, fig *eximius, praestans.*

celibacy, n. *caelibatus, -ūs.*

cell, n. *cella, cubiculum.*

cellar, n. *hypogeum (doliarium); a wine —, apotheca.*

cement, I. n. *gluten.* **II. v.tr. both lit. & fig.** *conglutinare.*

cemetery, n. *sepulc(h)ra, -orum.*

censer, n. *thuribulum.*

censor, n. 1, *censor*; 2, fig. *qui alqm reprehendit.* **censorious,** adj. *acerbus, severus.* Adv. *acerbe, severe.*

censure, I. v.tr. *reprehendĕre.* **II.** n. *reprehensio.* **censurable,** adj. *reprehendendus.*

census, n. *census, -ūs, aestimatio*; to take a —, *censēre.*

cent, n. 1, = a coin, *teruncius*; 2, = per —, *unciae usurae,* = ₁₂th per — per month, = 1 per — per ann.; *sextantes,* = 2 per — per ann.; *quadrantes,* = 3, etc.; *asses usurae* or *centesimae,* = 12 per — per ann.; *binae centesimae,* = 24, etc.

centaur, n. *centaurus.*

centenary, n. *festum saeculare.*

centre, I. n. *media pars*; the — of anything, expressed by *medius* (e.g. *media urbs*); the — of a government, *sedes imperii.* **II.** v.intr. (*ex* or *in*) *alqâ re constare*; to — in, see CONSIST.

century, n. *centum anni, saeculum.*

ceremonial, ceremony, n. *ritus, -ūs, caerimonia.* **ceremonious,** adj. *urbanus.* Adv. *urbane.*

certain, adj. 1, = fixed, *certus, firmus, stabilis, fidus* (= trustworthy), *exploratus* (= ascertained), *status* (= settled); a — income, *status reditus, -ūs*; to be — of a thing, *rem exploratam habēre*; 2, = someone known or unknown, *quidam; nescio qui, nescio quis.* Adv. *certe, certo, haud dubie, sine ullâ dubitatione, profecto, sane*; to know —, or for certain, *pro explorato or exploratum habēre.* **certainty, certitude,** n. *fides, res explorata.* **certificate,** n. *testimonium.* **certify,** v.tr. *certiorem facĕre, confirmare.*

cerulean, adj. *caeruleus.*

chafe, I. v.tr. *calefacĕre.* **II.** v.intr. *trasci, commoveri.*

chaff, n. *palea.*

chagrin, n. *aegritudo, maeror, sol(l)icitudo, dolor.*

chain, I. n. 1, *catena, vinculum*; 2, = an ornament, *catena*; 3, = a connected series, *series*; 4, = — of mountains, *montes, -ium,* m. **II.** v.tr. *vincire, catenas alci in(j)icĕre.*

chair, n. *sella, sedile, cathedra*; to set a — for, *sellam alci apponĕre.* **chairman,** n. *qui conventui praeest.*

chaise, n. *carpentum, pilentum.*

chalice, n. *calix, calathus.*

chalk, n. *creta.*

challenge, I. n. *provocatio.* **II.** v.tr. *alqm ad alqd provocare.*

chamber, n. *cubiculum.* **chamber-maid,** n. *serva.* **chamber-pot,** n. *matula, matella, trulla, scaphium.* **chamberlain,** n. *cubiculo praepositus* (Suet.).

champ, v.tr. *mandĕre, mordēre.*

champion, n. *propugnator.*

chance, I. n. *casus, -ūs, fors*; by —, *forte, casu*; game of —, *alea.* **II.** v.intr. *accidĕre.*

chancel, n. *absis, -īdis,* f. **Chancellor of the Exchequer,** n. *aerarii tribunus.*

chandler, n. *qui candelas sebat* (= candle-maker), *candelarum, propola* (= seller).

change, I. v.tr. (*com)mutare*; to — money, *permutare.* **II.** v.intr. (*com)mutari*; the weather changes, *tempestas commutatur, caelum variat.* **III.** n. (*com)mutatio, conversio, vicissitudo,*

varietas; = change of money, *permutatio,* or by verb *permutare.* **changeable,** adj. *mutabilis, mobilis, inconstans, varius.* Adv. *mutabiliter, mobiliter, inconstanter.* **changeableness,** n. *mutabilitas, varietas.* **changeling,** n. *puer subditus.*

channel, n. 1, lit. *fossa, canalis,* m.; 2, fig. *via, ratio.*

chant, v.tr. *canĕre, cantare.*

chaos, n. 1, lit. *chaos,* only in nom. and abl. sing.; 2, = confusion, *confusio, perturbatio.* **chaotic,** adj. *inordinatus, perturbatus.*

chapel, n. *aedicula, sacellum, sacrarium.*

chaps, n. = jaw, *jauces. -ium.* f.

chaps, n. on the hands, *rhagades* (Plin.).

chapter, n. of a book, *caput.*

character, n. 1, = a sign, *nota, signum*; 2, — of a person, *natura, indoles, -is,* f., *ingenium, animus, mores, -um*; weakness of —, *infirmitas, inconstantia*; strength of —, *constantia, gravitas*; 3, = a letter of the alphabet, *lit(t)era*; 4, = function, *munus, -eris,* n., or by apposition (e.g. to go in the — of ambassador, *legatum ire*); 5, = reputation, *fama, existimatio*; to give a — to a servant, *commendare.* **characteristic, I.** adj. *proprius.* Adv. *suo more.* **II.** n. *proprietas,* or by gen. (e.g. it is the — of the mind, *mentis est*). **characterize,** v.tr. *notare, designare.*

charcoal, n. *carbo.*

charge, I. n. 1, = office or trust, *munus, -eris,* n., *officium*; 2, = price, *pretium*; at a small —, *parvo pretio*; 3, = commission, *mandatum*; 4, = care of, *cura, custodia*; 5, = accusation, *accusatio, crimen*; 6, = attack, *impetus, -ūs, incursus, -ūs*; 7, = exhortation, *hortatio.* **II.** v.tr. 1, = order, *jubĕre, imperare*; 2, = to fix a price, *indicare*; 3, — with, = trust, *alqd alci committĕre, mandare, credĕre*; 4, take — of, *alqm curare*; 5, = accuse, *accusare*; 6, = attack, *impetum in alqm facĕre*; 7, = exhort, (*ad)hortari.* **chargeable,** adj. 1, *cui solvendum est*; 2, = with a fault, *culpae affinis* or *obnoxius.* **charger,** n. 1, = dish, *lanx*; 2, = horse, *equus* (*ecus*).

chariot, n. *currus, -ūs*; a two-horsed —, *bigae*; four —, *quadrigae.* **charioteer,** n. *auriga,* m. and f.

charity, n. 1, as a sentiment, *amor, benignitas*; 2, as conduct, *beneficentia, liberalitas*; 3, = alms, *stips.* **charitable,** adj. *benignus, liberalis, beneficus.* Adv. *benigne, liberaliter.*

charlatan, n. *circulator, jactator, ostentator.*

charm, I. n. 1, lit. *carmen, canticum, fascinum*; 2, fig. = an attraction, *delenimenta, -orum, blanditiae*; 3, = beauty, *venustas, amoenitas.* **II.** v.tr. 1, lit. *fascinare, incantare*; 2, fig. *capĕre.* **charming,** adj. *suavis, venustus, lepidus.* **charmer,** n. 1, = magician, *magus*; 2, = mistress, *deliciae.*

chart, n. *tabula.* **charter,** n. *privilegium* (e.g. to grant a —, *privilegia dare*).

chary, adj. *parcus.*

chase, I. v.tr. *venari*; see PURSUE. **II.** n. *venatio, venatus, -ūs.*

chasm, n. *hiatus, -ūs, specus, -ūs.*

chaste, adj. *castus.* **chastity,** n. *castitas.*

chastize, v.tr. *castigare.* **chastisement,** n. *castigatio.*

chat, v.intr. *fabulari cum alqo.*

chatter, I. v.intr. *garrire.* **II.** n. *garrulitas, loquacitas.* **chattering,** adj. *garrulus, loquax.*

cheap, adj. *vilis, parvi pretii.*

cheat, I. n. 1, *fraus, -dis,* f., *fallacia, dolus*; 2, = a man who —s, *circumscriptor* or *qui fallit.*

II. v.tr. *alqm fallĕre, decipĕre, circumvenīre, fucum facĕre.*

check, I. n. *impedimentum, mora.* **II,** v.tr. *alci obstare, impedimento esse, moram facĕre.*

cheek, n. *gena.*

cheer, n. 1, = joy, *hilaritas;* 2, = hospitality, *hospitium;* to entertain with good —, *hospitaliter* or *laute excipĕre.* **cheerful,** *hilaris, hilarus.* Adv. *hilariter, hilare.* **cheerless,** adj. *tristis, maestus.*

cheese, n. *caseus.*

chemistry, n. * *chemia, ars chemica.*

cheque, n. *perscriptio.*

cherish, v.tr. *curare, diligĕre, colĕre, observare.*

cherry, n. 1, the tree, *cerasus,* f. ; 2, = the fruit, *cerasum.*

chess, n. *lusus latrunculorum.*

chest, n. 1, = part of the body, *pectus, -oris,* n. ; 2,= a receptacle, *arca, cista.*

chestnut, n. *castanea.*

chew, v.tr. *mandĕre.*

chicanery, n. *dolus, praevaricatio.*

chicken, n. *pullus (gallinaceus).*

chide, v.tr. *alqm objurgare.* **chiding,** n. *objurgatio.*

chief, I. n. *caput, princeps, praefectus.* **II.** adj. *primus, praecipuus.* Adv. *praecipue.*

child, n. *filius, filia, liberi* (= children). **child-birth,** *partus, -ūs;* to be in —, *parturire.* **childhood,** n. *aetas puerilis.* **childlike,** adj. *puerilis.* **childish,** adj. *ineptus.* Adv. *pueriliter.* **childless,** adj. *(liberis) orbus.*

chill, I. adj. *frigidus.* **II.** n. *frigus, -oris,* n. **III.** v.tr. 1, lit. *refrigerare ;* 2, fig. *reprimĕre.*

chime, I. n. *concentus, -ūs.* **II.** v.intr. *concinĕre.*

chimera, n. *commentum, opinionum commenta, -orum.* **chimerical,** adj. *commenticius, inanis, vanus.*

chimney, n. (unknown in Roman houses) *compluvium* (= an opening in the roof of the *atrium*).

chin, n. *mentum.*

china, n. *murrha* (Mart.); made of —, *murrhinus.*

chine, n. *spina.*

chink, n. *rima.*

chip, n. *assula, scobis.*

chirp, v. *fritinnire, pipire, pipilare.*

chisel, I. n. *scalprum fabrile, caelum.* **II.** v.tr. *sculpĕre.*

chivalry, n. *ordo equester, res equestris;* = politeness, *summa comitas.* **chivalrous,** adj. *fortis et urbanus.*

choice, I. n. *delectus, -ūs, electio.* **II.** adj. *praecipuus, eximius.* **choose,** v.tr. *eligĕre, deligĕre.*

choir, n. 1, *chorus.* 2, = — of a church, *absis.* **chorister,** n. (*puer*) *symphoniacus.*

choke, I. v.tr. *suffocare, animam intercludĕre, praecludĕre.* **II.** v.intr. *suffocari, strangulare.*

choler, n. see ANGER. **cholera,** n. *pestis.*

chop, I. v.tr. *abscidĕre;* — a tree, — the hands, *amputare.* **II.** v.intr. *se vertĕre, verti.* **III.** n. *offa.*

chord, n. *nervus, fides, -ium,* pl.

chorus, n. *chorus ;* leader of —, *choragus.*

chough, n. *corvus.*

Christ, *Christus.* **Christendom,** n. * *popu-*

lus Christianus. **Christian,** adj. * *Christianus.* **Christianity,** n. * *lex* or *religio Christiana.*

chronic, adj. *longinquus, diuturnus.*

chronicle, I. v.tr. *in annales referre.* **II.** n. *annales, -ium,* m., *fasti.* **chronicler,** n. *annalium scriptor.* **chronology,** n. *temporum* or *annorum ratio.* **chronological,** adj. — errors, *temporum aetatumque errores.* Adv. *servato temporum ordine.*

church, n. *ecclesia.*

churl, n. *homo agrestis, rusticus, inurbanus.* **churlish,** adj. *inurbanus, agrestis, rusticus.* Adv. *rustice, inurbane.* **churlishness,** n. *rusticitas.*

churn, I. n. *labrum ad butyrum faciendum.* **II.** v.tr. *butyrum facĕre.*

cicatrice, n. *cicatrix.*

cider, n. *vinum ex malis confectum.*

cimeter, n. *acinaces, -is,* m.

cinder, n. *carbo ex(s)tinctus.*

cipher, I. n. 1, *nota, lit(t)era secretior ;* 2, a mere —, *nullo numero esse;* see NUMBER. **II.** v.intr. *computare.*

circle, n. 1, lit. *orbis, -is,* m., *circulus;* to describe a —, *circulum ducĕre ;* 2, = an assembly, *corona;* social —, *circulus;* family —, *familia.*

circuit, n. *circuitus, -ūs, ambitus, -ūs, orbis, -is,* m.

circular, I. adj. *orbiculatus, rotundus.* **II.** n. *lit(t)erae circum alqos dimissae.* **circulation,** n. *circuitus, -ūs;* there is a rumour in —, *rumor est.* **circulate, I.** v.tr. *circumagĕre.* **II.** v.intr. *circumagi, commeare;* of money, *in usum venīre.*

circumference, n. *orbis, -is,* m. *circuitus, -ūs.*

circumflex, n. When pronounced, *circumflexus accentus, -ūs* (Gram.); when written, *syllaba circumflexa* (Gram.).

circumlocution, n. *circuitio.*

circumnavigate, v.tr. *circumvehi (navi* or *classe).*

circumscribe, v.tr. *circumscribĕre, circumvenīre.*

circumspect, adj. *cautus, providus, prudens.* Adv. *caute, prudenter.* **circumspection,** n. *cautio, prudentia, circumspectio.*

circumstance, n. *res, caus(s)a, ratio ;* also by *hoc, id,* etc.; under these —s, *quae cum ita sint.* **circumstantial,** adj. — evidence, *testimonium e rebus collectum.* Adv. *accurate.*

circumvallation, n. *circummunitio.*

circumvent, v.tr. *circumvenīre.*

cistern, n. *cisterna, puteus.*

citadel, n. *arx, castellum.*

cite, v.tr. 1, = quote, *afferre, proferre, memorare ;* 2, = — before a court, *citare, in jus vocare.*

citizen, n. *civis,* m. and f. **citizenship,** n. *civitas;* to present or bestow —, *civitatem alci dare, impertire, tribuĕre, alqm in civitatem accipĕre* or *recipĕre.* **city,** n. *urbs* (= a town, as opp. to country), *oppidum, municipium* (= a free city which had received the *jus civile Romanum*), *colonia* (= a Roman settlement).

citron, n. *malum citrum.*

civic, adj. *civilis, civicus.*

civil, adj. 1,=civic, *civilis;* —process, *caus(s)a privata;* — rights, *jus civile ;* — war, *bellum civile* or *intestinum ;* 2, = polite, *urbanus, bene moratus.* Adv. *urbane.* **civilization,** n. *cultus, -ūs, humanus, humanitas.* **civilize,** v.tr. *expolire, ad humanitatem informare* or *effingĕre.*

clad, adj. *vestitus.*

claim, I. n. **l,** = a demand, *postulatio, petitio;* **2,** = a right, *jus, juris,* n. **II.** v.tr. *postulare, petĕre, poscĕre, flagitare, quaerĕre.* **claimant,** n. (at law), *petitor.*

clammy, adj. *lentus.*

clamour, I. n, *vociferatio, clamor, voces, -um,* f. **II.** v.intr. *(con)clamare alqd* or acc. and infin., or *vociferari.* **clamorous,** adj. see NOISY.

clan, n. *gens, tribus, -ūs,* f.

clandestine, adj. *clandestinus, furtivus.* Adv. *clam, furtim.*

clang, I. n. *sonus, -ūs, sonitus, -ūs.* **II.** v.intr. *(re)sonare.*

clank, I. n. *crepitus, -ūs.* **II.** v.tr. *crepitum alqd re dare.*

clap, I. n. *strepitus, -ūs, plausus, -ūs;* = — of the wings, *alarum crepitus, -ūs;* thunder —, *tonitrus, -ūs.* **II.** v.tr. **l,** = strike, *ferire;* 2, — the wings, etc., *alas quatĕre;* 3, = applaud, *alci (ap)plaudĕre;* — the hands, *manibus plaudum facĕre.*

claret, n. *vinum.*

clarify, v.tr. *deliquare.*

clash, I. v.tr. = strike, *pulsare, percutĕre.* **II.** v.intr. **l,** = strike together, *concurrĕre;* 2, = to disagree, *inter se (re)pugnare, dissidĕre, discrepare;* 3, = to sound, *sonare.* **III.** n. **l,** = collision, *concursus, -ūs;* 2, = sound, *sonus, -ūs, sonitus, -ūs.*

clasp, I. n. *fibula.* **II.** v.tr. **l,** *fibula conjungĕre;* 2, see EMBRACE, GRASP.

class, n. *classis* (Quint.), *ordo,* m. (= rank of citizens, etc.), *genus, -eris,* n. ; a — of learners, *discipuli.* **classic, I.** n. (= writer) *scriptor* or *scriptor optimus, praecipuus.* **II.** adj. *optimus, praecipuus, eximius.* **classify,** v.tr. *in genera describĕre.*

clatter, I. n. *crepitus, -ūs, sonus, -ūs.* **II.** v.intr. *sonare.*

clause, n. *pars, membrum, caput.*

claw, I. n. *unguis;* of a crab, *brachium.* **II.** v.tr. *ungues alci (rei) in(j)icĕre.*

clay, n. *argilla;* of —, *argillaceus.*

clean, I. adj. *purus, mundus.* **II.** v.tr. *purgare.* **III.** adv. = quite, *prorsus.* **cleanliness.** n. *munditia, mundities.*

clear, I. adj. **l,** *clarus, lucidus, perspicuus, planus, manifestus, evidens;* it is —, *apparet, liquet;* 2, see INNOCENT ; 3, see FREE. Adv. **l,** *distincte, perspicue, plane, manifeste, lucide;* 2, = without doubt, *sine dubio.* **II.** v.tr. **l,** *(ex)-purgare* = make clear; 2, see EXPLAIN ; 3, = free from a charge, *absolvĕre, liberare.* **III.** v.intr. it — s up, *tempestas fit serena.* **clearness,** n. **l,** *claritas;* 2, *serenitas* (of weather); 3, of a proof, *res explorata, fides.* **clear-sighted,** adj. *sagax, (sol)lers.* **clear-starch,** n. *amylum.*

cleave, I. v.intr. see ADHERE. **II.** v.tr. *(dif)findĕre, scindĕre.* **cleaver,** n. *cultellus.* **cleft,** n. *fissura, fissum, rima.*

clemency, n. *clementia, gratia, mansuetudo.* **clement,** adj. *clemens, mansuetus, indulgens.*

clench, v.tr. *manum comprimĕre.*

clergy, n. * clerus, * clerici ; — man, *sacerdos,* *clericus.* **clerical,** adj. *clericus, *ecclesiasticus.*

clerk, n. *scriba,* m. *librarius.*

clever, adj. *habilis, sol(l)ers, peritus alcjs rei.* Adv. *sol(l)erter, perite.* **cleverness,** n. *peritia, habilitas, sol(l)ertia.*

client, n. *cliens* (= both dependent in gen.

and client of a lawyer, in which sense also *consultor).* **clientship.** n. *clientēla.*

cliff, n. *scopulus, saxum.*

climate, n. *caelum, caeli status, -ūs, aër.*

climax, n. *gradatio;* in oratory, the — of happiness, *summa felicitas.*

climb, v.tr. *a(d)scendĕre, scandĕre, eniti in alqd.*

clinch, v.tr. *clavulo figĕre.*

cling, v.intr. *adhaerēre rei;* — to a person, *alqm amplecti, sectari.*

clink, I. v.intr. *tinnire, sonare.* **II.** n. *tinnitus, -ūs, sonitus, -ūs.*

clip, v.tr. *praecidĕre, circumcidĕre, resecare.*

cloak, I. n. **l,** *amiculum, pallium, sagum, lacerna, paenula;* 2, fig. *species.* **II.** v.tr. *tegĕre.*

clock, n. *horologium.*

clod, n. *glaeba (gleb).*

clog, I. n. *impedimentum.* **II.** v.tr. *impedire.*

cloister, n. **l,** = colonnade, *porticus, -ūs,* f. ; 2, = monastery, * monasterium.*

close, I. v.tr. **l,** = shut, *claudĕre, occludĕre;* 2, = finish, *finire, conficĕre;* 3, — a bargain, *de pretio cum algo pacisci;* 4, — with anyone, *manum conserĕre.* **II.** n. **l,** = inclosure, *saeptum;* 2, = end, *finis,* m. and *:., exitus, -ūs.* **III.** adj. **l,** = reserved, *taciturnus, tectus;* 2, = near, *propinquus, vicinus, finitimus;* — relationship, *propinquitas;* — friendship, *conjunctio;* 3, = solid, *densus, solidus;* 4, = compressed (of speech), *pressus, brevis.* Adv. l, *tecte;* 3, *solide;* 4, *presse, breviter.* **closeness,** n. l, *taciturnitas;* 2, *propinquitas, vicinitas;* 3, *soliditas.*

closet, n. *cubiculum.*

clot, I. n. *glaeba* (= lump) ; — of blood, *sanguis concretus.* **II.** v.tr. *congelare.*

cloth, n. *textum, pannus.* **clothes,** n. *vestitus, -ūs, vestes, -ium,* f. *vestimenta.* **clothe,** v.tr. *alqm vestire, amicire;* — oneself, *induĕre sibi vestem;* — with, *vestiri* or *amiciri re.*

cloud, I. n. *nubes, -is,* f. **II.** v.tr. *obscurare, tegĕre.* **III.** v.intr. *nubibus obducĕre.* **cloudy,** adj. *nubilus.* **cloudless,** adj. *nubibus vacuus, serenus.*

clover, n. *trifolium.*

clown, n. *homo rusticus, agrestis.* **clownish,** adj. *rusticus, agrestis.* Adv. *rustice.*

cloy, v.tr. *satiare.*

club, I. n. **l,** = cudgel, *clava;* 2, = society, *circulus, factio, sodalitas.* **II.** v.tr. *in medium proferre.* **club-foot,** n. *tali pravi.* **club-footed.** adj. *scaurus.*

cluck, v.intr. *singultire, glocire.*

clue, n. *glomus, filum* (of thread); fig. *vestigium, indicium.*

clump, n. *glaeba.*

clumsy, adj. *agrestis, inhabilis, ineptus, rusticus;* a — joke, *jocus illiberalis;* — manners, *mores rustici.* Adv. *laeve, illiberaliter, rustice;* to act —, *rustice facĕre.* **clumsiness,** n. *rusticitas, inscitia.*

cluster, I. n. **l,** = bunch, *fasciculus* (of flowers). *uva* (of grapes), *racemus, corymbus* (of any berries) ; 2, = a group, *circulus, corona.* **II.** v.intr. *(frequentes) convenire.*

clutch, I. v.tr. *comprehendĕre.* **II. n.,** to get into one's —es, *manus alci in(j)icĕre.*

coach, n. *carpentum, pilentum, cisium, raeda.* **coachman.** n. *raedarius, auriga.*

ooadjutor, n. *socius, collega,* m.

coagulate, v.intr. *coire, concrescĕre, coagulari.*

coal, n. *carbo.*

coalesce, v.intr. *coalescĕre, coire.* **coalition,** n. *conjunctio, consociatio.*

coarse, adj. 1, *crassus;* 2, = rude, *agrestis, rusticus, inurbanus.* Adv. *crasse, rustice, inurbane.* **coarseness,** n. 1, *crassitudo;* 2, *inhumanitas, mores inculti.*

coast, I. n. *litus, -ōris,* n. *ora;* lying on the —, *maritimus.* **II.** v.tr. *oram legĕre, praetervehi.*

coat, I. n. 1, *toga, tunica;* 2, = hide, *vellus, -ĕris,* n., *pellis;* 3, = of paint, *circumlitio.* **II.** v.tr. *alqd alci rei induĕre.*

coax, v.tr. *alci blandiri, alqm permulcēre, morem alci gerĕre.*

cobble, v.tr. 1, lit. *sarcire;* 2, fig. *inscienter facĕre alqd.* **cobbler,** n. *sutor.*

cock, v.tr. *erigĕre.*

cock, n. 1, as to the gender, *mas;* 2, = the male of the fowl, *gallus.* **cockcrow,** n. *cantus, -ūs, galli.* **cockroach, cockchafer,** *scarabaeus.* **cock-a-hoop,** to be —, *ex(s)ultare.*

cockle, n. = a fish, *pecten.*

cod, n. *asellus.*

code, n. *codex juris, corpus juris* (e.g. *Romani*), *leges.* **codify,** v.tr. *leges describĕre.*

coemption, n. *coëmptio.*

coequal, adj. *aequalis.*

coerce, v.tr. *coërcēre, cohibēre.* **coercion,** n. *necessitas.* **coercive,** adj. *validus* (= strong), or by verb (e.g. *qui cohibet*).

coexistent, adj. *quod eodem tempore est.*

coffer, n. *cista.*

coffin, n. *arca, loculus, sarcophagus.*

cog, n. of a wheel, *dens,* m.

cogent, adj. *firmus, validus.* **cogency,** n. *persuasio, ratio quae fidem facit.*

cogitate, v.intr. *cogitare.* **cogitation,** n. *cogitatio.* **cognition,** n. *cognitio, scientia.* **cognizance,** n. *cognitio.* **cognizant,** adj. *alcjs rei conscius.*

cohabit, v.intr. *concumbĕre.*

coheir, n. *coheres, -ēdis,* m. and f.

cohere, v.intr. *cohaerēre* (both lit. and fig.). **coherent,** adj. *cohaerens, contextus, continens, sibi congruens.* Adv. *contexte. continenter sibi constanter* or *convenienter.*

cohort, n. *cohors.*

coin, I. n. *nummus;* good —, *nummi boni;* bad —, *nummi adulterini.* **II.** v.tr. *cudĕre; ferire, signare.* **coinage,** n. *res nummaria.* **coiner,** n. *qui aes* or *nummos cudit.*

coincide, v.intr. 1, = to happen at the same time, *eodem tempore fieri,* or *incidĕre;* 2, see AGREE. **coincidence,** n. = chance, *fors, casus, -ūs.*

coition, n. *coitus, -ūs.*

cold, I. adj. 1, lit. *frigidus, gelidus* (= icy cold): in — blood, *consulto;* 2, fig. *fastidiosus, superbus.* Adv. 1, *frigide, gelide;* 2, *fastidiose, superbe.* **II.** 1, n. or **coldness,** n. *frigus, -oris,* n., *algor, gelu.* **cold-blooded,** adj. see CRUEL.

collapse, v.intr. *collabi, concidĕre, corruĕre.*

collar, I. n. *collare, monile, torques, -is,* m. and f.; dog —, *armilla;* horse —, *jugum.* **II.** v.tr. *prehendĕre.* **collar-bone,** n. *jugulum.*

collation, n. 1, = comparison, *collatio;* 2, = a meal, *cena.* **collate,** v.tr. *conferre.*

colleague, n. *collega,* m.

collect, I. v.tr. *colligĕre, conferre, comportare, conquirĕre, congerĕre;* — oneself, *se colligĕre;* — money, taxes, etc., *exigĕre, accipĕre.* **II.** v.intr. *convenire, coire.* **collection,** n. 1, of money, *collatio;* 2, = an assemblage, *thesaurus.*

college, n. 1, = body, *collegium, societas, sodalitas;* 2, = building, *schola.*

collier, n. 1, = a man, *carbonarius;* 2, = a ship, *navis oneraria.*

collocation, n. *collocatio, concursus, -ūs.*

colloquy, n. *colloquium.* **colloquial,** adj. — speech, *sermo communis.*

collusion, n. *collusio.*

colonel, n. *tribunus militum, praefectus.*

colony, n. *colonia, coloni.* **colonist,** n. *colonus.* **colonial,** adj. by gen. of *colonia.* **colonize,** v.tr. *coloniam constituĕre* or *collocare.*

colonnade, n. *columnarum ordo, -inis,* m., *porticus, -ūs,* f.

colossal, adj. *vastus, ingens, immanis.*

colour, I. n. 1, = a quality of bodies, *color;* 2, = a paint, *pigmentum;* 3, = pretext, *species;* 4, pl. = standards, *signum, vexillum.* **II.** v.tr. 1, lit. *colorare, tingĕre, inficĕre;* 2, fig. *speciem offerre.* **III.** v.intr., see BLUSH.

colt, n. *pullus equinus* (of horse), *asininus* (of ass).

column, n. 1, = a pillar, *columna;* 2, in printing, *pagina;* 3, in an army, *agmen;* in two —s, *bipartito;* in three —s, *tripartito.*

comb, I. n. *pecten;* (of a cock) *crista, juba.* **II.** v.tr. *pectĕre.*

combat, I. n. *pugna, certamen, dimicatio, concursus, -ūs, proelium;* (with the fists) *pugilatus, -ūs, pugilatio;* (in wrestling) *luctatus, -ūs, luctatio.* **II.** v.intr., see FIGHT.

combine, v.tr. *(con)jungĕre, consociare, cum alqo societatem inire.* **combination,** n. *(con)junctio, societas.*

combustion, n. *exustio.* **combustible,** adj. *quod comburi potest.*

come, v.intr. *(per)venire, advenire, accedĕre, appropinquare* (= to draw near); — on foot, *peditem venire;* — on horseback, *equo* (ad)*vehi;* — to a place often, *ad alqm (locum) ventitare, alqm (locum) frequentare;* it —s into my mind, *in mentem venit;* he —s to himself, *ad se redit, se colligit, animum recipit;* how —s it that? *qui factum est ut* etc., *qui eo fit ut, quo factum est ut;* I know not how it —s to pass, *fit nescio quomodo;* — as it may, *utcumque res ceciderit,* he has — to that audacity, *eo usque audaciae progressus est ut;* to — about = happen, *evenire, fieri;* — in the way of, *alci obstare;* — near, *appropinquare;* — off, or out, *evadĕre* (= escape); — round, *sententiam mutare;* — together, *convenire;* — to light, *in lucem proferri.* **coming, I.** n. *adventus, -ūs, reditio, reditus, -ūs.*

comedy, I. n. *comoedia.* **comic,** adj. 1, = belonging to comedy, *comicus;* 2, = ridiculous, *ridiculus, facetus.* Adv. *ridicule, facete.*

comely, adj. *bellus, venustus, pulcher.* **comeliness,** n. *venustas, decor, pulchritudo.*

comet, n. *cometes, -ae,* m.

comfort, I. v.tr. 1, = console, *alqm consolari;* 2, = refresh, *alqm alqā re reficĕre, recreare.* **II.** n. 1, = consolation, *solatium, consolatio;* 2, = ease, *copia, affluentia;* 3, comforts, *commoda, -orum.* **comfortable,** adj.

gratus (= agreeable), *jucundus* (= happy). Adv. *grate, jucunde.* **comfortless,** adj. 1, *sine spe ;* 2, = uncomfortable, *incommodus.* **comforter,** n. *consolator.*

command, I. v.tr. 1, *alqm alqd facĕre jubēre, alci alqd* or *ut imperare ; —* oneself, *sibi imperare ;* 2, = — a place, *alci loco imminēre.* **II.** n. 1, in war, *imperium ;* 2, = order, *jussum, mandatum ;* of the senate, *decretum ;* 3, = — of oneself, *continentia, temperantia.* **commander,** n. *dux, imperator ;* of a fleet, *praefectus classis.* See Order.

commemorate, v.tr. *commemorare, celebrare.* **commemoration,** n. *celebratio, commemoratio ;* in — of, *in memoriam alcjs.*

commence, v.tr. *incipĕre ;* see Begin.

commend, v.tr. 1, = recommend, *alqm alci commendare ;* 2, = praise, *laudare.* **commendation,** n. *commendatio, laus, -dis,* f. **commendable,** adj. *laudabilis.* Adv. *laudabiliter.* **commendatory,** adj. *commendaticius.*

comment, I. v.tr. *interpretari, explanare, enarrare, commentari.* **II.** n. and **commentary,** n. *interpretatio, explanatio, enarratio.* **commentator,** n. *interpres, -ētis,* m. and f., *explanator.*

commerce, n. 1, = business, *commercium, negotia, -orum, mercatura ;* 2, = intercourse, *usus, -ūs, commercium, consuetudo.* **commercial,** adj. *ad commercium pertinens.*

commingle, v.tr. see Mingle.

commiserate, v.tr. **commiseration,** n. see Pity.

commissariat, n. 1, = provision department, *res frumentaria ;* 2, = officer over this department, *rei frumentarii praefectus.* **commissary,** n. *procurator.*

commission, I. n. 1, *mandatum ;* to execute a —, *mandatum exsequi, conficĕre ;* 2 (as an office or charge) *munus, -ĕris,* n., *procuratio ;* to hold a — in the army, *ordines ducĕre ;* 3, = body of arbitrators, etc., *arbitri,* or *qui alqd investigant.* **II.** v.tr. *alqd alci* or *ut, mandare.* **commissioner,** n. *procurator.*

commit, v.tr. 1, = to intrust, *dare, mandare, committĕre ;* 2, = to send to prison, *in custodiam dare, in vincula con(j)icĕre ;* 3, = do, *facĕre, committĕre (in se) admittĕre, patrare ; —* a fault, *errare ; —* murder, *occidĕre.*

committee, n. *consilium ; —* of two, *duumviri ; —* of three, *triumviri,* etc.

commodious, adj. *commodus, opportunus, aptus.* Adv. *commode, opportune, apte.* **commodity,** n. 1, = convenience, *utilitas ;* 2, = an article, *res, commoditas, merx.*

common, I. adj. 1, = belonging to several people, *communis, publicus ; —* wealth, or weal, or good, *res publica ; —* sense, *communis sensus -ūs* (that which all men feel), = practical wisdom, *prudentia ;* in —, *communiter ;* 2, = ordinary, *plebeius, cot(t)idianus* (quot.), *vulgaris ;* 3, the —s, *plebs.* Adv. *communiter ;* = usually, *fere, ferme.* **II.** n. *ager publicus.* **commonplace, I.** adj. *vulgaris.* **II.** n. *alqd (sermone) tritum.* **commoner,** n. *unus e plebe.*

commotion, n. *tumultus, -ūs, motus, -ūs, agitatio.*

commune, v.intr. *colloqui cum alqo, alqd communicare* or *conferre inter se.* **communicate,** v.tr., see Share, Tell. **communication,** n. *communicatio, usus, -ūs, consuetudo.* **communicative,** adj. *loquax* (= talkative), *qui alqd (e)narrare vult.* **communion,** n. 1, = intercourse, *commercium, societas, consuetudo, conjunctio ;* 2, eccles. t.t. *communio,* *eucharistia,* *cena Domini.* **community,** n. 1, = Communion 1; 2, of goods, *vitae communitas ;* 3, = the state, *civitas, respublica.*

commute, v.tr. = to exchange, *(per)mutare, commutare.* **commutation,** n. *commutatio, redemptio.*

compact, I. n. *pactio, pactum, conventum ;* by —, *ex pacto, ex convento ;* to form a —, *pacisci cum alqo.* **II.** adj. *densus, crassus, confertus, solidus, pressus.* Adv. *solide, presse.*

companion, n. *comes, -ĭtis,* m. and f., *socius, sodalis,* m. ; *boon —, conviva,* m. and f. **companionable,** adj. *affabilis, facilis.* **companionship,** n. by *socius* (e.g. he gave me his —, *se mihi socium conjunxit*). **company,** n. *societas ;* to form a —, *societatem facĕre ;* to enter into — with, *alqm socium sibi jungĕre.*

compare, v.tr. *comparare, componĕre, conferre.* **comparable,** adj. *quod comparari potest, comparabilis.* **comparison,** n. *comparatio, collatio ;* in — of or with, *prae, ad ; comparatus ad alqd.* **comparative,** adj. *comparativus.* Adv. *comparate.*

compass, I. n. 1, * *acus magnetica nautarum ;* 2, = extent, *ambitus, -ūs, circuitus, -ūs, modus.* **II.** v.tr. 1, = surround, *alqd alci rei* or *alqā re circumdare, stipare ;* 2, = go round, *circumire ;* 3, see Attain.

compassion, n. *misericordia.* **compassionate,** adj. *misericors.* Adv. *cum misericordiā.*

compatible, adj. see Accordance.

compatriot, n. *civis,* m. and f.

compel, v.tr. *alqm ad alqd (faciendum)* or *accus.* and infin. *or ut, cogĕre, adigĕre.* **compulsory,** adj. *per vim.* **compulsion,** n. *vis, necessitas ;* by —, *vi, per vim.*

compendious, adj. *brevis, in angustum coactus.* **compendium,** n. *epitome, -es,* f., or *epitoma, excerpta, -orum.*

compensate, v.tr. *alqd (cum) alqā re compensare ; —* a loss, *damnum restituĕre.* **compensation,** n. *compensatio.*

compete, v.intr. 1, lit. *cum alqo contendĕre ; competĕre ;* 2, fig. *alqm* or *alqd aemulari.* **competent,** adj. see Able. Adv. *satis.* **competency,** n. *divitiae.* **competition,** n. *aemulatio.* **competitor,** n. *aemulus, competitor.*

compile, v.tr. *in unum conferre.* **compilation,** n. *epitome, -es,* f., *excerpta, -orum.*

complacent, adj. 1, see Complaisant ; 2, = self-satisfied, *qui sibi placet.* **complacency,** n. *voluptas, delectatio, amor sui.*

complain, v.intr. *(con)queri de re* or *alqd, expostulare de re.* **complaint,** n. 1, *questus, -ūs, querimonia, querela, expostulatio ;* 2, = illness, *morbus.*

complaisant, adj. *comis, indulgens, facilis ;* to be — to anyone, *morem alci gerere.*

complete, I. v.tr. *complēre, explēre, supplēre, absolvĕre* (= to finish), *conficĕre, cumulare.* **II.** adj. *absolutus, perfectus, justus, integer, plenus.* Adv. *absolute, perfecte, omnino, prorsus, plane* (the last three = altogether). **completion,** n. *confectio, absolutio, finis,* m. and f. **complement,** n. *complementum, supplementum.*

complex, adj. *multiplex.* **complexity,** n. *implicatio.* **complexion,** n. *color.*

complicate, v.tr. *implicare.* **complicated,** adj. *difficilis, involutus, impeditus.* **complication,** n. *res impedita et difficilis, difficultas.*

compliment, I. n. 1, *laus ;* to pay —s, *laudem alci tribuĕre ;* 2 = salutation, *salutatio, salus, -ūtis,* f. ; to send one's —s, *alqm valēre* *jubēre.* **II.** v.tr. *laudare, congratulari.* **complimentary,** adj. *honorificus.*

comply, v.intr. *alci obsequi, alci morem gerĕre ;* to — with one's requests, *alcjs precibus indulgēre.* **compliance,** n. *obsequium, indulgentia, officium.* **compliant,** adj. see COMPLAISANT.

components, n. *partes, -ium,* f.

compose, v.tr. 1, a book, *(con)scribĕre ;* in verse, *versibus scribĕre ;* 2, of music, *modos facĕre ;* 3, see ARRANGE ; 4, = to reconcile differences, *componĕre.* **composed,** adj. *tranquillus, quietus.* Adv. *tranquille, quiete.* **composer,** n. *scriptor.* **composition,** n. 1, = the act, *compositio ;* 2, = a writing, *scriptum.* **composure,** n. *tranquillitas.*

compound, I. v.tr. 1, lit. *componĕre, confundĕre ;* 2, fig. *componĕre ;* to be —ed of, *ex alqâ re constare ;* 3, — for, *satis habēre* with accus. and infin. **II.** adj. *compositus, multiplex.* **III.** n. 1, *res admixta ;* 2, = an enclosure, *saeptum.*

comprehend, v.tr. 1, = contain, *continēre, comprehendĕre ;* 2, = understand, *compr(eh)endĕre, intellegĕre (intellig.), perspicĕre.* **comprehensible,** adj. *facilis intellectu, "erspicuus, planus.* Adv. *plane, perspicue, aperte.* **comprehension,** n. *comprehensio, intellegentia.* **comprehensive,** adj. *late patens.* Adv. *penitus, prorsus.*

compress, I. v.tr. *comprimĕre, condensare, coartare.* **II.** n. = bandage, *penicillus* or *penicillum.* **compression,** n. *compressio, compressus, -ūs.*

compromise, I. v.tr. *compromittĕre* (i.e. agreement to abide by the decision of an arbitrator). **II.** n. *compromissum,* see AGREE.

compulsion, n. see COMPEL.

compunction, n. *poenitentia ;* I have — for, *poenitet me rei.*

compute, v.tr. *computare,* see RECKON.

comrade, n. = a fellow-soldier, *contubernalis, commilito, socius.* **comradeship,** n. *contubernium.*

concave, adj. *concavus.*

conceal, v.tr. *celare, occultare alqd alqm.*

concede, v.tr. *concedĕre.* **concession,** n. *concessio, concessus, -ūs.*

conceit, n. 1, = opinion, *opinio, sententia ;* 2, = pride, *arrogantia, fastidium.* **conceited,** adj. *arrogans, fastidiosus.* Adv. *arroganter, fastidiose.*

conceive, v.tr. 1, physically, *concipĕre ;* 2, fig. *cogitare, intellegĕre (intellig.) ;* see IMAGINE.

concentrate, v.tr. *colligĕre, contrahĕre, in unum conferre.*

conception, n. 1, = procreation, *conceptio, conceptus, -ūs ;* 2, in the mind, *notio, opinio ;* to form a —, *mente fingĕre alqd, notionem rei (animo) concipĕre.*

concern, I. n. 1, *res, negotium, cura ;* 2, fig. *anxietas, sol(l)icitudo, cura.* **II.** v.tr. 1, = to relate to, *pertinēre ad alqd ;* it —s, *refert, interest ;* to — oneself, *alci studēre ;* 2, to be —ed = troubled, *alqd aegre ferre.* **concerning,** prep. *de,* abl. *; per,* accus.

concert, I. n. 1, *symphonia, concentus, -ūs, certamen musicum ;* 2, = agreement, *consensus, -ūs, concordia.* **II.** v.tr. *inire consilium de alqâ re, paciscĭ alqd cum alqo.*

conciliate, v.tr. *conciliare.* **conciliation,** n. *conciliatio.* **conciliatory,** adj. *blandus.*

concise, adj. *brevis, pressus.* Adv. *presse, breviter.* **conciseness,** n. *brevitas.*

conclave, n., see ASSEMBLY.

conclude, v.tr. 1, = to finish, *finire, conficĕre, concludĕre ;* 2, = to draw a conclusion, *concludĕre ;* 3, = to decide, *statuĕre, constituĕre.* **conclusion,** n. 1, *finis,* m. and f. *;* 2, *conclusio.* **conclusive,** adj. *gravis.* Adv. *graviter.*

concoct, v.tr. 1, = to mix, *miscēre ;* 2, fig. *fingĕre, machinari.* **concoction,** n. *potus, -ūs.*

concomitant, adj., **-ly,** adv., *cum* with abl.

concord, n. *concordia, consensus, -ūs.* **concordant,** adj. *concors, congruens, conspirans.* Adv. *congruenter.*

concourse, n. *concursus, -ūs, concursio.*

concrete, adj. *concretus* (= grown together) *solidus* (= solid).

concubinage, n. *concubinatus, -ūs.* **concubine,** n. *concubina, pellex.*

concupiscence, n. *libido (luo.).*

concur, v.intr. *consentire, congruĕre, convenire.* **concurrence,** n. *consensio, consensus, -ūs.* **concurrent,** adj., **-ly,** adv. *una, simul.*

concussion, n. *concussio, concursus, -ūs.*

condemn, v.tr. 1, *damnare, condemnare ; —* to death, *alqm capitis damnare* or *condemnare ;* 2, = disapprove, *improbare, reprehendĕre, * culpare.* **condemnation,** n. 1, *damnatio ;* 2, *reprehensio, culpa.* **condemnable,** adj. *reprehendendus, reprehensione dignus.* **condemnatory,** adj. *damnatorius.*

condense, I. v.tr. *densare, spissare.* **II.** v.intr. *concrescĕre.* **condensation,** n. *densatio.*

condescend, v.intr., *comiter se gerĕre.* **condescending,** adj. *comis, facilis.* Adv. *comiter.* **condescension,** n. *comitas, facilitas.*

condign. adj. 1, = due, *debitus, meritus ;* 2, = severe, *acerbus, atrox.*

condiment, n. *condimentum.*

condition, I. n. 1, = state, *condicio, res, status, -ūs ;* 2, = stipulation, *condicio, pactum, conventum ;* under the —, *eâ condicione, eâ lege.* **II.** v.tr. *circumscribĕre.* **conditional,** adj. *incertus, condicionibus subjectus.* Adv. *eo pacto ut,* etc., *non sine exceptione.* **conditioned,** adj. *affectus ;* well, ill —, *bene, male moratus*

condole, v.tr. *casum alcjs dolēre.*

conduce, v.intr. *facĕre* or *efficĕre ut.* **conducive,** adj *utilis,* dat., or *ad.*

conduct, I. v.tr. 1, = to lead, *ducĕre, agĕre ;* in a procession, *deducĕre, prosequi ;* 2, = manage, *gerĕre, administrare ; —* oneself, *se gerĕre* or *praebēre.* **II.** n. 1, = behaviour, *vitae ratio, mores, -um ;* 2, = management, *administratio, procuratio.* **conductor,** n. *dux, procurator.* **conduit,** n. *aquaeductus, -ūs.*

cone, n. *conus.*

confectionery, n. *dulcia, -ium.* **confectioner,** n. *pistor dulciarius* (late).

confederacy, n. *foedus, -ĕris,* n., *societas* **confederates,** n. *socii, foederati.* **confederate,** adj. *foederatus.*

confer, I. v.intr. = to talk with, *deliberare, consultare de alqâ re* or *utrum.* **II.** v.tr. see GIVE. **conference,** n. *consilium, colloquium.*

confess, v.tr. *fateri, confiteri.* **confessedly,** adv. *sine dubio, plane.* **confession,** n *confessio.*

confide, I. v.tr. *alqd alci committĕre, tradĕre, mandare, credĕre.* **II.** v.intr. — in, *alci* or *alci rei* or *alqo* or *alqâ re (con)fidĕre.* **confidant,** n. *(alcjs rei) conscius, conscia.* **confidence,** n. *fides, fiducia, fidentia, confidentia* (= esp. self —) *;* to tell in —, *alci ut amico certissimo dicĕre.* **con-**

fident, adj. *alci (rei) confidens, alqâ re fretus,* or by *certus, confirmatus;* see CERTAIN. Adv. *(con)fidenter.* **confidential,** adj. 1, = trustworthy, *fidus, fidelis,* or *alcjs rei conscius;* 2, see SECRET. Adv. see SECRETLY. **confiding,** adj. *credulus.*

confine, I. n. *finis,* m. and f., *terminus, limes, -itis, confinium.* **II.** v.tr. 1, see RESTRAIN; 2, see IMPRISON; 3, to be —d in childbed, *parêre.* **confinement,** n. 1, = imprisonment, *custodia;* 2, = childbirth, *partus, -ûs.*

confirm, v.tr. *affirmare, confirmare, sancire, ratum facêre, ratum esse jubêre.*

confiscate, v.tr. *publicare.* **confiscation,** n. *publicatio.*

conflagration, n. *incendium, ignis,* m.

conflict, I. n. *certamen, pugna, proelium;* of opinions, *dissensio.* **II.** v.intr. 1, = to strike together, *concurrère;* 2, = to fight, *pugnare;* 3, = to differ, *dissentire, discrepare, repugnare.*

confluence, n. 1, = the place where rivers meet, *confluens* or *confluentes;* 2, see CONCOURSE.

conform, I. v.tr. *alqd ad alqd* or *alci rei accommodare.* **II.** v.intr. to — to, *alci* or *alci rei obsequi, obtemperare, inservire.* **conformable,** adj. *ad alqd accommodatus, alci rei* or *cum alqâ re congruens, conveniens, consentaneus.* Adv. *congruenter, convenienter.* **conformation,** n. *conformatio, forma.* **conformity,** n. *consensus, -ûs, consensio, convenientia.*

confound, v.tr. 1, see CONFUSE; 2, = to astonish, *percutère, consternare;* 3, = to bring to naught, *ad irritum redigère, evertère;* 4, as an exclamation, — it, *di perdant.*

confraternity, n. *fraternitas, societas, sodalitas.*

confront, v.tr. *adversus alqm stare, alci obviam ire.*

confuse, v.tr. *confundère, (per)miscère, (per)turbare.* **confusion,** n. *confusio, perturbatio.*

confute, v.tr. *refellère, redarguère, confutare, refutare.*

congeal, I. v.tr. *(con)gelare.* **II.** v.intr. *(con)gelari, frigère, algère.*

congenial, adj. *alci* or *alci rei* or *cum alqâ re congruens, conveniens;* = pleasant, *jucundus.*

congeries, n. *congeries.*

congratulate, v.tr. *alci de alqâ re,* or *alqd* or *quod, gratulari.* **congratulation,** n. *gratulatio.* **congratulatory,** adj. *gratulabundus.*

congregate, I. v.tr. *cogère, congregare.* **II.** v.intr. *cogi, congregari, convenire, coire, confluère.* **congregation,** n. *conventus, -ûs, coetus, -ûs, concio.*

congress, n. *conventus, -ûs, concilium.*

congruity, n. *convenientia,* see CONFORM.

congruous, adj., see CONFORMABLE.

conjecture, I. n. *conjectura, opinio, suspicio, divinatio.* **II.** v.tr. *conjecturâ augurari* or *consequi.* **conjectural,** adj. *quod conjecturâ prospici potest.* Adv. *conjecturâ.*

conjugal, adj. *conjugalis.*

conjugate, v.tr. *declinare* (Gram.). **conjugation,** n. *declinatio* (Gram.).

conjunction, n. (Gram.), *conjunctio,* see JOIN.

conjure, I. v.tr. 1, = to entreat, *obtestari, obsecrari per alqm* or *alqd;* 2, = to move by magic forms, *adjurare;* to — up, *(mortuorum) animas sitcère.* **II.** v.intr. = to act as a conjurer, *prae-*

stigias agère. **conjurer,** n. + *magus, ventilator,* + *praestigiator.*

connect, v.tr. *alqd ad alqd alligare, (con)jungère alqd* or *alqm cum re.* **connected,** adj. = *coherent, continens.* Adv. *continenter, uno tenore.* **connexion,** n. 1, *conjunctio, societas;* 2, = by marriage, *affinis.*

connive (at), v.intr. *co(n)nivère in alqâ re, alci rei* or *alci alqd ignoscère, alci* or *alci rei indulgère.* **connivance,** n. *indulgentia.*

connoisseur, n. *artium liberalium peritus, homo doctus.*

conquer, v.tr. *vincère, capère, expugnare, superare.* **conqueror,** n. *victor.* **conquest,** n. *victoria, occupatio, expugnatio.*

consanguinity, n. *sanguinis conjunctio.*

conscience, n. *conscientia virtutis et vitiorum, c. factorum, c. mentis, religio, fides;* a good —, *c. recte facti, mens bene sibi conscia;* to have a good —, *nullius culpae sibi conscium esse;* a bad —, *c. scelerum, mens male sibi conscia.* **conscientious,** adj. *religiosus, sanctus.* Adv. *religiose, sancte.* **conscientiousness,** n. *religio, sanctitas, fides.*

conscious, adj. *alcjs rei conscius, gnarus.* Adv. use adj. (e.g. I did it —, *gnarus feci*).

conscription, n. *delectus, -ûs, conquisitio militum.*

consecrate, v.tr. *(con)secrare, (de)dicare.* **consecrated,** adj. *sacratus, sacer.* **consecration,** n. *dedicatio.*

consecutive, adj. *continens, continuus.* Adv. *continenter.*

consent, I. v.intr. —, see AGREE. **II.** n. 1, *consensus, -ûs, consensio;* 2, *consensus, -ûs, assensus, -ûs,* see AGREEMENT; with your —, *te consentiente.*

consequent, adj. *consequens.* Adv., see THEREFORE. **consequence,** n. 1, = result, *consecutio, exitus, -ûs, eventus, -ûs;* the — was that, *ex quo factum est ut;* in — of, *ex* or *prae alqâ re, quae cum ita sint, itaque;* 2, = importance, *auctoritas, momentum, pondus, -ēris,* n; to be of —, *multum valère.*

conserve, I. v.tr. 1, see KEEP; 2, of fruit, *condire.* **II.** n. = jam, *fructus conditi.* **conservation,** n. *conservatio.* **conservative, I.** adj. *optimatibus addictus.* **II.** n. *unus ex optimatibus.* **conservatory,** n. *(locus) ad plantas colendas vitreis munitus.*

consider, v.tr. 1, = to look at, *spectare, intueri, contemplari;* 2, = to regard, *ducère, habère, existimare;* 3, see THINK; 4, = to be thoughtful for, *alqm respicère.* **considerable,** adj. *magnus, gravis;* also by *aliquantum* with genit. (al. praedae, — plunder; al. aeris alieni, — debt); a — number, *multitudo, vis.* Adv. *aliquanto* or *aliquantum.* **considerate,** adj. 1, = thoughtful, *providus, providens, prudens, cautus;* 2, = thoughtful for others, *alqm respiciens, alci consulens, benignus.* Adv. 1, *provide, providenter, prudenter, caute;* 2, *benigne.* **considerateness,** n. 1, *providentia, prudentia;* 2, *benignitas.* **consideration,** n. 1, with the eyes, *contemplatio, conspectus, -ûs;* 2, with the mind, *judicium, meditatio, commentatio, consilium;* 3, = thought for anyone, *alcjs respectus, -ûs;* 4, = motive, *ratio;* from these —s, *quae cum ita sint;* 5, see IMPORTANCE; with —, *considerate, consulto, consilio;* to act with good — *bono consilio facère alqd.*

consign, v.tr. *deferre alqd ad alqm, credère mandare alqd alci;* to — to the flames, *alqd in flammas con(j)icère.*

consist, v.intr. = to be made of, *in* or *ex alqd*

re *constare, compositum esse, consistĕre, alqd re contineri.* **consistent**, adj. 1,— with, *cum alqâ re congruens, conveniens, concors*, or by *esse* with the genit. (e.g. it is — with my character, *mei est*); 2, = unchanging, *constans*. Adv. *congruenter, convenienter, constanter.* **consistence, consistency**, n. 1, = thickness, *crassitudo, soliditas*; 2, = agreement, *constantia*.

console, v.tr. *consolari alqm, solatium afferre* or *solatio esse alci.* **consolation**, n. *solatium, consolatio.* **consoler**, n. *consolator.*

consonant, I. n. = a letter, *consonans (li(t)tera)*. **II.** adj. *consentaneus, congruus cum alqâ re.*

consort, I. n. *comes, -itis*, m. and f., *socius, socia*; = husband or wife, *maritus, marita; conju(n)x*, m. and f., *uxor*, f. **II.** v.intr. *alqo familiariter uti, alci socium esse.*

conspicuous, adj. 1, = visible, *conspicuus, clarus, manifestus*; 2, = remarkable, *insignis*. Adv. *clare, manifeste, mirum in modum.*

conspire, v.intr. *conjurare, conjurationem facĕre, conspirare.* **conspiracy**, n. *conjuratio, conspiratio.* **conspirator**, n. *conjuratus, -ûs, conjurationis socius.*

constable, n. *apparitor.*

constant, adj. 1, = incessant, *continuus, perpetuus*; 2, = faithful, *fidelis.* Adv. *perpetuo, continuo, fideliter.* **constancy**, n. 1, = patience, *patientia, constantia*; 2, = perseverance, *perseverantia, pervicacia*; 3, = continuance, *perpetuitas*; 4, = fidelity, *fides, fidelitas.*

constellation, n. *sidus, -ĕris*, n., *stella.*

consternation, n. see TERROR.

constipate, v.tr. med. t.t. *alvum a(d)stringĕre* or *cohibĕre.*

constitute, v.tr. *statuĕre, constituĕre, designare.* **constituent**, adj. *pars* or *res* (e.g. — parts, *alcjs rei partes, res e quibus alqd constat*). **constitution**, n. 1, of body, *corporis constitutio, affectio, habitus, -ûs*; a good —, *corpus bene constitutum*; a weak —, *corporis imbecillitas*; 2, of a state, *civitatis forma, reipublicae ratio.* **constitutional**, adj. 1, *innatus, insitus*; 2, *legitimus.* Adv. 1, *e naturâ*; 2, *legitime.*

constrain, v.tr. *alqm constringĕre, vi cogĕre, alci necessitatem imponĕre alcjs rei faciendae.* **constraint**, n. *vis*; to do by —, *alqd invitum facĕre.* **constrained**, adj. = unnatural, *invitus*; of speech, *oratio contorta, perplexa, difficilis*; a — look, *vultus fictus*; a — laugh, *risus invitus.*

construct, v.tr., see BUILD, MAKE. **construction**, n. 1, = act of —, *aedificatio, constructio*; 2, = interpretation, *interpretatio*; to put a good, bad — on, *alqd in bonam, malam partem accipĕre*; 3, = of a sentence, *compositio.*

construe, v.tr., see INTERPRET.

consult, v.tr. *alqm consulĕre, consilium petĕre ab alqo*; to — anyone's interests, *alci consulĕre.*

consume, v.tr. *edĕre.* **consumption**, n. *consumptio*; = the disease, *tabes, phthisis* (Plin.).

consummate, I. v.tr. *absolvĕre, cumulare, perficĕre, conficĕre.* **II.** adj. *summus, absolutus, perfectus*, or by superl. (e.g. *vir doctissimus*, of — learning). Adv. *summe, absolute, perfecte.* **consummation**, n. *absolutio, perfectio.*

contact, n. *tactio, (con)tactus, -ûs.* **contagion**, n. *contagio.* **contagious**, adj. *pestilens.*

contain, v.tr. *continĕre, complecti, comprehendĕre*; to — yourself, *se cohibĕre, temperare sibi quominus*, etc.

contaminate, v.tr. *contaminare, inquinare, polluĕre.* **contamination**, n. *contaminatio, macula, labes, -is*, f.

contemplate, v.tr. *contemplari.* **contemplation**, n. *contemplatio.* **contemplative**, adj. *in contemplatione (rerum) versatus*; see CONSIDER.

contemporaneous, adj. *quod eodem tempore est* or *fit.* Adv. *uno tempore, simul.* **contemporary**, n. *aequalis, qui ejusdem aetatis est.*

contempt, n. *contemptus, -ûs, fastidium.* **contemptible**, adj. *contemnendus, abjectus, turpis.* Adv. *turpiter.*

contend, v.intr. 1, = fight, *cum alqo certare, dimicare, pugnare, alci resistĕre*; 2, fig. *alci (rei) resistĕre*; 3, see ARGUE. **contention**, n. see STRIFE, QUARREL, ARGUMENT. **contentious**, adj. *aemulus.* Adv. *summâ vi.*

content, I. v.tr. *alci satisfacĕre.* **II.** adj. *sorte suâ contentus.* Adv. *tranquille.* **contentment**, n. *tranquillitas animi, animus tranquillus.* **contents**, n. *quod in libro continetur, argumentum, scripta, -orum.*

conterminous, adj. *alci loco confinis.*

contest, I. n. *certatio, certamen.* **II.** v.intr. *contendĕre*; see CONTEND.

context, n. *argumentum* or *ratio verborum* (opp. to *singula verba*).

contiguous, adj. *propinquus*; see CONTERMINOUS. **contiguity**, n. *propinquitas.*

continence, n. *continentia, temperantia, castitas, castimonia.* **continent, I.** adj. *continens, castus.* Adv. *caste.* **II.** n. *continens* **continental**, adj. by genit. of *continens.*

contingent, I. adj. *fortuitus, forte oblatus.* **II.** n. *quantum militum quaeque civitas mittĕre debet, auxilia, -orum.* **contingency**, n. *casus, -ûs* (= a chance).

continual, adj. *continuus, perpetuus, assiduus.* Adv. *continenter, assiduo, perpetuo.* **continuance**, n. *constantia, perpetuitas, assiduitas, continuatio, diuturnitas.* **continuation**, n. 1. see CONTINUANCE; 2, = the latter part, *reliqua pars.* **continue, I.** v.tr. 1, = carry on, *alqd extendĕre, producĕre, persequi, continuare*; to — after an interruption, *renovare.* **II.** v.intr. 1, = go on with, *in alqâ re perseverare*; 2, = last, *durare, manĕre, stare.* **continuity**, n. *continuatio, perpetuitas.*

contort, v.tr. *depravare, detorquĕre, distorquĕre.* **contortion**, n. *distortio, depravatio.*

contraband, n. *merces vetitae.*

contract, I. n. *pactum, conventio, condicio, conductio, locatio, syngrapha.* **II.** v.tr. 1, = draw in, *alqd contrahĕre* (in all meanings of Engl.); 2, = agree to do, *alqd redimĕre, alqd faciendum conducĕre* (opp. to *alqd faciendum locare*, to give out on —). **III.** v.intr. 1, *se contrahĕre*; 2, = grow shorter, *minui.* **contraction**, n. 1, *contractio* · 2, = in writing, *compendium.* **contractor**, n. *conductor, redemptor.*

contradict, v.tr. 1, = to speak against, *alci obloqui, contra dicĕre* (without dat. and in two words); 2, fig. (*inter se*) *repugnare, ab alqd re dissentire, discrepare.* **contradiction**, n. 1, *quod contra dictum est*; 2, *repugnantia, discrepantia, diversitas.* **contradictory**, adj. *contrarius, repugnans, diversus.* Adv. *contrarie, diverse.*

contrary, adj. *adversus*, (*alcjs rei*, dat., *inter se*) *contrarius*; a — wind, stream, *ventus adversus, flumen adversum*; on the —, *contra*, **es**

contrario; in answers *immo* (vero); — to, *praeter*, or *contra* with accus.

contrast, I. n. *asperitas* (in building, etc.). *diversitas, varietas, dissimilitudo, discrepantia.* **II.** v.tr. *alqd cum alqā re comparare, conferre.*

contravene, v.tr. *repugnare, alqd violare.*

contribute, v.tr. **1,** = to give towards, *pecuniam conferre, dare;* — to something, *ad* (or *in*) *alqd dare;* **2,** fig. = to assist, *vim habēre ad; valēre ad, prodesse, adjuvare ad, facēre ut, efficēre ut;* it —s much to glory, *magni interest ad laudem* (with infin. and accus. following). **contribution,** n. *stips, pecunia;* to levy a —, *pecuniam a civitatibus cogēre.* **contributor,** n. **1,** in gen. *qui alqd dat;* **2,** = — to a magazine, *scriptor.*

contrite, adj. see SORROWFUL. **contrition,** n. *poenitentia;* I feel —, *poenitet me rei.*

contrive, v.tr. *excogitare, invenire, fingēre;* — to do anything, *facēre or efficēre ut.* **contrivance,** n. **1,** = act of —, *inventio, excogitatio;* **2,** = thing contrived, *inventum;* **3,** = plan, *ratio, consilium.*

control, I. n. **1,** = power, *potestas, imperium, dicio;* **2,** self —, *moderatio, temperatio.* **II.** v.tr. *alqd moderari, cohibēre, coercēre, reprimēre;* — oneself, *sibi temperare, se continēre.*

controversy, n. *controversia, altercatio, disceptatio, contentio.* **controversial,** adj. *controversus* (= disputed). Adv. *per disputationem.* **controvert,** v.tr. *refellere, refutare.* **controvertible,** adj. *dubius, ambiguus.*

contumacy, n. *pertinacia, contumacia.* **contumacious,** adj. *contumax, pertinax.* Adv. *contumaciter, pertinaciter.*

contumely, n. *contumelia.* **contumelious,** adj. *contumeliosus, probrosus.* Adv. *contumeliose.*

convalescence, n. *sanitas restituta, valetudo confirmata.* **convalescent,** adj. use verb *convalescēre.*

convene, v.tr. *convocare.* **convenient,** adj. *commodus, opportunus, ad alqd* (or dat.) *accommodatus, idoneus.* Adv. *commode, opportune, accommodate.* **convenience,** n. *commoditas, commodum, occasio, opportunitas.* **convent,** see CLOISTER. **convention,** n. **1,** *conventus, -ūs, foedus, -ēris,* n., *pactio;* **2,** = custom, *mos.* **conventional,** adj. *tra(ns)laticius, a majoribus traditus, usu receptus;* it is —, *moris est, in more est.* Adv. *ex usu,* dat. *mos est.*

converge, v.intr. *se inclinare ad* or *in alqm* or *alqd.*

conversation, n. *sermo, sermo cot(t)idianus* (quot.), or *communis, colloquium;* to be the subject of —, *in ore omnium esse.* **converse,** I. v.intr. *colloqui cum alqo, serm. habēre cum alqo de re.* **II.** adj. see CONTRARY. **conversant,** adj. *in alqā re versatus or exercitatus, alcjs rei peritus.*

convert, I. v.tr. **1,** see CHANGE; **2,** = change anyone's opinion, *alqm in aliam mentem adducēre;* be —ed, *sententiam mutare.* **II.** n. *qui ad aliam opinionem* (e.g. *Christianam*) *adductus est.* **conversion,** n. **1,** = change, *(com)mutatio, conversio;* **2,** = change of opinion, *sententiae or morum mutatio,* = — to Christianity, *accessio ad Christi doctrinam.*

convex, adj. *convexus.*

convey, v.tr. **1,** see CARRY; **2,** legal t.t. *alqd alci transcribēre, (con)cedēre.* **conveyance,** n. **1,** see CARRIAGE; **2,** legal t.t. *cessio, transcriptio.* **conveyancer,** n. *scriba,* m.

convict, I. v.tr. **1,** *damnare, condemnare, alqm;* **2,** = show falsehood, etc., *alqd convincēre, redarguēre.* **II.** n. *damnatus, maleficus.* **conviction,** n. **1,** *damnatio;* **2,** *opinio, sententia, judicium.*

convince, v.tr. *persuadēre de re;* be convinced, *alci persuasum esse, exploratum or cognitum habēre.* **convincing,** adj. *ad persuadendum accommodatus, gravis.* Adv. *graviter.*

convivial, adj. *hilaris, jucundus.* **conviviality,** n. *hilaritas.*

convoke, v.tr. *convocare.*

convoy, I. n. **1,** *praesidium, custodia.* **II.** v.tr. *alqm praesidii caus(s)ā comitari.*

convulse, v.tr. *agitare, percutēre, (com)movēre;* — the state, *civitatem quassare, labefactare.* **convulsion,** n. *spasmus, convulsio* (Plin.). **convulsive,** adj. *spasticus* (Plin.).

cook, I. n. *coquus.* **II.** v.tr. *coquēre.* **cookery,** n. *res coquinaria.*

cool, I. adj. **1,** lit. *frigidus;* **2,** fig. *tranquillus* (of temperament), *superbus, fastidiosus* (= haughty), *fortis* (= brave), *impudens* (= impudent). **II.** n. *frigus, -oris,* n., *algor.* **III.** v.tr. *refrigerare.* **IV.** v.intr. **1,** lit. *frigescēre, frigēre* (= be —), *algēre* (= feel —); **2,** fig. *defervescēre, animum remittēre.* **coolness,** n. **1,** lit. *frigus, -oris,* n.; **2,** fig. *superbia, fastidium* (= pride), *fortitudo* (= courage), *inimicitia* (= unfriendliness). Adv. *frigide, aequo animo, tranquille, superbe, fastidiose, fortiter, impudenter* (= with effrontery).

cooper, n. *vietor.*

co-operate, v.intr. *unā agēre, alqm(ad)juvare.* **co-operation,** n. *opera, auxilium.* **coparter, co-operator,** n. *socius;* see COMPANION.

cope, v.intr. — with, *cum alqo* or *alqā re certare, alci resistēre.*

coping, n. *corona, fastigium.*

copious, adj. *copiosus, abundans, largus.* Adv. *copiose, abundanter, large.* **copiousness,** n. *copia, abundantia.*

copper, I. n. *aes, aeris,* n., *aes Cyprium;* — money, *rudera, -um;* — vessel, *a(h)eneum.* **II.** adj. *a(h)eneus.*

coppice, copse, n. *virgultum.*

copulation, n. *coitus, -ūs.*

copy, I. n. **1,** *exemplum, exemplar* (= model, — of a book, etc.); **2,** — (book), for a child, *lit(t)erae praeformatae.* **II.** v.tr. **1,** = imitate, *imitari;* **2,** of painters, writers, *pingēre, describēre;* — from the life, *similitudinem ex vero effingēre.*

coquet, v.tr. *viro spellicēre.* **coquette,** n. *quae viros pellicit.*

cord, I. n. *restis, funis,* m. **II.** v.tr. *constringēre, colligare.* **cordon,** n. *milites.*

cordial, adj. *ex animo amicus, benignus, comis.* Adv. *benigne, comiter, amice.* **cordiality,** n. *benignitas, comitas, amicitia.*

core, n. *nucleus, granum, semen* (= seed).

cork, I. n. *cortex.* **II.** v.tr. *obturare.*

corn, n. *frumentum, fruges, -um,* f., *annona,* — measure, *modius.*

corn, n. on the foot, *clavus.*

corner, n. *angulus;* done in a —, *in occulto.*

cornet, n. **1,** an instrument, *cornu, buccina;* **2,** military t.t. *vexillarius, signifer.*

cornice, n. *corona.*

corollary, n. *consectarium.*

coronation, n. *(dies ete) quo rex diadema accipit.*

coroner, n. *magistratus qui de mortuis in-quirit.*

corporal, I. n. *decurio.* **II.** adj. by genit. of *corpus, -ōris,* n. **corporal-punishment,** n. *verbera, -um ;* to inflict —, *verberibus casti-gare.*

corporation, n. *sodalitas* (religious), *muni-cipium, concilium, collegium.*

corps, n. *manus, -ūs,* f., *pars exercitūs, ala equitum, agmen.*

corpse, n. *cadaver, -ĕris,* m.

corpulent, adj. *obēsus.* **corpulence,** n. *corpus obesum.*

correct, I. v.tr. 1, = improve, *corrigĕre, emendare ;* — a book for the press, *menda libro tollĕre ;* 2, = punish, *punire, castigare.* **II.** adj. 1, of conduct, *honestus, rectus ;* 2, of style, *emen-datus, rectus, purus, accuratus ;* 3, = true, *verus.* Adv. *recte, honeste, pure, vere.* **correctness,** n. use adjectives (e.g. the — of a thing, *res recta).*

correspond, v.intr. 1, = agree, *respondēre alci rei* or *ad alqd, convenire alci rei ;* 2, to — by letter, *lit(t)eras dare et accipĕre ;* — with, *cum alqo per lit(t)eras colloqui.* **correspondent,** n. *qui alqd per lit(t)eras* (crebrius) *communicat.* **correspondence,** n. *per lit(t)eras.* **corres-ponding,** adj. *par.* Adv. *pariter.*

corroborate, v.tr. *ratum facĕre* or *efficĕre, confirmare, comprobare.* **corroboration,** n. *confirmatio.*

corrode, v.tr. *erodĕre.* **corrosive,** adj. *qui* (*quae, quod*) *erodit.*

corrupt, I. adj. *perditus, profligatus, turpis, corruptus.* Adv. *perdite, turpiter.* **II.** v.tr. *putrefacĕre, corrumpĕre* (lit. and fig.); *depravare, vitiare, perdĕre, pervertĕre* (lit.). **III.** v.intr. *putrefieri, corrumpi* (all fig.). **corrupter,** n. *corruptor, qui corrumpit,* etc. **corruptible,** adj. *quod corrumpi potest.* **corruption,** n. *cor-ruptio, depravatio, corruptela.* **corrupting,** adj. *perniciosus, exitiosus.*

corsair, n. *pirata,* m.

corslet, n. *thorax, lorica, pectoris teg(i)men* or *teg(i)mentum.*

cortege, n. *comitatus, -ūs.*

coruscation, n. *fulguratio, fulgor, splendor.*

cosmetic, n. *fucus.*

cost, I. n. *sumptus, -ūs, impensa, praemium, merces, -edis,* f. (=wages). **II.** v.tr. *alqd* (*con*)*stat* or *venit* or *venditur* or *emitur* (with genit. of the exact price); to — little, *parvo stare ;* very little, *minimo.* **costly,** adj. *sumptuosus, magno sump-tu, pretiosus.* **costliness,** n. *caritas.*

costume, n. *habitus, -ūs, ornatus, -ūs.*

cottage, n. *casa, tugurium.* **cottager,** n. *rusticus.*

cotton, n. *gossypion* (-*ium*) (Plin.).

couch, I. n. *lectus, lectulus.* **II.** v.tr. 1, = stretch out, *porrigĕre ;* to — spears, *hastas dirigĕre ;* 2, = express, (*con*)*scribĕre.* **III.** v.intr. *cubare, latēre, delitescĕre.*

cough, I. n. *tussis.* **II.** v.intr. *tussire.*

council, n. *concilium.* **council-chamber,** n. *curia.* **councillor,** n. *consiliarius, senator.*

counsel, I. n. 1, = consultation, *consultatio, deliberatio ;* 2, = advice, *consilium, auctoritas.* **II.** v.tr. see ADVISE.

count, n. *comes.* **county,** n. *comitatus, -ūs.*

count, v.tr. 1, *computare ;* 2, — upon, *alci confidĕre ;* see RECKON, CONSIDER. **counter,** n. 1. = — of a shop, use *mensa :* 2, = — for

reckoning, *calculus.* **countless,** adj. *innu-merabilis.*

countenance, I. n. 1, *vultus, os, oris,* n.; 2, = protection, *praesidium.* **II.** v.tr. *alci favēre, opem ferre.*

counter, adv. = against, *contra.* **counter-act,** v.tr. *alci resistĕre.* **counter-balance,** *parem esse alci.* **counterfeit, I.** v.tr. *simulare ;* **II.** adj. *simulatus ;* — money, *nummus adul-terinus.* **counterpane,** n. *lodix.* **counter-part,** n. *res alci simillima.* **counterpoise,** v.tr. *alqd cum alqā re* (*ad*)*aequare.*

country, n. 1, opp. to town, *rus ;* in the —, *ruri ;* 2, = one's native land, *patria ;* of what —? *cujas ?* of our —, *nostras ;* 3, = region, *terra, regio.* **country-house,** n. *villa.* **country-man,** n. 1, *homo rusticus ;* 2, = fellow —, *civis, nostras,* pl. *nostri.* **country-town,** n. *muni-cipium.*

couple, I. n. *par, bini ;* in married life, *conjuges, mariti.* **II.** v.tr. (*con*)*jungĕre ;* — with, *copulare cum re, miscēre re.*

courage, n. *animus, audacia, ferocia* (=fierce courage), *fortitudo, virtus, -ūtis,* f. **coura-geous,** adj. *fortis, audax, ferox, strenuus.* Adv. *fortiter, audacter, ferociter, strenue.*

courier, n. *nuntius.*

course, I. n. 1, (*de*)*cursus, -ūs ;* — of water, *lapsus, -ūs ;* — of the stars, *motus, -ūs ;* the — of nature, *naturae lex ;* fig. the — of life, *vitae cur-riculum ;* 2, = plan, *ratio, consilium ;* 3, = progress, *tenor, cursus, -ūs, via, progressus, -ūs ;* 4, = — of time, *in* (e.g. *in illo anno*); in — of a few, many days, *intra paucos, multos dies ;* 5, = — at a dinner, *ferculum ;* 6, = — of lectures, *alqm audire ;* 7, = manner of life, *mores, -um, vitae ratio.* **II.** v.tr. *venari.* **of course,** adv. *necessario, plane, prorsus ;* in answers, *sane.*

court, I. n. 1, = an open space, *area ;* 2, = royal —, *aula, regia ;* 3, = courtiers, *nobiles, -ium ;* 4, = — of justice, *forum, tribunal, sub-sellia, -orum.* **II.** v.tr. 1, of a lover, *alqam* (*in matrimonium*) *petĕre ;* 2, = to seek to obtain, *quaerĕre, captare.* **courtier,** n. *nobilis.* **cour-teous,** adj. *comis, communis.* Adv. *urbane, comiter.* **courtesy, courteousness,** n. *urbanitas, comitas.* **courtship,** n. *amor* or verb, *in matrimonium petĕre.*

cousin, n. (*con*)*sobrinus* (-*a*) (on the mother's side), *patruelis* (a father's brother's child).

covenant, I. n. *pactio, pactum, conventum.* **II.** v.tr. *pacisci cum alqo.*

cover, I. n. 1, of a bed, etc., *lodix, teg(i)men, stragulum, gausapa ;* = lid, *operimentum ;* 2, = shelter, *perfugium ;* under — of, *alqā re tectus ;* fig. = pretence, *per speciem alcis rei.* **II.** v.tr. 1, (*con*)*tegĕre, abtegĕre, operire, velare ;* 2 = pro-tect, *protegĕre, defendĕre ;* = to secure against loss, *cavēre alqd ;* 3, = overwhelm, fig. *alqd in alqm conferre,* or by special verbs (e.g. — with abuse, *alci maledicĕre*).

covert, I. n. 1, = shelter, *latebra, perfu-gium ;* 2, = thicket, *virgultum.* **II.** adj. *tectus.* See SECRET.

covet, v.tr. *alqd appetĕre, concupiscĕre, cupi-ditate rei flagrare.* **covetous,** adj. *avarus.* Adv. *avare.* **covetousness,** n. *avaritia.*

cow, n. *vacca.* **cow-herd,** n. *armentarius.* **cow-hide,** n. *corium vaccae.*

cowar d, n. *homo ignavus, timidus.* **cow-ardly,** adj. *ignavus, timidus.* Adv. *ignave, timide.* **cowardliness,** n. *metus, -ūs, ignavia.*

cower, v.intr. *perterritum esse.*

cowl, n. *cucullus.*

coxcomb, n. *homo ineptus.*

coy, adj. *verecundus.* **coyness,** n. *pudor, verecundia.*

cozen, v.tr. see CHEAT.

crab, n. *cancer.* **crabbed,** adj. 1, = ill-tempered, *morosus;* 2, = intricate, *difficilis, impedies.* Adv. *morose, difficulter.*

crack, I. n. 1, = noise, *crepitus, -ūs* (e.g. — of the fingers, *digitorum crepitus*), † *fragor;* 2, = fissure, *rima.* **II.** v.intr. *crepare, (dif)findi, dissilire, dehiscēre.* **III.** v.tr. 1, lit. = burst, *(dif)findēre, rumpēre;* 2, — a joke, *jocari;* to — a whip, *sonitum flagello edēre.*

cradle, I. n. *cunae, cunabula, -orum.* **II.** v.tr. *in cunabulis ponēre.*

craft, n. 1, = cunning, *dolus, astutia;* 2, = skill or trade, *ars, artificium;* 3, = ship, *cymba, scapha.* **crafty,** adj. *astutus, callidus, versutus, dolosus.* Adv. *astute, callide, versute, dolose.* **craftsman,** n. *opera.*

crag, n. see ROCK.

cram, v.tr. 1, with food, *farcire, refercire;* 2, fig. *alqd alqā re complēre, implēre;* = crowd, *stipare* (more common in pass.).

cramp, I. n. *spasmus, tetanus* (Plin.). **II.** v.tr. to be —ed, fig. *circumscribi.*

crane, I. n. 1, = bird, *grus, gruis,* m. and f.; 2, a machine, *troclea.* **II.** v.intr. — forward, *cervicem protendēre.*

crank, n. 1, of a machine, *uncus;* 2, = jest, *jocus.*

cranny, n. *rima.*

crash, I. n. *fragor.* **II.** v.tr. *crepare.*

crate, n. *crates, -is,* f.

crater, n. *crater, -ēris,* m.

crave, v.tr. see BEG, NEED. **craving,** n. *alcjs rei desiderium.*

crawl, v. *repēre, serpēre.*

crazy, adj. *mente captus;* see MAD.

creak, v. (con)crepare. **creaking,** n. *crepitus, -ūs.*

cream, n. *flos lactis.*

crease, I. n. *ruga.* **II.** v.tr. *rugare.*

create, v.tr. 1, lit. *(pro)creare, gignēre, facēre;* 2, fig. *praebēre, facēre, efficēre, fingēre,* or by special verbs (e.g. — confusion, *perturbare);* 3, = appoint, *creare, designare.* **creation,** n. 1, *procreatio* (= begetting), *initium* (= beginning); since the — of the world, *post mundum conditum;* 2, mental —, *poema, -ătis,* n. *fabula,* etc. **creative,** adj. *qui creare* (etc.)*potest.* **creator,** n. *(pro)creator, fabricator, auctor.* **creature,** n. *animal.*

credit, I. v.tr. 1, = to believe, *credēre;* 2, put to one's account, *alqd alci in acceptum conferre.* **II.** n. 1, = belief, *fides;* to give — to a thing, *alci* or *alci rei fidem habēre, tribuēre, adjungēre;* to withhold or refuse —, *fidem alci denegare;* 2, mercant. t.t. *fides;* to take up money on —, *pecuniam alcjs fide mutuam sumēre;* to purchase on —, *emēre in diem* (the time being fixed when payment has to be made), *emēre pecunià non praesenti;* his — is gone, *fides occidit, concidit;* 3, = authority, *auctoritas, gratia* (= influence), *opinio, existimatio;* 4, do — to, *gloriae* or *decori alci esse;* no —, *dedecori alci esse.* **credible,** adj. *fide dignus, credibilis, verisimilis.* Adv. *credibiliter.* **credibility,** *fides, auctoritas,* comb. *auctoritas et fides.* **credentials,** n. *auctoritas,* or *litt(t)erae.* **creditable,** adj. *honestus, honorificus.* Adv. *honorifice, honeste.* **creditor,** n. *creditor.* **credulous,** adj. *credulus.* Adv. *nimià cum*

creditate. **credulity,** n. *credulitas* (not in Cic.). **creed,** n. 1, = belief, *fides;* 2, = system believed, *doctrina.*

creek, n. *sinus, -ūs.*

creep, v.intr. see CRAWL.

crescent, n. *luna crescens.* **crescent-shaped,** adj. *lunatus.*

crest, n. *crista, juba.* **crested,** adj. *cristatus.* **crestfallen,** adj. *fractus, demissus.*

crevice, n. see CRACK.

crew, n. 1, *nautae;* 2, fig. *coetus, -ūs.*

crib, n. 1, for animals, *praesepe;* 2, see CRADLE.

crime, n. *delictum, maleficium, facinus, -inoris,* n., *scelus, -eris,* n., *nefas.* **criminate,** v.tr. *criminari.* **crimination,** n. *crimen, criminatio.* **criminal,** adj. *scelestus, sceleratus, nefarius.*

crimson, I. adj. *coccineus.* **II.** n. *color coccineus.* **III.** v.intr. *erubescēre.*

cringe, v.intr. — to, *alqm* or *alci adulari.*

cripple, n. *homo mancus, membris captus, homo debilis,* or *claudus manu, pedibus,* etc.

crisis, n. *discrimen, momentum.*

crisp, adj. 1, = curled, *crispus;* 2, = brittle, *fragilis.*

criterion, n. *discrimen.* **critic,** n. *criticus, homo alcjs rei peritus,* or simply *sapiens.* **criticism,** n. *judicium.* **criticize,** v.tr. *judicare.* **critical,** adj. 1, = belonging to criticism, *callidus, sol(l)ers, sapiens;* 2, = belonging to a crisis, *in discrimen adductus, anceps, dubius.* Adv. *accurate, callide, sol(l)erter, sapienter.*

croak, I. v.intr. *crocire* (of birds), *vocem emittēre.* **II.** n. *vox.*

crockery, n. *(vasa) fictilia.*

crocodile, n. *crocodilus.*

crocus, n. *crocus.*

crone, n. *vetula, anus, -ūs,* f.

crook, I. n. *pedum, lituus.* **II.** v.tr., see CURVE. **crooked,** adj. *curvatus, incurvus;* = bad, *pravus, distortus.* Adv. 1, *oblique,* or by adj.; 2, *prave.* **crookedness,** n. 1, *quod incurvum est;* 2, *pravitas.*

crop, I. n. 1, of corn, etc., *messis, fruges, -um,* f.; 2, of birds, *ingluvies.* **II.** v.tr. = cut short, *praecidēre, amputare, tondēre;* = to cut down, *depascēre,* † *tondēre.*

cross, I. n. 1, + *crux, ×* decussis; as instrument of punishment, *crux;* 2, fig. *mala, -orum,* or *calamitas.* **II.** adj. = transverse, *transversus, obliquus.* **III.** v.tr. 1, = lay across, *alqd alci rei transversum ponēre;* 2, = go across, *locum transire;* 3, = thwart, *alci obsistēre;* 4, = — the mind, *alqd alci subit;* 5, = — out, *delēre.* **cross-purpose,** n. be at —s, *alii alia putant,* or by adj. *contrarius.* **crosswise,** adv. *in transversum.* **crossing,** n. *transitus, -ūs.*

crouch, v.intr. *se demittēre.*

crow, I. n. *cornix.* **II.** v.intr. *canere.*

crowd, I. n. *turba, caterva, frequentia, multitudo.* **II.** v.tr. *(co)artare, stipare, premēre.* **III.** v.intr. *confluēre, congregari.*

crown, I. n. 1, = wreath, *corona;* diadem, *diadema, -ătis,* n.; 2, = kingly power, *regnum;* 3, = top, *summus* with noun (e.g. — of the mountain, *summus mons);* 4, = ornament, *decus, -ōris,* n. **II.** v.tr. *coronare;* — a king, *diadema regi imponēre.* **coronation,** n. *sollemnia quibus rex diadema accipit.*

crucible, n. *catinus* (Plin.).

crucify, v.tr. *alqm cruci affigĕre.* **cruci-fixion**, n. *crucis supplicium.*

crude, adj. 1, = raw or unripe, *crudus;* 2, fig. *informis, incultus, rudis.* Adv. *inculte.* **crudity**, n. *cruditas.*

cruel, adj. *crudelis, saevus, ferus, atrox.* Adv. *crudeliter, atrociter.* **cruelty**, n. *crudelitas, feritas, saevitia, atrocitas.*

cruise, v.intr. *(per)vagari;* — along the shore, *praeter oram vagari.*

crumb, n. 1, = the soft part of bread, *panis mollia (-ium);* 2, = a small piece, *mica, micula.* **crumble**, I. v.tr. *friare, comminuĕre, conterĕre.* II. v.intr. *friari, etc.*

crumple, I. n. *ruga.* II. v.tr. *rugare.* III. v.intr. *rugari.*

crupper, n. *postilena.*

crush, I. v.tr. 1, lit. *comprimĕre, contundĕre, conterĕre, conculcare* (by treading); 2, fig. *affligĕre, comprimĕre, obruĕre, frangĕre.* II. n. = crowd, *turba.* See CROWD.

crust, n. *crusta.* **crusty**, adj. *crustosus* (Plin.).

crutch, n. *baculum.*

cry, I. v.tr. 1, = call out, *(con)clamare, acclamare, proclamare, praedicare, clamitare;* 2, see WEEP. II. n. 1, *clamor, exclamatio, acclamatio;* 2, *proclamatio, praeconium;* 3, *lacrimae, vagitus, -ūs.* **crier**, n. *praeco.*

crystal, n. *crystallus.* **crystallize**, I. v.tr. *in crystallos formare.* II. v.intr. *in crystallos abire.*

cub, n. I. *catulus.* II. v.tr. *fetus edĕre.*

cube, n. *cubus.* **cubic**, adj. *cubicus.*

cubit, n. *cubitum.*

cuckoo, n. *cuculus.*

cucumber, n. *cucŭmis, -ĕris,* m.

cud, n. to chew the —, *ruminari, remandĕre.*

cudgel, I. n. *baculum, fustis,* m. II. v.tr. *ferire, percutĕre, fusti verberare.*

cue, n. 1, = hint, *signum;* to give a —, *alci innuĕre, signum alci dare;* 2, of an actor, *signum.*

cuff, I. n. 1, = blow, *alapa* (with the flat hand), *colaphus* (with the fist); 2, = sleeve, *manica extrema.* II. v.tr. *verberare alqm, plagam alci infligĕre, pugnis alci caedĕre.*

cuirass, n. *thorax.*

culinary, adj. *coquinarius.*

culmination, n. *fastigium.* **culminate**, v.intr. *in (summo) fastigio esse.*

culpable, adj. *culpâ dignus, reprehendendus, turpis, foedus.* **culprit**, n. see CRIMINAL.

cultivate, v.tr. 1, in agriculture, *(agrum) colĕre;* 2, fig. *fingĕre, (con)formare, instituĕre, expolire;* 3, = practise, *alci rei studĕre, se ad alqd applicare.* **cultivation, culture**, n. 1, *cultus, -ūs;* 2, mental —, *animi cultus, humanitas, lit(t)erarum or artium studia, -orum.* **cultivator**, n. 1, *agricola,* m.*, cultor;* 2, fig. by verb.

cumber, v.tr. *alqm or alqd impedire, praegravare, alci (rei) obstruĕre.* **cumbrous**, adj. *gravis, incommodus, inhabilis.* Adv. *graviter, incommode.*

cunning, I. adj. 1, *astutus, callidus, versutus, dolosus;* 2, = skilful, *peritus, dexter, habilis, expertus.* Adv. 1, *astute, callide, versute,* or abl. *dolo or per dolum or fraudem;* 2, = skilfully, *voll(l)erter, perite, callide.* II. n. 1, *astutia, calliditas, versutia, dolus;* 2, = skill, *ars, so(l)lertia.*

cup, I. n. 1, *poculum, scyphus, calix, calathus,*

phiala, patera, carchesium, scaphium, cymbium, cyathus, batiola, culullus; 2, fig. = — of sorrow, etc., *dolor;* to drain the —, *exhaurire dolorem,* etc. II. v.tr. *sanguinem alci (per cucurbitulas) detrahĕre.* **cup-bearer**, n. *minister or servus.* **cupboard**, n. *armarium.*

cupidity, n. *cupiditas, avaritia.*

cupola, n. *tholus.*

curator, n. *curator, custos.*

curb, I. n. *frenum.* II. v.tr. *frenare, coercēre, domare, comprimĕre, prohibēre.*

curd, n. *lac concretum.* **curdle**, v.tr. *L alqd coagulare.* II. v.intr. *coagulare, coire.*

cure, I. n. *curatio, medicina, sanatio.* II. v.tr. 1, *sanare alqm, mederi alci;* 2, = preserve, *condire.*

curiosity, n. 1, *nova noscendi studium, spectandi studium;* 2, = something rare or strange, *res nova or rara.* **curious**, adj. 1, = inquisitive, *curiosus, alcjs rei studiosus;* 2, = strange, *insolitus, novus, rarus, singularis;* 3, = accurate, *accuratus.* Adv. *anxie,* or adj.; *raro, accurate.*

curl, I. v.tr. *crispare, calamistro intorquĕre.* II. v.intr. 1, *crispari,* etc.; 2, = to be bent round, *torquēri, flecti.* III. n. *cirrus.* **curling-irons**, n. *calamister.* **curly**, adj. *crispus.*

currant, n. dried —s, *urae passae.*

current, I. adj. 1, = this, *hic* (e.g. — year, *hic annus);* 2, = common, *more or usu receptus;* to be — in, *esse, valēre.* Adv. *vulgo.* II. n. *flumen,* see STREAM. **currency**, n. *nummi or argentum.*

curry, v.tr. 1, to — leather, *conficĕre;* 2, to — favour, *alci blandiri.* **currycomb**, n. *strigilis.*

curse, I. n. 1, *exsecratio, imprecatio, maledictum;* 2, fig. *pestis.* II. v.tr. to — anyone, *exsecrari, alci male precari.*

cursory, adj. *rapidus, neglegens (neglig).* Adv. *breviter, strictim.*

curt, adj. *brevis.* Adv. *breviter.*

curtail, v.tr. *amputare, praecidĕre.*

curtain, n. *velum, aulaeum.*

curve, I. n. *(in)flexio, flexus, -ūs, sinus, -ūs.* II. v.tr. *(in)flectĕre.* III. v.intr. *flecti.*

cushion, n. *pulvinus, pulvinar.*

custard, n. *placenta ex ovis facta.*

custody, n. *custodia, carcer, -ĕris,* n., *vincula, -orum.*

custom, n. 1, = usage, *consuetudo, mos, institutum, usus, -ūs;* it is a — with us, *est institutum, mos or moris est;* 2, = duty, *vectigal, portorium.* **customer**, n. *emptor.* **customary**, adj. *usitatus, tritus, pervulgatus, vulgaris, cot(t)idianus* (quot.), *communis, tra(ns)laticius;* to be —, *mos or moris esse, solēre.* Adv. *ex consuetudine, vulgo, fere.*

cut, I. v.tr. 1, lit. *secare;* to — with a scythe, *(de)metĕre;* to — into planks, *in laminas secare;* to — the throat, *alqm jugulare;* to — on a gem, *in gemmâ scalpĕre;* to — the hair, *tondēre, praecidĕre;* to — down, lit. *excidĕre;* 2, fig. *trucidare;* to — short, = interrupt, *alqm interpellare;* = abridge, *contrahĕre;* to — up, *concidĕre.* II. n. 1, by verb (e.g. to receive a —, *cultro vulnerari),* if with a whip, *verber;* 2, of rivers, etc., *canalis,* m., *fossa;* 3, a short —, *via brevissima or proxima.* **cutting**, I. adj. *acerbus.* Adv. *acerbe.* II. n. of a plant, *propago.* **cutlery**, n. *cultri* (pl.). **cut-throat**, n. *sicarius.*

cuttlefish, n. *sepia.*

cycle, n. 1, = circular course, *orbis,* m., *cir-zulus;* 2, = revolution, *orbis,* or by verb *revolvi;* **see** REVOLVE.

cyclops, n. *cyclops.*

cygnet, n. *pullus cycnorum.*

cylinder, n. *cylindrus.*

cymbal, n. *cymbalum.*

cynic, n. 1, in philosophy, *cynicus;* 2, fig., *homo acerbus.* **cynical,** adj. *acerbus.* Adv. *acerbe.*

cynosure, n. 1, lit. *Ursa Minor;* 2, fig., *decus, -ōris,* n.

cypress, n. *cupressus,* f.

D.

dabble, I. v.tr. *alqd alqā re a(d)spergēre.* **II.** v.intr. 1, lit. *in aquā ludēre;* 2, fig. *alqd leviter attingēre.*

dad, daddy, n. *tata.*

daffodil, n. *narcissus.*

dagger, n. *pugio, sica.*

dainty, I. adj. 1, = — in choice of food, *fastidiosus;* 2, = elegant, *exquisitus, elegans;* see PRETTY. **II.** n. *cibus delicatus, cibi delicatiores.* **daintiness,** n. 1, = — in food, *cup(p)edia;* 2, = elegance, *venustas.*

dairy, n. *cella,* defining sense by context (e.g. *lacte repleta*).

dale, n. (*con)vallis.*

dally, v.intr. 1, = trifle, *nugari, lascivire;* 2, — with, *alci blandiri;* 3, see DELAY. **dalliance,** n. 1, *nugae, lascivia;* 2, *blanditiae.*

dam, n. = mother, *mater, matrix.*

dam, I. n. *agger, -ĕris,* m., *moles, -is,* f. **II.** v.tr. *molem alci rei ob(j)icēre, flumen coercēre.*

damage, I. n. *damnum, detrimentum, noxa.* **II.** v.tr. *alci nocēre, obesse, damno esse.* **damages,** n. pl., *impensa;* action for —, *judicium recuperatorium.*

dame, n. *mulier, matrona, domina.*

damn, v.tr. 1, *damnare, condemnare;* 2, theol. t.t., * *damnare, aeternis suppliciis addicēre.* **damnable,** adj. *damnandus.* **damnation,** n. *damnatio, condemnatio* (= the act).

damp, I. adj. *humidus.* **II.** v.tr. 1, lit. *humectare;* 2, fig. *deprimēre, comprimēre, restinguēre, sedare.* **III.** n. *vapor, nebula.*

damsel, n. *puella, ancilla, virgo.*

dance, I. n. *saltatio, chorēa.* **II.** v.intr. *saltare.* **dancer,** n. *saltator,* m. *saltatrix,* f.

dandle, v.tr. *manibus agitare.*

dandy, n., *homo elegans; de capsulā ætus* (Sen.).

danger, n. *periculum, discrimen.* **dangerous,** adj. *periculosus, anceps;* a — condition, *res dubiae.* Adv. *periculose.*

dangle, v.intr. *ex alqā re (de)pendēre.*

dank, adj. *humidus.*

dapper, adj. *pernix* (= quick), *nitidus* (= neat).

dapple, adj. *maculosus.*

dare, v.tr. *audēre.* **daring, I.** adj. *audax.* Adv. *audacter.* **II.** n. *audacia.*

dark, I. adj. 1, as opposed to daylight, *obscurus, caliginosus, caecus* (= blind); 2, = — in colour, *fuscus, niger, pullus;* 3, = difficult to the mind, *obscurus, abstrusus, impeditus, in-*

certus. Adv. *obscure, perplexe.* **II.** n. to be in the — about, *alqd ignorare.* **darkness,** n. *obscuritas, tenebrae, caligo, nox.* **dark-red,** adj. *ex rubro subniger.* **dark-black,** adj. *niger.* **darken, I.** v.tr. lit. and fig. *obscurare, tenebras alci rei obducēre.* **II.** v.intr. *obscurari;* it —s, *vesperascit.*

darling, n. *deliciae.*

darn, v.tr. *sarcire.* **darning-needle,** n. *acus, -ūs,* f. *grandior.*

dart, I. n. *pilum, hasta, telum, jaculum, tragula.* **II.** v.tr. *jaculari;* to throw —s, *tela (e)mittēre, con(j)icēre.* **III.** v.intr. *in alqm locum irrumpēre, se con(j)icēre.*

dash, I. v.tr. 1, lit. *alqd ad alqd offendēre, impingēre;* — out the brains, *caput perfringēre* or *elidēre;* 2, fig. *spem* (etc.) *reprimēre, comprimēre, ad irritum redigēre.* **II.** v.intr. see DART. **III.** n. 1, = rush, *impetus, -ūs;* 2, = something of, *aliquid, nescio quid;* 3, see DISPLAY.

dastard, n. *homo ignavus.*

date, n. (the fruit), *palmula* (Var.). **data,** n. *concessa, -orum.* **date, I.** n. *dies;* out of —, *obsoletus.* **II.** v.tr. *diem in epistolā a(d)-scribēre.* **dative,** n. (*casus*) *dativus* (Gram.).

daub, v.tr (*ob)linēre,* (*per)ungēre.*

daughter, n. *filia;* a little —, *filiola;* —-in-law, *nurus, -ūs,* f.

daunt, v.tr., see FRIGHTEN. **dauntless,** adj. *impavidus.* Adv. *impavide.*

daw, n. *monedula.*

dawdle, v.intr. *cessare.* **dawdler,** n. *cessator.*

dawn, n. *diluculum.* **it dawns,** v. (*di)-lucescit.*

day, n. 1, *dies, lux* (= daylight); the longest —, *dies solstitialis, solstitium* (= the time of the longest days); the shortest —, *dies brumalis;* before —, *ante lucem;* at break of —, (*cum) primā luce, luce oriente;* by —, *interdiu;* — and night, *diem noctem, diem noctemque, dies noctesque, noctes diesque, noctes et dies;* the — breaks, (*il)lucescit, dilucescit, lux oritur;* far on in the —, *multo die;* to wish one good —, *alqm salvum esse jubēre, alqm salutare;* good — ! *salve* (*salvete*); a lucky —, *dies albus* or *candidus;* an unlucky —, *dies ater;* the — star, *lucifer;* 2, = a period of time, *dies;* a period of two or three —s, *biduum, triduum;* to —, *hodierno die, hodie;* every other —, *tertio quoque die;* from — to —, *in dies;* — after —, *diem ex die, diem de die;* every —, *in dies singulos;* to pay to the —, *in diem solvēre;* the — before, after, *pridie, postridie* (*ejus diei*); in our —, *nostrā aetate, nostro tempore, nostris temporibus;* to pass one's —s, *vitam degēre;* the —time, *tempus diurnum.* **day-break,** n. *diluculum.* **day-labourer,** n. *operarius* (in pl. *operae*). **daily, I.** adj. *cot(t)idianus* (*quot.*), *diurnus;* — bread, *cibus diurnus.* **II.** adv. *cot(t)idie,* *omnibus diebus, in dies singulos.*

dazzle, v.tr. *caecare;* fig. *obstupefacēre;* to be —d, *obstupefieri, stupēre.*

deacon, n. * *diaconus.*

dead, adj. *mortuus, exanimis, exanimus;* fig. = dull, *languidus.* **deaden,** v.tr. *hebetare, obtundēre, enervare, debilitare, frangēre.* **deadly, I.** adj. 1, lit. *mortifer, exitialis;* 2, fig. of sin, etc., *capitalis, gravis.* **II.** adv. *usque ad mortem,* or by adj. **deadness,** n. *rigor, stupor, torpor.*

death, n., *mors, letum, obitus, -ūs, finis,* m. and f., or *exitus, -ūs, vitae, nex* (= violent —); to suffer —, *mortem subire;* he starved to —, *per inediam mori.* **death-bed,** n. use *adj. moriens* or *moribundus.*

deaf. adj. *surdus, auribus captus.* **deafen,** v.tr. *exsurdare, obtundĕre.*

deal, I. v.tr. *dividĕre, distribuĕre, dispertire.* **II.** v.intr. —with, see TREAT. **dealer,** n. *mercator, negotiator* (wholesale), *institor, tabernarius, caupo, propola* (retail). **dealing,** n. *commercium, negotium, usus, -ūs;* have —s with, *commercium cum algo habēre;* harsh —, *severitas;* upright —, *fides;* double —, *fraus.*

dear, adj. 1, *carus, magni pretii, pretiosus;* how — ? *quanti?* so —, *tanti;* 2, = beloved, *carus.* Adv. *care, magno pretio; maxime* or adj. **dearness,** n. *caritas, magnum pretium.* **dearth,** n. *inopia, caritas, fames, -is, f.*

debar, v.tr. *alqm alqā re excludĕre, alqd alci praecludĕre, alqm (ab) alqā re prohibēre,* or with *quominus* and subj.

debase, v.tr. *corrumpĕre, vitiare.* **debasement,** n. *ignominia.*

debate, I. n. *altercatio, disceptatio, contentio.* **II.** v.intr. *altercari, disceptare, disputare.*

debauch, I. v.tr. *corrumpĕre, depravare, vitiare, perdĕre.* **II.** n. *comissatio.* **debauchery,** n. *stuprum, mores dissoluti, pravi, perditi.*

debenture, n. *syngrapha.*

debility, n. *infirmitas, imbecillitas, infirma valetudo.*

debt, n. *debitum, pecunia debita, nomen, aes alienum;* to get into —, *aes alienum contrahĕre;* to be in —, *in aere alieno esse, obaeratum esse.* **debtor,** n. *debitor, qui debit, obaeratus.* **debit,** v.tr. *alqd alci expensum ferre.*

decade, n. *decem anni.*

decamp, v.intr. *discedĕre.*

decant, v.tr. *diffundĕre.* **decanter,** n. *lagena.*

decapitate, v.tr. *caput alci praecidĕre.*

decay, I. n. *deminutio, defectio virium, tabes, -is, f.* **II.** v.intr. *(de)minui, deficĕre, decrescĕre, senescĕre, tabescĕre;* a decayed tooth, *dens exesus* (Cels.).

decease, n. *obitus, -ūs;* see DEATH.

deceit, n. *fallacia, fraus, dolus.* **deceive,** v.tr. *decipĕre, frustrari, fallĕre, circumvenire.* **deceiver,** n. *fraudator.* **deceitful,** adj. *fallax, dolosus, vafer, fraudulentus.* Adv. *fraudulenter, fallaciter, dolose, per dolum.*

december, n. *(mensis) December.*

decent, adj. *quod decet, decōrus.* Adv. *decōre.* **decency,** n. *modestia, decorum.*

deception, n. 1, *fraus, dolus;* 2, see DELUSION.

decide, v.tr. 1, = settle a thing, *alqd* or *de alqā re statuĕre, constituĕre, decernĕre, alqd dijudicare;* 2, — to do, *constituĕre, statuĕre* with infin. or *ut.* **decided,** adj. 1, = fixed, *certus, exploratus;* I am —, *certum est mihi* with infin. ; 2, = resolute, *stabilis, constans, firmus.* Adv. *certo, certe, constanter;* in answers, *certe, vero, sane,* or by repetition of a word (e.g. *visne? volo).* **decision,** n. 1, *dijudicatio, judicium, sententia;* 2, of character, *constantia, stabilitas.* **decisive,** adj. *ultimus,* or *quod ad discrimen alqd adducit,* or *maximi momenti.*

deciduous, adj. *deciduus.*

decimate, v.tr. 1, lit. *decimare cohortes* (Suet.), *sorte decimum quemque (cohortis) ad supplicium legĕre;* 2, fig. see DESTROY.

decipher, v.tr. *explanare, interpretari, explicare.*

deck, I. n. *constratum navis* (Petr.). **II.** v, tr. 1. = COVER ; 2. = ADORN.

declaim, v.tr. *pronuntiare, declamare, declamitare.* **declamation,** n. 1, as an art, *pronuntiatio, declamatio;* 2, = speech declaimed, *declamatio.* **declamatory,** adj. *declamatorius, tumidus.* **declaimer,** n. *declamator.*

declare, v.tr. *dicĕre, profiteri, praedicĕre, declarare, asseverare, confirmare;* to — for anyone, *partes alcjs sequi.* **declaration,** n. *praedicatio, sententia, dictum;* — of war, *belli denuntiatio.*

decline, I. v.tr. 1, = refuse, *alqd recusare, negare;* 2, gram. t.t. *declinare.* **II.** v.intr. *deficĕre, (de)minui, (se)remittĕre, decrescĕre;* the day —s, *vesperascit.* **III.** n. 1, *(de)minutio, remissio;* in the — of life, *provectiore aetate;* 2, = consumption, *phthisis* (Plin.). **declension,** n. *declinatio* (Quint.).

declivity, n. *declivitas, acclivitas.*

decoction, n. *decoctum* (Plin.).

decompose, I. v.tr. 1, lit. *(dis)solvĕre, resolvĕre;* 2, fig. *(con)turbare, excitare, erigĕre.* **II.** v.intr. 1, *dissolvi, tabescĕre;* 2, *(con)turbari.* etc. **decomposition,** n. *(dis)solutio, tabes, -is, f.*

decorate, v.tr. *alqm alqā re (ex)ornare, distinguĕre, decorare.* **decoration,** n. *ornatus, -ūs, ornamentum.* **decorous,** adj. *decōrus.* Adv. *decōre.* **decorum,** n. *decōrum.*

decoy, I. v.tr. *allicĕre, pellicĕre.* **II.** n. *illex* (= a lure).

decrease, I. v.tr. *(de)minuĕre, imminuĕre, (sub)levare, mitigare.* **II.** v.intr. *remittĕre* (rare), *remitti, (de)minui,* etc. **III.** n. *deminutio.*

decree, v.tr. 1, of formal decrees, *alqd alci de alqā re,* with gerundive or *ut, decernĕre, alqd* or *ut, edicĕre, alqd de alqā re sciscĕre, alqd, de alqā re, ut, (lege) sancire;* impers. *alci placet ut* or accus. and infin. ; 2, see DETERMINE. **II.** n. *decretum, senatusconsultum, plebiscitum.*

decrepit, adj. *senectute confectus.* **decrepitude,** n. *senectutis imbecillitas.*

decry, v.tr. *vituperare.*

dedicate, v.tr. *alqd alci (de)dicare* (lit. and fig.), *consecrare* (only in religious sense).

deduce, v.tr. 1, = derive, *alqd ab* or *ex alqā re, ab alqo (de)ducĕre;* 2, logical t.t. *alqd ex alqā re concludĕre.* **deduct,** v.tr. *alqd alci rei* or *de alqā re detrahĕre, alqd de alqā re deducĕre.* **deduction,** n. 1, = abatement, *deductio, deminutio;* 2, logical t.t. *conclusio.*

deed, n. 1, *facinus, -ōris,* n. ; —s, *acta, facta;* 2, = document, *tabula, syngrapha.*

deep, I. adj. 1, lit. *altus, profundus;* ten feet —, *decem pedes altus;* 2, fig. *summus* (e.g. *summa eruditio,* — learning). Adv. 1, *alte, profunde;* 2, *penitus, prorsus, graviter* (e.g. *grav. commotus* — moved). **II.** n. *altum.* **deepen, I.** v.tr. 1, lit. *alqd altius fodĕre;* 2, = increase, *augĕre.* **II.** v.intr. = grow darker, *obscurari;* see also THICKEN. **depth,** n. 1, lit. *altitudo;* in —, *in altitudinem* (e.g. *triginta pedum* = thirty feet in —); 2, fig. of character, *summo ingenio,* etc., *praeditus;* in the — of night, *mediā nocte.*

deer, n. *cervus, dama.*

deface, v.tr. *deformare, in pējus fingĕre, foedare.*

defame, v.tr. *calumniari.*

default, n. 1, = error, *culpa, peccatum, error;* 2, = lack, *defectio, defectus, -ūs;* 3, lega t.t. = judgment, go by —, *vadimonium deserĕre.* **defaulter,** n. *qui vadimonium deserit.*

defeat, I. n. *clades, -is,* f., *strages, -is,* f.
II. v.tr., see CONQUER, BAFFLE.

defect, n. 1, *quod deest, desideratum;* the —s
of character, *vitia, -orum;* 2, *labes, -is,* f.,
vitium, mendum. **defective,** adj. *imperfectus,
mancus, vitiosus;* to be —, *deficĕre, deesse.* Adv.
imperfecte, vitiose. **defection,** n. *(ab alqo)
defectio.* **deficiency,** n. *defectio* (e.g. *virium,
animi*), *inopia.*

defend, v.tr. 1, *alqm* or *alqd ab alqo* or
alqd re defendĕre, alqm or *alqd tueri, tutari, alqd
ab alqo prohibĕre, pro alqo* or *alqâ re propugnare;*
2, legal t.t. *caus(s)am alejs dicĕre.* **defendant,** n. *reus.* **defence,** n. 1, in gen. *tutela,
praesidium, defensio, patrocinium;* 2, legal t.t.
patrocinium. **defenceless,** adj. *inermis,
sine praesidio.* **defensible,** adj. *quod defendi
potest.* **defensive,** adj. *ad alqm defendendum;*
— war, *bellum ad hostes repellendos susceptum;*
— weapons, *arma, -orum.*

defer, v.tr. 1, = to postpone, *differre, proferre, prorogare* (= to lengthen, e.g. the time for
payment, *diem ad solvendum*), *procrastinare,
producĕre, prolatare, re(j)icĕre;* 2, = to give
way to, *alci cedĕre, obsequi, morem gerĕre.*
deference, n. *observantia, obsequium.* **de-
ferential,** adj. *submissus;* see HUMBLE. Adv.
submisse.

deficient, adj., see DEFECTIVE.

defile, I. n. *angustiae, fauces, -ium,* f.
II. v.tr. *maculare, inquinare, (con)spurcare,
foedare, violare, polluĕre.* **defilement,** n.
macula, labes, -is, f.

define, v.tr. *(de)finire, describĕre, circumscribĕre.* **definition,** n. *(de)finitio.* **definite,**
adj. *certus, constitutus, status, definitus.* Adv.
certe, certo, definite.

deflect, v.intr. *declinare, errare.*

deform, v.tr. *deformare, depravare, in pejus
mutare* or *vertĕre.* **deformed,** adj. *distortus,
deformatus, deformis.* **deformity,** n. *deformitas, turpitudo.*

defraud, v.tr. *alqm alqâ re fraudare, fraudem* or *fallaciam alci facĕre, fraude* or *dolo
capĕre, fallĕre, circumscribĕre, circumvenire.* **defrauder,** n. *fraudator, circumscriptor.*

defray, v.tr. *sumptus suppeditare, solvĕre.*

defunct, adj. *mortuus, fato functus.*

defy, v.tr. *alqm provocare* (= to challenge),
spernĕre alqd (e.g. *imperia*), *contemnĕre alqd, alci
rei se offerre* or *resistĕre.* **defiance,** n. *provocatio* (Plin.), *contumacia* (= obstinacy).

degenerate, v.intr. *degenerare a parentibus,
mores mutare, depravari.* **degenerate,** adj.
degener, parentibus indignus.

degrade, v.tr. = to lower in rank or position,
in ordinem cogĕre (of soldiers), in gen. *alqm
gradu de(j)icĕre.* **degrading,** adj. *indecŏrus.*
degradation, n. *ignominia, dedecus, -ŏris,* n.

degree, n. 1, *gradus, -ūs;* having —s,
gradatus (= graduated); to such a —, *eo* with
noun in gen. *ut,* or *adeo ut;* by —s, *paul(l)atim,
sensim;* 2, = — in a university, *gradus.*

deify, v.tr. *alqm in caelum tollĕre, alqm inter
deos* or *in deorum numerum referre.* **deified,**
adj. *divus.* **deification,** n. *consecratio* (Tac.).

deign, v.intr. *dignari, velle* with infin.

deism, n. *Deum esse putare.* **deist,** n.
qui Deum esse putat. **Deity,** n. *Deus, numen.*

dejected, adj. *maestus, tristis, perculsus;*
to be —, *in maerore esse* or *jacĕre.* Adv.
maeste. **dejection,** n. *aegritudo, maestitia,
tristitia, maeror.*

delay, I. v.tr. 1, = retard, *(re)morari, detin-*

*ēre alqm, moram facĕre alci, moram alci afferre,
alqm (re)tardare, retinēre, reprimĕre, cohibēre;* 2,
= prolong, *ducĕre, (ex)trahĕre;* 3, = postpone,
differre. **II.** v.intr. *(com)morari, se tenēre,
continēre, se cunctari, cessare;* to — over a thing,
in alqâ re cessare. **III.** n. *mora, dilatio, cessatio*
(= idle —).

delectation, n. *delectatio, oblectatio.*

delegate, I. n. *legatus, nuntius.* **II.**
v.tr. 1, of formal delegation, *legare* (of state
embassy), *allegare* (private); 2, = commit to
anyone, *alqd alci committĕre, mandare, delegare.*

deleterious, adj. *mortifer, exitialis, perniciosus.* Adv. *perniciose.*

deliberate, I. v.intr. *deliberare, consulĕre,
consultare, consilium inire* or *c. capĕre de alqâ re;*
to — over anything, *alqd considerare, secum volvĕre.* **II.** adj. 1, = slow, *lentus;* 2, = careful,
prudens. Adv. *lente; prudenter, considerate,
consulto.* **deliberative,** adj. — assembly,
consilium, senatus, -ūs. **deliberation,** n. 1,
deliberatio, consultatio, consilium; 2, see
SLOWNESS.

delicate, adj. 1, = tender, *tener, mollis;* 2,
= weak, *imbecillus, infirmus;* 3, = fastidious,
fastidiosus, delicatus; 4, = requiring care,
difficilis, anceps, accuratus; 5, = fine, *exquisitus.* Adv. *molliter, infirme, fastidiose,
delicate, accurate, exquisite.* **delicacy,** n. 1,
mollitia, — of taste, style, etc., *humanitas,
subtilitas;* 2, *imbecillitas, infirmitas;* 3, *fastidium;* 4, = tact, *prudentia, cura;* 5, *venustas,
elegantia;* 6, = a dainty, *cibus delicatus.*

delicious, adj. *suavis, dulcis, amoenus.* Adv
suaviter, amoene.

delight, I. n. *voluptas, dulcedo.* **II.** v.tr.
delectare, oblectari. **III.** v. intr. *alqâ re delectari* or *oblectari.* **delightful,** adj. *jucundus,
suavis, acceptus, gratus.* Adv. *jucunde, suaviter,
grate.* **delightfulness,** n. *suavitas, amoenitas.*

delineate, v.tr. 1, lit. *designare, depingĕre;*
2, fig. *describĕre, depingĕre, adumbrare.* To
DESCRIBE. **delineation,** n. 1, *adumbratio,
descriptio;* 2, *deseriptio.*

delinquent, n. *maleficus, capite damnatus.*
delinquency, n., *delictum, scelus, -ĕris,* n.,
facinus, -inŏris, n.

delirium, n. *delirium, furor.* **delirious,**
v.tr. *delirus;* to be —, *mente alienari.*

deliver, v.tr. 1, see FREE; 2, = to utter,
pronuntiare; see SPEAK; 3, in childbirth, to
be delivered, *partum edĕre;* 4, — up, *prodĕre,
dedĕre, tradĕre.* **deliverer,** n. *liberator, vindex.* **delivery,** n. 1, *liberatio;* 2, *actio, elocutio, dictio;* 3, *partus, -ūs;* 4, *traditio, deditio.*

dell, n. *(con)vallis.*

delude, v.tr. *deludĕre.* See DECEIVE. **delusion,** n. 1, = cheat, *fraus, dolus, fallacia;*
2, = error, *error.* **delusive,** adj. *falsus, fallax,
vanus.* Adv. *fallaciter, vane.*

deluge, I. n. 1, lit. *eluvio;* 2, fig. *magna
vis alcjs rei.* **II.** v.tr. 1, lit. *(terram, etc.) inundare;* 2, fig. *magnam copiam alcjs rei dare;* be
deluged with, *alqâ re cumulari.*

delve, v.tr. *fodĕre.*

demagogue, n. *novarum rerum auctor;* to
be a —, *rebus novis studēre.*

demand, I. v.tr. *(de)poscĕre, exposcĕre, (ex)-
postulare, (ef)flagitare, implorare, requirĕre, flagitare, (ex)petĕre, exigĕre, requirĕre.* **II.** n. *postulatio, postulatum, flagitatio, preces, -um,* f.

demarcation, n. *terminus, limes, -ĭtis,* m.,
confinium.

dem 672 des

demean, v.tr. 1, = to conduct, *se gerĕre* in *e*; 2, = to lower oneself, *descendĕre ad alqd.*

demeanour, n. *mores, -um,* m.

demerit, n. *culpa.* See BLAME, FAULT.

demi, n. *semi,* in comp. (e.g. *semideus*).

demigod, n. *heros.*

demise, I. n. *obitus, -ūs;* see DEAD. **II.** v.tr. = leaving by will, *legare.*

democracy, n. *ratio popularis, civitas in quâ omnia per populum administrantur.* **democratical,** adj. *popularis.* **democrat,** n. *popularium fautor.*

demolish, v.tr. *alqd demoliri, de(j)icĕre (pro)-sternĕre, evertĕre.* **demolition,** n. *demolitio, eversio.*

demon, n. * *daemon* (Eccl.).

demonstrate, v.tr. *demonstrare, docēre, (con)firmare, probare.* **demonstration,** n. 1, = pointing out, *demonstratio;* 2, = proof, *argumentum, documentum;* 3, = political meeting, *contio.* **demonstrable,** adj. *quod doceri potest.* **demonstrative,** adj. 1, of argument, n. *argumentum;* 2, = eager, *fervidus, vehemens.* Adv. *vehementer.*

demoralize, v.tr. *mores corrumpĕre, moribus nocēre.* **demoralization,** n. *mores corrupti.*

demur, v.intr. 1, legal t.t. = to object to, *alci rei exceptionem facĕre, contra dicĕre;* 2, = to delay, *remorari, moram facĕre.* **demurrer,** n. 1, legal t.t. *exceptio;* 2, *mora, dilatio.*

demure, adj. *verecundus.*

den, n. *caverna, specus, -ūs, cavea, claustrum, latibulum.*

denizen, n. *incola,* m. & f.

denominate, I. v.tr. & **II.** n., see NAME. **denominator,** n. *index.*

denote, v.tr. *(de)notare, designare, notam imponĕre alci rei, alqd ostendĕre, significare.* **denotation,** n. *designatio, significatio.*

denounce, v.tr. 1, *denuntiare;* 2, — before a court, *nomen alcjs deferre, alqm accusare.* **denunciation,** n. 1, *denuntiatio;* 2, *delatio, accusatio.* **denouncer,** n. *accusator, index, delator.*

dense, adj. *densus, confertus, creber, crassus, solidus.* Adv. *dense, solide, confertim* (of soldiers). **density,** n. *densitas, soliditas;* see also STUPIDITY.

dent, I. n. *nota, injuria.* **II.** v.tr. *alci rei injuriam afferre.*

dentist, n. *medicus (dentium).*

deny, v.tr. 1, = to refuse to admit, *alqd (de)negare, recusare,* or with accus. and infin. or *quin, quominus;* it cannot be denied, *negari non potest quin;* 2, = to — oneself, *sibi temperare, se coercēre* or *continēre;* to — anything, *(ab) alqâ re temperare.* **denial,** n. *negatio, recusatio.*

depart, v. intr. 1, *abire ab* or *ex, abscedĕre ab* or *ex, decedĕre (de* or *ex) loco, discedĕre (ab) loco* or *ex loco, excedĕre loco* or *ex loco, egredi (ab) loco, digredi (ab, ex) loco;* fig. = to die, *decedĕre ex* or *a vitâ.* **departure,** n. *abitus, decessus. discessus* (all *-ūs*).

department, n. 1, *munus, -ēris,* n., *munia, -orum, provincia;* 2, = district, *pars, ager, regio.*

depend, v.intr. 1, = to be dependent on, *pendēre ex alqo* or *alqâ re, in alcjs dicione esse, esse in alcjs manu, in alcjs potestate verti, in alqo esse* or *positum* or *situm esse;* 2, = to rely on, *alci (con)fidĕre;* — upon it, *mihi crede.* **dependent,** adj. & n. use verb (e.g. *qui ex t*

dependence, n. 1, = subjec tion, *dicio;* 2, = trust, *fiducia.*

depict, v.tr. lit. & fig. *(de)pingĕre, (ef)fingĕre, exprimĕre, describĕre.*

deplore, v.tr. *deplorare, deflēre, complorare.* **deplorable,** adj. see MISERABLE.

deponent, n. 1, legal t.t. *testis, -is,* m. and f. ; 2, *gram.* t.t. *(verbum) deponens.*

depopulate, v.tr. *terram (de)vastare, (de)populari, vacuefacĕre.* **depopulation,** n. *populatio, vastatio.*

deport, v.tr. *se gerĕre.* **deportment,** n. 1, = carriage, *gestus, -ūs;* 2, = behaviour, *mores, -um,* m.

depose, v.tr. 1, = to remove from office, *loco suo alqm movēre;* see DETHRONE; 2, = — as a witness, *testari, testificari.* **deposition,** n. 1, use verb ; 2, *testimonium.*

deposit, I. v.tr. 1, = to lay down, *(de)ponĕre;* 2, of money, *pecuniam apud alqm (de)ponĕre, pecuniam collocare.* **II.** n. 1, *quod depositum est ; pecuniae apud alqm depositae;* 2, = pledge, *pignus, -ĕris,* n. See PLEDGE. **depository,** n. *apotheca, receptaculum.*

deprave, v.tr. *depravare, corrumpĕre, vitiare.* **depravation,** n. *depravatio, corruptio.* **depravity,** n. *pravitas, turpitudo, mores perditi, mores turpes.*

deprecate, v.tr. *deprecari alqd ab alqo* or *quin* with subj. **deprecation,** n. *deprecatio.*

depreciate, v.tr. *minuĕre, elevare (=lessen), obtrectare alci* or *alci rei.* **depreciation,** n. *obtrectatio.*

depredation, n. *latrocinium.* **depredator,** n. *praedator, latro.*

depress, v.tr. *deprimĕre, opprimĕre, alcjs animum affligĕre.* **depression,** n. *tristitia, maeror.*

deprive, v.tr. *alqm alqâ re privare, (de)spoliare, exspoliare, orbare, alqd alci adimĕre, detrahĕre, eripĕre.* **deprived,** adj. *orbus (orbatus) alqâ re;* — of the use of his limbs, *membris captus.* **deprivation,** n.*privatio, spoliatio.*

depth, n. see DEEP.

depute, v.tr. *legare* (in state affairs), *allegare* (in private). **deputy,** n. see AGENT. **deputation,** n. *legati.*

derange, v.tr. *(de)turbare, perturbare, conturbare.* **deranged,** adj. *demens, insanus.* **derangement,** n. 1, = confusion, *perturbatio;* 2, = madness, *dementia, insania.*

deride, v.tr. *alqm* or *alqd deridēre, irridēre.* **derider,** n. *irrisor.* **derision,** n. *irrisio.* **derisive,** adj. by verb.

derive, v.tr. *derivare* (= to draw off or turn aside a river), *(de)ducĕre;* to — a word, *verbum ex* or *ab alqâ re (de)ducĕre.*

derogate from, v.tr. *derogare* (e.g. *alqd de magnificentiâ, alqd sibi, fidem alci), alci* or *alci rei obtrectare.* **derogatory,** adj. to be — to, *alci dedecori esse;* to speak in a — manner of anyone, *alci obtrectare.*

descend, v.intr. 1, = to come down, *descendĕre ex* or *de;* 2, fig. *tradi;* to be —ed from, *ortum* or *oriundum esse ab alqo;* 3, see ATTACK. **descendant,** n. *prognatus;* pl. *progenies, posteri.* **descent,** n. 1, = going down, use the verb; 2, of a hill, *declivitas, locus declivis;* 3, = origin, *origo, genus, -ĕris,* n., *stirps, progenies;* 4, — upon = attack, *irruptio, incursio, incursus, -ūs.*

describe, v.tr. 1, *describĕre, verbis exsequi, scripturâ persequi, explicare alqd* or *de alqâ re, exponĕre alqd* or *de alqâ re, alqd enarrare*

enumerare, comprehendĕre, complecti, lit(t)eris mandare, memoriae prodĕre, tradĕre; 2, -= to draw, describĕre. **description**, n. descriptio, (e)narratio, expositio.

desecrate, v.tr. profanare, profanum facĕre, exaugurare (opp. inaugurare), polluĕre, maculare, violare. **desecration**, n. polluta sacra, -orum.

desert, n. dignitas, virtus, -ūtis, f., meritum.

desert, I. n. = wilderness, solitudo, vastitas, regio deserta, loca, -orum, deserta; to turn into a —, regionem (de)vastare. **II.** v.tr. 1, in gen. deserĕre, (de)relinquĕre, destituĕre, alci deesse, alqm prodĕre; 2, = to become a deserter, signa deserĕre or relinquĕre, ad hostem transfugĕre or perfugĕre. **desertion**, n. 1, (de)relictio; 2, transitio ad hostem. **deserter**, n. transfuga, desertor.

deserve, v.tr. (com)merēre, (com)merēri, (pro)merēre, (pro)merēri, dignum esse re; he — praise from me, dignus est quem laudem or qui a me laudetur; — well of a person or city, bene de alqo or erga alqm merēri. **deserving**, adj. alqd re dignus. Adv. merito, jure.

desideratum, n. quod deest, res necessaria.

design, n. and v.tr. 1, see SKETCH; 2, see PURPOSE. **designing**, adj. peritus, prudens, sciens or, in bad sense, fraudulentus. Adv. consulto.

designate, v tr. designare, notare, eligĕre, nominare. **designation**, n. 1, designatio, nominatio, notatio; 2, = purpose, finis, ratio.

desire, I. n. alcjs rei appetitio, appetitus, -ūs, appetentia, cupiditas, cupido, desiderium. **II.** v.tr. alqd appetĕre, expetĕre, cupĕre, concupiscĕre, desiderare, desiderio alcjs teneri, avēre (with infin., e.g. aveo scire, audire, etc.).; what do you —? quid vis? quid fieri jubes? **desirable**, adj. optabilis, expetendus. **desirous**, adj. alcjs rei appetens, cupidus, avidus. Adv. appetenter, cupide, avide.

desist, v.intr. desistĕre re (ab re and de re, or with infin.), absistĕre (a)re.

desk, n. mensa (= table), scrinium (= escritoire).

desolate, I. adj. 1, = waste, vastus, desertus; 2, = bereaved, orbus; 3, = despairing, spe destitutus, maestus. **II.** v.tr. vastare, (de)populari.

despair, I. n. desperatio. **II.** v.intr. desperare (— of, de re or alqd or alci rei, or with accus. and infin.); — of the cure of a sick person, aegrotum or aegroti salutem desperare. **despairing**, adj. see DESPERATE.

despatch, dispatch, I. v.tr. 1, = to do, conficĕre, perficĕre, absolvĕre, finire; with haste, maturare, accelerare; 2, = send off, (di)mittĕre, ablegare (on private), legare (on public business); 3, = kill, trucidare, caedĕre. **II.** n. 1, confectio, perfectio, festinatio, properatio; 2, missio; 3, trucidatio, caedes, -is, f. **despatches**, n.pl. lit(t)erae publice missae.

desperate, adj. 1, = hopeless, exspes, sine spe, desperatus (= despaired of); a — state of affairs, res desperatae or extremae; 2, = dangerous, periculosus; 3, = villainous, sceleratus, scelestus; 4, = brave, fortissimus. Adv. desperanter, periculose, sceleste, scelerate, or by superl. (e.g. — wicked, sceleratissimus), fortissime, acerrime. **desperation**, n. desperatio.

despise, v.tr. contemnĕre, contemptui habēre, despicĕre, aspernari, spernĕre. **despicable**, adj. contemnendus, turpis. Adv. turpiter, foede.

despite, I. n. odium, ma'ltia. **II.** prep. contra, adversus (e.g. contra leges, = in — of the laws); in, with abl., (contemptis precibus meis

Romam rediit, = (in) despite (of) my prayers he returned to Rome).

despond, v.intr. desperare de rebus suis, spe dejectum esse. **despondency**, n. see DESPAIR.

despot, n. tyrannus, dominus. **despotism**, n. dominatus, -ūs, tyrannis, -ĭdis, f., dominatio. **despotical**, adj. imperiosus, superbus. Adv. superbe, crudeliter.

dessert, n. mensa secunda.

destine, v.tr. alqd or alqm ad alqd or alci rei destinare, alqd constituĕre or statuĕre. **destined**, adj. destinatus, status, constitutus. **destination**, n. 1, = end, finis, m. and f.; 2, = end of journey, locum quem petimus, or the name of the town, etc. **destiny**, n. fatum, sors.

destitute, adj. inops, egens; of anything, alcjs rei inops, alqd re destitutus, privatus, or use sine with abl. **destitution**, n. inopia.

destroy, v.tr. perdĕre, destruĕre, diruĕre, demoliri, evertĕre, rescindĕre (e.g. pontem), intercidĕre (pontem), delēre, ex(s)tinguĕre (societatem vitae, potentiam), dissolvĕre, interrumpĕre; conficĕre, subvertĕre (e.g. imperium, leges et libertatem); to — oneself, mortem sibi consciscĕre. **destroyer**, n. evertor rei, qui alqd perdit, etc. **destructible**, adj. fragilis, quod perdi potest. **destructibility**, n. fragilitas. **destruction**, n. dissolutio, eversio, excidium, ex(s)tinctio. **destructive**, adj. perniciosus, exitiosus, funestus. Adv. perniciose.

desuetude, n. oblivio.

desultory, adj. inconstans, lēvis, mobilis, instabilis. Adv. parum diligenter.

detach, v.tr. alqd ab alqd re separare, sejungĕre, disjungĕre. **detachment**, n. = a body of troops, delecta manus, -ūs, delecti (milites).

details, n. singula, -orum, singulae res; to go into —, de singulis agĕre. **detail**, v.tr. res explicare, singula concisare et colligĕre.

detain, v.tr. (de)tinĕre. **detention**, n. impedimentum, mora; — in custody, custodia, comprehensio (= arrest).

detect, v.tr. alqm in alqd re deprehendĕre, alqd invenire, reperire, patefacĕre. **detection**, n. deprehensio, but better by verb (e.g. the — is due to him, ab eo res patefacta est).

deter, v.tr. deterrēre alqm ab or de re (or with ne, quin, quominus).

deteriorate, I. v.tr. deterius facĕre, in deterius mutare, in pejus mutare or vertĕre, corrumpĕre. **II.** v.intr. deteriorem (deterius) fieri, in pejorem partem verti et mutari, in pejus mutari. **deterioration**, n. deterior condicio or status, -ūs.

determine, v.tr. 1, = settle, alqd (di)judicare, (de)finire, alqd or de alqd re decernĕre, alqd statuĕre, constituĕre; 2, = decide to, statuĕre, constituĕre, decernĕre with infin.; I am —ed, certum est mihi alqd facĕre, or by fut. part. (e.g. — to die, moriturus). **determination**, n. 1, (de)finitio, (di)judicatio, arbitrium, judicium, sententia; 2, consilium, ratio; 3, = decision of character, constantia, gravitas. **determined**, adj. constans, gravis.

detest, v.tr. alqm or alqd detestari, aversari. **detestable**, adj. detestandus, detestabilis. Adv. foede, nefarie. **detestation**, n. odium.

dethrone, v.tr. alci regi imperium abrogare, regnum alci eripĕre or auferre.

detonate, v intr. crepitare, † fragorem dare.

detract, v.tr. detrahĕre de alqo or de alqd re, alqd minuĕre, alci obtrectare. **detraction**, n. obtrectatio.

detriment, n. *damnum, detrimentum, jactura.* **detrimental,** adj. *perniciosus, iniquus, adversus, † contrarius.* Adv. *perniciose.*

deuce, n. as exclamation, *malum, abi in malam rem* (or *crucem*).

devastate, v.tr. *(per)vastare, (de)populari, perpopulari.* **devastation,** n. *vastatio, (de)populatio.*

develop, I. v.tr. 1, = explain, *alqd explicare, evolvere, explanare;* 2, = educate, *educare, excolere;* 3, = improve, *augere* (e.g. the resources of a country), *excolere.* **II.** v.intr. *crescere, adolescere, augeri.* **development,** n. 1, *explicatio, explanatio;* 2, = growth, etc., *auctus, -ūs, progressus, -ūs.*

deviate, v.intr. *declinare, deflectere, digredi, discedere, ab alqā re (ab)errare.* **deviation,** n. *declinatio* (lit. or fig.), *digressio* (fig.). **devious,** adj. *devius, errabundus.*

device, n. 1, *ratio, consilium;* 2, = motto, *insigne, dictum, sententia;* as an inscription, *inscriptio.*

devil, n. * *diabŏlus* (Eccl.); go to the — ! *abi in malam partem!* **devilish,** adj. * *diabolicus* (Eccl.), *nefandus.* Adv. * *diabolice, foede.*

devise, v.tr. 1, *excogitare, invenire, fingere, machinari* (in a bad sense); 2, see BEQUEATH.

devoid, adj. *(ab) alqā re vacuus, liber;* — of care, *securus.*

devolve, I. v.tr. *alqd alci, (de)mandare, deferre.* **II.** v.intr. *alci (ob)venire, transmitti.*

devote, v.tr. 1, lit. *alqd alci (de)vovēre, (con)sĕcrare, (de)dicare;* 2, fig. *alqd alci (rei) addicĕre, ad alqd destinare;* to — oneself to, *se alci (rei) dedĕre, se ad alqd conferre.* **devoted,** adj. *alcjs rei studiosus.* Adv. *studiose,* or by superl. (e.g. —attached, *amantissimus*). **devotion,** n. 1, *devotio, dedicatio;* 2, *studium, obsequium, observantia, amor, benevolentia;* 3, = religious feeling, *pietas erga Deum.* **devotions,** n. *preces, -um, f.*

devout, adj. *pius erga Deum, venerabundus.* Adv. *pie.*

dew, n. *ros;* the — falls, *rorat, cadit ros.* **dewy,** adj. *roscidus.*

dewlap, n. *palearia, -ium, pl.*

dexterity, n. *habilitas, facultas, ingenii dexteritas ad alqd, sol(l)ertia, peritia, scientia rei.* **dexterous,** adj. *habilis, dexter, peritus, sol(l)ers, sciens.* Adv. *dext(e)re, perite, sol(l)erter, scienter.*

diadem, n. *diadema, -atis,* n., *insigne (regium).*

diagonal, adj. *diagonalis.*

diagram, n. *descriptio, forma (geometrica).*

dial, n. *solarium.*

dialect, n. *lingua* with special adj. (e.g. *rustica, Anglicana*); *dialectos, -i* (Suet.); to speak in the Doric —, *Dorice loqui.*

dialectics, n. *dialectica, -ae, dialectica, -orum,* n. *ars bene disserendi et vera ac falsa dijudicandi, disserendi ratio.*

dialogue, n. 1, =the philosophical, *dialogus, sermo;* 2, = in plays, *diverbium, sermones alterni;* 3, = conversation, *sermo.*

diameter, n. * *diametros, tinea media.*

diamond, n. *adamas.*

diaphragm, n. *diaphragma* (late), or *praecordia, -ium,* pl.

diarrhoea, n. *alvi profluvium, profusio, alvus cita, citatior, liquida, fluens, soluta* (διαρροία only as a Greek word, in Cicero).

diary, n. *ephemeris, -idis,* f. (= a merchant's —), *adversaria. -orum.*

dice, die, I. n. *talus, tessera;* to play at —, *talis* or *tesseris ludĕre, aleā* or *aleam ludĕre;* a — box, *fritillus, alveus, alveolus.* **II.** v.intr. *talos* or *tesseras jacĕre* or *mittĕre.* **dicer,** n. *aleo, aleator.*

dictate, v.tr. 1, = to read to one who writes down, *dictare;* 2, see ORDER. **dictation,** n. 1, see ORDER, SWAY; 2, = an exercise, *quod dictatum est.* **dictator,** n. *dictator.* **dictatorial,** adj. *imperiosus.* **dictatorship,** n *dictatura.*

diction, n. *dicendi* or *scribendi genus, -ēris,* n., *sermo.*

dictionary, n. * *thesaurus verborum.*

die, v.intr. *mori, vitā decedĕre, diem supremum obīre.*

diet, I. n. 1, *victus, -ūs, diaeta;* 2, = assembly, *conventus regum* or *principum.* **II.** v.tr. *alqm victum alci imponĕre.*

differ, v.intr. *discrepare cum alqo* or *alqā re, dissidēre, dissentire ab* or *cum alqo, differre ab alqo* or *alqā re.* **different,** adj. *discrepans, diversus, dissimilis, varius.* Adv. *aliter, alio modo.* **difference,** n. *varietas, diversitas* (in gen.); *discrepantia, dissensio* (= — in opinion and feeling).

difficult, adj. *difficilis, arduus, impeditus, magni negotii, laboriosus.* **difficulty,** n. *difficultas;* pecuniary difficulties, *pecuniae inopia,* with —, *vix.*

diffidence, n. *diffidentia.* **diffident,** adj. *timidus, diffidens.* Adv. *timide, modeste.*

diffuse, I. v.tr. *diffundĕre, differre, (di)vulgare.* **II.** adj. *copiosus, verbosus;* to be —, *longum esse.* Adv. *longe, diffuse, latius et diffusius, copiose, verbose.* **diffuseness,** n. by adj. (e.g. the — of a speech, *oratio longa*). **diffusion,** n. *propagatio,* or by adj.

dig, v.tr. *fodĕre;* to — up, *effodĕre, evellĕre.* **digger,** n. *fossor.*

digest, I. v.tr. *concoquĕre, conficĕre.* **II.** n. *digesta, -orum* (Jct.). **digestion,** n. *concoctio.* **digestible,** adj. *facilis ad concoquendum.*

dignity, n. 1, in gen. *honestas* (= moral dignity), *gravitas* (= earnestness of character), *auctoritas* (= influence), *amplitudo, majestas* (= rank), *dignitas* (= both of character and rank); to stand on one's —, *superbum se praebēre;* 2, = dignity of office, *dignitas;* official —, *magistratus, -ūs.* **dignify,** v.tr. *dignitatem deferre alci, (ex)ornare alqm.* **dignified,** adj. *gravis;* in a — way, *summā gravitate.*

digress, v.intr. *ab alqā re digredi, aberrare.* **digressive,** adj. *a proposito digredi.* **digression,** n. *digressio.*

dike, n. *moles, -is,* f., *agger, -ēris,* m.

dilapidation, n. *injuria, detrimentum.*

dilate, v.tr. 1, = to extend, *dilatare;* 2, fig. to — upon, *de alqā re latius dicĕre.*

dilatory, adj. *tardus, lentus.* **dilatoriness,** n. *cunctatio, tarditas, mora.*

dilemma, n. *complexio;* the horns of a —, *res in angustias deductae.*

diligence, n. *diligentia, industria, (g)navitas;* with —, *industrie, (g)naviter, sedulo, strenue, studiose, diligenter, cum diligentiā.* **diligent,** adj. *diligens, industrius, studiosus rei.*

dilute, v.tr. 1, lit. *aquā alqd (per)miscēre, diluĕre;* 2, fig. *diluĕre* (= an evil).

dim, I. v.tr. *obscurare.* **II.** adj. *obscurus.* **dimness,** n. *obscuritas.*

dimension, n. *dimensio.*

diminish, I. v.tr. *(im)minuĕre, sublevare*

II. v.intr. *se minuĕre, (im)minui.* **diminutive,** n. *nomen deminutivum* (Gram.), see SMALL.

dimple, n. *gelasinus* (Mart.).

din, I. n. *strepitus, -ūs, fremitus, -ūs;* to make a —, *strepĕre, strepitum edĕre.* **II.** v.tr. *alcjs aures obtundĕre.*

dine, v.tr. *prandĕre, cenare;* to — with one, *apud alqm cenare* or *accubare.* **dining-room,** n. *conclave.* **dinner,** n. (at noon) *prandium,* (the chief meal, at three or four o'clock) *cena.*

dingy, adj. *fuscus, sordidus.*

dint, n. 1, = a mark, *nota;* 2, **by — of,** by abl. (e.g. *ira,* = by — of anger).

diocese, n. ** diocesis* (Eccl.).

dip, I. v.tr. *(in)tingĕre in re, mergĕre in alqd.* **II.** v.intr. 1, *(im)mergi;* 2, see INCLINE; 3, to — into (of a book), *librum strictim attingĕre.* **III.** n. 1, = slope, *declinatio;* — of a hill, *declivitas;* 2, = into water, by verb (e.g. to take a —, *immergi*).

diploma, n. *diplomʌ, -ātis,* n. **diplomacy,** n. 1, *legatio* (e.g. to follow the profession of —, *legationes obire);* 2, = craft, *astutia.* **diplomat,** n. *legatus.* **diplomatic,** adj. = clever, *astutus, callidus.*

dire, adj. *dirus, atrox.* **direfulness,** n. *atrocitas.*

direct, I. v.tr. 1, = to manage, *alci rei praeesse, praesidĕre, alqd administrare, procurare, dirigĕre, regĕre, gubernare;* 2, see ORDER; 3, = to show the way, *viam alci monstrare;* 4, = to — one's course, etc., *iter dirigĕre, flectĕre, convertĕre;* 5, = to — a letter, *alci epistolam inscribĕre.* **II.** adv. see DIRECTLY. **III.** adj. (*di)rectus.* **direction,** n. 1, *cura, procuratio, administratio, moderatio, gubernatio;* 2, see ORDER; 3, use verb; 4, = course, *iter, itineris,* n., *cursus, -ūs, via;* in different —s, *in diversas partes;* 5, *inscriptio.* **directly,** adv. 1, = in a straight course, *recta viâ;* 2, = immediately, *statim, confestim.* **directness,** n. 1, of a route, *via recta;* 2, of speech, *sermo manifestus, clarus, planus.* **director,** n. *magister, præses, -ĭdis,* m. and f., *praefectus.*

dirge, n. *nenia.*

dirt, n. *caenum, sordes, -is,* f., *illuvies, squalor.* **dirty, I.** adj. 1, lit. *caenosus, lutulentus, spurcus, sordidus ʌnmundus;* to be —, *sordĕre, squalĕre;* 2, fig. *sordidus, turpis.* Adv. *spurce, sordide, immunde.* **II.** v.tr. *maculare, inquinare.*

disable, v.tr. *infirmare, enervare, debilitare, frangĕre.*

disabuse, v.tr. *alqm dedocĕre alqd.*

disadvantage, n. *incommodum;* see DAMAGE. **disadvantageous,** adj. *incommodus.* Adv. *incommode.*

disaffect, v.tr. *(ab)alienare, sol(l)icitare.* **disaffected,** adj. *(ab)alienatus, animo alieno* or *averso ab alqo* or *alqâ re.* **disaffection,** n. *alienatio, animus alienus* or *aversus.*

disagree, v.intr. *ab alqo, inter se,* etc., *discrepare, dissentire, dissidĕre;* of food, *non facile concoqui, stomacho gravem esse.* **disagreeable,** adj. *ingratus, gravis, molestus, injucundus.* Adv. *ingrate, graviter, moleste.* **disagreement,** n. *dissidium;* see QUARREL.

disallow, v.tr. *improbare, renuĕre, vetare.*

disappear, v.intr. *abire, auferri, tolli, obscurari, evanescĕre.* **disappearance,** n. by verb (e.g. after the disappearance of this hope, *hac spe sublatâ).*

disappoint, v.tr. *ad vanum* or *ad irritum redigĕre, frustrari, spem fallĕre;* to — a person in all his plans, *conturbare alci omnes rationes.*

disappointment, n. *frustratio,* better by verb (e.g. I have met with a —, *spes me fefellit*).

disapprove, v.tr. *improbare, reprobare, condemnare.* **disapproval,** n. *improbatio.*

disarm, v.tr. *alqm armis exuĕre, arma alci adimĕre.*

disarrange, v.tr. *(con)turbare, perturbare, confundĕre.* **disarrangement,** n. *perturbatio.*

disaster, n. *malum, clades, -is,* f., *calamitas, incommodum, casus, -ūs (adversus);* to be in —, *afflictâ condicione esse.* **disastrous,** adj. *calamitosus, funestus, adversus, gravis, tristis;* — state of things, *res adversae, fortunae afflictae.* Adv. *calamitose, funeste, adverse, graviter.*

disavow, v.tr. *diffiteri, infitiari, infitias ire, abnuĕre, repudiare, (de)negare.* **disavowal,** n. *infitiatio, repudiatio* (rare).

disband, v.tr. *exauctorare, missos facĕre dimittĕre, militiâ solvĕre, sacramento solvĕre.*

disbelieve, v.tr. *alci (rei) non credĕre.* **dis belief,** n. use verb.

disburden, v.tr. *alqm* or *alqd alqâ rʻ exonerare, levare, liberare, solvĕre, expedire.*

disburse, v.tr. see PAY.

discern, v.tr. *discernĕre;* — black from white, *atra et alba* or *ab albis discernĕre.* **discernible,** adj. *conspicuus.* **discerning,** adj. *intellegens, perspicax, sagax, prudens.* **discernment,** n. 1, = distinguishing, *distinctio;* 2, = insight, *intellegentia, prudentia, perspicientia;* a man of great —, *vir prudentissimus.*

discharge, I. v.tr. 1, as a soldier, *missum facĕre, alqm (di)mittĕre (ab exercitu), alqm militiâ solvĕre, exauctorare alqm, sacramento solvĕre alqm* (= to free a soldier from his oath), *alqm loco movĕre;* — a gladiator, *rude (rudis* = the foil given as a token of honour) *donare;* to — a civil officer or servant, *mittĕre alqm, missum facĕre alqm, removĕre alqm republicâ, alqm submovĕre administratione reipublicae* or *a republicâ;* 2, = unload, *navem,* etc., *exonerare;* 3, = pay, *solvĕre;* 4, = perform, *alqâ re fungi;* 5, = let off, *telum (e)mittĕre.* **II.** v.intr. of rivers, *in mare effundi* or *(ef)fluĕre;* of wounds, *pus exit,* or *effunditur.* **III.** n. 1, *(di)missio;* 2, by verb; 3, *solutio;* 4, *functio;* 5, *emissio;* 6, of wounds, rivers, etc., use verb.

disciple, n. *discipulus, auditor.*

discipline, I. n. *disciplina, regimen;* want of —, *licentia.* **II.** v.tr. *instituĕre, coercĕre, in officio continĕre.*

disclaim, v.tr. *repudiare.*

disclose, v.tr. *detegĕre, retegĕre, revelare, nudare, aperire, patefacĕre.* **disclosure,** n. *indicium, delatio.*

discolour, v.tr. *colorem mutare, decolorare.*

discomfit, v.tr. 1, *fundĕre, profligare,* in *fugam vertĕre;* 2, fig. *repellĕre, spem alci eripĕre.* **discomfiture,** n. 1, *clades, -is,* f., *strages, -is,* f., *fuga;* 2, by verb.

discomfort, n. *incommodum.*

disconcerted, adj. *perturbatus.*

disconsolate, adj. *spe destitutus, tristis.* Adv. *maeste.*

discontent, n. *molestia, taedium, fastidium.* **discontented,** adj. *sorte suâ non contentus;* to be —, *moleste ferre alqd.*

discontinue, v.tr. *interrumpĕre, intermittĕre, intercipĕre, omittĕre, dirimĕre.*

discord, n. 1, in music, *discrepans sonus, -ūs, dissonantia;* 2, fig. *dissensio, dissidium, discordia.* **discordant,** adj. 1, in music, *absonus;* 2, *dissidens ab* or *cum alqo, discors cum alqo.* **Adv.** *sine concentu, non congruenter.*

discount, I. n. *deductio;* without any —, *sine ullā deductione;* to pay without —, *solidum solvēre.* **II.** v.tr. *deductione facta pecuniam solvēre.*

discountenance, v.tr. *improbare, condemnare.*

discourage, v.tr. *animum alcjs infringĕre, deprimĕre, frangĕre, affligĕre;* to be discouraged, *affligi, de alqā re desperare;* to — anything, *alqd dissuadēre* or with *ne;* see DETER. **discouragement** n. *quod alcjs animum affligit.*

discourse, I. n. = conversation, *sermo, collocutio, colloquium, disputatio* (= discussion); = a speech or sermon, *contio.* **II.** v.intr. 1, *confabulari, colloqui cum alqo;* 2, *contionari* (= — to an assembly of the people), *orationem facĕre* or *habēre.*

discourteous, adj. *inurbanus, rusticus.* Adv. *inurbane, rustice.* **discourtesy,** n. *inurbanitas, rusticitas.*

discover, v.tr. *invenire, aperire, detegĕre* (= find), *indicare* (= point out), *in lucem proferre, enuntiare* (= make known). **discoverer,** n. *inventor, auctor, index, inventrix* (fem.). **discovery,** n. *inventio, investigatio* (as act); = the thing discovered, *inventum, res inventa.*

discredit, I. n. = disgrace, *dedecus, -ōris,* n., *ignominia, probrum, infamia.* **II.** v.tr. *alcjs fidem minuĕre, de famā detrahĕre, alcjs auctoritatem levare, alci invidiam facĕre.* **discreditable,** adj. *inhonestus, turpis.*

discreet, adj. *prudens, cautus, gravis, constans.* Adv. *prudenter, caute, graviter, constanter.* **discretion,** n. *prudentia, continentia* (= self-restraint), *cautio* (= wariness).

discriminate, v.tr. *di(j)udicare, discernĕre, distinguĕre* (alqd ab alqa re or two nouns joined by *et*). **discrimination,** n. *discrimen;* to make —, *discrimen facĕre.*

discursive, adj. *inconstans, varius, vagus.* Adv. *varie, inconstanter.* **discursiveness,** n. *error.*

discuss, v.tr. *disceptare, disputare* (alqd or *de re*). **discussion,** n. *disceptatio, disputatio.*

disdain, I. v.tr. *dedignari, spernĕre, fastidire, aspernari.* **II.** n. *fastigium, arrogantia.* **disdainful,** adj. *arrogans;* see HAUGHTY.

disease, n. *morbus;* to suffer from —, *aegrotare.* **diseased,** adj. *aeger, aegrotus.*

disembark, I. v.tr. *exponĕre;* — soldiers, *copias* (*e classe, navibus*) *exponĕre.* **II.** intr. *exponi* (*e nave*) *egredi.* **disembarkation,** n. *egressus, -ūs.*

disembarrass, v.tr. *alqm alqā re expedire, liberare, exonerare.*

disembodied, adj. *corporis sui expers.*

disenchant, v.tr. 1, lit. *alqm liberare* (allowing context to define from what); 2, fig. *alcjs animum convertĕre,* or *mutare.*

disengage, v.tr. *solvĕre, liberare.* **disengaged,** adj. *otiosus, vacuus.*

disentangle, v.tr. *expedire, explicare.*

disfavour, n. *odium, ira;* to fall into —, *alci in odium venire.*

disfigure, v.tr. *deformare.*

disfranchise, v.tr. *civitatem alci adimĕre, alqm suffragio privare.* **disfranchisement,** n. by verb (e.g. he suffered —, *suffragio privatus est*).

disgorge, v.tr. 1, (*e*)*vomĕre, e(j)icĕre;* 2, = give up, *reddĕre.*

disgrace, I. n. 1, = shame, *turpitudo, infamia, dedecus, -ōris,* n., *ignominia;* mark of —,

nota; 2, = shameful act, *dedecus, probrum, flagitium, opprobrium.* **II.** v.tr. *dedecorare, polluĕre, alci dedecori esse, dedecus inurĕre.* **disgraceful,** adj. *turpis, foedus, inhonestus, flagitiosus, probrosus, infamis.* Adv. *turpiter, foede, inhoneste, flagitiose.*

disguise, I. n. 1, in dress, *vestis mutata;* = mask, *persona, larva;* 2, = appearance, *species, simulacrum, imago, simulatio, persona.* **II.** v.tr. 1, *alqm alienā veste occultare, vestum mutare;* 2, fig. *alqd* (*dis*)*simulare, occultare.*

disgust, n. *fastidium, taedium, satietas* (from fulness), *nausea* (from a foul stomach). **disgusting,** adj. *teter, molestus* (= troublesome), *gravis, horribilis.* Adv. *tetre, moleste, graviter.*

dish, I. n. *patina, patella, lanx, scutula.* **II.** v.tr. — up, *apponĕre.*

dishearten, v.tr. *animum alcjs frangĕre, spem alci eripĕre.*

dishonest, adj. *malus, improbus, inhonestus, male moratus, fallax, fraudulentus.* Adv. *male, improbe, fallaciter, fraudulenter.* **dishonesty,** n. *improbitas, mores pravi* or *corrupti, fraus.*

dishonour, I. v.tr. *dedecorare, dedecore afficĕre, polluĕre.* **II.** n. *ignominia;* see DISGRACE.

disinclination, n. *declinatio rei* (opp. *appetitio*), *fuga, animus alienus* or *aversus.* **disinclined,** adj. *ab alqā re alienus, alienatus, aversus.*

disingenuous, adj. see DISHONEST.

disinherit, v.tr. *exheredare, exheredem facĕre, hereditate excludĕre.*

disinter, v.tr. *effodĕre, eruĕre.*

disinterested, adj. *suae utilitatis immemor.* Adv. *gratuito, liberaliter.* **disinterestedness,** n. *liberalitas, abstinentia.*

disjoin, v.tr. *disjungĕre, sejungĕre.*

disjoint, v.tr. = cut up, *scindĕre,* (*dis*)*secare, concidere, membratim caedĕre.* **disjointed,** adj. *interruptus, haud continuus, haud bene compositus.* Adv. *incomposite.*

disk, n. *discus, orbis,* m.

dislike, v.tr. *improbare, aversari, fastidire.*

dislocate, v.tr. *luxare* (only in past part.). **dislocation,** n. by verb.

dislodge, v.tr. (*de*)*pellĕre, expellĕre, propellĕre.*

disloyal, adj. *perfidus, infidelis.* Adv. *perfide.* **disloyalty,** n. *perfidia, infidelitas;* to show —, *perfide agĕre.*

dismal, adj. *maestus, luctuosus, tristis, miser.* Adv. *maeste, luctuose, misere.*

dismantle, v.tr. *alqd nudare, retegĕre;* — fortifications, *diruĕre.*

dismast, v.tr. *malo* or *malis privare.*

dismay, I. n. *terror.* **II.** v.tr. *terrēre alqm;* see FRIGHTEN.

dismember, v.tr. see DISJOINT.

dismiss, v.tr. (*di*)*mittĕre, missum facĕre alqm;* see DISCHARGE. **dismissal,** n. (*di*)*missio,* (to vote for —, e.g. *senatus Caelium ab rempublicā removendum censuit*) ; of soldiers, *missio militum, exauctoratio;* see DISCHARGE.

dismount, v.intr. *descendĕre, desilire ex equo* or *equis.*

disobey, v.tr. *alci non parēre* or *oboedire, alci dicto audientem non esse.* **disobedient,** adj. *non parens, dicto non audiens, minus oboediens.* Adv. *non oboedienter.* **disobedience,** n. *contumacia.*

disoblige, v.tr. *alci morem non gerĕre.*

disorder, I. n. 1, *confusio;* **2,** = — of the mind, *animi commotio, perturbatio;* **3,** = moral —, *licentia;* **4,** = *disease, morbus.* **II.** v.tr. *(con)-turbare, perturbare, miscēre, confundēre.* **disordered,** adj. 1, of *body, aeger;* 2, of mind, *alienatus.* **disorderly,** adj. 1, = *confused, confusus, (con)turbatus, perplexus, incompositus, inordinatus;* **2,** = of *conduct, effrenatus, dissolutus, pravus, corruptus.*

disorganize, v.tr. *(dis)solvēre, resolvēre.* **disorganisation,** n. *dissolutio.*

disown, v.tr. — a *person's authority, detrectare alcjs imperium;* — as a *judge, alqm judicem recusare;* — a *debt, infitiari debitum.*

disparage, v.tr. *extenuare, elevare, parvi facēre, alci obtrectare.* **disparagement,** n. *obtrectatio.* **disparaging,** adj. *invidiosus.*

disparity, n. *dissimilitudo, diversitas, differentia.*

dispassionate, adj. *placidus, placatus, tranquillus.* Adv. *placide, placate, tranquille.*

dispatch, v.tr. see DESPATCH.

dispel, v.tr. *discutēre* (= to shake off), *dissipare* (e.g. *ordines pugnantium*), *(de)pellēre, dispellēre, (dis)solvēre, resolvēre;* — *fear, metum alci depellēre.*

dispense, v.tr. 1, = *distribute, distribuēre, dividēre;* 2, — *with, (di)mittēre* (= get rid of), *alqd re carēre* (= be without). **dispensation,** n. *venia* (= pardon).

disperse, I. v.tr. *dis(j)icēre, dissipare, dispergēre, (dis)pellēre, fugare* (= put to flight). **II.** v.intr. *se dispergēre, dispergi, dilabi, discurrēre, diffugēre, effundi.* **dispersion,** n. *dissipatio, fuga.*

dispirit, v.tr. *animum alcjs affligēre or frangēre or infringēre.*

displace, v.tr. *loco suo movēre, transferre.*

display, I. v.tr. 1, *in conspectum dare, prae se ferre, proponēre, venditare, ostendēre, exhibēre;* **2,** = *do, agēre, facēre;* — *oneself, (se) praestare, se gerēre, or praebēre.* **II.** n. *ostentatio, venditatio.*

displease, v.tr. *alci displicēre, alqd habēre offensionis;* — *be displeased with, alci irasci.* **displeasure,** n. *offensio, ira, indignatio; without* —, *aequo animo.*

dispose, v.tr. 1, = *settle, statuēre, constituēre;* **2,** — of, *vendēre,* see SELL; *finire,* see FINISH; *alqd re uti,* see EMPLOY; *alqm interficēre,* see KILL. **disposal,** n. *institutio, ordinatio, arbitrium, potestas;* to *be at the* — of anyone, *penes alqm or ex alcjs arbitrio esse.* **disposed,** adj. *erga alqm animatus, ad alqd inclinatus, ad or in alqd propensus, ad alqd proclivis* (usu. in bad sense). **disposition,** n. 1, see DISPOSAL; 2, = *character, indoles, ingenium, mores, -um;* 3, = *frame* of mind, *voluntas, animi inclinatio, proclivitas.*

dispossess, v.tr. *de possessione dimovēre et de(j)icēre, possessione depellēre, deturbare.*

disproportion, n. *inaequalitas, dissimilitudo.* **disproportionate,** adj. *inaequalis, non aequalis, justo or solito major, impar.* Adv. *dissimiliter, justo or solito majus.*

disprove, v.tr. *refellēre, redarguēre.* **disproof,** n. *responsio* (= reply), *refutatio.*

dispute, I. v.tr. 1, *verbis contendēre, concertare, disputare, disceptare;* — about, *alqd in controversiam vocare or adducēre;* 2, = *quarrel, cum alqo rixari.* **II.** n. 1, *disputatio, contentio, controversia, concertatio, disceptatio;* 2, *rixa.*

disqualify, v.tr. 1, legal t.t. = make an

exception of, *excipēre;* **2,** = hinder, *alqm impedire or prohibēre ne or quominus, alci obesse.*

disquiet, n. *inquies, -etis, f., animi motus, -ūs, (animi) perturbatio.* **disquieted,** adj. *inquietus, anxius, sol(l)icitus.*

disquisition, n. *tractatio, oratio* (= speech), *scriptum* (= a writing).

disregard, I. n. 1, = neglect, *neglegentia;* 2, = disrespect, *contemptio;* to hold in —, *male de alqo opinari.* **II.** v.tr. *parvi, minimi facēre.* **disregardful,** adj. *alcjs rei neglegens, immemor.*

disrespect, n. *contemptio, despicientia;* comb. *contemptio et despicientia;* see DISREGARD. **disrespectful,** adj. *arrogans, insolens.*

dissatisfy, v.tr. *alci displicēre.* **dissatisfied,** adj. *tristis,* or by *alqd aegre ferre.* **dissatisfaction,** n. *molestia, taedium, indignatio, ira.*

dissect, v.tr. *(dis)secare.* **dissection,** n. *anatomia or anatomice* (late).

dissemble, v.tr. *(dis)simulare.* **dissembler,** n. *rei simulator ac dissimulator.*

disseminate, v.tr. *spargēre, dispergēre, jacēre, differre, serēre.* **dissemination,** n. use verb or *rumor* (e.g. the — of a report was great, *rumor percrebuit).*

dissension, n. *discordia;* see DISCORD.

dissent, I. v.intr. *ab alqo dissentire.* **II.** n. *dissensio.* **dissentient,** or **dissenter,** *qui ab alqo dissentit.*

disservice, n. *detrimentum, injuria.*

dissever, v.tr. *sejungēre, secernēre, segregare.*

dissimilar, adj. *dissimilis, diversus, diversi generis.* **dissimilitude,** n. *dissimilitudo.* **dissimulation,** n. *dissimulatio;* see DISSEMBLE.

dissipate, v.tr. *dissipare;* see DISPERSE. **dissipated,** adj. *effusus, pravus, dissolutus, luxuriosus, ad luxuriam effusus, libidinosus.* **dissipation,** n. *luxuria, licentia, pravitas.*

dissolve, v.tr. 1, = melt, *liquefacēre, liquari, (dis)solvēre, (re)solvēre, diluēre;* 2, = break up, *(dis)solvēre, di(s)jungēre.* **dissolute,** see DISSIPATED. **dissolution,** 1, *liquefactio;* 2, *dissolutio, dissipatio.* **dissoluteness,** n. *mores dissoluti, pravi,* etc.

dissonant, adj. *absōnus.* **dissonance,** n. *vox absōna.*

dissuade, v.tr. *dissuadēre alqd or de alqâ re, dehortari alqm ab alqâ re, deterrēre alqm ab alqâ re,* or with *ne, quin, quominus.* **dissuasion,** n. *dissuasio.*

dissyllable, n. *disyllăbus.*

distaff, n. *colus, f.*

distance, I. n. 1, of space, *spatium, distantia, intervallum, longinquitas;* at a *long* —, *longo spatio or intervallo interjecto;* 2, of time, *spatium, intervallum;* 3, fig. of manner, *superbia* (= pride). **II.** v.tr. *alqm superare;* see SURPASS. **distant,** adj. 1, *remotus, longinquus;* to be —, *distare, abesse ab;* to be far —, *distare longo intervallo or procul disjunctum esse ab;* he is far —, *longe abest;* 2, *praeteritus;* 3, = proud, *superbus.* Adv. *procul, superbe.*

distaste, n. *animus alienus, stomachus, taedium.* **distasteful,** adj. *molestus, injucundus, ingratus.* Adv. *moleste, injucunde, ingrate.*

distemper, n. see DISEASE.

distend, v.tr. *refercire* (= stuff full). **distention,** n. *distentio,* or by verb (e.g. *stomachus refertus).*

distil, I. v.tr. 1, = make by distillation,

(de)coquĕre ; 2, = pour out by drops, stillare.
II. v.intr. stillare. **distillation,** n. by verb.
distiller, n. qui alqd (de)coquit.

distinct, adj. 1, = separate, distinctus, separatus, di(s)junctus ; 2, = clear, distinctus, clarus, perspicuus. Adv. separatim, distincte, clare, perspicue. **distinction,** n. 1, = act of distinguishing, distinctio ; to draw a — between two things, aliud — aliud esse velle ; see DIFFERENCE ; 2, = rank, etc., honor, dignitas ; man of —, vir illustris or clarus ; a mark of —, insigne. **distinctive,** adj. proprius. Adv. proprie. **distinctiveness,** n. perspicuitas. **distinguish,** v.tr. 1, see DISCERN ; — between, (inter) alqas res dijudicare ; 2, = honour, alqm (alqâ re) ornare ; — oneself, gloriam adipisci. **distinguished,** adj. insignis, clarus, nobilis, eximius ; a — man, vir omnibus rebus ornatus or praecellens.

distort, v.tr. 1, detorquĕre, distorquĕre (e.g. oculos) ; 2, in pejus detorquĕre, vertĕre.

distract, v.tr. 1, = turn the attention, alqm (in plura studia, etc.) distrahĕre, distinĕre ; 2, in a bad sense, alqm (con)turbare, perturbare. **distracted,** adj. (con)turbatus, perturbatus, mente turbatâ. Adv. raptim atque turbate, or by adj. amens. **distraction,** n. 1, = interruption, impedimentum ; 2, = want of attention, animi conturbatio, incuria (= carelessness), neglegentia.

distrain, v.tr. in possessionem rerum debitoris mitti (Jct.), bona alcjs venum distrahĕre (Jct.), bona vendĕre. **distraint,** n. bonorum venditio (Jct.).

distress, I. v.tr. angĕre, vexare, urĕre, (dis)cruciare. II. n. 1, anxietas, timor, nimia cura ; 2, = poverty, res angustae, angustiae ; 3, = danger, periculum ; to be in —, laborare, in periculo versari ; 4, = DISTRAINT. **distressed,** adj. anxius, sol(l)icitus ; — in mind, anxius animo ; — circumstances, res afflictae or angustae. **distressing,** adj. gravis, acerbus. Adv. graviter, acerbe.

distribute, v.tr. distribuĕre, metiri, partiri, dispertire, dividĕre, (e)largiri, dispendĕre (=place here and there), assignare, describĕre. **distribution,** n. partitio, distributio, assignatio (of land), descriptio, largitio.

district, n. ager, regio, terra.

distrust, n. diffidentia (— in, alcjs rei), parva fides, suspicio. **distrustful,** adj. suspiciosus, diffidens, diffisus. Adv. diffidenter, suspiciose.

disturb, v.tr. (con)turbare, perturbare. **disturbance,** n. turbatio, tumultus, -ûs, motus, -ûs. **disturber,** n. turbator.

disunion, n. dissensio, discidium, discordia ; — in the State, civiles dissensiones ; to excite —, commovēre. **disunite,** v.tr. sejungĕre, secernĕre, disjungĕre, dissociare.

disuse, v.tr. dedocēre alqm alqd ; — yourself to, dediscĕre alqd, consuetudinem rei minuĕre.

ditch, n. fossa, incile. **ditcher,** n. fossor.

dithyrambic, adj. dithyrambicus.

ditty, n. carmen, cantus, -ûs.

diurnal, adj. cot(t)idianus (quot.), diurnus.

dive, v.intr. 1, urinari, se (de)mergĕre, (de)mergi, submergi ; — under, alqâ re or in alqd or in alqâ re sub alqd ; 2, — into, = examine, alqd explorare, investigare, cognoscĕre ; = read in parts, librum strictim attingĕre. **diver,** n. urinator.

diverge, v.intr. 1, lit. discedĕre, digredi ; of roads, in diversas partes ferre : 2, fig. ab alqo

discrepare, dissentire ; see DIFFER. **diver gence,** n. 1, declinatio ; 2, dissensio.

diverse, adj. diversus, dispar, impar, dissimilis. Adv. diverse, dissimiliter. **diversion,** n. 1, derivatio ; 2, avocatio ; 3, delectatio, oblectatio, voluptas, oblectamentum. **diversify,** v.tr. variare, distinguĕre. **diversity,** n. diversitas, discrepantia, dissensio. **divert,** v.tr. 1, a river, avertĕre, derivare ; 2, = lead aside, avocare, sevocare, distinĕre, diducĕre, flectĕre ; 3, = to amuse, delectare, oblectare. **diverting,** adj. jucundus, jocosus.

divest, v.tr. alqm exuĕre, alqm alqâ re nudare, detegĕre.

divide, I. v.tr. dividĕre, partiri, dispertire, dispertiri, distribuĕre, describĕre. II. v.intr. 1, dividi, discedĕre ; 2, of opinion, in contrarias sententias distrahi ; 3, = vote, in sententiam alcjs (pedibus) ire, in sententiam alcjs discedĕre. **dividend,** n. = interest, usura, foenus, -oris, n. **division,** n. 1, partitio, divisio ; 2, = a large part of an army, legio ; 3, = a part, pars, portio. **divisible,** adj. quod dividi potest.

divine, I. adj. 1, divinus, caelestis ; by — inspiration, divinitus ; to honour as —, alqm divino honore colĕre, alci divinos honores habēre ; 2, fig. praestans, eximius, pulcherrimus. Adv. divine, divinitus, eximie, pulcherrime. II. n. sacerdos, * clericus. III. v.tr. 1, lit. divinare, praesagire, praedicĕre, vaticinari, (h)ariolari ; 2, fig. praecipĕre, praesentire, conjecturâ consequi, conjectare. **divination,** n. 1, divinatio, vaticinatio, auguratio (= — by birds) ; the substance or result of —, vaticinium, oraculum ; to tell by —, divinare (= to divine), vaticinari (= to prophesy), (h)ariolari (= to tell fortunes), futura divinare ; 2, = conjecture, conjectura. **diviner,** n. vaticinator, vates, (h)ariolus. **divinity,** n. divinitas, natura divina, vis divina.

divorce, I. n. divortium, discidium (= separ ation), diffarreatio (= eating apart, opp. confarreatio), repudium (= putting away). II. v.tr. as the act of the man, divortium facĕre cum uxore, repudium remittĕre uxori, uxorem repudiare ; claves uxori adimĕre ; the woman was said divortium facĕre cum marito, repudiare virum, discedĕre a viro.

divulge, v.tr. (di)vulgare, in medium proferre, declarare, aperire.

dizzy, adj. vertiginosus ; a — height, immensa altitudo. **dizziness,** n. vertigo.

do, v.tr. facĕre (I fall at thy feet and beg, which I cannot — without the greatest pain, supplex te rogo, quod sine summo dolore facĕre non possum), agĕre, gerĕre, administrare ; to — too much, modum excedĕre in re ; I — not know what I shall —, quid agam or faciam nescio ; what have you to — here ? quid tibi hic negotii est ? to be done for, de re actum esse ; to — again, reficĕre, redintegrare, repetĕre, iterare ; — away with, see ABOLISH, KILL. **doer,** n. auctor.

docile, adj. docilis. Adv. dociliter. **docility,** n. docilitas.

dock, I. n. navale, or navalia, -ium. II. v.tr. = cut short, praecidĕre.

doctor, I. n. medicus. II. v.tr. alci mederi, alqm curare.

doctrine, n. = instruction, doctrina, institutio, praeceptum. **doctrinal,** adj. quod ad doctrinam pertinet.

document, n. lit(t)erae, tabulae.

dodge, I. v.tr. alqm huc illuc trahĕre, cir cumvenire, illudĕre. II. n. = trick, dolus.

doe, n. dama femina.

doff, v.tr. *exuĕre.*

dog, I. n. *canis;* a young —, *catulus;* of a —, *caninus;* to go to the —s, *pessum ire, corrumpi;* go to the —s! *ad malam crucem.* **II.** v.tr. *indagare, investigare.* **dogged,** adj. 1, (= sullen), *morosus, acerbus;* 2, (= determined), *constans, perseverans.* Adv. *morose, acerbe, constanter, perseveranter.* **doggedness,** n. *morositas; perseverantia.*

doggerel, n. *versus inculti.*

dogma, n. *dogma, placitum, scitum, praeceptum, institutum, sententia, judicium;* it is a — of the Stoics that all sins are alike, *placet Stoicis omnia peccata esse paria.* **dogmatical,** adj. 1, theol. t.t. **dogmaticus;* 2, =assertive, (con)-*fidens.* Adv. **dogmatice, (con)fidenter.*

doings, n. see ACTION.

dole, I. n. *stips,* see ALMS. **II. v. tr.** *demetiri, dividĕre, distribuĕre.* **doleful,** adj. *tristis, maestus.* Adv. *maeste.* **dolefulness,** n. *tristitia, maeror.*

doll, n. *pupa* (Pers.).

dollar, n. **thalĕrus.*

dolphin, n. *delphīnus.*

dolt, n. *stipes, -ītis,* m., *caudex (codex), homo rusticus, baro.* **doltish,** adj. *rusticus, stultus;* — conduct, *rusticitas.* Adv. *rustice, stulte.*

domain, n. *ager publicus, possessio.*

dome, n. *tholus* (= cupola).

domestic, I. adj. 1, *domesticus, familiaris, privatus;* 2, opp. to foreign, *intestinus, domesticus.* **II.** n. *servus, minister, serva, ministra.* **domesticate,** v.tr. see TAME.

dominion, n. 1, *potestas* (= civil authority), *jus, juris,* n. (= legal authority); *imperium* (= supreme power), *dicio, principatus, -ūs, regnum, dominatio, dominatus, -ūs* (= lordship), *tyrannis, -idis,* f. (τυραννίς, = usurped dominion in a free state); 2, = realm, *regnum.* **dominate,** v.tr. *dominari;* — over, *in algos.* **dominant,** adj. *summus, maximus, praecipuus* (= chief). **domination,** n. *dominatio;* see DOMINION. **domineering,** adj. *imperiosus, superbus.* **domineer,** v.intr. *ex arbitrio imperare.*

donation, n. *donum;* see GIFT.

doom, I. n. 1, = fate, *fatum, sors;* 2, = judgment, *judicis sententia, judicium.* **II.** v.tr. *damnare;* see CONDEMN, DESTINE. **doomsday,** n. *extremum judicium.*

door, n. *ostium, janua, fores, -um,* f., *valvae* (= folding-doors), *limen* (= threshold); to bolt the —, *ostio pessulum obdĕre;* to open a — to wickedness, *patefacĕre alci fenestram ad nequitiam.* **doorpost,** n. *postis,* m. **doorkeeper,** n. *janitor, janitrix,* f.

dormant, adj. *mortuus;* to be —, *jacĕre.*

dormitory, n. *cubiculum.*

dormouse, n. *glis, gliris,* m.

dose, I. n. *potio;* to take a —, *medicamentum sumĕre* or *accipĕre.* **II.** v.tr. *alci medicamentum dare.*

dot, I. n. *punctum.* **II.** v.tr. *pungĕre.*

dote, v.intr. *delirare;* — on, *perdite amare.* **dotage,** n. *senectus, -ūtis,* f. **dotard,** n. *senex,* fixing sense by context (e.g. *stultus*).

double, I. adj. 1, *duplex* (= twofold), *duplus* (in gen.), *geminus, geminatus* (= twins, double in nature), *bipartitus* (= having two parts), *anceps* (= two-headed, doubtful); 2, see TREACHEROUS. **II.** v.tr. 1, *duplicare;* 2, = sail round, *algd flectĕre, circumvehi;* 3, =

turn, *se flectĕre.* Adv. *bis, dupliciter, per fide, perfidiose.* **double-dyed,** adj. 1, lit. *bis tinctus;* 2, fig. use superl. (e.g a — villain, *homo sceleratissimus*). **double-faced,** adj. see DECEITFUL. **double mind,** n. *ambiguum ingenium.* **double sense,** n. *ambiguitas;* of —, *anceps, ambiguus, dubius.* **double-tongued,** adj. *bilinguis* (lit. and fig.). **doublet,** n. *tunica.*

doubt, I. n. *dubitatio (quin, ne, num, quidnam), scrupulus, difficultas, dubium,* (usu. after a prep., e.g. *in dubium vocare*); without —, *sine dubio, haud dubie, certe, non dubito quin* (with subj.); to be in —, *dubium esse, dubitare.* **II.** v.intr. *dubitare, dubium esse, in dubio esse* (to be doubtful), *animo* or *animi pendĕre; I* — whether, *dubito num; I* — not that, *non dubito quin.* **doubtful,** adj. 1, = doubting, *dubius, incertus;* 2, = open to doubt, *anceps, ambiguus, dubius, incertus.* Adv. *dubie, dubitanter, ambigue.* **doubtless,** adj. *sine dubio.*

dough, n. *farina.*

doughty, adj. *fortis.*

dove, n. *columba,* f. *columbus,* m. *palumbes, -is,* m. and f. **dove-cot,** n. *columbarium, turris.* **dovetail, I.** n. *securicula, subscus, -ūdis,* f. **II.** v.tr. *securiculd compingĕre.*

dower, n. *dos, dōtis,* f. **dowerless,** adj. *indotatus.*

down, I. prep. *de,* with abl. ; — the stream, *secundo flumine.* **II.** n. = grassy hill, *campus paul(l)o editus.* **downcast,** adj. *tristis, maestus.* **downfall,** n. *(oc)casus, -ūs, interitus, -ūs, exitium, ruina.* **downpour,** n. *imber, -bris,* m. **downright, I.** adj. 1, = altogether, *totus,* or *summus* (e.g. he is a — cheat, *totus e fraude factus est;* it is — folly, *summae stultitiae est*); 2, = straightforward, *simplex.* **II.** adv. *plane, prorsus, omnino, simpliciter.* **downwards,** adv. *desuper* (= from above), *deorsum;* in compounds by *de :* to go —, *descendĕre;* to bring —, *deferre, deducĕre.*

down, n. = plumage, *plumae;* on a plant, the chin, etc., *lanugo.* **downy,** adj. *plumeus, plumosus.*

doze, v.intr. *semisomnum esse;* dozing, *semisomnus.*

dozen, n. *duodecim.*

drab, adj. *ravus;* see BROWN.

drag, I. v.tr. *trahĕre, ducĕre, vehĕre;* — out, *educĕre;* see DRAW and PROTRACT. **II.** n. *sufflamen.*

dragon, n. *draco, serpens; anguis* (the constellation).

dragoon, I. n. *eques, -ītis,* m. **II.** v.tr. *dominari.*

drain, I. n. *fossa, incīle, cloaca, colliciae (colliquiae,* in fields, on roofs, etc.). **II.** v.tr. *siccare.*

drake, n. *anas mas;* see DUCK.

dram, n. 1, = a weight, *drachma;* 2, = — of liquor, *haustus, -ūs.*

drama, n. *fabula, drama, -ātis,* n. (late). **dramatic,** adj. *scaenicus;* the — art, *ars scaenica.* **dramatize,** v.tr. *ad scaenam componĕre* (Quint.).

draper, n. *qui pannos vendit.* **drapery,** n. 1 (as a business), *pannorum mercatura,* 2 (as hangings), *tapete;* 3, = cloth es, *vestitus, -ūs.*

draught, n. 1, = a drink, *haustus, -ūs;* 2, of air, *spiritus, -ūs.*

draw, I. v.tr. *trahĕre;* — a sword, *gladium e vaginā educĕre* (opp. *in vaginam recondĕre*), *gladium stringĕre;* with sword —n, *gladio stricto;* — a carriage, *currum vehĕre, ducĕre;* — out, *ex alqo loco educĕre, ab or ex alqo loco ducĕre* (persons, troops); — water, *ex puteo aquam trahĕre;* — wine, etc., *ex dolio promĕre, defundĕre;* — a line, *ducĕre lineam;* = to portray, *delineare, designare, describĕre* (always with an object, e.g. *delineare imagines*), *(de)pingĕre;* = to excite, *movēre* (e.g. *risum,* laughter, etc.); — a conclusion, *alqd concludĕre;* — a bill, *syngrapham conscribĕre;* — a lot, *sortem ducĕre;* — curtains, *velis alqd obtendĕre;* — aside, *alqm sevocare;* — down, 1, *deducĕre, elicĕre;* 2, = INCUR; — on, = entice, *pellicĕre;* — over, *in sententiam perducĕre;* — tight, *a(d)stringĕre;* — up, *scribĕre.* **II.** v.intr. — on or near, *accedĕre* = APPROACH; — back, *recedĕre, se recipĕre.* **draw-bridge,** n. use *pons,* m. **drawer,** n. 1 (of water), *aquarius;* 2, = chest of drawers, *armarium;* 3, = sketcher, *pictor.* **drawing,** n. *pictura, imago.* **drawing-room,** n. *atrium.*

drawl, v.intr. *in dicendo lentum esse.*

dray, n. *carrus, -ūs, carrum, vehiculum, plaustrum.*

dread, n. see FEAR.

dream, I. n. *somnium, species per somnum oblata* or *in quiete visa, visus, -ūs, nocturnus;* in a —, *per somnum;* someone appeared to me in a —, *imago alcjs in somnio mihi venit.* **II.** v.intr. *somniare, dormitare* (= to sleep away time); — of, *vidēre alqd in somnis* or *per somnum,* or *per quietem.* **dreamy,** adj. *somniculosus.*

dreary, adj. *tristis, miser, miserabilis, luctuosus, maestus.* Adv. *misere, miserabiliter, maeste.* **dreariness,** n. *tristitia, maestitia.*

dregs, n. 1, *faex;* 2, fig. the — of the population, *faex populi, sordes, -is, et faex urbis, infima plebs;* the — of the state, *sentina reipublicae.*

drench, v.tr. 1, = to give to drink, *alci potum praebēre;* 2, = to cover with water, *irrigare, madefacĕre.*

dress, I. n. *vestis, vestitus, -ūs, cultus, -ūs, ornatus, -ūs,* comb. *vestis atque ornatus;* to adopt the — of the Romans, *Romano habitu uti.* **II.** v.tr. 1, *vestire, veste tegĕre, veste induĕre alqm, vestem induĕre alci, veste alqm amicire;* 2, = prepare food, *(com)parare.* **III.** v.intr. *vestiri, amiciri alqā re.* **dressed,** adj. *indutus;* — in black, *sordidatus;* — white, *albatus.* **dressing-gown,** n. *vestis.* **dressing-room,** n. *cubiculum.* **dressing-table,** n. *mensa.*

dresser, n. 1, = table, *mensa;* 2, = of wool, *lanarius;* of plants, etc., *cultor.* **dressing,** n. med. t.t. *fomentum, cataplasma* (Plin.); (= the whole treatment) *curatio.*

drift, I. v.intr. *(de)ferri,* †*fluitare.* **II.** n. = tendency or aim, *consilium, ratio, propositum, ad quod spectat mens* or *animus;* what is the —? *quo spectat oratio?* what is your —? *quid vis?*

drill, I. v.tr. 1, = to bore, *perforare, terebrare;* 2, = to exercise, *exercēre* (e.g. *milites*), *militare;* *omni disciplinā militari erudire.* **II.** n. 1, *terebra;* 2, *exercitatio.*

drink, I. n. 1, = a drinking, *potio;* 2, = a draught, *potio, potus, -ūs.* **II.** v.tr. *bibĕre, potare, haurire* (=drink up), *sorbēre* (=suck in); — too much, *vino se obruĕre;* — in, *bibĕre;* — to, *alci alqd* or *salutem propinare.* **drinker,** n. *potor, potator* (=habitual —), *combibo, compōtor* (=a cup-companion). **drinking,** n. *potio;* in the act of —, *inter bibendum;* to be addicted to —, *vino indulgēre, deditum esse.* **drinking-bout,** n. *comissatio.*

drip, v.intr. *stillare.*

drive, I. v.tr. *agĕre, pellĕre* (= — by force); to — forward, *propellĕre* (e.g. *navem*); — from, *abigĕre ab* or *ex alqā re, exigĕre* (e) *re* (e.g. *domo, e civitate, hostem e campo*), *(ex)pellĕre alqm (de) re (domo, ex urbe, a patriā), depellĕre alqm re or de re (urbe, ex urbe, de provinciā), e(j)icĕre alqm (de) re (de fundo), exturbare ex re;* — hither and thither, *agitare (fluctibus agitari);* necessity —s, *necessitas urget* or *cogit alqm ut alqd faciat;* — too far, *modum excedĕre in re.* **II.** v.intr. 1, (in) *curru vehi;* 2, — at, *alqd petĕre;* 3, of the rain, *in alqm ferri.* **III.** n. 1, *gestatio;* to take a —, *curru vehi;* 2, = the approach to a house, *aditus, -ūs.* **driver,** n. = of a carriage, *raedarius, -ūs.* **driver,** n. = of a carriage, *raedarius, auriga;* of animals, *agitator;* a donkey —, *asinarius.*

drivel, v.intr. 1, lit. *salivare, salivam fluĕre pati;* 2, fig. *ineptire, nugari.* **II.** n. 1, *saliva;* 2, *nugae, ineptiae.*

drizzle, v.intr. *leniter pluĕre;* it —s, *rorat.*

droll, adj. *lepidus, jocularis, ridiculus.* Adv. *lepide, ridicule.* **drollery,** n. *lepor (lepos), ludus, jocus, nugae, tricae, ineptiae.*

dromedary, n. *(camelus) dromas, -ădis,* m.

drone, n. *fucus.* **droning,** n. *bombus.*

droop, I. v.tr. *demittĕre,* †*inclinare.* **II.** v.intr. 1, lit. *demitti;* 2, = fade, *languēre, languescĕre, flaccescĕre;* 3, = fail, *animo concidĕre, affligi.*

drop, I. n. *gutta, stilla;* not a —, *ne minimum quidem.* **II.** v.intr. 1, *lippire* (= — from the eyes), *(de)stillare de re;* — with, *stillare re* (e.g. *sanguine*), *madefactum esse re;* 2, see FALL. **III.** v.tr. 1, = let fall, *alqd de(j)icĕre, (manu) emittĕre, demittĕre;* 2, = cease, *alqd omittĕre, dimittĕre.*

dropsy, n. *aqua intercus, -ūtis, hydrops.* **dropsical,** adj. *hydropicus.*

dross, n. 1, = slag, *scoria;* 2, = rust, *robigo, aerugo* (= — of copper), *ferrugo* (= — of iron); 3, fig. *faex, sentina.*

drought, n. *caelum siccum, siccitas, siccitates, -um.*

drove, n. *grex, armenta, -orum.* **drover,** n. *pecuarius, armentarius, bubulcus.*

drown, I. v.tr. 1, *(de)mergĕre in aquam, summergĕre* (esp. in pass. part. *summersus), aquā suffocare;* fig. *se in alqā ingurgitare;* 2, = overspread, *inundare;* 3, fig. by special verbs (e.g. — the memory of, *oblivisci* = forget).

drowsy, adj. *dormitans, somni plenus, somno gravis, oscitans* (= yawning). Adv., by adj. **drowsiness,** n. *somno affectum esse.*

drudge, I. n. *servus, verna,* m. and f. **II.** v.intr. *servire.* **drudgery,** n. *officium servile.*

drug, I. n. *medicamentum;* — poisonous —, *venenum.* **II.** v.tr. 1, = administer drugs, *alci medicamentum praebēre, dare;* 2, put a —, into, *medicamentum alci rei addĕre, (cum) alqd re miscēre.* **druggist,** n. *medicamentarius* (Plin.).

drum, n. *tympanum;* to beat the —, *tympanum pulsare.*

drunk, adj. *ebrius, bene potus, temulentus, vino gravis, crapulae plenus.* **drunkenness,** n. *ebriositas, vinolentia, ebrietas.* **drunkard,** n. *ebriosus, vinolentus.*

dry, I. adj. 1, *siccus, aridus* (= withered), *sitiens* (= thirsty), †*siticulosus, (ex)siccatus, torridus;* 2, fig. *exilis, frigidus, jejunus, aridus.* Adv. *sicce, jejune, exiliter, frigide.* **II.** v.tr. *(ex)siccare, arefacĕre, torrefacĕre;* — tears, *abstergēre lacrimas.* **III.** v.intr. *siccari, siccescĕre, (ex)arescĕre.* **dryness,** n. 1, *siccitas, ariditas, 2, jejunitas, exilitas.* **dry-nurse,** n *assa.*

dual, adj. gram. t.t. *dualis numerus.*

dubious, see DOUBTFUL.

duck, I. n. *anas, -ātis, f.;* as term of endearment, *deliciae, corculum;* to play —s and drakes with, *alqd pessum dare.* **II.** v.tr. **1,** under water, *alqd (sub)mergĕre, demergĕre in aquam;* **2,** the head, *caput demittĕre.* **III.** v.intr. **1,** *se (sub)mergĕre, (sub)mergi;* **2,** *caput demittĕre.* **ducking,** n. to get a —, *madidum esse, madefieri.*

ductile, adj. **1,** *ductilis* (Plin.), *flexibilis;* **2,** fig. *obsequens, facilis.* **ductility,** n. **1,** by adj.; **2,** *habilitas, facilitas.*

dudgeon, n. *ira;* in —, *iratus.*

due, I. adj. **1,** = owed, *debitus;* to be —, *debēri;* to pay money before it is —, *pecuniam repraesentare;* **2,** = fit, *ad alqm idoneus, congruens, alqo dignus, alci debitus.* **II.** n. **1,** *debitum;* **2,** = tax, *vectigal;* harbour —, *portorium.*

duel, n. *certamen.*

duet, n. *versus altex*

duke, n. * *dux.*

dulcimer, n. *sambuca.*

dull, I. v.tr. **1,** = blunt, *hebetare; obscurare* (anything bright); **2,** = astound, *(ob)stupefacĕre, obtundĕre.* **II.** adj. **1,** lit. *hebes;* **2,** fig. *obtusus, (ob)stupefactus, hebes;* **3,** = sluggish, stupid, *tardus, iners, frigidus;* **4,** = uninteresting, *aridus, jejunus.* Adv. *tarde, frigide; jejune, aride.* **dulness,** n. **1,** = — of mind, *obtusior animi acies* or *vigor, mens tarda, imbecillitas ingenii, ingenium hebes, ingenii tarditas, stupor;* **2,** = sluggishness, *inertia, segnitia;* **3,** of colour; see PALENESS.

dumb, adj. *mutus, elinguis* (lit. and fig.); to become —, *obmutescĕre* (lit. and fig.); to be —, i.e. silent, *tacēre.* **dumbfounder,** v.tr. *obstupefacĕre.* **dumbness,** n. use adj. or verb (e.g. — seizes me, *obmutesco*).

dun, I. adj. *fuscus, subfuscus.* **II.** v.tr. *alqm alqd flagitare, alqd ab algo exposcĕre.* **III.** n. *flagitator.*

dunce, n. *stipes, -ĭtis, m., truncus.*

dung, n. *stercus, -ŏris, n., fimus.* **dunghill,** n. *sterquilinium, fimetum* (Plin.).

dungeon, n. *carcer, -ĕris, m.*

dupe, I. n. *homo credulus, fatuus, ludibrium.* **II.** v.tr. *alqm ludibrio habēre;* see DECEIVE.

duplicate, n. *alqd eodem exemplo.*

duplicity, n. *ambiguitas, fraus;* see DECEIT.

durable, adj. **1,** *firmus, solidus, duraturus, stabilis;* **2,** of time, *diuturnus, longinquus, perpetuus.* Adv. *firme, solide, stabiliter, perpetuo.* **durability,** n. **1,** *firmitas, stabilitas, perennitas;* **2,** *diuturnitas, longinquitas, perpetuitas.* **duration,** n. *temporis spatium;* long —, *diuturnitas;* short —, *brevitas.* **during,** prep. per with accus. = throughout, *in* with abl. = time within which, *inter* with accus. (e.g. *inter cenam* = — dinner, or *inter cenandum*), abl. abs. (e.g. — the reign of Augustus, *Augusto imperatore*), *dum* with pres. indic., *cum* with indic. in primary, subj. in secondary tenses.

dusk, n. *crepusculum;* at —, *primo vespere, jam obscurā luce;* it grows —, *advesperascit.* **dusky,** adj. *fuscus;* see DARK.

dust, I. n. *pulvis, -ĕris, m.;* to raise the —, *pulverem movēre* or *excitare;* to lay the —, *p. sedare;* to throw — in the eyes, *verba alci dare.* **II.** v.tr. *alqd abstergĕre, detergĕre.* **duster,** n. *penicillum* (or *-us*). **dustman,** n. *qui purgamenta tollit.* **dusty,** adj. *pulverulentus, pulveris plenus.*

duty, n. **1,** *officium, debitum, pietas, religio,*

22 *

munus, -ĕris, n., *partes, -ium;* it is the — of, *est alcjs;* it is my —, *meum est;* a sense of —, *pietas erga alqm* or *alqd, religio;* **2,** = tax, *vectigal.* **dutiful, duteous,** adj. *pius erga alqm, alci oboediens, dicto audiens.* Adv. *pie, oboedienter.* **dutifulness,** n. *pietas erga alqm, oboedientia.*

dwarf, n. *nanus* (Juv.), *pumilio.* **dwarfish,** adj. *pusillus.*

dwell, v.intr. **1,** *habitare in loco, (in)colĕre locum, domicilium habēre in loco;* **2,** fig. — upon, *alqd longius prosequi.* **dwelling,** n. *domicilium, sedes, -is, f., habitatio, aedes, -is, f.*

dwindle, v.intr. *(con)tabescĕre, (de)minui, extenuari,* † *rarescĕre.*

dye, I. v.tr. *alqā re tingĕre; alqā re inficĕre, imbuĕre, colorare, inducĕre colorem alci rei;* — with blood, *cruentare, sanguine inficĕre;* — oneself with something, *se inficĕre alqā re* (e.g. with woad, *vitro*). **II.** n. color or verb; the blossom of the pomegranate is a —, *flos Punici mali tingendis vestibus idoneus.* **dyer,** n. *infector.*

dynasty, n. *domus regnatrix, imperium, regnum.*

dyspepsia, n. *cruditas.* **dyspeptic,** adj. *crudus.*

E.

each, I. adj. *singuli, omnis, quisque* only after its noun, *uterque* (of two); on — side, *utrimque;* — other, *alii alios,* or *inter se.* **II.** pron. *quisque* after noun, *unusquisque, uterque* (of two), by distributive adjs. (e.g. *unicuique bina jugera,* = two acres each); see EVERY.

eager, adj. **1,** for anything, *alcjs rei cupidus, avidus, studiosus;* **2,** = keen, *acer, ardens, fervidus.* Adv. *cupide, avide, studiose, acriter, fervide.* **eagerness,** n. **1,** *cupiditas, cupido, aviditas, studium, appetentia;* **2,** *ardor, impetus, -ūs, fervor, concitatio, aestus, -ūs.*

eagle, n. *aquila;* — eyed, *cui oculus acer.*

ear, n. **1,** part of the body, *auris;* attentive —s, *aures applicatae;* to box a person's —s, *colaphum* (with the fist), *alapam* (with the palm) *alci ducĕre* or *impingĕre;* to pull the —s, *aures vellĕre;* to be over head and —s in debt, *aere alieno demersum esse;* **2,** of corn, *spica, arista.*

earring, n. *aurium insigne, inaures, -ium, f.*

earl, n. * *comes.*

early, I. adj. **1,** *matutinus* (= in the morning), *maturus;* **2,** of plants, etc., too —, *immaturus,* † *praecox, praematurus;* from — youth, *(jam inde) a puero, ab initio aetatis.* **II.** Adv. *mane, primā luce, sub lucem, mature.*

earn, v.tr. **1,** *merēre* and *merēri;* — much money, *grandem pecuniam quaerĕre;* — by labour, *manu;* — your subsistence, *alqd re pecuniam sibi facĕre* or *colligĕre, quaestum facĕre;* **2,** fig. *(pro)merēre, (pro)merēri.* **earnings,** n. *quaestus, -ūs, lucrum* (= gain); to make — by bad means, *turpi quaestu victum parare* or *quaerĕre.*

earnest, adj. *gravis, serius* (usu. of things); to take in —, *rem in serium vertĕre.* Adv. *serio, ex animo, graviter.* **earnestness,** n. **1,** = zeal, *studium, contentio, diligentia;* **2,** = seriousness, *gravitas, severitas, diligentia.*

earth, I. n. **1,** = soil, *terra, solum;* **2,** = the globe, *terra, orbis terrarum, tellus, -ūris, f.* (mostly poet.). **II.** v.tr. = — up, *terram aggerare.* **earth-born,** adj. † *terrigena, terrae*

Illius. **earthen,** adj. *terrenus.* **earthenware,** n. *fictilia, -ium.* **earthly,** adj. *terrestris;* — *life, haec vita;* — *goods res externae;* — *happiness, voluptas (humana);* — *minded,* ♁ *rebus divinis alienus.* **earthquake,** n. *terrae motus, -ūs.* **earthwork,** n. *agger, -ēris,* m. **earth-worm,** n. *vermis,* m.

ease, I. n. 1, *tranquillitas, quies, -ētis,* f., *otium* (=leisure), *vita otiosa, pax;* to be at —, *quiescěre;* to take your —, *requiescěre, quieti se dare;* at —, *tranquillo animo;* 2, = readiness, *facilitas.* **II.** v.tr. *exonerare, laxare, (al)levare, sublevare, expedire.* **easiness,** n. *facilitas,* esp. of temper, for which also *indulgentia;* — of belief, *credulitas.* **easy,** adj. 1, *ad algd faciendum or factu, facilis, nullius negotii, expeditus;* 2, = affluent, *dives;* — circumstances, *res secundae;* 3, = tranquil, *tranquillus, quietus, placidus;* 4, of temper, *facilis, indulgens;* 5, of manners, *simplex, comis.* Adv. in gen. *facile, nullo negotio;* = tranquilly, *tranquille, quiete, placide;* of temper, *facile, indulgenter;* of manners, *simpliciter, comiter.*

east, n. *oriens, regio orientis* (as a district of the heavens), *orientis solis partes, -ium* (= the East). **eastward, eastern, easterly,** adj. *ad orientem vergens, in orientem spectans;* (as adverbs) *ad orientem versus, ad or in orientem, ad regionem orientis;* — nations, *Asiatici;* — land, *orientis terrae,* or *regiones.*

eat, I. v.tr. = to take food, *eděre, manducare* (= to chew), *comeděre* (= to eat up), *vesci algd re* (= to eat up as nutriment), *vorare* (= to swallow, particularly to swallow unmasticated), *gustare* (= to taste); to — anyone out of house and home, *algm sumptibus perděre;* to — away, *(e)roděre.* **II.** v.intr. to — well = taste, *jucunde sapěre.* **eatable,** adj. *esculentus.* **eatables,** n. *cibus* (= food), *cibi* (= meats, that is, several kinds of food), *esca* (= prepared food); *victus, -ūs* (= living, victuals). **eating-house,** n. *popina.*

eaves, n. *suggrunaa.* **eaves-dropper,** n. *qui algd subauscultat.*

ebb, I. n. *aestûs decessus, -ūs,* or *recessus, -ūs;* at —, *minuente aestu;* — and flood, *aestus maritimi accedentes et recedentes.* **II.** v.intr. *receděre;* — and flow, *affluěre et remeare.*

ebony, n. *(h)eběnus,* f. (or *ebenum*).

ebriety, n. *ebrietas, temulentia;* see DRUNK.

ebullition, n. 1, lit. use *effervescěre;* 2, fig. *aestus, -ūs;* — of anger, *ira effervescit.*

eccentric, adj. *inauditus, inusitatus, novus, mirus, insolens.* **eccentricity,** n. *quod mirum est,* etc.

ecclesiastical, adj. * *ecclesiasticus.*

echo, I. n. *imago vocis;* to give an —, *voci responděre, vocem redděre, remittěre;* a place which —es, *locus clamoribus repercussus.* **II.** v.intr. and tr. see "give an echo" above.

eclat, n. *laus, splendor, ostentatio.*

eclipse, I. n. *obscuratio, defectus (solis* etc.). **II.** v.tr. 1, *obscurare;* to be eclipsed, *obscurari, deficěre;* 2, fig. *algm superare;* see EXCEL.

eclogue, n. *ecloga* (late).

economy, n. 1, = house-management, *rei familiaris administratio, diligentia;* political —, *rei publicae administratio;* 2, = frugality, *parsimonia;* from —, *rei familiaris tuendae studio.* **economical,** adj. *attentus ad rem, frugi, diligens, parcus.* Adv. *diligenter, parce.* **economist,** n. 1, *qui rem suam bene administrat;* 2, = political —, *qui rei publicae opes investigat.*

ecstasy, n. 1, = elevation and abstraction of mind, *secessus, -ūs, mentis et animi a corpore, animus abstractus a corpore, mens sevocata a corpore; furor;* 2, = great delight, *summa voluptas.* **ecstatic,** adj. *mente incitatus, fanaticus, furens.* Adv. *per furorem.*

eddy, n. *vertex, vorago* (= whirlpool).

edge, n. 1, = a sharp line, *acies, labrum* (of a cup, etc.); 2, = margin, *margo,* m. and f., *ora, crepido* (of quays, etc.); 3, = — of a dress, † *limbus, clavus, fimbriae,* † *instita.*

edible, adj. *esculentus.*

edict, n. *edictum, decretum, consultum, jussum.* **edify,** v.tr. 1, lit. *aedificare;* 2, fig. *docěre, monēre.* **edifying,** adj. *ad bonos mores docendos aptus, idoneus;* see EXCELLENT.

edit, v.tr. *librum edēre.* **editor,** n. *editor.* **edition,** n. *editio.*

educate, v.tr. *alěre* (= to support), *instituěre, erudire, docēre* (= teach), *educare* (= bring up); to be well educated, *bene doctum et educatum esse, institutum esse.* **education,** n. *educatio, disciplina, doctrina, eruditio;* a man of good —, *homo (e)doctus, eruditus, homo bene doctus et educatus;* without —, *(politioris) humanitatis expers.* **educator,** n. *educator* (= one who brings up), *magister, magistra, praeceptor, praeceptrix.* **educational,** adj. *ad disciplinam,* etc., *pertinens.*

educe, v.tr. *protrahěre, producěre, educěre.*

eel, n. *anguilla.*

efface, v.tr. *delēre, (e)raděre.*

effect, I. n. 1, = consequence, *effectus, -ūs, eventus, -ūs, consecutio;* 2, = influence, *vis, effectus, -ūs, vis et effectus;* to have great —, *multum (apud algm) valēre;* without —, *frustra, nequi(c)quam;* 3, = purpose, to this —, *his verbis, hoc consilio;* 4, in —, *re (verā), reapse;* 5, —s, *res, rerum,* f., *bona, -orum.* **II.** v.tr. *efficěre, facěre, conficěre, perficěre.* **effective,** adj. *alcjs rei efficiens, valens, efficax,* or by verb *qui,* etc., *efficit.* Adv. *efficienter, prospere.* **efficacy,** n. *efficientia.*

effeminate, adj. *mollis, effeminatus, delicatus,* † *semivir, muliebris.* Adv. *molliter, effeminate, muliebriter.* **effeminacy,** n. *mollitia, mollities, vita delicata.*

effervesce, v.intr. *fervēre, effervescěre.* **effete,** adj. *effetus, obsoletus.*

effigy, n. *effigies, imago, simulacrum.*

efflux, n. *effluvium, profluvium.*

effort, n. *opera, labor, studium, contentio, conatus, -ūs;* to make an —, *operam dare, (e)niti.*

effrontery, n. *impudentia, os, oris,* n. (*impudens*).

effulgence, n. *splendor, fulgor.*

egg, n. *ovum;* a fresh —, *ovum recens;* to lay —s, *ova parěre, eděre, gigněre;* ycke of —, *vitellus;* white of —, *album or albumen ovi* (Cels. & Plin.); teach your grandmother to suck —, *sus Minervam, ut aiunt* (i.a. *docet*). **egg-shell,** n. *ovi putamen* (Plin.).

egoism, n. *sui ostentatio, jactatio* (= display); *sui amor* (= love of self). **egoist,** n. *qui sibi soli studet.* **egoistical,** adj. use n.

egregious, adj. *maximus, summus, mirus, singularis.* Adv. *maxime, summe, mirum in modum.*

egress, n. 1, = going out, *egressus, -ūs, exitus, -ūs;* 2, = place through which you go out, *exitus, egressus, effugium;* 3, = mouth of a river, *os, oris,* n., *ostium.*

eider-down, n. *plumae* (*anatum*) *mollissimae.*

eight, adj. *octo ; octoni, -ae, -a* (= eight each).
eighteen, adj. *duodeviginti.* **eighteenth,** adj. *duodevicesimus, octavus decimus.* **eighty,** adj. *octoginta, octogeni* (distrib.). **eightieth,** adj. *octogesimus.*

either, I. pron. *alteruter* (more rarely *uter*), *utervis, uterlibet* ; not —, *neuter* (fem. and neut. of all, *-ra, -rum*). **II.** conj. either... or, *aut... aut, vel ... vel, sive* (*seu*)... *sive* (*seu*), not either ... nor, *neque* (*nec*) ... *neque*(*nec*).

ejaculate, v.tr. *voces interruptas* (*et inconditas*) *mittĕre* or *edĕre.* **ejaculation,** n. *voces interruptae.*

eject, v.tr. *e*(*f*)*icĕre, emittĕre, extrudĕre.* **ejection,** n. *expulsio,* but more usu. by verb; legal t.t. *dejectio.*

eke, v.tr. to — out, *alci rei parcĕre.*

elaborate, I. v.tr. *conficĕre, perficĕre, expolire.* **II.** adj. *elaboratus, expolitus, exquisitus, accuratus.* Adv. *exquisite, accurate.* **elaboration,** n. use the verb.

elapse, v.intr. *transire, praeterire, peragi.*

elastic, adj. 1, lit. *qui* (*quae, quod*) *product potest ;* 2, fig. see HOPEFUL.

elated, adj. *alqá re elatus ;* to be —, *efferri.* **elat'on,** n. *gaudium* (= joy), *arrogantia, superbia* (= pride).

elbow, n. *cubitum.*

elder, I. adj. (*natu*) *major, superior, prior.* **II.** n. eccl. t.t. **presbyter.* **elderly,** adj. *aetate provectus.*

elect, I. v.tr. *creare, capĕre, legĕre, eligĕre,* comb. *eligĕre et creare, deligĕre, cooptare* (as a colleague), *designare, declarare ;* — into a premature vacancy, *sufficĕre.* **II.** adj. *designatus, suffectus* (= to an unexpected vacancy). **election,** n. 1, act of choice, *electio, suffragia, -orum* (= the votes) ; 2, a popular —, *comitia, -orum ;* to hold an —, *comitia habĕre ;* day of —, *dies comitialis ;* day of your —, *tua comitia.* **electioneering,** adj. *candidatorius.* **elective,** adj. *suffragiis creatus.* **elector,** n. *qui jus suffragii habet, suffragator* (= partisan).

elegant, adj. *elegans, venustus, bellus* (= graceful), *lautus, nitidus, comptus, mundus* (= neat), *urbanus* (= refined). Adv. *eleganter, venuste, belle, nitide, urbane.* **elegance,** n., *elegantia, urbanitas, venustas, munditia.*

elegy, n. *elegia, elĕgi.* **elegiac,** adj. *elegiacus* (late).

element, n. 1, = original material, *elementum, natura ;* the —s, *principia rerum e quibus omnia constant, primordia rerum ;* the four —s,*qua*(*t*)*uor elementa, initia rerum ;* 2, = a part, *membrum ;* 3 = the rudiments of knowledge, *elementa, -orum, rudimenta, -orum ;* 4, fig. to be in one's —, *alqá re familiariter uti ;* to be out of one's —, *in alqá re peregrinum ac hospitem esse.* **elementary,** adj. *primus* (e.g. — knowledge, *prima lit*(*t*)*erarum studia*) ; — school, *schola in quá lit*(*t*)*erarum elementa traduntur.*

elephant, n. *elephantus* (*elephas*).

elevate, v.tr. 1, = raise, (*at*)*tollĕre, extollĕre,* (*at*)*levare ;* 2, fig. *tollĕre, evehĕre ;* to be raised, *efferri.* **elevated,** adj. 1, of places, *editus, altus,* (*ex*)*celsus, praecelsus ;* 2, fig. (*ex*)*celsus.* **elevation,** n. = a raising, *elatio,* but usu. by verb ; fig. *elatio, magnitudo ;* — of character, *magnanimitas ;* = of the voice, *vocis contentio ;* = a rising ground, *locus editus* or *superior.*

eleven, adj. *undecim ;* — each, *undēni ;* — times, *undecie*(*n*)*s.* **eleventh,** adj. *undecimus.*

elf, n. see FAIRY.

elicit, v.tr. *elicĕre, eblandiri* (by coaxing), *extorquēre* (by force), *evocare* (to call or bring forth) ; to — tears, *lacrimas movēre alci.*

eligible, adj. *opportunus, idoneus ad alqd, dignus alqá re,* or *qui* with subj. Adv. *opportune, bene.* **eligibility,** n. *opportunitas* (e.g. *loci*) ; = — to office, *dignus qui eligatur.*

elixir, n. **elixir*(*ium*).

elk, n. *alces, -is,* f.

ell, n. *ulna* (= a cloth measure), *cubitum.*

elm, *ulmus,* f. ; of an —, *ulmeus.*

elocution, n. (*e*)*locutio* (= selection or words), *pronuntiatio* (= delivery) ; as an art, *elocutoria, elocutrix* (Quint.).

elongate, v.tr. see LENGTHEN.

elope, v.intr. *cum algo* or *alqá* (*pro*)*fugĕre, effugĕre.* **elopement,** n. *fuga.*

eloquence, n. *facultas* or *vis* or *copia dicendi, facundia, eloquentia.* **eloquent,** adj. *facundus, eloquens, copiosus, dicendi peritus, in dicendo exercitatus, in dicendo suavis et ornatus.* Adv. *copiose, ornate, facunde.*

else, I. adj. *alius.* **II.** adv. 1, = besides, *praeterea, praeter* (prep. with accus., e.g. nothing —, *praeter hoc nihil*) ; see EXCEPT ; 2, = otherwise, *aliter, alioqui*(*n*), *alio modo, aliá ratione ;* it could not — happen, *fieri non potuit quin ;* —where, *alibi.*

elucidate, v.tr. see EXPLAIN.

elude, v.intr. *alci* or *de* or (*e*) *alcjs manibus elabi, de alcjs manibus effugĕre, alcjs manibus evadĕre, alqm eludĕre,* (*e*)*vitare,* (*ef*)*fugĕre, declinare.* **elusive,** adj. *fallax.* Adv. *fallaciter.*

Elysium, n. *Elysium,* see PARADISE. **Elysian,** adj. *Elysius* (e.g. *campi, domus*).

emaciate, v.tr. *attenuare, macerare, enervare, exhaurire.* **emaciated,** adj. *maceratus, macer, enervatus, enervatus et exsanguis, enectus, effetus* (= exhausted, of soils). **emaciation,** n. *macies.*

emanate, v.intr. *emanare.* **emanation,** n. by verb.

emancipate, v.tr. *liberare re* or *a re ;* as slaves, etc., *manumittĕre, servitute liberare, servitio eximĕre, e servitute in libertatem restituĕre* or *vindicare.* **emancipation,** n. *liberatio ; =* — of slaves, *manumissio.* **emancipator,** n. *liberator.*

embalm, v.tr. *condire.*

embank, v.tr. *molem opponĕre fluctibus, flumen arcēre, coërcēre.* **embankment,** n. *agger, -ĕris,* m., *terra ad aggerem exstruendum congesta, moles, -is,* f.

embark, I. v.tr. *imponĕre in navem* or *naves.* **II.** v.intr. 1, lit. *conscendĕre* (*navem*) ; 2, fig. — upon, *consilium* or *rationem inire.*

embarrass, v.tr. 1, = disturb, (*con*)*turbare ;* 2, = hinder, *algm impedire, alci obstare, obesse, officĕre.* **embarrassed,** adj. *impeditus ;* — cir cumstances, see EMBARRASSMENT. **embarrassing,** adj. *difficilis, dubius, anceps.* **embarrassment,** n. *implicatio, perturbatio ; =* — of mind, *mens turbata ;* = pecuniary —, *rei familiaris implicatio, angustiae.*

embassy, n. 1, = the office of an ambassador, *legatio, legationis munus, -ĕris,* n. ; 2, = the persons sent, *legatio, legati, qui missi sunt ;* see AMBASSADOR.

embattled, adj. *instructus.*

embellish, v.tr. (*ad*)*ornare, exornare, alci decori* or *ornamento esse, excolĕre.* **embellishment,** n. *decus, -oris,* n., *ornamentum, insigne.*

embers, n. *cinis, -ĕris,* m., *favilla.*

embezzle, v.tr. *avertĕre, intervertĕre, inter-vertĕre ad seque transferre, intercipĕre, supprim-ĕre, retinĕre ac supprimĕre.* **embezzlement,** n. *peculatus, -ūs.* **embezzler,** n. *pecuniae aver-sor, interceptor.*

embitter, v.tr. *exasperare, infestum facĕre, exacerbare.* **embittered,** adj. *irā accensus, iratus, infensus, infestus.*

emblem, n. *imago, signum, simulacrum.* **em-blematic,** adj. *alqd significans,* or *referens.*

embody, v.tr. 1, = to enroll troops, *milites conscribĕre;* 2, = to join one thing to another, *adjungĕre, ad(j)icĕre; inserĕre* (= to plant in, e.g. *alqm familiae);* — in a society, *in societatem a(d)scribĕre, recipĕre;* — the young soldiers with the veterans, *tirones immiscēre veteribus militi-bus;* — a speech in a letter, *epistulae orationem includĕre.* **embodiment,** n. *imago, simula-crum* (= *imago*).

embolden, v.tr. *alci animum addĕre, alqm accendĕre, confirmare.*

emboss, v.tr. *caelare (alqd auro, argento,* also *in auro).* **embossed,** adj. *caelatus;* arti-ficer in — work, *caelator.*

embrace, I. v.tr. 1, *amplecti, amplexari, complecti;* 2, = contain, *comprehendĕre, com-plecti;* 3, = seize, *capĕre* (e.g. *occasionem), uti;* 4, = encircle, *complecti;* 5, — an opinion, *ad alcjs partes transire, sententiae assentiri.* **II.** n. *amplexus, -ūs, complexus, -ūs.*

embrocation, n. *fomentum.*

embroider, v.tr. *(acu) pingĕre, acu facĕre;* — with gold, *auro alqd distinguĕre.* **embroid-ery,** n. *ars acu pingendi;* a piece of —, *opus acu pictum* or *factum, pictura acu facta.*

embroil, v.tr. *implicare alqm re, alqm con-turbare.*

embryo, n. *partus, -ūs.*

emendation, n. *emendatio (et correctio).*

emerald, n. *smaragdus,* m. and f.; of —, *smaragdinus.*

emerge, v.intr. *emergĕre, ex(s)istĕre.* **em-ergency,** n. *casus, -ūs, discrimen.*

emetic, n. *vomitorius,* with n. (e.g. *bulbus).*

emigrant, n. *patriā* or *domo profugus, pa-triā extorris, advena, incola* (= foreign resident). **emigrate,** v.intr. *(e)migrare, demigrare ex loco in locum, transmigrare alqo* (e.g. *Veios), domo emigrare, solum (exsilii caus(s)ā) vertĕre.* **emi-gration,** n. *(e)migratio.*

eminent, adj. *insignis, praestans, clarus, nobilis, egregius, excellens, praecellens, eximius, singularis* (= sole of its kind), *summus.* Adv. *egregie, eximie, summe, praecipue, singulariter;* by superl. with *ex omnibus* or *omnium,* or posit. with *prae ceteris* (e.g. *ex omnibus optimus, prae ceteris bonus).* **eminence,** n. 1, of place, *locus editus, clivus* (= a hill), *tumulus* (= a mound); 2, = moral —, *praestantia, excellentia, summa gloria;* 3, = — of rank, *amplissimus gradus, -ūs.*

emissary, n. *emissarius, speculator.*

emit, v.tr. *(e)mittĕre, jacĕre.* **emission,** n. *(e)missio, jactus, -ūs.*

emollient, n. *malagma, -ătis* (Cels.).

emolument, n. *emolumentum, lucrum, quaes-tus, -ūs, fructus, -ūs.*

emotion, n. *animi motus, -ūs, commotio, concitatio;* a strong —, *animi perturbatio;* to be under —, *perturbatum esse.*

emperor, n. *imperator, Caesar, Augustus, princeps.* **empress,** n. *domina, Augusta, uxor imperatoria.*

emphasis, n. *emphasis* (Quint.), *vis;* with —, *cum vi;* to have —, *vim habēre, multum valēre;* to have more —, *plus gravitatis* or *auctoritatis ha-bēre;* without —, *jejunus, frigidus.* **emphatic,** adj. *gravis, vehemens.* Adv. *graviter, vehementer.*

empire, n. *imperium, potestas, dicio, princi-patus, -ūs, dominatio, dominatus, -ūs, regnum* (= monarchical despotism), *tyrannis, -idis,* f. (= power usurped in a free state).

empirical, adj. *in usu tantum et experimen-tis positus* (Cels.).

employ, v.tr. 1, = to engage in any work or office, *occupare, occupatum tenēre, detinēre; alqo* or *alqā re uti; alqd usurpare, adhibēre alqd* or *alqm ad alqd,* etc.; 2, = to spend in, or on, *in alqm* or *alqd insumĕre, ad alqd conferre, in* or *ad alqd impendĕre, in alqd* or *in alqā re consumĕre, in alqā re collocare, alqd alci rei tribuĕre.* **employment,** n. 1, act of —, *usus, -ūs, occupatio, tractatio, pertractatio;* 2, = business, *res, negotium, studium, cura.* **em-ployer,** n. *qui operas conducit.*

emporium, n. *emporium, forum rerum ven-alium.*

empower, v.tr. *alci alcjs rei faciendae potestatem facĕre, alci mandare ut,* etc.; to be empowered by, *mandata habēre ab alqo, alcjs nomine, alqo auctore facĕre alqd.*

empty, I. adj. 1, *inanis* (opp. *plenus* or *in-structus), nudus* (opp. *(ex)ornatus), vacuus;* 2, fig. *inanis, vanus, omnis eruditionis expers* (*atque ignarus), omnium rerum rudis* (the two last in regard to learning and culture); — words, *verba inania, voces inanes, sermo inanis, sermo vanus.* **II.** v.tr. *vacuefacĕre, exinanire, exonerare* (= — a cargo, etc.), *exhaurire, exsiccare;* — itself (of a river), *se effundĕre, in mare (in)fluĕre.* **emptiness,** n. 1, = empty space, *inanitas, inane vacuum, vacuitas;* 2, fig. *inanitas, vanitas.*

empyrean, n. *caelum,* †*igneae arces,* †*ae-therea domus,* †*ignifer aether.*

emulate, v.tr. *(con)certare, contendĕre cum alqo, aemulari alqm.* **emulation,** n. *studium, certamen, certatio, aemulatio.* **emulator,** n. *aemulus,* m., *aemula,* f. **emulous,** adj. *aemulus.* Adv. *certatim.*

enable, v.tr. *facultatem alci alcjs rei facien-dae dare.*

enact, v.tr. 1, of a deliberative body, *alqd sancire, sciscĕre, jubēre;* 2, in a wider sense, *jubēre, accus.* and infin.; *statuĕre, constituĕre,* infin. or *ut.* **enactment,** n. = law, *sanctio. lex, plebiscitum, senatusconsultum.*

enamoured, adj. see LOVE.

encamp, v.intr. *castra ponĕre.*

enchant, v.tr. 1, *(ef)fascinare* (= by the evil eye), *incantare* (= — by charms); 2, fig. *capĕre, rapĕre, delinire, permulcēre.* **enchantment,** n. *(ef)fascinatio, carmen.*

encircle, v.tr. see ENCLOSE.

enclose, v.tr. *concludĕre, includĕre in, cingĕre, saepire, continēre, circumdare alqd alci rei,* or *alqd alqā re;* to be enclosed by, *alqā re cingi, circumdari, continēri.* **enclosure,** n. 1, = act of —, *inclusio;* 2, = enclosed place, *saeptum, locus saeptus, saepimentum, cohors.*

encomium, n. *laus, laudatio;* to pronounce an — on, *alqm laudare, dicĕre de alcjs laudibus.*

encompass, v.tr. see ENCLOSE.

encore, v.tr. *revocare.* **encore!** interj. *revoco.*

encounter, I. n. *congressio, concursio, con-cursus, -ūs* (as soldiers in fight). **II.** v.tr. *inter se concurrĕre, (inter se) congredi, signa inter se conferre* (of armies); — a person, *concurrĕre* or *congredi cum alqo* (hostilely), *incidĕre in alqm* (= to meet by chance), *convenire*, *congredi cum alqo* (= to meet by design).

encourage, v.tr. *(ad)hortari, cohortari ad alqd* or with *ut,* (con)*firmare, excitare, impellĕre, alqm stimulare, alci stimulos admovēre;* — to concord, *concordiam suadēre.* **encouragement,** n. = act of —, *confirmatio,* (ad)*hortatio, cohortatio, impulsus, -ūs, hortamen(tum), incitamentum.*

encroach, v.intr. *alqd occupare, in alqd invadēre;* — on one's rights, *alqd de jure alcjs deminuĕre.* **encroachment,** n. as an act, *vis, violatio;* as a result, *injuria illata.*

encumber, v.tr. †*gravare, onerare, praegravare, impedire;* — with burdens, *onera alci imponĕre.* **encumbrance,** n. *onus, -ĕris,* n. (= load), *impedimentum, molestia.*

end, I. n. 1, = termination, *finis,* m. and f., *extremum, terminus* (= boundary), *exitus, -ūs, modus* (e.g. *nullus modus caedibus fuit,* there was no — to the slaughter), *clausula* (= the conclusion of a period, of a letter, etc.), *caput* (e.g. *capita funis), extremus* (e.g. *in extremā oratione,* in the — of the speech); at the —, *in extremo* (in space), *ad extremum* (= lastly), *denique;* to bring to an —, *finem alci rei afferre, alqd ad finem adducĕre* or *perducĕre, alqd absolvĕre, alqd transigĕre, perficĕre, conficĕre, consummare;* the war has come to an —, *debellatum est;* 2, = aim or object, *finis, consilium, propositum.* **II.** v.intr. *finem, exitum habēre, evenire, exire, terminari, finiri,* †*finire, desinĕre.* **III.** v.tr. *alqd finire, terminare;* — a speech, *finem facĕre orationis* or *dicendi;* — life, *vitam finire, vitam deponĕre, mortem sibi conscicĕre* (= by suicide); — a strife, *controversiam dirimĕre.* **ending,** n. *finis, terminatio, exitus, -ūs.* **endless,** adj. *infinitus, perpetuus, aeternus, sempiternus.* Adv. *infinīte, perpetuo, perpetuum.* **endlessness,** n. *quod finem non habet, perpetuitas.*

endanger, v.tr. *alqm in periculum, in discrimen adducĕre* or *vocare, periclitari.*

endear, v.tr. *alqm alci devincire.* **endearments,** n. *blanditiae.*

endeavour, I. n. *nisus, -ūs, contentio, opera, conatus, -ūs, studium;* — after honours, *honorum contentio, ambitio, ambitus, -ūs;* my — tends, *id ago, hoc specto ut,* etc. **II.** v.intr. (e)*niti, contendĕre,* comb. *eniti et contendĕre ut,* etc., *operam dare ut,* etc., *studēre, conari* (the two last with infin.).

endorse, v.tr. 1, *syngrapham inscribĕre;* 2, fig. see **Allow, Sanction. endorsement,** n. use verbs.

endow, v.tr. 1, = — a daughter, *alci dotem dare;* 2, in gen. *alqm alqā re* or *alci alqd donare, alqm re instruĕre, augēre, ornare.* **endowed,** adj. *ornatus, praeditus, instructus.* **endowment,** n. *donatio,* or any word = property, *res,* etc. ; see **Property.**

endue, v.tr. see **Endow.**

endure, v.tr. *ferre, sustinēre, tolerare, pati, perpeti,* comb. *ferre et perpeti, pati ac ferre, perpeti ac perferre.* **endurance,** n. *toleratio, tolerantia, perpessio,* comb. *perpessio et tolerantia.* **endurable,** adj. *tolerabilis, tolerandus, patibilis;* to make a thing —, *lenire, mitigare, levare* (*consuetudine levior fit labor*). **enduring,** adj. *perpetuus, perennis.*

enemy, n. *hostis* (= public —), *inimicus* (= private —); the —, *hostis,* sing. or pl.

energy, n. *vis, vigor, virtus, -ūtis,* f., *impetus, -ūs, contentio* (e.g. *vocis*). **energetic,** adj. *acer, strenuus, impiger, vehemens.* Adv. *acriter, strenue, impigre, vehementer.*

enervate, v.tr. *enervare, debilitare,* (e)*mollire, frangĕre.* **enervation,** n. *debilitatio.*

enfeeble, v.tr. see **Enervate.**

enforce, v.tr. 1, = — an argument, confirmare; 2, in gen. *vim alci rei dare* or *praebēre.*

enfranchise, v.tr. 1, *alci civitatem dare, alqm in civitatem* or *civitati* a(d)*scribĕre, in civitatem* a(d)*sciscĕre, accipĕre, recipĕre, civitate donare;* 2, = set free, *manumittĕre.* **enfranchisement,** n. 1, *civitas,* or *civitatis donatio;* 2, = setting free, *manumissio.*

engage, v.tr. 1, = to fight with, *confligĕre cum alqo;* 2, = to bind, *alqm obligare, obstringĕre;* 3, = to secure the services of, *alqm mercede conducĕre;* 4, = ask, *alqm invitare, excitare* (e.g. *ad saltandum*); 5, — in conversation, *alqm appellare* (= address); *sermonem cum alqo incipĕre, instituĕre, conferre, se sermoni intermiscĕre;* 6, = undertake, *spondēre, promittĕre, recipĕre* (accus. and infin.); 7, — in, = enter upon, *alqd ingredi, inire, obire, suscipĕre.* **engaged,** adj. 1, *occupatus;* 2, = — in marriage, *sponsus, pactus.* **engagement,** 1, = battle, *pugna, proelium;* 2, = pledge, *sponsio, stipulatio, pactum, pactio, conventus, -ūs* (= agreement), *promissum* (= promise); to keep an —, *fidem praestare, servare;* = — in marriage, *pactio nuptialis;* 3, = appointment, *constitutum,* or by verb; 4, = business, *occupatio, negotium.* **engaging,** adj. *suavis;* — manners, *mores urbani.* Adv. *suaviter.*

engender, v.tr. —, *gignĕre, generare,* (pro)*creare,* comb. *creare et gignĕre, gignĕre et procreare;* 2, fig. *facĕre, creare;* see **Cause, Produce.**

engine, n. *machina, machinatio, machinamentum, tormentum.* **engineer,** n. *faber* (= workman), *architectus, machinator, operum* (pub *licorum) curator.*

engrave, v.tr. 1, *scalpĕre, in alqā re* or *alci rei* (e.g. *auro*) *incidĕre* (e.g. *leges*); 2, fig. *in mentibus alqd insculpĕre.* **engraving,** n. as an art or work of art, *scalptura* (Plin.). **engraver,** n. *scalptor* (Plin.).

engross, v.tr. 1, = buy up, *coëmĕre;* 2, = to write in large letters, *magnis lit(t)eris scribĕre;* 3, = occupy, *alqm occupare, tenēre.*

engulf, v.tr. 1, *absorbēre,* (de)*vorare;* 2, fig. *absorbēre,* (ex)*haurire.*

enhance, v.tr. 1, = increase, *augēre, amplificare;* 2, fig. *augēre, amplificare, ornare, exaggerare.* **enhancement,** n. *accessio, amplificatio.*

enigma, n. *aenigma, -ātis* n., *ambages, -um;* you speak in —, *ambages narras.* **enigmatical,** adj. *obscurus, perplexus, ambiguus.* Adv. *ambigue, per ambages, perplexe.*

enjoin, v.tr. see **Command.**

enjoy, v.tr. *frui, gaudēre, uti re* (e.g. *prosperrimā valetudine), florēre re* (e.g. *justitiae famā), voluptatem capĕre* or *percipĕre ex re.* **enjoyment,** n. *gaudium, fructus, -ūs, usus, -ūs, voluptas, suavitas, oblectatio, delectatio.*

enkindle, v.tr. *accendĕre, incendĕre, inflammare* (scil. *animos, discordiam, odium,* etc.).

enlarge, v.tr. *amplificare, dilatare* (opp. *coartare,* e.g. *castra, aciem, imperium), proferre, prolatare* or *propagare* (= to extend, e.g. *imperii fines, imperium), augēre* (= to increase); — one's knowledge, *alqd addiscĕre;* — upon, *alqā re pluribus (verbis) disputare.* **enlargement,** n. *amplificatio, propagatio, prolatio, incrementum.*

enlighten, v.tr. 1, lit. *illustrare, illuminare;* 2, fig. *alqm docēre, erudire, fingĕre.* **enlightenment,** n. *humanitas, mens exculta* or *perpolita.*

enlist, I. v.tr. *milites conscribĕre, comparare, sacramento adigĕre, obligare, conquirĕre.* **II.** v.intr. *nomen dare, profitĕri, sacramentum dicĕre.*

enlistment, n. use verbs.

enliven, v.tr. *alqm (ex)hilarare, laetificare.*

enmity, n. *inimicitia, odium, simultas.*

ennoble, v.tr. 1, *alqm nobilium ordini a(d)scribĕre ; in the Roman sense, transitio fit a plebe ad patricios ;* 2, fig. *ornare, excolĕre, illustrare.*

ennui, n. *taedium.*

enormous, adj. *ingens, immanis, immensus, mirâ or incredibile magnitudine.* Adv. *praeter modum,* or by superl. of adj. (e.g. — high, *altissimus).* **enormity,** n. *res atrox* or *nefanda, scelus, -ĕris,* n., *facinus, -ŏris,* n.

enough, adj. *sat, satis* (e.g. *satis consilii), affatim ;* more than —, *abunde, satis superque ;* not —, *parum* (opp. *nimis) ;* but — ! *sed haec hactenus.*

enquire, v.tr. 1, see ASK ; 2, — *into, de alqâ re quaerĕre, in alqd, (de) alqâ re inquirĕre, alqd* or *de alqâ re cognoscĕre.* **enquiry,** n. 1, see QUESTION ; 2, legal t.t. *quaestio, inquisitio, cognitio ;* 3, = investigation, *inquisitio, investigatio ;* see ENQUIRE.

enrage, v.tr. *alcjs exasperare, inflammare, alqm lacessĕre ;* to be enraged, *furore incendi* or *inflammari.*

enrapture, v.tr. *alqm oblectare, capĕre.*

enrich, v.tr. *locupletare, locupletem facĕre, ditare, divitiis ornare.*

enrobe, v.tr. *induĕre alci vestem* or *alqm veste.*

enroll, v.tr. *inscribĕre, consignare ;* see ENLIST.

enshrine, v.tr. *dedicare* (lit.), *(con)secrare* (lit. and fig.).

ensign, n. 1, *signum (militare), vexillum ;* 2, an officer, *signifer, aquilifer, vexillarius.*

enslave, v.tr. *alqm in servitutem redigĕre, alci servitutem injungĕre, alqm servitute afficĕre.* **enslaved,** adj. *alci rei addictus ;* to be —, *alci rei (in)servire.*

ensnare, v.tr. 1, *illaqueare* (lit. late) ; fig. Hor.), *laqueo capĕre, irretire ;* 2, fig. *irretire, illicĕre, capĕre.*

entail, v.tr. 1, *terram heredi ita addicĕre ut nunquam alienari possit ;* 2, fig. see CAUSE.

entanglement, n. *implicatio.*

enter, I. v.intr. *introire, inire, ingredi ;* — a port, *in portum venire, invehi, deferri ;* — upon, *inire, suscipĕre ;* — into, *coire, facĕre* (e.g. *societatem) ;* — public life, *ad rempublicam accedĕre, remp. capessĕre ;* — an office, *munus inire, ingredi, capessĕre, suscipĕre.* **II.** v.tr. = — accounts, *in tabulas referre ;* — as paid, *alqd alci expensum (re)ferre.* **entrance,** n. 1, = act of —, *ingressio, introitus, -ūs ;* 2, = place of —, *aditus, -ūs, os, ostium, janua* (= gate), *limen* (= threshold), *introitus, -ūs ;* 3, = beginning, *initium ;* at — of spring, *primo vere.* **entry,** 1, see ENTRANCE ; 2, = — in accounts, *nomen* (e.g. *nomen in tabulas referre,* make an —).

enterprise, n. *inceptum, conatus, -ūs, conata, -orum, opus, -ĕris,* n., *facinus, -ŏris,* n. **enterprising,** adj. *acer, strenuus, impiger, audax.*

entertain, v.tr. 1, = to have, *habēre ;* 2, = to amuse, *delectare, oblectare ;* 3, = to give hospitality to, *hospitio accipĕre, recipĕre, excipĕre.* **entertainer,** n. *hospes, -ĭtis,* m. and f. **entertainment,** n. 1 = hospitality, *hospitium ;* 2, = banquet, *epulae, † daps* or *dapes, convivium ;* 3, see AMUSEMENT. **entertaining,** adj., see AMUSING.

enthusiasm, n. *inflammatio animi, mentis incitatio et permotio, mens incitata, aestus, -ūs,* or *fervor (ingenii), ardor (animi), furor divinus.* † *mens furibunda.* **enthusiast,** n. 1, = religious —, † *homo entheus, divino spiritu tactus, homo fanaticus ;* 2, = given to anything, *alci rei addictus, deditus.* **enthusiastic,** adj. 1, † *entheus, fanaticus, † furens ;* 2, *ardens, acer, vehemens.* Adv. *ardenter, acriter, vehementer.*

entice, v.tr. *allicĕre, illicĕre, pellicĕre.* **enticement,** n. *illecebrae.* **enticing,** adj. *blandus, dulcis* or pres. part. of verb. Adv. *blande.*

entire, adj. *totus, integer, solidus.* Adv. *omnino, plane, prorsus.* **entireness, entirety,** n. by *totus.*

entitle, v.tr. 1, = to name, *inscribĕre* (a writing) ; 2, = to give a title to, *jus* or *potestatem alqd faciendi dare ;* I am entitled to, *facĕre alqd possum, mel est alqd facĕre.*

entomb, v.tr. *humare.*

entrails, n. *intestina, -orum, viscera, -um, exta, -orum.*

entrap, v.tr. 1, *irretire* (= — by a net), *inescare* (= — by bait) ; 2, fig. *irretire, illicĕre.*

entreat, v.tr. *precari, rogare, orare, petĕre, supplicare ;* see ASK.

entrust, v.tr. *(con)credĕre, commendare et concredĕre, committĕre, permittĕre, mandare, commendare* (all with *alqd alci), deponĕre alqd apud alqm.*

entwine, v.tr. *innectĕre alqd alci rei, alqd alqâ re redimire.*

enumerate, v.tr. *(an)numerare, dinumerare, enumerare.* **enunciate,** v.tr. *edicĕre, indicare, pronuntiare, enuntiare.* **enunciation,** n. *enuntiatio.*

envelope, I. v.tr. *involvĕre, obducĕre.* **II.** n. *involucrum, integumentum.*

envenom, v.tr. 1, *alqd veneno imbuĕre ;* 2, fig. *alqm exasperare, exacerbare.* **envenomed,** adj. see SPITEFUL.

environ, v.tr. *circumdare, circumstare.* **environs,** n. *loca quae circumjacent alci loco, quae circum alqm locum sunt.*

envoy, n. *legatus ;* see AMBASSADOR.

envy, I. n. *invidia, livor, malignitas, obtrectatio, malevolentia.* **II.** v.tr. *invidēre alci ;* — something, *alci alqd invidēre* (e.g. *invidēre alci honorem ; nullius equidem invideo honori,* = I — no one's honour) ; I am envied, *invideor mihi, in invidiâ sum, invidiae sum.* **enviable,** adj. † *invidendus, fortunatus, beatus.* **envious,** adj. *invidus, lividus, malignus.* Adv. *cum invidiâ, maligne.*

ephemeral, adj. *unius diei, caducus, bvevis.*

epic, adj. *epicus, herŏus, herŏicus ;* — poem, *epos* (in nom. and accus. only).

Epicurean, n. 1, = a follower of Epicurus, *Epicurēus ;* 2, = a lover of pleasure, *homo delicatus* or *luxuriosus.*

epidemic, adj. and n. *morbus, pestilentia, lues, -is,* f.

epigram, n. *epigramma, -ătis,* n. **epigrammatic,** adj. *epigrammaticus* (late), *salsus.*

epilepsy, n. *morbus comitialis.*

epilogue, n. *epilŏgus.*

episcopal, adj. * episcopalis* (eccl.). **episcopacy,** n. *episcopatus, -ūs* (eccl.).

episode, n. *embolium, excursus, -ūs, digressio, digressus, -ūs* (= digression).

epistle, n. *epistula.* **epistolary,** adj. *lit(t)eris* or *per lit(t)eras.*

epitaph, n. *titulus, elogium.*

epithalamium, n. *epithalamium, carmen nuptiale.*

epithet, n. *epitheton* (Quint.).

epitome, n. *epitome, summarium* (Sen.). **epitomize,** v.tr. *epitomen facĕre.*

epoch, n. *tempus, -ŏris,* n., *tempestas, aetas, saeculum.*

equal, I. adj. *aequus, similis, geminus* (= twin), comb. *aequus et par, aequalis et par, par et aequalis, par et similis, par atque idem, par atque unus; —*to each other, *compar* (scil. † *connubium*), † *parilis, inter se aequales;* not —, *dispar, impar, dissimilis;* to divide into twelve — *parts, in duodecim partes aequaliter dividĕre;* — to doing anything, *ad alqd faciendum sufficiens.* Adv. *aeque, aequaliter, pariter.* **II.** n. *par.* **III.** v.tr. *alqd cum alqā re a(d)aequare, aequiparare* (more rarely with dat.). **equality,** n. *aequalitas, aequabilitas.* **equable,** adj. *aequus, aequabilis, aequalis sibi, constans* (sibi), *stabilis.* Adv. *aequo animo, aequabiliter, constanter, aequaliter.* **equability,** n. *constantia, aequus animus, aequabilitas, stabilitas.* **equalize,** v.tr. *alqm* or *alqd alci* (*rei*) (*ex*)*aequare, adaequare.*

equanimity, n. *aequus animus, aequitas animi, aequa mens, constantia.*

equator, n. *circulus aequinoctialis.*

equerry, n. *equiso, tribunus stabuli* (under the emperors).

equestrian, I. adj. *equester, equestris.* **II.** n. *eques, -itis.*

equiangular, adj. *angulis aequis* or *paribus.*

equidistant, adj. *pari intervallo, aequis* or *paribus intervallis distantes inter se.*

equiformity, n. *aequabilitas.*

equilateral, adj. *aequis* or *paribus lateribus.*

equilibrium, n. *aequilibrium* (Sen.); in —, *pari momento libratus.*

equinox, n. *aequinoctium.* **equinoctial,** adj. *aequinoctialis.*

equip, v.tr. *armare, instruĕre, ornare.* **equipment,** n. *arma, -orum, armatura instrumenta, -orum, navalia* (of ships).

equipoise, n. see EQUILIBRIUM.

equitable, adj. *aequus, justus, meritus* (= deserved); it is —, *aequus, par, jus, fas est* (with infin. or infin. and accus.). **equity,** n. *aequitas, aequum bonum, justitia, moderatio;* contrary to —, *contra fas, contra quam fas est, contra jus fasque.*

equivalent, adj. see EQUAL.

equivocal, adj. *aequivocus, ambiguus, anceps, dubius, dubius et quasi duplex.* **equivocation,** n. *ex ambiguo dictum, ambiguitas, amphibolia.* **equivocate,** v.intr. *tergiversari.*

era, n. *temporum ratio.*

eradicate, v.tr. *eradicare* (ante-class.), *ex-(s)tirpare, (e)vellĕre, extrahĕre, evellĕre et extrahĕre, eruĕre, delĕre, exstinguĕre, excidĕre, eradĕre, tollĕre.* **eradication,** n. *ex(s)tirpatio, ex(s)tinctio, excidium.*

erase, v.tr. *delĕre, inducĕre* (= to cover with the broad end of the stylus), (*e*)*radĕre.* **erasure,** n. *litura.*

ere, adv. *priusquam, ante quam;* see BEFORE.

erect, I. adj. (*e*)*rectus.* **II.** v.tr. *erigĕre* (= set straight up), *aedificare* (= build), *exstruĕre* (= raise). **erection,** n. **1,** as act, *aedificatio, ex(s)tructio;* **2,** = building, *aedificium.*

erotic, adj. *amatorius.*

err, v.intr. *errare, vagari, in errore versari, errore captum esse* (= to be in error), *falli* (= to be misled), *peccare* (= to sin). **error,** n. *error, erratum* (= a single act), *lapsus, -ūs* (= a slip or fall), *peccatum* (= a sin); to commit —, *errare, peccare.* **erratic,** adj. *inconstans.* **erroneous,** adj. *falsus.* Adv. *falso.* **erroneousness,** n. see ERROR.

errand, n. *mandatum;* an —*-boy, nuntius, tabellarius.*

erst, adv. *quondam, olim.*

erudite, adj. *lit(t)eratus, doctus, doctrinā instructus, eruditus, eruditione ornatus;* comb. *doctus atque eruditus.* **erudition,** n. *doctrina, eruditio.*

eruption, n. *eruptio* (e.g. *Ætnaeorum ignium*).

escape, I. v.tr. *alqd* (*ef*)*fugĕre, subterfugĕre* (secretly), *evadĕre ex alqā re, ab alqo, elabi ex alqā re;* — a danger, *periculum vitare, effugĕre;* it —s me, *me praeterit, me fugit alqd.* **II.** v.intr. (*ef*)*fugĕre, elabi, evadĕre.* **III.** n. *vitatio, devitatio, fuga, effugium.*

escarpment, n. *vallum.*

escheat, I. n. *hereditas caduca* (Jct.). **II.** v.intr. *caducum esse* (Jct.).

eschew, v.tr. *vitare;* see AVOID.

escort, I. n. *comitatus, -ūs;* under someone's —, *alqo comite* or *comitante, comitatu* or *cum comitatu alcjs, cum alqo, ab alqo deductus* (as mark of honour). **II.** v.tr. *alqm comitari, deducĕre, prosequi, alci* (*rei*) *praesidio esse* (as a defence).

esculent, adj. *esculentus.*

esoteric, adj. *arcanus, occultus.*

especial, adj. *praecipuus, maximus, summus;* he had an — *care for, nihil antiquius habuit quam ut.* Adv. *praesertim, praecipue, maxime, in primis* (*imprimis*), *summe.*

esplanade, n. *ambulatio.*

espouse, v.tr. **1,** see BETROTH; **2,** see MARRY; **3,** fig. see EMBRACE.

esquire, n. * armiger.*

essay, I. v.tr. *conari.* **II.** n. **1,** = an attempt, *experimentum, conatus, -ūs, conata, -orum;* **2,** = treatise, *libellus.* **essayist,** n. *scriptor.*

essence, n. *natura, vis, proprietas;* it is the — of affection, *amicitia vera est,* or *amicitiae* (*proprium*) *est.* **essential,** adj. *verus, primus, praecipuus, proprius, in alcjs rei naturā positus.* Adv. *reapse, vere, praecipue, imprimis, necessario;* to be — different, *ipsā rei naturā diversum esse.*

establish, v.tr. **1,** = to set up, *statuĕre, constituĕre;* **2,** = to make strong, *confirmare, stabilire;* **3,** = to prove, *probare, confirmare.* **establishment,** n. **1,** = act of —, *constitutio, conciliatio* (e.g. *gratiae*), *confirmatio;* **2,** = household, *familia.*

estate, n. **1,** = condition, *ratio, status, -ūs, habitus, -ūs, condicio, res, fortuna, sors;* **2,** = property, *res, fundus, praedium, ager, pos sessio.*

esteem, I. n. **1,** = opinion, *aestimatio, opinio, existimatio;* **2,** = reverence, *observantia* (shown outwardly); to feel —, *alqm verĕri.* **II.** v.tr. **1,** = think, *aestimare, existimare, putare, habēre;* **2,** = reverence, *alqm respicĕre, verēri, magni facĕre alqm;* to be esteemed, *magni haberi* (the genitives *maximi, minimi, nihili, pluris,* etc., may be employed). **estimable,** adj. *dignus alqā re,* or *qui* with subj., *laudatus, bonus, optimus, honestus, gravis, probus.*

estimate, I. n. **1,** = in money, *aestimatio,*

2, = judgment, *judicium, aestimatio.* **II.** v.tr. **1,** *alqd aestimare* (with genit. or abl. of price), *censēre;* 2, see ESTEEM. **estimation,** n. see ESTEEM.

estrange, v.tr. *(ab)alienare;* — from yourself, *alqm* or *alcjs voluntatem a se alienare, alienare sibi alcjs animum.* **estrangement,** n. *alienatio, discidium.*

estuary, n. *aestuarium.*

eternal, adj. *aeternus, sempiternus, immortalis, perpetuus;* — enmity, *odium inexpiabile.* Adv. *in aeternum, perpetuo, semper.* **eternity,** n. *aeternitas;* for —, *in aeternum, in perpetuum, in omne tempus.*

ether, n. *aether.* **ethereal,** adj. *aetherius (aethereus).*

ethics, n. *de moribus,* or *officiis, ethice* (Quint.). **ethical,** adj. *de moribus* or *officiis, quod ad mores pertinet, moralis* (invented by Cicero).

etiquette, n. *mos, moris,* m., *usus, -ūs.*

etymology, n. = derivation, *etymologia, etymologice, explicatio verborum.*

eucharist, n. ** eucharistia.*

eulogy, n. *laudatio, laus.* **eulogist,** n. *laudator.* **eulogize,** v.tr. *laudare.*

eunuch, n. *eunūchus.*

euphemism, n., **euphemistic,** adj. *ut bona de his loquar.*

euphony, n. *sonus, -ūs, dulcis* or *suavis.*

evacuate, v.tr. *(de)relinquēre locum, (de)-cedēre loco* or *de* or *ex loco, discedēre a loco* or *loco* or *ex loco, excedēre loco* or *ex loco;* to — a town (with troops), *ab alqo loco milites deducēre.*

evade, v.tr. *de* or *ex alcjs manibus elabi, de alcjs manibus effugēre, alcjs manibus* or *alci evadēre, alqm subterfugēre.* **evasion,** n. *ambages, -is,* f., usu. in pl., *tergiversatio.* **evasive,** adj. *ambiguus.* Adv. *ambigue.*

evangelist, n. ** evangelista.* **evangelical,** adj. ** evangelicus.*

evaporate, I. v.tr. *(e)vaporare, exhalare, ex(s)pirare.* **II.** v.intr. *(e)vaporari, exhalari, ex(s)pirari.* **evaporation,** n. *(e)vaporatio, exhalatio, ex(s)piratio.*

even, adj. *aequus, planus,* comb. *aequus et planus;* of temper, *aequus, aequabilis;* of numbers, par. Adv. *aequaliter, aequabiliter, pariter.* **evenness,** n. *aequalitas* (Plin.); — of temper, *aequus animus.*

even, adv. *etiam, vel* (esp. with superl. or single words), *adeo, ipse* (e.g. *ipsa amicitia);* not —, *ne ... quidem;* — now, *jam nunc.*

evening, I. n. *vesper, -ĕris,* or *-ĕri,* m. *tempus vespertinum, occasus, -ūs, solis* (= sunset); towards —, *ad* (*sub*) *vesperum, sub occasum solis;* in the —, *vesperi;* the — before, *pridie vesperi;* yesterday —, *heri vesperi;* good — ! *salve;* I wish good — to anyone, *salvēre alqm jubeo.* **II.** adj. *vespertinus;* — star, *Hesperus, Vesper.*

event, n. **1,** = issue, *eventus, -ūs, exitus -ūs;* **2,** = occurrence, *res (gesta), factum, casus, -ūs, eventus, -ūs.* **eventful,** adj. *memorabilis, ille* (e.g. *ille dies =* that — day), *magni* or *maximi momenti.*

ever, adv. **1,** = always, *semper, perpetuo;* the best is — the rarest, *optimum quidque rarissimum est;* **2,** = at any time, *umquam (unq), (ali)quando;* if —, *si quando;* — so great, *quantumvis* or *quamvis magnus;* for —, *in aeternum.*

everlasting, adj. see ETERNAL.

every, adj. *quisque, quique, quilibet, quivis, omnis;* — one, each separately, *unusquisque;* — five days there were two days for hunt-

ing, *binae venationes per dies quinque;* — day, etc., *singulis diebus, mensibus, annis,* also *quot diebus, mensibus, annis,* and *in singulas horas* or merely *in horas;* each of two, *uterque;* — person, — one, *nemo non* or *nemo est quin* or *nemo est qui non* (e.g. — one holds, *nemo est quin existimet);* — one knows, *nemo est qui nesciat;* — where, *ubique, ubivis, nusquam.*

evict, v.tr. *alqo loco (ex)pellĕre, de alqo loco detrudĕre, deturbare.* **eviction,** n. *evictio* (Jct.), or by verb.

evident, adj. *certus, manifestus, apertus, evidens, perspicuus;* it is —, *constat, certum est, liquet* (with accus. and infin.). Adv. *aperte, manifeste, perspicue, evidenter.* **evidence,** n. 1, legal t.t. *testimonium, indicium;* 2, in gen. *argumentum,* or by verb *probare.*

evil, I. adj. *malus, perversus, maleficus.* **II.** n. *malum, incommodum* (= inconvenience); to be in —, *in malis esse;* to suffer under some —, *laborare ex alqâ re* (e.g. *ex pedibus).* **evil-doer,** n. *maleficus.* **evil-speaking,** adj. *maledicus.*

evince, v.tr. *ostendĕre, probare, (e)vincĕre.*

evoke, v.tr. *evocare, elicĕre, excitare.*

evolve, v.tr. *evolvĕre, explicare.* **evolution,** n. **1,** = — of soldiers, *decursus, -ūs;* **2,** = — of nature, *rerum progressio.*

ewe, n. *ovis femina.*

ewer, n. *urceus, hydria, urna.*

exacerbate, v.tr. see EMBITTER.

exact, I. adj. *exactus, accuratus, expressus.* **II.** v.tr. *alqd ab alqo exigĕre, alci alqd* or *alqd ab alqo extorquĕre; alqd alci imperare.* Adv. *accurate;* — so, *ita plane,* or *prorsus.* **exacting,** adj. *rapax.* **exaction,** n. *exactio.* **exactitude, exactness,** n. *diligentia, accuratio* (rare).

exaggerate, v.tr. *verbis exaggerare, multiplicare verbis* (e.g. *copias), verbis augēre, in majus (verbis) extollĕre, in majus accipĕre.* **exaggeration,** n. *(nimia) amplificatio, veritatis superlatio, trajectio.*

exalt, v.tr. *augēre, majus reddĕre, verbis* or *laudibus efferre* or *extollĕre.* **exaltation,** n. *dignitatis accessio.* **exalted,** adj. *altus (ex)celsus;* of — position, *gradu amplissimo.*

examine, v.tr. *explorare, ponderare, inquirĕre, (per)scrutari.* **examination,** n. *scrutatio, inquisitio, probatio.* **examiner,** n. in gen. *investigator;* of a school, *qui quid profecerint pueri exquirit.*

example, n. *exemplum, exemplar, documentum;* to set an —, *exemplum praebēre.*

exasperate, v.tr. see EXASPERATE.

excavate, v.tr. *(ex)cavare, effodĕre.* **excavation,** n. *cavum.*

exceed, v.tr. *transgredi, excedĕre, transire fines* (lit. and fig.), *terminos egredi* (fig.), *modum egredi* or *excedĕre, ultra modum egredi.* **excess,** n. *intemperantia, licentia, luxuria.* **excessive,** adj. *nimius, immodicus, immoderatus.* Adv. *nimis, immodice, immoderate, praeter modum.*

excel, v.tr. *excellĕre (ingenio, virtute, animi magnitudine, dignitate,* also *in alqâ re), alqm in re (ex)superare, alci (in) alqâ re praestare.* **excellent,** adj. *excellens, praestans, egregius, bonus, optimus, laudatus, praecipuus.* Adv. *excellenter, egregie, bene, optime, praecipue, imprimis (in primis).* **excellence,** n. *excellentia, praestantia.*

except, I. v.tr. *excipĕre, eximĕre, excludĕre;* — from military service, *vacationem militiae alci dare;* not one excepted, *ad unum omnes* or *omnes ad unum.* **II. prep.** *praeter, extra,* accus. past partic. of *excipĕre* in abl. abs. (e.g. *te excepto*), nisi after a neg. (e.g. *nisi in te nullam spem habeo*). **exception,** n. *exceptio.* **exceptional,** adj. *rarus.* Adv. *praeter modum.*

exchange, I. v.tr. *(per)mutare; —* letters, *lit(t)eras dare et accipĕre.* **II.** n. 1, = changing, *(per)mutatio, vices* (= turns); 2, of money, *collybus;* 3, = the place of —, *forum, mensa publica.*

exchequer, n. *aerarium, fiscus.*

excite, v.tr. *excitare, concitare,* (com)*movēre; —* pity, etc., *misericordiam, seditionem, bellum mov.* or *com., conflare* (e.g. *bellum, alci invidiam); —* a controversy, *controversiam inferre.* **excitable,** adj. *iracundus, fervidus.* **excited,** adj. *commotus.* **excitement,** n. *concitatio, commotio, motus, -ūs.*

exclaim, v.tr. *exclamare, conclamare* (of several). **exclamation,** n. *exclamatio, acclamatio, vox.*

exclude, v.tr. *excludĕre, prohibēre,* (ab) *alqo loco arcēre.* **exclusion,** n. *exclusio* (rare), or by verb. **exclusive,** adj. = — in choice of acquaintance, *parum affabilis, qui rari aditus est; —* property, *quod alci proprium est.* Adv. by adj. *proprius.* **exclusiveness,** n. *rari aditus esse.*

excommunicate, v.tr. *sacrificiis interdicĕre alci, alqm *excommunicare.* **excommunication,** n. *sacrificiorum interdictio,* *excommunicatio.*

excrement, n. *excrementum, stercus, -ōris,* n. **excrescence,** n. *gibber, -ēris,* m. (Plin. = a hunch), *tuber, -ĕris,* m. (= protuberance).

excruciating, adj. *acerbissimus.*

exculpate, v.tr. *excusare,* (ex)*purgare; —* with someone, *alci* or *apud alqm excusare; —* yourself, *se excusare de re.* **exculpation,** n. *excusatio, purgatio.*

excursion, n. *iter, -ineris;* to make an —, *excurrĕre* (e.g. *rus*).

excuse, I. v.tr. 1, = ask for pardon, *veniam petĕre, rogare, se alci* or *apud alqm excusare,* (ex)*purgare;* 2, = grant pardon, *veniam alci dare, alci ignoscĕre.* **II.** n. 1, *excusatio;* 2, *venia;* 3, see PRETEXT. **excusable,** adj. *cui ignosci potest.*

execrate, v.tr. *exsecrari, detestari, abominari;* see CURSE. **execrable,** adj. see ABOMINABLE.

execute, v.tr. 1, = to carry into effect, *exsequi, persequi* (e.g. *alcjs mandata; —* a command, *imperium), efficĕre, perficĕre, ad effectum adducĕre;* 2, = to inflict punishment, *poenam capĕre* or *poenas exigĕre de alqo, supplicium de alqo sumĕre, necare.* **execution,** n. 1, *effectio,* or by verb; 2, *supplicium;* 3, = on goods, *bonorum venditio, emptio;* 4, = slaughter, *caedes, -is.* **executive,** n. *penes quos est administratio rerum.*

exegesis, n. *explanatio, interpretatio.*

exemplary, adj. see EXCELLENT; — punishment, *exemplum severitatis.*

exempt, I. v.tr. *excipĕre, eximĕre, immunem facĕre, vacationem dare, gratiam facĕre alci alcjs rei.* **II.** adj. (ab *alqā re) immunis, alqā re liber, solutus; —* from further service (of a soldier), *emeritus.* **exemption,** n. *immunitas, vacatio.*

exercise, I. v.tr. 1, = carry on, *exercēre, facĕre, agĕre, alqā re fungi;* 2, physically, *exercēre;* e.g. *se, milites,* etc.). **II.** n. 1, *munus, -ĕris,* n.; 2, *exercitatio;* 3, = theme, *thema, -ātis* (Quint.).

exert, v.tr. 1, *contendĕre, intendĕre; —* yourself. (*con)niti, eniti, conari;* 2, see USE, EMPLOY.

EXERCISE. exertion, n. *contentio, intentio, conatus, -ūs.*

exhale, v.tr. *exhalare;* odours are exhaled, *odores (e floribus) afflantur;* see EVAPORATE. **exhalation,** n. *exhalatio.*

exhaust, v.tr. *exhaurire* (lit. and fig.), *conficĕre.* **exhausted,** adj. see WEARY. **exhaustion,** n. see FATIGUE.

exhibit, v.tr. 1, *proponĕre, ante oculos ponĕre, edĕre, celebrare;* 2, = manifest, *praebēre.* **exhibition,** n. 1, = act of —, by verb; 2, = show, *spectaculum, ludi.*

exhilarate, v.tr. (ex)*hilarare* (e.g. *vultum), hilarem facĕre.* **exhilaration,** n. *animi relaxatio, oblectatio.*

exhort, v.tr. *hortari;* see ADMONISH, ENCOURAGE.

exigence, n. *necessitas, angustiae.*

exile, I. n. 1, = banishment, *ex(s)ilium, relegatio;* 2, = person banished, *exsul, extorris,* *profugus.* **II.** v.tr. *e(j)icĕre, exterminare, relegare, deportare* (Tac.), (ex)*pellĕre, alci aquā et igni interdicĕre.*

exist, v.intr. *ex(s)istĕre, esse, exstare.* **existence,** n. use *esse* (e.g. to believe in the — of gods, *deos esse putare*); I have means of —, *habeo unde utar.*

exit, n. 1, = going away, *exitus, egressus, abitus,* all *-ūs;* 2, = way out, *exitus, effugium, janua.*

e~onerate, v.tr. see EXCULPATE.

exorbitant, adj. *immodicus, immoderatus.* Adv. *immodice, immoderate.*

exordium, n. *exordium, exorsus, -ūs, proemium.*

exoteric, adj. *quod ἐξωτερικὸν vocant, extotericus* (Gell.).

exotic, adj. *peregrinus, externus.*

expand, v.tr. see SPREAD. **expanse,** n. *spatium.*

expatiate, v.tr. *uberius* or *pluribus* (*verbis) disputare, dicĕre, longum esse in alqā re.*

expatriate, v.tr. see BANISH.

expect, v.tr. *ex(s)pectare, opperiri alqm* or *alqd; sperare* (with *fore ut, spem habēre alcjs rei,* or with accus. and infin.); a less slaughter than might have been —ed, *minor clades quam pro tantā victoriā fuit.* **expectant,** adj. use *spes* or *ex(s)pectatio,* or verb, or *arrectus.* **expectation,** n. *ex(s)pectatio, spes, opinio.*

expectorate, v.tr. *exscreare* (e.g. *sanguinem), exspuĕre.* **expectoration,** n. 1, *exscreatio* (= act of —) (Plin.); 2, *sputum* (= matter of —) (Cels.).

expedient, I. adj. *commodus, utilis;* it is —, *expedit.* **II.** n. *ratio;* no useful — is at hand, *nullum consilium in promptu est;* to find an —, *viam invenire, viam consilii invenire.* **expediency,** n. *utilitas.*

expedite, v.tr. *expedire, maturare.* **expedition,** n. 1, = speed, *celeritas;* 2, = military —, *expeditio.* **expeditious,** adj. *celer, promptus, maturus.* Adv. *celeriter, prompte, mature.*

expel, v.tr. *(ex)pellĕre re* or *a re* or *ex re, depellĕre alqm re, de re* or *ex re, exigĕre re* or *ex re, e(j)icĕre re, de, ex* or *ab re.* **expulsion,** n. *exactio, expulsio.*

expend, v.tr. *expendĕre, impendĕre, erogare* (of public money); — much money, *magnos sumptus facĕre; pecuniam profundĕre.* **expense,** n. *impensa, impendium, dispendium, sumptus, -ūs.*

expensive, adj. *sumptuosus, carus, pretiosus, magni pretii.* Adv. *sumptuose, pretiose.* **expenditure,** n. *rogatio, sumptus, -ūs.*

experience, I. n. *usus, -ūs, experientia, prudentia* (= wisdom that is the result of —); — in nautical matters, *scientia atque usus rerum nauticarum;* I write from —, *expertus scribo quod scribo.* **II.** v.tr. *experiri,* (*usu*) *discēre* or *cognoscēre, experientiá discēre, usu alqd mihi venit.* **experienced,** adj. (*usu*) *peritus, usu atque exercitatione praeditus, multarum rerum peritus; peritus alcjs rei, exercitatus, versatus in re.* **experiment,** n. *experimentum, periclitatio, periculum;* an unfortunate —, *res infeliciter tentata.* **experimental,** adj. and adv. *usu* or *experimentis cognitus.*

expert, adj. & n. *alci rei* or *ad alqd aptus, idoneus, alcjs rei compos, alcjs rei peritus, in alqâ re exercitatus, callidus, sol(l)ers.* **expertness,** n. *calliditas, sol(l)ertia.*

expiate, v.tr. *alqd luēre, expiare, poenas alcjs rei dare, pendēre, dependēre, †expendēre, solvēre.* **expiation,** n. *satisfactio, poena, piaculum.* **expiatory,** adj. *piacularis.*

expire, v.intr. *ex(s)pirare; animam, extremum spiritum edēre;* see **DIE.** **expiration,** n. by abl. abs. (e.g. at the — of the year, *anno exeunte, finito jam anno*).

explain, v.tr. *exponēre, expedire, explanare, explicare, interpretari, aperire, enodare, illustrare.* **explanation,** n. *explicatio, explanatio, interpretatio, enodatio.* **explanatory,** adj. use verb.

explicit, adj. *apertus, dilucidus, definitus.* Adv. *dilucide, plane, diserte, definite.*

explode, I. v.intr. (*di*)*rumpi.* **II.** v.tr. (*di*)*rumpēre, refellēre, confutare, refutare* (an opinion). **explosion,** n. †*fragor, crepitus, -ūs.*

export, v.tr. *exportare* (opp. *importare*). **exportation,** n. *exportatio.* **exports,** n. *merces* (*quae exportantur*).

expose, v.tr. 1, *exponēre;* — a child, *infantem exponere;* — to anything, *opponēre, ob(f)icēre, offerre alci rei;* 2, = to lay open, *detegēre* (e.g. *latentem culpam*); 3, = make bare, *nudare.* **exposition,** n. *expositio;* see EXPLANATION. **exposure,** n. by verb.

expound, v.tr. see EXPLAIN.

express, I. v.tr. *exprimēre, significare, declarare, demonstrare, verbis consequi, exsequi;* — oneself, *loqui, dicēre.* **II.** adj. 1, = EXACT ; 2, = quick, *celer.* Adv. *his ipsis verbis.* **expression,** n. 1, *verbum, sententia, vocabulum, dictum, vox;* 2, of the features, etc., *vultus, -ūs, argutiae* (= animation); void of —, *languens, languidus* (as in the countenance, the voice, etc.). **expressive,** adj. *significans, gravis* (= with strength, of a speaker); by *vis* (e.g. it is most —, *vim habet magnam*). Adv. *significanter* (Quint.), *plane, diserte.* **expressiveness,** n. *argutiae* (= lively —, of face, etc.), *gravitas* (= — of speech).

expunge, v.tr. *delēre, inducēre,* (*e*)*radēre* (Tac.).

expurgate, v.tr. (*ex*)*purgare.* **expurgation,** n. (*ex*)*purgatio* (= freeing from blame).

exquisite, adj. *exquisitus, conquisitus, egregius, venustus;* — tortures, *supplicia exquisita, pulcher.* Adv. *exquisite, egregie, pulchre, venuste.*

extant, adj., to be — (*superstitem*) *esse, exstare, ex(s)istere.*

extemporary, adj. *subitus, subitus et fortuitus;* power of — speaking, *ex tempore dicendi facultas.*

extend, I. v.tr. = stretch out, enlarge, *extendēre, distendēre, augēre, propagare, amplificare.* **II.** v.intr. *patēre, extendi, distendi,* etc. **extension,** n. *porrectio* (e.g. *digitorum*), *productio, prolatio, propagatio.* **extensive,** adj.

magnus, amplus, late patens, latus. Adv. *late extent,* n. *ambitus, -ūs, spatium, circuitus, -ūs.* to have a wide —, *latius patēre.*

extenuate, v.tr. *attenuare, extenuare* (opp to *amplificare*); — guilt, (*culpam,* etc.) *levare, mitigare.* **extenuation,** ᴍ. *extenuatio, levatio, mitigatio.*

exterior, I. adj. see EXTERNAL. **II.** n. *facies, forma, species, figura.*

exterminate, v.tr. *ad unum interfícēre, interimēre* (= kill), *eradicare, ex(s)tirpare* (= root out).

external, adj. *externus, exterior;* — advantages, *bona externa, bona corporis.* Adv. *extrinsecus.*

extinct, adj. *exstinctus, obsoletus.*

extinguish, v.tr. — a fire, *ex(s)tinguēre, restinguēre, compescēre, delēre* (= blot out).

extirpate, v.tr. *ex(s)tirpare ;* see EXTERMINATE.

extol, v.tr. *augēre, ornare, laudibus* (*ef*)*ferre, extollēre, verbis efferre.*

extort, v.tr. *exprimēre alci alqd* or *alqd ab alqo, expugnare alqd alci, alqd expilare, alci alqd extorquēre.* **extortion,** n. *res repetundae.*

extortionate, adj. *rapax, avarus.* Adv. *avare.* **extortioner,** n. *immodici fenoris exactor.*

extra, adv. *praeterea.*

extract, I. v.tr. 1, *extrahēre,* (*e*)*vellēre ;* 2, = to make an extract, *excerpēre ;* 3, = to press out, *exprimere.* **II.** n. 1, = — of a book, *excerptio* (Gell.), *quod excerptum est ;* 2, = — of a plant, etc., *sucus qui expressus est, quod expressum est.* **extraction,** n. as to origin, *origo, genus, -ēris,* n. ; of good —, *honesto loco ortus, honesto genere* (*natus*); of poor —, *tenui loco ortus, humili* or *ignobili loco natus.*

extraneous, adj. see EXTERNAL.

extraordinary, adj. *extraordinarius, inusitatus, insolitus, insolens, novus inauditus, incredibilis, mirus, insignis, summus.* Adv. *extra ordinem, praeter morem* or *consuetudinem, incredibiliter, mire, mirifice.*

extravagant, adj. 1, = lavish, *prodigus, effusus, sumptuosus;* 2, = excessive, *immoderatus, immodicus;* 3, = foolish, *insulsus.* Adv. *prodige, effuse, sumptuose, immoderate, immodice, insulse.* **extravagance,** n. 1, *prodigentia* (Tac.), *sumptus, -ūs* (*profusus*); 2, *intemperantia, immoderatio ;* 3, *insulse factum.*

extreme, adj. *extremus* (= farthest), *ultimus* (= last), *summus* (= highest); — part, *pars extrema ;* the — price, *summum pretium ;* to come into — danger, *in ultimum discrimen adduci ;* to go to —s, *modum excedēre* (so *ad extremum perventum est, ventum jam ad finem est, res est ad extremum perducta casum*). Adv. *summe, summopere, quam* or *vel maxime,* or by superl. (e.g. — good, *optimus*). **extremity,** n. 1, = furthest part, *extremus,* with n. ; 2, = top, *cacumen, vertex, fastigium, extremitas ;* of the body, *extremae partes ;* 3, = distress, etc., by special word (e.g. *inopia* = poverty), with *summus,* or *extrema, -orum,* pl.; to be brought to —s, *in extremum discrimen adductum esse.*

extricate, v.tr. see RELEASE.

extrude, v.tr. *extrudēre, expellēre, e(f)icēre,* comb. *extrudere et e(f)icēre.* **extrusion,** n. *expulsio;* see EXPEL.

exuberant, adj. *luxuriosus, laetus ;* of style, *redundans;* to be —, *exuberare* (e.g. *pomis, foliorum luxuriâ,* etc.). Adv. *ubertim, luxuriose.* **exuberance,** n. *ubertas, luxuria.*

exude, v.intr. (ex)sudare.

exulcerate, v.tr. exulcerare.

exult, v.intr. exsultare, gestire, comb. exsultare et gestire, laetitiā efferri, laetari, gloriari. **exultant,** adj. laetus. Adv. laete. **exultation,** n. laetatio.

eye, I. n. oculus, † ocellus, † lumen (dimin.), = sight, conspectus, -ūs (e.g. before the —s, in con spectus), = keen sight, acies; blear-eyed, lippus; — in trees, etc., oculus, gemma; bull's- —, use medius (e.g. scopum medium ferire, = hit the —); — in peacock's tail, oculus; mind's —, acies or oculus mentis, of ′ needle, foramen. ǁ I. v.tr. a(d)spicĕre, contemplari ;—askance, oculis limis a(d)spicĕre. **eye-ball,** n. pupula, pupilla. **eye-brow,** n. supercilium. **eye-lash,** n. pili pupillas tegentes. **eye-lid,** n. palpebra (usu. pl.). **eyesight,** n. acies, oculus. **eyesore,** n. res foeda or tetra; see UGLY. **eye-witness,** n. testis, m. and f. ; I was an —, ipse vidi.

F.

fable, n. 1, fabula (usu. with ficta or composita or commenticia); 2, = untruth, commentum, mendacium. **fabulous,** adj. fabulosus, fictus, commenticius, falsus, comb. fictus et commenticius.

fabric, n. 1, of carpenters, and in gen., fabrica ; of weavers, textum, textile ; 2, = structure, aedificium. **fabricate,** v.tr. fabricari, texĕre, conficĕre. **fabrication,** n. 1, = making, fabricatio ; 2, = falsehood ; see FABLE, 2. **fabricator,** n. opifex, fabricator (always with gen.), artifex, textor ; = inventor, auctor.

face, I. n. facies (= the front of the head), vultus, -ūs (= the countenance), os, oris (properly, = the mouth), comb. os vultusque or os et vultus; frons, -ntis, f. (= the forehead) ; — to —, coram ; to make —s, os (dis)torquēre. **II.** v.tr. and intr. 1, = be opposite, ad alqd spectare ; 2, = to cover, alqd alqā re or alci inducĕre ; 3, = encounter, alci obviam ire; 4, — about, signa convertĕre. **facial,** adj. quod ad faciem pertinet.

facetious, adj. jocosus, jocularis, lepidus, facetus. Adv. jocose, lepide, facete. **facetiousness,** n. lepos, -ōris, facetiae, or by sal.

facilitate, v.tr. alcjs rei expedire. **facility,** n. facilitas ; with —, facile, nullo negotio.

facing, prep. contra alqd, ex adverso rei.

facsimile, n. descriptio imagoque (e.g. lit(t)erarum).

fact, n. res, factum; that is a —, hoc certo auctore comperi ; in —, reapse, etenim, enim or quidem (enclit.), sane, profecto.

faction, n. factio. **factious,** adj. factiosus, partium studiosus, turbulentus, seditiosus. Adv. seditiose. **factiousness,** n. factio.

factitious, adj. see FALSE.

factor, n. negotiorum (pro)curator.

factory, n. fabrica, officina ; — hands, operae.

faculty, n. ingenium (= natural talent) comb. animus ingeniumque ; sol(l)ertia (= skill), facultas, e.g. dicendi (also poëtica facultas).

fade, v.intr. evanescĕre, † pallescĕre, marcescĕre. **faded,** adj. see PALE. **fading, I.** n. coloris mutatio. **II.** adj. caducus.

fagot, n. fascis, -is, m., sarmenta, -orum, pl.

fail, I. v.intr. 1, = to fall or come short of, non ferire ; 2, = to err or to do wrong, errare, labi, peccare, peccatum admittĕre (= to sin), delinquĕre ; 3, = to fall short, alci deesse, deficĕre ; 4, = — in a lawsuit, cadĕre; 5, = be bankrupt, foro cedĕre. **II.** n. e.g. without—, by certo,

omnino. **failing,** n. error, peccatum, delictum. **failure,** n. defectio (e.g. virium), ruinae or naufragium fortunarum, or use verb.

fain, adv. libenter (lub-), by a participle, as volens ; I would — believe that, hoc credĕre voluerim (vellem).

faint, I. adj. languidus, use sensu carēre if unconsciousness be implied. **II.** v.intr. 1, = swoon, † collabi, animus alqm relinquit ; 2, = be weary, languēre. **faint-hearted,** adj. timidus. **faintness,** n. 1, languor ; 2, by verb.

fair, I. adj. 1, = beautiful, pulcher, venustus ; the — sex, sexus, -ūs, muliebris ; 2, of weather, serenus ; of wind or tide, secundus ; 3, opp. to dark, candidus ; 4, morally, aequus, integer ; 5, = moderately good, mediocris. Adv. aeque, mediocriter, haud ita multum. **II.** n. nundinae, mercatus, -ūs. **fairness,** n. 1, pulchritudo, venustas ; 2, serenitas ; 3, aequitas, integritas ; 4, mediocritas.

fairy, n. = — of the stream, nympha ; = — of the tree, dryas (usu. pl. dryades) ; = — of the wood, faunus.

faith, n. 1, = fidelity, fidelitas, fides, pietas (= discharge of duty towards God, parents, etc.) ; 2, = belief, opinio, persuasio, fides ; to have — in, alci credĕre ; 3, see RELIGION ; 4, as exclamation, nae, Hercle, medius fidius. **faithful,** adj. fidelis, fidus (e.g. in suā sententiā). Adv. fideliter. **faithfulness,** n. fidelitas, fides, constantia. **faithless,** adj. perfidus, perfidiosus, infidelis, infidus. Adv. perfide, perfidiose, infideliter. **faithlessness,** n. perfidia, infidelitas.

falchion, n. † acinaces, -is, m.

fall, I. v.intr. cadĕre, decidĕre, delabi, defluĕre ; to — away, desert, or abandon, deficĕre, ab alqo desciscĕre, alqm deserĕre ; to — in battle, in acie cadĕre ; — by ambush or snares, per insidias interfici ; to — into, die, mori, perire ; = to be captured, expugnari, delēri ; to — out (= disagree), dissentire ; to — on, in alqm invadĕre, irruĕre ; to — into a person's arms, ruĕre in alcjs amplexus ; to — into suspicion, suspicio cadit in alqm ; = to sink, delabi, desidĕre ; of the wind, cadĕre, concidĕre ; of the voice, cadĕre ; = in price, cadĕre res fit vilior ; — of an army, pedem referre ; — at the feet of, se ad pedes alcjs pro- (j)icĕre ; — in with, in alqm incidĕre ; — in love with, amare. **II.** n. 1, casus, -ūs, lapsus, -ūs, ruina, labes, -is ; 2, = ruin, ruina, excidium ; a — from rank or dignity, dignitas amissa, gratia principis amissa ; 3, = the lessening of a height or level of a fluid body, decessus, -ūs, recessus, -ūs ; 4, = lessening, deminutio.

fallacy, n. error, fallacia, vitium, captio. **fallacious,** adj. fallax, vanus, fucosus, falsus, vitiosus. Adv. fallaciter, falso. **fallible,** adj. qui errare potest.

fallow, adj. the field lies —, ager cessat, quiescit, (re)quiescit, cultu vacat. **fallow soil,** n. novalis or novale, novactum.

false, adj. 1, = not genuine, falsus (opp. verus), subditus, suppositus (= forged), alienus (= under another name, e.g. libellum sub alieno nomine edĕre), simulatus (= pretended), fucatus, fucosus (= having a fair exterior, opp. sincerus, probus), fallax (= deceptive), mendax (= lying) ; — teeth, † dentes empti ; a — note, dissonum quiddam ; 2, = treacherous, perfidus, † dolosus, fraudulentus, a — oath, perjurium ; to swear —, perjurare, pejerare. Adv. falso, fallaciter simulate, perperam, perfide, fraudulenter. **falsehood,** n. mendacium, commentum, falsum. **falseness,** n. fallacia, dolus, perfidia. **falsify,** v.tr. vitiare, corrumpĕre, adulterare (e.g. nummos, gemmas), interpolare, depravare, tabulas interpolare (= to erase some letters and substitute others), *tabulas interlinĕre* (= to erase or to put out letters). **falsification,** n. use verb.

falter, v.intr. *haesitare, haerēre, titubare.* Adv. *titubanter, timide.*

fame, n. *laus, gloria, claritas, fama.* **famous,** adj. *celebratus,* (*prae*)*clarus, illustris.* Adv. (*prae*)*clare, bene* (= well).

familiar, adj. 1, *familiaris ; notus* = a bosom friend, *homo intimus, homo quo alqs intime utitur ; amicus conjunctissimus* ; 2, = acquainted with, *alcjs rei sciens, gnarus, non ignarus, peritus, non expers* ; — with a language, *linguam bene nosse, linguam intellegĕre* ; — with danger, *in periculis versatum esse.* Adv. *familiariter.* **familiarity,** n. *familiaritas, familiaris* or *intima amicitia.*

family, I. n. 1, *familia* (orig. = the slaves in a house), *domus, -ūs* ; 2, = race or clan, *gens,* also *genus* and *familia* (= a branch of a *gens,* thus the *gens Cornelia* comprised the families of the Scipios and Lentuli), *cognatio, stirps, propinqui* ; of good —, *nobilis, nobili genere* or *nobili loco natus, haud obscuro loco natus, honesto loco natus ; gentilis, gentilicius* (= belonging to a *gens*), *familiaris* (= belonging to a *familia*), domesticus (= belonging to the house). **II.** adj. *privatus* (opp. to *publicus*), *intestinus* (= in the interior of the — (opp. to *externus*).

famine, n. *fames, -is, inopia et fames.* **famish, I.** v.tr. *alqm fame enecare, conficĕre.* **II.** v.intr. *fame mori, confici, absumi* or *perire* or *interire.*

fan, I. n. 1, = an agricultural instrument, *vannus,* f. *ventilabrum* (Col.) ; 2, = a toy used by ladies, *flabellum.* **II.** v.tr. 1, *evannere, ventilare* ; 2, *flabello uti.*

fanatic, adj. *fanaticus.* **fanaticism,** n. *animus fanaticus,* or *superstitionibus deditus.*

fancy, I. n. *opinio* (*falsa*) ; as a faculty, *cogitatio ;* a mere —, *somnium ;* according to — (= liking), *ex libidine* (*lub*-) ; a glowing —, *fervidum ingenium, calor et impetus ;* to belong to — and not to fact, *opinionis esse, non naturae ;* — merely, *falsus, fictus.* **II.** v.tr. *cogitatione sibi alqd depingĕre, in opinione esse, opinari, alqd fingĕre ;* I — I am ill, *aegrotare mihi videor ;* what is fancied, *opinatus ;* what may be —, *opinabilis.* **fanciful,** adj. 1, = imaginative, *facilis et copiosus,* or *summo ingenio praeditus ;* 2, *morosus* (= captious). Adv. *morose.*

fang, n. *dens,* m. **fanged,** adj. *dentatus.* **fangless,** adj. *sine dentibus.*

far, adv. *procul, longe* (= to a great distance, e.g. *longe vidēre, prospicĕre*), *e longinquo* (=from afar), *eminus* (opp. *comminus*) ; to be —, *procul* or *longe abesse ;* — be it ! *di meliora* (scil. *dent*) ; so — is it that, etc., *tantum abest ut ;* to go too —, *modum excedĕre ;* as — as, *quatenus, quantum, quod* (e.g. *quod suam*) ; so —, *hactenus ;* — fetched, *longe repetitus.* **farther,** adv. *longius, ultra.*

farce, n. *mimus, fabula Atellana.* **farcical,** adj. *mimicus, ridiculus, scurrilis.* Adv. *ridicule.*

fare, I. v.intr. 1, *se habēre ;* — well, *bene, commode, recte valēre, bene, belle se habēre, bonā valetudine uti ;* 2, to — well, *laute vivĕre.* **II.** n. 1, *cibus potusque* (*potus, -ūs*), *victus, -ūs ;* poor —, *tenuis victus ;* good —, *lautus victus ;* 2, = money paid for journey, *vectura* (ante and post class.) ; 3, see PASSENGER. **farewell !** interj. *ave ! aveto ! avete ! vale ! valete !* to bid —, *salvēre* or *valēre alqm jubēre ;* a hearty —, *multam salutem alci dicĕre.*

farinaceous, adj. *farinaceus.*

farm, I. n. *ager, fundus, praedium ;* belonging to a —, *agrarius.* **II.** v.tr. 1, = till, *arare,*

colĕre ; 2, = let out on contract, (*e*)*locare* (*alqd faciendum*), opp. to *conducĕre.* **farm-work,** n. *aratio, opus rusticum, agricultura, agrorum cultus, -ūs.* **farmer,** n. 1, *agricola, arator ;* 2, = of the revenues, *publicanus,* in gen. *redemptor.* **farming,** n. 1, *agricultura* (or as two words) *cultus, -ūs, agrorum, res rusticae ;* 2, *redemptio, conductio.*

farrago, n. *farrago.*

farrier, n. (*faber ferrarius*) *qui equis soleas ferreas suppingit* (= one who shoes horses), *medicus equarius* (late = horse-doctor).

farrow, I. n. *fetus, -ūs.* **II.** v.tr. *fetum edĕre.*

farthing, n. *quadrans, teruncius ;* I do not care a — for, *haud flocci facio.*

fascinate, v.tr. †*fascinare* (= — by the look, e.g. *agnos*), *tenēre, capĕre* (fig.). **fascination,** n. 1, lit. *fascinum, fascinatio* (Plin.) ; 2, fig. *blanditiae, dulcedo.*

fashion, I. n. *mos* (as custom, e.g. *mos vestis*), *ritus, -ūs* (e.g. after the — of men, *hominum ritu*), *habitus, -ūs, ornatus, -ūs ;* a new —, *habitus novus ;* to be in the — (of things), *moris esse, usu receptum esse.* **II.** v.tr. see MAKE. **fashionable,** adj. *elegans, quod moris est.* Adv. *eleganter.*

fast, I. adj. 1, = quick, *celer, citus, properus, properans, festinans, citatus, incitatus, velox, pernix* (= brisk), *alacer* (= alive, energetic, opp. *languidus*), *agilis* (= in movement), *promptus* (= ready), *rapidus ;* 2, = fixed or firm, *firmus, stabilis ;* to hold —, *tenēre, retinēre ;* to stick —, *adhaerēre alci rei* or *ad alqd* or *in alqā re ;* to make —, *firmare, stabilire.* **II.** adv. *citato gradu, celeriter, rapide, prompte, firme, mordicus* (colloquial). **III.** v.intr. *cibo abstinēre.* **IV.** n. *jejunium, inedia.* **fasten,** v.tr. (*af*)*figĕre ad alqd* or *alci rei ;* see TIE, BIND ; — together, *configĕre, con*(*n*)*ectĕre, conjungĕre.* **fastening,** n. *vinculum, compages, -is,* f. (= fitting together), *claustra, -orum,* pl. (= bars), *pessulus, repagula, -orum* (= bolt). **faster !** interj. *propera !*

fastidious, adj. *fastidiosus, delicatus, mollis.* Adv. *fastidiose, delicate, molliter.*

fat, I. adj. *pinguis* (opp. *macer*), *opimus* (= full, rich, opp. *gracilis* or *sterilis,* of a field), *obesus* (= filled up, opp. *gracilis*), *nitidus* (= shining), *saginatus* (= fed up), *adipatus* (= supplied with grease), *luculentus* (= productive, e.g. *munus*). **II.** n. †*pingue, adeps, sebum* (*sevum*) ; to live on the — of the land, *delicatissimis cibis uti.* **fatten,** v.tr. *saginare, farcire.* **fatted,** adj. *saginatus, altilis.* **fatness,** n. *obesitas* (Suet.), *pinguitudo* (ante and post class.). **fatty,** adj. *pinguis.*

fate, n. *fatum, necessitas, sors* (= one's lot) ; the —s, *Parcae.* **fated,** adj. †*fatalis,* †*fatifer, funestus, mortifer* (*us*). Adv. *funeste, fato* or *fataliter* (= by fate). **fatalism,** n. use *fatum* (e.g. *omnia fato fieri credĕre,* to be a —). **fatality,** n. 1, = power of fate, *fatum ;* 2, = accident, *casus, -ūs.*

father, I. n. *pater, parens,* † *genitor,* † *sator ;* — and mother, *parentes ;* the —s, *patres* (=forefathers, senators). **II.** v.tr. — upon, *alqd alci tribuĕre.* **fatherhood,** n. *paternitas* (eccl.) or by *pater* (e.g. he learns it by his —, *hoc cum pater fit, tum discit*). **father-in-law,** n. *socer.* **fatherless,** adj. *orbus.* **fatherly,** adj. *paternus.*

fathom, I. n. *ulna.* **II.** v.tr. *explorare.*

fatigue, I. n. (*de*)*fatigatio, lassitudo, defectio virium.* **II.** v.tr. (*de*)*fatigare.* **fatigued,** adj. *fessus,* (*de*)*fatigatus, defessus, lassus, lassitudine confectus.*

fatuous, adj. *fatuus, ineptus, insicetus* (*in-*

facetus), *insulsus.* Adv. *inepte, inficete, insulse, stulte.* **fatuity,** n. *ineptiae, stultitia, insulsitas,* *fatuitas* (rare).

fault, n. 1, = wrong-doing, *vitium, peccatum, culpa, delictum ;* 2, = blame, *reprehensio* (opp. *probatio*), *vituperatio* (opp. *laus*); find — with, *accusare, reprehendĕre.* **faultiness,** n. *pravitas ;* see FAULT, 2. **faultless,** adj. *innocens, emendatus.* Adv. *innocenter, emendate.* **faultlessness,** n. *innocentia.* **faulty,** adj. *mendosus, vitiosus* (in gen.), *pravus* (morally). Adv. *mendose, vitiose, prave.*

favour, I. v.intr. *alci* or *alci rei favēre, alcjs rebus* or *partibus favēre* (= to be of his party), *alci indulgēre* (= to consult a person's wishes), *alci propitium esse* (= to be favourable or well-disposed, used generally of the gods), *alci studēre, alcjs esse studiosum* (= to be attached to), *juvare, adjuvare* (= to assist), *esse alci adjumento, afferre alci adjumentum* (= to give aid), *alqm fovēre, sustinēre ac fovēre, gratiā et auctoritate suā sustentare* (= to support with your influence), *suffragari alci* (= to vote for or recommend), *gratiosus alci* or *apud alqm* (= e.g. to stand in favour with someone). **II.** n. 1, = goodwill, *favor, gratia, voluntas, studium, benevolentia (beniv-);* by your —, *pace tuā ;* 2, = benefit, *beneficium, gratia.* **favourable,** adj. 1, = inclined to, *propitius* (of the gods), *amicus, benignus ;* 2, = advantageous, *commodus, prosperus ;* of wind or tide, *secundus.* Adv. *amice, benigne, commode, prospere.* **favourer,** n. *fautor.* **favourite, I.** n. *deliciae* (= pet); to be a — with, *apud alqm gratiā valēre, gratiosum esse.* **II.** adj. *gratiosus, gratus, acceptus.* **favouritism,** n. *gratia* (= influence) or circumloc. (e.g. he showed his — to Gaius, *Gaio se nimis indulgentem praebuit*).

fawn, I. n. *hinnuleus.* **II.** v.tr. — on, fig. *alqm adulari, alci blandiri.* **fawning,** n. *adulatio.* Adv. *blande.*

fealty, n. *fides, fidelitas ;* to swear — to, *in verba alcjs jurare.*

fear, I. n. *metus, -ūs, timor, verecundia* (of what is wrong), *terror* (= sudden fear), *pavor, trepidatio* (= trembling), *horror, formīdo, timiditas, ignavia* (= cowardice). **II.** v.tr. *alqm metuĕre, timēre, verēri* (= reverence), *extimescĕre, pertimescĕre.* **fearful,** adj. 1, = afraid, *timidus, trepidus, ignavus, pavidus, verecundus ;* 2, = dreadful, *metuendus, dirus, horribilis, terribilis, formidulosus (formidol-).* Adv. *timide, ignave, pavide, verecunde, dire, trepide, formidulose.* **fearless,** adj. *metu vacuus* or *solutus, impavidus, intrepidus ;* — as to, *securus de alqā re* (e.g. *bello*). Adv. *sine metu, sine timore, impavide, intrepide.* **fearlessness,** n. see COURAGE.

feasible, adj. *quod fieri* or *effici potest.* **feasibility,** n. *potestas* or *facultas alcjs rei faciendae.*

feast, I. n. 1, = holy day, *dies festus, dies sol(l)emnis, dies feriatus,* † *festum ;* 2, = a bountiful meal, *convivium, epulum, epulae, daps.* **II.** v.intr. 1, lit. *epulari ;* 2, fig. — on, *alqā re pasci* (both in good and bad sense).

feat, n. *facinus, -ŏris,* n., *factum, res mira, res difficilis.*

feather, I. n. *penna (pinna), pluma* (= down). **II.** v.tr. — one's nest, *res suas augēre ;* one who has — ed his nest, *bene peculiatus.* **feather-bed,** n. *culcita plumea.* **feathery,** adj. † *plumeus,* † *plumosus.*

feature, n. 1, of the face, *lineamentum, ductus, -ūs,* or *habitus, -ūs, os, ōris ;* the —s, *vultus, -ūs, os, ōris,* n. ; 2, = peculiarity, *proprietas, quod proprium est ;* it is a — of anyone, *alcjs est.*

febrile. adj. *febricolosus*

February, n. (*mensis*) *Februarius.*

fecund, adj. *fecundus.* **fecundate, v.tr.** † *fecundare.* **fecundity,** n. *fecunditas, fertilitas.*

federate, federal, adj. *foederatus, foederi junctus, foedere sociatus.*

fee, I. n. *merces, -ēdis,* f., *honos* (*honor*). **II.** v.tr. *alci mercedem dare.*

feeble, adj. *imbecillus, tenuis, infirmus, invalidus, languidus, debilis ;* of sight, etc., *hebes.* Adv. *infirme, imbecille* (rare), *languide.* **feebleness,** n. *imbecillitas, debilitas, infirmitas, languor.*

feed, I. v.tr. 1, *cibum praebēre alci, cibare* (of animals) (Col.), *pabulum dare alci* (oxen, etc.), *alĕre* (= to nourish), *pascĕre* (= to pasture, e.g. *sues, greges*) ; 2, fig. *alĕre ;* 3, of rivers, etc., *in mare,* etc., *influĕre.* **II.** v.intr. see EAT, GRAZE. **feeder,** n. 1, *qui aves,* etc., *alit ;* 2, = eater, *qui edit ;* 3, = a river, (*rivus*) *qui in mare influit.*

feel, I. v.tr. 1, physically, = touch, *tangĕre, tentare, alqā re affici ;* 2, mentally, *sentire, percipĕre, concipĕre, intellegĕre, capĕre, alqā re affici ;* — joy, *laetari ;* — pain, *dolēre.* **II.** v.intr. 1, = appears (by touch, etc.), *esse videri* or *esse ;* 2, = be, by special verb (e.g. — glad, *laetari ;* — thirsty, *sitire ;* — for, *alcjs misereri*). **feeler,** n. *crinis, corniculum* (Plin.). **feeling, I.** n. *sensus, -ūs* (= sensibility), *animus* (mental) ; the power or method of —, *sentiendi ratio ; tactus, -ūs* (= the touch), *gustatus, -ūs* (= taste), *judicium* (= power of judging), *conscientia* (= consciousness), *affectus, -ūs* (= the permanent condition or —); tender moral —, *pudor ;* thankful —, *gratus animus, pietas ;* humane —, *humanitas ;* joyous —, *laetitia ;* — for truth, *veritatis studium ;* — for the beautiful, *elegantia.* **II.** adj. *humanus, humanitatis plenus, multum humanitatis habens, humanitatis sensu praeditus, misericors.* Adv. *miserabiliter, magnā cum misericordiā.*

feign, v.tr. *fingĕre, simulare, dissimulare* (e.g. that a thing is not). **feigned,** adj. *fictus, simulatus.* Adv. *ficte, simulate.* **feint,** n. see PRETENCE.

felicitate, v.tr. *gratulari alci alqd* or *de alqā re.* **felicitation,** n. *gratulatio.* **felicity, felicitousness,** n. 1, *vita beata, beatum, beate vivēre ;* 2, = appropriateness, *proprietas.* **felicitous,** adj. 1, = happy, *felix, beatus ;* 2, = appropriate, *aptus.* Adv. *feliciter, beate, apte.*

fell, v.tr. 1, of timber, *caedĕre, excidĕre ;* 2, = knock down, (*con*)*sternĕre.*

fell, n. *clivus* (= hill).

fell, adj. *crudelis, saevus.*

fellow, n. = associate, *socius, comes, -itis,* m. and f., *sodalis,* m. and f. ; a good —, *homo festivus* or *lepidus ;* a bad —, *homo dissolutus ;* a trumpery —, *homuncio, homunculus.* **fellow-citizen,** n. *civis, municeps.* **fellow-countryman,** n. *civis.* **fellow-feeling,** n. *societas* (e.g. *aegritudinis,* in — sorrow, etc.). **fellow-heir,** n. *coheres, -ēdis,* m. and f. **fellow-servant,** n. *conservus.* **fellow-soldier,** n. *commilito.* **fellowship,** n. *societas ;* — in plans, *societas consiliorum ; collegium* (= a corporation, e.g. of merchants, artisans, priests) ; to take into —, *alqm in collegium cooptare ;* in a university, *socius* (e.g. to get a —, *socium a(d)scribi*) ; human —, *societas humana, societas hominum ;* good —, *comitas.*

felon, n. see CRIMINAL.

female, I. adj. *muliebris, femineus* (in fem. also *femina*) ; — sex, *sexus, -ūs ; muliebris* or *femineus.* **II.** n. *femina, mulier.* **feminine,** adj. 1, = FEMALE ; 2, Gram. t.t. *femininus.*

fen, n. *terra uliginosa, loca, -orum, uliginosa* or *palustria, palus, -ūdis,* f., *uligo.* **fenny,** adj. *uliginosus, paluster.*

fence, I. n. *saepes, -is, saepimentum, (con)saeptum* (usu. pl.). **II.** v.tr. 1, = hedge in, *saepire, saepto circumdare* ; 2, = to fight in fencing, *armis uti, batuěre.* **fencer,** n. *gladiator* ; a good —, *armorum peritissimus* ; to be a good —, *armis optime uti.* **fencing,** n. *ars gladii, ars gladiatoria* ; skilled in —, *armorum peritus* ; a —master, *lanista,* m. ; — school, *ludus.*

ferment, I. n. 1, lit. *fermentum* ; 2, fig. *tumor, fervor, aestus, -ūs.* **II.** v.tr. **fermentare.* **III.** v.intr. 1, **fermentari, fervěre, *fermentescěre* ; 2, fig. *fervēre, tumēre, turgescěre.*

fern, n. *filix.*

ferocious, adj. *ferox* ; see FIERCE.

ferret, n. *viverra* (Plin.).

ferruginous, adj. *ferrugineus* (= iron-coloured), *ferratus* (= holding or tasting of iron, scil. *aquae* (Sen.)).

ferry, I. n. *trajectus, -ūs* ; — -boat, *scapha* ; — -man, *portitor* ; the charge of —, *portorium.* **II.** v.tr. *tra(j)icěre, transmittěre.*

fertile, adj. *ferax, fecundus, fertilis, opimus, uber* (= rich), comb. *uber et fertilis, fecundus et uber, fetus.* **fertility,** n. *fertilitas, ubertas, fecunditas, copia.*

ferule, n. *ferula* (= a reed or staff).

fervent, fervid, adj. *fervidus* (= glowing, e.g. *pars mundi*) ; fig. *animus, fervens* (= heated, hot, e.g. *rota, aqua*), *ardens, flagrans* ; to make —, *fervefacěre* ; to be —, *fervēre.* Adv. *fervide, ardenter, ferventer.* **fervency, fervour,** n. *fervor* (e.g. *oceani,* or fig. *aetatis*).

festival, n. *dies festus, dies sol(l)emnis, sol-(l)emne, hilaritas.* **festive,** adj. *hilaris, festus, festivus* (ante and post class.). Adv. *hilariter, hilare, festive.* **festivity,** n. 1, = FESTIVAL ; 2 = mirth, *festivitas, hilaritas.* **festoon,** n. *serta, -orum.*

fetch, v.tr. *afferre, apportare, adducěre, arcessěre* (= to send for), *advehěre* ; — breath, *spirare, spiritum ducěre.*

fetid, adj. *teter, graveolens, foetidus, putidus.* **fetidness,** n. *foetor.*

fetter, I. n. 1, *compes, -ēdis,* f., *pedica, vinculum* (= chain) ; 2, fig. *vincula, -orum.* **II.** v.tr. 1, *vincula alci in(j)icěre, alci compedes indere* ; 2, fig. *impedire.*

feud, n. = enmity, *simultas* ; *bellum* (=public war) ; *inimicitia* (private), *rixa* (= quarrel).

feud, n. = property held of a lord, **feudum* (Mediæval Lat.). **feudal,** adj. **feudalis.*

fever, n. *febris.* **feverish,** adj. 1, *febriculosus* (Gell.) ; 2, fig. *(com)motus, ardens.*

few, adj. *pauci, rari* ; *ary* —, *perpauci* ; see LITTLE.

fiat, n. see COMMAND.

fib, n. *mendaciunculum* (once in Cicero).

fibre, n. *fibra.* **fibrous,** adj. by the gen. *fibrae.*

fickle, adj. *inconstans, varians, varius, lěvis, mutabilis,* comb. *varius et mutabilis, mobilis* (e.g. *ingenium, animus, voluntas*). **fickleness,** n. *inconstantia, levitas, mutabilitas, mobilitas, varietas.* **fictile,** adj. *fictilis.*

fiction, n. 1, *(con)fictio* (= the act) ; 2, *res ficta,* or *fictum, falsum, fabula, commentum.* **fictitious,** adj. *commenticius* ; see FABULOUS.

fiddle, n. *fides, -ium,* pl. **fiddler,** n. *fidicen.*

fidelity, n. *fidelitas* ; see FAITH.

fidget, I. v.tr. see DISTURB. **II.** v.intr. *quiescěre non posse.* **fidgetty,** adj. *inquietus.*

fie! interj. *phui pro(h)* (with nom. or accus.).

field, n. 1, = a plain, *campus* ; 2, = a piece of land, *ager,* or pl. *agri, arvum,* or pl. *arva* ; *seges, -ětis,* f. (= a sowed field) ; *pratum* (= meadow) ; relating to —, *agrarius* ; 3, fig. in relation to an army, to be in the —, *militiae esse* (opp. *domi*), *in castris esse, bellum gerěre* ; to take the — against, *arma capěre* or *ferre adversus alqm* ; in gen. — of history, etc., by special noun (e.g. *historia*), but *locus* and *area* are used in this sense. **field-day,** n. *dies quo milites lustrantur.* **field-piece,** n. *tormentum (bellicum).*

fiend, n. **diabolus* (Eccl.). **fiendish,** adj. **diabolicus, nefandus, foedus, immanis, crudelis, ferox, atrox.* Adv. *nefande, foede.* **fiendishness,** n. *(summa) ferocitas.*

fierce, adj. *ferox, ferus, saevus, atrox,* † *trux,* † *truculentus, immanis.* Adv. *ferociter, saeve, atrociter, immane, immaniter.* **fierceness,** n. *ferocitas, atrocitas, saevitia, immanitas.*

fiery, adj. 1, lit. *igneus,* † *ignifer, flammeus, ardens, fervens, fervidus* ; 2, fig. see FIERCE, IMPETUOUS.

fife, n. *tibia.* **fifer,** n. *tibicen.*

fifteen, adj. *quindecim* ; — apiece, *quini deni* ; — times, *quindecie(n)s.* **fifteenth,** adj. *quintus decimus.* **fifth,** adj. *quintus.* **fifty,** adj. *quinquaginta* ; — apiece, *quinquageni.* **fiftieth,** adj. *quinquagesimus.*

fig, n. 1, the tree, *ficus,* f. ; 2, the fruit, *ficus* ; dried —, *Carica, Cauneae* ; 3, not to care a — for, *non flocci facěre.*

fight, I. n. *pugna, certamen* ; — with the fist, *pugilatus, -ūs, pugilatio.* **II.** v.intr. *(de)pugnare, dimicare, proeliari, digladiari, bellare.* **fighter,** n. *pugnator, gladiator, proeliator.*

figment, n. see FICTION.

figure, I. n. 1, = form or shape, *figura, forma, species, facies, statura* (= the stature), *habitus, -ūs* (corporis, = the natural bearing, opp. *cultus*), *conformatio* ; a beautiful —, *dignitas corporis, venustas* ; 2, = an image or representation, lit. *schema, -ātis, figura, formo, imago* ; geometrical —s, *formae geometricae, schemata geometrica, descriptiones, -um* ; 3, fig. a — in rhetoric, *figura* (Quint.) ; rhetorical —s, *orationis ornamenta, -orum, verborum exornationes, -um* ; 4, = a cipher, *lit(t)era* ; 5, = sculpture, *signum.* **II.** v.tr. 1, = draw, *describěre* ; 2, = FORM ; 3, = IMAGINE. **figurative,** adj. *translatus.* Adv. *per translationem.*

figured, adj. *sigillatus* (of cups (Cic.), late of silk).

filament, n. *fibra* (in bodies and plants).

file, I. n. 1, *lima* (of smiths), *scobina* (of carpenters) ; 2, of soldiers, *ordo* ; of the rank and —, *milites.* **II.** v.tr. *limare, limā polire.* **filings,** n. *scobis.*

filial, adj. *pius* (erga parentes). Adv. *pie.*

fill, v.tr. 1, *implēre* (generally), *explēre* (= to fill up), *complēre* (to make quite full), *replēre* (= to fill again, or merely fill), *supplēre* (= to supply what is lacking), *opplēre* (= to fi.l so as to cover), *refercire* (= to stuff), *cumulare alqd alqd re* (= to heap up) ; 2, fig. (e.g. an office), *alqd re fungi.*

fillet, n. *fascia (fasciola), redimiculum, mitella, vitta* (round the head as an ornament), *infula* (used by priests).

filly, n. *equula (ecula).*

film, n. 1, = thin skin, *membrana* ; 2, = thread, *filum* ; 3, fig. = darkness, *caligo, nubes, -is.*

filter, I. n. *colum.* **II.** v.tr. *(per)colare, liquare.*

filth, n. 1, lit. see DIRT; 2, fig. *impuritas;* to utter —, *foeda loqui;* see OBSCENITY. **filthy,** adj. 1, see DIRTY; 2, *impurus;* see OBSCENE. Adv. 1, see DIRTY; 2, *impure.* **filthiness,** n. *squalor;* see FILTH.

fin, n. *pinna* (Plin.).

final, adj. *ultimus, extremus.* Adv. *ad extremum, denique, postremo, quod superest, restat, rel(l)iquum est.*

finances, n. 1, of a private person, *res familiaris;* see INCOME; 2, of a state, *vectigalia, -ium, aerarium* (= treasury), *respublica* (= the general pecuniary condition). **financial,** adj. *ad vectigalia or aerarium pertinens.*

find, v.tr. 1, *invenire, reperire; offendĕre* (= to fall on), *deprehendĕre in alqâ re* (= to catch); he found admirers, *erant or non deerant qui eum admirarentur;* to — out, *excogitare, explorare, exquirĕre;* 2, = to experience, *experiri, or* by special verb (e.g. death, *perire;* — favour, *gratiam conciliare*). **finder,** n. *inventor, repertor.*

fine, I. adj. 1, *bellus, elegans;* the — arts, *artes liberales;* see BEAUTIFUL; very —! *belle! pulchre! bene dicis! bene facis!* 2, = thin, *tenuis, subtilis;* 3, = pure, *purus;* 4, of weather, *serenus, sudus.* Adv. *belle, eleganter, tenuiter, subtiliter.* **II.** n. 1, = end, *finis,* m. (f. ante and post class., and poet. in sing.); in —, *denique;* 2, = penalty, *multa.* **III.** v.tr. *multare.* **fineness,** n. 1, *elegantia;* see BEAUTY; 2, *tenuitas, subtilitas;* 3, *serenitas.* **finery,** n. *lenocinium* (in bad sense), *munditia, apparatus, -ûs, lautitia.* **finesse,** I. n. *artificium.* **II.** v.intr. *artificiis uti.*

finger, I. n. *digitus* (also = a measure, e.g. *quatuor digitis longus, latus, crassus*), *pollex* (= the thumb); to count by the —*s, in digitos digerĕre, digitis or per digitos numerare, digitis computare;* to turn round your —, *nihil est tractibilius illo;* to regard as the — of God, *divinitus alqd accidisse putare.* **II.** v.tr. *tangĕre.*

finical, adj. *putidus.* Adv. *putide.*

finish, I. v.tr. *finire, ad exitum adducĕre, ad finem perducĕre, conficĕre, consummare, absolvĕre, perficĕre.* **II.** n. *absolutio, perfectio, lima* (=polish, lit. = file). **finished,** adj. *limatus* (=polished), *absolutus, perfectus.* **finisher,** n. *confector, perfector.* **finishing,** adj. = FINAL.

finite, adj. *finitus* (= having an end), *circumscriptus* (= limited). Adv. *finite.*

fir, n. *abies, -ĕtis,* f., *pinus.*

fire, I. n. 1, *ignis,* m., *flamma, ardor, incendium, scintillae* (= sparks), *focus* (= fireside); 2, = conflagration, *incendium;* to be on —, *ardēre, flagrare;* to waste with — and sword, *ferro ignique vastare;* to put out —, *ignem reprimĕre, incendium restinguĕre;* to be between two —*s, lupum auribus tenēre;* 3, fig. *ignis, ardor;* to set a person's mind on —, *vehementius incendĕre alcjs animum;* mental —, *vis, vigor, impetus, -ûs, spiritus, -ûs, calor, ardor, fervor,* all with *animi;* — of youth, *juvenilis ardor;* poetic —, *impetus divinus;* — of discourse, *vis orationis;* to be without — (of speakers), *languĕre, frigĕre;* 4, = — of soldiers, *teli conjectus, -ûs;* to stand —, *ignis ictu esse;* to be out of —, *extra teli conjectum esse.* **II.** v.tr. *incendĕre.* **III.** v.intr. *incendi;* he readily fires up, *natura ejus praeceps est in iram.* **fire-arms,** n. *tormenta, -orum.* **fire-brand,** n. 1, *torris,* m., *fax* (= torch); 2, fig. *incitator et fax.* **fire-brigade,** n. *excubiae nocturnae vigilesque adversus incendia instituti* (Suet.). **fire-engine,** n. *sipho(n)* (Plin. Min.). **fire-escape,** n. *scalae.* **fire-place, fire-side,** n. *caminus, focus.* **fire-wood,** n. *lignum* (usu. pl.). **fire-worshipper,** n. *qui ignem pro Deo veneratur.*

firm, adj. 1, *firmus, stabilis, solidus, immobilis, immotus;* 2, fig. *constans, firmus.* Adv. *firme, solide, constanter.* **firmness,** n. *firmitas, firmitudo* (e.g. *vocis, animi*), *obstinatio, soliditas* (lit.), *constantia, perseverantia.*

first, I. adj. *primus, prior* (of two), *princeps* (= chief). **II.** Adv. *primum, primo.* **first-born,** n. *natu major* (of two), *maximus* (of several). **first-fruits,** n. *primitiae.* **first-ling,** n. *primus genitus.*

fiscal, adj. *fiscalis* (J ct.).

fish, I. n. *piscis,* m., *piscatus, -ûs* (collectively); — of the sea, *piscis maritimus;* river —, *p. fluviatilis.* **II.** v.intr. 1, *piscari;* 2, fig. — for, *captare, aucupari.* **fishbone,** n. *spina piscis.* **fisher,** n. *piscator, piscatrix.* **fishery,** n. *mare or flumen in quo pisces capiuntur.* **fishhook,** n. *hamus.* **fishmonger,** n. *qui pisces venditat.* **fishing,** n. *piscatus, -ûs;* — line, *linum;* a — net, *rete, funda, jaculum* (= a casting-net); — boat, *scapha or cymba piscatoria* (small); — vessel, *navis piscatoria;* — rod, *arundo piscatoria.* **fishy,** adj. by gen. *piscium* (e.g. *odor,* a fishy smell).

fissure, n. *fissura, fissum, rima* (= a leak); to make a —, *diffindĕre.*

fist, n. *pugnus.* **fisticuffs,** n. *pugilatus, -ûs, colaphus;* to give—, *colaphum alci impingĕre.*

fistula, n. *fistula* (Cels.).

fit, I. adj. *ad alqd aptus, idoneus* (= proper), *commodus, opportunus, habilis, appositus;* comb. *opportunus et idoneus, commodus et idoneus, habilis et aptus.* Adv. *apte, commode, opportune, apposite.* **II.** v.intr. 1, lit. *aptum esse, apte convenire ad or in alqd;* the shoes —, *calcei ad pedes apte conveniunt;* 2, fig. *alci or ad alqd aptum esse, alci rei or ad alqd accommodatum esse, alci rei or cum re convenire, alci rei or cum alqâ re congruĕre.* **III.** v.tr. *alqd alci rei aptare, accommodare;* — out, *(ex)ornare, instruĕre.* **IV.** n. 1, of illness, *impetus, -ûs, accessio* (Plin.); 2, of anger, etc., *impetus, -ûs, or* by special word (e.g. *ira, amicitia*); by —s and starts, *modo ... modo* (e.g. good by —, *modo bonus, modo improbus*). **fitness,** n. *habilitas, opportunitas, convenientia.*

five, adj. *quinque; quini, -ae, -a* (= five each), *quinquennium,* a period of — years, also *lustrum; quinto quoque anno,* every — years; — times, *quinquie(n)s;* — fold, *quincuplex, quinquepartitus* (= of — parts). **fifth,** adj. *quintus, -a, -um.* **fives,** n. use *pila* (e.g. *pilis ludĕre*).

fix, v.tr. 1, *alci rei or ad alqd (af)figĕre;* 2, = APPOINT. **fixed,** adj. *certus.* Adv. *intentis oculis.* **fixture,** n. *res quae moveri non potest.* **fixedness,** n. *constantia* (animi, consilii); see FASTEN.

flabby, flaccid, adj. *marcidus, fluidus.* **flaccidity,** n. *resolutio* (Cels., e.g. *nervorum stomachi*).

flag, I. n. = standard, *signum, vexillum;* of a ship, *insigne, vexillum;* a — ship, *navis praetoria.* **II.** v.intr. *languescĕre* (= grow feeble), *frigēre* (of conversation, etc.), *refrigescĕre* (of preparations, etc.). **flagstaff,** n. *vexillum.*

flag, I. n. = flat stone, *quadratum saxum.* **II.** v.tr. *(viam) quadratis saxis sternĕre or munire.*

flagitious, adj. *flagitiosus, nefarius, foedus.* Adv. *flagitiose, nefarie, foede.*

flagon, n. *lagēna, ampulla.*

flagrant, adj. *impudens, apertus, manifestus.* Adv. *impudenter, aperte, manifeste.* **flagrancy,** n. *impudentia.*

flail, n. *pertica* (Plin.), or *fustis,* m. (Col.) (= cudgel used in thrashing).

flake, n. of snow, use in pl. *nives.*

flambeau, n. *fax, taeda.*

flame, I. n. 1, *flamma* (lit. and fig.), *ignis,* m. ; 2, fig. the — of war spreads in Africa, *Africa ardet bello.* **II.** v.intr. *ardēre, flagrare.* **flame-coloured**, adj. *flammeus, rutilus.* **flaming,** adj. *flammeus ;* — eyes, *oculi ardentes.*

flank, n. *latus, -ēris,* n. (of men, beasts, a camp, an army); on both —s, *ab utroque latere.*

flap, I. n. *lacinia.* **II.** v.tr. *alis plaudēre.* **III.** v.intr. *fluitare.*

flare, v.intr. *fulgēre, splendēre.*

flash, I. n. *fulgur.* **II.** v.intr. *fulgurare, fulgēre,* (*e*)*micare, coruscare, splendēre ;* the eyes —, *oculi scintillant.*

flask, n. *ampulla.*

flat, I. adj. 1, *planus, aequus* (=even), *pronus* (=on the ground) ; — nose, *nasus simus ;* 2, of wine, etc., *vapidus* (Col.) ; — bottomed boats, *naves plano alveo ;* 3, = insipid, *insulsus, frigidus.* Adv. fig. *plane.* **II.** n. *planities ;* — of the hand, *palma.*

flatter, v.tr. *alqm adulari, alci assentari* or *blandiri.* **flatterer**, n. *adulator, assentator.* **flattering**, adj. *blandus, blandiens, jucundus, gratus* (= acceptable). Adv. *assentatorie, per blanditias.* **flattery**, n. *adulatio, assentatio, ambitio* (= effort to gain favour), *blanditiae* (= smooth words, caresses, etc.); *blandimentum.*

flatulence, n. *inflatio.* **flatulent,** adj. use *inflatio.*

flaunt, I. v.intr. *se ostentare ;* — in gold and purple, *insignem auro et purpurâ conspici.* **II.** v.tr. = to display, *jactare alqd.*

flavour, I. n. *sapor.* **II.** v.tr. *alqd condire alqâ re.*

flaw, n. *vitium.* **flawless**, adj. *emendatus, sine culpâ.* Adv. *emendate.*

flax, n. *linum, carbasus,* f. **flaxen,** adj. 1, = of flax, *lineus ;* 2, = of colour, *flavus.*

flay, v.tr. lit. *pellem detrahēre alci* or *alcjs corpori, deglutēre alqm* (alive, *vivum*).

flea, n. *pulex.*

fledged, adj. †*plumatus ;* to be —, *pennas habēre.*

flee, I. v.intr. *fugam petēre, capere, capessēre, fugae se mandare, se committēre, in fugam se dare, se con(f)icēre, terga vertēre* (of soldiers), *in fugam effundi* or *se conjicēre ;* — from, *fugēre ab* or *ex alqo loco ;* — a person, *alqm fugēre ;* — to, *fugâ petēre alqd* (e.g. *arborem*), *confugēre* or *fugam capessēre alqo, confugēre* or *profugēre ad alqm.* **II.** v.tr. see Above. **flight,** n. *fuga.*

fleece, I. n. *vellus, -ēris,* n. **II.** v.tr. 1, *tondēre ;* 2, = rob, *expilare, spoliare.* **fleecy,** adj. † *laniger.*

fleet, I. adj. *velox, volucer, pernix.* **II.** n. *classis.* **fleeting**, adj. *fugax, caducus, fluxus.* **fleetness**, n. *velocitas, pernicitas.*

flesh, n. *caro, -nis,* f. (= on the body and cooked), *viscera, -um,* n. (= everything under the skin of an animal), *corpus, -ōris,* n. (opp. *ossa*); in speaking of the flesh of animals the Latins omit *caro* (e.g. *vitulina,* = veal ; *canina,* = dog's flesh). **fleshy,** adj. *carnosus.*

flexible, adj. 1, *lentus ;* 2, of character, *mollis, facilis.* **flexibility**, n. of character, *mollitia, mollitudo, facilitas.*

flicker, v.intr. *volitare* (of birds), *fluitare* (of things, as sails), *trepidare* (of flames, etc.).

flight, n. 1, *fuga ;* see FLEE ; to put to —, *fugare ;* 2, = way of flying, *lapsus, -ûs, volatus,*

-*ûs ;* 3, of stairs, *scalae.* **flighty,** adj. *volatilis, mobilis, levis, inconstans.* **flightiness,** n. *mobilitas, levitas.*

flimsy, adj. 1, = thin, *tenuis ;* 2, = worthless, *inanis.* **flimsiness,** n. 1, *tenuitas ;* 2, *inanitas.*

flinch, v.intr. (*re*)*cedēre, retro cedēre.*

fling, v.tr. *jactare, mittēre, jaculari, con(j)icēre ;* — at, *alci rei* or *in alqd in(j)icēre, alqm alqâ re petēre.*

flint, n. *silex ;* heart of —, *siliceus.*

flippant, adj. *lascivus, petulans.* **flippancy,** n. *petulant.*

flirt, I. v.intr. *alqm specie amoris illicēre.* **II.** n. *amator* or *amatrix inconstans.* **flirtation,** n. *species amoris.*

flit, v.intr. *volitare.*

flitch, n. *succidia.*

float, v.intr. *innare, innatare, aquâ sustinēri, fluctuare, fluitare, pendēre* (in the air).

flock, I. n. *grex, pecus, -ōris,* n. ; = a great number of persons, *caterva, multitudo.* **II.** v.intr. *affluēre, confluēre ;* — together, *concurrēre, convolare.*

flog, v.tr. *verberare ;* be —ged, *vapulare.* **flogging**, n. *verbera, -um, verberatio.*

flood, I. n. 1, as contradistinguished from ebb, *accessus, -ûs, maris* (opp. *recessus aestuum*), *aestûs commutatio* (=change of tide from the ebb) ; the — (tide) rises, *aestus crescit, aestus ex ulto se incitat ;* the — falls, *aestus minuit ;* 2, = overflow, *eluvio, diluvies ;* 3, fig. *vis* (e.g. *lacrimarum*). **II.** v.tr. 1, lit. *inundare ;* 2, fig. *alqd alqâ re cumulare.* **flood-gate,** n. 1, lit. *cataracta* (or *cataractes, -ae*) (Plin. Min.) ; 2, fig. *vis, impetus, -ûs.*

floor, n. *solum, coaxatio* (coass-); to make or lay —, *coaxationem facēre, coaxare ; pavimentum,* p. *tessellatum* or *vermiculatum* (= mosaic) ; *area* (= a barn-floor) ; *tabulatum,* (*con*)*tabulatio, contignatio* (= a storey).

floral, adj. *floreus.*

florid, adj. 1, of complexion, *rubicundus ;* 2, fig. *floridus.*

flounce, n. (of a woman's gown), *instita, segmenta, -orum,* pl. **flounced,** adj. *segmentatus.*

flounder, v.intr. 1, lit. *volutari, fluitare ;* 2, fig. *titubare.*

flour, n. *farina.*

flourish, I. v.intr. 1, *florēre, vigēre ;* 2, = make a display, *se jactare.* **II.** v.tr. see BRANDISH.

flout, v.tr. *ludificari, cavillari, deridēre, irridēre.*

flow, I. v.intr. (as a fluid) *fluēre, labi, manare ;* — into the sea, *effundi in mare ;* — between, *interfluēre ;* — past, *praeterfluēre ;* — together, *confluēre.* **II.** n. 1, *fluxio, lapsus, -ûs ;* 2, fig. *volubilitas, copia* (e.g. *verborum*); 3, of the tide, *accessus, -ûs* (opp. *recessus*). **flowing,** adj. 1, *fluens, manans ;* 2, = speech, (*pro*)*fluens, volubilis.* Adv. (*pro*)*fluenter, volubiliter.*

flower, I. n. 1, *flos, flosculus* (dim.) ; the goddess of —s, *Flora ;* 2, fig. — of life, *aetas florens ;* = best part of, *flos, robur ;* — of speech, *flos verborum.* **II.** v.intr. *florēre,* (*ef*)*florēscēre, flores mittēre.* **flowery,** adj. 1, lit. † *floreus ;* 2, fig. *floridus.*

fluctuate, v.intr. *fluctuare* (*animo*) or *fluctuari, pendēre animi* or *animo* (of several, *animis*), *incertum, dubium, ancipitem esse, haesitare, dubitare, in dubio esse.* **fluctuation**, n. *animus incertus* or *dubius* or *suspensus, dubitatio.*

flue, n. *camīnus;* the — smokes, *domus fumat.*

fluency, n. *oratio volubilis, facundia, volubilitas.* **fluent,** adj. *volubilis* (opp. *stabilis*); a — style, *genus orationis (pro)fluens.* Adv. (*pro*)-*fluenter, volubiliter;* to speak —, *commode verba facĕre.*

fluid, I. n. *liquor, humor, aqua.* **II.** adj. *liquidus, fluidus, fluens.*

flummery, n. 1, = a dish, *avēnae puls, -tis,* f.; 2, = empty talk, *gerrae, nugae, nugatoria, -orum.*

flurry, n. and v.tr.; see EXCITE.

flush, I. n. *rubor.* **II.** v.intr. *rubor* or *pudor alci suffunditur.*

fluster, v.tr. *percutĕre, agitare, commovēre.*

flute, n. *tibia* or *tibiae,* †*arundo.* **flute-player,** *tibicen.* **fluted,** adj. *striatus.*

flutter, I. v.intr. *trepidare, volitare.* **II.** v.tr. *agitare, commovēre.* **III.** n. *trepidatio.*

flux, n. *fluxio* (in gen.); — and reflux of the sea, *marinorum aestuum accessus et recessus* (both *-ūs*).

fly, I. n. *musca, cantharis, -ĭdis,* f. **II.** v.intr. *volare, volitare;* to — to, *advolare;* to — in, *involare;* to — out, *evolare;* to — away, *avolare;* to let —, *emittĕre e manibus, ventis dare.* **flying,** adj. *volatilis, volucer;* — (= dishevelled) hair, *crines passi.*

foal, I. n. *pullus equi, pullus equinus.* **II.** v.tr. *parĕre.*

foam, I. n. *spuma.* **II.** v.intr. *spumare,* (*ex*)*aestuare.* **foamy,** adj. *spumans,* †*spumeus.*

fodder, n. *pabulum, pastus, -ūs.*

foe, n. *hostis* (= a public —), *inimicus* (= a private —).

fog, n. *nebula.* **foggy,** adj. *nebulosus.*

foible, n. *vitium.*

foil, I. n. *rudis.* **II.** v.tr. *ad vanum* or *ad irritum redigĕre, eludĕre.*

foist, v.tr. — on, *alqd alci supponĕre, subdĕre, sub(j)icĕre.*

fold, I. n. †*sinus, -ūs, ruga* (= a wrinkle or small fold in plants, dresses, etc. (Plin.)). **II.** v.tr. *alqd* (*com*)*plicare;* to — the hands, *digitos pectinatim inter se implectĕre* (Plin.); with —ed hands, *compressis manibus.* **III.** as suffix, *plex* (e.g. three—, *triplex*). **folding-doors,** n. *valvae* (*bifores*), *fores, -ium,* f.

fold, n. = — for sheep, *ovile, saeptum,* usu. pl.; = — for cattle, *stabulum.*

foliage, n. *frons,* f., or pl. *frondes* (=branches); *folia, -orum* (= leaves).

folk, n. see PEOPLE.

follow, v.tr. 1, *alqm* (*con*)*sequi, insequi, subsequi* (= very close), *prosequi* (= at a distance), *alqm persequi* (= to follow out), *comitari* (=to accompany); he was —ed by an unusually large company, *stipatus est non usitatā frequentiā;* to — after or succeed, *alci* and *alci rei sucēdĕre, alqm* and *alqd excipĕre;* = — as a successor, *succēdĕre in alcjs locum;* to — from, *effici, confici ex re* (in argument, e.g. *ex propositis efficitur*); hence it —s, *sequitur, sequitur igitur* or *enim, ex quo efficitur;* what —s? *quid igitur?* thus it —s, *ita fit ut,* etc.; 2, = regard as a teacher, etc., *alqm* or *alqd sequi, auctoritate alcjs movēri, alci obtemperare* (= to listen to the wishes of), *dicto alcjs audientem esse* (= to — or obey his command); to — an opinion, *sententiam alcjs sequi* or *probare;* to — your own judgment, *suo ingenio uti.* **following,** adj. *sequens, secutus;* for the — year (e.g. *in insequentem annum*); *alci proximus, secundus ab alqo* (of persons in a

series), *futurus, venturus, posterus;* the — day, *dies posterus;* on the —, *postero die, postridie* (*ejus diei*). **follower,** n. = disciple, *discipulus, auditor,* (*as*)*sectator, unus e suis* (of the followers of a leader); —s of Socrates, *Socratici* (and so with many other names).

folly, n. see under FOOL.

foment, v.tr. 1, *alqd fovēre, fomenta alci rei adhibēre* or *admovēre;* 2, fig. *sol(l)icitare, excitare.* **fomentation,** n. *fomentum* (Cels.). **foment,** n. *fax, concitator, instimulator.*

fond, adj. 1, = foolish, *stultus;* 2, = loving, *amans, amator, cultor, studiosus alcjs rei;* very —, *alcjs rei* or *alcjs amantissimus* or *studiosissimus, consectator alcjs rei* (e.g. *voluptatis*); — of literature or learning, *lit(t)erarum studiosus;* — of hunting, *venandi studiosus.* Adv. *stulte, amanter.* **fondness,** n. 1, *stultitia;* 2, *studium, amor, caritas.* **fondle,** v.tr. *blandiri alci,* (*per*)*mulcēre alqm, amplexari et osculari alqm.* **fondling,** n. *blanditiae.*

food, n. *cibus, esca, cibaria, -orum* (= whatever may be eaten by men or beasts), *edulia, -ium* (= eatables), *alimentum* (or in pl., esp. in poets); *penus, -ūs* or *-i,* m. and f., and *-ōris,* n. (= supplies of food); to digest —, *cibum concĕere, concoquĕre;* a food-shop, *popina;* of animals, *pabulum, pastus, -ūs.*

fool, I. n. *homo stultus, fatuus, sannio* (= a maker of grimaces); to put a —'s cap on a person, *ludibrio habēre;* to play the —, *nugari, ineptire, desipĕre.* **II.** v.tr. *alqm ludĕre.* **foolery,** n. *ineptiae, nugae.* **fool-hardy,** adj. *temerarius;* see RASH. **foolish,** adj. *stultus, stolidus* (= silly), *ineptus* (=one who acts out of place and time and reason), *insulsus* (= witless), *demens* (= one who has lost his head), *fatuus.* Adv. *stulte, stolide, inepte, insulse.* **folly,** n. *stultitia* (= stupidity, a foolish act), *fatuitas* (= silliness), *insipientia* (= want of prudence), *amentia* (= unreason), *dementia* (= loss of faculty), *stulte factum* (as an act).

foot, I. n. 1, = member of the body, *pes, pedis,* m.; to go on —, *pedibus ire, venire, iter facĕre;* to serve on —, *pedibus merēre,* or *stipendia facĕre;* to tread under —, *pedibus conculcare, proculcare;* — by —, *pedetentim, gradatim* (= step by step); 2, = the lowest part, *pes* (of articles of furniture), or by *imus, infimus* with n. (e.g. *infimus mons*); *radix* (e.g. *montis*); the town lies at the — of the mountain, *urbs monti subjecta est;* 3, = a measure, *pes;* a — in size, *pedalis* (in longitudinem, in altitudinem), *pedem longus;* half a —, *semipedalis;* one and a half —, *sesquipedalis;* two —, *bipedalis;* three —, *tripedalis;* five — deep, *quinque pedes altus;* 4, (in versification) *pes.* **II.** v.intr. see TREAD, DANCE. **III.** adj. *pedester;* — soldier, *pedes, -itis.* **footing,** n. = way or manner, *modus, ratio, status, -ūs;* to place an army on the — of the Roman, *exercitum ad Romanae disciplinae formam redigĕre;* to place on the old —, *ad antiquum morem revocare;* to be on a very friendly — with, *valde familiariter alqo uti.* **footman,** n. *pedis(s)equus.* **foot-pad,** n. *latro.* **foot-path,** n. *semita, trames, -itis,* m., *callis.* **foot-print,** n. *vestigium.* **footstool,** n. *scamnum, scabellum.*

fop, n. *homo ineptus, homuncio.* **foppery,** n. *ineptiae* (= absurdities).

for, I. prep. 1 = in behalf of, in return for, *pro* (with the ablative); *dimicare pro legibus* (so *pro libertate, pro patriā*), = to fight — the laws; *Cato est mihi unus pro multis milibus,* = Cato alone is to me — (= as good as) many thousands; *huic ille pro meritis gratiam retulit,* = he returned him thanks — his deserts; 2, = *a⌐ alqm virum bo-*

num habēre, = to hold him — a good man (so vir
bonus habetur); "for" and "as" in such phrases
do not appear in Latin (e.g. dux electus est, = he
was chosen — (as) general); yet, pro nihilo
putare, = to think nothing of; 3, "for" denoting
value, by the genitive of indefinite price and
the ablative of the definite (e.g. quanti emisti?
— how much did you buy it?; viginti assibus,
= — twenty pence); 4, = by reason of, prae
with abl., propter with acc., to die — fear, prae
metu mori; — this reason, propter hoc; 5, of
time, in with accus., — the next day, in posterum diem; = during, accus., he had been away
— a year, annum jam aberat, or by per with
accus.; 6, expressing purpose, ad with accus.,
money — building a bridge, pecunia ad pontem
aedificandum data; to live — the day, in diem
vivĕre; 7, to watch or consult —, alci consulĕre;
love —, amor alcjs or erga algm; means or
remedy —, remedium adversus algd, or the genitive alone, as, care — you, vestri cara; —, as
denoting according to, pro suā quisque parte,
pro viribus (= according to your strength); according to your wisdom, quae tua est prudentia,
or quā es prudentiā; — the present, in praesens;
to live — yourself (that is, your own interests),
sibi vivĕre. II. conj. nam(que), enim (enclit.),
etenim, quippe, quod, cum (with subj.), quoniam,
quia; see BECAUSE, FORASMUCH, FOR 1., 2.

forage, I. n. pabulum. **II.** v.tr. pabulari; to send soldiers to —, pabulatum or pabulandi caus(s)ā milites mittĕre. **forager,** n. pa-
bulator. **foraging,** n. pabulatio.

forbear, v.tr. 1, = to abstain, se tenēre, se continēre, se cohibēre, (se) algā re abstinēre, alci rei
parcĕre; 2, = to endure patiently, patientiā uti,
patientiam adhibēre alci rei, patienter atque aequo
animo ferre, pati ac ferre, pati ac perferre, perferre
patique algd. **forbearance,** n. abstinentia,
continentia, patientia. **forbearing,** adj. abstinens, continens, temperatus.

forbid, v.tr. vetare (with accus. and inf.),
interdicĕre alci algā re (or with ne); to — one
your house, interdicĕre alci domo suā; it is
—den, vetitum est, non licet.

force, I. n. vis, violentia, impetus, -ūs, momentum; to use —, vim facĕre, vim adhibēre. **II.**
v.tr. see COMPEL. **forcible,** adj. 1, = by
force, per vim; 2, = physically strong, validus,
nervosus; 3, = morally strong, energetic, gravis,
vehemens. Adv. vi, per vim, valide, nervose,
graviter, vehementer.

forcemeat, n. insicia (Varr.).

ford, n. vadum.

fore, adv. ante, antea. **forearm, I.** n.
brachium. **II.** v.tr. see WARN, PREPARE; to
be —ed, praecavēre. **forebode,** v.intr. and
tr. 1, portendĕre, praesagire; 2, = have a
presentiment of, praesagire, praesentire. **foreboding,** n. praesensio. **forecast,** v.tr. (animo) praevidēre, providēre, prospicĕre. **forefather,** n. proăvus; pl. priores, majores, patres.
forefinger, n. digitus index. **forego,** v.tr.
(con)cedĕre algd. **forehead,** n. frons, -ntis, f.
foreknow, v.tr. praenoscĕre. **foreknowledge,** n. by providēre. **foreland,** n. promontorium. **foreman,** n. procurator. **fore-
mast,** n. malus anterior. **foremost,** adj.
primus. **forenoon,** n. dies antemeridianus. **forerunner,** n. praenuntius. **foresee,** v.tr. praevidēre, providēre, prospicĕre.
foresight, n. providentia, prospicientia.
forestall, v.tr. praevenire; see ANTICIPATE.
foretell, v.tr. praedicĕre. **forethought,** n.
providentia; by —, consulto; to do —, algd consulto or meditatum or praeparatum facĕre. **forewarn,** v.tr. praemonēre.

foreign, adj. peregrinus, externus, barbarus,
adventicius; — to, (ab) algā re, or alci rei
alienus; — to each other, res sibi repugnantes.
foreigner, n. peregrinus, alienigena, m. and f.,
advena, m. and f. (= new settler).

forensic, adj. forensis.

forest, n. silva, saltus, -ūs (wild and on
bills).

forfeit, I. v.tr. amittĕre, algā re multari.
II. n. poena, multa, damnum.

forge, v.tr. 1, = to form, tundĕre (= to beat,
e.g. ferrum), procudĕre (e.g. gladium), fabricari
(e.g. fulmina, fallaciam), fingĕre (e.g. fallacias),
2, = to falsify, — documents, tabulas corrumpĕre,
vitiare, interpolare, (= — parts in a document)
sub(j)icĕre; of money, cudĕre. **forger,** n.
subjector (of wills, etc.), qui nummos adulterinos
cudit; forged coin, nummus adulterinus. **for-
gery,** n. subjectio (= — of wills, etc.). For —
of money, use verb.

forget, v.tr. alcjs rei or algd oblivisci, neglegĕre (neglig-), neglegentiā praeterire; I have forgotten, algd fugit me, algd e memoriā excessit; to
be forgotten, e memoriā excidĕre; to — yourself,
sui oblivisci; to — your dignity, dignitatis suae
immemorem esse. **forgetful,** adj. obliviosus,
immemor. **forgetfulness,** n. oblivio.

forgive, v.tr. algd alci ignoscĕre, veniam
dare alcjs rei (= to give mercy instead of
justice), gratiam facĕre alcjs rei, algd alci
concedĕre, condonare, alci indulgēre. **forgiveness,** n. venia, poenae (meritae) remissio. **forgiving,** adj. facilis, clemens, exorabilis.

fork, n. furca, furcilla (used in making hay;
forks for eating were unknown). **forked,** adj.
bifurcus.

forlorn, adj. spe dejectus, relictus, destitutus.

form, I. n. 1, figura, forma, facies; of a
fine —, formosus, dignitate corporis praeditus or
insignis; human —, species humana; things
have taken a new —, magna rerum commutatio
facta est; 2, see FORMULA; 3, = bench, scamnum; 4, = appearances, for —'s sake, dicis
caus(s)ā. **II.** v.tr. 1, = to give — to, fingĕre,
figurare, formare, fabricari, facĕre, efficĕre; to —
intellectually and morally, fingĕre, (ex)colĕre,
expolire, instituĕre; 2, = troops, instruĕre,
ordinare; 3, = — plans, etc., (consilia) inire; —
friendship, amicitiam cum algo conjungĕre. **III.**
v.intr. 1, = constitute, ex alga re consistĕre; 2, of
troops, se explicare. **formal,** adj. = for the sake
of appearances, dicis caus(s)ā; = artificial, compositus, frigidus, simulatus; = stiff (of manners), urbanus ac perpolitus. Adv. rite (=
duly), composite, urbane. **formality,** n. 1, see
CEREMONY; 2, of manners, mores perpolitiae.
formation, n. 1, as act, conformatio; 2, =
form, conformatio, forma. **formless,** adj. informis, rudis. **formula,** n. formula, verba,
-orum.

former, adj. prior, pristinus (= ancient),
superior (e.g. annus); the —, the latter, hic
... ille, or ille ... hic. Adv. antea, olim, quondam.

formidable, adj. metuendus, timendus, horrendus, terribilis, formidulosus (formidol-). Adv.
formidulose, terribilem in modum.

fornication, n. stuprum.

forsake, v.tr. (de)relinquĕre, deserĕre, destituĕre, comb. deserĕre et relinquĕre, destituĕre et
relinquĕre.

forsooth! interj. scilicet (iron.), sane.

forswear, v.tr. 1, = to deny on oath, abjurare, ejurare (= to renounce); 2, = to swear
falsely, perjurare, pejurare.

fort, n. *locus munitus, arx, castellum, castrum.*
fortification, n. *munitio, munitiones, munimenta, -orum, opera, -um* (= works). **fortify**, v.tr. *(com)munire, praemunire, operibus munire, munitionibus firmare, muris munire, vallo et fossâ circumdare locum, vallum et fossam circumdare alci loco.*

forth, adv. 1, of place, *foras;* in combination it is expressed by *e, ex,* and *pro,* with the several verbs (e.g. to bring —, *efferre;* to cast —, *e(j)icĕre;* to go —, *exire;* to lead —, *educĕre, producĕre*) ; 2, of time, *inde.* **forthcoming**, adj. by fut. (e.g. — book, *liber quem alqs editurus est*) ; to be —, *in eo esse ut.* **forthwith**, adv. *extemplo, statim, confestim, protinus.*

fortitude, n. *fortitudo, animus forti., virtus, -ūtis,* f.

fortune, n. 1, *fortuna, fors, casus, -ūs;* changeful —, *fortunae vicissitudines, varietates temporum,* comb. *temporum varietates fortunaeque vicissitudines, casus varii;* to be content with your —, *sorte suâ contentum vivĕre;* the goddess of —, *Fortuna;* 2, =wealth, *divitiae, res familiaris, facultates, opes, pecuniae, bona, -orum, fortunae.* **fortune-teller**, n. *sortilegus, (h)ariolus;* a female —, *saga.* **fortuitous**, adj. *fortuitus, in casu positus, forte oblatus.* Adv. *forte, fortuito, casu.* **fortunate**, adj. *felix, fortunatus, prosper(us), secundus;* — condition, *res secundae.* Adv. *feliciter, fortunate, prospere.*

forty, adj. *quadraginta, quadrageni* (= — each), *quadragesie(n)s* (= — times).

forum, n. *forum.*

forward, I. adv. *porro;* to go —, *pergĕre.* II. v.tr. 1, = send on, *perferendum curare* (e.g. *lit(t)eras perferendas curavit);* 2, =help, *(ad)juvare, alci adjumento esse.* III. adj. 1, = early, *praecox;* 2, = rude, *protervus, inurbanus.*

foss, n. *fossa (incilis), incile.* **fossil**, n. *fossilia, -ium.*

foster, v.tr. *curare, nutrire, sustinēre, alĕre.* **foster-brother**, n. *collacteus* (late). **foster-child**, n. *alumnus, alumna.* **foster-father**, n. *nutricius.* **foster-sister**, n. *collactea* (Juv.).

foul, adj. *putidus, putridus, foetidus* (=stinking), *foedus, turpis* (= morally foul), *obscenus* (= impure), *immundus* (= dirty). **foul-play**, n. *dolus malus.* Adv. *putide, foede, turpiter.* **foulness**, n. *foeditas, obscenitas.*

found, v.tr. 1, *fundamentum alcjs rei jacĕre* or *ponĕre, fundamenta locare, condĕre, instituĕre, constituĕre, civitatem funditus tollĕre;* 2, fig. to be founded on, *niti alqâ re* or in *alqâ re,* also *niti fundamento alcjs rei, positum esse in alqâ re;* = cast, *fundĕre.* **foundation**, n. *fundamenta, -orum, sedes, -is;* — (of a pillar), *basis.* **founder**, I. n. *conditor, auctor.* II. v.intr. *submergi.* **foundling**, n. *infans expositus, expositicius.*

fount, or **fountain**, n. 1, lit. *fons* (= the place and the water), *caput* (= the spring); 2, fig. *fons, caput, principium,* comb. *fons et caput, principium et fons, origo, caus(s)a* (= the primary cause), comb. *caus(s)a atque fons.*

four, adj. *quat(t)uor, quaterni* (= — each) ; — or five, *quat(t)uor (aut) quinque;* — years old, *quadrimus;* a period of — years, *quadriennium;* every — years, *quarto quoque anno;* going on — feet, *quadrupes;* — fold, *quadruplex;* — times as much, *quadruplum;* — times, *quater.* **four-teen**, adj. *quat(t)uordecim, quaterni deni* (distributively); — times, *quater decies.* **fourteenth**, adj. *quartus decimus.* **fourth**, I. adj. *quartus, -a, -um;* every —, *quartus quisque;* the — time, *quartum;* in the — place, *quarto.* II. n. *quadrans.*

fowl, n. 1, *avis, volucris, ales, -itis,* m. and f. 2, = a hen, *gallina;* flesh of —, *(caro) gallinacea.* **fowler**, n. *auceps.* **fowling**, n. *aucupium.*

fox, n. 1, *vulpes, -is,* f. ; of a —, *vulpinus;* 2, fig. = a cunning man, *homo versutus* or *callidus.*

fraction, n. *pars.* **fractious**, adj. *morosus.* Adv. *morose.* **fractiousness**, n. *morositas.* **fracture**, I. n. med. t.t. *fractura* (Cels.). II. v.tr. *frangĕre.*

fragile, adj. *fragilis.* **fragility**, n. *fragilitas.* **fragment**, n. *fragmentum, re(l)liquiae* (= remains); —s of the plays of Menander, *trunca quaedam ex Menandro* (Gell.). **fragmentary**, adj. *fractus.*

fragrance, n. *odor suavis, suaveolentia.* **fragrant**, adj. *suavis,* † *suaveolens,* † *odorifer,* † *odoratus,* † *odorosus.*

frail, adj. *infirmus, debilis, imbecillus.* **frailty**, n. *infirmitas, imbecillitas* (lit. and fig.).

frame, I. n. 1, of a window, picture, etc., *forma* (Plin.); 2, = body, *corpus, -ŏris;* 3, see — of mind, *animus.* II. v.tr. 1, = put into a frame, *in formâ includĕre;* 2, = compose, *componĕre;* 3, see MAKE. **framework**, n. *compages, -is, contignatio.*

France, n. *Gallia.* **French**, adj. *Gallicus.* **franchise**, n. *civitas, jus, juris,* n., *suffragium.*

frank, adj. *sincerus, apertus, simplex.* Adv *sincere, candide, aperte, simpliciter.* **frank-ness**, n. *sinceritas, simplicitas.*

frankincense, n. *t(h)us, t(h)uris,* n.

frantic, adj. *insanus, delirus, fanaticus, amens, demens.* Adv. *insane.*

fraternal, adj. *fraternus.* Adv. *fraterne.* **fraternity**, n. 1, *fraternitas, necessitudo fraterna, germanitas;* 2, = society, *sodalitas, sodalitium, collegium, corpus, -ŏris.* **fraternize**, v.intr. *amicitiâ inter se conjungi.*

fratricide, n. 1, = the murder of a brother, *parricidium fraternum;* 2, = the murderer of a brother, *fratricida,* m.

fraud, n. *fraus, dolus (malus), circumscriptio, fallacia;* comb. *doli atque fallaciae;* to devise - against anyone, *dolum alci struĕre, nectĕre, confingĕre, fraude alqm tentare, fallaciam in alqm intendĕre.* **fraudulent**, adj. *fraudulentus, qui totus ex fraude et fallaciis constat* (opp. *homo sine fuco et fallaciis), dolosus.* Adv. *dolo malo, dolose, fraudulenter, contra (jus ac) fidem.*

fraught, adj. *alqâ re refertus, repletus, oneratus.*

fray, n. *pugna.*

freak, n. see CAPRICE.

freckle, n. *lenticula, lentigo* (Plin.). **freckled**, adj. *lentiginosus* (Val. Max.).

free, I. adj. 1, = — from burdens, etc., *liber, solutus; vacuus (a) re, expers rei;* from taxes, *immunis;* from guilt, *innocens;* from military service, *immunis militiâ;* from danger, *tutus;* from care, *securus;* to make —, *liberare;* to — from guilt, *absolvĕre alqm;* to be — from, *alqâ re carēre;* 2, = not subject to, *liber;* 3, = not restricted, as in space, *patens, apertus;* 4, = without cost, *gratuitus;* to have a — dwelling, *grati(i)s habitare;* 5, = — to do or to act, *liber, solutus;* I am = to say, *audeo dicĕre;* 6, = generous, *largus, munificus, liberalis.* Adv. *libere, solute, tuto, secure, aperte, grati(i)s, gratuito, large, munifice, liberaliter.* II. v.tr. *alqm alqâ re liberare, eximĕre. solvĕre, expedire. manumit-*

tēre (of a slave) ; to make — with, ., = to indulge in, *alci rei indulgēre* ; 2, = to treat disrespectfully, *algo parum honorifice uti*. **free-agent,** n. *qui sui juris est.* **freebooter,** n. *latro.* **free-born,** adj. *ingenuus.* **freedman,** n. *libertus, libertinus.* **freedom,** n. 1, = — from limits, *vacuitas, vacatio* ; from business, *otium* ; from taxes, *immunitas* ; from punishment, *impunitas* ; 2, = independence, *libertas* ; to give —, *libertatem alci dare, in libertatem alqm vindicare* ; — from slavery, *alqm manumittēre* ; — from prison, ı *custodia emittēre* ; to restore —, *libertatem alci reddēre* ; to restore yourself to —, *e vinculis se expedire* ; moral —, *arbitrium (liberum)* ; 3, = rights or privileges, *jus, juris,* n., *privilegium, beneficium* ; 4, = license, *licentia* ; to take —, *licentiam sibi sumēre, audēre* ; to take great —, *multa sibi sumēre* ; = great license, *licentia, arrogantia, procacitas.* **free-hearted,** adj. see GENEROUS. **freehold,** n. *praedium liberum* or *immune.* **freeholder,** n. *qui praed. lib. habet,* or simply *possessor.* **free-liver,** n. *qui licentius agit.* **free-living,** n. *licentia.* **freeman,** n. *civis, homo liber.* **free-speech,** n. *sermo liberior.* **free-thinking,** adj. see SCEPTICAL. **free-will,** n. *voluntas* ; to have —, *sponte suā agēre.*

freeze, I. v.tr. *glaciare, urēre.* **II.** v.intr. *gelare, gelari* (Plin., etc.) ; it —s, *gelat* ; = to feel cold, *frigēre, algēre.* **frozen,** adj. † *rigidus* ; to be —, *rigēre.*

freight, I. n. *onus, -ĕris,* n. **II.** v.tr. *onerare.* **freighted,** adj. *onustus.*

frenzy, n. *vesania, delirium, furor, amentia, dementia.*

frequent, adj. *frequens* (= many present, e.g., *frequens senatus*), *creber* (= thickly filled, opp. *rarus*), *multus* (= many), *celeber* (= numerous). Adv. *frequenter, crebro, saepe.* **II.** v.tr. *celebrare, frequentare, in alqo loco versari.* **frequency,** n. *frequentia, crebritas, celebritas.* **frequented,** adj. *frequens, celeber, tritus* (= well trodden).

fresh, adj. 1, = cool, *frigidus* ; 2, = recent, *recens, novus* ; — sod, *caespes vivus* ; 3, = unused, and therefore vigorous, *recens, integer, viridis,* comb. *recens integerque, vegetus, alacer* ; *vivus* ; a — complexion, *nitidus color.* Adv. use *frigidus* (*frigide* not in this sense), *recenter* (ante and post class.), *nove, integre, vegete.* **freshen,** v.tr. *refrigerare* (= to cool), *recreare, reficēre* (= to revive), *relaxare, integrare.* **freshness,** n. *viriditas* = vigour, use *novus,* with n. = novelty (e.g. the — of a book, *liber novus*).

fret, I. v.tr. 1, rub, *fricare, terēre* ; 2, = wear away, *atterēre* ; 3, fig. *sol(l)icitare, vexare, angēre.* **II.** v.intr. *alqd aegre ferre, angi, dolēre* ; see GRIEVE. **III.** n. *molestia* (or pl.), *angor, vexatio.* **fretful,** adj. *morosus, stomachosus* (rare). Adv. *morose, stomachose.* **fretfulness,** n. *morositas.*

fricassee, n. *sartago* (Pers.).

friction, n. *tritus.*

Friday, n. * *dies Veneris.*

friend, n. *amicus, amica, sodalis* (= companion), *necessarius* (= relation), *familiaris* (= intimate), *studiosus, amans, amator alcjs* ; my — ! *O bone ! sodes !* to be a — (patron) to, *alcjs fautorem esse, alci favēre* or *bene velle* ; those who are —s to a cause, etc., *qui stant ab* or *cum algo.* **friendless,** adj. *sine amicis, amicorum expers* or *inops.* **friendly, I.** adj. *amicus, benevolus, humanus, benignus, comis, urbanus.* **II.** Adv. *comiter, amice, benigne, urbane.* **friendliness,** n. *comitas, humanitas, benignitas, benevolentia (beniv-), affabilitas, urbanitas.* **friendship,** n. *amicitia, necessi-*

tudo, conjunctio, familiaritas ; to form a —, *amicitiam cum algo facēre, (con)jungēre, instituēre, conciliare, inire, sibi parare, ad am. alcjs se conferre, se applicare, se adjungēre, amicitiā alqm sibi conjungēre.*

frieze, n. 1, in architecture, *zoophorus* ; 2, = rough cloth, *gausapa (gausapes, gausape,* or *gausapum).*

fright, n. *terror, pavor* ; to take —, *pavescēre.* **frighten,** v.tr. *alqm (ex)terrēre, terrorem alci afferre, inferre, offerre, in(j)icēre, incutēre, alqm in terr. con(j)icēre.* **frightful,** adj. *terribilis, horribilis, foedus* (= disgusting), *horrendus, horrificus, ingens, immanis.* Adv. *terribilem in modum, foede, immane, immaniter.* **frightened,** adj. *terrore perculsus, territus, exterritus, trepidus* (= afraid, trembling).

frigid, adj. *frigidus* ; see COLD.

frill, n. *segmenta, -orum* (but this = flounce).

fringe, n. *fimbriae, limbus.*

frisk, v.intr. *salire, lascivire.* **frisky,** adj. *lascivus.* Adv. *lascive.* **friskiness,** n. *lascivia.*

frith, n. *fretum.*

fritter, I. v.tr. e.g. to — away time, *tempus (con)terēre* ; property, *dissipare.* **II.** n. *laganum.*

frivolous, adj. *nugax, levis, inanis, frivolus.* Adv. *maximā cum levitate.* **frivolousness,** **frivolity,** n. *nugae, levitas.*

fro, adv., e.g. to and —, *huc (et) illuc, ultro citro(que).*

frock, n. see GOWN.

frog, n. *rana* ; a small —, *ranunculus.*

frolic, I. n. *ludus et jocus, lascivia.* **II.** v.tr. *joca agēre, lascivire, ludēre* ; to — with, *cum algo jocari, joco uti, joculari.* **frolicsome,** adj. *hilaris (hilarus), jocularis, lascivus, ludibundus.*

from, prep. 1, = denoting severance and distance, is expressed by *a, ab* ; the force sometimes being increased by *procul* ; *decedĕre ab algo,* = to depart from ; *absunt a Dyrrachio,* = they are far from Dyrrachium ; *conscia mihi sum a me culpam hanc esse procul,* = I know that this fault is far from me. "From," denoting the place out of which, by *e, ex* (e.g. *ex urbe venit*). "From," denoting order, by *a* ; *quartus ab Arcesila,* = the fourth from Arcesilas ; with towns and small islands abl. alone, so *rure, domo* ; 2, = aversion, *alieno a te animo fuit,* = his mind was hostile to (from) you ; = transference, *per manus tradēre,* = from hand to hand. *A, ab,* denotes the beginning, e.g. *ab fundamento interire,* = to perish from the foundation, and has *ad* for its antithesis, e.g. *a minimo ad maximum,* = from the least to the greatest ; 3, = of time, *a, ab,* e.g. *ab horā tertiā bibebatur,* = they drank from three o'clock ; the force is increased by *jam, inde,* etc., *jam inde ab adolescentia,* = from youth up ; *a puero,* = from boyhood ; *a mane ad noctem,* = from morning to night ; *ab incenso Capitolio,* = from the burning of the Capitol ; *ab urbe conditā,* = from the foundation of the city ; 4, denoting a cause or source, is expressed by *a, de,* or *ex* ; e.g. *discĕre a patre, perire a peste, plaga ab amico,* = a snare from a friend ; *certe scio me ab singulari amore ac benevolentiā tibi scribĕre,* = I well know that I write to thee from singular love and good-will ; *a metu,* from fear ; *ex irā,* from anger.

front, I. n. *frons, -ntis,* f. ; — of the camp, *pro castris* ; to place the troops in —, *copias in fronte constituĕre* ; to attack in —, *hostes adversos aggredi.* **II.** adj. *prior, anticus,* opp. to *posticus.* **III.** v.tr. 1, = to look towards, *alqm a(d)spectare* ; 2, = to oppose, *alci adversari.* **frontage,** n.

frons. frontispiece, n. *libri prima tabula.*

fronting, adj. *alci (rei) adversus, oppositus.*

frontier, n. *confinium.* **frontlet,** n. *frontalia, -ium.*

frost, n. *frigus, -ĕris,* n., *gelu, pruina.*

frosty, adj. *frigidus* (lit. and fig.).

froth, I. n. *spuma.* **II.** v.intr. *spumare.*

frothy, adj. † *spumosus.*

froward, adj. *contumax, pertinax, pervicax.* Adv. *contumaciter, pertinaciter.* **frowardness,** n. *contumacia, pertinacia, pervicacia.*

frown, I. n. *frontis* or *superciliorum contractio.* **II.** v.intr. *frontem contrahĕre, vultum adducĕre.*

frowsy, adj. *sordidus, immundus.*

fructify, v.tr. see FERTILIZE.

frugal, adj. *parcus, restrictus* (opp. *largus*), comb. *parcus et restrictus* (in housewifery, opp. *neglegens*), *frugi* (indecl., comp. *frugalior,* sup. *frugalissimus*), comb. *homo frugi et diligens.* Adv. *parce, frugaliter.* **frugality,** n. *parsimonia, frugalitas, diligentia.*

fruit, n. 1, *fructus, -ūs, fruges, -um* (= fruit collectively), *fetus, -ūs*(= fruit, usu. as produced by generation), *pomum* (= tree-fruit), *baca* (= berry) ; to bear —, *fructum ferre* or *reddĕre* ; to bear no —, *sterilem esse* ; 2, fig. = good and bad results, *fruges, fructus, commoda, -orum, merces, -ēdis, pretium* (= reward). **fruitful,** adj. *ferax, fecundus, fertilis, opimus* (= rich, rank), *uber, fructuosus,* † *frugifer,* † *fructifer,* † *pomifer.* Adv. *fecunde, utiliter* (= profitably). **fruitfulness,** n. *fertilitas, ubertas.* **fruition,** n. *usus, -ūs, fructus, -ūs.* **fruitless,** adj. *inutilis, sterilis, cassus, irritus.* Adv. *incassum, frustra, nequi(c)quam, ad irritum, re infectā.* **fruit-tree,** n. *pomum, pomus,* f.

frustrate, v.tr. *ad vanum* or *ad irritum* or *ad vanum et irritum redigĕre, frustrari* (rather in sense of deceive) ; to be frustrated, *irritum fieri, ad irritum cadĕre* or *recidĕre* or *venire* ; — a hope, *spem fallĕre.* **frustration,** n. *frustratio.*

fry, I. n. 1, of fish, *examen, fetus, -ūs* ; 2, of men, common —, *plebs, plebecula.* **II.** v.tr. *assare, frigĕre.* **frying - pan,** n. *sartago* (Juv.), *frixorium* (Plin.) ; out of the — into the fire, *ne praeter casam, ut aiunt,* or *de fumo ad flammam.*

fudge! interj. *gerrae! nugas!*

fuel, n. *lignum* (or pl.).

fugitive, I. adj. *fugiens, fugax.* **II.** n. *domo* or *patriā profugus, fugitivus, extorris.*

full, I. adj. *alcjs rei* or *alqā re plenus, alqā re completus, oppletus, confertus, refertus, abundans* or *affluens, frequens* (= well attended, e.g. *theatrum, senatus*) ; to go with — sails, *passis velis vehi* ; at — pace, *gradu pleno* ; a — year, *annus solidus, integer* or *totus.* Adv. *plene* ; see ALTOGETHER, QUITE ; = copiously (of speech, etc.), *copiose, latius, fuse, abundanter, uberius.* **II.** v.tr. of cloth, *durare, curare.* **full-blown,** adj. 1, lit. *apertus* ; 2, fig., *superbus, tumidus.* **full-grown,** adj. *adultus, pubes (puber).* **full-moon,** n. *luna plena.* **fulness,** n. = abundance, *ubertas, copia.* **fulfil,** v.tr. *conficĕre, efficĕre, ad effectum adducĕre, exsequi, persequi, peragĕre, patrare, perpetrare* (e.g. *facinus*), *consummare* (= to finish), *alqā re fungi* (= — an office). **fulfilment,** n. *confectio.*

fuller, n. *fullo* (Plin.) ; —'s earth, *creta fullonica* (Plin.).

fulminate, v.tr. 1, † *fulminare* (= to hurl thunderbolts and to cast down by) ; 2, fig. *minas jactare.* **fulmination.** n. *minae.*

fulsome, adj. *putidus* ; — flattery, *nimia adulatio.* Adv. *putide.* **fulsomeness,** n. *molestia, nimia adulatio.*

fumble, v.intr. see FEEL.

fume, I. n. *fumus, vapor, faetor* (. = bad smell), *halitus, -ūs.* **II.** v.intr. *(ex)aestuare.*

fumigate, v.tr. *suffumigare.*

fun, n. *jocus, ludus.* **funny,** adj. *ridiculus.* Adv. *ridicule.*

function, n. *munus, -ĕris,* n., *officium, magistratus, -ūs, procuratio.*

fund, n. 1, *pecunia* ; 2, fig. by some special noun (e.g. — of knowledge, *doctrina*). **fundamental,** adj. *primus, principalis.* Adv. *funditus, penitus.* **fundamentals,** n. *elementa, -orum, principia, -orum.*

funeral, I. n. *funus, -ĕris,* n., *exsequiae, pompa funeris* or *pompa* (= the procession), *justa, -orum, justa funebria* (= the last tribute), *sepultura* (= interment). **II.** adj. *funebris,* † *funereus* ; — pile, *rogus, pyra.* **funereal,** adj. *funebris, lugubris.*

fungus, n. *fungus, agaricon* (Plin.). **fungous,** adj. *fungosus* (Plin.).

funnel, n. *infu(n)dibulum, cornu.*

fur, n. *pellis.* **furry,** adj. *vellosus.* **furrier,** n. *pellio.*

furbelow, n. *instita.*

furbish, v.tr. *interpolare, expolire.*

furl, v.tr. *vela legĕre.*

furlong, n. *stadium.*

furlough, n. *commeatus, -ūs* ; to give —, *alci commeatum dare* ; on —, *in commeatu esse.*

furnace, n. *fornax.*

furnish, v.tr. 1, = to provide with, *alqm alqā re instruĕre, ornare* ; 2, = to supply, *suppeditare, praebēre* ; 3, = to fit up (as a house, with furniture), *instruĕre, exornare et instruĕre.* **furnished,** adj. *alqā re instructus, praeditus.* **furniture,** n. of a house, *supellex, -lectilis,* f., *apparatus, -ūs.*

furrow, I. n. *sulcus.* **II.** v.tr. *sulcos facĕre, agĕre, ducĕre, sulcare.*

further, I. adj. *ulterior.* **II.** adv. 1, *ulterius, amplius* ; 2, = in fut. *porro, posthac* ; 3, = yet more, *praeterea, ad hoc, jam, autem, accedit* (quod), *huc accedit quod, addendum eodem est quod, ad(j)ice quod* ; what —? *quid vis amplius? quid porro?* **III.** interj. *perge! pergite! pergamus!* **IV.** v.tr. *alqm* or *alqd* (adj)uvare, *alci* or *alci rei consulere.* **furtherance,** n. *auxilium.* **furtherer,** n. *adjutor.* **furthest,** adj. *ultimus.*

furtive, adj. *furtivus.* Adv. *furtim, furtive.*

fury, n. *furor, rabies* ; a —, *Furia, Erinnys.* **furious,** adj. *rabidus, furiosus, furens, furibundus.* Adv. *rabide, furiose, furenter.*

furze, n. *ulex* (Plin.).

fuse, v.tr. *liquefacĕre, fundĕre.* **fusible,** adj. *fusilis.* **fusion,** n. *fusio* (= outpouring).

fuss, I. n. *tumultus, -ūs.* **II.** v.intr. *tumultuari.* **fussy,** adj. *curiosus.*

fustian, n. *gausapa* or *gausapes.*

fusty, adj. see MOULDY.

futile, adj. *futilis, inanis, vanus.* **futility,** n. *futilitas, inanitas, vanitas.*

future, I. adj. *futurus, posterus* ; a — governor, *imperaturus.* **II.** n. *futura, -orum* (e.g. *scire, prospicĕre*). **futurity,** n. *tempus futurum* or *posterum.*

G.

gabble, I. v.intr. garrire. II. n. garrulitas.
gable, n. fastigium.
gad, v.intr. vagari.
gadfly, n. oestrus, asilus, tabanus.
gag, I. v.tr. os alci alqa re obvolvĕre et prae-
ligare. II. n. use noun describing the material
of which gag is made (e.g. linteum in os injectum).
gage, n. pignus, -ŏris, n.; see PLEDGE.
gain, I. n. lucrum (opp. damnum, = loss or
injury), quaestus, -ūs (= profit), commodum (=
advantage), emolumentum (opp. detrimentum),
compendium (= savings), fructus, -ūs (= natural
growth), praeda, or in pl. (= booty), praemium
(= a prize). II. v.tr. alqd lucrari (opp. perdĕre),
consequi, assequi, capĕre; — a place (that is, to
reach it after effort), locum capĕre, in alqm
locum eniti or evadĕre; — a battle or
victory, superiorem discedĕre, vincĕre; the
enemy has —ed the day, hostis vicit or victor
evasit; — a wager, sponsione or sponsionem
vincĕre; — a lawsuit, caus(s)am, judicium (or
judicio) vincĕre, caus(s)am tenēre or obtinēre; —
a prize, praemium auferre; — a person's friendship, in amicitiam alcjs recipi; — over, conciliare; to try to — over, alqā re hominum (plebis,
etc.) animos ad benevolentiam allicĕre, conciliare
ad benevolentiam erga alqm. gainful, adj.
quaestuosus, lucrosus.
gainsay, v.tr. see CONTRADICT.
gait, n. incessus, -ūs.
gaiters, n. ocreae (= leather coverings for
soldiers, etc.).
gala, n. see FESTIVAL.
galaxy, n. orbis, -is, m., or circulus lacteus,
† via lactea.
gale, n. 1, ventus magnus, aura (= breeze);
2, fig. aura (e.g. popularis).
gall, I. n. fel, bilis. II. v.tr. 1, = rub, terĕre;
2, fig. mordĕre. galling, adj. mordax.
gallant, I. adj. 1, = brave, fortis, animosus,
strenuus; 2, = attentive to females, amori
deditus, amatorius. Adv. fortiter, animose,
strenue. II. n. 1, juvenis fortis; 2, amator.
gallantry, n. 1, virtus, -ūtis, f., fortitudo; 2,
amores, -um.
gallery, n. porticus, f. (= an open — with pillars), xystus (= walk or alley formed by two lines
of trees), pinacothēca (= picture —), superior locus
(as in a theatre, e.g. ex superiore loco spectare), cavea
summa or ultima (= the last row in a theatre; to
address the —, verba ad summam caveam spec-
tantia dicĕre); underground —, cuniculus.
galley, n. navis actuaria (= swift sailing
ship); navis longa, biremis, triremis (= ship of
war); to condemn to the —s, alqm dare ad remum
publicae triremis.
gallipot, n. ollula (aul-).
gallon, n. congius.
gallop, I. n. gradus, -ūs, citatus; at a —,
equo admisso or laxatis habenis. II. v.intr.
equo admisso, etc., vehi or currĕre.
gallows, n. crux (crucifixion and strangling
were the Roman equivalents for hanging, see
HANG).
gamble, v.intr. ludĕre; — with dice, tesseris
or talis ludĕre, aleā ludĕre. gambler, n.
aleator. gambling, n. alea; to gain at —,
prosperā aleā uti.
gambol, v.intr. ludĕre, lascivire.
game, I. n. 1, ludus, lusio, ludicrum (esp.
= public —); — of chance, alea; 2, = animal,

ferae, on table, caro ferina; to make — oi, alqm
ludibrio habēre, alqm ludĕre or illudĕre. II.
v.intr. see GAMBLE. gamesome, adj. see
PLAYFUL. gamester, gaming, see GAMBLE.
gaming-table, n. alveus.
gammon, n. = — of bacon, perna.
gammon, interj. = nonsense! gerrae! nugas!
gander, n. anser (mas or masculus, opp. anser
femina).
gang, n. caterva, operae (= of roughs).
gangway, n. forus.
gangrene, n. ossium caries, gangraena.
gaol, n. carcer, -ĕris, m., vincula, -orum.
gaoler, n. (carceris) custos.
gap, n. lacuna, hiatus, -ūs. gape, v.intr.
hiare.
garbage, n. purgamentum, quisquiliae.
garble, v.tr. = to falsify, corrumpĕre, vitiare.
garden, I. n. hortus; a small —, hortulus.
II. v.intr. in horto fodĕre, hortum colĕre. gar-
den-stuff, n. olus, -ĕris, n. gardening, n.
hortorum cultus, -ūs. gardener, n. qui hortum
colit.
gargle, I. n. 1, gargarizatio (= the act,
Cels.); 2, for the fluid use verb. II. v.intr.
gargarizare (ex) alqā re (Cels.).
garish, adj. 1, = bright, clarus, splendidus;
2, = gay, nitidus (= spruce), fucatus (= rouged).
garland, n. sertum.
garlic, n. a(l)lium.
garment, n. vestis; see CLOTHES.
garner, I. n. horreum. II. v.tr. condĕre.
garnish, v.tr. (ex)ornare, instruĕre.
garret, n. cenaculum superius; to live in
a —, sub tegulis habitare, in superiore habitare
cenaculo, tribus scalis habitare (= up three pair
of stairs).
garrison, I. n. praesidium, milites praesi-
diarii. II. v.tr. urbi praesidium imponĕre, in
urbe pr. (col)locare.
garrulity, n. garrulitas, loquacitas. garrulous, adj. garrulus, loquax, verbosus. Adv.
loquaciter.
garter, n. *periscĕlis (mediæval), in pl.
† genualia, -ium (Ov.).
gas, n. spiritus, -ūs, vapor, *gas quod dicitur.
gasconade, n. jactatio, ostentatio, venditatio (sui), venditatio quaedam atque ostentatio.
gash, I. n. vulnus, -ĕris, n. II. v.tr. vulnerare.
gasp, I. v.intr. aegre spiritum ducĕre, anhelare, † singultare. II. n. anhelitus, -ūs, singultus, -ūs. gasping, n. anhelitus, -ūs.
gastric, adj. ad stomachum pertinens. gas-
tronomy, n. quae ad gulam pertinent.
gate, n. janua, porta (= — of a city). gate-
keeper, n. janitor. gate-post, n. postis.
gather, I. v.tr. 1, legĕre (= to pick up), colligĕre, conquirĕre (= to search out), congerĕre (=
to heap up), coacervare (= flowers, flores carpĕre;
— grapes, vindemiare; 2, = conjecture, con(j)i-
cĕre. II. v.intr. 1, = assemble, convenire, congregari; 2, of a sore, suppurare. gathering,
n. 1, = assembly, coetus, -ūs; 2, = a sore, suppuratio (Cels.).
gaudy, adj. fucatus, magnificus. Adv. mag-
nificenter.
gauge, v.tr. metiri; see MEASURE.
gaunt, adj. exilis; see THIN.
gauntlet, n. manicae; to run the — per
militum ordines currentem virgis caedi.

gauze, n. *vestis coa.*

gay, adj. 1, of mind, *hilaris (hilarus), laetus;* 2, of colour, etc., *splendidus, nitidus.* Adv. *hilare, laete.* **gaiety,** n. *hilaritas, laetitia.*

gaze (at), I. v.intr. *in obtutu alcjs rei haerēre defixum, alqm* or *alqd intueri, contueri, contemplari.* II. n. *obtutus, -ūs, conspectus, -ūs.* **gazing-stock,** n. *spectaculum.*

gazette, n. *acta (diurna), acta publica, -orum.*

gear, n. *ornatus, -ūs, vestitus, -ūs, supellex, -lectilis,* f. (= household).

geld, v.tr. *castrare.* **gelding,** n. *can-t(h)erius.*

gem, n. *gemma,* †*lapis,* †*lapillus* (both also with *generosus*).

gender, n. *genus, -ěris,* n. **genealogy,** n. *origo, stirps* (= the branches of a family). **genealogical,** adj. *de origine,* etc., *scriptus, ad originem pertinens.*

general, I. n. *dux, imperator* (= g.-in-chief); the —'s tent, *praetorium;* to be —, *exercitui praeesse;* to appoint anyone —, *alqm exercitui praeficěre.* II. adj. *generalis* (= relating to the genus or whole), *communis* (= common to all, opp. *singularis,* = individually), *vulgaris,* comb. *vulgaris communisque; omnium rerum,* or merely *omnium;* — want, *inopia omnium rerum;* — conversation, *omnium hominum sermo;* a — idea, *notio universa* or *summa, notio communis;* the — good, *omnium salus;* to devote to the — good, *in commune conferre;* in —, *ad summam, in universum, universe* (opp. *proprie, nominatim), omnino* (opp. *separatim), generatim* opp. *si(n)gillatim, per singulas species), communiter.* Adv. = usually, *fere, ferme, vulgo, plerumque.* **generality,** n. = most people, *vulgus, -i,* n., *plerique.* **generalization,** n. *quod de omnibus rebus dictum est.* **generalship,** n. *ductus, -ūs;* under the — of Caesar, *Caesare duce;* to act with good —, *summo consilio rem gerěre.*

generate, v.tr. 1, *gigněre, generare, (pro)creare, parěre;* 2, = cause, *facěre, efficěre.* **generation,** n. 1, *generatio, procreatio* (e.g. *liberorum);* 2, = age, *saeculum, aetas;* the present —, *hujus aetatis homines, qui nunc vivunt homines.* **generator,** n. *genitor, procreator.* **generative,** adj. † *genitalis;* — organs, *genitalia, -ium.*

generous, adj. 1, = good of its kind, + *generosus, nobilis, eximius;* 2, = of a large heart, *generosus, magnificus, benignus, liberalis;* 3, = liberal, *largus, liberalis.* Adv. *bene, eximie, magnifice, benigne, liberaliter, large.* **generosity,** n. 1, see EXCELLENCE; 2, *magnificentia, magnanimitas, benignitas, liberalitas;* 3, *liberalitas, benignitas, beneficentia.*

genesis, n. see ORIGIN.

genial, adj. *comis, genialis* (of things, e.g. *hiem(p)s).* Adv. *comiter, genialiter.* **geniality,** n. *comitas.*

genitive, n. *(casus) genitivus* (Gramm.).

genius, n. 1, = an imaginary spirit, *genius;* 2, = high, natural ability, *ingenium, indoles, -is;* of rude —, *crassā Minervā;* a man of —, *vir magni* or *elati ingenii, vir ingenio praestans, magno ingenio praeditus homo.*

genteel, adj. *honestus, elegans, urbanus.* Adv. *honeste, eleganter, urbane.* **gentility,** n. *honestas, elegantia, urbanitas.*

gentle, adj. 1, = well-born, *generosus, ingenuus, nobilis;* 2, = in disposition, *mitis, clemens, mansuetus, placidus;* 3, of wind, *lenis;* of a hill, *mollis, lenis.* Adv. *nobili loco ortus* or *natus, placide, leniter, molliter.* **gentleman,**

n. 1, *homo generosus, ingenuus, nobilis, honesto* or *nobili loco natus;* 2, = well-bred, *homo urbanus, liberalis, ingenuus, generosus.* **gentlemanly,** adj. *liberalis, urbanus, ingenuus, generosus, honestus.* **gentleness,** n. 1, *nobilitas;* 2, *clementia, mansuetudo;* 3, *lenitas.* **gentry,** n. *nobilitas, nobiles, -ium, optimates, -(i)um.* **gentlewoman,** n. see LADY.

genuflexion, n. see KNEEL.

genuine, adj. *sincerus, merus, germanus.* Adv. *reapse, sincere, vere.* **genuineness,** n. *auctoritas, fides;* many doubt of the — of this book, *multi dubitant hunc librum ab eo ad quem refertur conscriptum esse.*

geography, n. * *geographia, terrarum* or *regionum descriptio.*

geology, n. * *geologia.* **geological,** adj. * *geologicus;* — time, *immensae antiquitatis.*

geometry, n. *geometria.* **geometrical,** adj. *geometricus (γεωμετρικός).* **geometer,** or **geometrician,** n. *geometres, -ae,* m.

germ, n. 1, = — of plants, † *germen;* 2, fig. *semen* (e.g. *malorum, discordiarum).* **germinate,** v.intr. *germinare* (Plin.). **germination,** n. *germinatio.* **germane,** adj. *affinis.*

Germany, n. *Germania.* **German,** adj. *Germanicus.*

gestation, n. *partus gerendi tempus* (Plin.). **gesture,** n. *gestus, -ūs* (= the mode of carrying the body), comb. *motus gestusque (gestus* is used especially of speakers, players, etc.). **gesticulate,** v.intr. *se jactare, gesticulari* (Suet.), *gestus facěre* or *agěre.* **gesticulation,** n. *jactatio, gestus, -ūs, motus, -ūs.*

get, v.tr. *acquirěre, conquirěre, consequi, capěre, adipisci, nancisci, (com)parare, lucrari* (= to get gain); — anything done, *alqd faciendum curare;* — abroad, *percrebrescěre;* — off, *disceděre;* — up, *surgěre;* — down, *descenděre;* — forward, *proficěre, provehi;* — in, *introire;* — near, *acceděre;* — out, *egredi;* — round, *circumvenire;* — by heart, *memoriae alqd mandare;* — with child, *gravidam facěre;* — to, *pervenire;* — away! *aufer te hinc.*

gewgaws, n. *nugae, lenocinium.*

ghastly, adj. 1, *exsanguis, pallidus, cadaverosus, luridus;* 2, see TERRIBLE. **ghastliness,** n. 1, *pallor;* 2, see HORROR.

ghost, n. 1, = breath, *spiritus, -ūs, anima;* the Holy —, * *Spiritus Sanctus,* * *Paracletus;* 2, = in pl. imaginary spirits, or the spirits of the dead, *lemures* (in gen.), *manes* (= the shade or ghost of a particular person), *lares* (= the good spirits worshipped in the home), **of a single person,** *larva, umbra* (= the shade).

ghoul, n. *larva teterrima.*

giant, n. *homo ingentis* or *immanis magnitudinis, homo eximiā corporis magnitudine, vir major quam pro humano habitu;* the giants, *gigantes;* one of the —, *gigas.* **gigantic,** adj. *eximiae* or *ingentis* or *immanis magnitudinis, eximiā* or *ingenti* or *immani magnitudine;* a — labour, *moles, -is.*

gibbet, n. see GALLOWS.

gibe, I. n. *ludibrium, sanna* (Juv.). II. v.tr. *ludibrio habēre.*

giddy, adj. 1, lit. *vertiginosus* (Plin.), *vertigine correptus;* 2, fig. *lěvis, inconstans.* Adv. *inconstanter.* **giddiness,** n. 1, *vertigo,* 2, *animus lěvis.*

gift, n. *donum;* see GIVE.

gig, n. *cisium.*

giggle, v.intr. *effuse ridēre, inepte ridēre. furtim cachinnare.*

gild, v.tr. *inaurare, alci rei aurum illinĕre or alqd auro illinĕre.*

gill, n. = a measure, *hemina.*

gills, n. *branchiae* (Plin.).

gimlet, n. *terebra.*

gin, n. = trap, *laqueus, tendicula.*

gingerly, adv. *pedetentim (pedetempt-), sentim.*

gipsy, n. * *Cingarus,* * *Cingara,* fem.

giraffe, n. *camēlŏpardălis* (Plin.).

gird, v.tr. 1, *(suc)cingĕre, accingĕre; —* yourself, *(suc)cingi* or *accingi* (e.g. *gladio, ferro);* 2, fig. — oneself to, = to apply to, *se accingĕre* or *accingi ad alqd,* or *alci rei.* **girder**, n. *trabs.* **girdle,** n. *zona, cingulum, cestus, balteus* (= belt).

girl, n. *puella, virgo.* **girlish,** adj. *puellaris, virginalis.* Adv. *more puellarum.* **girlhood,** n. *aetas puellaris;* she did it in her —, *puella fecit.*

girth, n. 1, = distance or space round, *ambitus, circuitus, complexus,* all *-ūs;* 2, of a horse, † *cingula.*

give, v.tr. *alqd alci dare, praebēre, reddĕre, tradĕre, impertire, largiri,* or *alqm alqā re* or *alqd alci donare, ad alqd conferre* (= contribute); to — for = to buy at, *rem emĕre tanti;* to — word for word, *exprimĕre verbum de verbo;* — up, see Cease; to — up for lost, *desperare de alqo* or *alqa re;* to — little attention to, *parum curare, neglegĕre (neglig-) alqd;* to — up yourself = to surrender, *se dare, manus dare, (con)cedĕre; —* in (of accounts), *rationem reddĕre, referre;* = to yield, see " — up yourself" above; — a blow, *plagam alci in(f)icĕre.* **gift,** n. *donum, munus, -ĕris,* n., *praemium* (= a reward or prize); to make a —, *alci donum dare, alqm dono donare.* **gifted,** adj. *alqā re praeditus;* a — man, *vir summi ingenii.* **giver,** n. *qui donum dat, largitor.*

gizzard, n. *ingluvies, guttur.*

glad, adj. *laetus, hilaris* or *hilarus;* — at, *alqā re laetari, gaudēre.* Adv. *laete, hilare, hilariter.* **gladden,** v.tr. *alqm (ex)hilarare.* **gladness,** n. *laetitia, hilaritas.*

glade, n. *silva.*

gladiator, n. *gladiator.* **gladiatorial,** adj. *gladiatorius;* a trainer of —s, *lanista.*

glance, I. n. (of the eyes), *oculorum conjectus, -ūs.* II. v.intr. 1, = shine, *splendēre, fulgēre, nitēre;* 2, — at, *oculos con(f)icĕre in alqd, alqd leviter* or *strictim attingĕre* or *dicĕre, perstringĕre.*

gland, n. *glans* (Cels.).

glare, I. v.intr. *fulgēre* (= be bright); — at, *alqm* or *alqd intentis oculis tueri.* II. n. *fulgor, intenti (ut aiunt) oculi.*

glass, n. *vitrum.* **glazier,** n. *vitrarius qui fenestris vitrum inserit.* **glassy,** adj. *vitreus.*

gleam, I. n. 1, *fulgor;* 2, fig. *aura;* — of hope, *specula.* II. v.intr. *fulgēre.*

glean, v.tr. *spicilegium facĕre (= —* in the field), *racemari (= —* in the vineyard). **gleaning,** n. *spicilegium.*

glee, n. *hilaritas, laetitia.* **gleeful,** adj. *hilaris, laetus.* Adv. *hilariter, laete.*

glen, n. *(con)vallis.*

glib, adj. *loquax, garrulus, volubilis.* Adv. *loquaciter, volubiliter.* **glibness,** n. *loquacitas, garrulitas, volubilitas.*

glide, v. *(pro)labi.*

glimmer, v.intr. *sublucēre.*

glimpse, n. see Sight, n.

glisten, glitter, v.intr. *micare, candēre, fulgēre, nitēre, lucēre, splendēre.* **glistening, glittering,** adj. *lucidus, candidus* (= — white, opp. to *niger,* = — black), † *coruscus, nitidus, splendidus, splendens, fulgens.*

gloat, v.intr. — over, *se a(d)spectu alcjs rei delectare.*

globe, n. *globus, sphaera, orbis terrarum.* **globular,** adj. *globosus.*

gloom, n. 1, lit. *obscuritas, caligo, tenebrae;* 2, fig. *animus dejectus, afflictus, caligo, tenebrae tristitia, maeror, maestitia.* **gloomy,** adj. 1, *obscurus,* † *tenebrosus, caliginosus;* 2, *tristis, maestus.* Adv. *obscure, per tenebras or caliginen* (e.g. *visus), maeste.*

glory, I. n. *gloria, honos (honor), decus, -ōris,* n. ; to be a — to, *laudi* or *gloriae esse alci, laudem alci afferre.* **II.** v.intr. *(de) alqā re gloriari* (or with *quod*). **glorify,** v.tr. *laudibus ornare* or *efferre* or *tollĕre, alqm gloriā afficĕre, alqm (laudibus) celebrare.* **glorious,** adj. *gloriosus, (prae)clarus, amplus* (esp. in superl.), *illustris.* Adv. *gloriose, (prae)clare, ample.* **glorying,** n. *gloriatio, praedicatio.*

gloss, I. n. 1, = a shining, *nitor, candor;* 2, = an explanation, *interpretatio.* **II.** v.tr. — over, *extenuare, mitigare.* **glossary,** n. *glossae.* **glossy,** adj. *nitidus.*

glove, n. *manicae* (= sleeves).

glow, I. n. *ardor, fervor, aestus, -ūs.* **II.** v.intr. *candēre, ardēre, fervēre;* to begin to —, *(ex)ardescĕre, incandescĕre, excandescĕre.* **glowing,** adj. *candens, ardens, fervens, fervidus;* to have a — desire for, *desiderio alcjs flagrare.* **glow-worm,** n. *cicindēla, lampyris* (Plin.).

glue, I. n. *glutinum, gluten.* **II.** v.tr. *(con)glutinare.* **glutinous,** adj. *glutinosus, lentus, viscosus.*

glut, I. v.tr. 1, lit. *satire, saturare, explēre;* 2, fig. — the market, *vilitatem annonae efficĕre.* **II.** n. *satias, satietas.*

glutton, n. *homo edax, vorax, gurges, -ĭtis,* m., *hel(l)uo;* comb. *gurges et helluo.* **gluttonous,** adj. *edax, vorax, gulosus* (Juv. Sen.). Adv. *avide.* **gluttony,** n. *hel(l)uatio, edacitas.*

gnarled, adj. see Knotty.

gnash, v.tr. *dentibus (in)frendĕre, dentibus stridĕre* or *stridēre.* **gnashing,** n. *stridor dentium* (Cels.).

gnat, n. *culex.*

gnaw, v.tr. 1, *alqd (ar)rodĕre, circumrodĕre;* 2, fig. *pungĕre, cruciare, mordēre.* **gnawing,** adj. *mordax.*

gnome, n. 1, see Maxim; 2, see Fairy.

go, v.intr. *ire, gradi* (= to step), *ingredi* (= to step into), *incedĕre* (= to enter), *vadĕre, ambulare* (= to walk), *spatiari* (= to strut), *commeare ad alqm (in locum), procedĕre* (= to — forth); to — out, *prodire* (of the harbour, *e portu), exire, excedĕre, egredi; —* in, *inire, introire, intrare, ingredi; —* over, *transire, praeterire locum* (= to pass by a place); — on board, *(navem) a(d)scendĕre, conscendĕre; —* down, *descendĕre; —* up, *a(d)scendĕre; —* before, *anteire, antegredi* (with accus.); — through, *transire; =* to set out, proceed, march, *proficisci (= —* on foot or horseback); = to betake yourself, *conferre se alqo;* = to make for, *contendĕre alqo.* In imper. as command, *abi! abi hinc! apage sis!* to let one —, *alqm demittĕre;* where are you —ing? *quo tendis?* what are you —ing to do? *quid cogitas?* to — and come, *venire et redire, ire et redire;* to — after, *alqd petĕre; —* to see, *spectatum ire; —* for someone, *alqm arcessĕre;* the affair begins to — better, *incipit* *res melius ire;* how goes it? how is it? how are you? *quomodo habes te?* or *est tibi?* the answer is made by *bene, recte, male,* etc. ; so of health, *quomodo vales?* of action, *quid agis? quid agitur?* is all well? answers, *valeo, bene mecum agitur;* — for, = be sold at, *emi* or *vendi,* with genit. of price; — about, = attempt, *alqd experiri, moliri;* — beyond, *excedēre;* — off (of a weapon), *emitti* (with the thing shot as subj.).

go-between, n. *conciliator, interpres, -ētis,* m. and f., *internuntius.*

goad, I. n. *stĭmŭlus;* to kick against a —, *stimulum pugnis caedēre, adversum stimulum calcare.* **II.** v.tr. *alqm ad* or *in alqd stimulare, incitare.*

goal, n. *meta* (= the pillar at the end of the course; then in poets, fig.), *calx* (lit. and fig.).

goat, n. *capra, capella.* **he-goat,** n. *caper, hircus.* **goatherd,** n. *caprarius.*

gobble, v.tr. *(de)vorare.*

goblet, n. *scyphus;* see CUP.

goblin, n. *umbra quae homines inquietat;* • *daemon, larva,* in pl. *lemures.*

God, n. *Deus* (as the highest being, often with title *Optimus, Maximus*), *numen divinum, numen* (= the nod, i.e. the supreme will), † *divus;* the —s, *di(i),* † *caelestes,* † *caelites,* † *caelicolae, di(i) superi, superi* also (opp. *inferi*); — of the house, *lares, penates;* to raise to the honours of a —, *alqm in deorum numerum referre, alqm inter deos referre, alqm consecrare;* to call — to witness, *Deum testari;* for —'s sake I beg, *Deum testans oro te, pro Deum fidem!* by the —s, *per deos;* so help me —, *ita me Deus* (adj)*uvet* or *amet, hercule* or *mehercule,* so also *Deus me perdat!* may — be favourable, *di(i) propitii sint;* in —'s name, *quod bonum, faustum, felix fortunatumque sit! quod bene vertat!* — grant, *faxit Deus! utinam di(i) ita faxint! utinam Deus ratum esse jubeat!* — forbid! *quod Deus prohibeat! quod omen Deus avertat! di meliora!* **goddess,** n. *dea,* † *diva.* **Godhead,** n. *numen.* **godless,** adj. 1, *impius* (*erga Deum,* so *erga patriam, erga parentes*); 2, *atheus* or *atheos* (=God-denying). **godlessness,** n. *impietas erga deos.* **godlike,** adj. *divinus.* **godly,** adj. *pius erga deos.* **godliness,** n. *pietas erga deos.* **godsend,** n. ἕρμαιον *ut ita dicam* (in colloquial passage); *quod quasi divinitus oblatum est.*

gold, n. *aurum.* **gold-dust,** n. *ballux* (Plin.). **gold-leaf,** n. *bractea, auri lamina.* **gold-mine,** n. *aurifodina* (Plin.). **goldsmith,** n. *aurifex.* **golden,** adj. *aureus, ex auro factus.*

good, I. adj. *bonus,* (in gen.) *jucundus, suavis, dulcis* (= pleasant), *probus* (= what it ought to be), *commodus* (= having the right quantity or quality), *opportunus* (= suitable), *prosper, secundus* (*res prosperae,* = — circumstances), *utilis* (= useful), *salutaris* (=healthful), *honestus* (=morally —), honourable), *simplex* (= unpretending), *benignus* (= kind); — health, *bona valetudo;* — for anything, *ad alqd utilis, commodus, opportunus, idoneus, aptus;* — eyes, *oculi acres et acuti;* my — friend, *o bone! sodes! a* — many, *plerique, aliquot, complures;* a — part, *bona pars* (= a considerable part); a — while, *aliquantum temporis;* to be — for, as a remedy, *alci rei* or *contra alqd prodesse, alci rei mederi, contra alqd efficacem esse;* to make —, *alqd sarcire* (e.g. *detrimentum acceptum*), *alqd restituēre.* **II.** interj. — bye, *vale, valete, avete,* pl.); *bene* (*agis*), *bene fecis! bene fecisti! bene habet! euge,* (well!) *non repugno! nihil impedio!* **III.** n. *bonum;* the highest—, *summum bonum;* external —s, *externa bona, -orum, res externae* or *humanae;* —s, = possessions, *bona;* = wares or merchandise, *merx;* to do much —, *de multis bene*

merēri; — to, *conferre in alqm beneficia (multa), bene de alqo mereri;* to turn to —, *alqd in bonum vertēre.* **good-breeding,** n. *humanitas.* **good-fellowship,** n. *comitas.* **good-for-nothing,** adj. *nequam.* **good-humour,** n. *comitas, facilitas.* **good-humoured,** adj. *comis, facilis, benignus.* Adv. *comiter, benigne.* **good-looking,** adj. *pulcher, venustus.* **goodly,** adj. 1, see GOOD-LOOKING ; 2, = large, *magnus.* **good-nature,** n. see GOOD-HUMOUR.

goodness, n. 1, = excellence, *bonitas;* 2, moral —, *probitas, virtus, -ūtis,* f.; 3, = kindness, *benignitas, bonitas.*

goose, n. *anser,* m., or *anser femina;* — flesh, *caro anserina.*

gore, I. n. *cruor.* **II.** v.tr. *transfīgēre, confodēre.* **gory,** adj. *cruentus, cruentātus.*

gorge, I. n. 1, = throat, *gula, guttur;* 2, = a narrow pass, *angustiae, saltus, -ūs.* **II.** v.tr. *alqm (ex)satiare, alqm (ex)saturare;* — oneself, *exsatiari (vino ciboque).*

gorgeous, adj. *splendidus, magnificus, lautus.* Adv. *splendide, magnifice, laute.* **gorgeousness,** n. *splendor, magnificentia.*

gormandize, v.intr. *hel(l)uari.* **gormandizer,** n. *hel(l)uo.*

gospel, n. * *evangelium.*

gossamer, n. *aranea* (= spider's web).

gossip, I. n. 1, = idle talk, *sermo, rumor;* 2, = talkative person, *homo garrulus, femina garrula;* 3, = friend, *familiaris.* **II.** v.intr. *sermonem cum algo conferre.*

gouge, v.tr. *scalpro eximēre* or *exsecare.*

gourd, n. *cucurbita.*

gout, n. *arthrītis;* — in the hands, *chīrāgra;* — in the feet, *podāgra.* **gouty,** adj. *arthrīticus.*

govern, v.tr. 1, = — a province, etc., *gubernare, administrare, gerēre, temperare, curare, reipublicae praeesse;* 2, in gen. = — temper, etc., *alci rei moderari, alqd temperare, regēre, coercēre.* **government,** n. 1, = governing, *administratio, procuratio, cura;* 2, = power, *imperium, regnum, dicio;* 3, as place, *provincia;* 4, = rulers, *ii penes quos est reipublicae administratio.* **governor,** n. 1, in gen. *gubernator, rector;* 2, state —, *praefectus, propraetor, proconsul, legatus.*

gown, n. *toga, vestis;* a lawyer's —, *toga forensis;* the manly —, *toga virīlis;* a morning —, *toga cubicularis* or *domestica;* a woman's —, *palla, stola.*

grace, I. n. 1, = favour, *gratia, favor,* comb. *gratia et favor, studium,* comb. *studium et favor, voluntas* (= inclination), *benevolentia* (= kindness), *indulgentia* (= special favour), *beneficium, venia* (= pardon); he grows in —, *mactus est virtute;* by the — of God, *Dei beneficio, Deo favente;* — in speaking, *facundia, lepos;* — at meals, *gratiarum* (=thanks) *actio;* to be in the good —s of, *apud alqm plurimum gratiā pollēre;* to gain the — of, *alcjs gratiam sibi conciliare;* your —, * *Clementia tua;* the —s, *Gratiae;* with a good, bad —, *cum bonā, malā gratia* (Ter.); 2, = gracefulness, *venustas* (=attraction, charm), *elegantia; lepos* (= — in words); feminine —, *muliebris venustas;* — of expression, *suavitas dicendi.* **II.** v.tr. *honestare,* (ad)*ornare, decorare.* **graceful,** adj. *venustus, decorus, elegans, lepidus.* Adv. *venuste, decore, eleganter, lepide.* **graceless,** adj. *improbus.* Adv. *improbe.* **gracious,** adj. *propitius* (esp. of gods); see KIND.

grade, n. = a step, *gradus, -ūs, a(d)scensus, -ūs* (= a step up); there are many —s in human society, *gradus plures sunt societatis hominum;*

— of honour, *gradus honoris* or *dignitatis.*
gradual, adj., **gradually,** adv. *per gradus,*
gradatim, or *paul(l)atim, sensim.* **graduate,**
I. v.intr. ** ad gradum (Baccalaurei in artibus,*
= as B.A., etc.) *admitti.* **II.** n. ** ad gradum*
(Baccalaurei, etc.) *admissus.*

graft, I. n. *surculus.* **II.** v.tr. *surculum*
arbori inserĕre.

grain, n. 1, = a seed, etc., *granum, mica*
(e g. *salis*); 2, = corn, *frumentum.*

graminivorous, adj. (*animal*) *quod herbis*
pascitur.

grammar, n. 1, = the science of —, *gram-*
matica, -ae, or *grammatica, -orum,* or *gramma-*
tice ; 2, = a book on —, *liber grammaticus* or
ad grammaticam rationem pertinens. **gram-**
matical, adj. *grammaticus.* Adv. *grammatice*
(Quint.). **grammarian,** n. *grammaticus.*

granary, n. *horreum, granaria, -orum.*
grand, adj. *grandis, eximius, magnificus,*
amplus. Adv. *eximie, magnifice, ample.* **gran-**
deur, n. *amplitudo, majestas.* **grandees,** n.
proceres, optimates. **grandiloquent,** adj.
grandiloquus, magniloquus (late in prose), *tumi-*
dus. Adv. *tumide.* **grandiloquence,** n.
oratio tumida. **granddaughter,** n. *neptis.*
grandfather, n. *avus.* **grandmother,** n.
avia. **grandson,** n. *nepos.* **great-grand-**
daughter, n. *proneptis.* **great - grand-**
father, n. *proävus* (so backward, *abävus, atävus,*
tritävus). **great-grandmother,** n. *proävia.*
great-grandson, n. *pronĕpos.*

grange, n. 1, = barn, *horreum* ; 2, =
country-house, *villa.*

granite, n. *lapis, lapĭdis,* m., *saxum.*

grant, I. n. *gratia, beneficium, donum, prae-*
mium, venia, concessio (= the granting). **II.** v.tr.
concedĕre ; see GIVE ; *sinĕre* (= allow); this —ed,
hoc dato or *concesso* ; —ed that, or that not, *ut*
sit, ne sit, ut non sit.

grape, n. *acinus* or *acinum* (=a single grape),
uva (= a bunch of grapes).

graphic, adj. *expressus* ; to give a — description, *alqd tanquam sub oculos sub(j)icĕre.*
Adv. *clare.*

grapple, v.tr. *cum alqo luctari.* **grap-**
pling-iron, n. *ferrea, manus, -ūs, harpago.*

grasp, I. v.tr. 1, (*ap)prehendĕre, compre-*
hendĕre, prensare ; — anyone's hand, *manum*
alcjs amplecti ; 2, fig. *concipĕre, intellegĕre* ; see
COMPREHEND ; — at, *alqd (ap)petĕre, captare.*
II. n. 1, *complexus, -ūs* ; to wrest from the —, *de*
manibus alqd extorquēre ; 2, *mens, captus, -ūs.*
grasping, adj. *avarus.*

grass, n. *gramen, herba* (= the young and
fresh grass). **grassy,** adj. *herbidus, †herbosus,*
gramineus. **grasshopper,** n. *gryllus (grillus)*
(Plin.).

grate, n. *focus, caminus.*

grate, v.tr. 1, = rub, *conterĕre* ; 2, fig. see
ANNOY. **grating,** n. *cancelli, clathri.*

grateful, adj. 1, = pleasant, (*per)gratus,*
acceptus, comb. *gratus acceptusque, jucundus,*
perjucundus, suavis ; 2, = thankful, *gratus,*
beneficii or *beneficiorum memor,* comb. *memor*
gratusque. Adv. *grate, grato animo.* **grati-**
tude, n. *gratus animus, memor beneficii* or
beneficiorum animus, gratus animus et beneficii
memor, grata beneficii memoria. **gratify,** v.tr.
alci gratificari, alqm delectare, morem alci gerĕre.
gratification, n. *expletio* (= satisfaction),
delectatio ; to have — from, *voluptatem ex alqā*
re percipĕre. **gratifying,** adj. *gratus.* **gratis,**
adv. *grat(i)is, sine mercede,* comb. *grat(i)is et sine*
mercede, gratuito, sine pretio. **gratuitous,**

adj. *gratuïtus.* Adv. see GRATIS. **gratuity,** n.
see ALMS, GIFT.

grave, adj. *gravis* (=full of excellence), *serius,*
severus. **gravity,** n. 1, *gravitas, severitas* ; to
have — of face (= look grave), *vultum ad severi*
tatem componĕre, also *vultum componĕre* ; 2,
(in physics) *gravitas.* **gravitation,** n.
vis et gravitas alcjs rei, pondus, -ĕris, n., *et*
gravitas.

grave, I. n. 1, *sepulc(h)rum, bustum, tumulus*
(=a mound); to carry to the —, *sepelire, exsequias*
alcjs funeris prosequi ; 2, = death, *mors, inferi* ;
he took the hope with him into the —, *moriens*
ferebat secum spem. **II.** v.tr. see ENGRAVE.

gravel, n. *glarea.*

gravy, n. *jus, juris,* n., *sucus.*

gray, adj. *canus* (= turning white, as the hair
from age), *ravus* (of the sea, the eyes), *caesius*
(= blue-green, esp. of the eyes), *glaucus* (of the
eyes, etc.), (*capilli*) *cani* (= gray hairs). **gray-**
beard, n. *senex.* **grayness,** n. *canities.*

graze, I. v.tr. *pascĕre.* **II.** v.intr. *pasci.*
grazier, n. *pecuarius.*

— **graze,** v.tr. = touch, *stringĕre, radĕre.*

grease, I. n. *adeps, lardum.* **II.** v.tr.
ung(u)ĕre, alqd alqā re illinĕre, perlinĕre (Col.),
oblinĕre. **greasy,** adj. *unctus* (= rubbed with
grease), *pinguis* (= fat).

great, adj. *magnus, grandis, amplus, vastus,*
immanis, spatiosus (= roomy), *procērus* (= tall),
altus (= high or deep), (*ex)celsus* (=lofty) ; a —
assembly, *conventus, -ūs, celeber* ; a — man, *vir*
magnus, clarus, or *illustris* ; a — statesman, *rei-*
publicae gerendae scientissimus ; too —, *nimius* ;
extraordinarily —, *ingens, praegrandis* ; very —,
maximus (maxu-) (in reference to contents and
quantity), *summus* (= the highest in regard to
rank or position), *suprēmus* (in relation to rank
and to inferiors). Adv. *magnopere, valde, vehe-*
menter (e.g. *veh. commotus,* — disturbed).
"Greatest" must often be expressed by superlatives ; the — enemy, *alcjs* or *alci inimicissimus* ;
— chatterer, *homo loquacissimus* or *omnium lo-*
quacissimus ; so —, *tantus* ; how —, *quantus* ;
soever —, *quantuscunque, quantusvis, quantus-*
libet ; as — again, *altero tanto major* ; twice as
—, *duplo major, duplus* ; as — as, *tantus,* followed by *quantus* or *instar* (e.g. *instar montis*) ;
the —, *nobiles, optimates* ; — grandfather, see
under GRAND. **greatcoat,** n. *pallium, lacerna,*
paenula (all = cloak). **greatness,** n. 1, *mag-*
nitudo, amplitudo ; 2, — of mind, *animi digni-*
tas, gravitas, amplitudo, magnitudo, magnani-
mitas.

greaves, n. *ocreae.*

Greece, n. *Graecia.* **Greek,** adj. *Graecus.*

greedy, adj. *alcjs rei avidus, cupidus.* Adv.
avide, cupide. **greediness,** n. *aviditas, cu-*
piditas. See GLUTTONY.

green, I. adj. 1, *viridis* (in gen.), *virens*
(= still green), *glaucus* (= sea-green) ; 2, =
fresh, *recens, vivus, crudus* (not ripe). **II.** n. 1,
viriditas, color viridis ; 2, = grassy spaces,
campus. **greens,** n. *olera, -um.* **green-**
grocer, n. *qui olera vendit.* **greenhouse,**
n. perhaps *sub vitro esse* or *habere* (= to be or
keep in a —). **greenness,** n. *viriditas.*

greet, v.tr. (*con)salutare, alqm liberaliter*
appellare, salutem alci dare, alqm salvēre jubēre.
greeting, n. (*con)salutatio, salus, -ūtis,* f.,
appellatio (= address).

gregarious, adj. *qui congregari solent.*

gridiron, n. *craticula* (Mart.).

grief, n. *aegritudo* (for any disturbance of

mind), **sol(l)icitudo** (= anxiety), *dolor* (= pain of heart), *maeror* (=sadness), *luctus, -ūs* (= sorrow, esp. the display of it), *angor*. **grieve, I.** v.tr. *alqm dolore afficēre, dolorem alci afferre, alqm alcjs rei piget.* **II.** v.intr. *maerēre alqd, dolēre alqd* (de or ex) *alqd re, alqm alcjs rei piget.* **grievance,** n. *injuria* (= wrong done), *querimonia, querel(l)a* (=complaint). **grievous,** adj. *acerbus, gravis, molestus.* Adv. *acerbe, moleste, graviter.* **grievousness,** n. *acerbitas, molestia, gravitas.*

griffin, n. *gryps.*

grill, v.tr. see ROAST.

grim, adj. †*torvus,* †*trux, saevus.* Adv. *saeve, ferociter.* **grimness,** n. *saevitia, ferocia, ferocitas.*

grimace, n. *os distortum;* to make —s, *os ducēre, os* (dis)*torquēre.*

grimy, adj. see DIRTY.

grin, I. n. use *rictus, -ūs.* **II.** v.intr. use *rictu ridēre.*

grind, v.tr. 1, *molēre;* to — the teeth, *dentibus frendēre;* 2, — the face of the poor, *egentes vexare, premēre.* **grinder,** n. 1, *qui alqd molit;* 2, of teeth, *dens genuinus.* **grindstone,** n. *cos.*

grip, I. v.tr. see SEIZE. **II.** n. *manus, -ūs,* f. **gripe,** v.tr. = to give pain, *alqm torminibus afficēre;* to be —ed, *torminibus* or *ex intestinis laborare, torminibus affectum esse.* **gripes,** n. *tormina, -um.*

grisly, adj. *foedus, teter.* **grisly-bear,** n. *ursus.*

grist, n. *farina;* to bring — to his own mill, *quaestum ad se redigēre.*

gristle, n. *cartilāgo* (Plin.). **gristly,** adj. *cartilagineus* (Plin.).

grit, n. *ptisāna* (= — of barley) (Cels.), *arena* (= — of sand).

groan, I. v.intr. *gemēre, gemitus edēre.* **II.** n. *gemitus, -ūs.*

grocer, n. *qui aromata vendit.* **grocery,** n. *aromata, -um* (= spices (Col.)).

groin, n. *inguen.*

groom, I. n. *agāso, equiso;* — of the chamber, *cubicularius.* **II.** v.tr. *curare.*

groove, n. *canālis, canaliculus, stria.*

grope, v.intr. *errare;* — one's way, *iter explorare.* Adv. *pedetemptim (pedetent-).*

gross, I. adj. 1, = thick, *crassus, densus;* 2, = too great, *nimius, incredibilis;* 3, = disgraceful, *turpis, foedus, indecōrus.* Adv. *dense, nimium, incredibiliter, turpiter, foede, indecore.* **II.** n. 1, = 144, *duodecies duodecim;* 2, in the —, *fere, ferme* (= generally), *in universum* (= altogether). **grossness,** n. 1, *crassitudo, densitas;* 2, *nimia magnitudo;* 3, *turpitudo, foeditas;* — of manners, *inhumanitas.*

grotesque, adj. *immanis, mirus.* Adv. *mire.* **grotesqueness,** n. *mira species.*

grotto, n. *antrum.*

ground, I. n. 1, *humus,* f., *solum, terra;* on the —, *humi;* 2, = reason of a thing, *fundamentum, ratio, caus(s)a, principium;* 3, = — of a battle, *locus;* 4, to gain —, *proficēre;* of a rumour, *percrebescēre.* **II.** v.tr. = teach, *alqm alqd docēre.* **III.** v.intr. of a ship, *sidēre.* **groundless,** adj. *vanus, futilis, fictus.* Adv. *sine caus(s)ā, temere, ex vano.* **groundlessness,** n. *vanitas.* **groundwork,** n. 1, of a building, *substructio, fundamentum;* 2, fig. *fundamentum, principium.*

group, I. n. *caterva, globus, circulus.* **II.** v.tr. *disponēre.* **grouping,** n. *dispositio.*

grove, n. *lucus, nemus, -ŏris,* n., *arbustum.*

grovel, v.intr. *humi jacēre, humi serpēre.* **grovelling,** adj. *abjectus, humilis, sordidus, submissus, servilis, turpis.* Adv. *humiliter, sordide, submisse, serviliter, turpiter.*

grow, I. v.intr. *crescēre, augeri, ingravescēre* (— worse); to let the beard —, *barbam promittēre;* — up, *adolescēre, pubescēre.* **II.** v.tr. *alēre, colēre.* **grower,** n. *cultor.* **grown-up,** adj. *adultus, pubes, grandis.* **growth,** n. *auctus, -ūs, incrementum.*

growl, I. n. *fremitus, -ūs.* **II.** v.intr. *fremere.*

grub, I. n. *vermiculus.* **II.** v.tr. —up, *eruēre.*

grudge, I. n. *simultas, invidia* (= a dislike). **II.** v.tr. *alci alqd invidēre;* see ENVY.

gruel, n. *cremor avenae, ptisana, pulticula.*

gruff, adj. *acerbus, raucus, asper.* Adv. *raucā voce.* **gruffness,** n. *rauca vox.*

grumble, v.intr. *murmurare, mussare.*

grunt, I. n. *grunnītus, -ūs.* **II.** v.intr. *grunnire.*

guarantee, I. n. 1, = surety, *sponsio, vadimonium* (= recognizance), *fides;* 2, = guarantor, *vas, praes, sponsor, obses, -idis,* m. and f. (= hostage). **II.** v.tr. *alqm* or *alqd* or de *alqā re praestare, fidem alci dare* or *interponēre, pro alqo* (pecuniam) *intercedēre.*

guard, n. 1, = a watch for the security of others, *custodia, praesidium, excubiae, vigiliae, statio* (= a post or file of men); to keep —, *excubare, excubias habēre* or *agēre, vigilias agēre, stationem agēre* or *habēre, in statione esse;* others mount —, *alii succedunt in stationem* (all of military matters); 2, = the persons forming the guard, *custodes, excubiae, excubitores* (= —s for the security of a place), *vigiliae, vigiles* (= —s by night), *statio;* to place the —, *custodias* or *vigilias* or *stationes disponēre.* **II.** v.tr. *custodire, alci* (rei) *praesidēre;* see PROTECT; — against, *alqd* or *ab alqā re praecavēre.* **guardian,** n. 1, in gen. *defensor, praeses, custos, propugnator;* 2, = — of a ward, *tutor, curator.* **guardianship,** n. 1, *custodia, praesidium, fides, tutela;* 2, *tutela.* **guarded,** adj. *cautus.* Adv. *caute.*

guerdon, n. *praemium, merces, -ēdis,* f.

guess, I. v.tr. *alqd* (opinione or conjecturā) *augurari, con(j)icēre, conjecturā consequi, opinari, suspicari.* **II.** n. *conjectura.*

guest, n. *hospes, -ĭtis,* m., *hospita,* f. (= one who is received into the home and entertained there); to receive as —, *alqm hospitio excipēre;* one brought uninvited, *umbra.* **guest-chamber,** n. *cubiculum hospitale.*

guide, I. n. 1, lit. *dux;* 2, fig. *dux, auctor, suasor.* **II.** v.tr. 1, *ducēre;* 2, *regēre, gubernare, moderari.* **guidance,** n. *ductus, -ūs, consilium,* or use *dux, auctor* (e.g. te duce). **guide-post,** n. *lapis* or *milliarium* (= mile-stone).

guild, n. *collegium.* **guildhall,** n. *curia.*

guile, n. *dolus, astutia.* **guileful,** adj. *dolosus, astutus.* Adv. *dolose, astute.* **guileless,** adj. *simplex, sincerus.* Adv. *simpliciter, sincere, sine fuco ac fallaciis.* **guilelessness,** n. *simplicitas.*

guilt, n. *vitium, culpa, noxia* (= — as a condition), *noxa* (= injury), *delictum* (= crime). **guilty,** adj. *noxius, sons, sceleratus.* Adv. *scelerate.* **guiltless,** adj. *innocens, insons, culpā vacuus* or *carens;* to be —, *extra noxiam esse, extra culpam esse, integer.*

guise, n. *mos, moris,* m., *habitus, -ūs, species.*

gulf, n. *sinus, -ūs* (= a bay), *gurges, -itis,* m., *vorago* (= a whirlpool).

gull, I. n. *gavia*. II. v.tr. *alqm decipĕre, alci verba dare*. **gullible**, adj. *credulus*.

gullet, n. *gula, guttur*.

gully, n. *alveus* (= bed of a stream).

gulp, I. n. *haustus, -ūs*. II. v.tr. *haurire, absorbēre*.

gum, I. n. 1, of the mouth, *gingiva*; 2, of trees, etc., *gummi* (Plin.). II. v.tr. *glutinare* (Plin.). **gummy**, adj. *gummosus* (Plin.), *glutinosus* (Cels.).

gun, n. * *sclopetum*, where possible use *tormentum* (= engine for hurling stones, etc.). **gunpowder**, n. * *pulvis pyrius*.

gurgle, v.intr. *murmurare*, † *susurrare*.

gush, v.intr. — out, *effundi* or *se effundĕre ex alqâ re*.

gust, n. *venti impetus, -ūs, ventus violens, procella*. **gusty**, adj. *turbidus, procellosus*.

gut, n. I. *intestinum*. II. v.tr. 1, *exenterare* (ante and post class.); 2, fig. *exinanire*.

gutter, n. *canalis, cloaca*.

guttural, adj. (*sonus*) *gravis*.

guzzle, v.intr. (*per*)*potare*. **guzzler**, n. *homo ebriosus*.

gymnasium, n. *gymnasium, palaestra*. **gymnastic**, adj. *gymnicus, palaestricus*. **gymnastics**, n. *ars gymnastica, palaestra*.

gypsum, n. *gypsum*.

gypsy, n. see GIPSY.

H.

ha! interj. *ha!*

haberdasher, n. *qui pannos vendit*. **haberdashery**, n. *panni*.

habiliment, n. *vestis, vestitus, -ūs*.

habit, n. 1, *consuetudo, mos, moris*, m., *usus, -ūs*; 2, of body, *habitus, -ūs*; 3, see HABILIMENT. **habitable**, adj. *habitabilis*. **habitation**, n. *domicilium, sedes, -is*, comb. *sedes et domicilium, habitatio*. **habitual**, adj. *inveteratus, usitatus, usu receptus*; — drunkard, *ebriosus*. Adv. *de* or *ex more*. **habituate**, v.tr. *alqm assuefacĕre* (with infin. or *ad*).

hack, v.tr. *caedĕre*; — in pieces, *concīdĕre*. **hackneyed**, adj. *tritus*.

haft, n. *manubrium, capulus* (= hilt of a sword).

hag, n. *anus, -ūs*, or *anicula*; an old —, *vetula*. **haggard**, adj. *morbo* or *maerore confectus*.

haggle, v.tr. 1, in buying, *minore pretio alqd emĕre velle, pretium facĕre* (= set a price); 2, see QUARREL.

hail, I. n. *grando*. II. v.intr. it —s, *grandinat* (Sen.).

hail, I. v.tr. *alqm salutare, appellare*. II. interj. *salve! ave!* — to you! *macte esto! macte virtute esto! o te felicem!*

hair, n. *pilus* (= a single —), *pili* (= — in general), *seta* (= a bristle), *crinis, coma* (= the hair of the head), *caesaries* (= flowing —), *villus, villi*, (= the thick hair of beasts, e.g. *villosissimus animalium lepus*); a fine —, *pilus tenuis*; thick —, *pilus crassus*; thin —, *pili rari*; downy —, *lanugo*; — of the eyebrows, *supercilia, -orum*; to cut —, *pilos recidĕre, tondĕre*; to a —, *rem acu tetigisti, rem ipsam putasti*; the account tallies to a —, *ratio ad nummum*

convenit; not a — 's breadth, *ab alqâ re non transversum, ut aiunt, digitum discedere*; false —, *capillamentum* (Suet.), *alieni capilli*; a — band, *redimiculum, vitta*. **hair-cloth**, n. *cilicium*. **hairdresser**, n. *tonsor, cinerarius*. **hairpin**, n. *crinale*. **hairsplitting**, n. *disserendi spinae, minuta subtilitas*. **hairy**, adj. *crinītus, capillatus, comatus* (opp. *calvus*), *intonsus* (= unshaved), *pilosus, setosus, capillosus, comosus* (= having much hair); to be —, *pilos habēre*.

halcyon, I. n. (*h*)*alcedo*, (*h*)*alcyon*. II. adj. *serenus*; — days, *dies sereni et tranquilli*, (*h*)*alcedonia, -orum*, (*h*)*alcyonei dies*.

hale, adj. *sanus, validus, robustus*; comb. *salvus et sanus, sanus et salvus*.

hale, v.tr. *rapĕre, trahĕre*.

half, I. adj. *dimidius, dimidiatus*. II. n. *dimidium, dimidiu pars, semis* (e.g. heir to — an estate, *heres ex semisse*). III. adv. *semi* as prefix, e.g. **half-asleep**, adj. *semisomnus* or *semisomnis*. **half-brother**, n. *eodem patre, eâdem matre natus*. **half-circle**, n. *semicirculus*. **half-hour**, n. *semihora*. **half-moon**, n. *luna dimidiata*. **half-open**, adj. *semiapertus*. **half-ounce**, n. *semuncia*. **half-pound**, n. *selibra*. **half-sister**, n. *eodem patre* or *eâdem matre nata*. **halve**, v.tr. in *aequas partes dividĕre*. **halved**, adj. *bipartitus, dimidiatus*. **halves!** interj. in *commune!* (Sen.); to go —, *dimidiam cum alqo partem dividĕre*.

hall, n. *atrium, vestibulum*; — for public meetings, *forum, conciliabulum*.

halloo, I. n. = the — of hunters, *venantium voces*; (in gen.) *clamor, clamores*. II. v.intr. *clamare, vociferari*. **halloo!** interj. *heus! ohe!*

hallow, v.tr. *consecrare, dedicare, inaugurare*. **hallowed**, adj. *sacer, sanctus*.

hallucination, n. *error*.

halm, n. *culmus, calamus* (= reed).

halo, n. *corona* (*lunae*), *area* (*lunae*) (Sen.).

halt, I. adj. *claudus*. II. v.intr. 1, = to walk as a lame person, *claudicare, claudum esse*; 2, = to stop, *subsistĕre, consistĕre*; 3, = to hesitate, *dubitare, animo pendēre, animo esse suspenso, haerēre, claudicare* (e.g. *si quid in nostrâ oratione claudicat*). III. n. use verb.

halter, n. *capistrum* (= — for a horse); to put on a —, *capistrare* (e.g. *equum, boves*); *laqueus* (= noose and — for strangling, e.g. *gulam laqueo frangĕre*).

ham, n. 1, = back of the knee, *poples, -itis*, m.; 2, = salted —, *perna*. **hamstring**, I. n. *poplitis nervus*. II. v.tr. *poplitis nervum secare*.

hamlet, n. *viculus, parvus vicus*.

hammer, I. n. *malleus*; a small —, *malleolus*. II. v.tr. *malleo* (*con*)*tundĕre*; — out, *ducĕre*.

hamper, n. *corbis*; see BASKET.

hamper, v.tr. *implicare, alqm impedire*.

hand, I. n. 1, *manus, -ūs*, f.; the hollow of the —, *palma*; —s off! *heus tu, manum de tabulâ!* to give a person the —, *alci dextram porrigĕre*; to join —s, *dextram jungĕre cum alqo*; — with one another, *dextras jungĕre, dextrae dextram jungĕre*; to strike —s on —, *fidem de alqâ re dextrâ dare, dextram fidemque dare*; put the last — on, *extremam* or *summam manum imponĕre alci rei* or *in alqâ re*; to lay —s on a person, *alci manus afferre* or *admovēre* or *in(j)icĕre, alci vim afferre, alci vim et manus in(j)icĕre*; to lay —s on yourself, *manus sibi afferre* (= to destroy oneself); to fall from —, *excidĕre de manibus*; to be at —, *ad manum, prae manibus* or *praesto esse,* *adesse;* to take in —, *in manum* or *manus sumĕre, in manum capĕre* (e.g. *hunc librum nemo in manus sumit*), = undertake, *suscipĕre;* to hold in the —, *manu tenēre;* to have in —, *in manibus habēre* (e.g. *victoriam;* the state is in the —s of the nobles, *respublica apud optimates est;* all is in the —s of the enemy, *omnia hostium sunt;* it is in my —, *alqd in mei manu* or *in meâ potestate est* or *positum est, alqd in me situm est;* with my (thy, his) own —, *meâ (tuâ, suâ) manu;* on the one —, on the other, *et ..et; quidem* (enclit.) ...*sed* or *autem; alter ..alter; alius . alius;* I have in —, *habeo alqd in manibus* or *inter manus, mihi alqd in manibus est;* the letter is not to —, *epistulam non accepi;* 2, = — of a clock, dial, etc., *index;* 3, = - -writing, n. *manus, -ūs,* f., *chirographum;* to write a good —, *bene ac velociter scribĕre;* 4, = workman, *opera,* usu. in pl. **II.** v.tr. *alqd alci dare, tradĕre, porrigĕre;* — down, *tradĕre, prodĕre;* — round, *circumferre.* **hand-bill,** n. *libellus.* **hand-breadth,** n. *palmus.* **handcuff, I.** n. —s, *manicae.* **II.** v. tr. *manicas alci in(j)icĕre.* **hand¡ful,** n. 1, lit. *manipulus, pugillus;* 2, fig. *exigua manus, -ūs,* f. (= small band) *pauci* (e.g. a — of men, *pauci* (*homines*)). **handicraft,** n. *artificium;* —sman, *artifex.* **handiwork,** n. *opus. -ĕris,* n., *opificium.* **handkerchief,** n. *sudarium.* **handlabour,** n. *opera;* I live by —, *operâ mihi vita est.* **handle, I.** n. 1, *capulus, manubrium* (= — of a sword, etc.), *ansa* (= — of a cup, etc.); 2, fig. *tanquam ansa, ad alqd faciendum;* see OPPORTUNITY. **II.** v.tr. 1, lit. *tractare;* 2, fig. *alqd tractare* or *disputare, disserĕre de alqd re.* **handling,** n. *tractatio.* **handwriting,** n. *manus, -ūs,* f., *chirographum.* **handy,** adj. 1, *habilis;* see SKILFUL; 2, *promptus;* see READY.

handsome, adj. 1, *formosus, venustus, bellus, speciosus, pulcher;* 2, fig. *amplus, magnus* (= great), *liberalis* (= freehanded). Adv. *venuste, belle, ample, magnopere, liberaliter.* **handsomeness,** n. *pulchritudo, venustas.*

hang, I. v.intr. 1, *pendēre* (*ab, de, ex*) *alqâ re;* 2, fig. — on anyone's lips, *oculos in vultu alcjs defigĕre,* or *in alqo* or *alqâ re.* **II.** v.tr. *suspendĕre alqd* (*de, ab, ex*) *alqâ re;* — the head, *caput demittĕre.* **hangdog, I.** n. *verbero, furcifer, -eri.* **II.** adj. *impudicus, scelestus.* **hanger,** n. *gladius.* **hanger-on,** n. *assec-(u)la,* m. **hanging, I.** n. *suspendium.* **II.** adj. *pendens, †pensilis, †pendulus.* **hangman,** n. *carnifex.*

hanker, v.tr. to — after, *alqd desiderare, desiderio alcjs rei teneri* or *flagrare.*

haphazard, adv. at —, *temere.* **hapless,** adj. *infelix;* see UNLUCKY. **haply,** adv. *forte.* **happen,** v.intr. *fieri, accidĕre, contingĕre, evenire.* **happy,** adj. 1,*felix,fortunatus*(=fortunate), *beatus* (= blessed), *faustus*(= of good omen), *secundus* (= favourable), *prosper* (= corresponding to hope), *bonus* (= good); may it have a — issue, *quod bonum, faustum, felix fortunatumque sit!* I am — to see you, *gratus acceptusque venis;* 2, of language, *aptus, accommodatus ad alqm rem.* Adv. *feliciter, fortunate, bene, fauste, prospere, bene, ex sententiâ* (= to your wish), *apte, accommodate.* **happiness,** n. *vita beata* or *beate vivĕre, felicitas, beatitas, beatitudo* (both in a philosophical sense).

harangue, I. n. *contio.* **II.** v.intr. *contionari.*

harass, v.tr. 1, *fatigare, vexare, sol(l)icitare;* 2, military term, *carpĕre, premĕre*

harbinger, n. *praenuntius, antecursor.*

harbour, I. n. 1, lit. *portus, -ūs;* steer for —, *portum petĕre;* — toll or dues, *portorium;* 2, fig. (*tanquam*) *portus, -ūs, refugium, perfugium.*

II. v.tr. 1, = receive, (*hospitio*) *excipĕre;* 2, fig. *colĕre, in se admittĕre.*

hard, I. adj. 1, *durus, solidus, rigidus* (=stiff), *crudus* (= unripe); 2, to feelings, *asper, acerbus* (= bitter), *iniquus* (= unfair), *indignus* (= unworthy); 3, =difficult, *difficilis, arduus.* **II.** adv. *summâ vi, enixe;* to go — with, *alqd aegre ferre.* **harden, I.** v.tr. *durum facĕre* or *reddĕre, durare* (ante and post class.). **II.** v.intr. *obdurescĕre* (lit. and fig.). **hardened,** adj. *inveteratus.* **hard-hearted,** adj. *durus, ferreus.* **hardihood,** n. *audacia.* **hardly,** adv. 1, = scarcely, *vix, aegre;* 2, = cruelly, etc., *dure, duriter, aspere, acerbe.* **hardness,** n. 1, lit. *duritia* (or *durities*); 2, fig. = severity, *iniquitas, crudelitas, saevitia;* 3, see HARDSHIP. **hardship,** n. 1, = toil, *labor;* 2, = trouble, *molestia, aerumna, injuria.* **hardy,** adj. 1, lit. *durus, robustus, laborum patiens;* 2, fig. *strenuus, audax.* Adv. *duriter.* **hardiness,** n. *robur, -ōris;* see STRENGTH.

hardware, n. *ferramenta, -orum.*

hare, n. *lepus, lepŏris,* m. **hare-brained,** adj. *temerarius.* **hare-lip,** n. *labrum fissum.*

hark! interj. *heus!*

harlequin, n. *sannio,* m.

harlot, n. *scortum, meretrix.*

harm, I. n. *damnum, detrimentum;* great —, *clades, -is, calamitas.* **II.** v.tr. *alci nocēre, alqm laedĕre.* **harmful,** adj. *nocens, noxius.* **harmless,** adj. *innoxius, innocuus.* Adv. by adj. **harmlessness,** n. *innocentia.*

harmony, n. 1, (*vocum,* etc.) *concentus, -ūs, concordia;* science of —, *harmonice* or *harmonica;* 2, fig. *consensus, -ūs, consensio, concordia, convenientia.* **harmonious,** adj. 1, of sounds, *consors, consonus, canorus;* 2, fig. *concors, congruens, consentiens, conveniens.* Adv. *consonanter, concorditer, congruenter, convenienter* **harmonize, I.** v.tr. 1, *alqas res concordes facĕre* or *reddĕre;* 2, *componĕre,* (*re*)*conciliare.* **II.** v.intr. *concinĕre* (lit. and fig.).

harness, I. n. *ornamenta equi, arma equestria.* **II.** v.tr. *instruĕre, equum ornare, equum ad currum jungĕre* (Plin.).

harp, n. *lyra, fides, -ium, psalterium.* **harper,** n. *fidicen, fidicina, fidicines, psaltes, -ae* (Quint.), *psaltria,* f.

harpy, n. 1, *harpyia;* 2, fig. *homo rapax.*

harrow, I. n. 1, *crates, -is, (h)irpex, (urpex) -icis,* m., *rastrum.* **II.** v.tr. 1, *occare;* 2, fig. — the feelings, *alqm (ex)cruciare, torquēre.* **harrowing,** adj. *terribilis.*

harry, v.tr. *vexare, torquēre, cruciare.*

harsh, adj. 1, *asper, austerus, severus, morosus, crudelis, saevus, durus;* 2, — in taste, *acer, asper;* 3, — in sound, *absonus, auribus ingratus, dissonus, raucus.* Adv. *aspere, austere, severe, crudeliter, saeve, morose, duriter, acriter;* in sound, use adj. **harshness,** n. 1, *asperitas, severitas, crudelitas, saevitia;* 2, *acerbitas;* 3, *asperitas.*

hart, n. *cervus.*

harvest, I. n. 1, *messis;* 2, fig. *quaestus. -ūs, fructus, -ūs.* **II.** v.tr. *messem facĕre.* **harvester,** n. *messor.*

hash, I. v.tr. *concīdĕre.* **II.** n. *minutal* (Juv.).

hasp, n. see LOCK, BOLT.

hassock, n. †*scirpea matta* (of rushes), *pulvinus* (= cushion).

haste, n. *festinatio, properatio, properantia, celeritas* (*festinatioque*), *maturatio, trepidatio* (= confused hurry, nervous haste); excuse —, *ignoscas velim festinationi meae* (in a letter);

you must make —, *properato* or *maturato opus est*; to be in —, *festinare*; more — less speed, *omnis festinatio tarda est.* **hasten, I.** v.intr. *aigo* or infin. *properare, contendĕre, advolare* al or *in alqm locum* (= — to a place, e.g. to the scene of action); *festinare, maturare* (both with infin.). **II.** v.tr. *accelerare, maturare, properare, festinare, praecipitare, repraesentare.* **hasty,** adj. 1, = hurried, *(prae)properus, citus, citatus, festinans, properans, praeceps*; 2, = irritable, *vehemens* or *acer* (e.g. *vehemens acerque,* opp. *placidus mollisque* = gentle and mild); = easily excited to wrath, *iracundus, stomachosus*; = passionate, *praeceps in iram, pronus in iram, vir* or *homo vehementis* or *violenti ingenii, vir violentus ingenio.* Adv. *propere, properanter, raptim, festinanter, vehementer, acriter, stomachose.* **hastiness,** n. 1, see HASTE; 2, of temper, *iracundia, stomachus.*

hat, n. a broad-brimmed —, *petăsus, causia; pileus* or *pileum* (more especially = a skull-cap of felt without brim); to take the — off to a person (as a mark of respect), *alci caput nudare.*

hatch, v.tr. 1, *parĕre, procreare* (=to produce young); 2, fig. = to brood, concoct, *moliri, machinari, (con)coquĕre.* **hatches,** n. *clat(h)ri, claustra, -orum.*

hatchet, n. *securis, ascia, dolabra.*

hate, hatred, I. n. *od'um* (also in the pl. *odia*), *invidia, simultas, ira* (=passion), *inimicitia.* **II.** v.tr. (both with and without accus.) *odisse;* to bear — against, *odium in alqm habēre, gerĕre, odio in alqm ferri, odium in alqm concepisse;* to be hated by, *odio alci esse, in odio apud alqm esse.* **hater,** n. *qui odit;* a — of, *inimicus, infensus alci.* **hateful,** adj. *odiosus, invisus.* Adv. *odiose, invidiose.*

haughty, adj. *superbus, insŏlens, contumax, arrogans;* comb. *minax atque arrogans* (= threatening and haughty); *sermo plenus arrogantiae* (= a — speech), *fastidiosus, alqā re tumens.* Adv. *superbe, insolenter, arroganter;* to behave —, *insolentius se gerĕre, se superbum praebēre, superbire.* **haughtiness,** n. *superbia, insolentia;* comb. *superbia et insolentia, insolentia et superbia; contumacia, arrogantia;* comb. *superbia et arrogantia; fastidium* (=contempt), comb. *superbia et fastidium; fastus, -ūs* (mostly poet.), *spiritus, -ūs* (usu. in pl.), *superbia et elatio quaedam animi.*

haul, I. v.tr. *trahĕre, ducĕre* (= to draw, to carry along with, gently), *subducĕre* (= — down to the sea, of ships), *rapĕre.* **II.** n. (in gen.) *tractus, -ūs* (= the act of pulling along).

haulm, n. see STALK.

haunch, n. *clunis,* m. and f.

haunt, I. v.tr. 1, *frequentare* (as *alcjs domum*), *(con)celebrare;* 2, of spirits, *alqm agitare, sol(l)icitare;* 3, of thoughts, etc., *urgēre, vexare, sol(l)icitare.* **II.** n. 1, of men, *locus quem alqs frequentare solet;* in bad sense, *latibulum;* = retreat, *receptaculum;* 2, of animals, *latibulum,* † *lustrum, cubile.* **haunted,** adj. — house, *domus ab umbris frequentata.*

have, v.tr. 1, = to hold, carry, *habēre, tenēre* (= to hold); *gestare* (= to carry); to hold in the hand, *(in) manibus habēre* or *tenēre;* to hold by the hand, *manu ducĕre;* to — with, carry with, *secum habēre* or *portare* or *gestare, esse cum alqā re* (i.e. *cum telo*); 2, as auxiliary by tenses of special verb, e.g. take it! — you got it? Yes, I — got it, *prehende! jam tenes? teneo;* 3, = to possess, *habēre alqd* (as *auctoritatem, potestatem); est mihi alqd* (e.g. *liber,* I — a book); *esse alqā re* (of a man's qualities, as *Hortensius tanta erat memoriā, ut,* etc. = Hort. had such a memory,

that, etc.), or *esse alcjs rei, alqd possidĕre,* to possess (lit. and of qualities, as *ingenium, magnam vim); tenēre alqd* (= to hold in possession, to hold an office, a rank, as *tenēre loca, summam imperii), alqā re praeditum* or *instructum* or *ornatum esse* (e.g. *animi nobilitate,* to — nobleness of heart), or *inest ei animi nobilitas, est in eo an. nob.; affectum esse alqā re;* to — an illness, *morbo correptum* or *affectum esse;* to — anyone or a thing = to use, *uti alqo* or *alqā re;* to — favourable wind, *uti vento secundo;* to — success in war, *uti praeliis secundis;* to — a great deal of money, *divitiis* or *opibus et copiis affluēre;* to — children, *liberis auctum esse;* to — a friend in, *habēre alqm amicum, uti alqo amice;* those whom I had with me (i.e. my companions), *qui erant mecum;* 4, = to be obliged, i.e. everybody has to use his own judgment, *suo cuique judicio utendum est;* see BE, DO, TAKE, GET, POSSESS.

haven, n. *portus, -ūs* (lit. and fig.); *refugium, perfugium* (fig. refuge); *asylum* (= refuge); see HARBOUR.

havoc, havock, n. *vastatio, (de)populatio* (= complete devastation); *eversio, excidium* (= destruction, e.g. of a town); *strages, caedes, -is,* f. (= slaughter).

haw, v.intr. *balbutire* (in Latin both trans. and intr.), *balbum esse, lingua haesitare.*

haw, v.tr. = spit up (*ex)screare* (Cels.).

hawk, v.tr. = sell, *venditare.*

hawk, n. *accipiter, -tris,* m. **hawk-eyed,** adj. *lyncēus.*

hay, n. *faenum (fe-);* make — while the sun shines, *vento, ut aiunt, uti secundo.* **hay-cock, hay-rick,** n. *faeni acervus* or *meta.* **haycutter,** n. *faenisex, -icis,* m. **hay-fork,** n. *furca.*

hazard, I. n. 1, *fors -tis,* f.; *sors, -tis,* f. (= lot), *casus, -ūs* (= chance, accident), *fortuna* (= luck), *periculum* (= risk, peril), *alea* (i.e. gambling); scil. *alea alcjs rei* = uncertainty); at —, *temere, forte, fortuito ac temere, temere ac fortuito.* **II.** v.tr. *audēre* or *tentare alqd* (= — with danger), *periculum facĕre alcjs rei;* see RISK, VENTURE. **hazardous,** adj. *periculosus, anceps, dubius* (= doubtful, uncertain), comb. *periculosus et anceps; difficilis* (= difficult), *lubricus* (= slippery), comb. *periculosus et lubricus.* Adv. *periculose.*

haze, n. *nebula* (= fog), *caligo* (= thick, dense fog); see FOG. **hazy,** adj. 1, *nebulosus;* 2, fig., *dubius, anceps.*

hazel, n. *corylus,* f. **hazel-nut,** n. (*nux) avellana* (Plin.).

he, pron. 1, expressed by the form of the verb, as *amat* (= he loves); 2, when used emphatically = *ille, is, iste* (referring to a third person); *ipse* (= he himself, himself), e.g. *Pythagoraeos ferunt respondēre solitos, Ipse dixit* = it is said that the Pythagoreans used to answer, He has said it. He, him, when = man, expressed by *homo,* e.g. *nosti hominem?* = do you know him? *valde hominem diligo;* (prefixed to the names of animals) *mas,* e.g. *caper* (= he-goat), by special form (e.g., *ursus* = — bear; *ursa* = she-bear.

head, I. n. 1, *caput* (= uppermost part of the human body); *cacumen* (= the top of anything), scil. *c. ovi); vertex, -icis,* m. (= top of the —); *bulla* scil. *c. ovi); vertex, -icis,* m. (= top of the —, scil. *bulla clavi* = (= the thick part at the top, scil. *bulla clavi* = — of a nail); *occipitium, occiput* (= hinder part of the —); *biceps* (adj. = with two —s); *capita aut navim* = head or tail (a game of boys: very late); *a capillo usque ad unguem; a vestigio ad verticem* (= from — to foot, from top to bottom);

alqm totum oculis perlustrare or *pererrare* (= to examine from — to foot, all over) ; *praeceps* (adj. = — foremost) ; *capitis longitudine alqm superare* (to be a — taller) ; 2, = animal, individual, *quot homines, tot sententiae,* as many opinions as —s ; *numerus eorum, qui in eum locum convenerant, fuit quinquaginta capitum* (= the company was composed of fifty —) ; *viritim* (= according to the number of —s) ; 3, = life, *res capitis alci agitur, caput alcjs agitur* (= it costs his —) ; 4, = chief, *caput* (= the head, chief, in gen.), *princeps* (= principal, the most influential), *dux* (= commander), comb. *dux et princeps; auctor* (= instigator), comb. *dux et auctor; fax, facis,* f., *tuba* (= signal, then = author of a conspiracy) ; *caput conjuratorum, princeps conjurationis* (= ring-leader of a conspiracy) ; 5, = understanding, faculties, memory, *mens, animus, ingenium, judicium; animo sum conturbato et incerto* (= I don't know where my — stands, I am quite confused) ; *multa simul cogito* (= my — is quite full); *opinionis errore sibi fingĕre alqd* (= to get a foolish notion into one's —) ; *alqd memoriā tenēre* (= to have a thing in the —) ; 6, = forepart of a thing, *superior* (*pars*) or *summus* (with noun) ; *pars prior* (= the first part), *prora* (= prow or fore-part of a ship); *fons, -tis,* m., *caput,* or comb. *fons et caput* (= — of a stream); *caput* (= — of a discourse) ; — of the table, *lectus summus* (see Smith "Dict. Antiq." art. *triclinium*) ; 7. = countenance, resistance, resolution ; to make — against, *alci resistĕre, alqm superare.* **II.** adj. in compound words, to be rendered with *primus* (= the first); *primarius, praecipuus* or *potissimus* (= particular, special) ; *summus* or *maximus* (= chief, original). **III.** v.tr. *alqm ducĕre, alei ducem* or *auctorem esse, alci* or *alci rei praeesse.* **head-ache,** n. *capitis dolor.* **head-band,** n. *infula, vitta, redimiculum.* **head-dress,** n. *vitta, redimiculum, mitra.* **header,** n. see DIVE. **headland,** n. *promontorium.* **headless,** adj. *capite praeciso.* **headlong,** adj. *inconsideratus, inconsultus* (= foolish), *incautus* (= incautious); *improvidus* (= thoughtless), comb. *improvidus incautusque; imprudens; temerarius* (= rash, e.g. *vox temeraria,* a rash expression), comb. *inconsultus et temerarius, temerarius atque inconsideratus; demens, praeceps.* Adv. *temere,* or by adj. *praeceps.* **head-man,** n. *praefectus* (with gen. or dat.), *magister, praeses, -idis* (= president, chairman). **head-piece,** n. *cassis, -idis,* f. (of metal), *galea* (of leather). **head-quarters,** n. *praetorium.* **headship,** n. *locus princeps* or *primus, principatus, -ūs.* **headstrong,** adj. *pertinax, contumax*(= obstinate), *pervicax.* **head-wind,** n. *ventus adversus.* **heady,** adj. 1, = headstrong, *vehemens* (= vehement, opp. *lenis, placidus*) ; 2, = intoxicating, *fervidus.*

heal, I. v.tr. 1, *alqm* or *alqd sanare, sanum facĕre, alci* or *alci rei mederi* (=to apply medicines, to restore), *alqm* or *alqd curare* (= to treat a complaint, take care of a person, nurse) ; 2, fig. *alqm* or *alcjs animum sanare, alqm ad sanitatem reducĕre* or *perducĕre* or *revocare, alci rei mederi.* **II.** v.intr. † *coire* (of wounds), *consanescĕre, sanum fieri* (= to get better). **healable,** adj. *sanabilis, quod sanari potest.* **healing, I.** adj. *saluber, salutaris* (= conducive to health, lit. and fig.), *utilis* (= useful, lit. and fig.). **II.** n. 1, *sanatio* (= art of curing), *curatio* (= treatment of a complaint, but not cure) ; 2, fig. *sanatio.* **health,** n. *sanitas; bona, commoda, firma, prospera valetudo* (= good health ; *valetudo* alone = state of health), *salus, -utis,* f., *corporis* or *valetudinis integritas* (= sound constitution), *salubritas, salutem alci propinare* (= to propose, drink the — of). *bene te! bene tibi!* (= your good — !). **healthful, healthy,** adj.

---

sanus, salvus (= in good condition, in good health), *integer* (= uninjured, sound), *valens, validus, firmus* (= strong), *robustus* (= robust, stout), comb. *robustus et valens, firmus et valens; saluber* or *salubris* (= of a place), *salutaris* (= salutary, wholesome, opp. *pestilens*), *sanus et salvus, salvus et sanus* (= safe and sound), *aër saluber* (= atmosphere, opp. *aër pestilens*), *mens sana* (= sound mind). Adv. *salubriter. belle.*

heap, I. n. *acervus, strues, -is,* f., *cumulus agger* (= a mass, mound) ; to fall all in a —, *collabi, corruĕre.* **II.** v.tr. 1, *acervum construĕre, cumulum exstruĕre, coacervare, aggerare, congerĕre* ; 2, fig. *alqm alqā re cumulare, alqd in alqm con-* (or *in-*) *gerĕre* (e.g. *convicia* = abuse), *alqd alci rei addĕre.*

hear, v.tr. and intr. 1. *audire, auscultare,* to — badly, *surdum esse* (never *male audire* = to be in bad re..ate) ; 2, = to listen, *audire, auscultare* (= to be a listener), *alqd audire* (= to listen to), *alcjs rei rationem non habēre* (= to make no account of), *alci aures dare* (= to lend an attentive ear), *alqm audire, alci auscultare* (= to follow an advice), *ausculta mihi* (= follow my advice); 3, = to learn, (*ex*)*audire* (of gods hearing prayer, etc.), *percipĕre* (= to — distinctly, to understand), *accipĕre* (= to learn from hearsay), *excipĕre* or *excipĕre auribus* (= to — with pleasure, to receive, to catch), *alqd* or *de alqā re cognoscĕre* (= to become acquainted with), *comperire* (= to receive information); to — a cause, *caus(s)am cognoscĕre* ; — a lecturer, *alqm audire ; quantum audio* (= from what I —), *quod nos quidem audierimus* (= at least as far as I have heard), *de rebus suis alqm facĕre certiorem* (= to let a person — from one). **hearer,** n. *auditor* (to be an attentive —, *diligenter audire alqm, studiosum esse alcjs audiendi, multam operam dare alci, se alci atientum praebēre auditorem.* **hearing,** n. 1, *auditus, -ūs,* scil. *auditus acutus* ; 2, = audience, *audientia;* to get a — for, *alci audientiam facĕre* (for a public speaker) ; *facĕre sibi audientiam* (for oneself), *audiri* (= to find hearers); 3, = judicial trial, *cognitio, interrogatio, interrogatio testium* (= — of witnesses) ; see TRIAL. **hearsay,** n. *rumor.*

hearken, v.intr., see HEAR.

hearse, n. *plaustrum* or *vehiculum.*

heart, n. 1, lit. *cor, cordis,* n., *pectus, -ōris,* n. (= the chest, breast); † *praecordia, -orum, cor palpitat* (= the heart beats); 2, fig. of a country, *interior alcjs terrae regio, interiora* (-*um*) *alcjs terrae,* or *intimus* with n. (e.g. *India intima*) ; 3, the — morally, inwardly, *animus; mens, -ntis,* f. (= mind, disposition), comb. *animus et mens* (= — and mind); *voluntas* (= inclination); *ingenium* (= natural disposition); *natura* (= human nature) ; *naturā vir bonus* (= good in —) ; *pectus, -ōris,* n. (= breast); *bonitas* (= good —); *animus benignus, benignitas* (= kindness); *animus mitis* (= gentleness of —); *animus improbus, improbitas* (= depravity of —); *animus fractus* or *afflictus* (= a broken —); *ex animo* (= from the —); *ex* (*animi*) *sententia* (= from my —'s desire); I have at —, *alqd* or *alqs mihi curae* or *cordi est; alqd mihi summae curae est, alqd mihi in medullis est; nihil est mihi alqā re antiquius* (= I am particularly anxious); *nihil mihi potius est, quam ut,* etc. (= I have nothing more at — than that); to take to —, *alqā re* (com)*moveri* ; to be grieved at — about, *alqd aegre ferre;* 4, as endearing term, *= my dear, meum cor* or *anime mi, meum corculum;* 5, = courage, *animus;* 6, = memory ; by —, *memoriter, ex memoriā;* to know by —, *memoriā tenēre* or *complecti, in memoria habēre;* to learn by —, *ediscĕre, memoriae mandare, tradĕre, committĕre;* to say off by —, *memoriter pronuntiare* or *recitare, ex memoriâ exponĕre.* **heart-ache,** n. *dolor;* see GRIEF, SORROW. **heart-break,** n. *dolor.* **heart-breaking, heart-rending,** adj. *miserabilis, maestus, acerbus, flebilis.* **heart-broken,** adj. *animo fractus* or *afflictus.* **heart-burning,** n. fig. *odium occultum* or *inclusum* (= secret hatred); *simultas obscura* (= secret dislike, political enmity, Cic.); *dolor* (= pain). **heartfelt,** adj. *verus, sincerus, sine fuco ac fallaciis.* **heartless,** adj. 1, = without courage, *timidus, humilis, demissus,* comb. *humilis atque demissus* (= low, downcast); *abjectus* or *abjectior, afflictus, fractus,* comb. *demissus fractusque, fractus et demissus* (= with a broken heart, spirit); *perculsus, pröfligatus,* comb. *perculsus et abjectus* (= prostrated); *tristis, maestus* (= sad, sorrowful); 2, = cruel, *crudelis, ferreus, immitis, inhumanus, saevus, severus.* Adv. *timide, humili animo, demisse, demisso animo, humili atque demisso animo; abjecte, abjecto* or *fracto* or *afflicto animo, demisso fractoque animo; timido animo, tristi animo; crudeliter, saeve, severe, inhumane.* **heartlessness,** n. *crudelitas, severitas, inhumanitas, saevitia.* **heart-shaped,** adj. *ad cordis speciem factus.* **heart-sick,** adj. *animo aeger.* **heart-whole,** adj. *nondum amore captus.* **hearty,** adj. 1, *verus* (= true, opp. *falsus*), *sincerus* (opp. *fucatus*); comb. *sincerus atque verus; incorruptus* (= genuine, not bribed, opp. *corruptus*); *candidus* (= candid); *simplex* (= upright); *integer* (= pure); *apertus* (= open-hearted, opp. *tectus*), comb. *apertus et simplex;* 2, = vigorous, *vegetus, vividus, vigens* (= fresh in mind and body), *alacer* (= lively); *valens, robustus, fortis, firmus* (= strong); 3, = cordial, *benignus, benevolus, amicus;* to receive a — welcome, *summo studio excipi;* to give one a — welcome, *alqm summo studio excipĕre.* Adv. *sincere, vere, simpliciter, sine fuco ac fallaciis, alacriter, fortiter, firme, firmiter, benigne, amice.* **heartiness,** n. 1, *veritas, sinceritas, simplicitas;* 2, *alacritas, fortitudo;* 3, *benignitas, amicitia, benevolentia, studium.*

hearth, n. *focus.*

heat, I. n. 1, *calor* (in gen. opp. *frigus*); *ardor* (= burning —), *fervor* (= roaring —), *aestus, -ûs* (= scorching, fever —); all these also in the pl. 2, fig. = ardour, *impetus, -ûs, ardor, fervor (animi), vis; gravitas* (= powerfulness, scil. *belli*); *incitatio* (= vehemence, impetus), *violentia* (= violence), *ardor juvenilis, ardor* or *fervor aetatis* (= fieriness of youth); *ira* (= anger); *impetus et ira, impotentia* (= ungovernableness, excess of passion); *iracundia* (= hastiness of temper); 3, = course at a race, *cursus, -ûs.* **II.** v.tr. 1 (lit.), (*per*)*calefacĕre, fervefacĕre* (esp. in past. part.); 2 (fig.), † *cal*(*e*)*facĕre, accendĕre, incendĕre, inflammare.* **heated,** adj., see HOT.

heath, n. 1, = a plant, *erīce, -es,* f. (Plin.); 2, = a place overgrown with heath, *loca (-orum) deserta* or *inculta, campi inculti* (= barren country); 3, = a place overgrown with shrubs of any kind, *silva.*

heathen, adj. *ethnicus, gentilis, paganus* (Eccl.); otherwise *sacrorum Christianorum expers;* the —, *barbarae gentes.*

heave, I. v.tr. = to move upwards, (*at*)*tollĕre, extollĕre,*(*al*)*levare; sustinēre* (= to hold up, scil. *arma*); — a sigh, *gemitum dare, edĕre.* **II.** v.intr. † *aestuare, fluctuare,* † *tumescĕre,* † *tumēre* (of the waves, etc.), *anhelare* (of the breast).

heaven, n. 1, *caelum,* † *polus* (= sky); † *Olympus* (= abode of the gods); to praise anyone or anything to the skies, *alqm* or *alqd in caelum tollĕre;* **by** —! *medius fidius!* 2, = God, *Deus*

(*Optimus Maximus*), *di*(*i*), (*dei*) † *supert;* **may** — fulfil your wishes! *di*(*i*) *tibi dent* (or *Deus tibi det*); if — pleases, *si di*(*i*)*s* (or *Deo*) *placet;* thank —! *di*(*i*)*s* (or *Deo*) *gratia!* in the name of —, *per Deum* (or *deos*); for —'s sake! *per deos immortales! proh deûm fidem! proh deûm atque hominum fidem;* — forbid, *di meliora.* **heaven-born,** adj. † *caeligenus, caelestis, divinus.* **heavenly,** adj. 1, *caelestis, divinus;* 2, = very charming, *venustus, bellus.* **heavenward,** adv. *in* or *ad caelum.*

heavy, adj. 1, lit. *gravis* (opp. *levis*), *ponderosus;* 2, fig. *gravis, difficilis, molestus* (= troublesome); it is — to bear, *aegre id fero;* it is a — task for me, *grave mihi est alqd;* = of weighty material, *gravis* (opp. *levis*); — (= indigestible) food, *cibus difficilis ad concoquendum;* of air, *caelum crassum, pingue;* a — (= rich) soil, *solum pingue;* a — (= hard) soil, *solum spissum;* = oppressive, *gravis* (opp. *levis*); *magnus* (= great, e.g. *imber magnus,* — rain); of speech, *jejunus, frigidus;* *periculosus* (= dangerous); *mortifer*(*us*) (= fatal, causing death); *atrox* (fearful); to labour under a — disease, *graviter aegrotare.* Adv. *graviter, difficiliter, moleste, aegre; vasto corpore* (= — built); *magnopere.* **heavy-armed,** adj. *qui gravi armatu sunt, gravioris armatûs.* **heaviness,** n. 1, *gravitas, pondus, -ēris,* n.; 2, *gravitas, difficultas, molestia; crassitudo* (of the air), *solum pingue* or *spissum* (of ground); — of mind, *sol*(*l*)*icitudo; anxietas, maeror, maestitia, tristitia.*

Hebrew, adj. *Hebraeus* or *Hebraicus.*

hecatomb, n. *hecatombe*

hectic, adj. *febriculosus.*

hector, v.intr. *se jactare.* **hectoring,** adj. *gloriosus.*

hedge, I. n. *saepes, -is,* f. (*sep*-), *saepimentum.* **II.** v.tr. *saepire.* **hedge-born,** adj. *tenui loco ortus; humili* or *obscuro* or *ignobili loco natus.* **hedge-hog,** n. *ericius, erinaceus* (Plin.), *echinus.*

heed, I. v.tr. 1, = take care, *alqd curare, observare;* 2, = obey, *alci oboedire* (*obed*-), *parēre.* **II.** n. *cura;* take —, (*prae*)*cavēre alqd, ab alqâ re, ut* or *ne.* **heedful,** adj. 1, *cautus, circumspectans;* 2, *oboediens.* Adv. *caute, oboedienter.* **heedless,** adj. 1, = neglectful, *neglegens* (*negligens*); 2, = rash, *temerarius.* Adv. *neglegenter, temere.* **heedlessness,** n. 1, *neglegentia;* 2, *temeritas.*

heel, I. n. 1, = the hind part of the foot or man and of quadrupeds, *calx;* 2, = whole foot, to be at one's —s, *alcjs vestigiis instare, alcjs vestigia premĕre, alqm vestigiis sequi;* to fall head over —s, *ire praecipitem per caput pedesque;* **II.** v.intr. of a ship, *labare* or *in latus labi.*

heft, n. *manubrium.*

heifer, n. *juvenca.*

height, n. 1, lit. *altitudo* (e.g. *hominis, montis,* etc.), *proceritas* (= tallness); 2, fig. *altitudo, sublimitas,* or by adj. *summus* with special n. (e.g. — of glory, *summa gloria*); 3, = high place, *locus editus* or *superior.* **heighten,** v.tr. 1, = to raise higher, *altius efferre;* 2, = to improve, *efferre;* = to raise, to increase, *augēre;* = to enlarge, *amplificare, exaggerare,* (*ex*)*ornare;* = to raise the price of an article, *pretium alcjs rei efferre;* = to sell at a higher price, *carius vendĕre alqd.*

heinous, adj. *foedus* (= foul, loathsome, lit. and fig.); = impious, *impius* (*erga Deum, erga patriam, erga parentes*); = detestable, *abominandus, detestandus, detestabilis;* = wicked, *nefarius, nefandus, scelestus, sceleratus, immanis, atrox, flagitiosus.* Adv. *foede, nefarie,* comb. *impie* *nefarieque, nefande, sceleste, scelerate, impie, atrociter, flagitiose.* **heinousness,** n. *impietas, atrocitas, scelus, -ĕris,* n., or *facinus, -ŏris,* n. (= the act).

heir, n. *heres,-ēdis,* m. & f.; the — to the whole fortune, sole —, *heres ex asse;* — to half the property, *heres ex dimidiā parte;* to name one his —, *alqm heredem instituĕre, alqm heredem* (*testamento*) *scribĕre, facĕre.* **heiress,** n. *heres,* f. **heirloom,** n. *alqd paternum (et avitum).* **heirship,** n. *hereditas.*

hell, n. 1, *inferi, Tartarus(os)* or pl. *Tartara;* 2, eccl. t.t. *Gehenna, Infernus.* **hellhound,** n. *Furia, Erin(n)ys.* **hellish,** adj. *infernus* (lit.); = dreadful, *terribilis;* = diabolical, *nefandus.*

hellebore, n. (*h*)*elleborus, veratrum.*

Hellenic, adj. *Graecus.*

helm, n. lit. and fig. *gubernaculum;* the handle of the —, or the — itself, *clavus.* **helmsman,** n. *gubernator* (lit. and fig.).

helmet, n. *cassis, -ĭdis* (of metal); *galea* (originally of skin).

help, I. n. *auxilium* (= increase of power, aid in need, in pl. *auxilia,* = auxiliaries); *subsidium* (= aid ready to be supplied; in pl. = the reserves), *ops,* f. (only *opis, opem, ope* in use, = power to assist), *adjumentum* (= a means), *ornamentum* (= a supply or support), *praesidium* (= something set before to shield you), *suppetiae* (= present aid, succour, of troops, etc.), *salus, -utis,* f. (= rescue, sustentation of existence), *opera* (= — in act and deed); with any-one's —, *alcjs auxilio* or *ope* or *operā, alqo adjuvante, alqo adjutore, divinā ope;* "with the — of a thing" may be expressed by the ablative (e.g. with the — of genius and reflection, *ingenio et cogitatione*). **II.** v.tr. 1, *alqm in alqā re* or *ad alqd faciendum* (*ad*)*juvare, alci subesse,* and *subvenire, succurrĕre, auxiliari* (rare); *so* — me God, *ita me Deus adjuvet;* — ! *subveni,* or pl. *subvenite!* 2, of food, *alqd alci dare, porrigĕre, dividĕre;* 3, = hinder, I can't — telling, (*facĕre*) *non possum quin dicam,* so *fieri non potest quin.* **helper,** n. *adjutor, adjutrix.* **helpful,** adj. *utilis, aptus, idoneus;* he is — to me, *auxilio mihi est;* to be —, = HELP. Adv. *utiliter, apte.* **helping,** adj. *auxiliaris, auxiliarius* (more usually = belonging to auxiliary forces). **helpless,** adj. *inermis* (or -*us*), *inops* or *auxilii inops, auxilio orbatus;* thoroughly —, *ad summam omnium rerum inopiam redactus.* **helplessness,** n. *inopia.* **helpmeet,** n. *socius, consors, -tis,* m. and f., *maritus* (= husband), *uxor,* f. (= wife).

helter-skelter, I. adj. *praeceps.* **II.** adv. *raptim.*

hem, I. n. *limbus, instita* (both, however, = fringe or border sewn on). **II.** v.tr. 1, *suĕre* (= sew); 2, fig. — in, *circumsedĕre, obsidĕre, circumvallare* (with entrenchments).

hem, I. v.intr. to — and haw, *haesitare, dubitare.* **II.** interj. (*e*)*hem!*

hemisphere, n. *hemisphaerium.*

hemorrhage, n. *haemorrhagia* (Plin.).

hemp, n. *cannabis, -is,* f. **hempen,** adj. *cannabinus.*

hen, n. 1, opp. to male, *femina;* 2, domestic fowl, *gallina.* **hen-coop,** n. *cavea.* **henhouse,** n. *gallinarium* (Plin.). **hen-pecked,** adj. (*maritus*) *cui uxor imperat.*

hence, adv. 1, of place, *hinc;* as interj., *apage, procul;* 2, of time, by abl. (e.g. *paucis diebus,* a few days —), or *post* (e.g. *post paucos dies*); 3, = for this reason, *hinc, ita, quam ob*

rem (or, as one word, *quamobrem*). **henceforth, henceforward,** adv. *dehinc, posthac.*

her, I. pers. pron., see SHE. **II.** adj. *ejus, illius, suus* (only in ref. to subj. of sentence).

herald, I. n. 1, *caduceator,* (*legatus*) *fetialis* (= belonging to a college of priests instituted to declare war or to ratify a peace); 2, = public crier, *praeco;* 3, = forerunner, *praenuntius.* **II.** v.tr. *nuntiare.*

herb, n. 1, *herba;* 2, = kitchen-stuff, *olus, oleris,* n. **herbage,** n. *herba* or *herbae,* † *gramen.* **herbalist,** n. *herbarius.*

herculean, adj. *fortissimus* (= very strong).

herd, I. n. 1, *grex;* of large cattle, etc., *armentum;* of a —, *gregalis, gregarius;* in —*s, gregatim;* 2, = a company of people, *grex, multitudo, caterva;* the common —, *vulgus, -i,* n. **II.** v.tr. *pascĕre.* **III.** v.intr. *congregari.* **herdsman,** n. in gen. *pastor;* = keeper of large cattle, *armentarius.*

here, adv. *hic* (= where the speaker is); not far from —, *haud procul;* *hoc loco, hac regione* (= in this place); from — (hence), *hinc;* only — and there, *rarus* (adv. *raro*); they fought only — and there, *rari praeliabantur;* — and there, in this and that place, *hac atque illac;* —(that is, in this thing), *hac in re.* **hereafter,** adv. *posthac, aliquando.* **herein,** adv. *in hac re.* **hereupon,** adv. *ad haec* (e.g. *ad haec* or *adversus haec respondit*).

hereditary, adj. *hereditarius, paternus* (as transmitted from a parent to a child). **heritage,** n. = an inherited estate, *heredium, hereditas, patrimonium.*

heresy, n. *haeresis* (Eccl.). **heretic,** n. *haereticus.* **heretical,** adj. *haerĕticus* (Eccl.).

hermaphrodite, n. *androgynos, homo utrusque sexûs.*

hermetically, adv. *arte clausus.*

hermit, n. *homo solitarius, eremĭta, anachoreta, -ae,* m. (Eccl.).

hero, n. 1, (= demigod, son of the gods, illustrious person), *heros, -ois,* m.; 2, = brave man, *vir fortis* or *fortissimus, dux fortissimus;* 3, = the principal person in a poem, *de quo* (*fabula*) *scripta est;* — of the drama, *persona prima.* **heroic,** adj. 1, *heroicus* (e.g. the — age, *aetas heroica, tempora,-um, heroica*), *praestans;* 2,= brave, valiant, *fortis, fortis et invictus;* = godly, *divinus;* = superhuman, *major quam pro homine* or *plus quam humanus;* = incredible, *incredibilis.* Adv. *fortiter, invicte, praestanter.* **heroine,** n. 1, = demi-goddess, *heroina, herois;* 2, = brave woman, *femina fortissima, praestantissima,* etc.; 3, — of a story, *de quā* (*fabula*) *scripta est.* **heroism,** n. *virtus, -ūtis, animus fortis* or *fortis et invictus* (= brave spirit); = greatness of soul, *animi magnitudo.*

heron, n. *ardea.*

hers, pron. *suus* (in reference to the main subject); *ejus, illius* (not in reference to the main subject).

herself, pron. (*ea*) *ipsa, se,* etc. (in ref. to subj. of sentence).

hesitate, v.intr. 1, *dubitare* with infin. (but *non dubitare quin*), *dubito* (= doubtful) or *incertum* (= uncertain) *esse;* I — what to do, *dubius* or *incertus sum quid faciam;* 2, = to get confused in speaking, *haerĕre, haesitare.* **hesitation,** ₁ 1, *dubitatio, haesitatio;* 2, *haesitatio, haesitan, tia linguae.*

heterogeneous, adj. *diversus et dissimilis.* **heterogeneousness,** n. *natura diversa et dissimilis.*

hew, v.tr. *caedĕre, concīdĕre* (scil. *lignum*). **hewer**, n. *qui ligna caedit*. **hewn**, adj. *quadratus* (e.g. *saxum*).

hexameter, n. *hexameter* (or *-trus*).

hey, interj. *eja! age!* **heyday**, n. (*aetatis*) *flos, floris*, m., *robur, -ŏris*, n.

hiatus, n. *hiatus, -ūs* (in sound); there is an — (in MS.), *alqd deest*.

hibernal, adj. *hibernus*. **hibernate**, v.intr. 1, = to pass the winter, *hibernare*; 2, = to sleep through the winter, *per hiemem dormire* or *quiescĕre*.

hiccough, hiccup, n. *singultus, -ūs* (Plin.).

hide, **I.** n. *corium, tergum, vellus, -ĕris*, n., *pellis*. **II.** v.tr. *abdĕre, abscondĕre, condĕre, celare, occulĕre, occultare*; — and seek, (*pueros*) *latitantes conquirĕre*. **hidden**, adj. *abditus*, etc.; to lie —, *latēre*. **hiding-place**, n. *latibulum*.

hideous, adj. *foedus, deformis*; see UGLY. Adv. *foede*. **hideousness**, n. *foeditas, deformitas*.

hierarchy, n. of priests, *sacerdotium*.

hieroglyphical, adj. **hieroglyphicus,*hierographicus*.

higgle, v.intr., see HAGGLE. **higgledy-piggledy**, adv. *confuse*.

high, **I.** adj. 1, *altus* (= the distance from the ground, opp. *humilis, profundus*), (*ex*)*celsus*, (*in*) *altum*) *editus* (= raised, opp. *planus*), *elatus* (= lifted up, and specially of words and manner), *erectus* (= straight up, hence lofty in thought), (*aditu*) *arduus* (= hard of ascent), *procērus* (= stretching up, opp. *brevis*, used only of things high by growth), *sublimis* (= rising from below up to heaven), *acutus* (= sharp, clear, of tones); most —, *summus* (opp. *imus, infimus*), *supremus* (in rank, opp. *infimus*); the —est God, *Deus supremus, Deus optimus maximus*; fifty feet —, *quinquaginta pedes altus*; to be fifty feet —, *in altitudinem quinquaginta pedum eminēre*; 2, a — price, *pretium magnum*; to be of — price, *magni pretii esse, magno constare*; to buy at — price, *magno* or (*pretio*) *impenso emĕre* (dear); to rise, to bid —er (at an auction), *contra liceri*; to set a — value on, *alqd magni aestimare, alqd magno aestimare, alci rei multum tribuĕre*; to stand —, *magnum pretium habēre*; to stand —er than, *praestare alci rei*; 3, fig. it is too — for me, *alqd mente meā assequi* or *capĕre non possum*; 4, = bad, of meat, etc., *rancidus, puter* (*putris*). **II.** adv. *alte*; to aim —. *magnas res* (*ap*)*petĕre*. **high-born**, adj. *generosus, nobili loco ortus*. **high-bred**, adj. 1, by birth, *generosus*; 2, fig. *generosus, urbanus*. **high-day**, n. *dies festus*. **high-flown**, adj. *tumidus*; to use — words, *ampullari, nullum modum habēre*. **high-handed**, adj. *superbus, imperiosus*. **high-heeled**, adj. — boot, *cothurnus* (of tragedy). **highlands**, adj. *loca mont*(*u*)*osa, -orum*. **highlander**, n. *homo montanus*. **highly**, adv. *magni* (e.g. *magni aestimare*, to value —), *valde, magnopere*. **high-mettled**, adj. *acer*. **high-minded**, adj. *magnanimus, generosus*. **high-mindedness**, n. *magnanimitas*. **highness**, n. *altitudo*; of price, *caritas*. **high-priced**, adj. *carus*. **high-priest**, n. *Pontifex Maximus*. **high-shouldered**, adj. *gibber* (= hunchbacked). **high-spirited**, adj. *generosus, fortis, animosus*. **high-treason**, n. *majestas, perduellio*. **high-water, high-tide**, n. *plurimus aestus, -ūs, accessus, -ūs*. **highway**, n. *via*. **highwayman**, n. *latro, grassator*.

hilarity, n. *hilaritas* (= merriness); = joy, *laetitia, animus laetus* or *hilaris*.

hill, n. *collis*, m. ; = height, *clivus*; = mound.

tumulus; = elevated spot, *locus editus* or *superior*; up —, *acclivis*, adj. ; *adverso colle*, adv. ; down —, *declivis* (opp. *acclivis*). **hillock**, n. *tumulus*. **hilly**, adj. † *clivosus, mont*(*u*)*osus*.

hilt, n. *capulus*.

hind, n. = female stag, *cerva*.

hind, n. 1, = servant, *domesticus* (= house-servant), *servus*; 2, = peasant, *agricola, rusticus, arator* (= ploughman).

hind, adj. *aversus* (= wrong side, opp. *adversus*); = that is behind, *posterior* (= hinder). **hindermost**, adj. *postremus*; (of two) *posterior*; = the last of a number, *ultimus*; = the most remote, *extremus*.

hinder, v.tr. *impedire, prohibēre alqm* or *alqd*, (*ab*) *alqa re, quin* or *quominus*; — in a thing, *impedimento esse alci* (*alci rei*) *ad alqd* ; in gen. *impedimentum afferre alci rei faciendae*; = to be in the way of, *obstare alci* and *alci rei*, = to oppose, *officĕre alci* and *alci rei, prohibēre* or *arcēre alqm alqā re* or *ab alqā re* ; = to retard, *retardare alqm ad alqd faciendum* or *ab alqā re facienda* or *in alqā re* ; = to delay a thing, *moram facĕre alci rei. alci obstare, officĕre*, or with *quominus* or *quin*. **hinderer**, n. *turbator* (e.g. *pacis*), = who interrupts anyone in speaking, *interpellator* (e.g. *sermonis*); = interrupter, *interventor*. **hindrance**, n. *impedimentum* ; = interruption, *interpellatio*; = delay, *mora*; = difficulty, *difficultas*.

hinge, **I.** n. 1, *cardo*, m.; 2, = a leading principle, *caput*; = the main thing in anything, *summa alcjs rei*; the — on which a question turns, *cardo*; = the deciding point, *momentum*. **II.** v.intr. *alqā re contineri, in alqā re versari*; see above.

hint, **I.** n. *significatio*; a — is sufficient, *rem ostendisse satis est*. **II.** v.intr. *alqd alci sub*(*j*)*icĕre* (= to remind privily).

hip, n. *coxendix*.

hire, **I.** n. 1, = hiring, *conductio*; 2, = wages, *merces, -ēdis*; see WAGES. **II.** v.tr. *conducĕre*; to — oneself out, *se* or *operam suam locare* (Plautus). **hireling**, **I.** n. = one who serves for wages, *homo conducticius, mercenarius* (i.e. serving for wages), *homo* (*miles*) *mercede conductus* (= engaged for hire). **II.** adj. *venalis*; see VENAL. **hirer**, n. *conductor*.

his, adj. *suus* (in reference to the subject of the same sentence, and if in a dependent sentence the subject of the principal sentence is referred to); *ejus, illius* (if not referring to the subject); — own, *suus* (*proprius*) (if referring to the subject); is not expressed in Latin, unless we wish to speak emphatically.

hiss, **I.** v.intr. *sibilare* (resembling the noise made by serpents), *sibilum mittĕre* or (*ef*)*fundĕre*; to utter a shrilling sound, *stridĕre* (*stridēre*). **II.** v.tr. (an actor or speaker) *sibilare*; to — off (a bad actor off the stage)(*e scaenā sibilis*) *explodĕre*. **III.** n. *sibilus* (poet. pl. *sibila*).

hist! interj. *st!*

historian, n. *rerum* (*gestarum* or *antiquarum*) *scriptor* or *auctor*, in the context only *scriptor* ; *historicus*. **historic**, adj. *historicus* ; — style of writing, *genus historicum* (opp. *genus oratorium*, etc.); by *historiae rerum* (e g. — *fidel-ity*,authority, *rerum* or *historiae fides, fidshistorica*) ; — writings, *libri ad historiam pertinentes* ; according to — truth, *ad historiae fidem*. Adv. *historice* (Plin. Min.). **history**, n. *historia, rerum gestarum memoria, res* (*gestae*), *annales*.

histrionic, adj. *scaenicus* (*scen-*); = what occurs on the scene of action, *theatralis* ; — art, *ars ludicra*.

hit, I. v.tr. 1, lit. *ferire, tundĕre, percutĕre ;* = not to miss, *tangĕre* (in gen. = to touch); to — with a blow, *icĕre ;* to be — by lightning, *de caelo tangi* or *ici ;* to — the mark, *collineare,* or *scopum ferire* (lit. and fig. but rare) ; 2, — it off = to agree, *convenire ;* to be hard —, *probe tactum esse ;* — upon, *alqm* or *alqd offendĕre, in alqm* or *alqd incidĕre, incurrĕre ;* Prov. "you have — the nail on the head," *acu tetigisti ;* the word —s us, *sermo nos tangit ;* to be — by calamities, *calamitate affligi.* **II.** n. 1, *ictus, -ūs ;* 2, = a casual event, *fors, fortis, f. ;* a lucky —, *fortuna secunda, felicitas ;* = injury, *plaga ;* "a —," *hoc habet* (= "he has caught it "); 3, = a sudden idea, *cogitatio repentina.*

hitch, I. v.tr. = to join together, *conjungĕre ;* = to tie to, *annectĕre ad* or dat. **II.** n. = hindrance, *impedimentum.*

hither, adv. of place, *huc* (where the speaker is) ; — and thither, *huc illuc, huc et illuc, ultro et citro ;* by *ad* in composition (e.g. to bring —, *afferre, apportare ;* to fly —, *advolare*) ; —! *huc ades!* **hitherto,** adv. = up to this time, *adhuc, adhuc usque, ad hoc tempus, ad hunc diem.*

hive, I. n. 1, (*apium*) *examen ;* 2, = box for the reception of a swarm of honey-bees, *alvus* or *alveus.* **II.** v.tr. = to — bees, *in alveum congerĕre.*

ho! interj. *heus!*

hoar, adj. *canus, † incanus ;* — antiquity, *antiquitas ultima.* **hoar-frost,** n. *pruina, pruinae* (the latter esp. of continued frost). **hoary,** adj. *canus, † incanus.*

hoard, I. n. (= a large stock) *copia, †acervus ;* to have a — of anything, *alqā re abundare.* **II.** v.tr. e.g. to — money, *pecuniam* or *opes undique conquirĕre* (= to collect), *coacervare.*

hoarse, adj. *raucus ;* a little —, *subraucus ; asper* (in gen. opp. *lenis*) ; to demand till one becomes —, *usque ad ravim poscĕre.* Adv. *raucā voce.* **hoarseness,** n. *rauca vox ;* — of throat, *fauces raucae.*

hoax, I. n. *ludificatio,* or circumloc. by verb. **II.** v.tr. *alci illudĕre, alqm* (*lepide*) *ludificari.*

hobble, v.intr. *claudicare* (lit. and fig.). **hobblingly,** adv. *claudo pede.*

hobby, n. 1, = a stick or figure of a horse, on which boys ride, † *arundo ;* to ride on a —, † *equitare in arundine longa ;* 2, = favourite object, everyone has his —, *trahit quemque sua voluptas ;* to be on one's —, *ineptiis suis plaudĕre.*

hobgoblin, n. *larva.*

hobnob, v.intr. *alqo familiariter uti.*

hock, n. *poples, -itis,* m.

hockey, n. *pila ;* to play —, *pilis ludĕre.*

hodge-podge, n. *farrāgo* (Juv.).

hoe, I. n. = a rake for hoeing the ground, *ligo, ligōnis,* m., *marra* (Plin.) ; = a rake, harrow to break clods with, *rastrum ;* (if a small one) *rastellus ;* = a weeding-hook, *sarculum.* **II.** v.tr. *sarrire* (= to weed with a hook).

hog, n. *sus, suis,* m. and f., *porcus.* **hoggish,** adj. 1, lit. *suillus ;* 2, fig. see GLUTTONOUS.

hogshead, n. *dolium* (= cask).

hoist, v.tr. *sublevare, tollĕre ;* — sails, *vela dare.*

hold, I. n. 1, = grasp, *manus, -ūs,* f. ; to take —, *prehendĕre ;* 2, see PRISON ; 3, of a ship, *alveus* (= hull), *caverna ;* 4, fig. to have a — over, *alqm devinctum* or *obligatum habēre, multum apud alqm valēre.* **II.** v.tr. 1, = to have, *tenēre ; habēre, obtinēre, possidēre* (= to possess), *gestare* (= to carry) ; — an office, *gerĕre* (e.g. *praeturam*);

2. = to contain, *capĕre, continēre ;* 3, = to uphold, *sustinēre, sustentare ;* 4, = to keep against attack, *defendĕre ;* 5, = to conduct, *agĕre, habēre* (e.g. *comitia,* an election) ; — a festival, *celebrare ;* 6, see CONSIDER, THINK. **III.** v.intr. = to hold good, *certum esse ;* it —s, (*res*) *convenit cum alqā re, in* or *ad alqd ut* or acc. and infin.; — back, *retinēre, cunctari* (= to delay); — forth (= to extend) *porrigĕre, extendĕre ;* = to propose, fig. *proponĕre, proferre, praebēre ;* = to discourse, *contionari ;* — in, lit. *equum inhibēre ;* fig. *re-primĕre, cohibēre ;* — on, — one's course, *cursum tenēre ;* — out (= to endure) *durare, (alqd) sustinēre, perferre ;* — up, see HOLD, II. 3 ; — with, *cum alqo consentire, convenire.* **holder,** n. 1, *is qui tenet ;* — of land, *possessor ; conductor* (= tenant), *colonus ;* 2, = something by which a thing is held, *retinaculum, capulus* (= handle). **hold-fast,** *fibula* (= clasp), *retinaculum.* **holding,** n. = possession, *possessio.*

hole, n. 1, *cavum* (= hollow place in gen., mouse's —, etc.), *foramen* (= an opening in or through a solid body), *rima* (= a chink), *lacuna* (= a pit, a pool); to bore a —, *pertundĕre ;* 2, = a small, miserable hut, a wretched —, *gurgustium.*

hollow, I. adj. 1, (*con*)*cavus ;* eaten up, hollowed out, *exesus* (e.g. *exesae arboris truncus*); — teeth, *dentes exesi* (Plin.) ; the—hand, *manus cava* or *concava* (e.g. of a beggar holding his hands in that way); to make —, *alqd* (*ex*)*cavare ;* 2, = deep, hoarse in sound, *fuscus* (= the tone of the voice. opp. *candidus*), *asper, raucus ;* 3, = not sincere, *vanus* (= empty), *simulatus, fucatus, fucosus* (= with only the outward appearance) ; see FALSE. **II.** n. *cavum, foramen ;* see HOLE ; = valley, *convallis, valles* (*vallis*), *-is,* m. **III.** v.tr. (*ex*)*cavare.*

holy, adj. *sacer* (= sacred to the gods, opp. *profanus*) ; = under divine protection, inviolable, *sanctus ;* inviolable (i.e. protected by the sanction of a heavy penalty), *sacrosanctus* (e.g. *memoria*) ; = what is held in veneration, *religiosus* (e.g. tombs, oaths) ; = august, venerable, *augustus ;* = with godly fear, *pius erga Deum ;* = reverend, *venerandus, venerabilis.* Adv. *sancte, religiose, pie, auguste.* **Holy Ghost,** n. * *Spiritus Sanctus.* **holiness,** n. *sanctitas, religio* (attaching to an object of regard), *caerimonia* (rare), *pietas erga Deum.*

homage, n. *cultus, -ūs* (e.g. *Dei*), *observantia ;* in feudal times, * *homagium.*

home, I. n. *domus, -ūs* (irreg.), *domicilium* (= household), *familia, patria* (= mother-country), *sedes* et *domicilium ;* at —, *domi, inter suos ;* to be at —, *domi esse, in patriā esse ;* at my —, *domi meae* (*tuae,* etc.) ; at — and abroad, *domi militiaeque ;* from —, *domo ;* at Cæsar's —, *in domo Cæsaris, domo Cæsaris ;* to remain at —, *domi (re)manēre ;* to keep at —, *publico carēre* or *se abstinēre, in publicum non prodire, domi sedēre ;* he is not at —, *est foris* (= he is out); he is at—, *est intus ;* to sup from —, *foris cenare ;* to go —, *ire domum.* **II.** adj. *domesticus, familiaris ;* to strike —, *ferrum adigĕre ;* to come — to one, *alqd sibi dictum putare.* **home-baked,** adj. *domi coctus.* **home-bred,** adj. *domesticus, intestinus, vernaculus.* **homeless,** adj. *profugus, extorris* (= exiled), *patriā* or *domo carens.* **homely,** adj. *simplex, inornatus.* **homeliness,** n. *simplicitas.* **home-made,** adj. *domesticus.*

homicidal, adj. see MURDEROUS. **homicide,** n. 1, = murder, *caedes, -is ;* 2, = murderer, *homicida,* m. and f. ; see MURDER, MURDERER.

homily, n. *oratio quae de rebus divinis habetur.*

homœopathy. n. *ea modendi ratio quae*

Similia **morbis** adhibet remedia (Riddle and Arnold).

homogeneous, adj. ejusdem generis, eodem genere. **homogeneity,** n. natura similis, genus simile.

homologous, adj. by par, similis, similis in algâ re ratio.

homonymous, adj. eodem nomine.

honest, adj. bonus, probus; = without trickishness, sincerus, sine fuco et fallaciis; = one in whose words and actions we may trust, fidus; = frank, simplex, candidus; = genuine, antiquâ fide; = pure, unstained, integer, sanctus, incorruptus; to lose one's — name, boni viri nomen amittēre. Adv. probe, integre, sancte, sine fraude; sine fuco et fallaciis (= without deceit); simpliciter, candide (= candidly). **honesty,** n. := uprightness, probitas; = moral purity, rectitude, integrity, integritas, sanctitas; = innocent heart, innocentia; = sincerity, sinceritas; = trustworthiness, fides, comb. integritas et fides; = noble mind, animus ingenuus, ingenuitas; = carefulness (as regards other people's property), abstinentia; to show —, fidem adhibēre in algâ re; = candour, simplicitas; = decency, discreetness, castitas, sanctitas, pudicitia.

honey, n. mel; his language is as sweet as —, loquenti illi mella profluunt, hence also sweetness of language, dulcedo orationis or suavitas (= mildness); my — (= my darling), deliciae meae, voluptas mea. **honeycomb,** n. favus; to take the —, favum eximēre; the cell of a —, cavum. **honeymoon,** n. dies conjugio facto laeti. **honeyed, honied,** adj. 1, mellitus; 2, fig. dulcis.

honorary, adj. honorarius (= for the sake of giving honour). **honorarium,** n. see FEE.

honour, I. n. 1, = official distinction, dignitas, honos (honor), honoris gradus, -ūs; highest —, amplissimus dignitatis gradus; 2, = moral quality, honestas, honos; 3, = reputation, fama, existimatio; of a woman, = chastity, pudor, pudicitia; 4, = respect felt, verecundia; 5, = mark of respect, honos; to pay the last —, justa alci facēre or solvēre. **II.** v.tr. 1, = celebrate, honorare, decorare, celebrare; 2, = esteem, colēre, diligēre, vereri. **honourable,** adj. honoratus (= very much honoured, e.g. the army, militia); causing or bringing honour, honestus, honorificus, honorabilis (very seldom, although once in Cic.); = proper, decōrus; = praiseworthy, laudabilis, laude dignus, praedicabilis; = glorious, gloriosus (e.g. mors); = excellent, distinguished, egregius; to thank a person in the most — terms, alci gratias agēre singularibus or amplissimis verbis. Adv. honeste, cum dignitate; = in a manner conferring honour, honorifice; most —, honorificentissime, summo cum honore; to die —, bene mori; = in a manner deserving of praise, laudabiliter, cum laude; gloriose; egregie, eximie.

hood, n. = covering for the head used by females, mitra, mitella; a fillet of net-work for covering the hair, reticulum. **hoodwink,** v.tr. alci illudēre, algm ludificari, fallēre.

hoof, n. ungula; cloven —, ungula bisulca (Plin.).

hook, I. n. 1, hamus (piscarius), uncus (= a large iron —); by — or by crook, quocunque modo; 2, = a sickle, falx. **II.** v.tr. to — a fish, hamo piscari, hamo pisces capēre; to — on, alci rei or in algâ re suspendēre. **hooked,** adj. aduncus; = having —s, hamatus.

hoop, n. circulus (= anything circular); an iron — set round with rings as an amusement for boys, trochus.

hoopoe, n. upupa, epops, -opis, m.

hoot, v.intr. (of owls), canēre; (of men), vociferari, alci obstrepēre; — off the stage, algm explodēre. **hooting,** n. cantus, -ūs, carmen (of owls), voces, vociferatio, clamor (of men).

hop, v.intr. (of birds), salire (Plin.); (of men), altero pede saltuatim currēre.

hope, I. n. spes (opp. fiducia = confidence); meton. Cicero our last —, spes reliqua nostra, Cicero; — (from the fact of a thing being considered likely), opinio; = expectation, ex(s)pectatio; a gleam of —, specula; — of, spes alcjs rei (e.g. of immortality, immortalitatis); = probability of, opinio alcjs rei; I have — that, etc., spero fore ut, etc.; I have no — in, despero de algâ re (e.g. de republicâ); if there is, or will be, —, si est, or erit, spes (e.g. of returning, reditûs). **II.** v.tr. sperare, accus. or accus. and (fut.) infin., confidēre. **hopeful,** adj. 1, = full of hope, spe animoque impletus (= filled with hope and courage); 2, = having qualities which excite hope (e.g. a son, daughter, pupil, etc.), bonae spei, qui spem bonae indolis dat. de quo bene sperare possis; very —, optima or egregiae or summae spei, eximiâ spe. Adv. cum magnâ spe. **hopeless,** adj. spe carens, spe orbatus, spe dejectus, † exspes (= one who has no hope); = one who must be given up, deperatus. Adv. sine spe, desperanter (rare). **hopelessness,** n. desperatio (as mental quality), res desperatae (= of affairs).

horde, n. grex, gregis, m.; caterva (of people); = wandering tribe, vagus with noun (e.g. — of Gaetulians, Gaetuli vagi).

horizon, n. 1, lit. *horizon, finiens circulus; the sun passes the —, sol emergit de subterraneâ parte, sol emergit supra terram; 2, fig. = the sky in gen. caelum (e.g. a clear — or sky, caelum vacuum); = view, a(d)cpectus, -ūs (= view from a mountain); conspectus (= sight); a thing limits our —, alqd a(d)spectum nostrum definit; 3, fig. = limits of the understanding (e.g. a thing goes, lies beyond my —, alqd in intelligentiam meam non cadit). **horizontal,** adj. aequus, libratus. Adv. ad libram.

horn, n. 1, lit. cornu; 2, fig. = the horns of the moon, cornua lunae; 3, = drinking-cup, poculum; 4, = musical instrument, cornu, buccina, tuba; to blow the —, cornu or buccinam inflare. **horned,** adj. corniger, cornutus. **hornless,** adj. non cornutus; (of an animal by nature without horns, or if it has lost them through butting) mutilus (cornibus).

horny, adj. corneus.

hornet, n. crabro.

horn-pipe, n. saltatio.

horoscope, n. horoscopus (Pers.); to cast a —, sidera natalicia notare.

horrible, horrid, adj. horrendus, horribilis, terribilis, nefarius, nefandus, foedus. Adv. terribilem in modum, nefarie, foede. **horribleness,** n. foeditas, better use adj. with n. (e.g. the — of the thing, res horrenda). **horrify,** v.tr. (ex)terrēre, perterrēre, obstupefacēre; to be horrified, obstupescēre. **horror, I.** n. = fear, horror, timor, pavor; 2, = hatred, odium; 3, = a monster, a perfect —, monstrum portentum.

horse, n. 1, equus (ecus), equa (the name of the species); common —, caballus; a Gallic —, mannus; a swift fleet —, veredus; a gelding, canterius; a nag, caballus; 2, = cavalry, equites, -um, equitatus, -ūs; to ride on —, equo vehi, equitare; to fight on —, ex equo pugnare. **horsebreaker,** n. equorum domitor; higher groom, for breaking in horses, equiso (ante and post class.). **horse-cloth,** n. stratum. **horse-dealer,** n. qui equos vendit. **horse-flesh,** n. 1 = meat, car *œquina; 2,* = horses, *equi.* **horse-fly,** n. *œstrus, tabannus.* **horse-hair,** n. *pilus equinus.* **horse-laugh,** n. *mirus risus, -ûs, cachinnus.* **horseman,** n. *eques, -itis,* m. **horsemanship,** n. *equitandi ars.* **horse - race,** n. *curriculum equorum, cursus (-ûs) equorum* or *equester; equorum certamen* (as a contest). **horse - shoe,** n. *solea ferrea* (in ancient times *solea spartea* or simply *spartea,* because they were only like slippers put on and taken off, and made of broom). **horse-soldier,** n. *eques, -itis,* m. **horse - stealer,** n. *fur.* **horse-whip,** n. see WHIP.

hortative, adj. *hortans, monens;* see EXHORTATION. **hortatory,** adj. *monens.*

horticulture, n. *hortorum cultura* or *cultus, -ûs.*

hose, n. see STOCKINGS.

hospital, n. *nosocomîum (νοσοκομεῖον,* Jct.); *valetudinarium* (Jct.).

hospitality, n. *hospitium* (= the relation of —). **hospitable,** adj. *hospitalis, liberalis.* Adv. *hospitaliter, liberaliter.*

host, n. 1, *hospes, -itis,* m., or *cenae pater* (at a feast); 2, for gain, *caupo* (= a tavern-keeper); to reckon without your —, *spe frustrari.* **hostess,** n. *hospita.*

host, n. 1, = number, *multitudo;* a — of, *sescenti* (sexc-); 2, = army, *exercitus, -ûs.*

hostage, n. *obses, -idis,* m.

hostel(ry), n. *caupona.* **hostler,** n. *stabularius* (in gen.), *agâso* (= groom).

hostile, adj. = belonging to a public enemy, by the gen. pl. *hostium, hostilis* (class. only in the meaning of acting as an enemy in times of war; hence, a — country, *hostilis terra* or *regio);* = anything in the possession of the enemy, *hosticus;* = unfriendly, *inimicus, infestus,* comb. *infensus atque inimicus, inimicus infensusque.* Adv. *hostiliter, inimice, infeste, infense.* **hostility,** n. *animus infestus, inimicitia; =* hatred, aversion, *odium;* in the pl. hostilities, *hostilia, -ium,* n.; *bellum* (= war); to commence —, *bellum facêre.*

hot, adj. 1, lit. *calidus, fervidus, fervens* (= seething), *candens* (= of a white heat), *aestuosus, ardens,* †*flagrans;* 2, fig. *calidus, fervidus, fervens, flagrans, acer, avidus;* see EAGER; to be —, *fervêre, candêre, aestuare;* to become —, *fervescêre,* †*effervescêre, incalescêre, (in)candescêre;* to make —, *calefacêre, fervefacêre.* Adv. *calide, fervide, ferventer, acriter, avide.* **hotbed,** n. 1, lit. *locus stercoratus;* 2, fig. *semen* (= seed). **hotheaded,** adj. *iracundus, ingenio praeceps, temerarius, imprudens.* **hothouse,** n. see HOTBED, GREENHOUSE.

hotel, n. *deversorium, caupona* (=a tavern), *hospitium.*

hound, I. n. *canis (venaticus), canis venator;* to keep a pack of —s, *canes alêre ad venandum.* **II.** v.tr. to — on, *alqm instigare, urgêre, lacessêre, stimulare, incitare.*

hour, n. *hora;* the space of an —, *horae spatium;* the —s of the night, *nocturna tempora, -um;* half an —, *semihora;* what — is it? *quota hora est?* his last —, *hora novissima* or *suprema;* in his last —, *eo ipso die, quo e vitâ excessit;* leisure —s, *tempus otiosum; tempus subsicivum,* to spare a few —s from one's studies, *alqd subsicivi temporis studiis suis subtrahêre;* from — to —, *in horas.* **hour-glass,** n. *horologium.* **hourly,** adj. *singulis horis.*

house, I. n. *domus, -ûs,* f. (irreg.), (= the place of abode, also those who inhabit it, the family), *aedes, aedificium, domicilium* (specially

the dwelling); *villa* (= country —); *insula* (= — let out in portions), *tectum* (= a covering or roof), *familia* (= the family), *stirps, -is,* f., *genus, -êris,* n. (= the race or clan), *res familiaris* (= house affairs); from — to —, *per domos, ostiatim* (= from door to door). **house-servants,** n. *familia* (= slaves, as with the ancients), *famuli domestici* (as now). **II.** v.tr. 1, = to take into one's —, *domo excipêre;* 2, = to store, *condêre.* **housebreaker,** n. *fur.* **household, I.** n. *domus, -ûs,* f., *familia, omnes sui (mei,* etc.). **II.** adj. *domesticus; —* gods, *lares, -um,* m., *penates, -ium.* **householder,** n. *paterfamilias.* **house-keeper,** n. *quae res domesticas dispensat.* **house-keeping,** n. *cura rei domesticae.* **house-maid,** n. *ancilla.* **house-warming,** n. to give a —, *domum amicis exceptis tanquam inaugurare.* **house-wife,** n. *hera.* **house-wifery,** n. *diligentia, cura domestica.*

hovel, n. *tugurium, gargustium.*

hover, v.intr. *circum volitare* (lit. and fig.).

how, adv. 1, as interrog. particle, *qui? quid?* = in or according to what manner? *quomodo? quemadmodum?* (to express surprise), *quid? quidvis? —* are you? — do you do? *= quomodo vales? ut vales?* — does it happen that, etc. ? = *qui tandem fit, ut,* etc. ? = what now, or what then? *quid porro?* = but what? *quid vero?* = — many? = *quot?* — few! = *quotusquisque!* (e.g. — few philosophers are there that, etc. ! *quotusquisque philosophus est, qui,* etc. !) — often? = *quotie(n)s?* — great? = *quantus?* — dear? — much? what price? = *quanti? quanto?* 2, in exclamations, *quam, quantopere;* — well you have done! = *quam bene fecisti!* — much could I wish? = *quam* or *quantopere vellem!* — dissatisfied he was, felt with himself! = *ut sibi ipse displicebat!* Very often merely the accus. of the noun (e.g. — blind I am that I could not foresee that! = *me caecum, qui haec ante non viderim!* — treacherous are the hopes of men! — short their earthly happiness! — vain all their efforts! = *o fallacem hominum spem! o fragilem fortunam et inanes nostras contentiones!)* 3, as a relative adv. = by what means, *quemadmodum* (= according to what, etc.); = by what means, *quomodo;* = in what manner, *quâ ratione;* — under what conditions, circumstances, *quo pacto;* they fix — to carry out the remainder = *reliqua, quâ ratione agi placeat,* constituunt; I don't know — this always happens, = *nescio quo pacto semper hoc fit.* **howbeit,** adv. *(at)tamen.* **however, I.** adv. *quamvis, quamlibet, quantumvis* (e.g. — great, *quamvis magnus).* **II.** conj. *sed, autem, (at)tamen, nihilominus.*

howl, I. v.intr. *ululare* (from the sound, referring to dogs, wolves, human beings); of the roaring of the sea, *fremêre;* of the loud cries of women at funerals, *ejulare;* to weep aloud, moan, *plorare, lamentari;* comb. *ejulare atque lamentari.* **II.** n. *ululatus; ejulatus, ploratus* (all, *-ûs), ejulatio;* or, of several together, *comploratio, lamentatio.*

hubbub, n. *tumultus, -ûs.*

huckster, I. n. *caupo, institor.* **II.** v. intr. *cauponam exercêre.*

huddle, n. *turba;* huddled together, *conferti.*

hue, n. *color.*

hue, n. = exclamation, *voces, -um,* pl., *clamor, vociferatio;* see CRY; to raise (= order) a — and cry by land and by water, *terrâ marique ut alqs conquiratur, praemandare.*

huff, n. impetus, -ūs (= fit); ira, iracundia; be in a —, irasci, moleste ferre.

hug, I. v.tr. amplecti, complecti; — the shore, litus † amare; — oneself, se jactare, gloriari. **II.** n. complexus, -ūs.

huge, adj. immanis, vastus (= immense in gen.); immensus (= unusually great), large = ingens (e.g. tree, arbor; sum of money, pecunia; genius, talent, ingenium); of — depth, immensâ, infinitâ altitudine. Adv. valde, magnopere. **hugeness, n.** magnitudo, moles (= bulk).

hulk, n. (= the body of a ship), alveus navis.

hull, n. the — of a nut, cortex; folliculus (= little bag, hence husk).

hum, I. v.intr. fremĕre, strepĕre, † susurrare, murmurare, murmur edĕre; stridorem edĕre; = to buzz, bombum facĕre; = sing softly, secum canĕre, cantare. **II.** n. fremitus, -ūs (in gen.); murmur, -ūris, n. (of men and bees), † susurrus, stridor, bombus, comprobatio (= applause). **III.** interj. hem!

human, adj. humanus; by the gen. pl. hominum (e.g. — vices and errors, hominum vitia et errores); = mortal, mortalis; — feelings (in gen.), humanitas. Adv. humano modo (= after the manner of men). **humane, adj.** = kind, affable, misericors, clemens. Adv. clementer. **humaneness, n.** clementia, misericordia. **humanity, n.** 1, = peculiar nature of man, natura or condicio humana; 2, = mankind, human race, humanum or hominum genus, -ĕris, n., gens humana; 3, = kind feelings, humanitas, clementia, misericordia. **humanize, v.tr.** = to make a person more civilized, alqm humanum reddĕre, excolĕre; see CIVILIZE. **humankind, n.** genus humanum.

humble, I. adj. humilis; = lowly, meek, submissus, demissus (opp. elatus); = modest, modestus, moderatus, verecundus; = suppliant, supplex, comb. humilis et supplex (e.g. oratio); = low, humilis (e.g. humili loco ortus); to show oneself —, submisse se gerĕre. Adv. demisse, submisse, simpliciter, humiliter (= meanly), modeste, moderate, comb. modeste ac moderate (= without ostentation); to be — disposed, animo esse submisso; to request —, supplicibus verbis orare; to entreat very —, multis verbis et supplicem orare. **II.** v.tr. = to break anyone's bold spirit, infringĕre, frangĕre alqm or alcjs audaciam, comprimĕre alcjs audaciam, comb. frangĕre alqm et comminuĕre; to — oneself, se or animum submittĕre, submisse se gerĕre, comprimĕre animos suos. **humbling, humiliating, adj.** use n. dedecus, -ōris, n. (e.g. he found it —, quod dedecori esse putavit). **humiliation, n.** dedecus, -ōris, n.; see DISGRACE. **humility, n.** = lowness of spirits, animus submissus, demissus = lowness of origin, humilitas; = modesty, modestia; * humilitas (as a Christian virtue).

humbug, I. n. gerrae, nugae, tricae. **II.** v.tr. alci illudĕre, alqm ludificare, alci verba dare, alqm circumvenire, circumducĕre.

humdrum, adj. iners, tardus, segnis (= sluggish).

humid, adj. humidus, humectus (ante and post class.). **humidity, n.** humor.

humour, I. n. 1 (= fluids of animal bodies), humor; 2, = temper, (animi) affectio or affectus, -ūs; ingenium, natura; arbitrary —, libido (lub-); in gen., = propensities, studia, -orum; = general temper of the mind, animi habitus, -ūs; temporary —, animi motus, -ūs; disposition in gen., animus; = inclination, voluntas; = a quiet disposition, animus tranquillus; the best — towards, summa in alqm voluntas; to be in good- —, bene affectum esse; to be in ill- —,

male affectum esse, morosum esse; ill- —, naturâ difficilis, morositas; violent —, asperitas (i.e. harshness); in the —, ex libidine, ad arbitrium suum; = as one thinks proper, arbitrio suo; comb. ad arbitrium suum (nostrum, etc.) libidinemque; I am in the —, libet (lub-) mihi alqd facĕre; 3, = that quality by which we give to one's ideas a ludicrous turn, lepos (lepor), -ōris, m. (in the whole character, also in a written work), festivitas (= mirth, wit; also in a written work); facetiousness or — in speech, cavillatio (= raillery); jocus; facetiae. **II.** v.tr. alci obtemperare; indulgĕre, alci morem gerĕre, morigerari. **humourist, n.** 1, homo jocosus, lepidus, facetus, festivus; 2, = an ill-tempered man, homo difficilis, morosus. **humoursome, adj.** difficilis, morosus, difficilis ac morosus.

hump, n. tuber, -eris, n. (Plin., e.g. of a camel); a bunch in any part of the body (espec. on the back), gibber, -eris, n. (Plin.). **humpbacked, adj.** gibber.

hunch, n. see HUMP.

hundred, adj. centum; every —, centeni, -ae, -a (also = — at once); a subdivision of the Roman people into centuries or —s, centuria; of a —, — years old, centenarius; a — times, centie(n)s; a — thousand, centum mil(l)ia; — years, centum anni; a space of one — years, centum annorum spatium; a century, a generation, saeculum. **hundred-fold, adj.** † centuplus, † centuplicatus; to bear fruit a —, cum centesimo efferre. **hundred-handed, adj.** † centimanus. **hundred-headed, adj.** † centiceps. **hundredweight, n.** centu(m)pondium (ante class.).

hunger, I. n. fames, -is; lit. and fig., — after gold, fames auri; = starvation, inedia; — is the best cook, cibi condimentum fames. **II.** v.intr. esurire; to — after, alqd sitire, alcjs rei avidum esse. **hungry, adj.** esuriens, jejunus, famelicus (ante and post class.). Adv. avide; see EAGERLY.

hunt, I. v.tr. venari; — after, alqd (con)sectari. **II.** n. venatio, venatus, -ūs. **hunter, huntsman, n.** venator. **huntress, n.** venatrix.

hurdle, n. crates, -is.

hurl, v.tr. jacĕre, jaculari, con(j)icĕre. **hurling, n.** conjectus, -ūs.

hurly-burly, n. tumultus, -ūs; see TUMULT, NOISE.

hurrah, see HUZZA.

hurricane, n. tempestas (foeda), turbo, -inis, m. (= whirlwind), procella.

hurry, I. v.tr. accelerare; impellĕre, incitare, excitare (= to rouse), rapĕre (= to carry off), urgĕre (= to press on), stimulare, stimulos alci admovere. **II.** v.intr. festinare, properare, maturare; whither are you —ing? quo te agis? — about, discurrĕre (in different directions), trepidare; — away, abripĕre, rapĕre, trahĕre (= to drag); — on, matu-rare, urgĕre, festinare. **III.** n. festinatio, tre-rare, urgĕre, festinare. **III.** n. festinatio, tre-pidatio (= alarm). **hurried, adj.** properus, citatus, citus, praeceps. Adv. festinanter, propere, cursim, raptim.

hurt, I. v.tr. 1, lit. alqm laedĕre, alci nocĕre; 2, fig. laedĕre; to be —, alqd aegre ferre. **II.** v.intr. dolēre (e.g. it —s, dolet, mostly ante class. and colloquial). **III.** n. 1, = a wound, vulnus, -ĕris, n.; 2, = injury, damnum. **IV.** adj. 1, sancius (= wounded); 2, fig. conturbatus, tristis. **hurtful, adj.** nocens, noxius, perniciosus, exitiosus, exitialis, damnosus. Adv. perniciose. **hurtfulness, n.** pernicies.

husband, I. n. maritus, vir, conju(n)x, -ūgis. m. and f.; a young married man, novus maritus. **II.** v.tr. rem familiarem curare, alci rei parcĕre.

husbandman, n. *agricola,* **m.** *arator* (= ploughman). **husbandry,** n. 1, *res rustica, res rusticae* (= the occupations of a farmer); = agriculture, *agricultura, agricultio* (or as two words); 2, = care of domestic affairs, *cura rerum domesticarum;* 3, = economy, as, good —, *frugalitas.*

hush, I. interj. *st! tace,* pl. *tacēte.* II. v.tr. *restinguĕre, ex(s)tinguĕre* (e.g. *tumultum,* to — the crowd); to — cares, *alcjs animum lenire et placare, placare et mitigare;* to — up a rumour, *rumorem opprimĕre;* see SUPPRESS.

husk, n. *folliculus, gluma.* **husky,** adj. *(sub)raucus;* see HOARSE.

hustings, n. *suggestus, -ūs (suggestum)* (= platform), *comitium* (= place of election).

hustle, v.intr. *alqm cubito offendĕre, premĕre.*

hut, n. *casa* (= a small —, cottage), *tugurium.*

hutch, n. *cavea* (= cage).

huzza, I. interj. *eja! eje! evoë! io! io!* II. n. (= a shout of joy), *clamor et gaudium.* III. v.intr. *(ac)clamare, conclamare, succlamare;* see SHOUT.

hyacinth, n. *hyacinthus (hyacinthos).*

Hyades, n. *Hyades, -um,* f. ; *suculae* (mistranslation of *ὑάδες,* as though from *ὗς* = pig, instead of *ὑειν* = to rain).

Hymen, n. *Hymen* or *Hymenaeus.* **Hymeneal,** adj. *nuptialis.*

hymn, I. n. *hymnus;* = in honour of Apollo or other gods, a song of triumph, *paean, -ānis,* m. II. v.tr. *cantu alcjs laudes prosequi.*

hyperbole, n. *hyperbole* (or *hyperbola), -es,* f., *veritatis superlatio et trajectio.* **hyperbolical,** adj. *veritatis modum excedens.*

Hyperborean, adj. †*Hyperboreus.*

hypercritical, adj. *iniquus, severus.* Adv. *nimid cum severitate.* **hypercriticism,** n. *nimia severitas.*

hypochondria, n. *atra* or *nigra bilis.* **hypochondriacal,** adj. *melancholicus.*

hypocrisy, n. *(dis)simulatio, fraus, -dis,* f., *mendacium;* without —, *ex animo.*

hypocrite, n. *(dis)simulator.* **hypocritical,** adj. *simulatus, fictus.* Adv. *simulate, ficte.*

hypothesis, n. *opinio, sententia* (= opinion), *ratio, condicio* (= condition), *conjectura* (= conjecture); on this —, *quo posito, quibus positis.* **hypothetical,** adj. *opinabilis.* Adv. to speak —, *ex conjecturâ* or *de re opinabili dicĕre;* if this be — granted, *hoc concesso* or *posito.*

hysteria, n. 1, med. t.t. **hysteria;* 2, = excitement, *furor, animi* or *mentis motus, -ūs, commotio, animus (com)motus.* **hysterical,** adj. 1, *hystericus* (Plin.); 2, †*furens, mente (com)motus.*

I.

I, pron. *ego, egomet.* It is generally only expressed in Latin when we wish to speak emphatically. The plural is frequently used in Latin for I. — myself, *ego ipse, egomet ipse, ipse;* — at least, *ego quidem, equidem.*

iambic, I. adj. *iambeus.* II. n. *iambus.*

ice, n. *glacies, gelu;* to break the —, fig. *viam aperire.* **ice-berg,** n. *glaciei moles, -is.* **icicle,** n. †*stiria.* **icy,** adj. 1, lit. *glacialis, gelidus, frigidus;* 2, fig. use *superbus.* Adv. *superbe.*

idea, n. = — of anything, *notio (notionem*

appello, quod Graeci tum ἔννοιαν, tum πρόληψιν dicunt. Ea est insita, et ante percepta cujusque formae cognitio, *enodationis indigens,* Cic.); = the apprehension of anything, *intellegentia (intellig-), intellectus, -ūs* (Quint.); the — which we form therefrom, opinion, *opinio;* = the picture we have of anything, *imago, effigies;* = the expectation we base upon the latter, *ex(s)pectatio;* = the — formed of anything, *informatio;* the — we form, an image to the mind, *species, idea,* (= thought) *cogitatio;* = the meaning of anything, *vis, vis,* f., *sententia;* an original, innate —, *notio in animis informata; notio animis impressa; insita et quasi consignata in animis notio; innata cognitio; praenotio insita* or *insita praeceptaque cognitio; quod natura insculpsit in mentibus;* = an innate — of God, *informatio Dei animo antecepta;* obscure —, *cognitio indagationis indigens;* to form a correct — of, *recte sentire de alqâ re;* to have no — of, *notionem alcjs rei nullam habēre, alqd ignorare;* to have a false, wrong — of, *prava de alqâ re sentire;* to have a clear — of, *perspectum habēre alqd;* much depends on what — you have of the office of a tribune, *plurimum refert quid esse tribunatum putes;* we have not all one and the same — about what is honourable and dishonourable, *non eadem omnibus honesta sunt ac turpia;* that — of Aristippus, *illud Aristippeum; (idea, iδέα,* in the meaning of Plato's system of mental philosophy, is generally rendered by Cic. by *iδέα,* with *species,* e.g. *hanc illi iδέαν appellant, jam a Platone ita nominatam, nos recte speciem possumus dicĕre;* and in Senec. by *idea* or *exemplar rerum);* to raise the mind to the — (in the sense of modern metaphysics), *a consuetudine oculorum mentis aciem abducĕre;* = definition of fear, *metus, -ūs* (e.g. to be subordinate to the — of fear, etc., *sub metum subjectum esse).* **ideal,** I. adj. 1, *optimus, summus* (= the best, most excellent); = most perfect, *perfectissimus* (rare), *perfectus et omnibus numeris absolutus;* = most beautiful, *pulcherrimus;* 2, = intellectual, *quod tantummodo ad cogitationem valet; quod non sensu, sed mente cernitur.* II. n. *singularis quaedam summae perfectionis species animo informata, singularis quaedam summae perfectionis imago animo et cogitatione concepta* (i.e. the idea of the highest perfection as conceived in the mind); anything in the most accomplished form, *undique expleta et perfecta forma alcjs rei, optima et perfecta alcjs rei species, optimum;* = what we picture in our minds as the — of anything, *effigies, imago, simulacrum* (also = the highest idea of anything, which is constantly in our mind), *species, forma;* — of beauty, *species pulchritudinis eximia quaedam;* = a pattern, model, *exemplar (et forma);* = a pattern (in a moral sense), *specimen* (e.g. *prudentiae specimen pontifex maximus, Qu. Scaevola).* Very often an — may also be rendered by adjs., *summus, optimus, pulcherrimus;* — of a state, *civitas optima* or *perfectissima;* — of a wise man (in mental philosophy), *sapiens, perfectus homo planeque sapiens;* — of an orator, *imago perfecti oratoris, simulacrum oratoris, orator summus, norma et regula oratoris* (e.g. *Demosthenes ille, norma oratoris et regula);* a bean — of a state, *imago civitatis, quam cogitatione tantum et mente complecti, nullo autem modo in vitam hominum introducĕre possumus* (= an — state); a state of the highest perfection, *civitas perfectissima;* = pattern, model of a state, *exemplar reipublicae et forma;* — of a state in Plato, *illa commenticia Platonis civitas; civitas, quam finxit Plato, cum optimum reipublicae statum exquireret.* **idealism,** n. *ars* or *vis animo sibi fingendi alqd.* **idealist,** n. *qui alqd sibi animo fingit.* **idealize,** v.tr. *speciem alcjs rei animo sibi fingĕre, concipĕre, informare, a consuetudine oculorum mentis aciem abducĕre;* see IDEAL.

identical, adj. *ejusdem generis* (= of the same kind); *idem, unus et idem, idem et par, nihil aliud nisi;* at the very same time, *eodem* or *uno eodemque tempore;* to be —, *nihil differre;* exertion and grief are not —, *interest alqd inter laborem et dolorem.* **identify,** v.tr. *ad eandem notionem* (or *vim* or *rationem*) *referre,* = to recognize, *agnoscēre.* **identity,** n. *eadem vis* or *ratio; nullum omnino discrimen.*

ides, n. *idus, -uum,* f.pl.

idiom, n. 1, = mode of expression peculiar to a language, *proprietas; quae Latinae linguae propria sunt; loquendi ratio;* 2, = genius or peculiar cast of a language, *idiōma, -ătis,* n. (Gram.). **idiomatic,** adj. *proprius.* Adv. *proprie.*

idiot, n. lit. and fig. (*homo*) *stultus;* see FOOL. **idiocy,** n. *fatuitas, stultitia.*

idle, I. adj. 1,= inactive, unemployed, *otiosus, vacuus, ignavus, piger, iners, segnis, deses, -ĭdis;* 2,= useless, *inutilis, vanus, irritus;* see USELESS, VAIN; 3, = trifling, unprofitable, *lēvis, vilis;* see INSIGNIFICANT. Adv. *ignave, segniter, frustra, incassum* (or as two words). **II.** v.intr. *cessare, nihil agēre.* **idleness,** n. 1, *cessatio, otium;* 2, = laziness, *segnitia, pigritia, desidia.* **idler,** n. *homo deses;* = one who loiters, *cessator;* I am the greatest — in the world, *nihil me est inertius.*

idol, n. 1, * *idolum* (= an image or likeness, = "idol" in the Christian Fathers); 2, fig. *amores, deliciae,* comb. *amores et deliciae* (of a beloved person). **idolator,** n. *deorum fictorum cultor.* **idolatrous,** adj. * *idolatricus, fictos deos colens.* **idolatry,** n. *deorum fictorum* (or *simulacrorum*) *cultus, -ūs;* to practise —, *colĕre deos fictos, alqd pro deo venerari.*

idyl, n. *carmen bucolicum, bucolica, -orum* (of a poem). **idyllic,** adj. by circumloc. (e.g. an — future of leisured life, *pulcherrima quaedam vitae umbratilis descriptio*).

if, conj. *si* (with the indic. mood if we merely speak about the reality of a thing; with the subj. if we represent anything as possible, probable, or doubtful); — every event is determined by fate, we cannot be too cautious, *si fato omnia fiunt, nihil nos admonēre potest ut cautiores simus;* a whole day would not be sufficient, — I were to enumerate, *dies deficiat, si velim numerare;* in comparisons (e.g. — anything of that kind delights me, it is painting, *si quid generis istiusmodi me delectat, pictura delectat*); *quod si* is often used instead of *si,* owing to a tendency in Latin to connect sentences by relatives. Very often we render — by a participle (e.g. I should never have thought of it, — you had not reminded me, *non mihi, nisi admonito, in mentem venisset*); but —, *sin, sin autem, si vero;* but — not, but unless, *si non, si minus, sin minus, sin aliter;* — not, unless, *nisi, ni, si non* (a negative condition, where *non* must be taken together with the verb); — not perhaps, *nisi forte;* namely —, *si quidem;* that is — (in correcting or modifying an expression previously used), *si modo,* and simply *si* (e.g. God only gives us reason, that is, — we have any, *a Deo tantum rationem habemus, si modo habemus;* — only, *dum modo, dummodo* (with the subjunctive); — perhaps, *si forte* (not *si fortasse;* see PERHAPS); — anyone, *si(ali)quis;* — anything, *si (ali)quid;* — at any time, — some day, *si (ali)quando* (*si aliquis, si aliquid, si aliquando* are only used if we lay a particular stress on the word "some"); even—(=although), *quamquam, quamvis licet, etsi, etiamsi* (see ALTHOUGH); whether ... or —, *sive (seu) ... sive (seu);* as —, *quasi, tamquam (tanq-), ac si, velut si,* (with conj.), (e.g. the Sequani feared the cruelty

of Ariovistus the same in his absence as — he were present, *Sequani Ariovisti absentis crudelitatem, velut si coram adesset, horrebant*); —, after many words, especially after to seem, to pretend, to feign, to suspect, to doubt, etc., by the accus. with inf. (e.g. with some I create a suspicion, as — I intended to sail, *moveo nonnullis suspicionem velle me navigare;* he did as — he were mad, *simulavit se furĕre*); as —, after *videor* (= it looks, appears to me), rendered with the nominative with inf. (e.g. it looks as — you were angry, *iratum esse videris*); not as —, *non quo* (not as — I had anything to write to you, *non quo haberem, quod tibi scriberem*).

ignite, I. v.tr. = to kindle or set on fire, *accendĕre, incendĕre, inflammare* (rare); see FIRE, HEAT. **II.** v.intr. *exardescĕre, accendi, incendi,* etc. (lit. and fig.); *ignem* or *flammam concipĕre;* see KINDLE, EXCITE. **igneous,** adj. *igneus.* **ignition,** n. *incensio,* but better use verb.

ignoble, adj. *ignobilis* (= of low birth); = of unknown origin, *obscuro loco natus, obscuris ortus majoribus;* = of low rank and character, *humilis* (of persons and things, e.g. speech, *oratio;* style, *verbum*); = of low descent, *humili loco natus;* = illiberal, *illiberalis;* = low, despicable, *abjectus, turpis;* — disposition, meanness of action, *humilitas, illiberalitas.* Adv. *humiliter, illiberaliter, turpiter.*

ignominy, n. *ignominia, infamia, dedecus, -ōris, probrum, contumelia, turpitudo;* to throw — upon, *algm ignominia afficĕre, ignominiam alci imponĕre* or *injungĕre* or *inurĕre.* **ignominious,** adj. *ignominiosus, contumeliosus, turpis, probrosus.* Adv. *contumeliose, turpiter.*

ignoramus, n. *homo inscius alcjs rei.* **ignorance,** n. *imprudentia, inscientia;* = want of abilities, *inscitia;* — of facts, *ignoratio;* = want of education, *ignorantia* (all with gen.); to confess one's — in many things, *confiteri multa se ignorare.* **ignorant,** adj. *insciens* (opp. *sciens*), *inscitus;* = unawares, *imprudens* (opp. *sciens*); *inscius alcjs rei* (= illiterate), = unskilful in, *ignarus alcjs rei;* = inexperienced in, *imperitus alcjs rei,* comb. *inscius imperitusque;* quite — of, *rudis alcjs rei* or *in alqd re,* or comb. *alcjs rei inscius et rudis;* = not learned, *indoctus;* = illiterate, *illit(t)eratus, indoctus;* a pupil who is only a beginner, *rudis et integer discipulus;* to be — of, *alqd nescire, alqd ignorare;* = not to be skilled in, *alqd non callēre.* Adv. by adj. or *imprudenter, inscienter, inscite, imperite, indocte.* **ignore,** v.tr. *praeterire.*

Iliad, n. *Ilias.*

ill, I. adj. 1, *aeger, aegrotus, morbidus* (= seized by disease), *valetudine affectus, invalidus, infirmus, imbecillus;* very —, *gravi et periculoso morbo aeger;* to be —, *aegrotare, morbo affici* or *laborare;* to fall —, *morbo corripi;* *in morbum incidĕre;* 2, in gen. *malus;* of an — reputation, *male audire, pravus, nequam* (= wicked). **II.** Adv. *male, prave, misere, miseriter;* it goes — with me, *male mecum agitur;* to brook a thing —, *alqd aegre* or *moleste ferre.* **III.** n. *malum, pestis, pestilentia* (= plague), *incommodum; casus, -ūs* (= misfortune). **ill-advised,** adj. *inconsultus, temerarius;* see RASH. **ill-affected,** adj. 1, = unfriendly, *inimicus, infestus;* 2, = disloyal, *infidelis;* — citizens, *cives turbulenti et mali.* **ill-bred,** adj. *humanitatis expers, inurbanus.* **ill-breeding,** n. *mores inurbani; inhumanitas.* **ill-fated,** adj. *infelix, miser;* see UNHAPPY. **ill-favoured,** adj. see UGLY. **ill-gotten,** adj. *male partus.* **ill-health,** n. *valetudo infirma.* **ill-made,** adj. *informis, deformis* (by nature, opp. to *formosus*), *male factus* (by art). **ill-matched,** adj. *impar;* see UN-

EQUAL. ill-mannered, adj. see ILL-BRED. **ill-nature.** n. *malignitas.* **ill-natured,** adj. *morosus, difficilis, malignus.* **illness,** n. *morbus, aegrotatio, valetudo infirma, adversa, incommoda* or *tenuis.* **ill-omened,** adj. *dirus, infaustus, inauspicatus.* **ill-temper,** n. *stomachus, morositas, malignitas, iracundia.*

illegal, adj. *legi repugnans, contrarius, quod contra leges fit;* = contrary to the law of God and man, *contra jus fasque, contra fas et jus.* Adv. *contra legem* or *leges; praeter leges* or *jus;* **illegality,** n. by the adj.

illegible, adj. *qui, quae, quod legi non potest;* to be —, *legi non posse.*

illegitimate, adj. 1, *incerto patre natus, spurius* (Jct.); *pellice ortus, nothus* (νόθος = a bastard) (Quint.), *(h)ibrida (hyb-)*, (= a person whose parents were of different countries, or one of whose parents was a slave); 2, in gen. = unlawful, *non legitimus* (not *illegitimus*), *quod contra leges fit; haud ex legibus;* 3, = not genuine, *adulterated, adulterinus.* Adv. *non legitime, haud ex legibus, contra leges.*

illiberal, adj. *illiberalis* (= unworthy of a free man, e.g. a joke, *jocus*), = mean, ungenerous, *sordidus, parcus, avarus, malignus.* **illiberality,** n. *illiberalitas, avaritia, parsimonia (parc-), malignitas.*

illicit, adj. *inconcessus, vetitus* (=prohibited), *nefas,* n. indecl. (= contrary to human and divine law, impious); — means, *artes malae.*

illimitable, adj. *infinitus.*

illiterate, adj. *illiteratus, indoctus, ineruditus;* to be —, *nescire lit(t)eras.* Adv. *indocte.*

illogical, adj. *quod haud necessario consequitur, inconstans, quod vitiose conclusum est.* Adv. *inconstanter, vitiose.*

illume, illumine, illuminate, v.tr. 1, = to throw light on, *collustrare, illustrare* (lit. and fig.); *illuminare* (lit. = illuminate, fig. = to throw light upon a matter; none of these verbs used in reference to the mind); the light of the sun —s all things, *sol cuncta luce suâ illustrat;* to be —d by the sun, *sole illustrem esse;* to — a town, *in urbe pernoctantia lumina accendêre* (Ammian, said of the lighting of the streets); 2, = to enlighten the mind, *colêre, docêre, erudire;* 3, = to adorn with pictures (as to — manuscripts or books, according to ancient practice), *varie pingêre, alci rei vivos colores inducêre.* **illumination,** n. 1, of MSS., use verb ILLUMINATE, 3; 2, = the picture itself, *pictura, tabula;* 3, mental —, *eruditio, doctrina.*

illusion, n. *(opinionis) error, somnium, opinio falsa* or *vana.* **illusive, illusory,** adj. *vanus, falsus, commenticius.*

illustrate, v.tr. 1, *illustrare;* see ILLUMINATE; 2, = — a book, *librum tabulis* or *picturis ornare;* 3, = to explain, *illustrare;* see EXPLAIN. **illustration,** n. 1, *explicatio;* see EXPLANATION; 2, of a book, *pictura, tabula;* 3, = example, *exemplum.* **illustrious,** adj. *(prae)clarus, amplus* (usu. in superl.), *splendidus, illustris, insignis, egregius, eximius, spectatus, nobilis, praestans.* **illustrative,** adj. *quod alqd illustrat, explicat,* etc.

image, n. 1, *imago, simulacrum. effigies;* = painting, *tabula picta, pictura;* = statue, *statua;* to form an — or likeness, *imaginem alcjs exprimêre;* 2, = a conception, *imago, species;* to form an — of, *animo alqd effingêre;* 3, in rhetoric, *translatio, figura.* **image-worshipper,** n. *qui imagines pro Deo veneratur.* **imagery,** n. 1, = sensible representations, pictures, statues,

imago; 2, = forms of the fancy, *imago;* see FANCY. **imaginable,** adj. *quod cogitari potest, quod cogitatione comprehendi* or *percipi potest, quod in cogitationem cadit, cogitabilis* (Sen.); with all — pains, *maximo, quod fieri potest, studio.* **imaginary,** adj. *cpinatus* (e.g. a good, *bonum;* an evil, *malum), opinabilis, commenticius, imaginarius, fictus, falsus, inanis;* — misfortunes, *malorum opinio;* — difficulties, *difficultates, quas sibi alqs ipse fingit;* see FANCY. **imagination,** n. *cogitatio* (= a thought, the faculty of thinking); an idle —, *metus, -ûs, inanis, species inanis;* = an idea without foundation, *opinio (falsa);* to exist in —, not in reality (e.g. of an evil), *opinionis esse, non naturae;* what lies only in one's —, *opinatus;* only based upon —, *opinabilis;* = false, fictitious, *falsus, fictus;* = the faculty of understanding, *mens,* comb. *cogitatio et mens.* **imaginative,** adj. *ingeniosus* (of one who has always new ideas); *sol(l)ers* (of one who understands the art of following out an idea); one who is —, *ingenium ad excogitandum acutum.* Adv. *ingeniose, sol(l)erter, acute.* **imagine,** v.tr. and intr. *animo concipêre, cogitare, complecti,* or simply *cogitare, fingêre, conjecturâ consequi;* = invent, *comminisci, excogitare, fingêre, machinari;* I — (parenthetically), *ut opinor.*

imbecile, adj. *fatuus, stultus;* see FOOLISH. **imbecility,** n. *imbecillitas animi* or *ingenii, fatuitas* (rare), *stultitia.*

imbibe, v.tr. *bibere, combibêre, imbibêre;* fig. *se alqâ re imbuêre, alqâ re infici;* — errors with your mother's milk, *errores cum lacte nutricis sugêre.*

imbrue, v.tr. *imbuêre, madefacêre;* — with blood, *cruentare.*

imbue, v.tr. 1, = to dye, *ting(u)êre, inficêre;* 2, fig. *alqm alqâ re inficêre, imbuêre, alqd docêre.*

imitable, adj. *imitabilis, quod imitari possumus.* **imitate,** v.tr. *imitari* (e.g. the human voice, *voces hominum);* to — in dress, manners, to — a statue, painting, sound, action, *(imitando* or *imitatione) exprimêre, imitando effingêre;* = to emulate, endeavour to equal or excel, *aemulari alqm* or *alqd* and *alci* or *cum alqo (aemulans* = imitating a rival; *imitans* = imitating one who is a pattern to us, who is our superior in that wherein we try to imitate him; *aemulari alqm* in a good sense; *aemulari alci* until Quint. only in a bad sense, i.e. to contend with a spirit of rivalry); to — (i.e. to tread in anyone's footsteps), *(per)sequi.* **imitation,** n. 1, the act of imitating, *imitatio* (in gen.); the desire of —, *imitatio, imitandi studium;* = emulation, *aemulatio;* also circumlocution with *imitari* (e.g. to devote oneself to the — of a person, *ad imitationem alcjs se conferre* or *ad imitandum alqm se conferre);* 2, = the thing itself that is imitated, *res imitatione* or *imitando expressa, res imitando effecta; effigies, imago, simulacrum;* to be an — of anything, *imitatione ex alqâ re expressum esse;* see IMAGE. **imitative,** adj. *qui alqd facile imitatur.* **imitator,** n. *imitator;* a zealous —, *aemulus, aemulator.*

immaculate, adj. *purus, sanctus, incorruptus, innocens, integer;* = chaste, pure, innocent, *castus,* comb. *castus et integer, integer castusque, castus purusque.* Adv. *pure, sancte, incorrupte, caste.*

immanent, adj. *in alqâ re inhaerens, interior.*

immaterial, adj. 1, = incorporeal (e.g. spirits), *corpore vacans, quod cerni tangique non potest;* 2, = unimportant, by *nullius momenti, nullo momento, lêvis;* to consider as —, *non flocci facêre.* **immateriality,** n. by circumloc.,

Plato asserts the — of the Deity, *Plato sine corpore ullo Deum esse vult.*

immature, adj. lit. and fig. *immaturus, crudus* (lit., poet., and late fig.).

immeasurable, adj. *immensus;* = endless, *infinitus* (e.g. multitude); = immense, extremely large, *vastus, ingens* (e.g. fortune); a mountain of — height, *mons in immensum editus.* Adv. *in* or *ad immensum.*

immediate, adj. 1, = without the intervention of anyone else, *ipse, proximus;* an — cause, *caus(s)a efficiens* or *proxima;* 2, = without delay, *praesens.* Adv. use adj. (e.g. to apply — to anyone, *alqm ipsum adire); statim* (followed by *ab alqâ re* or *ut* or *simulac), protinus, confestim, extemplo, e(x) vestigio;* not — from the field of battle, *non ex ipsâ acie;* — after anyone (in order, rank, or time), *secundum alqm;* — after, *sub alqd* (e.g. — after these words he threw himself at his feet, *sub haec dicta ad genua ejus procubuit);* — after (i.e. as a sequel to, and in consequence of), *ex alqâ re* (e.g. — after the dictatorship made into a consul, *consul ex dictaturâ factus).*

immemorial, adj. = beyond memory, e.g. from time —, *ex omni memoriâ aetatum,* or *temporum* (i.e. throughout all ages); = as long as we can think, *post hominum memoriam ;* = from the remotest times, *inde ab antiquissimis temporibus,* also by *priscus, antiquissimus, perantiquus* (= from ancient times, opp. *novus,* of persons and things); *avitus* (= from the times of our grandfathers); it is an — custom, *ex antiquis temporibus inveteravit.*

immense, adj. *ingens, vastus, immensus, infinitus.* Adv. *ad* or *in immensum;* = very much, *maxime, valde.* **immensity,** n. *immensitas, vastitas.*

immerge, v.tr. 1, *(im)mergĕre, demergĕre; submergĕre* (*in*) *alqâ re* or *in alqâ ;* 2, fig. *alqm in alqd demergĕre ;* = to fall into deep meditation about, *se totum in alcjs rei cognitione collocare.* **immersion,** n. by the verb.

immethodical, adj. = not properly arranged, *incompositus ;* = disordered, irregular, not put in order, *inordinatus* (e.g. soldiers, *milites) ;* = without method, † *indigestus ;* = careless, *neglegens (neglig-).* Adv. *sine ordine, incomposite, neglegenter.*

immigrate, v.intr. *(im)migrare.* **immigrant,** n. *advena,* m. and f. **immigration,** n. *adventus, -ûs* (e.g. of foreign tribes, *aliarum gentium).*

imminent, adj. *praesens, maximus, summus* with n. (e.g. to be in — danger, *in summo periculo esse);* by *subesse* (= to be at hand, near), *instare* (= to draw nigh, threaten, e.g. winter, war), *imminēre, impendēre* (to be —, e.g. evils, calamities).

immitigable, adj. *qui se mitigari non patitur.*

immobility, n. *immobilitas,* or by adj. ; see IMMOVABLE.

immoderate, adj. *immodicus* (= exceeding bounds, also in a moral sense) ; = intemperate, *immoderatus* (e.g. in drink ; also in a moral sense) ; *intemperans ;* = incontinent, unchaste, *incontinens ;* = impotent, ungovernable, *impotens* (e.g. joy, *laetitia), in anything, alcjs rei ;* = immodest (of persons and things), unrestrained, fierce, *effrenatus ;* — boldness, *audacia ;* = profuse, *effusus, profusus ;* = immense, *immanis* (e.g. size, *magnitudo);* sums of money, *pecuniae);* = extravagant, *luxuriosus.* Adv. *immoderate, intemperanter, immodeste, effuse,*

profuse, immodice, luxuriose; to drink —, *vino* **⁊** *obruĕre.* **immoderation,** n. *intemperantia, incontinentia ;* — in speaking, *immoderatio verborum.*

immodest, adj. = arrogant, *arrogans ;* = insolent, haughty, *insolens ;* = indiscreet, *impudicus, inverecundus.* Adv. *immodeste, arroganter, insolenter, impudice.* **immodesty,** n. = arrogance, *arrogantia ;* = haughtiness, *insolentia ;* = indiscretion, *impudicitia.*

immolate, v.tr. *immolare.* **immolation,** n. *immolatio.*

immoral, adj. *pravus, depravatus, perditus, inhonestus* (= base, nasty) ; = infamous, *turpis,* comb. *turpis atque inhonestus ; flagitiosus, nequam, corruptus;* see WICKED ; a person of bad principle, *male moratus, malis* of *corruptis moribus ;* — conduct, *mores turpes, mores corrupti.* Adv. *inhoneste, turpiter, flagitiose, perdite, prave.* **immorality,** n. *mores corrupti* or *perditi* (= immoral habits) ; *turpitudo, morum pravitas* or *depravatio,* or by *vitia, scelera, -um* (= crimes), *libidines* (= lusts) ; a life addicted to —, *vita vitiis flagitiisque omnibus dedita.*

immortal, adj. *immortalis* (opp. *mortalis ;* of persons and things, also in gen. = imperishable, e.g. glory) ; = eternal, *aeternus* (of things, e.g. life) ; = everlasting, unceasing, *sempiternus* (e.g. soul, life, glory) ; to be —, *immortalem* or *sempiternum esse, non interire* (in gen., e.g. of the soul) ; to have — life, *vitâ sempiternâ frui ;* to have — glory, *memoriâ omnium saeculorum vigēre.* **immortality,** n. *immortalitas* (opp. *mortalitas) ;* = eternity, hence eternal glory, *aeternitas ;* — of the soul or souls, *immortalitas* or *aeternitas animi* or *animorum ;* = immortal glory, *immortalis* or *sempiterna gloria ;* to assert the — of the soul, *dicĕre animos hominum esse immortales* or *sempiternos.* **immortalize,** v.tr. *alqd immortali gloriae tradĕre ;* see IMMORTAL.

immovable, adj. *immobilis, immotus, stabilis* (all lit. and fig.) ; — property, *res* or *bona quae moveri non possunt ;* to be — (lit.), *loco suo non moveri ;* see FIRM. Adv. use adj. **immovableness,** n. *immobilitas.*

immunity, n. 1, *vacatio, immunitas* (e.g. *tributorum) ;* 2, see FREEDOM.

immure, v.tr. *muro saepire, cingĕre* (= to enclose with a wall) ; see SHUT.

immutability, n. *immutabilitas* (Cic.); = firmness, consistency, *constantia ;* = steadfastness, *stabilitas* (e.g. *amicitiae) ;* = continuance, *perpetuitas ;* — of anyone's disposition, *constans in alqm voluntas.* **immutable,** adj. *immutabilis ;* = constant, *constans ;* = fixed, unchangeable, *ratus* (e.g. the course of the moon, *cursus lunae ;* the order of the stars, *astrorum ordines) ;* = undisturbed, *perpetuus* (e.g. right, *jus).* Adv. *constanter, perpetuo.* **immutation,** n. *mutatio ;* see CHANGE.

imp, n. 1, = child, *progenies ;* an — of mischief, *puer lascivus ;* 2, = demon, * *daemon.*

impair, v.tr. *alqd (im)minuĕre, imminuĕre, comminuĕre, debilitare, frangĕre, infringĕre ;* — an argument, *elevare ; deteriore statu* or *condicione esse, pejore loco esse.*

impale, v.tr. *(hastâ* or *palo) transfigĕre.*

impalpable, adj. *quod tangi non potest.*

impart, v.tr. 1, = to bestow on another a share or portion of something, *impertire alci alqd* or *alqm alqâ re* (lit. and fig.) ; *communicare alqd cum alqo* (= to share with anyone, lit., and to make a communication to) ; *participem facĕre alqm* (= to allow anyone to participate in) ; = to pour into, diffuse. *infundĕre alqd in* (with accus., e.g.

evils in a state, *mala in civitatem);* **2,** = to grant, confer (e.g. honour), *dare, tribuĕre, donare alci alqd* or *alqm algâ* r. ` = to present with); *afferre* (= to procure).

impartial, adj. *medius* (= in the middle, of persons), *tanquam medius nec in alterius favorem inclinatus* (= neutral, of persons only); = disinterested, *integer;* = not bribed, *incorruptus* (of persons and things, e.g. judge, witness, sentence); ✕ equitable, *aequus* (of persons and things, e.g. prætor, law); *aequitabilis* (of things); = free from partisanship, *studio et irâ vacuus* (of persons in gen.); = free from spite and ill-will, *obtrectatione et malevolentiâ liberatus;* to be —, *neutri parti favēre; neque irâ, neque gratiâ teneri.* Adv. *aequo animo, integre* or *incorrupte, sine irâ et studio.* **impartiality,** n. *animus ab omni partium studio alienus, animus studio et irâ vacuus;* = equity, *aequitas, aequabilitas.*

impassable, adj. *invius, insuperabilis, impeditus.* **impassibility, impassibleness,** n. *torpor* (= torpor, stupor); = hardness of heart, *durus animus;* = slowness, apathy, *lentitudo, lentus animus.* **impassible,** adj. *quod nullo dolore affici potest.*

impassioned, adj. *concitatus, fervidus, ardens, vehemens.*

impatience, n. *impatientia morae, festinatio;* to expect anything with the greatest —, *acerrime alqd ex(s)pectare.* **impatient,** adj. **1,** *impatiens morae* or *mararum, ardens, vehemens, acer;* to be — at a thing, *alqd aegre* or *moleste ferre;* **2,** = angry, *iracundus, iratus.* Adv. *ardenter, acriter, vehementer, iracunde;* see EAGER.

impeach, v.tr. *accusare.* **impeachable,** adj. *quem in jus vocare possumus.* **impeacher,** n. *accusator,* n. **impeachment,** n. *accusatio;* see ACCUSE.

impede, v.tr. *impedire;* see HINDER. **impediment,** n. **1,** *impedimentum;* see HINDRANCE; **2,** = stammer, *haesitantia linguae;* to have an —, *linguâ haesitare, balbutire.* **impedimental,** adj. *quod impedimento est, quod impedit, quod obstat et impedit;* to be — to anyone or anything, *obesse alci and alci rei;* it was very — for, a great hindrance to the Gauls in battle, that, etc., *Gallis magno ad pugnam erat impedimento, quod,* etc.; I will not be — to prevent his going, *nulla in me* or *per me est mora, in me non erit mora, non moror, quominus abeat.*

impel, v.tr. **1,** lit. *impellĕre, urgēre;* **2,** fig. *impellĕre, incitare, concitare, stimulare, (ad)hortari alqm ad alqd.*

impend, v.intr. **1,** lit. *impendēre, imminēre;* **2,** = to be near, *instare in alqm* or *alci impendēre.*

impenetrable, adj. **1,** *impenetrabilis* (Plin.); — against a thing, *alci rei;* = impervious, *impervius* (Tac., e.g. fire-proof, *ignibus impervius*) *impeditus;* see IMPASSABLE; **2,** = thick, *caligino sus* (of darkness); **3,** fig. *ambiguus* (= doubtful).

impenitence, impenitency, n. *obstinatio, animus obstinatus* or *offirmatus.* **impenitent,** adj. *obst:natus, offirmatus;* to become —, *obdurescĕre.* Adv. *obstinate.*

imperative, adj. **1,** = expressive of command, (e.g. — commands), by circumloc. with *imperare alci alqd* or with *ut,* or by *necessarius;* **2,** (in gram. = the — mood of a verb), *imperativus modus* (gram.).

imperfect, adj. *imperfectus* (= not completed); = only in its beginning, *inchoatus;* = only superficial, drawn out in general sketches, *adumbratus* (e.g. an idea, *intellegentia, opinio);* ✕ faulty, *vitiosus. mendosus;* = rough, *rudis;* =

defective, maimed, *mancus;* — tense, *tempus imperfectum* (gram.). Adv. *imperfecte, vitiose, mendose.* **imperfection, imperfectness,** n. *vitium, mendum, culpa,* or by adj. (e.g. the — of our nature, *natura hominum imperfecta et mendosa).*

imperial, adj. *imperatorius, Caesareus* (Imperial Rome); often by the genit. *imperatoris* or *Caesaris* or *Augusti; principalis,* or with the gen. *imperatoris* or *principis;* your — Majesty, * majestas* or *magnitudo tua.* **imperious,** adj. *imperiosus;* = haughty, *superbus;* = disdainful, *insolens;* = arrogant, *arrogans.* Adv. *imperiose, superbe, insolenter, arroganter.*

imperil, v.tr. *in discrimen adducĕre.*

imperishable, adj. *immortalis;* see ETERNAL, IMMORTAL.

impermeable, adj. see IMPENETRABLE.

impersonal, adj. gram. t.t. *impersonalis.* **impersonate,** v.tr. *partes alcjs agĕre.*

impertinence, n. *insolentia;* see ARROGANCE, RUDENESS. **impertinent,** adj. **1,** *insolens;* **2,** = not to the point, *quod nihil ad rem est.* Adv. *insolenter.*

imperturbable, adj. *stabilis, constans, firmus, gravis, immobilis.* Adv. *constanter, firme, graviter, tranquille.*

impervious, adj. *impervius;* see IMPENETRABLE.

impetuous, adj. *violentus,* = violent (e.g. attack, *impetus);* = strong, intense, *vehemens* (e.g. wind, *ventus,* then of individuals), comb. *vehemens et violentus* (e.g. homo); = eager, *acer, fervidus, fervens, intentus.* Adv. *magno impetu* (e.g. to attack the enemy, *hostem aggredi); violenter* (e.g. to demand, *poscĕre); vehementer* (= strongly, e.g. to insist upon it, *flagitare); acriter, ferventer.* **impetuosity,** n. *violentia* (lit. and fig.), *vis* (= strength), *incitatio* (= impulse); = intemperateness, *intemperies* (e.g. *caeli;* then = want of moderation); violence, *impetus, -ûs,* of persons and things (e.g. of the fever, *febris).* **impetus,** n. *impetus, -ûs, vis.*

impiety, n. *impietas erga Deum;* = wicked, criminal deed, *nefas, scelus, -ĕris, res scelesta* or *nefaria;* he has committed many —s against God and man, *multa et in deos et in homines impie nefarieque commisit.* **impious,** adj. *impius* (erga deum, erga patriam, erga parentes, etc.); = wicked (the general disposition), *nefarius;* = wicked, heinous, *nefandus* (of a deed). Adv. *impie, nefarie,* comb. *impie nefarieque, nefande.*

impinge, v.intr. to — against, *incidĕre in alqd, impingi alci rei* (so as to cause a violent shock), *offendĕre in algâ re* or *ad alqd.*

implacability, n. *odium implacabile* or *inexorabile.* **implacable,** adj. *implacabilis;* — against anyone, *alci* or *in alqm;* = inexorable, *inexorabilis* (all of persons and things, e.g. hatred, anger), against anyone, *in* or *adversus alqm;* = cruel, *atrox, saevus;* see CRUEL. Adv. *atrociter, saeve.*

implant, v.tr. **1,** lit. = to set, *alqd in alqâ re inserĕre, ponĕre;* **2,** fig. *ingenerare, ingignĕre* (at the time of one's birth, as it were); = to engraft, *inserĕre, animo infigĕre.*

implead, v.tr. *alqm in jus vocare;* see SUE, ACCUSER.

implement, n. **1,** = tools. *instrumentum, ferramentum;* **2,** fig. *minister;* see INSTRUMENT, TOOL.

implicate, v.tr. *implicare* or *impedire* (lit. and fig.); — in a thing, *alqd alqâ re illaqueare, admiscēre* or *immiscēre* (only the former in Cic.)

(fig.); intr. *in alqd re;* to implicate in a war, *alqm bello implicare;* to be—d in a war, *bello implicitum* or *illigatum* or *occupatum esse;* with anyone, *bellum gerère cum alqo;* to — oneself, *implicari alqd re* (lit. and fig.); to — oneself in (i.e. to meddle), *se immiscère alci rei* (fig.). **implicated,** adj. by past. part. *implicatus,* etc., *alcjs rei conscius, alci rei affinis.* **implication,** n. *implicatio;* to say a thing by —, see HINT. **implicit,** adj. 1, ⚹ implied, *tacitus;* an — compact, *assensio, consensus, -ūs, conventio;* he has an — faith, *est homo credulus, est nimis facilis ad credendum;* 2, = complete, *totus, omnis;* to have — faith in anyone, *alci maximam fidem adhibēre, totum se alci committēre.* Adv. *tacite, prorsus;* see ALTOGETHER.

implore, v.tr. *alqm* or *alqd implorare* (urgently), *alqd ab alqo petēre* (= to endeavour to obtain by entreaties); *alqm alqd rogare* (= to request); *deprecari* (= to pray for, entreat earnestly), comb. *petēre ac deprecari, ne,* etc.; *(precibus) impetrare,* or *alqd ab alqo exposcēre* (= to obtain by entreaties); = to induce by entreaties, *exorare;* = to beseech anyone on one's knees to help, to supplicate, beg humbly, *supplicare* or *supplicem esse alci, se alci supplicem ab(j)icēre;* = to beseech by everything sacred, to pray earnestly, *alqm obsecrare;* = to conjure, *alqm obtestari;* to — anyone for, to pray urgently, *alqd voce supplici postulare; orare multis et supplicibus verbis, ut,* etc.; *alqd ab alqo exposcēre;* to — anyone to help, *alqm ad* or *in auxilium implorare, auxilium implorare ab alqo;* to — God and man, *deûm atque hominum fidem implorare.*

imply, v.tr. *in se habēre;* to be implied in, *alci rei inesse,* or *subesse.*

impolite, adj. *inurbanus, rusticus, agrestis, inhumanus, illepidus.* Adv. *inurbane, rustice, illepide, inhumane, inhumaniter.* **impoliteness,** n. *rusticitas, inhumanitas.*

impolitic, adj. 1, in the state, *alienus* or *abhorrens a prudentia civili;* 2, fig. *imprudens.*

import, I. v.tr. 1, (that is, to bring goods into a country for sale) *invehēre, importare;* 2, = signify, *declarare, significare, valēre.* **II.** n. 1, *quod importatur;* 2, *significatio, sententia, vis.* **import-duty,** n. *portorium.* **importance,** n. 1, *auctoritas, discrimen, momentum, pondus, -ēris, vis;* to be of no —, *nullo esse numero;* 2, = of high position, *amplitudo, dignitas, auctoritas.* **important,** adj. *gravis;* to be —, *magni* (so *alcjs, maximi, minimi, pluris,* etc.) *momenti esse; valēre, vim habēre, alqo esse numero;* to deem anything more —, *antiquius alqd habēre.* **importation,** n. *invectio.* **importunate,** adj. *molestus, improbus;* see TROUBLESOME. **importune,** v.tr. *molestum esse alci, exposcēre, (ef)flagitare;* see TROUBLESOME, MOLEST. **importunity,** n. = pressing solicitation, *(ef)flagitatio.*

impose, v.tr. *alqd alci imponēre, injungēre;* — a punishment, *multam alci irrogare;* — upon; see CHEAT. **imposing,** adj. *conspicuus* (= drawing the attention); = showy, *speciosus;* = majestic, *magnificus* (e.g. form, *forma*); = deceitful, *fallax.* **imposition,** n. *irrogatio* (e.g. *multae,* = the infliction of a penalty); also by circumloc. with *imponēre* (e.g. to extract the poison by — of hands, *manu impositâ venena extrahēre*); *fraus* (= deceit, deception), *fallacia.* **impost,** n. *onera, -um, vectigal, tributum.* **impostor** n. *fraudator.* **imposture,** n. *fraus, -dis,* f., *fallacia, praestigiae* (= tricks).

impossibility, n. usu. *fieri non posse,* etc. (e.g. to prove the — of anything, *probare alqd fieri non posse*). **impossible,** adj.

by *quod fieri* or *quod effici non potest,* and the adv. by *nullo pacto* or *plane non;* nothing is — to kindness, *nihil est quod benevolentia efficēre non possit;* I believe this to be —, *non puto hoc fieri posse;* it is — for me to, etc., *fieri non potest, ut,* etc.

impotence, n. *imbecillitas, infirmitas corporis,* or *animi.* **impotent,** adj. *invalidus, infirmus, imbecillus, imbecillus.*

impound, v.tr. 1, in gen. *pignus, -ōris, capēre* or *auferre; alqm pignore cogēre* (of the consul who —ed a senator); 2, *in alqo loco includēre* (= to confine, e.g. cattle).

impoverish, v.tr. *alqm in egestatem reducēre.* **impoverishment,** n. *egestas, inopia, paupertas* = poverty.

impracticable, adj. 1, = impossible, *quod fieri non potest;* 2, = intractable, *contumax;* see IMPOSSIBLE, REFRACTORY.

imprecate, v.tr. *alqd alci (im)precari, ex(s)ecrari;* see CURSE, EXECRATE. **imprecation,** n. *dirae, preces, -um,* f., *ex(s)ecratio;* see EXECRATION.

impregnable, adj. 1, = not to be stormed, e.g. an — fortress, *inexpugnabilis;* 2, fig. = not to be moved, *stabilis.*

impregnate, v.tr. 1, = to make pregnant, *alqm gravidam* or *praegnantem facēre;* 2, fig. = to render prolific, † *fecundare, fertilem reddēre;* 3, gen. = to communicate the virtues of one thing to another, *complēre alqd alqā re* (= to fill with); *addēre alqd alci rei* (= to add); *(com)miscēre cum alqā re,* or simply *alqā re* (= to mix); see FILL. **impregnation,** n. (applied to animals or plants), by verb.

impress, v.tr. 1, lit. *alqd alci rei imprimēre;* 2, fig. *alqd alci inurēre, inculcare, in animo insculpēre* or *imprimēre.* **impression,** n. 1, the act of taking an —, *impressio;* = the copy, *exemplum* (= copy in general), *imago expressa, vestigium* (= footstep); to take or make an —, *exprimēre alqd alqā re* or *in alqā re, imprimēre alqd in alqā re;* 2, the working or effect of any influence on the mind, *animi motus, -ūs,* or by special word (e.g. *visa, -orum,* — of sight); *visis ad actionem excitamur,* we are excited to action by visible —s); to make an — on anyone, *alqm movēre.* **impressive,** adj. *gravis, vehemens.* Adv. *graviter, vehementer.* **impressiveness,** n. *gravitas.*

imprint, v.tr. *in alqā re imprimēre;* see IMPRESSION.

imprison, v.tr. *in custodiam dare, tradēre, in(j)icēre; custodiae* or *vinculis mandare, comprehendēre* (= arrest). **imprisonment,** n. *custodia, carcer, -eris,* m., *vincula, -orum.*

improbable, adj. *non verisimilis, non probabilis.* Adv. *non verisimiliter.* **improbability,** n. use adj.

improbity, n. *improbitas.*

impromptu, adv. *ex tempore.*

improper, adj. *improprius* (Plin. Quint.) (e.g. *verba* = unsuitable); = unbecoming, *indecent, indecōrus;* = silly, *ineptus* (e.g. laughter, *risus*); = unworthy, *indignus* (of anyone, *alqo*); = unsuitable, not suited, *alienus* (of things, place, and time, *ab alqo* or *ab alqā re* and *alci* or *alci rei; alcjs rei,* not Cic.); = inelegant, awkward in one's manners, *inconcinnus* (e.g. roughness of manners, want of polish, *asperitas i.*); = absurd, *absonus;* it is — to, etc., *indecorum est* (with inf.); to be — for anyone, *dedecēre* or *non decēre alqm, indignum esse alqo.* Adv. *indecore, perperam, inepte, indigne.* **impropriety,** n. *quod indecorum est.*

improvable, adj. *quod est ejusmodi ut corrigi*

possit. **improve, I.** v.tr. *alqd melius facĕre;* see CORRECT; *excolĕre.* **II.** v.intr. *meliorem fieri, se colligĕre* (morally), *convalescĕre* (= to — in health), *augēri* (= to rise in price), *proficĕre* (= to make progress). **improvement,** n. *correctio, emendatio,* comb. *correctio et emendatio;* — of circumstances, *amplificatio rei familiaris;* morally and mentally, *cultus, -ūs, educatio, disciplina* (= mental and moral training); *institutio* (= instruction in any particular branch); *humanitas* (= general moral and mental and physical — of the whole man), comb. *cultus (-ūs) atque humanitas;* I perceive an — in my general health, *meas vires auctas sentio.*

improvidence, n. *inconsiderantia, temeritas, imprudentia.* **improvident,** adj. *improvidus* (= not looking forward), *incautus* (= heedless, opp. *prudens*), comb. *improvidus incautusque, improvidus et neglegens* (neglig-); = inconsiderate, *inconsideratus;* = thoughtless, *temerarius;* = imprudent, *imprudens* (opp. *paratus*); = indifferent, negligent, *neglegens* (neglig-). Adv. *improvide, incaute, temere, imprudenter, inconsiderate, neglegenter* (neglig-).

imprudence, n. *imprudentia, temeritas* (= rashness); see IMPROVIDENCE. **imprudent,** adj. *imprudens, temerarius, inconsultus;* see IMPROVIDENT. Adv. *imprudenter, temere, inconsulte.*

impudence, n. *impudentia, os impudens* (or *durum* or *ferreum*); *confidentia* (= boldness, in a bad sense). **impudent,** adj. *impudens* (= void of feeling of shame), *procax* (= saucy), *confidens* (= having assurance), *improbus* (= saucy). Adv. *procaciter* (not in Cic.), *impudenter, confidenter.*

impugn, v.tr. *impugnare* (e.g. to — anyone's honour, *impugnare alcjs honorem*); *oppugnare; negare* (= to deny absolutely, opp. *aio*); *improbare* (= to prove to be void, e.g. a will, *testamentum*); *repugnare* (= to contend against, e.g. anyone's opinion, *alcjs opinioni*); = to contradict everything, *contra omnia disserĕre.*

impulse, n. 1, as a term of mechanical philosophy, *impulsio, impulsus, -ūs* (better by verbs, e.g. *agĕre, pellĕre,* etc.); see DRIVE, PROPEL, MOVE; 2, = motive, *impulsus, -ūs, caus(s)a,* or by circumloc. (e.g. ambition is the — of all his actions, *quidquid agit, gloriae cupiditate impulsus agit*); 3, = impression, *impulsus, -ūs, impulsio;* external —, *pulsus (-ūs) externus;* at anybody's —, *algo auctore, alcjs impulsu, alcjs auctoritate;* from one's own —, *sponte* or *suā sponte,* also *ipse* (i.e. from one's own free will); not influenced by anybody else, *per se;* willingly, *ultro;* — from without, *incitamentum, stimulus.* **impulsive,** adj. by verb; see IMPEL.

impunity, n. with —, *impunitus, inultus* (= unrevenged, unpunished, scot-free), *incastigatus* (= unchastised), *impune;* to have done with —, by *impune esse, non puniri; impune abire;* to be able to do with —, *alqd impune ferre* or *impune habēre* or *impune facĕre.*

impure, adj. *impurus* (fig. = immoral, unchaste, of persons and things, e.g. manners, morals, life, *mores*); *obscenus* (obscoen- or obscaen-), (= unchaste); = stained, *contaminatus* (opp. *integer*), with anything, *alqā re* (e.g. with blood, *sanguine*); = unchaste, *incestus;* = low, *inquinatus* (= spotted, e.g. a speech, a verse); *foedus, spurcus, turpis, teter* (= foul); — desires, *libidines.* Adv. *impure, obscene* (obscoen- or obscaen-), *inquinate, foede, spurce, turpiter.* **impurity,** n. *impuritas,* or *incestum, incestus, -ūs, obscenitas* (obscoen- or obscaen-), *libido, stuprum, foeditas, turpitudo.*

imputable, adj. by *cujus rei culpa alci*

assignari potest, and by verbs; see below. **imputation,** n. 1, by verb; 2, = charge, *crimen, culpa, accusatio.* **impute,** v.tr. *alqd alci assignare* (in a good and bad sense); to — to anyone the fault of anything, *culpam alcjs rei alci assignare; culpam alcjs rei conferre* or *transferre* or *derivare in alqm; culpae alqd alci dare, alqd alci a(d)scribĕre, attribuĕre, affingĕre;* see ATTRIBUTE.

in, prep. 1, of place, by old locative (e.g. — Rome, — Corinth, *Romae, Corinthi,* where — = at), *in* with abl. (e.g. *in Italiā*), *in* (e.g. *in loco, hac regione, his terris*), — a letter, *epistulā quādam,* with verbs implying motion, *in* with accus. (to place — a ship, *in navem imponĕre*); — the assembly, *pro contione* (= before); — breadth, *in latitudinem;* — height, *in altitudinem;* 2, of time, *in* with abl., or *inter* or *intra* with accus. (of time within which), *per* with accus. (= throughout), *de* with abl. (= — the course of), simply abl. (e.g. — the night, *nocte* or *de nocte*), by the noun in apposition (e.g. I did it — my boyhood, *puer feci*), to have a friend — so-and-so, *alqm amicum habēre;* 3, of anger); abl., *hoc modo* = in this way (so too *in hunc modum, ad hunc modum*); — respect of (e.g. — wisdom = *sapientiā*); 4, other uses, — an author, *apud* with accus. (e.g. — Cicero, *apud Ciceronem*); — the hands of, *penes alqm;* — the beginning, *ab initio* (when the act continues); to be — our favour, *a nobis stare,* with gerund (e.g. — loving, *amando*); — living, etc., *cum,* with indic. (e.g. you do well — saying, *bene facis cum dicis*).

inability, n. *imbecillitas, infirmitas* (= bodily weakness), *inopia* (= want of means), or use *non posse;* see WEAKNESS.

inaccessibility, n. by **inaccessible,** adj. *inaccessus;* = impassable, surrounded, *invius;* = difficult to pass, *impeditus* (e.g. forest); of persons difficult to be seen, *rari aditūs.* Adv. — situated, *quo non aditus est.*

inaccuracy, n. *indiligentia, pravitas* (when anything has been done totally wrong); = untruth, it must be circumscribed by *falsus* (e.g. to show the — of anything, *alqd falsum esse probare*); see FALSEHOOD. **inaccurate,** adj. *indiligens.* Adv. *indiligenter;* see INCORRECT.

inaction, inactivity, n. *segnities (segnitia), inertia, ignavia,* comb. *segnities et inertia* or *ignavia et inertia* (= laziness); inclination to be idle, *desidia* (opp. *industria, labor*), comb. *inertia atque desidia* or *desidia segnitiesque;* = cessation (of labour from fear of work), *cessatio;* = leisure, *otium, desidia;* = rest, *quies, -ētis.* **inactive,** adj. *ignavus, desses, segnis, iners, quietus.* Adv. *ignave, segniter, quiete.*

inadequacy, n. by **inadequate,** adj. *alienus ab alqā re, non sufficiens;* = not adapted, not answering the purpose (e.g. a witness, evidence given), *non satis idoneus, impar.* Adv. *parum, haud satis.*

inadmissibility, n. circumloc. by **inadmissible,** adj. *quod admitti non potest.*

inadvertence, n. *neglegentia* (neglig-); = want of care, *incuria;* = laziness, *socordia.* **inadvertent,** adj. *neglegens* (neglig-), (opp. *diligens*); = lazy, *socors,* comb. *socors neglegensque* (neglig-). Adv. *neglegenter* (neglig-); = unintentionally. *sine consilio.*

inalienable, adj. *quod abalienari non potest.*

inane, adj. *inanis.*

inanimated, adj. *inanimus, inanimatus.*

inanition, inanity, n. *inanitas* (lit. and fig.), *inane, vacuitas, vacuum;* = hollowness (fig.), *vanitas.*

inapplicability, n. by **inapplicable,**

adj. with *non pertinēre ad,* or *non cadēre in* (with acc.); *non valēre.*

inapposite, adj. *quod non aptum est.*

inappreciable, adj. *quod sentiri non potest,* or by *minimus.*

inapprehensive, adj. *neglegens (neglig-).*

inappropriate, adj. *non idoneus.*

inaptitude, n. 1, *inutilitas* (= uselessness); 2, see INABILITY.

inarticulate, adj. *non satis distinctus.* Adv. *parum distincte.*

inartificial, adj. *simplex* (e.g. food, speech, language).

inattention, n. *animus non attentus, neglegentia (neglig-), incuria, indiligentia.* **inattentive,** adj. *non attentus.*

inaudible, adj. *quod audiri non potest.*

inaugural, adj. *aditialis* (ante and post class.); to deliver an — discourse, *oratione munus auspicari.* **inaugurate,** v.tr. 1, *inaugurare, auspicare, dedicare* (in respect of the worship of the gods, e.g. statues, images, altars, temples, etc.); *consecrare* (anything, e.g. an animal, a field, etc.); to initiate, *initiare* (= to admit to a knowledge of the sacred rites); 2, = to begin, *coepisse;* see BEGIN. **inauguration,** n. *dedicatio, consecratio.*

inauspicious, adj. in gen. *infelix,* † *infaustus, laevus,* † *sinister, nefastus;* an — day, *dies ater.* Adv. *infeliciter, malis ominibus, inauspicato.*

incalculable, adj. *major* (e.g. *numerus,* etc.) *quam qui calculari possit.*

incandescent, adj. *candens.*

incantation, n. *carmen.*

incapability, n. *inscitia,* but better use *non posse* (e.g. — for action, *qui agěre non potest).*
incapable, adj. *indocilis* (= indocile, — of instruction); = dull, *hebes;* = unfit, incompetent, *inutilis* or *inhabilis ad alqd;* = too dull for, *hebes ad alqd.* **incapacitate,** v.tr. *inutilem redděre.* **incapacity,** n. see INCAPABILITY.

incarcerate, v.tr. *(in carcerem* or *in custodiam) in(j)icěre, includěre.* **incarceration,** n. *custodia, vincula, -orum,* n.

incarnate, adj. eccl. t.t. * *incarnatus* (Eccl.), *specie humana* or *corpore indutus.* **incarnation,** n. * *incarnatio.*

incautious, adj. *imprudens, incautus, inconsultus, inconsideratus, temerarius.* Adv. *imprudenter, incaute, inconsulte, inconsiderate, temere.*

incendiarism, n. *incendium* (e.g. he was tried for —, *de incendiis postulatus est).* **incendiary,** n. *incendiarius* (Tac.), *incendii auctor* (referring to one case only).

incense, I. n. *tus, turis;* of —, † *tureus;* carrying —, † *turifer.* **II.** v.tr. *tus accendēre.* **incense,** v.tr. *accendēre, incendēre* (lit. and fig.); see EXASPERATE.

incentive, I. adj. *quod instigat;* see INCITE. **II.** n. *instigatio, irritatio, incitatio, concitatio, impulsus, -ūs, instinctus, -ūs, stimulus;* = means of inciting, *irritamentum, invitamentum* (chiefly in the pl.), *illecebra, lenocinium* (= allurement); see IMPULSE.

inception, n. *initium;* see COMMENCEMENT. **inceptive,** adj. *incipiens.*

incessant, adj. *perpetuus, assiduus, continuus;* see CONTINUOUS. Adv. *perpetuo, assidue, continuo.*

incest, n. *incestus, -ūs, incestum.* **incestuous,** adj. *incestus.*

inch, n. 1, = a lineal measure, *digitus, uncia* (Plin.); 2, fig. = a small quantity; degree; not to yield, depart an — from, *ab alqo re non transversum digitum* or *non digitum discedēre;* to an —, almost, *tantum non, non multum* (not *parum) abfuit quin,* etc.; not an — better, *nihilo melius;* not an — different, *plane idem;* by —es, *paul(l)atim, sensim.*

inchoate, adj. *inchoatus.*

incident, I. adj. *quod ad alqd pertinet,* or *in alqd re consistit,* or *alqd re continetur, proprius,* with gen. or dat. **II.** n. *casus, -ūs, eventus, -ūs, res;* see CIRCUMSTANCE. **incidental,** adj. *fortuitus, forte oblātus.* Adv. *forte, fortuito;* I chanced to mention —, *in mentionem (alcjs rei) incidi.*

incipiency, n. *initium;* see BEGINNING. **incipient,** adj. *initium faciens.*

incision, n. *incisura* (Plin.) (= the act of making an —, and also the — made by the hand, the insects, leaves); the — made by the wheel, furrow, or ship, *sulcus.* **incisive,** adj. *mordens, mordax, asper.* **incisor,** n. (= foreteeth), *dentes qui digerunt cibum, dentes qui secant.*

incite, v.tr. *instigare* (= to instigate, set on); = to excite, animate, *incitare, excitare, concitare, (com)movēre, permovēre;* = to irritate, *irritare;* = to stimulate, *stimulare;* = to rouse, kindle, *inflammare, incendēre, accendēre;* = to urge, *impellēre* (all *alqm* or *alcjs animum ad alqd); stimulos alci admovēre* or *addēre* (= to prick), *calcaria alci adhibēre* or *admovēre* (= to give the spur), *alqm (ex)acuēre* (= to sharpen), *ignem alci sub(j)icěre* (= to kindle a fire underneath, i.e. to rouse one's desires, esp. envy). **incitement,** n. *impulsus, -ūs;* see IMPULSE.

incivility, n. *inurbanitas, rusticitas, inhumanitas.*

inclemency, n. 1, *inhumanitas, severitas, crudelitas, saevitia;* 2, of the weather, † *asperitas* (e.g. *hiemis),* or *gravis* with n. (e.g. *tempestas gravis);* — of winter, *hiemis difficultas.* **inclement,** adj. 1, *inclemens* (Liv.), *inhumanus, severus, crudelis, saevus;* 2, *gravis, asper;* see also COLD, STORMY, SEVERITY.

inclination, n. 1, lit. *inclinatio;* 2, in geom. and mech. (= leaning of two bodies, lines, planes, towards each other, so as to make an angle) *fastigium* (= slope); = declivity, *proclivitas, declivitas* (both considered from the top), *acclivitas* (considered from the bottom, = a bending upwards); 3, = leaning of the mind, — to a subject, *inclinatio animi;* for anything, *ad alqd voluntas;* = a propensity, *proclivitas ad alqd* (in a bad sense); a favourable — for anything or anybody, *studium alcjs rei* or *alcjs;* a favourable — towards a person, *propensa in alqm voluntas, propensum in alqm studium;* = love, *amor,* towards anybody, *in* or *erga alqm;* = — from a wish, *studio, propenso animo* (e.g. to do anything, *alqd facēre);* from free —, *ex animo;* to have an — for anything, *ad alqd inclinatum, proclivem, pronum esse, alci rei studēre, alcjs rei esse studiosum, alcjs rei studio teneri;* to be guided by one's own —, *studiis suis obsequi.* **incline, I.** v.intr. 1, = to slope, *proclivem* or *declivem esse;* to be rising, *acclivem esse* (in looking upwards); neither to — one way nor the other, *in nullā parte habēre proclinationes* (e.g. of walls, etc.); 2, = to lean (in a moral sense), to have a tendency (of times, circumstances, etc.), *inclinari, (se) inclinare;* to — towards anything, *(se) inclinare ad* or *in alqd* (of persons and things), *inclinatione voluntatis propendēre in alqm* (= to feel oneself from — drawn towards anybody); to — more towards peace, *inclinatiorem esse ad pacem.* **II.** v.tr. *inclinare, submittĕre, demittĕre* (e.g. *caput*). **inclined,** adj. for anybody for anything, *inclinatus ad alqm, alqd ;* = easy to persuade, *propensus ad* or *in alqd* (e.g. to pardon, enjoyment) ; — to fall into anything, *proclivis ad alqd, pronus in alqd* or *ad alqd ;* I am more — to think, *eo magis adducor ut putem ;* = merciful, *propitius* (especially of the gods, seldom of man) ; = benevolent, *benevolus* (of man).

inclose, v.tr. *saepire (sep-) ;* see ENCLOSE.

include, v.tr. = to comprehend, *comprehendĕre, complecti, continēre, annumerare, a(d)scribĕre alci rei* or *in* or *ad ;* to — among the accused, *in reos referre ;* without including you, *te excepto ;* to be included in anything, *comprehendi, continēri alqā re ;* to be included in that number, *in eo numero esse* or *haberi.* **inclusive, included,** adj. that matter —, *additā eā re ;* often simply by *cum* or *in ;* there were 300 soldiers, the prisoners —, *milites erant trecenti cum captivis* (or *captivis annumeratis*). Adv. that one —, *eo comprehenso ;* — all those, *omnibus comprehensis* or *additis.*

incogitable, adj. to be —, *ne cogitari quidem posse.*

incognito, adv. *incognitus, ignoratus, alieno* or *dissimulato nomine.*

incoherence, incoherency, n. by circumloc. with **incoherent,** adj. *interruptus* (= interrupted), *dissipatus* (= scattered, torn, e.g. a speech), *sibi non constans.* Adv. *interrupte, haud constanter* or *congruenter ;* **to speak —,** *haud cohaerentia dicĕre.*

incombustibility, n. by **incombustible,** adj. *qui ignibus non absumitur.*

income, n. *vectigal, -alis,* n. (including public and private —, as taxes, tithes, rent), *reditus, -ūs* (in the sing. = the returns), *fructus, -ūs* (= the produce), *pecunia,* also *reditus pecuniae* (= a pecuniary return) ; public —, *fructus publici,* (if in mere money) *pecuniae vectigales ;* — from lands, *praediorum fructus, fructus quem praedia reddunt ;* — from gain, *quaestus, -ūs ;* to make an —, *quaestum facĕre ;* he has an — to live upon, *habet unde vivat.*

incommode. v.tr. *incommodum alci afferre.* **incommodious,** adj. *incommodus ;* = troublesome, *molestus ;* see INCONVENIENT.

incomparable, adj. *incomparabilis* (Plin.) ; = unequalled, *sine exemplo maximus* (e.g. *Homerus*) ; *divinus* (of persons and things, e.g. a legion, *legio ;* a voice, *vox ;* works, *opera*) ; *singularis* (= unique, of persons and things, e.g. daughter, *filia ; virtus*) ; *eximius, egregius, praestans* (= uncommon, distinguished in particular respects, of things) ; Cicero, this man who, as regards his diction, can be equalled to none, *Cicero, caelestis hic in dicendo vir.* Adv. *sine exemplo, divine, eximie, egregie, praestanter.*

incompatibility, n. *repugnantia, diversitas ;* — of temper, rudeness, *importunitas ;* see RUDENESS. **incompatible,** adj. of anything that cannot subsist with something else, *alienus ab alqā re, alci rei contrarius ; adversarius, adversus, infensus* (= hostile), (*ab alqā re*) *diversus ;* to be — with anything, *abhorrēre ab alqā re ; pugnare inter se* (= to contradict each other, of things), *repugnare alci rei* (of two things that cannot be reconciled together).

incompetence, incompetency, n. *inscitia ;* see INABILITY. **incompetent,** adj. **1,** legally, to be — for anything, *faciendi alqd jus* or *potestatem non habēre, jure alqd facĕre non posse ;* **2,** in gen., *inscitus, inhabilis, nescius, :nutilis ;* see FOOLISH, INCAPABLE. Adv. *inscite.*

incomplete, adj. *imperfectus.* Adv. *imper. fecte.* **incompleteness,** n. *quod imperfectum est ;* see IMPERFECT.

incompliance, n. *recusatio ;* with anything, *alcjs rei.*

incomprehensibility, n. by **incomprehensible,** adj. *quod comprehendi* or *intellegi (intelligi) non potest.*

incompressible, adj. *quod comprimi, condensari non potest* (e.g. water).

inconceivable, adj. *quod (mente* or *cogitatione) comprehendi non potest, quod intellegi non potest, quod in intellegentiam non cadit, quod cogitare non possumus, quod cogitari non potest ;* =inexplicable, immense, *inexplicabilis* (e.g. kindness, *facilitas*) ; =incredible, *incredibilis.* Adv. *incredibiliter, mirum in modum.*

inconclusive, adj. (*argumentum*) *quo nihil efficitur.*

incongruity, n. *repugnantia ;* see ABSURDITY, CONTRADICTION. **incongruous,** adj. *alienus ab alqo* or *ab alqā re, incongruens* (Plin. Min.), *inconveniens.* Adv. *non apte.*

inconsequence, n. see ABSURDITY. **inconsequent,** adj. see INCOHERENT.

inconsiderable, adj. *lēvis* (= without weight, unimportant) ; *mediocris* (= mediocre, common, e.g. a man, a family ; then = not very great, light, etc.) ; *minutus* (= trifling) ; *exiguus* (= small in comparision with others, e.g. troops, *copiae ;* fortune, property, *res familiaris*) ; =small in gen., *parvus* (opp. *magnus,* e.g. sum of money, *pecunia ;* troop of soldiers, *manus*) ; not —, *non-nullus.* **inconsiderate,** adj. **1,** *inconsideratus* (= without thinking) ; *inconsultus* (= rash) ; = incautious, *incautus ;* = improvident, *improvidus,* comb. *improvidus incautusque ;* = imprudent, *imprudens ;* **2,** = not regardful of others, *alqm non observans* or *respiciens, alci non consulens.* Adv. *inconsiderate, incaute, imprudenter ; nullius ratione habitā* (= without regard to persons).

inconsistency, n. *discrepantia, inconstantia, mutabilitas ;* see CONTRADICTION. **inconsistent,** adj. *ab alqā re alienus, inconstans, alci rei contrarius, ab alqā re* or *alci rei absonus, alci rei repugnans, ab* or *cum alqā re* or *alci rei discrepans.* Adv. *inconstanter.*

inconsolable, adj. + *inconsolabilis,* (*dolor* or *luctus, -ūs*) *qui nullo solatio levari potest.*

inconspicuous, adj. *quod vix sentiri* or *sensibus percipi potest.* Adv. *sensim.*

inconstancy, n. *inconstantia* (of persons and things, physical and moral, e.g. of the wind, *venti*) ; = changeableness, *varietas* (e.g. of the army) ; = infidelity of a person, *infidelitas ;* = levity, *levitas ;* in one's resolutions, *mutabilitas* (*mentis*), comb. *inconstantia mutabilitasque mentis ;* = movableness, variableness, *mobilitas* (also of anything personified, e.g. of fortune, *fortunae*). **inconstant,** adj. *inconstans* (= not remaining always the same, physical, e.g. the wind, and in a moral sense, of persons and things) ; = changing, *varius ;* = unfaithful, *infidelis* (of persons) ; = vacillating, wavering, *infirmus* (of persons and things, opp. *firmus*) ; = volatile, *lēvis* (of persons) ; = changeable, fickle in one's resolutions, *mutabilis* (of persons), comb. *varius et mutabilis ;* = fickle, one who goes easily from one thing to another, *mobilis* (of persons and things, e.g. character, mind, disposition, *ingenium, animus ;* will, resolution, *voluntas*) ; = uncertain, not to be relied upon, *fluxus* (of things, e.g. faith, *fides ;* fortune, *fortuna*) ; see CHANGEABLE.

incontestable, adj. *quod refutari non potest*

incontinence, n. *incontinentia* (= want of power to rule one's passions); *intemperantia* (= Intemperance). **incontinent,** adj. *incontinens, intemperans.* Adv. *incontinenter;* = immediately, *statim.*

incontrovertible, adj. *quod refutari non potest.*

inconvenience, inconveniency, n. *incommoditas* (e.g. of anything, *rei;* of time, *temporis*); *incommodum* (= an — to anyone); = a disadvantage, *molestia;* to cause — to anyone, *alci incommodare* or *molestum esse, alci incommodum afferre, alci negotium exhibēre, facessēre.* **inconvenient,** adj. *inopportunus, intempestivus* (= in undue season), *incommodus* (= not quite convenient). Adv. *intempestive, incommode.*

inconvertible, adj. *immutabilis;* see IMMUTABLE.

incorporate, v.tr. see UNITE, 1; ESTABLISH, 2.

incorrect, adj. *non justus* (= not according to order, opp. *justus*), *pravus* (= perverse, contrary to reason, improper, opp. *rectus*); *vitiosus, mendosus* (= full of mistakes, opp. *rectus*); = false, not true, *falsus* (opp. *verus*); the account is —, *ratio non convenit* or *non constat;* a very — work, with many mistakes, *in quo multa vitia insunt;* in which many statements are —, *in quo multa perperam dicta sunt.* Adv. *perperam* (= wrong, contrary to the real nature of anything, opp. *recte;* e.g. to pronounce, *pronuntiare*); = with many mistakes, *vitiose, mendose* (opp. *recte,* e.g. to infer, argue, *concludēre*); = falsely, untruly, *falso* (opp. *vere* or *vero*); = not as it should be, *secus* (e.g. to judge, *judicare*). **incorrectness,** n. by adj. INCORRECT. **incorrigibility,** n. *pravitas.* **incorrigible,** adj. *qui corrigi non potest;* = saucy, *improbus.*

incorrupt, adj. **1,** *incorruptus;* **2,** fig. *integer, incorruptus, purus, sanctus, castus, innocens.* Adv. *incorrupte, sancte, integre, caste, pure, sancte.* **incorruptibility,** n. **1,** lit. *quod corrumpi* or *putrescēre non potest;* **2,** fig. *integritas, sanctitas, castimonia, castitas, innocentia.*

increase, I. v.intr. **1,** = to grow, (ac)*crescēre, succrescēre, gliscēre, incrementum capēre, augeri, augescēre, se corroborare* or *corroborari, ingravescēre* (in bad sense), *increbrescēre* (= to become more frequent), *invalescēre* (= to get the upper hand), *proficēre* (= to advance); the evil increases, *malum ingravescit* or *corroboratur.* **II.** v.tr. = to augment, *amplificare* (= to make wider), *dilatare* (= to spread out), *extendēre, propagare* or *proferre alqd* (= to extend the limits, e.g. *imperium* or *fines imperii*), *augēre, amplificare, multiplicare* (= to multiply). **III.** n. = augmentation, *amplificatio* (e.g. *gloriae rei familiaris*), *propagatio* or *prolatio finium, accretio, accessio, augmentum, auctus, -ūs, incrementum.*

incredible, adj. *incredibilis;* it is — (*auditu, dictu, memoratu*) *incredibile est.* Adv. *incredibiliter, incredibilem in modum.* **incredulous,** adj. *qui non facile adduci potest ut credat, incredulus.* **incredulity,** n. by circumloc. (e.g. *se incredulum praebuit,* = he showed his —).

increment, n. *incrementum;* see INCREASE. **incriminate,** v.tr. *alqm suspectum reddēre,* — oneself, *se scelere alligare.*

incrust, v.tr. *crustare.* **incrustation, n.** *crusta.*

incubate, v. intr. *incubare* (Plin.); **see** HATCH. **incubus, n.** *incubo.*

inculcate, v.tr. *alqm alqd docēre;* **to — that,** etc., *alci inculcare ut,* etc.; *imprimēre* (= to impress, imprint a mark upon) or *insculpēre* (= to engrave) *alqd in alqā re* (the two latter verbs both lit. and fig.); to have been —d on the heart, *in animo insculptum esse* or *in animo insculptum habēre.*

incumbency, n. **1,** = a relying on something, *officium* (in gen.), *munus, -eris* (as the duty of an office); **2,** = state of holding an ecclesiastical benefice, * *possessio beneficii.* **incumbent, I.** adj. = lying on (as duty or obligation), anything is — upon me, *debeo alqd facēre,* or *alqd mihi faciendum est,* or *est* with genit. (e.g. it is — upon, the duty of the pupil, *est discipuli;* it is — upon me, you, etc., *meum, tuum est*). **II.** n. = a clergyman, * *beneficiarius.*

incur, v.tr. **1,** lit. = to run against, hence to become subject to, *incurrēre in alqm* or *alci rei, incidēre in alqd;* **2,** fig. *colligēre* (e.g. hatred, *invidiam,* by anything, *alqā re*), or *alci in odium venire, in alcjs odium incurrēre; alcjs odium sibi contrahēre;* to — disgrace, *dedecus in se admittēre.*

incurability, n. by **incurable,** adj. *insanabilis,* † *immedicabilis;* = hopeless, *desperatus* (e.g. a patient given up by the medical attendant). Adv. use adj. (e.g. he was — ill, *morbus erat insanabilis*).

indebted, adj. **1,** = being in debt, *obaeratus;* to be — to, *alci pecuniam debēre* or *pecuniam acceptam referre;* **2,** = obliged by something received; to be — to anyone, *alci obnoxium esse, alcjs beneficiis obligatum esse;* to be greatly — to anybody, *alci multum* or *multa beneficia debēre, alqd alci acceptum referre.*

indecency, n. *turpitudo* (= — in anyone's language or behaviour), *obscenitas* (*obscoen-, obscaen-;* see OBSCENITY. **indecent,** adj. *indecōrus* (= unbecoming, opp. *decōrus,* e.g. laughter, *risus*); *obscenus* (= obscene), *inhonestus* (= dishonourable); *turpis; parum verecundus* (= offensive to modesty and delicacy, not feeling ashamed, e.g. words, *verba*); an — expression, *quod turpe dictu videatur* (e.g. to make use of, *dicēre*). Adv. *indecore, turpiter, obscene.*

indeciduous, adj. (*folia,* etc.) *quae non cadunt,* or *non decidua sunt.*

indecision, n. *dubitatio, inconstantia, haesitantia.* **indecisive,** adj. *dubius, anceps.* Adv. by adj.; see INDEFINITE.

indeclinable, adj. use *verbum quod casibus immutari non potest, quod declinari non potest, indeclinabilis* (gram.); — nouns, *aptota,* pl. (gram.).

indecorous, adj. *indecōrus;* see INDECENT. **indecorum,** n. *deformitas* (= ugliness); = an evil, a mistake, *vitium;* by the adj. *turpis* or *indecōrus,* also by *dedecet* (e.g. that is an —, *hoc turpe est* or *dedecet*); see INDECENCY.

indeed, adv. = in reality, *quidem* or *enim* (enclit.), *adeo, profecto, enimvero, vere* (= truly); *vero, re verā, re* (= in reality, indeed, opp. *nomine,* i.e. nominally, merely in appearance), I —, *equidem; —? itane vero?* (in an ironical sense), you don't say so? If used in an emphatic sense, e.g. this is true, it is indeed, = *sane* (referring to particular expressions), *vero?* both also = yes, certainly (i.e. *sane quidem* and *ita sane*); *quidem, enim* (to note concession); *credo* (= I think so; with reserve); *atqui* (= yes; if however, etc.); *nempe, nimirum, scilicet, videlicet* (all = a concession in a familiar kind of way; *nempe* = surely); *nimirum* = no doubt; *scilicet, videlicet* = of course; all four also used in an ironical sense; e.g. very difficult; *sane difficilis.* I could —

wish, Servius, *Ego vero, Servi, vellem;* I should — serve my fellow-citizens very badly, *Male, credo, mererer de meis civibus;* and —, *et sane;* surely —, *immo vero;* — ... but nevertheless, *etsi ... tamen;* or *by ille quidem, is quidem ... sed tamen;* — not, *neque* (at the beginning of a sentence, with *sed* following); then —, *tum vero.*

indefatigable, adj. *assiduus* (= constantly active), *impiger* (= unwearied); *indefessus,* comb. *assiduus et indefessus.* Adv. *assidue, impigre.*

indefatigability, n. *assiduitas, assiduitas et diligentia, impigritas.*

indefeasible, adj. *in perpetuum ratus.*

indefectible, indefective, adj. *vitio carens.*

indefensible, adj. *quod defendi non potest* (in gen.); of a military position, *(locus) qui teneri non potest.*

indefinable, adj. *quod definiri non potest;* an — sense of danger, *nescio quid periculi.* **indefinite,** adj. *incertus* (= uncertain, e.g. answer, *responsum*) ; = doubtful, *dubius, anceps;* = ambiguous, *ambiguus* (e.g. oracle, *oraculum,* = of doubtful meaning); for an — period, *in incertum;* the — pronoun, *pronomen infinitum or indefinitum* (gram.). Adv. *ambigue, incerte or incerto* (both ante class.), *dubie.*

indelibility, n. by circumloc. with adj. **indelible,** adj. † *indelibilis, quod deleri non potest; quod elui non potest* (= what cannot be wiped off); *inexpiabilis, implacabilis* (e.g. hatred, fig.) ; *sempiternus, perpetuus* (fig., e.g. hatred).

indelicate, adj. *parum verecundus, inurbanus, inhonestus* (= ungentlemanly), *impudicus* (= indecent). Adv. *parum verecunde, inurbane, impudice.* **indelicacy,** n. by adj.

indemnification, n. *damni restitutio;* in the connexion of a sentence, *compensatio,* or circumloc. by *damnum (com)pensare or (re)sarcire or restituĕre.* **indemnify,** v.tr. *damnum alci restituĕre, (re)sarcire, pensare;* to — by anything for a thing, *alqd alqâ re compensare.* **indemnity,** n. see INDEMNIFICATION ; act of —, *lex oblivionis;* see AMNESTY.

indent, v.tr. *alqd incidĕre.* **indenture, n.** *pactum.*

independence, n. *libertas* (opp. *servitus*), *arbitrium liberum* (i.e. liberty of using one's own judgment); = exemption from burdens, *immunitas.* **independent,** adj. *liber, solutus* (often = free in bad sense); *sui juris* (of one who is his own master, of age) ; *sui potens* (= who does as he thinks proper); *liber et solutus, solutus et liber* (= free and unbound, tied by nobody); = exempt from burdens, *immunis, legibus solutus;* to be —, *sui juris or suae potestatis or in suâ potestate esse;* to obey nobody, *nemini parēre;* to live as one thinks proper, — from others, *ad suum arbitrium vivĕre.* Adv. *libere, solute,* comb. *libere et solute, suo arbitrio* (= at one's own will).

indescribable, adj. *inenarrabilis* (= what cannot be estimated properly, e.g. trouble, labour); *incredibilis* (= incredible, e.g. joy, *laetitia*) ; *mirus* (= wonderful) ; *singularis* (e.g. faithfulness, *fides*), or by *nescio quid* (= what is so extraordinary that we can hardly comprehend it, e.g. that wonderful thing, *illud nescio quid praeclarum*). Adv. *inenarrabiliter, incredibiliter, singulariter, mirum in modum.*

indestructible, adj. *quod dirui or everti non potest, or perennis, perpetuus* (= lasting).

indeterminate, adj. *incertus;* see INDEFINITE. **indetermination,** n. by circumloc. with INDEFINITE. **indetermined,** adj. *dubius* (= doubtful), *incertus* (= uncertain); I am —

what to do, *dubius or incertus sum quid faciam;* I am — whether to stay or to go, *incertum mihi est quid agam, abeam an maneam;* I am — whether, etc., *incertus sum utrum,* etc. Adv *dubitanter;* see INDEFINITE.

index, n. 1, in gen. = that which points out, *index, -icis,* m. and f. (in a good or bad sense); 2, = the hand that points to the hour of the day, use *gnomon,* or *horarum index;* 3, = table of the contents of a book, *index or epitome.*

indexterity, n. *inscitia.*

Indian, adj. *Indianus, Indicus.*

indicate, v.tr. *indicare, indicio or indicium esse;* in reference to future things, *significare, praenuntiare, portendĕre;* = to announce, *nuntiare, nuntium alcjs rei afferre;* = to declare anything that is to be kept a secret, *enuntiare;* = to denounce, inform, *deferre;* = to declare, state what is to be done, *denuntiare* (e.g. war); = to prove, *arguĕre;* see DECLARE.

indication, n. *indicium, index, argumentum, vestigium, documentum, significatio, signum.* **indicative,** adj. 1, *indicans;* see DECLARE ; 2, = mood, *modus indicativus* (gram.). **indicatory,** adj. *significans;* see DECLARE.

indict, v.tr. = to accuse, *accusare, postulare, nomen alcjs deferre;* see ACCUSE, ACTION. **indictment,** n. bill of —, *libellus, accusatio* (inasmuch as the speaker appears before the public with it). **indictable,** adj. *accusabilis, quod lege animadvertendum est.* **indicter,** n. *accusator.*

indifference, n. 1, lit. *lēvitas, vilitas* (= slightness of a matter); 2, = carelessness about anything, taking no notice of it, *neglegentia (neglig-) alcjs or alcjs rei;* *neglectio alcjs rei, contemptio alcjs rei, despicientia alcjs rei, incuria;* 3, = calmness, *aequus animus, aequitas animi;* = coldness, *lentitudo;* = hardness of heart, *animus durus, animus alienatus ab alqo* (= coldness towards a friend); 4, = impartiality, *aequabilitas, aequitas;* see IMPARTIALITY. **indifferent,** adj. 1, in the proper sense, *idem valens, ejusdem pretii* (= of the same value); = neither good nor bad, *nec bonus nec malus ; indifferens* (attempted by Cicero as a translation of the Greek ἀδιάφορος) ; = keeping the middle course, neither to blame nor to praise, *medius, qui (quae, quod) neque laudari per se neque vituperari potest ;* = trifling, insignificant, *lĕvis, vilis;* = too sure of anything, *securus;* = careless about anything, *remissus, dissolutus;* (e.g. whoever, in seeing these things, could be so — as to remain silent? *quis tam dissoluto animo est, qui haec quum videat tacēre possit?);* = slow, sluggish, *lentus;* = hard-hearted, *durus;* it is — to me whether, etc., *nihil med interest or refert;* I have become — against any fresh grief, affliction, *obduruit animus ad dolorem novum;* to remain — to anything, to bear, put up with, *aequo animo ferre or pati alqd, lente* (= easily) *ferre alqd;* see IMPARTIAL ; 2, neither good nor the worst, *tolerabilis;* = middling, *mediocris, modicus;* = pretty fair, *satis bonus or sat bonus* (e.g. *accusator*). Adv. = without distinction, *promiscue, promiscam* (ante class.); = carelessly, *dissolute or remisso animo, neglegenter (neglig-);* = coolly, *lente;* = hard - heartedly, *duriter;* = impartially, *aequo animo, aequabiliter;* = middlingly, *mediocriter, modice.*

indigence, n. *inopia;* = want, *egestas, mendicitas;* = poverty, *inopia;* to be reduced to extreme —, *ad extremum inopiae venire;* to be reduced to complete poverty, to become a pauper, *in mendicitatem detrudi.* **indigent.** adj. *inops, egens, mendicus;* see NEEDY.

indigenous, adj. **1,** applied to persons, *indigĕna* (opp. *alienigena, advena, peregrinus*), or circumloc. by *in eâ* or *illâ terrâ natus*; the — inhabitants (= natives), *indigĕnae*; **2,** applied to animals, vegetables, etc., *indigĕna, vernaculus*; see NATIVE.

indigested, adj. **1,** = not concocted in the stomach, *crudus*; **2,** = not regularly disposed and arranged; see UNARRANGED; **3,** = not reduced to due form, *immaturus.* **indigestible,** adj. *difficilis concoctu* or *ad concoquendum, gravis.* **indigestion,** n. *cruditas* (e.g. of the stomach).

indignant, adj. *indignabundus* (= full of indignation); = half-angry, *subiratus*; = angry, *iratus, iracundus*; = with a hostile feeling, *iniquus*; to be — against anyone, *alci stomachari* or *iratum esse.* Adv. *irate, iracunde.* **indignation,** n. *indignatio* (in gen.), *indignitas* (= indignity, then dissatisfaction we feel), at anything, *alcjs rei*; = displeasure, sensitiveness, *stomachus*; = anger, *ira, iracundia, bilis*; rather in —, *subiratus*; in —, *animo iniquo* or *irato, indignabundus, iratus.* **indignity,** n. *ignominia, indignitas, contumelia*; see INSULT.

indirect, adj. **1,** lit. not straight, *non rectus, devius*; **2,** — fig., can only be rendered by circumloc.; there are direct and — causes, *caus(s)arum aliae sunt adjuvantes, aliae proximae*; if — means through a third party, it is rendered by *per* (e.g. *per senatum*); **3,** Gram. t.t. *obliquus* (e.g. *oratio obliqua*). Adv. *obscure, tecte, clam, occulte,* or by *per* with acc. as above, *circuitione quâdam.*

indiscernible, adj. *quod cerni non potest.*

indiscoverable, adj. *quod inveniri non potest.*

indiscreet, adj. see INCONSIDERATE, IMPROVIDENT, IMMODEST. **indiscretion,** n. see IMPROVIDENCE, IMMODESTY.

indiscriminate, adj. *promiscuus.* Adv. *omni discrimine sublato, promiscue.*

indispensable, adj. *necessarius*; it is —, *necesse est* (with acc. and inf. or with subjunc.). Adv. *necessario.*

indispose, v.tr. by circumloc. *alqd ad alqd inutile reddĕre, alqm ab alqâ re avocare.* **indisposed,** adj. **1,** to be, feel —, *lĕviter aegrotare*; to become —, see SICKLY; **2,** = unwilling, *aversus ab alqo* or *ab alqâ re* (= feeling averse), *alienatus, alienus* (= hostile to a cause); not to be — to believe a thing, *inclinato ad credendum esse animo*; not to feel — to do a thing, *haud displicet* (with inf.). **indisposition,** n. **1,** *commotiuncula*; **2,** *animus aversus, invitus, alienus*; see AVERSION, DISINCLINATION.

indisputable, adj. *certus, perspicuus, manifestus, clarus*; see CERTAIN. Adv. *sine (ullâ) controversiâ* (= without the least controversy); = undoubtedly, *certo, sine dubio*; = without fail, *haud dubie, certe*; = by far, *longe,* with adj. (e.g. Demosthenes was — the finest orator, *oratorum longe princeps Demosthenes*).

indissoluble, adj. *indissolubilis* (lit. e.g. knot, *nodus*); *inexplicabilis* (lit. = what cannot be unfolded, untwisted, e.g. chain, *vinculum*; hence fig. = unexplainable); = everlasting, *aeternus.*

indistinct, adj. *parum clarus* (both for the eye and the ear); *obscurus* (e.g. speech, *oratio*); = perplexed, *perplexus* (= difficult to make out, e.g. an answer, a reply, *responsum*); an — voice, *vox obtusa* (= weak, Quint.). Adv. *minus clare, obscure, perplexe, confuse*; see DOUBTFUL, DOUBTFULLY. **indistinguishable,** adj. *quod discerni non potest.*

indite, v.tr. *scribĕre.*

individual, I. adj. *proprius, singularis,*

singuli; to remain true to one's — character, *naturam propriam sequi.* Adv. *viritim, in singulos, si(n)gillatim.* **II.** n. an —, *homo.* **individuality,** n. *natura alcjs propria.*

indivisibility, n. by adj. **indivisible,** adj. *individuus, quod dividi non potest*; small — bodies, *corpuscula individua.*

indocile, adj. *indocilis.* **indocility,** n. *ingenium indocile.*

indoctrinate, v.tr. *erudire in alqâ re.*

indolence, n. *ignavia, inertia, desidia, segnitia (segnities), pigritia (pigrities).* **indolent,** adj. *ignavus, iners, deses, segnis* (in posit. rare in classical Lat.), *piger.* Adv. *ignave, segne, segniter*; see IDLE.

indomitable, adj. *quod vinci non potest, invictus, indomitus.*

in-door, adj. *umbratilis.* **in-doors,** adv. *domi.*

indorse, v.tr. **1,** *syngrapham inscribĕre*; **2,** fig. see SANCTION, ALLOW.

indubitable, adj. *non dubius*; = certain, *certus.* Adv. see CERTAIN.

induce, v.tr. anybody to a thing, *alqm in* or *alqd inducĕre* (= to lead into, e.g. an error, *in errorem*; to a war, *ad bellum*); = to urge anyone to a thing, *alqm impellĕre ad* or *in alqd* (e.g. to a war, *ad bellum*); = to allure anyone to a thing, *alqm illicĕre* or *pellicĕre in* or *ad alqd* (e.g. *in fraudem*); = to try to — a person to do a thing, *alqm sol(l)icitare ad alqd faciendum* or *sol(l)icitare ut,* etc. **inducement,** n. *caus(s)a, impulsus, -ûs, incitamentum, illecebrae, praemium.* **inducer,** n. *auctor.* **induct,** v.tr. *inaugurare.* **induction,** n. in logic, *inductio* (Quint.); logical t.t. *ratio per inductionem facta.*

indulgence, n. *indulgentia, clementia, benignitas, venia* (= the overlooking of faults); in the middle ages, *indulgentia* (= remission of sins). **indulge, I.** v.tr. *alci* or *alci rei indulgĕre, alci* or *alci rei veniam dare, alqm indulgentiâ tractare, alqd alci concedĕre* or *condonare*; = gratify, *(voluptabilis) se dedĕre (in)servire.* **II.** v.intr. *nimis sibi indulgĕre.* **indulgent,** adj. *indulgens* (= showing kindness or favour, opp. of *severus*), *clemens* (= merciful, opp. of *severus, crudelis*), *benignus* (= kindness of heart, opp. of *malignus*), *facilis.* Adv. *indulgenter, clementer, benigne.*

industry, n. *industria, (g)navitas* (rare, opp. *ignavia*), *labor, opera, assiduitas, sedulitas.* **industrious,** adj. *industrius, (g)navus, acer, sedulus, assiduus, strenuus, diligens.* Adv. *industrie, (g)naviter, acriter, assidue, strenue, diligenter.*

indweller, n. *incola,* m. and f.; see INHABITANT. **indwelling,** adj. = remaining within (e.g. sin), *qui intus est, insitus*; = natural, innate, *innatus, naturâ insitus.*

inebriate, v.tr. *ebrium facĕre, temulentum facĕre.* **inebriated,** adj. *ebrius, temulentus.* **inebriation,** n. *ebrietas*; see DRUNKENNESS.

inedited, adj. *ineditus.*

ineffability, n. by **ineffable,** adj. by *quod verbis exprimi non potest, inauditus*; = too horrible to utter, *infandus* (e.g. deed, grief); = incredible, *incredibilis* (e.g. pleasure, desire, longing); = unheard of, *inauditus* (e.g. greatness, size, cruelty). Adv. *supra quam enarrari potest* (= indescribably); *incredibiliter* (= incredibly).

ineffective, inefficient, adj. *invalidus* (lit. not strong, weak), (e.g. medicine, opp. *fortis, valens*); = unfit, unwholesome, *inutilis*; to remain, to be —, *effectu carēre* (e.g. plans, etc.).

Adv. *frustra, nequi(c)quam (nequidq-)*. **in-effectiveness, inefficiency**, n. use adj.

inelegance, inelegancy, n. circumloc. by *sine elegantiâ; inconcinnitas* (e.g. of the ideas, *sententiarum*); see ELEGANCE. **inelegant**, adj. *invenustus* (= ungraceful), *inelegans* (= without taste), *inconcinnus* (= slovenly, improper), *illepidus* (= without grace), *inurbanus, agrestis, inhumanus, rusticus* (= boorish), *inornatus* (= without ornament) ; *incomptus* (lit. uncombed, e.g. head, hair ; then fig., unpolished, e.g. speech, style). Adv. *ineleganter, illepide, inurbane, rustice.*

ineligible, adj. *qui per leges non eligendus est*, = unsuitable, *inopportunus ;* see UNFIT, UN-SUITABLE.

inept, adj. *ineptus ;* see ABSURD.

inequality, n. *inaequalitas, dissimilitudo* (= unlikeness, e.g. of character, *morum*). **in-equitable**, adj. *iniquus* (of pers. and things, opp. *aequus*, e.g. judge, law, condition); *injustus* (= unjust, of pers. and things, opp. *justus, meritus, debitus*, e.g. interest of money); *improbus* (= dishonest); *immeritus* (= undeserved ; especially with a negation before it, e.g. praise not undeserved, *laudes haud immeritae*). Adv. *inique, injuste.*

inert, adj. *iners, immobilis, tardus;* see IDLE, INDOLENT. Adv. *tarde.* **inertness**, n. *inertia;* see INDOLENCE.

inestimable, adj. *inaestimabilis* (lit. = what cannot be estimated, Liv.); *unicus* (= alone of its kind), *mirus, mirificus, incredibilis* (= wonderful); *eximius, praestans, excellens, singularis* (= excellent). Adv. *eximie, excellenter, unice, praestanter, mire, mirifice, incredibiliter.*

inevitable, adj. *quod vitari* or *fugari non potest, inevitabilis, necessarius.* Adv. *necessario.*

inexact, adj. *haud exquisitus* or *accuratus* (of things), *indiligens* (of persons). **inexactness**, n. *indiligentia; —* of expression, *verba non accurata.*

inexcusable, adj. *quod excusari non potest, quod nihil excusationis habet.* Adv. use adj.

inexhaustible, adj. *quod exhauriri non potest, infinitus.*

inexorability, inexorableness, n. circumloc. by **inexorable**, adj. *inexorabilis;* = with unflinching severity, *severissimus, durus.* Adv. use adj.

inexpediency, n. *inutilitas,* or by adj. **inexpedient**, adj. *inutilis, inopportunus.*

inexperience, n. *imperitia* (= want of knowledge and experience); *inscitia, inscientia, insolentia* (= ignorance in gen.), *alcjs rei.* **inexperienced**, adj. *imperitus,* in anything, *alcjs rei;* = ignorant, *ignarus* (*alcjs rei*), = only a beginner, *rudis in alqâ re;* to be — in anything, *alqd nescire, in alqâ re non versatum esse, in alqâ re peregrinum,* or *hospitem,* or comb. *peregrinum atque hospitem esse.* **inexpert**, adj. = INEX-PERIENCED.

inexpiable, adj. *inexpiabilis.*

inexplicable, adj. *inexplicabilis.* Adv. use adj.

inexpressible, adj. *inauditus, inenarrabilis;* see INEFFABLE.

inexpugnable, adj. *inexpugnabilis.*

inextinguishable, adj. † *inex(s)tinctus* (e.g. *ignis, fames, nomen*), *quod reprimi* or *ex(s)tingui non potest.*

inextricable, adj. *inexplicabilis,* † *inextricabilis.* Adv. use adj.

infallibility, n. (e.g. of a remedy) *certum*

remedium. **infallible**, adj. 1, = certain, *certus, non dubius; exploratus;* 2, = one who is incapable of erring, *qui errare non potest.* Adv. *certo;* to be —, *omni errore carêre.*

infamous, adj. *infamis, turpis, flagitiosus, sceleratus, foedus.* Adv. *turpiter, flagitiose, scelerate, foede.* **infamy**, n. *infamia, turpitudo, dedecus, -oris, ignominia.*

infant, n. *infans, filiolus, filiola.* **infancy**, n. *infantia* (Plin., Tac.), or by *infans* (e.g. in his —, *cum esset infans*). **Infanta**, n. *filia regis Hispaniae.* **infanticide**, n. *infantium caedes.* **infantine**, adj. *puerilis.*

infantry, n. *pedites, -um;* or collectively, *pedes,* also *peditatus, -ûs.*

infatuate, v.tr. *infatuare* (= to lead, entice to an absurdity); *occaecare* (= to make blind, to blind); *pellicëre* (= to inveigle, wheedle, e.g. a girl). **infatuated**, adj. *amens, demens.* **in-fatuation**, n. *amentia, dementia, furor.*

infect, v.tr. = to infuse into a healthy body the virus of a diseased body, *facëre ut alqd transeat in alios* (i.e. lit. to pass over into others, of diseases) ; = to communicate bad qualities to anyone ; e.g. others became likewise —ed, *contagio morbi etiam in alios vulgata est;* fig. to — a person through one's bad qualities, *alqm vitiis suis inficëre;* to become —ed by errors, *inficî* or *imbui vitiis, imbui erroribus.* **infection**, n. *contagio* (lit. and fig. in pl.), † *contagium, contactus, -ûs;* see CONTAGION. **infectious, infective**, adj. in good Lat. circ. by *contagio morbi;* — *disease, pestilentia.*

infecundity, n. *sterilitas* (opp. *fertilitas*).

infelicitous, adj. *infelix;* see UNHAPPY. **infelicity**, n. *malum;* see UNHAPPINESS.

infer, v.tr. *concludëre, colligëre.* **inference**, n. 1, = the art of inferring, *argumentatio, conjectura;* 2, = conclusion drawn, *conclusio* (of a syllogism), *conjectura* (on general grounds); *quod colligi potest* (from, etc., *ex,* etc.); see CON-CLUSION.

inferior, I. adj. *inferior, deterior, minor.* **II.** n. (e.g. anyone's —), *inferior; ii qui inferiores sunt.*

infernal, adj. *infernus* (lit.); the — regions, *inferi,* † *Orcus;* = frightful, *terribilis* (fig.); = diabolical, *nefandus* (fig.).

infertile, adj. *sterilis;* see BARREN. **infertility**, n. *sterilitas.*

infest, v.tr. *infestum reddëre;* to — (the high seas) by piracy, *mare infestare latrociniis; vexare.* **infested**, adj. *infestus.*

infidelity, n. (in a Christian sense), *impietas;* = unfaithfulness, *infidelitas; perfidia* (= treachery); = to commit a breach of faith, *fidem movêre* or *violare* or *frangëre;* = to show —, *perfide agëre.*

infinite, adj. *infinitus* (= without limits), *immensus;* — mood, *verbum infinitum, modus infinitus* (gram.). Adv. *infinite, ad* or *in infinitum, ad* or *in immensum;* see ENDLESS. **infini-tesimal**, adj. *minimus, quam minimus.* **infinitude, infinity**, n. *infinitas* (= infinite extent), *infinitum tempus* (= endless time); *magna copia* (= great quantity).

infirm, adj. *infirmus, imbecillus, invalidus, debilis;* see WEAK. **infirmary**, n. *nosocomium* (νοσοκομεῖον) *valetudinarium* (Jct.). **infirmity**, n. 1, *infirmitas, imbecillitas, debilitas;* 2, a complaint, *vitium;* = a bodily complaint, *vitium corporis, morbus;* the —, the defects of the state, *reipublicae vitia.*

inflame, v.tr. 1, = to set on fire in a lit. sense, *accendëre, incendëre, inflammare;* 2 = to

excite or increase (e.g. passions), *incitare, inflammare, accendere, incendere;* see INCITE; 3, = to heat, as to — with wine, to exasperate (e.g. the enmity of parties), *inflammare;* to be inflamed, to grow hot, angry, and painful, *inflammari, ardere, flagrare.* **inflammable,** adj. *facilis ad exardescendum, quod celeriter accenditur.* **inflammation,** n. *inflammatio* (Plin.). **inflammatory,** adj. 1, *inflammans;* 2, fig. *seditiosus, turbulentus* (of speech).

inflate, v.tr. 1, = to swell or distend by injecting air, *inflare, sufflare;* to become inflated, *inflari;* 2, = to distend by blowing in, *spiritu distendere* (e.g. a bladder); 3, = to become inflated, *se inflare* or *sufflare* (e.g. of the frog); = to puff up (e.g. to — anyone), *inflare alcjs animum ad superbiam.* **inflated,** adj. 1, *inflatus, sufflatus;* 2, of speech, *tumidus, turgidus, inflatus.* **inflation,** n. *inflatio; fastus, -ūs,* = idle vanity, conceit, *superbia inanis.*

inflect, v.tr. 1, = to bend, *(in)flectere;* see BEND; 2, (in the grammat. sense) *declinare.* **inflection,** n. *flexus, -ūs,* = in the grammat. sense, *declinatio.* **inflexibility,** n. (of the temper), *obstinatio, pertinacia, pervicacia, perseverantia.* **inflexible,** adj. *rigidus* (lit. = stiff with cold, then fig. = rigid, inexorable), *obstinatus, pertinax, pervicax.* Adv. *obstinate, pertinaciter, pervicaciter, perseveranter.*

inflict, v.tr. *alci alqd afferre, inferre* (esp. evil); *alqm alqd re afficere* (= to affect anyone, make an impression with anything); to — ignominy, disgrace, *alci turpitudinem inferre* or *infligere, ignominiā alqm afficere* or *notare; alci ignominiam injungere;* to — wrong, *injuriam alci facere, inferre, injungere, imponere;* — punishment upon, *poenam de alqo capere* or *sumere, alqm poenā afficere, alqm punire;* see PUNISH. **infliction,** n. = an evil, *malum, incommodum.*

inflorescence, n. *flos.*

influence, I. n. *vis; effectus, -ūs* (i.e. *vis efficiendi,* e.g. of the moon), *pondus, -eris, auctoritas, momentum* (= weight), *potentia* (= power), *gratia* (= personal or political —); *amplitudo* (= greatness acquired through the office which a person holds); *dignitas* (= personal — through one's high social position); = — of a whole party, or of one person, through power and wealth, *opes, -um,* f.; = power of one body by coming in contact with another, *tactus, -ūs* (e.g. of the sun, *solis;* of the moon, *lunae);* = — of the stars and the moon, *vis stellarum ac lunae;* divine —, *afflatus, -ūs, instinctus* or *divinus;* to exercise an — upon anything, *valere, conducere, vim habere ad alqd* (= to contribute to, etc.); = to extend to, *pertinere ad alqd;* to have —, weight with a person, *multum auctoritate valere* or *posse, apud alqm multum gratiā valere;* to have no —, to be of no avail, *nihil posse, nihil valere, sine auctoritate esse;* to have a beneficial — upon anyone, *prodesse alci (rei);* an injurious —, *nocere alci (rei).* **II.** v.tr. *alqm movere, permovere, alci persuadere;* see above, to have —. **influential,** adj. *(alcjs rei) potens* (of animate and inanimate objects); = strong, through means, resources, favour, *validus* or *potens opibus, gratiā* (of persons); an — person, *qui multum valet; gravis* (= weighty), *amplus* (= — in position), *magna auctoritate.* **influx,** n. by *influere* (e.g. *influentes in Italiam Gallorum copias reprimere,* = to check the — of the Gauls into Italy).

inform, v.tr. 1, (lit. = to give form or shape to), *(ef)fingere, facere, efficere, conformare, informare;* hence, = to animate, † *animare;* 2, = to acquaint anyone with a fact, *alci alqd nuntiare* (= to announce in writing, or by a messenger); = to announce through a messenger, *alqd alci per nuntium declarare;* = to communicate a fact (as a certainty), *certiorem facere alqm alcjs rei* or *de alqā re; alqm alqd* or *de alqā re docere; alqd ad alqm deferre, praeferre;* — by a hint, *alci alqd significare;* 3, — against, *accusare nomen alcjs de alqā re,* or *alci alcjs rei deferre.* **informal,** adj. *inusitatus, irritus, insolitus;* of an election, by *vitium* (e.g. *consul vitio creatus).* Adv. *vitio, haud more.* **informality,** n. 1, *vitium* (in an election, etc.); 2, = without formality, *amice.* **informant,** n. *auctor alcjs rei.* **information,** n. 1, = intelligence, *nuntius;* written —, *lit(t)erae;* = the authority (for the truth of anything), *auctoritas;* = a doubtful —, rumour, *fama;* = indication of anything, *significatio alcjs rei;* to receive —, *nuntium accipere, certiorem fieri,* about anything, *alcjs rei* or *de alqā re;* to learn, hear —, *alqd accipere, audire, comperire;* 2, = knowledge, *scientia, doctrina;* see KNOWLEDGE; 3, = accusation, *delatio, indicium.* **informer,** n. *delator, index, -icis,* m. and f.

infraction, n. = non-observance, by *violatus* (e.g. of a treaty, *violatum* or *ruptum foedus).* **infrangible,** adj. *quod frangi non potest.*

infrequency, n. *raritas;* see RARE, RARITY. **infrequent,** adj. *rarus.*

infringe, v.tr. = to break (e.g. contracts), *frangere, violare.* **infringement,** n. *immunitio, diminutio* (= lessening, e.g. *gloriae); violatio alcjs rei* (e.g. of the international law, *juris gentium;* of a treaty, *foederis);* — of the law, *peccatum, delictum.* **infringer,** n. *qui alqd non (ob)servat, qui alqd violat, alcjs rei violator.*

infuriate, I. adj. *rabidus;* see FURIOUS. **II.** v.tr. *exasperare;* see ENRAGE.

infuse, v.tr. 1, = to pour in (e.g. a liquid), *infundere;* 2, see INSTIL. **infusion,** n. 1, = the act of pouring in, *infusio;* 2, = the thing itself in which a thing is steeped, *dilutum, decoctum* (Plin.).

ingathering, n. = collecting fruits, *perceptio frugum* or *fructuum.*

ingenerate, v.tr. *generare, gignere, parere.*

ingenious, adj. = subtle, *subtilis;* = one who shows taste and refinement, *luculentus, sol(l)ers, callidus* (= dexterous or clever), *artificiosus* (= highly finished both by nature and art); = of great talent, *ingenio praestans, ingenio summo, elati ingenii;* = acute, ready, *argutus* (e.g. an idea, *sententia).* Adv. *subtiliter, luculente(r), sol(l)erter, callide, artificiose, argute;* see CLEVER, DEXTEROUS, ACUTE. **ingenuity,** n. = quickness of invention (of persons), *(ingenii) acumen* or *acies;* = clearness of mind, *perspicacitas, prudentia;* = subtlety, *subtilitas;* = sagaciousness, *sagacitas;* = clearness in arguing, *acumen* or *subtilitas disserendi; ars* (= cleverness), *sol(l)ertia* (= dexterity), *machinatio* (=contrivance). **ingenuous,** adj. an — mind, *liber* (= without reserve); = open, straightforward, *ingenuus;* an —, candid letter, *epistula liberior; apertus* (= open), *simplex* (= simple). Adv. *libere, ingenue, aperte, simpliciter;* to speak —, *libere dicere.* **ingenuousness,** n. = openness of heart, *libertas* (also of speech); — in conversation, *sermo liberior;* with —, *libere, ingenue; ingenuitas* (= the character of a gentleman).

ingestion, n. *indere alqd alci rei* or *in alqd, ingerere in alqd.*

ingle-nook, n. *domus (intima);* in the —, *domi.*

inglorious, adj. *inglorius* (e.g. life); = ugly, *turpis* (morally); e.g. deed). Adv. *sine gloria;* = dishonourably, *turpiter.*

ingot, n. — of gold, *later,* *-eris,* m., *aureus;* — of silver, *later argenteus.*

ingraft, v.tr. = to insert a scion of one tree or plant into another for propagation, *inserēre;* ingrafted, *insitus.*

ingrained, adj. *insitus;* = produced by habit, *inveteratus.*

ingrate, I. adj. = ungrateful ; *ingratus* (= both —, and what does not pay), = unmindful of kindness received, *beneficii, beneficiorum immemor.* **II.** n. *homo ingratus.* **ingratiate,** v.tr. = to commend oneself to another's goodwill (of persons), *alcjs favorem* or *benevolentiam sibi conciliare* or *colligēre, gratiam inire ab alqo, ad* or *apud alqm; alcjs benevolentiam captare* (= to seek favour), *alcjs gratiam aucupari, alcjs favorem quaerēre;* to try to — oneself with the people, *aurem popularem captare, alcjs gratiam sequi;* to have ingratiated himself with anybody, *gratiosum esse alci* or *apud alqm;* very much, *gratiā florēre* or *multum gratiā valēre apud alqm;* to have ingratiated oneself very much with everybody, *apud omnes in summā gratiā esse.* **ingratitude,** n. *animus ingratus, beneficiorum immemor.*

ingredient, n. *pars;* = member, limb, component part, *membrum* (e.g. *hujus otiosae dignitatis haec fundamenta sunt, haec membra*); —s, *elementa alcjs rei;* that of which anything is an —, *res ex quibus conflatur et efficitur alqd;* or by n. pl. (e.g. the following —s, *haec*).

ingress, n. *ingressus, -ūs.*

ingulf, v.tr. 1, = to swallow up in a vast deep, *(de)vorare, haurire;* 2, = to cast into a gulf, *alqm in alqd detrudēre, de(j)icēre, (alqā re) obruēre* (e.g. *fluctibus*).

inhabit, v.tr. *habitare alqm locum, (in) alqo loco;* = to be resident anywhere, *(in)colēre alqm locum;* = to occupy, *tenēre alqm locum* (e.g. places, countries); densely inhabited, *frequens (tectis;* opp. *desertus*). **inhabitable,** adj. *habitabilis.* **inhabitant,** n. *incōla,* m. and f. (= resident in a town, country); *sessor* (in the same sense, in Nepos); *habitator* (= one who has his residence in a country, etc.); = tenant, *inquilinus* (opp. landlord, *dominus*); = citizen, *civis* (opp. *peregrinus,* a foreigner); = colonist, *colōnus; homo,* esp. in the pl. *homines* (= mankind); — of a town, *oppidi incōla, oppidanus;* — of a village, *incola vici, vicanus, paganus;* — of an island, *insulanus* (Cic.); — of a province, *provincialis.*

inhale, v.tr. *spiritu (spirando) ducēre, spiritu haurire.*

inharmonious, adj. 1, *discors, absonus, dissonus;* 2, = on bad terms, *dissentaneus, discrepans.* Adv. *haud consonanter, haud congruenter.*

inherent, adj. *insitus, innatus, proprius;* to be —, *in alqā re inesse.* Adv. *naturā,* in or per *se* (e.g. the thing is — evil, *quod in se malum est*).

inherit, v.tr. and intr. *heredem esse* (= to be heir), to anyone, *alci* (not *alcjs*), *hereditatem accipēre ab alqo, hereditatem consequi;* I have inherited, *hereditas venit ad me, hereditas mihi obvenit;* to have inherited a thing, *alqd hereditate possidēre* (= to possess a thing by virtue of a will); =to succeed, come to property, *hereditatem adire, cernēre* (the legal declaration of acceptance, *cretio*); to — everything, *heredem ex asse esse;* to — one-half, *heredem esse ex dimidiā parte;* to — onesixth, *heredem in sextante esse.* **inheritance,** n. *hereditas* (= right of —, and the — itself); I come to the property by —, *hereditas mihi venit, obtingit, obvenit, hereditas ad me venit* or *per-*

venit. **inherited,** adj. *patrius, paternus, avitus.*

inhibit, v.tr. *interdicēre;* see FORBID. **inhibition,** n. *interdictum;* see PROHIBITION.

inhospitable, adj. † *inhospitalis,* † *inhospitus.* **inhospitality,** n. *inhospitalitas* or by *inhospitalis;* see CHURLISH.

inhuman, adj. *inhumanus* (= unfeeling, e.g. character, *ingenium;* cruelty, *crudelitas;* man, *homo*); = monstrous, *immanis* (of things and persons); = unfeeling, *ferus* (of persons), comb. *ferus et immanis, crudelis, saevus, atrox, durus, ferreus.* Adv. *inhumane, crudeliter, saeve, atrociter, dure, duriter.* **inhumanity,** n. *inhumanitas, immanitas, feritas, crudelitas, saevitas, atrocitas.*

inimical, adj. *inimicus;* see HOSTILE.

inimitability, n. by **inimitable,** adj. *non imitabilis, inimitabilis* (Quint.), or by *quod nulla ars* (or *nemo*) *consequi potest imitando.* Adv. by adj.

iniquitous, adj. = unfair, *injustus, iniquus.* Adv. *injuste, inique.* **iniquity,** n. *injustitia, iniquitas;* see WICKED.

initial, I. adj. by *initio positus,* or *primus.* **II.** n. = the first letter of a name, *prima lit(t)era.* **initiate,** v.tr. 1, in religious sense, *initiare;* 2, = to begin, *coepisse;* see BEGIN. **initiation,** n. 1, by *initiare;* 2, *initium.* **initiative,** adj. 1, by verb INITIATE; 2, *quod initio factum est, primus.*

inject, v.tr. *(siphonis ope) infundēre.*

injudicious, adj. *nullius consilii* (=without judgment); *imprudens* (= without caution), *stultus* (= silly); *inconsultus* (= without considering); = inconsiderate, *inconsideratus* (e.g. desires); = rash, *temerarius* (e.g. expression, *vox*). Adv. *inconsulte, inconsiderate* or *parum considerate, temere.* **injudiciousness,** n. *imprudentia, stultitia,* or by adj.

injunction, n. *interdictum.*

injure, v.tr. *laedēre, sauciare, vulnerare,* comb. *laedēre et vulnerare, lacerare* (=to tear to pieces), fig. *alci nocēre* (e.g. *optimum virum verborum contumeliis*), *violare* (= to treat with violence); the storm —s the ship, *tempestas afflictat navem.* **injury,** n. 1, as act, *vulneratio, sauciatio;* without — to duty, *salvo officio;* 2, = harm, *detrimentum, incommodum, damnum* (= loss), *malum* (= evil), *vulnus, -ēris* (=wound), *noxia* (= trespass); to do anyone an —, *injuriam alci facēre;* to forgive an —, *injuriam condonare.* **injurer,** n. *qui injuriam facit.* **injurious,** adj. *noxius, injuriosus, damnosus, gravis* (of air), *malus, adversus,* † *contrarius, iniquus;* — words, *contumeliae* or *verba contumeliosa.* Adv. *injuriose, damnose, graviter, male, contumeliose.*

injustice, n. *injustitia* (of unjust proceedings); — done, *injuria factum;* to commit an —, *injuriam facēre, injuste facēre.*

ink, n. *atramentum;* an —horn, —stand, —pot, * *atramentarium.* **inky,** adj. *atramento foedatus.*

inkling, n. *susurrus;* see WHISPER, HINT.

inland, adj. *mediterraneus.*

inlay, v.tr. *inserēre, variare, distinguēre;* see ADORN.

inlet, n. 1, *aditus, -ūs;* 2, of the sea, *aestuarium.*

inly, adv. *penitus.*

inmate, n. = lodger, *deversor, inquilinus;* of a country, *incola,* m. and f.; see INHABITANT.

inmost, innermost, adj. *intimus;* the — part, *intima pars; intima, -orum; viscera, -um,* pl. (=entrails, bowels, fig. = the noblest parts, e.g. of the heart, the state, etc.); a thing is impressed in my — heart, *alqd haeret mihi in visceribus;* also by *intimus* or *penitus* (e.g. he proceeded to the — parts of Macedonia to conceal himself, *se abdidit in intimam Macedoniam, penitus se abdidit in Macedoniam*), or, if speaking of forests, by *densissimus* (e.g. to retreat into the — parts of the forests, *se in densissimas silvas abdidit*).

inn, n. *deversori(ol)um, hospitium, caupona* (= a tavern). **innkeeper,** n. *caupo.*

innate, adj. *innatus, ingeneratus, insitus,* comb. *insitus et innatus; proprius;* = natural, *naturalis, nativus* (opp. *assumptus, adventicius,* i.e. artificially acquired); = inherited, *congeneratus; avitus* (e.g. an evil, *malum);* the old and — pride of the Claudian family, *vetus atque insita Claudiae familiae superbia;* — ideas, *notiones (in animo insitae).*

inner, adj. = interior, *interior* (opp. *exterior);* = what is going on in the interior of the country, etc., *intestinus* (opp. *externus,* foreign); = what is going on at home, in one's own country, *domesticus* (opp. *foris,* abroad), comb. *intestinus ac domesticus;* the — man, *animus;* the interior affairs, *res domesticae* (= home affairs); = intellectual (e.g. qualities, *bona animi, virtutes animi;* = natural feeling, *natura.* Adv. *intus;* within, *interius* (opp. *exterius).*

innocence, n. *innocentia;* = purity, incorruptness, *integritas,* comb. *integritas atque innocentia;* = simplicity, sincerity, *simplicitas;* to prove one's —, *se purgare alci;* = modesty, *pudicitia;* = chastity, *castitas,* comb. *integritas pudicitiaque;* — of the heart, *castus animus purusque.* **innocent, I.** adj. **1,** = without crime, *innocens* (= doing no harm), †*immerens,* †*immeritus* (= free from guilt, guiltless, *insons, culpâ vacuus* or *carens;* = pure, free from all sin, not to be seduced, *integer, sanctus;* to be — of a thing, *insontem esse alcjs rei* (e.g. of a public decree, *consilii publici);* **2,** = chaste, *integer* (= who leads a moral life); = discreet, *pudicus;* = chaste, who does nothing unchaste, *castus et integer.* Adv. *integre, pudice, caste,* comb. *pure et caste, caste integreque;* = without bad intention, *imprudenter, per inscitiam.* **II.** n. = idiot, *(homo) stultissimus.* **innocuous,** adj. = harmless, *innocuus* (= not able to do harm), to anyone, *alci;* = doing no harm, *innoxius,* to anyone, *alci;* = innocent, *innocens* (all three of persons and things); to be —, *non* or *nihil nocêre.*

innovate, v.tr. *novare, mutare* (=to change); see INNOVATION hereafter. **innovation,** n. **1,** = renewing, *renovatio;* **2,** = the thing itself, *res nova;* to be fond of making —s (in the state), *rerum novarum cupidum esse, rerum commutandarum* or *evertendarum cupidum esse;* fondness of making —s in the state of government, *rerum novarum studium.* **innovator,** n. = fond of innovations, *novitatis cupidus* (in gen.).

innumerable, adj. *innumerabilis,* †*innumerus;* = endless, *infinitus,* comb. *infinitus prope et innumerabilis;* an indefinite number, *sescenti.*

inobservance, n. *neglegentia (neglig-);* see INADVERTENCY, DISOBEDIENCE. **inobservant,** adj. *neglegens (neglig-).*

inoculate, v.tr. **1,** in gardening, *inoculare* (Col.); **2,** med. t.t. * *variolas inserêre* has been suggested.

inodorous, adj. *odore carens.*

inoffensive, adj. *quod nihil habet offensionis;* simple, *simplex.* Adv. *simpliciter.* **inoffen-**

siveness, n. by adj. INOFFENSIVE; see INNOCENT.

inopportune, adj. *inopportunus;* see INCONVENIENT. Adv. *haud opportune.*

inordinate, adj. *immoderatus, immodicus, nimius, incredibilis, singularis, mirificus, mirus.* Adv. *praeter modum, immoderate, immodice, nimis, nimium, incredibiliter, singulariter, mirifice, mire.*

inorganic, adj. e.g. — bodies, *corpora nullâ cohaerendi naturâ* (Cic.).

inquest, n. *quaestio;* to hold an —, *de alqâ re* (e.g. *de morte) quaerêre.*

inquietude, n. *sol(l)icitudo;* see DISQUIET.

inquire, v.intr. = to ask a question, *alqd* or *de alqâ re quaerêre* (= to ask in general); to — strictly after, *alqd requirêre, exquirêre, perquirêre; de alqâ re sciscitare; percontari (percunct-) alqd* or with *utrum* or *ne;* = to make oneself acquainted with a thing, *cognoscêre de alqâ re;* to — of persons after a thing, *alqd ab* or *ex alqo quaerêre, requirêre, exquirêre, alqm de alqâ re interrogare;* — about anything in writing, *sciscitari per lit(t)eras de alqâ re;* — into, *de alqâ re cognoscêre* or *quaerêre, de alqâ re* or *in alqd inquirêre, alqd investigare, indagare.* **inquiry,** n. **1,** = act of inquiring, *indagatio; investigatio* (=tracing); = examination, *cognitio; percontatio (percunct-)* (= questioning); — of the truth, *investigatio veri, veri inquisitio atque investigatio;* =the critical examination of the truth, *cognitio;* to be entirely bent upon the — of a thing, *totum se in alqâ re exquirendâ collocare;* = a diligent research, *diligentia;* to find by —, *inquirendo reperire;* **2,** legal t.t., = examination, *cognitio* (= inspection with the view of becoming acquainted with a thing, e.g. of the town, *urbis;* then = — by a magistrate or jury); *quaestio* (in gen., and in a court); *inquisitio* (lit. = examination of anything, e.g. of the truth, *veri;* in the law = — about a person's life and any crime committed by him); — for a capital offence, *cognitio rei capitalis;* to demand a judicial —, *inquisitionem in alqm postulare* (= to inquire into the conduct of, in order to accuse); to institute an —, *quaestionem habêre* or *instituêre, cognitionem constituêre,* about, into anything, *alqd* or *de alqâ re quaerêre, quaestionem de alqâ re habêre;* to come to an — (e.g. it will come to a trial), *venire in quaestionem* or *in cognitionem, cognosci.* **inquisition,** n. **1,** see INQUIRY; **2,** in some Catholic countries = a tribunal for trying heretics, *quaesitores;* a trial of this kind, *inquisitio de fide habita.* **inquisitive,** adj. *audiendi cupidus* or *avidus,* or *studiosus, curiosus.* Adv. *curiose.* **inquisitiveness,** n. *cupiditas, studium,* or *aviditas audiendi* or *cognoscendi.* **inquisitor,** n. = one who inquires by virtue of his office, *quaesitor;* to be the —, to be the person charged with an inquiry, an examination, trial, *cognoscêre, into,* of a thing, *alqd.*

inroad, n. *irruptio, incursio, incursus, -ûs* (the latter also of rivers); to make an —, *irruptionem* or *incursionem facêre in alqd;* = a sally, attack, excursion, *excursio, excursus, -ûs;* = a single expedition, movement in a campaign, *expeditio;* — into the enemy's land, *incursio in fines hostium facta.*

insalubrious, adj. *insaluber;* = oppressive, hence unfavourable to health, *gravis* (e.g. temperature, *caelum),* comb. *gravis et pestilens;* — air or climate, *pestilentia* or *gravitas caeli; intemperies caeli.* **insalubrity,** n. — of a place, *pestilens loci natura;* — of the air, *pestilentia* or *gravitas* or *intemperies caeli;* see UNHEALTHY.

insane, adj. *insanus* (lit. and fig.), *mente captus,* (of one who is out of his mind, silly,

foolish, and of anything that is so) *amens, demens* (lit. and fig., e.g. a scheme, *consilium, ratio*); = mad, raving, *furiosus, excors, vecors* (also = foolish), *secors* (rare), (of persons and things, e.g. a desire, *cupiditas*); = absurd, childish, *stultus, ineptus* (of persons and things). Adv. *dementer, insane, furiose, stulte, inepte.*

insanity, n. *insania* (of lunatics, or in gen. of extreme passion), *furor* (= fury, of anyone that flies into a passion), *amentia, dementia, vecordia* (= madness or silliness), *secordia* (rare), *stultitia* (= silliness).

insatiable, adj. *insatiabilis, inexplebilis* (lit. and fig.), *insaturabilis* (lit., e.g. belly, *abdomen*); an — desire for reading, *legendi aviditas.* Adv. by adj.

inscribe, v.tr. = to mark with letters, *inscribĕre, adscribĕre, consignare.* **inscription,** n. on monuments, coins, statues, *inscriptio, index, -icis,* m. and f. (both in gen.), (of a book, picture, statue); *titulus* (= *inscriptio* and *index*; then = epitaph, *titulus (sepulc(h)ri)*; also = a note, card, as a sign that a certain thing is to be sold or let); *epigramma, -ătis,* n., an — at the foot of a statue, a gift, a tombstone, etc. ; *carmen* (in verses, e.g., over the entrance of a temple) ; to place an — upon anything, *titulum inscribĕre alci rei, alqd inscribĕre.*

inscrutability, n. *obscuritas,* or by **inscrutable,** adj. *inexplicabilis, obscurus.*

insect, n. *insectum* (Plin.); *bestiola* (= a small animal, e.g. the wire-worm).

insecure, adj. *non* with *tutus, munitus* or *firmus, infestus* (of roads, etc., = beset by robbers), *instabilis, incertus, lubricus* (of footing). Adv. *non* with *tuto, firme, firmiter.* **insecurity,** n. by adj. (e.g. the — of the roads, *itinera infesta*).

insensate, adj., see INSANE, INSENSIBLE.

insensible, adj. 1, *sensûs expers;* to be —, *sensu carēre;* 2, fig., *durus, lentus.* Adv. *sensim, pedetemptim (pedetent-);* see FEELING. **insensibility,** n. 1, *torpor;* 2, *animus durus, lentitudo;* see also CRUELTY.

inseparability, n. by **inseparable,** adj. = *indissoluble, indissolubilis;* = indivisible, *individuus;* an — friend, *amicus fidissimus.* Adv. use adj. INSEPARABLE.

insert, v.tr. *inserĕre alci rei,* or *in alqd, includĕre alci rei,* or *in alqd, inter(j)icĕre, interponĕre* (= to put in between, e.g. intercalary months, *intercalatos menses;* then in general as a parenthesis, either in speaking or in writing) ; *supplēre* (= to supply, add, what was still wanting); *addĕre alqd alci rei,* or *in* with accus. (in general, = to add anything, e.g. I have inserted something in my speech, *in orationem addidi quaedam*) ; *adscribĕre alqd in alqd,* or *in alqd re* (e.g. *diem in lit(t)eris,* the date in a letter) ; = to fasten in, *infigĕre alci rei* or *in alqd;* = to fix in the ground, plant, *defigĕre in alqd* or *in alqd re.* **insertion,** n. 1, by verb INSERT; 2, in rhet., the — of a clause = parenthesis, *interpositio.*

inside, I. n. *pars interior.* **II.** adv. *intus.* **III.** prep. *in* with abl., *intra* with accus.; see WITHIN.

insidious, adj. *insidiosus, fallax, dolosus, fraudulentus.* Adv. *insidiose, fallaciter, dolose, fraudulenter.* **insidiousness,** n. *fallacia, dolus, fraus;* see DECEITFUL.

insight, n. = discernment, *intellegentia (intellig-);* = perfect knowledge, understanding, seeing through, *perspicientia;* of the truth, *veri;* a deeper — into, knowledge of things (in the highest sense), *sapientia;* = judgment, the opinion based upon judgment, *judicium, consilium;* = a clear knowledge and —, *cognitio,*

of and into, *alcjs rei;* no —, want of judgment, *imprudentia;* a man of deep —, *vir prudentissimus, vir multi* or *magni consilii plenus;* men of — and talent, *viri docti et eruditi;* see KNOWLEDGE.

insignia, n. *fasces, -ium,* m., *insignia, -ium.*

insignificant, adj. 1, = small, *parvus, exiguus, minutus;* 2, = unimportant, *lēvis, nullius momenti.* **insignificance,** n. 1, *exiguitas;* 2, *mediocritas* (rare), *nullius* or *parvi momenti.*

insincere, adj. *falsus, simulatus, fucosus, fucatus, fallax, fraudulentus, dolosus, infidus* or *infidelis* (rare). Adv. *falso, fallaciter, simulate, fraudulente, dolose.* **insincerity,** n. *fucus, fallacia* (e.g. *sine fuco et fallaciis*), *fraus, -dis,* f., *dolus, simulatio, infidelitas.*

insinuate, v.tr. and intr. 1, = to push, work oneself into favour, *se insinuare, arrepĕre, irrepĕre, obrepĕre,* † *surrepĕre in alqd* (e.g. *amicitiam*), *gratiam sibi parĕre apud alqm* (= to ingratiate oneself); 2, = to suggest by remote allusion, *alci alqd significare* (= to give to understand); see HINT. **insinuation,** n. 1, *blanditiae;* 2, *significatio.* **insinuating,** adj. *blandus* (= bland). Adv. *blande.*

insipid, adj. 1, *nihil sapiens, insulsus,* † *elutus;* 2, fig., *insulsus, absurdus, ineptus, frigidus, jejunus, inanis, exilis;* (= tasteless, lit. *insipidus* is quite late); = not seasoned, *non conditus;* see ABSURD. Adv. *insulse, absurde, inepte, frigide, jejune, inaniter, exiliter.* **insipidity,** n. by INSIPID, (e.g. the — of the food, *cibi voluptate carentes;* if fig. see ABSURDITY.

insist, v.intr. *alqd suadēre, hortari;* = to ask for, *alqd exigĕre, postulare, (ex)poscĕre, (ef)flagitare;* = to state strongly, *declarare, asseverare, dicĕre, ab alqo contendĕre ut* or *de alqâ re faciendâ.*

insnare, v.tr. *irretire* (lit. and fig.); see ENSNARE.

insobriety, n. *intemperantia;* see DRUNKENNESS.

insolence, n. *insolentia;* = pride, *superbia, contumacia, audacia, impudentia, arrogantia.* **insolent,** adj. *insolens, contumax, audax, impudens, arrogans.* Adv. *insolenter, contumaciter, audaciter, impudenter, arroganter, superbe.*

insoluble, adj. 1, *quod liquefieri non potest;* 2, fig. *inexplicabilis, difficilis et inexplicabilis.*

insolvent, adj. *qui non est solvendo* or *ad solvendum.* **insolvency,** n. *non solvendo esse,* or *foro cedĕre;* see BANKRUPT.

insomuch, adv. *sic, ita, hoc* or *eo modo, adeo;* under this condition, *hâc* or *eâ condicione, hâc lege;* so far, *eo usque;* see So.

inspect, v.tr. *visĕre, invisĕre* (= to view, lit.); *a(d)spicĕre* (= to look on); *inspicĕre, introspicĕre, perspicĕre* (= to look through, examine); = to examine, *intueri, contemplari oculis, (col)lustrare;* to —, superintend anything, *alqd curare, regĕre, moderari;* see EXAMINE. **inspection,** n. 1, = *r* looking on, by verbs; 2, = watch, guardianship, superintendence, *cura* (= care over anything, e.g. the treasury, *aerarii*); *custodia,* comb. *cura custodiaque;* = protection, protecting care, *tutela;* = superintendence, — of a chairman, an officer, *praesidium;* = watch over the public morals, *praefectura morum;* to have the —, superintendence over anything, *alci rei praeesse, praefectum esse, alci rei praesidēre* (as chairman, e.g. over public games, the affairs of the town); to have anyone under one's —, *alqm custodire.* **inspector,** n. *custos, -ōdis* (m. and f.), *curator* (= keeper, librarian); = one who is set over a thing, *praeses, -ĭdis,* m. and f., *praefectus, -i,* m. and f.), *praeses, -ĭdis,* m. and f., *praefectus,* one who superintends the public morals, *praefectus moribus, censor;* — of the public high-ways, *curator viarum;* = superintendent of a certain district of a town (as regards its clean-liness, etc.), *magister vici, vicomagister* (Suet.); — of the public buildings and chief constable, *aedilis* (in Rome). **inspectorship,** n. *custodis munus, -ēris, cura, praefectura.*

inspiration, n. 1, = the inhaling of air, *spiritus, -ūs;* 2, = — by the Holy Spirit, *instinctus (-ūs) divinus, instinctus divinus afflatusque, inspiratio* (Eccl.) ; by divine ⁻, through God's command, *divinitus;* 3, = counsel, *monitus, -ūs, consilium* (= advice, what has been suggested); at anyone's ⁻, see SUGGESTION. **inspire,** v.tr. = to infuse ideas, *suggerĕre, sub(j)icĕre alci algd* (= to suggest); as theol. t.t., to — by the Holy Spirit, *inspirare;* = to warn, advise, *monēre alqm algd* or *monēre alqm ut,* etc. ; to — with, instil, *alci in(j)icĕre;* to excite, — with, instil into anyone courage, vigour, *excitare, incitare, incendĕre, inflammare;* = to delight, *laetitiā or gaudio perfundĕre.* **inspired,** adj. *divino spiritu inflatus* or *tactus, mente incitatus* (in gen.); = fanatic, of enthusiasm approaching to madness, *fanaticus, furens, furibundus.* **inspirer,** n. see INSPIRE. **inspirit,** v.tr. *animum alci addĕre;* see ENCOURAGE.

instability, n. *inconstantia;* see INCONSTANCY. **instable,** adj. *inconstans;* see INCONSTANT.

install, v.tr. *inaugurare* (under the celebration of auguries). **installation,** n. by *inaugurare.* **instalment,** n. *prima (secunda,* etc.) *pensio, pars, portio;* to pay by —, *in antecessum dare;* to receive, to be paid by —, *in antecessum accipĕre* (Sen.).

instance, I. n. 1, = request, *preces, -um,* more usually by abl. abs. (e.g. at the — of these men, *his petentibus,* or *his auctoribus);* 2, = example, *exemplum, specimen;* for —, *verbi* or *exempli caus(s)ā or gratiā.* II. v.tr. *referre, dicĕre;* see MENTION. **instant,** I. adj. 1, = urgent, *vehemens, intentus, acer, magni momenti, gravis* (= serious); 2, = immediate, *praesens.* II. n. *punctum temporis* (= the smallest point in duration); = a moment, as part of an hour, *momentum* or *vestigium temporis, momentum horae;* in an —, *momento temporis;* to the —, *ad tempus;* not an —, *ne minimam partem temporis;* in every —, *omni puncto temporis, nullo temporis puncto intermisso;* the, this very —, by *ipse* (e.g. the very — of his departure, *suā ipsā profectione;* at the very —, *ipso tempore);* to an —, *ad tempus;* for the —, *ad tempus, temporis caus(s)ā;* for the present —, *in praesens, in praesentiā* (opp. *in posterum);* = a favourable opportunity, *tempus opportunum, temporis opportunitas or occasio;* not to allow the — to pass, *tempori or temporis occasioni non deesse;* during the last —, *in ipsā morte.* Adv. = immediately, *statim, confestim, protinus, e vestigio, extemplo, continuo;* = urgently, *intente, acriter, vehementer, impense, etiam atque etiam, magnopere.* **instantaneous,** adj. *brevissimus* (= of very short duration); = transient, *fugax* (= swift); sudden, *subitus* (e.g. *consilia);* = present, momentary, *praesens* (e.g. possibility, *facultas).* Adv. *puncto* or *momento temporis, e vestigio;* = by-and-by, immediately, *extemplo.*

instate, v.tr. = to establish in a rank or condition, by *constituĕre;* to — in an office (in general), *munus alci mandare* or *assignare* or *deferre, muneri alqm praeficĕre* or *praeponĕre;* to — in any particular office, *apponĕre* (e.g. in the office of guardian, *alqm custodem alcjs);* see [INSTALL.

instead, prep. *loco* or *in locum alcjs* or *alejs rei;* = in the place of, *vice* (Plin.), *in vicem* or *vicem alcjs* or *alcjs rei (meum, tuam, nostram, vicem,* in my, etc., stead ; — of you all, *vestram omnium vicem) ; pro* with the abl., (= for, as good as, in comparison with, in proportion to) ; I was invited — of him, *in locum ejus invitatus sum;* he had called them Quirites — of soldiers, *Quirites eos pro militibus appellaverat;* — of, = rather than, with the pres. part., *tantum abest ut ... ut,* etc. (= so far from ... he rather, sooner, etc.) ; = not only did not ... but, *non modo non ... sed etiam;* instead of ... he rather, *adeo non, adeo nihil ... ut;* instead of ... he only, *magis quam* (in Lat. the second clause comes first; e.g. — of frightening him, it only brought him into greater rage, *accenderat eum magis quam conterruerat);* — of taking to flight, *omissā fugā;* sometimes also by *cum* (e.g. — of praising him, he reproved him, *cum laudare deheret, eum vituperavit).*

instep, n. *pes superior.*

instigate, v.tr. *instigare* (e.g. *canes in alqm,* = to set on, and fig.), *concitare, incitare.* **instigation,** n. *impulsus, -ūs, stimulus, instinctus, -ūs;* at your —, *te auctore.* **instigator,** n. *auctor, concitator, impulsor, suasor, machinator, princeps, -ipis.*

instil, v.tr. 1, = to infuse by drops, in general, *in os alcjs in(j)icĕre or indĕre or ingerĕre; instillare* (by drops, e.g. milk); 2, = to fill with, *alqm alqā re implēre;* to — admiration, fig., *alqm admiratione imbuĕre, admirationem alci in(j)icĕre*

instinct, I. n. animal —, *natura;* from one's own —, *natura duce;* = natural desire, *appetitio* (= the act of striving, e.g. after knowledge, *cognitionis); appetitus, -ūs* (= natural feeling, especially animal); (both *appetitio* and *appetitus* are used by Cic. for the Greek ὁρμή = desire in general); a sudden impulse, *impetus, -ūs;* = inward desire, inclination, taste, *studium;* sensual —, *studia prava* or *turpia* or *humilia.* II. adj. — with anything, *alqā re imbutus.* **instinctive,** adj. *naturalis, duce naturā suā* (e.g. to do anything, *facĕre alqd).* Adv. *naturā (duce), naturaliter.*

institute, I. v.tr. = to found (e.g. a court), *condĕre* (lit. to put together, hence to accomplish the building or the establishing of anything, e.g. an empire, *imperium);* to — a thing, *instituĕre;* to — a monarchy, *regnum statuĕre, regem creare* (= to create a king); to — erect, place, *constituĕre* (e.g. a monument, *monumentum);* to — friendship, *conciliare amicitiam;* a union, wedding, *nuptias ;* peace, *pacem;* to — again, re-establish, *reconciliare* (e.g. peace, *pacem);* to effect, *facĕre* (e.g. a treaty, alliance, *foedus, -ĕris,* n. ; peace, *pacem).* II. n. see INSTITUTION. **institution,** n. 1, = foundation, *initium* (= beginning), or *verb* (e.g. after the — of the state, *post quam civitas instituta est,* or *post civitatem institutam,* or by abl. abs., *civitate institutā);* 2, = custom, *institutum, lex, mos, moris,* m. ; 3, = society, *societas, collegium, sodalitas ;* 4, = school, *ludus (lit(t)erarum), schola;* see SCHOOL.

instruct, v.tr. 1, *erudire* (= to draw out of a state of comparative rudeness and ignorance), in anything, *in alqā re;* = to teach, *alqm alqd docēre;* comb. *erudire atque docēre, docēre atque erudire;* = to prepare anyone for a certain avocation, *instituĕre alqd alqd;* or by *instruĕre* (lit. to provide anyone with what is necessary, *doctrinis, artibus,* = to instruct in); to lecture, *praecipĕre* or *tradĕre alqd* or *de alqā re, tradĕre praecepta alcjs rei;* to — anyone in elocution, *alqm ad dicendum instituĕre;* see ORDER ; to be instructed by anyone, *discĕre ab alqo;* to **be** instructed in

anything by anyone, *discĕre alqd* (or **with in-fin.**); 2, = order, *alqd alci praescribĕre* (e.g. *quae sint agenda*), *alci committĕre* or *mandare ut ;* see ORDER, CHARGE. **instructed,** adj. *eruditus* (= brought out of a state of ignorance, educated); one who has received a learned, a literary education, *doctus, doctrinâ instructus.* **instruction,** n. 1, = the act of teaching, *institutio* (= — in gen., information), in anything, *alcjs rei ;* = the bringing up of anyone from a state of ignorance, *eruditio ;* = education in a school, or from a master, *disciplina ; —* given by a teacher, *doctrina ; praeceptum* (= lesson); 2, = direction, *praeceptio* (= the act of prescribing), *praeceptum* (= precept), *praescriptum, mandatum* (= charge given to anyone, e.g. an ambassador); his —s, *alci mandare ut ;* see INSTRUCT, 2. **instructive,** adj. *utilis.* Adv. *utiliter.* **instructor,** n. *magister, doctor, praeceptor, dux* (= leader).

instrument, n. 1, = tool, *utensilia, -ium,* n. (= utensils in a household, and in general); = furniture, *supellex ;* = vessels, culinary —s, a soldier's cooking apparatus, *vasa, -orum ;* = tools for carrying on trade, *instrumentum* (collectively or in pl., e.g. agricultural, *rusticum) ;* = some large, artificial —, machine, *machina ;* an iron —, *feramentum ;* musical — with strings, *fides, -ium ;* = horn, *cornu ;* = trumpet, *tuba ;* = pipe, *tibia ;* to sing to an —, *ad chordarum sonum cantare ;* 2, = means, *minister* (fig.); to use anyone **as an** — for anything, *alcjs operâ alqd efficĕre ;* **3,** in law and in gen. (= a deed), *lit(t)erae, tabulae* (= anything in writing); to draw up an — in writing, *lit(t)eris alqd consignare.* **instrumental,** adj. 1, = contributing aid, *utilis* (= useful); convenient, *commodus, accommodatus, aptus ;* you were — in hindering, *per te stetit quominus,* etc., or te *auctore ;* to be —, *ad alqd valēre, alcjs operâ effici, alci prodesse ;* 2, = pertaining to music, — music, *cantus tibiarum nervorumque* or *nervorum et tibiarum ;* — vocal music, *chordarum sonitus et vocis cantus, vocum nervorumque cantus, -ûs.* **instrumentality,** n. *opera, ministerium,* or by *per* or *alcjs operâ* or abl. abs. (*e.g. per te* or *tuâ operâ* or *te auctore*).

insubordination, n. *disciplina nulla* (= no order, discipline); = licentiousness, *licentia, nimia licentia,* comb. *intemperantia et nimia licentia.* **insubordinate,** adj. *nullâ disciplinâ coercitus, intemperans, seditiosus, turbulentus,* male or *parum oboediens (obed-)* or *obtemperans.* Adv. *seditiose, turbulente(r).*

insufferable, adj. *intolerabilis ;* see INTOLERABLE.

insufficient, adj. *haud sufficiens, haud satis (magnus,* etc.), *impar* (= unequal); see INADEQUATE. Adv. *haud satis, parum.* **insufficiency,** n. *inopia, imbecillitas* (= weakness), *angustiae, egestas, paupertas* (= poverty).

insular, adj. by *insula* (e.g. through our — position, *eo ipso quod insulam incolimus*).

insult, I. n. *injuria, injuria alci illata, ab alqo illata, contumelia, probrum, maledictum ;* = disgrace, *dedecus, -ŏris,* n., *ignominia, indignitas.* **II.** v.tr. *alci maledicĕre* (= abuse), *contumeliam alci imponĕre ;* without any —, *sine ullâ contumeliâ ;* to be insulted, *injuriam accipĕre* or *pati ;* easily insulted, *animus mollis ad accipiendam offensionem ;* to feel yourself insulted, *injuriam sibi factam putare ;* insulted by something, *alqd in* or *ad contumeliam accipĕre* (= to take as an —). **insulting,** adj. *contumeliosus, probrosus, maledicus, maledicens ;* — words, *voces contumeliosae, verborum contumeliae.* Adv. *contumeliose, maledice, per ludibrium.*

24

insuperable, adj. *in(ex)superabilis* (lit., = what cannot be surmounted, of mountains), *quod superari non potest* (lit. and fig.); = invincible, *invictus* (of persons).

insupportable, adj. see INTOLERABLE.

insurance, n. *fides de damno resarciendo interposita.* **insure,** v.tr. and intr. *damnum praestare, de alqâ re cavēre.*

insurgent, adj. and n. *seditiosus, turbulentus.* **insurrection,** n. *rebellio, seditio, motus, -ûs, tumultus, -ûs.* **insurrectionary,** adj. *seditiosus ;* see INSURGENT.

insusceptibility, n. by **insusceptible,** adj. see INSENSIBLE.

intact, adj. *intactus ; integer* (= untouched), *salvus, incolumis* (= unharmed).

intangible, n. *quod sentire* or *sensibus percipĕre non possumus.*

integral, adj. *pars ac totum necessaria.* **integrity,** n. 1, = entireness (e.g. — of the empire), adj. *regnum integrum ;* 2, = incorruptness, *integritas, probitas, abstinentia, innocentia, sanctitas, castitas* (= purity).

integument, n. (= that which naturally covers a thing, but chiefly a term in anatomy), *cutis* = skin or —), *teg(u)men, (in)teg(u)mentum, operimentum* (= a covering, protection), *velamentum, velum* (= a covering, cloak), *involucrum* (= a wrapper).

intellect, n. *mens, -ntis,* f., *ingenium, ingenii vis, animus, cogitatio, intellegentia, quae pars animi rationis atque intellegentiae particeps est ;* acuteness of —, *ingenii acumen* or *acies, subtilitas, sagacitas.* **intellectual,** adj. by genit. of *mens,* etc. **intelligence,** n. 1, *perspicacitas, sol(l)ertia ;* see INTELLECT ; 2, = news, *nuntius ;* see NEWS. **intelligencer,** n. = one who sends or conveys intelligence, *nuntius, legatus* (= an ambassador); = one who gives notice of transactions in writing, a newspaper-writer, journalist, *diurnorum scriptor.* **intelligent,** adj. *mente praeditus* (= gifted with understanding); one who has understanding, and uses it, *mentis compos, sanus ;* = wise, *intellegens, sapiens, prudens, sciens,* comb. *prudens et sciens,* (*per)acutus, astutus, sol(l)ers ;* a very — man, *homo ingenio prudentiâque acutissimus ;* to be —, *sapĕre.* Adv. *intellegenter, sapienter, prudenter, scienter, acute, astute, sol(l)erter.* **intelligible,** adj. *quod facile intellegi potest ;* = well explained, *explicatus ;* = clear, *perspicuus ;* = plain, not confused, *planus ;* = manifest, *apertus* (lit., open to everybody, also of the speaker); = distinct, *distinctus* (= well arranged, e.g. of the language, also of the person who speaks it, e.g. *utroque distinctior Cicero,* Tac.). Adv. *perspicue, plane, aperte, distincte, explicate.*

intemperance, n. *intemperantia, immoderatio, impotentia ;* in drink, *ebrietas.* **intemperate,** adj. *intemperans, impotens, immodicus, immoderatus ;* — in drink, *ebriosus, temulentus ;* = angry, *iracundus.* Adv. *intemperanter, immodice, immoderate, iracunde.*

intend, v.tr. and intr. = to purpose, *propositum habēre* or by *propositum est mihi alqd* (or with infin.); = to think of, *cogitare alqd* (or with infin.); = to look forward to a thing, to direct one's attention to, (*animo) intendĕre* (with the accus. of a pron., or with *ut* or with infin.), *animum intendĕre ad* or in *alqd ;* = to design, to be trying to, *id agĕre ut,* etc., *alqd agitare ;* he could not do what he intended, *quod intenderat, non efficĕre poterat ;* = to prepare anything, *parare ;* = to attempt something difficult, *alqd moliri ;* = to devise, *alqd comminisci* (something bad, e.g. a fraud, *fraudem*); = to be about to, *velle, cogitare,* *in animo habēre, destinare* (all with infin. ; also very often by using the fut., e.g. *nunc scripturus sum,* = I am just about to write). **intense,** adj. *magnus, acer, ardens, summus, intentus;* to take — pains with, *incumbēre ad* or *in alqd* or *alci rei,* or by *animum intendĕre ad alqd.* Adv. *valde, magnopĕre, acriter, summe.* **intensify,** v.tr. *majorem,* etc., *reddĕre, amplificare, exaggerare, augēre;* see INCREASE. **intensity,** n. *vis, vis, f., gravitas;* — of cold, *rigor.* **intensive,** adj. = serving to give emphasis (e.g. an — particle), *intentivus* (e.g. *intentiva adverbia,* gram.). **intent, I.** adj. (lit., = having the mind strained, bent on a subject, eager, e.g. on business), *studiosus alcjs rei, intentus, attentus ad alqd or (in) alqd re; erectus;* to be — upon, *animum ad alqd, in alqd* or *alci rei intendĕre, incumbēre in* or *ad alqd* or *alci rei, studēre alci rei.* Adv. by adj. **II.** n. see INTENTION ; to all — and purposes, *omnino.* **intention,** n. = design, *consilium, propositum, mens, animus* (e.g. *in animo habēre, esse in animo alci*), *institutum, sententia, studium, voluntas.* **intentional,** adj. by adv. *quod consulto* or *de industriâ,* or *deditâ operâ fit.*

inter, v.tr. *sepelīre* (= to bury in general; also *sepelīre dolorem*), *humare* (= to cover with earth). **interment,** n. *sepultura, humatio;* place of —, *sepulc(h)rum;* see BURY.

interact, n. = interlude in a play, *embolium* (ἐμβόλιον, fig., *embolia amoris,* Cic.).

intercalary, adj. *intercalaris* or *intercalarius.* **intercalate,** v.tr. *intercalare.*

intercede, v.intr. = to plead, *(de)precari pro alqo* (= to — for anyone); see ENTREAT, BEG. **intercession,** n. *deprecatio* (= praying earnestly to turn off some evil); at anyone's request, *algo deprecatore* (e.g. to obtain pardon, *veniam impetrare);* to make — for anyone, *rogare pro alqo* (so as to obtain something); on account of anything, *alci adesse ad alqd deprecandum ;* with anyone, *deprecari alqm pro alqo, deprecatorem alci adesse apud alqm;* alci *supplicare pro alqo.* **intercessor,** n. one who entreats, *deprecator.* **intercessory,** adj. by verbs ; see INTERCEDE.

intercept, v.tr. 1, = to seize on by the way (e.g. a letter, a prince), *intercipĕre, excipĕre;* 2, = to cut off, *intercludĕre, circumvenire, officĕre* (e.g. — the light, *luminibus officĕre);* see INTERRUPT, HINDER.

interchange, I. v.tr. 1, = to reciprocate (e.g. places), by *(com)mutare, (per)mutare inter se;* see ALTERNATE, EXCHANGE. **II.** n. *(com)mutatio, permutatio, vicissitudo.* **interchangeable,** adj. *quae inter se (com)mutari possunt.* Adv. *invicem.*

intercolumniation, n. *intercolumnium.*

intercommunicate, v.intr. 1, *alqd communicare inter se* or *conferre inter se ;* see COMMUNICATE ; 2, of rooms, etc., *commeatus, -ûs, continēre.*

intercourse, n. *conversatio* (social), *usus, -ûs* (frequent) ; *commercium* (commercial and in gen.) ; habitual —, *consuetudo ;* —, inasmuch as parties live, reside together, *convictus, -ûs ;* family —, *usus domesticus* or *consuetudo ;* familiar —, *usus familiaris, familiaritas ;* I have — with anyone, *est mihi consuetudo cum alqo ;* to have familiar — with anyone, *alqo familiariter* or *intime uti, conjunctissime vivĕre cum alqo, usu cum alqo conjunctissimum esse ;* to avoid all — with men, *congressus hominum fugĕre, fugĕre colloquia et coetus hominum.*

interdict, I. v.tr. 1, = to forbid, *interdicĕre alci alqâ re,* or with *ne;* see FORBID ; 2, see EXCOMMUNICATE. **II.** n. *interdictum.*

interest, I. v.tr. 1, = to excite an interest, (e.g. a book), *jucundum esse* (lit. = to be pleasing); to delight, *delectare;* = to fascinate, *capĕre* (= to prepossess) ; to — anyone, *alci placēre ;* = to attract delight, *alqm delectare* or *delectatione allicĕre ;* = to enlist anyone's attention, *tenēre* (e.g. *audientium animos*); if it —s you to know this likewise, *si etiam hoc quaeris ;* 2, = to have a share, to be concerned in ; anything —s me, *alqd meâ interest, alqd ad me pertinet ;* 3, = to give a share in ; I — anyone in anything, *alci alqd commendo* (e.g. *alci gloriam alcjs);* I feel an — in anything, *alqd mihi curae* or *cordi* (but *curae* in anything, *alqd mihi curae* or *cordi* (but *curae cordique) est ;* I — myself for anyone, *alci studeo, consulo, alcjs sum studiosus ;* to take — in, *participem esse alcjs rei ;* = to be an accomplice in a bad action, *affinem esse rei* (lit. = to be related to anyone). **II.** n. 1, = causing interest, in gen. *studium;* the divided — of the hearers, *deductum in partes audientium studium ;* = attraction, *voluptas ;* = pleasantness, *jucunditas ;* = delight, *delectatio, oblectatio;* to give an — to a matter, *voluptatem dare alci rei ;* 2, = advantage ; to have an — in, by *interest* or *refert ;* the — anyone has in a thing, *res* or *rationes* or *caus(s)a alcjs ;* = advantage, *commodum; bonum, usus, -ûs, utilitas ;* = emolument, *emolumentum ;* the common —, *res* or *caus(s)a communis, communis omnium utilitas ;* in anyone's —, *ex usu alcjs;* anything is in my —, *alqd est e re meâ ;* my — requires it, *rationes meae ita ferunt ;* it is conducive to my —, *expedit mihi, meis rationibus conducit ;* not all have, feel the same —, *aliis aliud expedit ;* to defend anyone's —, *alcjs caus(s)am defendĕre ;* to consider, study anyone's —, *alcjs rationibus consulĕre ;* 3, *usura* or *usurae, faenus (Je-);* — added to the capital, *anatocismus ;* — of —, *usurae usurarum ;* to lend out money on —, *pecuniam faenerari, pecuniam dare faenore* or *faenori, ponĕre in faenore nummos ;* to invest capital at —, *pecuniam apud alqm occupare ;* to lend out money at high —, *pecuniam grandi faenore occupare ;* money lent without —, *pecunia gratuita ;* the act of lending money on —, *faeneratio ;* the — mounts up, *usurae multiplicantur ;* to return, repay an act of kindness with —, *beneficium cum usuris reddĕre ;* to return kindness with —, *debitum alci cumulate reddĕre.* **interested,** adj. *attentus, erectus ;* — in, *alcjs rei studiosus* (= fond of) ; I am — in anything, *alqd e re meâ est, mihi expedit, meâ interest* or *refert.* **interesting,** adj. by *quod ad se attrahit* or *illicit* (of a person), or by *alqm tenēre* (of a writer), or by *multum habēre* or *plenum esse delectationis* (of a book), *jucundus ;* see AGREEABLE.

interfere, v.intr. *alci rei* or *in alqd intercedĕre, admiscēre, intervenire, se interponĕre,* or *se immiscēre ;* I shall not — with it, *per me licet ;* to — on anyone's behalf (i.e. to guarantee for anyone), *intercedĕre pro alqo ;* to hinder, *alqm interpellare* or *prohibēre* or *impedire* (with *quominus* or *quin* or *ne), alci officĕre, obesse, alci obstare quominus* or *quin ;* see HINDER. **interference,** n. by verb, or by *intercessio* (of the tribunes).

interim, n. *tempus interjectum, spatium, temporis intervallum, tempus quod interea est ;* ad —, *interim ;* ad *tempus* (= for a time); *temporis gratiâ* (= for the present time); a decree ad —, *edictum ad tempus propositum.*

interior, I. adj. *interior, internus.* **II.** n. *pars interior ;* see INNER, INTERNAL.

interjacent, adj. 1, by *interjacēre, interce dĕre ;* 2, *interjacens, interjectus.*

interject, v.tr. *interpōnĕre, interjicĕre.*
interjection, n. (in grammar) *interjectio.*

interlace, v.tr. *implicare* = to intermix (e.g. remarks), *intexĕre algd alci rei* (fig., e.g. poetry in a discourse, *versus orationi*; see EN-TWINE.

interlapse, I. v.intr. *interjici, interponi.*
II. n. by verb; in the — of a year, *anno circum-acto* or *praeterito, anno interjecto,* also *anno post,* or *post annum.*

interlard, v.tr. see MIX.

interleave, v.tr. *libri singulis paginis in-ter(j)icĕre singulas chartas puras.*

interline, v.tr. *interscribĕre* (Plin. Min.).

interlocution, n. see CONVERSATION. **in-terlocutory,** adj. (= consisting of dialogue, e.g. discourses), *in sermone* ; to mention to any-one by way of conversation, *alci in sermone in-(j)icĕre* (with acc. and infin., Cic.); a thing is mentioned as an — remark, *incidit mentio de algd re.*

interlude, n. see INTERACT.

intermarriage, n. *connubium.* **inter-marry,** v.intr. *inter se matrimonio conjungi.*

intermeddle, v.intr. *se interponĕre alci rei* or *in algd, se admiscĕre* or *immiscĕre* ; not to —, *abesse* or *se abstinĕre ab algd re* ; you may do as you like, I shall not —, *quod voles facies, me nihil interpono.* **intermediate,** adj. *medius (intermedius,* ante class.).

interment, n. see INTER.

interminable, adj. *infinitus.* Adv. *in-finite.*

intermingle, v.tr. *alci algd (inter)miscĕre* ; see MINGLE, MIX.

intermission, n. *intermissio* (e.g. of duty, *officii*); see INTERRUPTION, PAUSE. **intermit,** v.tr. *algd intermittĕre* ; see OMIT, CEASE, INTER-RUPT. **intermittent,** adj., med. t.t. *febris intermittens* (Cels.). Adv. *tempore* or *inter-vallo interposito,* or *certis temporibus* (= at fixed times, or *incertis temp.* = at irregular intervals), *aliquando, nonnumquam (nonnunq-,* = some-times).

intermix, I. v.tr. see INTERMINGLE. **II.** v.intr. *(com)miscēri, permiscēri, intermiscēri.*
intermixture, n. *mistio, permistio* (the act); see COMPOUND, MIXTURE.

internal, see INNER. Adv. *intus, penitus.*

international, adj. — law, *jus (juris,* n.) *gentium.*

internecine, adj. *internecivus* ; see FATAL.

internuncio, n. = messenger between two parties, *internuntius.*

interpellation, n. *interpellatio* (Cic.).

interpolate, v.tr. = to insert, *algd alci rei addĕre, inserĕre* ; = to falsify, *corrumpĕre.* **in-terpolation,** n. use verb.

interpose, I. v.tr. = to place between (e.g. to — a body between the earth and the sun), *interponĕre, interjicĕre.* **II.** v.intr. = to mediate, *se interponĕre in rem* ; see INTERFERE.
interposition, n. 1, = a placing between (e.g. the — of the Baltic sea between, etc.), *in-terjectus, interpositus* (both -*ūs,* only common in abl. however), *interventus, -ūs* ; better use abl. abs. (e.g. *mari interjecto* = by the — of the sea ; 2, (in general = mediation, anything interposed), *vis, impulsus, -ūs* (= instigation), or by *auctor* (e.g. by my —, *me auctore*); see INTERFERENCE ; by divine —, influence, *divinitus.*

interpret, v.tr. 1, = to — for anyone, *interpretari* ; see TRANSLATE ; 2, = to unfold

the meaning of anything (e.g. a dream), *algd interpretari, esse interpretem alcjs rei* (e.g. the law, a dream); *con(j)icĕre, algd conjecturá expla-nare, conjecturam alcjs rei facĕre, algd enarrare* (= to conjecture, explain by conjecture, e.g. a dream, a wonder, etc.); = to take anything that is said, *accipĕre* (either in a good or bad sense); = to explain, *explanare* ; to — in a wrong sense, *misinterpret, detorquĕre in* (with accus.), *trahĕre ad* or *in* (with accus., = — on purpose); to — any-thing that is not clear, *rem obscuram interpre-tando explanare* ; to get anyone to — anything for, *de algd re uti interprete* ; to — anything in good part, *algd in bonam partem accipĕre* or *bene interpretari* ; to — anything as an offence, *algd in malam partem accipĕre* or *male interpretari* ; to — anything from anyone as haughtiness, *algd alci tribuĕre superbiae, trahĕre algd in superbiam* ; as an insult, as disgracing anyone, *in contumeliam convertĕre* ; to — a thing differently from what anyone said, *aliter algd ac dictum erat accipĕre.*
interpretation, n. *interpretatio, explanatio* (= explanation); an — by conjecture, a conjec-ture, hypothesis, *conjectio, conjectura* ; = critical explanations of an author, *enarratio* (Quint.); to be liable to have a bad — put upon, *in malam partem accipi.* **interpretative,** adj. *quod explanat.* **interpreter,** n. an — of a foreign tongue, *interpres, -ētis,* m. and f. ; to converse through the medium of an —, *per interpretem colloqui,* with anyone, *cum algo.*

interregnum, n. *interregnum.* **interrex,** n. *interrex.*

interrogate, v.tr. and intr. *quaerĕre, ex-quirĕre, requirĕre ex* or *ab algo* ; see ASK, IN-QUIRE ; = to — again and again, *rogitare* ; see ASK. **interrogation,** n. *interrogatio* (= the act of interrogating, hence anything in the form of a question), *percontatio (percunct-)*; = the question asked, *(inter)rogatum* ; = investigation, *quaestio.* **interrogative, I.** adj. use verb (e.g. in an — manner, *percontando (percunct-) et interrogando).* **II.** n. *particula interrogativa* (gram.). **interrogator,** n. *qui interrogat.* **interrogatory, I.** adj. by IN-TERROGATE. **II.** n. *interrogatio.*

interrupt, v.tr. *interrumpĕre* (e.g. a speech, *orationem* ; sleep, *somnum* ; order, succession, *ordinem*); *interpellare* (lit., to — a speaker by speaking, by addressing the meeting ; then in general, to disturb); = to rest, cease for a while from anything, *intermittĕre* (e.g. the march, journey, *iter* ; the battle, *praelium*); to intercept, arrest suddenly, *intercipĕre* (e.g. the march, *iter* ; a conversation, *sermonem medium*); to — by interfering, *intervenire alci rei* (e.g. a deliberation, *deliberationi*); = to cut short, *incidĕre* (lit. = to cut into, to cut away a piece as it were, e.g. a discourse, the conver-sation, speech, *sermonem*); = to speak whilst others are speaking, *algm interfari* ; = to cause to cease, separate, put off, *dirimĕre* (e.g. *sermo-nem, praelium* ; both of persons and circum-stances); to — by speaking against, *alci obloqui* ; — noisily, *alci obstrepĕre.* **interrupted,** adj. *interruptus, interceptus, intermissus.* Adv. *in-terrupte.* **interruption,** n. *interpellatio* (= of one who speaks by others ; then in gene-ral = disturbance); = the act of speaking whilst someone else speaks, *interfatio* ; = the act of ceasing for a while, *intermissio* (e.g. of the correspondence, *lit(t)erarum* or *epistolarum*); = the interval whilst an — takes place, *inter-capedo* (e.g. *scribendi*); without —, *uno tenore sine ullá intermissione* ; to carry on the war with —, *per dilationes bellum gerĕre.*

intersect, v.tr. *secare* (lit. and fig.); = to cleave, divide, *scindĕre* (lit. and fig.); to cut

across, thus, X, *decussare* (e.g. a line); to cut right in the middle, *medium secare*; by ditches, *fossis concidĕre* (e.g. a field, a piece of land). **intersection**, n. *sectio* (the act); the — (X) of two lines that cross each other, *decussatio, decussis, -is,* m. ; = diameter, *diametros*; see DIAMETER.

intersperse, v.tr. *immiscēre*; in anything, *alci rei*; to — poetry in a discourse, speech, sermon, *versus admiscēre orationi*; see MIX.

interstice, n. *rima, foramen.*

intertwine, v.tr. see ENTWINE.

interval, n. *intervallum, spatium interjectum* (in general; *distantia*, for — between two places, distance, seldom used, as in Vitruv.); — of time, *tempus interjectum*; to leave an —, a space between, *spatium relinquĕre* or *intermittĕre*; after a brief —, *interjecto haud magno spatio*; in the —, *interim*; at —s, *aliquando, nonnumquam* (*nonnung-*).

intervene, v.intr. = to be between, *interjacēre*; = to come between, *intercedĕre, interfluĕre, interponi, intervenire*; *supervenire alci rei* (of persons and things, e.g. of the night, *ni nox praelio intervenisset*, Liv.; to — (of obstacles), *ob(j)ici.* **intervention**, n. *interventus, -ūs* (of persons and things); see INTERFERENCE.

interview, n. *congressio* (= the act), *congressus, -ūs* (= the — itself, friendly meeting); an — for a stated purpose, *conventus, -ūs*; = conversation, *colloquium, sermo.*

interweave, v.tr. *interxēre alci rei* or *in algā re* (lit. and fig.); see ENTWINE.

intestate, n. of a person who dies without making a will, *intestatum* (Cic.) or *intestato* (Cic.) *decedĕre.*

intestine, **I.** adj. *intestinus*; see INTERNAL. **II.** n. *intestinum*, usu. pl. *ilia, viscera, exta* (all pl.).

intimacy, n. *familiaritas, usus (-ūs), familiaris, consuetudo, necessitudo.* **intimate**, **I.** adj. *familiaris* (e.g. conversation, *sermo*), *intimus* (*inter*), *conjunctus*; to have an — knowledge of anything, *algd penitus perspectum cognitumque habēre.* Adv. *familiariter, intime, conjuncte, penitus, prorsus*; see WHOLLY. **II.** v.tr. *significare* (in gen.); = to indicate, *indicare* (both *alci algd*); = to inform anyone about a matter, *docēre alqm alqd, alqm de alqā re certiorem facĕre, alqd alci nuntiare, declarare*; to — by words, *voce significare*; to — in a roundabout way, *alqd circuitu plurium verborum ostendĕre*; as a prediction, a wonder, *alqd portendĕre*; to — (in a threatening manner), *denuntiare.* **intimation**, n. *significatio, nuntius, denuntiatio.*

intimidate, v.tr. *metum (timorem, terrorem, pavorem, formidinem) alci in(j)icĕre, incutĕre; metum (timorem, terrorem) alci afferre, inferre, offerre*; *alqm in metum compellĕre, con(j)icĕre*; see FRIGHTEN, TERRIFY. **intimidated**, adj. *timefactus* (e.g. liberty). **intimidation**, n. *minae* = threats; by *pavorem* or *metum alci incutĕre.*

into, prep. as denoting motion towards or entrance, *in* with accus. ; *in meridiem*, = southwards ; *in Galliam*, = towards Gaul ; so of time, *to*, or up to, *dormiet in lucem*, = he will sleep till daybreak ; *in multam noctem*, = deep into the night. An adverb may be added, *usque in senectutem*, = down to old age ; *mihi in mentem venit*, = it occurs to me. *In*, as equivalent to into, may signify change or conversion, as *in lapidem verti*, = to be changed — stone ; *in aquam solvi*, = to be melted — water. With verbs compounded with preps., into is often not expressed, to go — the city, *urbem ingredi.*

intolerable, adj. *intolerabilis, intolerandus, vix tolerabilis, non ferendus* (of persons and things, e.g. woman, cold, pain); = odious, disagreeable, troublesome, *odiosus* (of persons and things, e.g. you are — to me, *odiosus mihi es*); = disobliging, disagreeable, *importunus* (of persons and things, e.g. avarice, *avaritia*.) Adv. *intoleranter*; to boast —, *intolerantissime gloriari*; it is — cold, *intolerabile est frigus.* **intolerance**, n. *animus aliorum de rebus divinis opiniones haud ferens*, or by some word = pride, *intolerantia, superbia, arrogantia.* **intolerant**, adj. *moribus immitis* (= of a harsh disposition); = intractable, difficult to deal with, obstinate, *difficilis*; = proud, *superbus, alcjs rei intolerans*; in religion, *erga alqos parum indulgens.*

intone, v.tr. = to sound the notes of a musical scale, *incipĕre* (= to begin to sing, Virg.); *voce praeire* (= to lead, of a precentor, to sound the first note); to — prayers, *preces canĕre.*

intoxicate, v.tr. *inebriare* (lit.), *ebrium reddĕre.* **intoxicated**, adj. *ebrius, temulentus.* **intoxicating**, adj. (*potus*) *qui alqm ebrium reddit.* **intoxication**, n. *ebrietas, temulentia*; see DRUNK.

intractable, adj. *indocilis, difficilis.* **intractability**, n. by adj.

intransitive, adj. *intransitivus* (gram.).

intrench, v.tr. = to cut a trench, (*com*)*munire* (= to fortify, in gen.); = to surround with fortifications, *operibus et munitionibus saepire, operibus munire*; = to surround with palisades, *vallare, obvallare, vallo* or *fossā saepire* (*sep-*), or *cingĕre*, or *circumdare*, or *munire*; *alqm locum munitionibus saepire, castra in algo loco communire.* **intrenchment**, n. *vallum, munitio, munimentum, opera, -um.*

intrepid, adj. *intrepidus*; see FEARLESS. **intrepidity**, n. *animus intrepidus* or *impavidus* or *fortis*; *fortitudo*; see COURAGE.

intricacy, n. *implicatio, contortio* (e.g. *orationis*); the — of the road, *iter impeditum.* **intricate**, adj. *contortus, implicatus, inexplicabilis, perplexus, tortuosus, impeditus.*

intrigue, **I.** n. = a plot of a complicated nature, *dolus* (= a trick played to do harm); a secret —, *clandestinum consilium, artificia, -iorum*; = a snare, *fallacia*; = a deception, *fraus, -dis*; *ambush, insidiae.* **II.** v.tr. *fallacias fabricari,* (*con*)*coquĕre* (e.g.*consilia*); see PLOT, CONSPIRE. **intriguer**, n. *doli* or *fallaciarum machinator.* **intriguing**, adj. *callidus et ad fraudem acutus, fraudulentus* (= deceitful); = cunning, crafty, *astutus, vafer*; = malicious, knavish, *malitiosus*; a crafty fellow, *veterator.*

intrinsic(al), adj. = real, *verus*, or *per se*, or *ipse.* Adv. *re verā, per se, vere*; see REAL.

introduce, v.tr. lit. *invehĕre, importare* (by carriers, by ship, goods, etc.); to — anyone to one, *alqm introducĕre ad alqm* (usu. to the great, to an audience, Curt., or to a house); to — anyone to a person (for making his acquaintance) by letter, *alqm alci commendare*; = to make acquainted with someone, *praesentim praesenti alci commendare*; = to induct anyone to an office, *alqm inaugurare*; in a fig. sense, e.g. to — anyone as speaking, *alqm loquentem* or *disputantem inducĕre*; = to bring up (e.g. customs, etc.), *inducĕre, introducĕre*; to have been introduced, *usu receptum esse*; to — many changes, *multa mutare* or *novare.* **introduction**, n. *invectio* (= importation of goods, etc.), *inductio* (= the act of letting go in, e.g. of armed soldiers, *inductio armatorum*); — of persons, *introductio* (e.g. *adolescentulorum nobilium*); to give an — to, *alqm alci commendare*; an — to a book, etc.

proemium, principium, exordium, praefatio (Plin., Quint.) ; say something in — to, *dicěre alqd ante rem;* after a short — respecting old age, *pauca praefatus de senectute.* **introductory,** adj. by v., e.g. to make — remarks, *praefari.*

intromission, n. *aditus, -ūs,* or by verb, *intromittěre.*

introspect, v.tr., **introspection,** n. *ipsum se inspicěre;* for gen. sense, see INSPECT.

intrude, v.intr. = to — on a person or family, *se intruděre, se inferre et intruděre, se inculcare alcjs auribus* (in order that one may be heard). **intruder,** n. by *importunus, molestus.* **intrusion,** n. *importunitas;* = troublesomeness, or by verb, *se inferre et intruděre.* **intrusive,** adj. *qui se infert et intrudit.* Adv. *moleste, importune.*

intrust, v.tr. *fidei alcjs alqd committěre* or *permittěre, traděre alqd in alcjs fidem;* see ENTRUST.

intuition, n. poetical, philosophical —, *anticipatio, cognitio, perceptio, comprehensio, anticipatio* (κατάληψις). **intuitive,** adj. = clear, *perspicuus, dilucidus;* = clearly expressed, *expressus* (of images); in philosophy use n. (e.g. — knowledge, *alqd per quandam animi perceptionem cognitum*). Adv. *perspicue, dilucide,* (*celeri*) *quādam animi perceptione.*

intumescence, inturgescence, n. by verbs, (*in*)*tumescere, extumescěre* (in gen.); *turgescěre;* see SWELL, SWELLING.

inundation, n. better expressed by verb, *inundare,* or by *magnae aquae.*

inurbanity, n. *inurbanitas, rusticitas.*

inure, v.tr. *assuefacere;* see ACCUSTOM.

inurn, v.tr. *in urnam conděre;* see INTER.

inutility, n. *inutilitas.*

invade, v.tr. *irruptionem* or *incursionem facěre in,* etc., *invaděre* (the enemy, a town, a harbour, etc., *in alqm, in alqd;* also of an evil); *alci* or *in alqm incurrěre, bellum alci inferre;* of a large body of troops, *in terram infundi* or *influěre;* to — a country with an army, *terram invaděre cum copiis;* the enemy's land, *copias in fines hostium introducěre,* or *inducěre, impressionem facěre in fines hostium;* see ATTACK, ASSAIL. **invader,** n. *hostis.* **invasion,** n. *irruptio, incursio.*

invalid, I. adj. in law, = having no effect, *irritus* (= without legal force, opp. *ratus,* e.g. a will); = fruitless, *vanus* (= vain, without effect, of things), comb. *irritus et vanus* (e.g. a will); = unfit, *parum idoneus*(= not suited to the purpose, e.g. authority, witness, excuse); of arguments, *infirmus, nugatorius, vitiosus;* to make anything —, *alqd irritum facěre* (e.g. a will), = to rescind, to annul, *alqd rescinděre* (e.g. a will, a compact, a sentence), comb. *rescinděre et irritum facěre* or *ut irritum et vanum rescinděre* (of a will). **II.** n. *aeger* = ill; to be a confirmed —, *tenui aut potius nullā valetudine esse;* an — soldier, *causarius.* **invalidate,** v.tr. *alqd irritum facěre, tollěre* (= to destroy), *infirmare* (= to weaken), *labefactare* (e.g. *opinionem*), *rescinděre, refigěre* (of laws); see ABROGATE, ABOLISH. **invalidish,** adj. *ad alqm morbum proclivior.* **invalidity,** n. use adj. INVALID or v. INVALIDATE.

invective, n. *convicium, contumelia, maledictum, probrum, invectio* (rare), verba with adj., e.g. *acerba* (= bitter); *maligna* (= sharp), *aculeata* (= stinging), *mordacia* (= reproachful), *criminosa* (of a speech). **inveigh,** v.intr. *in alqm invehi, incurrěre, incessěre, alqm jurgio adoriri, con-*

tumeliosis verbis or *verbis vehementioribus pro sequi, alqm* or *alqd objurgare;* = to scold, *alqm increpare, castigare.*

inveigle, v.tr. see MISLEAD, SEDUCE.

invent, v.tr. *invenire, reperire;* to — (in the mind), *excogitare;* = to contrive, hatch, *comminisci* (gen. something bad). **invention,** n. **1,** = act of —, *inventio, excogitatio,* or by verb (e.g. *hamis repertis,* = by the — of hooks) ; **2,** = thing invented, *alqd inventum* or *repertum;* **3,** = fiction, *commentum, fabula, mendacium* (= lie). **inventive,** adj. *ingeniosus* (= who has always new ideas); *sol(l)ers* (= clever, who knows how to make use of, how to apply new ideas to some purpose); sharp, deep,*acutus*(= who can conceive a thing in its depth); an — person, *ingenium ad excogitandum acutum;* the — faculty, *inventio, excogitatio.* **inventor,** n. *inventor* (chiefly poet., or late *repertor*), fem. *inventrix;* = author, *auctor, architectus* (lit. architect), comb. *architectus et princeps;* the —s of the art of sculpture, *fingendi conditores.* **inventory,** n. *repertorium, inventarium* (Jct.).

inverse, adj. *inversus, conversus.* Adv. *retro, permutato ordine.* **inversion,** n. *conversio* (lit., e.g. ôf the bladder, *vesicae;* fig. = destruction, *eversio*); = of words, *inversio verborum.* **invert,** v.tr. = to turn into a contrary direction, (*con*)*vertěre;* = to turn round, *invertěre* (e.g. the ring, *anulum;* hence fig., to change entirely, e.g. the order of the words, *ordinem verborum*); to — the order of words, † *ultima primis praeponěre;* = to alter, *commutare* (fig., e.g. the constitution of the state, *rempublicam*); = to change entirely, *permutare* (e.g. *omnem reipublicae statum;* = to upset completely, *evertěre* (fig., e.g. the state, *rempublicam*); = to turn everything topsyturvy, *omnia miscēre, summa imis miscēre, omnia sursum deorsum versare.*

invest, v.tr. **1,** see CLOTHE; **2,** = to — with an office, *magistratum alci dare, mandare, deferre, muneri alqm praeficěre;* to — anyone with the highest power, *deferre alci summam imperii;* **3,** = to lend (e.g. — with a charm), *alqd alci adděre, impertire, alqm alqd re* (*ex*)*ornare;* see ADORN, GIVE ; **4,** of money, *pecuniam collocare, occupare, ponēre,* with *in alqā re* or *apud alqm;* **5,** = to besiege, *circumsedēre, obsiděre, vallo* or *fossā cingēre* or *circumdare;* see BESIEGE. **investiture,** n. = the right of giving possession of any manor, office, or benefice. * *ritus inaugurationis feudalis.* **investment,** n. **1,** with an office, *inauguratio,* or by verb; see INSTALL ; **2,** of money, by verb INVEST ; **3,** = siege, *obsessio.*

investigate, v.tr. *exquirěre, indagare,* (*per*)*scrutari, investigare, quaerěre, cognoscěre* (the last two also of judicial investigation), *percontari* (*percunct*-), *sciscitari;* to — the true reason of anything, *veram rationem alcjs rei exsequi;* to — the truth, *quid verum sit exquirěre.* **investigation,** n. *investigatio, indagatio, percontatio* (*percunct*-) (= questioning), *inquisitio, quaestio, cognitio;* see INQUIRY. **investigator,** n. *investigator, indagator, quaesitor* (only in judicial matters), *inquisitor.*

inveteracy, n. *inveteratio.* **inveterate,** adj. *inveteratus, confirmatus* (fig., = deeply rooted), *penitus defixus* (of bad habits), *penitus insitus* (of opinions) ; to become —, *inveterascěre.* Adv. *penitus.*

invidious, adj. **1,** = envious, *invidus, invidiosus, lividus, malignus, malevolus;* **2,** = exposed to envy, *invidiosus, odiosus.* Adv. *maligne, invidiose.* **invidiousness,** n. **1,** *invidia, malevolentia, malignitas;* **2,** *invidia, odium.*

invigorate, v.tr. *corroborare* (e.g. anyone through constant work, employment, *alqm assiduo opere*); = to revive anyone, (*con*)*firmare* (e.g. the body through food, *corpus cibo firmare*); to become invigorated, *se corroborare, se confirmare, se recreare,* or *vires reficĕre* (= to recruit one's strength). **invigorating,** adj. *aptus ad corpus* (etc.) *reficiendum.* **invigoration,** n. *confirmatio animi,* for — of the body, use verb.

invincible, adj. *invictus, in(ex)superabilis, inexpugnabilis* (= impregnable, of places); *quod superari non potest* (fig., e.g. obstacles, *impedimenta*). Adv. *quod superari non potest.*

inviolability, n. *sanctitas* (of God and men, = sanctity), *caerimonia, religio* (= sacredness, of the gods and of everything consecrated to them, e.g. tombs). **inviolable,** adj. *inviolabilis, inviolatus; =* sacred, holy, consecrated, *sanctus, sacrosanctus.* Adv. *inviolate.* **inviolate,** adj. *integer* (of a thing remaining in its former state); = without having received any injury, unhurt, *illaesus, inviolatus,* comb. *integer atque inviolatus, intactus inviolatusque; =* entire, undamaged, *incorruptus; =* without any accident, safe, *incolumis* (opp. *afflictus, vitiosus*), comb. *integer incolumisque; =* safe, in safety, *salvus, c* ⏞ *salvus atque incolumis.*

invisibility, n. by **invisible,** adj. *caecus* or *nihil cernendus,* or *quem* (*quam, quod*) *cernĕre et vidēre non possumus, quem* (*quam, quod*) *non possumus oculis consequi;* to be —, *sub oculos non cadĕre; non comparēre* (= not to appear, of persons and things); the — world, *caelum, superi;* see HEAVEN. Adv. *quod cerni non potest.*

invitation, n. *invitatio;* at your —, *invitatus* or *vocatus a te, invitatu* or *vocatu tuo.* **invite,** v.tr. 1, (in the usual sense) *invitare alqm ad alqd* (any invitation, of persons and things); *vocare alqm ad alqd* (the usual phrase in inviting anyone to dinner through a slave); then in gen. of an invitation to take part in anything, e.g. *ad bellum, ad quietem,* etc.); to — oneself to dinner, *condicĕre ad cenam, condicĕre alci* (the latter in gen. in the sense, I'll be your guest); 2, = to allure; to — to the pleasures of rural life, *ad fruendum agrum invitare;* see ALLURE. **inviting,** adj. *blandus, gratus, amoenus, dulcis.* Adv. *blande, grate, amoene, dulciter.*

invocation, n. *imploratio* (= imploring), *testatio* (= calling as a witness).

invoice, n. (*mercium*) *libellus* or *index, -icis,* m. and f.; see ACCOUNT.

invoke, v.tr. *invocare, implorare;* to — the Muses, *invocare Musas;* to — the gods, *implorare* or *invocare Deos, invocare atque obtestari Deos, comprecari Deos* (the latter esp. = to pray for help); to — anyone's assistance, *implorare fidem alcjs, invocare subsidium alcjs, auxilium alcjs implorare et flagitare;* to — God as a witness, *Deum testari, Deum invocare testem.*

involuntary, adj. *invitus et coactus* (= unwilling and forced), *non voluntarius* (= not made to please us, e.g. death). Adv. *invite,* or by adj. or *haud sponte suā.* **involuntariness,** n. *necessitas,* or by adj. (e.g. — of my action, *quod coactus feci*).

involution, n. *implicatio, involutio* (Vitruv.), better by INVOLVE, which see. **involve,** v.tr. 1, = to envelop (e.g. to — one in smoke), *involvĕre;* see ENVELOP; 2, = to implicate, *alqm alqā re implicare, illaqueare, illigare;* to be involved in debt, *aere alieno obrutum, oppressum,* or *demersum esse;* see IMPLICATE; 3, = to imply, *continēre, habēre;* it is involved in the nature of the

case, *rei inest alqd, ex alqā re sequitur;* see IMPLY, FOLLOW.

invulnerable, adj. *invulnerabilis* (Sen.); to be —, *vulnerari non posse.*

inwall, v.tr. *saxo consaepire* (*consep-*).

inward, adj. = internal, interior, *interior;* see INNER. Adv. *introrsus* or *introrsum, intus, intrinsecus;* bent —, *incurvus.*

inweave, v.tr. *intexĕre alci rei* or in *alqā re* (lit. and fig.).

inwrought, adj. by *intextus;* see WEAVE, ENGRAVE.

irascible, adj. *iracundus, in iram praeceps. stomachosus, irritabilis.* Adv. *iracunde, iratē, stomachose.* **irascibility,** n. *iracundia, stomachus;* see IRRITATION. **ire,** n. see ANGER, WRATH. **ireful,** adj. see ANGRY.

iris, n. 1, see RAINBOW; 2, = the flag-flower, *iris* (Plin.).

irks, v.tr. impers.; it —, *alqm alcjs rei piget, taedet,* or with infin.; *alci molestum est,* with infin. **irksome,** adj. = annoying, *gravis, molestus;* = full of labour, tiring, *operosus; =* hateful, *odiosus.* Adv. *graviter, moleste, aegre.* **irksomeness,** n. *molestia, molestia;* see DISAGREEABLE.

iron, I. n. *ferrum;* of —, made of —, *ferreus;* ironed, *ferratus;* to put anyone in —s, *alqm in vincula con(j)icĕre* or *mittĕre;* we must strike the — whilst it is hot, *utendum est animis dum spe calent,* Curt.; *matura dum libido manet* (Ter.). **II.** adj. *ferreus* (both lit. and fig.); an — instrument, —ware, *ferramentum;* I must have a heart of —, *ferreus essem;* oh you with your heart of —! o te *ferreum!* **III.** v.tr. 1, = to smooth with an instrument of —, *ferro cal(e)facto vestes premĕre;* 2, = chain; see IRON, n. above. **ironmaster, ironmonger,** n. *negotiator ferrarius.* **ironmongery,** n. *ferramenta, -orum.*

ironical, adj. *alqd per ironiam seu dissimulationem dictum;* an — man, *simulator* (e.g. *in omni oratione simulatorem, quem εἴρωνα Graeci nominarunt, Socratem accepimus* (Cic.). Adv. *per ironiam.* **irony,** n. *ironīa* (εἰρωνεία, a word which Cic. borrowed from the Greek), *dissimulatio* (= dissimulation).

irradiate, v.tr. = to illuminate, lit. *irradiare* (post-Aug. poets), *luce suā collustrare* (of the sun, etc.), *illustrare;* see ILLUMINATE.

irrational, adj. = without reason, *rationis expers, brutus* (esp. of animals); *amens, demens, insanus* (= mad), *stolidus, stupidus, stultus, fatuus* (= stupid), *caecus* (= mentally blind). Adv. *insane, stolide, stulte.* **irrationality,** n. by adj. or some word = stupidity or madness (e.g. *stultitia, stupor, stupiditas, socordia, amentia, dementia*).

irreclaimable, adj. *quod emendari non potest.*

irreconcilable, adj. 1, = not to be appeased, *implacabilis, inexorabilis;* 2, of propositions, (res) *inter se repugnantes, contrariae;* see INCONSISTENT. Adv. by adj.

irrecoverable, adj. *irreparabilis;* an — loss, *damnum quod nunquam resarciri potest; irrevocabilis.* Adv. by adj.

irrefragable, adj. *certus, firmus, gravis, ratus, confirmatus,* or (*argumentum*) *quod refelli non potest,* or *quod vim affert in docendo.* Adv. by adj. or *necessario, necessarie* (rare, but found in Cic.), *necessarie demonstrari.*

irrefutable, adj. see IRREFRAGABLE.

irregular, adj. *enormis* (Tac., of streets, etc.), *incompositus* (= not well put together), *insitatus* (= unusual), *inaequalis, inaequabilis* (=

unequal); as gram. t.t., *anŏmalus*; of an election, *vitiosus*; — conduct, *licentia, mores dissoluti* or *pravi*. Adv. *enormiter, incomposite, inusitate, inaequaliter, inaequabiliter*; of conduct, *dissolute, prave*; of an election, *vitio* (e.g. *consules vitio creati*). **irregularity,** n. *enormitas* (Quint.), *inaequalitas*; gram. t.t., *anŏmalia*; — of conduct, *licentia, mores dissoluti* or *pravi, pravitas*; in an election, *vitium*.

irrelevant, adj. *alci rei, (ab) algâ re alienus*; it is —, *nihil ad rem* or *ad haec*.

irreligion, n. *impietas erga Deum* or *Deos*; = want of devotion, *Dei* or *Deorum neglegentia* (neglig-). **irreligious,** adj. *impius erga Deum* or *Deos, contemptor religionis*. Adv. *impie*.

irremediable, adj. see INCURABLE.

irremovable, adj. *immobilis*; see IMMOVABLE; = that cannot be changed, *immutabilis* (e.g. the tracks of the stars, *spatia*); *certus, ratus*.

irreparable, adj. see IRREVOCABLE.

irreprehensible, adj. *non reprehendendus, non vituperandus* (= blameless); = as it ought to be, *probus* (e.g. goods, an article; hence also of persons); = virtuous, good, *integer, sanctus*. Adv. *sancte, probe, integre*.

irreproachable, adj. see IRREPREHENSIBLE.

irresistible, adj. *cui nullâ vi resisti potest, invictus, in(ex)superabilis*. Adv. *necessario* or *necessarie* (rare), or *ita ut nullo modo resisti possit*.

irresolute, adj. *dubius* (= doubtful); = uncertain, *incertus*; = changeable, *mutabilis, mobilis, varius, parum stabilis, firmus* or *constans, inconstans, haesitans, cunctans*; to be —, *magnâ consilii inopiâ affectum esse*. Adv. *dubitanter, inconstanter*. **irresolution,** n. *dubitatio, haesitantia, cunctatio* (cont-).

irrespective, adj. by Adv. *nullâ ratione (alcjs rei) habitâ*.

irresponsible, adj. *cui nulla ratio reddenda est*. **irresponsibility,** n. use adj.

irretrievable, adj. see IRRECOVERABLE.

irreverence, n. *impietas erga Deum* or *Deos, nulla rerum divinarum reverentia*. **irreverent,** adj. *inverecundus, parum verecundus* (= immodest), *impius erga Deum* or *Deos*. Adv. *impie*; to behave — towards anyone, *reverentiam alci non praestare*.

irrevocable, adj. *irrevocabilis, irreparabilis, immutabilis*; an — loss, *damnum quod nullo modo resarciri potest*. Adv. *in perpetuum*.

irrigate, v.tr. *irrigare*. **irrigation,** n. *irrigatio, inductio aquarum*. **irriguous,** adj. + *irriguus*, or by *rigare, irrigare*.

irritable, adj. *irritabilis, stomachosus, iracundus*. Adv. *stomachose, iracunde*. **irritate,** v.tr. 1, e.g. to — a wound, *inflammare* (Plin.); 2, in a fig. sense, *alqm irritare, alcjs iram concitare* or *irritare*. **irritation,** n. *ira, stomachus*; see ANGER.

irruption, n. 1, e.g. of the sea, by *irrumpĕre*; e.g. of the enemy, *irruptio, incursio*. **irruptive,** adj. by *irrumpĕre*.

isinglass, n. *ichthyocolla* (Plin.).

island, n. *insula* (also = the inhabitants of the —, e.g. *insulas bello persequi*, Nep.). **islander,** n. *insulanus* (Cic.), *insulae incŏla*; the —s, *ii qui insulam*, or *insulas, incolunt*. **isle,** n. see ISLAND. **islet,** n. *parva insula*.

isolate, v.tr. *secernĕre, sejungĕre, separare* (= separate). **isolated,** adj. *remotus* (= distant), *solus* (= alone). **isolation,** n. *solitudo*.

isosceles, n. **isosceles*.

issue, I. n. 1, = the act of ↕ owing (e.g. — of blood), by verb; 2, = a sen..ling o*t* (e.g. the — of an order, money), by v*a*rb; 3, = the result of a thing, *exitus, -ūs, eventus, -ūs*; a good —, *successus, -ūs*; to know the —, *scire quos eventus res sit habitura*; the point at —, *res de quâ agitur*; see END, CONCLUSION, DECISION; 4, = offspring, *filius, filia* (= son, daughter); *progenies, stirps* (the latter lit. stem, in the sing. = children, — in gen.); one of the later —, *unus e posteris* (= one of those who were later born, down from the great-grandson, opp. *unus e majoribus*); = the descendants, *progenies* or *progenies liberorum, stirps* or *stirps liberorum* (as regards the coming generation); = the whole posterity, in a wide sense, *posteritas*; + *suboles*; male —, *stirps virilis, virilis sexûs stirps*; to leave —, *stirpem relinquĕre*. **II.** v.intr. 1, = to flow out, *effluĕre, emanare*; 2, = to go out, *egredi, evadĕre*; = to rush out (e.g. troops), *erumpĕre* (expressing wherefrom, of buds, leaves, etc., also of soldiers that make a sally, e.g. from the camp, *ex castris*); *prorumpĕre, prorumpi* (= to rush, expressing the direction whereto, e.g. a fountain, fire, also of soldiers); = to make a sally, *eruptionem facĕre*; = to rush forth, *procurrĕre* (of troops rushing forth from their position to attack the enemy); = to march out hastily, *provolare, evolare* (from, *ex*, etc.; with all troops, with the whole force, *omnibus copiis*); = to emerge, *emergĕre* (from, *ex*, etc.; lit. to dive forth, from under); to — suddenly from the ambush, *ex insidiis subito consurgĕre*; 3, = to proceed (as income), by *fructum reddĕre*; 4, = to end, *finire, terminari* (= to come to an end); = to cease, *desinĕre*. **III.** v.tr. 1, = to send out (e.g. money), *promĕre* (e.g. money from the treasury); to — a new coinage, *distribuĕre*; 2, = to send out, deliver from authority (e.g. to — an order, a book), *edĕre, proponĕre* (by placards), *pronuntiare* (by heralds, public criers); to be issued, *exire, emanare*; to — an order, *edicĕre, edictum proponĕre*; to — too severe orders, *nimis severe statuĕre*; to — a decree, *rescribĕre* (of the sovereign); to — a written order to anybody, *lit(t)eras dare* or *mittĕre ad alqm*; 3, = to deliver for use, to — voting papers, voting tablets, *diribĕre tabellas*; one who does this, *diribitor*; to — provisions, *dispensare* (of the *dispensator*, = the manager of the house).

isthmus, n. *isthmus* (*isthmos*).

it, pers. pron. 1, as a demons. pron. by *hic, haec, hoc*, or *is, ea, id*; 2, before a verb, not rendered at all; if used emphatically, by *ille, illa, illud*, or, pointing to a third party, *iste, ista, istud*, or if = self, itself, by *ipse, ipsa, ipsum*, or by *res, ipsa res*.

Italian, adj. *Italicus,* + *Italus*. **italics,** n. *lit(t)erae tenuiores et paullum inclinatae*.

itch, I. n. 1, as a disease, *scabies*; to suffer from the —, *scabie laborare*; 2, = sensation caused from that disease, *scabies* (rare), *prurigo, pruritus, -ūs* (Plin.), *formicatio* (μυρμηκία, = an — like the crawling of ants, Plin.). **II.** v.intr. lit. *prurire* (in gen.), *formicare* (Plin., as if ants were running about on the part of the body which itches), *verminare* (Mart., as if the part which itches was full of vermin).

item, I. adv. = also; (used when something is to be added) see FURTHER. **II.** n. in an account, —s of expenditure, *rationes sumptuariae*; in a gen. sense, = article, *pars, caput* (e.g. of a law, a treaty); an — in a contract, agreement, *condicio, caput*; or often *res* would be sufficient; or by adj. *singuli* (e.g. the —s of expenditure, *pecuniae singulae*).

iterate, v.tr. *iterare.* **iteration,** n. *ase* verb.

itinerant, n. and adj. *viator, circumfora-neus.* **itinerary,** n. *itineris descriptio.*

ivory, I. n. *ebor.* **II.** adj. *eburneus,* † *eburnus, eboreus.*

ivy, n. *hedera ;* — -mantled (of towers, etc.), *haberá obsitus.*

J.

jabber, v.intr. *blaterare, garrire, strepĕre, crepare ;* see PRATTLE. **jabberer,** n. *qui blate-rat.* **jabbering,** n. *clamor, strepitus, -ūs.*

jack, n. 1, as term of contempt, — of all trades, *qui se ad omnia aptum esse putat ;* 2, = boot—, *instrumentum ad caligas detrahen-das aptum ;* kitchen —, *machina quá utimur ad carnem circumagendam.* **jackanapes,** n. *homo stolidus.* **jackass,** n. *asinus* (lit. and fig.). **jackdaw,** n. *monedula,* perhaps *gra-culus.*

jacket, n. *vestis* or *vestimentum.*

jade, n. 1, = a poor horse, *caballus ;* 2, of a woman, *mulier importuna, puella proterva.* **jaded,** adj. *fatigatus, (de)fessus ;* see WEARY.

jag, v.tr. = to cut into notches like those of a saw, *incīdĕre* (= to make incisions) ; see INDENT. **jagged, jaggy,** adj. *serratus* (Plin.), with teeth like those of a saw) ; — rocks, *saxa praerupta ;* see RUGGED.

jail, n. *furcifer ;* see GAOL, PRISON.

jam, I. n. *fructus condīti.* **II.** v.tr. *com-primĕre.*

jamb, n. (in architecture) *postis,* m.

jangle, v. see QUARREL.

janitor, n. *janitor, ostiarius ;* fem. *janitrix.*

January, n. *Januarius (mensis).*

jar, I. v.intr. 1, = to strike discordantly, or if the jarring sound is repeated, *stridēre* (or *stridĕre,* = to whiz), *absonum esse, dissonare, dis-crepare ;* 2, = to disagree with, *discrepare, dis-sonum esse ;* see DISAGREE. **II.** n. = quarrel, *rixa, jurgium ;* see QUARREL. **jarring,** adj. *dissonus, discors ;* see DISCORDANT.

jar, n. = a vessel, *olla* (orig. *aula), cadus* (esp. for wine), *dolium* (= cask), *seria* (= large —) ; *urceus* (in gen.) ; *urna* (lit., = a jug for water, then an urn for the ashes of dead bodies, a lottery-box, a money-box, etc.) ; *hydria* (ὑδρία), *situlus* and *situla* (= a water-pot, also used as a lottery-box, in this sense usu. *sitella) ; amphora* (ἀμφορεύς = a large vessel, usually with two ears or handles, esp. used for wine).

jargon, n. *strepitus, -ūs,* or *sermo barbarus, ut ita dicam.*

jasper, I. n. *iaspis.* **II.** adj. *iaspideus* (Plin.).

jaundice, n. *morbus regius* or *arquatus* (Cels.). **jaundiced,** adj. fig. *lividus, invidus.*

jaunt, n. *iter, excursio* (Plin. Min.) ; to take a —, *excurrĕre* (Plin. Min.).

javelin, n. *pilum, iaculum ;* see DART.

jaw, n. 1, *maxilla* (Cels.) ; jaws, *fauces, -ium* (= the larynx) ; to tear out of the —s, *eripĕre e faucibus* (lit. and fig.). **jaw-bone,** n. *maxilla.*

jealous, adj. *aemulus* (= rival) ; = envious, *invidus, lividus ;* to be — of anyone, *aemulari*

alci or *cum algo, invidēre alci.* Adv. use adj. **jealousy,** n. in gen. *aemulatio* (Cic., Tusc.) ; *zelo-typia* (Plin., by Cic. written in Greek, ζηλοτυπία = — in love).

jeer, I. v.tr. and intr. *in ludibrium vertĕre* (Tac.) ; the people — at anything, *algd in orā omnium pro ludibrio abiit* (Liv.) ; = to deride any-thing or anyone, *ludibrio sibi habēre, ludificare, deridēre ;* = to mock, *irridēre,* all with *algm, illu-dĕre alci,* or *in algm ;* = to cavil, *algm cavillari.* **II.** n. *ludificatio, cavillatio, irrisio, irrisus, -ūs, ludibrium.* **jeerer,** n. *irrisor, derisor, cavil-lator.* **jeering,** adj. by adv. *cum irrisione.*

jejune, adj. *jejunus, aridus, exilis, siccus, exsanguis.* Adv. *jejune, exiliter, jejune et exiliter.* **jejuneness,** n. *jejunitas, siccitas,* comb. *je-junitas et siccitas et inopia.*

jeopardize, v.tr. *algd in aleam dare, algd in discrimen committĕre* or *vocare* or *adducĕre ; algd discrimini committĕre, algd ad ultimum discrimen adducĕre.* **jeopardy,** n. see DANGER, ADVEN-TURE.

jerk, I. v.tr. *offendĕre algm algá re* (e.g. *capite, cubito, pede aut genu) ;* see HIT, BEAT. **II.** n. 1, *impetus, -ūs ;* see HIT ; 2, see LEAP.

jerkin, n. 1, see JACKET ; a buff —, *lorica ;* 2, *vestis.*

jest, I. v.intr. *jocari, joco uti, joca agĕre cum algo, joculari, cavillari.* **II.** n. *jocus,* in the plur. *joca* in Cic. and Sall., *joci* in Liv., = a joke, amusement, *ludus,* comb. *ludus et jocus ;* = fun, wit, *facetiae ;* in —, *per jocum, per ludum et jocum ;* for —, *per ridiculum, joco, joculariter ;* do you mean that in earnest or in —? *jocone an serio hoc dicis?* without —, no —, *amoto* or *remoto joco, omissis jocis, extra jocum ;* to put a — upon anyone, *algm ludĕre, ludi-ficari.* **jester,** n. *qui jocatur ;* = buffoon, *scurra, sannio, balatro.*

jet, n. = the mineral, *gagates, -ae,* m. (Plin.) ; — -black, *nigerrimus.*

jet, n. of water, *aqua saliens* or *exsiliens* (or in pl.).

jetsam, n. *res naufragio ejectae.*

jetty, n. *moles, -is.*

Jew, n. *Judaeus.* **Judaism,** n. *Judaismus, religio Judaica, doctrina Judaica.* **Jewish,** adj. *Judaicus, Judaeus.* **Jewry,** n. *vicus Ju-daicus, regio Judaica.*

jewel, n. *gemma ;* see GEM. **jewelled,** adj. *gemmeus, gemmatus.* **jeweller,** n. *qui gemmas vendit* or *sculpit.*

jig, n. and v.tr. see DANCE.

jilt, v.tr. *repudiare.*

jingle, I. v.intr. (as in jingling chains or bells), *tinnire* (= to ring). **II.** n. or **jingling,** n. *tinnītus, -ūs.*

job, n. 1, = work, *opus, -ĕris,* n. ; 2, = a small lucrative business or office, *munus exiguum* or *parvum ;* see WORK, PERFORMANCE ; 3, = work carried on unfairly, *fraus, -dis,* f. **jobber,** n. 1, = one who does small jobs, *operarius* (= one who assists, servant, labourer) ; 2 (= a stock-jobber), *argentarius ;* see BROKER ; 3, = one who does anything unfairly, *fraudator, circum-scriptor.*

jockey, I. n. *agaso* (= groom). **II.** v.tr. (= to cheat), *circumvenire* (= to surround, fig. to take in) ; see CHEAT.

jocose, jocular, adj. *jocosus, jocularis, jocularius, ridiculus* (of persons and things) ; = laughable, *ridendus* (of things) ; *facetus, salsus, festivus, hilaris* (hilarus = gay) ; *ludicer, lascivus* (= sportive). Adv. *jocose, joculariter, festive, las-cive, hilariter, hilare, jacete, salse ;* see GAY.

**MERRY. jocoseness, jocularity, jocund-
ity,** n. *facetiae, hilarus animus et ad jocandum
promptus, hilaritas, laetitia, alacritas, lascivia.*

jog, I. v.tr. = to push off, *propellěre* (e.g.
alqm, or the vessel with the oar, *navem remis*);
impellěre; see PUSH. **II.** v.intr. (= to move
by jogs) *promověri, lente progredi.* **III.** n. **1,** =
a push intended to awaken attention, in general,
offensio; (= the impression from without) *(im)-
pulsus, -ūs;* a violent —, *impetus, -ūs;* see PUSH.

join, I. v.tr. lit. = to bring one thing in
contiguity with another, *(con)jungěre* (in general);
nectěre, con(n)ectěre (= to connect, lit. and fig.);
= to unite things so that they belong together,
comparare (all *cum alqā re or alci rei*); = to glue
together, cement, fig. = to unite closely together,
conglutinare (e.g. *verba*); =to tie, fasten together,
colligare, copulare, comb. *jungěre et copulare, continuare* (lit. and fig.); — without a break, *ad-
jungěre, ad alqd or alci rei;* — battle, *proelium
or pugnam committěre.* **II.** v.intr. **1,** = to be
connected with, *committi, continuari, (con)jungi,
adjungi;* **2,** = in partnership, etc., *se (con)jun-
gěre, or societatem inire or coire, cum alqo;* **3,** = to
meet, *se alci adděre, alci occurrěre, alcjs rei participem esse.* **joiner,** n. *faber.* **joint, I.** n.
(in anatomy = the joining of two or more bones),
commissura (in general, also in the human
body); *artus, -ūs, articulus,* comb. *commissurae
et artus;* — of a plant, *nodus;* in particular the
joints of the spine, *vertebrae,* so too *nodus,* and
comb. *nodi articulique;* a — of a chain, *annulus;*
(in architecture and joinery) = a binding or
tying together (in architecture), *colligatio, verti-
cula* (to cause motion); in joinery, *coagmentum,
coagmentatio, compages, -is, compactura, junctura*
(= the joining in general). **II.** adj. (as in —
property), *communis;* see COMMON. Adv. *conjuncte, conjunctim, una, communiter.* **joint-
heir,** n. *coheres, -ēdis,* m. and f. **joint-stock
company,** n. *societas.* **jointure,** n. *annua*
(quae viduae praebentur).

joist, n. *tignum transversum or transversarium.*

joke, see JEST.

jolly, adj. *hilaris (hilarus), lascivus ;* see
MERRY. **jollity,** n. *hilaritas, lascivia.*

jolt, I. v.tr. *jactare, concutěre, quassare;* see
SHAKE. **II.** v.intr. *jactari, concuti, quassari;* to
— against (e.g. the carriage —s), by *offenděre
alqm, alqd* (= to run accidentally against one, of
persons and things; hence to fall in with, meet);
incurrěre in alqm or in alqd (= to run violently
against anyone or anything, of persons and
things ; hence to fall in with anyone); *illidi alci
rei or in alqd, allidi ad alqd* (= to be knocked,
to dash upon anyone or against anything so as
to be hurt, of persons and things, e.g. against
the wall, *parieti illidi;* against the rocks, *ad
scopulos allidi*); see SHAKE. **III.** n. *jactatio,
quassatio,* or by verb.

jostle, v.intr. *alqm offenděre;* see JOLT, II.

jot, I. n. not a—, *nihil, ne minimā quidem
re, ne transversum unguem or digitum;* not to
care a —, *alqd non flocci, or nihili or nauci
facěre.* **II.** v.tr. to — down, *annotare or scribere.*

journal, n. **1,** = diary, *ephemĕris, -idis,* f.
(ἐφημερίς); **2,** in commerce, *rationes* (= accounts),
codex accepti et expensi, or, in the connexion of
the sentence, simply *codex or tabulae* (= a cash-
book for putting down income and expenditure);
= the waste-book, *adversaria, -orum;* **3,** = newspaper, *acta (diurna), -orum.* **journalist,** n.
diurnorum scriptor.

journey, I. n. *iter, itineris,* n. (to a place);
via (= the way, road); = the departure, *profectio*
(never in the sense of the—itself); = the act of

travelling and the stay in foreign countries, *peregrinatio;* = a voyage, *navigatio;* to be on a —,
in itinere esse; to make, undertake a —, *iter
facěre;* into foreign countries, *peregrinationes
suscipěre;* to get ready for the —, *omnia quae
ad proficiscendum pertineant comparare; profectionem or iter parare;* a march, *iter* (= in
gen.); a day's —, march (of troops), *diei or
unius diei iter;* — or march, *prima, secunda,
tertia, quarta, quinta castra, -orum :* — by sea,
cursus, -ūs, navigatio ; in speaking in the ordinary
sense of a — or voyage of so many days, the
number of days is added in the genitive case,
e.g. one day's —, *diei iter or cursus, -ūs,* or *navigatio ;* of two days, *bidui iter or cursus or navigatio ;* of nine days, *novem dierum iter, cursus,
navigatio ;* to be distant one day's —, *diei
itinere or cursu or navigatione abesse;* two days'
—, *bidui spatio or* simply *bidui abesse ;* the
forest extends in breadth a nine days' —, *latitudo
silvae patet novem dierum iter ;* the distance was
about a ten days' —, *via dierum fere erat decem.*
II. v.intr. *iter facěre, conficěre, progredi* (= to set
out), *peregrinari* (= to — abroad); see TRAVEL,
MARCH.

journeyman, n. in a trade, *opifex, -icis,* m.
and f. (= artisan); *opera* (usually in pl.), *mercenarius, operarius.*

Jove, n. *Jupiter,* gen. *Jovis* (as god and
planet); by — ! *mehercle !*

jovial, adj. *hilaris, lascivus;* see MERRY.
Adv. *hilariter, lascive.* **joviality,** n. *hilaritas,
lascivia;* see MIRTH.

joy, I. n. *gaudium* (= the state of the mind,
i.e. *cum ratione animus movetur placide atque constanter, tum illud gaudium dicitur,* Cic.), *laetitia,*
(when we show it outwardly, *laetitiā gestiens,*
Cic.); the sensation of —, = pleasure, *voluptas;*
comb. *laetitia ac voluptas,* = delight, *delectatio,
deliciae* (= the object of —; poets use also
gaudium and voluptas in this sense); to gratify
anyone, *gratificari alci* (by a present, etc.);
you have given me great pleasure, caused me
great —, by, etc., *magnam mihi gaudium attu-
listi, quod,* etc. ; it gives me great pleasure, *alqd
mihi gaudio, laetitiae, or voluptati est; delector
alqā re, alqd mihi in deliciis est;* anything gives
me great pleasure, *magnā laetitiā, magno gaudio
me afficit alqd; alqd summae mihi voluptati est :
magnum gaudium, magnam laetitiam voluptatemque capio (percipio) ex alqā re; alqd cumulum
gaudii mihi affert* (used when we wish to express
a still higher degree of —, caused by something
additional); to express one's — in words, *gaudium verbis prodere;* to jump with — (in succeeding, in hearing joyous news), *laetitiā se
efferre, gaudio exsilire, ex(s)ultare;* to be delighted
with —, *laetum esse omnibus laetitiis* (a phrase
which Cic. borrowed from a comedy of Caecilius
and uses very often); on his arrival they all
received him with expressions of —, *eum adveni-
entem laeti omnes accepēre.* **II.** v.intr. *gaudēre,
gaudio affici, gestire, ex(s)ultare, laetificari* (=
to show signs of —); see REJOICE. **joyous,
joyful,** adj. **1,** = glad, *laetus, hilaris or hilarus*
(= in a merry humour); *libens (lub-)* (=with pleasure); **2,** = giving joy, *laetus, laetabilis ; gratus*
(as regards anything for which we ought to be
thankful) ; = pleasing, *jucundus, dulcis;* = welcome, *exoptatus.* Adv. *laete, hilariter, hilare,
libenter (lub-), jucunde.* **joyless,** adj. *maestus ;*
see SAD. **joyousness, joyfulness,** n. see JOY.

jubilant, adj. = rejoicing, by *laetitiā or
gaudio ex(s)ultare, laetitiā or alacritate gestiens ;
ex(s)ultans et gestiens;* see EXULT. **jubilee,**
n. = a season of great public joy and festivity,
festi dies laetissimi; the — year, *annus qui est
quinquagesimus or centesimus post rem gestam.*

judge, I. n. 1, *judex, -icis*, m. (for the exact meaning of the term *judex* see Smith, "Dict. of Antiquities," art. JUDEX), *assessor*; in Cic. often *qui judicat* or *qui judicium exercet* or *qui est judicaturus* (when he is about to —); = arbitrator, *arbiter*; =delegate, *recuperator*; — of the circuit, *quaesitor* (lit. of criminal offences); = a mediator, umpire, *disceptator* (fem. *disceptatrix*); to bring anything before the —, *alqd ad judicem deferre*; verdict, sentence of the —, court, *judicis sententia, judicium*; a decree of a —, *edictum*; an injunction, *interdictum*; to appeal to the —, *ad judicem confugere*; belonging to the office of a —, *judicialis*; 2, in gen. *judex, aestimator, existimator*, comb. *existimator et judex, censor* (censor *castigatorque*); see CRITIC. **II.** v.intr. *judicare*, about anything, *alqd*, about anyone, *de alqo* (also in a judicial sense), *facere judicium*, about anything, *alcjs rei* or *de ulqâ re*, about anyone, *de alqo*; = to think, *existimare* (= to have an opinion), about anything, *alqd* or *de alqâ re*, about anybody, *de alqo*; = to think well, have a good or bad opinion of anyone, *bene* or *male existimare de alqo*; =to give a formal judgment, a decision, esp. in the Senate, *censēre*. **III.** v.tr. (= to hear and determine a case), *judicare de alqo, judicium edēre in alqm*; to — between, *dijudicare* (e.g. *vera et falsa*, or *vera a falsis*). **judgment,** n. = the process of examining facts in court, *judicium*; to administer justice, give —, *jus dicēre, agēre*; as a faculty of the mind, *judicium, sapientia, prudentia*; to show —, *judicium habēre*; see UNDERSTANDING, WISDOM; =determination, *arbitrium, decretum* (= decree), *sententia* (= opinion); the opinion which anyone forms after having first inquired into the value of anything, estimation, *existimatio*; the public opinion, *existimatio vulgi* (Caes.); to give one's —, *sententiam dicēre* (of the author, senator, judge); in my —, *meo judicio, quantum ego judico, (ex* or *de) meâ sententiâ, ut mihi quidem videtur*; — seat, *tribunal, judicium*; to bring anything before the —, *alqd (e.g. alcjs factum) in judicium vocare* (Cic.); see also OPINION. **judicature,** n. *jurisdictio, jurisdictionis potestas*; to be subject to anyone's —, *sub alcjs jus et jurisdictionem subjunctum esse*; it comes under my —, *jurisdictio mea est, hoc meum est, hujus rei potestas penes me est.* **judicial,** adj. 1, *judicialis*; = belonging to the judge, *judiciarius*; = what belongs to the forum, *forensis* (e.g. *contentiones*); a — opinion, *sententia*; a — decree, *edictum*; injunction, *interdictum* (of anything prohibited by the praetor, until the cause was tried); to demand a — inquiry against anyone, *judicium postulare in alqm, judices petēre in alqm*; 2, fig. (e.g. a — habit of mind), *aequus*; see IMPARTIAL; 3, sent by Heaven (e.g. — blindness), *a Deo* or *divinitus missa (caecitas,* etc.). Adv. *jure, lege* (e.g. to proceed — against anyone, *lege agēre cum alqo, jure* or *lege experiri cum alqo*). **judiciary,** adj. *judiciarius.* **judicious,** adj. *sagax, maximis consiliis, sapiens, prudens* (= sagacious). Adv. *sagaciter, sapienter, prudenter, aequo animo.* **judiciousness,** n. *sagacitas, prudentia, sapientia, aequanimitas* (i.e. without bias), *consilium.*

jug, n. *urceus, urceolus* (= little —), *hirnea, hirnula* (= little —), *amphora* (large, with two handles, esp. for wine); see JAR.

juggle, I. v.intr. 1, in the lit. sense, *praestigias agere*; 2, see DECEIVE. **II.** n. 1, = trick by legerdemain, *praestigiae*; 2, deception, *deceptio* (the act), *error* (= mistake); = fallacy, treachery, *fallacia*; = simulation, *simulatio, dissimulatio* (the former = pretending what one is not, the latter = pretending not to be what one really is). **jugglery, juggling,** n. = artifice, *ars, artificium, dolus.* **juggler,** n. 1, lit. *prae-* *stigiator* (in gen.), f. *praestigiatrix, circulator* or *planus* (= a conjuror who travels about, the former exhibiting snakes); 2, see DECEIVER.

jugular, adj. — vein, * *vena jugularis.*

juice, n. *sucus* (also fig. = energy, e.g. in speech); = poison, *virus,* n.; the — of the grape, *suci uvae* (in gen.), *melligo uvae* (when still unripe). **juicy,** adj. *suci plenus, sucosus* (= full of juice); *sucidus* (= with juice in).

jujube, n. 1, *zizyphus* (= the tree), *zizyphum* (= the fruit); 2, = a medicine which melts in the mouth, *ecligma* (all three Plin.).

July, n. *Julius (mensis)*; in the times of the Republic, *Quinctilis (mensis).*

jumble, I. v.tr. *(per)miscēre*; to make a regular —, *omnia miscēre, omnia miscēre et turbare*; see CONFOUND. **II.** v.intr. *(per)misceri.* **III.** n. *mistura* (lit. and fig., e.g. of virtues and vices, *mistura vitiorum et virtutum,* Suet.); = mixture of different kinds of corn, *farrago* (also of the contents of a book, *nostri libelli,* Juv.); — of words, *sartago*; = conflux of different things, *colluvies, colluvio* (e.g. *exercitus mixtus ex colluvione omnium gentium, colluvies illa nationum*); *varietas* (e.g. *sermonum opinionumque*); generally by *miscēre* (e.g. *bona mixta malis*).

jump, I. v.intr. lit. *salire*; = to exercise oneself in jumping, *saliendo se exercēre*; to — up, *exsilire*; with joy, *ex(s)ultare gaudio, exsilire*; to — upon or into, *insilire in alqd*; to — from a wearied horse upon a fresh one, *ex fesso in recentem equum transultare*; to — over anything, *transilire alqd*; to — down from, *desilire ex,* etc. (from the horse, *ex equo*). **II.** n. = leap, *saltus, -ūs.* **jumper,** n. *qui salit.*

junction, n. *conjunctio, junctio.* **juncture,** n. *status, -ūs*; — of affairs, *tempora, -um*; happy —, *temporum felicitas.*

June, n. *(mensis) Junius.*

jungle, n. *silva.*

junior, adj. and n. *junior* or *minor aetate*; the —, *(natu) minor.*

juniper, n. *juniperus,* f.

junk, n. 1, = pieces of old cable, *by funis, -is,* m.; see CABLE, ROPE; 2, = Chinese vessel, *navis serica.*

junket, n. *placenta* (= cake), *cup(p)edia, -orum,* or *cup(p)ediae* (ante and post class. = dainties). **junketting,** n. *iter, -inēris, voluptatis caus(s)â susceptum.*

juridical, adj. see JUDICIAL. **jurisconsult,** n. *juris peritus, juris* or *jure consultus* (both also written as one word), *juris sciens,* in *jure prudens.* **jurisdiction,** n. see JUDICATURE. **jurisprudence,** n. *juris civilis prudentia*; anyone's knowledge in —, *juris civilis scientia.* **jurist,** n. see JURISCONSULT. **juror,** n. as judge, *judex (selectus)* (selected in Rome from the senators, knights, i.e. *equites,* and the *tribuni aerarii*). **jury,** n. *judices, -um,* or *consilium* (e.g. *judicum*).

just, I. adj. = upright, *justus* (e.g. judge, complaint, fears, punishment, etc.), *aequus* (= equitable, reasonable, of persons), *legitimus* (= lawful, of things); to have — claims upon a thing, *alqd jure suo* (or *recte*) *postulare*; *meritus* (= deserved). **II.** adv. 1, = exactly, *diligenter* (e.g. I can't — tell, *hanc rem non ita diligenter teneo*); 2, in reference to a particular moment, *commodum, commode*; (colloquial) — now, *tantum quod (tantum quod cum (quum),* — when); — now, this moment, for the present, *in praesentia*; only — lately, *modo, proxime* (e.g. the piece which he had written — lately, *fabula quam proxime scripserat*); also by the adj. *recens* (with

ab or *ex* and ablat., or simply by the local ablat.); to have only — arrived from the province, the country, *e provinciâ recentem esse;* the people that had only — come from Rome, *homines Româ recentes;* = accidentally, *forte, forte fortunâ* (e.g. the king was — here, *rex forte aderat);* **3,** in comparison, — as, *aeque, perinde, pariter, similiter, item* (or *idem, eadem, idem,* in reference to subject and object), *itidem, juxta, eodem* or *pari modo* (= — in the same manner); to speak — in the same manner, *in eandem sententiam disputare;* to love anyone — as much, *aeque amare alqm;* to be — as old and as popular, *pari esse aetate et gratiâ;* — as well ... as, *aeque ... ac (atque, et, ut), perinde ... ac (atque, ut, quasi); proinde ... ac (quasi), similiter ... ac (atque, et, ut), item ... ut (uti, quemadmodum, quasi), itidem ... et (quasi), juxta ... ac (atque, quasi, cum* [with the ablat. of the persons to whom we compare anyone]); *non secus ... ac; ut ... ita, non minus ... quam* (the latter if there is no negation connected with it), *talis ... qualis, is* with *qui* following (if — as ... as, = — the same ... as, — such a one ... as); — as if, *aeque (pariter, perinde), ac si; similiter, ut si* or *ac si; juxta ac si;* — as well ... as, *tam ... quam, item ... ut;* — as well ... as anyone else, *tam ... quam qui maxime,* also *ita, ut cum maxime;* not ... — as little, *non ... non magis, non ... nihilo plus* (or *non plus*), — as little ... as, *non magis ... quam* (= no more ... than); *non plus ... quam; nec ... nec,* or *neque ... neque (nec inferendo injuriam, nec patiendo);* — as much ... as, *non magis ... quam* (i.e. no less ... than), *non nimis ... quam;* — as great, large, *tantusdem, idem* (e.g. *eadem impudentia);* — as much, *tantidem, tantundem (... as, quantum,* as regards the quality), *totidem (... as, atque, ac,* or the correlative *quot,* as regards the quantity); — as many vessels, *totidem naves, par navium numerus;* — as far, *pari spatio;* — that one, the same, *idem, hic idem, hic is, idem hic, idem ille, idem iste* (if the subject has already been mentioned before, = likewise the same); by *solus* (e.g. *capiti solo ex aquâ exstant,* only — their heads out from the water); **4,** to express emphasis, *imprimis,* or as two words (*in primis*), *potissimum, maxime, praesertim, praecipue;* = certainly, *quidem* (enclit.); = indeed, *utique, sane;* — now, *modo, jam cum maxime;* — now, of what has long been desired, *vixdum, vix tandem;* — at that time, *tum cum* maxime, *eo maxime tempore;* — then, then —, *tum maxime;* not —, not exactly, *haud ita, non ita* (e.g. *sunt ea* [*simulacra*] *praeclara, sed non ita antiqua*), also simply *haud,* or *non, parum* (= not so very); = not exactly, but, etc., *immo vero;* — that which,*id quod;* exactly, *quidem;* but that is — exactly what is considered wicked, *at id quidem nefas habetur;* with the superlative by *quisque,* — exactly the best, *optimus quisque;* but —, *nunc denique;* in answers, — so, *inquam, ita plane* or *prorsus;* sometimes expressed by *sub* with accus. (e.g. *sub lucem,* — before daybreak). Adv. *juste, jure, legitime, merito.* **justice,** n. *justitia* (= the virtue itself, and the love of —); = equity, equitability, *aequitas* (especially as a quality inherent in a person or thing); = right, law, *jus* (= that which is considered right); — requires that, etc., *aequum est* (with accus. and infin.); to exercise —, *justitiam exercēre* or *colēre;* to see — done to anyone, *alci jus dare* or *reddēre* (in court); *ea quae alci debentur tribuēre* (in gen., in daily life, to give anyone what is due to him); in —, *jure.* **justiciary,** n. perhaps *praetor urbanus;* see JUDGE. **justifiable,** adj. *justus;* = lawful, *legitimus,* comb. *justus et legitimus;* see LAWFUL; in more gen. sense, *alqd recte ac jure factum;* see EXCUSABLE. Adv. *recte ac jure.* **justifica-**

tion, n. **1,** *purgatio, excusatio, satisfactio;* to accept anyone's —, *excusationem* or *satisfactionem accipēre;* for his or her —, *sui purgandi caus(s)â;* **2,** Theol. t.t. *justificatio.* **justify,** v.tr. **1,** in the ordinary sense, *alqm* or *alqd purgare* (= to prove one's innocence); = to excuse, *alqm* or *alqd excusare* (e.g. that anything was not done on purpose, that anything was neglected through other engagements, or through an oversight, or through ignorance, etc.); = to free from guilt, *alqm culpâ liberare;* to — anyone on account of, *alqm purgare de alqâ re* (seldom *alcjs rei*), *culpam alcjs rei demovēre ab alqo;* to — oneself, *se purgare, se excusare;* to — oneself before anyone, *se purgare alci;* sufficiently, *satisfacēre alci;* to — one's conduct before anyone, *facti sui rationem alci probare;* **2,** Theol. t.t. *justificare.*

jut, v.intr. — out, *exstare, eminēre, prominēre;* of peninsulas and other portions of land, *excurrēre.*

juvenile, adj. *puerilis,* or by the genit. *pueri* or *puerorum, adolescentis* or *adolescentium, juvenilis.* **juvenility,** n. see YOUTH.

juxtaposition, n. by verbs (e.g. *quod una positum est*)

K.

kale, n. *crambe, -es,* f.

kalendar, n. *fasti, ephemeris, -idis,* f.

keel, n. *carina* (in poetry = the whole ship).

keen, adj. = sharp (lit. and fig.) *acer, acerbus* (= poignant); = acute, *acutus, astutus* (often in bad sense), *subtilis, perspicax, sagax, argutus* (= sagacious or witty). Adv. *acriter, acerbe, acute, astute, subtiliter, sagaciter, argute;* to feel a sorrow —, *summo dolore affici.* **keenness,** n. *acerbitas* (in such phrases as the — of winter, better use adj.), *astutia, subtilitas, sagacitas, perspicacitas;* — of wit, *argutiae.*

keep, I. v.tr. *servare, custodire, tenēre, continēre, habēre* (= to have); to — house, i.e., to remain in it, *domi* (re)*manēre;* to — one's bed, *in lecto esse, lecto tenēri;* to — a position, *locum tenēre;* = to store up, *condēre;* = to preserve, *conservare;* = to support (animals), *alēre;* = to observe, *tenēre, servare, observare;* to — faith, *fidem servare* or *praestare,* or *exsolvēre;* to — a secret, *alqd occultum tenēre;* to — apart, *distinēre;* to — back, = to retain, *retinēre;* I generally — it in this way, *ita facēre soleo, sic est meus mos.* **II.** v.intr. *continēri* (of a dam), *firmum esse* (of a door); *frangi non posse* (of what cannot be broken open, e.g. a door), *non rumpi* (of what cannot burst, e.g. a vessel), *manēre, non evanescēre* (of things that will — their colour); to — to a thing, *retinēre alqd (justitiam, officium);* always to — in the path of duty and honour, *officii et existimationis rationem semper ducēre;* who — to, upholds a thing, *retinens alcjs rei* (e.g. *sui juris dignitatis que);* to — in a certain track, *tenēre alqm locum, cursum tenēre alqo;* to — down, *reprimēre, comprimēre;* to — in, *claudēre, includēre, concludēre, continēre, cohibēre;* to — off, *arcēre, prohibēre, propulsare;* to — from, *(se) abstinēre;* to — up, *conservare, tuēri;* to — up with, *subsequi.* **III.** n. arx. **keeper,** n. *custos, curator.* **keeping,** n. *custodia* (= custody), *tutela* (= protection), to be in —, *convenire, congruēre;* see AGREE. **keepsake,** n. *donum,* or more accurately defined, *memoriae caus(s)â datum os acceptum.*

keg, n. *dolium* (of earthenware), *ligneum vas circulis vinctum* (of wood (Plin.)).

ken, n. *conspectus, -ūs.*

kennel, n. 1, a house for dogs, *stabulum canis* or *canum; tugurium canis* (for a watchdog, etc.); 2, = a pack of hounds, *canes;* 3, = a water-course of a street, *emissarium* (for the water), = a drain, *cloaca.*

kerb, n. *crepido,* better defined by *viae* or *itineris.*

kerchief, n. see HANDKERCHIEF, NECKKERCHIEF.

kernel, n. 1, of fruits, *nucleus* (large or small); 2, in a fig. sense, *medulla* (= marrow); = the blossom, *flos, floris,* m. (of a flower, youth, nobility); = the select portions, *robur, -oris,* n., *robora* (e.g. of Italy, of the Roman people, of the troops, the foot-soldiers, etc.); that was the real — of the army, *hoc erat robur exercitūs, id roboris in exercitu erat.*

kettle, n. *a(h)enum, cortina* (for cooking and dyeing); *lebes, -ētis,* m. **kettle-drum,** n. *tympanum.*

key, n. 1, *clavis, -is,* f. ; 2, fig. *janua* (rare, e.g. *urbs janua Asiae);* 3, of a musical instrument, * *clavis.*

kick, I. v.intr. and tr. *calcitrare, calces remittēre, calcibus caedēre;* a horse that —s, *equus calcitro.* **II.** n. *pedis* or *calcis ictus, -ūs;* to give anyone a —, *alqm pede* or *calce percutēre.*

kid, n. *haedus, haedulus.*

kidnap, v.tr. see STEAL. **kidnapper,** n. *plagiarius.*

kidney, n. *renes, renum,* m. **kidneybean,** n. *phasēlus,* m. and f.

kill, v.tr. *occīdēre* (e.g. *ferro, veneno,* but generally of an honourable death), *caedēre* (= to fell, especially in battle, in a fight; if of several, also *alqm caedes facēre);* *interficēre* (= to cause anyone's death, to murder, also in general like *occīdēre,* but implying a design and the act of destroying), *conficēre* (= to put to the sword, in case of resistance), *necare* (in a cruel manner and wilfully, implying cruelty and want of feeling), *enecare* (stronger than *necare); interimēre, e medio tollēre* (= to get rid, especially of an adversary); *vitam adimēre alci, vitā* or *luce alqm privare* (in general = to deprive of life), *alci vim afferre* (= to lay hands on), *trucidare* (= to murder), *jugulare* (= to cut the throat), *obtruncare* (= to attack anyone and assassinate him); *percutēre* (with the sword, axe, stick, etc., generally with the abl. of the instrument whereby a person is killed, e.g. *gladio,* hence *securi percutēre,* the proper term to express the act of executing one); to — oneself, *se interficēre, se occīdēre, se interimēre, mortem* or *necem sibi consciscēre, mortem* or *vim sibi inferre, vim afferre vitae suae, manus sibi afferre* or *inferre, seipsum vitā privare;* to — the time, *horas* or *tempus perdēre;* to — (of beasts), *caedēre* (cattle), *jugulare, mactare* (only = to slay victims, never = to butcher), *trucidare* (also of slaughter of men).

kiln, n. *fornax, -acis,* f. ; a lime- —, *fornax calcaria;* see STOVE, OVEN.

kimbo, n. (i.e. a—); see CROOKED, CURVE.

kin, n. see RELATION, RELATIVE. **kind, I.** n. *genus, -ēris,* n., *species* (= the single species of the genus); *modus* (esp. in gen. *ejusdem modi,* etc.); *forma* (= characteristic form, feature, e.g. *orationis, eloquentiae, dicendi, loquendi,* etc.); in logic, *species, forma, pars, -tis,* f. (opp. *genus);* of the same —, *ejusdem generis, congener ;* to arrange everything accord-

ing to its —, *singula generatim disponēre ;* Theocritus is wonderful in his — of poetry, *admirabilis in suo genere Theocritus ;* very often by *quidam* or *quasi* (e.g. for slaves the house is a — of republic, and they are all citizens in it, *servis respublica quasi civitas domus est ;* to make a — of will, *quasi testamentum facēre);* every — of, *omne genus* (with the gen., e.g. *herbarum radicumque),* or simply by *omnes* (e.g. every — of danger, *omnia pericula).* **II.** adj. *benignus* (in character and in actions); = charitable, *beneficus ;* = benevolent, *benevolus ;* = amiable, *facilis, humanus ;* = friendly, *amicus ;* = indulgent, *indulgens ;* = liberal, *liberalis ;* = obliging, *comis ;* = gentle, mild, *clemens ;* = well, favourably disposed, *propitius* (of the gods); you are too good ! very — ! *benigne ! benigne!* also *recte!* no, thank you (when we decline taking more — at table, thanking for any act of kindness), *facis amice !* Adv. *benigne, liberaliter,* comb. *benigne ac liberaliter, comiter, clementer, indulgenter* (e.g. to treat, deal with anyone —, *alqm habēre), amice, humane.* **kindness,** n. 1, = kindliness, *benignitas, benevolentia, comitas, humanitas, liberalitas* (= generosity), *clementia, indulgentia, facilitas* (= affability); 2, = a benefit, *beneficium ;* see FAVOUR. **kindred,** n. see RELATION, RELATIVE. **kinsman,** n. see RELATIVE.

kindle, I. v.tr. 1, *accendēre, inflammare* (= both to make light and to burn); *incendēre, inflammare et incendēre, succendēre* (from below), *alci rei ignem in(f)icēre, inferre* (= to throw fire in), *alci rei ignem sub(f)icēre, subdēre* (= to put fire under anything); 2, fig. *accendēre, incendēre, † succendēre, inflammare, concitare, excitare, incitare;* see EXCITE. **II.** v.intr. 1, *(ex)ardescēre;* 2, fig. = to glow with, *ardēre, flagrare.*

king, n. *rex, regis,* m. ; = a prince of a small territory, *regulus;* the — of —s, *rex regum ;* to be —, *regem esse, regnum obtinēre, regiam potestatem habēre;* to make oneself into a —, *to* occupy, usurp the throne, *regnum occupare; regium ornatum nomenque sumēre* (of one who had been before governor of a province, etc.), I shall be as happy as a —, if, etc., *rex ero, si,* etc. **kingcraft,** n. *ars regendi.* **kingdom,** n. *regnum.* **kingfisher,** n. *(h)alcedo,* later form *(h)alcyon.* **kingly,** adj. *regius, regalis.* **kingship,** n. *regia potestas, regnum.*

kiss, I. v.tr. *alqm osculari, suaviari, basiare;* to — a stranger, *osculis alqm excipēre;* to — each other, *osculari inter se ;* — Attica from me, *Atticae meae meis verbis suavium des;* to throw a — to anyone, *manum a facie jacēre;* in the plural, *oscula jacēre, basia jactare.* **II.** n. *osculum* (lit., = a little mouth, used as a nobler expression), *suavium* (= a tender — upon the mouth of cheek), *basium* (= a loud —); to give anyone a —, *osculum* or *suavium* or *basium alci dare; osculum alci ferre* or *offerre, basium* or *suavium alci imprimēre;* to steal a —, *suavium alci surripēre.*

kitchen, I. n. 1, = place for cooking, *culina ;* 2, = the dishes themselves, *cena* (coen-); to keep a good —, *laute cenitare.* **II.** adj. *culinarius ;* = materials, *res culinaria* (in gen.); vegetable, *olus, -ēris,* n., or in the plur. *olera, -um.* **kitchen-garden,** n. *hortus olitorius* (Jct.).

kitten, I. n. *catulus felinus.* **II.** v.intr. *feles parēre.*

knapsack, n. *pera* (= bag), *mantica* (= portmanteau), *sarcina* (= baggage of soldiers).

knave, n. *(tri)furcifer, veterator* (colloquial terms), *homo nequam* or *sceleratus;* see ROGUE. **knavery,** n. *nequitia, malitia, fraus, dolus.*

improbitas; see DECEPTION. **knavish,** adj. *nequam* (= worthless), *malitiosus* (= crafty), *perfidus* (= treacherous); *fraudulentus* (= fraudulent, deceitful), *lascivus* (= full of tricks). Adv. *perfide, malitiose, fraudulenter.*

knead, v.tr. (con)*depsĕre, subigĕre.*

knee, n. *genu;* to bend the —, *genua flectĕre,* or *curvare* (in general); to fall upon one's —s, (*in genu*) *procumbĕre* (unintentionally, or from admiration, or out of respect, or as suppliant); to fall upon one's —s before anyone, *alci procumbĕre, ad genua alcjs procumbĕre, ad genua alci or genibus alcjs accidere, prosternĕre se et supplicare alci* (= to prostrate oneself). **knee-deep,** adj. *genibus tenus.* **knee-pan,** n. *patella* (Cels.). **kneel,** v.intr. *genibus niti;* to — down (*in genu*) *procumbĕre;* see KNEE.

knell, n. *campana funebris.*

knife, n. *culter;* a small —, *cultellus.*

knight, n. *eques, -itis,* m. **knighthood,** n. *ordo equester* (= the whole order); *dignitas equestris, locus equester* (= the rank). **knightly,** adj. *equester;* = worthy of a knight, *equite dignus.*

knit, v.tr. *acubus texĕre;* fig., see TIE, UNITE; to — the brow, *frontem contrahĕre or adducĕre.*

knob, n. *bulla* (of a door, etc.); *nodus* (in plants). **knobbed, knobly,** adj. †*nodosus.*

knock, I. v.tr. and intr. *alqd pulsare* (e.g. *fores, ostium*); to — with the fist, *pulsare, tundĕre,* see BEAT, KILL; to — against, *alqd ad or in alqd offendĕre* (e.g. *pedem in saxum*); to — down, *sternĕre,* —ed up, *fatigatus* (through a combat), *fessus* (through suffering, e.g. illness, poverty, etc.); = fit to sink, *defatigatus, defessus, lassus, lassitudine confectus* (= worn out). **II.** n. *pulsatio* (e.g. *forium*); there is a — against the door, *pulsantur fores.* **knocker,** n. by circumloc. (e.g. he raised the —, *fores pulsavit*), or *tintinnabulum* (= bell). **knock-kneed,** adj. *varus.*

knot, I. n. *nodus* (in gen.), *articulus* (= joint), = a tie, *nodus, vinculum;* = difficulty, *nodus, difficultas;* = a group of people, *circulus;* to make a —, *nodum facĕre, nectĕre;* to draw the —, *nodum a(d)stringĕre;* to loosen the —, *nodum solvĕre, expedire* (lit. and fig.). **II.** v.tr. *nodare, nectĕre;* see TIE. **knotty,** adj. 1, *nodosus, geniculatus;* 2, fig. *difficilis, spinosus* (= thorny); a — point, *nodus.*

know, v.tr. *scire, novisse* (= to have learnt to know); = to have a knowledge of, *alcjs rei scientiam habēre, alqd cognitum habēre;* = to have had a good knowledge, of experience in a matter, *non nescire, non ignorare, alcjs rei non ignarum esse; didicisse* (= to have learnt); I —, a thing does not escape me, *me non fugit or non praeterit;* = to comprehend, *tenēre, intellegĕre, cognoscĕre* (= to experience, learn); I don't —, *nescio, haud scio, ignoro, me fugit, me praeterit;* not to — that the dictator had arrived, *ignorare venisse dictatorem;* I don't — where to turn, to whom to apply, *nescio quo me convertam;* I don't — what to say, *nescio or non habeo or nihil habeo, quod dicam;* I don't — who, *nescio quis;* I read I don't — what, *legi nescio quid;* I don't — whether … (a modest assertion), *haud scio an,* etc., *nescio an,* etc. (e.g. I don't — whether this road is the shorter of the two, *haud scio an or nescio an haec via brevior sit*); you must —, *scito* (not *sci*), *scitote* (not *scite*); do you — perhaps? *scin? scisne? nostin'?* as far as I —, *quod scio, quantum scio, quod sciam;* I should like to — (in questions, the answer to which

would create surprise), *miror, miror unde sit;* to — for certain, *certo and certe scire, pro certo scire, certum habēre, pro certo habēre, exploratum or cognitum habēre, certum est mihi alqd and de alqâ re, exploratum or notum exploratumque mihi est alqd and de alqâ re, cognitum compertumque mihi est alqd, certis auctoribus comperisse* (on good authority); let me —, *fac me certiorem, fac ut sciam;* I wished you to —, *id te scire volui;* to get to —, *audire* (= to hear), *accipĕre* (= to receive intelligence), *comperire* (= to understand), *discĕre* (= to learn); he knew how to maintain his dignity, *auctoritatem suam bene tuebatur;* = to have a clear idea about anything, *novisse, cognovisse, cognitum habēre* (in gen.), *alcjs rei notitiam habēre or tenēre* (= to have a conception of a thing), *didicisse* (through having learnt, opp. *ignorare), vidisse* (through outward perception), *tenēre* (= to hold), *intellegĕre* (*intellig-*) *alqm* or *alqd* (with regard to a thing, = to understand its peculiar features; with regard to persons, to understand their motives, etc.); = to learn to —, *noscĕre, cognoscĕre* (esp. through experience), *discĕre* (by study, inquiry, *μανθανειν); percipĕre* (= to obtain a clear perception); to get a taste of anything, *degustare* (fig., = to get a knowledge of anything, e.g. *ingenium alcjs*); to — anyone, *noscĕre or novisse alqm,* opp. *ignorare;* = to become most intimately acquainted with a thing, *alqd familiariter nosse* (*novisse*); they — each other perfectly well, *erant notissimi inter se;* to — oneself thoroughly, *penitus ipsum se nosse;* to — a person by sight, *alqm de facie nosse;* not to — anyone, *alqm non nosse, alqs mihi est ignotus, alqm ignorare* (seldom); = to recognise, *cognoscĕre;* in order that nobody might — me, *ne quis me cognosceret; agnoscĕre ex alqâ re* (e.g. anyone by his works, *alqm ex operibus suis*), *noscitare alqd ex re* (e.g. anyone by the voice, *voce;* by his countenance, *facie*). **knowable,** adj. *insignis,* by anything, *alqâ re* (e.g. *armis*), *conspicuus alqâ re* (= conspicuous, e.g. *armis*); to make a thing — by, *alqd insignire alqâ re* (e.g. *notâ*); to make anything —, intelligible by words, *alqd explanare.* **knowing, I.** n. = KNOWLEDGE. **II.** adj. *sciens, prudens,* comb. *sciens ac prudens* (with regard to the person who does a thing, opp *insciens*), *quod consulto et cogitatum fit, quod de industriâ fit* (= on purpose); = clever, *callidus, versutus, astutus.* Adv. *consulto* (= with consideration, calmly); *de industriâ* (= on purpose); to sin wilfully, —, *scientem peccare* (opp. *inscientem peccare*); I have done it —, *sciens or sciens prudensque feci, consulto or de industriâ feci.* **knowledge,** n. *scientia, notitia, cognitio* (in a subjective sense); in an objective sense, = a branch of learning, *ars)* = art), *doctrina, disciplina;* sciences, literature, *doctrinae, disciplinae, disciplinae studia, -orum;* to inform anyone, bring anything to his —, *alqm certiorem facĕre alcjs rei or de alqâ re, docēre alqm alqd or de alqâ re* (= to teach), *erudire alqm de alqâ re* (= to instruct), comb. *alqm erudire atque docēre;* to gain — about a thing, *cognoscĕre de alqâ re;* to have anything brought to one's —, *certiorem fieri de alqâ re, docēri alqd;* the — of anything spreads to, reaches, *auditur alqd;* to have no — of, *alqd ignorare;* a clear perception, *notitia alcjs rei; notio alcjs rei* (= the idea which we have of anything, e.g. the — of God, *notitia* or *notio Dei*); = the knowing about anything, *scientia alcjs rei;* = the act of having got into a thing with the understanding, *cognitio* or *intellegentia* (*intellig-*) *alcjs rei;* — about the past, *memoria praeteritorum;* about the future, *prudentia futurorum;* to have only a superficial — of, in, *alqd primoribus labris* or *leviter attigisse, primis labris gustasse;* to have scarcely a superficial — of, *alqâ re ne imbutum quidem* esse; if I possess any — in it, *si in me est huiusce rei ratio alqa;* void of —, *rerum rudis* or *ignarus* (in gen.); illiterate, *lit(t)erarum expers, non lit(t)eratus, illit(t)eratus;* with regard to the fine arts and sciences, *liberalium artium nescius;* = quite illiterate, *omnium rerum rudis* (in gen.), *omnis eruditionis expers.* **known,** adj. *notus;* it is —, *constat, certum est,* with accus. and infin.; to make —, *declarare;* see PUBLISH.

knuckle, n. *articulus (digiti).*

L.

label, I. n. *scheda (sc(h)ida)* = strip of papyrus bark, leaf of paper; *tessera* (= a square, a square piece of stone or wood); *pittacium* (late, — on necks of bottles, etc.). **II.** v.tr. *pittacium affigēre* or *titulum inscribĕre.*

labial, n. = letter pronounced by the lips. *litera labialis* (only as t.t.).

laborious, adj. *laboriosus, operosus, industrius, (g)navus, diligens, sedulus;* to be —, *magni esse laboris, laboriosum esse.* Adv. *laboriose, operose, industrie, (g)naviter, sedulo, diligenter.*

labour, I. n. 1, *labor, opus, -ĕris,* n., *opera, occupatio, pensum* (= task); *moles,-is,* f.(esp. poet., but also in prose, e.g. *haud magnâ mole,* = without great —); to undertake a —, *laborem suscipĕre;* to wear down with —, *alqm labore conficĕre;* to pay by —, *pecuniam debitam operâ suâ (com)pensare;* learned —s, *studia;* — by night, *lucubratio;* —s at spare time, *operae subscivae;* without —, free from —, *otiosus;* 2, in childbirth, *partus, -ûs* (= bringing forth), † *nisus, -ûs (nixus).* **II.** v.intr. 1, = to be active, *laborare;* — in study, *studēre lit(t)erîs;* — on or at anything, *elaborare in re* or *in alqd* or *ut, operam dare alci rei, incumbēre in* or *ad alqd,* or *alci rei;* to be employed in —, *in opere esse, laborem subire;* — day and night, *opus continuare diem et noctem;* — for pay, *operam suam locare;* 2, = to be troubled, *laborare;* — under, *alqâ re laborare* (of trouble); — under a delusion, *decipi;* 3, = to strive, *(e)niti;* see STRIVE; 4, of childbirth, *parturire.* **laboured,** adj. *nitidius valde et affectatius* (Quint.), *nimis exquisitus.* **labourer,** n. *qui opus facit, operarius, opera;* — for pay, a hireling, *mercenarius;* — in a vineyard, *vinitor;* to engage —s, *conducĕre operas;* skilled —s, *artifices.* **laboratory,** n. *locus cameratus ubi metallorum experimenta aguntur.*

labyrinth, n. *labyrinthus* (of the Cretan —); fig. *difficultates summae, res inexplicabiles;* to fall into a —, *in summas difficultates incurrĕre;* to be in a —, *in summis difficultatibus esse* or *versari.* **labyrinthine,** adj. † *labyrinthēus, inexplicabilis.*

lace, I. n. 1, *texta reticulata, -orum;* 2, of a boot, *li(n)gula* (Juv. = shoe-latchet). **II.** v.tr. *nectĕre;* see TIE.

lacerate, v.tr. *lacerare,* † *dilacerare, laniare* (fig., e.g. the heart, *acerbissimo dolore afficĕre alcjs animum).* **laceration,** n. *laceratio, laniatus, -ûs.*

lachrymose, adj. = breaking into tears, *lacrimabundus;* = full of tears, *lacrimosus (lac(h)ru-)* (e.g. *oculi* or *lumina, voces);* = causing tears, *lacrimosus.*

lack, I. n. = not having, *defectio* (esp. *defectio virium,* — of strength), *inopia* (= — of means), *penuria* (= — of necessaries). **II.** v.tr. *re carēre, egēre, indigēre, inopiâ rei laborare* or *premi, alqâ*

alci deesse, abesse, deficĕre; — nothing, *nihil deessi alci.* **lack-a-day !** interj. *ah ! o ! proh !* generally with accus., also without exclamation, e.g. *me miserum !* **lack-lustre,** adj. *decolor.*

lackey, n. *pedissequus, famulus.*

laconic, adj. 1, *Laconicus* = Spartan; 2, = brief, *brevis.* Adv. *breviter, paucis (verbis).*

lacquer, I. n. *lacca.* **II.** v.tr. *laccâ alqd obducĕre* (not class.).

lacteal, adj. † *lacteus.*

lad, n. *puer.*

ladder, n. *scalae;* the step of a —, *scalarum gradus, -ûs.*

lade, v.tr. = to load, *onerare;* — anyone, *onus alci imponĕre.* **laden,** adj. *onustus, oneratus, gravis,* † *gravidus;* — with debt, *aere alieno obrutus;* — with business, *occupationibus distentus.* **lading,** n. *onus, -ĕris,* n.

ladle, I. n. = large spoon, *cochlear (cochlearium* or *cochleare,* Plin.); *trulla* (= small —), *cyathus.* **II.** v.tr. *haurire.*

lady, n. *domina, hera, matrona, materfamilias* (= lady of the house). **lady-like,** adj. *honestus, quod matronâ dignum est.* **ladyship,** n. *domina.* **lady's-maid,** n. *famula,* † *ornatrix.*

lag, v.intr. *contari (cunct-), cessare, morari.* **lagging,** n. *mora, contatio.* **laggard,** n. *cessator, contator.*

lagoon, n. *lacuna.*

laic, lay, adj. *laicus.* **laity,** n. *laici* (Eccl. t.t.). **layman,** n. *laicus.*

lair, n. *latibulum, cubile;* see DEN.

laird, n. *dominus, possessor.*

lamb, I. n. *agnus, agna;* a small —, lambkin, *agnellus;* of a —, *agninus;* — like, *placidior agno;* as meat (*caro*) *agnina.* **II.** v.tr. *agnum edĕre* or *procreare.*

lambent, adj. use † *lambĕre* (e.g. *flamma quae lambit alqd.).*

lame, I. adj. *claudus, mancus* (= short of a limb), *debilis* (= feeble); to be — of a wound, *vulnere debilitatum esse;* to be —, *claudum esse, claudicare;* — in speech, *si quid in oratione claudicat;* — in one foot, *altero pede claudum esse;* a — excuse, *excusatio vana.* **II.** v.tr. *alqm claudum reddĕre.* Adv. by adj. or v. (e.g. to walk —, *claudicare).* **lameness,** n. *claudicatio.*

lament, I. n. or **lamentation,** *lamentum* (usu. in pl.), *lamentatio* (= act of —), *fletus, -ûs* (= weeping), *gemitus, -ûs* (= groaning), *comploratio, (com)ploratus, -ûs, ejulatus, ejulatio* (the latter rare = wailing), *quiritatio (quir-), questus, -ûs, querimonia, querela* (= complaint), *nenia* (= dirge), *plangor* (= beating of the breast, loud —). **II.** v.tr. *alqd lamentari, deflēre, (con)queri,* † *flēre, deplorare* (= — bitterly), *complorare* (rare), † *plorare.* **III.** v.intr. *lamentari, flēre, (de)plorare, ejulare, (con)queri.* **lamentable,** adj. *deflendus,* † *lamentabilis, flebilis, miserandus, miserabilis.* Adv. *miserandum in modum, miserabilius, flebiliter.* **lamented,** adj. past part. of v. or *divus* (of the dead, Tac.).

lamp, n. *lucerna, lych̆us.* **lamp-black,** n. *fuligo.*

lampoon, I. n. *libellus famosus* (Suet.), *famosum carmen* or *famosi versus, -ûs,* pl. **II.** v.tr. *libellum ad infamiam alcjs edĕre.*

lance, I. n. *lancea, hasta;* to break a — with, *hastâ pugnare cum alqo;* fig. *certare, contendĕre cum alqo.* **II.** v.tr. med. t.t. *incidĕre.* **lancer,** n. *eques hastatus.* **lancet,** n. (or little lance), *scalpellum (scalpellus).*

land, I. n. 1, opp. to the sea, *terra*, †*tellus, ūris*, f.; to gain the —, *terram capĕre*; to quit —, (*navem*) *solvĕre*; to sail along —, *oram legĕre*; 2, a fruit-bearing country, *ager, fundus, solum, terra*; a cultivated —, field, *arvum*; to culti-vate —, *agrum colĕre*; relating to the culture of —, *agrarius*; 3, = a particular part of the earth, *terra, regio, provincia, ager, pagus, civitas, patria*; in the — of the Etruscans, *in Etrus-corum finibus*; to drive out of the —, *alqm civi-tate pellĕre, in exsilium pellĕre, agĕre alqm*; of what —? *cujas*; out of our —, *nostras*; the law of the —, *lex* (*publica*). **II.** adj. *terrestris, ter-renus, pedester* (e.g. *pugna pedestris,* — battle). **III.** v.intr. *e nave* or *navem egredi, e nave evadĕre* or *exire.* **IV.** v.tr. *alqos* or *alqd e nave* or *in terram exponĕre*; to — a fish, *piscem capĕre*. **landed,** adj. — property, *agrum, possessio* (usu. in pl.); — proprietor, *agrorum possessor.* **land-ing,** n. *e(x)scensio, egressus, -ūs, litoris appvl-sus, -ūs*; to make a —, *navi exire*; to forbid anyone a —, *alqm navi egredi prohibĕre*; a — place, *aditus, -ūs.* **landlord,** n. *agrorum possessor* (= proprietor), *caupo* (= "mine host"). **landmark,** n. *lapis, -ĭdis,* m. **landscape,** n. *regio, terra*; in painting, *regio in tabulā picta.* **landslip,** n. *terrae lapsus, -ūs.*

lane, n. *angiportum* (or *-us, -ūs*), = narrow street; country lane, *via.*

language, n. 1, = the faculty of speech, *vox, oratio, lingua*; 2, = the act and manner of speak-ing, *vox, lingua, oratio, dictio*; the — of common life, *sermo cot(t)idianus* (*quot-*); — of polite life, *sermo urbanus*; to speak a —, *alqā linguā uti* or *loqui.*

languid, adj. *languidus, languens, remissus, lassus* (= weary), *fessus* (= worn out), *defessus* (= worn down); to be —, *languĕre*; fig. *iners* (= inactive), *frigidus, languidus* (of style). Adv. *languide.* **languidness** or **languor,** n. *languor.* **languish,** v.intr. *languĕre, langues-cĕre*; = to pine away, *tabescĕre*; — in prison, *in carcere vitam miserrimam trahĕre.*

lank, lanky, adj. *prolixus, procĕrus* (= tall), *gracilis, tenuis* (= thin). **lankness,** n. *procĕritas, gracilitas, tenuitas.*

lantern, n. *laterna* (*lanterna*).

lap, I. n. 1, *gremium* (= bosom), *sinus, -ūs* (properly = a fold of the gown); 2, of a racecourse, *spatium.* **II.** v.tr. 1, = to lick up, *ligur(r)ire, lingĕre*; 2, = to touch (as waves), *lambĕre.* **lap-dog,** n. *catellus.* **lappet,** n. *lacinia.*

lapidary, n. *scalptor.*

lapse, I. n. 1, *lapsus, -ūs* (= a gliding or fall); 2, fig. *lapsus, -ūs, error, peccatum*; 3, = flight, expiry, †*fuga*; after the — of a year, *interjecto anno.* **II.** v.intr. 1, *labi, defluĕre*; 2, *errare* (= to go wrong); 3, of property, *cad-ucum fieri, reverti* (*ad dominum*).

larboard, adj. *laevus*; see LEFT.

larceny, n. *furtum*; to commit —, *furtum facĕre.*

lard, I. n. *adeps, -ĭpis,* m. and f., *lar(i)dum.* **II.** v.tr. *alqd adipe ad coquendum parare.* **larder,** n. *armarium promptuarium, cella pen-aria, carnarium* (for keeping meat, Plaut.).

large, adj. 1, = of great size or bulk, *magnus, grandis, amplus*; a — assembly, *celeber conven-tus, -ūs*; 2, — of heart (= liberal), *largus* (e.g. *argus homo, largus animo* or *promissis*). Adv. *magnopere, large.* **large-hearted,** adj. 1, = magnanimous, *magnanimus*; 2, = generous, *liberalis, benignus, benevolus.* **large-hearted-ness,** n. 1, *magnanimitas*; 2, *liberalitas, benignitas, benevolentia.* **largeness,** n. 1,

magnitudo, amplitudo, proceritas (= tallness), *altitudo* (= in height), *ambitus, -ūs* (= in girth), *spatium* (= in surface); 2, fig. see LARGE-HEARTEDNESS. **largess,** n. *largitio, congiar-ium* (of corn, oil, or money).

lark, n. *alauda.*

larynx, n. *guttur, -ūris,* n.

lascivious, adj. *lascivus* (= playful), *im-purus, impudicus, libidinosus.* Adv. *parum caste, impudice.* **lasciviousness,** n. *lascivia* (= playfulness), *impudicitia, libido.*

lash, I. n. 1, = a whip, *flagrum, lorum* (usu. in pl.), *flagellum, scutica* (= light —); 2, = a blow or stroke, *verber, -ēris,* n. (*huic homini parata erunt verbera*); — of the tongue, *verbera linguae*; — of fortune, *verbera fortunae.* **II.** v.tr. 1, *flagel-lare, verberare, virgā* or *virgis caedĕre*; 2, = to bind, *alligare, colligare*; see BIND, FASTEN. **lashing,** n. *verberatio.*

lassitude, n. *lassitudo, languor, (de)fatigatio.*

last, n. of a shoemaker, *forma*; let the shoe-maker stick to his —, *ne ultra crepidam sutor.*

last, I. adj. *ultimus, extremus, postremus, proximus, summus* (= the highest), *novissimus* (= latest); when used of two, *posterior, supe-rior*; to the —, *ad ultimum.* **II.** n. by *extre-mus* (e.g. the — of the letter, *epistula extrema*); at —, (*tum*) *demum, denique, ad extremum* or *postremum.* **III.** v.intr. *durare, (per)man-ēre, stare, longum* or *diuturnum esse.* **last-ing,** adj. *firmus, solidus, duraturus, stabilis, diuturnus, (per)mansurus, perennis*; not —, *fra-gilis* (=frail), *caducus* (=falling), *fluxus.* **lastly,** adv. *postremo, postremum, ad extremum, denique, quod superest* or *restat* or *extremum est, novissime* (esp. in Quint.).

latch, n. *pessulus* (= bolt). **latchet,** n. *corrigia.*

late, adj. 1, *serus*; I went away —, *serus abii*; too — repentance, *sera paenitentia*; *tardus* (= slow), *serotinus* (= — coming or growing, e.g. *hiems, pira, pulli*); the —, *defunctus,* = *mortuus, divus* (of an emperor); — in the day, *multo die*; — at night, *multā nocte,* or by neut. *serum,* used as n. (e.g. *serum erat diei,* it was — in the day); 2, = recent, *recens, novus, inferior* (e.g. of a — age, *inferioris aetatis*). Adv. *nuper, modo.* **lateness,** n. use adj.

latent, adj. *occultus, abdĭtus, abscondĭtus, reconditus.*

lateral, adj. *lateralis* (ante and post class.), *a latere.* Adv. *a latere.*

lath, n. *asser, -eris,* m., *asserculus.*

lathe, n. *tornus*; to work at the —, *tornare.*

lather, n. *spuma a sapone facta.*

Latin, adj. *Latinus*; the — tongue, *latinitas, oratio* or *lingua Latina, sermo Latinus*; to translate into —, *alqd Latine reddĕre*; to know —, *Latine scire, linguam Latinam callĕre*; to be ignorant of —, *Latine nescire.* **latinity,** n. *latinitas.*

latitude, n. 1, = breadth, *latitudo*; in —, *in latitudinem*; fig. — of speech, *latitudo verborum*; 2, = liberty, *licentia* (=) to have great —, *late patēre.*

latter, adj. *posterior*; the former, the —, *hic . . . ille.* Adv. see LATELY.

lattice, n. *cancelli, clathri.*

laud, I. n. *laus.* **II.** v.tr. *alqm laudare, extollĕre*; see PRAISE. **laudable,** adj. *landa-bilis, laudatus, laude dignus.* Adv. *laudabiliter, laudabili in modo.* **laudatory,** adj. *honorificus.*

laugh, laughing, or **laughter, I.** n. *risus, -ūs*; immoderate —, *cachinnatio*; a horse —, *cachinnus*; a — at, *irrisus, -ūs, derisus, -ūs*; a — to scorn, *derisus*; a — -stock, *ludibrium*;

to be a — -stock, *esse alci ludĭbrĭo*. **II. v.intr.** *rīdēre ;* to — at, *arridēre* (= to smile upon in a friendly way, e.g. *non alloqui amicos, vix notis familiariter arridēre) ; alqm deridēre, irridēre ;* = to burst into —, *cachinnare, cachinnari.* **laughable,** adj. *ridiculus, ridendus.* Adv. *ridicule.* **laughter,** n. see LAUGH, I.

launch, v.tr. 1, *navem deducĕre ;* 2, = to hurl, *torquēre ;* to — out, *in aequor efferri ;* to — out in praise of, *alqm efferre laudibus.*

laundress, n. *mulier quae lintea lavat.* **laundry,** n. *aedificium quo lintea lavantur.*

laurel, n. *laurus (-i* and *-ūs),* f. ; belonging to —, *laureus ;* fig.*gloria, laus, honos* (= honour); decorated with —, *laureatus ;* to strive for —s, *gloriae cupidum esse ;* to win new —s in war, *gloriam bello augēre.* **laurelled,** adj. *laureatus.*

lava, n. *massa ardens, saxa liquefacta,* pl.

lave, v.tr. *lavare* (= to wash), *abluĕre* (= to wash off), *irrigare.* **lavatory,** n. *bal(i)neum* (= bath). **laver,** n. *aqualis,* m. and f. (ante class.), *pelvis* (Plin.).

lavish, I. adj. *prodigus* (e.g. *aeris), profusus* (e.g. *profusissima largitio), in largitione effusus ; a — giver, largitor.* Adv. *large, prodige, effuse, profuse.* **II.** v.tr. *profundĕre, effundĕre, largiri.* **lavishness,** n. *effusio* (= prodigality), *largitas, munificentia ;* see LIBERALITY.

law, n. *lex, regula* (= a rule), *norma* (= a standard); body of —s, *jus* (e.g. *jus civile,* = civil —); a —, *lex, edictum, institutum ; lex* is also used in a wider sense, as is our " law," e.g. *versibus est certa lex, hanc ad legem formanda est oratio* (= to or by this model); a divine —, *fas ;* a — of nature, *lex naturae.* **law-breaker,** n. *legis violator.* **lawful,** adj. *legitimus* (= according to —); *legalis* (Quint.) (e.g. *pars civitatis, vita,* = conformable to —). Adv. *legitime, lege, per leges.* **lawfulness,** n. use adj. **lawgiver,** n. see LEGISLATOR. **lawless,** adj. *effrenatus.* Adv. *effrenate, licenter, contra legem, praeter jus.* **lawlessness,** n. *(effrenata) licentia.* **lawsuit,** n. *lis, litis,* f., *controversia.* **lawyer,** n. *jurisconsultus, juris peritus ;* see ADVOCATE.

lawn, n. 1, = fine linen, *sindon ;* see LINEN ; 2, = grass plat, *pratulum* or *herba* (= grass).

lax, adj. 1, = loose, *laxus, fluxus ;* 2, med. t.t. *solutus, liquidus* (e.g. *alvus liquida,* — bowels, Cels.) ; 3, fig. *(dis)solutus, remissus, laxus, neglegens (neglig-).* Adv. fig. *(dis)solute, remisse, laxe, neglegenter (neglig-).* **laxness, laxity,** n. *neglegentia (neglig-,* = carelessness) ; — of spirit, *remissio animi ac dissolutio,* or adj.

lay, adj. see LAIC.

lay, n. see SONG.

lay, v.tr. 1, = to place, *ponĕre, (col)locare* : 2, fig. — the foundations, *fundamenta jacĕre ;* — an ambush, *insidiari, insidias collocare, facĕre, ponĕre, struĕre, parare, tenděro alci ;* — siege, *obsidēre ;* — a wager, *sponsione provocare* or *lacessĕre ;* — a plan, *consilium* or *rationem inire* or *capĕre ;* — hands on, *manus alci inferre ;* — waste, *vastare ;* 3, = — eggs, *(ova) parĕre ;* — aside, *ab(j)icĕre, (se)ponĕre ;* — before, *alqd alci proponĕre ;* — oneself open to, *alqd in se admittĕre ;* — down, = to put down, *(de)ponĕre ;* — down an office, *magistratu abiri,* **se** *abdicare ;* — down arms, *ab armis discedĕre ;* — down a proposition, *sententiam dicĕre, alqd affirmare, confirmare ;* see STATE ; — out money, see SPEND ; — out a corpse, *mortuum lavare* (= to wash), *alci omnia justa solvĕre* would include the laying out ; — up, *condĕre, reponĕre ;* see STORE ; — commands, blame, etc., upon, see COMMAND, BLAME, etc. **layer,** n. 1, in build-

ing, etc., *corium* (of lime, etc.) *ordo* (= row) ; 2, of a plant, *propago.*

lazar, n. see LEPER.

lazy, adj. *piger, ignavus, segnis, iners, otiosus* (= having leisure). Adv. *pigre, ignave, segniter, otiose.* **laziness,** n. *ignavia, segnitia, pigritia.*

lead, I. v.tr. 1, *ducĕre, agĕre ;* — an army, *exercitum ducĕre, exercitui praeesse* (= to command) ; — the way, *alci praeire* (= to go before) ; 2, fig. = to pass, — a life, *vitam agĕre ;* = to induce, *alqm ad alqd faciendum* or *ut alqd faciat, adducĕre ;* in bad sense, *inducĕre ;* see PERSUADE ; 3, with omission of object, e.g. the road —s, *via fert ;* the matter —s to, etc., *res spectat ;* see TEND ; — away, *abducĕre, seducĕre ;* — into, *inducĕre ;* — out, *educĕre ;* — a colony, *coloniam deducĕre.* **II.** n. or **leadership,** *ductus, -ūs ;* under your —, *te duce.* **leader,** n. *dux, ducis,* m. (lit. and fig.), *auctor, princeps, -icis,* m. and f. (fig.). **leading,** adj. *princeps, primarius* (of men), *summus* (of men and things); see CHIEF. **leading-strings,** n. *alci obtemperare (tanquam puer).*

lead, n. *plumbum ;* of —, *plumbeus.* **leaden,** adj. *plumbeus.*

leaf, n. of a tree, *folium, frons ;* a — of paper, *scheda (sc(h)ida), pagina, charta ;* of metal, wood, etc., *bractea, lamina.* **leafless,** adj. *foliis carens* or *nudatus.* **leafy,** adj. †*frondosus,* †*frondeus,* †*frondifer.*

league, I. n. *foedus, -eris,* n. (= treaty), *pactum* (= agreement), *societas* (= alliance or union). **II.** v.tr. *foedus cum alqo inire.*

league, n. *tria mil(l)ia passuum.*

leak, n. *rima ;* to spring a —, *rin:as agĕre.* **leakage,** n. *rima.* **leaky,** adj. *rimosus, rimarum plenus ;* ships that have become —, *quassatae naves.*

lean, I. adj. *macer* (opp. *pinguis), macilentus* (ante and post class.) ; *strigosus* (of horses, etc.) ; see THIN. **II.** v.intr. *niti ;* — on, *(in)niti ; inhaerēre* (= to adhere to), *pendēre* (= to hang from), *confugĕre* or *sese conferre ad alcjs praesidia* (= to seek support with), *fulciri re* (= to depend on or be supported by), *ad alqd acclinare* (= to — towards), *se applicare, in alqd* or *alci rei incumbĕre ;* to — backward, *se reclinare ;* to — to (in opinion), *sententiae favēre.* **leaning,** adj. — on, *innixus ;* — towards, †*acclinis ;* — backwards, †*reclinis ;* — against or on, *incumbens.* **leanness,** n. *macies.*

leap, I. n. *saltus, -ūs ;* to take a —, *salire ;* by —s, *per saltus, saltuatim.* **II.** v.intr. *salire ;* — back, *resilire ;* — down, *desilire ;* — forward, *prosilire ;* — for joy, *gestire, ex(s)ultare ;* — on horseback, *in equum insilire ;* — over, *tran(s)silire.* **leaping,** n. *saltus, -ūs.* **leapfrog,** n. *(pueri) alius alium transilit.* **leap-year,** n. *annus intercalaris, annus bisextus* (late).

learn, v.tr. 1, *discĕre, ediscĕre* (by heart), *memoriae mandare* (= to commit to memory), *perdiscĕre* (thoroughly) ; word for word, *ad verbum ediscĕre ;* — something more, *addiscĕre ;* **2,** = to hear, *discĕre, cognoscĕre* (esp. by inquiry), *certiorem fieri, audire.* **learned,** adj. *doctus, eruditus, lit(t)eratus.* Adv. *docte, erudite, lit(t)erate.* **learner,** n. *discipulus.* **learning,** n. *doctrina, eruditio.*

lease, I. n. *conductio.* **II.** v.tr., to hire on —, *conducĕre ;* to let on —, *locare.*

leash, n. *lorum* (= a strip of leather) ; — of hounds, *tres canes.*

least, I. adj. *minimus ;* see LITTLE. **II.** adv. *minime ;* at —, *saltem, certe, (at)tamen ;* not in the —, *nihil omnino, ne minimum quidem.*

leather, I. n. *corium* (= the hide); *aluta* (tanned). **II.** adj. *scorteus.*

leave, n. *concessio* (= yielding), *permissio* (= permission), *potestas* (= authority), *copia* (= allowance), *venia* (= favour), *arbitrium* (= freedom of action); to give —, *potestatem alci facĕre*; with your —, *pace tuâ*; against —, *me invito*; — to say, *sit venia verbo*; I have —, *mihi licet*; through you, *per te*; give me — to clear myself, *sine me expurgem.*

leave, I. n. = departure, by verb, to take —, *salvĕre alqm jubĕre*; see FAREWELL. **II.** v.tr. 1, = to desert, abandon, *(de)relinquĕre, deserĕre, destituĕre*; 2, — property, *relinquĕre, legare*; see BEQUEATH; 3, = to depart from, *(ex) alqo loco (ex)cedĕre, discedĕre, proficisci, egredi, digredi*; — a province on expiration of office, *(de or ex) provinciâ decedĕre*; — behind, *relinquĕre*; — off, *alqd omittĕre, desinĕre* with infin., *desistĕre alqâ re* or infin.; — out, *omittĕre, praetermittĕre.*
leavings, n. *quae reliqua sunt.*

leaven, I. n. *fermentum*; bread without —, or unleavened, *panis nullo fermento or sine fermento coctus.* **II.** v.tr. *fermentare*; *panis fermentatus,* = leavened bread (Plin.).

lecture, I. n. *schola* (= disputation), *oratio* (= address), *sermo* (= speech). **II.** v.tr. 1, *scholam habĕre de alqâ re*; 2, fig. see REPROVE.
lecturer, n. *qui scholas habet.* **lecture-room,** n. *schola.*

ledge, n. *projectura*; — of rocks, *dorsum.*

ledger, n. *codex accepti et expensi.*

lee, n. (of a ship), *navis latus a vento tutum.*

leech, n. 1, see DOCTOR; 2, = bloodsucker, *hirudo, sanguisuga* (Plin.).

leek, n. *porrum* and *porrus* (of two kinds, one called *capitatum* the other *sectivum*, also *sectilis*).

leer, v.intr. *oculis limis intueri, limis oculis a(d)spicĕre* or *limis (oculis) spectare.* **leering,** adj. *limus.* Adv. *limis oculis.*

lees, n. *faex* (= dregs of wine; so *faex populi*).

leet, n. as in court-leet, *curia.*

left, adj. *rel(l)iquus*; to be —, *restare*; see LEAVE.

left, adj. *sinister, laevus*; the — hand, *sinistra* (i.e., *manus*); on the —, *a sinistrâ, ad laevam.* **left-handed,** adj. *qui manu sinistrâ pro dextrâ utitur.*

leg, n. *crus, cruris,* n.; — of mutton, *caro ovilla*; — of a table, *pes mensae.* **leggings,** n. *ocreae.*

legacy, n. *legātum*; to make a —, *alci legare alqd.*

legal, adj. *legitimus, quod ex lege* or *legibus* or *secundum leges fit.* Adv. *legitime, lege.*
legality, n. *quod ex lege fit.* **legalize,** v.tr. *legibus constituĕre, sancire ut, ferre, ut alqd fiat* (= to propose a law).

legate, n. *legatus, nuntius.* **legation,** n. *legatio.*

legend, n. on coin, *inscriptio, titulus*; — history of a saint, *vita hominis sancti, res ab homine sancto gesta*; = fable, *fabula.* **legenda.'y,** adj. *commenticius, fictus, fabulosus, falsus* (= untrue).

legerdemain, n. *ars praestigiatoria*; — tricks, *praestigiae* (ante and post class.).

legible, adj. *quod facile legi potest.* Adv. by **legibility,** n. *quod facile legi potest.*

legion, n. *legio*; legionary, *legionarius*

(e.g. *cohors, miles*); fig. *ingens numerus, magna vis.* **legionary,** adj. *legionarius.*

legislate, v.intr. *leges dare, constituĕre, condĕre, scribĕre*; see also LAW. **legislation,** n. *legis (legum) datio, legis latio* (= proposal of a law); so by circuml. *leges dare, leges condĕre*; see LAW. **legislator,** n. *legis* or *legum lator.* **legislative,** adj. — body, *senatus, -ûs.* **legislature,** n. *comitia, -orum (centuriata, tributa,* etc.), *senatus, -ûs.*

leisure, n. *otium* (opp. *negotium,* that is, *nec* and *otium*); to be at —, *otiari, vacare, cessare*; at —, *otiosus, vacuus*; not at —, *occupatus*; — time, *tempus subsicivum (subsec-).* **leisurely,** adj. *lentus, otiosus*; see SLOW. Adv. *otiose.*

lend, v.tr. 1, *mutuum dare, commodare alci alqd*; — on interest, *fenerari, (fenore) occupare, (col)locare*; 2, fig. *dare, praebēre.*

length, n. *longitudo*; = extension in height, *proceritas*; — in time, *longinquitas, diuturnitas*; — of the way, *longinquitas viae*; in —, *per longitudinem*; — of time, *in longinquum, diu*; to run all —s, *extrema audēre*; at —, *tandem, denique, tum (tunc) demum*; = fully, *copiose, fuse.* **length-wise,** adv. *in longitudinem.* **lengthy,** adj. — in words, *verbosus, longus*; not to be —, *ne in re multus sim.* **lengthen,** v.tr. *alqd longius facĕre, producĕre*; — in time, *prorogare*; — for payment, *diem ad solvendum prorogare*; — the war, *bellum prorogare*; — the service, *militiam continuare*; — a feast, *convivium producĕre.*

lenient, adj. *mitis, clemens, misericors.* Adv. *clementer.* **leniency,** n. *clementia, lenitas, misericordia.*

lens, n. *vitrum lenticulari formâ* (in no sense class.).

lentil, n. *lens, -ntis,* f., *lenticula* (Cels.).

leonine, adj. *leoninus.*

leopard, n. *leopardus* (very late).

leprosy, n. *lepra* (usu. in pl., Plin.). **leper,** n. *homo leprosus* (late).

less, I. adj. *minor.* **II.** adv. *minus*; see LITTLE. **lessen,** v.tr. *(de)minuĕre, imminuĕre.* **lessening,** n. *deminutio, imminutio.*

lessee, n. *conductor.*

lesson, n. 1, *discenda* (= things to be learned; if by heart, *ediscenda*); dictated —s, *dictata, -orum*; to take —s of anyone, *audire magistrum* (= proof); 2, fig. *praeceptum, monitum, documentum* (= proof).

lest, conj. *ne* with subj.

let, v.tr. = to hinder; see HINDER.

let, v.intr. 1, = to cause or make; I will — you know, *te certiorem faciam* (also by *monēre*); — Socrates say, *Xenophon Socratem disputantem facit*; 2, = to command, *jubēre, curare, alci negotium dare*; 3, = as a sign of the imperative, — us go, *eamus*; 4, in various phrases, e.g. to — blood, *sanguinem mittĕre*; to — go, *missum facĕre, mittĕre, dimittĕre*; — alone, — that alone, or be quiet, *missa isthaec fac*; — down, *demittĕre*; — fly, = shoot, *jaculari, telum in alqm jacĕre*; — loose, *emittĕre*; — in, *admittĕre*; — off, *absolvĕre*; = absolve; *pila (e)mittĕre, tela con(j)icĕre*; = discharge weapons; — into your secrets, *secreta consilia alci impertire*; — slip, *omittĕre, praetermittĕre*; — an opportunity, *facultatem alqd agendi omittĕre*; — that pass, *ut ista omittamus*; 5, = to allow, *sinere* acc. and infin. or *ut, pati* acc. and infin., *concedĕre* infin., *permittĕre alci ut* or infin.; — not, *cave ne* (e.g. — him not go out, *cave ne exeat*); my business

will not — me, *per negotium mihi non licet;* **6,** = to lend or give the use of; see LEASE.

lethal, adj. *mortifer, exitialis, exitiabilis, funestus.*

lethargic, adj. *veternosus, torpidus.* **lethargy,** n. *torpor* (Tac.), *veturnus.*

letter, n. **1,** (of the alphabet) *lit(t)era;* capital —, *lit(t)era grandis;* —s of the alphabet, *lit(t)erarum notae;* to the —, *ad verbum, ad lit(t)eram;* the — of the law, *verba legis;* to hold to the —, *scriptum sequi;* **2,** == an epistle, *lit(t)erae, epistula (epistola);* by —, *lit(t)eris, per lit(t)eras.* **letter-carrier,** n. *tabellarius, qui lit(t)eras perfert.* **letters,** n. = learning, *doctrina, eruditio, humanitas, lit(t)erae;* a man of —, *homo doctus, eruditus, lit(t)eratus, doctrinâ ornatissimus.* **lettered,** adj. *lit(t)eratus.*

lettuce, n. *lactuca.*

levant, n. *oriens, solis ortus, -ûs.*

levee, n. *salutatio.*

level, I. adj. *aequus, planus,* comb. *aequus et planus, libratus* (= balanced). **II.** n. *aequum* (e.g. *in aequum descendĕre), planities;* to be on a — with, *pari esse condicione cum algo, parem or aequalem esse alci.* **III.** v.tr. **1,** *aequare, coaequare, exaequare, complanare* (e.g. *terram);* **2,** = to destroy, *solo urbem aequare;* — to the ground, *diruĕre, evertĕre, sternĕre;* see RAZE.

lever, n. *vectis, -is,* m.

leveret, n. *lepusculus.*

levity, n. **1,** = lightness, *lēvitas;* **2,** = in character, *inconstantia, lēvitas* (with *hominis, animi, opinionis);* = jesting, *jocus, jocatio.*

levy, I. v.tr., — soldiers, *milites scribĕre, milites consoribĕre;* — tribute, *tributum imponĕre, vectigal exigĕre.* **II.** n. *delectus, -ûs;* to make a —, *delectum habĕre or agĕre;* see ENLIST.

lewd, adj. *impudicus, incestus, impurus.* Adv. *incaste, impure.* **lewdness,** n. *impudivitia, impuritas, libidines, -um,* pl. f.

lexicon, n. ** lexicon, * onomasticon.*

liable, adj. *obnoxius* (e.g. *irae, bello);* to be —, *cadĕre in* (e.g. *cadit ergo in bonum hominem mentiri?* Cic.). **liability,** n. use adj.

libation, n. *libatio, libamentum, libamen;* to make a —, *libare.*

libel, I. n. *libellus famosus, carmen famosum* (in verse). **II.** v.tr. *libellum ad infamiam alcjs edĕre.* **libellous,** adj. *famosus, probrosus.*

liberal, adj. *liberalis, largus, munificus, benignus, beneficus;* too —, *prodigus, profusus;* the — arts, *artes liberales, artes ingenuae.* Adv. *liberaliter, large,* comb. *large et liberaliter, munifice, benigne, prodige, profuse;* to give —, *largiri.* **liberality,** n. *liberalitas, munificentia, largitas, beneficentia, benignitas;* of thought, etc., *animus ingenuus, liberalis.*

liberate, v.tr. *liberare;* to — a slave, *manumittĕre;* see DELIVER. **liberator,** n. *liberator* (e.g. *patriae), vindex.* **liberation,** n. *liberatio;* = of a slave, *manumissio.*

libertine, n. *homo dissolutus.* **libertinism,** n. *licentia morum, mores dissoluti.*

liberty, n. *libertas;* too much —, *licentia;* = leave, *copia, potestas;* = of will, *arbitrium, liberum arbitrium;* at —, *liber;* you are at — to do it, *nihil impedit quominus facias, algd facĕre tibi licet or integrum est.*

library, n. *bibliotheca;* a considerable —, *bona librorum copia.* **librarian,** n., to be a —, *bibliothecae praeesse.*

libration, n. *libratio.*

license, I. n. = permission, *copia, potestas;*

= liberty, *licentia* (also in bad sense, *licenti. Sullani temporis; licentia militum; magna gla diatorum est licentia).* **II.** v.tr. *algm privilegio munire.* **licentious,** adj. *dissolutus, libidinosus (lub-).* Adv. *per licentiam, dissolute.* **licentiousness,** n. *libido, libidines, vita dissoluta;* see LEWD.

lick, v.tr. *lingĕre, lambĕre;* to — up, *ligur(r)ire.*

lickerish, adj. *fastidiosus, delicatus.*

licorice, n. *glycyrrhiza, -ae,* f., *dulcis radix* (Plin.).

lid, n. *operculum, operimentum.*

lie, I. n. *mendacium, commentum, falsum;* to tell a —, *mendacium dicĕre alci de algâ re;* to give a person the —, *mendacii algm coarguĕre.* **II.** v.intr. *mentiri.* **liar,** n. (homo) *mendax, homo fallax, falsiloquus* (Plaut.).

lie, v.intr. = to be in a certain place or position, *jacēre* (e.g. *jacēre humi,* to lie or be on the ground; so *jacēre in gramine, jacēre ad alcjs pedes, jacēre sub arbore, jacēre per vias); cubare* (in bed, etc.); *situm esse, positum esse;* as far as —s in me, *quantum est in me (te, vobis,* etc.), *pro viribus meis (tuis,* etc.); to — in, *puerperio cubare* (of childbirth (Plaut.)); *parturire;* to — in this, *contineri re, situm esse, versari, cerni in re;* on whom does it —? *per quem stat?* where —s the hindrance? *quid impedit?* to — between, *interjacēre;* with accus. or with dat.; — in wait, *alci insidiari;* — down, *procumbĕre, decumbĕre, quieti se dare;* — hid, *latēre;* — still, *quiescĕre;* — under an obligation, *alci gratiâ devinctum esse.*

lief, adj. e.g. I had as —, *malim;* — die as endure it, *mortuum me quam ut id patiar malim.*

liege, adj. *imperio or dicione alcjs subjectus, or parens, obnoxius alci;* to be —, *esse in alcjs dicione, parēre alci.*

lieu, n. in — of, *pro, loco, vice.* **lieutenant,** n. in gen. *legatus;* in the army, perhaps *centurio* (infantry), and *praefectus* (cavalry); the lord-lieutenant of a country, *praefectus provinciae.*

life, n. **1,** *vita, anima, spiritus, -ûs;* physical —, *vita quae corpore et spiritu continetur;* in my —, *dum vivo;* to have —, *vivĕre, in vitâ esse;* to come to —, *nasci, in lucem edi;* to put an end to —, *mortem sibi consciscĕre;* to take away —, *vitam alci adimĕre;* to give —, *procreare, parēre algm;* to call into —, *gignĕre, procreare, facĕre, efficĕre;* he can scarcely sustain —, *vix habet unde vivat;* as to the manner in which men live, *mode of —, victus, -ûs;* in public duty, *in republicâ gerendâ;* private —, *vita cot(t)idiana (quot-);* early —, *iniens aetas;* the prime of —, *bona or constans aetas;* (as a word of affection), *mea vita! mea lux!* while there is —, there is hope, *aegroto dum anima est spes est;* to restore to —, *ad vitam revocare or reducĕre, e mortuis excitare;* to come to — again, *reviviscĕre;* to venture your —, *capitis periculum adire;* to cost a person his —, *morte stare;* to try a person for his —, *de capite quaerĕre;* to lead a —, *vivĕre, vitam agĕre;* to flee for one's —, *fugâ salutem petĕre;* to lose —, *perire, vitam perdĕre;* if I could without losing my —, *si salvo capite potuissem;* to depart this —, *diem obirs supremum;* all one's —, *per totam vitam;* loss of — by law, *ultimum supplicium;* to the —, *ad vivum;* full of —, *vividus, vegetus, alacer;* to put — into, *alci animum facĕre or addĕre;* **2,** fig., see VIGOUR; in oratory, *sucus,* comb. *sucus et sanguis;* **3,** = the reality (e.g. paint from the --), *ipse* with the noun mentioned; **4,** = time, *aetas, tempora -um* (e.g. this —, *haec aetas).* **life-blood,** n. **1,** *sanguis, -inis,* m.; **2,** fig.

see LIFE. **life-boat,** n. *scapha ad naufragos excipiendos facta.* **life-guards,** n. *milites* or *cohortes praetoriani* (of the emperor). **lifeless,** adj. 1, *exanimis, exanimus, inanimus* (opp. *animatus, animans*); 2, *frigidus, exsanguis, exilis, aridus,* comb. *aridus et exsanguis, jejunus* (all of speech). Adv. fig., *languide, frigide, exiliter,* comb. *frigide et exiliter* (of speech); *jejune,* comb. *jejune et exiliter.* **lifetime,** n. *aetas, †aevum.* **lively,** adj., **liveliness,** n., **livelihood,** n., see LIVE.

lift, I. v.tr. *(at)tollĕre, extollĕre, (sub)levare;* — upright, *erigĕre;* he —s his hands to heaven, *manus ad sidera tollit;* —ed up, *levatus, allevatus, arrectus;* — with pride, etc., *superbiā, rebus secundis,* etc., *elatus.* **II.** n., use verb.

ligament, n. *ligamentum* (Tac.). **ligature,** n. *ligatura* (late).

light, I. n. = luminous matter, or the result of (as daylight), *lumen, lux;* with the —, *cum primā luce, die illucescente, sub lucis ortum;* the — of the eyes, *lumina (oculorum);* — of a precious stone, *lux gemmae;* to give —, *lucem edĕre, fundĕre;* to see the — of day (or be born), *in lucem edi* or *suscipi, nasci;* to come to —, *in lucem proferri, protrahi, detegi, patefieri* (= to be uncovered, made manifest); to bring to —, *in lucem proferre, protrahĕre, aperire, patefacĕre, detegĕre;* to stand in or intercept a person's —, (lit.) *alcjs luminibus officĕre, obstruĕre,* (fig.) *alci officĕre, obesse;* to stand in your own —, *sibi* or *utilitati suae* or *commodis suis male consulĕre, sibi deesse;* to place in an odious —, *algd in invidiam adducĕre, in summam invid. adduc., alci rei ad(f)icĕre invidiam;* to see in a false —, *algd fallaci judicio vidēre;* — lamp, *lumen* (in gen.), *lucerna* (espec. = a lamp), *candela* (= a taper or torch of wax, tallow, etc.), *cereus* (= a wax taper or torch); to light a —, *lumen, lucernam, candelam accendĕre;* to write or work by —, *ad lucernam (cum lucernā) scribĕre, algd lucubrare* or *elucubrari* (e.g. *epistulam*); to study by —, *lucubrare;* a study by —, *lucubratio.* **II.** adj. as opposed to what is dark, *clarus* (= light in itself), *illustris, lucidus* (= light-spreading), *luminosus, albidus* (= white), *candidus* (= dazzling), *pellucidus* (= shining through). **III.** v.tr. 1, = to set light to, *algd accendĕre;* 2, = to fill with light, *illustrare, collustrare.* **lighten, I.** v.intr. *fulgēre, fulgurare* (usu. impers. *fulget, fulgurat*). **II.** v.tr. see LIGHT, III. 2. **lighthouse,** n. *pharus (pharos).* **lightning,** n. *fulmen, fulgur.*

light, adj. as opposed to heavy, *lĕvis* (opp. *gravis*); — soil, *solum tenue;* = inconsiderable, *lĕvis* (opp. *gravis,* weighty), *parvus* (opp. *magnus*); — pain, *dolor levis* or *parvus* (= slight); — armed infantry, *equites lĕvis armaturae;* — troops, *milites levis armaturae* or merely *levis armaturae, milites leves, velĭtes* (as a regular part of the Roman army, early called *rorarii*), *milites expediti* (= all soldiers who have laid aside their kit, consequently we find *expediti levis armaturae*); — clad or armed, *expeditus, nudus* (=one who has laid aside his overcoat); a —-foot-soldier, *pedes expeditus;* — of foot, *velox* (opp. *tardus*), *pernix* (= nimble); he is very — of foot, *inest in eo praecipua pedum pernicitas;* — of colour, *pallidus;* see PALE; — -hearted, *hilaris, curis vacuus, curis liber solutusque animus;* it is something — (= trivial), *nihil est negotii;* —-minded, *lĕvis, vanus.* Adv. *leviter* (lit. and fig.), *tenere, inconsulte (inconsulto)* (= without consideration); to think — of anything, *algd non magni facĕre.* **lighten,** v.tr. lit. *exonerare* (not in Cic. or Caes.), *jacturam facĕre* (of a ship). **lightness,** n. *lĕvitas* (lit. and fig.). **lightsome,** adj. *hilaris,*

alacer (= cheerful). **lightsomeness,** n. *laetitia, hilaritas;* see GAY.

like, I. adj. = similar, *similis, consimilis,* with gen. or dat., *par,* dat. ; *instar* (indecl., n.), gen.; to make —, *ad similitudinem rei fingĕre;* he is no longer — what he was, *prorsus alius est factus ac fuit antea;* that is — him, *hoc dignum est illo.* **II.** adv. *similiter, simili modo* with *ut atque* (ac), *modo, instar, ritu* with gen. (*ad instar, post* class.) ; see As. **III.** v.tr. *amare, diligĕre, carum habēre alqm, delectari alqā re;* I — that, *hoc arridet* or *cordi est* or *datum* or *acceptum est mihi, libet mihi;* I do not — that, *hoc displicet mihi* (with infin. following); I — it well, *magnopere probo;* if you —, *si isthuc tibi placet;* as you —, *arbitratu tuo.* **like-minded,** adj. *consors, congruens, conveniens, consentaneus.* **likely,** adj. *veri similis* (often written as one word, sometimes *similis veri*), *probabilis;* it is — that, *veri simile est,* with accus. and infin. **likelihood,** n. *veri similitudo* (also in one word, or *similitudo veri*), *probabilitas.* **liken,** v.tr. *algd alci rei* or *cum alga re comparare;* see COMPARE. **likeness.** n. 1, = resemblance, *similitudo,* or by adj. ; see LIKE; 2, = portrait, *effigies, imago;* painted —, *picta imago.* **liking,** n. *amor, voluptas* (= pleasure); *libido;* to one's —, *gratus, acceptus, jucundus.* **likewise,** adv. *item, itidem, et,* or by *idem;* see ALSO.

liliputian, adj. see LITTLE, INSIGNIFICANT.

lily, n. *lilium;* of or from a —, *lilaceus.*

limb, n. *membrum, artus, -uum* (= a member).

limber, adj. *flexibilis, mollis, lentus.*

lime or **limestone, I.** n. *calx, -cis,* f. and (rarely) m.; to burn —, *calcem coquĕre;* quick- —, *calx viva;* slaked —, *calx ex(s)tincta;* bird- —, *viscum.* **II.** v.tr. = to smear with bird—, *visco illinĕre.* **lime-burner,** n. *calcarius.* **lime-kiln,** n. (*fornax*) *calcaria.* **limed,** adj. *viscatus.*

lime-tree, n. *tilia.*

limit, I. n. *terminus, finis, -is,* m., *limes, -itis,* m., *circumscriptio.* **II.** v.tr. *finire, limitare* (= to separate by a boundary-stone or line, thus *limitati agri*), *terminare* (= to put an end to), *certis limitibus* or *terminis circumscribĕre.* **limitation** or **limiting,** n. *determinatio, circumscriptio, definitio, limitatio;* = exception, *exceptio.* **limited,** adj. 1, = short, *brevis;* see BRIEF; 2, fig. a — monarchy, *condiciones regiae potestati impositae,* or *potestas certis cond. circumscriptā.* **limitless,** adj. *immensus, infinitus.*

limn, v.tr. see PAINT.

limp, adj. *languidus, flaccus, flaccidus.* **limpness,** n. *languor.*

limp, v.intr. *claudicare, claudum esse* (= to be lame); see LAME.

limpet, n. *lepas.*

limpid, adj. *limpidus* (rare), *pellucidus;* see TRANSPARENT.

linch-pin, n. *axis fibula.*

linden-tree, n. *tilia.*

line, I. n. 1, *linea;* a straight —, *recta linea;* curved —, *curva linea;* the — of the circle, *linea circumcurrens;* to draw a —, *lineam ducĕre* or *scribĕre;* 2, a boundary —, *finis,* m. and f. ; 3, — (in poetry), *versus, -ūs, versiculus;* in letters, to write a few — in reply, *pauca rescribĕre;* 4, of soldiers, *acies* (in battle), *agmen* (on the march); the front —, *prima acies, hastati, principia, -iorum;* the second —, *principes, -um;* the third —, *triarii;* — of skirmishers, *velites;* to advance in equal —, *aequā fronte procedĕre;* a soldier of the —, (*miles*) *legionarius;* to draw up the army in

three —s, *aciem triplicem instruĕre;* **5,** in the father's —, *a patre;* in the mother's —, *a matre;* to be connected with one in the direct —, *artissimo gradu contingĕre alqm;* **6,** (in fortification), *fossa* (= trench), *vallum* (= entrenchment), *opus,-eris,* n., *munitio* (=fortification), *agger,-eris,* m. (= mound); **7,** = a thin rope, *funis, funiculus, linea;* a carpenter's —, *amussis, -is,* m., *linea;* a chalked—, *linea cretâ descripta;* a fishing—, *linea;* a plumb —, *perpendiculum;* by —, *ad amussim, examussim* (ante and post class.). **II.** v.tr. **1,** — a dress, perhaps *vesti alqd assuĕre;* **2,** = to fill, *complēre.* **lineal,** adj. better not expressed, (e.g. a — descendant, *unus e posteris alcjs).* **lineage,** n. *stirps, -is,* f., *genus, -eris,* n., *origo, progenies.* **lineament,** n. used generally in the pl., as in English, *lineamenta (similitudo oris vultûsque ut lineamenta,* Liv.), but applied to the mind (e.g. *animi lineamenta sunt pulchriora quam corporis);* see FEATURE. **linear,** adj. *linearis* (Plin.).

linen, n. as the material, *linum* (λίνον, flax; *linum tam factum quam infectum, quodque netum quodque in telâ est,* Cic.); *linteum, lintea, -orum,* n. (properly of —, i.e. — cloth, e.g. *lintea, vestis, vela);* clad in —, *linteatus.*

linger, v.intr. *cessare, morari, contari (cunct-);* he —s (i.e. dies slowly), perhaps *paul(l)atim moritur.* **lingerer,** n. *cessator, contator (cunct-).* **lingering, I.** n. *cessatio, contatio (cunct-), mora.* **II.** adj. *tardus, lentus, contabundus (cunct-)* (of people); a — death, *tabes, -is,* f. (= consumption), perhaps *tarda mors, -tis,* f.; see SLOW. Adv. *tarde, contanter (cunct-), lente;* see SLOWLY.

linguist, n. *homo multarum linguarum sciens.* **linguistic,** adj. *grammaticus* or *de ratione linguarum.*

liniment, n. *unguentum.*

link, I. n. **1,** = torch, *fax, taeda, funale;* **2,** = bond, *vinculum, conjunctio, societas, familiaritas* (of friendship), *affinitas* (by marriage), *necessitudo* (any close tie); **3,** of a chain, *annulus* (Mart.). **II.** v.tr. *conjungĕre, (con)(n)ectĕre;* see UNITE.

lint, n. *linamentum* (Cels.).

lintel, n. *limen (superum* or *superius).*

lion, n. **1,** *leo;* of a —, *leoninus;* a —'s skin, *pellis leonina;* · —'s claw, *unguis leoninus;* **2,** fig. (e.g. the — of the season) *deliciae, -um.* **lion-hearted,** adj. *magnanimus.* **lioness,** n. *leaena.*

lip, n. *labrum;* the upper —, *labrum superius;* the lower —, *labrum inferius;* primoribus *labris* (= the tip of the —s) *gustasse* = to get a taste of; *labellum* (esp. in endearing sense), *labium* (rare). **lip-salve,** n. *unguentum.* **lip-service,** n. see FLATTERY. **lip-wisdom,** n. *verbo tenus sapientia.*

liquid, I. adj. *liquidus, fluens;* to grow —, *liquescĕre, liquefieri;* to make —, *liquefacĕre.* **II.** n. *liquor, humor,* + *latex, sucus* (=juice). **liquidate,** v.tr. see PAY. **liquefy,** v.tr. *liquefacĕre.* **liquor,** n. see LIQUID, II.

lisp, v.intr. *balbutire* (= to stammer).

list, n. = catalogue, *tabula, index* (Quint.).

list, v.tr. see WISH, DESIRE, PLEASE.

listen, v.intr. see HEAR. **listener,** n. *auscultator.*

listless, adj. *socors, deses, languidus, piger.* Adv. *torpide, stupide, languide.* **listlessness,** n. *torpor* (Tac.), *socordia, desidia.*

lists, n. *campus, hippodromus, spatia, -orum;* to enter the — against (fig.), *cum alqo contendĕre.*

litany, n. *litania* (Eccl.), or *preces, -um,* f. (= prayers).

literal, adj. to employ a word in its — sense, *verbum proprie dicĕre;* a — translator, *ad verbum interpres;* the—sense, *propria vis.* Adv. *lit(t)eratim, proprie, ad lit(t)eram, ad verbum.* **literary,** adj. *lit(t)eratus* (= lettered or learned), *lit(t)erarum studiosus;* — leisure, *otium lit(t)eratum;* — monuments, *lit(t)erarum monumenta.* **literature,** n. *lit(t)erae, lit(t)erarum monumenta, -orum;* to entrust to the care of —, *lit(t)eris mandare* or *consignare;* to learn from —, *lit(t)eris percipĕre;* we have no history in our —, *abest historia lit(t)eris nostris;* the study of —, *lit(t)erarum studium;* the knowledge of —, *lit(t)erarum scientia;* to be acquainted with —, *lit(t)eras scire;* to be without —, *lit(t)eras nescire.*

lithe, adj. *mollis, flexibilis.*

lithographer, n. *lithographus* (in no sense class.).

litigate, v.tr. and intr. *litigare cum alqo pro alqo, inter se de algâ re (noli pati fratres litigare)* (Cic.), *lites sequi.* **litigant,** n. *qui cum alqo litigat.* **litigation,** n. *lis.* **litigious,** adj. *litigiosus* (=full of strife, given to lawsuits). **litigiousness,** n. use an adj. (e.g. the — of the man, *homo litium cupidus).*

litter, I. n. **1,** *lectica;* a small —, *lecticula;* **2,** *fetura, fetus, -ûs, suboles (sob-)* (= a brood); — of pigs, *porcelli uno partu editi;* **3,** — for cattle, *stramentum;* = confusion, *turbae;* to make a —, *res turbare.* **II.** v.tr. **1,** *parĕre, fetum edĕre* = to bring forth; **2,** see STREW.

little, I. adj. *parvus, parvulus* (dim.), *exiguus, minutus, modicus;* often rendered by diminutives, as — (small) coins, *nummuli;* — book, *libellus;* — present, *munusculum;* — used as a noun, e.g. a little gain, *paul(l)um lucri;* also by *aliquid,* e.g. a — pride, *alqd superbiae;* to sell by — and —, or by retail, *divendĕre;* the — ones, *parvi, liberi;* a — time, *tempus breve;* for a —, *parumper, paul(l)isper;* in a —, *brevi;* a — after, *paul(l)o post;* by — and —, *paul(l)isper, sensim, gradatim, minutatim;* a — soul, *animus pusillus;* not a —, *valde, vehementer, magnopere;* he is a — too much given to money, *aliquanto ad rem est avidior;* these things are a — troublesome to me, *nonnihil molesta haec sunt mihi;* a — before sunset, *sub occasum solis;* how — quantillus* (Plaut.), *quantulus;* how — soever, *quantuluscunque;* so —, *tantulus;* he lacked — of being killed, *haud multum a(b)fuit quin occideretur.* **II.** adv. *paul(l)um, aliquantulum, nonnihili* (=somewhat), *parum* (= too —). **III.** n. *aliquantum, nonnihil, parum* (= too —), *paul(l)um, paul(l)ulum;* see LITTLE I. **littleness,** n. *parvitas, exiguitas.* **less,** adj. *minor.* **least,** adj. *minimus; minimum,* at least.

liturgy, n. *liturgia* (Eccl.).

live, I. v.intr. **1,** *vivĕre, in vitâ esse;* yet to —, *in vivis esse, superstitem esse;* to let one —, *alcjs vitae parcĕre;* cannot — without, *alqâ re carēre non posse;* so long as I —, *me vivo, dum (quoad) vivo;* if I —, *si vita suppetit;* as I —! *ita vivam!* — for a thing, *deditum esse rei;* — in a thing, *totum esse in re;* — for self, *sibi vivĕre;* **2,** to — on anything, *vivĕre re, vesci re, ali re, vitam sustentare alqâ re;* **3,** to — luxuriously, *laute vivĕre;* — poorly, *parce vivĕre;* to — at or in a place, *locum incolĕre, locum* or *in loco habitare;* see DWELL; as to your condition, to —, *vitam agĕre* or *degĕre;* — happily, etc., *bene, feliciter, misere,* etc.*. vivĕre.* **II.** adj. or **living,** adj. *vivus.* **livelihood,** n. *victus, -ûs* (= provisions). **livelong,** adj. *totus.* **lively,** adj

l, = active, *strenuus, acer ;* see ACTIVE ; 2, = sprightly, *alacer, vegetus, hilaris, festivus, lepidus;* see MERRY, WITTY ; 3, of places, = frequented; *celeber ;* 4, = keen, *vehemens ;* to feel a — joy, *valde* or *vehementer gaudēre ;* to form a — idea of anything, *rem tanquam praesentem contemplari.* **liveliness,** n. *alacritas, hilaritas, festivitas.*

liver, n. *jecur, -(in)oris,* n.

livery, n. *vestis quam alcjs famuli gerunt.* **liveryman,** n. *sodalis, -is,* m., or *socius alcjs societatis.* **livery-stables,** n. *stabulum (mercenarium).*

livid, adj. *lividus ;* a — colour, *livor.*

lizard, n. *lacerta, stellio.*

lo ! interj. *en, ecce.*

load, I. n. *onus, -ēris,* n.; a cart—, *vehes, -is,* f.(Plin.); a — on the mind, *tristitia, molestia, animi dolor* or *aegritudo.* **II.** v.tr. 1, *onerare, gravare* (properly = to make heavy or weigh down, e.g. *membra gravabat onus, gravatus vino somnoque, oculi morte gravati) ;* he —ed the people excessively, *nimium oneris plebi imposuit ;* oppriměre (= to press down or oppress) ; — with reproaches ; see REPROACH ; 2, of firearms, *arma parare, instruěre.* **loaded,** adj. *onustus, oneratus.*

loaf, n. *panis, -is,* m.

loam, n. *lutum.* **loamy,** adj. *lutosus* (= muddy), *cretosus, argillosus* (of chalk).

loan, n. *res mutuata* or *mutuo data* or *commodata ; pecunia mutua* or *credita.*

loath, adj. *invitus ;* I am —, *piget me* (e.g. *referre piget me, piget me dicěre).* **loathe,** v.tr. *alqd fastidire, aversari, a re abhorrēre.* **loathing,** n. *fastidium* (for food, fig. = disdain), *odium* (= hatred), *taedium* (= disgust, mostly post class.). **loathsome,** adj. *teter, foedus, obscenus (obscaen-), odiosus.* **loathsomeness,** n. *foeditas, obscenitas (obscaen-).*

lobby, n. *vestibulum.*

lobster, n. *cancer* (= crab).

local, adj. by the genitive *loci, regionis,* etc. (e.g. *locorum difficultates,* = — difficulties ; *loci opportunitas,* = a — advantage or convenience). **locality,** n. *locus,* or *loci natura* or *situs, -ūs.*

loch, n. *lacus.*

lock, I. n. *claustra, -orum* (properly = a shutter or fastener) ; to be under — and key, *esse sub claustris* or *clavi ;* — in a river, *piscina* (Plin.) or *emissarium* (= outlet of a lake). **II.** v.tr. *obserěre, occluděre ;* to — in, *claustro includěre ;* to — out, *claustro foras excluděre ;* to — up, *alqm concluděre.* **locker,** n. *armarium.* **locket,** n. *collare ;* see NECKLACE. **lock-jaw,** n. *tetanus* (Plin.).

lock, n. of hair, *cirrus ;* of wool, *floccus.*

locomotion, n. *motus, -ūs.* **locomotive,** adj. *suâ vi motus ;* — engine, *machina ad currus trahendos facta.*

locust, n. *locusta* (Plin.).

lodge, I. n. *casa* (= a cot). **II.** v.intr. 1, *deversari apud alqm, apud alqm devertěre ;* 2, = in, (in) *alqâ re haerěre.* **III.** v.tr. 1, *hospitio excipěre, tecto recipěre ;* 2, — a complaint, *alqm* or *nomen alcjs deferre ;* — a spear, etc., *adigěre.* **lodger,** n. *deversor* (at an inn), *inquilinus, incquilina* (= one who lives in another's house). **lodgings,** n. *cenaculum meritorium* (= hired room, Suet.), or by *domus,* = house. **lodging-house,** n. *insula.* **lodgment,** n. to effect a —, see LODGE II. and III.

loft, n. *caenaculum (coen-) ;* hay—, *faenilia, ium (fen-) ;* corn—, *horreum.* **lofty,** adj. 1, = high, *altus, (ex)celsus, editus* (of places), *sublimis* (= aloft, mostly poet.) ; 2, fig. *(ex)celsus, elatus, sublimis, erectus ;* of speech, *grandis ;* of pride, *superbus.* Adv. *alte, excelse* (lit. and fig.), *sublime* (lit.), *elate* (fig.) ; = proudly, *superbe.* **loftiness,** n. 1, *altitudo ;* 2, (fig.) *altitudo, elatio, excelsitas,* comb. of speech, *altitudo et elatio oratoris* (Cic.), *sublimitas et magnificentia et nitor* (Quint.) ; — of mind, *altitudo animi.*

log, n. 1, *lignum* (or *ligna,* pl. = firewood) ; *stipes, -ĭtis,* m. (= trunk of tree) ; 2, fig. = blockhead, *stipes, caudex, -icis,* m., *truncus.* **logbook,** n. *tabulae.* **loggerhead,** n. 1, = blockhead ; see LOG ; 2, to be at —s, see QUARREL.

logic, n. *logica, -orum,* or *dialectica* (or *dialectice), logica* (or *logice,* or written in Greek, ἡ λογική). **logical,** adj. *logicus, dialecticus* (= connected with logic) ; — questions, *dialectica, -orum ;* — conclusion, *consequentia, -ium,* or *ea quae ex concessis consequuntur* Adv. *dialectice* or *quod ex concessis consequitur,* or *quod necessarie demonstratur.* **logician,** n. *dialecticus.*

loin, n. *lumbus.*

loiter, v.intr. *cessare ;* see LINGER.

loll, v.intr. and tr. *recumběre, recubare ;* to — out the tongue, *linguam exserěre.*

lonely, lonesome, lone, adj. *solus, solitarius, avius, reductus* (of situation). **loneliness,** n. *solitudo.*

long, I. adj. 1, = extension in space, *longus, procērus* (= tall), *promissus* (= hanging down), *longinquus* (= distant) ; exceedingly —, *praelongus ;* — hair, *capillus promissus ;* to defer for a — time, *in longinquum tempus differre rem ;* the measure or degree of length is put in the accusative (e.g. six feet —, *longus pedes sex* or *in longitudinem sex pedum ;* a foot —, *pedalis, pedem longus)* ; 2, = extension in time, *longus, longinquus, diuturnus, diutinus ;* during a — while, *diu ;* a — time before, *multum ante alqd ;* a — time after, *multum post alqd ;* 3, = slow or dilatory, *tardus, lentus, segnis, piger ;* a — business, *lentum negotium.* **II.** adv. *diu ;* — ago, *pridem, jampridem* (or as two words), *jamdudum* (or in two words) ; not — ago, *haud dudum, modo, olim ;* how —, *quamdiu ;* as — as, *quamdiu … tamdiu ;* — after, *multo post* or *post multos annos ;* — before, *ante multos annos.* **III.** v.intr. and tr. to — for, *avēre alqd* or with infin., *cupěre alqd* or with infin. or *ut, gestire* with infin., *avēre, cupěre, gestire, desiderare* (= to regret the loss or want of) *alqd* or *alqm, alqd ab alqo, alqd in alqo ; desiderio alcjs rei teneri* or *flagrare, concupiscěre* (= to desire). **longevity,** n. by *circumloc. ;* see OLD. **longing, I.** n. *alcjs rei desiderium* (= desire), *appetitus, -ūs, appetitio* (= passionate desire). **II.** adj. — after anything, *alcjs rei cupidus,* or *avidus.* Adv. *cupide, avide.* **long-suffering,** adj. see PATIENT.

look, I. n. 1, as act, *(oculorum) obtutus, -ūs ;* to direct a — at, *aspectum* or *oculos convertěre* or *con(j)icěre in rem ;* — at a person, *intueri, a(d)spicěre alqm ;* 2, = appearance of the countenance, *vultus, -ūs ;* a severe —, *vultus severus ;* in gen. *species, facies.* **II.** v.tr. to — at, *a(d)spicěre, intueri, contemplari.* **III.** v.intr. *speciem alcjs (rei) praebēre, videri ;* see SEEM ; to — about, *circumspicěre ;* to — back, *(alqd) respicěre ;* to — down, *despicěre ;* to — down upon, *alqm despicěre ;* to — for, see SEEK ; = to expect, *ex(s)pectare ;* to — out, = to be on the — out, *speculari ;* **to** — out for, = to take care of, *alci rei consulĕre*; **to** — towards, *in or ad algm locum spectare*; **to** — up, *suspicĕre*; **to** — up to, *algm verēri*. **looking-glass**, n. *speculum*. **look-out**, n. use verb.

loom, n. *tela*.

loom, v.intr. *in conspectum e longinquo dari.*

loop, **I.** n. *laqueus* (= noose). **II.** v.tr. *annectĕre*; see TIE. **loophole**, n. *foramen* (= hole), *fenestra* (= — in the wall of a tower for the discharge of missiles).

loose, **I.** adj. **1**, = slack, *laxus, fluxus, remissus*; — reins, *laxae* or *fluxae habenae*; with — hair, *passis crinibus*; **2**, of soil, *rarus* (opp. *densus*), *solutus* (opp. *spissus*), *facilis* (Col.); **3**, of teeth, *mobilis* (Plin.); **4**, = at liberty, (*carcere*, etc.) *liberatus, solutus*; **5**, of morals, (*dis*)*solutus, effrenatus, remissus*. Adv. *laxe*, (*dis*)*solute*. **II.** v.tr. (*re*)*laxare, remittĕre*, (*re*)*solvĕre*; see UNTIE. **looseness**, n. use adj. LOOSE.

lop, v.tr. *tondēre*, (*de*)*putare, amputare* (= to prune), *praecidĕre* (= to — off). **lopsided**, adj. *uno latere grandis.*

loquacious, adj. *loquax, garrulus* (= chattering), *verbosus*. Adv. *loquaciter, verbose*. **loquacity**, n. *loquacitas, garrulitas.*

lord, n. *dominus*. **lordly**, adj. **1**, of high rank, *illustris, nobilis, illustri* or *nobili loco natus*; **2**, = proud, *superbus, arrogans*; see PROUD, ARROGANT. **lordliness**, n. *superbia, arrogantia*; see PRIDE, ARROGANCE. **lordship**, n. = power, *imperium, dominatus, -ūs.*

lore, n. *eruditio, doctrina.*

lorn, adj. *solus, desertus*; see LONELY, FORLORN.

lose, v.tr. *amittĕre, perdĕre, jacturam rei facĕre* (of loss purposely incurred); one who has lost a member, *captus* (e.g. *oculo, auribus*); **to** = to be bereaved, *privari, orbari re*; **to** — hope, *spe excidĕre*; **to** — a battle, *vinci*; **to** — patience, *patientiam rumpĕre*; **to** — time, *tempus perdĕre*; **to** — sight of one, *algm e conspectu amittĕre*; **to** never — sight of, *algd nunquam dimittĕre*; **to** be lost, *amitti, perdi, perire, absumi*; **to** give up for lost, *desperare de re*; **to** — colour, *evanescĕre, pallescĕre*; **to** be lost in thought, *in cogitatione defixum esse*; the mountain —s itself in the plain, *mons in planitiem se subducit*; I am lost, *perii*; the ships were lost at sea, *mersae sunt naves* (*in*) *mari*. **loser**, n. *qui damno afficitur*; he was a great —, *magno damno affectus est*. **losing**, n. *amissio.*

loss, n. *damnum, detrimentum, jactura, dispendium*; **to** sustain a —, *damna pati, calamitates subire, incommodis affici*; **to** repair a —, *damnum resarcire*; the — of a battle, *pugna adversa*; I am at a —, *dubius sum*; see UNCERTAIN.

lot, n. **1**, *sors, -tis*, f., *sortitio, sortitus, -ūs*; by —, *sorte, sortito*; **2**, = fortune, *sors, fortuna*; casting of —s, *sortitio, sortitus, -ūs*. **lottery**, n. *sors, sortitio, alea* (= game of dice); 'tis all a —, *nihil incertius est.*

loth, adj. see LOATH.

lotion, n. *liquida quae alci illinuntur.*

loud, adj. *clarus* (= clear), *magnus* (= strong); — cry, *magnus clamor*; — voice, *vox clara, vox magna*. Adv. *clare, clarā voce, magnā* or *summā voce*. **loudness**, n. *magnitudo, vox clara.*

lounge, v.intr. *nihil agĕre, desidēre*. **lounger**, n. *homo deses, iners, contator* (*cunct-*), *cessator, ambulator.*

louse, n. *pediculus* (Plin.). **lousy**, adj. *pediculosus* (Mart.).

lout, n. *homo rusticus, agrestis, stipes, caudex*

(*cod-*). **loutish**, adj. *rusticus, agrestis*; see RUDE. Adv. *rustice.*

love, **I.** n. *amor, caritas* (= affection), *pietas* (= reverent devotion), *studium*; = a favourable disposition, *studium alcjs rei*; **to** have —, *alcjs rei amantem esse*; worthy of —, *amandus, amore dignus*; — affair, *amor*; — potion, + *philtrum*; the god of —, *Cupido, Amor*; the goddess of —, *Venus*; my — ! *mea voluptas! meum cor!* delight of my heart, *deliciae meae*. **II.** v.tr. *amare* (with natural affection), *diligĕre* (as friends), *carum habēre algm, studēre alci, amore complecti algm, prosequi algm, amore alcjs teneri, amore alcjs captum esse, alcjs amore deperire*; **to** — learning, *lit(t)erarum studiosum esse*. **loves**, n. *amores.*

loved, adj. *carus, acceptus, gratus, jucundus, suavis*. **loving**, adj. *alcjs amans, studiosus, blandus, benignus, dulcis, suavis, indulgens*. Adv. *amanter.*

loving-kindness, n. *misericordia*; see MERCY. **lovely**, adj. **1**, *bellus, venustus* (of persons and things), *amoenus* (of things); see BEAUTIFUL; **2**, = worthy of love, *amore dignus, amandus, amabilis*. **loveliness**, n. *venustas, amoenitas*. **lover**, n. *amator*, f. *amatrix*; **a** — of literature, *lit(t)erarum studiosus.*

low, **I.** adj. **1**, of position, *humilis, demissus*; **2**, of voice, *gravis, submissus, suppressus*; **3**, of price, *vilis*; **to** buy at a — price, *parvo* or *vili* (*pretio*) *emĕre*; **4**, in regard to condition, *humilis* (= humble), *ignobilis, obscurus* (as to birth and ancestors), *tenuis* (as to property); lower, *inferior* (in position), *sordidus* (as to origin); of — birth, *humili* or *ignobili, obscuro* or *tenui loco ortus, humili fortunā ortus*; of the lowest birth, *infimae condicionis et fortunae, infimus, sordido loco ortus*; of the lower orders, *tenuioris ordinis*; the lowest of the people, *infima plebs*; the lowest class of men, *ultimae sortis homines, infimi ordinis* (*generis*) *homines, infimum genus hominum, faex, vulgus, -i, n., plebs, plebecula*; **5**, = having a — tone, *humilis, illiberalis* (= unworthy a gentleman), *abjectus* (= despicable, employed with *animus*), *turpis*; see BASE; — expressions, *verba ex triviis petita*; **6**, = sad, *maestus, tristis*. **II.** adv. *humiliter* (lit. post class., but class. = basely), *demisse, abjecte* = basely, *illiberaliter* (= unbecomingly to a gentleman); **to** speak —, *submisse, submissā voce dicĕre*. **lowly**, adj. **1**, see LOW, 4; **2**, = humble, *modestus, moderatus*; see HUMBLE. **lowliness**, n. **1**, *humilitas, obscuritas*; **2**, *modestia*; see HUMILITY. **lowness**, n. **1**, *humilitas* (of position or stature); **2**, of birth, *humilitas, ignobilitas, obscuritas*; **3**, of price, *vilitas*; **4**, of the voice, *vox gravis*; **5**, of mind, *humilitas, animus humilis* or *abjectus, turpitudo*; of expression, *verba ex triviis petita*. **low-born**, adj. *ignobili* or *obscuro loco natus*. **low-lands**, n. *loca* (*-orum*) *plana*. **low-spirited**, adj. *animus demissus et oppressus, afflictus, maestus, tristis*; see SAD. **lower**, **I.** adj. *inferior*; the — world, *apud inferos*, † *Tartarus* (*-os*), † *Tartara, -orum*, pl.; — orders, see LOW, 4. **II.** v.tr. *demittĕre*; **to** — the voice, *submittĕre* (Quint.); **to** — oneself, *se ab(j)icĕre*. **lowering**, adj. see DARK, THREATENING.

low, v.tr. of cattle, *mugire*. **lowing**, n. *mugitus, -ūs.*

loyal, adj. *fidelis, fidus*. Adv. *fideliter*. **loyalty**, n. *fides, fidelitas.*

lozenge, n. *pastillus* (Plin.).

lubber, n. **lubberly**, adj. see LOUT.

lubricate, v.tr. *ung(u)ĕre.*

lucid, adj. *lucidus* (= bright, distinct of speech, etc.; in the latter sense, also *dilucidus*). Adv. (*di*)*lucide*. **lucidness, lucidity**, n. *perspicuitas* (Quint.), better use adj. or adv. (e.g.

he expressed himself with —, *dilucide rem expli-cavit).

Lucifer, n. 1, the morning star, *Lucifer,* † *Phosphorus,* † *Eous;* 2, = Satan, *Lucifer* (Eccl.).

luck, n. *fortuna, fors, sors, casus, -ūs;* good —, *fortuna secunda, res secundae;* bad —, *adversa fortuna, res adversae;* good — to it! *bene vertat!* **lucky,** adj. *felix, fortunatus, faustus, auspica-tus.* Adv. *feliciter, ex animi sententiâ, auspicato.*

lucre, n. *lucrum* (= gain), *quaestus, -ūs* (= ac-quirement); for —'s sake, *lucri caus(s)â.* **lucra-tive,** adj. *lucrosus, quaestuosus.*

lucubration, n. *lucubratio.*

ludicrous, adj. *(de)ridiculus, perridiculus, ridendus, deridendus.* Adv. *(per)ridicule.* **ludi-crousness,** n. *stultitia, insulsitas* (= folly), or by adj.

lug, v.tr. *trahĕre, vehĕre.* **luggage,** n. *impedimenta, -orum,* n.; the — (collectively), *vasa, -orum,* n.; *sarcinae* (= the knapsacks, etc., of the individual soldiers).

lugubrious, adj. *lugubris* (mostly poet., belonging to mourning), *flebilis, maestus, tristis* (= sad); see SAD. Adv. † *lugubre,* † *lugubriter, flebiliter, maeste;* see SADLY.

lukewarm, adj. *tepidus* (lit. and fig.); = indifferent, *languidus, frigidus, lentus, remissus, neglegens* (neglig-). Adv. *languide, frigide, lente, remisse, neglegenter* (neglig-). **lukewarmness,** n. *tepor* (lit.), *languor,* or by adj.

lull, I. v.tr. *sedare* (e.g. *ventos, insolentiam,* etc.); to — to sleep, *sopire,* † *somnum suadēre.* **II.** v.intr., the wind —s, *venti vis cadit, venti se-dantur.* **III.** n. use verb. **lullaby,** n. *cantus, -ūs,* or verb *lallare* (= to sing a —, Pers.).

lumber, n. *scruta, -orum.*

luminous, adj. *luminosus* (= having light), *lucidus* (= giving light); — narration, *narratio lucida* or *perspicua* or *aperta* or *dilucida;* the thoughts of, etc., are not —, *sententiae alcjs lucem desiderant.* Adv. *(di)lucide, perspicue, aperte, plane,* comb. *aperte atque dilucide, dilucide et perspicue.* **luminary,** n. 1, lit. *sol, -is,* m., *luna* (= sun, moon, etc.); 2, fig. *lumen.*

lump, n. *massa, glaeba* (gleba). **lumpish,** adj. *hebes, stupidus* (= stupid). **lumpy,** adj. *glebosus* (Plin.).

lunar, adj. *lunaris* (with *cursus, cornua,* etc.); a — year, *annus lunaris.* **lunatic,** adj. *lunaticus* (very late); see MAD, MADMAN.

lunch, n. *prandium.*

lung, n. *pulmo;* —s, *pulmones.*

lunge, n. and v.tr. see STAB.

lupine, n. *lupinus, lupinum.*

lurch, I. n. 1, see ROLL; 2, to leave in the —, *deserĕre;* see ABANDON. **II.** v.intr. see ROLL.

lure, I. n. = decoy-bird, or fig. *illecebra.* **II.** v.tr. *allicĕre, illicĕre, pellicĕre.*

lurid, adj. *obscurus, caliginosus* (luridus = pale yellow, ghastly).

lurk, v.intr. *latēre, latitare* (intensive of *latēre*).

luscious, adj. *(prae)dulcis.* **luscious-ness,** n. *dulcedo.*

lust, I. n. *libido* (lub-), *cupiditas.* **II.** v.tr. to — after, *concupiscĕre* (= to desire earnestly).

lusty, adj. = full of vigour, *valens, validus, vegetus;* = large and stout, *robustus;* to be —, *vigēre.* **Adv. valide. lustiness,** n. *vigor, robur.*

lustration, n. *lustratio* (= a purifying, e.g. *municipiorum*). **lustral,** adj. *lustralis.*

lustre, n. 1, *nitor, fulgor, splendor;* to throw a — on, *splendorum addĕre alci;* 2, = space of five years, *lustrum.* **lustrous,** adj. *splendidus, splendens, clarus, lucidus;* see BRIGHT.

lute, n. *lyra,* † *barbitos,* m. and f. (only nom., voc. and accus.), *fides, -ium,* f. pl., *cithara, testudo.*

luxuriant, adj. *laetus, luxuriosus.* Adv. *laete.* **luxuriate,** v.intr. *luxuriare.* **luxu-rious,** adj. *luxuriosus, sumptuosus, mollis, delicatus, lautus* (lot-). Adv. *luxuriose, delicate, molliter.* **luxury,** n. *luxus, -ūs, luxuria* or *luxuries, lautitia, apparatus, -ūs, deliciae.*

lye, n. *lixivia* (Plin.).

lynx, n. *lynx.* **lynx-eyed,** adj. *lynceus.*

lyre, n. *lyra, cithara, fides, -ium,* f. pl., *testudo, barbitos,* m. and f. (only nom., voc. and accus.). **lyrical,** adj. *lyricus.* **lyrist,** n. *lyricen, citharista,* m.

M.

macaroon, n. *placenta* (= cake).

mace, n. *fasces, -ium,* m. **mace-bearer,** n. *lictor.*

macerate, v.tr. *macerare* (e.g. flax, fish) (Plin.). **maceration,** n. *maceratio* (of flax, fish).

machination, n. = a secret, malicious de-sign, *machina, conatus, -ūs, dolus;* to make —s, *consilia (con)coquĕre;* to do a thing through anyone's —, *algo auctore facĕre alqd.* **ma-chine,** n. *machina, machinatio, machinament-um* (= machinery); *compages, -is,* f. (= frame-work); the —, fabric of the human body, *com-pages corporis.* **machinery,** n. *machinatio, machinamenta, -orum,* n.; *machinae.*

mackerel, n. *scomber.*

mad, adj. 1, lit. *insanus, vecors, furiosus, demens, mente captus,* + *rabidus* (usu. of animals), *phreneticus* (phrenit-); 2, fig. *insanus, vecors, vesanus, furiosus, amens, demens.* Adv. *insane, furiose, rabide, dementer.* **madcap,** n. *homo* or *juvenis ingenio praeceps.* **madden,** v.tr. 1, *mentem alienare;* 2, fig. *exacerbare, exasperare, incendĕre;* see EXCITE. **madhouse,** n. *domus publica quâ curantur insani.* **madman,** n. *homo insanus,* etc.; see MAD. **madness,** n. 1, lit. *insania, amentia, dementia, vecordia, furor, rabies* (esp. of animals); 2, fig. *insania, amen-tia, dementia, vecordia, furor, rabies.*

madam, n. *domina.*

madder, n. *rubia* (Plin.).

magazine, n. 1, = store, granary, *horreum, receptaculum alcjs rei* (= repository for corn, goods, etc.), *armamentarium* (for arms); 2, = pamphlet, *acta, -orum;* see JOURNAL.

maggot, n. *vermis, -is,* m., *vermiculus.* **maggoty,** adj. *verminosus* (Plin.).

magi, n. *magi.* **magic, I.** n. *ars magica,* or *magice* (Plin.). **II.** adj. 1, *magicus;* 2, fig. by *mirus* (e.g. a — power, *mira quaedam vis*); see also JUGGLERY.

magistracy, n. *magistratus, -ūs.* **magis-trate,** n. *magistratus, -ūs.* **magisterial,** adj. *ad magistratum pertinens;* in his — capacity, *quippe qui magistratus erat.*

magnanimity, n. see GENEROUS. **mag-nanimous,** adj. see GENEROUS.

magnet, n. *(lapis) magnes, -ētis,* m. **mag-netic, magnetical,** adj. *magnesius* (e.g. *magnesia saxa,* Lucret.); — power, *attrahendi quae dicitur vis* (in a lit. sense), *mira quaedam vis* (in a fig. sense). **magnetism,** n. ** magnetisma* (t.t., not class.).

magnificent, adj. *magnificus* (= splendid), *splendidus,* comb. *splendidus et magnificus; prae-clarus* (= eminent through exterior and inward qualities, excellent), comb. *magnificus et prae-clarus; lautus* (*lot-*) (of banquets); *sumptuosus* (= expensive); *amplus* (e.g. *amplissimae divitiae*). Adv. *magnifice, splendide, praeclare, laute, sumptuose, ample.* **magnificence,** n. *magnificentia, splendor* (= outward splendour, also inward excellency); *res magnifica, splendida* (= a splendid thing); *cultus, -ūs* (as regards dress and costly household utensils); *lautitia* (*lot-*) (of an expensive mode of living); *apparatus, -ūs* (= preparations). **magnifier,** n. = one who magnifies, *laudator* (in gen.), fem. *laudatrix;* also simply by verbs, to be the — of anything, *laudare alqd, praedicare alqd* or *de alqâ re.* **magnify,** v.tr. *augēre* (lit., e.g. the number of praetors, *numerum praetorum;* fig. to represent a thing greater than it is, in this sense comb. *amplificare et augēre*), *amplificare* (= to make greater in extent, e.g. a town, *urbem;* the property, *rem familiarem;* then fig. = by our actions to make a thing appear greater than it is); *(verbis) exaggerare* (= to make in words much of a thing, e.g. a kindness); *verbis augēre, in majus (verbis) extol-lēre* (= to impair the truth by exaggeration); *in falsum augēre* (= to exaggerate falsely); *in majus accipēre* (= to take a thing in a greater light than one ought). **magniloquence,** n. *magniloquentia.* **magnitude,** n. *magnitudo* (in gen., both lit. and fig.), *amplitudo* (= great extent, also fig. = importance of anything and high authority of a person), *ambitus, -ūs, spatium* (= circumference, extent of a thing in gen.).

magpie, n. *pica.*

mahometan, n. and adj. ** Muhamedanus.*

maid, n. 1, = an unmarried woman, see GIRL; 2, = servant, *ancilla, famula.* **maiden, maidenly,** adj. *virgineus* (= pertaining to virgins), *virginalis* (= peculiar, natural to virgins, e.g. bashfulness, *verecundia*). **maiden-hood,** n. *virginitas.* **maid-servant,** n. see MAID, 2.

mail, n. 1, armour, *lorīca, thorax, -acis,* m.; 2, a letter-bag, *folliculus* (= bag) with descriptive epithet (e.g. *ad lit(t)eras perferendas*); = the letters themselves, *lit(t)erae.* **mail-coach,** n. *raeda (r(h)eda) cursualis publica.* **mailed,** adj. *loricatus.*

maim, n. *mutilare, truncare;* see INJURE. **maimed,** adj. *mancus, truncus.*

main, I. adj. *primus, princeps;* see CHIEF, PRINCIPAL, GREAT; (= the greater part), *pars prima* (= first part), *caput* (= chief point); his — intention is, *id maxime (praecipue) sequitur* or *agit* or *spectat;* — point, *summa* (sc. res), *res magni momenti* or *magni discriminis, caput alcjs rei* or *summa;* the — question is, *id maxime quaeritur, quaeritur de,* etc. (in a metaphysical question), *agitur de alqâ re, cardo alcjs rei* (= hinge); to give, state only the — points of anything, *summatim alqd exponēre;* *summas tantummodo attingēre;* to review briefly the — points, *per capita decurrēre;* to stray, wander from the — question, *a proposito aberrare* or *declinare;* to return to the — point, *ad propositum reverti* or *redire, ad rem redire, prae ceteris*

alqd agēre or *spectare;* — road, *via;* — object, *finis;* to make anything one's — object, *omnia ad alqd referre* or *revocare;* his — object is, *id potissimum spectat* or *sequitur;* in the —, *si veram rei rationem exigis, vere* (= in reality). Adv. *praecipue;* see PRINCIPALLY, UNCOMMONLY. **II.** n. 1, = the great sea, *altum;* see OCEAN; 2, = the main-land, *(terra) continens.* **main-land,** n. *terra (continens).* **main-mast,** n. *malus.* **main-sail,** n. *velum.*

maintain, v.tr. 1, *sustinēre, sustentare* (e.g. the world, health), through anything, *alqâ re;* *(con)servare* (= to preserve, e.g. one's property, *rem familiarem conservare;* then = to save) *tueri* (= to see that anything is in a good condition), comb. *tueri et conservare; alēre* (by care and nursing), comb. *alēre et sustentare, sustentare et alēre;* to — one's physical strength, *valetudinem tueri;* 2, = to keep in the necessaries of life, *sustinēre, sustentare, alēre;* 3, = not to lose or surrender, *tenēre, retinēre, obtinēre, (con)servare;* 4, = to — an argument, *contendēre, confirmare;* see ASSERT. **maintainable,** adj. *munitus, firmatus* (= fortified), *firmus* (= firm, durable, lit. and fig. = not easy to be overthrown), *stabilis* (= stable, fig. = unalterable), comb. *stabilis et firmus* (e.g. a ship), *perennis* (= what does not easily go bad, e.g. fruit). **maintainer,** n. *(con)servator, salutis auctor* (= one who restores, saves), *vindex* (= one who claims), or by verbs. **maintenance,** n. 1, *victus, -ūs* (= food for the necessary support of the body), *alimenta, -orum* (= food in gen.; then in the meaning of the law, what anyone subsists on, subsistence); to give to anyone his —, *alci victum* or *alimentum* (often in pl.) *praebēre;* 2, = protection, continuance, *conservatio, tuitio* (= the act), *salus, -ūtis,* f., *incolumitas* (= the state of being preserved).

maize, n. *far.*

majestic, adj. *augustus, sanctus* (= very reverend), *magnificus* (= splendid). Adv. *auguste.* **majesty,** n. *majestas* (later of the Roman emperor); *dignitas, numen* (= high power, will, both of God and man, e.g. of the emperor); surrounded with —, *augustus;* to violate the —, *majestatem* (of the people, *populi* ; of the emperor, *imperatoris) minuēre* or *laedēre;* your — *l majestas tua l* (late).

major, I. adj. 1, = greater in number, extent, e.g. the — part, *major* (e.g. *major pars*); see MORE; 2, in music (the — mode, opp. the minor mode), *modus major;* 3, in logic, the — premiss, *propositio.* **II.** n. 1, = a military rank, *centurio, praefectus;* *optio* (= assistant to and immediately under the *centurio*); 2, in law = a person of full age to manage his own concerns, *sui juris, suae potestatis* (no longer under the parent's control), *suae tutelae* (not longer requiring to be represented in court by a guardian), *sui potens* (= one who can do as he likes). **major-domo,** n. = steward, *qui res domesticas dispensat, dispensator.* **majority,** n. 1, = the greater number, *major pars, major numerus* (both = a greater number in comparison with another number), or *plures* (= several), *plurimi* (= most); *plerique* (= a large number); the — of historical writers, *plures auctores;* Servius took care that the — did not prevail, *Servius curavit ne plurimum plurimi valerent;* — of votes, *sententiae longe plurimae* (of the senators, judges), *suffragia longe plurima,* (of the citizens in the *comitia*); to have the — of votes, *vincēre* (of persons), *valēre* (of a motion, etc.), *longe plurimum valēre, magnis suffragiis* or *per suffragia superare;* to be acquitted by a great —, *sententiis fere omnibus absolvi;* the — rules, carries the victory, *major pars vincit;* the — (in the senate) decided in favour of the same opinion, *pars major in ean-*

dem sententiam ibat; 2, = full age, *aetas quâ sui juris alqs fit;* he entrusted him with the government until the children should come to their —, *regnum ei commendavit quoad liberi in suam tutelam pervenirent.*

make, I. v.tr. 1, = to form, in the ordinary sense in gen. *facĕre;* = to accomplish, *conficĕre, efficĕre, perficĕre;* 2, = to create, *creare* (of God and nature); made for, *ad alqd factus, alci rei or ad alqd natus,* comb. *alci rei or ad alqd natus factusque* (opp. as regards persons, *ad alqd doctus or institutus*); a spot almost made for an ambuscade, *loca insidiis nata;* 3, in an arithmetical sense, *efficĕre,* or by *esse, fieri;* 4, = to — by art, *arte imitari or efficĕre, alqd fingĕre* (= to invent); 5, = to do, to perform, *facĕre, agĕre* (*agĕre,* the Greek πράττειν, = to act without reference to the result); = to choose anyone as one's model, *auctore uti alqo;* the ambassadors — haste to get to Africa, *legati in Africam maturantes veniunt;* he made haste to get to Rome, *Romam proficisci maturavit;* 6, = to cause to have any quality (e.g. wealth —s man proud), *facĕre, efficĕre, reddĕre alqm* (with the accus.); *facĕre* and *efficĕre* denoting the producing of a certain condition in a thing, whilst *reddĕre* implies a change of the previous condition, e.g. to — anyone useless, *alqm inutilem facĕre,* e.g. of a wound; to — anyone better, *alqm meliorem reddĕre;* to — the people from wild savages into gentle and civilised beings, *homines ex feris mites reddĕre or homines feros mites reddĕre;* very often, however, the verb "to —," with its accus. of the predicate, must be rendered in Latin by one verb; to — equal, *aequare,* etc. (see under the adjs.); to — much, a great deal of a person, *alqm magni facĕre* (= to esteem), *multum alci tribuĕre* (= to think very highly of anyone), *alqm colĕre* (= to have great regard for, to respect a person); not to — much regard for, to — light of a person, *alqm parvi facĕre* (= to treat with indifference), *alqm contemnĕre* (= to despise); to — much of a thing, *alqd magni facĕre, existimare* (= to value highly), *alqd in honore habĕre* (= to honour); not to — much of a thing, *alqd neglegĕre* (*neglig-,* = to disregard, neglect); to — much, be eager for, etc., *alcjs rei esse appetentissimum;* = to be fond of, *alqm carum habĕre;* see FOND; 7, = to bring into any state, to constitute, *facĕre, instituĕre* (= to appoint to an office), *constituĕre* (= to institute anyone as), *creare* (= to create, to elect) *alqm* (with accus., e.g. to — anyone the heir, *heredem alqm facĕre, instituĕre*); 8, = to establish, e.g. to — friendship, *conciliare* (e.g. *amicitiam;* a wedding, *nuptias; pacem*), *facĕre* (e.g. a treaty, *foedus; pacem*); to — harmony, peace, *concordiam reconciliare;* between two, *alqm in gratiam reconciliare cum alqo;* to — quarrels, *discordiam concitare* (= to cause discord); *causam jurgii inferre, jurgia excitare* (= to begin, excite quarrels); between two, *discordes reddĕre;* between the citizens, *discordiam inducĕre in civitatem;* 9, = to settle, in the phrase, to — one's abode, *in alqm locum migrare, in alium locum demigrare or transmigrare, in alqm locum immigrare* (= to go to live in, to remove to); see also RESIDE, LIVE; 10, = to raise to good fortune (e.g. he is made for this world); to — a man, *alqm gratiâ et auctoritate suâ sustentare* (= to get anyone forward); *alcjs fortunae auctorem esse;* 11, = to gain (e.g. to — money of), see MONEY, GAIN; 12, = to discover, to — land, *capĕre* (e.g. *insulam or portum*); see LAND; *ex alto invehi in portum, decurrĕre in portum;* 13, to — one's way to, = to arrive at, see PENETRATE, ADVANCE; 14, = to convert, *alqâ re uti* (e.g. to — anything an instrument of, etc.); 15, = to put into a suitable form for use, to — a bed, *lectum sternĕre;* 16, = to compose (e.g. to — verses), *facĕre, scribĕre,* see COM-

POSE; 17, to — hay, *fenum secare, caedĕre, succidĕre;* 18, = to contribute (e.g. this argument —s nothing in his favour), *magni (parvi,* etc.) *momenti esse* (= to matter); impers. it —s nothing, *nihil est ad rem;* 19, to — amends, *satisfacĕre alci de alqâ re, alqd expiare, alqd (cum) alqâ re compensare;* 20, to — arrangements, (*ap-*) *parare, comparare, praeparare, adornare alqd, facĕre,* comb. *parare et facĕre, se comparare or praeparare ad alqd;* 21, to — away with, = to kill, *interficĕre;* see KILL. **II.** n. = formation of the body, *omnis membrorum et totius corporis figura,* or simply *corporis figura, cor poris conformatio et figura,* in the connection of a sentence also simply *corpus;* of strong —, *maximi corporis* (of a man), of immensely strong —, *immani corporis magnitudine;* see also SHAPE. **maker,** n. in gen. *qui facit,* etc., or *auctor* (e.g. *pacis*), *suasor* (= adviser), *factor, fabricator.* **making,** n. *factio, fabricatio,* but better use verb. **makeshift, makeweight,** n. *ad tempus* (e.g. of an edict, a decree, *edictum ad tempus propositum*).

maladjustment, n. *incompositus* (e.g. the — of parts, *partes incompositae*).

maladministration, n. *prava rerum administratio.*

malady, n. see ILLNESS.

malapert, n. *petulans, procax, protervus, parum verecundus* (= not very discreet); see SAUCY.

malapropos, adv. *intempestive.*

malaria, n. *aër pestilens, caelum grave et pestilens.*

malcontent, n. *rerum mutationis or rerum novarum* or *rerum evertendarum cupidus.*

male, adj. *virilis* (only of man), *mas, masculus, masculinus* (Plin.) (both of man, but more frequently of animals); the — sex, *virilis sexus, -ûs.*

malediction, n. *ex(s)ecratio, dirae, -arum,* f. (= curses); see CURSE.

malefactor, n. *homo maleficus (malif-)* (= perpetrator of a wicked act). **maleficence,** n. *malitia* (= roguery), *improbitas* (= wickedness, opp. *probitas*), *malignitas* (= malignity); see MALICE. **malefic,** adj. *maleficus (malif-), malitiosus* (= roguish, esp. in law proceedings), *improbus* (= wicked, of persons, opp. *probus*), *malignus* (= evil-disposed, jealous, of persons, opp. *benignus*). **malevolent,** adj. see MALICE, MALICIOUS. **malformation,** n. *quod informe est.* **malice,** n. = envy, *malignitas, invidia, malevolentia (maliv-)* = a wicked pleasure in trying to do others harm, *malitia* (= roguery); = a wicked act, *scelus, -ēris,* n. **malicious,** adj. *malitiosus, malevolus (maliv-,* = malevolent); +*malignus* (never used in the sense of malicious, only = ill-natured, ill-willed), *invidus;* = saucy, *procax.* Adv. *malitiose* (not so strong as the English). **maliciousness,** n. see MALICE. **malign, I.** adj. see MALICIOUS and UNFAVOURABLE. **II.** v.tr. see SLANDER. **malignant,** adj. see MALICIOUS. **maligner,** n. *obtrectator.* **malignity,** n. 1, *malevolentia (maliv-);* 2, of a disease, *vis morbi.* **malpractice,** n. see MISDEED. **maltreat,** v.tr. *male tractare;* see INJURE. **maltreatment,** n. see INJURY. **malversation,** n. *peculatus, -ûs.*

mallard, n. *anas (-ātis) mas or masculus.*

malleability, n. by **malleable,** adj. *quod malleis extendi potest, lentus* (= tough), *ductilis* (Plin.).

mallet, n. 1, *fistuca* (for driving anything

with force), *pavicula* (= a rammer), *fustis* (= a club), *malleus* (= a hammer), *pistillum* (= a pestle).

mallow, n. *malva, malache, -es* (Plin.).

malt, n. *hordeum aquâ perfusum et sole tostum.*
malt-liquor, n. see BEER.

mama, mamma, n. *mamma.*

mammal, n. *animal.*

mammon, n. *divitiae, opes, -um;* see RICHES.

man, I. n. *homo* (in gen.), *vir* (esp. = a brave man); men, in a collective sense, *homines, genus humanum, hominum universum genus* (= the whole human race), *mortales, -ium;* a young —, (*homo*) *adulescens* (*adol-*); quite a young —, (*homo*) *adulescentulus* (*adol-*), *juvenis;* very often it is not expressed at all in Latin, especially with adjs., and when it is contained as subject in the verb, e.g. many men, people, *multi;* there are men who, etc., *sunt qui,* etc., *non desunt qui,* etc., *inveniuntur* or *reperiuntur qui,* etc. (in all these phrases use the indicative mood after *qui,* when the class of men is clearly defined; but the subjunctive mood when the class of men is described in an indefinite sense, so as to require a qualification; there are men who will have it that, etc., *sunt qui dicant,* i.e. who mean to say, who seem to say, to think; but *sunt qui dicunt* = there are men who assert, i.e. in a positive manner); no —, *nemo, nullus* (= no one, nobody); he is not a — (i.e. he is a brute), *homo non est, omnis humanitatis expers est;* this — (referring to some name mentioned immediately before, without laying any emphasis on the word this), simply *hic* (but *hic vir,* if with emphasis); — by —, every —, *viritim* (= to every — individually, e.g. to distribute anything, to grant, *tribuěre* or *dare*); altogether, everyone up to the very last —, *universi, ad unum omnes;* so much —, or every — gets so much, *singuli auferunt* with the accus. of the sum; = soldier, *miles, -ītis,* m.; his men, *sui;* our men, *nostri;* men may also be expressed by *exercitus, -ūs, copiae, manus, -ūs;* newly recruited men, *tirones;* with commendation, *vir;* to march in a file three men together, three abreast, *triplici ordine inceděre;* they marched thirty men abreast, *triginta armatorum ordines ibant;* with — and horse, *viris equisque* (i.e. with infantry and cavalry); an army of ten thousand men, *exercitus decem mil(l)ium;* **a** — from a country town, a countryman, but a — of the right sort, *rusticanus vir, sed plane vir* (Cic.); show yourself a —, *virum te praesta:* in chess, *latro, latrunculus* (Sen.), *miles;* in draughts, *calculus;* — of money, *pecuniosus;* — of the world, *homo urbanus,* or *pervolitus;* merchant- —, *navis* (*mercatoria*), *navis rotunda;* —-of-war, *navis longa, navis rostrata, quinqueremis* (= different kinds of Roman men-of-war, in opp. to *navis rotunda,* = merchant- —). **II.** v.tr. 1, = to furnish with soldiers, *navem* or *classem militibus* or *propugnatoribus instruěre* or *complěre;* — to sufficiently, *navem* or *classem armatis ornare;* to be sufficiently —ned, *suum numerum habēre.* **manful,** adj. see MANLY. **manhood,** n. 1, = adult age, *pubertas* (Plin.), *aetas adulta;* to reach —, *togam virilem suměre;* 2, = humanity, *humana natura, humanitas.* **mankind,** n. *homines, genus humanum.* **manly,** adj. 1, = belonging to men, *virilis;* 2, = brave, *virilis, fortis;* see BRAVE. **manliness,** n. *virtus, -ūtis,* f., *animus virilis* or *fortis;* see COURAGE. **mannikin,** n. *homuncio, homunculus, humullus.* **manservant,** n. *servus, famulus.* **manslaughter,** n. *hominis caedes;* guilty of —, by *hominem caeděre, interficěre.* **man-trap,** n. *stimulus* (Caes.).

manacle, I. n. *manica.* **II.** v.tr. *vincire, catenis.*

manage, v.tr. = to conduct, *tractare* (= to treat, handle), *regěre* (lit. = to conduct, e.g. *domesticam disciplinam regěre*), *administrare* (= to have a thing under one's hands), *perfungi alqâ re* (= to discharge the duties of an office), *gerěre* (= to hold a public office, with reference to the general conduct), *praeesse alci rei* (= to act as presiding officer, to superintend the management of affairs), *procurare* (= to act for an absent person, e.g. anyone's business, *alcjs negotia*), *dispensare.* **manageable,** adj. 1, = easy to be used, *habilis* (opp. *inhabilis*), or transl. by verbs; 2, = that may be made subservient to one's views, *qui regi potest* (both lit. and fig.), *tractabilis* (fig., of persons), *docilis, facilis* (= compliant); see FLEXIBLE. **management,** n. = manner of carrying on, *administratio, tractatio* (e.g. of the war), *cura* (care, e.g. of a family, of a household, *rei domesticae cura*); the — of anyone's affairs (in his absence), (*pro*)*curatio; dispensatio* (of a steward). **manager,** n. = one who has the direction of anything, *negotiorum* (*pro*)*curator;* to be the — of anyone's business, *alcjs rationes negotiaque procurare, alcjs rem* or *negotia gerěre), praefectus* (= one who discharges the duties of an office, in good Latin always with the gen. or dat. of the office), *magister* (= principal of an establishment, director of a company).

mandate, n. *edictum* (e.g. to issue a —, *edictum proponěre* or *edicěre, ut,* etc., of a public body); in gen. *imperatum, jussum, mandatum.*

mandible, n. *maxilla.*

mandrake, mandragora, n. *mandrăgoras, -ae,* m. (Plin.).

mane, n. *juba, coma (comae cervicum,* of lions' —s, Gell.); with a —, *jubatus, comatus.*

manes, n. *Manes, -ium,* m.

mange, manginess, n. *scabies, scabrities* or *scabritia* (Plin.). **mangy,** adj. † *scaber.*

manger, n. *praesaepe, praesaepis, praesaepium* (*praesep-*).

mangle, I. n. *machina quâ lintea aut panni lēvigantur.* **II.** v.tr. 1, = to smooth clothes with a —, *lēvigare;* 2, fig. (*di*)*laniare.* **mangled,** adj. *truncus, mutilus.*

mania, n. *insania* (lit. and fig.). **maniac,** n. *homo insanus;* see MAD.

manifest, I. adj. *apertus* (= open before one), *manifestus* (= apparent), comb. *apertus et manifestus; perspicuus* (= clear), comb. *apertus et perspicuus; evidens* (= evident), *testatus* (= shown, proved by witnesses), *notus, cognitus* (= known); a — crime, *facinus manifesto compertum et deprehensum* (when anyone is caught in the act); it is —, *patet, apparet, manifestum est, perspicuum est omnibus;* to make —, *aperire* (= to open), *patefacěre.* Adv. *aperte, manifesto, sine dubio, perspicue, evidenter, palam* (= openly), *scilicet* (ironically). **II.** v.tr. *aperire* (= to open), *patefacěre* (= to make clear), *manifestum facěre* (= to make —), (*in medium*) *proferre* (= to make generally known), comb. *proferre et patefacěre;* *enuntiare, declarare, ostenděre, evulgare, divulgare* (= to divulge). **manifestation,** n. *significatio, declaratio, demonstratio, indicium;* see DECLARATION. **manifesto,** n. if of the government, *edictum;* in gen. to issue a —, perhaps *alqd proponěre.*

manifold, adj. *multiplex* (= various), *multiformis* (= many-shaped); may also be rendered by *varietas* with the gen. following (e.g. — learning, *varietas doctrinarum;* — sounds, *varietas sonorum*); to possess — learning, *multiplici* *variáque doctrinâ esse ;* or it may be rendered by *multi* (= many), *creber* (= frequent) ; at the — requests of, *saepe rogatus.*

maniple, n. *manipulus.* **manipulate,** v.tr. *tractare ;* see TREAT. **manipulation,** n. *tractatio.*

manliness, n. **manly,** adj. see MAN.

manna, n. *manna* (Eccl.).

manner, n. = way of performing, *ratio, modus* (= mode, guide), *via* (= way, sure mode), comb. *ratio et via, ratio et modus ; genus, -eris* (= mode of proceeding, e.g. *argumentandi genus,* — of arguing ; *dicendi genus,* — of expressing one's sentiments) ; = custom, habitual practice, *ratio, consuetudo* (= custom according to which one is wont to act), *ritus, -ûs* (= mode of acting as established by custom or habit, or by the law ; hence the instinctive habit of animals), comb. *ratio et consuetudo ; institutum,* comb. *consuetudo et institutum ;* = sort, kind, *genus ;* = certain degree or measure, *quodammodo ;* in a —, in like —, *eodem* or *pari modo ;* = mien, carriage, *ratio* (in gen.), *mos* (= — in gen., distinct mode), *mores, -um,* m. (= the whole — of a person) ; = anybody's general way, *ingenium alcjs moresque* (= character) ; that is my —, *ita sum, eo sum ingenio, ita ingenium meum est* (= that is my character), *sic meus est mos* (= my —, mode), *mea sic est ratio* (= my — of proceeding) ; as it is my —, your —, in my —, *sicut meus est mos,* also *meo more, ex* or *pro consuetudine meâ, tuâ, consuetudine meâ ;* it is not my —, *non est meae consuetudinis ;* to live in his —, *suo more* or *suo instituto vivêre ;* what — is that ? *qui istic mos est ?* after, in the — or way of, etc. (= like), *more alcjs* (e.g. in the — of parents, wild beasts, a torrent, *more parentum, ferarum, torrentis, fluminis* ; *in morem alcjs* (e.g. in the — of cattle, *in morem pecudum*) ; in the — of slaves, *servilem in modum ;* *modo* or *ritu alcjs* (e.g. in the — of robbers, women, beasts, *ritu latronum, mulierum, pecudum*) ; in this —, *hoc modo, hac ratione, ita* or *sic* (= thus) ; in an equal —, *pari modo ;* = style, *stilus* (of a writer), *manus, -ûs* (of an artist, painter ; e.g. written in the Attic —, *Attico stilo scriptus*). **manners,** n. in the pl. = established customs, *mores ;* good —, *boni mores ;* a person of good —, *homo bene moratus, modestus ;* to follow anyone's —, *alcjs mores induêre* or *imitari ;* = decent deportment, *mores ;* refined, elegant —, *morum elegantia, mores elegantes* (in gen.), *urbanitas* (= courteous —), *humanitas* (= gentlemanly —), that show a man of good education) ; without —, *rudis et moris omnis ignarus* (= rude and ignorant) ; *vitae communis ignarus* (= one who knows nothing of the rules of society), *rusticus, agrestis* (= rude, rough, clumsy), *inurbanus* (= without refinement), *humanitatis expers, inhumanus.* **mannerism,** n. *ratio,* or any word = manners, and define it by context (e.g. **a new** — in speaking, *nova ratio loquendi*), or by adj. or adv. *putidus, putide* (e.g. *putide dicêre* = to speak with —s) ; see AFFECTED, AFFECTATION. **mannerist,** n. *pictor qui tabulas suo* (or *alcjs*) *more pingit.* **mannerly, I.** adj. *urbanus, humanus, perpolitus ;* see POLITE. **II.** adv. *urbane, humane, humaniter, perpolite ;* see POLITELY.

manœuvre, I. n. 1, military, *decursio, decursus, -ûs* (*decursio* always as the act of manœuvring, *decursus* = the — itself) ; *militibus decursionem* or, if for amusement, *certamen ludicrum indicêre* (= to give the order for holding **a —,** to announce a —) ; *milites in decursione*, or *in certamen ludicrum educêre* (= to let the troops march out for a —, Veget.), *certamen ludicrum committêre ;* to hold a — (at sea), *proelium navale committêre* (of the commander) ;

2, see SCHEME, TRICK. **II.** v.intr. **1, to** —, *in decursionem exire* (= to march out to a —), *in armis decurrêre,* or simply *decurrêre* (= to make evolutions for exercise), *inter se in modum justae pugnae concurrêre* (= to hold a sham fight for exercise and amusement) ; 2, see SCHEME, TRICK.

manor, n. *fundus, praedium.*

mansion, n. in gen., *aedes, -ium,* f. ; see HOUSE.

mantelet, n. *vinea, pluteus, testudo.* **mantle,** n. *amiculum, palla* (for women), *pallium, palliolum* (= Greek —), *lacerna* (= thick —), *chlamys* (= light —), *paenula* (with a hood for travelling), *sagum, sagulum* (= soldier's or servant's —), *paludamentum* (= general's —). **mantel-piece,** n. by *mensa* (= table), *pluteus* or *tabula* (= shelf).

manual, I. adj. = performed by the hand, *manu meâ, tuâ,* etc., *factus ;* — labour, *opera* (opp. *ars*), or by *manus* (e.g. to get a bare living from the earnings of one's — labour, *manuum mercede inopiam tolerare*). **II.** n. = small book, *libellus.*

manufactory, n. = the building, *officina.* **manufacture, I.** n. = operation of manufacturing, *artis opus, -êris, opera fabrilis ;* — is at a standstill, *op. jacet ;* = the article —d, *opus quod arte* or *manu factum est.* **II.** v.tr. *fabricare ;* see also MAKE. **manufacturer,** n. *opifex, -icis, fabricator* (always with the gen. of the thing that is manufactured), *artifex, -icis* (of artificial objects), *textor* (= a weaver). **manufacturing-town,** n. *urbs officinis nobilis* (= known by its manufactures).

manumission, n. *missio* (in gen.), *manumissio* (of a slave). **manumit,** v.tr. *alqm manu mittêre,* or as one word, *manumittêre.*

manure, I. n. *stercus, -ôris, fimus.* **II.** v.tr. *stercorare.*

manuscript, n. 1, = anything in one's own handwriting intended for recital or for the press, *chirographum ;* 2, = a written work, *liber, libellus,* or further defined as opp. to printed book, *manu scriptus* or *nondum editus.*

many, n. *multi, haud pauci ;* see MUCH ; *creber* or *frequens* (= — together) ; an assembly of — people, *magna frequentia (hominum) ;* a good —, *complures, plerique ;* as — as, *quot . . . tot ;* — a thing, — things, *nonnulli, aliquot, quidam* (= some), *sunt qui . . . ;* — a time, *nonnunquam* (= now and then), *interdum* (= sometimes) ; — times indeed, perhaps *aliquando ;* not — things, but much (i.e. not much, but well), *non multa, sed multum ;* — ways, — a way, *varie, vario modo, multis modis ;* these — years, *abhinc multos annos ;* to make — words, *verba facêre, longum esse ;* — men, — minds, *quot homines, tot sententiae* (Ter.) ; of — meanings, *ambiguus* (= ambiguous, equivocal, e.g. a word, *verbum ;* an oracle, *oraculum*) ; with — corners, *polygonius* (Vitruv.), in pure Latin, † *multangulus* (Lucret.) ; to have — corners, *plurium angulorum formam exhibêre ;* with — feet, *multis pedibus,* † *multipes,* † *multiformis ;* — times, *saepe, saepenumero* (= often), *crebro* (= frequently, repeatedly), *persaepe, saepissime* (= very often), *iterum atque iterum* (= again and again), *etiam atque etiam ;* how — times, *quotie(n)s ;* so — times, *totie(n)s ;* as — times . . . as, *toties . . . quot . . . ;* however — times, *quotiescunque, quotiescumque ;* — times greater, *multiplex.* **many-coloured,** adj. *variis coloribus distinctus, multicolor* (Plin.). **many-headed,** adj. *multa capita habens.* **many-sided,** lit. † *multangulus, polygonius.*

map, I. n. *tabula ;* a — of a certain part of a country, **a** — of a country, *regio* (e.g. *in Germa-*

map   764   mar

niá) *in tabulá* or *in membraná* or *in chartá picta* or *depicta.* **II.** v.tr. *terrarum situs pingĕre;* to — out, *designare, describĕre.* **mapping,** n. *graphis, -idos,* f.

maple, n. *acer;* of —, *acernus.*

mar, v.tr. *deformare, corrumpĕre;* see SPOIL.

marauder, n. *praedator, direptor.* **marauding,** adj. *praedatorius, praedabundus.*

marble, I. n. *marmor;* — -*cutter,* (*faber*) *marmorarius;* statue, bust in —, *signum marmoreum.* **II.** adj. *marmorius.*

march, n. (*mensis*) *Martius.*

march, I. v.intr. *ambulare* (in gen.), *incedĕre* (= of marching exercise, and in war); to — out, set out, *progredi, proficisci;* to be on the —, *iter facĕre;* to — off, forward, to decamp, *castra movĕre, promovĕre,* or simply *movĕre;* to -- three men abreast, *triplici ordine incedĕre;* they were marching thirty men abreast, *triginta armatorum ordines ibant;* to be marching quicker, to accelerate one's —, *accelerare iter;* to — behind, to — in the rear, to close the rear, *agmen claudĕre, cogĕre.* **II.** v.tr. *ducĕre* (e.g. *exercitum*); — back, *reducĕre;* — across, *tra(ns)ducĕre;* see LEAD. **III.** n. **1,** in a military sense, = movement of soldiers, *iter, profectio* (= the marching off) on the —, *iter faciens* (e.g. he was killed on the —, *occisus est in itinere*), *ex itinere* (= from the —, i.e., whilst the — is being interrupted for a time); to make a —, *iter facĕre, conficĕre;* to direct the — a place, *iter algo facĕre, contendĕre, convertĕre, intendĕre;* to change the route of the —, *iter* (*com*)*mutare, iter* or *viam flectĕre;* the troops on the —, *agmen;* **2,** (= signal to move), to sound the —, *classicum canĕre* (= to sound the trumpet); —! (as a word of command) *procede!* (for one); *procedite!* (for several); **3,** (= — of intellect); see PROGRESS; **4,** (= a day's journey), *iter;* one day's —, *iter unius diei, castra, -orum* (the latter inasmuch as the Romans always pitched a camp after every day's —); after a five days' —, *quintis castris;* to make forced —es, *magnis itineribus contendĕre* (in gen.), *dies noctesque iter facĕre, die et nocte continuare iter* (= day and night). **marches,** n. *fines, -ium,* m., *confinium;* see BOUNDARY.

mare, n. *equa.*

margin, n. *margo,* m. and f. **marginal,** adj. *quod ad marginem pertinet, in margine scriptus.*

marine, I. adj. = belonging to the sea, *marinus, ad mare pertinens.* **II.** n. *nauta,* m. (= sailor), *miles* (-*tis*) *classicus;* the —s, *epibatae.* **mariner,** n. *nauta.* **maritime,** adj. *maritimus* (= situated near the sea), — state, *civitas maritima* (= situated near the sea), *civitas* or *gens mari pollens, civitas* or *gens navibus* or *classe multum valens* (= powerful at sea, having a large navy); to be a — state, *classe* (*classibus*) *multum valēre.*

marjoram, n. *amarăcus* (Plin.).

mark, I. n. **1,** *nota, signum, signa et notae* (Cic.), *indicium, vestigium* (= trace); it is the — of a wise man, *est sapientis* (followed by infin.); to make one's —, *clarum algá re fieri;* **2,** = thing aim'd at, *scopos, -i* (Suet.); see AIM; **1,** = goal (fig.); see PURPOSE. **II.** v.tr. (*de*)*signare, notare;* = to take notice of, *observare, animadvertĕre;* — or mind, *animum advertĕre, animum* or *animo attendĕre;* — out, lit. *metiri metari;* fig. *designare,* (*de*)*notare;* see PURPOSE. **marked,** adj. = distinguished, *illustris;* in a bad sense *infamis, insignis* (e.g. *turpitudine*

insignis). **marker,** n. **1,** in a book, *nota* (= mark); **2,** = one who marks at a game, *minister* or *servus* (= assistant). **mark-land,** n. see MARCHES. **marksman,** n. *homo jaculandi peritus, jaculator.*

market, I. n. **1,** *macellum* (= provision —), *forum* (= — -place), *emporium* (= — town), *nundinae* (= fair); the cattle —, *forum boarium;* the vegetable —, *forum olitorium;* **2,** = sale, *venditio;* to find a —, *vendi.* **II.** v.intr. *nundinari.* **marketable,** adj. *venalis.* **market-day,** n. *nundinae.* **market-garden,** n. *hortus.* **market-place,** n. *forum.* **marketing,** n. to go —, *nundinari.*

marl, n. *marga* (Plin.).

marmalade, n. *fructus decocti.*

marmoset, n. *simiolus.*

marmot, n. perhaps *mus.*

marriage, n. *conjugium, matrimonium, nuptiae, con*(*n*)*ubium;* a legal, lawful —, *conjugium legitimum, matrimonium justum* or *legitimum, nuptiae justae et legitimae;* to contract a —, to enter into the state of matrimony. *in matrimonium ire* (Plaut.), *ducĕre uxorem* (of the man), *nubĕre alci* (of the woman); *matrimonio jungi* or *conjungi, nuptiis inter se jungi* (of man and wife); to demand anyone in —, *sibi algam in matrimonium petĕre,* also simply *petĕre algam;* to be united to anyone in —, *algam in matrimonio habēre;* to give one's daughter in — to anyone, *alci filiam* (or *virginem*) *in matrimonium dare* or *nuptum dare, alci filiam collocare* or *nuptum locare.* **marriage-contract,** n. *sponsalia, -ium, pactio nuptialis;* to make a —, *pactionem nuptialem facĕre;* the written document , deed containing the — written on tablets, *tabulae legitimae, tabulae nuptiales, dotis tabulae.* **marriage-feast,** n. *nuptiae.* **marriage-settlement,** n. *dos, dotis,* f. **marriageable,** adj. *pubes, -ēris* (in an age of puberty, in both sexes), *nubilis, adultus* (= grown up), *sponsae* or *marito †maturus.* **marry, I.** v.tr. **1,** = to unite in matrimony; by the clergyman or the person taking his place, *sol*(*l*)*ennibus* (*solenn*-) *dictis con*(*n*)*ubium sancire;* **2,** = to dispose of (of females only), *alci algam* (*in matrimonium*) *collocare, alci in matrimonium dare* or *tradĕre;* **3,** = to take for husband or wife, in gen., *matrimonio se* (*con*)*jungĕre cum algo* or *algá, in matrimonium accipĕre* or *recipĕre;* to — a woman (of a man), *ducĕre algam uxorem in matrimonium,* or simply *ducĕre algam* (*uxorem*), *matrimonio algam secum conjungĕre, algam uxorem sibi adjungĕre;* to — a man (of a woman), *nubĕre alci;* to — each other, *matrimonio jungi* or *conjungi, nuptiis inter se jungi;* to — again, *novum matrimonium inire;* to — to advantage, *virginem bene dotatem ducĕre* (of a man), *in luculentam familiam collocari* (of a female); to be married, to be a married man, *uxorem duxisse;* to be a married woman, *nuptam esse viro.* **II.** v.intr. = to enter into the conjugal state, *ux orem ducĕre* (*in matrimonium*) (see above), *nubĕre viro* (of the woman). **marrying,** n. *nuptiae.*

marrow, n. **1** *medulla;* **2,** = the essence, the best part of anything, *medulla* (seldom in this sense, e.g. *medulla verborum,* Aul. Gell.), *flos, floris,* m. (= the best part of anything). **marrow-bone,** n. *os medullosum* (not class.).

marry! interj. *medius fidius, mehercle.*

marsh, n. *palus, -udis,* f. (= morass). **marshy,** adj. *paluster* (= swampy), *caenosus* (= miry), *uliginosus* (= swampy).

marshal, I. n. use *dux* for field — ; = one who directs the order of the feast, procession, etc., *ductor pompae*. **II.** v.tr. *instruěre, disponěre*.

mart, n. see MARKET.

martial, adj. *militaris, bellicosus;* a — look, *oculi truces;* — law, *jus* (between nations in a state of war), or in the pl. *jura belli, lex belli* (= the laws of war); according to the — law, *jure* or *lege belli;* — law, in its theory, *leges militares*.

martyr, I. n. *martyr* (Eccl.); to become a — for, to die a — to a cause, *pro algâ re mortem occumběre*. **II.** v.tr. *alqm pro algâ re interficěre*. **martyrdom,** n. = death of a martyr, *martyrium* (Eccl.). **martyrology,** n. *historia martyrum*.

marvel, n. *miraculum, portentum*. **marvellous,** adj. (*per*)*mirus,* (*ad*)*mirandus, mirificus, stupendus,* (*ad*)*mirabilis* (= astonishing, e.g. *audacia*), *ingens, immanis*. Adv. *mirum in modum, mire, mirifice,* (*ad*)*mirabiliter, stupendum in modum* (= in an astonishing manner), *valde* (= very), *vehementer* (= violently).

masculine, adj. *masculus, masculinus*.

mash, I. n. *farrago*. **II.** v.tr. (*con*)*tunděre,* (*con*)*terěre*.

mask, I. n. 1, = cover for the face, *persōna* (esp. on the stage), *larva* (= an ugly —, often used at pantomimes); to put on a — (in a lit. sense), *personam sibi accommodare* or *sibi aptare, personam induěre;* to take anyone's — off, *alci personam deměre, alcjs capiti personam detrahěre;* 2, fig. to have put on a different —, *alienam personam ferre* or *gerěre, simulare algd;* to unmask oneself, to take off the —, *simulationem deponěre;* to take off the — from a person or thing, to unmask, fig. *alci* or *alci rei personam deměre et redděre suam* (Sen.); to strip off the — which anyone wears, and show him in his real light, *alqm nudare;* to retain the — of friendship, *speciem amicitiae retiněre;* to betray anyone under the — of friendship, *alqm per simulationem amicitiae proděre*. **II.** v.tr. 1, lit. *personam alci aptare, personam alcjs capiti imponěre;* to — oneself, *personam sibi accommodare* or *sibi aptare, personam induěre; se velare* (= to cover oneself with a veil); 2, fig. *tegěre* (= to cover; with anything, *algâ re*), *occultare* (= to conceal; e.g. one's intentions, *inceptum suum*).

mason, n. 1, *structor* (= builder), *faber* (= carpenter), *caementarius;* 2, a free—, * *latōmus*. **masonry,** n. *structura* (*caementicia*).

masquerade, n. *convivium a convivis personalis celebratum*. **masquerader,** n. *homo personatus*.

mass, I. n † *massa, moles, -is,* f., *summa* (= the whole); a great —, *magnum pondus, -eris,* n., *magna copia* or *vis alcjs rei ;* in the —, *per saturam; —* of people, *multitudo, frequentia ;* see CONCOURSE, ASSEMBLY. **II.** v.tr. *colligěre* (= collect), (*ac*)*cumulare* (= — together); see COLLECT, ACCUMULATE. **massive,** adj. 1, *solidus* (= dense), *magnus* (= great), *gravis* (= heavy); 2, fig. of character (e.g. simplicity), *gravis*. **massiveness,** n. 1, by adj.; 2, *gravitas*.

mass, n. = Catholic service, * *missa*.

massacre, I. n. *caedes, -is, trucidatio, internecio*. **II.** v.tr. *caeděre, irucidare, trucidando occiděre* (= to butcher); a great number of enemies were —d, *magna caedes fugientium est facta*

mast, n. on ships, *malus,* † *arbor mali ;* the —head, *malus summus;* lower end of the —, *malus imus*.

mast, n. = fruit of the beech, *glans fagea,* oak —, *glans querna*.

master, I. n. 1, as a title, *dominus* (e.g. a learned man, *vir doctissimus, illustrissimus,* etc.) ; 2, = one who rules- either men or business, *pater familias* or *familiae* (or in one word, *paterfam-*), *herus* (of the house, the former as regards the family, the latter in reference to the servants and the entire household), *possessor* (= one who possesses anything); the young — of the house, *filius herilis, filius familiae* (the latter with reference to the family. the former as regards the servants); 3, = lord, ruler, *dominus, princeps, -ipis,* m. (the first in a state, as opp. to *dominus*), *tyrannus* (τύραννος, = ruler in the most absolute sense), *dynastes, -is,* m. (δυνάστης, = potentate; then especially sovereign of a small principality); to be — over anything or anybody, *imperare alci rei* and *alci, potentem esse alcjs rei* (both lit. and fig.) ; *praeesse alci rei* and *alci* (= to preside over, in a lit. sense); Prov., like —, like man, *plane qualis dominus talis et servus;* — of, *potens* with genit. ; to be — of anything, *algd in suâ potestate habēre, alqm locum teněre;* to get — of, *potiri* (in good prose, *algâ re, algd, alcjs (rei) potiri, rerum potiri,* to seize the government); 4, = the — under whom a youth serves his apprenticeship, *magister, paterfamilias, herus* (Com.) ; 5, = teacher, *magister;* 6, of a man perfectly skilled in any occupation, a — in anything, *artifex* (with the genit., especially with the genit. of the gerund); *antistes, -itis,* m. and f., *princep alcjs rei* (= one of the first, a man of importance in anything), *perfectus et absolutus in algâ re* (= perfect in any art or science), *algâ re* or *in algâ re excellěre* (= to be foremost, excel in anything); Horace is a — in the art of portraying the human character, *Horatius ad notandos hominum mores praecipuus;* 7, fig. = over oneself, *sui potens* or *compos;* — of arts, * *magister liberalium artium* (abbreviated *M.A.* or *A.M.*); — of the ceremonies at court, *comes, -itis, officiorum, magister officiorum* or *aulae* (in gen.) ; at audiences, levees, *magister admissionum* (all under Roman emperors); — builder, *architectus;* —-piece, *opus summo artificio factum;* — ship, = superior skill, *summa alcjs rei peritia;* = office of a governor, *magisterium*. **II.** v.tr. 1, = to subdue, *domare, vincěre, superare;* see SUBDUE, CONQUER; to — all one's passions, *continēre omnes cupiditates;* the fire (the flames) was —ed, *vis flammae oppressa est;* 2, to — a thing, = to understand, *intellegěre* (*intellig-*), *discěre* (= to learn), *consequi* (= to attain), *algd cognitum habēre, perspicěre, alqa re instructum esse*. **masterful,** adj. *insolens, superbus, contumax, arrogans*. Adv. *insolenter, superbe, contumaciter, arroganter*. **masterfulness,** n. *insolentia, superbia, contumacia, arrogantia*. **masterly,** adj. *artificiosus* (= executed or executing with — skill, of persons and things), *artifex* (= of persons), *summâ* or *singulari arte, summo artificiú factus, callidissimo artificio factus, singulari opere artificioque* or *politissimâ arte perfectus* (= made in a — manner, of things); a speech delivered in a — manner, *oratio artis plena*. **mastery,** n. 1, = victory, *victoria ;* see also POWER ; 2, = attainment of eminent skill, to obtain the — of a thing, *perdiscěre* (= to learn a thing accurately, thoroughly); see also MASTER, I. 7, and II.

mastic, mastich, n. *mastiche* (Plin.), *resina lentiscina* (Plin.).

masticate, n. *manducare, manděre*. **mastication,** n. use verb.

mastiff, n. perhaps *canis Molossus*.

mat. I. n. = texture of sedge, etc., *storea* or

storia, teges, -ĕtis, f., *tegeticula.* **II.** v.tr. — together, *implicare.*

match, n. for getting a light, *sulphurata,*
-orum (Mart.), *igniarium* (Plin.); a — box, *pyxis*
or *theca* (*sulphuratorum*).

match, I. n. 1, = one's equal (in a contest,
etc.); a — for . . , *par alci* or *alci rei* (opp.
impar); to be a — for anyone, *alci parem esse*
(e.g. *bello*), *non inferiorem esse algo*; to be a —
for a thing, *alci rei parem* (e.g. a business, *negotiis*), *alqd sustinēre* (e.g. a burden, a load,
molem); 2, = contest, *certamen*; 3, see MAR-
RIAGE. **II.** v.tr. — oneself with, *cum algo in
certamen descendĕre, congredi cum algo* (= to
try one's strength against anyone, e.g. in a duel),
parem esse alci, non inferiorem esse algo; =
to compare, *aequare alqm* and *alci rei* or
alqd; = to suit, *adaequare, exaequare alqd cum
alqâ re* or *alci rei*; = to join, *(con)jungĕre,
copulare cum alqâ re.* **III.** v.intr. = to be like,
alci rei similem or *parem esse.* **matchless,**
adj. *singularis, incomparabilis* (Plin.) *unicus,
praestans* (or in superl. *praestantissimus*), *egregius*; see EXCELLENT. **match-maker,** n.
nuptiarum conciliator, -trix.

mate, I. n. 1, = one that eats at the same
table, mess—, *convictor* (= one who constantly
associates and lives, eats and drinks with
another), *socius* (= companion), *conju(n)x* (=
husband or wife); 2, in a merchant ship
or ship of war, *(sub magistro) nautis praepositus.* **II.** v.tr. 1, in chess, *alqm vincĕre* or *ad
incitus redigĕre*; 2, in gen., see MATCH II.

material, I. adj. 1, = consisting of matter,
not spiritual, *corporeus*; the spirit is not —,
mens ab omni mortali concretione segregata est;
2, = not trivial, substantial, — point, *res* (opp.
sententia, argumentum); — gain, *lucrum, quaestus, -ūs*; — wants, *indigentia, inopia* (as the
want felt); — pleasure, *voluptas.* Adv. *in omni
genere* (= in all respects), *multum valde* (=
greatly), *re(vera)* (= really). **II.** n. = anything
composed of matter, *materia* (*materies,* lit. and
fig.), *res* (= what is —, opp. *verba*), *silva* (often
quasi silva; in a fig. sense, plenty of —, e.g.
*primum silva rerum ac sententiarum comparanda
est*); the — for a rampart, *agger, -eris,* m.; a
stock of — and of words, *copia rerum et verborum*; to collect —s, *silvam rerum comparare*;
to leave —s about anything historical, in
commentariis alqd relinquĕre; —s for war, *belli
apparatus, -ūs.* **materialism,** n. *opinio eorum
qui nihil in naturâ esse statuunt nisi corpora.*
materialist, n. *qui nihil in rerum naturâ
esse statuit nisi corpora.*

maternal, adj. *maternus*; — feelings, *animus maternus*; — affection, love, *amor maternus,
amor matris erga liberos, materna indulgentia*
(= — indulgence). **maternity,** n. *animus maternus*; see also above.

mathematical, adj. *mathematicus, accuratus, certus* (fig., = exact, accurate, certain); —
calculation, *mathematicorum ratio*; to infer with
— exactness, *necessariâ mathematicorum ratione
concludĕre alqd*; with — certainty, *certissimus.*
Adv. by adj. **mathematician.** n. *mathematicus,* or by circumloc., *mathematicarum artium peritus.* **mathematics,** n. *mathematica,
-ae* (Sen.).

matins, n. *matutinae preces, -um* (= morning prayer).

matricide, n. 1, *matricidium* (= the crime);
2, *matricida,* m. and f. (= the person).

matriculate, v.tr. (a student), *alqm civitati academicae* or *in civitatem academicam a(d)-
scribĕre.* **matriculation,** n. see above.

matrimony, n. *matrimonium*; see MAR-
RIAGE. **matrimonial,** adj. see CONJUGAL,
CONNUBIAL.

matron, n. *matrona*; — of a workhouse,
etc., *custos, -odis, procuratrix.* **matronly,**
adj. *matronalis.*

matter, n. 1, (= substance excreted from living animal bodies), *pus, puris,* n. (Cels.); full of
—, *purulentus*; 2, (= visible, tangible —), *corpus,
-ŏris,* n., *res corporeae, quae cerni tangique possunt*;
3, (in a more general and philosophical sense),
*rerum natura, principia rerum ex quibus omnia
constant*; 4, (= thing treated of), *res, propositum*
(= that of which the speaker intends to treat);
that has nothing to do with the —, *hoc nihil est
ad rem*; to come to the —, *ad propositum* or *ad
rem ipsam venire*; but let us return to the — in
hand (after a digression), *jam ad instituta pergamus*; (after an introduction) *sed ad propositum
revertamur,* or simply *sed ad propositum*; but to
return to the — in hand, *sed ut eo revertar, unde
sum egressus*; *ut eo unde egressa est referat se
oratio*; to cut the — short, *ut paucis dicam, ut
in pauca conferam, ne longum fiat, ne longus
sim*; it is a difficult — to, etc., *difficile est*
(with infin. or with supine in *-u*); = material,
materia (*materies*), *silva* (often *quasi silva*);
= event, occurrence, *res, res gesta*; = affair,
cause, *res* (in gen., also = disputed point in a
lawsuit, the lawsuit itself); *negotium* (= a business to perform, engagement), *caus(s)a* (in a
war, in a lawsuit, or in a literary discussion);
to meddle with the —s of other people, *aliena
negotia curare*; how is it with the —? how do
—s stand? *quo loco res est? ut res se habet?* how
stands your —? *quomodo tibi res se habet?* the
— is settled, *judicata res est*; concerning the —,
quod rem or res spectat; pith of the —, *res*; —
of fact, *factum*; what's the —? *quid* or *quidnam
est? quid rei est? quid accidit?* what's the —
with her? *quid tristis est?* (of one who seems
sorrowful), *quo morbo laborat?* (of one who is
ill); upon the whole —, *denique*; a small —,
paul(l)ulum, aliquantum. **it matters,** v.imp.
interest, refert; with genit. if used of a person
to whom it matters; but if the person is expressed by a personal pronoun, we use the abl.
meâ, tuâ, nostrâ, vestrâ, e.g. to me it —s, *meâ
interest* or *refert*; the thing in which we feel an
interest can never be expressed by a noun, but
must be rendered with the accus. and infin.,
the simple infin., or by a relative clause (oblique
interrogation), or with *ut*; how much it matters
is expressed by *magnopere, magis, maxime,
minime, multum, permultum, plurimum, nihil,*
etc., or by the genit. of value, e.g. *magni,
permagni, parvi, pluris, tanti, quanti,* etc., e.g.
it —s a great deal to me whether you are with
me or not (I am very anxious for you to be
present with me), *maxime nostrâ interest te esse
nobiscum*; at Rome, *permagni nostrâ interest te
esse Romae.*

matting, n. see MAT.

mattock, n. *dolabra.*

mattress, n. *stragulum*; a — of goat's hair,
cilicium.

mature, I. adj. 1, *maturus* (= ripe, of full
age), *tempestivus* (= seasonable); 2, of judgment,
etc., *consideratus, sapiens, prudens, sagax, perspicax, intellegens* (*intellig-*). Adv. *mature* (=
soon), *tempestive* (= seasonably), *considerate,
sapienter, prudenter, sagaciter, intellegenter* (*in-
tellig-*). **II.** v.tr. 1, = ripen, *maturare, coquĕre*;
2, fig. *parare, efficĕre, fingĕre*; see DEVISE, PRE-
PARE. **III.** v.intr. *maturescĕre.* **mature-
ness, maturity,** n. *maturitas* (= timeliness,
lit. and fig.); to bring to —, *ad maturitatem
perducĕre* (lit.); to come to —, *maturescĕre* (also

fig. = **to be** brought to a state of perfection, Plin.).

matutinal, adj. *matutinus.*

maudlin, adj. see DRUNKEN, SILLY

maul, v.tr. *laedĕre* (= injure).

maunder, v.intr. *nugari.*

mausoleum, n. *mausoleum* (Suet.); see TOMB.

maw, n. *ingluvies, venter;* see STOMACH.

mawkish, adj. *putidus.* Adv. *putidē.*
mawkishness, n. use adj.

maxim, n. *dogma* (δόγμα), or in pure Latin *decretum* (= principle established by a philosopher, doctrine), *praeceptum* (= precept, whereby we determine an action, a rule or any doctrine, also said of a philosopher), *institutum, sententia* (in gen. = an opinion founded upon reasons), *judicium* (= conviction, anyone's view of a matter, arrived at after mature consideration), *regula alcjs rei* or *ad quam alqd dirigitur* (= rule, principle upon which we act in a matter; never without the genit. of the object, e.g. the same — applies with regard to gain, as, etc., e.g. *eadem utilitatis quae honestatis est regula)* ; *lex* (= law, stated rule, e.g. *primam esse historiae legem).*

maximum, n. *quod maximum est;* the — gain, *quaestus (-ūs) maximus.*

May, n. *(mensis) Maius.* **May-day,** n. *Kalendae Maiae.*

may, verb aux. **1,** = to be possible; see POSSIBLE, CAN ; **2,** = to have physical power; see ABLE, CAN ; **3,** = to have moral power; see ALLOW, DARE ; **4,** see PERHAPS ; however, as no precise mode in which this verb is to be rendered can be stated, each person's individual judgment, formed by attentive reading, must be the guide; — . . . ever so, still, etc., *tametsi . . . tamen;* if — expresses a conjecture, it is rendered by *videri,* e.g. you — not be fully aware of his boldness, *parum perspexisse ejus videris audaciam;* he — be twenty years old, *viginti annos natus esse videtur;* a thing that — be done, etc., or — in forms of prayer and petition, should be rendered simply by the subjunctive mood, or sometimes by the inf., e.g. he — go, *eat;* somebody might say, *forsitan quispiam dixerit* or *forte aliquis dicet* (= perhaps someone will say); however they — grumble, I shall say what I think, *fremant, dicam quod sentio;* whoever he — be, etc., *quicunque is est;* as fast as — be, *quam celerrime;* you — for me, (*per me) licet;* if I — say so, *si ita loqui* or *dicere licet, sit venia verbi;* — be, see PERHAPS.

mayor, n. *urbis praefectus, -ūs* (Suet.).
mayoralty, n. *urbis praefectura.*

maze, n. *labyrinthus (qui itinerum ambages occursusque ac recursus inexplicabilis continet,* Plin.). **mazy,** adj. *inexplicabilis* (Plin.), † *inextricabilis.*

mead, n. *mulsum.*

mead, meadow, n. *pratum;* belonging to, growing on the —, *pratensis;* — land, — ground, *pratum.* **meadowy,** adj. *multa prata habens.*

meagre, adj. **1,** of flesh ; see LEAN ; **2,** as **in** — soil, *exilis;* see BARREN ; **3,** = wanting strength of diction, *jejunus, exilis, aridus.* Adv. *jejune, exiliter.* **meagreness,** n. **1,** see LEANNESS ; **2,** *exilitas;* **3,** *jejunitas exilitas.*

meal, n. *farina* (of wheat or any other kind of grain) ; see FLOUR. **mealy,** adj. *farinarius.*

meal, n. in gen. *cibus* (= food) ; *epulae* (= banquet); properly only two among the Romans, viz., the morning —, *prandium;* and the chief

— of the day, *cena (coen-),* taken in the decline of the day. Besides these, the *jentaculum,* taken on rising in the morning, was a very slight refreshment. The *prandium* was taken about noon, hence *cibum meridianum sumĕre.* Between the *prandium* and the *cena* the Romans sometimes took a luncheon *(gustare).* To take a — is *edĕre, cibum capĕre, prandĕre, prandium comedĕre, gustare* (= to lunch), *cenare, cenitare, epulari* (= to feast, to banquet) ; to take a — at anyone's table, *accubare apud alqm.*

mean, adj. = low and unworthy, *illiberalis, sordidus* (= unworthy a free man), *abjectus* (= contemptible), *turpis* (= base), *improbus* (= dishonest), of clothing, etc., *sordidus* ; of rank, *humilis, ignobilis, obscurus* (= morally bad and low), *foedus* (= foul, of things) ; — plan, *foedum consilium.* Adv. *illiberaliter, sordide, abjecte, abjecte et sine dignitate, turpiter, turpiter et nequiter, foede.* **meanness,** n. *illiberalitas, animus abjectus, improbitas, sordes, -(i)um, indignitas;* of rank, *humilitas, ignobilitas, obscuritas;* to bear all —es, *omnes indignitates (per)ferre;* to lead anyone to —, *alqm ad nequitiam adducĕre;* I fear to commit a —, *extimesco ne quid turpiter faciam.*

mean, or **medium,** n. *res media, modus;* there is no — between peace and war, *inter pacem et bellum medium nihil est.* **means,** n. = whatever serves to the attainment of an object, *via, ratio, consilium, facultas, auxilium, adjumentum;* a — which leads to your end, *id quod eo quo intendas fert deducitque;* ways and —, *via atque ratio;* to select or take a —, *rationem* (or *viam) inire* (or *nihil capĕre* or *sequi)* ; to try all —, *omnia experiri, nihil inexpertum omittĕre;* to try the last —, *extrema experiri* or *audēre, ad extrema* (ad *ultimum auxilium) descendēre;* to endeavour by all —, *omni ope atque operâ eniti* (with *ut* or *ne)* ; by fair —, *recte;* by foul —, *foede, turpiter;* by all —, *omnino, prorsus, plane;* concessively, *(ita) sane, vero, utique;* by no —, *neutiquam, haudquaquam, minime, nullo modo;* =̈ resources (see the word), *opes, facultates, divitiae;* I have — to live, *habeo unde vivam;* I have no — to, etc., *ad alqd perficiendum mihi desunt facultates;* out of your own —, *tuis opibus, privato sumptu;* by — of, *ope* (or *auxilio) alcjs, alqo juvante, per alqm;* (if a thing, the ablative alone is generally employed), to mount the wall by — of ladders, *scalis murum a(d)scendĕre;* by participles, *praeliis secundis usus,* = by — of successful engagements. If you wish to represent a cause, operation, or occasion, employ *per; mulieres per aetatem ad pugnum inutilis,* = women useless for fight by — (= on account of) their age ; *per se cognitus,* by his own — or efforts ; *per Caeciliam agĕre,* = to carry on by — of Caecilia ; *eorum operâ plebs concitata est,* = by their — the people were stirred up ; *ejus beneficio in curiam venerant,* = by his — (or favour) they had entered the senate.

mean, v.tr. **1,** = to have in contemplation, *velle, cogitare;* see INTEND ; **2,** = to design with reference to a future act, e.g. to — well to anyone, *bonâ fide agĕre cum alqo, alci bene velle, alci cupĕre* (but never *alci bene cupĕre* in this sense), *alci favēre,* comb. *alci favēre et cupĕre;* *alci amicum esse, alci cupĕre et amicum esse ;* **3,** = to signify, *dicĕre alqm* or *alqd, significare, designare, denotare,* also with the addition *oratione suâ* (= to allude to anyone in one's speech, words) ; I — Hilarus, *Hilarum dico;* *intellegĕre (intellig-,* = to understand by), what does he — ? *quid sibi vult?* what does he — by these words? *quid sibi vult haec oratio? quid sibi volunt verba ista?* = to be a sign for expressing an idea, *significare, declarare, sonare* (lit. to sound), *valēre* (= to contain such and such a meaning) ; this word (the word *becco*) —s the bill of a cock, *id gallinacei rostrum valet.* **meaning,** n. **1,** = that which exists in the mind (e.g. yes, that is my —, *mihi vero sic placet, sic hoc mihi videtur ;* see INTENTION, WISH, OPINION ; **2,** see PURPOSE, AIM ; **3,** = signification, *significatio* (of a word), *vis* (= force of an expression), *sententia* (= the idea which the person speaking attaches to a certain word), *notio* (= original idea of a word ; see IDEA), *intellectus, -ūs* (how a word is to be understood, post Aug. t.t., Quint.) ; it is necessary to fix the — of the verb "to be in want of," *illud excutiendum est, quid sit* CARERE ; to give a — to a word, *verbo vim, sententiam, notionem sub(j)icĕre ;* well- —, see BENEVOLENT.

meander, v.intr. *flexuoso cursu fluĕre.*

measles, n. **1,** = disease in man, * *morbilli* (t.t.) ; **2,** = disease in pigs, * *hydātis finna* (not class.).

measurable, adj. *quod metiri possumus.* **measurableness,** n. render by adj. **measure, I.** n. **1,** *mensura* (= that by which extent or dimension is ascertained, lit. and fig., in an abstract and concrete sense), *modus* (= proportion, limit as to how far a person ought or is allowed to go), *moderatio* (= moderation) ; weights and —s, *mensurae et pondera, -um* (Plin.) ; to take the — of anything, *mensuram alcjs rei inire ;* with full—, *pleno modio, cumulate ;* according to the — of, *pro modo, pro ratione* (but generally by *pro* with ablat., according to, e.g. *pro viribus agĕre, pro se quisque,* i.e. everyone according to his strength) ; beyond —, *out of all —, sine modo, praeter* or *extra* or *supra modum, immodice, immoderate, majorem in modum* (= beyond the usual —), *nimis* (= too much), *admodum* (= exceedingly), *longe* (= by far, with superl., e.g. *longe omnium maximus*), *sic ut nihil supra possit, adeo ut nihil supra ;* in such a —, *hoc modo, tali modo, sic ;* in some —, *algo modo, algâ ratione, algâ ex parte, algd, nonnihil* (= somehow, in some way ; this relieves me in some —, *me res algd sublevat*) ; in a certain —, *quodam modo ;* also when it modifies an expression, by *ut ita dicam, quasi, quidam* with the word the meaning of which it modifies (e.g. all arts have in some — a common tie, *omnes artes habent quoddam commune vinculum*) ; in such a — as, *prout* ; — for —, *par pari referre* or *respondēre ;* **2,** = steps taken, *ratio* (= mode of acting), *consilium* (= plan), *remedium* (= remedy) ; a wise —, *consilium prudens ;* to take a —, *rationem inire, consilium capĕre ;* to take — according to time and circumstances, *consilium pro tempore et pro re capĕre ;* to take good, practical or effective —, *bonis consiliis uti ;* to take joint —, *consilia communicare ;* **3,** in music, *modi, numeri ;* see also METRE. **II.** v.tr. **1,** = to ascertain extent, degree, (di)*metiri, emetiri, permetiri, mensuram alcjs rei inire ;* **2,** = to ascertain the degree of anything (e.g. of heat), *emetiri ;* **3,** = to travel over, *emetiri ;* see PASS, v.tr. ; **4,** = to judge of distance, etc., by anything (also fig. = to judge by, etc.), (di)*metiri algd algâ re ;* **5,** = to adjust, proportion, lit. *metiri ;* fig. = to determine the ratio of one thing to another, *algd dirigĕre ad algm rem* or *algâ re ;* with what judgment ye judge, ye shall be judged, and with what — ye mete, it shall be measured to you again, *in quo judicio judicaveritis, judicabimini, et in quâ mensurâ mensi fueritis, remetietur vobis* (Vulgate). **III.** v.intr. render by *magnitudine esse* (with genit., e.g. *quinque pedum*). **measured,** adj. see MODERATE. **measurer,** n. *qui metitur, mensor.* **measureless,** adj. *immensus, infinitus.* **measurement,** n. *mensio* (= the act), *mensura* (= the manner) ; see MEASURE. **measuring-rod.** n. *decempĕda.*

meat, n. **1,** = anything eaten by man or beast, see FOOD ; **2,** = flesh, *caro, -nis,* f. ; a small piece of —, *caruncula ;* a piece of roast —, *caro assa* or *assum,* with distinguishing adj. (e.g. *assum vitulinum* = veal) ; boiled —, *caro elixa ;* cooked —, *caro cocta ;* salt —, *caro sale conspersa* or *conditanea ;* horse —, *equorum pabulum* (= food for the horses) ; — market, *macellum* (= general market).

mechanic, n. *faber, opifex.* **mechanical,** adj. *machinalis* (Plin.), *mechanicus* (Aul. Gell.), *organicus* (architectural term) ; to possess — skill, *manibus exercitatum esse.* Adv. *sine mente ac ratione.* **mechanics,** n. as a science, *scientia machinalis* (= knowledge of —, mechanical science, Plin.). **mechanism,** n. *machinatio.*

medal, n. *nummus in memoriam alcjs rei cusus* (to commemorate an event). **medallion,** n. *clipeus* or *clipeum* (in the form of a shield) ; see also MEDAL.

meddle, v.intr. see INTERFERE. **meddler,** n. *ardelio* (Phaed., Mart.), *homo importunus, molestus.* **meddling,** adj. see INQUISITIVE.

mediæval, adj. *ad medium aevum* or *ad patrum tempora pertinens.*

mediate, I. adj. opp. to immediate ; in philosophy, causes so termed are thus discriminated by Cicero, *caus(s)arum aliae sunt adjuvantes, aliae proximae,* of causes, some are mediate, others immediate. Adv. *per caus(s)as adjuvantes.* **II.** v.intr. *se interponĕre ad algd faciendum ;* see also RECONCILE. **III.** v.tr. — a peace, *pacem conciliare.* **mediation,** n. use *deprecator* (e.g. *me deprecatore,* by my —). **mediator,** n. *qui se* (or *auctoritatem suam*) *interponit, arbiter, qui arbitri partes agit* or *sustinet, interpres, -ētis* (= one who, as a translator, represents the interests of his party), *conciliator alcjs rei* (= he who brings about an object, e.g. a marriage, *conciliator nuptiarum*), *deprecator* (in gen.).

medicable, adj. see CURABLE. **medical,** adj. † *medicus, medicinus, medicinalis ;* — properties, by *vis medendi ;* — man, *medicus* (in gen.). **medicament, medicine,** n. **1,** *medicina, medicamen tum), remedium* (as a remedy for some complaints, *ad, contra algd*) ; counteracting —, *antidōtus* (*antidotum*) ; pertaining to —, *medicinalis ;* **2,** = medical science, *medicina, ars medicinalis, ars medendi ;* to practise —, *medicinam exercēre.* **medicine-bottle,** n. *poculum* (= cup). **medicine-box,** n. *narthecium, pyxis.* **medicinal,** adj. *saluber, salutaris.* Adv. *remedio* (dat. = as a remedy).

mediocre, adj. *mediocris.* **mediocrity,** n. *mediocritas.*

meditate, v.intr. **1,** *cogitare, meditari, commeniuri ;* see THINK ; **2,** see INTEND. **meditation,** n. *cogitatio, commentatio, meditatio,* comb. *commentatio atque meditatio ;* see THOUGHT. **meditative,** adj. by adv. *attento animo, in cogitatione defixus.*

medium, n. a middle course, fig. *media consilia, -orum, media consilii via ;* to pursue a —, *mediam consequi consilii viam. mediam quandam sequi viam ;* see MEANS.

medlar, n. *mespilum ;* — -tree, *mespilus,* f. (Plin.).

medley, n. *farrago* (Juv.), *colluvio rerum,* so too *colluvio omnium scelerum.*

meed, n. *praemium ;* see REWARD.

meek, adj. *demissus, modestus, verecundus.* Adv. *modeste, verecunde.* **meekness,** n. *animus demissus, modestia, verecundia.*

meet, adj. see FIT, PROPER, USEFUL.

meet, I. v.tr. 1, *alci occurrĕre, obviam venire, obvium se dare, obvium esse, obviam or obvium fieri, (obviam) se offerre* (all in gen. = to — a person), *congredi cum algo* (of two meeting each other on the way), *offendĕre alqm, incidĕre alci* or *in alqm* (accidentally), *improviso alci incidĕre* (unexpectedly), *obviam ire* (intentionally) ; somebody —s me on the road, *se inter viam offert alqs ;* = to go to —, *obviam ire* (out of politeness, or from hostile motives), *occurrĕre, occursare, obviam procedĕre, obviam venienti procedĕre, obviam venire* or *progredi, obviam egredi* (all with dat. ; in Plaut. and Ter.); = to come together in any place, *invenire, reperire alqm* (or *alqd,* = to find anyone whom we wish to see), *offendĕre alqm* (or *alqd,* = accidentally, unexpectedly to fall upon anything or upon a person), *nancisci* (= to — accidentally, to catch, e.g. anyone alone, without a witness, *alqm sine arbitris*), *convenire alqm* (= to — anyone by appointment to whom we wish to speak) ; to be met (e.g. he can be met at, etc.), *inveniri, reperiri ;* to be met at a certain place, *frequentare locum ;* 2, fig. = to encounter (e.g. to — danger), *periculo obviam ire, se offerre, se opponĕre, se committĕre ;* to — death, *mortem oppetĕre, morti se offerre* or *se ob(j)icĕre ;* = to receive with kindness (e.g. to — anyone's views), *consentire de alqā re ;* to — kindly, to — halfway, *urbanum* or *liberalem se praebēre alci.* II. v.intr. 1, of two persons, *inter se obvios esse, inter se congredi* or *convenire, concurrĕre inter se* (accidentally) ; to — by appointment, *congredi cum algo, convenire alqm* (e.g. on the road, *ex itinere*) ; *confluĕre* (in large numbers), *concurrĕre, convolare* (= to hasten together) ; 2, of lines, circumstances, etc., *convenire ;* 3, = to — in a hostile manner, *(inter se) concurrĕre* (of bodies, and of those who fight), *(inter se) congredi* (in a single combat, and of troops), *signa inter se conferre, cum infestis signis concurrĕre* (of two armies), *collidi inter se* (of two ships). **meeting**, n. = assembly, *congressio, conventus, -ūs* (= a friendly —), *coetus, -ūs (coit-)* (= a gathering), *concursus, -ūs, concursio* (= any coming together) ; a large, numerous —, *celeber conventus, celebritas* (= a gathering of many persons at a place), *frequentia* (= a — that is well attended). **meeting-house**, n. 1, *conveniendi locus, locus quo conveniunt ;* 2, *aedes, -ium.*

melancholy. melancholic. I. adj. 1, = hypochondriacal, *melancholicus* (μελαγχολικός); 2, fig. *tristis* (= sorrowful, also of things, e.g. countenance), *maestus* (= downcast, opp. to *laetus*). II. n. = hypochondria, *atra bilis,* or the Greek μελαγχολία, in Cic., e.g. *Graeci volunt illi quidem, sed parum valent verbo ; quem nos furorem,* μελαγχολίαν *illi vocant ; quasi vero atra bile solum mens, ac non saepe vel iracundiā graviore, vel timore, vel dolore moveatur ;* = sorrowful disposition, *tristitia, maestitia.*

melée, n. *concursus, -ūs* (= charge), or *pugna, praelium* (= battle).

melliferous, adj. † *mellifer.* **mellifluence**, n. *mel* (e.g. *Homerici senis mella,* = the — of Homer, Plin. Min.). **mellifluent, mellifluous**, adj. *mellitus.*

mellow, I. adj. 1, of fruit, *mītis, mollis* (= mild, soft ; *mollis* also of meat) ; of wine, *lenis* (Ter.), *mollis* (Verg.) ; = ripe, *maturus,* comb. *maturus et coctus ;* 2, fig. *sapiens, sagax, prudens ;* see WISE, SAGACIOUS. II. v.tr. *coquĕre.* III. v.intr. *maturescĕre.*

melodious, adj. *canōrus, sonōrus, numerosus* (= harmonious, tuneful, of a speech and of the

speaker) *numerose cadens* (= with graceful periods, of a speech). Adv. *numerose.* **melodiousness**, n. use adj. (e.g. — of the voice, *vox canora*). **melody**, n. *modus, modulus* (Plin.), *melos, -i,* n., *cantus, -ūs ;* — and time, *cantus numerique ;* — of the voice, *vocis modulatio.* **melodrama**, n. *drama musicum.* **melodramatic**, adj. *mirificus ;* see WONDERFUL.

melon, n. *melo* (Plin.).

melt, I. v.tr. 1, = to make liquid, *liquidum facĕre, liquefacĕre, dissolvĕre,* †*resolvĕre* (= to dissolve snow, pearls, *nivem, margaritas,* etc.), *diluĕre* (= to dilute, e.g. a pearl in vinegar, *baccam aceto*) ; 2, = to soften to tenderness, *alcjs mentem ad misericordiam revocare, alqm ad misericordiam vocare* or *adducĕre* (= to move to compassion). II. v.intr. 1, = to become liquid, to — away, *liquescĕre, liquefieri, dissolvi, tabescĕre* (of snow, then fig. of man, e.g. from desire, *desiderio,* from love, *amore*) ; 2, fig. to — into tears, *in lacrimas effundi ;* 3, = to lose substance (e.g. corporeal things — as breath into the wind), *dilabi* (= gradually to — so as to disappear). **melting**, adj. by adv. *mollis et delicatus* (of sounds, e.g. *quanto molliores sunt et delicatiores in cantu flexiones*) ; see also PITEOUS.

member, n. 1, *membrum, artus, -ūs* (both of the body) ; see LIMB ; 2, = part of a discourse or of a verse, a clause, *membrum* (e.g. of the body, of a speech), *pars* (= part of a whole, = a part which is a whole by itself) ; *articulus* (*articulus dicitur cum singula verba intervallis distinguuntur,* Cic.), *incisio, incisum* (κόμμα = part of a sentence), *membrum* (= a greater part of a sentence, e.g. *quae Graeci* κόμματα *et* κῶλα *nominant, nos recte incisa et membra dicimus*) ; 3, = an individual of a community or society ; a — of a council, senate, *vir* or *homo senatorius, senator ;* — of a community, *civis ;* — of a race, *gentilis ;* — of a family, *homo de alcjs stirpe ;* — of a society, *socius, sodalis, -is,* m. ; see PART. **membership**, n. render by circumloc. with **member.**

membrane, n. *membrana.*

memoir, n. a private —, *dicta factaque alcjs, memoria* (= tradition, narrative); an historical —, *commentarii ;* Socrates' —, as Xenophon gives them, *ea quae a Socrate dicta Xenophon retulit.* **memorable**, adj. = worth mentioning, *(com)memorabilis* (rare), *memoratu dignus* = deserving to be handed down to posterity, *memoriā dignus, memorabilis, memoriae prodendus ; insignis* (= of special note) ; no — event occurred, *nihil memoriā dignum actum ;* this year will be — on this account, *hic annus insignis erit hac re.* **memorandum**, n. = remark, see NOTE ; = list of goods, *index, -icis,* m. and f. ; = a sign whereby to remember anything, *nota* (= characteristic, a mark made with the pen ; to make a — with chalk against anything, *cretā notare alqd*) ; — -book, *adversaria, -orum* (= waste-book, day-book). **memorial**, I. n. *monumentum ;* a — in writing, *lit(t)erarum monumenta, -orum, lit(t)erae.* II. adj. — coin, *nummus in memoriam alcjs cusus ;* — column, *cippus.* **memoirs**, n. *commentarii.* **memory**, n. *memoria, recordatio* (= recollection) ; to keep in —, *memoriā tenēre alqd ;* to the — of, *in memoriam alcjs ;* from —, *ex memoriā, memoriter ;* to commit to —, *alqd memoriae mandare, ediscĕre ;* in the — of man, *post hominum memoriam ;* to hand down to —, *memoriae tradĕre,* or *prodĕre.*

menace, v. and n., and **menacing**, adj. and adv., see THREATEN, THREAT, THREATENING.

menagerie, n. *vivarium, leporarium* (both = preserve), or *ferae saeptis (sept-) inclusae.*

25

mend, I. v.tr. 1, = to repair, *reflcēre, reparare, reconcinnare*(=to — again what was whole before), *(re)sarcire* (= to patch up anything damaged, or that is torn to pieces, a tub, house, roof, coat, etc.), *emendare, corrigĕre* (= to free a written treatise from mistakes); 2, fig. *emendare, corrigĕre;* = to — one's life, *mores suos mutare;* to — one's pace, *gradum addĕre.* **II.** v.intr. 1, physically, *(ex morbo) convalescĕre;* 2, = to improve, *melius ire* (e.g. things —, *res melius it*).

mendacious, adj. *mendax.* Adv. *falso, per mendacium.* **mendacity,** n. *mendacium;* see LIE.

mendicancy, mendicity, n. *mendicitas, egestas* (= neediness), comb. *egestas ac mendicitas* (all = beggary). **mendicant,** adj. *mendīcus;* see BEG, BEGGAR.

menial, I. adj. 1, = pertaining to domestic servants, *servilis;* 2, fig. *servilis, humilis, sordidus, illiberalis.* **II.** n. see SERVANT, DOMESTIC.

menstrual, adj. *menstruus.*

mensuration, n. *dimensio* (= measuring), *ars metiendi;* see SURVEYING.

mental, adj. by the genitives *animi, ingenii;* — gifts, *animi facultates* (= talents), *ingenium* (= natural talent); to possess excellent — gifts, *ingenio valēre, ingenio abundare* (= to abound in), *praestantissimo ingenio praeditum esse* (= to be endowed with excellent — gifts); —debility, *morbus animi* or *mentis, aegritudo animi* (as affliction, etc.). Adv. *mente, anime, cogitatione.*

mention, I. n. *commemoratio* (when the idea existed already in the mind previously), *mentio* (in reference to the idea in general, whether quite new or —ed a second time); to make — of a matter, *mentionem facēre alcjs rei.* **II.** v.tr. *(com)memorare alqd, alcjs rei meminisse* (= to remember, if anyone shows by his words that he has not forgotten a thing, also to — in anything written), comb. *meminisse et commemorare; mentionem facēre alcjs rei* or *de alqâ re* (= to make — of); to — accidentally, or in passing, *(casu) in mentionem alcjs rei incidere;* to — frequently, *mentionem alcjs rei agitare, crebro* or *crebris sermonibus alqd usurpare;* not to — that, etc., *ut omittam* or *ne dicam, quod,* etc.; not to — all these things, *omissis his rebus omnibus;* above—ed, *de quo (quâ) supra commemoravimus, quem (quam, quod) supra commemoravimus* or *diximus, quem (quam, quod) supra scripsi, qui (quae, quod) supra scriptus (-a, -um) est, de quo (quâ) a nobis antea dictum est, cujus supra meminimus,* also simply by *ille;* as we have —ed above, before, *ut supra dictum est, ut supra scripsi* or *scriptum est;* see STATE, DECLARE.

mentor, n. see ADVISER.

mephitic, n. *mephiticus* (late), *foetidus.*

mercantile, adj. *mercatorius,* generally by the genit. *mercatoris* or *mercatorum* (= of the merchants); or by *commercium, mercatura* (e.g. *mercaturas facēre,* = to be engaged in — transactions); see COMMERCIAL. **mercenary,** adj. *mercenarius* (= for hire, e.g. *testis* = a paid witness, *miles* = — soldier), *(mercede* or *pretio) conductus; quaestuosus* (= eager for gain), *avarus* (= avaricious), *venalis* (= readily bribed). **mercer,** n. = general dealer in cotton, etc., *tabernarius* (= shopkeepers in general), *qui pannos vendit* or *venditat* (= a hosier in a small way). **merchandise,** n. 1, = goods, *merx, -cis,* f., *res venales;* 2, = commerce, *commercium, mercatura, negotia, -orum.* **merchant,** n. *mercator.* **merchantman,** n. *navis mercatoria* (Plaut.), or *oneraria,* also simply *oneraria.*

mercurial, adj. 1, by circuml. with mercury; 2, fig. *mobilis, lĕvis.* **mercury,** n. 1, the god, *Mercurius;* 2, the planet, *stella Mercurii, Mercurius;* 3, the metal, *argentum vivum* (Plin.).

mercy, n. *misericordia, clementia, mansuetudo, venia* (= pardon), *lenitas* (= mildness). **merciful,** adj. *misericors, clemens, mansuetus, exorabilis* (= easily entreated), *lenis, mitis.* Adv. *clementer, mansuete.* **merciless,** adj. *immisericors, inexorabilis, immitis, inclemens, inhumanus, crudelis, durus, atrox, saevus, ferreus;* see CRUEL. Adv. *inclementer, inhumane, crudeliter, duriter (dure), atrociter, saeve.* **mercilessness,** n. *inclementia, inhumanitas, duritia (durities), crudelitas, atrocitas, saevitia;* see CRUELTY.

mere, adj. *merus* (= not mixed, opp. *mixtus,* in prose generally only in reference to wine, then also = nothing but), *solus, unus* (= sole); also by *ipse* (before the noun, e.g. by the — sight, *ipso aspectu);* in a wider sense, by *merus* (in good prose only of things); — trifles, *merae nugae;* not to be able to sleep with — joy, *prae magno gaudio somnum capēre non posse.* Adv. *(tantum)modo, solum, tantum;* see ONLY.

meretricious, adj. 1, see UNCHASTE; 2, fig. of style, *fucatus.*

merge, v.tr. 1, see DIP; 2, see MIX, MINGLE.

meridian, I. n. in astron. *circulus meridianus;* = the highest point, see HEIGHT, SUMMIT. **II.** adj. *meridianus.*

merit, I. n. 1, = excellence which claims reward, *dignitas, virtus* (= excellence); according to —, *pro merito, merito, pro dignitate;* 2, = value (applied to things), *excellentia, praestantia;* see EXCELLENCE, VALUE, WORTH; 3, see REWARD; to make a — of necessity, *necessitati parēre.* **II.** v.tr. see DESERVE. **merited,** adj. *meritus, debitus,* comb. *meritus ac debitus.* **meritorious,** adj. by circumloc. (e.g. *laude dignus, laudabilis,* or, that is a very — act of yours, *hāc re optime meruisti);* to act in a — manner, *bene merēre;* towards any body, *de alqo.* Adv. *bene, optime.*

merle, n. *merula.*

mermaid, n. *nympha quae faciem mulieris et piscis caudam habet.*

merriment, n. *hilaritas, alacritas, lascivia, animus hilaris* (= merry disposition, mood). **merry,** adj. *hilarus, hilaris, lascivus* (= frolicsome), *festivus;* see GAY. Adv. *hilariter, hilare, festive.* **merry-andrew,** n. *homo jocosus, ridiculus, coprea* (= jester), *sannio* (= mimic, and in gen. sense), *scurra* (= droll). **merrymaking,** n. *voluptas;* see PLEASURE, FEAST.

mesh, n. *macula.* **meshy,** adj. *reticulatus.*

mesmerize, v.tr. *manuum contractatione somnum alci inducĕre.* **mesmerism, mesmerist,** n. use verb.

mess, I. n. 1, = portion of food, *cibus* or some special n. (e.g. a — of veal, *caro vitulina);* 2, = common meal, *convivium;* 3, = soldiers dining together, use *convivae, sodales, -ium.* **II.** v.intr. *cenare (coen-).* **messmate,** n. *conviva,* m. and f., *sodalis,* m. and f.

mess, n. 1, = dirt, squalor, *illuvies, paedor, sordes, -ium,* f.; see FILTH; 2, fig. *res afflictae, perturbatio* or *confusio rerum;* his affairs are in a —, *pessime cum illo agitur;* see TROUBLE.

message, n. *nuntius, mandatum, legatio* (of an ambassador, e.g. to undertake a — to anyone, *legationem ad alqm suscipĕre),* or by *mittĕre* (e.g. the reason of the — sent was, *caus-*

(*)a *mittendi erat*); see ANSWER, REPORT; to send a —, *alqm certiorem facĕre alcjs rei* or *de alqâ re*. **messenger,** n. 1, *nuntius (nunc-)* (as bearer of a piece of news, by word of mouth ; fem. *nuntia), tabellarius* (= letter-carrier) ; to inform anyone by letter or by a —, *per lit(t)eras aut per nuntium certiorem facĕre alqm ;* 2, in a political sense, *nuntius* (= — in general), *legatus* (= ambassador, deputy) ; 3, — of a court of law, *viator, apparitor* (= usher).

Messiah, n. *Messias, -ae* (Eccl.).

metal, n. *metallum* (in gen.), *aes, aeris*, n. (= copper, brass, bronze) ; like —, *metallo* or *aeri similis*. **metallic,** adj. *metallicus* (Plin., in gen.), *aereus, a(h)eneus* (= of brass). **metalliferous,** adj. † *metallifer*. **metallurgy,** n. use *ars metallica* ; see MINE.

metamorphose, v.tr. *mutare in alqd ;* see TRANSFORM. **metamorphosis,** n. *metamorphosis* (only as title of Ovid's poem, *ut Ovidius lascivire in Metamorphosi solet,* Quint.) ; use verb.

metaphor, n. and adj. *translatio, verba translata,* Cic., *modus transferendi, metaphora* (post Aug. ; Quint. states it to be a Greek term, *translatio quae metaphora Graece dicitur*). **metaphoric,** adj. *translatus*. Adv. by *translatis verbis* (e.g. to speak) ; to use a word —, *verbum transferre ;* see FIGURATIVE.

metaphysic, metaphysical, adj. *metaphysicus* (not class.). **metaphysics,** n. *metaphysica, -ae* (not class.) ; where possible use *philosophia*.

mete, v.tr. see MEASURE.

metempsychosis, n. *animarum ab aliis post mortem ad alios transitio*.

meteor, n. *fax (caelestis)*. **meteoric,** adj. by circumloc. **meteoric-stone, meteorolite, meteorite,** n. *lapis qui caelo decidit*.

method, n. *ratio, via,* comb. *ratio et via, via et ratio* (= the particular — which we follow in anything), *modus* (= mode in which anything is done) ; — of teaching, *docendi, disserendi ratio, docendi modus* (= manner of explaining a thing). **methodic, methodical,** adj. by circumloc. with *ratio, ratio et via*. Adv. *ratione et viâ, viâ et ratione* (= according to a particular method), *artificio et viâ, viâ et arte* (= according to the rules of art).

metonymic, metonymical, adj. *(im)-mutatus*. Adv. *verbis mutatis, immutatis* (e.g. to speak) ; to use an expression —, *verbum mutare, immutare, verbum pro verbo* (or *verba pro verbis) quasi submutare*. **metonymy,** n. *immutatio, verba mutata, denominatio* or *metonymia* (better written as Greek, μετωνυμία).

metope, n. *metopa, intertignium*.

metre, n., as regards poetry, = short and long syllables in verse, *metrum* (Quint.). **metrical,** adj. *metricus*.

metropolis, n. *caput ;* see CAPITAL. **metropolitan, I.** adj. by circumloc. with *caput*. **II.** n. *episcopus metropolitanus* (Eccl.).

mettle, n. *audacia* (= boldness), *ferocitas* (= high spirit) ; — of youth, *fervor adolescentiae, fervor juvenilis ;* man of —, *homo acer, homo fervidioris animi ;* see COURAGE. **mettlesome,** adj. *audax, ferox ;* see COURAGEOUS.

mew, I. n. = a cage for hawks, *cavea*. **II.** v.tr. to shed (e.g. a hawk) ; see MOULT. **mews,** pl., see STABLE.

mew, v.intr. (of a cat) perhaps *vagire* (used of young goats or hares).

miasma, n. *noxius terrae halitus, -ûs* (Plin.).

mica, n. *phengites (lapis)* (Plin., Suet.).

microcosm, n. * *microcosmus* (or in Greek μικρόκοσμος).

microscope, n. * *microscopium* (as t.t.). **microscopic,** adj. (i.e. very small), *minimus, mirâ quâdam corporis exiguitate*.

midday, n. *meridies, tempus meridianum ;* about —, *ad meridiem ;* at —, *meridie, tempore meridiano, meridianis temporibus ;* before —, forenoon, *dies antemeridianus, tempus antemeridianum, ante meridiem, tempore antemeridiano ;* after —, afternoon, *dies postmeridianus* (or *pomeridianus)*. **midland,** adj. *mediterraneus*. **midnight,** n. *media nox ;* at —, *mediâ nocte, concubiâ nocte* (= at the dead of night) ; shortly after —, *de mediâ nocte*. **midriff,** n. *diaphragma, -ātis,* n. (very late), or written as Greek διάφραγμα (Cels.), *praecordia, -ium*. **midst,** prep. *in, inter, medius, in medio ;* in the — of the preparation for war, *in ipso apparatu belli ;* so in *ipso itinere,* in the — of the march ; — of dinner, *inter cenandum (coen-) ;* see MIDDLE. **midsummer,** n. *media* or *summa aestas*. **midway,** adv. *medius ;* — between, *medius inter*. **midwife,** n. *obstetrix*. **midwinter,** n. *bruma*.

midden, n. *sterquilinium ;* see DUNGHILL.

middle, adj. and n. (between two), *medius*. The Latins used *medius* in concord with its nouns, e.g. in the — of the slaughter, *media caedes* (lit. = the — slaughter ; so we employ mid, e.g. midnight, *media nox);* so *media acies,* = the — of the army ; the king was in the —, *medius omnium rex erat ;* to strike in the —, *medium ferire ;* to seize by or round the —, *medium alqm* (or *alqd) arripĕre ;* the — class (or social condition), *ordo plebeius* (opp. to *patres, equites)*, *plebs, plēbis,* f. **middling,** adj. *mediocris*.

mien, n. (oris) *habitus, -ûs, lineamenta, -orum* (= features), comb. *habitus oris lineamentaque, os (oris,* n.) *et vultus, -ûs* (= face and looks), *facies* (= countenance).

might, I. n. = bodily strength, *vis, vis,* f., *ops, -is,* f. (sing. only in genit., accus., and ablat. = physical means), *robur, -oris,* n., *nervi* (= muscles, as seat of the physical strength) ; with all one's —, *omni vi, summâ vi, omni ope, omnibus viribus* or *opibus* or *nervis, omnibus viribus atque opibus, omnibus opibus ac nervis ;* — is right, *fortiori cedendum est*. **II.** v.intr. *poteram, potuissem,* or by imperf. subj. (e.g. I — go, *irem, ≈ i* was permitted, *licuit mihi* with infin., *ut,* or simple subj.) ; see MAY. **mighty,** adj. *potens, validus ;* see POWERFUL, STRONG. Adv. *magnopere, valde, summâ vi, vehementer*.

migrate, v.intr. = to remove from one country to another, *abire, discedĕre* (= in gen. to go away from a place), *proficisci* (= to set off ; of soldiers, to march), *migrare, emigrare* (from a place, *ex,* etc. ; to, *in,* etc.), *demigrare* (from, *de* or *ex,* etc.) ; *e terrâ excedĕre, solum mutare* or *vertĕre* (= to leave one's own country, esp. of an exile). **migration,** n. *mutatio loci*. **migratory,** adj. by *(de)migrare, vagari* (= to rove), *huc illuc migrare* (= to change one's abode very often), by the genit. *nomâdum ;* — bird, *advena avis* or *volucris*.

milch, adj. *lac habens ;* — cow, *vacca (quae lac praebet) ;* see MILK.

mild, adj. 1, of the taste, *mollis* (= soft for the tongue and the palate, opp. *acer,* = harsh, of food in gen.), *mitis* (= not tart, of fruit that is quite ripe, opp. *acerbus), lenis* (= pleasant, opp. *asper* and *acer,* of wine, food), *dulcis* (= sweet) ; to make —, *mollire, mitigare, lenire ;* to grow — (of fruit, etc.), *mitescĕre ;* 2, = pleasantly affecting the senses, *mollis* (= soft, flexible, e.g. name, speech, opp. *durus, acer), mitis* (= not hard, harsh, e.g. winter, summer, climate ; then speech, words, opp. *asper*), *lenis* (= gentle), *temperatus* (= not too warm and not too cold, of the climate, the seasons, opp. *frigidus*, = cold, or *calidus*, = warm), *tepidus*, = warm ; — winter, *tepida bruma* (Hor.), *lēvis* (= light, e.g. punishment, opp. *gravis*); 3, of men and their dispositions, and of that which shows mildness, *mollis* ; *mitis* (= not harsh, of a — disposition, opp. *asper*), *clemens* (= gentle), *misericors* (= compassionate, opp. *durus*), *facilis* (= easy in granting requests, forgiving),*indulgens* (= indulgent, of persons, towards anyone, *alci*, opp. *acerbus et severus*), *placidus* (= peaceful, opp. *fervidus*, *iracundus*), *mansuetus* (= gentle, lit. tame), comb. *mitis et mansuetus*, *lenis et mansuetus*, *placidus et lenis*. Adv. *leniter*, *clementer*, *placide*, *mansuete*. **mildness**, n. 1, — of the climate, etc., *lenitas* (of anything, e.g. *doloris*) ; opp. *asperitas*) ; 2, of the character, *lenitas* ; *animus lenis* or *mitis*, *ingenium lene* or *mite* (= — of character), *mansuetudo morum* (= — of manners), *clementia* (= — in treating others), *indulgentia* (= indulgence), *modestia* (= moderation), in Tac. and Plin. of the weather (e.g. *hiemis*).

mildew, n. of vegetables, corn, plants, *robigo* (*rub-*), *mucor* (Plin., = mouldiness, mustiness), *situs*, *-ūs* (= filth arising from mouldiness), *uredo* (= blasting of trees, herbs).

mile, n. of a Roman —, *mille* (*passuum*) (1,000 paces ; in the pl. *mil(l)ia* (*passuum*) ; — -stone, as the point where the — terminates, hence as a measurement of distance, *mil(l)iarium*, or *lapis*, *-ĭdis*, m. ; he lies interred five —s from the city, *sepultus est ad quintum lapidem*. **mileage**, n. *vectīgal quod in singula mil(l)ia exigitur*. **milestone**, n. *mil(l)iarium*, *lapis*.

militant, adj. by *pugnare*, etc. ; the church —, *ecclesia militans* (Eccl.). **military, I.** adj. *militaris* (= belonging to a soldier or to war), *bellicus* ; — service, *militia* ; — preparations, *apparatus*, *-ūs*, *belli* ; — skill, *rei militaris peritia*, *usus*, *-ūs*, *belli* ; — school, *ludus militaris*. **II.** n. the —, = soldiers, *milites*, or collect. *miles*, *copiae*. **militate**, v.intr., to — against, *alci adversari*. **militia**, n. perhaps *cives ad hostem propulsandum armati*.

milk, I. n. 1, lit. *lac*, *-tis*, made of —, looking like —, *lacteus* ; goat's —, *lac caprinum* ; new —, *lac recens* ; curdled —, *la concretum* ; 2, fig. — of human kindness, *benŭnitas*, *comitas* ; see KINDNESS. **II.** v.tr. *mulgēre*. **milker**, n. *qui mulget*. **milking**, n. *mulctus*, *-ūs* (Var.). **milkmaid, milkman**, n. *puella quae vaccas mulget* ; (*homo*) *qui lac venditat*. **milk-pail**, n. *mulctra*, *mulctrum*. **milk-sop**, n. *homo effeminatus et mollis* ; see EFFEMINATE. **milk-white**, adj. *lacteus*. **milky**, adj. *lactens* (= full of milk), *lacteus* (= like milk). **milky-way**, n. *orbis* or *circulus lac*ᵗᵉᵘˢ, *via* † *lactea* (Ov.).

mill, I. n. as a machine, — for grinding, *mola* (= — stone), *pistrinum* (= the place where the mills are, with the ancients = tread- —, in which the slaves worked) ; belonging to the —, *molaris pistrinalis* ; hand —, *mola trusatilis*. **II.** v.tr. see GRIND. **mill-dam**, n. (*molae*) *agger*. **miller**, n. *qui molam habet*, *pistor*. **mill-hopper**, n. *infundibulum*. **mill-pond**, n. *piscina* ; as smooth as a —, *tranquillus*, *placidus* ; see SMOOTH. **mill-stone**, n. *mola* (every mill had two such *mola*, the upper one of which was called *catillus*, the lower *meta*). **mill-stream**, n. *rivus qui molam agit*.

millenary, adj. *millenarius* (Eccl.). **millennial**, adj. *mille annorum*. **millennium**, n. *mille annorum spatium*.

miller, n. *milium*.

milliner, n. *quae mundum muliebrem facit*. **millinery**, n. *mundus* or *vestitus* (*-ūs*) *muliebris*.

million, n. *decies centena mil(l)ia* ; two, three millions, *vicies*, *tricies centena mil(l)ia* ; a — times, *decies centies millie(n)s* (lit.), *sescenties* (= our colloquial phrase, a — times). **millionaire**, n. *vir magnis opibus praeditus* ; see RICH.

milt, n. 1, in anatomy, *splen*, *lien* ; 2, = roe of fishes, *ova*, *-orum*. **milter**, n. *piscis mas*.

mimic, I. adj. *mimicus* (= belonging to mimes ; post class. = imitative), *simulatus*, *fictus* (= imitative). **II.** n. *artis mimicae peritus*, *mimus* (= player in a mime or farce). **III.** v.tr. *alqm imitari* ; see IMITATE. **mimicry**, n. *ars mimica*.

minaret, n. *turricula*.

mince, I. v.tr. 1, lit. *concidĕre*, *consecare* ; 2, fig. *extenuare*, comb. *extenuare et diluĕre* ; not to — matters, *sine fuco ac fallaciis dicĕre*. **II.** v.intr. *mollius incedĕre*. **III.** n. *minutal* (Juv.). **mincemeat**, n. 1, lit. *minutal* ; 2, fig. to make — of, *concidĕre* (= cut up), *trucidare* (= slaughter). **mincing**, adj. *putidus*. Adv. *putide*.

mind, I. n. 1, *animus* (= the whole of man as an intelligent being, the higher nature in man, opp. *corpus*), *mens* (as that which represents the power of thinking ; then the faculty of thinking itself), *spiritus*, *-ūs* (almost synonymous with *anima*, = breath of life, life itself, then = qualities of the —, energy, enthusiasm, courage, pride, etc.), *ingenium* (= natural abilities, genius, power of invention, production) ; in one's own —, imagination, *spe et opinione*, or *spe atque animo* ; the workings of the —, *animi motus*, *-ūs* ; a philosophical —, *sapientia*, *sagacitas*, *subtilitas* (*in disputando*), *vir subtilis*, *sagax* (of the person) ; = an inclination, *studium* (= inclination, zeal), *appetitus*, *-ūs*, *appetitio* (= instinctive longing after anything), *cupiditas*, *cupido*, *desiderium*, *aviditas* (=desire), *alacritas* (= the state of feeling inclined), comb. *alacritas studiumque*, *alacritas et cupiditas* (after all these words, that which we have a — for in the genit.) ; I have a —, *animus mihi est*, *mihi libet* (*lub-*) ; I have no —, *nolo* ; I have a greater —, *malo* ; to have a — to do anything, *alcjs rei studio captum esse*, *teneri*, *alcjs rei studiosum*, *appetentem*, *cupidum esse*, *alqd appetĕre*, *concupiscĕre* ; to have a great — to, *alcjs rei studio* or *cupiditate ardēre*, *flagrare* ; *mirā alacritate esse ad alqd faciendum* (= to be very much disposed for, e.g. for disputing, *ad litigandum*) ; to have no — to, *abhorrēre*, *alienum esse ab alqā re* ; 2, *memoria*, see MEMORY, THOUGHT ; to keep in —, = to think about, *cogitare cum* or *in animo*, or simply *cogitare alqd* or *de alqā re* ; *considerare in animo* or *cum animo* or *secum*, or simply *considerare alqd* or *de alqā re* (= to consider maturely), *deliberare alqd* and *de alqā re* (= to deliberate with oneself), *alqd agitare mente* or *animo*, or *in mente* or *cum animo* (= to think over), *perpendĕre*, *pensitare* (not in Cic. or Caes.), *alqd* (= to consider on all sides), *secum meditari de alqā re* or *alqd* ; only keep this one thing in —, *hoc unum cogita* ; I keep many important things in —, *versantur animo meo multae et graves cogitationes* ; to be against one's —, *longe alia mihi mens est* ; to be of a —, *opinari*, *opinione duci*, *opinionem habēre* ; with one —, *in hoc omnes consentiunt* ; see UNANIMOUS ; to make up one's —, *certum consilium capĕre* ; to put one in — of, = to warn, (*com*)*monēre*, *admonēre*, *commonefacĕre alqm de alqā re* (or *with ut*, or *with ne* and the subj.

mood); it comes into my —, *in mentem mihi alqd venit, mihi in opinionem alqd venit, subit animum cogitatio, in mentem* or *in cogitationem mihi incidit alqd* (= a thought comes into my —), *mihi* or *animo,* or *in mentem occurrit alqd, mihi succurrit alqd* (= a sudden thought strikes me), *subit recordatio* or *recordor* or *reminiscor* (= I remember); the thing had come into my —, *tetigerat animum hujus rei memoria.* **II.** v.tr. 1, = to attend to, *animum advertĕre (advort-)* or *alqd animadvertĕre, animum attendĕre ad alqd* or *alqd attendĕre, animum intendĕre ad* or *in alqd, alcjs rei rationem habēre* (= to regard); *alqd agĕre;* — your own business, *tuum negotium gere, res tuas cura;* 2, = to obey, *alci oboedire, parēre;* 3, = to object to, *alqd recusare;* I do not —, *non recuso quin* or *quominus;* 4, = to remind, *alci alqd ad animum revocare;* see REMIND. **III.** v.intr. = to remember, *alcjs rei miminisse, alqd recordari;* see REMEMBER. **mindful,** adj. 1, *diligens alcjs rei* and *in alqd re* (= accurate, punctual, cautious in anything, opp. *neglegens), sedulus* (= earnest in anything, very attentive, opp. *piger,* e.g. *spectator). alcjs rei studiosus, amans* (e.g. *veritatis);* see ATTENTIVE, CAREFUL; 2, = remembering, *memor, haud immemor* (both *alcjs rei);* to be —, *meminisse* (e.g. *mortis).* **mindless,** adj. *neglegens (neglig-)* (= negligent), *socors* (= thoughtless), comb. *socors neglegensque;* see CARELESS, UNMINDFUL; *insanus* (= not in his senses), *excors* (= stupid, a simpleton), *amens, demens;* see IRRATIONAL.

mine, possess. pron. *meus, mea, meum.*

mine, I. n. 1, *metallum,* or pl. *metalla, -orum;* a silver —, *fodina argenti* or *argentifodina;* a gold —, *aurifodina* (Plin.); 2, in fortification, *cuniculus;* to sap, dig a —, *cuniculum agĕre;* 3, fig. *fons uberrimus,* or by *thesaurus* (e.g. *memoria thesaurus omnium rerum).* **II.** v.tr. 1, = to dig a —; see above; 2, fig. = to practise secret means of injury, *insidias alci parare* or *instruĕre* or *ponĕre, perniciem alci moliri;* 3, milit. term, by *cuniculos agĕre.* **miner,** n. 1, *metallicus* (Plin.); 2, in fortification, *qui cuniculum agit.* **mineral,** I. n. *metallum.* **II.** adj. *fossilis, metallicus;* — kingdom, *fossilia, -ium,* n.; — spring, — waters (as the place), *fons medicae salubritatis, aquae medicatae* (Sen.), *aquae salubres,* in the context also simply *aquae.* **mining,** n. use *metallum* (e.g. useful for —, *ad metalla exercenda utilis).*

mingle, v.tr. and intr., see MIX.

miniature, n. *tabella* or *pictura,* fixing the sense by the context (e.g. *tabellas pinxit parvas);* in — (e.g. Rome in —, *quasi* or *tanquam (tamq-) Roma minor).*

minimum, n. *minimum, pars minima.*

minion, n. 1, = favourite, *deliciae;* 2, = minister, *minister, servus.*

minister, I. n. 1, = servant in a higher sense, *minister,* or by circumloc.; see INSTRUMENT; 2, of a state, *principis socius et administer omnium consiliorum, socius consiliorum principis et particeps, consiliarius* (as his adviser); state —, *ille penes quem est cura administrandae reipublicae;* — of foreign affairs (= foreign secretary), *rerum externarum administer;* — of war, *qui res bellicas administrat;* 3, — of the Gospel; see CLERGYMAN, PRIEST. **II.** v.tr. to — an occasion, *alci occasionem dare, praebēre;* see GIVE, AFFORD, SUPPLY. **III.** v.intr. 1, see ATTEND, SERVE; 2, to — to, *facultates* or *opes praebēre;* see SERVE, SUPPORT, ASSIST. **ministerial,** adj. 1, *ad servum* or *ministrum pertinens;* see ATTEND, SERVE; 2, in a political sense by cir-

cumloc. (e.g. his — duties, *rerum publicarum administratio);* see OFFICIAL, EXECUTIVE; 3, see CLERICAL, PRIESTLY. **ministration,** n. 1, see SERVICE, OFFICE; 2, see CO-OPERATION, INTERCESSION. **ministry,** n. 1, = means, *interventio,* etc., *administratio, ministerium, (pro)curatio;* 2, political, *qui rempublicam administrant;* see MINISTER; 3, clerical, ** ministerium.*

minium, n. *minium.*

minor, I. adj. see LITTLE, SMALL; the — premiss, *assumptio* (opp. *propositio* = the major). **II.** n. gen. *infans* (if a little child), or by *nondum adultā aetate* (= not yet of age); sons that are —s, *filii familiarum;* with regard to the guardian, a ward, *pupillus;* = not able to reign, *nondum maturus imperio.* **minority,** n. 1, *aetas nondum adulta* (in gen.), *aetas pupillaris* (= age of the ward); 2, = the smaller number, *pars* or *numerus minor.*

minotaur, n. *minotaurus.*

minstrel, n. see SINGER, perhaps *poēta amatorius* (as a poet), *citharaedus* (κιθαρῳδός, = singer to the lyre); see MUSICIAN, PLAYER. **minstrelsy,** n. *chorus canentium* (= chorus of singers); *concentus, -ūs.*

mint, n. in botany, *ment(h)a.*

mint, I. n. = place where money is coined by public authority, *monēta* (a surname of Juno, in whose temple money was coined); everything relating to the —, *res nummaria.* **II.** v.tr. see COIN.

minuet, n. *saltatio;* see DANCE.

minus, prep. *sine* with abl.

minute, I. adj. 1, see LITTLE, SMALL; 2, fig. *minutus* (= trifling and contemptible), *subtilis, diligens, accuratus* (= exact). Adv. *subtiliter, minute, accurate, diligenter.* **II.** n. 1, of time, *horae sexagesima pars* (= 60th part of an hour); 2, fig. see MOMENT. **minutes,** n. pl. = short sketch of an agreement, etc., *breviarium* (= a summary, Suet.), *exemplum* (= draught of a theme), *scriptum, libellus, commentarii, acta, -orum* (of the Senate); — of a speech, *oratio scripta, sermo scriptus* (Suet.); to make — of anything, *alqd lit(t)eris consignare* (in gen. = to write down); see NOTE; —-book, see MEMORANDUM. **III.** v.tr. *notare, annotare,* in *tabulas referre, lit(t)eris consignare;* see DRAW UP, NOTE, WRITE. **minuteness,** n. 1, = smallness, *exiguitas, brevitas* (of stature); 2, = carefulness, *subtilitas, accuratio* (rare), *diligentia.* **minutiae,** n. by *omnia, -ium,* or *singula, -orum;* see DETAIL, TRIFLE, PARTICULAR.

minx, n. *puella putita* (= an affected girl), *filiola* (= little daughter, expressing affection).

miracle, n. 1, = a wonderful thing, *res mira, miraculum* (= thing exciting astonishment); see WONDER; 2, in theology, ** miraculum.* **miraculous,** adj. *mirus, mirificus, mirandus, mirabilis;* in a — manner, *mirum in modum, mirandum in modum, mirabiliter.* Adv. see above, in a — manner.

mirage, n. *(vana) species (urbis,* etc.) *oculis oblata.*

mire, miriness, n. *lutum;* see MUD. **miry,** adj. *lutosus, lutulentus;* see MUDDY.

mirror, n. *speculum.*

mirth, n. *hilaritas, laetitia* (= gladness), *gaudium* (= joy), *lascivia* (= sportiveness), *risus, -ūs* (= laughter), *jocus* (= jest), *lusus, -ūs* (= sport); see GAIETY, JOY. **mirthful,** adj. *hilaris (hilarus), laetus, lascivus, jocosus.* Adv. *hilare, hilariter, laete, lascive, jocose.*

misacceptation, n. *interpretatio perversa* or *perperam facta;* see MISUNDERSTANDING.

misadventure, n. *casus, -ūs (adversus), incommodum* (= something unpleasant, adversity, especially misfortune in war); see MISFORTUNE.

misadvised, adj. *imprudens* (= without foresight), *inconsideratus,inconsultus*(=thoughtless).

misanthrope, n. *qui genus humanum or hominum universum genus odit.* **misanthropic, misanthropical,** adj. *hominibus inimicus.* **misanthropy,** n. *animus hominibus inimicus.*

misapplication, n. *usus (-ūs) perversus.* **misapply,** v.tr. *algā re abuti* (= to make a bad use of), *male interpretari or accipĕre* (= to misinterpret).

misapprehend, v.tr. see MISUNDERSTAND. **misapprehension,** n. see MISUNDERSTANDING.

misbecome, v.tr. *alqm alqd dedecet, or alqd facĕre dedecet.*

misbehave, v.intr. *indecōre, indigne se gerĕre.* **misbehaviour,** n. *rusticitas, mores rustici;* see RUDENESS, FAULT.

misbelief, n. see UNBELIEF. **misbelieve,** v.tr. *perperam judicare, falso sibi persuasum habēre.*

miscalculate, v.tr. 1, *male computare alqd or rationem alcjs rei, or by ratio me fefellit ;* 2, fig. *errare, decipi.* **miscalculation,** n. 1, *mendum, rationes falsae;* 2, *error.*

miscarriage, n. 1, = ill conduct, *delictum* (= act of misbehaviour); 2, = failure, by *res ad* (or *in*) *irritum cadit, ad irritum redigitur ;* 3, of an untimely birth, *abortus, -ūs, abortio.* **miscarry,** v.intr. 1, = not to succeed, *non or parum or secus procedĕre* (= not to lead to the desired result), *praeter spem evenire, secus cadĕre, praeter opinionem cadĕre* (= to end worse than one expected), *ad irritum cadĕre, redigi* (= to be frustrated) ; 2, by *abortum facĕre* (of an untimely birth).

miscellaneous, adj. by *varius et diversus ;* — kinds, *varia et diversa genera* (sc. *operum*). **miscellany,** n. *liber de diversis rebus scriptus.*

mischance, n. see MISFORTUNE.

mischief, n. *malum, incommodum, damnum, maleficium* (= intentional —), *calamitas, turbae* (= noise and confusion). **mischief-maker,** n. *mali auctor.* **mischievous,** adj. 1, = harmful, *noxius, calamitosus, perniciosus ;* see HURTFUL ; 2, = full of tricks, *lascivus.* Adv. *calamitose, perniciose, lascive.* **mischievousness,** n. 1, = injuriousness, by *circuml.* (e.g. who does not see the — of the thing? *quis non intelligit rem nocēre or rem esse noxiam ?*) ; 2, *lascivia.*

misconceive, v.tr. and intr. *perperam accipĕre.* **misconception,** n. *opinionis error, opinio falsa.*

misconduct, n. 1, see MISBEHAVIOUR ; 2, see FAULT.

misconjecture, I. n. *falsa suspicio.* **II.** v.tr. and intr. *falso suspicari.*

misconstruction, n. see MISINTERPRETATION. **misconstrue,** v.tr. see MISINTERPRET.

miscreant, n. 1, = unbeliever, *doctrinae falsae studiosus, apostăta* (Eccl.) ; 2, = a vile wretch, *homo illiberalis, sordidus* (= unworthy of a free-born man), *abjectus* (= contemptible), *turpis* (= disreputable).

misdeal, v.intr. perhaps *paginas male distribuĕre.*

misdeed, n. *facinus, -ŏris, n. scelus, -ĕris, n., maleficium, malefactum, delictum, peccatum.*

misdemeanour, n. 1, = ill behaviour, *mores pravi ;* see MISCONDUCT ; 2, in law, an offence of a less atrocious character than a crime, *peculatus, -ūs, publicus* (= defalcation), *scelus, -ĕris,* n. (= crime) ; to be guilty of —, *scelus suscipĕre, admittĕre, facĕre.*

misdirect, v.tr. 1, a letter, *epistulam perperam inscribĕre ;* 2, a passenger, *a recta viā abducĕre* (lit.) ; 3, fig. *inducĕre alqm in errorem* (= to lead anyone into an error).

misemploy, v.tr. *abuti algā re*(=to misuse). **misemployment,** n. *usus, -ūs, perversus.*

miser, n. *homo tenax, homo avarus.* **miserable,** adj. *miser, misellus, miserabilis, miserandus* (= to be pitied, in poor circumstances), *infelix* (= unhappy), *afflictus, aerumnosus ; calamitosus ;* see UNHAPPY ; = worthless, *nequam, nihili, improbus, turpis* (= wicked, of persons and things), *vilis* (= vile) ; to lead a — life, *in miseriā esse or versari ; — food, tenuis victus, -ūs ;* to live in — circumstances, *parce ac duriter vitam agĕre, tenuiter vivĕre, vitam in egestate degĕre.* Adv. *misere, miserabiliter, infeliciter, calamitose, improbe, nequiter, turpiter ;* see MISER. **miserliness,** n. *avaritia, sordes, -is,* f. (or in pl.). **miserly,** adj. *avarus, tenax, sordidus, parcus, malignus.* **misery,** n. = great unhappiness of mind and body, *miseria, res miserae or afflictae* (= depressed circumstances), *calamitas* (= caused through losses), *aerumna, vexatio* (= trouble), *angor, maeror, tristitia* (= sorrow), *egestas* (= great poverty), *angustiae* (= bad times), *tempora luctuosa* (= distressing, gloomy times).

misformed. adj. *deformis, deformatus, distortus.*

misfortune, n. *malum, and* pl. *mala, calamitas* (= attended with loss and injury, also in war), *casus, -ūs (adversus or tristis* = unfortunate accident, *incommodum, res adversae, fortuna* (adversa, = casualties caused by bad luck), *acerbitates, -um* (= great hardships) ; he had the — to, etc., *accidit ei ut,* etc. ; one — after another, *aliud ex alio malo.*

misgive, v.intr. perhaps *malum praesagire, praesentire or diffidĕre* (= to distrust) ; see DOUBT. **misgiving,** n. *metus, -ūs, timor* (= fear), *sol(l)icitudo* (= anxiety), *praesensio* (= foreboding).

misgovern, v.tr. *male regnare, male rem gerĕre.* **misgovernment,** n. *mala reipublicae gubernatio or moderatio, mala alcjs rei administratio.*

misguidance, n. *error, or by falso alcjs consilio regi.* **misguide,** v.tr. *in errorem inducĕre ;* see MISLEAD.

mishap, n. see ACCIDENT, MISFORTUNE.

misinform, v.tr. by *alqm falsa docēre.*

misinterpret, v.tr. *falso explicare, in malam partem accipĕre or male interpretari alqd, perverse, perperam interpretari.* **misinterpretation,** n. *interpretatio perversa or perperam facta.*

misjudge, v.tr. *male judicare.*

mislay, v.tr. see LOSE.

mislead, v.tr. *corrumpĕre alcjs animum et mores, alqm ad nequitiam adducĕre, alqm in errorem inducĕre ;* to be misled, *labi, errare, in errorem induci.* **misleading,** adj. *falsus.*

mismanage, v.tr. see MISGOVERN.

misnomen, n. *falsum nomen.*

misogamist, misogynist, n. *qui mulieres odit.*

misplace, v.tr. (in) alieno loco collocare; to
— confidence, etc., alqd re falli.

misprint, I. v.tr. typis mendose exscribĕre.
II. n. mendum typographicum.

mispronounce, n. male pronuntiare.

misproportion, n. ratio impar.

misquotation, n. verba falso allata, falsa
commemoratio (= mention), verba haud accurate
prolata. **misquote,** v.tr. verba alcjs haud accurate proferre.

misreckoning, n. falsae rationes.

misrepresent, v.tr. fig. alqd narrando depravare (= to represent any fact in a wrong light),
perversa interpretari (= to interpret wrongly, fig.),
verbum in pejus detorquēre (= to dissemble the true
meaning of an expression so as to cause it to be
taken in a bad sense). **misrepresentation,**
n. use verb.

misrule, n. see Misgovern.

miss, n. as title, domina.

miss, I. n. 1, see Loss, Want; 2, error;
see Fault, Mistake. **II.** v.tr. 1, carēre alqd re
(= not to have got a thing), alqd desiderare (=
to feel the want of it); 2, = to discover that
something is wanting, desiderare, quaerĕre, requirĕre (= to look for anything that we have had,
although in vain); to — with regret, desiderio
alcjs rei angi, magnâ molestiâ desiderare alqd; see
Lose; 3, = to fail of finding the right way,
deerrare; to — anyone on the road, ab alqo deerrare or aberrare; 4, = to fail in aim, destinatum non ferire (in shooting, etc.); 5, = to omit,
transire, omittĕre, praetermittĕre; see Omit.
III. v.intr. 1, = to fail to hit, see II. 4;
2, = not to succeed; see Fail. **missing,**
adj. to be —, deesse, desiderari. **missile, I.**
n. (telum) missile, jaculum; hasta (longer or
shorter for throwing), pilum (short, used by the
Roman infantry); to cast a —, missile or jaculum
mittĕre. **II.** adj. missilis.

misshapen, adj. deformis; see Misformed.

mission, n. 1, = sending out, missio; 2,
legatio (= deputation, ambassadors); 3, see
Destiny. **missionary,** n. missus qui gentes
barbaras alqd doceat.

misspell, v.tr. non recte scribĕre, prave
scribĕre.

misspend, v.tr. 1, money, perdĕre; see
Squander; 2, time, perdĕre; see Waste.

misstate, v.tr. see Misrepresent. **mis-
statement,** n. quod falsum est; deliberate —,
mendacium.

mist, n. 1, nebula (subtilis, in opp. to fog =
caligo, nebula densa, when the — is very thick);
2, fig. caligo (e.g. the — of those calamitous
days, caligo illorum temporum); to be in a —,
attonitum, perculsum esse. **misty,** adj. 1, nebulosus, caliginosus; 2, fig. obscurus.

mistake, I. v.tr. 1, = to take one thing or
person for another, e.g. you — me for another, me
alium esse putas; ignorare alqm (= not to know
a person, lit. and fig.), parum intellegĕre (intelligi-)
alqd or alqm (= to know too little of anything,
not to know sufficient of a person's character);
2, see Misunderstand. **II.** v.intr. = to be
—n, errare, per errorem labi (= to commit a
slight error), in errore versari (= to be in
error), falli (= to deceive oneself), peccare (= to
fall into an error, commit a sin owing to a —),
dubium or incertum esse (= to be uncertain);
if I am not —n, nisi fallor, nisi animus (me)
fallit, nisi quid me fallit or fefellerit; I may
be —n, potest fieri ut fallar. **III.** n. 1, in gen.
error, erratum (from want of thought, by being
misled; error, = the condition one is in after

having committed a —; erratum, = the — itself;
both also representing any literary work),
lapsus, -ûs (= a single —), peccatum (= anything
done wrong); in — for, pro (e.g. pro illo culpavit,
= he blamed the one in — for the other); to
make a —, errare, peccare (in a thing, alqd in alqd
re), labi in alqâ re; to be under a —, in errore
esse or versari, errore captum esse, errore vagari;
to see one's —, errorem suum agnoscĕre; 2, a —
in writing, mendum; to correct a — in writing,
mendum tollĕre; full of written —s, mendosus.
mistaken, adj. see Wrong. Adv. per errorem,
perperam.

mistress, n. 1, = a woman who governs,
domina (also as title), hera (as regards the servants), quae imperio regit (= one who rules, e.g.
a town, urbem), dominatrix, moderatrix, gubernatrix (in a fig. sense, of desires and passions;
dominatrix, in an absolute sense; the two latter
= guide); 2, = head of a family, materfamilias
(materfamiliae, or as two words), hera (with
reference to the servants), matrona (on account
of the high veneration in which she was held as
head of the family, therefore chiefly of women
of higher rank), domina; 3, = governess,
praeceptrix, magistra (also fig., e.g. practice is
the best — to teach us to speak a language,
certissima loquendi magistra consuetudo; or magister if the Latin noun is masculine, e.g.
experience, an excellent —, usus, egregius
magister); 4, = a woman beloved and courted,
amata, dilecta, amica (in a bad sense), amor
noster, deliciae meae; 5, = a woman in keeping
(i.e. a kept —), amica, concubina, pellex.

misunderstand, v.tr. non recte intellegĕre
(intellig-); see Misinterpret. **misunderstanding,** n. error (= mistake); = difference
of opinion, dissensio; dissidium.

misuse, I. n. usus, -ûs, perversus, abusus,
-ûs (rare). **II.** v.tr. alqd re perverse (ab)uti, immodice or immoderate or intemperanter or insolenter et immodice abuti re (e.g. alcjs indulgentiâ,
alcjs patientiâ), male uti re; see Abuse, Use.

mite, n. minimus in agreement with noun
(e.g. a — of a thing, res minima).

mitigate, adj. quod mitigari potest. **mitigate,** v.tr. lenire (e.g. illness, pain, hatred,
anger, grief, taste, etc.), mitigare, mitiorem
facĕre (e.g. pain, fevers, sorrows, taste, etc.),
mollire (= to cause anything, e.g. anger, violence,
iram, impetum, to abate, also to make milder in
taste), levare (= to afford relief, alleviate, e.g. care,
alqm curâ levare; — cares with wine, curas levare
vino), alqd remittĕre ex alqâ re (= to diminish).
mitigation, n. mitigatio, levatio (al)levamen-
um; to afford anyone a — of anything, lenire
alci alqd, levare alqm alqâ re; — of anger, placatio (e.g. deorum immortalium), mitigatio; or
by verbs, see above.

mitre, n. = a sacerdotal ornament, mitra
(Eccl.).

mitten, n. see Glove.

mix, I. v.tr. 1, temperare; to — one thing
with, among another, (per)miscēre alqd cum alqâ
re, alqd alqâ re or alqd alci rei, temperare alqd
alqâ re; to — a thing, admiscēre alqd alci rei or
in alqd (gen. in the passive, admisceri alqâ re,
to be —n with); to — poison, etc., venenum,
etc., parare, coquĕre (= to prepare, to boil in
gen.); 2, see Confuse; 3, = to associate oneself with in company, se (con)jungĕre cum
alqo, (com)misceri, permisceri. **II.** v.intr. 1,
= to become blended promiscuously in a
mass or compound (e.g. oil and water will not
—), by the passive of the verbs above; 2, to —
in society, hominum coetus et celebrationes obire;
see Society. **mix up,** v.tr. 1, see Mix; 2,

see IMPLICATE. **mixed**, adj. *(per)mixtus, promiscuus.* **mixture**, n. 1, *(per)mistio (mixt-*, = the act and the thing itself), *mistura (mixt-*, = modes of mixing and the thing itself, mostly post class.), *temperatio* (as act and as the quality of —); the — of the metal, *temperatio aeris;* 2, in pharmacy, see MEDICINE, 3; 3, lit. and fig. ≍ a mass of things without order; *farrago* (= a — of different kinds of corn, fig. a book containing a — of things, *farrago libelli, Juv.*), *colluvio, colluvies*(fig., when different things flow together, e.g. the army, a — of all kinds of nations, *exercitus mixtus ex colluvione omnium gentium*); *varietas* (= a mixed variety, e.g. of words and opinions, *sermonum opinionumque*); but more frequently it is expressed by *miscēre;* e.g. a — of good and evil, *bona mixta malis.*

mnemonic, mnemonical, adj. *ad memoriae artem pertinens.* **mnemonics**, n. *ars* or *artificium* or *disciplina memoriae.*

moan, I. v.intr. *gemĕre.* **II.** n. *gemitus, -ūs;* see GROAN, LAMENT.

moat, n. *fossa;* to surround with a — for defence, *fossam castris circumdare, castra fossā cingĕre.*

mob, I. n. *vulgus, -i,* n. (= the mass of the people; see PEOPLE), *turba* (= crowd), *multitudo de plebe, multitudo obscura et humilis* (as regards the origin); *sentīna reipublicae* or *urbis* (= the lowest of the low, rabble), *faex populi* (= the dregs of the people). **II.** v.tr. see SURROUND. **III.** v.intr. *concurrĕre, concursare.*

mobile, adj. *mobilis;* see also FICKLE. **mobility**, n. 1, *mobilitas* (e.g. of the tongue, *linguae;* also fig. of the mind, *animi;* — of character, *mobilitas hominis* or *ingenii*), *agilitas* (= nimbleness, swiftness); 2, = fickleness, *lēvitas, ingenium mobile;* see FICKLENESS.

mock, I. v.tr. 1, see IMITATE, MIMIC; 2, = to deride, *alqm, alqd deridēre, irridēre;* 3, in a less evil sense = to ridicule, *alqm ludĕre* (= to banter), *alqm ludibrio habēre, ludificari* (= to make a fool of), *cavillari* (= to censure in a sarcastic manner; one who does this, *cavillator*); 4, = to disappoint, *ludĕre, ludificari, ad irritum redigĕre;* see FRUSTRATE. **II.** v.intr. to — at, *in ludibrium vertĕre,* or by *cavillari,* at anybody, *alqm;* see above. **III.** n. see MOCKERY; to make a — of; see MOCK, I. 3. **IV.** adj. *simulatus, fictus, falsus;* see FALSE. **mocker**, n. = one who scorns, *derisor, irrisor, cavillator* (= who cavils). **mockery**, n. 1, *irrisio, irrisus, -ūs, cavillatio* (= scoff), *ludibrium, ludus, jocus, ludificatio* (= the act of mocking), *petulantia, lascivia;* 2, = that which disappoints, *inceptum irritum;* 3, = counterfeit appearance, *species, simulacrum, fallacia* (= deceit), *oculorum ludibrium* (= mere outward show), *falsa imago* (= a false image), *fabula* (= a fable); to make a — of . . . , to turn into —, *deridēre alqd* (also *alqm*), *in risum vertēre alqd.*

mode, n. 1, *natura* (= nature of a thing), *ratio* (= systematic — of proceeding, relation between two things), *modus* (= rule to go by, — of doing anything), *via* (= manner in which one thing is derived from another), comb. *ratio et via, ratio et modus,* (— of proceeding, e.g. of arguing, *argumentandi genus*), *mos, consuetudo* (= custom); see MANNER; 2, in music, *modi, moduli* (= musical —); 3, — of dress, *habitus, -ūs;* see DRESS; —s of speaking; see EXPRESSION.

model, I. n. *proplasma, -ătis,* n. (Plin., or as Greek πρόπλασμα,— an artist's—); *exemplar, -aris, exemplum* (= a pattern in gen.); to give a — of anything, *alcjs rei modum formamque de*

monstrare; to take the — from anything, to take anything as a —, *exemplum sumĕre ab alqd re;* to work by a — or pattern, *alqd ad imitandum proponĕre, alqd in exemplum assumĕre.* **II.** v.tr. 1, = to shape out of a raw material, *fingĕre;* = to bring into a proper shape, *formare,* comb. *fingĕre et formare;* = to copy, *exprimĕre imaginem alcjs* (in gen. = to represent, express anyone's features); 2, fig. = to arrange according to a certain rule, *ex lege* or *ratione quādam instituĕre alqd* (e.g. *rempublicam*). **III.** adj. *optimus.*

moderate, I. adj. = keeping the middle path, avoiding extremes, *moderatus, modicus* (opp. to *effrenatus*), *modestus* (in moral feeling, opp. to *cupidus, petulans*), *temperans, temperatus, mediocris* (= mediocre), *sobrius.* Adv. *moderate, modeste, modice, temperate, mediocriter;* to live —, *continentem esse in omni victu cultuque.* **II.** v.tr. = *moderari* (= to impose a limit to, with dat.), = to direct (with accus.); *modum* (or *moderationem*) *adhibēre alci rei, alqd continēre, coërcēre* (= to restrain). **moderation, moderateness**, n. *modus* (= due measure), *continentia* (= self-restraint), *temperantia* (= self-government, both opp. to *libido (lub-)*), *moderatio* (= the middle course, in conduct), *modestia* (= the moral feeling to avoid excess), *sedatio alcjs rei* (e.g. of the passions); *abstinentia* (= keeping from what belongs to others). **moderator**, n. see PRESIDENT.

modern, adj. *recens, novus, ad nova exempla* (= in the new style, according to the new fashion, opp. *vetus*), *qui nunc est, ut nunc fit, hujus aetatis, elegans* (= elegant), *hic, haec, hoc,* = the present, e.g. *haec* or *nostra aetas, homines nostrae aetatis, homines qui nunc sunt* or *vivunt* (all = our — days), *praesens* (= at the present moment, opp. that which takes place at any other time; if we say our —, etc., *praesens* is seldom used, but generally *hic, haec, hoc*); — *Capua, Capua quae nunc est;* the —, our age, *haec aetas;* our — times, *haec tempora.*

modest, adj. *modicus* (= slight, middling), *modestus* (= moderate, under control, opp. *immodestus*), *pudens* (opp. *impudens*), *verecundus* (= full of respect), *demissus* (= lowly, opp. *acerbus*). Adv. *modice, modeste, prudenter, verecunde.* **modesty**, n. *modestia* (opp. *superbia*), *pudor* (= a feeling of shame or respect), *verecundia* (bashfulness).

modicum, n. *pau(l)lulum.*

modifiable, adj. *res de quâ alqd immutari potest.* **modification**, n., with this —, that, etc., *cum eo ut,* etc. or by *ita definire, ut,* etc. **modify**, v.tr. = to change the form or external qualities, *immutare alqd de alqâ re* (= to make a change in anything), *temperare alqd* (= to moderate).

modulate, v.tr. *vocem per vices tollĕre atque remittĕre* (= to raise and to lower the voice, in speaking), *vocem* or *cantum modulari.* **modulation**, n. *flexio (vocis), numerus* (or in pl.).

moiety, n. see HALF.

moist, adj. *humidus* (= moderately wet). **moisten**, v.tr. *conspergĕre* (= to sprinkle), (*ir)rigare* (= to water); † *humectare.* **moisture**, n. *humor.*

molar, adj. (e.g. tooth) *dens genuinus.*

mole, n. = mound, *moles, -is,* f., *agger, -ĕris,* m. **molecule**, n. see PARTICLE.

mole, n. = mark on the body, *naevus.*

mole, n. = animal, *talpa.* **mole-hill**, n. 1, lit. perhaps (*talpae*) *grumus;* 2, fig. to make mountains out of —s, *difficilia ex facillimis re digĕre.*

molest, v.tr. *alqm sol(l)icitare, vexare, molestiam alci afferre* or *exhibēre, molestum esse alci, alci incommodum afferre, conciliare* (= to give trouble), *alci negotium exhibēre, facessēre* (= to cause unpleasantness to anyone). **molestation, n.** 1, *molestia, onus, -ĕris, n.* (= a burthen); 2, = trouble, *molestia, onus, -ĕris, n., cura* (= anxiety), *incommodum* (= adversity), *vexatio.*

mollifiable, adj. *quod molliri potest.* **mollification, n., mollify, v.tr.** (e)*mollire* (= to make soft, lit. and fig.), *mitigare* (in a lit. sense, e.g. food by boiling it ; then fig.), *lenire* (= to appease), *frangēre* (= to subdue anyone's hardheartedness), *movēre alqm* or *alejs animum* (= to make an impression upon anyone, by exhortations, entreaties, etc.).

molten, adj. *liquefactus ;* see MELT.

moment, n. 1, *punctum* or *vestigium* or *momentum temporis ;* in a —, *statim, e vestigio, confestim ;* for the —, *in praesens ;* 2, = impulsive power ; see MOMENTUM ; 3, = importance ; of great —, *magni momenti ;* see IMPORTANCE. **momentary, adj.** *brevissimus* (= of a short duration); see INSTANTANEOUS. **momentous, adj.** *magni momenti ;* see IMPORTANT. **momentousness, n.** see IMPORTANCE. **momentum, n.** (in mechanics) *vis quâ alqd movetur.*

monarch, n. *rex, regis* (= king), *princeps, -ĭpis,* m. (= prince, sovereign, post Aug.), *imperator, Caesar, Augustus* (= emperor, Imperial Rome), *dominus* (= an absolute —), *tyrannus* (τύραννος, = one who has usurped the highest power in a state, which was free before) or by circumloc., to express an absolute —, a despot, the only ruler, *qui solus regnat, qui unus consilio et curâ gubernat civitatem, penes quem est summa rerum omnium* (all = rex), *qui solus imperio potitus est* (= tyrannus) ; to be the —, *regnare ;* to proclaim oneself as the —, = to usurp the throne, *dominatum* or *tyrannidem occupare, dominatum invadēre.* **monarchical, adj.** *regius ;* a — government, use *rex* (e.g. *regi parent,* they have a —). **monarchist, n.** *defensor imperii regii.* **monarchy, n.** 1, as the kind of government, *imperium quod ab uno sustinetur* or *sub uno stat, principatus, -ūs* (= the government of him who is the head of the state), *imperium regum* or *regium, imperium quod penes regem* or *reges est, potestas regia, tyrannis, -ĭdis* (τυραννίς, of one who has usurped the government of a free state) ; 2, = the state itself that is under a monarchical government, *civitas quae ab uno regitur, respublica, civitas in quâ penes unum est summa omnium rerum* (in gen.) ; *regnum, civitas regia.*

monastery, n. *monasterium, coenobium* (Eccl.).

Monday, n. *dies lunae* (not class.).

monetary, adj. *quod ad pecuniam pertinet, pecuniarius, nummarius, argentarius.* **money, n.** *pecunia* (= sum of —), *argentum, aes* (= coined from silver or copper, silver coin, copper coin); good —, *nummi probi ;* bad —, *nummi adulterini ;* for very little —, for a deal of —, *parvo, magno* (*pretio*) ; prov., — makes —, *dat census honores* (Ov.) ; to pay — down, out of hand, by *praesentem pecuniam solvēre, repraesentare ; praesenti pecuniâ solvēre ;* ready —, *pecunia praesens* or *nummi praesentes* or *numeratum* or *pecunia ;* — transactions, *negotium,* more distinctly *negotium nummarium, negotiatio* (on a large scale), *argentaria* (= banking business, — exchanging); to carry on — transactions, *argentariam facēre.* **money-bag, n.** see PURSE. **money-broker, n.** *argentarius.* **money-making, n.** *quaestus, -ūs.* **money-market, n.** *res nummaria.* **moneyed, adj.** *dives, pecuniosus ;* see RICH. **moneyless, adj.** *inops ;* see POOR.

mongrel, I. adj. *nothus.* **II. n.** (h)*ibrida* (*hyb-*), m. and f.

monition, n. *monitio* (= the act), *monitum* (= the warning given). **monitor. n.** *moniter.*

monk, n. *monăchus* (Eccl.).

monkey, n. *simia.*

monody, n. use Greek μονῳδία.

monograph, n. *liber* (= book); see BOOK.

monologue, n. *sermo ;* to hold a —, *solum loqui.*

monomaniac, n. *de unâ modo re insanire.*

monopolize, v.tr. perhaps *solum habēre* or *exercēre alqd.*

monosyllable, n. only in pl. *monosyllaba, -orum* (Quint.).

monotheism, n. *credēre unum modo Deum esse.* **monotheist, n.** *qui unum modo Deum esse credit.*

monotone, n. use Greek μονοτονία.

monotony, n., monotonous, adj. by *oratio omni varietate carens.* Adv., use adj.

monsoon, n. *ventus qui* (*certo tempore*) *flare consuevit.*

monster, n. *monstrum, portentum, belua* (lit. = beast). **monstrosity, n.** 1, *deformitas* (= deformity) ; 2, see MONSTER. **monstrous, adj.** *deformis* (opp. *formosus*), *immanis* (e.g. *belua, praeda, facinus,* etc.), *portentosus, monstr(u)osus, naturae repugnans.* Adv. *praeter naturam, monstr(u)ose.*

month, n. *mensis, -is,* m. **monthly, adj.** *singulis mensibus, in singulos menses, menstruus.*

monument, n. *monumentum* (*moni-*) ; see MEMORIAL. **monumental, adj.** 1, *ad monumentum pertinens ;* 2, fig. *gravis, magni momenti ;* see IMPORTANT.

mood, n. 1, of mind, *animus ;* 2, *modus* (Gram.). **moodiness, n., moody, adj.** see PEEVISH.

moon, n. *luna ;* eclipse of the —, *lunae defectus, -ūs.* **moonlight, I. n.** *lunae lumen.* **II. adj.** *lunâ illustris.*

moor, n., moorland, n. *loca* (-*orum*) *palustria.* **moor-hen, n.** *fulica* (*fulex*).

moor, v.tr. *navem ad terram* (*ripam,* etc.) *religare,* or *deligare.* **moorings, n.** use verb (e.g. he found convenient —, *loco opportuno navem relegavit*).

moot, v.tr. see SUGGEST, ARGUE. **moot-point, n.** it is a —, *incertum* or *dubium est an.*

mop, I. n. *pēniculus.* **II. v.tr.** *alqd peniculo detergēre.*

mope, v.intr. *tristem* or *maestum esse.* **moping, adj.** *tristis, maestus ;* see SAD.

moral, I. adj. 1, = relating to morals, *moralis ;* — philosophy, *de moribus,* or *philosophia ;* 2, = upright, *honestus, probus, bene moratus,* or perhaps *gravis ;* see UPRIGHT ; 3, it is a — certainty, *verisimillimum est* with acc. and infin. Adv. *honeste, probe* = uprightly, *verisimiliter ;* see PROBABLY. **II. n.** = teaching of a story, etc., *res ad quam fabula spectat.* **morals, n.** = moral conduct, *mores, -um ;* = ethics, *de moribus* or *de officiis* or *philosophia.* **moralist, n.** *qui de moribus praecipit.* **morality, n.** *mores, -um ;* see MORALS. **moralize, v.intr.** *de moribus praecipēre.*

morass, n. *palus, -ūdis,* f.

morbid, adj. 1, *aeger ;* a — condition of body, *aegrotatio ;* 2, fig. *aeger, aegrotus ;* a — condition of mind, *aegritudo.* Adv. *maeste*

(= sadly); see SADLY. **morbidness**, n. 1, physical, *aegrotatio*; 2, fig. *aegritudo*; see SADNESS.

more, I. adj. *plures* (neut. *plura*), *plus* (either as a n., alone or with genit., e.g. — money, *plus pecuniae*), or by **II.** adv., *plus* = — in quantity or degree (e.g. *plus umare, diligĕre*), *amplius* (as neuter adj. = a greater extent, value, etc., e.g. I am *aedilis*, that is, — than a private individual, *ego sum aedilis, hoc est, amplius quam privatus*); if without comparison = increase, addition, = "*davantage*" of the French, *quid vultis amplius?* — than 6 hours, *amplius sex horis*; *magis* (adv. in reference to the quality of the things compared, and expresses that one thing possesses a certain quality in a higher degree than another, e.g. to be — offended at a thing than another, *alqd in contumeliam accipĕre magis*), *potius* (= rather, sooner, has a subjective meaning, when a choice, a selection is made between two objects, actions, opinions, etc. ; it always excludes one of two things chosen, whilst *magis* attributes a higher value to one of the two things, without excluding the other, e.g. he would rather have stayed — in Utica than in Rome, *Uticae potius quam Romae esse maluisset*); *ultra* (as prepos. with accus. = exceeding a certain measure, proportion, etc., e.g. — than half-a-pint, *ultra heminam*); "than" after — is rendered in Latin after *plus* and *amplius* by *quam* or by the ablat. ; if numbers are stated *quam* is generally left out, and the numeral with the noun is rendered by the same case as if *quam* had been used ; after *magis* and *potius* we use always *quam* (e.g. to conquer rather through cunning device than through bravery, *magis ratione et consilio quam virtute vincĕre*); in connexion with a noun or adj. in an adj. or adv. sense — is often rendered by a comparative (e.g. with — attention, care, *attentius, diligentius*); if two adjs. or advs. are compared in reference to a certain thing, we use either *magis* . . . *quam*, — . . . than, or both are expressed by the comparative, the second being preceded by *quam* (e.g. — passionate than cautious, with — passion than prudence, *calidus magis quam cautus* or *calidior quam cautior*; with — bravery than luck, *fortiter magis quam feliciter, fortius quam felicius*); after negations — is rendered 1, when = in addition to, further, by *amplius, ultra* (e.g. I demand nothing —, *nihil amplius* or *ultra flagito*); but **2**, if = no longer, by *jam* (e.g. nobody will say that any —, *hoc jam nemo dicet*); I am not doing a certain thing any —, by *desino* (= I cease) or *desisto* (= I leave off) with inf. (e.g. I cannot see any —, *desino vidēre*); and what is — (in a climax), *et quod plus est*; still —, *plus etiam* (as regards the amount, e.g. he owes me that much and — still, *tantum et plus etiam mihi debet*), *amplius* (= still besides, e.g. what do you want — ? *quid vis amplius?*); so much —, *tanto plus* (as regards the quantity, etc.), *eo magis* (implying intensity); once — again, *alterum tantum, bis tantum*; the — . . . the — . . . , *quo . . . hoc, quanto . . . tanto*, or *eo . . . quo, tanto . . . quanto*; the — people possess, the — they wish to have, *homines quo plura habent, eo ampliora cupiunt.* **III.** n. *plus*; see I. **moreover**, adv. *praeterea, insuper, ultro, ad hoc, ad haec, accedit quod* with indic. ; see BESIDES.

moribund, adj. *moribundus.*

morn, morning, I. n. *mane* (indecl.), *tempus matutinum* (the time in the —) ; in the pl., the —s, *tempora matutina*; towards —, *sub luce* or *lucem*; in the —, *mane, matutino tempore*; the early — ; *primum mane, prima lux* or *lux* (= the first light of the —); early in the —, *primo mane, multo mane, bene mane prima luce, ubi primum illuxit,* *ad lucem, primo diluculo* (= with the — dawn); with subst. by *antelucanus* (e.g. working by candlelight early in the —, before daylight, *lucubratio antelucana*); until —, *ad lucem* (e.g. to watch, *vigilare*); this —, *hodie mane, hodierno mane*; yesterday —, *hesterno mane, hesterno die mane*; good —! *salve!* or (to several) *salvete!* to wish anyone a good —, *salvēre alci dicĕre.* **II.** adj. *matutinus*; see above. **morning-star**, n. *Lucifer*, † *Phosphorus.*

morose, adj. *morosus* (= never satisfied with oneself and with others), *acerbus* (= harsh with those around one), *stomachosus* (= churlish), *difficilis* (= ill-tempered). Adv. *morose, acerbe.* **moroseness**, n. *morositas, acerbitas.*

morrow, n. *dies posterus* or *crastinus.* Adv. to- —, *cras, crastino die* ; in letters the writers express "to- —" by *postridie ejus diei, qui erat tum futurus, cum haec scribebam* (Cic.); early to- — morning, *cras mane*; for to- —, *in crastinum diem*; to-day or to- —, some time, *aliquando* ; rather to-day than to- —, as soon as possible, *quam primum*; the day after to- —, *perendie.*

morsel, n. *offa* (= mouthful), *pars exigua*; see PARTICLE.

mortal, adj. **1**, *mortalis* (= subject to death, opp. *immortalis*), *humanus* (= of human, not of divine origin, opp. *divinus, divus*), *fragilis, cadūcus* (= fragile, perishable, opp *firmus, stabilis*); —s, *homines, mortales*; all men are —, *omnibus moriendum est*; **2**, = deadly, *mortifer*; see FATAL ; **3**, = complete, by superl. (e.g. — enemy, *homo infensissimus*). Adv. to be — wounded, *mortiferum vulnus accipĕre* ; = very, *valde, vehementer, magnopere.* **mortality**, n. **1**, *condicio mortalis, mortalitas* ; **2**, = number of deaths, by circumloc. (e.g. there was a great —, *plurimi morte absumpti sunt*).

mortar, n. = a vessel, *pila, mortarium.*

mortar, n. = cement, *arenatum, mortarium.*

mortgage, I. n. *hypotheca, pignus, -ōris,* n. **II.** v.tr. *pignori dare, obligare.*

mortification, n. **1**, in surgery, *gangraena* (Cels.); **2**, fig. see VEXATION. **mortify, I.** v.intr. in surgery, by *putrescĕre.* **II.** v.tr. see HUMBLE.

mortmain, n. * *mortua manus* (Mediæval Lat.).

mosaic, I. adj. *tessellatus, vermiculatus.* **II.** n. *opus tessellatum, vermiculatum.*

mosque, n. *aedes sacra Turcica.*

mosquito, n. *culex.*

moss, n. *muscus.* **mossy**, adj. *muscosus.*

most, I. adj. *maximus, plurimus* ; — people, *plerique* ; see MUCH. **II.** adv. *maxime, plurimum, valde, vehementer* ; see VERY. **mostly**, adv. *fere, plerumque, saepe* ; see GENERALLY.

mote, n. see PARTICLE.

moth, n. *tinea, blatta* (= mite).

mother, n. 1, lit. *mater* (also as address to an aged female), *matrix* (of an animal); 2, fig. = preserver, *mater* (in gen.), *parens, -tis,* m. and f., *procreatrix, genitrix* (*parens* must chiefly be used when the noun which is expressed as the — of anything is masculine). **mother-country**, n. *terra patria.* **motherhood**, n. *mater, maternus* (e.g. the feeling of —, *animus maternus*). **mother-in-law**, n. *socrus, -ūs,* f. **motherless**, adj. *matre orbus* or *carens.* **motherly**, adj. *maternus.* **mother-tongue**, n. *patrius sermo.* **mother-wit**, n. to do a thing by —, *crassâ* or *pingui Minerva alqd facĕre* (= without art); *summo ingenio* (= cleverly).

motion, I. n. 1, (in gen.) *motus, -ūs, motio*
(= the act of setting in —), *agitatio* (= moving
up and down); to be in —, *movēri, agitari* ; to set
anyone in —, *agēre alqm* ; to set in quick —,
incitare, concitare (e.g. a horse, etc.); **2,** = proposal, *rogatio* (of the tribunes), *sententia* (in the
senate); to bring forward a —, *rogationem or
legem (re)ferre.* **II.** v.tr. *annuĕre, significare.*
motionless, adj. *immotus.*

motive, I. n. *caus(s)a, ratio* ; to act from
any —, *alqâ ratione adductus alqd facĕre.* **II.**
adj. *qui (quae, quod) agitat or movet.*

motley, adj. *coloris maculosi, maculosus*
(= spotted in gen.), *maculis albis* (= with white
spots), *varii or disparis coloris* (= of different
colours).

motto, n. *sententia* (as an idea which we
have pronounced, a sentiment), *dictum* (= a saying, anything uttered), *verbum, vox* (as a short
sentiment).

mould, n. = shape, *forma.*

mould, n. = soil, *terra* ; see EARTH. **mould-
er,** v.intr. *mucescĕre, putrescĕre.* **mouldiness,**
n. *mucor.* **mouldy,** adj. *mucidus* (Juv.).

moult, v.intr. *plumas ponĕre.*

mound, n. *tumulus, agger, -ĕris, m.*

mount, I. v.intr. 1, see RISE ; 2, = to get
on horseback, *conscendĕre (equum).* **II.** v.tr.
1, = to furnish with horses, *milites equis imponĕre* ; —ed, *equo vectus* ; 2, to — guard, by
*excubiae in stationem procedunt, milites in sta-
tiones succedunt* ; = to ascend, *scandĕre, a(d)s-
cendĕre, conscendĕre, escendĕre.*

mountain, n. *mons, -tis,* m. ; what belongs
to, lives, grows upon the —, *montanus* ; full of
—s, *montuosus or montosus* ; situate on this side
of the —s, *cismontanus* ; on the other side of
the —s, *transmontanus* ; on, along the —, *sub
montem, in or sub radicibus montis* (= close to the
foot of the —). **mountaineer,** n. *homo montanus.* **mountainous,** adj. *montosus, montuosus* (opp. *planus*), *montanus.*

mountebank, n. *circulator* (in gen.), fem.
circulatrix, pharmacopōla circumforaneus (=
quack).

mourn, I. v.intr. *maerēre, in maerore esse or
jacēre* (= to be deeply afflicted), *lugēre, in luctu
esse* (= to show one's grief outwardly), *squal-
ēre, in squalore esse* (of extreme grief, which
shows itself by entire neglect of one's own self
and of outward appearance, e.g. *luget senatus,
maeret equester ordo, squalent municipia,* Cic.),
comb. *luctu atque maerore affectum esse, in luctu
et squalore esse* ; *cultu lugubri indutum* (= to
go into —ing), for anyone, *pro alqo.* **II.** v.tr.
see LAMENT, GRIEVE. **mournful,** adj. *tristis*;
maestus (= sad), *lugubris, flebilis, lamentabilis,
acerbus, luctuosus* (= causing sorrow). Adv.
maeste, †lugubriter, flebiliter, acerbe, luctuose.
mournfulness, n. *maeror, tristitia*; see
SADNESS. **mourning,** n. *maeror, maestitia*
(= grief), *luctus, -ūs* (= grief shown outwardly
by dress, etc.); — dress, *vestis or cultus, -ūs,
lugubris, squalor* (referring to the neglect
shown in one's outward appearance, with a view
to excite sympathy), *sordes, -ium* (forgetting all
dignity and decency); to be in —, *in luctu
esse, pullatum or sordidatum esse.*

mouse, n. *mus, muris,* m. and f., *musculus*
(= a little —). **mouse-hole,** n. *cavis or cavum
muris.* **mouse-trap,** n. *muscipula* (Sen.).

moustache, n. perhaps *barba labri superioris.*

mouth, n. 1, *os, oris,* n. ; with open —,
hians ; anything makes my — water, *alqd salivam mihi movet* ; to have a thing in one's —,

alqd in ore habēre (lit. of food, **fig. of words**): to
be in anyone's —, *in omnium ore or in omnium
ore et sermone esse, omni populo in ore esse, per
omnium ora ferri* ; 2, — of a river, etc., *os, oris,*
n., *ostium* (in gen.); *caput* (= a single — of a
river); = entrance, in gen. *aditus, -ūs.*

move, I. v.tr. *(com)movēre, ciēre* (= to set in
motion), *agitare* (= to — up and down), *versare* (=
to turn round), *quatēre* (= to shake), *moliri* (=
to — with exertion), *rotare, circumagēre* (= to —
round ; *rotare* more poet.) ; fig. *commovēre, permovēre, turbare, conturbare* (= to agitate one's mind);
to — heaven and earth, *caelum ac terras miscēre* ;
= to guide anyone, influence anyone's will,
(com)movēre (in gen.), *flectĕre* (= to persuade anyone who was of a different mind before), *vincĕre*
or *expugnare precibus, precibus lacrimisque* (= to
persuade anyone to yield). **II.** v.intr. **1, se**
(com)movēre, (com)moveri (= to be in motion), *incitari* (quickly, opp. *retardari*), *ferri* (suddenly,
violently, opp. *labi,* particularly of celestial
bodies), *micare, vibrare* (= to vibrate, e.g. of the
light) ; to — in a circle, *in orbem circumagi* ; to
— round anything, *ambire alqd, versari circa
alqd* (e.g. round the axis of the earth,
of the universe, etc.), *ferri circum alqd, volvi
circa alqd* ; 2, in an assembly, *(re)ferre* ; see
MOTION, I. 2. **moveable,** adj. *mobilis* (lit.
and fig., e.g. of the mind), *agilis* (of what
can be easily moved about, e.g. a ship,
then fig. of the mind, etc.). **movement,** n.
motus, -ūs ; to observe the enemy's —s, *quae ab
hostibus agantur cognoscĕre* ; see MOTION.

mow, v.tr. *demetĕre, secare* (= to cut).
mower, n. *faenisex (fen-).* **mowing,** n. *faen-
isicium, faenisicia (fen-).*

much, adj. and adv. *multus* ; — trouble
and labour, *plurimum laboris et operae* ; — also
rendered by subst., such as *copia, vis, multitudo,
magnus numerus* ; to have — of a thing, *abundare alqâ re* (e.g. *otio,* leisure) ; to have — intercourse with anyone, *multum esse cum alqo* ; —
more — less, *multo magis, multo minus* ; sometimes also *multis partibus* (e.g. to be — greater,
multis partibus majorem esse); — beloved, *dilec-
tissimus, carissimus* ; as — as, *tantus . . . quantus*
(adv. *tantum . . . quantum*) ; — less, *nedum, ne
dicam, tantum abest ut.*

muck, n. see DIRT. **muck-heap,** n. *ster-
quilinum.*

mucous, adj. *mucosus* (Cels.). **mucus,** n.
pituita (= phlegm, rheum), *mucus* (= filth of
the nose).

mud, n. *lutum, caenum.* **muddy,** adj.
lutosus (of soil), *lutulentus* (= besmeared with
mud) ; see DIRTY.

muddle, I. n. *turba, confusio* ; see CON-
FUSION. **II.** v.tr. 1, *miscēre, turbare,* comb.
miscēre ac turbare ; see CONFUSE ; 2, with drink,
†inebriare ; to be —d, *vino madēre* (Plaut.).

muff, n. *manĭca* (= a long sleeve).

muffin, n. see CAKE.

muffle, v.tr. *velare, obvolvĕre.* **muffler,** n.
tegumentum, teg(i)mentum ; wearing a —, *capite
obvoluto.*

mug, n. see CUP.

muggy, adj. *humidus* (= damp), *densus* (=
thick), *calidus* (= warm).

mulberry, n. *morum* ; —-tree, *morus,* f.

mulct, v.tr. *multare.*

mule, n. *mulus, mula.*

mull, v.tr. —ed wine, *vinum fervidum.*

mullet, n. *mullus.*

multifarious, adj. *multiplex, varius.* Adv.
varie, multis modis.

multiform, adj. *multiformis.*

multiplication, n. *multiplicatio.* **multiply, I.** v.tr. 1, in arithmetic, *multiplicare ;* 2, in gen. = to increase, *multiplicare ;* see IN-CREASE. **II.** v.intr. *augeri, crescĕre.*

multitude, n. *multitudo* (of persons and things), *vis, vis,* f. (e.g. *magna vis hominum*), *vulgus, -i,* n. (= the —, in contemptuous sense), by *multi* and n. (e.g. *multi homines, multae naves, frequentia, coetus, -ūs* (= number of people together). **multitudinous,** adj. *creber, frequens, multus, numerosus.*

mumble, v.intr. see MUTTER.

mummer, n. *qui personam* or *partes agit.* **mummery,** n. *persona* or *partes, -ium.*

mummy, n. *homo mortuus arte medicatus* (Tac.).

munch, v.tr. *manducare.*

mundane, n. 1, lit. *mundanus ;* 2, fig. = worldly, *alcjs rei* (e.g. *divitiarum*), *studiosus, alci rei deditus.*

municipal, adj. *municipalis.* **municipality,** n. *municipium.*

munificence, n. *munificentia, largitas, liberalitas ;* see GENEROSITY. **munificent,** adj. *munificus, liberalis ;* see GENEROUS. Adv. *munifice, large, liberaliter.*

muniment, n. *munimentum.* **munition,** n. *instrumenta, -orum,* or *apparatus, -ūs, belli.*

mural, adj. *muralis.*

murder, I. n. *caedes* (in gen.), *occisio, homicidium* (= homicide), *nex* (= violent death), *scelus alci allatum* (= crime committed upon anyone), *parricidium alcjs* (on a father, mother, brother, etc.) ; to commit a —, *caedem, homicidium facĕre, parricidium committĕre, parricidio se obstringĕre ;* on anyone, *caedem alcjs facĕre* or *efficĕre* or *perpetrare, mortem per scelus alci inferre, necem alci inferre, offerre, alci vim afferre* (= to lay hands upon anyone), *algm interficĕre* or *occidĕre* (= to kill anyone) ; accomplice in a —, *caedis socius,* in the context also *sceleri affinis* (as participating in the —). **II.** v.tr. *caedĕre, occidĕre, interficĕre, trucidare, jugulare, necare, de* or *e medio tollĕre.* **murderer,** n. *homicīda,* m. and f. (in gen.), *parricīda* (of a father, mother, brother, sister, a free citizen, a public officer, one's sovereign, etc.), *fratricīda* (of a brother), *matricīda* (of a mother), *sicarius* (= who makes a trade of it), *percussor* (= who pierces, slaughters anyone) ; — of a despot, tyrant, *tyrannicīda, tyranni interfector.* **murderous,** adj. *sanguinarius* (= bloodthirsty, e.g. man, thought), † *cruentus* (when much blood is shed, e.g. *bellum, dies ;* also bloodthirsty, e.g. thought), *atrox* or (stronger) *atrocissimus* (= fearful, most fearful, e.g. battle, *pugna ;* bloodshed, slaughter, *caedes*).

murmur, I. n. 1, *murmur, -ūris,* n., *fremitus, -ūs* (especially of a seditious mob), *susurrus* (= whispering, and of a river) ; to bear a thing without a —, *sedate* or *quiete* or *aequo animo ferre alqd ;* 2, = complaint, *querela ;* see COMPLAIN. **II.** v.intr. 1, *murmurare,* † *susurrare* (of a low continued noise) ; to — (as a sign of approbation or disapproval), *admurmurare ;* as a sign of applause or indignation, *fremere* (also = to — at, with accus. and infin.) ; to — at with a hissing noise, *mussare, mussitare ;* 2, = to complain, *queri ;* see COMPLAIN.

muscle, n. 1, in anatomy, *musculus* (Cels.) ; the — in the arm, *lacertus ;* 2, a shell-fish, *mytilus* (mit-). **muscular,** adj. *lacertosus ;* see STRONG.

muse, n. *Musa.*

museum, n. *musēum* (as a place where men

of learning meet, not in the sense of a repository) ; natural history —, *thesaurus rerum naturalium exemplis refertus, thesaurus quo res naturales continentur.*

mushroom, n. *fungus, boletus* (= edible —).

music, n. 1, as art, *ars musica, musice, -es,* f. (μουσική, ἡ), *musica, -orum, res musica ;* 2, of musical productions, = composed pieces, *modi* (*musici*) ; = made with instruments, *cantus, -ūs, concentus, -ūs, symphonia* (of several instruments) ; to make — with an instrument, *canĕre* (with the abl. of the instrument) ; to enter a town with —, *urbem ad classicum introire* (of soldiers) ; pieces of —, *modi exscripti* (instrumental). **musical,** adj. 1, = concerning, referring to music, *musicus, aptatus ad usus canendi* (= adapted for making music, e.g. instrument, *organum*) ; 2, = understanding music, by circumloc. *musicis eruditus, artis musicae peritus ;* to have a — ear, in the context by *aures eruditas habēre, aurium judicio valēre ;* 3, = melodious, *canōrus ;* of speech, *numerosus ;* see MELODIOUS. Adv. by adjs. ; *numerose.* **musician,** n. 1, if he plays in public, *servus* or *puer symphoniacus* (= a slave), *fidicen, -icinis,* m. (= who plays the lyre), *tibicen, -icinis* (= who plays the flute or clarionet), *cornicen* (= who plays the horn) ; 2, in a higher sense, *artis musiciae peritus.*

musket, n. see GUN.

muslin, n. *sindon, coa, -orum, byssus.*

must, differently expressed, 1, by gerundive = a necessity inferred from the circumstances of the case, e.g. people, we, you, etc. — die, *moriendum est ;* one — confess that every living creature is mortal, *confitendum est omne animal esse mortale ;* the person by which a thing is to be done in the dative, very seldom by *ab,* and only when a second dative would make the meaning ambiguous and obscure ; e.g. everyone — use his own judgment, *suo cuique judicio utendum est ;* the property of many citizens is at stake, of which you — take every care, *aguntur bona multorum civium, quibus a vobis consulendum est* (here *a vobis* on account of *quibus,* Cic., who in another passage has also two datives with the gerundive) ; we — take the same road, *haec via (nobis) ingredienda ;* one — know nature, *noscenda est natura ;* the speaker — consider three points, *tria videnda sunt oratori ;* 2, by *oportet* (impersonal δεῖ, expressing a necessity inferred from reason, or from the law, or from prudence or justice), with the accus. and infin., or merely with the subjunctive mood ; 3, = by *debēre* (ὀφείλειν), to express a moral obligation, e.g. you — honour him like your father, *eum patris loco colēre debes ;* if we were affected in seeing the misery of our allies, what — we now do when we see our own blood shed? *sociorum miseriā commovebamur, quid nunc in nostro sanguine facĕre debemus ? Debēre,* therefore, is nearly = *officium,* so that we can also express — by *officium est alcjs* and simply *est alcjs,* e.g. a stranger — mind only his own affairs, *peregrini officium est* (i.e. *peregrinus debet*) *nihil praeter suum negotium agĕre ;* a good orator — have heard much, *est boni oratoris* (i.e. *bonus orator debet*) *multa auribus accepisse. Officium* is gen. left out in I, you —, *meum, tuum, vestrum est ;* 4, by *putare* and *existimare,* in the rhetorical style, as a form of politeness, so that the hearers may be allowed to come to a conclusion themselves about a point, e.g. you see to what a pitch the republic — proceed, *videte quem in locum rempublicam perventum putetis ;* 5, by *opus est* (impersonal χρή), in speaking of any event subjectively felt, and from the supplying of which we expect great advantages ; either with accus. and infin., or if the person who — do, etc., a thing is added in the dative, *ut* with subjunctive mood, e.g. if anything should happen which you — know (which it is useful for you to know), I'll write to you, *si quid erit, quod te scire opus est, scribam ;* I — go and wash myself, *mihi opus est ut lavem.* Also, I — have so and so may be rendered by *mihi opus est,* either impersonally with abl., or personally with the nominative of the person or thing that — be had, e.g. we — have a guide. *dux et auctor nobis opus est ;* we — use your authority, *auctoritate tuâ nobis opus est ;* 6, by *necesse est* (impersonal, ἀνάγκη ἐστί), expressing necessity, either with accus. and infin., or simply with subjunctive mood, e.g. this mortal frame of ours — (necessarily) perish some time, *corpus mortale alqo tempore perire necesse est ;* 7, by *facĕre non possum,* or simply *non possum* with *quin,* etc., or *fieri non potest* with *ut non,* etc., or *non possum non* with infin., to express what cannot be avoided, inward necessity, e.g. I — exclaim, *non possum quin exclamem ;* 8, simply by the verb: in the indicative, inasmuch as in Latin we often leave it for the reader to supply in his own mind under what circumstances an action took place, e.g., I — confess, *confiteor* (Ter.), *fateor* (Cic.); I — regret, *doleo* (Cic.); I — express my surprise, *miror* (Liv.); this one thing I — remark, *unum illud dico ;* in the subjunctive, if we only speak of a supposed necessity, e.g. a circumstance, at which not only all educated people, but even savages — blush, *o rem dignam, in quâ non modo docti, verum etiam agrestes erubescant ;* 9, you — (as urgent appeal), either simply by the imperative mood, or by *fac ut,* e.g. if you are not satisfied with that, you — accuse your own injustice, *haec si vobis non probabuntur, vestram iniquitatem accusatote ;* you — not (as an urgent warning, not to a thing), *fac ne,* etc. (= mind that not, etc.), *cave ne* (= take care lest, or not to, etc.), *noli* with infin., e.g. you — not wish, *cave ne cupias.*

must, n. *mustum.*

mustard, n. *sinapi* (in the genit. *sinapis,* in the dat., accus., and abl. *sinapi ;* the nom. seldom) ; — plaster, *sinapismus* (very late).

muster, I. v.tr. **1,** *recensēre* (= to examine through one by one, to ascertain the condition, number, etc., of the army, cavalry, the senate, the people), *inspicēre* (= to inspect, e.g. the legions, *arma, viros, equos cum curâ inspicĕre,* Liv.); *numerum alcjs inire* (of a crowd), comb. *recensēre et numerum inire*(of a mass of people); **2,** fig. to — courage, *animum erigĕre.* **II.** v.intr. *congregari, coire, convenire, adesse ;* see ASSEMBLE. **III.** n. see ASSEMBLY.

musty, adj. *mucidus* (Juv., of bread and wine), in gen. perhaps *obsoletus ;* see also OLD.

mutable, adj. (com)*mutabilis, inconstans, mobilis ;* see CHANGEABLE. **mutability,** n. *mutabilitas ;* see CHANGE, LEVITY.

mute, I. adj. *mutus.* **II.** n. *servus,* defining sense by context, or *unus ex iis qui funus ducunt.*

mutilate, v.tr. *mutilare* (gen. of trifling mutilations, e.g. nose, ears, finger), *truncare* (= to make into a stump as it were, to — entirely, cut off anyone's head, arms, feet, hands, etc., singly or all at once ; e.g., a body, *corpus ;* a statue, *simulacrum).* **mutilated,** adj. *mutilatus, mutilus, truncus, truncatus* (*mutilus* and *truncatus* are used also of mutilation by nature), *debilis* (= infirm, inasmuch as the person that is mutilated is deprived of the use of the — limb), *curtus* (= cut wrong, too small, too short, not

having sufficient size or perfection and completeness, e.g. *eorum omnium, multa praetermittentium, quasi curta sententia).* **mutilation,** n. by verb.

mutiny, I. n. *conspiratio* (= a plot against the superior), *conjuratio* (= conspiracy), *seditio, motus, -ûs* (= insurrection). **II.** v.intr. *inter se conspirare, inter se conjurare* (= to conspire), *seditionem facĕre.* **mutineer,** n. *conjuratus, homo seditiosus.* **mutinous,** adj. *seditiosus.* Adv. *seditiose.*

mutter, v.intr. and tr. *mussari, mussitare.*

mutton, n. *caro (carnis) ovilis.*

mutual, adj. *mutuus.* Adv. *mutuo.*

muzzle, n. = fastening for the mouth, *fiscella.*

my, pron. *meus ;* but only expressed if it is required to avoid ambiguity, e.g. I have seen — brother, *fratrem vidi ;* I am — own master, *meus sum, mei juris sum ;* it is — business, — duty, *meum est ;* I for — part, *quod ad me attinet, ego quidem* (often *noster* is used for *meus,* as *nos* for *ego).*

myriad, n. **1,**= ten thousand, *decem mil(l)ia ;* **2,** = an indefinitely large number, *sescenti.*

myrmidon, n. *emissarius, satelles, -ĭtis,* m. (*et administer).*

myrrh, n. *murra (myrrha) ;* of —, *murrinus ;* anointed with —, † *murreus.*

myrtle, I. n. *myrtus (mur-).* **II.** adj. † *myrteus ;* — berry, *myrtum ;* — grove, *myrtetum.*

myself, pron. see I, SELF.

mysterious, adj. *arcanus ;* a — affair, *res arcana, mysterium ;* see SECRET. **mystery,** n. **1,** in a religious sense, *mysteria, -orum, sacra, -orum* (= worship, e.g. *Cereris) ;* to initiate into the mysteries, *mysteriis initiari ;* to celebrate, perform the mysteries, *mysteria facĕre ;* these are mysteries to me (which I don't understand), *haec non intellego ;* = sacred, secret, *arcanum ;* **2,** = a secret in gen., *res occulta.* **mystic, I.** adj. **1,** = belonging to religious mysteries, *mysticus, mysticis disciplinis initiatus ;* **2,** = see STRANGE. **II.** n. *homo mysticus, homo studio mystico deditus.* **mysticism,** n. *studium mysticum* (= mysterious doctrine). **mystification,** n. *ludus, ludificatio* (= tricks, fun) ; = fraud, *fraus.* **mystify,** v.tr. *alqm fraudare* (= to deceive).

myth, n. *fabula.* **mythical,** adj. † *fabulosus.* **mythology,** n. *fabulae.* **mythological,** adj. *quod ad fabulas pertinet.*

N.

nag, n. *caballus ;* see HORSE.

naiad, n. *naias.*

nail, I. n. **1,** (on the fingers and toes) *unguis, -is,* m.; dirty —s, *ungues sordidi* (e.g. and see that your —s be not dirty, *et sint sine sordibus ungues,* Ov.) ; to cut the —s, *ungues recidĕre* or *resecare ;* to bite one's —s, *ungues rodĕre ;* **2,** an iron or wooden —, to be driven into a board, etc., *clavus ;* to drive a —, *clavum (de)figĕre ;* you have hit the — on the head, *acu tetigisti ;* a small tack, *clavulus ;* head of a —, *clavi bulla.* **II.** v.tr. = to fasten with —s on anything, (*clavis) affigĕre,* or *configĕre alci rei, suffigĕre in alqd ;* —ed, *fixus.*

naive, adj. perhaps *simplex* Adv. perhaps *sine fuco ac fallaciis.*

naked, adj. *nudus* (lit. and fig.); half-—, *seminudus ;* to make or strip —, *nudare* (e.g.

corpus). Adv. *aperte* (= openly), *sine fuco ac fallaciis* (= without dissimulation). **nakedness**, n. 1, *nudatum corpus*; 2, fig. of style, *jejunitas, inopia ac jejunitas, exilitas, siccitas*.

name, I. n. 1, *nomen* (of a person), *vocabulum* (= the sign of an object or person), *appellatio* (= the calling, the title), *cognomen* (= the family name); my — is Balbus, *est mihi nomen Balbo* or *Balbus*; give him a kiss in my —, *suavium des ei meis verbis*; in the — of the state, *publice* (opp. *privatim*); in — (or appearance) only, *verbo* (*tenus*), *verbo non re* or *reverâ*; under the — of, *nomine alcjs rei, sub titulo alcjs rei, specie alcjs rei* (= under the excuse, pretence, or pretext); 2, fig. *nomen*; to have a —, *magnum nomen* or *magnam famam habēre*; to obtain a —, *nomen consequi, famam colligēre*; *nomen* also = nation or people, e.g. hostile to the Roman — (= everything Roman), *nomini Romano inimicum* or *infestum*; the terror of the Gallic —, *terror Gallici nominis*. **II.** v.tr. *alqm nominare, alci nomen dare, indēre, facēre, alci rei nomen imponēre, alqm appellare, dicēre, nuncupare*; to — after a person, *ab nomine alcjs appellare* (with the appellation in the accus.); see CALL, APPOINT. **nameless**, adj. *nominis expers*; a certain person who shall be —, *homo quidam*. **namely**, adv. if inserted to add something to a previous statement, by apposition (e.g. if you wish to destroy avarice you must destroy its parent, — luxury, *avaritiam si tollere vultis, mater ejus est tollenda, luxuries*); sometimes it may be rendered by rel. and *est* (e.g. *maxime illa movens eloquentia quae est naturalis*); more expressive is *dico* or *inquam*, = I mean, e.g. *superiores oratores, Crassum dico et Antonium*. **namesake**, n. *eodem nomine appellatus*.

nap, I. n. *somnus brevis, somnus meridianus* (= sleep in the middle of the day). **II.** v.intr. *paul(l)um conquiescēre*; see SLEEP.

nap, n. (of cloth), perhaps *villus*.

nape, n. *cervix*.

napkin, n. *mappa, mantele, -is*, n.

narcissus, n. *narcissus* (Plin.).

narcotic, I. adj. by (*con*)*sopire, somnum alci afferre*. **II.** n. *medicamentum somnificum* (Plin.).

nard, n. *nardus* (Plin.).

narrate, v.tr. (lit.) (*e*)*narrare, referre, memorare, exponēre alqd alci*; see TELL, RELATE, RECITE. **narration, narrative, I.** n. *narratio* (= the act of telling, and the — itself), *relatio* (Quint.), *memoria* (= account of any event as handed down to us), *expositio* (= exposition, representation), *historia* (= story). **II.** adj. by *narrare*, etc. **narrator**, n. *narrator: auctor, rerum gestarum pronuntiator*.

narrow, I. adj. 1, = of little breadth, *angustus* (= not broad, not wide, leaving little distance from side to side, opp. *latus*, generally as censure), *artus* (= tightened, opp. *laxus*, generally expressing praise, hence also fig. = intimately connected, of friendship, etc.), *contractus* (= drawn together); 2, = not liberal, *angusti animi et parvi, pusilli animi et contracti*; 3, = difficult; to have a — escape, *vix* or *aegre periculum effugēre*. Adv. = nearly, *aegre, vix* (= scarcely), *fere, ferme* (= almost); = closely, *accurate, diligenter*. **II.** v.tr. (*co*)*artare, contrahēre*. **III.** v.intr. *in artius coire, cogi*. **IV.** n. or **narrows**, *aditus, -ūs* (= access in gen.), *angustiae locorum* or simply *angustiae* (= — passage through a mountain, hollow, etc.), *fauces, -ium*, f. (= — entrance and outlet). **narrowness**, n. *angustiae* (lit. of narrow pass, fig. = embarrassment, difficult circumstances, deficiency of understanding); — of mind, *animus angustus et parvus*.

nasal, adj. *narium* (gen. of *nares*, = nose).

nascent, adj. *nascens*.

nasty, adj. 1, of taste, *amarus* (= bitter), *injucundus, gravis* (= unpleasant); see UNPLEASANT; 2, = foul, *spurcus, teter, immundus, foedus, obscenus* (*obscaen-*): see FOUL. Adv. *amare, graviter, spurce, tetre, foede, obscene* (*obscaen-*). **nastiness**, n. 1, of taste, *amaritas, amaritudo*; of smell, *gravitas* (Plin.); 2, *foeditas, obscenitas* (*obscaen-*).

natal, adj. *natalis, natalicius*.

nation, n. *populus, gens, -ntis*, f. (= the people of a country as a whole), *natio*; my, your —, *cives nostri, vestri*. **national**, adj. *gentis proprius* (= peculiar to a people), *domesticus* (= referring to one's own country), *popularis* (= peculiar to the great mass of the people), *togatus* (= only of the Romans, e.g. *fabula togata*, = the — drama); it is —, *est gentis proprium* (= it is peculiar to the whole people); — character, mind, of a people, in the context, *natura insita, ingenium, ingenium hominum, mores, mos alcjs gentis*. **nationality**, n. *mores populi* or *civitatis, mores domestici* (= customs at home); the — of the Greeks, *mores* or *omnis mos Graecorum*; to preserve the —, *mores, leges, et ingenium sincerum integrumque a contagione accolarum servare*.

native, I. adj. *indigēna*, or by circuml. *in eâ* or *illâ terrâ natus*; — land, *patria*. **II.** n., the —s, *indigenae*; the —s of an island, *in insulâ nati*. **nativity**, n. in astrology, *thema, -ātis*, n. (Suet.), *positus, -ūs, siderum et spatia* (= place of the stars at the time of anyone's birth), *sidus* (*-ēris*, n.) *natalicium* (= the sign under which anyone is born); to cast a —, *notare sidera natalicia*.

natural, I. adj. *naturalis* (= coming from nature, opp. *artificiosus*; = founded upon the nature of things, opp. *arcessitus* or *quaesitus*); *nativus* (= what is so by nature, in its — condition, of things, e.g. wall, dam, hair, colour, grotto, heat, opp. *artificiosus*, also of innate qualities, opp. *quaesitus*), *naturaliter innatus* or *insitus*, also simply *innatus* or *insitus*, comb. *innatus atque insitus* (= innate by nature, only of qualities), *proprius et naturalis* (= peculiar by nature, to anyone, *alcjs*), *simplex, sincerus* (= simple, without a mixture, of things outwardly seen; hence also = not artificial, of words, and sincere, not hypocritical, of man, opp. *fucatus*), *verus* (= true, sincere, opp. *simulatus*, of words, etc.), comb. *sincerus atque verus* (opp. *fucatus et simulatus*); *filius non legitimus*, a — son; *filius nothus, filius e concubinâ natus, filius naturalis* (Jct.); a — death, *mors, -tis*, f.; to die a — death, *naturae concedēre*; to be a — consequence of anything, *ex ipsâ rei naturâ sequi*; quite —! of course! *minime mirum id quidem*; — philosophy, *physica, -orum, investigatio rerum naturae* (= study of nature); the Greeks studied — philosophy, nature, *Graeci studium collocabant in rebus naturalibus scrutandis explicandisque*; — sciences, *disciplinae quae naturae investigatione continentur, disciplinae quae in mundi leges atque in corporum naturam inquirunt*; — products, *quae terra gignit* or *parit, quae gignuntur in* or * *terrâ, res naturales*; — gift, *ingenium, indoles, -is*. Adv. *secundum naturam, naturaliter, naturas convenienter*; = unaffectedly, *simpliciter, sincere, sine fuco ac fallaciis*; = clearly, *manifesto, necessario*. **II.** n. *stultus*; see FOOL, IDIOT. **naturalisation,** n., by **naturalize**, v.tr., to — someone, *alci civitatem dare* (see CITIZEN); to be —d, *civem esse, in civitate* or *civitati a(d)scriptum esse*; to — an animal or plant, *importare*. **naturalist**, n. *qui rerum naturalium exempla* (*undique conquirit, et*) *investigat*. **nature, n.** *natura, ingenium, indoles*,

-is, f., *proprietas* (= peculiar to anyone or anything)*; natura rerum, mundus* (= of things, world), *agri, campi, rus* (= open air, fields)*; by —, naturâ, naturaliter*; according to —, *secundum naturam* (= in the course of —), opp. *contra naturam*, i.e. contrary to —), *naturae convenienter* (= in accordance with —, both with *vivēre* = to live); the — of a thing, *natura* or *ratio alcjs rei*; to draw, picture anything from —, *ad verum exprimēre alqd* (with the pencil or in writing); phenomenon of —, *quod in rerum naturâ fit, ostentum, prodigium, portentum*; agreeable to —, *naturae conveniens* or *congruens, naturae* or *ad naturam accommodatus, ad naturam aptus* (opp. *naturae* or *a naturâ alienus*), *naturalis* (opp. *fucatus*)*;* to be in conformity with —, *naturae convenire, secundum naturam esse*; law of —, *lex naturae* or *naturalis* (in gen.), *ratio profecta a rerum naturâ* (= law based upon the — of things); people living in a state of —, *populus nullo officio aut disciplinâ assuefactus.*

naught, n. *nihil*; to set at —, *parvi facēre* (= to make little of); see Mock.

naughty, adj. *improbus, immodestus* (= behaving, in an improper manner), *rusticus* (= rude). **naughtiness**, n. *immodestia* (= improper behaviour), *rusticitas* (= rudeness).

nausea, n. *nausea, fastidium* (= disgust). **nauseous**, adj. see Loathsome, Disgusting.

nautical, naval, adj. *navalis* (e.g. *pugna*), *nauticus* (= nautical); *maritimus* (= belonging to the sea).

nave, n. **1**, of a wheel, *modiolus*; **2**, of a building, *spatium medium.*

navel, n. *umbilīcus.*

navigable, adj. *navigabilis, navium patiens* (= being able to carry vessels). **navigate**, v.tr. *navigare in alqo loco* or *per alqm locum* or simply *alqm locum.* **navigation**, n. *navigatio* (= the voyage itself), *ars navalis* (as art, skill). **navigator**, n. *nauta*; see Sailor. **navy**, n. *copiae navales, naves* (= ships), † *naves bellicae* (= men-of-war), *classis.*

nay, adv. *im(m)o* (*vero*); *quin etiam, atque etiam, atque adeo* (= — even); he is living, — he comes into the senate, *vivit, im(m)o vero etiam in senatum venit*; see No.

neap-tide, n. perhaps *aestus (-ūs) minor.*

near, I. adv. *prope, juxta, propter* (rare); — two hundred men, *ad ducentos homines*; see Nearly. **II.** prep. *ad, prope, propter* with accus., *secundum* (= along or by with accus.). **III.** adj. **1**, *propinquus* (= — to with gen.); —er, *propior*; —est, *proximus*; *vicinus* (= neighbouring); a — friend, *familiaris*; — relationship, *necessitudo*; **2**, see Mean. **nearly**, adv. *prope, paene, fere, ferme*; he was — doing it, *in eo erat ut*; to be — related, *alqm genere contingēre, alci propinquum* (et *necessarium*) *esse.* **nearness**, n. *propinquitas* (of place or relationship). **nearsighted**, adj. **1**, *non longe prospicēre posse*; **2**, fig. *parum prudens.*

neat, adj. **1**, = very clean, *nitidus* (= — -looking, of the outside), *comptus* (= dressed smartly, also *nitidus*, = of — appearance), comb. *nitidus et comptus, elegans* (= elegant in dress, appearance, manners); a — little gentleman, *ad unguem factus homo* (Hor., Sat.), *juvenis barbâ et comâ nitidus, totus de capsulâ* (Sen.); **2**, = free from impure words and phrases, *nitidus, comptus* (of the style, the speaker, the writer), comb. *nitidus et comptus.* Adv. *nitide, compte, eleganter*; see Clean, Elegant. **neatness**, n. *nitor, elegantia* (= — as regards outward appearance and manners), *munditia, munditiæ* (= cleanliness).

neat-cattle, n. *armenta, -orum.* **neatherd**, n. *armentarius.*

nebula, n. *nebula.* **nebulous**, adj. *nebulosus.*

necessaries, n. *res quibus carēre non possumus, res quibus homines utuntur, res ad vitam necessariae, usus vitae necessarii, quae sunt ad vivendum necessaria, quae ad victum cultumque pertinent* (for our daily sustenance; e.g. wheat, wood, and other —, *frumentum lignaque et cetera necessaria usibus*). **necessary**, adj. *necessarius*; — things, *res necessariae* (in gen.); to provide with everything —, *omnibus rebus ornare atque instruĕre*, or simply *ornare atque instruĕre*; it is —, *necessarium est*; it is — to, etc., or that, etc., *opus est* (gen. with infin., sometimes but not often with *ut* and subj. mood), *necesse est* (with accus. and infin., or with subj. mood; see Must); *est quod* or *cur* (= there is a reason why); despatch is —, *maturato* or *properato opus est, properes* or *festines necesse est* (= it is — for us to be quick), *est quod festines* or *festinemus* (= it is desirable to be quick); if it should be —, *si usus fuerit, si quis usus venerit, si res postularit* (= if circumstances require it); I consider it — to do a certain thing, *alqd faciendum puto, necesse est me alqd facĕre* (= I must necessarily do a thing). Adv. *necessario, utique* (= at any rate); often by *necesse est* with subjunctive mood (e.g. out of dissipation must — come avarice, *ex luxuriâ exsistat avaritia necesse est*). **necessitarian**, n. *qui omnia fato fieri putat.* **necessitate**, v.tr. by *cogĕre*; see Oblige. **necessity**, n. **1**, *necessitas*; to be placed in the —, *cogi* with *ut*, etc. (= to see, find oneself compelled), *necessario cogi* with infin. (= to find oneself necessarily compelled); if anyone should be placed in this —, *si quae necessitas hujus rei alci obvenerit*; to perceive the — of a thing, *vidēre alqd necessarium esse*; **2**, = need; see Want.

neck, n. **1**, = part of an animal's body, or of the human body, *collum, cervix* (before Aug. almost always used in the pl., *cervices*), *gula, fauces, -ium* (= throat, gullet); fig. to bend anyone's —, *animum* or *ferociam alcjs frangĕre*; to bend anyone's — under the yoke of servitude, *alci jugum servitutis injungĕre*; **2**, = a long, narrow tract of land, *cervix* (e.g. *Peloponesi, Plin.*), *isthmus* or *isthmos*; **3**, = the long, slender part of a vessel, plant, instrument, *collum, cervix*, or pl. *cervices* (of a bottle, etc.)*; os, oris*, n. (= opening of a bottle, etc.). **neck-cloth**, n. *focale, -is*, n. **necklace**, n. *monile, -is, torques* (*torquis*), *-quis*, m.

necromancer, n. *qui animas mortuorum excitat.*

nectar, n. *nectar.*

need, I. n. = occasion for something, *necessitas*; there is — of anything, *alqâ re opus est.* **II.** v.tr. **1**, = to be without, *alqâ re carēre, egēre*; **2**, = to want, *alqd requirēre, desiderare, alci opus est alqâ re*; it —s a strong man to do this, *strenui est hoc facĕre.* **needful**, adj. *necessarius.* **needless**, adj. see Unnecessary. **needy**, adj. of persons, = having but scanty means to live upon (opp. *locuples, copiosus*), *egens, indigens, inops* (of persons; see Poor), comb. *pauper et tenuis, tenuis atque egens.* **neediness**, n. *rei familiaris angustiae* (in a higher degree, *rei familiaris inopia*), *egestas, indigentia* (= want), *inopia* (= want of what is necessary); see Poverty.

needle, n. *acus, -ūs*, f. **needlework**, n. *opus acu factum.*

nefarious, adj. *nefarius*; see Abominable, Wicked. Adv. *nefarie.*

negation, I. n. *negatio.* II. adj. *negans, privans.*

neglect, I. v.tr. *neglegere* (*neglig-*), *deesse alci rei* (= to — doing a thing), *intermittĕre* (= to intermit, discontinue for a time, e.g. studies, *studia*), *omittĕre* (= to omit, give up altogether), *deserĕre* (= to have nothing more to do with anyone). II. or **negligence,** n. *neglegentia* (*neglig-*) (= want of attention), *indiligentia* (= want of accuracy), *incuria* (= a want of the care which one ought to bestow upon a thing), *neglectio* (= act of neglecting), by a participle (e.g. through the — of everything else, *relictis rebus omnibus*). **neglectful, negligent,** adj. *neglegens* (*neglig-*), *indiligens* ; see CARELESS.

negotiate, v.tr. *agĕre alqd, agĕre de alqâ re,* or with *ut* (= to speak about a thing ; with anyone, *cum alqo*) ; to — a peace, *agĕre de condicionibus pacis* or *de pace* ; to — with anyone for a thing, *colloqui cum alqo de alqâ re* (by word of mouth), *colloqui per internuntios cum alqo et de alqâ re mentionem facĕre* (by intermediators). **negotiation,** n. *actio de alqâ re* (e.g. *de pace,* before a war breaks out), *pactio* (= treaty), *condiciones* (= conditions of a treaty), *colloquium* (= counsel between two generals by word of mouth) ; to break off the —s for anything, *infectâ pace dimittĕre legatos, dimittĕre pacis internuntios.* **negotiator,** n. *internuntius conciliator* (e.g. *pacis*), *legatus* (= ambassador).

negro, n. *Aethiops, Afer.* **negress,** n. *femina Aethiops, Afra.*

neigh, v.intr. *hinnire, hinnītum edĕre.* **neighing,** n. *hinnītus, -ūs.*

neighbour, n. in gen. *vicinus,* fem. *vicina* (of a house, farm, place), *finitimus, confinis* (= close to the boundary), *propinquus* (who stands, sits, etc., next to a person) ; to be a —, *vicinum esse.* **neighbouring,** adj. *vicinus, propinquus, confinis* (of states), *proximus* ; — country, *terra vicina* or *finitima* (= — territory), *civitas finitima* (= a — state). **neighbourhood,** n. *vicinia, vicinitas* (= the relation of neighbours to each other), *propinquitas* (opp. *longinquitas*) ; — neighbours, *vicini* (e.g. all the — sees him, *omnes vicini eum vident*). **neighbourly,** adj. *vicinis conveniens* or *dignus, ut decet vicinum.*

neither, I. pron. *neuter* ; in — direction, on — side, *neutro.* II. conj. *nec .. nec, neque ... neque, neve* (*neu*, .. *neve* (*neu*).

nephew, n. *filius fratris* (= brother's son), *filius sororis* (= sister's son).

ne-plus-ultra, n. *quod optimum est.*

nepotism, n. by *qui suos colit.*

nereid, n. *Nereis.*

nerve, n. 1, *nervus* (= sinew, not class. in modern sense) ; 2, fig. *nervi* (of oratory, etc.) ; see VIGOUR. **nervous,** adj. 1, = nervy, *nervosus* (lit. of limbs of the body ; then = full of vigour, of the style of a writer, speaker, and of the writer or speaker himself) ; 2, = of weak nerves, perhaps *infirmus, imbecillis, debilis* ; see WEAK ; 3, = frightened, *timidus* ; see TIMID. Adv. = vigorously, *nervose, infirme, timide.* **nervousness** n. 1, = strength (in speech, etc.), *nervi* ; 2, see WEAKNESS ; 3, fig. perhaps *animus infirmus, imbecillus* ; 4, *timor* ; see FEAR.

nest, n. *nidus* ; a little —, *nidulus* ; to build a —, *nidum facĕre,* (*con*)*fingĕre, nidificare.* **nestle,** v.intr. in *gremio alcjs esse* (= to lie in the lap), *alqm amplecti* (= to embrace) ; see EMBRACE. **nestling,** n. *pullus.*

net, I. n. in gen. *rete, -is,* or *reticulum* (made of fine thread with meshes) ; to knit a —, *reta* or *reticulum texĕre ;* = an ornament for the head, *reticulum ;* a — for catching fish, *rete,* † *funda, jaculum, everriculum* (= a drag- —) ; a — for catching birds, *rete, plaga,* or in pl. *plagae* ; *casses, -ium* (for catching animals). II. v.tr. *reti capĕre ;* see above.

nettle, n. *urtica* (= stinging —), *galeopsis, lamium* (= dead —) (Plin.). **nettled,** adj. *iratus.*

neuter, adj. — gender, *neuter, neutralis* (Quint.). **neutral,** adj. *medius, neutrius partis,* comb. *medius et neutrius partis, qui est in neutris partibus, non in alterius, ullius partem inclinatus* (in gen.), *otiosus* (= one who remains quiet) ; to be —, *medium esse, in neutris partibus esse, neutram partem sequi, non alterius, ullius partis esse ;* to be perfectly —, *nullius partis esse ;* to remain —, *medium se gerĕre, neutri parti se adjungĕre.* **neutrality,** n. *neutrius partis* or *neutrarum partium studium,* in the connexion of the sentence also simply *quies* or *otium* (= the state of quietness). **neutralize,** v.tr. see COUNTERBALANCE ; to — a state, *facĕre ut regio neutrius partis sit.*

never, adv. *numquam* (*nunquam*), *non umquam, nullo tempore ;* that he would either return home as a pontifex or —, *domum se nisi pontificem non reversurum ;* as a strong negation, *minime, minime vero, minime gentium.* **nevertheless,** adv. *nihilominus, nihilo setius,* (*at*)*tamen ;* see HOWEVER.

new, adj. *novus* (of what did not exist before, opp. *antiquus* = what has already been in existence a long time) ; in a wider sense also = not customary hitherto, unusual, unheard of, as synonymous with *inauditus,* hence comb. *novus et inauditus ; recens* (of what has only been made recently, a short while ago, fresh, young, opp. *antiquus,* what existed in former times) ; also comb. *recens ac novus* or *novus ac recens* (to express both the newness of the thing itself and the short existence of it) ; what is still — to a person (= unaccustomed), *insolitus* (e.g. dwelling, *domicilium*) ; is there anything —? *num quidnam novi ?* **new-born,** adj. *recens natus* (Plaut.), *catuli recentes* (= puppies, Var.). **new-comer,** n. *advena,* m. and f. ; see STRANGER. **new-fangled,** adj. *mirus* (= strange), *novus* (= new), *inauditus* (= unheard of). **new-fashioned,** adj. *novus* or *novo ritu.* **newly,** adv. *nuper, modo,* (= lately) *recens* (ante and post class.) ; see LATELY. **newness,** n. *novitas, insolentia* (of what is uncommon). **news,** n. *alqd novi, novae res, nuntius ;* what —? *quid novi ?* that is no — to me, *mihi nihil novi affers.* **newspaper,** n. *acta publica, -orum ;* see JOURNAL.

newt, n. *lacertus, lacerta* (= lizard).

next, I. adj. *proximus ;* in the — year, *proximo* or *insequenti anno.* II. adv. *deinceps, deinde, post haec, postea* (= afterwards). III. prep. see NEAR.

nib, n. = point of a pen, *acumen.*

nibble, v.intr. *admordēre, ambedēre* (= to gnaw at), *gustare* (= to taste).

nice, adj. 1, = delicious, *suavis, dulcis ;* 2, = fastidious, by *delicatus ;* 3, of judgment, etc., *accuratus, diligens, subtilis ;* see ACCURATE. Adv. *suaviter, delicate, accurate, diligenter, subtiliter.* **niceness, nicety,** n. 1, of taste, etc., *suavitas, dulcitas* (rare) ; 2, *fastidium ;* 3, *diligentia, subtilitas ;* to a —, *ad unguem.*

niche, n. *aedicula* (for statues).

nick, n. in the — of time, *in* (*ipso*) *tempore, opportunissime.* **nickname,** I. n. *nomen* or *nomen per ludibrium datum.* II. v.tr. *nomen alci per ludibrium dare.*

niece, n. *fratris filia* (= brother's daughter), *sororis filia* (= sister's daughter).

niggardly, adj. see MISERLY. **niggardliness,** n. see MISERLINESS.

night, n. *nox, tenebrae* (= darkness); till —, *in noctem;* by —, *nocte, noctu, nocturno tempore;* early in the —, *concubiâ nocte;* in the dead of —, *nocte intempestâ.* **night-cap,** n. *galerus;* see CAP. **night-dress, nightgown, night-shirt,** n. *vestis nocturna.* **nightfall,** n. see EVENING, NIGHT. **nightingale,** n. *luscinia.* **nightlight,** n. see LAMP. **nightly,** adj. *nocturnus.* **nightmare,** n. *suppressio nocturna* (Plin.). **nightshade,** n. *solanum* (Plin.).

nimble, adj. *mobilis;* see LIGHT, QUICK, SWIFT.

nimbus, n. † *radii.*

nine, adj. *novem;* — times, *novie(n)s.* **nineteen,** adj. *undeviginti,* distrib. *undeviceni.* **nineteenth,** adj. *undevicesimus, nonus decimus.* **ninety,** adj. *nonaginta,* distrib. *nonageni.* **ninth,** adj. *nonus.*

nipple, n. *papilla.*

nitre, n. see SALTPETRE.

no, I. adv. *non, minime vero, minime . . . . quidem* (= —, not at all), *im(m)o, im(m)o vero, im(m)o enimvero, im(m)o potius* (= —, rather to the contrary); instead of our — in answer to a question, we generally repeat the verb of the preceding question (e.g. is your brother within? — ! *istne frater intus? non est?* you are not angry, I hope? *non iratus es?* — ! *non sum iratus!* don't you believe that? *an tu haec non credis?* —, not at all ! *minime vero!* are we at fault then? *num igitur peccamus?* —, not you ! *minime vos quidem!* so then you deceive him? *viccine hunc decipis?* — ! on the contrary he deceives me, *im(m)o enimvero hic me decipit;* — ! that is not it, ye judges; — ! it is not indeed ! *non est ita, judices! non est profecto !);* to say yes or —, *aut etiam aut non respondēre;* one says yes, the other —, *hic ait, ille negat;* to say — to anything that is offered us, to decline, *abnuēre* or *recusare alqd* or *de alqâ re, negare se alqd facturum esse.* **II. (none),** adj. *nullus, nemo (nullus* of persons and things, *nemo* of persons only), *non ullus, non quisquam* (= not one, if a greater stress is to be laid upon the negative; the former as an adj., the latter as a pronoun), *neuter* (= neither, must always be used if we speak of two individuals or of two parties); if *nullus* and *nemo* are used in a partitive sense, that is, if — stands in opp. to the remaining parts or the whole, they govern the genit. (e.g. — mortal, *nemo mortalium;* — animal is more prudent, *nulla beluarum prudentior est);* the genit. may also sometimes be expressed by a circumloc. with *de, ex* (e.g. — man of our army was killed, *nemo de nostris cecidit);* sometimes it would appear that instead of *nullus* and *nemo* we use in Latin *nihil* (with genit. when it stands for *nullus*) ; however, *nihil* expresses the negative more strongly than *nullus* = none at all (e.g. there is — one (at all) more miserable than I am, and — one more happy than Catulus, *nihil me infortunatius, nihil fortunatius est Catulo;* to have — doubt (at all), *nihil dubitationis habēre);* very often we use — when the negative does not refer to anything in general, but to something particular; in this case, which takes place principally when — belongs as an adj. to a noun or refers as a predicate to a noun previously mentioned, we use in Latin the negative *non* instead of *nullus* (e.g. you ordered them — ship, *navem iis non imperasti).* We likewise use *non* in Latin for

— when the object in English is expressed by a verbal noun (e.g. to have — fear, *non timēre;* to feel — doubt, *non dubitare;* to feel — hatred against anyone, *non odisse alqm,* etc.); — one, *nemo;* at — place, *nusquam;* at — time, *numquam (nunq-), nullo tempore;* and at — time, *nec umquam;* in — respect, *nihil;* in — wise, *nullo modo, nullâ ratione.* **nobody,** n. *nemo, nullus* (= no; as the genit. of *nemo, neminis* was little used, *nullius* was used instead), *nemo homo;* and — *nec ullus, nec quisquam;* that —, *ne quid;* a — *terrae filius.* **nowhere,** adv. *nusquam.*

noble, I. adj. 1, by birth, *nobilis, generosus, nobili* or *illustri loco natus;* 2, morally, *ingenuus, magnanimus, praeclarus, honestus, liberalis, elatus, excelsus.* Adv. — born, *nobili loco natus* or *ortus, ingenue, praeclare, honeste, liberaliter, elate.* **II.** n. *unus e nobilibus,* or by *homo nobilis* or *generosus;* in pl. the nobles, *optimates, nobiles.* **nobility,** n. 1, by birth, *nobilitas, genus nobile, generosa stirps, -pis;* — by lofty position, *summo loco natum esse;* 2, — the nobles; see NOBLE, II. ; 3, moral —, *magnanimitas, animus ingenuus,* etc. ; see NOBLE, I. 2.

nocturnal, adj. *nocturnus.*

nod, I. v.intr. *nutare;* to — in approbation, *annuēre;* to —, = to doze, *nictare.* **II.** n. *nutus, -ûs.*

noise, I. n. *strepitus, -ûs* (= loud —), *fremitus, -ûs* (= low, hollow —, of bees, horses, etc.), *crepitus, -ûs* (= clattering, clashing), *sonitus, -ûs* (= loud, clear sounds, e.g. of a trumpet), *stridor* (= the whizzing, e.g. of a saw), *fragor* (= the crackling, e.g. of a house that falls), *murmur* (= murmuring of water), *turba* (= confusion), *tumultus, -ûs* (= uproar with clamour; then in general any — caused by a mob or by a single individual), *convicium;* to make a —, *strepere, strepitum edēre, fremēre, concrepare, strepitum facēre alqâ re, tumultum facēre, tumultuari* (= to shout, also in a camp, when the enemy is approaching), *clamare, clamitare* (= to cry with a loud voice) ; to march out with great —, *magno strepitu et tumultu castra movēre.* **II.** v.tr. to — abroad ; see PUBLISH. **noiseless,** adj. *quietus* (= quiet), *tacitus* (= silent). Adv. *quiete, tacite, (cum) silentio* (= in silence). **noiselessness,** n. *silentium* (e.g. of the night, *noctis*). **noisy,** adj. *strepens, fremens, tumultuosus* (= full of shout and uproar, e.g. *contio*), † *argutus.* Adv. *cum strepitu.*

noisome, adj. *foedus, teter.*

nomades, n.pl. *nomādes* (νομάδες), in pure Latin, *vagae gentes.* **nomadic,** adj. by the genit. *nomādum,* or by *vagus.*

nomenclature, n. *index nominum* or *nomen.*

nominal, adj. and adv. opp. to real, *nomine, verbo, per speciem, specie.*

nominate, v.tr. *nominare, dicēre, facēre, designare, (con)salutare* (= to greet as), *creare;* see APPOINT. **nomination,** n. *nominatio, designatio.* **nominative,** n. *casus, -ûs, nominativus* or *rectus.* **nominee,** n. use *nominatus* (e.g. the — of Caesar, *a Caesare nominatus*).

non, in comp. (e.g. —-residence, see ABSENCE). **nonentity,** n. *nihil;* perfect eloquence is no —, *est certe alqd consummata eloquentia.* **nonsense, I.** n. *ineptiae;* to talk —, *inepta dicēre, aliena loqui.* **II.** interj. *nugas' gerrae!* **nonsensical,** adj. see FOOLISH.

none, adj. see NO.

nook, n. see ANGLE, CORNER.

noon, n. = midday, *meridies.*

noose, n. *laqueus.*

nor, conj. *neque;* see NEITHER.

normal, adj. see REGULAR.

north, or **northern,** or **northernly, I.** adj. septentrionalis (septem-), aquilonaris; — lights, lumen a septentrionibus oriens; — wind, †Boreas, septentriones venti. **II.** n. septentrio, or pl. septentriones, †aquilo, †Boreas. **north-east,** adj. inter septentriones et orientem spectans; the — wind, Aquilo. **north pole,** n. †polus glacialis, gelidus, or simply †polus (Ov.) or axis (septentrionalis). **northwards,** adv. septentrionem versus. **north-west,** adj. inter septentriones et occasum solis spectans; — wind, Caurus (Cor-).

nose, n. nasus, nares, -ium (=nostrils, hence the —, an organ for breathing and smelling; also the sing., naris, if we speak of one nostril); to blow the —, nares or se emungēre; to turn up the —, naribus contemptum or fastidium ostendēre; to turn up the — at anyone (from contempt), alqm suspendēre naso (Hor.).

nosegay, n. fasciculus.

nostrils, n. nares, -ium, f.

nostrum, n. medicamentum.

not, adv. non, haud (the former in gen., the latter only in certain comb., chiefly before adv. and adj., to modify their meaning, e.g. — much, haud multum; — far, haud longe); nullus, as frequently used by modern writers, in ancient writers not merely = non, but = — at all (e.g. Philotimus non modo nullus venit, sed, etc., Cic.); minus (= less, notas strong as non), nihil (stronger than —, = by no means), neutiquam, haudquaquam, nequaquam, minime (also stronger than —), ne (expresses a request, wish, command, e.g. do — resist, if, etc., ne repugnatis, si, etc.; dare —, ne audeto); fac ne, with subjunctive mood (see LEST, etc.), or cave (ne) with subj. (= take care lest, etc.), or noli (with infin. = do — wish, all three only = an invitation, a request, etc., uttered in a modest manner, instead of ne; do — be tempted to, cave cupias; do — believe it, cave credas); in double prohibitions, neve (neu) ... neve (neu); after verbs of fearing, — = ut (e.g. vereor ut veniat = I fear that he will — come. In questions, — is expressed by annon (= perhaps —), when an affirmative answer is expected (e.g. did I — say perhaps that it would happen so? annon dixi hoc futurum?); or nonne, if we put a question with a view to convince anyone that we are right (e.g. what, does — the dog resemble the wolf? quid, canis nonne lupo similis?); by ne (enclit.), esp. with verbs that express a perception, if we are not certain whether the person spoken to perceives the thing (e.g. do you — see that in Homer Nestor makes a boast of his virtues? videsne ut apud Homerum saepissime Nestor de virtutibus praedicet?); by non, if we think that the person does — at all perceive the thing to which we wish to direct his attention (e.g. do you — see how great the danger is when, etc., non vides quanto periculo, etc., by num, when a negative answer is expected; — on any account, minime, minime gentium, fac or cave ne with subj., noli with infin.; — by any means, nullo pacto, nullo modo (= in no wise), nihil; — at all, neutiquam; — so very (before an adj. or adv.), haud or non ita (e.g. — so very far, haud (non) ita longe); — sufficiently, — quite, non satis, parum (= too little); — even, ne ... quidem (the word upon which the stress lies must be placed between ne and quidem, e.g. I do — even consider this profitable, ne utile quidem hoc esse arbitror); so, = — in this manner, non ita, non sic; = less, minus (e.g. — to stray so far, minus late vagari; but —, non vero, neque vero, non autem (the second in passing to something else; non autem sometimes separated by a word which is put between, e.g. but I can—tell you, non possum autem dicēre; if "but —" is merely used to introduce an antithesis, non alone is used, e.g. I mean the father, but — the son, dico patrem, non filium); — either, nec or neque (e.g. Epicurus says, we do — require understanding, nor words either, Epicurus negat opus esse ratione, neque disputatione; fortune does — give us virtue, and therefore does — take it away either, virtutem fortuna non dat, ideo nec detrahit); but also ... —, nec ... quidem (the word upon which the stress lies is placed between nec and quidem, especially in opp. to something else, e.g. but also Jugurtha did — remain quiet in the meantime, sed nec Jugurtha quidem quietus interea); and —, et non (when the negative refers to one word only, as when the stress lies upon the negative), neque (to connect two sentences or two parts of the same sentence, e.g. via certa et non longa = a safe road and one that is — very long, but via certa neque longa = a road both safe and short); and so —, and therefore —, ac non (to express an inference, e.g. there was nobody who would have taken him to be accused of a crime, and who would — therefore think that he had been condemned over and over again, nemo erat qui illum reum, ac non millies condemnatum arbitraretur); and — rather, ac non potius, or simply ac non; and — less, atque etiam, itemque (= and so also, likewise also); to say —, by negare; my friend said that he would — do it, meus amicus negabat se hoc facturum esse; in connexion with an adj., — is often rendered in Latin by one word, containing — and the adj., e.g. — prudent, amens (= silly), demens (= foolish); — pleasant, injucundus, ingratus.

notable, adj. see REMARKABLE.

notary, n. scriba (publicus).

notation, n. inscriptio alcjs rei (upon); = the act of noting down, (per)scriptio, subscriptio (= the writing down of one's name, nominis). **note, I.** n. 1, in music, soni or vocis signum; to play or sing from —s, ex libello canēre (not from memory); 2, = letter, epistula (epistola), lit-(t)erae. **II.** v.tr. 1, by scribēre, exarare (= to — down, in letters of Cic.); 2, see NOTICE. **notes,** n. pl., dictata, -orum (= dictations of a professor written down by the student). **note-book,** n. adversaria, commentarii (Plin. Min.), pugillares (Plin.); see JOURNAL. **noted,** adj. see FAMOUS. **noteworthy, notable,** adj. see REMARKABLE. **notice, I.** n. observatio, animadversio, notatio, comb. notatio et animadversio; to take —, animadvertēre; to give —, see PROCLAIM, DISMISS. **II.** v.tr. animadvertēre; see REMARK. **noticeable,** adj. see REMARKABLE. **notify,** v.tr. alqm alcjs rei certiorem facēre, alqd (de)nuntiare; see INFORM. **notification,** n. promulgatio (of laws), denuntiatio (in gen.). **note-of-hand,** n. chirographum.

notch, I. n. see INDENT, INCISION. **II.** v.tr. striare (in architecture), incidēre (= to make incisions, e.g. in a tree).

nothing, n. nihil (nil), nihilum, nulla res; since nihil must be considered as a noun, it is used with adjectives or with a gen. (e.g. — of the kind, nihil tale; to think — mean, nihil humile cogitare; he has done — new, nihil novi fecit; to anticipate — good, nihil boni divinare); to rise from —, ex nihilo oriri; out of — comes —, de nihilo nihil fit, de nihilo nihil creari potest; to be as good as —, pro nihilo esse; with comparatives, nihilo, e.g. — greater, nihilo majus; — less, nihil minus, nihil vero minus; — but, nihil nisi (but not nihil quam); — else but, *nihil aliud nisi, nihil aliud quam* (the latter if in the words preceding, *tam*, so much, is to be understood) ; and —, *nec quidquam*; I have — to fear, *nihil est quod timeam* ; I have — to say in reply, *nihil est quod respondeam* ; to care — for, *alqd non flocci* or *parvi facĕre*, or *pro nihilo ducĕre* ; good for —, *inutilis* (= useless); *nequam* (of a good-for- — fellow).

notice, n., **notify,** v.tr., see under No-TATION.

notion, n. see CONCEPTION, IDEA.

notorious, adj. **1,** = well known, *notus, manifestus, clarus, tritus, celebratus,* comb. *tritus ac celebratus* (= commonplace); **2,** in a bad sense, *insignis* or *infamis alqâ re,* or by superl. (e.g. a — evil-doer, *homo sceleratissimus*). Adv. *manifestum est,* with acc. and infin. **notoriety,** n. *fama* (in gen.), *infamia* (in bad sense).

notwithstanding, adv. *nihilominus* (or in two words, *nihilo minus*), *tamen, attamen, verumtamen,* often not expressed after *etsi,* etc. = although.

nought, n. see NOTHING.

noun, n. *nomen* (Gram.); see SUBSTANTIVE.

nourish, v.tr. *nutrire.* **nourishing,** adj. *in quo multum alimenti est, magni cibi* (= containing much nutritious matter, opp. *parvi cibi*), *valens* (= strong, opp. *imbecillus, infirmus*). **nourishment,** n. *alimentum.*

novel, I. adj. *novus*; see NEW, UNCOMMON. **II.** n. *fabula, fabella* (= a short story). **novelist,** n. *qui fabulas componit.* **novelty,** n. 1, as quality, *novitas, insolentia* ; 2, = a new thing, *res nova.*

November, n. *(mensis) Novembris* or *November.*

novice, n. *novicius, novellus* (= one who has just arrived, established himself, settled at a place, Liv.); a — in military service, *tiro, miles, -ĭtis, novus* (opp. *miles veteranus*) ; a — in anything, *tiro* or *rudis,* or comb. *tiro et rudis* in *alqâ re* (= a mere beginner in anything), *peregrinus* or *hospes,* or comb. *peregrinus atque hospes in alqâ re* (= inexperienced). **novitiate,** n. *tempus ad alcjs facultates experiendum constitutum* or *tempus tirocinii.*

now, adv. *nunc* (opp. *tunc*; **at this moment,** the time present with the writer, as *tunc* refers to time present in regard to the person or thing referred to) ; *jam* (a particle of transition, up to —, from —), *hoc tempore, in praesentiâ, in hoc tempore, in praesenti ; hodie* (= to-day) ; *nunc demum* (that is, — for the first time, — at length, in contradistinction to *tum* or *tunc primum*) ; — especially, *(nunc) cum maxime ; but* —, *modo ; just —, nunc ipsum, hoc ipso tempore ; from* —, *jam inde, ab hoc tempore ;* — (as a particle of connexion or inference), *igitur,* or by a periphrasis, *quae cum ita sunt* (= as these things are so). As a particle of mere transition, *autem* or *vero* or *quidem, equidem, sed ;* but sometimes no particle at all is used, e.g. whatever he may — say, *quidquid dicat;* you may — (or then) be present or not, *adsis necne.* As a particle of affirmation or concession use *vero* or *nunc ; nunc vero,* — in fact ; *nunc autem,* = but now. With a question, *quid vero?* — what? or *quid autem?* — what in the world? *quid tandem?* In exhortations, e.g. come —, *age, agite ;* — four years ago, *quat(t)uor abhinc annis, ante hos quatuor annos ;* — and then, *aliquando, nonnunquam (nonnumq-).* **nowadays,** adv. *hodie, hodierno tempore;* see Now.

nowhere, adv. *nusquam.*

nude, adj., **nudity,** n., see NAKED.

nudge, v.tr. *alci latus fodicare* (Hor.).

nugatory, adj. *nugatorius;* see VAIN.

nugget, n. perhaps *later, -ĕris,* m. (Var.).

nuisance, n. by *molestus* (e.g. the man is a —, *homo molestus est*).

null, adj. *vanus* (= not to be depended on, e.g. *promissum*), *inanis* (= without a meaning, e.g. *promissum*), *fut(f)ilis* (= futile, e.g. *sententia,* opinion), *nullus* (= as good as nothing, e.g. *nulla est haec amicitia*), *fragilis* (= fragile), *caducus* (= perishable) ; to declare anything — and void, *alqd irritum esse jubere, alqd rescindĕre* (= to rescind, e.g. a will) ; fig. by *nihil valēre, nihil auctoritatis habēre* (= to have no authority), *nulla alcjs habetur ratio* (= anyone is not considered at all). **nullify,** v.tr. *ad irritum redigĕre.* **nullity,** n. *vanitas, inanitas, fragilitas ;* see INVALIDITY.

numb, I. adj. *torpens;* to be —, *torpēre;* to grow —, *torpescĕre.* **II.** v.tr. *alqm torpore afficĕre.* **numbness,** n. *torpor.*

number, I. n. 1, *numerus* (in most senses of the Eng. = several people or things ; mere — or cypher, grammatical —, musical measure); an equal —, *numerus par;* unequal —, *numerus impar ;* to be one of a —, *esse numero* or *in numero ;* **2,** = many, *copia, multitudo,* or by *multus* (e.g. a — of men, *multi homines*). **II.** v.tr. *numerum inire; alqd numerare, dinumerare, numerum alcjs rei inire* or *exsequi* or *efficĕre, computare* (= to reckon), *(enumerando) percensēre* (= to go over in numbering) ; to — the stars, *stellas dinumerare ;* to — on the fingers, *numerare digitis* or *per digitos, computare digitis ;* to — among the gods, *referre in numerum deorum.* **numbering,** n. — of the people, *census, -ûs;* see CENSUS. **numberless,** adj. *innumerus, innumerabilis.* **numerable,** adj. *numerabilis.* **numerical,** adj. — signs, *numerorum notae* or *signa, -orum.* Adv. *numero.* **numerous,** adj. *creber* (= frequent), *celeber* (= full of people), *frequens* (= quite full), *multo, magnus, multiplex* (= manifold) ; a — assembly of the senate, *frequens senatus.* Adv. *magno numero.*

numismatics, n. and adj. *nummorum doctrina.*

nun, n. *monacha, nonna* (Eccl.).

nuptial, adj. *nuptialis, genialis* (e.g. *lectus*); see CONNUBIAL. **nuptials,** n. *nuptiae ;* see WEDDING.

nurse, I. n. 1, *nutrix* (in gen. or = wet- —), *nutricula* (dimin.) ; a sick —, by verb *quae alqm curat;* 2, fig. *altrix.* **II.** v.tr. 1, *nutrire* (= to suckle), *gestare* (= to carry in the arms), *fovēre* (= to fondle); 2, in sickness, *alqm curare, alci assidēre.* **nursery,** n. *parvulorum diaeta ;* — in a garden, *seminarium* (lit. and fig. ; *plantarium,* Plin.) ; — of vines, *vitiarium.* **nursery - gardener,** n. *qui seminarium habet.* **nursling,** n. *alumnus* (= adopted son) ; *alumna* (= adopted daughter) ; see DARLING.

nurture, n. see EDUCATION.

nut, n. *nux;* to crack a —, *nucem frangĕre;* you have only one more — to crack, but a hard one, *unus tibi restat nodus,* sed Herculaneus (Sen.). **nutshell,** n. lit. *putamen;* fig. to put the thing in a —, *ne multa dicam.*

nutriment, nutrition, n. see FOOD, NOURISH.

nymph, n. *nympha, Nerëis, -idis,* f. (= sea —), *Oreas, -ădis,* f. (= mountain —), *Dryas, -ădis,* f., and *Hamadryas* (= tree —), forest —), *Naïs* and *Naïas* (= river —).

O.

ô ! oh ! interj. *o!* (in gen., as exclamation whenever we feel affected), *proh !* (chiefly implying indignation), *heu !* (in complaining, lamenting), *ohe !* expressive of weariness after having attended to a thing for some time) ; after an interjection we use either the voc., when we invoke the thing itself, or the accus., when we say, e.g. —, unfortunate that I am ! *o* (or *heu) me miserum* or *me perditum !* or *me miserum !* —, certainly, *sane quidem, scilicet quidem* (in gen. Ironically) ; —, no, *minime vero ;* —, I shall come, *ego vero veniam ;* —, it is already done, *atqui jam factus est.*

oak, n. *quercus, -ûs,* f. (= the common —) ; of —, oaken, *querneus* or *quernus, querceus* (= of the common —). **oak-apple,** n. *galla* (Plin.).

oakum, n. *stuppa ;* made of —, *stuppeus.*

oar, n. *remus* (in gen., = — of a ship, boat), *scalmus* (= a round piece of wood, a thole, to which the — was fastened ; then fig. for the — itself), *nullum scalmum vidit,* he saw no —, i.e. boat ; † *palma* (lit. = blade) ; bank of —s, seat for rowers, *transtrum,* also *sedile ;* hole for an —, *columbarium* (late) ; stroke of the —, *pulsus, -ûs, remorum.*

oath, n. *jusjurandum,* gen. *jurisjurandi* (= the — taken by subjects and soldiers), *sacramentum* (military), *religio, jusjurandi verba* (= the form of an —) ; a false —, *falsum jusjurandum, perjurium ;* to put one to his —, *jusjurandum ab algo exigère, jusjurandum alci deferre ;* to swear or take an —, *jusjurandum dare* or *jurare, sacramentum* or *sacramento dicère* (Liv.) ; to swear a false —, *falsum jurare, pejerare* or *perjurare ;* to take the truest —, *verissimum jusjurandum jurare, ex animi sententiâ jurare ;* to take the — (i.e. according to the usual form), *verbis conceptis jurare* (so *pejerare) ;* to swear allegiance, *in verba alcjs* (to his dictation) *jurare* (used of citizens, officials, and soldiers ; also fig.), *sacramentum dicère apud alqm, sacramento* or *sacramentum dicère alci* (of soldiers) ; to administer the — of fidelity, *alqm in sua verba jusjurandum adigère ;* to refuse to take the —, *sacramentum detrectare* (of soldiers) ; to bind by —, *jurejurando alqm a(d)stringère, obstringère, obligare ;* to bind oneself by an —, *se jurejurando obstringère.*

oats, n. *avêna.* **oatmeal-porridge,** n. *avenae puls.* **oatmeal-gruel,** n. *cremor avenae.*

obdurate, adj. see OBSTINATE.

obedient, adj. *oboediens, dicto audiens, dicto audiens atque oboediens, obtemperans, obsequens* (all with dat.). Adv. *oboedienter.*

obedience, n. *oboedientia* (= submission to masters, etc.), *obtemperatio* (to anything, *alci rei ;* = the act of complying with, *alci rei ;* = the act of complying with, e.g. the laws, *legibus), obsequium, obsequentia* (= resignation to another's will, fulfilling instructions), *officium* (inasmuch as it is the result of duty to superiors, the allegiance of tributary states) ; to remain in —, *in officio retinêri* or *continêri ;* to bring back to —, *ad obsequium redigère.* **obey,** v.tr. *alci parère, alci obtemperare, alci oboedire* (strictly), *oboedire* (obed-), *dicto audientem esse* (= to — anyone's commands), *obtemperare* (= to comply with anyone's wishes), *obsequi* (= to yield to anyone's advice), *alqm audire, alci auscultare* (= to listen to anyone's entreaties), *alci morem gerère, morigerari* (= to gratify), very often comb. to increase the force, *parère et oboedire, oboedire et parère, obtemperare et oboedire, obsequi et oboedire, dicto audientem atque oboedientem esse.*

obeisance, n. see Bow.

obelisk, n. *obeliscus* (Plin.).

obelus, n. *obelus* (late) *vergula censoria* (Quint.).

obese, adj. see FAT.

obituary, n. perhaps *ratio Libitinae ;* to be registered in the —, *in rationem Libitinae venire* (Suet.).

object, I. n. 1, = something presented to the mind by the senses, *res ;* the —s around us, *res externae ;* to be the — of is variously rendered ; by *esse* and dat. (e.g. to be an — of care, hatred, contempt to anyone, *alci esse curae, odio, contemptui),* by *esse* and *in* (e.g. to be an — of hatred with anyone, *in odio esse apud alqm ;* to become an — of hatred, *in odium venire, pervenire),* by nouns already involving the idea (e.g. — of love, *amor, deliciae ;* — of desire, *desiderium),* by circumloc. with verbs (e.g. to be the — of anyone's love, *ab algo amari, diligi) ;* 2, = ultimate purpose, *finis, -is,* m. (and f. mostly poet. or ante and post class.), *consilium,* by circumloc. with *id quod volo* or *cupio* (= the design) ; *propositum,* or by circumloc. with *quod specto* or *sequor* or *peto* (= end, aim) ; *finis* (= the main purpose, e.g. the — of a house is usefulness, *domus finis est usus ;* but not = *propositum* = the aim or — we have in view) ; the — of anything, *consilium alcjs rei* (in a subjective sense), *id cujus caus(s)â alqd facimus* (in an objective sense) ; with what —, *quo consilio ;* with the — of, *eo consilio ut ;* to have an —, *consilium sequi, certum alqd consilium proposuisse* (of persons), *agère, petère* (= to seek), *velle* or *spectare alqd* (= to regard, also of things) ; to have a great — in view, *magnum quidquam spectare* (of persons): the laws have this — in view, *hoc spectant leges, hoc volunt ;* to lose sight of the — one had in view (in a speech, etc.), *a proposito aberrare ;* to make anything one's —, *alqd sibi proponère ;* 3, in metaphysics, *quod sub sensus cadit.* **II.** v.tr. *contra dicère,* in *contrariam partem afferre* (= to have something to say on the other side), *respondère* (= to answer) ; I have nothing to — against it, *nihil impedio, non repugnabo* (with *quominus* and subj. ; also *ne,* and after a negative *quin,* with subj. *non recusabo quin* or *quominus) ;* but someone may —, *sed fortasse quispiam dixerit, dicat alqs forte ;* but one might —, simply *at* (enim). **objection,** n. *quod contra dicitur, excusatio* (= excuse against accusations and orders), *exceptio* (= exception taken in a law-court) ; without the least —, *sine morâ, sine ullâ dubitatione, haud contanter* (cunct-), *non dubitanter ;* to raise an —, *contra dicère ;* I'll hear no — ! *nihil audio !* (Com.) ; see also HINDRANCE. **objectionable,** adj. *malus* (= evil) ; see BAD. **objective,** adj. *sub sensus cadère* or *res externae ;* — case, *casus accusativus* (direct), *casus dativus* (indirect). Adv. *res externas* (e.g. the world) ; — considered, *res externas dico.* **objector,** n. *qui alqd alci contra dicit.*

objurgate, v.tr. *objurgare.*

oblation, n. see SACRIFICE.

oblige, v.tr. 1, = to constrain by moral force or necessity, or by law, *obligare alqm alci rei,* or with *ut ; alligare, obstringère* (strictly), *devincire* (so that we cannot escape it) ; also by *cogi* (e.g. he was —d (= compelled by force) to destroy himself, *coactus est ut vitâ se ipsâ privaret) ;* the Campanians were —d to march out at the gates, *coacti sunt Campani portis egredi ;* or by the active *cogère* (e.g. not as he wished, but as the will of the soldiers —d him to do, *non ut voluit, sed ut militum cogebat voluntas) ;* 2, = to do anyone a favour, *alqm sibi obligare* or *obstrin-*

ēre o1 *devincire* (by a friendly act, *beneficio*; by acts of kindness, *officiis*); to be very much —d to anyone, *alci multum* or *multa beneficia debēre*; I am very much —d to you (as answer), *gratissimum illud mihi fecisti*, or (in declining an offer) simply *benigne*. **obligation,** n. = what constitutes legal or moral duty, *officium, debitum, religio* (= moral —); I am under the —, *meum est, debeo;* to impose the — upon anyone, *imponēre alci officium, obligare* or *obstringēre alqm;* see DUTY. **obligatory,** adj. render by OBLIGE. **obliging,** adj. *humanus, comis* (= courteous), *facilis* (= easy), *officiosus* (= ready to oblige); an — letter, *lit(t)erae humaniter scriptae* or *humanitatis plenae;* see KIND. Adv. *humane, humaniter, comiter, facile, officiose*. **obligingness,** n. *humanitas, comitas, facilitas;* see COURTEOUSNESS.

oblique, adj. 1, *obliquus* (= slanting, opp. *rectus*); 2, fig. *per ambages;* 3, in gram. — cases, *casus obliqui; —* narrative, *oratio obliqua* (Quint.). Adv. *oblique, ex obliquo,* in *obliquum*. **obliquity,** n. *obliquitas, iniquitas;* see INIQUITY.

obliterate, v.tr. = to erase, *delēre* (lit. and fig.); see ERASE, BLOT OUT, EFFACE, DESTROY.

oblivion, n. *oblivio,* † *oblivium*. **oblivious,** adj. *immemor, obliviosus;* see FORGETFUL.

oblong, adj. *oblongus* (Plin.).

obloquy, n. *odium* (= hatred), *opprobrium, convicium, maledictum* (= abuse); see ABUSE.

obnoxious, adj. 1, = subject, *alci rei obnoxius;* 2, = hurtful, *noxius;* see HURTFUL.

obol, n. *obolus*.

obscene, adj. *obscenus;* see FOUL. Adv. *obscene*. **obscenity,** n. *obscenitas* (e.g. *verborum* or *orationis*); see FILTH, FILTHY.

obscure, I. adj. 1, lit. = without light; see DARK; 2, fig. = not easily understood, *obscurus* (e.g. *narratio*), *caecus* (e.g. *morbus, carmen), involutus* (= involved), *reconditus* (= hidden), *ambiguus, dubius* (= doubtful), *perplexus* (= confused, perplexing, e.g. *sermones, carmen), incertus* (= vague, e.g. *rumor), subobscurus* (= rather —, e.g. of an author); he is very —, *valde obscurus est* (of a philosopher, etc.); 3, = not noted, *obscurus*. Adv. *obscure, perplexe, ambigue, dubie; —* born, *obscuro loco natus.* **II.** v.tr. *obscurare* (lit. and fig.), *alci rei tenebras offundēre, obducēre* (fig. = to make indistinct). **obscurity,** n. 1, *obscuritas;* see DARKNESS; 2, fig. *obscuritas, oratio involuta,* etc.; see OBSCURE, 2; 3, of birth, *obscuritas, humilitas, ignobilitas*.

obsequies, n. see FUNERAL.

obsequious, adj. and adv. by *alci adulari* (= to flatter). **obsequiousness,** n. *adulatio*.

observe, v.tr. 1, *(ob)servare, asservare* (= carefully), *animadvertēre* (= to attend to a thing), *spectare, contemplari* (= to — as a quiet spectator), *considerare* (= to look at carefully); *to —* the enemy, *hostium consilia speculari* (= to spy out his plans); 2, = to keep to, maintain, *(ob)servare, conservare, custodire* (= to adhere strictly to a certain course), *colēre* (= to — duly); to — one's duty, *officium suum servare* (opp. *off. praetermittēre*); to — order, a custom, an oath, *ordinem, morem, jusjurandum (con)servare;* 3, = to remark; see REMARK, MENTION. **observance,** n. *mos* (= habit), *ritus, ūs* (= manner), *conservatio* (= maintenance); see HABIT. **observant,** adj. see OBEDIENT, ATTENTIVE, and under OBSERVE. **observation,** n. 1,

observatio, *animadversio* (= act of attending to); — of the stars, *observatio siderum; —* of nature, *notatio naturae et animadversio;* power of —, *ingenii acumen* or *acies* (= acuteness), *sagacitas* (= sagacity); 2, = remark, *dictum;* see REMARK. **observatory,** n. *specula astronomica.* **observer,** n. *custos, -ōdis,* m. and f. (= guard, keeper), *animadversor* (= who gives heed to, e.g. *vitiorum,* Cic.), *spectator* (= a looker-on), *speculator* (= who spies out; fem. *speculatrix*); an — of nature, *speculator venatorque naturae; —* of the sky and stars, *spectator caeli siderumque;* an acute —, *homo acutus, sagax* (of quick perception); a conscientious — of all his duties, *omnium officiorum observantissimus*.

obsolete, adj. *obsoletus* (lit. = worn out, cast off, e.g. *vestis;* fig. *verba), ab usu quotidiani sermonis jam diu intermissus* (= long since out of use in ordinary language), *ab ultimis et jam obliteratis temporibus repetītus* (= far-fetched from bygone times; both of words).

obstacle, n. *impedimentum.*

obstinate, adj. *pertinax* (of persons, and things which continue unabated, e.g. an illness), *pervicax* (= resolute), *obstinatus, offirmatus* (= steadfastly persevering, the latter in a bad sense); an — illness, *morbus longinquus* (= long); to observe an — silence, *obstinatum silentium obtinēre.* Adv. *pertinaciter, pervicaciter, obstinate, obstinato animo, offirmatā voluntate.* **obstinacy,** n. *pertinacia, pervicacia, obstinatio, animus obstinatus, voluntas offirmatior.*

obstreperous, adj. *tumultuosus.*

obstruct, v.tr. 1, = to block up, *obstruēre, obstare, officēre* (with dat.), *obsaepire* (obsep-), *intersaepire;* to — the light, *obstruēre* or *officēre luminibus alcjs;* 2, = to retard (e.g. progress), see HINDER, OPPOSE. **obstruction,** n. *impedimentum;* see STOPPAGE, HINDRANCE. **obstructive,** adj. *quod impedimento est, quod impedit, quod obstat et impedit.*

obtain, I. v.tr. *compotem fieri alcjs rei, potiri alqā re* (= to get possession of), *adipisci* (= to — what one desires), *alqd assequi, consequi* (by an effort), *nancisci* (by chance or through an opportune circumstance), *impetrare* (= to get what was requested), *obtinēre* (= to — and keep what we claimed), *auferre* (as the fruit of exertion), *acquirēre* (in addition to what one has), *exprimēre* (= to extort, e.g. money, *nummulos ab alqo);* to — by entreaties, *exorare* (anything from anyone, *alqd ab alqo*); to — the highest power, *rerum potiri.* **II.** v.intr., see PREVAIL. **obtaining,** n. *adeptio, impetratio* (of what we requested).

obtrude, v.tr. see INTRUDE.

obtuse, adj. *hebes* (dull; lit. of a sword, angle, fig. of persons, mental qualities, the senses, etc., e.g. *homo, ingenium), obtusus, retusus* (lit. = blunted, of a sword, angles, etc.; then fig. of things, e.g. *ingenium;* all three lit. and fig., opp. *acutus*), comb. *obtusus et hebes* (e.g scythe, *falx*). **obtuseness,** n. see DULNESS STUPIDITY.

obverse, n. (of a coin, opp. reverse), *nummus aversus.*

obviate, v.tr. *alci rei occurrēre* or *obviam ire* (= to prevent), *praecavēre alqd* (= to prevent by precaution); see HINDER.

obvious, adj. *apertus, manifestus, clarus, perspicuus;* see CLEAR, EVIDENT. Adv. *aperte, manifeste, clare, perspicue.*

occasion, I. n. 1, see TIME, OPPORTUNITY; 2, = incidental cause, *occasio, caus(s)a, auctor* (= author, of persons); to give an — for, *insam* dare or *praebēre alcjs rei* or with *ad alqd faciendum* (= to afford a handle for), *occasionem dare* or *praebēre alcjs rei* (e.g. *sui opprimendi*, of suppressing him), *locum dare* or *facēre alci rei* (= to give room for) ; on every —, *quotie(n)scumque* (*-cunque*) *potestas data est.* **II.** v.tr. *auctorem esse alcjs rei* (= to be the author of, e.g. a war, *belli ;* anyone's return, *alcjs reditūs*), *creare* (= to create, e.g. an error, *errorem ;* war, *bellum*), *movēre* (= to excite, e.g. laughter, *risum ;* war, *bellum*), *caus(s)am alcjs rei inferre* (= to give the first cause, e.g. for a quarrel, *jurgii*) ; see CAUSE.

occasional, adj. render by *occasione datâ* or *oblatâ, si occasio fuit* or *tulerit,* or by *per occasionem ;* see ACCIDENTAL, CASUAL. Adv. *raro* (= seldom), *subinde, aliquando* '= now and then).

occident, n. see WEST.

occiput, n. *occipitium* (Plin., opp. *sinciput*), *aversa pars capitis.*

occult, adj. *occultus ;* see ABSTRUSE, OBSCURE.

occupy, v.tr. **1,** = to hold or possess, *habēre, tenēre,* in *manibus habēre, possidēre ;* **2,** = to take, *capēre, occupare, expugnare* (*urbem*), *potiri re ;* to be quite occupied with anything, *studio alcjs rei teneri* or *trahi, studio* or *amore alcjs rei captum esse.* **occupancy,** n. *possessio.* **occupation,** n. **1,** (of a place) *occupatio, expugnatio* (= storming); **2,** (in business) *negotium ;* see BUSINESS, OCCUPIER, POSSESSOR.

occur, v.intr. **1,** = to come into one's mind, render by *in mentem mihi alqd venit, mihi in opinionem alqd venit* (as a conjecture), *subit animum cogitatio,* in *mentem* or *in cogitationem mihi incidit alqd* (= the thought comes into my mind), *mihi* or *animo* or *in mentem occurrit alqd, mihi succurrit* (= it just strikes me), *subit recordatio, recordor* or *reminiscor alcjs rei ;* **2,** of passages in books, *reperiri* (= to be found), *legi ;* **3,** = to happen, *fieri* (= to become), *accidēre, evenīre* (= to happen). **occurrence,** n. *casus, -ūs, res gesta* (= thing that has happened, in context also *res*), *eventum* (= event).

ocean, n. *oceanus.*

ochre, n. *ochra* (Plin.).

octagon, n. *octogōnos* (*octag-*). **octagonal,** adj. *octagōnos, -on.*

octave, n. (in music) **1,** = an interval of an eighth, *diapāson ;* **2,** = the eight notes, *octo voces* or *soni.*

octennial, adj. *octo annorum.*

October, n. (*mensis*) *October.*

octogenarian, n. *octoginta annorum* (in gen.), *octoginta annos natus* (= 80 years old).

ocular, adj. by *oculus* (e.g. to give — evidence of, *alci alqd ante oculos proponēre*) ; see VISIBLE. **oculist,** n. *medicus qui oculis medetur.*

odd, adj. **1,** = uneven, *impar* (e.g. number); **2,** = remaining, left over ; — moments, *tempora subsiciva* (*subsec-*) ; see SURPLUS ; **3,** see SINGULAR, STRANGE, EXTRAORDINARY. **oddity,** n. **1,** = ODDNESS ; **2,** = queer fellow, *homo mirabiliter moratus.* **oddness,** n. see SINGULARITY, etc. **odds,** n. see ADVANTAGE, SUPERIORITY.

ode, n. *ode* or *oda* (late), *carmen ;* see SONG, POEM.

odious, adj. *odiosus* (= hateful), *invisus* (= detested), *invidiosus* (= exciting envy and dislike), *offensus* (of what has given offence and is therefore hated) ; to be —, *odium* or *invidiam habēre* (of things) ; not to be —, *odii* or *invidiae*

nihil habēre (of persons and things) ; to be — to anyone, *alci esse odiosum* or *invisum* or *offensum, alci esse odio* or *in odio, apud alqm esse in odio, alci esse invidiae.* Adv. *odiose, invidiose.* **odiousness,** n. *odium,* or render by ODIOUS. **odium,** n. *invidia.*

odour, n. = smell, *odor ;* see SMELL. **odoriferous, odorous,** adj. † *suaveolens,* † *odorus, odoratus* (= sweet-smelling ; poet.).

Odyssey, n. *Odyssēa.*

of, prep., by the genitive ; after a verb or an adjective by the case or preposition the Latin word requires ; after partitive words, including comparatives and superlatives, by the genit. or a prep. according to the rules of syntax ; by an adjective (e.g. a basin — marble, *labrum marmoreum*) ; this preposition is sometimes used for others (e.g. a temple constructed — (out of) marble, *aedes ex marmore exstructa ;* I have heard nothing — (about) that affair, *eâ de re nihil audivi*).

off, adv. = away from, out of, *ab, de, ex ;* to go —, *decedēre ;* to go — secretly, *subterfugēre ;* to bring —, *auferre ;* to slip —, *elabi ;* to get —, *evadēre ;* to bear, carry —, *auferre ;* to be well —, *divitem* or *locupletem esse, alqâ re abundare ;* to lie — (of geographical position), *adjacēre alci loco ;* far —, *longe* or *procul ;* to be far —, *longe abesse.*

offal, n. of meat, perhaps *caro ad vescendum non apta.*

offend, v.tr. *offendēre* (= to put a stumbling-block in a person's way), *laedēre* (= to wound the feelings), *violare* (= to outrage), *pungēre* (= to sting), *mordēre* (= to bite) ; without — , ing you, *pace tuâ dixerim ;* to be —ed, *aegre* or *moleste ferre ;* to have in it something which —s, *habēre alqd offensionis.* **offence,** n. **1,** = anger, etc., *offensio, ira ;* to take —, *irasci ;* to give — , *laedēre ;* see ANGER ; **2,** = a fault, *peccatum, delictum, culpa ;* see FAULT. **offender,** n. *reus* (= accused person) ; see CULPRIT. **offensive,** adj. **1,** *quod offensionem alci affert, odiosus* (= hateful), *putidus* (= — to good manners) ; that is more — to me, *id aegrius patior ;* see LOATHSOME, ODIOUS ; **2,** of war, *bellum* alone, except where opposition to defensive is strongly expressed, then by verb (e.g. *bellum arcebant magis quam inferebant* = they waged a defensive rather than an — war). Adv. *putide,* or by adj. **offensiveness,** n. by adj.

offer, I. v.tr. *offerre, profiteri* (= to propose voluntarily), *polliceri* (= to promise ; all *alci alqd*), *porrigēre* (= to — with the hand held out, e.g. a small coin, *assem*), *praebēre* (= to hold out, e.g. *manum, os ;* then fig. = to proffer), *praestare* (= to afford, e.g. fowls — a lighter kind of food, *aves leviorem cibum praestant*), *dare* (= to give) ; to — violence to, *vim alci offerre ;* to — one's services to anyone, *alci operam suam offerre ;* to — one's services in, at anything, *ad rem* or *in alqâ re operam suam profiteri ;* to — one's goodwill, *studium profiteri ;* to — anything to a person of one's own free will, *alqd alci ultro offerre* or *polliceri ;* to — battle to the enemy, *hostem ad pugnam provocare ;* to — hospitality to anyone, *alqm invitare hospitio* or *in hospitium ;* to — up, *afferre* (= to bring as a contribution), *offerre.* **II.** v.intr. = to present itself, *offerri, dari* (of things, e.g. of an opportunity), *ob(f)ici* (accidentally), *suppetēre* (= to be in store, at hand). **III.** n. *condicio* (also = an — of marriage) ; to make an — to anyone, *condicionem alci ferre, deferre* or *offerre* or *proponēre.* **offering,** n. see SACRIFICE.

office, n. **1,** *munus, -eris,* n. (= function), *officium* (= what one has to do), *partes, -ium* (= particular sphere), *provincia* (duty imposed upon

one), sors, -tis, f. (= duty allotted to one), *locus* (= appointment), *magistratus, -ūs* (= magisterial —, opp. *imperium*, a military command during war), *honos* (honor); that is my —, *hoc meum est;* 2, = a kindness, *beneficium, officium;* see KINDNESS, DUTY; 3, = place of business, *domus, -ūs* (irreg.); at anyone's —, *apud alqm.*
officer, 1, n. = military —, *praefectus militum* or *militaris, praepositus militibus,* or by some special term (e.g. *centurio, tribunus*); naval —, *praefectus classis* or *navis;* 2, = civil —, rendered by *magistratus, -ūs;* for particular —s, see their titles. **official, I.** adj. = pertaining to a public office, e.g. — report, *lit(t)erae publicae;* to make an — report, *referre de al̩á re, deferre de alqâ re.* **II.** n. = officer, render by OFFICE, or a special title. Adv. *publice, publicâ auctoritate.* **officiate,** v.intr. render by OFFICE, e.g. to — instead of another, *alcjs officio fungi;* see OFFICE. **officious,** adj. *molestus, alcjs studiosus* (= desirous of serving one). Adv. *moleste.* **officiousness,** n. *studium* (towards one, *erga* or *in alqm*).
offing, n. (*mare*) *altum.*
offscourings, n. *purgamenta, -orum* (lit. and fig.).
offspring, n. *progenies, stirps, liberi* (= children).
oft, often, adv. *saepe, saepenumero* (= oftentimes), *crebro* (= repeatedly), *multum* (= many times); to be — with a person, *multum esse cum alqo;* I do a thing —, *soleo alqd facĕre;* also by the adjs. *creber* and *frequens;* see FREQUENT (e.g. he was — in Rome, *erat Romae frequens*); in many cases the idea of — is expressed by frequentative verbs (e.g. to read —, *lectitare;* to visit —, *frequentare*); more —, *saepius, crebrius;* very —, *saepissime, persaepe, creberrime, frequentissime.*
ogle, v.tr. *oculis limis intueri* or *a(d)spicĕre* (= to look sideways).
ogre, n. *umbra quaedam teterrima.*
oil, I. n. *oleum* (in gen., but lit. = olive —), *olivum* (= olive —); belonging to olive —, *olearius;* to paint with — colours, *pigmentum oleatum inducĕre alci rei.* **II.** v.tr. *oleo ungĕre, oleo perfundĕre* (all over). **oilman,** n. (*mercator*) *olearius* (Plin.). **oilpainter,** n. *pictor qui pigmentis oleatis utitur.* **oil-painting,** n. *pictura pigmentis oleatis facta.* **oily,** adj. *olearius* (= of oil), *oleaceus* (= like oil; Plin.), *oleosus* (= full of oil; Plin.).
ointment, n. *unguentum, nardus* (of nard oil); — for the eyes, *collyrium.*
old, adj. = that which has long been, *vetus, vetustus, inveteratus, antiquus* (= ancient), *priscus* (= primitive), *pristinus* (= at the first), *obsoletus* (= gone out of use); in comparative, — *er* (that which was before another thing), *prior, superior* (e.g. Dionysius the elder, *Dionysius superior*); an — soldier, *veteranus miles;* an — evil, *malum inveteratum;* an — custom, *mos a patribus acceptus;* as applied to men, in the sense of having lived long, *grandis,* comp. *grandior* (with or without *natu*), *aetate gravis* (= weighed down with years), † *grandaevus, vetulus* (contemptuous term); an — man, *senex;* an — woman, *anus, anicula, vetula;* to be of a certain age, *natum esse* (with the time in the accus.); *octo annos natus est,* = he is eight years old, or *octo annorum est;* see ELDERS, ANCIENT. **old age.** n. *senectus, -ūtis.* **old-fashioned,** adj. *obsoletus* (= out of fashion), *antiquus, priscus* (= old). **olden,** adj. *priscus;* see OLD. **older,** comp. *major* (with or without *natu*); the oldest (or eldest), *maximus natu.*
olfactory, adj. *quod ad odorem pertinet.*

oligarchy, n. *paucorum potentia* or *potestas* or *administratio* or *dominatio, respublica quae paucorum potestate regitur* (as a state). **oligarchical,** adj. e.g. to become —, *in paucorum jus ac dicionem cedĕre.*
olive, I. n. *oliva, olea;* — -tree, *olea, oliva;* the wild — -tree, *oleastris;* — grove, *olivētum;* — season, harvest, *oleītas, olivitas.* **II.** adj. *oleaginius.*
Olympiad, n. *Olympias, -iădis,* f. **Olympic,** adj. *Olympicus;* the — games, *Olympia, -orum.*
omelet, n. *lagānum.*
omen, n. *omen* (in gen. = a prognostic token), *ostentum* (= a portentous prodigy), *auspicium, augurium* (= augury), *portentum, monstrum, prodigium* (= prodigy). **ominous,** adj. *ominosus.* Adv. *ominose.*
omit, v.tr. 1, = to neglect, *mittĕre* or *omittĕre alqd,* or with infin. ; see NEGLECT; 2, = to leave out, *omittĕre, praetermittĕre, praeterire, transire* (= to pass over), *intermittĕre* (for a time). **omission,** n. = neglect, *intermissio* (for a time, e.g. of a duty, *officii*); = leaving out, *praetermissio.*
omnipotent, adj. see ALMIGHTY. **omnipresent,** adj. *ubique praesens.* **omnipresence,** n. to feel God's —, *Dei numen et spiritum ubique diffusum sentire.* **omniscient,** adj. *cujus notitiam nulla res effugit, qui omnia videt et audit* (= who sees and hears all things), *omnia providens et animadvertens* (= who foresees and perceives all things; all three of God). **omniscience,** n. by adj.
on, I. prep. of place, *in* with ablat. (e.g. *in saxo,* — the rock; *in terrâ,* — the ground, e.g. *fructus in terrâ est*); *in scaenâ* (scen-), — the stage; *in capite,* — the head; *in equo,* — horseback; *in limite,* — the borders; "on" is sometimes rendered by *ex* (e.g. to hang — the tree, *pendēre ex arbore*); as denoting time, — is expressed by the ablat. without a preposition (e.g. — the fourth day, *quarto die*); = after, by *ex* (e.g. *statim ex consulatu,* — the expiration of his consulship), or by abl. abs. ; *a* or *ab* often represents — (e.g. — the side, *a parte;* — the left hand, *ab laeva;* — the wing, *a latere;* to be — anyone's side, *stare ab alqo* [= to take part with one]); bad — the part of = in disposition, *ab ingenio improbus;* = near, or in the direction of, *ad, juxta* (e.g. *ad meridiem,* — the south; *ad Tiberim,* — the Tiber); to speak — or upon anything, *de alqâ re loqui;* — account of, *propter, ob, per alqd, de, pro, prae alqâ re; caus(s)â, gratiâ, ergo* (*alcjs rei,* the two former also with pers. pron., e.g. *meâ gratiâ,* all placed after their case, *ergo* only ante class.); — account of fear, *propter timorem* (*prae metu*); to provide *pecuniam; propter hereditatem contentio oritur,* a strife arises — the inheritance; *amicitia propter se expetenda,* friendship is to be sought for — its own account; — account of business I cannot, etc., *per negotia mihi non licet;* — certain reasons, *certis de caus(s)is;* — account of the noise it can scarcely be heard, *prae strepitu vix audiri potest.* **II.** adv. or **onwards,** *porro.* **onward!** interj. *perge, pergite.*
one, adj. as a numeral, *unus, -a, -um;* a certain —, *quidam;* some—, *aliquis;* some — of you, *aliquis ex vobis;* any—, *quispiam* (e.g. *forsitan quispiam dixerit,* any— may perhaps say; *so dicet aliquis forte,* some— will perchance say); each —, *quisque;* after *si, nisi, ne, num, quando, ubi,* and generally in conditional prepositions, even without a conjunction, use *quis* instead of *aliquis* or *quispiam* (e.g. *ubi semel quis pejeraverit, ei postea credi non oportet* = when once

any— has sworn falsely, he ought not afterwards to be believed); in negative sentences, and in such as contain a negative sense, "any —" is to be rendered as a noun by *quisquam*, and "any" alone as adjective by *ullus* (e.g. *estne quisquam omnium mortalium de quo melius existimes tu?* is there any — of all mortals of whom you think better? so *an est ulla res tanti?* is there anything so important?); "as any—" is rendered *quam qui maxime* (e.g. *tam sum amicus reipublicae quam qui maxime,* = I am as friendly to the state as any—); no —, *nemo; — = alter* when there are only two objects (e.g. *altero pede claudus,* = lame in— foot); *unus ille,* = that — (e.g. *unum illud addam,* = I will add only that — thing); *uno verbo,* = in — word; not even —, *ne unus quidem, non ullus, nemo unus* (= not a single person); not — of us, *nemo de nobis unus;* not — of them, *ii nulli;* — and another, *unus et alter, unus alterque* (= both together); some—, several, *non nemo, unus et item alter;* — after the other, *alius post alium, alius ex alio; singuli, = — by —; —* as much as the other, *uterque pariter, ambo pariter;* the — ... the other, *alter ... alter; hic ... ille; prior ... posterior; alii ... alii; alii ... pars* (or *partim) pars ... alii; quidam ... alii; —* ... the other, *alter alterum* (of two), *alius alium* (e.g. *alter alterum* or *alius alium adjuvat,* = the — assists the other); so *inter se* (e.g. *timent inter se,* = they fear — another); if "other" refer to a substantive, repeat the substantive (e.g. *manus manum lavat, = —* hand washes the other; so *civis civi paret);* at — time ... at another, *alias ... alias* (e.g. *alias beatus, alias miser);* — and the same, *unus atque idem, unus idemque; uno eodemque tempore, = at —* and the same time; it is — and the same, *idem est, par est; —* ... and other, *aliud ... aliud;* to be — and the same, *nihil differre, nihil interesse;* labour and pain are not — and the same, *interest alqd inter laborem et dolorem;* it is all — to me, *meâ nihil interest; —* might have thought, *crederes, putares;* — or the other, *alteruter.*

once, adv. 1, as numeral, *semel; —* and for all, *semel; —* more, *iterum* (= again, for the second time), *denuo, de novo* (= anew, afresh); more than —, *semel atque iterum, semel iterumve, semel et saepius, non semel* (= not —, but often, e.g. *pati alqd);* — or, at all events, not often, *semel, aut non saepe certe;* not —, *non semel, ne semel quidem* (= not even —); at —, all at —, *repente, subito* (= suddenly, e.g. why has this been done all at — ? *quid repente factum?); statim, il(l)ico simul* (= at the same time, e.g. *trium simul bellorum victor,* Liv.); all the people at —, *omnes simul* (= at the same time), *(omnes) universi, cuncti* (together); one at a time (or at —), *singuli;* many at —, *multi simul;* 2, of time, *aliquando,* and after *ne* or *si* simply *quando* (= some time, past or future, which we are not able or willing to specify, e.g. did you — hear of him ? *num ex eo audivisti aliquando?); quandoque* (= some time or other, e.g. he will — (i.e. some time) remember the kindness he received, *quandoque beneficii memor futurus est); quondam* (= some time past, e.g. that virtue — existed in this republic, *fuit ista quondam in hac republicâ virtus), olim* (= at some remote time past or future, opp. *nunc, nuper;* hence in fables or narratives = — upon a time); — at last, *tandem aliquando;* if —, *si quando.* **one-eyed,** adj. *uno oculo captus, luscus.* **oneself,** pron. *ipse.* **one-sided,** adj. see UNEQUAL, UNFAIR.

onion, n. *caepa (caepe).*

only, I. adj. *unus, solus, unicus, solus, singularis* (also = distinguished); (he said that) he was the — person, etc., who, *unum se ex omni civitate Aeduorum qui.* **II.** adv. *solum, tandum*

(modo); not — ..., but also, non tantum (solum) ..., sed etiam.

onset, onslaught, n. *incursio;* see ATTACK, ASSAULT.

ontology, n. *ontologia* (t.t.), or by circumloc. (e.g. *scientia illius quod per se ex(s)istit).* **ontological,** adj. *ontologicus* (technical).

onward, adv. see ON.

onyx, n. *onyx* (Plin.).

ooze, v.intr. *manare,* † *(de)stillare,* † *sudare, emanare* (also fig.). **oozy,** adj. *uliginosus.*

opal, n. *opalus* (Plin.).

opaque, adj. *haud pellucidus* or *translucidus.*

open, I. adj. 1, = not closed, *(ad)apertus* (= not shut, not cloaked or covered, opp. *clausus, involutus), patens* (= standing —, wide —; also = extending far and wide), comb. *patens et apertus; (pro)patulus* (= lying —, free of access), comb. *apertus ac propatulus; hians* (= wide —, yawning); an — door, *fores apertae* (= not shut), *fores patentes* (= wide —); an — field, *campus apertus* or *patens* (with a distant view), *locus planus* or simply *campus* (= a plain); in the — street, *in aperto ac propatulo loco* (= in an —, public place), *in publico* (= in the middle of the street, in public); the — sea, *mare apertum* (poet. *aperta oceani* = not surrounded by lands), *altum* (= the high sea); — eyes, *oculi patentes;* — mouth, *os hians;* to be, stand —, *apertum esse, patère* (= wide —; fig. his ear is — to the complaints of all, *patent aures ejus querulis omnium);* 2, = accessible, e.g. anything is — to me, *patet mihi alqd* (e.g. a post of honour); 3, = manifest, *apertus, manifestus, clarus* (e.g. to catch anyone in the — act, *in manifesto facinore deprehendère, in re manifestâ tenère);* see CLEAR; 4, = candid, *apertus, simplex, candidus;* see CANDID. Adv. *aperte, manifesto, simpliciter, candide, palam, propalam.* **II.** v.tr. 1, *aperire* (= to uncover, unclose), *patefacère* (= to lay —, both opp. to *operire), reserare* (= to unbolt, opp. to *obserare), recludère* (= to unlock, opp. to *occludère;* all these of a door, gate, etc.), *(ex)pandère* (= to expand, — wide), *evolvère, revolvère* (= to unroll, e.g. a book); to — a letter, *lit(t)eras aperire, resignare, solvère; insecare, incidère* (= to cut —); to — one's hand, *digitos porrigère* (opp. *digitos contrahère);* to — one's eyes, lit. *oculos aperire;* fig. *meliora alqm docère,* = to teach anyone better; to — one's ears to flatterers (fig.), *aures patefacère assentatoribus;* to — a vein, *venam secare, incidère;* to — the entrance to anything, *aditum ad alqd patefacère* (lit. and fig.); to — a way by force of arms, *iter sibi aperire ferro;* to — one's heart to anyone, *se* or *sensus suos alci aperire, se alci patefacère;* 2, = to explain, etc., *aperire, detegère, retegère* (e.g. *conjurationem), explicare, interpretari* (=to expound); see EXPLAIN; 3, med. t.t., to — the bowels, *alvum de(j)icère, purgare;* 4, to — a church, etc., *inaugurare, consecrare, dedicare;* 5, = to begin, *exordiri;* see BEGIN. **III.** v.intr. *se aperire, aperiri* (in gen.), *patefieri* (of a gate), *pandi, se pandère* (= to — wide, to unfold oneself; also of blossoms, Plin.), *discedère* (of heaven, of the earth, etc.), *dehiscère* (= to burst —, of the earth); to — again (of wounds), *recrudescère;* to — out, *patescère* (e.g. *campus);* to — outside, *aperturam habère in exteriorem partem.*

opening, n. 1, as an act, *apertio (patefactio* only fig. = public announcement); the — of the hand, *digitorum porrectio* (opp. *digitorum contractio);* also rendered by verbs (e.g. at the — of the body, *in aperiendo corpore);* 2, = aperture, *apertura* (in architecture), *foramen* (in gen.), *os, oris,* n. (= mouth of a river, etc.); to make

an — in anything, *alqd aperire* (in gen.), *alqd perforare* (= to make a hole through); to have an —, *patēre* (= to stand open), *hiare* (= to yawn); see HOLE, BREACH, FISSURE; **3,** the — of a church, etc., *consecratio, dedicatio ;* **4,** = opportunity, *occasio, opportunitas* (= opportunity); to see a good — in business, etc., *quaestum petēre ;* see GAIN ; **5,** = beginning, *initium, exordium ;* **6,** med. t.t. — of the bowels, *purgatio (alvi).* **openness,** n. *simplicitas* (rare in class. period), † *candor, animus simplex* or *candidus.*

opera, n. *drama (-ătis, n.) musicum* or *melicum.*

operate, v.intr. **1,** *vim habēre ad alqd* or *in alqā re ;* see ACT ; **2,** in war, *rem agēre ;* **3,** in surgery, to — upon, render by *secare alqm* or *alqd* (= to cut a person or thing), *scalpellum admovēre, adhibēre alci rei* (= to apply the lancet to, e.g. a limb, Cels.). **operation,** n. **1,** *res agenda, res gerenda* or *gesta* (= an act either to be performed or already performed), *negotium* (as an obligation undertaken); by the — of anyone, *per* with accus. (= by means of) or *a(b)* with ablat. (= by); see PROCESS ; **2,** in war, *res bello gerenda,* or in the context *res gerenda* (when the — is not yet performed), *res bello gesta,* or in the context *res gesta* (when performed) ; plan of —s, *omnis* or *totius belli ratio* (in war) ; to draw up a plan of —s, *rei agendae ordinem componēre, totius belli rationem describēre ;* **3,** in surgery, see OPERATE. **operative, I.** adj. see PRACTICAL. **II.** n. see WORKMAN, LABOURER.

ophthalmia, n. *oculorum inflammatio*(Cels.), *lippitudo.*

opiate, n. *medicamentum somnificum* (Plin.).

opinion, n. *opinio, sententia, existimatio, judicium* (= decision), *dogma, -ătis,* n., *praeceptum* or *decretum* or *placitum* (of a philosopher, teacher, etc. ; see MAXIM); a false —, *opinio falsa, pravum judicium, error* (= error) ; false —s, *opiniones falsae, opinionum commenta* (= dreams); a firmly-rooted but false —, *opinio confirmata ;* the general —, *opinio vulgaris* or *vulgi, sententia vulgaris ;* the general — respecting anything, *omnium opinio de alqā re ;* public —, *existimatio vulgi ;* according to the general —, *ad vulgi opinionem, ex vulgi opinione ;* in my —, *meā quidem opinione, (ex* or *de) meā sententiā, ut mihi quidem videtur, ut opinor, ut puto, quantum equidem judicare possum* (= as far as I can judge); to have a correct — of anything, *vere* or *recte judicare de alqā re ;* to form an — of anything merely by guess, *de alqā re conjecturā judicare ;* to have a good — of anyone, *bene de algo existimare ;* to have a high — of a person or thing, *magnam de algo habēre opinionem, magna est alcjs de alqā re opinio ;* to have a high (no mean) — of oneself, *multum sibi tribuĕre, se alqm esse putare, magnifice de se statuĕre ;* to be of —, *opinionem habēre, opinari ;* that is indeed my —, *mihi vero sic placet, sic hoc mihi videtur ;* to give one's —, *sententiam dicĕre, dare, sententiam ferre* (by voting tablets), *dico quod sentio, sententiam meam aperio, expono quae mihi videntur* (= I say what I think of a thing) ; to ask anyone his —, *quaerĕre quid alqs sentiat ;* to speak in favour of anyone's —, *in alcjs sententiam dicĕre ;* to turn a person from his —, *alqm de sententiā movēre, deducĕre ;* I bring someone over to my —, *alqm in sententiam meam adduco, alqm ad sententiam meam traduco ;* to get an — into one's head, *in sententiam venire.* **opinionated,** adj. render by *homo opinionibus inflatus.* **opine,** v.tr. see THINK, IMAGINE.

opium, n. *opium (opion,* Plin.).

opponent, n. *adversarius,* in speeches of an advocate *iste ;* see ANTAGONIST.

opportune, adj. *opportunus* (in gen.), *commodus* (= convenient), *idoneus* (= suitable) ; *tempestivus.* Adv. *opportune, commode, tempestive.* **opportuneness,** n. *opportunitas, commoditas* (= advantage). **opportunity,** n. *opportunitas* (in gen.), *occasio* (= unexpected — ; *opp.* exists before an action and leads to it, whereas *occ.* presents itself during an action and facilitates it ; *occ.* should therefore be used in speaking of the events of a war, etc.), *casus, -ūs* (= a casual —), *potestas, facultas, copia* (all three = suitableness for carrying out anything), *ansa* (lit. = handle, fig. = occasion, in the connexion *ansam praebēre* or *dare alcjs rei* or *ad alqd ;* all these nouns are construed with gen. of the object); a good, favourable —, *opportunitas idonea, occasio commoda et idonea, occasio bona et optata, temporis opportunitas, tempus opportunum,* also simply *occasio, opportunitas, tempus ;* when the — serves, *per occasionem, occasione datā* or *oblatā, si occasio fuerit* or *tulerit ;* at the first —, *ut primum occasio* or *potestas data est* (*erit*), *primo quoque tempore dato, ubi primum opportunum* (Sall.) ; to seek an —, *occasionem quaerĕre* or *circumspicĕre ;* to find an — for anything, *alcjs rei (faciendae) caus(s)am reperire* (= to find a cause, e.g. for making a war, *bellandi) ;* to seize an —, *occasionem arripĕre ;* to avail oneself of an —, *opportunitate* or *occasione uti ;* to lose an —, *occasioni deesse, occasionem amittĕre, praetermittĕre, dimittĕre.*

oppose, v.tr. *alqd alci (rei) ob(j)icĕre* (lit. and fig. = to oppose anything to anyone or anything), *adversari alci, repugnare alci rei* or *contra alqd* (= to fight against a thing), comb. *adversari et repugnare, resistĕre* (= to resist), *obsistĕre* (= to place oneself against), *obniti* (= to strive against with all one's might), *obesse, obstare* (= to stand in the way); (all the above with dat.) ; † *obluctari,* † *reluctari ;* I don't — it, *per me licet, nihil impedio ;* to be —d to each other, *repugnare inter se* (of two things that contradict each other), *obtrectare inter se* (of two rivals in a state); to — in public disputation, *adversario respondĕre.* **opposer,** n. see OPPONENT.

opposite, adj. **1,** *adversus, oppositus, objectus ;* an island — to Alexandria, *insula objecta Alexandriae ;* — to, *e regione* (with gen. or dat., e.g. us, *nobis*); on, to the — side of, *trans, ultra* (see BEYOND, OVER); **2,** see ADVERSE, CONTRARY. **opposition,** n. **1,** = the act of opposing, *oppositio,* = difference, *repugnantia, discrepantia ;* see RESISTANCE ; without —, *nemine obloquente ;* **2,** = the body of opposers, *pars adversa* (in gen.), or *factio adversa* or *adversaria* (during a revolution) ; where possible use special terms (e.g. *optimates, -(i)um,* pl. = the Tory —).

oppress, v.tr. *premĕre, opprimĕre, vexare, affligĕre.* **oppression,** n. *vexatio, injuria* (= injustice, e.g. of the authorities, *magistratuum*); — in a state, *dominatio crudelis ;* see TYRANNY. **oppressive,** adj. *molestus* (= troublesome), *magnus* (= great), *iniquus* (= unjust), *gravis* (= heavy), — cold, *frigorum vis ;* to be burdened with an — debt, *aere alieno premi ;* — government, *dominatus (-ūs) crudelis.* Adv. *moleste, graviter, inique.* **oppressor,** n. *qui dominatum crudelem exercet, tyrannus* (= sole ruler, may at times serve).

opprobrium, n. *(op)probrium ;* see IGNOMINY. **opprobrious,** adj. *probrosus* (= disgraceful); see IGNOMINIOUS.

optative, adj., the — mood, *modus optativus* (Gram.).

optics, n. *optice, -es,* f. **optical,** adj. in gen. by *oculus* (e.g — deception, *oculorum mendacium ;* — nerve, *nervus oculorum*). **optician,** n. *optices gnarus.*

option, n. *optio,* (*eligendi*) *optio et potestas,* *potestas optioque* (all = right of choice), *arbitrium* (= free-will) ; see CHOICE. **optional,** adj., render by *alcjs rei eligendae optionem alci dare, alci permittère arbitrium alcjs rei, facère alci potestatem optionemque ut eligat, facère alci arbitrium in eligendo.*

opulent, adj. *opulentus;* see RICH, WEALTHY.
opulence, n. *opulentia;* see RICHES, WEALTH.

or, conj. *aut* (excludes one or other of the suppositions expressed, e.g. here, soldiers, we must conquer — die, *hic vincendum aut moriendum, milites, est*) ; *vel* (implies that it is indifferent which of two or more than two things is chosen ; considered by themselves they may be of the same or a different kind. If several ideas are proposed, *vel* generally denotes a climax, = " — even," e.g. — shall I say even, *vel dicam;* — rather, *vel potius;* — even indeed, *vel etiam*), *ve* (enclit., generally separates single words, seldom sentences, and expresses that the nominal or real difference is not very great, e.g. merriment — laughter, *hilaritas risusve;* hence with numerals it is = " — at most," e.g. four — five each, *quaterni quinive*), *sive, seu* (arising from *vel* and *si,* always with a verb expressed or understood ; implying that two or more expressions amount to the same, or that the speaker is undecided about them, and leaves the choice to others, e.g. the mother — the stepmother, *mater seu noverca;* be it accidentally — intentionally, *sive casu sive consilio*) ; in negative sentences the disjunctive particles are generally changed into *neque* or *neve* (e.g. laziness — idle dreaming is out of place here, *nihil loci est segnitiae neque socordiae*) ; — not, *neve, neu* (after *ut* or *ne* and a verb) ; — at least, *aut certe* (or *aut* alone), *vel certe;* — rather, — more correctly, *vel ut verius dicam, atque adeo* (= nay even), or simply *aut;* either . . . —, *aut . . . aut, vel . . . vel, sive . . . sive* (with the distinction stated above), e.g. they thought either to induce the Allobrogians by persuasion, — to compel them by force, to allow, etc., *Allobrogibus sese vel persuasuros existimabant, vel vi coacturos, ut paterentur, etc.* (i.e. it was indifferent to them which way they did it) ; the laws of the Cretans, whether given by Jupiter — Minos, educate youth by means of physical exercise, *Cretum leges, quas sive Juppiter sive Minos sanxit, laboribus erudiunt juventutem ;* respecting " — " in double questions, see WHETHER.

oracle, n. *oraculum* (in gen.), *sors oraculi* or, in the context, simply *sors* (lit. = by drawing lots, then in gen. = prophecy) ; *responsum oraculi* or *sortium,* or *responsum* alone in the context (as answer to a question) ; to give an —, *oraculum dare* or *edère;* to pronounce anything as an —, *alqd oraculo edère;* to seek an —, *oraculum* or *responsum* (as answer to a question), *petère* (from someone, *ab alqo*) ; to seek an — at Delphi (through ambassadors), *mittère Delphos consultum* or *deliberatum;* according to an —, *oraculo edito;* = the place where an — was given, *oraculum* (also fig. of any place we seek for obtaining advice, e.g. a lawyer's house is an — for the whole state, *domus juris consulti est oraculum totius civitatis*) ; god of an —, *deus qui oracula edit.* **oracular,** adj. *qui oracula edit.*

oral, adj. *praesens;* to have — communication, *coram sermonem cum alqo habère,* or *praesens cum praesenti colloqui.*

orange, n. *malum aurantium* (Linn.).

oration, n. *oratio, contio* (before a popular meeting). **orator,** n. *orator.* **oratorical,** adj. *oratorius.* **oratory,** n. 1, *doctrina dicendi*

(Cic.), *ratio dicendi, ars oratoria* (Quint.) ; see RHETORIC ; 2, = house for prayer, *aedes sacra.*

orb, n. *sphaera, globus, orbis.* **orbed,** adj. *in orbem circumactus.* **orbit,** n. in astronomy, *orbis, -is,* m., or less exactly *cursus, -ūs, circulus, ambitus, -ūs,* comb. *circulus et orbis.*

orchard, n. *pomarium.*

orchestra, n. 1, = the place, *suggestus* (*-ūs*) *canentium;* 2, = the music, *symphonia;* = the singers, *symphoniaci;* to sing with the accompaniment of the —, *ad symphoniam canère;* the accompaniment of the —, *symphonia.*

orchid, n. *orchis* (Plin.).

ordain, v.tr. 1, see DECREE, ESTABLISH, APPOINT, INSTITUTE ; 2, *in sacerdotum numerum recipère, ordinare* (Eccl.). **ordinance,** n. see DECREE, EDICT, RULE. **ordination,** n. *ritus quo alqs in sacerdotum numerum recipitur, ordinatio* (Eccl.).

ordeal, n. 1, ** judicium Dei* (Med. Lat.) ; 2, fig. by circumloc., one who has passed through many — s, *multis periculis spectatus;* see PROOF.

order, I. n. 1, *ordo, -ĭnis,* m. ; the — of words in a sentence, *verborum quasi structura;* to set in —, *disponère, digerère;* to march in —, *compositos et instructos procedère;* to march without —, *sine ordine iter facère;* in, according to —, *ordine, ex ordine, per ordinem;* out of —, *extra ordinem* (generally = in an extraordinary way) ; = regular mode of proceeding, acting, *disciplina bona;* love, spirit of —, *bonae disciplinae studium;* — in one's mode of living, *certus vivendi modus ac lex;* to live according to —, *vitae institutum* or *rationem servare, a vitae ratione non discedère;* — in one's affairs, *rerum suarum modus quidam et ordo;* to keep anyone in —, under strict discipline, *alqm severā disciplinā coërcère, alqm in officio continère* (in submission) ; 2, = division, class ; — in architecture, *columnarum genus, -ĕris,* n. ; the Doric —, *columnae Doricae;* see CLASS, KIND, RANK ; 3, = rank, *ordo* (e.g. *senatorius, equestris*) ; = fraternity, *collegium;* an — of knights, *ordo equestris;* 4, = command, *jussum, mandatum, imperatum* (= military —), *edictum* (= decree), *senatus consultum* (= — of Parliament), *praeceptum* (= maxim) ; to follow an —, *jussum exsequi;* to reject an —, *jussum spernère, abnuère;* to execute, accomplish an —, *jussum efficère, patrare, peragère;* see COMMAND, DECREE, PRECEPT ; 5, in business, *mandatum* (= commission) ; to give an — at a shop, *alqd emère.* "In — to or that" is rendered by *ut* or *qui* with subj. or by the fut. act. part., e.g. we eat in — to live, but we do not live in — to eat, *edimus ut vivamus, sed non vivimus ut edamus;* he sent an ambassador in — to make inquiry, *legatum misit qui rogaret;* by the gerundive, or by the gerundive in *di* with *caus(s)ā,* e.g. Antigonus handed over the body of Eumenes to his friends in — to bury him, *Antigonus Eumenen mortuum propinquis ejus sepeliendum tradidit;* he sent off three legions (in —) to procure forage, *pabulandi caus(s)ā tres legiones misit;* Gracchus marched out with the legions in — to devastate Celtiberia, *Gracchus duxit ad depopulandam Celtiberiam legiones;* by the supine in *um* after verbs of motion (e.g. they came in — to ask, *venerunt rogatum*) ; "in — not to" is rendered by *ne* with subj. (e.g. in — not to say, mention it, *ne dicam, ne commemorem*). **II.** v.tr. 1, = to arrange, *ordinare, componère, disponère;* see above ; 2, = to command, *jubère, praecipère* (= to enjoin), *imperare, praescribère* (= to direct, prescribe), *edicère ut* (= to decree) ; to

— the army to any place, *exercitum in alqm locum indicĕre*; to — a person to prepare dinner, *cenam (caen-) alci imperare*; he —ed his soldiers not to, etc., *militibus suis jussit, ne*, etc. (with subj.). **orderly, I.** adj. = well arranged (of things), *compositus, dispositus, descriptus* (= arranged with precision), *honestus* (= honourable), *modestus* (= unassuming), *diligens, accuratus* (= painstaking), *sobrius* (= temperate) ; see METHODICAL. **II.** n. perhaps *minister* (= servant), or better *optio* (= adjutant).

ordinal, I. adj., — number, *numerus ordinalis* (Gram.). **II.** n. *formula sacrorum.* **ordinance,** n. see EDICT, DECREE.

ordinary, I. adj. 1, *usitatus* (= usual), *cot(t)idianus (quoti-, = daily), vulgaris, communis* (= belonging to all); **2,** = mediocre, *mediocris*; see CUSTOMARY, COMMON, REGULAR, USUAL. **II.** n. 1, see JUDGE, CHAPLAIN ; **2,** = meal, *cena.* **ordinarily,** adv. *ferme, fere.*

ordnance, n. see ARTILLERY.

ordure, n. *stercus, -ōris,* n.

ore, n. *aes.*

oread, n. *oreas.*

organ, n. 1, in anatomy ; — **of the voice,** *vox*; interior —s of the body, *viscera, -um;* the — of speech, *lingua*; see MEANS, INSTRUMENT ; **2,** in music, * *organum pneumaticum* (the nearest class. equivalent is perhaps *lyra* = lyre). **organic,** adj. (e.g. — bodies, *animantia, -ium*, or *nascentia, -ium;* — disease, *vitium naturae,* or *insitum*); see NATURAL. Adv. *naturâ, per naturam.* **organize,** v.tr. *ordinare, constituĕre, componĕre* (= to arrange); to — a state, *civitatis statum ordinare, describĕre, rempublicam constituĕre* or *componĕre, rempublicam legibus temperare*; a well-—d state, *civitas bene constituta, civitas legibus temperata, civitas quae commodius rem suam publicam administrat.* **organisation,** n. *descriptio, temperatio;* — of the body, *corporis temperatio, natura et figura corporis;* — of the state, republic, *reipublicae forma.* **organism,** n. *compages, -is* (= framework, e.g. *corporis*), *natura* (= nature), *figura, forma* (= form), comb. *natura ac figura.*

orgies, n. *bacchanalia, -ium;* see REVELRY.

Orient, n., **Oriental,** adj. see EAST, EASTERN.

orifice, n. see HOLE.

origin, n. *orīgo, ortus, -ûs, fons, -ntis,* m. (= source), *principium* (= first beginning), *caus(s)a, figura* (= cause), *unde fit alqd* (= whence a thing arises); to derive its — from, *ortum* or *natum esse ab alqâ re;* the — of the soul is not of this world, *animarum nulla in terris origo inveniri potest;* see BEGINNING, BIRTH, CAUSE, SOURCE. **original, I.** adj. 1, *primus, principalis* (= the first, e.g. cause, *caus(s)a*, meaning, *significatio ; primigenius,* ante and post class.), *pristinus* (= former), *nativus* (= natural, e.g. barrenness, *sterilitas*); **2,** = one's own, *proprius* or *(sui) ipsius,* = new, *novus,* or perhaps *mirus* (= wonderful); a history from — sources, *historia ab ipsîs temporibus repetīta;* **3,** = clever, *ingeniosus;* — genius, *ingenium, indoles, -is.* Adv. *initio, principio* (= at the beginning), *primum, primo* (= at first), *mirum in modum* (= wonderfully). **II.** n. Cic. uses ἀρχέτυπον, and Pliny *archetypum;* = — text, *chirographum* (= the author's own manuscript), *exemplum* (= pattern in general); in a metaphysical sense, *species* (= an ideal, first in Cic. for the Platonic ἰδέα). **originality,** n. render in gen. by ORIGINAL ; — of genius, *proprietas* (= peculiarity), *indoles, -is* (= natural

talent); see ORIGINAL, I. **originate, I.** v.tr. see CREATE, PRODUCE, BEGIN. **II.** v.intr. to — in or from a thing, *(ex)oriri ab alqâ re, emanare* or *fluĕre de* or *ex alqâ re, proficisci ab alqâ re* (= to proceed, spring from), *fieri* or *effici* or *sequi* or *consequi ex alqâ re* (= to be the consequence of) ; to — with a person, *originem accepisse ab algo.* **originator,** n. *auctor*; see AUTHOR.

orisons, n. *prĕces, -um,* f.

ornament, I. n. *decus, -ŏris,* n. (= adorning by its innate beauty), *ornatus, -ûs* (= ornaments in gen., then of speech, *afferre ornatum orationi*, Cic.), *ornamentum* (by its lustre and costliness ; both of persons and things), comb. *decus et ornamentum, insigne* (= honorary decoration, of things), comb. *insigne atque ornamentum; lumen* (lit. = light, fig. what constitutes the excellence, glory, i.e. of persons or towns), comb. *lumen et ornamentum,* or *decus et lumen;* the —s in the temples, *decora et ornamenta fanorum;* Pompey, the — of the state, *Pompeius, decus imperii;* the —s of the republic, *lumina civitatis;* Corinth, the — of all Greece, *Corinthus, Graeciae totius lumen;* virtue is the only real —, *verum decus in virtute positum est;* to be the — of our age (of persons), *exornare nostrae aetatis gloriam;* to be an — to any person or thing, *alci* or *alci rei decori* or *ornamento esse, decus afferre alci* or *alci rei.* **II.** v.tr. *(ex)ornare, decorare;* see ADORN. **ornamental,** adj., render by verbs. **ornate,** adj. *(per)ornatus;* an — style, *nitidum quoddam verborum genus et laetum;* or *genus orationis pictum et expolitum.* Adv. *ornate.*

ornithology, n. by *aves, -ium,* f. (= birds, e.g. a book on —, *liber de avibus scriptus*).

orphan, I. n. *orbus,* fem. *orba* (= bereft of parents), an — in respect of father, mother, *orbus (orba) patre, matre;* —s, *orbi;* to become an —, *orbari parentibus;* asylum for —s, *orphanotrophium* (Jct.). **II.** adj. *orbus, orbatus, parentibus orbatus* (= bereft of parents).

orthodox, adj. *orthodoxus* (Eccl.), *veram Christi legem sequens, legis Christianae studiosus* (both of persons), *legi Christianae conveniens* (of things, e.g. doctrine). **orthodoxy,** n. *orthodoxia* (Eccl.), *in Christianam legem studium.*

orthoepy, n. *vera loquendi ratio.*

orthography, n. *recte scribendi scientia* (= knowledge of —), *formula ratioque scribendi* (as a system, Quint.).

oscillate, v.intr. 1, lit. *agitari;* 2, fig. see DOUBT, HESITATE. **oscillation,** n. 1, *agitatio;* 2, *dubitatio.*

osier, I. n. *vimen.* **II.** adj. *vimineus.*

osprey, n. *ossifragus* (Plin.).

osseous, adj. *osseus* (Plin.).

ossify, I. v.tr. *in os mutare.* **II.** v.intr. *in os mutari* or *transire.* **ossification,** n. use verb.

ostensible, adj. *simulatus, fictus* (= feigned). Adv. *simulate, ficte, per speciem.* **ostentation,** n. *sui jactatio, ostentatio, venditatio.* **ostentatious,** adj. *gloriosus, jactans.* Adv. *gloriose.*

ostler, n. *agaso;* see GROOM.

ostracism, n. *testarum suffragia, -orum;* of the Athenian custom ; = expulsion, in gen. by *expelli.*

ostrich, n. *struthiocamēlus* (Plin.).

other, adj. *alius* (in gen.), *alter* (the — **one** of the two, opp. *uterque,* = both; also indefinitely = another, but only as a second party, e.g. if you enter into an agreement with an—, *si cum altero contrahas*), *ceteri, rel(l)iquus,* = the — (*ceteri* represents the — part as acting reciprocally with the first; *reliquus* or *reliqui*, simply = remainder; the nom. sing. masc. *ceterus* not used, sing. in gen. rare), *secundus* (= second), *diversus* (= quite different), *alienus* (= belonging to someone else); —s, *alii*; the —s, *ceteri, reliqui*. If — = one of the same or a similar kind, we use *alter* or *novus* (e.g. another Hannibal, *alter Hannibal*; another Camillus, *novus Camillus*); all —s, *omnes alii, ceteri* (= all the remainder); on the — hand, *rursus* (= again), *e contrario* (= on the contrary). **otherwise**, adv. *aliter* (also =in the other case), *alioqui(n)* (= in other respects), *cetera, ceteroqui(n)* (= in other respects), *quod nisi ita est* or *fit, quod nisi ita esset* (= if this be, were not so; in hypothetical sentences); see ELSE.

otter, n. *lutra* (*lyt-*, Plin.).

ottoman, n. *lectus;* see COUCH.

ought, v.aux. *debēre*, or by gerund. or gerundive (e.g. *virtus colenda est*, = virtue — to be practised; *parendum est mihi*, I — to obey); by *oportet*, by *officium est* or *est* only with gen. (see MUST), or by *licet* (of persons, e.g. you — not to have done that, *non tibi licebat hoc facĕre*); you either — not to have commenced the war at all, or you — to have carried it on in a manner befitting the dignity of the Roman people, *aut non suscipi bellum oportuit, aut pro dignitate populi Romani geri;* you — to have taken this road, *haec via tibi ingredienda erat;* upon him whom you — to have honoured as a father, you have heaped all kinds of insults, *omnibus eum contumeliis onerasti quem patris loco colĕre debebas;* — to have been, etc., is expressed by past tense of *debēre* or *oportet* with pres. infin. (e.g. I — to have gone, *ire debui*); see MUST, OBLIGE.

ounce, n. *uncia;* half- —, *semuncia;* two —s, *sextans;* three—s, *triens;* four —s, *quadrans;* five —s, *quincunx;* six —s, *semis;* seven —s, *septunx;* eight —s, *bes;* nine —s, *dodrans;* ten —s, *dextans;* eleven —s, *deunx;* twelve —s, *as.*

our, pron. adj. *noster;* — people, *nostri* (= those of — party, household, country, etc.); *nostrates* (= — countrymen); — Cicero just mentioned, *hic, ille;* for — sake, *nostrā* (or *nostri*) *caus(s)a, propter nos;* for — part, *per nos* (e.g. for — part, as far as we are concerned, it shall be allowed, *per nos licitum erit*), of — country, *nostras.* **ourselves**, pron. see WE, SELF.

ousel, n. *merula.*

out, I. adv. *extrinsecus* (opp. *intrinsecus*, = in, on the inside); — or —wards may be also rendered by *foris, foras, peregre;* to be —, *foris esse;* to go —, *exire foras* (= out of doors); to work —, *perficĕre;* to breathe —, *exspirare, respirare;* to blow —, *efflare;* to break —, *ex loco, vinculo carceris rumpĕre;* to break — in anger, *stomachum, iram effundĕre;* a fire breaks —, *incendium oritur;* to break — into laughter, *in risus* or *cachinnos* *effundi;* to break — into reproaches, *ad verborum contumeliam descendĕre;* in comp. by *e(x)* (e.g. *excogitare*, to think —; *exire*, to go —); to spread —, *(ex)pandĕre.* II. **'of**), prep. (denoting a coming forth from locally), *e* or *ex* (e.g. *exire ex navi*, to go — of the ship; so *ex urbe, e vitā; extorquēre arma e manibus; e(f)licĕre alqm e civitate; milites ex eo loco deducĕre*), *extra* (properly = —side of, opp. *intra*, = within, e.g. *aut intra muros aut extra;* so *extra limen, ordinem, noxiam, teli jactum* (= — of range), *consuetudinem, numerum*, etc.). Sometimes " — of" has no corresponding Latin term, the relation being indicated by the case (e.g. *navi egredi*, = to go — of the vessel; so with the names of towns, and with *domus*); —, as signifying the cause, *e, ex, a, ab,* also *propter* and *prae* (e.g. — of fear, *prae metu*), or by a participle and the ablative, *metu coactus* (so *pudore adductus*); to

be — of one's mind, *sui* or *mentis non compotem esse, non apud se esse* (Ter.); to be — of one's mind for joy, *laetitia ex(s)ultare, efferri;* from anger, *prae iracundia non esse apud se.* from fright, *metu exanimatum esse;* to put a person — of his mind, *perturbare alqm;* to be put — of one's mind, *perturbari;* to go — of the country, *peregre abire.*

outbid, v.tr. *licitatione vincĕre.*

outbreak, n. *eruptio* (= act of breaking forth), *initium, principium* (= beginning, e.g. *belli*, — of war), *seditio* (= sedition); — of illness, *morbo opprimi, affligi.*

outcast, n. *exsul, extorris, profugus.*

outcry, n. *clamor, vociferatio, voces;* expressing disapproval, *acclamatio.*

outdo, v.tr. *superare, vincĕre alqm.*

outer, adj. *externus* (*externae nationes*), *externus* (*res externae*, Cic.; so *externa, -orum*, = outer things, opp. *interiora*); see EXTERIOR, EXTERNAL.

outface, v.tr. *impudentiā vincĕre.*

outflank, v.tr. *circumire, circumvenire.*

outgrow, v.tr. use circumloc. (e.g. he outgrew his clothes, *illi vestitus grandior jam opus erat*).

outhouse, n. *pars aedibus adjecta.*

outlandish, adj. *peregrinus, barbarus.*

outlast, v.tr. *diutius durare.*

outlaw, I. n. *proscriptus, relegatus, ex(s)ul* (= exile). II. v.tr. *proscribĕre, aqud et igni alci interdicĕre.* **outlawry**, n. *proscriptio, aquae et ignis interdictio.*

outlay, n. *sumptus, -ūs;* see EXPENSE.

outlet, n. *exitus, -ūs, egressus, -ūs* (in gen.), *effluvium* (Plin., Tac.; rare), *emissarium, os, oris, ostium, caput* (of rivers).

outline, I. n. *lineamentum* (e.g. *tu operum lineamenta perspicis*, Cic.); the —s of a face, *lineamenta* (e.g. *similitudo oris vultūsque ut lineamenta*, Liv.; compare *animi lineamenta sunt pulchriora quam corporis*); *adumbratio* (= sketch). II. v.tr. *describĕre, adumbrare* (lit. and fig.); see SKETCH.

outlive, v.tr. *alci superesse.*

outlook, n. 1, to have an — of a place, *ad, in* or *inter alqd spectare;* 2, to be on the —, *omnia circumspectare;* 3, fig. *spes* (e.g. *bona* = good —, *nulla* = poor —).

outlying, adj. *longinquus* (= far removed); — districts, *regiones quae circa alqm locum sunt.*

outnumber, v.tr. *numero* (*numeris*) or computatione superare, multitudine superare.

outpost, n. *statio* (of troops), *propugnaculum* (scil. *navium; propugnaculum oppositum barbaris; propugnacula imperii*).

outrage, I. n. *injuria, contumelia* (= affront). II. v.tr. *alci afferre injuriam, alqm injuriā afficĕre, probris conficĕre.* **outrageous**, adj. *immanis, contumeliosus, immoderatus, indignus;* see MONSTROUS. Adv. *indigne, immoderate.*

outride, v.tr. *equitando alqm superare.* **out riders**, n. *qui alci equitando praeeunt* or *alqm equitando deducunt.*

outright, adv. *penitus, prorsus, omnino.*

outrun, v.tr. *alqm cursu superare* or *vincĕre.*

outsail, v.tr. *navigando superare alqm.*

outset, n. *initium;* see BEGINNING.

outside, I. adj. *externus;* as a noun, use —, *externa, -orum, superficies* (= the surface; e.g. *aquae, testudinum, corporum*), *forma, species.*

(=show; lit. and fig.). **II.** adv. *extra, extrinsecus, foris* (with verbs of rest; *foras,* with verbs of motion); on the —, *extrinsecus.*

outskirts, n. see SUBURB.

outspoken, adj. see FRANK.

outspread, adj. *passus;* with — sails, *passis ƀr plenis velis;* with — hands (in entreaty), *supplicibus manibus.*

outstanding, adj. of debt, by *aes alienum;* see DEBT.

outstrip, v.tr. 1, *alqm cursu superare* or *vincěre, alqm † praevertěre;* 2, fig. see EXCEL.

outtalk, v.tr. *multiloquio vincěre alqm.*

outvote, v.tr. *alqm suffragiis vincěre.*

outwalk, v.tr. *ambulando alqm praevertěre.*

outward, I. adj. *exterus, externus;* an — show, *species.* **II.** adv. *extra, extrinsecus;* a ship — bound, *navis ad exteras nationes destinata;* see OUTSIDE, II.

outweigh, v.tr. *graviorem esse alqâ re* (lit.) ; *vincěre* (fig. of opinions) ; Cato alone —s in my opinion hundreds of thousands, *unus Cato mihi pro centum millibus est; praeponderare* (lit. and fig.; rare).

outwit, v.tr. *circumvenire* (= to deceive); see DECEIVE.

outworks, n. *munimenta (exteriora).*

oval, I. adj. *ovatus* (= like an egg, Plin.). **II.** n. *figura ovata.*

ovation, n. *ovatio* (= a Roman lesser triumph); fig. to receive an —, *magnis clamoribus excipi.*

oven, n. *furnus* (for baking), *clibănus* (= small portable —).

over, I. adv. *super, supra;* to be — (= remaining), *superesse, rel(l)iquum* (relic-) *esse;* = to be done with, *actum esse de alqo* or *alqâ re;* when the battle was —, *confecto proelio;* — and — again, *etiam atque etiam;* —much, *praeter modum;* often expressed in comp., — timid, *timidior;* a little — or under, *haud multo plus minusve.* **II.** prep. *super, supra* with accus. (*super* also with ablat., but chiefly poet.), *trans* (= across) with accus., *amplius* (with numerals; e.g. — a hundred, *amplius centum); inter cenam* (*coen-*), — dinner ; *per* with accus. (= through, of place); to make a bridge — a river, *pontem in flumine facěre.*

overawe, v.tr. *alqm metu complěre, terrěre, coërcěre, compriměre.*

overbalance, v.tr. *praeponderare;* see OUTWEIGH.

overbear, v.tr. *alqm vincěre, superare, compriměre, coërcěre.* **overbearing,** adj. *arrogans, insolens, superbus.*

overbid, v.tr. *pluris licitari.*

overboard, adj. to throw anything —, *alcjs rei jacturam facěre;* to fall —, *in mare exciděre.*

overboiled, adj. (or part.) *nimis coctus.*

overbold, adj. *temerarius, audax.*

overburdened, adj. *praegravatus, nimio ænere oppressus.*

overcast, adj. † *(ob)nubilus* (of the sky).

overcharge, v.tr. 1, = to put too high a price, *nimio venděre;* 2, = to load too heavily, *nimio pondere onerare;* to — the stomach, *se vino ciboque onerare.*

overcoat, n. *amiculum;* see CLOAK.

overcome, v.tr. *(de)vincěre, superare, profligare;* not to be —, *inexpugnabilis* (both of place and persons), *insuperabilis, invictus.*

overdo, v.tr. *nimio labore se fatigare* (= your-

self); to — a thing, *nimium laborem in rem conferre, modum exceděre in alqâ re;* = to overcook, *nimis coquěre.*

overdraw, v.tr. 1, see EXAGGERATE ; 2, to — an account, *aes alienum contrahěre* or *conflare* (= to incur debt).

overdress, v.tr. *nimis splendide se ornare.*

overdrink, v.intr. *vino se obruěre.*

overdrive, v.tr. *(de)fatigare.*

overdue, adj. *pecunia quam alqs jam solvěre debuit.*

overeat, v.reflex. *heluari* (=to be gluttonous).

overfill, v.tr. *supra modum implěre.*

overflow, I. n. *inundatio fluminis,* (col) *luvio ;* the river produces an —, *flumen extra ripas diffluit, flumen alveum excedit.* **II.** v.tr. *inundare ;* the Tiber —ed the fields, *Tiberis agros inundavit.* **III.** v.intr. 1, *effundi, † inundare ;* the fountain —s, *fons exundat ;* 2, fig. *alqâ re abundare, suppeditare, redundare.*

overgrow, v.intr. 1, see OUTGROW; 2, to be —n with foliage, *frondibus contextum, obsitum esse.*

overhang, v.intr. *imminěre, impenděre.*

overhasty, adj. *praeproperus.* Adv. *praepropere.*

overhaul, v.tr. see EXAMINE, INSPECT.

overhead, adv. *supra, desuper, insuper ; see* OVER, I.

overhear, v.tr. *excipěre, subauscultare.*

overheat, v.tr. *alqd nimis cal(e)facěre;* to — oneself, by *sudare* (= to perspire).

overjoyed, adj. *laetitiâ affectus* or *ex(s)ultans.*

overland, adj. *terrâ* (opp. *mari*).

overlap, v.tr. *alci rei imminěre* or *impenděre* (= to overhang).

overlay, v.tr. 1, = to smother, *incubando oppriměre* or *suffocare ;* 2, = to spread over, *alqd alci rei inducěre, † illiněre;* to — with gold, *inaurare.*

overload, v.tr. *nimis* or *nimium onerare, onus nimis grave alci (rei) imponěre.* **overloaded,** adj. *nimis oneratus, pondere nimis gravi oppressus ;* to be — with business, *negotiis obrutum esse ;* see OVERCHARGE.

overlong, adj. *praelongus.*

overlook, v.tr. 1, = to oversee, *servare, observare* (= to watch), *custodire* (= to guard), *praeesse alci* or *alci rei* (= to superintend), *inquirěre in alqd, scrutari, inspicěre alqd* (= to examine thoroughly) ; 2, = to command a view of, *alci rei imminěre, alqd prospicěre* (e.g. *ex superioribus locis prospicěre in urbem);* 3, = to pardon, *alci rei* or *alcjs alci rei veniam dare* or *condonare, alci rei* or *alci alqd ignoscěre, co(n)nivěre in alqd re* (= to shut one's eyes, wink at) ; see INDULGENCE, PARDON ; 4, = to pass by inadvertently, *praeterire, omittěre, praetermittěre* (= to leave unnoticed ; also of a fault, to let it pass unpunished). **overlooker,** n. *custos, -ôdis,* m. and f., *curator, praeses, -ĭdis,* m. and f., *praefectus, exactor* (= one who sees that things are done carefully), *magister, rector* (= instructor), *curator viarum* (= surveyor of the public roads), *aedilis* (in Rome, = superintendent of the public buildings and police).

overmuch, I. adj. *nimius.* **II.** adv. *nimis, nimium.*

overnight, adv. *vesperi* (= in the evening).

overpay, v.tr. *plus quam debetur solvěre.*

overpeopled, adj. *use circumloc.* (e.g. *tanta erat multitudo hominum quantas victus non suppeditabat).*

overplus, n. see SURPLUS.

overpower, v.tr. *opprimĕre, frangĕre, profligare, vincĕre, debellare.* **overpowering,** adj. see OVERWHELMING.

overprize, v.tr. *pluris quam par est aestimare.*

overrate, v.tr. *nimium alci rei tribuĕre;* to — oneself, *immodicum sui esse aestimatorem.*

overreach, v.tr. *circumvenire, circumscribĕre, fraude capĕre alqm;* see CHEAT.

overripe, adj. *qui jam maturitatem excessit.*

overrule, v.tr. = to bear down, *(de)vincĕre.* **overruling Providence,** n. *Providentia omnia administrans* or *gubernans.*

overrun, v.tr. 1, = to outrun, *cursu praeterire;* 2, = to swarm over, *(per)vagari;* 3, to be — with (of plants), *alqā re obsitum esse.*

overscrupulous, adj. use compar., *diligentior,* etc.; see SCRUPULOUS.

oversee, v.tr. *(pro)curare.* **overseer,** n. *custos, (pro)curator;* — of the highways, *curator viarum.*

overshadow, v.tr. 1, † *obumbrare,* † *inumbrare alqd;* 2, fig. *alci rei officĕre.*

overshoes, n. *tegumenta calceorum.*

overshoot, v.tr. *jactu* or *sagittā scopum transgredi;* to — oneself, *consilio labi.*

oversight, n. *error, erratum, incuria;* — of a business, *curatio, procuratio, cura.*

oversleep, v.intr. *diutius dormire.*

overspread, v.tr. 1, *obducĕre, inducĕre;* see OVERLAY; 2, see OVERRUN, 2.

overstrain, v.tr. *nimis contendĕre;* to — one's strength, *vires nimis intendĕre.*

overt, adj. *apertus, manifestus.*

overtake, v.tr. *assequi, consequi;* = to surprise, *opprimĕre, deprehendĕre alqm, supervenire alci.* **overtaken,** adj. *praeventus;* to be — with sleep, *somno opprimi.*

overtask, v.tr. *majus justo pensum alci in(j)ungĕre.*

overtax, v.tr. *iniquis oneribus premĕre.*

overthrow, I. v.tr. 1, = to cast down, *profligare, de(j)icĕre;* 2, = to demolish, *diruĕre, subvertĕre, demoliri;* 3, = to defeat, *(de)vincĕre, prosternĕre, opprimĕre.* **II.** n. *clades, -is, strages, -is.*

overtop, v.tr. *eminĕre,* † *supereminĕre.*

overture, n. 1, *condiciones ad alqd agendum propositae;* — of peace, *pacis condiciones;* to make —s, *condiciones ferre* or *proponĕre;* 2, to an opera, *(dramatis musici) exordium.*

overturn, v.tr. *evertĕre, subvertĕre alqd.*

overvalue, v.tr. *nimis magni aestimare.*

overweening, adj. *superbus;* see PROUD.

overwhelm, v.tr. *obruĕre, opprimĕre, demergĕre, (sub)mergĕre.* **overwhelmed,** part. *obrutus, mersus, demersus, submersus;* — with grief, *dolore* or *tristitiā oppressus.* **overwhelming,** adj. by superl. of adj. or circumloc. (e.g. = grief, *magno dolore affectus*).

overwise, adj. *qui peracutus videri vult.*

overwork, I. n. *labor immoderatus.* **II.** v.intr. and reflex. *nimis laborare;* see WORK.

overworn, adj. e.g. = with age, *aetate* or *senio confectus.*

overwrought, adj. or part. *nimis elaboratus* (=wrought too highly), *laboribus confectus* (= worn down by labours).

overzealous, adj. *nimis studiosus.*

owe, v.tr. *debĕre* (= to be in debt; to anyone, *alci);* to — something to a person, *debēre alci alqd* (in gen., of any kind of obligation, e.g. money, *pecuniam;* gratitude, *gratiam;* compassion, *misericordiam);* to — much money, *aere alieno demersum* or *obrutum esse;* to — anyone a great deal, *grandem pecuniam alci debēre* (lit.), *multa alci debēre* (fig.); owing to, by *per;* it was owing to you, *per te stetit quominus* or *tibi alqd acceptum refero,* or by *propter* with accus. or *alcjs beneficio.* **owing,** adj. see DUE.

owl, n. *ulula, noctua, strix, -gis,* f., *bubo;* like an —, *noctuīnus* (e.g. *oculi,* Plaut.).

own, I. adj. 1, = belonging to one by nature or by one's course of action, *proprius;* but generally by *meus, tuus, suus,* etc., or by *ipsius* or *meus ipsius,* etc. (e.g. it was written by his — hand, *ipsius* (or *suā ipsius) manu scriptum erat, ipse scripserat);* I saw it with my — eyes, *ipse vidi, hisce oculis egomet vidi* (Com.); I quote the emperor's — words, *ipsa principis verba refero;* through my — fault, *meā culpā;* 2, = what we have for our — use, *proprius* (opp. *communis* or *alienus;* in Cic. with genit., in other writers also with dat.), *peculiaris* (of what one has acquired for his — use), *privatus* (of private property, opp. *publicus), domesticus* (= relating to one's family or home), comb. *domesticus et privatus* (e.g. *domesticae et privatae res,* one's — private matters, opp. *publicae), privus* (= belonging to any one individual); my, your — people, servants, *mei, tui,* etc.; he has taken from us everything that was our —, *ademit nobis omnia quae nostra erant propria.* **II.** v.tr. 1, see ACKNOWLEDGE, CONFESS; 2, see POSSESS, CLAIM.

owner, n. *possessor, dominus;* to be the — of anything, *possidēre alqd.* **ownership,** n. *possessio* (in gen.), *dominium* (Jct.), *auctoritas* (= right of possession), *manicipium* (= right by purchase); the obtaining of — by long use or possession, *usucapio.*

ox, n. *bos, bovis,* m. and f.; a young —, *juvencus;* a driver of —en, *bubulcus.* **oxherd,** n. *armentarius.*

oyster, n. *ostrea,* † *ostreum.* **oyster-bed,** n. *ostrearium* (Plin.). **oyster-shell,** n. *testa.*

P.

pabulum, n. *pabulum;* see FOOD.

pace, I. n. *gradus, -ūs, passus, -ūs* (= the act of stepping out in walking; in the prose of the golden age only the step; as Roman measure of length = 5 Roman feet); *gressus, -ūs* (= the act of making strides, walk); to keep — with anyone, *alcjs gradus aequare* (lit.), *parem esse alci* (fig., = to be equal to anyone); at a quick —, *pleno* or *citato gradu;* at a slow —, *tarde, lente;* see STEP. **II.** v.intr. *gradi* (= to walk with an equal and bold step), *vadēre* (quickly and easily), *incedere, ingredi, ambulare, spatiari* (= to walk about); see MARCH, WALK. **III.** v.tr. *passibus metiri alqd.* **pacer,** n. perhaps *Asturco* (= an Asturian horse).

pacific, adj. by *pacis* (e.g. — propositions, *pacis condiciones), pacificus,* † *pacifer;* see PEACEABLE. **pacification,** n. *pacificatio, compositio, pax.* **pacificator,** n. *pacificator, pacis auctor* (Liv.), *pacis reconciliator* (Liv.). **pacify,** v.tr. *placare* (= a man when angry); to — a country, *pacare;* = to restore peace (e.g. to a province), *sedare, componĕre.*

pack, I. v.tr. 1, *imponĕre in alqd* (= to put or load into), *condĕre in alqd* or *alqā re* (= to put into

anything for the purpose of preservation); to — in a parcel with something else, *alqd in eundem fasciculum addĕre*; to — one's things for a journey, for a march, *sarcinas* or *sarcinulas colligĕre* or *expedire*, *sarcinas aptare itineri*, *vasa colligĕre* (in the camp, of soldiers); to give orders for the troops to — up, *vasa conclamare jubĕre*; to — goods, *merces in fasciculos colligĕre*; to — together, *colligĕre* (= to collect in a lump, into a bundle, e.g. one's things, baggage, furniture, *sarcinas, vasa*), *colligare, alligare, constringĕre* (= to tie together, e.g. one's knapsack, *sarcinam*; household effects, *vasa*), *stipare* (= to — closely); to — together in bundles or bales, *in fasciculos, in fasces colligare*; to — into a small compass, to crowd, *stipare,* (*co*)*artare, complēre* (= to fill); 2, to — a jury, a meeting, etc., *suos inter judices coetum introducĕre*, etc. **II.** n. 1, = bundle, *fasciculus, sarcina, sarcinula;* — of cards, *chartae;* 2, = a crowd, (*magna*) *frequentia* (*hominum*); = a mob, *turba, grex, gregis,* m. ; see CROWD ; 3, of dogs, *canes, -um.* **pack-ass,** n. *asinus clitellarius* (lit.), *homo clitellarius* (fig. of men, = drudge). **pack-horse,** n. *equus clitellarius.* **pack-saddle,** n. *clitellae.* **pack-thread,** n. *linea.* **package,** n. *sarcina, sarcinula, fasciculus;* see PARCEL, BAGGAGE, LUGGAGE. **packer,** n. *qui alqas res in sarcinam colligit.* **packet,** n. *fasciculus;* = a ship, *navis;* see PARCEL.

pact, n. *pactio, pactum* (= agreement entered into between two litigant parties ; *pactio,* = the **act**; *pactum,* = the terms of the agreement); see COMPACT, CONTRACT.

pad, n. see CUSHION, BOLSTER.

paddle, I. n. *remus;* see OAR. **II.** v.intr. 1, *navem remo impellĕre*; 2, with the hand, etc., *aquam manu,* etc., *agitare.*

padlock, n. in the context, *claustrum.*

pæan, n. † *paean.*

pagan, adj. *paganus* (Eccl.).

page, n. *puer ex aulâ, minister ex pueris regiis, puer regius, puer nobilis ex regiâ cohorte* (at a king's court), *puer paedagogianus* (Imperial Rome).

page, n. of a book, *pagina.*

pageant, n. *spectaculum* (= show) *pompa* (= procession), *apparatus magnifici* (= great preparations at public processions, etc.). **pageantry,** n. see above.

pagoda, n. *templum* or *aedes, -is,* f. (= temple).

pail, n. *situla* (*situlus*); see BUCKET.

pain, I. n. *dolor* (in gen., of body and mind), *maestitia* (= grief), *desiderium* (= grief for the absent or the dead); violent —, *cruciatus, -ūs* (of body and mind); to cause —, *dolorem facĕre* (*efficĕre, afferre, commovĕre, excitare* or *incutĕre;* to anyone, *alci*). **II.** v.tr. *alqm cruciare* or *dolore afficĕre* (lit. and fig.). **III.** v.intr. *dolēre;* see above. **painful,** adj. *vehemens* (= causing violent feeling, e.g. an evil, a wound), *gravis* (= serious, severe, i.e. complaint, wound), *acerbus* (= heartfelt, e.g. death); — sensation, *dolor;* wherever a man is, he has the same — feeling at the complete ruin both of public affairs and of his own private circumstances, *quocumque in loco quisquis est, idem est ei sensus et eadem acerbitas, ex interitu rerum et publicarum et suarum;* that is — to me, *hoc mihi dolet* (ante class.). Adv. *vehementer, graviter, acerbe, dolenter, summo* or *magno cum dolore.* **painless,** adj. *sine dolore, doloris expers, dolore vacuus, vacans* or *carens.* Adv. by adj. **painlessness,** n. *indolentia,* or by circumloc. *dolore vacare* or *carēre, non* or *nihil dolēre* (e.g. — is, according to Epicurus, the

highest pleasure, *summa voluptas est, ut Epicuro placet, nihil dolēre,* or *Epicuro placuit omni dolore carēre summam esse voluptatem,* Cic.). **pains,** n. = toil, *opera* (of one's own), *virium contentio* (= exertion of power), *labor,* comb. *opera et labor* (see LABOUR), *negotium* (from *nec* and *otium,* = absence of leisure, through work that we are executing, etc. ; then the performance of the work, particularly of that which causes uneasiness of mind, trouble), *studium* (= zeal, assiduity) ; with a great deal of —, *non facile;* only with the greatest —, *aegerrime, vix* (= hardly) ; with great —, *multâ operâ, magno labore, multo labore et sudore, multo negotio;* with all possible —, *omni virium contentione, omni ope atque operâ;* with very little —, without the least —, *facile,* generally *nullo negotio* or *sine negotio;* carefully, and with great —, *fide et operâ;* to take —, *multam operam consumĕre;* to take — in order to, etc., *operam dare, niti, eniti, contendĕre, ut,* etc. ; to take all possible — in order to, etc., *omni ope atque operâ* or *omni virium contentione niti* (or *eniti*), *ut,* etc., *contendĕre et laborare, ut,* etc., *eniti et contendĕre, ut,* etc., *eniti et efficĕre, ut,* etc. ; see TOIL, TROUBLE, ANXIETY. **painstaking,** adj. *operosus;* see LABORIOUS, INDUSTRIOUS.

paint, I. v.tr. 1, *pingĕre* (intr. and tr.), *depingĕre* (tr., = to depict, with the pencil or with words, describe), *effingĕre* (= to portray, with the pencil) ; to — from nature, from life (in an absolute sense), *similitudinem effingĕre ex vero;* to — anyone's likeness, *alqm pingĕre;* to — anyone's likeness with a striking resemblance, *veram alcjs imaginem reddĕre;* to — anything in different colours and in light sketches, *varietate colorum adumbrare;* 2, = to besmear with colour, *illinĕre alqd alqâ re, sublinĕre alqd alqâ re* (= to lay on a ground colour), *inducĕre alqd alqâ re* or *alci rei* (e.g. *parietes minio,* = to — the walls red) ; with different colours, *coloribus* (*variare et*) *distinguĕre;* to — blue, *colorem caeruleum inducĕre alci rei;* all the Britons — their bodies with woad, *omnes se Britanni vitro inficiunt;* to — white (to whitewash), *dealbare* (e.g. *parietem*), *polire albo* (e.g. pillars, *columnas*) ; to — the face, *fucare.* **II.** n. *pigmentum, color, fucus* = cosmetic; see COLOUR. **paint-brush,** n. *penicillus.* **painter,** n. *pictor;* a — of houses, *qui* (*parietes,* etc.) *colore inducit.* **painting,** n. *pictura* (in gen. also = that which is painted), *ars pingendi* or *picturae* (= art of —, also *pictura*).

pair, I. n. *par* (of two persons or things in close connection), *jugum* (lit. = a yoke of oxen ; then two persons joined together for an evil purpose, e.g. *jugum impiorum nefarium,* Cic.); *bini* (= two at a time, two together, e.g. *binos* [*scyphos*] *habebam;* *jubeo promi utrosque,* I had a — [of glasses]; I want this —); *utrique* (= this —, the — mentioned); see COUPLE, BRACE. **II.** v.tr. (*con*)*jungĕre.* **III.** v.intr. *jungi, conjungi,* (*con*)*jungĕre, coire* (= to copulate).

palace, n. *domus, -ūs, regia,* or simply *regia* (= royal mansion, *palatium* only in poetry and late prose), *domus, -ūs,* f. (house in gen., very often sufficient in the context).

palate, n. *palatum;* a fine —, *subtile palatum, doctum et eruditum palatum;* a very fine —, *palatum in gustatu sagacissimum;* he has a fine —, *sapit et palatum* (Cic.) ; see TASTE, RELISH. **palatable,** adj. *jucundi saporis* (= of pleasant taste), *jucundus, suavis, dulcis* (= sweet, pleasant) ; see SAVOURY, RELISH. **palatal,** adj. *palatilis* (Gram. t.t.).

palatinate, n. *palatinatus.*

palaver, n. *nugae;* see NONSENSE.

pale, I. adj. *pallidus, luridus* (= black and

blue), *albus* (= white), *decolor* (= discoloured); — colour, *pallidus color, pallor ;* to be —, *pallēre ;* of colours, expressing shade by *sub* (e.g. *subflavus,* = — yellow, Suet.). **II.** v.intr. *pallescĕre ;* see above ; to — before, *alqā re* or *ab alqo vinci.* **paleness,** n. *pallor, pallidus color, macula* †*alba* (= a white spot).

pale, paling, I. n. *palus, -udis,* f. (in gen.), *sudes, -is,* f. (= a stake to prop up trees ; in fortification, a pile driven into the ground for defence), *stipes, -itis,* m. (= stem of a tree used as a stake), *vallus* (= pole for fortifying a rampart, etc., palisade); see STAKE, POST. **II.** v.tr. *ad palum alligare* (trees); to — the vine, *vites palis adjungĕre ;* = to surround, *palis cingĕre ;* see SURROUND. **palisade**, n. *vallum, palus ;* to surround with a —, *vallo munire* or *cingĕre* or *circumdare, vallare.* **palisading,** n. *vallum, valli ;* see PALE.

palette, n. *patella* or *discus colorum.*

palfrey, n. *equus* or *caballus.*

palimpsest, n. *palimpsestus.*

palinode, n. *palinodia* (better written as Greek παλινῳδία).

pall, n. 1, *pallium ;* see MANTLE ; 2, = covering thrown over the dead, *tegumentum* or *involucrum feretri.*

pall, v.intr., to — upon anyone, *alqm alcjs rei taedet.*

palladium, n. *palladium.*

pallet, n. = a small bed, *lectulus, grabatus.*

palliasse, n. *lectus stramenticius.*

palliate, v.tr. *alqd excusare, extenuare ;* to — anything with, *praetendĕre alqd alci rei, tegĕre* or *occultare alqd alqā re, excusatione alcjs rei tegĕre alqd* (= to cover, varnish by means of an excuse, Cic.), *alqd in alcjs rei simulationem conferre* (= to hide under pretence, Caes.); see EXCUSE. **palliation,** n. use verb (e.g. the — of his fault, *culpam excusavit*).

pallid, adj. see PALE.

palm, I. n. 1, *palma ;* see HAND ; 2, a plant, *palma* (= — -tree, also a branch of it worn in token of victory); to present the — to anyone (as token of victory), *dare alci palmam ;* adorned with —, *palmatus.* **II.** v.tr. to — off upon anyone, *centonem alci sarcire* (Com.), *imponĕre alci* (absolute), *alqd alci supponĕre ;* he has —ed anything upon him, *verba illi dedit ;* see IMPOSE. **palmary,** adj. *palmaris.* **palmer,** n. see PILGRIM. **palmistry,** n. either use χειρομαντεία in Greek characters, or *ars eorum qui manuum lineamenta perscrutantur.* **palmy,** adj. *florens* (= flourishing), *optimus* (= best).

palpable, adj. 1, lit. *quod sentire possumus, a(d)spectabilis* (= visible), *tractabilis* (= that may be touched); see PERCEPTIBLE ; *quod manu tenēre possumus, quod manu tenetur ;* 2, fig. *quod comprehensum animis habemus, manifestus* (= manifest), *evidens* (= evident), *apertus* (= open, clear), comb. *apertus ac manifestus* (e.g. *scelus*). Adv. *manifesto, evidenter, aperte.*

palpitate, v. intr. *palpitare ;* see BEAT. **palpitation,** n. *palpitatio* (Plin.).

palsy, n. see PARALYSIS.

paltry, adj. *vilis ;* see PETTY.

pamper, v.tr. *alci nimis indulgēre ;* see FEED, GLUT, INDULGE.

pamphlet, n. *libellus.* **pamphleteer,** n. *libellorum scriptor.*

pan, n. *sartago* (Plin.), *patina, patella ;* see DISH. **pancake,** n. *laganum* or *placenta.*

panacea, n. lit. *panchrestum medicamentum* (Ht. in Plin., fig in Cic.); *panacea* (= a plant, the heal-all).

pandects, n. *pandectae* (Imperial Rome).

pander, I. n. *leno.* **II.** v.intr. to — to, 1, lit. *lenocinari ;* 2, fig. *alci inservire,* or perhaps *blandiri ;* see FLATTER.

pane, n. *vitreum quadratum* (square).

panegyric, n. *laudatio,* upon anyone, *alcjs* (of a speech, oration, and the praise contained in it), *laus, laudes,* upon anyone, *alcjs ;* — upon one deceased, *laudatio (mortui)* in gen. **panegyrist,** n. *laudator* (in gen. ; fem., *laudatrix*), *praedicator* (loud and in public).

panel, n. (in architecture) *tympanum* (= square — of a door), *abacus* (in wainscoting), *intertignium, intercolumnium* (= square compartment on the ceilings of rooms) ; a panelled ceiling, *lacunar,* †*laquear.*

pang, n. *dolor, doloris stimulus ;* see STING, ANGUISH, AGONY.

panic, n. *pavor, terror.*

pannier, n. *clitellae.*

panoply, n. see ARMOUR.

panorama, n. perhaps *tabula in modum circi picta ;* see also PROSPECT.

pant, v.intr. of the heart ; see PALPITATE, BEAT ; to — for breath, *aegre ducĕre spiritum, anhelare ;* to — for, fig. *sitire, concupiscĕre alqd.* **panting,** n. *anhelitus, -ūs.*

pantaloon, n. perhaps *sannio, scurra,* m.

pantheism, n. *ratio eorum qui deum in universā rerum naturā situm esse putant.* **pantheist,** n. *qui deum,* etc., *putat ;* see above.

panther, n. *panthēra* (Plin.), *pardus* (Plin.).

pantomime, n. *mimus, pantomīmus* (Suet.).

pantry, n. *cella penaria, promptuarium* (where victuals are kept).

pap, n. 1, *papilla, uber, -ĕris,* n. ; see BREAST ; 2. = soft food for infants, *puls, pulticula* (= gruel) (Plin.).

papa, n. *pater ;* see FATHER.

papacy, n. *papatus* (= dignity of the Pope). **papal,** adj. *papalis.* **papist,** n. *sacra a pontifice Romano instituta sequens, legis pontificis Romani studiosus.*

paper, I. n. 1, as material for writing upon, *charta* (made from the papyrus, then any kind of writing material), †*papyrus,* f. ; 2, = — written on, writing, *charta, scriptum ;* papers (i.e. written —), *scripta, -orum, lit(t)erae, epistulas (epistol-), libelli, tabellae ;* public —s, *tabulae publicae ;* — money, currency, *pecunia chartacea,* or *syngrapha publica ;* — -hanging, *tapete, -is (tapetum,* = tapestry) ; = newspaper, *acta (diurna), -orum.* **II.** v.tr. to — a room, *conclavis parietes tapetibus ornare.* **III.** adj. *chartaceus* (Jct.). **paper-hanger,** n. *qui conclavium parietes tapetibus ornat.*

papyrus, n. *papyrus,* f. (*papyrum*).

par, n. (in gen.) see EQUALITY (in commerce) by *aequalis ;* — of exchange, *vicissitudines rei argentariae aequales, pecunias permutandae pretium aequale.*

parable, n. *parabŏla* (class. = a comparison), or in pure Latin *collatio, tra(ns)latio, similitudo ;* see ALLEGORY, SIMILE. **parabolical,** adj. *per similitudinem,* or *tra(ns)lationem* or *collationem ;* to speak —ly, *ut similitudine utar.*

parade, I. n. 1, in military affairs, *decursus, -ūs, decursio ;* 2, = show, *ostentatio, apparatus, -ūs ;* see SHOW, DISPLAY. **II.** v.intr. (of troops), *decurrĕre.* **III.** v.tr. *ostentare ;* see DISPLAY.

paradigm, n. in Gram., *paradigma.*

Paradise, n. 1, *paradisus* (Eccl.); 2, = a

very delightful spot, *locus amoenissimus;* **3,** = the blissful seat after death, *sedes (-is,* f.) *beatorum.*

paradox, n. *quod est admirabile contraque opinionem omnium,* in the pl. *quae sunt admirabilia,* etc., also simply *admirabilia* or *mirabilia quaedam,* in pl. *paradoxa.* **paradoxical,** adj. see above.

paragon, n. *specimen;* see PATTERN.

paragraph, n. *caput* (= section).

parallel, I. adj. 1, *parallēlos;* 2, fig. *(con)similis;* a — passage, *locus congruens verbis et sententiis.* **II.** n. 1, *linea parallela;* 2, fig., perhaps *similitudo;* to draw a —, *alqd cum alqā re conferre;* see COMPARE, COMPARISON. **III.** v.tr. *alqd cum alqā re aequare, comparare, conferre;* see COMPARE. **parallelogram,** n. * parallelogrammon.

paralogism, n. (in logic) *falsa ratio;* to make a —, *vitiose concludĕre;* see SOPHISM.

paralysis, n. 1, *paralysis* (Plin.), in pure Latin *nervorum remissio;* 2, fig. perhaps by *impotens, invalidus;* see POWERLESS. **paralytical,** adj. *paralyticus* (Plin.). **paralyse,** v.tr. 1, lit. *pede (manu,* etc.) *captum* or *debilem esse* (to be —d); see LAME; 2, fig. *invalidum reddĕre, affligĕre, percellĕre* (Cels.).

paramount, adj. and n. see CHIEF, SUPERIOR.

paramour, n. see LOVER, MISTRESS.

parapet, n. *pluteus, lorica* (milit. term.).

paraphernalia, n. *apparatus, -ūs;* see DRESS, ORNAMENT.

paraphrase, I. n. *circuitio, circuitus, -ūs, eloquendi, circuitus plurium verborum, circumlocutio* (all = circumlocution rather than simply —), *paraphrasis, -is,* f. (Quint.). **II.** v.tr. and intr. *pluribus alqd exponĕre et explicare* (Cic., Quint.), *pluribus vocibus et per ambitum verborum alqd enuntiare* (Suet.), *circuitu plurium verborum ostendĕre alqd* (Quint.).

parasite, n. 1, *parasĭtus,* fem. *parasita* (= a trencher friend), *assec(u)la, parasĭtaster* (= a wretched —); 2, = a plant, *planta parasitica.* **parasitic, parasitical,** adj. *parasiticus* (παρασιτικός). **parasitism,** n. *parasitatio, ars parasitica* (Com.).

parasol, n. *umbella* (Juv.), *umbraculum.*

parboiled, adj. *semicoctus* (Plin.).

parcel, I. n. 1, see PART, PORTION; 2, see QUANTITY, MASS; 3, = package, *fascis, -is,* m., *fasciculus* (= a bundle, containing several things together), *sarcina* (= burden, carried by a man or a beast); see PACKET. **II.** v.tr. *partiri* (= to divide), *dividĕre, distribuĕre, metiri* (= to measure); see DIVIDE.

parch, I. v.tr. *(ex)siccare, arefacĕre, torrefacĕre, (ex)urĕre.* **II.** v.intr. *(ex)siccari, siccescĕre, arefieri, arescĕre* (the latter two = to become dry); see BURN, DRY. **parched,** adj. *aridus;* see DRY.

parchment, n. *membrana.*

pardon, I. v.tr. *ignoscĕre alci rei* or *alci alqd, veniam alcjs rei dare alci;* to — an oath, *jurisjurandi gratiam alci facĕre, solvĕre alqm sacramento* (= to free from the obligation); to — a debt, *pecuniam creditam condonare* or *remittĕre, creditum condonare, debitum remittĕre alci.* **II.** n. *venia, remissio* (e.g. the foregoing of a payment, *remissio tributi);* to ask —, *remissionem petĕre, veniam praeteritorum precari;* see FORGIVE, INDULGENCE, OVERLOOK. **pardonable,** adj. †*excusabilis, cui alqa venia dare potest.*

pare, v.tr. *(de)secare, resecare, circumsecare* (= to cut off in gen.), *subsecare* (= to cut off a

26

little), *circumcīdĕre* (= to cut off all round). **parings,** n. *praesegmina, -um* (ante and post class.).

parent, n. see FATHER, MOTHER; *parens* (in gen.), *procreator* (= creator), *genitor.* **parentage,** n. *stirps, genus, -ĕris,* n.; see EXTRACTION, BIRTH. **parental,** adj., by the genit. *parentum,* e.g. — love, *parentum amor.* Adv. *parentum more.* **parentless,** adj. *orbatus* or *orbus (parentibus).*

parenthesis, n. *interpositio, interclusio (quam nos interpositionem vel interclusionem dicimus, Graeci* παρένθεσιν *vocant, dum continuationi sermonis medius alqs sensus intervenit,* Quint.); to put anything in —, *alqd continuationi sermonis medium interponĕre.* **parenthetical,** adj. a — remark, *verba (orationi) interposita.*

parhelion, n. *parelion, sol alter* or *imago solis* (Sen.).

pariah, n. *unus e faece populi.*

parietal, adj. by circuml. with *paries;* see WALL.

parish, n. *paroecia (parochia)* (Eccl.). **parishioner,** n. *parochianus* (Eccl.).

parity, n. see EQUALITY.

park, n. 1, *vivarium* (= preserve, Plin.), *saeptum* (sep-) *venationis* (Var.) or perhaps *saeptum* alone (= enclosure); 2, *horti* (= gardens), *viridarium* (= garden planted with trees).

parley, I. v.intr. *colloqui alqd cum alqo,* gen. *colloqui de alqā re* (= to speak with another about anything), *conferre alqd, consilia conferre de alqā re, communicare cum alqo de alqā re* (= to communicate about anything), *appropriately agĕre, disceptare cum alqo de alqā re* (= to confer on some point of mutual concern), *coram conferre alqd;* (in a military sense), to — (respecting the surrender of a town), *legatum* or *legatos de condicionibus urbis tradendae mittĕre.* **II.** n. *colloquium, sermo.*

parliament, n. (in England) *senatus, -ūs;* to convoke the —, *senatum convocare* or *cogĕre;* an act of —, *senatus consultum;* house of —, *curia;* member of —, *senator.* **parliamentary,** adj. *senatorius, quod ad senatum pertinet.*

parlour, n. see ROOM.

parochial, adj. * *parochialis;* see PARISH.

parody, I. n. (of a poem) *poëtae verba et versus ad aliud quoddam idque ridiculum argumentum detorta,* or Greek παρωδία. **II.** v.tr. (a poem) *poëtae verba et versus ad aliud quoddam idque ridiculum argumentum detorquēre.*

parole, n. (in military affairs) *fides (data);* see WORD.

paroxysm, n. 1, *febris accessio* (Cels.), or *accessus, -ūs;* 2, fig. *vis* or *impetus,* or by part. (e.g. *irā impulsus,* = under a — of anger).

parricide, n. 1, *parricīda,* m. and f., the person *(parentis sui);* 2, the act, *parricidium.* **parricidal,** adj. see MURDEROUS.

parrot, n. *psittacus.*

parry, v.tr. and intr. 1, in fencing, to — a thrust or stroke, *ictum* (or *petitionem) vitare, cavēre, cavēre et propulsare,* also simply *cavēre, vitare* (with the sword), *ictum declinare, petitionem declinatione et corpore effugĕre,* also simply *ictum effugĕre* (by a movement of the body); to — well, *recte cavēre;* to try to —, or to — anyone's thrust with the shield, *ad alcjs conatum scutum tollĕre;* to — and strike again, *cavēre et repetĕre;* —ing, *ictus propulsatio;* 2, fig. to — an evil blow, etc., *amovēre* (= to avert), *depellĕre, repellĕre, propellĕre, propulsare, defendĕre* (= to ward off), *deprecari* (lit. by entreaties); see FENCE, AVOID.

parse, v.tr. *sententiam* or *locum quasi in membra discerpĕre*; to — words, *quae sint singula verba explicare*. **parsing**, n. use verb.

parsimonious, adj. (gen. in an ill sense, but sometimes in a good sense = frugal) *parcus* (= who is always afraid to give too much, esp. in expenditure, opp. *nimius*, who goes too far in anything, Plin.), *restrictus* (= who does not like to give, opp. *largus*), comb. *parcus et restrictus*, *tenax* (= tight, opp. *profusus*), also comb. *parcus et tenax*, *restrictus et tenax*; *malignus* (= niggard, who grudges everything); see MEAN. Adv. *parce*, *maligne* (= too sparingly, e.g. *laudare*, Hor.), *restricte*. **parsimony**, n. *parsimonia alcjs rei* (= being careful with anything, then in avoiding expenditure; e.g. *parsimonia temporis*); too great —, *tenacitas* (= being close, never coming out with anything, Liv.), *malignitas* (= niggardliness); see MEANNESS.

parsley, n. *apium*, *oreoselinum* or *petroselinum* (Plin.).

parsnip, n. *pastināca* (Plin.).

parson, n. *presbyter*, *clericus*, or by *sacerdos*. **parsonage**, n. *aedes presbyteri*.

part, I. n. *pars*, *membrum* (= limb, e.g. of the body, of a discourse), *locus* (= important passage, point in a science, treatise); the middle, furthest, lowest, highest — of anything is rendered by *medius*, *extremus*, *infimus*, *summus*, in the same case as the thing itself (e.g. the middle — of a line of battle, *acies media*; the highest — of the mountain, *mons summus*); for the most —, *magnam partem*, *plerumque* (= in most cases, as regards time); in two, three —**s**, etc., *bifariam*, *trifariam*, *bipartito*, *tripartito*, etc.; the greater —, *aliquantum* with genit. (e.g. *viae*); the one —, the other —, *pars . . . pars*, *partim . . . partim* (also with genit. or with the prep. *ex*), *pars* or *partim . . . alii* (*-ae, -a*), *alii* (*-ae, -a*) . . . *alii* (*-ae, -a*) (all of persons and things); partly . . . partly, *partim . . . partim* (but the latter particles can only be used when we speak of a real division into parts), *quā . . . quā* (= on the one hand . . . on the other hand), *et . . . et*, *cum . . . tum*, *tum . . . tum* (= both . . . and); I for my —, *ego quidem*, *equidem* (= if I must give my own opinion, etc.; for which moderns often put badly, *quod ad me attinet*), *pro meā parte* (= according to my power); to divide into —s, *in partes dividĕre* or *distribuĕre*; to receive a — of anything, *partem alcjs rei accipĕre*; to take a — in anything, *alcjs rei participem* or *in parte* or *in societate alcjs rei esse*, *partem* or *societatem in alqā re habēre* (in some good act), *alcjs rei socium esse* (in some good and in some wicked action), *affinem esse alcjs rei* or *alci rei* (in something that is bad); to take — in anything, *partem alcjs rei capĕre* (e.g. in the government of a republic, *administrandae reipublicae*), *in partem alcjs rei venire*, *interesse alci rei* (= to be present at anything, to take — in or exercise influence, e.g. in the battle, *pugnae*), *attingĕre* (by action, in a business transaction, in the carrying out of anything); to have no — in anything, *alcjs rei expertem esse*, *partem alcjs rei non habēre*; to allow anyone to take a — in consultations, *alqm in consilium adhibēre* or *ad consilium admittĕre*; in —, partly, *per partes*, *particulatim* (mostly post class.); *carptim* (= in pieces, when one — is taken now, and another at some other time, and so on, opp. *universi*, e.g. *seu carptim partes* [i.e. partly and in different lots], *seu universi* [*convenire*] *mallent*, Liv.); *ex parte*, *alqā ex parte* (= in —, when only a — of the whole is taken at a time, or only a few parts at a time, etc. opp. *totus*, e.g. to conquer a town —, *urbem ex parte*

capĕre; to please —, *ex parte placēre*; to be changed —, *alqā ex parte commutari*), *nonnullā parte* (inasmuch as the parts do not form a connected whole, but are isolated, "here and there," e.g. *summotis sub murum cohortibus ac nonnullā parte propter terrorem in oppidum compulsis*); to take one's — with one, or to take — with one, *in alcjs partes transire*, *transgredi*, *alqm defendĕre*, *pro alcjs salute propugnare* (the latter two = to defend, e.g. very eagerly, *acerrime*), against anyone, *stare cum algo adversus alqm*; to take in good —, *in bonam partem accipĕre*; to act a —, *agĕre alqm* or *alcjs partes*, *alcjs personam tueri*; on the — of . . ., *ab algo* (e.g. on his — nothing will be done, *ab eo* or *ab illo nihil agitur*; on his — we have nothing to fear, *ab eo nihil nobis timendum est*, also by *alcjs verbis*, *alcjs nomine*, in anyone's name; see NAME); a — (music), *modi musici compluribus vocibus descripti*; — singing, *complurium vocum cantus*; in these —s, *hāc regione*, *hic*; good —s; see ABILITY, SPEECH. **II.** v.tr. *dividĕre*, *partiri*; see DIVIDE, SEPARATE. **III.** v.intr. *digredi*, *discedĕre*. **parting**, n. *digressio*, *digressus*, *-ūs*, *discessus*, *-ūs*. **partly**, adv. *partim*, (*alqā*) *ex parte*; see PART, I.

partake, v.tr., to — of, *participem esse alcjs rei*; of food, see EAT; also PART, I. **partaker**, n. *socius*; — of or in anything, *particeps* or *socius alcjs rei*, *affinis alcjs rei* or *alci rei*; fem. *socia*, in anything, *particeps* or *socia alcjs rei*, *affinis alcjs rei* or *alci rei*.

parterre, n. perhaps *area floribus consita*.

parthenon, n. *Parthenon* (Plin.).

partial, adj. 1, *alterius partis studiosus*, *cupidus* (= acting under the influence of one's passion), *ad gratiam factus* (= what is done to insinuate oneself, *iniquus* (= unfair); 2, = partly, *ex* (*alqā*) *parte*; see PARTLY. Adv. *cupide*, *inique*, *ex* (*alqā*) *parte*. **partiality**, n. *studium* (= the leaning towards one party), *gratia* (= favour shown to one party, e.g. *crimen gratiae*, i.e. accusation of —), *cupiditas* (= bias, esp. of a judge, etc.); to act with —, *cupidius agĕre*; to approve anything through —, *studio quodam comprobare alqd*.

participate, v.intr. and tr., by *particeps alcjs rei* (= anyone who receives a share of anything or takes part in anything, e.g. *ejusdem laudis*; in a conspiracy, *conjurationis*; in a pleasure, *voluptatis*), *consors*, *socius alcjs rei* (= who has joined with others, e.g. *socius sceleris*), *affinis alcjs rei* or *alci rei* (in anything, esp. in a bad action, e.g. *affinis facinori*, *noxae*, *culpae*), *compos alcjs rei* (= who possesses anything, is in the possession of, e.g. anything pleasant, e.g. the consulate, praise), *alcjs rei potens* (= who possesses a thing and is the master over it); to come to — in a thing, *participem* or *compotem fieri alcjs rei*; to — in a crime, *se obstringĕre alqā re*. **participation**, n. *societas*, *communicatio* (in anything, *societas alcjs rei* (= joint — in, e.g. *belli*). **participator**, n. *socius*, *affinis*, *consors*; see PARTICIPATE.

participle, n. *participium* (Gram.).

particle, n. 1, *particula* (in gen.), *frustum* (= a little bit of food, otherwise rare); 2, in gram., *particula*.

particoloured, adj. *versicolor*, *varius*.

particular, adj. *separatus*; everyone has his own — place and his own table, *separatos singulis sedes et sua cuique mensa* (Tac.); = peculiar to anyone, *proprius* (of which we are the only possessors, opp. *communis*); *praecipuus* (in possessing which we have an advantage over others), *peculiaris* (when one thing is to

be distinguished from another, of **a** thing peculiar in its kind), *singularis* (= single, isolated, excellent), *praecipuus* (= excellent), *eximius* (= exceeding ; see EXCELLENT) ; = strange, wonderful, *singularis*, *novus* (= new, what was never seen before), *mirus* (= striking) ; a — case, *mirus quidam casus;* see PECULIAR, EXACT, SINGULAR ; = exacting, *diligens, accuratus;* a — friend; see INTIMATE, PRIVATE. **particulars,** n., in the pl., to go into —, *singula sequi ; scribēre de singulis rebus* (in letters) ; *rem ordine, ut gesta est, narrare.* **particularity,** n. *diligentia.* **particularize,** v.tr. *nominare* (= to name), *enumerare* (= to enumerate), *per nomina citare* (= to mention several persons by name). **particularly,** adv., by *quod curae* or *cordi est; gravis* (= important), or with the advs. *sedulo* (= assiduously), *studiose* (= with zeal), *diligenter* (= with care), *cupide* (= eagerly), *impense* (= urgently), *vehementer* (= vehemently, very much), *magnopēre* (= with all one's mind), *praesertim, praecipue* (= especially), *maxime* (= chiefly), *imprimis (in primis* = above all), *etiam atque etiam* (= over and over), also *vehementer etiam atque etiam ;* to court anyone's friendship most —, *cupidissime alcjs amicitiam appetēre.*

partisan, n. *homo alcjs studiosus fautor.*
partisanship, n. *studium, favor.*

partisan, n. a weapon, *bipennis.*

partition, n. 1, see DIVISION, SEPARATION ; 2, a — in a house, *paries, -ētis,* m. (= wall), *paries intergerinus (intergerivus,* Plin., = common wall between neighbouring houses), *saeptum (sep-,* = fence or place fenced off), *loculamentum* (used of the —s in an aviary).

partitive, adj. in Gram., *partitivus.*

partner, n. 1, lit., by verbs, see PARTAKER, ASSOCIATE ; 2, in commercial business, *socius* (in every sense) ; 3, in marriage, *conju(n)x, -jugis,* m. and f. ; see HUSBAND, WIFE. **partnership,** n. *consortio* (rare), *societas* (as society and persons united in —, Cic.), *socii* (= persons associated together); to form a —, *societatem facĕre ;* to enter into — with anyone, *alqm sibi socium adjungĕre.*

partridge, n. *perdrix.*

parturition, n. *partus, -ūs.*

party, n. 1, *pars,* or pl. *partes* (in gen.), *factio* (lit. = any number of persons who entertain the same sentiments, then esp. in a political sense), *secta*(prop.of philosophers or learned men in gen.); the opposite —, see OPPOSITION ; to belong to anyone's —, *alcjs partis* or *partium esse, alcjs partes sequi, alcjs sectam sequi, cum algo facĕre, ab* or *cum algo stare, alcjs rebus studēre* or *favēre, alcjs esse studiosum ;* not to belong to either, any —, *neutrius partis* or *nullius partis esse* (see NEUTRAL); to favour different parties (of several), *aliorum* (*alias*) *partes fovēre ;* to get anyone over to one's own —, *alqm in suas partes trahĕre, ducĕre ;* to divide into two parties, *in duas partes discedĕre, in duas factiones scindi ;* — zeal in the contest, *studium ;* — leader, *dux* or *princeps partium, princeps* or *caput factionis ;* in the context also simply *dux, caput ;* — spirit (*partium*) *studium ;* — struggle, — dispute, in the State, *certamen partium* or *factionum ;* 2, = company, *aliquot* (= a few, in an indefinite sense), *complures* (=a large number) ; a large —, *copia, multitudo,* also by *alii—alii;* pleasure —, into the country, by *excurrĕre ;* on the water, by *navigare ;* to be one of the —, *una esse cum aliis ;* he who is one of the —, *socius* (= who joins), *comes* (= companion); to be one of the — invited by anyone, to go with a — somewhere, *alci comitem se addĕre* or *adjungĕre ;* a card —, *lusus, -ūs* (= game) ; see

CAUSE, COMPANY. **party-wall,** n. see PARTITION.

parvenu, n. *novus homo.*

paschal, adj. *paschalis* (Eccl.).

pasha, n. *satrapes, -ae* and *-is,* m.

pasquinade, n. *libellus famosus* (= a libel); see LIBEL ; if a poem, *carmen probrosum, famosum, carmen maledicum, elogium* (= verses written at anyone's door, Plaut.); a — upon anyone's voluptuousness, *versus in alcjs cupiditatem facti.*

pass, I. v.intr. 1, *transire, transgredi* (= to go past), *ire* or *venire per alqm locum* (= to — through a place), *alqm locum inire* or *ingredi* or *intrar* (= to enter into a place, of persons), *importari, invehi* (= to be imported, of things), *algo loco exire* or *egredi* (from a place, of persons), *exportari, evehi* (= to be transported away from a place, of things), *alqm locum transcendĕre* or *superare* (= to — through, over a place which lies high, e.g. a mountain) ; to — through the gate, *portā exire* (in going out), *portā introire* (in going in); to — across a river, *flumen transire* or *tra(j)icĕre* or *transmittĕre ;* to let the troops — across a river, *copias flumen* or *trans flumen tra(j)icĕre;* not to allow anyone to —, *alqm aditu prohibēre* (in going past or in going in), *alqm egressione prohibēre, alqm egressu arcēre* (in going out); not to allow anyone to — backwards and forwards, *nec aditu nec reditu alqm prohibēre ;* see Go, etc.; 2, to — into possession of, see GET ; 3, of the time, *transire, praeterire* (= to — by), *abire* (= to go away), *circumagi, se circumagĕre* (= to come round), *exire, praeterire* (= to elapse); the time —es quickly, *tempus fugit, aetas volat;* 4, *perferri* (= to be carried, of a law) ; see ENACT ; 5, = to be tolerated, *probari* (of that which can be approved), *ferri posse* (of what can be tolerated); to let a thing —, *alqd non plane improbare* (= not to disapprove altogether), *alqd ferre* (= to bear); see ALLOW, PERMIT ; 6, = to be considered, *haberi alqm* or *pro algo* (the latter if we consider anyone to be a person of a certain character, etc.); to — as rich, *haberi divitem* (if the person really is so), *haberi pro divite* (if considered as such); 7, = to come to —, *accidĕre ;* see HAPPEN ; 8, in fencing, *alqm petĕre ;* 9, as I —ed along, in —ing, *in transitu, transiens, praeteriens* (also fig. = by-the-bye; the two former in a fig. sense only post-Aug. (e.g. Quint.), but *quasi praeteriens* in Cic.), *strictim* (fig., but superficially, after Seneca also *obiter*); to mention in —ing, *in mentionem alcjs rei incidĕre* (Liv.); 10, to — by, *praeterire* or *praetergredi,* a place, *alqm locum ; transire alqm locum* (= to go beyond a place) ; to let none — by, go past, *neminem praetermittĕre ;* = to cease, *abire ;* of time, *praeterire, transire ;* to — through, *transire* (absol., or with the accus. of the place), *iter facĕre per* (with accus. of the place), *pervadĕre, penetrare* (= to penetrate), *transvehi, vehi per locum* (in a carriage, on board a vessel). **II.** v.tr. 1, = to go beyond, *transgredi* (only lit., e.g. *flumen*), *transire* or *egredi alqd* or *extra alqd* (lit. and fig.), *excedĕre* (fig.); to — the boundaries, limits, *transire fines* (both in entering and leaving a country ; then also fig. *alcjs rei*), *egredi extra fines* (lit., in leaving a country, *terminos egredi,* fig.); to — the fifth year, *egredi quintum annum ;* see SURPASS ; 2, of time, *degĕre, agĕre, transigĕre* (e.g. *diem, vitam,* or *aetatem*) ; with anything or with a person, *ducĕre alqā re* (e.g. the night with interesting conversation, *noctem jucundis sermonibus*), *consumĕre* or *contĕrĕre alqā re* or *in alqā re* (in a good or bad sense), *absumĕre alqā re* (= to waste time, e.g. with talking, *tempus dicendo); extrahĕre alqā re* (when we talk instead of act-

ing), *fallĕre alqd re ;* to — whole days by the fireside, *totos dies juxta focum atque ignem agĕre ;* to — the night, *pernoctare ;* see SPEND ; **3,** to — an examination, *alci satisfacĕre ;* (= to satisfy), *probari* (= to be considered competent, *stare* (= not to fall through in carrying out anytning) ; very honourably, *pulcherrime stare,* in **1** disgraceful manner, *turpem inveniri ;* **4,** of a business, to — accounts, *rationes ratas habĕre ;* see TERMINATE, SETTLE, DIVIDE ; **5,** = to allow to —, *transitum dare alci* (a person), *transmittĕre ;* **6,** = to put through a narrow hole, *tra(j)icĕre, immittĕre, inserĕre* (the latter two = to put into, e.g. one's hand, the key into the keyhole) ; to — thread through a needle, *filum in acum inserĕre ;* **7,** = to — sentence, *sententiam dicĕre* (by word of mouth) or *ferre* (by votes) ; upon anyone, *judicium facĕre de alqo* (e.g. *optimum*) ; to — sentence of death upon anyone, *alqm capitis damnare ;* see SENTENCE ; **8,** to — a law, *decernĕre* (of the Senate), *legem esse jubĕre* (of the people) ; see ENACT. — **away,** v.intr. **1,** see PASS, I. 3 ; **2,** see DIE. — **by,** v.tr. **1,** see PASS, I. 10 ; **2,** see PASS OVER. — **off, I.** v.tr. to — anyone or anything on anyone for anyone or anything, *dicĕre* (= to say), *perhibĕre* (= to call), *ferre* (= to bring forward), *mentiri* (= to say falsely) ; to — anyone, report as being dead, *falsum nuntium mortis alcjs afferre ;* to — anything as one's own, *suum esse alqd dicĕre ;* to—as truth, *verum esse alqd dicĕre, simulare alqd esse verum ;* to — anyone as one's father, *patrem sibi alqm assumĕre ;* to — anyone (falsely) as the author of anything, *alqm auctorem esse alcjs rei mentiri ;* to — anyone by a false report as the founder, *alqm conditorem famâ ferre ;* to — oneself for, *se ferre alqm* (= to report up and down), *se profiteri alqm* (= to declare oneself to be so and so), *simulare, alqm se esse velle* (he will have it that he is so and so), to — himself off as a king, *regis titulum usurpare.* **II.** v.intr. *abire* (used by Cic. of sea-sickness) ; see CEASE. — **on,** v.intr. *pergĕre ;* let us — (in speaking), *pergamus (ad alqd).* — **over, I.** v.tr. any person or thing in speaking (= not to remember), *praeterire* with or without *silentio, relinquĕre,* comb. *praeterire ac relinquĕre, mittĕre, omittĕre* (of one's own free will and with intent. e.g. *omitto jurisdictionem contra leges ; relinquo caedes ; libidines praetereo*) ; to — over, that, etc., *ut omittam, quod,* etc., *ne dicam, quod,* etc. ; —ing over all these circumstances, *omissis his rebus omnibus ;* to be —ed over, *praeteriri* (in gen.), *repulsam ferre* or *accipĕre* (= to be rejected, in the election of an office) ; see NEGLECT. — **round,** v.intr. *tradĕre.* **III.** n. **1,** = a narrow passage, *aditus, -ûs* (= access in gen.), *angustiae locorum,* or simply *angustiae* (= narrow —), *fauces, -ium* (= narrow entrance and exit into a more open country), *saltus, -ûs* (= woody mountain-pass, e.g. near Thermopylae, *Thermopylarum*) ; **2,** see PASSAGE, ROAD ; **3,** = an order to —, *libellus, -ûs, qui alci aditum aperiat ;* **4,** = condition, *eo ventum est ut ;* see CONDITION. **passable,** adj. **1,** *pervius, tritus* (= much frequented) ; or *transitu facilis ;* **2,** = tolerable, *tolerabilis, mediocris.* Adv. *mediocriter.* **passage,** n. **1,** = the act of passing, *transitus, -ûs, transitio, transvectio* (= transit of goods) ; *transgressio, transgressus, -ûs, tra(n)smissio, tra(n)smissis, -ûs, trajectio, trajectus, -ûs* (the substs. in *-io* express the act, those in *-us* the condition, the — itself) ; — across a river, *transitus* or *transvectio fluminis ;* in the — of such large sums of the royal treasure into Italy, *in tantâ pecuniâ regiâ in Italiam trajiciendâ ;* = to grant a — to anyone, *dare alci transitum* or *iter per agros urbesque, alqm per fines suos ire pati, alqm per fines*

regni transirĕ sinĕre (to an army, **to a general** with the army through a country) ; a — across, *transitio, transitus, -ûs ;* **2,** = way, road, *iter, via, aditus, -ûs ;* **3,** — of a book, *locus, caput* (= chapter) ; bird of —, *avis advena ;* see MIGRATORY. **passenger,** n. **1,** on the road, *viator* (on foot), *vector* (on horseback, by carriage, ship) ; **2,** after he has arrived, *hospes, -itis.* **passing,** n. **1,** see PASSAGE ; **2,** in commerce, *permutatio* (= exchange), *venditio* (= sale). **passport,** n. by *facultas (alcjs loci adeundi) data.* **password,** n. *tessera* (= a token). **past, I.** adj. and n., *praeteritus, ante actus* (or as one word, *anteactus,* = done before), *prior, superior* (= last, e.g. last week) ; the —, *praeterita, -orum ;* the — time, tense, *tempus praeteritum ;* pardon for what is —, *venia praeteritorum, rerum praeteritarum* or *ante actarum oblivio ;* the — years, *anni praeteriti* (e.g. since one's birth, etc.), *anni priores* (= the last few years) ; during the — year, *priore* or *superiore anno ;* during the time —, *tempore praeterito* (= the whole of it), *prioribus annis* (= during the last few years) ; during, in the — night, *nocte priore* or *superiore.* **II.** adv. *praeter* (gen. only in comp. with verbs ; when in Lat. we form compounds with *praeter* and *trans, praeter* denotes the direction in which an object moves — another and at the same time removes from it, whilst *trans* expresses the direction from a certain point to the furthest end) ; to hurry —, *praetervolare ;* to drive —, v.tr. *praetervehĕre* or *transvehĕre,* anything, *praeter alqd ;* v.intr. *praetervehi* or *transvehi,* anything, *alqd ;* the driving —, *praetervectio ;* to fly —, *praetervolare ;* to flow —, *praeterfluĕre ;* to lead —, *praeterducĕre* (Plaut.), *transducĕre,* — any place, *praeter alqm locum ;* to go — a place, *praeterire* or *transire alqm locum ;* to let go —, to allow to pass, *praetermittĕre* (lit. persons and things, then = not to avail oneself of, through carelessness, e.g. an opportunity for, *occasionem alcjs rei ;* the day appointed, the term, *diem), transitum alcjs rei exspectare* (= to wait until anything is over, e.g. a storm, *tempestatis), omittĕre* (fig. = to lose, e.g. an opportunity, *occasionem), dimittĕre* (fig. = to allow to pass, because one fancies he is not in want of it, e.g. an opportunity, *occasionem, occasionem fortunâ datam), amittĕre* (= not to heed, through carelessness, so as to be unable to make use of, e.g. *occasionem ;* the favourable moment, *tempus), intermittĕre* (e.g. not a moment, *nullum temporis punctum ;* not a day, without, etc., *nullam diem, quin,* etc.). **III.** as prep. *praeter,* trans. with accus. ; see above II. **pastime,** n. *ludus* (= game), *oblectamentum, oblectatio, delectamentum* (rare).

passion, n. **1,** = suffering, *perpessio, toleratio* (Cic., both with the genit. of that which causes us to suffer) ; — of Christ, **passio* or **perpessio ;* see SUFFERING ; **2,** = excitement, *animi concitatio, animi impetus, -ûs ;* stronger, *animi perturbatio, motus, -ûs, animi turbatus* or *perturbatus* (= violent emotion in gen. ; *animi affectio* = disposition ; affection of the mind ; *animi motus, commotio* or *permotio* = mental excitement in gen.), *cupiditas, cupido* (= longing), *libido* (lubchiefly = sensual desire), *temeritas* (= rashness), *intemperantia* (= want of moderation, licentiousness, opp. *aequitas*) ; = anger, *ira, iracundia ;* = fondness for, *alcjs rei studium ;* violent —, *acerrimus animi motus, -ûs, vehemens animi impetus, -ûs ;* disorderly, unruly —, *libidines, -um ;* without —, *aequo animo ;* to rule over one's —, to conquer —, *perturbatos animi motus cohibĕre, cupidates coërcĕre, cupiditatibus imperare, continentem esse* (esp. with regard to sensuality) ; to be free from —, *ab orni animi concitatione* *vacare, omni animi perturbatione liberum* or *liberatum esse;* **to act** under the influence of —, *cupide agĕre;* **to go so far in one's** — as, etc., *studio sic efferri.* **passionate,** adj. *cupidus* (=greedy, eager), *concita̅ us. incitatus* (=excited), *impotens* (of one who cannot master his passion, always with the genit., e.g. *irae, laetitiae;* then that cannot be restrained, excessive, e.g. *laetitia, postulatum), vehemens, ardens, flagrans* (= eager, ardent), *iracundus, cerebrosus* (= hot-tempered, hasty), *studiosissimus alcjs rei* (= very much given to anything). Adv.*cupide,cupidissime* (=eagerly), *studiose* (=with zeal), *vehementer, ardenter, studio flagranti* (= with extreme zeal), *iracunde* (=hastily), *effuse* or stronger *effusissime* (= beyond all bounds); **to be** — fond of anything, *alci rei effuse indulgēre* (beyond all bounds, e.g. feasting, *conviviis), alcjs rei esse studiosissimum, magno alcjs rei studio teneri* (=to be a great admirer of anything), *alqā re maxime delectari* (= to be quite delighted in); **to love anyone** —, *effusissime alqm deligĕre* (as a friend, etc.). **passionateness,** n. *animi ardor, fu̅or* (in a high degree); — in contending for anything, *ira et studium.* **passionless,** adj. *cupiditatis expers, omni animi perturbatione vacuus* or *liber.* **passive,** adj. 1, by *pati* (e.g. *affectus), accipiendi et quasi patiendi vim habēre* (= to have aptness to suffer, opp. *movendi vim habēre et efficiendi,* Cic.); **to remain** —, *quiescēre;* in anything, *alqā patiender ferre;* under an insult, *acceptā injuriā alci ignoscēre;* one who remains —, *quietus;* 2, — verb, *verbum patiendi* (opp. *verbum agens,* Aul. Gell.), *patiendi modus* (Quint.), *verbum passivum* (late Gram.). Adv. *aequo animo, patienter;* see PASSIVE, 1; in Gram., *passive.* **passiveness,** n. *patientia;* see PATIENCE.

Passover, n. * *Pascha.*

paste. I. n. *farina quā chartae glutinantur* (Plin.). **II.** v.tr. *farinā glutinare.*

pastor, n. 1, see SHEPHERD; 2, * *pastor;* see PREACHER. **pastorship,** n. see MINISTRY. **pastoral, I.** adj. 1, *pastoralis, pastoricius;* in wider sense, *agrestis, rusticus;* 2, *quod ad pastorem pertinet.* **II.** n. = — poem, *carmen bucolicum.*

pastry, n. *panificium* (= bread-making), *opus pistorium, crustum;* = meat-pie, *artocreas* (Pers.). **pastry-cook,** n. *crustulareus* (Sen.); see BAKER.

pasturage, n. 1, = business of feeding cattle, *res pecuaria* or *pecuaria;* 2, see PASTURE. **pasture. I.** n. *pascuum, locus pascuus* (in gen.), *ager pascuus* (= — land); common — land, *ager compascuus.* **II.** v.tr. *pascĕre* (lit. and fig.). **III.** v.intr. *pastum ire, pabulari* (= to graze), *pasci* (= to feed).

pat, I. n. *plaga lĕvis.* **II.** v.tr. perhaps *permulcēre* (= to soothe, of patting a horse). **III.** adv. *in tempore, opportune;* see FIT, CONVENIENCE.

patch, I. n. *pannus.* **II.** v.tr. (re)*sarcire, pannum alci rei assuĕre.* **patchwork,** n. *cento* (= a coat patched together; in modern writers also a written work patched together from different sources).

patent, I. adj. 1, *manifestus, apertus, clarus, certus;* see OPEN; 2, *res cui diploma datum est.* **II.** n. 1, a letter —, = a public order, *edictum;* to issue a —, *edicĕre* or *edictum proponĕre,* with *ut* or *ne* (when anything is prohibited); 2, for some new invention, use *diploma, -ătis,* or *libellus quo beneficium alqd datur* (e.g. *dare alci beneficium salis vendendi,* or *potestas alcjs rei faciendae* or *vendendae.* **III.** v.tr. by n. with *dare;* see above.

paternal, adj. *paternus, patrius* (=fatherly); — property, *res paterna, bona (-orum) paterna, patrimonium;* —disposition, *animus paternus in alqm* (so *animus maternus, fraternus);* — love, *amor paternus* or *patrius.*

path, n. *via* (= way in gen.), *semita, trames, -ĭtis,* m. (= by-road), *callis,* m. and f. (=footpath through a wood, etc.); the — of life, *via vitae;* **to** stray from the — of virtue, *de viā decedĕre;* **to** follow the — of virtue, *virtutem sequi, virtuti operam dare;* **to lead anyone away** from the — of virtue, *alqm transversum agĕre* (in gen.), *alqm ad nequitiam adducĕre* (= to lead to extravagances). **pathless,** adj. *invius;* see WAY, PASSAGE.

pathetic, pathetical, adj. *misericors* (= pitiful), *flebilis, maestus, tristis* (= sad). Adv. *flebiliter, maeste.* **pathos,** n. *maestitia, maeror, tristitia;* there was such — in his speech, *tanta maestitia inerat orationi.*

pathologist, n. *medicus qui valetudinis genera novit.* **pathology,** n. * *pathologia* (t.t.).

patience, n. *patientia, tolerantia* (= strength and perseverance in enduring calamity, etc.; generally with genit., e.g. *tolerantia doloris,* in enduring pain), *perseverantia* (if we shrink from no difficulties, however great), *aequus animus, aequitas animi* (= a quiet mind not disturbed by anything); **to have** — with anyone, *alqm* and *alcjs mores* or *naturam patienter ferre,* or simply *alqm ferre;* — ! i.e. wait ! *exspecta ! mane !* see PERSEVERANCE. **patient, I.** adj. *patiens, tolerans, tolerabilis* (rare, not in Cic., who, however, uses the adv. *tolerabiliter),* in anything, *alcjs rei, placidus;* **to be** —, *ex(s)pectare, manēre* (=to wait), *quiescēre* (= to be quiet). Adv. *patienter, toleranter, tolerabiliter, aequo animo* (= with a calm mind, e.g. **to put up with** anything); **to look at a thing** —, *aequo animo spectare alqd;* **to endure** —, *patienter* or *toleranter ferre alqd, patienter atque aequo animo ferre,* and with *pati ac ferre, pati et perferre, perferre ac pati, perferre patique alqd.* **II.** n. *aeger* (= the sick person).

patois, n. *sermo rusticus.*

patriarch, n. *patriarcha* (Eccl.). **patriarchal,** adj. 1, *patriarchalis* (Eccl.); 2, fig. * *grandaevus;* see OLD.

patrician, adj. and n. *patricius* (opp. *plebeius);* the —s, *patricii.*

patrimony, n. *hereditas* (= inheritance), *patrimonium* (= inherited from the father).

patriot, n. *patriae* or *reipublicae amans, reipublicae amicus* (= who loves his own native country), *civis bonus* (= a good citizen, in general); **to be a** —, *amare patriam, bene de republicā sentire.* **patriotic,** adj. *patriae* or *reipublicae amans.* Adv. *patriae caus(s)ā.* **patriotism,** n. *patriae amor* or *caritas* (= love of one's own country), *pietas erga patriam,* in the context only *pietas* (= the duty which we have towards our own native country), *reipublicae studium;* **if** — is a crime, I have already sufficiently atoned for it, *si scelestum est patriam amare, pertuli poenarum satis;* **to possess** —, *patriam amare, bene de republicā sentire.*

patristic, adj. *patrum* or *quod ad patres pertinet.*

patrol, I. n. *circitores, circuitores* (late). **II.** v.intr. *circumire stationes* (= to examine and watch the outposts), *circumire vigilias* (= to examine the sentinels), *circumire urbem* (= to go round the town).

patron, n. 1, = protector, *patrōnus, fautor, cultor, amator, praeses, -idis,* m. and f. (= guardian); — of the learned, *doctorum cultor* · 2, = a

superior, as a feudal lord, *dominus feudi,* or holder of church property, *patronus ;* — saint, *praeses, -ĭdis,* m. **patronage,** n. = the system of patron and client, *patrocinium, clientela, praesidium,* to be under the —, *sub alcjs fĭde et clientelā esse.* **patroness,** n. *patrona.* **patronize,** v.tr. *alqd gratiā et auctoritate suā sustentare.*

patronymic, adj. and n. *patronymicum nomen* (Gram.).

patten, n. *lignea solea* (= mere wooden sole tied under the feet), *sculponea* (= a kind of higher wooden shoe).

patter, I. v.intr. *crepare, crepitare, crepitum dare* (= to clatter), *strepĕre, strepitum dare* (= to rattle). **II.** n. *crepitus, -ūs, strepitus, -ūs.*

pattern, n. 1, = example, *exemplum, exemplar, specimen, documentum, proplasma, -ătis,* n. (of a sculptor, Plin.) ; to set a —, *exemplum proponere ad imitandum ;* a — of excellence, *excellentiae specimen ;* 2, = sample, *exemplum.*

paucity, n. *paucitas,* or by adj. *pauci.*

paunch, n. *abdōmen* (proper term), *venter* (= stomach in gen.).

pauper, n. see POOR. **pauperism,** n. see POVERTY.

pause, I. n. *mora* (= delay), *respiratio, interspiratio* (= interval in speaking, in order to take breath), *distinctio* (in music, Cic.), *intervallum* (= interval, e.g. to make a pause in speaking, *intervallo dicĕre,* e.g. *distincta alias et interpuncta intervalla, morae respirationesque delectant,* Cic. ; but as regards music = stop), *intermissio* (when anything stops for a while), *intercapēdo* (= interval, interruption, e.g. to make a — in writing letters, in one's correspondence, *intercapedinem scribendi facĕre*). **II.** v.intr. *moram facĕre* (= to make a delay), *intersistĕre* (= to stop for a while, during a speech, etc., Quint.) ; to — in anything, *moram facĕre in alqā re* (in paying, *in solvendo*), *intermittĕre alqd* (= to discontinue for a time), *alqd faciendi intercapedinem facĕre ;* I do not — a single moment in my work during the night, *nulla pars nocturni tempori ad laborem intermittitur ;* see CEASE, INTERMIT.

pave, v.tr. *lapide* or *silice (con)sternĕre* or *persternĕre* (in gen.), *munire* (= to make a road). **pavement,** n. *pavimentum,* † *strata viarum, via strata* (= paved road). **paving,** n. *stratura* (Suet.). **paving-stone,** n. *saxum quadratum.*

pavilion, n. *papilio* (= a tent erected for pleasure in summer ; late) ; see TENT.

paw, I. n. *pes, pedis,* m. (= foot), *ungula* (= claw). **II.** v.tr. *(solum,* etc.) *pedibus ferire.*

pawn, I. n. *pignus, -ĕris,* n. ; see PLEDGE. **II.** v.tr. *alqd pignori dare* or *opponĕre.* **pawnbroker,** n. *pignerator* or *qui pignora quaestus caus(s)ā accipit.* (The Romans had no system of pawnbroking.)

pawn, n. at chess, *latrunculus, latro.*

pay, I. v.tr. *(per)solvĕre, exsolvĕre, dissolvĕre, pendĕre, dependĕre* (= to weigh out), *pensitare, numerare, numerato solvĕre* (in ready money) ; not to be able to —, *non esse solvendo* or *ad solvendum ;* to — cash, *praesenti pecuniā solvĕre, repraesentare ;* to — a penalty, *poenas dare* or *solvĕre ;* to — for, = to give money for, *alqd pro alqā re solvĕre ;* = to atone for, *luĕre ;* to — for with one's life, *alqd capite luĕre ;* see ATONE. **II.** v.intr. *fructum ferre, quaestuosum, fructuosum esse.* **III.** n. *merces, -ēdis,* f. (= wages), *stipendium* (of a soldier), *quaestus, -ūs* (= gain). **payable,** adj. *solvendus ;* a bill is — at sight, *pecunia ex syngraphā solvenda est.* **pay-day,** n. *dies quo merces solvenda est,* or *dies* alone if fixed by con-

text. **paymaster,** n. 1, in gen. *qui alqd solvit ;* see STEWARD ; 2, in the army, *tribunus aerarius.* **payment,** n. *solutio, repraesentatio* (= ready-money —).

pea, n. *pisum* (Plin.), *cicer, -ĕris,* n. (= chick-pea).

peace, I. n. *pax, otium* (= leisure), *concordia* (= agreement) ; in —, *in pace ;* to treat for —, *agĕre de pacis condicionibus ;* to enter on —, *inire pacem ;* to make —, *facĕre pacem ;* to keep or preserve —, *pacis fĭdem servare ;* to break —, *pacem frangĕre, violare ;* to have no —, *turbari, vexari,* from someone, *ab algo ;* to leave a person in —, *alqm non turbare ;* to dismiss in —, *alqm cum pace demittĕre ;* articles of —, *pacis leges, condiciones ;* to bring —, *ferre ;* to prescribe —, *dicĕre ;* to accept —, *accipĕre ;* love of —, *pacis amor.* — one who studies —, *pacis amans, congruens ;* to bind over to keep the —, *pecuniā de vi cavēre.* **II.** interj. *tace, tacete ! Pax !* **peaceable,** adj. *placidus, placabilis, concors.* Adv. *placide, concorditer, congruenter.* **peaceful,** adj. *pacatus, placidus, quietus, tranquillus.* Adv. *placide, quiete, tranquille, cum (bonā) pace.* **peacefulness,** n., **peacemaker,** n. see PEACE. **peace-offering,** n. *piaculum, placamen ;* see TREATY, TRUCE.

peacock, n. *pavo.*

peak, n. 1, generally by *summus* or *extremus* (= the uppermost or furthest part, etc., e.g. the — of the mountain, *summum montis jugum*) ; see SUMMIT, TOP ; 2, = the end of anything that terminates in a point, *apex ;* see POINT.

peal, I. n. *sonitus, -ūs, comparanum* (of bells) ; — of laughter, *cachinnus ;* — of applause, *plausūs clamores ;* — of thunder, *tonitrus, -ūs, fragor* (mostly poet.). **II.** v.tr. perhaps *campanas movēre* or *ciēre.* **III.** v.intr. *sonare.*

pear, n. *pirum.* **pear-tree,** n. *pirus,* f.

pearl, n. *margarita.* **pearly,** adj. *margaritam similis.*

peasant, n. *agricola,* m., *agricultor,* in the context also simply *cultor* (= countryman, in reference to his occupation ; poetic, *ruricola), rusticus* (both in reference to his occupation and to his manners, hence = an uncultivated person, without refinement, in opp. to *urbanus,* a refined civilian), *agrestis* (in reference to his dwelling in the country ; also with regard to his rude manners), *rusticanus* (= brought up in the country), *paganus, vicanus* (= villager, opp. *oppidanus).* **peasantry,** n. *rustici, agrestes.*

pease, n. see PEA.

pebble, n. *calculus, lapillus.*

peccadillo, n. *culpa, delictum ;* see FAULT.

peccant, adj. *peccans.*

peck, I. n. = a measure, perhaps *semodius.* **II.** v.tr. *rostro tundĕre* (= to strike) or *caedĕre, vellicare.*

pectoral, adj. *pectoralis* (Cels.).

peculation, n. *peculatus, -ūs (publicus) ;* to commit —, *pecuniam avertĕre, peculari ;* to be accused of —, *peculatūs accusari ;* see EMBEZZLE.

peculiar, adj. 1, = belonging to a person, *proprius* (= both what belongs to anyone as his property and what is — to him, in Cic. only with genit.), *meus, tuus, suus* (= *proprius*), comb. *proprius et meus, praecipuus et proprius* (= particular and —), *peculiaris* (= what anyone possesses as his own, esp. of one's own earnings), comb. *peculiaris et proprius, privatus* (= what belongs to anyone as his own property, opp. *publicus), singularis* (= what belongs to anyone as his characteristic feature) ; this failing is not merely — to old people, *id quidem non proprium* *senectutis est vitium;* it is — to man, etc., *est naturâ sic generata hominis vis,* etc. (Cic.), to every man, *cujusvis hominis est* (e.g. to err, *errare,* Cic.); see PARTICULAR, SPECIAL; 2, = singular, *mirus, novus;* see STRANGE. Adv. *praesertim, maxime, imprimis (in primis), mirum in modum, mire.* **peculiarity,** n. *proprietas* (= peculiar nature of anything), *natura* (= natural state, characteristic feature); what is a noble — in his style, *quod orationi ejus eximium inest;* everyone should as much as possible preserve his own —, *id quemque maxime decet quod est cujusque maxime suum.*

pecuniary, adj. *pecuniarius, praemium pecuniae* or *rei pecuniariae;* to make large — rewards to anyone, *munera pecuniae magna alci dare, praemia rei pecuniariae magna alci tribuēre.*

pedagogue, n. *paedagogus* (= the slave who accompanied a child to school; used also by Plaut. in something of the modern sense of —); *magister* (= master); see PEDANT, EDUCATE, SCHOOL.

pedant, n. *homo ineptus (qui aut tempus quid postulet, non videt, aut plura loquitur, aut se ostentat, aut eorum, quibuscum est, vel dignitatis vel commodi rationem non habet, aut denique in alqo genere inconcinnus aut multus est, is ineptus esse dicitur,* Cic.); *homo putidus* (= who tries the patience of his hearers or readers to the utmost, through his pedantic manner). **pedantic,** adj. *ineptus, putidus, molestus;* to have nothing —, *nihil habēre molestiarum nec ineptiarum;* see AFFECTED. Adv. *inepte, putide, moleste.* **pedantry,** n. *ineptiae* (in gen.), *jactatio putida* (= idle ostentation), *molestia* (= affectation), *morositas* (= niceness), *molesta* or (stronger) *molestissima diligentiae perversitas* (= unnecessary care and trouble, so as to be wearisome to others); exact, conscientious, but without —, *diligens sine molestiâ;* see AFFECTATION.

pedestal, n. of a column, etc., *basis, stylobātes, -is,* m.

pedestrian, adj. and n. a —, *pedes, -ĭtis,* m.; — tour, *iter pedestre;* to begin a — tour, *iter pedibus ingredi;* to make a — tour, *iter pedibus facēre, conficēre.*

pedigree, n. *stemma gentile* or simply *stemma* (Sen.); to repeat one's whole — off by heart, *memoriter progeniem suam ab avo atque atavo proferre.*

pedlar, n. *institor.*

peel, I. n. *cutis* (Plin.), *corium* (Plin.), *tunica, crusta* (e.g. *glandis,* Plin.), *putamen* (= shell of nuts, etc.). **II.** v.tr. *putamen, cutem,* etc., *alci rei detrahēre* (fruit, eggs); to — a tree, *corticem arbori in orbem* (all round) *detrahēre, decorticare arborem* or *delibrare arborem.* **III.** v.intr. *cutem (paul(l)atim) (de)ponēre* **peeling,** n. *decorticatio.*

peep, I. v.intr. *prospicēre* (= forth, *enitēre, emicare* (= to shine), *apparēre, conspici, conspicuum esse* (= to be seen, the latter two esp. of objects that are very conspicuous); to — at anything, *alqd intueri, oculis percurrēre.* **II.** n. 1, *a(d)spectus, -ûs, conspectus, -ûs;* to take a — at, *alqd oculis percurrēre, oculos in alqd con(j)icēre;* see LOOK; 2, = beginning at — of day, *diluculo, primâ luce.*

peep, v.intr., of chickens, *pipare, pipire.*

peer, n. 1, = equal, *par;* 2, = noble, *unus e patriciis* or *nobilibus;* house of —s, *senatus, -ûs.* **peerage,** n. by *gradus, -ûs* (e.g. to raise to the —, *alqm ad amplissimum gradum producēre.* **peerless,** adj. *cui par inveniri non potest, unicus.* Adv. *unice.*

peer, v.intr. *(per)scrutari alqd;* see EXAMINE.

peevish, adj. *stomachosus, morosus, difficilis, iracundus;* see ILL-TEMPER. Adv. *stomachose, morose, iracunde;* see SENSITIVE, IRRITABLE. **peevishness,** n. *stomachus, morositas, difficultas, ira, iracundia.*

peg, I. n. *paxillus* (small, for driving into the ground), *cultellus ligneus.* **II.** v.tr. see FASTEN.

pelf, n. *lucrum.*

pelisse, n. *pallium* or *pallium ex peltibus factum.*

pell-mell, adv. *promiscue* (= promiscuously), *confuse, permixte* (= without order), *passim* (= in all directions); lying there —, *promiscuus, confusus, permixtus;* we may also form compounds with *per* or *cum* (e.g. to mix —, *miscēre, permiscēre, commiscēre*), to mix — everything, *miscēre omnia ac turbare.*

pellucid, adj. †*pellucidus;* see TRANSPARENT.

pelt, v.tr. *lapides in alqm jacēre, con(j)icēre, alqm lapidibus petēre.* **pelting,** adj. (of rain) *maximus,* or less strongly *magnus imber.*

pen, I. n. 1, **penna (scriptoria)* (not in use till the 7th century), *calamus, stilus* (of metal); to dip a — in ink, *calamum intingēre* (Quint.); 2, = fold, *saeptum (sep-).* **II.** v.tr. 1, *scribēre;* see WRITE; 2, = to fold, *saeptis (sep-) includēre.* **pen-knife,** n. see KNIFE. **penman,** n. *qui scribit.* **penmanship,** n. *ars bene scribendi.*

penal, adj. — law, *lex poenalis* (Jct.). **penalty,** n. *poena, damnum, multa (mulcta)* (the two latter = the — inflicted upon anyone, *damnum* as a punishment inflicted, *multa* = both the loss the person suffers, and the indemnification for the person aggrieved); to inflict a —, *alqm alqâ re multare.* **penance,** n. *satisfactio* (= penalty for injuries done, Eccl. term = penance), *multa (mulcta)* (= penalty), *poena* (in gen. = penalty paid by anyone), *piaculum* (= atonement); to order anyone to do —, *piaculum ab alqo exigēre.* **penitence,** n. *paenitentia* (in gen.); see REPENTANCE. **penitent,** adj. *paenitens* (= repenting); Alexander was so — after he had murdered Clitus, that he was about to kill himself, *interempto Clito Alexander manus vix a se abstinuit, tanta vis erat paenitendi.* **penitential,** adj. (quod) *paenitentiam declarat.* **penitentiary,** n. *carcer, -eris,* m. (= prison), defining further sense by context.

pence, n., see PENNY.

pencil, n. 1, of painter, *penicillus* (or *-um);* see PAINTER; 2, for writing, *stilus* (see PEN).

pendant, n. *stalagmium* (Plaut.), *inaures, -ium,* f. (= ear-ring).

pending, I. adj. 1, in law, *res delata est ad judicem;* the matter is still —, *adhuc sub judice lis est;* 2, in commerce, *nondum expeditus* or *confectus.* **II.** prep. *per* with accus. (= during), *nondum* with part. (e.g. — the decision of the court, *lis nondum judicata), dum, donec* (= until, e.g. — his return, *dum redeat).*

pendulous, adj. *pendulus.*

pendulum, n., perhaps *perpendiculum* (not class.).

penetrability, n., by **penetrable,** adj. *penetrabilis, pervius* (where there is a road through, opp. *invius).* **penetrate, I.** v.tr. *penetrare, permanare* in with accus., *pervadēre per* or simply with accus. (to — all parts of the body; poison —s every limb of the body, *vene-*

rum *cunctos artus pervadit* or *in omnes partes permanat*); the draught —s the veins, *potio venas occupat*; to — the mind, *penetrare in animos* (of a speaker's address, etc.); —d (with grief, joy, etc.), *commotus, ictus, percussus, perfusus.* **II.** v.intr. (with an effort) *penetrare*, through a place, *per alqm locum*, to a place, *ad alqm locum* or *in alqm locum*; *pervadĕre algm locum* or *per alqm locum* (= to go through a place, both of persons and things), *exaudiri* (=to be heard), *ad aures pervadĕre* (of the echo, e.g. *clamor urbem pervadit*), *translucĕre* (of the light), imperceptibly, *perferri in alqm locum* (= to spread as far as); with **force,** *irruĕre, irrumpĕre in alqm locum* (the latter two of a large number; all three of persons and **things),** *descendĕre in* or *ad alqd* (= to descend down to —, of persons and things); the cry —s into their ears, *clamorem exaudiunt*; the cry —s into the camp, *clamor in castra perfertur*; to — into the future, *futuri temporis gnarum esse*; to — into a country, *progredi, procedĕre, prorumpĕre* (the latter = to rush forth with violence); *se insinuare* (by stealth, e.g. into the affections, etc., also lit.). **penetrating,** adj. 1, of cold, etc., *penetralis, penetrabilis, acutus, acer, maximus, gravis*; 2, fig. *sagax, acutus, astutus, callidus, sol(l)ers, perspicax*; see SAGACIOUS, ACUTE. **penetration,** n. *acies, acumen* (e.g. *ingenii*), *sagacitas, sol(l)ertia, perspicacitas.* **penetrative,** adj. *gravis, vehemens* (of a sermon, etc); see IMPRESSIVE. **penetrativeness,** n., the — of judicial pleadings, *aculei oratorii ac forenses* (Cic.).

peninsula, n. *peninsula.* **peninsular,** adj., by circuml. with *peninsula.*

penny, n. *as, nummus* (*sestertius*); not a — (I give, etc.), *ne mummum quidem*; to the last — (or farthing), *ad nummum* (i.e. to agree, *convenire*); to pay to the last —, *ad assem solvĕre.*

pension, I ᴜ. *annuum* (= yearly payment, Plin. Min., Suet., more usual in pl.). **II.** v.tr. *annua*, etc., *alci praebĕre.* **pensioner,** n. *cui annua praebentur.*

pensive, adj. *in cogitatione* (or *cogitationibus*) *defixus, subtristis* (= somewhat sad, ante and post class.) : see THOUGHTFUL. Adv. use adj. **pensiveness,** n. *cogitatio* (= thought), *tristitia* (= sadness).

pentagon, n. *pentagon(i)um* (or *pentagonion*, late). **pentagonal,** adj. *quinquangulus* (Gram.).

pentameter, n. (*versus*) *pentameter* (Quint.).

pentateuch, n. *pentateuchus* (Eccl.).

Pentecost, n. *dies pentacostes, pentacoste* (Eccl.).

penthouse, n. *tugurium parieti affixum*, as milit. term, *vinea.*

penultima, n. by *penultimus* (opp. *ultimus*, Aul. Gell. ; *penultima*, sc. *syllaba*).

penurious, adj. *parcus, sordidus, avarus, tenax*; see NIGGARDLY. Adv. *sordide, avare, parce, parce ac tenuiter.* **penuriousness,** n. *sordes, -is*, f. (usu. in pl.), *tenacitas, tenuitas victus* (in one's mode of living); see NIGGARDLINESS, MEANNESS, PARSIMONY. **penury,** n. *inopia, egestas* (*victus* or *rerum necessariarum penuria*); see POVERTY.

peony, n. *paeonia* (Plin.).

people, I. n. as a large number in gen., *vis* (=crowd, of men and animals), *copiae* (=troops, soldiers), *vulgus, -i*, n. (= the great mass of the —, in opp. to those of a higher position, e.g. the soldiers in opp. to the commissioned officers), *plebs, -is*, f. (= the common —); the —, *homines*

(= men in gen.), *homunculi, homunciones* (in a contemptuous sense); the young —, *adolescentuli*; the — of Greece, *Graeci*; the towns—, *oppidani* (= the inhabitants of the town), *cives* (= citizens); the — in the village, *vicani*; the — in the country, *rustici, pagani* (= peasants); before the —, *palam* (= not in secret), *coram omnibus* (= in the presence of all), *in oculis* or *ante oculos omnium*; very often in Latin the gen. term *homines* is left out with adjs., e.g. many —, *multi*; all the —, *omnes*; good —, *boni*; when *qui* follows, e.g. there are — who say, *sunt qui dicant*; there are — who believe, *sunt qui existimant*; when we make a wide and general statement, when " —" = "one," e.g. — say, *dicunt*; — report, *narrant*; the —, = those who belong to anyone, anyone's household, or servants or relations, etc., *alcjs familia* (= anyone's servants, etc., all together, Caes.), *alcjs famuli, ministri* (= servants), *alcjs comitas, qui alqm comitantur* (= those who accompany anyone, attendants), *alcjs milites* (=soldiers); my, your, etc., —, *mei, tui*; *plebecula* (contemptuous), in the name of the —, *publice*; a man of the lower orders, of the —, *homo plebeius* (according to his descent), *homo de plebe* (according to his rank); the language of the common —, *sermo plebeius*; a number of — forming one body as it were, *gens, natio* (e.g. *exterae nationes et gentes*, Cic.); *populus* (forming a State, all the free-born citizens together who are united through the same form of government, e.g. *Scipio Hergetum gentem cum infesto exercitu invasisset, compulsis omnibus*, Athanagiam urbem, quae caput ejus populi erat, circumsedit, Liv.; where *gentem* = a — of the same origin or race, but which as a State, *populus*, had a capital; one gens may comprise several *populos*), in the pl. also comb. *populi nationesque*; when we speak of one particular — or nation, we may also render — in Latin by *nomen* (=name, i.e. anything, everybody who has or goes by that name, e.g. Hannibal the mortal enemy of the Roman —, *Hannibal inimicissimus nomini Romano*, Nepos), also comb. *gens ac nomen* (e.g. *Nerviorum*, Caes.); belonging to our —, nation, *nostras*; see NATION ; a riot caused by the —, *tumultus, -ūs*; a decree of the whole —, *populi scitum, plebiscitum* (decreed by the great mass of the — [in opp. to a decree of the senate], and which had been adopted by majority, after it had been proposed by the presiding magistrate), *populi jussum* (inasmuch as the — collectively had the right of commanding the senate to confirm a decree adopted by them, after which every citizen was obliged to obey the same), comb. *populi scitum jussumque*; the power of the —, *populi* or *popularis potestas* (see POWER). **II.** v.tr. *coloniam* or *colonos deducĕre* or *mittĕre alqo* (= to send out a colony), or *locum incolis frequentare* (in sense of filling a place with inhabitants); 2, fig. *complĕre* (= to fill); 3, = INHABIT; see POPULATE. **peopled,** adj. see POPULOUS. **populace,** n. *plebs* (= commons), *vulgus, -i*, n. (= mob); dregs of the —, *populi faex* or *sentina.* **popular,** adj. 1, = belonging to the people, *popularis*; the — party, *populares*; 2, = a general favourite, *popularis* (rare), *populo* or *in vulgus gratus* or *acceptus*; to be —, *gratia multum apud alqm valēre*, or *gratiā plurimum posse*; to become —, *gratiam ab alqo* or *in* or *apud alqm inire*; 3, = suited to the common understanding, of style, etc., *ad commune judicium accommodatus.* Adv. *populariter.* **popularity,** n. *gratia* (= influence), *populi favor* or *studium*; breath of —, †*aura popularis*; to gain —, *gratiam ab alqo, ad* or *apud alqm inire.* **populate,** v.tr. *frequentare* (*incolis*); to — a place with settlers, *coloniam* or *colonos deducĕre, mittĕre alqo* (the former if the

person himself lead a colony anywhere); see
People II. **population,** n. 1, *colonorum
deductio in locum* (when a colony is established
anywhere); 2, *multitudo* (= multitude), *frequentia* (= large multitude), *civium* or *incolarum numerus* (= number of resident inhabitants), *cives*
(= citizens), *incolae* (= inhabitants); see People;
the town has a sufficient —, *urbi frequentia
suppetit.* **populous,** adj. *frequens* (opp.
desertus), *celeber* (of a place through which there
is a heavy traffic, much visited, e.g. a street, etc.,
opp. *desertus*). **populousness,** n. *celebritas
hominum* or *civium frequentia* (where there is a
large attendance).

pepper, I. n. *piper, -ĕris,* n. — -cruet, —-
box, *pyxis piperis.* **II.** v.tr. *pipere condire.*

per, a Latin prep., which, as a prefix in
English, means 1, = Thorough, Thoroughly,
which see; 2, = by; *per annum,* a year, see
Annual; — week; see Weekly.

peradventure, adv. *forte, fortasse, forsitan;*
see Perhaps.

perambulate, v.tr. *transire, iter facĕre per
alqm locum* (= to travel through, *peragrare*
(= to wander through, in gen.), *obire* (=
through a country, etc., in order to see it,
on foot, *pedibus*), (*per*)*lustrare* (in order to
look about), *percurrĕre* (quickly, also *percurrĕre
celeriter*), *pervolare* (in a hurry), *circumire* (all
round), *pervagari* (in a place). **perambulation,** n. *lustratio, peragratio, transitus, -ūs* (=
passage through, etc.).

perceivable, adj. *quod sentiri* or *sensibus
percipi potest, sensibilis* (= what can be felt, the
latter first in Vitruv.). **perceive,** v.tr. *sentire,
sensibus percipĕre* (with the senses, in gen.),
auribus percipĕre, audire (with the ears), *oculis
percipĕre, vidēre* (= to see), *cernĕre* (= to see
more distinctly); to — the course of the stars,
cursus stellarum notare; fig. with the understanding, *animadvertĕre* (= to direct one's thoughts
to a certain thing; with the part. when I — a
thing in a particular state; with the accus. and
infin. when I — through what I have heard, etc.),
cognoscĕre (= to learn, to know; to obtain a clear
perception of anything), *sentire* (= to feel, to see,
alqd or *de alqâ re*), *vidēre* (= to see, to understand); to — clearly, *perspicĕre, conspicĕre* (=
to behold), *observare* (= to observe), *intellegere* (*intellig-*) (= to comprehend). **perceptibility,** n. by **perceptible,** adj. *insignis,
conspicuus* (= conspicuous), *manifestus* (=manifest); see Clear. Adv. *manifeste;* see Clearly.
perception, n. gen. by verbs, by *percipĕre;*
see Sensation, Notion, Idea. **perceptive,**
adj. by verbs.

perch, I. n. 1, a measure of length = 5¼
yards; *pertica* (very late); 2, for hens, *pertica
(gallinaria).* **II.** v.intr. *alci rei insidēre* (=
to settle on), *alci rei insidēre* (= to remain on).

perch, n. = a fish, *perca* (Plin.).

perchance, adv. see Peradventure.

percolate, I. v.tr. see Strain. **II.** v.intr.
permanare. **percolation,** n. *percolatio,* or by
verb.

percussion, n. *ictus, -ūs* (= blow), *pulsus,
-ūs* (= push); see Shock.

perdition, n. *exitium, interitus, -ūs, pernicies.*

peremptory, adj. 1, *confidens, arrogans;*
to give — orders, *definite praecipere* or *diligenter
mandare alqd,* or in a stronger sense, *arroganter
praecipĕre;* 2, a — judgment, *judicium plenum
arrogantiae;* to judge in a — manner, *arrogantius judicare.* Adv. *confidenter, arroganter;*
see Absolute, Positive, Decisive.

perennial, adj. *perennis.* Adv. by adj. or
perpetuo; see Always.

perfect, I. adj. *plenus* (in gen. of anything
that is neither deficient as regards the contents,
nor in number or size), *integer* (= not mutilated,
complete), *absolutus, perfectus,* comb. *absolutus
et perfectus, perfectus atque absolutus, expletus et
perfectus, perfectus cumulatusque, perfectus completusque* (= having the highest perfection, completed), *verus, germanus* (= real, genuine); to
make anything —, *alqd absolvēre* (so that nothing can be said to be wanting, e.g. *beneficium,*
kindness), *cumulare alqd* (= to crown, fig., e.g.
the pleasure, *gaudium*). Adv. *plene, absolute,
perfecte,* or by superl. in sense of "quite"
(e.g. — right, *rectissime.* **II.** v.tr. *excolēre* (= to
develop further, e.g. the art of oratory, *orationem*), *conficĕre, perficĕre;* to — anyone in knowledge, *augēre alqm scientiâ.* **III.** n. Gram. t.t.
praeteritum perfectum (Quint.). **perfection,**
n. *integritas* (= completeness), *absolutio, perfectio, absolutio perfectioque* (= highest degree of
— ; — of virtue, *virtus, -ūtis, perfecta cumulataque;* to bring anything to —, *alqd absolvēre*
or *perficēre.*

perfidious, adj. *perfidus, perfidiosus* (=
faithless, opp. *fidelis*), *infidus* (= not trustworthy, opp. *fidus*). Adv. *perfide, perfidiose;*
see Treacherous. **perfidy,** n. *perfidia* (=
faithlessness, with which anyone breaks a
solemn promise), *infidelitas* (= want of faith);
to show —, *perfide* or *fraudulenter agĕre.*

perforate, v.tr. = to bore through, *terebrare* (with a borer, and also otherwise, e.g. an
apple with the finger), *perterebrare* (with the
borer), *perforare* (= to make holes in, in gen.).

perforce, adv. *vi, per vim, necessario,* or by
invitus or *compulsus, coactus.*

perform, v.tr. (*per*)*agĕre* (= to do, e.g. business, *negotium*), *gerĕre* (= to be the support of
anything, as it were, e.g. *negotium*), *obire* (= to
undergo), *alqd praestare* (= to discharge, e.g. *officium*), (*per*)*fungi alqâ re* (= to discharge, to discharge with zeal), *administrare* (= to administer), *exsequi* (= to carry out; all these, *negotium,
munus*), *conficĕre* (= to accomplish, e.g. *negotium*); to — one's duties, *res suas obire, officia sua
exsequi;* to — a business for anyone (at anyone's
request), *negotium alcjs procurare;* to — a part,
partes agĕre, in scaenâ (scen-) esse (on the stage);
to — the part of an accuser, *partes accusatoris
obtinēre;* to — sacred rites, *sacra facĕre;* see
Do, Execute, Accomplish, Discharge, Fulfil.
performance, n. = the act of —, *actio, administratio* (=the administering), *confectio* (=the
accomplishing), *perfunctio;* — of a business for
another (at his request), *procuratio;* — the
thing itself which is performed, *actio, negotium*
(= business), *officium* (= duty), *ministerium* (=
service); a — on the stage, *fabula* (= the piece
played), with *agi* (e.g. during the —, *dum fabula
agitur*); to give a —, *fabulam dare.* **performer,**
n. 1, in gen. *actor, auctor, confector,* or by Perform; 2, *artis musicae peritus,* or, in gen. *alcjs rei
artifex* (e.g. *canendi*), *alcjs rei peritissimus* (e.g.
cantandi), *acroăma, -ătis,* n. (lit. = a concert,
then also the person who gives it, singer, minstrel, player).

perfume, I. n. *odor* (*odos*), *unguentum* (=
ointment). **II.** v.tr. *odoribus perfundĕre* (with
sweet smells); † *suffire* (by burning —). **perfumer,** n. 1, who perfumes, by verbs; 2, *qui
merces odorum venditat, myropola, -ae,* m. (Plaut.),
unguentarius.

perfunctory, adj. *negligens* (*neglig-*); see
Negligent.

perhaps, adv. *fortasse, forsitan,* † *forsan*

(*fortasse* also with numbers; the latter generally with subj.; *fortassis* is very little used, and *forsan* is poetical; we cannot say *forte* for *fortasse* in gen., as *forte* can in gen. only be used after *si*, *nisi*, *ne* [not after *num*], in which case we could not say *fortasse*), *haud scio an*, *nescio an* (= I don't know whether, etc.), to express a modest assertion, with which we must use *nullus*, *nemo*, *numquam* (*nunq-*), whilst according to the English " — someone, etc., or I don't know whether anyone, etc.," we might be led to say, *ullius*, *quisquam*, *umquam*; whether — someone, somebody, after the verbs "to ask (*quaerere*)" and "to search, explore (*percontari*)," by *ecquis* (or *ecqui*), *ecquae* (or *ecqua*), *ecquid*; you ask whether — there be any hope? *quaeris ecqua spes sit?* — someone, — anyone, *forsitan quispiam*, *alqs forte*; — may also be rendered by *aliquando* (some time, or *quando* after *si* or *ne*), *circiter*, *fere*, or *ferme* (in approximate estimations as regards time and numbers; see ALMOST); *fere* and *ferme* also in gen. when we speak in an uncertain manner, e.g. he spoke — in this way, *in hanc fere sententiam locutus est;* unless —, *nisi forte*, *nisi si*; if —, *si forte*; — because, etc.? *an quod*, etc.? — not, etc.? (at the beginning of a principal sentence, in a direct question, which serves as an answer at the same time), *an.*

pericardium, n. **pericardium* (not class.).

peril, n. see DANGER, RISK. **perilous,** adj. see DANGEROUS.

period, n. **1,** in astronomy, *ambitus*, *-ūs*, *circuitus*, *-ūs*; **2,** = a portion of time, *tempus* (= time, space of time in gen.), or *tempora*, *tempestas* (= a time with regard to certain signs, circumstances, epoch), *aetas* (= age), *spatium temporis* (= space of time); no — of my life, *nullum aetatis meae tempus*; **3,** in chronology; see TIME, EPOCH; **4,** in gram. *periodus* (Quint.), in Cic. only in Greek, περίοδος, rendered by him by (*verborum*) *ambitus*, or (*verborum* or *orationis*) *circuitus*, or (*verborum*) *comprehensio* or *circumscriptio* or *continuatio*, or *verborum* or *orationis orbis*, or *circuitus et quasi orbis verborum*; a well-flowing and rounded —, *apta et quasi rotunda constructio;* structure of the —, (*verborum*) *compositio* (Quint.). **periodical,** adj. what returns at stated intervals, *sollemnis* (*sol(l)enn-*), e.g. — diseases, *morbi tempore certo* or *stato recurrentes*; — writings, papers, periodicals, *ephemerides*, *-um*; see JOURNAL; — winds, *venti qui magnam partem temporis in certis locis flare consueverunt.* Adv. *certis temporibus.*

peripatetic, adj. *peripateticus;* the **—s,** *Peripatetici.*

periphery, n. *perimetros* (Vitr.).

periphrasis, n. see PARAPHRASE.

perish, v.intr. *perire* (e.g. by illness, *morbo*), *interire* (stronger than *perire*, = complete annihilation), *cadere* (= to fall, principally in battle), *occidere* (= to die in the presence of others, e.g. in battle), *occidi*, *interfici*, *necari* (= to be killed; see KILL); to — in the war, *bello cadere*, *in bello occidere;* *absumi alqā re* (= to be swept away through, etc., e.g. *fame*, *veneno*; through illness, through pestilence, *morbo*, *pestilentiā*); more — from hunger than by the sword, *plures fames quam ferrum absumpsit.* **perishable,** adj. *quod corrumpi potest*, *fluxus* (= inconstant, e.g. *gloria*), *fragilis* (= frail), comb. *fluxus et* (or *atque*) *fragilis*, *caducus*, *infirmus* (= weak), comb. *caducus et infirmus*, *brevis* (= short, e.g. *omnia quae habent speciem gloriae contemne*, *brevia*, *fugacia*, *caduca existima*, Cic.). **perishable-**

ness, n. *fragilitas*, *brevitas* (= shortness, e.g. of life), *infirmitas* (= weakness).

peristyle, n. *peristyl(i)um.*

periwinkle, n. a plant, *vinca pervinca* (or as one word, *vincapervinca*, Plin.).

perjure, v.tr. *falsum jurare* (in gen.), *pejerare* or *perjurare*, *perjurium facere.* **perjured,** adj. *perjurus.* **perjury,** n. *falsum jusjurandum* (in gen.), *perjurium.*

perky, adj. *protervus;* see SAUCY.

permanency, n. *perpetuitas* (= without interruption), *perennitas*, *diuturnitas*, *longinquitas* (= for a length of time), *stabilitas.* **permanent,** adj. by *permanere*, or by *perpetuus*, *perennis*, *diuturnus*, *longinquus*, *stabilis*; see CONSTANT. Adv. *perpetuo.*

permeability, n., **permeable,** adj. † *penetrabilis;* see PENETRATE.

permissible, adj. *licitus* (= allowed), *concessus* (= granted); to be —, *licitum esse*, *licere.* **permission,** n. *concessio* (= concession), *permissio* (very rare; the substs. *concessus* and *permissus* only in the abl. sing.); *potestas*, *copia* (= power given anyone); *arbitrium* (= free will to do a thing), *licentia* (= entire liberty to do what one likes); to give anyone —, *veniam*, *potestatem*, *licentiam alci dare*, for or to, *alcjs rei faciendae*, *potestatem alci facere*, *concedere*, *licentiam alci concedere*, *licentiam alci permittere ut*, etc., *alci alqd permittere*, *concedere* (see PERMIT); to give children — to play, *pueris ludendi licentiam dare;* to have the —, *mihi licet*, *permissum*, *concessum est;* with your —, *permissu et concessu tuo*, *si per te licitum erit*, *pace tuā;* without anyone's — (to do a thing, etc.), *injussu alcjs;* contrary to my —, *me invito.*

permissive, adj. by verbs. **permit,** v.tr. *sinere* (with infin.), *concedere alqd alci* or *ut* (= to concede, generally after a request has been made, opp. *repugnare*), *permittere* (dat. or *ut*, = to allow anything to be done, opp. *vitare*), *facultatem dare* or *potestatem facere alcjs rei*, *alcjs rei veniam dare* or *dare hanc veniam ut* (= to show indulgence in anything); see ALLOW.

permutation, n. (*per*)*mutatio.*

pernicious, adj. *perniciosus* (= ruinous), *exitiosus* (= leading to a tragical end, e.g. conspiracy), *exitialis*, *exitiabilis* (of such a kind as to be likely to lead to a tragical end, e.g. war), *funestus* (= bringing grief over a great many, e.g. tribuneship), *damnosus*, to anyone, *alci* (= causing injury, e.g. *bellum*). Adv. *perniciose*, *exitiose*, *funeste.* **perniciousness,** n. *vis nocendi*, also by circumloc. with *nocere;* who does not see the — of this thing? *quis non intellegit hanc rem nocere?*

peroration, n. *peroratio*, *epilogus*, *conclusio.*

perpendicular, adj. *directus* (*ad perpendiculum*).

perpetrate, v.tr. *alqd committere* or *in se admittere;* see COMMIT. **perpetration,** n. by verb. **perpetrator,** n. of a crime, *auctor facinoris* or *delicti*, in the context *auctor;* by circumloc. *qui*, *quae facinus* or *flagitium* or *scelus commisit;* *qui*, *quae facinus in se admisit.*

perpetual, adj. *perpetuus;* see CONTINUAL. Adv. *perpetuo;* see ALWAYS. **perpetuate,** v.tr. *alqd perpetuum reddere*, *continuare* (= to carry on beyond the usual time). **perpetuation,** n. by verb. **perpetuity,** n. *perpetuitas;* see DURATION, ETERNITY.

perplex, v.tr. **1,** of matters; see CONFUSE; **2,** of persons, *alcjs mentem animumque perturbare*, *percutere*, *distrahere*, *sol(l)icitare*, *in perturbationem con(j)icere;* with talking, *oratione* *differre.* **perplexing**, adj. *difficilis, perplexus,* *impeditus, anceps, dubius.* **perplexity**, n. *sol(l)icitudo* (= anxiety), *dubitatio* (= doubt); see DOUBT.

perquisite, n. by *reditus extraordinarii, pecunia extraordinaria,* or in the plur. *pecuniae extraordinariae* (of a public functionary, Cic.), *peculium* (= the private property of a child or slave).

perry, n. *vinum ex piris factum.*

persecute, v.tr. *insectari* (= to pursue with hostile intentions), *insequi* (= to pursue close at one's heels), *vexare* (= to vex, to tease unceasingly); violently, *vehementius premĕre* or *vexare ulqm*; to — with insults, *alqm verbis contumeliosis prosequi, alqm maledictis* or *contumeliis insectari, alqm probris et maledictis vexare.* **persecution**, n. *insectatio* (= pressure), *vexatio* (= vexation). **persecutor**, n. *vexator* (= who teases), *insectator.*

perseverance, n. *perseverantia* (= not shrinking from any difficulty, however great), *permansio (in sententiâ), constantia* (= consistency, constancy), *assiduitas* (= assiduity), *pertinacia* (= pertinacity, in defending an opinion), *pervicacia* (= utmost — in trying to accomplish a thing or to gain a victory), *obstinatio, obstinatior voluntas, obstinatus animus* (= firm, obstinate in a resolution once formed; in a bad sense = obstinacy), *patientia* (= patience; e.g. in one's work, *laboris), virtus, -ūtis* (= in undergoing trouble in gen.). **persevere**, v.intr. *perseverare* (proper term), *constare* (with and without *sibi,* = to be always the same), *perstare, consistĕre, persistĕre* (= to insist upon), *(per)manēre* (= to remain firm in; all these generally *in alqâ re), pergĕre.* **persevering**, adj. *perseverans, constans, assiduus* (= who does not lose his hold, e.g. an enemy, an accuser), *tenax alcjs rei* (= clinging fast to anything), *pertinax, pervicax, obstinatus.* Adv. with pers., *perseveranter, constanter, firmiter, affirmato animo, pertinaciter, pervicacius, obstinate, obstinato animo.*

persist, v.intr. see PERSEVERE. **persistence**, n. see PERSEVERANCE.

person, n. 1, in widest sense, *homo;* in mere enumeration, or contemptuously, *caput; persona* (lit., = the mask of the dramatic actor, then fig., = the part which he acts; *persona* never = the individual); by the name of a — we understand that by which we denote his individuality, so that every — may have a peculiar nomination of his own, = *nomen est, quod unicuique personae apponitur, quo suo quaeque proprio vocabulo appelletur* (Cic.); in his, etc., own —, *ipse* (= he himself), *praesens, coram* (= he himself being present, oral); e.g. he came in his own —, *ipse venit;* to be there in his own —, *praesentem* or *coram adesse;* —s of higher rank, *homines nobiles;* a handsome — (= woman), *mulier formosa;* 2, = body, *corpus, -ōris,* n., *species* (= exterior in gen.), *forma, facies;* 3, = a — represented on the stage, *persona* (lit. = mask), *partes, -ium* (= part); to appear in the — of, *alcjs personam ferre* or *sustinēre* or *tueri* (= to act), *alcjs partes agĕre, obtinēre* (all lit. and fig.); 4, = — in gram., *persona* (e.g. *tertia,* Quint.). **personage**, n. 1, = PERSON; 2, = great man, *homo nobilis.* **personal**, adj., **personally**, adv. *personalis, personaliter* (Imperial Rome, t.t.); a — verb, *verbum personale* (Gram.); in other instances than these we must render it by *ipse, per se* (= himself), or by *praesens, coram* (= present, in his own person, opp. *per lit(t)eras* (= by letter, and such like), or by *proprius* (=not in common with others, opp. *com-*

munis), or by *privatus* (= referring to one as a private individual, opp. *publicus),* or by other terms, e.g. he appeared —, *ipse aderat;* I have a — interview with anyone, *ipse* or *praesens cum alqo colloquor;* Cæsar made a speech as his own — dignity and the respect of his ancestors required, *orationem habuit Caesar, sicut ipsius dignitas et majorum ejus amplitudo postulabat;* to know anyone —, *alqm ipsum nosse, alqm de facie nosse;* not to know anyone —, *alqm non nosse, alqm* or *alcjs faciem ignorare;* not to mind — offences, *omittĕre privatas offensiones;* in the sense of rude, see RUDE and PERSONALITY, 2; — occupations, *studia privata* (opp. *opera publica).* **personality**, n. 1, if = "existence as a person," or "the person itself," it must be rendered by circumloc. (e.g. in our days people deny the — of the devil, *recentiores diabolum esse negant;* he always mixes his own — up with it, *se ipse semper praedicat);* 2, = direct offensive application to a person, perhaps *contumeliae, privatae offensiones* (= personal offences, insults), *maledicta, -orum.* **personalty**, n. *(bona) sua.* **personate**, v.tr. *alcjs partes agĕre,* or *personam gerĕre, tueri* or *sustineri;* see REPRESENT, COUNTERFEIT, FEIGN, RESEMBLE. **personification**, n. *prosopopoeïa* (Quint.), pure Lat. *conformatio,* or *personarum fictio* or *confictio,* or *ficta alienarum personarum oratio.* **personify**, v.tr. a thing, 1, in a writing, as acting or speaking, *rem tanquam loquentem inducĕre, alci rei orationem (at)tribuĕre;* 2, to represent as a human being, *alqd humanâ specie induĕre, alqâ alci rei tanquam vitam (at)tribuĕre.*

perspective, n. (= the science) *scaenographia* (= theatrical drawing, Vitr.); pleasing —, *ea ars pictoris quâ efficit ut quaedam eminēre in opere, quaedam recessisse credamus* (Quint.).

perspicacious, adj. lit. *perspicax* (= who can see everything at one glance), *sagax* (= sagacious), *acutus* (= sharp), comb. *acutus et perspicax, acer* (= keen). **perspicacity**, n. (with regard to the understanding) *perspicacitas, acies* or *acumen ingenii, ingenium acre* or *acutum.* **perspicuity**, n. by adj. **perspicuous**, adj. *(di)lucidus, luculentus, clarus, evidens, illustris, perspicuus, apertus, distinctus, planus;* see CLEAR, INTELLIGIBLE. Adv. *(di)lucide, clare, evidenter, luculenter, perspicue, aperte, distincte, plane.*

perspiration, n. *sudor;* to be in a —, *sudare, sudorem emittĕre;* to be in a great —, *multo sudore manare, sudore madēre* (in gen., Plin.). **perspire**, v.intr. *sudare* (also fig. = to work hard), *sudorem emittĕre* (lit.); I —, *sudor mihi erumpit;* to — a great deal, *multum sudare* (with fear), *multo sudore manare, sudore madēre* (= to drop with perspiration).

persuade, v.tr. = to convince by argument, *persuadēre alci de alqâ re,* or with accus. and infin. (the accus. alone can only be used with *persuadēre* when it is a pronoun in the neuter gender, such as *hoc, illud, nihil);* he can easily be —d, *facile adducitur ad credendum;* = to influence by entreaty, etc., *commodis verbis delenire, ut,* etc. (= to talk over), *permovēre* (with *ut* when we want to state the intention; with the infin. alone or with the accus. and infin. when this is not the case; with the accus. alone simply, when it is a neut. pronoun); *alqm impellĕre* (= to urge) or *adducĕre* (= to bring) or *inducĕre* (= to induce) *ad alqd* or with *ut, alci auctorem esse alcjs rei* or with *ut* (= to cause anyone to); they —d me to it, *persuadetur mihi* (not *persuadeor);* to allow oneself to be —d, *persuaderi sibi pati;* to — anyone to believe a thing, *fidem alcjs rei facĕre alci, alqm adducĕre ad opinionem;* to be easily —d to believe a thing, *facile induci ad credendum;* I am not easily —d to believe, *non adduci possum, ut credam;* see CONVINCE. **persuasion,** n. *persuasio;* — was not difficult, *non difficilis persuasio fuit;* gift of —, *virtus ad persuadendum accommodata, vis persuadendi;* see CONVICTION, BELIEF. **persuasive,** adj., **persuasiveness,** n., by circumloc. with the verb (e.g. a — speech, *oratio ad persuadendum accommodata).*

pert, adj. *protervus, procax.* Adv. *proterve, procaciter.* **pertness,** n. *protervitas, procacitas.*

pertain, v.intr. = to belong or relate to, *pertinère ad alqd, spectare ad alqd, referri, alcjs juris esse* (= to be his of right) ; with the genit. *nullius est artis,* it —s to no art ; *proprium esse;* what —s to this, *quod pertinet* or *attinet ad hoc,* or *refertur,* or *referendum est.*

pertinacious, adj. *obstinatus, pervicax, pertinax.* Adv. *obstinate, pertinaciter;* to act — in anything, *obstinato animo agère alqd.* **pertinacity,** n. *animi obstinatio,* in a thing, *alcjs rei* (= obstinacy, contumacy), *pervicacia, animus pervicax* (= great perseverance), *pertinacia* (in holding an opinion or entertaining a plan), *contumacia* (= contumacy).

perturbation, n. see AGITATION, DISTURBANCE.

perusal, n. *lectio, perlectio (pell-).* **peruse,** v.tr. *perlegère, evolvère, pervolvère, pervolutare.*

pervade, v.tr. 1, lit. *permanare, alqa re perfunli;* 2, fig. *permanare, perfundère;* to — the mind, *ad animum descendère, in animum penetrare.*

perverse, adj. *perversus* (lit.= diverted; fig., not as it ought to be), *pravus* (fig. = contrary to the object intended, e.g. meaning, *mens, opinio).* Adv., fig. *perverse, perperam* (= not right, opp. *recte) ;* see OBSTINATE, STUBBORN. **perverseness,** n. *perversitas* (e.g. *hominum, opinionum, morum).* **perversion,** n. *corruptio*(= spoiling), *depravatio;* — of meaning, *verbi depravatio, verbum in pejus detortum* (Sen.). **pervert, I.** v.tr. 1, in gen. *depravare, corrumpère;* 2, as Theol. t.t., perhaps *a fide Christianâ abducère.* **II.** n. perhaps *qui a fide Christianâ abductus est.*

pervious, adj. *pervius* (of places, etc.), †*penetrabilis;* to the air, *aëri expositus.*

pest, n. 1, lit., see PESTILENCE ; 2, fig., of anything or person very obnoxious, *pestis, pernicies,* comb. *pestis ac pernicies;* —house, *aedificium ad pestilentiae contagia prohibenda exstructum.* **pester,** v.tr. see TROUBLE, DISTURB, ANNOY.

pestilence, n. lit. *pestilentia* (as an epidemic disease), *lues, -is* (as obnoxious matter likely to spread disease), *morbus pernicialis*(= dangerous illness; also fig.). **pestilential,** adj. *pestilens* (lit., opp. *saluber), foedus* (fig.= abominable, horrible, e.g. smell, opp. *suavis).* **pestle,** n. *pilum, pistillum* (Plin.).

pet, I. n. *deliciae, amores, -um;* see FAVOURITE. **II.** v.tr. *fovère,* in *deliciis habère.*

petard, n. in phrase, he is hoist with his own —, perhaps *in suos laqueos ipse incidit.*

petition, I n. 1, in gen. see PRAYER, REQUEST ; 2, a formal —, *petitio* (= petitioning for, *alcjs rei), quae alqs petit, lit(t)erae* (supplices) *libellus* (supplex) ; to sign a — (along with others), *libellum subscribère;* to grant a —, *alci petenti satisfacère, annuère;* to present a — containing a request that, etc., *libello oblato petère, ut,* etc. **II.** v.tr. *petère alqd ab alqo, rogare alqd,* anyone, *alqm* or *ab alqo* (= to demand anything as a favour), in an urgent manner, *implorare et exvoscère alqd, contendère ab alqo ut, flagitare or efflagitare alqm a!qd* (= to request, to urge); to —

anyone for **a** person or thing, *ab alqo alqd alci petère ;* to — an authority (e.g. parliament), *petère alqd per lit(t)eras.* **petitioner, n.** *qui libellum affert, qui libello petit oblato, qui supplicat.*

petrify, v.tr. 1, in *lapidem (con)vertère, mutare ;* to be petrified, *lapidescère* (Plin., rare); 2, fig. *alqm obstupefacère ;* to be petrified (with astonishment, etc.), *obstupescère, attonitum esse.*

petticoat, n. *tunica interior, corporis velamentum interius* (the Romans had no equivalent) ; — government, *imperium uxorium* or *muliebre.* **pettifogger,** n. *rabula, causidicus rabiosus et ineptus.* **pettifogging,** adj. a — attorney, *causidicus* (opp. to *orator*); in wider sense, see PALTRY. **petty,** adj., see LITTLE, TRIFLING, PALTRY.

petulance, n., see PASSION, SAUCINESS, IMPUDENCE. **petulant,** adj., see SAUCY, IMPUDENT.

pew, n. *sedes quae est in aede sacrâ.*

pewter, n. see TIN.

phaeton, n. see CARRIAGE.

phantom, n. 1, *somnium, opinionis commenta, -orum ;* they are mere —s, *et falsa et inania sunt ;* 2, see GHOST.

Pharisee, n. *Pharisaeus* (Eccl.) ; fig., see HYPOCRITE. **Pharisaical,** adj., lit. by the gen. *Pharisaeorum* (Eccl.) ; see HYPOCRITICAL.

pharmacy, n. *(ars) medicamentaria* (Plin.).

phase, n. *status, -ûs, condicio* or *ratio,* or by circumloc. (e.g. the thing has passed into **a** new —, *res mutata est,* or *nova fit).*

pheasant, n. *(avis) Phasiana* (Plin.) ; *Phasianus (Fas-,* Suet.).

phenomenon, n. in gen. *ostentum, prodigium, portentum, miraculum* (= any marvellous sight seen, and relating to some future event); in the sky, *phaenomenon* (very late, or as Greek φαινόμενον), *res mira* or *mirifica* or *nova* (= strange).

phial, n. see BOTTLE.

philanthropy, n. *caritas generis humani, humanitas.* **philanthropist,** n. **philanthropical,** adj. *hominibus* or *generi humano amicus, humanus.* Adv. *humane.*

Philippic, n. 1, lit. *(oratio) Philippica;* 2, fig. *oratio in alqm habita.*

Philistine, n. 1, lit. *Philistinus;* 2, fig. *homo humanitatis expers.*

philologist, n. *grammaticus, philologus.* **philology,** n. *grammatica* (or *grammatice), philologia* (= literary studies). **philological,** adj. *grammaticus.*

philosopher, n. *philosophus,* fem. *philosopha;* the true —, *sapiens* (i.e. a wise man); theoretical —, *qui in rerum contemplatione studia ponit ;* practical —, *qui de vita ac moribus rebusque bonis et malis quaerit.* **philosophy,** n. *philosophia.* **philosophical,** adj. by the genit. *philosophiae, philosophorum ;* = wise, *sapiens, prudens;* — writings, *philosophiae scriptae, libri qui sunt de philosophiâ;* — precepts, *philosophiae* or *philosophorum praecepta;* that is not a common, but a — term, *quod non est vulgi verbum, sed philosophorum.* Adv. *philosophorum more, sapienter, prudenter.* **philosophize,** v.intr. *philosophari* (lit.), *argumentari, ratiocinari* (= to argue), *disputare* (= to expound).

philtre, n. *philtrum, amatoris poculum, virus amatorium,* or *amatorium* alone (Plin.).

phlegm, n. 1, *pituita* (t.t.) ; 2, = dulness, *tarditas ingenii* or *animi,* also merely in the

context *tarditas, patientia* (= indolence), *inertia* (= inertness), *lentitudo* (= indifference). **phlegmatic,** adj. *tardus, patiens, iners, lentus.* Adv. *patienter, lente,* or perhaps *aequo animo.*

phœnix, n. *phoenix.*

phonetic, adj. by circumloc. (e.g. *sonum verbi ipsum lit(t)eris exprimĕre*).

phosphorus, n. *phosphorus* = the morning star ; also as scientific t.t., but not, in this sense, class. **phosphorescent,** adj., **phosphorescence,** n. by *lux in undis lucens* or *fulgens.*

photograph, n. use where possible *pictura* or *imago ;* perhaps where closer definition is necessary *imago alcjs per solis radios depicta.*

phrase, n. *locutio* (Aul. Gell.); these are mere —s, *verba sunt.* **phraseology,** n. *locutio, dicendi genus, -ēris,* n.ˈ

phthisis, n. *phthisis* (Cels.). **phthisical,** adj. *phthisicus* (Plin.).

physic, I. n. see MEDICINE. **II.** v.tr. see PURGE, CURE. **physical,** adj. 1, = natural, must generally be rendered by the genit. *naturae* (if we speak of nature), or *corporis* (if we speak of the animal body) ; — complaints, *mala naturae, mala quae natura habet* (in gen.), *vitia corporis* (= bodily defects) ; — strength, *vires corporis ;* to be of good — constitution, *corporis valetudine uti bonā ;* 2, referring to science, *physicus ;* — science, *physica* or *physice, physiologia* (the theory) ; see PHYSICS. Adv. *naturā, physice.* **physician,** n. see DOCTOR. **physics,** n. *physica, -orum.* **physiognomist,** n. *physiognomon,* by *qui se profitetur hominum mores naturasque ex corpore, oculis, vultu, fronte, pernoscĕre* (Cic.). **physiognomy,** n. *oris habitus, -ūs, lineamenta, -orum,* n. (= features), comb. *habitus oris lineamentaque, os vultusque, os et vultus* (= countenance and features), *facies* (= face).

physiology, n. *naturae ratio, quam Graeci* φυσιολογίαν *appellant,* or *natura rerum quae Graece* φυσιολογία *dicitur,* or simply *physiologia.* **physiological,** adj. *ad naturae rationem pertinens.* Adv. *e rerum naturā.*

piacular, adj. *piacularis.*

piano, n. use some known instrument, *lyra, cithara.*

pick, I. v.tr. and intr. *rostro tundĕre* or *caedĕre alqd* (of birds) ; to — a bone, by *rodĕre alqd ;* to — one's teeth, *dentes spinā perfodĕre* (with a tooth — of wood, silver, etc., Petron.) ; = to gather, *carpĕre ;* see PLUCK ; to — wool, *lanam carpĕre* or *purgare ;* to — one's pocket, see ROB ; to — a quarrel, see QUARREL ; to — out, see SELECT, CHOOSE ; to — up, *legĕre, colligĕre, tollĕre,* see GATHER, RAISE. **II.** n. —axe, *dolābra ;* a —pocket, *sector zonarius* (Plaut.), or by *fur* = thief. **picked,** adj. *delectus* (of troops), *eximius, praestans,* etc. ; see EXCELLENT. **picking,** n. see CHOICE ; in the pl. see REMAINS.

pickle, I. n. *salsura.* **II.** v.tr. to - fish, *pisces muriā condire.*

picnic, n. and v.intr. *symbola* (συμβολή, ante class.) = a contribution to a common feast (e.g. *aliquot adolescentuli coimus in Piraeo in hunc diem ut de symbolā essemus,* = we went to a —, Ter.), or *excurrĕre* may be used (e.g. *excurro in Pompeianum,* Cic.).

picquet, n. *statio ;* to post —s, *stationes disponĕre.*

pictorial, adj. and adv. *tabulis ornatus* or *(de)pictus, per tabulas*

picture, I. n. *pictura, tabula (picta);* = likeness, *imago (picta);* word —, by circumloc. (e.g. *ita rem verbis exprimit ut paene ob oculos posita esse videatur*). **II.** v.tr. to — in the mind, *alqd mente, animo* or *cogitatione fingĕre* or *concipĕre ;* in words, *depingĕre, expingĕre, exprimĕre ;* see EXPRESS, PAINT. **picture-frame,** n. *forma in quā includitur pictura.* **picture-gallery,** n. *pinăcōthēca.* **picturesque,** adj. *graphicus* (= very beautiful, as if it had been painted, rare), *amoenus* (= delightful) ; to be —, *graphicam in aspectu efficĕre delectationem* (Vitr. = to present a most beautiful aspect) ; see BEAUTIFUL. Adv. *graphice, amoene.* **picturesqueness,** n. see BEAUTY.

pie, n. see PASTRY.

piebald, adj. † *bicolor.*

piece, I. n. 1, part of a whole, *pars* (= part in gen.), *fragmentum* (poet. *fragmen* = a — broken off), *segmen* (= a — cut off), *frustum* (= a bit), *truncus* (= a — cut off or struck off, e.g. a — of the same stone, *truncus ejusdem lapidis*), *crusta* (= a — of marble cut off, for mosaic work) ; a — (bit) of cloth, *pannus ;* a pretty large — of anything (i.e. = a considerable quantity, a good deal), *aliquantum* with genit. (e.g. of land, *agri*) ; a very large — (i.e. much), *multum* with genit. ; to tear into —s, *dilacerare, dilaniare, discerpĕre ;* see TEAR ; to fall to —s, *dilabi ;* 2, = a single thing, which belongs to a whole species, in gen. *res* (thing in gen.) ; *pars* (= part, e.g. *plura de extremis loqui pars ignaviae est,* Tac., a — of cowardice) ; whenever we say a — of, the word — is not expressed, e.g. a — of money, *nummus* (a single coin), *alqd nummorum* (an indefinite sum of money) ; a — of land, *ager,* dim. *agellus ;* a — of meat, *caruncula ;* a — of wood, *lignum,* made out of one —, or into one —, *solidus* (= not interrupted, solid, massive [e.g. ring]) ; a boat made out of one — of timber, *linter ex unā arbore excavatus ;* = an artificial production, *opus, -ēris,* n. (in gen.), *tela* (= a — of woven cloth), *pictura, tabula* (= a picture), *fabula* (= a theatrical —), *cantus, -ūs* (= a — of music), *tormentum* (= a field- —) ; in — s, —meal, *minutatim* (lit. in small —s, then also fig. = by degrees), *membratim* (lit. = limb by limb, then fig. = one part after the other, e.g. to relate, *enumerare,* i.e. to enumerate), *carptim* (= by detached parts, fig. = partly), *pedetentim (pedetemt-)* (= one thing after the other, step by step, gradually) ; also by *singuli* (if = the single things) ; —work, by circumloc. (e.g. to pay by —, *ut res quaeque confecta est, solvĕre*). **II.** v.tr. *consuĕre ;* to — a garment, by *assuĕre alqd alci rei ;* see PATCH, MEND.

pied, adj. *maculosus.*

pier, n. 1, *pila (pontis);* see PILLAR ; 2, *moles (-is), (opposita fluctibus) moles lapidum* (= mole).

pierce, v.tr. 1, see THRUST, DRIVE ; 2, = to — through, *transfigĕre ;* see STAB ; 3, see ENTER, PENETRATE. **piercing,** adj. 1, of sounds, *acer, acutus ;* see SHRILL ; 2, of the mind, *acutus, acer, sagax ;* see ACUTE.

piety, n. *pietas erga Deum* (= reverence and love to God, *religio* (= religious feeling), *sanctitas* (= holiness of life), *sanctimonia* (= virtuous sentiment, innocence). **pious,** adj. *pius erga Deum* (also *erga patriam, parentes,* etc.), *religiosus* (= conscientious), *sanctus* (= approved of God), *religiosus sanctusque, sanctus et religiosus.* Adv. *pie, sancte,* comb. *pie sancteque.*

pig, n. *porcus* (Eng. pork), *sus, suis,* m. and f. ; a small —, *porcellus ;* a sucking —, *porcus lactens, porcellus.* **piggery,** n. *suile* (Col.), *hara.* **piggish,** adj. 1. *suillus, porcinus ;* 2, fig. see

GREEDY. piggishness, n. *spurcitia, spurcities* (= foulness); see also **GREEDINESS. pigheaded,** adj. see **OBSTINATE.**

pigeon, n. *columba* (a cock —, *columbus*), *palumbes, -is* (*palumba*); see **DOVE**; — house, *columbarium; turris, turricula* (= — tower).

pigment, n. see **PAINT.**

pigmy, n. see **DWARF**; the Pigmies, *Pigmaei* (Plin.).

pike, n. *hasta*; see **LANCE.**

pilaster, n. *parastăta* or *parastas, -ădis*, f.

pile, I. n. *strues, -is,* f. (of things collected in an elevated form), *cumulus, acervus* (= heap of things, in gen.); *rogus* (= funeral —, also — of wood); a — of books, *acervus librorum*; a — of buildings, see **EDIFICE**; a — driven into the ground (for building on), *sublĭca*; a bridge built on —s, *pons sublĭcius*; to drive down —s, *palos* or *stipites* or *sudes demittĕre, defigĕre*; see **HEAP, STAKE. II.** v.tr. (co)*acervare, cumulare, congerĕre*; see **ACCUMULATE**; to — up, *facĕre struem alcjs rei* (e.g. *lignorum*), *exstruĕre* (e.g. *rogum*); see **HEAP.**

pilfer, v.tr. and intr.; see **STEAL.**

pilgrim, n. *viator* (= traveller in gen.), or *qui in loca sacra migrat*; —'s staff, *baculum.* **pilgrimage,** n. *iter, itineris,* n. (= journey in gen.), or *iter in loca sacra, peregrinatio sacra.*

pill, n. *catapotium* (Plin.) (that which is swallowed), in pure Latin *pilula* (Plin.); fig. to give one a — to swallow, *alqm tangĕre* (Com.); he swallowed the —, *haec concoxit.*

pillage, I. n. *rapīna, direptio* (implying destruction of property), *expĭlatio* (for the sake of robbing), *depopulatio* (= laying waste). **II.** v.tr. *diripĕre, populari* (= to lay waste), *compilare, expilare, spoliare.* **III.** v.intr. *praedari*; see **PLUNDER. pillager,** n. *praedator, direptor, populator*; see **PLUNDER.**

pillar, n. *columen* (fig. = foundation, e.g. *columen reipublicae*), *pila* (= support of a bridge, etc.), *columna* (= column); see **COLUMN, POST. pillared,** adj. *columnatus, columnis instructus.*

pillory, n. *numella* (= fetter for criminals); to punish with the —, *alqm ad palam in aliorum exemplum alligare*; fig. *alqm cruciare*; see **TORMENT.**

pillow, I. n. *cervĭcal* (Juv.), *pulvīnus.* **II.** v.tr. (*suf*)*fulcire*; see **SUPPORT.**

pilot, I. n. *gubernator* (lit. and fig.). **II.** v.tr. *gubernare* (lit. and fig.)

pimp, n. *lēno.*

pimple, n. *varus* (Plin., on the face, Greek ἴονθος), *pustula* (in gen., Plin.). **pimpled, pimply,** adj. *pustulosus* (Cels.).

pin, I. n. *acus, -ūs,* f. **II.** v.tr. *alqd acu* (*af*)*figĕre.* **pin-cushion,** n. *thēca* (= case). **pin-money,** n. *peculium* (Jct.), or *pecunia uxori data.*

pincers, n. pl. *forceps.* **pinch, I.** v.tr. I, = to nip, perhaps *alqd* or *alqm digitis comprimĕre, vellĭcare* (Quint.); 2, fig. (co)*artare* = to crowd, to — for room, *urēre* (of a shoe, frost, etc.); to — oneself, *fraudare se victu suo*; to —, of poverty, *urgēre.* **II.** n. 1, lit. use verb; 2, fig. *aculeus* (= sting), *morsus, -ūs* (= bite); see **STING**; at a —, by circumloc. (e.g. he would only do it at a —, *coactus modo hoc fecerit*). **pinching,** adj. of poverty, etc., by *extremus, summus,* etc.; see **EXTREME.**

pinchbeck, n. 1, *aes facticium*; 2, fig., see **SHAM.**

pine, n. *pīnus,* f.

pine, v.intr. *tabescĕre, confĭci alqā re*: to — for anything, *alqd desiderare,* or more strongly, *alcjs desiderio tabescĕre.* **pining,** n. *tabes, -is* (= wasting away); see also **SORROW.**

pinion, I. n. 1, of a bird, *penna* (*pinna*); see **WING**; 2, *compes, -ĕdis,* f.; see **FETTER. II.** v.tr. *manus post tergum religare, alci compedes in(j)icĕre, alqm (re)vincire.*

pink, adj. *puniceus*; — colour, *color puniceus.*

pinnace, n. *navis actuaria* or *lembus.*

pinnacle, n. *fastigium* (lit. and fig.).

pint, n. *sextarius* (both as a measure of liquids and as the vessel containing it); half a —, *hemina*; a quarter of a —, *quartarius.*

pioneer, n. *qui primus alqd facit.*

pious, adj. *pius, sanctus*; see **PIETY.**

pip, n. *pituita* (= disease of chickens, Plin.).

pip, v.intr. *pipare, pipire* (Col.).

pip, n. of fruit, *semen, granum, nucleus* (Plin.), *acinus* (esp. of the grape).

pipe, I. n. 1, for water, etc., *tubus, tubulus, canalis, fistula*; 2, = a musical instrument, *fistula, tibia,* † *arundo,* † *calamus,* † *avēna*; 3, for smoking, perhaps, if context is clear, *fistula* or *tubulus,* or adding *fumum edens.* **II.** v.intr. *fistulā* or *tibiā canĕre* or *cantare.* **pipe-clay,** n. *creta fig(u)līna.* **piper,** n. *tibicen.*

pipkin, n. *olla* (old form *aula*).

piquant, adj. *acutus* (lit. = stimulating to the senses; then also fig., e.g. of the speaker, Quint.), *salsus* (lit. = seasoned with salt, — in taste; then fig. pertinent, to the point, interesting, esp. through wit, of persons, of things said or written, etc.); *facetus* (= facetious). Adv. *acute, salse.* **piquancy,** n. *sal, vis.* **pique, I.** n. *simultas*; see **ANGER, IRRITATION. II.** v.tr. see **OFFEND, IRRITATE, EXASPERATE**; to — oneself, *gloriari alqā re, jactare se de alqā re.*

piracy, n. *latrocinium maris*; to carry on —, *latrocinio maris vitam tolerare* (= to get one's living by —); to make the sea unsafe through —, *mare infestum facĕre navibus piraticis*; *latrociniis et praedationibus infestare mare.* **pirate,** n. *praedo (maritimus), pīrāta.* **piratical,** adj. *piraticus*; — State, *gens latrociniis assueta.*

piscatory, adj. *piscatorius.*

pistil, n. *pistillum* (only as t.t.).

pistol, n., where possible by *arcus, -ūs* (= bow), otherwise *sclopetus minor*; see **GUN.**

piston, n. (in machines) *fundulus* (moving up and down, *fundulus ambulatilis*), *embolus* (= sucker of a pump).

pit, I. n. *puteus* (in gen.), *fovea* (deep, open at the top, for catching wild beasts; then also fig. = a snare), *scrobs* or (small) *scrobiculus* (= a hole dug for planting a tree or for interring a dead body), *fossa* (= a long ditch for the defence of a place or for the purpose of drainage), *fodīna, specus, puteus* (in a mine); to dig a —, *facĕre foveam* (*fossam*), *fodĕre scrobem, specum sub terrā fodĕre*; to fall into a —, *in foveam incidĕre* (the latter also fig. = to fall into a snare); in the theatre, *cavea* (= the seats assigned to the spectators, *cavea ima* was reserved for the nobility, *cavea media* and *summa* more nearly = pit). **II.** v.tr. to mark (e.g. with small-pox), *distinguĕre*; see **MARK. pit against,** v.tr. *alqm alci opponĕre, alqm cum algo committĕre.* **pit-a-pat,** adv. to go —, *palpitare.* **pitfall,** n. *fovea.* **pitman,** n. see **MINER.**

pitch, I. n. *pix*; of —, *piceus*; as black as —, *picĕus, vicīnus, omnium nigerrimus* (=

quite black, in gen.); — pine, *picea;* — dark, (*tenebris*) *obductus* (= quite covered with darkness, e.g. *nox*). **II.** v.tr. (*op*)*picare.* **pitchy, adj.** *picatus* (= besmeared with pitch).

pitch, I. n. 1, = degree, *fastigium, gradus, -ūs,* or by *summus, extremus,* or *ultimus* with n. (i.e. to the highest — of madness, *ad summam amentiam*); to this, that, what a — of, *huc, eo, quo* with gen. ; 2, in music, *sonus, vox ;* at the highest — of the voice, *voce summā ;* a high —, *vox acuta;* medium —, *vox media;* low —, *vox gravis.* **II.** v.tr. 1, to — a tent, *tabernaculum statuēre* or *constituēre* or *collocare, tentorium statuēre* or *ponēre, tabernaculum tendēre,* or simply *tendēre;* 2, = to throw, *jacēre, con*(*j*)*icēre;* see THROW; 3, in music, to — a note, *canendo praeire.* **III.** v.intr. to — upon, *incidēre, incurrēre in alqm* or *alqd.* **pitchfork,** n. *furca.*

pitcher, n. see JAR.

piteous, pitiable, adj. *miser, miserabilis, miserandus, dolendus, flebilis,* (*e*)*lamentabilis.* Adv. *misēre, miserabiliter, flebiliter, miserandum in modum.* **piteousness,** n. use adj., or circuml. (e.g. the — of the story greatly moved me, *narratio mire me commovit*). **pitiful,** adj. 1, = full of pity, *clemens, misericors;* see MERCIFUL; 2, see PITEOUS; 3, = mean, *abjectus, vilis, humilis, contemptus;* see CONTEMPTIBLE. Adv. *clementer, misere, abjecte, humiliter;* see CONTEMPTIBLY. **pitifulness,** n. 1, *clementia, misericordia;* 2, see PITEOUSNESS; 3, by adj. (PITIFUL 3), or *humilitas.* **pitiless,** adj. *immisericors, durus, ferreus, inhumanus, crudelis, saevus;* see CRUEL. Adv. *immisericorditer, inhumane, inhumaniter, crudeliter, saeve.* **pitilessness,** n. *crudelitas, inhumanitas, saevitia.* **pity, I.** n. *misericordia* (*misericordia est aegritudo ex miseriā alterius injuriā laborantis,* Cic.), *miseratio;* out of —, *propter misericordiam, misericordia captus* or *permotus ;* to feel —, *misericordiam habēre, misericordem esse* (= to have a feeling heart), *se misericordem praebēre* (= to show oneself merciful in one single case) ; to have — on anyone, *misereri alcjs, miseret me alcjs;* it is a — that, etc., *dolendum est, quod,* etc., *incommode accidit, ut,* etc. ; it is a — that he died, *mors ejus dolenda est;* it is a — that the money was lost, *dolenda est jactura pecuniae ;* it is a great —, it is a thousand pities, *valde, magnopere dolendum est;* deserving —, *miserandus, miseratione dignus.* **II.** v.tr. *miserēri, miseret me alcjs, misericordiā alcjs commotum* or *captum esse* (= to feel —). **pitying,** adj. and adv. see PITIFUL 1.

pith, n. *medulla* (lit. and fig.). **pithy,** adj. 1, lit. *medullosus* (Cels.) ; 2, fig. *sententiosus* (= full of meaning), *nervosus* (= vigorous), *densus* (Quint.).

pittance, n. *mercedula* (= poor pay), *pecunia exigua.*

pivot, n. 1, lit. *cnŏdax* (Vitr., rare) ; 2, fig. see HINGE.

placable, adj. *exorabilis, placabilis.* **placability,** n. *placabilitas.*

placard, I. n. *libellus;* see ADVERTISEMENT. **II.** v.tr. *libellum proponēre;* see ANNOUNCE, ADVERTISE.

place, I. n. = a free, open space, *locus, campus* (= open —, field, e.g. in the middle of a town), *area* (= a free, open — not occupied with buildings) ; the — in front of a dwelling-house, *propatulum* (in gen.), *vestibulum* (= entrance court) ; — of battle, *locus pugnae ;* = an inhabited —, *locus, oppidum* (= — surrounded with walls), *regio* (= district), *pagus, vicus* (= village) ; a fortified —, *locus munitus* (in gen.), *castrum, castellum* (= castle, fort) ; = natural

position, *seaes, -is;* = a certain portion of space in gen., inhabited —, the —, *loca ;* at this —, *hic, hoc loco;* at which —, where, *ubi, quo loco ;* at what —? *ubinam ?* from which —, whence, *unde, a* or *ex quo loco;* at every —, *ubique, omnibus locis;* from every —, *undique, ab omnibus locis;* at different —s, *passim;* at both —s, *utrobique;* at another —, see ELSEWHERE; fig. — in a book, *locus* (pl. *loci*); this has been stated in another — (= in another part of the book), *alio loco dictum est;* about this in another —, *de quo alibi;* = a separate — allotted anywhere, lit. *locus* (in gen.), *sedes* (where one sits), *spatium* (= — which anything occupies) ; to assign, show to a person his or her — (in the theatre), *alqm sessum ducēre* (Plaut.); to give up one's — to a person, *alci locum dare, cedēre;* to take a — on the seats allotted (in front of the rostrum of the curia, etc.), *locum in subselliis occupare;* to sit in the first —, *in primā caveā sedēre* (in the theatre), *summum* or *supra* or *superiorem accubare* (at table) ; in the last —, *in ultimā caveā sedēre* (in the theatre), *infra* or *inferiorem accubare* (at table) ; to get up from one's —, (*ex*)*surgēre* (principally of several) *consurgēre;* to rise from one's — before anyone (out of respect), *alci assurgēre;* to bring anyone from his — (= seat), *alqm loco movēre;* description of —s (towns, etc.), *descriptio locorum* (Cic. uses τοποθεσία = the stating of the locality of a —) ; commander of a —, *praefectus urbi;* = situation, office, *munus, -ĕris,*n.,*magistratus, -ūs;* of a servant,use circuml. (e.g. to change a —, *in aliam familiam ingredi*); to appoint in — of, *alqm sufficēre;* in — of, *loco alcjs;* in the first —, *primo, primum;* in the next —, *deinceps;* primo and primum are followed by *deinde, tum, praeterea, postremo.* **II.** v.tr. *statuĕre* (lit., to make a thing stand, e.g. *vas in loco frigido, juvencum ante aram*), *constituĕre;* to — in different spots, *disponĕre;* to — in line of battle, *ordinare, instruĕre;* to — anything round a thing, *cingĕre alqd alqā re* (e.g. watchmen round a house, *domum custodibus*) ; to — anything before, *alqd apponĕre alci rei* or *ad alqd* (before the hearth, *foci;* before the fire, *ad ignem*), *proponĕre alqd alci rei* (e.g. *igni*); to — oneself at or near a spot or anything, *consistĕre in algo loco* (e.g. at the door, *in aditu*), by the side of, near anything, *consistĕre ad alqd* (e.g. *ad mensam*), *assistĕre ad alqd* (e.g. *ad fores,* near the door) ; to — one's money with anyone, *pecuniam collocare* or *occupare apud alqm ;* to — behind, *postponĕre* or *posthabēre* or *postferre alqd alci rei ;* to — over (i.e. in command of, *alci rei* or *loco alqm praeficĕre*); to — round, *alqm* or *alqd alci* (*rei*), or *alqm* or *alqd alqā re circumdare ;* to — under, *alqd alci* (*rei*) *sub*(*j*)*icēre;* to — upon, *alqd alci* (*rei*) *imponĕre, superponĕre.*

placid, adj. *placidus;* see GENTLE, QUIET, CALM.

plagiarism, n. *furtum* or by *auctorem ad verbum transcribĕre neque nominare* (= to copy a passage from an author without naming him), or by *alcjs scripta furantem pro suis praedicare* (i.e. in so doing to pass oneself off as the author of such a passage, etc.). **plagiarist,** n. *qui aliorum scrinia compilat* (Hor.), *qui auctorem ad verbum transcribit neque nominat.*

plague, I. n. 1, lit. (as the disease) *pestis, pestilentia;* see PESTILENCE ; 2, fig., *malum* (= evil in gen.); *pestis* (= pest); the — take you ! *in malam crucem !* What the — is it? *Quid, malum, est ?* to be a — to anyone, *molestiae esse alci.* **II.** v.tr. *vexare* (= to let anyone have no peace), *sol*(*l*)*icitare* (= to disquiet), *angēre* (of cares, etc.), *exercēre, cruciare,* (*ex*)*agitare;* with re-

quests, *alqm precibus fatigare;* with questions, *alqm obtundĕre rogitando;* to — anyone to do, etc. (= to bother), *alci instare de algā re* or with *ut;* see VEX, WORRY.

plain, I. adj. 1, = smooth, *aequus, planus;* **see** FLAT; 2, = manifest, *clarus, planus, apertus, perspicuus, evidens, manifestus;* see CLEAR, MANIFEST; 3, = unadorned, *simplex, inornatus, incomptus* (of dress), *(di)lucidus, inornatus, subtilis, pressus, ʳᵖressus, distinctus, attenuatus* (of speech); 4, — candid, *sincerus, liber;* see FRANK; 5, = without beauty, perhaps *haud formosus* or *venustus;* see UGLY. Adv. = clearly, *clare, plane, aperte, perspicue, evidenter, manifeste;* = without ornament, *simpliciter, inornate* (of dress, etc.), *(di)lucide, subtiliter, (ex)presse, distincte, attenuate;* = frankly, *sincere, libere, aperte.* **II.** n. *planities* (= every —, also the — surface of a mirror); as an open country, *planities, aequus et planus locus* (wide, where one has unlimited view and a free scope, in opp. to hills and mountains), *campus* with and without *planus* or *apertus* (= an open field, in opp. to mountains); an extended —, *aequor* (also surface of the sea, often in the poets, but also in Cic.); of what is, grows, has its abode, is situate in the —, *campester* (e.g. *campestris urbs*).

plainness, n. 1, = clearness, by *evidentia, perspicuitas,* or adj. ; see PLAIN; 2, = lack of ornament, *simplicitas* (of dress, etc.), or by adj. PLAIN, 3 (of style); 3, of speech; see FRANKNESS; 4, = lack of beauty; see UGLINESS.

plaint, n. see LAMENTATION, COMPLAINT, ACTION. **plaintiff,** n. *accusator* (if a female, *accusatrix*); *qui* (or *quae*) *accusat* (= accuser, who brings anyone up before the court in a criminal prosecution); *qui* (or *quae*) *petit* (= who makes a claim, in a civil action); to appear as the principal — against anyone, *suo nomine accusare alqm;* as the second — or jointly with another, *subscribens accusare alqm;* — in error, *appellator* (Cic.), *qui appellat* or *provocat.* **plaintive,** adj. *miserabilis, flebilis, lamentabilis, queribundus, querulus* (mostly poet.). Adv. *miserabiliter, flebiliter.* **plaintiveness,** n. by adj.

plait, I. n. 1, *sinus, -ūs, ruga,* but both = fold rather than — ; see FOLD; 2, = a braid of hair, *gradus, -ūs* (Quint., Suet.). **II.** v.tr. 1, see FOLD; 2, to — the hair, *comam in gradus formare* or *frangĕre.*

plan, I. n. 1, = a sketch drawn on paper, *forma, conformatio, figura, species* (= a draught), *imago* (= outline), *designatio* (= design), *forma rudis et impolita* (= rough sketch), *descriptio, ichnographia* (the former = first sketch, then like the latter = ground - plan); to draw a — of anything, *speciem operis deformare, imaginem* or *formam operis delineare;* of a building, *aedificandi descriptio;* 2, in idea, *consilium, cogitatio* (as a mere idea which we hope to realize), *propositum* or *inceptum* (as intention, or as anything first begun, undertaken), *ratio* (= — and decision, wherein the means of doing it and the possible result are considered), *descriptio* (as regards all the particulars of it), *ordo* (= the order in which a thing is to be done); — of an operation, *rei agendae ratio;* a — agreed upon, *ratio rei compositae* (Liv.); — for carrying on a war, *totius belli ratio;* a decided —, *ratio stabilis ac firma;* without any decided —, *nullo consilio, nullā ratione;* to draw up, make a — for anything, *instituĕre rationem alcjs rei* (e.g. *operis*), *describĕre rationem alcjs rei* (e.g. *belli, aedificandi*); to conceive the — to, etc., *consilium capĕre* or *inire alcjs rei faciendae,* or with inf. or with *ut;* concerning a thing, *consilium capĕre* or *inire de algā re.* **II.** v.tr. 1, = to form a draught, *speciem* or *imaginem alcjs*

operis lineis deformare, formam alcjs operis lineis describĕre, imaginem alcjs operis delineare; see DESIGN; 2, in idea, *algd (ex)cogitare, moliri, consilium inire alcjs rei faciendae;* see above, PLAN, I. 2.

plane, I. n. 1, = a geometrical figure, *forma plana;* 2, = a tool, *runcina* (Plin.). **II.** v.tr *runcinare.*

plane, n. = a tree, *platanus,* f.

planet, n. *stella errans, sidus, -ĕris,* n., *errans;* in pl. also *stellae quae errantes et quasi vagae nominantur;* the five —s, *quinque stellae eosdem cursus constantissime servantes.* (*Planeta, planetes,* is not found in good prose.)

plank, I. n. *tabula* (= board), *axis, -is,* m. (*assis*); to nail —s, *coaxare* (*coass-*). **II.** v.tr. *contabulare, coaxare* (*coass-*). **planking,** n. *contabulatio, coaxatio* (*coass-,* = boarded floor, etc.), or by pl. of PLANK.

plant, I. n. *herba* (in gen.), *planta* (= slip). **II.** v.tr. 1, *serĕre, (de)ponĕre* (trees, etc.), *conserĕre, obserĕre* (a place with trees, etc.); 2, = to set up, *statuĕre, constituĕre, infigĕre* (e.g. *signum,* a standard); see SET UP; 3, to — a colony, *coloniam deducĕre.* **plantation,** n. *plantarium* (= nursery garden), *seminarium* (= nursery garden, lit. and fig.), *arbustum* (= orchard, esp. the trees round which vines were planted), *vitiarium* (= nursery for vines), *quercētum* (= oak wood), *locus arboribus consitus* (gen. term). **planter,** n. *sator, qui serit;* —s of a colony, *coloni.* **planting,** n. *satio, satus, -ūs* (= the act of —).

plash, I. n. *murmur, fremitus, -ūs* (e.g. *aequoris,* perhaps *sonus, sonitus, -ūs.* **II.** v.tr. *murmurare, fremĕre, fremitum edĕre.*

plaster, I. n. 1, *gypsum, arenatum, tectorium;* see CEMENT, MORTAR; 2, in medicine, *emplastrum.* **II.** adj. a — cast, *imago* (*e*) *gypso expressa.* **III.** v.tr. *gypsare* (Col.), *gypso illinĕre* or *obducĕre.* **plasterer,** n. = who whitewashes the walls, *tector;* see PAINT.

plastic, adj. *plasticus.*

plate, I. n. 1, *bractea, lam(i)na* (lit. = a thin piece of metal; the latter stronger than the former, then also of wood, anything veneered); 2, = a copper— print, *pictura linearis* or *imago per aeneam lam(i)nam expressa, figura aenea,* or in the context merely *imago;* 3, a — at table, *catillus,* pl. *catilla, -orum,* n. (a smaller one made of clay), *patella;* 4, collectively, — used at table, *vasa* (*-orum*) *argentea* or *aurea* (silver or gold), *argentum.* **II.** adj. — glass, perhaps use *vitrum densatum.* **III.** v.tr. to — with silver, *argento inducĕre.*

platform, n. *suggestus, -ūs.*

Platonic, adj. *Platonicus, Academicus* (= pertaining to the Academy, i.e. the — philosophy, *academia, ἀκαδημία*). **Platonist,** n. *Platonicus philosophus;* the —s, *academici* (= the followers of the Academy).

platter, n. *catillus* (pl. *catilla*), *patella.*

plaudit, n. *plausus, -ūs;* see APPLAUSE.

plausible, adj. 1, = probable, *veri similis* (or as one word *verisim-*), *probabilis;* 2, in bad sense, *fucatus, fucosus, simulatus, speciosus.* Adv *veri similiter* (*verisim-*), *probabiliter, simulate, speciose* (Quint.), *ad speciem, in* or *per speciem, specie.* **plausibility,** n. 1, *verisimilitudo, probabilitas;* 2, *simulatio, species.*

play, I. v.intr. and tr. to — an instrument of music, *canĕre, †modulari,* with the abl.·. of the instrument played (e.g. on a stringed instrument, *fidibus*), *psallĕre* (on a stringed instrument, esp. the guitar, hence often comb.

cantare et psallere, canere voce et psallere, = to sing to the sound of the —); = to amuse oneself, *ludere* (either absol. or with the ablat. of the game); the fishes — in the water, *pisces in aquâ ludunt;* to — at dice, *tesseris* or *talis ludere, aleâ* or *aleam ludere;* to — at cricket, ball, *pilâ ludere;* to — for anything, *ludere in alqd* (e.g. for money, *in pecuniam,* Jct.); = to act in any particular character, on the stage and in real life, *agere alqm* or *alcjs partes, alcjs personam tueri;* to — a piece (in the theatre), *fabulam agere;* not to let the actors — any longer, *histrionibus scaenam interdicere;* to — the fool with anyone, to — anyone a trick, *alqm ludere* or *ludificari, alci imponere;* to — the rogue with anyone, *fraudem* or *fallaciam alci facere, dolum alci nectere* or *confingere.* **II.** n. = amusement, *ludus* (= game, **see** the word), *lusus, -ûs* (= playing), *lusio* (= the act), *ludicrum* (= a farce for amusement), *ludibrium* (= the carrying on a joke with anyone; the joke itself, sport), *spectaculum* (= a theatrical piece), *fabula* (dimin. *fabella,* = a piece at the theatre), *comoedia* (= comedy), *tragoedia* (= tragedy); mere —, *ludus, jocus* (= joke); that is but — for him, *hoc ei ludus* or *jocus est;* = room for acting, *campus* (opp. *angustiae;* e.g. he has full — in his speech, *est campus, in quo ex(s)ultare possit oratio,* Cic.); to have —, *late vagari posse;* = action, *motus, -ûs, gestus, -ûs* (of the limbs, etc.), *vultus, -ûs* (= face), *argutiae* (= lively expression of the countenance); fair —, *ex aequo et bono* (e.g. to see —, *curare ut omnia ex aequo et bono fiant).* **play-bill,** n. *libellus.* **player,** n. 1, (on a musical instrument) *canens* (both male and female), *psaltes,* in pure Latin *fidicen,* on a stringed instrument; if a female, *psaltria,* in pure Latin *fidicina, citharista,* m., *citharoedus; cornicen* (= who blows a horn or cornet), *tibicen* (= a — on the flute, a piper), *tubicen* (= a trumpeter); for amusement in gen., *lusor,* a female, *ludens;* 2, see GAMBLER; 3, — on the stage, *actor;* see ACTOR. **playfellow, playmate,** n. *aequalis* (= of the same age). **playful,** adj. *lascivus, jocosus.* Adv. *jocose.* **playfulness,** n. *lascivia.* **playground,** n. *locus quo pueri ludendi caus(s)â conveniunt.* **playhouse,** n. see THEATRE. **playthings,** n. *quae pueris in lusum oblata sunt;* see TOY. **playwriter, playwright,** n. *qui fabulas scribit.*

plea, n. 1, defendant's —, *defensio, oratio pro se* or *alqo habita* (= a speech made in one's own defence, or for others); to make a — in court, *orare* or *dicere pro se, se defendere, caus(s)am dicere* (for oneself), *orare et dicere pro algo, defendere alqm* (for someone); *exceptio* (= exception taken by defendant to plaintiff's statement, and inserted in a praetor's edict); in a gen. sense, see LAWSUIT, CAUSE, APOLOGY; 2, = excuse, *excusatio;* see EXCUSE. **plead,** v.intr. 1, in law, *cau(s)sam agere, actitare* (frequentative), *dicere, (per)orare,* or *alqm se fecisse defendere, alqm defendere, versari in foro* (= to be a pleader); 2, in gen. *alqd excusare;* see BEG, ALLEGE. **pleader,** n. *orator, causidicus* (term rather of contempt); see ADVOCATE.

pleasant, or **pleasing,** adj. *acceptus* (=that which you are glad to see or hear), *gratus* (= very —, *pergratus,* of value to us), comb. *gratus acceptusque, jucundus, suavis* (= lovely), *dulcis* (= attractive), *mollis* (= gentle), *carus* (= dear), *gratiosus alci* and *apud alqm* (= in favour with), *urbanus* (= polite), *lepidus, facetus, festivus* (= humorous, witty), *laetus* (= joyous), *amoenus* (= charming, of place), *voluptarius* (= delightful), *commodus* (= suitable, e.g. *mores*); — conversation, *sermo festivus, venustus et urbanus;* — places, *loca amoena* or *voluptaria;* to be — to

the eyes, *oculos delectare;* to be — to the ears, *aures (per)mulcere, auribus blandiri;* to have a — taste, *jucunde sapere.* Adv. *jucunde, suaviter, dulce, dulciter, commode, lepide, festive, facete, amoene* or *amoeniter.* **pleasantness.** n. *jucunditas, dulcedo, amoenitas, suavitas, commoditas* (ante class. in Ovid.), *lepos,* or by adj.; see also LOVELINESS. **pleasantry,** n. *facetiae, lepos, festivitas,* or by *jocus* (=joke). **please,** v.intr. *alci placere, alqm delectare, alci gratum, acceptum* or *cordi esse,* or *arridere;* it —s, *placet* (of a decree of the senate); if you —, *vis (si vis);* to be —d, *delectari, gaudere re;* to be dis—d, *abhorrere re;* I am —d with this, *hoc mihi gratum est;* this dis—s me, *displicet mihi hoc;* you are —d to say, *libet (lubet) tibi dicere;* to — yourself, *gratificari sibi;* to — another, *gratificari alci, morem gerere alci;* eagerness to — (another), *immodica placendi cupido.* **pleasing,** adj., see PLEASANT. **pleasure,** n. *voluptas;* = will, *arbitrium; libido (lub-,* = passion, caprice), *delectatio, oblectatio, deliciae* (= delight), *delectamentum* (rare), *oblectamentum* (= object of —); according to —, *ex libidine, ex arbitrio ejus* (or *suo*); to do his —, *gratum facere alci;* = gross pleasures (lust), *cupiditates, libidines (lub-), corporis voluptates;* it is the — of the gods, the senate, etc., *dis, senatui placet;* a journey of —, *gestatio* (Sen.); to take — in the country, *excurrere rus,* in the gardens, *horti;* to walk for —, *ambulare.*

plebeian, I. n. *homo plebeius, homo de plebe;* the —s, *plebeii, plebs;* the order of the —s, *ordo plebeius, plebs;* from the order of the —s, *de plebe, plebeii generis, plebeius.* **II.** adj. *plebeius* (opp. *patricius*).

pledge, I. n. *pignus, -ĕris,* n., *hypotheca, arrhabo, -ōnis,* m., *arrha.* **II.** v.tr. *(op)pignerare* or *obligare alqd;* to — your word, *fidem interponere* or *obligare.*

Pleiades, n. *Pleiades* or *Vergiliae.*

plenary, adj. see FULL, ENTIRE, COMPLETE.

plenipotentiary, n. merely *legatus* (= ambassador); plenipotentiaries arrived from Sicily, *Siculi veniunt cum mandatis.*

plenitude, n. see FULNESS.

plenteous, plentiful, adj. *uber, abundans, copiosus, largus, affluens, opimus;* see ABUNDANT. Adv. *uberius, uberrime* (not in posit.), *abunde, abundanter, copiose, satis superque, large, cumulate, prolixe, effuse.* **plenty,** n. *ubertas* (without reference to the use we make of it), *copia* (of anything, for a certain purpose, opp. *inopia,* Cic.), *abundantia* (= abundance, more than we wish), *affluentia* (= profusion), *magna vis* (great quantity); — of anything, *satis* with genit.; to have — of anything, *suppeditare* or *abundare alqa re.*

pleonasm, n. *pleonasmus* (late, or as Greek πλεονασμός), better use circumloc. (e.g. *nimiâ abundantiâ verborum uti).* **pleonastic,** adj. by circumloc. (e.g. *verba plura sunt quam pro re*).

plethora, n. *sanguinis abundantia.* **plethoric,** adj. *plenus sanguinis.*

pleurisy, n. *pleuritis.*

pliant, pliable, adj. 1, *lentus, flexibilis;* 2, fig. *mobilis, inconstans, mollis, flexibilis.* **pliancy, pliability,** n. 1, *lentitia, lentor* (Plin.); 2, *mobilitas, inconstantia, mollitia.*

plight, I. n. see CONDITION, STATE. **II.** v.tr. see PLEDGE.

plinth, n. *plinthus, plinthis, -ĭdis,* f.

plod, v.intr. 1, = to go slowly, *tardius progredi;* 2, = to toil, *omni ope atque operâ eniti, ut,* etc.*, contendere et laborare, sudare et laborare;*

see Toil. **plodding,** adj. *esse industriâ singulari* (of persons).

plot, plat, n. of ground, *agellus, area.*

plot, I. n. 1, *consensio, conspiratio, consensionis* or *conspirationis globus* (in gen.), *conjuratio* (= conspiracy), *coitio* (= a secret combination, esp. of two candidates for an office, for the purpose of getting rid of their competitors); to form a —, *consensiones* or *coitionem facĕre, conspirare;* to form a — against anyone, *in alqm conspirare, contra alqm conjurare, ad alqm opprimendum consentire* (in order to oppress anyone); see Conspiracy; **2,** in dramatic writings, *argumentum fabulae.* **II.** v.tr. and intr. see above and Plan, Devise, Contrive, Conspire. **plotter,** n. see Conspirator.

plough, I. n. *aratrum;* —boy, *bubulcus,* in fig. sense a mere —boy, *agrestis, rusticus;* —man, *arator* (who tends the oxen); —share, *vomer;* —handle, *stiva.* **II.** v.tr. *arare* (absol. and with accus.), *inarare* (e.g. *semen,* = to cover by —ing), *exarare alqd* (= to dig up, to —), *aratro subigĕre* (= to break up, to till), *subvertĕre aratro alqd* (= to overturn with the plough); to — a field after it has been lying fallow, *proscindĕre.* **ploughing,** n. *proscissio* (= first —, Col.).

pluck, I. v.tr. *vellĕre* (= to tear up or away); stronger, *vellicare;* to — out a hair, *pilum evellĕre;* to — flowers, *flores carpĕre;* see Tear; to — up, *evellĕre, eruĕre;* to — up courage, *animum recipĕre.* **II.** n. 1, = heart, liver and lights of a sheep, etc., *intestina, -orum;* **2,** = courage, *animus, virtus, -ūtis,* f.

plug, n. *epistomium.*

plum, n. *prunum.* **plum-tree,** n. *prunus,* f. (Col.).

plumage, n. *plumae, pennae (pinnae).* **plume, I.** n. *pluma, penna (pinna).* **II.** v. reflex. to — oneself on, *alqd ostentare, jactare, prae se ferre.* **plumy,** adj. *plumis obductus, plumatus, pennatus* (= winged, also of an arrow; *plumiger* and *penniger* are both poetic).

plumber, n. *artifex plumbarius.*

plummet, plumb-line, n. *linea, perpendiculum.*

plump, adj. *pinguis;* see Fat. **plumpness,** n. *pinguitudo.*

plunder, I. v.tr. *praedari, praedam facĕre, diripĕre* (the enemy's territory, etc., also = to destroy the enemy, to ransack; in good prose only as t.t. representing warfare), *compilare, expilare* (= to rob by —), *(de)spoliare, exspoliare* (in gen. = to rob), *nudare* (= to strip), *depeculari* (rare, = to embezzle, in a contemptuous sense = to —; all these of one person or thing, also of several, e.g. to — men, to — houses, etc.), *depopulari* (= to lay waste, districts, etc.); to — out and out, *exhaurire, exinanire, nudum atque inane reddĕre* (= to clear a house, etc.), *everrĕre et extergĕre* (= to sweep and wipe clean, jocular instead of to — completely, to strip; a temple, *fanum,* Cic.). **II.** n. *praeda, rapina* (= act of —ing) to live by —, *rapto vivĕre.* **plunderer,** n. *direptor, spoliator, populator, praedator, expilator.*

plunge, I. v.tr. to — into, *mergĕre in alqd* or *in alqâ re,* or merely *alqâ re* (into anything liquid, e.g. into the water, *in aquam, aquâ;* into the sea, *in mari), demergĕre* or *submergĕre, immergĕre* (*in alqd* or *alqâ re*). into, *in alqd* or *in alqâ re* or *sub alqâ re;* to — a dagger, etc., see Thrust; to — anyone, a State, into difficulties, see Precipitate, Throw. **II.** v.intr. to — in, 1, *(im)mergĕre, demergĕre, submergĕre;* **2,** fig. see *mergĕre* or *ingurgitare in alqd.*

pluperfect, n. *tempus plusquam perfectum* (Gram.).

plural, adj. in Gram., the — number, *numerus pluralis, numerus multitudinis.* **plurality,** n. by *plures* (= more) or *multitudo* (= a number).

ply, v.tr. *exercēre.*

poach, I. v.tr. e.g. eggs, perhaps *fricare* (= to fry); —ed eggs, perhaps *ova assa* or *fricata.* **II.** v.intr. *furtim feras intercipĕre.* **poacher,** n. *fur* (= thief).

pocket, I. n. *sacculus* (= small bag, Juv.), *marsupium* (ante and post class.; = bag for holding money), *crumēna* (= a purse for containing small coin, a bag worn over the shoulders); the ancients had no —s in their garments, but they used the folds in their toga, *sinus, -ūs* (lit. = bosom, in sense of —, poet. and post Aug.). **II.** v.tr. = to take away, *auferre;* to — dishonestly, *pecuniam avertĕre.* **pocket-book,** n. *pugillares, -ium* (Plin.). **pocket-handkerchief,** n. *sudarium.* **pocket-knife,** n. *culter;* see Knife. **pocket-money,** n. *pecunia alci data.*

pod, n. *siliqua.*

podagra, n. *podagra, podagrae morbus.*

poem, n. *carmen* (= a short —, esp. a lyric —, a — composed according to metrical rules, such as the odes of Horace), *pŏēma, -ătis,* n.; to make a —, *carmen (poema) facĕre, fingĕre, scribĕre* (in gen.), *carmen fundĕre* (= to make verses extempore, with ease). **poesy,** n. see Poetry. **poet,** n. *pŏēta,* m., *carminum auctor, scriptor, conditor,* † *vates* (= inspired —). **poetaster,** n. *pŏēta malus.* **poetess,** n. *pŏētria.* **poetical,** adj. *pŏēticus.* Adv. *pŏētice, pŏētarum more.* **poetry,** n. *pŏētice* or *pŏētica, pŏēsis* (Quint.), or by poem; see Poem.

poignant, adj. *acer;* see Keen.

point, I. n. 1, *acumen* (in gen.), *cuspis, -ĭdis,* f. (of a weapon, an arrow, etc.), *spiculum* (= head or point of a dart, pike-head, the dart or arrow itself, opp. *hastile* = shaft), *cacumen, culmen, fastigium, vertex, -icis,* m. (= the highest = of anything, also by *summus);* see Summit; **2,** of land, *promontorium;* see Cape; **3,** in writing, see Stop; **4,** a small particle (as regards space or time), *pars* (= part in gen.), *locus* (= spot), *punctum temporis* (= minute); to draw the troops together at one —, *copias in unum locum contrahĕre* or *cogĕre;* the highest — of the mountain, *summus mons;* I am on the — of, etc. (I am about to, etc.), *in eo est, ut,* etc., *prope est, ut,* etc. (= the time is near at hand, when, etc.); to be on the — of conquering, *prope in manibus victoriam habēre;* **5,** = a circumstance, *res* (in gen.), *locus* (= a single subject of which we speak), *caput* (= main —, principal part, one particular portion, e.g. *a primo capite legis usque ad extremum), cardo, -inis,* m. (= main — on which anything hinges), *quaestio* (= the — in dispute), or *de quo agitur, nomen* (= an item in an account, outstanding debt); in this particular —, *hac in re;* the right —, *res ipsa;* to hit the right —, *rem acu tangĕre* (Plaut.); not to the —, *nihil ad rem;* an important —, *res magni momenti;* the most important —, *res maximi momenti, res gravissima, caput rei.* **II.** v.tr. and intr. 1, of sharp instruments, *(prae)acuĕre;* see Sharpen; **2,** with the finger at anyone or anything, *digito monstrare alqd* or *alqm, digitum intendĕre ad alqd* or *ad alqm* (= to stretch, hold out, etc.); see Notice; **3,** see Punctuate. **point-blank, I.** adj. *directus;* to give a — refusal, *alqd prorsus negare.* **II.** adv. *plane, prorsus, omnino;* see Altogether. **pointed,** adj. 1, *(prae)acutus;* **2,** fig. of speech, *salsus, aculeatus* (= stinging), *ad alqd appositus* (= directed to); see Clear. Adv. *salse, apposite.* **pointer,** n. = a

dog, *canis* (*venaticus*). **pointless**, adj. 1, see
BLUNT; 2, fig. *insulsus, frigidus, ineptus, inanis*.
poise, v.tr. *librare*.
poison, I. n. *venēnum, virus, -i*, n. (= poisonous vegetable or animal juice or liquid);
fig. *venenum*. **II.** v.tr. *alqd venenare* (rare),
alqd veneno imbuĕre; to slay many, to —
many, *multos veneno occidĕre ;* to strangle the
wife and — the mother, *laqueo uxorem interimĕre
matremque veneno ;* fig. to — the minds of the
young, *animos adolescentium inficĕre malis libidinibus*. **poisoned**, adj. *venatus* (= dipped in
poison, mixed with poison, e.g. an arrow, javelin,
sagitta, telum; meat, *caro*), *veneno necatus* or *ab-
sumptus* (= killed by poison); — words, perhaps
verba acerba or *aculeata*. **poisoner**, n. *veneficus* (if female, *venefica*). **poisoning**, n. *veneficium* (= mixing poison, as a regular occupation,
and as a crime). **poisonous**, adj. *venenatus* (in
gen.), *veneno imbutus* or *infectus* or *tinctus* (=
dipped in poison), *veneno illitus* (= besmeared
with —).

poke, I. v.tr. anyone, *alqm fodĕre* or *fodicare;*
to — the fire, *ignem excitare*. **II.** v.intr. to — about,
alqd rimari, perscrutari. **poker**, n. perhaps *ferramentum* (= iron tool) *quo ignis excitatur*.

pole, n. 1, = long rod, *contus, pertica, lon-
gurius, asser, vectis;* 2, of the earth, *axis, cardo,
† polus*, and *† vertex ;* the south —, *axis meridianus ;* the north —, *axis septentrionalis* (septemt-).
polar, adj. *septentrionalis* (septemt-) (= northern).
poleaxe, n. see AXE. **polecat**, n. *feles*.

polemical, adj. by circumloc., e.g. *qui cum
alqo de alqâ re disceptat* or *concertat, qui alqd in
controversiam vocat*. **polemics**, n. *disputationes*.

police, n. 1, matters relating to public
security, no exact term, use *publicae* or *urbanae
securitatis cura;* 2, = constables, etc., the
aediles had charge of many of the functions of
the police ; in gen. *ii quibus publicae securitatis
cura delata est* (= — officers). **policeman**, n.
unus e publicae securitatis custodibus.

policy, n. *ratio rei publicae gerendae, cīvīli-
tas* (in Quint. as trans. of πολιτική), *disciplina
reipublicae;* fig. *prudentia, calliditas, consilium*.
politic, adj. *prudens, sagax, astutus, callidus,
circumspectus, providus ;* see CUNNING, WISE,
PRUDENT. **political**, adj. referring to the
State, *cīvīlis* (as trans. of the Greek πολιτικός,
which does not exist in Latin, = referring to
the State or to State affairs ; e.g. *oratio civilis*),
publicus (= relating to public affairs), *polīticus*
(= relating to — science) ; — storms, *tempora
turbulenta, turbulentae in civitate tempestates ;* a
— discussion, *sermo de republicâ habitus ;* —
writings, *scripta quae ad rempublicam gerendam
pertinent ;* — science in gen., *ratio civilis, reipublicae gerendae ratio ;* see STATE. Adv., use
adj. **politician**, n. *vir rerum civilium peritus,
vir regendae civitatis peritus* or *sciens*. **politics**,
n. *respublica*, or in pl. *res publicae* (e.g. *ad rempublicam accedĕre*, = to take up —). **polity**, n.
respublica, genus, -ĕris, n., or *forma reipublicae,
ratio civilis*.

polish, I. v.tr. (*ex*)*polire, perpolire* (lit. and
fig., in fig. sense also *limare*). **II.** n. 1, lit.
nitor, candor ; see BRIGHTNESS ; 2, fig. circumloc. with *lima* (his writings lack —, *scriptis ejus
lima deest*); see POLITENESS. **polished**, adj. lit.
by past part. of POLISH, I. ; see also POLITE.

polite, adj. *urbanus, comis, humanus, affabilis, blandus, officiosus* (esp. towards superiors).
Adv. *urbane, comiter, humane, humaniter, blande,
officiose*. **politeness**, n. *urbanitas, comitas,
humanitas, affabilitas*.

poll, I. n. 1, see HEAD ; 2, = register of

heads, perhaps *index nominum ;* **3,** = entry
of the names of electors, see VOTE, ELECT,
REGISTER. **II.** v.tr. 1, lit. (*am*)*putare, praecidĕre ;* 2, = to give votes, see VOTE. **pollard**,
n. *arbor, -ōris*, f., (*am*)*putata*. **polling**, n.
see VOTING. **polling-booth**, n. *saeptum,
ovile*. **poll-tax**, n. to impose a —, *tributum
in singula capita imponĕre*.

pollute, v.tr. *polluĕre*. **pollution**, n. *pol-
lutio*.

poltroo⌐ ⌐. see COWARD.

polygamy, n. to live in a state of —, *solēre
plures uxores habēre* (of a man), *pluribus nuptam
esse* (of a woman).

polyglot, adj. *pluribus linguis scriptus*.

polygon, n. * *polygōnum*. **polygonal**, adj.
polygonius (Vitr.), † *multangulus* (Lucr.).

polypus, n. *polypus, -ōdis*, m. (as animal,
Plin., and as tumour in the nose, Cels.).

polytheism, n. *multorum deorum cultus, -ūs*.
polytheist, n. *qui multos deos colit*.

pomatum, n. *capillare* (in gen., Mart.).

pomegranate, n. *mālum granātum* or
Punicum (Col.).

pommel, I. n. of a saddle, *umbo sellae*. **II.**
v.tr. see BEAT.

pomp, n. *apparatus, -ūs ;* = show of magnificence, *venditatio, venditatio atque ostentatio* (=
boasting, swaggering) ; — of words, *inanis verborum strepitus, -ūs, quaedam species atque pompa ;*
to speak with a show of —, *in dicendo adhibēre
quandam speciem atque pompam*. **pompous**,
adj. 1, *magnificus, jactans, gloriosus, arrogans,
insolens ;* see BOASTFUL ; 2, of style, *inflatus,
tumidus ;* see INFLATED. Adv. *magnifice, gloriose,
arroganter, insolenter*. **pompousness, pomposity**, n. 1, *magnificentia, arrogantia, insolentia ;* 2, of words, *insolentia verborum*, or by
adj. ; see INFLATION.

pond, n. *stagnum* (= any stagnant pool of
water, also fish—), *piscina* (= fish—), *lacus, -ūs*
(= a lake, whether by nature or artificial).

ponder, v.tr. and intr. *ponderare, secum reputare ;* see CONSIDER. **ponderous**, adj. see
WEIGHTY.

poniard, n. see DAGGER.

pontiff, n. *pontifex ;* see PRIEST, POPE.

pontoon, n. *ponto*.

pony, n. *mannus, mannulus* (of Gallic race,
Plin. Min.), or *equus parvus*.

poodle, n. *canis*.

pool, n. *lacuna* (= a body of stagnant water),
† *volutabrum* (= a muddy place in which swine
delight to roll) ; see POND.

poop, n. *puppis*.

poor, adj. = in kind or nature, deficient in its
proper qualities, *malus, vilis* (= of small worth),
mediocris (= middling), *deterior* (= less good, superl. *deterrimus*), *pejor* (superl. *pessimus*) ; — living, *tenuis victus, -ūs ;* — speech, *oratio jejuna ;* —
cottage, *casa exigua ;* = barren, *inops alcjs rei* (or
alqâ re or *ab alqâ re*), *sterilis* (= unproductive) ;
— in words, *inops verborum ;* = not rich, *pauper*
(πένης, opp. *dives*), *tenuis* (= of small means, opp.
locuples), *egens, indigens* (= needy, wanting necessaries, opp. *abundans*), *tenuis atque egens ;* *inops*
(= without resources, opp. *opulentus*), *mendicus*
(= a beggar) ; somewhat —, *pauperculus ;* the
—, *pauperes, tenuis vitae homines* (= having a
slender income), *capite censi* (so called because the poorest were in the census taken
by numbers, without regard to property), also
proletarii (from *proles* = offspring) ; = wretched,
pitiable, *miser, misellus, infelix, miserandus : a*

— fellow, *homo misellus;* — fellow! *vae, me (te) miserum!* **poorhouse,** n. *ptōchotrophĭum* (Jct.), or by circumloc. (e.g. *aedes publicae pro indigentibus aedificatae).* **poor-laws,** n. *leges de indigentibus factae.* **poorly, I.** adv. *tenuiter, mediocriter, misere.* **II.** adj. see ILL.

poverty, n. *paupertas, angustiae rei familiaris* (= narrow means), *difficultas domestica, tenuitas, egestas* (= want), *inopia* (= destitution), *mendicitas* (= mendicity), in comb. *egestas ac mendicitas;* — of mind, *animi egestas, tenuis et angusta ingenii vena* (Quint.); — of words, *verborum inopia, inopia ac jejunitas, sermonis inopia;* — in your mother tongue, *egestas patrii sermonis.*

pop, I. n. *crepitus, -ūs.* **II.** v.intr. *crepare;* to — out, *evadĕre, ex(s)ilire.*

pope, n. * *pontifex Romanus,* * *papa.* **popish,** adj. * *papisticus.*

poplar, n. *pōpulus,* f.; of the —, *pōpuleus.*

poppy, n. *papāver, -ĕris,* n.

popular, adj. *in vulgus gratus;* see under PEOPLE. **populate,** v.tr. see under PEOPLE.

porch, n. *vestibulum;* in a temple or church, *pronaos* (πρόναος).

porcupine, n. *hystrix* (Plin.).

pore, n. *foramen* (e.g. *foramina invisibilia corporis* (Cels.). **porosity,** n. *raritas.* **porous,** adj. *fistulosus* (Plin., = full of holes), *spongiosus, rarus.*

pore, v.tr. to — over a book, *in libro alqo haerēre;* to — over, *totum se abdēre in alqd.*

pork, n. (*caro*) *suilla* or *porcina.* **porker,** n. *porcus.*

porphyry, n. *porphyrites* (Plin.).

porpoise, n. *porculus marinus* (Plin.).

porridge, n. *puls, -tis,* f.; see BROTH, SOUP, OATMEAL.

porringer, n. see PLATE.

port, n. 1, *portus, -ūs;* see HARBOUR; 2, see GAIT.

portable, adj. *quod portari* or *gestari potest.*

portcullis, n. *cataracta.*

portend, v.intr. *portendĕre, augurari, significare, praemonstrare, praenuntiare.* **portent,** n. *portentum, ostentum, prodigium, monstrum, signum, omen, augurium, auspicium,* † *avis.* **portentous,** adj. *portentosus, monstr(u)osus,* † *prodigiosus.* Adv. *monstr(u)ose.*

porter, n. 1, = keeper of a lodge, *janitor* (female, *janitrix), ostiarius;* see DOOR-KEEPER, GATE-KEEPER; 2, = one who carries burdens, *bajŭlus;* 3, see BEER.

portfolio, n. *scrinium.*

porthole, n. *fenestra.*

portico, n. *porticus, -ūs,* f.

portion, I. n. *pars, portio;* see PART, SHARE. **II.** v.tr. see DIVIDE.

portly, adj. see STOUT.

portmanteau, n. *vidulus, averta* (= cloakbag carried behind a horse, late Imperial Rome).

portrait, n. *imago (picta);* anyone's —, *effigies ex facie ipsius similitudine expressa.* **portrait-painter,** n. *pictor qui homines coloribus reddit.* **portray,** v.tr. *depingĕre* (in words or colours); see DESCRIBE, PAINT.

position, n. *collocatio* (= mode in which anything is placed, e.g. of the stars, *siderum,* Cic.), *status, -ūs, habitus, -ūs,* or by *positum esse;* fig. = circumstances, *status, -ūs* (= state in which anything is), *condicio* (= condition, rank in society, circumstances), *locus* (= — in which a person is placed, Cæs.), *tempus, tempora* (= change in one's circumstances which from time to time takes

place; hence often = bad, difficult circumstances), *res* (= affairs, etc., in gen.), *fortuna* (= outward circumstances, fortune).

positive, adj. a — law, *lex scripta* (opp. *lex nata);* the — right, *jus civīle* (opp. *jus naturale),* also merely *leges;* = certain, *certus;* a — statement, *affirmatio;* I make a— statement, *aio, affirmo;* the — degree, *positivus (gradus, -ūs)* (Prisc.). Adv. *affirmate, certo;* to know —, *certo* or *certis auctoribus comperisse;* to assert —, *affirmare, confirmare.* **positiveness,** n. = positive assertion, *affirmatio;* = certainty, by circumloc. (e.g. *alqd certum habēre, alqd affirmare).*

possess, v.tr. *possidēre (ingenium, magnam vim,* etc.), *alqd* or *possessionem rei habēre* or *tenēre, in possessione rei esse, habēre (auctoritatem), tenēre* (= to hold, e.g. *tu meum habes, tenes, possides), alqd re praeditum, instructum, ornatum* or *affectum esse* (= to be gifted with), *inesse alci* or *in alqo;* with *est* and genit. or dat., *virtus est virium* (= virtue - es strength), *est mihi liber* (= I — a book), or with the ablat. (e.g. *Hortensius erat tantā memoriā ut,* etc., = Hortensius —ed such a memory, that, etc.); — partitively, *alcjs rei participem esse;* all men cannot — all things, *non omnes omnium participes esse possunt;* not to —, *carēre re;* to — not at all, *alcjs rei expertem esse;* to — richly, *alqd re abundare* or *valēre.* **possession,** n. *possessio;* a taking —, *occupatio;* = the object possessed, *possessio, bona, -orum, res sua.* **possessive,** adj. *possessivus (casus)* (Gram.). **possessor,** n. *possessor, dominus.*

possible, adj. *quod esse, fieri* or *effici potest, quod per rerum naturam admitti potest;* a — case, *condicio quae per rerum naturam admitti potest* or simply *condicio* (Cic.); if it is, were —, if —, *si potest, si posset;* as much as —, *quantum potest (poterit,* etc.); it is — that, etc., *fieri potest, ut,* etc.; as much as it is —, *quoad fieri potest* or *poterit;* as . . . as —, *quam* with superl. (e.g. as early as —, *quam maturrime;* as quick as —, *quam celerrime;* as shortly as —, *quam brevissime);* he joined his colleague with his army in as rapid marches as —, *quantis maximis poterat itineribus exercitum ducebat ad collegam;* to show every — care, *omnem, quam possum, curam adhibēre;* every —, often merely *omnis.* Adv. *fieri potest ut,* etc.; see PERHAPS. **possibility,** n. *condicio* (= possible case, Cic.), *potestas* or *facultas* or *copia alqd faciendi* (= possession; *potestas,* as permission, power; *facultas* and *copia* = the opportunities), *locus alcjs rei* (= opportunity given through circumstances; e.g. he denies the — of this idea, *negat esse posse hanc notionem);* also when — implies that a thing can be done, by *fieri* or *effici posse* (e.g. they deny the — of anything, *alqd fieri posse negant).*

post, I. n. 1, *postis* (of a gate, etc.); *arrectaria, -orum,* n. (lit. what stands erect, opp. *transversaria,* Vitr.); *palus* (= a stake), *cippus* (esp. gravestone); 2, = military station, *locus* (= place in gen.), *statio* (= outpost, guard), *praesidium* (= any place taken by the troops, and which is to be defended); 3, = office, *locus, munus, -ĕris,* n., *partes, -ium;* 4, = system of public conveyance, *res veredaria, res vehicularia* (= the whole institution, Imperial Rome), *rei vehiculariae curatores* (= the persons connected with it); 5, system of conveyance of letters, *tabellarii* (= letter-carriers); to send through the —, *alqd per tabellarios mittēre;* to put into the —, *alqd tabellario perferendum committēre.* **II.** v.tr. 1, of travelling, letters, etc.; see I. 4, 5; 2, of troops, *(dis)ponĕre, (col)locare, constituĕre;* 3, = to affix a notice, etc., *proponĕre.* **postage,** n. *vecturae pretium;* to pay the —, *pro vecturā solvere.* **post-chaise,** n. *vehiculum publicum.*

raeda cursualis (Imperial Rome). **postern,** n. *postica, posticum.* **posthaste,** adv. *summâ celeritate* or *quam celerrin.e.* **postillion,** n. see RIDER, GROOM. **postman,** n. *tabellarius* (= private messenger; see POST I. 5. **postscript,** n. *algd epistulae additum.*

posterior, adj. *posterior.*

posterity, n. *posteritas* (in a wide sense, but only poetic for *progenies* or *stirps*), *posteri,* † *minores.*

posthumous, adj. *post patrem mortuum natus*

postmeridian, adj. *postmeridianus* or *pomeridianus, post meridiem* (opp. *ante meridiem*), *tempore pomeridiano, horis pomeridianis.*

postpone, v.tr. *differre, proferre, re(j)icĕre;* see DEFER.

postulate, n. *sumptio.*

posture, n. 1, of body, *status, habitus, gestus* (all *-ūs*); 2, = condition of affairs, *status, -ūs, res, condicio, ratio;* see STATE.

pot, n. *olla;* a small —, *ollula.* **potbellied,** adj. *ventriosus.* **potherb,** n. *olus, -ĕris,* n. **pothook,** n. *uncus;* in writing, *uncus quem dicunt.* **pothouse,** n. *caupona.* **potsherd,** n. *testa.* **pottage,** n. *jus, juris,* n.

potent, adj. see POWERFUL, EFFICACIOUS.

potentate, n. *res, tyrannus;* see SOVEREIGN.

potential, adj. *potentialis* (Gram.); see also POSSIBLE.

potion, n. *potio;* see PHILTRE.

potter, n. *figulus;* a —'s work, *opus figlinum, opera figlina* or *fictilia,* n. pl. (of several pieces); —'s vessels, earthenware, *(opus) figlinum, opera figlina;* —'s wheel, *rota figularis* or *figuli;* —'s workshop, *figlina* (Plin.). **pottery,** n. 1, the art, *ars figularis;* 2, = things made; see under POTTER.

pouch, n. *sacculus, saccus;* see BAG.

poultice, n. *cataplasma, -ătis,* n. (Cels.); *malagma, -ătis,* n. (= an emollient —, Cels.); a mustard —, *sinapismus.*

poultry, n. *aves cohortales* (kept in the yard) (Col.), *altiles, -ium* (= fattened —). **poulterer,** n. *qui altiles vendit.*

pounce, v.intr. to — upon; see SEIZE.

pound, I. n. 1, *libra, (libra) pondo* (in weight, of hard substances), *libra mensurâ* (of liquids); a bowl the gold of which weighs five —s, *patera ex quinque auri (libris) pondo;* 2, of money, use *libra Anglicana* as t.t., but use *argentum* or *pecunia* where possible; 3, = enclosure for stray animals, *saeptum publicum.* **II.** v.tr. *(con)tundĕre, (con)terĕre.*

pour, I. v.tr. 1, *fundĕre;* to — into, *infundĕre in algd;* to — upon or over, *superfundĕre alci rei.* **II.** v.intr. 1, of rain, *(ef)fundi;* 2, fig. to — forth, *(ef)fundi,* or *se (ef)fundĕre;* 3, to — along, *ferri;* 4, to — off, *defundĕre.* **pouring,** adj. *effusus* (of rain).

pout, v.intr. perhaps *frontem contrahĕre* (= to frown).

poverty, n. see POOR.

powder, I. n., in gen., *pulvis, -ĕris;* a medicine, *pulvis medicatus.* **II.** v.tr. 1, to reduce to —, *in pulverem conterĕre* (Plin.); 2, = to sprinkle with —, *pulvere conspergĕre.*

power, n. if internal, *potentia* or *vires, -ium,* (= strength); if external, *vis* (= force) or *potestas* (= authority from office), *jus, juris,* n., *potestasque, potestas ac dicio* or *dicio* alone (= authority), *facultas alcjs rei faciendae* (= —

of doing anything), *copiae, opes, -um, facultates, -um* (= resources), *robur, nervi, lacerti* (= physical —); to strive with all one's —, *omni ope eniti ut;* it is in my —, *est* or *positum* or *situm est in meâ manu,* or *potestate;* to reduce under one's —, *suae dicionis facĕre;* to be under the — of, *sub alcjs dicione atque imperio esse;* to do anything by —, *per vim facĕre algd;* to possess —, *vim habēre;* to compel anyone by —, *manus inferre alci;* — over persons or a nation, *potestas, imperium* (= military — or command); unlimited —, *dominatio, summum imperium, summa rerum.* **powerful,** adj. 1, physically, *validus, viribus pollens, robustus, valens, lacertosus, firmus;* 2, in influence, etc., *potens, valens, validus, gravis* (= weighty, of character); 3, of medicine, *efficax, potens* (Plin.); 4, of speech, *gravis, nervosus, validus* (Quint.). Adv. *valide* (not in Cic. or Caes.), *graviter, vehementer, valde* (= very —). **powerless,** adj. *invalidus, impotens, infirmus, imbecillus, languidus, irritus;* in political sense, *cui opes non suppeditant;* see WEAK. **powerlessness,** n. *imbecillitas, infirmitas;* in political sense by circumloc. (e.g. he felt his —, *sensit sibi opes deesse);* see WEAKNESS.

practicable, adj. *quod fieri* or *effici potest, facilis* (= easy, opp. *difficilis);* anything is —, *res facilitatem habet;* it is not —, *fieri* or *effici non potest.* **practicability,** n. *facultas, potestas.* **practical,** adj. *in agendo positus, usu peritus, ipso usu perdoctus;* — knowledge, *usus, -ūs;* to have a — knowledge of anything, *algd usu cognitum habēre, algd usu didicisse, alcjs rei usum habēre;* — use, *utilitas* (as regards public life). Adv. *(ex) usu;* to learn a thing —, *usu discĕre algd.* **practice,** n. 1, = exercise, etc., *usus, -ūs, usus rerum* (= exercise and experience); *exercitatio, tractatio,* comb. *usus et exercitatio, usus et tractatio;* to have more — than theory, *minus in studio quam in rebus et usu versatum esse;* we must combine theory and —, *discas oportet et quod didicisti agendo confirmes;* the — of an attorney, *caus(s)arum actio;* of a physician, surgeon, *medicinae usus et tractatio;* 2, = habit, *mos, consuetudo;* to make a — of, *solēre;* see CUSTOM. **practise,** v.tr. *algd facĕre, exercēre, factitare, tractare;* see PRACTICE. **practitioner,** n. *medicus.*

praetor, n. *praetor.* **praetorian,** adj. *praetorius, praetorianus* (Tac.). **praetorship,** n. *praetura.*

pragmatical, adj. *molestus, qui res alienas tractat.*

prairie, n. *campus.*

praise, I. v.tr. *laudare* (in gen.), *laudem alci tribuĕre, laudem alci impertire* or *laude algm impertire, laude algm afficĕre* (= to give — to), *collaudare* (with others), *dilaudare* (very much, almost too much), *praedicare algm* or *de algo* (aloud and openly). **II.** n. *laus, -dis,* f. (in a subjective and objective sense), *laudatio* (= a laudatory oration), *praedicatio* (= the act of recommending one for a meritorious deed, esp. openly and in public, e.g. *quae praedicatio de meâ laude praetermissa est);* they give — and thanks unto the gods, *diis laudes gratesque agunt.* **praiseworthy,** adj. *laudabilis, laude dignus, laudandus, collaudandus, praedicandus;* to be —, *laudi esse;* to be considered —, *laude dignum duci, laudi duci.* Adv. *laudabiliter.*

prance, v.intr. perhaps *magnifice incedĕre* (of a person), *ex(s)ultare* (of a horse).

prank, n. to play —s, perhaps *lascivire.*

prate, prattle, v. see BABBLE, CHATTER.

pray, v.intr. and tr. 1, *precari, preces* or *precationem facĕre* (generally; more poet. *preces*

fundĕre), *supplicare* (humbly, upon one's knees);
to God, *precari Deum* or *ad Deum, orare* or *invocare Deum* (= to invoke), *Deo supplicare* (= to
entreat humbly) ; to — unto God that He, etc.,
precari a Deo, ut, etc.; to — for, *alqd a Deo precari*
or *petĕre ;* 2, = to entreat for, in more gen. sense,
(*ef*)*flagitare, petĕre,* (*ex*)*poscĕre, implorare, rogare,
orare alqd ;* to — and beseech, *rogare atque
orare, petĕre ac deprecari.* **prayer,** n. *precatio,
supplicatio, preces, -um* (= the formulary, book
of common —), *votorum nuncupatio* (in which
we make promises). **prayerful,** adj. **prayer-
fully,** adv. *supplex.* **praying,** n. *precatio, preces, -um, supplicatio* (humble) ; a day of — and
thanksgiving, *supplicatio et gratulatio ;* to appoint —, *supplicationem decernĕre.*

preach, v.tr. and intr. * *contionar* (the
usual term in writers after the Reformation),
* *praedicare,* or *orationem* (*sacram*) *habĕre, e*
(*sacro*) *suggestu dicĕre,* in *caetu Christianorum
verba facĕre, de rebus divinis dicĕre ;* to — about,
in the context, *dicĕre de alqā re, oratione explicare alqd.* **preacher,** n. * *praedicator ;* —
to deaf ears, *monitor non exauditus.*

preamble, n. *exordium ;* see INTRODUC-
TION.

precarious, adj. *incertus.* Adv. *parum* or
non certo.

precaution, n. *cautio,* or by verb *providĕre,
praecavēre.*

precede, v.tr. *anteire, antegredi, antecedĕre,
praeire, praegredi.* **precedence,** n. *prior
locus ;* to have the — before anyone, *alci antecedĕre ;* to let anyone have the —, *alci cedĕre,
alqm priore loco ire jubēre.* **preceding,** adj.
antecedens, praecedens ; = last, *prior, superior ;*
= the one immediately before, *proximus.* **precedent,** n. see EXAMPLE.

precentor, n. *praecantor* (late).

precept, n. *praeceptum* (beforehand, what
and how it is to be done), *praescriptum, praescriptio* (= rule, made by a higher authority, and
which we have to follow, e.g. *naturae, rationis ;*
the former the — itself, the latter the act of
prescribing), *lex* (made into law).

preceptor, n. *magister ;* see TEACHER.

precincts, n. *ambitus, -ūs ;* see LIMIT, DIS-
TRICT.

precious, adj. *magnificus, splendidus, egregius, eximius, pulcherrimus, jucundissimus, suavissimus ;* — stones, *gemmae.*

precipice, n. *locus praeceps.*

precipitate, I. v.tr. *praecipitare* (from, *ex*
or *de alqo loco,* into, etc., *in alqm locum,* headlong,
lit. and fig.), *de*(*j*)*icĕre,* from (*ab* or *de*) *alqo loco,*
into, *in alqm locum, deturbare, de* or *ex alqo loco,
in alqm locum ;* to — oneself, *sese praecipitare,* or
merely *praecipitare,* or, in the sense of the
middle voice in Greek, *praecipitari,* from, etc.,
alqo loco, de or *ex alqo loco ;* into, *in alqm locum ;*
(e.g. into ruin, *in exitium*), over, *super alqm
locum, se de*(*j*)*icĕre, se ab*(*j*)*icĕre* (= to throw
oneself down from the wall into the sea, *e
muro in mare se abjicĕre*), *inferri* or *se inferre
in alqd* (= to rush into, e.g. *in flammas, in
medios ignes,* also fig., e.g. *se inferre in capitis
periculum*). **II.** adj. *temerarius, praeceps ;* see
HASTY, RASH. Adv. *temere.* **precipitancy,**
precipitation, n. *temeritas ;* see RASHNESS.
precipitous, adj. *praeceps, praeruptus.*

precise, adj. (*de*)*finitus* (= marked out), *accuratus* (= accurate), *subtilis* (= accurate in the
choice of words). Adv. *subtiliter ;* = altogether,
plane ; by *ipse* (e.g. *ipso in tempore,* = — at the
right time); see EXACT, ACCURATE. **preci-**

sion, n. *subtilitas, proprietas verborum ;* see
ACCURACY.

preclude, v.tr. see HINDER, EXCLUDE.

precocious, adj. *praecox* (lit. of fruit, and
fig. post Aug. of talents) ; see PREMATURE.

preconceived, adj. *praejudicatus.* **preconception,** n. *sententia praejudicata.*

preconcerted, adj. *ex composito* (*factus,* etc.).

precursor, n. *praecursor* (lit., Plin.), *praenuntius,* fig.

predatory, adj. *praedatorius.*

predecessor, n. in office, *decessor* (*anteces-
sor,* only by Jct.) ; he is my —, *succedo ei.*

predestination, n. *praedestinatio* (Eccl.).
predestine, v.tr. *praedestinare* (Liv.) ; in a
theol. sense, *praefinire.*

predetermine, v.tr. *praefinire.*

predicable, adj. *quod alci rei attribui
potest.*

predicament, n. an awkward —, *difficultas.*

predicate, I. n. *attributio, attributum, res
attributa, id quod rebus* or *personis attribuitur*
or *attributum est* (= to attribute). **II.** v.tr. *alqd
de alqā re praedicare, dicĕre ;* see SAY.

predict, v.tr. *praedicĕre ;* see PROPHESY.
prediction, n. *praedictio ;* see PROPHECY.

predilection, n. see AFFECTION.

predispose, v.tr. *animum ad alqd praeparare* or *componĕre.* **predisposed,** adj. *propensus* or *proclivis ad alqd.* **predisposition,**
n. *animi ad alqd proclivitas, voluntatis inclinatio,
studium.*

predominance, n. 1, = power, *potentia ;*
see POWER ; 2, = greater number of, by *plures.*
predominate, v.intr. 1, *dominari ;* 2, *plures
esse.* **predominating,** adj. see CHIEF.

preeminence, n. *praestantia, excellentia,
eminentia.* **preeminent,** adj. *praestabilis,
praestans, excellens, praecipuus, summus, optimus,
conspicuus, insignis.* Adv. *praecipue ;* see ES-
PECIALLY.

preexist, v.intr. *antea exstare* or *esse.* **pre-
existence,** n. by verb.

preface, I. n. *prooemium* (= introduction),
praefatio (in disputations, to ask permission or
to apologise, etc. ; then = written — to a book) ;
— to a book, *prooemium libri* (not *ad librum*),
prooemium libro additum. **II.** v.tr. *praefari* (=
both to write a — and to make one in speaking),
praefationem dicĕre (in speaking), *prooemium
scribĕre* (= to write). **prefatory,** adj. to make
a few — remarks, *pauca praefari.*

prefect, n. *praefectus.* **prefecture, n.**
praefectura.

prefer, v.tr. 1, *praeponĕre, anteponĕre, praeferre, anteferre* (in gen.), *alqm potissimum diligĕre*
(= to esteem very highly), *alqd alci rei posthabēre*
(= to hold one thing inferior to another) ; *prae-
optare* with infin. (= to wish rather), *malle*
with infin. (to wish rather, e.g. *mori maluit*) ;
2, see PROMOTE ; 3, see ACCUSE. **preferable,**
adj. *potior, praeoptandus, praestabilior,* or by
compar. of any adj. = excellent ; see GOOD,
EXCELLENT. Adv. *potius.* **preference,** n.
by verb PREFER. **preferment,** n. by special
name of office (e.g. *consulatus*), or by *honos* (=
office).

prefix, n. **I.** v.tr. *praeponĕre, anteponĕre ; praescribĕre* (in writing). **II.** n. *syllaba ante-
posita.*

pregnancy, n. *praegnatio* (of a female with
child), *graviditas* (more advanced, Cic.). **pregnant,** adj. 1, *praegnans* (in gen. of women and

animals, fig. = full of anything), *gravida* (in a more advanced state), *gravidata* (fig.); to be —, *gravidam* or *praegnatum esse, ventrem ferre, partum ferre* or *gestare*; to be — by anyone, *gravidam esse ex alqo*; 2, of language, *pressus* (concise); of events, *magni* or *maximi momenti*; see IMPORTANCE.

prehensile, adj. *quod ad prehendendum xptum* or *accommodatum est.*

prejudge, v.tr. *prius judicare quam alqs alqd sciat.*

prejudice, I. n. *opinio praejudicata, alqd praejudicati, opinio praesumpta* (preconceived); *opinio prava* (= wrong opinion), *opinio ficta* (= a false opinion, in the context often simply *opinio* = erroneous opinion), *opinionis commentum* (= fanciful dream); a — still more confirmed through the teaching of others, *opinio confirmata*; to have a — against anyone, *male* de *algo opinari*; to come anywhere with a —, *alqd praejudicati afferre.* **II.** v.tr. *alqm alci suspectum reddĕre, alqm* or *alcjs animum alienum reddĕre* or *alienare ab alqo*; to become —d against anyone, *ab alqo alienari*; to become —d, *ab alqo alienatum esse, ab alqo animo esse alieno* or *averso*, very much, *ab alqo animo esse aversissimo.* **prejudicial,** adj. see INJURIOUS.

prelate, n. *• episcopus.*

preliminary, adj. see PREFATORY.

prelude, I. n. 1, *prooemium*; 2, fig. *prolusio, praelusio atque praecursio* (Plin. Min.). **II.** v.tr. 1, perhaps *prooemium canĕre* (fixing sense by context); 2, fig. *nuntiare*; see ANNOUNCE.

premature, adj. **1,** lit. *praematurus, praecox* (Plin.), *immaturus*; 2, fig. *praematurus,* † *praecox, immaturus, praeproperus.* Adv. *praemature.*

premeditate, v.tr. *praemeditari* (= to think over beforehand); —d act, *quod ex consulto fit.* **premeditation,** n. *praemeditatio*; see PURPOSE.

premier, n. = prime minister, perhaps *penes quem est summa reipublicae.*

premise, v.tr. *praefari.* **premises,** n. *aedificium* (or in pl.), *domus, -ūs* (irreg.); see HOUSE, BUILDING.

premiss, n. *propositio* (major), *assumptio* (minor). **premisses,** n. *concessa, -orum,* or *ea quae antecesserunt.*

premium, n. *praemium.*

premonition, n. *monitio, monitum.* **premonitory,** adj. *quod praemonet.*

preoccupy, v. *praeoccupare* (= to seize beforehand), in pass. to be —ied, *totum alci rei deditum esse.* **preoccupation,** n. *praeoccupatio* (lit.), *animus alci rei deditus* (fig.).

preparation, n. *praeparatio* (in gen.) *apparatio* (= a getting ready everything), *praemeditatio* (= premeditation, e.g. *futurorum malorum*), *meditatio* (= the preparing of a lesson, etc.), *commentatio* (= the thinking over anything, e.g. a play, a speech); — for a war, *apparatus, -ūs, belli*; to make — for a war, *bellum* (*ap*)*parare.* **preparatory,** adj. *quod alqd parat*; see PREPARE. **prepare,** v.tr. *praeparare* (for a future object), (*ap*)*parare* (= to get everything ready), *instruĕre* (= to provide everything necessary); to — oneself for, *se parare, se praeparare ad alqd* (in gen.), (*ap*)*parare alqd* (= to make preparation for), *animum praeparare ad alqd, se* or *animum componĕre ad alqd* (to — one's mind), *ante meditari alqd, praemeditari alqd* (= to think over, a lesson, etc.), *commentari alqd* (= to think over,

e.g. a plan, a sermon); to — for war, *se parare ad bellum, bellum parare* or *apparare, belli apparatum instruĕre.*

preponderance, preponderate, n., v.intr., see PREDOMINANCE, PREDOMINATE.

prepossess, v.tr. *capĕre* or *occupare* (= to preoccupy, to get the start of anything, to cause it to be in one's favour), *delenire, permulcēre* (to win over); to — anyone's mind for anyone, *animum alcjs conciliare ad benevolentiam erga alqm.* **prepossessing,** adj. see AGREEABLE, CHARMING. **prepossession,** n. *sententia praejudicata*; see PREJUDICE.

preposterous, adj. *praeposterus*; see PERVERSE.

prerequisite, n. see REQUISITE.

prerogative, n. *quod alci proprium est.*

presage, I. v.tr. *portendĕre* (= to foreshow), *praesagire* (= to forebode); see FORETELL, PROPHESY, FOREBODE. **II.** n. *praesagium*

Presbyter, n. *• presbyter.*

prescient, adj. † *praesciens,* or *sagax*; see WISE.

prescribe, v.tr. *praescribĕre* (= to order, and of a doctor). **prescription.** n. 1, = custom, *usus, -ūs*; 2, = medical, *medicamenti praescriptio.* **prescriptive,** adj. — right, perhaps *jus ex usu factum.*

presence, n. 1, *praesentia*; frequent —, *assiduitas*; in anyone's —, *coram alqo praesente* (but *apud alqm* when addressing anyone, e.g. *dicĕre, loqui, verba facĕre apud alqm*); 2, — of mind, perhaps *animus ad omnia paratus.* **present, I.** adj. render by circumloc., as *qui nunc est, qui hodie est*; the — Consul, *qui nunc Consul est*; my scholar and now my friend, *discipulus meus, nunc amicus*; the — state of things, *hic rerum status. Praesens,* = that which prevails and continues now in contrast with that which prevailed or will prevail at another time. *Instans,* to signify that which is imminent or at hand; "the —" is represented by *hic*; *haec tempora,* = the — time; according to the — silly custom, *more hoc insulso*; at —, *in praesenti*; for the —, *in praesens* (*tempus*); the — tense, *praesens tempus* (Gram.); to be —, *adesse, interesse.* Adv. *mox* (= soon), *statim* (= immediately). **II.** v.tr. to — arms, *telum erigĕre honoris caus(s)a*; see GIVE, INTRODUCE. **III.** n. see GIFT.

presentiment, n. † *praesagium* (absolute or with gen.) and *praesagitio* (absolute as a faculty within us); see FOREBODE.

preserve, I. v.tr. 1, *sustinēre, sustentare* (in gen. to keep up, e.g. the world, health), by anything, *alqā re*; *servare, conservare* (= to — so as to keep it, e.g. property, *rem familiarem cons.,* = to save), *tueri* (= to have an eye upon, to guard from falling, also to keep a building in repair, also = to entertain, keep), comb. *tueri et conservare,* *alĕre* (through nursing; then in gen. = to keep), comb. *alĕre et sustentare, sustentare et alĕre,* one's health, *valetudinem tueri*; see KEEP, SAVE; 2, = to conserve, *condire.* **II.** n. = conserve, *fructus, -ūs, conditus.* **preserver,** n. (con)*servator* (fem. *conservatrix*), *salutis auctor.* **preservation,** n. *conservatio, tuitio* (= the act), *salus, -ūtis,* f., *incolumitas* (= safety); the desire of self— is innate in every being, *omni animali primus ad omnem vitam tuendam appetitus a naturā datus est, se ut conservet* (Cic.).

preside, v.intr. *praesidēre*; to — at, *alci rei praesidēre, alci rei praeesse.* **presidency,** n. *praefectura* or in certain cases (e.g. the Indian Presidencies), *provincia.* **president,** n. *praeses,*

-ĭdis (= who presides), *princeps, caput* (= head);
— at a trial, *qui judicio praeest.*

press, I. n. 1, = a machine for pressing, *prelum* (in gen. use it also for printing —), *torcular* (for wine, etc.); 2, fig. e.g. freedom of the —, *libertas or licentia alcjs rei scribendae or edendae.* **II.** v.tr. 1, in a machine, *prelo premĕre, prelo alqd sub(j)icĕre;* 2, = to squeeze, *premĕre, comprimĕre;* 3, = to urge, to — upon, *alqm urgēre, premĕre, alci instare, alqm vexare* (= to worry), *propellĕre* (= to drive forward); his creditors —ed him, *ei instabant creditores;* to be —ed by business, *occupationibus distinēri;* 4, = to persuade, *alei instare, alqd ab alqo* (*ex*)*petĕre;* 5, = to enlist by force, *nautas vi comparare.* **III.** v.intr. to — forward, *contendĕre* (e.g. to the camp, *in castra;* to go to Rome, *Romam ire*); see HASTEN. **press-gang,** n. *qui nautas vi comparant.* **pressing,** adj. *magni or maximi momenti, gravis;* see IMPORTANT, URGENT. **pressure,** n. 1, lit. *pressio* (Vitr.), *pressus, -ūs, compressio,impetus,nisus,-ūs;* 2,fig.by circumloc., e.g. under — of danger, *instante periculo or periculo coactus.*

prestige, n. *nomen* (= mere name), *gloria, fama;* see FAME, REPUTATION.

presume, v.intr. 1, = to take liberties, be arrogant, *sibi arrogare, sumĕre ut;* 2, = to assume (a thing to be true, etc.), *putare;* see SUPPOSE. **presumption,** n. 1, *arrogantia;* see INSOLENCE; 2, = conjecture, *conjectura;* there is a — in favour of anyone, perhaps *hoc pro or ab alqo stat.* **presumptive,** adj. *quod ex conjecturā cognitum est, opinabilis.* Adv. *ex conjecturā.* **presumptuous,** adj. *arrogans;* see INSOLENT. Adv. *arroganter.* **presumptuousness,** n. see PRESUMPTION.

pretence, n. *simulatio, species, verba, -orum* (mere words, opp. to reality); without —, *sine fuco ac fallaciis.* **pretend,** v.tr. and intr. *simulare;* they —ed that they wanted to go hunting, and left the town, *per speciem venandi urbe egressi sunt.* **pretended,** adj. *simulatus, opinatus* (= imaginary), *fictus;* see FALSE, IMAGINARY. **pretender,** n. 1, *simulator;* 2, one who claims the throne, *qui regnum sibi arrogat.* **pretension,** n. 1, *postulatio;* just —, *jus;* 2, *ostentatio;* see POMP, DISPLAY.

preterite, n. *praeteritum* (*tempus*) (Gram.).

preternatural, adj. and adv. *quod praeter naturam, praeter modum or mirabili quodam modo fit.*

pretext, n. *caus(s)a, praescriptio, titulus, nomen* (= title, false name), *simulatio* (= the pretending of something), *species* (when we make anything bad appear as if it was something very innocent); under the — of, *per caus(s)am alcjs rei, nomine or simulatione or simulatione atque nomine alcjs rei, per simulationem alcjs rei, simulatā re, specie or per speciem alcjs rei.*

pretty, adj. *bellus* (proper term), *pulcher, pulchellus* (= rather —, both of persons and things), *formosus* (= well-shaped, of persons), *lepidus* (= neat, of persons and things), *venustus* (= charming, of persons and things), *festivus* (= graceful, elegant), *bonus* (= not inconsiderable, of a quantity). Adv. *belle, pulchre, formose, lepide, festive, venuste.* **prettiness,** n. see BEAUTY.

prevail, v.intr. *esse* (= to be), *obtinēre* (*fama obtinuit,* Liv.), *adducĕre alqm ut* (= to persuade), *multum, plus valēre or pollēre* (= to have much force),with anyone, *apud alqm; morbus crescit,*the disease —s; to — on oneself, *se ipsum vincĕre;* I cannot — on myself to, etc., a me impetrare non possum ut faciam, etc. (so *non possum adduci ut credam;* = I cannot be —ed upon to believe); to

— over, *superare, vincĕre;* to be —ed upon by entreaties, *precibus flecti* (Liv.); a —ing or prevalent opinion, *opinio vulgata.* **prevalent,** adj. (*per*)*vulgatus, communis.*

prevaricate, v.intr. *tergiversari.* **prevarication,** n. *tergiversatio* (= shift); see LIE.

prevent, v.tr. *prohibēre ne or quominus impedire, obstare;* see HINDER. **prevention,** n. *prohibitio* (rare, or by verb). **preventive,** adj. *quod alqd impedit or alci rei obstat.*

previous, adj. see PRECEDING.

prey, I. n. *praeda;* beast of —, *fera.* **II.** v.intr. *praedari;* to — upon, *alqm bestiam venari, alqā bestiā vesci* (= to feed upon); fig. *animum,* etc., (*ex*)*edĕre, consumĕre.*

price, I. n. *pretium; annona* (= — of corn); to fix the —, *pretium facĕre, indicare* (of the seller); the — asked with the abl.; so at a high, low —, *magno, parvo* (*pretio*), so too gen. *magni, parvi,* etc.; what is the —? *quanti indicas? quanti hoc vendis?* (when we ask the seller); *quanti hoc constat?* (= what does that cost? when we ask a person the value of anything); I agree with him about the —, *convenit mihi cum algo de pretio;* the — has fallen, *pretium alcjs rei jacet;* to raise the —, *pretium alcjs rei efferre or augēre.* **II.** v.tr. *pretium alci constituĕre, pretium merci statuĕre, pretium enumerare or pacisci.* **priceless,** adj. *inaestimabilis.*

prick, I. v.tr. *pungĕre* (of anything that stings, also gen. of sharp pain), *stimulare* (with a sharp-pointed stick, e.g. *bovem*), *mordēre* (= to bite, of a pain, e.g. of a flea or a fly); to — with a needle, *acu pungĕre;* to — up one's ears, *aures erigĕre or arrigĕre.* **II.** n. *punctus, -ūs* (Plin.), or by verb. **prickle,** n. *aculeus, spina* (= thorn). **prickly,** adj. *aculeatus, spinosus.*

pride, n. *superbia* (= haughtiness), *spiritus, -ūs* (= high spirit), *insolentia* (= arrogance, insolence), *contumacia* (= obstinacy), *arrogantia* (= arrogance), *fastidium* (when we treat those around us with contempt), *fastus, -ūs* (= behaviour of a person towards one with whom he disdains to have any intercourse).

priest, n. *sacerdos* (in gen. also = priestess), *antistes* (also = priestess), *flamen* (of one particular god, e.g. *flamen Dialis*); high —, *pontif, pontifax maximus.* **priestcraft,** n. *ratio sacerdotum.* **priestess,** n. see PRIEST. **priesthood,** n. *sacerdotium.* **priestly,** adj. by the genit. *sacerdotis or sacerdotum.* **priestridden,** adj. *sacerdotibus subjectus.*

prig, n. perhaps *qui se nimium jactat.*

prim, adj. perhaps *de se nimium sol(l)icitus* or *de moribus diligentior.*

primal, primeval, adj. see ANCIENT.

primary, adj. *primus, principalis;* the — meaning of a word, *naturalis et principalis verbi significatio* (Quint.); = chief, *praecipuus.* Adv. *primo* (= at first), *praecipue* (= chiefly).

primate, n. *primas* (Eccl.).

prime, I. adj. 1, *primus* = first; 2, = excellent, *eximius, optimus.* **II.** n. 1, = the best of anything, *flos;* 2, — of life, *aetas vigens.* **prime-minister,** n. *is penes quem summa rerum est.*

primitive, adj. 1, = original, *priscus, antiquus;* 2, see PRIMARY.

primogeniture, n. *aetatis privilegium* (Jct.).

prince, n. 1, *adulescens* (*adol-*) or *juvenis regii generis, puer or juvenis regius* (= a young man of royal blood, son of a king, etc.), *filius principis, filius regis or regius;* 2, = king, *rex;*

see SOVEREIGN. **princess,** n. *mulier regii generis, mulier regio semine orta, regia virgo;* daughter of a king, etc., *filia regis* or *regia.*

principal, I. adj. *primus, princeps, principalis, praecipuus* (= chief). Adv. *maxime, praecipue, ante omnia, imprimis, praesertim, maximam partem* (= for the most part). **II.** n. 1, = head of a school, *magister;* 2, = capital, opp. to interest, *caput, sors, pecuniae, nummi.* **principality,** n. *terra principis imperio subiecta.*

principle, n. 1, = beginning, *principium, elementum, primordia, -orum;* 2, = rule of conduct, *dogma, -ātis,* n., *decretum* (in anyone's mode of action) ; *consilium* (= a rule to act upon, and which is based upon sound reasoning), *praeceptum* (= precept, rule, to serve as a guide in our actions, also of a philosopher, Hor.), *disciplina, institutum, institutio* (= what has become a — through habit), comb. *ratio et institutio mea, praecepta institutaque philosophiae, sententia* (= opinion), *judicium* (= judgment), *regula alcjs rei* or *ad quam alqd dirigitur* (never without genit. of object, e.g. *eadem utilitatis quae honestatis est regula*), *lex* (= law) ; the highest moral —, *summum bonum, ultimum* or *finis bonorum;* a man of firm —, *homo constans* (= true to his character), *homo gravis* (always acting upon —, and according to what is right), so *gravitas* = — ; a man of vacillating —, *homo lēvis;* a man of strict —, *homo sevērus;* a man who acts according to his own —, *vir sui judicii* (because it is his conviction), *vir sui arbitrii* (because he thinks fit) ; from —, *ratione* (= according to the adopted —), *judicio, animi quodam judicio* (= from a certain conviction), *doctrinā* (as the result of one's studies, inquiries, etc., opp. *naturā,* from a natural feeling) ; always to remain true to one's —, *sibi constare.*

print, I. n. = an impression, *impressio.* **II.** v.tr. *exprimĕre alqd alqā re* or *in alqā re;* to — a book, *librum typis describĕre, exscribĕre, exprimĕre.* **printer,** n. *typographus.* **printing-press,** n. *prelum typographicum.*

prior, I. adj. *prior;* see EARLY, BEFORE, PRECEDING. **II.** n. (of a monastery), in gen. *antistes, -ĭtis,* m., * *prior,* or *magister.* **prioress,** n. *priorissa.*

prism, n. * *prisma, -ătis,* n. (late). **prismatic,** adj. * *prismaticus* (as t.t.).

prison, n. *custodia* (lit. = act of guarding ; then the place), *carcer, -ĕris,* m. (= a public —), *ergastulum* (= a place commonly below ground, where slaves were made to work in chains), *vincula, -orum,* n. (= chains) ; to cast into —, *in custodiam* or *in vincula* or *in ergastulum mittĕre, in custodiam* (or *in vincula*) *mittĕre, tradĕre, condĕre, con(j)icĕre, in custodiam* (or *in carcerem*) *dare, includĕre, custodiae* or *vinculis mandare;* to take to —, *in custodiam* or *in vincula,* (*de)dŭcĕre;* to be (confined) in —, *in custodiā esse* or *servari, custodiā tenēri, in carcere* or *in vinculis esse.* **prisoner,** n. *captus, -a* (in gen.) ; taken — (in war), *bello captus, captivus, -a;* by the police, *comprehensus, -a.*

pristine, adj. *pristinus, priscus* (= ancient), *prior* (= former).

prithee! interj. (*die*) *quaeso, tandem, cedo.*

privacy, n. *solitudo;* see SECRECY. **private, I.** adj. *privatus* (referring to a single individual, etc., opp. *publicus*), *proprius* (only referring to the person himself, not to all, opp. *communis*), *domesticus* (= domestic, opp. *forensis*), comb. *domesticus et privatus, secretus* (= secret, without witnesses, opp. *apertus*) ; — affairs, *res privata* or *domestica* or *domestica et privata; peculium, quod sui juris est* (Jct.) ; — enemy,

inimicus (opp. *hostis*) ; a — life, *vita privata* (in gen.), *historia vitae privatae* (= history of one's — life), *vita otiosa* (= having no business to attend to), *vita umbratilis* (= easy life in retirement). Adv. *clam, secreto, occulte, remotis arbitris* (= without spectators), *privatim* (= in a private capacity). **II.** n. in the army, *miles.* **privateer,** n. *navis* (*praedatoria*). **privation,** n. *privatio* (= act of —), *inopia, egestas, paupertas* (= need) ; see POVERTY. **privative,** adj. *privativus* (Gram.).

privilege, n. 1, = a particular right, *privilegium* (granted by special authority), *beneficium, commodum* (= any right, whereby a person derives a particular benefit ; *benef.* when it is granted, *comm.* when it has been obtained ; all three Jct.) ; 2, = exemption from a burden, *immunitas, gratia, munus, -ēris,* n., *beneficium* (= favour) ; see FAVOUR. **privileged,** adj. *privilegiarius* (Jct.) ; = exempt from, *immunis.*

privy, I. adj. see PRIVATE, SECRET. **II.** n. *sella* (*familiarica*). **privy-council,** n. in imperial times *consistoriani.* **privy-purse,** n. *fiscus.*

prize, I. n. *praemium, palma;* to fix a —, *praemium* (*pro*)*ponĕre.* **II.** v.tr. *magni aestimare* or *facĕre.* **prize-fighter,** n. *qui praemio proposito contendit,* or *pugil* (= boxer).

pro and con, in *utramque partem.*

probable, adj. *probabilis, veri similis* (or as one word, *verisim-*). Adv. *probabiliter, verisimiliter* (*verisim-*). **probability,** n. *probabilitas, verisimilitudo* (*verisim-*).

probation, n. *probatio;* a time of —, *tempus ad alcjs facultates experiendas constitutum.* **probationer,** n. *alumnus* (fem. *-a*).

probe, I. n. *specillum.* **II.** v.tr. see EXAMINE.

probity, n. *probitas.*

problem, n. *quaestio.* **problematical,** adj. *dubius, incertus;* see DOUBTFUL.

proboscis, n. *proboscis* (Plin.), *manus, -ūs,* f. (of an elephant).

proceed, v.intr. 1, *progredi;* see GO ; 2, = to come from, *oriri;* 3, = to act, *agĕre, facĕre;* see ACT ; 4, to — against, *litem alci intendĕre.* **proceeding,** n. *ratio;* legal —, *actio;* to commence —s, *actionem alci intendĕre;* = transactions, *acta, -orum.* **proceeds,** n. *reditus, -ūs, fructus, -ūs.*

process, n. *ratio* = course of proceedings, *actio* (= — at law) ; in — of time, (*procedente*) *tempore.*

procession, n. in gen. *pompa;* at a funeral, *pompa funebris;* to hold a —, *pompam ducĕre.*

proclaim, v.tr. *declarare* (e.g. public shows, *munera, edicĕre* (lit. of authorities = to make known a law, etc., but also = to decree in gen.), *promulgare* (= to make generally known, a law, etc.), *proponĕre* (= to placard, e.g. *edictum,* etc.), *praedicĕre* (through the herald), *pronuntiare* (= to announce). **proclamation,** n. 1, the act of —, *pronuntiatio, declaratio, praedicatio;* 2, = the thing proclaimed, *edictum; libellus* (= a written —).

proclivity, n. *proclivitas,* but better by circumloc. (e.g. he has a — to do anything, *est ejus alqd facĕre*).

proconsul, n. *pro consule* (also, but less often, *proconsul*). **proconsular,** adj. *proconsularis.*

procrastinate, v.tr., **procrastination,** n. see DELAY.

procreate, v.tr. *procreare.* **procreation,** n. *procreatio.*

procure, v.tr. *(com)parare* (= to see that any-thing is ready, for oneself or for others, e.g. *auctoritatem, gloriam, servos,* also money), *afferre* (= to bring, also of things, e.g. *auctoritatem, utili-tatem, consolationem), acquirere* (after difficulty, e.g. *quod ad vitae usum pertinet, dignitatem, opes, divitias), conciliare* (= to collect together, e.g. *legiones pecuniâ, sibi benevolentiam alcjs, alci favorem ad vulgus), expedire* (= to manage to get, e.g. *pecunias), prospicere* (= to provide for, e.g. *alci habitationem, alci maritum);* see GET, GAIN, OBTAIN. **procurator,** n. *procurator;* see MANAGE, MANAGER. **procurer,** n. *leno.* **procuring,** n. *comparatio, conciliatio.*

prodigal, adj. see EXTRAVAGANT. **pro-digality,** n. *effusio* (as act), *sumptus effusi* or *profusi* (as luxury), *profusa luxuria* (= great luxury); see EXTRAVAGANCE.

prodigious, adj. *ingens;* see ENORMOUS. **prodigy,** n. *res mira* or *mirabilis, miraculum.*

produce, I. v.tr. 1, = to bring forward, *pro-ferre, exhibere; edere* (= to publish); 2, = to bring into existence, *(pro)creare* (of living beings and of the earth ; then = to cause, e.g. danger), *gignere, parere, generare* (= to bring forth, of living beings), *(ef)ferre, (ef)fundere* (of nature, also of the earth, of a field, etc. ; *fundere, effun-dere,* always with the idea of abundance), *facere, efficere* (with the hand, by art and skill). **II.** n. of the earth, *quae terra gignit* or *parit, ea quae gignuntur e terrâ* (in gen.), *fructus, -ûs, reditus, -ûs,* by circumloc. *id quod agri efferunt* (of the fields). **product,** n. in arithmetic, *summa quae ex multiplicatione effecta est;* see also PRODUCTION. **production,** n. *opus, -eris,* n. (= work); of art, *opera et artificia;* whether this is a — of nature or of art, *sive est naturae hoc sive artis.* **productive,** adj. 1, *fertilis;* see FRUITFUL; 2, — of, *alcjs rei effi-ciens.* **productiveness,** n. see FERTILITY.

proem, n. *procemium.*

profane, I. v.tr. † *profanare, profanum facere, violare, polluere.* **II.** adj. *profanus* (opp. *sacrum), impius* (= impious); — history, *his-toria rerum a populis gestarum.* Adv. *impie.* **profanation, profaneness, profanity,** n. *impietas.*

profess, v.tr. *profiteri;* to — the Christian religion, *Christum sequi, doctrinam Christianam sequi;* to — to belong to a certain school, *persequi* with accus. (e.g.*Academiam);* =to assert that one is something that one is not, *se alqd esse simu-lare.* **professed,** adj. by circumloc. (e.g. a — Christian, *qui se Christianum esse dicit),* or by *manifestus, apertus;* see MANIFEST. Adv. *per speciem, simulatione alcjs rei* (= by pretence). **profession,** n. 1, = declaration, *professio* or by *se alqd (esse) profiteri* (e.g. *Christianum (esse);* — in opp. to practice, *verbo* (opp. *re(verâ));* 2, = employment, *munus, -eris,* m. **professor,** n. *professor (eloquentiae,* etc., Plin., Suet.), better *qui alqd docet.* **professorship,** n. by PRO-FESSOR.

proffer, v.tr. *promittere ;* see OFFER.

proficiency, n. by *scientia* (= knowledge), *facilitas* (= readiness). **proficient,** adj. *eru-ditus, doctus* (= learned), *sciens alcjs rei* (= skil-ful); to be —, *multum, parum,* etc., *proficere;* see SKILFUL.

profile, n. *faciei latus alterum, imago obliqua* (= likeness in —, Plin.); in the pl. also by the **t.**t. *catagrapha, -orum,* n. (καтáγραφα (= — por-trait, Plin.).

profit, I. n. 1, = material (= *lucrum, quaest-us, fructus, reditus* (all *-ûs), emolumentum, com-pendium* (by saving); 2, fig. *compendium, fructus,*

quaestus (rare); to make much —, *multum profi-cere ;* see PROGRESS. **II.** v.intr. 1, = to be ser-viceable to, *ad alqd proficere, alci (rei) prodesse, conducere, adesse* (of men =to support, so *alqm ju-vare);* 2, = to make progress, *proficere ;* 3, = to make gain, *quaestuosum esse, fructum ferre;* see PROFITABLE. **profitable,** adj. 1, lit. *quaes-tuosus, fructuosus, lucrosus, frugifer* (of lands); see FRUITFUL; 2, fig. *fructuosus, frugifer, utilis.* Adv. *utiliter.* **profitless,** adj. = useless, *inu-tilis, vanus, futilis, irritus;* see USELESS. Adv. *frustra, incassum* (= in vain).

profligacy, I. n. *animus perditus, nequitia, flagitium;* see VICE. **II.** n. *homo flagitiosus,* etc. ; *homo scelestus, (con)sceleratus* (= one who has committed crime), *homo perditus* or *profli-gatus* (= incorrigible). **profligate,** adj. *flagiti-osus, vitiosus, malus, turpis, libidinosus, perditus, nequam, sceleratus, scelestus.* Adv. *flagitiose, male, libidinose, perdite, nequiter, turpiter, ne-farie, scelerate, sceleste.*

pro formâ, adv. *dicis caus(s)â.*

profound, adj. *altus, profundus* (lit. and fig.). Adv. *penitus, prorsus ;* see ALTOGETHER. **profundity,** n. *altitudo* (lit. and fig.).

profuse, adj. see EXTRAVAGANT, LAVISH.

progenitor, n. *parens.*

progeny, n. *progenies ;* see OFFSPRING.

prognostic, n. *signum ;* to be a — of, *alqd praenuntiare.* **prognosticate,** v.tr. see FORE-BODE.

programme, n. *libellus.*

progress, I. n. 1, = journey, *iter, itineris,* n. ; quite a royal —, *velut rex iter faciebat ;* 2, = advance, *progressus, -ûs, progressio, processus, -ûs ;* to make much or little —, *multum* or *parum proficere.* **II.** v.intr. 1, *progredi ;* see AD-VANCE ; 2, = to improve, *proficere.* **progres-sion,** n. *progressio, progressus, -ûs ;* see PRO-GRESS. **progressive,** adj. *qui, quae, quod progreditur.* Adv. *gradatim, pedetemtim (pede-tent-).*

prohibit, v.tr. *vetare ;* see FORBID. **pro-hibition,** n. *interdictum ;* to issue a —, *in-terdicere alci alqâ re* or *ne.* **prohibitive, prohibitory,** adj. *qui, quae, quod vetat.*

project, I. n. *consilium* (= plan), *inceptum, propositum* (= proposal), *institutum.* **II.** v.intr. *prominere, eminere, exstare, pro(j)ici, projectum esse.* **projectile,** n. *(telum) missile.* **projec-tion,** n. by verb. **projector,** n. *auctor.*

proletariat, n. *proletarii.*

prolific, adj. see FRUITFUL.

prolix, adj. *longus* (= long, opp. *brevis,* of persons and things), *copiosus* (= full), *verbosus* (= making too many words), *multus* (only of per-sons) ; see LONG. **prolixity,** n. by adj. PROLIX.

prologue, n. *prologus.*

prolong, v.tr. *prorogare, propagare* (= to — the time of, e.g. *imperium in annum), producere* (= to draw out), *extendere* (= to extend, e.g. *alqd ad noctem), continuare* (= to continue, e.g. *mili-tiam, alci consulatum magistratum), trahere* (= to — more than we should, e.g. *bellum), proferre* (= to put off, e.g. *diem), prolatare* (= to protract, e.g *comitia).* **prolongation,** n. *productio* (in gen.), *prorogatio, propagatio* (e.g. *vitae), pro-latio* (e.g. *diei).* **prolonged,** adj. *longus, diuturnus.*

promenade, n. *ambulatio* (both of act and place).

prominence, n. 1, *prominentia, eminentia* (= a standing out); 2, fig. of rank, etc. *fama, gloria* or by *alqm alqâ re praes'are ;* see SUB-

PASS. prominent, adj. and adv. by *promi-ěre, eminēre* (= to be raised above; also fig. = to distinguish oneself, e.g. *inter omnes*), *exstare* (= to stand out, lit. e.g. *capite solo ex aquâ*), *excellēre* [fig. = to excel in, *algâ re* or *in alqâ re*), *praestare* or *superare alqm alqâ re* (fig. = to be superior in).

promiscuous, adj. *promiscuus.* Adv. *promiscue.*

promise, I. v.tr. *alci alqd* or *de alqâ re pro-mittēre, polliceri, alqd (in se) recipēre;* = to take upon oneself, *pollicitari* (frequent.), *(de)spon-dēre* (formally, by being legally bound), *alci alqd;* also comb. *promittēre et spondēre, pro-ponēre* (as reward, e.g. *servis libertatem*), *pro-nuntiare* (publicly); "I — that," or "I — to," rendered in Latin by the accus. and infin. (gen. the fut. infin., seldom the pres. infin.), e.g. *pro-mitto* or *polliceor me hoc facturum esse.* **II.** v.intr. = to be likely (e.g. he —s to be a great speaker, *veri simile est eum futurum esse oratorem.* **III.** n. *promissio, pollicitatio* (the act), *fides* (=word), *pro-missum* (= the thing promised); to give anyone a — to, etc., *alci promittēre* or *polliceri,* with accus. and fut. infin.; to keep, redeem a —, *promissum* or *fidem fucēre* or *efficēre* or *praestare* or *servare* or *(ex)solvēre* or *persolvēre, promisso stare* or *satis-facēre, quod promisi* or *pollicitus sum* or *quod promissum est (ob)servare* or *efficēre, quod promis-sum est tenēre, promissi fidem praestare.* **prom-ising,** adj. by circumloc. (e.g. a — pupil, *puer industrius;* a — crop, *seges fertilis).* **promis-sory,** adj. — note, *chirographum.*

promontory, n. *promontorium,* a small —, *lingua, li(n)gula.*

promote, v.tr. *(ad)juvare alqm* or *alqd, adjumento esse alci rei, adjutorem* or (in the fem.) *adjutricem esse alcjs rei* or *in alqâ re* (in gen. = to give any assistance); *alcjs rei esse (ad)-ministrum* (in a bad sense = to be an abettor), *augēre alqm* or *alqd* (= to increase), *alci* or *alci rei favēre, fovēre alqd* (= to favour), *alci* or *alci rei consulēre, prospicēre* (= to take care of), *alci pro-desse* (= to be of use), *consilio, studio, operâ adesse alci* (= to assist anyone by advice and by acting); to — anyone's interest, *servire alcjs commodis, rebus* or *rationibus alcjs consulēre, prospicēre;* to — the common interest, *saluti reipublicae consulēre, rempublicam juvare, tueri, reipublicae salutem suscipēre* (= to try to —); = to — in office, anyone, *tollēre, augēre, attollēre* (anyone's reputation among his fellow-citizens), *fovēre* (by actually favouring him), *(ex)ornare* (= to dis-tinguish), *gratiâ et auctoritate suâ sustentare* (to raise through one's personal influence), *pro-ducēre ad dignitatem* (= to — to a higher rank), *promovēre ad* or *in munus* or *ad (superiorem) locum* (= to — to an office, Imperial Rome), *mu-neri praeficēre* (= to appoint to an office, to set over); *tra(ns)ducēre alqm in ampliorem ordinem* or *ex inferiore ordine in superiorem ordinem* (a military office). **promotor,** n. *auctor, adjutor, fautor.* **promotion,** n. — of our welfare, *amplificatio nostrarum rerum;* — to a higher office, *amplior honoris gradus, -ûs, dignitatis accessio, officium amplius.*

prompt, I. adj. *promptus.* Adv. *cito;* see QUICKLY. **II.** v.tr. *alqd alci sub(f)icēre.* **promp-ter,** n. *qui alqd alci sub(j)icit.* **promptitude, promptness,** n. *celeritas;* see QUICKNESS, READINESS.

promulgate, v.tr. *promulgare.* **promul-gation,** n. *promulgatio.*

prone, adj. 1, = flat, *pronus;* 2, = tending to, *pronus, proclivis, propensus ad alqd.* **prone-ness,** n. *proclivitas* (rare), or by adj.

prong, n. *dens, -tis,* m. (of a fork).

pronoun, n. *pronomen* (Gram.).

pronounce, v.tr. letters, etc., *enuntiare, ex-primēre, dicēre* (= to utter with the voice), *lit(t)era sonis enuntiare;* to — one word after the other, *verba continuare;* it is difficult to —, *haud facile dictu est;* = to utter formally, *efferre verbis; ex-plicare, explanare verbis* (= to explain in words); to — a sentence, an opinion, *sententiam dicēre, sen-tentiam pronuntiare* (= to announce the verdict of the judge). **pronunciation,** n. *appellatio* (= the — of a letter, etc.); *pronuntiatio* (Quint., always = *actio,* i.e. the whole recitation); *locutio* (= the act of speaking), *vox* (= the voice of the person that speaks), *vocis sonus,* in the context *sonus* (= the tone of the voice).

proof, n. *tentamen* (= trial); = the act of prov-ing, *probatio, demonstratio* (= a strict — of any-thing; also in mathematics), *argumentatio* (= by giving clear reasons); the — of it is difficult, *difficile est probatu;* = that by which anything is proved (sign in gen.), *signum, indicium, documen-tum, specimen* (the foregoing two = specimen, ex-ample, sample; but *specimen* never in the plur. in ancient writers); = reasons which serve as a —, *argumentum* (= reason founded upon facts); *ratio* (= reasonable grounds); to give —, *argumenta* or *rationes afferre;* to bring forward many —s for the existence of a Supreme Being, *multis argu-mentis Deum esse docēre;* very often *argumentum* is left out in Latin when an adj. is used in English (e.g. the strongest — is, *firmissimum hoc afferri videtur, quod,* etc.). **prove, I.** v.tr. = to show, *significare, ostendēre, declarare, (com)-probare, praestare* (= to perform what we are ex-pected to do); to — anything by one's actions, *alqd praestare re, alqd comprobare re;* to — one-self as, etc., *se praebēre alqm, exhibēre alqm* (e.g. as a friend of the people, *exhibēre virum civilem*), *se praestare alqm* (= to — oneself really to be, etc.); = to show by reasoning, *docēre, (argu-mendis) demonstrare* (= to show, demonstrate in every point, by logical reasons), *(con)firmare,* generally *firmare* (= to assert, affirm by reason), *probare alci alqd* (= to — to anyone the possi-bility of a thing), *efficēre* (= logically to — that anything can be done), *evincēre* (= to — beyond all doubt); this is —d by showing that, etc., *ejus rei testimonium est, quod,* etc.; this —s no-thing, *nullum verum id argumentum;* the result —d it, *exitus approbavit;* the mode of proving anything, *probationis genus, -ēris,* n., *argumen-tationis genus, via, ratio probandi* (= way in which anything can be —d), *argumentatio* (= argumentation), *ratio* (= manner in which we proceed in proving anything, Cic.). **II.** v.intr. = to turn out, *fieri, evadēre.* **proven,** p.part. e.g. not —, *non liquet.*

prop, I. n. 1, lit. *adminiculum* (in gen.), *pedamen(tum)* (for vines), *statumen* (for vines, etc.); 2, fig. *adminiculum, firmamentum, subsi-dium, praesidium;* see HELP. **II.** v.tr. 1, lit. *fulcire* (in gen.); 2, fig. *alci adesse,* to be —ped by, *alqâ (re) niti;* see SUPPORT.

propagate, v.tr. 1, applied to plants; to — by layers, *propagare;* to — by grafting, *in-serēre;* = to produce, *gignēre;* 2, fig. *gignēre (et propagare), serēre* (= to sow). **propagation,** n. 1, by layers, *propagatio;* 2, of a report, etc., *rumorem serēre.*

propel, v.tr. *propellēre.*

propensity, n. *proclivitas* or *animus pro-clivis ad alqd;* see INCLINATION.

proper, adj. 1, *proprius* (= peculiar, opp. *communis*), *verus* (= true, real, opp. *falsus*), *ger-manus* (= genuine); if we add — in order to lay a stress upon the noun, we use *ipse* (e.g. *ipsi Ar-gentini*); the — word, *verbum proprium* (opp.

verbum translatum); the — Metellus, *verus et germanus Metellus;* **2,** = becoming, *decōrus, honestus;* = suitable, *aptus, idoneus, accommodatus ad alqd.* Adv. *proprie, vere,* comb. *proprie vereque, germane.* **property,** n. 1, *dominium* (Jct., = the — or the legal title to anything, different from *possessio,* possession), *patrimonium* (= patrimony; also fig. with *tamquam* before it, of mental, etc., qualities), *peculium* (= the stock or money which a son with the consent of his father, or a slave with the consent of his master, had of his own; private—), *possessiones* (= landed —), *bona, -orum,* n., *fortunae* (= effects); *census, -ūs* (in gen.); by *res* (sing. or plur.) in a gen. sense (e.g. moveable —, *res moventes, res quae moveri possunt);* or by *proprius, -a, -um,* also comb. with poss. pron. *proprius meus* (*tuus,* etc.), and often by poss. pron. alone (e.g. that is my —, *hoc meum* or *hoc meum proprium est);* to consider anything as one's —, *suum alqd ducěre;* **2,** = peculiarity, *proprietas, quod alcjs (rei) proprium est.* **property-tax,** n. *tributum ex censu collatum.* **proprietary,** adj. by *proprius.* **proprietor,** n. *possessor, dominus.* **proprietorship,** n. *dominium, possessio.*

prophecy, n. **1,** as the act, *praedictio* (e.g. *rerum futurarum*), *vaticinatio;* **2,** that which is prophesied, *praedictum, vaticinium.* **prophesy, I.** v.tr. *praedicěre, praenuntiare* (in gen. = to foretell), *vaticinari, caněre, augurari* (= to augur). **II.** v.intr. *futura praedicěre* or *praenuntiare, vaticinari* (= to act the part of a *vates,* to — by divine inspiration). **prophet,** n. *vates, -is,* m. and f., † *vaticinator,* † *fatiloquus.* **prophetess,** n. *vates, -is.* **prophetic,** adj. *divinus, praesagiens, fatidicus, vaticinus* (= concerning prophecies, e.g. writings). Adv. *divinitus, caelesti quodam instinctu mentis, instinctu divino afflatuque* (all = inspired).

propinquity, n. *propinquitas* (= relationship), *affinitas* (= by marriage).

propitious, adj. *propitius, aequus,* † *secundus, faustus* (of things). Adv. by adj. **propitiousness,** n. by adj. **propitiate,** v.tr. see CONCILIATE. **propitiation,** n. *placatio* (e.g. *deorum*). **propitiatory,** adj. by verb.

proportion, I. n. *proportio, commensus, -ūs,* (= measure or size of a thing in — to another, Vitr.), *symmetria* (Vitr.); in a general sense it is best rendered by *ratio* (= the relation of one thing to another), or by *comparatio* (when two or more things are in a certain relation to each other); an arithmetical, geometrical —, *ratio arithmetica, geometrica;* in — to, *pro portione alcjs rei, pro ratâ parte, pro* with abl. (e.g. *pro viribus,* in — to one's power); see PROPORTIONATE. **II.** v.tr. *alqd dirigěre ad alqum rem.* **proportional, proportionate,** adj. *pro portione, pro, prae* with abl., or by *ad* with acc., or by *ut est* with the object compared in the nomin. (e.g. *pro viribus, prae aliis, pro numero, ad cetera, ut tum erant tempora);* see PROPORTION.

proposal, n. = what anyone proposes, *condicio;* — of a law, *legis latio* (in the forum), *rogatio* (in the comitia to be accepted by the assembly of the people); to vote for a — in the senate, *pedibus ire in alcjs sententiam;* = suggestion, plan, *consilium, ratio, propositum;* to make a —, *condicionem ferre* or *proponěre;* to make the — of anything, *alqd proponěre* (= to move), *alqd suaděre* (= to try to recommend, to advise), *alqd commendare* (= to recommend). **propose,** v.tr. 1, *proponěre;* to — a law, *legem ferre* or *rogare, rogationem* or *legem ferre;* 2, in marriage, perhaps *alqam in matrimonium petěre;*

3, see PURPOSE, INTEND. **proposer,** n. of a law, *(legis)lator,* in gen. *auctor alcjs rei.* **proposition,** n. 1, see PROPOSAL; 2, in logic, *thesis* (Quint.); in a wider sense *propositum.*

propriety, n. *convenientia, decōrum, honestas.*

prorogue, v.tr. *prorogare.* **prorogation,** n. *prorogatio.*

proscribe, v.tr. *proscriběre.* **proscription,** n. *proscriptio.*

prose, n. *prosa (oratio)* (Quint.), *oratio soluta* (in opp. to *oratio astricta, devincta*), or merely *oratio* (in opp. to *poëmata*). **prosaic,** adj. *jejunus, frigidus.*

prosecute, v.tr. 1, = to carry out, *gerěre, facěre, exsequi, perficěre;* see Do; 2, = to bring an action against, *alqm accusare, reum facěre de alqâ re, alqm postulare.* **prosecution,** n. 1, use verb PROSECUTE, 1; 2, *accusatio.* **prosecutor,** n. *accusator.*

proselyte, n. *discipulus.* **proselytism,** n., **proselytize,** v.tr. *alqm discipulum facěre.*

prosody, n. *versuum lex et modificatio* (Sen.).

prospect, n. 1, = view, *prospectus, -ūs, conspectus, -ūs;* to have a —, *spectare ad* or *in alqm locum;* 2, = hope, *spes* (e.g. *mercedis*); some —, *specula.* **prospective,** adj. *futurus;* see FUTURE. Adv. *in futurum.*

prospectus, n. *libellus.*

prosper, v.intr. *crescěre* (lit. and fig. = to grow), *provenire* (lit. and fig.), *bonâ fortunâ uti.* **prosperity,** n. *res secundae* or *prosperae* or *florentes, copiae (rei familiaris)* (= good circumstances); general —, *salus, -utis, communis, omnium felicitas.* **prosperous,** adj. *secundus, prosper(us), fortunatus.* Adv. *secunde, prospere, fortunate.*

prostitute, I. n. *mulier impudica* (= any unchaste woman), *amica, meretrix, prostibulum.* **II.** v.tr. 1, *publicare;* 2, fig. *alqâ re abuti.* **prostitution,** n. 1, *vita meretricia;* 2, use PROSTITUTE, II. 2.

prostrate, I. v.tr. 1, = to throw down, *(pro)sternere;* 2, to — oneself before anyone, *ad pedes alcjs procumběre* or *se ab(j)icěre* or *se submittěre* or *prosterněre, ad genua alcjs procumběre, supplicem se ab(j)icěre alci* (as a suppliant); 3, fig. *alqm* or *animum affligěre, percellěre, frangěre.* **II.** adj. by part. of verb, to lie —, *(humi) jacěre.* **prostration,** n. by the verb.

protect, v.tr. *tuěri, tutari, defenděre* (= to ward off, *ab alqâ re, contra alqd);* *(pro)tegěre* (= to cover, *ab alqâ re, contra alqd), munire* (= to fortify), *custodire* (= to guard), *praesidēre alci rei, praesidem esse alcjs rei, alci praesidio esse, prohibēre alqd* (= to keep off) or *prohibēre alqd ab algo* or *alqm ab alqâ re.* **protection,** n. *tutela, praesidium, defensio, patrocinium, clientēla* (= relation of patron and client), *fides, arx, portus, -ūs, perfugium;* to take under your —, *alqm in fidem recipěre* (as a lord or sovereign), *alcjs patrocinium suscipěre* (as a defender at law). **protective,** adj. use verb. **protector,** n. *defensor, tutor* (rare), *propugnator* (e.g. *quasi propugnator patrimonii sui,* Cic.), or by verb.

protest, I. v.intr. *asseverare* (= to affirm with assurance), *affirmare* (= to assure), *adjurare* (upon oath); by the gods, *(ab)testari deos;* to — against, *interceděre, intercessionem facěre* (esp. of a magistrate), against anything, *alci rei interceděre* (= to interfere in a thing by virtue of one's office, officially), *interpellare* (= to interrupt a speaker). **II.** n. *interpellatio* (= interruption of a speaker), *intercessio* (by the authorities, etc.)

Protestant, adj. and n. *a lege pontificis Romani abhorrens.* **Protestantism,** n. *Protestantismus.*

protocol, n. *tabulae, commentarii* (in gen.).

prototype, n. *exemplum.*

protract, v.tr. *producĕre;* see DELAY, PROLONG.

protrude, I. v.tr. *protrudĕre.* **II.** v.intr. *protrudi, prominĕre;* see PROJECT.

protuberance, n. *tuber, gibber* (Plin.). **protuberant,** adj. *eminens, prominens* (= projecting).

proud, adj. *superbus, arrogans, fastidiosus* (= disdainful), *contumax* (= stubborn); to be —, *alqd re inflatum* or *elatum esse* or *tumēre;* — flesh, (med. t.t.) *caro fungosa* *(Plin.). Adv. *superbe, arroganter, contumaciter, fastidiose.*

prove, v.tr. see PROOF.

provender, n. *pabulum;* FORAGE, FOOD.

proverb, n. *proverbium, verbum* (= word); to become a —, *in proverbii consuetudinem venire, in proverbium venire, cedĕre;* according to the —, *ut aiunt.* **proverbial,** adj. *proverbii loco celebratus* (= well known, e.g. *versus*), *quod proverbii locum obtinet, quod in proverbium* or *in proverbii consuetudinem venit* (= what has become —); see PROVERB. Adv. *proverbii loco* (= as a proverb), *ut est in proverbio, ut proverbii loco dici solet;* see PROVERB.

provide, I. v.tr. *instruĕre* or *ornare alqm alqā re* (= to — with), *alci rei providĕre, alqd* (com)*parare, praeparare, alqd alci praebēre* (= to give). **II.** v.intr. **1,** = to order, *jubēre, edicĕre* (of an edict); **2,** = to — for anyone, *alci consulĕre, providēre* (= to consult the interests of); = to make adequate provision for, *alqm re familiari* or *copiis* or *pecuniā instruĕre;* he is —d for, *habet unde vivat;* to — against, (pro)*vidēre, praecavēre ne quid fiat.* **provided, I.** adj. — with, *alqā re instructus, ornatus, praeditus.* **II.** conj. — that, (dum)*modo* with subj., *eā lege* or *condicione ut* or *ne.* **providence,** n. = forethought, *providentia;* = divine —, *deorum providentia* (*providentia* alone in Quint., Sen.), or use *deus* or *dei* (di(i)). **provident,** adj. *providus, diligens* (= careful); see CAREFUL. Adv. *diligenter,* or by adj.; see PROVIDENT. **providentially,** adv. *dis faventibus, divinitus.* **providing that,** conj. see PROVIDED, II. **provision, I.** v.tr. to — a town, *oppidum cibo* or *rebus necessariis instruĕre.* **II.** n. **1,** to make — for; see PROVIDE, II. 2; **2,** = stipulation, *condicio;* see STIPULATION. **provisional,** adj. by adv. use *ad* or *in tempus.* **provisions,** n. *cibus, cibaria, -orum, alimentum, victus, -ūs, commeatus, -ūs, frumentum, res frumentaria* (the last three esp. of — for an army).

province, n. **1,** = duty, *provincia, officium;* **2,** = district, *regio* (in gen.), *provincia.* **provincial,** adj. *provincialis* (= belonging to a province); — (manners), etc., *rusticus, agrestis, inurbanus.*

proviso, n. see PROVISION, II. 2.

provocation, n. **provocative,** adj. by PROVOKE.

provoke, v.tr. **1,** = to call forth, (com)*movēre* (e.g. *iram*), *ciēre, concitare;* **2,** = to make angry, *alci stomachum movēre* or *facĕre;* see VEX, IRRITATE; **3,** to — to anything, *alqm ad alqd incitare, concitare, impellĕre, irritare;* see URGE. **provoking,** adj. *molestus.* Adv. *moleste.*

provost, n. *praeses, -idis,* m., or *alci rei praepositus.*

prow, n. *prora, pars prior navis.*

prowess, n. *virtus, -ūtis,* f.; see VALOUR.

prowl, v.intr. *vagari, peragrare;* to — for plunder, *praedari.*

proximate, adj. by *proximus;* see NEAR, NEXT. **proximity,** n. see NEARNESS.

proxy, n. = agent, *procurator, vicarius;* by —, *per procuratorem;* to vote by —, perhaps *per alium suffragium ferre.*

prude, n. *mulier putida* (= affected).

prudence, n. *providentia* (= foresight), *cautio, circumspectio, prudentia, diligentia, gravitas* (as moral characteristic). **prudent,** adj. *providus, cautus, circumspectus, consideratus, prudens, diligens.* Adv. *provide, caute, circumspecte, considerate, diligenter;* see WISDOM.

prune, v.tr. **1,** to — trees, *arbores* (am)*putare* (= to lop off), *tondēre* (e.g. hedges), *purgare, intervellēre* (Col., = to tear off branches here and there), *pampinare* (of vines); **2,** fig. *amputare, resecare.* **pruner,** n. of trees, *putator, frondator.* **pruning-hook,** n. *falx.*

prurience, n. see LUST.

pry, v.tr. and intr. to — into, *alqd rimari, investigare, scrutari.*

psalm, n. *psalmus* (Eccl.). **psalmist,** n. *psalmista,* m. (Eccl.). **psalter,** n. *psalterium* (Eccl.). **psaltery,** n. *psalterium.*

pshaw! interj. *phui!*

psychical, adj. *de animā* (e.g. — research, *investigatio quae de animā fit*).

psychology, n. *psychologia* (as t.t.), or *investigatio quae de animo* or *mente fit.* **psychological,** adj. *psychologicus;* see above. **psychologist,** n. *humani animi investigator.*

puberty, n. *aetas puber.*

public, I. adj. **1,** before everyone's eyes, *quod in aperto ac propatulo loco est* or *fit* (= in an open place), *quod palam* or *coram omnibus fit* (= before everybody's eyes), *publicus;* not to appear in —, *publico carēre* or *se abstinēre;* a — house, *caupona* (cop-), *deversorium;* **2,** concerning the State, etc., *publicus* (in gen.), opp. *privatus, forensis* (referring to — life, opp. *domesticus*); at the — expense, *sumptu publico, de publico, publice, impendio publico;* by — measures, *publico consilio, publice;* the — credit, *fides publica;* the — opinion, *vulgi opinio.* Adv. *aperte, palam, coram omnibus, in propatulo, in publico, foris.* **II.** n. the —, *homines* (= the people in gen.), *populus* (= all the people), *vulgus, -i,* n. (= the great mass), *spectatores* (= spectators), *auditores* (= the audience), *lectores* (= the readers). **publican,** n. **1,** *publicanus* (= farmer of the public taxes); **2,** = inn-keeper, *caupo* (who keeps a public-house). **publication,** n. *editio libri* (Plin.); = the book itself, *liber.* **publicity,** n. e.g. of proceedings, *consilia palam* or *coram omnibus inita;* to shun —, *celebritatem odisse* or *fugĕre homines* (= not to like to go out), *lucem fugĕre* (in gen. = to shun the light of day, fig. not to like to appear before the public). **publish,** v.tr. a work, etc., (*in lucem*) *edĕre, emittĕre, foras dare.* **publisher,** n. of a book, *qui librum edendum curat.*

pudding, n. *placenta* (= cake).

puddle, n. see POOL.

puerile, adj. *puerilis* (= both childlike and foolish).

puff, I. v.tr. *inflare* (lit. and fig.); to — up with pride, *alqm* to —ed up, *superbire, tumescĕre.* **II.** v.intr. **1,** = to blow, *flare, spirare;* see BLOW; **2,** to pant, *anhelare.* **puffy,** adj. *inflatus.*

pugilism, n. *pugilatus, -ūs, pugilatio.* **pugilist,** n. *pugil.*

pug-nosed, adj. *simus*.

pull, I. v.tr. 1, = to tweak, *vellĕre* (e.g. *aurem*, to — the ear), *vellicare* (Plaut., Quint.); 2, = to drag, *trahĕre, ducĕre, vehĕre;* to — down, *demoliri, dis(j)icĕre, diruĕre;* to — out, *(e)vellĕre, eripĕre.* **II.** n. *tractus, -ūs* (mostly poet.), *nisus, -ūs, vis, impetus, -ūs,* or by verb.

pullet, n. *pullus gallinaceus*.

pulley, n. *trochlea, machina tractatoria* (Vitr.).

pulmonary, adj. *quod ad pulmones pertinet*.

pulp, n. *caro* (Plin., of fruits).

pulpit, n. in the context merely *suggestus, -ūs*.

pulsate, v.intr. *palpitare, agitari, moveri*. **pulsation**, n. *palpitatio, motus, -ūs;* see MOVEMENT. **pulse**, n. *arteriarum* or *venarum pulsus, -ūs* (Plin., = the beating of the —), *venae* (the — itself); the — does not beat equally, *venae non aequis intervallis moventur*.

pulse, n. as a vegetable, *legumen* (or in pl.).

pulverize, v.tr. 1, *in pulverem redigĕre;* 2, fig. *percellĕre*.

pumice, n. *pumex*.

pump, I. n. *antlia, tympanum.* **II.** v.intr. *antliā exhaurire;* to — a ship, *sentinam exhaurire*.

pumpkin, n. *pepo* (Plin.).

pun, n. *logi* (λόγοι, Cic. in Non.), *facetiae*.

punch, n. = a drink, *cal(i)dum* (= hot water and wine).

Punch, n. see PUPPET.

punch, I. n. 1, = drill, *terebra;* 2, see BLOW. **II.** v.tr. 1, *terebrare;* 2, *tundĕre, fodĕre*.

punctilio, n. perhaps *dīligentia* (= carefulness), *dubitatio* (= doubt, where — keeps from action), *fastidium* (= pride), *sol(l)icitudo* (= anxiety). **punctilious**, adj. *sol(l)icitus* (= anxious), *dīligens* (= careful), *accuratus* (= exact). Adv. *dīligenter, accurate*. **punctiliousness**, n. *sol(l)icitudo, dīligentia, religio* (in religious matters).

punctual, adj. *dīligens* (= exact, careful); to be — to an appointment, *ad* or *in tempus advenire.* Adv. *dīligenter, ad tempus* (= at the appointed time), *ad diem* (= on the day appointed). **punctuality**, n. *dīligentia* (care).

punctuate, v.tr. *notis distinguĕre, interpungĕre* (Sen.). **punctuation**, n. *interpunctio;* — mark, *interpunctum*.

puncture, I. n. *punctum* (Plin.). **II.** v.tr. *pungĕre, compungĕre*.

pungent, adj. *acer, acutus, acerbus, mordax*, all lit. and fig. Adv. *acriter, acute, acerbe*.

punish, v.tr. *punire, poenā afficĕre* (= to inflict punishment), *in alqm animadvertĕre, multare, castigare* (= to correct, chastise, *verbis, verberibus*); to — anything, *alqd vindicare* (= to avenge), *alqd ulcisci, persequi,* or comb. *ulcisci et persequi;* to — anyone very severely, *gravissimum supplicium de alqo sumĕre;* to — anyone with exile, fine, or imprisonment, *exilio, pecuniā,* or *vinculis multare;* to — any infringement of the law, any violation of one's rights, *delicta, violata jura exsequi;* to be —ed, *puniri,* also *poenas dare, solvĕre, pendĕre, expendĕre,* by anyone, *alci,* for anything, *alcjs rei* (= to pay). **punishable**, adj. *poenā dignus.* **punisher**, n. *castigator, vindex* (= avenger), *ultor* (= revenger). **punishment**,

n. 1, the act, *castigatio, multatio, animadversio* (e.g. *vitii*); 2, the — itself, *poena* (as **an** atonement), *noxa* (as loss or injury) *multa* (more particularly = fine: the latter the act), *damnum* (= penalty), *supplicium* (= cruel —, torture, violent death), *animadversio* (= reproof, in order to correct anyone), also comb. *animadversio et castigatio;* — by confiscation of property, *multatio bonorum;* capital —, *poena vitae* or *capitis, supplicium capitis, ultimum supplicium, extremum supplicium;* fear of —, *metus, -ūs, poenae* or *animadversionis;* to inflict — on anyone, see PUNISH; to suffer —, *poenam* or *supplicium (de)pendĕre, expendĕre, solvĕre, persolvĕre, dare, subire, perferre, luĕre* or *ferre*.

puny, adj. *pusillus* (e.g. *animus*); a man of — stature, *homo brevi staturā;* a — fellow, *homuncio*.

pupil, n. 1, *pupula, pupilla, acies* (= **a** sharp eye); 2, at a school, etc., *alumnus* (m.), *alumna* (f.), *discipulus, discipula*. **pupilage**, n. *status, -ūs,* or *condicio pupilli*.

puppet, n. *neurospaston* (Aul. Gell.) (better written as Greek νευρόσπαστον); see DOLL.

puppy, n. 1, *catulus, catellus;* 2, fig. *adulescentulus ineptus*.

purchase, I. v.tr. 1, lit. *(co)emĕre, mercari;* 2, fig. *emĕre, redimĕre, mercari.* **II.** n. 1, act of —, *emptio;* 2, thing bought, *merx* (= merchandise), *quod emptum est* (in gen.). **purchasable**, adj. *venalis.* **purchaser**, n. *emptor*.

pure, adj. see CLEAR; 1, = free from moral guilt, *purus, integer,* comb. *purus et integer* (= without a stain in his moral character, etc.), *castus* (= chaste), comb. *purus et castus, castus purusque* (e.g. body, mind), *integer castusque, sanctus* (= pleasing to God, holy), *insons* (= free from guilt, whose conscience does not accuse him of any crime, etc.), innocent, opp. *sons*), comb. *purus et insons, emendatus* (= spotless, perfect, e.g. morals, a man), *incorruptus;* — virgin, *virgo casta;* 2, = not mixed with anything, lit., *purus* (in gen.), *'merus* (= mere, not mixed with, opp. *mixtus*); — water, *aqua pura;* — wine (*vinum*) *merum;* — gold, *aurum purum* (*putum*); 3, fig. *purus, sincerus;* — language, *sermo purus* or *rectus* or *bonus* or *emendatus;* — joy, *sincerum gaudium;* — clean, *mundus, purus.* Adv. *pure, integre, caste;* = entirely, etc., *prorsus, plane;* — spiritual, *ab omni concretione mortali segregatus* (e.g. a being, *mens,* Cic.); the — spiritual state of the soul, is *animi status in quo sevocatus est a societate et contagione corporis* (Cic.). **purity**, n. fig. *castitas;* — of a language, *sermo purus* or *emendatus* or *purus et emendatus;* —of expression, *incorrupta integritas, quasi sanitas* (i.e. healthy vigour), *sanitas* (Quint.); *munditia verborum, mundities orationis* (= free from foul language, Aul. Gell.); moral —, *castitas* (as quality), *castimonia* (= abstinence from that which is bad, (chiefly in a religious sense), *sanctitas* (= holiness, as virtue), *sanctimonia* (= innocence of character), *integritas* (= integrity), *innocentia* (= disinterestedness, opp. *avaritia*), *gravitas* (= dignity).

purify, v.tr. *(re)purgare, expurgare, purum facĕre* (in gen.); *purificare* (Plin.); *lustrare* (=to — by offering an expiatory sacrifice), *emendare* (= to — from faults); to — the language (from bad words, etc.), *expurgare sermonem, emendare, consuetudinem vitiosam et corruptam purā et incorruptā consuetudine emendare.* **purification**, n. *purgatio* (in gen.), *lustratio* (= — by an expiatory sacrifice); festival of —, *Februa, -orum* (on 15th Feb.). **Purism**, n. *in scribendo* (or *dicendo*) *elegantia.* **Purist**, n. *in* *scribendo* or *dicendo dīligens.* **Puritan,** n., **Puritanism,** n. *qui de sacris dīligentior or religiosior est.* **Puritanically,** adv. *severius;* see STRICTLY.

purgatory, n. *purgatorium* (Eccl.). **purgation,** n. *purgatio, lustratio.* **purgative,** adj. and n. *medicina alvum purgans, inaniens, bonam faciens, movens.* **purge,** v.tr. and intr. 1, of the medical man, *alvum purgare, bonam facĕre, movēre, de(j)icĕre;* 2, see PURIFY.

purl, v.intr. *murmurare, sonare, susurrare.*

purloin, v.tr. *avertĕre;* see EMBEZZLE, STEAL.

purple, I. n. 1, = purple colour, *purpura, ostrum* (= the liquor of the shell-fish used for dyeing purple), *conchylium* (= purple proper), *color purpureus;* 2, *purpura, vestis purpurea* (= garments, covering, etc.). **II.** v.intr. to grow —, † *purpurare.*

purport, I. n. see MEANING, OBJECT. **II.** v.tr. see MEAN.

purpose, I. n. *propositum, consilium, institutum, sententia, animus, mens* (our "mind"), *voluntas* (= wish), or by *velle* (e.g. my — was to go, *ire volui*), with this —, *eo consilio, ut,* or by *ad* with gerund or gerundive (e.g. I was sent for the — of seeking him, *ad eum petendum missus sum*); on —, *consulto, de industria, dedita opera;* to what —, *quo consilio;* see WHY; to no —, *without* —, *nullo* or *sine consilio, temere;* to the —, *ad rem, apposite.* Adv. *consulto;* see ON PURPOSE, PURPOSE, I. **II.** v.tr. *statuĕre;* see INTEND. **purposeless,** adj. *vanus, inanis, irritus, cassus, inutilis.*

purr, v.intr. perhaps *sonitum edĕre,* or *gaudium sonitu exhibēre.*

purse, n. *marsupium, zona, crumena, sacculus.* **purse-proud,** adj. *pecuniā superbus.*

pursuant, prep. — to, in pursuance of, *secundum alqd* (e.g. of a law, *ex lege, ex decreto*).

pursue, v.tr. *alqm persequi, prosequi, consectari, insequi, insectari, alci insistĕre, instare,* all lit. and fig. **pursuit,** n. *studium, cupiditas* (= desire for anything), *ars, quaestus, -ūs;* to make a — of anything, *alqd factitare* or *exercēre.*

purveyor, n. *obsonator,* or by *providēre.*

pus, n. *pus* (Cels.). **pustule,** n. *pustula* (Cels.).

push, I. v.tr. *pellĕre, trudĕre, offendĕre, pulsare, alqm,* with, *alqā re* (e.g. *capite, cubito, pede aut genu*), *fodĕre alqm* or *alqd,* with, *alqā re;* to — forward, *propellĕre, impellĕre;* to — back, *repellĕre;* to — down, *depellĕre.* **II.** v.intr. to — on, *contendĕre, instare;* see HASTEN. **III.** n. *(im)pulsus, -ūs, impetus, -ūs;* to make a —, *instare.* **pushing,** adj. *acer;* see EAGER.

pusillanimous, adj. *timidus, abjectus, humilis, demissus, fractus.* Adv. *timide, abjecte, humiliter, demisse, animo abjecto,* etc. **pusillanimity,** n. *timiditas, formīdo* (= fear), *animus timidus,* etc. (see above), *animi demissio, infractio,* or *imbecillitas.*

put, v.tr. in gen., *ponĕre* (e.g. *calculum*), to — to or near, *apponĕre alqd alci rei* or *ad alqd, proponĕre alqd alci rei, admovēre alqd alci rei, inferre alqd ad alqd;* to — a thing in its proper place, *alqd suo loco ponĕre;* to — away, *abdĕre, ponĕre* (the latter fig. = to lay aside); to — upon, *alqm* or *alqd imponĕre* or *inferre in alqd* (e.g. *puerum in equum*), *collocare alqd in alqā re,* seldom *in alqd* or merely *alqā re, alqd accommodare alci rei* or *ad alqd;* to — before anything, *proponĕre alqd alci rei;* to — anything anywhere, *ponĕre* (in gen.), *(col)locare* (at a certain place);

to — on one side, to — by, *seponĕre, reponĕre,* to — down, *deponĕre, demittĕre* (= to let down); fig. *de(j)icĕre, ex(s)tinguĕre;* see DESTROY; to — forward, *producĕre* (e.g. a candidate), *afferre* (a proof); to — off, *differre;* see DELAY; to — off a dress, *ponĕre, eruĕre;* to — on, *induĕre;* to — out, *e(j)icĕre, extrudĕre, expellĕre* (= to expel), *ex(s)tinguĕre* (= to quench); to — over, *imponĕre, superponĕre* (lit.), *praeficĕre* (fig. of office); to — under, *alqd alci rei supponĕre* or *sub-(j)icere;* to — the horses to, etc., *equos currui jungĕre, carpento subjungĕre;* to — to flight, *fugare;* to be — to flight, *fugĕre, se in fugam dare;* to — to death, *interficĕre;* see KILL; to — up at, *devertĕre,* or *deverti,* at anyone's house, *ad alqm,* at a place, *ad* or *in* with accus. of the place (e.g. *ad hospitem,* and *ad alqm in Albanum,* and *ad* or *in villam suam*); to — up with, see BEAR, TOLERATE; to — in, *appellĕre, portum petĕre;* see ENTER; to — out to sea, *navem* or *classem solvĕre;* see LEAVE.

putative, adj. *falsus* or *qui dicitur esse.*

putrefaction, n. by verb PUTREFY, I. **putrefy, I.** v.tr. *putrefacĕre.* **II.** v.intr. *putrefieri, putrescĕre.* **putrid,** adj. *putridus, puter* (*putris*). **putridness,** n. *putor* (ante and post class.).

putty, n. *gluten* (*vitreariorum*).

puzzle, I. n. 1, a game, *nodus quidam in lusum oblatus, quaestio lusoria* (Plin.), *aenigma, -ātis,* n.; 2, a difficulty, *nodus.* **II.** v.tr. *animum distrahĕre, impedire.* **III.** v.intr. *in alqā re haerēre, in angustiis esse.* **puzzling,** adj. *difficilis, ambiguus.*

Pygmy, n. *pygmaeus* (= one of the Pygmies, Plin, etc.); = dwarf, *nanus* (Juv.).

pyramid, n. *pyramis, -idis,* f. **pyramidal,** adj. *in pyramidis formam factus.*

pyre, n. † *pyra, rogus.* **pyrites,** n. *pyrites, -ae* (Plin.).

pyrotechnics, pyrotechny, n. as t.t. *ars pyrotechnica.*

pyrrhic, adj. 1, *in metre pes pyrrhichius* (Quint.); 2, — victory, perhaps *victoria, ut aiunt, Pyrrhi regis modo incassum relata.*

pyx, n. *pyxis* (Eccl.).

Q.

quack, I. n. 1, of a duck, by verb QUACK, II.; 2, an itinerant seller of medicine, *pharmacopola circumforaneus;* 3, see IMPOSTOR. **II.** v.intr. *tetrinnire.* **III.** adj. *falsus.* **quackery,** n. *ars pharmacopolarum.*

quadrangle, n. 1, a figure, * *quadrangulum;* 2, a courtyard, *area* (Plin. Min.). **quadrangular,** adj. *quadrangulus* (Plin.).

quadrennial, adj. *quat(t)uor annorum.*

quadrille, n. *saltatio.*

quadripartite, adj. *quadripartitus.*

quadruped, n. *quadrupes.*

quadruple, adj. *quadruplex.*

quaff, v.tr. see DRINK.

quag(mire), n. *palus, -udis,* f.; see BOG. **quaggy,** adj. *paluster;* see BOGGY.

quail, n. (a bird), *coturnix.*

quail, v.intr. *animo deficĕre;* see TREMBLE.

quaint, adj. *lepidus* (= pretty) ; see CURIOUS, AFFECTED ; *insolitus*, *novus*, *mirus* (= new, strange), *facetus*, *argutus* (= witty) ; see STRANGE, HUMOROUS. Adv. *novo* or *insolito* or *miro quodam modo*, *mire*, *facete*, *argute*. **quaintness,** n. use adj.

quake, v.intr. *tremĕre* ; see TREMBLE. **quaker,** n. *unus ex iis qui se amicos appellant.*

qualify, v.tr. 1, *instituĕre*, *instruĕre*, *fingĕre* (of men) ; to — oneself, *se praeparare* ; 2, = to modify a remark, etc., *extenuare*, *attenuare*, *deminuĕre* ; see LESSEN. **qualification,** n. *jus, juris*, n. (= right), *potestas* (= power), comb. *jus potestasque* (e.g. *provinciae administrandae*, for administering a province) ; in gen. sense = fit, by adj. QUALIFIED. **qualified,** adj. *idoneus*, *accommodatus*, *aptus*, *utilis*, *opportunus ad alqm rem*, *dignus alqâ re* (e.g. *honore*).

quality, n 1, *proprietas*, *proprium* (= peculiarity), *natura* (= natural condition), *genus*, *-ĕris* (= kind), *ratio*, *vis* (= state, condition), *qualitas* (ποιότης = particular condition, coined by Cic. as a metaphysical t.t.), *res quae est alcjs rei propria* (= what is the peculiar nature of anything, Cic.) ; often by *esse* with the genit. of the noun which possesses the — we mention (but *proprium* must be added when we speak more emphatically) ; it is one — of a good orator, etc., *est boni oratoris*, etc. ; one — of a wise man is to do nothing he may repent, *sapientis est proprium, nihil quod paenitĕre possit, facĕre* ; or by the neut. gen. of an adj. instead of the genit. (e.g. one — of a human being is, *humanum est*) ; of what —, *qualis* ; of such a — or kind, *talis* ; a good, noble —, *virtus*, *-ŭtis* ; a bad —, *malum*, *vitium* ; 2, = kind, sort, *nota* (e.g. wine of good —, of the best —, *vinum bonae, optimae notae* ; of the second —, *secundae notae* ; of different —, *diversae notae*).

qualm, n. 1, lit. *defectio* (*virium*, Plin., = faintness), *fastidium* (= loathing) ; 2, fig., use *circuml.* (e.g. I have a — of conscience, *mens mihi angitur*).

quantity, n. 1, *numerus* (= number), *copia* (= plenty), *aliquot* (= a few, several, a considerable number) ; a great —, *multitudo*, *magnus numerus*, *acervus* (= a heap, mass), *turba* (= a confused mass of things or people), *nubes, -is* (= a cloud of things, e.g. *pulveris*), *silva* or *quasi silva* (= an abundance, esp. with regard to literary objects, e.g. *silva rerum et sententiarum*), *vis* (= a large —, of persons and things, in an emphatic sense), *pondus, -ĕris*, n. (= —, according to weight, e.g. *pondus auri*) ; a very large indefinite — is expressed by *sescenti* (e.g. I received a great — of letters all at one time, *sescentas literas uno tempore accepi*) ; 2, time of syllables in prosody, *mensura*, *quantitas* (Gram.).

quantum, n. *portio* ; see PORTION, SHARE.

quarantine, n. *tempus valetudini spectandae praestitum.*

quarrel, I. n. *jurgium, rixa, altercatio.* **II.** v.intr. *jurgare* (with one, *cum algo*), *rixari, altercari* ; see DISPUTE. **quarrelsome,** adj. *rixis deditus.*

quarry, I. n. = a stone —, *lapicidĭnae, lautumia* or *lautomia* (Plaut.). **II.** v.tr. *caedĕre, excidĕre.*

quarry, n. = game, *praeda.*

quart, n. (as a measure) *duo sextarii.*

quartan, n. *febris quartana.* ●

quarter, I. n. 1, = fourth part, *quarta pars* (post Aug., also *quarta* alone ; every — of a year, *tertio quoque mense* ; 2, = part, district, *vicus* ; 3, = mercy, e.g. to grant a person —. *alcjs*

vitae parcĕre, alci (*victo*) *vitam dare.* **II.** v.tr. **1,** *quadrifariam dividĕre* or *dispertire* (in gen., = to divide into four parts) ; to — a man (as a punishment), in *quat(t)uor partes distrahĕre* (Sen.) ; 2, *collocare* in *algo loco* or *apud alqm* ; to — the troops, *milites per hospitia disponĕre* or in *hospitia dividĕre* or in *hospitia deducĕre* (upon the ratepayers) ; *milites per oppida dispertire, militibus hospitia* in *oppidis praestare* (upon the towns). **quarter-day,** n. perhaps *dies constitutus, dictus* or *certus*, or by exact date. **quarter-deck,** n. *puppis.* **quartering,** n. *milites per hospitia dispositi* or in *hospitia divisi* (as to the troops), *milites tecto* (*tectis*) or *ad se recepti* (as to the person upon whom the troops are quartered). **quarterly,** adj. and adv. *trimestris* ; money to be paid —, *pecunia tertio quoque mense solvenda.* **quarters,** n.pl. *habitatio* (in gen.), *tectum* (= roof, shelter), *deversorium* (= a lodging-place for travellers, an inn), *hospitium* (= place where strangers were entertained, guest-chambers), *mansio* (Plin., place to stop at for the night) ; my — are at Mr So-and-so's, *habitare apud alqm* ; of troops, *castra, -orum* ; to place the troops in the winter —, *copias* in *hibernis collocare* ; to be in winter —, in *hibernis esse* ; —, in the usual military sense, *stativa, -orum* ; to take up —, *stativa ponĕre* ; to be in —, in *stativis esse* ; close —, *cominus* ; to come to —, *manum conserĕre.*

quash, v.tr. 1, see SQUEEZE, CRUSH ; 2, in law, to — an indictment, etc., *rescindĕre.*

quaver, I. v.intr. 1, in gen., see TREMBLE, VIBRATE ; 2, in music, *vibrassare.* **II.** n. *octava* (with or without *pars*) ; a semi-—, *pars sextadecima.*

quay, n. *margo, -ĭnis*, m., *crepido.*

queen, n. *regina* (also fig.) ; — bee, *rex apium.* **queenly,** adj. *reginae similis*, † *regius.*

queer, adj. *novus*, *insolitus* ; see STRANGE, HUMOROUS.

quell, v.tr. *opprimĕre* (e.g. *tumultum*), *comprimĕre* (e.g. *tumultum, seditionem*) ; see CONQUER.

quench, v.tr. *sedare* (e.g. *sitim, iram*), *restinguĕre*, *ex*(*s*)*tinguĕre*, *explēre*, *reprimĕre*, *depellere.*

querimonious, querulous, adj. *queribundus, querulus*, or by the verb (*con*)*queri* (*alqd* or *alqâ re*).

query, v.intr., **querist,** n. see QUESTION.

quest, n. to go in — of, see SEEK, SEARCH.

question, I. n. 1, *interrogatio* (= the act of asking a —, and the — itself) ; (*inter*)*rogatum* (= the — asked) ; *quaestio* (= strict inquiry, and esp. a search, in literature, or a judicial inquiry or trial) ; *controversia* (esp. = legal controversy) ; *lis* (= lawsuit), *res, caus*(*s*)*a* (= the matter in dispute), *percontatio* (= inquiry), *disceptatio* (= a debate on a disputable point, in order to arrive at the exact truth) ; to ask anyone a —, *interrogare alqm de alqâ re* (see INTERROGATE) ; a short —, *interrogatiuncula, rogatiuncula, quaestiuncula* ; a — about morals, etc., *de moribus*, etc. ; a captious —, *captio, interrogatio captiosa* ; to bother, confuse anyone with —s, *rogitando alqm obtundĕre* ; to answer a —, *ad rogatum respondēre* ; there is no — about, *non est dubium quin* or *accus.* and infin. ; without —, *sine dubio, procul dubio, certe, certo* ; the — arises, *quaeritur, oritur disputatio, existit quaestio* ; now the — is, *nunc id agitur* ; it is a very important —, *magna quaestio* (i.e., which it will take a long time to settle, Cic.) ; 2, = torture, *quaestio* ; to put to the —, *de algo* in *alqm quaerĕre* (e.g. *de servo* in *dominum*, to torture the slave respecting his

master) ; *quaestionem de alqo habēre* (the object of the inquiry in the genitive case). **II.** v.tr. (*inter*)*rogare, exquīrĕre, quaerĕre, percontari* ; to — anything, *ad incertum revocare* ; to — anyone, *alqm interrogando urgēre, alqm rogitando obtundĕre* (in a troublesome manner) ; see ASK, EXAMINE. **questionable**, adj. *is* or *id de quo* or *ea de quā quaeritur* or *quaestio est, incertus, anceps, dubius.* **questioning**, n. (*inter*)*rogatio, percontatio, quaestio.*

quibble, I. n. *captio, cavillatio* (esp. in Quint.), *ambāges, -is, calumnia.* **II.** v.intr. *cavillari.* **quibbler**, n. *cavillator.* **quibbling**, adj. *captiosus.*

quick, I. adj. 1, see LIVE, ALIVE ; 2, see FAST, SPEEDY ; 3, *acer, alacer, alacer et promptus* (= active and ready) ; 4, = sharp, *subtilis* ; see SHARP, ACUTE ; 5, — with child ; see PREGNANT. Adv. 1, *cito, celeriter* ; see FAST ; 2, *mox, mature* ; see SOON. **II.** n. to cut to the —, *ad vivum resecare* (lit.), *mordēre* (fig.). **quicken**, v.tr. 1, *animare* (poet., also fig.) ; 2, see ACCELERATE ; 3, = to stimulate, *accendĕre, incendĕre, inflammare alqm.* **quicklime**, n. *calx viva.* **quickness**, n. 1, *velocitas, pernicitas* ; see SPEED ; 2, of intellect, *perspicacitas, sol(l)ertia, ulliditas, ingenii alacritas, celeritas.* **quicksand**, n. *syrtis* (lit. and fig.). **quick-scented**, adj. *sagax.* **quick-sighted**, adj. *perspicax* (lit. and fig.). **quick-sightedness**, n. *perspicacitas, ingenii acies* or *acumen.* **quicksilver**, n. *argentum vivum.* **quick-tempered**, adj. *iracundus* ; see IRRITABLE. **quick-witted**, adj. *acer, acutus, argutus, perspicax.*

quiescent, adj. by *quiescĕre.* **quiescence**, n. see QUIETNESS.

quiet, I. adj. *quiētus* (= abstaining from exertion), *tranquillus* (= with little motion, esp. of the sea), comb. *tranquillus et quietus, pacatus* (= reduced to peace and obedience, esp. of countries), *sedatus* (= not excited, calm, e.g. *gradus, tempus*), *placidus* (= placid, undisturbed), *otiosus* (= free from business) ; a — life, *vita quieta* or *tranquilla* or *tranquilla et quieta, vita placida, vita otiosa* ; to lead a — life, *vitam tranquillam* or *placidam* or *otiosam degĕre, quiete vivĕre, otiose vivĕre, vitam umbratilem colĕre* ; a — province, *provincia quieta* (in gen.), *provincia pacata* (= reduced to a peaceful state). Adv. 1, *tacite, silentio* (= in silence) ; 2, *quieto animo, tranquille, quiete, placide, sedate, otiose.* **II.** n. 1, (*re*)*quies, -ētis, f., tranquillitas, remissio* (the two latter after exertion), *otium* (= freedom from business), *silentium* (= silence) ; 2, fig. *quies, -ētis, otium, tranquillitas* (of mind), *pax* (= peace, only polit.). **III.** v.tr. *quietum reddĕre, tranquillare* or *sedare* or *placare* (= to calm), *pacare* (= to pacify). **quietness**, n. see TRANQUILLITY, QUIET, II.

quill, n. 1, = pen, *penna* ; 2, of a porcupine, etc., *spina* ; 3, of a musical instrument, *plectrum.*

quilt, n. *stragulum.*

quinquennial, adj. *quinquennis, quinque annorum* (in gen. = lasting five years), *quinquennalis* (= done every five years, also = lasting five years).

quinsy, n. *cynanche* (Cels.), in pure Latin *angina.*

quintessence, n. *flos, floris,* m. (the proper term) ; *medulla* (= marrow).

quintette, n. *cantus* (*-ūs*) *e quinque symphoniacis editus.*

quip, n. *facetiae.*

quire, n. *scapus* (Plin., with the ancients *=* 20 sheets).

quirk, n. see QUIBBLE, I.

quit, v.tr. see LEAVE, DESERT.

quite, adv. *prorsus, plane, omnino* (= altogether, perfectly), *plane, in* or *per omnes partes, per omnia* (= in every respect), *penitus, funditus* (= entirely, completely) ; *satis* (= enough, e. g. *satis scio,* = I am — certain), *valde* (= very), *magnopēre* (= greatly) ; that is — wrong, *falsum est id totum* ; I am — in love, *totus in amore sum* ; to be of — a different opinion, *longe aliter sentire* ; — right ! *ita est !* (as answer) ; — certain, *haud dubie* (= no doubt) ; not —, *minus* (e.g. not — so many) ; *parum* (= too little).

quits, adv. render by *fidem suam solvisse* ; we are —, *nihil rel(l)iqui est.*

quiver, I. n. *pharĕtrae* ; wearing a —, † *pharetratus.* **II.** v.intr. † *trepidare, tremĕre.*

qui-vive, n. on the —, by *alacer* ; see ALERT.

quoit, n. *discus.*

quota, n. (*rata*) *pars* (usu. *pro ratā parte*).

quote, v.tr. *afferre, proferre* (= to bring forward), *referre* (= to report), *laudare* (with praise), (*pro*)*ponĕre* (as an example), *notare* (with censure), (*com*)*memorare* (= to mention), *transcribĕre* (= to copy off) ; to — an instance, *exemplum afferre* ; *commemorare* ; from which letters I have —d a few passages as an example, *ex quibus lit(t)eris pauca in exemplum subjeci.* **quotation**, n. 1, = act of quoting, *prolatio, commemoratio* ; 2, = passage quoted, *locus allatus,* etc. ; see QUOTE.

quoth, v.intr. *inquit, ait.*

quotidian, adj. *cot(t)idianus.*

R.

rabbi, n. **rabbi.*

rabbit, n. *cuniculus.*

rabble, n. *sentīna reipublicae* or *urbis* (= the lowest of the people), *faex populi* (= the dregs), *colluvio, quisquiliae* (= refuse), *turba* (= crowd) ; see MOB.

rabid, adj. *rabidus* ; see MAD. Adv. *rabide.*

race, n. *genus, -ĕris,* n. (also = *gens,* more particularly when we speak of the — to which a certain tribe belongs) ; *gens* (in a more gen. sense = all who belong to a certain tribe ; in a more narrow sense, all who bear the same generic name [*nomina*] in opp. to *familia,* i.e. the subdivisions of a *gens*) ; *stirps* (= the lineage of a family descended from a *gens*) ; *progenies* (lit. = descent ; then also = posterity) ; *prosapia* (= stock), *semen* (lit. = seed, meton. for *genus*), *proles, -is,* f. (= progeny), *nomen* (= name), † *propago,* † *sanguis* ; see BREED, KIND. **raciness**, n. *sucus,* comb. *sucus et sanguis, sapor vernaculus* (= idiomatic —). **racy**, adj. *habens quemdam sucum suum* ; *habens nescio quem saporem vernaculum* ; *salsus* (= pungent).

race, I. n. = contest, *cursus, -ūs, certamen, curriculum* ; to hold —s, *cursu certare* ; horse —, *cursus, -ūs, equorum* or *equester.* **II.** v.intr. (*cursu*) *certare* or *contendĕre, pedibus contendĕre* (on foot). **race - course**, n. *curriculum* (in gen.), *stadium* (the ancient στάδιον), *circus* (= circus), *hippodromos.* **race-horse**, n. *equus, celes, -ētis,* m. **racer**, n. on foot, *cursor* ; = a horse, *equus.*

rack, I. n. 1, = manger, *faliscae* ; 2, an instrument of torture, *equuleus, tormentum,*

quaestio (= examination by torture); **to put to**
the —, *in equuleum alqm imponĕre, equuleo*
torquĕre, dare alqm in quaestionem. **II.** v.tr.
1, lit., see above; 2, fig. *torquĕre, vexare;* see
TORMENT, VEX.

racket, n. 1, = a bat, *reticulum* (not class.);
2, = noise, *strepitus, -ūs;* see NOISE.

racquets, n. by *pilâ ludĕre;* see BALL.

radiance, n. *fulgor* (= brightness), *claritas,*
candor, splendor, nitor. **radiant,** adj. 1, =
bright, *clarus, candidus, splendidus, nitens, niti-*
dus, fulgens; 2, of expression of face, *felix,*
laetus; see HAPPY, GLAD. Adv. *clare, splen-*
dide, nitide, feliciter, laete. **radiate,** v.tr.
and v.intr. *radiare.* **radiation,** n. *radiatio*
(Plin.).

radical, adj. and n. 1, = innate, *insitus;*
it is a — fault, *culpa hominibus naturâ est insita,*
or by *praecipuus* (= chief), *maximus* (= very
great); see THOROUGH; 2, Gram. — word,
verbum nativum, primigenium, primitivum; 3,
in politics, *novarum rerum cupidus* or *studio-*
sus; a red —, *novarum rerum avidus.* Adv.
radicitus, funditus, penitus, prorsus, omnino;
see ALTOGETHER.

radish, n. *raphanus* (Plin.).

radius, n. *radius.*

raffle, I. v.intr. *aleâ ludĕre;* **to — for,** *de*
lqâ re aleae jactu contendĕre. **II.** n. *alea.*

raft, n. *ratis.*

rafter, n. *canterius, tignum transversarium,*
transtrum, dim. *transtillum.*

rag, n. *pannus.* **ragamuffin,** n. *homo*
pannosus or *nequam.* **ragged,** adj. (of men)
pannosus (Cic.), *pannis obsitus* (Ter.).

rage, I. n. *rabies, furor, saevitia, ira, ira-*
cundia (see under MADNESS); *alcjs rei cupiditas,*
cupido, studium, aviditas (= violent desire for,
e.g. *gloriae*). **II.** v.intr. *furĕre* (of men, in poets
also of personified objects), *saevire* (= to be cruel,
also fig. of things, e.g. of the wind); against
anyone or anything, *in alqm* or *in alqd.* **rag-**
ing, adj. see VIOLENT.

rail, I. n. = bar, *tignum transversum;* on a
railway, *ferrum;* see BAR. **II.** v.tr. **to — off,**
saeptis claudĕre, (con)saepire. **railing,** n.
palus (= stake, fence), *clathri* (= trellis-work);
see FENCE. **railway,** n. *via ferro strata;* **to**
construct a —, *viam ferro sternĕre.*

rail, v.intr. *conviciis* or *contumeliis uti;* **to —**
at, *alqm conviciis consectari, alci maledicĕre,*
maledicta in alqm dicĕre or *conferre.* **raillery,**
n. *jocus, cavillatio.*

raiment, n. *vestis, vestītus, -ūs, vestimentum,*
cultus, -ūs, ornatus, -ūs, habitus, -ūs (esp. in
Suet.).

rain, I. n. *pluvia, imber, nimbus* (with storm);
-- bow, *arcus pluvius* (Hor.); in prose, gen.
xelestis arcus, -ūs, and in the context simply *ar-*
cus. **II.** v.impers. it —s, *pluit;* it —s fast,
magnus effunditur imber, magna vis imbrium
effunditur. **rainy,** adj. *pluvius,* † *aquosus,*
† *imbrifer.*

raise, v.tr. 1, *(at)tollĕre;* 2, *erigĕre* (e.g.
malum); 3, see ERECT, BUILD; 4, to — the
price, etc., by *efferre* (e.g. *pretium alcjs rei),*
carius vendĕre alqd; to — the salary, *stipendium*
augēre; see INCREASE; 5, = to cause to grow,
educĕre (e.g. *flores semine sparso);* 6, = to elevate anyone in condition, *augēre, ornare, pro-*
ducĕre ad dignitatem or *ad honores;* to a high
condition, *amplis honoribus ornare* or *decorare;*
7, = to stir up, *excitare* (e.g. *animos), erigĕre,*
recreare; 8, = to bring together, *colligĕre, (com)-*

parare, (con)scribĕre; see COLLECT; **9,** = **to**
— the voice, by *tollĕre* (e.g. *clamorem*); **10,** =
to — a siege, *oppugnatione desistĕre, oppugna-*
tionem relinquĕre.

raisin, n. *acinus passus,* † *racēmus passus,* in
pl. *uvae passae* (Col.).

rake, I. n. 1, *pecten, rastrum, rastellum,*
irpex (to break clods or to pull up weeds); 2,
= good-for-nothing fellow, *ganeo, nepos, -ōtis,* m.
(= prodigal), *homo dissolutus* or *perditus.* **II.**
v.tr. *pectine verrĕre* (hay, etc.), *radĕre* (= to — the
ground). **rakish,** adj. *perditus, profligatus,*
dissolutus.

rally, I. v.tr. 1, to — troops, *aciem* or *ordines*
restituĕre, milites in ordinem revocare; 2, = to
banter, *alqm ludĕre, irridĕre.* **II.** v.intr. 1, of
troops, *se colligĕre;* 2, in gen. *se reficĕre, colli-*
gĕre, convalescĕre (from illness); see RECOVER.
III. n. use verb.

ram, I. n. *aries, -ĕtis,* m. (both of sheep and
battering —). **II.** v.tr. *alqd fistucâ adigĕre,*
fistucare. **rammer,** n. *fistuca, pavicula.*

ramble, I. v.intr. *errare* (lit. and fig.),
about, *circum alqd* (having lost the right road),
vagari, palari, a proposito aberrare (fig.). **II.**
n. *ambulatio;* to go for a —, *ire ambulatum.*
rambler, n. *homo vagus, erro* (= vagrant).
rambling, adj. *vagus* (lit. and fig.).

ramification, n. 1, lit. by *ramis diffundi;*
2, fig. *pars.* **ramify,** v.intr. *dividi;* see also
EXTEND.

rampant, adj. in gen. *ferox, superbus*
(= proud); to be —, *superbire;* in heraldry,
erectus or *arrectus.*

rampart, n. 1, *vallum* (properly speaking),
agger, -ĕris, m. (= a mound, mole); 2, fig. *val-*
lum, propugnaculum, praesidium.

rancid, adj. *rancidus.*

rancour, n. *odium* (*occultum*); see HATRED.
rancorous, adj. *iratus, iracundus* (= angry),
malevolus, malignus (= spiteful), *invidus* (= envious), *infestus, inimicus* (= hostile). Adv. *irate,*
iracunde, maligne, infeste, inimice.

random, adj. *in casu positus, fortuitus,* **or**
by adv.; at —, *temere,* or comb. *temere ac for-*
tuito (e.g. *agĕre* or *facĕre alqd*).

range, I. v.tr. 1, see RANK, II. 2; 2, **see**
ROAM. **II.** n. 1, *ordo, series* (in gen.), *montes*
continui (= — of mountains), *teli jactus, -ūs,* or *con-*
jectus, -ūs (— of missiles); 2, — of thought, etc., by
circumloc. (e.g. *sententiarum varietate abun-*
dantissimum esse); — of subjects, *rerum fre-*
quentia.

rank, I. n. 1, of troops, *ordo, -inis,* m.; **the**
—s, *ordines militum;* to break through the **—s,**
ordines perrumpĕre; to throw the —s into confusion, *ordines (con)turbare;* in their —, *ordi-*
nati (of troops), *ordinatim;* 2, degree in
military affairs, *ordo (militandi),* or by *gradus*
honoris or *dignitatis* (e.g. *gradu honoris* or *dig-*
nitatis, and merely *honore superiorem esse algo);*
to reduce to the —, *in ordinem cogĕre;* **3,** in
civil life = degree, *locus* (*honoris* or *dignitatis*),
dignitas (= position in society); a Spaniard of—,
Hispanus nobilis. **II.** v.tr. 1, to — the soldiers,
ordines or *aciem instruĕre;* 2, = to place in a
particular class, *ordinare, disponĕre* (= to arrange), (*in numero*) *habēre* (= to consider, e.g.
alqm in amicorum numero); see CONSIDER. **III.**
v.intr. by *in ordinem redigi;* to — with, *eodem*
loco esse cum algo (in gen.), *pares ordines ducĕre*
(of two military officers).

rank, adj. of plants, *luxuriosus;* of smell,
† *graveolens, foetidus;* = very great, *magnus,*
maximus.

rankle, v.intr. perhaps *mordēre* (= to bite), or *pungēre* (= to prick).

ransack, v.tr. 1, a house, *exhaurire, exinanire, nudum atque inane reddēre;* a temple, *fanum everrēre et extergēre, spoliare expilareque, nudare ac spoliare;* 2, = to search thoroughly, *rimari, scrutari.*

ransom, I. n. 1, = the money paid as —, *pecuniae quibus alqs redimitur,* or by *pretium, pecunia* (e.g. *alqm sine pretio dimittēre, reddēre);* 2, = release from captivity, *redemptio.* **II.** v.tr. *redimēre (pecuniā).*

rant, I. n. *sermo tumidus, turgidus, inflatus.* **II.** v.tr. perhaps *sermone tumido uti,* or simply *declamare.* **ranter,** n. *orator tumidus, turgidus, inflatus.*

rap, I. v.intr. at the door, *pulsare (fores).* **II.** n. *pulsatio.*

rapacious, adj. *rapax, furax* (= thievish).

rapacity, n. *cupiditas rapinarum* or *praedae* or *praedae rapinarum, spoliandi cupido, rapacitas* (the latter as inherent quality).

rape, n. *stuprum mulieri oblatum.*

rapid, I. adj. *rapidus* (of wind), † *rapax;* see SWIFT, QUICK. Adv. *rapide.* **II.** n. *vertex, gurges, -itis,* m. **rapidity,** n. *rapiditas;* see SPEED, QUICKNESS.

rapier, n. *gladius* (= sword).

rapture, n. *summa voluptas.* **rapturous,** adj. *beatus* (= blessed), *felicissimus* (= very happy); see HAPPY.

rare, adj. *rarus* (= not often met with), *inusitatus* (= unusual), *infrequens* (= that is not often met); = thin, *rarus, tenuis, singularis, eximius* (= exceedingly fine, etc.). Adv. *raro;* I am — at Rome, *Romae sum infrequens.* **rarefaction,** n. use adj. (e.g. the — of the atmosphere, *aer extenuatus).* **rarefy,** v.tr. *extenuare.* **rarity,** n. *raritas, res rara, res rara visu* or *inventu.*

rascal, n. *homo scelestus, sceleratus.* **rascality,** n. *scelus, -ēris,* n. **rascally,** adj. *scelestus, turpis, sceleratus;* see BASE.

rase, v.tr. = to level with the ground, *solo aequare* or *adaequare.*

rash, adj. *praeceps, praecipitatus* (= headlong, etc.), *inconsultus* (= inconsiderate, e.g. *certamen), temerarius* (= thoughtless). Adv. *inconsulte (inconsulto), inconsiderate, temere, nimis festinanter, praepropere;* to act —, *festinantius agere.* **rashness,** n. *temeritas.*

rash, n. *eruptio(nes)* (Plin.), *scabies* (= itch).

rasher, n. of bacon, *lardi offula.*

rasp, I. v.tr. *scobinā radēre.* **II.** n. *scobina.*

raspberry, n. *morum Idaeum.*

rat, n. *mus.* **rat-trap,** n. *muscipula* (Phaed.).

rate, I. n. 1, at the —, *pro modo, pro ratione,* but generally *pro;* to buy at a high or low —, *magno* or *parvo emēre;* — of interest, *usura, fenus, -ōris,* n. ; 2, = tax, *vectīgal, tributum;* to lay a —, *vectīgal, tributum imponēre alci* (= to — anyone) and *alci rei, tribuum indicēre alci;* 3, = manner, *modus;* at this —, *in hunc modum;* at any —, *certe, utique;* — of going (of a watch), *motus, -ūs.* **II.** v.tr. 1, *aestimare alqd, aestimationem alcjs rei facēre;* see ESTIMATE; 2, *alci imponēre tributum;* see TAX; 3, = to scold, *increpare;* see SCOLD. **rateable,** adj. *cui vectīgal imponi potest.*

rather, adv. 1, *potius* (if we select), *prius* (= before), *multo magis* (= so much the more, in a higher degree), *quin etiam, quin potius, quin immo* (when we substitute something still

stronger, etc.), *immo* (= nay even; also comb. *immo potius, immo vero, immo enimvero, immo etiam);* and not —, *ac non potius,* also *ac non;* I did not . . . , — . . . (or in similar phrases), *tantum abest, ut . . . ut;* I would —, by *malo,* with infin. ; 2, = somewhat, *aliquantum, aliquanto.*

ratification, n. *sanctio,* or by **ratify,** v.tr. a treaty, *sancire pactum, fidem foederis firmare, foedus ratum facēre.*

ratio, n. *pro ratā portione;* see PROPORTION.

ratiocination, n. see REASONING.

ration, n. *demensum, cibus* or *victus, -ūs, diuturnus* (= daily allowance of food).

rational, adj. 1, = having reason, *rationis praeditus* or *utens, rationis particeps;* 2, = agreeable to reason, *(rationi) consentaneus.* Adv. *ratione;* to act —, *ratione uti, prudenter* or *considerate agēre.* **rationalism,** n. *opinio eorum qui in investigatione veri ratione suā (neque divinā quiddam lege) utendum esse putent.* **rationalist,** n. *qui,* etc., *putet;* see above. **rationality,** n. *ratio.*

rattle, I. v.intr. 1, *crepare, crepitum dare* (= to make a crackling, clattering noise), *strepēre, strepitum dare* (= to make a loud noise), *sonare* (= to sound) ; 2, *blaterare* (= to talk idly). **II.** v.tr. to — the chains, *vincula movēre;* see before. **III.** n. 1, *crepitus, -ūs, strepitus, -ūs, sonitus, -ūs, fragor* (of thunder); 2, a child's plaything, † *crepitaculum.* **rattlesnake,** n. *serpens.*

ravage, I. v.tr. *vastare, populari.* **II.** n. *vastatio, populatio.*

rave, v.intr. *furēre, insanire, bacchari, delirare,* comb. *delirare et mente captum esse;* = to talk irrationally, † *ineptire* (= to do and say things which are irreconcileable with commonsense), *(h)ariolari* (lit., = to prophesy, then = to talk nonsense; ante class.); *nugari* (= to talk and do silly things), *(h)al(l)ucinari* (= to blunder, to talk as if one were dreaming).

raven, n. *corvus.*

ravening, adj. *rapax, vorax, edax.* **ravenous,** adj. 1, see RAVENING ; 2, = very hungry, *cibi avidus.* Adv. *summā cibi aviditate, voraciter.* **ravenousness,** n. *cibi aviditas, voracitas, edacitas.*

ravine, n. *angustiae viarum* (in gen. = narrow passage, path), *fauces, -ium* (= defile), *saltus, -ūs* (= mountain pass).

raving, adj. see RAVE, MAD.

ravish, v.tr. 1, *algam (per vim) stuprare;* 2, = to charm, *oblectare;* see DELIGHT. **ravisher,** n. *raptor,* or by verb. **ravishing,** adj. *dulcis, suavis;* see DELIGHTFUL.

raw, adj. *crudus* (opp. *coctus,* also of wounds), *incoctus* (= not yet boiled, opp. *coctus* ante Aug.); half —, *subcrudus, rudis* (of anything in its natural state), *impolitus* (= unpolished, e.g. stone), *incultus* (= not manufactured, worked up, cultivated, e.g. field, vine); — gold, silver, *aurum, argentum infectum* (opp. *argentum factum);* — hands, troops, *rudis;* of weather, *frigidus* (= cold), *humidus* (= damp). **raw-boned,** adj. see THIN.

ray, n. *radius;* a — of hope, *spes, specula,* or by *lux* (e.g. *lux quaedam civitati affulsisse visa est).*

ray, n. a fish, *raia* (Plin.).

razor, n. *culter tonsorius, novacula.*

reach, I. v.tr. and intr. 1, see EXTEND, STRETCH ; 2, = to touch by extending, *contingēre, attingēre;* 3, = to deliver with the hand, *porrigēre, praebēre;* 4, = to arrive at, *pervenire ad* or *in* with accus. (in gen.), *attingēre locum,* *capĕre alqm locum* (esp. by sea) ; **to** — the harbour, *portum capĕre, in portum pervenire, pervehi ;* **5,** = to arrive at by effort, *assequi ;* **6,** of reports, *pervenire, accedĕre, deferri ad alqm.* **II. 1.** within —, *quod manu prehendi, quod conlingi potest ;* out of — of gunshot, *extra teli jactum* or *conjectum.*

reach, retch, v.intr. *nauseare.* **reaching,** n. *nausea.*

react, v.tr. **1,** tc — a play, *fabulam iterum or denuo dare* (of the author), or *edĕre* (of the manager of a theatre), or *agĕre* (of the actors) ; **2,** to — upon, *alqm afficĕre* (with adv. of the manner in which the affection takes place). **reaction,** n. *commutatio* (= change).

read, v.tr. and intr. *legĕre* (in gen. ; lit. = to pick up, gather, e.g. *spicas*), *recitare* (= to — aloud, recite), *praeire* or *praeire voce* (= to — to anyone in order that he may repeat it after him) ; to — anything often, *lectitare ;* to — anything in a cursory manner, to glance at, *pervolvĕre, pervolutare ;* fig. to — in the future, *praesagire futura ;* to — the future in the stars, *e siderum positu et spatiis conjecturam facĕre de rebus futuris ;* to — it in anyone's looks, by *alqd in alcjs vultu* or *ex toto ore eminet* (e.g. *pigritia et desperatio in omnium vultu eminet, toto ex ore crudelitas eminet*) ; a person that is well —, *homo satis lit(t)eratus, eruditus, disertus ;* fairly well —, *tinctus lit(t)eris ;* to be much —, in *manibus esse.* **readable,** adj. *jucundus ;* see DELIGHTFUL. **reader,** n. *lector, recitator* (= one who reads aloud), *anagnostes* (= a slave who reads aloud). **reading,** n. *lectio, pellectio, recitatio* (aloud to anyone = recital) ; want of —, *inscitia lit(t)erarum ;* worth —, *dignus qui legatur, legendus ;* a true or false — in an author, *vera* or *falsa lectio.* **reading-desk,** n. perhaps *pulpitum.*

ready, adj. **1,** *instructus, paratus* (ad *alqd* or with infin.), *promptus* (= quick, ad *alqd* or *in alqd* or *in alqâ re*), comb. *promptus et paratus, expedītus* (= always prepared, in readiness) ; — to do a thing, *paratus facĕre alqd* or *ad alqd faciendum ;* simply with the part. fut. act. (e.g. *moriturus, periturus*) ; to be —, ad *manum esse, praesto adesse,* for, *ad alqd ;* at anybody's command, *ad nutum alcjs expeditum esse ;* to get or make —, *parare, instruĕre alqd ;* to get oneself — for, *se parare ad alqd, se expedire ad alqd,* (com)*parare, instruĕre alqd ;* = finished, *perfectus, absolutus ;* — money, *pecunia praesens* or *numerata ;* to pay — money, *pecuniam repraesentare ;* **2,** = obliging, *officiosus, facilis.* Adv. *prompte, prompto* or *parato animo, libenter, libentissimo animo* or (of several) *libentissimis animis ;* = easily, *facile.* **readiness,** n. **1,** to be in —, *paratum, promptum, promptum paratumque, expeditum esse* (of persons), *sub manibus esse* (of servants, etc., at hand, etc.), *ad manum esse* (of persons and things), *in promptu esse, paratum* or *provisum esse, suppetĕre* (= to be in sufficient quantity, of corn, etc.) ; to hold in —, *habĕre paratum, in expedito ;* **2,** *animus promptus* or *paratus, facilitas, officium, studium.*

real, adj. **1,** = not fictitious, *verus* (= true, e.g. *gloria, laus*), *certus* (= certain, *sinc̄rus* (= unalloyed), *germanus* (= true, e.g. brother ; hence = genuine, e.g. *Stoicus, patria*) ; a — scholar, *vere doctus,* sometimes by *ipse* (e.g. the — man, *homo ipse*) ; **2,** in law, *quod ad rem* or *res spectat, ad res pertinens ;* a — estate, *solum, fundus.* Adv. = truly, *vere, re, revera* (or as two words, *re vera*), *profecto,* (enim)*vero ;* ironically *scilicet,* in question, *itane vero?* **reality,** n. *quod est seu quod esse potest* (Vitr.), *res, res verae, verum realities,* facts, what really exists, opp. *res*

fictae), *veritas, natura* (both these words **in an** abstract sense) ; in —, *re, re verâ, reapse ;* to become a —, *fieri, effici, ad effectum adduci.* **realize,** v.tr. **1,** = to carry into effect, *facĕre, efficĕre, perficĕre, ad effectum adducĕre* or *perducĕre, ad verum perducĕre ;* **2,** = to grasp mentally, *intellegĕre* (animo), *repraesentare, ante oculos* or *sibi proponĕre ;* **3,** of money, *pecuniam redigĕre* or *alqd alqo pretio vendĕre.* **realization,** n. *effectus, -ûs, inventio et excogitatio* (= discovery), or by *mente concipĕre.*

realm, n. *civitas, respublica* (= state), *regnum* (= kingdom).

ream, n. of paper, *viginti scapi* (*scapus* = a cylinder on which twenty sheets were rolled).

reanimate, v.tr. **1,** lit. perhaps *alqm a* † *morte revocare* or *mortuo vitam reddĕre* or *restituĕre ;* **2,** fig. to — anyone's hope, and *novam spem alqm excitare* or *erigĕre, novam spem alci ostendĕre.*

reap, v.tr. **1,** (*de*)*metĕre ;* **2,** prov., as you sow, so you will —, *ut sementem feceris, ita metes ;* to — where we have not sown, *alienos agros demetĕre, sub arbore quam alius consevit legĕre fructum* (Liv.) ; fig. = to gain, *fructum capĕre, percipĕre,* the fruit of, *ex alqâ re, fructum alcjs rei ferre.* **reaper,** n. *messor.* **reaping-hook,** n. *falx.*

reappear, v.intr. *redire* (= to return).

rear, n. *agmen extremum* or *novissimum, acies novissima* or *extrema ;* the — of the enemy, *hostes novissimi, postremi ;* to form the —, *agmen claudĕre, cogĕre.*

rear. I. v.tr. **1,** see RAISE, LIFT ; **2,** to — up, plants, etc., *alĕre* (in gen.) ; children, *educare, educĕre ;* see EDUCATE ; **3,** fig., see EXALT, ELEVATE. **II.** v.intr. of horses, *ex(s)ultare, tollĕre* or *arrectum.*

reason, I. n. **1,** = cause, *principium, initium, fons, -ntis,* m. (= source, origin), *causa* (= cause), comb. *causa et semen* (e.g. *belli*), *ratio ;* to state a —, (*causam* or *rationem*) *afferre* (e.g. *cur credam, afferre possum, firmissimum argumentum afferri videatur*) ; not without a —, *non sine causâ,* (cum causâ) for this —, that, etc., *propterea* (*quod*), *quod, quoniam, quamobrem, quapropter, quare, idcirco, itaque ;* by — of, *ex alqâ re ;* there is no —, I have no — to, etc., or why, etc., *non est, nihil est, quod* or *cur ; non habeo, nihil habeo, quod* or *cur,* with subj. (e.g. you have no — to make yourself uneasy, *nihil est quod te moveat*) ; I have — to feel ashamed, *est quod me pudeat ;* what — has he (to say, etc.) ? *quid est quod,* etc. ? I have more — to congratulate you than to request you, *magis est quod tibi gratuler, quam quod te rogem ;* = fact, proof, *argumentum, res* (generally in the pl., opp. *verba*) ; **2,** *ratio* (as that which calculates), *mens* (= understanding), *prudentia, consilium* (= prudence) ; void of —, *ratione carens, rationis expers ;* **3,** see RIGHT, JUSTICE ; **4,** = moderation, *aequitas* (also = feeling of justice), *justitia, fas* (of what is right according to the voice of anyone's conscience), *moderatio, liberalitas ;* in —, *ex aequo, sicut aequum est, ut par est.* **II.** v.intr. *ratiocinari* (in gen.), *disputare* or *disserĕre de alqâ re* (about any thing, *animo* or *secum reputare* (with oneself) ; see ARGUE. **reasonable,** adj. **1,** *rationis particeps* (= rational), *modestus* (= unassuming), *rationi conveniens, consentaneus* (= in accordance with reason ; **2,** = moderate, *aequus* (= according to — demands), *justus* (= according to what is right, both of persons and things), *meritus* (= rightly deserved, e.g. praise), *modicus* (= moderate, in price, etc.) ; to buy at a — cost, *bene emĕre.* Adv. *rationi convenienter,* *merito, jure, bene, parvo pretio* (= cheaply).

reasonableness, n. *ratio ;* = moderation, *aequitas, justitia, moderatio, modestia;* see REA-SON. **reasoner,** n. *disputator,* or use verb. **reasoning,** n. *ratiocinatio, argumentatio;* see also REASON.

reassemble, I. v.tr. *recolligĕre.* **II.** v.intr. *iterum cogi* or *convenire;* see ASSEMBLE.

reassert, v.tr. **1,** = to repeat, *iterare, iterum confirmare;* see ASSERT; **2,** = to re-establish, *restituĕre* (= to restore), *vindicare* (= to claim).

reassume, v.tr. *recipĕre.*

reassure, v.tr. *confirmare, recreare, erigĕre.*

rebel, I. v.intr. *seditionem movēre* (= to cause a revolt), *imperium auspiciumque abnuĕre* (= to refuse obedience, of soldiers), *rebellare, rebellionem facĕre* (of a tribe recently subdued), *imperium alcjs detrectare* (= to refuse to obey anyone), *defi-cĕre ab alqo* or *ab alcjs imperio, desciscĕre ab alqo* (= to desert anyone). **II.** n. *homo seditiosus, novorum consiliorum auctor.* **rebellion,** n. *seditio, motus, -ūs, tumultus, -ūs, rebellio.* **re-bellious,** adj. *seditiosus, turbulentus, novarum rerum cupidus* or *studiosus.* Adv. *seditiose, tur-bulente(r).*

rebellow, v.intr. *reboare, resonare.*

rebound, v.intr. *repeɪcuti, repelli* (= to be driven back), *residēre* (= to fall back, of persons and things), *resilire* (= to jump back), *resultare* (= to leap back, of things); of echo, *resonare, vocem reddĕre* or *remittĕre, voci respondēre.*

rebuff, I. v.tr. *repellĕre, re(j)icĕre.* **II.** n. *repulsa* (of a candidate: only poet. in wider sense), or by *repelli;* see REFUSAL.

rebuild, v.tr. *alqd totum denuo* or *de in-tegro aedificare, restituĕre, reficĕre, renovare* (= to beautify).

rebuke, I. v.tr. *alqm reprehendĕre de* or *in alqā re, alqm vituperare de alqā re, alqm objur-gare de* or *in alqā re, alqm (verbis) castigare, alqm* or *alqd increpare, alqm increpitare, alqm alcjs rei incusare;* see BLAME. **II.** n. *reprehensio, vitu-peratio, objurgatio, convicium* (= scolding), *casti-gatio.* **rebuker,** n. *reprehensor, castigator, ob-jurgator.*

rebut, v.tr. *redarguĕre, repellĕre, refellĕre;* see CONFUTE.

recall, I. v.tr. **1,** *revocare* (the proper term, e.g. an opinion, *sententiam;* a promise, *promis-sum*), *retractare* (= to recant, e.g. words, *dicta*), *alqd irritum esse jubēre* (e.g. *largitiones*), *rescindĕre* (= to rescind, e.g. a decree, a will), *mutare* (= to change, e.g. one's opinion, *sententiam*); **2,** = to call back, *revocare* (verbally and in writing, lit. and fig.), *alqm reverti jubēre* (= to order anyone to return); to — an ambassador, *alqm e legatione revocare;* to — troops from the battle, *signum re-ceptui dare;* to — to their (the people's) minds, *memoriam alcjs rei renovare* or *redintegrare;* to — to anyone's mind, *alci alqd in memoriam re-digĕre* or *reducĕre, alqm in memoriam alcjs rei revocare* or *reducĕre;* to — to one's mind, *me-moriam alcjs rei repetĕre* or *revocare.* **II.** n. *revocatio,* or by verbs, *receptus, -ūs* (= signal for — of troops).

recant, v.tr. *se sententiam revocare dicĕre.* **recantation,** n. use verb.

recapitulate, v.tr. *enumerare, referre* (= to relate) or more exactly *colligĕre et commonēre qui-bus de rebus verba fecerimus breviter.* **reca-pitulation,** n. *enumeratio, rerum repetitio et congregatio.*

recapture, I. v.tr. *recipĕre.* **II.** n. by verb.

recast, v.tr. **1,** lit. *recoquĕre, conflare* (= to melt down); **2,** fig. *totum denuo fingĕre* (lit. = to

mould all anew, Plaut.), *fingĕre* or *formare in aliud* (lit. = to make into something quite dif-ferent), *recoquĕre* (lit. and fig.), *commutare* (= to transform, e.g. *rempublicam*), *renovare* (= to give a new shape, e.g. *alqd in legibus);* see TRANSFORM.

recede, v.intr. *recedĕre, retro cedĕre.*

receipt, n. **1,** *acceptio,* or by circumloc. with *accipĕre* (e.g. after the — of the money, etc., *pecuniā acceptā;* after the — of your letters, *lit(t)eris tuis acceptis* or *allatis);* to acknowledge the — of, *testari se accepisse alqd;* to sign the — in a book, *acceptum referre alqd;* **2,** of money, a —, *apocha* (Jct., ἀποχή) or *accepti latio* (or as one word *acceptilatio,* when the money has really been paid; *ac. lat.* = a discharge, Ulp. Dig.), *antapocha* (= a written acknowledgment by the party who paid the money, to the effect that he paid it and got a — for it, Jct.); to enter the — of anything, *alqd habēre accep-tum;* to give a — for, *acceptum alqd testari* (= to acknowledge to have received); **3,** = a recipe, a medical prescription, *praeceptum;* to make up a — (of the druggist), *medicamen-tum ex medici formulā diluĕre.* **receive,** v.tr. **1,** *accipĕre* (in the widest sense; also = to take a drink, medicine, poison, etc.), *ferre, nancisci* (of good and evil, accidentally or by chance, without any effort on our part); **2,** to — a per-son, *accipĕre, excipĕre, salutare* (= to greet, wel-come), *recipĕre;* to — kindly, *benigne* or *benigno vultu excipĕre, benigne salutare;* to — one who arrives (in going to meet him), *alci obviam venienti procedĕre;* to — anyone in a ship, car-riage, to take in, *tollĕre alqm;* **3,** in one's house, *recipĕre* (as a benefactor), *excipĕre* (as a friend), *hospitio accipĕre* or *excipĕre tecto, ad se* (*domum*) *recipĕre;* **4,** anywhere, to — as citizen, *a(d)scis-cĕre in numerum civium, facĕre civem;* into a family, *in familiam assumĕre;* among the patri-cians, *inter patricios* or *in numerum patriciorum assumĕre;* into a society, etc., *cooptare* (in *colle-gium et in ordinem*); among (the number of) one's friends, *in amicitiam recipĕre, accipĕre, ad amicitiam a(d)scribĕre, amicum sibi adjungĕre;* not to —, *re(j)icĕre;* **5,** to —, take anything said or done in a certain manner, *accipĕre, ex-cipĕre, interpretari* (= to put an interpretation upon it); well, in *bonam partem accipĕre, boni* or *aequi bonique facĕre, boni consulĕre;* not well, badly, ill, in *malam partem accipĕre; aegre, graviter, moleste, indigne ferre, male interpre-tari.* **receiver,** n. **1,** *qui alqd accipit, receptor* (esp. in bad sense, of thieves, etc.); **2,** *exactor* (of taxes), *portitor* (of customs). **receptacle,** n. *receptaculum* (= any place where things may be deposited or kept), *cella, cellula* (= store-room, cellar), *horreum* (= store-room, barn), *apo-thēca* (= repository for wine), *armarium* (for clothes), *claustrum* (for wild beasts), *piscina* (for fish; also in gen. = water reservoir), *cavea* (for birds). **reception,** n. **1,** in gen. *acceptio,* or by verbs; **2,** *receptio, hospitium* (in anyone's house and at his table), *aditus, -ūs* (= access to anyone), *cooptatio* (into a body, so-ciety, etc.); to meet with a good, bad —, *bene, male accipi, benigne, male excipi, at, ab alqo.* **receptive,** adj. *aptus ad discendum, docilis.* **receptiveness, receptivity,** n. *docilitas.* **recipient,** n. *qui accipit.*

recent, adj. *recens* (of what came only recently, of late, into existence, fresh, = young, opp. *anti-quus,* i.e. what existed in former times), also comb. *recens ac novus* or *novus ac recens* (of a thing that is but new, as well as of that which has but lately begun to exist). Adv. *nuper, recens* (ante and post class.).

receptacle, see under RECEIVE.

recess, n. **1,** = retired place, *recessus, -ūs*

recessus, -ūs, penetrale (usu. pl. and mostly poet.);
— in a room, perhaps *angulus;* **2,** = holidays, *feriae.*

recipe, n. see RECEIPT, 3.

reciprocal, adj. *mutuus.* Adv. *mutuo, invicem.* **reciprocate,** v.tr. *inter se dare.* **reciprocity,** n. *vicissitudo* (= alternation), or by verb.

recital, n. *enumeratio, narratio, commemoratio.* **recite,** v.tr. 1, = to repeat aloud, *pronuntiare, recitare;* **2,** = to narrate, *enumerare,* (com)-*memorare, dicěre, (e)narrare, referre, exponěre;* see NARRATE, SAY. **recitation,** n. *lectio, recitatio.* **recitative,** n. *recitatio notis signisque composita.* **reciter,** n. *recitator.*

reckless, adj. 1, = rash, *neglegens, temerarius, incautus, imprudens;* **2,** = of anything, *neglegens alcjs.* Adv. *neglegenter* (= carelessly), *temere* (= rashly), *imprudenter* (= inconsiderately). **recklessness,** n. *imprudentia, socordia, neglegentia, temeritas;* see RASHNESS, CARELESSNESS, or by verbs.

reckon, v.tr. 1, *computare, computare rationem rei;* **2,** see CONSIDER. **reckoning,** n. *ratio;* to form a —, *rationem habēre rei, aestimare rem, rationem inire;* by my —, *meā opinione;* to run your pen through the —, *alci rationes conturbare;* to find your — in, *quaestum facěre in re.*

reclaim, v.tr. 1, *repetěre* (by request), *reposcěre* (imperatively), *exigěre* (= to collect money that is owing, e.g. *credita,* anything lent), *auqd recipěre* (= to recover), *alqm or alqd ab alqā re vindicare;* **2,** fig. to call back from error, vice, etc., *alqm revocare ad virtutem (a perditā luxuriā,* etc.), *alqm ad officium reducěre.*

recline, I. v.tr. *reclinare;* to — the head upon the elbow, *niti or initi cubito, initi in cubitum.* **II.** v.intr. *jacēre* (= to lie), *accumběre, (ac)cubare* (at table). **reclining,** adj. *(re)supinus* (on the back).

recluse, n. *homo solitarius;* see also HERMIT.

recognise, v.tr. 1, *a(d)gnoscěre, (re)cognoscěre* (= to make the acquaintance of anyone a second time); to — anyone by anything, *noscitare alqm alqā re* (e.g. *facie, voce);* **2,** = to acknowledge, *cognoscěre* (in gen.), *appellare alqm* with accus. of the title (= to declare anyone), *(com)probare* (= to approve), *accipěre* (= to receive). **recognition,** n. 1, in gen., see RECOGNISE; **2,** *comprobatio.* **recognizance,** n. *sponsio, vadimonium;* to enter into —s, *vadimonium facěre.*

recoil, v.intr. *repercuti, resilire* (lit. and fig.), † *resultare, recellěre;* to — at, *refugěre et reformidare alqd.*

recollect, v.tr. *alcjs rei* (com)*meminisse, reminisci, alqd recordari,* comb. *reminisci et recordari,* or by *memoriam alcjs rei tenēre or habēre, memorem or haud immemorem esse alcjs rei* (all = *meminisse*)*, memoriam alcjs rei repetěre, revocare, renovare, redintegrare, memoriā repetěre alqd, subit animum alcjs rei memoria, alqd mihi in memoriam, venit mihi in mentem alqd, alcjs rei, de alqā re* (all = *reminisci*)*;* to — anything quite well, *commeminisse* with genit.; I cannot — it, *memoriā alqd excessit, delapsum est, e memoriā alqd mihi exiit, excidit, ex animo alqd effluxit, fugit* or *refugit alqd meam memoriam.* **recollection,** n. *memoria* (= memory, and remembrance), *recordatio* (the act), comb. *recordatio et memoria, memoria ac recordatio;* to bring to one's —, *in memoriam redigěre, reducěre, revocare.*

recommence, I. v.tr. *de integro instaurare* (= to set on foot again), *(red)integrare* (= to

begin afresh), *renovare* (= to renew), *iterare* (= to begin a second time), *repetěre* (= to repeat, after an interruption). **II.** v.intr. *renasci,* or by pass. of verbs given above.

recommend, v.tr. *commendare;* to — oneself, *gratum esse, placēre, probari* (all of persons and things), to anyone, *alci;* by, *se commendare alqā re* (of persons), *commendari alqā re* (of things). **recommendable,** adj. *commendandus, commendatione dignus, commendabilis.* **recommendation,** n. *commendatio, laudatio, suffragatio* (by voting in favour); to give anyone a — to anyone, *alqm commendare alci, ad alqm de alqo scriběre;* his — is of great use to me with, *maximo usui mihi est alcjs commendatio apud alqm;* a letter of —, *litt(t)erae commendaticius;* to give anyone a letter of — to, *alqm commendare alci per litt(t)eras.* **recommendatory,** adj. *commendaticius.*

recompense, I. n. *pretium, merces, -ēdis,* f., *remuneratio, munus, -ěris,* n.; see REWARD. **II.** v.tr. *compensare, remunerari;* see REWARD.

reconcile, v.tr. 1, *placare* (by reconciliatory means, in gen., e.g. *numen divinum), expiare* (anything polluted by a crime, e.g. *numen, manes);* to — a person with anyone, *alqm cum algo or alqm or alcjs animum alci reconciliare or reducěre or restituěre in gratiam,* also *alqm in alcjs gratiam reconciliare or restituěre;* to — oneself with, to anyone, *reconciliari alci, reconciliare sibi alqm or alcjs animum or alcjs gratiam, in gratiam cum algo redire or reverti;* **2,** = to make congruous, *alqd ad alqd or alci rei accommodare, facěre ut alqd cum alqā re conveniat or congruat;* fig. of things, to be —d together, *congruěre, congruentem esse alci rei, aptum esse alci rei, non alienum esse ab alqā re,* both with genit. (e.g. *sapientis est)*; **3,** = to submit to, *se sub(j)icěre, obtemperare or parēre,* with dat., *alqd subire or perferre;* see YIELD. **reconcilable, reconciliatory,** adj. 1, *placabilis;* **2,** *qui (quae, quod) alci rei accommodari potest.* **reconciler,** n. *reconciliator gratiae.* **reconciliation,** n. 1, *reconciliatio concordiae or gratiae;* **2,** see ATONEMENT; **3,** = agreement of things seemingly opposite, by verb RECONCILE, 2.

recondite, adj. *reconditus.*

reconduct, v.tr. *reducěre.*

reconnoitre, v.tr. to — a locality, etc., *cognoscěre qualis sit natura alcjs loci, naturam alcjs loci perspicěre* (accurately), *situm alcjs loci speculari* (= to explore), *visěre alqd* (in gen. = to inspect anything, e.g. *copias hostium), explorare alqd* (= to spy out, e.g. *itinera hostium);* one sent out to —, *explorator.* **reconnoitring,** n. by verbs.

reconquer, v.tr. *recipěre, reciperare (recup-).*

reconsider, v.tr. *denuo, rursus or iterum considerare, reputare,* etc.; see CONSIDER.

record, I. v.tr. *referre in tabulas, libellum,* etc., *litt(t)eris or memoriae mandare.* **II.** n. *lit(t)erae, tabulae, historia, monumentum, memoria alcjs rei.* **records,** pl. *annales, -ium,* m. (= annals), *acta (publica or diurna or urbana,* = journal), *fasti* (= calendar), *tabulae (publicae)* (= official state —), *acta Senatūs* (= — of the Senate). **record-office,** n. *tabularium.* **recoruer,** n. = keeper of records, *chartularius* (legal, Jot.), *componendis patrum actis delectus* (Tac., of records of the Senate); = a judge, *judex.*

recount, v.tr. *referre;* see RELATE.

recourse, n. to have — to anyone or to anything, *confugěre or perfugěre ad alqm or alqd* (lit. and fig.), *alcjs rei perfugio uti* (fig. e.g. *aquarum), decurrěre ad alqm or alqd, se ad alqm conferre;* in bad sense, *ad alqd descenděre.*

recover, I. v.tr. *recipĕre*, (e.g. *res amissas*) *reciperare, reparare, repetĕre*; to — one's debts, *evincĕre* (Jct.), *nomina sua exigĕre* (e.g. *amissa*). **II.** v.intr. 1, *convalescĕre, sanescĕre* (*in sanitatem*) *recipĕre* or *reciperare, restitui in sanitatem*; to — from illness, *convalescĕre e morbo*; 2, in gen. = to regain a former condition, *se* or *animum colligĕre, se reficĕre, se* or *animum recipĕre* with and without *ex* (*a*) *pavore, se recreare ex timore, respirare a metu, respirare et se recipĕre* (from fright), *se* or *animum erigĕre* (from a desponding state of mind), *vires, auctoritatem, opes reciperare, pristinam fortunam reparare* (= to regain influence, etc.); in law, see above. **recoverable,** adj. *quod restitui* or *reparari,* etc., *potest,* † *reparabilis*; in law, *quod evinci potest* (Jct.). **recovery,** n. 1, in gen. *recipe ratio*; 2, *sanitas restituta, valetudo confirmata*; to have, to entertain, no hopes for anyone's —, *alqm* or *alcjs salutem desperare* (Cic.); all 'the medical men doubt of his —, *omnes medici diffidunt*; 3, in law, *evictio* (Jct.).

recreant, n. 1, = apostate, *apostata* (Eccl.); 2, see COWARD.

recreate, v.tr. 1, = to create anew, *renovare, recreare*; see RENEW; 2, = to amuse, etc., oneself, *requiescĕre* (= to rest), *animum relaxare, remittĕre, mentem reficĕre et recreare* (= to revive). **recreation,** n. *requies, -ētis* (= rest); — of the mind (after hard work, care, etc.), *animi remissio, relaxatio, oblectatio, requies*; for —, *laxandi levandique animi gratiâ*; to allow oneself a few moments' —, *aliquantulum sibi parcĕre*.

recriminate, v.intr. *culpam, crimen,* etc., *in alqm regerĕre.* **recrimination,** n. *accusatio mutua* (Tac.).

recruit, I. v.tr. and intr. 1, one's strength, *se* or *vires recreare, reficĕre*; 2, to — the army, *supplēre, explēre, delectibus supplēre, supplementum scribĕre alci, reficĕre, milites conscribĕre, delectum habēre.* **II.** n. *novus miles* (in gen.), *tiro* (not drilled), opp. *vetus miles, veteranus*); the —s, *milites tirones, milites in supplementum lecti,* also *supplementum* (= reserve); a —ing officer, *conquisitor.* **recruiting,** n. *conquisitio, delectus, -ûs.*

rectangle, n. *figura orthogōnia.* **rectangular,** adj. *orthogonios.*

rectification, n. *correctio, emendatio.* **rectify,** v.tr. *corrigĕre, emendare* (mistakes in writing, copying, printing); see CORRECT.

rectilineal, adj. (*di*)*rectus.*

rectitude, n. *aequitas, probitas, integritas, honestas, simplicitas, ingenuitas* (in one's actions), *animus ingenuus.*

rector, n. of a grammar-school or college, *scholarum, gymnasii, academiae, rector* or *moderator;* to be — of, etc., *praeesse, praefectum esse alci rei;* of a parish, *paroeciae rector,* or, where possible, *sacerdos* (= priest).

recumbent, adj. (*re*)*supīnus,* † *reclīnis,* or by *reclinari;* see RECLINE.

red, adj. *ruber, rubens* (= bright —), *rufus* (= light —, auburn), *rutilus* (= fire-red); *rubicundus* (= ruddy), *rubidus* (= dark —), *puniceus* (= purple), † *sanguineus* (= blood- —), † *flammeus* (= flame-coloured); — hair, *capillus rufus* or *rutilus;* the — sea, *Sinus Arabicus.* **redden, I.** v.tr. † *rubefacĕre.* **II.** v.intr. (*e*)*rubescĕre* (= to blush). **red-hot,** adj. *candens, fervens.* **red-lead,** n. *minium.* **redness,** n. *rubor, pudor.*

redeem, v.tr. *redimĕre, liberare* (= to set free); a pledge, *repignerare quod pignori datum est* (Jct.); see also FREE. **redeemer,** n. *liberator, -index,* from anything, *alcjs rei* (= deliverer); *re- emptor* (by ransom; * *mundi redemptor,* the — of

the world), * *servator;* see SAVIOUR. **redemption,** n. 1, *redemptio, liberatio* (= deliverance); 2, in theology, * *salus* (= salvation), * *redemptio.*

redolent, adj. *alqd redolens.*

redouble, v.tr. *reduplicare,* † *ingeminare.*

redoubt, n. *castellum, propugnaculum.*

redound, v.intr. *redundare*; to anyone's credit, *esse* with double dat. (e.g. it —s to my credit, *est mihi honori*). **redundancy,** n. *redundantia.* **redundant,** adj. *redundans, supervacaneus.*

redress, I. v.tr. = to amend, *corrigĕre, emendare, restituĕre, alci rei mederi, alci satisfacĕre de alqâ re;* to — a wrong, *injuriam sarcire.* **II.** n. *satisfactio, remedium,* or by verb.

reduce, v.tr. 1, = to bring to any state, to — to order, *in integrum reducĕre* (civil affairs, etc.); to — a man to poverty, *alqm ad inopiam redigĕre;* to — to ashes, *incendio delēre* (a house, town, etc.), *incendiis vastare* (e.g. *omnia*); to — one to despair, *alqm ad desperationem adducĕre* or *redigĕre;* 2, = to diminish in length, quantity, etc., (*im*)*minuĕre, deminuĕre* (in gen.); to — the price of, *pretium alcjs rei* (*im*)*minuĕre;* 3, = to conquer, *vincĕre, expugnare* (of a stronghold). **reduction,** n. 1, by verbs; 2, *expugnatio;* 3, in arith. and logic, *reductio.*

reduplication, n. *reduplicatio* as gram. t.t.

reecho, v.intr. *resonare alqd* or *alqâ re* or *remittĕre, alqâ re resultare.*

reed, n. *carex* (= sedge, shear-grass), *arundo* (= cane), *canna* (= small —), *calamus.* **reedy,** adj. *arundinĕus.*

reef, I. n. 1, *scopuli, saxa* (= rocks); see ROCK; 2, = portion of a sail, *velum.* **II.** v.tr. *vela subducĕre.*

reek, v.intr. *fumare.*

reel, I. n. 1, = a winder, *glomus* (= ball, e.g. *lini*); 2, = a dance, *saltatio.* **II.** v.intr. *titubare, vacillare.*

reelect, v.tr. *reficĕre.*

reestablish, v.tr. *restituĕre, reficĕre.* **reestablisher,** n. *restitutor.* **reestablishment,** n. *restitutio, refectio;* see RENEWAL.

refectory, n. *cenaculum.*

refer, I. v.tr. 1, = to direct, etc., anyone or anything to another person, *alqm* or *alqd delegare ad alqm* or *ad alqd, revocare alqm ad alqm* or *ad alqd* (e.g. *alqm ad Graecorum poëtarum fabulas), re*(*j*)*icĕre* or *remittĕre alqd ad alqm* (e.g. *causam ad senatum*); 2, fig. to — anything to a thing, *referre* or *deferre alqd ad alqd;* anything to another matter, *alqd ad aliam rem transferre;* everything to sensual pleasure, *omnia ad voluptatem corporis referre.* **II.** v.intr., to anyone or to anything, *spectare ad alqd* (intended), *pertinĕre, referri ad alqd* (really), *alqm* or *alqd attingĕre* or *perstringĕre, alcjs rei mentionem facĕre;* it —s to this, that, etc., *hoc eo spectat, ut,* etc.; it —s to those who, etc., *hoc illis dictum est, qui,* etc.; to — a speech, a sermon, etc., to anyone, *oratione designatur alqs;* = to appeal to anyone, *provocare ad alqm, appellare alqm* and *alqd* (both also = to appeal to a higher tribunal), *alqm testari, alqm testem citare* (= to — to anyone as a witness), *delegare, re*(*j*)*icĕre alqm ad alqd* (for better information), *afferre alqd* (= to — to, as a proof), *alcjs rei excusationem afferre, alcjs rei excusatione uti* (= to — to anything, as an excuse for, etc.). **referable,** adj. *qui* (*quae, quod*) *ad alqm* or *alqd referri potest.* **referee,** n. *arbiter.*

reference, n. 1, to anyone, by verbs; 2, allusion to books, persons, etc.; see QUOTATION; 3, = relation, by *ratio;* to have — to *pertinēre, referri ad alqd;* having **no — to** the matter, *alienus ab alqâ re;* with **— to,** etc., by *quod attinet ad* (e.g. *quod ad librum attinet quem tibi filius dabat,* Cic.), or by *ad* (e.g. *adornatum ad specimen magnifico ornatu,* Cic.); or by *de* with abl. (= on account of, concerning, e.g. *recte non credis de numero militum,* Cic.).

refill, v.tr. *replēre.*

refine, v.tr. 1, *liquare* (*vinum*), *purgare* (Plin., gold, silver, etc.); 2, fig. (*ex*)*polire, excolēre.* **refined,** adj. (*ex*)*polītus, urbanus, comis* (= courteous), *humanus, liberalis, elegans;* **a —** palate, *palatum subtile;* **—** torture, *exquisitum supplicium.* **refinement,** n. 1, of liquids, etc., by verb REFINE, I.; 2, of manners, etc., *urbanitas, comitas, humanitas, elegantia;* of language, etc., *subtilitas,* comb. *subtilitas et elegantia, argutiae.*

reflect, I. v.tr. **to —** the rays of light, *radios repercutēre, regerēre.* **II.** v.intr. 1, of the mind, *remittēre;* the mind is —ed in the face, *mens in facie tanquam in speculo cernitur,* or *imago mentis est vultus;* **to —** on, *secum in animo considerare,* or simply *considerare alqd* or *de alqâ re* (= to dwell on), *commentari alqd* or *de alqâ re* (= to think over in private); *alqd* or *de alqâ re secum meditari, alqd secum reputare, alqd (re)volvēre, memoriam alcjs rei repetēre* or *revocare;* see THINK; 2, to — upon, *culpare;* see BLAME. **reflection,** n. 1, of rays, etc., *repercussus, -ûs* (Plin.); 2, = image reflected, *imago;* 3, = thought, *meditatio, commentatio, cogitatio, consideratio, deliberatio, reputatio;* 4, as quality *mens, ratio, consilium;* 5, = blame, *reprehensio* see BLAME. **reflective,** adj. 1, *magni consilii;* see THOUGHTFUL; 2, Gram. *reciprocus.*

reflux, n. *recessus, -ûs.*

reform, I. v.tr. 1, = to make anew, *renovare, restituēre;* of scattered troops, *ordines restituēre;* 2, = to amend, *corrigēre, emendare.* **II.** v.intr. *se corrigēre, mores suos mutare, in viam redire.* **III.** n. *correctio, emendatio* (in gen.); of manners, *morum mutatio.* **reformation,** n. 1, see REFORM, III.; 2, Eccl., *reformatio.* **reformatory,** n. by circuml. (e.g. *carcer ad scelestos corrigendos destinatus*), or, where context allows, by *carcer* alone. **reformer,** n. *corrector, emendator.*

refract, v.tr. *radii infringuntur* or *refringuntur.* **refraction,** n. *refractio radiorum.* **refractory,** adj. *contumax* (= contumacious), *imperium detrectans* (= refusing to obey, of soldiers, subjects), *detrectans militiam* (= of soldiers). **refractoriness,** n. *contumacia.*

refrain, v.tr. (*se*) *abstinēre, se continēre ab alqâ re,* (*sibi* or *animis*) *temperare ab alqâ re* or *quin* or *quominus;* **to —** from tears, *lacrimas tenēre, temperare a lacrimis.*

refresh, v.tr. *refrigerare* (= to cool), *recreare, reficēre* (= to revive, to renew one's physical strength), comb. *reficēre et recreare, recreare et reficēre;* **to —** anyone by giving him something to eat, *cibo juvare alqm;* **to —** with meat and drink, *cibo ac potione firmare alqm;* **to —** oneself, *animum reparare, relaxare, integrare* (in gen.); by mental recreation, *animo relaxari.* **refreshing,** adj. *reficiens, recreans, suavis, dulcis.* **refreshment,** n. 1, *refectio* (as act), *id quod corpus reficit* (= what refreshes the body), *delectatio* (= delight, as a condition), *laxamentum* (for the mind); 2, —s, *cibus.*

refrigerate, v.tr. *refrigerare.*

refuge, n. *perfugium, refugium, asylum* (= an asylum for everybody **gen. a** sacred grove or

temple), *recessus, -ûs, secessus, -ûs* (=retreat), **r**- *ceptaculum* (= a place where one may find **shelte** from prosecution, etc.), *portus, -ûs* (lit. = harbour; hence fig. = any place of shelter), comb. *portus et perfugium, praesidium,* comb. *perfugium et praesidium salutis;* to seek a — at a place, (con)- *fugēre* or *perfugēre* or *refugēre ad* or *in alqm locum, alqo loco perfugio uti;* to have **a —,** *perfugium* or *receptum habēre.* **refugee,** n. *fugitivus* (= a runaway slave, or a deserter), *exul, extorris, profugus* (= exile).

refulgent, adj. see BRIGHT.

refund, v.tr. *reddēre* (e.g. *ad assem alci impensum,* (*dis*)*solvēre* (e.g. a debt, *nomen;* **to —** a sum of money lent, *aes alienum*), *rescribēre* (= to pay money by bill).

refuse, I. v.tr. *alqd recusare* (or with accus and infin., *quin* or *quominus* = **to —** to do anything, *alqd* (*de*)*negare* (or with accus. and futinfin.), *alqd detrectare, repudiare, renuēre, respuēre;* **to —** anything to anyone, *alqd alci recusare.* **II.** n. *ramentum* (Plin., = shavings, etc.), *scobis* (= sawdust, smaller than *ramentum*), *retrimentum* (of olives, metals, etc.), *intertrimentum* (of metals, etc., in melting), *purgamen*(*tum*) (= dirt swept off), *faex* (= dregs, lit. and fig.), *quisquiliae* (= sweepings, usu. fig.), *sentina* (= bilgewater; also fig.). **refusal,** n. *recusatio, repudiatio, repulsa* (= rejection of a candidate); to give anyone the — of anything, *alci potestatem alcjs rei emendae facēre.*

refute, v.tr. *refellēre* (anyone's opinion by arguments, a person or thing), *redarguēre* (= to convince of the contrary, a person or thing), comb. *refellēre et redarguēre, convincēre* (= to convince anyone that he is wrong, to prove the fallacy of anything, e.g. *errores*), *revincēre* (= to prove the contrary of an assertion), *confutare,* e.g. *argumenta Stoicorum*), *diluēre* (= to weaken, e.g. *crimen*), comb. *refutare ac diluēre, diluēre at refellēre, diluēre alqd et falsum esse docēre, dissolvēre;* **to —** anything by testimonies, evidence, *alqd testimoniis refutare.* **refutation, n.** *confutatio, refutatio, responsio.*

regain, v.tr. *recipēre, reciperare.*

regal, adj. see ROYAL.

regale, v.tr. see ENTERTAIN; **to —** oneself, see FEAST.

regalia, n. *ornatus, -ûs, regius, insignia regia* (pl.).

regard, I. v.tr. 1, *animum intendēre in alqd* or *alci rei, alqd animadvertēre* (or *animum advertēre,* = to direct one's attention to), *observare alqd* (= to notice), *intueri* (*in*) *alqd* (= to look at), *respicēre alqd* (= to mind), *spectare alqd* (= not to lose sight of); as —s so-and-so, by *pertinēre ad,* etc. (= to concern), *attinēre ad,* etc. (= to belong to), *spectare alqd* or *ad alqd* (= to refer to), *attingēre alqm* (= to have reference to anyone); not to —, *neglegēre;* 2, = to care for, *alqm* or *alqd carum habēre, colēre, diligēre* (= to esteem), *magni alqm aestimare;* 3, = to consider, *ducēre, habēre;* see CONSIDER. **II.** n. 1, *respectus, -ûs* (lit., = the looking back); hence consideration of thoughts and sentiments), *ratio* (=reference), *cura* (= care); to have —, etc., *respectum habēre ad alqm, respicēre alqm* or *alqd, rationem habēre alcjs* or *alcjs rei, rationem ducēre alcjs rei;* for oneself, *suam rationem ducēre;* so as to cogitare;* out of — for, in Latin often by the dative of the person, e.g. *animadversionem et supplicium remittēre alci;* with — to anything, see REFERENCE; 2, = esteem, *alcjs caritas, studium, amor* (= love), *pietas erga alqm* (= dutiful affection); see AFFECTION; kind —s (*etiam atqu etiam*) *vale* (*valete*); Cicero sends his —s, *Cicero tibi salutem plurimam dicit.* **regardful,** adj.

see ATTENTIVE. **regardless**, adj. *in quo nullius ratio habetur, in quo delectus omnis et discrimen omittitur, neglegens;* see CARELESS. Adv. *neglegenter, nullius ratione habitâ, delectu omni et discrimine omisso.*

regatta, n. see RACE.

regency, n. *regni administratio, interregnum* (= interreign), *procuratio regni* (= the office of a viceroy)*;* to entrust anyone with the —, *administrationem regni in alqm transferre.* **regent**, n. *procurator regni* or *imperii, interrex.*

regenerate, v.tr. *regenerare;* to be —d, *renasci.* **regeneration**, n. *regeneratio* (Eccl.).

regicide, n. 1, = murder of a king, *regis caedes, -is,* f., in the context also *parricidium* (*regis*)*;* to commit —, *regem interficĕre;* 2, = the murderer, *regis interfector* or *percussor* or *patricida.*

regiment, n. *legio* (of infantry), *turma equitum* (of cavalry).

region, n. *regio* (in gen.), *tractus, -ûs* (= tract of a country, referring to the distance), *plaga* (only of the — of the sky, also *plaga caeli*), *ora* (lit. = tract on the coast), *pars* (= part, district, also of the sky), *loca,* pl. (places, gen. with an adj. expressing the nature of the soil, e.g. *loca amoena*).

register, **I.** n. *liber* (as note-book), *tabulae* (= tables), *album* (= an official account, report, e.g. of the judges, suitors, applicants, etc.)*;* to enter in a —, *in album referre.* **II.** v.tr. *in acta publica referre* (of public —s), *in tabulas referre* (in gen.). **registrar**, n. in gen. *qui alqd in acta publica refert.* **registration**, n. use verb.

regret, **I.** n. (*com*)*miseratio* (= the giving vent to one's compassion), *dolor* (= grief), *desiderium* (= longing), *paenitentia* (= repentance). **II.** v.tr. *dolēre, aegre* or *moleste ferre, lugēre* (= to mourn)*;* it is to be —ted, *dolendum est quod;* I —, *doleo;* hence = to repent, *paenitet* or *piget me alcjs rei;* = to feel the loss of, *desiderare, desiderio alcjs teneri.*

regular, adj. *ordinatus* (= ordered), *omnibus membris aequalis et congruens* (of the — shape of the human body, also of a — building), *omnibus partibus absolutus et perfectus* (= perfect in gen.), *aequabilis* (= equable), *constans* (= not deviating from the — course, e.g. the course of the stars)*; certus* (= fixed), *rectus* (= correct)*;* — troops, *milites legionarii* (in the ancient sense, opp. *velites* = light troops)*;* = legitimate, ordinary, *justus* (in gen.), *legitimus* (= legitimate)*;* a — battle, *justa pugna;* in — array, *acie* (in battle), *composito agmine* (of line of march)*;* the — consuls, *consules ordinarii;* — revenue, income, *status reditus, -ûs* (opp. *reditus extraordinarius*). Adv. *ordine, constanter* (e.g. *cursus suos servare*), *recte, ordinate, composite, juste, aequabiliter, legitime.* **regularity**, n. *ordo, constantia, aequabilitas, symmetria* (= proportion, Vitr.), *apta compositio* (of words in a sentence). **regulate**, v.tr. *ordinare, componere, dirigĕre, formare, fingĕre;* to — oneself by anything, *se ad alqd accommodare;* see ARRANGE. **regulation**, n. *ratio, ordo, -inis,* m., *mos, consuetudo, institutum* (of what is customary), *lex* (of what has become almost a law)*;* domestic —, *victus cultusque, privatae vitae ratio;* = order, *jussum, praeceptum, edictum* (= edict)*;* —s, *instituta et leges;* to make a few fresh —s, *quaedam nova instituĕre;* a few useful —s, *quaedam utilia instituĕre,* also *quasdam utilitates instituĕre;* it is a wise — in nature that, etc., *salubriter a naturâ institutum est, ut* or *quod.*

rehabilitate, v.tr. anyone's character, *culpâ alqm liberare.*

rehearsal, n. *meditatio* (= previous study)*;* to have a —, *praeludĕre fabulae* (of the actor). **rehearse**, v.tr. see above*; praeludĕre concentui* (of the orchestra and the singer).

reign, **I.** v.intr. *regnare* (as a king), *imperium tenēre, imperare, imperium alcjs terrae obtinēre.* **II.** n. *regnum, dominatio, principatus, -ûs, imperium;* in the — of, *regnante* or *rege alqo;* see RULE.

reimburse, v.tr. see INDEMNIFY, REFUND. **reimbursement**, n. see INDEMNITY.

rein, **I.** n. *habena, frenum* (lit. and fig.), *lorum,* pl. *frena* or *freni;* to pull the —s, *habenas adducĕre* (lit. and fig.), to loosen the —s, *frenos dare* (lit. and fig.)*;* to take the —s of government, *clavum imperii tenēre.* **II.** v.tr. *frenare* (lit. and fig.)*;* to — in, *habenas adducĕre.*

reindeer, n. *reno.*

reinforce, v.tr. *amplificare* (= to cause to be of greater extent, strength, e.g. a tone), *augēre* (= to increase, e.g. an army)*;* to — an army, *auxiliis confirmare, copiis firmare;* to — one's army (of the commander), *novis copiis se renovare* (after the army had been reduced in numbers). **reinforcement**, n. *supplementum, novae copiae* (= new forces), *auxilium* (= allies), *subsidium* (= reserve)*;* somebody receives —, *copia alci augetur, subsidium alci mittitur.*

reins, n. *renes, -um,* m.

reinstate, v.tr. *in* (*regnum,* etc.) *reducĕre,* or by *restituĕre* (= to restore).

reinvigorate, v.tr. see REFRESH.

reiterate, v.tr. see REPEAT.

reject, v.tr. *re*(*j*)*icĕre, improbare, reprobare* (the two foregoing = to disapprove), *repudiare* (= to repudiate), *respuĕre* (= to spit out), *spernĕre, aspernari* (= to throw away, *asp.* implies disdain), *contemnĕre* (= not to consider worth having)*;* to — entirely, *omnino non probare, funditus repudiare, legem suffragiis repudiare* (different from *legem abrogare,* i.e. to rescind)*;* a condition, a proposal, *condicionem repudiare* or *respuĕre;* to — prayers, *preces aversari.* **rejection**, n. *rejectio* (e.g. *judicum*)*, improbatio, repudiatio, aspernatio, repulsa* (of a candidate).

rejoice, **I.** v.intr. *gaudēre* (= to be glad), *laetari* (= to be merry), *gestire* (the strongest expression, when we manifest our joy in our looks, etc.), *subridēre* (= to smile as a sign of joy)*;* to — at anything, *gaudēre, laetari alqâ re* (the latter construction is used to denote that the joy continues*;* the simple accus. only with a neuter pron. with accus. and infin., and *gaudēre* also with *quod*), *delectari alqâ re;* very much, *gaudēre vehementerque laetari;* very much at, *magnam laetitiam voluptatemque capĕre* (or *percipĕre*) *ex alqâ re, magnae laetitiae mihi est alqd, alqd re gaudio exultare* (= to jump with joy)*;* with anyone, *unâ gaudēre, gaudio alcjs gaudēre;* see GLAD. **II.** v.tr. (*ex*)*hilarare, hilarem facĕre* (= to cheer up), *laetificare* (e.g. *sol laetificat terram*), *laetitiâ afficĕre, laetitia et voluptate afficĕre, laetitiam alci afferre* or *offerre* (= to fill with joy). **rejoicing**, n. *voluptas, delectatio, gaudium, laetitia.*

rejoin, v.intr. 1, see RETURN; 2, see ANSWER.

relapse, **I.** v.intr. *recidĕre* (in gen., of illness, *in graviorem morbum*)*;* to — into, *recidĕre in alqd* (e.g. into former slavery), *relabi.* **II.** n. use verb.

relate, v.tr. 1, = to tell in detail, *alqd* (*e*)*narrare, dicĕre,* (*com*)*memorare, referre, prodĕre, tradĕre* (= to hand down)*;* see TELL; 2, = to pertain to, *spectare, attingĕre ad, contingĕre alqm,* or

by impersonals *attinet, pertinet ad, med, tud refert,* etc.; see NARRATE. **related,** adj. 1, = connected by birth, marriage, etc., *propinquus alci, necessarius, cognatus, agnatus* (only on the father's side), *affinis* (by marriage), *consanguineus, consanguinitate propinquus* (= near by blood), *non alienus sanguine alci;* to be most nearly —, *proximum esse;* 2, fig. *cognatus, propinquus.* **relation,** n. 1, = connexion, *ratio, conjunctio;* in — to, *ad alqm* or *alqd, quod ad alqm* or *alqd attinet, prae alqo* or *alqâ re;* 2, relative, person connected with you by birth, marriage, etc., *propinquus, genere proximus, necessarius;* comb. *propinquus et necessarius, propinquus et cognatus, propinquus et affinis, cognatus atque affinis;* a near —, *artâ propinquitate* or *propinquâ cognatione conjunctus;* 3, see NARRATION. **relationship,** n. 1, *necessitudo, propinquitas* (in gen.), *cognatio* (by birth), *agnatio* (on the father's side), *affinitas* (by marriage), *germanitas* (of brothers and sisters, or cities springing from the same mother city), *consanguinitas* (by blood); 2, fig. *cognatio, conjunctio;* to have — with anything, *alci rei finitimum esse.* **relative, I.** adj. opp. to absolute, *quod non simpliciter et ex suâ vi consideratur; quod in comparatione (rerum,* etc.) *positum est, quod ad alqd refertur* or *spectat.* Adv. *comparate, ex comparatione (rerum,* etc.). **II.** n. 1, see RELATION; 2, *relativum* (Gram.).

relax, I. v.tr. 1, *(re)laxare, remittĕre, concedĕre;* 2, in medicine, see OPEN. **II.** v.intr. = to remit in close attention, *(re)languescĕre, se remittĕre, remitti, animum remittĕre* or *relaxare, requiescĕre curamque animi remittĕre* (after hard work), *alqd remittĕre* (e.g. *industriam);* to — for a little while, *alqd intermittĕre;* in anything, *desistĕre* or *(de) alqâ re* (e.g. *incepto;* in a contest, *de contentione).* **relaxation,** n. 1, *solutio* (principally of the parts of the body); 2, see MITIGATION (of the law); 3, = remission of application, *animi relaxatio, remissio* (of the mind), *oblectatio* (= amusement), *oblectamentum* (= anything to amuse oneself with or to while away the time). **relaxing,** adj. *gravis.*

relay, n. *equi recentes* or *per viam dispositi.*

release, I. v.tr. 1, anyone, *dimittĕre alqm* (= to let anyone go), *libertatem alci dare, largiri* (= to set anyone at liberty), *manu mittĕre alqm* (a slave), *emancipare* (= to emancipate, to free anyone from one's power, e.g. a son), *mittĕre* or *missum facĕre alqm, missionem alci dare, exauctorare* (= to dismiss from the service, soldiers), *vinculis exsolvĕre, e custodiâ emittĕre* (from prison, a state prisoner); to — anyone from anything, *solvĕre alqm alqâ re* (e.g. from service, *militiâ), liberare alqm alqâ re* (e.g. *servitute);* 2, = to free from obligation, *(ex)solvĕre, liberare alqâ re; remittĕre, condonare alci alqd, gratiam alcjs rei facĕre alci* (from the payment of a sum of money, penalty, etc.; *gratiam facĕre* in Sall.). **II.** n. *missio* (= dismission), *liberatio, remissio* (e.g. *poenae), apocha* (= receipt for money, Jct.).

relent, v.intr. *molliri* or *moveri pati.* **relentless,** adj. *immisericors, saevus, durus, crudelis;* see CRUEL. Adv. *saeve, crudeliter.* **relentlessness,** n. *saevitia, crudelitas*

relevant, adj. *quod ad rem est.*

reliance, n. see RELY.

relics, n. *reliquiae* (= remains). **relict,** n. *vidua;* see WIDOW.

relief, n. fig. *(al)levatio, sublevatio* (= the — given), *levamen(tum), allevamentum* (= the — which one gets), *remedium* (= remedy), *auxilium* (= help), *subsidium* (of soldiers), *delenimentum* (= anything calculated to soothe, e.g. *vitae),*

laxamentum (= relaxation), *deminutio* (= diminution of taxes, *onerum), beneficium* (= — in money); — of a sentinel, see RELIEVE, below; in painting, *eminentia, asperitas;* high —, *alto* relievo, *imago ectypa* (Sen., as image). **relieve,** v.tr. *exonerare* (= to exonerate, to ease), *levare, allevare* (fig. = to ease), *sublevare* (fig. = both to mitigate and to support), *laxare* (fig. = to relax, to soften), or *adesse alci, (de)minuĕre* (= to lessen, e.g. taxes, *onera), subvenire* (= to assist, e.g. *necessitatibus);* to — a sentinel, *revocare* (= to recall, e.g. *vigilias, milites ab opere), deducĕre* (e.g. *milites ab opere);* of the soldiers themselves, *alqos excipĕre, alqis succedĕre.*

religion, n. *religio* (= reverence towards the holy, the sentiment of — and the consequent services), *pietas erga Deum* (in the sense of the ancients, *erga deos* = fear of the gods), *res divinae* (= divine things), *caerimonia, caerimoniae* (= prescribed observances), *sacra, -orum* (= external rites), *lex* (= religious law or doctrine, as *lex Christiana);* a man without —, or irreligious, *homo impius erga Deum* or *deos, homo neglegens deorum, religionum omnium contemptor, religionum neglegens* (= inattentive to outer usages); to change your —, *sacra patria deserĕre.* **religious,** adj. *pius* (= reverent) *erga Deum, sanctus, religiosus* (= conscientious); — observances, *ritus, religiones, caerimoniae.* Adv. *pie, sancte, religiose;* to be — brought up, *sanctissimo modo educari.*

relinquish, v.tr. *relinquĕre;* see ABANDON.

relish, I. n. 1, a — for (i.e. a disposition to taste), *gustatus, -ûs;* he has no — for, *abest desiderium alcjs rei;* 2, something tasty, *promulsis, -idis,* f., *condimentum.* **II.** v.tr. see ENJOY.

reluctance, n. I have a great — to anything, *magnum alcjs rei odium me cepit;* with —, *coactus* or *invitus, animo invito* or *averso.* **reluctant,** adj. *invitus, coactus.*

rely, v.intr. *(con)fidĕre alci rei* or *alqâ re* (= to trust in), *niti alqâ re* (= to depend on); —ing upon, *fretus alqâ re, nixus (nisus) alqâ re, ferox alqâ re* (= boldly trusting, e.g. *eâ parte virium).* **reliance,** n. *fides, fiducia;* see CONFIDENCE.

remain, v.intr. *(per)manēre, durare* (= to endure), *stare* (= to stand or stay); to — in health and uninjured, *salvum atque incolumem conservari;* to — faithful, *fidum manēre;* to — in your opinion, *in sententiâ tuâ (per)manēre* or *perseverare* (opp. to *a sententiâ decedĕre);* to — unchanged in your custom, *in consuetudine perseverare;* to — unchanged in your plan, *institutum suum tenēre;* to — faithful to your promise, *promissis stare;* to — a secret, *tacēri, tacitum tenēri;* let that — with yourself, *haec tu tecum habeto, hoc tu tibi soli dictum puta.* "It —s" (used as the final result of an argument), *manet;* to — snug, *nidum servare* (= to keep in your nest, Hor.); to — in the camp, *castris se tenēre;* = to be left, *reliquum esse, relinqui, superesse* (= to survive); *ex multis filiis hunc unum fortuna reliquum esse voluit,* fate allowed only this one son to — out of many; = to be left, to be over and above, *restare, superare, superesse.* **remainder,** n. *residuum, reliquum, quod restat;* to get the — by adding and subtracting, *addendo deducendoque vidēre quae reliqui summa est.* **remaining,** adj. *reliquus, residuus.* **remains,** n. 1, of anything, *reliquum,* or pl. *reliqua* or *reliquiae;* of eatables, *reliquiae ciborum,* in the context merely *reliquiae;* "the remainder of anything" is also rendered by *quod superest* or *restat* or *reliquum est;* e.g. *quod membrorum reliquum est);* 2, = a dead body, *cadaver, -eris,* n. (= corpse), *cineres, -um* (= ashes).

remand, I. v.tr. 1, = to send back, *remittĕre;* 2, in law, *comperendinare reum* (= to

defer the sentence until the third day and further), *ampliare reum* (= to adjourn a trial). **II. n.** *comperendinatio* (or *-ātus, -ūs*).

remark, I. v.tr. 1, see OBSERVE, PERCEIVE; 2, = to express in words, etc., *dicĕre;* see SAY. **II. n.** 1, see OBSERVATION; 2, a — expressed, *dictum* (= anything that is said, an opinion), often merely by a pron. in the neuter gender, e.g. that — of Plato's is excellent, *praeclarum illud Platonis est;* or by the adj. in the neuter gender, e.g. I must first make a few introductory —s, *pauca ante dicenda sunt.* **remarkable,** adj. *notabilis, mirus* (= wonderful), *notandus, memorabilis* (= worth noticing), *memoratu dignus, commemorabilis, commemorandus* (= worth mentioning), *insignis* (= very —, lit. distinguished, of persons and things); *conspicuus* (=striking), *singularis* (= especial), *illustris* (= illustrious), *egregius, optimus* (= excellent); nothing happened that was very —, *nihil memorid dignum actum.* Adv. *mire, insigniter, singulariter, egregie, optime;* = very, *valde,* by superl. (e.g. — beautiful, *pulcherrimus);* see VERY.

remedy, n. 1, in medicine, *medicina* (lit. and fig.), *medicamen(tum)* (lit., e.g. *dare contra alqd), remedium* (= — against, for, lit. and fig.); to apply a — for a complaint, *morbo medicinam adhibēre;* 2, in gen., for counteracting an evil, *remedium,* for, to, against anything, *alcjs rei, ad* or *adversus alqd* (lit. and fig.), *medicina,* for, *alcjs rei* (lit. and fig.), *auxilium, subsidium,* against, *alcjs rei* (to effect a — in case of anyone being placed in a difficult position, in distress, etc.; *auxilium* also of persons being ill), †*lenimen* (= soothing —). **remedial,** adj. *quod ad remedium pertinet; salutaris;* — measures or legislation, perhaps *leges salutares.* **remediless,** adj. †*insanabilis.*

remember, v.tr. *meminisse alcjs, alcjs rei, de alqā re,* accus. and infin., rel. clause, or subj., *alqd* or *de alqā re recordari, alqd (memoriā) repetĕre, alcjs* or *alcjs rei memorem,* or *haud immemorem esse;* I don't — it, *memoriā delapsum est, e memoriā alqd mihi exiit, excidit, ex animo alqd effluxit, (re)fugit alqd meam memoriam;* he won't — it (implying intention), *nullam alcjs rei adhibet memoriam;* to — anyone, anything with a grateful heart, *grato animo alcjs nomen prosequi, gratissimum alcjs nomen retinēre, gratā memoriā prosequi alqd;* to — anyone with a kind feeling, *memoriam alcjs cum caritate et benevolentiā usurpare;* as far as I can —, *ut mea memoria est, quantum memini, nisi animus* or *memoria me fallit.* **remembrance,** n. *memoria, recordatio;* see RECOLLECTION, MEMORY.

remind, v.tr. *(ad)monēre, commonēre, commonefacĕre, alqm alcjs rei* or *de alqā re;* to — one to do anything, *(ad)hortari, (ad)monēre ut.* **reminiscence,** n. see REMEMBRANCE.

remit, v.tr. = to send back, *remittĕre;* to — money, etc., *mittĕre, emittĕre, condonare alci alqd, gratiam alcjs rei facĕre alci;* to — an oath, *jurisjurandi gratiam facĕre, solvĕre alqm sacramento;* to — a sum of money, *pecuniam creditam condonare* or *remittĕre, creditum condonare, debitum remittĕre alci;* to — taxes, *vectigalia omittĕre;* to — a part of a sum, *remittĕre alci de summā;* to — a punishment, *poenam remittĕre;* to — sins, *peccata* or *delicta alci ignoscĕre, peccata alci concedĕre.* **remiss,** adj. see CARELESS, NEGLIGENT. **remission,** n. *remissio* (of tribute, *tributi);* to seek —, *remissionem petĕre;* to seek — for the past, *veniam praeteritorum precari;* see PARDON, SIN. **remittance,** n. by *pecunia.*

remnant, n. see REMAINDER.

remodel, v.tr. see ALTER, RENEW.

remonstrance, n. *(ad)monitio, monitus,*

-ūs. **remonstrate,** v.intr. *alqm de alqā re (ad)monēre, commonēre,* or with *ut* or *ne,* etc. (= to warn), *agĕre cum alqo de alqā re* (in gen. = to treat, speak with anyone about).

remorse, n. *peccati dolor;* to feel —, *conscientiā (peccatorum) morderi, conscientiā animi (ex)cruciari, cruciari conscientiā scelerum suorum;* see also SORROW. **remorseless,** adj. *immisericors;* see PITILESS.

remote, adj. 1, *remotus, amotus, semotus, disjunctus* (= isolated), *longinquus* (= a long way off); 2, fig. *ab alqā re remotus, disjunctus, alienus;* see DISTANT. Adv. *remote, procul* (= far), *vix* (= hardly). **remoteness,** n. *longinquitas.*

remount, v.tr. anu intr. *equum iterum conscendĕre.*

remove, I. v.tr. *amovēre* (= to carry, to move away, further), *avehĕre* (in a cart, ships, by horses, etc.), *abducĕre* (living beings), also *deportare* (then = to — an exile under military escort, esp. also of bringing anything from the provinces), *asportare* (= to carry away), *demovēre, removēre, submovēre* (on one side, persons and things), *tollĕre, auferre* (= to take away, things; *tollĕre* also = to erase, e.g. *maculas), eluĕre* (= to wash out, e.g. *maculas), depellĕre* (= to drive away, e.g. a complaint, pains, etc.); *subportare* (= to carry to a place), *subtrahĕre* (e.g. baggage belonging to an army, *impedimenta);* to — the things (after a meal), *tollĕre, auferre* (e.g. *mensam);* to — anyone, *transducĕre* (e.g. *populum Albanum Romam), collocare in alqo loco* (= to assign another residence, e.g. *gentem Allobrogum in vestigiis hujus urbis), rescribĕre ad* with accus., *transcribĕre in* with accus. (= to place into another class, e.g. *peditem ad equum rescribĕre, equitum turmas in funditorum alas transcribĕre, alqm alii muneri praeficĕre* or *praeponĕre* (to another office, situation, etc.); to — anything to a distance, *amovēre, removēre, abducĕre, deducĕre, ablegare* (= to send anyone away, in order to get rid of him, under a pretence), *amandare, relegare* (anyone on account of some misdemeanour, the latter to a certain spot; but both imply something disgraceful), *amoliri* (anyone or anything, when it causes great difficulty), *avertĕre* (of what is unpleasant to the senses), *subducĕre, submovēre* (by degrees), *depellĕre, repellĕre, propulsare* (by force), *emovēre* (e.g. *multitudinem e foro,* esp. in Liv.). **II.** v.intr. 1, in gen. *se (a)movēre;* = to go away, *abire, discedĕre;* = to go out of one's sight, *ex oculis* or *e conspectu abire, e conspectu recedĕre;* from a place, *excedĕre, evadĕre, se subducĕre* (imperceptibly, also with the addition of *clam,* e.g. *de circulo);* 2,= to change the place of residence, *(e)migrare (ex) loco, demigrare, commigrare, transmigrare, de* or *ex loco,* to, *in locum* (= to emigrate to another place, *in alium locum* or *in alia loca), migrare, emigrare domo* or *e domo* (from a house), *secedĕre in locum* (in a spirit of rebellion), *proficisci.* **III.** n. *gradus, -ūs* (= step). **removal,** n. 1, in gen. *deportatio* (in gen., and in particular the — of an exile to the place of his destination, Jct.), *depulsio* (= the removing a pain, *doloris), amandatio* (= the sending anyone away, in order to get rid, etc.), *relegatio,* or rarely *ablegatio* (= banishment), *amotio* (= a complete removing, e.g. *omnis doloris), remotio* (the repelling, e.g. *criminis);* 2, to — to another place or house, *migratio, demigratio* (= emigration, Liv., Nep.; of a whole order of the plebeians, Liv.), *profectio* (= starting).

remunerate, v.tr. *referre, reddĕre alqd* (in gen.), *remunerari alqm* (in a good sense), for anything with, by, *(com)pensare alqd alqā re* (= to weigh one against the other, e.g. *beneficia bene-*

ficiis, merita beneficiis), rependĕre alqd alqâ re (= to weigh back, fig. = to repay, e.g. *damnum alqâ re*). **remuneration,** n. *remuneratio, compensatio;* for a —, *pretio* (for money); without any —, *sine pretio, gratis, gratuito;* see REWARD.

rend, v.tr. *(dis)scindĕre* (= to tear), *(dis)rumpĕre* (lit. and fig.), *(di)lacerare* (= to lacerate, lit. and fig.), *distrahĕre, divellĕre* (= to pull in pieces, lit. and fig.), *diripĕre* (= to tear asunder). **rending,** n. *disscidium, diruptio, distractio, laceratio.* **rent,** n. = tear, use verb.

render, v.tr. 1, *reddĕre, referre* (= to return, e.g. *gratias* = thanks), *praebĕre, dare, praestare, tribuĕre* (= to give); to — service, *operam alci navare;* to — an account, *rationem reddĕre or referre;* 2, = to make, *facĕre, efficĕre, reddĕre,* or by special verbs, e.g. *augēre* (= to — greater), *minuĕre* (= to — less); 3, see TRANSLATE. **render up,** v.tr. see SURRENDER. **rendering,** n. 1, by verb; 2, see TRANSLATION.

rendezvous, n. *constitutum* (= an appointment made), *locus ad conveniendum* (= the place appointed for the —); to appoint a — with, *tempus locumque constituĕre cum algo.*

renegade, n. *qui sacra patria deserit or deseruit, apostăta* (Eccl.); = a deserter, *is qui deficit, desciscit ab algo, transfuga,* m. and f.

renew, v.tr. *(re)novare;* = to restore, to repair, *reconcinnare, reficĕre* (more particularly by rebuilding); = to begin afresh, to repeat, *renovare, renovare et instaurare, instaurare (de integro), integrare, redintegrare* (= to begin quite from the beginning), *repetĕre* (= to repeat), *iterare* (= to do a second time), *refricare* (= to excite again), *referre* (= to bring back), *reconciliare (pacem, gratiam,* etc.); to — the war, *bellum renovare, redintegrare, de integro instaurare, rebellare, rebellionem facĕre, bellum reparare, restituĕre* (two foregoing only of a conquered nation, without any odious meaning); to — the friendship, *amicitiam renovare,* with anyone, *se restituĕre in alcjs amicitiam;* to — the remembrance of anything in one's mind, *memoriâ alqd repetĕre.* **renewable,** adj. *qui(quae,quod) renovari potest.* **renewal,** n. *renovatio, instauratio, redintegratio;* of a war, *rebellio.*

renounce, v.tr. *renuntiare alqd* or (post class.) *alci rei, se alqâ re abdicare* (e.g. *magistratu), alqm or alqd ejurare, re(j)icĕre, repudiare* (= to reject), *remittĕre alqd* (that is, to let it go), *decedĕre or desistĕre alqâ re or de alqâ re* (= to stand away from); to — an opinion, *sententiâ or de sententiâ decedĕre;* to — your right, *de jure suo cedĕre or decedĕre, jus demittĕre or remittĕre;* to — honour and glory, *honorem et gloriam ab-(j)icĕre.* **renunciation,** n. *cessio* (= the yielding of a thing to another), *repudiatio, rejectio.*

renovate, v.tr. see RENEW. **renovation,** n. see RENEWAL.

renown, n. *fama* (chiefly in a good sense), *gloria, laus, nomen, claritas, claritudo.* **renowned,** adj. *clarus, illustris;* see CELEBRATED, FAMED, FAMOUS.

rent, I. n. 1, = profits derived annually from lands, etc., *quaestus, -ûs* (= what we can gain by anything), *reditus, -ûs, fructus, -ûs* (= profit), *vectigal* (= tax, then of private rent), *merces, -ēdis,* f. (= the — which the property brings in); 2, — of a house, *merces habitationis, habitatio;* what — does he pay? *quanti habitat?* to pay much —, *magni habitare.* **II.** v.tr. 1, to let out, *locare;* 2, = to hire, *conducĕre, redimĕre;* cheaply, *parvo conducĕre, bene redimĕre;* dear, *magno conducĕre, male redimere.* **rental,** n. see RENT, I.

reobtain, v.tr. *recipĕre, reciperare.*

reopen, I. v.tr. *iterum recludĕre* (in gen). **II.** v.intr. *of* wounds, *recrudescĕre* (also fig.).

repair, I. v.tr. *reficĕre, reparare, (re)sarcire, restituĕre, restaurare, reconcinnare.* **II.** n. *to* keep in good —, *alqd sartum tectum tueri.* **repairs,** pl. use verb REPAIR.

repair, v.intr. *se alqo conferre or recipĕre;* see also GO.

reparation, n. see INDEMNIFICATION, SATISFACTION.

repartee, n. perhaps *alqd acute responsum,* or *quod alqd salsi or salis habet;* see WIT.

repast, n. see MEAL.

repay, v.tr. *reddĕre, referre, reponĕre, solvĕre;* to — anyone what is due, *alci satisfacĕre, alci debitum or pecuniam debitam solvĕre;* fig. *pensare or compensare alqd alqâ re, rependĕre alqd alqâ re* (e.g. *damnum alqâ re*); with the same coin, *par pari referre;* see PAY. **repayment,** n. *solutio (pecuniae alci creditae),* or by verb.

repeal, I. v.tr. *rescindĕre* (e.g. a decree, a will), *tollĕre* (= to do away with), *abolēre* (= to abolish), *abrogare* (= a law, a decree, also a power), *derogare legi or alqd de lege* (partly), *obrogare legi* (= to substitute one law partially for another). **II.** n. *abrogatio, derogatio, obrogatio.*

repeat, v.tr. 1, *repetĕre* (in the widest sense), *iterare* (= to do, to say a second time, e.g. *saepe eadem), redintegrare* (= to do, bring forward, say quite afresh), *retractare* (= to go through again what has been learnt, read), *decantare* (gen. in bad sense, = to keep repeating); 2, = to recite, of lessons, etc., perhaps *alqd memoriâ pronuntiare;* to — with the same words, *alqd iisdem verbis reddĕre.* **repeated,** adj. *repetitus, iteratus.* Adv. *iterum atque iterum, saepenumero, etiam atque etiam, identidem.* **repeater,** n. a watch, *horologium sonis tempus indicans.* **repetition,** n. 1, *repetitio, iteratio, redintegratio* (all three e.g. *verbi); —* of the same word at the end of a sentence (in rhetoric), *conversio, regressio* (of the same words in different clauses, Quint.); 2, of a lesson, see REPEAT, 2.

repel, v.tr. *repellĕre, propulsare* (= to drive away by force), *re(j)icĕre* (= to throw back), *deterrēre* (= to deter, e.g. *verberibus), fugare* (= to put to flight); on an accusation, *culpam a se amovēre, crimen dissolvĕre or diluĕre, suspicionem a se propulsare.*

repent, I. v.intr. *mores suos mutare, in viam redire, ad virtutem redire or revocari, ad bonam frugem se recipĕre.* **II.** v.tr. I —, *paenitet me alcjs rei,* or with infin., or with *quod* and subj., *subpaenitet me alcjs facti* (a little). **repentance,** n. *paenitentia* (in gen.). **repentant,** adj. *paenitens.*

repertory, n. *thesaurus.*

repetition, n. see REPEAT.

repine, v.intr. to — at, *(con)queri alqd or de alqâ re.* **repining,** n. *maeror* (= sorrow), *querēla* (= complaint).

replace, v.tr. 1, = to put back, *reponĕre;* 2, to put in place of, *alqm alci, alqd alci rei substituĕre, alqm in alcjs locum sufficĕre* (= to elect in place of another magistrate).

replant, v.tr. *reserĕre.*

replenish, v.tr. *implēre* (in gen. what is empty, hollow), *explēre* (so that no space remains empty), *complēre* (= to fill quite full), *replēre* (= to fill to the brim), *opplēre* (= to cover a surface by filling up; also to fill to the top, so that it will not hold any more).

replete, adj. see FULL. **repletion,** n. *satietas.*

reply, I, v.intr. *respondēre* (to a thing, *alci rei*); to — to a charge, *criminibus respondēre, se defendēre,* or *purgare;* to — by letter, *rescribēre;* but I —, simply *ego autem* or *ego vero.* **II.** n. *responsio, responsum* (in gen.), *excusatio, defensio, purgatio* (to a charge), *oraculum, sors* (of an oracle).

report, I. v.tr. *nuntiare* (= to announce), *renuntiare* (= to send back information, both *alci alqd*), *certiorem alqm facēre de alqā re* (= to inform), *afferre, deferre, referre ad alqm de alqā re* (= to give information, etc., more particularly to an authority), *per lit(t)eras significare* (= to inform in writing), *(e)narrare* (in gen. = to relate), *memoriae tradēre* or *prodēre; ferre, perhibēre* (= to say); *renuntiare alci* (in consequence of an order to that effect, or in reply to information received); it is —ed, *dicitur, dicuntur,* etc., with personal subj., or simply *prodēre* (of the historian); to — the whole proceedings, *omnem rem ordine enarrare, ordine edocēre omnia* (orally), *omnia perscribēre* (in writing). **II.** n. 1, *relatio* (= formal — to the senate; in gen. sense post Aug.), *narratio* (= narration), *rei gestae expositio, renuntiatio* (of an ambassador), *lit(t)erae* (in the form of a letter); 2, = rumour, *fama, rumor, auditio;* I know it by —, *auditu illud accepi;* 3, = noise, *fragor, crepitus, -ūs;* see NOISE. **reporter,** n. *qui defert ad alqm* (= who makes a report to anyone), *auctor rerum* (= voucher, authority), *notarius* (= shorthand writer, Plin. Min.).

repose, I. v.tr. *reponēre.* **II.** v.intr. *quiescēre.* **III.** n. *quies, -ētis,* f.; see REST. **repository,** n. *receptaculum;* see RECEPTACLE.

reprehend, v.tr. *reprehendēre;* see REBUKE. **reprehensible,** adj. *culpā dignus, reprehendus, vituperabilis, vituperandus.* **reprehension,** n. *reprehensio, vituperatio, culpa.*

represent, v.tr. 1, *repraesentare* (= to place clearly before one's eyes, Plin.), *exprimēre, (ef)fingēre* (= to express, picture, of the plastic art), *pingēre, depingēre* (= to paint, of the painter), *adumbrare* (= to sketch), *imitari,* + *simulare* (= to imitate), *indicare, significare* (= to indicate); 2, = to describe in words, *(de)pingēre* (= to paint, of the painter; then also of the orator, etc., = to picture, illustrate), *(ef)fingēre* (of the sculptor, also of the orator, writer); *eloqui* (= to utter, of the speaker, e.g. *cogitata*), *dicendo effingēre, alcjs rei imaginem exponēre, adumbrare alqd* or *speciem et formam alcjs rei* (= to shade, sketch, of the painter and speaker), *describēre* (= to describe in its characteristic features); to — anyone in a bad, wrong light, *deformare alqm* (Cic.); to — anything in a clear, lively manner, *alqd paene sub aspectum sub(j)icēre, alqd sub oculos sub(j)icēre* (= to show by reasoning, *alqm de alqā re monēre* or with *ut* or *ne* (= to warn), *alqm alqd docēre* (= to inform), *ostendēre alci alqd,* or with accus. and infin. (= to show in words), *memorare* with accus. and infin. (= to mention); to — the advantage of, *alqm docēre quanta sit alcjs rei utilitas;* 3, = to show by action, *agēre;* to — a person, *alcjs partes agēre, alcjs personam induēre* or *suscipēre* or *gerēre* (all both on the stage and in daily life); to — a person of rank, *nobilem virum agēre;* to — a drama, *fabulam dare;* 4, = to supply the place of another, to — one's country, *gerēre personam civitatis atque ejus decus et dignitatem sustinēre.* **representation,** n. 1, = the act of describing, by the verb; 2, = that which exhibits by resemblance, image; see IMAGE, LIKENESS, PICTURE; 3, = an exhibition of the form of a thing, *repraesentatio* (t.t. of the elder Pliny); 4, of a play, *actio* (= the act), *fabula* (= the play); 5, = exhibition of a character in a play, by *agēre;* see PART; 6, = verbal description, *expli-*

catio, descriptio (in gen. in words, *descriptio* most particularly = a characteristic —), *adumbratio* (= sketch), *narratio* (of the state of things, how a matter stands, in a speech), *oratio, sermo* (= diction); 7, in politics, by the verb; 8, = the standing in the place of another, by circumloc. (e.g. by *alienā vice fungi,* or by *senatores a civibus delecti).* **representative, I.** adj. by *vice alcjs* or *officio;* — government, *civitas per quosdam a civibus delectos cives administrata.* **II.** n. *vicarius* (= substitute, deputy), *procurator;* a parliamentary —, *senator suffragiis civium delectus.*

repress, v.tr. *opprimēre, comprimēre* (e.g. *tumultum*).

reprieve, I. v.tr. 1, = to respite after sentence of death, perhaps by *vitam alci prorogare;* 2, fig. = to relieve for a time from suffering, by *differre, proferre* (= to postpone), *prolatare* (= to delay), *prorogare* (= to delay, put off). **II.** n. by *temporis intervallum, spatium* (= space of time, period in gen.), *prolatio* (= the act of —), *mora* (= delay).

reprimand, I. v.tr. *alqm reprehendēre de* or *in alqā re, alqm vituperare de alqā re, alqm objurgare.* **II.** n. *reprehensio, vituperatio, objurgatio* (= blame), *convicium* (= scolding); see BLAME.

reprint, I. v.tr. a book, *librum denuo typis exscribendum curare.* **II.** n. see EDITION.

reprisal, n. 1, see RETALIATION; 2, —s, *vis vi repulsa;* to make —s, *vim vi repellēre, par pari referre.*

reproach, I. n. as act, *maledictio* (rare), *exprobatio, animadversio;* the actual —, *opprobrium* (not in Cic. or Caes.); *probrum, maledictum, convicium, vox contumeliosa, verbum contumeliosum, contumelia.* **II.** v.tr. *convicium facēre, alqm increpitare* or *incusare, in alqm invehi, alci maledicēre, alqd alci ob(j)icēre, objectare;* see REPROVE, BLAME, REVILE. **reproachful,** adj. *contumeliosus* (= abusive), or by verb. Adv. *contumeliose,* or by verb.

reprobate, I. adj. *perditus* (= lost to virtue or grace), *profligatus* (= morally ruined), comb. *profligatus et perditus, damnatus* (lit. = condemned; hence meton. = criminal, e.g. *quis te miserior? quis te damnatior?), sceleratus, scelerosus* (= burdened with crime). **II.** n. *homo perditus,* etc. **reprobation,** n. 1, see CONDEMNATION; 2, Eccl. *damnatio, reprobatio.*

reproduce, v.tr. *denuo generare* or *ferre;* to — a piece, *fabulam iterum referre* (Ter.). **reproduction,** n., **reproductive,** adj. by verb.

reproof, n. as act, or actual —, *vituperatio, culpa, castigatio, reprehensio, objurgatio, contumelia, animadversio, exprobatio;* to be a ground of —, *opprobrio* or *crimini esse alci;* to be open to the — of treachery, *in (summā) perfidiae infamiā esse;* see BLAME. **reprove,** v.tr. *alqm vituperare, reprehendēre, exprobrare alci alqd* or *de alqā re, objurgare alqm de alqā re, alqm increpare, increpitare, incusare;* to — severely, *alqm graviter accusare;* to make a thing a ground to —, *crimini dare alci alqd, vitio dare* or *vertēre alci alqd.* **reprover,** n. *reprehensor, vituperator, objurgator, castigator.*

reptile, n. *animal reptans,* or, where possible, by *serpens* (= serpent).

republic, n. *civitas libera et sui juris, respublica libera,* in the context also merely *respublica* (= a free constitution and a state which has such). **republican, I.** adj. generally by the genit. *reipublicae liberae* or simply *reipublicae* (e.g. a — government, *reipublicae (liberae) forma);*

to give a country a — constitution, *reipublicae formam civitati dare, a regis dominatione in libertatem populi vindicare rempublicam* (if the State was a monarchy before). **II.** n. *reipublicae liberae civis* (= citizen of a republic), *reipublicae liberae studiosus, communis libertatis propugnator* (= one who is or speaks in favour of a — government).

republish, v.tr. *librum denuo edĕre.* **republication,** n. **1,** as act, use verb; **2,** the book itself, *liber (denuo editum).*

repudiate, v.tr. see REJECT. **repudiation,** n. *repudiatio* (in gen., but rare); of a son, *abdicatio filii* (= disowning and disinheriting); *divortium, repudium* (of a wife); see REJECTION.

repugnant, adj. *pugnans, repugnans* (of things), *diversus* (= quite contrary), *aversus, alienus ab algâ re, alci rei contrarius, odiosus* (= hateful); see CONTRARY. **repugnance,** n. *repugnantia rerum* (= incompatibility), *odium* (= hatred); to feel —, *abhorrēre ab algâ re, algd fastidire, spernĕre, aspernari.*

repulse, I. v.tr. *repellĕre* (= to drive back), from, etc., *ab,* etc., *propulsare* (away), *re(j)icĕre* (= to throw back). **II. n. 1,** by the verbs; of a candidate, *repulsa;* **2,** see REFUSAL. **repulsive,** adj. *odiosus* (= hateful), *putidus* (= affected), *intolerabilis* (= unbearable); see DISGUSTING.

repurchase, v.tr. *redimĕre.*

reputable, adj. see RESPECTABLE.

reputation, n. *bona fama,* generally merely *fama, bona existimatio,* in the context simply *existimatio, gloria* (= glory), *laus* (= praise), *nomen* (= name), *honor* (= esteem); bad —, *mala fama, infamia.* **repute,** n. see REPUTATION; to be in good —, *bene audire;* to be in bad —, *mala audire, in infamiâ esse, infamem esse, in invidiâ esse, invidiam habēre.* **reputed,** adj. *qui (quae, quod) dicitur, fertur.*

request, I. n. *preces, -um* (= the act and the thing itself), *rogatus, -ûs* (only in ablat. sing.), *rogatio* (as act), *supplicium* (= humble —, praise to God), *postulatio* (= urgent —, demand); at your —, *te petente, te auctore;* at my —, *rogatu meo, a me rogatus;* what is your —? *quid petis* ? **II.** v.tr. *precari* (absolute), anything of anyone, *algd ab algo, alqm ut,* etc., *orare, rogare,* anything of anyone, *alqm alqd* (= to apply for), *algd petĕre, poscĕre* (of a formal application, = to demand), *contendĕre ut* (urgently, = to insist), *flagitare, efflagitare* (violently, *algd ab algo*), *precibus exposcĕre* (= to violently demand, anything, *algd,* e.g. *pacem*), *deprecari* (= to — on behalf of, anything, *algd*), *implorare* (= to implore anyone, *alqm;* anything, *algd*), *supplicare;* anyone on behalf of, *alci pro algâ re, petĕre, postulare suppliciter;* anything of anyone, *algd ab algo, orare alqm supplicibus verbis, orare or rogare alqm suppliciter* (all = humbly, on one's knees); stronger by comb. *rogare atque orare, petĕre et contendĕre, orare obtestarique, orare atque obsecrare, implorare atque obtestari, obsecrare atque obtestari, obtestari atque obsecrare, precari atque orare, petĕre ac deprecari;* = to invite, *invitare, vocare.*

requiem, n. *missa defunctorum* (= mass for the dead, Eccl.).

require, v.tr. *poscĕre, postulare, requirĕre, desiderare* (= to demand, to consider necessary), (= to need, *esse* with genit. of a noun along with an adj., e.g. *multi laboris est), egēre algâ re, ferre* (= to bring about necessity), *imperare,* from anyone, *alci* (= to command), *exigĕre* (= to exact, e.g. *vehicula);* to be —d, *opus esse;* if circumstances —, *si res or tempus postulat, cum res postulabit, si res cogit;* as time may —, *si tempus postulaverit, pro rerum statu or condicione.*

requirement, n. *postulatio, postulatum,* or by verbs. **requisite, I.** adj. *necessarius;* to be —, *necessarium esse, opus esse* (= to be necessary), *requiri, desiderari* (of what would be missed). **II.** n. *necessitas* (= necessity), *usus, -ûs* (= use), *res necessaria;* a principal — for anything, *res maxima necessaria ad algd;* the first — is that, etc., *primum est, ut,* etc. **requisition,** n. *petitio, rogatio, imperatum, quod imperatur.*

requite, v.tr. *reddĕre, referre* (= to give back), *algd algâ re compensare* or *rependĕre;* to — like for like, *par pari referre.* **requital,** n. use verb.

rescind, v.tr. *rescindĕre, abrogare, tollĕre, abolēre, legi algd derogare* (= to partly —), *obrogare* (= to — by substitution of another law); see REPEAL, ABOLISH.

rescript, n. *responsio, responsum* (= answer in gen.; the former, the act; the latter, the contents of the answer), *sententia* (= a lawyer's decision), *decretum* (= decree), *res judicata* (= decision arrived at in reference to a matter), *rescriptum* (of the emperor, prince, etc.), *codicilli* (= Ministerial decree, order of the Cabinet, Imperial Rome).

rescue, I. v.tr. *liberare algâ re* or *ab algâ re, exsolvĕre algâ re, servare ex algâ re* (e.g. *periculo* or *ex periculo, alqm alci rei* or *ab, ex, de algâ re eripĕre;* to — one's country from slavery, *patriam in libertatem vindicare.* **II.** n. *liberatio,* or by circumloc. with *(con)servare.*

research, n. *eruditio* (= learning), *investigatio* or *cognitio* (rerum, = inquiry); a man of much —, *vir eruditissimus.*

resemblance, n. *similitudo, convenientia, congruentia, analogia* (in reference to words and ideas, in Cic., written in Greek ἀναλογία, or rendered by *proportio), congruentia morum* (in manners); — with, etc., *similitudo* with genit. (e.g. *morborum, animi).* **resemble,** v.tr. *similem esse* with genit. or dat., *ad similitudinem alcjs rei accedĕre* (instead of which we also find *prope, propius,* = nearer; *proxime,* = nearest), *accedĕre ad algd* (of interior and exterior likeness), *facie alcjs similem esse, os vultumque alcjs referre* (as regards the countenance and the looks), *mores alcjs referre* (in character).

resent, v.tr. *aegre* or *moleste ferre, in malam partem accipĕre.* **resentful,** adj. *iracundus, iratus* (= angry). Adv. *iracunde.* **resentment,** n. *ira, iracundia, stomachus.*

reservation, n. *condicio, exceptio;* with this —, that, etc., *hac lege* or *hac condicione* or *cum hac exceptione ut, his exceptis.* **reserve, I.** v.tr. *retinēre* (= to keep back), *algd excipĕre* (= to except), *algd reservare, algd reponĕre* (= to store up). **II.** n. **1,** in gen., *copia;* **2,** = troops, *subsidia, -orum, copiae subsidiariae, cohortes subsidiariae, (milites) subsidiarii* (in gen.); to keep in —, lit. *in subsidio ponĕre* or *collocare,* fig. *algd recondĕre;* **3,** see RESERVATION; **4,** in manners, *verecundia* (= bashfulness), *modestia* (= modesty), *taciturnitas* (= silence), *cautio* (= caution); without —, *aperte, simpliciter* (= straightforwardly, openly), *sincere, libere, ingenue* (= freely). **reserved,** adj. *taciturnus* (= taciturn), *occultus, tectus* (= secret), comb. *occultus et tectus, modestus* (= modest), *verecundus* (= bashful), *cautus* (= cautious), towards anyone, *tectus ad alqm.* **reservoir,** n. *lacus, -ûs* (= a large receptacle for water, lake), *castellum* (= — of an aqueduct), *cisterna* (= a hollow place under ground for holding rain-water, Plin.), *piscina* (= pond), *aquae receptaculum* (Vitr.).

reside, v.intr. **1,** *habitare (locum, in loco, apud alqm,* etc.), *sedem* or *sedem ac domicilium habēre algo loco;* see LIVE; **2,** fig. *esse* or *versari* *in alqâ re, alci inesse rei.* **residence,** n. 1, *habitatio* (= the residing); if for a time, *mansio, commoratio;* 2, *domus, -ûs,* f. (irreg.), *domicilium, aedes, -ium,* f. (= house). **resident,** n. 1, by verbs ; 2, = a minister at a foreign court, perhaps *procurator rerum* or *legatus.*

residue, n. *pecunia residua, quod residuum* or *reliquum est.* **residuary,** adj. — legatee, *heres, -edis,* m. and f.

resign, v.tr. 1, an office, *deponère (provinciam, dictaturam,* etc.), of an officer of state, *abdicare se magistratu,* (a consul) *consulatu,* (a dictator) *dictaturâ,* etc. ; also *abdicare magistratum (consulatum), abire magistratu (consulatu,* etc.), *decedère (provinciâ* or *ex* or *de provinciâ,* = to retire after the expiration of the term of office) ; 2, = to give up, *(con)cedère, deponère, omittère ;* to — oneself to, to be —ed, *alqd aequo animo ferre* or *pati, se ad alqd submittère.* **resignation,** n. 1, *abdicatio, ejuratio (dictaturae,* etc.); 2, morally, *animus submissus* or *demissus* (in opp. to *animus elatus*).

resin, n. *rēsīna* (Plin.). **resinous,** adj. *resinaceus, resinosus* (Plin.).

resist, v.tr. *alci resistère, obstare, repugnare, obsistère, adversari, obniti;* to — the enemy, *hostibus resistère, hosti se opponère;* to — bravely, *fortiter repugnare* or *resistère ;* anyone's request, *preces alcjs respuère* or *re(j)icère* or *repudiare.* **resistance,** n. *pugna, certamen* (= contest, fight), *defensio* (= defence) ; to render —, *resistère* (a person or thing, with arms or in words), *repugnare* (see above), *se defendère* (in battle) ; to prepare for —, *ad resistendum se parare.* **resistless,** adj. and adv. *cui nullo modo resisti potest.*

resolute, adj. *fortis* (= brave), *firmus, constans, stabilis, obstinatus, obfirmatus, promptus* (= ready), *gravis* (= serious). Adv. *fortiter, praesenti animo, firme, firmiter, constanter, obstinate, graviter.* **resoluteness,** n. *animi praesentia ;* see Resolution, 2. **resolution,** n. 1, = dissolution, *(dis)solutio, dissipatio* (of a whole into parts), *explicatio* (= explanation) ; 2, = determination, as quality, *constantia, stabilitas, firmitas, firmitudo, gravitas, obstinatio ;* 3, = purpose, *sententia, consilium, propositum ;* 4, — of a deliberative body, *sententia, decretum, scitum* (of a popular assembly, esp. *scitum plebis* or *plebiscitum*). **resolve,** v.intr. *decernère* (of magistrates, then in gen.), *consilium capère ; statuère, constituère ; destinare, animo proponère* (in one's own mind); *censère, placet alci* (of the senate); *sciscère, jubère,* comb. *sciscère jubèreque* (= to make a law, decree, of the people).

resonant, adj. *resonans.*

resort, I. v.intr. *locum celebrare, frequentare, ad locum ventitare, se conferre, commeare ;* = to use, *uti ;* to — to extremes, *ad extrema decurrère.* **II.** n. 1, *conveniendi locus, locus ubi conveniunt;* 2, = recourse, use verb.

resound, v.intr. *resonare, vocem reddère* or *remittère.*

resource, n. *auxilium, subsidium, praesidium, adjumentum.* **resources,** n. = means for an object, *facultates, opes,* pl., *pecunia* (= money), *bona, -orum* (= goods), *res familiaris* (= private property), *fortunae* (= prosperous condition), *patrimonium* (= inheritance), *census, -ûs* (= property legally valued).

respect, I. v.tr. 1, *alqm suspicère, verēri* (= to fear), *reverēri* (ante and post class.); *colère, observare, magni aestimare ;* 2, = to pay attention to, *alcjs rationem habère, alci morem gerère ;* 3, = to relate ; see Relate, 2. **II.** n. *observantia* (= esteem), *reverentia* (= reverence), *honor* (= esteem); to have, feel — for, *alqm verēri ;* in every

—, *omnio, ab omni parte, omni ex parte, in omni genere, omnibus rebus ;* in — to, *de alqâ re ;* see Regard, II. **respectable,** adj. *honestus, spectatus* (= tried), *bene moratus* (= moral), *vir bonae existimationis.* Adv. *honeste, bene.* **respectability,** n. *dignitas, honestas.* **respectful,** adj. *observans, venerabundus.* Adv. *reverenter* (Plin.). **respecting,** adj. *de* with abl. ; see About. **respective,** adj. and adv. *proprius, suus,* etc. (e.g. our — brothers, *nostri fratres*), or by *quisque* (e.g. each has his — duties, *sua cuique sunt officia*); by *alter . . . alter, hic . . . ille.*

respire, v.intr. *respirare ;* see Breathe. **respiration,** n. *respiratio, respiratus, -ûs, spiritus, -ûs.* **respiratory,** adj. *qui (quae, quod) ad respiratum pertinet ;* — organs, *pulmones,* pl. (= lungs).

respite, n. and v.tr. see Reprieve.

resplendent, adj. *splendidus ;* see Bright.

respond, v.intr., **response,** n. see Answer. **respondent,** n. *reus* (in a criminal trial), *is unde petitur* (in a civil) ; see Defendant. **responsible,** adj. by *alci ratio reddenda est;* to be —, *alqd praestare* (= to guarantee for) ; to make oneself — for anyone, *alqd in se recipère.* **responsibility,** n. by the adj. **responsive,** adj. *apertus* (= open), by circumloc. (e.g. *qui amorem pro amore reddit,* — to affection ; not —, *taciturnus*) ; see also Frank.

rest, I. n. 1, = quiet, *tranquillitas, (re)quies, -ētis,* f., *otium,* †*pax ;* 2, see Prop. **II.** v.intr. 1, *(con)quiescère* (in gen.) ; = to sleep, *(con)quiescère, requiescère, quieti se dare* or *tradère, acquiescère, cessare* (= to be unemployed) ; 2, to — upon, *alqâ re (in)niti, suffulciri ;* fig. *in alqâ re niti, in alqo* or *alqâ re positum,* or *situm esse ;* see Depend. **III.** v.tr. see Prop, Support. **resting-place,** n. *tranquillus ad quietem locus* (from the troubles of life), *deversorium* (= inn, also fig.), *sepulcrum* (= grave). **restive,** adj. *contumax.* **restless,** adj. *inquietus, commotus, sollicitus* (= anxious), *turbidus, turbulentus, tumultuosus* (of the sea, etc.). Adv. use adj. **restlessness,** n. *inquies, -ētis* (Plin.), *commotio* (e.g. *animi,* = — of mind), *sollicitudo.*

rest, n. = remainder, *quod restat, reliquum, residuum.* **restitution,** n. use verb. **restoration,** n. *refectio, reconciliatio* (e.g. *gratiae*), or by verb. **restorative,** adj. and n. *medicina.* **restore,** v.tr. *restituère, reficère* (in gen.), *reducère* (= to bring back, e.g. *regem*), *reddère* (= to give back) ; to — to health, *sanare, sanum facère, sanitatem alci restituère ;* see Renew. **restorer,** n. *restitutor, reconciliator* (e.g. *gratiae*).

restrain, v.tr. *reprehendère* (= to seize behind), *retrahère* (= to pull back, fig. to detain anyone against his will), *tenère* (lit. = to hold in one's hand), *retinère* (= to keep back a person or thing, e.g. *naves tempestatibus retinentur*), *continère* (= to hold fast on all sides), *retardare* (= to retard the progress of a person or thing, lit. and fig.), *arcère alqm* or *alqd* (= to refuse access to a person or thing), *cohibère* (= to hinder the free motion of a person or thing, hence fig. to check, e.g. *iram*), *comprimère* (lit. = to press together, hence fig. violently to suppress, put a stop to, actions, intentions, passion), *reprimère, supprimère* (= to repress, hence = violently to check, e.g. *fletum*), *refrenare* (= to bridle), *circumscribère* (= to restrict), *(de)finire* (= to set bounds to) ; to — anyone from, by *cohibère alqd ab alqâ re, defendère alqd* or *alqm ab alqâ re, arcère alqm* (*ab*) *alqâ re* (e.g. *hostes Galliâ, homines ab injuriâ poena arcet*), *alqm revocare ab alqâ re* (e.g. *a scelere*); to — oneself, *se tenère, se continère* (= to check oneself), *se cohibère,* (e.g. in affliction). **restraint,** n. *moderatio,*

..mperatio, modestia, continentia (opp. _luxuria_), _impedimentum, mora_ (= hindrance), _modus_ (= measure).

restrict, v.tr. _coercēre, reprimēre, circumscribere, (de)finire, restringere;_ see RESTRAIN. **restriction,** n. see RESTRAINT, LIMIT. **restrictive,** n. _qui (quae, quod) coercit._

result, I. v.intr. _oriri_ (in gen.), _fieri, evenire, evadēre_ (= to turn out), _consequi (alqd or ut), proficisci, nasci, gigni, ex(s)istēre, ex alqd re._ **II.** n. _exitus, -ūs, eventus, -ūs, effectus, -ūs, consequentia;_ to lead to a —, _exitum habēre;_ general —, _summa._

resume, v.tr. see RECOMMENCE. **resumption,** n. use verb.

resurrection, n. *a morte ad vitam revocatio, resurrectio_ (Eccl.).

resuscitate, v.tr. †_resuscitare, alqm ab inferis excitare;_ see REVIVE.

retail, v.tr. _divendēre, distrahēre._ **retaildealer,** n. _propōla._

retain, v.tr. _tenēre, retinēre, obtinēre, (con)servare._ **retainer,** n. 1, _cliens_ (= client), _unus e suis_ (= one of a bodyguard); 2, = fee, _ärr(h)a(bo)._

retake, v.tr. _reciperare, recipēre;_ to — from, _alqd alci auferre._

retaliate, v.tr. _par pari referre._ **retaliation,** n. use verb.

retard, v.tr. _(re)morari, (re)tardare_ (all of a person or thing, and of the person or thing that is the cause), _detinēre_ (a person or thing, e.g. _naves tempestatibus detinebantur), producēre, differre, proferre_ (= to protract); to — from one day to the other, _alqd procrastinare._

retire, v.intr. _recedēre_ (persons and things), _concedēre, abcedēre, excedēre, secedēre_ (all with _a,_ etc.), _decedēre de_ or _ex (provinciā,_ etc., of a magistrate), _se subtrahēre_ (imperceptibly), _recedēre in otium, se removēre a negotiis publicis, se subtrahēre a curiā et ab omni parte reipublicae_ (from public business); to — to a place, _algo recedēre, secedēre, se referre_ (= to go back), _se abdēre in alqm locum_ (= to conceal oneself from anything), _recedēre ab,_ etc. (in gen.), _se recipēre ab,_ etc., _se removēre ab,_ etc., _se retrahēre ab alqd re_ (e.g. from a banquet, _a convivio_). **retired,** adj. _secretus, remotus, reductus, solitarius;_ a — life, _vita umbratilis._ **retirement,** n. _solitudo, vita a rebus publicis remota, vita otiosa, umbratilis, privata ac quieta._ **retiring,** adj. see MODEST.

retort, I. v. _regerēre alqd alci._ **II.** n. _quod alqs alci regerit;_ see REPLY.

retrace, v.tr. = to seek again, _alqd ab alqd re repetēre;_ to — one's footsteps, _pedem referre;_ see RETURN.

retreat, I. n. 1, _reditus, -ūs_ (= return), _receptus, -ūs_ (of soldiers, etc.), _fuga_ (= flight); 2, = place of refuge; see REFUGE. **II.** v.intr. _se recipēre_ (of soldiers and others), _pedem_ or _gradum referre_ (in fighting), _castra referre_ (e.g. _in tutiora loca,_ of the general), _exercitum_ or _copias reducēre algo_ (e.g. _in castra, ad mare_).

retrench, v.tr. _sumptus minuēre, circumcidēre, contrahēre._ **retrenchment,** n. use verb.

retribution, n. _poena_ (= punishment). **retributive,** adj. _pro poenā_ (= in place of punishment).

retrieve, v.tr. see RECOVER. **retriever,** n. _canis._

retrograde, I. v.intr. 1, = to retire, _se recipēre, pedem referre;_ 2, = to grow worse, _in pejus mutari, deteriorem fieri._ **II.** adj. _pejor, deterior_ (=

wors(/); a — movement, use _retro_ (= backwards)- **retrogression,** n. _recessus, -ūs, regressus, -ūs._

retrospect, n. _respectus, -ūs_ (lit. = looking back), _(praeteritorum) memoria._ **retrospective,** adj. _qui (quae, quod) alqd respicit;_ to have a — effect, _ad praeterita pertinēre._ Adv. by _retro._

return, I. v.intr. _reverti_ (in the perfect and pluperfect, _reverti, reverteram,_ seldom _reversus sum,_ etc.; but as part. _reversus_ with active meaning), _redire_ (of persons and things, e.g. of ships, rivers), _reducem esse_ (of persons and things, e.g. ships, etc.), _revenire_ (e.g. _domum), remeare_ (= to wander back), _alqd repetēre_ (= to seek again); _recurrēre, revolare_ (= to fly back). **II.** v.tr. _reddēre, restituēre._ **III.** n. 1, = going back, _reditus, -ūs, regressus, -ūs, reversio_ (before a journey is finished); 2, formal —, _renuntiatio, professio;_ to make a —, _renuntiare, profiteri;_ 3, = giving back, by verb, see II.; 4, see PROFIT, INCOME. **returned,** adj. _redux._

reunite, v.tr. 1, lit. _iterum conjungēre;_ see UNITE; 2, fig. _reconciliare alqm cum alqo_ or _alci._ **reunion,** n. _reconciliatio_ (= reconciliation); see also ASSEMBLY.

reveal, v.tr. _patefacēre, manifestum reddēre, aperire, retegēre_ (rare before Aug.), _(in medium_ or _lucem) proferre, evulgare, divulgare;_ see DISCLOSE, BETRAY, PUBLISH. **revelation,** n. _patefactio,_ or by verb; Eccl. _revelatio,_ the book of —, _Apocalypsis._

revel, I. v.intr. 1, _comis(s)ari;_ 2, see DELIGHT. **II.** n. and **revelry,** n. _comis(s)atio._ **reveller,** n. _comis(s)ator._

revenge, I. n. _ultio_ (= the act of —), _vindicatio_ (by the gods, the law, magistrates, and others through the law), _ulciscendi cupiditas, ira, iracundia._ **II.** v.tr. _ulcisci alqm_ or _alqd, vindicare alqm_ or _alqd in alqm_ (of laws and magistrates), comb. _ulcisci et persequi, poenas capēre pro alqo_ or _alcjs rei, poenas alcjs rei expetēre_ (= to claim — for anybody or anything). **revengeful,** adj. _ultionis cupidus, iratus_ (= angry). Adv. _irato animo._

revenue, n. _vectigal, reditus, -ūs._

reverberate, I. v.tr. to — the rays, _radios repercutēre, regerēre._ **II.** v.intr. see RESOUND. **reverberation,** n. _repercussus, -ūs_ (Plin., Tac.).

reverence, I. n. 1, _observantia, reverentia, veneratio, verecundia_ (stronger than _reverentia);_ religious —, _religio_ or _pietas erga Deum;_ as a title use in gen. _vir reverendus;_ of a king, _augustus;_ 2, to make a —, _(reverenter) alqm salutare._ **II.** or **revere,** v.tr. _alqm observare, colēre et observare,_ or _verēri et colēre, alqm reverēri, reverentiam adversus alqm adhibēre, reverentiam alci habēre_ or _praestare._ **reverend,** adj. _reverendus_ in gen. (or Eccl.). **reverent,** adj. _verecundus_ (= shy, modest), _religiosus, venerabundus_ (= devout), _pius_ (= dutiful). Adv. _verecunde, religiose, pie;_ they went — into the temple, _venerabundi templum iniēre_ (Liv.).

reverie, n. _cogitatio_ (= thought); lost in a —, _in cogitatione defixus, nescio quid meditans._

reverse, I. v.tr. _invertēre, (com)mutare, convertēre;_ see CHANGE. **II.** n. 1, = change, _(com)mutatio, vicissitudo, vicis_ (gen.), pl. _vices_ more common (mostly poet.), _conversio;_ 2, = contrary, _contrarium;_ 3, = defeat, _clades, -is, f.;_ see DEFEAT; 4, = hind part, _pars aversa._ **reversible,** adj. _qui (quae, quod) facile inverti potest._ **reversion,** n. 1, see REVERSE, II.; 2, legal t.t. _hereditas._ **revert,** v.intr. _redire ad alqm, cedēre alci._

review, I. v.tr. _inspicēre, perspicēre, cognos-_

cere, percensere, recensēre, corrigĕre ; to — an **army**, *recensēre* (i.e. to number), *inspicĕre* (e.g. the legions, *arma, viros, equos cum curā, singulos milites*), *numerum alcjs inire* (e.g. troops), comb. *alqd recensēre et numerum inire, lustrare* (of the censor, then the army by the general, with religious rites), *oculis lustrare, oculis obire* (with a glance) ; to — a book, perhaps *de libro judicium exprimĕre.* **II.** n. 1, *conspectus, -ūs*, or by verbs ; 2, of troops, *recensio* (with a view to numbering), *lustratio* (= rites at beginning of a —), in gen. *simulacrum pugnae, ludicrum certamen, imago pugnae, justa belli species* (all in Liv. xl. 6) ; 3, see JOURNAL. **reviewer**, n. *qui de libro judicium suum exprimit.*

revile, v.tr. *conviciari, convicium alci facĕre, alqm conviciis consectari or incessĕre, alci maledicĕre, alqm maledictis insectari, maledicta in alqm dicĕre or conferre, probris et maledictis alqm vexare, maledictis or probris alqm increpare, contumeliosis verbis alqm prosequi.* **reviler**, n. *conviciator, maledicus.* **reviling**, n. *maledictio, verborum contumelia, probrum, convicium.*

revise, **I.** v.tr. see REVIEW, CORRECT. **II.** n. *plagula de prelo emendanda,* or by verb. **revision**, n. *lima* (lit. = file), *emendatio, correctio* ; see CORRECTION.

revisit, v.tr. *revisĕre.*

revive, **I.** v.intr. *reviviscĕre, ad vitam redire* (lit. and fig., of persons and things), *renasci* (fig. of things), *revirescĕre, recreari, respirare.* **II.** v.tr. *vitam alcjs restituĕre, vitam alci reddĕre.*

revoke, v.tr. *irritum esse jubēre, abrogare, rescindĕre (legem,* etc.) ; see ABOLISH, RESCIND. **revocable**, adj. † *revocabilis, qui (quae, quod) facile mutari potest.* **revocation**, n. *revocatio* (in gen.), *abrogatio, rescissio* (of a law) ; see ABROGATION.

revolt, **I.** v.intr. *seditionem movēre, imperium auspiciumque abnuēre* (= to refuse obedience, of soldiers), *rebellare, rebellionem facĕre, imperium alcjs detrectare, deficĕre ab alqo or ab alcjs imperio, desciscĕre ab alqo.* **II.** n. *seditio, defectio, rebellio, tumultus, -ūs.* **revolter**, n. *(homo) seditiosus, qui ab alqo desciscit.* **revolting**, adj. *taeter (tet-), nefandus, foedus, turpis* ; see DISGUSTING.

revolution, n. 1, = turning, *conversio, orbis, anfractus, -ūs (solis), ambitus, -ūs* ; 2, political —, *novae res* ; see also REVOLT. **revolutionary**, adj. lit. *seditiosus, novarum rerum studiosus* or *cupidus* ; fig. *novissimus* (= very strange). **revolutionist**, n. *(homo) novarum rerum cupidus.* **revolutionize**, v.tr. *commutare* (lit. and fig.).

revolve, **I.** v.intr. *se (re)volvĕre* or *(re)volvi, se circumagĕre* or *circumagi, circumverti.* **II.** v.tr. *alqd animo volvĕre* or *volutare.* **revolver**, n. see PISTOL.

revulsion, n. *(com)mutatio* ; see CHANGE.

reward, **I.** v.tr. *praemium alci dare, tribuĕre, (per)solvĕre, pretium alci deferre, praemio alqm ornare* or *decorare, renumerari alqm praemio.* **II.** n. *remuneratio,* for, *alcjs rei* ; (= the thing itself, *praemium* or *pretium, fructus, -ūs* (= fruit). **rewarder**, n. *qui alci praemium dat,* etc.

rewrite, v.tr. *iterum scribĕre.*

rhapsody, n. perhaps *dictum grandiloquum,* or *ampullae* (i.e. *ampullae et sesquipedalia verba*).

rhetoric, n. *rhetorica* or *rhetorice* (ῥητορική), pure Latin *ars orandi* or *bene dicendi scientia* (Quint.). **rhetorical**, adj. *rhetoricus* (ῥητορικός), *oratorius.* Adv. *rhetorice.*

rheum, n. *gravedo, humor.* **rheumatism**, n. *cruciatus, -ūs,* or *dolor* in gen.

rhinoceros, n. *rhinoceros* (Plin.).

rhubarb, n. *radix pontica* (Cels.).

rhyme, **I.** n. *extremorum verborum similis sonitus, -ūs.* **II.** v.intr. *versus extremis verbis inter se consonantes,* or *versus qui extremis verbis similiter sonant, facēre.*

rhythm, n. *numerus* or in the pl. *numeri, modus, modi,* pl., *rhythmus* (Quint. ; Cic. uses Greek ῥυθμός). **rhythmical**, adj. *numerosus.* Adv. *numerose.*

rib, n. *costa* ; of a ship, *statumen.*

ribald, adj. *obscenus* ; see FILTHY. **ribaldry**, n. *sermo obscenus, obscenitas.*

riband, ribbon, n. *redimiculum* (= anything to tie round the head, forehead), *taenia, fascia* (= small bit of cloth, etc., for a headdress), *lemniscus* (for garlands, also for an order), *vitta* (= head-band), *infula* (= fillet, also badge of honour).

rice, n. *oryza* ; as a dish, by *puls ex oryzâ cocta.*

rich, adj. *dives (dis,* opp. *pauper), locuples* (= having much property and in a flourishing condition), *opulentus* (= who has means, money, influential), *copiosus, copiis dives* or *locuples* (= rich in provisions of all kinds, *copiosus* also of a fertile mind), *pecuniosus, magnae pecuniae, bene nummatus, argento copiosus* (= having much money), *fortunatus* (= fortunate, wealthy), *beatus* (= who has everything he can wish for), *abundans* (= who has so much that he can give unto others ; also of a fertile mind, opp. *inops), opimus* (= rich, abundant, e.g. booty, profit, kingdom, etc.), *amplus* (= considerable, splendid in a gen. sense, e.g. reward, funeral), *uber* (= ample, in large quantities, or yielding a great deal), *opimus* (= sumptuous), *pretiosus* (=costly), *lautus* (= luxurious) ; — in, *dives alqâ re* (poetic with gen.), *opulentus alqâ re, uber alqâ re* or *alcjs rei, ferax alcjs rei* (= yielding, etc., of countries, fields, etc.), *frequens alqâ re* (where anything exists in large numbers, e.g. *Nilus feris et beluis frequens*). Adv. *copiose, beate* (= with all blessings), *abundanter, ample* (often in superl. *amplissime), pretiose* (expensively), *laute* (= well, luxuriously).

riches, n. *divitiae* (= large fortune), *opulentia* (= ample means, as regards money, property, etc.), *opes,* f. pl. (= means wherewith to accomplish a thing), *fortunae* (= blessing of Providence), *facultates, -um,* pl., *copiae* (= means of all kinds). **richness**, n. *copia, abundantia, ubertas* (of soil, etc.) ; see ABUNDANCE, FERTILITY.

rick, n. *meta* (Col.).

rid, get rid of, v.tr. *alqm liberare, expedire alqâ re, alqm eripĕre ex* or *ab alqâ re* (all three = to free from danger, and esp. from any unpleasant position, etc.), *alqd deponĕre* (= to lay aside), *dimittĕre* (= to dismiss) ; to have got — of, *solutum, vacuum esse alqâ re* (e.g. fear) ; see FREE, DISMISS. **riddance**, n. *liberatio* ; good —, *abi (abite).*

riddle, **I.** n. *aenigma, -ătis,* n., *ambāges, -um,* f. (= ambiguity in speech or action) ; you talk in —s, *ambāges narras.* **II.** v.intr. *enigmata loqui.* **riddled**, adj. e.g. — with wounds, *graviter vulneratus, multis vulneribus oppressus.*

ride, v.intr. *equitare, equo vehi* (in gen.) ; to — up to, *equo vehi ad alqm* or *ad alqd, adequitare ad alqm* or *ad alqd, obequitare alci rei* ; to — quickly, *equo concitato* (of several, *equis citatis) advehi* or *advolare, equo admisso (equis admissis) accurrĕre* ; to — at anchor, *in ancoris consistĕre.* **rider**, n. *eques, -itis,* m. ; to be a very good —, *equitandi* *peritissimum esse.* **riding,** n. *equitatio, equitatus, -ūs* (Plin.). **riding-master,** n. *qui alqm equitare docet.*

ridge, n. *montis dorsum, jugum.*

ridicule, I. n. *(de)ridiculum;* see MOCK-ERY. **II.** v.tr. anyone or anything, *irridēre, deridēre alqm* or *alqd, in risum vertēre* (e.g. *cognomen);* see MOCK. **ridiculous,** adj. *ridiculus, ridendus, deridiculus, perridiculus, subridiculus;* see ABSURD. Adv. *(per)ridicule, subridicule, joculariter, deridendus, jocularis* (= facetious). **ridiculousness,** n. by adj.

rife, adj. to be — (e.g. a report), *fertur, fama* or *res percrebescit* or *percrebuit.*

rifle, n. see GUN.

rifle, v.tr. see PLUNDER.

rift, n. *rima;* see CRACK.

rig, v.tr. *armare.* **rigging,** n. *armamenta, -orum.*

right, I. adj. 1, (in geometry) *rectus;* — angled, *orthogonios;* see STRAIGHT; = not left, *dexter* (opp. *sinister)* ; the — hand, *(manus) dextra;* 2, = morally —, *aequus, rectus, verus* (= true), *accuratus, diligens* (= careful, accurate), *justus;* it is —, *fas (jusque) est;* it is not — of you to, etc., *non recte fecisti quod,* etc. ; it serves me —, *jure plector* (Cic.); it serves you —, *merito tibi accidit;* 3, = correct, *rectus, verus* (true), *justus* (just as it should be, e.g. measure, size), often also *by ipse;* the — word for anything, *verum rei vocabulum;* to go the — road, *rectam viam ingredi* (lit.); to go the — way about it, *rectam rationem inire* (= to choose the — remedy); I have got to the — house, *ad eam ipsam domum pervenio quo tendo;* at the — time, *in tempore, opportune, opportuno tempore* (= convenient), *tempore suo, tempore ipso* (= in due time); *ad tempus* (= at the right moment); to make the — use of anything, *recte* or *bene* or *sapienter uti alqd re;* you are —, *res ita est ut dixisti, sunt ista ut dicis;* to do what is —, *recte agēre.* 1. adv. *recte, vere, juste, rite* (= duly), *jure, merito* (= deservedly), *bene* (= well), *diligenter, accurate* (= accurately), *plane, prorsus* (= altogether, I do not — understand, *non satis* or *plane intellego).* **III.** n. = — to do anything, *jus, potestas alcjs rei* (= power, as a —, to do so); I have a — to do it, *jus est alqd facēre, potestatem habeo alqd faciendi; fas* (= the divine law, what is — in the sight of God, hence, what is in the course of nature, what our conscience allows us to do); contrary to all —s, *contra jus fasque, contra jus ac fas;* by —s, *jure, suo jure* (= from his own personal —), *merito* (= deservingly); with the greatest —, *justissime, justo jure, optimo jure, merito atque optimo jure, jure meritoque, jure ac merito, merito ac jure.* **righteous,** adj. *bonus, probus, sanctus, aequus, justus.* Adv. *bene, probe, sancte, juste.* **righteousness,** n. *probitas, sanctitas.* **rightful,** adj. *legitimus, justus, debitus* (= due), or *quo de jure est.* Adv. *lege, legitime, juste, jure;* see LEGALLY, RIGHT, II.

rigid, adj. *rigidus, rigens* (lit., = stiff with cold; then fixed in gen., e.g. eyes, hair; *rigidus* also fig. inflexible, unsociable, e.g. *mores rigidi), immobilis* (= immovable, of persons and things), *durus* (= without grace, delicacy, opp. *mollis), severus* (= severe). Adv. *rigide, dure, severe.* **rigidity,** n. *rigor.* **rigorous,** adj. see RIGID. **rigour,** n. *rigor* (opp. *clementia,* also of a thing, e.g. *animi, veteris disciplinae,* mostly post Aug.), *severitas, duritia.*

rill, n. *rivus (rivulus* very late, except in fig. sense).

rim, n. *labrum* (= lip), *ora* (of a shield, etc.); see EDGE.

rime, n. *pruina.*

rind, n. *cortex* (of trees), *liber* (= the inward bark); see SKIN.

ring, I. n. *circulus, orbis, -is,* m. (in gen.), *an-(n)ulus* (= — on a finger, of curtains, chains, hair), *inaures, -ium,* f. (= ear—s); = circle, fig. *corona, orbis, -is,* m., *circulus.* **II.** v.tr. and intr. *tinnire;* to — at the door, *pulsare fores* or *januam* (= to knock), to — for anyone, *(aeris) tinnitu alqm arcessēre* (lit.), *digitis concrepare* (= to snap with the fingers, as the Romans did when they wished to call a slave); of bells, *sonare* (intr.); to — the bells, *campanam pulsare;* = to resound, *resonare;* to — the changes, *alqd iterare;* = to surround, *circumdare;* see SURROUND. **ring-dove,** n. *columba* (= blue rock), *palumbes, -is,* m. and f. (= stock-dove). **ringing, I.** adj. † *sonorus, canorus.* **II.** n. † *tinnitus, -ūs,* or by *sonus.* **ringleader,** n. *auctor, princeps, caput, dux, fax* (lit. = torch), *tuba* (lit. = trumpet). **ringlet,** n. *cirrus;* see CURL. **ringworm,** n. *lichen* (Plin.).

rinse, v.tr. *eluěre, colluěre, perluěre.*

riot, I. n. 1, *seditio, motus, -ūs, concitatio* (e.g. *plebis contra patres), tumultus, -ūs* (of slaves, peasants, allies against the Romans themselves), *vis repentina* (= sudden rising); 2, = extravagant conduct, *comis(s)atio* (= feasting), *rixa* (= brawling). **II.** v.intr. 1, *seditionem (tumultum,* etc.) *movēre* or *concitare;* 2, = to run riot, *comis-(s)ari* (= to revel), *bacchari* (= to rave), *luxuriare* (= to live riotously). **rioter,** n. *(homo) seditiosus, turbulentus,* etc. **riotous,** adj. 1, *seditiosus, rerum eventendarum* or *rerum novarum cupidus, rerum mutationis cupidus, turbulentus,* comb. *seditiosus ac turbulentus* (e.g. *civis);* 2, *comis(s)-abundus;* = living, *luxuria.* Adv. *turbulente, seditiose, luxuriose.*

rip, v.tr. 1, *scindēre, divellēre* (= to tear) see TEAR, CUT; 2, *dissuěre* (a seam; rare).

ripe, adj. *maturus, tempestivus* (lit. and fig.), *coctus;* a — old age, *senectus, -ūtis;* — judgment, *judicium.* **ripen, I.** v.tr. *maturare* (lit. and fig.). **II.** v.intr. *maturari, maturescěre, ad maturitatem pervenire, maturitatem assequi* or *adipisci.* **ripeness,** n. *maturitas* (lit. and fig.), *maturitas tempestiva* (lit.), *tempestivitas* (lit. and fig.).

ripple, I. v.intr. perhaps *leni murmure defluěre,* or *delabi, susurrare, leniter* † *sonare.* **II.** n. perhaps *unda;* the — of the waves, *lene undarum murmur.*

rise, I. v.intr. 1, = to get up, *(ex)surgěre, consurgěre* (esp. of a number of people), *assurgěre* (esp. as a mark of honour to anyone, *alci) ;* to — in the morning, *expergisci* (= to awake), *(e lectulo* or *lectulo* alone) *surgěre;* from table, *a cenā;* to — from illness, *e morbo assurgěre;* of the sun, stars, etc., of sunrise, *(di)lucescěre, illuscěre, (ex)-oriri;* of the wind, tempest, etc., *consurgěre, cooriri;* 2, = to increase, *surgěre, increbescěre, crescěre;* to — in the air, *(in) sublime ferri;* of a river, *nasci* (Plin.), *proficisci, gigni, (ex)oriri;* to — from beneath, *emergěre;* of thoughts, *subire mentem* or *animum, alci succurrěre;* of prices, *augēri, crescěre, ingravescěre;* to — in dignity, in the world, etc., *ad honores ascendēre, altiorem dignitatis gradum consequi;* 3, = to rebel, *cooriri* (e.g. *ad bellum);* see REBEL; to — again, *resurgěre* (Eccl.). **II.** n. and **rising,** n. *(ex)ortus, -ūs* (of the sun, etc.), *a(d)scensus, -ūs* (= place where one ascends); — of a hill, so *clivus leniter assurgens* (of a gentle —); = origin, *ortus, -ūs, caus(s)a, fons, -ntis,* m., *origo;* to give — to, *locum alci rei dare* or *prae-bēre, efficěre;* see CAUSE; — in price, *annona carior* (of corn), in gen. use verb; = insurrection; see REBELLION. **rising,** adj. of ground, *(collis) paul(l)ulum ex planitie editus* or *assurgens*

fig. perhaps *qui gratiâ (in ates) augetur* (of reputation, etc.); see PROSPEROUS.

risible, adj. *quod ad ridendum pertinet.*
risibility, n. by *ridēre* (e.g. I have nothing to excite my —, *non habeo quod rideam*).

risk, I. n. *periculum* (= danger), *discrimen, alea alcjs rei* (= danger, uncertainty in anything); at my —, *meo periculo*; to take anything at one's own —, *alqd periculi sui facĕre.* **II.** v.tr. *alqd in aleam dare, alqd in periculum* or *discrimen adducĕre* or *vocare*; to — one's life, *committĕre se periculo mortis.*

rite, n. by *ritus, -ūs*; see CEREMONY. **ritual, I.** adj. *de ritu.* **II.** n. *liber* or *formula sacrorum.*
ritualist, n. *homo de sacris (rite faciendis) diligentissimus.*

rival, I. n. *aemulus,* fem. *aemula* (in gen.), *rivalis* (as a lover), *competitor* (political). **II.** adj. *aemulans cvm alqo.* **III.** v.tr. *(con)certare* or *contendĕre cum alqo* (= to contest), *aemulari alqm* or *cum alqo* (= to strive for anything which another tries to gain). **rivalry,** n. *aemulatio.*

river, I. n. *fluvius, flumen, amnis, rivus* (= rivulet, any small river which flows), *torrens* (= torrent); the — flows quickly, *fluvius citatus* (or *incitatus) fertur*; slowly, *fluvius placide manat*; the — is rapid, *fluvius violentus invehitur*; is low, *amnis tenui fluit aquâ*; a swollen —, *rivus ̄nflatus*; to direct a — into another channel, *amnem in alium cursum deflectĕre.* **II.** adj. *fluviaticus, fluviatilis, fluvialis.* **river-basin,** n. *locus ubi omnia flumina in unum defluunt.*
river-god, n. *numen fluminis.* **river-horse,** n. *hippopotamus* (Plin.).

rivet, I. v.tr. *clav(ul)o figĕre.* **II.** n. *fibula ferrea, clavus* (nail).

road, n. 1, *via* (= the way for going or travelling), *iter* (= the going, or the — itself); on the —, *in* or *ex itinere*; a — goes to, *iter fert alqo*; 2, fig. the right —, *via*; the wrong —, *error.*
roads, n. pl. = anchorage for ships, roadstead, *statio.* **roadside,** adj. by *in itinere.* **roadster,** n. *caballus.*

roam, v.intr. *palari* (e.g. *per agros*), *vagari.*
roaming, adj. *vagus.*

roan, adj. *badius albis maculis sparsus.*

roar, I. v.intr. of beasts, *mugire* (of an ox, also of thunder, etc.), *rudĕre* (= to bray like an ass, also of lions, stags, etc.), *rugire, fremĕre* (of lions), *vociferari* (of men). **II.** n. *mugītus, rudītus, rugītus* (all *-ūs), vociferatio.*

roast, I. v.tr. *assare, torrēre, frigĕre* (the two foregoing = to fry). **II.** adj. *assus*; — meat, *assum, caro assa, assa,* n. pl. (several pieces); — beef, *assum bubulum*; — veal, *assum vitulinum.*

rob, v.tr. *rapĕre, latrocinari* (= to — on the highway); *alqm alqâ re depeculari* (men, temples, etc., rare), *alqm alqâ re (ex)spoliare, despoliare, expilare, compilare* (= to strip temples, the public treasury, etc., the latter also *alqd alqâ re), fraudare alqm re* (by cheating), *alqd alci eripĕre* (= to snatch away), *adripĕre, au-ferre* (= to take away); to — of children, *or-bare.* **robber,** n. *ereptor* (plunderer), *praedo* (= who seeks after booty both by sea and by land), *latro* (= burglar), *pirata* (= pirate), *fur* (= thief); band of —s, *latronum* or *praedonum globus, latronum* or *praedonum turba,* or simply *latrones, praedones,* or *latrocinium* (Cic., and fig. of Catiline and his associates). **robbery,** n. *rapina, spo-liatio* (the act), *latrocinium* (= highway —; *la-trocinium* alone or *latrocinium maris* also = piracy), *praedatio* (= taking booty); robberies of all kinds, *latrocinia et raptus*; to commit —, *rapĕre, rapinas facĕre, latrocinari, piraticam facĕre* or *exercēre* (by sea).

robe, I. n. *vestis* (= dress in gen.), *amictus, -ūs* (= anything thrown over), *stola, palla* (= dress for the Roman ladies), *trabea* (= robe of state); see DRESS, GOWN. **II.** v.tr. *vestire.*

robust, adj. *robustus*; see STRONG.

rock, n. *saxum* (= any mass of stones), *rupes, -is* (= steep —, on the land and in the sea), *scopulus* (in prose, = dangerous — in the water, cliff), *cautes, -is,* f. (= ragged —, crag), comb. *saxa et cautes*; fig. *arx* (= castle, —, e.g. *arx est illa spei salutisque nostrae*). **rocky,** adj. *scopulosus, saxosus, saxeus* (= made of —).
rock, I. v.tr. *movēre, quatĕre.* **II.** v.intr. *movēre.*

rocket, n. by *radius pyrius.*

rod, n. *virga* (in gen.), *ferula* (= fennel-giant, for chastising children), *arundo* (cane), *decem-pēda* (in land-surveying).

roe, n. of fish, *ova, -orum,* pl.
roe, n. = female deer, *caprea.* **roebuck,** n. *capreolus, caprea.*

rogation, n. *rogatio* (= the proposal of a law; Eccl. = prayer), *supplicatio* (= prayer).

rogue, n. (homo) *perfidus, nequam, scelestus, sceleratus, fraudulentus, veterator, (tri)furcifer* (Com.). **roguery,** n. *fraus, -dis,* f., *dolus.*
roguish, adj. 1, *perfidus, fraudulentus*; see under ROGUE; 2, = saucy, *protervus, lascivus.* Adv. *perfide, nequiter, sceleste, scelerate, fraudu-lenter, proterve, lascive.*

roll, I. v.tr. *volvĕre, devolvĕre* (down), *evol-vĕre* (out), *provolvĕre* (forward), *convolvĕre* (to-gether), *volutare, versare* (over and over); to — round anything, *alqd alci rei circumvolvĕre, in-volvĕre.* **II.** v.intr. *convolvi, se volutare, volu-tari*; tears — down his cheeks, *lacrimae per genas manant.* **III.** n. *orbis, cylindrus* (= cylin-der); = what is rolled up, *volumen* (of paper); = a — of bread, *panis*; — of a drum, *tympani pulsatio* (= beating), or *sonus* (= sound); = list, *album* (e.g. *senator, -ium,* Tac.). **roller,** n. *cylindrus* (for rolling things round, or for levelling ground), *phalangae* (put under ships).
roll-call, n. *album*; to answer to the —, *ad nomina respondēre.*

Roman Catholic, adj. * *Catholicus,* * *qui fidem Romanae Ecclesiae tenet.*

romance, I. n. *fabula.* **II.** v.intr. *fabulari.*
romantic, adj. *fictus* (= feigned), *mirus, novus* (= wonderful), *amoenus* (= pretty, of a place). Adv. *ut in fabulis fit, ficte, mire, amoene.*

romp, v.intr. see PLAY.

roof, I. n. *tectum, culmen*; buildings without —, *aedificia hypaethra*; to receive under your —, *hospitio excipĕre alqm.* **II.** v.tr. to —, *tecto tegĕre*; to unroof, *nudare tecto.* **roofless,** adj. *hypae-thrus, nudatus*; = homeless, *sine tecto.*

room, n. 1, *locus, spatium* e.g. to make —, *viam* or *locum dare, locum dare et cedĕre; popu-lum* or *turbam submovēre* (e.g. for the consul by the lictors), *partem sedis* or *subselli vacuam facĕre* (= to give up one's seat); see SPACE; 2, = apartment, *conclave, cubiculum* (= chamber, bed—); *hospitalia, -ium,* n. (= guest cham-bers); dining-—, *cenaculum*; (all the —s above the ground-floor were *cenacula)*; *cenatio*; a small —, *cenatiuncula*; bed—, *cubiculum* (see Smith, "Dict. Antiq. Art.," *Domus*). **roomy,** adj. *spatiosus*; see SPACIOUS.

roost, I. n. *pertica gallinaria.* **II.** v.intr. *stabulari.*

root, I. n. 1, *radix* (= — of a tree: then — of the tongue, hair, feather, mountain, hill, etc.; fig. = origin); by the —s, *radicitus, radicibus*; 2, fig. *stirps, fons, -ntis,* m., *caus(s)a* (= cause,

origin, source); with the —, *radicitus, radicibus.*
II. v.intr. *radicari* (lit. Col.), *radices capĕre*
or *mittĕre* (lit.), *inhaerescĕre in mente* (fig. of
that which one does not forget), *radices agĕre*
(= to take —, also fig. = to gain a firm footing),
insidĕre, inveterascĕre (both fig., the former of a
superior, the latter of a habit, an evil, etc.).
III. v.tr. *fovēre, alĕre* (fig. = to foster); to — up,
evellĕre. **rooted,** adj. *inveteratus, confirmatus*
(fig.); deeply —, fig. *penitus defixus.*

rope, n. *restis* (= a thin —), *funis, -is,* m. (=
a thick —), *rudens* (= a cable), *retinaculum* (of
a ship), *funis ancorarius, ancorale* (= anchor —),
funis extenitus (= tight —).

rosary, n. 1, = garden of roses, *rosarium,
rosetum ;* 2, = beads, *rosarium* (Eccl.). **rose,**
n. *rosa.* **rosy,** adj. *roseus.*

rosemary, n. *ros marinus.*

rosin, n. *resina.*

rostrum, n. *rostra, -orum.*

rot, I. v.intr. *putrescĕre, putrefieri, tabescĕre.*
II. n. *tabes, -is.* **rotten,** adj. *putrefactus,
putridus.*

rotate, v.intr. *se volvĕre, volvi, se circumagĕre, circumagi ;* see REVOLVE. **rotation,** n.
ambitus, -ūs, circuitus, -ūs, circumactio (e.g. *rotarum*), *circulatio* or *circinatio* (of the planets),
cursus, -ūs (= course); in —, *ordine ;* see SUC-
CESSION. **rotatory,** adj. † *versātilis.*

rotundity, n. *figura rotunda,* **rotunditas**
(Plin.).

rouge, I. n. *fucus.* **II.** v.intr. *fucare.*

rough, adj. *asper* (e.g. road, places, climate,
voice, life or mode of living, man), *salebrosus* (=
rugged, uneven), *confragosus* (= craggy, stony),
hirsutus (lit. = shaggy ; then of thorns, etc.),
asper, gravis (of weather), *turbidus* (of weather
or wind); see STORMY ; *horridus* (= standing on
end ; hence void of refinement, of things and
persons, e.g. *verba*), *raucus* (= hoarse); of character, *inhumanus, inurbanus, agrestis, rusticus;*
see SKETCH. Adv. *aspere, dure, duriter, inhumane, inurbane, rustice.* **roughen,** v.tr. (*ex*)-
asperare (lit. and fig.). **roughness,** n. *asperitas* (in gen., e.g. of the climate, *caeli, animi*),
duritia ; of manners, *inhumanitas, inurbanitas, rusticitas.*

round, I. adj. *rotundus, globosus* (=globular),
orbiculatus (lit. = orbicular, like a disk ; then
— like a ball, — in gen.), *teres* (rounded),
comb. *teres* or *rotundus.* **II.** v.tr. 1, *rotundare,
curvare, conglobare ;* 2, fig. *polire, concludĕre.*
III. n. 1, see CIRCLE ; 2, in fighting, *certamen ;*
in music, *cantus, -ūs* (song); to go to the —s,
vigilias circumire. **IV.** adv. and prep. *circa,
circum* (*alqd*). **roundabout,** adj. and adv. *devius ;* a — way, *ambāges, -um, circuitus, -ūs.*
rounded, adj. *teres* (lit. and fig.), *rotundatus,
rotundus, conglobatus ;* of style, *quasi rotundus,
concinnus.* **roundelay,** n. see SONG. **roundly,** adv. *plane, prorsus* (= altogether).

rouse, v.tr. *excitare.*

rout, I. v.tr. to — the enemy, *hostes dissipare*
or *hostes in fugam dissipare.* **II.** n. see MOB,
DEFEAT.

route, n. see WAY, ROAD, JOURNEY.

routine, n. *habitus, -ūs* (= any art or virtue
in which we feel at home, as it were), *usus, -ūs*
(= practice), *ordo* (= order).

rove, v.intr. see RAMBLE. **rover,** n. *qui
errat, etc ; =* pirate, *pirata,* m., *praedo.*

row, n. *ordo, -inis,* m., *series ;* first, second,
&c. — of seats, *sedilia prima, secunda,* etc. ;
in a —, (*ex*) *ordine, in ordinem, deinceps.*

row, n. 1, see QUARREL ; 2, see NOISE.

row, I. v.intr. *remigare ;* to — with all one's
might, *remis contendĕre.* **II.** v.tr. *remis propellĕre.*

royal, adj. *regius,* or by the gen. *regis* (= belonging to a king), *regalis* (= according to the
dignity of a king). Adv. *regie, regaliter, regio*
more. **royalist,** n. *qui regis partibus studet.*
royalty, n. 1, *regia potestas ;* 2, on a book,
fructus, -ūs, reditus, -ūs.

rub, v.tr. *terĕre* (= to — off, to — to pieces),
atterĕre (= to — against), *conterĕre* (= to pound),
fricare (e.g. a floor), *demulcĕre, permulcĕre* (= to
stroke); to — out, *delēre.*

rubber, n. at whist, by *paginis ter contendĕre.*

rubbish, n. 1, *rudus* (= rubble); see REFUSE ;
2, *nugae, gerrae ;* see NONSENSE.

rubble, n. *rudus.*

rubric, n. *rubrica* (Eccl.).

ruby, I. n. *carbunculus* (Plin.). **II. adj.**
purpureus.

rudder, n. *gubernaculum, clavus.*

ruddy, adj. *rubicundus.* **ruddiness,** n.
use adj. (e.g. *color rubicundus*).

rude, adj. *rudis* (= inexperienced); — verses,
versus inconditi or *incompositi* (= unmannerly,
agrestis, rusticus, inurbanus, inhumanus ; = insolent, *insolens.* Adv. *incondite, incomposite,
rustice, inurbane, inhumane, insolenter.* **rudeness,** n. *rusticitas, inhumanitas, inurbanitas,
insolentia, mores rustici,* etc.

rudiments, n. pl. *rudimenta ;* see ELE-
MENTS. **rudimentary,** adj. *inchoatus.*

rue, n. *ruta.*

rue, v.tr. see REGRET, REPENT. **rueful,**
adj. see SORROWFUL. **ruth,** n. see PITY.

ruff, n. see COLLAR.

ruffian, n. *latro* (= bandit), *sicarius* (= assassin), *homo nefarius,* etc. **ruffianly,** adj.
nefarius, nequam, perditus, sceleratus ; see
WICKED.

ruffle, v.tr. 1, *agitare ;* to be —d, *inhorres-
cĕre* (also of a hen, to — her feathers, *gallinae
inhorrescunt edito ovo, excutiuntque sese,* Plin.);
2, fig. see EXCITE, IRRITATE.

rug, n. *stragulum.* **rugged,** adj. see ROUGH,
UNEVEN.

ruin, I. n. 1, —s, *ruinae, parietinae* (e.g.
Corinthi), *muri diruti* (= walls partly destroyed);
2, *ruina* (lit. = the falling in, then fig.), *interitus,
-ūs, exitium ;* the — of one's fortune, *ruina
fortunarum ;* that was his —, *hoc ei exitio fuit ;*
see DESTRUCTION. **II.** v.tr. *pessumdare* (lit. and
fig.), *perdĕre, alqm* or *alqd praecipitare* (e.g. the
State), *conficĕre* (= completely to wear out, exhaust, e.g. *partem plebis tributo*), *prosternĕre
alqm* or *alqd* (e.g. the enemy), *affligĕre* (e.g. the
State, etc.), *profligare* (entirely, a person, the
State, one's health), also comb. *affligĕre et perdĕre, affligĕre et prosternĕre, affligĕre et profligare*
(all = *funditus perdĕre* or *evertĕre*). **ruinous,**
adj. 1, see PERNICIOUS ; 2, = very great (of
expense), *maximus, effusus.*

rule, I. v.tr. and intr. 1, *regĕre, civitatem regĕre,
imperium tractare, regnare, rempublicam regĕre* or
moderari, reipublicae praeesse ; see REIGN ; 2, to
— passions, *alqd* or *alci rei temperare ;* see RE-
STRAIN. **II.** n. *lex* (e.g. *leges dicendi*), *praescriptum,
praeceptum, ars, ratio, regula* (= a ruler or instrument for ruling lines or deciding cases,
as *regula sermonis, regula ad quam alqd dirigitur*), *norma ;* to give a —, *legem dare, scribĕre,
praeceptum dare* or *tradĕre ;* to lay down as a —,

praecipĕre, praescribĕre; in **a** court of law, *edicĕre.* **ruler,** n. 1, *rector, moderator, qui alci rei praeest ;* 2, for drawing, *regula.*

rumble, v.intr. *(in)sonare, mugire, murmurare.*

rum'nate, v.intr. *ruminare* or *ruminari* (tr. **and** intr., lit. and fig.), *remandēre* (tr. and intr., Plin.); see MEDITATE. **ruminant,** adj. *ruminalis* (Plin.). **rumination,** n. *ruminatio* (lit. and fig.).

rummage, v.intr. *alqd perscrutari.*

rumour, I. n. *rumor, fama, sermo* (= talk), *ōpinio* (= opinion), *auditio* (= what we know by hearsay), comb. *rumor* (or *fama*) *et auditio.* **II.** v.tr., it is —ed, *fertur, (res, fama,* etc.) *percrebescit.*

rump, n. *clunes, -ium,* m. and f.

rumple, v.tr. *immundum* (in gen.), *incomptum* (of hair) *facĕre.*

run, I. v.intr. *(de)currĕre*(from a higher place to one that lies lower, *ab, de =* down from, *ex =* out of, *per,* with accus. or the simple accus. = through, *ad =* as far as), *cursu ferri, aufugĕre* (= to — away), *cursu tendĕre algo* (= to — anywhere), *occurrĕre* (= to — up to), *percurrĕre* (= to — to a place), *procurrĕre* (= to — out of), *se proripĕre* (= to dash forth, e.g. into the street, *in publicum ;* out of the house, *foras*), *effundi, se effundĕre* (of **a** large crowd, e.g. *in castra), transcurrĕre alqd* (= to — over anything ; then absolute = to — across to, over to anyone, e.g. *ad alqm), circumcurrĕre, circumcursare alqm locum* (= to — about in a place), *cursare, trepidare* (= to — about), *pervagari alqm locum* (= to ramble about in a place) ; **to** — against each other, *inter se concurrĕre ;* to — a race, *cursu certare, certatim currĕre ;* to — against anyone, *incurrĕre* or *incurrĕre et incidĕre in alqm ;* against anything, *impingi alci rei, se impingĕre in alqd,* so of a ship, *scopulo,* etc., = to — aground ; to — down, fig. see DECRY ; to — after anyone, *cursu effuso tendĕre* or *currĕre ad alqm, cupide appetĕre alqd* (fig. = to long for) ; of rivers (= to flow), *inferri, (in)fluĕre in alqd ;* to — into, *influĕre* in, etc., *effundi, se effundĕre* (e.g. *in mare);* **to** — into = to enter, *intrare alqd, alqm locum* (e.g. *portum);* to — out of, *exire (ex) algo loco* (e.g. of ships, carriages) ; to — round, *ferri, moveri, circa alqd* (e.g. *circa terram,* of the sun); tears — over his cheeks, *lacrimae manant per genas;* to — over, *equum,* etc., *agĕre in alqm =* to treat lightly, *alqd (oratione,* etc.) *percurrĕre, perstringĕre ;* **to** — to seed, *in semen ire.* **II.** n. *cursus, -ūs, citatus* or *effusus.* **runaway,** n. *fugitivus.* **runner,** n. *cursor.* **running, I.** adj. — water, *aqua viva.* **II.** n. see RUN, II.

rupture, I. n. 1, *fractura* (e.g. *ossis);* 2, fig. *discordia* (= disagreement) ; *dissidium.* **II.** v.tr. *frangĕre, confringĕre, diffringĕre ;* see BREAK.

rural, adj. *rusticus, agrestis* (= in the country ; also = simple, plain, etc.), *rusticus* (= peculiar to the country, e.g. — life).

rush, n. *juncus, s(c)irpus;* made of —, *junceus* or *juncinus, s(c)irpeus;* full of —es, *juncosus;* a place covered with —es, *juncetum.* **rushlight,** n. see LAMP.

rush, v.intr. **see** RUN.

rusk, n. perhaps *panis tostus.*

russet, adj. *fuscus* (= dusky).

rust, I. n. *robigo (rub-,* in gen. ; also in reference to corn), *situs, -ūs* (= mould, mustiness), *ferrugo* (= — of iron), *aerugo* (= — of copper). **II.** v.intr. *robiginem trahĕre* or *sentire, robigine obduci, robigine infestari* (all in Plin.), fig. *corrumpi.* **III.** v.tr. *alqd robigine obducĕre,* etc. (Plin., Quint.). **rusty,** adj. *robi-*

ginosus (rub-, in gen.), *aeruginosus* (in Sen., of brass and copper).

rustic, adj. *rusticus, rusticanus, agrestis.* **rusticate, I.** v.tr. perhaps *rus relegare.* **II.** v.intr. *rusticari, rure vivĕre* or *degĕre.*

rustle, I. v.intr. *crepare, crepitum dare* (of a clattering noise), *strepĕre, strepitum dare* or *edĕre* (loud), *sonare* (= to sound loud) ; to — (of leaves), perhaps †*susurrare* (= to whisper). **II.** n. *crepitus, -ūs, strepitus, -ūs, sonus.*

rut, n. *orbita.*

ruth, n. see RUE.

rye, n. *secale* (Plin.).

S.

Sabbath, n. *sabbata, -orum.*

sable, adj. *niger, ater ;* see BLACK.

sabre, n. *acinaces, -is.*

saccharine, adj. by *dulcis.*

sacerdotal, adj. *quod ad sacerdotes* or *sacerdotium pertinet.*

sack, I. n. 1, *saccus;* — of leather, *culeus,* see BAG ; 2, see PLUNDER. **II.** v.tr. see PLUNDER. **sackbut,** n. *buccina.* **sackcloth,** n. by *toga sordida ;* in — and ashes, *sordidatus.*

sacrament, n. *sacramentum* (Eccl.).

sacred, adj. *sacer, sanctus, sacrosanctus, religiosus, augustus;* nothing is more — to me than, etc., *nihil antiquius est quam,* etc. ; to declare —, *sancire.* Adv. *sancte, religiose, auguste.* **sacredness,** n. *sanctitas,* or by *religio.*

sacrifice, I. n. *sacrificium, sacra, -orum,* n., *res divina* (the act), *victima, hostia* (= the victim); = loss, *jactura, damnum.* **II.** v.tr. 1, *sacrificare, (sacra,* or *rem divinam) facĕre* with ablat. of victim, *hostiam immolare, litare* (under favourable auspices), *caedĕre* (= to slaughter); 2, fig. *alcjs rei jacturam facĕre, alqd alci dare, dedĕre* (= to give up); to — one's life for, *pro alqd re* or *alqd occumbĕre, vitam profundĕre.* **sacrificer,** n. *immolator* (rare), or by verb. **sacrificial,** adj. by genit. of *sacrificium,* † *sacrificialis.*

sacrilege, n. *sacrilegium.* **sacrilegious,** adj. *sacrilegus.* Adv. by adj.

sacristan, n. *aedituus.* **sacristy,** n. *sacrarium.*

sad, adj. 1, = sorrowful, *maestus, tristis, maerens, afflictus* (= cast down); 2, = causing sadness, *gravis, acerbus, tristis, miserabilis, miserandus, luctuosus.* Adv. *maeste,* † *triste, miserabiliter, luctuose.* **sadden,** v.tr. *maestitiā, dolore, alqm afficĕre.* **sadness,** n. *maestitia, tristitia, dolor* (= pain), *maeror, aegritudo, aegrimonia, miseria* (often in pl.); see SORROW.

saddle, I. n. *ephippium.* **II.** v.tr. *equum sternĕre ;* to — anyone with anything, *alqd alci imponĕre, injungĕre.* **saddle-bags,** n. *hippoperae* (Sen.). **saddle-horse,** n. *equus.* **saddler,** n. *ephippiorum artifex.*

safe, I. adj. *tutus (ab alqā re), salvus sospes* (= — and sound), *integer* (= whole), *incolumis* (= unharmed), *periculo vacuus* (= free from danger). Adv. *tuto, tute.* **II.** n. *cella penaria.* **safe-conduct,** n. *fides (publica).* **safeguard,** n. *propugnaculum ;* see PROTECTION. **safety,** n. *salus, -utis,* f., *incolumitas ;* in —, *tutus,* etc. **safety-valve,** n. 1, lit. perhaps *foramen per quod vapor calidus emittitur ;* 2, fig. *salutis certa via atque ratio.*

saffron, I. n. *crocus.* **II.** adj. *croceus.*

sagacious. adj. *sagax, prudens, perspicax, rationis et consilii plenus.* Adv. *sagaciter, prudenter.* **sagacity,** n. *sagacitas, prudentia, perspicacitas.*

sage, n. *salvia* (Plin.).

sage, I. adj. see WISE. **II.** n. *sapiens.*

sail, I. n. *velum ;* to set —, *vela dare ;* = to set out —, (*navem*) *solvěre ;* to furl —, *vela subducěre.* **II.** v.intr. *navigare ;* to — over, *transvehi, transmitti ;* to — past, *praetervehi ;* to — round, *circumvehi.* **sailing,** n. *navigatio.* **sailor,** n. *nauta,* m.

saint, n. (*vir*) *sanctus,* (*femina*) *sancta, beatus, beata* (Eccl.). **saintly,** adj. *sanctus.*

sake, n. for the — of, *ob, propter, per* (with accus.), *prae, pro, de* (with ablat.), *caus*(*s*)*â* or *gratiâ* (with genit., and more rarely *ergo,* which follows the genit.), or by part. *motus, affectus, coactus alqâ re.*

salaam, n. by *corpus humi prosterněre.*

salad, n. *acetaria, -orum* (Plin.).

salamander, n. *salamandra* (Plin.).

salary, I. n. *merces, -ēdis,* f. **II.** v.tr. *mercedem alci dare ;* to be salaried, *mercedem accipěre.*

sale, n. *venditio* (in gen.), *hasta* (= auction); to offer for —, *alqd venum dare.* **saleable,** adj. *vendibilis* (= on sale), *quod facile vendi potest.* **salesman,** n. *venditor.*

salient, adj. *praecipuus* (= chief); see PRINCIPAL.

saline, adj. *salsus.*

saliva, n. *saliva.*

sallow, adj. *pallidus.*

sally, I. v.tr. *erumpěre, eruptionem facěre.* **II.** n. 1, *eruptio ;* 2, fig. *alqd argute dictum.*

salmon, n. *salmo* (Plin.).

saloon, n. *atrium, exēdra, oecus.*

salt, I. n. *sal.* **II.** adj. *salsus.* **III.** v.tr. *sale condire, salire.* **salt-cellar,** n. *salinum, concha salis.* **salt-mine, salt-pit, salt-works,** n. *salifodina, salinae.* **saltness,** n. *salsitudo.*

salubrious, adj. *saluber,* or *salubris.* Adv. *salubriter.* **salubriousness,** n. *salubritas.* **salutary,** adj. *salutaris ;* see USEFUL.

salute, I. v.tr. *salutare, consalutare* (of several); in letters, *alci multam* or *plurimam salutem dīcěre, impertire, a*(*d*)*scrīběre ;* of sending a message, so *salutem nuntiare,* or simply *salutem.* **II.** n. 1, see KISS ; 2, milit. t.t. perhaps by *tela alci erigěre honoris caus*(*s*)*â* (= by presenting arms), *missilibus effusis alqm excipěre* (= by discharge of guns). **salutation,** n. *salutatio, salus* (see above), *alqm salvěre jubēre.*

salvation, n. *salus, -utis,* f., *conservatio* (in gen.).

salve, I. n. *unguentum ;* for the eyes, *collyrium.* **II.** v.tr. (*in*)*ungěre.*

salver, n. see DISH.

salvo, n. with this —, *hoc excepto, hac lege or condicione.*

same, adj. *īdem, eadem, īdem ;* = — as, followed by *et, ac, que ut, qui* (*quae, quod*), *quam, quasi, cum* with ablat. (*alci rei*), *unus et idem, ipse, ipsa, ipsum* (=self), *ejusdem generis* (=of the same kind); it is not the — whether, *multum interest utrum . . . an ;* it is the — to me, *meâ nihil interest* or *refert ;* in the — way, *eodem modo ;* at the — time, *eodem tempore ;* in the — place, *ibidem ;* to the — place. *eodem.* **sameness,** n. see MONOTONY.

sample, n. *exemplum, specimen, documentum ;* see EXAMPLE.

sanatory, adj. *quod alci rei meâetur ;* see also SALUTARY.

sanctify, v.tr. (*con*)*secrare, dedicare* (= to consecrate), *sanctificare* (Eccl.). **sanctification,** n. *sanctificatio* (Eccl.). **sanctimonious,** adj. perhaps by *qui se sanctissimum esse simulat.*

sanction, I. n. *confirmatio, auctoritas, fides ;* with, without the — of, *jussu, injussu alcjs.* **II.** v.tr. *sancire, ratum facěre, ratum esse jubēre ;* see also ALLOW. **sanctity,** n. *sanctitas* (both as moral quality and sacredness of a thing, in which latter sense also *caerimonia* and *religio*).

sanctuary, n. *templum, penetralia, -ium, delubrum, fanum,* † *adytum, asylum* (in the sense of refuge).

sand, n. *arēna, sabulum* (*sabulo,* coarse), *saburra* (for ballast). **sand-bank,** n. *syrtis.* **sand-glass,** n. *clepsydra.* **sand-heap,** n. *acervus arenae.* **sandstone,** n. *tofus.* **sandy,** adj. *arenosus, sabulosus* (= full of sand).

sandal, n. *sandalium* (very rare), *crepĭda, solea ;* wearing —s, *crepidatus, soleatus.*

sane, adj. *sanus, sanus et salvus, mentis compos, animi integer ;* to be —, *mentis compotum esse ;* not to be —, *mente captum esse, mente alienari* or *alienatum esse, nullius consilii esse.* **sanity,** n. use adj.

sanguinary, adj. *sanguinem sitiens* (= thirsting for blood), *cruentus,* † *sanguineus* (= bloody); see CRUEL, BLOODY. **sanguine,** adj., **sanguineness,** n. see HOPE, HOPEFULNESS.

sap, I. n. *sucus.* **II.** v.tr. 1, = to undermine, *cuniculos agěre ;* 2, fig. *corrumpěre* (= to spoil), *haurire* (=to drain away). **sapless,** adj. 1, lit. *suco carens ;* 2, fig. *exsucus* (Quint.). **sapling,** n. *arbor novella.* **sapper,** n. *qui cuniculos agit.*

sapient, adj. *sapiens, sapientiâ praeditus ;* to be —, *sapěre.*

sapphire, n. *sapp*(*h*)*īrus* (Plin.).

sarcasm, n. *facetiae acerbae* or *dictum aculeatum.* **sarcastic,** adj. *acerbus.* Adv. *acerbe.*

sarcophagus, n. *sarcophagus* (Juv.).

sardonyx, n. *sardonyx* (Plin.).

sash, n. *cingulum ;* see BELT ; a — window, *fenestra ex ligneâ compage confecta.*

Satan, n. *Satānas, -ae.* **satanic,** adj. see DEVILISH.

satchel, n. *pera, sacculus* (Plin.).

satellite, n. *satelles, -ĭtis,* m. and f.

satiate, v.tr. (*ex*)*satiare, explēre, saturare :* to — oneself with food, *cibo satiari.* **satiation** or **satiety,** n. *satietas, saturitas.*

satin, n. *pannus sericus densior ac nitens.*

satire, n. *satira* (*satura*), *carmen satiricum, carmen probrosum, carmen* † *famosum, carmen maledicens, carmen refertum contumeliis, versus in alcjs cupiditatem facti.* **satirical,** adj. *acerbus ;* see above. Adv. *acerbe.* **satirist,** n. *qui libellum* or *libellos ad infamiam alterius edit, satirarum scriptor, satirici carminis scriptor.* **satirize,** v.tr. *alqm perstringěre, acerbis facetiis alqm irridēre, carmen probrosum facěre in alqm, carmen ad alcjs infamiam eděre.*

satisfaction, n. *satisfactio* (originally = payment of a creditor, then amends to any-one injured), *expletio* (= fulfilment), *voluptas* (= pleasure), *poena* (=penalty). **satisfactory,** adj. *idoneus* (= suitable); see GOOD, EXCELLENT. Adv. *bene, ex sententia.* **satisfy,** v.tr. *satisfa-*

vēre alci, placēre alci, ex(s)pectationem or *desiderium explēre.*

satrap, n. *satrapes, -ae* and *-is,* m.

saturate, v.tr. see SOAK.

Saturday, n. ** dies Saturni.*

Saturnalia, n. *Saturnalia, -ium,* n.

satyr, n. *satyrus.*

sauce, n. *jus, juris,* n., *embamma, -ātis,* n. (Plin.), *condimentum.*

saucepan, n. *vas ad condimenta paranda accommodatum.*

saucer, n. *patella;* see PLATE.

saucy, adj. *petulans, insolens, protervus, procax, immodestus.* Adv. *petulanter, insolenter, proterve, procaciter, immodeste.* **sauciness,** n. *impudentia, os impudens, insolentia, protervitas, procacitas.*

saunter, v.intr. *ambulare, morari;* to — about, *vagari;* see LOITER.

sausage, n. *tomaculum* (Juv.), *farcīmen, hillae.*

savage, adj. *ferus, agrestis, indomitus, efferatus* (= wild), *incultus, vastus* (= waste), *ferox, immanis, saevus, trux, atrox* (= cruel), *incultus ferusque.* Adv. *ferociter, immaniter, saeve, atrociter.* **savageness,** n. *feritas, ferocitas, immanitas, saevitia, atrocitas.*

save, I. v.tr. 1, = to preserve, *(con)servare;* 2, = to deliver, *liberare, vindicare alqm ab alqâ re;* see FREE; 3, to — money, *compendium* (opp. *dispendium) facēre;* to — time, *sequi compendium temporis;* to — health, *parcēre valetudini;* to — labour, *laborem diminuēre;* God — you, *salve, ave, salvēre te jubeo* (at meeting), *salve et vale* (at parting); —d or laid by, *repositus, sepositus.* **II.** prep. and conj. see EXCEPT. **saving,** adj. *parcus, frugi* (indecl.). **savings,** n. *quod alqs parsimoniâ collegit, peculium* (= the — of a slave; what a father gives to sons and daughters). **savings-bank,** n. by *mensa publica apud quam alqs pecuniam collocat.* **savingness,** n. *parsimonia* (= sparingness), *frugalitas.* **saviour,** n. *(con)servator, liberator;* of Christ, *Salvator* (Eccl.).

savour, I. n. *sapor* (= taste), *odor* (= smell); an ill —, *foetor;* to be in ill —, *male audiri;* to be in good —, *bene audiri.* **II.** v.tr. *sapēre* (= to have a taste), *alqd redolēre* (= to smell of). **savoury,** adj. *suavis.*

saw, n. = saying, *dictum, verbum, vox, sententia, proverbium.*

saw, I. n. *serra;* a tooth of a —, *dens serrae.* **II.** v.tr. *serrâ (dis)secare.* **III.** v.intr. *serram ducēre.* **sawdust,** n. *scob(i)s.* **sawed,** adj. *serratus.* **sawing,** n. *serratura.*

say, v.tr. *dicēre, (e)loqui, (e)narrare, profiteri, fari, praedicare, asseverare;* to — that not, *negare;* I — yes, *aio, affirmo;* I — no, *nego;* to — not a word, *tacēre;* they, people —, *dicunt, tradunt, ferunt* (with accus. and infin.), or *dicitur, traditur, fertur* (with nomin. and infin.); I will not —, *ne dicam;* — I, *inquam* (so *inquit, ait,* —s he); as they, people —, *ut aiunt, ut dicitur.* **saying,** n. *dictio* (= act of —, as in Quint., the thing said), *verbum, proverbium, sententia, dictum, quod aiunt, illud.*

scab, n. *scabies.* **scabby,** adj. *scabiosus.*

scabbard, n. *vagina.*

scaffold, n. *machina, catasta* (= a place where slaves were exposed for sale); to come to the —, *ad mortem duci;* see EXECUTION.

scald, I. v.tr. *aquâ ferventi perfundēre* (= to burn). **II.** n. use verb.

scale, I. n. 1, of a fish, *squama;* 2, of a

balance, *lanx;* pair of —s, *libra, trūtina.* **II.** v.tr. to — a fish, *desquamare.* **III.** v.intr. = to weigh, † *pendēre.* **scaly,** adj. *squamosus.*

scale, I. n. 1, = gradation, *gradus, -ūs;* on the — of, *(ad) instar alcjs rei;* on a larger, smaller —, *major, minor,* with noun; 2, in music, *diagramma, -ātis,* n. **II.** v.tr. *(positis scalis) a(d)scendēre, scalas moenibus applicare* or *admovēre;* see CLIMB. **scaling-ladder,** n. *scalae.*

scallop, I. n. *pecten.* **II.** v.tr. see SCOOP.

scalp, I. n. *cutis capitis.* **II.** v.tr. *cutem capiti detrahēre.*

scalpel, n. *scalpellum.*

scamp, n. see KNAVE. **scamper,** v.intr. see HURRY.

scan, v.tr. 1, *inspicēre, (per)scrutari, contemplari;* see EXAMINE; 2, in prosody, *pedibus versum metiri* (Gram.). **scansion,** n. use verb.

scandal, n. 1, see DISGRACE; 2, see SLANDER. **scandalize,** v.tr. see SHOCK, HORRIFY. **scandalous,** adj. *mali* or *pessimi exempli, probrosus, turpis;* see DISGRACEFUL.

scant, scanty, adj. *angustus, artus* (= narrow), *exiguus, parvus;* see SMALL. Adv. *anguste, arte, exigue.* **scantiness,** n. *angustiae, exiguitas.*

scar, n. *cicatrix.*

scarce, adj. *rarus, singularis.* Adv. *vix, aegre.* **scarcity,** n. *raritas, res rara, paucitas, inopia, penuria, difficultas* (e.g. = — of money, *difficultas nummaria*); — of provisions, *caritas* (= dearth) *rei frumentariae* (so *vini, nummorum*).

scare, v.tr. *terrēre;* see TERRIFY. **scarecrow,** n. perhaps *formido.*

scarf, n. *fascia, mitella.*

scarlet, I. adj. *coccineus* (Plin.). **II.** n. *coccum.* **scarlet-fever,** n. *febris* (= fever).

scathe, v.tr. = to harm, *laedēre, nocēre, damnô esse alci, detrimentum afferre;* of words, *mordēre, pungēre;* a scathing remark, *verba quasi aculei, verba aculeata.* **scatheless,** adj. *sine damno, salvus, incolumis.*

scatter, I. v.tr. 1, = to throw about, *spargēre, serēre* (= to sow, of seeds); 2, = to drive away, *dispergēre, dis(j)icēre, dissipare, dispellēre, discutēre, fundēre* (of an army). **II.** v.intr. *dissipari, dilabi, diffugēre.*

scavenger, n. *qui vicos urbis purgare solet.*

scene, n. *scaena* (properly = the stage; hence *in scaenam prodire, in scaenâ esse, scaenam tenēre* = to be master or chief of the stage); the place before the —, *proscaenium;* belonging to —s, *scaenicus* (used with *artifices, actores, poëtae);* = place of action, *locus ubi alqd agitur;* fig. *res, spectaculum, rerum status, -ūs;* to be behind the —s, *alqd penitus novisse* or *exploratum habēre.* **scenery,** n. 1, of a theatre, *apparatus, -ūs, ad scaenam pertinens;* 2, = prospect, *locus* (or pl. *loca*).

scent, I. n. 1, = sense of smell, *odoratus, -ūs,* or by *nasus* (nose); of dogs, *narium sagacitas;* keen-scented, *sagax;* 2, = an odour, *odor, nidor;* to get — of, *alqd* (e.g. *nummum olfacēre*); to put on the wrong —, *alqm in errorem inducēre;* 3, = a perfume, essence, *unguentum.* **II.** v.tr. = 1, to find by —, *alqm* or *alqd odorari* (of dogs, etc.), *olfacēre;* see SMELL; 2, = to perfume, *odoribus perfundēre.* **scent-bottle,** n. *arcula* (= box for scents); see BOTTLE. **scented,** adj. *odoratus.*

sceptical, adj., **sceptic,** n. *qui se de omnibus rebus dubitare dicit.* **scepticism,** n. *dubitatio de omnibus rebus.*

sceptre, n. *sceptrum;* to wield the —, *regnare;* see REIGN.

schedule, n. *libellus;* see LIST.

scheme, I. n. *consilium, ratio;* to form a —, *rationem inire;* see PLAN. **II.** v.intr. see above and PLAN.

schism, n. *schisma, -ātis,* n. (Eccl.). **schismatic,** n. * *schismaticus.*

school, I. n. 1, *schola, ludus lit(t)erarum, ludus discendi;* to go to — to anyone, *in alcjs scholam ire, alcjs scholam frequentare;* 2, fig. that is a — of patience, *in hāc re tentatur patientia nostra;* philosophy, the — of life, *philosophia dux vitae, et officiorum magistra;* a — of wisdom, *sapientiae officina;* 3, = body of disciples, *schola, secta;* = teaching, *disciplina.* **II.** v.tr. *docēre;* see TEACH, TRAIN. **school-fellow,** n. *condiscipulus.* **schoolmaster,** n. *magister.* **school-mistress,** n. *magistra.* **scholar,** n. *discipulus, alumnus, audītor* (= a listener), *tiro* (= a beginner); my —, *alumnus disciplinae meae; alqm magistrum habēre, alqm audire.* **scholarly,** adj. *eruditus.* **scholarship,** n. 1, = learning, *lit(t)erae, doctrina, eruditio;* 2, = prize, *praemium.*

science, n. *scientia, notitia, cognitio* (= knowledge), *ars, doctrina, disciplina* (= system of knowledge); the — of music, grammar, etc., *musica, grammatica, -orum.* **scientific,** adj. *quod in artibus versatur;* — principles, *artis praecepta;* = learned or taught, *doctrinā eruditus.* Adv. *erudite,* or by some special noun (e.g. to treat music —, *e musicorum rationibus disserēre).*

scimitar, n. *acīnāces, ensis †falcatus;* see SABRE.

scintillation, n. *scintilla* (= spark). **scintillate,** v.intr. *scintillare* (e.g. *scintillant oculi).*

sciolist, n. *semidoctus* (e.g. *apud doctos et semidoctos ipse percurro,* Cic.).

scion, n. 1, of plants, *surculus;* 2, fig. *progenies.*

scissors, n. *forfices* (= shears, barber's —, Mart.), *forficulae* (= small shears or —, Plin.).

scoff, I. n. *ludibrium;* see MOCK. **II.** v.tr. to — at anyone or anything, *alqm* or *alqd in ludibrium vertēre, ludibrio habēre;* to be —ed at, *alci ludibrio esse;* see MOCK. **scoffer,** n. *irrisor;* see MOCKER. **scoffing,** n. *ludificatio, cavillatio;* see MOCKERY.

scold, I. v.tr. *jurgare cum alqo, objurgare, increpare alqm.* **II.** n. *objurgator;* of a woman, *jurgiis addicta.* **scolding,** n. *objurgatio, convicium.*

scoop, I. n. see LADLE. **II.** v.tr. *(ex)cavare.*

scope, n. 1, = the purpose or drift, *propositum, consilium;* 2, = room or space, *spatium;* 3, = liberty, *copia, potestas.*

scorch, I. v.tr. *amburēre, adurēre, torrēre, torrefacēre.* **II.** v.intr. *torrēri, arescēre* (e.g. *herbae arescunt et interficiuntur,* Cic.). **scorched,** adj. *torridus.* **scorching,** adj. *torridus;* see HOT.

score, I. n. 1, = account, *ratio, nomen;* on the — of friendship, *amicitiae nomine;* to pay a —, *pecuniam solvēre;* to quit —s, *par pari referre;* 2, in music, *cantilena cum musicis notis annexis;* 3, in number, *viginti.* **II.** v.tr. *notare, signare* (= to mark); see also RECKON; to underscore, *lineas sub verbis ducēre.*

scorn, n. *contemptus, -ūs, contemptio, fastidium.* **II.** v.tr. *contemnēre, fastidire, spernēre, aspernari.* **scorner,** n. *contemptor, animus*

contemptor. scornful, adj. *fastidiosus;* see also PROUD, INSOLENT. Adv. *fastidiose.*

scorpion, n. *scorpio, scorpius.*

scot, n. 1, in reckoning, *symbola* (ante and post class.); 2, in law, — and lot, *vectīgal;* — free, *immunis, inultus.*

scoundrel, n. *homo nefarius, nequam;* see RASCAL.

scour, v.tr. *(de)tergēre, tergēre* (or *tergēre), (ex)purgare* (= to cleanse); to — the land, *pervagari, percurrēre, (de)vastare* (in war).

scourge, I. n. = whip, *flagrum, flagellum, lora, -orum;* = plague, *pestis* (lit. and fig.); see PLAGUE. **II.** v.tr. *virgis* or *verberibus caedēre, verberare.* **scourging,** n. by verb.

scout, n. *explorator, speculator.*

scowl, I. v.intr. *frontem contrahēre, corrugare.* **II.** n. *frons, -ntis,* f., *asperior, vultus, -ūs,* † *torvus, truculentus.*

scraggy, adj. *strigosus;* see THIN.

scramble, v.tr. = for anything, *alqd certatim arripēre;* to — up, *manibus pedibusque a(d)scendēre.*

scrap, n. *frustum, fragmentum;* the —s, *frusta, rel(l)iquiae* (of food, *cibi).*

scrape, I. n. *angustiae, difficultas;* to be in a —, *in angustiis esse.* **II.** v.tr. *radēre;* to — off, *abradēre, defringēre;* to — together, *congerēre.* **scraper,** n. flesh —, *strigil* or *strigilis.*

scratch, v.tr. *scabēre, scalpēre, fricare, radēre;* to — out, *delēre.*

scrawl, I. n. *litterae male factae.* **II.** v.tr. = to scribble, *lit(t)eris male factis scribēre.*

scream, I. n. *clamor, vociferatio, ululatus, -ūs;* of an infant, *vagitus, -ūs.* **II.** v.intr. *clamare, clamitare, vociferari, ululare, vagire* (of children).

screech, v.intr. *ululare;* —owl, *ulula* (scil. *avis).* **screeching,** n. *ululatus, -ūs.*

screen, I. n. *umbraculum* (= a shady place; a parasol), *praesidium* (= a protection). **II.** v.tr. *defendēre* (= to ward off, e.g. *defendēre ardores solis,* Cic.); see PROTECT.

screw, I. n. *cochlea* (for drawing water); *clavus* (= nail). **II.** v.tr. *clavis adigēre alqd.*

scribe, n. *scriba,* m., *librarius*

scrip, n. see PURSE, WALLET.

scripture, n. (*sancta) scriptura* (Eccl.), *libri divini, lit(t)erae.* **scriptural,** adj. *ad normam librorum divinorum, libris sacris conveniens.*

scrivener, n. *scriba,* m.; see NOTARY.

scrofula, n. *struma.* **scrofulous,** adj. *strumosus* (Col.).

scroll, n. *volumen.*

scrub, v.tr. *(de)fricare, (de)tergēre, tergēre* (*tergēre).*

scruple, I. n. 1, as a weight, *scrupulum;* 2, = hesitation or difficulty, *dubitatio, haesitatio, cunctatio, religio, scrupulus.* **II.** v.intr. *animo haerēre, haesitare, suspenso esse animo;* to — to, *dubitare* with infin.; not to —, *non dubitare quin;* see HESITATE; in stricter sense *religione ac metu teneri, religione obstrictum esse, alqd religioni habēre;* he —s to, *religio ei obstat ne.* **scrupulous,** adj. *religiosus, sol(l)icitus, anxius, accuratus, diligens.* Adv. *religiose, anxie, accurate, diligenter,* or sometimes by superl. (e.g. — clean, *mundissimus).*

scrutiny, n. *scrutatio.* **scrutineer,** n. *scrutator.* **scrutinize,** v.tr. *scrutari;* see EXAMINE.

scud, v.intr. see HASTEN.

scuffle, n. *rixa.*

scull, I. n. (of the head) *calvāria* (Plin.); = an oar, *remulus, palma.* **II.** v.intr. *remigare.* **sculler,** n. *remex.*

scullery, n. *culina* (= kitchen). **scullion,** n. *puer culinarius.*

sculpture, I. n. 1, *ars fingendi* (as a science), *sculptura, sculptura* (for distinction see Smith's " Dict. Antiq.," art. Scalptura); 2,= work carved, *opus, -ēris,* n., *signum, marmor.* **II.** v.tr. = to work in statuary, *scalpēre, sculpēre.* **sculptor,** n. *sculptor, statuarum artifex.*

scum, n. 1, *spuma* (= foam; so of silver, Plin.), *scoria* (Plin., = — of metals); 2, fig. *faex, sentina (reipublicae,* etc.).

scurf, n. *furfur, furfures* (Plin.), *porrigo.* **scurfy,** adj. *porriginosus* (Plin.).

scurrilous, adj. *contumeliosus, probrosus, scurrīlis.* Adv. *contumeliose, scurrīliter* (Plin.). **scurrility,** n. *contumelia* (or in pl.), *scurrīlitas* (Quint.).

scurvy, I. n. by *ulcus, -ēris,* n. **II.** adj. *humilis, ignobilis, obscurus, infimus.*

scutcheon, n. *insigne* (or in pl.).

scuttle, n. *area, cista* (= box).

scuttle, v.tr. and intr. *navem perforare.*

scythe, n. *falx.*

sea, I. n. *mare* (in gen.), *oceanus, pelagus, -i,* n., *pontus,* †*aequor;* the high —, *altum* (= the "deep"); the open —, *salum;* the Mediterranean —, *Mare Magnum, * Mare Mediterraneum;* the Black —, *Pontus (Euxinus);* the Adriatic —, *Adriaticum;* the Red —, *Sinus Arabicus;* the Dead —, *Lacus Asphaltītes;* lying on or near the —, *maritimus;* beyond the —, *transmarinus;* an arm of the —, *aestuarium;* —breeze, *afflatus, -ūs, maritimus* (Plin.); —calf, *phoca;* —coast, *ora (maritima);* —faring, *maritimus;* —fight, *pugna navalis;* —girt, *circumfluus;* —green, †*thalassinus, thalassicus* (Plaut.); —gull, * larus* (Linn.); —man, *nauta;* —manship, *ars navigandi;* —sand, *arena (maritima);* —sickness, *nausea;* —water, *aqua marina* (Plin.); —weed, *alga.* **II.** adj. *marinus, maritimus,* (*maritu-*).

seal, I. n. *signum.* **II.** v.tr. *(con)signare, obsignare alqd;* —ing-wax, *cera.*

seal, n. (an animal) *phoca.*

seam, n. *sutura.* **seamstress,** n. *quae acu victum quaeritat.*

sear, I. adj. *aridus* (= dry), *serus* (= late). **II.** v.tr. *arefacĕre* (ante and post class., = to dry), *(ad)urēre* (= to burn).

search, I. n. *indagatio, investigatio, inquisitio, exploratio, inspectio.* **II.** v.tr. *investigare, inquirēre, explorare, indagare, scrutari, quaerēre, (ex)petĕre, sequi, persequi, sectari, captare, aucupari, studēre rei;* see SEEK.

season, I. n. (e.g. *anni,* of the year) *tempus, tempestas* (= time), *occasio, opportunitas, locus* (= occasion). **II.** v.tr. *condire.* **seasonable,** adj. *tempestivus, opportunus, ad tempus.* Adv. *tempestive, opportune;* not —, *non opportune, alieno tempore.* **seasoning,** n. *condimentum* (= the material employed), *conditio* (= the act).

seat, I. n. *sella, sedile, cathedra* (= chair); — at the theatre, etc., *subsellia;* = dwelling, *domicilium, sedes, -is;* to have a — in the royal council, *omnibus consiliis principis interesse;* to put a — for anyone, *sellam alci apponēre.* **II.** (or set), v.tr. *ponēre, statuēre, collocare, constituēre;* to — yourself, *considēre, assidēre, subsidēre;* to — yourself on, *assidēre in re;* to — yourself on horseback, *conscendēre equum;*

see SET. **III.** (to be seated or to sit), v.intr. *sedēre;* to be — on anything, *sedēre in re;* to be — on the soil, *humo sedēre;* to be — in school, *in scholā sedēre.* **seated,** adj. = rested, *penitus defixus, inveteratus.*

secede, v.intr. *abire, decedēre, secedēre* (e.g. *secedant improbi,* Cic. ; *secedēre in sacrum montem,* Liv.); so as to take up another opinion, *secedēre et alia parte considēre* (Sen.), or by *sententiam mutare.* **seceder,** n. *transfuga,* m. **secession,** n. *secessio.*

seclude, v.tr. *secludēre, segregare, removēre, excludēre, eximēre, excipēre.* **secluded,** adj. see LONELY. **seclusion,** n. *solitudo;* a life of —, *vita umbratilis.*

second, I. adj. *secundus, alter* (e.g. —father, *alter parens);* in the first place, in the —, *primum, deinde.* Adv. *secunde, deinde.* **II.** n. 1, in a fight, *qui alci adest;* 2, of time, *momentum (temporis).* **III.** v.tr. 1, = to support, *alci adesse, auxilio esse, subvenire;* 2, = to help, *adjuvare;* see HELP; 3, to — a motion, *in alcjs sententiam dicēre; alci adesse.* **secondary,** adj. *secundarius* (in rank or position), *inferior, minoris momenti.* **seconder,** n. *suasor* (e.g. *legis).* **second-hand,** adj. *usu inferior factus.* **second-rate,** adj. *inferior.* **second-sight,** n. *praesagitio.*

secrecy, n. perhaps *taciturnitas* (= strict silence), or *solitudo*(= solitude); to keep anything in —, *rem occultam* or *abditam* or *secretam habēre.*

secret, I. adj. 1, = hidden, *arcanus* (of plans, etc.), *secretus, abditus, tectus, occultus, absconditus, latens* (all of places, etc.); 2, = furtive, *clandestinus, furtivus.* Adv. *clam, furtim, secreto, in occulto, occulte.* **II.** n. *res occulta* or *arcana,* in pl. *arcana, -orum; mysterium* (e.g. *epistulae nostrae tantum habent mysteriorum,* Cic.). **secrete,** v.tr. see HIDE. **secretion,** n. *excrementum* (Plin.).

secretary, n. *scriba,* m. **secretaryship,** n. *scribae munus, -ēris.*

sect, n. *secta, schola, disciplina.* **sectary, sectarian,** n. *homo sectae studiosus.*

section, n. *pars, portio.*

secular, adj. *saecularis* (= occurring every age, also Eccl. = temporal, for which in gen. use *civilis).* **secularize,** v.tr. *profanum facĕre,* or *ad profanum usum redigēre, exaugurare* (of a temple, or anything consecrated).

secure, I. adj. 1, = careless, *securus* (i.e. *sine curā), incautus;* to be — or free from care about anything, *alqd non timēre;* 2, = safe, *tutus;* see SAFE. Adv. *secure, incaute, tuto.* **II.** v.tr. 1, = to make safe, *tutum reddēre;* see PRESERVE; 2, = to strengthen, *confirmare;* 3, = to tie up, etc., see FASTEN; 4, = to arrest; see SEIZE. **security,** n. 1, = safety, *salus, -utis,* f., *incolumitas;* see SAFETY; 2, = pledge, *pignus, -ēris,* n., *cautio, satisdatio, vadimonium* (= bail); to give —, *satis dare, cavēre.*

sedan, n. *lectīca.*

sedate, adj. *sedatus, placidus, gravis;* to be —, *quietum esse, animo esse tranquillo.* Adv. *sedate, placide, graviter.* **sedateness,** n. *gravitas.* **sedative,** n. *sedatio* (e.g. *animi),* of a medicine, *medicina quae dolorem compescit.*

sedentary, adj. *sedentarius;* see SEAT, SIT.

sedge, n. *ulva.* **sedgy,** adj. *ulvis obductus.*

sediment, n. *faex, sedimentum* (Plin.).

sedition, n. *seditio;* to raise —, *seditionem concitare, concire* or *conflare;* to put down —, *seditionem sedare* or *componēre.* **seditious,** adj. *seditiosus;* see REBELLIOUS. Adv. *seditiose.*

seduce, v.tr. **1,** = to lead astray, *a rectâ viâ abducĕre, corrumpĕre, sol(l)icitare* (= to tamper with), *in errorem inducĕre* ; see PERVERT ; **2,** to — a woman, *stuprum cum alqâ,* or *alci facĕre*. **seducer,** n. *corruptor,* or by verb. **seduction,** n. *stuprum, corruptēla* (of women, etc.) ; = charm, *illecebrae, lepos*. **seductive,** adj. = pleasant, *amoenus, qui (quae, quod) alqm corrumpit,* etc.

sedulous, adj. *sedulus, assiduus, industrius, acer, diligens, accuratus*. Adv. *sedulo, assidue, industrie, acriter* (= eagerly), *diligenter, accurate*. **sedulity,** n. *sedulitas, assiduitas, industria, diligentia*.

see, n. bishop's —, * *diocesis*.

see, I. v.tr. *vidēre, cernĕre, a(d)spicĕre, conspicĕre, spectare, intellegĕre* (= to understand); to — anything from, *cognoscĕre* or *intellĕgĕre alqd ex re* ; to let a person —, *ostendĕre alqd, se ostendĕre, conspici* ; not to let oneself be —n in public, *in publicum non prodire* ; = to understand, *perspicĕre, intellegĕre*. **II.** v.intr. = to have the faculty of sight, *vidēre, cernĕre* ; to — further (in mind), *plus vidēre* ; to — to, *alci rei prospicĕre, consulĕre* (or *ut, ne*). **seeing that,** conj. see SINCE. **seer,** n. *vates, -is*.

seed, n. *semen* ; to run to —, *in semen exire* (Plin.) ; fig. *semen, stirps*. **seed-plot,** n. *seminarium,* lit. and fig. **seed-time,** n. *sementis*. **seedling,** n. *arbor novella*.

seek, v.tr. *quaerĕre, petĕre, (in)vestigare, indagare* ; to — to do, *studēre, cupĕre, operam dare ut,* etc. ; to — out, *exquirĕre* ; = to endeavour, *conari* ; to — a person's ruin, *alci insidias struĕre* or *parare*. **seeker,** n. *indagator, investigator*. **seeking,** n. *indagatio, investigatio*.

seem, v.intr. *vidēri,* used personally, e.g. it —s that you are good, *videris bonus* ; to — good, fit, *videri* (e.g. *eam quoque, si videtur, correctionem explicabo*). **seeming, I.** n. *species*. **II.** adj. *fictus, speciosus, falsus*. Adv. *in speciem, specie, ut videtur*. **seemly,** adj. *decens, decōrus, honestus* ; not —, *indecens, indecorus* ; it is —, *decet* ; it is not —, *dedecet, non decet, indecorum est*.

seethe, v.tr. *coquĕre* ; see BOIL.

segment, n. *segmentum* (Plin.).

segregate, v.tr. *segregare, seponĕre, semovēre, removēre, sejungĕre*. **segregation,** n. *segregatio, sejunctio*.

seignior, n. *dominus* ; see LORD.

seize, v.tr. *(ap)prehendĕre, comprehendĕre* (= to arrest), *rapĕre, arripĕre, corripĕre* ; = to fall on and take. *occupare, invadĕre* ; to be —d by illness, *morbo affici* ; to be —d with fear, *timore percelli* ; to be —d with anger, *ira incendi*. **seizure,** n. *comprehensio* ; of illness, *tentatio*.

seldom, adv. *raro*.

select, I. v.tr. *legĕre, eligĕre, deligĕre* ; see CHOOSE. **II.** adj. *delectus*. **selection,** n. *electio, delectus, -ûs, optio* (= choice) ; = a number chosen, *res selectae* ; — of passages, *ecloga*.

self, pron. *se, ipse, ipse se* ; I my—, *egomet* (so *tute, ipsemet*) ; of him—, *suâmet sponte* ; we our-selves, *nos ipsi, nosmet, nosmet ipsi* ; by one—, *solus* ; he is beside him—, *mente est captus* ; — command, *imperium sui, moderatio, continentia* ; to possess — -command, *in se ipsum habēre potestatem* ; — -deceit, *error* ; — -denial, *animi moderatio, temperantia* ; — -destruction, *mors voluntaria* ; to be guilty of — -destruction, *manus sibi inferre* ; — -evident, *(quasi) ante oculos positus* ; by — -exertion, *suâ ipsius manu* ; — -love, *amor sui* ; to have — -love, *se ipsum amare* ; — -preservation, *tuitio sui, corporis nostri tutela* ; — -seeking, *cu-*

piditas. **selfish,** adj. and adv. *suarum rerum cupidus*. **selfishness,** n. *cupiditas mea (tua,* etc.), *privatae utilitatis studium, avaritia*. **self-willed,** adj. *suae opinioni addictus, pertinax* ; see OBSTINATE.

sell, v.tr. *vendĕre, divendĕre* (by retail), *venditare* (= to live by selling), *venundare* (*venum dare*) ; to be sold, *vendi, vēnire, venum ire* ; to — yourself, *se venditare, se vendĕre alci* (= to take a bribe), *pecuniam accipĕre ab alqo* ; to — at a dear rate, *vendĕre alqd alci grandi pretio* ; he —s cheaper than others, *vendit minoris quam alii* ; how much do you — that for? *hoc quanti vendis?* **seller,** n. *venditor, institor, negotiātor, nundinator, mercator, propōla*. **selling,** n. *venditio* ; see SALE, AUCTION.

semblance, n. *species, imago* ; see APPEARANCE.

semicircle, n. *hemicyclium*. **semicircular,** adj. by noun.

seminary, n. *schola* (= school), *seminarium* (= seed-plot, fig.).

senate, n. *senatus, -ûs*. **senate-house,** n. *curia*. **senator,** n. *senator*. **senatorial,** adj. *senatorius*.

send, v.tr. *mittĕre, legare, ablegare, amandare* ; to — across, *transmittĕre* ; to — away, *ablegare, amandare, relegare, dimittĕre* ; to — back to, *remittĕre* ; to — for, *arcessĕre, (ac)cire* ; to — out, *edĕre, emittĕre* ; to — for soldiers from their winter quarters, *milites ex hibernis evocare* ; to — forward, *praemittĕre* ; I have nobody to —, *neminem habeo quem mittam* ; to — us word with all speed, *fac nos quam diligentissime certiores* (Com.) ; God — him health, *salvus Deum quaeso ut sit* (Com.).

senior, adj. *prior, superior, grandior (natu,* = older), *major (natu)* ; to be a person's —, *alci aetate anteire, antecedĕre*. **seniority,** n. by adj.

sensation, n. **1,** = a feeling, *sensus, -ûs,* or by some special noun (e.g. — of pain, *dolor* ; — of joy, *gaudium*) ; to have no —, *omni sensu carēre, nihil sentire* ; **2,** = an excitement, per-haps *(animi) commotio* ; to make a —, *alci admirationem movēre*. **sensational,** adj. *mirificus, mirus, admirabilis*. Adv. *mire, mirifice, admirabiliter*. **sense,** n. **1,** *sensus, -ûs* (= the faculty, properly of feeling, that is *facultas or vis sentiendi*) ; — of sight, *sensus videndi* or *visûs* ; the —s, *sensus* ; — of taste, *gustatus, -ûs* ; — of hearing, *audītus, -ûs* ; — of smell, *odoratus, -ûs* ; **2,** = mental or moral feeling, *judicium, conscientia, prudentia, sapientia* ; **3,** = faculty of will, *mens, voluntas* ; **4,** = meaning (of a word), *vis, significatio, sententia* ; to ascribe a — to a word, *verbo notionem sub(j)icĕre*. **senseless,** adj. **1,** lit. (*omni*) *sensu carens* ; **2.** *rationis expers* ; see FOOLISH, MAD. **sensible or sensuous,** adj. **1,** *quod sensibus percipi potest, sub sensus cadens, perspicuus, evidens* ; **2,** = having sound or good sense, e.g. a — man, *animus* or *homo sapiens, prudens*. Adv. *ita ut sentiri possit, sapienter, prudenter*. **sensitive,** adj. **1,** = SENSIBLE, I. ; **2,** fig. of quick feeling, perhaps *acer* (= eager), *anxius, sol(l)icitus* (= anxious), *accuratus, diligens* (= scrupulous, i.e. in discharge of duty), *tener* (= delicate). **sensitiveness or sensibility,** n. **1,** physical, *qui alqd facile sentit* ; **2,** moral, *anxietas, sol(l)icitudo, diligentia,* or by adj. **sensitive-plant,** n. *aeschynomene* (Plin.). **sensual,** adj. *cupiditatibus serviens, libidinosus*. Adv. *libidinose*. **sensuality,** n. *libido* ; see LUST. **sentient,** adj. see SENSIBLE, I.

sentence, I. n. **1,** = logical statement, *sententia* (lit. = opinion ; then also the words in which it is expressed) ; 2, = a judicial decision, *judicium, decretum, sententia ;* to pronounce —, *sententiam ferre de alqo, sententiam pronuntiare, alqm damnare, condemnare, judicium facĕre de re, de alqo.* **II.** v.tr. see above. **sententious,** adj. *verbosus* (= prolix), *sententiosus* (= pithy), *opinionibus inflatus* (= conceited).** Adv. *verbose, sententiose.*

sentiment, n. 1, = opinion, *sententia, opinio, judicium ;* see THOUGHT ; 2, = feeling, *sensus, -ūs, animus ;* a pleasurable —, *voluptas ;* an unpleasant —, *dolor ;* to have a —, *sentire alqd ;* without —, *sensu carens.* **sentimental,** adj. *mollis, effeminatus,* comb. *mollis ac effeminatus.*

sentinel or **sentry,** n. *excubitor, vigil, statio, miles stationarius ;* to stand —, *excubias* or *vigilias agĕre, in statione esse ;* to place —, *stationes disponĕre ;* to relieve —, *in stationem succedĕre ;* see GUARD.

separable, adj. *separabilis, dividuus, qui* (*quae, quod*) *separari potest.* **separate, I.** v.tr. *separare, sejungĕre, disjungĕre, secernĕre, discernĕre, dividĕre ;* we are —d by a great distance, *magno locorum intervallo disjuncti sumus.* **II.** adj. and adv. *separatus,* etc., or by *proprius, suus, viritim, separatim* (e.g. each had his — place, *stationem propriam* or *suam habuit ; stationes viritim datae sunt*). **separation,** n. *separatio, disjunctio.* **separatist,** n. *qui a publicis ecclesiae ritibus secedit.*

September, n. (*mensis*) *September.*

septennial, adj. *qui* (*quae, quod*) *septimo quoque anno fit.*

sepulchre, n. *sepulc(h)rum.* **sepulchral,** adj. *sepulc(h)ralis.* **sepulture,** n. *sepultura, funus, ex(s)equiae* (= rites of burial).

sequel, n. *quod sequitur, eventus, -ūs, exitus, -ūs.* **sequence,** n. *ordo, series.*

seraph, n. *seraphus* (Eccl.).

serenade, I. v.tr. *alqm concentu honorare.* **II.** n. *concentus, -ūs* (*nocte factus*).

serene, adj. 1, see CLEAR ; 2, see TRANQUIL.

serf, n. *servus.* **serfdom,** n. *servitus, -ūtis,* f.

serge, n. *pannus.*

serious, adj. 1, = grave, *serius* (of things), *gravis, severus, austerus, tristis* (= sad) ; 2, = important, *magni* or *maximi momenti.* Adv. *graviter, severe, triste.* **seriousness,** n. 1, *gravitas* (= moral weight), *severitas, tristitia* (= sadness) ; 2, see IMPORTANCE.

sermon, n. * *contio,* or *oratio de rebus divinis facta.*

serpent, n. *serpens ;* see SNAKE.

serried, adj. *densus, confertus.*

serve, v.tr. 1, = to do or render service to, *servire alci, deservire alci, operam alci navare* or *praestare ;* 2, = to wait at table, *famulari, ancillari* (ante and post class.), *ministrare ;* to — meat, *inferre cibos, instruĕre mensam cibis ;* to — wine to the company, *praebēre pocula convivis ;* to — as a soldier, *mereri, stipendia facĕre, militare ;* to — under, *sub duce merēri ;* to — God, *Deum colĕre ;* to benefit, *ad alqm* or *alci conducĕre, proficĕre.* **servant,** n. *servus, famulus, verna* (= slave), *ancilla* (= a waiting-woman), *assecla* (contemptuous term), *minister, mancipium* (= bought slave), *pedis(s)equus* (= a footman), *servitium* (collective term, = slaves), *puer.* **service,** n. *opera, servitium, ministerium, obsequium, officium, observantia, cultus, -ūs ;* — of God, *cultus Dei, pietas erga Deum ;* to confer a — or kindness on a person, *in alqm officia conferre.* **serviceable,** adj. *opportunus, utilis, aptus rei* or *ad rem, ad usum comparatus, aecommodatus ;* see USEFUL.

servile, adj. 1, *servīlis ;* 2, fig. see ABJECT, LOW, MEAN. **servility,** n. *adulatio ;* see also MEANNESS. **servitude,** n. *servitudo, servitium, servitus, -ūtis,* f. ; to free anyone from —, *in libertatem alqm vindicare, servitute alqm eximĕre.*

session, n. — of Parliament, *senatus, -ūs* (e.g. during a —, *cum senatus habetur*). **sessions,** n. pl. *cum de alqā re quaeritur.*

set, I. v.tr. 1, = to place (*im*)*ponĕre, statuĕre, sistĕre ;* 2, = to plant, *serĕre* (e.g. *arbores ;* see PLANT) ; to — in order, *parare* (= to prepare) ; see ARRANGE ; to — jewels, † *auro includĕre ;* to — about, *incipĕre ;* see BEGIN ; to — anyone against another, *inimicitias inter alqos serĕre ;* to — apart, *seponĕre ;* to — aside, see REJECT ; to — forth, *exponĕre* (= to expose for sale, etc., and explain) ; to — on, see INCITE ; to — on fire, *incendĕre* (lit. and fig.) ; to — over, *alci* (*rei*) *praeficĕre.* **II.** v.intr. of the sun, etc., *occidĕre ;* to — out, *proficisci ;* to — forward, see PROMOTE ; to — off, see EMBELLISH ; to be — over, *praeesse ;* to — up, see ERECT, APPOINT. **III.** adj. *status, constitutus* (= settled), *praescriptus* (= prescribed) ; a — speech, *oratio ;* of — purpose, *consulto.* **IV.** n. see NUMBER, COLLECTION, COMPANY. **settee,** n. *lectulus.* **setting,** n. *occasus, -ūs* (e.g. *solis*).

settle, I. v.tr. 1, = to fix or determine, *statuĕre, constituĕre, definire ;* 2, = to fix your abode in, *sedem et domicilium collocare alqo loco ;* 3, = to put an end to, *dirimĕre* (e.g. *jurgium* or *iras,* a dispute, quarrel ; so with *controversiam, praelium, bellum*) ; to — accounts, *rationes conficĕre ;* to — a debt, etc., *solvĕre, expedire ;* 4, = to put in order, e.g. to — the State, *rempublicam componĕre.* **II.** v.intr. 1, *considĕre, consistĕre, sedem habēre,* se *collocare ;* 2, see SINK ; 3, see ALIGHT. **settlement,** n. *constitutio ;* — of a daughter, *filiae collocatio ;* = agreement, *pactum, foedus, -ēris,* n. ; = of a colony, *coloniae deductio ;* = fixed abode, *domicilium, aedes, -ium* (of private persons), *colonia* (= colony) ; = of a debt, use verb. **settler,** n. *advena,* m. and f., *colonus.*

seven, adj. *septem, septeni, -ae, -a* (= — each*;* of — years, *septennis, septem annorum ;* — years old, *septem annos natus ;* — times, *septie(n)s.*

seventh, adj. *septimus.* **seventhly,** adv. *septimum.* **seventeen,** adj. *septemdecim, decem et septem* or *decem septem* or *septem et decem, septeni deni* (— each) ; — times, *septie(n)s decie(n)s.* **seventeenth,** adj. *septimus decimus.*

seventy, adj. *septuaginta, septuageni* (— each) ; — letters, *septuagenae lit(t)erae,* not *septuaginta* (i.e. — alphabetical letters) ; — times, *septuagie(n)s.* **seventieth,** adj. *septuagesimus ;* the — time, *septuagesimum.*

sever, v.tr. *dividĕre, dirimĕre, separare, secernĕre, disjungĕre.*

several, adj. *nonnulli, plures, aliquot.* Adv. by *unusquisque,* or by *si(n)gillatim ;* — may also be rendered with the aid of the distributive numerals (e.g. *uxores habent deni duodenique inter se communes,* = sets of ten or twelve have — wives in common), also by *quisque* (e.g. *prout quisque monitione indigerent,* as they — required admonition), and lastly by *singuli* (e.g. *duodena describit in singulos homines jugera,* he allotted to the men — twelve acres), so too *viritim.*

severe, adj. *severus, austerus, durus, acerbus* (the two last of winter, also in gen.), *gravis.* Adv. *severe, rigide, austere, dure, duriter, acerbe, graviter.* **severity,** n. *severitas, gravitas* (of climate and in gen.), *duritia.*

sew, v.tr. *suĕre.* **sewing,** n. *suendi ars.*

sewer, n. *cloaca.*

sex, n. *sexus, -ūs ;* male —, *virīlis sexus ;* female —, *muliebris sexus.* **sexual,** adj. *quod ad sexum pertinet ;* — intercourse, *coitus, -ūs.*

sexagenarian, adj. *sexagenarius;* see SIXTY.

sexton, n. *aedituus.*

shabby, adj. 1, *obsoletus, sordidus* (e.g. *amictus, homo*); 2, fig. see MEAN. **shabbiness,** n. 1, use adj.; 2, *sordes, -ium* (of conduct).

shackles, n. *vincula, catenae, compedes, -um;* — for the feet, *pedicae;* for the hands, *manicae.* **shackle,** v.tr. *vinculis colligĕre, catenis vincire;* fig. *impedire, impedimento esse.*

shade, I. n. *umbra;* in the —. *in umbrā;* under the —, *sub umbrā;* to be afraid of —s, *umbras timēre;* fig. "shadow," = a mere appearance or pretext, *umbra* (e.g. *gloriae, libertatis, honoris; sub umbrā foederis aequi servitutem pati*); *umbra* also = — in painting (opp. *lumen*); further, a person's shadow or companion is in Latin *umbra,* "shade," = ghosts, †*umbrae;* in pl., *manes.* **II.** v.tr. †*umbrare;* see DARKEN. **shady,** adj. *umbrosus, opacus* (= dark). **shadow, I.** n. *umbra.* **II.** v.tr. see SHADE, II. **shadowy,** adj. 1, = SHADY; 2, see VAIN, UNREAL.

shaft, n. 1, = arrow, *sagitta;* 2, = handle, *hastile;* 3, in architecture, *truncus;* 4, of a carriage, *temo* (= pole), or by *lora* (= reins); of a mine, etc., *puteus* (Plin.).

shake, I. v.tr. *quatĕre, tremefacĕre, labefactare, quassare* (= to — often); to — hands, *jungĕre dextras;* they — the foundations, *labefactant fundamenta reipublicae;* to — off, *excutĕre.* **II.** v.intr. *quassari, agitari, tremĕre.* **shaking,** n. *quassatio* (in act. sense), *tremor* (in pass. sense).

shallow, I. adj. *tenuis;* —s or shoals, *vada-·orum,* pl.; full of —s, *vadosus;* fig. *parum subtilis.* **II.** n. *vadum.*

sham, I. n. *fallacia, dolus;* without —, *sine fuco ac fallaciis.* **II.** v.intr. *simulare* (to pretend); see FEIGN, PRETEND. **sham-fight,** n. *simulacrum pugnae;* see REVIEW.

shambles, n. *laniēna.*

shame, I. n. 1, = modesty, *pudor, verecundia,* comb. *pudor et verecundia; pudicitia,* comb. *pudor et pudicitia;* to have lost the sense of —, *pudorem posuisse;* he who has lost his sense of —, *pudoris oblitus;* 2, = moral turpitude, *turpitudo* (baseness), *ignominia,* comb. *ignominia et turpitudo; infamia,* comb. *turpitudo et infamia; dedecus, -ōris,* n., comb. *ignominia et dedecus, dedecus et infamia, macula* (= a spot or brand) *et dedecus; probrum,* comb. *probrum et dedecus; flagitium* (= a crime), comb. *flagitium et dedecus;* to our —, *cum nostro dedecore;* — I *proh pudor! o indignum facinus!* it is a — to say that, *hoc est turpe dictu.* **II.** v.tr. *pudore,* etc., *alqm afficĕre.* **shamefaced,** adj. see MODEST. **shameful,** adj. *turpis, foedus* (in gen.), *obscenus* (= obscene), *ignominiosus, probrosus, inhonestus* (= dishonourable), *flagitiosus, nefarius* (= criminal). Adv. *turpiter, foede, obscene, ignominiose, inhoneste, flagitiose, nefarie.* **shamefulness,** n *turpitudo, foeditas, obscenitas, ignominia.* **shameless,** adj. *impudens, impudicus* (= unchaste), *inverecundus;* a — (or brazen) face, *os impudens* (so *durum, ferreum*). Adv. *impudenter.* **shamelessness,** n. *impudentia, impudicitia.*

shank, n. *crus, cruris,* n., *tibia.*

shape, I. n. *forma, figura, species;* to give — to, *formare, fingĕre alqd.* **II.** v.tr. *(con)formare, figurare, fingĕre, alqd in formam rei redigĕre;* to — itself differently, *mutari.* **shapeless,** adj. *informis, deformis.* **shapely,** adj. *formosus.* **shapeliness,** n. see BEAUTY. **shaping,** n. *(con)formatio.*

share, I. n. 1, *pars, portio, sors;* 2, of a plough, *vomer.* **II.** v.tr. *partiri* (e.g. *partiuntur inter se;* so *partiri praedam in socios, bona cum algo, curas cum algo, copias inter se*), *sortiri, dare* (e.g. *perinde ut cuique data sunt*), *dividĕre* (e.g. *dividĕre equitatum in omnes partes*), *algd cum algo communicare.* **sharer,** n. *particeps, socius, consors;* in a thing, *alcjs rei.*

shark, n. *pristis;* spelling also *p(r)ist(r)is, p(r)ist(r)ix.*

sharp, adj. 1, lit. *acutus;* — to the taste, *acutus, acer, acerbum;* 2, fig. = working strongly on the feelings, *acer, acerbus, severus;* there is — fighting, *acriter pugnatur;* 3, = penetrating, *acutus, sagax;* — eyes, *oculi acuti;* — nose, *nasus sagax;* 4, of mental faculties, *acer, acutus, subtilis* (e.g. *ingenium acre*); 5, of words, *iracundus, mordax* (= biting), *severus, gravis* (= severe); — witted, *perspicax, sagax.* Adv. *acute, acriter, sagaciter, subtiliter* (= wisely), *iracunde, severe, graviter* (= severely). **sharpen,** v.tr. *(ex)acuĕre* (lit. and fig.). **sharper,** n. *veterator, fraudator, praestigiator.* **sharpness,** n. 1, of edge, by adj., *acutus;* 2, fig. *severitas;* see STERNNESS; 3, — of intellect, *(ingenii) acus, -ūs,* f., *acumen, ingenium acutum, perspicacitas, subtilitas.*

shatter, v.tr. 1, *frangĕre, confringĕre, diffringĕre, discutĕre, elidĕre, quassare;* 2, fig. *frangĕre, quassare.*

shave, v.tr. *(ab)radĕre, barbam alcjs tondēre* (= to clip); to get —d, *tondēri.* **shavings,** n. *scob(i)s* (= sawdust), *assulae, schidiae* (= chips).

shawl, n. see MANTLE.

she, as a personal pronoun, is expressed only when emphasis requires it (e.g. *illa, ista, haec, ea*); as an adjective, is expressed by the feminine (e.g. a —-friend, *amica;* a —-wolf, *lupa*).

sheaf, n. *manipulus* (= a handful), *fascis.*

shear, v.tr. *tondēre* (e.g. *oves*). **shearer,** n. *qui tondet.* **shearing,** n. *tonsura.* **shears,** n. *forfices* (Mart.).

sheath, n. *vagina;* to draw a sword from its —, *gladium e vaginā educĕre.* **sheathe,** v.tr. *in vaginam recondĕre.*

shed, n. *tugurium, taberna;* as military term, *pluteus, vinea.*

shed, v.tr. *(dif)fundĕre, effundĕre, profundĕre;* to — tears, *lacrimas profundĕre, lacrimare;* to — blood, see KILL. **shedding,** n. *effusio, profusio;* — of tears, *fletus, -ūs;* — of blood, *caedes, -is;* — of leaves, by *decidĕre.*

sheep, n. *ovis* (ŏis). **sheep-fold,** n. *ovile.* **sheepish,** adj. *insulsus;* see STUPID; a — fellow, *ovis* (Plaut.). **sheepishness,** n. *insulsitas, nimia verecundia.* **shepherd,** n. *pastor.*

sheer, adj. 1, see STEEP; 2, *merus;* — folly, *mera* or *maxima stultitia.*

sheet, n. 1, of a bed, *lodix* (= blanket, Juv.); 2, a — of paper, *scheda, sc(h)ida, schedula, plagula* (Plin.); 3, a — of lead, *(plumbi) lamina;* 4, of a sail, *pes.* **sheet-anchor,** n. *ancora.* **sheet-lightning,** n. *fulgur, fulmen.*

shelf, n. *pluteus* (Juv.), *pegma, -ătis,* n.

shell, n. *testa, concha* (of fish), *putamen, cortex* (of fruit, etc.). **shell-fish,** n. *concha, conchylium.*

shelter, I. n. 1, = covering, *teg(i)men;* 2, = protection, *perfugium, asylum, patrocinium, defensio.* **II.** v.tr. 1, *tegĕre, defendĕre;* 2, *tutari alqm, defendĕre, auctoritate tueri, in suam fidem et clientelam suscipĕre, protegĕre, receptum tutum praebēre alci;* see PROTECT.

shelving, adj. *declivis;* see SLOPING.

shepherd, n. see under SHEEP.

sheriff, n. perhaps by *praetor*, in mediæval Latin by * *vicecomes* or *geraeſa*.

shew, v.tr. = to bring forward, *edēre, ostendēre, explicare;* = to prove or explain, *demonſtrare, declarare, ostendēre, exponēre, narrare;* to — mercy, *alci misericordiam impertiri.*

shield, I. n. 1, *scutum, clipeus, parma, pelta, ancile* (esp. of the sacred — which fell from heaven); a —-bearer, *armiger;* 2, fig. see PROTECTION. **II.** v.tr. *scuto defendēre, clipeo protegēre;* to — from danger, *a periculo defendēre;* see PROTECT.

shift, I. n. 1, = refuge or resource, *effugium, ambāges, -um, remedium, ratio, consilium, latebra;* a dishonest —, *fraus, doli* (pl.), *ambāges;* everyone made — for himself, *sibi quisque consulebat;* 2, = an under-garment, *tunica interula.* **II.** v.tr. = to change, (*per*)*mutare;* to — one's clothes, *mutare vestem;* to — off, *eludēre, evitare, subterfugēre;* see CHANGE. **shifty,** adj. 1, see CUNNING; 2, see CHANGEABLE.

shilling, n. *quadraginta octo asses.*

shin, n. *tibia, crus, cruris,* n.

shine, v.intr. (*col*)*lucēre, splendēre, fulgēre, nitēre, micare* (= to glitter); to — forth, *elucēre, effulgēre;* to — upon, *alci affulgēre;* it —s with a borrowed light, *luce lucet alienâ.*

ship, I. n. *navis, navigium* (used of smaller vessels), *navis longa* or *rostrata* (= a — of war), (*navis*) *biremis* (= — having two banks of oars, so *triremis, quadremis, quinqueremis,* having three, four, five), *navis praedatoria* or *piratica* (= a pirate vessel); belonging to a —, *navalis, nauticus;* shipping, *naves,* pl.; —wreck, *naufragium;* one who has suffered —wreck, *naufragus;* to suffer —wreck, *naufragium facēre;* a —'s captain, *navarchus;* a —-owner, *navicularius* (who lets out —s); —'s crew, *remigium classicique milites;* master of a —, *magister.* **II.** v.tr. *in navem* (*naves*) *imponēre.*

shire, n. *provincia, ager,* * *comitatus.*

shirt, n. *subucula.*

shiver, I. v.tr. = to break in pieces, *frangēre, confringēre, diffringēre, elidēre.* **II.** v.intr. = to tremble, *tremēre* (with fear), *algēre* (= to be cold).

shoal, n. 1, *vadum, vada,* pl.; see SHALLOW; 2, = a large quantity or number, *turba, grex, caterva.*

shock, I. n. 1, in battle, etc., *impetus, concursus, congressus,* all -*ûs;* to bear the —, *sustinēre impetum;* at the first —, *ad primum impetum;* 2, fig. of the feelings, etc., *offensio;* see OFFENCE; 3, of corn, *frumenti manipulorum acervus.* **II.** v.tr. *offendēre, commovēre;* to be —ed, *commovēri.* **shocking,** adj. *quod offensioni est, quod offensionem habet or affert, odiosus;* a — life, *vita turpis;* see DISGUSTING; to be —, *offensioni esse.* Adv. = very badly, *pessime,* or by superl. (e.g. *pessimus* = bad).

shoe, I. n. *calceus, calceamentum, solea* (= sandal); horse- —, *solea ferrea* (—s nailed were unknown); —s that fit, *calcei apti ad pedem;* the — pinches, *calceus urit.* **II.** v.tr. *calceare;* to — a horse, *affigēre equo soleas ferreas.* **shoeblack,** n. *puer qui calceos deterget.* **shoemaker,** n. *sutor.*

shoot, I. n. = sprout, † *germen, surculus, planta, virga, propago* (= layer). **II.** v.intr. 1, to — out, as ears of corn, *spicas, surculos,* etc., *emittēre;* 2, of pains, etc., *angēre* (= to torture), or *angi* (= to be tortured); of stars, *volare.* **III.** v.tr. = to cast forth, *jaculari, emittēre, jacēre;* to — arrows out of a bow, *arcu sagittas* (*e*)*mittēre;* to — at, *sagittis* or *telis petēre;* see FIRE. **shooting-star,** n. see METEOR.

shop, I. n. *taberna, officina* (= work—); * bookseller's —, *libraria;* a barber's —, *taberna tonsoris.* **II.** v.intr. to go a-shopping, *concursare circum tabernas,* or by *emēre* (= to buy). **shopkeeper,** n. *qui alqas res vendit,* in pl. *tabernarii.*

shore, I. n. 1, *litus, -ōris,* n., *ora, aeta* (ἀκτή), *ripa* (= the declining bank or margin), *arena* (= sand); 2, = support, *fulcrum.* **II.** v.tr. *fulcire.*

short, adj. *brevis, concisus* (= pruned), *angustus* (= within a small space), *contractior* (= somewhat drawn in), *compressus* (= squeezed together), *paucioribus verbis expressus* (of a writing); — of stature, *humilis* (opp. *procerus*); a — cut, *compendium, via compendiaria* (lit. and fig.); to be —, *ac ne multa, ut in pauca referam, ne multis, ne plura;* in —, *summatim, ad summam, summa illa sit, in brevi;* cut it —, *verbo dicas;* a — syllable, *syllaba brevis;* — hair, *capilli tonsi;* a — memory, *memoria hebes;* the —est day, *dies brumalis, bruma;* the —est night, *nox solstitialis.* **short-legged,** adj. *cruribus brevibus.* **short-sighted,** adj. *myops* (Jct.), *qui oculis non satis prospicit;* fig. *stultus, imprudens.* **shortcoming,** n. *delictum.* **shorten,** v.tr. *praecidēre, breviorem facēre or reddēre;* to — a syllable, *syllabam corripēre;* see CONTRACT. **shorthand,** n. *notae.* **shortly,** adv. 1, = compendiously, *summatim, strictim, compresse, paucis verbis, breviter;* 2, = within a short time, *brevi, propediem, paucis diebus, exiguo spatio;* — before, *brevi ante, paul*(*l*)*o ante, proxime, nuper;* — after, *brevi post, paul*(*l*)*o post, non ita multo post;* — before a person's death, *haud multum ante* (so *post*) *alcjs mortem.* **shortness,** adj. *brevitas, exiguitas, angustiae, compendium, contractio* (= a drawing in).

shot, n. *teli jactus, -ûs,* or *conjectus, -ûs, ictus, -ûs,* (*telum*) *missile* (= what is fired), *glans* (= ball); to fire a —, *telum emittēre;* they were now within —, *jam ad teli jactum pervenerant;* out of —, *extra teli jactum.*

shoulder, I. n. *humerus;* —-blade, *scapula.* **II.** v.tr. *alqd in humeros tollēre.*

shout, I. n. *clamor, vociferatio, vox, acclamatio;* to raise a —, *clamorem tollēre.* **II.** v.tr. (*con*)*clamare, vociferari.*

shove, I. v.tr. *trudēre, impellēre.* **II.** n. *impulsus, -ûs.*

shovel, I. n. *pala, batillum.* **II.** v.tr. *batillo tollēre.*

show, I. n. 1, = an exhibition, *spectaculum, pompa, ludi* (= games); 2, *ostentatio* (= display), *species* (= appearance); to make — of or pretend, *simulare, prae se ferre;* for some time there was some — of fight, *exiguum temporis alqa forma pugnae fuit;* under a — of friendship, *per simulationem amicitiae.* **II.** v.tr. *proponēre, ostentare alqd, prae se ferre;* to — off, *se ostentare;* see SHEW. **showy,** adj. see BEAUTIFUL, OSTENTATIOUS.

shower, I. n. *pluvia repentina, imber, pluvia;* a plentiful —, *largus imber;* a — of stones, *lapidum imber.* **II.** v.tr. *effundēre.* **showery,** adj. *pluvius, pluvialis.*

shred, I. n. *frustum* (= a scrap), *segmentum* (Plin.). **II.** v.tr. *minutatim dissecare or concidēre.*

shrew, n. *mulier jurgiis dedita.* **shrewd,** adj. *prudens, sol*(*l*)*ers, callidus, astutus, perspicax, sagax.* Adv. *callide, astute, sagaciter, sol*(*l*)*erter, prudenter.* **shrewdness,** n. *calliditas, astutia, perspicacitas, sagacitas, prudentia, sol*(*l*)*ertia.* **shrewish,** adj. see QUARRELSOME. **shrewmouse,** n. *sorex.*

shriek, I. n. *ejulatus, -ûs, ululatus, -ûs.* **II.** v.intr. *ululare.* **III.** v.tr. *clamare;* see SCREAM.

shrift, n. a short —, *confestim alqm necare;* see also CONFESSION, SHRIVE.

shrill, adj. *acutus, argutus.* Adv. *acute, argute.*

shrimp, n. 1, **cancer pagurus* (Linn.); 2, fig. see DWARF.

shrine, n. *aedicula, delubrum, sacellum.*

shrink, v.intr. *se contrahĕre;* to — through fear, *pedem referre;* to — from duty, *abhorrēre, recedĕre (ab officio nunquam recedemus,* Cic.); to — from fight, *pugnam detractare.* **shrinking**, n. 1, *alcjs rei contractio;* 2, see FEAR.

shrive, v.tr. *peccata sua sacerdoti fateri (=* to confess), *peccata confitentem absolvĕre (=* to absolve).

shrivel, I. v.tr. *rugosum facĕre.* II. v.intr. *(cor)rugari, contrahi.*

shroud, I. n. *mortui vestimentum.* II. v.tr. *involvĕre, velare, tegĕre, mortuum vestimento induĕre.*

shrub, n. *frutex.* **shrubbery**, n. *arbustum.*

shrug, v.tr. to — the shoulders, *humeros movēre.*

shudder, I. n. *horror, tremor.* II. v.intr. *horrēre, tremĕre;* to — greatly, *perhorrescĕre.*

shuffle, I. v.tr. 1, = to mix, *(com)miscēre;* to — cards, *paginas (per)miscēre;* 2, = to act deceitfully, *fraudare.* II. v.intr. *tergiversari* (of conduct), *claudicare (=* to limp). **shuffler**, n. *fraudator, homo fallax.* **shuffling**, n. *fraus, -dis,* f., *dolus, tergiversatio.*

shun, v.tr. *(de)fugĕre, vitare, declinare, aversari.* **shunning**, n. *devitatio, fuga, declinatio, vitatio.*

shut, v.tr. *claudĕre, operire;* to — the eyes, *oculos operire;* to — the hand, *manum comprimĕre;* to — in, *includĕre;* to — out, *excludĕre.* **shutter**, n. (for a window), *foricula, valvae.*

shuttle, n. *radius (textorius).* **shuttlecock**, n. *pila pennata.*

shy, I. adj. *timidus, pavidus, verecundus (=* modest); to be — of expense, *sumptibus parcĕre.* II. v.tr. of a horse, *terrēri, saltum in contraria facĕre.* Adv. *timide, verecunde.* **shyness**, n. *timor, pavor, verecundia, pudor.*

sibilant, adj. *sibilans.*

sibyl, n. *sibylla.* **sibylline**, adj. *sibyllinus.*

sick, adj. *aeger* (used of disorders of mind and body; see ILL); to rise from a — bed, *assurgĕre ex morbo;* a — man, *aeger, aegrotus;* to feel —, *nauseare;* to be —, *vomĕre,* fig. by impers. *taedet alqm alcjs rei;* see ILL. **sicken**, I. v.tr. see DISGUST. II. v.intr. *in morbum incidĕre.* **sickly**, adj. *morbosus;* see ILL, WEAK. **sickness**, n. = sensation of —, vomiting, nausea, *vomitus, -ūs (=* illness), *morbus (=* disorder), *aegrotatio (=* condition of —), *valetudo* (properly = state of health or strength; used alone = —, or with *adversa, infirma,* etc.); a contagious —, *contagio, lues, -is,* f. (= the impure cause of the disease); an epidemic, = *pestilentia.*

sickle, n. *falx.*

side, I. n. *latus, -ēris,* n. (of the body, a hill, etc.), *pars (=* part, party), *regio (=* district), *pagina (= —* of a leaf); on that —, *illinc, ultro;* on this — and on that, *citra ultroque;* on all —s, *quoquoversus, omnibus partibus;* towards all —s, *in omnes partes;* on this —, *hinc;* on both —s, *utrimque;* on each of two —s, *utrobique;* on his — nothing takes place, *ab eo nihil agitur.* II. adj. *obliquus, transversus;* a — blow, *ictus obliquus;* to give anyone a — blow, *gladio alqm ob-*

lique petĕre. III. v.intr. to — with, *alcjs partibus* or *alci favēre, studēre, alcjs studiosum esse.* **sideboard**, n. *abacus.* **sidelong**, adj. *obliquus.* **sideways**, adv. *oblique, ab obliquo, ex obliquo.*

sidereal, adj. by gen. *siderum, sideralis* (Plin.).

siege, n. *oppugnatio, obsessio, obsidio.*

sieve, n. *cribrum.* **sift**, v.tr. *cribrare* (Plin.), *cribro secernĕre;* fig. *investigare, (per)scrutari, explorare.*

sigh, I. n. *suspirium.* II. v.intr. *suspiria ducĕre, suspirare.* **sighing**, n. *suspiratus, -ūs.*

sight, I. n. 1, *visio, visus, -ūs, videndi facultas, oculus, conspectus, -ūs (=* view), *a(d)spectus, -ūs,* — of the eye, *oculi acies;* at first —, *primo a(d)spectu;* 2, = spectacle, *species (=* an appearance), *spectaculum (=* a show); in —, *in conspectu, ante oculos,* in or *sub oculis;* he was in —, *sub oculos erat;* to take out of —, *oculis subducĕre, ex hominum conspectu subtrahĕre;* I knew him by —, *de facie novi;* to pay at —, *pecunias repraesentare;* to catch — of, *conspicĕre.* II. v.tr. *conspicari, conspicĕre.*

sign, I. n. *signum, significatio, indicium, vestigium (=* footmark), *nota (=* mark), *insigne (=* badge), *nutus, -ūs (=* nod); the peculiar — of a thing, *proprium alcjs rei (=* characteristic); it is the — of a wise man, *est sapientis;* — of the future, *signum, omen, ostentum, portentum;* a good —, *omen faustum;* a bad —, *omen sinistrum.* II. v.tr. 1, to — a document, *(con)signare alqd, alci rei (nomen) subscribĕre,* as witnesses, *scribendo adesse;* 2, see SIGNAL.

signal, I. adj. *insignis, notabilis, maximus, insignatus, egregius.* Adv. *insigniter, notabiliter, maxime, insignite, egregie.* II. n. *signum, symbolum;* to give the — for an attack, *signum dare;* for battle, *classicum canĕre, tubā signum dare.* III. v.tr. see above, SIGNAL, II. **signalize**, v.tr. *declarare (=* to show), *alci* or *alci rei decori esse (=* to be an honour) to), *insignire (=* to make remarkable, e.g. *tot facinoribus foedum annum etiam dii tempestatibus et morbis insignivere,* Tac.); to — yourself, *se clarum reddĕre.* **signature**, n. *nomen, -inis,* n., *subscriptio, nomen subscriptum.* **signet**, n. *signum (=* seal). **significance, signification**, n. *significatio;* see MEANING. **significant**, adj. see EXPRESSIVE. **signify**, v.tr. *significare (=* to make signs), *valēre (=* to be equivalent, e.g. *verbum quod idem valet), velle (=* to wish); see also MEAN, ANNOUNCE, PORTEND.

silence, n. *silentium, taciturnitas (=* not speaking); to keep —, *tacēre, conticēre, conticescĕre, obticēre, obmutescĕre.* **silent**, adj. *tacitus, silens, taciturnus (=* taciturn); to be —, *silēre, tacēre, linguis favēre* (at religious rites); to be — about, *celare, silentio praeterire alqd;* be —! *quin taces!* Adv. *tacite, silentio.*

silk, n. *bombyx* (Plin.), or *vestis serica.* **silk-worm**, n. *bombyx* (Plin.). **silken**, adj. *sericus, bombycinus* (Plin.). **silky**, adj. see SMOOTH.

sill, n. *limen.*

silly, adj. *stultus, fatuus, stolidus, infacetus absurdus, excors, vecors, ineptus, insulsus, amens, ridiculus (=* exciting laughter). Adv. *stulte, stolide, infacete, absurde, inepte, insulse, ridicule.* **silliness**, n. *stultitia, fatuitas, stoliditas, ineptiae, vecordia, amentia, insulsitas, ridiculum.*

silt, I. n. *limus.* II. v.tr. *limo opplēre.*

silver, I. n. *argentum;* wrought —, *argentum factum.* II. adj. and **silvery**, *argenteus;* plated with —, *argentatus;* — mine, *argenti metalla,*

-*orum*, **n.** ; — foil, *bractea argentea*, *argenti fodina* (or as one word), *argentaria (fodina)* ; — money, *nummi argentei* ; — plate, *argentum (factum)*, *vasa argentea*, pl. **III.** v.tr. *alqd argento inducĕre.*

similar, adj. *similis* (used with the genit. of internal bodily or mental relations, with dat. otherwise, e.g. *non tam potuit patris similis esse quam ille fuerat sui*, Cic.). Adv. *similiter*. **similarity**, n. = resemblance, *similitudo (est homini cum Deo similitudo*, Cic. ; *habet honestatis similitudinem* ; *similitudines*, = similar objects). **simile**, n. *similitudo, translatio, collatio.* **similitude**, n. = comparison, *similitudo* ; see LIKE, SIMULATE.

simmer, v.intr. *fervescĕre, lente bullire.*

simony, n. *simonia* (Eccl.).

simper, v.intr. *subridēre, stulte ridēre.*

simple, adj. *simplex* (in gen.) ; = harmless, *innoxius* ; = sincere, *sincerus, probus, integer, sine fuco* ; = silly, *stolidus, insulsus* ; = without ornament, *simplex, sine ornatu* ; = sheer, *merus.* Adv. *simpliciter* ; see also ONLY. **simples**, n. pl. *herbae (medicinales).* **simpleton**, n. *homo crassi ingenii, stultus, fatuus, ineptus* ; see FOOL. **simplicity**, n. *simplicitas* (in gen.), *stultitia* (= folly), *innocentia* (= guilelessness). **simplify**, v.tr. *explicare, simplicem reddĕre.*

simulate, v.tr. = to imitate or pretend, *simulare* (e.g. *mortem, lacrimas, simulavit se furēre*). **simulation**, n. *simulatio* (e.g. *fallax imitatio simulatioque virtutis*).

simultaneous, adj. *quod uno et eodem tempore est* or *fit.* Adv. *eodem tempore, simul, una.*

sin, I. n. *peccatum, delictum* (= omission), *flagitium, nefas* ; to commit a —, *peccare, delinquĕre, peccatum committĕre.* **II.** v.intr. *peccare (in se, erga alqm, in re ; multa peccantur), delinquĕre.* **sinful**, adj. *pravis cupiditatibus deditus, impius, improbus, flagitiosus.* **sinless**, adj. *integer, sanctus.* **sinlessness**, n. *vitae sanctitas.* **sinner**, n. *qui peccavit, peccator* (Eccl.).

since, I. adv. *abhinc* (e.g. he died two years —, *abhinc annos duos,* or *annis duobus, mortuus est)*; long —, *jamdudum, jampridem.* **II.** prep. by *e, ex, a, ab, post* (e.g. — the foundation of the city, *post urbem conditam)* ; — that time, *ex eo tempore* ; many years —, *multis abhinc annis* ; — when, *ex quo* ; a long time —, *jamdiu* ; — childhood, *a pueritiâ, a puero.* **III.** conj. 1, of time, *cum (quom, quum), postquam* (or as two words) ; this is the third day — I heard it, *tertius hic dies quod audivi* ; it is a long time — you left home, *jamdudum factum est cum abiisti domo* ; — he died this is the three-and-thirtieth year, *cujus a morte hic tertius et trigesimus annus* ; 2, of cause, may be rendered by *cum* with subj., or *quandoquidem, quia, quoniam* with indic., thus frequently in Cic. *quae cum ita sint*, — this is so, but observe *quandoquidem tu istos oratores tantopere laudas* (in the indic., Cic.) ; so *urbs quae, quia postrema aedificata est, Neapolis nominatur* (Cic.) ; *quoniam res in id discrimen adducta est* ; — may also be rendered by the relative with a causal force, and so requiring the subj., e.g. *maluimus iter facĕre pedibus, qui incommodissime navigassemus*, Cic. ; so too *quippe qui* with indic. or subj. (all these conjs. follow the ordinary rules of mood) ; see BECAUSE.

sincere, adj. *sincerus* (opp. *fucatus, simulatus), integer* (e.g. *te sincerum integrumque conserves*, Cic.), *probus, purus, candidus, verus* ; see HONEST. Adv. *sincere, integre* (= justly), *probe, pure, candide, vere, ex animo, simpliciter* ; *yours* —, in letters, *vale (valete).* **sincerity**, n. *sinceritas, candor, integritas, probitas, veritas* (= truthfulness), *simplicitas.*

sinecure, n. *munus omni labor vacuum.*

sinew, n. *nervus* ; the —s, as = strength, *nervi.* **sinewy**, adj. *nervosus.*

sing, v.tr. and intr. *canĕre, cantare, modulari* ; to — much, *cantitare* ; to — to the harp, *ad citharam canĕre* ; to — in harmony, *servare modum, ad numerum canĕre.* **singer**, n. †*cantor, cantrix, cantator, cantatrix.* **singing**, n. *cantus, -ūs, concentus, -ūs* (of a number of persons).

singe, v.tr. *ustulare, amburēre, adurēre.*

single, I. adj. *unus, solus, singularis, ūnicus* ; a — or unmarried man, *caelebs* (a bachelor) ; — combat, *certamen unius cum uno.* Adv. *singillatim.* **II.** v.tr. to — out, *eligĕre* ; see SELECT. **singular**, adj. 1, as opp. to plural, *singularis* ; the — number, *numerus singularis* (gram.) ; see SINGLE, I. ; 2, = out of the common way, *singularis* (=very superior, e.g. *Aristoteles meo judicio in philosophiâ prope singularis,* = almost standing alone, Cic. ; also in a bad sense, e.g. *singularis crudelitas, nequitia), unicus* (= unique), *egregius, eximius, praestans* (= excellent), *maximus* (= very great) ; 3, = strange, *mirus, mirificus, mirabilis, novus, inusitatus, insolens.* Adv. *singulariter, unice, egregie, eximie, praestanter, insolenter, maxime, mire, mirifice, mirabiliter, nove, inusitate.* **singularity**, n. *insolentia, praestantia* (= excellence), or use adj.

sinister, adj. *sinister* (lit. = left-handed ; fig. with *mores, natura, interpretatio*, etc.), †*infaustus* (= unlucky) ; see ILL-OMENED, CORRUPT.

sink, I. v.tr. *(sub)mergĕre, demergĕre, immergĕre, deprimĕre.* **II.** v.intr. *(con)sidĕre, desidĕre, residĕre, submergi, demergi, immergi* ; to — in ruins, *collabi, corruĕre, mergi* ; to — morally, *in (omnia) flagitia se ingurgitare* ; **w** — into sleep, *somno opprimi* ; the price —s, *pretium imminuitur* ; his courage —s, *animus cadit* ; to let one's courage —, *sibi diffidĕre* ; to — into the mind, *in animum penetrare* ; to be sunk in debt, *aere alieno obrui.* **III.** n. *sentina.*

sinuous, adj. *sinuosus.*

sip, I. v.tr. *(primis labris) degustare, sorbillare* (ante and post class.). **II.** n. use verb.

sir, n. 1, as title, *dominus* ; 2, in addresses, *vir optime.*

sire, n. 1, *pater, genitor* ; see FATHER ; 2, see SIR.

siren, n. *siren.*

sirocco, n. *auster.*

sister, n. *soror, germana* ; father's —, *amita* ; mother's —, *matertera* ; grandfather's —, *amita magna* ; grandmother's —, *matertera magna* ; — in-law, *glos, gloris,* f. (Jct.). **sisterhood**, n. *sororum societas* (Eccl.). **sisterly**, adj. *ut sorores solent.*

sit, v.intr. *sedēre, alqâ re insidēre, considĕre* (= to —down) ; to — near, *considĕre rei* or *alci* ; to — on, *sedēre in re* ; to — at table, *accumbĕre, discumbĕre, recumbĕre* ; to — above at table, *superior accumbĕre* (e.g. of a court, *haběri* (e.g. *conventus), sedēre* (of the magistrates) ; we sat up talking till late at night, *sermonem in multum noctem produximus* (Cic.) ; he —s up till daylight, *usque ad lucem vigilat* ; of fowls, *(ovis) incubare* (Plin.) ; as milit. term, to — down before a place, *oppidum circumsedēre.* **sitting**, n. *sessio* (lit. of a court), *consessus, -ūs* (of a court, etc.) ; to break up the —, *consessum*, etc., *dimittĕre.*

site, n. *situs, -ūs, situate,* adj. *situs, positus, collocatus* ; to be — near, *adjacēre.* **situation**, n. 1, = position, *situs, -ūs, sedes, -is, locus* ; if he were in that —, *si eo loco esset* ; 2, = office, *munus, -eris,* n. ; see OFFICE.

six, adj. *sex, seni* (= — each); — or seven, *sex septem*, *sex aut septem*; to throw — (at dice), *senionem mittĕre*; — times, *sexie(n)s*. **sixth**, adj. *sextus*; the — time, *sextum*. **sixteen**, adj. *sedecim (sexd-), decem et sex, seni deni* (= — each); — times, *sedecie(n)s*. **sixteenth**, adj. *sextus decimus*; one —, *pars sexta decima*. **sixty**, adj. *sexaginta, sexageni* (= — each); — times, *sexagie(n)s*. **sixtieth**, adj. *sexagesimus*; the — time, *sexagesimum*; sixty thousand, *sexaginta milia*; the — thousandth, *sexagie(n)s millesimus*.

size, n. 1, = measure, *mensura, amplitudo* (= largeness), *parvitas* (= smallness), *proceritas* (= tallness), *altitudo* (= height), *ambitus, -ūs* (= girth), *spatium* (= extent of surface); to take the — of (di)metiri; of the —, of, (ad) instar alcjs rei; of great, small —, etc., magnus, parvus; 2, = glue, gluten (glutinum).

skate, I. n. *solea ferrata*. II. v.intr. *soleis ferratis glaciem transcurrĕre*.

skein, n. *filia volumen* or *filorum glomus*.

skeleton, n. *ossa, -ium, n., ossium compages*; he is a mere —, *vix ossibus haeret*.

sketch, I. n. *adumbratio*; see OUTLINE. II. v.tr. *describĕre, designare, adumbrare* (esp. fig.).

skewer, n. *veru* (= spit).

skiff, n. *scapha, cymba, navicula*.

skill, n. *peritia, scientia, ars, artificium, sol(l)ertia, calliditas, prudentia, habilitas*. **skilful**, adj. *peritus rei, arte insignis, exercitatus in re, dexter, sol(l)ers, sciens, callidus, habilis* (= handy); *prudens* (= with insight), *bonus* (= good); — in the law, *juris consultus*. Adv. *perite, dext(e)re, callide, scienter, prudenter, habiliter, bene*.

skim, I. n. *spuma*; to form —, *spumescĕre*; full of —, *spumosus*. II. v.tr. 1, *despumare, spumam eximĕre*; 2, = to read quickly, *algd (legendo) percurrĕre*. III. v.intr. *volare* (= to fly).

skin, I. n. *cutis, pellis, membrana, corium* (= hide); to get off with a whole —, *integrum abire*. II. v.tr. *corium detrahĕre, pelle* or *corio exuĕre*; to — over, *cicatricem inducĕre, (ob)ducĕre*. **skin-deep**, adj. *levis*. **skinny**, adj. see THIN.

skip, I. n. *saltus, -ūs*. II. v.intr. *salire* (= to leap); to — with joy, *ex(s)ultare*. III. v.tr. = to pass over, *transilire, praeterire*. **skipping-rope**, n. *restis*.

skipper, n. *navis magister*; see CAPTAIN.

skirmish, I. n. *praelium lĕve*. II. v.intr. to engage in —es, *praeliis parvulis cum hoste contendĕre*. **skirmisher**, n. *veles, -ĭtis*, m. (= light-armed soldier, or by verb).

skirt, I. n. *limbus, ora*. II. v.tr. to — the shore, *legĕre oram*; to — or border on, *affinem esse* (e.g. *gens affinis Mauris*).

skittish, adj. *protervus, lascivus*; to be —, *lascivire*. Adv. *proterve, lascive*. **skittishness**, n. *protervitas, lascivia*.

skulk, v.intr. *latĕre*.

skull, n. *calvaria*.

sky, n. *caelum*; a bright —, *caelum serenum*; an open —, *caelum patens*; under the open —; *sub divo, in publico*; from the —, *de caelo, xaelitus*. **skylark**, n. *alauda*. **skylight**, n. *fenestra*.

slack, adj. *laxus, fluxus, remissus* (= loose), *entus, tardus* (= slow), *segnis, piger* (= idle); — in duty, *neglegens*. **slacken**, v.tr. *laxare*; so — the reins, *laxare habenas*; to — work, *opus remittĕre*. Adv. *lente, tarde, segniter, neglegenter*. **slackness**, n. *segnitia, pigritia* (= laziness), *neglegentia* (= negligence); — of reins, etc., by *laxus, remissus*.

slake, v.tr. *sitim ex(s)tinguĕre* or *explēre, sitim depellĕre* or *sedare*; to — lime, *calcem macerare*.

slander, I. n. *calumnia, (falsa) criminatio, falsum crimen, obtrectatio, maledictio*. II. v.tr. *calumniari, criminari, diffamare, alci obtrectare, maledicĕre, alqm calumniis* or *ignominiis afficĕre, insectari, alci probrum, convicium, contumeliam*, etc., *facĕre*. **slanderer**, n. *obtrectator*. **slandering**, n. *criminatio, obtrectatio*. **slanderous**, adj. *maledicus, famosus*. Adv. *maledice, per calumniam*.

slant, adj. *obliquus, transversus*. Adv. *oblique*.

slap, I. n. *alapa* (Juv.). II. v.tr. *palmā percutĕre*.

slash, I. n. *incisura* (= incision, Col.), *vulnus, -ēris* (= wound), *ictus, -ūs* (= blow). II. v.tr. *caedĕre, incidĕre, gladio percutĕre* (with a sword).

slate, I. n. to write on, use *tabula*; for a roof, *tegula* (= tile, usu. in pl.); a —, *quarry, lapidis fissilis fodina*. II. v.tr. *tegulis obtegĕre* or *consternĕre*.

slattern, n. *mulier sordida*.

slaughter, I. n. *caedes, -is*, f. (= a cutting down), *occidio, occisio, clades* (fig. = discomfiture, severe loss), *strages, -is*, f. (fig. = overthrow, destruction); a general —, *internecio*; *trucidatio* (= butchery), *nex* (= violent death); man—, *homicidium*. II. v.tr. *caedĕre, concidĕre* (of a number), *jugulare* (= to cut the throat), *mactare* (= to slay a victim); see SLAY; *trucidare*. **slaughterhouse**, n. *laniēna*. **slaughterer**, n. *lanius*.

slave, n. *servus* (considered as property), *ancilla* (= female —), *verna* (= a slave born in the house), *famulus* (= household —), *mancipium* (= one obtained by war or purchase); the —s, *servitium, servitia, corpora servilia, familia*; to sell as a —, *sub coronā vendĕre*; a — of lusts, *servus libidinum*; to be a — to anything, *alci rei oboedire, inservire*. **slave-dealer**, n. *venalicius, mango* (Quint.). **slave-labour**, n. *opus servile*. **slave-market**, n. *forum* or *lapis* (e.g. *de lapide emptus, Cic.*). **slavery**, n. *servitus, -ūtis*, f., *servitudo, servitium*; to be in —, *in servitute esse*. **slave-trade**, n. *venditio* (= selling) or *emptio* (= buying) *servorum*. **slave-war** or **-rising**, n. *tumultus, -ūs, servīlis, bellum servile*. **slavish**, adj. *servilis* (lit. and fig.), *vernilis* (lit. and fig., esp. in Tac.). Adv. *serviliter, vernīliter*.

slaver, I. n. *sputum* (Cels.). II. v.intr. *salivam ex ore demittĕre, salivā madēre*.

slay, v.tr. *interficĕre, occidĕre, interimĕre, tollĕre, ferire, percutĕre, absumĕre, ex(s)tinguĕre, trucidare, jugulare, necare* (= to put to death). **slayer**, n. *interfector, occisor, percussor*; — of men, *homicīda*, m. and f. so *tyrannicīda, etc.*).

sledge, n. *traha* (= a drag). **sledge-hammer**, n. *malleus*.

sleek, adj. *lēvis* (= smooth), *nitidus* (= shining); to be —, *nitēre*.

sleep, n. *somnus* (= sleep), *sopor* (= heaviness), *quies, -ētis* (= rest); — falls on me, *somnus me opprimit*; to fall to —, *dormitare*. II. v.intr. *dormire, quiescĕre*; to go to — or bed, *cubitum ire, se somno dare*. **sleepiness**, n. *veternus* (of the lethargy of the aged), or by adj. **sleepless**, adj. *insomnis, exsomnis, vigilans*. **sleeplessness**, n. *insomnia, vigilia, vigilantia*. **sleepy**, adj. *semisomnus (-somnis), somni plenus, somno gravis, veternus, somniculosus* (= sluggish). Adv. *somniculose*, or better by adj.

sleet, n. *nix grandine mixta*.

sleeve, n. *manica*; to laugh in one's — . .

furtim ridēre; in sinu gaudēre (= to rejoice in secret).

sleight, n. *ars, artificium, dolus;* — of hand, *praestigiae.*

slender, adj. *tenuis* (lit. and fig.), *gracilis* (lit.), *exīlis* (lit. and fig.); — provision, *victus, -ūs, tenuis.* Adv. *tenuiter* (= poorly), *exīliter.* **slenderness,** n. *tenuitas, exīlitas* (lit. and fig.), *gracilitas* (lit.).

slice, I. n. — of bread (*panis*) *frustum.* **II.** v.tr. *concidēre, secare.*

slide, I. v.intr. *labi.* **II.** n. — on ice, by *in glacie labi.*

slight, I. adj. *lēvis* (in gen. of clothing, etc., also fig.), *parvi momenti* (= of little account), *tenuis, gracilis, exīlis* (= slender), by diminutive (e.g. *opusculum,* = — work). **II.** v.tr. *parvi, flocci facēre, nullam curam alcjs habēre, contemnēre.*

slim, adj. *exīlis;* see SLENDER. **slimness,** n. *exīlitas.*

slime, n. *limus.* **slimy,** adj. *limosus.*

sling, I. n. *funda;* — for the arm, *fascia, mitella* (Cels.); to have the arm in a —, *brachium mitellā involutum habēre.* **II.** v.tr. *mittēre, torquēre;* to — at, *fundā petēre.*

slink, v.intr. to — away, *sese subducēre.*

slip, I. n. **1,** lit. *lapsus, -ūs;* **2,** fig. *lapsus* (rare), *culpa* (= fault), *error* (= mistake); there's many a — between the cup and the lip, *inter os et offam* (sc. *multa intervenire possunt*); **3,** of a plant, *surculus;* see SHOOT. **II.** v.intr. *vestigio falli, labi;* to — away, *aufugēre;* to let —, *amittēre, omittēre;* to — from the memory, *de memoriā excidēre.* **slipper,** n. *solea, crepida.* **slippery,** adj. *lubricus.*

slit, I. n. *fissura* (= a split, Plin.), *rima* (= an opening or leak), *scissura* (= a slit, Plin.). **II.** v.tr. *incidēre* (= to cut into), *findēre* (= to cleave), *scindēre* (= to tear).

sloe, n. *prunum silvestre* (Plin.); —-tree, *prunus,* f., *silvestris* (Col.).

sloop, n. see SHIP.

slop, n. and v.tr. see WET

slope, I. n. *declīvitas* (downwards), *acclīvitas* (upwards). **II.** v.intr. *vergēre, se dimittēre.* **sloping,** adj. *declīvis, acclīvis.*

sloth, n. *desidia, inertia, segnitia, segnities, ignavia, socordia, pigritia.* **slothful,** adj. *desidiosus* (rare), *iners, ignavus, segnis, socors, piger.* Adv. *inerter, segniter, ignave.*

slouch, v.intr. *discinctum esse.*

slough, n. *palus, -ūdis,* f.; (for swine), *volutabrum;* — of a snake, *vernatio* (Plin.).

sloven, n. *homo sordidus, discinctus.* **slovenliness,** n. *sordes* (= filth), *incuria, neglegentia* (= carelessness).

slow, adj. *tardus, lentus, segnis, piger, serus* (= late); — to learn, *tardus ad discendum.* Adv. *tarde, lente, segniter, paul(l)atim, pedetentim* (*pedetemt-*). **slowness,** n. *tarditas, segnitas, pigritia;* — of a river, *lēnitas.*

slug, n. *limax* (Plin.). **sluggard,** n. *homo ignavus.* **sluggish,** adj. *segnis, piger, socors.* Adv. *segniter, socorditer.* **sluggishness,** n. *pigritia, ignavia, socordia.*

sluice, n. *emissarium.*

slumber, n. and v. see SLEEP.

slur, I. n. *macula, labes, -is, dedecus, -ŏris,* n. **II.** v.tr. to — over, *extenuare.*

slut, n. *mulier sordida, immunda.*

sly, adj. *vafer, subdolus, astutus, versutus;* — old fellow, *veterator.* Adv. *vafre, subdole, astute, versute.* **slyness,** n. *dolus, astutia.*

smack, I. n. a taste, *sapor, gustus, -ūs.* **II.** v.intr. to — of, *sapēre* (e.g. *mella herbam eam sapiunt,* = the honey —s of the grass).

smack, I. n. = a blow, *alapa.* **II. v.tr.** *alapam alci ducēre* (Phaedr.).

small, adj. *parvus, exiguus, minutus, tenuis* (= thin), *gracilis* (= slender), *angustus* (= narrow); a — soul, *animus pusillus;* that betrays a — mind, *illud pusilli est animi;* too —, *justo minor, parum magnus;* as —as, how—! *quantulus.* **smallness,** n. *parvitas, exiguitas, tenuitas, gracilitas, angustiae.*

small-pox, n. *variolae,* or by *pestilentia.*

smart, I. n. *dolor, morsus, -ūs, cruciatus, -ūs.* **II.** v.intr. *dolēre;* to — for, *paenas alci pendēre, paenas subire, perferre or luēre.* **III.** adj. **1,** = keen, *acer, acerbus, gravis, acutus;* **2,** = active, *impiger, callidus* (= clever); **3,** = witty, *salsus;* see WITTY; **4,** = dressy, *lautus, nitidus.* **smartness,** n. **1,** = wit, *sal;* **2,** dressiness, use adj. SMART III., 4.

smatterer, n. *homo leviter lit(t)eris imbutus.* **smattering,** n. *lēvis artis alcjs scientia.*

smear, v.tr. (*il)linēre.*

smell, I. n. *odoratus, -ūs* (the sense), *odoratio* (the act), *odor* (the result); an ill —, *foetor;* to have a bad —, *male* (good, *bene*) *olēre.* **II.** v.intr. to — of, (re)*dolēre alqd;* to —, or have the sensation, *odorari, olfacĕre.* **smelling-bottle,** n. *vasculum olfactoriolum.*

smelt, v.tr. *fundēre, coquēre* (Plin.), *liquefacēre.*

smile, I. n. *rīsus, -ūs;* with a —, *subridens.* **II.** v.intr. (*sub)rīdēre, irridēre alci rei;* fortune —s on me, *fortuna mihi effulget.*

smirk, I. n. by *rīsus, -ūs, contortus.* **II.** v.intr. *vultum ad alqd componēre.*

smite, v.tr. *ferire, percutēre.*

smith, n. *faber ferrarius* (= a blacksmith). **smithy,** n. *officina ferraria.*

smoke, I. n. *fumus.* **II.** v.intr. *fumare, vaporare, exhalare.* **III.** v.tr. to — (tobacco), *herbae Nicotianae fumum ducēre;* see FUMIGATE. **smoky,** adj. *fumosus* (= full of smoke, discoloured by smoke).

smooth, I. adj. *lēvis, teres;* of words, etc., *blandus;* of the sea, etc., *tranquillus, placidus;* of the temper, *aequus, aequabilis, aequalis.* Adv. in gen. by adj.; of words, etc., *blande;* of the sea, etc., *tranquille, placide;* of the temper, *aequo animo, aequabiliter, aequaliter.* **II.** v.tr. *lēvare, lēvigare* (in gen.), *limare* (with file), *runcinare* (with plane); of the sea, *tranquillare, sedare;* fig. to — a person's way, *aditum alci ad alqm dare.* **smoothness,** n. *lēvitas, tranquillitas, aequanimitas;* — of diction, *aequabilitas.*

smother, v.tr. *suffocare, animam intercludēre;* fear —s his voice, *metus vocem praecludit;* see STRANGLE.

smouldering, adj. *fumans.*

smuggle, v.tr. *merces furtim or porterio non soluto importare or invehēre.* **smuggler,** n. *qui merces vetitas importat.*

smut, n. *fuligo, robigo* (= blight). **smutty,** n. *fumosus* (= smoky).

snack, n. *pars, portio, gustus, -ūs* (= a taste).

snaffle, n. *frenum.*

snail, n. *cochlea.* **snail's-shell,** n. *cochleae testa.*

snake, n. *anguis, serpens, coluber, vipera, draco.* **snaky,** adj. *+vipereus, +anguineus.*

snap, I. v.intr. *crepitum edĕre, crepare;* = to break asunder, *frangi, diffringi;* = to scold.

alqm increpare. **II.** v.tr. *frangĕre, (prae)rumpĕre, diffringĕre, infringĕre;* to — the fingers, *digitis concrepare;* to — at, lit. and fig. *petĕre, arripĕre;* to — up, see SEIZE. **III.** n. *crepitus, -ūs.*

snappish, adj. *morosus, difficilis, mordax, iracundus.* Adv. *morose, iracunde.*

snare, I. n. lit. and fig. *laqueus, plaga, insidiae, -arum;* to set a — for anyone, *alci insidias facĕre;* to get one's head out of a —, *se expedire (ex laqueo).* **II.** v.tr. lit. and fig. *illaqueare, irretire.*

snarl, v.intr. 1, lit. *fremĕre;* 2, fig. *(sub)ringi.*

snatch, v.tr. and intr. *rapĕre, corripĕre;* to — away, *surripĕre;* to — at, *captare;* see SEIZE.

sneak, I. v.tr. *irrepĕre;* to — into anything, e.g. *ad amicitiam reptare* (= to creep); to — away, *furtim se subducĕre.* **II.** n. *homo nequam, abiectus;* see CONTEMPTIBLE.

sneer, I. n. *derīsus, -ūs, irrīsus, -ūs.* **II.** v.tr. *deridēre, irridēre.*

sneeze, v.intr. *sternuĕre.* **sneezing,** n. *sternutamentum.*

sniff, n. and v.tr. and intr. see SMELL.

snip, v.tr. *circumcidĕre, amputare.*

snipe, n. *scolopax* (late).

snob, n. *homo putidus.*

snore, v.intr. *stertĕre.*

snort, I. v.tr. *fremĕre.* **II.** n. *fremitus, -ūs.*

snout, n. *rostrum.*

snow, I. n. *nix, nivis;* a — -ball, *nivis glebula* (late); —flake, *nix;* — -storm, *nivis casus, -ūs,* or *nives.* **II.** v.tr. *ning(u)ĕre,* gen. impers.; it —s, *ningit.* **snowy,** adj. *nivosus;* — -white, *niveus, colore niveo.*

snub, I. v.tr. **II.** n. see REBUKE. **snub-nosed,** adj. *simus.*

snuff, I. n. 1, of a candle, *fungus;* 2, = comminuted tobacco, *pulvis sternutatorius;* — -box, *pyxis.* **II.** v.tr. *candelae fungum demĕre;* to — out, *ex(s)tinguĕre;* to — up anything, *alqd naribus haurire.* **snuffers,** n. *forfices* (scissors, Mart.) *candelarum.* **snuffle,** v.intr. *vocem naribus proferre.*

snug, adj. see COMFORTABLE.

so, adv. *sic, ita, hunc in modum, hoc modo, ut . . . sic, ut . . . ita, tam . . . quam;* — then, *itaque, ergo;* see THEREFORE; — that (= in order that), *ut;* — not, *ne,* or by rel. *qui, quae, quod* with subj. ; — that, of consequence, *ut;* — not, *ut non;* — much, *tam valde, tam vehementer, tantum, tantopere, adeo;* twice — much, *bis tanto, alterum tantum;* not — much, *minus, non ita;* — much . . . as, *tantopere . . . quantopere;* — great, *tam multus, tantus, tantum;* — great . . . as, *tantum . . . quantum;* — again, *alterum tantum;* — many, *tot;* — many . . . as, *tot . . . quot;* just — many, *totidem;* — far, *eo, eo usque, in tantum, quoad, hactenus;* to carry a thing — far, *rem eo adducĕre;* — far as I can look back, *quoad longissime potest mens mea respicĕre;* — little food, *tantulus cibus;* — few, *tam pauci;* as . . . —, *et . . . et, tum . . . tum, tam . . . quam, vel . . . vel;* not — . . . as, *non tam . . . quam;* is it —? *itane? siccine?* — quickly, *tam cito, tam celeriter;* — quickly as possible, *quam primum, primo quoque tempore, simul ac, ut primum;* as that was painful, — this is pleasant, *ut illud erat molestum, sic hoc est jucundum* (Cic.); — uncivil as, *tam inurbanus ut* (Cic.); did you think me — unjust as to be angry with you? *adeone me injustum esse existimasti ut tibi irascerer?* (Cic.); — far from, *tantum abest ut . . . non;* — often, *totie(n)s . . . quotie(n)s;* grant it —, *fac ita esse;* if it had been done (— cour-

teous are you), you would have written it, *et si esset factum (quae tua est humanitas), scripsisses;* — called, *quem, quam, quod dicunt, qui,* etc., *dicitur.* **so-so,** adv. *mediocriter.*

soak, v.intr. *macerare;* to — up, *bibĕre;* to — through, *permanare* (= to trickle through), *madefacĕre* (= to wet). **soaking,** adj. of rain, *effusus.*

soap, I. n. *sapo* (Plin.). **II.** v.tr. *sapone illinĕre.*

soar, v.intr. *sublime ferri, se tollĕre* (lit. and fig.), *subvolare* (of birds, etc.).

sob, I. n. *singultus, -ūs.* **II.** v.intr. *singultire.*

sober, I. adj. *sobrius* (opp. *vinolentus,* used lit. and fig.), *temperans, temperatus, modestus, modicus, moderatus* (all = moderate in desires), *severus* (= grave). Adv. *sobrie, temperate, modeste, modice, moderate, severe.* **sobriety, soberness,** n. *sobrietas, temperantia, moderatio, modestia, severitas.*

sociable, adj. *sociabilis, comis, affabilis;* see COURTEOUS, FRIENDLY. **social,** adj. *socialis, communis, civilis* (in political sense), *sociabilis, congregabilis* (= disposed to meeting together, of bees), *facilis* (= easy of approach, as a quality of character); — life, *vitae societas, communitas vitae.* Adv. *quod ad societatem vitae pertinet.* **socialism,** n. by *forma civitatis in quā summa aequalitas inter cives exstat.* **socialist,** n. *qui summam inter cives aequalitatem appetit.* **sociality,** n. *socialitas, mores faciles* (= sociability). **society,** n. = the union of several persons for a common end, *societas* (of learned and commercial men), *sodalitas* (= a brotherhood or fraternity), *factio* (= a union which makes a party, esp. in a bad sense), *collegium* (= a corporation of merchants, artisans, priests); to form — with someone, *societatem cum alqo facĕre, inire, coire, rationem cum alqo communicare* (= to make common cause), *societatem contrahĕre cum alqo;* to take into —, *alqm in societatem assumĕre (ad)scribĕre, alqm in collegium cooptare* (by election); = to the associated persons, *socii* (of a craft), *grex* (= a band, e.g. a company of actors); = society in general, *societas humana (hominum* or *generis humani);* civil —, *societas civilis;* = as an assemblage, *coetus, -ūs, conventus, -ūs (virorum feminarumque* or *mulierumque), circulus* (= a circle or gathering, whether in the streets or in houses, a club); to go into —, *in circulum venire;* to avoid —, *vitare coetus, hominum conventus fugĕre, homines fugĕre, abstinēre congressu hominum,* se a *congressu hominum segregare.*

sock, n. see STOCKING.

socket, n. of a candlestick, *myxa;* of the eye, * *cavum oculi.*

Socratic, adj. *Socraticus.*

sod, n. *caespes, -itis,* m. ; a green —, *caespes vivus* or *viridis.*

soda, n. *nitrum.*

sodden, adj. *madidus.*

sofa, n. *lectulus.*

soft, adj. *mollis, lēnis* (= gentle), *effeminatus* (= effeminate). Adv. *molliter, leniter, effeminate.* **soften,** I. v.tr. *(e)mollire, mitigare, lenire* (lit. and fig.). **II.** v.intr. *molliri, mollescĕre.* **softness,** n. *mollitia* or *mollities.*

soho, interj. *heus! heus tu! ehe!*

soil, I. n. *solum;* a good —, *solum pingue;* poor —, *solum exile.* **II.** v.tr. *inquinare, polluĕre, maculare;* see DEFILE.

sojourn, I. v.intr. *cum alqo* or *in alqā terrā commorari* (= to tarry), *sedem habēre in loco, per-*

grinari in urbe or in gente (as a foreigner). **II.**
n. mora, commoratio, peregrinatio. **sojourn-
er,** n. hospes (= guest), peregrinus (= foreigner),
advena, m. and f. (= alien).

solace, I. n. solatium, solatio (= the act),
† solamen, levamen(tum) (= an alleviation). **II.**
v.tr. alqm (con)solari, alci solatium praebēre,
dare, afferre.

solar, adj. solaris, or by genit. solis (= of
the sun).

solder, I. n. ferrumen (Plin.). **II. v.tr.**
conferruminare (Plin.), (im)plumbare.

soldier, n. miles, -itis; common —, miles
gregarius, manipularis; foot —, pedes; horse
—, eques; to serve as a —, stipendia facĕre,
merēre or merēri, with genit. or dat. **soldierly,** adj. militaris, rei militaris peritus.
soldiery, n. milites, or as collect. miles.

sole, adj. solus, unus, unicus; — survivor,
superstes, -itis, m. Adv. solum (modo), tantum
(modo). **solitary, I.** adj. solus, solitarius (of
persons), solus, desertus, avius, devius, secretus
(of places). **II.** n. see HERMIT. **solitude,**
n. solitudo (both as state and lonely place).

sole, n. of the foot (pedis) planta, solum; —
of a shoe, (calcei) solea (= a sandal), solum.

sole, n. = fish, solea.

solecism, n. soloecismus (= offence against
grammar); see also IMPROPRIETY.

solemn, adj. sol(l)emnis, originally = yearly
or annual, and hence festal and customary, but
not solemn in our sense, which may be expressed
by summā religione imbutus, and by sanctus,
religiosus. Adv. sol(l)emniter, sancte, religiose. **solemnize,** v.tr. celebrare. **solem-
nization,** n. celebratio. **solemnity,** n. 1,
sol(l)emne (e.g. sollemne clavi figendi, Liv.; nostrum illud sollemne servemus, Cic. = an established custom); = profound religious sentiment,
reverentia; 2, see GRAVITY, SERIOUSNESS.

solicit, v.tr. sol(l)icitare, poscĕre, deposcĕre,
expetĕre, comb. deposcĕre atque expetĕre, obsecrari,
orare alqm alqd. **solicitation,** n. preces, -um,
(ef)flagitatio, rogatio, obsecratio; at the — of,
alcjs rogatu, alqo rogante, precando. **solicitor,**
n. 1, qui rogat, qui poscit; 2, advocatus; see
ADVOCATE. **solicitous,** adj. sol(l)icitus (=
concerned, moved with anxiety), anxius; see
ANXIOUS. Adv. sol(l)icite, anxie. **solicitude,**
n. sol(l)icitudo, cura, anxietas; to be an object
of —, curae esse alci.

solid, adj. solidus (in most senses of the
English; = firm, lasting), stabilis, firmus; see
STABLE; — food, cibus, caro (= meat). Adv.
solide, stabiliter, firme; — ground, solidum, n.;
— bodies, solida, -orum. **solidity,** n. soliditas.

soliloquy, n. meditatio (= meditation),
cum alqs secum loquitur. **soliloquize,** v.tr.
ipsum secum loqui.

solitary, adj. see under SOLE.

solo, n. unius cantus, -ūs; on an instrument,
quod alqs solus fidibus, etc., canit.

solstice, n. solstitium (= summer —), bruma
(= winter —); relating to the —, solstitialis,
brumalis.

solve, v.tr. (dis)solvĕre (properly = to loosen,
and hence to — knotty points), enodare (=
to undo a knot); see EXPLAIN. **solubility,** n.
use verb. **soluble,** adj. 1, lit. quod dissolvi
potest; 2, fig. quod explanari potest. **solution,**
n. 1, = act of dissolving (dis)solutio; 2, = what
is dissolved, dilutum (Plin.); 3, = explanation,
enodatio, expositio, (dis)solutio, explicatio. **sol-
vent, I.** adj. qui solvendo (par) est. **II.** n.
quod ad alqd dissolvendum vim habet.

some, adj. used with nom. aliquis (aliqua,
aliquod), quis (after si, e.g. si quis hoc dicit),
aliquot with gen. (e.g. aliquot hominum); —
. . . others, alii . . . alii, quidam . . . alii;
—one, aliquis, quispiam, quisquam; when the
relative follows, aliquis is dropped (e.g. habeo
quem quem amem); —one, I know not who, nescio
qui or quis; — (as a softening term), e.g. —
fifteen, etc., homines ad quindecim Curioni
assenserunt; abhinc menses decem fere, = —
ten months ago; nactus equites circiter triginta,
= having obtained — thirty horsemen; in —
way or other, quācumque; there is — reason,
non sine caus(s)a; it is — comfort to me, nonnihil me consolatur (Cic.); for — time, aliquando, aliquandiu. **somehow,** adv. nescio
quomodo, nescio quo pacto. **something,** n.
see SOME; when emphatic, aliquid, nonnihil.
sometimes, adv. aliquando, nonnunquam,
subinde, interdum. **somewhat,** n. aliquan-
tu(lu)m, nonnihil. **somewhere,** adv. alicubi, alqo loco, nonnusquam. **somewhither,**
adv. aliquo.

somersault, n. saltus, -ūs (= leap); to
turn a —, dare saltus.

somnambulist, n. qui in somnis ambulat.

somniferous, adj. † somnifer, somnificus.

somnolent, adj. see SLEEPY.

son, n. filius, † natus; a little —, filiolus;
foster—, alumnus; a —-in-law, gener; a step-
—, privignus; —s and daughters, liberi.

song, n. cantus, -ūs, canticum, cantilēna (contemptuously, e.g. eadem cantilena, = the same
old —), carmen, modus. **songster,** n. cantor,
vocis et cantūs modulator; f. cantrix, poëtria.

sonorous, adj. sonorus, canorus, clarus; see
CLEAR. Adv. sonore, canore, clare.

soon, adv. cito; brevi tempore (= in a short
time), mox, jam, propediem; very —, extemplo
(= straightway); — after, paul(l)o post, non ita
multo post; —, mature (= shortly), mane; too
—, ante tempus; to do —, maturate alqd
facĕre; as — as possible, quam maturrime;
as — as, quam primum, simul ac or atque, ut
(primum); as — as, simul ac. **sooner,** adv. =
rather, potius, libentius; I had —er, mallem.

soot, n. fūligo. **sooty,** adj. fuligine oblĭtus.

sooth, n. verum, veritas; in —, vere, certe;
for —, sane, profecto. **soothsay,** v.tr. praedicĕre. **soothsayer,** n. (h)aruspex, m.; see
PROPHET. **soothsaying,** n. auguratio, augurium.

soothe, v.tr. mulcēre, lenire, placare, sedare,
levare, mitigare, tranquillare. **soothing,** adj.
by part. or by blandus. Adv. blande.

sop, I. n. frustum, offa (panis). **II. v.tr.**
macerare (= to soak).

sophism, n. sophisma (Sen.), captio. **sophist,** n. 1, sophista, m.; 2, fig. homo captiosus.
sophistical, adj. captiosus. Adv. captiose.
sophistry, n. ars sophistica, fallaces dicendi
artes.

soporific, adj. † soporifer, soporus, somnificus (Plin.).

sorcerer, n. veneficus. **sorceress,** n.
venefica, maga, saga. **sorcery,** n. ars magica.

sordid, adj. sordidus (= unclean, mean), abjectus, humilis (= despicable), avarus (= greedy);
see MEAN. Adv. sordide, abjecte, humiliter,
avare. **sordidness,** n. sordes, avaritia.

sore, I. n. 1, ulcus, -ēris, n.; see ABSCESS; 2,
fig. molestia; see TROUBLE. **II.** adj. quod alqm
dolore afficit; fig. to be — about anything, alqd
graviter ferre. **III.** adv. aegre, graviter, moleste;
— wounded, compluribus confectus vulneribus.

sorrel, n. *oxys.*

sorrel, adj. *spadix.*

sorrow, I. n. *dolor, aegritudo, maestitia, molestia, tristitia, acerbitas, paenitentia (agĕre paenitentiam rei,* = to have — for), *desiderium*(=longing), *luctus, -ūs* (= mourning). **II.** v.intr. *dolēre, maerēre, dolore affici, lugēre, desiderare, contristari, alqm paenitet alcjs rei.* **sorrowful,** adj. *tristis, maestus, lugubris, dejectus, afflictus, molestiâ affectus;* to be —, *dolēre, aegritudine affici, se maerori tradĕre, contristari.* Adv. *maeste;* see SADLY.

sort, I. n. *mos, modus, ratio, genus, -ĕris,* n. (= kind or manner); after a —, *quodammodo;* after the same —, *similiter;* in what —? *quomodo?* in like —, *pari ratione;* of what —? *cujusmodi? qualis?* of this —, *hujuscemodi;* of that —, *ejusmodi, istiusmodi;* he is not the — of man to, *non is est qui* with subj. **II.** v.tr. *(in genera) digerĕre;* see SEPARATE. **III.** v.intr. = to be suitable, *aptum esse;* see SUIT. **sorting,** n. *diribitio.*

sortie, n. *excursio, eruptio;* to make a —, *erumpĕre.*

sot, n. by *homo ebriosus.* **sottish,** adj. *ebriosus, vinulentus.*

soul, n. *anima* (= the living principle), *animus* (= the emotional nature), *spiritus, -ūs* (= breath, spirit), *mens* (= the intelligence); by my —, *ita vivam ut,* etc., *ne vivam si,* etc.; from my —, *ex animo;* with all my —, *toto animo;* (as a living being), *anima, caput, homo;* not a —, *nemo.*

sound, adj. (as opposed to unsound or rotten) *sanus* (= in a natural state, hence our sane, opp. insane), *salvus* (= safe), *incolumis* (= uninjured), *sospes* (= escaped from peril), *integer* (= entire, whole), *firmus, robustus* (= strong), *saluber* (*locus*), *salutaris* (*herba, ars*), comb. *sanus et salvus;* to be — in health, *bonâ* or *prosperâ valetudine uti,* valēre; = deep, of sleep, *altus, artus;* of knowledge, etc., *altus, accuratus.* Adv. *sane, salve, integre, firme, robuste, alte, arte, accurate.* **soundness,** n. *sanitas, bona* or *firma* or *prospera valetudo* (of health), *salus, -ūtis* (in gen.), of argument, *gravitas.*

sound, I. n. = noise, *sonus, sonitus, -ūs, vox, clamor, strepitus, -ūs, fremitus, -ūs* (= din); a high —, *sonus acutus;* deep —, *sonus gravis;* soft —, *sonus levis.* **II.** v.tr. *sonare* (in gen.); to — a trumpet, *tubam inflare;* to — an alarm, *tubâ signum dare;* to — a march, *(vasa) conclamare;* to — a retreat, *receptui canĕre* or *signum dare.* **III.** v.intr. *sonare, sonitum edĕre, canĕre* (of trumpets).

sound, v.tr. = to test depth, perhaps *tentare quae sit altitudo (maris, fluminis,* etc.); fig. see EXAMINE.

sound, n. = strait, *fretum;* see STRAIT.

soup, n. *jus.*

sour, I. adj. *acidus*(= sharp), *acerbus, amārus* (=bitter), *acer;* somewhat —, *subacidus;* to be —, *acēre;* to turn —, *acescĕre.* Adv. *acerbe, acide, acriter, morose.* **II.** v.tr. *alqm exacerbare;* see EMBITTER. **sourness,** n. *acerbitas, amaritudo* (lit. and fig.), *morositas* (fig.).

source, n. *fons, -ntis,* m., *caput;* to take its — in, *profluĕre ex algo loco,* fig. *fons, caus(s)a, principium, stirps;* see FOUNTAIN.

south, n. *meridies, plaga* (or *regio*) *australis* or *meridiana, pars meridiana, regio in meridiem spectans;* — wind, *ventus meridianus, ventus australis* (opp. to *ventus septentrionalis*), *auster* (= the — wind properly); the —-east, *regio inter ortum brumalem et meridiem spectans;* —-east wind, *euronōtus* (=——-east), *vulturnus* (=——-east one-third —); —-western, *inter occasum bru-*

malem et meridiem spectans; —-west wind, *africus;* ——-west, *inter meridiem et occasum solis spectans;* ———-west wind, *libonōtus* (Plin.); west—-west wind, *subvesperus.* **southern,** adj. *meridianus* (in later writers *meridionalis* or *meridialis*), *in meridiem spectans, australis.*

southwards, adv. *in* or *ad meridiem.*

southernwood, n. *abrotonum (abrotonus).*

sovereign, I. adj. *sui juris, alii non subjectus;* — remedy, *remedium efficacissimum.* **II** n. *rex, dominus, princeps, imperator, tyrannus.* **sovereignty,** n. *summa rerum* or *imperii,* (*summum*) *imperium, dominatio, dominatus, -ūs, principatus, -ūs, regnum, tyrannis, -idis,* f. ; to rise to the —, *rerum potiri.*

sow, n. *sus.*

sow, v.tr. *serĕre* (lit. and fig.), *semen spargĕre, seminare* (from *semen,* = a seed); as you —, so shall you reap, *ut sementem feceris, ita metes.* **sower,** n. *sator.* **sowing,** n. *satio, satus, -ūs, sementis.*

space, n. *spatium, locus;* fig., to give — to, *locum dare, indulgēre rei.* **spacious,** adj. † *spatiosus, amplus.* **spaciousness,** n. *amplitudo.*

spade, n. *pala.*

span, I. n. *palmus* (Plin.); the — of life, *exigua vitae brevitas;* the — of the arch was 20 ft., *arcus viginti pedes latus erat.* **II.** v.tr. *jungĕre* (e.g. *flumen ponte,* = to — the river).

spangle, I. n. *bractea.* **II.** v.tr. *(bracteis) distinguĕre.*

spaniel, n. by *canis.*

spar, n. *lapis (-idis) specularis* (= a stone, Plin.).

spar, n. *vectis,* m. ; see STAKE.

spar, v.intr. *pugnis certare.*

spar, n. *obex, vectis,* m.

spare, v.tr. *alci* or *alci rei parcĕre.*

spark, n. *scintilla, igniculus;* a — of hope, *spes exigua, spĕcula.* **sparkle,** v.intr. † *scintillare, fulgēre, nitēre;* see GLITTER. **sparkling,** n. *nitor.*

sparrow, n. *passer, -ĕris,* m. ⸲

spasm, n. *spasmus, spasma, -ătis,* n. (Plin.), *tetanus* (of the neck). **spasmodic,** adj. by adv. = by fits and starts, perhaps *haud uno tenore.*

spatter, v.tr. *a(d)spergĕre.*

spawn, I. n. *piscium ova, -orum.* **II.** v.tr. *ova gignĕre.*

speak, v.intr. *fari, loqui, dicĕre, sermocinari* (= to converse); to — Greek, *Graecâ linguâ uti, Graece loqui;* = to make a speech, *dicĕre, loqui, verba facĕre, orationem habēre contionari;* to — of, *alqm* or *algd dicĕre, de algâ re,* = to — about ; to — to, *alqm affari, appellare, compellare, alloqui;* to — together, *colloqui;* to — for, or to, something, *testem esse alci rei;* to — for and against, *in utramque partem disputare.* **speaker,** n. *orator* (= orator), *qui dicit* (= person speaking).

speaking, I. n. *locutio, sermo.* **II.** adj. (e.g. a — likeness, *vera alcjs imago*). **speech,** n. 1, *oratio;* the faculty of —, *oratio* (whence *ratio et oratio*); 2, = a set —, *oratio; contio* (before a popular assembly). **speechless,** adj. see DUMB.

spear, I. n. *hasta;* see LANCE. **II.** v.tr. *hastâ transfigĕre.*

special, adj. *praecipuus, eximius, egregius* (= excellent), *proprius, peculiaris* (= — to anyone or anything). **speciality,** n. *quod alci* or *alci rei proprium est.* **specially,** adv. *praecipue, eximie, egregie, imprimis* (*in primis*), *maxime, prae ceteris, praesertim, valde,* or by superl. (e.g — good, *optimus*).

specie, n. *aurum* or *argentum signatum.*

species, n. *genus, -ēris,* n., *species;* the human
—, *genus humanum.* **specific, I.** adj. *proprius,
peculiaris;* — charges, etc., *singuli* (= one by
one). **II.** n. see REMEDY

specify, v.tr. *si(n)gillatim enumerare, denotare.* **specification,** n. *enumeratio.*

specimen, n. *specimen, documentum, exemplum.*

specious, adj. having a fair appearance,
speciosus, fucatus, simulatus (= feigned).

speck, n.*macula*(= a spot), *labes,-is*(= a stain),
nota (= a mark) ; = a fault, *vitium.* **speckle,**
v.tr. *(com)maculare, maculis alqm conspergēre.*
speckled, adj. *maculis distinctus, maculatus.*

spectacle, n. *spectaculum.* **spectacles,**
n. perhaps *vitrea ad (oculorum) aciem adjuvan-
dum apta.*

spectator, n. *spectator.*

spectre, n. see GHOST.

speculate, v.intr. 1, *cogitare, quaerĕre, inquirĕre de alqâ re;* see INQUIRE ; 2, in business,
quaestui servire. **speculation,** n. 1, *cogitatio*
(= thought); to be sunk in —, *in cogitatione defixum esse;* scientific —, *rerum contemplatio;* philosophical —, *philosophia;* 2, — in business, *negotium;* to be absorbed in —, *emendi et vendendi
quaestu et lucro duci.* **speculative,** adj. e.g. philosophy, *philosophia contemplativa* (Sen.). **speculator,** n. *qui quaestui servit, quaestuosus.*

speech, n. see SPEAK.

speed, I. n. *celeritas, velocitas, properatio,
festinatio.* **II.** v.tr. see PROSPER. **speedy,**
adj. *celer, velox, properus.* **speedily,** adv. *cito,
celeriter, velociter, propere, festinanter, festinans.*

spell, I. n. *incantamentum, carmen.* **II.**
v.tr. *syllabas lit(t)erarum ordinare.* **spell-
bound,** adj. *defixus, stupens, stupefactus.* **spelling,** n. *ars lit(t)erarum recte ordinandarum.*

spend, v.tr. *pecuniam erogare* (esp. of public
money), *(in)sumĕre (in alqm rem), in alqâ re
sumptum* or *impensam facĕre;* to — time, *tempus,
diem, aetatem,* etc., *agĕre, degĕre, consumĕre, (con)-
terĕre* (= to waste); to — the night, *pernoctare;*
I spent three days with him, *triduum cum eo
fui;* fig. to — oneself, *alci rei deditum esse;* to
— itself, see ABATE. **spendthrift,** n. *nepos.*

spew, v.tr. *(e)vomĕre.* **spewing,** n. *vomitus,
-ūs.*

sphere, n. *sphaera, globus;* fig. = an office,
munus, -ēris, n., *officium* (= duty); to keep in
one's own —, *se rerum suarum finibus continēre.*
spherical, adj. *globosus.*

sphinx, n. *sphinx, -ngis,* f.

spice, I. n. *condimentum* (lit. and fig.); a —
of anything (e.g. of the Devil), *nonnihil alcjs
rei.* **II.** v.tr. *aromatibus* or *aromatis condire.*
spicy, adj. 1, *(aromate) condītus;* 2, fig. *salsus.*

spider, n. *aranea.* **spider's-web,** n.
aranea (Plaut.), *texta aranea* (Plin.).

spike, I. n. *clavus* (= nail), *cuspis, -ĭdis,* f.
(= head of a weapon). **II.** v.tr. (e.g. cannon),
tormenta bellica clavis adactis inutilia reddĕre.

spikenard, n. *nardus* (Plin.).

spill, v.tr. *effundĕre.* **spilling,** n. *effusio.*

spin, I. v.tr. 1, *nēre,* † *stamina ducĕre, texĕre
telam;* 2, *versare* (= to turn), *circumagĕre, in orbem agĕre.* **II.** v.intr. *circumagi.* **spinning,**
n. use verb. **spinner,** n. *qui* or *quae stamina
net.* **spindle,** n. *fusus.*

spine, n. *spina* (properly = a thorn, then
the backbone). **spinal,** adj. *qui (quae, quod)
ad spinam pertinet.*

spinster, n. *innupta, virgo.*

spiral, adj. *tortuosus* (of a line); see CROOKED.

spire, n. *turris;* a — on a tower, perhaps
fastigium (= gable).

spirit, n. *spiritus, -ūs* (properly = breath or
air), = animation or vigour, *spiritus, sanguis;* =
soul, *animus, mens, spiritus, ingenium;* a lofty
—, *animus excelsus;* of little —, *homo parvi
animi;* = the prevailing feeling, *mens;* = the
peculiar tone of thought, *ingenium, natura;* =
temper, disposition, *animus, studium, indoles,
-is,* f., *ingenium;* — of the age, *horum temporum*
or *hujus aetatis ratio,* or *mores, -um,* m. ; =
meaning, *sententia, voluntas;* = strong drink,
vinum or *liquor acrior;* to understand the —
of a writer, *mentem scriptoris assequi;* a disembodied —, *anima;* the Holy —, **Spiritus*
Sanctus or *Sacer;* an evil —, *daemon;* the —s
of the departed, *manes, -ium.* **spirited,** adj.
animosus, generosus, fortis; see BRAVE. **spiritless,** adj. *ignavus, demissus, fractus; =* empty,
inanis; see COWARDLY. **spiritual,** adj. (not sensuous) by the gen. *animi* or *ingenii; =* without
body, *corpore carens, ab omni concretione mortali
segregatus;* — mind, *animus religiosus, pius erga
Deum;* opp. to secular, * *ecclesiasticus.* Adv.
animo, mente; = religiously, *caste, religiose,
pure, pie.* **spiritualism,** n. by *credĕre animas
mortuorum cum hominibus communicare.* **spi-
ritualist,** n. *qui inter mortuos ac vivos commercium esse putat.* **spirituality,** n. *animus
rerum divinarum studiosus.* **spiritualities,**
n. *reditus ecclesiastici.*

spit, n. (= utensil to roast meat on), *veru.*

spit, v.intr. *(ex)spuĕre.* **spittle,** n. see SALIVA.

spite, I. n. *odium occultum, simultas obscura,
malevolentia, livor;* to have or show a —, *suc-
censēre alci, odium occultum gerĕre adversus alqm;*
in — of, *adversus,* or in with accus., or by *cum*
(e.g. *ivit cum manēre illi liceret*), or by abl. abs.
(e.g. in — of the laws, *legibus contemptis*). **II.**
v.tr. see ANNOY. **spiteful,** adj. *malignus,
malevolus, lividus.* Adv. *maligne, malevole.*

splash, v.tr. *a(d)spergĕre.*

spleen, n. *lien, splen;* fig. *odium, livor, invidia.* **splenetic,** adj. 1, *lienosus;* 2, *malevolus, malignus.*

splendid, adj. *splendidus, splendens, fulgens,
nitens, nitidus, (prae)clarus.* Adv. *splendide,
nitide, magnifice, (prae)clare.* **splendour,** n.
splendor, fulgor, nitor; lit. and fig. *apparatus,
-ūs* (= pomp).

splice, v.tr. *partes inter se texĕre.*

splint, n. *canalis, ferulae* (Cels.). **splinter,**
n. *ossis fragmentum* (of a bone), *ligni assula* or
fragmentum (of wood).

split, I. n. *fissura* (Plin.), *scissura* (Plin.).
II. v.tr. *(dif)findĕre, scindĕre.* **III.** v.intr.
(dif)findi, dissilire (= to leap apart).

spoil, I. n. *praeda;* the — of war, *spolia,
-orum;* — taken from the person of an enemy,
exuviae. **II.** v.tr. 1, *spoliare;* see PLUNDER ; 2,
= to injure, *corrumpĕre;* see DESTROY ; 3, = to
indulge too much, *nimis alci morigerari.* **spoil-
er,** n. *praedator, spoliator.* **spoiling, spoliation,** n. *spoliatio, expilatio, direptio.*

spoke, n. (of a wheel), *radius (rotae).*

spondee, n. *spondēus* (scil. *pes*).

sponge, I. n. *spongia.* **II.** v.tr. *spongiâ abstergēre.* **sponge-cake,** n. *placenta.* **spongy,**
adj. *spongiosus* (Plin.).

sponsor, n. *sponsor.*

spontaneous, adj. *libens.* Adv. *ultro, sponte*
(suâ), suo motu. **spontaneousness, spon-**

taneity, n. by *arbitrium* (e.g. *quod alcjs arbi-trio factum est*).

spoon, n. *cochlear (cochleare, cochlearium,* Plin.), *ligula* (= ladle). **spoonful,** n. *cochlear.*

sport, I. n. 1, *ludus* (= game), = to hunting, *venatio;* 2, = mockery, *ludibrium;* to make — of, *alci illudere;* see MOCK. **II.** v.intr. *ludere;* to — about, *lascivire.* **sportive,** adj. *lascivus* (= playful), *jocosus* (= jocose) ; see PLAYFUL, JOCOSE. Adv. *lascive, jocose.* **sportiveness,** n. *lascivia, jocus.* **sportsman,** n. *venator.*

spot, I. n. 1, *macula* (lit. and fig.), *nota* (= mark ; also = disgrace) ; see STAIN ; 2, = place, *locus.* **II.** v.tr. *notare* (lit.), *maculare, inquinare* (fig.). **spotless,** adj. *sine maculis, castus, purus, sanctus, integer.* Adv. *sine maculis, caste, pure, sancte, integre.* **spotted,** adj. *maculosus.*

spouse, n. *maritus* (the husband), *uxor* (the wife), *co(n)junx* (the husband or the wife).

spout, I. n. *os ;* = pipe, *fistula.* **II.** v.intr. *erumpere, exsilire.*

sprain, n. and v.tr. pernaps by *convellere* (Col.), *manare, serpere* (fig.).

sprawl, v.intr. *humi prostratum jacere.*

spray, n. of the sea, *spuma* (= foam).

spray, n. of a tree, perhaps *virgula ;* see SPRIG.

spread, I. v.tr. *(ex)pandere* (= to lay open), *explicare* (= to unfold), *extendere* (= to stretch out), *sternere* (= to lay out or flat), *spargere* (= to scatter), *serere, disseminare* (= to sow seed broad-cast), *differre, (di)vulgare* (= to make common), *dilatare* (= to stretch out). **II.** v.intr. *patere, extendi* (lit.), *percrebescere, increbescere, (di)vulgari* (fig.). **spreading,** adj. † *fatulus.*

sprig, n. *surculus, virgula.*

sprightliness, n. *alacritas* (= eagerness), *facetiae, sal, -is,* m. (= wit) ; see EAGERNESS, WIT. **sprightly,** adj. *alacer, facetus, salsus.*

spring, I. n. 1, = origin, *origo, ortus, -ūs, fons, -ntis,* m. (= source), *principium, caus(s)a* ; = fountain, *fons, scaturigo* (rare) ; 2, = first season of the year, *ver, tempus vernum ;* the — of life, *iniens aetas ;* 3, = — in machinery, perhaps by *machinatio* (e.g. *machinatio quādam moveri,* Cic.). **II.** v.intr. *salire* (= to leap); to — down, *desilire ;* to — forward, *prosilire ;* to — from, to take origin in, *ex alqo* or *alqā re (e)nasci, (ex)oriri, proficisci ;* to — out, *prosilire, prorumpere ;* to — up, *crescere* (= to grow), *surgere* (= to rise, of winds, etc.). **III.** v.tr. to — a leak, *rimas agere ;* to — a mine, *cuniculum igni explodere.* **spring-tide,** n. *aestus, -ūs, maximus.*

sprinkle, v.tr. *alqm alqā re spargere, a(d)spergere, conspergere.*

sprite, n. *faunus* (= faun), or *nympha* (= nymph).

sprout, I. n. *surculus ;* see SHOOT. **II.** v.intr. *germinare* (Plin.).

spruce, adj. *comptus, bellus, ornatus, concinnus, nitidus, elegans.* Adv. *compte, belle, ornate, nitide, eleganter.*

spur, I. n. *calcar* (lit. and fig.). **II.** v.tr. *equo calcaria subdere* or *equum calcaribus concitare* or *stimulare.*

spurious, adj. *adulterinus, falsus.*

spurn, v.tr. *fastidire, aspernari, repudiare ;* to — with the foot ; see KICK.

spurt, I. v.intr. *summā vi contendere.* **II.** n. *nisus, -ūs ;* see EFFORT.

sputter, v.tr. *spuere;* to — out, *balbutire* (=to stammer).

spy, I. n. *explorator, speculator, emissarius.* **II.** v.intr. *explorare, speculari.*

squabble, I. n. *rixa, altercatio.* **II.** v.intr. *rixari.*

squadron, n. *equitum turma, ala ;* — of ships, *classis.*

squalid, adj. *sordidus, squalidus, spurcus ;* see DIRTY.

squall, I. n. *subita tempestas ;* = crying, *vāgitus, -ūs.* **II.** v.intr. *vagire.*

squalor, squalidity, squalidness, n. *sordes, -is,* f., usu. in pl., *squalor, spurcitia, spurcities.* Adv. *sordide, squalide, spurce.*

squander, v.tr. *profundere, effundere, perdere, dissipare.* **squanderer,** n. *nepos, -ōtis,* m.

square, I. adj. *quadratus.* **II.** n. *quadratum,* n. **III.** v.tr. *quadrare.*

squash, v.tr. see CRUSH.

squat, I. v.intr. *subsidere.* **II.** adj. *habitu corporis brevis atque obesus.*

squeak, I. n. *stridor.* **II.** v.intr. *stridere.*

squeamish, adj. *fastidiosus, delicatus.* **squeamishness,** n. *fastidium.*

squeeze, I. n. *compressio.* **II.** v.tr. *premere, comprimere ;* to — out, *exprimere.*

squib, n. see LAMPOON.

squint, v.intr. *limis* or *perversis oculis esse, limis spectare, strabonem esse;* to — at, *limis oculis intueri alqd* or *alqm.*

squire, n. * *armiger.*

squirrel, n. *sciūrus* (Plin.).

squirt, n. and v.tr. see SYRINGE.

stab, I. n. *ictus, -ūs* (= a blow), or *vulnus, -ēris, sicā factum.* **II.** v.tr. *(con)fodere,* or *sicā* or *pugione ferire, sicā conficere* (= to slay by stabbing, etc.). **stabber,** n. *sicarius.*

stable, I. adj. *stabilis, firmus ;* fig. *constans, propositi tenax.* **II.** n. *stabulum* (= stall, or in pl.). **III.** v.tr. *stabulare.* **stability,** n. *stabilitas, firmitas, constantia.*

stack, I. n. *meta* (of hay), *cumulus, acervus, strues, -is,* f. **II.** v.tr. *cumulare ;* see PILE.

staff, n. *baculum, bacillum, scipio* (carried before officials), *fustis,* m. (= cudgel) ; an augur's —, *lituus ;* the — of a spear, *hastile ;* shepherd's —, *pedum ;* herald's —, *caduceus ;* to lean on a —, *baculo inniti ;* — of officers, *legati et praefecti et tribuni militum ;* any other —, (of assistants) *socii,* (= colleagues) *adjutores, ministri.*

stag, n. *cervus.*

stage, n. 1, of a theatre, *proscaenium, scaena* (lit. = the wall which closed the — behind) ; 2, fig. *scaena* (e.g. to go upon the —, *in scaenam prodire*) ; 3, = degree, *gradus, -ūs ;* — part of a journey, *iter, itineris,* n. **stage-coach,** n. *vehiculum publicum.*

stagger, I. v.intr. *titubare, vacillare, incertis ire pedibus.* **II.** v.tr. *animum movēre, percutēre.* **staggers,** n. *vertigo.*

stagnant, adj. 1, *stagnans ;* 2, fig. see SLOW. **stagnate,** v.intr. 1, † *stagnare ;* 2, perhaps *hebescēre, languēre.*

staid, adj. see SOBER.

stain, I. n. 1, *macula, labes, -is, decoloratio* (the act) ; 2, fig. *macula, labes, -is,* f., *nota* (= mark), *dedecus, -ōris,* n. ; see SHAME. **II.** v.tr. 1, see DYE, DIRTY ; 2, fig. *maculare, foedare, polluere ;* to — a reputation, *alcjs existimationem violare, alcjs famae* or *alci notam turpitudinis inurēre, alqm infamiā a(d)spergere ;* = to discolour, *decolorare ;* = to dye, *tingēre, inficēre.* **stainless,** adj. *purus ;* see PURE.

stair, n. *gradus, -ūs;* a —case, *scalae (scalis habito tribus,* = I dwell up three pair of —s).

stake, I. n. *palus, stipes, -ĭtis,* m. ; as instrument of punishment, *palus* (= — to which criminals were bound ; where burning is implied, better use *igni interficĕre*); a — at play or gambling, *pignus, -ĕris,* n. (= a bet), *quod ponitur ;* to be at —, *agi, periclitari, in discrimen adduci;* my honour is at —, *fama agitur mea.* **II.** v.tr. *(de)ponĕre.*

stale, adj. *vetus, obsolētus, exsolētus* (= worn out) ; to become —, *obsolescĕre.*

stalk, I. n. *caulis* (of a herb), *caudex* (or a tree), *scapus, culmus* (= green stalk), *calamus* (= reed) ; see STEM. **II.** v.intr. *(magnifice) incedĕre,* † *spatiari.*

stall, I. n. *stabulum ;* = a little shop, *taberna ;* = a seat in a choir, *sella.* **II.** v.tr. *stabulare.*

stallion, n. *(equus) admissarius.*

stamen, n. *stamen.*

stammer, I. v.intr. *balbutire.* **II.** n. use verb.

stamp, I. n. *nota, signum, imago (impressa);* persons of that —, *ejusmodi homines ;* the — or blow of the foot, *(pedis) supplosio.* **II.** v.intr. *pedibus calcare, pulsare, pedem supplodĕre.* **III.** v.tr. to — under foot, *conculcare ;* = to mark, *signare, notare, signum* or *notam imprimĕre ;* to — money, *nummos signare* or *cudĕre.*

stanch, v.tr. see STAUNCH.

stand, I. n. *mora* (= delay), *locus, statio* (= place for standing) ; = prop, *statumen, adminiculum ;* = sideboard, etc., *abacus ;* to come to a —, *subsistĕre ;* to make a — against, *resistĕre ;* to take a —, *locum capĕre ;* to be at a —, *haerēre, animi pendēre.* **II.** v.intr. *stare, consistĕre ;* to let a thing —, *non movēre alqd ;* it —s written, *lit(t)eris consig-\;tum est, legimus ;* to — good, *obtinēre ;* to — against, *alci resistĕre ;* to — still, *quiescĕre ;* to — aside, *recedĕre ;* to — by anyone, *alci adesse ;* to — fast, *consistĕre ;* to — for an office, *munus petĕre* or *ambire ;* to — good in law, *lege valēre ;* to — on ceremony, *cum algo comiter sed haud familiariter agĕre ;* not to — on ceremony, *cum algo amicissime agĕre ;* to — in the way, *alci obstare ;* to — out, *eminēre, prominēre ;* to — out to sea, *vela dare ;* to — up, *surgĕre, erectum stare, horrēre* (= to bristle) ; to — before a person, *assurgĕre* (or of several, *consurgĕre*) *alci.* **III.** v.tr. see ENDURE. **standing, I.** adj. or part. *stans ;* = lasting, *diuturnus, perpetuus ;* = erect, *erectus ;* = water, *aqua stagnans ;* — camp, *castra stativa ;* — army, *milites.* **II.** n. *gradus, -ūs, locus, ordo ;* see RANK ; of long —, *vetus ;* of short —, *recens.* **standstill,** n. to be at a —, *haerēre.*

standard, n. 1, = flag, *vexillum ;* to raise a —, *vexillum tollĕre ;* to hoist or display a —, *vexillum proponĕre; aquila* (i.e. the eagle of the legion) ; 2, = measure, *regula, norma.* **standard-bearer,** n. *vexillarius, signifer, aquilifer.*

stanza, n. *versuum series.*

staple, I. n. 1, *emporium* (= market) ; 2, see HOOK. **II.** adj. — commodities, by *res alcjs terrae propriae.*

star, n. *astrum, sidus, -ĕris,* n.(= a collection of —s, also = *astrum), signum* (= a sign in the skies), *stella ;* = a distinguished person, e.g. *Africanus sol alter ;* = a — of the first magnitude ; the —s of the State, *lumina civitatis ;* = a critical sign or mark, *asteriscus* (Gram.) ; the — under which one is born, *sidus natalicium.* **star-gazer,** n. *astrologus* (= interpreter of stars). **starlight,** adj. *sideribus illustris* (Tac.). **starry,** adj. *stellifer, astris distinctus et ornatus.*

starboard, adj. and n. *latus navis dextrum.* **starch,** n. *amylum* (Plin.).

stare, I. n. *obtutus, -ūs.* **II.** v.intr. *obtutum in re figĕre, conspicari, intueri, stupēre* (with astonishment).

stark, adj. *rigens* (with cold) ; see STIFF.

starling, n. *sturnus* (Plin.).

start, I. n. 1, *saltus, -ūs*(= jump) ; by fits and —s, *haud uno tenore ;* 2, see BEGINNING, COMMENCEMENT ; 3, = setting out, *profectio ;* to get the — of anything, *alqm antecedĕre* (lit.), *alqm superare* (fig.). **II.** v.intr. 1, *trepidare, expavescĕre ;* 2, see BEGIN ; 3, = to set out, *proficisci.* **III.** v.tr. *initium alcjs rei facĕre, alqd instituĕre.*

startle, v.tr. (dim. of START) *alci metum in(ji)cĕre, alqm improviso, de improviso, imprudentem* or *necopinantem opprimĕre.* **startling,** adj. *mirandus, mirificus.*

starve, I. v.tr. *fame* or *inediā necare, consumĕre.* **II.** v.intr. *fame* or *inediā necari, consumi.*

state, I. n. 1, *status, -ūs, condicio, locus, res, fortuna ;* a good —, *res secundae ;* a bad —, *res adversae ;* 2, = rank, *homo mei loci atque ordinis ;* 3, = a city or commonwealth, *civitas, respublica, regnum, imperium ;* at the cost of the —, *sumptu publico ;* a maxim of —, *ratio civilis ;* a minister of —, *socius et administer reipublicae gerendae ;* council of —, *consilium publicum ;* 4, = grandeur, *cultus, ornatus, apparatus* (all -ūs), *magnificus.* **II.** v.tr. *narrare, praedicare, dicĕre, profiteri, affirmare, confirmare, asseverare.* **stately,** adj. of carriage, *erectus* (= upright), *nobilis* (noble) ; of banquets, etc., *lautus, magnificus.* **stateliness,** n. use adj. **statesman,** n. *vir reipublicae peritus.* **statesmanship,** n. *ars reipublicae regendae.* **station, I.** n. 1, see POSITION ; 2, see RANK. **II.** v.tr. see PLACE, SET. **stationary,** adj. *stativus (stativa castra), immobilis, immotus, quod non movetur, fixus.* **stationer,** n. *chartarius* (= a paper-seller ; very late). **stationery,** n. use PAPER.

statistics, n. by *res (singulae),* (of details) : *omnia* (of information collectively).

statue, n. *statua, simulacrum* (= likeness), *signum, imago.* **statuary,** n. see SCULPTOR, SCULPTURE.

stature, n. *statura ;* a man of low, etc., —, *homo parvae, magnae, procerae staturae.*

statute, n. *lex.* **statutable,** adj. *legitimus.*

staunch, I. adj. *firmus, solidus, bonus ;* a — friend, *amicus certus, fidus, fidelis.* **II.** v.tr. *sanguinem sistĕre, cohibēre* (Cels.).

stay, I. v.tr. 1, = to prop, *fulcire, fulcire et sustinēre, statuminare* (by a post or beam), *adminiculari* (as the vine is trained on supports) ; to — yourself on, *niti* (or *inniti*) *alqā re* (*in alqā re), in alqd* (*in alqm*); 2, = to stop, arrest, *(de)morari, detinēre, cohibēre ;* see CHECK. **II.** v.intr. = to abide or tarry, *commorari, manēre, versari ;* to — with, *apud alqd manēre ;* to — much anywhere, *locum frequentare.* **stays,** n. use *mamillare* (Mart.).

stead, n. in — of, *pro, loco, vice, in locum, in vicem alcjs ;* in — of, etc., *tantum abest, ut,* etc., *non modo non . . . sed etiam ;* in — of the consul, *pro consule ;* to be in — of a father, *pro patre esse alci, cum debeat* or *debēret* (e.g. in — of going, he did this, *hoc facet, cum ire deberet*).

steady, steadfast, adj. *stabilis, firmus* (lit. and fig.), *constans, gravis, fidus, fidelis* (fig.). Adv. *firme, graviter, firmiter, constanter, fide, fideliter.* **steadiness, steadfastness,** n. *stabilitas, firmitas, constantia, gravitas, sobrietas* (in regard to drink).

steak, n. *offella, offula;* **a beef—,** *offula cornis bubulae.*

steal, v.tr. *furtum facēre, furari, surripēre* (*subr-*), *avertēre, intercipēre;* to — out of the city, *clam se urbe subducēre;* to — over anyone (of sleep, etc.), *alqm subire.* **stealer,** n. *fur.*

stealth, n. by —, *furtim, clam.* **stealthy,** adj. *furtivus* (e.g. *amor*), *clandestinus, occultus, tectus.* Adv. *furtive, furtim, clam, occulte, tecte.*

steam, I. n. *vapor, nīdor* (from anything cooked), *fumus* (= smoke). **II.** v.tr. *vaporare.* **steamboat,** n. *navis vi vapōris* (*neque velis*) *impulsa.* **steam-engine,** n. *machina vi vaporis impulsa.*

steed, n. *equus.*

steel, I. n. *chalybs;* = sword, *ferrum.* **II.** v.tr. see HARDEN.

steep, I. adj. *praeruptus, praeceps, arduus.* **II.** n. *locus praeceps.* **III.** v.tr. *aquā macerare* or *mollire;* see SOAK. **steepness,** n. use adj.

steeple, n. *turris* (= tower), perhaps *fastigium turri superpositum* (for a — on a tower). **steeplechase,** n. see RACE.

steer, v.tr. *gubernare, regēre;* to — a ship, *navem gubernare* (so *gubernare rempublicam*). **steerage,** n. and adj. *puppis* (e.g. — passengers, *qui in puppi vehuntur*). **steering,** n. *gubernatio.* **steersman,** n. *gubernator* (so *rei publicae*), *rector* (fig.).

steer, n. = young bull, *juvencus.*

stem, I. n. *arboris stirps* or *truncus* (of a tree), *caulis, calamus* (of a plant); = race, *progenies, stirps, prosapia, familia, genus, -ēris,* n. **II.** v.tr. *cohibēre, sistēre, coercēre, reprimēre;* to — the tide, *aestum marinum sistēre;* to — the sedition, *seditionem sedare, compescēre;* see also RESIST.

stench, n. *foetor, putor* (ante and post class.).

step, I. n. = a stair, *gradus, -ūs;* = a pace, *gradus, passus, gressus, all -ūs;* to take —s, *agēre, agēre et moliri, consilium capēre;* extreme —, *ultima experiri;* to keep — with, *alejs gradus aequare;* fig. *parem esse alci;* — by —, *gradatim, pedetentim.* **II.** v.intr. *gradi, vadēre;* to — forwards, *progredi, pergēre;* to — over, *transire, superare alqd.* **step-brother,** n. *filius vitrici* (on the father's side), *filius novercae* (on the mother's). **step-daughter,** n. *privigna.* **step-father,** n. *vitricus.* **step-mother,** n. *noverca.* **step-sister,** n. *filia vitrici* or *novercae.* **step-son,** n. *privignus.*

stereotype, n. *formae lit(t)erarum fixae.* **stereotyped,** adj. *tritus;* see TRITE.

sterile, adj. *sterilis* (lit. and fig.). **sterility,** n. *sterilitas* (lit. and fig.).

sterling, adj. *verus, bonus.*

stern, adj. † *torvus, durus, severus, austerus.* Adv. *dure, duriter, severe.* **sternness,** n. *severitas.*

stern, n. *puppis* (= poop).

stew, I. v.tr. *carnem* (*igne lento*) *coquēre.* **II.** n. *caro* (*igne lento*) *cocta.*

steward, n. *procurator, curator, dispensator, administrator, villicus* (of the farm); — of the house, *rerum domesticarum curator.* **stewardship,** n. *cura, procuratio, dispensatoris munus, -ēris,* n., *administratio.*

stick, I. n. *baculum, bacillum, radius* (= wand), *virga* (= rod), *clava, fustis, -is* (= cudgel), *palus.* **II.** v.intr. 1, *haerēre, adhaerēre, cohaerēre* (= to — together); 2, fig. *haerēre, haesitare, dubitare.* **III.** v.tr. *(af)figēre* (= to — to), *defigēre, praefigēre* (= before), *infigēre;* see STAB. **sticking-plaster,** n. *implastrum* (Plin.). **stickle,** v.intr. *summo studio in or ad alqd in-*

cumbēre. stickler, n. *qui summo studio in alqd incumbit.* **sticky,** adj. *lentus, tenax.*

stiff, adj. *rigidus, rigens, durus;* — in character, *pertinax, inexorabilis, rigidus;* in manners, perhaps *rusticus, agrestis, parum comis;* to be —, *rigēre.* Adv. *rigide, dure, duriter, pertinaciter, rigide, rustice, parum comiter.* **stiffen,** v.tr. *durare, indurare, rigidum facēre.* **stiffness,** n. *rigor, rigiditas* (lit. and fig.), *rusticitas* (fig.).

stifle, v.tr. 1, *suffocare, spiritum intercludēre;* 2, fig. *opprimēre, ex(s)tinguēre.*

stigma, n. *nota.* **stigmatize,** v.tr. *notam* (*turpitudinis*) *inurēre alci.*

stile, n. *claustra, -orum* (= barrier).

still, I. adj. *tranquillus, quietus, placidus, sedatus, tacitus, silens, lenis* (= gentle), *immotus* (= motionless); — night, *nox tacita;* be —, *taceas, quaeso! quiesce!* **II.** v.tr. *sedare, reprimēre, restinguēre, ex(s)tinguēre, lenire, permulcēre;* to — hunger, *famem explēre.* **III.** Adv. 1, = up to this time, *adhuc, etiam, etiamnunc* (or *etiamnum*); 2, with compar. (e.g. — more), *etiam magis* = especially, *praesertim;* 3, see NEVERTHELESS. **stilling,** n. *sedatio.* **stillness,** n. *silentium, tranquillitas, quies.*

still, n. * *alembicum.*

stilts, n. *grallae.* **stilted,** adj. see INFLATED.

stimulant, n. *vinum* (= wine). **stimulate,** v.tr. *stimulare, excitare;* see ENCOURAGE.

stimulus, n. *stimulus, incitamentum, irritamentum* (mostly in pl.), *calcar* (= spur).

sting, I. n. *aculeus;* the wound from a —, *ictus, -ūs.* **II.** v.tr. *pungēre* (lit. and fig.), *aculeos infigēre.* **stinging,** adj. *mordens, mordax, acerbus, aculeatus.*

stingy, adj. *parcus, sordidus, tenax, malignus.* Adv. *parce, sordide, maligne.* **stinginess,** n. *parsimonia, tenacitas, malignitas;* see MEANNESS.

stink, n. and v.intr. see SMELL.

stint, I. n. *inopia;* see NEED. **II.** v.tr. *alqd alci parce dare;* *alqm alqā re privare* (= to deprive of).

stipend, n. see SALARY. **stipendiary,** adj. *mercenarius, stipendiarius.*

stipulate, v.intr. *stipulari, pacisci.* **stipulation,** n. *stipulatio, pactum, condicio.*

stir, I. n. *motus, -ūs, tumultus, -ūs, turba, strepitus, -ūs;* to be in a —, *movēri, agitari.* **II.** v.tr. (com)*movēre;* to — oneself, *moveri.* **III.** v.intr. *moveri, progredi;* see GO, ADVANCE.

stirrup, n. perhaps *lorum ad pedem sustinendum ex ephippio pendens.* (The Romans rode without stirrups, see Smith's "Dict.Antiq.," art. Ephippium.)

stitch, I. n. — in the side, *lateris dolor.* **II.** v.tr. (con)*suēre.*

stock, I. n. (*arboris*) *truncus, stirps, stipes, -itis,* m.; —s for ship-building, *navalia, -ium* (= a dock); the —s (as instrument of punishment), by *pedicae* (= fetters); a — or family, *gens, stirps;* descended from a noble —, *claro* or *honesto loco natus;* = quantity, *magna copia;* — of money, *ingens num(m)orum vis;* — dove, *palumbes, -is,* m. and f.; — jobber, *argentarius.* **II.** v.tr. *instruēre;* see PROVIDE. **III.** adj. see COMMON, TRITE. **IV.** adv. —-still, *immotus.*

stockade, n. *vallum.*

stocking, n. *tibiale, -is,* n. (Suet.).

stoic, adj. and n. *stoicus.* **stoical, stoically,** adj. and adv. *stoico, ut aiunt, more.* **stoicism,** n. *ratio stoicorum.*

stomach, I. n. 1, *stomachus;* 2, = anger, *stomachus.* **II.** v.tr. *stomachari, alqd indigne ferre.* **stomacher,** n. *mamillare* (Mart.).

stone, I. n. *lapis, -ĭdis,* m., *saxum;* — in the human body, *calculus* (Cels.); — of fruit, *nucleus,* see KERNEL ; precious —, *gemma;* to throw —s at, *lapides con(j)icĕre in alqm;* a — breaker, *lapicīda,* m. ; — quarry, *lapicīdīnae;* a —'s-throw, *lapidis jactus, -ūs.* **II.** v.tr. *lapides in alqm con(j)icĕre.* **stoning,** n. *lapidatio.* **stony,** adj. *lapideus* (of stone), *saxeus, lapidosus, saxosus* (= abounding in stones). **stonyhearted,** adj. *durus, ferreus.*

stool, n. *scabellum.*

stoop, v.intr. *se inclinare, proclinare, se demittĕre.* **stooping, I.** n. *corporis inclinatio.* **II.** adj. *pronus, inclinatus.*

stop, I. v.intr. *(con)sistĕre, resistĕre, subsistĕre, gradum sistĕre* (= to stay), in a place, *alqo* (or in *algo) loco, versari in algo loco, morari;* = to cease, *ab alqd re cessare, alqd omittĕre.* **II.** v.tr. *sistĕre;* = to hinder, *prohibĕre, inhibēre, coercēre, impedire;* a sedition, etc., *ex(s)tinguĕre, compescĕre;* = to block up, *viam intercludĕre,* a bottle, etc., *obturare, occludĕre;* = to punctuate, *interpungĕre* (Sen.). **III.** n. *impedimentum, mora;* see HINDRANCE ; — (in printing), *interpunctum;* without —, *sine morā.* **stoppage,** n. *obstructio, impedimentum, retentio* (= holding back), of the bowels, *alvus a(d)stricta* (Cels.). **stopper,** n. *obturamentum* (Plin.).

store, I. n. *copia, magna vis, abundantia* (= plenty) ; to have a —, *abundare, affluĕre re;* — of provisions, *commeatus, -ūs* (for the army), *alimenta, -orum, annona;* — -house, *apothēca, horreum* (= granary); — -room, *cella promptuaria* or *penaria.* **II.** v.tr. *coacervare, reponĕre, condĕre, instruĕre, ornare re;* to — yourself with, *sibi comparare alqd, providēre rei.*

storey, n. *tabulatio, tabulatum.*

stork, n. *ciconia.*

storm, I. n. *tempestas, procella;* fig. *tempestas, fluctus, -ūs;* = a violent attack, *impetus, -ūs, vis;* a — cloud, *nimbus.* **II.** v.tr., e.g. *urbem vi oppugnare, expugnare;* to take by —, *vi capĕre.* **III.** v.intr. *furĕre, saevire;* see RAGE. **storming, I.** n. *expugnatio.* **II.** adj. — party, *(milites) ad urbem oppugnandam missi.* **stormy,** adj. 1, lit. *turbidus, procellosus;* 2, fig. *iratus* (= angry), *tumultuosus.* Adv. *irate, turbide.*

story, n. *res, narratio, narratiuncula, fabula* (= fable) ; to tell a —, *narrare;* = a falsehood, *mendacium;* a — -teller, *narrator, mendax* (= liar).

stout, adj. *crassus, obēsus* (= fat), *vastus, amplus* (= large), *fortis, constans, virilis, valens, validus, firmus, robustus, potens* (= strong) ; see FAT, STRONG. Adv. *fortiter, constanter, acriter, pro viribus suis, valide, robuste.* **stoutness,** n. 1, see CORPULENCE ; 2, see COURAGE, ENDURANCE.

stove, n. *focus, caminus.*

stow, v.tr. see STORE. **stowage,** n. *locus.*

straddle, v.tr. *varicare* (ante and post class.). **straddling,** adj. *varicus.*

straggle, v.intr. *vagari, deerrare, palari.*

straight, I. adj. *(di)rectus, erectus* (= upright) ; a — line, *linea directa;* a — way, *recta via.* **II.** adv. —way, *recto itinere, statim, confestim* (= immediately), *protinus* (= both —forward and immediately). **straighten,** v.tr. *corrigĕre* (lit. and fig., in former sense mostly ante and post class.). **straightforward,** adj. *simplex;* see FRANK, UPRIGHT.

strain, I. n. *intentio, contentio (corporis,*

nervorum; opp. *remissio);* = tune, see TUNE ; in this —, *ita, sic* (= thus), or by rel. sentence (e.g. *quae cum dixisset, abiit,* having spoken in this —, he went off). **II.** v.tr. *(in)tendĕre, intentare, contendĕre in* or *ad alqd, contra alqm* or *alqd;* = to sprain, see SPRAIN ; = to filter, see FILTER.

strait, I. adj. *artus (arctus), angustus, strictus* (= bound up). **II.** n. *fretum;* the — of Gibraltar, *fretum Gaditanum;* — of Constantinople, *Bosporus Thracius;* = a narrow path, *viarum* or *locorum* or *itineris angustiae;* = a difficulty, *angustiae;* = poverty, *inopia, res durae* or *angustae.* **straiten,** v.tr. *in angustias adducĕre.*

strand, I. n. *litus, -oris,* n., *ripa, acta.* **II.** v.tr. *navem vadis* or *litoribus illidĕre* or *impingĕre, in litus e(j)ici.*

strange, adj. 1, = foreign, *peregrīnus, externus, exterus* (= outward, the first, of persons and things, opp. *intestinus;* the second, of persons, esp. with *gentes* and *nationes,* as opp. to *socii), extraneus* (= not belonging to the family), *adventicius* (= coming from abroad, opp. *vernaculus), barbarus* (= not Roman); 2, = unversed in, a stranger to, *in alqā re peregrinus* or *aliēnus, hospes,* or *rudis;* — in this city, *ignarus hujus urbis;* 3, = unusual, *insolitus, insolens, novus, mirus;* that seems — to me, *mirum hoc mihi videtur, miror, admiror hoc;* 4, = not belonging to one, *alienus;* to fall into — hands, *in alienas manus incidĕre;* 5, = unsuitable, averse, *aliēnus;* to be —, *alienum esse, abhorrēre ab.* Adv. *mirum in modum, mirifice, mirabiliter, inusitate.* **strangeness,** n. *novitas, insolentia,* or by adj. **stranger,** n. *hospes, -ĭtis,* m. (in gen.), *externus* (opp. *civis), aliēnigĕna,* m. (opp. *indigena), advena,* m. and f. (= incomer), *barbarus.*

strangle, v.tr. *strangulare, laqueo interimĕre, gulam laqueo frangĕre.*

strap, I. n. *lorum* (of leather). **II.** v.tr. *loris (con)stringĕre* (= to bandage).

stratagem, n. *ars, dolus, consilium, astus, -ūs, insidiae.* **strategic,** adj. *quod ad prudentem ducem pertinet.* **strategist,** n. *dux prudens* or *peritus.* **strategy,** n. *ars belli gerendi.*

stratum, n. perhaps *stratum* as t.t., or by circumloc. (e.g. *genus aliud alci impositum).* **stratify,** v.tr. perhaps by *digerĕre, disponĕre.*

straw, I. n. *stramentum.* **II.** adj. *stramenticius.* **strawberry,** n. *fragum.*

stray, v.intr. *(ab)errare, vagi, pali.*

streak, I. n. *linea, nota* (= mark). **II.** v.tr. *lineis* or *variis coloribus distinguĕre.*

stream, I. n. *flumen* (= flowing water); down the —, *flumine secundo;* up the —, *flumine adverso.* **II.** v.intr. *fluĕre, effundi in rem;* to — together, *undique convenire.*

streamer, n. *vexillum, signum.*

street, n. *via, vicus* (= the street as running between two lines of houses), *platea* (= the broad open roads or promenades in a city), *angiportus, -ūs* (= narrow crossways, streets, or alleys) ; a public —, in contrast with the homes, was called *publicum; in publico* (opp. to *in privato;* = in public, on the high road) ; to remain all night in the —, *jacēre et pernoctare in publico.*

strength, n. *vis* (or in pl. *vires), nervi, robur -oris,* n., *opes* (= resources), as passive quality, — of resistance, *firmitas;* to feel your —, *sibi confidĕre;* to have — in, *multum valēre re, excellĕre in re.* **strengthen, I.** v.tr. *corroborare, (con) firmare;* to — yourself, *se reficĕre.* **II.** v.intr. by pass. *corroborari*, etc. ; see also INCREASE. **strengthened**, adj. *confirmatus*. **strengthening**, n. *confirmatio* (e.g. *perpetuae libertatis, animi*).

strenuous, adj. *strenuus* (*o. iners, ignavus*), *impiger, acer* ; see ACTIVE. Adv. *strenue, impigre, acriter*. **strenuousness**, n. (*g*)*navitas, studium*.

stress, n. *rei momentum, vis, vis et pondus, -ĕris*, n. ; with —, *cum vi, graviter* ; to lay — on, *alqâ re niti* or *confidĕre, in re spem* or *fiduciam ponĕre* ; — of weather, *tempestas, procella*.

stretch, I. v.tr. (*ex*)*tendĕre, contendĕre, intendĕre* ; to — forth or out, *protendĕre, porrigĕre* ; to — the iron under the hammer, *ferrum producĕre incude*. **II.** v.intr. see REACH. **III.** n. *contentio, intentio, nisus, -ûs* (= effort) ; at a —, *ino tenore* ; — of land, *campus*. **stretcher**, n. *see* LITTER.

strew, v.tr. *sternĕre* (= to lay on the ground), *spargĕre* (= to scatter).

strict, adj. 1, = accurate, *accuratus, dīligens* ; to tell in — confidence, *alqd alci in aurem dicĕre* ; 2, *severus, rigidus* ; see SEVERE. Adv. = truly, *re verâ, reapse* ; = accurately, *accurate, dīligenter* ; = severely, *severe, rigide*. **strictness**, n. *accuratio, diligentia, severitas* ; see SEVERITY. **stricture**, n. *animadversio, reprehensio* ; see BLAME.

stride, I. n. *ingens gradus, -ûs*. **II.** v.intr. *ingentes gradus ferre*.

strife, n. *certatio, certamen, contentio* (in gen.), *disceptatio, controversia, altercatio* (= dispute), *jurgium, rixa* (= quarrel) ; — in a lawsuit, *lis*. **strive**, v.intr. (*e*)*niti, coniti, contendĕre, operam dare, conari, studĕre, ut* ; to — after, (*co*)*niti, contendĕre ad alqd,* (*ex*)*petĕre, affectare, captare alqd, rei studĕre, sequi* or *persequi alqd* ; to — against, *obniti, resistĕre* ; to — with or against, *configĕre, concertare*. **striving**, n. *see* EFFORT ; — after, *alcjs appetitio, contentio*.

strike, v.tr. *ferire, percutĕre, pulsare, verberare* (= to lash), *caedĕre* ; to be struck, *vapulare* ; to — (as a clock), *sonare* ; to — twelve, *horologium indicat horam duodecimam* ; to — a flag or yield, *vexillum demittĕre* ; the lightning —*s, de caelo tangitur alqd* ; to be struck blind, *captum esse oculis* ; to — a coin, *cudĕre* ; see COIN ; to — the mind, *percutĕre, percellĕre* (=!to shock) ; to — a bargain, *pacisci* ; to — against, *alqd offendĕre, in alqd incurrĕre* ; to — against rocks (of a ship), *saxis illidi*. **striking**, adj. *see* REMARKABLE.

string, I. n. *linum, linea, filum, funiculus* or *vinculum* (= cord) ; — of leather, shoe—, *corrigia* ; a bow—, *nervus* ; — of a dart, *amentum* ; — of a musical instrument, *chorda, nervus, fides, -ium*. **II.** v.tr. to — an instrument, *lyrae, citharae*, etc., *nervos aptare* ; to — together ; *see* BIND. **stringent**, adj. *see* SEVERE.

strip, I. v.tr. *spoliare, nudare, denudare, exuĕre, alci vestem detrahĕre* ; to — a person of his wealth, *alqm opibus spoliare*. **II.** n. *pars* ; — of paper, *scidula chartae* ; — of cloth, *lacinia*.

stripe, I. n. 1, see STREAK ; 2, see STROKE. **II.** v.tr. see STREAK.

stripling, n. *adulescens*.

stroke, I. n. 1, *verber* ; see BLOW ; 2, see LINE ; 3, of lightning, *fulmen* ; 4, of fortune, etc., *eventus, -ûs* (*felix* = lucky, etc.) ; = artifice, *ars* (e.g. a master—, *summa ars*) ; to put the finishing — to, *alqd ad finem perducĕre*. **II.** v.tr. *alqm permulcĕre, demulcĕre*.

stroll, I. n. *ambulatio*. **II.** v.intr. *ambulare* ; see WALK, WANDER.

strong, adj. *valens, validus, firmus, 1 robustus, lacertosus, fortis* ; to be — (in influence), *pollēre*. Compare *Etruria tantum pollens terrâ marique*, Liv. ; *pollēre pecuniâ, scientiâ, armis, gratiâ, nobilitate* ; comb. *potens pollensque*, Sall. ; a — wind, *ventus vehĕmens* ; of arguments, *gravis, firmus* ; — memory, *memoria* (*alcjs rei*) *tenax* ; a — position, *locus munitus*. Adv. *valide, firme, firmiter, fortiter* ; = very, *valde* or *vehementer*, or by compound (e.g. *movēri*, = to be moved ; *commovēri*, = to be — moved).

strophe, n. *stropha* (late).

structure, n. *aedificium, aedes, -is*, f., *opus, -ĕris*, n., *monumentum* (= a building), *structura* (= the kind of building ; *structura parietum, structurae antiquae genus*, Liv. ; also = the substance) ; fig. *structura verborum* or *vocum* ; — of a sentence, *forma, ratio*.

struggle, I. n. *luctatio* ; see CONTENTION. **II.** v.intr. *luctari* ; to — with each other, *luctari inter se* ; to — with the difficulty, *luctari cum difficultate* ; see CONTEND, FIGHT.

strumpet, n. *scortum, meretrix*.

strut, v.intr. *superbe incedĕre*.

stubble, n. *stipulae*.

stubborn, adj. *pertinax, pervicax, obstinatus, contumax*. Adv. *pertinaciter, pervicaciter, obstinate, contumaciter, obstinato animo*. **stubbornness**, n. *pertinacia, pervicacia, contumacia, obstinatio* (usually of a good quality), *obstinatus animus*.

stucco, n. see PLASTER.

stud, I. n. *bulla* ; = button, *fibula* (= clasp) ; = a number of horses, *equi, equaria*. **II.** v.tr. *alqâ re distinguĕre*.

study, I. n. *studium, studia, meditatio* (= thought) ; = room for —, *conclave*. **II.** v.tr. *lit*(*t*)*eris studĕre, lit*(*t*)*eras tractare* ; to — something, *alci rei studĕre, incumbĕre* or *operam dare*. **student**, n. *alcjs rei studiosus*. **studio**, n. *conclave* (*pictoris*, of a painter, etc.). **studious**, adj. *lit*(*t*)*erarum studiosus, in studiis literarum versatus*. Adv. *summo studio*.

stuff, I. n. *materia, materies* ; = baggage, *impedimenta, -orum, sarcinae* ; household —, *supellex, -lectilis*, f. ; kitchen —, *culinaria* ; — gown, etc., *textile* ; as an exclamation, *nugas! gerrae!* **II.** v.tr. (*re*)*fercire, replēre* ; see FILL. **stuffing**, n. *fartum* (Plin., of food), *tomentum* (of cushions).

stultify, v.tr. *alqm stultitiae coarguĕre* or *convincĕre*.

stumble, v.intr. *offendĕre*. **stumbling**, n. *offensio* ; to cause or be a —-block to, *esse offensioni alci* ; things which are —-blocks, *quae habent offensionem* (Cic.).

stump, n. *caudex, stipes, -ĭtis, truncus*.

stun, v.tr. 1, lit. perhaps *alqm sensu privare* ; 2, fig. *obtundĕre, stupefacĕre, perterrēre, percellĕre*. **stunned**, adj. 1, *sensu privatus* ; 2, fig. *stupefactus*.

stunt, v.tr. *alcjs incrementum impedire*.

stupefy, v.tr. *stupefacĕre, sopire, torporem afferre, habetare* ; to be stupefied, *torpescĕre, stupescĕre, torpēre, stupēre*. **stupefaction**, n. *stupor, torpor*.

stupendous, adj. *ingens, immanis* ; see WONDERFUL.

stupid, adj. *stupidus, stolidus* ; see FOOLISH. Adv. *stupide, stolide*. **stupidity**, n. *stupiditas, animus stolidus*, or *stupidus*. **stupor**, n. *stupor, torpor*.

sturdy, adj. 1, see STRONG; 2, see CONFIDENT.

sturgeon, n. *acipenser.*

stutter, v.intr. *balbutire;* see STAMMER.

sty, n. *hara, suile.*

style, I. n. 1, in gen. *genus,-ĕris,* n., *ratio, habitus, -ūs* (of dress, etc.), *mos* (= custom); 2, in language, *dicendi* or *scribendi genus, orationis* or *sermonis genus, oratio, sermo, elocutio ;* the — is the man, *qualis est ipse homo, talis est ejus oratio.* II. v.tr. *appellare;* see NAME. **stylish**, adj. *speciosus, elegans, nitidus, lautus, magnificus.* Adv. *speciose, eleganter, nitide, laute, magnifice.* **stylishness**, n. *elegantia, magnificentia, lautitia.*

suave, adj. *urbanus, blandus;* see COURTEOUS. **suavity**, n. *urbanitas;* see COURTESY.

subaltern, I. adj. *inferioris loci.* II. n. perhaps *subcenturio.*

subcommissioner, n. *procurator, vicarius.*

subdivide, v.tr. *iterum dividĕre;* see DIVIDE. **subdivision**, n. *pars.*

subdue, v.tr. *in imperium alcjs redigĕre, dicioni suae sub(j)icĕre alqm, sui juris facĕre, subigĕre, domare.*

subject, I. v.tr. *sub(j)icĕre;* to — yourself, *se imperio alcjs sub(j)icĕre;* see also EXPOSE. II. n. 1, *civi* or *regi subjectus,* or by *civis;* 2, in grammar or logic, *subjectum;* 3, = matter discussed, etc., *res, quaestio, argumentum.* III. adj. *imperio* or *dicioni alcjs subjectus, parens, obnoxius alci;* to be —, *esse in alcjs dicione;* to become —, *sub alcjs imperium cadĕre.* **subjection**, n. *servitus, -ūtis,* f.; to hold in —, *alqm in officio retinĕre, alqm oppressum tenĕre.* **subjective**, adj., according to one's own view, e.g. viewed —ly to myself, *meo quidem judicio;* so *tuo* or *ejus* or *eorum quidem judicio;* as opposed to objective, *opinio,* opp. to *res.* **subjectivity**, n. *quod in opinione constat,* or *quoad per hominum judicium perspici potest.*

subjoin, v.tr. *sub(j)icĕre, subjungĕre.*

subjugate, v.tr. *domare, in dicionem suam redigĕre;* see SUBDUE.

subjunctive, adj. — mood, *modus subjunctivus* or *conjunctivus* (Gram., and in Quint. fig.).

sublime, adj. *sublimis, elatus, excelsus;* see LOFTY. Adv. *sublime* (usually lit.), *elate, excelse.* **sublimity**, n. *sublimitas* (Quint.), *elatio, excelsitas.*

sublunary, adj. *infra lunam positus.*

submarine, adj. *quod sub mari (positum) est.*

submerge, v.tr. *submergĕre.* **submersion**, n. use verb.

submit, v.tr. *submittĕre; submittĕre se alci, se alejs imperio sub(j)icĕre, in alcjs potestatem te permittĕre, alci cedĕre* or *concedĕre, alci dare manus.* **submission**, n. *obsequium* (as act), *animus submissus* (as state). **submissive**, adj. see OBEDIENT.

subordinate, I. adj. *inferior, alci subjectus.* II. v.tr. 1, see SUBDUE ; 2, to give an inferior place to, *alqd alci rei posthabĕre.* **subordination**, n. 1, = obedience, *obsequium, disciplina* (of soldiers); against —, *contra morem obsequii;* want of — among the soldiers, *intemperantia militum;* see OBEDIENCE ; 2, = placing below, *alqd alci rei posthabĕre.*

suborn, v.tr. *subornare.*

subpœna, n. *denuntiatio testimonii.*

subscribe, v.tr. *subscribĕre;* = to agree to, *assentiri ;* = to give one's name or support to, *nomen profitĕri.* **subscriber**, n. *subscriptor* (= one who writes under), *qui se alqd daturum profitetur* (to a charity, etc.). **subscription**, n. *subscriptio* (= that which is written under), *stips* (= alms), *collatio* (= collection).

subsequent, adj. *(sub)sequens.* Adv. *postea;* see AFTERWARDS.

subserve, v.tr. *alci subservire, alci esse usui, auxilio esse alci, adjumento alci esse, alci obtemperare.* **subservience**, n. *obtemperatio, obsequium.*

subside, v.intr. *residĕre, considĕre, remitti, cadĕre* (= to fall).

subsidy, n. *subsidium, vectīgal, tributum* (= tax).

subsist, v.intr. *subsistĕre, stare in re;* to — on, *vesci* (e.g. *lacte et carne,* Sall.). **subsistence**, n. *victus, -ūs, alimenta, -orum.*

substance, n. *natura, corpus, -ōris,* n., *res;* = property, *res, bona, -orum.* **substantial**, adj. *verus, solidus, gravis, magni momenti* (= important), *aliquid* (e.g. — victory, *aliquid victoriae*). Adv. *magnā ex parte.* **substantiate**, v.tr. see PROVE. **substantive**, n. *nomen* (Gram.).

substitute, I. n. *vicarius.* II. v.tr. *alqm in alterius locum substituĕre, sufficĕre* (of the election of a magistrate as —). **substitution**, n. use verb.

substruction, **substructure**, n. *substructio.*

subterfuge, n. *deverticulum, latebra, ars, tergiversatio.*

subterranean, adj. *subterraneus.*

subtle, adj. *subtilis,* † *tenuis* (= thin, slender); *argutus, acutus ;* see CLEVER, CUNNING. Adv. *subtiliter, tenuiter, argute, acute.* **subtlety**, n. 1, = fineness, *tenuitas, subtilitas;* 2, of intellect, etc., *acies, acumen, subtilitas, captio.* **subtleties**, n. *argutiae.*

subtract, v.tr. *deducĕre* (e.g. *addendo deducendoque vidēre quae reliqua summa fiat*). **subtraction**, n. by *deducĕre.*

suburb, n. *suburbium* (very rare). **suburban**, adj. *suburbanus.*

subvert, v.tr. *subvertĕre.* **subversion**, n. *eversio ;* see DESTRUCTION.

succeed, v.intr. *alci succedĕre;* so *in locum alcjs, in paternas opes;* (also in time, *aetas aetati succedit*), *alqm (sub)sequi ;* = to have success, *succedĕre, bene, prospere, optime cedĕre, evenire.* **success**, n. *exitus, -ūs, bonus, res secundae, felicitas, prosperitas, successus, -ūs.* **successful**, adj. *felix, faustus,* comb. *felix faustusque.* Adv. *feliciter, fauste, prospere, bene, ex sententiā.* **succession**, n. *successio* (in office, etc.) ; = order, *series, continuatio ;* in —, *ex ordine.* **successive**, adj. *alii post alios, continuus.* Adv. *(ex) ordine, in ordinem, deinceps.* **successor**, n. *successor.*

succinct, adj. *brevis.* Adv. *brevi, breviter.*

succour, I. n. *auxilium, subsidium.* II. v.tr. *auxiliari, succurĕre, juvare alqm, auxilio alci esse* or *venire alci, succurĕre ;* see HELP.

succulent, adj. *sucosus* (Plin.), *suci (suci) plenus.*

succumb, v.intr. *succumbĕre alci rei* (e.g. *somno, senectuti, labori*).

such, adj. pron. *talis* followed by *qualis, ejusmodi, ejus generis ut,* etc. ; — is your courtesy, *quae tua est humanitas;* nor am I — a fool, *nec tam sum stultus* (Cic.); are you — a stranger as that . . .? *adeone es hospes hujusce urbis ut . . .?*

st *nos ii sumus qui esse debemus* (= if we are — as we ought to be); *videndum est ut eâ liberalitate utamur quae prosit amicis, noceat nemini* (= we must take care to use — liberty as may benefit our friends and injure none).

suck, I. v.tr. *sugĕre, bibĕre* (= to drink). **II. 1.** *suctus, -ûs* (as act); to give —, *mammam alci praebēre, ad ubera admittĕre* (of animals). **sucker,** n. *surculus, planta.* **suckle,** v.tr. *mammam alci dare* or *praebĕre.* **suckling,** n. (*infans*) *lactens.* **suction,** n. *suctus, -ûs.*

sudden, adj. *subitus, repens, repentinus, inopinatus, necopinatus.* Adv. *subito, ex tempore, inopinato, necopinato, improviso, de improviso;* to attack anyone —, *opprimĕre imprudentem.* **suddenness,** n. use adj.

sue, v.tr. *postulare, citare, litem auci intendĕre, judicio alqm persequi, in jus vocare* (at law); = to make suit for, *ambire;* to — for an office, *ambire magistratum;* to — for the consulship, *petĕre consulatum;* = to entreat, *sol(l)icitare, efflagitare;* see ENTREAT, BEG; to — for payment, *nomina exigĕre.*

suet, n. *sebum* (= tallow); beef —, *sebum bovillum* (so *ovillum,* etc.).

suffer, I. v.tr. *pati, sufferre, perferre, tolerare, sustinēre* (= to bear); = to permit, *permittĕre, sinĕre, concedĕre;* see ALLOW, PERMIT; to — grief, *e dolore animi laborare, angi animo;* to — loss, *detrimentum capĕre* or *pati; damnum, detrimentum,* or *jacturam facĕre;* to — shipwreck, *naufragium facĕre;* to — pain, etc., *dolorem accipĕre;* to — a disgrace, *dedecus* (*in se*) *admittĕre* (Caes.); to — harm or inconvenience, *alqo affici incommodo;* to — or undertake many labours, *multos subire* or *adire labores;* I — for my rashness, *do poenas temeritatis meae* (Cic.). **II.** v.intr. *dolorem ferre* or *pati, dolore affici,* (*ex*)*cruciari, poenas dare* (as punishment), *laborare, aegrotare* (= to be ill). **sufferance,** n. *patientia;* see PATIENCE. **sufferer,** n. *aeger, aegrotatus* (in illness), *qui alqd patitur* (in gen.). **suffering,** n. *dolor* (=pain), *miseria* (= misery), *res adversae, casus, -ûs, calamitas.*

suffice, v.intr. *sufficĕre* (e.g. *non sufficiebant muri, nec vires sufficĕre cuiquam*); *satis esse alci rei* or with infin., *suppeditare alci ad alqd.* **sufficient,** adj. *satis, quantum satis est;* it is —, *satis est* (so *satis superque est*); — for, *ad,* e.g. *ad dicendum temporis satis habēre.* **sufficiency,** n. *quod satis est.*

suffocate, v.tr. *suffocare.*

suffrage, n. *suffragium* (*alci,* for anyone); to give one's —, *ferre suffragium* (= to vote), *suffragium inire;* = the right of —, *suffragium.*

suffuse, v.tr. *suffundĕre.*

sugar, n. *saccharum* or *saccharon* (Plin.); — candy, *saccharum crystallinum;* — plum, *cup-*(*p*)*edia, -orum.*

suggest, v.tr. *monēre alqm alqd,* or with *ut, sub*(*j*)*icĕre alqd alci;* see MENTION. **suggestion,** n. *admonitio, monitum, consilium.* **suggestive,** adj. *qui* (*quae, quod*) *alqd repraesentat* (of what recalls something else); see SUGGEST.

suicide, n. *mors voluntaria;* to commit —, *manus sibi inferre, sibi mortem* or *necem consciscĕre.*

suit, I. n. **1,** *actio, lis, caus*(*s*)*a;* see ACTION; **2,** of clothes, *vestis, vestitus, -ûs;* of cards, *chartae* or *paginae ejusdem generis;* **3,** = petition, *rogatio;* in love, use verb Woo. **II.** v.tr. *congruĕre;* they —, *bene illis inter se convenit;* or *by decet, convenit,* impers. **suitable,** adj. *congruens, idoneus, aptus, accommodatus, consentaneus, conveniens,* all with *ad* and accus., etc.,

dignus with abl., or *qui* with subj.; **of time,** *opportunus;* see APPROPRIATE. **suitableness,** n. *congruentia, convenientia, opportunitas* (of time). Adv. *congruenter, idonee, apte, accommodate, convenienter, digne, opportune.*

suite, n. **1,** of persons, *comitatus, -ûs, comites, -um;* **2,** of rooms, *conclavia, -ium;* see ROOM.

suitor, n. **1,** see CANDIDATE; **2,** see LOVER.

sulky, sullen, adj. *morosus, contumax, tetricus.* Adv. *morose, contumaciter.* **sulkiness, sullenness,** n. *morositas, contumacia.*

sully, v.tr. *maculare, inquinare.*

sulphur, n. *sulfur;* dipped in —, *sulfuratus.*

sultan, n. *imperator Turcicus.*

sultry, adj. *aestuosus.* **sultriness,** n. *aestus, -ûs.*

sum, I. n. *summa;* of money, *pecunia,* once in Cic. *summa pecuniae;* for a large, small, etc., —, *magni, parvi* (*pretii*), *magno, parvo* (*pretio*); this is the — of what I have to say, *haec summa est.* **II.** v.tr. *summam facĕre, computare, rationem alcjs rei inire, ducĕre,* of speech, etc., to — up, *breviter repetĕre.* **summary, I.** n. see EPITOME. **II.** adj. **1,** *brevis;* see CONCISE; **2,** = hasty, arrogant, *inconsideratus, arrogans.* Adv. *breviter, sine morâ, inconsiderate, arroganter.*

summer, adj. and n. *aestas, tempora, -um, aestiva;* at the beginning of —, *aestate ineunte;* at the end of —, *aestate extremâ;* — house, see ARBOUR.

summersault, n. see SOMERSAULT.

summit, n. **1,** *cacumen* (= peak), *culmen, vertex,* also by *summus* (e.g. *summus mons*); **2,** fig. *culmen, fastigium,* or by *summus* (e.g. *summa gloria,* = the — of glory).

summon, v.tr. **1,** *alqm appellare, citare, diem alci dicĕre;* see CITE; **2,** in gen. (*ad*)*vocare, convocare, arcessĕre, citare;* to — to surrender, *invitare ad deditionem;* to — up one's courage, *animum colligĕre.* **summons,** n. by verb or in abl., *arcessitu, accitu* (= at the — of); as legal t.t. use verb.

sumptuary, adj. *sumptuarius.* **sumptuous,** adj. *sumptuosus* (Cic.); see COSTLY, MAGNIFICENT. Adv. *sumptuose.* **sumptuousness,** n. (*magnus*) *apparatus, -ûs;* see MAGNIFICENCE, LUXURY.

sun, n. *sôl, -is,* m. ; the rising —, *sol oriens;* setting —, *sol occidens;* rising, setting of the —, *ortus, -ûs, occasus, -ûs, solis;* from —rise to — set, *ab orto usque ad occidentem solem;* the —rises, *sol exoritur, dies appetit,* or by impers. *lucescit, dilucescit, illucescit;* the —'s disk, *orbis solis.* **sunbeam,** n. *radius solis.* **sunburnt,** adj. *adustus.* **Sunday,** n. *Dies Dominica* (Eccl.). **sundial,** n. *solarium.* **sunrise, sunset,** n. see under SUN. **sunshine,** n. *sôl.* **sunny,** adj. **1,** lit. *apricus;* **2,** fig. *hilaris, felix.*

sunder, v.tr. *separare, disjungĕre;* see SEVER.

sundry, adj. *diversi, -ae, -a, plures, nonnulli.*

sup, v.tr. *sorbēre;* = to take supper, *cenare.*

superable, adj. *superabilis.*

superabound, v.intr. *superare, superesse.*

superannuate, v.tr. *alqm loco suo senectutis causâ movēre, rude donari.* **superannuated,** adj. *ob senectutem muneribus exsolutus.*

superb, adj. *magnificus, lautus;* see SPLENDID.

supercilious, adj. *superbus* (= proud), *fasti*

diosus (= **dis**dainful); see HAUGHTY. **super-ciliousness**, n. *fastus, -ūs, superbia.*

supererogation, n. *quod alqs sponte suā (neque officio coactus) facit* (= work of —).

superficial, adj. *exterior, externus ;* poor or inconsiderable, *lēvis, parvi momenti ;* = inaccurate, *parum dīligens.* Adv. *strictim, lēviter ;* a man — learned, *homo lēviter lit(t)eris imbutus.* **superficiality**, n. *lēvitas.*

superficies, n. *summus* with a noun ; *superficies (aquae, testudinis, corporum).*

superfine, adj. *subtīlissimus, tenuissimus* (= very fine).

superfluous, adj. *supervacaneus, supervacuus* (mostly post Aug.) ; to be —, *superesse.* **superfluity**, n. *quod supervacaneum est.*

superhuman, adj. *divinus, major quam pro homine ;* a — task, *opus quod ultra hominis vires est ;* — size, *humanā specie amplior.*

superintend, v.tr. *alqd (pro)curare, praeesse alci* or *alci rei.* **superintendence**, n. *(pro)curatio, administratio alcjs rei.* **superintendent**, n. *qui rebus praeest; (pro)curator;* see AGENT.

superior, adj. *superior, praestantior, melior* (e.g. comp. of good) ; see GOOD, EXCELLENT. **superiority**, n. *prior locus, priores partes.*

superlative, adj. *superlativus* (gram.), *excellens, praestans, praestantissimus, optimus* (e.g. superl. of good) ; see GOOD, EXCELLENT.

supernal, adj. †*supernus, caelestis ;* see HEAVENLY.

supernatural, adj. *naturam superans, supra naturae leges* or *vires positus,* or by *caelestis, divinus ;* to happen by — agency, *divinitus fieri.* Adv. *divinitus.* **supernaturalism**, n. *ratio eorum qui divinitus de rebus divinis edoctos esse homines dicunt.*

supernumerary, adj. in gen. *justum numerum superans* or *excellens ;* of soldiers, *a(d)-scriptivus, a(d)scripticius, accensus.*

superscribe, v.tr. *inscrībere in alqā re.* **superscription**, n. *inscriptio* (also = the title of a book).

supersede, v.tr. *in locum alcjs substitui, alci succedere.*

superstition, n. *superstitio.* **superstitious**, adj. *superstitiosus, superstitione imbutus, superstitioni obnoxius.* Adv. *superstitiose.*

superstructure, n. *aedificium ;* see BUILD-ING.

supervene, v.intr. see FOLLOW, SUCCEED.

supervise, v.tr. *(pro)curare ;* see SUPERIN-TEND. **supervision**, n. *(pro)curatio.*

supine, I. n. *supīnum* (gram.). II. adj. 1, *supīnus* (on the back) ; 2, = indolent, *socors, neglegens.* Adv. *socorditer, neglegenter.* **supineness**, n. *socordia, neglegentia.*

supper, n. *cena.*

supplant, v.tr. 1, lit. *supplantare ;* 2, fig. *in alterius locum irrepere.*

supple, adj. *mollis, flexibilis, lentus.*

supplement, n. *supplementum* (quite class. only of — to troops), in gen. *id quod additum est.*

suppliant, adj. and n. *supplex.* **supplicate**, v.tr. *supplicare, obsecrare alqm.* **supplication**, n. *supplicatio* (only of formally decreed state —), *obsecratio.*

supply, I. v.tr. *supplēre, suppeditare* (= to furnish) ; see FURNISH. II. n. *subsidium, supplementum* (of troops) ; in gen. *copia, suppeditatio ;* — of provisions, *commeatus, -ūs.*

support, I. v.tr. 1, = to bear up, *sustinēre, ferre, fulcire ;* see PROP ; 2, = to keep, to feed, etc., *alere, sustinēre, sustentare* (quite class. in this sense) ; 3, = to help, *ulci adesse ;* see HELP ; 4, at an election, *alci suffragari* (= to vote for), in wider sense, *alci favēre.* II. n. 1, lit. see PROP ; 2, = maintenance, *sustentatio* (as act), *alimentum, victus, -ūs* (= food, etc.) ; 3, = help, *adjumentum, auxilium ;* see HELP ; 4, at an election, *suffragium,* in wider sense, *favor.* **supporter**, n. *adjutor ;* at an election, *suffragator,* in wider sense, *fautor ;* see HELPER, PARTISAN.

suppose, v.tr. *ponēre* (= to lay down), *opinari, opinione praecipere ;* — it is so, *pone* or *fac ita esse, esto ;* — the soul to die, *fac animam interire ;* I — he is drunk, *ebrius est, ut opinor ;* see also BELIEVE, IMAGINE, THINK. **supposing that**, conj. *fac ita esse ;* see above. **supposition**, n. *opinio, conjectura.* **supposititious**, adj. *subditus.*

suppress, v.tr. *supprimēre, reprimēre, abolēre ;* to — sedition, *restinguēre seditionem.* **suppression**, n. use verb.

suppurate, v.intr. *suppurare.* **suppuration**, n. *suppuratio* (Plin.).

supreme, adj. *supremus, summus ;* the — Being, *Deus, Optimus, Maximus.* **supremacy**, n. *principatus, -ūs* (in gen.), *regnum* (= kingship), *imperium* (= supreme power), *dominatus, -ūs, dominatio* (= lordship) ; see POWER. Adv. *praecipue, maxime.*

sure, adj. *certus* (= certain), *tutus* (= safe), *securus* (= free from apprehension), *firmus* (= trustworthy), *fidēlis* (= faithful) ; it is —, *constat ;* I am —, *certo scio ;* who is — of it? *quis est cui exploratum sit?* to be —, he had the rods, *fasces certe habebat ;* are you — of it? *satin hoc certum, persuasum est vobis, exploratum* or *compertum habetis ;* I am —, *compertum est mihi.* Adv. *certe, certo* (= certainly), *nimirum, profecto,* or more strongly *im(m)o (enim)vero* (= really), *saltem* (= at least). **surety**, n. *vas, -dis,* m., *praes, -dis,* m., *sponsor* (of a person), *vadimonium* (= money given as bail).

surf, n. see FOAM, WAVE.

surface, n. *superficies* (Plin.), or by *summus* with noun (e.g. — of water, *summa aqua*).

surfeit, I. n. *satietas, fastidium* (lit. and fig.), comb. *satietas et fastidium, crapula* (= — after a debauch) ; = too much food, *nimius cibus.* II. v.tr. 1, *fastidium alci alcjs rei movēre ;* to — oneself, *se ingurgitare ;* 2, fig. *satiare, saturare.*

surge, I. n. *fluctus, -uum.* II. v.intr. *fluotuare,* lit. and fig.

surgery, n. *chirurgia* (Cels.). **surgeon**, n. *chirurgus, vulnerum medicus* (Plin.).

surly, adj. *morosus ;* see ILL-TEMPERED. Adv. *morose.* **surliness**, n. *morositas.*

surmise, I. n. *conjectura, praesagium* (tempestatis futurae, malorum). II. v.tr. *suspicari, augurari, praesagire.*

surmount, v.tr. *transcendēre* (lit.), *superare* (lit. and fig.). **surmountable**, adj. *(ex)superabilis.*

surname, n. *cognomen* (as Cicero in *Marcus Tullius Cicero*) ; he has a —, *alci cognomen Flacco* or *Capitoni est.*

surpass, n. *alci* or *alqm antecellēre, excellēre, alqm (ex)superare, alqm* or *alci praestare* (lit. and fig.).

surplice, n. *vestis sacerdotalis.*

surplus, n. *rel(l)iquum, quod superest.*

surprise, I. n. *(ad)miratio ;* of a sudden attack, *subita incursio, adventus, -ūs, repentinus.*

II. v.tr. *alqm necopinantem opᵖᵣrĭmĕre, alqm de proviso excĭpĕre;* see also ASTONISH. **surprising,** adj. see WONDERFUL.

surrender, I. v.tr. *se dare, se dedĕre in alcjs fĭdem, se tradĕre.* II. n. *dedĭtio;* to make a —, (*oppidi*) *deditionem hosti* or *ad hostem facĕre, in deditionem venire* (so *alqm in deditionem accipĕre*); = giving up, *traditio.*

surreptitious, adj. *furtīvus, subreptīcius* (Plaut.). Adv. *furtive, furtim, clam.*

surrogate, n. *vicarius.*

surround, v.tr. *circumdare* (e.g. *exercitum castris, brachia collo, alqd alqā re, regio circumdata insulis,* Cic.; *amiculo circumdatus*); *circumvenire, circumcludĕre, circumvallare* (in a siege); fig. *alcjs pueritiam robore circumdare.*

survey, I. v.tr. *spectare, contemplari, considerare, intuēri, intuēri et contemplari, contuēri* (with fixed attention), *oculis collustrare* or *perlustrare* (= to — carefully, to go over), (*in*)*visĕre* (= to look closely at, esp. things which interest us), *perspicĕre* (= to look at in all its parts), *contuēri perspicĕreque, circumspicĕre* (= to look all round a thing); to — hastily, *oculis percurrĕre;* to — in mind, *contemplari animo* or *animo et cogitatione, considerare secum in animo,* or merely *contemplari* or *considerare, contemplari et considerare;* (*per*)*lustrare animo* or *mente animoque, circumspicĕre mente, expendĕre, perpendĕre* (= to weigh); = to measure land, *agrum metīri.* II. n. *contemplatio, observatio, conspectus, -ūs;* see VIEW. **surveyor,** n. (of land) *decempedator, metator.*

survive, v.intr. *superstitem esse.* **survival,** n. use verb. **survivor,** n. *superstes, -ĭtis.*

susceptible, adj. *capax* (e.g. *capax amicitiae, animus ad praecepta capax), inclinatus, pronus, proclivis* (mostly in bad sense), *ad alqd,* comb. *inclinatus et pronus.* **susceptibility,** n. use adj.

suspect, I. v.tr. *suspicari* (*alqd de alqo, alqm), suspicĕre* (usu. in past part.) II. n. *alci suspectus.* **suspicion,** n. *suspĭcio.* **suspicious,** adj. *suspiciosus* (= causing suspicion and ready to suspect). Adv. *suspiciose* (= in a way to excite suspicion); = with suspicion, use adj. or *curiosus* (= inquisitive).

suspend, v.tr. *suspendĕre* (*nidum tigno, columbam ab alqo malo, alqd collo* or *e collo* or *in collo*); to — oneself, *se suspendĕre;* = to interrupt, delay, *differre;* to — anyone from office, *alqm alqo loco* (*sub*)*movēre.* **suspense,** n. *dubitatio, haesitatio;* to be in —, *in dubio esse, animo fluctuare.* **suspension,** n. *dilatio* (= delay); — of hostilities, *indutiae.*

sustain, v.tr. *sustinēre* (= to support, *ager hominum quinque millia sustinēre potest,* Cic.); *re frumentariā ali et sustinēri;* see SUPPORT. **sustenance,** n. *alimentum, victus, -ūs.*

sutler, n. *lixa.*

swaddle, v.tr. *fasciis involvĕre.* **swaddling-bands,** n. *fasciae.*

swagger, v.intr. *gloriari, se jactare.*

swain, n. *agrestis, rusticus, colonus.*

swallow, n. *hirundo.*

swallow, v.tr. *sorbēre* (fig. † *odia, alqd animo*), (*de*)*vorare* (lit. and fig.).

swamp, I. n. *palus, -ūdis, ūlĭgo;* —s, *palustria, -ium.* II. v.tr. (*de*)*mergĕre, immergĕre.* **swampy,** adj. *paluster, -tris, -tre,* and *palustris, -e, uliginosus.*

swan, n. *cygnus.*

sward, n. see GRASS.

swarm, I. n. *conventus, -ūs, frequentia;* — of bees, *examen, agmen apium.* II. v.intr. con-

fluĕre; to — as bees, *examinare* (Col.); see ASSEMBLE.

swarthy, adj. *fuscus, furvus, adustus.*

sway, I. n. *imperium, dominatio, dominium, dicio.* II. v.tr. *regĕre, imperare, imperium habēre* or *exercēre;* see RULE.

swear, v.tr. and intr. *jurare, jusjurandum jurare* or *dare;* to — falsely, *falsum jurare* (an oath I do not think binding), *pejerare, perjurare.* **swearing,** n. *exsecrationes, maledicta, -orum.*

sweat, I. n. *sudor.* II. v.intr. and tr. *sudare.*

sweep, I. v.tr. 1, *verrĕre;* 2, fig., see EXAMINE. II. v.intr. to — along, *verrĕre, percurrĕre.* **sweeper,** n. *qui scopis converrit.* **sweepings,** n. *quisquiliae, -arum,* f.

sweet, adj. *dulcis* (= — to the taste, e.g. *dulcior melle,* Ov.), *suavis* (= agreeable to the smell, e.g. *odor suavis et jucundus), jucundus, blandus* (= pleasant). Adv. *dulciter, dulce, suaviter, jucunde, blande;* to taste —, *dulci esse sapore.* **sweeten,** v.tr. *dulcem reddĕre.* **sweetheart,** n. *deliciae.* **sweetness,** n. *dulcedo, dulcitudo, suavitas, jucunditas.*

swell, I. v.intr. (*in*)*tumescĕre, turgescĕre, crescĕre, augēri* (= to increase); to be swollen, *tumēre.* II. v.tr. *inflare* (e.g. *spem alcjs inflare), tumefacĕre;* to — the sails, *vela tendĕre.* **swelling,** n. *tumor, struma* (= scrofulous —), *tuber* (Plin., both natural, as hump on camel, and of disease), *panus* (Plin.), *scirrhoma, -ătis,* n. (Plin.).

swerve, v.intr. *declinare de* or *a* (*a proposito, a malis,* opp. *appetĕre bona).*

swift, adj. *citus, properus* (= making haste, hurrying), *velox* (= brisk, fast; e.g. *pedites velocissimi), celer* (= active, expeditious), *pernix* (= brisk), *alacer* (= sprightly). Adv. *cito, citato gradu, celeriter, rapide, perniciter.* **swiftness,** n. *celeritas, rapiditas, velocitas, pernicitas.*

swill, v.tr. *ingurgitare* (*se, se vino;* so fig. *se in flagitia*).

swim, v.intr. *nare, natare;* to — over, *tranare.* **swimmer,** n. *natator, nandi perītus.* **swimming,** n. *natatio, ars natandi, scientia natandi.*

swindle, v.tr. *fraudare* (*alqm pecuniā).* **swindler,** n. *fraudator.* **swindling,** n. *fraudatio.*

swine, n. *sus, percus* (= pig); —-herd, *subulcus, suarius* (Plin.).

swing, I. v.tr. *agitare, vibrare, jactare.* II. v.intr. *agitari, vibrari, jactari.* III. n. *funiculus quo se jactat alqs.* **swinging,** n. use verb.

switch, n. *virga, vimen.*

swoon, v.intr. and n. *animo linqui;* see FAINT.

swoop, I. n. *impetus, -ūs.* II. v.intr. to — upon, *impetum in alqm* or *alqd facĕre.*

sword, n. *gladius, ensis* (mostly used in poetry), *ăcĭnăces* (= a Persian —); to have a — at one's side, *gladio succinctum esse;* to draw the —, *gladium* (*e vaginā*) *educĕre;* to sheathe the —, *gladium in vaginam recondĕre;* to put to the —, *interficĕre;* see KILL.

sycophant, n. *delator* (Tac. ; = an accuser), *assentator, adulator* (= a flatterer). **sycophancy,** n. *sycophantia, assentatio, adulatio.*

syllable, n. *syllaba.*

syllogism, n. *syllogismus, ratiocinatio* (Sen.). **syllogistic,** adj. *syllogisticus* (Quint.).

sylvan, adj. *silvester.*

symbol, n. *symbolum, signum, imago;* see SIGN. **symbolic,** adj. by circumloc. (e.g. *quod per imaginem alcjs rei fit*).

symmetry, n. *symmetria, proportio, congruentia, aequalitas;* — of the limbs, *apta membrorum compositio;* — in style, *concinnitas.* **symmetrical,** adj. *par, similis, aequalis, congruens.* Adv. *pariter, similiter, congruenter, aequaliter.*

sympathy, n. **l,** = attraction of bodies, etc., *sympathia* (= agreement among things, in Cic. always written as Greek συμπάθεια), *consensus, -ūs,* or *concordia rerum;* **2,** as mental feeling, *societas* (e.g. *laetitia cum alqo,* with anyone's joy), *animus dolore, laetitiā,* etc., *alcjs affectus.* **sympathetic,** adj. and adv. *dolore or laetitiā alcjs affectus.* **sympathize,** v.intr. *unā gaudēre et dolēre, eadem sentire.*

symphony, n. *symphonia.*

symptom, n. *alcjs morbi nota* **or** *indicium* **or** *signum.*

synagogue, n. *synagoga* (Eccl.).

synchronism, n. *aequalitas temporum.*

syncope, n. see FAINT.

syndicate, n. *societas;* see COMPANY.

synod, n. *synodus* (Eccl.).

synonym, n. *vocabulum idem significans* or *declarans.* **synonymous,** adj. *idem significans* or *declarans.*

synopsis, n. *synopsis* (Jct.); see EPITOME.

syntax, n. *syntaxis* (Gram.), *orationis constructio, verborum quasi structura.* **syntactical,** adj. *quod ad orationis constructionem pertinet.*

syringe, I. n. *sipho* (Suet.). **II.** v.tr. *per siphonem in(j)icĕre.*

syrup, n. *potio dulcis.*

system, n. *formula* or *descriptio* (e.g. *philosophiae, reipublicae), instituta, praecepta, -orum* (= rules). **systematic,** adj. *ad artem redactus, per artem compositus.* Adv. *ordinate,* (*ex*) *ordine, composite.* **systematize,** v.tr. *in artem redigĕre;* see ARRANGE.

T.

tabby, adj. *maculosus;* see also GREY.

tabernacle, n. **1,** see TENT, HABITATION; **2,** *tabernaculum* (Eccl.).

table, n. **1,** *tabula* (= a board for various purposes, e.g. with an account, a will, a law, etc., written upon it; a list of things to be sold by auction, and which were written on boards, and hung outside the stalls of money-changers); **2,** = an article of furniture, *mensa* (= — for holding dishes and for other purposes; then meton., the contents of the dishes, the fare, meal, e.g. the Emperor's —, *mensa principis), monopodium* (μονοπόδιον, = a — with only one foot of ivory, generally made of the wood of the citrus of Africa); to set or lay the —, *mensam* (ap)*ponĕre;* to sit down at —, *accubare;* to rise, get up from —, *surgĕre a cenā;* at —, *apud mensam, super mensam, inter cenam, super cenam, inter epulas;* **3,** = fare, *cena, victus,* -*ūs;* a good —, *lauta cena, lautus victus;* a bad —, *tenuis victus;* for general arrangement of — at feasts, see Smith "Dict. Antiq.," art. Triclinium; at the head of the —, *medius* (= the middle position, *medius* seems to have been the highest); above or below anyone, *supra, infra alqm;* foot of the —, *pes mensae;* — cover, —-cloth, *linteum in mensā ponendum* or *positum;* —-linen, *mappa* (= —-napkin); — service, *vasa, -orum;* — talk,

sermo; **4,** = tablet, *tabula;* — of laws, *legis* or *legum tabula;* **5,** the Lord's —, * mensa Domini;* see SACRAMENT, SUPPER, COMMUNION, ALTAR; **6,** = many particulars, *index.* **table-land,** n. *planities magna et edita.* **tableau,** n. see PICTURE. **tablet,** n. *tabula, tabella* (also = voting —), *cera* (= smeared with wax), *aes* (of bronze), *pugillares, -ium* (Plin.), *codicilli* (= — consisting of several leaves, a kind of memorandum-book). **tabular,** adj. = set down in tables, *per indices expositus;* to give a — view of anything, *per indices exponĕre alqd.*

tacit, adj. *tacitus* (both of persons and of things); see SECRET. Adv. *tacite.* **taciturn,** adj. *taciturnus.* **taciturnity,** n. *taciturnitas.*

tack, I. n. **l,** = a small nail, *clavulus;* see NAIL; **2,** = plan, *consilium, ratio;* to try a fresh —, *novum consilium experiri.* **II.** v.tr. see NAIL. **III.** v.intr. *navem flectĕre.* **tackle,** n. for fishing, *instrumenta piscatoria, -orum.* **tackling,** n. *armamenta, -orum,* n.; see RIGGING.

tact, n. *dexteritas;* see CLEVERNESS, TALENT. **tactics,** n.pl. *res militaris.* **tactician,** n. *rei militaris peritus.*

tadpole, n. *ranunculus.*

taffeta, taffety, n. *pannus sericus.*

tail, n. *cauda;* to wag the —, *caudam movēre;* — of a comet, *stellae crines, -ium.*

tailor, n. *sartor.*

taint, I. v.tr. **l,** in gen., *imbuĕre alqā re;* **2,** = to impregnate with something obnoxious, *corrumpĕre, inquinare;* *vitiare* (fig.; e.g. corn, *frumentum).* **II.** v.intr. *corrumpi, vitiari* (e.g. the atmosphere, *aurae;* meat, fruit), *putrescĕre* (= to become bad). **III.** n. **l,** = tincture, *color* (e.g. *veritatis, urbanitatis, antiquitatis), fucus* (e.g. *alcjs rei fuco illitus, tinctus), species* (e.g. *alci rei species imponĕre, inducĕre);* **2,** *contagio* (lit. and fig.); see CORRUPTION. **tainted,** adj. *vitiatus,* or by *putrescĕre.*

take, I. v.tr. *sumĕre* (= to — anything in order to make use of it), *capĕre* (= to lay hold of, to seize); then to — possession of anything in order to keep it; hence = to storm, e.g. a town), *rapĕre* (= to seize quickly), *arripĕre* (= to — up, to snatch away), *accipĕre* (= to accept, receive), *tollĕre* (to — up, to lift up, in order to — a thing away from its former place), (*de*)*promĕre* (= to —, fetch anything from a place where it had been kept hitherto), *auferre* (= to have carried away, —n up, away), *eripĕre* (= to — by force), *expugnare* (= to storm, always with the idea of the victory being obtained after resistance); not to — anything, *alqd non accipĕre, deprecari* (e.g. *manus);* to — anyone on one side, *alqm secretum adducĕre;* to — money from one (i.e. a person is bribed), *pecuniam ab alqo accipĕre;* to — from, = to quote, *transferre;* this passage I have — verbally from Dicæarchus, *istum ego locum totidem verbis a Dicaearcho transtuli;* to —, lay hold of anyone, *alqm medium arripĕre* (= to put one's arm round anyone's waist and hold him fast); to — anyone round the neck, *in alcjs collum invadĕre* (= to embrace him); to — anyone in custody, *alqm comprehendĕre;* = to receive, *recipĕre in alqd* (e.g. *in ordinem senatorium), assumĕre in alqd* (e.g. *in societatem);* to — anyone in, into one's house, *alqm ad se* or *ad se domum, alqm domum suam recipĕre; = to accept, claim from anyone, *accipĕre ab alqo, poscĕre ab alqo;* to — anything or anyone to, for, as (i.e. to fabricate anything from a material), *facĕre* or *fingĕre* or *effingĕre* or *exprimĕre alqd ex alqā re;* anyone as, for (i.e. to appoint), *alqm,* with the accus. of the office to which anyone is elected (e.g. *alqm arbitrum, alqm imperatorem).*

sŭměrĕ accipĕre, eligĕre, habēre; **to — back again,** *redŭcĕre;* to partake of, *sŭmĕre* (something to **eat** or to drink, e.g. *cibum potionemque), potare* or *bibĕre* (=to drink, e.g. *medicamentum), accipĕre* (when it is given); to — (= to understand) the word (term) in various meanings, *verbum in plures partes accipĕre;* —n as a whole, *omnino,* or by *universus;* to — in good part, *in bonam partem accipĕre, belle ferre, boni* or *aequi bonique facĕre;* to — it ill, amiss, *in malam partem accipĕre, aegre* (or *graviter* or *moleste* or *indigne) ferre, male interpretari;* to — anyone's part, *ad alcjs partes transire, sequi alqm, facĕre cum alqo;* **to** — to be true, as such, *ponĕre* (= to state), *sŭmĕre* (= to — for granted, admit, in speech, in a disputation), *velle,* with accus. and infin. (= to be of opinion, to mean); to — for certain, *sŭmĕre* or *habēre* or *putare pro certo, fingĕre, facĕre* (the foregoing two = to suppose, to — a case); to — away, *alqd alci auferre, eripĕre;* to — down (in writing), *lit(t)eris consignare, lit(t)eris mandare, scripturā persequi;* to — off, *alqd alci* or *alci rei* or *ex alqā re detrahĕre* (e.g. *tegumentum humeris);* to — oneself off, *furtim degredi, clam se subducĕre* (secretly), *se abripĕre, se proripĕre* (quickly); **to** — out, *eximĕre,* out of, *alci rei, de* or *ex alqā re* (out of a place), *excipĕre de* or *ex* (= to — away from a place), *promĕre ex* (e.g. arrows out of the quiver; money out of the public treasury, medicine out of a box, etc.), *educĕre ex;* fig. = to select, *excerpĕre ex,* etc. (e.g. *verba ex orationibus);* to — up, *tollĕre;* to — upon oneself, *subire* (anything dangerous), *in se recipĕre* (= to — the responsibility for anything). **II.** v.intr. **to** — to, *se conferre, concedĕre alqo* (= to retreat); to — to books, *lit(t)eris studēre, urgēre alqd* (e.g. *studia,* = eagerly to be engaged in); see APPLY, RESORT, LIKE; to — after, see IMITATE, RESEMBLE; **to** — up with, *satis habēre, contentum esse alqā re* (= to be contented with), *acquiescĕre in alqā re.* **taking,** n. *expugnatio* (of a city).

tale, n. *narratio* (= the act of telling, and the — itself), *historia* (= narrative), *memoria* (= recorded event), *expositio* (= exposition, description; concise, *circumcisa;* short, *brevis), fabella* (= a short fable, brief tale, or story). **tale-bearer,** n. *delator* (= informer), *sycophanta* m. (= sycophant). **tell, I.** v.tr. (*e)narrare alqd alci, referre* (= to report), (*com)memorare* (= to mention), *dicĕre* (= to say), *enumerare* (= to recount), *prodĕre (memoriae), posteris tradĕre, scriptum relinquĕre* (= to hand down to posterity, of historians), *alcjs rei auctorem esse* (= to vouch for the truth), *exponĕre, explicare* (= to describe), *persequi* (from beginning to end); = to count, *numerare.* **II.** v.intr. = to have effect, *valēre;* a telling speech, etc., *oratio gravis.* **teller,** n. 1, = anyone who tells anything, *narrator, auctor rerum gestarum;* 2, = one who numbers, *qui alqas res numerat.*

talent, n. 1, = a weight and a coin, *talentum;* 2, = mental faculties, *ingenium* (= natural gift), *indoles, -is* (= —s in a moral sense, insomuch as they may be improved by dint of exertion, etc.), *virtus, -ūtis,* f. (= cleverness, skill), comb. *ingenium et virtus, facultas* (= power, capability of doing a thing), more clearly defined *ingenii facultas;* who has —, *ingeniosus, eximii ingenii, magno ingenio praeditus.* **talented,** adj. a very — man, a great genius, *homo ingeniosus, homo eximii ingenii;* to be —, *ingenio abundare, incredibili magnitudine consilii atque ingenii esse.*

talisman, n. *amulētum* (Plin.).

talk, I. v.intr. familiarly, of several, *sermocinari;* together, *loqui* or *colloqui inter se,* (*con)fabulari* (mostly ante class.); to — nonsense, *garrire* (= to — too much, familiarly and in a

contemptuous sense), *blaterare* (= to — unceasingly, making many words about nothing), (*h)ariolari* (like a soothsayer), *alucinari* (without thinking), *nugari* (= to — foolery; all these generally in a transitive sense, with accus.); to — over, see DISCUSS. **II.** n. = familiar conversation, *sermo, colloquium, sermonis cum alqo communicatio;* foolish —, *gerrae, nugae, ineptiae.* **talkative,** adj. *garrulus, loquax.* Adv. *loquaciter.* **talkativeness,** n. *garrulitas, loquacitas.* **talker,** n. (*homo) garrulus* or *loquax.*

tall, adj. of a man, *longus* (opp. *brevis), procērus, procērā staturā,* (*ex)celsus;* a — man, *homo magni corporis, homo grandis, homo staturā procērā.* **tallness,** n. *procēritas,* or by adjs.

tallow, n. *sebum;* a — candle, *sebaceus* (late).

tally, v.intr. *convenire alci rei;* see FIT. SUIT.

Talmud, n. **Talmudum.*

talon, n. *unguis.*

tamarisk, n. *tamārix* (Col.).

tambourine, n. *tympanum.*

tame, I. adj. 1, *cicur* (by nature, of animals), *mansuetus, mansuefactus* (= tractable, of animals and of men), *placidus* (= mild, gentle, peaceable, of men and of animals), *mitis* (= meek, who easily yields, of men and animals); to grow —, *mansuescĕre, mansuefieri, mitescĕre* (opp. *feritatem servare);* 2, fig. *demissus, abjectus, ignavus* (e.g. *animus);* of language, etc., *jejunus, frigidus.* Adv. *demisse, abjecte, ignave, jejune, frigide.* **II.** v.tr. *mansuefacĕre, mansuetum facĕre* or *reddĕre, domare* (= to subdue wild beasts and tribes; then also fig. passions), *frangĕre* (lit. = to break; then fig. = to break, weaken the strength, force, of a person or passions), *frenare* (lit. = to bridle; hence fig. = to curb, rule passions), *refrenare* (lit. = to check with the bridle; thence fig. to restrain persons and passions, e.g. *juventutem), coërcēre* (fig. = to keep within bounds, persons and passions, e.g. *juventutem), comprimĕre, reprimĕre* (lit. = to press together or back, repress; fig. forcibly to restrain passions), *compescĕre* (= not to allow to become too strong, to check, *querelas), moderari alci rei* (fig. = to moderate), *placidum reddĕre* (= to make gentle, men and beasts), *mitem reddĕre* (= to soften), *mitem reddĕre et mansuetum* (= to make tractable, the two foregoing of men), *delenire* (= to soothe, to gain, e.g. *alqm argento, plebem munere).* **tameness,** n. by adjs. and verbs. **tamer,** n. *domitor,* fem. *domitrix.* **taming,** n. *domitus, -ūs* (of animals).

tamper, v.intr. see MEDDLE; = to tempt, *sol(l)icitare.*

tan, I. n. *cortex coriarius.* **II.** v.tr. to — skins, *subigĕre, depsĕre* (= to knead, work anything well till it is soft), *conficĕre* (= to get up, ready); to — (of the sun), *colorare.* **tanner,** n. *coriarius* (Plin.).

tangent, n. *linea circulum contingens.*

tangible, adj. fig. *quod manu tenēre possumus, quod manu tenetur* or *prehenditur, tractabilis.*

tangle, I. v.tr. see ENTANGLE. **II.** n. *nexus, -ūs, nodus.*

tank, n. see RESERVOIR.

tantalize, v.tr. see TEASE.

tantamount, adj. as regards the quantity, *totidem;* as regards the value, *tantidem, tantundem;* see SAME.

tap, I. n. = a light blow, *plaga lĕvis.* **II.** v.intr. *lĕviter ferire.*

tap, I. n. of a cask, *obturamentum* (Plin.,

= stopper). **II.** v.tr. (*vinum*, etc.) *de dolio pro-mĕre, dolium relinĕre* (= to take the pitch off).
taphouse, n. *taberna.*

tape, n. see RIBBON.

taper, n. *cereus.*

tapestry, n. *pictura acu facta, stragulum pictum* or *aulaeum, velum* (= curtain).

tapis, n. to bring on or upon the —, by *commemorare alqd, mentionem alcjs rei facĕre, in medium proferre.*

tar, n. *pix liquida* (Plin.).

tardy, adj. *tardus, lentus.* Adv. *tarae, lente.*
tardiness, n. *tarditas.*

tare, n. a vetch, *vicia.*

target, n. 1, see SHIELD; 2, a — to shoot at, *scopos, -i* (Suet.).

tariff, n. *formula* (*ex quâ portoria* [= harbour dues, etc.] *exiguntur*).

tarnish, I. v.tr. 1, lit. *inquinare;* see STAIN; 2, fig. *inquinare, obscurare;* to — one's honour, *nomini* or *decori officĕre.* **II.** v.intr. of metals, *inquinari.*

tarpaulin, n. *linteum pice munītum.*

tarry, v.intr. *cunctari* (from fear), *cessare* (from idleness), *morari, commorari, moram facĕre* (when one ought to proceed), *tergiversari* (= to try to evade, make evasions), comb. *cunctari et tergiversari, dubitare* (when one is un-decided), *haesitare* (from timidity, perplexity, or on account of difficulties, to hesitate); we must not —, *nulla mora est, maturato opus est* (= no time is to be lost); without —ing, *sine morâ, propere, festinanter.*

tart, n. *scriblita, crustulum.*

tart, adj. 1, of the taste; see SOUR; 2, of the temper, *acerbus, amarus, morosus, stomacho-sus.* Adv. see SOURLY; *acerbe, morose, stoma-chose.* **tartness,** n. 1, see SOURNESS; 2, *acer-bitas, morositas, stomachus.*

tartar, n. in chemistry, **tartărus* (= salt of —, **sal tartari.*

task, I. n. = what is imposed by another, *pensum* (lit. of women spinning wool, then in gen.), *opus, -ĕris,* n. (= work); it is a difficult —, *res magna est;* = lesson, *pensum,* see, however, LESSON; to take anyone to — on account of, *rationem alcjs rei ab alqo* (*re*)*petĕre* or *reposcĕre.* **II.** v.tr. *pensum alci dare* or *imponĕre;* to — oneself with, *alqd faciendum sibi provonĕre.* **task-master,** n. *operis exactor.*

tassel, n. perhaps *fimbriae* (= fringe).

taste, I. v.tr. = to try by eating a little, *gustatu explorare, gustare* (= to take a little of anything; then fig. to become acquainted with, e.g. *suavitatem vitiae*), of anything, (*de*)*gustare alqd, gustare de alqâ re* (a little off the top; then fig. to — the pleasures of anything, e.g. *degustare vitam, honorem*); to — first, before, **†praegustare* (lit.), (*de*)*libare alqd* (lit. and fig.). **II.** v.intr. *sapĕre, alqo sapore esse;* to — like, of, *sapĕre* or *resipĕre alqd* (lit.), *redolēre alqd* (fig., e.g. of the school, *doctrinam,* Cic.); bitter, *amaro esse sapore;* pleasant, *jucunde sapĕre.* **III.** n. 1, objectively, lit. as quality of things, *sapor;* anything loses its —, *alcjs rei sapor non permanet;* fig., e.g. good —, *elegantia* (e.g. in a poem); bad —, *insulsitas;* 2, subjectively, lit. the ability to —, *gustatus, -ûs, gustus, -ûs* (how-ever, Cic. only uses *gustatus,* mostly post class.); = sense of beauty, delighting in that which really is beautiful, *gustatus,* for, *alcjs rei* (Cic.), *elegantia* (= refined — for what is fine, inasmuch as it shows itself by the out-ward appearance), *venustas* (= grace in any-one, Plin.), *judicium* (= judgment in matters of

—), *intellegentia* (of one who is a great judge in matters of —), also *aures, -ium,* and comb. *aures et judicium alcjs* (as far as the — depends upon the ear, e.g. *alcjs* or *temporis auribus accom-modatus*); a good, correct, refined —, *elegantia* (in gen.), *subtile* or *exquisitum* or *politum judi-cium* (= acute judgment), *judicium intellegens* (of a connoisseur); without —, *homo parum elegans;* with —, *scite;* commode (e.g. to dance, *saltare*), *scienter* (e.g. *tibiis cantare*); according to my —, *quantum ego sapio, quantum equidem judicare possum.* **tasteful,** adj. *politus* (= refined, e.g. judgment, letter, man), *elegans, venustus* (= graceful; both the foregoing of persons and things). Adv. *polite, eleganter, venuste.* **taste-less,** adj. 1, lit. *nihil vapidus* (of wine, Col.), *sine sapore;* anything is —, *alcjs rei sapor nul-lus est;* 2, fig. *inelegans, insulsus, infacētus* (*infic-*); see RUDE. Adv. *ineleganter, insulse, infacēte* (*infic-*). **tastelessness,** n. 1, lit. *cui nullus sapor est;* 2, fig. *insulsitas.*

tatter, n. *pannus;* see RAG. **tattered,** adj. *pannosus.*

tattle, I. v.tr. *garrire.* **II.** n. *sermunculus* (rare), or perhaps *sermo stultus.* **tattler,** n. *homo garrulus.*

tattoo, v.tr. *notis compungĕre.*

taunt, I. v.tr. *alqd* or *de alqâ re alci ob*(*jỳ-cĕre, conviciari, cavillari alqm* (= to satirize). **II.** n. *convicium;* see INVECTIVE. **taunting,** adj. *contumēliosus.* Adv. *contumēliose.*

tautology, n. *ejusdem verbi aut sermonis iteratio* (Quint.). **tautological,** adj. *idem verbum aut eundem sermonem iterans.*

tavern, n. *caupona.* **tavern-keeper,** n. *caupo.*

tawdry, adj. *speciosior quam decet* (= too showy); see also VULGAR.

tawny, adj. *fulvus.*

tax, I. n. *vectīgal, tributum;* to lay on a —, *vectīgal, tributum imponĕre alci* and *alci rei, tributum indicĕre alci;* to collect a —, *vectīgalia* (etc.) *exigĕre;* to exempt from a —, *tributis vindi-care alqm, tributis liberare alqm;* exempt from a —, *immunis tributorum,* in the context *immunis* (opp. *vectigalis*). **II.** v.tr. *tributum* (= income-or poll-—) or *vectigal* (= property-—) *imponĕre alci* or *alci rei;* to — every individual, *tributa in singula capita imponĕre.* **taxable,** adj. *vectī-galis.* **taxation,** n. *tributorum in singula capita distributio.* **tax-gatherer,** n. *vecti-galium exactor.*

tea, n. the plant, **thea* (Linn.; necessary as t.t., not class.).

teach, v.tr. anything, (*e*)*docēre* (in gen., also = to show, explain, prove), *praecipĕre, praecepta dare de alqâ re* (= to give precepts), *tradĕre* (= to lecture upon, to —, e.g. history, the rules of an art, etc.), *profitēri* (= to profess, to — publicly what we profess), *ostendĕre, declarare* (= to show, declare); to — anyone, *alqm instituĕre, instruĕre, erudire,* (*e*)*docēre alqm alqd* or *de re, instituĕre, erudire alqm alqâ re, in alqâ re, tradĕre alci alqd* (see before), *imbuĕre alqm alqâ re.* **teachable,** adj. *qui* (*quae*) *docēri potest, docilis.* **teach-ableness,** n. *docilitas.* **teacher,** n. *doctor, magister* (= master, in reference to the influence, authority which he has over his pupils), *prae-ceptor* (giving instruction, Cic.), *auctor* (*alcjs rei*), *explicator alcjs rei* (of one who explains), *pro-fessor* (= a public —, Quint., Suet.), *ludimagister,* or as two words, *ludi magister* (= schoolmaster, principal of a school), comb. *magister atque doctor, praeceptor et magister, dux et magister.* **teaching,** n. *doctrina, eruditio, institutio, disciplina, professio* (= public —).

team, n. *jugum.*

tear, n. *lacrima, flētus, -ūs* (= weeping, constant flowing of —s); with many —s, *cum or non sine multis lacrimis, magno (cum) fletu;* to shed —s, *lacrimas effundere* or *profundere, lacrimare, flēre* (= to weep). **tearful,** adj. *lacrimans, lacrimosus, flebilis.* Adv. *flebiliter, multis cum lacrimis, magno (cum) fletu.* **tearless,** adj. *siccus* (e.g. eyes), *sine lacrimis.*

tear, I. v.tr. to — into pieces, *(di)scinaēre, conscindere* (very rare), *concerpere, discerpere, (di)laniare, (di)lacerare* (= to lacerate), *vellere, eruēre* (e.g. *oculos,* = to — up by the roots), *convellere, divellere* (= to — in pieces), *distrahēre, differre* (= to — in different directions), *diripere, eripere* (= to — away from, *alqd alci;* see SEIZE); to be torn by passion, etc., *differri, distrahi,* or by special verb (e.g. to be torn by anguish, *angui;* by apprehension, *sol(l)icitum esse);* = to — down, *rescindere;* to — open, *resignare* (= to — open a letter), *rescindēre* (lit. and fig.), *diripēre, dirumpēre* (= to break in two, forcibly). **II.** v.intr. see HURRY, RUSH.

tease, v.tr. *alqm fatigare* (= to plague), *vexare* (= to worry), *negotium alci facessēre, alqm algâ re* (e.g. *rogitando), obtundēre.*

teasel, n. *dipsacus (dipsacos, Plin.).*

teat, n. *mamma.*

technical, adj. a — term, *artis vocabulum, vocabulum apud artifices usitatum;* — terms, language, terminology, *vocabula quae in quâque arte versantur;* Zeno and the Peripatetics differ merely in their new — terms, *inter Zenonem et Peripateticos nihil praeter verborum novitatem interest.* **technicality,** n. use adj. **technology,** n. *ars officinarum.*

tedious, adj. *longus, longinquus* (of what lasts long and hence becomes troublesome), *molestus, taedii plenus* (= wearying), *lentus* (= slow; of a war, *lentum et diuturnum);* it would be —, *longum est;* not to be —, *ne longus sim.* Adv. *moleste, lente, cum taedio.* **tediousness,** n. of anything, *molestia quam* (or *taedium quod) alqd alci affert.*

teem, v.intr. *turgēre* (= to swell); to begin to —, *turgescēre; plenum esse alcjs rei* (e.g. *succi,* as a human body, Ter.), *distentum esse algâ re* (= to be extended as it were through anything, e.g. *lacte,* as an udder); see ABOUND. **teeming,** adj. see FRUITFUL.

teethe, v.intr. *dentire* (Plin.); see TOOTH.

teetotal, etc. *vino exempli caus(s)â (se) abstinēre;* see ABSTAIN, ABSTINENCE.

telegraph, n. as t.t. *telegraphum quod dicitur.*

telescope, n. **telescopium.*

tell, v.tr. see under TALE.

temerity, n. *temeritas.*

temper, I. v.tr. *temperare* (lit. and fig.); to — with anything, *alqd alqd re miscēre* (lit. and fig.); see MIX. **II.** n. 1, = character, *ingenium* (= peculiar disposition of the mind), *natura* (of the body, of the mind), *animus* (= character); 2, = anger, *ira, iracundia;* to be in a —, *irasci, iracundum esse.* **temperament,** n. *temperatio;* see TEMPER, DISPOSITION. **temperance,** n. *continentia* (= abstaining), *temperantia* (= being moderate in the enjoyment of sensual pleasure, both in opp. to *libido, libidines), moderatio, modestia, frugalitas* (= moderation), *abstinentia* (= abstinence from anything). **temperate,** adj. *temperans, temperatus, continens* (= moderate in the enjoyment of anything), comb. *moderatus ac temperatus, temperatus moderatusque, continens ac temperans, moderatus, modestus* (= moderate), *sobrius* (= sober), *frugi* (= frugal), *abstinens* (= abstinent), *abstēmius* (= abstemious); of climate,

temperatus. Adv. *temperanter, temperate, continenter, moderate, modeste, sobrie, frugaliter.* **temperateness,** n. *temperantia;* see TEMPERANCE. **temperature,** n. *temperatio* (= the blending of —, so, mild —, *aeris, caeli,* etc.), *temperies* (e.g. of the atmosphere, *aeris),* or by *caelum* (e.g. *salubre, serēnum,* or with noun, *caeli clementia,* etc.). **tempered,** adj. good-—, *mītis;* ill-—, *morosus.*

tempest, n. *tempestas* (= unfavourable weather, boisterous weather in general, storm on the land and on the sea; then also fig.), *procella* (= hurricane, storm on the sea; also fig. of storms in a State); a — arises, *tempestas* (or *procella) venit* or *oritur* or *cooritur;* a — threatens, *tempestas* (or *procella) imminet* or *impendet, alci* (lit. and fig.). **tempestuous,** adj. *procellosus* (lit.), *turbidus, turbulentus* (lit. and fig.), *violentus* (lit., e.g. weather, *tempestas;* then fig. = violent, e.g. attack, *impetus;* character, *ingenium; homo), vehemens* (= vehement, violent, having a high degree of inward strength, e.g. *ventus;* then of man = passionate). Adv. *procellose* (lit.), *turbide, turbulente, violenter, vehementer.* **tempestuousness,** n. *violentia* (e.g. *venti, maris);* then = roughness, boisterous manners, *vehementia.*

templar, n. **(eques) templarius, -is, f.*

temple, n. *aedes sacra* (of a god; *aedes* alone can only be said if the genit. of the deity is added, or if it is sufficiently clear from the context), *templum, fanum, delubrum, aedicula, sacrarium* (= shrine); in poetry sometimes the name of a god stands for his — (e.g. *Jupiter, Vesta), sacellum* (surrounded with a wall and containing an altar; used as a place of refuge).

temples, n. (part of the head) *tempora, -um.*

temporal, adj. = pertaining to this life, *externus* (referring to the world without), *humanus* (referring to a man and man's destiny; *terrenus* and *terrester,* Eccl.); — affairs, *res externae;* — things, treasures, *fortunae, res familiaris, opes, -um,* f.; — welfare, *hujus vitae felicitas;* if opposed to "spiritual," *profanus* (opp. *sacer),* in gram., — augment, *augmentun temporale.* **temporality,** n. *res externa.*

temporary, adj. *temporarius* (very rare before Aug.), *temporalis,* better by *ad* or *in tempus.* **temporarily,** adv. *ad* or *in tempus* (= for the time being). **temporize,** v.intr. *temporibus inservire.*

tempt, v.tr. anyone, *alqm* (at)*tentare, alcjs sententiam tentare* (= to sound anyone, what his opinion is), *so(l)licitare alqm* or *alcjs animum* (= to try to persuade anyone to do a certain thing, e.g. *pretio* or *pecuniâ), alqm ad* or *in alqd invitare, illicēre, pellicēre, allicēre, vocare, adducēre* or *inducēre.* **temptation,** n. *tentatio* (= the act of trying anyone or a thing), *so(l)licitatio* (= the act of tempting anyone to, etc.), *corruptelarum illecebrae* (= allurements wherewith to tempt anyone); to lead anyone into —, *alqm in discrimen vocare* or *adducēre, alqm sol(l)icitare. pellicēre.* **tempter,** n. *tentator* (Hor., and Eccl. of the Devil).

ten, adj. *decem; deni, -ae, -a* (= — each, also = — at once); containing —, *denarius;* the number —, *decussis;* — o'clock, *hora quarta;* of — years, *decennis* (Plin.); — times, *decie(n)s* (also = as in English, I have told you — times, *decies dixi).* **tenth,** adj. *decimus.*

tenable, adj. *quod tenēri potest.*

tenacious, adj. *tenax alcjs rei* (lit. and fig., mostly poet. and in post-Aug. prose); see FIRM. Adv. *tenaciter.* **tenaciousness, tenacity,** n. *tenacitas.*

tenant, I. n. *conductor, incola,* m. and f., *habi-*

tator (in gen.), *inquilinus* (of a house). **II.** v.tr.
see INHABIT. **tenancy,** n. *alcjs rei conducendae condicio.* **tenantry,** n. use pl. of TENANT, or *clientes, -ium.*

tend, v.tr. *curare, colĕre.*

tend, v.intr. 1, = to go, *tendĕre ;* see GO ; 2, = to relate, *ad alqd pertinēre, spectare, tendĕre.* **tendency,** n. *inclinatio, proclivitas ad alqm, studium alcjs rei ;* see INCLINATION. **tender,** v.tr. and n. see OFFER.

tender, adj. *tener, mollis, delicatus* (= delicate), *misericors* (= — -hearted), *amans* (= affectionate), *indulgens* (= indulgent). Adv. *molliter, delicate,* comb. *delicate ac molliter, indulgenter.* **tenderness,** n. 1, = softness, etc., *teneritas, mollitia (mollities) ;* 2, = affection, *indulgentia, amor.*

tendon, n. *nervus* (Cels.).

tendril, n. *clavicula, caulis, pampinus,* m. and f. (of a vine), *viticula* (Plin.).

tenement, n. see HOUSE.

tenet, n. *praeceptum, placitum, decretum ;* the —s, *disciplina, ratio* (Stoicorum, etc.).

tennis, n. *pila.* **tennis-court,** n. *locus quo pilā luditur.*

tenour, n. *tenor* (= uninterrupted course, e.g. *vitae, consulatūs), sententia* (= meaning) ; see MEANING.

tense, n. *tempus, -oris,* n. (Gram.).

tension, n. *intentio.*

tent, n. *tentorium, tabernaculum* (often = a hut), *contubernium ;* general's —, *praetorium ;* to pitch a —, *tabernaculum collocare, ponĕre, constituĕre.*

tentacle, n. *corniculum* (in gen., Plin.).

tentative, adj. and adv. *experientia, probatio, tentatio* (e.g. *tentatione usus),* or by verb *qui (quae, quod) tentat.*

tenterhooks, n. to be on —, *ex(s)pectatione angi.*

tenuity, n. see THINNESS.

tenure, n. *possessio* or *possidēre.*

tepid, adj. *tepidus, tepens ;* to become —, *tepescĕre ;* to be —, *tepēre ;* to make —, *tepefacĕre.* Adv. *tepide* (Plin.). **tepidness,** n. *tepor* (also fig. = lukewarmness, e.g. in writings ; Tac.).

tergiversation, n. *tergiversatio.*

term, I. n. 1, see LIMIT, BOUNDARY ; 2, = limited time, *dies* (in gen., in this sense generally feminine), *dies certa, dies stata* or *statuta* or *constituta* (or in masc.) ; a time named, fixed, e.g. to fix a —, *diem statuĕre* or *constituĕre* (by mutual appointment, e.g. when a sum is to be paid), *diem dicĕre* (for settling a law dispute) ; 3, in Gram., see EXPRESSION, WORD ; 4, the arts, see TECHNICAL ; 5, see CONDITION ; to be on good —s with anyone, *cum alqo familiariter vivĕre, alcjs familiaritate uti.* **II.** v.tr. see NAME. **terminal,** adj. *quod certis diebus fit.* **terminate, I.** v.tr. see LIMIT, END. **II.** v.intr. *finiri, terminari ;* see END. **termination,** n. *confectio, finis, -is, exitus, -ūs.* **terminology,** n. *artis vocabula, -orum ;* — of a sect, etc., *verba, -orum* (*sua* or *alcjs propria*).

termagant, n. *mulier jurgiis addicta.*

terrace, n. *pulvinus* (= flower-bed raised in the form of pillows, a plantation that gradually rises), *solarium* (= a place on the top of the house for basking in the sun), *ambulatio* (= a covered or open place for walking).

terrestrial, adj. *qui (quae, quod) terram incolit, ad terram pertinens, terrestris, terrēnus* (= of the earth, opp. to *caelestis.* e.g. of animals, etc.) ;

as opp. to heavenly, *terrestris* (Eccl.), **better** expressed by *humanus* (opp. to *divinus*).

terrible, adj. *terribilis* (= exciting terror), †*terrificus, horribilis, horrendus* (= horrible), *atrox* (= fearful, e.g. man, deed, bloodshed), *immanis* (= monstrous, unnatural, cruel), *dirus* (= portentous), *formidulosus* (= causing fear), *foedus* (= detestable, abominable, e.g. plots, war, fire), *incredibilis* (= incredible, not to be believed, imagined, e.g. *stupiditas*). Adv. *terribilem* or *horrendum in modum, atrociter, foede, foedum in modum.* **terrific,** adj. see DREADFUL, TERRIBLE. **terrify,** v.tr. *alqm (per)terrēre,* see FRIGHTEN. **terror,** n. *terror* (in a subjective sense = fear, in an objective sense, that which causes —) ; also in the pl. *formido, metus, -ūs, pavor* (all in subjective sense) ; with —, *terrore percussus, terrore coactus.*

territory, n. *territorium* (= field belonging to a town) ; in a wider sense = boundaries, dominions, etc., by *ager, terra, regio.* **territorial,** adj. *qui (quae, quod) ad agrum pertinet.*

terse, adj. e.g. style, by *pressus, brevis, angustus, densus* (e.g. *densior hic, ille copiosior,* Quint.), *strictus* (Quint.), or by *paucis verbis (uti,* etc.). Adv. *presse, breviter, paucis verbis.* **terseness,** n. *brevitas,* or by *oratio pressa,* etc.

tertian, n. *(febris) tertiana.*

tesselated, adj. *tessellatus.*

test, I. n. see TRIAL, EXAMINATION. **II.** v.tr. *tentare, experiri, periclitari alqd* (also *alqm), periculum facĕre alcjs rei* (also *alcjs), explorare ;* to be —ed, to stand the —, *usu* or *re probari.*

testaceous, adj. *testaceus* (Plin.).

testament, n. 1, *testamentum* (= will) ; see WILL ; 2, the New —, *Testamentum Novum ;* the Old —, *Testamentum Vetus* (Eccl.). **testamentary,** adj. by *testamento institutus,* etc., *testamentarius* (in Cic. *lex test.* = a law about wills ; in Plin. *adoptio test.*). **testator,** n. *testator* (Suet. and Jct.), or *is qui testamentum facit.* **testatrix,** n. *testatrix* (Jct.). **testify,** v.tr. *testari* (in gen.), *testificari, testimonio confirmare* (= to confirm by testimony), *testimonio esse, testem esse* (= to be a witness ; the former of a thing, the latter of a person), *affirmare* (= to affirm, or *testificari* in this sense). **testimonial,** n. perhaps by *testimonium honorificum ; lit(t)erae commendaticiae ;* = letters of recommendation ; see CERTIFICATE. **testimony,** n. *testimonium.*

testy, adj. *morosus ;* see PEEVISH.

tether, v.tr. and n. see TIE.

tetrameter, n. *tetrametrus* (very late).

tetrarch, n. *tetrarcha,* m. **tetrarchy,** n. *tetrarchia.*

text, n. 1, = the words of a writer, *verba, -orum* (= the words of an author quoted by a commentator) ; 2, — of Scripture, *exemplum Sacrae Scripturae propositum.*

textile, adj. *textorius.* **textual,** adj. *quod ad verba scriptoris pertinet.* **texture,** n. †*textura, textus, textus, -ūs* (both poet. and post Aug.) ; see WEB.

than, conj. after a comparative and after verbs containing the idea of a comparison (e.g. after *malo,* I would rather ; *praestat,* it is better), *quam ;* or by the ablat., e.g. *virtus est praestantior quam aurum* or *praestantior auro ;* if there is a number before the noun, — after the comps. *amplius* and *plus, minus, minor, major* is left out altogether, and the numeral is still expressed in the same case as if it had been used, e.g. *amplius sunt sex menses, plus ducentos milites desideravit* (= more —, etc.), *minus trecenti*

— less —) *perierunt ;* more (less) — eight years old, *major (minor) quam octo annos natus, major (minor) octo annos natus, major (minor) octo annis natu, major (minor) octo annis, major (minor) octo annorum ;* = — that, *quam ut* or *qui (quae, quod)* with subj. (e.g. the pain was greater — he could bear, *dolor major erat quam quem ille ferre posset) ;* — one could expect from, etc., considering, etc., expressed by Liv. and later writers simply by *quam pro* (which we however never read in Cic. and Caes.), e.g. *praelium atrocius erat quam pro pugnantium numero ;* in negative and interrogative sentences, also when we state anything the words "nothing else —," by *praeter, praeterquam, excepto* (with n. as abl. abs.), *nisi,* e.g. *praeter illum vidi neminem, tibi nihil deesse arbitror praeter voluntatem, philosophi negant quemquam esse bonum nisi sapientem ;* — here may be rendered either by *nisi* or *quam,* but *nisi* implies that everything else is excluded, whilst *quam* is only used in a comparative sense, e.g. *erat historia nihil aliud nisi annalium confectio* (i.e. history was this only and nothing else besides, Cic.), *virtus nihil aliud est quam in se perfecta et ad summum perducta natura* (i.e. as much as, the same as, Cic.).

thane, n. *dominus ; * thanus* (mediæval term).

thank, v.tr. *gratias alci agĕre ;* that, for, by *quod* or *qui,* not *pro alqâ re ; gratiam habēre, persolvēre, referre, reddēre, tribuĕre, gratiam habēre, gratum esse erga alqm, beneficii memoriam conservare, memori mente gratiam persolvēre, gratâ memoriâ beneficium (beneficia) prosequi* (in one's heart), *re ipsâ atque animo esse gratum* (by deed, and in one's own heart) ; heartily, most sincerely, *maximas, incredibiles, singulares gratias agĕre alci,* also *amplissimis* or *singularibus verbis gratias agĕre alci ;* — you ! (in accepting) *benigne dicis !* I have to — you for it, *alci alqâ debēre* (something good), *alci alqd acceptum referre ;* no, — you ! *benigne (dicis) ! benigne ac liberaliter !* also *recte !* (all right ! no ! as answer to a question) ; I — you for your kind invitation, *bene vocas ; jam gratia est ;* the act of —ing, *gratiarum actio* (words). **thankful,** adj. *gratus ;* see GRATEFUL. Adv. *grate, grato animo.*
thankfulness, n. *animus gratus ;* see GRATITUDE. **thankless,** adj. *ingratus* (= both ungrateful and bringing no thanks). Adv. *ingrate.*
thanks, n. *gratiae* (often in the pl. with *agĕre*) ; to return —, *gratias agĕre* or *gratiam persolvĕre quod* or *qui, gratiam alci referre, reddĕre,* for, *pro alqâ re ;* — God ! *est diis gratia !*
thanksgiving, n. *gratiarum actio* (in gen.), *supplicatio, supplicium* (= public — for victories, for deliverance from sickness). **thankworthy,** adj. *laudabilis, gratiâ* or *laude dignus, gratus.*

that, I. demonstr. pron. *ille, illa, illud, iste, ista, istud (ille,* without being in opp. to *hic,* often used when we speak of something very well known, very celebrated, of any thing or person remote as regards time or place, but present in the mind of the speaker ; *iste* = —, often when we speak of a third person or thing, with the idea of contempt or disapproval, — man there), *alter* (= the other of two ; pl. *alteri,* if we speak of several on the other side) ; *is, ea, id, hic, haec, hoc ;* those who, *illi qui* or (the relative clause preceding) *qui, ii ;* — or, the word — not expressed, e.g. *jacet corpus dormientis ut mortui* (= as — of a dead man) ; — is my father, *hic est meus pater ;* — only is true friendship, *haec demum est amicitia firma ;* often by *sic,* e.g. — is his way, *sic est ingenium ejus ;* — such a one, etc., *is, ea, id ;* of — age, *id aetatis ;* at — time, *id temporis ;* we are at — age, *id jam aetatis sumus.* **II.** rel. pron. *qui, quae, quod ;* see

Who. III. conj. to connect the main clause **1** A, when the sentence with — contains the subject of the copula in the main sentence ; 1, when the sentence with — conveys a general idea, render by the inf., e.g. *officii est,* etc., or by another noun, e.g. *nihil suavius est quam amari* or *amor,* = nothing is more pleasing than — one should be loved ; 2, use the accus. and inf., after "it is pleasing, grievous, probable, clear, manifest, evident, true, it appears, it is useful, right, reasonable, necessary, lawful, it is allowed —"; after several of these impersonal verbs, use also *quod* and *ut,* see under C and D (e.g. it is pleasing to hear — you are well, *gratum est te valēre) ;* 3, than —, as —, inf. with an adv. or another noun with an adj. or part., e.g. *nulla res tanto erat damno,* etc., *quam* (a noun with an adj. or part.). B, when the sentence with — contains the object of the verb of the main clause, use acc. and infin. ; 1, this is the case after all *verba sensuum et affectuum,* to which belong also " to know, conceive, remind, expect, hope, fear, believe," etc. ; then also after *fac,* when it is = *finge,* fancy —, etc., *fac qui ego sum esse te ;* after the verbs " to hope, swear, promise, threaten," we use the accus. and fut. infin., only after " to hope" we use the accus. and pres. infin. when we speak of anything referring to the present time, and the accus. and perf. infin. when we speak of anything past ; 2, after the so-called *verba declarandi,* as " to say, tell, indicate, remember, convince, teach, prove *(efficere),*" etc. ; 3, also after " to fix, determine, wish, forbid, impose, concede (that anything is so)," etc., the infin., if the sentence with — declares the object, whilst if it contains a wish or intention, we use *ut ;* after "they," "the people say," "it is reported," etc. *(dicunt, tradunt, ferunt, produnt, perhibent),* either by accus. and infin., or the nom. and indic. (of the passive voice), e.g. *dicunt Romulum primum regem Romanum fuisse,* or *Romulus primus rex Romanorum fuisse dicebatur ; dicunt vos adfuisse,* or *vos dicebamini adfuisse ;* after *dubito,* in the sense "I doubt not," we find in Cic. always *quin.* C, when the sentence with — contains a description of anything or a circuml., 1, of the subject, when we can put "which" instead of "—," by *quod,* as after "there is reason," or "there is no reason," (which, etc.), *est (habeo), non est, nihil est quod* (we may also use *cur,* as in English) ; also after "it is pleasing, rejoicing, I am glad, it is painful," etc. (e.g. *nihil est quod* [i.e. *illud quod] timeas) ;* also after " we must add *(eo* or *huc accedit),*" where we use *quod* when we speak of a matter of fact, and *ut* when we refer to anything that is only in progress, always when the thing is only about to happen ; 2, of the object when — = "because ;" also by *quod* after " to be glad, rejoice *(gaudēre),* to feel sorry, grieve *(dolēre),* to wonder *(mirari),*" etc., where we use *quod* when we speak of a definite fact, but *si,* if we speak of something merely imaginary or as we suppose it ; 3, when — stands for "inasmuch as, inasfar as." D, always *ut* or *qui (quae, quod)* when the sentence with — expresses the purpose, condition, aim, effect, surmise, permission, encouragement, wish or command, as subject or object, or as additional clause ; after *is sum, non is sum, talis, qualis, is* (such a one), *ejusmodi,* etc. ; also *qui,* etc. *(ut is,* etc.), after *tam, tantus,* generally after negations, after *quis ?* and after comparatives with *quam,* when these words express the degree, measure, up to which anything is said to possess a certain quality ; and after nouns to express a purpose (e.g. Caesar sent messengers — they might say, *Caesar nuntios misit qui dicerent) ;* but *ut is,* etc., to express result ; — not, after " to fear, to be afraid," etc., *ne non,* seldom *ut,* and — alone,

as; only — not, — by any means, *ut ne* (*ne* being placed before — which is prevented), e.g. *ut hoc ne facerem* (= he took care —, etc.); I say — . . . not, etc., by *nego* with accus. and infin., e.g. he asserts — there are no gods, *deos esse negat.* E, — in exclamations, 1, when we express a wish, oh — ! *ut! utinam! o si* (see OH); God grant —, etc., *faxit Deus, ut,* etc. ; — not ! *utinam ne!* 2, in general exclamations, by accus. and infin. (which apparently is not governed by any preceding verb), e.g. *me miserum! te in tantas aerumnas propter me incidisse!*

thatch, n. *stramentum.* **thatched,** adj. — house, *casa stramento tecta.*

thaw, I. v.tr. (*dis*)*solvĕre, liquefacĕre.* **II.** v.intr. (*dis*)*solvi, liquefiĕri, liquescĕre, et tabescĕre calore, glaciem tepefactam molliri.* **III.** n. use verb.

the, def. art. not expressed in Latin ; but if we speak emphatically, sometimes by the demonstr. pron. *hic, haec, hoc; ille, illa, illud; iste, ista, istud* (see THAT); — more, etc.,. . . . more, etc, *quo . . . eo* or *hoc, quanto . . . tanto, eo . . . quo, tanto . . . quanto,* e.g. *homines quo plura habent, eo ampliora cupiunt,* = more they have, — more they want ; in general sentences we use the superlative with *ut quisque . . . ita,* e.g. *ut quisque est vir optimus, ita difficillime alios improbos suspicatur* (= — better a man is, with — more difficulty he suspects, etc., . . .); sometimes in sentences of the latter kind the connecting particles *ut* and *ita* are altogether omitted, e.g. *sapientissimus quisque aequissimo animo moritur :* — sooner — better, *quam primum, primo quoque tempore* or *die;* — with an adj. or adv., e.g. — better, *hoc, eo, tanto ;* so much — greater, *eo* or *hoc major;* so much — better, *tanto melius.*

theatre, n. *theatrum, scaena.* **theatrical,** adj. *scaenicus, theatralis* (= belonging to the theatre; very late = also low, vulgar), (e.g. dress, *habitus, venustas,* in this sense), also by the genit. *histrionum* (in reference to the actors), e.g. — gestures, *histrionum gestus inepti.* Adv. *more histrionum.*

theft, n. *furtum.* **thief,** n. *fur.* **thieve,** v.intr. see STEAL. **thievish,** adj. *furax.—* Adv. *furaciter.*

their, poss. pron. *suus* (if referring to the main subject in the sentence), *eorum, illorum* (if referring to any other subject); on — account, for — sake, *suâ caus(s)â, eorum caus(s)â, propter eos* (see before). **theirs,** poss. pron. *suus* or *illorum.*

them, pers. pron. *eos* or *eas, illos* or *illas, ipsos* or *ipsas;* = to them, *eis* or *iis,* etc. **themselves,** see SELF.

theme, n. = subject to write or speak on, *propositio, propositum, id quod propositum est, quaestio, id quod quaerimus* (=question proposed, leading idea for a metaphysical inquiry), *argumentum* (= material, contents, e.g. *epistulae*).

then, adv. *tunc* (corresponds to *nunc,* now), *tum* (denoting continuity, as *jam* in the present; — that is at that time, after something foregoing), *illo* (*eo*) *tempore.*

thence, adv. *illinc* (*illim*), *istinc, abhinc* (= from that place ; *hinc et illinc,* hence and —, hither and thither). **thenceforth,** adv. *inde, ex ea tempore.*

theocracy, n. *regnum quo Deus ipse rex habetur,* or θεοκρατία.

theogony, n. *deorum generatio.*

theology, n. *theologĭa* (Eccl.), or *rerum divinarum scientia.* **theologian,** n. *theŏlŏgus* or *lit(t)erarum sanctarum studiosus.* **theo-**

logical, adj. *theologicus,* **or by the** genit. *lit(t)erarum sanctarum.*

theorem, n. *perceptum* (translation of the Greek θεώρημα, Cic.).

theory, n. *ratio* (= science of anything in gen., e.g. *belli*), *doctrina* (= literary or theoretical knowledge), *ars, praecepta, -orum* (= rules); — of moral duties or obligations, *conformatio officiorum* (Cic.); — and practice, *ratio atque usus, -ūs ;* to combine —, *doctrinam ad usum adjungĕre.* **theoretical,** adj. *quod in cognitione versatur, in spectione* or *in cognitione et aestimatione positus* (Quint.), *quod ab artis praeceptis proficiscitur* (= according to the rules of art, analogous to, Cic.); — knowledge, *ratio* (e.g. *belli*); to possess — of, *alqd ratione cognitum habēre ;* to have a — and practical bearing, *ad cognoscendi et agendi vim rationemque referri.* Adv. *ratione, ex artis praeceptis.* **theorist,** n. *qui artem ratione cognitam habet.*

theosophy, n. * *theosophĭa* (as t.t.). **theosophist,** n. * *theosŏphus.*

therapeutics, n. *ars medendi, medicina.*

there, adv. = in that place, *ibi ; illic, isthic;* to be —, *adesse ;* to stand —, *adstare;* — where, *ibi ubi, illic ubi ;* — you have, — you see, not rendered, but simply *habes, accipe, vides* (e.g. *librum*); = thither, *illuc ;* see THITHER. **thereabouts,** adv. *prope* (= near), *ferme, fere* (= nearly). **thereafter, thereupon,** adv. (*ex*)*inde* (*exin*), *deinde* (*dein*), *statim* (= immediately) ; see AFTERWARDS, THEN.

therefore, adv. *igitur, itaque, ergo* (*igitur* never at the beginning), *ideo, eo, idcirco, propterea* (= for that reason), *proin(de)* (= hence), *quare, quamobrem, quapropter, quocirca* (= wherefore). **therein,** adv. *in eo, in eis* (*iis*), etc.

thermometer, n. * *thermometrum* (as t.t.).

thesis, n. see THEME.

they, pers. pron. *ii* or *eae, illi* or *illae, ipsi* or *ipsae;* but it is only expressed in Latin when we speak emphatically.

thick, adj. *crassus* (= stout, compact, opp. *tenuis* (= thin) and *macer* (=meagre)), *pinguis* (= fat, stout, opp. *macer*), *opimus* (= who looks like one that lives well, opp. *gracilis*), *obēsus* (= well-fed, opp. *gracilis* and (of animals) *strigosus*), *corpore amplo* (= of large-sized body), *turgens, turgidus* (= swollen, e.g. eyes, etc.), *densus* (= dense, opp. *rarus,* = single, scarce, solitary), *spissus* (= impenetrable, of the soil, of darkness, etc., opp. *solutus,* loose), *confertus* (=crowded, of a mass, opp. *rarus*), *concretus* (= curdled, of milk, also of air); when we express the measure of anything, — is either rendered by *crassus* with accus., or by *crassitudine* with the genit. of the measure (e.g. *quat(t)uor pedes crassus, quat(t)uor pedum crassitudine*); *creber, frequens* (= many) ; a — voice, *vox obtusa* (Quint.) ; — skin, med. *callosus* (lit.), *durus* (fig.). Adv. *dense, spisse, confertim, crebro, frequenter.* **thicken, I. v.tr.** *densare,* † *spissare.* **II. v.intr.** *densari, spissari, concrescĕre* (= become like one mass, to curdle, e.g. of milk, etc.). **thicket,** n. *dumētum, fruticētum,* or *locus sentibus obsitus.* **thickness,** n. *crassitudo, spissitas* (so as to become impenetrable), *obesitas* (= fatness, opp. *gracilitas*), *corpus amplum, crebritas, frequentia.* **thick-set,** adj. see THICK, STOUT.

thief, n. see THEFT.

thigh, n. *femur.*

thimble, n. *digiti munimentum.*

thin, I. adj. *tenuis* (opp. *crassus*), *subtilis* (= fine, tender, e.g. of leather), *gracilis, exilis, macer* (=meagre, opp. *obesus*), *strigosus* (=lean, of animals), *rarus* (= not close together, e.g. hair,

opp. *densus*), *angustus* (= narrow), *liquidus* (of anything liquid), *dilutus* (= diluted, e.g. wine, colour). **II.** v.tr. *attenuare*; of trees, *collucare* (of clearing the ground of trees, post-Aug. of a single tree); *interlucare* (Plin.). Adv. *tenuiter*, *graciliter*, *rare*. **thinness**, n. *tenuitas*, *exilitas*, *gracilitas* (= slenderness), *raritas* (= looseness of texture), *macies* (= leanness).

thine, pron. *tuus*.

thing, n. 1, = event, *res*, *negotium*; —**s**, *res*, *rerum natura*; —**s**, with an adj. before it, often rendered merely by the adj. n.pl. (e.g. wonderful —s, *mira*), or by some noun (e.g. foolish —s, *nugae*, *ineptiae*); a tiresome —, *lentum* (= slow), *molestum negotium*; above all —s, *ante omnia*, *imprimis* (*in primis*), *praecipue*; 2, = any substance, *res*, *supellex* (= household furniture), *vasa*, -*orum* (= vessels, pots, also of soldiers), *sarcinae* (= effects which we carry with us when travelling); = clothes, *vestis*, *vestitus*, -*us*.

think, v.intr. and tr. 1, abs. = to have ideas and to be conscious of it (in an absolute sense), *cogitare*, *intellegĕre* (= to have clear ideas); 2, with an object, anything, *alqd cogitare*, *alqd cogitatione comprehendĕre* or *percipĕre* or *complecti*, *alqd cogitatione et mente complecti*, *alqd mente concipĕre*, *alqd cogitatione or (de)pingĕre* (= to picture anything in one's mind); — about, *de alqa re cogitare*; 3, = to suppose, *opinari*, *putare*, *arbitrari*, *censēre*, *credĕre*; 4, see PURPOSE; 5, = to judge, *judicare*, *sentire* (= to have a certain opinion), comb. *sentire et judicare*, *statuĕre* (= to fix). **thinker**, n. = a speculative, philosophical —, *philosophus* (in this sense always in Cic.); a deep —, *subtilis disputator*, *homo acutus ad excogitandum*. **thought**, n. *cogitatio* (= the act of —, what we have been thinking of), *cogitatum* (= what we have been thinking about), *mens* (=disposition, then = opinion, view), *memoria alcjs rei* (= memory), *sententia* (= opinion), † *sensus*, -*ūs*, *mens*, *animus* (= mind), *notio* (= notion), *opinio* (= opinion, founded upon conjecture), *suspicio* (= conjecture as suspicion), *consilium* (= view, plan), *conjectura* (= conjecture), *dictum* (= — as expressed); —s, *cogitata mentis*, or by circumloc. *quae mente concipimus*, *quae animo cogitamus*, *sentimus*, *versamus*, or often simply by the neut. pl. of the pron. or adj. (e.g. *ista tua*); to be in deep —, *in cogitatione defixum esse*. **thoughtful**, adj. *in cogitatione defixus* (= lost in thought), *sapiens*, *prudens* (= wise). Adv. *sapienter*, *prudenter*. **thoughtfulness**, n. see THOUGHT. **thoughtless**, adj. *socors* (= who does not think), *stupidus* (= slow from stupidity), *inconsultus*, *neglegens*, *indiligens* (= neglectful), *imprudens* (= without foresight), *temerarius* (= rash). Adv. *inconsulte* (or *inconsulto*), *neglegenter*, *indiligenter*, *imprudenter*, *temere*. **thoughtlessness**, n. *..cordia* (= slowness to think), *stupiditas* (= stupidity, habitual), *neglegentia*, *indiligentia*; see CARELESSNESS.

third, adj. see THREE.

thirst, I. n. *sitis* (lit. and fig.). **II.** v.intr. *sitire* (also of plants, fields, etc.); fig. to — after, *sitire alqd*. **thirsty**, adj. *sitiens* (lit. and fig.; after, *alcjs rei*). Adv. *sitienter* (fig.).

thirteen, adj. *tredecem*, more frequently (always in Cic.) *decem et tres* or *tres et decem*; — each, *terni deni* or *deni terni*; — times, *tredecie(n)s*. **thirteenth**, adj. *tertius decimus* or *decimus et tertius*. **thirty**, adj. *triginta*; — each, *triceni*, -*ae*, -*a*; — times, *tricie(n)s*, *trigesie(n)s*. **thirtieth**, adj. *trigesimus* (*tric.*), -*a*, -*um*.

this, dem. pron. *hic*, *haec*, *hoc* (or *qui*, *quae*, *quod* at the beginning of a new sentence, if —

refers to persons or things, in "and —, for —, but —, hence —, — therefore, now —," etc.; the conjs. are left out when we use *qui*); — one, *hicce*, *haecce*, *hocce*; —... that, *alter*... *alter* (of two); this... that? *uter*... *uter* (of two), *hic*... *ille* or *iste*; on — side, *cis*, *citra*; what is on — side, *citerior*.

thistle, n. *carduus*.

thither, adv. *eo*, *in eum locum*, *ad id loci*, *huc* (= hither), *illuc*, *illo*, *isthuc*, *isto*; hither and —, *huc et (atque) illuc*.

thong, n. *lorum*; see STRAP.

thorax, n. *thorax* (Plin.); see CHEST.

thorn, n. *spina* (= — of plants, also — bush), *sentis*, -*is*, m. and f., *vepres*, -*is*, m. (= — bush); — bushes, *senticetum* (ante class.), and in the pl. in this sense, *vepres*, *sentes* (= hedge of —), *dumetum*, *dumi* (= a place full of brambles, a thicket). **thorny**, adj. *spinosus* (lit., fig. = of perplexed meaning), † *sentus* (= rough with thorns), *laboriosus*, *arduus*, *aerumnosus* (fig.); — paths, etc., of the Stoics, *dumeta Stoicorum* (Cic.).

thorough, adj. see COMPLETE. Adv. *penitus*, *prorsus*, *omnino*, *plane*, *funditus*; see COMPLETELY. **thoroughbred**, adj. *generosus*.

thoroughfare, n. by *transitus*, -*ūs*, *transvectio* (= a passing through), *iter* (*pervium*), *via* (*pervia*, = road), or by the verbs *transire*, *transvehi*.

thou, pers. pron. *tu*, *tute* (emphatic).

though, conj. see ALTHOUGH.

thousand, adj. *mille* (properly speaking a noun, not declined in the sing., but used only as nom. or accus.; as a noun, it governs the genit. (e.g. *mille passuum*); but *mille* is also considered as an adj., which however is not declined), *mil(l)ia*, -*ium*; several —s, the pl. of *mille*, and declined; with the cardinal or distributive numerals (e.g. 2,000, *duo* or *bina mil(l)ia*; 10,000, *decem* or *dena mil(l)ia*, the noun in the genit. (e.g. 30,000 armed men, *trecenta mil(l)ia armatorum*), except when we say 3,300, and so on (e.g. *habuit tria mil(l)ia trecentos milites*); = innumerable, *mille* (= 1,000) or *sescenti* (*sexc.*, = 600; both = immense); a — times, *mil(l)ie(n)s*. **thousandth**, adj. *mil(l)esimus*.

thraldom, n. see SLAVERY, BONDAGE, SERVITUDE.

thrash, v.tr. to — corn, *e spicis grana excutĕre* or *exterĕre*, *frumentum deterĕre* (Col.), *messem perticis flagellare*, *spicas baculis excutĕre* (with long sticks); = beat; see BEAT. **thrashing**, n. *tritura*. **thrashing-floor**, n. *area*, or more explicitly, *area in quā frumenta deteruntur*. **thrashing-machine**, n. *tribulum*.

thread, I. n. 1, lit. *filum*, *linea*, *linum*, *licium*, † *subtemen*, *stamen*; 2, fig. of a narrative, *filum* (= quality, kind), better use *narratio*. **II.** v.tr. to — a needle, *filum per acumen con(j)icĕre*; to — one's way; see Go. **threadbare**, adj. *obsolētus* (of clothes), *tritus* (of topics, etc.).

threat, n. *(com)minatio*, *denuntiatio*. **threaten**, v.tr. *minas jacĕre*; to — anyone with, *alci alqd minitari*, *(com)minari*, *denuntiare alci alqd* (in words, e.g. war, murder); it —s to, etc., *in eo est ut*, etc., or by the periphrastic conjugation, with part. fut. act. (e.g. *odia in novas pugnas eruptura sunt*); to — = to be near at hand (of war, etc.), *(im)minēre*, *impendēre*, *instare*, *ingruĕre* (poet., and in Tac.). **threatening**, adj. *minax*, *miniabundus* (lit. of persons), *instans*, *imminens* (= near at hand, e.g. war, danger), *praesens* (= near, e.g. persecution, danger). Adv. *mināciter*.

three, adj. *tres, tria; trini, trinae, trina* (= three together); a period **of** — days, *triduum;* –fold, *triplex;* — footed, *tripes;* — hundred, *trecenti;* — thousand, *tria mil(l)ia.* **threefold, triple,** adj. *triplus, triplex, tripartitus (pert.) in tres partes divisus.* **thrice,** adj. *ter;* twice or —, *bis terque, iterum ac tertium;* — more, *triplo plus.* **third, I.** adj. *tertius;* a — time, *tertium, tertio;* in the — place, *tertio;* there is no — course, *nihil tertium est, nihil habet ista res medium.* Adv. *tertio.* **II.** n. *tertia pars;* heir to a —, *heres ex triente;* two —s, *e tribus duae partes, bes, bessis* (= two —s of a whole (e.g. the *as*) consisting of twelve parts, consequently 8–12ths or 2–3rds, e.g. *alqm relinquĕre heredem ex besse*).

threshold, n. *limen* (lit. and fig.).

thrift, n. *frugalitas, parsimonia.* **thrifty,** adj. *frugi, parcus.* Adv. *frugaliter, parce.*

thrill, I. v.tr. *commovēre.* **II.** v.intr. 1, of notes, *resonare;* see RESOUND; 2, — with joy, **etc.,** *ex(s)ultare, (laetitiā) gestire, efferri, commovēri.* **thrilling,** adj. 1, see SHRILL; 2, = exciting, *mirificus, mirus, horrendus;* see WONDERFUL.

thrive, v.intr. by *crescĕre;* see PROSPER.

throat, n. *jugulum, guttur;* to cut any one's —, *alqm jugulare.*

throb, I. v.intr. by *salire, palpitare;* see BEAT. **II.** n. *cordis palpitatio* (Plin.).

throe, n. *dolor.*

throne, n. *solium* (lit. = an elevated seat, — in gen., in particular = the royal —), *suggestus, -ūs* (= elevated seat, elevation in gen.), *sedes, -is,* **f.,** or *sella regia* (lit. = the king's —), *regnum* (fig. = royal dignity, reign), *imperium* (fig. = the highest power); to sit on the —, *sedēre in solio or in sede regiā* (lit.), *regem esse, regnare* (fig. = to reign, to be king); to ascend the —, *regnum occupare* (fig.), *regnum or imperium adipisci* (= to come upon the —).

throng, I. n. *frequentia.* **II.** v.tr. *frequentare;* see CROWD.

throstle, n. *turdus.*

throttle, I. n. see WINDPIPE. **II.** v.tr. *suffocare, animam or spiritum intercludĕre.*

through, prep. *per* with accus. of place and time (e.g. *per tres dies, or tres dies* anno, = — three days; *per Africam,* = — Africa; *per te,* = — you); as denoting the instrument or means, it was = — you (i.e. on account of), *propter te erat or te auctore;* — and —, *penitus, prorsus, omnino;* see ALTOGETHER. **throughout, I.** prep. see THROUGH. **II.** adv. see THROUGH AND THROUGH **a**bove; see BY.

throw, I. v.tr. *jacĕre, jactare* (repeatedly or constantly), *mittĕre* (= to let go), *con(j)icĕre* (= hurl), *in(j)icĕre* (= to — into) *alci rei or in alqd;* — anything at anyone, *petĕre alqm alqā re* (e.g. *alqm malo*); to — stones at anyone, *lapides mittĕre or con(j)icĕre in alqm, lapidibus petĕre alqm, lapidibus alqm prosequi;* to — dice, *talos or tesseras jacĕre;* let the die be thrown (fig.), *jacta alea esto;* to — about, *jactare* (e.g. *tempestate jactari in alto*); to — anything, *spargĕre, dispergĕre;* to — across, *trans(j)icĕre alqd trans alqd or* double accus. (e.g. *exercitum (trans) Rhodanum*); **to** — a bridge across a river, *flumen ponte jungĕre;* to — away, *ab(j)icĕre;* to — oneself into, *se alci rei dedĕre, alci rei studēre;* to — open, *patefacĕre;* to — out; see REJECT, REMARK; to — up; see BUILD, VOMIT. **II.** n. *jactus, -ūs* (in gen. and of dice), *conjectus, -ūs* (in gen.), *alea* (= — of the dice, fig.), *missus, -ūs* (of stones, etc.). **thrower,** n. *jaculator.* **throwing,** n. † *conjectio:* see THROW, II.

thrust, I. v.tr. see PUSH, DRIVE, PIERCE; to — oneself; see INTRUDE. **II.** n. *ictus, -ūs, plaga* (= blow), *petitio* (=attack).

thumb, I. n. *(digitus) pollex.* **II.** v.tr. *pollice terĕre.* **thumbscrew,** n. by *circumloc.* (e.g. to apply the —, *pollicem (paul(l)atim) contundĕre.*

thump, I. n. see BLOW. **II.** v.tr. see BEAT.

thunder, I. n. *tonitrus, -ūs, tonitruum, -i, fragor* (of any loud noise, e.g. *fragor caeli or caelestis*); fig. = noise, clamor, *sonitus, -ūs.* **II.** v.intr. *(in)tonare* (impers., trans., and intr.) also fig. of a strong voice). **thunder-bolt,** n. *fulmen;* struck by a —, *de caelo tactus.* **thunder-storm,** n. *tonitrua et fulmina, tempestas cum tonitribus.* **thunder-struck,** adj. *obstupefactus.*

Thursday, n. * *dies Jovis.*

thus, adv. *ita, sic* (in this manner); see So.

thwart, I. v.tr. see HINDER. **II.** n. *transtrum.*

thy, pron. *tuus;* see YOUR.

thyme, n. *thymum.*

tick, ticking, I. n. of a clock, *sonus or sonitus, -ūs (aequalibus intervallis factus).* **II.** v.intr. perhaps *tempus sonitu indicare, sonare.*

ticket, n. *tessera* (Suet.), probably the best word for a ticket for theatre, etc. (Admission to Roman theatres was free).

tickle, v.tr. *titillare alqd* (also fig. e.g, *sensus;* but Cic. always says *quasi titillare); quasi titillationem adhibēre alci rei* (e.g. *sensibus); to* — the palate, *palatum tergēre* (Hor., of anything we eat). **tickling,** n. *titillatio.* **ticklish,** adj. 1, lit. *titillationis minime patiens;* 2, fig. of persons; he is very — in that respect, *hac re facile offenditur;* of things, *lubricus et anceps.*

tide, n. 1, *aestus, -ūs (maritimus),* or in pl., *marinorum aestuum accessus et recessus* (both *-ūs), aestus maritimi mutuo accedentes et recedentes;* the — comes in twice every twenty-four hours, *bis affluunt bisque remeant aestus maris vicenis quaternisque semper horis* (Plin.); 2, fig. *mutatio* (= change), or by *crescĕre ac decrescĕre.* **tidal,** adj. *quod ad aestum pertinet;* — wave, *unda (aestu facta).*

tidings, n. *nuntius alcjs rei;* see NEWS.

tidy, adj. *nitidus;* see NEAT.

tie, I. v.tr. see BIND; to — a knot, *nodum facĕre, in nodum colligĕre.* **II.** n. 1, *nodus* (= knot), *vinculum;* 2, of friendship, etc., *vinculum, nodus, conjunctio, necessitudo* (also of kinship).

tier, n. *ordo, -inis,* m.; see Row.

tiger, n. *tigris.*

tight, n. *strictus, a(d)strictus* (= fitting —)**,** *angustus, artus* (= narrow); a — shoe, *calceus urens* (when it hurts); — rope, *funis contentus.* **tighten,** v.tr. *stringĕre, a(d)stringĕre* (e.g. chain, *vinculum;* a shoe, *calceum), intendĕre, contendĕre* (= to bend, draw —, what was loose before, e.g. *arcum intendĕre or contendĕre;* the skin, *cutem intendĕre*), comb. *contendĕre et adducĕre;* to — the reins, *habenas adducĕre* (opp. *remittĕre*). Adv. and **tightness,** n. use adj.

tile, n. *tegula, imbrex* (for roof), *tessera* (for paving).

till, I. prep. 1, to express the limit, *ad, usque ad* with accus. (= to a certain point), *in, usque in* with accus. (= about as far as), *tenus* with ablat. (put after the noun to fix the end); 2, as regards the time, *ad, usque ad, in, usque in;* — when? *quo usque* (continuing)? *quem ad finem* (= — what time)? — to-day, *usque ad* *hunc diem, hodie quoque;* — to-morrow, *in crastinum;* — late at night, *ad multam noctem;* — daylight, *ad lucem.* **II.** conj. *dum, donec, quoad* (= as long as; but *quoad* defines the time more precisely); not —, *non prius quam, non ante quam;* see UNTIL.

till, v.tr. *arare* (= plough), *colĕre* (= cultivate); see CULTIVATE. **tillage,** n. *aratio, cultus, -ūs, cultura.* **tiller,** n. *arator* (= ploughman), *agricola, (agri)cultor.*

till, n. = money —, *arca.* **tiller,** n. *clavus.*

tilt, see COVER.

tilt, I. v.tr. *invertĕre.* **II.** v.intr. = fight, by *hastis ex equis pugnare;* see TOURNAMENT.

timber, n. *materia* or *materies* (= to fell —, *materiam caedĕre, materiari* (once in Caes.).

time, I. n. 1, *tempus, -ŏris,* n. *dies* (= the day), *spatium* (= — as a period) † *aevum, intervallum* (= interval), *aetas* (= age), *tempestas* (= season), *saeculum* (= a long —, a generation), *otium* (= leisure), *occasio, opportunitas* (= opportunity); the most celebrated general of his —, *clarissimus imperator suae aetatis;* in our —, *nostrā memoriā;* at the right —, *tempore (tempori, temperi) ad tempus, tempestive, opportune, in tempore;* in ancient —s, *antiquitus;* from the — when, *ex quo (tempore);* at every —, *omni tempore;* from — to —, *interdum* (= now and then); for all —, *in omne tempus;* in good —, *mature* (e.g. to rise, *surgĕre*); against the —, *sub* or *ad tempus;* in the mean —, *interea, interim;* according to — and circumstance, *pro tempore et pro re, ex re et tempore;* to require — for, *tempus postulare ad;* it is — to go, *tempus est ut eamus* or *ire;* eight —s eight, *octo octies multiplicata;* 2, in music, *tempus, numerus, modus;* to beat —, *manu intervalla signare;* in —, *numerose.* **II.** v.tr. *tempus observare finem certo tempore alci rei imponĕre.* **timely, I.** adj. *maturus* (of fruits, etc., fig. *aevi maturus,* Verg.), *tempestivus, opportunus.* **II.** adv. *mature, tempestive, opportune.* **timepiece,** n. see CLOCK. **time-server,** n. *adulator, assentator* (= flatterer).

timid, adj. *timidus, pavidus, trepidus, verecundus* (= bashful), *formidinis plenus* (= full of fear), *ignavus* (= cowardly); to be —, *timidum,* etc., *esse, metuĕre, timēre;* don't be —, *omitte timorem.* Adv. *timide, pavide, trepide, verecunde, ignave.* **timidity,** n. *timiditas, pavor, trepidatio, ignavia.* **timorous,** adj. see TIMID.

tin, n. *plumbum album, stannum* (Plin.).

tincture, n. (in med.) *liquor medicatus;* = a slight colouring, *color, fucus* (lit. and fig.).

tinge, v.tr. *imbuĕre, colorare, inficĕre, tingĕre alqd alqā re, alqd alci rei inducĕre.*

tinder, n. *fomes, -itis,* m.

tingle, v.intr. 1, in the ears, *aures tinnire;* 2, see ITCH.

tinker, n. *a(h)enorum refector.*

tinkle, v.intr. *tinnire;* see RESOUND. **tinkling,** n. † *tinnitus, -ūs.*

tinsel, n. 1, lit. *bractea* (= metal leaf); — cloth, *pannus auro intextus;* 2, fig. *fucus, species.*

tip, I. n. *cacumen, summa, ultima pars;* see POINT. **II.** v.tr. *(prae)acuĕre* (= sharpen), *alqd alci rei praefigĕre;* — over, *invertĕre;* see OVERTURN. **tiptoe,** n. 1, lit. *in digitos erecti* (from Quint.); 2, fig. *(ex)spectatione,* etc.) *intentus.*

tipple, v.intr. see DRINK. **tippler,** n. *potor;* see DRUNKARD. **tipsy,** adj. *temulentus, ebrius.* Adv. *temulenter,* or by adj.

tire, I. v.tr. *(de)fatigare.* **II.** v.intr. *(de)fatigari.* **tired,** adj. *(de)fatigatus, defessus,*

lassus, lassitudine confectus. **tiresome,** adj. *importunus, molestus* (lit. and fig.), *lentus* (= slow). **tiring,** adj. *quod (de)fatigat,* or by *laboriosus;* see LABORIOUS.

tiro, n. *tiro; rudis et tiro.*

tissue, n. 1, † *textus, -ūs;* see TEXTURE; 2, fig. *series,* or by *totus* (e.g. the thing is a — of falsehoods, *tota res e mendaciis constat*).

tit-bit, n. *cup(p)edia, -orum,* or *cup(p)ediae.*

tithe, I. n. *decuma, decima pars.* **II.** v.tr. *decumas imponĕre.*

title, n. *titulus* (in gen.), *inscriptio, index* (= — of a book), *nomen* (= name), hence comb. *titulus nomenque* (Ov.), *praescriptio* (= introduction to a senatorial decree, etc.); to give a book a —, *inscribĕre librum;* a — (as an honour), *nomen, appellatio* (in addressing anyone); to give anyone a —, *alqm appellare* with accus. of the title (e.g. *regem*); = right, *vindiciae;* see RIGHT. **titled,** adj. by birth, etc., *nobilis.* **titular,** adj. by *nomine,* opp. to *re.*

titter, v.intr., see LAUGH.

tittle, n. *minima pars, aliquid ex alqā re;* **tittle-tattle,** n. see CHATTER, GOSSIP.

tittle, n. to a —, by circumloc., e.g. by *subtiliter, acu* (e.g. *rem acu tetigisti*), *res ipsa.*

to, prep. (denoting motion towards) *ad* (in gen.) *in* (= into) with accus. *(ad eum locum proficisci,* to go — that place; *ad alqm venire,* to come — someone), with towns and small islands accus. without *ad,* but not if *urbem, oppidum* be used in apposition with the name of the place, *ad* also with *usque* (e.g. *usque ad Romam profectus est,* he went (i.e. as far as) Rome); with *a, ab,* it denotes the extreme points of motion or distance *(Aquitania a Garumnā ad Pyraneos montes pertinet,* A. extends from the Garonne — the Pyrenees), the direction of a word or speech *(invitare ad cenam*) limit in time *(Sophocles ad summam senectutem tragoedias fecit,* = Sophocles made tragedies down — extreme old age; *ad diem solvĕre,* = to pay — the day); — is properly the sign of the Latin dative *(mihi dedit librum,* = he gave a book — me; *mihi venit auxilio,* = he came — my aid); sometimes the force of — is given by the genit. *(desiderium edendi,* = desire to eat), also by an infin. *(me jussit ire,* = he commanded me — go), by the supine *(spectatem ivit,* = he came — behold), or by the gerundive with *ad (profectus est ad ludos spectandos,* = he has gone — see the games); after *dignus,* worthy, use *qui* and the subj. *(dignus est qui laudetur,* = he is worthy — be praised); = in order to, *ut* or *ne* with subj. *In* with the accus. properly means "into," denoting entrance (as *in domum intravit,* = he went into his house), but sometimes the idea of entrance or of penetration, is dropped, so that the Latin *in* corresponds with our — or till (e.g. *in aram confugit,* = he fled — the altar; *in eandem sententiam loquitur,* = he speaks — the same effect; *indulgens in* or *erga patrem, severus in filium,* = indulgent — [or towards] his father, severe — his son). Special phrases — my, thy house, *ad me, ad te,* — this or that place, *huc* or *illuc;* — the temple of Vestae, Jupiter, *ad Vestae, Jovis;* — the country, — home, *rus, domum;* to look — the west, *in occidentem spectare;* = a man, *ad unum;* to compare anyone — anyone, *alqm cum alqo comparare.* **to-day, I.** n. *hodiernus dies.* **II.** adv *hodie.* **to-morrow, I.** n. *crastinus dies.* **II.** adv. *cras.*

toad, n. *būfo;* —stool, *fungus.* **toady,** n. and v.tr. see FLATTER.

toast, I. v.tr. 1, = scorch bread, *torrēre;* 2, = drink health, *salutem alci propinare.* **II.** n. 1, *panis tostus;* 2, use verb, see above I. 2.

tobacco, n. *herba nicotiana,* = the plant, *tabacum* (as smoked).

toe, n. *(pedis) digitus.*

together, adv. *unā (cum), simul,* comb. *unā simul, eodem tempore simul, conjunctim;* all —, *ad unum omnes, cuncti, universi* (opp. *singuli*).

toil, I. n. *magnus labor.* **II.** v.intr. *multo sudore et labore facēre alqd;* see LABOUR, WORK.

toilsome, adj. *laboriosus, operosus;* see LABORIOUS, DIFFICULT. Adv. *laboriose, operose.*

toilet, n. *cultus, -ūs, ornatus, -ūs;* to make one's —, *se vestire.*

token, n. *signum;* see SIGN.

tolerable, adj. **1.** = what can be tolerated, *tolerabilis, tolerandus, patibilis;* **2.** = middling, *tolerabilis, mediocris, modicus.* Adv. *tolerabiliter, mediocriter, modice, satis* (= sufficiently). **tolerate,** v.tr. *tolerare, ferre,* with sense of acquiescence, *aequo animo ferre;* in religious matters, *aliena sacra alci permittēre;* see BEAR; = to allow anything being done, *pati alqd fieri, sinēre, permittēre.* **tolerance,** n. *indulgentia* (= indulgence), *tolerantia, toleratio* (= bearing of anything); in matters of religion, *indulgentia erga sacra aliena.*

toll, n. *vectīgal* (in gen.), *portorium* (as excise duty, transit, at a —bar); — keeper, *exactor portorii, portitor.*

toll, v.intr. and tr. by *sonare.*

tomb, n. *sepulc(h)rum, tumulus* (lit. = mound). **tomb-stone,** n. *lapis, -ĭdis,* m., *cippus, monumentum.*

tome, n. *liber;* see BOOK.

ton, tun, n. as a vessel, *seria* (oval), *dolium* (round); as a measure, of liquids, *centum urnae* (liquid measure), perhaps *maximum pondus, -ēris,* n. (in avoirdupois weight). **tonnage,** n. calculated by the number of *amphorae* (i.e. Roman cubic feet), e.g. *navis plus quam trecentarum amphorarum est.*

tone, n. **1,** *sonus, sonitus, -ūs, vox* (from the mouth or a musical instrument); **2,** fig. see CHARACTER.

tongs, n., fire —, *forceps,* m. and f.

tongue, n. *lingua* (also fig. = neck of land, language), *ligula* (= neck of land), *examen* (of a scale), *sermo* (= language).

tonic, n. *medicina quae stomachum corroborat.*

tonsils, n. *tonsillae.*

too, adv. *etiam, quoque, praeterea* (e.g. *unum etiam vos oro,* = one thing — I ask of you; *non sophistae solum, sed philosophi quoque,* = not the sophists only, but the philosophers —); — much, *nimium, nimio;* — great, *nimis magnus;* by comparative, he is — learned to have said that, *doctior est quam qui hoc dixerit;* to act — hastily, *festinantius agēre, per imprudentiam facēre alqd.*

tool, n. in sing. use special word (e.g. *rastrum,* = rake, gardener's —); pl. as collective, *instrumentum* (e.g. *rusticum*).

tooth, n. *dens, -ntis,* m. (in the mouth, also of an anchor); a hollow —, *dens cavus or cavatus* (Plin.); false —, *dentes empti* (Mart.); — ache, *dolor dentium;* to have —, *laborare ex dentibus;* —pick, *dentiscalpium* (Mart.); — powder, *dentifricium* (Plin.); —some, *dulcis.*

top, I. n. **1,** *summus* with noun (e.g. *summus mons*); from — to toe, *totus,* or by adv. *penitus, omnino, prorsus* (= altogether); see SUMMIT; **2,** a child's —, *turbo.* **II.** adj. *summus* (= highest); — heavy, *gravior* (= heavier than is right).

topaz, n. *topazius* or *chrysolithus* (Plin.).

toper, n. *potator, potor.*

topic, n. *argumentum;* see SUBJECT.

topography, n. *locorum descriptio.*

topsy-turvy, adv. to turn —, *omnia turbare et miscēre.*

torch, n. *fax, taeda* (= a piece of wood), *funale* (= wax candle).

torment, I. v.tr. *(ex)cruciare* (lit. and fig.), *torquēre* (lit. = to torture; then fig., both of man and of bodily and mental pain), *stimulare* (= to prick, then fig., e.g. of the conscience), *angēre* (= to distress), *vexare* (= to let anyone have no rest and peace); to — anyone with questions, *alqm rogitando obtundēre.* **II.** n. *cruciatus, -ūs* (lit. and fig.), *tormentum* (lit. = torture; then fig. excruciating pain, of body or mind), comb. *cruciatus et tormentum, doloris stimuli* (= excruciating pain). **tormentor,** n. *vexator* (fig.).

tornado, n. *turbo.*

torpedo, n. *torpēdo* (= the fish, and perhaps as t.t. for the explosive).

torpid, adj. *torpens* (lit. and fig.).

torpor, n. *torpor.*

torrent, n. *torrens;* —of rain, *imber torrentis modo effusus;* — of words, *flumen verborum.*

torrid, adj. *torridus.*

tortoise, n. *testudo;* — shell, *testudinis putamen* (Plin.), *testudinis testa* (Var.).

torture, I. n. *tormenta, -orum,* n. (lit. and fig., as a measure to compel prisoners to confess; then the instruments used for that purpose, such as *equuleus* (= rack); *cruciatus, -ūs* (of the pain suffered; also fig., e.g. of the conscience), *quaestio* (of slaves), *verbera, -um* (= lashes). **II.** v.tr. **1,** lit. *(ex)torquēre, excarnificare* (rare), *in equuleum imponēre, (ex)cruciare;* to — anyone at a trial, *(tormentis) quaerēre de alqo,* also *de alqā re;* **2,** fig. *(ex)cruciare;* see TORMENT. **torturer,** n. *tortor, carnifex* (= executioner).

toss, I. v.tr. *mittēre, jaculari, jactare;* see THROW, HURL. **II.** n. *jactus, -ūs, jactatio.*

total, I. adj. *totus, cunctus, universus, omnis.* Adv. *omnino, plane, prorsus, funditus* (with verbs of destroying, etc.), *penitus* or by *totus* (e.g. *totus ex fraude factus*). **II.** n. *summa* (of a debt; also *in summā exercitus tuendā,* the whole, i.e. the main part of the army, Caes.), *solidum* (of a debt). **totality,** n. *universitas, summa* or by adj. TOTAL.

totter, v.intr. *labare,* † *nutare, vacillare* (to vacillate), *titubare* (like one that is drunk, asleep, etc.).

touch, I. v.tr. **1,** lit. *tangēre, attingēre, contingēre* (all three also = to border, of countries, etc.); **2,** fig. = affect, *(com)movēre, alqm dolore,* etc., *afficēre;* = relate to, *pertinēre ad;* — at (of a ship), *(navem) appellēre, appelli ad* or *in;* to — upon, *leviter tangēre, breviter* or *strictim attingēre, breviter perstringēre.* **II.** n. *tactio, tactus, -ūs* (= the act or sense); fig. a — of art, etc., perhaps *aliquid,* with gen. of noun. **touching, I.** adj. *animum (com)movens, miserationem* or *misericordiam movens.* **II.** prep. *de;* see CONCERNING. **touchstone,** n. *cōticula, lapis Lydius* (Plin.); fig. *obrussa* (= test, whether anything is first-proof). **touchy,** adj. *mollis ad accipiendam offensionem* (e.g. *animus,* Cic.), *irritabilis* (= irritable), *iracundus.*

tough, adj. *lentus* (lit. and fig.). **toughness,** n. *lentitia.*

tour, n. *iter, itinĕris,* n.; to make —, etc., *iter facēre.* **tourist,** n. see TRAVELLER.

tournament, n. by *certamen equitum hastis concurrentium.*

tow, n. *stuppa.*

tow, v.tr. *trahĕre;* to — line, *funis, -is.*

toward, I. prep. *ad, in, versus* (always after its noun) with accus. (e.g. *ad orientem,* — the east, *Brundisium versus*); also *adversus* (e.g. *adversus montem,* = [motion] — the mountain) ; to go — anyone, *obviam ire alci;* with a wider application of the idea of direction, denoting dispositions, inclinations, etc., as, — a person, *adversus, erga, in* with accus. (*est enim pietas justitia adversus deos,* = piety is justice — the gods); genit. merely (*caritas patriae,* = love — one's native land); *ad meridiem,* = — midday ; *sub vesperum,* = — evening. **II.** adj. see DOCILE, OBEDIENT.

towel, n. *mantēle* (*mantile*).

tower, I. n. *turris;* a — of strength, fig., *arx* or *praesidium.* **II.** v.intr. *ex algo loco eminēre, exstare;* to — over, *alci loco imminēre;* to be in a —ing rage, *iracundiā efferri.*

town, I. n. *urbs* (also = capital, more particularly Rome itself), *oppidum, municipium* (= a free city, esp. in Italy); —'s-people, *oppidani;* — hall, *curia;* —ship, *urbis ager.* **II.** adj. *urbanus.*

toy, I. n. see PLAYTHING, = trifles, *nugae.* **II.** v.intr. see PLAY.

trace, I. n. *vestigium, indĭcium* (= sign), in the pl. comb. *indicia et vestigia* (e.g. *veneni*), *significatio alcjs rei* (= indication, e.g. *timoris*). **II.** v.tr. 1, = to draw, mark out, *delineare, designare* (with the pencil; *des.* also fig. *verbis*), *describĕre* (with the pencil or pen), *adumbrare* (= to shadow out) ; 2, = to follow by footsteps, (*odore*) *persequi alqd* or *alqd* (lit. of dogs, etc. ; then of men), *odorari* (lit. and fig.), *indagare* or *investigare alqd* (lit. and fig.). **tracer,** n. *investigator* (fem. *investigatrix,* late), *indagator.* **tracing,** n. *investigatio, indagatio.* **track, I.** n. 1, see PATH ; 2, see TRACE. **II.** v.tr. *alcjs* or *alcjs rei vestigia persequi,* also *persequi alqm* or *alqd;* see TRACE.

tract, n. **I.** *spatium* (= space in gen.), *tractus, -ūs* (= district) ; see REGION, DISTRICT ; **II.** = treatise, *libellus.* **tractable,** adj. *tractabilis, docilis, obsequens, obsequiosus, oboediens facilis* (= willing). Adv. *obsequenter, oboedienter.* **tractableness,** n. *obsequium, oboedientia, docilitas, facilitas, obsequium.*

trade, I. n. 1, see COMMERCE ; 2, = the business anyone has learnt, *ars* (= art, also any mechanical skill, as in Liv. of the — of a butcher, *artificium* ; *ars operosa* (=an art which produces something), *negotium servile* (of the lower —s, e.g. of a shoemaker, smith, etc., and which were carried on by slaves), *ars sordida, quaestus, -ūs sordidus* (inasmuch as the lower trades and the gains made by them were considered below the dignity of a free Roman and of the patricians, opp. *ars liberalis*). **II.** v.tr. *rem gerĕre et lucrum facĕre* (= to do a good —, Plaut.), *mercaturam* or (of several) *mercaturas facĕre* (as a merchant, more esp. wholesale), *negotiari* (of a money-lender, banker, corndealer, etc.). **tradesman, trader,** n. *caupo* (= huckster); see MERCHANT.

tradition, n. *traditio* (= handing over, down); in the sense of "handing down by verbal —', by *memoria* if = remembrance in gen.), *lit(t)erae* (in writing), *sermo* or *fama* (oral). **traditional, traditionary,** adj. *posteris traditus* or *proditus* (in gen.), *lit(t)eris custoditus* (in writing).

traduce, v.tr. see SLANDER.

traffic, I. n. *commercium;* see COMMERCE. **II.** v.intr. *mercaturam facĕre;* see TRADE.

tragedy, n. 1, *tragoedia;* to perform a —, *tragoediam agĕre;* 2, fig. *casus, -ūs.* **tragedian,** n. = tragic actor, *tragoedus, tragicus actor.* **tragic,** adj. *tragicus;* in a — manner, *tragico more;* fig. *tristis* (= sad), *luctuōsus* (= mournful, e.g. *exitium*), *miserabilis* (= wretched, e.g. *aspectus*), *atrox* (= frightful, e.g. *res,* event). Adv. *tragice, miserabiliter, atrociter.* **tragicomedy,** n. *tragicomoedia.*

train, I. v.tr. 1, see DRAW ; 2, = to educate, (*e*)*docēre, instituĕre;* to — soldiers or athletes, *exercēre;* see EDUCATE. **II.** n. 1, of a gown, etc., *syrma, -atis,* n. (= robe with —), or by *quod trahitur, quod verrit terram* (= sweeping the ground, of long dresses); 2, = procession, *pompa;* 3, = series, *ordo, series.* **trainer,** n. of horses, *equorum domitor;* of athletes, *magister* (*gladiatorum magister,* Cic.). **training,** n. *disciplina* (in the widest sense); in war, *militiae* or *militaris disciplina;* in law, *juris civilis discip.;* in philosophy, *philosophiae discip.;* exercitatio (= exercise, both physical and other, e.g. *exerc. dicendi,* in speaking); see EDUCATION.

trait, n. 1, = a touch, *linea* (e.g. *primis velut lineis alqd designare*); 2, in a person's character, by adjs. ; an excellent —, *praeclarum* (e.g. *praec. hoc quoque Thrasybuli*), or by *proprius,* followed by genit. (e.g. *quod oratoris proprium est*), or by genit. and *est* (e.g. *sapientis est,* = it is the — of a wise man).

traitor, n. *proditor, majestatis* or *perduellionis reus* (= one accused of high treason). **traitorous,** adj. see TREACHEROUS.

trammel, n. and v.tr. see FETTER.

tramp, I. v.intr. see TRAVEL, WALK. **II.** n. 1, *iter* (= journey); 2, *grassator* (= footpad).

trample, v.tr. and intr. (*pedibus*) (*con*)*culcare alqd;* fig. to — under foot, *deridēre* (= to turn into ridicule, persons or things, e.g. religion, *res divinas*), *opprimĕre;* see TREAD, DESPISE, OPPRESS.

trance, n. *secessus, -ūs mentis et animi a corpore, animus a corpore abstractus.*

tranquil, adj. *tranquillus.* **tranquillity,** n. *tranquillitas* (lit. and fig.); see QUIET, CALM. **tranquillize,** v.tr. *tranquillare.*

transact, v.tr. business, *rem gerĕre, agĕre, transigĕre;* see DO. **transaction,** n. *res, negotium;* see BUSINESS.

transcend, v.tr. *praestare alci alqā re,* (*ex*)*superare alqm, excellĕre alci* (*in alqā re*) or *inter alqos;* see EXCEL, SURPASS. **transcendent,** adj. *praestans, singularis, eximius;* see EXCELLENT. **transcendental,** adj. *quod sensu oi sensibus percipi non potest, quod sub sensus non cadit, quod sensibus non subjectum est.*

transcribe, v.tr. *transcribĕre;* see COPY. **transcript,** n. *exemplum* (= copy).

transfer, I. v.tr. *tra*(*ns*)(*j*)*icĕre,* (lit. *legiones in Siciliam*), *tra*(*ns*)*ducĕre* (lit.), *transportare* (lit.), *transferre* in with accus. (lit. *bellum in Italiam;* then = to translate into another tongue, e.g. *ex Graeco in Latinum;* then = to use in a fig. sense, e.g. a word, *verbum;* = to put on another, e.g. *culpam in alqm*), *transmittĕre* in with accus. (= to send over, across as it were, e.g. the war into Italy), *transfundĕre in* or *ad* with accus. (= to pour out of one vessel into another, e.g. *amorem in alqm, omnes suas laudes ad alqm*) ; = to make over, as a right, (*con*)*cedĕre alqd alci, transcribĕre alqd,* to anyone, *alci* (in writing, Jct.); to — a part of, *cedĕre alci alqd de alqā re.* **II.** n. *translatio* (= the act of —ing), *mancipium* (of property).

transferable, adj. *quod in alqm concedĕre licet.*
transference, n. *tra(ns)latio.*

transfiguration, n. *transfiguratio* (Eccl.).
transfigure, v.tr. *(com)mutare;* his countenance was—d at these words, *quibus dictis ejus facies serēnior facta est; transfigurare* (Eccl.).

transfix, v.tr. 1, *transfigĕre, (con)fodĕre;* 2, fig. *defigĕre (alqm gladio).*

transform, v.tr. *totum denuo fingĕre* (lit. = to form anew); to — into *transformāre in alqm* or *in aliud, (con)vertĕre in alqm* or *algd* (e.g. *in canem), (com)mutare;* see CHANGE. **transformation**, n. use verb.

transfuse, v.tr. *transfundĕre.* **transfusion**, by the verb.

transgress, **I.** v.tr. *transcendĕre* (e.g. *jus gentium, morem), violare* (e.g. *foedus, jus gentium).* **II.** v.intr. *ab officio discedĕre, algd contra leges facĕre.* **transgression**, n. *violatio* with gen. (= the act of —, e.g. *juris gentium, foederis), peccatum, delictum* (= fault, etc.); see CRIME, FAULT. **transgressor**, n. *violator alcjs rei,* or by verb; see also CRIMINAL.

transient, adj. *brevis, fugax, caducus, instabilis, mutabilis, fluxus, incertus.* **transit**, n. *transitus, -ūs* (in gen. = the best word for — of a planet); goods for —, *merces ad alios populos transeuntes;* — duty, *portorium;* — in a general sense, see PASSAGE. **transition**, n. *transitio* (from one party to another, etc.), *transitus, -ūs* (lit., and in Quint. fig. of words, etc.), *transgressio* (lit. rare), *trajectio, tra(ns)jectus, -ūs* (lit.). **transitive**, adj. in gram., a — verb, *verbum transitivum.* **transitory**, adj. see TRANSIENT.

translate, v.tr. into another language, *(con)vertĕre* (in gen.), *transferre* (word for word, Quint.), *reddĕre* (= to render accurately), *interpretari* (= to interpret); to — into Latin, *in Latinum (con)vertĕre, Latine reddĕre;* lit., faithfully, exactly, *verbum e verbo* or *de verbo exprimĕre, verbum pro verbo reddĕre.* **translation**, n. *liber scriptoris conversus* or *tra(ns)latus;* — of a speech, *oratio conversa.* **translator**, n. *interpres, -ētis,* m. and f.

translucent, adj. *pellucidus;* see TRANSPARENT.

transmarine, adj. *transmarinus.*

transmigration, n. by circumloc. (e.g. — of souls, *animarum in nova corpora (quasi) migratio).*

transmit, v.tr. *mittĕre alci* or *ad alqm.* **transmission**, n. *missio,* or by verb.

transmute, v.tr. see CHANGE.

transom, n. *tignum transversum* or *transversarium, transtrum.*

transparent, adj. 1, *pellucidus, tra(ns)lucidus, perspicuus;* to be —, *pellucēre, lucem transmittĕre;* 2, fig. *evidens, manifestus;* see CLEAR. Adv. *evidenter, sine dubio, manifeste.* **transparency**, n. *vitri pelluciditas* (Vitr.), *perspicuitas.*

transpire, v.intr. 1, *exhalari, emanare;* 2, = to escape from secrecy, *(di)vulgari, pervulgari, efferri (foras* or *in vulgas), percrebrescĕre.*

transplant, v.tr. *transferre* (= to remove persons and things elsewhere, e.g. *omnes nobiles familias Romam;* also plants, e.g. *brassicam), tra(ns)ducĕre* (e.g. *populum Albanum Romam, gentem in Galliam).* **transplantation**, n. *tra(ns)latio.*

transport, **I.** v.tr. 1, *transportare* (by land and by water, persons and things), *transferre* (= to bring across, things), *transmittĕre, tra(ns)jicĕre* (= to send across the water, persons and things);

= to send to penal settlement, *relegare;* see BANISH; 2, fig. to be —ed (with delight, etc.), *efferri, ex(s)ultare,* or by special verb (e.g. *gaudēre).* **II.** n. 1, *navigium vectorium, navicula vectoria* (= a ship for crossing), *navis oneraria* (= ship of burden); 2, *animus gaudio* or *laetitiā gestiens;* see RAPTURE. **transportation**, n. 1, by verb; 2, see BANISHMENT.

transpose, v.tr. *transmutare* (e.g. words, letters, Quint.). **transposition**, n. *tra(ns)jectio* (of words), *transmutatio* (Quint.).

transubstantiation, n. by *transubstantiatio* (Eccl.).

transverse, adj. *transversus, transversarius* (lying across). Adv. *transverse, e transverso.*

trap, **I.** n. *muscipulum* or *muscipula* (Phaed., mouse- —), *laqueus* (= noose, —, lit. and fig.); see SNARE. **II.** v.tr. *irretire* (lit. and fig.); see ENSNARE. **trap-door**, n. *(parva) janua.*

trappings, n. *ornamentum, ornatus, -ūs, equorum* (in gen.), *phalerae* (= horses' head and neck ornaments).

trash, n. 1, *quisquiliae* (= sweepings), *viles* or *vilissimae res;* see WASTE; 2, = nonsense, *gerrae, nugae.* **trashy**, adj. see WORTHLESS.

travail, **I.** v.tr. *parturire.* **II.** n. *dolor quem in puerperio alqs perpetitur,* in the context simply *dolores* (Ter.); in —, by *parturire.*

travel, **I.** v.tr. *iter facĕre* (in gen.), *peregrinari* (abroad), *proficisci in* or *ad* or *circa, obire, circumire* (with accus.), *peragrare, perlustrare.* **II.** n. *iter, itĭneris,* n. (in gen.), *peregrinatio* (abroad). **traveller**, n. *iter faciens, viator* (= wanderer on foot), *vector* (= passenger on board a vessel), *peregrinator, peregrinans* (= one who travels or resides abroad).

traverse, v.tr. 1, see CROSS; 2, = to wander over, *pervagari* (intentionally), *obire,* † *pererrare* (without a defined purpose), *peragrare. lustrare, perlustrare.*

travesty, n. see PARODY.

tray, n. *ferculum.*

treacherous, adj. *perfĭdus, perfidiosus, infĭdēlis, infĭdus, fallax, dolosus* (= cunning), *subdolus* (in a bad sense, = sly). Adv. *perfĭdiose, dolose;* see FAITHLESS. **treachery**, n. *proditio* (= betrayal of a town, etc.; also *amicitiarum,* Cic.), *perfĭdia, fraus, -dis,* f., *dolus (malus), infidēlitas.*

treacle, n. *condimentum ex saccharo factum.*

tread, **I.** v.intr. *ingredi;* to — in the footsteps of anyone, *alcjs vestigiis ingredi;* see WALK. **II.** v.tr. to — upon, *calcare;* to — under foot, fig. *obterĕre (et calcare)* (e.g. *libertatem), conculcare, proculcare* (lit. = to trample down; then fig., e.g. *senatum, Italiam).* **III.** n. *(in)gressus, -ūs, vestigium, pēs, pĕdis,* m. ; trodden path, *via trita.*

treason, n. *majestas, majestatis (laesae* or *minutae) crimen;* to commit —, *majestatem minuĕre* or *laedĕre.* **treasonable**, adj., adv. by circumloc. with *majestas* (e.g. accused of treason, *laesae majestatis accusatus).*

treasure, **I.** n. *thesaurus, gaza* (lit. = treasury of the Persian king, then of any foreign prince), *opes, -um, divitiae* (= riches), *copia* (= quantity, store). **II.** v.tr. *accumulare, coacervare* (= to heap up money, —s), *condĕre, repōnĕre* (= to store). **treasure-house**, n. *thesaurus.* **treasurer**, n. *praefectus aerarii* (Plin.). **treasury**, n. *aerarium.*

treat, **I.** v.tr. = to be engaged in anything, *tractare alqm* or *algd, curare alqm* or *algd* (= to attend to), *disputare, disserĕre de algā re, prosequi algd* (on a learned subject); to — a case (of illness), *curare morbum;* to — a patient, *alqm tractare, curare;* = to behave towards anyone, *alqm habēre, alqd re afficēre, alqo uti;* to — well, ill, etc., *bene, male,* etc. ; to — as an enemy, *(in) hostium numero habēre alqm, pro hoste habēre* or *ducēre alqm;* = to entertain, *invitare* (in gen.) ; see ENTERTAIN. **II.** v.intr. to — with (= to negotiate), *agēre cum alqo de alqâ re.* **III.** n. *delectatio* (= delight), *spectaculum* (= a show) ; to give anyone a —, perhaps *alqm* (*delectandi caus(s)â*) *invitare;* see ENTERTAINMENT. **treatise,** n. *disputatio, dissertatio* (on a learned topic ; class. only of oral discussion), *liber, libellus* (= the book in which a subject is treated). **treatment,** n. *tractatio, curatio* (= attending to) ; kind —, *comitas, humanitas;* cruel, unkind —, *saevitia;* mode of —, *tractatio, curatio.* **treaty,** n. *pactio, pactum* (= a legal contract between two contending parties, *pactio* as act, *pactum* = what has been stipulated), *conventio, conventus, -ūs* (= agreed upon, although not legally binding), *sponsio* (= a — of peace or alliance concluded between the generals of two belligerent States, but as yet without the sanction of the latter), *foedus, -ěris,* n. (= alliance sanctioned by the senate and the people) ; according to the —, *ex pacto, ex convento* (Cic.), *ex conventu,* comb. *ex pacto et convento;* to conclude a — with, *facěre* or *inire, icěre, ferire* or *pangěre;* to break a —, *foedus violare, rumpěre.*

treble, I. adj. 1, see THREE, TRIPLE ; 2, — voice, *vox* †*summa* or *acuta.* **II.** v.tr. *alqd triplex facěre.*

tree, n. *arbor,* f. ; apple-—, pear-—, etc., *malus,* f., *pirus,* f., etc. ; see under name of special fruit ; 2, see PEDIGREE.

trefoil, n. *trifolium* (Plin.).

trellis, n. see LATTICE.

tremble, v.intr. *treměre* (in gen.), *contremiscěre, intremiscěre* (all these, with fright, and both of persons and things), *micare* (= to have a tremulous motion, like flames, e.g. of the veins), *vacillare* (= to shake), *horrēre* (= to shudder with cold, fear, of persons); to — for fear of anything, *treměre alqd* (e.g. *virgas ac secures dictatoris*), *contremiscěre alqd* (e.g. *vincula*), *extimescěre alqd* (e.g. *periculum*); to cause to —, *alqd tremefacěre.* **trembling, I.** adj. *tremens, tremebundus* (in a single case), *tremulus* (= constantly). **II.** n. *tremor;* with —, *tremens;* without —, *intrepide.*

tremendous, adj. 1, *terribilis;* see TERRIBLE ; 2, *ingens, immanis.* Adv. *valde, vehementer, magnopere, maxime.*

tremulous, adj. see TREMBLING, I.

trench, I. n. *fossa;* see DITCH. **II.** v.tr. *fossam foděre* or *facěre;* to — upon, see ENCROACH.

trencher, n. see PLATE.

trepan, I. n. *modiolus* (Cels.). **II.** v.tr. *calvarium* or *os capitis modiolo perforare.*

trespass, I. v.intr., lit. *in alienum fundum ingredi* (Jct.); fig., see TRANSGRESS. **II.** n. 1, lit. use verb; 2, fig. *alcjs rei violatio* (the act), *injuria alci rei illata* (as a fact); see TRANSGRESS. **trespasser,** n. lit. *qui in alienum fundum ingreditur;* fig. *alcjs rei violator.*

tress, n. *comae* (= hair).

trial, n. *tentatio* (*tempt-*), *experimentum, experientia* (= the experience gained by the — one has made), *periclitatio* (with a risk), *periculum* (= experience gained with respect to anything, even with attending danger), *conatus, -ūs* (=attempt); to make a —, *periculum facěre alcjs rei;* — in law, *judicium, interrogatio* (= examination in court, e.g. of a witness), *quaestio* (as a whole) ; put on his —, *alqm postulare* or *accusare alcjs rei.* **try, v.tr.** *tentare* (= to — to find a thing out, what it

is, etc.), *expertri* (= to see how it answers, as the result of *tentare*), *periclitari* (with a risk, all the foregoing *alqm* or *alqd*), *periculum facěre alcjs* or *alcjs rei, explorare* (= to examine, to explore), *gustatu explorari alqd* (by tasting, wine, etc.); = to attempt, *tentare* (*tempt-*), *conari* (generally with infin. ; with respect to the beginning of an undertaking), (e)*niti ut* or *ne;* in law, to — a case, *judicare, cognoscěre* or *quaerěre de alqâ re.* **tried,** adj. *spectatus, cognitus, probatus,* comb. *spectatus et probatus.* **trying,** adj. *gravis, molestus;* see TROUBLESOME.

triangle, n. *trigōnum, triangulum.* **triangular,** adj. *triangulus, triquetrus* (= three-sided).

tribe, n. 1, *tribus, -ūs,* f. (= a division of the people among the Romans) ; by tribes, *tributim;* *fellow* —sman, *tribulis;* 2, in wider sense, *gens, populus;* see NATION. **tribal,** adj. by genit. of *tribus, -ūs,* or *gens.*

tribulation, n. *miseria, res miserae* or *afflictae;* see TROUBLE.

tribunal, n. 1, *tribunal* (= platform for the magistrates in the forum, e.g. in Rome for the praetor) ; 2, *judicium* (= COURT, which see); to summon anyone before a —, *alqm in judicium vocare.*

tribune, n. *tribunus militum* or *militaris* (= military —), *tribunus plebis* (of the people). **tribuneship,** n. *tribunatus, -ūs, tribunicia potestas.*

tribute, n. *tributum, vectīgal* (often in kind), *stipendium* (in money). **tributary, I.** adj. *vectigalis* (= paying taxes), *tributarius* (= paying poll and land tax), *stipendiarius* (= paying a certain sum annually, of persons, more particularly of States that pay —). **II.** n. — of a river, by circumloc. (e.g. a — of the Rhone, *flumen quod in Rhodanum influit*).

trick, I. n. *dolus* (=cunning), *fraus* (=deception), *ars, artificium* (=artifice), *machīna* (= stratagem), *techna* (Com.); all manner of —s, *astutiae;* conjuror's —, *praestigiae;* to play anyone a —, *dolum alci nectěre.* **II.** v.tr. and intr. see DECEIVE, DECEPTION. **trickery,** n. *fallacia;* see DECEPTION. **trickish,** adj. *versutus.*

trickle, v.intr. *manare,* †*rorare, stillare alqd re.*

trident, n. *tridens.*

triennial, adj. †*trietēricus.* **triennium,** n. *triennium.*

trifle, I. n. *res parva* or *parvula, res minuta, munusculum* (= a small present), *res parvi momenti* (= a matter, thing of trifling importance), often also by the adjs. *parvus, lēvis, perlevis;* —s, *res parvae* or *minutae, nugae* (the latter also of insignificant —) ; to buy anything for a —, *parvo* or *vili eměre.* **II.** v.intr. *lascivīri* (= to play), *nugari* (= to talk nonsense), *luděre* (= to play, to frolic), †*ineptire* (=to play the fool) ; to — opp. to act seriously, *alqd negligěre.* **trifler,** n. *nugator.* **trifling, I.** adj. *lēvis, parvus;* see UNIMPORTANT. **II.** n. *lascivia* (= playfulness), *nugae, ineptiae* (= absurdities), *ludus* (= game).

trigonometry, n. *trigonometria* (as t.t. not class.).

trilateral, adj. *tribus lateribus.*

trill, I. n. perhaps *vox* or *sonus vibrans* (Plin.). **II.** v.tr. the voice in singing, *vibrissare* (late).

trim, I. adj. see NEAT. **II.** v.tr. in gen. *alqd curare* (= to put in due order); = to decorate the body, etc., (*ex*)*ornare* (e.g. *variâ veste*); to — the hair, *reciděre* (= to lop off what is too long, e.g. *capillos*), (*de*)*tondēre* (= to cut off, shave, e.g.

the hair, hedges, etc.); to — trees, *arbores (amputare;* to — timber, etc. (in carpentry) *(asciâ) dolare, asciâ polire;* to — the sails, *vela facĕre, vela pandĕre.* **III.** v.intr. in politics, *consilia mutare,* or *fortunae inservire.* **IV.** n. 1, see DRESS, ORNAMENT; 2, of a ship, perhaps by *navis suis ponderibus librata.* **trimmer,** n. *qui consilia mutat.* **trimming,** n. *clavus* (= a stripe of purple on the robes of the senators and equites), *ornatus, -ûs, ornamentum* (= ornament).

trimeter, n. *versus (-ûs) trimetrus (trimetros).*

Trinity, n. *trinitas* (Eccl.). **Trinitarian,** n. *qui triplicem Dei naturam esse dicit.*

trinket, n. *an(n)ulus* (= ring), *torques, -is,* m. and f. (= necklace), or by other special noun; in pl. *mundus (muliebris)* collectively.

trio, n. = three together, *tres, tria;* in music, *concentus (-ûs) trium vocum.*

trip, I. v.intr. 1, *offendĕre;* 2, fig. *errare, labi, labi et cadĕre, offendĕre;* to — along, *celeriter ire.* **II.** v.tr. *supplantare alqm.* **III.** n. 1, see STUMBLE; 2, ERROR; 3, = a journey, *iter;* see JOURNEY, EXCURSION.

tripartite, adj. *tripartītus (triper-).*

tripe, n. *omāsum* (= the thick fat intestines of a bullock, Schol. Hor. Ep.), *omentum porci* (Juv.).

triple, adj. *triplex;* see under THREE.

tripod, n. *tripus.*

trireme, n. *(navis) trirēmis.*

trisyllable, n. *trisyllābum verbum.*

trite, adj. (= often repeated, worn), *(con)trītus, communis, communis et contritus.*

triumph, I. n. 1, in honour of a Roman victory, *triumphus;* to celebrate a —, *triumphare, triumphum agĕre* or *habĕre, ovare* (if inferior to a —); to celebrate a — over anybody or over a people, *de alqo* or *ex alqâ terrâ triumphare;* 2, fig. *victoria* (= a victory), *ex(s)ultatio, laetitia, gaudium* (= joy). **II.** v.intr. 1, *triumphare, triumphum agĕre* or *habĕre, ovare* (of a lesser triumph), over, *de alqo;* 2, fig. *ex(s)ultare, laetari;* over anyone, *vincĕre alqm.* **triumphal,** adj. 1, = belonging to a Roman triumph, *triumphalis;* — procession, *triumphus;* in a —, *in triumpho, per triumphum, triumphans;* 2, fig. or **triumphant,** = victorious, *victor;* = in high spirits, *gestiens, elatus, ex(s)ultans.*

triumvir, n. *triumvir.* **triumvirate,** n. *triumviratus, -ûs.*

trivial, adj. by *(con)trītus, communis, lēvis, parvi momenti;* see TRIFLING. **triviality,** n. by adj.

trochee, n. *trochaeus.*

troop, I. n. *caterva, grex;* —s, *globus, manus, copiae, milites, manus, -ûs,* f., *ala* (of horse), *cohors* = cohort). **II.** v.intr. *convenire, coire, confluĕre.* **trooper,** n. *eques, -itis,* m.; see CAVALRY, HORSE.

trope, n. *verbum tra(ns)latum, verbi tra(ns)latio, tropus* (Quint.).

trophy, n 1, *tropaeum;* 2, fig. see MEMORIAL.

tropical, adj. 1, = fig. *tra(ns)latus;* 2, = belonging to the Tropics, by genit. of noun; see TROPIC; — heat, *aestus, -ûs, ardentissimus.* **tropic,** n. in astronomy, *circulus, orbis,* m. ; — of Cancer, *circulus solstitialis;* of Capricorn, *circulus brumalis;* the —s, = very hot countries, *regiones torridae.*

trot, I. v.tr. *citato gradu* or perhaps *tolutim ire* (of a horse), *citato equo vehi* (of the rider). **II.** n. *gradus, -ûs, citatus, gradus tolutilis.*

troth, n. *fides;* to plight —, *fidem alci dare.*

troubadour, n. *poëta amatorius* (as poet), *citharoedus* (as singer).

trouble, I. v.tr. *agitare* (= to set in motion, e.g. water, wind; hence of the mind, to torment), *exagitare* (= to drive from one place to another, neighbours, the State, also of the conscience), *commovēre* (= to disturb), *(con)turbare, perturbare* (= to confuse anyone, or anyone's mind) ; = to afflict, *sol(l)icitare, sol(l)icitum habēre, sol(l)icitudine* or *aegritudine afficĕre, sol(l)icitudinem* or *aegritudinem alci afferre, alqm vexare, angĕre, excruciare alcjs animum et sol(l)icitare;* may I — you to hand me this book, *des mihi, quaeso, hunc librum;* to — oneself about anything, *alqd curare;* not to — about anything, *alqd neglegĕre;* to — anyone with entreaties, *alqm precibus obtundĕre* or *fatigare.* **II.** n. 1, = disturbance of mind, *animi motus, -ûs, perturbatio, sol(l)icitudo* (= painful anxiety), *angor* (= anxiety, anguish); 2, = molestation, *labor, molestia, onus, -ĕris* (= burden), *incommodum* (= inconvenience), *difficultas* (= difficulty); see ANNOYANCE; to give — to, *molestiam alci afferre;* see under I. ; 3, = pains, *opera;* to take — over anything, *alci rei operam dare;* great —, *omnibus viribus contendĕre ut;* with great —, *aegre, vix;* without —, *sine negotio.* **troubler,** n. *turbator,* or by verb. **troublesome,** adj. *molestus, gravis* (= giving great trouble), *incommodus, iniquus* (= inconvenient), *durus* (= hard), *operosus, laboriosus* (= laborious), *odiosus* (of what we hate), *difficilis* (of what has its difficulties), comb. *gravis et incommodus, gravis et odiosus, laboriosus molestusque, odiosus et molestus.*

trough, n. *alveus.*

trousers, n. *brac(c)ae.*

trowel, n. *trulla* (late, but *trullissare,* = to use a —, Vitr.).

truant, adj. and n. by *qui ludo lit(t)erarum abest.*

truce, n. *indutiae.*

truck, n. 1, = barter, *(per)mutatio rerum;* 2, see BARROW.

truckle, v.intr. *morem alci gerĕre* (= to please), *alci assentire.*

trudge, v.intr. see WALK.

true, adv. *vērus; sincērus, germanus* (the two foregoing = genuine), comb. *verus et sincerus, verax* (= veracious), *fidus, fidēlis* (= faithful); in answers, — ! *certe;* see YES ; as — as I live, I know, *ita vivam, ut scio;* as — as I live, I don't know, *ne vivam si scio.* Adv. *vere, sincere, profecto* (= certainly), *sane, certe, certe quidem;* see REALLY. **trueborn, truebred,** adj. (e.g. Englishman), *verus et sincerus* (e.g. Stoicus), *germanus.* **truehearted,** adj. *fidelis, simplex.* **trueheartedness,** n. *(animi) fidelitas, simplicitas.* **truth,** n. *vēritas* (as quality), *vērum* (= what is —) ; to speak —, *verum, vera dicĕre;* strict —, *summa veritas;* historical —, *historiae fides* (Ov.) ; according to —, *ex re;* in —, *vero, sine dubio, profecto, plane, enimvero,* or as two words, *enim vero;* see INDEED, REALLY. **truthful,** adj. *verus, verax, veridicus* (rare). Adv. see IN TRUTH above. **truthfulness,** n. *veritas, veritatis studium* or *amor.*

trump, v.tr. and n. where possible use word from dice (e.g. *Venus, jactus, -ûs, venereus* or *basilicus*) ; a —, = good fellow, *optimus (homo).* **trump up,** v.tr. *fingĕre;* see INVENT.

trumpery, n. see TRASH, TRIFLE.

trumpet, I. n. *tuba* (straight), *bucina, lituus, cornu* (curved), *classicum* (usually = signal given by *cornu*) ; the — sounds, *classicum canit* (*canĕre* also in pass., *classicum cani jubet, Caes.*

so also *bellicum, canĕre* and *cant); to sound the — for retreat, receptui canĕre.* **II. v.tr. fig. =** to propagate praise, *bucinatorem esse alcjs rei, alqd praedicare.* **trumpeter,** n. *tubicen, bucinator;* fig. *bucinator.*

truncheon, n. *scipio;* = cudgel, *fustis,* m.

trundle, v.tr. *volvĕre.*

trunk, n. 1, of a tree, *truncus, stirps;* 2, of the body, *truncus* (often *corpus* can be used); 3, = chest, *arca;* see CHEST; 4, of an elephant, *manus, -ūs* (Cic.), *proboscis* (Plin.).

truss, n. = bandage, *fascia;* — of hay, *fascis.*

trust, I. n. 1, = confidence, *fiducia, fides, spes firma* or *bona;* — in oneself, *fīdentia;* 2, anything —ed to anyone, *quod alci mandatum* (in gen.), *creditum* or *depositum est;* 3, = credit, i.e. to take on —, *fide suā emĕre.* **II. v.intr.** (*con)fīdĕre, credĕre, alci fretum esse algo* or *alqā re* (= to build on); not to —, *alci diffīdĕre.* **III. v.tr.** *alqd alci* (*con)credĕre, committĕre, commendare;* to — yourself altogether to, *se totum alci committĕre, omnia consilia tlci credĕre.*

trustee, n. *custos, administrator, procurator;* see TRUSTY. **trustworthiness,** n. *constantia, fides;* see under TRIAL. **trustworthy,** adj. *certus, firmus, constans* (opp. *varius, mobilis*), *certus et constans, firmus et constans, fīdus, fidēlis.*

tub, n. *dolium, mulctra* (= milk-pail), *labrum* (= vat).

tube, n. *tubus;* see PIPE.

tuber, n. *tuber, -ēris,* n. (= anything that protrudes, more esp. a bump, swelling). **tubercle, n.** (in anatomy), *tuberculum* (Cels.). **tuberous, adj.** *tuberosus.*

tuck, I. v.tr. to — up a garment, *succingĕre;* the hair, *comam in nodum † religare, capillos in nodum † colligĕre.* **II.** n. see FOLD.

Tuesday, n. **dies Martis.*

tuff, n. *tophus* (*tofus*).

tuft, n. e.g. a — of hair, *crinis* (or pl. *crines*), of wool, *floccus;* a — of grass, *fasciculus* (of flowers, also of flax); a — of feathers, *crista* (= — or plume on the head of a bird, comb of a cock, crest or plume of a helmet). **tufted,** adj. *cristatus.*

tug, I. v.tr. *trahĕre.* **II.** n. *navis quae aliam navem trahit.*

tuition, n. see INSTRUCTION.

tulip, n. **tulipa.*

tumble, I. v.intr. = to roll about, *volutari* (e.g. *in luto*), *se volvere;* see FALL. **II.** v.tr. *omnia perturbare* or *miscēre.* **III.** n. see FALL.

tumbler, n. 1, = acrobat, *petaurista,* m.; 2, = glass, *poculum;* 3, see PIGEON.

tumid, adj. *tumidus, inflatus, turgens, tumens;* — words, *ampullae* (Hor.).

tumour, n. *tumor, tuber, -ēris,* n. (= any swelling), *struma* (= scrofulous —).

tumult, n. 1, = great noise, *tumultus, -ūs, tumultuatio* (rare), *strepitus, -ūs;* see NOISE; 2, = excitement of the mass, *seditio, motus, -ūs, concitatio* (e.g. *plebis contra patres), tumultus, -ūs* (in the Roman sense, of any rising of a conquered tribe, e.g. of the slaves, the country people, the allies, etc., against the Romans themselves); see REBELLION. **tumultuary, tumultuous,** adj. *tumultuosus, turbulentus* (= turbulent), comb. *seditiosus et turbulentus* (e.g. *civis);* see DISORDERLY, NOISY. Adv. *tumultuose, turbulente.*

tumulus, n. *tumulus.*

tun, n. *dolium, cupa* (= cask), **as liquid measure** use *centum urnae;* see TON.

tune, I. n. = a short air, *cantus, -ūs, carmen* (= song), *modi, numeri, moduli;* to be in —, *concentum servare;* out of —, *absonus.* **II. v.tr.** a musical instrument, *fides ita contendĕre nervis ut concentum servare possint* (Cic.). **tuneful,** adj. *canōrus, musicus;* see MUSICAL. **tuner, n.** by the verb. **tuning,** n. by the verb.

tunic, n. *tunica.*

tunnel, I. n. *cuniculus.* **II. v.tr.** *cuniculum facĕre.*

tunny, n. *thynnus* or *thunnus* (Plin.).

turban, n. *mitra.*

turbid, adj. *turbidus* (= disturbed, **e.g** *aqua;* well, *scaturigo;* weather, sky, *caelum*).

turbot, n. *rhombus.*

turbulence, n. *omnium rerum perturbatio, tumultus, -ūs;* see TUMULT. **turbulent, adi** *turbulentus.*

tureen, n. *patina.*

turf, n. *caespes, -ĭtis,* m. (= sward, sod).

turgid, adj. *tumidus;* see TUMID.

turmoil, n. *turba;* see TUMULT.

turn, I. v.tr. to — a wheel, etc., (*con)torquēre, circumagĕre* (round, e.g. hand-mills), *distorquēre* (in different directions); to — anything round, *in orbem torquēre* or *circumagĕre, † rotare* (like a wheel); *vertĕre* (e.g. *navem, currum), convertĕre* (quite round, stating the *terminus ad quem,* hence with *ad* or *in* with accus.), *versare* (lit. = to twirl about, fig. *mentem ad omnem malitiam,* etc.), *flectĕre* (= to bend, lit. and fig.), *circumvertĕre, intorquēre* (round towards one side, e.g. *oculos ad alqd), retorquēre* (back, e.g. *oculos ad alqd);* to — one's back, (*con)verti, se* (*con)vertĕre* (lit. *terga* (*con)vertĕre* = to take to flight, of soldiers), *abire, decedĕre, discedĕre* (= to go away); to — the mind to, *animum ad alqd advertĕre,* **or** in one word *alqd animadvertĕre;* to — the scale, by *facĕre ut altera lanx deprimatur* (lit. or fig.); to — a coat, *vestem refĭcĕre;* to — with a lathe, *tornare;* = to change, e.g. to — goods into money, *vendĕre;* see SELL, TRANSFORM, CHANGE; to — one's eyes upon, *oculos con(ĵ)icĕre in alqd;* to — away, *dimittĕre* (= send away); see DISMISS; to — out; see EXPEL; to — over; see TRANSFER, CONSIDER. **II.** v.intr. *se* (*con)vertĕre,* (*con)verti;* to — from side to side, *se versare* (of one who does not know what to do or to say); see CHANGE, BECOME; to — away, *se avertĕre;* to — back, *redire, reverti;* to — in, *cubitum ire;* see BED; to — into; see CHANGE, BECOME; to — off, *deflectĕre, declinare de alqā re;* to — out; see BECOME; to — out well (of a thing), *bene* or *belle evenire, bene* or *prospere cadĕre, prospere procedĕre* or *succedĕre;* very well, *alci res fauste, feliciter prospereque evenire;* head —s round, by *vertigine laborare;* of leaves, *colorem mutari.* **III.** n. 1, *rotatio* (of a wheel); see TURNING; 2, see WINDING; 3, see CHANGE; 4, of affairs, things take a good —, *res in meliorem statum conversa est;* things take a bad —, *res male vertit, omnia in pejorem partem vertuntur et mutantur;* 5, it is your —, *nunc tuae sunt partes;* 6, in a fig. sense, e.g. the — of thought; see FORM, CAST, SHAPE, MANNER; 7, in writing, etc., to give a good shape, etc., *sententiam apte conformare;* to give a more elegant —, *alqd elegantius dicĕre;* different —s, *variae figurae et verba.* **turn against, I.** v.tr. *alqm ab alqo alienare.* **II.** v.intr. *ab algo alienari.* **turn over, v.t.** see UPSET; to — a book, *librum evolvĕre;* to — a new leaf, *mores emendare.* **turncoat, n.** *qui de sententiā decedit, qui sententiam* or *consilium mutat.* **turner,** n. *qui alqd tornat.* **turning,** n. 1, *versatio* (e.g. *machinarum,*

Vitr.), *rotatio* (Vitr.), *circumactio* (round, Vitr.), *conversio, circumactus, -ūs, flexus, -ūs*(= bending), *declinatio* (= — aside, e.g. of the body); see DE-VIATION; **2,** = the art of —, *ars tornandi* ; **3,** of a road, or *flexus viae*, or *iter* or *via*. **turnkey,** n. *janitor* or *custos carceris*. **turnpike,** n. *taberna ad viarum vectigal exigendum constructa*, or perhaps *taberna vectigalis*.

turnip, n. *rapum*.

turpentine, n. *resina terebinthǐna* (Cels.).

turpitude, n. *turpitudo* ; see DISGRACE, SHAME.

turret, n. *turricula*.

turtle, n. 1, — -dove, *turtur* ; **2,** a fish, *tes-tudo* (= tortoise).

tush, interj. *st !*

tusk, n. *dens*.

tutelage, n. *tutēla* ; see PROTECTION. **tu-telary,** adj. — god, of a place, *deus praeses loci, deus qui loco praesidet, deus cujus tutelas or cujus in tutelā locus est* ; of a family, *penates, -ium*, m. (= the private gods in each separate home ; there were also *penates publici*, as pro-tectors of the city, the temples, etc.), *lares, -(i)um*, m. (= the house or family gods of the Romans). **tutor,** n. 1, see GUARDIAN ; 2, *magister, praeceptor* ; private —, *praeceptor do-mesticus* ; see TEACH.

twang, I. v.intr. e.g. bows, *crepare, crepi-tare, sonare*. **II.** n. *crepitus, -ūs, sonus, sonitus, -ūs*.

tweak, v.tr. *vellĕre, vellicare*.

tweezers, n. *volsella*.

twelve, adj. *duodecim, duodeni* (= — each), — times, *duodecie(n)s* ; — hundred, *mille et ducenti, milleni et ducenti* (= 1200 each, also 1200 in one sum, hence always with nouns that are used only in the pl.), — hundred times, *mil-lie(n)s et ducentie(n)s*. **twelfth,** adj. *duo-decimus* ; heir to the — part, *heres ex uncia*. **twelvemonth,** n. *annus*.

twenty, adj. *viginti, vicēni* (= — each). **twentieth,** adj. *vicēsimus*.

twig, n. *virga, surculus, rāmulus*.

twilight, n. *crepusculum* ; in the —, *crepus-culo, primo vespere*.

twin, n. and adj. *geminus* ; —s, *gemini*.

twine, I. v.tr. *circumvolvĕre, flectĕre, (in)tor-quēre* ; see TWIST. **II.** v.intr. *implicari, im-plecti* ; to — round anything, *alqd circumplecti, se circumvolvĕre alci rei* (= to wind round, e.g. *arbori*, of a plant). **III.** n. *linum* ; see STRING.

twinge, I. v.tr. *urĕre* ; see PINCH. **II.** n. *dolor, cruciatus, -ūs* ; sharp —s of pain, *acres dolorum morsus* ; — of conscience, *dolor*.

twinkle, v.intr. † *coruscare* (of a flame, a flash of lightning, of the rays of light), *micare* (= to glitter, of arms, stars, etc.), *fulgēre* (= to shine, to reflect rays of light, of arms, etc.), *scin-tillare* (= to sparkle, of the eyes, etc.). **twink-ling,** n. 1, *fulgor* (= brightness, e.g. *armorum*) ; 2, in the — of an eye, *temporis puncto*.

twirl, v.tr. *versare* ; see SPIN.

twist, I. v.tr. *(in)torquēre, obtorquēre* (in past part. *obtorta gula*, = twisted neck), *(in)flec-tĕre, nectĕre, texĕre* (= to form, put together, weave). **II.** v.intr. *se torquēre, flectĕre, torquēri, flecti*.

twit, v.tr. anyone with anything, *alqd alci ob(j)icĕre*.

twitch, v.intr. *vellĕre, vellicare*.

two, adj. *duo, bini* (= — each) ; a period of — days, *biduum* ; a period of — years, *biennium* ;

— -footed, † *bipes* ; —fold, *duplex* ; — -coloured, † *bicolor* ; —-headed, *biceps* ; —-edged, *bipennis* ; —-handed, *duas manus habens* ; — hundred, *ducenti, duceni* (= — hundred each). **twice,** adv. *bis* ; — as much, *bis tantum* ; — as great, *altero parte major*.

type, n. 1, = model, *exemplar, exemplum, forma* ; 2, = symbol, *figura, significatio, imago* (Eccl.) ; 3, = letters, *lit(t)erarum formae*. **typical,** adj. *typǐcus* (Eccl.). **typify,** v.tr. *alqd sensibus sub(j)icĕre, oculis* or *sub oculis (alcjs) sub(j)icĕre* ; see REPRESENT. **typogra-phical,** adj. e.g. — error, * *mendum typogra-phicum, erratum typographicum* (not class.).

tyrant, n. *tyrannus* (= a usurper) ; after-wards = a despot, anybody that is cruel, but in the latter sense always with an adj., such as *crudēlis, intolerandus, saevus et violentus*, e.g. *tyrannus saevissimus et violentissimus in suos,* Cic.), *dominus* (= sovereign ruler), comb. *dominus et tyrannus* ; in gen. sense, = cruel person, *homo crudelis (saevus,* etc.). **tyrannical,** adj. *tyran-nicus* (of usurpers, despotic, e.g. laws, deeds, cruelty), *crudēlis* (= cruel). Adv. *tyrannice* (= in a despotic manner, e.g. *statuĕre* = to act as master, judge, etc. *in alqm,* Cic.), *crudēliter* (= cruelly). **tyrannize,** v.intr. to — over anyone, *tyrannicā crudelitate importune vexare alqm* (of a people, a country, Just.), *tyrannice in alqm statuĕre* ; to — over a State, *civitatem servitute oppressam tenēre*. **tyranny,** n. *tyrannis, -idis,* f., or in pure Latin *dominatio* or *dominatus, -ūs,* or *domi-natus regius* (of a usurper), *dominatio crudēlis* or *impotens* or *superba* or *crudelis superbaque* (implying a cruel government), *crudelitas* (= cruelty in gen.).

tyro, n. see TIRO.

U.

ubiquity, n. *omnipraesentia* (Eccl.), or by *qui (quae, quod) omnibus locis praesens est*. **ubiquitous,** adj. *omnibus locis praesens*.

udder, n. *uber, -ěris,* n.

ugly, adj. *dēformis* (= disfigured), *turpis* (= shameful), *tēter* (= nasty), *obscēnus* (= ob-scene), *foedus* (= abominable, horrible : all both lit. and fig., of persons and things). Adv. *dē-formiter* (e.g. *sonare*), *turpiter, tēterrime, obscēne, foede*. **ugliness,** n. *dēformitas, turpitudo* (= moral —), *obscēnitas foeditas*.

ulcer, n. *ulcus* ; see ABSCESS. **ulcerate, I.** v.intr. *suppurare* (Plin.). **II.** v.tr. *ulcerare*. **ulcerous,** adj. *ulcerosus* (Tac.).

ulterior, adj. = further, *ulterior* ; see FURTHER ; of places, objects, etc., *quae rel(l)iquae sunt, quae restant,* or by *alia, cetera*.

ultimate, adj. *extrēmus, ultimus* ; see FUR-THEST, LAST, FINAL. Adv. *ad extrēmum, ad ultimum, postremo* ; see LAST, END. **ultima-tum,** n. perhaps *extrēma conditio*.

ultra, Latin, only in composition ; to be —-Tory, *ultra modum optimatium partes am-plecti*.

ultramarine, n. *color caeruleus* or *cyaneus* (Plin.).

umbrage, n. 1, see SHADE ; 2, fig. to give — to, by *alqs alqd aegre* or *moleste fert* or *parti-tur, in offensionem alcjs cadĕre* ; to take — at, *fastidire alqd* (= to disdain) ; see OFFENCE. **umbrageous,** adj. see SHADY.

umbrella, n. *umbella* (= parasol, Mart., **Juv.**), † *umbraculum* (Ov.).

umpire, n. *arbiter* (= arbitrator); decision of an —, *arbitrium.*

un-, a prefix, as a particle of negation or of privation; by the prefix *in* (e.g. *ingratus*), or by *non* (when a thing cannot and does not exist), or by *sine* with a noun in the ablat.

unabashed, adj. 1, = firm, *constans, firmus, interritus;* 2, = shameless, *impudens.*

unabated, adj. *integer* (= whole).

unable, adj. by circumloc. with *non posse, nequire.*

unaccented, adj. *syllaba sine accentu enuntiata.*

unacceptable, adj. *ingratus.*

unaccompanied, adj. 1, *solus, incomitatus, sine comitatu;* see ALONE; 2, of the voice, *sine symphoniâ* (Plin.).

unaccomplished, adj. *imperfectus, inchoatus* (= only commenced); to leave anything —, *alqd inchoatum* or *imperfectum ac rude relinquĕre.*

unaccountable, adj. see INEXPLICABLE.

unaccustomed, adj. *insuetus* (of persons and things), to anything, *alcjs rei* or *ad alqd, insolitus* (of persons and of things, opp. *solitus,* e.g. *labor, spectaculum, verba*), *insolens* (of persons, also = unusual, e.g. *verbum*), to anything, *alcjs rei* or *in alqâ re* (e.g. *vera audiendi,* and *in dicendo*), *inexpertus,* to anything, *ad alqd.*

unacquainted, adj. with anything, *alcjs rei ignarus* (= who does not understand how to do any particular thing), *imperitus alcjs rei* (= inexperienced), *inscius* (= ignorant of anything), *rudis alcjs rei* or *in alqâ re.*

unadorned, adj. *inornatus* (in gen.), *incomptus* (e.g. *caput;* then = without rhetorical ornament, e.g. speech), *simplex* (e.g. *crinis*), *parus* (of style, language, in Cic. generally = free from foreign terms and constructions).

unadulterated, adj. *sincĕrus* (= quite genuine), *integer* (= free from spurious mixtures), opp. *vitiatus*), comb. *sincerus integerque, incorruptus* (= incorrupt, pure, e.g. *sensus, fides*).

unadvisable, adj. *inutilis* (= useless), *temerarius, inconsultus* (= rash), *quod sine consilio fit, quod alci parum prodest.* **unadvised,** adj. *inconsideratus, imprudens, temerarius, inconsultus.* Adv. *sine consilio, inconsiderate, imprudenter, temere, inconsulte.*

unaffected, adj. 1, = simple, *simplex* (e.g. *cibus,* also of words), *candidus* (= clear, without hypocrisy, of words and of the speaker), *inaffectatus* (of an orator, *jucunditas alcjs,* Quint.); — ease and grace (in speeches, etc.), *genus dicendi candidum, simplicitas* (in manners); 2, = not moved, *immotus, constans;* to remain — under, etc., *non affici,* or more strongly (*com*)*moveri alqâ re.* Adv. *simpliciter, sine fuco ac fallaciis.*

unaffrighted, adj. *interritus.*

unaided, adj. *sine auxilio, nullius auxilio adjutus, non adjutus.*

unalienable, adj. *qui* (*quae, quod*) *alienari non potest.*

unalleviated, adj. *non mītigatus;* see ALLEVIATE.

unallowable, adj. *illicitus.*

unalloyed, adj. *purus* (lit.), *sincĕrus* (fig.).

unaltered, adj. *immutatus, integer* (as before), or by *non mutari.*

unambitious, adj. *modestus,* or by circumloc. *qui honores non petit.*

unamiable, adj. *difficilis;* see ILL-TEMPERED.

unanimity, n. *consensio, consensio sententiarum, concordia;* see AGREE, CONCORD.

unanimous, adj. *concors, unanimus.* Adv. *unâ voce, unâ mente;* to defend a person —, *uno animo atque unâ voce alqm defendĕre;* — to demand battle, *proelium poscĕre; communi sententiâ statuĕre alqd; ad unum omnes decernunt,* = they all to a man determine; *cunctis populi suffragiis consulem declarari,* = to be appointed Consul —; *omnium in unum congruerunt sententiae,* = all were of one opinion; *omnibus sententiis absolvi, condemnari,* = to be acquitted, to be condemned —.

unanswerable, adj. *qui* (*quae, quod*) *refelli non potest.* **unanswered,** adj. to leave or remain —, by *ad alqm non respondĕre* (of anything said or written), *ad alqd non rescribĕre* (with regard to something written).

unappalled, adj. *interritus.*

unappeased, adj. *non satiatus.*

unapproachable, adj. of places, *invius;* of persons, *ad quem aditus, -ûs, difficilis est.*

unarmed, adj. *inermis, inermus* (of things), *nudus.*

unasked, adj. (*suâ*) *sponte, ultro.*

unassuming, adj. *modestus;* see MODEST.

unattainable, adj. *quod attingi non potest.*

unattempted, adj. to leave nothing —, *nihil inexpertum omittĕre, omnia experiri.*

unattended, adj. *incomitatus, sine comitibus.*

unauthentic, adj. *sine auctore editus* (e.g. a tale, *fabula*), *ab haud idoneis auctoribus vulgatus* (e.g. *fabula*), *sine ullo satis certo auctore allatus* (e.g. *rumor*), *incertus* (e.g. *rumor*).

unauthorized, adj. *illicitus;* to be — to do a thing, *faciendi alqd jus* or *potestatem non habēre, jure alqd facĕre non posse.*

unavailable, adj. *haud in medium prolatus, inutilis* (= useless). **unavailing,** adj. *irritus, vanus, fut(t)ilis.*

unavenged, adj. *inultus.*

unavoidable, adj. *inevitabilis,* better by *quod evitari non potest, quod evitare* or *effugĕre non possumus.*

unavowed, adj. see SECRET.

unaware, adj. *inscius, nescius, ignarus.*

unaware, unawares, adv. *inexpectatus, inopinatus* (when we least think of it or expect it), *inopinans* (= who does not suppose a thing to happen), *necopinatus* (= what we do not think even possible), *necopinans* (= who cannot suppose that such a thing would happen), *improvisus* (= unforeseen), comb. *improvisus atque inopinatus, insperatus* (of what we did not hope, unexpected), *subitus* (= sudden), *repentinus* (= sudden, what happens quickly and to our surprise), or by *praeter ex(s)pectationem* or *opinionem,* (*ex*) *inopinato, improviso,* (*ex*) *insperato.*

unawed, adj. *interritus.*

unbaked, adj. *crudus* (of bricks, Plin.), *panis non bene coctus* (of bread).

unbar, v.tr. *reserare.*

unbearable, adj. see INTOLERABLE.

unbeaten, adj. e.g. path, *non trītus.*

unbecoming, adj. see INDECOROUS.

unbefriended, adj. *auxilio* or *amici carens.*

unbeliever, n. *qui non credit* (*alqd esse,* etc.). **unbelieving,** adj. *incrēdulus;* see

ıbove. unbelief, n. see INCREDULITY, INFIDELITY.

unbeloved, adj. *non amatus.*

unbend, v.tr. 1, a bow, *arcum † retendĕre, remittĕre;* 2, the mind, *animum remittĕre, (re)laxare.* **unbendable,** adj. see INFLEXIBLE, FIRM.

unbewailed, adj. *† inflētus, † indēflētus, † indeploratus.*

unbiassed, adj. *simpler* (= without prejudice), *liber* (e.g. *liber in consulendo*), *solutus,* and chiefly comb. *liber et solutus* (= not bound by anything), *integer* (= free from partiality, e.g. *judicium*), comb. *integer ac liber* (e.g. *animus*), *impavidus* (= fearless).

unbidden, adj. *invocatus;* an — guest (whom anyone brings), *umbra* (Hor.); see SPONTANEOUS.

unbind, v.tr. *(dis)solvĕre, laxare* (= to loosen).

unblamable, adj. *integer, sanctus;* see BLAMELESS.

unbleached, adj. *nondum candidus.*

unblemished, adj. *purus, integer, in(con)taminatus* (= not stained by having been in contact), *innocens* (= innocent), *castus* (= morally pure).

unbloody, adj. *incruentus.*

unblushing, adj. 1, see BLUSH; 2, see IMPUDENT.

unborn, adj. *nondum natus.*

unborrowed, adj. see ORIGINAL, GENUINE.

unbosom, v.tr. *confitēri alqd, se alci patefacēre.*

unbought, adj. *non emptus, † inemptus.*

unbound, adj. of hair, *passus;* see also LOOSE.

unbounded, adj. 1, *infīnītus;* 2, fig. — passion, see IMMODERATE.

unbrace, v.tr. *(re)laxare.*

unbred, adj. *male moratus.*

unbribed, adj. *incorruptus, integer* (= impartial).

unbridled, adj. 1, of a horse, *infrēnatus, ɛffrēnatus, † infrēnis* or *infrēnus, † effrēnus;* 2, fig. *effrenatus;* see LICENTIOUS.

unbroken, adj. *integer* (= whole); of horses, *indomitus.*

unbrotherly, adj. *parum fraternus.*

unbuckle, v.tr. *diffibulare* (Stat.), *refībulare* (Mart.), *solvĕre* (e.g. knapsack, *sarcinas*).

unburden, v.tr. *exonerare* (lit. and fig.), *līberare, levare, solvĕre alqā re.*

unburied, adj. *inhumatus, insepultus.*

unburnt, adj. *crudus* (of bricks; Plin.).

unbutton, v.tr. the coat, *vestem discingĕre* (= ungirdle); see also UNDO.

uncalled, adj. *invocatus;* — for, *non petītus;* see UNNECESSARY.

uncancelled, adj. see CANCEL.

uncared, adj. — for, *neglectus.*

uncarpeted, adj. *sine stragulo.*

uncaused, adj. *sine caus(s)ā.*

unceasing, adj. *perpetuus, continuus, assiduus;* see INCESSANT.

unceremonious, adj. *simplex* (= natural), *parum comis* (= not polite), *agrestis, rusticus, inurbanus* (= rude); — habits, etc., *(morum) simplicitas.* Adv. *simpliciter, rustice, inurbane.*

29

uncertain, adj. *incertus* (also = indefinite), *dubius* (= doubtful), *anceps* (= doubtful as regards the issue, e.g. of a war; but never in the sense of a battle, etc.; see UNDECIDED), *ambiguus* (= ambiguous, not to be depended on, e.g. *fides*); to be —, *incertum* or *dubium esse* (in gen., of persons and things), *dubitare, vacillare, haerēre, haesitare, animi* or *animo pendēre, suspensum esse* (= to hesitate), *incertum alci esse, in incerto habēre* (in gen. of persons), *dubitatione aestuare* (= to be hesitating what to do), *in incerto* or *in dubio esse* (in gen. of things), *non satis constare* (= not to be quite certain yet, of things); all these verbs generally with an interrogative, such as *quid* and *utrum . . . an;* — what to do, *incertus quid faceret;* to make anything —, *alqd ad* or *incertum revocare, alqd in dubium (re)vocare;* to leave anything —, *alqd in medio* or *in incerto* or *in dubio relinquĕre;* to walk with — steps, *titubare;* see STAGGER. Adv. *incerte, incerto, temere* (= rashly). **uncertainty,** n. see UNCERTAIN.

unchain, v.tr. *e vinculis eximĕre, vincula solvĕre;* see LOOSEN.

unchangeable, adj. *stabilis, constans;* see IMMUTABLE. Adv. *stabiliter, constanter.* **unchangeableness,** n. *stabilitas, constantia;* see IMMUTABILITY. **unchanged,** adj. *immutatus, integer.*

uncharitable, adj. *durus* (in gen. = hard-hearted), *inhumanus, humanitatis expers* (= unkind, harsh). Adv. *inhumane, inhumaniter.* **uncharitableness,** n. *animus durus, ingenium inhumanum, inhumanitas.*

unchaste, adj. *impurus* (= impure), *incestus* (with regard to religion and moral purity), *impudicus* (= having no shame, indecent), *libidinosus* (= sensual, of persons and things, e.g. *amor*), *parum verēcundus* (= indiscreet, improper), *obscenus* (= obscene, foul); — love, *amor libidinosus, libīdines.* **unchastity,** n. *impuritas, impudicitia, libīdo.*

unchecked, adj. *liber.*

unchristian, adj. *contra legem Christianam.*

uncivil, adj. see IMPOLITE. **uncivility,** n. see IMPOLITENESS. **uncivilized,** adj. *rudis, fērus* (= wild), *barbarus* (= foreign, and so rude), *agrestis* (= uncultivated), *incultus* (= without culture), *inerudītus* (= uneducated, untaught), *indoctus* (= without literary education).

unclasp, v.tr. *refībulare* (Mart.); see LOOSEN.

uncle, n. *patruus* (= a father's brother), *avunculus* (= a mother's brother); great-—, *patruus* or *avunculus magnus.*

unclean, adj. 1, see DIRTY; 2, see UNCHASTE, FOUL.

unclouded, adj. *serēnus* (lit. and fig.).

uncoil, v.tr. *evolvĕre.*

uncoined, adj. *infectus.*

uncoloured, adj. 1, lit. *purus;* 2, fig. *sine fuco ac falaciis.*

uncombed, adj. *† impexus, horridus, in com(p)tus.*

uncomfortable, adj. *molestus, incommodus;* see UNEASY. Adv. *incommode.* **uncomfortableness,** n. *molestia.*

uncommanded, adj. *injussus, injussu alcjs, ultro, sponte (suā)* (= of one's free will).

uncommissioned, adj. 1, see UNCOMMANDED; 2, an — officer, *succenturio* or *o*

uncommon, adj. *rarus, insolitus, inusitatus* (= rare), *singulāris, mīrus, inaudītus* (= extraordinary); see RARE, EXCELLENT, EXTRAORDINARY. Adv. *raro, singulāriter, mīre;* see SELDOM.

uncommunicative, adj. *tectus;* see RESERVED.

uncomplaining, adj. *patiens.*

uncompleted, adj. *imperfectus.*

uncompounded, adj. *simplex.*

unconcerned, adj. *securus* at, about, for anything, *de alqā re* or *pro alqā re* (e.g. *de bello, bello, pro salute*), *neglegens alcjs rei* (e.g. *legis, amicorum*); to be —, *securum esse;* to be — about, *neglegēre* with accus. or by *bono esse unimo;* see INDIFFERENT.

unconditional, adj. *simplex, absolutus* (= Independent of anything else), mostly comb. *simplex et absolutus, purus* (= without any exception, e.g. *judicium,* Cic.). Adv. *simpliciter, absolute* (= without any limitation, Jct.).

uncongenial, adj. see UNPLEASANT.

unconnected, adj. **1,** lit. see SEPARATE; **2,** in speaking, *dissolutus, inconditus.*

unconquerable, adj. see INVINCIBLE. **unconquered,** adj. *invictus.*

unconscionable, adj. see UNREASONABLE. **unconscious,** adj. **1,** = insensible (*omni*) *sensu carens;* **2,** = ignorant, *inscius, ignārus;* I am not — of it, *non sum inscius, non me fugit, non me praeterit, non ignoro.* **unconsciousness,** n. **1,** by circumloc. with *sensu carēre;* **2,** by adj.

unconsecrated, adj. *non consecratus* (opp. *sacratus*), *profānus* (opp. *sacer*).

unconsidered, adj. *neglectus,* e.g. to leave nothing —, *omnia dīligenter circumspicĕre.*

unconstitutional, adj. *non legitimus, quod contra legem fit.*

unconstrained, adj. *līber.*

uncontaminated, adj. *in(con)taminatus.*

uncontested, adj. *quod sine certamine fit;* an — election, *comitia quibus alqs nullo competitore deligitur.*

uncontrollable, adj. *impotens* (of persons and things), *effrenatus* (= unbridled); see VIOLENT. **uncontrolled,** adj. *līber* (= free); — sovereignty, *dominatus, -ūs.*

unconverted, adj. *nondum ad legem Christianam adductus.*

unconvinced, adj. *non adductus ad credendum.*

uncooked, adj. *crudus, incoctus.*

uncork, v.tr. *relinĕre* (Plaut. and Ter. = to take the pitch off with which a jar was sealed), or perhaps *obturamentum extrahĕre.*

uncorrupt, adj. *incorruptus* (lit. and fig.).

uncourteous, adj. see RUDE.

uncouth, adj. of expression, *insolitus, insolens;* of manners, *incultus* (= inelegant, opp. *cultus,* e.g. *homo, mores*), *incultus moribus* (of persons), *immānis* (= savage), *agrestis, rusticus* (= rude). **uncouthness,** n. *immānitas, inhumanitas;* see KINDNESS.

uncover, v.tr. *detegĕre, retegĕre, aperire* (all also fig. of secrets, crimes, etc.), *nudare* (lit. = to strip off clothes; fig. to lay open); to — the head, *caput aperire* or *adaperire.*

unction, n. *unctio;* extreme —, *unctio extrema* (Eccl.); to speak with —, perhaps *speciose* or *speciosus dicĕre.* **unctuous,** adj. *pinguis;* of speech. perhaps *speciosus.*

uncultivated, adj. of soil, *incultus* (opp. *cultus* or *consitus*), *vastus* (*ab naturā et humanē cultu* = quite barren, e.g. mountain, Sall.); fig. *indoctus, rudis, agrestis.*

uncurbed, adj. see UNBRIDLED.

uncut, adj. † *immissus* (= suffered to grow, of trees, opp. *amputatus*), *intonsus* (= unshorn of the hair, then also of trees), *integer* (= from which nothing has been taken, whole).

undamaged, adj. *inviolatus* (= inviolate), *integer* (= still entire, whole).

undaunted, adj. *intrepidus;* see INTREPID.

undecayed, adj. *incorruptus.*

undeceive, v.tr. *errorem alci extrahĕre, eripĕre, extorquēre.*

undecided, adj. *nondum dijudicatus* (= not yet settled in court, e.g. *lis*), *integer* (= still unsettled, of a thing), *dubius* (= doubtful, both of the mind and of events), *incertus* (both of persons and things), *ambiguus, anceps* (= doubtful as regards the result, e.g. *belli fortuna, in dubio esse,* of things); I am — what to do, *dubius* or *incertus sum quid faciam;* I am — whether, etc., *incertus sum, utrum,* etc.; the lawsuit is still —, *adhuc de eā re apud judicem lis est;* h.s fate is still —, *non habet exploratam rationem salutis suae.*

undecked, adj. (= unadorned) *inornatus.*

undefended, adj. *indefensus* (of a city, also in Tac. of a lawsuit), *nudus* (= exposed to attack).

undefiled, adj. see UNBLEMISHED.

undefined, adj. *infīnitus.*

undeniable, adj. *ēvidens* (opp. *dubius*). Adv. *certe, certo, sine dubio.*

under, prep. expressing rest: **1,** standing — any place, *sub* (with ablat., e.g. *sub terrā, sub arbore;* with accus. it expresses the direction toward the lower part of anything; hence we use, with several verbs of motion, *sub* with accus., e.g. *sub ipsos muros aciem instruĕre,* = to draw up the army in order of battle — the very walls), *subter* with ablat. and accus., *infra* with accus. (of the direction of anything below towards the lower part of anything above the former, beneath, e.g. *infra lunam nihil nisi mortale*), *in* with ablat. (e.g. — the shade, *in umbrā*); to have a thing — the coat, *alqd veste tectem tenēre;* **2,** expressing dependence, etc., *sub* with ablat. (in gen.), *cum* (= — the superintendence and in company of, etc.); — Hannibal, *sub Hannibale;* — the leadership of Hannibal, ablat. abs. *Hannibale magistro;* **3,** expressing a lower measure and rank, as regards rank and merit, *infra,* to be —, below anyone, *infra alqm esse, inferiorem esse alqo, alci cedĕre;* in anything, *alqā re ab alqo vinci;* see BELOW; as regards the quality and quantity, *minor* with ablat. (= less, younger than, etc.); — seven years old, *minor septem annis, nondum septem annos natus, septimum annum nondum egressus;* not to sell, etc. — (the price), *minori pretio alqd non vendĕre;* **4,** in determining the manner in which anything is done, *sub* with ablat., *per* with accus. (= by means of); **5,** expressing simultaneity, e.g. — the reign of Romulus, *regnante Romulo, sub Romulo;* — this condition, *eā condicione;* — these circumstances, *quae cum ita sint;* — the cloak of, *alcjs rei specie;* — sail, *passis velis;* to be — anyone's eyes, *sub alcjs oculis esse;* to be — age, *impubem esse, haud sui juris esse.* "Under" in such phrases is often to be rendered by *inferior* with special noun, e.g. —servant, *usa famulus inferior.* **under-current,** n. **1,** of water, *flumen*, etc., *subterfluens*, or *sub terrâ fluens;* 2, fig., by circumloc. (e.g. there was an — of feeling in his words, *haec obscurâ quâdem significatione indicavit*). **under-garment,** n. *tunica (inferior), subûcula* (of a man).

underdone, adj. *semicoctus* (Plin.).

undergo, v.tr. *alqd subire, sustinēre* (= to carry anything as a burden, to attend to a thing); = to pass through, *pati, perpeti* (to the end), *(per)ferre* (= to — to the end), *tolerare, perfungi alqâ re* (= to go through it); to — punishment, *poenas dare* or *pendēre*.

underground, adj. see SUBTERRANEOUS.

undergrowth, n. *virgulta, -orum;* see UNDERWOOD.

underhand, adj. *clandestīnus;* see SECRET.

underlay, v.tr. *supponēre, sub(j)icēre, subdēre, substernēre* (all four with *alci rei* or *sub alqd*). **underlayer,** n. 1, *qui sub(j)icit,* etc.; 2, = something laid under, *fundamentum.*

underlet, v.tr. *minore pretio locare alqd.*

underlie, v.tr. e.g. the suggestion —s the speech, *haec per orationem tacite significantur.*

underline, v.tr. *lineam ducēre subter alqd.*

underling, n. *(ad)minister, satelles, -itis,* m.

undermaster, n. *hypodidascalus.*

undermine, v.tr. 1, *(cuniculo* or *cuniculis) subruēre* (e.g. a wall, a rampart), *suffodēre* (e.g. a mountain, a wall, a town); 2, fig. *subruēre* (= to ruin, e.g. *libertatem*), *evertēre* (= to overthrow, e.g. *rempublicam, fundamenta reipublicae*), *labefactare* (= to cause to fall, e.g. *rempublicam, amicitiam*).

undermost, adj. *infimus* (= the lowest), *imus* (= the deepest); see Low.

underneath, I. adv. *subter, infra;* see BENEATH. **II.** prep. see UNDER.

under-officer, n. perhaps *optio, succenturio.*

underpart, n. *pars inferior* (= lower part), *(partes) secundae* (lit. and fig.).

underpin, v.tr. *alqd substruēre* (e.g. *saxo quadrato);* see SUPPORT.

underrate, v.tr. *minoris aestimare;* see LOWER.

undersell, v.tr. *minoris (quam ceteri) vendēre.*

undersigned, adj. the —, *qui nomen subscripsit.*

understand, v.tr. = to comprehend (with the ear or with the intellect); 1, with the ear, *accipēre;* 2, with the intellect, *accipēre* (= to receive in the mind), *intellegēre* (= to form an idea of anything, hence to comprehend, more particularly *intellegēre alqm,* i.e. his character, his motives, opp. *alqm ignorare); comprehendēre* or *amplecti* or *complecti,* all with or without *mente* (= to form an idea of), *percipēre* (= to perceive with the understanding), *perspicēre* (clearly), *alqd certum* or *exploratum habēre* (= to — thoroughly); I don't — you, *nescio quid velis;* how am I to — that? *quid hoc sibi vult?* hence, to — by it, i.e. to put a construction on, etc., *intellegēre* or *intellegi velle* (both with double accus.), *dicēre, vocare, appellare* (all with double accus.); = I mean this, *dicēre* with double accus., *interprětari* with accus., *significare* with accus.; see MEAN; = to have acquired knowledge in anything, *alqd intellegēre* (of an accurate knowledge, e.g. *multas linguas), scire alqd* or with infin. (= to have a clear idea of

anything, and to remember it, e.g. *multas linguas), instructum esse alqâ re* (= to be versed in anything), *alcjs rei non ignārum esse* (= not to be unacquainted with anything), *peritum esse alcjs rei* (= experienced, skilled in); to — anything tolerably, *mediocriter adeptum esse alqd* (e.g. *singularum rerum singula,* Cic.); not to —, *alqd nescire* or *ignorare, alcjs rei ignarum esse;* to — Latin, *Latine scire, doctum esse Latinis lit(t)eris, Latinae linguae perītum esse;* not to — Latin, *Latine nescire;* to — riding on horseback, *equitandi perītum esse.* **understand¹ng,** n. *mens;* see INTELLECT.

undertake, v.tr. *incipēre* (= to begin), *subire, aggredi alqd* or *ad alqd* (= to get to it), *sumēre, suscipēre* (= to take a business into one's own hands), *(in se) recipēre* (if we take it off anyone's hands), *moliri* (= to try to accomplish anything difficult, also with infin.), *conari* (if very laborious, gen. with infin.), *audēre* (at one's own risk, peril, gen. with infin.); to — a journey, *iter incipēre* or *aggredi* or *inire* (on business), *iter facēre* (in gen.); to — to make, etc., anything, *alqd faciendum conducēre;* to — to do (i.e. to pledge oneself), *se facturum esse alqd promittēre.* **undertaker,** n. 1, in gen. by verbs; 2, of funerals, *libitinarius; designator* (who arranged the procession, Sen.); to be an —, *libitinam exercēre* (Val. Max.). **undertaking,** n. *inceptio, inceptum, conatus, -ûs,* m., *conata, -orum,* n., *opus, -ēris,* n., *facinus, -ōris,* n. (= a crime).

undervalue, v.tr. *parvum* or *parvi ducēre, parvi aestimare, contemnēre, despicēre* (= to despise), comb. *contemnēre* (or *despicēre) et pro nihilo ducēre, vīle habēre* (= to consider as trifling).

underwood, n. *virgulta, -orum, arbusta, -orum, silva caedua.*

underwriter, n. *qui cavet de* or *pro alqd re.*

undeserved, adj. *immeritus* (of what we have not deserved, e.g. praise), *indignus* (= unworthy), *falsus* (= false, unfounded, e.g. *invidia).* Adv. *immerito.* **undeserving,** adj. *immerens;* see UNWORTHY.

undesigned, adj. *fortuitus;* see ACCIDENTAL. Adv. *fortuito, casu, imprudenter.* **undesigning,** adj. *simplex, candidus.*

undesirable, adj. by *vīlis* (= poor); see WORTHLESS. **undesired,** adj. *ultro oblatus* (= freely offered), or by adv. *ultro.*

undetected, adj. *secrētus;* see SECRET.

undeveloped, adj. *immaturus, nondum adultus.*

undigested, adj. 1, of food, *crudus;* 2, of plans, etc., *imperfectus.*

undiminished, adj. *integer;* see WHOLE.

undiscerning, adj. *hebes;* see STUPID.

undisciplined, adj. *inexercitatus, rudis, tiro (in alqâ re),* comb. *tiro ac rudis.*

undisguised, adj. *sincērus.* Adv. *sincēre.*

undisturbed, adj. *otiosus* (= at leisure), *liber (ab) arbitris* (= free from ear or eye witnesses, spies, e.g. *locus);* to live in — peace, in *otio et pace vivēre;* to leave anyone —, *alqm non vexare, alqm non interpellare* (= not to interrupt anyone in his work, etc.); they allowed him to pass through their territory —, *cum bonâ pace eum per fines suos transmiserunt.*

undivided, adj. *indīvisus* (e.g. *ungula equi), communis* (= in common). Adv. *pro indivīso* (ante and post class.; e.g. *possidēre alqd).*

undo, v.tr. 1, to — a knot, etc., (dis)solvĕre, resolvĕre, expedire; 2, see RUIN. **undone,** adj. infectus; to consider as —, pro infecto hatĕre; what is done cannot be —, factum infectum fieri non potest; = ruined, perditus (e.g. perditus sum, perii, = I am —). \

undoubted, adj. non dubius, indubitatus (= not doubted, post Aug.), certus. Adv. haud dubie, sine dubio.

undress, I. v.tr. to — anyone, exuĕre alqm veste (in gen.), detrahĕre alci vestem (= to take off), nudare (= to strip anyone), alqm veste or vestibus spoliare (= to rob). **II.** v.intr. exuĕre (vestem), (de)ponĕre vestem; a room for —ing, apodytĕrium (esp. in baths). **III.** n. vestis nocturna (= night-dress), vestis domestica (= housedress, house-coat, in gen.). **undressed,** adj. 1, non vestītus, nudus (both = quite naked, and without a coat or dress on); 2, of bricks, etc., crudus; of food, non coctus.

undue, † indebitus, immodicus (= immoderate). Adv. nimis, nimium; see DUE, RIGHT, PROPER.

undulate, v.intr. † undare (= to rise in waves, in gen., also of boiling water); see WAVE. **undulating,** adj. undatus (Plin. of marks on shells).

undutiful, adj. impius (erga alqm); see DISOBEDIENT.

unearthly, adj. non mortalis; of spirits, perhaps caelestis.

uneasy, adj. anxius, so(l)licitus; to be, feel — (in one's mind), angi (for fear of some accident or misfortune), so(l)licitum esse (= to be troubled), dubitatione aestuare (= to be in great uncertainty what to do, Cic.). **uneasiness,** n. (animi) perturbatio; to feel —, perturbari, commovēri, permovēri. Adv. anxie (rare), moleste, aegre (e.g. alqd ferre).

unedifying, adj. frigidus, insulsus (of a discourse, etc.), in worse sense, turpis; see SHAMEFUL.

uneducated, adj. indoctus, inerudītus

unembarrassed, adj. liber; see FREE.

unemployed, adj. negotiis vacuus (in gen. = free from business), otiosus (of one who has leisure to follow his own inclinations, both of persons and things), nullis occupationibus implicatus (= not engaged in any particular business), munerum publicorum expers (= not holding a public office), ab omni munere solutus ac liber (of one who holds no office of any kind).

unencumbered, adj. liber.

unendowed, adj. indōtatus.

unenlightened, adj. humanitatis expers, indoctus.

unenterprising, adj. iners, socors, piger.

unenviable, adj. miser, tristis; see PITIFUL.

unequal, adj. inaequalis (of the inward state of anything), impar (= uneven; then, not equal in strength, attainments, etc.), dispar (= void of equality, not quite equal, both outwardly and inwardly), dissimilis (= dissimilar, as to quality, etc.), diversus (= wholly different, in kind and manner), dissonus (of sounds), inīquus (of a battle, etc.). Adv. inaequaliter, impariter, inīque. **unequalled,** adj. summus.

unerring, adj. certus.

unessential, adj. ad rem ipsam or ad rei naturam non pertinens, quod ad rem non pertinet, a re alienus, adventicius.

uneven, adj. non aequus, inīquus, inaequa-

bilis, inaequalis, asper (= rough, opp. levis); an — number, nůmerus impar. **unevenness,** n. inīquitas, asperitas; — of temper, inconstantia mutabilitasque mentis.

unexamined, adj. inexploratus.

unexampled, adj. inīcus, singulāris, nōvus (of what has not been heard or seen before), inauditus.

unexceptionable, adj. e.g. — witness, testis locuples or probus; — testimony, testimonium firmum or certum.

unexecuted, adj. non perfectus, imperfectus; to leave —, omittĕre (e.g. a plan, consilium).

unexercised, adj. inexercitatus.

unexhausted, adj. 1, = untired, † indefessus, integer; 2, = not used up, integer, solidus.

unexpected, adj. in(ex)spectatus, inopīnatus, necopīnatus, improvīsus. Adv. (ex) improviso, contra ex(s)pectationem.

unexplored, adj. inexploratus.

unextinguishable, adj. † inexstinctus.

unfading, adj. e.g. — laurels, gloria immortalis.

unfailing, adj. perpetuus (= perpetual), certus (= sure).

unfair, adj. inīquus (of persons and things, opp. aequus, e.g. judge, law, condition), injustus, (= unjust, of persons and things, opp. justus, meritus, dēbitus, e.g. interest on money), immeritus (= not deserved, chiefly with a negative before it, e.g. laudes haud immeritae); it is —, inīquum or injustum est, with accus. and infin.; to make — demands, iniqua postulare; to be — towards anyone, iniquum esse in alqm. Adv. inīque, injuste. **unfairness,** n. inīquitas (in conduct; also in the pl.), inique or injuste factum (of any act).

unfaithful, adj. infidēlis (opp. fidelis), infīdus (= not to be depended upon, trusted, opp. fīdus), perfīdus, perfidiosus (the latter of one whose nature it is to be —); to be —, fidem fallĕre. Adv. infidēliter. **unfaithfulness,** n. infidēlitas, perfidia.

unfamiliar, adj. nŏvus, inusitatus; see STRANGE.

unfashionable, adj. qui (quae, quod) contra consuetudinem fit.

unfasten, v.tr. (re)solvĕre (= to untie), (re)laxare (= to loosen), avellĕre, revellĕre (= to tear off), refigĕre (of what is nailed fast).

unfathomable, adj. immensus, infīnītus.

unfavourable, adj. = averse, inīquus, to anyone, alci or in alqm (= hostile), malignus (= jealous, opp. benignus), adversus (= contrary), aversus (= turned away), aliēnus, inopportunus (= not suitable), of omens, infaustus, funestus, sinister (used both of lucky and unlucky omens; see Andrew's Lat. Dict., SINISTER); — circumstances, conditions, res adversae, tempora inīqua. Adv. inīque, maligne, male, inopportune. **unfavourableness,** n. inīquitas (e.g. temporum), inopportunitas, or by adj.

unfeathered, adj. implūmis.

unfeeling, adj. sensūs expers, a sensu or a sensibus aliēnatus, nihil sentiens (lit.), durus, ferus, ferreus, comb. saxeus ferreusque, inhumanus (fig.); to be —, sensu carēre, nihil sentire, nullius rei sensu movēri, a sensu abesse or aliēnatum esse (lit.), durum, ferreum, inhumanum esse, inhumano esse ingenio (fig.). Adv. dure, duriter, inhumane, inhumaniter, crudēliter.

unfeigned, adj. *vērus* (opp. *simulatus*), *sinzērus* (opp. *fucatus*), *simplex.* Adv. *vere, sincēre, simpliciter, ex animo.*

unfeminine, adj. † *masculus.*

unfermented, adj. *sine fermento (factus).*

unfilial, adj. *impius (erga parentes).* Adv. *impie (erga parentes).*

unfit, I. adj. *inutilis alci rei* or (generally) *ad alqd;* see UNSUITABLE. **II.** v.tr. *inutilem reddĕre.* **unfitness,** n. *inutilitas.* **unfitting,** adj. see IMPROPER.

unfix, v.tr. *refīgĕre;* see UNFASTEN. **unfixed,** adj. *mobilis.*

unfledged, adj. *implumis.*

unfold, v.tr. *explicare* (lit. and fig.), *aperire* (= to open; also fig.), *explanare* (fig., in words).

unforeseen, adj. *improvīsus.*

unforgiving, adj. *implacabilis, inexorabilis;* see IMPLACABLE.

unforgotten, adj. by circumloc. (e.g. of an act of kindness) *immortali memoriā retinēre beneficium perceptum;* what you have done for me will be —, *meam tuorum erga me meritorum memoriam nulla umquam delebit oblivio.*

unformed, adj. *informis* (= without shape), *nondum perfectus* (= not finished), of character, perhaps *adhuc puerīlis.*

unfortified, adj. *immunītus.*

unfortunate, adj. see UNLUCKY.

unfounded, adj. *vanus, fictus.*

unfrequented, adj. *minus celeber, inceleber, desertus.*

unfriendly, adj. *inimīcus, inīquus, aliēnus,* towards anyone, *ab alqo;* to have — feelings towards anyone, *alieno animo esse ab alqo* or *in alqm.* **unfriendliness,** n. *inimicitia, simulias.*

unfruitful, adj. *infēcundus, sterilis* (opp. *fertilis* and, as regards the soil, *omnis);* see BARREN. **unfruitfulness,** n. *sterilitas.*

unfulfilled, adj. *irritus, vanus, fallax;* to remain —, *exitum* or *eventum non habēre, non ēvenire;* to leave no duty —, *nullum ducis officium remittĕre.*

unfurl, v.tr. to — the sails, *vela pandĕre.*

unfurnished, adj. *ab alqā re imparatus;* an — house, *domus nuda atque inanis.*

ungainly, adj. *inhabilis;* see UNCOUTH.

ungenerous, adj. *illiberalis;* — act, *illiberalitas.* Adv. *illiberaliter.*

ungenial, adj. *tristis, asper.*

ungenteel, adj. *ignobilis.* **ungentle,** adj. *asper* (= rough, e.g. *verba).* **ungentleman-like, ungentlemanly,** adj. *incultus, indecōrus* (e.g. *laughter);* see INDECOROUS.

ungird, v.tr. *discingĕre,* † *recingĕre.*

ungodly, adj. see IMPIOUS, IMPIETY.

ungovernable, adj. *qui regi non potest* (lit. and fig.), *indomitus* (= untamed, of living beings and of things), *effrēnatus* (= unbridled, of persons and things), *ferox* (of temper, of persons and of anything showing such a disposition), *impotens* (of persons and things), comb. *ferox impotensque.* Adv. *effrēnate, impotenter.* **ungoverned,** adj. see UNBRIDLED.

ungraceful, adj. *invenustus;* see INELEGANT. **ungracefulness,** n. by the adjs.

ungracious, adj. *iniquus, petulans, īratus* (= angry). Adv. *inīque, iniquo animo, petulanter, īrate.*

ungrateful, adj. *ingratus* (of an — spirit, and of what is a thankless task), *beneficii, beneficiorum immemor.*

ungrounded, adj. *vanus, irritus, inanis.*

ungrudging, adj. see LIBERAL.

unguarded, adj. 1, *incustodītus, sine custodiis* (= not guarded by anyone), *indēfensus;* 2, = imprudent, *incautus, imprudens.* Adv. *incaute, imprudenter, temere* (= rashly); see IMPRUDENT.

unguent, n. *unguentum.*

unhallowed, adj. *profanus;* see also SACRILEGIOUS.

unhappy, adj. *infelix, infortunatus, miser* (= miserable), *non prosper* (= not prosperous, of things), † *infaustus* (= ill-fated, e.g. day, omen, etc.), also comb. *infaustus et infelix, calamitosus* (e.g. war, conflagration), *funestus* (= mournful, causing mischief, e.g. war, omen), *sinister* (lit. = on the left-hand side, opp. *dexter), adversus* (= not as we wish it, e.g. battle, circumstances, result of an undertaking, opp. *secundus), malus* (= in a bad condition, opp. *bonus), calamitosus, aerumnosus* (= full of calamity); — position, *res adversae, fortunae afflictae.* Adv. *infēliciter, misere, male, calamitose* (rare). **unhappiness,** n. *miseria;* see MISERY.

unharmed, adj. *inviolatus, salvus* (= safe).

unharness, v.tr. *disjungĕre, solvĕre.*

unhatched, adj. *nondum (ex ovo) exclusus.*

unhealthy, adj. 1, = disposed to illness, *valetudine affectus, ad aegrotandum proclīvis, infirmā valetudine, infirmus, invalidus, aeger, imbecillus;* see WEAK, ILL; 2, see UNWHOLESOME. **unhealthiness,** n. *mala, infirma, tenuis, aegra* or *incommoda, valētudo;* see also UNWHOLESOMENESS.

unheard, adj. *inaudītus;* to punish, to condemn anyone —, *alqm inaudītum punire, damnare;* — of, *inauditus, nŏvus.*

unheated, adj. *non cal(e)factus.*

unheeded, adj. *neglectus.*

unheroic, adj. *ignavus;* see COWARDLY.

unhesitating, adj. *strenuus, confīdens;* see PROMPT. Adv. *strenue, confidenter.*

unhewn, adj. *rudis.*

unhindered, adj. *non impedītus, līber* (= free, without constraint), *sine morā.*

unhinge, v.tr. 1, to — a door, *postes cardine* † *emovēre;* see UNFIX; 2, fig. with the mind —d, *mente captus.*

unhistorical, adj. *contra historiae fidem scriptus, commentīcius, fictus.*

unholy, adj. (man, place) *profanus* (opp. *sacer);* see IMPIOUS.

unhonoured, adj. *inhonoratus.*

unhook, v.tr. *refīgĕre* (from a wall), *refībulare* (Mart. = to unbuckle).

unhoped for, adj. *insperatus.*

unhurt, adj. *integer, incolumis, salvus, intactus* (= untouched), comb. *integer intactusque, inviolatus* (= not hurt), comb. *integer atque inviolatus, intactus inviolatusque, invulneratus, incorruptus* (where nothing is spoiled or destroyed).

unicorn, n. *monocĕros, -ōtis* (Plin.).

uniform, I. adj. *unius generis, semper eodem modo formatus, constans, aequabilis* (e.g. *motus).* Adv. *constanter, aequabiliter, uno tenore.* **II.** n. of soldiers, *vestitus, -ūs, militaris.* **uniformity,** n. *aequabilitas, constantia* (of persons and things).

unimaginable, adj. *supra quam quod cogitari potest.*

unimpaired, adj. *integer.*

unimpassioned, adj. e.g. an — address, *animi perturbatione liber* or *vacuus* (= without violent emotion), *cupiditatis* or *cupiditatum expers, omni cupiditate carens, sine irâ et studio* (= without passion).

unimpeachable, adj. see TRUSTWORTHY.

unimportant, adj. *lĕvis, nullius momenti.*

uninformed, adj. *indoctus, humanitatis expers.*

uninhabitable, adj. *inhabitabilis ;* to be quite —, *omni cultu vacare.* **uninhabited,** adj. *habitatoribus vacuus* (e.g. a town), *cultoribus vacuus* (=without anybody to cultivate), *desertus* (= deserted).

uninitiated, adj. 1, lit. *profanus ;* 2, fig. *alcjs rei expers.*

uninjured, adj. *incolumis, integer, salvus.*

uninspired, adj. *divino spiritu haud afflatus.*

uninstructed, adj. *indoctus.*

unintelligible, adj. *obscurus* (e.g. *narratio*). Adv. *obscure* (e.g. *narrare alqd*), or by the noun *obscuritas* (e.g. *verborum*).

unintentional, adj. *insciens.* Adv. *forte, casu ;* I did it —, *insciens feci.*

uninteresting, adj. *jejunus, frigidus.*

unintermitting, adj. *continuus, assiduus.*

uninterred, adj. *inhumatus, insepultus.*

uninterrupted, adj. *continens, continuus* (= continuous), *assiduus* (= constant, e.g. rain, work), *perpetuus, perennis* (=lasting), comb. *con·tinuus et perennis* (e.g. *motio*) ; my connection with anyone is —, *by in consuetudine cum algo permanēre.* Adv. *continenter, uno tenore, perpetuo.*

uninured, adj. see UNACCUSTOMED.

uninvestigated, adj. *inexploratus.*

uninvited, adj. *invocatus ;* see UNASKED. **uninviting,** adj. *injucundus.*

union, n. see under UNITE.

unique, adj. *unicus, singularis.*

unison, n. (in music) *concordia vocum.*

unit, n. *monas, -ădis,* f. (μονάς).

unitarian, n. *qui simplicem Dei naturam esse arbitratur.* **unitarianism,** n. *ratio eorum qui simplicem esse Dei naturam dicunt.*

unite, I. v.tr. *(con)jungĕre, alci rei* or *cum algâ re ;* with anybody, *cum algo ; congregare* (= to collect two or more things to one flock as it were), *copulare* (so that two or more things are closely tied together), with anything or anyone, *cum algâ re* or *cum algo,* *(con)sociare* (as companions), with, etc., *cum,* etc., *miscēre alci rei* or *cum algâ re*(=to mix, lit. and fig.) ; see JOIN. **II.** v.intr. *se (con)jungĕre* (of two corps), with anyone, *alci* or *cum algo ; miscēri* (of two rivers, etc.), *cum algo coire,* with anything, *alci rei* or *cum algâ re ; consentire* (= to agree) ; **to** — in a partnership, *societatem cum algo inire ;* see JOIN, AGREE. **union,** n. 1, *(con)junctio, congregatio, consociatio ;* 2, = agreement, *consensio, consensus, -ūs, concordia ;* see AGREEMENT ; 3, = united body, *societas, sodalitas ;* see SOCIETY, CONCORD. **unity,** n. 1, opp. to multiplicity, by *unus* (e.g. there was — of opinion among them all, *sententia inter omnes una erat) ;* 2, see UNION, 2.

universal, adj. *universus ;* — history, *res in orbe terrarum actae ;* see GENERAL. **Adv.** *universe, in universum ; —* beloved, *ab omnibus dilectus.* **universality,** n. *qui (quae, quod) latissime patet* or *ad universos pertinet.* **universe,** n. *(rerum) universitas, rerum natura.*

university, n. ** academia.*

univocal, adj. of a word, etc., *unam tantum significationem habens.*

unjust, adj. *injustus, injurius, injuriosus* (= of an — mind), *iniquus* (= unreasonable) ; *(injuriosus,* = contrary to right and to the civil law ; *iniquus,* = contrary to the moral law). Adv. *injuste, inique, injuriose, contra jus (fasque).* **unjustifiable,** adj. *iniquissimus ;* see INEXCUSABLE. Adv. *iniquissimo modo.*

unkempt, adj. *neglectus.*

unkind, adj. *inhumanus, severus ;* see STERN. Adv. *inhumane, severe.* **unkindness,** n. *inhumanitas, severitas ;* see CRUELTY.

unknowing, adj. *inscius ;* see IGNORANT. **unknown,** adj. *ignotus* (in gen., of persons and things, opp. *notus), incognitus* (= not yet learned, of things, opp. *cognitus), incompertus* (=not yet certain, fully ascertained, opp. *compertus), inexploratus* (= not yet inquired into, opp. *exploratus), ignobilis* (= to the world, of places and persons ; hence also = of obscure birth, opp. *nobilis), obscurus* (= obscure) ; a person — to me, *nescio quis.*

unlace, v.tr. see UNTIE, LOOSEN.

unlamented, adj. to die —, *non deploratum mori.*

unlatch, v.tr. see OPEN.

unlawful, adj. *non legitimus, vetitus, qui (quae, quod) contra legem* or *leges est.* Adv. *contra legem* or *leges, injuriâ, per injuriam.*

unlearn, v.tr. *dediscĕre.* **unlearned,** adj. *illit(t)eratus, indoctus, ineruditus.* Adv. *indocte.*

unleavened, adj. *sine fermento* (Cels.).

unless, conj. *nisĭ* (contracted *nĭ*), with indic. where the statement is definite, with subj. where possibility is implied ; in certain cases *si non* is used (e.g. *libertas si aequa non est, ne libertas quidem est),* esp. with fut. (e.g. *si te vidēre non potero, discedam*).

unlettered, adj. see UNLEARNED.

unlevelled, adj. *asper ;* see UNEVEN.

unlicensed, adj. *cui jus alcjs rei vendendae non est concessum.*

unlike, adj. *dissimilis.* **unlikely,** adj. see IMPROBABLE.

unlimited, adj. *infinitus.*

unload, v.tr. *exonerare* (lit., e.g. *plaustrum ;* also fig. = disburden), *liberare, levare, solvĕre alqâ re* (fig. = to disburden).

unlock, v.tr. *recludĕre, reserare.*

unlooked for, adj. *inex(s)pectatus, insperatus.*

unloose, v.tr. *solvĕre* (a ship, etc.), *liberare* (= to set free) ; see FREE, v.tr.

unlucky, adj. *infelix* (of omens) ; see UNFAVOURABLE.

unmade, adj. *non factus* or *non confectus ;* of a bed, *non stratus.*

unman, v.tr. *enervare.* **unmanned,** adj. *fractus, perculsus.*

unmanageable, adj. see UNGOVERNABLE.

unmanly, adj. *viro indignus, effeminatus* (= effeminate), *mollis* (= soft), comb. *effeminatus et mollis.*

unmannerly, adj. *male moratus* (of persons, opp. *bene moratus*), *rusticus* (= rude, opp. *urbanus*); see RUDE.

unmarried, adj. *caelebs.*

unmask, v.tr. to — anyone, *personam capiti alcjs detrahĕre* (lit. and fig., Mart.), *animum alcjs nudare, evolvĕre alqm integumento dissimulationis suae nudareque* (fig. = to find him out).

unmatched, adj. *unicus.*

unmeaning, adj. *inanis.*

unmelodious, adj. *non canorus;* see INHARMONIOUS.

unmentioned, adj. to remain —, *omitti, praetermitti;* to leave —, *omittĕre, praetermittĕre.*

unmerciful, adj. *immisericors.* Adv. *immisericorditer.*

unmindful, adj. *immemor,* of a thing, *alcjs rei.*

unmingled, unmixed, adj. *merus,* fig. *simplex.*

unmistakable, adj. see CLEAR, CERTAIN.

unmitigated, adj. by circumloc.; often the superlat. of an adj. will suit (e.g. the war was waged with — cruelty, *bellum atrocissimum gerebatur*).

unmolested, adj. to leave anyone —, *alci molestiam non exhibēre.*

unmoor, v.tr. *solvĕre.*

unmotherly, adj. *non maternus.*

unmoved, adj. *immotus;* to be, remain —, *non* (com)*movēri alqā re, repudiare alqd* (e.g. *alcjs preces*), *non laborare de alqā re* (e.g. *de alcjs morte*).

unnatural, adj. *quod praeter naturam ex-*(s)*istit, monstr*(u)*osus, portentosus, immanis* (= vast). Adv. *contra naturam, praeter naturam.*

unnavigable, adj. *innavigabilis.*

unnecessary, unneedful, adj. *non necessarius, quod non opus est, supervacaneus, vanus* (= idle, e.g. *metus*) ; it is — to mention these, *eos nihil attinet nominare.* Adv. *praeter rem, praeter necessitatem, nimis;* see TOO.

unnerve, v.tr. see UNMAN.

unnoticed, adj. to leave —, *praetermittĕre, praeterire* (*silentio*), *neglegere* (= not to mind).

unnumbered, adj. see INNUMERABLE.

unobserved, adj. see UNNOTICED.

unoccupied, adj. see UNEMPLOYED, UNINHABITED.

unoffending, adj. *innocens.*

unopened, adj. *non apertus ;* of a letter, *li*(t)*erae non resignatae.*

unorganized, adj. e.g. — bodies, *corpora nullā cohaerendi naturā* (Cic.).

unorthodox, adj. *fidei Christianae parum conveniens* (of a doctrine), *fidei Christianae parum obediens* (of a person).

unostentatious, adj. see MODEST.

unpack, v.tr. *alqd vacuum reddĕre ;* see UNLOAD.

unpaid, adj. *non solutus* (of money, debts), *residuus* (=outstanding, e.g. money not received by the creditor), *cui non satisfactum est* (of the creditor).

unpalatable, adj. *amarus* (=bitter).

unparalleled, adj. *unicus, singularis.*

unpardonable, adj. *quod nihil excusationis habet* (e.g. *vitium*), *inexpiabilis* (e.g. *scelus, fraus*).

unpatriotic, adj. *patriae immemor* (of a person), (*injuria*) *in patriam illata* (of an act).

unperceived, adj. see UNNOTICED.

unphilosophical, adj. *philosophiae expers.*

unpitying, adj. see UNMERCIFUL. **unpitied,** adj. by circumloc. with *misericordia* (e.g. they fell —, *nullius misericordiam adepti interfecti sunt*).

unpleasant, adj. *molestus, ingratus, injucundus;* see DISAGREEABLE. Adv. *moleste, ingrate.* **unpleasantness,** n. *incommodum, molestia;* to cause anyone —, *molestiam alci afferre* or *exhibēre, incommodo alqm afficĕre, incommodum alci* (*af*)*ferre;* to cause yourself —, *molestiam ex alqā re capĕre* or *accipĕre.*

unpoetic, adj. *a poētarum ratione alienus.*

unpolished, adj. *impolītus* (lit. and fig.).

unpolluted, adj. *impollutus, castus.*

unpopular, adj. *invidiosus, plebi* (*populo,* etc.) *ingratus,* or *haud gratus* or *acceptus ;* to be (very) —, *in* (*magnā*) *invidiā esse ;* to become —, *in invidiam venire.* **unpopularity,** n. *invidia;* see above.

unpractised, adj. *inexercitatus.*

unprecedented, adj. *novus, inaudītus.*

unprejudiced, adj. *integer, integer ac liber.*

unpremeditated, adj. (*verba,* etc.) *extemplo* or *sine consilio dicta.*

unprepared, adj. *imparatus,* with anything, *ab alqā re.*

unprepossessing, adj. see DISAGREEABLE.

unpretending, adj. see MODEST.

unprincipled, adj. *male moratus ;* see WICKED.

unproductive, adj. *infecundus ;* see UNFRUITFUL.

unprofitable, adj. *qui nullum fructum fert.* Adv. by adj. or *incassum.*

unpromising, adj. *qui* (*quae, quod*) *nullam spem affert.*

unpronounceable, adj. *qui* (*quae, quod*) *enuntiari non potest.*

unpropitious, adj. see UNFAVOURABLE.

unprotected, adj. *indefensus, non custoditus.*

unproved, adj. *argumentis non* (*con*)*firmatus.*

unprovided, adj. *imparatus ;* — for (e.g. children), (*liberi*) *quibus nondum prospectum est.*

unprovoked, adj. *non lacessītus, ultro* (= of one's own accord).

unpublished, adj. *nondum editus.*

unpunished, adj. *impunītus, inultus, incastigatus* (also with words); to remain —, *impune esse, non puniri ;* — for anything, *alqd impune facĕre.*

unpurchased, adj. *non emptus.*

unqualified, adj. 1, see UNSUITABLE ; **2,** = very great, *summus, maximus.*

unquestionable, adj. *non dubius, certus.* Adv. *sine dubio.*

unravel, v.tr. 1, lit. *retexĕre ;* 2, fig. *explanare, explicare, enodare.*

unread, adj. *non lectus ;* an — man, by *li*(t)*erarum expers ;* see UNEDUCATED.

unreasonable, adj. it is —, *iniquum est,* with accus. and infin. Adv. *inique.*

unreconciled, adj. *non placatus;* see RECONCILE.

unrefined, adj. 1, lit. *crudus;* 2, fig. see RUDE.

unrelenting, adj. see CRUEL, HARD.

unremitting, adj. *continuus* (e.g. *labor*); see CONSTANT.

unrepaid, adj. e.g. kindness, by (*beneficia*) *non reddita.*

unrepentant, adj. *quem non poenitet alcjs rei.*

unrepining, adj. see PATIENT.

unreprovable, unreproved, adj. *non reprehensus.*

unrequested, adj. *ultro oblatus* (= freely offered), *ultro.*

unresented, adj. *inultus, impunitus.*

unreserved, adj. *liber;* see FRANK.

unrest, n. *inquies, -ētis,* f.

unrestrained, adj. *effrenatus.*

unrevenged, adj. *inultus.*

unrewarded, adj. *sine praemio, inhonoratus.*

unriddle, v.tr. *solvēre, explicare.*

unrighteous, adj. *impius, improbus.* Adv. *impie, improbe.* **unrighteousness,** n. *impietas, improbitas.*

unripe, adj. *immaturus* (lit. of fruit, fig. of man, opp. *maturus*), *crudus* (= raw, opp. *maturus et coctus*). **unripeness,** n. *immaturitas.*

unrivalled, adj. *eximius, praestans;* see EXCELLENT.

unrobe, v.tr. see UNDRESS.

unroof, v.tr. see UNCOVER.

unroot, v.tr. *eradicare* (ante-class. lit. and fig.), *radicitus evellēre.*

unruffled, adj. of the sea, temper; see CALM, TRANQUIL.

unruly, adj. see UNGOVERNABLE. **unruliness,** n. *effrenatio, impotentia, ferocitas.*

unsafe, adj. *infestus, intutus;* fig. = exposed to danger, *instabilis* (lit. = unstable, e.g. step, *gradus, incessus*), *lubricus* (lit. = slippery), *incertus* (fig. = uncertain).

unsaid, adj. *indictus.* **unsay,** v.tr. see RECANT.

unsalable, adj. *qui* (*quae, quod*) *vendi non potest.*

unsalted, adj. *sale non conditus.*

unsatiated, adj. *nondum saturatus.*

unsatisfactory, adj. *non idoneus* (= unsuited), or by some positive adj., as *malus* (= evil). Adv. *minus bene.* **unsatisfied,** adj. *cui non satisfactum est.*

unsavoury, adj. see TASTELESS, UNPALATABLE.

unscrew, v.tr. *solvēre.*

unscriptural, adj. *non ut sanctae lit(t)erae docent.*

unseal, v.tr. *resignare alqd.*

unsearchable, adj. *inexplicabilis, inexploratus.*

unseasonable, adj. *intempestivus, importunus, immaturus* (lit. = unripe, of fruits; then fig. = before the right time). Adv. *intempestive, importune.* **unseasoned,** adj. *non conditus;* of wood, *viridis.*

unseemly, adj. see INDECOROUS.

unseen, adj. *invisus.*

unselfish, adj. *suae utilitatis immemor;* see also TEMPERATE. **unselfishness,** n. *abstinentia, continentia,* or by adj.

unserviceable, adj. *inutilis.*

unsettle, v.tr. *labefacēre, labefactare* (lit. and fig.); see SHAKE. **unsettled,** adj. accounts, see UNPAID; — weather, *caelum varians;* in a moral sense, *inconstans, varius, mobilis voluntas,* comb. *varius et mutabilis, incertus.*

unshackled, adj. *liber.*

unshaved, adj. *intonsus.*

unsheathe, v.tr. *gladium e vaginā educēre.*

unship, v.tr. *exponēre* (passengers and goods).

unshod, adj. *pedibus nudis.*

unshorn, adj. *intonsus.*

unshrinking, adj. *impavidus, intrepidus.*

unsightly, adj. see UGLY.

unsisterly, adj. *quod sororis non est.*

unskilful, unskilled, adj. *inhabilis* (*alci rei* or *ad alqd*), *inscitus, imperitus, rudis in alcjs rei* (= ignorant, in an art or science), *imperitus,* in, *alcjs rei* (= without practical experience), *ignarus alcjs rei.* Adv. *inepte, inscite* (= without judgment), *imperite.* **unskilfulness,** n. *imperitia, inscitia, alcjs rei.*

unslaked, adj. e.g. lime, *vivus;* of thirst, *non ex(s)tinctus.*

unsocial, adj. *insociabilis.*

unsolicited, adj. see UNASKED, VOLUNTARY.

unsolved, adj. *non solutus.*

unsophisticated, adj. *simplex.*

unsorted, adj. *incompositus, inordinatus.*

unsought, adj. *non petitus.*

unsound, adj. (timber) *cariosus* (= worm-eaten, bones, etc.), *puter, putris* (= rotten); — in health, see UNHEALTHY; of mind, see INSANE; of opinions, *falsus.* **unsoundness,** n. see UNHEALTHINESS, INSANITY.

unsown, adj. *non satus.*

unsparing, adj. 1, *inclemens, acer, acerbus;* 2, see LIBERAL.

unspeakable, adj. *infandus.*

unspoiled, adj. *incorruptus, integer.*

unstable, unsteady, adj. *mobilis, inconstans, instabilis.* **unsteadiness,** n. *inconstantia.*

unstained, adj. see UNSPOILED, PURE.

unstring, v.tr. a bow, † *arcum retendēre,* † *remittēre.* **unstrung,** adj. of the nerves, etc., *fractus, debilitatus.*

unstudied, adj. (of style) *simplex.*

unsubdued, adj. *indomitus;* see UNTAMED.

unsuccessful, adj. *cui eventus deest, irritus, infelix;* see UNFORTUNATE. Adv. *infeliciter.*

unsuitable, unsuited, adj. by *alienus ab alqā re, inutilis ad alqd, incommodus;* see UNFIT. Adv. *inutiliter, incommode.* **unsuitableness,** n. *inutilitas, incommoditas.*

unsuspected, adj. *non suspectus, in quem nulla suspicio cadit.* **unsuspicious,** adj. *simplex, candidus, simulationum nescius.* Adv. *simpliciter, candide.* **unsuspiciousness,** n. *simplicitas, animus simplex,* or *apertus.*

untainted, adj. *incorruptus, non infectus.*

untamed, adj. *indomitus* (lit. and fig.), *effrenatus* (fig.).

untasted, adj. *ingustatus.*

untaught, adj. *indoctus.*

unteachable, adj. *indocilis.*

untenable, adj. *infirmus, lēvis.*

unterrified, adj. *interritus.*

unthankful, adj. see UNGRATEFUL. **un-thankfulness**, see INGRATITUDE.

unthinking, adj. see THOUGHTLESS.

untie, v.tr. *(dis)solvĕre, laxare.*

until, I. prep. *ad* or *in* with accus. II. conj. *dum, donec, quoad* with indic. when mere time is expressed; subj. when the idea is of contingency, purpose, etc.

untilled, adj. *inaratus.*

untimely, adj. see UNSEASONABLE.

untinged, adj. *purus.*

untiring, adj. see INDEFATIGABLE.

unto, prep. see TO.

untold, adj. 1, *non dictus;* 2, see COUNT-LESS, INNUMERABLE.

untouched, adj. by *intactus;* see also UN-MOVED.

untoward, adj. see UNFAVOURABLE.

untranslatable, adj. *quod verbis reddi non potest.*

untried, adj. *inexpertus.*

untrodden, adj. e.g. path, *via non trita.*

untroubled, adj. *nullo motu perturbatus* or *tranquillus, placidus;* see CALM.

untrue, adj. *falsus.* Adv. *falso, ficte.* **un-truth**, n. (as quality, character) *vanitas* or by adjs., e.g. *alqd falsum esse probare;* = the thing itself, *falsum, mendacium.*

unturned, adj. to leave no stone —, *omnibus modis alqd aggredi.*

untwine, **untwist**, v.tr. *(re)solvĕre, retexĕre.*

unused, adj. 1, see UNACCUSTOMED; 2, *novus, integer;* see FRESH. **unusual**, adj. *involutus, insolens.*

unutterable, adj. *infandus, inenarrabilis.* Adv. *supra quam quod enuntiari potest.*

unvanquished, adj. *invictus.*

unvaried, **unvarying**, adj. see UN-CHANGED, IMMUTABLE.

unvarnished, adj. 1, lit. *fuco non illitus;* 2, fig. *simplex, sine fuco ac fallaciis;* see PLAIN.

unveil, v.tr. by *caput aperire.*

unversed, adj. *non versatus, peregrinus atque hospes, tiro ac rudis in alqā re.*

unviolated, adj. *inviolatus.*

unwalled, adj. *muris non circumdatus, sine muris* (in gen.), *immunitus* (of fortifications).

unwarlike, adj. *imbellis.*

unwarrantable, adj. *iniquus.* **unwarranted**, adj. *sine auctore editus.*

unwary, adj. *incautus, imprudens.* Adv. *incaute, imprudenter.* **unwariness**, n. *imprudentia.*

unwashed, adj. *illotus.*

unwatched, adj. *incustoditus.*

unwavering, adj. see FIRM.

unwearied, adj. *indefessus, integer* (= still fresh), *assiduus.*

unweave, v.tr. *retexĕre.*

unwelcome, adj. *alcī non acceptus, ingratus.*

unwell, adj. see ILL.

unwholesome, adj. *insalubris* (Plin.), *pestilens, gravis.*

unwieldy, adj. *inhabilis* (= difficult to manage), *vasti corporis* (= of a great size).

unwilling, adj. *invitus.* Adv. by *algo in vito.* **unwillingness**, n. see RELUCTANCE.

unwind, v.tr. *retexĕre.*

unwise, adj. *insipiens, stultus.* Adv. *insipienter, stulte.*

unwitting, adj. and adv. *inscius.*

unwomanly, adj. *quod non mulieris est.*

unwonted, adj. see UNUSUAL.

unworthy, adj. *indignus,* of anything, *alqd re,* to, etc., by *qui* with subj. **unworthiness**, n. *indignitas.*

unwounded, adj. *invulneratus* (once in Cic., where we read *invulneratus inviolatusque), sine vulnere, integer.*

unwrap, v.tr. *evolvĕre.*

unwrinkle, v.tr. *erugare* (Plin.).

unwritten, adj. still —, *non scriptus.*

unwrought, adj. *rudis.*

unyielding, adj. see INFLEXIBLE.

unyoke, v.tr. *disjungĕre* (e.g. cattle, *jumenta, equos).*

up, adv. *sursum* (= upwards, in contrast with *deorsum,* = downwards); in combination it may be rendered by *ad, e, in, sub, trans;* — the river, *adverso flumine* (opp. to down the river, *secundo flumine);* — the hill, *in adversum montem;* to look —, *suspicĕre* (e.g. to heaven, *caelum);* to press —, *eniti (conniti) in alqd;* to burn —, *extorrēre, adurĕre;* to dry —, *exarescĕre;* to dig —, *effodĕre, eruĕre;* to deliver —, *tradĕre;* to go —, *a(d)scendĕre;* — from boyhood, etc., *a puero, a pueris;* — to, *tenus* with ablat. (always after the case); — ! *age! surge!* **upwards**, adv. *sursum;* see also MORE.

upbraid, v.tr. to — anyone with, *reprehendĕre alqm de alqā re.* **upbraiding**, n. *objurgatio, convicium* (= scolding).

uphill, I. adv. *adverso colle, adversus collem.* II. adj. 1, lit. *acclivis, arduus;* 2, fig. *arduus, difficilis.*

uphold, v.tr. lit. and fig. *sustinēre, sustentare, fulcire* (= to prop).

upholsterer, n. by *qui (domum,* etc.) *instruit,* or *(ex)ornat.*

upland, adj. *editus;* see MOUNTAINOUS.

upon, prep. *super* with accus. with verbs of motion, ablat. with verbs of rest; *in* with accus. or ablat. (often in comp., e.g. *incidĕre* = to light —): = after, *e(x)* (e.g. directly — the consulship of Caesar, *statim e consulatu Caesaris),* or by ablat. abs. (— this, *quo* or *hoc facto),* or by *cum (quum),* with subj. (e.g. *quae cum secum reputasset, dixit,* he said — reflection); — this condition, *eā condicione,* or *hac lege ut;* — the whole, *plerumque* (= usually), *ad summam* (= in a word); see ON.

upper, adj. (as regards the position) *superus, superior, summus, supremus* (the two last = highest); (as regards the order) *primoris* (not used in the nom.), *superior;* (as regards rank, dignity) *superior (loco* or *dignitate);* to get the — hand, *superare, vincĕre;* — storey of a house, *pars superior aedium;* — part, *pars superior;* also by *superior* or (if the highest part) by *summus* (in the same gender as the noun, e.g. — of a ship, *navis summa;* — world, in Cic. always called *haec loca quae nos incolimus.*

uppermost, adj. *summus* (in gen.), *primus*

(= according to order in rank), *princeps* (in rank or dignity).

upright, adj. (*di*)*rectus* (*directus* = straight, perpendicularly as well as horizontally), *erectus* (in a moral sense), *probus, honestus, integer, gravis.* Adv. lit. *recte,* or use adj. ; fig. *recte, probe, honeste, sincere, ingenue, integre, graviter.* **uprightness,** n. *probitas.*

uproar, n. see NOISE.

upset, I. v.tr. (*sub*)*vertĕre, evertĕre.* **II.** v.intr. *everti, subverti, corruĕre.*

upshot, n. *exitus, -ūs, eventus, -ūs.*

upsidedown, adj. to turn —, *omnia turbare et miscēre.*

upstart, n. *novus homo.*

urbanity, n. *urbanitas ;* see POLITENESS.

urchin, n. 1, see HEDGEHOG ; 2, see CHILD, BOY.

urge, v.tr. *impellĕre, incitare, excitare, stimulare alqm, stimulos alci admovēre* (all these lit. and fig.), *accendĕre, inflammare* (fig.), anyone to, *alqm ad alqd ; (ad)hortari ad alqd* or with *ut* or *ne ;* to — anyone with requests, *instare alci* (with *ut* or *ne*), *alqm urgēre,* comb. *instare et urgēre* (absolute), *alqm orare obsecrareque, precibus fatigare alqm, ab alqo petĕre et summe contendĕre, ut* or *ne,* etc. **urgent,** adj. *urgens* (lit.), *gravis, vehemens, magni momenti, necessarius, maximus, summus ;* at my — request, *orante me atque obsecrante.* Adv. *vehementer, magnopere.* **urgency,** n. *necessitas.*

urine, n. *urīna, lotium.*

urn, n. *urna.*

usage, n. *mos, consuetudo ;* see CUSTOM. **use, I.** n. 1, = application of a thing to your wants, *usus, -ūs, usurpatio, usura* (= using) ; to make — of, *alqā re uti ;* to come into —, *in usum venire, in consuetudinem or morem venire, more recipi* (= to become usual) ; to be of —, *utilem usi esse ;* to be of great —, *magno usui esse ;* 2, see USEFULNESS. **II.** v.tr. *uti alqā re ;* — for, *ad alqd, abuti re, ad alqd or in alqā re* (= to consume), *usurpare alqd, adhibēre alqd,* for anything, *ad alqd, conferre ad or in alqd ;* — in a certain sense, *vocabulo alqd significare, declarare ;* see also TREAT. **useful,** adj. *utilis, aptus, idoneus, accommodatus, commodus* (all *ad alqd*) ; to be —, *utilem esse, usui esse, alci prodesse or proficēre.* Adv. *utiliter, apte, commode.* **usefulness,** n. *utilitas, usus, -ūs, commoditas ;* see USE. **useless,** adj. *inutilis ad alqd* (or *alci rei*), *vanus, inanis, irritus.* Adv. *inutiliter* (only after negative), *frustra, ad irritum, incassum* (or as two words, *in cassum*).

usher, I. n. perhaps *apparitor ;* gentleman — (at court), *magister admissionum* (Imperial Rome) ; **2,** = under-teacher, *hypodidascalus.* **II.** v.tr. 1, *ad alqm introducĕre ;* 2, fig. see BEGIN.

usual, adj. *usitatus, solitus, consuetus, nequi*(*c*)*quam, inaniter, sol*(*l*)*emnis* (= habitual), *tritus* (of language, = commonplace), *vulgaris,* more or *usu receptus* (= customary) ; it is —, *solet ;* more than —, *plus quam solet, plus solito ;* see COMMON, CUSTOMARY. Adv. *ferme, fere, plerumque, ut solet.*

usucaption, n. *usucapio.*

usufruct, n. *usus, -ūs, et fructus, -ūs, ususfructus* (both parts of the word declined).

usurp, v.tr. (*as*)*sumĕre alqd, invadĕre in alqd, occupare* (e.g. *regnum,* = — the government). **usurper,** n. *qui regnum occupat.* **usurpation,** n. *occupatio,* or by the verbs.

---

usury, R. *fenerari.* **usurer,** n. *fenerator, tocullio.* **usurious,** adj. *avarus ;* see AVARICIOUS. **usury,** n. *usura* (paid by the debtor), *feneratio* (= lending on interest), *fenus, -ōris,* n. (= interest received).

utensil, n. *vas, -is* (in pl. *vasa, -orum,* = vessel), in farming, *instrumentum* (*rusticum,* as collective noun always in the sing.) ; —s, *utensilia, -ium,* n. (= everything necessary in daily life), *supellex, -ectilis,* f. (= household furniture).

uterine, adj. *uterinus* (Jct.).

utility, n. see USEFULNESS. **utilitarian,** adj. *qui omnia ad utilitatem confert.*

utmost, adj. *extremus, ultimus, summus ;* misery, *summae angustiae, extremae res, extrema or ultima, -orum, summa inopia ;* see EXTREME.

utter, uttermost, adj. see EXTREME, COMPLETE. Adv. *penitus, funditus ;* see ENTIRELY.

utter, v.tr. *significare* (= to give to understand), *indicare* (= to point out), *ostendĕre* (to show), *profitēri* (= to profess), *prae se ferre or gerēre* (= to declare openly) ; to — a sound, *sonitum edĕre, emittĕre ;* see PRONOUNCE. **utterance,** n. see PRONUNCIATION, DELIVERY.

uvula, n. *uva* (Plin.).

V.

vacancy, n. 1, = void space, *vacuum, inane, inanitas* (= emptiness) ; 2, with regard to office, by *vacuus ;* chosen to fill a —, *suffectus ;* 3, see LEISURE ; 4, of mind, *inanitas, stupiditas.* **vacant,** adj. 1, see EMPTY ; 2, of an office, *vacuus ;* to be —, *vacuum esse, vacare ;* 3, = unoccupied by business, by *vacuus labore or negotiis ;* 4, = empty, of thought, *stupidus ;* see FOOLISH ; 5, in law, *vacuus* (= having no heir, e.g. a house, field). **vacate,** v.tr. 1, = make empty, *vacuefacĕre ;* 2, = to make vacant, an office, *se abdicare alqā or* (but not in Cic. or Caes.). **vacation,** n. *feriae.* **vacuity, vacuum,** n. see VACANCY. **vacuus,** adj. see VACANT.

vaccinate, v.tr. anyone, *variolas alci inserĕre* (not class.). **vaccination,** n. *insitio variolarum.*

vacillate, v.intr. *vacillare* (lit. and fig.). **vacillating,** adj. *dubius, incertus, ambiguus ;* see DOUBTFUL. **vacillation,** n. *dubium, dubitatio ;* see DOUBT, HESITATION.

vagabond, vagrant, I. adj. *vagus.* **II.** n. *erro, grassator.* **vagary,** n. *nugae* (= tricks), *ineptiae* (= silliness) ; see WHIM.

vague, adj. *incertus, dubius, ambiguus, anceps ;* see INDEFINITE, UNCERTAIN. Adv. *incerte, dubie, ambigue.* **vagueness,** n. *dubium, dubitatio ;* see DOUBT, OBSCURITY.

vain, adj. 1, = empty, worthless, *inanis ;* see IDLE ; 2, = fruitless, *vanus, irritus ;* to labour in —, *operam perdĕre, operam frustra consumĕre or conterĕre, oleum et operam perdĕre* (prov., Cic.) ; 3, = proud, *inanis, vanis* (= foolishly —), *laudis avidus* (= ambitious), *superbus* (= proud), *gloriosus* (= boastful), *putidus* (= affected) ; to be —, *rebus inanibus delectari.* Adv. **in vain,** *frustra, incassum* (or *in cassam,* as two words), *nequi*(*c*)*quam ;* see VAIN ; = proudly, etc., *gloriose, putide, superbe.* **vainglorious,** adj. *gloriosus.* **vanity,** n. = emptiness, *inani-*

tas, vanitas, fragilitas; = empty pride, *ambitio, ostentatio.*

vale, n. see VALLEY.

valediction, valedictory, n. and adj. see FAREWELL.

valentine, n. *epistula amatoria.*

valet, n. *cubicularius.*

valetudinarian, n. *suae valetudinis (nimis) studiosus.*

valiant, valorous, adj. *fortis, animosus,* comb. *fortis et animosus* or *animosus et fortis, strenuus,* comb. *fortis atque strenuus* or *strenuus et fortis, acer* (= full of energy), comb. *acer et fortis;* see BRAVE. Adv. *fortiter, animose,* comb. *animose et fortiter, strenue, acriter.* **valour,** n. *fortitudo, virtus, -ūtis,* f.; see BRAVERY.

valid, adj. *gravis* (= important); in point of law, *bonus* (e.g. witness), *justus* (= right), *idoneus* (= fit, sufficient, e.g. witness, excuse), *ratus* (= confirmed, what has become a law), *firmus, certus,* comb. *ratus ac firmus* (e.g. *jussum);* to be —, *valēre* (of a coin, a law, etc.); to make anything —, *ratum facēre alqd, ratum esse alqd jubēre.* **validity,** n. (of reasons, etc.), *gravitas, pondus, -ĕris,* n.; in point of law (of a witness, etc.), *fides.*

valley, n. *(con)vallis.*

value, I. v.tr. (= to determine the worth of an object) *aestimare* (of gen. import), something greatly, *censēre* (of the censor), to be —d, *censēri* (used of citizens and their possessions); fig. = to think well of, *aestimare* (with genit. or abl.), *facēre, ducēre, pendēre, habēre* (with gen. *magni,* etc.), *deligēre;* to — not at all, *alqd nullo loco, nihilo, pro nihilo* or *nihil numerare, alqm nullo loco putare, alqm despicĕre;* to — highly, *magni facēre* or *ducēre,* or *pendēre,* or *habēre;* to — more than, *pluris aestimare;* to — little, *parvi facēre,* etc. **II.** n. *aestimatio* (= estimated value), *pretium* (= price), *virtus, -ūtis,* f. (= inner worth, of a person or thing); great (intrinsic) —, *praestantia;* moral —, worth, *virtus, honestas;* things without —, *res viles* or *leves.* **valuable,** adj. *pretiosus* (lit.), *magni pretii* (lit. and fig.), *alci acceptus, gratus* (of what does one good to see, hear, etc.). **valuation,** n. *aestimatio.* **valuer,** n. *qui alqd aestimat, aestimator.* **valueless,** see WORTHLESS.

valve, n. *epistomium.*

vampire, n. *vespertilio (qui sanguinem sugit).*

van, n. of an army, *primum agmen* (in marching order); *acies prima* (in battle order).

van, n. = winnowing-fan, *vannus,* f.

van, n. see CART, WAGGON.

vane, n. see WEATHERCOCK.

vanish, v.intr. *(e)vanescĕre.*

vanity, n. see under VAIN.

vanquish, v.tr. *(de)vincĕre, superare,* comb. *vincĕre et superare, domare* (= to subdue), *profligare* (= to drive an army off the field), *subigĕre* (= to subjugate). **vanquisher,** n. *victor* (f. *victrix), expugnator* with gen. (e.g. *urbis), domitor* with gen. (e.g. *Hispaniae).*

vapid, adj. **1,** *vapidus* (of wine); **2.** fig. see INSIPID.

vapour, n. *vapor,* †*halitus, -ūs, nebula* (= both arising from the ground and from the water); *terrae anhelitus, -ūs, ex(s)piratio,* or *exhalatio, ex terrā afflatus, -ūs* (more particularly

that ascending from the bottom of a cavern, whereby Pythia became inspired, both Cic. de Div. ii. 57, 117); — bath, *assa sudatio* (Cels.).

variable, adj. see CHANGEABLE. **variableness,** n. see CHANGE. **variance,** n. *discordia;* to set at —, *discordiam concitare;* to be at — with each other, *inter se discordare, inter se dissidēre;* see ENMITY. **variation,** n. *varietas* (= accidental change, e.g. *caeli);* see ALTERATION, CHANGE, DEVIATION. **vari-coloured, variegated,** adj. *varius, varii coloris, versicolor.* **variegate,** v.tr. *variare, distinguĕre.* **variety,** n. *varietas* (e.g. *caeli,* of the weather; *eloquendi,* of style), *diversitas, vicissitudo;* a — of things, *res multae* or *variae.* **various,** adj. *varius, diversus, multiplex* (= manifold). Adv. *varie, diverse.* **vary, I.** v.tr. *variare;* see ALTER, CHANGE. **II.** v.intr. *variare, variari, (com)mutari, immutari.*

varicose, adj. and n. *varix* (e.g. vein).

varlet, n. see SERVANT, ROGUE.

varnish, I. n. **1,** *atramentum tenue* (of a dark colour, for paintings, Plin.): **2,** = fair appearance, *color, fucus, species.* **II.** v.tr. **1,** *atramento tenui illinĕre;* **2,** fig. e.g. errors or deformity, *praetendĕre alqd alci rei, tegĕre* or *occultare alqd alqā re.*

vase, n. *vas, vasis,* n. see JAR.

vassal, n. *cliens.* **vassalage,** n. *clientela.*

vast, adj. *vastus, immanis,* comb. *vastus et immanis, magnus, ingens, incredibilis, amplus;* see GREAT. Adv. *magnopere, incredibiliter, valde;* see VERY. **vastness,** r. *amplitudo, magnitudo, immensitas.*

vat, n. *cupa, dolium.*

vaticinate, v.tr. see FORETELL.

vault, I. n. **1,** = arched roof, *camera, concameratio, fornix;* see ARCH; **2,** = —ed chamber, *fornix;* — underground, *hypogēum;* **3,** see TOMB. **II.** v.tr. **1,** *confornicare, concamerare;* see ARCH; **2,** *salire;* see LEAP.

vaunt, v.intr. and n. see BOAST.

veal, n. *(caro) vitulina.*

veer, v.intr. *se vertĕre, verti.*

vegetable, adj. *qui (quae, quod) ad plantas pertinet;* — kingdom, perhaps *plantae et arbores.* **vegetables,** n. *olus* or pl. *olera, -um,* n.; — garden, *hortus olitorius;* — gardener, *olitor;* — market, *forum olitorium.* **vegetate,** v.intr. **1,** lit. see GROW; **2,** fig. *hebescĕre, languēre.* **vegetation,** n. *herbae, plantae.* **vegetative,** adj. circ. by *crescĕre.*

vehemence, n. *vis, incitatio* (e.g. of a smell, of a disease, of a war, etc.), *impetus, -ūs* (= haste), *violentia* (= violence), *ardor, aestus, -ūs* (of a fever, of the passions), *impotentia* (= unbridled passion), *iracundia* (= hastiness), *studium* (= eagerness). **vehement,** adj. *vehemens* (= not calm, opp. *lenis, placidus), gravis* (= violent, e.g. *morbus, odor, verbum* [= offensive]), *magnus, acer* (= acting in a passion, opp. *lenis,* also e.g. *bellum),* comb. *acer et vehemens, acerbus* (= bitter), *animosus* (= spirited), *concitatus, incitatus* (= spurred on), *intentus* (= intent, anxious), *rapidus* (= quick, hasty), *violentus* (= violent), *atrox* (= dreadful, shocking), *ardens, flagrans* (of fever and of the passions), *iracundus* (= angry); — desire, *cupiditas magna* or *acris, ardens* or *flagrans.* Adv. *vehementer, valde, graviter, acriter, acerbe, contente, intente, animose, ardenter, violenter.*

vehicle, n. **1,** see CARRIAGE, WAGGON; **2.** MEANS.

veil, I. n. *rica* (among the Roman ladies, Plaut.), *flammeum* (Plin.), *flammeolum* (Juv., = bridal —) ; the — of oblivion, by *alqd velare, alqd occultare.* **II.** v.tr. *velare, tegĕre* (both lit. and fig.).

vein, n. *vena* (used also of veinlike marks in an object, and fig. as — of humour), *arteria* (= artery), *alqd alcjs rei* (fig. e.g. he has a — of strength, *alqd virium ei inest*).

vellicate, v.tr. *vellĕre, vellicare.*

vellum, n. *membrana.*

velocity, n. *velocitas ;* see SWIFTNESS.

velvet, n. see SILK. **velvety,** adj. see SMOOTH.

venal, adj. *venalis* (of merchandise, etc., or persons), *nummarius* (e.g. *judices, judicium*). **venality,** n. *animus venalis.*

vend, v.tr. *vendĕre.* **vender,** n. *venditor.* **vendible,** adj. *vendibilis.*

veneer, v.tr. *sectilibus laminis operire* or *vestire.*

venerable, adj. *venerabilis ;* see REVEREND. **venerate,** v.tr. *colĕre* (= to worship, revere), *observare* (= to revere), comb. *colĕre et observare, observare et diligĕre, in honore habĕre* (a man), *admirari, venerari* (a person or thing). **veneration,** n. *cultus, -ūs, veneratio* (of a god or of a man), *religio* (= awe).

venereal, adj. *venereus.*

vengeance, n. *ultio ;* see REVENGE.

venial, adj. *veniâ dignus.*

venison, n. (*caro*) *ferina.*

venom, n. 1, *venenum* (lit. and fig.); see POISON. **venomous,** adj. *venenatus* (lit. and fig.) ; see POISONOUS.

vent, I. n. 1, *spiramentum,* †*spiramen,* †*spiraculum* (in gen. = —-hole), *aestuarium* (= hole to let in air, e.g. in digging wells), *foramen ;* 2, by *effundĕre,* see below. **II.** v.tr. to — one's passion, *stomachum in algm erumpĕre, odium exprimĕre, iram,* etc., *in algm effundĕre, evomĕre.* **vent-hole,** n. see VENT I.

ventilate, v.tr. 1, *ventulum facĕre alci* (Com. by fanning), *ventilare* (= to fan); to — a room, *ventum* (*in cubiculum,* etc.), *immittĕre ;* 2, fig. *in medium proferre.* **ventilation,** n. use verb. **ventilator,** n. see VENT, I.

ventricle, n. *ventriculus.*

ventriloquist, n. *ventriloquus* (late ; in Plutarch's time, about A.D. 70, a — was termed in Greek πύθων, and, if a female, πυθώνισσα), perhaps *qui sonos alienos suâ voce imitatur.*

venture, I. n. = experiment, *experimentum, periculum* (= risk), *alea* (= hazard), *facinus, -ŏris,* n. (= bold act) ; at a —, *temere, forte, temere, fortuito ac temere, temere ac fortuito.* **II.** v.intr. and tr. *periclitari* (both *alqd,* and = to be endangered); to — to do a thing, *audēre* (courageously), *conari* (= to attempt, both with infin., never with *ut*); he —d to ask him, *ausus est eum rogare;* to — upon, at, on anything, *audēre alqd* (e.g. an undertaking, *facinus*), *periculum facĕre alcjs rei ;* into battle, by *se committĕre in aciem ;* nothing —, nothing win, prov. *dimidium facti, qui cœpit, habet* (Hor.), *fortes fortuna adjuvat* (Ter.). **venturesome, venturous,** adj. *audax, temerarius.* Adv. *audaciter, temere.* **venturousness,** n. *audacia, temeritas.*

veracious, adj. *verus, verax ;* see TRUTHFUL. **veracity,** n. *veritas.*

verandah, n. *subdialia, -ium* (= open galleries, Plin.), *podium* (= balcony), or *porticus,*

verb, n. *verbum* (gram.). **verbal,** adj. by *verbum* or *vox.* Adv. by *praesens* (= present), or *ipse* or *coram* (= face to face); see also VERBATIM. **verbatim,** adv. *ad verbum, totidem verbis.* **verbose,** adj. *verbosus.* **verboseness, verbosity,** n. *copia* or *ubertas verborum,* or by *copiose et abundanter de alqâ re dicĕre* or *loqui, in dicendo adhibĕre quandam speciem atque pompam.*

verdant, adj. *viridis.* **verdure,** n. *viriditas* (e.g. *pratorum*).

verdict, n. in law, *responsum* (= answer), *arbitrium* (= decision of an arbitrator, in gen.), *judicium* (= judgment of a judge); to pronounce a —, *decernĕre* (= to decide, of magistrates), *judicare, sententiam dicĕre* (of a judge).

verdigris, n. *aerugo* (Plin., *aeris* or *cypria*).

verge, n. 1, = brink, *margo, ora ;* see MARGIN ; 2, fig. by circumloc. (e.g. on the — of danger, *cum periculum jam instaret* or *imminente periculo,* or *minimum abfuit quin periculum adesset*). **verger,** n. *apparitor.*

verge, v.intr. *vergĕre ad alqd* (= to slope towards); to — upon, *tangĕre, attingĕre alqd* (= to touch), *alci rei finitimum esse* (lit. and fig.).

verification, n. *confirmatio ;* see PROOF. **verify,** v.tr. (*ap*)*probare, comprobare.* **verily,** adv. *profecto, sane, certe, nē* (*nae*). **verity,** n. see TRUTH.

verisimilitude, n. *verisimilitudo* (also as two words, *veri sim.*). **veritable,** adj. *verus ;* see TRUE, GENUINE.

vermilion, I. n. *minium.* **II.** adj. *miniatus* (= coloured with red-lead), *miniaceus* (= — coloured, Vitr.); see RED.

vermin, n. *bestiolae molestae* (in gen.), *pediculi* (= lice).

vernacular, adj. — tongue, *sermo patrius, sermo nativus, sermo noster, lingua nostra, verba -orum, nostratia.*

versatile, adj. *versatĭlis* (of that which may be turned round, lit.) ; of genius, *agilis, mobilis, varius et multiplex.* **versatility,** n. of genius, *facilitas, ingenium facile* or *mobile, agilitas, mobilitas.*

verse, n. *versus, -ūs, versiculus ;* to make —, *versus facĕre* or *scribĕre, versus fundĕre ;* = a short division of any composition, *pars.* **versification,** n. *versuum ratio.* **versify,** v.tr. *carmina facĕre.*

versed, adj. *versatus in alqâ re, exercitatus in alqâ re, perĭtus, gnarus alcjs rei.*

version, n. *liber scriptoris conversus.*

vertebra, n. *vertebra* (Plin.).

vertex, n. *vertex,* or by *summus ;* see SUMMIT. **vertical,** adj. (*di*)*rectus ;* a — line, *linea, perpendiculum.* Adv. *recte, directo, ad lineam, ad perpendiculum.*

vertiginous, adj. 1, e.g. motion, *quod in orbem circumagitur* or *circumfertur ;* 2, *vertiginosus* (= suffering from giddiness, Plin.). **vertigo,** n. *vertīgo* (*oculorum*).

very, I. adj. see TRUE, REAL, **II.** adv. *summe* (= in the highest degree, with verbs and adjs.), (*quam*) *maxime* (= most, with adj. and verbs), *magnopere* or *magno opere, maximopere* or *maximo opere, summopere* or *summo opere* (only with verbs), *impense* (= without fearing any trouble, only with verbs), *admodum* (= completely), *valde* (= with great strength ; the foregoing with verbs and adjs.), *sane quam* (= — much indeed, e.g. *gaudēre, brevis*), *oppido* (with adjs. and advs., more used in the colloquial style), *satis* (= sufficient, with regard to a certain end, to circumstances, to a position, etc., with adjs. and advs., e.g. *non satis se tutum in Argis videbat*), *enixe* (= with great exertion, e.g. to try, *operam dare*), *vehementer*, with *rogare, dolēre, gaudēre*, etc. ; (often = in the highest degree), *graviter* (with verbs and partic., e.g. to be ill, *aegrotare ; iratus*), *mire, mirifice, mire quantum* (= extraordinarily, with verbs and adjs.), *apprime* (mostly ante and post class. = extremely, with adjs., e.g. *apprime gnarus alcjs rei*), *perfecte* (= perfectly, e.g. *perfecte sapiens, eloquens*), *in primis* (*inprimis*, = foremost; instead of *in primis*, we find also *inter primos, in paucis, cum paucis, inter paucos, ante alios, praeter ceteros, super omnes*), *bene* (= well, with adjs., advs., and verbs, e.g. *bene mane, bene potus*), *probe* (= right, right well, with adjs. and verbs, but only in colloquial style), *egregie, eximie* (= exceedingly, with adjs. and verbs ; *egregie* also in daily intercourse, in the epistolary style and in conversation), *longe* (= by far, e.g. *longe superare*); " — " also by *per* or *prae* in composition with an adj., adv., or verb (e.g. — few, *perpauci* or *perquam pauci*; it pleases me — much, *mihi perplacet* or *mihi perquam placet, mihi valde placet ;* — hard, *praedurus ;* by a superl., which may be strengthened by adding *longe* or *multo* (e.g. *(longe) fertilissimus, multo ditissimus*); not —, before adj. and advs., by *non ita, haud ita* (e.g. not so — many, *non ita multi ;* not — long after, *haud ita multo post*).

vesicle, n. *vesica* (Plin.).

vesper, n. = evening star, *Hesperus, Vesper.* **vespers,** n. in the Romish Church, *Preces Vespertinae.*

vessel, n. = utensil, *vas, vasis* (in the pl. *vasa, -orum*, n.); in anatomy, blood —, *arteriae, venae ;* = ship, *navis.*

vest, I. n. *subucula*, or *tunica ;* see GARMENT. **II.** v.tr. 1, *vestire ;* see CLOTHE ; 2, see INVEST. **vested,** adj. e.g. rights, by *jus, juris*, n. (e.g. — interests are sacred, *jus alcjs est sacrosanctum*). **vestry,** n. *sacrarium.* **vesture,** n. see GARMENT.

vestal, I. adj. see PURE, CHASTE. **II.** n. *Vestalis (virgo).*

vestibule, n. *vestibulum, pronaus, -aos* (of a temple).

vestige, n. *vestigium.*

vetch, n. *vicia.*

veteran, adj. and n. *veteranus* (esp. of soldiers ; in the agricultural writers, also of animals and plants); a — soldier, *(miles) veteranus* or *emeritus ;* in wider sense, *veterator* (of a lawyer, Cic.).

veterinary, adj. *veterinarius* (Col.).

veto, I. n. *intercessio* (of the tribunes), in gen. by circumloc. ; see FORBID. **II.** v.tr. *rogationi intercedĕre* (of the tribunes); see FORBID.

vex, v.tr. *stomachum facĕre alci, indignationem movēre alci, offendĕre, pungĕre, sol(l)icitare, vexare, mordēre, commovēre alqm ;* to be —ed at, *alqd aegre* or *moleste ferre ;* I am —ed at, *me piget alcjs rei ;* see ANNOY. **vexation,** n. *aegritudo animi, indignatio, stomachus, molestia ;* full of —, *indignabundus.* **vexatious,** adj. *molestus, gravis ;* see TROUBLESOME. Adv. *moleste, graviter.*

viaduct, n. by *ponte jungĕre* (e.g. *flumen*).

vial, n. see BOTTLE.

viands, n. *cibus.*

viaticum, n. *viaticum.*

vibrate. v.intr. *vibrare ;* of sound, *tinnire*

(e.g. *aures tinniunt*), *vocalem sonam reddĕre* (e.g. of a column). **vibration,** n. *motus, -ūs.*

vicar, n. in gen. *vicarius.* **vicarage,** n. see BENEFICE, PARSONAGE. **vicarious,** adj. and adv. *alcjs loco.*

vice, prep. in composition, by *pro* or *sub* (e.g. *subpraefectus, proconsul*).

vice, n. *vitiositas, turpitudo* (= the quality of —), *libidines* (= lust), *vitia, -iorum* (= habitual sins ; one such, *vitium*), *flagitium, scelus, -ĕris*, n. (= as a wicked act). **vicious,** adj. *vitiosus* (= defective, unsound), *turpis* (= shameful), *flagitiosus* (= profligate, all of persons and things, e.g. *vita*), comb. *vitiosus ac flagitiosus* (e.g. *vita*), *cujus in animo improbitas versatur* (of man's heart, of man in general), *vitiis contaminatus, inquinatus* (= polluted with —, of persons and things), *scelestus, sceleratus, perditus* (= criminal ; the former of the disposition, the latter of an act of persons and things) ; very —, *vitiis, flagitiis, sceleribus obrutus* (of persons), *vitiis flagitiisque omnibus deditus* (also of things, e.g. *vita*). Adv. *vitiose, turpiter, flagitiose,* comb. *flagitiose et turpiter, scelerate, perdite, sceleste.* **viciousness,** n. see VICE.

vicissitude, n. *vicissitudo, vicissitudines* (= a change that takes place regularly, e.g. of the times, *vicissitudo* or *varietas temporum ;* of day and night, *dierum noctiumque vicissitudines ;* of fortune, *fortunae vicissitudo, mutatio rerum humanarum*).

victim, n. *victima, hostia, piaculum* (in expiation) ; see SACRIFICE. **victimize,** v.tr. see CHEAT.

victor, n. *victor ;* see CONQUEROR. **victorious,** adj. *victor, victrix* (with nouns of the fem. and neuter gender). Adv. by adj. **victory,** n. *victoria, tropaeum, triumphus* (= the triumph decreed by S^nate, hence = — itself) ; to gain —, *vincĕre, victoriam consequi, adipisci, victoriâ potiri.*

victuals, n. *cibus, cibaria, -orum, alimenta, -orum ;* see PROVISIONS. **victual,** v.tr. *rem frumentarium providēre, comparare, frumentum (com)parare, conferre ;* see FOOD.

vie, v.intr. *aemulari alqm* or *cum alqo ;* see RIVAL.

view, I. v.tr. see INSPECT, LOOK, SEE. **II.** n. 1, *(ad)spectus* (= vision), *acies* (= glance), *oculus* (= eye), *prospectus* (at a distance), *despectus* (from a high place), *conspectus* (= sight ; all *-ūs*) ; to be in —, *in conspectu esse ;* to come into —, *in conspectum venire ;* in — of, *in oculis situm esse ;* see SIGHT ; 2, see DESIGN ; point of —, *ratio ;* to consider in the right point of —, *vere* or *recte judicare de alqâ re.*

vigil, n. 1, see WATCH ; 2, in church affairs, *pervigilium ;* 3, see EVE. **vigilance,** n. *vigilantia ;* see CARE. **vigilant,** adj. *+ vigil, vigilans, intentus, providus, diligens.* Adv. *vigilanter, intente, diligenter.*

vigour, n. *vis* (physical and mental, pl. *vires*), *robur, -ŏris*, n. (= physical strength), *nervi, lacerti* (= nerve), *vigor* (= energy). **vigorous,** adj. *valens, validus* (= possessing physical strength), *strenuus, impiger, acer* (= energetic), *vegetus* (= fresh), *firmus,* comb. *firmus et robustus* (e.g. *respublica*), *valens et firmus* (e.g. *civitas*), *robustus* (= robust ; man, state, food), comb. *robustus et valens* (e.g. *homo*), *lacertosus* (= muscular, man and animal), *corpore vigens, corpore validus, corpore robusto* (the first of youthfulness, the second of physical strength, the third of a stout, healthy body), *fortis* (= strong), *acer* (= eager); see STRONG, ENERGETIC. Adv. *fortiter, acriter ;* see STRONGLY, EAGERLY.

vile, adj. *abjectus, nequam, turpis, detestabilis, inquinatus, illiberalis, sordidus, foedus.* Adv. *abjecte, nequiter, turpiter, inquinate, illiberaliter, sordide, foede.* **vileness,** n. *turpitudo, nequitia, illiberalitas, foeditas;* see DEPRAVITY. **vilify,** v.tr. *alqm ignominiâ afficere;* see SLANDER.

villa, n. *villa.*

village, n. *pagus, vicus.* **villager,** n. *paganus, vicanus, rusticus, agrestis.*

villain, n. 1, in Mediaeval Latin, * *villanus;* 2, *homo scelestus, sceleratus, nefarius, nequam, flagitiosus,* as a term of reproach, also *scelus, -ĕris,* n., *flagitium;* see ROGUE. **villanous,** adj. *scelestus, sceleratus, nefarius, nequam, flagitiosus.* **villany,** n. 1, as disposition, see WICKEDNESS; 2, as act, *scelus, -ĕris,* n., *facinus, -ŏris,* n., *dedecus, -ŏris,* n., *consilium foedum, flagitium.*

vindicate, v.tr. a right, *jus tenēre, obtinēre, retinēre;* one's character, *sibi constare, a se non desciscĕre;* to — one's liberty, *se in libertatem vindicare.* **vindication,** n. see DEFENCE. **vindictive,** adj. *ulciscendi cupidus;* a — spirit, *ulciscendi* or *ultionis cupidita*. Adv. use adj.

vine, I. n. *vitis, labrusca (vitis)* (= wild —); a small —, *viticula.* **II.** adj. *vinearius* (Col.), or by genit. of *vitis;* — dresser, *vinitor;* — yard, *vinea, vinetum, arbustum.* **vinegar,** n. *acetum;* — bottle, *acetabulum;* — leaf, *pampinus,* m. and f. **vinery,** n. perhaps *vites sub vitreis consitae.* **vinous,** adj. *vinosus* (mostly post class.). **vintage,** n. *vindemia, vindemiola* (small); to gather the —, *vindemiare uvas* or *vinum* (Plin). **vintner,** n. *vinarius* (ante and post class.).

violate, v.tr. *violare, rumpĕre.* **violable,** adj. † *violabilis.* **violation,** n. 1, *violatio;* 2, see RAPE. **violence,** n. *violentia, vis, ardor* (of heat), *fervor* (of heat or passion), *impotentia* (= lack of restraint), *acerbitas, morositas, immanitas* (all three of temper), (*caeli*) *intemperies,* (*caeli, morbi,* etc.) *gravitas, aestus, -ûs* (of a fever, etc.). **violator,** n. *violator, ruptor.* **violent,** adj. † *violens, violentus* (= boisterous, of mind, etc.), *acer, vehemens, impotens, gravis* (of illness, weather, etc.); see SEVERE, CRUEL. Adv. *violenter, acriter, vehementer, impotenter, graviter.*

violet, I. n. *viŏla, iŏn* (Plin.); a bed of —s, *violarium;* the colour, † *viola.* **II.** adj. *violacĕus, ianthinus* (Plin.).

violin, n. *fides, -ium,* f. (e.g. to play on the —, *fidibus canĕre.*)

viper, n. *vipera* (lit. and fig.), *aspis, -idis,* f.

virago, n. 1, = female warrior, † *virago, mulier* or *virgo bellicosa, animosa, fortis;* 2, = quarrelsome woman, *mulier jurgiosa.*

virgin, I. n. *virgo.* **II.** adj. † *virgineus, virginalis* (e.g. *verecundia*), *virgo* in app. to noun (e.g. *id ego virgo feci*); — soil, *terra rudis* (ante class.). **virginity,** n. *virginitas.*

virile, adj. (e.g. age) *virilis;* see MANLY. **virility,** n. *virilitas* (Plin., Quint.).

virtue, n. *virtus, -ûtis,* f., *laus* (= praiseworthy condition), *honestum, rectum* (= what is right), *honestas* (= probity), *sanctimonia* (= guiltlessness), *pudicitia* (= modesty of a woman, as her first —); = efficacy, *virtus, -ûtis, vis;* to have — in anything, *ad alqd alci prodesse;* by — of, *per* with accus. or *ex* with ablat. (e.g. he does it by — of his wealth, *per opes* or *(ex) opibus hoc facit*). **virtual,** adj. and adv. *re non verbo.* **virtuous,** adj. *virtute praeditus* or *ornatus, sanctus* (= pleasing to God, of persons and things), *honestus, probus* (= upright, of men), *castus* (= chaste); a — life, *vita honesta* or *sancta.* **virtuoso,** n. *alcjs rei artifex, alcjs rei peritissimus.*

virulence, n. 1, *vis, gravitas* (e.g. *morbi*); see POISON; 2, fig. *acerbitas, virus,* n. **virulent,** adj. *gravis* (e.g. climate, *caelum*); fig. *acerbus;* see BITTER. Adv. *graviter, acerbe.*

visage, n. see FACE, COUNTENANCE.

viscera, n. *viscera, -um, exta, -orum.*

viscid, adj. † *tenax, glutinosus* (= sticky, like glue, Col.); see STICKY.

visible, adj. *a(d)spectabilis, quod cerni potest, quod a(d)spectu semĭtur, conspectus, conspicuus* (= clear to be seen), *expressus* (= clearly expressed, e.g. *vestigia, indicia*), *apertus* (= open, opp. *occultus,* e.g. discord, *simultas;* dolor), *manifestus* (= manifest), *latens, occultus* (e.g. *caedes*). Adv. *manifesto;* see CLEARLY, EVIDENTLY. **vision,** n. (in optics) *visus, -ûs, a(d)spectus, -ûs, sensus, -ûs videndi, cernendi;* an optical illusion, *res objecta* (= what appears to the eye, Cic.), *visus, -ûs, visum, visio* (= anything seen, a — in a dream), *species* (both awake and in a dream), *simulacrum* (= anything we fancy as resembling a certain thing). **visionary,** adj. opp. to real, *inanis, fictus, vanus;* of character, *fanaticus* (= enthusiastic), perhaps *cogitationi deditus* (= unpractical), by circumloc., see DREAM, IMAGE.

visit, I. n. *salutatio, salutationis officium* (in the Roman sense, of friends and clients in the morning); to come on a —, *visendi caus(s)â venire;* to accept the — of anyone, *alqm admittĕre;* your — will be welcome to all, *carus omnibus exspectatusque venies.* **II.** v.tr. *alqm (in)visĕre* or *visitare, visendi caus(s)â venire* (to see how anyone is), *adire, convenire alqm* (in order to speak to or transact business with anyone), *salutare alqm, salutatum* or *salutandi caus(s)â ad alqm venire, ad alqm salutandum venire* (out of politeness, = to wait upon), *obire, adire, venire ad,* etc., *frequentare* (= attend, as a school); to — a fair, *obire nundinas;* to go on a round of —s, = anyone's country-seats, *obire villas suas;* (in a Scriptural sense) *alqm urgēre, vexare, punire.* **visitation,** n. (of Divine Providence) *poena.* **visitor,** n. *salutans, salutator, qui visendi (ac salutandi) caus(s)â venit (or veniunt) ad alqm, hospes, -ĭtis* (=guest); I have —s, *habeo alqm mecum;* I have no —, *solus sum, neminem mecum habeo;* I shall have many —s, *multi apud me erunt.*

visor, n. *buccula* (= cheek-piece)

vista, n. *prospectus, -ûs;* see VIEW.

visual, adj. (e.g. nerve) *oculorum nervus.*

vital, adj. *vitalis* (= belonging to life); = very important, *maximi momenti.* Adv. *maximi momenti;* see VERY. **vitality,** n. *animus, vis vitalis;* see LIFE.

vitiate, v.tr. *vitiare, corrumpĕre.* **vitiation,** n. *corruptio, depravatio.*

vitreous, adj. *vitreus.*

vitriol, n. * *vitriŏlum.*

vituperate, v.tr. see SCOLD. **vituperation,** n. *vituperatio, reprehensio.* **vituperative,** adj. see ABUSIVE.

vivacious, adj. *vividus;* see ACTIVE, CHEERFUL. **vivacity,** n. *vigor;* see LIVELINESS, CHEERFULNESS. **vivid,** adj. see LIVELY.

viviparous, adj. — animals, *bestiae quae partum edunt (vivum).*

vixen, n. 1, = she-fox, *vulpes, -is;* 2, =quarrelsome woman, *mulier jurgiosa.*

vizier, n. *cui summa imperii delegata est.*

vocabulary, n. *index verborum* (= list of words), *verba (nostra)* (= abundance of words).

vocal, adj. *vocalis;* — music, *vocum, cantus, -ûs;* — and instrumental music, *vocum nervorumque cantus.*

vocation, n. *officium, partes, -ium, munus, -èris,* n.

vocative, n. *casus, -ûs, vocativus* (Gram.).

vociferate, v.intr. *vociferari.* **vociferation,** n. *vociferatio.* **vociferous,** adj. and adv. *magno (cum) clamore.*

vogue, n. to be in —, *expeti* (of what has a sale), *moris esse* (= to be the custom).

voice, I. n. *vox* (= the faculty of uttering sounds ; then the sound produced), *cantus, -ûs,* (= song), *sonus* (= sound of the — and of musical instruments), *vocis sonus;* a clear —, *clara vox* (opp. *vox obtusa*), *vox canora* (opp. *vox fusca*) ; a high —, *vox acuta* (opp. *vox gravis*) ; with a loud —, *clarâ voce, magnâ voce ;* to raise the —, *attollère sonum;* to lower the —, *submittère vocem;* the general —, *omnium consensus, -ûs, consensus publicus;* there is but one —, *omnes uno ore in alqâ re consentiunt;* in Gram. a verb in the active, passive —, *verbum activum, passivum.* **II.** v.tr. see UTTER.

void, I. adj. 1, see EMPTY ; 2, lacking anything, *vacuus (ab) alqâ re, carens alqâ re, egens alcjs rei* or *alqâ re; —* of, *inops alcjs rei* or *alqâ re, privatus* or *spoliatus alqâ re.* **II.** n. *inanitas, inane, vacuitas, vacuum.* **III.** v.tr. see EMPTY, v.tr., VACATE.

volatile, adj. *volaticus* (lit. and fig.) ; fig. (of anyone's character, *lēvis, mobilis* (opp. *constans*). **volatility,** n. (of fluids, etc.) by *fugère ;* fig. *lēvitas, ingenium mobile, animus lēvis, vanitas, mobilitas (ingenii* or *animi,* opp. *constantia),* comb. *mobilitas et lēvitas animi.*

volcano, n. *mons e cujus vertice ignes erumpunt,* or *mons flammas eructans.* **volcanic,** adj. *flammas eructans, ignes* or *flammas evomens.*

volition, n. *voluntas.*

volley, n. *tormenta, -orum, emissa; —* of words, *flumen* or *turba (inanium) verborum.*

voluble, adj. see FLUENT.

volume, n. = book, or division of book, *liber, volumen* (= a roll of parchment), *pars* (as a part) ; — of smoke, etc., † *volumen,* or by noun with or without adj. (e.g. *fumus,* = smoke, *aqua* = water). **voluminous,** adj. by *multus* (e.g. he has left — writings on this, *multa* or *plurima de hâc re reliquit).*

voluntary, adj. *voluntarius, volens* (opp. *coactus), non coactus, non invitus,* or by *sponte (meâ,* etc.). Adv. *(meâ,* etc.) *voluntate, sponte* (= of one's own accord), comb. *suâ sponte et voluntate, ultro* (= without being asked). **volunteer, I.** n. *voluntarius (miles) ; —s, (milites) voluntarii.* **II.** v.intr. *voluntate facère alqd;* of soldiers, *nomen* (pl. of several, *nomina) dare.*

voluptuous, adj. *voluptarius, libidinosus, ad voluptates propensus, voluptatibus* or *rebus venereis deditus, impudicus* (= unchaste), *delicatus* (= effeminate). **voluptuousness,** n. *voluptas, libido,* or in the pl. *libidines.*

vomit, I. n. *vomitus, -ûs, vomitio* (both of the act and the matter thrown up ; mostly post class.). **II.** v.tr. and intr. *(e)vomère, vomitare* (frequently or much, Col. Sen.).

voracious, adj. *edax, cibi avidus, gulosus* (who is always eating), *vorax* (lit. and fig.). Adv. *avide* (lit. or fig.). **voracity,** n. *edacitas, cibi aviditas, voracitas.*

vortex, n. *vertex, turbo.*

votary, n. *(con)secratus, sacer* (= sacred, as belonging to the gods), in a gen. sense, *admirator, studiosus alcjs* or *alcjs rei;* a — of any science, by *alci rei se tradère.* **vote, I.** n. *sententia* (in gen. = opinion ; — of the senator, of the judge and the people), *suffragium* (of a citizen in the comitia; also of the voting tablet), *punctum* (= the vote which a candidate gained in the comitia), *tabella* (= voting tablet) ; to obtain the greatest number of —s in a tribe, *longe plurima in alqâ tribu puncta ferre* (Cic.) ; the right to a —, *suffragium,* or *jus suffragii.* **II.** v.intr. *sententiam ferre* (e.g. of a judge), *in sententiam alcjs discedère* (= to go over to another's opinion), *suffragium ferre* (by single individuals among the people in the comitia), *in suffragium ire* or *suffragium inire* (of the people in the comitia) ; *censère, decernère, jubère* (of the formal decrees of the senate) ; to — for anyone's opinion, *in sententiam pede* or (of several) *pedibus ire;* to — for anyone, *suffragari alci (ad munus)* (when anyone applies for a post) ; for anything, *suffragari alci rei* (also fig. = to approve, e.g. *alcjs consilio).* **voter,** n. *suffragator* (= one who votes in favour of anyone), *qui suffragium fert* (who gives a vote), *qui suffragium habet* (who has the right of voting). **voting-tablet,** n. *tabella* (in gen.), *suffragium* (in the comitia).

votive, adj. *votivus* (e.g. *ludi).*

vouch, I. v.tr. *asseverare, testari, affirmare, confirmare, adjurare* (e.g. with accus. and infin., = swear that a thing is so). **II.** v.intr. *testificari* (but often with accus.) ; to — for anything, by *praestare alqd* or *de alqâ re* (e.g. *damnum, periculum), alqd in se recipère, spondère futurum ut,* etc. **voucher,** n. 1, see WITNESS ; 2, see RECEIPT. **vouchsafe,** v.intr. *concedère.*

vow, I. n. *votum, voti sponsio* or *nuncupatio* (in the presence of proper witnesses), *devotio alcjs rei* (e.g. *vitae) ; religio* (= duty, constraint, etc. imposed by a vow). **II.** v.tr. *(de)vovère alqd alci* (also with fut. infin.) ; — to do anything, *spondère, promittère se alqd facturum esse;* see PROMISE, UNDERTAKE.

vowel, n. *lit(t)era vocalis.*

voyage, I. n. *navigatio, cursus, -ûs.* **II.** v.intr. *navigare ;* see SAIL, TRAVEL.

vulgar, adj. *vulgaris* (belonging to the mass), *plebeius* (= peculiar to the *plebs,* plebeian), *illiberalis, sordidus, rusticus ;* see RUDE. Adv. *illiberaliter, sordide, rustice, more rustico.* **vulgarism,** n. *sermo vulgaris.* **vulgarity,** n. see RUDENESS.

vulnerable, adj. *qui (quae, quod) vulnerari potest.*

vulpine, adj. *vulpinus* (Plin.).

vulture, n. *vultur(ius)* (lit. and fig.), *milvus.*

W.

wabble, v.intr. *vacillare* (both lit. and fig.). **wabbling,** n. *vacillatio.*

wad, v.tr. to — a dress, *vesti xylinum* (= cotton, Plin.) *insuère.* **wadding,** n. *xylinum vestibus insuendum.*

waddle, v.intr. *anatis in modum incedère.*

wade, v.intr. (through a river, etc.), *vado transire alqm locum.*

wafer, n. 1, in the eucharist, *panis cenae sacrae ;* 2, for fastening letters, *cera* or *signum* (= seal).

waft, v.tr. *sublime ferre.*

wag, I. v.tr. *movēre, quassare;* see SHAKE;
— the tail, *caudam movēre.* **II.** n. *homo jocosus, joculator.* **waggery,** n. *joca, -orum,
facetiae.* **waggish,** adj. *jocosus.*

wage, v.tr. *bellum gerĕre cum alqo;* — war;
see WAR. **wager, I.** n. *sponsio;* to lay a —,
sponsionem facĕre cum alqo. **II.** v.intr. see BET.
wages, n. *merces, -ēdis,* f., *stipendium.*

waggle, v.tr. and intr. see WAG.

wagon, n. *plaustrum, vehiculum, currus, -ūs.*
wagoner, n. *plaustri ductor.*

wagtail, n. *motacilla.*

waif, n. of persons, *inops, egens;* of things,
abjectus.

wail, I. v.intr. *plangĕre;* see LAMENT. **II.**
n. *planctus, -ūs;* see LAMENTATION.

wain, n. *plaustrum.*

wainscot, n. *r. . ries, -ētis,* m.

waist, n. *corpus, -ŏris,* n., *medium.* **waist-
band,** n. see BELT. **waistcoat,** n. *thorax
laneus* (= under — of wool (Suet.) worn by in-
valids), *subucula* (worn under the tunic).

wait, v.intr. *manēre;* to — for, *opperiri,
ex(s)pectare, alqm* or *alqd, praestolari alci* or *alqm,
manēre alqm* (so esp. of fate, etc., awaiting any
one, but not with accus. in Cic. or Caes.), or
dum alqs adveniat; to — on, *alci famulari* (so
ministrare alci pocula) = to salute, *salutare
alqm, alqm salutatum venire.*

wait, n. 1, lie in —; see AMBUSH; 2, a
nightly musician, *qui nocte fidibus canit.*
waiter, n. 1, *famulus* (in the house), *minister*
(who assists in any certain thing), *puer* (= boy);
2, see TRAY. **waiting,** n. 1, = delay, etc.;
mora, ex(s)pectatio, mansio, commoratio; 2, at
table, etc., *ministerium;* 3, = calling, *salutatio;*
lord, lady in —, by *unus (una) ex eis qui circa
alqm sunt;* see ATTENDANCE. **waitress,
waiting-maid,** n. *famula, ministra, ancilla*
(= servant). (N.B. Waiting at table in Roman
times was carried on by men).

waive, v.tr. *alqd concedĕre, de alqā re decedĕre.*

wake, I. v.tr. *exsuscitare, expergefacĕre (e
somno), excitare (e somno), (ex)suscitare (e) somno.*
II. v.intr. *excitari,* etc. **III.** n. *pervigilium*
(funebre). **wakeful,** adj. *vigil, † exsomnis,
† insomnis.* **wakefulness,** n. *insomnia, vigilantia, vigilia.*

walk, I. v.intr. *ire* (in gen., also for pleasure, e.g. *ibam forte viā sacrā,* Hor.), *gradi,
ingredi* (in a quiet manner), *incedĕre* (sometimes
= affectedly or majestically), *cedĕre;* to —
about, *deambulare* (till one is tired, e.g. *in litore*), *inambulare* (up and down in a place, e.g.
in gymnasio), *obambulare alci loco;* in front of
the rampart, *ante vallum;* in the fields, *in
herbis; spatiari* (for exercise, *in alqo loco*), to —
out, take a —, besides the preceding general
terms, more particularly by *ire* or *abire (deam-
bulatum, delectationis caus(s)ā ambulare* (up and
down a little, etc.); to — (opp. to ride, etc.) on
a journey, *pedibus ire, venire, iter facĕre, pedibus
incedĕre.* **II.** n. 1, = the act or state of —ing,
(de)ambulatio, inambulatio, itio; 2, = manner
of —ing, *incessus, -ūs, ingressus, -ūs;* 3, to take
a —, *alqo ire;* to go for a —, *(de)ambulatum ire;*
to go for a — to any one's house, *viam facĕre ad
alqm;* for pleasure or exercise, *ambulatio* (as act,
then as the place along which we walk), *inambulatio;* a short —, *ambulatiuncula* (act and place);
= avenue, *ambulacrum* (= planted with trees;
ante and post class.), *xystus* (= alley, Vitr.);
covered —, *tecta ambulatio* or *ambulatiuncula.*

walker, n. (masc. and fem.), *qui, quae (de)-
ambulat, ambulator* (fem. *ambulatrix,* who makes
a business of it, e.g. *villicus ambulator esse non
debet,* Col. ; *villica ne sit ambulatrix,* Cato de
R. R.). **walking,** n. see WALK, II. 1.

wall, I. n. *murus, moenia, -ium* (= walls of a
city), *maceria* (of clay, etc., as a fence round
gardens, farmyards, vineyards, parks, etc.),
paries, -ētis, m. (= party —, partition in a
building, house), *propugnacula, -orum,* n. (=
bulwarks); the ruins of an old —, *parietinae.*
II. v.tr. *muro cingĕre* or *circumdare, munire*
(= to fortify).

wallet, n. *pera* (Mart.), *saccus, mantica.*

wallow, v.intr. — in the mire, *in luto* (lit.
and fig.), *volutari.*

walnut, n. *juglans;* — tree, *juglans.*

wan, adj. *pallidus;* see PALE.

wand, n. *virga;* see ROD, STAFF.

wander, v.intr. *vagari, palari, errare, peregre abire* (= to go abroad), *peregrinari* (= to
travel abroad); to — over any place, *alqm locum
pervagari;* to — from the subject, *deerrare, aberrare (ab) alqā re;* to — from (in a moral sense),
de viā decedĕre (all = to stray from the right
path); to — in mind, *delirare.* **wanderer,** n.
erro, peregrinator (abroad). **wandering,** adj.
1, *errabundus, vagus;* 2, fig. *neglegens* (= inattentive), *delirus* (= crazy).

wane, v.intr. *decvescĕre* (of the moon, day,
etc.), *senescĕre* (of the moon, and fig. of life,
praise, etc.); see DECREASE, DECLINE.

want, I. n. = deficiency, *penuria,* opp. *copia,*
generally with genit.), *inopia* (with genit.), *egestas*
(= destitution), *desiderium* (= the — of a thing
previously possessed), *defectio, defectus, -ūs* (the
latter rare, except in Plin.), *difficultas, angustiae;* by compounds (e.g. — of temperance,
intemperantia; inertia (of activity); to be in
— of anything, *alqā re carēre* (in gen. = not
to have a thing), *alqā re egēre, indigēre* (= to
feel the lack of), *alcjs rei inopiā laborare,
premi,* or simply *ab alqā re laborare, alqā re
premi* (= to be pressed for it); to come to —,
ad inopiam venire; to suffer —, to live in
poverty, *vitam inopem colĕre, in egestate esse*
or *versari.* **II.** v.intr. *alqd alci dᵢ esse* (of
what we should have), *abesse* (when we do not
feel the —, e.g. *hoc unum ille, si nihil utilitatis
habeat, abfuit; si opus erat, defuit,* Cic.), *deficĕre*
(= to be short of anything); *alqd ab alqo desiderari*
(of what we do not like to miss); I shall not be
—ing, *(alci) non deero.* **III.** v.tr. 1, = to require,
egēre alqā re, seldom *alcjs rei, indigēre alqā re*
or *alcjs rei, opus* or *usus est alqā re* (when it
would be useful), *desiderare alqd, requirĕre alqd;*
I — so and so, *careo alqā re* (= I have not got it),
egeo alqā re (I should like to have it), *deficit mihi
alqd* or *deficit me alqd* (= it has left me, i.e. I am
short of it), *alqd non suppetit* (= it is not sufficient); I — nothing further, *nihil ultra flagito;*
see LACK; 2, = wish; see WISH. **wanting,**
adj. by *deesse;* see WANT, II.

wanton, I. adj. e.g. boys, *lascivus* (in play),
protervus, petulans (= bold); grown — by prosperity, *superbus* (e.g. *in fortunā*), *dissolutus* (= dissolute), *intemperans* (= indulging in sensuality),
effrenatus (= licentious); — injuries, *injuriae
ultro factae.* Adv. *ultro* (= without provocation)
*lascive, petulanter, proterve, dissolute, intemper-
anter, effrenate.* **II.** v.intr. *lascivire, lascivum,*
etc., *esse;* see above. **wantonness,** n. *lascivia, petulantia, protervitas, intemperantia.*

war, I. n. *bellum* (= — by land, *b. terrestre;*
by sea, *navale;* civil, intestine, *intestinum, domesticum, civile;* with the Gauls, *Gallicum;* with

slaves, *servile; for* life and death, *internecinum*), *arma*, *-orum* (= arms), *militia* (= military service, strategy), *tumultus*, *-ūs* (= outbreak in provinces, or close at home), † *Mars* (poet., except in phrases *meo*, *suo*, etc. *Marte*); in —, (*in*) *bello*; in time of —, *belli tempore*; in — and in peace, *domi bellique* or *bellogue*, *domi militiaeque*; to seek an occasion for —, *bellum quaerēre*; to cause or stir up —, *bellum movēre*, *concitare*, *excitare*, *ciēre*; to carry on a —, *bellare*, *bellum gerēre*, against, *cum alqo*; see ARMS, MILITARY, SOLDIER. **II.** v.intr. *bellare*, *bellum gerēre*; see above. **war-cry**, n. *clamor*, *bellicus*; to raise the —, *clamorem tollēre*. **warfare**, n. see WAR, I. **war-horse**, n. *equus militaris* or † *bellator*, or simply *equus*. **warlike**, adj. *militaris* (e.g. *inerat in eo habitus virilis vere ac militaris*), *bellicosus*, *ferox* (= inclined to war), *belliger* (= martial). **warrior**, n. *miles*.

warble, v.tr. *canēre*. **warbling**, n. *cantus*, *-ūs*.

ward, I. v.tr. to — off a blow, in fencing, *ictum* (or *petitionem*) *vitare*, *cavēre*, *cavēre et propulsare*, also simply *cavēre*, *vitare* (with the sword), *ictum declinare*, *petitionem declinatione corporis effugēre*, also simply *ictum effugēre* (by turning); fig. *amovēre*, *depellēre*, *repellēre*, *propellēre*, *propulsare*, *arcēre*, *avenēre*, *defendēre* (*alqd*, from anyone, *ab alqo* or *alcjs*), *deprecari* (by entreaties, e.g. *a se calamitatem*). **II.** n. 1, = quarter of a town, *regio*, *vicus* (as t.ts. both prob. post Aug.); **2,** = custody, *custodia*, *carcer*, *-ēris*, n. (= prison); see CUSTODY; **3,** = a minor, *pupillus*, *pupilla*; **4,** = part of a key, *clavis dens*. **warden**, **warder**, n. *custos*. **wardrobe**, n. *vestiarium* (= place and the garments together, Plin., Col.), *vestis*, *vestimenta*, *-orum* (= garments in gen.). **wardship**, n. *tutela*; see GUARDIANSHIP.

ware, n. 1, *merx*; see GOODS, MERCHANDISE; 2, see POTTERY. **warehouse, I.** n. *horreum*, *receptaculum mercium*, *cella* (= stores), *apotheca*. **II.** v.tr. *condēre*.

warm, I. adj. *calidus* (opp. *frigidus*); — water, *cal(i)da*; a — desire, *desiderium ardens* or *flagrans*; luke- —, *tepidus*; to be —, *calēre*; to become —, *calescēre*, *calefieri*. **II.** v.tr. *calefacēre*, *tepefacēre* (= to make tepid), *fovēre* (by the heat of the body). **warming-pan**, n. *vas excalfactorium*. **warmth**, n. *calor* (e.g. *solis*; fig., in Quint., Plin. *esp.*, *dicentis*, *dicendi*), *fervor* (lit. and fig.), *tepor* (lit); he speaks with —, *iratus dicit*.

warn, v.tr. (*prae*)*monēre* or *admonēre alqm ut* (or *ne*). **warning**, n. (*ad*)*monitio* (the act), *monitus*, *-ūs* (= — from heaven, by oracles, etc.), (*ad*)*monitum* (= notice given), *exemplum*, *documentum* (= example); to listen to a —, *audire* or *facēre ea quae alqs sapienter monuit*; to take anything as a —, *habēre alqd sibi documento*; to take anyone as a —, *exemplum sibi capēre de algo*; of a master, perhaps *missum* (*missam*) *facēre* (metaph. from dismissing soldiers; as the Roman servants were slaves, *vendēre* may be used at times); of a servant's —, *alci renuntiare* or *ab alqo discedēre* or *abire* (= leave).

warp, I. n. (in manufacture) *stamen*. **II.** v.intr. (of wood, etc.) *pandare*, *pandari*. **III.** v.tr. of wood, *pandum facēre*, fig. *torquēre*; see DISTORT.

warrant, 1. v.t. to — an officer, etc., *alci copiam dare* or *potestatem facēre*, to do a thing, *alcjs rei faciendae*; to a purchaser, *praestare alqd* or *de alqā re*, *to* anyone, *alci*; to feel —ed in anything, *magnam fiduciam alcjs rei habēre*; I — you, *meherc(u)le*, *medius fidius*; see also PROMISE, UNDERTAKE. **II.** n. (a written instru-

ment, in gen.), *auctoritas* (also in the pl.), *potestas*, *mandatum*, or by *auctor* (e.g. *Caesare auctore*, under the — of Caesar). **warrantable**, adj. *quod excusari potest*; see ALLOW. **warranty**, n. *satisdatio*; see GUARANTEE.

warren, n. *leporarium* (Var.).

warrior, n. see under WAR.

wart, n. *verrūca*; covered with —s, *verrucosus*.

wary, adj. *consideratus*, *cautus*. **wariness**, n. *cautio*, *circumspectio*.

wash, I. v.tr. *lavare*, *abluēre*; to — spots out of a garment, *maculas vestis eluēre*. **II.** v.intr. *lavari*. **III.** n. 1, *lavatio*; to take a —, *lavari*; 2, = ointment, *fucus*; —hand-basin, *aqualis* (Plaut.); —handstand, *abacus*; —house, *cella in qua lintea lavantur*; —tub, *labrum eluacrum* (Cato); washerwoman, *mulier* (or where possible, *serva*) *quae lintea lavat*.

wasp, n. *vespa*. **waspish**, adj. † *mordax*; see IRRITABLE.

waste, **I.** v.tr. *vastare*, (*de*)*populari*, *perpopulari* (= to lay —), see DESTROY; *consumēre*, *absumēre*, *conficēre* (all of sorrow, disease, etc.); = to squander, *dissipare*, *perdēre*, *profundēre*, *effundēre*, *exedēre* (= to eat away, lit. and fig.); to — time, *tempus perdēre*; see SPEND. **II.** v.intr. e.g. the body, (*con*)*tabescēre* (e.g. *morbo*, *desiderio*), *consumi*, *confici*. **III.** n. 1, = lonely place, *vastitas*, *solitudo*, *loca deserta* or *deserta*, *-orum*; 2, of expenditure, *sumptus effusi* or *profusi*; 3, in manufactures, *ramenta*, *-orum*, (of metals, etc.), *scobis* (= sawdust or filings); 4, = loss in gen. *jactura*, *damnum*; see LOSS; 5, fig. moral —, by special nouns (e.g. — of energy, *intemperantia*; of time, *inertia* [= laziness]). **IV.** adj. (e.g. country) *vastus*, *incultus* (opp. *cultus*, *consitus*, of the field), comb. *desertus et incultus* or *incultus et desertus* (e.g. *solum*). **wasteful**, adj. *profusus*, *effusus* (of persons and things), *prodigus* (usu. of persons). Adv. *profuse*, *effuse*, *prodige*. **wastefulness**, n. *profusio*, *effusio*; see WASTE, III. 2. **waste-book**, n. *adversaria*, *-orum*.

watch, I. n. 1, = a watching, *excubiae*, *vigilia*; to keep —, *vigilare*; 2, military term, men set to —, *vigilia* (e.g. *vigilias ponēre*, = to set a —), *statio* (of sentinels, *sentries*), *excubitores* (= sentinels), *excubiae* (Tac.); a —man, *vigil* (regular term for city policeman in Imperial Rome); 3, a division of time, *vigilia* (e.g. *primā*, *secundā vigiliā*, = in the first, second, etc. There were 4 —es in the night); 4, pocket timepiece, *horologium parvulum*; see CLOCK. **II.** v.intr. (*per*)*vigilare*, *excubare*; to — till late at night, *ad multam noctem*, *de multā nocte*; = to lie observant, *attentum esse*. **III.** v.tr. 1, = to observe, *alqd tuēri*, (*ob*)*servare*, *spectare* (= to have in view), *speculari*, *explorare* (= to examine); see OBSERVE, EXAMINE; 2, = to guard, *custodire*; see GUARD; to — for, *ex(s)pectare*, *opperiri* (*alqm*, or *alqd*), *alci insidiari* (in ambush, then metaph. in gen.); to — an opportunity, *occasionem captare*; to — over, *alqd tuēri*, *observare*. **watchfire**, n. *ignis*. **watchful**, adj. † *vigil*, *vigilans*. Adv. *vigilanter*. **watchfulness**, n. *vigilantia*, *vigilia*; see also CARE. **watchman**, n. *vigil* (see WATCH I., 2), *excubitor*, *custos*. **watchtower**, n. *specula* (also fig. *tanquam e speculā prospexi tempestatem futuram*). **watchword**, n. *tessera* (= tablet on which the — was written), *signum* (lit. and fig.), this was the — of the Stoics, *hoc Stoici praeceperunt*.

water, I. n. *aqua* (plur. *aquae* of a larger quantity, also of medicinal springs), † *latex*, † *lympha* and † *unda*; running —, *aqua viva*, *flumen vivum*; fresh —, *aqua dulcis*; salt- —, *aqua* *talsa;* sea- —, *aqua marina;* rain- —, *aqua pluvia-tilis, aqua caelestis;* to go for, fetch —, *aquam petĕre, aquatum ire, aquari* (in a larger quantity, i.e. of soldiers for the army); to lay under —, *irrigare* (e.g. a field), *inundare* (= to inundate); by land and —, *terrâ marique;* to travel by —, *navigare;* prov., still —s run deep, *altissima quaeque flumina minimo sono labuntur* (Curt.); the — under the skin, *aqua intercus* (= dropsy); = urine, *urina;* = colour of a diamond, *splendor;* — -bearer, in gen., *aquarius,* in the army, *aquator,* = a sign of the zodiac, *Aquarius;* — -bottle, *ampulla, lagena;* — -butt, -cask, *dolium;* — -clock, *clepsydra;* — -closet, *latrina, sella familiarica;* — -colour, *pigmentum aquâ dilutum;* — -fall, *aqua ex edito desiliens* (Plin.); — -fowl, *avis aquatica* (Plin.). **II.** adj. *aquatilis, aquarius;* — animals, *aquatilia, -ium,* pl. **III.** v.tr. and intr. *irrigare* (*rigare*); see also SPRINKLE, MIX; it makes my teeth or my mouth —, *salivam mihi alqd movet* (Sen.). **watering,** n. *aquatio* (= fetching of —, or by verb, e.g. *aquatum ire*); — of plants, by *aquâ conspergĕre;* — -place (of inland places, i.e. mineral springs), *aquae;* of seaside, circumloc. with *maritimus* (e.g. *oppidum maritimum);* — -pot, *hydria, urceus;* see JAR. **waterproof,** adj. *aquae vi resistens.* **watersnake,** n. *hydrus.* **waterspout,** n. 1, *fistula* (= waterpipe); 2, = sheet of water, *typhon* (Plin.). **waterworks,** n. *aquaeductus, -ûs* (= an aqueduct, the nearest class. equivalent to our —). **watery,** adj. *aquatilis* (Plin.), = having a — taste), *aquosus* (= abounding in water).

wattle, I. n. 1, = hurdle, *crates, -is,* f. ; 2, of a cock, *palea.* **II.** v.tr. *contexĕre;* see WEAVE.

wave, I. n. *unda, fluctus, -ûs.* **II.** v.tr. *agitare, jactare,* † *rotare.* **III.** v.intr. *undare, fluctuare,* † *fluitare, agitari, jactari.*

waver, v.intr. *fluctuare* (*animi* or *animo*), *dubitare;* see HESITATE. **waverer,** n. (*homo*) *inconstans, incertus.* **wavering,** n. *inconstantia, animus incertus* or *dubius* or *suspensus, dubitatio.*

wax, n. *cera;* to mould in —, *e cerâ fingĕre;* — candle, — light, *cereus.* **waxen,** adj. *cereus.* **wax,** v.intr. *crescĕre;* see GROW.

way, n. *via* (lit. and fig.), *iter, -inĕris,* n. (= the going from one place to another, hence a march), *aditus, -ûs* (= access), *cursus, -ûs* (= the direction or course), *semita* (= a small way, a path), *trames, -itis,* m. (= a subordinate way running along beside the highway, a foot-road or path), *callis* (= a hilly road), *deverticulum* (= a side road leading off from the chief or high road), *meatus, -ûs* (post Aug. = a channel or course), *limes, -itis,* m. (= a boundary path or line), *angiportus, -ûs* (= a narrow — or street between two rows of houses), *ratio* (= plan or manner), *mos* (= custom, e.g. in the — of the Romans, *more Romanorum*), *consilium, institutum* (= plan); a straight — or path, *via recta;* a short —, *compendiaria* (most often fig., with *quasi,* e.g. *via ad gloriam proxima et quasi compendiaria,* Cic.), *compendium viae;* when there are two —s, *bivium;* three, *trivium;* four, *quadrivium;* — there is none, *avia, -orum;* by- —s *iter devium;* out of the —, *avius, remotus* (lit.), *reconditus, exquisitus* (fig.); to go the direct — or road, *rectâ viâ ire;* on the —, *inter viam, ex itinere;* to make —, see PROGRESS; to form a — or plan, *rationem inire;* to get out of the —, *de viâ decedĕre alci, alcjs congressum fugĕre;* —s and means, *opes, -ûm,* f. (= resources), *ratio* (= plan); by the —, in passing (of a speaker), *strictim* (= cursorily), *ut hoc dicam;* see ROAD; to get under — (of a ship), *absolvi, ancorâ* (*ancoram*) *solvĕre.* **way-farer,** n. *viator.* **waylay,** v.tr. *alci insi-*

diari or *insidias facĕre.* **wayside,** n. and adj. *ad viam.* **wayward,** adj. see WILFUL, F.CKLE.

we, pron. *nos;* — ourselves, *nos ipsi, nosmet ipsi;* frequently not expressed.

weak, adj. *tenuis* (= thin, opp. *crassus;* then fig., e.g. *sonus, spes), exilis* (= fine, e.g. *vox,* Quint.), *parvus, exiguus* (= inconsiderable), *lēvis* (of what cannot be maintained, opp. *gravis,* e.g. *argumentum), imbecillus* (late *imbecillis,* = — in bodily strength or mind); a — head, *ingenium imbecillum;* *infirmus* (of one who can stand nothing) *debilis* (= frail, opp. *robustus), invalidus* (opp. *validus), enervatus* (= unnerved, with *velut* before it, also of the state), *languidus, iners* (= sluggish) *mollis* (= effeminate), *fractus* (= broken), *confectus* (= worn out, of a man and his body), *hebes* (= dull, opp. *acer,* e.g. sight, hearing, memory). **weakly, I.** adv. *tenuiter, exiliter, exigue, imbecille, infirme, molliter.* **II.** adj. see WEAK. **weaken,** v.tr. *imbecillum* or *infirmum* (e.g. *stomachum) reddĕre, debilitare* (lit. and fig., e.g. anyone's rage), *delumbare* (fig., e.g. an idea; very rare), *enervare* (= to unnerve), *infirmare* (lit., to make loose what was firm; then fig., to — a thing, e.g. *fidem testis), attenuare, extenuare* (lit., to make thin, = to diminish in gen.), (*com)minuĕre* (= to lessen), *frangĕre* (lit., = to break), *hebetare, obtundĕre* (= to make dull), *labefactare* (= to shake, lit. and fig.). **weakening,** n. *debilitatio, infractio, deminutio, imminutio,* or by verb. **weakness,** n. *tenuitas* (opp. *crassitudo,* e.g. of a thread), *exilitas* (e.g. *in dicendo), imbecillitas, infirmitas* (of body and mind), *debilitas* (of body and mind), *virium defectio, languor, lēvitas* (of arguments, etc.), *vitium, error* (= fault).

weal, n. the public —, *salus publica, respublica.*

weal, n. = mark on the body, *vibex.*

wealth, n. *res secundae* or *prosperae* or *florentes, divitiae, opes, -um,* pl., *copia* (esp. with genit., e.g. *rei familiaris), abundantia alcjs rei, opulentia.* **wealthy,** adj. *bene nummatus, pecuniosus, copiis rei familiaris locuples et pecuniosus, opulentus, opulens, copiosus.*

wean, v.tr. 1, † *infantem lacte depellĕre, a matre prohibēre;* 2, fig., *alqm alqd dedocēre.*

weapon, n. *arma, -orum,* n., *telum.*

wear, I. v.tr. 1, = to waste, (*usu)* (*at)terĕre* or *deserĕre;* very much, *conterĕre* (e.g. *librum legendo);* 2, = to have on the body, *gerĕre, gestare, indutum esse alqâ re, indui alqâ re, ornatum esse alqâ re* (as ornament), (*sue)cinctum esse alqâ re, uti alqâ re* (= to make use of), *tractare alqd* (= to handle, e.g. *arma);* to — the toga, *togatum esse;* to — away or out, see before, also CONSUME. **II.** v.intr. *usu atteri* or *delēri;* to — off, *evanescĕre.* **III.** n. *usus, -ûs* (e.g. *margaritarum);* to stand — and tear, of things, *usu non attritum esse,* of persons, *omnia fortiter perferre.* **wearing,** n. *usus, -ûs;* — apparel, *vestimentum.* **worn,** adj. *usu detritus* (Plin., of a garment); — out (= hackneyed), *contritus, obsoletus* (often used, and hence old, e.g. *vestis,* fig. *verba);* — out (= tired out), (*de)fatigatus, lassus, fessus;* with illness, wounds, etc., *morbo, vulneribus,* etc., *confectus* or *fractus.*

weary, I. adj. 1, = fatigued, (*de)fatigatus, lassus, fessus;* 2, = disgusted with, by *taedet* or *pertaesum est alqm alcjs rei.* **II.** v.tr. *alqm* (*de)fatigare;* = — with, *alqm obtundĕre;* see BORE. **III.** v.intr. by *taedet* or *pertaesum est alqm alcjs rei.* **weariness,** n. 1, = fatigue, (*de)fatigatio, lassitudo;* 2, fig. *taedium.* **wearisome,** adj. *longus, laboriosus.*

weasel, n. *mustela.*

weather, I. n. caelum, caeli status, -ūs, tempestas (good or bad); fine, clear —, tempestas bona or serena, caelum sudum or serenum; dry —, siccitas; to depend upon the —, to be guided by the —, by tempestatis rationem habēre; — cock, gallus a(h)eneus; — wise, caeli mutationum peritus. **II.** v.tr. **1,** lit. alqm locum circumvehi; **2,** fig. superare; — a storm, vim tempestatis perferre.

weave, v.tr. (con)texēre (lit. and fig.). **weaver,** n. textor. **web,** n. textum, textura, tela; — footed, quibus pedes ad nandum accommodati sunt.

wed, v.tr. see MARRY. **wedlock,** n. see MARRIAGE. **wedding.** n. see MARRIAGE; — day, dies nuptiarum; to fix the — day, diem nuptiis dicēre.

wedge, I. n. cuneus; — shaped, cuneatus; seats in the theatre in — shape, cunei; troops drawn up in — shape, cuneus. **II.** v.tr. cuneare; — together, see CROWD.

Wednesday, n. *dies Mercurii.

weed, I. n. herba inutilis or iners. **II.** v.tr. (e)runcare.

weed, n. =garment, vestis; in —s of peace, (cives) togati; widows' —s, viduarum more vestita.

week, n. septem dierum spatium, septem dies or hebdomas; one —, septem dies; a fortnight, quindecim dies (Caes.). **week-days,** n. dies profesti (opp. dies fasti), dies negotiosi (Tac.), opp. dies sacri). **weekly,** adj. by circumloc. (e.g. — wages, merces quae in singulas hebdomades habentur).

weep, v.intr. and tr. lacrimare or lacrimari, lacrimas fundere (=to shed tears), (de)plorare (loudly), lamentari (of sustained weeping), ejulare (pitifully, e.g. of female mourners), vagire (of little children); — over anything, alci rei illacrimare or illacrimari. **weeping,** n. fletus, -ūs, lacrimae (=tears), ploratus, ejulatus, vagitus (all -ūs), lamentatio.

weevil, n. curculio.

weigh, I. v.tr. **1,** (ex)pendēre, perpendēre, examinare; **2,** fig. (ex)pendēre, perpendēre, ponderare, examinare (e.g. quădam populari trutină examinari, Cic.), considerare cum or in animo, secum reputare, mente agitare or volutare; — deeply, multa (etiam atque etiam) secum reputare; — down, opprimēre (lit. and fig.). **II.** v.intr. pondo pendēre or pondo valēre with acc. of the weight; to — heavily, magni ponderis esse; to — ten pounds, decem libras explēre. **weight,** n. pondus, -eris, n., gravitas, momentum (lit. and fig.; e.g. terrae, armorum); see IMPORTANCE, PRESSURE, **weighty,** adj. gravis (lit. and fig.). Adv. graviter (lit. and fig.).

weir, n. moles, -is, f., agger, -ēris, m. (= dam), cataracta (καταρράκτης = sluice lock, Plin. Min.).

welcome, I. adj. acceptus, gratus, ex(s)pectatus, exoptatus; to bid —, alqm salvēre jubeo, benigne alqm excipēre; you will be — to all, carus omnibus ex(s)pectatusque venies; be —, salve. **II.** n. salutatio. **III.** v.tr. salutare alqm, benigne alqm accipēre. **IV.** interj. salve (pl. salvete).

welfare, n. salus, -ūtis, f., incolumitas (= safety), bonum (= anyone's interests, or of a thing), felicitas (= happiness); to try to promote anyone's —, alcjs commodis or utilitatibus servire, alcjs saluti prospicēre, consulēre, servire.

well, I. adv. bene, recte; very —, optime, praeclare; as exclamation, esto! (expressing consent), bene! recte! pulc(h)re! (acclamation); very —! quam maxime! (general exclamation), ita est! (in reply); — then! age! recte vero! to take a thing —, alqd in bonam partem accipēre; to do —, bene or recte facēre or agēre or gerēre rem. **II.** adj. salvus, sanus, integer, valens; to be —, (bene, commode, or recte) valēre, belle, recte, pulc(h)re, bene (se) habēre; to get —, convalescēre; not to be —, male se habēre. **well-affected,** adj. benevolus erga alqm. **well-being,** n. salus, -ūtis, f., bona valetudo. **well-born,** adj. nobilis; see NOBLE. **well-bred,** adj. urbanus; see POLITE. **well-built,** adj. bene aedificatus (of structures), formosus (of persons). **well-disposed,** adj. see WELL-AFFECTED. **well-educated, well-informed,** adj. doctus, eruditus; see LEARNED. **well-fed,** adj. corpore amplo, pinguis (opp. macer), opimus(opp. gracilis), obesus(opp. gracilis, strigosus). **well-known,** adj. omnibus notus. **well-meaning,** adj. benevolus, amicus (both of persons), fidelis (e.g. friend; consilium, advice). **well-meant,** adj. e.g. advice, consilium benevole dictum. **well-spent,** adj. e.g. life, vita bene acta. **well-wisher,** n. studiosus alcjs.

weld, v.tr. (con)ferruminare (Plin.).

well, I. n. puteus. **II.** v.intr. — up, scatēre; see SPRING, v.intr.

welter, v.intr. se volutare, volutari.

west, I. n. regio ad occidentem vergens, occidens (= the setting sun), occidens, occasus, -ūs (solis). **II.** adj. occidentalis (Plin.), †occiduus; — wind, Zephyrus, Favonius; North — wind, Caurus (Cor.); South — wind, Africus. **westward,** adj. ad occasum, ad occidentem vergens, in occidentem spectans. **western,** adj. occidentalis (Plin.). **westerly,** adj. (wind) ab occidente, in occidente.

wet, I. adj. humidus, madens (mostly poet. and post Aug.), madidus, *† uduw, uvidus (mostly poet. and post Aug.); see MOIST. **II.** n. caeli status, -ūs, humidus or uvidus or pluvius; see RAIN. **III.** v.tr. madefacēre, madidum reddēre, perfundere; to get — through, madefieri, madidum reddi; — nurse, nutrix. **wetness,** n. humor.

wether, n. vervex, -ēcis, m.

whale, n. balaena, cetus (in pl. cete) (= sea-monster in gen.; Plin.); —bone, balaenae maxilla.

wharf, n. navale, crepido.

what, pron. interrog. quid? — do you want? quid vis? — does that mean? quid hoc sibi vult? As a conjunctive or adj. pronoun, qualis, qui; he wrote to me — books he had read, scripsit mihi quos libros legerit; in reference to an antecedent by qui; — you told me, id quod or ea quae mihi dixisti. **whatever,** pron. quicunque (quicum), quisquis.

wheal, n. vibex (ante and post class.).

wheat, n. triticum, siligo (= very fine white —, ante and post class); of —, wheaten, triticeus; a — field, ager tritico consitus; — meal, farina triticea.

wheedle, v.tr. and intr. illicēre.

wheel, I. n. rota, tympanum (τύμπανον, of water-mills, etc.), radii (= spokes of —); as instrument of torture, equuleus; see RACK. **II.** v.tr. **1,** = push forward, propellēre; **2,** = turn round, convertēre, circumagēre; = push, propulsare; —barrow, vehiculum (= cart) or corbis (= basket). **III.** v.intr. signa convertēre (of soldiers); right, left —, in hastam, in scutum. **wheelwright,** n. qui rotas facit.

wheeze, v.intr. anhelare; see PANT. **wheezy,** adj. †anhelus.

whelm, v.tr. see OVERWHELM.

whelp, n. catulus.

when, adv. and conj. = at the time that, *cum* (*quom*) (in this sense with the indic. ; the subj. is used only when we speak hypothetically or state the opinion of another), *quo tempore, ubi* (= then —, etc., generally with indic.; with the subj. only when we represent anything as uncertain, casual, etc.), *quando* (= — once, interrog. and indefinitely as well as in a relative sense ; with subj. only in indirect questions when we represent circumstances as repeatedly occurring ; otherwise always with indic.), *ut* (= as soon as, of any result, after which another result immediately takes place, always with indic.); often by the particip. of the verb; = at what time, interrogatively, *quando?* *quo tempore?* = at which time; see WHO, WHICH; = after the time that, *cum, ut, ubi* (the last two always with indic. *cum* also with present and perfect indic., and when the action is represented as occurring repeatedly [as often as], with the imperf. indic. ; however in the narrative style in past tenses always with imperf. and pluperf. subj.; often "when" in this sense is rendered by a partic. in the same case as the noun to which it refers, if the subject is the same both in the main and in the dependent clause ; but if the latter has a different subject from that in the main cl̄ause, then by the ablat. abs.). **whence**, adv. as interrog., *unde?* *ex quo loco?* = from whom? whereby? *unde? a, ex quo homine? ex quâ re?* — have you got that? *a quo hoc accepisti?* (in gen.) ; *unde id scis?* (= — do you know that?); — does it come that, etc., *unde fit ut*, etc. **whenever, whensoever**, conj. *quandocunque* (*cumq.*), *quotie(n)scunque* (*cumq.*), or simply *utcunque, quotie(n)s.*

where, adv. and conj. as interrogative, *ubi? ubinam? quo loco? quo loci?* —ever? *ubi gentium? ubi terrarum?* as relative particle, *ubi, quâ.* **whereas**, adv. *quoniam, quod, cum, quippe qui* (*quae, quod*); see BECAUSE, SINCE. **whereby**, adv. *ex quo* (*quâ*, etc.) *fit* ; as interrog. *quâ ratione? quâ re?* **wherefore**, adv. 1, interrog. *cur?* see WHY ; 2, *quamobrem;* see THEREFORE. **wherein**, adv. *in quo, in quâ re, in quibus, ubi.* **wherever**, adv. *ubivis* (= at any p̄lace, whichever it may be), *ubicunque* (*cumq.*), *quacumque* (= at any place). **whereof**, adv. *cujus quorum* (*quarum,* etc.) or *e quo* (*quâ*, etc.). **whereon**, adv. *quo facto, cum quibus verbis.* **whereto**, adv. *quo(rsum), quem ad finem.*

wherry, n. see BOAT.

whet, v.tr. (*ex*)*acuĕre* (lit. and fig.). **whetstone**, n. *cos.*

whether, I. pron. *uter.* II. conj. *ne* (appended to that word in the interrog. sentence upon which the stress lies), *num* (= — perhaps), *utrum* (seldom in simple questions), *an* (only after *nescire* and similar verbs of doubting), in double questions, — . . . or (" or —") *utrum . . . an* (or *anne* or *ne*), *num . . . an, ne* (as an enclitic) ; sometimes *ne* is appended to *utrum,* sometimes also *ne* is put, a few words intervening, after *utrum,* esp. when in the two clauses there occur two words opposed to each other, e.g. *utrum taceamne, an praedicem?* sometimes "—" in the first question is not at all expressed in Latin, e.g. *interrogatur, pauca sint, anne multa;* sometimes, in two interrog. clauses where two words are directly opposed to each other, the interrog. particles may be left out altogether, e.g. *velit, nolit, scire difficile est ;* if " or" in the second question appears as more a copulative than an interrog. particle, it is simply rendered by *aut,* e.g. *quaesierunt necne ille aut ille defensurus esset; — . . .* or not, *utrum* (*num* or *ne*) . . . *necne* or *annon* (*necne* generally in indirect

questions and without any verb at all, whilst *annon* is chiefly used in direct and but seldom in indirect questions, both with and without a verb), e.g. *quaeritur sintne dii, necne sint;* or *dii utrum sint, necne, quaeritur;* or even *dii necne sint quaeritur* (sometimes for *annon, anne* is found, e.g. *cum interrogetur tria pauca sint anne multa,* Cic.)*;* where the alternatives are presented as on an equality, either of which may be true, *sive—sive* (*seu—seu*) (e.g. *sive eum ex paludibus elicĕre, sive obsidione premĕre posset.* Caes).

whey, n. *serum.*

which, pron. see WHO.

whiff, n.*halitus, -ūs* (= breath).

while, I. n. *tempus, -ŏris,* n., *spatium, mora* (= delay), *otium* (= leisure) ; a little, short —, *breve spatium, pau(l)lulum* (*temporis*) : for a short —, *parumper, pau(l)lisper* ; a little — after, *paul(l)o post, non ita multo post, pau(l)lo post ;* a long — after, *post longum tempus.* II. (**whilst**) conj. *dum* (nearly always with present indic. even when the verb in the main clause is in the past tense), *donec* (with indic. or subj. according to the regular rules of mood), *cum* (*quom,* with pres. and perf. indic. and imperf. and p̄luperf. subj.), or by part. (e.g. *haec lacrimans dixit,* she said — weeping), or by *inter* with gerund in phrases (*inter bibendum, = —* drinking; *inter cenandum, = —* dining). III. v.tr. to — away the time, *tempus fallĕre alqâ re.*

whim, n. *libido.* **whimsical**, adj. *difficilis, naturâ difficilis, morosus* (= ill-tempered), *inconstans, lēvis* (= fickle) ; see FICKLE.

whimper, v.tr., **whine**, v.intr. *vagire* (of a child or animal). **whimpering**, n. **whining**, n. *vagitus, -ūs.*

whinny, v.intr. *hinnire.*

whip, I. n. *scutica, -ae,* f., or *tora, -orum,* n. (made of cords tied together), *flagrum, flagellum.* II. v.tr. *verberare.*

whirl, I. v.tr. (*con*)*torquēre, quassare, quatĕre* (= to shake). II. v.intr. as in dancing, *in gyrum agi.* III. n. *vertigo* (mostly post Aug.), or by verb. **whirlpool**, n. *turbo, vertex, vorago, gurges, -ĭtis,* m. **whirlwind**, n. *turbo, vertex.*

whirr, I. v.tr. *stridĕre* (*stridĕre*). II. n. *stridor.*

whisk, v.tr. see SNATCH.

whiskers, n. by *genae pilosae* or †*hirsutae.*

whisper, I. v.intr. *susurrare,* to anyone, *cum* †*alqo.* II. v.tr. anything into anyone's ear, *insusurrare alci alqd ad aurem* or *in aures.* III. n. *susurrus.* **whisperer**, n. *susurrator* (very rare).

whist, I. n. by *chartarum ludus,* but where possible translate by *alea* (= dice). II. interj. *st! tace, tacete.*

whistle, I. v.intr. and tr. *sibilare ;* to — anyone, *alqm sibilo advocare.* II. n. *sibilus;* pl. also *sibila, -orum.* **whistler**, n. *qui sibilat* (with the mouth), *tibicen* (on the pipe).

whit, n., not a —, *ne minimum quidem, minime.*

white, I. adj. *albus* (opp. *ater*), *candidus* (= fair, opp. *niger*), *canus* (= hoary), *purus* (= not dirty, not stained), *niveus* (= white as snow), *lacteus* (= white as milk). II. n. *album, candor* — of an egg, of the eye, *album ovi, oculorum* (Cels.). **white-haired** adj. *albis capillis, canis capillis.* **white-lead**, n. *cerussa.* **whiten**, I. v.tr. *dealbare, candefacĕre* (ante and post class.). II. v.intr. *albescĕre, canescĕre* (= grow hoary) **whiteness**, n. *albitudo* (Plaut.), *candor*

whitewash, I. n. *albarium (opus).* **II.** v.tr. *dealbare.*

whither, I. adv., as interrog., *quo? quem in locum? quorsum (quorsus)? in quam partem?* — then? *quonam?* **II.** conj. with reference to the antecedent, *quo: — ever, quoquo, quocunque (-cumque), quacunque, quovis, † quolibet.*

whitlow, n. *paronychium, paronychia* (Plin.).

Whitsuntide, n. * *Pentecoste* (Eccl.).

whiz, I. v.intr. *stridēre (stridĕre)* (of serpents). **II.** n. *stridor.* **whizzing, I.** adj. *stridens.* **II.** n. *stridor.*

who, I. rel. pron. *qui, quae, quod.* **II.** interrog. pron. *quis, quis, quid?* Which of two? *uter, utra, utrum?* **whoever,** n. *quicunque (quicum.), quisquis.*

whole, I. adj. *integer* (= uninjured), *tot us* (in opp. to part.), *solidus* (esp. in enumeration, e.g. *usurâ, nec eâ solidâ, contentus erat), cunctus* (e.g. *Gallia, civitas), omnis* (e.g. *omne caelum), universus, plenus* (e.g. *annus plenus atque integer); =* healthy, *sanus.* **II.** n. the —, *totum, tota res* (opp. *partes), unum* (in so far as anything is a —), *omnia, -ium, universum, universa res, universitas* (= all together), *summa* (= the sum, e.g. *summa exercitûs,* = the sum total of the army), *solidum* (= the capital); the — of may also be expressed by adj. (e.g. *tota Gallia,* = the — of Gaul), on the —, by *paene, fere, ferme* (= mostly, almost). **wholly,** adv. *plane, omnino, prorsus. penitus* (= thoroughly), *funditus* (= to the foundation), *radicitus* (= root and branch); see ALTOGETHER. **wholesale,** n. *mercatura magna.* **wholesome,** adj. *saluber, salutaris* (lit. and fig.), *utilis;* to be — for, *alci salutarem esse, alci prodesse.* **wholesomeness,** n. *salubritas, utilitas* (lit. and fig.).

whoop, n. *clamor;* see SHOUT, n.

whore, n. *scortum, meretrix.*

whose, adj., rel. and interrog. pron. *cujus.*

why, I. adv. as interrog. *cur? quamobrem (quam ob rem)? quare? quapropter? quâ de caus(s)â? quid est cur,* etc.? *quid est quod,* etc.? *quid?* — not? *cur non* (with indic.), *quidni* (with subj. implying surprise)? *quin* (with indic., request to do a thing). **II.** conj. *cur, quamobrem, quapropter, propter quod.* **III.** interj. (at answering an objection expressed or implied), *immo, enimvero.*

wick, n. *ellychnium.*

wicked, adj. *impius (erga Deum, patriam,* etc.), *nefarius, scelestus, sceleratus, flagitiosus, dissolutus, perditus* (= abandoned), *pravus* (= irregular), *malus, malitiosus* (= bad), *corruptus* (= corrupted), *deterrimus* (= very bad), *nequam* (= worthless), *turpis, foedus* (= shameful). Adv. *impie, nefarie, sceleste, scelerate, flagitiose, dissolute, perdite, prave, male, malitiose, nequiter, turpiter, foede.* **wickedness,** n. *impietas (erga alqm), scelus, -ĕris,* n., *facinus, -oris,* n., *flagitium* (= a — deed, then —), *pravitas, nequitia, turpitudo, foeditas, vitium, malitia, vitiositas.*

wicker, adj. *vimineus, craticius;* — work, *crates, -is,* f. usu. in pl.).

wide, adj. *latus* (e.g. *planities), laxus* (of dress, shoes, house), *capax* (= containing much), *amplus* (= of large size), *patens* (= — stretching). Adv. *late, laxe.* **widen, I.** v.tr. *amplificare (urbem, rempublicam,* fig. *auctoritatem), dilatare* (e.g. *castra, aciem;* power of a state, *imperium), laxare* (a garment, lines of troops). **II.** v.intr. *se dilatare* (the sea), *patescĕre* (a plain). **width,** n. 1, lit. *amplitudo, latitudo, laxitas;* 2, fig. perhaps *in omnes opiniones indulgens.*

widow, n. *vidua.* **widowed,** adj. *viduus.* **widower,** n. *viduus.* **widowhood,** n. *viduitas.*

wield, v.tr. *tractare* (e.g. *ferrum, arma, tela).*

wife, n. *conju(n)x, uxor, marita;* to take a —, *uxorem ducĕre.*

wig, n. *capillamentum* (Suet.), *crines † empti, galerum (galerus,* Juv.).

wight, n. see MAN.

wild, adj. *ferus* (of living and inanimate beings), *agrestis* (= growing — in the field, of plants; hence also rude in manners), *silvester* (= growing, living — in the woods, of plants, animals, men), *indomitus* (= untamed, of animals, opp. *mansuetus), rudis* (= still unprepared, of things, e.g. of the soil, etc.; hence = still uncivilized, of men), *incultus* (= untilled, of the soil, hence uncivilized, of men), *vastus* (= isolated, barren, of a country, opp. *celeber), ferox* (= acting like a savage), *immanis* (= cruel, of character), *saevus* (= ferocious, all four of men), *insanus, amens* (= mad), *lascivus* (= playful); a —, beast, *fera.* Adv. *ferociter, immaniter, saeve* (= fiercely), *insane* (= madly). **wilderness,** n. *locus desertus, loca deserta, -orum, solitudo, vastitas.* **wildness,** n. *feritas, ferocia, ingenium ferox, animus ferox* (= fierceness), *immanitas* (= cruelty), *lascivia* (= playfulness).

wile, n. *ars, dolus;* see TRICK. **wily,** adj. *astutus, versutus;* see CUNNING, adj.

wilful, adj. *contumax, pertinax, pervicax, obstinatus;* a — act, *quod consulto or cogitatum fit,* comb. *quod consulto et cogitatum fit.* Adv. *contumaciter, pertinaciter, pervicaciter, consulto, consilio, de or ex industriâ, datâ or deditâ operâ, voluntate et judicio,* or also by *sciens or prudens et sciens.* **wilfulness,** n. *contumacia, pertinacia, pervicacia, obstinatio* (= inflexibility).

will, I. n. 1, *voluntas* (= volition in gen., and also exercise of —), *animus* (= disposition of mind), *consilium, propositum* (= purpose), *arbitrium* (= decision), *auctoritas* (= command, esp. — of the senate as expressed in a decree), or by *auctor* (e.g. he did it at the — of Caesar, *hoc Caesare auctore fecit), nutus, -ûs* (lit. = nod, fig. = command), comb. *arbitrium et nutus, auctoritas nutusque, libido* (= fancy, caprice, in good or bad sense), *studium* (= good —); he has a — to, *est alci in animo alqd facĕre;* 2, = testament, *testamentum, tabulae (testamenti);* to make a —, *testamentum facĕre,* in favour of any one, *alqm heredem suum facĕre.* **II.** v.tr. *velle, cupĕre,* with infin. or subj., with or without *ut; alqd or* with accus. and infin. or *ut; avēre alqd or* with infin. **willing,** adj. *libens, volens, paratus, promptus* (the last two *ad alqd).* Adv. *libenter, animo libenti, animo libenti prolixoque, animo prompto paratoque.* **willingness,** n. *animus libens or promptus, voluntas.*

wily, adj. see WILE.

willow, n. *salix.*

win, I. v.tr. see GET, GAIN. **II.** v.intr. *vincĕre.* **winner,** n. *victor.*

winning, adj. *pulcher, venustus* (= beautiful), *suavis* (= sweet), *blandus* (= persuasive), *comis* (= courteous).

wind, I. n. 1, *ventus, aura* (both of gentle and violent blasts), *flatus, -ûs* (mostly poet., all three lit. and fig.); favourable, unfavourable —, *ventus secundus, adversus;* the — rises, *ventus increbrescit or cooritur;* — sinks, *cessat, cadit;* to speak to the —, *dare † verba in ventos;* 2, = flatulency, *ventus, inflatio.* **II.** v.tr. (e.g. a horn, *cornu), inflare;* see BLOW, PLAY, v.tr. **windfall,** n. *alqd alci forte oblatum* (e.g. the money was a great — to me, *pecunia casu*

oblata multum mihi proderat.). **wind-mill,**
n. *mola venti* (Jct.). **wind-pipe,** n. *aspera
arteria.* **wind-ward,** adj. *ad ventum conversus.*
windy, adj. *ventosus;* fig. *vanus, ventosus, inanis.*

wind, I. v.tr. *torquēre* (e.g. *funem*), *glomer-
are* (into a ball); — up, *trochleā tollēre* (lit. i.e.
with a pulley), *ad finem perducēre* (fig.); see
END. **II.** v.intr. *se sinuare, sinuari.* **winding,
I.** adj. *flexuosus, tortuosus.* **II.** n. *flexus, -ūs.*
windlass, n. *ergata,* m.

window, n. *fenestra* (with shutters, curtains,
or bars; only under the emperors made of the
transparent *lapis phengites* or *specularis*).

wine, n. *vinum;* sour —, *vappa;* — not
diluted with water, *merum;* the — god *Bacchus*
(poet. = wine). **wine-bibber,** n. *homo vinulentus.* **wine-cellar,** n. *apotheca.* **wine-
merchant,** n. *vinarius.*

wing, I. n. *ala, pennae;* — of an army, *cornu,
ala;* the soldiers who form the —s, *alarii;*
to be posted in the right —, *dextrum tenēre;*
the — of a house, *ala;* — of a door, *foris;*
door with —s, folding-doors, *fores, -ium, valvae.*
II. v.tr. *volare;* see FLY. **winged,** adj. *penniger,* † *pennatus,* † *alatus,* † *aliger.*

wink, I. n. *nictus, -ūs.* **II.** v.intr. *nictare,*
at any one, *alci;* to — at, *indulgēre alci, con-
(n)ivēre in alqā re.*

winnow, v.tr. corn, *frumentum ventilare* or
evannēre. **winnowing-fan,** n. *ventilabrum,
vannus,* f.

winter, I. n. *hiem(p)s, tempus* (*anni*) *hibernum, tempora hiberna, -orum, tempus hiemale,
bruma, tempus brumale* (= time of the shortest
days), a hard —, *hiems gravis* or *acris;* a mild
—, *hiems* † *mollis, mitis, tepida* (Hor.). **II.** adj.
hiemalis, hibernus, brımalis, or by genit. of
hiem(p)s; — quarters, *hiberna, -orum.* **III.**
v.intr. *hiemare, hibernare, hiberna agēre* (of
troops); for — in gen. *hiemem agēre.* **winterly,**
adj. *hiemalis.*

wipe, v.tr. (*abs*)*tergēre, detergēre, extergēre;*
— out (fig.), *abolēre;* see ABOLISH.

wire, n. *filum* or *filum ferreum.*

wise, I. adj. *sapiens, sapientiā praeditus,
prudens* (= with practical insight); to be —,
sapēre, sapientem esse. **II.** n. *ratio, modus, via;*
in no —, *nullo modo;* see MANNER, WAY. Adv.
sapienter. **wisdom,** n. *sapientia, prudentia;*
with —, *sapienter, ratione ac consilio.* **wise-
acre,** n. *qui se sapientem esse jactat.*

wish, I. v.tr. and intr. *velle, cupēre;* if you
— it, *si vis, si tibi placet;* I don't — it, by
nolo; I — rather, by *malo;* I could —, *velim*
(with pres. subj. if we speak as though the —
were likely to be fulfilled), *vellem* (with imperf.
subj. if there are difficulties, so that the speaker
doubts the fulfilment); to — for anything, *alqd
cupēre, desiderare,* (*ex*)*optare, sitire* (= thirst for).
II. n. *optatio* (= the act), *optatum* (= the thing we
— for), *desiderium* (= the desire), *voluntas* (= will,
demand), *votum* (in consequence of a vow taken;
then = —; prayer to the gods that a certain —
may be fulfilled); according to my —, *ex sententiā;* according to anyone's —, *ad alcjs voluntatem.*

wistful, wistfully, wistfulness, adj.
use circumloc. (e.g. his face bore a — expression, *ille desiderium vultu expressit;* he appeared
to be a prey to —, *desiderio movēri visus est*).

wit, n. (*ingenii*) *acumen, dicacitas* (= quick,
ingenious answer), *lepos* (= tasteful, elegant), *facetiae* (= witticisms), comb. *lepos facetiaeque, sal,
-is,* m.; also in the pl. *sales,* comb. *sal et facetiae,
facete dictum;* to —, *nempe, nimirum, scilicet.*
witless, adj. see FOOLISH. **witticism,** n.

quod facete dictum est; see WIT. **witty,** adj.
dicax, facetus, non infacetus, lepidus, salsus,
Adv. *facete, salse, lepide.*

witch, n. *venefica, maga, saga.* **witch-
craft,** n. *veneficium, ars* † *magica, magica*
(Plin.); see MAGIC.

with, prep. (A) = in union, 1, *cum, una cum;*
often simply rendered by the ablat. with an
adj. (e.g. *omnibus copiis egredi*); **2,** in friendly
intercourse, *cum;* after verbs compounded with
cum, either *cum* with ablat. or simply the
dat. (e.g. what have I to do — you? *quid tibi
mecum est rei?*), after words expressing similarity or equality, the simple dat. (but after
similis and its compounds, also the genit.);
when two things are represented as being
equal to one another, by *idem* (= the same, etc.),
the prep. "—" is rendered by *qui* or a copulative conj., seldom by *cum* with ablat. (only in
poets simply by the dat.; a Graecism); **3,** = in
participation, in confederacy with, *cum* (e.g.
cum alqo bellum gerēre adversus alqm); = by
means of, *per* with accus. *alcjs operā, alcjs ope,
auxilio, alqo auctore;* also sometimes by the
simple ablat. (e.g. *Caesar eā legione, quam secum
habebat, murum perduxit in altitudinem,* etc.);
4, in a hostile sense, *cum, contra, adversus* with
accus. (the two latter used when *cum* might be
misunderstood, as it might also mean "in union
—," etc.), e.g. *bellum gerēre cum alqo* or *contra
(adversus) alqm;* (B) = in company and accompanied by, 1, of persons, *cum* (= along —); but if
only expressing that one particular action refers
to more than one person, it is generally rendered in Latin simply by a copulative conjunction (*et, ac, atque*), (e.g. the women — their
children were killed, *mulieres atque infantes
occisi sunt*); **2,** of things, *cum;* it is often rendered in this sense (armed, furnished —, etc.)
more clearly by participles or adjs. or by a
relative clause (e.g. armed — a dagger, *cum sicā,*
or *sicā instructus;* at the same time as some
phenomenon that takes place in the course of
time, *cum,* or (but less expressive) by the simple
ablat. (e.g. — daybreak, (*cum*) *primā luce*),
hence also of effects and consequences that are
simultaneous and immediate or direct; = not
without, *cum, non sine* (e.g. to hear, etc. —
pleasure, *cum voluptate;* — the help of the
gods, (*cum*) *dis adjuvantibus*); in many instances by particular expressions (e.g. — care,
diligenter), or by construction with a partic.
(e.g. — quickness, *adhibitā celeritate;* — that,
inde, deinde, ad haec; — all your diligence, *pro
or ex tuā diligentiā;* — all men truth is to be
held in honour, *apud omnes veritas colenda est*).

withal, adv. *simul.*

withdraw, I. v.tr. *alqd ab alqo* or *ab alqā
re avertēre, avocare, revocare, removēre, alqd ex*
or *de alqā re detrahēre* (also from a place, e.g.
inimicum ex Galliā), *retrahēre, abstrahēre, alqd
alci tollēre, auferre;* of troops, *deducēre, revocare,
subducēre;* of money, *deducēre* (*de summā,* etc.);
see TAKE AWAY. **II.** v.intr. (*re*)*cedēre, discedēre, ab,* etc., *se recipēre ab,* etc., *se removēre
ab,* etc., *se retrahēre ab alqā re;* from a person,
se removēre ab alqo or *ab alcjs amicitiā, alqm
or alcjs aditum sermonemque effugēre;* to — from
duty, allegiance, etc., *ab officio recedēre;* to —
from office, *magistratu abdicare, se magistratum
ejurare.*

wither, I. v.tr. 1, lit. (*ad*)*urēre, torrēre;* **2,**
fig. *perdēre* (= destroy). **II.** v.intr. (*ex*)*arescēre,
inarescēre* (Plin.). **withered,** adj. *marcidus.*

withhold, v.tr. *detinēre, retinēre, supprimēre, comprimēre;* I cannot — my praise **of** him
facēre non possum quin eum laudem.

within, I. prep. *intra, inter* (both of space and time), *in* with abl. = in the course of (*in eo anno natus est* = sometime in that year), often by the abl. only (e.g. *alqm finibus suis recipĕre*), or with verbs expressing motion by *in* with accus. (e.g. *in fines suos recipĕre*), he did it — the year, *hoc abhinc nondum uno anno exacto fecit;* if the time be future, *ante annum exactum.* **II.** adv. *intus* (in gen.), *domi* (= at home).

without, I. prep. *extra* (with accus. of place), *sine* (with abl.), *sine alcjs operā;* not —, *non sine, cum;* by *nullus* in the abl. with the noun (e.g. — danger, *nullo periculo*); by adjs., such as *expers alcjs rei, carens alqā re, nudus alqā re, inops ab,* etc.; by adjs. expressing a deficiency, etc., chiefly compounded with *in,* e.g. — trouble, *facilis;* — clothes, *nudus;* — injury, *integer;* — a will, *intestatus;* — caution, *incautus;* — my, etc., knowledge, by *inscius, insciens, alqo insciente, alqo inscio;* — an invitation, *invocatus;* by the negative with participles, mostly by the ablat. abs. (e.g. — many words, *missis ambagibus,* Hor.); — anybody or anything, = if somebody has not been there, or if such or such a thing had not happened, but for, *nisi* or *ni fuisset* (only Com. say here *absque algo esset*); by *nec (neque)* (e.g. many praise the orators and poets — understanding them, *multi oratores et poëtas probant neque intellegunt*); sometimes by *ut non* or (but only when the preceding clause contains already a negation) *quin* (e.g. *Augustus numquam filios suos populo commendavit, ut non adjiceret* [= — adding] *si merebuntur*); *nunquam accedo, quin abs te doctior abeam,* = I never came — going away better; by *praeter* (e.g. *praeter consulem amicum habeo nullum,* = — counting the consul I have no friend). **II.** adv. *extra, extrinsecus, ex* or *ab exteriore parte, ab exterioribus partibus* (= from —, also = from abroad); *foris* (= out of doors).

withstand, v.tr. *resistĕre;* see RESIST.

withy, n. *vimen.*

witness, I. n. 1, *testis,* to call as a —, *alqm testari* or *contestari, alqm antestari;* to appeal to anyone as —, *testificari alqm;* to be a —, *testem esse, testari;* to appear as a —, *testem ex(s)istĕre;* *arbiter* (= one who has heard anything), *auctor* (= —ing an act, e.g. at a marriage); without —, in private, *sine arbitris, arbitris remotis, sine auctoribus;* in the presence of (before) many —es, *multis audientibus, coram multis; spectator* (= onlooker); 2, = testimony, *testimonium.* **II.** v.tr. and intr. 1, *testari, attestari, testificari, testimonio confirmare, testimonio esse, testem esse* (the former of the two of a thing, the latter of a person); 2, = behold, *vidēre, spectare;* see SEE.

wizard, n. *magus, veneficus.*

wizened, adj. *retorridus* (mostly post Aug.).

woad, n. *isatis, vitrum.*

wobble, v.intr. see WABBLE.

woe, wo, I. n. *dolor, mala, -orum, res adversae, luctus, -ūs, maeror;* see SORROW. **II.** interj. *vae! —* to me! *vae mihi! vae mihi misero! pro dolor! perii!* **woeful,** adj. see SAD, UNHAPPY, SORROWFUL.

wolf, n. *lupus,* fem. *lupa;* of the —, *lupinus.* **wolfish,** adj. *saevus.*

woman, n. *femina* (opp. *vir*), *mulier* (= grown up —), a young —, *puella, virgo, adulescens* (e.g. *filia adulescens*), *juvenis;* an old —, *anus, -ūs,* f. *vetula;* a little — (as endearing term), *muliercula, adulescentia;* = the sex, — kind, *sexus (-ūs) muliebris, mulieres, -um.* **womanish,** adj. *muliebris, mollis, effeminatus;* see EFFEMINATE. **womanly,** adj. *muliebris.*

womb, n. *alvus, uterus.*

wonder, I. n. 1, = the feeling, *(ad)miratio;* to see anything with —, *alqd stupefactus* or *attonitus vidēre;* see ASTONISHMENT; 2, = a wonderful thing, *casus, -ūs, mirificus, res mira* or *inusitata, monstrum, portentum, miraculum.* **II.** v.intr. *(ad)mirari, admiratione stupēre,* at anything, *alqd, alqd mihi mirum est* or *videtur;* I — that, etc. *miror* with accus. and infin.; I — whether, etc. *miror si,* etc.; I — what may have been the cause, *miror quid causae fuerit;* for our colloquial, I —, *demiror* is used (e.g. I — what it is, *demiror quid sit*). **wonderful,** adj. *mirus, mirificus, (ad)mirabilis, (ad)mirandus, novus, inusitatus, portentosus, monstr(u)osus.* Adv. *mire, mirifice, (ad)mirabiliter, nove, inusitate, monstr(u)ose;* see ADMIRE.

wont, I. n. *usus, -ūs, mos, consuetudo;* see CUSTOM. **II.** adj. *(as)suetus;* to be —, *solēre.*

woo, v.tr. *amare* (= to love), *in matrimonium petĕre* (Suet.); fig. = seek, *petĕre.* **wooer,** n. *amator, procus.*

wood, n. *lignum,* or pl. *ligna* (for burning), *materia (materies,* = —fit for use, in opp. to *liber,* = bark, and when cut up, in opp. to *lignum,* = — for fuel), *silva* (= forest), *nemus, -ŏris,* n., *lucus* (= grove), *saltus, -ūs* (= glade, defile), *silvestris locus* (= plantation with —, shrubs); of —, *ligneus.* **wooden,** adj. *ligneus.* **wood-cutter,** n. *qui ligna caedit.* **wood-engraving,** n. *tabula in lignum incisa et in chartam impressa.* **woodland,** n. *silvae, nemora, -um, saltus, -ūs.* **wood-louse,** n. *oniscus, multipeda* (Plin.). **woodman,** n. see WOOD-CUTTER. **wood-nymph,** n. *(Hama)dryas.* **wood-pecker,** n. *picus.* **wood-pigeon,** n. *palumbes, -is,* m. and f. **wooded, woody,** adj. *silvestris, silvosus* (e.g. *saltus*), *silvis vestitus* (e.g. *mons*), †*nemorosus, saltuosus* (e.g *regio, loca*).

woof, n. *subtemen, trama.*

wool, n. *lana.* **woollen, woolly,** adj. *laneus.*

word, I. n. 1, = part of speech and (particularly the pl. "words") speech in gen., *vocabulum,* as a name for one particular object (e.g. *conservatoris sibi nomen, Graeco ejus rei vocabulo assumpsit*); in the pl. *vocabula* = "words, vocabulary," unconnected, *nomen* (= name), *verbum* (= something spoken, a —); hence a short sentence, saying); — for —, *verbum pro verbo, ad verbum; vox* (inasmuch as it is spoken or heard, whether by itself or in the context). *sermo, oratio* (= speech); *dictum* = saying (e.g. *dicto alcjs obtemperare* = to obey anyone's —); in one — (in enumerating), *uno verbo, ut paucis dicam, quid multa? quid opus est verbis? ne multa! ne plura;* the — of God (i.e. the Holy Scriptures), *libri divini, lit(t)erae divinae* or *sanctae* (Eccl.); 2, = promise, *fides;* upon my —, *meā fide.* **II.** v.tr. see EXPRESS. **wordy,** adj. *verbosus.*

work, I. n. = anything completed, *opus, -ĕris,* n., *factum* (= deed), *pensum* (= task), *monumentum* (= monument), *munitio, munimentum* (= fortification); a little —, *opusculum* (also = — of art); *opus, liber, libellus* (= a literary —); = toil, *opera, labor* (with an effort), *occupatio* of a scholar, *studia, -orum;* by candle-light, *lucubratio* (esp. before daybreak); done in leisure hours, *operae subsicivae;* it is the — of a good man to do this, *boni (hominis) est hoc facĕre;* the —s (in machinery, etc.), *machina, machinatio.* **II.** v.intr. to — at, *(e)laborare in alqa re, operam dare alci rei, incumbĕre in* or *ad alqd; opus facĕre,* in opere esse, *laborem subire* or *obire;* by candlelight, *lucubrare;* to — all night, *ad laborem nullam partem noctis intermittĕre;* to — night and day, *opus continuare diem et noctem;* to — for wages, *operam suam locare.* **III.** v.tr. *facĕre, conficĕre, efficĕre, perficĕre, fingĕre*

(= to fashion), *fabricari*; see MAKE. **work-basket,** n. *quasillum (quasillus).* **work-house,** n. *ptōtchōtrophium* (Jct.), or by circuml. (e.g. *domus in quâ indigentes publico sumptu aluntur*). **working, I.** adj. — days, *dies negotiosus* (Tac.), *dies profestus.* **II.** n. *tractatio* (in gen.) ; — of the ground, *cultio* or *cultus* (-*ūs*) *agrorum.* **workman,** n. *agri cultor* (in the field), *operarius,* in the pl. *operae* (if for wages, *mercenarius*; pl. *operae conductae* or *mercenariae*), *artifex* (= artist), *opifex* (= manual —), *faber* (= — in wood, stone, etc.), *vinitor* (in a vineyard). **workmanship,** n. *ars, opus, -ĕris,* n. **workshop,** n. *officina* (the place), *fabrica* (of a *faber,* i.e. one who works in hard material), *artificium* (of an *artifex,* = a studio).

world, n. *mundus* (= the universe, *opus universum, universitas rerum, rerum natura* = universe, only in the sing.) ; = the globe, *orbis* (*tĕrrarum*) (as known to the Romans), *terrae* (= countries in gen.) ; rulers of the —, *terrarum* or *omnium terrarum principes* (of a nation) ; to be brought into the —, *nasci* ; to leave the — (i.e. die), *ex vitâ discedĕre, e vitâ excedĕre* ; what in the —? *quid tandem?* everything in the —, *quodvis, nihil non* ; I am the most miserable man in the —, *prorsus nihil est quin sim miserrĭmus* ; the next —, *caelum* (Heaven), *vita caelestis* or *futura* ; = mankind, *homines* or *omnes* (= all men) ; the present —, *homines qui nunc sunt or vivunt, homines hujus aetatis* ; the ancient —, *antiquitas, aetas vetus, veteres, -um* ; the learned —, *docti homines.* **worldly,** adj. **worldliness,** n. *qui (quae) utilitatem suam (neque veram laudem) petit.*

worm, n. *vermis,* m. (in gen.), *vermiculus* (= little —), *lumbricus* (= earth —, the — in the intestines), *terēdo* (in wood, meat, clothes), *tinea* (in wood and books). **worm-eaten,** adj. *cariosus* (of wood) ; to be —, *vermiculari* (of trees, Plin.).

worn, part. and adj. ; see WEAR.

worry, v.tr. 1, (*di*)*laniare* (= tear, of dogs, etc.) ; 2, fig. *vexare, sol(l)icitare, cruciare* (the two last metaph. as from baiting of wild beasts) ; see TEASE, VEX.

worse, I. adj. *pejor, deterior.* **II.** adv. *pejus, deterius.* **worst, I.** adj. *pessimus, deterrimus.* **II.** adv. *pessime.* **III.** v.tr. *vincĕre* ; see DEFEAT.

worship, I. n. *adoratio, veneratio* (as act) ; divine —, *Dei cultus, -ūs, divinus cultus, res divinae, sacra, -orum* ; secret — (as in Eleusis that of Ceres, etc.), *initia, -orum* ; to perform —, *sacra facĕre* ; to attend —, *sacris adesse* ; your — (as title), *vir optime.* **II.** v.tr. *colĕre, venerari.* **worshipful,** adj. *optimus,* e.g. the — Company of Carpenters, *fabri consociati, viri optimi,* or *societas clarissima fabrorum.* **worshipper,** n. *cultor, venerator.*

worsted, I. n. *lana* (= wool). **II.** adj. *laneus.*

worth, I. n. 1, = value, *aestimatio* (= value which anyone puts on a thing), *pretium* (= the value itself) ; see VALUE ; 2, = moral —, *virtus, -ūtis,* f. ; see EXCELLENCE. **II.** adj. see WORTHY ; it is — while, *operae pretium est,* with infin. **worthy,** adj. *dignus* with abl. of thing ; — to, with infin. *dignus qui* with subj. ; — of confidence, *fide dignus* or *dignus cui fides habeatur* ; — of praise, *laude dignus, laudandus, dignus qui laudetur* ; to render one's self — of a thing, *alqd merēri or merēri* or *promerēre* or *promerēri* ; = venerable, *venerandus, venerabilis, veneratione dignus* ; to be — much, little, etc., *multum valēre, agni, parvĭ pretii esse, magno, parvo pretio*

vendi or *emi.* Adv. *digne, pro dignitate.* **worthiness,** n. *dignitas, honestas* ; see DIGNITY. **worthless,** adj. 1, *vilis* (= cheap), *inutilis* (= useless) ; 2, morally —, *corruptus, perditus, inhonestus* ; see WICKED. **worthlessness,** n. 1, *vilitas* (Plin.), or by adj. ; 2, see WICKEDNESS.

wound, I. n. *vulnus, -ĕris,* n. (in gen.), *plaga* (from a blow, etc.), *ulcus, ĕris,* n. (= a sore, an ulcer), *cicatrix* (= scar). **II.** v.tr. *vulnerare* (lit. and fig.), *sauciare* (lit., fig. only in Plaut.). **wounded,** adj. *vulneratus, saucius* (= deeply —), fig. *dolore affectus.*

wrangle, v.intr. see QUARREL.

wrap, v.tr. — up, *alqâ re involvĕre, velare* (= veil). **II.** n. see WRAPPER. **wrapper,** n. *tegumentum* (= cover, e.g. of a shield).

wrath, n. *ira, iracundia, bilis* (lit. = bile), *stomachus* (lit. = stomach = what revolts us), *indignatio.* **wrathful,** adj. *iratus, iracundus* ; see ANGRY. Adv. *irate, iracunde.*

wreak, v.tr. see REVENGE.

wreath, n. *corona, sertum* (= garland). **wreathe,** v.tr. *nectĕre* (= twine), (*con*)*torquēre* (= twist) ; to — anyone, *coronare, sertis redimire* (e.g. a victim).

wreck, I. n. *naufragium* (= wrecking of a ship, or of fortune) ; = the remnants of a ship, *navis fracta, navis* or *navigii reliquiae, tabulae navis fractae* ; after a —, *naufragio facto.* **II.** v.tr. *frangĕre* (= break, lit. and fig.), *navem in scopulos,* etc., or *scopulis + illidĕre* ; to be —ed, *naufragium facĕre.* **wrecked,** adj. *naufragus* (lit. and fig.).

wren, n. *regulus* (late).

wrench, v.tr. see TEAR, PULL.

wrest, v.tr. *eripĕre, extorquēre* (e.g. *alqd alci de manibus*) ; fig., — the sense of anything, *alqd perverse interpretari.*

wrestle, v.intr. *luctari* (lit. of the wrestler ; then also = resist in gen.), *cum alqo.* **wrestler,** n. *luctator* (in gen.), *athleta,* m. **wrestling,** n. *luctatio, luctatus, -ūs* (Plin.).

wretch, n. *homo malus, improbus, nequam, improbus ac nefarius* ; poor —, *homo miserrimus* (for other adjs. see WICKED). **wretched,** adj. *miserabilis, miserandus* (= pitiable), *miser* (better in superl. *miserrimus*), *maestus, tristis* (= unhappy), *aerumnosus* (= full of care), *afflictus, fractus* (= broken down), *malus, nequam* (= worthless) ; see PITIABLE, SAD, WICKED. Adv. *miserabiliter, misere, miserrime, maeste, male, nequiter.* **wretchedness,** n. *miseria* ; see MISERY.

wriggle, v.intr. *se torquēre, torquēri.*

wring, v.tr. one's hands, *manus tollĕre* (= raise the hands in astonishment) ; — the neck, *gulam frangĕre* ; — the soul, *cruciare alqm* or *animum* ; to — out clothes, *aquam exprimĕre linteis.*

wrinkle, I. n. *ruga* ; full of —s, *rugosus.* **II.** v.tr. *rugare* ; — the face, forehead, *frontem contrahĕre* or *adducĕre.* **wrinkled,** adj. *rugosus.*

wrist, n. *prima palmae pars* (Cels.).

writ, n. 1, anything written, *scriptum* ; Holy —, *Lit(t)erae Sanctae, Sacrae* or *Divinae* (Eccl.) ; 2, in law, *lit(t)erae* ; to issue a —, perhaps *alqm citare.*

write, v.tr. *scribĕre* (metaph. *exarare,* from ploughing, in letters of Cic. and post Aug.) ; to know how to (read and) —, *lit(t)eras scire* ; he who is unable to —, *lit(t)erarum nescius* ; to — a good hand, *lepidâ manu conscribĕre* ; = to — on something, *describĕre in alqâ re* (e.g. figures on the sand, *figuras in arenâ*). *inscribĕre alci rei*

or *in alqd re* (e.g. one's name on a monument, *nomen suum in monumento, in statuâ*), *incidĕre alci rei* or *in alqâ re, referre in alqd* (= enter in a journal); = to make or compose by —ing, *(con)scribĕre, lit(t)eris mandare, consignare* (= to consign to —ing), *libros edĕre* (= to put forth), *alqd scribĕre*; to — to anyone, *alci scribĕre* (= to do anything with *ut*), *lit(t)eras ad alqm dare* **or** *mittĕre*; to inform by —ing, *alqm per lit(t)eras, certiorem facĕre de alqâ re*; to one another, *lit(t)eras dare et accipĕre*; to — often, *scriptitare*; to —back, *lit(t)eris rescribĕre* or *respondĕre*; to — a letter, *scribĕre* or *conscribĕre epistulam.* **writer,** n. = one who performs the mechanical operation, *qui lit(t)eras facit; scriba,* m. (= one who takes writing as a profession), *scriptor* (= a secretary of a private person), *auctor, scriptor* (= author). **writing,** n. 1, = the act of, *scriptio, scriptura*; 2, as a learned occupation, *scribendi studium*; 3, = the thing written, *scriptum, codicilli* (= a note, inquiry, order), *lit(t)erae epistula* (= letter); art of —, *ars scribendi.* **writing-case,** n. *scrinium.* **writing-desk,** n. *mensa* (= table), or simply *scribĕre* (e.g. *ad scribendum me confero,* I betake myself to my —). **writing-master,** n. *qui alqm artem scribendi docet.* **writing-paper,** n. *charta.* **writing-tablet,** n. *cera* (= — smeared with wax), *tabula* (or pl. *tabulae*).

writhe, v.intr. *torquēri.*

wrong, I. adj. *falsus* (= false, opp. *verus*), *alienus* (= foreign, opp. *meus,* etc.; hence unfavourable, e.g. time, place); morally —, *pravus*; see **Wicked**; to be —, *perperam judicare* or *statuĕre.* **II.** adv. see **Wrongly. III.** n. = an unjust act, *injuria.* **IV.** v.tr. *injuriam alci inferre* or *facĕre, injuriâ alqm afficĕre, fraudare alqm alqâ re* (= cheat). **wrongdoer,** n. *homo maleficus, scelerosus,* etc.; see **Wicked. wrongly,** adv. *male* (in gen.), *perperam* (= falsely, opp. *recte*), *falso* (= falsely), *inique, injuriâ, per injuriam* (= unjustly), *immerito* (= without desert), *prave* (= improperly), *nequiter* (= wickedly), comb. *male, prave, nequiter, turpiter.* **wrongful,** adj. **wrongfully,** adv. see **Wrong** and **Unjust.**

wroth, adj. *irae plenus, iracundus*; see **Angry.**

wrought, adj. of metals or of deeds, *factus, confectus.*

wry, adj. *distortus* or *perversus* (e.g. *oculi*).

wryneck, n. *iynx* (Plin.).

Y.

yacht, n. *celox.*

yard, n. (= a measure) by adj. *tripedalis* (in *longitudinem,* = measuring three feet) or *tres pedes longus*; see **Ell.**

yard, n. = court-yard, *area* (= any free open place in front or at the back of a house; the *area* in front of the house together with the side-wings formed the *vestibulum,* where the clients assembled when waiting upon their patron), *(aedium) propatulum* (= open space in front of a house, entry, porch), *cohors* (for cattle); in a ship, *antenna.*

yarn, n. *linum netum* (= linen, Jct.), *lana neta* (woollen —, Jct.).

yawl, n. *navis, scapha*; see **Ship.**

yawn, I. v.intr. = to gape, *oscitare, oscitari*; = to open wide, *scindi, hiare*; see **Open. II. n.** *oscitatio* (Plin.); = opening, *hiatus, -ūs.*

ye, pron. *vos*; see **You.**

yea, adv. (Plin.); see **Yes.**

year, n. *annus, annuum tempus, anni spatium, annuum spatium*; half a —, by adj. *semestris* (e.g. *semestre regnum,* Cic., = rule lasting six months), after the reign of a —, *cum annum jam regnasset*), for a —, *in annum* (e.g. *comitia in annum prolata sunt,* = the elections have been put off for a —); two —s ago, *abhinc annis duobus,* or *annos duos*; a — after, *post annum*; at the end of a —, *anno circumacto*; last —, *anno superiore* or *proximo*; at the end of the —, *extremo anno*; after the lapse of a —, *anno praeterito, exacto anno*; every other —, *alternis annis*; every, each —, *singulis annis, quotannis*; from — to —, *per annos singulos*; every three —s, *tertio* (so *quarto, quinto,* etc.) *quoque anno*; within a —, *intra annum*; it is more than three —s, *amplius triennium est, amplius trienno*; it is a — since, *annus est cum, postquam,* etc.; it is not yet ten —s since, *nondum decem anni sunt cum,* etc.; scarcely a — had passed, *annus vix intercesserat*; a period of two —s, *biennium*; three —s, *triennium*; four —, *quadrennium*; five —s, *quinquennium*; six —s, *sexennium*; seven —s, *septennium*; ten —s, *decennium* (instead of which *anni duo, anni tres,* etc., may be used); to be in —s, *aetate provectum esse*; to be getting into —s, *senescĕre, longius aetate procedĕre* or *provehi*; a —'s pay, *merces, -edis, annua.* **yearly** (or annual), **I.** adj. *annuus, anniversarius* (= returning after the lapse of a year). **II.** adv. *quotannis, singulis annis, in singulos ann.os* (= for every year).

yearn, v.tr., to — for, *alqd desiderare.* **yearning,** n. *desiderium.*

yeast, n. *fermentum* (Cels.).

yell, v.intr., **yelling,** adj., see **Cry, Scream, Shriek.**

yellow, I. adj. *flavus, flavens* (= of gold colour), *fulvus* (= brownish —), *luteus* (= orange red or like sulphur; *flavus, fulvus,* and *luteus* denote a — inclining to red), *luridus* (= sallow, of the complexion, dirty teeth, etc.), *ravus* (= greyish —, of the eyes, etc., rare), †*aureus* (= of gold-like —), †*croceus* (= of saffron colour), †*sulfureus* (= of sulphur colour), *gilvus* (= pale —, only of the colour of horses), *helvus* (= light —, of cows); to be —, *flavēre*; to grow —, †*flavescĕre.* **II.** n. — yolk of an egg, *luteum* (Plin.), *vitellus.* **yellow-haired,** adj. *flavus.* **yellowish,** adj. *subflavus, sufflavus.*

yelp, v.intr. *gannire* (lit. and fig.). **yelping,** n. *gannitus, -ūs*; see **Bark.**

yeoman, n. see **Farmer, Soldier. yeomanry,** n. see **Cavalry.**

yes, adv. (to express affirmation or consent), *ita, ita est, sic est* (= it is so), *recte* (as a word of politeness, = certainly), *certe* (= assuredly), *vero* (= indeed, when we affirm with greater emphasis), *etiam,* strengthened *quin etiam* (= — indeed), *sane, sane quidem* (= of course), *immo* (*vero*) (implies an antithesis, either strengthening the affirmation, or correcting what has been said immediately before); gen. however use none of these particles to express consent, repeat either the word or that word upon which the stress lies in a question, e.g. will you come? *veniesne?* —! *veniam!* are you going to my house? *mene vis?* —! *te!* Clitipho came here; did he come alone? *Clitipho huc adiit; solus?* —! *solus:* I say —, *aio, affirmo, annuo* (in nodding); you say —, but I say no, *tu dis, ego nego*; to answer — or no, *aut etiam aut non respondēre.*

yesterday, I. adv. *heri, hesterno die*; in writing the Romans expressed it by *pridie ejus diei quo haec scribebam*; — evening, last night, *heri vespĕri; —* morning, *heri mane.* **II.** n. *dies hesternus.*

yet, I. conj. *(at)tamen, verumtamen* (or as two words), *sed, at, etsi, quamquam (quanq.* the last four answering objections raised or implied by the speaker); see NEVERTHELESS, NOTWITHSTANDING. **II.** adv. = still, even now, *etiam, etiamnunc (etiamnum)*; = up to this time, *adhuc, ad id (tempus), hactenus;* not —, *nondum, non . . . etiam; adhuc non* (= not up to this moment).

yew, I. n. — tree, *taxus,* f. **II.** adj. *taxicus* (Plin.).

yield, I. v.tr. see PRODUCE, AFFORD, CON-CEDE; to — the breath; see EXPIRE, DIE; = surrender (e.g. a fortress); see SURRENDER. **II.** v. intr. to anyone's request, *alcjs precibus cedĕre, alci obsequi, (con)cedĕre, morem gerĕre* or *obsequi.* **yielding,** adj. (of temper) *facilis* (opp. *difficilis*), *indulgens* (opp. *durus*).

yoke, I. n. *jugum* (lit. and fig.), *servi-tutis jugum, jugum servile, servitus, -ūtis* (fig.); to bring anyone under the — of slavery, *alci jugum servitutis injungĕre;* to keep under —, *alqm servitute oppressum tenēre;* metonym. = a couple (e.g. of oxen), *(boum) jugum;* = — of marriage, † *jugum.* **II.** v.tr. *(con)jungĕre.* **yokefellow,** n. *socius* (= companion), *con-ju(n)x* (in marriage).

yolk, n. (of an egg) *ovi luteum,* Plin., *vitellus.*

yonder, I. adj. *ille, iste.* **II.** adv., *illic, istic;* see THERE.

yore, adv. in times or days of —, *olim* (= a long time back), *quondam* (= formerly), opp. *nunc.*), *antea, antehac* (=in former days), *patrum memoriā* (= in the memory of our ancestors, of old), *antiqui, veteres, viri prisci.*

you, pron. 1, see THOU; 2, pl. *vos;* it is generally not expressed, except when we speak emphatically, or when it stands in opposition to another personal pronoun. **your,** adj. 1 (in addressing a person), *tuus, -a -um;* see THY; 2, in the pl. *vester (vestra, vestrum).* **your self, yourselves,** pron. reflex. *tu ipse, tute-(met) ipsi, vos ipsi, vosmet (ipsi).*

young, I. adj. 1, of men, *parvus, parvulus* (= little, not yet grown up, opp. *adultus*); — person, *infans* (before he has learnt to talk, up to the end of the seventh year; his — son, *filius infans*), *puer, puella* (=boy, girl, till about the seventeenth year), *adulescens, adulescentulus* (= growing youth, or grown up, until the thirtieth year and beyond), *juvenis* (=young man in his best years, between twenty and forty; see under YOUTH), *filius* (= a son, in opp. to the father, e.g. the — Marius, *Marius filius);* the — people; see YOUTH; 2, of animals, *novellus* (e.g. a — fowl, *novella gallina), pullus* (as a noun, so that the name of the animal is expressed in the form of an adj. e.g. a — fowl, *pullus gallinaceus;* a — horse, a foal, *pullus equinus), catulus* (of the canine or feline race, e.g. a — dog, *catulus [canis];* a — cat, kitten, *catulus feles;* also of the — of other animals, e.g. of pigs, ser-pents, etc.), *juvencus, juvenca* (= a — bull, a heifer); 3, of trees, etc., *novellus;* a — vine, *vitis novella.* **II.** n. (collective), *partus, - ūs,*

proles, -is, f. (mostly poet.), † *suboles, -is,* f. *pul li, -orum;* to bring forth —, *fetus edĕre o: procreare;* see above. **younger,** adj. *junior,* (natu) *minor;* the — of two sons, *minor natu e filiis;* a whole year —, *toto anno junior;* a few years —, *aliquot annis minor.* **youngest,** adj. (natu) *minimus;* the — of the sons, *minimus natu* (of several) *e filiis.*

youth, n. 1, in an abstract sense lit. *pueri-itia, aetas puerilis* (= the age of boys until the young Roman received the *toga virilis,* that is, till the fifteenth year of age), *adulescentia* (from the fifteenth until the end of the twenty-fifth year, the time during which the youth grew into a man), *juventus, -ūtis,* f.(strictly up to the fortieth year), † *juventas* (= in its first spring as it were, the age of a young man), *juventa* (not very often in prose); in —, gen. by *puer* or *adulescens* (= when a boy, a —); from —, *a puero, a parvo, a parvulo, a pueris, a parvis, a parvulis* (the three last of several, all = from early child-hood), *ab adulescentiā, ab ineunte aetate* or *adulescentiā, a primā aetate* or *adulescentiā, ab initio aetatis;* in a fig. sense = young people, *pu-eri, puellae* (= boys, girls), *adulescentes, virgines* (=young men, maidens), *juventus, -ūtis,* f., *juve-nes, -um, juvenes utriusque sexūs* (=young people of both sexes), the goddess —, *Juventas;* 2, a young man, *puer, adulescentulus, adulescens, juvenis.* **youthful,** adj. see YOUNG. Adv. *juveniliter, puerorum, adulescentium ritu* or more.

yule, n. see CHRISTMAS.

Z.

zeal, n. *studium, industria;* ardent —, *ardor, fervor;* with —, *studio, studiose;* with great —, *summo studio, studiosissime.* **zealot,** n. *acer-rimus fidei* (etc.). **zealous,** adj. *studiosus* (with genit.), *acer* (fiery), *ardens* (= burning with zeal); a — patriot, *civis acerrimus* or *patriae amans;* see EAGER. Adv. *studiose, acriter, ardenter, enixe, intente* (=intently).

zenith, n. * *zenith* (t.t.); in the —, *supra verticem.*

zephyr, n. *Zephyrus, Favonius.*

zero, n. by *nihil;* to be at — (fig.), *nihil valēre* (= worth nothing); his spirits were at —, *animus suus fractus* or *demissus est.*

zest, n. = relish, by *sapor* (e.g. *sapor vinosus);* fig. *studium.*

zigzag, n. *discursus torti vibratique* (of light-ning, Plin. Min.; the term can be used in gen.).

zodiac, n. *orbis* or *circulus signifer;* sign o: —, *sidus, -ĕris,* n.

zone, n. 1, see GIRDLE; 2, in geog. † *zona, cingulum* (terrestrial and celestial, *caeli regio o: ora* or *plaga;* torrid —, *zona torrida* (Plin.) : frigid —, *regio glacialis* (Col.); temperate —, *temperatae caeli regiones.*

zoology, n. *animantium descriptio.* **zoo-logical,** adj. by gen. *animantium* · — gardens *ferarum saeptum.*

GEOGRAPHICAL GLOSSARY

OF THE

ENGLISH NAMES OF IMPORTANT PLACES

WITH CLASSICAL OR LATER LATIN EQUIVALENTS.

AAR, R., Arola, Arula, Abrinca.
Africa, Africa; African, adj. Africanus; subst.
Afer.
Aix, Aquae Sextiae.
Aix-la-Chapelle, Aquisgranum, Urbs Aquensis.
Aleppo, Aleppum.
Algiers, Algerium.
Alsace, Alsatia.
America, America; American, adj. Americanus.
Amiens, Ambianum, Samarobriva.
Amsterdam, Amstelodamum.
Andalusia, Vandalitia.
Angers, Andegavum.
Angoulême, Engolisma.
Anhalt, Anhaltinum.
Anjou, Andegavensis Ager.
Antwerp, Antwerpia.
Arras, Atrebatum.
Artois, Artesia.
Asia, Asia; Asiatic, adj. Asiaticus, Asianus.
Atlantic Ocean, Oceanus Atlanticus.
Augsburg, Augusta Vindelicorum.
Austria, Austria.
Autun, Augustodunum.
Auvergne, Arvernia.
Avignon, Avenio.

BADAJOZ, Pax Augusta.
Baltic Sea, Mare Suebicum.
Bamberg, Bamberga, Papeberga.
Barcelona, Barcino.
Basle, Basilea.
Bavaria, Bojaria, Bajoaria.
Bayonne, Lapurdum.
Beauvais, Bellovacum.
Berlin, Berolinum.
Berne, Berna, Arctopolis.
Besançon, Vasontio.
Black Sea, Pontus Euxinus.
Blois, Blesae.
Bohemia, Boiohaemum.
Bologna, Bononia.
Bonn, Bonna.
Bordeaux, Burdigala.
Boulogne, Bolonia, Gesoriacum.
Bourges, Avaricum.
Braganza, Bragantia.

Bremen, Berma.
Brescia, Brixia.
Breslau, Vratislavia.
Bristol, Venta Silurum.
Brunswick, Brunsviga.
Brussels, Bruxellae.
Bulgaria, Bulgaria.
Burgundy, Burgundia.

CADIZ, Gades.
Calais, Caletum.
Cambray, Camaracum.
Cambridge, Cantabrigia.
Canterbury, Cantuaria, Durovernum.
Carinthia, Carinthia.
Carlisle, Carleolum, Brovoniacum.
Carlsbad, Thermae Carolinae.
Carlsruhe, Hesychia Carolina.
Carpathian M., Carpathus.
Carthagena, Carthago Nova.
Caspian Sea, Mare Caspium.
Cassel, Cassula, Cassellae.
Castile, Castilia.
Cattegat, Sinus Codanus.
Champagne, Campania.
Chester, Cestria.
Clairvaux, Claravallis.
Clausenburg, Claudiopolis.
Cleves, Clivis.
Coblentz, Confluentes.
Coburg, Coburgum.
Cologne, Colonia Agrippina, Augusta Ubiorum
Constance, Constantia.
Constantinople, Byzantium, Constantinopolis
Copenhagen, Hafnia, Codania.
Cordova, Corduba.
Corfu, Corcyra.
Cornwall, Cornubia.
Coventry, Conventria.
Cracow, Cracovia.
Croatia, Croatia.
Cronstadt, Corona.
Cyprus, Cyprus.

DALMATIA, Dalmatia; adj. Dalmaticus.
Damascus, Damascus; adj. Damascenus.
Dantzig, Gedanum, Dantiscum.

Danube, R., Danubius.
Darmstadt, Darmstadium.
Dauphiné, Delphinatus.
Dead Sea, Lacus Asphaltites.
Denmark, Dania.
Dessau, Dessavia.
Devonshire, Damnonia.
Dijon, Divia, Diviodunum.
Dnieper, R., Borysthenes, Danapris.
Dniester, R., Danastris.
Don, R., Tanais.
Dorchester, Durnovaria, Durnium.
Dover, Dubrae, Portus Dubris.
Dresden, Dresda.
Dublin, Dublinum.
Düsseldorf, Dusseldorpium.

Ebro, R., Iberus.
Edinburgh, Edinum.
Eisenach, Isenacum.
Elba, Ilva, Aethalia.
Elbe, R., Albis.
England, Anglia ; English, adj. Anglus, Anglicus.
Erfurt, Erfurdia, Erfurtum.
Esthonia, Estonia, Aestonia.
Exeter, Isca, Exonia.

Faenza, Faventia.
Ferrara, Ferraria.
Fiesole, Faesulae.
Finland, Finnia, Fennonia, Venedia.
Flanders, Flandria.
Florence, Florentia.
France, Gallia.
Franche Comté, Comitatus Burgundiae.
Franconia, Franconia.
Frankfort-on-the-Main, Francofurtum ad Moenum.
Frankfort-on-the-Oder, Francofurtum ad Oderam.
Freiburg, Friburgum.
Frejus, Forum Julii.
Friesland, Frisia.

Garda, Lago, Lacus Benacus.
Garonne, R., Garumna.
Gascony, Vasconia.
Geneva, Geneva.
Geneva, Lake of, Lacus Lemanus.
Germany, Germania.
Ghent, Ganda, Gandavum.
Girgenti, Agrigentum.
Glasgow, Glasgua.
Gloucester, Claudia Castra.
Goslar, Goslaria.
Gothenburg, Gothoburgum.
Göttingen, Gottinga.
Greece, Graecia.
Grenoble, Gratianopolis.
Guadalquivir, Baetis.
Guadiana, R., Anas.
Guienne, Aquitania.

Haarlem, Harlemum.
Hague, The, Haga Comitis.
Halle, Hala Saxonum.
Hamburg, Hamburgum.
Hanover, Hanovera.
Harz Mountains, Sylva Hercynia.
Havre de Grace, Portus Gratiae.
Heidelberg, Heidelberga.
Holland, Hollandia, Batavia.
Holstein, Holsatia.
Hungary, Hungaria.

India, India.
Ingolstadt, Ingolstadium.
Inn, R., Oenus.
Inspruck, Oenipontum.
Ireland, Hibernia.
Istria, Histria.
Italy, Italia.

Jaen, Jaenum.
Japan, Japonia.
Jena, Jena.
Jericho, Hiericho.
Jerusalem, Hierosolyma.
Juliers, Juliacum.
Jutland, Jutia, Jutlandia.

Kent, Cantium.
Kiel, Kilia, Kilonium.
Königsberg, Regiomontanum.

Lancaster, Longovicum.
Landau, Landavium.
Langres, Lingones.
Languedoc, Langedocis.
Lapland, Lapponia.
Lausanne, Lausodunum.
Leghorn, Liburnus Portus.
Leicester, Ratae Coritanorum.
Leipzig, Lipsia.
Lerida, Ilerda.
Leyden, Lugdunum Batavorum.
Liège, Leodium.
Limoges, Limovicum.
Lincoln, Lindum Colonia.
Linz, Lentia, Lintia.
Lisbon, Olisipo.
Lithuania, Lithuania.
Loire, R., Ligeris.
Lombardy, Longobardia.
London, Londinium, Londinum.
Loretto, Lauretum.
Lorraine, Lotharingia.
Louvain, Lovanium.
Lübeck, Lubeca.
Lucca, Luca.
Lucerne, Lucerna.
Lüneberg, Luneburgum.
Luneville, Lunaris Villa.
Luxemburg, Luciburgum.
Lyons, Lugdunum Segusianorum.

Maas, R., Mosa.
Madrid, Madritum, Mantua Carpetanorum.
Maestricht, Trajectum ad Mosam.
Magdeburg, Magdeburgum, Parthenopolis.
Main, R., Moenis.
Majorca, Insula Balearis Major.
Malaga, Malaca.
Malta, Malta, Melita.
Man, Isle of, Mona.
Manchester, Mancunium.
Mannheim, Manhemium.
Marburg, Marburgum.
Marne, R., Matröna.
Marseilles, Massilia.
Mayence, Moguntia, Moguntiacum.
Mechlin, Mechlinia.
Mecklenburg, Megalopolis.
Mediterranean Sea, Mare Internum, Mare Mediterraneum, Mare Nostrum, Mare Magnum.
Melun, Melodunum.
Merida, Augusta Emerita.
Messina, Massana.
Metz, Divodurum.
Milan, Mediolanum.
Mincio, R., Mincius.
Modena, Mutina.
Montpellier, Mons Pessulus.
Moravia, Moravia.
Morea, Peloponnesus.
Moscow, Moscovia.
Moselle, R., Mosella.
Munich, Monacum.
Munster, Monasterium.

Namur, Namurcum.
Nancy, Nancejum.
Nantes, Nannetes, Nantetum.
Naples, Neapolis, Parthenope.
Narbonne, Narbo Martius.
Nassau, Nassavia.
Navarre, Navarra Alta.
Neckar, R., Nicer, Nicrus.
Netherlands, Belgica.
Nevers, Nivernum, Nevidunum Aeduorum.
Newcastle, Novum Castrum.
Nismes, Nemausus.
Normandy, Normannia, Neustria.
North Sea, Oceanus Septentrionalis.
Northumberland, Northumbria.
Norway, Norvegia.
Norwich, Norvicum.
Nüremberg, Norimberga.

Oder, R., Odera, Viadrus.
Orange, Arausio.
Orkney Islands, Orcades.
Orleans, Aurelianum.
Orvieto, Urbs Vetus.
Osnabrück, Osnabruga.
Ostend, Ostenda.
Otranto, Hydruntum.
Oviedo, Ovetum.
Oxford, Oxonia.

Padua, Patavium.
Palatinate, Palatinatus.
Palermo, Panormus.
Pamplona, Pompeiopolis.
Paris, Lutetia, Lutetia Parisiorum.
Parma, Parma.
Pavia, Ticinum.
Perpignan, Perpinianum.
Perugia, Perusia.
Pesth, Pestinum.
Petersburg, St., Petropolis.
Piacenza, Placentia
Picardy, Picardia.
Piedmont, Pedemontium.
Plymouth, Plymuthum.
Po, R., Padus.
Poitiers, Limonum Pictavium
Poitou, Terra Pictavensis.
Poland, Polonia.
Pomerania, Pomerania.
Portugal, Lusitania.
Posen, Posnania.
Pozzuoli, Puteoli.
Prague, Praga.
Provence, Provincia.
Prussia, Borussia, Prussia.

Raab, Arrabona.
Ratisbon, Ratisbona, Reginoburgum.
Red Sea, Sinus Arabicus.
Reggio, Rhegium.
Rheims, Remi.
Rhine, R., Rhenus.
Rhone, R., Rhodanus.
Riga, Riga.
Rimini, Ariminum.
Rochelle, Rupella, Santonum Portus.
Rochester, Durobrivae.
Rome, Roma.
Rotterdam, Roterodamum.
Rouen, Rothomagus.
Roussillon, Russilio, Russino.
Russia, Russia.
Ryswick, Rysvicum.

Saxony, Saxonia.
Saint Cloud, Fanum S. Clodoaldi.
Saint Denis, Dionysiopolis.
Saint Malo, Maclovium.
Saint Omer, Audomaropolis
Salamanca, Salamantica
Salerno, Salernum.
Salisbury, Sarisberia, Sarum.
Salzburg, Salisburgum.
Sambre, R., Sabis.
Saone, R., Araris.
Saragossa, Caesarea Augusta.
Sardinia, Sardinia.
Saumur, Salmurium.
Savoy, Sabaudia.
Scheldt, R., Scaldis.
Schleswig, Slesvicum.
Schwerin, Suerinum.

Scilly Isles, Silures, Cassiterides.
Scotland, Scotia, Caledonia.
Seine, R., Sequana.
Sens, Agendicum Senonum.
Seville, Hispalis.
Shrewsbury, Salopia.
Sicily, Sicilia.
Sienna, Sena.
Silesia, Silesia.
Slavonia, Slavonia.
Soissons, Augusta Suessionum.
Sorrento, Sorrentum.
Spain, Hispania.
Spires, Spira, Augusta Nemetum.
Spoleto, Spoletum.
Stettin, Stetinum.
Stockholm, Stockholmia.
Strasburg, Argentoratum.
Stuttgardt, Stutgardia.
Styria, Styria.
Swabia, Suevia.
Sweden, Suecia.
Switzerland, Helvetia.

TANGIERS, Tingis.
Taranto, Tarentum.
Tarragona, Tarraco.
Tartary, Tartaria.
Tessin, R., Ticinus.
Thames, R., Tamesis, or Tamesa.
Theiss, R., Tiscus.
Thuringia, Thuringia.
Tiber, R., Tiberis.
Tivoli, Tibur.
Toledo, Toletum.
Toulon, Tullonum.
Toulouse, Tolosa.
Tournay, Tornacum.
Tours, Turones, Caesarodunum.
Trent, Tridentum.
Trèves, Augusta Trevirorum.
Trieste, Tergeste.

Tripoli, Tripolis.
Tübingen, Tubinga.
Tunis, Tunetum.
Turin, Augusta Taurinorum.
Turkey, Turcia.
Tuscany, Etruria.
Tyrol, Teriolis.

ULM, Ulma.
Upsala, Upsalia.
Urbino, Urbinum.
Utrecht, Trajectum.

VALLADOLID, Vallisoletum.
Valois, Valesia.
Venice, Venetiae.
Vercelli, Vercellae.
Verdun, Verodunum.
Verona, Verona.
Versailles, Versalia.
Vicenza, Vicentia.
Vienna, Vindobona.
Vienne, Vienna.
Vincennes, Ad Vicenas.
Vistula, R., Vistula.
Viterbo, Viterbium.

WALLACHIA, Valachia.
Warsaw, Varsovia.
Weimar, Vinaria.
Weser, R., Visurgis.
Wiesbaden, Thermae Mattiacae.
Wight, Isle of, Vectis.
Winchester, Venta Belgarum
Wittenberg, Vitemberga.
Worcester, Vigornia.
Worms, Wormatia.

YORK, Eboracum.

ZANTE, Zacynthus.
Zürich, Turicum, Tigurium.

GLOSSARY

OF

A FEW COMMON ENGLISH NAMES

WITH CLASSICAL OR LATER LATIN EQUIVALENTS.

ALBERT, Albertus.
Alexander, Alexander.
Alfred, Aluredus.
Anna }
Anne } Anna.
Antony, Antonius.
Arthur, Arturus.
Augustine, Augustinus.

BEATRICE, Beatrix.
Benedict, Benedictus.
Bernard, Bernardus.

CECIL, Caecilius.
Cecilia, Caecilia.
Celia, Celia.
Charles, Carolus.
Claude, Claudius.
Clement, Clemens.
Constance, Constantia.
Cyprian, Cyprianus.
Cyril, Cyrillus.

EDMUND, Edmundus.
Edward, Eduardus.

Ellen }
Eleanor } Helena.
Elinor }
Emily, Aemilia.

FELIX, Felix.
Florence, Florentia.
Francis }
Frank } Franciscus.
Frederic, Fredericus.

GEORGE, Georgius.
Gregory, Gregorius.

HELEN, Helena.
Henry, Henricus.
Hilary, Hilarius.
Horace, Horatius.

JAMES, Jacobus.
John, Johannes.
Joseph, Josephus.
Julia, Julia.
Julian, Julianus.
Justin, Justinus.

LAWRENCE, Laurentius.
Lewis, Ludovicus.
Lucy, Lucia.

MARGARET, Margarita.
Mark, Marcus.
Mary, Maria.

PATRICK, Patricius.
Paul, Paulus.
Peter, Petrus.
Philip, Philippus.

RALPH, Radulfus.
Randolph, Randolphus
Richard, Ricardus.
Robert, Robertus.

STEPHEN, Stephanus.

THOMAS, Thomas.
Timothy, Timotheus.

VALENTINE, Valentinus.
Vincent, Vincentius.

WALTER, Gualterus.
William, Gulielmus.

16 Y 3.75

91070